W9-AFO-521

THE INTERNATIONAL FILM INDEX 1895-1990

Edited by
Alan Goble

Bowker-Saur
London Melbourne Munich New Jersey

All rights reserved. No part of this publication may be reproduced or transmitted in any form or by any means (including photocopying and recording) without the written permission of the Copyright Act 1956 (as amended) or under the terms of the licence issued by the Copyright Licensing Agency, 7 Ridgemount Street, London WC1E 7AE, UK. The written permission of the copyright holder must be obtained before any part of his publication is stored in a retrieval system of any nature. Applications for the copyright holder's written permission to reproduce, transmit or store in a retrieval system any part of this publication should be addressed to the publisher.

Warning: The doing of an unauthorised act in relation to a copyright work may result in both a civil claim for damages and criminal prosecution.

©Bowker-Saur, 1991.

Published by Bowker-Saur
60 Grosvenor Street, London W1X 9DA
Tel: 071-493 5841 Fax: 071-580 4089

Bowker-Saur is part of the Professional Publishing Division of
Reed International Books.

British Library Cataloguing in Publication Data
Goble, Alan
The international film index : titles and directors, 1895-1990
1. Cinema films
I. Title
791.430321

ISBN 0-86291-623-2

Library of Congress Cataloguing in Publication Data
available on request

Cover Design by Robin Caira, Typographics, Whitstable, Kent.
Printed and bound by Antony Rowe Ltd.
Printed on acid free paper.

To Valerie

Contents

Foreword

The industry which produced the extraordinary range and variety of films indexed in these volumes has also encouraged the growth of a substantial library of reference works. Even ignoring those publications that just signpost a pleasant ramble through the trivia of popular entertainment and stardom, the search for basic film detail relies on a rich choice of information sources - rich but frustrating. A bulky handbook of films available on television or video will not list many foreign language films or documentaries; lavish encyclopedias of genres such as film noir, westerns, or science fiction are just that; while the catalogues of the major national film institutes, splendid for their full-dress cataloguing detail, are still in the process of catching up with nearly a century of production.

Alan Goble's index, with its simple aim - but monumental achievement - of recording the world's first century of film production, has been twenty years in the making. Its compilation, as the bibliography testifies, has encompassed the existing mosaic of reference works, and much more. Even in the areas where the difficulties of collating the total output are most extreme, such as the floodtide of the Indian film industry, this index still achieves a standard rare in international works: thus some 2,000 film titles from the Indian sub-continent will be found here.

For the first time, and of use to every sort of enquirer from the home video watcher to the researcher of archive copy, there is a single reference work on films which offers the basic information previously scattered among many shelves of encyclopedias, directories, yearbooks and indexes. And in providing filmographies for some 25,000 directors, *The International Film Index* redresses the emphasis on 'known' figures repeated by too many reference works.

The rarity or other special interest of certain printed books is often indicated by their omission from standard bibliographies. In the same way I expect the phrase 'Not in Goble' to be as much a reflection on the importance of this major historical reference work for film studies as an encouragement for the next edition.

Alex Noel-Tod
Film Studies Librarian
University of East Anglia

Preface

This is the first major attempt to provide a comprehensive index to films by title and director on a worldwide basis. It has taken some twenty years to compile but, as with any such work, there remains more to be done. I feel, however, that it has reached a stage where it can fill a niche in the literature of the cinema that has remained empty for too long.

My objective at the beginning was to index all feature films, together with their directors and alternative titles, but difficulties led me to decide that I would record all (theatrical) films found and add information as it came to hand. The effect, therefore, was cumulative. At a later stage I decided to include silent films, so making *The International Film Index* a record of the productions in nearly one hundred years of cinema.

It is generally felt that the director is the key person in the production of a film and I realised that the logging of the director's name with the film would provide an index of directors that would be second to none. This has resulted in filmographies for some 25,000 directors, ranging from those who have made only one film to those that have made several hundred.

I opted to include documentaries, shorts and animated films, initially in order to assist in completing feature directors' filmographies. There is, however, a whole body of directors whose main work is in the former areas, and who have left their mark on the industry, so these types of film are also included.

I decided that the basic information required to identify a film should include the original title, year of release, director, country of origin, type of film and any alternative titles. To provide further information such as running times, colour or acting credits, would have required a great deal more time to research and probably resulted in an index too large to be practicable in book form. Twenty years ago a personal computer was not a possibility, but now I can take advantage of the technology, and so the possibility of adding further fields to the existing entries is a real one; but that will depend on the success of this first edition.

While compiling *The International Film Index*, I have maintained two parallel indexes, one arranged by title and one by director. This has produced a cross-check which has helped to resolve many anomalies. It has also assisted in identifying the original titles of foreign films shown in the USA and the United Kingdom.

I have set no parameters for the standard of film contained in this work or made any judgement on the artistic merit of a director. Inclusion has been determined by the fact that in some book, magazine or newspaper, someone has felt it necessary to give details on the film and/or the director.

A work of this size and scope cannot hope to be without errors. While my system has enabled me to carry out a considerable amount of cross-checking, the vagaries and inconsistencies of recorded information on the cinema as well as time limitations will mean that some errors and gaps remain. In addition, the reader may not necessarily agree that I have selected the right information in a particular case. Quite often, one source will say authoritatively that this is the position, while another will say the opposite, just as authoritatively. In such cases I have made a judgement but generally I have assumed nothing. It is likely, for instance, that two titles listed are in fact the same film, but unless I have found reasonable evidence to confirm that, I have left them as separate entries. This 'duplication' of titles occurs mainly with foreign titles. With so many languages and standards of transliteration, it has not been feasible to check all spelling variants. Where I found what I could confirm to be the same film title in different spellings I have included both spellings under a master title.

The making of motion pictures has been carried on now for nearly one hundred years. In a park within a mile or so from where I write today, as early as 1896, a few dedicated people produced some of the first films to be made in the United Kingdom. From humble beginnings such as those the cinema has developed to the exciting international industry it is today. I am pleased that, with the publication of this book, those pioneers take their place alongside the others mentioned within, the famous and not so famous, but who have all contributed to making the cinema one of the great pleasures of the twentieth century.

Alan Goble
September 1991

User's Guide

INTRODUCTION

This Index contains some 232,000 film titles from 25,000 directors covering the period 1895 to 1990, of which some 177,000 are master titles and the remainder alternative titles. It includes the vast majority of feature films made in the USA, Canada, the UK, France, Germany, Italy, Australia and New Zealand as well as films from more than a hundred other countries. 129 countries or territories (some no longer in existence) are covered in all. Most directors are included and certainly all the better known figures.

Also included are art films, alternative cinema, documentaries, shorts, serials and animated films. A number of feature length films made for television are covered as well as films that have been funded by television.

The International Film Index contains two main listings, Film Titles and Directors' Filmography, both in alphabetical order. Each film title is given in Volume I with up to six other vital identifying pieces of information (see below). Then there follows in Volume II a listing of film directors, including up to four other categories of data about the director, plus a chronological listing of the director's filmography. Essential film data are repeated in the filmography so as to increase the user-friendliness of the publication. The second volume also contains two subsidiary indexes, Directors by Country and Directors of Animated Films, as well as the Select Bibliography.

For the reader's interest, we give below a breakdown of the contents of *The International Film Index.*

THE INTERNATIONAL FILM INDEX: Breakdown of Contents

Films (master titles)	USA	Canada	UK	France	Germany[a]	Italy
Feature[b]	35352	2102	9476	9147	9879	8435
Short	34371	422	7077	3916	633	497
Animated	6341	379	441	468	226	78
Documentary	918	1948	888	622	151	258
Television	2801	461	406	78	54	81
Serial	477	-	37	25	-	6
Total	80260	5312	18325	14256	10943	9355
of which: Silent	40219	24	8299	3563	4046	829
Film Directors Total	5679	844	2194	2020	1422	1343

Films (master titles)	Other Europe[c]	Australia/ New Zealand	Japan	Rest of World	TOTAL
Feature[b]	17402	1033	4367	13393	110586
Short	2105	531	20	484	50056
Animated	1561	54	170	69	9787
Documentary	1482	474	55	481	7277
Television	175	104	4	33	4197
Serial	7	1	-	-	553
Total	22732	21927	4616	14460	182456
of which: Silent	1677	448	39	536	59680
Film Directors Total	5135	506	603	4942	24688

[a]Including the former East Germany. [b]Feature or category not identified. [c]Including USSR.

EXPLANATORY NOTES

Sort Order

Film titles are listed alphabetically according to the principles laid down in the *American Library Association Filing Rules* (1980). Titles beginning with numbers are filed at the beginning of the index.

I. Film Titles

The following information may be given for a title (see explanations below)

- Master Title
- Year
- Director(s)
- Additional Credits
- Type of Film
- Country of Film Origin
- Alternative Title(s)

Master Title

The 232,000 film titles have been obtained from various published sources, a bibliography of which is included at the end of Volume II. The inclusion of a title is no guarantee that the film still exists, or ever existed, but indicates that a source included a film of that name which was at one time at some stage of production. The master title is the original language release title, where identifiable. However, the title may be the re-release title, working title, title for television, literal translation or any title that the film was known by for some purpose, if the master title is not clear.

Cross references are given from alternative film titles to the master title entry.

Year

The year generally indicates the first date of release but in cases whether the film was produced some years before being released, the earlier date is shown. In some cases it was not possible to determine the exact date of release and the date given is the probable one.

Director(s)

The entry for the director is usually under the best-known name. Thus the films of Mihaly Kertesz are listed under Michael Curtiz although his early work was credited to Kertesz. However, all alternative names are cross-referenced in the Directors' Filmography listing.

Where available, major co-directors are also given.

Additional Credits

For some films it has not been possible to determine the director and so another aid to identifying the film has been given in italics if one was found. This may be the production company, the producer, a leading actor, writer or other person connected with the film. Many have a key in brackets following the name to indicate the nature of their involvement (see list of ABBREVIATIONS below).

Type of Film

A film may be annotated to indicate whether it is a short, a documentary, a serial, an animation, a television film etc - see full list of ABBREVIATIONS below. A "short" is defined as being 30 minutes or under. This description has not been given to films prior to 1915 as before that date the majority of films were in this category. Films with no type-annotation are feature films (the majority) or films where the category has not been identified.

A film described as an "Anthology" (ANT) is a collection of short films which have been combined and shown as a feature.

A film has been described as a "Compilation" (CMP) where the source has indicated that it had been produced from segments of several films or newsreels, usually linked by a commentary.

Films which are denoted "Made for Television" (MTV) are those which have been funded by television and may or may not have been shown in the cinema. They may be documentaries or films made from editing television series.

"Series" (SER) is used to describe a group of films, each complete on its own, which may have, for instance, a common theme or cast.

Nearly all films made before 1928 were silent. However, the abbreviation "SIL" is only given to distinguish a silent film where both a sound and a silent version was made.

"Serials" (SRL) are films composed of several episodes and were made predominantly in the USA during the period 1914-1936. They were invariably action melodramas and were usually shown in weekly instalments. Some films were made in serial form in Mexico in the 1960s but these comprised only three or four episodes and were made in this form to subvert legislation. These have not been classified as Serials.

Films which are denoted "Television Films" (TVM) are almost exclusively American and relate to films produced for transmission on television. Occasionally these have been shown in the cinema, invariably in the United Kingdom, but are now being marketed on video without their origin being too apparent. They do, however, serve to make a director's filmography more complete as many now work in both film and television environments simultaneously.

Country of Film Origin

The country of film origin is generally the country in which the film was made and/or the country which financed the production. See COUNTRY CODES below for a full list of countries covered. If a source has indicated that a film is claimed by a particular country, i.e. it is shown in its yearbook, then it has been noted as of that origin. Films made in the United Kingdom with American funds often fall within this category as one source calls it a British film and another an American one. Where the film is a co-production, the country given relates to the director's origin.

The country of film origin retains the West and East German and the North and South Korean distinctions, with pre-war films listed under West Germany and South Korea respectively.

Alternative Titles

The alternative film title may be a title used when the film was shown in another country (i.e. foreign language title or alternative original language title), when transmitted on television or released on video, a working title, a literal translation or a title used when re-released.

An alternative title may be followed by a country code in brackets, e.g. "(FRN)". This denotes the country in which the alternative title was used.

II. Directors' Filmography

The following information may be given in an entry for a director (see explanations below):

- Name
- Country of Director's Origin
- Date(s)
- Occupation
- Alternative name(s)
- Films:
  - Master Title
  - Year
  - Type of Film
  - Alternative Title(s)

Name

The director's best-known name is used. Cross-references are given from alternative names. Please note that all names are given with surname first, then first name.

Country of Director's Origin

Country refers to the director's place of birth, which is usually but not always the country in which the majority of the director's films were made. If birthplace information is not available, this has been assumed to be the same as the main country of film-making.

The country name is given as so known at the time of the director's birth, which may refer to a state or territory no longer existing (such as Palestine). All Germans, whether from the former West or East German states, are listed under Germany. Similarly, all Koreans, whether from North or South Korea, are listed under Korea.

Date(s)

The dates of birth and death, if given, are those most often attributed in the sources.

Occupation

The main occupation of the director is sometimes given where this is not directing, such as Henri Decae, Cinematographer.

Alternative Names(s)

This includes any variations in a director's signature, including pseudonyms and alternative spellings. The latter are fairly common with directors from countries such as the USSR and are given in italics.

Films

Traceable films attributed to the director are given by master title in chronological order. Additional information given includes year, type of film and alternative titles (see above for explanations). Co-directors are not included, though they are indicated in the Film Title listing.

Directors by Country

All directors are regrouped in alphabetical order in a separate index in Volume II by country (as defined above). Life dates are also given where available.

Directors of Animated Films

All directors of animated films - who have created a distinctive artistic medium - are regrouped in straight alphabetical sequence in a separate index in Volume II. Country (as defined above) and life dates are also given as well as alternative names.

Select Bibliography

This includes all the major printed sources consulted, sorted in alphabetical order by title. Author, publisher, publisher location and publication date are also given.

ABBREVIATIONS

ANM animated
ANS animated short
ANT anthology
ASS animated short series
C/D co-director
CMP compilation
DCS short documentary
DOC documentary
DSS documentary short series
EDT editor
M composer (music)
MTV made for television
P producer
PH photographer
SER series
SHS short series
SHT short
SIL silent
SND sound
SPV supervision
SRL serial
TVM television film
U/C uncredited

COUNTRY CODES

AFG Afghanistan
ALB Albania
ALG Algeria
ANG Angola
ARG Argentina
ASL Australia
AUS Austria
BLG Belgium
BLV Bolivia
BNG Bangladesh
BNN Benin
BRK Burkina Faso
BRM Burma
BRZ Brazil
BUL Bulgaria
CHL Chile
CHN China
CLM Colombia
CMR Cameroon
CND Canada
CNG Congo
CPV Cape Verde Islands
CRC Costa Rica
CUB Cuba
CYP Cyprus
CZC Czechoslovakia
DMN Dominican Republic
DNM Denmark
ECD Ecuador
EGY Egypt
ETH Ethiopia
FNL Finland
FRG West Germany
FRN France
GBN Gabon
GDR East Germany
GHN Ghana
GIB Gibraltar
GNB Guinea Bissau
GRC Greece
GRM Germany
GTM Guatemala
GUM Guam
GUN Guinea
GYN Guyana
HKG Hong Kong
HNG Hungary
ICL Iceland
INC Indochina
IND India
INN Indonesia
IRL Ireland
IRN Iran
IRQ Iraq
ISR Israel
ITL Italy
IVC Ivory Coast
JMC Jamaica
JPN Japan
JRD Jordan
KMP Kampuchea (Cambodia)
KNY Kenya
KOR Korea
KWT Kuwait
LAO Laos
LBN Lebanon
LBY Libya
LCH Liechtenstein
LTH Lithuania
LTV Latvia
LXM Luxembourg
MDG Madagascar
MLI Mali
MLT Malta
MLY Malaysia
MNC Monaco
MNG Mongolia
MRC Morocco
MRT Mauretania
MXC Mexico
MZM Mozambique
NCR Nicaragua
NGR Nigeria
NKR North Korea
NPL Nepal
NRW Norway
NTH Netherlands
NZL New Zealand
PHL Philippines
PKS Pakistan
PLN Poland
PLS Palestine
PNM Panama
PRC Puerto Rico
PRG Paraguay
PRT Portugal
PRU Peru
RMN Romania
SAF South Africa
SDN Sudan
SKR South Korea
SLN Sri Lanka
SLV El Salvador
SML Somalia
SNG Singapore
SNL Senegal
SPN Spain
SRN Surinam
SWD Sweden
SWT Switzerland
SYR Syria
T&T Trinidad & Tobago
THL Thailand
TNS Tunisia
TRK Turkey
TWN Taiwan
UAR United Arab Republic
UGN Uganda
UKN United Kingdom
UNN United Nations
URG Uruguay
USA United States of America
USS Union of Soviet Socialist Republics
VEN Venezuela
VTN Vietnam
WIN West Indies
YGS Yugoslavia
ZIM Zimbabwe
ZMB Zambia
ZRE Zaire

Vorwort

Die Branche, die ein solch außergewöhnliches Volumen und eine solche Vielfalt an Filmen produzierte, wie sie in den vorliegenden Bänden aufgeführt sind, führt ebenso zur Erarbeitung einer umfangreichen Bibliothek von Nachschlagewerken. Selbst wenn man diejenigen Veröffentlichungen außer Acht läßt, die lediglich den Weg für einen vergnüglichen Streifzug durch die Bagatellen der populären Unterhaltung und der Stars weisen, kann man bei der Suche nach grundlegenden Einzelheiten über einen Film auf eine reichhaltige Auswahl an Informationsquellen zurückgreifen -zwar reichhaltig, doch gleichzeitig frustierend. Ein behäbiges Handbuch über Fernseh- oder Videofilme führt nicht die vielen fremdsprachigen Spiel- oder Dokumentarfilme auf; verschwenderisch aufgemachte Enzyklopädien über verschiedene Filmgenres wie etwa den Schwarzen Film, Western oder Science Fiction beschränken sich auf ein einzelnes Thema; und die Kataloge der bedeutenden nationalen Filminstitute, die mit ihren formellen Katalogangaben ausgezeichnet sind, sind noch mit der Aufarbeitung von fast einem Jahrhundert der Filmproduktion beschäftigt.

Alan Gobles Verzeichnis verfolgt ein einfaches Ziel - und stellt eine monumentale Leistung dar - nämlich das erste Jahrhundert der Filmproduktion festzuhalten, und seine Zusammenstellung nahm zwanzig Jahre in Anspruch. Die Auflistung, wie die Bibliographie belegt, berücksichtigt die vielen vorhandenen Nachschlagewerke, und noch vieles mehr. Selbst in den Bereichen, wo die Schwierigkeiten der Erfassung der Gesamtproduktion sich am deutlichsten stellen, wie etwa bei der Flut der Filme aus dem indischen Raum, erreicht dieser Index dennoch ein Niveau, das bei internationalen Werken selten ist: man findet hier etwa 2.000 Filmtitel aus dem indischen Subkontinent.

Erstmals gibt es ein einzelnes Nachschlagewerk für Filme, das für alle Arten der Informationssuchenden vom Videofreund bis zum Forscher im Archiv von Nutzen ist, und das die grundlegende Information bietet, die zuvor auf vielen Regalen voller Enzyklopädien, Handbücher, Jahrbücher und Indexe verstreut war. Durch die Hinzufügung von Filmographien von etwa 25.000 Regisseuren stellt *The International Film Index* den Ausgleich zu 'bekannten' Persönlichkeiten wieder her, die in zu vielen Nachschlagewerken wiederholt werden.

Die Seltenheit oder spezialisierte Interessenlage gewisser Bücher im Druck zeigt sich oft durch deren Fehlen in den Standard-Bibliographien. Auf die gleiche Art erwarte ich die Wendung 'Nicht im Goble' zu einem Spiegel der Bedeutung dieses bedeutenden historischen Nachschlagewerkes für Filmstudien zu werden, sowie eine Ermutigung für die nächste Auflage.

Alex Noel-Tod
Bibliothekar für Filmstudien
Universität East Anglia

Einleitung

Das vorliegende Werk stellt den ersten bedeutenden Versuch dar, einen umfassenden Filmindex nach Titel und Regisseur auf weltweiter Basis zusammenzustellen. Die Erstellung nahm fast zwanzig Jahre in Anspruch, und doch bleibt noch immer mehr zu tun, wie das bei all diesen Werken der Fall ist. Ich bin jedoch der Ansicht, daß ein Stadium erreicht wurde, wo es in der Literatur über das Kino eine Lücke füllen kann, die schon viel zu lange klafft.

Zu Anfang war es mein Bestreben, alle Spielfilme mit Angabe des Regisseurs und anderen Titeln aufzuführen, doch führten Schwierigkeiten zu der Entscheidung, alle (theatralischen) gefundenen Filme aufzunehmen und die entsprechende Information hinzuzufügen, so wie sie auftaucht. Die Vorgehensweise war somit kumulativ. Zu einem späteren Zeitpunkt entschloß ich mich zur Aufnahme von Stummfilmen, wodurch *The International Film Index* zu einer Zusammenstellung der Produktionen in fast einhundert Jahren des Kino wurde.

Man ist gemeinhin der Ansicht, daß der Regisseur die Schlüsselperson bei der Produktion eines Films ist, und mir wurde klar, daß die Angabe des Namens des Rgeisseurs mit dem Film einen Index von Regisseuren liefern würde, der keinem anderen nachsteht. Dies führte zu Filmographien von etwa 25.000 Regisseuren, angefangen bei denen, die nur einen Film drehten bis zu denjenigen, die mehrere hundert hervorbrachten.

Ich entschloß mich, Dokumentarfilme mitaufzunehmen, Kurzfilme und Trickfilme, was ursprünglich geschah, um die Filmographien der Spielfilmdirektoren zu vervollständigen. Es gibt jedoch eine ganze Reihe von Regisseuren, deren hauptsächliche Arbeit in den ersteren Bereichen liegt und die der Branche ihren Stempel aufgedrückt haben, somit wurden diese Filmarten ebenso mitaufgenommen.

Ich kam zu der Überzeugung, daß die grundlegende Information, die vonnöten ist, um einen Film zu identifizieren, den Originaltitel, das Veröffentlichungsjahr, den Regisseur, das Herkunftsland, die Filmart und etwaige Alternativtitel einschließen sollte. Die Angabe weiterer Informationen wie Laufzeit, Farbe oder Schauspielerangaben hätte sehr viel mehr Zeit und Nachforschungen in Anspruch genommen und hätte unter Umständen zu einem Index geführt, der zu umfangreich gewesen wäre, um in Buchform handlich zu sein. Vor zwanzig Jahren lag ein Personalcomputer noch nicht im Bereich der Möglichkeiten, doch nun kann ich mir die Technik zunutze machen und somit wird die Möglichkeit der Hinzufügung von weiteren Bereichen zu den vorhandenen Einträgen zur Wirklichkeit; doch hängt dies von dem Erfolg der ersten Auflage ab.

Bei der Zusammenstellung des *International Film Index* benutzte ich zwei parallele Indexsysteme, eines nach Titel und eines nach Regisseur. Dadurch wurde eine gegenseitige Überprüfung möglich, was zur Bereinigung vieler Unregelmäßigkeiten führte. Es half ebenso dabei, die Originaltitel von ausländischen Filmen, die in den USA und in Großbritannien gezeigt wurden, zu ermitteln.

Für den Standard eines Films, der in diesem Werk aufgeführt wird, setzte ich keine Parameter fest, noch beurteile ich die künstlerische Leistung eines Regisseurs. Die Aufnahme wird durch den Umstand bestimmt, daß in einem Buch, einer Zeitschrift oder Zeitung, es jemand für angebracht hielt, Einzelheiten über den Film und/oder den Regisseur anzugeben.

Ein Werk von diesem Umfang und Ausmaß kann nicht darauf hoffen, fehlerfrei zu bleiben. Obgleich meine Arbeitsweise mich in die Lage versetzte, eine beträchtliche Menge von Überprüfungen durchzuführen, bedeuten die Grillen und Schwankungen aufgezeichneter Information über das Kino sowie die zeitlichen Beschränkungen, daß sich einige Fehler und Lücken einschleichen. Außerdem wird der Leser nicht unbedingt der Meinung sein, daß ich in gewissen Fällen die relevante Information aufgenommen habe. Relativ häufig wird eine bestimmte Quelle ganz eindeutig das Eine behaupten, während eine andere sich ebenso sicher auf das Gegenteil versteift. In solchen Fällen traf ich eine Entscheidung, doch ließ ich mich im allgemeinen nicht zu Mutmaßungen verleiten. So ist es zum Beispiel wahrscheinlich, daß es sich bei zwei aufgeführten Titel in der Tat um ein und denselben Film handelt, doch habe ich dies als zwei gesonderte Einträge belassen, es sei denn, es war zuverlässige Information vorhanden, die die Annahme belegte. Diese "Verdoppelung" der Titel tritt vor allem bei ausländischen Titeln auf. Bei so vielen verschiedenen Sprachen und Arten der Übertragung erwies sich die Überprüfung der unterschiedlichen Schreibweisen nicht als machbar. In den Fällen, in denen es möglich war, den gleichen Filmtitel in unterschiedlichen Schreibweisen festzustellen, nahm ich beide Schreibweisen unter dem Haupttitel auf.

Die Produktion von Filmen existiert seit fast einhundert Jahren. In einem Park, der etwa einen Kilometer von dem Ort entfernt ist, an dem ich heute schreibe, produzierte eine Gruppe engagierter Menschen bereits im Jahr 1896 einen der ersten Filme, die in Großbritannien entstanden. Aus solch bescheidenen Anfängen entwickelte sich das Kino in die aufregende internationale Industrie, die sie heutzutage darstellt. Es ist mir eine Freude, daß diese Pioniere durch die Veröffentlichung dieses Buches ihren Platz neben den anderen dort Aufgeführten einnehmen, den Berühmten und den minder Berühmten, die jedoch alle dazu beigetragen haben, das Kino zu einem der größten Vergnügen des zwanzigsten Jahrhunderts zu machen.

Alan Goble
September 1991

Benutzungsanleitung

EINFÜHRUNG

Dieser Index enthält etwa 232.000 Filmtitel von 25.000 Regisseuren aus dem Zeitraum 1895 bis 1990, wovon es sich bei etwa 177.000 Einträgen um Haupttitel und bei dem Rest um alternative Titel handelt. Er umfaßt den Großteil von Spielfilmen, die in den USA, Kanada, Großbritannien, Frankreich, Deutschland, Italien, Australien und Neuseeland produziert wurden, sowie Filme aus mehr als hundert anderen Ländern. Insgesamt werden 129 Länder beziehungsweise Territorien (von denen einige nicht mehr existieren) abgedeckt. Die meisten Regisseure sind erfaßt und sicher alle bekannteren Persönlichkeiten.

Außerdem wurden Kunstfilme, das alternative Kino, Dokumentarfilme, Kurzfilme, Filmserials und Trickfilme aufgenommen. Eine Reihe von Fernsehfilmen von Spielfilmlänge erscheinen ebenso, sowie Filme, die vom Fernsehen finanziert wurden.

The International Film Index enthält zwei Hauptlisten, Filmtitel und die Filmographien der Regisseure, beide in alphabetischer Reihenfolge. Die Filmtitel sind in Band I mit bis zu sechs anderen, wichtigen Angaben (siehe unten) aufgeführt. Darauf folgt in Band II eine Liste von Filmregisseuren, einschließlich bis zu vier weiteren Kategorien von Daten über den Regisseur, sowie eine chronologische Liste der Filmwerke des Regisseurs. Wichtige Filmdaten werden in der Filmographie wiederholt, um diese Veröffentlichung benutzerfreundlicher zu gestalten. Der zweite Band enthält weiterhin zwei Unterverzeichnisse, Regisseure nach Land und Regisseure von Trickfilmen, sowie die Ausgewählte Bibliographie.

Als Orientierungshilfe für die Leser geben wir nachstehend eine Aufgliederung des Inhalts des *International Film Index*.

THE INTERNATIONAL FILM INDEX: Aufgliederung des Inhalts

	USA	Kanada	GB	Frankreich	Deutschland[a]	Italien
Filme (Haupttitel)						
Spielfilm[b]	35352	2102	9476	9147	9879	8435
Kurzfilm	34371	422	7077	3916	633	497
Trickfilm	6341	379	441	468	226	78
Dokumentarfilm	918	1948	888	622	151	258
Fernsehen	2801	461	406	78	54	81
Serials	477	-	37	25	-	6
Insgesamt	80260	5312	18325	14256	10943	9355
Davon Stummfilme	40219	24	8299	3563	4046	829
Filmregisseure Insgesamt	5679	844	2194	2020	1422	1343

	Sonstiges Europa[c]	Australien/ Neuseeland	Japan	Restliche Welt	INSGESAMT
Filme (Haupttitel)					
Spielfilm[b]	17402	1033	4367	13393	110586
Kurzfilm	2105	531	20	484	50056
Trickfilm	1561	54	170	69	9787
Dokumentarfilm	1482	474	55	481	7277
Fernsehen	175	104	4	33	4197
Serial	7	1	-	-	553
Insgesamt	22732	2197	4616	14460	182456
Davon Stummfilme	1677	448	39	536	59680
Filmregisseure Insgesamt	5135	506	603	4942	24688

[a]Einschließlich der ehemaligen DDR. [b]Spielfilm oder nicht identifizierte Kategorie. [c]Einschließlich der UdSSR

ERLÄUTERUNGEN

Reihenfolge der Einträge

Die Filmtitel sind in alphabetischer Reihenfolge aufgeführt, gemäß der Prinzipien, die in den *American Library Association Filing Rules* (1980) (Ablagevorschriften des amerikanischen Bibliotheksverbandes) festgelegt sind. Die Titel, die mit Zahlen beginnen, erscheinen zu Beginn des Index.

I. Filmtitel

Die folgende Information ist unter Umständen bei einem Titel angegeben (siehe nachstehende Erklärungen)

- Haupttitel
- Jahr
- Regisseur(e)
- Zusätzliche Angaben
- Filmart
- Herkunftsland des Films
- Alternative Titel

Haupttitel

Die 232.000 Filmtitel stammen aus unterschiedlichen veröffentlichten Quellen. Eine entsprechende Bibliographie findet sich am Ende des II. Bandes. Die Aufnahme eines Titel ist keine Garantie, daß der Film noch existiert, oder jemals existierte, sondern gibt lediglich an, daß eine Quelle einen Film mit diesem Titel aufführte, der sich irgendwann in einem Produktionsstadium befand. Der Haupttitel ist der Titel in der Originalsprache der Veröffentlichung, wo identifizierbar. Doch handelt es sich bei diesem Titel unter Umständen um den Veröffentlichungstitel, Arbeitstitel, Titel für das Fernsehen, eine genaue Übersetzung oder einen Titel, unter dem der Film für einen bestimmten Zweck bekannt war, falls der Haupttitel nicht klar ist.

Es werden Querverweise von alternativen Filmtiteln zu den Einträgen der Hauptttitel angegeben.

Jahr

Das Jahr gibt im allgemeinen das erste Veröffentlichungsdatum an. In Fällen, wo der Film mehrere Jahre vor der Veröffentlichung entstand, wird das frühere Datum angegeben. In einigen Fällen war es nicht möglich, das genaue Veröffentlichungsdatum festzustellen, und das angegebene Datum ist daher eine mutmaßliche Angabe.

Regisseur(e)

Der Eintrag für den Regisseur erfolgt gewöhnlich unter dem am besten bekannten Namen. Demzufolge werden die Filme von Mihaly Kertesz unter dem Namen Michael Curtiz aufgeführt, obgleich seine frühen Arbeiten unter dem Namen Kertesz erschienen. Allen alternativen Namen wird in der Filmographie der Regisseure ein Querverweis beigegeben.

Falls zutreffend sind außerdem bedeutende Ko-Regisseure angegeben.

Zusätzliche Angaben

Bei manchen Filmen war es unmöglich, den Regisseur ausfindig zu machen. In diesen Fällen werden anderweitige Hilfen zur Identifizierung des Films zur Verfügung gestellt, falls vorhanden. Dabei kann es sich um die Produktionsgesellschaft handeln, den Produzenten, einen Hauptdarsteller, Autor oder eine andere Person, die mit dem Film in Zusammenhang steht. Vielen Einträgen folgt ein Schlüssel in Klammern, der das Wesen dieses Zusammenhangs bezeichnet (siehe nachstehende Liste der ABKÜRZUNGEN).

Filmart

Ein Film trägt unter Umständen eine Anmerkung, ob es sich um einen Kurzfilm, einen Dokumentarfilm, ein Serial, einen Trickfilm, einen Fernsehfilm etc. handelt - vergleichen Sie bitte die nachstehende vollständige Liste der ABKÜRZUNGEN. Ein "Kurzfilm" ist durch eine Höchstdauer von 30 Minuten definiert. Diese Beschreibung trifft nicht auf Filme vor dem Jahr 1915 zu, da vor diesem Zeitpunkt die meisten Filme in diese Kategorie fielen. Filme ohne Artangabe sind Spielfilme (der Großteil) oder Filme, bei denen die Kategorie nicht festzustellen war.

Ein Film, der als "Anthologie" (ANT) beschrieben wird, ist eine Sammlung von Kurzfilmen, die zusammengefaßt und als Spielfilm gezeigt wurden.

Ein Film, wird als "Kompilationsfilm" (CMP) beschrieben, wenn die Quelle angibt, das er aus Teilen von verschiedenen Filmen oder Archivmaterial zusammengeschnitten wurde. Diese Filme haben für gewöhnlich einen Begleitkommentar.

Filme, die die Angabe "Für das Fernsehen produziert" (MTV) tragen, sind Filme, die vom Fernsehen finanziert wurden, ungeachtet der Tatsache, ob sie im Kino gezeigt wurden oder nicht. Dabei kann es sich um Dokumentarfilme handeln, oder um Filme, die aus einem Zusammenschnitt von Fernsehserien entstanden.

Der Begriff "Serie" (SER) wird benutzt, um eine Filmgruppe zu beschreiben, die ein gemeinsames Thema oder die gleiche Besetzung haben können, obgleich sie jeweils in sich abgeschlossen sind.

Fast alle Filme, die vor 1928 entstanden, waren Stummfilme. Doch wird die Bezeichnung "SIL" nur gegeben, um einen Stummfilm zu identifizieren, wenn eine Fassung als Stummfilm und als Tonfilm existiert.

"Serials" (SRL) sind Filme, die aus verschiedenen Episoden bestehen. Sie wurden vornehmlich 1914-1936 in den USA produziert. Es handelt sich hierbei vorwiegend um Aktions-Melodramen, die gewöhnlich in wöchentlichen Episoden gezeigt wurden. Einige Filme wurden in Serial-Form in Mexiko in den 60er Jahren produziert, doch umfassen diese lediglich drei oder vier Episoden und entstanden in dieser Form, um die Gesetzgebung zu umgehen. Diese Filme wurden nicht als "Serials" eingestuft.

Filme, die als "Fernsehfilme" (TVM) bezeichnet sind, sind fast ausschließlich amerikanisch, und der begriff bezieht sich auf Filme, die für die Übertragung im Fernsehen gedreht wurden. Gelegentlich wurden diese im Kino gezeigt, im allgemeinen in Großbritannien, und werden inzwischen als Videos vertrieben, ohne daß ihre Herkunft unbedingt offensichtlich wäre. Sie tragen jedoch dazu bei, die Filmographie eines Regisseurs vollständiger zu gestalten, da viele Regisseure inzwischen gleichzeitig für Film und Fersehen arbeiten.

Herkunftsland eines Films

Das Herkunftsland des Filmes ist im allgemeinen das Land, in dem der Film entstand und/oder das Land, das die Produktion finanzierte. Siehe die nachstehende Liste der LÄNDERBEZEICHNUNGEN, in der die vollständige Liste der abgedeckten Länder angegeben ist. Falls eine Quelle angab, daß ein Film von einem bestimmten Land beansprucht wird, d.h. er erschien im entsprechenden Jahrbuch, so wurde dieses Land als Herkunftsland aufgeführt. Filme, die in Großbritannien mit amerikanischen Mitteln hergestellt wurden, fallen in diese Kategorie, da eine Quelle sie einen britischen Film und eine andere einen amerikanischen nennt. Falls es sich bei einem Film um eine Ko-Produktion handelt, bezieht sich das angegebene Land auf das Herkunftsland des Regisseurs.

Das Herkunftsland eines Filmes behält die Bezeichnungen Bundesrepublik und DDR sowie Nord- und Südkorea bei, wobei Vorkriegsfilme jeweils unter Bundesrepublik und Südkorea aufgeführt werden.

Alternative Titel

Beim alternativen Filmtitel kann es sich um einen Titel handeln, der benutzt wurde, als der Film in einem anderen Land gezeigt wurde (d.h. ein fremdsprachiger Titel oder ein alternativer Titel in der ursprünglichen Sprache), als er im Fernsehen ausgestrahlt wurde oder als Video erschien, oder um einen Arbeitstitel, eine genaue Übersetzung oder einen Titel, der bei der Neu-Veröffentlichung benutzt wurde.

Ein alternativer Titel kann von einer Länderbezeichnung in Klammern gefolgt sein, z.B. "(FRN)". Dies gibt das Land an, in dem der alternative Titel benutzt wurde.

II. Filmographie der Regisseure

Die nachstehende Information kann beim Eintrag für einen Regisseur erscheinen (siehe nachstehende Erklärungen):

- Name
- Herkunftsland des Regisseurs
- Datum/Daten
- Beruf
- Andere(r) Name(n)
- Filme:
  - Haupttitel
  - Jahr
  - Filmtyp
  - Alternative(r) Titel

Name

Es wird der Name des Regisseurs benutzt, unter dem er am besten bekannt ist. Bei anderen Namen werden Querverweise gegeben.

Herkunftsland des Regisseurs

Das Herkunftsland bezieht sich auf das Geburtsland des Regisseurs, das größtenteils, jedoch nicht immer, das Land ist, in dem der Großteil der Filme des Regisseurs entstand. Falls Angaben über den Geburtsort des Regisseurs nicht vorliegen, so wird angenommen, daß dies mit dem Hauptentstehungsland seiner Filme identisch ist.

Der Name des Landes wird angegeben, wie er zum Zeitpunkt der Geburt des Regisseurs bekannt war, und kann sich auf einen Staat oder ein Territorial beziehen, das nicht mehr existiert (wie etwa Palästina). Alle Deutschen, gleichgültig, ob sie aus der ehemaligen DDR oder der Bundesrepublik stammen, werden unter Deutschland aufgeführt. In gleicher Weise werden alle Koreaner, gleichgültig, ob sie aus Nord- oder Südkorea stammen, unter Korea aufgeführt.

Datum/Daten

Bei den Geburts- und Todesdaten, falls angegeben, handelt es sich um diejenigen, die in den Quellen am häufigsten angeführt werden.

Beruf

Die hauptsächliche Beschäftigung des Regisseurs wird manchmal angegeben, wenn es sich dabei nicht um die Regie handelt, wie etwa bei Henri Decae, Kinematograph.

Andere(r) Name

Dies umfasst etwaige Abweichungen bei der Namenszeichnung eines Regisseurs, einschließlich Pseudonyme und abweichende Schreibweisen. Letzteres ist bei Regisseuren aus Ländern wie der UdSSR relativ häufig.

Filme

Auffindbare Filme, die dem Regisseur zugeschrieben werden, sind nach Haupttitel und in zeitlicher Reihenfolge angegeben. Zusätzliche gegebene Information umfaßt das Jahr, den Filmtyp und alternative Titel (siehe Erklärungen oben). Ko-Regisseure sind nicht eingeschlossen, obgleich diese in der Liste der Filmtitel aufgezeigt werden.

Regisseure nach Land

Alle Regisseure wurden in alphabetischer Reihenfolge in einem gesonderten Index in Band II nach Land zusammengefaßt (wie oben angegeben). Lebensdaten werden wo verfügbar ebenso angegeben.

Regisseure von Trickfilmen

Alle Regisseure von Trickfilmen - die ein charakteristisches künstlerisches Medium geschaffen haben - werden in alphabetischer Reihenfolge in einem gesonderten Index in Band II zusammengefaßt. Das Land (wie oben angegeben) und die Lebensdaten werden neben den anderen Namen angegeben.

Ausgewählte Bibliographie

Dies umfaßt alle bedeutenden Quellen im Druck, die zu Rate gezogen wurden, in alphabetischer Reihenfolge nach Titel aufgeführt. Der Autor, der Herausgeber, der Sitz des Herausgebers und das Veröffentlichungsdatum werden außerdem angegeben.

ABKÜRZUNGEN

ANM animated (Trickfilm)
ANS animated short (Kurztrickfilm)
ANT anthology (Anthologie)
ASS animated short series (Kurztrickfilmserie)
C/D co-director (Ko-Regisseur)
CMP compilation (Kompilationsfilm)
DOC documentary (Dokumentarfilm)
DCS short documentary (Kurzdokumentarfilm)
DSS documentary short series (Kurzdokumentarserie)
EDT editor (Montage)
M composer (music) Komponist (Musik)
MTV made for television (Für das Fernsehen produziert)
P producer (Produzent)
PH photographer (Fotograf)
SER series (Serie)
SHS short series (Kurzserie)
SHT short (Kurzfilm)
SIL silent (Stummfilm)
SND sound (Tonfilm)
SPV supervision (Leitung)
SRL serial (Serial)
TVM television film (Fernsehfilm)
U/C uncredited (keine Angaben)

LÄNDERANGABEN

AFG Afghanistan
ALB Albanien
ALG Algerien
ANG Angola
ARG Argentinien
ASL Australien
AUS Österreich
BLG Belgien
BLV Bolivien
BNG Bangladesch
BNN Benin
BRK Burkin Faso
BRM Burma
BRZ Brasilien
BUL Bulgarien
CHL Chile
CHN China
CLM Kolumbien
CMR Kamerun
CND Kanada
CNG Kongo
CPV Kapverden
CRC Costa Rica
CUB Kuba
CYP Zypern
CZC Tschechoslowakei
DMN Dominikanische Republik
DNM Dänemark
ECD Equador
EGY Ägypten
ETH Äthiopien
FNL Finnland
FRG Bundesrepublik Deutschland
FRN Frankreich
GBN Gabun
GDR DDR
GHN Ghana
GIB Gibraltar
GNB Guinea Bissau
GRC Griechenland
GRM Deutschland
ATM Guatemala
GUM Guam
GUN Guyana
HKG Hongkong
HNG Ungarn
ICL Island
INC Indochina
IND Indien
INN Indonesien
IRL Irland
IRN Iran
IRQ Irak
ISR Israel
ITL Italien
IVC Elfenbeinküste
JMC Jamaika
JPN Japan
JRD Jordanien
KMP Kampuchea (Kambodscha)
KNY Kenia
KOR Korea
KWT Kuwait
LAO Laos
LBN Lebanon
LBY Libyen
LCH Liechtenstein
LTH Litauen
LTV Lettland
LXM Luxemburg
MDG Madagaskar
MLI Mali
MLT Malta
MLY Malaysien
MNC Monaco
MNG Mongolien
MRC Marokko
MRT Mauretanien
MCX Mexiko
MZM Mosambik
NCR Nicaragua
NGR Nigeria
NRK Nordkorea
NPL Nepal
NRW Norwegen
NTH Niederlande
NZL Neuseeland
PHL Philippinen
PKS Pakistan
PLN Polen
PLS Palästina
PNM Panama
PRC Puerto Rica
PRG Paraquay
PRT Portugal
PRU Peru
RMN Rumänien
SAf Südafrika
SDN Sudan
SKR Südkorea
SLN Sri Lanka
SLV El Salvador
SML Somalia
SNG Singapur
SNL Senegal
SPN Spanien
SRN Surinam
SWD Schweden
SWT Schweiz
SYR Syrien
T&T Trinidad & Tobago
THL Thailand
TNS Tunesien
TRK Türkei
TWN Taiwan
UAR Vereinigte Arabische Republik
UGN Uganda
UKN Großbritannien
UNN Vereinte Nationen
URG Uruguay
USA Vereinigte Staaten von Amerika
USS Union der sowjetischen sozialistischen Republiken
VEN Venezuela
VTN Vietnam
WIN Westindien
YGS Jugoslawien
ZIM Simbabwe
ZMB Sambia
ZRE Zaire

Avant-propos

L'industrie qui a réalisé les films dont la liste extraordinaire et variée est indexée dans ces volumes a également encouragé le développement d'une bibliothèque considérable d'ouvrages de référence. Même si l'on ignore ces publications qui dépeignent superficiellement ces variétés et spectacles populaires d'une grande banalité, la recherche de données de référence détaillées sur des films repose sur un choix riche en sources d'informations: riche mais frustrant. Un recueil épais de films disponibles sur bandes vidéo ou présentés à la télévision ne donnera pas la liste de nombreux films ou documentaires en langues étrangères; les superbes encyclopédies du genre film noir, westerns ou film de science fiction sont simplement décevantes; même si les catalogues des principaux instituts cinématographiques nationaux présentent un catalogage splendide dans les règles de l'art, ils ont un retard de près d'un siècle de production qui est toujours en train d'être rattrapé.

L'index d'Alan Goble est une réussite monumentale et son simple objectif consiste à noter les réalisations cinématographiques mondiales du premier siècle du cinéma mais il a demandé vingt années de travail. Sa rédaction, comme la bibliographie en témoigne, comprend une mosaïque d'ouvrages de référence et bien d'autres. Même dans les domaines où les difficultés rencontrées dans la collation des données globales sont les plus sévères, telles que l'afflux de films de l'industrie cinématographique indienne, cet index est d'une qualité qui est rare en matière d'ouvrages internationaux: ainsi on retrouvera ici quelques 2000 titres de film du sous-continent indien.

Pour la première fois, il existe un ouvrage cinématographique à référence simple présentant des informations essentielles qui étaient autrefois dispersées dans les bibliothèques d'encyclopédies, de répertoires, d'indexes et de livres annuels. Utile à toute personne cherchant des renseignements, du spectateur de bandes vidéo à la maison au chercheur de films d'une cinémathèque, *The International Film Index* fournit des filmographies sur quelques 25.000 directeurs et valorise l'importance attachée aux chiffres "connus", répétés dans de trop nombreux ouvrages de référence.

La rareté ou l'intérêt spécial de certains livres sont souvent indiqués par leur omission des bibliographies standard. De la même manière, je m'attends à ce que l'observation "Pas dans Goble" soit autant une remarque sur l'importance de ce principal ouvrage de référence historique sur la filmologie qu'un encouragement pour la préparation de l'édition suivante.

Alex Noel-Tod
Bibliothècaire de filmologie
Université d'East Anglia

Préface

C'est la première grande tentative de constitution d'un index cinématographique complet présentant un classement par titre et par directeur de film du monde entier. Vingt années de rédaction ont été nécessaires mais comme pour tout autre ouvrage similaire, il reste beaucoup de travail à faire. Cependant, je pense qu'il a atteint un niveau lui permettant de combler un créneau dans la littérature du cinéma qui est demeuré vide pendant de trop nombreuses années.

Au début, j'avais pour objectif de cataloguer tous les longs métrages ensemble avec leurs directeurs et les titres de film du monde entier, mais les difficultés que j'ai rencontrées m'ont amené à prendre la décision de classer tous les films (théatraux) que j'ai trouvés et d'ajouter des informations au fur et à mesure de leur venue. L'effet était par conséquent cumulatif. J'ai décidé ultérieurement de compter les films sans parole et de faire de *The International Film Index*, un dossier des productions des cent années du cinéma.

Il est d'opinion générale que le directeur est la personne clé dans la réalisation d'un film et je me suis rendu compte que l'inscription du nom du directeur au côté de son film permettrait de présenter un index inégalable. Ceci a donné lieu à des filmographies sur quelques 25.000 directeurs, allant de ceux qui ont réalisé un seul film à ceux qui en ont produit plusieurs centaines.

J'ai choisi d'y faire figurer les documentaires, les courts métrages et les films d'animation afin de participer, tout d'abord, à l'achèvement des filmographies des directeurs réalisant des films à long métrage. Cependant, il existe un groupe de directeurs dont le principal travail, spécialisé dans les domaines précédemment cités, a marqué l'industrie; ces types de film ont été également comptés.

J'ai décidé que les informations de base nécessaires à l'identification d'un film devraient comprendre le titre original du film, l'année de sortie, le directeur, le pays d'origine, le type de film et tous les autres titres prêtés au film. Pour fournir davantage de renseignements tels que la durée, la couleur et les crédits d'interprétation, il aurait fallu consacrer un temps bien plus considérable à la recherche et l'index aurait été sans doute trop gros pour pouvoir être imprimé sous la forme d'un livre. Il y a vingt ans, je n'avais pas la possibilité de travailler sur un ordinateur individuel mais je peux désormais profiter de cette technologie et ainsi, le fait de pouvoir ajouter d'autres domaines aux entrées existantes constitue un véritable avantage; mais cela dépendra du succès de la première édition.

Tout en rédigeant *The International Film Index*, j'ai conservé deux indexes parallèles, un classé par titre et l'autre par directeur. J'ai pu ainsi établir un recoupement qui m'a permis de résoudre les nombreuses anomalies. Cela a également facilité l'identification des titres d'origine des films étrangers projetés aux Etats-Unis et en Grande-Bretagne.

Je n'ai fixé aucun critère quant à la qualité des films se trouvant dans cet ouvrage et je n'ai porté aucun jugement sur la valeur artistique du directeur du film. Ce cataloguage est basé sur l'opinion d'une personne exprimant dans un livre, une revue ou un journal la nécessité de donner les particularités du film et/ou du directeur.

On ne peut espérer qu'un ouvrage de cette taille et de cette portée soit irréprochable. Même si ma méthode m'a permis d'effectuer un nombre considérable de recoupements, les bizarreries et l'inconsistance des informations conservées sur l'industrie cinématographiques ainsi que les limitations imposées par le temps se traduiront par l'occurrence d'erreurs et de blancs. En outre, le lecteur peut ne pas être nécessairement d'accord avec la sélection des informations dans certains cas. Une source d'information se déclarera péremptoire alors qu'une autre la contredira tout aussi péremptoirement. Dans de tels cas, j'ai porté un jugement mais je n'ai généralement rien supposé. Par exemple, il est possible que deux titres figurant sur la liste représentent en fait le même film mais à moins que je trouve des preuves bien fondées me permettant de confirmer ceci, je les ai fait figurer comme entrées particulières.

Cette duplication de titres se produit principalement avec les titres étrangers. Avec des normes de translitération et des langues étrangères si nombreuses, la vérification de toutes les variantes orthographiques n'a pas été faisable. Lorsque j'ai pu confirmer que le même titre de film est orthographié différemment, j'ai inscrit les deux noms sous le titre original.

Cela fait presque cent ans que la production de films de cinéma se poursuit. Dans un parc se trouvant à environ 2 km du lieu où je vous écris aujourd'hui, quelques personnes passionnées pour leur métier ont réalisé dès 1896 quelques-uns des premiers films tournés en Grande-Bretagne: des modestes débuts tels que ceux que le cinéma a connu pour en arriver à l'industrie cinématographique internationale aussi captivante qu'elle l'est de nos jours. Par la parution de ce livre, je suis heureux que ces pionniers se rangent aux côtés d'autres mentionnés ici, les célèbres et les moins célèbres mais qui ont tous contribué à faire du cinéma un des grands plaisirs du vingtième siècle.

Alan Goble
septembre 1991

Principes d'utilisation

Introduction

Cet index contient quelques 232.000 titres de films réalisés par 25.000 auteurs depuis 1895 jusqu'à 1990. 177.000 de ces titres sont originaux, les autres sont des titres de substitution. L'index inclut la vaste majorité des films faits aux Etats-Unis, Canada, en Grande-Bretagne, France, Allemagne, Italie, Australie et Nouvelle-Zélande ainsi que des films en provenance de plus d'une centaine d'autres pays. En tout 129 pays et territoires (certains d'entre eux n'existe même plus) sont répertoriés. La plupart des réalisateurs connus, et bien entendu tous ceux de renommée, sont inclus.

Les films d'art, le cinéma d'avant-garde, documentaires, court-métrages, séries et films d'animation sont également inclus.

The International Film Index comprend deux rubriques principales, Titres de Films et Filmographies des Réalisateurs, le tout classé par ordre alphabétique. Dans le premier tome, le titre est suivi par des données essentielles (6 au maximum, voir ci-dessous) servant à identifier le film. On peut également trouver, dans le second tome, une liste des réalisateurs; cette liste est accompagnée de une à quatre séries de données concernant le réalisateur et la chronologie de ses films. Toute information essentielle se rapportant au film est répétée dans la filmographie afin de rendre plus aisé l'usage de cet ouvrage. Le second tome contient également deux répertoires subsidiaires: celui des réalisateurs selon leurs pays d'origine et celui des auteurs de films d'animation ainsi qu'une bibliographie.

Pour l'information du lecteur nous détaillons, ci-dessous, le contenu du *International Film Index*.

THE INTERNATIONAL FILM INDEX: Détail du Contenu

USA Films (titres originaux)	Canada	GB	France	Allemagne[a]	Italie	
Long métrage[b]	35352	2102	9476	9147	9879	8435
Court métrage	34371	422	7077	3916	633	497
Film d'animation	6341	379	441	468	226	78
Documentaire	918	1948	888	622	151	258
Télévision	2801	461	406	78	54	81
Séries	477	-	37	25	-	6
Total	80260	5312	18325	14256	10943	9355
parmi lesquels: film muets	40219	24	8299	3563	4046	829
Réalisateurs						
Total	5679	844	2194	2020	1422	1343

Films (titres originaux)	Autres pays européens[c]	Australie/ Nelle Zélande	Japon	Autres	TOTAL
Long métrage[b]	17402	1033	4367	13393	110586
Court métrage	2105	531	20	484	50056
Film d'animation	1561	54	170	69	9787
Documentaire	1482	474	55	481	7277
Télévision	175	104	4	33	4197
Séries	7	1	-	-	553
Total	22732	21927	4616	14460	182456
parmi lesquels: film muets	1677	448	39	536	59680
Réalisateurs					
Total	5135	506	603	4942	24688

[a]Ceci inclut l'ancienne Allemagne de l'Est. [b]Long métrage ou film n'appartenant à aucune catégorie. [c]URSS incluse.

NOTICE EXPLICATIVE

Organisation

Les titres de films classés par ordre alphabétique selon les principes établis par l'*American Library Association Filing Rules* (1980) (règlements de classification de l'association américaine des bibliothèques). Les titres commençant avec un chiffre sont placés en début de l'index.

I. Titres de films

Un titre peut être accompagné des détails suivants (voir explications ci-dessous).

- Titre original
- Année
- Auteur(s)
- Autres contributions
- Catégorie
- Pays d'origine
- Autre(s) titre(s)

Titre original

Diverses publications ont été consultées pour rassembler ces 232.000 titres (on en trouvera une bibliographie à la fin du second tome). La présence d'un titre dans cet ouvrage n'indique pas nécéssairement que le film soit toujours en existence ou ait même jamais existé; elle signifie simplement que l'ouvrage de référence a signalé qu'à un moment donné un film portant ce titre a été en production. Le titre est donné dans la langue dans laquelle il est originellement sorti.

Toutefois si le titre original n'est pas clair, peuvent être donnés selon les circonstances le titre sous lequel le film est sorti, le titre provisoire, celui adopté pour la télévision, une traduction litérale ou simplement le titre sous lequel le film a été connu quelle qu'en soit la raison.

La liste des titres originaux et "Autres titres" est à double entrée.

Année

L'année indiquée est, en général, celle de la sortie. Dans les cas où le film fut produit bien avant sa sortie, la date la plus ancienne est donnée. Dans certains cas il a été impossible de déterminer la date exacte de sortie; une date probable a été fournie.

Réalisateur(s)

Les réalisateurs sont inclus sous les noms pour lesquels ils étaient mieux connus. Ainsi les films de Mihaly Kertesz apparaissent sous "Michael Curtiz" bien qu'il ait réalisé ses premiers films sous le nom de Kertesz. Toutefois des renvois sont établis entre les différents noms d'un auteur.

Lorsque l'information était disponible, le nom des assistants réalisateurs est aussi indiqué.

Autres contributions

Pour certains films il n'était possible de déterminer le nom du réalisateur. En conséquence d'autres moyens ont été fournis pour aider à l'identification du film. Ils peuvent inclure la compagnie de production, le producteur, l'acteur principal, le scénariste ou bien toute autre personne ayant rapport au film. Dans la plupart des cas la nature de leur contribution est indiquée entre parenthèses.

Catégorie

Certains titres sont annotés afin d'indiquer s'il s'agit d'un court métrage, d'un documentaire, d'un feuilleton, d'un film d'animation, de télévision etc (pour une liste complète des abréviations, voir ci-dessous). Un court métrage est un film durant moins de trente minutes. Cette définition ne s'applique pas aux films réalisés avant 1915 puisqu'avant cette date la majorité des films étaient de courte durée. Les films non annotés sont ou bien des longs métrages ou bien des films dont l'exacte catégorie n'a pas été determinée.

Un film décrit comme étant une "Anthologie" (ANT) est un long métrage constitué de plusieurs courts métrages.

Le terme "compilation" (CMP) se réfère à tout film composé de diverses sections d'autres films ou de reportages; ces sections sont reliées entre elles par des commentaires.

Le terme "réalisé pour la télévision" (MTV) se réfère aux films qui ont été financés par la télévision. Il se peut que certains soient sortis en salle. Il peut s'agir de documentaires ou de films montés à partir de divers épisodes d'une série.

Le terme "séries" (SER) décrit un groupe de films indépendants les uns des autres mais ayant un thème ou des personnages en commun.

La presque totalité des films réalisés avant 1928 étaient muets. L'abréviation "SIL" n'est utilisée que pour distinguer la version muette de la version parlante lorsque le film existe dans les deux versions.

Le terme "Feuilleton" (abréviation SRL) représente les films composés de plusieurs épisodes, réalisés principalement aux Etats-Unis de 1914 à 1936. Il s'agissait de films d'action/mélodrames montrés chaque semaine à la télévision. Certains films furent réalisés au Mexique sous ce format dans les années soixante mais ils ne comprenaient que trois ou quatre épisodes et le format ne servait qu'à détourner les lois en vigueur. Ces films n'ont pas été répertoriés sous le terme "Feuilleton".

Le terme "Téléfilm" (TVM) s'applique principalement à des films américains et se rapporte aux films produits pour passer à la télévision. Certains ont pu sortir au cinéma, invariablement en Grande-Bretagne, mais sont maintenant présents sur le marché vidéo et il n'est pas toujours aisé d'identifier leur origine. Ils servent toutefois à fournir des renseignements plus détaillés sur les réalisateurs qui travaillent à la fois au cinéma et à la télévision.

Pays d'origine

Ceci représente généralement le pays dans lequel le film fut réalisé et/ou le pays qui a financé la production (voir la rubrique "Codes des Pays" ci-dessous pour une liste complète de pays répertoriés). Lorsqu'un ouvrage de référence indique que tel ou tel pays revendique la création d'un film (ainsi que le signale sa revue annuelle), ce pays est considéré comme le pays d'origine. Les films faits en Grande-Bretagne à l'aide de fonds américains échouent souvent dans cette catégorie; tel ouvrage de référence le signalera comme film américain, tel autre comme film britannique. Dans le cas d'une co-production, le pays indiqué est celui dont le réalisateur est originaire.

La distinction entre Allemagne de l'Est et Allemagne de l'ouest est conservée; il en est de même avec la Corée du Nord et la Corée du Sud.

Autres Titres

Il s'agit ici du titre substitué au titre original - par exemple lorsqu'un film est sorti dans un pays différent de celui d'origine (titre en langue étrangère ou simplement autre titre) à la télévision, en vidéo; il peut également s'agir d'un titre provisoire, d'une traduction litérale ou d'un nouveau titre donné au film lors d'une seconde sortie.

Un "autre titre" peut être suivi du code d'un pays, par exemple "(FRN)". Ceci indique le pays dans lequel ce nouveau titre fut utilisé.

II. Filmographie des Réalisateurs

Une rubrique concernant un réalisateur peut contenir les renseignements suivants:

- Nom
- Pays d'origine
- Date(s)
- Profession
- Autre patronyme
- Films:
  - Titre d'origine
  - Année
  - Catégorie
  - Autre titre

Nom

Le nom le mieux connu du réalisateur est utilisé. Des renvois aux "autres noms" ont été établis.

Pays d'origine

Il s'agit du lieu de naissance du réalisateur qui souvent, mais pas toujours, se trouve être le pays dans lequel la majorité de ses films ont été faits. Dans les cas où les détails concernant le lieu de naissance est manquant, le pays indiqué est celui où ses films ont été réalisés.

Dates

Lorsqu'elles sont mentionnées, les dates de naissance et de décès sont celles indiquées dans les ouvrages de référence.

Profession

Il arrive que l'auteur ne soit pas réalisateur par profession, par exemple Henri Decae, cinéaste.

Autre Patronymes

Cette rubrique inclut toute variation dans le nom de l'auteur, y compris pseudonymes et orthographe différente. Celle-ci est courante parmi les metteurs en scéne originaires de pays comme la Russie.

Films

Tous les films répertoriés et attribués à un auteur sont présentés chronologiquement et le titre original en est donné. Sont également indiqués l'année, la catégorie, les autres titres (voir explications ci-dessus). Les noms des assistants réalisateurs ne sont pas inclus bien qu'ils soient présents au sein de la rubrique "Titres de Films".

Réalisateurs par Pays

Tous les réalisateurs sont regroupés par ordre alphabétique et selon leur pays d'origine (index distinct dans le second tome). Les dates, lorsqu'elles sont disponibles, sont également indiquées.

Réalisateurs de films d'animation

Tous ces auteurs - qui ont contribués à la création d'un genre artistique à part - sont classés séparément par ordre alphabétique (voir index dans le second tome). Pays d'origine (voir définition ci-dessus), dates et autres patronymes sont également indiqués.

Bibliographie

Cette bibliographie inclut tous les principaux ouvrages consultés. Les titres sont classés par ordre alphabétique. Le nom de l'auteur, de l'éditeur, la société d'édition et la date sont également indiqués.

ABREVIATIONS

ANM animated (animé)
ANS animated short (court métrage animé)
ANT anthology (anthologie)
ASS animated short series (série de courts métrages animés)
C/D co-director (co-directeur)
CMP compilation (rédaction)
DOC documentary (documentaire)
DCS short documentary (court métrage documentaire)
DSS documentary short series (série de courts métrages documentaires)
EDT editor (éditeur)
M composer (music) compositeur (musique)
MTV made for television (réalisé pour la télévision)
P producer (réalisateur)
PH photographer (photographe)
SER series (série)
SHS short series (série de courts métrages)
SHT short (court métrage)
SIL silent (sans parole)
SND sound (son)
SPV supervision (direction)
SRL serial (feuilleton)
TVM television film (film télévisé)
U/C uncredited (sans générique)

CODES DE PAYS

AFG Afghanistan
ALB Albanie
ALG Algérie
ANG Angola
ARG Argentine
ASL Australie
AUS Autriche
BLG Belgique
BLV Bolivie
BNG Bangladesh
BNN Bénin
BRK Burkina Faso
BRM Birmanie
BRZ Brésil
BUL Bulgarie
CHL Chili
CHN Chine
CLM Colombie
CMR Cameroun
CND Canada
CNG Congo
CPV Iles du Cap-Vert
CRC Costa Rica
CUB Cuba
CYP Chypre
CZC Tchécoslovaquie
DMN République Dominicaine
DNM Danemark
ECD Ecuador
EGY Egypte
ETH Ethiopie
FNL Finlande
FRG Allemagne de l'Ouest
FRN France
GBN Gabon
GDR Allemagne de l'Est
GHN Ghana
GIB Gibraltar
GNB Guinée Bissau
GRC Grèce
GRM Allemagne
GTM Guatemala
GUM Guam
GUN Guinée
GYN Guyane
HKG Hong Kong
HNG Hongrie
ICL Islande
INC Indochine
IND Indonésie
INN Indonésie
IRL Irlande
IRN Iran
IRQ Irak
ISR Israël
ITL Italie
IVC Côte d'Ivoire
JMC Jamaïque
JPN Japon
JRD Jordanie
KMP Cambodia (Cambodge)
KNY Kenya
KOR Corée
KWT Kuweit
LAO Laos
LBN Liban
LBY Libye
LCH Liechtenstein
LTH Lithuanie
LTV Lettonie
LXM Luxembourg
MDG Madagascar
MLI Mali
MLT Malte
MLY Malaysia
MNC Monaco
MNG Mongolie
MRC Maroc
MRT Mauritanie
MXC Mexique
MZM Mozambique
NCR Nicaragua
NGR Nigéria
NKR Corée du Nord
NPL Népal
NRW Norvège
NTH Pays-Bas
NZL Nouvelle-Zélande
PHL Philippines
PKS Pakistan
PLN Pologne
PLS Palestine
PNM Panama
PRC Puerto Rico
PRG Paraguay
PRT Portugal
PRU Pérou
RMN Roumanie
SAF Afrique du sud
SDN Soudan
SKR Corée du sud
SLN Sri Lanka
SLV Salvador
SML Somalie
SNG Singapour
SNL Sénégal
SPN Espagne
SRN Surinam
SWD Suède
SWT Suisse
SYR Syrie
T&T Trinité-et-Tobago
THL Thaïlande
TNS Tunisie
TRK Turquie
TWN Taiwan
UAR République Arabe Unie
UGN Uganda
UKN Royaume-Uni
UNN Nations unies
URG Uruguay
USA États-Unis
USS Union des Républiques Socialistes Soviétiques
VEN Venezuela
VTN Viet-nam
WIN Antilles
YGS Yougoslavie
ZIM Zimbabwe
ZMB Zambie
ZRE Zaïre

Proemio

L'industria che ha creato la straordinaria e svariatissima gamma di film elencati in questi volumi ha anche stimolato la realizzazione di un'ampia biblioteca di libri di consultazione. Anche scontando quelle pubblicazioni che non rappresentano che rassegne delle trivialità del mondo dello spettacolo e delle celebrità del cinema, per la ricerca di dati sul mondo cinematografico bisogna fare affidamento ad un ricco assortimento di fonti d'informazione - ricco ma frustrante. Anche il più grande dei manuali dei film disponibili in televisione o su videocassetta non comprende molti film e documentari stranieri; le lussuose enciclopedie dei film noir, western o di fantascienza si limitano a descrivere solo i film di questi generi; mentre i cataloghi dei principali istituti cinematografici nazionali, pur essendo precisi nei più minuziosi dettagli, hanno un secolo di produzioni cinematografiche alle spalle e sono ancora in ritardo di molti anni nel lavoro di catalogazione.

La guida di Alan Goble ha un solo semplice scopo di proporzioni monumentali, cioè di catalogare il primo secolo di produzioni cinematografiche, un lavoro che è durato vent'anni. Come testimonia la bibliografia, nella realizzazione della guida si è fatto riferimento anche all'enorme mosaico di opere di consultazione già esistenti. Anche in quei campi dove è particolarmente difficile raccogliere informazioni sulla produzione totale, come ad esempio la marea crescente di film prodotti dall'industria cinematografica indiana, questa guida, che contiene i titoli di 2.000 film del subcontinente indiano, ha conseguito un'ampiezza di trattazione che le altre pubblicazioni internazionali stentano ad eguagliare.

Per la prima volta esiste, ed è disponibile a chiunque, dall'amante della videocassetta al ricercatore di dati archiviati, un'unico libro di consultazione sui film, che offre le informazioni di base che si trovavano precedentemente sparse lungo numerosi scaffali di enciclopedie, indici, guide ed annuari. Le filmografie di pressoché 25.000 registi contenute nel *International Film Index* ristabiliscono l'equilibrio troppo spesso sbilanciato dai libri di consultazione che concentrano l'attenzione solo sui personaggi "conosciuti".

La rarità o altro interesse speciale di certe pubblicazioni stampate è spesso indicata dal fatto che vengono omesse dalle normali bibliografie. In modo analogo penso che la frase "not in Goble" non solo rifletterà l'importanza di questo storico ed importantissimo libro di consultazione per lo studio dei film ma servirà da incoraggiamento alla pubblicazione della prossima edizione.

Alex Noel-Tod
Film Studies Librarian
University of East Anglia

Prefazione

Questa nuova opera è il primo tentativo di realizzare un esauriente indice di film di tutto il mondo, classificati per titolo e nome del regista. Il lavoro di compilazione dei dati è durato venti anni ma, come per qualsiasi altra opera di questo genere, c'è ancora molto lavoro da fare. Penso però che sia giunta al punto in cui possa riempire una lacuna che esiste da troppo tempo nel campo della letteratura dedicata al mondo del cinema.

Lo scopo iniziale fu semplicemente di elencare tutti i lungometraggi, indicando inoltre i nomi dei registi ed i titoli alternativi. Alcune difficoltà mi condussero però ad elencare tutti i film (teatrali) che trovavo, aggiungendo allo stesso tempo tutte le relative informazioni raccolte. L'effetto era dunque cumulativo. Più tardi decisi di includere anche i film muti, il che mi permise di creare *The International Film Index* che comprende le produzioni di oltre cento anni di storia del cinema.

Nella produzione dei film, il regista è in genere considerato la persona chiave. Mi resi conto che elencando assieme al titolo di ogni film anche il nome del relativo regista avrei prodotto inoltre un indice di registi di ineguagliata completezza. Il risultato di questo lavoro è stato una serie di filmografie relative a circa 25.000 registi, da coloro che non hanno realizzato che un solo film a coloro che ne hanno prodotti centinaia e centinaia.

Scelsi anche di includere documentari, cortometraggi e film d'animazione, in primo luogo per rendere più complete le filmografie dei registi dei lungometraggi. Vi sono però moltissimi registi le cui opere principali sono dei suddetti tipi e che hanno lasciato il loro segno sull'industria cinematografica, e per questo motivo ho deciso di includere le loro opere.

Decisi che le informazioni essenziali necessarie per identificare un film dovessero comprendere il titolo originale, l'anno di messa in circolazione, il regista, il paese di origine, il tipo di film e gli eventuali titoli alternativi. Fornire anche altre informazioni come la durata, colore e nomi dei realizzatori, avrebbe prolungato il lavoro di ricerca e prodotto forse un indice troppo voluminoso da essere pratico come libro di consultazione. Venti anni fa non esisteva l'alternativa del personal computer ma ora posso approfittare di questo sviluppo tecnologico, il che mi permetterà di aggiungere altre categorie alle inserzioni già esistenti, benché tutto dipenda dal successo della prima edizione.

Nel realizzare *The International Film Index* ho creato due indici paralleli, uno contenente i titoli dei film e l'altro contenente i nomi dei relativi registi, i quali mi hanno permesso di controllare attentamente le informazioni, di risolvere molte anomalie, e di identificare i titoli originali dei film stranieri distribuiti negli Stati Uniti e nel Regno Unito.

Non ho né applicato criteri di qualità ai film elencati in quest'opera né giudicato le abilità artistiche dei registi. I film sono stati inseriti semplicemente per via del fatto che a un certo momento qualcuno ha sentito la necessità di fornire informazioni e/o il nome di un regista in uno dei libri, delle riviste e dei giornali che ho consultato.

Un'opera di queste dimensioni e di questa portata non potrà mai essere completamente libera da errori. Benché il metodo che ho impiegato mi abbia permesso di eseguire numerosi riscontri, le incertezze e le incoerenze delle informazioni che esistono sul mondo del cinema, oltre ai limiti di tempo, saranno indubbiamente fonti di errori e lacune. Il lettore potrebbe inoltre pensare che in alcuni casi non abbia scelto le informazioni giuste. Mi è accaduto spesso di trovare che in una fonte di informazioni veniva fatta un'affermazione categorica che in un'altra veniva smentita da un'affermazione altrettanto categorica ma totalmente opposta. In questi casi ho dovuto fare una scelta tra le due ma in generale non ho fatto alcuna supposizione. infatti possibile che abbia inserito due titoli che corrispondano allo stesso film, ma a meno che non abbia trovato informazioni atte a sostanziare questa ipotesi, li ho inseriti come se fossero due titoli diversi. Dato l'enorme numero sia di lingue diverse che di criteri di traslitterazione non è stato possibile controllare tutte le varie grafie. Nei casi in cui ho trovato conferma che due titoli scritti diversamente corrispondevano infatti allo stesso film li ho inclusi ambedue sotto ad un titolo principale.

L'inizio della storia del cinema risale a quasi cento anni fa. Già nel 1896, in un parco a qualche chilometro da dove scrivo oggi queste parole, un gruppetto di devoti del cinema realizzò alcuni dei primi film mai prodotti nel Regno Unito. Partendo da queste origini modeste il cinema si è sviluppato ed è divenuto l'appassionante industria internazionale che è oggi. Sono lieto di garantire, mediante la pubblicazione di questo volume, che quei pionieri si affianchino oggi agli altri nomi più o meno famosi che hanno contribuito a fare del cinema una delle più grandi fonti di piacere del ventesimo secolo.

Alan Goble
settembre 1991

Guida per l'utente

INTRODUZIONE

Questo elenco contiene i titoli di circa 232.000 film realizzati da 25.000 registi tra il 1895 ed il 1990, 177.000 dei quali sono titoli originali e gli altri titoli alternativi. Comprende la stragrande maggioranza dei film realizzati negli Stati Uniti, Canada, Regno Unito, Francia, Germania, Italia, Australia e Nuova Zelanda, come pure film realizzati in oltre cento paesi diversi. L'elenco ricopre la produzione di ben 129 paesi e territori diversi (alcuni ormai defunti), comprende la grande maggioranza dei registi e senza dubbio tutti i maggiori esponenti del settore.

L'elenco comprende anche i film d'arte, il cinema alternativo, documentari, cortometraggi, serie e film d'animazione, come pure lungometraggi realizzati per e/o finanziati da emittenti televisive.

The International Film Index contiene due elenchi, uno dei titoli dei film ed uno delle filmografie dei registi, ambedue disposti in ordine alfabetico. Ogni titolo appare nel 1º volume assieme ad altre sei informazioni essenziali all'identificazione del film (v. a seguito). Il 2º volume contiene invece un elenco dei registi oltre ad un massimo di quattro categorie d'informazioni su ogni regista ed un elenco cronologico della relativa filmografia. I dati essenziali sui film vengono ripetuti nella filmografia per garantire la facilità di consultazione dell'opera. Il secondo volume contiene inoltre due indici supplementari: Directors by Country (registi divisi per paese di origine) e Directors of Animated Films (registi di film d'animazione), ed una bibliografia.

Per informazione del lettore, pubblichiamo qui a seguito una scomposizione del contenuto dell'*International Film Index.*

THE INTERNATIONAL FILM INDEX: Scomposizione del contenuto

Film (titoli originali)	Stati Uniti	Canada	Regno Unito	Francia	Germania[a]	Italia
Lungometraggi[b]	35352	2102	9476	9147	9879	8435
Cortometraggi	34371	422	7077	3916	633	497
Animazione	6341	379	441	468	226	78
Documentari	918	1948	888	622	151	258
Televisione	2801	461	406	78	54	81
Film a episodi	477	-	37	25	-	6
Totale	80260	5312	18325	14256	10943	9355
de quali:						
Muti	40219	24	8299	3563	4046	829
Registi						
Totale	5679	844	2194	2020	1422	1343

Films (master titles)	Resto dell'Europa[c]	Australia/ Nuova Zelanda	Resto del Giappone	mondo	TOTAL
Lungometraggi[b]	17402	1033	4367	13393	110586
Cortometraggi	2105	531	20	484	50056
Animazione	1561	54	170	69	9787
Documentari	1482	474	55	481	7277
Televisione	175	104	4	33	4197
Film a episodi	7	1	-	-	553
Totale	22732	21927	4616	14460	182456
de quali:					
Muti	1677	448	39	536	59680
Registi					
Totale	5135	506	603	4942	24688

[a]Compresa l'ex-Repubblica Democratica Tedesca. [b]Lungometraggio o categoria non identificati. [c]Compresa l'URSS

NOTE ESPLICATIVE

Ordine di classifica

I titoli dei film sono elencati in ordina alfabetico secondo i principi del *American Library Association Filing Rules* (1980) [le regole di archiviazione dell'associazione delle librerie americane]. I titoli che iniziano con delle cifre vengono elencati all'inizio del volume.

I. Titoli dei film

Per ogni titolo vengono fornite le seguenti informazioni (v. spiegazioni che seguono):

- Titolo originale
- Anno
- Regista/i
- Altri riconoscimenti
- Tipo di film
- Paese di origine del film
- Titolo/i alternativo/i

Titolo originale

I 232.000 titoli dei film sono tratti da varie pubblicazioni, che vengono elencate in una bibliografia alla fine del 2º volume. Il fatto che appaia nell'elenco non garantisce però che il film esista ancora, né che sia mai esistito, ma significa solo che una delle fonti d'informazioni utilizzate indica il titolo del film e che in un dato momento il film si trovava in una determinata fase di produzione. Il titolo originale è il titolo del film nella lingua originale, ove sia identificabile. Il titolo può essere tuttavia il titolo di messa in circolazione, il titolo provvisorio, il titolo dell'emissione televisiva, una traduzione letterale o qualsiasi altro titolo con il quale è stato identificato il film per uno scopo od un'altro, se il titolo originale non è chiaro.

Accanto ai titoli alternativi appare un riferimento al titolo originale.

Anno

L'anno indica in genere la prima data in cui è

stato messo in circolazione il film, benché venga indicata, nei casi in cui il film è stato realizzato qualche anno prima della messa in circolazione, la prima data. In alcuni casi non è stato possibile determinare la data esatta di messa in circolazione e la data indicata corrisponde dunque alla data più probabile.

Regista/i

L'inserzione del regista viene fatta con il suo nome più conosciuto. I film di Mihaly Kertesz vengono dunque elencati sotto Michael Curtiz, benché nelle sue prime realizzazioni cinematografiche apparisse il cognome Kertesz. Tutti i nomi alternativi vengono comunque riferiti all'elenco delle filmografie dei registi.

Se disponibili, vengono anche inclusi i nomi degli eventuali co-registi.

Altri riconoscimenti

Per alcuni film non è stato possibile determinarne il regista ed ho dunque fornito un'altro dato, purché disponibile, per assistere nell'identificazione del film. Il dato in questione è, in alcuni casi, la società produttrice, ed in altri il produttore, uno dei principali attori, lo sceneggiatore o un'altra persona collegata alla produzione del film. Accanto a molti di questi nomi appare un riferimento tra parentesi che indica in che modo abbiano partecipato alla realizzazione del film.

Tipo di film

Troverete accanto ai titoli dei film un'annotazione che indica se si tratta di un cortometraggio, di un documentario, di un film a episodi, di un film d'animazione, di un telefilm ecc. - v. la lista completa delle abbreviazioni che segue. Un "cortometraggio" è un film di durata non superiore ai 30 minuti. Questa descrizione non è stata applicata ai film realizzati prima del 1915, dato che prima di questa data la maggior parte dei film era di questo tipo. I film per i quali non appare un'annotazione che ne descriva il tipo sono per la maggior parte lungometraggi o film per i quali non viene identificata la categoria di appartenenza.

Un film che viene definito "antologia" (ANT) è una raccolta di cortometraggi messi assieme e distribuiti come lungometraggio.

I film definiti "raccolta" (CMP) sono film per i quali la fonte ha indicato che sono stati realizzati usando segmenti di vari film o cinegiornali, normalmente collegati l'uno all'altro da una narrazione.

I film definiti "realizzato per la televisione" (MTV) sono quelli finanziati dalle emittenti televisive potendo o meno essere stati proiettati nelle sale cinematografiche. Possono essere documentari o film realizzati mediante il montaggio di scene tratte da una serie televisiva.

Il termine "serie" (SER) viene usato per descrivere un gruppo di film, ognuno indipendente dall'altro ma che hanno, per esempio, una trama o un cast in comune.

Pressoché tutti i film realizzati prima del 1928 sono film muti. L'abbreviazione "SIL" viene aggiunta solo per distinguere la versione muta nei casi in cui esiste sia una versione muta che una versione sonora dello stesso film.

I "film a episodi" (SRL) sono film composti da vari episodi e realizzati predominantemente negli Stati Uniti tra il 1914 ed il 1936. Sono invariabilmente melodrammi di azione e venivano generalmente proiettati a episodi settimanali. Anche in Messico negli anni 60 alcuni film furono realizzati ad episodi. Sono film che non durano più di tre o quattro episodi realizzati in questo modo per sovvertire la legislazione in vigore. Questi film non sono stati definiti "film a episodi".

I film definiti "film per la televisione" (TVM) sono quasi esclusivamente americani e realizzati per essere trasmessi in televisione. A volte vengono anche stati proiettati nelle sale cinematografiche, invariabilmente nel Regno Unito, ma vengono oggi distribuiti su videocassetta senza una chiara indicazione delle loro origini. Servono però a rendere più completa la filmografia dei registi, dato che molti lavorano contemporaneamente sia per la televisione che per il cinema.

Paese di origine del film

Il paese di origine del film è in genere il paese in cui è stato realizzato il film e/o il paese che ne ha finanziato la produzione. L'elenco delle ABBREVIAZIONI PER I PAESI indica i paesi compresi. Se una fonte ci ha indicato che la produzione di un film è rivendicata da un paese in particolare, se cioè appare nel relativo annuario, sarà questo il paese indicato nell'elenco. Ricadono generalmente in questa categoria i film realizzati nel Regno Unito con finanziamenti americani, dato che in alcune fonti vengono definiti film britannici ed in altre film americani. Se il film è una coproduzione, il paese indicato è il paese di origine del regista.

La definizione del paese di origine del film conserva le distinzioni tra Germania Federale e Democratica e tra Corea del Nord e del Sud. I film del periodo prima della guerra vengono elencati rispettivamente sotto Germania Federale e Corea del Sud.

Titoli alternativi

Il titolo alternativo di un film può essere il titolo usato per distribuire il film in un altro paese (cioè il titolo tradotto o un altro titolo originale), per trasmetterlo in televisione o distribuirlo su videocassetta, un titolo provvisorio, una traduzione letterale o un titolo utilizzato per una seconda messa in circolazione del film.

Ai titoli alternativi viene in alcuni casi aggiunto il nome abbreviato di un paese, p.es. "(FRN)", che indica il paese nel quale è stato utilizzato il titolo alternativo.

II. Filmographie dei registi

Le inserzioni relative ai registi possono contenere le seguenti informazioni (v. spiegazioni che seguono):

- Nome
- Paese di origine del regista
- Data/e
- Professione
- Nomi alternativi
- Film:
  - Titolo originale
  - Anno
  - Tipo di film
  - Titolo/i alternativo/i

Nome

Viene utilizzato il nome più conosciuto del regista. Accanto ai nomi alternativi appaiono riferimenti al nome utilizzato.

Paese di origine del regista

Il paese di origine si riferisce al luogo di nascita del regista, che è normalmente, ma non sempre, il paese in cui ha realizzato la maggior parte di suoi film. Se non sono disponibili informazioni sul luogo di nascita ho presunto che sia il paese in cui ha realizzato il maggior numero dei suoi film.

Il nome del paese viene indicato come era all'epoca della nascita del regista, il che potrebbe corrispondere ad uno stato od a un territorio ormai defunto (come per esempio la Palestina). Tutti i registi tedeschi, originari sia della Germania Federale che della Germania Democratica, vengono elencati sotto il titolo di Germania. In modo analogo, i registi coreani, sia del Nord che del Sud, vengono elencati sotto il titolo di Corea.

Date

Le date di nascita e di morte sono quelle più spesso indicate nelle fonti d'informazione consultate.

Professione

Laddove il mestiere principale del regista non sia la regia, ne viene indicata la professione, come per esempio Henri Decae, Cineasta.

Nome/i alternativo/i

Sono comprese le varianti dei nomi dei registi: pseudonimi e grafie alternative che sono particolarmente comuni in Unione Sovietica.

Film

Tutti i film realizzati dal regista che sono riuscito ad identificare, elencati in ordine cronologico secondo il titolo originale. Tra le informazioni viene fornito l'anno, il tipo di film ed i titoli alternativi (v. sopra per le relative spiegazioni). I co-registi non sono inclusi, benché vengano indicati nell'elenco dei titoli dei film.

Registi per paese

Tutti i registi vengono rielencati in ordine alfabetico e per paese in un indice separato nel 2º volume (come definito sopra). Vengono indicate ove appropriato anche le date di nascita e di morte.

Registi di film di animazione

Tutti i registi di film di animazione - che abbiano creato un particolare mezzo di espressione artistica - vengono elencati in ordine alfabetico in un indice separato nel 2º volume, assieme al paese di origine (come definito sopra), date di nascita e di morte e nomi alternativi.

Bibliografia

Questo elenco comprende tutte le principali pubblicazioni consultate, disposte in ordine alfabetico secondo i titoli. Vengono inoltre indicati l'autore, l'editore, il paese di origine dell'editore e la data di pubblicazione.

ABBREVIAZIONI

ANM animated (animato)
ANS animated short (cortometraggio animato)
ANT anthology (antologia)
ASS animated short series (breve serie animata)
C/D co-director (co-regista)
CMP compilation (raccolta)
DOC documentary (documentario)
DCS short documentary (documentario breve)
DSS documentary short series (breve serie di documentari)
EDT editor (tecnico del montaggio)
M composer (music) compositore (musica)
MTV made for television (realizzato per la televisione)
P producer (produttore)
PH photographer (fotografo)
SER series (serie)
SHS short series (miniserie)
SHT short (cortometraggio)
SIL silent (muto)
SND sound (sonoro)
SPV supervision (supervisione)
SRL serial (film a episodi)
TVM television film (telefilm)
U/C uncredited (anonimo)

ABBREVIAZIONI PER I PAESI

AFG Afghanistan
ALB Albania
ALG Algeria
ANG Angola
ARG Argentina
ASL Australia
AUS Austria
BLG Belgio
BLV Bolivia
BNG Bangladesh
BNN Benin
BRK Burkina Faso
BRM Birmania
BRZ Brasile
BUL Bulgaria
CHL Cile
CHN Cina
CLM Colombia
CMR Camerun
CND Canada
CNG Congo
CPV Isole del Capo Verde
CRC Costa Rica
CUB Cuba
CYP Cipro
CZC Cecoslovacchia
DMN Repubblica Dominicana
DNM Danimarca
ECD Ecuador
EGY Egitto
ETH Etiopia
FNL Finlandia
FRG Germania Federale
FRN Francia
GBN Gabon
GDR Repubblica Democratica Tedesca
GHN Ghana
GIB Gibilterra
GNB Guinea Bissau
GRC Grecia
GRM Germania
GTM Guatemala
GUM Guam
GUN Guinea
GYN Guyana
HKG Hong Kong
HNG Ungheria
ICL Islanda
INC Indocina
IND India
INN Indonesia
IRL Irlanda
IRN Iran
IRQ Iraq
ISR Israele
ITL Italy (Italia)
IVC Costa d'Avorio
JMC Giamaica
JPN Giappone
JRD Giordania
KMP Cambodia (Cambogia)
KNY Kenya
KOR Corea
KWT Kuwait
LAO Laos
LBN Lebano
LBY Libia
LCH Liechtenstein
LTH Lithuania
LTV Lettonia
LXM Lussemburgo
MDG Madagascar
MLI Mali
MLT Malta
MLY Malaysia
MNC Monaco
MNG Mongolia
MRC Morocco
MRT Mauritania
MXC Messico
MZM Mozambico
NCR Nicaragua
NGR Nigeria
NKR Corea del Nord
NPL Nepal
NRW Norvegia
NTH Paesi Bassi
NZL Nuova Zelanda
PHL Filippine
PKS Pakistan
PLN Polonia
PLS Palestina
PNM Panama
PRC Puerto Rico
PRG Paraguay
PRT Portogallo
PRU Perú
RMN Romania
SAF Sudafrica
SDN Sudan
SKR Corea del Sud
SLN Sri Lanka
SLV El Salvador
SML Somalia
SNG Singapore
SNL Senegal
SPN Spagna
SRN Surinam
SWD Svezia
SWT Svizzera
SYR Siria
T&T Trinidad & Tobago
THL Tailandia
TNS Tunisia
TRK Turchia
TWN Taiwan
UAR Emirati Arabi Uniti
UGN Uganda
UKN Regno Unito
UNN Nazioni Unite
URG Uruguay
USA Stati Uniti d'America
USS Unione delle Repubbliche Socialiste Sovietiche
VEN Venezuela
VTN Vietnam
WTN Caraibi
YGS Iugoslavia
ZIM Zimbabwe
ZMB Zambia
ZRE Zaire

Film Titles

Film Titles

Numerics

. . . • 1971 • Cozarinsky Edgardo • ARG • DOT DOT DOT ○ ELLIPSIS ○ . . . (DOT DOT DOT)
. . . • 1972 • de Anchieta Jose • BRZ • RETICENCIAS ○ BREAKS
. . . (DOT DOT DOT) see . . . • 1971
@ • 1979 • Brakhage Stan • SHT • USA
? see **F FOR FAKE** • 1977
0, 1, 2, 3 • 1967 • Miesseu V. • ANS • BLG
00–2 MOST SECRET AGENTS (USA) see **002 AGENTI SEGRETISSIMI** • 1964
0 – 18 • 1915 • *London Film Co.* • UKN • MESSAGE FROM THE SKY, A
0–18 OR A MESSAGE FROM THE SKY (USA) see **ON HIS MAJESTY'S SERVICE** • 1914
00/CIAK OPERAZIONE MONDO • 1967 • Marzano Marino • ITL
00 SEX AM WOLFGANGSEE • 1966 • Antel Franz • AUS
0 UHR 15, ZIMMER 9 • 1950 • Rabenalt Arthur M. • FRG
1 • Strombeck Grant • SHT • USA
1 + 1 (EXPLORING THE KINSEY REPORTS) • 1961 • Oboler Arch • USA, CND
1 + 1 + 1 see **TAVERNA ROSSA** • 1940
1 + 1 + 3 • 1980 • Genee Heidi • FRG
1, 2, 3.. see **SZAMOK TORTENETE, A** • 1962
1, 2, 3 see **UNO, DOI, TREI..** • 1975
1–2–3 GO! • 1941 • Cahn Edward L. • SHT • USA
1, 2, 3 RHAPSODIE • 1964 • Daalder Renee • SHT • NTH
1.42.08 • Lucas George • SHT • USA
1 APRIL 2000 • 1952 • Liebeneiner Wolfgang • AUS, FRG • APRIL 1, 2000 (USA)
1' DE ABRIL, BRASIL • 1988 • Leticia Maria • BRZ • APRIL 1ST, BRAZIL
1 MAJA • 1938 • Alexandrov Grigori • USS • MAY 1ST
001 OPERACION CARIBE see **A–001 OPERAZIONE GIAMAICA** • 1965
1 POLSKI KONGRES POKOJU • 1950 • Bossak Jerzy • DOC • PLN • FIRST POLISH PEACE CONGRESS
1 X 1 DER EHE • 1949 • Jugert Rudolf • FRG
1A IN OBERBAYERN • 1939 • Seitz Franz • FRG • 1A IN UPPER BAVARIA (USA)
1A IN OBERBAYERN • 1956 • Albin Hans • FRG
1A IN UPPER BAVARIA (USA) see **1A IN OBERBAYERN** • 1939
1c see **BOOT POLISH** • 1954
1ST TRADE UNION CONGRESS • 1945 • Bossak Jerzy • DOC • PLN
002 AGENTI SEGRETISSIMI • 1964 • Fulci Lucio • ITL • 00–2 MOST SECRET AGENTS (USA) ○ OH! THOSE MOST SECRET AGENTS ○ WORST SECRET AGENTS
2 AOUT 1914 • 1914 • Linder Max • FRN
2–BOULDY–2 see **DVA, BOULDEJ, DVA** • 1930
2–BULDI–2 see **DVA, BOULDEJ, DVA** • 1930
2 CONVICTS, THE see **EVENTYR PAA FODREJSEN** • 1911
2½ DADS see **TWO AND A HALF DADS** • 1986
2 GIRLS WANTED • 1927 • Green Alfred E. • USA
2 MAL 2 IM HIMMELBETT • 1964 • Balling Erik • FRG, DNM
002 OPERATION MOON see **002 OPERAZIONE LUNA** • 1965
002 OPERAZIONE LUNA • 1965 • Fulci Lucio • ITL, SPN • DOS COSMONAUTAS A LA FUERZA (SPN) ○ 002 OPERATION MOON ○ TWO COSMONAUTS AGAINST THEIR WILL
2 PE CAL, 1 PE MAGAR • 1973 • Bokor Pierre • MTV • RMN
2 + 5 MISSIONE HYDRA • 1966 • Francisci Pietro • ITL • STAR PILOTS (USA) ○ DUE + CINQUE MISSIONE HYDRA ○ TWO + FIVE MISSION HYDRA
2 X 2 • Razutis Al • SHT • USA
2 X 2 + 4 • 1945 • Bohdziewicz Antoni • PLN
2 X ADAM –1 X EVE • 1959 • Lang Franz M. • FRG
3 • 1955-56 • Jordan Larry • SHT • USA
3.10 TO YUMA • 1957 • Daves Delmer • USA
3.15 • 1985 • Gross Larry • USA • 3.15: MOMENT OF TRUTH ○ MOMENT OF TRUTH
3.15: MOMENT OF TRUTH see **3.15** • 1985
3.30 ESCAPE FROM THE HAIDARI CAMP see **HAIDHARI 3.30' APODRASATE** • 1967
3 A.M. see **THREE A.M.** • 1976
3 CARS • 1988 • Kybartas • SHT • USA
3 CODONAS, DIE • 1940 • Rabenalt Arthur M. • FRG
3 COMRADES, THE see **TRE KAMMERATER, DE** • 1912
3–D DYNASTY • 1977 • Chang Mei-Chun • HKG
3 DEADLY SHOOTERS see **3 KILABOT SA BARILAN** • 1968
3 DIMENSION • 1953 • Spottiswoode Raymond • CND
3 GLOCKEN VON SAN MARTINO, DIE • 1915 • Albes Emil • FRG
3 IN THE CELLAR see **UP IN THE CELLAR** • 1970
3 INVENTEURS, LES • 1980 • Ocelot Michel • FRN • THREE INVENTORS, THE
3 KILABOT SA BARILAN • 1968 • Garces Armando • PHL • 3 DEADLY SHOOTERS
3 NOVEMBER 1918 • 1965 • Zbonek Edwin • AUS
3–RING WING–DING • 1968 • Lovy Alex • ANS • USA
3 SISTERS, THE • 1930 • Sloane Paul • USA
3 SUNRISES, 4 SUNSETS • 1972 • Dippel Lidmilla • ANS • USA
3 TO 1 FOR LOVE (USA) see **3:1 A SZERELEM JAVARA** • 1939
3 WOMEN • 1977 • Altman Robert • USA
3:1 A SZERELEM JAVARA • 1939 • Vaszary Janos • 3 TO 1 FOR LOVE (USA)
3RD PATHETIQUE • 1960 • Yermakov A. • MTV • USS
4.. 3.. 2.. 1.. DEAD see **PERRY RHODAN –SOS AUS DEM WELTALL** • 1967
4.. 3.. 2.. 1.. MORTE (ITL) see **PERRY RHODAN –SOS AUS DEM WELTALL** • 1967
4 FOIS 2 • 1969 • Labro Philippe • SHT • FRN
4 GESELLEN, DIE • 1938 • Froelich Carl • FRG
4½ MUSKETIERE • 1935 • Kardos Leslie • HNG, AUS
4 RAGAZZE SOGNANO • 1943 • Giannini Guglielmo • ITL
4 X 4 see **FYRA GANGER FYRA** • 1965
4 x 8 + 16 • Hornisher Christina • USA
4D MAN, THE • 1959 • Yeaworth Irvin S. Jr. • USA • EVIL FORCE, THE (UKN) ○ MASTER OF TERROR ○ FOUR D MAN, THE
4D SPECIAL AGENTS • 1980 • Orton Harold • UKN
$5.20 AN HOUR DREAM, THE • 1980 • Mayberry Russ • TVM • USA
5 A 7 TRES PARTICULIERS • Love John • FRN
5 COPIES see **FEM KOPIER** • 1913
5% DE RISQUE see **CINQ POUR CENT DE RISQUES** • 1979
5 DESPORPISTAS VENEZOLANOS • 1973 • Blanco Javier • DOC • VNZ • 5 VENEZUELAN SPORTSMEN
5 JUNI, DER • 1942 • Kirchhoff Fritz • FRG • EINER UNTER MILLIONEN
£5 MAN, THE • 1937 • Parker Albert • UKN
5 MINUTES TO LOVE see **ROTTEN APPLE, THE** • 1963
£5 NOTE, THE • 1910 • Coleby A. E. • UKN
5 + 1 • 1969 • Job Guy, Taittinger Michel • DOC • FRN
5 SINNERS (USA) see **NACHTLOKAL ZUM SILBERMOND, DAS** • 1959
5 VENEZUELAN SPORTSMEN see **5 DESPORPISTAS VENEZOLANOS** • 1973
5,4,3,2,1. • 1969 • Brault Francois • DCS • CND
5:30 COLLECTION, THE • 1907 • Cooper Arthur? • UKN
5:48, THE • 1979 • Ivory James • TVM • USA
6.5 SPECIAL • 1958 • Shaughnessy Alfred • UKN • CALLING ALL CATS
6–9 THE DAILY DOUBLE • 1970 • *Kirt Films International* • USA • DAILY DOUBLE, THE
6.18.67 • Lucas George • SHT • USA
6 DAGESLOBET • 1958 • Roos Jorgen • DOC • DNM • SEKSDAGESLOBET ○ SIX DAY RACE, THE ○ SIX DAYS, THE
6 GENDARMI IN FUGA (ITL) see **GENDARME EN BALLADE, LE** • 1970
6 GIRLS AND A BRIDEGROOM see **SETT BANAT WA ARISS** • 1968
6 JUIN A L'AUBE, LE • 1945 • Gremillon Jean • DOC • FRN
6 P.M. 1944 see **V SHEST CHASOV VECHERA POSLE VOINY** • 1944
6, RUE DU CALVAIRE • 1973 • Daskalides Jean • BLG
6–TAGE–KRIEG, DER (FRG) see **HA'MATARAH TIRAN** • 1968
6 x 2: SUR ET SOUS LA COMMUNICATION see **COMMUNICATION, LA** • 1976
6:30 COLLECTION • 1936 • Watt Harry • DOC • UKN
7–9–13 • 1934 • Sandberg Anders W. • DNM
7 BROTHERS MEET DRACULA, THE see **LEGEND OF 7 GOLDEN VAMPIRES, THE** • 1974
7 BULLETS FOR GRINGO • 1967 • Navarro Marcelino D. • PHL
07 CON EL 2 ADELANTE • 1966 • Iquino Ignacio F. • SPN
007 DOWN SHE GOES see **NEVER SAY DIE** • 1988
7 FACES DE UM CAFAJESTE, AS • 1968 • Valadao Jece • BRZ • SEVEN FACES OF A NO–GOOD, THE
7 FRATELLI CERVI, I • 1967 • Puccini Gianni • ITL • SEVEN CERVI BROTHERS, THE
7 JAHRE PECH see **SCHERBEN BRINGEN GLUCK** • 1957
7 KLEIDER DER KATHRIN, DIE • 1954 • Deppe Hans • FRG
7 MAN ARMY • 1977 • Chang Chen • HKG
7 NOTAS • 1973 • Oteyza Carlos • VNZ • SEVEN NOTES
07.. TASSI • 1943 • Pagliero Marcello • ITL • 07 TAXI
07 TAXI see **07.. TASSI** • 1943
7 VOLTE 7 • 1968 • Lupo Michele • ITL • SEVEN TIMES SEVEN (USA)
7 WISE DWARFS • 1941 • Beebe Ford, Lyford Dick • USA
7e COMPAGNIE AU CLAIR DE LUNE, LA • 1978 • Lamoureux Robert • FRN
7TH CAVALRY see **SEVENTH CAVALRY** • 1956
7TH COMMANDMENT, THE • 1961 • Berwick Irvin • USA
7TH HEAVEN • 1927 • Borzage Frank • USA
7TH THUNDERBOLT (UKN) see **SETTE FOLGORI DI ASSUR, LE** • 1962
8½ see **OTTO E MEZZO** • 1963
8 BALL BUNNY • 1950 • Jones Charles M. • ANS • USA
8 HOURS DON'T MAKE A DAY see **ACHT STUNDEN SIND KEIN TAG** • 1972
8 MADELS IM BOOT • 1932 • Waschneck Erich • FRG
8 MILLION WAYS TO DIE • 1986 • Ashby Hal • USA
008 OPERAZIONE RITMO • 1965 • Piacentini Tullio • ITL
8 TO 4 see **EIGHT TO FOUR** • 1981
8–WHEEL BEAST, THE see **BESTIONE, IL** • 1974
8 X 8 see **ACHT MAL ACHT** • 1957
08/15 I • 1954 • May Paul • FRG
08/15 II • 1955 • May Paul • FRG
08/15 IN DER HEIMAT • 1955 • May Paul • FRG
8A. BIENAL DE SAO PAULO, A • 1965 • Diegues Carlos • SHT • BRZ
8e MERVEILLE, LA • 1964 • *Misonne Claude (Pr)* • BLG • EIGHTH WONDER, THE
8H A.M. • 1988 • Beaudry Jean, Bouvier Francois • CND
8TH DAY • 1985 • Humaloja Timo • MTV • FNL
8TH HOUSE, THE • Beattie Paul • SHT • USA
9.2 INCH GUN, THE • 1947 • Cutts Graham • DCS • UKN
9 DEATHS OF THE NINJA see **NINE DEATHS OF THE NINJA** • 1985
9–ES KORTEREM • 1955 • Makk Karoly • HNG • WARD NO.9 ○ KILENCES KORTEREM, A
9 MILES TO NOON • 1963 • Leder Herbert J. • USA
9 MINUTES • 1967 • Vamos Thomas, Bobet Jacques • DCS • CND
9 TO 5 • 1980 • Higgins Colin • USA • NINE TO FIVE
9½ WEEKS • 1984 • Lyne Adrian • USA
9/30/55 see **SEPTEMBER 30, 1955** • 1977
9TH SESSION OF THE HOME NATIONAL COUNCIL see **IX SESJA KRN** • 1946
10 • 1979 • Edwards Blake • USA
10.30 P.M. SUMMER • 1966 • Dassin Jules • USA, SPN
10.32 • Dreifuss Arthur • NTH • TEN THIRTY–TWO IN THE MORNING ○ MURDER IN AMSTERDAM
10 GENTLEMEN FROM WEST POINT • 1942 • Hathaway Henry • USA
10 KORKUSUZ ADAM • 1964 • Basaran Tunc • TRK
10 MILLES / HEURE • 1970 • Carriere Marcel • DCS • CND
$10 RAISE • 1935 • Marshall George • USA • MR. FAINTHEART (UKN)
10, RILLINGTON PLACE • 1971 • Fleischer Richard • UKN
10 SECOND FILM • 1965 • Conner Bruce • SHT • USA
10 TO MIDNIGHT see **TEN TO MIDNIGHT** • 1983
10½ WEEKS see **TEN AND A HALF WEEKS** • 1986
10TH VICTIM, THE (USA) see **DECIMA VITTIMA, LA** • 1965
11–A IN BERLIN • 1956 • Albin Hans • FRG
11 DAYS 11 NIGHTS: PART 3 –THE FINAL CHAPTER see **ELEVEN DAYS ELEVEN NIGHTS: PART 3** • 1988
11 HARROWHOUSE • 1974 • Avakian Aram • USA • ANYTHING FOR LOVE
11, RUE DES SAUSSAIES see **RUE DES SAUSSAIES** • 1950
11 X 14 • 1977 • Benning James • USA
11:35 AB HAMBURG • 1919 • Carstennsen Carlo • FRG
11:50 FROM ZURICH • 1970 • van der Heyde Nikolai • SHT • NTH
11TH COMMANDMENT, THE • 1988 • Leder Paul • USA
12 + 1 (FRN) see **UNA SU TREDICI** • 1969
12–10 • 1919 • Brenon Herbert • UKN • TWELVE: TEN
12 DESPERATE HOURS see **EXTRA DAY, THE** • 1956
12 GOLDEN COMMANDOS, THE • 1967 • Marquez Artemio • PHL
12 GRAVES OF THE KHOJA NASREDDIN, THE see **12 MOGIL KHODZHI NASREDDINA** • 1967
12 MADCHEN UND EIN MANN • 1959 • Quest Hans • AUS
12 MILLION DOLLAR BOY, THE see **DYNAMITE JOHNSON** • 1978
12 MINUTEN NACH 12 • 1939 • Guter Johannes • FRG
12 MOGIL KHODZHI NASREDDINA • 1967 • Mints Klimenti • USS • 12 GRAVES OF THE KHOJA NASREDDIN, THE
12 STUNDEN ANGST • 1960 • von Radvanyi Geza • FRG, FRN
12 TO THE MOON see **TWELVE TO THE MOON** • 1960
12 UHR MITTAGS KOMMT DER BOSS • 1968 • Hartmann Siegfried • GDR • BOSS ARRIVES AT MIDDAY, THE
13 see **EYE OF THE DEVIL** • 1966
13–13, EL • 1943 • Lucia Luis • SPN
13 CHAIRS see **13 STOLAR** • 1945
13 CHAIRS see **UNA SU TREDICI** • 1969
13 CLOCKS, THE • 1970 • Leroy Mervyn • USA
13 EAST STREET • 1952 • Baker Robert S. • UKN
13 EAST STREET see **13 WEST STREET** • 1962
13 FEMMES POUR CASANOVA (FRN) see **CASANOVA E COMPAGNI** • 1978
13 FRIGHTENED GIRLS see **THIRTEEN FRIGHTENED GIRLS** • 1963
13 GHOSTS see **THIRTEEN GHOSTS** • 1960
13 GOLDEN NUNS see **SHIH–SAN NU NI** • 1977
13 JOURS EN FRANCE • 1968 • Lelouch Claude, Reichenbach Francois • DOC • FRN • CHALLENGE IN THE SNOW (UKN) ○ GRENOBLE (USA)
13 KLEINE ESEL UND DER SONNENHOF • 1958 • Deppe Hans • FRG
13 LEAD SOLDIERS • 1948 • Mcdonald Frank • USA
13. MARZ, DER see **SILBERKONIG 1, DER** • 1921
13 MEN AND A GUN (UKN) see **TREDICI UOMINI E UN CANNONE** • 1936
13 MOST BEAUTIFUL WOMEN, THE • 1964 • Warhol Andy • USA
13 REVIR see **TRINACTY REVIR** • 1945
13 RUE MADELEINE • 1947 • Hathaway Henry • USA
13 STEPS TO DEATH (UKN) see **WHY MUST I DIE?** • 1960
13 STOLAR • 1945 • Larsson Borje • SWD • 13 CHAIRS
13 STUHLE • 1938 • Emo E. W. • FRG

13 UNTER EINEM HUT • 1950 • Meyer Johannes • FRG
13° UOMO, IL (ITL) see **HOMME DE TROP, UN** • 1967
13 WASHINGTON SQUARE • 1928 • Brown Melville • USA
13 WEST STREET • 1962 • Leacock Philip • USA • 13 EAST STREET ○ TIGER AMONG US, THE
13e CAPRICE, LE • 1967 • Boussinot Roger • FRN
13TH FLOOR, THE • 1988 • Loach Chris • ASL • THIRTEENTH FLOOR, THE
13TH HOUR, THE • 1947 • Clemens William • USA
13TH LETTER, THE • 1951 • Preminger Otto • USA
13TH MAN, THE see **THIRTEENTH MAN, THE** • 1937
13TH OCTOBER, THE • 1949 • Thorndike Andrew • DOC • GDR
14-18 • 1962 • Aurel Jean, Saint-Laurent Cecil • FRN • OVER THERE 1914-1918 (USA)
14, THE • 1973 • Hemmings David • UKN • WILD LITTLE BUNCH, THE ○ EXISTENCE ○ FOURTEEN, THE
14 AMAZONS, THE • 1972 • Cheng Kang • HKG
14 ANOS DE POLITICA DO ESPIRITO • 1940 • Ribeiro Antonio Lopes • SHT • PRT
14 ANS D'AURELIE, LES • Ricaud Michel • FRN
14 CARROT RABBIT • 1952 • Freleng Friz • ANS • USA
14 DAGE I JERNALDEREN • 1977 • Roos Jorgen • DOC • DNM
14 GAST, DER • 1915 • Bolten-Baeckers Heinrich • FRG
14 GOING ON 30 • 1988 • Schneider Paul • TVM • USA • FOURTEEN GOING ON THIRTY
14 YEAR OLD GIRL, THE see **HEDY** • 1965
14'S GOOD, 18'S BETTER • 1982 • Armstrong Gillian • SHT • ASL
15 AOUT, LE • 1973 • Akerman Chantal • BLG
15 FACONS DE REGARDER L'HIVER ET D'EN RIRE • 1977 • Lavoie Richard • SER • CND
15 FROM ROME see **MOSTRI, I** • 1963
15 JAHRE SCHWEREN KERKER see **FRAUEN AUS DER WIENER VORSTADT** • 1925
15 MAIDEN LANE • 1936 • Dwan Allan • USA
15-MINUTE LAP • 1910 • *Ambrosio* • ITL
15 MINUTES ON 15 YEARS see **15 PERC 15 EVROL** • 1965
15 PERC 15 EVROL • 1965 • Meszaros Marta • DCS • HNG • 15 MINUTES ON 15 YEARS
15e, PRELUDE DE CHOPIN, LE • 1922 • Tourjansky Victor • FRN
16 ANOS DESPUES • 1979 • Nunez Sergio • DOC • CUB • SIXTEEN YEARS LATER
16 DAYS OF GLORY • 1985 • Greenspan Bud • DOC • USA
16 FATHOMS DEEP • 1948 • Allen Irving • USA
17 OP • 1988 • Wielopolska Brita • DNM • SALLY'S BIZNIZ
17e CIEL, LE • 1965 • Korber Serge • FRN
17e PARALLELE see **17e PARALLELE: LE VIETNAM EN GUERRE, LE** • 1968
17e PARALLELE: LE VIETNAM EN GUERRE, LE • 1968 • Ivens Joris • DOC • FRN, VTN • 17TH PARALLEL: VIETNAM IN WAR (USA) ○ VIETNAM EN GUERRE, LE ○ 17TH PARALLEL ○ 17e PARALLELE
17TH MAY, A FILM ABOUT RITUALS • Breien Anja • SHT • NRW • MAY 17
17TH PARALLEL see **17e PARALLELE: LE VIETNAM EN GUERRE, LE** • 1968
17TH PARALLEL: VIETNAM IN WAR (USA) see **17e PARALLELE: LE VIETNAM EN GUERRE, LE** • 1968
17TH POLISH BOXING CHAMPIONSHIPS IN LODZ see **XVII BOKSERSKIE MISTRZOSTWA POLSKI W LODZI** • 1946
18 AGAIN! • 1988 • Flaherty Paul • USA • EIGHTEEN AGAIN!
18 BRONZE GIRLS OF SHAOLIN, THE see **EIGHTEEN BRONZE GIRLS OF SHAOLIN, THE** • 1983
18 BRONZEMEN, THE see **SHAOLIN SZU SHIH-PA T'UNG JEN** • 1976
18 FATAL STRIKES • 1981 • Yang Ching • HKG
18 TO 45 • 1918 • Walsh Raoul • USA
18 YEARS OLD SCHOOLGIRLS, THE (UKN) see **CHEERLEADERS, THE** • 1973
19 BOATS AND THE CRIMINAL • Shindo Kaneto • JPN
19 DECEMBER • 1966 • Celis Louis • BLG
19 RED ROSES see **19 RODE ROSER** • 1973
19 RODE ROSER • 1973 • Carlsen Esben Hoilund • DNM • 19 RED ROSES ○ NITTEN RODE ROSER
19TH HOLE CLUB, THE • 1936 • *Terry Paul/ Moser Frank (P)* • ANS • USA
£20.000 KISS, THE • 1963 • Moxey John Llewellyn • UKN
£20 A TON see **20 POUNDS A TON** • 1955
$20 A WEEK • 1935 • Ford Wesley • USA
$20 A WEEK see **TWENTY DOLLARS A WEEK** • 1924
20 ANS EXPRESS • 1963-64 • Portugais Louis • SER • CND
20 FACES see **SHONEN TANTEIDAN -KABUTOMUSHI NO YOKI & TETTO NO KAIJIN** • 1957
20 JAHR VRIJ • 1966 • Stip Kees • SHT • NTH
20 JULI, DER • 1955 • Harnack Falk • FRG • PLOT TO ASSASSINATE HITLER, THE (USA)
20 LET SOVETSKOGO KINO see **KINO ZA DVADTSAT LET** • 1940
20 MILLION MILES TO EARTH • 1957 • Juran Nathan • USA • GIANT YMIR, THE
20-MULE TEAM • 1940 • Thorpe Richard • USA • TWENTY-MULE TEAM
20 POUNDS A TON • 1955 • Anderson Lindsay • DCS • UKN • £20 A TON
20TH CENTURY CHOCOLATE CAKE, A • 1984 • Siegel Lois • CND
20TH CENTURY ILLUSTRATIONIST, THE (UKN) see **ILLUSIONS FUNAMBULESQUES** • 1903
20TH OF JULY, THE • 1989 • Vollmar Wolf • FRG
21 - 87 • 1963 • Lipsett Arthur • SHT • CND
$21 A DAY (ONCE A MONTH) • 1941 • Lantz Walter • ANS • USA
21 CARAT SNATCH, THE see **POPSY POP** • 1970
21 DAYS see **FIRST AND THE LAST, THE** • 1937
21 DAYS TOGETHER (USA) see **FIRST AND THE LAST, THE** • 1937
21 HOURS AT MUNICH • 1976 • Graham William A. • TVM • USA • TWENTY-ONE HOURS AT MUNICH
21 JUMP STREET see **TWENTY-ONE JUMP STREET** • 1987
21 MILES • 1942 • Watt Harry • DOC • UKN
21 TODAY • 1936 • Taylor John H. • UKN
21:12 PIANO BAR • 1981 • Jimenez Mary • BLG
22 LIPCA • 1949 • Bossak Jerzy • DOC • PLN • JULY 22ND
22 LIPCA -SWIETO ODRODZENIA POLSKI • 1945 • Bossak Jerzy • DOC • PLN • 22ND JULY -THE NATIONAL DAY OF THE REBIRTH OF POLAND
22 MISFORTUNES see **DVADZATDVA NESHCHASTIA** • 1930
22ND JULY -THE NATIONAL DAY OF THE REBIRTH OF POLAND see **22 LIPCA -SWIETO ODRODZENIA POLSKI** • 1945
22ND JUNE 1897 • 1979 • Nachiket, Patwardhan Jayoo • IND
23½ HOURS LEAVE • 1919 • King Henry • USA
23½ HOURS LEAVE • 1937 • Blystone John G. • USA
23 MINUTOS COM FERNANDO LOPES GARCA • 1969 • Vasconcelos Antonio-Pedro • SHT • PRT
23 PACES TO BAKER STREET see **TWENTY THREE PACES TO BAKER STREET** • 1956
23 SKIDOO • Biggs Julian • SHT • USA
23RD PSALM BRANCH • 1967 • Brakhage Stan • USA • SONG XXIII ○ SONG 23
24 CARAT • 1914 • Thornton F. Martin • UKN
24-DOLLAR ISLAND • 1926 • Flaherty Robert • DCS • USA
24 EYES see **NIJUSHI NO HITOMI** • 1988
24 HEURES DE LA VIE D'UN FAUX-COL • 1928 • Greville Edmond T. • SHT • FRN
24 HEURES DE LA VIE D'UNE FEMME • 1968 • Delouche Dominique • FRN, FRG • 24 STUNDEN IM LEBEN EINER FRAU (FRG) ○ 24 HOURS IN A WOMAN'S LIFE ○ TWENTY-FOUR HOURS OF A WOMAN'S LIFE
24 HEURES D'UN AMERICAIN A PARIS • 1964 • Benazeraf Jose • FRN, USA • PARIS OOH-LA-LA! (USA) ○ PARIS EROTIKA
24 HORAS DE SONHO • 1941 • de Garcia Eduardo Chianca • BRZ
24-HOUR LOVER (USA) see **BENGELCHEN LIEBT KREUZ UND QUER** • 1968
24 HOURS see **TWENTY-FOUR HOURS** • 1931
24 HOURS IN A WOMAN'S LIFE see **24 HEURES DE LA VIE D'UNE FEMME** • 1968
24 HOURS IN AN UNDERGROUND MARKET see **CHIKAGAI NIJUYO-JIKAN** • 1947
24 HOURS OF A WOMAN'S LIFE • 1952 • Saville Victor • UKN • AFFAIR IN MONTE CARLO (USA)
24 HOURS OF RAIN • 1983 • Ikonomov Vladislav • BUL
24 HOURS OF THE REBEL see **SEPTEMBER 30, 1955** • 1977
24 HOURS TO KILL • 1965 • Bezencenet Peter • UKN
24 IMAGENS POR MINUTO • 1976 • de Almeida Manuel Faria • SHT • PRT
24-JIKAN NO JOJI (JPN) see **HIROSHIMA MON AMOUR** • 1959
24 ORE DI TERRORE • 1964 • Brighouse Tony • ITL
24 STUNDEN AUS DEM LEBEN EINER FRAU • 1931 • Land Robert • FRG
24 STUNDEN IM LEBEN EINER FRAU (FRG) see **24 HEURES DE LA VIE D'UNE FEMME** • 1968
25 • 1976 • Correa Jose Celso Martinez, Lucas Celso • BRZ
25 BASANT • 1986 • Shah Aleer • NPL • PERIOD OF TWENTY-FIVE YEARS, A
25, FIREMAN'S STREET (USA) see **TUZOLTO UTCA 25** • 1973
25 OCTOBER, FIRST DAY • 1968 • Norshtein Yuri • ANM • USS
25 YEARS • 1976 • Morley Peter • DOC • UKN • 25 YEARS - IMPRESSIONS
25 YEARS -IMPRESSIONS see **25 YEARS** • 1976
25 YEARS OF PLANICA • Povh Dusan • SHT • YGS
25TH HOUR, THE (USA) see **VINGT-CINQUIEME HEURE, LA** • 1966
26 COMMISSARS see **DVADTSAT SHESJ KOMISSAROV** • 1936
27 DOWN see **SATTAWIS DOWN** • 1973
27 HORAS • 1985 • Armendariz Montxo • SPN • 27 HOURS
27 HOURS see **27 HORAS** • 1985
27A • 1973 • Storm Esben • ASL
27TH DAY, THE • 1957 • Asher William • USA
28 MINUTES FOR 3 MILLION DOLLARS see **28 MINUTI PER 3 MILIONI DI DOLLARI** • 1967
28 MINUTI PER 3 MILIONI DI DOLLARI • 1967 • Pradeaux Maurizio • ITL • 28 MINUTES FOR 3 MILLION DOLLARS
28 UP • 1985 • Apted Michael • DOC • UKN
29 ACACIA AVENUE • 1945 • Cass Henry • UKN • FACTS OF LOVE, THE (USA) ○ FACTS OF LIFE, THE
29-CENT ROBBERY, A • 1910 • *Thanhouser* • USA
-30- • 1959 • Webb Jack • USA • DEADLINE MIDNIGHT (UKN) ○ THIRTY
30 BELOW ZERO • 1926 • Kerr Robert, Hillyer Lambert • USA
30-FOOT BRIDE OF CANDY ROCK, THE • 1959 • Miller Sidney • USA • LOU COSTELLO AND HIS 30-FOOT BRIDE
30 IS A DANGEROUS AGE, CYNTHIA • 1967 • Mcgrath Joseph • UKN
30 MINUTES, MISTER PLUMMER • 1962 • Poirier Anne-Claire • DCS • CND
30 PINNAR MUCK • 1966 • Frisk Ragnar • SWD
31° IN THE SHADE see **TRICET JEONA VE STINU** • 1965
31 STUPNU VE STINU see **TRICET JEONA VE STINU** • 1965
32 DICEMBRE • 1988 • De Crescenzo Luciano • ITL • DECEMBER 32ND
32° GIRO D'ITALIA • 1949 • Simonelli Giorgio C. • DOC • ITL
32, RUE DE MONTMARTRE see **DERRIERE LA FACADE** • 1939
33.333 • 1924 • Molander Gustaf • SWD
33.333 • 1936 • Lindlof John • SWD
33e CHAMBRE • 1947-51 • Verneuil Henri • SHT • FRN
35, BOULEVARD GENERAL KOENIG • 1971 • Markopoulos Gregory J. • USA
36 CHOWRINGHEE LANE • 1981 • Sen Aparna • IND
36 FILLETTE • 1987 • Breillat Catherine • FRN • VIRGIN
36 HOURS • 1964 • Seaton George • USA
36 HOURS OF TERROR see **OLGA'S HOUSE OF SHAME** • 1964
36 HOURS TO KILL • 1936 • Forde Eugene J. • USA
36, LE GRAND TOURNANT • 1970 • de Turenne Henri • FRN
36 ORE ALL'INFERNO • 1969 • Montero Roberto Bianchi • ITL
36TH CHAMBER OF SHAOLIN, THE see **SHAO-LIN SAN-SHIH-LIU FANG** • 1977
37.2 DEGREES IN THE MORNING see **37'2 LE MATIN** • 1985
37'2 LE MATIN • 1985 • Beineix Jean-Jacques • FRN • BETTY BLUE (UKN) ○ 37.2 DEGREES IN THE MORNING
38 • 1986 • Gluck Wolfgang • AUS, FRG
38 - 24 - 36 (USA) see **CANZONI NEL MONDO** • 1963
38 CALIBRE FRIENDSHIP • 1914 • *Nestor* • USA
39 EAST • 1920 • Robertson John S. • USA
39 STEPS, THE • 1935 • Hitchcock Alfred • UKN
39 STEPS, THE • 1959 • Thomas Ralph • UKN
40 AMATE TUTTE, LE • 1965 • Damiani Damiano • ITL
40 AR MED KUNGEN • 1947 • Werner Gosta • SHT • SWD
40-HORSE HAWKINS • 1924 • Sedgwick Edward • USA
40 QUADRATMETER DEUTSCHLAND • 1987 • Baser Tecfik • FRG
40 SKIPPER'S STREET see **SKEPPARGATAN 40** • 1925
40TH DOOR, THE • 1924 • Seitz George B. • USA
41 JIKAN NO KYOFU see **DAI SANJI SEKAI TAISEN-YONJI-ICHI JIKAN NO KYOFU** • 1960
42:6 (BEN GURION) • 1969 • Perlov David • SWT • BEN-GURION STORY, THE
42ND STREET • 1933 • Bacon Lloyd • USA • FORTY-SECOND STREET
44 see **QUARANTE-QUATRE** • 1981
44-CALIBRE MYSTERY, THE • 1917 • Kelsey Fred A. • SHT • USA
45 CALIBRE ECHO • 1932 • Mitchell Bruce • USA • MYSTERIOUS RIDER, THE (UKN)
45 CALIBRE WAR • 1929 • Maloney Leo • USA
45 FATHERS • 1937 • Tinling James • USA
45 MINUTES FROM BROADWAY • 1910 • *Kalem* • USA
45 MINUTES FROM BROADWAY • 1920 • De Grasse Joseph • USA
47 MORTO CHE PARLA • 1950 • Bragaglia Carlo Ludovico • ITL
47 RONIN, THE see **GENROKU CHUSHINGURA PART I** • 1941
47 RONIN, THE see **CHUSHINGURA** • 1962
47 RUE VIEILLE-DU-TEMPLE • 1960 • Jallaud Sylvia • SHT • FRN
47 SAMURAI see **CHUSHINGURA** • 1962
48 AVENUE DE L'OPERA • 1916 • Bernard-Deschamps • FRN
48-HOUR PRISON BREAK see **SHUTSUGOKU YONJUHACHI JIKAN** • 1969
48 HOURS • 1982 • Hill Walter • USA
48 HOURS OF LOVE see **QUARANTE HUIT HEURES D'AMOUR** • 1968
48 HOURS TO ACAPULCO see **48 STUNDEN BIS ACAPULCO** • 1967
48 HOURS TO LIVE (USA) see **MED FARA FOR LIVET** • 1959
48 HOURS (USA) see **WENT THE DAY WELL** • 1942
48 STUNDEN BIS ACAPULCO • 1967 • Lemke Klaus • FRG • 48 HOURS TO ACAPULCO
'49 - '17 • 1917 • Baldwin Ruth Ann • USA
49 DNEY • 1962 • Gabay Gennadiy • USS • FORTY-NINE DAYS (USA) ○ SOROK DEVYAT DNEI
49TH MAN, THE • 1953 • Sears Fred F. • USA
49TH PARALLEL • 1941 • Powell Michael • UKN • INVADERS, THE (USA) ○ FORTY-NINTH PARALLEL, THE
50-50 • 1923 • Florey Robert • USA
50/50 • 1981 • Tuhus Oddvar Bull • NRW
50 FANTASTICS • 1965 • Warhol Andy • USA
$50 FOR A KISS • 1915 • *Cressey Will M.* • USA
50 JAHRE -HEITER BETRACHTET see **HERRLICHE ZEITEN** • 1950
$50 MILLION CAN'T BE WRONG • 1933 • Santley Joseph • SHT • USA
50 PERSONALITIES • 1965 • Warhol Andy • USA
50 YEARS KLM • 1970 • Erends Ronny • SHT • NTH
50,81% • 1974 • Depardon Raymond • DOC • FRN
52 MILES TO MIDNIGHT see **HOT RODS TO HELL** • 1967
52 MILES TO TERROR see **HOT RODS TO HELL** • 1967
52 PICK-UP • 1987 • Frankenheimer John • USA • FIFTY-TWO PICK-UP
52ND STREET • 1937 • Young Harold • USA
54 CAMINOS HACIA EL FUTURO • 1979 • Garayucochea Oscar • DOC • VNZ • 54 ROADS TOWARDS THE FUTURE
54 ROADS TOWARDS THE FUTURE see **54 CAMINOS HACIA EL FUTURO** • 1979
55 DAYS AT PEKING • 1963 • Ray Nicholas • USA, SPN, UKN
56, RUE PIGALLE • 1948 • Rozier Willy • FRN
58 MASODPERC • 1966 • Gyarmathy Livia • DCS • HNG • 58 SECONDS
58 SECONDS see **58 MASODPERC** • 1966
60 CYCLES • 1964 • Labrecque Jean-Claude • DCS • CND • SIXTY CYCLES
60 MINUTOS CON EL PRIMER MUNDIAL DE BOXEO AMATEUR • 1974 • Alvarez Santiago • DOC • CUB
63 DAYS see **63 DNI** • 1969
63 DNI • 1969 • Wionczek Roman • MTV • PLN • 63 DAYS
65, 66 OCH JAG • 1936 • Henrikson Anders • SWD • PRIVATES 65, 66 AND I
66 • 1966 • Breer Robert • SHT • USA
£66.13.9 3/4 FOR EVERY MAN, WOMAN AND CHILD • 1916 • Collins Edwin J. • UKN
66 SCENER FRA AMERIKA • 1981 • Leth Jorgen • DNM • 66 SCENES IN AMERICA
66 SCENES IN AMERICA see **66 SCENER FRA AMERIKA** • 1981
67 DAYS see **UZICKA REPUBLIKA** • 1974
'68 • 1988 • Kovacks Steven • USA • SIXTY-EIGHT ○ 68
68 see **'68** • 1988
69 • 1968 • Breer Robert • SHT • USA
69 see **SIXTYNINE** • 1969
69:AN, SERGEANTEN OCH JAG • 1952 • Husberg Rolf • SWD • PRIVATE 69, THE SERGEANT AND I
69 LIEBESSPIELE (ENGEL DER SUNDE) • 1968 • Rieger August • FRG • 69 LOVE GAMES (ANGELS OF SIN)
69 LOVE GAMES (ANGELS OF SIN) see **69 LIEBESSPIELE (ENGEL DER SUNDE)** • 1968
70 • 1970 • Breer Robert • USA
70-TALETS MANNISKOR • 1975 • Watkins Peter • SWD • SEVENTIES PEOPLE, THE
72 DESPERATE REBELS, THE see **SEVENTY-TWO DESPERATE REBELS, THE**
72 HOURS OR DIE see **POWER GAME** • 1982
72.KOGUS • 1987 • Tokatli Erdogan • TRK • WARD NO.72
75 YEARS OF CINEMA MUSEUM • 1972 • Hershon Eila, Guerra Roberto • DOC • FRN
77 • 1977 • Breer Robert • USA
077: FURY IN ISTANBUL see **AGENTE 077, DALL'ORIENTE CON FURORE** • 1965
077, INTRIGO A LISBONA (ITL) see **MISION LISBOA** • 1965

077: SPECIAL MISSION LADY CHAPLIN see **MISSIONE SPECIALE LADY CHAPLIN** • 1966

79 A.D.–THE DESTRUCTION OF HERCULANEUM see **ANNO 79, LA DISTRUZIONE DI ERCOLANO** • 1963

79 A.D. (USA) see **ANNO 79, LA DISTRUZIONE DI ERCOLANO** • 1963

79 PRIMAVERAS • 1969 • Alvarez Santiago • DOC • CUB • 79 SPRINGTIMES FO HO CHI MINH

79 SPRINGTIMES FO HO CHI MINH see **79 PRIMAVERAS** • 1969

80 CHANNELS UNDER THE SEA • 1962 • Lemon Max • DOC • ASL

80 HUSZARS see **NYOLCVAN HUSZAR** • 1978

80 MILLION WOMEN WANT..? • 1913 • *Dumbrille Douglas* • USA

81ST BLOW, THE • 1975 • Bergman David, Guri Haim • DOC • ISR

83:AN I LUMPEN see **KUNGLIGA JOHANSSON** • 1934

84 CHARING CROSS ROAD • 1987 • Jones David • USA

84 CHARLIE MOPIC • 1988 • Duncan Patrick • USA

84 PREND DES VACANCES, LE • 1949 • Joannon Leo • FRN

087 MISION APOCALIPSIS (SPN) see **MISSIONE APOCALISSE** • 1966

087 MISSION APOCALISSE see **MISSIONE APOCALISSE** • 1966

087 MISSION APOCALYPSE see **MISSIONE APOCALISSE** • 1966

90 DAYS • 1985 • Walker Giles • CND

90 DAYS A YEAR see **90 DNI W ROKU** • 1968

90 DEGREES IN THE SHADE (UKN) see **TRICET JEONA VE STINU** • 1965

90 DNI W ROKU • 1968 • Gryczelowska Krystyna • DOC • PLN • 90 DAYS A YEAR

90 JAHRE DEUTSCHER GESCHICHTE –90 JAHRE KONRAD ADENAUER • 1968 • Viktor Herbert • DOC • FRG • 90 YEARS OF GERMAN HISTORY –90 YEARS KONRAD ADENAUER

90 JOURS, LES • 1959 • Portugais Louis • CND

90 MINUTEN AUFENTHALT • 1936 • Piel Harry • FRG

90 NOTTI IN GIRO PER IL MONDO • 1963 • Loy Mino • DOC • ITL

90 YEARS OF GERMAN HISTORY –90 YEARS KONRAD ADENAUER see **90 JAHRE DEUTSCHER GESCHICHTE – 90 JAHRE KONRAD ADENAUER** • 1968

91:AN KARLSSON • 1946 • Bolander Hugo • SWD

91:AN KARLSSON MUCKAR (TROR HAN) • 1960 • Gronberg Ake • SWD • PRIVATE 91 KARLSSON IS DEMOBBED OR SO HE THINKS

91:AN KARLSSON RYCKER IN • 1956 • Ragneborn Arne • SWD

91:AN KARLSSON SLAR KNOCKOUT • 1958 • Lewin Gosta • SWD

91:AN KARLSSONS BRAVADER • 1951 • Bernhard Gosta • SWD • EXPLOITS OF PRIVATE 91 KARLSSON

091, POLICIA AL HABLA • 1960 • Forque Jose Maria • SPN

91:AN KARLSSONS PERMIS • 1948 • Bolander Hugo, Bernhard Gosta • SWD

92° IN THE SHADE • 1975 • Mcguane Thomas • USA • NINETY–TWO IN THE SHADE

92 MINUTER AF I GAAR • 1977 • Brandt Carsten • DNM • 92 MINUTES OF YESTERDAY

92 MINUTES OF YESTERDAY see **92 MINUTER AF I GAAR** • 1977

99 AND 44/100% DEAD • 1974 • Frankenheimer John • USA • CALL HARRY CROWN (UKN)

99 DONNE (ITL) see **HEISSE TOD, DER** • 1969

99 FRAUEN see **HEISSE TOD, DER** • 1969

99 MUJERES (SPN) see **HEISSE TOD, DER** • 1969

99 RIVER STREET • 1953 • Karlson Phil • USA

99 WOMEN (USA) see **HEISSE TOD, DER** • 1969

100 A DAY • 1974 • Armstrong Gillian • SHT • ASL

$100 A NIGHT (USA) see **MADCHEN FUR DIE MAMBO–BAR** • 1959

100 ADVENTURES see **STET PRIKLYUCHENNI** • 1929

100% AMERICAN • 1918 • *Pickford Mary* • SHT • USA

100% BRAZILIAN FILM, A see **FILM 100% BRASILEIRO, UM** • 1986

100 CRIES HAS THE NIGHT see **MIL GRITOS TIENE LA NOCHE** • 1982

100 CRIES OF TERROR (USA) see **CIEN GRITOS DE TERROR** • 1964

100 GLIMPSES OF SALVADOR DALI • 1961 • Mekas Jonas • USA

100 GRAMS OF IMMORTALITY see **TIZ DEKA HALHATATLANSAG** • 1967

100 JAHRE JOHANN STRAUSS • 1925 • *Humboldt-Film* • FRG

100 KIDS WAITING FOR A TRAIN see **CIEN NINOS ESPERANDO UN TREN** • 1988

100 MEN AND A GIRL • 1937 • Koster Henry • USA

100 METERS WITH CHAPLIN see **CIEN METROS CON CHARLOT** • 1967

100 MILLIONS DE JEUNES • 1967 • Bertolino Daniel, Floquet Francois • DSS • CND

100 MONSTERS see **YOKAI HYAKU MONOGATARI** • 1968

100% NYLON • 1974 • Basov Vladimir • USS

100 PYGMIES AND ANDY PANDA • 1940 • Lovy Alex • ANS • USA

100 RAGAZZE PER UN PLAYBOY (ITL) see **BEL AMI 2000 ODER: WIE VERFUHRT MAN EINEN PLAYBOY?** • 1966

£100 REWARD • 1908 • Williamson James? • UKN

100 RIFLES • 1969 • Gries Tom • USA, SPN

100 TO 1 SHOT • 1906 • Blackton J. Stuart • USA

100 YEARS HENCE see **AIRSHIP, THE** • 1908

101 ACTS OF LOVE • 1970 • Haims Eric Jeffrey • USA

105% ALIBI • 1959 • Cech Vladimir • CZC

108–GO–SHA • 1959 • Murayama Shinji • JPN • POLICE MURDERER

108 HEROES FROM LIANG SHAN, THE • Chang Ch'Eh • HKG

113, EL • 1938 • Sevilla Raphael J. • MXC

120 ADVENTURES OF THE GULLIBLE KID • SER • PLN

120 DECIBELS • 1988 • Vafeas Vassilis • GRC

120 KILOMETERS AN HOUR • Kardos Leslie

120, RUE DE LA GARE • 1945 • Daniel-Norman Jacques • FRN

125, RUE MONTMARTRE • 1959 • Grangier Gilles • FRN

140 DAYS UNDER THE WORLD • 1966 • Fowler Kell • DOC • NZL

148 MINUTES FROM THE UNFINISHED SENTENCE see **148 PERC A BEFEJEZETLEN MONDATBOL** • 1974

148 PERC A BEFEJEZETLEN MONDATBOL • 1974 • Fabri Zoltan • HNG • 148 MINUTES FROM THE UNFINISHED SENTENCE ○ UNFINISHED SENTENCE, THE ○ UNFINISHED SENTENCE IN 148 MINUTES, THE

$200.00 • 1911 • Melies Gaston • USA

200 MOTELS • 1971 • Zappa Frank, Palmer Tony • USA, UKN • TWO HUNDRED MOTELS

210 VS. 213 • 1914 • *Melies* • USA

222 NO. LU DOSYA • 1967 • Havaeri Seyfi • TRK • FILE 222

240–ROBERT • 1979 • Krasny Paul • TVM • USA

250 GRAMMAA • 1984 • Honkasalo Pirjo, Lehto Pekka • FNL • 250 GRAMMES –A RADIOACTIVE TESTAMENT

250 GRAMMES –A RADIOACTIVE TESTAMENT see **250 GRAMMAA** • 1984

273 DAYS BELOW ZERO see **273 DNI PONIZEJ ZERA** • 1968

273 DNI PONIZEJ ZERA • 1968 • Bossak Jerzy (c/d) • DOC • PLN • 273 DAYS BELOW ZERO

288 STOURNARA ST. • 1961 • Simopoulos Dinos • GRC

300 DIN KE BAAD • 1938 • *Biswas Anil (M)* • IND

300 MIL TIL HIMLEN • 1989 • Dejczer Maciej • DNM, PLN, FRN • 300 MILES TO HEAVEN

300 MILES FOR STEPHANIE • 1981 • Ware Clyde • TVM • USA • THREE–HUNDRED MILES FOR STEPHANIE

300 MILES TO HEAVEN see **300 MIL TIL HIMLEN** • 1989

300 SPARTANS, THE • 1962 • Mate Rudolph • USA • LION OF SPARTA

300 YEAR WEEKEND, THE • 1977 • Stoloff Victor • USA • THREE–HUNDRED YEAR WEEKEND, THE

300 YEARS AGO • 1956 • Petrov Vladimir • USS

317e SECTION, LA see **317eme SECTION, LA** • 1965

317eme SECTION, LA • 1965 • Schoendoerffer Pierre • FRN, ITL, SPN • 317e SECTION, LA ○ TROIS CENT DIXSEPTIEME ○ PLATOON 317

322 • 1969 • Hanak Dusan • CZC

353 AGENTE ESPECIAL see **AGENTE 3S3 MASSACRO AL SOLE** • 1966

365 DAYS • 1922 • Roach Hal • SHT • USA

365 NIGHTS IN HOLLYWOOD • 1934 • Marshall George • USA

400 BLOWS, THE see **QUATRE CENT COUPS, LES** • 1959

400 BLOWS OF THE DEVIL, THE see **400 FARCES DU DIABLE, LES** • 1906

400 cm3 see **FOUR HUNDRED CUBIC CENTIMETRES** • 1966

400 FARCES DU DIABLE, LES • 1906 • Melies Georges • FRN • MERRY FROLICS OF SATAN, THE (USA) ○ 400 BLOWS OF THE DEVIL, THE ○ QUATRE CENT FARCES DU DIABLE, LES ○ PILLULES DU DIABLE, LES

400 LAT POCZTY POLSKIEJ • 1958 • Ziarnik Jerzy • DOC • PLN • 400 YEARS OF POLISH POST

400 MILLION, THE • 1939 • Ivens Joris • USA • CHINA'S FOUR HUNDRED MILLION

400 MILLION MILES FROM EARTH see **HIMMELSKIBET** • 1917

400 YEARS OF POLISH POST see **400 LAT POCZTY POLSKIEJ** • 1958

413 • 1914 • Ince Ralph • USA

491 (FYRAHUNDRANITTIOETT) • 1964 • Sjoman Vilgot • SWD

500 HATS OF BARTHOLOMEW CUBBINS, THE • 1943 • Pal George • ANS • USA

500 POUND JERK, THE • 1972 • Kronik William • USA

$500 REWARD • 1911 • Sennett Mack • USA

$500 REWARD • 1915 • Macdonald Donald • USA

£500 REWARD • 1918 • Flemming Claude • ASL

501 NUMARALI HUCRE • 1967 • Eraslan Nusret • TRK • CELL NO.501

600–LECIE BYDGOSZCZY • 1946 • Bossak Jerzy • DOC • PLN • 600TH ANNIVERSARY OF BYDGOSZCZ, THE ○ SIX HUNDRED YEARS OF BYDGOSZCZ

600 MILLION PEOPLE ARE WITH YOU • 1958 • Ivens Joris • CHN • WAR OF 600 MILLION PEOPLE, THE

600TH ANNIVERSARY OF BYDGOSZCZ, THE see **600–LECIE BYDGOSZCZY** • 1946

625 • 1969 • Hein Wilhelm, Hein Birgit • FRG

633 SQUADRON • 1964 • Grauman Walter • UKN

681 A.D. –THE GLORY OF KHAN • Staikov Lyudmil • BUL

711 OCEAN DRIVE • 1950 • Newman Joseph M. • USA

800 HEROES see **PA–PAI CHUANG–SHIH** • 1977

800 LEAGUES OVER THE AMAZON (USA) see **OCHOCIENTAS MIL LEGUAS POR EL AMAZONAS** • 1958

806 / THE BEGINNING • 1972 • Lofven Chris • ASL

"813" • 1920 • Sidney Scott • USA • EIGHT–THIRTEEN

813 see **813: THE ADVENTURES OF ARSENE LUPIN** • 1922

813: THE ADVENTURES OF ARSENE LUPIN • 1922 • Mizoguchi Kenji • JPN • RUPIMONO ○ 813

976 EVIL • 1988 • Englund Robert • USA • HOROSCOPE ○ NINE SEVEN SIX: EVIL

984: PRISONER OF THE FUTURE see **NINE EIGHTY FOUR – PRISONER OF THE FUTURE** • 1979

999.. ALIZA MIZRACHI • 1967 • Golan Menahem • ISR

999 NACHT, DIE • 1919 • Sauer Fred • FRG

$1000 A MINUTE • 1935 • Scotto Aubrey • USA

$1000 A TOUCHDOWN • 1939 • Hogan James P. • USA

1000 CARAT DIAMOND, THE (UKN) see **SUPERCOLPO DA SETTE MILIARDI** • 1967

1000 CHILOMETRI AL MINUTO • 1940 • Mattoli Mario • ITL • MILLE AL MINUTO

1000 CONVICTS AND A WOMAN • 1971 • *Hay Alexandra* • USA

1000 EYES OF DR. MABUSE, THE (USA) see **TAUSEND AUGEN DES DR. MABUSE, DIE** • 1960

1000 FEMALE SHAPES see **1000 SHAPES OF A FEMALE** • 1963

$1000 PANTS, THE • 1914 • *Melies* • USA

1000 PLANE RAID, THE see **THOUSAND PLANE RAID, THE** • 1969

$1000 REWARD • 1913 • *Wilbur Crane* • USA

£1000 REWARD • 1913 • Heath Harold • UKN

$1000 REWARD • 1915 • *Fairbanks Marion* • USA

$1000 REWARD • 1923 • Seeling Charles R. • USA

1000 SHAPES OF A FEMALE • 1963 • Mahon Barry • USA • 1000 FEMALE SHAPES

$1000 SHORT • 1920 • *West Billy* • SHT • USA

£1000 SPOOK, THE • 1907 • Booth W. R. • UKN • THOUSAND POUND SPOOK, THE

1000 WORTE DEUTSCH • 1930 • Jacoby Georg • FRG

1000 YEARS FROM NOW see **CAPTIVE WOMEN** • 1952

1001 ARABIAN NIGHTS • 1959 • Kinney Jack • ANM • USA

1001 CRTEZ • 1961 • Vukotic Dusan • YGS • 1001 DRAWINGS

1001 DRAWINGS see **1001 CRTEZ** • 1961

1001 NIGHTS see **FINALMENTE LE MILLE E UNA NOTTE** • 1972

1001 RABBIT TALES • 1982 • Freleng Friz, Jones Charles M. • ANM • USA

1001 WAYS TO LOVE (UKN) see **COMMENT LES SEDUIRE** • 1967

1776 • 1972 • Hunt Peter H. • USA

1776 OR THE HESSIAN RENEGADES • 1909 • Griffith D. W. • USA

1789 • 1974 • Mnouchkine Ariane • FRN

1810 O LOS LIBERTADORES DE MEXICO • 1916 • *Cimar* • MXC • 1810 OR THE LIBERATORS OF MEXICO

1810 OR THE LIBERATORS OF MEXICO see **1810 O LOS LIBERTADORES DE MEXICO** • 1916

1812 • 1912 • Goncharov Vasili M., Hansen Kai, Uralsky A. • USS

1812 • 1929 • Waschneck Erich • FRG

1812 • 1965 • Strangeway Stan • UKN

1812 see **KUTUZOV** • 1944

"1812" (GRAFIN VANDIERES) • 1923 • Berger Josef • FRG

1848 • 1948 • Risi Dino • SHT • ITL

1857 • 1981 • Elder Bruce • CND • FOOL'S GOLD

1860 see **MILLE DI GARIBALDI, I** • 1933

1861 • 1911 • *Selig* • USA

1895–1945 CINQUANT'ANNI DI SESSO • 1970 • Messeri Gian Maria • ITL

1896, OR THE MOVIES MOVE • Makinen Aito • DOC • FNL

1900 • Devensky David • SHT • USA

1900 see **NOVECENTO** • 1976

1904 MELBOURNE CUP • 1904 • Barrett Franklyn • DOC • NZL

1905 see **MAT** • 1956

1914 • 1915 • Tucker George Loane • UKN

1914, DIE LETZTEN TAGE VOR DEM WELTBRAND • 1931 • Oswald Richard • FRG • 1914: THE LAST DAYS BEFORE THE WAR (USA)

1914: THE LAST DAYS BEFORE THE WAR (USA) see **1914, DIE LETZTEN TAGE VOR DEM WELTBRAND** • 1931

1917 • 1970 • Weeks Stephen • UKN

1918 • 1958 • Roshal Grigori • USS

1918 • 1984 • Harrison Ken • USA

1919 • 1983 • Betancor Antonio Jose • SPN

1919 • 1984 • Brody Hugh • UKN • NINETEEN NINETEEN

1919, A RUSSIAN FUNERAL • 1971 • Le Grice Malcolm • UKN

1922 see **NOUMERO, TO** • 1978

1922: A MINER'S STRIKE see **CORONATION DEEP 1922** • 1984

1933 • 1967 • Wieland Joyce • SHT • USA

1939 • 1989 • Carmbeck Goran • SWD

1940, FUOCO NEL DESERTO • 1958 • Ferroni Giorgio • ITL

1941 • 1941 • Lee Francis • SHT • USA • FILM 1941

1941 • 1979 • Spielberg Steven • USA

1943: UN INCONTRO • 1971 • Giannetti Alfredo • ITL

1950 BRITISH EMPIRE GAMES • 1950 • NZL

1953 FLOOD DISASTER, THE • 1977 • Breyer Charles • SHT • NTH

1954 ARS VINTER–VM I SVERIGE • 1954 • *Gunwall Per (Edt)* • SWD

1958 • 1959 • Ramello Catone • ITL

1958 –A VERY EXCEPTIONAL YEAR see **1958 –ET GANSKE ALMINNELIG AR** • 1980

1958 –ET GANSKE ALMINNELIG AR • 1980 • Tuhus Oddvar Bull • NRW • 1958 –A VERY EXCEPTIONAL YEAR

1963. JULIUS 27. SZOMBAT • 1963 • Meszaros Marta • DCS • HNG • SATURDAY, JULY 27, 1963

1967 see **PENIS** • 1965

1968 • 1969 • Schaal Hans • USA

1969 • 1988 • Thompson Ernest • USA

1984 • 1956 • Anderson Michael • UKN

1984 • 1984 • Radford Michael • UKN

1985 • 1970 • *Ccm* • USA

1988: A REMAKE see **1988: THE REMAKE** • 1978

1988: THE REMAKE • 1978 • Schmidt Richard R. • USA • 1988: A REMAKE ○ SHOWBOAT NINETEEN EIGHTY EIGHT

1989 • 1963 • Leenhardt Roger • DCS • FRN

1990: I GUERRIERI DEL BRONX • 1982 • Castellari Enzo G. • ITL • 1990: THE BRONX WARRIORS (USA) ○ BRONX WARRIORS

1990: THE BRONX WARRIORS (USA) see **1990: I GUERRIERI DEL BRONX** • 1982

1999–NEN NO NATSU YASUMI • 1988 • Kaneko • JPN • SUMMER VACATION 1999 (UKN)

2000 B.C. • 1931 • *Terry Paul/ Moser Frank (P)* • ANS • USA

2000 BELOW • 1939 • Heyer John • DOC • ASL

2,000 MANIACS see **TWO THOUSAND MANIACS!** • 1964

2000 WEEKS • 1969 • Burstall Tim • ASL

2000 WOMEN • 1944 • Launder Frank • UKN • HOUSE OF 1000 WOMEN, THE

2000 YEARS LATER • 1969 • Tenzer Bert • USA

2001: A SPACE ODYSSEY • 1968 • Kubrick Stanley • USA, UKN • JOURNEY BEYOND THE STARS

2010 • 1984 • Hyams Peter • USA • 2010: THE YEAR WE MAKE CONTACT

2010: THE YEAR WE MAKE CONTACT see **2010** • 1984

2019: DOPO CAPUTA DI NEW YORK see **AFTER THE FALL OF NEW YORK** • 1983

2019: THE FALL OF NEW YORK see **AFTER THE FALL OF NEW YORK** • 1983

2020 TEXAS FREEDOM FIGHTERS see **2020 TEXAS GLADIATORS** • 1982

2020 TEXAS GLADIATORS • 1982 • Mancuso Kevin, D'Amato Joe • ITL • 2020 TEXAS FREEDOM FIGHTERS ○ TEXAS GLADIATORS 2020 ○ SUDDEN DEATH

2069 A.D. see **2069 A.D.: A SENSATION ODYSSEY** • 1969

2069 A.D.: A SENSATION ODYSSEY • 1969 • Kopetsky Sam • USA • 2069 A.D. –A SEX ODDITY ○ 2069 A.D.

2069 A.D. –A SEX ODDITY see **2069 A.D.: A SENSATION ODYSSEY** • 1969

2069: A SEX ODYSSEY (USA) see **STOSSTRUPP VENUS –5 MADCHEN BLASEN ZUM ANGRIFF** • 1974

2069: A SPACE ODYSSEY see **ACH JODEL MIR NOCH EINEN – STOSZTRUPP VENUS BLAST ZUM ANGRIFF** • 1973
2076 OLYMPIAD • 1977 • *Zafer Jerry* • USA
2084 see **LORCA AND THE OUTLAWS** • 1985
$2500 DOLLAR BRIDE, THE • 1912 • *Pathe* • USA
2889 see **IN THE YEAR 2889** • 1966
3000 A.D. (UKN) see **CAPTIVE WOMEN** • 1952
3,000 MILE CHASE, THE • 1977 • Mayberry Russ • TVM • USA • THREE-THOUSAND MILE CHASE, THE
4,000 FRAMES • 1970 • Cantrill Arthur, Cantrill Corinne • ASL
5000 DOLARES DE RECOMPENSA • 1972 • *Churubusco Azteca* • MXC
5000 DOLLAR FUR DEN KOPF VON JONNY R. (FRG) see **BALADA DE JOHNNY RINGO, LA** • 1966
5000 DOLLARI SULL'ASSO • 1965 • Balcazar Alfonso • SPN, ITL, FRN
5000 FINGERS OF DR.T., THE • 1952 • Rowland Roy • USA • CRAZY MUSIC
5000 MARK BELOHNUNG • 1942 • Mayring Philipp L. • FRG
$5000 REWARD • 1918 • Gerrard Douglas • USA
$5000 REWARD see **DAREDEVIL'S REWARD** • 1928
$5000 REWARD, DEAD OR ALIVE • 1911 • Dwan Allan • USA
6,000 ENEMIES • 1939 • Seitz George B. • USA
6,000 KM PI PAURA see **SEIMILA CHILOMETRI DI PAURA** • 1978
7362 • 1966 • O'Neill Patrick • SHT • USA
8000 LI OF CLOUD AND MOON see **BAQIAN LI LU YUN HE YUE** • 1947
10,000 B.C. • *O'Brien Willis* • ANS • USA
$10,000 DOLLAR BRIDE, THE • *Powers* • USA
10,000 DOLLARS BLOOD MONEY see **DIECIMILA DOLLARI PER UN MASSACRO** • 1967
10,000 REWARD see **RUBBER TIRES** • 1927
11,000 SEXES, THE see **ONZE MILLE VIERGES, LES** • 1975
12,000 MEN • 1978 • Duckworth Martin • DOC • CND
£20,000 • 1916 • SAF
20,000 B.C. • 1931 • SHT • USA
$20,000 COROT, THE • 1913 • *Joyce Alice* • USA
20,000 DOLLARI SPORCHI DI SANGUE • 1969 • Cardone Alberto • ITL • KIDNAPPING (PAGA O UCCIDIAMO TUO FIGLIO)
20,000 DOLLARI SUL 7 • 1967 • Cardone Alberto • ITL • 20, 000 DOLLARS ON 7
20,000 DOLLARS ON 7 see **20,000 DOLLARI SUL 7** • 1967
20,000 EYES • 1961 • Leewood Jack • USA
20,000 LEAGUES ACROSS THE LAND (USA) see **VINGT MILLE LIEUES SUR LA TERRE** • 1960
20,000 LEAGUES UNDER THE SEA • 1916 • Paton Stuart • USA
20,000 LEAGUES UNDER THE SEA • 1954 • Fleischer Richard • USA
20,000 LEAGUES UNDER THE SEA see **TWENTY THOUSAND LEAGUES UNDER THE SEA** • 1973
20,000 LEGS UNDER THE SEA • 1917 • Beaudine William • USA
20,000 MEN A YEAR • 1939 • Green Alfred E. • USA
20,000 YEARS IN SING SING • 1933 • Curtiz Michael • USA
$24,000 MILLION FOR THE MOON • 1971 • Gross Yoram • ANS • ASL
$30,000 • 1920 • Warde Ernest C. • USA • THIRTY THOUSAND DOLLARS ○ THIRTY THOUSAND
30,000 MILES UNDER THE SEA see **KAITEI 30,000 MAIRU** • 1970
36,000 BRASSES • 1962 • Dufaux Georges • DCS • CND
50,000 B.C.(BEFORE CLOTHING) • 1963 • Rose Warner • USA • NUDES ON THE ROCKS
$50,000 JEWEL THEFT, THE • 1915 • Macquarrie Murdock • USA
$50,000 POLICY, THE • 1915 • *Mina* • USA
$50,000 REWARD • 1924 • Elfelt Clifford S. • USA • WINNING A WOMAN
55,000 FOR BREAKFAST • 1949 • Garceau Raymond • DCS • CND • 55,000 PETIT DEJEUNERS
55,000 PETIT DEJEUNERS see **55,000 FOR BREAKFAST** • 1949
70,000 WITNESSES • 1932 • Murphy Ralph • USA
80,000 SUSPECTS • 1963 • Guest Val • UKN
$100,000 • 1915 • Lloyd Frank • USA
$100,000 BILL, THE • 1915 • Edwards Walter • USA
100,000 COBBERS • 1942 • Hall Ken G. • DOC • ASL
100,000 DOLLARI PER LASSITER (ITL) see **DIEZ MIL DOLARES PARA LASSITER** • 1965
100,000 DOLLARI PER RINGO • 1965 • De Martino Alberto • ITL, SPN
120,000 V GOD • 1931 • Kuleshov Lev • USS
150,000 VOLTS • 1965 • Essid Hamadi • SHT • TNS
200,000 LEAGUES UNDER THE SEA (USA) see **DEUX CENT MILLE LIEUES SOUS LES MERS: OU, LE CAUCHEMAR D'UN PECHEUR** • 1907
300,000 HEROES • 1977 • Carbonell Maria L. • VNZ
500,000 (USA) see **GOJUMAN-NIN NO ISAN** • 1963
660124, THE STORY OF AN IBM CARD • 1961 • De Palma Brian • SHT • USA
1,000,000 EYES OF SUMURU, THE (USA) see **SUMURU** • 1967
$1,000,000 PEARL MYSTERY (USA) see **MYSTERY OF THE £500, 000 PEARL NECKLACE, THE** • 1913
$1,000,000 REWARD • 1920 • Lessey George A. • SRL • USA
$5,000,000 COUNTERFEITING PLOT, THE • 1914 • Harrison Bertram • USA
40,000,000 SHOES • 1961 • Leiterman Douglas • CND
100,000,000 WOMEN • 1942 • Weiss Jiri • DOC • UKN

A

A • 1964 • Lenica Jan • SHT • FRN, FRG
A-001 OPERAZIONE GIAMAICA • 1965 • del Amo Antonio • SPN, ITL, FRG • OUR MAN IN JAMAICA ○ SCHARFE SCHUSSE AUF JAMAICA ○ ACTION IN JAMAICA ○ 001 OPERACION CARIBE
A-008 OPERATION EXTERMINATE see **A 008 OPERAZIONE STERMINIO** • 1965
A 008 OPERAZIONE STERMINIO • 1965 • Lenzi Umberto • ITL, EGY • A-008 OPERATION EXTERMINATE ○ SUSPENSE A CAIRO POUR AGENT 008
A-009 MISSIONE HONG KONG (ITL) see **GEHEIMNIS DER DREI DSCHUNKEN, DAS** • 1965
A 45 KILOMETRES DE PARIS • 1934 • Bohdziewicz Antoni • SHT • FRN
A 077 DEFIE LES TUEURS (FRN) see **A 077, SFIDA AI KILLERS** • 1965
A 077, SFIDA AI KILLERS • 1965 • Margheriti Antonio • ITL, FRN • A 077 DEFIE LES TUEURS (FRN) ○ MISSION CASABLANCA
A 300KM POR HORA • 1972 • Farias Roberto • BRZ
A.A.A. MASSAGGIATRICE BELLA PRESENZA OFFRESI • 1972 • Fidani Demofilo • ITL
A AND B IN ONTARIO • 1984 • Wieland Joyce (c/d) • CND
A... AY • 1989 • Erdem Reha • TRK
A B C • 1950 • Hofman Eduard • ANS • PLN
A.B.C. • 1958 • Ferno John • SHT • UKN • ARUBA, BONAIRE, CURAZAO
A.B.C.INEMA • 1975 • Bertolucci Giuseppe • ITL • ABICINEMA
A.B.C. OF LOVE, THE • 1919 • Perret Leonce • USA
A.B.C. STAVELEG I AFRIKA • 1963 • Barfod Bent • SHT • DNM • AFRICAN ALPHABET (USA)
A BANNA • 1980 • Dienta Kalifa • MLI • C'EST FINI ○ IT'S FINISHED ○ IT'S ALL OVER
A BELLES DENTS • 1966 • Gaspard-Huit Pierre • FRN, FRG
A BIENTOT, J'ESPERE • 1968 • Marker Chris • DOC • FRN
A BIRIBI • 1906 • Nonguet Lucien, Heuze Andre • FRN
A BON PIED, BON OEIL see **GREAT CANADIAN SHOE-OFF, THE** • 1972
A BOUT DE SOUFFLE • 1960 • Godard Jean-Luc • FRN • BREATHLESS (USA)
A-BRIENDO BRECHA • 1984 • Agazzi Paolo • BLV
A BRIGLIA SCIOLTA (ITL) see **BRIDE SUR LE COU, LA** • 1961
A BYAHME MLADI • 1961 • Zheljazkova Binka • BUL • YET WE WERE YOUNG ○ WE WERE YOUNG
A.C. ASTOR WITH SENTIMENTAL MAC • 1928 • *De Forest Phonofilm* • SHT • UKN
A CANNE MOZZE • 1977 • Zaccariello Giuseppe • ITL
A CAUSE, A CAUSE D'UNE FEMME • 1962 • Deville Michel • FRN
A CAUSE DE L'AMOUR see **BI AMR AL-HUBB** • 1965
A CAVALLO DELLA TIGRE • 1961 • Comencini Luigi • ITL • JAIL BREAK (UKN) ○ ON THE TIGER'S BACK ○ ASTRIDE THE TIGRESS
A CHACUN SON ENFER • 1977 • Cayatte Andre • FRN, FRG • AUTOPSIE D'UN MONSTRE
A CHACUN SON PARADIS • 1951 • Emmer Luciano, Enrico Robert • ITL • IL PARADISO TERRESTRE ○ RITUAL OF LOVE
A CHE SERVONO QUEST QUATTRINI • 1942 • Pratelli Esodo • ITL
A CHEVAL • 1950 • Decae Henri • SHT • FRN
A CHI TOCCA...TOCCA! • 1978 • Baldanello Gianfranco, Golan Menahem (Spv) • ITL, FRG, ISR • AGENTEN KENNEN KEINE TRANEN ○ URANIUM-VERSCHWORUNG, DIE ○ KESHER HAURANIUM ○ YELLOWCAKE OPERAZIONE URANO ○ URANIUM CONSPIRACY, THE
A CIASCUNO IL SUO • 1967 • Petri Elio • ITL • WE STILL KILL THE OLD WAY (USA) ○ TO EACH HIS OWN
A COEUR JOIE • 1938 • Masson Jean • SHT • FRN
A COEUR JOIE • 1967 • Bourguignon Serge • FRN, UKN • TWO WEEKS IN SEPTEMBER (UKN)
A... COME ASSASSINO • 1966 • Harrison R. • ITL
A. CONSTANT see **ALICE CONSTANT** • 1976
A CONTRATIEMPO • 1981 • Ladoire Oscar • SPN • ON THE OFFBEAT
A CORPS PERDU • 1988 • Pool Lea • CND, SWT • STRAIGHT TO THE HEART
A CORPS PERDU see **SEUL A CORPS PERDU** • 1961
A COUP DE CROSSE (FRN) see **FANNY PELOPAJA** • 1984
A COUTEAUX TIRES • 1963 • Girard Charles • FRN • DAGGERS DRAWN (USA)
A CRIS PERDUS • 1972 • Dufaux Georges, Beaudet Marc • DOC • CND
A CUARENTA Y CINCO REVOLUCIONES POR MINUTO • 1969 • Lazaga Pedro • SPN
A CUORE FREDDO • 1971 • Ghione Riccardo • ITL
A DENTI STRETTI (ITL) see **SAIGNEE, LA** • 1971
A DIVINE COMEDY -PURGATORY see **SKARSELD** • 1975
A DONDE VAN NUESTROS HIJOS • 1956 • Alazraki Benito • MXC
A DOPPIA FACCIA • 1969 • Freda Riccardo • ITL, FRG • PUZZLE OF HORROR (USA) ○ GESICHT IM DUNKELN, DAS (FRG) ○ DOUBLE FACE
A DOPPIA MANDATA (ITL) see **A DOUBLE TOUR** • 1959
A DOUBLE TOUR • 1959 • Chabrol Claude • FRN, ITL • WEB OF PASSION (UKN) ○ A DOPPIA MANDATA (ITL) ○ LEDA (USA)
A-DUCKING THEY DID GO • 1939 • Lord Del • SHT • USA
A DUE PASSI DAL CONFINE • 1962 • Vernuccio Gianni • ITL
A DUO-TRIO see **DUETT ZU DRITT** • 1977
A, EN SAN ADVOKAT • 1940 • Rodin Gosta • SWD • OH, WHAT A LAWYER
A, EN SA'N NATT see **O, EN SA'N NATT** • 1937
A ESLI ETO LYUBOV? • 1961 • Raizman Yuli • USS • WHAT IF IT IS LOVE? ○ AND WHAT IF IT IS LOVE? ○ IF THIS BE LOVE ○ WHAT IF IT BE LOVE ○ HOW COULD IT HAPPEN
A ESTRADA DA VIDA see **ESTRADA DA VIDA** • 1968
A-FEI TSINGCHUN • 1990 • Wong Ka-Wai • HKG
A FIL DI SPADA • 1953 • Bragaglia Carlo Ludovico • ITL • AT SWORD'S POINT (USA) ○ DON RUY
A FLEUR DE PEAU • 1962 • Bernard-Aubert Claude • FRN
A FLEUR D'EAU • 1969 • Reichenbach Francois • SHT • FRN • VICHY 1969
A FORCE D'HOMME • 1969 • Audy Michel • DOC • CND
A FORCE ON S'HABITUE • 1979 • Gallepe Jean-Pierre • DOC • FRN • BELLE VIE, LA
A FORZA DI SBERLE • 1974 • Corbucci Bruno • ITL
A FOST PRIETENUL MEU • 1961 • Blaier Andrei • RMN • HE WAS MY FRIEND
A FUEGO LENTO • 1977 • Ibanez Juan • MXC
A FUERZA DE ARRASTRARSE • 1924 • Buchs Jose • SPN
A GHENTAR SI MUORE FACILE • 1967 • Klimovsky Leon • ITL, SPN • EN GHENTAR SE MUERE FACIL (SPN) ○ YOU DIE EASILY AT GHENTAR
A GO GO see **PERVERSOS, LOS** • 1965
A HAUNTING WE WILL GO • 1939 • Gillett Burt • SHT • USA
A-HAUNTING WE WILL GO • 1942 • Werker Alfred L. • USA
A-HAUNTING WE WILL GO • 1949 • Kneitel Seymour • ANS • USA
A-HAUNTING WE WILL GO • 1966 • Mckimson Robert • ANS • USA
A HAUTEUR D'HOMME • 1977 • Piquint Jean-Marie • BLG
A HIERRO MUERE • 1962 • Saslavsky Luis • SPN
A HJARA VERALDAR • 1983 • Johannesdottir Kristin • ICL • RAINBOW'S END
A HUNTING WE WILL GO • 1932 • Fleischer Dave • ANS • USA
A HUNTING WE WILL GO • 1960 • *Halas John (P)* • ANS • UKN
A HUNTING WE WON'T GO • 1943 • Wickersham Bob • ANS • USA
A.. IS FOR APPLE • 1963 • Burrows John, Hudson Hugh • SHT • UKN
A IS FOR ARCHITECTURE • 1959 • Verrall Robert A. • ANM • CND
A.K. • 1985 • Marker Chris • DOC • FRN
A.K.A. CASSIUS CLAY • 1970 • Jacobs Jim • DOC • USA • AKA CASSIUS CLAY
A LA BELLE FREGATE • 1942 • Valentin Albert • FRN
A LA CABARET • 1916 • Wright Walter • SHT • USA
A LA CONQUETE DE L'AIR • 1901 • Zecca Ferdinand • FRN • CONQUEST OF THE AIR (USA) ○ FLYING MACHINE, THE
A LA CONQUETE DE L'AIR • 1906 • Velle Gaston • FRN • CONQUEST OF THE AIR (USA)
A LA CONQUETE DE L'ESPRIT HUMAIN see **WAR FOR MEN'S MINDS, THE** • 1943
A LA CONQUETE DE L'OR • 1952 • Novik William • SHT • FRN
A LA CONQUETE DU POLE • 1912 • Melies Georges • FRN • CONQUEST OF THE POLE, THE ○ CONQUETE DU POLE, LA ○ VOYAGE AU POLE, LE
A LA CROISEE DES CHEMINS • 1943 • Poitevin Jean-Marie • CND
A LA CULOITE DE ZOUAVE • 1947-51 • Verneuil Henri • SHT • FRN
A LA FRANCAISE (FRN) see **IN THE FRENCH STYLE** • 1963
A LA GARE • 1925 • Saidreau Robert • FRN
A LA GUERRE COMME A LA GUERRE • 1969 • Tregubovich Viktor • USS
A LA GUERRE COMME A LA GUERRE • 1971 • Borderie Bernard • FRN, ITL, FRG • ECCITANTI GUERRE DI ADELEINE, LE (ITL)
A LA JAMAIQUE • 1956 • Berthomieu Andre • FRN • LOVE IN JAMAICA (USA)
A LA LEGION LE GUSTAN LAS MUJERES • 1975 • Gil Rafael • SPN
A LA MANIERE DE SHERLOCK HOLMES • 1955 • Lepage Henri • FRN
A LA MEMOIRE DU ROCK • 1962 • Reichenbach Francois • SHT • FRN
A LA MEMOIRE D'UNE HEROS • 1951 • Ventura Ray • FRN
A LA MOD • 1968 • Clark Barry • USA
A LA ORILLA DE UN PALMAR • 1937 • Sevilla Raphael J. • MXC • AT THE EDGE OF A PALM GROVE (USA)
A LA PALIDA LUZ DE LA LUNA • 1985 • Gonzalez Sinde Jose Maria • SPN • BY THE PALE LIGHT OF THE MOON
A LA POURSUITE DU VENT • 1943 • Leenhardt Roger • DCS • FRN
A LA QUEUE LEU LEU • 1955 • Blais Roger • SHT • CND
A LA RECHERCHE DE L'INNOCENCE • 1963 • Forest Leonard • DCS • CND • IN SEARCH OF INNOCENCE
A LA RECHERCHE D'UN APPARTEMENT • 1906 • Blache Alice • FRN
A LA SALIDA NOS VEMOS • 1985 • Palau Carlos • CLM • SEE YOU OUTSIDE
A LA SOMBRA DEL PUENTE • 1946 • Gavaldon Roberto • MXC
A LA SOMBRA DEL SOL • 1965 • Enrique Taboada Carlos • MXC, PRU
A LA SOMBRE DEL SOL • 1978 • Caiozzi Silvio • CHL • IN THE SHADOW OF THE SUN
A LA SOURCE, LA FEMME AIMEE • 1966 • Kaplan Nelly • FRN
A L'AISE DANS MA JOB • 1973 • Moreau Michel • DCS • CND
A LAS CINCO DE LA TARDE • 1960 • Bardem Juan Antonio • SPN • AT FIVE O'CLOCK IN THE AFTERNOON
A L'ASSAUT DES AIGUILLES DU DIABLE • 1942 • Ichac Marcel • DCS • FRN
A L'AUBE DU TROISIEME JOUR • 1962 • Bernard-Aubert Claude • FRN • POLLIORKA ○ MOUTONS DE PRAXOS, LES ○ POLYORCHIA
A L'AUBE D'UN MONDE • 1956 • Lucot Rene • SHT • FRN
A L'AUTOMNE DE LA VIE • 1988 • Chouinard Ivan • CND
A L'AUTRE BOUT DE MON AGE • 1975 • Tetreault Roger • CND
A L'EAU see **GET WET** • 1966
A L'ECOLE DU TROTTOIR • Ricaud Michel • FRN
A L'EST DE BERLIN • Frank A. M. • FRN
A L'EST DU RIO CONCHO • 1976 • Roussel Gilbert • FRN
A L'HEURE DE LA COLONISATION • 1963 • Fortier Monique • DOC • CND
A L'HORIZON DU SUD • 1924 • de Gastyne Marco • FRN
A L'INTENTION DE MADEMOISELLE ISSOUFOU A BILMA • 1979 • de Bendern Caroline • FRN
A L'ITALIENNE (FRN) see **MADE IN ITALY** • 1965
A LO MACHO • 1939 • de Anda Raul, de Lucenay Martin • MXC • IN ROUGH STYLE (USA)
A L'OMBRE DES HOMMES see **ENFER DES ANGES, L'** • 1939
A L'OMBRE DU DEUXIEME BUREAU see **NADIA, LA FEMME TRAQUEE** • 1939
A L'OMBRE DU VATICAN • 1921 • Ravel Gaston • FRN
A L'OMBRE D'UN ETE • Van Belle Jean-Louis • FRN
A L'OMBRE D'UNE FEMME see **FORT-DOLORES** • 1938

A LOS CUATRO VIENTOS • 1954 • Fernandez Bustamente Adolfo • MXC

A LOS CUATROS VIENTOS • 1988 • Zorrilla Jose Antonio • SPN

A.M. AND P.M. • 1933 • *Van Buren* • ANS • USA

A ME MI PLACE • 1985 • Montesano Enrico • ITL • I LIKE IT

A MEDIA LUZ • 1946 • Momplet Antonio • MXC

A MEDIA LUZ LOS TRES • 1957 • Soler Julian • MXC

A MEZZANOTTE VA LA RONDA DEL PIACERE • 1975 • Fondato Marcello • ITL • MIDNIGHT PLEASURES (USA)

A MI-CHEMIN DU CIEL • 1930 • Cavalcanti Alberto • FRN

A MI LA LEGION! • 1942 • de Orduna Juan • SPN

A MI LAS MUJERES, NI FU NI FA • 1971 • Ozores Mariano • SPN

A MI NO ME MIRE USTED! • 1941 • Saenz De Heredia Jose Luis • SPN

A MI QUE ME IMPORTA QUE EXPLOTE MIAMI • 1975 • Cano Manuel • SPN

A MINUIT, LE 7 • 1936 • de Canonge Maurice • FRN

A MINUIT.. L'INDEPENDANCE • 1960 • DOC • BRK

A MOI LE JOUR, A TOI LA NUIT • 1932 • Heymann Claude, Berger Ludwig • FRN • LIT DE MME LEDOUX, LE

A MORT L'ARBITRE • 1984 • Mocky Jean-Pierre • FRN

A MOSCA CIECA • 1965 • Scavolini Romano • ITL

A NOI PIACE FREDDO..! • 1960 • Steno • ITL • SOME LIKE IT COLD

A NOS AMOURS • 1983 • Pialat Maurice • FRN • TO OUR LOVES

A NOUS DEUX • 1979 • Lelouch Claude • CND, FRN • ADVENTURE FOR TWO, AN (USA) ○ US TWO

A NOUS DEUX, FRANCE see **A NOUS DEUX, LA FRANCE!** • 1970

A NOUS DEUX, LA FRANCE! • 1970 • Ecare Desire • IVC, FRN • FEMMES NOIRES, FEMMES NUES ○ A NOUS DEUX, FRANCE ○ TAKE CARE! FRANCE

A NOUS DEUX, MADAME LA VIE • 1936 • Mirande Yves, Guissart Rene • FRN • C'EST LA VIE ○ GAGNANT, LE

A NOUS DEUX PARIS • 1953 • Kast Pierre • SHT • FRN

A NOUS DEUX PARIS • 1965 • Vierne Jean-Jacques • FRN

A NOUS LA LIBERTE • 1931 • Clair Rene • FRN • LIBERTY FOR US (USA) ○ LIBERTE CHERIE ○ FREEDOM FOR US

A NOUS LA RUE • 1986 • Dao Moustapha • SHT • BRK • STREET IS OURS, THE

A NOUS LES MINETTES • Villeneau Henri • FRN

A NOUS LES MINETTES see **GRANDE FRIME, LA** • 1976

A NOUS LES PETITES ANGLAISES • 1975 • Lang Michel • FRN • LET'S GET THOSE ENGLISH GIRLS

A NOUS QUATRE, CARDINAL! • 1973 • Hunebelle Andre • FRN

A NYNI HRAGE DECHOVKA • 1953 • *Stallich Jan (Ph)* • SHT • CZC

A.O.S. see **AOS** • 1964

A.P.O. OF THE PRIMITIVE • 1977 • Meulman Wim • NTH

A PARIS TOUS LES DEUX (FRN) see **PARIS HOLIDAY** • 1958

A PARIS UN SOIR see **FAUSSE ALERTE** • 1940

...A PATY JEZDEC JE STRACH • 1964 • Brynych Zbynek • CZC • FIFTH RIDER IS FEAR, THE (UKN) ○ ...AND THE FIFTH RIDER IS FEAR ○ FIFTH HORSEMAN IS FEAR, THE (USA)

A PIED, A CHEVAL ET EN SPOUTNIK • 1958 • Dreville Jean • FRN • HOLD TIGHT TO THE SATELLITE (UKN) ○ SPUTNIK ○ DOG, A MOUSE AND A SPUTNIK, A (USA) ○ BY FOOT, BY HORSE AND BY SPUTNIK

A PIED, A CHEVAL ET EN VOITURE • 1957 • Delbez Maurice • FRN • ON FOOT, ON HORSE, AND ON WHEELS (USA)

A PLEIN SEXE • 1977 • Vernier Gerard • FRN

A PLEINE BOUCHE • 1976 • Roy Jean-Claude • FRN

A PLEINES MAINS • 1960 • Regamey Maurice • FRN

A-PLUMBING WE WILL GO • 1940 • Lord Del • SHT • USA

A POINGS FERMES • 1949 • Martin Marcel • SHT • FRN

A PORTE CHIUSE • 1961 • Risi Dino • ITL • BEHIND CLOSED DOORS

A POZDRAVUJTE VLASTOVKY • 1972 • Jires Jaromil • CZC • ...AND REMEMBER ME TO THE SWALLOWS ○ MY LOVE TO THE SWALLOWS ○ GREETINGS TO THE SWALLOWS

A PRENDRE OU A LAISSER • 1971 • Bendeddouche Jamal • ALG

A PRENDRE OU A LECHER • 1980 • Baudricourt Michel • FRN

A PROPOS DE JEAN VIGO • 1983 • de Oliveira Manoel • SHT • PRT

A PROPOS DE JIVAGO • 1962 • Alexeieff Alexandre • SHT • FRN

A PROPOS DE LA FEMME • 1969 • Pierson Claude • CND, FRN • ALL ABOUT WOMEN (UKN)

A PROPOS DE LA SUITE.. • 1984 • Cornellier Robert • MTV • CND

A PROPOS DE METHODES • 1973 • Lamothe Arthur • CND

A PROPOS DE NICE • 1929 • Vigo Jean • FRN

A PROPOS D'UN COLLOQUE • 1968 • Dansereau Fernand • DCS • CND

A PROPOS D'UN MEURTRE • 1966 • Ledieu Christian • SHT • FRN

A PROPOS D'UNE PLAGE • 1964 • Dufaux Georges • SHT • CND

A PROPOS D'UNE RIVIERE • 1955 • Franju Georges • SHT • FRN • AU FIL D'UNE RIVIERE ○ SAUMON ATLANTIQUE, LE

A PROPOS OF THE TRUCE WITH FINLAND see **K VOPROSU O PEREMIRII S FINLJANDIEJ** • 1945

A PROPOSITO DI QUELLA STRANA RAGAZZA CHE E VENUTA AD ABITARE DA ME • 1981 • Loy Nanni • ITL

A PROPOSITO LUCKY LUCIANO see **LUCKY LUCIANO** • 1973

A PUGNI NUDI (PER UNA TRISTE ESPERIENZA IN UN CARCARE MINORILE) • 1975 • Zeani Marcello • ITL

A PUNTA DE LATIGO • 1949 • Perla Alejandro • SPN

A QUALCUNO PIACE CALVO • 1959 • Amendola Mario • ITL

A QUALSIASI PREZZO • 1968 • Miraglia Emilio Paolo • ITL, FRG • VATICAN AFFAIR, THE (USA) ○ VATICAN STORY ○ AT ANY PRICE

A QUELLE HEURE TU TE LEVES DEMAIN? • 1980 • Bailly Jean-Pierre • FRN

A QUELQUES JOURS PRES • 1968 • Ciampi Yves • FRN, CZC • O PAR DNU (CZC) ○ MATTER OF DAYS, A (USA) ○ TECH NEKOLIK DNU.. ○ TOO LATE BY A FEW DAYS.. ○ FEW MORE DAYS, A

A QUI APPARTIENT CE GAGE? • 1973 • Warny Clorinda, Blackburn Marthe, Gibbard Susan, Morazain Jeanne, Saia Francine • CND

A QUI LA BEBE? • 1947-51 • Verneuil Henri • SHT • FRN

A QUOI REVENT LES JEUNES FILMS • 1925 • Chomette Henri • FRN

A RAS DEL RIO • 1961 • Aguirre Javier • SHT • SPN

A REBROUSSE-POIL • 1959 • Armand Pierre • FRN

A RITMO DE BOSSA NOVA see **QUIERO MORIR EN CARNAVAL** • 1961

A RITMO DE TWIST • 1962 • Alazraki Benito • MXC

A SABLAZO LIMPIO • 1958 • Cortes Fernando • MXC

A SAINT-HENRI LE CINQ SEPTEMBRE • 1962 • Aquin Hubert • CND • SEPTEMBER FIVE AT SAINT-HENRI

A SAN FRANCISCO • 1914 • Serena Gustavo • ITL

A SANGRE FRIA • 1959 • Bosch Juan • SPN

A SIX ANS.. UN MAGNETOPHONE • 1970 • Moreau Michel • DCS • CND

A SOIR ON FAIT PEUR AU MONDE • 1969 • Brault Francois, Dansereau Jean • DOC • CND

A SORI SDESI TIBJE see **A ZORI ZYDES TIKHIYE..** • 1973

A SUD NIENTE DI NUOVO • 1956 • Simonelli Giorgio C. • ITL

A SUIVRE • 1970 • Zarifian Christian • FRN

A SUON DI LUPARA • 1967 • Petrini Luigi • ITL • TO THE SOUND OF GUNFIRE

A TEAM, THE • 1982 • Holcomb Rod • TVM • USA

A-TEAM: THE COURT MARTIAL, THE • 1985 • Mordente Tony, Sheldon Les, O'Herlihy Michael • TVM • USA • A-TEAM: TRIAL BY FIRE ○ LAST COURT MARTIAL, THE

A-TEAM: THE JUDGEMENT DAY, THE • 1985 • Hemmings David • TVM • USA

A-TEAM: TRIAL BY FIRE see **A-TEAM: THE COURT MARTIAL, THE** • 1985

A TEPYER SUDI.. • 1967 • Dovgan Vladimir • USS • AND NOW PASS JUDGEMENT..

A TIRO LIMPIO • 1958 • Cardona Rene • MXC

A TIRO LIMPIO • 1963 • Perez-Dolc Francesc • SPN

A TO Z see **A - Z** • 1956

A TODA MAQUINA see **ATM** • 1951

A TOI DE FAIRE, MIGNONNE • 1963 • Borderie Bernard • FRN, ITL • YOUR TURN, DARLING (USA)

A TOI DE JOUER CALLAGHAN • 1954 • Rozier Willy • FRN

A-TOMINABLE SNOWMAN • 1966 • Levitow Abe • ANS • USA

A TOUS LES VENTS • 1945 • Decae Henri • SHT • FRN

A TOUT CASSER • 1953 • Dupont Jacques • SHT • FRN • STOCK-CARS ○ STOCK CAR

A TOUT CASSER • 1968 • Berry John • FRN, FRG • GREAT CHASE, THE (UKN) ○ BREAKING IT UP

A TOUT PRENDRE • 1963 • Jutra Claude • CND • TAKE IT ALL (USA) ○ WAY IT GOES, THE

A TOUTE ALLURE • 1982 • Kramer Robert • FRN

A TOUTE HEURE EN TOUTE SAISON • 1961 • Fellous Roger, Manchon Charley • SHT • FRN

A TUTTA BIRRA see **BOLIDI SULL'ASFALTO A TUTTA BIRRA** • 1970

...A TUTTE LE AUTO DELLA POLIZIA • 1975 • Caiano Mario • ITL

A UM PULO DA MORTE • 1969 • Lima Victor • BRZ • AT THE SIDE OF DEATH

A 'UN • 1989 • Furuhata Yasuo • JPN

A UN DIOS DESCONOCIDO • 1977 • Chavarri Jaime • SPN • TO AN UNKNOWN GOD

A VALPARAISO • 1963 • Ivens Joris • SHT • CHL, FRN

A VASEN VITEZI • 1918 • Binovec Vaclav • CZC • PASSION WINS

A VENDRE • 1978 • Drillaud Christian • FRN

A VENEZIA UN DICEMBRE ROSSO SHOCKING (ITL) see **DON'T LOOK NOW** • 1973

A VENISE, UNE NUIT • 1937 • Christian-Jaque • FRN

A VENT'ANNI E SEMPRE FESTA • 1957 • Duse Vittorio, Corbucci Sergio • ITL

A VI GIFTA? • 1936 • Ibsen Tancred, Arvedson Ragnar • SWD • NASTAN GIFTA ○ ARE WE MARRIED?

A VIUVA VIRGEM • 1972 • Rovai Pedro Carlos • BRZ

A VOL D'OISEAU • 1962 • Miles Christopher • SHT • FRN • VOL D'OISEAU ○ FLIGHT OF THE BIRD

A VOLAR JOVEN • 1947 • Delgado Miguel M. • MXC

A VOTRE ORDRES, MADAME • 1942 • Boyer Jean • FRN

A VOTRE SANTE! • 1950 • Thevenard Pierre • SHT • FRN

A VOTRE SANTE • 1973 • Dufaux Georges • DOC • CND

A.W.S. • 1916 • Buss Harry • UKN

A.W.O.L. • 1973 • Freed Herb • SWD, USA

A WOPBOPALOOBOP AT LOPBAMBOOM • 1989 • Bausch Andy • LXM

A.Y. JACKSON: A PORTRAIT • 1970 • Macartney-Filgate Terence • DOC • CND

A YAY TAW BON • Aung Myint • BRM

A - Z • 1956 • Snow Michael • ANM • CND • A TO Z

A & Z • 1967 • Schubert Dietrich • FRG

A ZIVOT JDE DAL.. • 1935 • Junghans Karl • CZC, FRG • UND DAS LEBEN GEHT WEITER (FRG) ○ LIFE GOES ON ○ LIFE CONTINUES

A ZORI ZYDES TIKHIYE.. • 1973 • Rostotsky Stanislav • USS • DAWNS HERE ARE QUIET, THE (USA) ○ AND THE DAWNS ARE QUIET HERE.. ○ DAWNS ARE QUIET HERE, THE ○ AT DAWN IT'S QUIET HERE ○ A SORI SDESI TIBJE

AA DOKI NO SAKURA • 1967 • Nakajima Sadao • JPN • DIARIES OF KAMIKAZE, THE

AA FURUSATO • 1938 • Mizoguchi Kenji • JPN • AH, MY HOME TOWN (USA)

AA KAIGUN • 1969 • Murayama Mitsuo • JPN • GATEWAY TO GLORY

AA KIMI GA AI • 1967 • Nomura Yoshitaro • JPN • BARREN LOVE

AA KOE NAKI TOMO • 1972 • Imai Tadashi • JPN • AH! MY FRIENDS WITHOUT VOICE

AA RIKUGUN HAYABUSA SENTOTAI • 1969 • Murayama Mitsuo • JPN • FALCON FIGHTERS, THE (USA)

AA YOKAREN • 1968 • Murayama Shinji • JPN • YOUNG EAGLES OF THE KAMIKAZE, THE

AAAMOUR see **LAAASKA** • 1978

AABROO • 1968 • Rawal C. L. • IND • COVER

AADARSHA NAARI • 1983 • Lama Hem B. • NPL • IDEAL WOMAN

AADHI RAAT KE BAAD • 1965 • *Kumar Ashok* • IND

AADI HAQEEQAT AADHA FASANA • 1990 • Ghosh Dilip • IND • CHILDREN OF THE SILVER SCREEN

AADMI • 1958 • IND • MAN, THE

AADMI • 1968 • Bhimsingh A. • IND • MAN

AAG • 1945 • Kapoor Raj • IND • FIRE

AAG • 1968 • Kumar Naresh • IND • FIRE

AAG AUR SHOLEY • 1987 • PKS, BNG, NPL • FLAMES

AAG HI AAG • 1988 • PKS • FIRE

AAH.. BELINDA • 1985 • Yilmaz Atif • TRK

AAH.. TAMARA • 1964 • de la Parra Pim, Verstappen Wim • SHT • NTH

AAJ KA MLA • 1984 • *Khanna Rajesh* • IND • TODAY'S MLA

AAKALER SANDHANE see **AKALER SANDHANE** • 1980

AAKASH • 1953 • *Biswas Anil (M)* • IND

AAKHRI KHAT • 1967 • Anand Chetan • IND • LAST LETTER, THE

AAKRONT • 1972 • Vaidya Girish • IND

AAKROSH • 1978 • Nihalani Govind • IND • CRY OF THE WOUNDED ○ AKROSH

AALAM MODHEK GEDDAN • 1968 • Mustafa Hassam Eddin • EGY • IT'S A MAD WORLD

AALAYAM • 1967 • Thirumalai-Mahalingam • IND • TEMPLE, THE

AALTJES • 1966 • van Gelder J. A. • SHT • NTH

AAMNE SAMNE • 1967 • Prakash Suraj • IND • NEIGHBOURS

AAMUA KAUPUNGISSA • 1954 • Donner Jorn • SHT • FNL • MORNING IN THE CITY

AAN • 1952 • Khan Mehboob • IND • SAVAGE PRINCESS (UKN) ○ PRIDE

AANASI YIGIT DOGURMUS • 1966 • Kurthan Nazif • TRK

AANDHI • 1989 • Islam Nazaral • PKS • STORM

AANDHIYAN • 1952 • Ahand Chetah • IND • CRUEL WIND

AANMELDING • 1964 • Houwer Rob • SHT • NTH, FRG • APPLICATION ○ ANMELDUNG

AANSLAG, DE • 1986 • Rademakers Fons • NTH • ASSAULT, THE

AANSLAG OP KARIBA • 1973 • Hall Ivan • SAF

AAR PAAR • 1954 • Dutt Guru • IND

AARAAM • 1951 • *Biswas Anil (M)* • IND

AARAVALLI • 1957 • Krishnan S. V. • IND

AARDOLIE • 1953 • Haanstra Bert • NTH • CHANGING EARTH, THE ○ ONTSTAAN EN VERGAAN

AARGHAT • 1985 • Nihalani Govind • IND

AAROHI • 1965 • Sinha Tapan • IND • ASCENT

AARON LOVES ANGELA • 1975 • Parks Gordon Jr. • USA

AARON SLICK FROM PUNKIN CRICK • 1951 • Binyon Claude • USA • MARSHMALLOW MOON (UKN)

AARON'S ROD • 1923 • Coleby A. E. • UKN

AASE CLAUSEN • 1932 • Gade Svend • FRG

AASHIK • 1962 • *Kapoor Raj* • IND

AASHIYANA • 1952 • *Kapoor Raj* • IND

AASMAN • 1990 • Hussnain • PKS • SKY

AASMAN MAHAL • 1965 • Kapoor Prithviraj • IND

AASRA • 1967 • Bose Satyen • IND • HOPE

AASRAA • 1941 • *Biswas Anil (M)* • IND

AATAMIN PUVUSSA JA VAHAN EEVANKIN • 1971 • Kassila Matti • FNL • IN ADAM'S DRESS AND A LITTLE IN EVE'S TOO ○ IN ADAM'S CLOTHES AND A LITTLE IN EVE'S TOO

AATH DIN • 1946 • *Burman S. D. (M)* • IND

AAZAM TEFL FIL AALAM • 1976 • Sharkawi Galal • LBN • GREATEST CHILD IN THE WORLD, THE

AB DILLI DUR NAHIN • 1957 • *Kapoor Raj (P)* • IND

AB HEUTE ERWACHSEN • GDR • GROWN UP -AS FROM TODAY

AB MITTERNACHT • 1938 • Hoffmann Carl • FRG

AB MORGEN SIND WIR REICH UND EHRLICH • 1977 • Antel Franz • AUS, FRG • AS OF TOMORROW WE'LL BE RICH AND HONEST ○ RICH AND RESPECTABLE (USA)

ABA IBRAHIM KOUMANBAEF see **PESNI ABAYA** • 1945

ABACHURINA POST-OFFICE • 1973 • Lakshminarayan N. • IND • POST OFFICE AT ABACHURINA

ABADIA MASSABNI • 1975 • el Imam Hassan • EGY

ABAFANA • 1978 • SAF

ABAJO EL TELON • 1954 • Delgado Miguel M. • MXC

ABAJO ESPERA LA MUERTE • 1964 • de Orduna Juan • SPN

ABAKANOWICZ OF AUSTRALIA • 1976 • Mcgill Chris • DOC • ASL

ABALONE INDUSTRY, THE • 1913 • Sennett Mack • DOC • USA

ABANDERADO, EL • 1943 • Ardavin Eusebio F. • SPN

ABANDERADOS DE LA PROVIDENCIA, LOS • 1966 • Perez De Rozas Jose Luis • SPN

ABANDON ALL HOPE see **LASCIATE OGNI SPERANZA** • 1937

ABANDON SHIP (USA) see **SEVEN WAVES AWAY** • 1956

ABANDONADAS, LAS • 1944 • Fernandez Emilio • MXC • ABANDONED ONES, THE

ABANDONADO, EL • 1949 • Urueta Chano • MXC

ABANDONED • 1949 • Newman Joseph M. • USA

ABANDONED ONES, THE see **ABANDONADAS, LAS** • 1944

ABANDONED WELL, THE • 1913 • Vale Travers? • USA

ABANDONMENT, THE • 1916 • Macdonald Donald • USA

ABANDONS SUCCESSIFS, LES • 1975-77 • Moreau Michel • CND

ABANG • 1980 • Razali Rahim • MLY

ABANICO DE LADY WINDERMERE, EL • 1944 • Ortega Juan J. • MXC

ABARE GOEMON • 1966 • Inagaki Hiroshi • JPN • RISE AGAINST THE SWORD

ABAREBISHA • 1960 • Watanabe Kunio • JPN

ABAREMBO SAMBAGARASU • 1960 • Bansho Yoshiaki • JPN • WILD TRIO

ABARENBO KAIDO • 1957 • Uchida Tomu • JPN

ABASHEHEY • 1962 • Sen Mrinal • IND • AND AT LAST

ABASHIRI BANGAICHI: AKU ENO CHOSEN • 1967 • Ishii Teruo • JPN • ABASHIRI PRISON: CHALLENGE TO THE EVIL

ABASHIRI BANGAICHI: FUBUKI NO TOSO • 1967 • Ishii Teruo • JPN • ABASHIRI PRISON: DUEL IN SNOW STORM ○ STORY FROM ABASHIRI, A

ABASHIRI BANGAICHI: KETTO REIKA SANJU DO • 1967 • Ishii Teruo • JPN • ABASHIRI PRISON: DUEL IN HOKKAIDO

ABASHIRI PRISON: CHALLENGE TO THE EVIL see **ABASHIRI BANGAICHI: AKU ENO CHOSEN** • 1967

ABASHIRI PRISON: DUEL IN HOKKAIDO see **ABASHIRI BANGAICHI: KETTO REIKA SANJU DO** • 1967
ABASHIRI PRISON: DUEL IN SNOW STORM see **ABASHIRI BANGAICHI: FUBUKI NO TOSO** • 1967
ABASHOKOBEZI • 1978 • SAF
ABASTECIMENTO, NOVA POLITICA • 1968 • dos Santos Nelson Pereira • SHT • BRZ
ABASTECIMIENTO • 1973 • Ruiz Raul • SHT • CHL • SUPPLY
ABATHAKATHI • 1985 • SAF
ABATHUMBI • 1985 • SAF
ABATIS, L' • 1952 • Devlin Bernard, Garceau Raymond • SHT • CND • SETTLER, THE
ABAZURE NO KARAKU • 1967 • Kobayashi Satoru • JPN • PLEASURE OF A BITCH, THE
ABBA –THE MOVIE • 1977 • Hallstrom Lasse • SWD
ABBANDONO • 1940 • Mattoli Mario • ITL
ABBAS THE FLOWER see **CICEK ABBAS** • 1982
ABBASE SULTAN • 1968 • Demirag Turgut • TRK • ABBASE THE SULTANA ○ SULTANA ABBASE, THE
ABBASE THE SULTANA see **ABBASE SULTAN** • 1968
ABBASSO IL ZIO • 1962 • Bellocchio Marco • DCS • ITL
ABBASSO LA FORTUNA see **SCIOPERO DEI MILIONI, LO** • 1948
ABBASSO LA MISERIA • 1945 • Righelli Gennaro • ITL
ABBASSO LA RICCHEZZA • 1946 • Righelli Gennaro • ITL
ABBE CONSTANTIN, L' • 1925 • Duvivier Julien • FRN
ABBE CONSTANTIN, L' • 1933 • Paulin Jean-Paul • FRN
ABBE CONSTANTIN, L' see **BETTINA LOVED A SOLDIER** • 1916
ABBE PIERRE, L' • 1955 • Devlin Bernard • DCS • CND
ABBES' MOTHER see **OM ABBES** • 1969
ABBESS, THE see **NASTY HABITS** • 1976
ABBEY GRANGE, THE • 1922 • Ridgwell George • UKN
ABBIAMO VINTO • 1951 • Stemmle R. A. • ITL
ABBOTT AND COSTELLO GO TO MARS • 1953 • Lamont Charles • USA • ON TO MARS
ABBOTT AND COSTELLO IN HOLLYWOOD • 1945 • Simon S. Sylvan • USA
ABBOTT AND COSTELLO IN THE FOREIGN LEGION • 1950 • Lamont Charles • USA
ABBOTT AND COSTELLO IN THE NAVY • 1941 • Lubin Arthur • USA • IN THE NAVY
ABBOTT AND COSTELLO LOST IN ALASKA (UKN) see **LOST IN ALASKA** • 1952
ABBOTT AND COSTELLO MEET CAPTAIN KIDD • 1952 • Lamont Charles • USA
ABBOTT AND COSTELLO MEET DR. JEKYLL AND MR. HYDE • 1953 • Lamont Charles • USA
ABBOTT AND COSTELLO MEET FRANKENSTEIN • 1948 • Barton Charles T. • USA • ABBOTT AND COSTELLO MEET THE GHOSTS ○ BRAIN OF FRANKENSTEIN, THE ○ MEET THE GHOSTS
ABBOTT AND COSTELLO MEET THE GHOSTS see **ABBOTT AND COSTELLO MEET FRANKENSTEIN** • 1948
ABBOTT AND COSTELLO MEET THE INVISIBLE MAN • 1951 • Lamont Charles • USA
ABBOTT AND COSTELLO MEET THE KEYSTONE KOPS • 1955 • Lamont Charles • USA
ABBOTT AND COSTELLO MEET THE KILLER BORIS KARLOFF • 1949 • Barton Charles T. • USA
ABBOTT AND COSTELLO MEET THE MUMMY • 1955 • Lamont Charles • USA
ABBUFFATORE, L' see **SPORCA GUERRA, UNA** • 1965
ABBY • 1974 • Girdler William • USA
ABBY AND THE BOMB, THE • 1911 • Haldane Bert? • UKN
ABC A PRETO E BRANCO • 1964 • Fraga Augusto • SHT • PRT
ABC DA GREVE • 1989 • Hirszman Leon • DOC • BRZ • STRIKE'S ABC
ABC DEL AMOR, EL • 1967 • Coutinho Eduardo, Kuhn Rodolfo, Soto Helvio • CHL, BRZ, ARG • ABC DO AMOR, EL (BRZ) ○ ABC OF LOVE, THE
ABC DO AMOR, EL (BRZ) see **ABC DEL AMOR, EL** • 1967
ABC LIFELINE see **SEIKATSUSEN ABC** • 1931
ABC MURDERS, THE • 1966 • Tashlin Frank • UKN • ALPHABET MURDERS, THE
ABC OF FEAR, THE see **ABECEDA STAHA** • 1961
ABC OF FIRST AID • 1966 • Larkin Ryan • ANS • CND
ABC OF LOVE, THE see **LIEBES-ABC, DAS** • 1916
ABC OF LOVE, THE see **ABC DEL AMOR, EL** • 1967
ABC OF LOVE AND SEX – AUSTRALIA STYLE • 1978 • Lamond John • ASL
ABC OF THE FERGUSON SYSTEM, THE • 1949 • UKN
ABC PIN UP • 1944 • *O'Brien Joseph/ Mead Thomas (P)* • SHT • USA
ABC'S OF MARRIAGE, THE • 1970 • DOC • USA
ABDICATION, THE • 1974 • Harvey Anthony • UKN
ABDUCTED • 1987 • Collins Boon • CND
ABDUCTION • 1975 • Zito Joseph • USA
ABDUCTION IN YELLOW • 1980 • Evstatieva Marianna • BUL
ABDUCTION OF BANKER FUXE, THE see **UNOS BANKERE FUXE** • 1923
ABDUCTION OF KARI SWENSON, THE • 1987 • Gyllenhaal Stephen • TVM • USA
ABDUCTION OF LORELEI, THE • 1978 • Rank Richard • USA
ABDUCTION OF PARSON JAMES, THE • 1911 • *Yankee* • USA
ABDUCTION OF PINKIE, THE • 1913 • *Selig* • USA
ABDUCTION OF SAINT ANNE, THE • 1975 • Falk Harry • TVM • USA • THEY'VE KIDNAPPED ANNE BENEDICT
ABDUCTORS, THE • 1956 • Mclaglen Andrew V. • USA
ABDUCTORS, THE • 1972 • Schain Don • USA
ABDUL TAPANG • 1968 • Garces Armando • PHL • ABDUL THE BRAVE
ABDUL THE BRAVE see **ABDUL TAPANG** • 1968
ABDUL THE BULBUL AMEER • 1941 • Harman Hugh • ANS • USA
ABDUL THE DAMNED • 1935 • Grune Karl • UKN
ABDULLA THE GREAT • 1954 • Ratoff Gregory • UKN • ABDULLA'S HAREM (USA)
ABDULLAH • 1981 • *Kapoor Raj* • IND
ABDULLA'S HAREM (USA) see **ABDULLA THE GREAT** • 1954
ABE CLAN, THE see **ABE ICHIZOKU** • 1938
ABE GETS EVEN WITH FATHER • 1911 • Sennett Mack • USA
ABE-HAYAT • IND
ABE ICHIZOKU • 1938 • Kumagai Hisatora • JPN • ABE CLAN, THE
ABE LINCOLN IN ILLINOIS • 1939 • Cromwell John • USA • SPIRIT OF THE PEOPLE (UKN) ○ SO GREAT A MAN
ABECEDA STAHA • 1961 • Hadzic Fadil • YGS • ABC OF FEAR, THE
ABEL • 1985 • van Warmerdam Alex • NTH
ABEL GANCE ET SON NAPOLEON • 1984 • Kaplan Nelly • DOC • FRN
ABEL GANCE, HIER ET DEMAIN • 1963 • Kaplan Nelly • FRN • ABEL GANCE, YESTERDAY AND TOMORROW
ABEL GANCE –THE CHARM OF DYNAMITE • 1968 • Brownlow Kevin • DOC • UKN • CHARM OF DYNAMITE, THE
ABEL GANCE, YESTERDAY AND TOMORROW see **ABEL GANCE, HIER ET DEMAIN** • 1963
ABEL MIT DER MUNDHARMONIKA • 1933 • Waschneck Erich • FRG
ABEL SANCHEZ • 1946 • Serrano De Osma Carlos • SPN
ABEL –TWOJ BRAT • 1970 • Nasfeter Janusz • PLN • ABEL, YOUR BROTHER
ABEL, YOUR BROTHER see **ABEL –TWOJ BRAT** • 1970
ABELARDO'S SHORT STORIES see **CUENTOS DE ABELARDO** • 1989
ABELARDO'S STORIES see **CUENTOS DE ABELARDO** • 1989
ABELHA NA CHUVA, UMA • 1971 • Lopes Fernando • PRT
ABEND - NACHT - MORGEN • 1920 • Murnau F. W. • FRG • EVENING.. NIGHT.. MORNING
ABENTEUER AM LIDO • 1933 • Oswald Richard • AUS
ABENTEUER AUS 1001 NACHT, EIN see **ABENTEUER DES KLEINEN MUCK** • 1953
ABENTEUER DER KATJA NASTJENKO, DAS see **BEGIERDE** • 1920
ABENTEUER DER SCHONEN DORETTE, DIE • 1921 • Rippert Otto • FRG
ABENTEUER DER SIBYLLE BRANT, DAS • 1925 • Froelich Carl • FRG • UM EIN HAAR..
ABENTEUER DER THEA ROLAND, DAS • 1932 • Koster Henry • FRG • THEA ROLAND (UKN) ○ STORCH HAT UNS GETRAUT, DER ○ ABENTEUER EINER SCHONEN FRAU, DAS
ABENTEUER DES DR. DOLITTLE, DAS see **DOKTOR DOLITTLE UND SEINEN TIEREN** • 1928
ABENTEUER DES DR. KIRCHEISEN, DAS • 1921 • Biebrach Rudolf • FRG
ABENTEUER DES KAPITAN HASSWELL, DIE • 1925 • *Ranneg Film* • FRG
ABENTEUER DES KARDINAL BRAUN, DIE (FRG) see **OPERAZIONE SAN PIETRO** • 1967
ABENTEUER DES KAY HOOG, DIE see **SPINNEN, DIE** • 1919
ABENTEUER DES KLEINEN MUCK • 1953 • Staudte Wolfgang • GDR • ABENTEUER AUS 1001 NACHT, EIN
ABENTEUER DES KONIGS PAUSOLE, DIE • 1933 • Granowsky Alexis • FRG, AUS • KONIGS PAUSOLE
ABENTEUER DES PRINZEN ACHMED, DIE • 1926 • Reiniger Lotte, Koch Carl • FRG • ADVENTURES OF PRINCE ACHMED (USA) ○ WAK-WAK, EIN MARCHENZAUBER ○ GESCHICHTE DES PRINZEN ACHMED, DIE
ABENTEUER DES TIL ULENSPIEGEL, DIE see **AVENTURES DE TILL L'ESPIEGLE, LES** • 1956
ABENTEUER DES VAN DOLA, DAS • 1915 • Del Zopp Rudolf • FRG
ABENTEUER DES WERNER HOLT, DIE • 1963 • Kunert Joachim • GDR • ADVENTURES OF WERNER HOLT, THE (UKN)
ABENTEUER EINER BALLNACHT, DAS • 1918 • Larsen Viggo • FRG
ABENTEUER EINER BRAUTNACHT, DAS see **ABENTEUERLICHE HOCHZEIT, DIE** • 1925
ABENTEUER EINER NACHT • 1923 • Piel Harry • FRG
ABENTEUER EINER NACHT, DAS see **GEHEIMNIS VON BOMBAY, DAS** • 1920
ABENTEUER EINER SANGERIN, DAS • 1916 • Philippi Siegfried • FRG
ABENTEUER EINER SCHONEN FRAU, DAS see **ABENTEUER DER THEA ROLAND, DAS** • 1932
ABENTEUER EINES ERMORDETEN 1, DIE • 1921 • Ralph Louis • FRG • FLUCHT AUS DEM LEBEN, DIE
ABENTEUER EINES ERMORDETEN 2, DIE • 1921 • Ralph Louis • FRG • SMARAGD DES RADJAH VON PANLANZUR, DER
ABENTEUER EINES JUNGEN HERRN IN POLEN • 1934 • Frohlich Gustav • FRG • LIEBE UND TROMPETENKLANG
ABENTEUER EINES SOMMERS • 1974 • Pfandler Helmut • AUS • SUMMER ADVENTURE
ABENTEUER EINES ZEHNMARKSCHEINES, DIE • 1926 • Viertel Berthold • FRG • UNEASY MONEY (USA) ○ ADVENTURES OF A TEN MARK NOTE ○ K13 S13
ABENTEUER GEHT WEITER, DAS • 1939 • Gallone Carmine • FRG • JEDE FRAU HAT EIN SUSSES GEHEIMNIS
ABENTEUER IM GRANDHOTEL • 1943 • Marischka Ernst • FRG • VERGISS, WENN DU KANNST
ABENTEUER IM INDISCHER DSCHUNGEL see **KRISCHNA** • 1941
ABENTEUER IM NACHTEXPRESS • 1925 • Piel Harry • FRG
ABENTEUER IM SUD EXPRESS • 1934 • Marischka Ernst • FRG
ABENTEUER IN ENGADIN • 1932 • Obal Max • FRG
ABENTEUER IN MAROKKO • 1939 • Lapaire Leo • FRG, SWT • FRAU UND DER TOD, DIE
ABENTEUER IN WARSCHAU • 1937 • Boese Carl • FRG, PLN
ABENTEUER IN WIEN see **GEFAHRLICHES ABENTEUER** • 1953
ABENTEUER MIT FUNFZEHN HINDEN, EIN see **SIEN BESTER FREUND** • 1929
ABENTEUER TEGUAN • 1967 • Scholl Romeo • DOC • SWT
ABENTEUERIN VON MONTE CARLO 1, DIE • 1921 • Gartner Adolf • FRG • GELIEBTE DES SCHAH, DIE
ABENTEUERIN VON MONTE CARLO 2, DIE • 1921 • Gartner Adolf • FRG • MAROKKANISCHE NACHTE
ABENTEUERIN VON MONTE CARLO 3, DIE • 1921 • Gartner Adolf • FRG • MORDPROZESS STANLEY, DER
ABENTEUERIN VON TUNIS, DIE • 1931 • Wolff Willi • FRG • TREFFPUNKT AFRIKA!
ABENTEUERLICHE HOCHZEIT, DIE • 1925 • Seitz Franz • FRG • ABENTEUER EINER BRAUTNACHT, DAS
ABENTEURER, DER • 1921 • Mendes Lothar • FRG
ABENTEURER, DER • 1925 • Walther-Fein Rudolf • FRG
ABENTEURER, EIN • 1919 • Schomburgk Hans • FRG
ABENTEURER G.m.b.H., DIE • 1929 • Sauer Fred • FRG
ABENTEURER VON PARIS, DER • 1920 • Sauer Fred • FRG
ABENTEURER VON PARIS, DER • 1936 • Martin Karl Heinz • FRG
ABENTEURER VON SAGOSSA, DAS • 1923 • Seitz Franz • FRG
ABERDEEN ANGUS • 1947 • Harper Campbell • UKN
ABERDEEN –BY SEASIDE AND DEESIDE • 1969 • O'Leary Hans Neiter • DCS • UKN
ABERFAN • 1968 • Woods Grahame • CND
ABERGLAUBE • 1919 • Jacoby Georg • FRG
ABERGLAUBE • 1940 • Ruttmann Walter • FRG
ABERNATHY KIDS TO THE RESCUE • 1910 • *Champion* • USA
ABESALOM AND ETERI see **ABESALOM I ETERI** • 1967
ABESALOM I ETERI • 1967 • Esakia Leo • USS • ABESALOM AND ETERI
ABESSINIEN VON HEUTE –BLICKPUNKT DER WELT • 1935 • Rikli Martin • FRG
ABGERECHNET WIRD NACHTS • 1985 • *Rudolph Claude-Oliver* • FRG • ALPHA CITY
ABGRUND DER SEELEN, DER • 1920 • Gad Urban • FRG
ABGRUNDE • 1915 • Oberlander Hans • FRG
ABGRUNDE DER LIEBE • 1922 • Berger Friedrich • FRG
ABHAGIN • 1938 • *Roy Bhimal (Ph)* • IND
ABHIGYAN • 1938 • *Sircar B. N. (P)* • IND
ABHIJAN • 1962 • Ray Satyajit • IND • EXPEDITION, THE (UKN)
ABHILASHA • 1938 • *Biswas Anil (M)* • IND
ABHILASHA • 1968 • Bose Amit • IND • WISH
ABHIMAN • 1957 • *Biswas Anil (M)* • IND
ABHIMAN • 1973 • *Burman S. D. (M)* • IND
ABHIMANYU • *Ramachandran M. G.* • IND
ABHINETRI • 1940 • *Sircar B. N. (P)* • IND
ABHISHAPT • 1988 • Jha Prakesh • IND
ABHISHAPTA CHAMBAL • 1967 • Dey Manju • IND • CURSED VALLEY OF CHAMBAL ○ ACCURSED CHAMBAL VALLEY
ABHORRENCE • 1966 • Hintsch Gyorgy • HNG
ABI AND RABI • 1932 • Ohanian • IRN
ABI FAWQA ASH-SHAGARA • 1969 • Kamal Hussein • EGY • MON PERE LA-HAUT SUR L'ARBRE
ABIADH WA AL-ASWAD, AL– • 1970 • Fahmy Ashraf, Abdel-Aziz Muhammad, Sabaa Madqur • EGY • BLANC ET LE NOIR, LE
ABICINEMA see **A.B.C.INEMA** • 1975
ABID AL-MAL • 1953 • Wahab Fatin Abdel • EGY • ESCLAVES DE L'ARGENT, LES
ABIDE BY TRUTH see **SATHYAM THAVARATHE** • 1968
ABIDE WITH ME • 1914 • *Pathe* • USA
ABIDE WITH ME • 1914 • *Frontier* • USA
ABIDE WITH ME • 1915 • Malins Geoffrey H. • SHT • UKN
ABIDE WITH ME • 1916 • Watts Tom • UKN
ABIDE WITH ME • 1928 • Parkinson H. B., Edwards J. Steven • SHT • UKN
ABIE KABIBLE OUTWITTING HIS RIVAL • 1917 • *International Film Service* • USA
ABIERTO DE 18 A 24 • 1987 • Dinenzon Victor • ARG • OPEN FROM 6P.M. TO MIDNIGHT
ABIE'S IMPORTED BRIDE • 1925 • Calnek Roy • USA
ABIE'S IRISH ROSE • 1929 • Fleming Victor • USA
ABIE'S IRISH ROSE • 1946 • Sutherland A. Edward • USA
ABIGAIL DEAR HEART see **SONG OF SURRENDER** • 1949
ABIGAIL LESLIE IS BACK IN TOWN see **SEXPERT** • 1976
ABIGAIL WANTED see **STINGRAY** • 1978
ABIGAIL'S PARTY • 1977 • Leigh Mike • MTV • UKN
ABIJAN –PORT DE LA PECHE • 1962 • Rouch Jean • DCS • FRN
ABILENE TOWN • 1946 • Marin Edwin L. • USA
ABILENE TRAIL • 1951 • Collins Lewis D. • USA
ABIME DE PENITENCE, L' • 1924 • Bieganski Victor • PLN
ABISMO, O • 1982 • Sganzerla Rogerio • BRZ • ABYSS, THE
ABISMO DE PASION see **CUMBRES BORRASCOSAS** • 1953
ABISMOS • MXC
ABISMOS DA MEIA-NOTTE, OS • 1984 • de Macedo Antonio • PRT
ABITIBI • 1961 • Bonniere Rene • DCS • CND
ABITO NERO DA SPOSA, L' • 1945 • Zampa Luigi • ITL
ABLAKON • 1985 • M'Bala Gnoan • IVC
ABLE MAN, AN see **KARL FOR SIN HATT** • 1940
ABLE SEAMAN BROWN see **SINGLE-HANDED** • 1953
ABLEMINDED LADY, THE • 1922 • Sellers Oliver L.?, Gamble Don? • USA
ABNEGACION • 1937 • Portas Rafael E. • MXC
ABNER, THE BASEBALL • 1961 • Kneitel Seymour • ANS • USA
ABNORMAL see **HENTAI** • 1966
ABNORMAL BLOOD see **NIHON BOKO ANKOKUSHI –IJOSHA NO CHI** • 1967
ABNORMAL CRIMINAL see **HENTAIMA** • 1967
ABNORMAL FEMALE, THE • 1969 • Raders George • USA
ABNORMAL SEX CRIMES see **IJYO SEI HANZAI** • 1968
ABNORMAL VIOLATION see **IJOH BOHKOHZAI** • 1968
ABNORMAL VIRGIN see **HENTAI SHOJO** • 1968
ABNORMAL WIFE, AN see **HENTAIZUMA** • 1968
ABOGADO, EL ALCALDE Y EL NOTARIO, EL • 1968 • Font Espina Jose Maria • SPN
ABOITEAUX,LES • 1955 • Blais Roger • SHT • CND
ABOMINABLE COUNT YORGA, THE see **RETURN OF COUNT YORGA** • 1971
ABOMINABLE DR. PHIBES, THE • 1971 • Fuest Robert • UKN, USA • DR. PHIBES
ABOMINABLE HOMBRE DE LA COSTA DEL SOL, EL • 1969 • Lazaga Pedro • SPN
ABOMINABLE HOMME DES DOUANES, L' • 1963 • Allegret Marc • FRN
ABOMINABLE MAN, THE see **MANNEN PA TAKET** • 1977
ABOMINABLE MOUNTAINEERS, THE • 1968 • Bartsch Art • ANS • USA
ABOMINABLE SNOW RABBIT, THE • 1961 • Jones Charles M. • ANS • USA
ABOMINABLE SNOWMAN, THE • 1954 • *Panda* • SHT • USA

ABOMINABLE SNOWMAN, THE • 1957 • Guest Val • UKN • ABOMINABLE SNOWMAN OF THE HIMALAYAS, THE (USA)
ABOMINABLE SNOWMAN, THE see **JUJIN YUKI-OTOKO** • 1955
ABOMINABLE SNOWMAN OF THE HIMALAYAS, THE (USA) see **ABOMINABLE SNOWMAN, THE** • 1957
ABONGOUA-BENENE • 1956 • Regnier Michel • DCS • IVC
ABORIGINAL FAMILY EDUCATION • 1973 • Cowan Tom • DOC • ASL
ABORTAR EN LONDRES • 1977 • Carretero Gil • SPN
ABORTION! • 1967 • USA
ABORTION ISSUE, THE • 1980 • Waxman Albert • MTV • CND
ABORTO CRIMINAL • 1973 • Iquino Ignacio F. • SPN • CRIMINAL ABORTION
ABORTO: PARLANO LE DONNE • 1975 • Maraini Dacia • ITL
ABOU BEN BOOGIE • 1944 • Culhane James • ANS • USA
ABOU EL BANAT see **ANOUL BANAT** • 1973
ABOUT A COMB WHO DIDN'T WANT TO BRUSH HIS TEETH • 1967 • ANM • PLN
ABOUT A TAPESTRY • Hesse Isa • FRG
ABOUT BACHTALO • 1967 • Dobrowolska Krystyna • ANM • PLN
ABOUT FACE • 1942 • Neumann Kurt • USA
ABOUT FACE • 1952 • Del Ruth Roy • USA
ABOUT HUMAN MIRACLES see **PRO CHUDESA CHELOVYECHSKIYE** • 1968
ABOUT JOHNNY WHO MADE SHOES FOR DOGS • 1962 • Hornicka Lidia • ANM • PLN
ABOUT LAST NIGHT • 1986 • Zwick Edward • USA • SEXUAL PERVERSITY IN CHICAGO
ABOUT LIFE see **UBER LEBEN** • 1978
ABOUT LOVE see **PRO LIOUBOV** • 1932
ABOUT LOVE see **O LIUBVI** • 1971
ABOUT MRS. LESLIE • 1954 • Mann Daniel • USA
ABOUT PUBERTY AND REPRODUCTION • 1974 • Patel Ishu • ANS • CND
ABOUT SEVEN BROTHERS see **NOIN SEITSEMAN VELJESTA** • 1968
ABOUT SOMETHING ELSE see **O NECEM JINEM** • 1963
ABOUT THE WHITE BUS • 1968 • Fletcher John • DOC • UKN
ABOUT TIME • 1967 • Bonniere Rene • DCS • CND
ABOUT TRIAL MARRIAGE see **TRIAL MARRIAGE** • 1928
ABOUT TWENTY YEARS OLD see **NIJU-SAI ZENGO** • 1950
ABOUT TWO MEN WHO STOLE THE MOON see **O DWOCH TAKICH CO UKRADLI KSIEZYC** • 1962
ABOUT V.D. • 1974 • Patel Ishu • ANS • CND
ABOUT WARSAW BUT DIFFERENTLY see **O WARSZAWIE, ALE INACCZEJ** • 1960
ABOVE ALL LAWS (UKN) see **ADVENTURES IN SILVERADO** • 1948
ABOVE ALL THINGS (UKN) see **FLOOD TIDE** • 1958
ABOVE AND BELOW STAIRS • 1905 • Stow Percy • UKN
ABOVE AND BEYOND • 1952 • Panama Norman, Frank Melvin • USA
ABOVE PAR • 1915 • *Reliance* • USA
ABOVE RUBIES • 1932 • Richardson Frank • UKN
ABOVE SUSPICION • 1943 • Thorpe Richard • USA
ABOVE THE ABYSS • 1915 • *Travers Richard C.* • USA
ABOVE THE CLOUDS • Uher Stefan • CZC
ABOVE THE CLOUDS • 1933 • Neill R. William • USA • WINGED DEVILS (UKN)
ABOVE THE CLOUDS see **FOK EL SUHAB** • 1948
ABOVE THE HORIZONS • 1966 • Kroitor Roman, O'Connor Hugh • CND
ABOVE THE LAW • 1914 • *Lubin* • USA
ABOVE THE LAW • 1988 • Davis Andrew • USA • NICO: ABOVE THE LAW ○ NICO
ABOVE THE LAW see **INDISCHE GRABMAL I-II, DAS** • 1921
ABOVE US THE EARTH • 1977 • Francis Karl • UKN
ABOVE US THE WAVES • 1955 • Thomas Ralph • UKN
ABRA CADABRA • 1983 • Stitt Alexander • ANM • ASL
ABRACADABRA • 1952 • Neufeld Max • ITL
ABRACADABRA • 1957 • Vukotic Dusan • ANS • YGS
ABRAHAM BOSSE • 1972 • Leenhardt Roger • DCS • FRN
ABRAHAM GESNER • 1985 • Macgillivray William D. • MTV • CND
ABRAHAM LINCOLN • 1924 • Rosen Phil • USA • DRAMATIC LIFE OF ABRAHAM LINCOLN, THE
ABRAHAM LINCOLN • 1930 • Griffith D. W. • USA
ABRAHAM LINCOLN'S CLEMENCY • 1910 • *Pathe* • USA
ABRAHAMS GOLD • 1990 • Graser Jorg • FRG • ABRAHAM'S GOLD
ABRAHAM'S GOLD see **ABRAHAMS GOLD** • 1990
ABRAHAM'S SACRIFICE • 1979 • Hively Jack • MTV • USA
ABRANTES, A ARTE E A VIDA • 1971 • de Almeida Manuel Faria • SHT • PRT
ABRASASAS • 1984 • Volpato Reinaldo • BRZ • OPEN WINGS
ABRE TU FOSA, AMIGO, LLEGA SABATA • 1970 • Bosch Juan • SPN, ITL
ABREGEONS LES FORMALITES • 1916 • Feyder Jacques • FRN
ABRI 39 see **FAUSSE ALERTE** • 1940
ABRIGO A CUADROS, UN • 1956 • Hurtado Alfredo • SPN
ABRIL DE GIRON • 1966 • Alvarez Santiago • DOC • CUB
ABRIL DE VIETNAM EN EL ANO DEL GATO • 1975 • Alvarez Santiago • DOC • CUB
ABRIL DEL CARIBE • 1982 • Alvarez Santiago • CUB • APRIL FROM CARIBE
ABROAD WITH TWO YANKS • 1944 • Dwan Allan • USA
ABRUSTUNG see **WELT OHNE WAFFEN, DIE** • 1927
ABSALON • 1912 • Andreani Henri • FRN
ABSCHIED • 1930 • Siodmak Robert • FRG • SO SIND DIE MENSCHEN ○ ADIEU ○ FAREWELL
ABSCHIED • 1966 • Gunther Egon • GDR • ADIEU ○ FAREWELL
ABSCHIED VON DEN WOLKEN • 1959 • Reinhardt Gottfried • FRG • REBEL FLIGHT TO CUBA
ABSCHIED VON GESTERN • 1966 • Kluge Alexander • FRG • YESTERDAY GIRL
ABSCHIEDSWALZER • 1934 • von Bolvary Geza • FRG
ABSCHNITT: DIE KETTE see **MOREL, DER MEISTER DER KETTE 1** • 1920
ABSCHNITT: GLANZ UND ELEND see **MOREL, DER MEISTER DER KETTE 2** • 1920
ABSCONDED • 1953 • Whitaker Charles • UKN
ABSEITS • 1957 • Hart Wolf • FRG
ABSEITS VOM GLUCK • 1914 • Biebrach Rudolf • FRG
ABSEITS VOM GLUCK • 1916 • Biebrach Rudolf • FRG
ABSENCE • 1976 • Brakhage Stan • SHT • USA
ABSENCE, L' • 1976 • Sauriol Brigitte • CND
ABSENCE MAKES THE HEART GROW FONDER • 1925 • Butler Alexander • UKN
ABSENCE OF MALICE • 1981 • Pollack Sydney • USA
ABSENCES • 1988 • Katakouzinos George • GRC
ABSENCES REPETEES • 1972 • Gilles Guy • FRN
ABSENDER UNBEKANNT • 1950 • von Rathony Akos • FRG
ABSENT • 1928 • Gant Harry A. • USA
ABSENT see **NIEOBECNI** • 1963
ABSENT MINDED ABE • 1913 • *Brennan John* • USA
ABSENT-MINDED ARTHUR • 1910 • *Powers* • USA
ABSENT-MINDED BEGGAR, THE • 1909 • *Empire Films* • UKN
ABSENT-MINDED BOOTBLACK, THE • 1903 • Hepworth Cecil M. • UKN
ABSENT-MINDED BURGLAR, AN • 1912 • Henderson Dell • USA
ABSENT-MINDED CUPID, AN • 1909 • *Edison* • USA
ABSENT-MINDED CUPID, AN • 1914 • Miller Ashley • USA
ABSENT-MINDED JONES • 1910 • Rains Fred • UKN
ABSENT-MINDED LECTURER (USA) see **CONFERENCIER DISTRAIT, LE** • 1899
ABSENT MINDED MAN, THE • 1907 • Fitzhamon Lewin? • UKN
ABSENT-MINDED MR. BOOB • 1913 • France Charles H. • USA
ABSENT-MINDED MOTHER, AN • 1914 • France Charles H. • USA
ABSENT-MINDED PROFESSOR, THE • 1907 • Stow Percy • UKN
ABSENT-MINDED PROFESSOR, THE • 1961 • Stevenson Robert • USA
ABSENT-MINDED SURGEON, THE see **CHIRURGIEN DISTRAIT, LE** • 1909
ABSENT-MINDED VALET,THE • 1912 • Thompson Frederick A. • USA
ABSENT WITHOUT LEAVE • 1902 • *Gaumont* • UKN
ABSENTEE, THE • 1915 • Cabanne W. Christy • USA
ABSENTEE, THE see **REJTOZKODO, A** • 1985
ABSINTHE • 1913 • *Gem* • USA
ABSINTHE • 1914 • Brenon Herbert • USA, FRN
ABSINTHE see **MADAME X** • 1929
ABSOLUTAMENTE CERTO • 1957 • Duarte Anselmo • BRZ
ABSOLUTE BEGINNERS • 1985 • Temple Julien • UKN
ABSOLUTE FILM • 1947 • *Fischinger Oskar (P)* • SHT • USA
ABSOLUTE MAJORITY see **ZETTAI TASU** • 1965
ABSOLUTE QUIET • 1936 • Seitz George B. • USA
ABSOLUTION • 1978 • Page Anthony • UKN
ABSOLUTION, L' • 1922 • Kemm Jean • FRN
ABSORBING GAME, AN • 1911 • Fitzhamon Lewin? • UKN
ABSORBING TALE,AN • 1909 • Booth W. R. • UKN
ABSTRACT • 1927 • Duchamp Marcel • FRN
ABSTRACT ART EXHIBITION • 1962 • Kotowski Jerzy • ANS • PLN
ABSTRACT IN CONCRETE • Arvonio John • USA
ABSTRACTE KUNST IN VLAANDEREN, DE • Deses Greta • BLG
ABSTRONICS • 1954 • *Bute Mary Ellen* • ANS • USA
ABSTURZ, DER • 1922 • Wolff Ludwig • FRG • DOWNFALL
ABSURD • 1981 • Newton Peter • USA
ABSURD see **ANTHROPOPHAGOUS 2** • 1981
ABTRUNNIGE, DER • 1921 • Valentin Heinrich • FRG
ABU DHABI MARINE SURVEY • 1955 • UKN
ABUDASSE KALE • 1968 • Wickremasooriya Kumar • SLN • STRANGE TIME, A
ABUELA, EL • 1925 • Buchs Jose • SPN
ABUELA MADE IN SPAIN • 1969 • Lazaga Pedro • SPN
ABUELITA, LA • 1942 • Sevilla Raphael J. • MXC
ABUELITA ATOMICA, UNA • 1958 • Porter Julio • MXC
ABUELITA CHARLESTON • 1961 • Seto Javier • SPN • LITTLE GRANDMA CHARLESTON
ABUELITA DE ANTES DE LA GUERRA, UNA • 1974 • Escriva Vicente • SPN
ABUELO TIENE UN PLAN • 1972 • Lazaga Pedro • SPN
ABUNA MESSIAS • 1939 • Blasetti Alessandro • DOC • ITL
ABUS DE CONFIANCE • 1937 • Decoin Henri • FRN • ABUSED CONFIDENCE (USA) ○ ABUSE OF CONFIDENCE
ABU'S POISONED WELL • 1943 • Halas John, Batchelor Joy • ANS • UKN
ABUSAN • 1973 • Duparc Henri • IVC • FAMILLE, LA ○ FAMILY, THE
ABUSE • 1983 • Bresson Arthur Jr. • USA
ABUSE see **KATAHRISIS EXOUSIAS** • 1970
ABUSE OF CONFIDENCE see **ABUS DE CONFIANCE** • 1937
ABUSED CONFIDENCE (USA) see **ABUS DE CONFIANCE** • 1937
ABUSEMENT PARK • 1947 • Sparber I. • ANS • USA
ABUSO DE CONFIANZA • 1950 • Lugones Mario C. • ARG
ABUSO DI POTERE • 1972 • Bazzoni Camillo • ITL
ABWARTS see **ABWARTS: DAS DUELL UBER DER TIEFE** • 1984
ABWARTS: DAS DUELL UBER DER TIEFE • 1984 • Schenkel Carl • FRG • OUT OF ORDER ○ AUFZUG, DER ○ ABWARTS
ABWEGE • 1928 • Pabst G. W. • FRG • CRISIS ○ BEGIERDE ○ DESIRE
ABY KWILO ZYCIE • 1962 • Hoffman Jerzy, Skorzewski Edward • DOC • PLN • THAT LIFE MAY FLOURISH
ABYSMAL BRUTE, THE • 1923 • Henley Hobart • USA
ABYSS see **SZAKADEK** • 1955
ABYSS, THE • 1914 • Santschi Thomas • USA
ABYSS, THE • 1989 • Cameron James • USA
ABYSS, THE see **AFGRUNDEN** • 1910
ABYSS, THE see **ABISMO, O** • 1982
ABYSS, THE see **OEUVRE AU NOIR, L'** • 1988
ABYSS OF PASSION see **CUMBRES BORRASCOSAS** • 1953
ABYSSES, LES • 1963 • Papatakis Nico • FRN
AC KURTLAR • 1969 • Guney Yilmaz • TRK • HUNGRY WOLVES, THE
ACA LAS TORTAS • 1951 • Bustillo Oro Juan • MXC • HIJOS DE LOS RICOS, LOS
ACABARAM-SE OS OTARIOS • 1930 • de Barros Luis • BRZ
ACABEMOS DE UNA VEZ • 1975 • Cohen Rafael • ARG • AT LONG LAST COME
ACADAMUS • 1987 • Dyulgerov Georgi • BUL
ACADEMICIAN FROM ASKANIA, THE • 1962 • Gerasimov Vladimir • USS
ACADEMICIAN IVAN PAVLOV see **AKADEMIK IVAN PAVLOV** • 1949
ACADEMY AWARDS FILM, THE • 1951 • Carleton-Hunt • USA
ACADEMY DECIDES, THE • 1937 • Baxter John • UKN
ACADEMY FOR YOUNG LADIES see **LYCEE DE JEUNES FILLES, UN** • 1896
ACADEMY LEADER • 1965 • Malanga Gerard • USA
ACADEMY NEWSREEL • 1961 • Chytilova Vera • SHT • CZC
ACADEMY ROMANCE, AN • 1914 • *Powers* • USA
ACADIA ACADIA?!? see **ACADIE L'ACADIE?!?, L'** • 1971
ACADIE CONTEMPORAINE • 1966 • Forest Leonard • DOC • CND
ACADIE L'ACADIE?!?, L' • 1971 • Brault Michel, Perrault Pierre • CND • ACADIA ACADIA?!?
ACADIE LIBRE • 1969 • Forest Leonard • DCS • CND
ACADIENNE -CAPE BRETON • 1964 • Perry Margaret • DOC • CND
ACADIENS, LES • 1971 • Heroux Denis • CND
ACADIENS DE LA DISPERSION, LES • 1967 • Forest Leonard • DOC • CND
ACAPULCO • 1951 • Fernandez Emilio • MXC
ACAPULCO A GO GO • 1966 • Martinez Arturo • MXC
ACAPULCO EXPOSE see **ACAPULCO UNCENSORED** • 1968
ACAPULCO FIRST BEACH TO THE LEFT see **ACAPULCO PRIMA SPIAGGIA.. A SINISTRA** • 1983
ACAPULCO GOLD • 1978 • Brinckerhoff Burt • USA
ACAPULCO PRIMA SPIAGGIA.. A SINISTRA • 1983 • Martino Sergio • ITL • ACAPULCO FIRST BEACH TO THE LEFT
ACAPULCO UNCENSORED • 1968 • *Hollywood Cinema Associates* • USA • ACAPULCO EXPOSE
ACAPULQUENA • 1958 • Pereda Ramon • MXC
ACCADDE A DAMASCO see **ACCADDE A DAMASCO E FEBBRE** • 1943
ACCADDE A DAMASCO E FEBBRE • 1943 • Zeglio Primo, Rubio Jose L. • ITL • MERAVIGLIA DI DAMASCO, LA ○ ACCADDE A DAMASCO ○ FEBBRE
ACCADDE AL COMMISSARIATO • 1954 • Simonelli Giorgio C. • ITL
ACCADDE AL PENITENZIARIO • 1955 • Bianchi Giorgio • ITL
ACCADDE DI NOTTE • 1961 • Callegari Gian Paolo, Concini Franco • ITL
ACCADDE TRA LE SBARRE • 1955 • Cristallini Giorgio • ITL
ACCAO MISSIONARIA NO ORIENTE • 1956 • Spiguel Miguel • SHT • PRT
ACCATTONE! • 1961 • Pasolini Pier Paolo • ITL • BEGGAR, THE
ACCELERATION • Prochazka Pavel • ANS • CZC
ACCELERATION PUNK • 1977 • Glassman Robert • DOC • FRN, UKN
ACCENT, THE see **EKEZET** • 1977
ACCENT ON CRIME (UKN) see **DELINQUENT DAUGHTERS** • 1944
ACCENT ON GIRLS • 1936 • Waller Fred • SHT • USA
ACCENT ON LOVE • 1941 • Mccarey Ray • USA
ACCENT ON YOUTH • 1935 • Ruggles Wesley • USA
ACCEPTABLE LEVELS • 1984 • Davies John • UKN
ACCEPTABLE RISKS • 1986 • Wallace Rick • TVM • USA
ACCESS CODE • 1984 • Sobel Mark • USA
ACCESSION OF THE ROMANOV DYNASTY see **VOTSARENIYA DOMA ROMANOVIKH** • 1913
ACCETTA PER LA LUNA DI MIELE, UN' see **ROSSO SEGNO DELLA FOLLIA, IL** • 1969
ACCI-DENTAL TREATMENT • 1929 • Bentley Thomas • UKN
ACCIAIO • 1933 • Ruttmann Walter • ITL, FRG • ARBEIT MACHT FREI (FRG) ○ STEEL
ACCIDENT • 1967 • Losey Joseph • UKN
ACCIDENT • 1970 • Ben Salah Mohamed • SHT • ALG
ACCIDENT • 1973 • Duckworth Martin, Crawley Pat • DOC • CND
ACCIDENT • 1986 • Gelinov Ognyan • DOC • BUL
ACCIDENT, AN • 1948 • Tyrlova Hermina • CZC
ACCIDENT, L' • 1912 • Feuillade Louis • FRN
ACCIDENT, L' • 1963 • Greville Edmond T. • FRN • ACCIDENT, THE (USA)
ACCIDENT, THE • 1974 • Zalakevicius Vitautus • MTV • USS
ACCIDENT, THE • 1983 • Brittain Don • CND • ACCIDENT AT MEMORIAL STATION
ACCIDENT, THE see **WYPADEK** • 1971
ACCIDENT, THE see **JIKEN** • 1977
ACCIDENT, THE (USA) see **ACCIDENT, L'** • 1963
ACCIDENT AT MEMORIAL STATION see **ACCIDENT, THE** • 1983
ACCIDENT D'AUTO • 1907 • Feuillade Louis • FRN
ACCIDENT INSURANCE • 1913 • Smalley Phillips • USA
ACCIDENT IS THE BEST POLICY • 1916 • *Vitagraph* • SHT • USA
ACCIDENT OF WAR • 1976 • SAF
ACCIDENT POLICY, AN • 1915 • Mckim Edwin • USA
ACCIDENT TO TOMMY'S TROUSERS • 1905 • *Walturdaw* • UKN
ACCIDENTAL ACCIDENTS • 1924 • Mccarey Leo • SHT • USA
ACCIDENTAL ALIBI, AN • 1913 • *Phillips Augustus* • USA
ACCIDENTAL BANDIT, AN • 1913 • *Essanay* • USA
ACCIDENTAL BOMB, AN see **BOMBE PAR HASARD, UNE** • 1969
ACCIDENTAL CLUE, AN • 1913 • *Majestic* • USA
ACCIDENTAL DEATH • 1963 • Nethercott Geoffrey • UKN
ACCIDENTAL DENTIST, AN • 1913 • *Gains Eleanor* • USA
ACCIDENTAL HEROES • 1919 • *Field Elinor* • SHT • USA
ACCIDENTAL HONEYMOON, THE • 1918 • Perret Leonce • USA
ACCIDENTAL KILLER see **SKOTTET** • 1969
ACCIDENTAL LIFE, AN • 1969 • Peterlic Ante • YGS
ACCIDENTAL LOVE • 1971 • Shulman Iosif • USS
ACCIDENTAL MILLIONAIRE, AN • 1912 • *Lubin* • USA
ACCIDENTAL OUTLAW, AN • 1911 • *Standing Jack* • USA
ACCIDENTAL PARSON, AN • 1915 • *Luna* • USA
ACCIDENTAL SERVANT, AN • 1913 • *Eclair* • USA
ACCIDENTAL SHOT, THE • 1913 • *Gebhardt George* • USA
ACCIDENTAL SPY see **MR. STRINGFELLOW SAYS NO** • 1937

ACCIDENTAL TOURIST, THE • 1988 • Kasdan Lawrence • USA
ACCIDENTE 703 • 1962 • Forque Jose Maria • SPN
ACCIDENTI ALLA GUERRA • 1949 • Simonelli Giorgio C. • ITL
ACCIDENTI ALLE TASSE • 1951 • Mattoli Mario • ITL
ACCIDENTS, LES • 1967 • Bedjaoui Ahmed • DCS • ALG
ACCIDENTS CAN HAPPEN • 1925 • Lamont Charles • SHT • USA
ACCIDENTS DON'T HAPPEN • 1946-54 • Mulholland Donald • SHS • CND • PAS D'ACCIDENTS
ACCIDENTS NEVER HAPPEN SINGLY see **MALHEUR N'ARRIVE JAMAIS SEUL, UN** • 1903
ACCIDENTS WANTED (UKN) see **NUISANCE, THE** • 1932
ACCIDENTS WILL HAPPEN • 1903 • *Biograph* • USA
ACCIDENTS WILL HAPPEN • 1907 • Booth W. R.? • UKN
ACCIDENTS WILL HAPPEN • 1911 • Martinek H. O. • UKN
ACCIDENTS WILL HAPPEN • 1912 • *Kalem* • USA
ACCIDENTS WILL HAPPEN • 1915 • *Pyramid* • USA
ACCIDENTS WILL HAPPEN • 1938 • Clemens William • USA
ACCIDENTS WILL HAPPEN • 1964 • Kneitel Seymour • ANS • USA
ACCOMPANIED ON THE TOM-TOM • 1910 • Coleby A. E. • UKN
ACCOMPANIMENT, THE see **ACOMPANAMIENTO, EL** • 1988
ACCOMPLICE, THE • 1915 • Horne James W. • USA
ACCOMPLICE, THE • 1917 • Dean Ralph • USA
ACCOMPLICES see **UNTER EINER DECKE** • 1989
ACCOMPLICES, THE see **INFERNO ADDOSSO, L'** • 1959
ACCOMPLISHED MRS. THOMPSON, THE • 1914 • North Wilfred • USA
ACCORD FINAL • 1938 • Rosenkranz Ignacy, Sirk Douglas (U/c) • FRN
ACCORD PARFAIT • 1958 • Weinfeld Jean • SHT • FRN
ACCORDEON ET SES VEDETTES, L' • 1946 • Sevestre • SHT • FRN
ACCORDEON MYSTERIEUX, L' • 1906 • Velle Gaston • FRN • MYSTERIOUS ACCORDION, THE
ACCORDEON SONG see **PISEN O HARMONICE** • 1974
ACCORDEUR, L' see **GONZAGUE** • 1933
ACCORDING TO ADVICE • 1913 • *Vitagraph* • USA
ACCORDING TO HOYLE • 1922 • Van Dyke W. S. • USA
ACCORDING TO LAW • 1912 • *Selig* • USA
ACCORDING TO LAW • 1916 • Garrick Richard • USA
ACCORDING TO LAW see **ENLIGT LAG** • 1957
ACCORDING TO MRS. HOYLE • 1951 • Yarbrough Jean • USA
ACCORDING TO ORDERS see **WEDLUG ROZKAZU** • 1959
ACCORDING TO ORDERS see **ZGODNIE Z ROZKAZEM** • 1970
ACCORDING TO PONTIUS PILATE see **SECONDO PONZIO PILATO** • 1988
ACCORDING TO ST. JOHN • 1916 • Chatterton Thomas • SHT • USA
ACCORDING TO SENIORITY • 1913 • Lambart Harry • USA
ACCORDING TO THE CODE • 1916 • Calvert E. H. • USA
ACCORDING TO THE LAW see **ENLIGT LAG** • 1957
ACCORDING TO THEIR LIGHTS • 1915 • Nowland Eugene • USA
ACCORDING TO VALUE • 1915 • Lloyd Frank • USA
ACCORDION see **GARMON** • 1934
ACCORDION, AN • 1968 • Zaninovic Stejpan • DOC • YGS
ACCORDION JOE • 1930 • Fleischer Dave • ANS • USA
ACCOUNT OF MY BELOVED WIFE see **AISAIKI** • 1959
ACCOUNT RENDERED • 1932 • Gordon Leslie H. • UKN
ACCOUNT RENDERED • 1957 • Scott Peter Graham • UKN
ACCOUNTANT see **REVISOR** • 1933
ACCOUNTING, THE • 1915 • *Bushman Francis X.* • USA
ACCOUNTS • 1983 • Darlow Michael • TVM • UKN
ACCOUPLEMENTS POUR VOYAGEURS • 1979 • Roy Jean-Claude • FRN
ACCROCHE-COEUR, L' • 1938 • Caron Pierre • FRN • RIVIERA EXPRESS
ACCROCHE-TOI.. J'ARRIVE see **DIRTY TRICKS** • 1980
ACCROCHE-TOI, Y A DU VENT • 1961 • Bernard-Roland • FRN, ITL • SEGUGIO, IL (ITL)
ACCUMULATIONS • 1964 • van Faassen Frederice, van Faassen Henk • NTH
ACCURATE MAN, THE see **RICHTIGE MANN, DER** • 1982
ACCURSED, THE (USA) see **TRAITORS, THE** • 1957
ACCURSED CASTLE, THE see **KASR EL MALOUN, EL** • 1962
ACCURSED CHAMBAL VALLEY see **ABHISHAPTA CHAMBAL** • 1967
ACCURSED HANDCUFFS see **PASUNG PUAKA** • 1979
ACCURSED MARRIAGE • 1987 • *Ema Raja* • MLY
ACCURSED MOUNTAIN, THE see **MONT MAUDIT, LE** • 1920
ACCURSED TOWER, THE see **TOUR MAUDITE, LA** • 1901
ACCUSA DEL PASSATO, L' • 1957 • De Felice Lionello • SPN
ACCUSA E: VIOLENZA CARNALE E OMICIDO, L' see **VERDICT, LE** • 1974
ACCUSATION, THE • 1914 • Myers Harry • USA
ACCUSATION, THE see **ETTEHAM, EL** • 1937
ACCUSATION OF BRONCO BILLY, THE • 1913 • *Anderson Broncho Billy* • USA
ACCUSED • 1914 • *Kalem* • USA
ACCUSED • 1925 • Henderson Dell • USA
ACCUSED • 1936 • Freeland Thornton • UKN
ACCUSED • 1957 • Audley Michael, Gunn Gilbert • UKN • MARK OF THE HAWK (USA)
ACCUSED, THE • 1948 • Dieterle William • USA
ACCUSED, THE • 1967 • Marquez Artemio • PHL
ACCUSED, THE • 1988 • Kaplan Jonathan • USA
ACCUSED, THE see **TRAITORS, THE** • 1957
ACCUSED, THE see **OBZALOVANY** • 1964
ACCUSED INNOCENT, THE • 1928 • SYR
ACCUSED OF MURDER • 1956 • Kane Joseph • USA
ACCUSED PLEADS NOT GUILTY, THE see **KATIGOROUMENI, APOLOYISOU** • 1968
ACCUSEE, L' see **MUTTAHIMA, AL-** • 1942
ACCUSEE, LEVEZ-VOUS • 1930 • Tourneur Maurice • FRN • CRIME AU MUSIC-HALL, UN
ACCUSER, THE see **IMPRECATEUR, L'** • 1976
ACCUSING CONSCIENCE, THE • 1916 • *Puritan* • SHT • USA
ACCUSING EYES, THE • 1913 • *Gaumont* • USA
ACCUSING FINGER • 1915 • *Empire* • USA
ACCUSING FINGER, THE • 1915 • *Trump* • USA
ACCUSING FINGER, THE • 1936 • Hogan James P. • USA
ACCUSING HAND, THE • 1913 • Fielding Romaine • USA
ACCUSING PAST, THE see **PASADO ACUSA, EL** • 1938
ACCUSING PEN, THE • 1915 • Powell Paul • USA
ACCUSING SKELETON, THE • 1913 • *Warner'S Features* • USA
ACCUSING TOE, THE • 1918 • Vidor King • SHT • USA
ACCUSING VOICE, THE • 1916 • Davenport Harry • SHT • USA
AC/DC • 1969 • Winters Larry • USA
AC/DC: LET THERE BE ROCK • 1980 • Dionysius Eric, Mistler Eric • FRN • AC/DC THE FILM: LET THERE BE ROCK
AC/DC THE FILM: LET THERE BE ROCK see **AC/DC: LET THERE BE ROCK** • 1980
ACE, THE • 1985 • SAF
ACE, THE see **GREAT SANTINI, THE** • 1979
ACE CINEMAGAZINE • 1936 • Searle Francis • SHS • UKN
ACE DRUMMOND • 1936 • Beebe Ford, Smith Cliff • SRL • USA
ACE ELI AND ROGER OF THE SKIES • 1973 • Erman John • USA
ACE HIGH • 1917 • Terwilliger George W. • SHT • USA
ACE HIGH • 1918 • Reynolds Lynn • USA
ACE HIGH • 1919 • Holt George • SHT • USA
ACE HIGH see **QUATTRO DELL'AVE MARIA, I** • 1968
ACE IN THE HOLE • 1942 • Lovy Alex • ANS • USA
ACE IN THE HOLE (UKN) see **BIG CARNIVAL, THE** • 1951
ACE LUCKY (UKN) see **FEUDIN' RHYTHM** • 1949
ACE OF ACES • 1933 • Ruben J. Walter • USA
ACE OF ACES, THE • 1938 • USA • BIRDS OF PREY (UKN)
ACE OF ACTION • 1926 • Bertram William • USA
ACE OF CACTUS RANGE • 1924 • Dixon Denver, Andrus Malon • USA
ACE OF CADS, THE • 1926 • Reed Luther • USA
ACE OF CLUBS, THE • 1915 • Ayres Sydney • USA
ACE OF CLUBS, THE • 1926 • Mcgowan J. P. • USA
ACE OF DEATH, THE • 1915 • Haddock William F. • USA
ACE OF DIAMONDS, THE • 1915 • Reehm George E. • USA
ACE OF GOLD see **AS DE OROS** • 1968
ACE OF HEARTS, THE • 1910 • *Imp* • USA
ACE OF HEARTS, THE • 1913 • *Dragon* • USA
ACE OF HEARTS, THE • 1915 • *Edwards Walter* • USA
ACE OF HEARTS, THE • 1916 • Calvert Charles • UKN
ACE OF HEARTS, THE • 1921 • Worsley Wallace • USA
ACE OF SCOTLAND YARD, THE • 1929 • Taylor Ray, Horne James W. • SRL • USA
ACE OF SPADES • 1925 • Mcrae Henry • USA
ACE OF SPADES • 1984 • SAF
ACE OF SPADES see **OPERAZIONE CONTROSPIONAGGIO** • 1965
ACE OF SPADES, THE • 1912 • *Harte Betty* • USA
ACE OF SPADES, THE • 1931 • Fleischer Dave • ANS • USA
ACE OF SPADES, THE • 1935 • Pearson George • UKN
ACE OF THE LAW • 1924 • *Patton Bill* • USA
ACE OF THE SADDLE • 1919 • Ford John • USA
ACE OF THIEVES see **MASTERTJUVEN** • 1915
ACE UP MY SLEEVE see **CRIME AND PASSION** • 1975
ACE UP YOUR SLEEVE see **CRIME AND PASSION** • 1975
ACELGAS CON CHAMPAN Y MUCHA MUSICA • 1973 • Fons Angelino • SPN
ACEPHALE • 1968 • Deval Patrick • FRN
ACES • 1965 • Gass Karl • DOC • GDR
ACES AND EIGHTS • 1936 • Newfield Sam • USA
ACES GO PLACES see **TSUI-CHIA P'AI-TANG** • 1982
ACES GO PLACES 3 see **MAD MISSION 3: OUR MAN IN BOND STREET** • 1984
ACES GO PLACES V: TERRACOTTA HIT, THE • 1989 • Lau Kar-Leung • HKG
ACES HIGH • 1976 • Gold Jack • UKN, FRN
ACES OF TROUBLE, THE • 1934 • Samuelson G. B. • UKN
ACES WILD • 1936 • Fraser Harry L. • USA
ACH, BORIS • 1989 • List Niki • AUS
ACH, DU FROHLICHE.. • 1962 • Reisch Gunter • GDR • MERRY CHRISTMAS INDEED!
ACH EGON • 1961 • Schleif Wolfgang • FRG
ACH JODEL MIR NOCH EINEN -STOSZTRUPP VENUS BLAST ZUM ANGRIFF • 1973 • Sternbeck Hans • FRG, AUS • 2069: A SPACE ODYSSEY ○ SEX CHARGE
ACH LOUIE • 1915 • *Starlight* • USA
ACH! SUCH CRIMES • 1916 • *Starlight* • USA
ACHATMURMEL, DIE • 1960 • Bergman Barbl • GDR
ACHE IN EVERY STAKE, AN • 1941 • Lord Del • SHT • USA
ACHHUT KANYA • 1937 • Osten Franz • IND
ACHILLE see **MARI REVE, LE** • 1936
ACHILLES HAELEN ER MIT VABEN • 1978 • Rex Jytte • DNM • ACHILLES' HEEL IS MY WEAPON
ACHILLES' HEEL see **TENDRON D'ACHILLE, LE** • 1933
ACHILLES' HEEL IS MY WEAPON see **ACHILLES HAELEN ER MIT VABEN** • 1978
ACHILLES (UKN) see **IRA DI ACHILLE, L'** • 1962
ACHING VOID, THE • 1911 • *Vitagraph* • USA
ACHING YOUTH • 1928 • Guiol Fred • SHT • USA
ACHIT AND HER KO KO see **ACHIT NAI THI EU KO KO** • 1981
ACHIT NAI THI EU KO KO • 1981 • U Kyee Myint • BRM • ACHIT AND HER KO KO
ACHOO 302 • 1989 • Hussain Iltaf • PKS
ACHOO MR. KEROOCHEV • 1959 • Vanderbeek Stan • ANS • USA
ACHRAROUMES • 1978 • Paradjanov Sergei • SHT • USS • RETURN TO LIFE ○ RETOUR A LA VIE
ACHT ENTFESSELTEN, DIE • 1939 • Kautner Helmut • FRG
ACHT MADELS IM BOOT • 1959 • Bittins Alfred • FRG • EIGHT GIRLS IN A BOAT
ACHT MAL ACHT • 1957 • Richter Hans, de Vogel Willem, Cocteau Jean • SWT • 8 X 8
ACHT STUNDEN SIND KEIN TAG • 1972 • Fassbinder R. W. • FRG • 8 HOURS DON'T MAKE A DAY
ACHT TAGE GLUCK see **LIEBESEXPRESS, DER** • 1930
ACHT UHR DREIZEHN • 1921 • Werckmeister Hans • FRG
ACHTE GEBOT, DAS see **ACHTE GEBOT, DU SOLLST NICHT FALSCH ZEUGNIS REDEN WIDER DEINEN NACHSTEN** • 1915
ACHTE GEBOT, DU SOLLST NICHT FALSCH ZEUGNIS REDEN WIDER DEINEN NACHSTEN • 1915 • Mack Max • FRG • ACHTE GEBOT, DAS
ACHTE TAG, DER • 1989 • Munster Reinhard • FRG • EIGHTH DAY, THE
ACHTE WOCHENTAG, DER (FRG) see **OSMY DZIEN TYGODNIA** • 1958
ACHTGROSCHENMADEL 1, DAS • 1921 • Neff Wolfgang • FRG • JAGD AUF SCHURKEN 1
ACHTGROSCHENMADEL 2, DAS • 1921 • Neff Wolfgang • FRG • JAGD AUF SCHURKEN 2
"ACHTUNG! -AUTO-DIEBE!" • 1930 • Piel Harry • FRG • AUTOBANDITEN
ACHTUNG BANDITI • 1951 • Lizzani Carlo • ITL
ACHTUNG! FEIND HORT MIT! • 1940 • Rabenalt Arthur M. • FRG
ACHTUNG HARRY! AUGEN AUF!! • 1926 • Piel Harry • FRG • SECHS WOCHEN UNTER DEN APACHEN
ACHTUNG! LIEBE! LEBENSGEFAHR! • 1929 • Metzner Erno • FRG • RIVALEN IM WELTREKORD
ACHTUNG! WER KENNT DIESE FRAU? • 1934 • Seitz Franz • FRG
ACHTZEHNJAHRIGEN, DIE • 1927 • Noa Manfred • FRG
ACI • 1971 • Guney Yilmaz • TRK • PAIN
ACI GUNLER • 1967 • Gorec Ertem • TRK • BITTER DAYS
ACI HATIRALAR • 1978 • Yilmaz Atif • TRK • BITTER MEMORIES
ACI INANC • 1968 • Utku Umit • TRK • BITTER FAITH
ACI INTIKAM • 1968 • Atadeniz Yilmaz • TRK • BITTER REVENGE
ACI TURKU • 1967 • Palay Abdurrahman • TRK • BITTER SONG
ACI YILLAR • 1968 • Erakalin Ulku • TRK • BITTER YEARS
ACID • 1989 • Sangeeta • PKS
ACID CAMP • Van Meter Ben • USA
ACID (DELIRIO DEI SENSI) • 1967 • Scotese Giuseppe Maria • ITL • ACID (DELIRIUM OF THE SENSES)
ACID (DELIRIUM OF THE SENSES) see **ACID (DELIRIO DEI SENSI)** • 1967
ACID EATERS, THE • 1968 • Elliott B. Ron • USA • ACID PEOPLE, THE
ACID MANTRA • 1968 • Van Meter Ben • USA
ACID PEOPLE, THE see **ACID EATERS, THE** • 1968
ACID TEST, THE • 1913 • Martin E. A. • USA
ACID TEST, THE • 1914 • *Vitagraph* • USA
ACID TEST, THE • 1914 • *Victor* • USA
ACID TEST, THE • 1915 • *King Henry* • USA
ACID TEST, THE • 1924 • Hill Sinclair • UKN
ACID TEST, THE • 1970 • Benardos Peter • DOC • ASL
ACIERIES DANS UN PARC • Lust Georges • DOC • BLG
ACIERIES DE LA MARINE ET D'HOMECOURT, LES • 1925 • Gremillon Jean • SHT • FRN
ACK, DU AR SOME EN ROS • 1967 • Fischer Gunnar • SHT • SWD • OH, YOU ARE LIKE A ROSE
ACO PORTUGUES • 1961 • Queiroga Perdigao • SHT • PRT
ACOMA THE SKY CITY • 1929 • Flaherty Robert • DCS • USA
ACOMPANAME • 1964 • Amadori Luis Cesar • SPN
ACOMPANAMIENTO, EL • 1988 • Orgambide Carlos • ARG • ACCOMPANIMENT, THE
ACONCAGUA • 1962 • Fleider Leo • ARG
ACORES • 1957 • Mendes Joao • SHT • PRT
ACORES • 1972 • Spiguel Miguel • SHT • PRT
ACORES E A ALMA DO SEU POVO • 1956 • Mendes Joao • SHT • PRT
ACORN PEOPLE, THE • 1981 • Tewkesbury Joan • TVM • USA
ACORRALADO • 1975 • *Priego Alfonso Rosas* • MXC
ACOSADA • 1963 • Dubois Albert • ARG • PINK PUSSY (WHERE SIN LIVES), THE (USA) ○ PINK PUSSY CLUB, THE ○ EXPLOITEERS, THE ○ WHERE SIN LIVES ○ PINK PUSSY, THE ○ PINK PUSSY CAT, THE
ACOSO, EL • 1964 • Solas Humberto • CUB
ACOSTATES FOSTE OFFER see **KRIGENS FJENDE** • 1915
ACQUA, ACQUA, FUOCO, FUOCO • 1920 • D'Ambra Lucio • ITL
ACQUA CHETA • 1933 • Zambuto Gero • ITL
ACQUA E SAPONE • 1984 • Verdone Carlo • ITL • SOAP AND WATER
ACQUASANTA JOE • 1971 • Gariazzo Mario • ITL
ACQUE AMARE • 1955 • Corbucci Sergio • ITL
ACQUE DI PRIMAVERA • 1942 • Malasomma Nunzio • ITL
ACQUI ESTA PANCHO VILLA • 1958 • Rodriguez Ismael • MXC
ACQUITTAL, THE • 1923 • Brown Clarence • USA
ACQUITTED • 1916 • Powell Paul • USA
ACQUITTED • 1929 • Strayer Frank • USA
ACQUITTED see **AF ELSKOVS NAADE** • 1913
ACRE OF SEATS IN A GARDEN OF DREAMS, AN • 1973 • Furnham David • UKN
ACRE OF SUNDAY, AN • 1970 • Lewis David • DCS • UKN
ACRES OF ALFALFA • 1914 • Sennett Mack • DOC • USA
ACRO-BATTY • 1942 • Lewyn Louis • SHT • USA
ACROBATE, L' • 1940 • Boyer Jean • FRN
ACROBATE, L' • 1973 • Pollet Jean-Daniel • FRN
ACROBATIC PERFORMANCE -SELLS AND YOUNG • 1901 • *Paul R. W.* • UKN
ACROBATIC PILLS • 1908 • *Lubin* • USA
ACROBATIC TOYS see **FRERES BOUTDEBOIS, LES** • 1908
ACROBATIC TRAMPS, THE • 1902 • Williamson James • UKN
ACROBATTY BUNNY • 1946 • Mckimson Robert • ANS • USA
ACROSS 110TH STREET • 1972 • Shear Barry • USA
ACROSS ARCTIC UNGAVA • Wilkinson Douglas • DCS • CND
ACROSS AUSTRALIA IN THE TRACK OF BURKE & WILLS • 1915 • ASL
ACROSS AUSTRALIA WITH FRANCIS BIRTLES THE INTREPID OVERLANDER • 1912 • ASL
ACROSS DARKNESS see **YAMI O YOKOGIRE** • 1959
ACROSS THE ALLEY • 1913 • Avery Charles • USA
ACROSS THE ARAKS see **POTU STORONU ARAKSA** • 1947
ACROSS THE ARAX see **POTU STORONU ARAKSA** • 1947
ACROSS THE ATLANTIC • 1928 • Bretherton Howard • USA
ACROSS THE ATLANTIC (USA) see **SECRET OF THE AIR, THE** • 1914
ACROSS THE BADLANDS • 1950 • Sears Fred F. • USA • CHALLENGE, THE (UKN)
ACROSS THE BLUE SEA see **PRIKO SINJEG MORA** • 1980
ACROSS THE BORDER • 1913 • *Pilot* • USA
ACROSS THE BORDER • 1914 • *Mchugh Grace* • USA
ACROSS THE BORDER • 1922 • Seeling Charles R. • USA
ACROSS THE BORDER see **CALIFORNIA ROMANCE, A** • 1922
ACROSS THE BORDER see **SPECIAL INSPECTOR** • 1939

ACROSS THE BRIDGE • 1957 • Annakin Ken • UKN • ACROSS THE FORBIDDEN BRIDGE TO MEXICO
ACROSS THE BURNING TRESTLE • 1914 • Ridgely Richard • USA
ACROSS THE CHASM • 1913 • *Patheplay* • USA
ACROSS THE CHASM • 1920 • *Dalton Emmett* • SHT • USA
ACROSS THE CONTINENT • 1913 • *Pilot* • USA
ACROSS THE CONTINENT • 1922 • Rosen Phil • USA
ACROSS THE COURT • 1914 • *Asher Max* • USA
ACROSS THE DEADLINE • 1922 • Conway Jack • USA
ACROSS THE DEADLINE • 1925 • Maloney Leo • USA
ACROSS THE DESERT • 1915 • King Burton L. • USA
ACROSS THE DIVIDE • 1909 • *Selig* • USA
ACROSS THE DIVIDE • 1911 • *Nestor* • USA
ACROSS THE DIVIDE • 1921 • Holloway John • USA • ACROSS THE GREAT DIVIDE
ACROSS THE FJORD see **KJAERLEIKENS FERJEREISER** • 1979
ACROSS THE FOOTLIGHTS • 1915 • King Burton L. • USA
ACROSS THE FORBIDDEN BRIDGE TO MEXICO see **ACROSS THE BRIDGE** • 1957
ACROSS THE FRINGE see **SHIMANA PERIYE** • 1978
ACROSS THE GREAT DIVIDE • 1913 • *Essanay* • USA
ACROSS THE GREAT DIVIDE • 1915 • Taylor Edward C. • USA
ACROSS THE GREAT DIVIDE • 1976 • Raffill Stewart • USA
ACROSS THE GREAT DIVIDE see **ACROSS THE DIVIDE** • 1921
ACROSS THE HALL • 1914 • Sennett Mack, Avery Charles • USA
ACROSS THE HALL • 1916 • Davey Horace • SHT • USA
ACROSS THE ISTHMUS • 1909 • *Selig* • USA
ACROSS THE LAKE • 1989 • Maylam Tony • UKN
ACROSS THE LINE • 1916 • Jaccard Jacques • SHT • USA
ACROSS THE LINE • 1919 • *Lowell John* • SHT • USA
ACROSS THE LOCK GATE TO THE SEA see **MITO KOMONUMI O WATARU** • 1961
ACROSS THE MEXICAN BORDER • 1911 • *Powers* • USA
ACROSS THE MEXICAN LINE • 1911 • Blache Alice • USA
ACROSS THE PACIFIC • 1914 • Carewe Edwin • USA
ACROSS THE PACIFIC • 1926 • Del Ruth Roy • USA
ACROSS THE PACIFIC • 1942 • Huston John • USA
ACROSS THE PLAINS • 1910 • Boggs Frank • USA
ACROSS THE PLAINS • 1911 • *Anderson Broncho Billy* • USA
ACROSS THE PLAINS • 1928 • Horner Robert J. • USA
ACROSS THE PLAINS • 1939 • Bennet Spencer Gordon • USA
ACROSS THE PLAINS see **WAR ON THE PLAINS** • 1912
ACROSS THE RAPIDS see **SANGEN OM DEN ELDRODA BLOMMAN** • 1918
ACROSS THE RIO GRANDE • 1913 • *Essanay* • USA
ACROSS THE RIO GRANDE • 1916 • Jaccard Jacques • SHT • USA
ACROSS THE RIO GRANDE • 1933 • Binney Josh • USA
ACROSS THE RIO GRANDE • 1949 • Drake Oliver • USA
ACROSS THE RIVER • 1965 • Sharff Stefan • USA
ACROSS THE RIVER AND INTO THE TREES • 1987 • Frankenheimer John • USA
ACROSS THE RIVER OF WRATH see **KIMI YO FUNDO NO KAWA A WATARE** • 1975
ACROSS THE SAHARA • 1933 • Summers Walter • DOC • UKN
ACROSS THE SIERRAS • 1912 • *Gebhardt George* • USA
ACROSS THE SIERRAS • 1941 • Lederman D. Ross • USA • WELCOME STRANGER (UKN)
ACROSS THE TRACK OF ROSS SMITH see **THROUGH AUSTRALIAN WILDS** • 1919
ACROSS THE UNKNOWN see **WYCIECZKA W NIEZNANE** • 1968
ACROSS THE WAY • 1915 • *Farrington Renee* • USA
ACROSS THE WIDE MISSOURI • 1951 • Wellman William A. • USA
ACROSS THE WIRES • 1915 • Batley Ernest G. • UKN
ACROSS THE WORLD WITH MR. AND MRS. JOHNSON • 1930 • Meehan James Leo • USA
ACROSS THIS LAND WITH STOMPIN' TOM CONNORS • 1973 • Saxton John • DOC • CND
ACROSS TO SINGAPORE • 1928 • Nigh William • USA • CHINA BOUND
ACROSS ZANGEZUR • 1967 • Schneiderov Vladimir • DOC • USS
ACT, THE • 1983 • Shore Sig • USA • BLESS 'EM ALL
ACT FIVE, SCENE SEVEN. FRITZ KORTNER REHEARSES KABALE UND LIEBE see **FUNFTER AKT, SIEBTE SZENE. FRITZ KORTNER PROBT KABALE UND LIEBE** • 1965
ACT OF AGGRESSION (USA) see **AGRESSION, L'** • 1974
ACT OF BETRAYAL • 1988 • Clark Lawrence Gordon • TVM • UKN, ASL
ACT OF EVIL see **AKRIET** • 1980
ACT OF GOD • 1981 • Greenaway Peter • UKN
ACT OF KINDNESS, AN • 1911 • *Urban Trading Co* • UKN
ACT OF LOVE • 1980 • Taylor Jud • TVM • USA
ACT OF LOVE (USA) see **ACTE D'AMOUR, UN** • 1953
ACT OF MURDER • 1964 • Bridges Alan • UKN
ACT OF MURDER, AN • 1948 • Gordon Michael • USA • LIVE TODAY FOR TOMORROW ○ I STAND ACCUSED ○ CASE AGAINST CALVIN COOKE
ACT OF PASSION • 1984 • Langton Simon • TVM • USA • LOST HONOR OF KATHRYN BECK, THE
ACT OF PIRACY • 1969 • Graham William A. • TVM • USA
ACT OF PIRACY • 1989 • Cardos John Bud • USA
ACT OF REPRISAL, AN • 1965
ACT OF SEEING WITH ONE'S OWN EYES, THE • 1971 • Brakhage Stan • USA
ACT OF THE DONES AT GUINEA see **ACTO DOS FEITOS DE GUINE** • 1977
ACT OF THE HEART • 1970 • Almond Paul • CND • ACTE DE COEUR
ACT OF VENGEANCE • 1974 • Kelljan Bob • USA • VIOLATOR, THE (UKN)
ACT OF VENGEANCE • 1986 • Mackenzie John • TVM • USA, CND
ACT OF VIOLENCE • 1948 • Zinnemann Fred • USA
ACT OF VIOLENCE • 1979 • Wendkos Paul • TVM • USA • VICTIM: ANATOMY OF A MUGGING, THE
ACT OF VIOLENCE see **ATO DE VIOLENCIA** • 1981
ACT OF WILL • 1989 • Sharp Don • TVM • USA
ACT ONE • 1963 • Schary Dore • USA
ACT WITHOUT WORDS (USA) see **ACTE SANS PAROLES** • 1964
ACT YOUR AGE • 1939 • Roberts Charles E. • SHT • USA
ACTAS DE MARUSIA • 1974 • Littin Miguel • MXC • PROCEEDINGS IN MARUSIA ○ LETTERS FROM MARUSIA
ACTE D'AMOUR, UN • 1953 • Litvak Anatole • FRN, USA • ACT OF LOVE (USA)
ACTE DE COEUR see **ACT OF THE HEART** • 1970
ACTE SANS PAROLES • 1964 • Bettiol Bruno, Bettiol Guido • SHT • FRN • ACT WITHOUT WORDS (USA)
ACTEON • 1964 • Grau Jorge • SPN
ACTEUR, L' • 1976 • Laguionie Jean-Francois • ANS • FRN
ACTEUR EN RETARD, L' • 1908 • Melies Georges • FRN • WHY THE ACTOR WAS LATE ○ WHY THAT ACTOR WAS LATE ○ POURQUOI L'ACTEUR EN RETARD
ACTEUR, LA VOISINE, L' • 1982 • Rancourt Daniel • SHT • CND
ACTING ACTRESS see **SASHA -SASHENKA** • 1967
ACTING: LEE STRASBERG AND THE ACTORS STUDIO • 1981 • Kline Herbert • DOC • USA
ACTING OUT • 1983 • Sens Al • SHT • CND
ACTION • 1921 • Ford John • USA • LET'S GO
ACTION • 1969 • Baker Fred • USA
ACTION • 1979 • Brass Tinto • ITL
ACTION • 1990 • Farhang Darioush • IRN
ACTION AT MIRONOV, THE see **PROZESS MIRONOVA** • 1920
ACTION B • 1951 • Mach Josef • CZC
ACTION B see **AKCE B** • 1951
ACTION BRUTUS see **AKCJA "BRUTUS"** • 1970
ACTION CRAVER, THE • 1927 • Potel Victor • USA
ACTION FOR SLANDER • 1937 • Whelan Tim, Saville Victor • UKN
ACTION FORCE 3: PYRAMIDS OF DARKNESS • ANM • USA
ACTION FORCE: ARISE SERPENTOR, ARISE • ANM • USA
ACTION FORCE: THE MOVIE • ANM • USA
ACTION GALORE • 1925 • Eddy Robert • USA • MEN WITHOUT FEAR (UKN)
ACTION IMMEDIATE • 1956 • Labro Maurice • FRN • TO CATCH A SPY (USA)
ACTION IN ARABIA • 1944 • Moguy Leonide • USA
ACTION IN JAMAICA see **A-001 OPERAZIONE GIAMAICA** • 1965
ACTION IN THE NORTH ATLANTIC • 1943 • Bacon Lloyd • USA
ACTION J • 1963 • Heynowski Walter • DOC • GDR
ACTION JACKSON • 1988 • Baxley Craig R. • USA
ACTION MAN (USA) see **SOLEIL DES VOYOUS, LE** • 1967
ACTION OF THE TIGER • 1957 • Young Terence • UKN, USA
ACTION SET • 1968 • USA
ACTION STADIUM see **AZCIJA STADION** • 1978
ACTION STATIONS! • 1943 • Ivens Joris • CND • BRANLE-BAS DE COMBAT ○ ALARME!
ACTION STATIONS • 1962 • Brealey Gil • DOC • ASL
ACTION STATIONS see **HI-JACK** • 1957
ACTION: THE OCTOBER CRISIS OF 1970 • 1974 • Spry Robin • DOC • CND • EVENEMENTS D'OCTOBRE 1970, LES
ACTION UNDER ARSENAL see **AKCJA POD ARSENALEM** • 1977
ACTION USA • 1989 • Stewart John • USA
ACTIUNEA AUTOBUZUL • 1978 • Calotescu Virgil • RMN • BUS ACTION, THE
ACTIVATOR ONE • 1969 • Spotton John • CND
ACTIVE SERVICE • 1916 • Myll Louis • SHT • USA
ACTIVIST, THE • 1969 • Napoleon Art • USA
ACTIVISTS, THE see **AKTIVISTIT** • 1939
ACTO DA PRIMAVERA • 1963 • de Oliveira Manoel • PRT • PASSION OF JESUS, THE
ACTO DE POSESION • 1976 • Aguirre Javier • SPN
ACTO DOS FEITOS DE GUINE • 1977 • Silva Fernando Matos • PRT • ACT OF THE DONES AT GUINEA
ACTOR see **AKTOREN** • 1943
ACTOR, THE • 1913 • *August Edwin* • USA
ACTOR AND THE RUBE, THE • 1915 • *Chamberlain Riley* • USA
ACTOR AND THE SAVAGES, THE see **ACTORUL SI SALBATICII** • 1974
ACTOR BOOK AGENT, THE • 1913 • *Komic* • USA
ACTOR BURGLAR, THE • 1909 • *Phoenix* • USA
ACTOR DETECTIVE see **KUMONOSU YASHIKI** • 1959
ACTOR FINNEY'S FINISH • 1914 • Hopper E. Mason • USA
ACTOR IN A NEW ROLE, AN • 1911 • *Hopkins Jack* • USA
ACTORS, THE see **KOMODIANTEN** • 1941
ACTORS AND SIN • 1952 • Hecht Ben • USA
ACTOR'S ARTIFICE, THE • 1911 • Stow Percy • UKN
ACTORS' BOARDING HOUSE, THE • 1915 • *Rooney Pat* • USA
ACTOR'S CHILD, THE • 1908 • *Selig* • USA
ACTOR'S CHILDREN, THE • 1910 • O'Neil Barry?, Carleton Lloyd B.? • USA
ACTOR'S CHRISTMAS, THE • 1913 • *Baggot King* • USA
ACTORS' HEARTS • 1911 • *Pathe* • USA
ACTOR'S REVENGE, AN see **YUKINOJO HENGE** • 1963
ACTOR'S ROMANCE, AN • 1913 • *Garcia Al* • USA
ACTOR'S STRATEGY, AN • 1913 • *Lubin* • USA
ACTORUL SI SALBATICII • 1974 • Marcus Manole • RMN • PLAYER AND THE SAVAGES, THE ○ ACTOR AND THE SAVAGES, THE
ACTRA'S LIVE COMMAND PERFORMANCE • 1981 • Schulz Bob • MTV • CND
ACTRESS see **JOYU** • 1947
ACTRESS, AN see **JOYU** • 1956
ACTRESS, THE • 1910 • *Powers* • USA
ACTRESS, THE • 1911 • *Trunnelle Mabel* • USA
ACTRESS, THE • 1913 • *Rex* • USA
ACTRESS, THE • 1913 • Ridgely Richard, Miller Ashley • *Edison* • USA
ACTRESS, THE • 1914 • *Mason Edna* • USA
ACTRESS, THE • 1923 • Ivanovsky Alexander • USS
ACTRESS, THE • 1928 • Franklin Sidney A. • USA • TRELAWNEY OF THE WELLS
ACTRESS, THE • 1953 • Cukor George • USA
ACTRESS, THE • 1988 • Kuhn Siegfried • GDR
ACTRESS, THE see **AKTRISA** • 1943
ACTRESS, THE see **AKTORKA** • 1972
ACTRESS AND ANGEL (UKN) see **BUTTER AND EGG MAN, THE** • 1928
ACTRESS AND CHEESE HOUND, THE • 1915 • *Kalem* • USA
ACTRESS AND CHILD • 1909 • *Phoenix* • USA
ACTRESS AND HER JEWELS, THE • 1913 • *Hotely Mae* • USA
ACTRESS AND THE COWBOYS, THE • 1911 • Dwan Allan • USA
ACTRESS AND THE POET, THE see **JOYU TO SHINJI** • 1935
ACTRESS AND THE SINGER, THE • 1911 • Salter Harry • USA
ACTRESS PULLS THE STRINGS, THE • 1912 • *Tennant Barbara* • USA
ACTRESS' ROMANCE, AN • 1917 • Thayer Otis B. • SHT • USA
ACTRESSES see **KOKUHAKUTEKI JOYU-RON** • 1971
ACTRESS'S SON, AN • 1914 • *Melies* • USA
ACTS OF THE APOSTLES (USA) see **ATTI DEGLI APOSTOLI** • 1969
ACTUA-TILT • 1960 • Herman Jean • FRN
ACTUALITES • 1947 • Margaritis Gilles • SHT • FRN
ACTUALITES GAULOISES • 1952 • Remise Jac • ANS • FRN
ACTUALITES PREHISTORIQUES • 1947 • Remise Jac, Duvoir G., Guy C., Young M., Lamothe Arthur, Gelinas Pascal, Harel Pierre • ANS • FRN
ACTUALITES ROMAINES • 1947 • Remise Jac • ANS • FRN
ACUERDATE DE VIVIR • 1952 • Gavaldon Roberto • MXC
ACUSATION, LA • 1965 • Solas Humberto • CUB
AD OGNI CESTO OGNANO PER SE see **DITO NELLA PIAGA, IL** • 1969
AD OGNI COSTO • 1967 • Montaldo Giuliano • ITL, FRG, SPN • DIAMANTES A GO-GO (SPN) ○ TOP JOB (FRG) ○ GRAND SLAM (USA) ○ AT ANY COST
AD SOFF HALAYLA • 1985 • Green Eytan • ISR • WHEN NIGHT FALLS
AD UNO AD UNO.. SPIETATAMENTE (ITL) see **UNO A UNO SIN PIEDAD** • 1968
AD URBE CONDITA • 1966 • Lomnicki Jan • DOC • PLN
AD3 OPERAZIONE SQUALO BIANCO • 1966 • Ratti Filippo M. • ITL
ADA • 1919 • Raabeova Hedvika • SHT • CZC
ADA • 1961 • Mann Daniel • USA
ADA • 1977 • Jutra Claude • MTV • CND
ADA • 1985 • Kosovac Milutin • YGS
ADA • 1987 • Duru Sureyya • TRK • ISLAND, THE
ADA, TO NIE WYPADA • 1937 • Mayflower Z.
ADADA • 1988 • Lim Kwon-Taek • SKR
ADAGE, L' • 1964 • Delouche Dominique • SHT • FRN
ADAGIO • 1969 • Mogubgub Fred • ANS • USA
ADAGIO FOR ELECTION DAY • 1949 • Peterson Sidney • USA
ADAGIO PARA UNA ESTRELLA • 1978 • Aznar Tomas • SPN
ADAK • 1980 • Yilmaz Atif • TRK • SACRIFICE, THE ○ VOW, THE
ADALEN 31 • 1969 • Widerberg Bo • SWD • ADELEN RIOTS, THE
ADALENS POESI • 1928 • Berthels Theodor • SWD • POETRY OF ADALEN
ADALENS POESI • 1948 • Johansson Ivar • SWD
ADAM • Dai Yona • ISR
ADAM • 1977 • Gligorowski Petar • YGS
ADAM • 1983 • Tuchner Michael • TVM • USA
ADAM • 1987 • Ananiadis Iordanis • SHT • GRC
ADAM 2 • 1969 • Lenica Jan • ANM • FRG
ADAM AND EVA • 1923 • Vignola Robert G. • USA
ADAM AND EVALYN (USA) see **ADAM AND EVELYNE** • 1949
ADAM AND EVE • Vrbanic Ivo • ANS • YGS
ADAM AND EVE • 1912 • *Morey Harry T.* • USA
ADAM AND EVE • 1962 • Marek Dusan • ANS • CZC
ADAM AND EVE see **ADAM OCH EVA** • 1963
ADAM AND EVE see **ADEM ILE HAVVA** • 1967
ADAM AND EVE A LA MODE • 1920 • Robbins Jess • SHT • USA
ADAM AND EVE (USA) see **ADAMO ED EVA** • 1950
ADAM AND EVE (USA) see **ADAN Y EVA** • 1955
ADAM AND EVELYNE • 1949 • French Harold • UKN • ADAM AND EVALYN (USA)
ADAM AND EVIL • 1927 • Leonard Robert Z. • USA • HIS BROTHER FROM BRAZIL
ADAM AND HIS APPLE see **ADAM LOST HIS APPLE** • 1966
ADAM AND NICOLE see **EROTIC INFERNO** • 1975
ADAM AND SIX EVES • 1962 • Wallis John • USA
ADAM AND SOME EVES • 1918 • De Vonde Chester M. • SHT • USA
ADAM AS A SPECIAL CONSTABLE • 1918 • Leigh J. L. V. • UKN
ADAM AT 6A.M. • 1970 • Scheerer Robert • USA
ADAM BEDE • 1915 • Vale Travers • USA
ADAM BEDE • 1918 • Elvey Maurice • UKN
ADAM EST.. EVE • 1953 • Gaveau Rene • FRN • ADAM EST EVE -LA NOUVELLE LEGENDE DES SEXES ○ ADAM IS EVE -THE NEW LEGEND OF THE SEXES
ADAM EST EVE -LA NOUVELLE LEGENDE DES SEXES see **ADAM EST.. EVE** • 1953
ADAM ET EVE • 1973 • Gagne Jacques • SHT • CND
ADAM ET EVE • 1983 • Luret Jean • FRN
ADAM ET EVE • 1984 • Soutter Michel • SWT, FRN
ADAM HAD FOUR SONS • 1941 • Ratoff Gregory • USA • LEGACY
ADAM -HIS SONG CONTINUES • 1986 • Markowitz Robert • TVM • USA
ADAM I EVA • 1960 • Vrbanic Ivo • YGS
ADAM II • 1966 • von Borresholm Boris • FRG
ADAM IS EVE -THE NEW LEGEND OF THE SEXES see **ADAM EST.. EVE** • 1953
ADAM KHOCHET BYT CHELOVEKOM • 1959 • Zalakevicius Vitautus • USS • ADAM WANTS TO BE A MAN
ADAM LEDOLOMAC • 1990 • Lavanic Zlatko • YGS • ADAM THE ICEBREAKER
ADAM LOST HIS APPLE • 1966 • Wainwright Earl • USA • ADAM AND HIS APPLE
ADAM OCH EVA • 1963 • Falck Ake • SWD • ADAM AND EVE
ADAM THE ICEBREAKER see **ADAM LEDOLOMAC** • 1990
ADAM UND EVA • 1923 • Porges Friedrich • FRG
ADAM UND EVA • 1928 • Biebrach Rudolf • FRG
ADAM UND EVA • 1928 • Schunzel Reinhold • FRG

ADAM WANTS TO BE A MAN see **ADAM KHOCHET BYT CHELOVEKOM** • 1959

ADAM, WO BIST DU? • 1915 • Albes Emil • FRG

ADAM Y EVA see **ADAN Y EVA** • 1955

ADAMA HAMA • 1984 • Ankri Serge • ISR • BURNING LAND

ADAMAK • 1971 • Haritash Khosrow • IRN

ADAMANT, THE see **SANGE SABOUR** • 1968

ADAMANTS LETZTES RENNEN • 1917 • Mack Max • FRG

ADAMINTE VARIYELLU • 1984 • George K. G. • IND • ADAM'S RIB

ADAMLESS EDEN, AN • 1912 • *Essanay* • USA

ADAMO ED EVA • 1950 • Mattoli Mario • ITL • ADAM AND EVE (USA)

ADAM'S ANCESTORS • 1915 • *Rand John* • USA

ADAM'S APPLE • 1928 • Whelan Tim • UKN • HONEYMOON AHEAD (USA)

ADAM'S DREAM • 1990 • Pakarnyk Alan • ANS • CND

ADAM'S EVE • 1929 • Pearce A. Leslie • USA

ADAM'S FILM REVIEW • 1924 • Hughes Harry • UKN

ADAM'S RIB • 1923 • De Mille Cecil B. • USA

ADAM'S RIB • 1949 • Cukor George • USA

ADAM'S RIB see **REBRO ADAMOVO** • 1956

ADAM'S RIB see **ADAMINTE VARIYELLU** • 1984

ADAM'S TREE (USA) see **ALBERO DI ADAMO, L'** • 1936

ADAM'S TWO RIBS see **DWA ZEBRA ADAMA** • 1964

ADAM'S WOMAN • 1970 • Leacock Philip • ASL • RETURN OF THE BOOMERANG

ADAMSSON I SVERIGE • 1966 • Ericson Stig Ossian • SWD • I NEED A WOMAN

ADAN, EVA Y EL DIABLO • 1944 • Crevenna Alfredo B. • MXC

ADAN Y EVA • 1955 • Gout Alberto • MXC • ADAM AND EVE (USA) ◦ ADAM Y EVA

ADAN Y LA SERPIENTE • 1946 • Christensen Carlos Hugo • ARG

ADARAWANTHAYO • 1968 • Jayatilaka Amarnath • SLN • LOVERS

ADAUCHI • 1964 • Imai Tadashi • JPN • REVENGE, THE

ADAUCHI SANSHU • 1931 • Uchida Tomu • JPN • REVENGE CHAMPION, THE ◦ ADAUCHI SENSHU

ADAUCHI SENSHU see **ADAUCHI SANSHU** • 1931

ADAUCHI SOMATO • 1927 • Inagaki Hiroshi • JPN • CHANGEFUL REVENGE

ADAWIYA • 1968 • Salaheddin Kamal • EGY

ADD TOVABB, SZAMAR A VEGALLOMAS • 1973 • Jankovics Marcell • ANM • HNG

ADDAMS FAMILY, THE • 1972 • *Halas John (P)* • ASS • UKN

ADDED FUEL • 1915 • *Hunt Irene* • USA

ADDERLEY STREET, CAPETOWN • 1898 • Mitchell Robert A. • UKN

ADDICTED TO HIS LOVE • 1988 • Seidelman Arthur Allan • TVM • USA • SISTERHOOD

ADDICTION • 1985 • Khalik Ali Abdul • EGY

ADDICTION: A CRY FOR LOVE see **CRY FOR LOVE, A** • 1980

ADDING MACHINE, THE • 1969 • Epstein Jerome • UKN, USA

ADDIO ALEXANDRA! • 1969 • Battaglia Enzo • ITL • LOVE ME, LOVE MY WIFE (UKN)

ADDIO, AMORE! • 1944 • Franciolini Gianni • ITL

ADDIO ANNA • 1974 • Delubac Yves-Andre • FRN

ADDIO, FIGLIO MIO! • 1954 • Guarini Giuseppe • ITL

ADDIO FRATELLO CRUDELE • 1971 • Patroni Griffi Giuseppe • ITL • 'TIS PITY SHE'S A WHORE (USA)

ADDIO GIOVINEZZA • 1915 • Oxilia Nino • ITL

ADDIO GIOVINEZZA! • 1918 • Genina Augusto • ITL

ADDIO GIOVINEZZA! • 1927 • Genina Augusto • ITL • INCONSTANT YOUTH

ADDIO GIOVINEZZA! • 1940 • Poggioli Ferdinando M. • ITL

ADDIO JEFF (ITL) see **JEFF** • 1968

ADDIO, KIRA • 1942 • Alessandrini Goffredo • ITL

ADDIO MAMMA • 1967 • Amendola Mario • ITL

ADDIO, MIA BELLA NAPOLI! • 1946 • Bonnard Mario • ITL

ADDIO MIA BELLA SIGNORA! • 1954 • Cerchio Fernando • ITL

ADDIO, MIMI • 1947 • Gallone Carmine • ITL • HER WONDERFUL LIE ◦ BOHEME, LA

ADDIO NAPOLI! • 1954 • Montero Roberto Bianchi • ITL

ADDIO PER SEMPRE • 1958 • Costa Mario • ITL

ADDIO SOGNI DI GLORIA • 1956 • Vari Giuseppe • ITL

ADDIO ULTIMO UOMO • 1979 • Castiglioni Alfredo, Castiglioni Angelo • ITL

ADDIO ZIO TOM see **ZIO TOM** • 1971

ADDITION, L' • 1984 • Amar Denis • FRN • CAGED HEART, THE ◦ PATSY, THE

ADDITION AND SUBTRACTION (USA) see **TOM WHISKY OU L'ILLUSIONNISTE TOQUE** • 1900

ADDRESS BY LENIN see **ADRES LENINA** • 1929

ADDRESS UNKNOWN • 1944 • Menzies William Cameron • USA

ADEBAR • 1957 • Kubelka Peter • SHT • AUS

ADELA • 1984 • Veroiu Mircea • RMN

ADELA HAS HAD NO SUPPER YET see **ADELA JESTE NEVECERELA** • 1977

ADELA JESTE NEVECERELA • 1977 • Lipsky Oldrich • CZC • DINNER FOR ADELE (USA) ◦ ADELA HAS HAD NO SUPPER YET ◦ NICK CARTER IN PRAGUE ◦ ADELE HASN'T EATEN YET ◦ ADELE HASN'T HAD HER SUPPER YET

ADELAIDE • 1968 • Simon Jean-Daniel • FRN, ITL • FINO A FARTI MALE (ITL) ◦ DEPRAVED, THE (USA)

ADELAIDE see **ADELHEID** • 1969

ADELAIDE AS IT IS TODAY • 1911 • *West's* • ASL

ADELAIDE IN A HURRY • 1911 • *Wondergraph* • ASL

ADELAIDE SHOW • 1918 • ASL

ADELAIDE SHOW –DAILY COVERAGE • 1917 • *Krischock H. (Ph)* • ASL

ADELAIDE'S ELECTRIC TRAMS • 1915 • ASL

ADELE • 1919 • Worsley Wallace • USA

ADELE HASN'T EATEN YET see **ADELA JESTE NEVECERELA** • 1977

ADELE HASN'T HAD HER SUPPER YET see **ADELA JESTE NEVECERELA** • 1977

ADELEN RIOTS, THE see **ADALEN 31** • 1969

ADELE'S WASHDAY • 1909 • *Vitagraph* • USA

ADELHEID • 1969 • Vlacil Frantisek • CZC • ADELAIDE

ADELITA, LA • 1937 • Gomez Guillermo Hernandez • MXC

ADEM ILE HAVVA • 1967 • Saydam Nejat • TRK • ADAM AND EVE ◦ MADDENING DESIRE ◦ CILDIRTAN ARZU

ADEMAI AU MOYEN-AGE • 1935 • de Marguenat Jean • FRN

ADEMAI AU POTEAU-FRONTIERE • 1949 • Colline Paul • FRN

ADEMAI AVIATEUR • 1934 • Tarride Jean • FRN

ADEMAI BANDIT D'HONNEUR • 1943 • Grangier Gilles • FRN

ADEUS, ATE AO MEU REGRESSO • 1974 • Vasconcelos Antonio-Pedro • PRT

ADEUS PORTUGUES, UM • 1985 • Botelho Joao • PRT • PORTUGUESE GOODBYE, A

ADHEMAR LAMPIOT • 1932 • Christian-Jaque • FRN

ADHEMAR OU LE JOUET DE LA FATALITE • 1951 • Guitry Sacha, Fernandel • FRN

ADHESION • 1912 • Aylott Dave? • UKN

ADHIKAR • 1938 • Barua Pramathesh Chandra • IND • AUTHORITY

ADHIKI KATARA • 1968 • Tegopoulos Apostolos • GRC • UNJUST CURSE ◦ HUNTED

ADHWA' AL-MADINA • 1972 • Wahab Fatin Abdel • EGY • LUMIERES DE LA VILLE, LES

ADI SHANKARACHARYA • 1983 • Iyer G. V. • IND • PHILOSOPHER, THE

ADI VASFIYE • 1985 • Yilmaz Atif • TRK • HER NAME IS VASFIYE

ADIEU see **ABSCHIED** • 1930

ADIEU see **ABSCHIED** • 1968

ADIEU ALOUETTE: CHALLENGE FOR THE CHURCH • 1972 • Weintraub William • CND

ADIEU AU LYS, L' • 1971 • Danis Aime • CND

ADIEU BONAPARTE • 1984 • Shahin Youssef • EGY, FRN • WEDAA YA BONAPARTE, AL-

ADIEU CHERIE • 1945 • Bernard Raymond • FRN

ADIEU FILIPPI • 1968 • Kuypers Rik • NTH, BLG

ADIEU FOULARDS • 1983 • Lara Christian • FRN

ADIEU FRANCISKA see **AUF WIEDERSEHEN, FRANZISKA** • 1941

ADIEU L'AMI • 1968 • Herman Jean • FRN, ITL • DUE SPORCHE CAROGNE (ITL) ◦ FAREWELL FRIEND (USA) ◦ HONOR AMONG THIEVES ◦ SO LONG FRIEND ◦ CODE, THE

ADIEU, LEBWOHL, GOODBYE • 1961 • Martin Paul • FRG • BABYSITTER-BOOGIE

ADIEU LEONARD • 1943 • Prevert Pierre • FRN • BOURSE OU LA VIE, LA

ADIEU LES BEAUX JOURS • 1933 • Meyer Johannes, Beucler Andre • FRN • BEAUX JOURS D'ARANJUEZ, LES

ADIEU LES COPAINS • 1930 • Joannon Leo • FRN

ADIEU LES COPAINS • 1934 • Joannon Leo • FRN

ADIEU L'HIVER see **TOKEI** • 1987

ADIEU MASCOTTE • 1929 • Thiele Wilhelm • FRN • MODELL VON MONTPARNASSE, DIE

ADIEU, MONSIEUR LE PROFESSEUR • 1972 • Moreau Michel • DCS • CND

ADIEU NU, L' • 1976 • Meunier Jean-Henri • FRN

ADIEU PARIS • 1952 • Heymann Claude • FRN

ADIEU PHILIPPINE • 1961 • Rozier Jacques • FRN, ITL

ADIEU POULET • 1975 • Granier-Deferre Pierre • FRN • FRENCH DETECTIVE, THE (USA)

ADIEU SOLIDARITE see **ADJO SOLIDARITET** • 1984

ADIEU VIENNE • 1939 • Severac Jacques • FRN

ADIEU VOYAGES LENTS • 1978 • Ripeau Marie-Genevieve • FRN

ADIEUX, LES see **AFSCHEID, HET** • 1967

ADIK MANJA • 1979 • Hafsham Othman • MLY • BABY WOES

ADIOS ALICIA • 1977 • Perez Liko, San Miguel Santiago • VNZ, SPN • GOODBYE ALICIA

ADIOS AMIGO • 1975 • Williamson Fred • USA • NO SWEAT

ADIOS BUENOS AIRES • 1938 • Torres-Rios Leopoldo • ARG

ADIOS, CIGUENA, ADIOS • 1970 • Summers Manuel • SPN • GOODBYE STORK

ADIOS, CORDERA • 1966 • Herrero Pedro Mario • SPN

ADIOS CUNADO • 1966 • Gonzalez Rogelio A. • MXC

ADIOS DAVID • 1978 • Montero Rafael • MXC • GOODBYE DAVID

ADIOS GRINGO • 1965 • Stegani Giorgio • ITL, FRN, SPN

ADIOS JUVENTUD • 1943 • Pardave Joaquin • MXC

ADIOS, MARIQUITA LINDA • 1944 • Patino Gomez Alfonso • MXC

ADIOS MI CHAPARRITA • 1939 • Cardona Rene • MXC

ADIOS, MIMI POMPON • 1960 • Marquina Luis • SPN

ADIOS MUNECA • 1987 • *Belen Ana* • SPN • GOODBYE LITTLE GIRL

ADIOS NICANOR • 1937 • Portas Rafael E. • MXC

ADIOS, NINON • 1960 • Madrid Jose Luis • SPN

ADIOS PEQUENA • 1985 • *Belen Ana* • SPN • GOODBYE MY LOVELY

ADIOS PROBLEMAS • 1955 • Land Kurt • ARG

ADIOS, RIO • 1988 • Andonov Ivan • BUL

ADIOS, SABATA (USA) see **INDIO BLACK, SAI CHE TI DICO: SEI UN GRAN FIGLIO DI..** • 1970

ADIOS SE UN ARTISTA • 1910 • de Chomon Segundo • SPN

ADIOS SUI GENERIS • 1976 • Kamin Bebe • ARG • BYE BYE SUI GENERIS

ADIOS, TEXAS see **TEXAS ADDIO** • 1966

ADIOS (UKN) see **LASH, THE** • 1930

ADIPIPOPEX • 1920 • *Plagge Karl Viktor* • FRG

ADJ KIRALY KATONAT! • 1983 • Erdoss Pal • HNG • PRINCESS, THE

ADJA TIO • 1980 • Koula Jean-Louis • IVC

ADJACENT YES, BUT SIMULTANEOUS • 1965 • *Landow George (P)* • USA

ADJO SOLIDARITET • 1984 • Wam Svend, Vennerod Petter • NRW • GOODBYE SOLIDARITY ◦ ADIEU SOLIDARITE

ADJUDANT SEINER HOHEIT, DER (FRG) see **POPBOCNIK JEHO VYSOSTI** • 1933

ADJUSTING HIS CLAIM • 1916 • MacMackin Archer • USA

ADJUTANT DES ZAREN, DER • 1928 • von Strischewski Wladimir • FRG

AD'LAL ALA AL-JANIBI AL-AKHAR • 1972 • Shaath Ghalib • EGY

ADLER VON FLANDERN, DER see **IKARUS, IM HOHENFLUG DER LEIDENSCHAFTEN** • 1918

ADLER VON VELSATAL, DER • 1956 • Haussler Richard • FRG

ADMA –FOR SHORT • 1958 • Anscombe Ronnie • UKN

ADMAN, THE • 1979 • Alexander Mike • SHT • UKN

ADMI • 1939 • Shantaram Rajaram • IND • LIFE IS FOR LIVING

ADMINISTRATEURS, LES • 1960 • Dansereau Fernand, Godbout Jacques • DOC • CND

ADMIRABLE CRICHTON, THE • 1918 • Samuelson G. B. • UKN

ADMIRABLE CRICHTON, THE • 1957 • Gilbert Lewis* • UKN • PARADISE LAGOON (USA)

ADMIRABLE CRICHTON, THE (UKN) see **MALE AND FEMALE** • 1919

ADMIRAL • 1968 • Giersz Witold • ANS • PLN • ADMIRAL, THE

ADMIRAL, THE see **ADMIRAL** • 1968

ADMIRAL NAKHIMOV see **AMIRAL NAKHIMOV** • 1946

ADMIRAL USHAKOV, THE SHIPS ARE STORMING THE BASTIONS see **KORABLI SHTURMUYUT BASTIONY** • 1953

ADMIRAL WAS A LADY, THE • 1950 • Rogell Albert S. • USA

ADMIRAL YAMAMOTO see **RENGO KANTAI SHIREICHOKAN YAMAMOTO ISOROKU** • 1968

ADMIRAL YI AND HIS TURTLEBOAT ARMADA • 1976 • Chang Il-Ho • SKR

ADMIRALS ALL • 1935 • Hanbury Victor • UKN

ADMIRAL'S ORDERS • 1915 • Weston Harold • UKN

ADMIRAL'S SECRET, THE • 1934 • Newall Guy • UKN

ADMIRAL'S YARN, THE • 1929 • Aylott Dave, Symmons E. F. • SHT • UKN

ADMIRERS GALORE see **CHIT THU WAING WAING LAI** • 1982

ADMIRERS THREE • 1916 • *Dovoy Alice* • USA

ADMIRING FATHER, AN see **HAZOBABAS, O** • 1968

ADMISSION FREE • 1932 • Fleischer Dave • ANS • USA

ADMISSION TWO PINS • 1914 • *Victor* • USA

ADMITTANCE, THE • 1968 • Watson Patricia • CND

ADOLESCENCE • 1966 • Forgency Vladimir • FRN

ADOLESCENCE PERVERSE see **ADOLESCENCE PERVERTIE** • 1975

ADOLESCENCE PERVERTIE • 1975 • Benazeraf Jose • FRN, ITL • ADOLESCENZA PERVERSA (ITL) ◦ ADOLESCENCE PERVERSE

ADOLESCENCIA MARGINAL • 1979 • Bulbulian Maurice • DOC • CND • DELAISSES, LES

ADOLESCENT, THE • 1967 • Yamaskich Osamu, McLarty James E. • JPN

ADOLESCENT, THE see **ADOLESCENTE, L'** • 1978

ADOLESCENT CAIN see **CAIN ADOLESCENTE** • 1959

ADOLESCENT DAYS see **NO YUKI, YAMA YUKI, UMIBE YUKI** • 1987

ADOLESCENT GIRL, THE see **ADOLESCENTE, L'** • 1978

ADOLESCENTE, L' • 1976 • Brescia Alfonso • ITL

ADOLESCENTE, L' • 1978 • Moreau Jeanne • FRN, FRG • ADOLESCENT, THE ◦ ADOLESCENT GIRL, THE

ADOLESCENTES A DEPUCELER • 1980 • Love John • FRN

ADOLESCENTES AU PENSIONNAT • 1980 • Gregory Gerard • FRN

ADOLESCENTES, LAS • 1975 • Maso Pedro • SPN

ADOLESCENTES, LES (FRN) see **DOLCI INGANNI, I** • 1960

ADOLESCENTES, LOS • 1968 • Salazar Abel • MXC • ADOLESCENTS, THE

ADOLESCENTES TROP CURIEUSES • Reinhard Pierre B. • FRN

ADOLESCENTI, LE • 1964 • Baldi Gian Vittorio, Brault Michel, Teshigahara Hiroshi, Rouch Jean • ITL, CND, JPN • FLEUR DE L'AGE, OU LES ADOLESCENTES, LA ◦ THAT TENDER AGE ◦ VEUVES DE QUINZE ANS, LES ◦ SHISHUNKI ◦ ADOLESCENTS, THE

ADOLESCENTS, THE see **ADOLESCENTI, LE** • 1964

ADOLESCENTS, THE see **ADOLESCENTES, LOS** • 1968

ADOLESCENTUL RAUTACIOS • 1968 • Vitandis Gheorghe • RMN • MALICIOUS ADOLESCENT, THE

ADOLESCENZA PERVERSA (ITL) see **ADOLESCENCE PERVERTIE** • 1975

ADOLF ARMSTARKE • 1937 • Wallen Sigurd • SWD • ADOLF ARMSTRONG

ADOLF ARMSTRONG see **ADOLF ARMSTARKE** • 1937

ADOLF AS A FIREMAN see **ADOLF I ELD OCH LAGOR** • 1939

ADOLF HITLER –MY PART IN HIS DOWNFALL • 1972 • Cohen Norman • UKN

ADOLF HITLER: THE BUNKER see **BUNKER, THE** • 1981

ADOLF I ELD OCH LAGOR • 1939 • Branner Per-Axel • SWD • ADOLF AS A FIREMAN

ADOLF I TOPPFORM • 1952 • Aring Wilhelm, Stivell Arne • SWD

ADOLF IN PLUNDERLAND • 1940 • Porter Eric • ANS • ASL

ADOLF KLARAR SKIVAN • 1938 • Jahr Adolf • SWD • ADOLF MAKES IT

ADOLF MAKES IT see **ADOLF KLARAR SKIVAN** • 1938

ADOLF NI TSUGU • 1986 • Tezuka Osamu • ANM • JPN

ADOLF UND MARLENE • 1977 • Lommel Ulli • FRG • MANN VON OBERZALBERG – ADOLF UND MARLENE, DER

ADOLPHE OR THE AWKARD AGE see **ADOLPHE OU L'AGE TENDRE** • 1968

ADOLPHE OU L'AGE TENDRE • 1968 • Toublanc-Michel Bernard • FRN, FRG, PLN • TENDER AGE, THE (UKN) ◦ ADOLPHE OR THE AWKARD AGE

ADOLPHO ,FILS DU FUHRER see **COMMENT SE FAIRE VIRER DE L'HOSTO** • 1977

ADOM OU LE SANG D'ABEL • 1976 • Benhamou Gerard-Myriam • FRN

ADONDE MUERE EL VIENTO • 1975 • Siro Fernando • ARG • WHERE THE WIND DIES

ADOPTED BABY, THE • 1915 • Myll Louis • USA

ADOPTED BROTHER, THE • 1913 • Cabanne W. Christy? • USA

ADOPTED CHILD, THE • 1911 • Bouwmeester Theo • UKN

ADOPTED CHILD, THE • 1912 • *Pathe* • USA

ADOPTED DAUGHTER, THE • 1910 • *Lubin* • USA

ADOPTED DAUGHTER, THE • 1914 • Smallwood Ray C. • USA

ADOPTED FATHER, THE see **WORKING MAN, THE** • 1933

ADOPTED SON, THE • 1912 • *Williams Kathlyn* • USA

ADOPTED SON, THE • 1917 • Brabin Charles J. • USA

ADOPTING A BABY • 1909 • Coleby A. E. • UKN

ADOPTION • 1967 • Derkaoui Mustafa • SHT • PLN

ADOPTION see **OROKBEFOGADAS** • 1975

ADOPTION, L' • 1978 • Grunebaum Marc • FRN, SWT

ADOPTION, THE • 1910 • *Edison* • USA

ADOPTIVKIND, DAS • 1914 • Biebrach Rudolf • FRG
ADORABILI E BUGIARDE • 1959 • Malasomma Nunzio • ITL • ASSASSINIO COL BOTTO ○ MAGNIFICHE TRE, LE ○ RAGAZZE BRIVIDO
ADORABLE • 1933 • Dieterle William • USA
ADORABLE BLUNDERER see **ADORAVEL TRAPALHAO** • 1967
ADORABLE CHEAT, THE • 1928 • King Burton L. • USA
ADORABLE CORPS DE DEBORAH, L' (FRN) see **DOLCE CORPO DI DEBORAH, IL** • 1968
ADORABLE CREATURES (USA) see **ADORABLES CREATURES** • 1952
ADORABLE DECEIVER, THE • 1926 • Rosen Phil • USA
ADORABLE IMP see **KEMEKO NO UTA** • 1968
ADORABLE JULIA (FRN) see **JULIA, DU BIST ZAUBERHAFT** • 1962
ADORABLE JULIE see **JULIA, DU BIST ZAUBERHAFT** • 1962
ADORABLE LIAR see **ADORABLE MENTEUSE** • 1961
ADORABLE MENTEUSE • 1961 • Deville Michel • FRN • MENTEUSE, LA ○ ADORABLE LIAR
ADORABLE OUTCAST, THE • 1928 • Dawn Norman • USA
ADORABLE SAVAGE, THE • 1920 • Dawn Norman • USA
ADORABLE SINNER (USA) see **KATJA** • 1959
ADORABLES CANAILLES see **SEXY GANG** • 1967
ADORABLES CREATURES • 1952 • Christian-Jaque • FRN, ITL • QUANDO LE DONNE AMANO (ITL) ○ ADORABLE CREATURES (USA)
ADORABLES DEMONS • 1956 • Cloche Maurice • FRN
ADORABLES MUJERCITAS • 1973 • *Estudios Americas* • MXC
ADORADA ENEMIGA • 1963 • Cardona Rene Jr. • MXC, CLM
ADORATION • 1928 • Lloyd Frank • USA
ADORATION • 1929 • Stone Andrew L. • SHT • USA
ADORAVEL TIO MANECO • 1970 • Migliaccio Flavio • BRZ
ADORAVEL TRAPALHAO • 1967 • Tanko J. B. • BRZ • ADORABLE BLUNDERER
ADORED WIFE see **BAHU BEGUM** • 1967
ADORING AN AD • 1910 • *Lubin* • USA
ADOROBILE IDIOTA (ITL) see **RAVISSANTE IDIOTE, UNE** • 1964
ADRES LENINA • 1929 • Petrov Vladimir • USS • LENIN'S ADDRESS ○ ADDRESS BY LENIN
ADRESSATIN VERSTORBEN • 1911 • Stark Kurt • FRG
ADRESSE UNBEKANNT • 1938 • Martin Karl Heinz • FRG, CZC
ADREY • 1916 • Ford Hugh • USA
ADRIAN TROUPE OF CYCLISTS, THE • 1901 • Smith G. A. • UKN
ADRIANA LECOUVREUR • 1918 • Falena Ugo • ITL
ADRIANA LECOUVREUR • 1956 • Salvini Guido • ITL
ADRIEN • 1943 • Fernandel • FRN • BAR DU SOLEIL, LE
ADRIENNE LECOUVREUR • 1913 • Mercanton Louis, Desfontaines Henri • FRN
ADRIENNE LECOUVREUR • 1938 • L'Herbier Marcel • FRN
ADRIFT • 1912 • *Imp* • USA
ADRIFT • 1914 • *Tennant Barbara* • USA
ADRIFT see **HRST VODY** • 1971
ADRIFT IN A GREAT CITY • 1914 • *La Badie Florence* • USA
ADRIFT ON LIFE'S TIDE • 1913 • Buckland Warwick? • UKN
ADRUSHTA VANTHALU • 1968 • Madhusudhan Rao V. • IND • FORTUNATE, THE
ADUA AND HER COMPANIONS see **ADUA E LE COMPAGNE** • 1960
ADUA AND HER FRIENDS see **ADUA E LE COMPAGNE** • 1960
ADUA E LE COMPAGNE • 1960 • Pietrangeli Antonio • ITL • LOVE A LA CARTE (USA) ○ ADUA AND HER COMPANIONS ○ ADUA AND HER FRIENDS ○ HUNGRY FOR LOVE
ADUEFUE, THE LORDS OF THE STREET (UKN) see **GUERISSEURS, LES** • 1988
ADULT EDUCATION see **HIDING OUT** • 1987
ADULT FAIRY TALES (UKN) see **FAIRY TALES** • 1978
ADULT FUN • 1972 • Scott James • UKN
ADULT VERSION OF JEKYLL AND HYDE, THE • 1972 • Elliott B. Ron • USA
ADULTERA, L' • 1911 • Caserini Mario • ITL
ADULTERA, L' • 1946 • Coletti Duilio • ITL
ADULTERA, LA • 1955 • Demicheli Tulio • MXC
ADULTERA, LA • 1975 • Bodegas Roberto • SPN
ADULTERESS, THE • 1973 • Meisel Norbert • USA
ADULTERESS, THE see **YORU NO TSUZUMI** • 1958
ADULTERESS, THE see **INFIDELES, LES** • 1972
ADULTERESS, THE see **CHILD UNDER A LEAF** • 1974
ADULTERESS, THE (USA) see **THERESE RAQUIN** • 1953
ADULTERESS IN LOVE see **AMOUR AUX TROUSSES, L'** • 1974
ADULTERIO, EL • 1943 • Diaz Morales Jose • MXC
ADULTERIO A BRASILEIRA • 1970 • Rovai Pedro Carlos • BRZ
ADULTERIO A LA ESPANOLA • 1975 • Marcos Arturo • SPN
ADULTERIO ALL'ITALIANA • 1966 • Festa Campanile Pasquale • ITL • ADULTERY ITALIAN STYLE
ADULTERIO CASI DECENTE, UN • 1969 • Gil Rafael • SPN
ADULTERO, EL • 1975 • Fernandez Ramon • SPN
ADULTERO LUI, ADULTERA LEI • 1963 • Matarazzo Raffaello • ITL
ADULTEROUS AFFAIR • 1966 • Leversuch Ted • CND • ROOM FOR A STRANGER ○ LOVE BLACKMAILER, THE
ADULTERY see **OSWALT KOLLE: ZUM BEISPIEL: EHEBRUCH** • 1969
ADULTERY FOR FUN AND PROFIT • 1972 • USA
ADULTERY ITALIAN STYLE see **ADULTERIO ALL'ITALIANA** • 1966
ADULTS WITH OBJECTIONS see **MAYORES CON REPAROS** • 1967
ADVANCE AND BE MECHANIZED • 1967 • Washam Ben • ANS • USA
ADVANCE AUSTRALIA • 1916 • *Lorne Len* • ASL
ADVANCE INTO LIBYA • 1941 • Hurley Frank • DOC • ASL
ADVANCE TO GROUND ZERO see **NIGHTBREAKER** • 1989
ADVANCE TO THE REAR • 1964 • Marshall George • USA • COMPANY OF COWARDS
ADVANTAGE see **AVANTAZH** • 1978
ADVANTAGES OF HYPNOTISM, THE • 1911 • Coleby A. E. • UKN
ADVANTAGES OF LAGGING BEHIND, THE • 1972 • Severijn Jonne • DOC • NTH
ADVENT • 1956 • Vlcek Vladimir • CZC • GATES OF DAWN, THE
ADVENT • 1980 • Grubcheva Ivanka • BUL
ADVENT OF JANE, THE • 1912 • Salter Harry • USA
ADVENT OF THE MOTHER-IN-LAW, THE • 1905 • Green Tom? • UKN
ADVENTURE • 1925 • Fleming Victor • USA
ADVENTURE • 1945 • Fleming Victor • USA
ADVENTURE • 1965 • Doukov Stoyan • ANM • BUL
ADVENTURE see **AVENTYRET** • 1936
ADVENTURE 1 • 1990 • Alves Joe • USA
ADVENTURE, THE • 1964 • Richardson John • ASL
ADVENTURE, THE • Lee Shuch • HKG
ADVENTURE, THE see **HANS BROLLOPSNATT** • 1916
ADVENTURE, THE see **AVVENTURA, L'** • 1960
ADVENTURE, ADVENTURE see **BOKEN, BOKEN, MATA BOKEN** • 1968
ADVENTURE AT BRIARCLIFF, THE • 1915 • *Courtot Marguerite* • USA
ADVENTURE AT MARIENSZTAT see **PRZYGODA NA MARIENSZTACIE** • 1954
ADVENTURE AT THE BOTTOM OF THE SEA, AN • 1906 • *Pathe* • FRN
ADVENTURE AT THE CENTRE OF THE EARTH see **AVENTURA AL CENTRO DE LA TIERRA** • 1964
ADVENTURE BY THE SEA • 1964 • Bartsch Art • ANS • USA
ADVENTURE FOR TWO, AN (USA) see **A NOUS DEUX** • 1979
ADVENTURE FOR TWO (USA) see **DEMI-PARADISE, THE** • 1943
ADVENTURE GIRL • 1934 • Raymaker Herman C. • USA
ADVENTURE HUNTER, THE • 1915 • Martin E. A. • USA
ADVENTURE HUNTERS, THE see **ADVENTURE OF THE ACTION HUNTERS, THE** • 1986
ADVENTURE IN A HAREM, AN see **HAREMSEVENTYR, ET** • 1914
ADVENTURE IN BALTIMORE • 1949 • Wallace Richard, Cromwell John (U/c) • USA • BACHELOR BAIT (UKN) ○ BALTIMORE ESCAPADE
ADVENTURE IN BERLIN see **SPUR FAHRT NACH BERLIN, DIE** • 1952
ADVENTURE IN BLACKMAIL (USA) see **BREACH OF PROMISE** • 1941
ADVENTURE IN BLUE • Munteanu Stefan • ANM • RMN
ADVENTURE IN DIAMONDS • 1940 • Fitzmaurice George • USA • DIAMONDS ARE DANGEROUS
ADVENTURE IN HEARTS, AN • 1920 • Cruze James • USA • CAPTAIN DIEPPE (UKN)
ADVENTURE IN INDO-CHINA • 1957 • Pergament Andre • FRN
ADVENTURE IN IRAQ • 1943 • Lederman D. Ross • USA
ADVENTURE IN MANHATTAN • 1936 • Ludwig Edward • USA • MANHATTAN MADNESS (UKN)
ADVENTURE IN MUSIC • 1944 • Le Borg Reginald, Winston S. K., Matray Ernst • USA
ADVENTURE IN ODESSA • 1954 • Atamanov Lev • USS
ADVENTURE IN RHYTHM • 1961 • Shaindlin Jack • SHT • USA
ADVENTURE IN SAHARA • 1938 • Lederman D. Ross • USA
ADVENTURE IN SICILY, AN • 1911 • *Yankee* • USA
ADVENTURE IN SPACE • Wiemer Hans Ulrich • ANM • GDR
ADVENTURE IN STRIPES see **PRZYGODA W PASKI** • 1961
ADVENTURE IN TAKLAMAKAN see **KIGANJO NO BOKEN** • 1965
ADVENTURE IN TEHRAN see **TAHRAN MACERASI** • 1968
ADVENTURE IN THE AUTUMN WOODS, AN • 1913 • Griffith D. W. • USA
ADVENTURE IN THE COUNTRY see **PRZYGODA W TERENIE** • 1960
ADVENTURE IN THE GOLDEN TRIANGLE see **MI CHUANG JIN SANJIAO** • 1988
ADVENTURE IN THE HOPFIELDS • 1954 • Guillermin John • UKN
ADVENTURE IN THE NIGHT, AN see **AVENTURA EN LA NOCHE, UNA** • 1947
ADVENTURE IN THE STRANGE STONE CASTLE see **KIGANJO NO BOKEN** • 1965
ADVENTURE IN WARSAW (USA) see **PRZYGODA NA MARIENSZTACIE** • 1954
ADVENTURE IN WASHINGTON • 1941 • Green Alfred E. • USA • FEMALE CORRESPONDENT (UKN) ○ SENATE PAGE BOYS
ADVENTURE IS A HARD LIFE see **TEZKY ZIVOT DOBRODRUHA** • 1941
ADVENTURE ISLAND • 1947 • Newfield Sam • USA
ADVENTURE LIMITED • 1934 • King George • UKN
ADVENTURE MAD • 1928 • Mendes Lothar • USA
ADVENTURE OF A DIAMOND, THE • 1919 • SAF
ADVENTURE OF A FRENCH GENTLEMAN WITHOUT TROUSERS see **MESAVENTURE VAN EEN FRANSCH HEERTJE ZONDER PANTALON OP HET STRAND TE ZANDVOORT** • 1905
ADVENTURE OF A MILLIONAIRE • 1910 • *Powers* • USA
ADVENTURE OF A PICKPOCKET, THE • 1914 • *Edison* • USA
ADVENTURE OF A SUGAR DOLL, THE • 1965 • *Childrens Film Society* • ANS • IND
ADVENTURE OF AN HEIRESS, THE • 1913 • *Joyce Alice* • USA
ADVENTURE OF BARON MUNCHAUSEN (USA) see **AVVENTURE DEL BARONE DI MUNCHAUSEN** • 1914
ADVENTURE OF CHECHEMENI see **CHECHEMENI-GO NO BOKEN** • 1976
ADVENTURE OF FATHER CHRISTMAS, THE see **AVENTURE DU PERE NOEL, L'** • 1957
ADVENTURE OF FAUSTUS BIDGOOD, THE • 1987 • Jones Michael, Jones Andy • CND
ADVENTURE OF FLORENCE, THE • 1915 • *La Badie Florence* • USA
ADVENTURE OF KUROKI TARO see **KUROKI TARO NO BOKEN** • 1977
ADVENTURE OF ROB ROY, AN • 1911 • *Gaumont* • UKN
ADVENTURE OF SALVATOR ROSA, AN (USA) see **AVVENTURA DI SALVATOR ROSA, UN** • 1940
ADVENTURE OF SHERLOCK HOLMES' SMARTER BROTHER, THE • 1975 • Wilder Gene • USA • SHERLOCK HOLMES' SMARTER BROTHER
ADVENTURE OF THE 13TH SISTER, THE • 1959 • Li Han-Hsiang • HKG
ADVENTURE OF THE ABSENT-MINDED PROFESSOR, THE • 1914 • Seay Charles M. • USA
ADVENTURE OF THE ACTION HUNTERS, THE • 1986 • Bonner Lee • USA • ADVENTURES OF THE ACTION HUNTERS, THE ○ TWO FOR THE MONEY ○ ADVENTURE HUNTERS, THE
ADVENTURE OF THE ACTRESS' JEWELS, THE • 1914 • Seay Charles M. • USA
ADVENTURE OF THE ALARM CLOCK, THE • 1914 • Seay Charles M. • USA
ADVENTURE OF THE BUTTON, THE • 1912 • *Missimer Howard* • USA
ADVENTURE OF THE COUNTERFEIT BILLS, THE • 1912 • *Vitagraph* • USA
ADVENTURE OF THE COUNTERFEIT MONEY, THE • 1914 • Seay Charles M. • USA
ADVENTURE OF THE EXTRA BABY, THE • 1914 • Seay Charles M. • USA
ADVENTURE OF THE GOOD SOLDIER SCHWEIK, THE • 1953 • Saizescu Geo • RMN
ADVENTURE OF THE HASTY ELOPEMENT, THE • 1914 • Seay Charles M. • USA
ADVENTURE OF THE ITALIAN MODEL, THE • 1912 • Brooke Van Dyke • USA
ADVENTURE OF THE LOST WIFE, THE • 1914 • Seay Charles M. • USA
ADVENTURE OF THE MISSING LEGACY, THE • 1914 • Seay Charles M. • USA
ADVENTURE OF THE PICKPOCKET, THE • 1914 • Seay Charles M. • USA
ADVENTURE OF THE RETIRED ARMY COLONEL, THE • 1912 • Brooke Van Dyke • USA
ADVENTURE OF THE RIVAL UNDERTAKERS, THE • 1914 • Beggs Lee • USA
ADVENTURE OF THE SHOOTING PARTY, THE • 1913 • Trimble Larry • UKN
ADVENTURE OF THE SMELLING SALTS, THE • 1912 • *Vitagraph* • USA
ADVENTURE OF THE SMUGGLED DIAMONDS, THE • 1914 • Seay Charles M. • USA
ADVENTURE OF THE STOLEN SLIPPER, THE • 1914 • Seay Charles M. • USA
ADVENTURE OF THE THUMB PRINT, THE • 1912 • *Costello Maurice* • USA
ADVENTURE OF THE WRONG SANTA CLAUS, THE • 1914 • Seay Charles M. • USA
ADVENTURE OF THE YELLOW CURL PAPERS, THE • 1915 • *Garwood William* • USA
ADVENTURE OF WESTGATE SEMINARY, THE • 1913 • Trimble Larry • UKN
ADVENTURE ON THE MEXICAN BORDER, AN • 1913 • Fielding Romaine • USA
ADVENTURE SHOP, THE • 1918 • Webb Kenneth • USA
ADVENTURE STARTS HERE see **HAR BORJAR AVENTYRET** • 1965
ADVENTURE UNLIMITED (UKN) see **WHITE PONGO** • 1945
ADVENTURER see **AVENTYRARE, EN** • 1942
ADVENTURER, THE • 1915 • MacDonald Donald • USA
ADVENTURER, THE • 1917 • Blache Alice • USA
ADVENTURER, THE • 1917 • Chaplin Charles • USA
ADVENTURER, THE • 1920 • Edwards J. Gordon • USA
ADVENTURER, THE • 1920 • Hartigan P. C. • USA
ADVENTURER, THE • 1928 • Tourjansky Victor, Van Dyke W. S. (U/c) • USA • GALLANT GRINGO, THE (UKN)
ADVENTURER, THE • 1970 • Shahin Mohammed • SYR
ADVENTURER OF SEVILLE, THE (USA) see **AVENTURAS DEL BARBERO DE SEVILLA** • 1954
ADVENTURER OF TORTUGA see **AVVENTURIERO DELLA TORTUGA, L'** • 1965
ADVENTURERS, THE • 1951 • MacDonald David • UKN • FORTUNE IN DIAMONDS (USA) ○ GREAT ADVENTURE, THE
ADVENTURERS, THE • 1970 • Gilbert Lewis* • UKN, USA
ADVENTURES • 1965 • Dinov Todor • ANM • BUL
ADVENTURES • 1967 • Rubbo Michael • SHT • CND
ADVENTURES AND EMOTIONS OF EDGAR POMEROY, THE • 1920-21 • SER • USA
ADVENTURES AT RUGBY (USA) see **TOM BROWN'S SCHOOLDAYS** • 1940
ADVENTURE'S END • 1937 • Lubin Arthur • USA
ADVENTURES IN BABYSITTING • 1987 • Columbus Chris • USA • NIGHT ON THE TOWN, A
ADVENTURES IN BOKHARA see **NASREDDIN V BUKHARE** • 1943
ADVENTURES IN DIPLOMACY • 1914 • *Francis Alec B.* • USA
ADVENTURES IN PERCEPTION see **OOG OP AVONTUUR, HET** • 1970
ADVENTURES IN PYGMYLAND see **BY AEROPLANE TO PYGMYLAND** • 1927
ADVENTURES IN RAINBOW COUNTY • 1970 • Pearson Peter • CND, UKN, ASL
ADVENTURES IN SHARPS AND FLATS • 1963 • Spery Joseph C. • SHT • USA
ADVENTURES IN SILVERADO • 1948 • Karlson Phil • USA • ABOVE ALL LAWS (UKN)
ADVENTURES IN SPACE • *Ideal* • FRG
ADVENTURES IN SPACE • 1964 • *Capra Frank (P)* • USA • REACHING FOR THE STARS
ADVENTURES IN THE CREEP ZONE see **SPACEHUNTER: ADVENTURES IN THE FORBIDDEN ZONE** • 1983
ADVENTURES IN THE FAR NORTH • 1923 • *Kleinschmidt F. E.* • USA • CAPTAIN KLEINSCHMIDT'S ADVENTURES IN THE FAR NORTH
ADVENTURES OF *, THE see **ADVENTURES OF AN ASTERISK** • 1957
ADVENTURES OF A £5 NOTE, THE • 1910 • Fitzhamon Lewin? • UKN
ADVENTURES OF A BABY, THE • 1911 • *Bechtel William* • USA
ADVENTURES OF A BAD SHILLING, THE • 1913 • Collins Edwin J.? • UKN
ADVENTURES OF A BATH CHAIR • 1907 • Stow Percy • UKN
ADVENTURES OF A BILL POSTER, THE • 1903 • Stow Percy? • UKN

ADVENTURES OF A BOY SCOUT, THE • 1915 • Warren Edward • USA
ADVENTURES OF A BROKER'S MAN, THE • 1907 • Martin J. H.? • UKN
ADVENTURES OF A BROWN MAN IN SEARCH OF CIVILIZATION • 1971 • Ivory James • MTV • IND
ADVENTURES OF A COWPUNCHER • 1910 • *Bison* • USA
ADVENTURES OF A CUPBOARD • 1965 • Sturlis Edward • ANM • PLN
ADVENTURES OF A DENTIST, THE • 1967 • Klimov Elem • USS
ADVENTURES OF A DOLL • 1966 • *Winzentsen Franz* • SHT • FRG
ADVENTURES OF A DRUMMER BOY • 1909 • Blackton J. Stuart (Spv) • USA
ADVENTURES OF A FOOL see **GHARAMIATE MAGNOUN** • 1967
ADVENTURES OF A FOOTBALL, THE • 1914 • Kinder Stuart? • UKN
ADVENTURES OF A FRENCH GENTLEMAN WITHOUT HIS TROUSERS see **MESAVENTURE VAN EEN FRANSCH HEERTJE ZONDER PANTALON OP HET STRAND TE ZANDVOORT** • 1905
ADVENTURES OF A £IOO BANK NOTE, THE • 1905 • Martin J. H.? • UKN
ADVENTURES OF A JACKAROO, THE see **CALOOLA** • 1911
ADVENTURES OF A KITTY see **KONEKO MONOGATARI** • 1987
ADVENTURES OF A LITTLE SAMURAI see **SHONEN SARUTOBI SASUKE** • 1960
ADVENTURES OF A MADCAP • 1915 • *Saunders Jackie* • USA
ADVENTURES OF A MILLIONAIRE'S SON, THE see **NED MED MILLIONAERDRENGEN** • 1913
ADVENTURES OF A NOBLEMAN see **REKOPIS ZNALEZIONY W SARAGOSSIE** • 1965
ADVENTURES OF A PARAIBA see **AVENTURAS DE UM PARAIBA** • 1982
ADVENTURES OF A PERFORMING FLEA, THE • 1907 • Cooper Arthur • UKN
ADVENTURES OF A PLUMBER'S MATE • 1978 • Long Stanley • UKN
ADVENTURES OF A PRIVATE EYE • 1977 • Long Stanley • UKN
ADVENTURES OF A RAREBIT EATER see **DREAMS OF THE RAREBIT FIEND** • 1921
ADVENTURES OF A ROLL OF LINO, THE • 1907 • Collins Alf • UKN • FATHER BUYS SOME LINOLEUM
ADVENTURES OF A ROOKIE • 1943 • Goodwins Leslie • USA
ADVENTURES OF A SEA-GOING HACK, THE • 1915 • *Wilson Ben* • USA
ADVENTURES OF A TAXI DRIVER • 1976 • Long Stanley • UKN
ADVENTURES OF A TEN MARK NOTE see **ABENTEUER EINES ZEHNMARKSCHEINES, DIE** • 1926
ADVENTURES OF A WATCH, THE • 1908 • Booth W. R. • UKN
ADVENTURES OF A WATCH, THE • 1913 • Kirkland Hardee • USA
ADVENTURES OF A WATER IMP see **KAPPA NO PATARO** • 1957
ADVENTURES OF A WINDOW CLEANER, THE • 1904 • *Paul R. W.* • UKN
ADVENTURES OF A YOUNG MAN • 1962 • Ritt Martin • USA • HEMINGWAY'S ADVENTURES OF A YOUNG MAN (UKN)
ADVENTURES OF ALGY, THE • 1925 • Smith Beaumont • ASL
ADVENTURES OF AMERICAN JOE, THE • 1912 • *Kalem* • USA
ADVENTURES OF AN ALARM-CLOCK • 1962 • Hartwig Jania • ANM • PLN
ADVENTURES OF AN AMATEUR HYPNOTIST, THE • 1911 • *Lux* • ITL
ADVENTURES OF AN AMERICAN RABBIT, THE • 1986 • Moskowitz Steward • ANM • USA
ADVENTURES OF AN ANT • 1984 • Nazarov Eduard • ANS • USS
ADVENTURES OF AN ASTERISK • 1957 • Hubley John • ANS • USA • ADVENTURES OF *, THE
ADVENTURES OF AN EVERYDAY HERO see **AVONTUREN VAN ALLEDAAGSE HELD** • 1975
ADVENTURES OF AN INSURANCE MAN, THE • 1905 • Green Tom • UKN
ADVENTURES OF AN OCTOBERITE, THE (USA) see **POKHOZDENIYA OKTYABRINI** • 1924
ADVENTURES OF AN OLD FLIRT, THE • 1909 • Porter Edwin S. • USA
ADVENTURES OF ANTAR AND ALBA, THE see **MUGHAMMARAT ANTAR WA ALBA** • 1948
ADVENTURES OF ARCHIE, THE see **HOT TIMES** • 1974
ADVENTURES OF ARSENE LUPIN see **AVENTURES D'ARSENE LUPIN, LES** • 1956
ADVENTURES OF BARON CRAC see **BARON DE CRAC, LE** • 1910
ADVENTURES OF BARON MUNCHAUSEN, THE • 1927 • *Peroff Paul* • ANM • USA • NOTHING BUT THE TRUTH
ADVENTURES OF BARON MUNCHAUSEN, THE • 1929 • Ivanov-Vano Ivan, Cherkez D. • ANM • USS
ADVENTURES OF BARON MUNCHAUSEN, THE • 1947 • Dunning George • ANM • CND
ADVENTURES OF BARON MUNCHAUSEN, THE • 1988 • Gilliam Terry • UKN, FRG
ADVENTURES OF BARON MUNCHAUSEN, THE (USA) see **MUNCHHAUSEN** • 1943
ADVENTURES OF BARRY MCKENZIE, THE • 1972 • Beresford Bruce • ASL
ADVENTURES OF BIG AND LITTLE WILLIE, THE • 1915 • *Hazelden Mario-Toons* • UKN
ADVENTURES OF BILLY, THE • 1911 • Griffith D. W. • USA
ADVENTURES OF BORIVOJE SURDILOVIC see **AVANTURE BORIVOJA SURDILOVICA** • 1981
ADVENTURES OF BUCKAROO BANZAI, THE • 1984 • Richter W. D. • USA • BUCKAROO BANZAI ○ ADVENTURES OF BUCKAROO BANZAI ACROSS THE EIGHTH DIMENSION
ADVENTURES OF BUCKAROO BANZAI ACROSS THE EIGHTH DIMENSION see **ADVENTURES OF BUCKAROO BANZAI, THE** • 1984
ADVENTURES OF BUFFALO BILL • 1917 • *Essanay* • USA
ADVENTURES OF BULLWHIP GRIFFIN, THE • 1967 • Neilson James • USA
ADVENTURES OF BUSTY BROWN, THE • 1964 • *Mahon Barry (P)* • USA • ADVENTURES OF RUSTY BROWN, THE ○ LUSTY BUSTY BROWN ○ BUSTY BROWN ○ DUSTY BROWN
ADVENTURES OF CAPTAIN AFRICA, THE • 1955 • Bennet Spencer Gordon • SRL • USA
ADVENTURES OF CAPTAIN FABIAN • 1951 • Marshall William • USA
ADVENTURES OF CAPTAIN KETTLE, THE • 1922 • Milton Meyrick • UKN
ADVENTURES OF CAPTAIN MARVEL • 1941 • Witney William, English John • SRL • USA • RETURN OF CAPTAIN MARVEL
ADVENTURES OF CAROL, THE • 1917 • Knoles Harley • USA
ADVENTURES OF CASANOVA • 1947 • Gavaldon Roberto • USA, MXC • CAPITAN CASANOVA, EL (MXC)
ADVENTURES OF CHATRAN, THE • 1987 • JPN
ADVENTURES OF CHICO, THE • 1938 • Woodard Horace, Woodard Stacy • USA
ADVENTURES OF CHILDLIKE AND BLAND, THE • 1911 • *Sun Films* • UKN
ADVENTURES OF CHINESE TARZAN, THE • 1940 • *Ping Fei* • CHN
ADVENTURES OF CHOPPY AND THE PRINCESS, THE see **CHOPPY AND THE PRINCESS** • 1984
ADVENTURES OF CORPORAL KOCHEKOV, THE • 1955 • Rasumny Alexander • USS
ADVENTURES OF CURLEY AND HIS GANG, THE see **CURLEY** • 1947
ADVENTURES OF DANIEL BOONE see **DANIEL BOONE** • 1936
ADVENTURES OF DAVID GRAY see **VAMPYR** • 1931
ADVENTURES OF DEADWOOD DICK, THE • 1915 • Paul Fred, MacBean L. C. • SER • UKN
ADVENTURES OF DICK DOLAN, THE • 1917 • Wilson Frank • UKN
ADVENTURES OF DICK TURPIN -200 GUINEAS REWARD, DEAD OR ALIVE, THE • 1912 • Raymond Charles • UKN • TWO HUNDRED GUINEAS REWARD
ADVENTURES OF DICK TURPIN -A DEADLY FOE, A PACK OF HOUNDS, AND SOME MERRY MONKS, THE • 1912 • Raymond Charles • UKN
ADVENTURES OF DICK TURPIN -THE GUNPOWDER PLOT, THE • 1912 • Raymond Charles • UKN
ADVENTURES OF DICK TURPIN -THE KING OF HIGHWAYMEN, THE • 1912 • Raymond Charles • UKN
ADVENTURES OF DR. DOLITTLE, THE see **DOKTOR DOLITTLE UND SEINEN TIEREN** • 1928
ADVENTURES OF DOLLY, THE • 1908 • Griffith D. W. • USA
ADVENTURES OF DON COYOTE, THE • 1947 • Le Borg Reginald • USA
ADVENTURES OF DON JUAN, THE • 1948 • Sherman Vincent • USA • NEW ADVENTURES OF DON JUAN, THE (UKN)
ADVENTURES OF DON QUIXOTE see **DON QUICHOTTE** • 1932
ADVENTURES OF DORCAS DENE, DETECTIVE, THE • 1919 • Carlton Frank • SER • UKN
ADVENTURES OF DOROTHY DARE, THE • 1916 • SER • USA
ADVENTURES OF ELIAS MABROUK • 1929 • Pidutti Jordano • LBN
ADVENTURES OF EVE, THE • 1918 • Leigh J. L. V. • SER • UKN
ADVENTURES OF FIFINE, THE • 1909 • *Vitagraph* • USA
ADVENTURES OF FLUTTERGUY, THE • 1976 • Holwill Donald • UKN
ADVENTURES OF FORD FAIRLANE, THE • 1990 • Harlin Renny • USA
ADVENTURES OF FRANK AND JESSE JAMES • 1948 • Brannon Fred C., Canutt Yakima • USA
ADVENTURES OF FRANK MERRIWELL, THE • 1936 • Landers Lew • SRL • USA
ADVENTURES OF FREDDIE • 1977 • Averback Hy • USA • MAGNIFICENT MAGICAL MAGNET OF SANTA MESA
ADVENTURES OF FRONTIER FREEMONT, THE • 1976 • Friedenberg Richard • USA
ADVENTURES OF GALLANT BESS, THE • 1948 • Landers Lew • USA
ADVENTURES OF GERARD, THE • 1970 • Skolimowski Jerzy • UKN, ITL, SWT • AVVENTURE DI GERARD, LE (ITL)
ADVENTURES OF GIL BLAS (USA) see **AVENTURES DE GIL BLAS DE SANTILLANE, LES** • 1955
ADVENTURES OF GIRL REPORTER, THE • 1914 • *Grandin Ethel* • USA
ADVENTURES OF GOOPI AND BAGHI, THE see **GOOPI GYNE O BAGHI BYNE** • 1969
ADVENTURES OF GUCIO THE PENGUIN, THE see **PRZYGODY GUCIA PINGWINA** • 1953
ADVENTURES OF GUSTAVE THE PENGUIN see **PRZYGODY GUCIA PINGWINA** • 1953
ADVENTURES OF HAJJI BABA, THE • 1954 • Weis Don • USA
ADVENTURES OF HAL 5, THE • 1958 • Sharp Don • UKN
ADVENTURES OF HAMBONE AND HILLIE, THE see **HAMBONE AND HILLIE** • 1984
ADVENTURES OF HAWKEYE -INDIAN SCOUT, THE • 1963 • Newfield Sam • USA
ADVENTURES OF HERCULES, THE • 1984 • Cozzi Luigi • ITL • HERCULES II
ADVENTURES OF HUCKLEBERRY FINN • 1985 • Hunt Peter H. • TVM • USA
ADVENTURES OF HUCKLEBERRY FINN, THE • 1938 • Thorpe Richard • USA • HUCKLEBERRY FINN
ADVENTURES OF HUCKLEBERRY FINN, THE • 1960 • Curtiz Michael • USA • HUCKLEBERRY FINN
ADVENTURES OF HUCKLEBERRY FINN, THE • 1981 • Hively Jack • TVM • USA
ADVENTURES OF ICHABOD AND MR. TOAD, THE see **ICHABOD AND MR. TOAD** • 1949
ADVENTURES OF JACK LONDON see **JACK LONDON** • 1942
ADVENTURES OF JACQUES, THE • 1913 • Johnston Lorimer • USA
ADVENTURES OF JANE, THE • 1949 • Whiting Edward J., Goulding Alf • UKN
ADVENTURES OF JANE ARDEN, THE • 1939 • Morse Terry O. • USA
ADVENTURES OF JIMMY, THE • 1950 • Broughton James • SHT • USA
ADVENTURES OF JOE SLUDGE A. B., THE • 1913 • *Searchlight Films* • UKN
ADVENTURES OF JON AND GVENDUR see **AEVINTYRI JONS OG GVENDAR** • 1923
ADVENTURES OF JUAN QUIN QUIN, THE see **AVENTURAS DE JUAN QUIN QUIN, LAS** • 1967
ADVENTURES OF KATHLYN, THE • 1914 • Grandon Francis J. • SRL • USA
ADVENTURES OF KITTY COBB, THE • 1914 • *Swayne Marian* • USA
ADVENTURES OF KITTY O'DAY, THE • 1945 • Beaudine William • USA
ADVENTURES OF LIEUTENANT DARING RN -IN A SOUTH AMERICAN PORT, THE • 1911 • Aylott Dave • UKN
ADVENTURES OF LIEUTENANT PETROSINO, THE • 1912 • *Feature Photoplay Co* • USA
ADVENTURES OF LIMBURGER AND SCHWEITZER, THE • 1914 • *Powers* • USA
ADVENTURES OF LITTLE CRICKET AND PINOCCHIO see **AVENTURAS DE CUCURUCHITO Y PINOCHO** • 1942
ADVENTURES OF LITTLE JOE AND TOM THUMB see **AVENTURAS DE JOSELITO Y PULGARCITO** • 1959
ADVENTURES OF LITTLE TIGER see **TORACHAN NO BOKEN** • 1955
ADVENTURES OF LUCKY PIERRE, THE see **LUCKY PIERRE** • 1961
ADVENTURES OF MANDRIN, THE (USA) see **AVVENTURE DI MANDRIN, LE** • 1952
ADVENTURES OF MARCO POLO, THE • 1938 • Mayo Archie, Ford John • USA
ADVENTURES OF MARK TWAIN, THE • 1944 • Rapper Irving • USA
ADVENTURES OF MARK TWAIN, THE • 1985 • Vinton Will • ANM • USA • COMET QUEST
ADVENTURES OF MARTIN EDEN, THE • 1942 • Salkow Sidney • USA • MARTIN EDEN
ADVENTURES OF MAUD, THE see **LITTLE BIT OF SUGAR FOR THE BIRDS, A** • 1906
ADVENTURES OF MAYA (USA) see **BIENE MAYA, DIE** • 1929
ADVENTURES OF MAZIE, THE • 1926 • Ceder Ralph, Wilkinson Jimmy • SHT • USA
ADVENTURES OF MICHAEL STROGOFF see **SOLDIER AND THE LADY, THE** • 1937
ADVENTURES OF MR. NOBODY HOLMES • 1916 • Moser Frank • ANM • USA
ADVENTURES OF MR. PICKWICK, THE • 1921 • Bentley Thomas • UKN
ADVENTURES OF MR. PROKOUK (USA) see **DOBRODRUZSTVI PANA PROKOUKA** • 1947-58
ADVENTURES OF MR. PRY, THE • 1936 • Tyrlova Hermina, Dodel Karel • ANM • CZC
ADVENTURES OF MR. PUSHER LONG, THE • 1921 • Graeme Kenneth • SER • UKN
ADVENTURES OF MR. WONDERBIRD see **BERGERE ET LE RAMONEUR, LA** • 1953
ADVENTURES OF NELLIE BLY, THE • 1981 • Schellerup Henning • TVM • USA • LEGEND OF NELLIE BLY
ADVENTURES OF NEMO, THE • 1968 • Zeman Karel • CZC
ADVENTURES OF NICK CARTER, THE • 1972 • Krasny Paul • TVM • USA
ADVENTURES OF OCTYABRINI, THE see **POKHOZDENIYA OKTYABRINI** • 1924
ADVENTURES OF P.C.49 -THE CASE OF THE GUARDIAN ANGEL, THE • 1949 • Grayson Godfrey • UKN
ADVENTURES OF P.C. SHARPE, THE • 1911 • Coleby A. E. • UKN
ADVENTURES OF P.C. SHARPE -THE STOLEN CHILD • 1911 • Coleby A. E. • UKN
ADVENTURES OF PARKER, THE • 1946 • Elliott W. F. • UKN
ADVENTURES OF PEG O' THE RING, THE • 1916 • Ford Francis, Jaccard Jacques • SRL • USA • PEG O' THE RING
ADVENTURES OF PICASSO, THE see **PICASSOS AVENTYR** • 1978
ADVENTURES OF PICO AND COLUMBUS, THE • 1990 • Schoemann Michael • ANM • FRG
ADVENTURES OF PIMPLE -PIMPLE P.C., THE • 1913 • Evans Fred • UKN • PIMPLE JOINS THE POLICE FORCE
ADVENTURES OF PIMPLE -THE BATTLE OF WATERLOO • 1913 • Evans Fred, Evans Joe • UKN
ADVENTURES OF PIMPLE -THE INDIAN MASSACRE • 1913 • Evans Fred, Evans Joe • UKN
ADVENTURES OF PIMPLE -THE SPIRITUALIST, THE • 1914 • Evans Fred, Evans Joe • UKN
ADVENTURES OF PIMPLE -TRILBY, THE • 1914 • Evans Fred, Evans Joe • UKN • TRILBY BY PIMPLE AND CO
ADVENTURES OF PINOCCHIO, THE • 1936 • *Cartoni Animati* • ANM • ITL
ADVENTURES OF PINOCCHIO, THE see **PRIKLJUCENIJA BURATINO** • 1959
ADVENTURES OF PINOCCHIO, THE see **AVVENTURE DI PINOCCHIO, LE** • 1968
ADVENTURES OF PINOCCHIO, THE see **PINOCCHIOVA DOBRODRUZSTVI** • 1971
ADVENTURES OF POPEYE • 1935 • Fleischer Dave • ANS • USA
ADVENTURES OF PRINCE ACHMED (USA) see **ABENTEUER DES PRINZEN ACHMED, DIE** • 1926
ADVENTURES OF PRINCE COURAGEOUS, THE • 1921 • Becker Fred G. • USA
ADVENTURES OF QUENTIN DURWARD, THE • 1956 • Thorpe Richard • UKN • QUENTIN DURWARD (USA)
ADVENTURES OF RABBI JACOB, THE see **AVENTURES DE RABBI JACOB, LES** • 1973
ADVENTURES OF RED RYDER • 1940 • Witney William, English John • SRL • USA
ADVENTURES OF REMI, THE see **SANS FAMILLE** • 1957
ADVENTURES OF REX, THE • 1959 • Reeve Leonard • SRL • UKN
ADVENTURES OF REX AND RINTY, THE • 1935 • Beebe Ford, Eason B. Reeves • SRL • USA

ADVENTURES OF REYNARD see **ROMAN DE REYNARD, LE** • 1938
ADVENTURES OF ROBERT MACAIRE, THE (USA) see **AVENTURES DE ROBERT MACAIRE, LES** • 1925
ADVENTURES OF ROBIN HOOD, THE • 1938 • Curtiz Michael, Keighley William • USA
ADVENTURES OF ROBINSON CRUSOE see **ROBINSON CRUSOE** • 1922
ADVENTURES OF ROBINSON CRUSOE, THE see **AVENTURAS DE ROBINSON CRUSOE, LAS** • 1952
ADVENTURES OF ROBINSON CRUSOE, THE SAILOR OF YORK see **DOBRODRUZSTVI ROBINSONA CRUSOE, NAMORNIKA Z YORKU** • 1982
ADVENTURES OF RUSTY, THE • 1945 • Burnford Paul • USA
ADVENTURES OF RUSTY BROWN, THE see **ADVENTURES OF BUSTY BROWN, THE** • 1964
ADVENTURES OF RUTH, THE • 1919-20 • Marshall George • SRL • USA
ADVENTURES OF RUTH, THE • 1927 • Marshall George • USA
ADVENTURES OF SADIE (USA) see **OUR GIRL FRIDAY** • 1953
ADVENTURES OF SANDY MACGREGOR, THE • 1914 • Stow Percy • UKN
ADVENTURES OF SCARAMOUCHE,THE see **SCARAMOUCHE** • 1963
ADVENTURES OF SHEKHCHALLI • 1939 • *Navinchandra* • IND
ADVENTURES OF SHERLOCK HOLMES, THE • 1921 • Elvey Maurice • SER • UKN
ADVENTURES OF SHERLOCK HOLMES, THE • 1939 • Werker Alfred L. • USA • SHERLOCK HOLMES (UKN)
ADVENTURES OF SHORTY, THE • 1914 • Ford Francis • USA
ADVENTURES OF SHORTY HAMILTON, THE • 1917 • SER • USA
ADVENTURES OF SINBAD, THE • 1979 • Slapczynski Richard • ANM • USA
ADVENTURES OF SINBAD, THE (USA) see **SINBAD NO BOKEN** • 1962
ADVENTURES OF SINBAD THE SAILOR, THE see **POHADKY TISICE A JEDNE NOCI** • 1972
ADVENTURES OF SINDBAD, THE see **SHINDOBADDO NO BOKEN** • 1968
ADVENTURES OF SINDBAD THE SAILOR, THE see **PRZYGODY SINDBADA ZEGLARZA** • 1969
ADVENTURES OF SIR GALAHAD • 1949 • Bennet Spencer Gordon • SRL • USA
ADVENTURES OF SLIM AND PIM, THE • 1918 • *Dawson Leslie* • ASS • UKN
ADVENTURES OF SMILIN' JACK • 1943 • Taylor Ray, Collins Lewis D. • SRL • USA
ADVENTURES OF SPORTS BILLY, THE • 1982 • ANM • USA • SPORTS BILLY
ADVENTURES OF STINGAREE, THE • *Kalem* • SRL • USA
ADVENTURES OF SUFFY, THE • 1916 • *Eagle Film* • USA
ADVENTURES OF SUN KUNG see **SONGOKU** • 1959
ADVENTURES OF TAKLA MAKAN see **KIGANJO NO BOKEN** • 1965
ADVENTURES OF TARA PART 1, THE see **PRISON SHIP: THE ADVENTURES OF TARA** • 1987
ADVENTURES OF TARTU • 1943 • Bucquet Harold S. • UKN • TARTU (USA)
ADVENTURES OF TARZAN • 1921 • Hill Robert F. • USA
ADVENTURES OF TEDDY RUXPIN, THE see **TEDDY RUXPIN: THE ADVENTURES OF TEDDY RUXPIN** • 1985
ADVENTURES OF THE ACTION HUNTERS, THE see **ADVENTURE OF THE ACTION HUNTERS, THE** • 1986
ADVENTURES OF THE AMERICAN RABBIT, THE • 1986 • Wolf Fred, Nishiwaza Nobutaka • ANM • USA
ADVENTURES OF THE BENGAL LANCERS see **TRE SERGENTI DEL BENGALA, I** • 1965
ADVENTURES OF THE FLYING CADETS • 1943 • Taylor Ray, Collins Lewis D. • SRL • USA
ADVENTURES OF THE HEROES OF THE NESLE TOWER see **AVENTURES DES HEROS DE LA TOUR DE NESLE** • 1947
ADVENTURES OF THE JOLLY GLOBE TROTTER, THE see **PRZYGODY WESOLEGO OBIEZYSWIATA** • 1968
ADVENTURES OF THE KID AMBASSADOR • 1979 • Atakaiwanwati Panthep, Takeda Kazunari • THL, JPN
ADVENTURES OF THE LITTLE SAILOR, THE • Patrocka Jiri • ANS • CZC
ADVENTURES OF THE MASKED PHANTOM, THE • 1939 • Abbott Charles • USA
ADVENTURES OF THE NICKEL-PLATED FEET, THE see **AVENTURES DES PIED NICKELES, LES** • 1917
ADVENTURES OF THE NIMBLE DOLLAR • 1914 • *Powers* • USA
ADVENTURES OF THE PRINCE AND THE PAUPER, THE see **PRINCE AND THE PAUPER, THE** • 1969
ADVENTURES OF THE QUEEN • 1975 • Rich David Lowell • TVM • USA
ADVENTURES OF THE SPIRIT, THE • 1963 • *Glut Don (P)* • USA
ADVENTURES OF THE WILDERNESS FAMILY, THE • 1976 • Raffill Stewart • USA • WILDERNESS FAMILY, THE
ADVENTURES OF THE WILDERNESS FAMILY PART 2 see **FURTHER ADVENTURES OF THE WILDERNESS FAMILY, PART II** • 1978
ADVENTURES OF THREE NIGHTS, THE • 1913 • *Eiko* • USA
ADVENTURES OF TILL EULENSPIEGEL, THE see **AVENTURES DE TILL L'ESPIEGLE, LES** • 1956
ADVENTURES OF TINTIN: RED RACKHAM'S TREASURE, THE see **TINTIN: RED RACKHAM'S TREASURE** • 1987
ADVENTURES OF TINTIN: THE BLACK ISLAND, THE see **TINTIN: THE BLACK ISLAND** • 1987
ADVENTURES OF TINTIN: THE CALCULUS AFFAIR, THE see **TINTIN: THE CALCULUS AFFAIR**
ADVENTURES OF TINTIN: THE CALCULUS CASE, THE see **TINTIN: THE CALCULUS AFFAIR**
ADVENTURES OF TINTIN: THE CRAB WITH THE GOLDEN CLAWS see **TINTIN ET LE CRABE AUX PINCES D'OR** • 1987
ADVENTURES OF TINTIN: THE LAKE OF SHARKS, THE see **TINTIN ET LE LAC AUX REQUINS** • 1972
ADVENTURES OF TINTIN: THE SECRET OF THE UNICORN see **TINTIN: THE SECRET OF THE UNICORN** • 1987
ADVENTURES OF TINTIN: THE SEVEN CRYSTAL BALLS, THE see **TINTIN: THE SEVEN CRYSTAL BALLS**
ADVENTURES OF TINTIN: THE SHOOTING STAR, THE see **TINTIN: THE SHOOTING STAR** • 1987
ADVENTURES OF TOM JONES, THE see **BAWDY ADVENTURES OF TOM JONES, THE** • 1975
ADVENTURES OF TOM SAWYER, THE • 1938 • Taurog Norman, Potter H. C. • USA
ADVENTURES OF TOM THUMB, JR. • 1940 • Gillett Burt • ANS • USA
ADVENTURES OF TWO SWEDISH EMIGRANTS IN AMERICA, THE see **TVA SVENSKA EMIGRANTERS AVENTYR I AMERIKA** • 1912
ADVENTURES OF ULYSSES, THE see **ODISSEA, L'** • 1911
ADVENTURES OF ULYSSES, THE see **AVVENTURE DI ULISSE, LE** • 1969
ADVENTURES OF WERNER HOLT, THE (UKN) see **ABENTEUER DES WERNER HOLT, DIE** • 1963
ADVENTURES OF WILLIAM TELL see **AVENTURES DE GUILLAUME TELL** • 1898
ADVENTURES OF WILLIAM TELL (USA) see **GUILLAUME TELL ET LE CLOWN** • 1898
ADVENTURES OF WILLIE WOODBINE AND LIGHTNING LARRY -A JOYRIDE TO THE CANNIBAL ISLANDS, THE • 1915 • Aldridge Sidney • UKN
ADVENTURES OF X, THE • 1967 • Newman Michael, Fisher Andrew • UKN
ADVENTURES OF YOUNG DINK STOVER see **HAPPY YEARS, THE** • 1950
ADVENTURES ON THE RYUKYUS see **OGON KUJYAKU-JO** • 1961
ADVENTURES UNDER AND ABOVE • 1975 • Vetrov I. • USS
ADVENTURES WITH THE LYONS • 1954 • Guest Val • SRL • UKN
ADVENTURESS, THE • 1910 • *Essanay* • USA
ADVENTURESS, THE • 1920 • Balshofer Fred J. • USA
ADVENTURESS, THE (USA) see **I SEE A DARK STRANGER** • 1946
ADVENTURESS OF THE CHAMPS-ELYSEES, THE see **AVENTURIERE DES CHAMPS-ELYSEES, L'** • 1956
ADVENTURESS OUTWITTED, AN • 1912 • Stow Percy • UKN
ADVENTUROUS AMBROSE • 1918 • *Swain Mack* • SHT • USA
ADVENTUROUS AUTOMOBILE TRIP, AN see **RAID PARIS - MONTE CARLO EN 2 HEURES, LE** • 1905
ADVENTUROUS BLONDE • 1938 • McDonald Frank • USA
ADVENTUROUS BLONDE see **TORCHY BLANE, THE AMOROUS BLONDE** • 1937
ADVENTUROUS CAPTAIN, THE (USA) see **CAPITAN AVENTURERO, EL** • 1938
ADVENTUROUS KNIGHTS • 1935 • Roberts Charles E. • USA
ADVENTUROUS SEX, THE • 1925 • Giblyn Charles • USA
ADVENTUROUS SOUL, THE • 1927 • Carroll Gene? • USA • ADVENTUROUS SOULS (UKN)
ADVENTUROUS SOULS (UKN) see **ADVENTUROUS SOUL, THE** • 1927
ADVENTUROUS VOYAGE OF "THE ARCTIC", THE • 1903 • Booth W. R. • UKN • TRIP OF THE "ARCTIC", THE ○ VOYAGE OF THE "ARCTIC"; OR, HOW CAPTAIN KETTLE DISCOVERED THE NORTH POLE (USA)
ADVENTUROUS WOMAN see **AVENTURERA** • 1989
ADVENTUROUS YOUTH • 1928 • Godal Edward • UKN
ADVERSARY, THE • 1970 • Klein Larry • USA
ADVERSARY, THE (UKN) see **PRATIDWANDI** • 1970
ADVERSIDAD • 1944 • Iglesias Miguel • SPN
ADVERTISEMENT ANSWERED, AN • 1910 • *Essanay* • USA
ADVERTISEMENT GIRL, THE see **CHICA DE LOS ANUNCIOS, LA** • 1968
ADVERTISEMENTERS • 1916 • *Cooper Claude* • SHT • USA
ADVERTISING DID IT • 1915 • Fielding Romaine • USA
ADVERTISING FOR MAMA • 1911 • *Kalem* • USA
ADVICE TO THE LOVELORN • 1933 • Werker Alfred L. • USA
ADVICE TO THE LOVELORN • 1981 • Falk Harry • TVM • USA
ADVISE AND CONSENT • 1962 • Preminger Otto • USA
ADVISOR, THE • 1915 • King Burton L. • USA
ADVOCATE, THE • 1978 • SAF
ADVOKAT CHUDYCH • 1941 • Slavinsky Vladimir • CZC • LAWYER OF THE POOR, THE
ADVOKATKA VERA • 1937 • Fric Martin • CZC • VERA THE LAWYER
ADWITIYA • 1968 • Chatterjee Nabyendu • IND • IMCOMPARABLE
ADYASAKTI MAHAMAYA • 1968 • Choudhury Purnendu Roy • IND • DURGA AS THE GODDESS OF DESTRUCTION
AEDAL DAAD • 1911 • Gad Urban • FRG • STORE FLYVER, DEN ○ GENEROSITY
AEGEAN SAILOR, THE see **NAFTIS TOU EGEOU, O** • 1968
AEGEAN TRAGEDY, THE see **TRAGODIA TOU AEGAEOU** • 1965
AEGTESKAB OG PIGESJOV • 1914 • Blom August • DNM • MR. KING PAA EVENTYR ○ SURPRISE PACKET, A
AELITA • 1924 • Protazanov Yakov • USS • AELITA: THE REVOLT OF THE ROBOTS ○ REVOLT OF THE ROBOTS
'AELITA, DON'T MOLEST MEN see **AELITA, NE PRISTAVAI K MUZHCHINAM** • 1989
AELITA, NE PRISTAVAI K MUZHCHINAM • 1989 • Natanson Georgi • USS • AELITA, DON'T MOLEST MEN
AELITA: THE REVOLT OF THE ROBOTS see **AELITA** • 1924
AENIGMA • 1987 • Fulci Lucio • ITL
AENNCHEN VON THARAU • 1927 • Neff Wolfgang • FRG
AENNCHEN VON THARAU • 1954 • Schleif Wolfgang • FRG
AERELOSE, DEN • 1916 • Holger-Madsen • DNM • PRISON TAINT, THE ○ INFAMOUS, THE
AERESOPREJSNING, EN • 1914 • Holger-Madsen • DNM • MISUNDERSTOOD
AERIAL ANARCHISTS, THE • 1911 • Booth W. R. • UKN
AERIAL ANTICS see **HOG WILD** • 1930
AERIAL DEVELOPMENT, AN • 1911 • Booth W. R.? • UKN
AERIAL ELOPEMENT, AN • 1909 • Stow Percy • UKN
AERIAL GUNNER • 1943 • Pine William H. • USA
AERIAL INVASION FRUSTRATED • 1915 • Wilson Rex? • UKN
AERIAL JOYRIDE, AN • 1916 • *Plumb And Runt* • USA
AERIAL JOYRIDE, AN • 1917 • Reed Walter C.?, Reed Charles? • SHT • USA
AERIAL MILESTONES • 1948 • Martin-Jones John • DOC • UKN
AERIAL SUBMARINE • 1910 • Booth W. R. • UKN
AERIAL TORPEDO, THE see **AIRSHIP DESTROYER, THE** • 1909
AERIAL VIEW • 1979 • MacGillivray William D. • CND
AERO-ENGINE • 1934 • Elton Arthur • DOC • UKN
AERO-NUT, THE • 1920 • Griffin Frank C. • SHT • USA
AERO-NUTICS • 1953 • Kneitel Seymour • ANS • USA
AEROBICIDE • 1986 • Prior David A. • USA
AERODROME, THE • 1983 • Foster Giles • TVM • UKN
AEROGRAD • 1935 • Dovzhenko Alexander • USS • FRONTIER ○ AIR CITY
AEROGUAPAS, LAS • 1958 • Manzanos Eduardo, Costa Mario • SPN, ITL
AERONAUTICS • 1941 • Corby Francis, Harrison S. B. • SHT • USA
AERONAVE IN FIAMME, L' • 1918 • Campogalliani Carlo • ITL
AEROPLANE ELOPEMENT, AN • 1911 • Humphrey William • USA
AEROPLANE INVENTOR, THE see **OPFINDERS SKAEBNE, EN** • 1911
AEROPLANE LOVE AFFAIR, AN • 1912 • *Pates Gwendoline* • USA
AEROPLANIST'S SECRET, THE • 1910 • *Cosmopolitan* • USA
AEROPUERTO • 1953 • Lucia Luis • SPN
AEROPUERTO see **BARAJAS, AEROPUERTO INTERNACIONAL** • 1950
AERZTE • 1961 • Kohlert Lutz • GDR
AESOP see **EZOP** • 1969
AESOP'S FABLES • 1917 • Estabrook Howard • ANM • USA
AESOP'S FABLES • 1941-45 • Davis Mannie, Donnelly Eddie • ASS • USA
AESOP'S FABLES: FOILING THE FOX • 1950 • Rasinski Connie • ANS • USA
AESOP'S FABLES: GOLDEN EGG GOOSIE • 1951 • Donnelly Eddie • ANS • USA
AESOP'S FABLES: THE MOSQUITO • 1945 • Davis Mannie • ANS • USA
AESOP'S FABLES: THE TIGER KING • 1960 • Rasinski Connie • ANS • USA
AESTHETIC MATCH, AN • 1913 • *Majestic* • USA
AEVENTYRERSKEN • 1914 • Blom August • DNM • EXILED
AEVINTYRI JONS OG GVENDAR • 1923 • Gudmundsson Loftur • ICL • ADVENTURES OF JON AND GVENDUR
AF ELSKOVS NAADE • 1913 • Blom August • DNM • ACQUITTED
AF JORD ER DU KOMMET • 1984 • Vest Nils • DOC • DNM • YOU ORIGINATE FROM THE EARTH
AFACEREA PROTAR • 1956 • Boros Haralambie • RMN • PROTAR AFFAIR
AFANASI NIKITIN • 1957 • *Biswas Anil (M)* • IND
AFAQ • 1973 • Abdes-Salam Shadi • EGY • HORIZONS
AFAR OU LA DERIVE DES CONTINENTS • 1981 • Tazieff Haroun • DOC • FRN
AFERA PLUKOVNIKA REDLA • 1930 • Anton Karl • CZC • SCANDAL OF COLONEL REDL, THE
AFFAEREN BIRTE • 1944 • Lauritzen Lau Jr. • DNM
AFFAEREN I MOLLEBY • 1976 • Hedegaard Tom • DNM
AFFAIR, THE • 1972 • Cates Gilbert • TVM • USA
AFFAIR, THE see **JOEN** • 1959
AFFAIR, THE see **JOEN** • 1967
AFFAIR, THE see **THERE'S ALWAYS VANILLA** • 1972
AFFAIR AT AKITSU, AN see **AKITSU ONSEN** • 1962
AFFAIR AT ISCHIA • 1961 • Weiss Helmut • FRG
AFFAIR AT KAMAKURA see **KURUTTA KAJITSU** • 1956
AFFAIR AT NO. 26, THE • 1915 • Batley Ernest G. • UKN
AFFAIR AT THE NOVELTY THEATRE, THE • 1924 • Croise Hugh • UKN
AFFAIR AT THE VILLA FIORITA, THE see **BATTLE OF THE VILLA FIORITA, THE** • 1965
AFFAIR FOR THE POLICE, AN • 1914 • Humphrey William • USA
AFFAIR IN HAVANA • 1957 • Benedek Laslo • USA
AFFAIR IN LATE AUTUMN, AN see **MAN CHU** • 1983
AFFAIR IN MONTE CARLO (USA) see **24 HOURS OF A WOMAN'S LIFE** • 1952
AFFAIR IN RENO • 1957 • Springsteen R. G. • USA
AFFAIR IN THE MIST see **KIRI ARU JOJI** • 1959
AFFAIR IN THE SNOW see **JUHYO NO YOROMEKI** • 1968
AFFAIR IN TRINIDAD • 1952 • Sherman Vincent • USA
AFFAIR IN VERSAILLES see **SI VERSAILLES M'ETAIT CONTE** • 1955
AFFAIR LAFONT, THE see **CONFLIT** • 1938
AFFAIR OF ART, AN • 1909 • *Edison* • USA
AFFAIR OF DARTMOOR TERRACE, THE see **KENSINGTON MYSTERY, THE** • 1924
AFFAIR OF DRESS, AN • 1914 • Edwin Walter • USA
AFFAIR OF HEARTS, AN • 1910 • Powell Frank?, Griffith D. W.? • USA
AFFAIR OF HONOR, AN • 1913 • *Komic* • USA
AFFAIR OF HONOR, AN see **LOVAGIAS UGY** • 1937
AFFAIR OF HONOUR, AN • 1899 • *Warwick Trading Co* • UKN
AFFAIR OF HONOUR, AN • 1904 • Collins Alf • UKN
AFFAIR OF HONOUR, AN • 1914 • Williamson James • UKN
AFFAIR OF HONOUR, AN • 1922 • Greenwood Edwin • UKN
AFFAIR OF MADAME POMPADOUR, THE (UKN) see **AVVENTURE DI MANDRIN, LE** • 1952
AFFAIR OF OUTPOSTS, AN • 1904 • *Paul R. W.* • UKN
AFFAIR OF STATE, AN (USA) see **ZWEI GIRLS VOM ROTEN STERN** • 1966
AFFAIR OF SUSAN, THE • 1935 • Neumann Kurt • USA
AFFAIR OF THE DESERTED HOUSE, THE • 1915 • *Ridgley Cleo* • USA
AFFAIR OF THE FOLLIES, AN • 1927 • Webb Millard • USA • THREE IN LOVE
AFFAIR OF THE HEART see **LJUBAVNI SLUCAJ ILI TRAGEDIJA SLUZBENICE P.T.T.** • 1967
AFFAIR OF THE HEART see **ONNATACHI NO NIWA** • 1967
AFFAIR OF THE HEART, AN • 1934 • Samuelson G. B. • UKN
AFFAIR OF THE SKIN, AN • 1963 • Maddow Ben • USA • LOVE AS DISORDER
AFFAIR OF THE TERRACE, THE • 1915 • *Wilson Ben* • USA
AFFAIR OF THREE NATIONS, AN • 1915 • Daly Arnold, Miller Ashley • USA

AFFAIR OFF AN EGG, THE • 1910 • Powell Frank, Griffith D. W.? • USA
AFFAIR TO REMEMBER, AN • 1957 • McCarey Leo • USA
AFFAIR WITH A KILLER • 1965 • McCowan George • CND
AFFAIR WITH A STRANGER • 1953 • Rowland Roy • USA
AFFAIRE, L' • 1950 • Reinert Emile Edwin
AFFAIRE, L' • 1955 • Kazansky Gennadi • USS
AFFAIRE BERLINESE see **INTERNO BERLINESE** • 1985
AFFAIRE BLAIREAU, L' • 1931 • Wulschleger Henry • FRN
AFFAIRE BLAIREAU, L' see **NI VU, NI CONNU..** • 1958
AFFAIRE BLUM see **AFFARE BLUM** • 1948
AFFAIRE BOUDJELBANA, L' • 1967 • Riad Mohamed Slimane • SHT • ALG
AFFAIRE BRONSWIK, L' • 1978 • Awad Robert, Leduc Andre • SHT • CND
AFFAIRE BUREAU, L' • 1923 • Osmont Louis • FRN
AFFAIRE CLASSEE • 1932 • Vanel • SHT • FRN
AFFAIRE CLEMENCEAU, L' • 1918 • Serena Gustavo • ITL
AFFAIRE CLEMENCEAU, L' see **PROCESSO CLEMENCEAU, IL** • 1918
AFFAIRE COFFIN, L' • 1980 • Labrecque Jean-Claude • CND • COFFIN AFFAIR, THE
AFFAIRE COQUELET, L' • 1934 • Gourguet Jean • FRN
AFFAIRE CRAZY CAPO, L' • 1944 • Jamain Patrick • FRN, ITL
AFFAIRE DANTON, L' see **DANTON** • 1982
AFFAIRE DE FEMMES, UNE • 1988 • Chabrol Claude • FRN • STORY OF WOMEN, A
AFFAIRE DE LA RUE DE LOURCINE, L' • 1923 • Diamant-Berger Henri • FRN
AFFAIRE DES POISONS, L' • 1955 • Decoin Henri • FRN, ITL • PROCESSO DEI VELENI, IL (ITL) ○ CASE OF POISONS, THE (USA) ○ POISON AFFAIR, THE
AFFAIRE D'HOMMES, UNE • 1980 • Ribowski Nicolas • FRN
AFFAIRE DOMINICI, L' • 1972 • Bernard-Aubert Claude • FRN, ITL
AFFAIRE DREYFUS, L' • 1899 • Melies Georges • FRN • DREYFUS AFFAIR, THE ○ DREYFUS COURT MARTIAL
AFFAIRE DREYFUS, L' • 1902 • Zecca Ferdinand • FRN
AFFAIRE DREYFUS, L' • 1907 • Nonguet Lucien • FRN
AFFAIRE DU COLLIER DE LA REINE, L' • 1912 • de Morlhon Camille • FRN
AFFAIRE DU COLLIER DE LA REINE, L' • 1945 • L'Herbier Marcel, Dreville Jean (U/c) • FRN • QUEEN'S NECKLACE, THE (USA)
AFFAIRE DU COLLIER DE LA REINE, L' see **COLLIER DE LA REINE, LE** • 1929
AFFAIRE DU COURRIER DE LYON, L' • 1923 • Poirier Leon • FRN
AFFAIRE DU COURRIER DE LYON, L' • 1937 • Lehmann Maurice, Autant-Lara Claude • FRN • COURIER OF LYON, THE (USA) ○ AFFAIRE LESURQUES, L' ○ COURRIER DE LYON, LE
AFFAIRE DU GRAND-HOTEL, L' • 1945 • Hugon Andre • FRN
AFFAIRE DU GRAND THEATRE, L' • 1916 • Pouctal Henri • FRN
AFFAIRE DU TRAIN 24, L' • 1923 • Leprieur Gaston • FRN
AFFAIRE D'UNE NUIT, L' • 1960 • Verneuil Henri • FRN • IT HAPPENED ALL NIGHT (USA)
AFFAIRE EST DANS LE SAC, L' • 1932 • Prevert Pierre • FRN • IT'S IN THE BAG (UKN)
AFFAIRE LAFARGE, L' • 1937 • Chenal Pierre • FRN
AFFAIRE LESURQUES, L' see **AFFAIRE DU COURRIER DE LYON, L'** • 1937
AFFAIRE MANET, L' • 1950 • Aurel Jean • SHT • FRN
AFFAIRE MAURIZIUS, L' • 1953 • Duvivier Julien • FRN, ITL • CASO MAURITIUS, IL (ITL) ○ MAURIZIUS CASE, THE (USA) ○ ON TRIAL
AFFAIRE MOLYNEUX, L' see **DROLE DE DRAME** • 1937
AFFAIRE NINA B • 1961 • Siodmak Robert • FRG, FRN • NINA B AFFAIR, THE (USA)
AFFAIRE NO.306 • 1956 • Rybakov Anatoly • USS
AFFAIRE PERSONNELLE, UNE see **LICHNOYE DELO** • 1932
AFFAIRE STEINBERG, L' • 1933 • Peguy Robert • FRN
AFFAIRE SUISSE, L' • 1978 • Ammann Peter • SWT, ITL
AFFAIRE TOURNESOL, L' • Belvision • ANM • FRN
AFFAIRES DE COEUR • 1909 • Cohl Emile • ANS • FRN • AFFAIRS OF HEART
AFFAIRES DE COEUR see **COEUR DE COQ** • 1946
AFFAIRES DU COEUR • 1924 • Ibragimov Azhdar • USS
AFFAIRES PUBLIQUES, LES • 1934 • Bresson Robert • FRN
AFFAIRES SONT LES AFFAIRES, LES • 1942 • Dreville Jean • FRN
AFFAIRS IN THE WALLS see **KABE NO NAKANO HIMEGOTO** • 1965
AFFAIRS OF A GENTLEMAN • 1934 • Marin Edwin L. • USA
AFFAIRS OF A ROGUE (USA) see **FIRST GENTLEMAN, THE** • 1948
AFFAIRS OF A VAMPIRE see **CURSE OF THE UNDEAD** • 1959
AFFAIRS OF ADELAIDE, THE see **BRITANNIA MEWS** • 1948
AFFAIRS OF ANATOL, THE • 1921 • De Mille Cecil B. • USA • PRODIGAL KNIGHT, A (UKN) ○ FIVE KISSES ○ ANATOL
AFFAIRS OF ANNABEL, THE • 1938 • Stoloff Ben • USA
AFFAIRS OF APHRODITE, THE • 1970 • Patrick Alain • USA
AFFAIRS OF CAPPY RICKS • 1937 • Staub Ralph • USA
AFFAIRS OF CELLINI, THE • 1934 • La Cava Gregory • USA • FIREBRAND
AFFAIRS OF DOBIE GILLIS, THE • 1953 • Weis Don • USA
AFFAIRS OF DR. HOLL see **DOKTOR HOLL** • 1951
AFFAIRS OF GERALDINE, THE • 1946 • Blair George • USA
AFFAIRS OF HEART see **AFFAIRES DE COEUR** • 1909
AFFAIRS OF JANICE • 1976 • Colt Zebedy • USA
AFFAIRS OF JIMMY VALENTINE, THE • 1942 • Vorhaus Bernard • USA • UNFORGOTTEN CRIME
AFFAIRS OF JULIE, THE (USA) see **ZURCHER VERLOBUNG, DIE** • 1957
AFFAIRS OF MARTHA, THE • 1942 • Dassin Jules • USA • ONCE UPON A THURSDAY (UKN)
AFFAIRS OF MAUPASSANT, THE • 1938 • Koster Henry • USA
AFFAIRS OF MESSALINA, THE (USA) see **MESSALINA** • 1951
AFFAIRS OF ROBIN HOOD, THE • 1981 • Kanter Richard • USA
AFFAIRS OF SALLY, THE see **FULLER BRUSH GIRL, THE** • 1950
AFFAIRS OF SUSAN, THE • 1945 • Seiter William A. • USA
AFFAMEES, LES • Reinhard Pierre B. • FRN
AFFARE BECKET, L' • 1966 • Civirani Osvaldo • ITL • BECKET AFFAIR, THE (USA)
AFFARE BLUM • 1948 • Engel Erich • GDR • BLUM AFFAIR, THE ○ AFFAIRE BLUM
AFFARE DER BARONESSE ORLOWSKA, DIE • 1923 • *Bukan-Film* • FRG
AFFARE NABOB • 1962 • Habib Ralph • FRG, FRN
AFFARE ROEDERN, DIE • 1944 • Waschneck Erich • FRG
AFFARE SI COMPLICA, L' • 1941 • Faraldo Pier Luigi • ITL
AFFECTED DETECTIVE, THE • 1922 • Haldane Bert • UKN
AFFECTION see **MAMTA** • 1967
AFFECTION see **MAMATHE** • 1968
AFFECTION see **OBICH** • 1973
AFFECTIONATE SHARKS see **TENDRES REQUINS** • 1967
AFFECTIONATELY YOURS • 1941 • Bacon Lloyd • USA
AFFEDILMEYEN SUC • 1968 • Ozer Nazmi • TRK • UNFORGIVEN GUILT, THE
AFFENBRUCKE, DIE • 1927 • Reiniger Lotte • ANS • FRG
AFFENKRANKHEIT, DIE • 1928 • Reiniger Lotte • ANS • FRG
AFFENMENSCH, DER see **APACHENRACHE 4** • 1920
AFFERRA IL TEMPO • 1973 • Branca Antonello • ITL • SEIZE THE TIME
AFFET BENI • 1967 • Gorec Ertem • TRK • FORGIVE ME
AFFET BENI ALLAHIM • 1968 • Figenli Yavuz • TRK • FORGIVE ME, MY GOD
AFFICHE, L' • 1925 • Epstein Jean • FRN
AFFICHE CONTRE AFFICHE • 1972 • Alawiya Burhan • BLG
AFFICHE ROUGE, L' • 1977 • Cassenti Frank • FRN • RED POSTER, THE
AFFICHES ANIMEES, LES • 1908 • *Pathe* • FRN • ANIMATED POSTERS, THE (USA)
AFFICHES EN GOGUETTE, LES • 1906 • Melies Georges • FRN • HILARIOUS POSTERS, THE (USA)
AFFIDAVIT OF MATURITY see **CYROGRAF DOJRZALOSCI** • 1967
AFFINITA ELETTIVE, LE • 1979 • Amico Gianni • ITL
AFFINITIES • 1915 • *Grandin* • USA
AFFINITIES • 1915 • Calvert E. H. • *Essanay* • USA
AFFINITIES • 1922 • Lascelle Ward • USA
AFFISSIONI • 1950 • Bazzoni Luigi, Fenelli Mario • ITL • POSTERS
AFFITTACAMERE, L' • 1976 • Laurenti Mariano • ITL
AFFONDAMENTO DELLA VALIANT, L' (ITL) see **VALIANT, THE** • 1962
AFFRAY OF HONOR, AN • 1913 • *Nestor* • USA
AFFREUX, LES • 1959 • Allegret Marc • FRN
AFFRICA see **GRANDE APPELLO, IL** • 1936
AFGHANISTAN • 1929 • Erofeyev • USS
AFGRUNDEN • 1910 • Gad Urban • DNM • ABYSS, THE
AFGRUNDEN • 1911 • Dinesen Robert, Davidsen Hjalmar • DNM
AFIFE JALE • 1987 • Kaygun Sahin • TRK
AFLAME IN THE SKY • 1927 • McGowan J. P. • USA
AFONYA • 1975 • Daneliya Georgi • USS
AFRA • 1910 • *Cines* • ITL
AFRAH • 1968 • Badrakhan Ahmed • EGY • WEDDING, THE
AFRAH' ASH-SHABAB • 1964 • Salman Mohammed • LBN • FETES DE LA JEUNESSE, LES
AFRAID OF SOMETHING • 1979 • el Alamy Yehya • EGY
AFRAID TO DIE see **KARAKKAZE YARO** • 1960
AFRAID TO BE FALSE • 1917 • *Sims Milton* • SHT • USA
AFRAID TO DANCE • 1988 • Lawrence Denny • ASL • KICK START
AFRAID TO FIGHT • 1922 • Worthington William • USA
AFRAID TO LIVE see **BEKENNTNIS DER INA KAHR, DAS** • 1954
AFRAID TO LOVE • 1925 • West Reginald • UKN
AFRAID TO LOVE • 1927 • Griffith Edward H. • USA
AFRAID TO LOVE see **BEKENNTNIS DER INA KAHR, DAS** • 1954
AFRAID TO LOVE see **SEVMEKTEN KORKUYORUM** • 1968
AFRAID TO TALK • 1932 • Cahn Edward L. • USA
AFRAID TO TALK see **YOUNG FUGITIVES** • 1938
AFRICA • 1930 • Lantz Walter, Nolan William • ANS • USA
AFRICA • 1973 • SAF
AFRICA ABLAZE see **SOMETHING OF VALUE** • 1957
AFRICA ADDIO • 1966 • Prosperi Franco*, Jacopetti Gualtiero • ITL • AFRICA, BLOOD AND GUTS
AFRICA ADVENTURE • 1954 • Ruark Robert C. • DOC • USA
AFRICA AMA • 1971 • Guerrasio Guido, Pellini Oreste, Castiglioni Alfredo, Castiglioni Angelo • DOC • ITL
AFRICA BEFORE DARK • 1928 • Disney Walt • ANS • USA
AFRICA, BLOOD AND GUTS see **AFRICA ADDIO** • 1966
AFRICA DANCES see **AFRIKA TANZT** • 1967
AFRICA D'OGGI see **STREGONI IN TIGHT** • 1965
AFRICA EROTICA • 1970 • Sulistrowski Zygmunt • USA • HAPPENING IN AFRICA ○ KAREN, THE LOVEMAKER
AFRICA EXPRESS see **AFRICAN EXPRESS** • 1975
AFRICA MONOGATARI see **AFURIKA MONOGATARI** • 1981
AFRICA NERA AFRICA ROSSO • 1977 • Lizzani Carlo • MTV • ITL
AFRICA NO TORI • 1975 • Isomi Tadahiko • JPN • BIRD FROM AFRICA, THE
AFRICA NUDA, AFRICA VIOLENTA • 1974 • Gervasi Mario • ITL
AFRICA ON THE RHINE • 1988 • Seck Pape Badara • SNL, FRG
AFRICA ON THE SEINE see **AFRIQUE SUR SEINE** • 1955
AFRICA SCREAMS • 1949 • Barton Charles T. • USA
AFRICA SEGRETA • 1969 • Guerrasio Guido, Pellini Oreste, Castiglioni Alfredo, Castiglioni Angelo • DOC • ITL • SECRET AFRICA
AFRICA SEXY • 1963 • Montero Roberto Bianchi • DOC • ITL
AFRICA SHAKES • 1966 • SAF
AFRICA SOTTO I MARI • 1953 • Roccardi Giovanni • ITL • WOMAN OF THE RED SEA (UKN)
AFRICA SPEAKS • 1930 • Hoefler Paul L., Fuller Walter • DOC • USA
AFRICA SQUAWKS • 1939 • Rasinski Connie • ANS • USA
AFRICA SQUEAKS • 1932 • *Iwerks Ub (P)* • ANS • USA
AFRICA SQUEAKS • 1940 • Clampett Robert • ANS • USA
AFRICA STORY see **AFURIKA MONOGATARI** • 1981
AFRICA -TEXAS STYLE • 1967 • Marton Andrew • UKN, USA • COWBOY IN AFRICA
AFRICAIN, L' • 1982 • de Broca Philippe • FRN • AFRICAN, THE
AFRICAN, THE see **AFRICAIN, L'** • 1982
AFRICAN ADVENTURE • 1971 • *Stouffer Marty (P)* • DOC • USA
AFRICAN ALPHABET (USA) see **A.B.C. STAVELEG I AFRIKA** • 1963
AFRICAN AWAKENING • 1962 • Hopkinson Peter • UKN
AFRICAN DIARY • 1945 • Kinney Jack • ANS • USA
AFRICAN DREAM, AN • 1988 • Smallcombe John • SAF
AFRICAN ELEPHANT, THE • 1971 • Trevor Simon • DOC • USA • KING ELEPHANT
AFRICAN EXPRESS • 1975 • Lupo Michele • ITL, FRG • AFRICA EXPRESS ○ TROPICAL EXPRESS
AFRICAN FURY see **SKABENGA** • 1953
AFRICAN FURY (USA) see **CRY, THE BELOVED COUNTRY** • 1952
AFRICAN HOLIDAY • 1937 • Pearson Harry • USA • JUNGLE ADVENTURE
AFRICAN HUNT • 1912 • Rainey Paul • DOC • USA
AFRICAN IMAGE • 1975 • Boughedir Ferid • DOC • TNS
AFRICAN IN LONDON, AN • 1941 • Pearson George • DCS • UKN
AFRICAN JUNGLE • 1924 • Lantz Walter • ANS • USA
AFRICAN JUNGLE HUNT • 1957 • Rasinski Connie • ANS • USA
AFRICAN LION, THE • 1955 • Algar James • DOC • USA
AFRICAN LIONS AND AMERICAN BEAUTIES • 1919 • Fishback Fred C. • SHT • USA
AFRICAN MANHUNT • 1955 • Friedman Seymour • USA
AFRICAN PARADISE • 1942 • *Johnson Osa (P)* • USA
AFRICAN QUEEN, THE • 1952 • Huston John • UKN
AFRICAN QUEEN, THE • 1976 • Sarafian Richard C. • TVM • USA
AFRICAN RAGE see **TIGERS DON'T CRY** • 1976
AFRICAN RUN, THE see **TUXEDO WARRIOR** • 1985
AFRICAN SAFARI • 1968 • Shanin Ronald E. • DOC • USA • RIVERS OF FIRE AND ICE, THE
AFRICAN SANCTUS • Fanshawe David • USA
AFRICAN SICKNESS see **MAL D'AFRICA** • 1967
AFRICAN STORY • 1971 • Girolami Marino • ITL
AFRICAN TIMBER • 1989 • Bringmann Peter F. • FRG
AFRICAN TREASURE • 1952 • Beebe Ford • USA • BOMBA AND THE AFRICAN TREASURE (UKN)
AFRICANUS SEXUALIS see **BLACK IS BEAUTIFUL** • 1970
AFRIKA! • 1972 • SAF
AFRIKA • 1974 • Cavallone Alberto • ITL
AFRIKA TANZT • 1967 • von Collande Volker, Lind Klaus, Triyandafilidis Anton • FRG • AFRICA DANCES
AFRIKANDER GIRL, AN • 1912 • Noy Wilfred • UKN
AFRIQUE LIBRE • 1967 • Portugais Louis, Beaudet Marc • DOC • CND
AFRIQUE NOIRE D'HIER A DEMAIN • 1963-64 • Regnier Michel • DSS • CND
AFRIQUE SAFARI • 1972 • de Almeida Manuel Faria • SHT • PRT
AFRIQUE SUR SEINE • 1955 • Vieyra Paulin • SNL • AFRICA ON THE SEINE
AFRIT AM ABDU • Fawzi Hussein • EGY • UNCLE ABDU'S GHOST
AFRIT MERATI • 1968 • Wahab Fatin Abdel • EGY • MY WIFE'S SPIRIT ○ IFRITU 'IMRA'ATI
AFRIT SAMARA • 1959 • Reda Hassan • EGY • GHOST OF SAMARA, THE
AFRITET ISMAIL YASSINE • 1954 • el Saifi Hassan • EGY • ISMAIL YASSINE AND THE GHOST
AFRO-AMERICAN ARTIST, THE • 1976 • *Moss Carlton* • DOC • USA
AFRO-AMERICAN MUSIC: ITS HERITAGE • 1960 • Galanty Sidney • SHT • USA
AFRO-AMERICAN WORKSONGS IN A TEXAS PRISON • 1956 • Seeger Pete • USA
AFRODHITI • 1968 • Lois Giorgos • GRC • APHRODITE
AFRODITE, DEA DELL'AMORE • 1958 • Bonnard Mario • ITL • APHRODITE, GODDESS OF LOVE (USA)
AFSAR • 1950 • *Burman S. D. (M)* • IND
AFSCHEID, HET • 1967 • Verhavert Roland • BLG • FAREWELL, THE ○ ADIEUX, LES ○ FAREWELLS
AFSKEDENS TIME • 1973 • Holst Per • DNM • SACKED!
AFSPORET • 1942 • Ipsen Bodil, Lauritzen Lau Jr. • DNM
AFSPRAAK, DIE • 1974 • SAF
AFSPRAAK IN DIE KALAHARI • 1973 • SAF
AFTENLANDET • 1976 • Watkins Peter • DNM • EVENING LAND
AFTER see **DESPUES DE..** • 1981
AFTER A LIFETIME • 1971 • Loach Kenneth • UKN
AFTER A MILLION • 1924 • Nelson Jack • USA
AFTER A NIGHT OF LOVE (USA) see **DOPO UNA NOTTE D'AMORE** • 1935
AFTER ALL • 1912 • Salter Harry • USA
AFTER ALL see **NEW MORALS FOR OLD** • 1932
AFTER BEDTIME • 1920 • Frazee Edwin • SHT • USA
AFTER BUSINESS HOURS • 1925 • St. Clair Malcolm • USA
AFTER COOK • 1969 • Murray Don* • ASL
AFTER DARK • 1915 • Buckland Warwick • UKN
AFTER DARK • 1915 • Thompson Frederick A. • USA
AFTER DARK • 1923 • Noble Jack? • USA • HOODED MOB, THE ○ MEN IN MASKS ○ LAW AND ORDER
AFTER DARK • 1924 • Bentley Thomas • UKN
AFTER DARK • 1924 • Chapin James • USA
AFTER DARK • 1932 • Parker Albert • UKN
AFTER DARK see **AFTER DARKNESS** • 1985
AFTER DARK, MY SWEET • 1990 • Foley James • USA
AFTER DARK; OR, THE POLICEMAN AND HIS LANTERN • 1902 • Smith G. A. • UKN
AFTER DARKNESS • 1985 • Othenin-Giraud Dominique, Guerrez Sergio • UKN, SWT • NACH DER FINSTERNIS ○ AFTER DARK
AFTER DEATH (USA) see **DOPO LA MORTE** • 1913
AFTER EIGHT.. FOREVER see **SONHO DE VALSA** • 1988
AFTER FIVE • 1915 • Apfel Oscar • USA

AFTER FOOD OF THE GODS see **FOOD OF THE GODS II** • 1988
AFTER GIORGIONE • 1975 • Le Grice Malcolm • UKN
AFTER GRAD WITH DAD • 1980 • Egoyan Atom • CND
AFTER HENRY • 1918 • Drew Sidney, Drew Sidney Mrs. • SHT • USA
AFTER HER DOUGH • 1914 • *Tincher Fay* • USA
AFTER HER MILLIONS • 1915 • Lehrman Henry • USA
AFTER HIS OWN HEART • 1919 • Franklin Harry L. • USA
AFTER HOURS • 1985 • Scorsese Martin • USA
AFTER LAUGHTER • 1981 • Vanderbeek Stan • USA
AFTER LEONARDO • 1973 • Le Grice Malcolm • UKN
AFTER LESLIE WHEELER • 1973 • Le Grice Malcolm • UKN
AFTER LIFE see **AFTERLIFE** • 1978
AFTER LUMIERE • 1974 • Le Grice Malcolm • UKN
AFTER MANET • 1975 • Le Grice Malcolm • UKN
AFTER MANY DAYS • 1912 • *Dalberg Camilla* • USA
AFTER MANY DAYS • 1919 • Morgan Sidney • UKN
AFTER MANY YEARS • 1908 • Griffith D. W. • USA
AFTER MANY YEARS • 1910 • *Selig* • USA
AFTER MANY YEARS • 1912 • *Imp* • USA
AFTER MANY YEARS • 1912 • *Vitagraph* • USA
AFTER MANY YEARS • 1930 • Huntington Lawrence • UKN
AFTER MARRIAGE • 1925 • Dawn Norman • USA
AFTER MEIN KAMPF • 1961 • Porter Ralph • DOC • USA • RAVAGED
AFTER MIDNIGHT • 1921 • Ince Ralph • USA
AFTER MIDNIGHT • 1927 • Bell Monta • USA
AFTER MIDNIGHT see **NEW YORK AFTER MIDNIGHT** • 1983
AFTER MIDNIGHT (UKN) see **AFTER MIDNIGHT WITH BOSTON BLACKIE** • 1943
AFTER MIDNIGHT (UKN) see **CAPTAIN CAREY, U.S.A.** • 1950
AFTER MIDNIGHT WITH BOSTON BLACKIE • 1943 • Landers Lew • USA • AFTER MIDNIGHT (UKN)
AFTER MR. SAM • 1974 • Hammond Arthur • DOC • CND
AFTER MY LAST MOVE see **NACH MEINEM LETZTEN UMZUG** • 1970
AFTER NIGHTFALL see **GREAT JEWEL ROBBER, THE** • 1950
AFTER NINE HUNDRED DAYS • 1953 • Huisken Joop • DOC • GDR
AFTER OFFICE HOURS • 1932 • Bentley Thomas • UKN
AFTER OFFICE HOURS • 1935 • Leonard Robert Z. • USA
AFTER ONE HUNDRED YEARS • 1911 • *Selig* • USA
AFTER ONE YEAR see **NACH EINEM JAHR** • 1963
AFTER PILKINGTON • 1988 • Morahan Christopher • TVM • UKN
AFTER PRISON, WHAT? • Weyman Ron • DCS • CND
AFTER PROUST • 1970 • McGill Chris • SHT • ASL
AFTER RAIN, CLEAR SKY • 1931 • CHN
AFTER SCHOOL • 1912 • Dwan Allan • USA
AFTER SCHOOL see **VERBRECHEN NACH SCHULSCHLUSS** • 1959
AFTER SCHOOL see **PRIVATE TUTOR** • 1988
AFTER SEBEN • 1929 • Kaufman S. Jay • SHT • USA
AFTER SIX DAYS • 1922 • Vay Armando, Gariazzo Antonio • USA
AFTER THE ARGUMENT • 1986 • Ball Christopher • SHT • CND
AFTER THE AUTUMN LEAVES see **RUSKAN JALKEEN** • 1979
AFTER THE AXE • 1981 • Gunnarsson Sturla • CND
AFTER THE BACHELOR'S BALL • 1909 • *Lubin* • USA
AFTER THE BALL • 1910 • *La Badie Florence* • USA
AFTER THE BALL • 1914 • Kingsley Pierce • USA
AFTER THE BALL • 1921 • Parkinson H. B. • SHT • UKN
AFTER THE BALL • 1924 • Fitzgerald Dallas M. • USA
AFTER THE BALL • 1929 • Fleischer Dave • ANS • USA
AFTER THE BALL • 1932 • Rosmer Milton • UKN
AFTER THE BALL • 1956 • Smith Paul J. • ANS • USA
AFTER THE BALL • 1957 • Bennett Compton • UKN
AFTER THE BALL see **APRES LE BAL** • 1897
AFTER THE BALL see **AFTER THE BALL WAS OVER** • 1969
AFTER THE BALL WAS OVER • 1914 • Kellino W. P. • UKN
AFTER THE BALL WAS OVER • 1969 • *Noland Alice* • USA • AFTER THE BALL
AFTER THE BALLED-UP BALL • 1917 • Howe J. A. • SHT • USA
AFTER THE BATTLE • 1916 • *Forde Victoria* • SHT • USA
AFTER THE BAWL • 1919 • Seiter William A. • SHT • USA
AFTER THE BOMB • Brzezinski Tony • USA
AFTER THE CIRCUS • 1919 • Kellette John William • SHT • USA
AFTER THE CLUB • 1906 • Mottershaw Frank • UKN
AFTER THE DANCE • 1935 • Bulgakov Leo • USA
AFTER THE DELUGE see **DESPUES DEL DILUVIO** • 1968
AFTER THE EARTHQUAKE • 1935 • *Sircar B. N. (P)* • IND
AFTER THE EARTHQUAKE • Portillo Lourdes, Serrano Nina, Perez Luis • DOC • USA
AFTER THE ECLIPSE • 1967 • Sukhdev S. • DOC • IND
AFTER THE FALL see **PO UPADKU** • 1989
AFTER THE FALL OF MAN see **JALKEEN SYNTIINLANKEEMUKSEN** • 1953
AFTER THE FALL OF NEW YORK • 1983 • Dolman Martin • ITL, FRN • 2019: THE FALL OF NEW YORK ○ 2019: DOPO CAPUTA DI NEW YORK
AFTER THE FANCY DRESS BALL • 1907 • Williamson James? • UKN
AFTER THE FLOOD see **DESPUES DEL DILUVIO** • 1968
AFTER THE FOG • 1929 • De Cordova Leander • USA
AFTER THE FOX (UKN) see **CACCIA ALLA VOLPE** • 1965
AFTER THE HONEYMOON • 1912 • Henderson Dell • USA
AFTER THE HONEYMOON • 1913 • Sturgeon Rollin S. • USA
AFTER THE MASSACRE • 1913 • *Reliance* • USA
AFTER THE MATINEE • 1906 • Fitzhamon Lewin • UKN
AFTER THE MATINEE • 1918 • *Ruge Billy* • SHT • USA
AFTER THE 'OLIDAY • 1904 • Fitzhamon Lewin • UKN
AFTER THE PLAY • 1916 • Worthington William • SHT • USA
AFTER THE PROMISE • 1987 • Greene David • TVM • USA
AFTER THE RAIN • 1989 • Thompson Harry • USA • PASSAGE, THE
AFTER THE REHEARSAL • 1984 • Bergman Ingmar • MTV • SWD
AFTER THE REWARD • 1912 • *Essanay* • USA
AFTER THE SENTENCE see **PO WYROKU** • 1967
AFTER THE SHOW • 1921 • De Mille William C. • USA
AFTER THE STORM • 1915 • Eason B. Reeves • *American* • USA
AFTER THE STORM • 1915 • Vale Travers? • *Ab* • USA
AFTER THE STORM • 1928 • Seitz George B. • USA
AFTER THE STORM • 1956 • Knorre F., Pentzlin E. • USS
AFTER THE STORM see **DESERT GOLD** • 1914
AFTER THE STORM see **DESPUES DE LA TORMENTA** • 1988
AFTER THE THIN MAN • 1936 • Van Dyke W. S. • USA
AFTER THE VERDICT • 1929 • Galeen Henrik • UKN
AFTER THE VOTE • 1969 • Kreps Bonnie • CND
AFTER THE WAR • 1918 • De Grasse Joseph • USA
AFTER THE WELSH RABBIT • 1913 • Williams C. Jay • USA
AFTER THIRTY • 1920 • *Cumberland John* • SHT • USA
AFTER TOMORROW • 1932 • Borzage Frank • USA
AFTER TONIGHT • 1933 • Archainbaud George • USA • SEALED LIPS (UKN)
AFTER TWENTY YEARS • 1911 • *Fahrney Milton* • USA
AFTER TWENTY YEARS • 1915 • *Mackley Arthur* • USA
AFTER YEARS OF STUDY see **GAKUSO O IDETE** • 1925
AFTER YESTERDAY, BEFORE TOMORROW see **DUNDEN SONRA, YARINDAN ONCE** • 1988
AFTER YOU, COMRADE • 1966 • Uys Jamie • SAF • ALL THE WAY TO PARIS
AFTER YOUR OWN HEART • 1921 • Marshall George • USA
AFTERGLOW • 1923 • Samuelson G. B., Summers Walter • UKN
AFTERLIFE • 1978 • Patel Ishu • ANS • CND • APRES LA VIE ○ AFTER LIFE
AFTERMATH • 1914 • *Famous Players* • USA
AFTERMATH • 1979 • Barkett Steve • USA • ZOMBIE AFTERMATH
AFTERMATH • 1980 • Brakhage Stan • SHT • USA
AFTERMATH see **DDANACH** • 1970
AFTERMATH, THE • 1914 • Ayres Sydney • *American* • USA
AFTERMATH, THE • 1986 • van Eyck Robert • BLG
AFTERMATH OF WAR, THE see **TOKYO SHIGAISEN** • 1967
AFTERMATH (USA) see **BRENNENDE GRENZE** • 1926
AFTERNOON • 1965 • Warhol Andy • USA
AFTERNOON • 1969 • Zafranovic Lordan • SHT • YGS
AFTERNOON AFFAIR, AN see **SZERETOK** • 1984
AFTERNOON DELIGHT see **AFTERNOON DELIGHTS** • 1981
AFTERNOON DELIGHTS • 1981 • Evans Warren • USA • AFTERNOON DELIGHT
AFTERNOON FULL OF ADVENTURES, AN • Homoki-Nagy Istvan • HNG
AFTERNOON IN THE VILLAGE, AN see **DELUTAN KOPPANYMONOSTORBAN, EGY** • 1955
AFTERNOON MIRACLE, AN • 1920 • Smith David • SHT • USA
AFTERNOON OF A FAUN • 1952 • Richter Hans • AUS
AFTERNOON OF A PHEASANT see **POSLIJEPODNE JEDNOG FAZANA** • 1973
AFTERNOON OF WAR see **IN THE AFTERNOON OF WAR** • 1981
AFTERNOON RENDEZVOUS see **HIRUSAGARI NO AIBIKI** • 1967
AFTERSHOCK • 1989 • Harris Frank • USA • IF WE KNEW THEN
AFTERWARD...THE ADVENTURES OF A DOLL • 1957 • Winzentsen Franz • ANS • FRG
AFTERWARDS • 1928 • Butts W. Lawson • UKN
AFTERWARDS (UKN) see **THEIR BIG MOMENT** • 1934
AFTI I YI INE DIKI MAS • 1967 • Grigoriou Grigoris • GRC • THIS EARTH BELONGS TO US
AFTI POU DHEN LIYISE • 1967 • Kosteletos Odisseas • GRC • WOMAN'S VICTORY, A ○ SHE WHO DID NOT BEND
AFURIKA MONOGATARI • 1981 • Hani Susumu • JPN • GREEN HORIZON, THE ○ TALE OF AFRICA, A ○ AFRICA STORY ○ AFRICA MONOGATARI ○ GREEN HORIZONS
AFYON-OPIUM see **AFYON-OPPIO** • 1972
AFYON-OPPIO • 1972 • Baldi Ferdinando • ITL • SICILIAN CONNECTION, THE ○ AFYON-OPIUM
AFZIEN • 1985 • Verhage Gerrard • NTH
AFZWAAIEN • 1966 • Ceulemans J. • BLG
AG AND BERT • 1929 • Phillips Bertram • UKN
AGA DUSEN KADIN • 1967 • Ozer Nazmi • TRK • WOMAN IN THE NET, THE
AGADA • 1985 • Kim Hyeong-Myeong • SKR • AGATHA
AGADIR, MINUIT MOINS LE QUART • 1959 • Cauvin Andre • BLG
AGAIN • 1971 • Buchs Julio • SPN
AGAIN • 1975 • Kidder Margot • USA
AGAIN A LOVE STORY see **HOMME QUI ME PLAIT, L'** • 1969
AGAIN FOREVER • 1985 • Kotler Oded • ISR
AGAIN ONE NIGHT see **ARU YO FUTATABI** • 1956
AGAIN -PIONEERS! • 1950 • Beaudine William • USA
AGAIN THE WIZARD see **NEUES VOM HEXER** • 1965
AGAIN TO THE FRONT • 1952 • NKR
AGAIN (UKN) see **CALDI AMORE DI UNA MINORENNE, I** • 1969
AGAINST A CROOKED SKY • 1975 • Bellamy Earl • USA
AGAINST ALL see **PROTI VSEM** • 1957
AGAINST ALL FLAGS • 1952 • Sherman George • USA
AGAINST ALL OBSTACLES see **EDHIR NEECHAL** • 1968
AGAINST ALL ODDS • 1924 • Mortimer Edmund • USA
AGAINST ALL ODDS • 1984 • Hackford Taylor • USA
AGAINST ALL ODDS see **TODESKUSS DES DR. FU MAN CHU, DER** • 1968
AGAINST DESPERATE ODDS • 1913 • *Kalem* • USA
AGAINST HEAVY ODDS • 1914 • *Gebhardt George* • USA
AGAINST HEAVY ODDS • 1916 • *Pathe* • USA
AGAINST KING see **PROTIV KINGA** • 1975
AGAINST THE GRAIN • 1918 • Edwards Henry • UKN
AGAINST THE GRAIN • 1980 • Burns Tim • ASL
AGAINST THE LAW • 1913 • *Gem* • USA
AGAINST THE LAW • 1934 • Hillyer Lambert • USA • URGENT CALL (UKN) ○ POLICE AMBULANCE
AGAINST THE RULES • 1931 • Heath Arch B. • USA
AGAINST THE TIDE • 1912 • Collins Edwin J. • UKN
AGAINST THE TIDE • 1937 • Bryce Alex • UKN
AGAINST THE WIND • 1948 • Crichton Charles • UKN
AGAINST WIND AND TIDE: A CUBAN ODYSSEY • 1981 • Burroughs Jim • DOC • USA
AGAMEMNON THE LOVER • 1971 • Greenwald Barry (c/d) • CND
AGAMI • 1984 • Islam Morshedul • SHT • BNG
AGAPI KE EMA • 1968 • Foskolos Nikos • GRC • LOVE AND BLOOD
AGAPI MAS, I • 1968 • Karayannis Kostas • GRC • OUR LOVE
AGAPITIKOS TIS VOSKOPOULAS, O • 1956 • Dimopoulos Dinos • GRC • AMANT DE LA BERGERE, L'
AGARRANDO PAREJO • 1963 • Salvador Jaime • MXC
AGATHA • 1979 • Apted Michael • UKN, USA
AGATHA see **AGATHA ET LES LECTURES ILLIMITEES** • 1981
AGATHA see **AGADA** • 1985
AGATHA CHRISTIE'S A CARIBBEAN MYSTERY see **CARIBBEAN MYSTERY, A** • 1983
AGATHA CHRISTIE'S DEAD MAN'S FOLLY • 1986 • Donner Clive • TVM • USA • DEAD MAN'S FOLLY
AGATHA CHRISTIE'S ENDLESS NIGHT see **ENDLESS NIGHT** • 1971
AGATHA CHRISTIE'S MURDER IN THREE ACTS • 1986 • Nelson Gary • TVM • USA
AGATHA CHRISTIE'S MURDER WITH MIRRORS see **MURDER WITH MIRRORS** • 1985
AGATHA CHRISTIE'S ORDEAL BY INNOCENCE see **ORDEAL BY INNOCENCE** • 1984
AGATHA CHRISTIE'S SPARKLING CYANIDE see **SPARKLING CYANIDE** • 1983
AGATHA CHRISTIE'S THIRTEEN AT DINNER see **THIRTEEN AT DINNER** • 1985
AGATHA ET LES LECTURES ILLIMITEES • 1981 • Duras Marguerite • FRN • AGATHA
AGATHA, LASS DAS MORDEN SEIN • 1960 • Haugk Dietrich • FRG
AGATON AND FINA see **AGATON OCH FINA** • 1912
AGATON OCH FINA • 1912 • Jaenzon Julius • SWD • AGATON AND FINA
AGATON SAX • 1977 • Gissberg Jan • SWD
AGATON SAX OCH BYKOPINGS GASTABUD • 1976 • Lasseby Stig • SWD
AGAZA FI GAHANIM see **IGAZA FI GEHANNAM** • 1949
AGAZAT NUCF SANA • 1962 • Ridha Ali • EGY • SIX MOIS DE VACANCES
AGAZET GHARAM • 1967 • Zulficar Mahmoud • EGY • LOVE VACATION
AGE 18 see **USIA 18** • 1980
AGE DE CHAISE, L' • 1979 • Bedard Jean-Thomas • CND • CHAIRMEN
AGE DE LA MACHINE, L' • 1978 • Carle Gilles • DOC • CND
AGE DE LA TERRE, L' see **IDADE DA TERRA, A** • 1981
AGE DE L'AMOUR, L' (FRN) see **ETA DELL'AMORE, L'** • 1953
AGE DES ARTERES • 1959 • Berr • SHT • FRN
AGE DES MACHINES, L' • 1950 • Novik William • SHT • FRN
AGE D'OR, L' • 1930 • Bunuel Luis • FRN • GOLDEN AGE, THE (USA) ○ AGE OF GOLD, THE
AGE D'OR, L' • 1940 • de Limur Jean • FRN
AGE D'OR A VELO, L' • 1983 • Payer Roch Christophe • MTV • CND
AGE DU CASTOR, L' see **AGE OF THE BEAVER** • 1951
AGE DU COEUR, L' • 1906 • Heuze Andre • FRN
AGE DU METAL, L' • 1962 • Regnier Michel • DCS • CND
AGE FOR LOVE, THE • 1931 • Lloyd Frank • USA • AGE OF LOVE
AGE INGRAT, L' • 1964 • Grangier Gilles • FRN
AGE OF 18, THE see **USIA 18** • 1980
AGE OF ASSASSINS, THE see **SATSUJINKYOJIDAI** • 1967
AGE OF BAMBOO AT MENTAWEI, THE see **BAMBUALDERN PA MENTAWEI** • 1938
AGE OF CONSENT • 1932 • La Cava Gregory • USA • ARE THESE OUR CHILDREN? (UKN) ○ FRATERNITY HOUSE
AGE OF CONSENT • 1969 • Powell Michael • ASL
AGE OF CURIOSITY, THE • 1963 • *Farrow Mia* • SHT • USA
AGE OF DAYDREAMING, THE see **ALMODOZASOK KORA** • 1964
AGE OF DESIRE, THE • 1923 • Borzage Frank • USA
AGE OF GOLD, THE see **AGE D'OR, L'** • 1930
AGE OF ILLUSIONS see **ALMODOZASOK KORA** • 1964
AGE OF INDISCRETION • 1935 • Ludwig Edward • USA
AGE OF INDISCRETION, THE see **ETA DELL'AMORE, L'** • 1953
AGE OF INFIDELITY (USA) see **MUERTE DE UN CICLISTA** • 1955
AGE OF INNOCENCE • 1977 • Bridges Alan • CND, UKN • RAGTIME SUMMER ○ SUMMER RAIN
AGE OF INNOCENCE, THE • 1924 • Ruggles Wesley • USA
AGE OF INNOCENCE, THE • 1934 • Moeller Philip • USA
AGE OF INVENTION, THE • 1984 • Kish Albert • DOC • CND
AGE OF LOVE see **AGE FOR LOVE, THE** • 1931
AGE OF MACKENZIE KING, THE • 1959 • Leiterman Douglas • CND
AGE OF PEACE, THE see **ETA DELLA PACE, L'** • 1974
AGE OF REPTILES, THE • 1960 • *Glut Don (P)* • SHT • USA
AGE OF SUCCESS • 1988 • Chang Sun-Woo • SKR
AGE OF THE BEAVER • 1951 • Low Colin • CND • AGE DU CASTOR, L'
AGE OF THE EARTH, THE see **IDADE DA TERRA, A** • 1981
AGE OF THE GODS see **NIPPON TANJO** • 1959
AGE OF THE MEDICI (USA) see **ETA DI COSIMO DE' MEDICI, L'** • 1972
AGE OF THE SEA, THE see **ILIKIA TIS THALASSAS, I** • 1979
AGE OF UNEASINESS, THE see **ETA DEL MALESSERE, L'** • 1968
AGE OF YOUTH (USA) see **GODY MOLODYYE** • 1959
AGE TENDRE, L' • 1974 • Laumet • MTV • FRN
AGE VS. YOUTH • 1911 • Saiter Harry • USA
AGED FEET IN A CARPET HALL • 1970 • Channell David • UKN
AGEING see **OUDER WORDEN** • 1975
AGELESS SEX, THE • 1914 • Lambart Harry • USA
AGEMAN • 1990 • Itami Juzo • JPN
AGENCE BEAUSOLEIL • 1974 • Brault Francois, Gauvreau J. • SHT • CND
AGENCE CACAHUETE • 1912-14 • *Raimu* • FRN
AGENCE MATRIMONIALE • 1952 • Le Chanois Jean-Paul • FRN
AGENCY • 1979 • Kaczender George • CND
AGENT 000 AND THE CURVES OF DEATH • 1983 • Makinen Visa • FNL
AGENT 00 SEXY see **AGENTE 00 SEXY** • 1968

AGENT 003, OPERACION ATLANTIDA (SPN) see **AGENTE SO 3 OPERAZIONE ATLANTIDE** • 1965

AGENT 3S3, MASSACRE IN THE SUN see **AGENTE 3S3 MASSACRO AL SOLE** • 1966

AGENT 3S3: PASSPORT TO HELL (USA) see **AGENTE 3S3, PASSAPORTO PER L'INFERNO** • 1965

AGENT 8 3/4 (USA) see **HOT ENOUGH FOR JUNE** • 1963

AGENT 36-24-36 see **COME SPY WITH ME** • 1967

AGENT 38-24-36 (THE WARM-BLOODED SPY) see **RAVISSANTE IDIOTE, UNE** • 1964

AGENT 069 • 1970 • *Stacey Dist.* • USA

AGENT 69 see **I SKYTTENS TEGN** • 1978

AGENT 69 JENSEN -I SKORPIONENS TEGN • 1977 • Hedman Werner • DNM

AGENT 69 JENSEN I SKYTTENS TEGN see **I SKYTTENS TEGN** • 1978

AGENT 255: DESPERATE MISSION (USA) see **AGENTE Z55, MISSIONE DISPERATA** • 1965

AGENT 505 -TODESFALLE BEIRUT • 1965 • Kohler Manfred R. • FRG, ITL, FRN • AGENT 505 (UKN) ○ AGENT FIVEOFIVE

AGENT 505 (UKN) see **AGENT 505 -TODESFALLE BEIRUT** • 1965

AGENT, THE • 1922 • Semon Larry • SHT • USA

AGENT A LE BRAS LONG, L' • 1908 • Bosetti Romeo • FRN • AGENT WITH LONG ARMS, THE ○ INFLUENTIAL AGENT, THE

AGENT DE POCHE, L' • 1909 • Cohl Emile • ANS • FRN • POCKET POLICEMAN

AGENT ET LE VIOLINISTE, L' see **VIOLINISTE, LE** • 1908

AGENT FIVEOFIVE see **AGENT 505 -TODESFALLE BEIRUT** • 1965

AGENT FOR H.A.R.M. • 1966 • Oswald Gerd • USA • HARM MACHINE, THE

AGENT FOR PANIC • 1964 • *Newman Brad* • FRG

AGENT FOR THE PLAINTIFF, AN • 1968 • *Barry Gene* • TVM • USA

AGENT JOE WALKER OPERATION FAR EAST see **AGENTE JO WALKER OPERAZIONE ESTREMO ORIENTE** • 1966

AGENT KITSOS CALLS GASTOUNI see **PRAKTOR KITSOS KALI GASTOUNI** • 1967

AGENT LOGAN'S SECRET MISSION YPOTRON see **AGENTE LOGAN MISSIONE YPOTRON** • 1966

AGENT NO.13 • 1912 • de la Riva Alberto • GTM

AGENT NR.1 • 1971 • Kuzminski Zbigniew • PLN

AGENT OF DOOM (USA) see **SOIR.. PAR HASARD, UN** • 1964

AGENT ON ICE • 1986 • Worswick Clark • USA

AGENT PLONGEUR, L' • 1901 • Zecca Ferdinand • FRN

AGENT RIGOLO ET SON CHIEN POLICIER, L' • 1913 • Machin Alfred • NTH

AGENT S3S OPERAZIONE URANIO • 1966 • Cardone Alberto, Kohler Manfred R. • ITL

AGENT SIGMA 3 -MISSION GOLDWATHER see **AGENTE SIGMA 3 MISSIONE GOLDWATHER** • 1967

AGENT WITH LONG ARMS, THE see **AGENT A LE BRAS LONG, L'** • 1908

AGENTE 00 SEXY • 1968 • Cortes Fernando • MXC • AGENT 00 SEXY

AGENTE 3S3 MASSACRO AL SOLE • 1966 • Sollima Sergio • ITL, FRN, SPN • AGENTE 353 ENVIADO SPECIAL ○ 353 AGENTE ESPECIAL ○ HUNTER OF THE UNKNOWN ○ AGENT 3S3, MASSACRE IN THE SUN

AGENTE 3S3 -PASAPORTE PARA EL INFIERNO (SPN) see **AGENTE 3S3, PASSAPORTO PER L'INFERNO** • 1965

AGENTE 3S3, PASSAPORTO PER L'INFERNO • 1965 • Sollima Sergio • ITL, FRN, SPN • AGENTE 3S3 -PASAPORTE PARA EL INFIERNO (SPN) ○ PASSEPORT POUR L'ENFER (FRN) ○ AGENT 3S3: PASSPORT TO HELL (USA) ○ PASSPORT TO HELL (UKN)

AGENTE 077, DALL'ORIENTE CON FURORE • 1965 • Grieco Sergio • ITL, FRN, SPN • FROM THE ORIENT WITH FURY (UKN) ○ FUREUR SUR LE BOSPHORE ○ PARIS-ESTAMBUL SIN REGRESO ○ 077: FURY IN ISTANBUL ○ FURY IN ISTANBUL

AGENTE 077, MISION BLOODY MARY see **AGENTE 077 -MISSIONE BLOODY MARY** • 1965

AGENTE 077 -MISSIONE BLOODY MARY • 1965 • Grieco Sergio • ITL, FRN, SPN • MISSION BLOODY MARY (USA) ○ MUERTE ESPERA EN ATENAS, LA ○ OPERATION LOTUS BLEU ○ AGENTE 077, MISION BLOODY MARY ○ OPERACION LOTO AZUL

AGENTE 353 ENVIADO SPECIAL see **AGENTE 3S3 MASSACRO AL SOLE** • 1966

AGENTE 777 MISSIONE SUPERGAME (ITL) see **COPLAN FX18 CASSE TOUT** • 1965

AGENTE COPLAN: MISSIONE SPIONAGGIO (ITL) see **COPLAN PREND DES RISQUES** • 1963

AGENTE JO WALKER OPERAZIONE ESTREMO ORIENTE • 1966 • Parolini Gianfranco • ITL • AGENT JOE WALKER OPERATION FAR EAST

AGENTE LEMMY CAUTION MISSIONE ALPHAVILLE (ITL) see **ALPHAVILLE, UNE ETRANGE AVENTURE DE LEMMY CAUTION** • 1965

AGENTE LOGAN MISSIONE YPOTRON • 1966 • Stegani Giorgio • ITL, SPN • YPOTRON -FINAL COUNTDOWN (USA) ○ YPOTRON (SPN) ○ OPERATION "Y" (UKN) ○ AGENT LOGAN'S SECRET MISSION YPOTRON

AGENTE POSITIVO, O • 1972 • Sabag Fabio • BRZ

AGENTE SEGRETO 777 INVITO AD UCCIDERE • 1966 • Bomba Enrico • ITL

AGENTE SEGRETO 777 OPERAZIONE MISTERO • 1965 • Bomba Enrico • ITL • SECRET AGENT 777 OPERATION MYSTERY

AGENTE SIGMA 3 MISSIONE GOLDWATHER • 1967 • Callegari Gian Paolo • ITL, SPN • AGENT SIGMA 3 -MISSION GOLDWATHER

AGENTE SO 3 OPERAZIONE ATLANTIDE • 1965 • Paolella Domenico • ITL, SPN • AGENT 003, OPERACION ATLANTIDA (SPN) ○ OPERATION ATLANTIS (USA)

AGENTE SPECIALE L. K. • 1967 • Franco Jesus • ITL

AGENTE TIGRE: SFIDA INFERNALE • 1966 • Vernay Robert • ITL

AGENTE VIAJERO, EL • 1974 • *Filmadora Chapultepec* • MXC

AGENTE X-17 OPERAZIONE OCEANO (ITL) see **X-17 TOP SECRET** • 1965

AGENTE X-77 ORDINE DI UCCIDERE see **ORDEN: FX 18 DEBE MORIR** • 1965

AGENTE Z-55, MISION HONG KONG (SPN) see **AGENTE Z55, MISSIONE DISPERATA** • 1965

AGENTE Z55, MISSIONE DISPERATA • 1965 • Montero Roberto Bianchi • ITL, FRN, SPN • AGENTE Z-55, MISION HONG KONG (SPN) ○ DESPERATE MISSION ○ AGENT 255: DESPERATE MISSION (USA)

AGENTEN KENNEN KEINE TRANEN see **A CHI TOCCA...TOCCA!** • 1978

AGENTES DEL QUINTO GRUPO, LOS • 1954 • Gascon Jose • SPN

AGENTS MAGNETIQUES, LES • 1908 • Cohl Emile • ANS • FRN

AGENTS TELS QU'ON NOUS LES PRESENTE, LES • 1908 • Feuillade Louis • FRN

AGENTS WEN MANONG • 1968 • David Raul T. • PHL • AGENTS YES SIR

AGENTS YES SIR see **AGENTS WEN MANONG** • 1968

AGENTUR UBERSEE see **LIEBESHANDEL** • 1926

AGENZIA MATRIMONIALE • 1953 • Pastina Giorgio • ITL

AGENZIA RICCARDO FINZI.. PRATICAMENTE DETECTIVE • 1979 • Corbucci Bruno • ITL • FINZI DETECTIVE AGENCY, THE

AGES AND STAGES • 1949-57 • Crawley Judith • SER • CND

AGES OF LOVE, THE see **KING OF THE TURF, THE** • 1926

AGES OF MAN, THE • 1969 • Croitoru Alecu • RMN

AGETES KABSHADERNE • 1917 • Lauritzen Lau • DNM

AGGET AR LOST! EN HARDKOKT SAGA • 1975 • Alfredson Hans • SWD • EGG! EGG? A HARDBOILED STORY

AGGIE see **AGGIE -THE DIARY OF A NYMPH** • 1969

AGGIE APPLEBY, MAKER OF MEN • 1933 • Sandrich Mark • USA • CUPID IN THE ROUGH (UKN)

AGGIE -THE DIARY OF A NYMPH • 1969 • Kennedy Ken • USA • DIARY OF A NYMPH ○ AGGIE

AGGRESSIVE TEENAGERS, THE see **ZAGALATONES** • 1971

AGGRESSOR, THE • 1911 • Ince Thomas H., Tucker George Loane • USA

AGGRESSOR, THE • 1914 • Jones Edgar • USA

AGGRESSOR, THE see **MAD BULL** • 1977

AGGRESSOR, THE see **AGRESOR, EL** • 1988

AGGRIPPES A LA TERRE • 1968 • Ivens Joris • FRN

AGGRO SEIZEMAN • 1975 • Mannas James, Stuart-Young Brian • GYN

AGGUATO A TANGERI • 1958 • Freda Riccardo • ITL, FRN • GUET-APENS A TANGER (FRN) ○ TRAPPED IN TANGIERS ○ AMBUSH IN TANGIERS

AGGUATO DELLA MORTE, L' • 1919 • Palermi Amleto • ITL

AGGUATO SUL BOSFORO • 1969 • Batzella Luigi • ITL

AGGUATO SUL GRANDE FIUME (ITL) see **FLUSSPIRATEN VOM MISSISSIPPI, DIE** • 1963

AGGUATO SUL MARE • 1956 • Mercanti Pino • ITL

AGHA see **ZUGURT AGA** • 1985

AGI MURAD, IL DIAVOLO BIANCO • 1959 • Freda Riccardo • ITL, YGS • BELI DJAVO (YGS) ○ WHITE WARRIOR, THE (USA)

AGILOK & BLUBBO • 1969 • FRG

AGING OF NORTH AMERICA, THE • 1985 • Kennedy Michael • DOC • CND

AGIOUPA see **AYOUPA** • 1957

AGIR SUC • 1967 • Inanoglu Turker • TRK • PENALTY, THE

AGIT • 1971 • Guney Yilmaz • TRK • ELEGY ○ COMPLAINT

AGIT-TRAIN see **AGITPOEZHD VTSIKA** • 1921

AGIT-TRAIN OF THE CENTRAL COMMITTEE see **AGITPOEZHD VTSIKA** • 1921

AGITATED ADVERTS • 1917 • Dyer Anson • ANM • UKN

AGITATOR, THE • 1912 • Dwan Allan • USA • COWBOY SOCIALIST, THE

AGITATOR, THE • 1945 • Harlow John • UKN

AGITATORS see **SOVVERSIVI** • 1967

AGITPOEZHD VTSIKA • 1921 • Vertov Dziga • USS • TRAIN OF THE CENTRAL COMMITTEE, THE ○ TRAIN OF THE CENTRAL EXECUTIVE ○ V.T.I.K. TRAIN, THE ○ AGIT-TRAIN ○ TRAIN, THE ○ AGIT-TRAIN OF THE CENTRAL COMMITTEE ○ VTIK TRAIN, THE

AGLA GOZLERIM • 1968 • Dinler Mehmet • TRK • WEEP, MY EYES

AGLAYAN BIR OMUR • 1968 • Saydam Nejat • TRK • WEEP, MY LIFE

AGLAYAN KADIN • 1967 • Seden Osman, Evin Semih • TRK • WEEPING WOMAN, THE

AGLI ORDINI DEL RE (ITL) see **TOUR, PRENDS GARDE!, LA** • 1958

AGMAL IYUM HAYATI • 1973 • Barakat Henry • LBN • PLUS BEAUX JOURS DE MA VIE, LES

AGNALDO AND THE DANGER see **AGNALDO, PERIGO A VISTA** • 1969

AGNALDO, PERIGO A VISTA • 1969 • de Barros Reynaldo Paes • BRZ • AGNALDO AND THE DANGER

AGNES ARNAU UND IHRE DREI FREIER • 1918 • Biebrach Rudolf • FRG

AGNES CECILIA • 1990 • Gronroos Anders • SWD

AGNES DE RIEN • 1949 • Billon Pierre • FRN

AGNES KEMPLER'S SACRIFICE • 1915 • *Henley Hobart* • USA

AGNES OF GOD • 1985 • Jewison Norman • USA

AGNES OF THE PORT see **AGNI TOU LIMANIOU** • 1952

AGNESE VA A MORIRE, L' • 1976 • Montaldo Giuliano • ITL

AGNESE VISCONTI • 1910 • Pastrone Giovanni • ITL

AGNI • 1977 • Radhakrishnan C. • IND • FIRE

AGNI PARIKSHA • 1951 • Manickyam P. V. • IND • FIRE TEST

AGNI PARIKSHA • 1954 • Agradoot • IND

AGNI PUTHRI • 1967 • Krishnan M. • IND • PURIFIED BY FIRE

AGNI TOU LIMANIOU • 1952 • Tzavellas Georges • GRC • AGNES OF THE PORT

AGNIESZKA 46 • 1964 • Checinski Sylwester • PLN

AGNUS DEI (UKN) see **EGI BARANY** • 1970

AGONIA see **AGONIYA** • 1976

AGONIA, A • 1980 • Bressane Julio • BRZ • AGONY, THE

AGONIE DE BYZANCE, L' • 1913 • Feuillade Louis • FRN

AGONIE DE JERUSALEM, L' • 1927 • Duvivier Julien • FRN

AGONIE DES AIGLES, L' • 1921 • Duvivier Julien, Bernard-Deschamps • FRN

AGONIE DES AIGLES, L' • 1933 • Richebe Roger • FRN

AGONIE DES AIGLES, L' • 1951 • Alden-Delos Jean • FRN

AGONIES OF AGNES • 1918 • *Dressler Marie* • SHT • USA

AGONISTES • 1970 • Carayannis Costa • GRC • FIGHTERS

AGONIYA • 1976 • Klimov Elem • USS • AGONY ○ AGONIA ○ RASPUTIN ○ DEATH THROES

AGONIZANDO EN EL CRIMEN • 1967 • Eguiluz Enrique L. • SPN • SUFFERING IN CRIME

AGONIZING ADVENTURE see **ANGOISSANTE AVENTURE, L'** • 1919

AGONY see **AGONIYA** • 1976

AGONY, THE see **AGONIA, A** • 1980

AGONY AND THE ECSTASY, THE • 1965 • Reed Carol • USA

AGONY COLUMN, THE see **BLIND ADVENTURE, THE** • 1918

AGONY IN THE GARDEN • 1964 • Physick Gordon • UKN

AGONY OF FEAR • 1915 • Warren Giles R. • USA

AGONY OF LOVE see **LAWET EL HUB** • 1959

AGONY OF LOVE, THE • 1966 • Rotsler William • USA • FROM LADY TO TRAMP

AGONY ON THE FACE OF A CAROUSEL HORSE, THE • Dell Budd • USA

AGORA E QUE SAO ELAS • 1953 • Garcia Fernando • PRT

AGORA MEYHANESI • 1968 • Aslan Mehmet • TRK • AGORA TAVERN, THE

AGORA TAVERN, THE see **AGORA MEYHANESI** • 1968

AGOSTA • 1986 • Melo Jorge Silva • PRT

AGOSTINO • 1962 • Bolognini Mauro • ITL

AGOSTINO DI IPPONA • 1972 • Rossellini Roberto • MTV • ITL • AUGUSTINE OF HIPPO (USA)

AGOSTO DONNE MIE NON VI CONOSCO • 1960 • Malatesta Guido • ITL

AGRAHARATHIL KAZHUTHAI • 1977 • Abraham John • IND • DONKEY IN A BRAHMIN VILLAGE

AGREABLE SUEUR DE LA MORT, L' • 1972 • Vergez Gerard • FRN

AGRESOR, EL • 1988 • Fernandino Guillermo, Gutmann Luis • ARG • AGGRESSOR, THE

AGRESSION • 1965 • Foldes Peter • ANM • FRN

AGRESSION, L' • 1974 • Pires Gerard • FRN, ITL • APPUNTAMENTO CON L'ASSASSINO (ITL) ○ ACT OF AGGRESSION (USA) ○ SOMBRES VACANCES

AGRI DAGIN EFSANESI • 1976 • Un Memduh • TRK • LEGEND OF MOUNT ARARAT, THE

AGRIA PATHI • 1967 • Tatasopoulos Stelios • GRC • WILD PASSIONS

AGRICULTURAL AND INDUSTRIAL GROWTH • 1967 • Carter Donald* • DCS • CND

AGRICULTURAL EXPERIMENT IN ITALY, AN see **BORGO A MOZZANO** • 1958

AGRICULTURAL SHOW see **COUNTRY CATTLE SHOW, A** • 1897

AGRICULTURE, L' • 1955 • Dewever Jean • FRN

AGRICULTURE, L' • 1965-66 • Garceau Raymond • DCS • CND

AGRIPPINA • 1910 • Guazzoni Enrico • ITL

AGRONOME • 1955 • Palardy Jean • DCS • CND

AGRONOMISTS • 1978 • Kovachev Hristo • DOC • BUL

AGUA, EL • 1960 • Gomez Manuel Octavio • CUB

AGUA CLARA • 1974 • Varela Miguel Angel • VNZ • CLEAR WATER

AGUA EN EL SUELO, EL • 1935 • Ardavin Eusebio F. • SPN

AGUA SANGRIENTA • 1952 • Torres Ricardo • SPN

AGUAS BAJAN NEGRAS, LAS • 1948 • Saenz De Heredia Jose Luis • SPN

AGUAS BAJAN TURBIAS, LAS • 1951 • del Carril Hugo • ARG • DARK RIVER (USA) ○ MUDDY WATERS RUN DOWN ○ RIVER OF BLOOD, THE

AGUAS CRIADORAS • 1944 • Coelho Jose Adolfo • SHT • PRT

AGUAS VIVAS • 1969 • Tropa Alfredo • SHT • PRT

AGUAZET SEIF • 1967 • Arafa Saad • EGY • SUMMER HOLIDAYS ○ AJAZAT SAIF

AGUEDA, A LINDA • 1953 • Campos Henrique • SHT • PRT

AGUENTA CORACAO • 1984 • Farias Reginaldo • BRZ • HOLD ON, HEART

AGUIAS EM PATRULLA • 1969 • Fernandes Ary • BRZ • EAGLES ON PATROL

AGUILA A SOL • 1937 • Boytler Arcady • MXC

AGUILA CON LAS HERMANAS see **ESCUELA PARA SOLTERAS** • 1964

AGUILA DESCLAZA, EL • Arau Alfonso • MXC • BAREFOOT EAGLE, THE

AGUILA NEGRA CONTRA LOS ENMASCARADOS DE LA MUERTE, EL • 1956 • Peon Ramon • MXC

AGUILA NEGRA EN EL TESORO DE LA MUERTE, EL see **TESORO DE LA MUERTE, EL** • 1953

AGUILA NEGRA EN LA LEY DE LOS FUERTES, EL • 1956 • Peon Ramon • MXC

AGUILA NEGRA VS. LOS DIABLOS DE LA PRADERA, EL • 1956 • Peon Ramon • MXC

AGUILA NERA • 1953 • Peon Ramon • MXC

AGUILA NERA EN LA VENGADOR SOLITARIO, EL see **VENGADOR SOLITARIO, EL** • 1953

AGUILA ROJA • 1941 • Curwood Robert • MXC

AGUILAS DE ACERO • 1927 • Rey Florian • SPN • MISTERIOS DE TANGER, LOS

AGUILAS DE AMERICA • 1933 • Ojeda Manuel R. • MXC

AGUILAS FRENTE AL SOL • 1932 • Moreno Antonio • MXC

AGUIRRE, DER ZORN GOTTES • 1972 • Herzog Werner • FRG • AGUIRRE, WRATH OF GOD (UKN)

AGUIRRE, WRATH OF GOD (UKN) see **AGUIRRE, DER ZORN GOTTES** • 1972

AGUJERO EN EL TIEMPO, UN • 1976 • Atienza Juan G. • SPN

AGUJERO EN LA PARED, EL • 1982 • Kohon David Jose • ARG • HOLE IN THE WALL, THE

AGUSTINA DE ARAGON • 1928 • Rey Florian • SPN

AGUSTINA DE ARAGON • 1950 • de Orduna Juan • SPN

AGYU ES HARANG • 1915 • Balazs Bela • HNG

AH! AHH! TISHOO!!! • 1914 • Collins Edwin J. • UKN • SOME SNUFF

AH BU KADINLAR • 1967 • Inci Kemal, Palay Abdurrahman • TRK • AH, THOSE WOMEN

AH, C'EST BON • 1980 • von Puttkamer Peter • SHT • CND

AH CHONG STORY, THE • 1961 • Vogel Virgil W. • USA

AH, CRADLE • 1980 • Xie Jin • CHN
AH, EN SA'N GRABB • 1939 • Johansson Ivar • SWD • OH, WHAT A BOY
AH! ETJIMA • 1959 • Murayama Mitsuo • JPN
AH, EVE! see **AH MIN HAWA** • 1961
AH FEI see **YU-MA TS'AI-TZU** • 1983
AH GUZEL ISTANBUL • 1982 • Kavur Omer • TRK • OH, LOVELY ISTANBUL
AH HIMEYURI NO TO • 1968 • Masuda Toshio • JPN • MONUMENT OF MAIDENS LILY
AH, I MORRON KVALL • 1919 • Brunius John W. • SWD • OH TOMORROW NIGHT
AH JONAN • 1960 • Sugie Toshio • JPN • WEAKER SEX (USA)
AH KAITEN TOKUBETSU KOGEKITAI • 1968 • Ozawa Shigehiro • JPN • HUMAN TORPEDOES
AH! LES BELLES BACCHANTES • 1954 • Loubignac Jean • FRN • PEEK-A-BOO (USA) ○ FEMMES DE PARIS
AH MIN HAWA • 1961 • Wahab Fatin Abdel • EGY • AH MIN HAWWA ○ AH, EVE!
AH MIN HAWWA see **AH MIN HAWA** • 1961
AH! MY FRIENDS WITHOUT VOICE see **AA KOE NAKI TOMO** • 1972
AH, MY HOME TOWN (USA) see **AA FURUSATO** • 1938
AH! NANGO SHOSA • 1938 • Tsuburaya Eiji • JPN
AH! NOMUGI PASS see **AH! NOMUGI TOGE** • 1978
AH! NOMUGI TOGE • 1978 • Yamamoto Satsuo • JPN • AH! NOMUGI PASS
AH! NURTURE • 1948 • Peterson Sidney • USA
AH! QUEL COUREUR! see **CASSE-COU MADEMOISELLE** • 1954
AH! QUELLE EQUIPE • 1956 • Quignon Roland-Jean • FRN
AH! QUELLE GARE! • 1932 • Guissart Rene • FRN • PETOUCHE ○ CA ROULE..
AH SI? ..E IO LO DICO A ZZZORRO! • 1975 • Lo Cascio Franco • ITL
AH! SI MON MOINE VOULAIT.. • 1973 • Pierson Claude • FRN, CND
AH SING AND THE GREASERS • 1910 • *Lubin* • USA
AH -SWEET MOUSE STORY OF LIFE • 1965 • Jones Charles M. • ANS • USA
AH, THOSE WOMEN see **AH BU KADINLAR** • 1967
AH! VOUS DIRAIS-JE, MAMAN • 1985 • Desbiens Francine • ANS • CND
AH, WILDERNESS! • 1935 • Brown Clarence • USA
AH YING • 1983 • Fong Yuk-Ping • HKG • PAN-PIEN JEN
AHALYA • 1936 • Banerjee Jyotish • IND
AHAS GAUWA • 1974 • Pathirajah Dharmasena • SLN • REACHING FOR THE SKY
AHASIN POLA WATHA • 1976 • Peries Lester James • SLN • WHITE FLOWERS FOR THE DEAD ○ FROM HEAVEN TO EARTH ○ AHASIN POLOWATA
AHASIN POLOWATA see **AHASIN POLA WATHA** • 1976
AHASVER • 1915 • Kvapil Jaroslav • CZC
AHASVER • 1917 • Reinert Robert • FRG
AHASVER • 1920 • Reinert Robert • FRG
AHAVA BANAMAL • 1967 • Gorji Obadiah • ISR • HARBOUR OF LOVE ○ HANECH'SHEKET
AHAVA ILEMETH • 1982 • Silberg Joel • ISR • SECRET OF YOLANDA, THE
AHAVA LE ARBA YADAIYM see **HA'ISHA BACHEDER HASHENI** • 1967
AHDAB, EL • 1947 • Hilmy Ibrahim Hassan • EGY • HUNCHBACK, THE
AHDAT SANAWOUACH EL-DJAMR • 1975 • Hamina Mohamed Lakhdar • ALG • CHRONICLE OF THE HOT YEARS ○ CHRONIQUE DES ANNEES DE BRAISE ○ CHRONICLE OF THE YEARS OF THE BRAZIER ○ CHRONICLE OF THE YEARS OF EMBERS
AHEAD OF THE LAW • 1926 • Sheldon Forrest • USA
AHEAD OF THE SILENCE see **INAINTE DE TACERE** • 1979
AHI ESTA EL DETALLE • 1940 • Bustillo Oro Juan • MXC • THERE IS THE DETAIL
AHI VA OTRO RECLUTA • 1960 • Fernandez Ramon • SPN
AHI VIENE MARTIN CORONA • 1951 • Zacarias Miguel • MXC
AHI VIENE VIDAL TENORIO • 1948 • Cardona Rene • MXC
AHI VIENEN LOS ARGUMEDO • 1961 • Munoz Manuel • MXC
AHI VIENEN LOS GORRONES • 1952 • Martinez Solares Gilberto • MXC
AHI VIENEN LOS MENDOZA • 1948 • Peon Ramon • MXC
AHIBBAK YA HILWA • Shukry Abdel Moneim • EGY • JE T'AIME, MA CHERIE!
AHIJADO DE LA MUERTE, EL • 1946 • Foster Norman • MXC
AHKEA KKOTS • 1961 • Yongmin Lee • SKR • BAD FLOWER, THE
AHLAM • 1987 • Lledo Jean-Pierre • ALG • EMPIRE OF DREAMS
AHLAM AL MADINA • 1984 • Malass Mohamed • SYR • DREAMS OF THE CITY
AHLAM EL CHABAB • 1943 • Salim Kamel • EGY • DREAMS OF YOUTH
AHMED THE SHEIK • 1968 • Egilmez Ertem • TRK
AHNA AL-TALAMD'A • 1959 • Salem Atef • EGY • NOUS LES ETUDIANTS ○ WE STUDENTS
AHNFRAU, DIE • 1919 • Fleck Jacob, Fleck Luise • AUS
AHNUNGSLOSE ENGEL, DER • 1936 • Seitz Franz • FRG
AHO.. AU COEUR DU MONDE PRIMITIF • 1975 • Bertolino Daniel, Floquet Francois • DOC • CND
AHORA SEREMOS FELICES • 1940 • Molte William • NOW WE SHALL BE HAPPY (USA)
AHORA SOY RICO • 1952 • Gonzalez Rogelio A. • MXC
AHORA TE VAMOS A LLAMAR HERMANO • 1971 • Ruiz Raul • SHT • CHL • NOW WE WILL CALL YOU BROTHER
AHORTAGOS, O • 1968 • Dadiras Dimis • GRC • INSATIABLE, THE
AHWAR, AL • 1976 • Hawal Kasim • DOC • IRQ
AI • 1963 • Kuri Yoji • ANS • JPN • LOVE
AI-CH'ING CH'ANG P'AO • 1976 • Ch'En Yao-Ch'I • HKG • RUN LOVER RUN
AI FUTATABI • 1972 • Ichikawa Kon • JPN • TO LOVE AGAIN
AI-JEN NU-SHENG • 1983 • Hope Anthony • HKG • MY DARLING, MY GODDESS
AI MARGINI DELLA METROPOLI • 1953 • Lizzani Carlo • ITL
AI NI YOMIGAERU HI • 1922 • Mizoguchi Kenji • JPN • RESURRECTION OF LOVE, THE (USA) ○ DAY WHEN LOVE RETURNS, THE
AI NO BOREI • 1977 • Oshima Nagisa • JPN, FRN • EMPIRE DES PASSIONS, L' (FRN) ○ EMPIRE OF PASSION (UKN) ○ PHANTOM LOVE (USA) ○ PHANTOM OF LOVE, THE
AI NO CORRIDA • 1976 • Oshima Nagisa • JPN, FRN • IN THE REALM OF THE SENSES (USA) ○ EMPIRE DES SENS, L' (FRN) ○ EMPIRE OF THE SENSES
AI NO FUKEI • 1929 • Tasaka Tomotaka • JPN • GUARDIANS OF LOVE
AI NO KAWAKI • 1967 • Kurahara Koreyoshi • JPN • LONGING FOR LOVE ○ THIRST FOR LOVE, THE
AI NO MACHI • 1928 • Tasaka Tomotaka • JPN • STREET OF LOVE
AI NO NIMOTSU • 1956 • Kawashima Yuzo • JPN • BUNDLE OF LOVE
AI NO SANGA • 1950 • Koishi Eiichi • JPN • THIRD FLOOR LOVE ○ MOUNTAIN AND RIVER OF LOVE
AI NO SANKA • 1967 • Yamada Yoji • JPN • SONG OF LOVE
AI NO SANPUNKAN SHIATSU • 1968 • Yuge Taro • JPN • FINGER PRESSING TREATMENT
AI NO SENKUSHA • 1946 • Nakamura Noboru • JPN • PIONEER LOVE
AI SHA • 1981 • T'An Chia-Ming • HKG • LOVE MASSACRE
AI TEMPI DI CESARE BORGIA see **MASCHERA DI CESARE BORGIA, LA** • 1941
AI TO CHIKAI • 1945 • Imai Tadashi • JPN • LOVE AND PLEDGE
AI TO HONOHO TO • 1961 • Sugawa Eizo • JPN • CHALLENGE TO LIVE
AI TO KIBO NO MACHI • 1959 • Oshima Nagisa • JPN • TOWN OF LOVE AND HOPE, A
AI TO NIKUSHIME NO KANATA • 1951 • Taniguchi Senkichi • JPN • BEYOND LOVE AND HATE
AI TO SHI NO KIROKU • 1966 • Kurahara Koreyoshi • JPN • HEART OF HIROSHIMA, THE
AI TO SHI NO TANIMA • 1954 • Gosho Heinosuke • JPN • VALLEY BETWEEN LOVE AND DEATH, THE
AI TO SHI O MITSUMETE • 1964 • Saito Buichi • JPN • GAZING AT LOVE AND DEATH
AI VOSTRI ORDINA, SIGNORA! • 1939 • Mattoli Mario • ITL • AT YOUR ORDERS, MADAME (USA) ○ ORGIA DI SOLE ○ AL VOSTRI ORDINA, SIGNORA! ○ GIOCHI DI SOCIETA
AI WA CHIKARA DA • 1930 • Naruse Mikio • JPN • STRENGTH OF LOVE ○ LOVE IS STRENGTH
AI WA DOKO MADEMO • 1932 • Uchida Tomu • JPN
AI WA OSHIMINAKU • 1967 • Morinaga Kenjiro • JPN • SINGING FOR LOVE
AI-YE • 1950 • Hugo Ian • SHT • USA • MANKIND
AI YO HOSHI TO TOMONI • 1947 • Abe Yutaka • JPN • LOVE, LIVE WITH THE STARS
AIBO • 1966 • Ichikawa Kon • JPN • HEY, BUDDY!
AIBOLIT-66 • 1967 • Bykov Rolan • USS
AIBU • 1933 • Gosho Heinosuke • JPN • CARESS
AICHA • 1953 • Madqur Gamal • EGY
AID TO THE NATION • 1947 • *De Mille Cecil B.* • SHT • USA
AIDA • 1911 • Apfel Oscar, Dawley J. Searle • USA
AIDA • 1953 • Fracassi Clemente • ITL
AIDA • 1976 • Jourdan Pierre • FRN
AIDA • 1988 • Fellbom Claes • SWD
AIDANKAATAJAT • 1983 • Soinio Olli • FNL • BREAKING OUT ○ OVERTHROWERS
AIDE-TOI • 1918 • Feuillade Louis • FRN
AIDED BY THE MOVIES • 1915 • Douglass James • USA
AIDO • 1969 • Hani Susumu • JPN • AIDO -SLAVE OF LOVE
AIDO -SLAVE OF LOVE see **AIDO** • 1969
AIDS: MIRROR OF LONELINESS see **SIDA: ESPEJO DE LA SOLEDAD** • 1988
AIDS OF A NATION • 1918 • *Universal* • SHT • USA
AIENKYO • 1937 • Mizoguchi Kenji • JPN • STRAITS OF LOVE AND HATE, THE (USA) ○ GORGE BETWEEN LOVE AND HATE
AIEULE, L' • 1990 • Palardy Claude • SHT • CND
AIGEN KATSURA • 1937 • Nomura Kosho • JPN • TREE OF LOVE
AIGLE A DEUX TETES, L' • 1948 • Cocteau Jean • FRN • EAGLE WITH TWO HEADS, THE (USA) ○ EAGLE HAS TWO HEADS, THE (UKN)
AIGLE ET LA COLOMBE, L' • 1977 • Bernard-Aubert Claude • FRN
AIGLE NOIR, L' see **VENDICATORE, IL** • 1959
AIGLON, L' • 1914 • Chautard Emile • FRN
AIGLON, L' • 1926 • Bieganski Victor • PLN
AIGLON, L' • 1931 • Tourjansky Victor • FRN
AIGLON, L' see **NAPOLEON II L'AIGLON** • 1961
AIGRETTE, L' • 1917 • Negroni Baldassare • ITL
AIGRETTE HUNTER, THE see **EGRET HUNTER, THE** • 1910
AIGULLE ROUGE, L' (FRN) see **VERTRAUMTE TAGE** • 1951
AIJIN • 1953 • Ichikawa Kon • JPN • LOVER, THE ○ LOVERS
AIJO KAIGAN • 1967 • Kyodo Ichiro • JPN • AWAKENING FOR LOVE
AIJO NO KEIFU • 1961 • Gosho Heinosuke • JPN • RECORD OF LOVE ○ LOVE'S FAMILY TREE
AIJO NO KESSAN • 1956 • Mifune Toshiro • JPN • SETTLEMENT OF LOVE
AIJO NO MIYAKO • 1958 • Sugie Toshio • JPN • CITY OF LOVE
AIKA HYVA IHMISEKSI • 1977 • Mollberg Rauni • FNL • PRETTY GOOD FOR A HUMAN BEING
AIKALAINEN • 1984 • Linnasalo Timo • FNL • CONTEMPORARY, THE
A'ILA AL-KABIRA, AL- • 1964 • Wahab Fatin Abdel • EGY • GRANDE FAMILLE, LA
AILA, DAUGHTER OF THE NORTH see **AILA, POHJOLAN TYTAR** • 1951
AILA, POHJOLAN TYTAR • 1951 • Witikka Jack, Powell Michael • FNL • AILA, DAUGHTER OF THE NORTH
A'ILAT ZIZI • 1962 • Wahab Fatin Abdel • EGY • FAMILLE DE ZIZI, LA
AILE OU LA CUISSE, L' • 1976 • Zidi Claude • FRN
AILE SEREFI • 1977 • Aksoy Orhan • TRK • HONOUR OF THE FAMILY
AILEEN O' THE SEA • 1913 • *Bracken Mildred* • USA
AILES BLANCHES, LES • 1942 • Peguy Robert • FRN
AILES BRISEES, LES • 1933 • Berthomieu Andre • FRN
AILES DE LA COLOMBE, LES • 1981 • Jacquot Benoit • FRN, ITL
AILES DE LA GASPESIE, LES • 1950 • Proulx Maurice • DCS • CND
AILES QUI S'OUVRENT, LES • 1936 • Kapps Walter • FRN
AILILA • Lung Kong • HKG
AIM AT THE PIT see **ANA O NERAE** • 1968
AIMEE • 1979 • Farges Joel • FRN
AIMEE D'UN AUTRE, L' see **HABIBAT RIHALY** • 1975
AIMER PLEURER MOURIR • 1915 • Perret Leonce • FRN
AIMEZ-VOUS BRAHMS? see **GOODBYE AGAIN** • 1961
AIMEZ-VOUS LES CHIENS? • 1975 • Godbout Jacques • DOC • CND
AIMEZ-VOUS LES FEMMES? • 1964 • Leon Jean • FRN, ITL • TASTE FOR WOMEN, A (USA) ○ DO YOU LIKE WOMEN?
AIMLESS WALK see **BEZUCELNA PROCHAZKA** • 1930
AIN EL GHEZAL • 1924 • Chikly Scemana • TNS • GIRL FROM CARTHAGE, THE
AINA • Islam Nazaral • PKS
AINAMA • 1980 • Cassenti Frank • FRN • CINEMA-SALSA POUR GOLDMAN ○ SALSA POUR GOLDMAN
AINE DES FERCHAUX, L' • 1963 • Melville Jean-Pierre • FRN, ITL • JEUNE HOMME HONORABLE, UN ○ MAGNET OF DOOM ○ JEUNE HOMME, UN
AINO FAMILY • 1978 • *Sanrio* • JPN • FAMILY IN LOVE
AINSI FINI LA NUIT • 1948 • Reinert Emile Edwin • FRN
AINSI SOIENT-ILS • 1970 • Patry Yvan • CND
AIN'T HE GRAND? • 1916 • Clements Roy • SHT • USA
AIN'T IT AGGRAVATIN' • 1954 • Barclay David • SHT • USA
AIN'T IT SO? • 1918 • Seiter William A.? • SHT • USA
AIN'T IT THE TRUTH? • 1915 • *Beery Wallace* • USA
AIN'T LOVE FUNNY • 1927 • Andrews Del • USA
AIN'T LOVE GRAND • 1921 • St. John Al • SHT • USA
AIN'T MISBEHAVIN' • 1941 • Murray Warren • SHT • USA
AIN'T MISBEHAVIN' • 1955 • Buzzell Edward • USA
AIN'T MISBEHAVIN' • 1974 • Neal Peter, Stern Anthony • CMP • UKN
AIN'T NATURE GRAND? • 1927 • Roberts Stephen • SHT • USA
AIN'T NATURE GRAND • 1930 • Harman Hugh, Ising Rudolf • ANS • USA
AIN'T NATURE WONDERFUL? • 1920 • Lyons Eddie, Moran Lee • SHT • USA
AIN'T NO HEROES • 1983 • Kotcheff Ted • USA
AIN'T NO TIME FOR GLORY • 1957 • *Sullivan Barry* • TVM • USA
AIN'T NOBODY'S BUSINESS • 1977 • Barrett-Page Sally • USA
AIN'T SHE SWEET • 1933 • Fleischer Dave • ANS • USA
AIN'T SHE TWEETY • 1952 • Freleng Friz • ANS • USA
AIN'T THAT DUCKY • 1945 • Freleng Friz • ANS • USA
AIN'T WE GOT FUN • 1937 • Avery Tex • ANS • USA
AIR • 1972 • Driessen Paul • ANM • CND
AIR AMERICA • 1987 • Rush Richard • USA
AIR AMERICA • 1990 • Spottiswoode Roger • USA
AIR BEDS • 1980 • Taylor Richard • UKN
AIR CADET • 1951 • Pevney Joseph • USA • JET MEN OF THE AIR (UKN)
AIR CADETS • 1944 • Beveridge Jane Marsh • DOC • CND
AIR CAGE, THE see **LUFTBUREN** • 1973
AIR CIRCUS, THE • 1928 • Hawks Howard, Seiler Lewis • USA
AIR CITY see **AEROGRAD** • 1935
AIR CREW • 1943 • O'Reilly • SHT • USA
AIR DE FAMILLE, UN • 1963 • Carle Gilles • DCS • CND
AIR DE PARIS, L' • 1954 • Carne Marcel • FRN, ITL • ARIA DI PARIGI (ITL)
AIR DE RIEN, L' • 1989 • Jimenez Mary • BLG, FRN, CND • EASY IN MIND (UKN)
AIR DEVILS • 1938 • Rawlins John • USA
AIR DEVILS see **FLYING WILD** • 1941
AIR DU CRIME, L' • 1984 • Klarer Alain • SWT, FRN
AIR EAGLES • 1931 • Whitman Phil • USA
AIR EXPRESS, THE • 1937 • *Lantz Walter (P)* • ANS • USA
AIR FORCE • 1943 • Hawks Howard • USA
AIR FRIGHT • 1933 • Meins Gus • SHT • USA
AIR FURY see **AIR HAWKS** • 1935
AIR HAWK • 1981 • Eggleston Colin • MTV • ASL
AIR HAWK, THE • 1924 • Mitchell Bruce • USA
AIR HAWKS • 1935 • Rogell Albert S. • USA • AIR FURY
AIR HOPPERS • Boyle Joseph C. • SHT • USA
AIR HOSTESS • 1933 • Rogell Albert S. • USA
AIR HOSTESS • 1949 • Landers Lew • USA
AIR HOSTESS, THE • 1937 • *Mintz Charles (P)* • ANS • USA
AIR LEGION, THE • 1929 • Glennon Bert • USA
AIR MAIL • 1932 • Ford John • USA
AIR MAIL, THE • 1925 • Willat Irvin V. • USA
AIR MAIL PILOT, THE • 1928 • Carroll Gene • USA
AIR MAN, THE • 1980 • Kolarov Keran • BUL
AIR MARCH see **AVIO-MARS** • 1934
AIR NATAL see **HAUT LE VENT** • 1942
AIR OF A KILLING, THE see **AIRE DE UN CRIMEN, EL** • 1988
AIR OUTPOST • 1937 • Keene Ralph, Taylor John • DOC • UKN
AIR PATROL • 1962 • Dexter Maury • USA
AIR PATROL, THE • 1928 • Mitchell Bruce • USA
AIR PATROL, THE (UKN) see **AIR POLICE** • 1931
AIR PATROL (UKN) see **HAPPY LANDING** • 1934
AIR POLICE • 1931 • Paton Stuart • USA • AIR PATROL, THE (UKN)
AIR PUR • 1939 • Clair Rene • FRN
AIR RAID see **KUSHU** • 1938
AIR RAID WARDEN • 1943 • Lovy Alex • ANS • USA
AIR RAID WARDENS • 1943 • Sedgwick Edward • USA
AIR STRIKE • 1955 • Roth Cy • USA
AIR TIGHT • 1925 • Beaudine Harold • SHT • USA
AIR TIGHT • 1931 • Stevens George • SHT • USA
AIR TORPEDO, THE see **TORPILLE AERIENNE, LA** • 1912
AIR TORPEDO, THE (USA) see **LUFT-TORPEDO, DAS** • 1913
AIR TRANSPORT SUPPORT • 1945 • Cutts Graham • DCS • UKN
AIRBORN • 1970 • *Windham Charles (P)* • SHT • USA
AIRBORNE • 1962 • Landis James • USA
AIRBORNE see **SKYJACKED** • 1972
AIRCRAFT, THE • 1980 • Gelinov Ognyan • BUL
AIRCRAFT AT WORK • 1966 • Crombie Donald • DOC • ASL

AIRCRAFT MISSING see **FLYGPLAN SAKNAS** • 1965

AIRE DE UN CRIMEN, EL • 1988 • Isasi Antonio • SPN • AIR OF A KILLING, THE

AIRED IN COURT • 1917 • *Dillon Jack* • USA

AIRFORCE 80 • 1980 • Robertson Michael • DOC • ASL

AIRHAWK • 1981 • Baker David • MTV • ASL

AIRING THEIR TROUBLES • 1918 • *Triangle* • USA

AIRLIFT A LA CARTE • 1971 • Smith Paul J. • ANS • USA

AIRLINE STEWARDESS see **STEWARDESSES, THE** • 1969

AIRMAIL MYSTERY, THE • 1932 • Taylor Ray • SRL • USA

AIRMAN REMEMBERS, AN • 1960 • Holmes Cecil • DOC • ASL

AIRMAN'S BRIDE, THE • 1913 • *Patheplay* • USA

AIRMAN'S CHILDREN, THE • 1915 • Denton Jack • UKN

AIRMAN'S ENEMY, THE • 1913 • *Film De Paris* • FRN

AIRMAN'S LETTER TO HIS MOTHER, AN • 1941 • Powell Michael • UKN

AIRMEN, THE • 1975 • Vekhotko A., Troshchenko N. • USS

AIRPLANE! • 1980 • Abrahams Jim, Zucker David, Zucker Jerry • USA

AIRPLANE DRONE see **BAKUON** • 1939

AIRPLANE II -THE SEQUEL • 1982 • Finkleman Ken • USA

AIRPORT • 1934 • Lockwood Roy • UKN

AIRPORT • 1970 • Seaton George, Hathaway Henry (U/c) • USA

AIRPORT '77 • 1977 • Jameson Jerry • USA

AIRPORT '80 -THE CONCORDE (UKN) see **CONCORDE - AIRPORT '79, THE** • 1979

AIRPORT 1975 • 1974 • Smight Jack • USA

AIRPORT S.O.S. HIJACK see **THIS IS A HIJACK** • 1973

AIRS • 1976 • Brakhage Stan • SHT • USA

AIRSHAFT • 1967 • Jacobs Ken • USA

AIRSHIP see **LUFTSCHIFF, DAS** • 1983

AIRSHIP, THE • 1908 • Blackton J. Stuart • USA • 100 YEARS HENCE

AIRSHIP, THE see **HIMMELSKIBET** • 1917

AIRSHIP DESTROYER, THE • 1909 • Booth W. R. • UKN • BATTLE IN THE CLOUDS, THE (USA) ○ AERIAL TORPEDO, THE

AIRTIGHT SAFE, THE • 1910 • Coleby A. E. • UKN

AIRWOLF • 1984 • Bellisario Donald P. • TVM • USA

AIRWOLF 2 • 1984 • Corea Nick, Laidman Harvey • MTV • USA • AIRWOLF 2: THE SEARCH ○ AIRWOLF 2: DEADLY MISSION

AIRWOLF 2: DEADLY MISSION see **AIRWOLF 2** • 1984

AIRWOLF 2: THE SEARCH see **AIRWOLF 2** • 1984

AIRWOLF 3: FLIGHT INTO DANGER • 1984 • Dollinger Steve • MTV • USA

AIRWOLF: THE STAVOGRAD INCIDENT • 1986 • Jubenvill Ken • TVM • USA

AISAI MONOGATARI • 1951 • Shindo Kaneto • JPN • STORY OF A BELOVED WIFE ○ STORY OF MY LOVING WIFE

AISAIKI • 1959 • Hisamatsu Seiji • JPN • ACCOUNT OF MY BELOVED WIFE

AISHU NO RINGOEN • 1957 • Murayama Shinji • JPN • APPLEYARD ROMANCE

AISLIN • 1976 • Armstrong Mary • MTV • CND

AISUREBAKOSO • 1955 • Yamamoto Satsuo, Imai Tadashi, Yoshimura Kozaburo • JPN • BECAUSE I LOVE ○ IF YOU LOVE ME

AITANGA • 1942 • Lund Helge • NRW

AITSU TO WATASHI • 1961 • Nakahira Ko • JPN • THAT GUY AND I

AIUTAMI A SOGNARE • 1980 • Avati Pupi • ITL • HELP ME DREAM (USA)

AIYOKU • 1966 • Sato Junya • JPN • GRAPES OF PASSION

AIYOKU NO KI see **AIYOKU NO YORU** • 1930

AIYOKU NO YORU • 1930 • Gosho Heinosuke • JPN • DESIRE OF NIGHT ○ RECORD OF LOVE AND DESIRE ○ AIYOKU NO KI

AIZEN KATSURA • 1954 • Kimura Keigo • JPN • DOCTOR AND THE NURSE

AIZEN KATSURA • 1962 • Nakamura Noboru • JPN • FLOWER IN A STORM

AIZO TOGE • 1934 • Mizoguchi Kenji • JPN • PASS OF LOVE AND HATE, THE (USA) ○ GORGE BETWEEN LOVE AND HATE ○ MOUNTAIN PASS OF LOVE AND HATE, THE

AJAANTRIK • 1958 • Ghatak Ritwik • IND • PATHETIC FALLACY, THE ○ AJANTRIK ○ MECHANICAL MAN

AJAMIL • 1948 • Kapadia J. • IND

AJANDEK EZ A NAP • 1980 • Gothar Peter • HNG • PRICELESS DAY, A

AJANTRIK see **AJAANTRIK** • 1958

AJAZAT SAIF see **AGUAZET SEIF** • 1967

AJE, AJE, BARA AJE • 1989 • Lim Kwon-Taek • SKR • COME, COME, COME UPWARD ○ COME, COME TO A HIGHER PLACE

AJIA HIMITSU KEISATSU • 1966 • Matsuo Akinori • JPN • ASIAPOL SECRET SERVICE

AJISAI NO UTA • 1960 • Takizawa Eisuke • JPN • BLOSSOMS OF LOVE

AJKA ALLADIN • 1935 • *Honey Talkies* • IND

AJOLAHTO • 1981 • Niskanen Mikko • FNL • GOTTA RUN!

AJURICABA • 1977 • Caldeira Oswalda • BRZ

AJUSTE DE CUENTAS • 1973 • Demicheli Tulio • SPN, ITL • DIRTY MOB, THE (UKN) ○ RICCO ○ TIPO CON UNA FACCIA STRANA TI CERCA PER UCCIDERTI, UN (ITL) ○ RICO

AJUSTE DE CUENTAS • Kusmanich Dunav • CLM • RENDERING ACCOUNTS

AK ALTIN • 1957 • Akat Lutfu • TRK

AKA CASSIUS CLAY see **A.K.A. CASSIUS CLAY** • 1970

AKADEMIK IVAN PAVLOV • 1949 • Roshal Grigori • USS • ACADEMICIAN IVAN PAVLOV ○ IVAN PAVLOV

AKADHIBU HAWWA see **AKAZIB HAWA** • 1969

AKADO SUZUNOSUKE • 1958 • Mori Kazuo • JPN

AKAGE • 1969 • Okamoto Kihachi • JPN • RED LION

AKAHIGE • 1965 • Kurosawa Akira • JPN • RED BEARD

AKAI GURASU • 1966 • Nakahira Ko • JPN • RED GLASS, A

AKAI HANKACHI • 1964 • Masuda Toshio • JPN • RED HANDKERCHIEF

AKAI HATOBA • 1958 • Masuda Toshio • JPN • LEFT HAND OF JIRO

AKAI JINBAORI • 1958 • Yamamoto Satsuo • JPN • HIS SCARLET CLOAK ○ RED CLOAK, THE

AKAI JITENSHIA • 1954 • Fujiwara Sugio • JPN • RED BICYCLE

AKAI KAIRAKU • 1968 • Sasaki Moto • JPN • RED PLEASURE

AKAI KUCHIBIRU IMADA KIEZU • 1947 • *Sada Keiji* • JPN • RED LIPS

AKAI MIZU • 1963 • Yamamoto Satsuo • JPN • RED WATER

AKAI NIKU • 1967 • Tobita Yoshi • JPN • RED FLESH

AKAI PANTI • 1959 • Iwama Tsuruo • JPN • RED PANTIES

AKAI SATSUI • 1964 • Imamura Shohei • JPN • INTENTIONS OF MURDER ○ UNHOLY DESIRE

AKAI TANIMA KETTO • 1965 • Masuda Toshio • JPN • DUEL AT RED VALLEY

AKAI TENSHI • 1966 • Masumura Yasuzo • JPN • RED ANGEL, THE

AKAI YUKI NO TERASARETE • 1925 • Mizoguchi Kenji (c/d) • JPN • SHINING IN THE RED SUNSET (USA) ○ UNDER THE CRIMSON SUNSET ○ IN THE RED RAYS OF THE SLEEPING SUN

AKAKY TSERETELI'S JOURNEY ALONG THE RACHA AND LECHKHUMA • 1912 • Amashukeli Vasily • DOC • USS • TRAVELS OF AKAKI TSERETELI IN RACHA AND LECHKHUMI

AKALER SANDHANE • 1980 • Sen Mrinal • IND • IN SEARCH OF FAMINE ○ AAKALER SANDHANE

AKANEGUMO • 1967 • Shinoda Masahiro • JPN • CLOUDS AT SUNSET

AKANISHI KAKITA • 1936 • Itami Mansaku • JPN • KAKITA AKANISHI

AKASEN CHITAI • 1956 • Mizoguchi Kenji • JPN • STREET OF SHAME ○ RED-LIGHT DISTRICT

AKASEN KICHI • 1953 • Taniguchi Senkichi • JPN • RED-LIGHT DISTRICT ○ RED-LIGHT BASES

AKASEN NO HI WA KIEZU • 1958 • Tanaka Shigeo • JPN • TAINTED FLOWERS

AKASH KUSUM • 1965 • Sen Mrinal • IND • UP IN THE CLOUDS ○ HOUSE OF CARDS

AKASHWANI • 1934 • Pendharkar Bhal G. • IND • VOICE FROM THE SKY

AKATON MIES • 1983 • Laine Edvin • FNL • HOW TO FIND A WIFE FOR A FARMER ○ MAN WITHOUT A WIFE

AKATSUKI NO CHIHEISEN • 1959 • Inoue Kazuo • JPN • SHOWDOWN AT DAWN

AKATSUKI NO DASSO • 1950 • Taniguchi Senkichi • JPN • ESCAPE AT DAWN

AKATSUKI NO SHI • 1924 • Mizoguchi Kenji • JPN • DEATH AT DAWN (USA) ○ DEATH IN THE DAWN

AKATSUKI NO TSUISEKI • 1950 • Ichikawa Kon • JPN • PURSUIT AT DAWN

AKATSUKI NO YUSHI • 1927 • Kinugasa Teinosuke • JPN • BRAVE SOLDIER AT DAWN, A

AKAZIB HAWA • 1969 • Wahab Fatin Abdel • EGY • AKADHIBU HAWWA ○ MENSONGES D'EVE, LES

AKBULUT MALKOCOGLU VE KARAOGLAN A KARSI • 1967 • Aslan Mehmet • TRK • AKBULUT VS. MALKOCOGLU AND KARAOGLAN

AKBULUT VS. MALKOCOGLU AND KARAOGLAN see **AKBULUT MALKOCOGLU VE KARAOGLAN A KARSI** • 1967

AKCE B • 1951 • Fric Martin, Mach Josef • CZC • ACTION B

AKCE KALIMANTAN • 1961 • Sis Vladimir • CZC, INN • OPERATION KALIMANTAN

AKCIJA • 1960 • Kavcic Jane • YGS • ATTACK

AKCIJA STADION see **AZCIJA STADION** • 1978

AKCJA "BRUTUS" • 1970 • Passendorfer Jerzy • PLN • OPERATION BRUTUS ○ ACTION BRUTUS

AKCJA CZYSCIEC • 1967 • Passendorfer Jerzy • PLN • ON THE WAY TO PURGATORY

AKCJA POD ARSENALEM • 1977 • Lomnicki Jan • PLN • ACTION UNDER ARSENAL

AKE AND HIS WORLD see **AKE OCH HANS VARLD** • 1984

AKE KLARAR BIFFEN • 1952 • Redig Rune • SWD

AKE OCH HANS VARLD • 1984 • Edwall Allan • SWD • AKE AND HIS WORLD

AKELARRE • 1984 • Olea Pedro • SPN • SABBATH

AKEN SENSO • 1943 • *Tsuburaya Eiji (Ph)* • JPN

AKENFIELD • 1975 • Hall Peter • UKN

AKES LILLA FELSTEG see **MON PHOQUE ET ELLES** • 1951

AKH! AFTI I YINEKA MOU • 1967 • Skalenakis Giorgos • GRC • OH! THIS IS MY WIFE

AKH AL-KABIR, AL- • 1958 • Wahab Fatin Abdel • EGY • FRERE AINE, LE

AKHTAR RAGOL FIL ALAM • 1967 • Mustafa Niazi • EGY • MOST DANGEROUS MAN IN THE WORLD, THE

AKI TACHINU • 1960 • Naruse Mikio • JPN • APPROACH OF AUTUMN, THE ○ AUTUMN IS BEGINNING

AKIBIYORI • 1960 • Ozu Yasujiro • JPN • LATE AUTUMN

AKIKET A PACSIRTA ELKISER • 1959 • Ranody Laszlo • HNG • FOR WHOM THE LARKS SING

AKIKO • 1961 • D'Amico Luigi Filippo • ITL

AKIT KETTEN SZERETNEK • 1915 • Curtiz Michael • HNG • LOVED BY TWO

AKITSU ONSEN • 1962 • Yoshida Yoshishige • JPN • AFFAIR AT AKITSU, AN

AKKA NAGO • 1968 • David Vincent • SLN • SISTERS

AKKARA PAHA • 1969 • Peries Lester James • SLN • FIVE ACRES OF LAND ○ FIVE ACRES

AKLI MIKLOS • 1986 • Revesz Gyorgy • HNG • MIKLOS AKLI

AKMAR, EL • 1978 • el Nasr Hisham Abou • EGY

AKO LABAN SA LIPUNAN • 1967 • Marquez Artemio • PHL • I, AGAINST SOCIETY

AKOGARE • 1935 • Gosho Heinosuke • JPN • YEARNING ○ LONGING

AKOGARE • 1955 • Nakamura Noboru • JPN • YEARNING

AKOGARE • 1966 • Onchi Hideo • JPN • ONCE A RAINY DAY

AKOJO DANZETSU • 1978 • Fukasaku Kinji • JPN • FALL OF AKO-JO, THE

AKORD SMRTI • 1919 • Kolar J. S., Lamac Carl • CZC • CHORD OF DEATH ○ DEATH PACT

AKRAMANA • 1978 • Kasaravalli Girish • IND • CONQUEST

AKRAN • 1971 • Myers Richard • USA

AKRIET • 1980 • Palekar Amol • IND • ACT OF EVIL

AKROBAT NA HRAZDE • 1953 • *Stallich Jan (Ph)* • SHT • CZC

AKROBAT SCHO-O-ON • 1943 • Staudte Wolfgang • FRG

AKROSH see **AAKROSH** • 1978

AKSAM YILDIZI • 1967 • Evin Semih • TRK • NIGHT STAR

AKSAMCI • 1967 • Davutoglu Zafer • TRK • DRUNKARD, THE

AKSELI AND ELINA see **AKSELI JA ELINA POHJANTAHDEN** • 1970

AKSELI AND ELINA UNDER THE NORTH SEA see **AKSELI JA ELINA POHJANTAHDEN** • 1970

AKSELI JA ELINA POHJANTAHDEN • 1970 • Laine Edvin • FNL • AKSELI AND ELINA UNDER THE NORTH SEA ○ AKSELI AND ELINA

AKTENSKAPSBROTTAREN • 1964 • Ekman Hasse • SWD • MARRIAGE WRESTLER, THE

AKTENSKAPSBYRAN • 1913 • Sjostrom Victor • SWD • MARRIAGE BUREAU, THE ○ MARRIAGE AGENCY, THE

AKTENSKAPSLEKEN • 1935 • Hylten-Cavallius Ragnar • SWD • MARRIAGE GAME, THE

AKTIEBOLAGET HALSANS GAVA • 1916 • Klercker Georg • SWD • "GIFT OF HEALTH" LTD.

AKTION J • 1961 • Heynowski Walter • GDR

AKTIVISTIT • 1939 • Orko Risto • FNL • ACTIVISTS, THE

AKTOREN • 1943 • Frisk Ragnar • SWD • ACTOR

AKTORKA • 1972 • Lenartowicz Stanislaw • PLN • ACTRESS, THE

AKTORZY PROWINCJONALNI • 1979 • Holland Agnieszka • PLN • PROVINCIAL ACTORS

AKTRISA • 1943 • Trauberg Leonid • USS • ACTRESS, THE

AKU AKU • 1959 • Heyerdahl Thor • DOC • USA

AKU NO MONSHO • 1964 • Horikawa Hiromichi • JPN • MARK OF EVIL, THE ○ BRAND OF EVIL

AKU NO TANOSHISA • 1954 • Chiba Yasuki • JPN • TEMPTATION OF PLEASURE

AKUDOMA JUNEN • 1967 • Komori Haku, Watanabe Mamoru, Yamamoto Shinya • JPN • TEN YEARS OF EVIL

AKUJO • 1964 • Watanabe Yusuke • JPN • NIGHT SCANDAL IN JAPAN

AKUJO NO KISETSU • 1958 • Shibuya Minoru • JPN • DAYS OF EVIL WOMEN

AKUMA GA KITARITE FUE WO FUKU • 1978 • Saito Mitsumasa • JPN • DEVIL COMES AND THE WHISTLE BLOWS, THE

AKUMA GA YONDEIRU • 1970 • Yamamoto Michio • JPN • TERROR IN THE STREETS

AKUMA KARA NO KUNSHO • 1967 • Murayama Mitsuo • JPN • MEDAL FROM THE DEVIL ○ MEDAL FROM THE GENERAL

AKUMA NO HIDARITE • 1966 • Nakahira Ko • JPN • DEVIL'S LEFT HAND, THE

AKUMA NO KANPAI • 1947 • Marune Santaro • JPN • DEVIL'S DEFEAT ○ DEVIL'S TOAST

AKUMA NO KESHIIN • 1959 • Akasaka Chogi • JPN • SUPER GIANT 8 (USA) ○ DEVIL INCARNATE, THE

AKUMA NO MACHI • 1956 • Suzuki Seijun • JPN

AKUMA NO SATSUTABA • 1960 • Sekigawa Hideo • JPN • DEVIL'S BANKNOTES

AKUMA NO SEPPUN • 1959 • Maruyama Seiji • JPN

AKUMA NO TEMARI-UTA • 1977 • Ichikawa Kon • JPN • DEVIL'S BOUNCING-BALL SONG, THE ○ DEVIL'S SONG OF BALL, THE ○ DEVIL'S SONG, THE ○ RHYME OF VENGEANCE, A

AKUMA-TO see **AKURYO-TO** • 1982

AKUMA TO TENSHI NO KISETSU • 1958 • Horiiki Kiyoshi • JPN

AKUMYO • 1961 • Tanaka Tokuzo • JPN • BAD NAME

AKUMYO ICHIDAI • 1967 • Yasuda Kimiyoshi • JPN • NOTORIOUS MAN AND THE ISSEI, THE

AKUMYO JU-HACHI BAN • 1968 • Mori Kazuo • JPN • NOTORIOUS MAN RETURNS, THE

AKUMYO MUTEKI • 1965 • Tanaka Tokuzo • JPN • INVINCIBLE BAD NAMES

AKUMYO NAWABARI ARASHI • 1974 • Masumura Yasuzo • JPN • BAD NAMES' BREAKING OF TERRITORIES

AKUMYO NIWAKA • 1965 • Tanaka Tokuzo • JPN • SUDDENLY BAD NAMES

AKUMYO NOBORI • 1965 • Tanaka Tokuzo • JPN • TWO NOTORIOUS MEN STRIKE AGAIN

AKUMYO ZAKURA • 1966 • Tanaka Tokuzo • JPN • BAD NAMES' CHERRY BLOSSOM

AKURYO-TO • 1982 • Shinoda Masahiro • JPN • DEVIL'S ISLAND ○ AKUMA-TO

AKUSEN TAMANOI -NUKERAREMASU • 1974 • Kumashiro Tatsumi • JPN • STREET OF JOY

AKUTO • 1965 • Shindo Kaneto • JPN • CONQUEST, THE ○ SCOUNDREL, A

AKUTO SHAIN YUKYO-DEN • 1968 • Ichimura Hirokazu • JPN • CODE OF THE RUTHLESS

AKUZUKINCHAN KIOTSUKETE • 1970 • Moritani Shiro • JPN • BE CAREFUL RED RIDING HOOD

AKWARELE • 1978 • Rydzewski Ryszard • PLN • WATERCOLOURS

AL AI LA DELLA LEGGE • 1968 • Stegani Giorgio • ITL, FRG • BEYOND THE LAW

AL ASSIFA see **STORM, THE** • 1970

AL-AYYAM AL-TAWILLA • 1980 • Saleh Tewfik • IRQ • LONG DAYS, THE ○ AYYAM AL TAWWILA, AL

AL BUIO INSIEME • 1933 • Righelli Gennaro • ITL • AMIAMOCI COSI

AL CAER LA TARDE • 1948 • Portas Rafael E. • MXC

AL CAPONE • 1959 • Wilson Richard • USA

AL CHRISTIE'S "MADAME BEHAVE" see **MADAME BEHAVE** • 1925

AL COMPAS DE TU MENTIRA • 1950 • Canziani Hector • ARG

AL COMPAS DL ROCK'N ROLL • 1956 • Diaz Morales Jose • MXC

AL DI LA DEL BENE E DEL MALE see **OLTRE IL BENE E IL MALE** • 1977

AL DI LA DELL'ODIO • 1972 • Santini Alessandro • ITL

AL DIABLO CON AMOR • 1972 • Suarez Gonzalo • SPN • DEVIL WITH LOVE, THE

AL DIABLO CON ESTE CURA! • 1967 • Rinaldi Carlos • ARG • TO HELL WITH THIS PRIEST

AL DIABLO CON LA MUSICA • 1958 • Porter Julio • MXC

AL DIABLO CON LAS MUJERES • 1954 • Delgado Miguel M. • MXC

AL DIAVOLO LA CELEBRITA • 1949 • Steno, Monicelli Mario • ITL • FAME AND THE DEVIL (USA) ○ ONE NIGHT OF FAME ○ NIGHT OF FAME, A

AL DONAHUE AND HIS ORCHESTRA IN HARMONY HIGHWAY • 1944 • Keays Vernon • SHT • USA
AL ESTE DE MARACAIBO • 1972 • Oropeza Daniel • VNZ • EAST OF MARACAIBO
AL FIN, SOLOS • 1955 • Perla Alejandro • SPN
AL FIN SOLOS, PERO... • 1977 • Gimenez-Rico Antonio • SPN
AL FRESCO • 1930 • Oumansky Alexander • UKN
AL GRITO DE ESTE PUEBLO • 1972 • Rios Humberto • ARG • CRY OF THE PEOPLE, THE (UKN)
AL HAPANIM • 1989 • ISR • FLAT ON YOUR FACE
AL HILAL • 1935 • Khan Mehboob • IND
AL JENNINGS OF OKLAHOMA • 1951 • Nazarro Ray • USA
AL KHEVEL DAK • 1981 • Bat-Adam Michal • ISR • THIN LINE, A
AL MARGEN DE LA LEY • 1935 • Iquino Ignacio F. • SPN • CRIMEN DEL EXPRESO DE ANDALUCIA, EL
AL MARTIN'S GAME • 1911 • *Lubin* • USA
AL NEIL • 1979 • Rimmer David • CND • PORTRAIT, A
AL OTRO LADO DE LA CIUDAD • 1961 • Balcazar Alfonso • SPN
AL OTRO LADO DEL ESPEJO • 1973 • Franco Jesus • SPN
AL PAREDON • 1970 • Mitrotti Mario • VNZ • TO THE WALL
AL PIACERE DI RIVEDERLA • 1976 • Leto Marco • ITL
AL PONERSE EL SOL • 1967 • Camus Mario • SPN • SUNSET
AL PROPRIO POSTO • 1979 • Roselli Franco • ITL
AL-QAHIRA THALATHIN see **CAIRO 30** • 1966
AL QUENETRA, MY LOVE • 1974 • Bunni Amin Al- • DOC • SYR
AL SERVICIO DE LA MUJER ESPANOLA • 1978 • de Arminan Jaime • SPN • AT THE SERVICE OF THE SPANISH LADY
AL SERVIZIO DELL'IMPERATORE (ITL) see **SI LE ROI SAVAIT CA** • 1956
AL SOLE • 1935 • Gallone Carmine • ITL
AL SON DE LA MARIMBA • 1940 • Bustillo Oro Juan • MXC
AL SON DEL CHARLESTON • 1954 • Salvador Jaime • MXC
AL SON DEL MAMBO • 1950 • Urueta Chano • MXC
AL SUR DE MANIADERO • 1970 • Cortazar Octavio • DOC • CUB • SOUTH OF MANIADERO
AL TRELEOR MUSCLE EXERCISES • 1905 • *Bitzer Billy (Ph)* • USA
AL TROPICO DEL CANCRO • 1972 • Mulargia Edoardo, Lomi Gian Paolo • ITL • PEACOCK'S PLACE
AL VOSTRI ORDINA, SIGNORA! see **AI VOSTRI ORDINA, SIGNORA!** • 1939
AL-YEMEN • 1931 • Schneiderov Vladimir • USS
AL' YLI PAASTA PERHANAA • 1968 • Kassila Matti • FNL • LET NOT ONE DEVIL CROSS THE BRIDGE
ALA-ARRIBA • 1942 • de Barros Jose Leitao • PRT • ALLA ARIBA
ALA MAN NAT'LUQ AR-RACAC? • 1975 • el Sheikh Kamal • EGY • SUR QUI DOIT-ON TIRER? ○ WHO WE MUST SHOOT AT
ALA MODE • 1958 • Vanderbeek Stan • ANS • USA
ALA SOTTO IL PIEDE, L' • 1973 • Massi Stelvio • ITL
ALA WARAQU SILUFAN • 1974 • Kamal Hussein • EGY • COMME UNE FEUILLE DE CELLOPHANE
ALAAP • 1977 • Mukherjee Hrishikesh • IND
ALABAMA -2000 LIGHT YEARS • 1969 • Wenders Wim • SHT • FRG
ALABAMA'S GHOST • 1973 • Hobbs Fredric • USA
ALABASTER BOX, THE • 1917 • Withey Chet • USA
ALADDIN • 1898 • Smith G. A. • UKN
ALADDIN • 1906 • Capellani Albert • FRN
ALADDIN • 1915 • Evans Fred, Evans Joe • UKN
ALADDIN • 1922 • *Rock Joe* • USA
ALADDIN • 1923 • *Cramer Joseph* • USA • WONDERFUL LAMP, THE
ALADDIN • 1934 • *Kabuli* • IND
ALADDIN • 1936 • Pal George • ANS • NTH
ALADDIN • 1953 • Reiniger Lotte • ANS • UKN
ALADDIN • 1987 • Corbucci Bruno • ITL
ALADDIN AND HIS LAMP • 1952 • Landers Lew • USA
ALADDIN AND HIS MAGIC LAMP see **ALADINO Y LA LAMPARA MARAVILLOSA** • 1957
ALADDIN AND HIS MAGIC LAMP see **ALADIN ET LA LAMPE MERVEILLEUSE, UN CONTE DES MILLE ET UNE NUITS** • 1969
ALADDIN AND HIS WONDERFUL LAMP • 1906 • *Pathe* • FRN
ALADDIN AND HIS WONDERFUL LAMP • 1934 • Iwerks Ub • ANS • USA
ALADDIN AND HIS WONDERFUL LAMP • 1939 • Fleischer Dave • ANM • USA
ALADDIN AND HIS WONDERFUL LAMP • 1940 • Sreenivasarao P. S., Tharukshuvu • IND
ALADDIN AND HIS WONDERFUL LAMP • 1985 • Burton Tim • MTV • USA
ALADDIN AND THE MAGIC LAMP see **ALADIN ES A CSODASZONYEG** • 1955
ALADDIN AND THE WONDERFUL LAMP • 1899 • Smith G. A. • UKN
ALADDIN AND THE WONDERFUL LAMP • 1917 • Franklin Chester M., Franklin Sidney A. • USA
ALADDIN AND THE WONDERFUL LAMP see **ALADIN ET LA LAMPE MERVEILLEUSE, UN CONTE DES MILLE ET UNE NUITS** • 1969
ALADDIN FROM BROADWAY • 1917 • Wolbert William • USA
ALADDIN IN PEARLIES • 1912 • Rains Fred • UKN
ALADDIN JONES • 1915 • *Historical Feature Film* • USA
ALADDIN: OR, A LAD OUT • 1914 • Plumb Hay? • UKN
ALADDIN UP-TO-DATE • 1912 • Dawley J. Searle • USA
ALADDIN UP-TO-DATE • 1917 • Berthelet Arthur • SHT • USA
ALADDIN'S AWAKENING • 1913 • *Nestor* • USA
ALADDIN'S LAMP • 1931 • *Terry Paul / Moser Frank (P)* • ANS • USA
ALADDIN'S LAMP • 1935 • *Terry Paul / Moser Frank (P)* • ANS • USA
ALADDIN'S LAMP • 1943 • Donnelly Eddie • ANS • USA
ALADDIN'S LAMP see **MIGHTY MOUSE IN ALADDIN'S LAMP** • 1947
ALADDIN'S LANTERN • 1938 • Douglas Gordon • SHT • USA
ALADDIN'S MAGIC LAMP see **VOLSHEBNAYA LAMPA ALADDINA** • 1967
ALADDIN'S OTHER LAMP • 1917 • Collins John H. • USA
ALADDIN'S WONDERFUL LAMP see **ALADINO Y LA LAMPARA MARAVILLOSA** • 1957
ALADIN • 1900 • *Pathe* • FRN
ALADIN • 1906 • *Pathe* • FRN
ALADIN • 1947 • Salumbides Vicente • PHL
ALADIN ES A CSODASZONYEG • 1955 • ANS • HNG • ALADDIN AND THE MAGIC LAMP
ALADIN ET LA LAMPE MERVEILLEUSE see **ALADIN ET LA LAMPE MERVEILLEUSE, UN CONTE DES MILLE ET UNE NUITS** • 1969
ALADIN ET LA LAMPE MERVEILLEUSE, UN CONTE DES MILLE ET UNE NUITS • 1969 • Image Jean • ANM • FRN • ALADIN ET LA LAMPE MERVEILLEUSE ○ ALADDIN AND HIS MAGIC LAMP ○ ALADDIN AND THE WONDERFUL LAMP
ALADINO Y LA LAMPARA MARAVILLOSA • 1957 • Soler Julian • MXC • ALADDIN AND HIS MAGIC LAMP ○ ALADDIN'S WONDERFUL LAMP
ALAEDIN'S SONS see **PESARAN-E-ALAEDIN** • 1967
ALAGEYIK • 1958 • Yilmaz Atif • TRK • HIND, THE
ALAIN GRANDBOIS • 1971 • Frappier Roger • DCS • CND
ALAIN R. -EIN LEBEN UND EIN FILM • 1971 • Radanowicz Georg • DOC • SWT
ALAKAZAM THE GREAT (USA) see **SAIYU-KI** • 1960
ALAKH NIRANJAN • 1950 • Gunjal Dada • IND • RAJA GOPICHAND
ALALUIA, GRETCHEN! • 1978 • BRZ
ALAM ARA • 1931 • Arani A. M. • IND
ALAM ARA • 1931 • Kapoor Prithviraj • IND • BEAUTY OF THE WORLD
ALAM EYAL, EYAL • 1976 • Aziz Mahmud Abdel • EGY • WORLD OF CHILDREN, CHILDREN, A
ALAMAT NG KILABOT • 1967 • Herrera Armando A. • PHL • LEGEND OF THE TERROR
ALAMBRADAS DE VIOLENCIA • 1966 • Klimovsky Leon • SPN
ALAMBRISTA! • 1978 • Young Robert Malcolm • USA • ILLEGAL, THE
ALAMID • 1967 • Santiago Cirio H. • PHL • JUNGLE CAT
ALAMO, THE • 1960 • Wayne John • USA
ALAMO, THE see **ALAMO: THIRTEEN DAYS TO GLORY, THE** • 1987
ALAMO BAY • 1985 • Malle Louis • USA
ALAMO: THIRTEEN DAYS TO GLORY, THE • 1987 • Werner Peter • TVM • USA • ALAMO, THE
ALAMUT AMBUSH, THE • 1983 • Grier Ken • MTV • UKN • CHESSGAME: ENTER HASSAN
ALAN AND APPLE • 1967 • Warhol Andy • USA
ALAN AND DICKIN • 1967 • Warhol Andy • USA
ALAN COURTNEY'S 1280 CLUB • Lloyd Ted • USA
ALAN STIVELL • 1975 • Vautier Rene • FRN
ALARM • 1922 • St. John Al • SHT • USA
ALARM • 1938 • Lauritzen Lau Jr. • DNM
ALARM • 1941 • Fredersdorf Herbert B. • FRG
ALARM • 1965 • Badzian Teresa • ANM • PLN
ALARM see **TREVOGA** • 1951
ALARM, THE • 1914 • Arbuckle Roscoe, Dillon Eddie • USA
ALARM, THE see **NABAT** • 1917
ALARM AUF GLEIS B see **GLEISDREIECK** • 1936
ALARM AUF STATION III • 1939 • Mayring Philipp L. • FRG
ALARM CLOCK ANDY • 1920 • Storm Jerome • USA
ALARM IM WELTALL see **PERRY RHODAN -SOS AUS DEM WELTALL** • 1967
ALARM IM ZIRKUS • 1954 • Klein Gerhard • GDR
ALARM IN PEKING • 1937 • Selpin Herbert • FRG
ALARM OF ANGELON, THE • 1915 • *American* • USA
ALARM ON 83RD STREET • 1965 • Bernds Edward • USA
ALARM SHOT see **RIASZTOLOVES** • 1977
ALARMA • 1937 • Cardona Rene • MXC
ALARME! see **ACTION STATIONS!** • 1943
ALARMING MORNING see **TREVOZHNOYE UTRO** • 1967
ALARMSTUFE V • 1941 • Lippl Alois J. • FRG
ALARSCOBAL • 1917 • *Lugosi Bela* • HNG
ALAS ABIERTAS • 1920 • Lezama Luis • MXC
ALAS AND ALACK • 1915 • De Grasse Joseph • USA
ALAS DE JUVENTUD • 1949 • del Amo Antonio • SPN
ALAS DE MI PATRIA • 1940 • Borcosque Carlos • ARG • MY COUNTRY'S WINGS (USA)
ALAS DORADAS • 1976 • Duran Fernando • MXC
ALAS, I'M INVISIBLE see **HILFE, ICH BIN UNSICHTBAR** • 1951
ALAS! MY HEART see **HAYE MERA DIL** • 1968
ALAS, POOR BUNNY • 1911 • Kinder Stuart? • UKN
ALAS! POOR YORICK! • 1913 • Campbell Colin • USA
ALAS SOBRE EL CHACO • 1939 • Cabanne W. Christy • MXC • WINGS OVER THE CHACO (USA)
ALAS Y GARRAS • 1967 • Rodriguez De La Fuente Felix • DOC • SPN • WINGS AND CLAWS
ALASKA • 1919 • *Katterjohn* • USA
ALASKA • 1930 • Lantz Walter, Nolan William • ANS • USA
ALASKA • 1944 • Archainbaud George • USA
ALASKA • 1989 • van Diem Mike • SHT • NTH
ALASKA HIGHWAY • 1943 • McDonald Frank • USA
ALASKA HIGHWAY • 1944 • Finnie Richard S. • DOC • CND
ALASKA LOVE • 1932 • Stafford Babe • SHT • USA
ALASKA MONOGATARI • 1976 • Horikawa Hiromichi • JPN • ALASKA STORY, THE
ALASKA PASSAGE • 1959 • Bernds Edward • USA
ALASKA PATROL • 1949 • Bernhard Jack • USA
ALASKA SEAS • 1954 • Hopper Jerry • USA
ALASKA STORY, THE see **ALASKA MONOGATARI** • 1976
ALASKA SWEEPSTAKES • 1936 • *Lantz Walter (P)* • ANS • USA
ALASKAFUCHSE • 1964 • Wallroth Werner W. • GDR
ALASKAN, THE • 1924 • Brenon Herbert • USA
ALASKAN ADVENTURES • 1926 • Robertson Jack • USA
ALASKAN ESKIMO • 1953 • Algar James • DOC • USA
ALASKAN INTERLUDE, AN • 1914 • Lessey George A. • USA
ALASKAN KNIGHTS • 1930 • *Mintz Charles (P)* • ANS • USA
ALASKAN MOUSE HOUND, THE • 1916 • *Hamilton Lloyd V.* • USA
ALASKAN SAFARI • 1968 • Hayes Ron, Hayes Bev • USA
ALAUDDIN KHAN • 1963 • *Ghatak Ritwik* • DOC • IND
ALAVERDOBA • 1966 • Shengelaya Eldar • USS
ALAYAM, ALAYAM • 1977 • el Maanouni Ahmed • MRC • DAYS, DAYS ○ ALYAM, ALYAM ○ OH ,THESE DAYS
ALAZAN Y EL ROSILLO, EL • 1964 • Cardona Rene • MXC
ALAZAN Y ENAMORADO • 1963 • Martinez Solares Gilberto • MXC
ALBA DE AMERICA • 1951 • de Orduna Juan • SPN
ALBA DEI FALSI DEI, L' • 1978 • Tessari Duccio • ITL • QUINTO COMANDAMENTO, IL
ALBA DI DOMANI see **ORGOGLIO** • 1938
ALBA DI SANGUE • 1949 • Gil Rafael • ITL, SPN
ALBA, IL GIORNO E LA NOTTE, L' • 1955 • Trebitsch Fernando • ITL
ALBA PAGANA see **DELITTO A OXFORD** • 1970
ALBANIA • 1945 • Karmen Roman • DOC • USS
ALBANIA see **CAVALIERE DI KRUJA, IL** • 1940
ALBANIE, LE CAS DE L'EUROPE • 1977 • Bertolino Jean • DOC • FRN
ALBANILES, LOS • 1976 • Fons Jorge • MXC • BRICKLAYERS, THE
ALBANY BUNCH, THE • 1931 • Sennett Mack • SHT • USA
ALBANY NIGHT BOAT, THE • 1928 • Raboch Alfred • USA
ALBATROS, L' • 1971 • Mocky Jean-Pierre • FRN • ALBATROSS, THE ○ LOVE HATE
ALBATROSS, THE see **ALBATROS, L'** • 1971
ALBEDO • 1983 • Leduc Jacques, Roy Renee • CND
ALBENIZ • 1947 • Amadori Luis Cesar • ARG • SPANISH SERENADE
ALBERG DEGLI ASSENTI, L' • 1939 • Matarazzo Raffaello • ITL
ALBERGO LUNA, CAMERA 34 • 1947 • Bragaglia Carlo Ludovico • ITL
ALBERO DALLE FOGLIE ROSA, L' • 1974 • Nannuzzi Armando • ITL
ALBERO DEGLI ZOCCOLI, L' • 1978 • Olmi Ermanno • ITL • TREE WITH THE WOODEN CLOGS, THE (UKN) ○ TREE OF WOODEN CLOGS, THE
ALBERO DELLA MALDICENZA, L' • 1979 • Bonacquisti Giacinto • ITL
ALBERO DI ADAMO, L' • 1936 • Bonnard Mario • ITL • ADAM'S TREE (USA)
ALBERO DI NATALE, L' (ITL) see **ARBRE DE NOEL, L'** • 1969
ALBERO VERDE • 1966 • Rolando Giuseppe • ITL
ALBERT AND JUNO • 1971 • Carretero Amaro • ANS • SPN
ALBERT CARTER Q.O.S.O. • 1967 • Brims Ian • UKN
ALBERT ET LEO EN ALBINIE • 1979 • Forcier Andre • CND
ALBERT HAT PROKURA • 1919 • Krafft Uwe Jens • FRG
ALBERT PINTO KO GUSSA KYON AATA HAI • 1979 • Mirza Saeed • IND • WHY SHOULD ALBERT PINTO BE ANGRY?
ALBERT R.N. • 1953 • Gilbert Lewis* • UKN • BREAK TO FREEDOM (USA) ○ SPARE MAN
ALBERT SCHWEITZER • 1957 • Hill Jerome • DOC • USA
ALBERT -WARUM? • 1978 • Rodl Josef • FRG • ALBERT -WHY?
ALBERT -WHY? see **ALBERT -WARUM?** • 1978
ALBERTA NATURAL LANDSCAPES • 1985 • Woodland James • MTV • CND
ALBERTE • 1973 • Udnaes Sverre • NRW
ALBERTFALVAI TORTENET • 1955 • Meszaros Marta • DCS • HNG • HISTORY OF ALBERTFALVA, A
ALBERTINE • 1986 • Bronken Per • NRW
ALBERTINE, L'ETERNELLE JEUNESSE • 1980 • Lavoie Richard • CND
ALBERTO DELLA FELICITA, L' • 1934 • Sampieri G. V. • ITL
ALBERTO EXPRESS • 1989 • Joffe Arthur • FRN
ALBERTO IL CONQUISTATORE see **SCAPOLO, LO** • 1956
ALBERTS HOSE • 1915 • Paulig Albert • FRG
ALBERT'S SAVINGS • 1940 • Purcell Harold • UKN
ALBIE THE FROG • 1974 • Scott Michael • CND
ALBINA SI PORUMBELUL • 1951 • Popescu-Gopo Ion • ANS • RMN • BEE AND THE DOVE, THE
ALBINO see **WHISPERING DEATH** • 1975
ALBISOLA MARE SAVONA • 1963 • Verhavert Roland • SHT • BLG
ALBRECHT FOR YOU • 1978 • Brown Lou • SHT • ASL
ALBUM • 1970 • Perry Dave • ASL
ALBUM DE FAMILLE, L' • 1976 • Barouh Pierre • FRN
ALBUM DE FAMILLE DE JEAN RENOIR, L' • 1956 • Gritti Roland • DOC • FRN
ALBUM FLEISCHERA • 1963 • Majewski Janusz • PLN • HERR FLEISCHER'S ALBUM ○ FLEISCHER'S ALBUM
ALBUM POLSKI • 1970 • Rybkowski Jan • PLN • POLISH ALBUM ○ RETURN
ALBUMINABLE HOMME DES TIMBRES, L' see **TOMMY TRICKER AND THE STAMP TRAVELLER** • 1988
ALBUQUERQUE • 1948 • Enright Ray • USA • SILVER CITY (UKN)
ALBUR DE AMOR • 1947 • Patino Gomez Alfonso • MXC
ALBURY PYJAMA GIRL MYSTERY, THE • 1939 • Kathner Rupert • SHT • ASL
ALBY'S DELIGHT see **OVER THE BROOKLYN BRIDGE** • 1983
ALCADE'S CONSPIRACY, THE • 1912 • *Joyce Alice* • USA
ALCALDA DE ZALAMEA, EL • 1953 • Gutierrez Maesso Jose • SPN
ALCALDE POR ELECCION • 1976 • Ozores Mariano • SPN
ALCATRAZ EXPRESS • 1960 • Peyser John • MTV • USA • BIG TRAIN, THE
ALCATRAZ ISLAND • 1937 • McGann William • USA
ALCATRAZ: THE WHOLE SHOCKING STORY • 1980 • Krasny Paul • TVM • USA
ALCESTES • 1987 • Lykouresis Tonis • GRC
ALCESTIS • 1976 • Quinnell Ken • SHT • ASL
ALCHEMIST, THE • 1913 • *Kinemacolor* • USA
ALCHEMIST, THE • 1983 • Band Charles • USA
ALCHEMIST AND THE DEMON, THE see **ALCHIMISTE PARAFARAGAMUS OU LA CORNUE INFERNALE, L'** • 1906
ALCHEMIST'S HOURGLASS, THE • 1936 • Lipp Leo • USA
ALCHIMIE • 1952 • Gremillon Jean • SHT • FRN
ALCHIMIE, UNE • 1966 • Kupissonoff Jacques • SHT • BLG
ALCHIMIE NOUVELLE see **NEW ALCHEMISTS, THE** • 1974
ALCHIMIST, DER • 1918 • Heiland Heinz Karl • FRG
ALCHIMISTE PARAFARAGAMUS OU LA CORNUE INFERNALE, L' • 1906 • Melies Georges • FRN • MYSTERIOUS RETORT, THE (USA) ○ ALCHEMIST AND THE DEMON, THE

ALCOFRISBAS, THE MASTER MAGICIAN see **ENCHANTEUR ALCOFRISBAS, L'** • 1903

ALCOHOL-GAUGE see **ALKOHOLOMIERZ** • 1962

ALCOHOL, TOMORROW'S FUEL • 1986 • Nicolle Douglas • DOC • CND

ALCOHOLISMO • 1978 • Vera Oscar • VNZ

ALCOHOLMAKERS, THE see **SAMOGONSHCHIKI** • 1961

ALCOOL • 1979 • Tretti Augusto • ITL

ALCOOL TUE, L' • 1948 • Resnais Alain • DCS • FRN

ALCOOLISME, L' • 1956-57 • Devlin Bernard • SHT • CND

ALDEA MALDITA, LA • 1929 • Rey Florian • SPN

ALDEA MALDITA, LA • 1942 • Rey Florian • SPN

ALDEBARAN • 1935 • Blasetti Alessandro • ITL

ALDEIA DA ROUPA BRANCA • 1938 • de Garcia Eduardo Chianca • PRT

ALDEIA DOS RAPAZES DA RUA, A • 1947 • Coelho Jose Adolfo • SHT • PRT

ALDERDOM OCH DARSKAP • 1916 • Hansen Edmond • SWD • OLD AGE AND FOLLY

ALDERMASTON POTTERY • 1965 • Darlow Michael, Searle Tony • DOC • UKN

ALDEVARAN • 1975 • Thomopoulos Andreas • GRC

ALDILA, L' • 1981 • Fulci Lucio • ITL • E TU VIVRAI NEL TERRORE! L'ALDILA ○ BEYOND, THE ○ AND YOU'LL LIVE IN TERROR! THE BEYOND ○ SEVEN DOORS OF DEATH

ALDO ET JUNIOR • 1984 • Schulmann Patrick • FRN

ALDOZAT, AZ • 1980 • Dobray Gyorgy • HNG • VICTIM, THE

ALDRIG I LIVET • 1957 • Ragneborn Arne • SWD • NEVER IN YOUR LIFE ○ DET HANDER I NATT

ALDRIG MED MIN KOFOT • 1954 • Bernhard Gosta • SWD • NEVER WITH MY JEMMY

ALECHINSKY D'APRES NATURE • 1970 • de Heusch Luc • DCS • FRN, BLG

ALEGO see **ALEKO** • 1954

ALEGRE CARAVANA, LA • 1953 • Torrado Ramon • SPN

ALEGRE CASADA, LA • 1951 • Zacarias Miguel • MXC

ALEGRE DIVORCIADO, EL • 1975 • Lazaga Pedro • MXC, SPN

ALEGRE JUVENTUD • 1962 • Ozores Mariano • SPN

ALEGRE VOY! • 1934 • Nosseck Max • SPN

ALEGRES AGUILARES, LOS • 1965 • Zacarias Miguel • MXC

ALEGRES CHICAS DE EL MARINO, LAS • 1975 • de la Loma Jose Antonio • SPN

ALEGRES PLACERES DEL SEXO, LOS • 1978 • Carretero Gil • SPN

ALEGRES VACACIONES • 1948 • Blay Jose Maria, Moreno Arturo • SPN

ALEGRES VAMPIRAS DE VOGEL, LAS • 1974 • Perez Tabernero Julio • SPN

ALEGRIA DE VIVIR, LA • 1965 • Soler Julian • MXC

ALEJANDRA • 1941 • Benavides Jose Jr. • MXC

ALEKO • 1954 • Roshal Grigori, Sidelev Sergei • USS • ALEGO

ALEKSANDR POPOV see **ALEXANDER POPOV** • 1949

ALEKZA DUNDIC see **OLEKO DUNDICH** • 1958

ALENA • 1947 • Cikan Miroslav • CZC

ALENKA • 1961 • Barnet Boris • USS • ALYONKA

ALENS LIVSMYSTERIUM • 1940 • Holger-Madsen • DNM

ALENTEJO NAO TEM SOMBRA • 1953 • Vitorino Orlando • SHT • PRT

ALERT • 1943 • Monkman Noel • DOC • ASL

ALERT IN THE SOUTH see **ALERTE AU SUD** • 1953

ALERTA EN EL CIELO • 1961 • Amadori Luis Cesar • SPN

ALERTE AU DEUXIEME BUREAU • 1956 • Stelli Jean • FRN • NEST OF SPIES (USA)

ALERTE AU SUD • 1953 • Devaivre Jean • FRN, ITL • ALLARME A SUD (ITL) ○ ALERT IN THE SOUTH

ALERTE AUX CANARIES • 1955 • Roy Andre • FRN

ALERTE EN MEDITERRANEE • 1938 • Joannon Leo • FRN • S.O.S MEDITERRANEAN ○ HELL'S CARGO

ALERTEZ LES BEBES • 1978 • Carre Jean-Michel • FRN

ALESSANDRO PANAGULIS • 1979 • Ferrara Giuseppe • MTV • ITL

ALESSANDRO, SEI GRANDE! • 1941 • Bragaglia Carlo Ludovico • ITL • ISOLA DELL'INCANTO, L'

ALESSANDROWNA see **DIARIO DI UNA STELLA, IL** • 1939

ALESSIA...UN VULCANO SOTTO LA PELLE • 1979 • Rizzo Alfredo • ITL

ALEVLI YILLAR • 1968 • Dinler Mehmet • TRK • FLAMING YEARS

ALEX AND THE GYPSY • 1976 • Korty John • USA • LOVE AND OTHER CRIMES

ALEX BIG SHOT • 1967 • Buenaventura Augusto • PHL

ALEX COLVILLE • 1967 • Bonniere Rene • DCS • CND

ALEX FALLS IN LOVE • 1986 • Davidson Boaz • USA

ALEX IN WONDERLAND • 1970 • Mazursky Paul • USA

ALEX THE GREAT • 1928 • Murphy Dudley • USA

ALEX: THE LIFE OF A CHILD • 1986 • Markowitz Robert • TVM • USA

ALEXANDER see **ALEXANDRE LE BIENHEUREUX** • 1968

ALEXANDER AND THE CAR WITH A MISSING HEADLIGHT • 1966 • Fleischamman Peter • CND

ALEXANDER BILIS • 1967 • Feleo Ben • PHL • ALEXANDER, THE FAST ONE

ALEXANDER CALDER • 1963 • Richter Hans • SWT

ALEXANDER DEN STORE • 1917 • Stiller Mauritz • SWD • ALEXANDER THE GREAT

ALEXANDER GALT: THE STUBBORN IDEALIST • 1962 • Biggs Julian • CND

ALEXANDER GRAHAM BELL see **STORY OF ALEXANDER GRAHAM BELL, THE** • 1939

ALEXANDER HAMILTON • 1931 • Adolfi John G. • USA

ALEXANDER MATROSOV see **RYADOVOI ALEXANDER MATROSOV** • 1948

ALEXANDER NEVSKY • 1938 • Eisenstein Sergei, Vasiliev Dimitri • USS • ALEXANDR NEVSKII

ALEXANDER PARKHOMENKO • 1942 • Lukov Leonid • USS

ALEXANDER POPOV • 1949 • Rappaport Herbert, Eisimont Viktor • USS • ALEKSANDR POPOV

ALEXANDER, THE FAST ONE see **ALEXANDER BILIS** • 1967

ALEXANDER THE GREAT • 1956 • Rossen Robert • USA

ALEXANDER THE GREAT • 1964 • *Shatner William* • MTV • USA

ALEXANDER THE GREAT see **ALEXANDER DEN STORE** • 1917

ALEXANDER THE GREAT see **SIKANDAR** • 1941

ALEXANDER THE GREAT see **MEGALEXANDROS, O** • 1980

ALEXANDER THE GREATER AFFAIR, THE see **ONE SPY TOO MANY** • 1966

ALEXANDER: THE OTHER SIDE OF DAWN • 1977 • Erman John • TVM • USA

ALEXANDER ZWO • 1972 • Wirth Franz Peter • FRG

ALEXANDER'S RAGTIME BAND • 1931 • Fleischer Dave • ANS • USA

ALEXANDER'S RAGTIME BAND • 1938 • King Henry • USA

ALEXANDR NEVSKII see **ALEXANDER NEVSKY** • 1938

ALEXANDRA • 1914 • Biebrach Rudolf • FRG

ALEXANDRA • 1922 • Frenkel-Bouwmeester Theo • FRG

ALEXANDRA see **ALEXANDRA: QUEEN OF SEX** • 1983

ALEXANDRA: QUEEN OF SEX • 1983 • Freeman Robert • USA • ALEXANDRA

ALEXANDRE see **ALEXANDRE LE BIENHEUREUX** • 1968

ALEXANDRE E ROSA • 1978 • Botelho Joao, da Silva Jorge Alves • SHT • PRT

ALEXANDRE LE BIENHEUREUX • 1968 • Robert Yves • FRN • VERY HAPPY ALEXANDER (USA) ○ HAPPY ALEXANDER ○ ALEXANDER ○ ALEXANDRE

ALEXANDRIA MORE AND MORE see **ISKENDRIA KAMAN WAKAMAN** • 1989

ALEXANDRIA, POURQUOI? see **ISKINDIRIA.. LEH?** • 1978

ALEXANDRIA, WHY? see **ISKINDIRIA.. LEH?** • 1978

ALEXIA'S STRATEGY • 1913 • *Edison* • USA

ALEXIS, GENTLEMAN-CHAUFFEUR • 1937 • de Vaucorbeil Max • FRN • GRAND RAID, LE

ALEXIS LADOUCEUR, METIS • 1961 • Garceau Raymond • DCS • CND

ALEXIS TREMBLAY, HABITANT -THE STORY OF A FARMER IN QUEBEC • 1943 • Beveridge Jane Marsh • DOC • CND • TERRE DE NOS AIEUX

ALF • 1987 • Patchett Tom • MTV • USA

ALF, BILL AND FRED • 1964 • Godfrey Bob • ANS • UKN

ALF GARNETT SAGA, THE • 1972 • Kellett Bob • UKN

ALF 'N' FAMILY (USA) see **TILL DEATH US DO PART** • 1968

ALF YAD WA YAD • 1972 • Ben Baraka Sohail • MRC, ITL • THOUSAND AND ONE HANDS, A ○ MILLE ET UNE MAINS, LES

ALFA TAU! • 1942 • De Robertis Francesco • ITL

ALFABETO NOTTURNO • 1953 • Birri Fernando, Holland Peter • SHT • ITL

ALFALFA'S AUNT • 1939 • Sidney George • SHT • USA

ALFALFA'S DOUBLE • 1940 • Cahn Edward L. • SHT • USA

ALFIE • 1966 • Gilbert Lewis* • UKN

ALFIE DARLING • 1975 • Hughes Ken • UKN • OH! ALFIE (USA)

ALFONS ZITTERBACKE • 1966 • Petzold Konrad • GDR

ALFONSINA • 1957 • Land Kurt • ARG

ALFRED DESROCHERS, POETE • 1960 • Fournier Claude • DCS • CND

ALFRED HARDING'S WOOING • 1913 • Haldane Bert? • UKN

ALFRED HITCHCOCK PRESENTS • 1985 • De Jarnatt Steve, Walton Fred, Oliansky Joel, Haines Randa • TVM • USA

ALFRED J #1 • 1957 • Devlin Bernard • SHT • CND

ALFRED J #2 • 1957 • Devlin Bernard • SHT • CND

ALFRED LALIBERTE • 1985 • Beaudry Michel • MTV • CND

ALFRED LALIBERTE, SCULPTEUR • 1988 • Lefebvre Jean-Pierre • DOC • CND

ALFRED LOVED BY THE GIRLS see **FLICKORNAS ALFRED** • 1935

ALFRED NOCNI CUVAR • 1971 • Grgic Zlatko • ANS • YGS • NIGHTWATCHMAN MUST FALL, THE ○ ALFRED THE NIGHTWATCHMAN

ALFRED R. see **ALFRED R., EIN LEBEN UND EIN FILM** • 1972

ALFRED R., EIN LEBEN UND EIN FILM • 1972 • Radanowicz Georg • SWT • ALFRED R.

ALFRED THE GREAT • 1969 • Donner Clive • UKN

ALFRED THE NIGHTWATCHMAN see **ALFRED NOCNI CUVAR** • 1971

ALFRED VON INGELHEIMS LEBENSTRAUM • 1920 • Lund Erik • FRG

ALFREDO, ALFREDO • 1972 • Germi Pietro • ITL, FRN

ALFREDO CAMPOLI AND HIS ORCHESTRA • 1936 • Shepherd Horace • UKN

ALFREDS TECHTELMECHTEL • 1919 • Czerny Ludwig • FRG

ALF'S BABY • 1953 • Rogers Maclean • UKN

ALF'S BUTTON • 1920 • Hepworth Cecil M. • UKN

ALF'S BUTTON • 1930 • Kellino W. P. • UKN

ALF'S BUTTON AFLOAT • 1938 • Varnel Marcel • UKN

ALF'S CARPET • 1929 • Kellino W. P. • UKN

ALGARVE • 1960 • Mendes Joao • SHT • PRT

ALGARVE, O • 1972 • de Almeida Manuel Faria • SHT • PRT

ALGARVE DE ALEM-MAR • 1950 • Ribeiro Antonio Lopes • SHT • PRT

ALGARVE ENCANTADO • 1944 • Miranda Armando • SHT • PRT

ALGER • 1967 • Bendeddouche Ghaouti • DCS • ALG

ALGER DES CORSAIRES see **DJEZAIR AR-RAIS, AL-** • 1975

ALGER ET L'ALGERIE • 1966 • Tolbi Abdelaziz • ALG

ALGER INSOLITE see **TAHYA YA DIDU** • 1971

ALGER-LE CAP • 1951 • de Poligny Serge • FRN

ALGERIA • 1973 • Leduc Jacques • DCS • CND

ALGERIA ON FIRE see **ALGERIE EN FLAMMES**

ALGERIE 62, CHRONIQUE D'UN CONFLIT • 1962 • Portugais Louis, Martin M. • DOC • CND

ALGERIE EN FLAMMES • ALG • ALGERIA ON FIRE

ALGERIE: UNE EXPERIENCE • 1976 • Duchene Nicole • DOC • CND

ALGERIEN, LES • 1965 • Lorenzini Ennio • FRN, ALG

ALGERNON BLACKWOOD STORIES • 1949 • Gilkison Anthony • SER • UKN

ALGERNON'S BUSY DAY • 1912 • *Shamrock* • USA

ALGIE, THE MINER • 1912 • *Quirk Billy* • USA

ALGIERS • 1938 • Cromwell John • USA

ALGIE'S EXPENSIVE STICK • 1912 • Collins Alf • UKN

ALGIE'S SISTER • 1914 • Walker Gilmore • USA

ALGO AMARGO EN LA BOCA • 1967 • de la Iglesia Eloy • SPN

ALGO ES DIJO EL DIABLO • 1974 • *Diana* • MXC

ALGO FLOTA SOBRE EL AGUA • 1947 • Crevenna Alfredo B. • MXC

ALGO GRANDE • 1971 • *Cinema-Center* • MXC

ALGOL • 1920 • Werckmeister Hans • FRG

ALGUIEN NOS QUIERE MATAR • 1969 • Velo Carlos • MXC

ALGUNAS LECCIONES DE AMOR • 1965 • Zabalza Jose Maria • SPN

ALGY AND THE PIERRETTE • 1913 • Collins Edwin J. • UKN

ALGY, DID HE DESERVE IT? • 1912 • Thornton F. Martin • UKN

ALGY FORFEITS HIS CLAIM • 1913 • *Nestor* • USA

ALGY GOES IN FOR PHYSICAL CULTURE • 1914 • Birch Cecil • UKN

ALGY GOES ON THE STAGE • 1910 • Collins Alf • UKN

ALGY ON THE FORCE • 1913 • Sennett Mack • USA

ALGY THE PICCADILLY JOHNNY • 1900 • Gibbons Walter • UKN

ALGY THE WATCHMAN • 1912 • Lehrman Henry • USA

ALGY TRIES FOR PHYSICAL CULTURE • 1910 • Collins Alf • UKN

ALGY'S ALIBI • 1914 • *Chadwick Cyril* • USA

ALGY'S AWFUL AUTO • 1913 • *Princess* • USA

ALGY'S LITTLE ERROR • 1914 • Plumb Hay? • UKN

ALGY'S NEW SUIT • 1906 • *Warwick Trading Co* • UKN

ALGY'S TORMENTOR • 1913 • Fitzhamon Lewin • UKN

ALGY'S YACHTING PARTY • 1908 • Stow Percy • UKN

ALHAN HIND WA CAMILIA • 1987 • Khan Mohamed • EGY • DREAMS OF HIND AND CAMILIA

ALI see **ANGST ESSEN SEELE AUF** • 1973

ALI AND HIS BABY CAMEL • 1953 • Hagopian Michael • USA

ALI AND THE CAMEL • 1960 • Geddes Henry • SRL • UKN

ALI BABA • 1902 • Zecca Ferdinand • FRN • ALI BABA ET LES QUARANTE VOLEURS

ALI BABA • 1911 • *Cines* • ITL

ALI BABA • 1934 • *Madan* • IND

ALI BABA • 1936 • *Iwerks Ub (P)* • ANS • USA

ALI BABA • 1937 • Bose Modhu • IND

ALI-BABA • 1937 • Pal George • ANS • NTH

ALI BABA • 1939 • Khan Mehboob • IND • ALIBABA

ALI BABA • 1970 • Luzzati Emmanuele • ANM • ITL

ALI BABA AND THE FORTY THIEVES • 1907 • *Pathe* • FRN

ALI BABA AND THE FORTY THIEVES • *Pathe* • FRN

ALI BABA AND THE FORTY THIEVES • 1918 • Franklin Sidney A., Franklin Chester M. • USA

ALI BABA AND THE FORTY THIEVES • 1943 • Lubin Arthur • USA

ALI BABA AND THE FORTY THIEVES see **ALI BABA WA AL ARBAIN HARAME** • 1941

ALI BABA AND THE FORTY THIEVES see **ALI BABA ET LES 40 VOLEURS** • 1954

ALI BABA AND THE FORTY THIEVES OF BAGHDAD see **ALI BABA VA CHEHEL DOZD-E-BAGHDAD** • 1967

ALI BABA AND THE SACRED CROWN see **SETTE FATICHE DI ALI BABA, LE** • 1963

ALI BABA AND THE SEVEN SARACENS (USA) see **SINBAD CONTRO I 7 SARACENI** • 1965

ALI BABA BOUND • 1940 • Clampett Robert • ANS • USA

ALI BABA BUJANG LAPOK • 1960 • Ramlee P. • MLY • ALI BABA IN BURLESQUE

ALI BABA BUNNY • 1956 • Jones Charles M. • ANS • USA

ALI BABA ET LES 40 VOLEURS • 1954 • Becker Jacques • FRN • ALI BABA (USA) ○ ALI BABA AND THE FORTY THIEVES

ALI BABA ET LES QUARANTE VOLEURS see **ALI BABA** • 1902

ALI BABA GOES TO TOWN • 1937 • Butler David • USA

ALI BABA IN BURLESQUE see **ALI BABA BUJANG LAPOK** • 1960

ALI BABA (USA) see **ALI BABA ET LES 40 VOLEURS** • 1954

ALI BABA VA CHEHEL DOZD-E-BAGHDAD • 1967 • Amin-E-Amini • IRN • ALI BABA AND THE FORTY THIEVES OF BAGHDAD

ALI BABA WA AL ARBAIN HARAME • 1941 • Mizrahi Togo • EGY • ALI BABA AND THE FORTY THIEVES

ALI BARBOUYOU ET ALI BOUF A L'HUILE • 1907 • Melies Georges • FRN • DELIRIUM IN A STUDIO (USA) ○ DELIRE A L'ATELIER

ALI BOUF A L'HUILE • 1907 • Mesguich Felix • ALG

ALI CHE TRADISCONO, LE • 1912 • Lolli Alberto Carlo • ITL

ALI: FEAR EATS THE SOUL see **ANGST ESSEN SEELE AUF** • 1973

ALI, I'VE SEEN ALI see **ALIYI GORDUM ALIYI** • 1967

ALI SPEZZATE • 1920 • Maggi Luigi • ITL

ALI THE MAN -ALI THE FIGHTER • 1975 • Baxter Rick • DOC • USA

ALIANZA PARA EL PROGESO • 1971 • Luduena Julio • ARG • ALLIANCE FOR PROGRESS

ALIAS 1 2 3 see **ALYAS 1 2 3** • 1968

ALIAS A GENTLEMAN • 1947 • Beaumont Harry • USA

ALIAS ALADDIN • 1920 • Roach Hal • SHT • USA

ALIAS BILLY SARGENT • 1912 • *Bushman Francis X.* • USA

ALIAS BILLY THE KID • 1946 • Carr Thomas • USA

ALIAS BOSTON BLACKIE • 1942 • Landers Lew • USA

ALIAS BULLDOG DRUMMOND (USA) see **BULLDOG JACK** • 1935

ALIAS CHAIN GANG • 1967 • Feleo Ben • PHL

ALIAS EL ALACRAN • 1961 • Martinez Arturo • MXC

ALIAS EL RATA • 1964 • Gonzalez Rogelio A. • MXC • RATA, EL

ALIAS EL REY DE JOROPO • 1978 • Rebolledo Carlos, Urguelles Thaelman • VNZ • KING OF THE JOROPO-DANCE ○ REY DE JOROPO, EL ○ KING OF TROUBLE, THE

ALIAS FRENCH GERTIE • 1930 • Archainbaud George • USA • LOVE FINDS A WAY (UKN)

ALIAS FU MANCHU see **ALYAS FUMANCHU** • 1964

ALIAS GARDELITO • 1961 • Murua Lautaro • ARG

ALIAS GREASED LIGHTNING • 1915 • *Mina* • USA

ALIAS HOLLAND JINNY • 1915 • Mong William V. • USA

ALIAS JAMES, CHAUFFEUR • 1915 • Douglass James • USA

ALIAS JANE JONES • 1916 • Meyers Ray • SHT • USA

ALIAS JESSE JAMES • 1959 • McLeod Norman Z. • USA

ALIAS JIMMY BARTON • 1916 • *Hartman Gretchen* • SHT • USA

ALIAS JIMMY VALENTINE • 1915 • Tourneur Maurice • USA

ALIAS JIMMY VALENTINE • 1920 • Mortimer Edmund • USA

ALIAS JIMMY VALENTINE • 1929 • Conway Jack • USA

ALIAS JOHN LAW • 1935 • Bradbury Robert North • USA

ALIAS JOHN PRESTON • 1956 • MacDonald David • UKN

ALIAS JULIUS CAESAR • 1922 • Ray Charles • USA
ALIAS LADYFINGERS • 1921 • Veiller Bayard • USA • LADYFINGERS
ALIAS MARY BROWN • 1918 • D'Elba Henri, Dowlan William C. • USA
ALIAS MARY DOW • 1935 • Neumann Kurt • USA
ALIAS MARY FLYNN • 1925 • Ince Ralph • USA
ALIAS MARY SMITH • 1932 • Hopper E. Mason • USA
ALIAS MIKE FURY see **GAMBLING HOUSE** • 1950
ALIAS MIKE MORAN • 1919 • Cruze James • USA
ALIAS MISS DODD • 1920 • Franklin Harry L. • USA
ALIAS MR. JONES • 1916 • *Ross Budd* • USA
ALIAS MR. SMITH • 1915 • *Mcquarrie Murdock* • USA
ALIAS MR. TWILIGHT • 1946 • Sturges John • USA
ALIAS MRS. JESSOP • 1917 • Davis Will S. • USA
ALIAS NICK BEAL • 1948 • Farrow John • USA • CONTACT MAN, THE (UKN) ○ DARK CIRCLE ○ STRANGE TEMPTATION
ALIAS PHANTOM see **ALYAS PHANTOM** • 1965
ALIAS PHIL KENNEDY • 1922 • Bertram William • USA
ALIAS ST. NICK • 1935 • Ising Rudolf • ANS • USA
ALIAS SMITH AND JONES • 1970 • Levitt Gene • TVM • USA
ALIAS TEXAS PETE OWENS (UKN) see **SELL 'EM COWBOY** • 1924
ALIAS THE BAD MAN • 1931 • Rosen Phil • USA
ALIAS THE BANDIT • 1930 • Nelson Jack • SHT • USA
ALIAS THE CHAMP • 1949 • Blair George • USA
ALIAS THE DEACON • 1928 • Sloman Edward • USA
ALIAS THE DEACON • 1940 • Cabanne W. Christy • USA
ALIAS THE DEACON see **HALF A SINNER** • 1934
ALIAS THE DOCTOR • 1932 • Bacon Lloyd, Curtiz Michael • USA
ALIAS THE JESTER • 1985 • ANM • UKN
ALIAS THE LONE WOLF • 1927 • Griffith Edward H. • USA
ALIAS THE LONE WOLF see **LONE WOLF KEEPS A DATE, THE** • 1941
ALIAS THE NIGHT WIND • 1923 • Franz Joseph J. • USA
ALIAS THE PROFESSOR • 1933 • Horne James W. • SHT • USA
ALIAS WILL JAMES • 1988 • Godbout Jacques • DOC • CND
ALIAS YELLOWSTONE JOE • 1911 • *Mersereau Violet* • USA
ALIBABA see **ALI BABA** • 1939
ALIBABA AND THE FORTY THIEVES • 1926 • *Imperial* • IND
ALIBABA AND THE FORTY THIEVES (USA) see **ARIBARA TO YONJUPIKINO TOZOKU** • 1971
ALIBI • 1929 • West Roland • USA • PERFECT ALIBI, THE (UKN) ○ NIGHTSTICK
ALIBI • 1931 • Hiscott Leslie • UKN
ALIBI • 1938 • Chenal Pierre • FRN
ALIBI • 1942 • Hurst Brian Desmond • UKN
ALIBI • 1955 • Weidenmann Alfred • FRG
ALIBI, L' • 1968 • Gassman Vittorio, Lucignani Luciano, Celi Adolfo • ITL • ALIBI, THE
ALIBI, THE • 1912 • *Nestor* • USA
ALIBI, THE • 1913 • *Holmes Helen* • USA
ALIBI, THE • 1915 • Easton Clem • USA
ALIBI, THE • 1916 • Scardon Paul • USA
ALIBI, THE see **BROKEN TIES** • 1918
ALIBI, THE see **INVISIBLE POWER, THE** • 1921
ALIBI, THE see **ALIBI, L'** • 1968
ALIBI BABY • 1945 • Yates Hal • SHT • USA
ALIBI BREAKER see **DOUBLE EXPOSURES** • 1937
ALIBI BYE BYE • 1935 • Holmes Ben • SHT • USA
ALIBI CLUB, THE • 1912 • *Majestic* • USA
ALIBI FOR DEATH, AN (USA) see **ALIBI ZERBRICHT, EIN** • 1963
ALIBI FOR MURDER • 1936 • Lederman D. Ross • USA
ALIBI IKE • 1935 • Enright Ray • USA
ALIBI INN • 1935 • Tennyson Walter • UKN
ALIBI PER MORIRE, UN • 1962 • Montero Roberto Bianchi • ITL
ALIBI POUR UN MEURTRE • 1961 • Bibal Robert • FRN
ALIBI RACKET • 1935 • Seitz George B. • SHT • USA
ALIBI ZERBRICHT, EIN • 1963 • Vohrer Alfred • AUS, FRG • ALIBI FOR DEATH, AN (USA)
ALIBI,L' • 1914 • Pouctal Henri • FRN
ALIBIS • 1977 • Rissient Pierre • FRN, HKG • ONE NIGHT STAND
ALICE • 1980 • Gruza Jerzy, Bromski Yacek • BLG, PLN, UKN
ALICE • 1988 • Svankmajer Jan • ANM • FRG, UKN
ALICE • 1990 • Allen Woody • USA
ALICE ADAMS • 1923 • Lee Rowland V. • USA • FOOLISH DAUGHTERS
ALICE ADAMS • 1935 • Stevens George • USA
ALICE AND THE DOG CATCHER • 1924 • Disney Walt • ANS • USA
ALICE AND THE THREE BEARS • 1924 • Disney Walt • ANS • USA
ALICE AT THE CARNIVAL • 1927 • Disney Walt • ANS • USA
ALICE AT THE RODEO see **ALICE'S RODEO** • 1927
ALICE AU PAYS DES MERVEILLES • 1948 • Bonin Lou, Maurette Marc • FRN, UKN
ALICE BABS I TOPPFORM see **SANGEN OM STOCKHOLM** • 1947
ALICE BE GOOD • 1926 • Cline Eddie • SHT • USA
ALICE BRADY AT THE LIBERTY LOAN APPEAL • 1918 • *Select* • USA
ALICE CANS THE CANNIBALS • 1924 • Disney Walt • ANS • USA
ALICE CHARMS THE FISH • 1926 • Disney Walt • ANS • USA
ALICE CHOPS THE SUEY • 1925 • Disney Walt • ANS • USA
ALICE CONSTANT • 1976 • Laurent Christine • FRN, SWT • A. CONSTANT
ALICE CUTS THE ICE • 1926 • Disney Walt • ANS • USA
ALICE DOESN'T LIVE HERE ANYMORE • 1974 • Scorsese Martin • USA
ALICE DOWN WONDERLAND • 1973 • Cleve Bastian • FRG
ALICE FOILS THE PIRATES • 1927 • Disney Walt • ANS • USA
ALICE GETS IN DUTCH • 1924 • Disney Walt • ANS • USA
ALICE GETS STUNG • 1925 • Disney Walt • ANS • USA
ALICE GOODBODY see **GOSH** • 1974
ALICE HELPS THE ROMANCE • 1926 • Disney Walt • ANS • USA
ALICE HUNTING IN AFRICA • 1924 • Disney Walt • ANS • USA
ALICE IN ACIDLAND • 1969 • Donne John • USA • ALICE IN HIPPIELAND
ALICE IN CARTOON LAND • 1924-27 • Disney Walt • ASS • USA
ALICE IN DEN STADTEN • 1974 • Wenders Wim • FRG • ALICE IN THE CITIES (USA)
ALICE IN HIPPIELAND see **ALICE IN ACIDLAND** • 1969
ALICE IN MOVIELAND • 1928 • *Paramount* • SHT • USA
ALICE IN MOVIELAND • 1940 • Negulesco Jean • SHT • USA
ALICE IN SOCIETY • 1916 • *Howell Alice* • SHT • USA
ALICE IN SPANISH WONDERLAND see **ALICIA EN LA ESPANA DE LAS MARAVILLAS** • 1977
ALICE IN SWITZERLAND • 1939 • Cavalcanti Alberto • SHT • UKN
ALICE IN THE ALPS • 1927 • Disney Walt • ANS • USA
ALICE IN THE BIG LEAGUE • 1927 • Disney Walt • ANS • USA
ALICE IN THE CITIES (USA) see **ALICE IN DEN STADTEN** • 1974
ALICE IN THE JUNGLE • 1925 • Disney Walt • ANS • USA
ALICE IN THE KLONDIKE • 1927 • Disney Walt • ANS • USA
ALICE IN THE NAVY see **ALIKI STO NAFTIKO** • 1960
ALICE IN THE WOOLY WEST • 1926 • Disney Walt • ANS • USA
ALICE IN WONDERLAND • Nijgh Lennaert • SHT • NTH
ALICE IN WONDERLAND • 1903 • Hepworth Cecil M., Stow Percy • UKN
ALICE IN WONDERLAND • 1915 • Wheeler Dewitt C. • USA
ALICE IN WONDERLAND • 1916 • Young W. W. • USA
ALICE IN WONDERLAND • 1927 • *Pathe* • USA
ALICE IN WONDERLAND • 1931 • Pollard Bud • USA
ALICE IN WONDERLAND • 1933 • McLeod Norman Z. • USA
ALICE IN WONDERLAND • 1948 • Bower Dallas • UKN, FRN
ALICE IN WONDERLAND • 1951 • Bunin Louis • ANM • USA
ALICE IN WONDERLAND • 1951 • Geronimi Clyde, Luske Hamilton, Jackson Wilfred • ANM • USA
ALICE IN WONDERLAND • 1967 • Miller Jonathan • MTV • UKN
ALICE IN WONDERLAND • 1976 • Townsend Bud • USA
ALICE IN WONDERLAND • 1986 • Harris Harry • TVM • USA
ALICE LEAVES WONDERLAND • 1989 • Stevenson • SHT • UKN, ASL
ALICE LOSES OUT • 1925 • Disney Walt • ANS • USA
ALICE OF HUDSON BAY • 1915 • Bartlett Charles • USA
ALICE OF THE LAKE • 1915 • King Burton L. • USA
ALICE OF THE SAWDUST • 1917 • Blystone John G. • SHT • USA
ALICE OF WONDERLAND IN NEW ADVENTURES see **ALICE OF WONDERLAND IN PARIS** • 1966
ALICE OF WONDERLAND IN PARIS • 1966 • Deitch Gene • ANM • USA • ALICE OF WONDERLAND IN NEW ADVENTURES
ALICE ON THE FARM • 1925 • Disney Walt • ANS • USA
ALICE OR THE LAST ESCAPADE (USA) see **ALICE OU LA DERNIERE FUGUE** • 1977
ALICE OU LA DERNIERE FUGUE • 1977 • Chabrol Claude • FRN • ALICE OR THE LAST ESCAPADE (USA)
ALICE PICKS THE CHAMP • 1925 • Disney Walt • ANS • USA
ALICE PLAYS CUPID • 1925 • Disney Walt • ANS • USA
ALICE RATTLED BY RATS • 1925 • Disney Walt • ANS • USA
ALICE SOLVES THE PUZZLE • 1925 • Disney Walt • ANS • USA
ALICE STAGE STRUCK • 1925 • Disney Walt • ANS • USA
ALICE, SWEET ALICE • 1977 • Sole Alfred • USA • COMMUNION ○ HOLY TERROR
ALICE THE BEACH NUT • 1927 • Disney Walt • ANS • USA
ALICE THE COLLEGIATE • 1927 • Disney Walt • ANS • USA
ALICE THE FIREFIGHTER • 1926 • *Disney Walt (P)* • ANS • USA
ALICE THE GOLF BUG • 1927 • Disney Walt • ANS • USA
ALICE THE JAIL BIRD • 1925 • Disney Walt • ANS • USA
ALICE THE LUMBERJACK • 1926 • Disney Walt • ANS • USA
ALICE THE PEACEMAKER • 1924 • Disney Walt • ANS • USA
ALICE THE PIPER • 1924 • Disney Walt • ANS • USA
ALICE THE TOREADOR • 1924 • Disney Walt • ANS • USA
ALICE THE WHALER • 1927 • Disney Walt • ANS • USA
ALICE THROUGH A LOOKING GLASS • 1928 • Lang Walter • USA
ALICE TO NOWHERE • 1986 • Power John • TVM • ASL
ALICE WINS THE DERBY • 1925 • Disney Walt • ANS • USA
ALICENTE ANWESHANAM • 1989 • Chandran T. V. • IND • IN SEARCH OF ALICE
ALICE'S ADVENTURES IN WONDERLAND • 1910 • Porter Edwin S. • USA
ALICE'S ADVENTURES IN WONDERLAND • 1972 • Sterling William • UKN
ALICE'S AUTO RACE • 1927 • Disney Walt • ANS • USA
ALICE'S BALLOON RACE • 1925 • Disney Walt • ANS • USA
ALICE'S BROWN DERBY • 1926 • Disney Walt • ANS • USA
ALICE'S CHANNEL SWIM • 1927 • Disney Walt • ANS • USA
ALICE'S CHOICE • 1912 • Melies Gaston • USA
ALICE'S CIRCUS DAZE • 1927 • Disney Walt • ANS • USA
ALICE'S DAY AT SEA • 1924 • Disney Walt • ANS • USA
ALICE'S EGG PLANT • 1925 • Disney Walt • ANS • USA
ALICE'S FISHY STORY • 1924 • Disney Walt • ANS • USA
ALICE'S KNAUGHTY KNIGHT • 1927 • Disney Walt • ANS • USA
ALICE'S LITTLE PARADE • 1925 • Disney Walt • ANS • USA
ALICE'S MEDICINE SHOW • 1927 • Disney Walt • ANS • USA
ALICE'S MONKEY BUSINESS • 1926 • Disney Walt • ANS • USA
ALICE'S MYSTERIOUS MYSTERY • 1925 • Disney Walt • ANS • USA
ALICE'S ORNERY ORPHAN • 1925 • Disney Walt • ANS • USA
ALICE'S PICNIC • 1927 • Disney Walt • ANS • USA
ALICE'S RESTAURANT • 1969 • Penn Arthur • USA
ALICE'S RODEO • 1927 • Disney Walt • ANS • USA • ALICE AT THE RODEO
ALICE'S SACRIFICE • 1911 • *Lubin* • USA
ALICE'S SPANISH GUITAR • 1926 • Disney Walt • ANS • USA
ALICE'S SPOOKY ADVENTURE • 1924 • Disney Walt • ANS • USA
ALICE'S THREE BAD EGGS • 1927 • Disney Walt • ANS • USA
ALICE'S TIN PONY • 1925 • Disney Walt • ANS • USA
ALICE'S WILD WEST SHOW • 1924 • Disney Walt • ANS • USA
ALICE'S WONDERLAND • 1923 • Disney Walt • ANS • USA
ALICIA • 1974 • Verstappen Wim • NTH
ALICIA EN LA ESPANA DE LAS MARAVILLAS • 1977 • Feliu Jordi • SPN • ALICE IN SPANISH WONDERLAND
ALICIA IN CONCERT • van Zuylen Erik • NTH
ALIEN • 1979 • Scott Ridley • USA, UKN
ALIEN, THE • 1913 • *Vignola Robert* • USA
ALIEN, THE • 1915 • Ince Thomas H. • USA
ALIEN, THE • 1965 • Quinn Ron • USA
ALIEN, THE • 1980 • van den Berg Rudolf • NTH
ALIEN ATTACK • 1977 • Katzin Lee H., Crichton Charles, Lenny Bill • MTV • UKN • SPACE 1999: ALIEN ATTACK
ALIEN BASEBALL TEAM • 1986 • SKR
ALIEN BLOOD • 1917 • *Fortune* • USA
ALIEN CHICKEN AND THE SURREY FOWL, THE • 1903 • *Warwick Trading Co* • UKN
ALIEN CONTAMINATION • 1981 • Cozzi Luigi • ITL • CONTAMINATION
ALIEN DEAD, THE • 1980 • Ray Fred Olen • USA • IT FELL FROM THE SKY ○ SWAMP OF THE BLOOD LEECHES
ALIEN ENCOUNTER see **STARSHIP INVASIONS** • 1977
ALIEN ENCOUNTERS • 1979 • Flocker James T. • USA
ALIEN ENCOUNTERS see **UFOS ARE REAL** • 1979
ALIEN ENEMY, AN • 1918 • Worsley Wallace • USA
ALIEN FACTOR, THE • 1977 • Dohler Don • USA • ALIEN TERROR, THE
ALIEN FROM L.A. • 1988 • Pyun Albert • USA • ODEON
ALIEN FROM SPACESHIP EARTH • 1977 • *George Lynda Day* • USA
ALIEN LOVER • 1975 • Swift Lela • TVM • USA
ALIEN MASSACRE, HORRORS OF THE RED PLANET see **WIZARD OF MARS** • 1964
ALIEN NATION • 1988 • Baker Graham* • USA • OUTER HEAT
ALIEN ORO, THE • 1973 • *Koenig Walter* • MTV • USA
ALIEN PREDATOR see **ALIEN PREDATORS** • 1987
ALIEN PREDATORS • 1987 • Sarafian Deran • USA • FALLING, THE ○ MUTANT 2 ○ ALIEN PREDATOR
ALIEN PREY (USA) see **PREY** • 1984
ALIEN QUESTION, THE • 1905 • Collins Alf? • UKN
ALIEN SABOTAGE (UKN) see **PASSPORT TO ALCATRAZ** • 1940
ALIEN SHORE see **CHUZHOI BEREG** • 1930
ALIEN SOULS • 1916 • Reicher Frank • USA
ALIEN TERROR • 1977 • McNeil Chuck • USA
ALIEN TERROR see **INVASION SINIESTRA** • 1968
ALIEN TERROR, THE see **ALIEN FACTOR, THE** • 1977
ALIEN THUNDER • 1973 • Fournier Claude • CND • DAN CANDY'S LAW
ALIEN WARRIOR • 1985 • Hunt Ed • USA • KING OF THE STREETS
ALIEN ZONE • 1975 • Miller Sharron • USA • HOUSE OF THE DEAD
ALIENIST, THE see **ALIENISTA, O** • 1970
ALIENISTA, O • 1970 • dos Santos Nelson Pereira • BRZ • ALIENIST, THE
ALIENISTE, L' see **AZYLO MUITO LOUCO** • 1970
ALIENS • 1986 • Cameron James • USA
ALIENS see **UNWRITTEN CODE, THE** • 1919
ALIENS ARE COMING, THE • 1980 • Hart Harvey • TVM • USA
ALIENS FROM ANOTHER PLANET • 1966 • *Darren James* • MTV • USA
ALIENS FROM SPACESHIP EARTH • 1977 • Como Don • USA • ALIENS FROM SPACESHIP EARTH WANTED
ALIENS FROM SPACESHIP EARTH WANTED see **ALIENS FROM SPACESHIP EARTH** • 1977
ALIENS' INVASION, THE • 1905 • Fitzhamon Lewin • UKN
ALIEN'S RETURN, THE see **RETURN, THE** • 1980
ALIF LAILA • 1953 • Amarnath K. • IND
ALIF LAILA WA LEILA • 1941 • Mizrahi Togo • EGY • THOUSAND AND ONE NIGHTS, A
ALIJO, EL • 1976 • del Pozo Angel • SPN
ALIKE, UNALIKE see **PAREIL PAS PAREIL** • 1978
ALIKI see **ALIKI, MY LOVE** • 1963
ALIKI DIKTATOR • 1972 • Vouyouklakis Takis • GRC
ALIKI IN THE NAVY see **ALIKI STO NAFTIKO** • 1960
ALIKI, MY LOVE • 1963 • Mate Rudolph • USA, GRC • ALIKI
ALIKI STO NAFTIKO • 1960 • Sakellarios Alekos • GRC • ALIKI IN THE NAVY ○ ALICE IN THE NAVY
ALIMANAS, LAS • 1976 • de Ossorio Amando • SPN
ALIMENTE • 1929 • Boese Carl • FRG
ALIMENTS, GENTILS ALIMENTS • 1975 • Fournier Claude, Raymond Marie-Josee • DCS • CND
ALIMINIUM • 1952 • Ichac Marcel • DCS • FRN
ALIMONY • 1918 • Flynn Emmett J. • USA
ALIMONY • 1924 • Horne James W. • USA • WHEN THE CRASH CAME (UKN)
ALIMONY • 1949 • Zeisler Alfred • USA
ALIMONY see **JEEVANAMSAM** • 1968
ALIMONY ACHES • 1935 • Lamont Charles • SHT • USA
ALIMONY LOVERS • 1969 • Perkins Harold • USA
ALIMONY MADNESS • 1933 • Eason B. Reeves • USA
ALINA • 1950 • Pastina Giorgio • ITL
ALINA • 1985-89 • Osman Aziz M. • MTV • MLY
ALINE • 1967 • Weyergans Francois • FRN, BLG, SWT
ALIPIN NG BUSABOS • 1968 • de Guzman Armando • PHL • SLAVE OF SLAVE
ALISHAR NAVOI see **ALISHER NAVOI** • 1947
ALISHER NAVOI • 1947 • Yarmatov Kamil • USS • ALISHAR NAVOI
ALISON'S BIRTHDAY • 1979 • Coughlan Ian • ASL
ALISTAIR MACLEOD • 1984 • MacGillivray William D. • MTV • CND
ALITET GOES INTO THE MOUNTAINS see **ALITET UKHODIT V GORY** • 1949
ALITET LEAVES FOR THE HILLS see **ALITET UKHODIT V GORY** • 1949

ALITET UKHODIT V GORY • 1949 • Donskoi Mark • USS • ALITET LEAVES FOR THE HILLS ○ ALITET GOES INTO THE MOUNTAINS ○ ZAKONE BOLSHOI ZEMLI
ALIVE ALIVE O see **...AND NO ONE COULD SAVE HER** • 1972
ALIVE AND KICKING • 1958 • Frankel Cyril • UKN
ALIVE BY NIGHT see **EVIL SPAWN** • 1987
ALIVE ON SATURDAY • 1957 • Travers Alfred • UKN
ALIW • 1979 • Bernal Ishmael • PHL
ALIXE OR THE TEST OF FRIENDSHIP • 1913 • Ranous William V. • USA
ALIYI GORDUM ALIYI • 1967 • Utku Umit • TRK • ALI, I'VE SEEN ALI
ALKALI BESTS BRONCHO BILLY • 1912 • *Anderson Broncho Billy* • USA
ALKALI IKE AND THE HYPNOTIST • 1913 • *Carney Augustus* • USA
ALKALI IKE AND THE WILDMAN • 1913 • *Carney Augustus* • USA
ALKALI IKE IN JAYVILLE • 1913 • Hopper E. Mason • USA
ALKALI IKE PLAYS THE DEVIL • 1912 • Anderson G. M. • USA
ALKALI IKE STUNG • 1912 • Anderson G. M. • USA
ALKALI IKE'S AUTO • 1911 • *Carney Augustus* • USA
ALKALI IKE'S AUTO • 1913 • Anderson G. M. • USA
ALKALI IKE'S BOARDING HOUSE • 1912 • Anderson G. M. • USA
ALKALI IKE'S BRIDE • 1912 • *Carney Augustus* • USA
ALKALI IKE'S CLOSE SHAVE • 1912 • *Carney Augustus* • USA
ALKALI IKE'S GAL • 1913 • *Carney Augustus* • USA
ALKALI IKE'S HOMECOMING • 1913 • Anderson G. M. • USA
ALKALI IKE'S LOVE AFFAIR • 1912 • *Carney Augustus* • USA
ALKALI IKE'S MISFORTUNES • 1913 • Anderson G. M. • USA
ALKALI IKE'S MOTHER-IN-LAW • 1913 • *Carney Augustus* • USA
ALKALI IKE'S MOTORCYCLE • 1912 • Anderson G. M. • USA
ALKALI IKE'S PANTS • 1912 • Anderson G. M.? • USA
ALKESTE -DIE BEDEUTUNG PROTEKTION ZU HABEN • 1971 • Lepeniotis Antonis • AUS
ALKOHOL • 1919 • Lind Alfred, Dupont E. A. • FRG
ALKOHOLOMIERZ • 1962 • Hoffman Jerzy, Skorzewski Edward • PLN • ALCOHOL-GAUGE
ALKONY • 1971 • Szabo Istvan • DCS • HNG • TWILIGHT
ALKONYOK ES HAJNALOK • 1961 • Jancso Miklos • SHT • HNG • TWILIGHT AND DAWN ○ DUSKS AND DAWNS
ALL 33 DI VIA OROLOGIO FA SEMPRE FREDDO see **SHOCK TRANSFERT SUSPENCE HYPNOS** • 1977
ALL A MISTAKE • 1912 • *Imp* • USA
ALL ABIR-R-RD • 1950 • Freleng Friz • ANS • USA
ALL ABOARD • 1915 • Christie Al • USA
ALL ABOARD • 1917 • Roach Hal • SHT • USA
ALL ABOARD • 1927 • Hines Charles • USA
ALL ABOARD • 1937 • Schwarzwald Milton • SHT • USA
ALL ABOARD see **HOTOVO, JEDEM** • 1947
ALL ABOARD FOR RENO • 1911 • *Solax* • USA
ALL ABOARD FOR THE MOON • 1924 • *Bray J. R. (P)* • ANS • USA
ALL ABOUT A BABY • 1915 • *Superba* • USA
ALL ABOUT A PRIMA BALLERINA • 1982 • Sheybal Vladek • UKN
ALL ABOUT AL-LONG • 1989 • To Johnny • HKG
ALL ABOUT DOGS • 1942 • Rasinski Connie • ANS • USA
ALL ABOUT EMILY • 1949 • Sparling Gordon • DCS • CND
ALL ABOUT EVE • 1950 • Mankiewicz Joseph L. • USA
ALL ABOUT GLORIA LEONARD • 1978 • Leonard Gloria • USA
ALL ABOUT HASH • 1940 • Cahn Edward L. • SHT • USA
ALL ABOUT LOVING (UKN) see **DE L'AMOUR** • 1964
ALL ABOUT WOMEN • 1971 • Pierson Claude • FRN
ALL ABOUT WOMEN (UKN) see **A PROPOS DE LA FEMME** • 1969
ALL ALONE • 1911 • *Reliance* • USA
ALL ALONE see **SINGUR** • 1968
ALL AMERICAN see **OLYMPIC HERO, THE** • 1928
ALL-AMERICAN, THE • 1932 • Mack Russell • USA • SPORT OF A NATION (UKN)
ALL AMERICAN, THE • 1953 • Hibbs Jesse • USA • WINNING WAY, THE (UKN)
ALL AMERICAN BANDS, THE • 1943 • Negulesco Jean • SHT • USA
ALL-AMERICAN BLONDES • 1939 • Lord Del • SHT • USA
ALL-AMERICAN BOY, THE • 1973 • Eastman Charles • USA
ALL-AMERICAN CHUMP • 1936 • Marin Edwin L. • USA • COUNTRY BUMPKIN (UKN) ○ WHERE'S ELMER?
ALL-AMERICAN CO-ED • 1941 • Prinz Leroy • USA
ALL-AMERICAN KICKBACK • 1931 • Lord Del • SHT • USA
ALL AMERICAN PRO • 1948 • Dreifuss Arthur • USA
ALL-AMERICAN SWEETHEART • 1937 • Hillyer Lambert • USA
ALL-AMERICAN TOOTHACHE • 1936 • Meins Gus • SHT • USA
ALL AMERICANS • 1929 • Santley Joseph • SHT • USA
ALL AND NOBODY see **TODO Y NADIE** • 1977
ALL AROUND CURE, AN • 1916 • Curtis Allen • SHT • USA
ALL AROUND FRYING PAN • 1925 • Kirkland David • USA • OUT OF THE FRYING PAN
ALL AROUND MISTAKE, AN • 1915 • Lessey George A. • USA
ALL ASHORE • 1953 • Quine Richard • USA
ALL AT SEA • 1914 • *Keystone* • USA
ALL AT SEA • 1914 • *Albuquerque* • USA
ALL AT SEA • 1914 • *Nestor* • USA
ALL AT SEA • 1917 • *Triangle* • USA
ALL AT SEA • 1917 • *Black Diamond* • USA
ALL AT SEA • 1919 • Parrott Charles, Roach Hal • USA
ALL AT SEA • 1928 • Goulding Alf • USA
ALL AT SEA • 1929 • Baker Eddie • USA
ALL AT SEA • 1933 • Kleinert E. H. • SHT • USA
ALL AT SEA • 1935 • Kimmins Anthony • UKN
ALL AT SEA • 1939 • Smith Herbert • UKN
ALL AT SEA • 1969 • Fairbairn Kenneth • UKN
ALL AT SEA • 1977 • Auzins Igor • MTV • ASL
ALL AT SEA (USA) see **BARNACLE BILL** • 1957
ALL BAD see **SCHWARZE NYLONS -HEISSE NACHTE** • 1958
ALL BALLED UP • 1915 • *Kromann Ann* • USA
ALL BALLED UP • 1916 • Miller Rube • USA
ALL BEGINNINGS ARE DIFFICULT • 1964 • Mariassy Felix • HNG
ALL BEGINNINGS ARE HARD see **MINDEN KEZDET NEHEZ** • 1966
ALL BETS OFF • 1916 • Lyons Eddie, Moran Lee • SHT • USA
ALL BOUND 'ROUND • 1919 • Lyons Eddie, Moran Lee • SHT • USA
ALL BUSINESS • 1936 • Yarbrough Jean • SHT • USA
ALL BY MYSELF • 1943 • Feist Felix E. • USA • YOU GO TO MY HEART
ALL BY YOURSELF IN THE MOONLIGHT • 1929 • Aylott Dave, Symmons E. F. • SHT • UKN
ALL CLEAR: NO NEED TO TAKE COVER • 1917 • Denison James • UKN
ALL COLORED VAUDEVILLE SHOW • 1935 • Mack Roy • SHT • USA
ALL COOKED UP • 1915 • Ransom Charles • USA
ALL COONS LOOK ALIKE TO ME • 1909 • *Warwick Trading Co* • UKN
ALL COONS LOOK ALIKE TO ME (PARODY) • 1908 • Gilbert Arthur • UKN
ALL COPPERS ARE... • 1971 • Hayers Sidney • UKN
ALL CREATURES GREAT AND SMALL • 1974 • Whatham Claude • UKN
ALL CREATURES GREAT AND SMALL: THE HOMECOMING • 1983 • Dudley Terence • TVM • UKN
ALL DOGS GO TO HEAVEN • 1989 • Bluth Don • ANM • IRL
ALL DOLLED UP • 1915 • *Heinie & Louie* • USA
ALL DOLLED UP • 1921 • Sturgeon Rollin S. • USA • BOBBED SQUAD, THE
ALL DRAWINGS OF THE TOWN see **SVI CRTEZI GRADA** • 1959
ALL DRESSED UP • 1918 • *Compson Betty* • SHT • USA
ALL DRESSED UP • 1920 • Roach Hal • SHT • USA
ALL EINSTEIN'S FAULT see **MUZ Z PRVNIHO STOLETI** • 1961
ALL EXCITED • 1931 • Lamont Charles • SHT • USA
ALL FALL DOWN • 1962 • Frankenheimer John • USA
ALL FOOLS' DAY AFFAIR, AN • 1918 • *Jaxon* • USA
ALL FOR A BIG ORDER • 1911 • *Imp* • USA
ALL FOR A GIRL • 1912 • Thompson Frederick A. • USA
ALL FOR A GIRL • 1915 • Applegate Roy • USA
ALL FOR A GIRL • 1916 • *Plumb & Runt* • USA
ALL FOR A HUSBAND • 1917 • Harbaugh Carl • USA
ALL FOR A TOOTH • 1914 • Williams C. Jay • USA
ALL FOR A WOMAN (USA) see **DANTON** • 1920
ALL FOR BUSINESS • 1914 • Reehm George E. • USA
ALL FOR GOLD • 1911 • *Yankee* • USA
ALL FOR GOLD • 1918 • *Sedgwick Eileen* • SHT • USA
ALL FOR GOLD see **LIFE UNDER THE SOUTHERN CROSS** • 1911
ALL FOR HER • 1912 • Brenon Herbert • USA
ALL FOR HIS SAKE • 1914 • Merwin Bannister • USA
ALL FOR IRELAND • 1915 • Olcott Sidney • USA
ALL FOR JIM • 1912 • *Prior Herbert* • USA
ALL FOR LOVE • 1912 • Salter Harry • USA
ALL FOR LOVE • 1914 • *Fielding Romaine* • USA
ALL FOR LOVE • 1915 • *Heather Enid* • UKN
ALL FOR LOVE • 1986 • Volev Nikolai • BUL
ALL FOR LOVE see **VSE PRO LASKA** • 1930
ALL FOR LOVE see **ROMANZO D'AMORE** • 1950
ALL FOR LOVE see **KOSHOKU ICHIDAI OTOKO** • 1961
ALL FOR MARY • 1955 • Toye Wendy • UKN
ALL FOR MONEY see **ALLES FUR GELD** • 1923
ALL FOR NOTHING • 1907 • Collins Alf? • UKN
ALL FOR NOTHING • 1928 • Parrott James • SHT • USA
ALL FOR NOTHING see **TODO POR NADA** • 1989
ALL FOR NUTTIN' • 1916 • Walsh Phil • USA
ALL FOR OLD IRELAND • 1915 • Olcott Sidney • USA
ALL FOR PEGGY • 1915 • De Grasse Joseph • USA
ALL FOR SCIENCE • 1913 • O'Sullivan Tony • USA
ALL FOR THE BOY • 1915 • Physioc Wray • USA
ALL FOR THE DOUGH BAG • 1920 • Howe J. A. • SHT • USA
ALL FOR THE LOVE OF A GEISHA • 1904 • *Paul R. W.* • UKN
ALL FOR THE LOVE OF A GIRL • 1909 • *Powers* • USA
ALL FOR THE LOVE OF A GIRL • 1915 • Drew Sidney • USA
ALL FOR THE LOVE OF A LADY • 1911 • *Edison* • USA
ALL FOR THE LOVE OF GLORIA see **HIS MYSTERY GIRL** • 1923
ALL FOR THE LOVE OF LAURA • 1916 • *Gayety* • USA
ALL FOR YOU • 1965 • Barabanova M., Sukhobokov V. • USS
ALL FOWLED UP • 1955 • McKimson Robert • ANS • USA
ALL FRIENDS HERE see **SAMI SWOI** • 1967
ALL "FUR" HER • 1918 • Seiter William A.? • SHT • USA
ALL GIRL see **ALL WOMAN** • 1967
ALL GOD'S CHILDREN • 1980 • Thorpe Jerry • TVM • USA
ALL-GOLD SPHINX, THE see **SFINGE D'ORO, LA** • 1967
ALL GOOD AMERICANS see **PARIS INTERLUDE** • 1934
ALL GOOD CITIZENS see **VSICHNI DOBRI RODACI** • 1968
ALL GOOD FELLOW COUNTRYMEN see **VSICHNI DOBRI RODACI** • 1968
ALL GUMMED UP • 1947 • White Jules • SHT • USA
ALL HAIL TO THE KING • 1913 • Henderson Dell • USA
ALL-HAIRS see **VSEHOCHLUP** • 1979
ALL HALLOWE'EN • 1953 • Gordon Michael S. • SHT • UKN
ALL HALLOWS EVE see **ZADNUSZKI** • 1961
ALL HAMS ON DECK • 1970 • Smith Paul J. • ANS • USA
ALL HANDS • 1940 • Carstairs John Paddy • UKN
ALL HANDS ON DECK • 1961 • Taurog Norman • USA
ALL I DESIRE • 1953 • Sirk Douglas • USA
ALL IN • 1936 • Varnel Marcel • UKN
ALL IN A DAY • 1917 • *Essanay* • SHT • USA
ALL IN A DAY • 1920 • Newmeyer Fred, Roach Hal • SHT • USA
ALL IN A DAY'S WORK • 1914 • Plumb Hay? • UKN
ALL IN A DAY'S WORK • 1977 • Higgins Don • UKN
ALL IN A NIGHT'S WORK • 1961 • Anthony Joseph • USA
ALL IN A NUTSHELL • 1949 • Hannah Jack • ANS • USA
ALL IN GOOD FUN • 1956 • Anderson James M. • UKN
ALL IN GOOD TASTE • 1981 • Kramreither Anthony • CND
ALL IN GOOD TIME see **FAMILY WAY, THE** • 1966
ALL IN ORDER see **ORDNUNG** • 1980
ALL IN THE AIR • 1914 • Hotaling Arthur D. • USA
ALL IN THE FAMILY • 1912 • *Essanay* • USA
ALL IN THE SAME BOAT • 1915 • Christie Al • USA
ALL IN THE SEX FAMILY • 1975 • Losch Seaman • USA
ALL IN THE SWIM • 1919 • *Lyons Eddie* • SHT • USA
ALL IN THE WASH • 1912 • *Lubin* • USA
ALL IS FAIR • 1912 • Melies Gaston • USA
ALL IS FAIR IN LOVE AND WAR • 1911 • *Vitagraph* • USA
ALL IS LEFT TO THE PEOPLE see **VSE OSTAETSIA LYUDYAM** • 1963
ALL IS LOVE • 1980 • Shariliev Borislav • BUL
ALL IS NOT GOLD THAT GLITTERS • 1910 • Haldane Bert? • UKN
ALL IS VANITY see **MUJO** • 1970
ALL IS WELL see **TOUT VA BIEN** • 1972
ALL JAZZED UP • 1919 • *Christie* • SHT • USA
ALL JAZZED UP • 1919 • Watson William • *L-Ko* • SHT • USA
ALL JOKING ASTRIDE • 1950 • Sparling Gordon • DCS • CND
ALL JORDENS FROJD • 1953 • Husberg Rolf • SWD • ALL THE JOY OF EARTH
ALL KINDS OF A GIRL • 1918 • *Field Elinor* • USA
ALL LIT UP • 1920 • Roach Hal • SHT • USA
ALL LIT UP • 1959 • Halas John, Batchelor Joy • ANS • UKN
ALL LIVING THINGS • 1939 • Buchanan Andrew • UKN
ALL LIVING THINGS • 1955 • Gover Victor M. • UKN
ALL LOVE EXCELLING • 1914 • Mackenzie Donald • USA
ALL MAN • 1916 • Chautard Emile • USA
ALL MAN • 1918 • Scardon Paul • USA
ALL MEN ARE APES! • 1965 • Mawra Joseph P. • USA
ALL MEN ARE ENEMIES • 1934 • Fitzmaurice George • USA
ALL MEN ARE LIARS • 1919 • Morgan Sidney • UKN
ALL MEN ARE LIARS see **TRUTH ABOUT MURDER, THE** • 1946
ALL MINE TO GIVE • 1956 • Reisner Allen • USA • DAY THEY GAVE BABIES AWAY, THE (UKN)
ALL MIXED UP • 1914 • *Selig* • USA
ALL MIXED UP • 1918 • *Christie* • USA
ALL MIXED UP see **MANJI** • 1964
ALL MUST MARRY see **WOMAN-PROOF** • 1923
ALL MY DARLING DAUGHTERS • 1972 • Rich David Lowell • TVM • USA
ALL MY GOOD COUNTRYMEN see **VSICHNI DOBRI RODACI** • 1968
ALL MY LIFE • 1966 • Baillie Bruce • SHT • USA
ALL MY MEN • 1966 • USA
ALL MY SONS • 1948 • Reis Irving • USA
ALL NEAT IN BLACK STOCKINGS • 1968 • Morahan Christopher • UKN
ALL NIGHT • 1918 • Powell Paul • USA
ALL NIGHT LONG • 1924 • *Sennett Mack (P)* • SHT • USA
ALL NIGHT LONG • 1962 • Dearden Basil • UKN
ALL NIGHT LONG • 1981 • Tramont Jean-Claude • USA
ALL NIGHT LONG see **TOUTE UNE NUIT** • 1982
ALL NIGHT RIDER • 1969 • Findlay Michael • USA
ALL NIGHT THROUGH see **UNRUHIGE NACHT** • 1958
ALL NUDITY SHALL BE PUNISHED (USA) see **TODA NUDEZ SERA CASTIGADA** • 1973
ALL NUDITY WILL BE PUNISHED see **TODA NUDEZ SERA CASTIGADA** • 1973
ALL OF A SUDDEN NORMA • 1919 • Hickman Howard • USA
ALL OF A SUDDEN PEGGY • 1920 • Edwards Walter • USA
ALL OF ME • 1934 • Flood James • USA
ALL OF ME • 1963 • Martin Jay • USA
ALL OF ME • 1984 • Reiner Carl • USA
ALL OF MYSELF see **WATASHI NO SUBETE-O** • 1954
ALL OF OUR LIVES • 1984 • Sky Laura • DOC • CND
ALL ON A SUMMER'S DAY see **DOUBLE CONFESSION** • 1950
ALL ON ACCOUNT OF A BANANA • 1912 • *Majestic* • USA
ALL ON ACCOUNT OF A BIT OF STRING • 1913 • *Gerrard Film Co* • UKN
ALL ON ACCOUNT OF A DOUGHNUT • 1915 • *Alhambra* • USA
ALL ON ACCOUNT OF A JUG • 1914 • Ricketts Thomas • USA
ALL ON ACCOUNT OF A LAUNDRY MARK • 1910 • Porter Edwin S. • USA
ALL ON ACCOUNT OF A LIE • 1910 • *Essanay* • USA
ALL ON ACCOUNT OF A PHOTO • 1915 • *Wallace Irene* • USA
ALL ON ACCOUNT OF A PORTRAIT • 1913 • Williams C. Jay • USA
ALL ON ACCOUNT OF A RING • 1912 • *Frazer Robert* • USA
ALL ON ACCOUNT OF A SNEEZE • 1915 • *Pyramid* • USA
ALL ON ACCOUNT OF A TRANSFER • 1913 • Williams C. Jay • USA
ALL ON ACCOUNT OF A WIDOW • 1912 • *Powers* • USA
ALL ON ACCOUNT OF AN EGG • 1913 • *Eclair* • USA
ALL ON ACCOUNT OF AN OLIVE • 1916 • *Hippo* • USA
ALL ON ACCOUNT OF CHECKERS • 1912 • *Selig* • USA
ALL ON ACCOUNT OF DAISY • 1913 • Hotaling Arthur D. • USA
ALL ON ACCOUNT OF POLLY • 1913 • *Patheplay* • USA
ALL ON ACCOUNT OF POLLY • 1914 • *Balboa* • USA
ALL ON ACCOUNT OF THE CHEESE • 1914 • *Ab* • USA
ALL ON ACCOUNT OF THE MILK • 1910 • Powell Frank • USA
ALL ON ACCOUNT OF THE PORTER • 1911 • *Essanay* • USA
ALL ON ACCOUNT OF TOWSER • 1915 • Davis Ulysses • USA
ALL ONE NIGHT (UKN) see **LOVE BEGINS AT 20** • 1936
ALL OR NOTHING see **TODO O NADA** • 1984
ALL OUR ENEMIES see **PROTI VSEM** • 1957
ALL OUT see **TUTTO PER TUTTO** • 1968
ALL-OUT ATTACK ON SINGAPORE see **SHINGAPORU SOKOGEKI** • 1943
ALL OUT FOR V • 1942 • Davis Mannie • ANS • USA
ALL OVER A STOCKING • 1916 • Christie Al • SHT • USA
ALL OVER HIS BISCUITS • 1915 • *Nestor* • USA
ALL OVER RUSSIA see **PO RUSI** • 1968
ALL OVER THE TOWN (USA) see **ALL OVER TOWN** • 1949
ALL OVER THE WORLD • 1967 • Conde Conrado • PHL
ALL OVER TOWN • 1937 • Horne James W. • USA
ALL OVER TOWN • 1949 • Twist Derek • UKN • ALL OVER THE TOWN (USA)
ALL POINT TO HIM ALONE • 1974 • Preskanu V. • USS
ALL QUIET IN THE EAST • 1934 • Bianchi P. • ANM • FRN
ALL QUIET ON THE WESTERN FRONT • 1930 • Milestone Lewis • USA
ALL QUIET ON THE WESTERN FRONT • 1979 • Mann Delbert • TVM • USA
ALL RASCALS see **KOI TO TAIYO TO GANG** • 1962
ALL RED ROUTE, THE see **ROUND THE WORLD IN TWO HOURS VIA THE ALL RED ROUTE** • 1914
ALL RIOT ON THE WESTERN FRONT • 1930 • Knight Castleton • UKN

ALL RIVERS MEET AT THE SEA • 1913 • *Broncho* • USA
ALL ROADS LEAD TO CALVARY • 1921 • Foss Kenelm • UKN
ALL ROADS LEAD TO ROME see **TOUS LES CHEMINS MENENT A ROME** • 1948
ALL ROUND REDUCED PERSONALITY (REDUPERS), THE see **ALLSEITIG REDUZIERTE PERSONLICHKEIT -REDUPERS, DIE** • 1978
ALL RUSSIAN ELDER KALININ see **VSEROSSIISKII STAROSTA KALININ** • 1920
ALL SCOTCH • 1909 • Wormald S.? • UKN
ALL SCREWED UP see **TUTTO A POSTO E NIENTE IN ORDINE** • 1974
ALL-SEEING EYE, THE • 1912 • *Republic* • USA
ALL SET BACKSTAGE • 1975 • Cox Paul • SHT • ASL
ALL SHOOK UP! see **ODD BALLS** • 1984
ALL SORTS AND CONDITIONS OF MEN • 1921 • Treville Georges • UKN
ALL SORTS OF HEROES • 1976 • Megginson Rick, Hughes Steve • UKN
ALL SOULS DAY see **ZADNUSZKI** • 1961
ALL SOULS DAY see **SIMBATA MORTILOR** • 1968
ALL SOULS' EVE • 1921 • Franklin Chester M. • USA
ALL SPACED OUT see **TOUT ECARTILLE** • 1972
ALL SQUARE AFT • 1957 • Bryant Gerard • UKN
ALL SQUARE (UKN) see **GANG WAR** • 1928
ALL SQUARE (UKN) see **PINTO KID, THE** • 1941
ALL STAR BOND RALLY • 1944 • Dudley Michael • SHT • USA
ALL-STAR BOND RALLY • 1945 • Audley Michael • USA
ALL STAR MELODY MASTER(S) • 1945 • Negulesco Jean • SHT • USA
ALL-STAR MUSICAL REVUE • 1945 • Berkeley Busby • SHT • USA
ALL STARS • 1916 • Collins Edwin J.? • UKN
ALL STEAMED UP • 1929 • Taurog Norman • SHT • USA
ALL STONES FESTIVAL • 1980 • Smith John • USA
ALL STUCK UP • 1915 • *Pollard Jack* • USA
ALL STUCK UP • 1918 • Hotaling Arthur D. • SHT • USA
ALL TEED OFF • 1968 • Bartsch Art • ANS • USA
ALL TEED UP • 1930 • Kennedy Edgar • SHT • USA
ALL THAT FALLS HAS WINGS • 1989 • Jang Gil-Su • SKR
ALL THAT GLISTENS IS NOT GOLD • 1925 • Butler Alexander • UKN
ALL THAT GLITTERS • 1936 • Rogers Maclean • UKN
ALL THAT HEAVEN ALLOWS • 1956 • Sirk Douglas • USA
ALL THAT I HAVE • 1951 • Claxton William F. • USA
ALL THAT JAZZ • 1979 • Fosse Bob • USA
ALL THAT MONEY CAN BUY (UKN) see **DEVIL AND DANIEL WEBSTER, THE** • 1941
ALL THAT TROUBLE FOR A DRINK • 1908 • *Warwick Trading Co* • UKN
ALL THE ADVANTAGES • 1972 • Mason Christopher • UKN
ALL THE BROTHERS WERE VALIANT • 1923 • Willat Irvin V. • USA
ALL THE BROTHERS WERE VALIANT • 1953 • Thorpe Richard • USA
ALL THE COMFORTS OF HOME • 1912 • *Cosmopolitan* • USA
ALL THE DOG'S FAULT • 1914 • *Powers* • USA
ALL THE DOORS FLEW OPEN FOR KITSOS see **EBENE KITSO** • 1968
ALL THE DOORS WERE CLOSED • 1989 • Un Memduh • TRK
ALL THE DRAWINGS OF THE TOWN see **SVI CRTEZI GRADA** • 1959
ALL THE EVIDENCE see **STRANGE JUSTICE** • 1932
ALL THE EVILS OF S— see **ALL THE SINS OF SODOM** • 1968
ALL THE FINE YOUNG CANNIBALS • 1960 • Anderson Michael • USA
ALL THE FUN OF THE FAIR • 1904 • *Paul R. W.* • UKN
ALL THE GOLD IN THE WORLD see **TOUT L'OR DU MONDE** • 1961
ALL THE JOY OF EARTH see **ALL JORDENS FROJD** • 1953
ALL THE KIND STRANGERS • 1974 • Kennedy Burt • TVM • USA
ALL THE KING'S HORSES • 1935 • Tuttle Frank • USA
ALL THE KING'S MEN • 1949 • Rossen Robert • USA
ALL THE KING'S MEN • 1974 • Bonniere Rene • CND
ALL THE KING'S MEN see **T'IEN-HSIA TI-YI** • 1983
ALL THE LOVIN' KINFOLK • 1970 • Hayes John • USA • CLOSEST OF KIN, THE ○ KINFOLK ○ KIN FOLK
ALL THE LOVING COUPLES • 1969 • Bing Mack • USA • ALL THE LOVING NEIGHBORS
ALL THE LOVING NEIGHBORS see **ALL THE LOVING COUPLES** • 1969
ALL THE MARBLES • 1981 • Aldrich Robert • USA • CALIFORNIA DOLLS, THE (UKN)
ALL THE MEMORY OF THE WORLD see **TOUTE LA MEMOIRE DU MONDE** • 1956
ALL THE OTHER GIRLS DO (USA) see **OLTRAGGIO AL PUDORE** • 1965
ALL THE PRESIDENT'S MEN • 1976 • Pakula Alan J. • USA
ALL THE RIGHT MOVES • 1983 • Chapman Michael • USA
ALL THE RIGHT NOISES • 1969 • O'Hara Gerry • UKN
ALL THE ROMAN MUSCLES • 1970 • USA
ALL THE SAD WORLD NEEDS • 1918 • Herrick Hubert • UKN
ALL THE SAD YOUNG MEN see **WINDY CITY** • 1984
ALL THE SENATOR'S GIRLS • 1977 • Cognito En • USA
ALL THE SINS OF SODOM • 1968 • Sarno Joe • USA • SINS OF SODOM ○ ALL THE EVILS OF S—
ALL THE TEMPTATIONS OF THE EARTH • 1989 • Samandarrian Hamid • IRN
ALL THE THINGS YOU ARE see **LETTER FOR EVIE, A** • 1945
ALL THE TRICKS see **ANOTE KONOTE** • 1968
ALL THE TRICKS IN LIFE see **SHIN JINSEI YONJUHATTE URAMOMOTE** • 1968
ALL THE WAY see **JOKER IS WILD, THE** • 1957
ALL THE WAY BOYS see **PIU FORTE.. RAGAZZI!** • 1972
ALL THE WAY DOWN • 1968 • Spencer Zoltan G. • UKN
ALL THE WAY HOME • 1963 • Segal Alex • USA
ALL THE WAY TO JERUSALEM • 1968 • Perry Frank • DOC • USA
ALL THE WAY TO PARIS see **AFTER YOU, COMRADE** • 1966
ALL THE WAY UP • 1970 • McTaggart James • UKN
ALL THE WAY UP THERE • 1978 • Preston Gaylene • DOC • NZL
ALL THE WINNERS • 1920 • Malins Geoffrey H. • UKN
ALL THE WISHES OF THE WORLD see **SVE ZELJE SVIJETA** • 1966
ALL THE WORLD TO NOTHING • 1919 • King Henry • USA
ALL THE WORLD'S A STAGE • 1910 • Salter Harry • USA
ALL THE WORLD'S A STAGE • 1915 • Wilson Frank? • UKN
ALL THE WORLD'S A STAGE • 1917 • Weston Harold • UKN
ALL THE WORLD'S A STAGE • 1979 • *Moss Carlton* • USA
ALL THE WORLD'S A STOOGE • 1941 • Lord Del • SHT • USA
ALL THE WORLD'S WOMEN see **TODAS AS MULHERES DO MUNDO** • 1967
ALL THE WRONG CLUES see **KUEI-MA CHIH-TO HSING** • 1981
ALL THE YEARS OF HER LIFE • 1974 • Fortier Bob • MTV • CND
ALL THE YOUNG MEN • 1960 • Bartlett Hall • USA
ALL THE YOUTHFUL DAYS see **FENG-KUEI-LAI-TE JEN** • 1983
ALL THESE PEOPLE • 1960 • Darlow Michael, Searle Tony • UKN
ALL THESE WOMEN (USA) see **FOR ATT INTE TALA OM ALLA DESSA KVINNOR** • 1964
ALL THINGS BRIGHT AND BEAUTIFUL (USA) see **IT SHOULDN'T HAPPEN TO A VET** • 1976
ALL THINGS FLOW (UKN) see **PANTA RHEI** • 1951
ALL THIS AND GLAMOUR TOO see **VOGUES** • 1937
ALL THIS AND HEAVEN TOO • 1940 • Litvak Anatole • USA
ALL THIS AND MONEY TOO (UKN) see **LOVE IS A BALL** • 1962
ALL THIS AND RABBIT STEW • 1941 • Avery Tex • ANS • USA
ALL THIS AND RABBIT STEW • 1950 • Rasinski Connie • ANS • USA
ALL THIS AND WORLD WAR II • 1976 • Winslow Susan • DOC • USA
ALL THOSE GOOD COUNTRYMEN see **VSICHNI DOBRI RODACI** • 1968
ALL THOSE IN FAVOUR • 1941 • Alexander Donald • DOC • UKN
ALL THROUGH BETTY • 1916 • Noy Wilfred? • UKN
ALL THROUGH THE NIGHT • 1942 • Sherman Vincent • USA
ALL THROUGH THE PAGE BOY • 1904 • Collins Alf? • UKN
ALL TOGETHER NOW • 1970 • Allan William Louis • USA
ALL TOGETHER NOW • 1974 • Lehman Lewis • USA
ALL TOGETHER NOW • 1975 • Kleiser Randall • TVM • USA
ALL WE CHILDREN FROM BULLERBYN see **ALLA VI BARN I BULLERBYN** • 1960
ALL WEEKEND LOVERS see **JEU DE MASSACRE** • 1967
ALL WET • 1922 • St. John Al • SHT • USA
ALL WET • 1924 • McCarey Leo • SHT • USA
ALL WET • 1927 • Disney Walt • ANS • USA
ALL WET • 1930 • Newfield Sam • SHT • USA
ALL WOMAN • 1918 • Henley Hobart • USA
ALL WOMAN • 1967 • Warren Frank • USA • ALL GIRL ○ SCHIZO
ALL WOMEN ARE BAD • 1969 • Crane Larry • USA • WOMEN ARE BAD
ALL WOMEN HAVE SECRETS • 1940 • Neumann Kurt • USA
ALL WOOL • 1925 • Roach Hal • SHT • USA
ALL WOOL GARMENT, AN • 1908 • *Essanay* • USA
ALL WORK AND NO PAY • 1942 • Lord Del • SHT • USA
ALL WRONG • 1919 • Worthington William, West Raymond B. • USA
ALL YOU NEED IS CASH see **RUTLES, THE** • 1978
ALLA ARIBA see **ALA-ARRIBA** • 1942
ALLA CONQUISTA DELL'ARKANSAS (ITL) see **GOLDSUCHER VON ARKANSAS, DIE** • 1964
ALLA EN EL BAJIO • 1941 • Mendez Fernando • MXC
ALLA EN EL RANCHO CHICO • 1937 • Cardona Rene • MXC
ALLA EN EL RANCHO GRANDE • 1936 • de Fuentes Fernando • MXC • THERE AT THE BIG RANCH ○ OUT AT BIG RANCH
ALLA EN EL RANCHO GRANDE • 1948 • de Fuentes Fernando • MXC
ALLA EN EL TROPICO • 1940 • de Fuentes Fernando • MXC
ALLA LEJOS Y HACE TIEMPO • 1978 • Antin Manuel • ARG • FAR AWAY AND LONG AGO
ALLA MIA CARA MAMMA NEL GIORNO DEL SUO COMPLEANNO • 1974 • Salce Luciano • ITL
ALLA RICERCA DEL PIACERE • 1972 • Amadio Silvio • ITL • HOT BED OF SEX (UKN)
ALLA RICERCA DI GREGORY (ITL) see **IN SEARCH OF GREGORY** • 1970
ALLA RICERCA DI MAYRA • 1972 • Dahl Gustavo • ITL • SEARCHING FOR MAYRA
ALLA TIDERS 91:AN LARLSSON • 1953 • Bernhard Gosta • SWD
ALLA TIDERS KARLSSON • 1936 • Rodin Gosta • SWD • MARVELLOUS KARLSSON
ALLA VI BARN I BULLERBYN • 1960 • Hellbom Olle • SWD • ALL WE CHILDREN FROM BULLERBYN
ALLA VI BARN I BULLERBYN • 1986 • Hallstrom Lasse • SWD • CHILDREN OF BULLERBY VILLAGE, THE
ALLA VIENE EL TEMPORAL • 1988 • Casanova Luis Molina • PRC • HERE COMES THE HURRICANE
ALLABAD: THE ARABIAN WIZARD • 1902 • *Biograph* • USA
ALLADIN AND HIS MAGIC LAMP (USA) see **VOLSHEBNAYA LAMPA ALADDINA** • 1967
ALLADIN AND HIS WONDERFUL LAMP • 1951 • Wadia Homi • IND
ALLADIN AND THE MAGIC LAMP • *Indian Children Film Society* • IND
ALLADIN AND THE WONDERFUL LAMP • 1926 • IND
ALLADIN AND THE WONDERFUL LAMP • 1930 • IND
ALLADIN AND THE WONDERFUL LAMP • 1933 • IND
ALLADIN AND THE WONDERFUL LAMP • 1957 • Raghunath T. R. • IND
ALLADIN KA BETA • 1939 • *Shanker* • IND
ALLADIN KA BETA • 1955 • *Chitra* • IND
ALLAH 3311 • 1914 • *Tennant Barbara* • USA
ALLAH BE PRAISED -IT'S A BOY see **ALLAH VOERD LOVET -DET BLEV EN DRENG** • 1979
ALLAH KERIHM • 1955 • Schulz-Kampfhenkel O. • FRG • UTAS ABENTEUERLICHE REISE DURCH ALGERIEN
ALLAH MANA • 1954 • Badrakhan Ahmed • EGY • GOD IS ON OUR SIDE
ALLAH RAZI OLSUN OSMAN BEY • 1967 • Gulyuz Aram • TRK • THANK GOD, OSMAN BEY
ALLAH VOERD LOVET -DET BLEV EN DRENG • 1979 • Bovin Mette, Adler Barbara, Rue Nele • DOC • DNM • ALLAH BE PRAISED -IT'S A BOY
ALLAHA ADANAN TOPRAK • 1967 • Figenli Yavuz • TRK • GOD'S COUNTRY
ALLAMI ARUHAZ • 1952 • Gertler Viktor • USS • STATE DEPARTMENT STORE
ALLAN • 1966 • Shebib Donald • CND
ALLAN FIELD'S WARNING • 1913 • Haldane Bert? • UKN
ALLAN QUARTERMAIN • 1919 • SAF
ALLAN QUARTERMAIN AND THE LOST CITY OF GOLD • 1986 • Nelson Gary • USA
ALLARME A SUD (ITL) see **ALERTE AU SUD** • 1953
ALLARME DAL CIELO (ITL) see **CIEL SUR LA TETE, LE** • 1964
ALLARME IN CINQUE BANCHE (ITL) see **MILLIARD DANS UN BILLIARD, UN** • 1965
ALL'ARMI SIAM FASCISTI • 1962 • Del Fra Lino, Mangini Cecilia, Micciche Lino • DOC • ITL
ALLAUDDIN AND THE WONDERFUL LAMP • 1938 • Vakil Nanubhai • IND
ALLAUDDIN THE SECOND • 1934 • Muzumdar Nagendra • IND
ALLAVERDOBA • 1962 • Shengelaya Georgi • SHT • USS
ALLE ABENTEUER DIESER ERDE • 1970 • *Quinn Freddy* • FRG
ALLE DAGEN FEEST • 1975 • de Jong Ate, Seunke Orlow, Jongerius Otto, de Lussanets Paul • NTH • PARTY EVERY DAY, A
ALLE GAR RUNDT OG FORELSKER SIG • 1941 • Gregers Emanuel • DNM
ALLE JAHRE WIEDER • 1967 • Schamoni Ulrich • FRG • EVERY YEAR AGAIN ○ TIME AND TIME AGAIN
ALLE KANN ICH NICHT HEIRATEN • 1952 • Wolff Hans • FRG
ALLE KATZCHEN NASCHEN GERN • 1969 • Zachar Jozef • FRG • BLONDE AND THE BLACK PUSSYCAT, THE (UKN)
ALLE LIEBEN PETER • 1959 • Becker Wolfgang • FRG
ALLE MAN PA POST • 1940 • Henrikson Anders • SWD • EVERYBODY AT HIS STATION
ALLE MAND PA DAEK • 1943 • Schneevoigt George • DNM
ALLE MENSCHEN WERDEN BRUDER • 1973 • Vohrer Alfred • FRG
ALLE SCHULD RACHT SICH AUF ERDEN • 1912 • Rye Stellan • FRG
ALLE STEHEN KOPF • 1940 • Rabenalt Arthur M. • FRG • GENERAL CONFUSION (USA)
ALLE SUNDEN DIESER ERDE • 1958 • Umgelter Fritz • FRG
ALLE TAGE IST KEIN SONNTAG • 1935 • Janssen Walter • FRG
ALLE TAGE IST KEIN SONNTAG • 1959 • Weiss Helmut • FRG
ALLE WEGE FUHREN HEIM • 1957 • Deppe Hans • FRG
ALLEES DE LA TERRE, LES • 1973 • Theberge Andre • CND
ALLEGEMENT, L' • 1983 • Schuepbach Marcel • SWT
ALLEGHENY UPRISING • 1940 • Seiter William A. • USA • FIRST REBEL, THE (UKN)
ALLEGORIA DI PRIMAVERA • 1949 • Emmer Luciano, Gras Enrico • ITL • STORY OF SPRING, THE ○ BOTTICELLI
ALLEGORIE • 1974 • Paureilhe Christian • FRN
ALLEGORY • 1987 • Sfikas Kostas • GRC
ALLEGRA • 1985 • SAF
ALLEGRA REGINA, L' see **REGINA DI NAVARRA, LA** • 1942
ALLEGRETTO • 1936 • Fischinger Oskar • ANS • USA
ALLEGRI MASNADIERI • 1937 • Elter Marco • ITL
ALLEGRO • 1939 • McLaren Norman • ANS • USA
ALLEGRO BARBARO • 1979 • Jancso Miklos • HNG
ALLEGRO CANTANTE, L' • 1938 • Righelli Gennaro • ITL
ALLEGRO FANTASMA, L' • 1941 • Palermi Amleto • ITL • TOTO ALLEGRO FANTASMA
ALLEGRO MA TROPPO • 1962 • *De Roubaix Paul (P)* • SHT • FRN
ALLEGRO NON TROPPO • 1976 • Bozzetto Bruno • ITL
ALLEGRO SQUADRONE, L' • 1954 • Moffa Paolo • ITL, FRN • GAITES DE L'ESCADRON, LES ○ GIORNO IN CASERNA, UN
ALLEGRO VIVACE • 1965 • Radzinowicz Anatol • PLN
ALLEIN IM URWALD • 1922 • Wendt Ernst • FRG • RACHE DER AFRIKANERIN, DIE
ALLELUIA see **ALLELUYAHS, LES** • 1963-64
ALLELUJA E SARTANA, FIGLI DI...DIO • 1972 • Siciliano Mario • ITL
ALLELUYAHS, LES • 1963-64 • Fournier Claude, Portugais Louis • DCS • CND • ALLELUIA
ALLEMAGNE, ANNEE ZERO (FRN) see **GERMANIA, ANNO ZERO** • 1947
ALLEMAGNE, TERMINUS EST • 1964 • Buyens Frans • BLG
ALLEMAN • 1963 • Haanstra Bert • DOC • NTH • HUMAN DUTCH, THE
ALLEMANDE IM HERBST • 1962 • Verhavert Roland • DOC • BLG
ALLEMANDS REVIENNENT, LES see **YERMANI XANARHONTAI, I** • 1947
ALLER ET RETOUR • 1948 • Astruc Alexandre • SHT • FRN • ALLER-RETOUR
ALLER PLUS LOIN • 1973 • Gagne Jacques • DCS • CND
ALLER RETOUR • 1979 • Petrovic Aleksandar • YGS • TAMO I NATRAG ○ PUTNICI PASSENGERS ○ PASSENGERS
ALLER-RETOUR see **ALLER ET RETOUR** • 1948
ALLER-RETOUR see **DUS-INTORS**
ALLER SIMPLE, UN • 1970 • Giovanni Jose • FRN, ITL, SPN • SOLO ANDATA (ITL)
ALLERGIC TO LOVE • 1944 • Lilley Edward • USA
ALLERSEELEN • 1919 • Lund Erik • FRG
ALLES AUS LIEBE • 1943 • Marischka Hubert • FRG
ALLES DREHT SICH, ALLES BEWEGT SICH! • 1929 • Richter Hans • FRG • EVERYTHING TURNS, EVERYTHING REVOLVES
ALLES FUR DEN HUND • 1959 • Schamoni Peter • SHT • FRG
ALLES FUR DIE FIRMA • 1921 • Peukert Leo • FRG
ALLES FUR DIE FIRMA • 1950 • Dorfler Ferdinand • FRG
ALLES FUR GELD • 1923 • Schunzel Reinhold • FRG • FORTUNE'S FOOL ○ ALL FOR MONEY
ALLES FUR GLORIA • 1941 • Boese Carl • FRG
ALLES FUR PAPA • 1953 • Hartl Karl • FRG
ALLES FUR VERONIKA • 1936 • Harlan Veit • FRG

ALLES HORT AUF MEIN KOMMANDO • 1934 • Zoch Georg • FRG
ALLES LUGE • 1948 • Emo E. W. • AUS
ALLES SAL REGKOM • 1951 • SAF
ALLES SCHWINDEL • 1940 • Hoffmann Bernd • FRG
ALLES UM EINE FRAU • 1935 • Abel Alfred • FRG • KAMERADEN
ALLES VERKEHRT • 1919 • Moest Hubert • FRG
ALLES WEG'N DEM HUND • 1935 • Sauer Fred • FRG • VERUCKTE TESTAMENT, DAS
ALLEY CAT • 1984 • Victor Edward • USA
ALLEY CAT, THE • 1929 • Steinhoff Hans • UKN
ALLEY CAT, THE • 1941 • Harman Hugh • ANS • USA
ALLEY CAT, THE see **MATOU, LE** • 1985
ALLEY CATS, THE • 1966 • Metzger Radley H. • USA
ALLEY OF GOLDEN HEARTS, THE • 1924 • Phillips Bertram • UKN
ALLEY OF NIGHTMARES see **SHE FREAK** • 1967
ALLEY TO BALI • 1954 • Patterson Don • ANS • USA
ALLEY TRAMP • 1965 • Lewis Herschell G. • USA
ALLEY TRAMP(S) • 1968 • Parys Armand • USA
ALLEZ FRANCE! • 1964 • Dhery Robert, Tchernia Pierre • FRN • COUNTERFEIT CONSTABLE, THE (USA)
ALLEZ.. ON SE TELEPHONE • 1974 • Viard Philippe • FRN
ALLEZ OOP • 1933 • Cummings Jack • USA
ALLEZ OOP • 1934 • Lamont Charles • SHT • USA
ALLEZ VOUS PENDRE AILLEURS see **EMMERDEUR, L'** • 1973
ALLI SKINI, I • 1974 • Dimopoulos Michel • GRC • OTHER SCENE, THE
ALLIANCE, L' • 1970 • de Chalonge Christian • FRN • WEDDING RING, THE
ALLIANCE FOR PROGRESS see **ALIANZA PARA EL PROGESO** • 1971
ALLIES see **LOVE IN A HURRY** • 1919
ALLIES, THE • 1966 • Huisken Joop • DOC • GDR
ALLIGATOR • 1980 • Teague Lewis • USA
ALLIGATOR ALLEY see **HOOKED GENERATION, THE** • 1969
ALLIGATOR NAMED DAISY, AN • 1955 • Thompson J. Lee • UKN
ALLIGATOR PEOPLE, THE • 1959 • Del Ruth Roy • USA
ALLIGATOR SHOES • 1981 • Borris Clay • CND • SOULIERS EN CROCO, LES
ALLIGATORS • 1980 • Martino Sergio • ITL • GREAT ALLIGATOR, THE (USA) ○ BIG ALLIGATOR RIVER
ALLIMUNI AL-HUBB • 1957 • Salem Atef • EGY • APPRENEZ-MOI L'AMOUR
ALLMACHTIGE DOLLAR, DER • 1923 • Speyer Jaap • FRG
ALLNIGHTER, THE • 1987 • Hoffs Tamar Simon • USA • CUTTING LOOSE
ALLO, ALLO • 1961 • Popescu-Gopo Ion • ANS • RMN • HULLO, HULLO ○ HELLO, HELLO
ALLO BERLIN, ICI PARIS • 1931 • Duvivier Julien • FRN, FRG • HALLO HALLO! HIER SPRICHT BERLIN (FRG)
ALLO GRAMMA, TO • 1976 • Liaropoulos Lambros • GRC • OTHER LETTER, THE
ALLO I AM THE CAT • 1975 • Mahdy Nuzry • EGY
ALLO, JE T'AIME • 1952 • Berthomieu Andre • FRN
ALLO, MADEMOISELLE! • 1932 • Champreux Maurice • FRN
ALL'OMBRA DEL DELITTO (ITL) see **RUPTURE, LA** • 1970
ALL'OMBRA DELLA GLORIA • 1943 • Mercanti Pino • ITL
ALL'OMBRA DELLE AQUILE • 1966 • Baldi Ferdinando • ITL
ALL'OMBRA DI UNA COLT • 1965 • Grimaldi Gianni • ITL, SPN • IN A COLT'S SHADOW (UKN) ○ IN THE SHADOW OF A COLT
ALL'OMBRE DELLE FANCIULLE IN FIORE • 1952 • Rondi Brunello • SHT • ITL
ALL'ONOREVOLE PIACCIONO LE DONNE • 1972 • Fulci Lucio • ITL • EROTICIST, THE
ALLONS ENFANTS.. POUR L'ALGERIE • 1961 • Gass Karl • DOC • GDR
ALLONS Z'ENFANTS • 1980 • Boisset Yves • FRN
ALLONSANFAN • 1974 • Taviani Paolo, Taviani Vittorio • ITL
ALLOTMENT WIVES • 1945 • Nigh William • USA • WOMAN IN THE CASE (UKN)
ALLOTRIA • 1936 • Forst Willi • FRG
ALLOTRIA IN ZELL AM SEE • 1963 • Marischka Georg • AUS
ALL'OVEST DI SACRAMENTO • 1971 • Chentrens Federico • ITL
ALL'S FAIR • 1913 • Plumb Hay? • UKN
ALL'S FAIR • 1946 • Hughes Harry • UKN
ALL'S FAIR • 1989 • Lang Rocky • USA • SKIRMISH
ALL'S FAIR AT THE FAIR • 1938 • Fleischer Dave • ANS • USA
ALL'S FAIR AT THE FAIR • 1947 • Kneitel Seymour • ANS • USA
ALL'S FAIR IN LOVE • 1909 • *Edison* • USA
ALL'S FAIR IN LOVE • 1910 • Fitzhamon Lewin? • UKN
ALL'S FAIR IN LOVE • 1912 • Stow Percy • UKN
ALL'S FAIR IN LOVE • 1914 • *Kineto* • UKN
ALL'S FAIR IN LOVE • 1921 • Hopper E. Mason • USA • BRIDAL PATH, THE ○ LOOK BEFORE YOU LEAP
ALL'S FAIR IN LOVE AND WAR • 1909 • Fitzhamon Lewin? • UKN
ALL'S FAIR IN LOVE AND WAR • 1910 • *Capitol* • USA
ALL'S RIGHT WITH THE WORLD • 1911 • Fitzhamon Lewin? • UKN
ALL'S WELL • 1941 • Fleischer Dave • ANS • USA
ALL'S WELL see **TUDO BEM** • 1979
ALL'S WELL THAT ENDS WELL • 1904 • Williamson James • UKN
ALL'S WELL THAT ENDS WELL • 1906 • Collins Alf? • UKN
ALL'S WELL THAT ENDS WELL • 1910 • *Electrograff* • USA
ALL'S WELL THAT ENDS WELL • 1913 • Collins Edwin J.? • UKN
ALL'S WELL THAT ENDS WELL • 1914 • *Princess* • USA
ALL'S WELL THAT ENDS WELL • 1940 • Davis Mannie • ANS • USA
ALL'S WELL THAT ENDS WELL see **CASE OF SPIRITS, A** • 1909
ALLSEITIG REDUZIERTE PERSONLICHKEIT -REDUPERS, DIE • 1978 • Sander Helke • FRG • ALL ROUND REDUCED PERSONALITY (REDUPERS), THE
ALLT HAMNAR SIG • 1917 • Tallroth Konrad • SWD • REVENGE
ALLTAGLICHE GESCHICHTE • 1945 • Rittau Gunther • FRG
ALL'ULTIMO SANGUE • 1968 • Moffa Paolo • ITL • BURY THEM DEEP (UKN) ○ TO THE LAST DROP OF BLOOD
ALLUMETTES • 1963 • Georgi Katja, Georgi Klaus • ANS • GDR • MATCHES
ALLUMETTES ANIMEES, LES • 1908 • Cohl Emile • ANS • FRN • ANIMATED MATCHES, THE
ALLUMETTES FANTAISIES, LES see **ALLUMETTES FANTASTIQUES** • 1912
ALLUMETTES FANTASTIQUES • 1912 • Cohl Emile • ANS • FRN • ALLUMETTES FANTAISIES, LES ○ ALLUMETTES MAGIQUES, LES
ALLUMETTES MAGIQUES, LES see **ALLUMETTES FANTASTIQUES** • 1912
ALLUMORPHOSES • 1960 • Rhein • SHT • FRN
ALLURES • 1961 • Belson Jordan • SHT • USA
ALLVARSAMMA LEKEN, DEN • 1945 • Carlsten Rune • SWD • SERIOUS GAME
ALLVARSAMMA LEKEN, DEN • 1977 • Breien Anja • NRW, SWD • GAMES OF LOVE AND LONELINESS ○ LOVE AND LONELINESS
ALLY SLOPER • 1898 • Smith G. A. • UKN
ALLY SLOPER • 1900 • Barrett Franklyn • SER • NZL
ALLY SLOPER GOES BATHING • 1921 • Malins Geoffrey H. • SHT • UKN
ALLY SLOPER GOES YACHTING • 1921 • Malins Geoffrey H. • SHT • UKN
ALLY SLOPER RUNS A REVUE • 1921 • Malins Geoffrey H. • SHT • UKN
ALLY SLOPER'S ADVENTURES • 1921 • Malins Geoffrey H. • SHS • UKN
ALLY SLOPER'S HAUNTED HOUSE • 1921 • Malins Geoffrey H. • SHT • UKN
ALLY SLOPER'S LOAN OFFICE • 1921 • Malins Geoffrey H. • SHT • UKN
ALLY SLOPER'S TEETOTAL ISLAND • 1921 • Malins Geoffrey H. • SHT • UKN
ALM AN DER GRENZE, DIE • 1951 • Janssen Walter • FRG
ALMA see **CONDENADOS, OS** • 1974
ALMA ARAGONESA • 1960 • Ochoa Jose • SPN
ALMA CERCADA, EL • 1950 • del Amo Antonio • SPN
ALMA DE ACERO • 1956 • Morayta Miguel • MXC
ALMA DE BRONCE • 1944 • Murphy Dudley • MXC
ALMA DE GAUCHO • 1930 • Otto Henry • USA
ALMA DE LA COPLA • 1964 • Ballesteros Pio • SPN
ALMA DE SACRIFICIO • 1917 • Coss Joaquin • MXC
ALMA DE UMA CIDADE, A • 1954 • Mendes Joao • SHT • PRT
ALMA DEL BANDOLEON, EL • 1934 • Barth-Moglia Luis • SPN
ALMA DEL BANDONEON, EL • 1935 • Soffici Mario • ARG • SOUL OF THE ACCORDION, THE (USA)
ALMA EN UN TANGO, EL • 1945 • Irigoyen Julio • ARG
ALMA GRANDE • 1965 • Urueta Chano • MXC • YAQUI JUSTICIERO, EL
ALMA GRANDE EN EL DESIERTO • 1966 • Gonzalez Rogelio A. • MXC
ALMA JAROCHA • 1937 • Helu Antonio • MXC
ALMA LLANERA • 1964 • Martinez Solares Gilberto • MXC, VNZ
ALMA MATER • 1915 • Guazzoni Enrico • ITL
ALMA NORTENA • 1938 • Guzman Roberto • MXC
ALMA PROVINCIANA • 1926 • CLM
ALMA RIFENA • 1922 • Buchs Jose • SPN
ALMA SE SERENA • 1969 • Saenz De Heredia Jose Luis • SPN
ALMA TAYLOR • 1915 • *Hepworth* • CMP • UKN
ALMA VIDA • 1967 • Garces Armando • PHL
ALMA, WHERE DO YOU LIVE? • 1917 • Clarendon Hal • USA
ALMACITA DI DESOLATO • 1985 • de Rooy Felix • NTH
ALMADA NEGREIROS VIVO, HOJE • 1968 • de Macedo Antonio • SHT • PRT
ALMADA, NOME DE GUERRA • 1969-77 • de Sousa Ernesto • PRT
ALMADRABA ATUNEIRA, A • 1961 • Campos Antonio • SHT • PRT
ALMAFUERTE • 1949 • Amadori Luis Cesar • ARG
ALMANYA ACI VATAN • 1980 • Goren Serif • TRK • GERMANY, BITTER LAND
ALMA'S CHAMPION • 1912 • *Walker Lillian* • USA
ALMAS-E-33 • 1968 • Mehrjui Dariush • IRN • DIAMOND 33
ALMAS EN PELIGRO • 1951 • Santillan Antonio • SPN
ALMAS ENCONTRADAS • 1933 • Sevilla Raphael J. • MXC
ALMAS REBELDES • 1937 • Galindo Alejandro • MXC • REBEL SOULS (USA)
ALMAS TROPICALES • 1923 • Contreras Torres Miguel • MXC • TROPICAL SOULS
ALMATLAN EVEK • 1959 • Mariassy Felix • HNG • SLEEPLESS YEARS
ALMENRAUSCH see **IM BANNE DER BERGE** • 1931
ALMENRAUSCH UND EDELWEISS • 1918 • Kampers Fritz • FRG
ALMENRAUSCH UND EDELWEISS • 1928 • Seitz Franz • FRG
ALMENRAUSCH UND EDELWEISS • 1957 • Reinl Harald • AUS
ALMERIA AFFAIR, THE see **CASO ALMERIA, EL** • 1984
ALMIGHTY DOLLAR, THE • 1916 • Thornby Robert T. • USA
ALMO DE DIOS: EL DIFUNTO ES UN VIVO • 1941 • Iquino Ignacio F. • SPN
ALMODO IFJUSAG • 1974 • Rozsa Janos • HNG • DREAMING YOUTH
ALMODOZASOK KORA • 1964 • Szabo Istvan • HNG • AGE OF DAYDREAMING, THE ○ AGE OF ILLUSIONS
ALMOND-EYED MAID, AN • 1913 • Edwin Walter • USA
ALMOND-SCENTED see **DAKH NA BADEMI, S** • 1967
ALMONDS AND RAISINS • 1983 • Karel Russ • DOC • USA
ALMOS' A MAN • 1977 • Laleman Stan • MTV • USA
ALMOST • 1910 • Bouwmeester Theo? • UKN
ALMOST • 1920 • *Moranti Milburn* • USA
ALMOST A BIGAMIST • 1917 • Christie Al • SHT • USA
ALMOST A BRIDE see **KISS FOR CORLISS, A** • 1949
ALMOST A BRIDEGROOM • 1914 • *Crystal* • USA
ALMOST A CRIME • 1914 • *Sphinx Films* • USA
ALMOST A DESERTER • 1916 • *U.s.m.p.* • SHT • USA
ALMOST A DIVORCE • 1931 • Varney-Serrao Arthur • UKN
ALMOST A FRIAR • 1917 • *Kerrigan J. Warren* • USA
ALMOST A GENTLEMAN • 1928 • *Bennett Billy* • SHT • UKN
ALMOST A GENTLEMAN • 1938 • Mitchell Oswald • UKN
ALMOST A GENTLEMAN • 1939 • Goodwins Leslie • USA • MAGNIFICENT OUTCAST (UKN)
ALMOST A GHOST TOWN • 1957 • Anderson Robert • DOC • CND
ALMOST A HERO • 1910 • *Powers* • USA
ALMOST A HERO • 1910 • Porter Edwin S. • *Edison* • USA
ALMOST A HERO • 1913 • *Powers* • USA
ALMOST A HERO • 1915 • Davis Ulysses • USA
ALMOST A HERO • 1919 • *Strand* • SHT • USA
ALMOST A HEROINE • 1916 • Ellis Robert • SHT • USA
ALMOST A HONEYMOON • 1930 • Banks Monty • UKN
ALMOST A HONEYMOON • 1938 • Lee Norman • UKN
ALMOST A HUSBAND • 1919 • Badger Clarence • USA
ALMOST A HUSBAND • 1924 • Lamont Charles • SHT • USA
ALMOST A KING • 1915 • Beaudine William • *Kalem* • USA
ALMOST A KING • 1915 • Christie Al • *Nestor* • USA
ALMOST A KNOCKOUT • 1915 • Christie Al • USA
ALMOST A LADY • 1926 • Hopper E. Mason • USA
ALMOST A LOVE STORY • 1980 • Zahariev Edward • BUL
ALMOST A MAN • 1912 • *Steppling John* • USA
ALMOST A MAN see **UOMO A META, UN** • 1966
ALMOST A PAPA • 1915 • Webster Harry Mcrae • USA
ALMOST A RESCUE • 1913 • *Nestor* • USA
ALMOST A SCANDAL • 1915 • *Ritchie Billie* • USA
ALMOST A SCANDAL • 1917 • Christie Al • SHT • USA
ALMOST A SUICIDE • 1912 • *Lyons Edward* • USA
ALMOST A WHITE HOPE • 1914 • MacDonald Donald • USA
ALMOST A WIDOW • 1915 • Dillon John Francis • USA
ALMOST A WIDOW • 1916 • Davey Horace • SHT • USA
ALMOST A WILD MAN • 1913 • Henderson Dell • USA
ALMOST A WINNER • 1913 • *Crystal* • USA
ALMOST AN ACTRESS • 1913 • Curtis Allen • USA
ALMOST AN ANGEL • 1990 • Cornell John • USA
ALMOST AN ANGEL see **IT STARTED WITH EVE** • 1941
ALMOST AN OUTLAW • 1920 • *Ridgeway Fritzie* • SHT • USA
ALMOST AN OUTRAGE • 1914 • *Ab* • USA
ALMOST ANGELS • 1962 • Previn Steven • USA • BORN TO SING (UKN)
ALMOST BY ACCIDENT: OR, SAVED BY A SOCK • 1909 • *Walturdaw* • UKN
ALMOST DIVORCED • 1917 • *Compson Betty* • SHT • USA
ALMOST GOOD MAN, THE • 1917 • Kelsey Fred A. • SHT • USA
ALMOST GUILTY • 1916 • Chaudet Louis W. • SHT • USA
ALMOST HUMAN • 1914 • Nash Percy? • UKN
ALMOST HUMAN • 1927 • Urson Frank • USA • BEAUTIFUL BUT DUMB
ALMOST HUMAN (UKN) see **DEATH CORPS** • 1970
ALMOST HUMAN (USA) see **MILANO ODIA: LA POLIZIA NO PUO SPARARE** • 1974
ALMOST LUCK • 1915 • *Superba* • USA
ALMOST MARRIED • 1914 • *Sterling* • USA
ALMOST MARRIED • 1919 • Perez Marcel • *Wm. Steiner Prod.* • USA
ALMOST MARRIED • 1919 • Swickard Charles • *Metro* • USA
ALMOST MARRIED • 1932 • Menzies William Cameron • USA
ALMOST MARRIED • 1942 • Lamont Charles • USA
ALMOST MARRIED see **NO ROOM FOR THE GROOM** • 1952
ALMOST PERFECT AFFAIR, AN • 1979 • Ritchie Michael • USA
ALMOST RIGHT • 1916 • *Armstrong Billy* • USA
ALMOST SUMMER • 1977 • Davidson Martin • USA • DIRTY LOOKS
ALMOST WELCOME • 1918 • Lyons Eddie, Moran Lee • USA
ALMOST YOU • 1985 • Brooks Adam • USA
ALMOURAL • 1954 • Garcia Fernando • SHT • PRT
ALMURAHIKAT • 1961 • Din Ahmad Dia Ad- • EGY • TEENAGERS
ALNIMIN KARA YAZISI • 1968 • Gorec Ertem • TRK • MY DARK FATE
ALOCHAYA • 1940 • *Sircar B. N. (P)* • IND
ALOHA • 1931 • Rogell Albert S. • USA • NO GREATER LOVE (UKN)
ALOHA, BOBBY AND ROSE • 1975 • Mutrux Floyd • USA
ALOHA HOOEY • 1942 • Avery Tex • ANS • USA
ALOHA, LE CHANT DES ILES • 1937 • Mathot Leon • FRN
ALOHA MEANS GOODBYE • 1974 • Rich David Lowell • TVM • USA
ALOHA OE • 1915 • Stanton Richard • USA
ALOHA OE • 1933 • Fleischer Dave • ANS • USA
ALOHA SUMMER • 1988 • Wallace Tommy Lee • USA
ALOIS VYHRAL NA LOS • 1918 • Branald Richard F. • CZC • ALOIS WON THE SWEEPSTAKES
ALOIS WON THE SWEEPSTAKES see **ALOIS VYHRAL NA LOS** • 1918
ALOISE • 1975 • de Kermadec Liliane • FRN
ALOM A HAZROL • 1971 • Szabo Istvan • DCS • HNG • DREAM ABOUT A HOUSE
ALOMA OF THE SOUTH SEAS • 1926 • Tourneur Maurice • USA
ALOMA OF THE SOUTH SEAS • 1941 • Santell Alfred • USA
ALOMBRIGAD • 1983 • Jeles Andras • HNG • DREAM-BRIGADE
ALONA ON THE SARONG SEAS • 1942 • Sparber I. • ANS • USA
ALONE • 1963 • Dwoskin Stephen • USA
ALONE see **ODNA** • 1931
ALONE see **SAMAC** • 1958
ALONE see **SAM** • 1959
ALONE see **SOLA** • 1976
ALONE AGAINST ROME see **SOLO CONTRO ROMA** • 1962
ALONE AT DAYBREAK see **SOLOS EN LA MADRUGADA** • 1978
ALONE AT LAST see **ENDELIG ALENE** • 1914
ALONE I DID IT • 1914 • *Heron Andrew (P)* • UKN
ALONE IN A CITY see **SAM POSROD MIASTA** • 1965
ALONE IN LONDON • 1915 • Trimble Larry • UKN
ALONE IN MOSCOW • 1964 • Frez Ilya • USS
ALONE IN NEW YORK • 1914 • *Standing Mr.* • USA
ALONE IN THE CITY OF SIGHS AND TEARS • 1915 • McCully William • USA
ALONE IN THE DARK • 1982 • Sholder Jack • USA
ALONE IN THE EARLY HOURS OF THE MORNING see **SOLOS EN LA MADRUGADA** • 1978

ALONE IN THE JUNGLE • 1913 • Campbell Colin • USA
ALONE IN THE NEON JUNGLE • 1988 • Brown George Stanford • TVM • USA • COMMAND IN HELL
ALONE IN THE NIGHT see **NAYEDINYE S NOCHYU** • 1967
ALONE IN THE PACIFIC see **TAIHEIYO HITORIBOTCHI** • 1963
ALONE IN THE STREETS • 1956 • Stano Silvio
ALONE IN THE TOWN see **SAM POSROD MIASTA** • 1965
ALONE IN THE WORLD • 1916 • Weber Lois • SHT • USA
ALONE IN THE WORLD see **SAMI NA SWIECIE** • 1958
ALONE ON THE PACIFIC (USA) see **TAIHEIYO HITORIBOTCHI** • 1963
ALONE WITH THE DEVIL • 1914 • DNM
ALONE WITH THE MONSTERS • 1958 • Nour Nazli • SHT • UKN
ALONG CAME A CITY CHAP • 1914 • *Ab* • USA
ALONG CAME A DUCK • 1934 • Gillett Burt, Muffati Steve • ANS • USA
ALONG CAME A SPIDER • 1969 • Katzin Lee H. • TVM • USA
ALONG CAME A WOMAN • 1935 • Collins Lewis D. • USA
ALONG CAME AUNTIE • 1926 • Guiol Fred • SHT • USA
ALONG CAME DAFFY • 1947 • Freleng Friz • ANS • USA
ALONG CAME JONES • 1945 • Heisler Stuart • USA
ALONG CAME LOVE • 1936 • Lytell Bert, Mansfield Duncan • USA
ALONG CAME MURDER see **KID GLOVE KILLER** • 1942
ALONG CAME RUTH • 1924 • Cline Eddie • USA
ALONG CAME SALLY (USA) see **AUNT SALLY** • 1933
ALONG CAME YOUTH • 1930 • Corrigan Lloyd, McLeod Norman Z. • USA
ALONG FLIRTATION WALK • 1935 • Freleng Friz • ANS • USA
ALONG MY ROAD see **ROJO** • 1964
ALONG RUSSIAN PATHS see **PO RUSI** • 1968
ALONG THE BORDER • 1916 • Mix Tom • SHT • USA
ALONG THE FANGO RIVER see **AU LONG DE LA RIVIERE FANGO** • 1974
ALONG THE GALGU RIVER see **GALGA MENTEN** • 1954
ALONG THE GREAT DIVIDE • 1951 • Walsh Raoul • USA
ALONG THE MALIBU • 1916 • Madison Cleo, Mong William V. • SHT • USA • GUILTY ONE, THE
ALONG THE MOHAWK TRAIL • 1956 • Newfield Sam • USA
ALONG THE MOONBEAM TRAIL • 1920 • *Dawley Herbert M. (P)* • USA
ALONG THE NAVAJO TRAIL • 1945 • McDonald Frank • USA
ALONG THE OREGON TRAIL • 1947 • Springsteen R. G. • USA
ALONG THE PAVEMENT see **PO TROTOARA** • 1967
ALONG THE RIO GRANDE • 1941 • Killy Edward • USA
ALONG THE RIVER KAMA • Touloubieva Z. • DOC • USS
ALONG THE RIVER NILE • 1912 • Olcott Sidney • DOC • USA
ALONG THE SUNDOWN TRAIL • 1943 • Newfield Sam • USA
ALONG THE SUNGARI RIVER see **SONGHUA JIAN SHANG** • 1947
ALONG THESE LINES • 1974 • Dunning George • ANS • CND
ALONG THESE LINES • 1974 • Pearson Peter • CND
ALONG UNTRODDEN DUNES see **LANGS ONGEBAENDE KLINGEN** • 1948
ALONG WITH GHOSTS • 1969 • Yoshida Kimiyoshi • JPN • JOURNEY WITH GHOST ALONG TOKKAIDO ROAD
ALORS, HEUREUX? • 1979 • Barrois Claude • FRN
ALOUETTE • 1944 • Jodoin Rene, McLaren Norman • ANS • CND
ALOUETTE ET LA MESANGE, L' • 1922 • Antoine Andre • FRN
ALOUNAK • 1968 • Alkhas Mardouk • IRN • HUT
ALP ASLANIN FEDAISI ALPAGO • 1967 • Saydam Nejat • TRK • ALPAGO, ALP ASLAN'S BRAVE
ALPAGO, ALP ASLAN'S BRAVE see **ALP ASLANIN FEDAISI ALPAGO** • 1967
ALPAGUEUR, L' • 1976 • Labro Philippe • FRN • PREDATOR, THE
ALPAMYS-BATYR • Kitausov Gani, Danenov Zhaken • ANM • USS
ALPASLAN, THE HERO OF MALAZGIRT see **MALAZGIRT KAHRAMANI ALPASLAN** • 1967
ALPENGLUHEN • 1927 • Beck-Gaden Hanns • FRG
ALPENGLUHN IM DIRNLROCK • 1974 • Gotz Siggi • FRG
ALPENKONIG UND DER MENSCHENFEIND, DER • 1965 • Anders Gunther • AUS
ALPENTRAGODIE • 1927 • Land Robert • FRG
ALPES, LES • 1958 • Painleve Jean • SHT • FRN
ALPHA BETA • 1973 • Page Anthony • UKN
ALPHA BLUE • 1981 • Damiano Gerard • USA • SATISFIERS OF ALPHA BLUE
ALPHA CAPER, THE • 1973 • Lewis Robert Michael • TVM • USA • INSIDE JOB (UKN)
ALPHA CITY see **ABGERECHNET WIRD NACHTS** • 1985
ALPHA INCIDENT, THE • 1977 • Rebane Bill • USA
ALPHA OMEGA • 1961 • Bozzetto Bruno • ANS • ITL • ALPHA-OMEGA
ALPHA-OMEGA see **ALPHA OMEGA** • 1961
ALPHABET • 1966 • Lynch David • SHT • USA
ALPHABET • 1967 • Noyes Eliot • ANS • CND
ALPHABET CITY • 1984 • Poe Amos • USA
ALPHABET MURDERS, THE see **ABC MURDERS, THE** • 1966
ALPHABET -UPPER CASE • 1973 • Hale Jeffrey • USA
ALPHABETISATION, L' • 1974 • Al-Rawi Abdel-Hadi • SHT • IRQ
ALPHAVILLE, UNE ETRANGE AVENTURE DE LEMMY CAUTION • 1965 • Godard Jean-Luc • FRN, ITL • AGENTE LEMMY CAUTION MISSIONE ALPHAVILLE (ITL) ○ ALPHAVILLE (USA) ○ TARZAN VS. I.B.M.
ALPHAVILLE (USA) see **ALPHAVILLE, UNE ETRANGE AVENTURE DE LEMMY CAUTION** • 1965
ALPINE ANTICS • 1936 • King Jack • ANS • USA
ALPINE BALLAD • 1966 • Stepanov Boris • USS
ALPINE CABARET • 1937 • Schwarzwald Milton • SHT • USA
ALPINE CLIMBERS • 1936 • Hand David • ANS • USA
ALPINE ECHO, AN • 1909 • *Vitagraph* • USA
ALPINE FIRE see **HOHENFEUER** • 1985
ALPINE FOR YOU • 1951 • Sparber I. • ANS • USA
ALPINE LEASE, THE • 1911 • *Kalem* • USA
ALPINE MELODIES • 1929 • Jeffrey R. E. • UKN
ALPINE ROMANCE see **WHITE HOT** • 1982
ALPINE VICTORY see **ARUPUSU TAISHO** • 1934
ALPINE WORLD • 1970 • Pavel Eric • DOC • USA
ALPINE YODELER, THE • 1936 • *Terry Paul/ Moser Frank (P)* • ANS • USA
ALPINISME, L' • 1956-57 • Devlin Bernard • DCS • CND
ALPS NO WAKADAISHO see **ARUPUSU NO WADADAISHO** • 1966
ALQUEZAR • 1966 • Basterretxea Nestor, Larruquert Fernando • SHT • SPN
ALQUIMISTA, EL • 1968 • Berriatua Luciano • SHT • SPN
ALRAUNE • 1918 • Curtiz Michael • HNG • MANDRAKE
ALRAUNE • 1918 • Illes Eugen • FRG • MANDRAKE
ALRAUNE • 1927 • Galeen Henrik • FRG • DAUGHTER OF DESTINY, A ○ UNHOLY LOVE ○ MANDRAGORE ○ MANDRAKE
ALRAUNE • 1930 • Oswald Richard • FRG • DAUGHTER OF EVIL
ALRAUNE • 1952 • Rabenalt Arthur M. • FRG • MANDRAKE ○ UNNATURAL ○ VENGEANCE ○ MANDRAGORE
ALRAUNE AND THE GOLEM see **ALRAUNE UND DER GOLEM** • 1919
ALRAUNE, DIE HENKERSTOCHTER, GENNANT DIE ROTE HANNE • 1918 • Illes Eugen • FRG
ALRAUNE UND DER GOLEM • 1919 • Chrisander Nils (Spvn) • FRG • ALRAUNE AND THE GOLEM
ALRIGHT DARLING see **AYOS NA DARLING** • 1968
ALS DIE SABBATLICHER ERLOSCHEN... • 1915 • Matull Kurt • FRG
ALS GEHEILT ENTLASSEN • 1960 • von Cziffra Geza • FRG
ALS ICH TOT WAR • 1916 • Lubitsch Ernst • FRG
ALS ICH WIEDERKAM • 1926 • Oswald Richard • FRG
ALS IN EEN ROES • 1987 • de la Parra Pim • NTH • INTOXICATED
AL'S TROUBLES • 1925 • Lamont Charles • SHT • USA
ALS TWEE DRUPPELS WATER • 1963 • Rademakers Fons • NTH • LIKE TWO DROPS OF WATER ○ SPITTING IMAGE, THE
ALSACE • 1915 • Pouctal Henri • FRN
ALSELMO HA FRETTA see **SPOSA NON PUO ATTENDERE, LA** • 1950
ALSINO AND THE CONDOR (USA) see **ALSINO Y EL CONDOR** • 1982
ALSINO Y EL CONDOR • 1982 • Littin Miguel • NCR, CUB • ALSINO AND THE CONDOR (USA)
ALSKA MEJ! • 1986 • Pollak Kay • SWD • LOVE ME!
ALSKANDE PAR • 1964 • Zetterling Mai • SWD • LOVING COUPLES
ALSKARINNAN • 1962 • Sjoman Vilgot • SWD • SWEDISH MISTRESS, THE (USA) ○ MISTRESS, THE
ALSKLING, JAG GER MIG • 1943 • Molander Gustaf • SWD • DARLING I SURRENDER
ALSKLING PA VAGEN • 1955 • Bauman Schamyl • SWD • DARLING AT SEA
ALSKLING PA VIFT • 1964 • Gimtell Kage G. • SWD • MISS SEX
ALSO ES WAR SO.. • 1977 • Thome Karin • FRG, AUS • WILLIE -EINE ZAUBERPOSSE ○ WILLIE AND THE CHINESE CAT ○ THERE WAS A TIME
ALSO-RANS, THE • 1914 • Plumb Hay? • UKN
ALSORT BALLET • 1956 • Barton J. • ANM • UKN
ALSTER CASE, THE • 1915 • Haydon J. Charles • USA
ALT DETTE -OG ISLAND MED see **KVINNAN BAKOM ALLT** • 1951
ALT DETTE -OG ISLAND OGSA see **KVINNAN BAKOM ALLT** • 1951
ALT-HEIDELBERG • 1923 • Behrendt Hans • FRG • STUDENT PRINCE
ALT HEIDELBERG • 1959 • Marischka Ernst • FRG
ALT PA ET BRAEDT • 1977 • Axel Gabriel • DNM
ALT PAA ET KORT • 1912 • Blom August • DNM • GOLD FROM THE GUTTER ○ GULDMONTEN
ALTA COSTURA • 1954 • Marquina Luis • SPN
ALTA INFEDELTA • 1964 • Petri Elio, Rossi Franco, Monicelli Mario, Salce Luciano • ITL, FRN • HAUTE INFIDELITE (FRN) ○ SEX IN THE AFTERNOON ○ HIGH INFIDELITY
ALTA SCHUFITA ROSIE • 1969 • Bratescu Geta • ANS • RMN • ANOTHER LITTLE RED RIDING HOOD
ALTA TENSION • 1972 • Buchs Julio • SPN
ALTA VELOCIDADE • 1967 • de Macedo Antonio • SHT • PRT
ALTAIR • 1956 • De Mitri Leonardo • ITL
ALTAR BOYS, THE see **MINISTRATEN, DIE** • 1990
ALTAR CHAINS • 1916 • Merwin Bannister • UKN
ALTAR MAYOR • 1943 • Delgras Gonzalo • SPN
ALTAR OF AMBITION, THE • 1915 • MacMackin Archer • USA
ALTAR OF DEATH, THE • 1912 • West Raymond B. • USA
ALTAR OF LOVE, THE • 1910 • Costello Maurice, Gaillord Robert • USA
ALTAR OF THE AZTECS, THE • 1913 • McRae Henry • USA
ALTAR OF THE BRAVE see **DAMBANA NG KAGITINGAN** • 1968
ALTAR STAIR, THE • 1922 • Hillyer Lambert • USA
ALTARS OF DESIRE • 1926 • Cabanne W. Christy • USA
ALTARS OF THE EAST • 1955 • Ayres Lew • USA
ALTARS OF THE WORLD • 1976 • Ayres Lew • DOC • USA
ALTAS VARIEDADES • 1959 • Rovira Beleta Francisco • SPN
ALTE 79 see **LA ELVE LEVE!** • 1981
ALTE BALLHAUS, DAS • 1925 • Neff Wolfgang • FRG
ALTE FORSTERHAUS, DAS • 1956 • Philipp Harald • FRG
ALTE FRITZ 1, DER • 1927 • Lamprecht Gerhard • FRG • FRIEDE
ALTE FRITZ 2, DER • 1927 • Lamprecht Gerhard • FRG • AUSKLANG
ALTE GESETZ, DAS • 1923 • Dupont E. A. • FRG • ANCIENT LAW, THE ○ BARUCH
ALTE GOSPODAR, DER • 1922 • Randolf Rolf • FRG
ALTE KAMERADEN • 1934 • Sauer Fred • FRG • FAHNLEIN DER VERSPRENGTEN, DAS
ALTE LIEBE, EINE • 1959 • Beyer Frank • GDR
ALTE LIED, DAS • 1919 • Krause Karl Otto • FRG
ALTE LIED, DAS • 1930 • Waschneck Erich • FRG • ZU JEDEM KOMMT EINMAL DIE LIEBE
ALTE LIED, DAS • 1945 • Buch Fritz Peter • FRG
ALTE RECHT, DAS • 1934 • Anderson Igo M. • FRG
ALTE SCHERE, DIE • 1915 • Del Zopp Rudolf • FRG
ALTE SUNDER, DER • 1951 • Antel Franz • FRG
ALTE UND DER JUNGE KONIG, DER • 1935 • Steinhoff Hans • FRG • YOUNG AND THE OLD KING, THE
ALTE VAGABUND UND SEIN HUNDCHEN, DER • 1930 • Schwerdtfeger Heinz-Hermann • FRG
ALTEE SPIEL UM GOLD UND LIEBE, EIN see **SCHATZ, DER** • 1923
ALTEMER LE CYNIQUE • 1925 • Monca Georges, Keroul Maurice • FRN
ALTER EGO • 1941 • Ban Frigyes • HNG
ALTER EGO • 1990 • Lamarre Louise • SHT • CND
ALTER EGO see **BEWITCHED** • 1945
ALTER EGO see **CLONUS HORROR, THE** • 1979
ALTER EGO see **MURDER BY THE BOOK** • 1987
ALTER EGOIST • 1967 • Culhane Shamus • ANS • USA
ALTER ENGEL, EIN • 1967 • Hadaschik Joachim • DOC • GDR
ALTER KAHN UND JUNGE LIEBE • 1957 • Hinrich Hans • GDR
ALTERCATION AU CAFE, UNE • 1896 • Melies Georges • FRN • QUARREL IN A CAFE, A
ALTERED MESSAGE, THE • 1911 • Blache Alice • USA
ALTERED STATES • 1980 • Russell Ken • USA
ALTERNATIVA, LA • 1962 • Nunes Jose Maria • SPN
ALTERNATIVE 3 • 1978 • Miles Christopher • UKN
ALTERNATIVE, THE • 1913 • *Reliance* • USA
ALTERNATIVE, THE • 1915 • Maude Arthur • USA
ALTERNATIVE, THE • 1977 • Eddy Paul • MTV • ASL
ALTERNATIVE DE BAIE ST-PAUL, L' • 1977 • Dussault Louis • CND
ALTERNATIVE MISS WORLD, THE • 1980 • Gayor Richard • UKN
ALTERNATIVE WAR see **NO DRUMS, NO BUGLES** • 1971
ALTES HERZ WIRD WIEDER JUNG • 1943 • Engel Erich • FRG
ALTESTE GEWERBE DER WELT, DAS see **PLUS VIEUX METIER DU MONDE, LE** • 1967
ALTGERMANISCHE BAUERNKULTUR • 1934 • Ruttmann Walter • FRG
ALTHOUGH THERE ARE MILLIONS OF WOMEN see **ONNA WA IKUMAN ARITOTEMO** • 1966
ALTID BALLADE • 1955 • Axel Gabriel • DNM
ALTIN AVCILARI • 1968 • Davutoglu Zafer • TRK • GOLD HUNTERS, THE
ALTIN COCUK BEYRUTTA • 1967 • Gorec Ertem • TRK • GOLDEN BOY IN BEIRUT
ALTIN MEZAR • 1968 • Alpaslan Mumtaz • TRK • GOLDEN GRAVE, THE
ALTIN SHEER • 1979 • Aksoy Orhan • TRK • GOLDEN TOWN, THE
ALTISONIANS • 1967 • Blomdahl Karl-Birgir • SWD
ALTISSIMA PRESSIONE • 1967 • Trapani Enzo • ITL
ALTITUDE 3200 • 1938 • Benoit-Levy Jean, Epstein Marie • FRN • YOUTH IN REVOLT (USA) ○ GRAND REVE, LE ○ NOUS LES JEUNES
ALTO PARANO • 1958 • Catrani Catrano • ARG
ALTRA, L' • 1947 • Bragaglia Carlo Ludovico • ITL
ALTRA DONNA, L' • 1980 • Del Monte Peter • ITL
ALTRA FACCIA DEL PADRINO, L' • 1973 • Prosperi Franco • ITL
ALTRA FACCIA DEL PECCATO, L' • 1968 • Martino Luciano • ITL
ALTRA FACCIA DEL PECCATO, L' • 1969 • Avallone Marcello • ITL • QUEER.. THE EROTIC, THE (UKN)
ALTRA META DEL CIELO • 1977 • Rossi Franco • ITL
ALTRE, L' • 1969 • Maietto Renzo • ITL
ALTRI, GLI ALTRI E... NOI, GLI • 1966 • Arena Maurizio • ITL
ALTRI RACCONTI DI CANTERBURY, GLI • 1972 • Guerrini Mino • ITL • OTHER CANTERBURY TALES, THE (UKN)
ALTRI TEMPI • 1952 • Blasetti Alessandro • ITL • IN OLDEN DAYS (USA) ○ INFIDELITY (UKN) ○ TIMES GONE BY ○ ZIBALDONE N.1
ALTRIMENTI CI ARRABBIAMO • 1974 • Fondato Marcello • ITL, SPN • Y SI NO ENFADAMOS (SPN) ○ WATCH OUT, WE'RE MAD
ALTRIMENTI VI AMMUCCHIAMO • 1974 • Bange George • ITL, HKG
ALTRO DIO, L' • 1975 • Bartolini Elio • ITL
ALTRO INFERNO, L' • 1981 • Mattei Bruno • ITL • OTHER HELL, THE
ALTRO IO • 1924 • Bonnard Mario • ITL
ALTRO IO, L' • 1917 • Bonnard Mario • ITL
ALTRO PIATTO DELLA BILANCIA, L' • 1973 • Colucci Mario • ITL
ALTURA • 1951 • Sequi Mario • ITL • ROCCE INSANGUINATE
ALTYD IN MY DROME • 1952 • SAF
ALUCARDA • 1975 • Moctezuma Juan Lopez • MXC • ALUCARDA, HIJA DE LAS TINIEBLAS
ALUCARDA, HIJA DE LAS TINIEBLAS see **ALUCARDA** • 1975
ALUCINACAO • 1972 • Roucourt Wagner • BRZ
ALUM AND EVE • 1932 • Marshall George • SHT • USA
ALUMINITE, L' • 1910 • *Gance Abel* • FRN
ALUNISSONS • 1971 • Ansorge Ernest, Ansorge Giselle • ANS • SWT
ALVARADO VILLAGE DE PECHE • 1953 • Philippe Anne • SHT • BLG
ALVAREZ KELLY • 1966 • Dmytryk Edward • USA
ALVARO PIUTTOSTO CORSARO • 1954 • Mastrocinque Camillo • ITL
ALVERDENS PORNO • 1973 • Orsted Ole • DNM
ALVES & Co • 1974 • Semedo Artur • MTV • PRT
ALVIN AND KELVIN KEECH • 1926 • *De Forest Phonofilms* • SHT • UKN
ALVIN PURPLE • 1973 • Burstall Tim • ASL
ALVIN RIDES AGAIN • 1974 • Bilcock David Jr., Copping Robin • ASL • FOREPLAY: THE PREQUEL
ALVINO REY AND HIS ORCHESTRA • 1948 • Cowan Will • SHT • USA
ALVIN'S SOLO FLIGHT • 1961 • Kneitel Seymour • ANS • USA
ALVORADA -AUFBRUCH IN BRASILIEN • 1961 • Niebeling Hugo • FRG • ALVORADA -BRAZIL'S CHANGING WORLD
ALVORADA -BRAZIL'S CHANGING WORLD see **ALVORADA -AUFBRUCH IN BRASILIEN** • 1961
ALWAN • 1973 • Zubaydi Qays Al- • IRQ • COULEURS
ALWAYS • 1909 • *Warwick Trading Co* • UKN
ALWAYS • 1987 • Jaglom Henry • USA
ALWAYS • 1989 • Spielberg Steven • USA
ALWAYS see **DEJA VU** • 1984
ALWAYS A BRIDE • 1940 • Smith Noel • USA
ALWAYS A BRIDE • 1953 • Smart Ralph • UKN

ALWAYS A BRIDESMAID • 1942 • Kenton Erle C. • USA
ALWAYS A GENTLEMAN • 1928 • Taurog Norman • SHT • USA
ALWAYS A NEW BEGINNING • 1973 • Goodell John D. • DOC • USA
ALWAYS ANOTHER DAWN • 1947 • McCreadie Tom O. • ASL
ALWAYS AUDACIOUS • 1920 • Cruze James • USA
ALWAYS AWAY • 1911 • Salter Harry • USA
ALWAYS FOR PLEASURE • 1978 • Blank Les • USA
ALWAYS GAY • 1913 • Wilson Frank? • UKN
ALWAYS GOODBYE • 1931 • Menzies William Cameron, MacKenna Kenneth • USA
ALWAYS GOODBYE • 1938 • Lanfield Sidney • USA
ALWAYS IN MY HEART • 1942 • Graham Jo • USA
ALWAYS IN MY HEART see **DAIMAN FI KALBI** • 1947
ALWAYS IN MY HEART see **MR. IMPERIUM** • 1951
ALWAYS IN MY HEART see **KIMI NO NAWA** • 1954
ALWAYS IN THE WAY • 1915 • Dawley J. Searle • USA
ALWAYS IN TROUBLE • 1938 • Santley Joseph • USA
ALWAYS KICKIN' • 1939 • Fleischer Dave • ANS • USA
ALWAYS LEAVE THEM LAUGHING • 1949 • Del Ruth Roy • USA
ALWAYS LEAVE THEM LAUGHING see **NAUGHTY BUT NICE** • 1939
ALWAYS LOVE YOUR NEIGHBOURS • 1915 • Birch Cecil • UKN
ALWAYS ON MONDAY see **MY TALE IS HOT** • 1964
ALWAYS ON SATURDAY • 1966 • *Boxoffice International* • USA
ALWAYS ON SUNDAY • 1965 • Russell Ken • MTV • UKN
ALWAYS ON SUNDAY (USA) see **DOMENICA D'ESTATE, UNA** • 1962
ALWAYS READY IN THE DARKNESS see **SIEMPRE LISTO EN LAS TINIEBLAS** • 1939
ALWAYS RIDIN' TO TOWN • 1925 • Sheldon Forrest • USA
ALWAYS TELL YOUR HUSBAND • 1915 • Birch Cecil • UKN
ALWAYS TELL YOUR WIFE • 1913 • Bantock Leedham • UKN
ALWAYS TELL YOUR WIFE • 1923 • Croise Hugh, Hitchcock Alfred • UKN
ALWAYS THE WOMAN • 1922 • Rosson Arthur • USA
ALWAYS TOGETHER • 1913 • *Majestic* • USA
ALWAYS TOGETHER • 1947 • De Cordova Frederick • USA
ALWAYS TROUBLE WITH TEACHER see **IMMER ARGER MIT DEN PAUKERN** • 1968
ALWAYS UNTIL VICTORY see **HASTA LA VICTORIA SIEMPRE** • 1967
ALWAYS VICTORIOUS (USA) see **KANONEN-SERENADE** • 1958
ALWAYS WHEN NIGHT FALLS see **IMMER WENN ES NACHT WIRD** • 1961
ALWAYS YOURS see **SIEMPRE TUYA** • 1950
ALYAM, ALYAM see **ALAYAM, ALAYAM** • 1977
ALYAS 1 2 3 • 1968 • Reyes Efren • PHL • ALIAS 1 2 3
ALYAS FUMANCHU • 1964 • PHL • ALIAS FU MANCHU
ALYAS PHANTOM • 1965 • Toledo Paquito • PHL • ALIAS PHANTOM
ALYE PARUSA • 1961 • Ptushko Alexander • USS • CRIMSON SAILS ○ RED SAILS
ALYGISTOS, O • 1967 • Silinos Vangelis • GRC • NO SURRENDER
ALYONKA see **ALENKA** • 1961
ALYSE AND CHLOE (UKN) see **ALYSE ET CHLOE** • 1970
ALYSE ET CHLOE • 1970 • Gainville Rene • FRN • ALYSE AND CHLOE (UKN)
ALZIRE ODER DER NEUE KONTINENT • 1977 • Koerfer Thomas • SWT
AM ABEND AUF DER HEIDE • 1941 • von Alten Jurgen • FRG
AM ABEND NACH DER OPER • 1944 • Rabenalt Arthur M. • FRG
AM AMBOSS DES GLUCKS • 1916 • Hanus Emerich • FRG
AM ANDERN UFER • 1918 • Halm Alfred • FRG
AM ANFANG WAR ES SUNDE • 1954 • Cap Frantisek • FRG, YGS • BEGINNING WAS SIN, THE (USA) ○ V ZACETKU JE BIL GREH ○ GREH
AM BESTEN GEFALLT MIR DIE LORE • 1925 • *Boheme-Film* • FRG
AM BRUNNEN VOR DEM TORE • 1952 • Wolff Hans • FRG
AM ENDE DER WELT • 1943 • Ucicky Gustav • FRG • AT THE EDGE OF THE WORLD
AM GALGEN HANGT DIE LIEBE • 1960 • Zbonek Edwin • FRG
AM HOCKZEITSABEND • 1917 • *Kaiser-Titz Erich* • FRG
AM I A FEMALE? see **AM I FEMALE?** • 1970
AM I DREAMING? • 1920 • *De Haven Carter* • SHT • USA
AM I FEMALE? • 1970 • *St. Thomas Warren* • USA • AM I A FEMALE?
AM I HAVING FUN • 1936 • Black Preston • SHT • USA
AM I SO BAD? • 1967 • Tosheva Nevena • DOC • BUL
AM I TO BLAME? see **STORY OF ALFRED NOBEL, THE** • 1939
AM I TRYING! see **OTOKO WA TSURAIYO** • 1969
AM I TRYING PART II see **ZOKU OTOKOWA TSURAIYO** • 1969
AM KREUZWEG DER LEIDENSCHAFT • 1919 • *Kuhnberg Leontine* • FRG
AM LIEBESHOF DES SONNENKONIGS see **LOUISE DE LAVALLIERE** • 1920
AM NARRENSEIL • 1923 • Firmans Josef • FRG
AM NARRENSEIL 1 • 1921 • Firmans Josef • FRG • SCHRECKENSTAGE DER FINANZKREISE
AM NARRENSEIL 2 • 1921 • Firmans Josef • FRG • RATSEL DER KRIMINALISTIK
AM RANDE • 1963 • Radax Ferry • DOC • SWT • ON THE BRINK
AM RANDE DER GROSSTADT • 1922 • Kobe Hanns • FRG
AM RANDE DER SAHARA • 1930 • Rikli Martin, Biebrach Rudolf • FRG
AM RANDE DER WELT • 1927 • Grune Karl • FRG • AT EDGE OF WORLD (USA) ○ AT THE EDGE OF THE WORLD
AM RANDE DES LEBENS see **DUELL MIT DEM TOD** • 1949
AM ROTEN KLIFF • 1921 • Henning Hanna • FRG
AM RUDESHEIMER SCHLOSS STEHT EINE LINDE • 1927 • Guter Johannes • FRG
AM SCHWEIDEWEGE • 1918 • Halm Alfred • FRG
AM SEIDENEN FADEN • 1938 • Stemmle R. A. • FRG
AM SONNTAG WILL MEIN SUSSER MIT MIR SEGELN GEHN • 1961 • Marischka Franz • FRG, AUS • LEBEN WIE IM PARADIES, EIN
AM TAG ALS DER REGEN KAM • 1959 • Oswald Gerd • FRG • DAY IT RAINED, THE (USA) ○ DAY THE RAINS CAME, THE
AM TOR DES LEBENS • 1918 • Wiene Conrad • AUS • AM TOR DES TODES
AM TOR DES TODES see **AM TOR DES LEBENS** • 1918
AM VORABEND see **BLICK ZURUCK, EIN** • 1944
AM WEBSTUHL DER ZEIT • 1921 • Holger-Madsen • FRG • LABOREMUS
AM WEIBE ZERSCHELLT • 1919 • *Kaiser-Titz Erich* • FRG
AMA, EL • 1930 • Perojo Benito • MXC • MAMA (USA)
AMA A TU PROJIMO • 1958 • Demicheli Tulio • MXC
AMA LUR • 1966 • Basterretxea Nestor, Larruquert Fernando • SPN • TIERRA MADRE
AMA NO BAKEMONO YASHIKI • 1959 • Magatani Morehei • JPN • GIRL DIVER OF SPOOK MANSION ○ HAUNTED CAVE
AMA NO YUHGAO • 1948 • Abe Yutaka • JPN • EVENING GLORY OF HEAVEN
AMA ROSA • 1960 • Klimovsky Leon • SPN
AMACHUA KURABU • 1920 • Kurihara Kisaburo • JPN • AMATEUR CLUB
AMADERA MARUHI MONOGATARI • 1968 • Nakajima Sadao • JPN • SECRET OF THE MONASTERY, THE
AMADEUS • 1984 • Forman Milos • USA
AMADOR • 1965 • Regueiro Francisco • SPN, FRN
AMAGI GOE • 1983 • Mimura Haruhiko • JPN • ON MOUNTAIN PASS AMAGI
AMAGODUKA • 1985 • SAF
AMAHLAYA • 1985 • SAF
AMAI ASE • 1964 • Toyoda Shiro • JPN • SWEET SWEAT
AMAI HIMITSU • 1971 • Yoshimura Kozaburo • JPN • SWEET SECRET
AMAI SHOYA • 1968 • Okuwaki Toshio • JPN • SWEET BRIDAL NIGHT, A
AMAI YORU NO HATE • 1961 • Yoshida Yoshishige • JPN • BITTER END OF SWEET NIGHT
AMAKUSA SHIRO TOKISADA • 1962 • Oshima Nagisa • JPN • REVOLUTIONARY, THE (USA) ○ REBEL, THE (UKN) ○ SHIRO TOKISADA FROM AMAKUSA
AMAKUZURE • 1968 • Ikehiro Kazuo • JPN • DARING NUN, THE
AMALIA • 1936 • Barth-Moglia Luis • ARG
AMALIA, KARHU • 1982 • Olsson Claes • FNL • AMALIA, THE BEAR
AMALIA, THE BEAR see **AMALIA, KARHU** • 1982
AMAMI, ALFREDO! • 1940 • Gallone Carmine • ITL
AMAN • 1967 • Kumar Mohan • IND • PEACE
AMANAT • 1955 • Sen Arbind • IND
AMANDA, DAS KLUGE HIRTENMADCHEN • 1915 • Del Zopp Rudolf • FRG
AMANDUS • 1966 • Stiglic France • YGS
AMANECER EN PUERTA OSCURA • 1957 • Forque Jose Maria • SPN
AMANECER RANCHERO • 1942 • de Anda Raul • MXC
AMANECI EN TUS BRAZOS • 1966 • Portillo Rafael • MXC
AMANGELDY • 1938 • Levine Moissej • USS
AMANIE • 1973 • M'Bala Gnoan • IVC • WHAT IS THE NEWS?
AMANITA PESTILENS • 1963 • Bonniere Rene • CND
AMANSIZ OUL • 1985 • Kavur Omer • TRK • DESPERATE ROAD, THE
AMANSIZ TAKIP • 1967 • Evin Semih • TRK • MERCILESS CHASE
AMANT DE BORNEO, L' • 1942 • Feydeau Jean-Pierre, Le Henaff Rene • FRN
AMANT DE CHATTERLEY, L' • 1955 • Allegret Marc • FRN • LADY CHATTERLEY'S LOVER
AMANT DE CINQ JOURS, L' • 1960 • de Broca Philippe • FRN, ITL • AMANTE DI CINQUE GIORNI, L' (ITL) ○ FIVE DAY LOVER, THE (USA) ○ INFIDELITY (UKN)
AMANT DE LA BERGERE, L' see **AGAPITIKOS TIS VOSKOPOULAS, O** • 1956
AMANT DE LA LUNE, L' see **REVE A LA LUNE** • 1905
AMANT DE LADY CHATTERLY, L' (FRN) see **LADY CHATTERLEY'S LOVER** • 1981
AMANT DE MADAME VIDAL, L' • 1936 • Berthomieu Andre • FRN
AMANT DE PAILLE, L' • 1950 • Grangier Gilles • FRN
AMANT DE POCHE, L' • 1977 • Queysanne Bernard • FRN • LOVER BOY (UKN)
AMANT MAGNIFIQUE, L' • 1986 • Issermann Aline • FRN
AMANT POUR ELLES... ET POUR LUI • Ricaud Michel • FRN
AMANTE, L' • 1989 • Belmont Vera • FRN, FRG • BELOVED, THE
AMANTE, L' (ITL) see **CHOSES DE LA VIE, LES** • 1970
AMANTE DEL DEMONIO, L' • 1972 • Lombardo Paolo • ITL • DEVIL'S LOVER, THE (USA)
AMANTE DEL MALE, L' • 1952 • Montero Roberto Bianchi • ITL
AMANTE DEL PRETE, L' (ITL) see **FAUTE DE L'ABBE MOURET, LA** • 1970
AMANTE DEL VAMPIRO, L' • 1960 • Polselli Renato • ITL • VAMPIRE AND THE BALLERINA, THE (USA) ○ VAMPIRE'S LOVER, THE
AMANTE DELL'ORSA MAGGIORE, L' • 1971 • Orsini Valentino • ITL, FRG, FRN • LOVER OF THE GREAT BEAR, THE ○ SMUGGLERS
AMANTE DI CINQUE GIORNI, L' (ITL) see **AMANT DE CINQ JOURS, L'** • 1960
AMANTE DI GRAMIGNA, L' • 1968 • Lizzani Carlo • ITL, RMN • GRAMINA'S LOVER ○ BANDIT, THE
AMANTE DI PARIDE, L' • 1955 • Allegret Marc • ITL • FACE THAT LAUNCHED A THOUSAND SHIPS, THE (UKN) ○ LOVES OF THREE QUEENS (USA) ○ HELEN OF TROY ○ ETERNA FEMMINA ○ FEMMINA
AMANTE DI UNA NOTTE, L' (ITL) see **CHATEAU DE VERRE, LE** • 1950
AMANTE GIOVANE, L'(ITL) see **NOUS NE VIEILLIRONS PAS ENSEMBLE** • 1972
AMANTE INFEDELE (ITL) see **SECONDE VERITE, LA** • 1965
AMANTE INGENUA, LA • 1977 • Ulloa Jose • SPN
AMANTE ITALIANA, L' (ITL) see **SULTANS, LES** • 1966
AMANTE MUITO LOUCA • 1980 • de Oliveira Denoy • BRZ • VERY CRAZY LOVER, A
AMANTE PERFECTA, LA • 1975 • Romero-Marchent Rafael • SPN
AMANTE PERFECTA, LA • 1976 • Lazaga Pedro • SPN
AMANTE PURA, L' (ITL) see **CHRISTINE** • 1959
AMANTE SEGRETA, L' • 1941 • Gallone Carmine • ITL
AMANTES DE LA ISLA DEL DIABOLO, LOS • 1972 • Franco Jesus • SPN, FRN • AMANTS DE L'ILE DU DIABLE, LES (FRN) ○ LOVERS OF DEVIL'S ISLAND, THE
AMANTES DE VERONA, LOS (SPN) see **GIULIETTA E ROMEO** • 1964
AMANTES DEL DESIERTO, LOS • 1958 • Cerchio Fernando, Alessandrini Goffredo, Suay Ricardo Munoz, Klimovsky Leon, Vernuccio Gianni • ITL, SPN • AMANTI DEL DESERTO (SPN) ○ FIGLIA DELLO SCEICCO, LA ○ DESERT WARRIOR
AMANTES DEL DIABLO, LES • 1971 • Elorrieta Jose Maria • SPN, ITL • DEVIL'S LOVERS, THE (USA) ○ DIABOLICAL MEETINGS ○ LOVERS OF THE DEVIL, THE ○ SATAN'S LOVERS ○ DIABOLICI CONVEGNI
AMANTES, LOS • 1950 • Rivero Fernando A. • MXC
AMANTES, LOS • 1956 • Alazraki Benito • MXC
AMANTI • 1968 • De Sica Vittorio • ITL, FRN • TEMPS DES AMANTS, LE (FRN) ○ PLACE FOR LOVERS, A (USA) ○ LOVERS
AMANTI DEL CHIARO DI LUNA, GLI (ITL) see **BIJOUTIERS DU CLAIR DE LUNE, LES** • 1958
AMANTI DEL DESERTO (SPN) see **AMANTES DEL DESIERTO, LOS** • 1958
AMANTI DEL MOSTRO, LE • 1974 • Garrone Sergio • ITL
AMANTI DEL PASSATO • 1955 • Bianchi Adelchi • ITL
AMANTI DELL'INFINITO, GLI see **RICHIAMO NELLA TEMPESTA, IL** • 1952
AMANTI DI DOMANI, GLI (ITL) see **CELA S'APPELLE L'AURORE** • 1955
AMANTI DI RAVELLO, GLI • 1951 • De Robertis Francesco • ITL • FENESTA CA LUCIVE
AMANTI DI TOLEDO, GLI (ITL) see **AMANTS DE TOLEDE, LES** • 1953
AMANTI D'OLTRETOMBA • 1965 • Caiano Mario • ITL • NIGHTMARE CASTLE (USA) ○ FACELESS MONSTER, THE (UKN) ○ NIGHT OF THE DOOMED ○ LOVERS BEYOND THE TOMB
AMANTI FRA DUE GUERRE see **INVIATI SPECIALI** • 1943
AMANTI IN FUGA • 1947 • Gentilomo Giacomo • ITL
AMANTI LATINI, GLI • 1965 • Costa Mario • ITL • LATIN LOVERS (USA)
AMANTI MIEI • 1979 • Grimaldi Aldo • ITL • CINDY'S LOVE GAMES ○ TIGHT FIT
AMANTI SENZA AMORE • 1948 • Franciolini Gianni • ITL
AMANTI SENZA PECCATO • 1957 • Baffico Mario • ITL • SPOSA NON VESTITA DI BIANCO, LA
AMANTI, SENZA SOLE • 1922 • D'Ambra Lucio • ITL
AMANTS, LES • 1958 • Malle Louis • FRN • LOVERS, THE
AMANTS DE BRAS-MORT, LES • 1950 • Pagliero Marcello • FRN
AMANTS DE DEMAIN, LES • 1958 • Blistene Marcel • FRN
AMANTS DE L'ILE DU DIABLE, LES (FRN) see **AMANTES DE LA ISLA DEL DIABOLO, LOS** • 1972
AMANTS DE MINUIT, LES • 1931 • Allegret Marc, Genina Augusto • FRN
AMANTS DE MINUIT, LES • 1952 • Richebe Roger • FRN
AMANTS DE TERUEL, LES • 1962 • Rouleau Raymond • FRN • LOVERS OF TERUEL, THE (USA)
AMANTS DE TOLEDE, LES • 1953 • Decoin Henri, Palacios Fernando • FRN, SPN, ITL • TIRANO DE TOLEDO, EL (SPN) ○ AMANTI DI TOLEDO, GLI (ITL) ○ LOVERS OF TOLEDO, THE (USA)
AMANTS DE VERONE, LES • 1948 • Cayatte Andre • FRN • LOVERS OF VERONA, THE (USA)
AMANTS DE VILLA BORGHESE, LES (FRN) see **VILLA BORGHESE** • 1953
AMANTS DU PONT-NEUF, LES • 1989 • Carax Leos • FRN
AMANTS DU PONT SAINT-JEAN, LES • 1947 • Decoin Henri • FRN
AMANTS DU TAGE, LES • 1955 • Verneuil Henri • FRN • LOVER'S NET (USA) ○ LOVERS OF LISBON, THE ○ PORT OF SHAME
AMANTS ET VOLEURS • 1935 • Bernard Raymond • FRN
AMANTS MAUDITS, LES • 1951 • Rozier Willy • FRN • DAMNED LOVERS
AMANTS TERRIBLES, LES • 1936 • Allegret Marc • FRN
AMANTS TRAQUES, LES see **MISTER FLOW** • 1936
AMAPHOYISANA • 1985 • SAF
AMAPOLA DEL CAMINO • 1937 • Bustillo Oro Juan • MXC
AMAR • 1948 • Khan Mehboob • IND • IMMORTAL
AMAR, AKBAR, ANTHONY • 1977 • Desai Manmohan • IND
AMAR ES VIVIR • 1945 • Ortega Juan J. • MXC
AMAR FUE SU PECADO • 1950 • Gonzalez Rogelio A. • MXC
AMAR JYOTI • 1936 • Shantaram Rajaram • IND • ETERNAL LIGHT
AMAR LENIN • 1970 • *Ghatak Ritwik* • DOC • IND
AMARAMENTE • 1959 • Capuano Luigi • ITL
AMARANTH • 1916 • *Chrisander Nils* • FRG
AMARCORD • 1973 • Fellini Federico • FRN, ITL • FELLINI'S AMARCORD
AMARGO MAR • 1984 • Eguino Antonio • BLV
AMARGURA DE MI RAZA, LA • 1972 • *Estudios America* • MXC
AMARILLY OF CLOTHES-LINE ALLEY • 1918 • Neilan Marshall • USA
AMARSI MALE see **BRUCIA, AMORE, BRUCIA** • 1969
AMARTI E IL MIO DESTINO • 1957 • Baldi Ferdinando • ITL
AMARTI E IL MIO PECCATO • 1953 • Grieco Sergio • ITL
AMATEUR see **AMATOR** • 1979
AMATEUR, DER • 1916 • Reicher Ernst • FRG
AMATEUR, THE • 1982 • Jarrott Charles • CND
AMATEUR ADVENTURESS, THE • 1919 • Otto Henry • USA
AMATEUR ANIMAL TRAINER, AN • 1914 • *Bracy Sidney* • USA
AMATEUR ARCHITECT, THE • 1905 • Fitzhamon Lewin • UKN
AMATEUR BILL SYKES, AN • 1902 • Williamson James • UKN
AMATEUR BROADCAST • 1935 • *Lantz Walter (P)* • ANS • USA
AMATEUR BURGLAR, AN • 1915 • *Punchinello* • USA
AMATEUR BURGLAR, THE • 1911 • Fitzhamon Lewin? • UKN

AMATEUR BURGLAR, THE • 1913 • *Kalem* • USA
AMATEUR CAMERA MAN, THE • 1915 • *Novelty* • USA
AMATEUR CLUB see **AMACHUA KURABU** • 1920
AMATEUR CROOK • 1937 • *Victory* • USA • CROOKED BUT DUMB (UKN)
AMATEUR DADDY • 1932 • Blystone John G. • USA
AMATEUR DETECTIVE, THE • 1914 • *Hastings Carey L.* • USA
AMATEUR DETECTIVE (UKN) see **IRISH LUCK** • 1939
AMATEUR DEVIL, AN • 1920 • Campbell Maurice • USA
AMATEUR FILM, THE see **AMATORFILMEN** • 1922
AMATEUR GENTLEMAN, THE • 1920 • Elvey Maurice • UKN
AMATEUR GENTLEMAN, THE • 1926 • Olcott Sidney • USA
AMATEUR GENTLEMAN, THE • 1936 • Freeland Thornton • UKN
AMATEUR HIGHWAYMAN, THE • 1913 • *Fraunholz Fraunie* • USA
AMATEUR HOLD-UP, AN • 1909 • *Essanay* • USA
AMATEUR HOUR see **I WAS A TEENAGE TV TERRORIST** • 1987
AMATEUR ICEMAN, THE • 1912 • *Johnson Arthur* • USA
AMATEUR LIER, THE • 1919 • *Drew Sidney* • SHT • USA
AMATEUR LION TAMER, THE • 1913 • *Mack Hughie* • USA
AMATEUR NIGHT • 1910 • *Edison* • USA
AMATEUR NIGHT • 1915 • *Aubrey James* • USA
AMATEUR NIGHT • 1929 • Lantz Walter, Nolan William • ANS • USA • AMATEUR NITE
AMATEUR NIGHT • 1935 • *Terry Paul/ Moser Frank (P)* • ANS • USA
AMATEUR NIGHT • 1946 • Richardson Frank • UKN
AMATEUR NIGHT • 1975 • Goldman Thalma • UKN
AMATEUR NIGHT AT THE DIXIE BAR AND GRILL • 1979 • Schumacher Joel • TVM • USA
AMATEUR NIGHT IN LONDON • 1930 • Banks Monty • UKN
AMATEUR NITE see **AMATEUR NIGHT** • 1929
AMATEUR NURSE, THE • 1915 • *La Pearl Harry* • USA
AMATEUR ORPHAN, THE • 1917 • Brooke Van Dyke • USA
AMATEUR PAPER HANGER, THE • 1907 • Martin J. H.? • UKN
AMATEUR PHOTOGRAPHER see **DOBRE SVETIO** • 1985
AMATEUR PRODIGAL, AN • 1915 • *Stonehouse Ruth* • USA
AMATEUR SPORTSMAN, AN • 1914 • *Gaumont* • USA
AMATEUR WIDOW, AN • 1919 • Apfel Oscar • USA
AMATEUR WIFE, THE • 1920 • Dillon Eddie • USA
AMATEUR WILLIAM TELL, THE • 1909 • *Edison* • USA
AMATHAKA VUNADA? • 1967 • Das D. M. • SLN • HAVE YOU FORGOTTEN?
AMATHIKAMA • 1968 • Jayasinghe Nihal • SLN • CABINET MINISTER, A
AMATOR • 1979 • Kieslowski Krzysztof • PLN • CAMERA BUFF ○ AMATEUR
AMATORFILMEN • 1922 • Molander Gustaf • SWD • AMATEUR FILM, THE
AMAXAKI, TO • 1957 • Dimopoulos Dinos • GRC • HORSE AND CARRIAGE (USA) ○ PETIT FIACRE, LE ○ HANSOM CAB, THE
AMAYA • 1952 • Marquina Luis • SPN
AMAYAKUDU • 1968 • Rao Addola Narayana • IND • INNOCENT
AMAZING ADVENTURE see **AMAZING QUEST OF ERNEST BLISS, THE** • 1936
AMAZING ADVENTURE, THE • 1917 • George Burton • SHT • USA
AMAZING ADVENTURES OF ITALIANS IN RUSSIA, THE • 1973 • Ryazanov Eldar • USS
AMAZING BATTALION, THE see **BATALION** • 1927
AMAZING CAPTAIN NEMO, THE • 1978 • March Alex • USA • RETURN OF CAPTAIN NEMO, THE
AMAZING COLOSSAL MAN, THE • 1957 • Gordon Bert I. • USA
AMAZING COLOSSAL MAN, THE • 1965 • Andersen Yvonne • ANS • USA
AMAZING DOBERMANS, THE • 1976 • Chudnow David, Chudnow Byron • USA
AMAZING DR. CLITTERHOUSE, THE • 1938 • Litvak Anatole • USA
AMAZING DR. G., THE (USA) see **DUE MAFIOSI CONTRO GOLDGINGER** • 1965
AMAZING DREAMING OF DZIGA VERTOV, THE see **CUDESNI SAN DZIGE VERTOVA** • 1990
AMAZING DUEL see **DUEL ABRACADABRANT** • 1902
AMAZING ELOPEMENT, THE see **KAERLIGHEDSOEN** • 1924
AMAZING GRACE • 1974 • Lathan Stan • USA
AMAZING GRACE • 1983 • SAF
AMAZING GRACE AND CHUCK • 1987 • Newell Mike • USA • SILENT VOICE
AMAZING HOWARD HUGHES, THE • 1977 • Graham William A. • TVM • USA
AMAZING IMPOSTOR, THE • 1919 • Ingraham Lloyd • USA
AMAZING LOVERS, THE • 1919 • Rolfe B. A. • USA
AMAZING MR. BEECHAM, THE (USA) see **CHILTERN HUNDREDS, THE** • 1949
AMAZING MR. BLUNDEN, THE • 1972 • Jeffries Lionel • UKN
AMAZING MR. FORREST, THE (USA) see **GANG'S ALL HERE, THE** • 1939
AMAZING MISTER NO LEGS, THE • 1981 • Browning Ricou • USA • MISTER NO LEGS
AMAZING MR. NORDILL, THE • 1947 • Newman Joseph M. • SHT • USA
AMAZING MR. WILLIAMS • 1940 • Hall Alexander • USA • INCREDIBLE MR. WILLIAMS
AMAZING MR. X., THE • 1948 • Vorhaus Bernard • USA • SPIRITUALIST, THE
AMAZING MONSIEUR FABRE, THE see **MONSIEUR FABRE** • 1951
AMAZING MRS. HOLLIDAY, THE • 1943 • Manning Bruce • USA • FOREVER YOURS
AMAZING PARTNERSHIP, THE • 1921 • Ridgwell George • UKN
AMAZING QUEST, THE see **AMAZING QUEST OF ERNEST BLISS, THE** • 1936
AMAZING QUEST OF ERNEST BLISS, THE • 1936 • Zeisler Alfred • UKN • ROMANCE AND RICHES (USA) ○ AMAZING QUEST, THE ○ RICHES AND ROMANCE ○ AMAZING ADVENTURE
AMAZING QUEST OF MR. ERNEST BLISS, THE • 1920 • Edwards Henry • SRL • UKN
AMAZING SUNDAY • 1958 • Duba Cenek • USS, CZC
AMAZING TRANSPARENT MAN, THE • 1960 • Ulmer Edgar G. • USA
AMAZING TRANSPLANT, THE • 1970 • Silverman Louis • USA
AMAZING VAGABOND, THE • 1929 • Fox Wallace • USA
AMAZING WHAT COLOR CAN DO • 1954 • *Kaufman Boris (Ph)* • SHT • USA
AMAZING WIFE, THE • 1919 • Park Ida May • USA
AMAZING WOMAN, AN see **SENORA ESTUPENDA, UNA** • 1968
AMAZING WOMAN, THE • 1920 • Carleton Lloyd B. • USA
AMAZING WORLD OF GHOSTS • 1978 • Dixon Wheeler • USA
AMAZING WORLD OF PSYCHIC PHENOMENA • 1976 • Guenette Robert • USA
AMAZON • 1990 • Kaurismaki Mika • FNL
AMAZON PARADISE, THE see **PARAISO AMAZONICO, EL** • 1970
AMAZON QUEST • 1949 • Sekely Steve • USA • AMAZON (UKN)
AMAZON, THIS WORLD'S BUSINESS see **AMAZONAS, EL NEGOCIO DE ESTE MUNDO** • 1986
AMAZON TRADER, THE • 1956 • McGowan Tom • USA
AMAZON (UKN) see **AMAZON QUEST** • 1949
AMAZON WOMEN ON THE MOON • 1987 • Dante Joe, Gottlieb Carl, Horton Peter, Landis John, Weiss Robert K. • USA
AMAZONA • 1959 • Villar Felix • PHL
AMAZONAS • 1965 • Rocha Glauber • SHT • BRZ
AMAZONAS, EL NEGOCIO DE ESTE MUNDO • 1986 • Azpurua Carlos • DOC • VNZ • AMAZON, THIS WORLD'S BUSINESS
AMAZONE • 1951 • Vedres Nicole • SHT • FRN
AMAZONE, DIE • 1921 • Lowenbein Richard • FRG
AMAZONE, L' • 1912 • Fescourt Henri • FRN
AMAZONES DE LA LUXURE, LES • 1974 • Franco Jesus
AMAZONES, LES (FRN) see **GUERRIERE DAL SENO NUDO, LE** • 1974
AMAZONIA see **AMAZONIA INFERNO VERDE** • 1984
AMAZONIA INFERNO VERDE • 1984 • Gariazzo Mario • ITL • AMAZONIA: THE CATHERINE MILES STORY ○ AMAZZONE BIANCA, L' ○ AMAZONIA ○ WHITE AMAZON ○ WHITE SLAVE
AMAZONIA: THE CATHERINE MILES STORY see **AMAZONIA INFERNO VERDE** • 1984
AMAZONS • 1984 • Glaser Paul Michael • TVM • USA
AMAZONS • 1987 • Sessa Alejandro • USA
AMAZONS, THE • 1917 • Kaufman Joseph • USA
AMAZONS, THE (UKN) see **GUERRIERE DAL SENO NUDO, LE** • 1974
AMAZONS' MARCH AND EVOLUTIONS, THE • 1902 • Smith G. A. • UKN
AMAZONS OF ROME (USA) see **VERGINI DI ROMA, LE** • 1960
AMAZZONE BIANCA, L' see **AMAZONIA INFERNO VERDE** • 1984
AMAZZONE MACABRA, L' • 1916 • Campogalliani Carlo • ITL
AMAZZONE MASCHERATA, L' • 1914 • Ghione Emilio • ITL
AMAZZONE MASCHERATA, L' • 1914 • Negroni Baldassare • ITL
AMAZZONI, LE see **GUERRIERE DAL SENO NUDO, LE** • 1974
AMAZZONI BIANCHE • 1936 • Righelli Gennaro • ITL
AMAZZONI DONNE D'AMORE E DI GUERRA • 1973 • Brescia Alfonso • ITL, SPN • BEAUTY OF THE BARBARIANS
AMAZZONIA TERRA SCONOSCIUTA • 1955 • Dottesio Attilio • ITL
AMBAR • 1952 • *Kapoor Raj* • IND
AMBARA DAMA • 1981 • Rouch Jean, Dieterlen Germaine • FRN
AMBASCIATORE, L' • 1936 • Negroni Baldassare • ITL
AMBASSADEURS, LES see **SUFARA', AS-** • 1975
AMBASSADOR, THE • 1976 • Golan Menahem • ISR
AMBASSADOR, THE • 1984 • Thompson J. Lee • USA
AMBASSADOR BILL • 1931 • Taylor Sam • USA
AMBASSADOR FROM HELL, THE see **SAFIR GEHANNAM** • 1944
AMBASSADOR FROM INDIA, THE see **EMBAJADOR DE LA INDIA, EL** • 1989
AMBASSADOR FROM THE DEAD, AN • 1915 • Powell Paul • USA
AMBASSADOR OF HELL, THE see **SAFIR GEHANNAM** • 1944
AMBASSADOR TO THE SOVIET UNION see **POSOL SOVYETSKOVO SOIUZA** • 1970
AMBASSADORS, THE see **SUFARA', AS-** • 1975
AMBASSADOR'S DAUGHTER, THE • 1913 • Merwin Bannister • USA
AMBASSADOR'S DAUGHTER, THE • 1956 • Krasna Norman • USA
AMBASSADOR'S DESPATCH, THE see **VALISE DIPLOMATIQUE, LA** • 1909
AMBASSADOR'S DISAPPEARANCE, THE • 1913 • Costello Maurice • USA
AMBASSADOR'S ENVOY, THE • 1914 • *Borzage Frank* • USA
AMBER VASE, THE • 1915 • Ayres Sydney • USA
AMBER WAVES • 1980 • Sargent Joseph • TVM • USA
AMBICION SANGRIENTA • 1968 • Salvador Jaime • MXC • BLOODY AMBITION
AMBICIOSA • 1952 • Cortazar Ernesto • MXC
AMBICIOSA • 1976 • Lazaga Pedro • SPN
AMBICIOSOS, LOS (MXC) see **FIEVRE MONTE A EL PAO, LA** • 1959
AMBIENTE E PERSONAGGI • 1951 • De Sica Vittorio • DOC • ITL
AMBITIEUSE, L' • 1912 • de Morlhon Camille • FRN
AMBITIEUSE, L' • 1959 • Allegret Yves • FRN, ITL, AUS • CLIMBERS, THE (USA)
AMBITION • 1914 • *Wilson Ben* • USA
AMBITION • 1915 • *Hulette Gladys* • USA
AMBITION • 1916 • Vincent James • USA
AMBITION • 1917 • *Ruge Billy* • SHT • USA
AMBITION see **SCANDAL FOR SALE** • 1932
AMBITION see **GENDAI NO YOKUBO** • 1956
AMBITION OF THE BARON, THE • 1915 • *Bushman Francis X.* • USA
AMBITIOUS, THE see **BAKUMATSU** • 1970
AMBITIOUS ANNIE (UKN) see **FIVE AND TEN CENT ANNIE** • 1928
AMBITIOUS AWKWARD ANDY • 1916 • *Hiers Walter* • SHT • USA
AMBITIOUS BUTLER, THE • 1912 • Sennett Mack • USA
AMBITIOUS CHILDREN see **CHILDREN'S THOUGHTS FOR THE FUTURE** • 1912
AMBITIOUS ETHEL • 1916 • *Burton Ethel* • USA
AMBITIOUS PA • 1914 • *Ab* • USA
AMBITIOUS PEOPLE • 1931 • Grinde Nick • SHT • USA
AMBITUS • 1967 • Patris Gerard, Ferrari L. • SHT • FRN
AMBIZIONI SBAGLIATE • 1984 • Carpi Fabio • ITL • WRONG AMBITIONS
AMBIZIOSE, LE • 1961 • Amendola Toni • ITL
AMBIZIOSO, L' • 1975 • Squitieri Pasquale • ITL
AMBLER'S RACE, THE see **PRASHNAI GULSARA** • 1970
AMBLIN' • 1969 • Spielberg Steven • SHT • USA
AMBOY DUKES, THE see **CITY ACROSS THE RIVER** • 1949
AMBROSE AND HIS WIDOW • 1918 • Fredericks Walter S. • SHT • USA
AMBROSE APPLEJOHN'S ADVENTURE see **STRANGERS OF THE NIGHT** • 1923
AMBROSE, THE LION HEARTED • 1918 • Fredericks Walter S. • SHT • USA
AMBROSE'S CUP OF WOE • 1916 • Fishback Fred C., Raymaker Herman C. • SHT • USA
AMBROSE'S DAY OFF • 1919 • Fredericks Walter S. • SHT • USA
AMBROSE'S FIRST FALSEHOOD • 1914 • Henderson Dell • USA
AMBROSE'S FURY • 1915 • Wright Walter • USA
AMBROSE'S ICY LOVE • 1918 • Fredericks Walter S. • SHT • USA
AMBROSE'S LITTLE HATCHET • 1915 • Wright Walter • USA
AMBROSE'S LOFTY PERCH • 1915 • Wright Walter • USA
AMBROSE'S NASTY TEMPER • 1915 • Wright Walter • USA
AMBROSE'S RAPID RISE • 1916 • Fishback Fred C. • SHT • USA
AMBROSE'S SOUR GRAPES • 1915 • Wright Walter • USA
AMBULANCE • 1975 • Casson Barry • DOC • CND
AMBULANCE • 1990 • Cohen Larry • USA
AMBULANCE see **AMBULANS** • 1962
AMBULANCE CORPS DRILL • 1899 • *Bitzer Billy (Ph)* • USA
AMBULANS • 1962 • Morgenstern Janusz • SHT • PLN • AMBULANCE
AMBUSH • 1939 • Neumann Kurt • USA
AMBUSH • 1947 • Reinhardt John • USA
AMBUSH • 1949 • Wood Sam • USA
AMBUSH • 1965 • Forlong Michael • DCS • UKN
AMBUSH • 1968 • USA
AMBUSH • Ho Meng-Hua • HKG
AMBUSH see **ZASEDA** • 1969
AMBUSH, THE see **MACHI-BUSE** • 1970
AMBUSH AT CIMARRON PASS • 1958 • Copelan Jody • USA
AMBUSH AT DEVIL'S GAP • 1966 • Eastman David • SRL • UKN
AMBUSH AT IGU PASS see **IGA NO SUIGETSU** • 1958
AMBUSH AT IRIQUOIS POINT • 1979 • Thomas Ralph L. • TVM • CND
AMBUSH AT TOMAHAWK GAP • 1953 • Sears Fred F. • USA
AMBUSH BAY • 1966 • Winston Ron • USA
AMBUSH FOR A NUN see **ENCRUCIJADA PARA UNA MONJA** • 1967
AMBUSH IN LEOPARD STREET • 1962 • Piperno J. Henry • UKN
AMBUSH IN TANGIERS see **AGGUATO A TANGERI** • 1958
AMBUSH MURDERS, THE • 1982 • Stern Steven Hilliard • TVM • USA
AMBUSH TRAIL • 1946 • Fraser Harry L. • USA
AMBUSH VALLEY • 1936 • Ray Bernard B. • USA
AMBUSHED • 1914 • *Bushman Francis X.* • USA
AMBUSHED • 1926 • *Reeves Bob* • USA
AMBUSHED (UKN) see **TORNADO IN THE SADDLE, A** • 1942
AMBUSHERS, THE • 1967 • Levin Henry • USA
AME A VOILE, L' • Veilleux Pierre • ANS • CND
AME BELGE • 1918-19 • du Plessis Armand • BLG
AME CORSE • 1906 • Jasset Victorin • FRN
AME D'ARGILE • 1955 • Toublanc-Michel Bernard • SHT • FRN
AME D'ARTISTE • 1925 • Dulac Germaine • FRN • HEART OF AN ACTRESS
AME DE CLOWN • 1933 • Didier Marc, Noe Yvan • FRN
AME DE PIERRE, L' • 1918 • Burguet Charles • FRN
AME DE PIERRE, L' • 1927 • Roudes Gaston • FRN
AME DES MOULINS, L' • 1912 • Machin Alfred • NTH
AME DU BONZE, L' • 1918 • Roussell Henry • FRN
AME DU VIOLON, L' • 1911 • Perret Leonce • FRN
AME D'UNE GRANDE DAME, L' • 1954 • Lavoie Hermenegilde • CND
AME QUI VIVE • 1961 • Dasque Jean • FRN
AMEDEE • 1949 • Grangier Gilles • FRN
AMEDEE • 1978 • Nomikos Marie-Antoinette • FRN
AMEL, EL • 1943 • Kamel Morsi Ahmad • EGY • WORKER, THE
AMELIA • 1965 • Guerrero Juan • MXC
AMELIA AND THE ANGEL • 1957 • Russell Ken • SHT • UKN
AMELIA EARHART • 1976 • Schaefer George • TVM • USA
AMELIA LOPES O'NEILL • 1990 • Sarmiento Valeria • CHL, FRN
AMELIA OR THE TIME FOR LOVE see **AMELIE OU LE TEMPS D'AIMER** • 1961
AMELIE see **AMELIE OU LE TEMPS D'AIMER** • 1961
AMELIE OU LE TEMPS D'AIMER • 1961 • Drach Michel • FRN • AMELIA OR THE TIME FOR LOVE ○ AMELIE ○ TIME TO DIE, A
AMENAGEMENT REGIONAL, L' • 1966 • Garceau Raymond • DCS • CND
AMENAZA, LA see **POWER GAME** • 1982
AMENDMENT TO THE DEFENCE OF THE REALM ACT • 1976 • Staikov Lyudmil • BUL
AMENU'S CHILD • 1949 • Graham Sean • GHN
AMERE VICTOIRE • 1957 • Ray Nicholas • FRN, UKN • BITTER VICTORY (UKN)
AMERICA • 1924 • Griffith D. W. • USA • LOVE AND SACRIFICE (UKN) ○ AMERICA: 1776

AMERICA • 1986 • Downey Robert • USA

AMERICA see **AMERICAN ROMANCE, AN** • 1944

AMERICA: 1776 see **AMERICA** • 1924

AMERICA 3000 • 1985 • Engelbach David • USA • THUNDER WARRIORS

AMERICA, AMERICA • 1963 • Kazan Elia • USA • ANATOLIAN SMILE, THE

AMERICA AMERICA • 1988 • Chang Kil-Su • SKR

AMERICA AT THE MOVIES • 1976 • *Stevens George Jr. (P)* • CMP • USA

AMERICA BY NIGHT see **AMERICA DI NOTTE** • 1961

AMERICA.. COSI NUDA COSI VIOLENTA • 1970 • Martino Sergio • ITL • NAKED AND VIOLENT

AMERICA DI NOTTE • 1961 • Scotese Giuseppe Maria • DOC • ITL, FRN • NUITS D'AMERIQUE, LES (FRN) ○ AMERICA BY NIGHT

AMERICA DO SEXO • 1970 • Filho Luis Rosemberg, da Costa Flavio Moreira, Siqueira Jose Ruben, Hirszman Leon • BRZ

AMERICA - EUROPA I LUFTSKIB • 1913 • Lind Alfred • DNM

AMERICA FIRST • 1972 • Anderson Joseph L. • USA

AMERICA IS HARD TO SEE • 1969 • De Antonio Emile • DOC • USA

AMERICA IS WAITING • 1981 • Conner Bruce • SHT • USA

AMERICA, PAESE DI DIO • 1966 • Vanzi Luigi • DOC • ITL • SO THIS IS GOD'S COUNTRY? (UKN)

AMERICA PAGANA • 1955 • Patellani Federico, Buzzi Aldo • DOC • ITL

AMERICA PREPARING • 1916 • *Kemble*

AMERICA REVISITED • 1971 • Ophuls Marcel • MTV • FRG

AMERICA SIMULTANEOUS: THE ELECTRIC FAMILY • 1968 • Markson Morley • CND

AMERICA THROUGH THE KEYHOLE see **AMERIQUE INSOLITE, L'** • 1958

AMERICA, UNKNOWN LAND see **AMERIKA, TIERRA INCOGNITA** • 1987

AMERICAIN, L' • 1969 • Bozzuffi Marcel • FRN • AMERICAN, THE (USA)

AMERICAIN OU LE CHEMIN D'ERNOA, L' • 1920 • Delluc Louis • FRN • CHEMIN D'ERNOA, L'

AMERICAIN SE DETEND, L' • 1957 • Reichenbach Francois • SHT • FRN

AMERICAN 30'S SONG • 1969 • Brakhage Stan • SHT • USA

AMERICAN, THE (USA) see **AMERICAIN, L'** • 1969

AMERICAN AND THE QUEEN, THE • 1910 • *Thanhouser* • USA

AMERICAN ANTHEM • 1986 • Magnoli Albert • USA

AMERICAN ARISTOCRACY • 1916 • Ingraham Lloyd • USA

AMERICAN BEAUTY • 1927 • Wallace Richard • USA • BEAUTIFUL FRAUD, THE (UKN)

AMERICAN BEAUTY, AN • 1916 • Taylor William D. • USA

AMERICAN BORN • 1913 • *Ayres Sydney* • USA

AMERICAN BOY • 1978 • Scorsese Martin • DCS • USA

AMERICAN BOYFRIENDS • 1990 • Wilson Sandra • CND

AMERICAN BUDS • 1918 • Buel Kenean • USA

AMERICAN CHRISTMAS CAROL, AN • 1979 • Till Eric • TVM • USA

AMERICAN CITIZEN, AN • 1914 • Dawley J. Searle • USA

AMERICAN COMMANDO NINJA • 1988 • *L'Argent Patrick* • COMMANDO THE NINJA

AMERICAN COMMANDOS • 1985 • Suarez Bobby A. • USA • MISTER SAVAGE ○ HITMAN

AMERICAN CONNECTION, THE • 1984 • Berwick Ray • SAF

AMERICAN CONSUL, THE • 1917 • Sturgeon Rollin S. • USA

AMERICAN COUNT, AN • 1910 • *Lubin* • USA

AMERICAN COUSIN, THE see **CUGINO AMERICANO, IL** • 1986

AMERICAN CREED, THE • 1946 • Stevenson Robert • DCS • USA

AMERICAN DATE • 1987 • Bernstein Armyan • USA • CROSS MY HEART

AMERICAN DOES LONDON IN TEN MINUTES, AN • 1908 • *Tyler Walter* • UKN

AMERICAN DREAM, AN • 1966 • Gist Robert • USA • SEE YOU IN HELL, DARLING (UKN)

AMERICAN DREAM, THE • 1981 • Damski Mel • TVM • USA

AMERICAN DREAM, THE see **DROMMEN OM AMERIKA** • 1976

AMERICAN DREAMER • 1971 • Schiller Lawrence, Carson L. M. Kit • USA

AMERICAN DREAMER • 1984 • Rosenthal Rick • USA

AMERICAN DRIVE-IN • 1984 • Shah Krishna • USA

AMERICAN EAGLE • 1988 • Smawley Robert • USA

AMERICAN EAGLE, THE see **LONE EAGLE, THE** • 1927

AMERICAN EMPIRE • 1942 • McGann William • USA • MY SON ALONE (UKN)

AMERICAN FAMILY see **DAUGHTERS COURAGEOUS** • 1939

AMERICAN FARMERS VISIT RUSSIA • 1955 • Tuzova Z. • USS

AMERICAN FEVER • 1979 • De Molinis Claudio • ITL

AMERICAN FLEET IN MELBOURNE • 1925 • ASL

AMERICAN FLYERS • 1985 • Badham John • USA

AMERICAN FRENCH POSTCARDS see **FRENCH POSTCARDS** • 1979

AMERICAN FRIEND, THE (USA) see **AMERIKANISCHE FREUND, DER** • 1977

AMERICAN FRIENDS • 1990 • Powell Tristram • UKN

AMERICAN GAME, THE • 1979 • Freund Jay, Elfstrom Robert, Powell Peter, Wolf David • USA

AMERICAN GEISHA • 1986 • Philips Lee • TVM • USA

AMERICAN GENTLEMAN, AN • 1915 • Gorman John • USA

AMERICAN GIGOLO • 1979 • Schrader Paul • USA

AMERICAN GIRL, THE • 1911 • *Lubin* • USA

AMERICAN GIRL, THE • 1917 • SER • USA

AMERICAN GOTHIC • 1988 • Hough John • USA • HIDE AND SHRIEK

AMERICAN GRAFFITI • 1973 • Lucas George • USA

AMERICAN GUERRILLA IN THE PHILIPPINES, AN • 1950 • Lang Fritz • USA • I SHALL RETURN (UKN)

AMERICAN HARVEST • 1987 • Lowry Dick • TVM • USA • RACE AGAINST THE HARVEST

AMERICAN HEIRESS, THE • 1917 • Hepworth Cecil M. • UKN

AMERICAN HERO • 1986 • Lustgarden Steven • USA

AMERICAN HEROINE, THE • 1979 • Stevens Stella • DOC • USA

AMERICAN HOLIDAYS see **VACANZE IN AMERICA** • 1984

AMERICAN HOT WAX • 1978 • Mutrux Floyd • USA • ROCK'N ROLL HOT WAX

AMERICAN IN PARIS, AN • 1951 • Minnelli Vincente • USA

AMERICAN IN ROME, AN see **AMERICANO A ROMA, UN** • 1954

AMERICAN IN THE MAKING, AN • 1913 • *Thanhauser* • USA

AMERICAN INSURRECTO, THE • 1911 • *Hartman Ruth* • USA

AMERICAN INVASION, AN • 1912 • *Kinemacolor* • USA

AMERICAN INVASION, AN • 1912 • *Kalem* • USA

AMERICAN JOURNEY • 1982 • Clarke Malcolm • TVM • USA

AMERICAN JUSTICE see **JACKALS** • 1986

AMERICAN KING, AN • 1914 • Lessey George A. • USA

AMERICAN KNOCKABOUTS • 1902 • Collins Alf? • UKN

AMERICAN LIVE WIRE, AN • 1918 • Mills Thomas R. • USA

AMERICAN MADNESS • 1932 • Capra Frank • USA

AMERICAN MAID • 1917 • Capellani Albert • USA

AMERICAN MANNERS • 1924 • Horne James W. • USA

AMERICAN MARCH, AN • 1940 • Fischinger Oskar • ANS • USA

AMERICAN MARDI, AN • 1941 • Fischinger Oskar • USA

AMERICAN MATCHMAKER see **AMERICANER SCHADCHEN** • 1939

AMERICAN METHODS • 1917 • Lloyd Frank • USA

AMERICAN MOON, THE • 1960 • *Whitman Robert (P)* • USA

AMERICAN MURDER, AN • 1988 • Campbell Douglas • USA

AMERICAN MUSIC -FROM FOLK TO JAZZ AND POP • 1969 • Fleishman Stephen • USA • ANATOMY OF POP

AMERICAN NIGHTMARE • 1982 • McBrearty Don • CND

AMERICAN NIGHTMARES see **COMBAT SHOCK** • 1986

AMERICAN NINJA • 1985 • Firstenberg Sam • USA • AMERICAN WARRIOR

AMERICAN NINJA 2: THE CONFRONTATION • 1987 • Firstenberg Sam • USA

AMERICAN NINJA 3 see **AMERICAN NINJA 3: BLOODHUNT** • 1989

AMERICAN NINJA 3: BLOODHUNT • 1989 • Sundstrom Cedric • USA • AMERICAN NINJA 3

AMERICAN NINJA THE MAGNIFICENT • 1988 • Lee Charles • USA • NINJA OF THE MAGNIFICENCE

AMERICAN NITRO • 1979 • Kimberlin Bill • USA

AMERICAN ODDBALLS see **CRY UNCLE** • 1971

AMERICAN PIE • 1981 • Fairbanks Jeffrey • USA

AMERICAN PLACE, AN • 1988 • Schell Maximilian • USA, FRG

AMERICAN PLUCK • 1925 • Stanton Richard • USA • PLUCK

AMERICAN POP • 1981 • Bakshi Ralph • ANM • USA

AMERICAN PRINCESS, THE • 1913 • Neilan Marshall • USA

AMERICAN PRISONER, THE • 1929 • Bentley Thomas • UKN

AMERICAN QUEEN, AN • 1913 • Ball Eustace Hale • USA

AMERICAN RAMPAGE • 1988 • Decoteau David • USA

AMERICAN RASPBERRY • 1980 • Swirnoff Brad • USA • PRIME TIME

AMERICAN REVOLUTION 2 • 1969 • DOC • USA

AMERICAN ROMANCE, AN • 1944 • Vidor King • USA • AMERICA

AMERICAN ROULETTE • 1988 • Hatton Maurice • UKN

AMERICAN SECRET SERVICE (CRONACHE DE IERI E DI OGGI PRESENTATE DA DESY LUMINI) • 1968 • Di Gianni Enzo • ITL

AMERICAN SOLDIER, AN • 1908 • *Kalem* • USA

AMERICAN SOLDIER, THE • 1914 • *Selig* • USA

AMERICAN SOLDIER, THE (USA) see **AMERIKANISCHE SOLDAT, DER** • 1970

AMERICAN SOLDIER IN LOVE AND WAR • 1903 • *Bitzer Billy (Ph)* • USA

AMERICAN SPIRIT, THE see **FIGHTING THROUGH** • 1919

AMERICAN SPOKEN HERE • 1940 • Wrangell Basil • SHT • USA

AMERICAN STORIES FOOD FAMILY AND PHILOSOPHY see **HISTOIRES D'AMERIQUE** • 1989

AMERICAN STUD IN PARIS, AN • *Holmes John C.* • USA

AMERICAN SUCCESS see **AMERICAN SUCCESS COMPANY, THE** • 1979

AMERICAN SUCCESS COMPANY, THE • 1979 • Richert William • USA • AMERICAN SUCCESS ○ SUCCESS ○ RINGER, THE

AMERICAN SUICIDE CLUB, THE • 1910 • FRN

AMERICAN TABOO • 1983 • Lustgarden Steven • USA

AMERICAN TAIL, AN • 1986 • Bluth Don • ANM • USA

AMERICAN -THAT'S ALL • 1917 • Rosson Arthur • USA

AMERICAN TICKLER see **AMERICAN TICKLER OR THE WINNER OF 10 ACADEMY AWARDS** • 1976

AMERICAN TICKLER OR THE WINNER OF 10 ACADEMY AWARDS • 1976 • Vincent Chuck • USA • AMERICAN TICKLER ○ EJECTION ○ DRAWS

AMERICAN TORSO see **AMERIKAI ANZIKSZ** • 1976

AMERICAN TRAGEDY, AN • 1931 • von Sternberg Josef • USA

AMERICAN VENUS, THE • 1926 • Tuttle Frank • USA

AMERICAN VOYEUR see **GETTING IT ON** • 1983

AMERICAN WARRIOR see **AMERICAN NINJA** • 1985

AMERICAN WAY, THE • 1919 • Reicher Frank • USA

AMERICAN WAY, THE • 1961 • Starkman Marvin • USA

AMERICAN WAY, THE • 1986 • Phillips Maurice • UKN • RIDERS OF THE STORM (USA)

AMERICAN WEREWOLF IN LONDON, AN • 1981 • Landis John • USA

AMERICAN WIDOW, AN • 1918 • Reicher Frank • USA

AMERICAN YEARS • 1976 • *Hammid Alexander* • USA

AMERICANA • 1981 • Carradine David • USA

AMERICANER SCHADCHEN • 1939 • Ulmer Edgar G. • USA • MARRIAGE BROKER, THE ○ AMERICAN MATCHMAKER

AMERICANIZATION OF EMILY, THE • 1964 • Hiller Arthur • USA • EMILY

AMERICANO, L' see **YANKEE** • 1966

AMERICANO, THE • 1915 • Vale Travers • USA

AMERICANO, THE • 1917 • Emerson John • USA

AMERICANO, THE • 1955 • Castle William • USA

AMERICANO A ROMA, UN • 1954 • Steno • ITL • AMERICAN IN ROME, AN

AMERICANO EN TOLEDO, UN • 1957 • Arevalo Carlos, Monter Jose Luis • SPN

AMERICANO IN VACANZA, UN • 1946 • Zampa Luigi • ITL • YANK IN ROME, A (USA)

AMERICANS AFTER ALL • 1916 • Greene Clay M. • SHT • USA

AMERICA'S BIGGEST CIRCUS • 1925 • DOC • USA

AMERICA'S CHILDREN see **THEY LIVE IN FEAR** • 1944

AMERICA'S CUP RACE, THE • 1899 • Porter Edwin S. • USA

AMERICA'S HIDDEN WEAPON • 1944 • McGann William • DOC • USA

AMERICATHON • 1979 • Israel Neal • USA

AMERIGO TOT • Huszarik Zoltan • SHT • HNG

AMERIIKAN RAITTI • 1989 • Torhonen Lauri • FNL • SHORES OF AMERICA, THE ○ PARADISE AMERICA

AMERIKA • 1983 • Razutis Al • CND

AMERIKA • 1987 • Wrye Donald • TVM • USA

AMERIKA -RAPPORTS DE CLASSE • 1983 • Straub Jean-Marie, Huillet Daniele • FRN, FRG

AMERIKA, TIERRA INCOGNITA • 1987 • Risquez Diego • VNZ • AMERICA, UNKNOWN LAND

AMERIKAI ANZIKSZ • 1976 • Body Gabor • HNG • AMERICAN TORSO ○ AMERIKAI ANZIX ○ VIEW OF AMERICA, A

AMERIKAI ANZIX see **AMERIKAI ANZIKSZ** • 1976

AMERIKAI FLU, AZ (HNG) see **FILS D'AMERIQUE, UN** • 1932

AMERIKANER IN SALZBURG, EIN • 1958 • Weiss Helmut • FRG

AMERIKANISCHE DUELL, DAS • 1918 • Piel Harry • FRG

AMERIKANISCHE FREUND, DER • 1977 • Wenders Wim • FRG • AMERICAN FRIEND, THE (USA)

AMERIKANISCHE SOLDAT, DER • 1970 • Fassbinder R. W. • FRG • AMERICAN SOLDIER, THE (USA)

AMERIKANO, L' (ITL) see **ETAT DE SIEGE** • 1972

AMERINDIA • 1958 • Bravo Sergio, Zorilla Concha Enrique • CHL, ;

AMERIQUE DU SUD: LES INDIENS DES FORETS • 1976 • Dousseau Anik • DOC • CND

AMERIQUE INSOLITE, L' • 1958 • Reichenbach Francois • DOC • FRN • AMERIQUE VU PAR UN FRANCAIS, L' ○ AMERICA THROUGH THE KEYHOLE

AMERIQUE LUNAIRE, L' • 1962 • Reichenbach Francois • SHT • FRN

AMERIQUE VU PAR UN FRANCAIS, L' see **AMERIQUE INSOLITE, L'** • 1958

AMES DE FOUS • 1917 • Dulac Germaine • FRN • SOULS OF THE MAD

AMES D'ENFANTS • 1928 • Benoit-Levy Jean • FRN • SOULS OF CHILDREN, THE

AMES D'ORIENT • 1919 • Poirier Leon • FRN

AMES MORTES, LES • 1960 • Allio Rene • ANM • FRN

AMES QUI VIVENT see **DEMONS DE L'AUBE, LES** • 1945

AMES SAUVAGES • 1920 • Ravel Gaston • FRN

AMES TOURMENTEES see **NOUFOUSS HAIRA** • 1968

AMESHKUATAN -LES SORTIES DU CASTOR • 1978 • Bulbulian Maurice, Hebert Marc • DOC • CND

AMETRALLADORA, EL • 1943 • Robles Castillo Aurelio • MXC

AMETRALLADORA, LA see **QUEL CALDO MALEDETTO GIORNO DI FUOCO** • 1968

AMGHAR • 1966 • Derkaoui Mustafa • SHT • PLN

AMHI JATO AMCHYA GAVA • 1968 • Torne Kamalakar • IND

AMI DE LA FAMILLE, L' • 1957 • Pinoteau Jack • FRN

AMI DE MON AMIE, L' • 1987 • Rohmer Eric • FRN • BOYFRIENDS AND GIRLFRIENDS (USA) ○ MY GIRLFRIEND'S BOYFRIEND(UKN)

AMI DE VINCENT, L' • 1983 • Granier-Deferre Pierre • FRN

AMI FRITZ, L' • 1919 • Hervil Rene, Devoyod Suzanne • FRN

AMI FRITZ, L' • 1933 • de Baroncelli Jacques • FRN

AMI NO NAKANO BOKO • 1967 • Wakamatsu Koji • JPN • VIOLENCE IN THE NET

AMI VIENDRA CE SOIR, UN • 1945 • Bernard Raymond • FRN • FRIEND WILL COME TONIGHT, A (USA)

AMIAMOCI COSI • 1940 • Simonelli Giorgio C. • ITL

AMIAMOCI COSI see **AL BUIO INSIEME** • 1933

AMICA, L' • 1969 • Lattuada Alberto • ITL

AMICA DI MIA MADRE, L' • 1975 • Ivaldi Mauro O. • ITL

AMICAL SOUVENIR see **ROUTE DU BONHEUR, LA** • 1952

AMICHE, LE • 1955 • Antonioni Michelangelo • ITL • GIRL FRIENDS, THE (USA)

AMICHE ANDIAMO ALLA FESTA • 1975 • Trentin Giorgio • ITL • LET'S GO TO THE PARTY, GIRLS

AMICI DEGLIN AMICI HANNO SAPUTO, GLI • 1973 • Marcolini Fulvio • ITL

AMICI DELL'ISOLA, GLI • 1962 • Pupillo Massimo • ITL

AMICI DI NICK HEZARD, GLI • 1976 • Di Leo Fernando • ITL • NICK THE STING

AMICI DIVERSI • 1979 • Steno • ITL

AMICI MIEI • 1975 • Monicelli Mario • ITL • MY FRIENDS

AMICI MIEI ATTO II • 1983 • Monicelli Mario • ITL • MY FRIENDS ACT II ○ AMICI MIEI N.2

AMICI MIEI ATTO III • 1985 • Loy Nanni • ITL • MY FRIENDS 3

AMICI MIEI N.2 see **AMICI MIEI ATTO II** • 1983

AMICI PER LA PELLE • 1955 • Rossi Franco • ITL • WOMAN IN THE PAINTING, THE (USA) ○ FRIENDS FOR LIFE

AMICI PIU DI PRIMA • 1976 • Veo Carlo, Tommassi Vincenzo • CMP • ITL

AMICIZIA • 1938 • Biancoli Oreste • ITL • FRIENDSHIP (USA)

AMICO • 1949 • Buchholz Gerhard T. • FRG

AMICO, UN • 1968 • Guida Ernesto • ITL • FRIEND, A

AMICO DEL GIAGUARO, L' • 1959 • Bennati Giuseppe • ITL

AMICO DEL PADRINO, L' • 1974 • Agrama Frank • ITL

AMICO DELLE DONNE, L' • 1943 • Poggioli Ferdinando M. • ITL

AMICO DI FAMIGLIA, L' (ITL) see **NOCES ROUGES, LES** • 1972

AMICO MIO.. FREGA TU.. CHE FREGO IO! • 1973 • Fidani Demofilo • ITL

AMICO PUBBLICO N.1, L' see **ARRIVIAMO NOI!** • 1940

AMICO STAMMI LONTANO ALMENO UN PALMO • 1972 • Lupo Michele • ITL

AMID THE WONDERS OF THE DEEP see **TWENTY THOUSAND LEAGUES UNDER THE SEA** • 1905

AMIE D'ENFANCE, UNE • 1977 • Mankiewicz Francis • CND

AMIGA, LA • 1987 • Meerapfel Jeanine • ARG

AMIGAS, LAS • 1969 • Lazaga Pedro • SPN

AMIGOS, LOS • 1973 • Cavara Paolo • ITL • DEAF SMITH AND JOHNNY EARS (UKN)

AMIGOS MARAVILLA EN EL MUNDO DE LA AVENTURA, LOS • 1960 • Peon Ramon • MXC

AMIGOS MARAVILLA, LOS • 1960 • Peon Ramon • MXC

AMIGUITAS DE LOS RICOS, LAS • 1968 • Diaz Morales Jose • MXC • GIRL-FRIENDS OF THE RICH, THE

AMIN: THE RISE AND FALL see **RISE AND FALL OF IDI AMIN, THE** • 1981

AMINATA • 1971 • Vermorel Claude • FRN
AMINTIRI BUCURESTENE • 1970 • Gabrea Radu • RMN • BUCHAREST MEMORIES
AMINTIRI DIN COPILARIE • 1964 • Bostan Elisabeta • RMN • RECOLLECTIONS FROM CHILDHOOD
AMIR AD-DAHA • 1963 • Barakat Henry • EGY • PRINCE DEMONIQUE
AMIR AL-INTIQAM • 1950 • Barakat Henry • EGY • COMTE DE MONTE-CHRISTO, LE
AMIRA MY LOVE • 1975 • el Imam Hassan • EGY
AMIRA WAL NAHR, AL • 1986 • ANM • IRQ • PRINCESS AND THE RIVER
AMIRAL NAKHIMOV • 1946 • Pudovkin V. I. • USS • ADMIRAL NAKHIMOV
AMIS, LES • 1969 • Blain Gerard • FRN
AMIS, LES see **VRIENDEN, DE** • 1971
AMIS COMME AUTREFOIS see **CESSEZ LE FEU** • 1934
AMISK • 1977 • Obomsawin Alanis • CND
AMITIES HAITIENNES • 1958 • Forest Leonard • DCS • CND
AMITIES PARTICULIERES, LES • 1964 • Delannoy Jean • FRN • THIS SPECIAL FRIENDSHIP (USA)
AMITYVILLE 3D • 1983 • Fleischer Richard • USA • AMITYVILLE III: THE DEMON
AMITYVILLE CURSE, THE • 1990 • Berry Thomas • USA
AMITYVILLE HORROR, THE • 1979 • Rosenberg Stuart • USA
AMITYVILLE II: THE POSSESSION • 1982 • Damiani Damiano • USA
AMITYVILLE III: THE DEMON see **AMITYVILLE 3D** • 1983
AMLASH ENCHANTED FOREST, THE • 1973 • Soriano Shlomo • ISR
AMLETO • 1908 • Caserini Mario • ITL • HAMLET (USA)
AMLETO • 1910 • Caserini Mario • ITL • HAMLET
AMLETO • 1914 • *Revelle A. Hamilton* • ITL • HAMLET (USA)
AMLETO • 1917 • Rudolfi Eleuterio • ITL • HAMLET (USA)
AMLETO DI MENO, UN • 1973 • Bene Carmelo • ITL • ONE HAMLET LESS
AMLETO E I SUO CLOWN • 1920 • Gallone Carmine • ITL • ON WITH THE MOTLEY
AMMA • 1960 • Singh Hira • NPL • MOTHER
AMMA • 1968 • Panthalu B. R. • IND • MOTHER
AMMA ARIYAN • 1986 • Abraham John • IND • REPORT TO MOTHER
AMMAR FARHAT • 1963 • Essid Hamadi • DCS • TNS
AMMARRANDO EL CORDON • 1968 • Alvarez Santiago • DOC • CUB • TYING UP THE CORD
AMMAZZALI TUTTI E TORNA SOLO • 1969 • Castellari Enzo G. • ITL, SPN • KILL THEM ALL AND COME BACK ALONE (USA) ○ MATALOS Y VUELVE (SPN)
AMMAZZARE IL TEMPO • 1979 • Rafele Mimmo • ITL
AMMAZZATINA, L' • 1975 • Dolce Ignazio • ITL
AMMENKONIG, DER • 1935 • Steinhoff Hans • FRG • TAL DES LEBENS, DAS
AMMIE, COME HOME see **HOUSE THAT WOULD NOT DIE, THE** • 1970
AMMUTINAMENTO, L' • 1962 • Amadio Silvio • ITL, FRN • REVOLTEES DE L'ALBATROS, LES (FRN) ○ WHITE SLAVE SHIP (USA) ○ WILD CARGO
AMMUTINAMENTO NELLO SPAZIO (ITL) see **MUTINY IN OUTER SPACE** • 1965
AMNESIA • 1921 • Contreras Torres Miguel • MXC
AMO NON AMO • 1979 • Balducci Armenia • ITL • TOGETHER (USA) ○ I LOVE YOU, I LOVE YOU NOT
AMO TE SOLA • 1935 • Mattoli Mario • ITL • IDILLIO 1848
AMO UN ASSASSINO • 1952 • Bandini Baccio • ITL
AMOK • 1928 • Mardzhanishvili Kote • USS
AMOK • 1934 • Ozep Fedor • FRN
AMOK • 1944 • Momplet Antonio • MXC
AMOK • 1964 • Dimopoulos Dinos • GRC • RAPE, THE (USA)
AMOK • 1982 • Ben Baraka Sohail • MRC
AMONENHOF, DER • 1919 • Krafft Uwe Jens • FRG
AMONG BLOWS AND BOLEROS see **ENTRE GOLPES Y BOLEROS** • 1988
AMONG CLUB FELLOWS • 1913 • Henderson Dell • USA
AMONG HUMAN WOLVES see **SECRET JOURNEY, THE** • 1939
AMONG JEWS see **UNTER JUDEN** • 1923
AMONG PEOPLE see **V LYUDKYAKH** • 1939
AMONG PEOPLE see **WSROD LUDZI** • 1960
AMONG THE BREAKERS • 1910 • *Electrograff* • USA
AMONG THE BUSHES • Nehrebecki Wladyslaw • ANS • PLN
AMONG THE CANNIBAL ISLES OF THE SOUTH PACIFIC • 1918 • Johnson Martin E. • DOC • USA
AMONG THE CINDERS • 1983 • Hadrich Rolf • NZL
AMONG THE HEADHUNTERS • 1955 • Denis Armand, Denis Michaela • DOC • UKN • ARMAND AND MICHAELA DENIS AMONG THE HEADHUNTERS
AMONG THE IGLOO DWELLERS • 1931 • Finnie Richard S. • DOC • CND
AMONG THE LIVING • 1941 • Heisler Stuart • USA
AMONG THE LIVING DEAD • 1980 • *Vernon Howard* • USA
AMONG THE MARRIED see **MEN CALL IT LOVE** • 1931
AMONG THE MISSING • 1934 • Rogell Albert S. • USA
AMONG THE MOURNERS • 1914 • Henderson Dell • USA
AMONG THE REEDS OF THE VOLGA DELTA • 1950 • Schneiderov Vladimir • DOC • USS
AMONG THE ROSES • 1910 • *Imp* • USA
AMONG THE RUINS see **HAIKYO NO NAKA** • 1923
AMONG THE THORNS see **YOUNG SINNER, THE** • 1965
AMONG THOSE KILLED • 1915 • Morgan George • USA
AMONG THOSE PRESENT • 1917 • Windom Lawrence C. • SHT • USA
AMONG THOSE PRESENT • 1919 • Kenton Erle C., Grey Ray • SHT • USA
AMONG THOSE PRESENT • 1921 • Newmeyer Fred, Taylor Sam • SHT • USA
AMONG THOSE PRESENT (UKN) see **HEADLEYS AT HOME, THE** • 1938
AMONG VULTURES see **UNTER GEIERN** • 1964
AMONG WOLVES • 1985 • Giovanni Jose • FRN, SWT, MLT
AMONGST PEOPLE see **WSROD LUDZI** • 1960
AMONGST THE THIEVES (UKN) see **LONE STAR MOONLIGHT** • 1946
AMOOOOOR • 1968 • Gagne Jacques, Fournier Claude • DCS • CND
AMOOZIN' BUT CONFOOZIN' • 1944 • *Mintz Charles (P)* • ANS • USA
AMOR A BALAZO LIMPIO • 1960 • Alazraki Benito • MXC
AMOR A LA ESPANOLA • 1967 • Merino Fernando • SPN, ARG • LOVE SPANISH STYLE
AMOR A LA VIDA, EL • 1950 • Contreras Torres Miguel • MXC • EXTRANA AVENTURA DE UN HOMBRE, LA
AMOR A LA VUELTA DE LA ESQUINA • 1985 • Cortes Alberto • MXC • LOVE AROUND THE CORNER
AMOR A RITMO DE GO GO • 1966 • Delgado Miguel M. • MXC
AMOR A TODO GAS • 1968 • Torrado Ramon • SPN
AMOR ABRIO LOS OJOS, EL • 1946 • Sevilla Raphael J. • MXC
AMOR AM STEUER • 1921 • Janson Victor • FRG
AMOR AMERICA • 1989 • Cappelari • FRG
AMOR, AMOR, AMOR • 1965 • Gurrola Juan Jose, Ibanez Jose Luis, Barbachano Ponce Miguel, Ibanez Juan, Mendoza Hector • MXC
AMOR AN DER LEINE see **KIND, ICH FREU' MICH AUF DEIN KOMMEN** • 1933
AMOR AOS 40, O see **TARDE OUTRA TARDE, UMA** • 1975
AMOR AUDAZ • 1930 • Gasnier Louis J. • SPN
AMOR AUF SKI • 1928 • Randolf Rolf • FRG
AMOR BAJO CERO • 1960 • Blasco Ricardo • SPN
AMOR BANDIDO • 1980 • Barreto Bruno • BRZ • OUTLAW LOVE
AMOR BRUJO, EL • 1949 • Roman Antonio • SPN
AMOR BRUJO, EL • 1967 • Rovira Beleta Francisco • SPN • SORCERER'S LOVE ○ WITCH LOVE ○ EVIL LOVE
AMOR BRUJO, EL • 1985 • Saura Carlos • SPN • LOVE BEWITCHED, A ○ LOVE THE MAGICIAN
AMOR CASI LIBRE • 1975 • Merino Fernando • SPN
AMOR CHE UCCIDE • 1917 • Caserini Mario • ITL
AMOR CHINACO • 1941 • Sevilla Raphael J. • MXC
AMOR CON AMOR SE PAGA • 1940 • Navarro Carlos • MXC • LOVE FOR LOVE (USA)
AMOR CON AMOR SE PAGA • 1949 • Cortazar Ernesto • MXC
AMOR DE ADOLESCENTE • 1963 • Bracho Julio • MXC • DESNUDOS ARTISTICOS
AMOR DE ASSASSINO see **TEARS FOR A KILLER** • 1977
AMOR DE DON JUAN, EL (SPN) see **DON JUAN** • 1956
AMOR DE EXTRANO, EL • 1974 • *Churubusco Azteca* • MXC
AMOR DE LA CALLE • 1949 • Cortazar Ernesto • MXC
AMOR DE LEJOS • 1954 • Cardona Rene • MXC
AMOR DE LOCURA • 1952 • Baledon Rafael • MXC
AMOR DE LOS AMORES, EL • 1944 • Mediz Bolio Antonio • MXC
AMOR DE LOS AMORES, EL • 1960 • de Orduna Juan • SPN
AMOR DE MADRE see **TU HIJO** • 1934
AMOR DE MAE • 1977 • Monteiro Joao Cesar • PRT • MOTHER LOVE
AMOR DE MIS AMORES • 1940 • Cardona Rene • MXC
AMOR DE PERDICAO • 1943 • Ribeiro Antonio Lopes • PRT
AMOR DE PERDICAO • 1977 • de Oliveira Manoel • PRT • LOVE OF PERDITION ○ DOOMED LOVE ○ ILL-FATED LOVE
AMOR DEL BUENO • 1954 • Peon Ramon • MXC
AMOR DEL CAPITAN BRANDO, EL • 1974 • de Arminan Jaime • SPN • GREAT LOVE OF CAPTAIN BRANDO, THE ○ GRAN AMOR DE CAPITAN BRANDO,EL
AMOR DESCEU EM PARAQUEDAS, O • 1968 • Esteves Constantino • PRT • LOVE CAME DOWN BY PARACHUTE
AMOR DI LADRO • 1914 • Serena Gustavo • ITL
AMOR DI MI BOHIO, EL • 1946 • Orol Juan • MXC, CUB
AMOR DI UNA VIDA • 1945 • Morayta Miguel • MXC
AMOR EMPIEZA A MEDIANOCHE, EL • 1973 • Lazaga Pedro • SPN
AMOR EMPIEZA EN SABADO • 1958 • Aguado Victorio • SPN
AMOR EN CUATRO TIEMPOS • 1954 • Spota Luis • MXC
AMOR EN EL AIRE • 1967 • Amadori Luis Cesar • SPN, ARG • LOVE IN THE AIR
AMOR EN LA SOMBRA • 1959 • Davison Tito • MXC
AMOR EN LAS NUBES • 1968 • Dieguez Manuel Zecena • MXC, GTM • LOVE IN THE CLOUDS
AMOR EN UN ESPEJO • 1968 • Lorente German • SPN • LOVE IN A MIRROR
AMOR ES ESTRANY, EL • 1988 • Balague Carlos • SPN • LOVE IS STRANGE
AMOR ES UNA MUJER CORDA, EL • 1987 • Agresti Alejandro • ARG • LOVE IS A FAT WOMAN
AMOR ESTA EN ALGUNA PARTE, EL • 1971 • *Cima* • MXC
AMOR FATAL • 1911 • Brezeanu Grigore • RMN
AMOR GITANA • 1910 • de Chomon Segundo • SPN
AMOR IN DER KLEMME • 1918 • *Dorsch Kathe* • FRG
AMOR IN QUARTIER • 1915 • Halm Alfred • FRG
AMOR INDIO see **TIZOC** • 1956
AMOR INFIEL, EL • 1974 • David Mario • ARG • UNFAITHFUL LOVE
AMOR LAS VUELVE LOCAS, EL • 1945 • Cortes Fernando • MXC
AMOR LIBRE, EL • 1977 • Hermosillo Jaime Humberto • MXC • FREE LOVE
AMOR LLEGO A JALISCO, EL • 1962 • Salvador Jaime • MXC
AMOR MANDA, EL • 1940 • Vatteone Augusto Cesar • LOVE COMMANDS (USA)
AMOR MIO • 1972 • *A.a. Mexicanos* • MXC
AMOR MIO NON MUORE.., L' • 1938 • Amato Giuseppe • ITL
AMOR, MUJERES Y FLORES • 1989 • Rodriguez Martha, Silva Jorge • CLM, UKN • LOVE, WOMEN AND FLOWERS
AMOR NO ES CIEGO, EL • 1950 • Patino Gomez Alfonso • MXC
AMOR NO ES NEGOCIO, EL • 1949 • Salvador Jaime • MXC
AMOR NO ES PECADO, EL • 1964 • Baledon Rafael • MXC • CIELO ES DE LOS PORRES, EL
AMOR NON HO.. PERO, PERO • 1951 • Bianchi Giorgio • ITL
AMOR NUNCA MUERE, EL • 1955 • Amadori Luis Cesar • ARG
AMOR PERDIDO • 1950 • Morayta Miguel • MXC
AMOR PROHIBIDO • 1944 • Boytler Arcady • MXC
AMOR PROHIBIDO • 1955 • Amadori Luis Cesar • ARG
AMOR PROHIBIDO see **TIMANFAYA** • 1971
AMOR QUE HUYE, EL • 1917 • Arredondo Carlos Martinez • MXC
AMOR QUE MALO ERES! • 1952 • Diaz Morales Jose • MXC
AMOR QUE YO TE DI, EL • 1959 • Demicheli Tulio • MXC, SPN
AMOR SALVAJE • 1949 • Orol Juan • MXC • PASION SALVAJE
AMOR SE DICE CANTANDO • 1957 • Morayta Miguel • MXC, ARG
AMOR SOBRE RUEDAS • 1954 • Torrado Ramon • SPN
AMOR TIENE CARA DE MUJER, EL • 1973 • *Clasa* • MXC
AMOR UND DAS STANDHAFTE LIEBESPAAR • 1920 • Reiniger Lotte • ANS • FRG
AMOR VAGABUNDO • 1989 • Carvana Hugo • BRZ • VAGABOND LOVE
AMOR VENDIDO • 1950 • Pardave Joaquin • MXC
AMOR Y PECADO • 1955 • Crevenna Alfredo B. • MXC
AMOR Y SEXO • 1963 • Alcoriza Luis • MXC • SAFO 1963 ○ SAPHO 63
AMORCITO CORAZON • 1960 • Gonzalez Rogelio A. • MXC
AMORE • 1923 • Gallone Carmine • ITL
AMORE • 1935 • Bragaglia Carlo Ludovico • ITL
AMORE • 1973 • Chapier Henri • FRN • AMOUR
AMORE, L' • 1948 • Rossellini Roberto • ITL • WAYS OF LOVE ○ WOMAN ○ MIRACLE
AMORE, UN • 1965 • Vernuccio Gianni • ITL
AMORE A PALERMO see **ATTACO ALLA PIOURA** • 1985
AMORE A PRIMA VISTA • 1958 • Rossi Franco • ITL, SPN • BUENOS DIAS, AMOR (SPN) ○ RAGAZZE D'ESTATE
AMORE A ROMA, UN • 1960 • Risi Dino • ITL, FRN • INASSOUVIE, L' (FRN) ○ LOVE IN ROME
AMORE A VENT'ANNI see **AMOUR A VINGT ANS, L'** • 1962
AMORE AD ALTA VELOCITA see **BACIO A FIOR D'ACQUA, UN** • 1936
AMORE ALL'ARRABBIATA • 1977 • Veo Carlo • ITL
AMORE ALL'ITALIANA • 1966 • Steno • ITL • SUPERDIABOLICI, I ○ LOVE ITALIAN STYLE ○ SUPER DIABOLICAL, THE
AMORE AMARO • 1974 • Vancini Florestano • ITL
AMORE, AMORE • 1968 • Leonardi Alfredo • ITL • MY LOVE, MY LOVE
AMORE ATTRAVERSO I SECOLO, L' (ITL) see **PLUS VIEUX METIER DU MONDE, LE** • 1967
AMORE BREVE, L' • 1969 • Scavolini Romano • ITL • STATO D'ASSEDIO, LO ○ BESIEGED
AMORE CANTA, L' • 1941 • Poggioli Ferdinando M. • ITL
AMORE CHE NON TORNA • 1938 • Valetty Bruno • LOVE THAT DOESN'T RETURN (USA)
AMORE CONIUGALE, L' • 1970 • Maraini Dacia • ITL
AMORE COSI FRAGILE COSI VIOLENTA, UN • 1973 • Pittoni Leros • ITL
AMORE DI NORMA, L' • 1955 • Martin G. D. • ITL
AMORE DI UNA DONNA, L' (ITL) see **AMOUR D'UNE FEMME, L'** • 1954
AMORE DI USSARO (ITL) see **ULTIMO HUSAR, EL** • 1940
AMORE DIFFICILE, L' • 1962 • Sollima Sergio, Bonucci Alberto, Manfredi Nino, Lucignani Luciano • ITL, FRG • OF WAYWARD LOVE (USA) ○ SEX CAN BE DIFFICULT ○ EROTICA
AMORE E ANARCHIA see **FILM D'AMORE E D'ANARCHIA: OVVERO STAMATTINA ALLE IO IN VIA DEI FIORI NELLA NOTA CASA DI TOLLERANZA** • 1973
AMORE E CHIACCHIERE • 1957 • Blasetti Alessandro • ITL • SALVIAMO IL PANORAMA
AMORE E COME IL SOLE, L' • 1968 • Lombardi Carlo • ITL • LOVE IS LIKE THE SUN
AMORE E DENARO • 1937 • Brignone Guido • ITL
AMORE E DOLORE • 1937 • Brignone Guido • ITL
AMORE E FANGO see **PALUDE TRAGICA** • 1953
AMORE E GINNASTICA • 1973 • D'Amico Luigi Filippo • ITL
AMORE E GUAI • 1959 • Dorigo Angelo • ITL
AMORE E MORTE • 1932 • Romeo Rosario • ITL • LOVE AND DEATH
AMORE E MORTE NEL GIARDINO DEGLI DEI • 1972 • Scavolini Sauro • ITL
AMORE E RABBIA • 1969 • Lizzani Carlo, Pasolini Pier Paolo, Bertolucci Bernardo, Godard Jean-Luc, Bellocchio Marco • ITL, FRN • CONTESTATION, LA (FRN) ○ VANGELO '70 ○ LOVE AND ANGER
AMORE E SANGUE • 1951 • Girolami Marino • ITL • CAMORRA ○ CITY OF VIOLENCE
AMORE E SMARRIMENTO • 1954 • Ratti Filippo M. • ITL
AMORE FACILE • 1964 • Puccini Gianni • ITL
AMORE FORMULA 2 • 1970 • Amendola Mario • ITL
AMORE GRAND AMORE LIBERO • 1976 • Perelli Luigi • ITL
AMORE IMPERIALE • 1941 • Volkov Alexander • ITL
AMORE IN 4 DIMENSIONI • 1963 • Romain Jacques, Mida Massimo, Guerrini Mino, Puccini Gianni, Risi Dino, Fellini Federico, Antonioni Michelangelo, Maselli Francesco, Zavattini Cesare, Lattuada Alberto, Lizzani Carlo • ITL, FRN • AMOUR EN 4 DIMENSIONS, L' (FRN) ○ LOVE IN 4 DIMENSIONS (USA) ○ LOVE IN THE CITY
AMORE IN ITALIA, L' • 1978 • Comencini Luigi • MTV • ITL
AMORE IN PRIMO CLASSE • 1980 • Samperi Salvatore • ITL, FRN • AMOUR EN PREMIERE CLASSE, L' (FRN)
AMORE IN QUARANTENA • 1938 • Palermi Amleto • ITL • LOVE IN QUARANTINE (USA)
AMORE IN STOCKHOLM see **DIAVOLO, IL** • 1963
AMORE LIBRE • 1974 • Pavoni Pier Ludovico • ITL • FREE LOVE
AMORE MIEI • 1978 • Steno • ITL
AMORE MIO • 1964 • Matarazzo Raffaello • ITL
AMORE MIO AIUTAMI • 1969 • Sordi Alberto • ITL • HELP ME DARLING
AMORE MIO NON FARMI MALE • 1974 • Sindoni Vittorio • ITL
AMORE MIO SPOGLIATI CHE POI TI SPIEGO • 1975 • Pittorru Fabio • ITL
AMORE MIO UCCIDIMI! • 1973 • Prosperi Franco • ITL
AMORE NASCE A ROMA, L' • 1959 • Amendola Mario • ITL
AMORE NEL MONDO, L' • 1963 • Loy Mino • ITL
AMORE NELL'ARTE, L' • 1950 • Bava Mario • ITL
AMORE OGGI, UN • 1970 • Mulargia Edoardo • ITL
AMORE, PIOMBO E FURORE see **CHINA 9 LIBERTY 37** • 1978
AMORE PIU BELLO, L' • 1959 • Pellegrini Glauco • ITL, SPN • UOMO DAI CALZONI CORTI, L' ○ LAD IN SHORTS
AMORE POVERO, L' • 1963 • Andreassi Raffaele • ITL
AMORE PRIMITIVO, L' • 1964 • Scattini Luigi • ITL • PRIMITIVE LOVE (USA)

AMORE QUESTO SCONOSCIUTO, L' • 1969 • Pupillo Massimo • ITL
AMORE QUOTIDIANO (ITL) see **DONNEZ-NOUS NOTRE AMOUR QUOTIDIEN** • 1973
AMORE ROSSO • 1922 • Righelli Gennaro • ITL
AMORE ROSSO • 1953 • Vergano Aldo • ITL • MARIANNA SIRCA
AMORE SENZA FINE, UN • 1959 • Knaut Luis, Terribile Mario • ITL
AMORE SI FA COSI, L' • 1939 • Bragaglia Carlo Ludovico • ITL
AMORE TARGATO FORLI, UN • 1977 • Sesani Riccardo • ITL
AMORE TOSSICO • 1984 • Caligari Claudio • ITL • TOXIC LOVE
AMORE TRAGICO see **PAGLIACCI** • 1949
AMORE VEGLIA • 1914 • Negroni Baldassare • ITL
AMORE VUOL DIRE GELOSIA • 1975 • Severino Mauro • ITL
AMORES DE AYER • 1944 • Rodriguez Ismael • MXC
AMORES DE JUAN CHARRASQUEADO, LOS • 1968 • Delgado Miguel M. • MXC • LOVES OF JUAN CHARRASQUEADO, THE
AMORES DE KAFKA, LOS • 1987 • Feijoo Beda Ocampo • ARG • LOVES OF KAFKA, THE
AMORES DE MARIETA, LOS • 1963 • Gomez Landero Humberto • MXC • FABULOSOS VEINTES, LOS
AMORES DE TRES COLEGIALAS, LOS see **TRES COQUETONAS, LAS** • 1959
AMORES DE UN TORERO, LOS see **LUNA ENAMORADA, LA** • 1945
AMORES DE UNA VIUDA, LOS • 1948 • Soler Julian • MXC
AMORES DIFICILES, LOS • 1967 • Pena Raul • SPN • DIFFICULT LOVE
AMORI DI ANGELICA, GLI • 1966 • McWarriol J. • ITL
AMORI DI ERCOLE, GLI • 1960 • Bragaglia Carlo Ludovico • ITL, FRN • AMOURS D'HERCULE, LES (FRN) ○ LOVES OF HERCULES, THE ○ HERCULES AND THE HYDRA
AMORI DI MANON LESCAUT, GLI • 1955 • Costa Mario • ITL, FRN • AMOURS DE MANON LESCAUT, LES (FRN)
AMORI DI MEZZO SECOLO • 1954 • Germi Pietro, Rossellini Roberto, Pellegrini Glauco, Pietrangeli Antonio, Chiari Mario • ITL
AMORI DI UNA CALDA ESTATE (ITL) see **PIANOS MECANICOS, LOS** • 1965
AMORI E CANZONI see **ISOLA DEL SOGNO, L'** • 1947
AMORI E VELENI • 1950 • Simonelli Giorgio C. • ITL
AMORI IMPOSSIBILI, GLI (ITL) see **REMPART DES BEGUINES, LE** • 1972
AMORI, LETTI E TRADIMENTI • 1977 • Brescia Alfonso • ITL
AMORI PERICOLOSI • 1964 • Questi Giulio, Lizzani Carlo, Giannetti Alfredo • ITL, FRN
AMORINA • 1961 • del Carril Hugo • ARG
AMORISTS, THE see **JINRUIGAKU NYUMON** • 1966
AMOROSA • 1986 • Zetterling Mai • SWD
AMOROSA MENZOGNA, L' • 1949 • Antonioni Michelangelo • DOC • ITL
AMOROSAS, AS • 1968 • Khouri Walter Hugo • BRZ • LOVING ONES, THE
AMOROSE NOTTI DI ALI BABA, LE • 1973 • De Marchi Luigi • ITL
AMOROSEN ABENTEUER DE MR. O, DIE • 1977 • FRG
AMOROUS ADVENTURES OF A MILKMAN, THE see **AMOROUS MILKMAN, THE** • 1975
AMOROUS ADVENTURES OF A YOUNG POSTMAN, THE • Baker Anthony • USA
AMOROUS ADVENTURES OF BUX, THE • 1926 • Le Strange Norman • UKN
AMOROUS ADVENTURES OF DON QUIXOTE & SANCHO PANZA, THE • 1976 • Nussbaum Raphael • USA • WHEN SEX WAS A KNIGHTLY AFFAIR (UKN) ○ SUPERKNIGHTS ○ SUPERKNIGHT
AMOROUS ADVENTURES OF MOLL FLANDERS, THE • 1965 • Young Terence • UKN
AMOROUS ADVENTURES OF UNCLE BENJAMIN, THE (UKN) see **MON ONCLE BENJAMIN** • 1969
AMOROUS ARTHUR • 1912 • Fitzhamon Lewin • UKN
AMOROUS COOK, THE see **SOLDIER, POLICEMAN AND COOK** • 1899
AMOROUS DOCTOR, THE • 1911 • Bouwmeester Theo • UKN
AMOROUS GENERAL, THE see **WALTZ OF THE TOREADORS** • 1962
AMOROUS GHOST, AN see **ET SPOKELSE FORELSKER SEG** • 1947
AMOROUS GHOST, THE see **MAN ALIVE** • 1945
AMOROUS LIQUID see **TAJO NA NYUEKI** • 1967
AMOROUS MILITIAMAN, THE • 1904 • *Biograph* • USA
AMOROUS MILITIAMAN, THE • 1904 • Collins Alf? • UKN
AMOROUS MILKMAN, THE • 1975 • Nesbitt Derren • UKN • AMOROUS ADVENTURES OF A MILKMAN, THE
AMOROUS MR. PRAWN, THE see **AMOROUS PRAWN, THE** • 1962
AMOROUS NURSE, THE • 1908 • Fitzhamon Lewin? • UKN
AMOROUS POLICEMAN, THE • 1906 • Hough Harold • UKN
AMOROUS PRAWN, THE • 1962 • Kimmins Anthony • UKN • PLAYGIRL AND THE MINISTER, THE (USA) ○ AMOROUS MR. PRAWN, THE
AMOROUS SCOTCHMAN, THE • 1909 • *Empire Films* • UKN
AMOROUS SEX, THE (USA) see **SWEET BEAT** • 1959
AMORS HJAELPETROPPER • 1916 • Davidsen Hjalmar • DNM
AMOS • 1985 • Tuchner Michael • TVM • USA
AMOU SABZI FOROUSH • 1967 • Arjomand Homayoun • IRN • AMOU, THE GREENGROCER
AMOU SIBILOU • 1970 • Beyzai Bahram • IRN
AMOU, THE GREENGROCER see **AMOU SABZI FOROUSH** • 1967
AMOUGIES • 1970 • Laperrousaz Jerome, Roy Jean-Noel • DOC • FRN • EUROPEAN MUSIC REVOLUTION
AMOUR • 1970 • Axel Gabriel • DNM, FRN
AMOUR see **AMORE** • 1973
AMOUR, L' • 1968 • Balducci Richard • FRN, ITL
AMOUR, L' • 1973 • Morrissey Paul, Warhol Andy • USA
AMOUR, L' • 1989 • Faucon Philippe • FRN
AMOUR, L' see **LAMURU** • 1933
AMOUR A LA BOUCHE, L' • 1974 • Kikoine Gerard, Nubbar Alex, Van Damme Alain • FRN
AMOUR A LA CHAINE, L' • 1965 • de Givray Claude • FRN • TIGHT SKIRTS, LOOSE PLEASURES (USA) ○ LOOSE PLEASURES ○ CHAINWORK LOVE ○ VICTIMS OF VICE ○ TIGHT SKIRTS
AMOUR A LA MER, L' • 1963 • Gilles Guy • FRN
AMOUR A L'AMERICAINE, L' • 1931 • Heymann Claude, Fejos Paul • FRN
AMOUR A MORT, L' • 1984 • Resnais Alain • FRN
AMOUR A PARIS, UN • 1987 • Allouache Merzak • FRN • ROMANCE IN PARIS, A
AMOUR A TOUS LES ETAGES, L' • 1902 • Zecca Ferdinand • FRN
AMOUR A TRAVERS LES AGES, L' see **PLUS VIEUX METIER DU MONDE, LE** • 1967
AMOUR A VINGT ANS, L' • 1962 • Truffaut Francois, Ishihara Shintaro, Rossellini Renzo Jr., Ophuls Marcel, Wajda Andrzej, Aurel Jean • FRN, JPN • HATACHI NO KOI (JPN) ○ AMORE A VENT'ANNI ○ LOVE AT TWENTY (USA) ○ MILOSC DWUDZIESTOLATKOW ○ LIEBE MIT ZWANZIG (FRG)
AMOUR.. AMOUR.. • 1932 • Bibal Robert • FRN • POUR LES BEAUX YEUX
AMOUR AU FEMININ, L' see **FAIRE L'AMOUR: DE LA PILULE A L'ORDINATEUR*** • 1968
AMOUR, AUTOCAR ET BOITES DE NUIT • 1960 • Kapps Walter • FRN
AMOUR AUTOUR DE LA MAISON, L' • 1946 • de Herain Pierre • FRN
AMOUR AUX TROUSSES, L' • 1974 • Pallardy Jean-Marie • FRN • PIEGE POUR UN GARCE ○ ADULTERESS IN LOVE ○ HOT ACTS OF LOVE
AMOUR AVEC DES SI.., L' • 1963 • Lelouch Claude • FRN • AVEC DES SI..
AMOUR AVEUGLE • 1920 • de Carbonnat Louis • FRN
AMOUR BLESSE, L' • 1975 • Lefebvre Jean-Pierre • CND • CONFIDENCES DE LA NUIT ○ WOUNDED LOVE
AMOUR C'EST GAI, L'AMOUR C'EST TRISTE • 1969 • Pollet Jean-Daniel • FRN
AMOUR CHANTE, L' • 1930 • Florey Robert • FRN • VIE PARISIENNE
AMOUR CHEZ LES POIDS LOURDS, L' • 1978 • Pallardy Jean-Marie • FRN, ITL • GROSSI BESTONI, I (ITL) ○ EROTIC ENCOUNTERS ○ TRUCK STOP
AMOUR COMME LE NOTRE, UN • 1975 • Pierson Claude • CND, FRN, ITL • FRENCH LOVE (UKN)
AMOUR D'AUTOMNE • 1912 • Feuillade Louis • FRN
AMOUR DE FREDERIC CHOPIN, UN see **CHANSON DE L'ADIEU, LA** • 1934
AMOUR DE LA TERRE see **HANIN AL-ARD** • 1971
AMOUR DE MA VIE, L' see **HABIB AL-UMR** • 1946
AMOUR DE PLUIE, UN (FRN) see **MALE D'AMORE** • 1974
AMOUR DE POCHE, UN • 1957 • Kast Pierre • FRN • NUDE IN HIS POCKET (USA) ○ GIRL IN HIS POCKET ○ POCKET LOVE, A
AMOUR DE SABLE, UN • 1977 • Lara Christian • FRN
AMOUR DE SWANN, UN • 1983 • Schlondorff Volker • FRN, FRG • SWANN IN LOVE (UKN)
AMOUR D'EMMERDEUSE, UN • 1979 • Vandercoille Alain • FRN, BLG • PETITE MERVEILLE, LA
AMOUR DES FEMMES, L' • 1981 • Soutter Michel • SWT, FRN
AMOUR DESCEND DU CIEL, L' • 1956 • Cam Maurice • FRN
AMOUR D'ETUDIANT, UN see **GHARAM TALEB** • 1971
AMOUR DISPOSE, L' see **INCONSTANT, L'** • 1931
AMOUR DONT LES FEMMES ONT BESOIN, L' see **AMOUR QU'IL FAUT AUX FEMMES, L'** • 1933
AMOUR DU COUPLE, L' • 1973 • Belisle Benjamin • DOC • CND
AMOUR DU MORT, L' • 1921 • Maudru Charles • FRN
AMOUR D'UN METIER, L' • 1950 • Gerard • SHT • FRN
AMOUR D'UNE FEMME, L' • 1954 • Gremillon Jean • FRN, ITL • AMORE DI UNA DONNA, L' (ITL)
AMOUR EN 4 DIMENSIONS, L' (FRN) see **AMORE IN 4 DIMENSIONI** • 1963
AMOUR EN ALLEMAGNE, UN • 1983 • Wajda Andrzej • FRN, FRG • LIEBE IN DEUTSCHLAND, EINE (FRG) ○ LOVE IN GERMANY, A (USA)
AMOUR EN CAGE, L' • 1934 • Lamac Carl, de Limur Jean • FRN
AMOUR EN DOUCE, L' • 1984 • Molinaro Edouard • FRN
AMOUR EN FUITE, L' • 1979 • Truffaut Francois • FRN • LOVE ON THE RUN (USA)
AMOUR EN HERBE, L' • 1977 • Andrieux Roger • FRN
AMOUR EN LIBERTE, L' • 1976 • Kupissonoff Jacques • BLG
AMOUR EN PREMIERE CLASSE, L' (FRN) see **AMORE IN PRIMO CLASSE** • 1980
AMOUR EN QUESTION, L' • 1978 • Cayatte Andre • FRN
AMOUR EN VITESSE, L' • 1932 • Heymann Claude, Guter Johannes • FRN • QUATRE DE L'EQUIPE, LES ○ EQUIPE 13, L'
AMOUR EST LE PLUS FORT, L' (FRN) see **VIAGGIO IN ITALIA** • 1953
AMOUR EST REVENU, L' see **WA ADAL'HOB** • 1960
AMOUR EST UN JEU, L' • 1957 • Allegret Marc • FRN • MA FEMME, MA GOSSE ET MOI
AMOUR ET CARBURATEUR • 1926 • Colombier Piere • FRN
AMOUR ET CARREFOUR • 1929 • Peclet Georges • FRN
AMOUR ET CIE • 1949 • Grangier Gilles • FRN
AMOUR ET DISCIPLINE • 1931 • Kemm Jean • FRN • FUITE A L'ANGLAISE, LA
AMOUR ET HAINE • 1935 • Pronin Vassily • USS
AMOUR ET JALOUSIE • 1964 • Khalifa Omar • SHT • TNS
AMOUR ET KARATE see **HUBB WA KARATI** • 1973
AMOUR ET LA VEINE, L' • 1932 • Banks Monty • FRN
AMOUR ET L'ARGENT, L' • 1911 • Perret Leonce • FRN
AMOUR ET LARMES • 1955 • el Sheikh Kamal • EGY
AMOUR ET LE TEMPS, L' • 1910 • Carre Michel • FRN
AMOUR ET PEINE CAPITALE see **HUBBUN WA IDAM** • 1956
AMOUR ET QUADRILLE • 1932 • Tedesco Jean • FRN
AMOUR EXISTE, L' • 1960 • Pialat Maurice • SHT • FRN
AMOUR FOU, L' • 1969 • Rivette Jacques • FRN
AMOUR FUGITIF, L' • 1983 • Ortega Pascal • FRN
AMOUR GUIDE, L' • 1933 • Boyer Jean, Taurog Norman • FRN
AMOUR HANDICAPE, L' • 1979 • Graf Marlies • SWT • BEHINDERTE LIEBE
AMOUR HUMAIN, L' • 1970 • Heroux Denis • CND
AMOUR IMPOSSIBLE • 1984 • Chbib Bachar • CND
AMOUR INTERDIT, L' • 1984 • Dougnac Jean-Pierre • FRN, ITL
AMOUR L'APRES-MIDI, L' • 1972 • Rohmer Eric • FRN • LOVE IN THE AFTERNOON (UKN) ○ CHLOE IN THE AFTERNOON (USA)
AMOUR MADAME, L' • 1952 • Grangier Gilles • FRN
AMOUR MAITRE DES CHOSES, L' • Kemm Jean • FRN
AMOUR MENE LES HOMMES, L' • 1957 • Roussel Emile • FRN • DESIR MENE LES HOMMES, LE ○ DESIRE TAKES THE MEN
AMOUR MENSONGE, L' • 1979 • Peres Uziel • FRN, ISR • FALSE LOVE
AMOUR N'EST PAS UN PECHE, L' • 1952 • Cariven Claude • FRN
AMOUR NOIR ET AMOUR BLANC • 1927 • Starevitch Ladislas • FRN • BLACK LOVE AND WHITE (USA) ○ CUPIDS, BLACK AND WHITE ○ TWO CUPIDS, THE
AMOUR NU, L' • 1980 • Bellon Yannick • FRN
AMOUR PAR TERRE, L' • 1984 • Rivette Jacques • FRN • LOVE ON THE GROUND (USA)
AMOUR PAS COMME LES AUTRES, L' • Baroni Jeanne • FRN
AMOUR PASSE, L' • 1914 • Poirier Leon • FRN
AMOUR PERDU see **HUBB AD'-D'A'I** • 1970
AMOUR QUI FUT, L' see **HUBB AL-LADHI KAN, AL-** • 1971
AMOUR QU'IL FAUT AUX FEMMES, L' • 1933 • Trotz Adolf • FRN • AMOUR DONT LES FEMMES ONT BESOIN, L' ○ CHEMIN DU VRAI BONHEUR, LE
AMOUR QUOTIDIEN, L' • 1974 • Dansereau Fernand, Rossignol Yolande • SHS • CND
AMOUR SACRE • 1915 • Bernard-Deschamps • FRN
AMOUR SANS LENDEMAIN (FRN) see **TENTATIVO SENTIMENTALE, UN** • 1963
AMOUR TEL QU'IL EST, L' (FRN) see **IO LA CONOSCEVO BENE** • 1965
AMOUR TENACE • 1912 • Linder Max • FRN
AMOUR, TOUJOURS L'AMOUR, L' • 1952 • de Canonge Maurice • FRN
AMOUR TROP FORT, L' • 1981 • Duval Daniel • FRN, IND
AMOUR VEILLE, L' • 1937 • Roussell Henry • FRN
AMOUR VIOLE, L' • 1977 • Bellon Yannick • FRN • RAPE OF LOVE (USA) ○ VIOLATED LOVE
AMOUREUSE, L' • 1972 • Mesnil Christian • BLG
AMOUREUSE, L' • 1972 • Sassy Jean-Paul • CND
AMOUREUSE, L' • 1988 • Doillon Jacques • FRN
AMOUREUSE AVENTURE, L' • 1931 • Thiele Wilhelm • FRN
AMOUREUX, LES see **EPERVIER, L'** • 1933
AMOUREUX DE COLETTE, LES see **COLLETTE ET SON MARI** • 1932
AMOUREUX DE LA VIE, LES see **UCHCHAQ AL-HAYAT** • 1971
AMOUREUX DE MARIANNE, LES • 1953 • Stelli Jean • FRN • POURQUOI PAS TOI
AMOUREUX DU FRANCE, LES • 1963 • Grimblat Pierre, Reichenbach Francois • FRN, ITL • GIOCO DEGLI INNAMORATI, IL (ITL)
AMOUREUX SONT SEULS AU MONDE, LES • 1947 • Decoin Henri • FRN • MONELLE (USA) ○ NOIR SUR BLANC
AMOURS CACHES DE SYLVIE, LES • Love John • FRN
AMOURS CELEBRES • 1961 • Boisrond Michel • FRN, ITL
AMOURS DE BLANCHE NEIGE, LES (FRN) see **WINTERMELODIE** • 1946
AMOURS DE CASANOVA, LES see **CASANOVA** • 1933
AMOURS DE JEUNE DESSAUER, LES see **TAMBOUR BATTANT** • 1933
AMOURS DE LA BELLE FERRONIERE, LES see **FRANCOIS 1er** • 1937
AMOURS DE LA PIEUVRE • 1967 • Painleve Jean • SHT • FRN
AMOURS DE LA REINE ELISABETH, LES • 1912 • Desfontaines Henri, Mercanton Louis • FRN • QUEEN BESS –HER LOVE STORY ○ REINE ELISABETH, LA ○ ELISABETH REINE D'ANGLETERRE ○ QUEEN ELISABETH
AMOURS DE LADY HAMILTON, LES (FRN) see **LADY HAMILTON ZWISCHEN SCHMACH UND LIEBE** • 1968
AMOURS DE MANON LESCAUT, LES (FRN) see **AMORI DI MANON LESCAUT, GLI** • 1955
AMOURS DE MINUIT, LES • 1930 • Genina Augusto, Allegret Marc • FRN
AMOURS DE PARIS, LES • 1960 • Poitrenaud Jacques • FRN
AMOURS DE PERGOLESE, LES • 1932 • Brignone Guido • FRN
AMOURS DE ROCAMBOLE, LES • 1924 • Maudru Charles • FRN
AMOURS DE TONI, LES see **TONI** • 1935
AMOURS, DELICES ET ORGUES • 1946 • Berthomieu Andre • FRN • COLLEGE SWING
AMOURS D'HERCULE, LES (FRN) see **AMORI DI ERCOLE, GLI** • 1960
AMOURS DIFFICILES, LES • 1975 • Delpard Raphael • FRN
AMOURS DU MILLIONNAIRE, LES see **GHARAMU AL-MILLYUNIR** • 1957
AMOURS EN FAMILLE • Scotland Michael • FRN
AMOURS EXOTIQUES • 1927 • Poirier Leon • FRN
AMOURS FINISSENT A L'AUBE, LES • 1952 • Calef Henri • FRN
AMOURS TRAGIQUES see **ECHEC ET MAT** • 1931
AMOURS VIENNOISES • 1930 • Choux Jean, Land Robert • FRN
AMPELOPEDE, L' • 1973 • Weinberg Rachel • FRN
AMPHIBIAN MAN, THE (USA) see **CHELOVEK AMPHIBIA** • 1962
AMPHIBIOUS MAN, THE see **CHELOVEK AMPHIBIA** • 1962
AMPHITHEATRE, THE • 1964 • Mujica Rene • ARG
AMPHITRYON • 1935 • Schunzel Reinhold • FRG • AUS DEN WOLKEN KOMMT DAS GLUCK ○ LUCK COMES OUT OF THE CLOUDS
AMPHITRYON II see **DIEUX S'AMUSENT, LES** • 1935
AMPRENTA • 1967 • Doreanu Vladimir Popescu • RMN • FINGERPRINT
AMPUMARATA • 1970 • Kaarresalo-Kasari Eila • SHT • FNL • FINNISH FRUSTRATIONS
AMRIT MATHAN • 1934 • *Mohan Chanda* • IND
AMSEL VON LICHTENTAL, DIE see **VORSTADTVARIETE** • 1934
AMSTERDAM • 1964 • van der Horst Herman • DOC • NTH
AMSTERDAM AFFAIR • 1968 • O'Hara Gerry • UKN

AMSTERDAM BIJ NACHT • 1937 • Benno Alex • NTH • AMSTERDAM BY NIGHT
AMSTERDAM BY NIGHT see **AMSTERDAM BIJ NACHT** • 1937
AMSTERDAM KILL, THE • 1977 • Clouse Robert • HKG
AMSTERDAMNED • 1988 • Maas Dick • NTH
AMUCK • 1978 • Goslar Jurgen • FRG • MANIAC MANSION
AMUCK see **REPLICA DI UN DELITTO** • 1972
AMULET, THE • 1912 • USA
AMULET OF OGUM, THE see **AMULETA DA MORTE** • 1974
AMULETA DA MORTE • 1974 • dos Santos Nelson Pereira • BRZ • AMULETTO DE OGUM, A ○ AMULET OF OGUM, THE
AMULETTEN • 1911 • Linden Gustaf M. • SWD • TALISMAN
AMULETTO DE OGUM, A see **AMULETA DA MORTE** • 1974
AMUSEMENT OF SEVEN MARRIED COUPLES see **SHINKON NANATSU NO TANOSHIMI** • 1958
AMUSING CHANGES • *Pathe* • FRN
AMUSING HOAX, THE see **MYSTIFICATION AMUSANTE, LA** • 1903
AMUSING THE KIDS • 1915 • Batley Ernest G.? • UKN
AMY • 1976 • Noyce Phil • DCS • ASL
AMY • 1981 • McEveety Vincent • USA
AMY GOES TO BUY SOME BREAD • 1979 • Vukotic Dusan • ANS • YGS
AMY PRENTISS • 1974 • Sagal Boris • TVM • USA
AMY PRENTISS: BAPTISM OF FIRE • 1974 • Hayden Jeffrey • TVM • USA • PRIME SUSPECT
AN 01, L' • 1972 • Doillon Jacques, Resnais Alain, Rouch Jean • FRN
AN 40, L' • 1940 • Rivers Fernand, Mirande Yves • FRN
AN-AN-TE CHIA-CH'I • 1983 • Hou Hsiao-Hsien • TWN
AN DE NODO • 1980 • Traore Falaba Issa • MLI • WE ARE ALL GUILTY
AN DER BLAUEN ADRIA see **KORALLENPRINZESSEN, DIE** • 1937
AN DER DONAU, WENN DER WEIN BLUHT • 1965 • von Cziffra Geza • FRG, AUS
AN DER LIEBE NARRENSEIL see **AURI SACRA FAMES 1** • 1920
AN DER SCHONEN BLAUEN DONAU • 1955 • Schweikart Hans • AUS
AN DER SCHONEN BLAUEN DONAU • 1965 • Olden John • AUS
AN DER SCHONEN BLAUEN DONAU 1 • 1926 • Zelnik Friedrich • FRG
AN DER SCHONEN BLAUEN DONAU 2 see **TANZENDE WIEN, DAS** • 1927
AN DER WESER • 1927 • Philippi Siegfried • FRG
AN EINEM FREITAG IN LAS VEGAS (FRG) see **LAS VEGAS, 500 MILLONES** • 1968
AN EINEM FREITAG UM HALB ZWOLF • 1961 • Rakoff Alvin • FRG, FRN, ITL • MONDO NELLA MIA TASCA, IL (ITL) ○ WORLD IN MY POCKET, THE (USA) ○ TABULA RASA-FUNF, DIE TOTEN ○ VENDREDI 13 HEURES (FRN) ○ PAS DE MENTALITE ○ ON FRIDAY AT ELEVEN
AN EN GANG GOSTA EKMAN • 1940 • Bauman Schamyl • SWD • ONCE MORE WITH GOSTA EKMAN ○ FAR OCH SON
AN FRANZOSISCHEN KAMINEN • 1962 • Maetzig Kurt • GDR
AN' GOOD IN THE WORST OF US • 1911 • Haldane Bert? • UKN
AN HEILIGEN WASSER • 1952 • Waschneck Erich • FRG • SIEG DER LIEBE
AN HEILIGEN WASSERN • 1961 • Weidenmann Alfred • FRG
AN JEDEM FINGER ZEHN • 1954 • Ode Erik • FRG
AN JEUX, L' • 1975 • Cardinal Roger • DCS • CND
AN JUNG-GUN SHOOTS ITO HIROBUMI • NKR
AN KLINGENDEN UFERN • 1948 • Unterkircher Hans • AUS
AN LEVA DE GAMLA GUDAR • 1937 • Wahlberg Gideon, Bauman Schamyl • SWD • OLD GODS STILL LIVE, THE (USA) ○ OLD GODS ARE STILL ALIVE
AN-MAGRITT • 1969 • Skouen Arne • NRW
AN MILOUSE TO PARELTHON • 1967 • Kosteletos Odisseas • GRC • SPEAK OF THE PAST
AN OLES IYINEKES TOU KOSMOU • 1967 • Matsas Nestor • GRC • IF ALL THE WOMEN IN THE WORLD
AN TOILEANACH A DFHILL • 1971 • Mulkerns Jim • IRL • RETURN OF THE ISLANDER, THE
ANA • 1957 • Ichikawa Kon • JPN • LADY HAS NO ALIBI, THE ○ HOLE, THE ○ PIT, THE
ANA • 1967 • Akat Lutfu • TRK • MOTHER, THE
ANA • 1967 • Sawa Kensuke • JPN • PIT, A
ANA • 1983 • Reis Antonio, Cordeiro Margarida Martins • PRT
ANA AL DOCTOR • 1968 • Kamel Abbas • EGY • I.. THE DOCTOR
ANA AL-HUBB • 1953 • Barakat Henry • EGY • JE SUIS L'AMOUR
ANA DICE SI • 1958 • Lazaga Pedro • SPN
ANA HAKKI ODENMEZ • 1968 • Seden Osman • TRK • RIGHT OF A MOTHER, THE
ANA HURRA • 1959 • Abu Saif Salah • EGY • I'M FREE
ANA MARIA • 1943 • Rey Florian • SPN
ANA O NERAE • 1968 • Shindo Takae • JPN • AIM AT THE PIT
ANA, PASION DE DOS MUNDOS • 1989 • San Miguel Santiago • VNZ • ANA, PASSION OF TWO WORLDS
ANA, PASSION OF TWO WORLDS see **ANA, PASION DE DOS MUNDOS** • 1989
ANA TERRA • 1972 • Garcia Durval Gomes • BRZ
ANA WA HUWWA WA HIYYA • 1963 • Wahab Fatin Abdel • EGY • MOI, LUI, ET ELLE
ANA WAHDI • 1952 • Barakat Henry • EGY • JE SUIS SEULE
ANA Y GABRIEL • 1978 • Groce Ivan • VNZ • ANNA AND GABRIEL
ANA Y LOS LOBOS • 1972 • Saura Carlos • SPN • ANNA AND THE WOLVES (USA)
ANAADI ANANT • 1986 • Jha Prakesh • IND • END WITHOUT END
ANABELLE'S DREAM • 1967 • Djurkovic Dejan • SHT • YGS
ANACLETO AND THE POLECAT • 1942 • Sgrilli Roberto • ANS • ITL
ANACLETO SE DIVORCIA • 1950 • Rodriguez Joselito • MXC
ANACONDA • 1954 • Anderberg Torgny • SWD
ANACORETA, EL • 1976 • Estelrich Juan • SPN • ANCHORITE, THE
ANACRUSA see **ANACRUSA O DE COMOLA MUSICA VIENE DESPUES DEL SILENCIO** • 1978
ANACRUSA O DE COMOLA MUSICA VIENE DESPUES DEL SILENCIO • 1978 • Zuniga Ariel • MXC • ANACRUSIS ○ ANACRUSA
ANACRUSIS see **ANACRUSA O DE COMOLA MUSICA VIENE DESPUES DEL SILENCIO** • 1978
ANADA see **HRST VODY** • 1971
ANADI • 1959 • *Kapoor Raj* • IND
ANADOLU KIZI • 1967 • Canturk Husnu • TRK • GIRL FROM ANATOLIA, THE
ANAEMIC CINEMA • 1926 • Duchamp Marcel • SHT • FRN
ANAIC OU LE BALAFRE • 1908 • Melies Georges • FRN
ANAIT • 1948 • Bek-Nazarov Amo • USS
ANAJIGOKU • 1968 • Higashimoto Kaoru • JPN • INFERNO OF A PIT
ANAK KU SAZALI • Ramlee P. • MLY • MY SON SAZALI
ANAK KU SUAMI KU • 1971 • Rojik Omar • MLY • MY SON, MY LOVER
ANAK NG KIDLAT • 1959 • Barri Mario • PHL • DAUGHTER OF LIGHTNING
ANAK PONTIANAK • 1958 • Estella Ramon • MLY • SON OF THE VAMPIRE
ANAK SARAWAK • 1988 • Razali Rahim • MLY
ANAK SULUNG • 1982 • Azia Ali • MLY
ANAK TUNGGAL • 1979 • Osman M. • MLY • PRODIGAL SON, THE
ANAKATOSOURAS, O • 1967 • Grigoriou Grigoris • GRC • MEDDLER, THE
ANALFABETO, EL • 1960 • Delgado Miguel M. • MXC
ANALOGIES • 1955 • Davis James* • SHT • USA
ANALYSE • 1970 • Ledoux Patrick • BLG
ANALYZE YOUR SEX • 1970 • *Fleetan Films* • USA
ANAMESA SE DHIO YINEKES • 1967 • Karayannis Kostas • GRC • BETWEEN TWO WOMEN
ANAMNESIS • 1969 • Zwartjes Frans • SHT • NTH
ANANTARAM • 1986 • Gopalakrishnan Adoor • IND • REST OF THE STORY, THE ○ MONOLOGUE ○ ANANTHARAM
ANANTHARAM see **ANANTARAM** • 1986
ANAPARASTASIS • 1970 • Angelopoulos Theo • GRC • RECONSTRUCTION ○ RECONSTITUTION
ANAR-BALA • 1940 • Khan A. M. • IND • POMEGRANATE GIRL
ANARA QUARTER see **GORODOK ANARA** • 1976
ANARCHIE CHEZ GUIGNOL, L' • 1906 • Melies Georges • FRN • PUNCH AND JUDY
ANARCHIST, THE • 1913 • Brenon Herbert • USA
ANARCHIST AND HIS DOG, THE • 1907 • *Walterdaw* • UKN
ANARCHISTES, LES see **BANDE A BONNOT, LA** • 1969
ANARCHISTES OU LA BANDE A BONNOT, LES see **BANDE A BONNOT, LA** • 1969
ANARCHISTIC GRIP, THE • 1910 • *Lubin* • USA
ANARCHIST'S DOOM, THE see **TUBE OF DEATH, THE** • 1913
ANARCHIST'S SWEETHEART, THE • 1908 • Bouwmeester Theo? • UKN
ANARCHY IN ENGLAND • 1909 • Gobbett T. J. • UKN
ANARQUISTAS, LOS • 1912 • *Republic* • USA
ANASTASIA • 1956 • Litvak Anatole • UKN, USA
ANASTASIA • 1986 • Chomsky Marvin • TVM • USA • ANASTASIA: THE MYSTERY OF ANNA
ANASTASIA see **ANASTASIA -DIE LETZTE ZARENTOCHTER** • 1956
ANASTASIA, DIE FALSCHE ZARENTOCHTER • 1928 • Bergen Arthur • FRG
ANASTASIA -DIE LETZTE ZARENTOCHTER • 1956 • Harnack Falk • FRG • ANASTASIA, THE CZAR'S LAST DAUGHTER ○ IS ANNA ANDERSON ANASTASIA? ○ ANASTASIA
ANASTASIA MIO FRATELLO • 1973 • Steno • ITL • ANASTASIA MIO FRATELLO PRESUNTO CAPO DELL'ANONIMA
ANASTASIA MIO FRATELLO PRESUNTO CAPO DELL'ANONIMA see **ANASTASIA MIO FRATELLO** • 1973
ANASTASIA PASSED BY see **DUIOS ANASTASIA TRECEA** • 1979
ANASTASIA PASSING GENTLY see **DUIOS ANASTASIA TRECEA** • 1979
ANASTASIA, THE CZAR'S LAST DAUGHTER see **ANASTASIA -DIE LETZTE ZARENTOCHTER** • 1956
ANASTASIA: THE MYSTERY OF ANNA see **ANASTASIA** • 1986
ANASTENARIA, LA • Carbonell Maria L. • DCS • VNZ
ANATA KAIMASU • 1956 • Kobayashi Masaki • JPN • I'LL BUY YOU
ANATA NO BIRU • 1954 • Hani Susumu • DOC • JPN • YOUR BEER
ANATA TO TOMO NI • 1955 • Ohba Hideo • JPN • YOU AND YOUR FRIEND
ANATA WA NANI O KANGAETE IRU KA? • 1967 • Kuri Yoji • ANS • JPN • WHAT DO YOU THINK?
ANATAHAN • 1954 • von Sternberg Josef • USA, JPN • SAGA OF ANATAHAN, THE
ANATH ASHRAM • 1937 • *Sircar B. N. (P)* • IND
ANATHEMA • 1974 • Cenevski Kiril • YGS
ANATOL see **AFFAIRS OF ANATOL, THE** • 1921
ANATOLE • 1962 • Deitch Gene • ANS • USA
ANATOLE CHERI • 1951 • Heymann Claude • FRN
ANATOLE FAIT DU CAMPING • Dubout Albert • ANM • FRN • ANATOLE'S CAMPING TRIP
ANATOLE'S CAMPING TRIP see **ANATOLE FAIT DU CAMPING**
ANATOLIAN SMILE, THE see **AMERICA, AMERICA** • 1963
ANATOMIA DE UN CARNAVAL • 1982 • Alvarez Santiago • CUB • ANATOMY OF A CARNIVAL
ANATOMIA MIAS LISTIAS • 1973 • Karayannis Kostas • GRC • GANGSTERS, THE
ANATOMIA MILOSCI • 1972 • Zaluski Roman • PLN • ANATOMY OF LOVE
ANATOMIE DES LIEBESACKTS • 1971 • Schnell Hermann • FRG • ANATOMY OF LOVE (UKN)
ANATOMIE D'UN MEURTRE • Benazeraf Jose • FRN
ANATOMIE D'UN RAPPORT • 1976 • Moullet Luc, Pizzorno Antonietta • FRN
ANATOMIE STUNDE • 1977 • Zanussi Krzysztof • MTV • FRG • LEKCJA ANATOMII ○ ANATOMY LESSON
ANATOMIST, THE • 1961 • William Leonard • UKN
ANATOMY LESSON see **ANATOMIE STUNDE** • 1977
ANATOMY OF A CARNIVAL see **ANATOMIA DE UN CARNAVAL** • 1982
ANATOMY OF A HORROR • 1980 • Azzopardi Mario • TVM • CND • DEADLINE
ANATOMY OF A MARRIAGE see **VIE CONJUGALE, LA** • 1964
ANATOMY OF A MARRIAGE: MY DAYS WITH FRANCOISE (USA) see **VIE CONJUGALE: FRANCOISE, LA** • 1964
ANATOMY OF A MARRIAGE: MY DAYS WITH JEAN-MARC (USA) see **VIE CONJUGALE: JEAN-MARC, LA** • 1964
ANATOMY OF A MOTOR OIL • 1970 • De Normanville Peter • DCS • UKN
ANATOMY OF A MURDER • 1959 • Preminger Otto • USA
ANATOMY OF A PERFORMANCE see **TRIBUTE TO LOUIS ARMSTRONG** • 1970
ANATOMY OF A PSYCHO • 1961 • Peters Brooke L. • USA
ANATOMY OF A SEDUCTION • 1979 • Stern Steven Hilliard • TVM • USA
ANATOMY OF A SYNDICATE see **BIG OPERATOR, THE** • 1959
ANATOMY OF A TOWN • 1967 • Kidawa Janusz • DOC • PLN
ANATOMY OF AN ILLNESS • 1984 • Heffron Richard T. • TVM • USA
ANATOMY OF CINDY FINK, THE • 1965 • Leacock Richard • DOC • USA
ANATOMY OF LOVE see **ANATOMIA MILOSCI** • 1972
ANATOMY OF LOVE, THE (USA) see **TEMPI NOSTRI** • 1954
ANATOMY OF LOVE (UKN) see **ANATOMIE DES LIEBESACKTS** • 1971
ANATOMY OF POP see **AMERICAN MUSIC -FROM FOLK TO JAZZ AND POP** • 1969
ANAYURT OTELI • 1987 • Kavur Omer • TRK • MOTHERLAND HOTEL
ANBALIPPU • 1968 • Thirulokachander A. C. • IND • GIFT
ANBAR EL MAWI • 1988 • Fahmy Ashraf • EGY • DEATH WARD
ANBASSADRICE, L' • 1913 • Pouctal Henri • FRN
ANBU VAZHI • 1967 • Natesan M. • IND • WAY OF LOVE, THE
ANCESTOR, THE see **ANCETRE, L'** • 1909
ANCESTOR, THE see **ANTENATO, L'** • 1936
ANCESTOR'S LEGACY, THE • 1914 • *Ambrosio* • USA
ANCESTRAL ESTATE see **ODAL FEDRANNA** • 1980
ANCESTRY • 1915 • Otto Henry • USA
ANCETRE, L' • 1909 • Cohl Emile • ANS • FRN • ANCESTOR, THE
ANCHE GLI ANGELI MANGIANO FAGIOLI • 1973 • Clucher E. B. • ITL, FRN, SPN • EVEN ANGELS EAT BEANS
ANCHE GLI ANGELI TIRANO DI DESTRO • 1974 • Clucher E. B. • ITL
ANCHE L'ESTASI • 1978 • Tiso Ciriaco • ITL • PAGINE DI ORRORE QUOTIDIANO
ANCHE L'INFERNO TREMA • 1958 • Regnoli Piero • ITL • ORA PER VIVERE, UN'
ANCHE NEL WEST, C'ERA UNA VOLTA DIO • 1968 • Silvestri Dario • ITL, SPN • BETWEEN GOD, THE DEVIL AND A WINCHESTER (USA) ○ EVEN IN THE WEST THERE WAS GOD ONCE UPON A TIME
ANCHE PER DJANGO LE CAROGNE HANNO UN PREZZO • 1971 • Solvay Paolo • ITL
ANCHE SE VOLESSI LAVORARE, CHE FACCIO? • 1972 • Mogherini Flavio • ITL
ANCHIN TO KIYOHIME • 1960 • Shima Koji • JPN • PRIEST AND THE BEAUTY, THE
ANCHOR, THE (UKN) see **PIONEERS OF THE FRONTIER** • 1940
ANCHORITE, THE see **ANACORETA, EL** • 1976
ANCHORS AWEIGH • 1945 • Sidney George • USA
ANCIENNETE ET COMPETENCE see **SENIORITY VERSUS ABILITY** • 1968
ANCIENS CANADIENS, LES • 1950 • Devlin Bernard • DCS • CND
ANCIENS DE SAINT-LOUP, LES • 1950 • Lampin Georges • FRN
ANCIENT BLOOD, THE • 1916 • Bartlett Charles • SHT • USA
ANCIENT BOW, THE • 1912 • *Vitagraph* • USA
ANCIENT CITY see **KOTO** • 1980
ANCIENT CITY OF KOTO, THE see **KOTO** • 1980
ANCIENT COIN, THE • 1915 • *Courtot Marguerite* • USA
ANCIENT COIN, THE see **STARINATA MONETA** • 1965
ANCIENT CURES • 1953 • *Smith Pete* • SHT • USA
ANCIENT CUSTOMS OF EGYPT • 1921 • Urban Charles • USA
ANCIENT FISTORY • 1953 • Kneitel Seymour • ANS • USA
ANCIENT HIGHWAY, THE • 1925 • Willat Irvin V. • USA
ANCIENT LAW, THE see **ALTE GESETZ, DAS** • 1923
ANCIENT MARINER, THE • 1925 • Otto Henry, Bennett Chester • USA
ANCIENT MUSIC see **MUZYKA DAWNA** • 1964
ANCIENT ORDER OF GOOD FELLOWS, THE • 1913 • Lambart Harry • USA
ANCIENT ROMAN, THE • 1909 • ITL
ANCIENT SCULPTURE OF IRELAND • 1969 • Morrison George • DOC • IRL
ANCIENT TEMPLES OF EGYPT • 1912 • Olcott Sidney • DOC • USA
ANCILLAE DOMINI • 1959 • Lavoie Hermenegilde, Lavoie Richard • CND
ANCINES WOODS, THE see **BOSQUE DE ANCINES, EL** • 1969
ANCORA DOLLARI PER I MCGREGOR • 1970 • Merino Jose Luis • ITL
ANCORA UNA VOLTA.. A VENEZIA • 1976 • Giorgi Claudio • ITL
ANCORA UNA VOLTA PRIMA DI LASCIARCI • 1973 • Biagetti Giuliano • ITL
AND A LITTLE CHILD SHALL LEAD THEM • 1909 • Griffith D. W. • USA
AND A STILL, SMALL VOICE • 1918 • Bracken Bertram • USA
AND AGAIN I AM WITH YOU • Khrzhanovsky Andrei • ANM • USS
AND ALL THAT JAZZ • 1979 • Selfe Ray • UKN
AND ALL THESE WOMEN see **OCH ALLA DESSA KVINNOR** • 1944
AND ALL WILL BE QUIET see **POTEM NASTAPI CISZA** • 1966
AND ALONG CAME MARY • 1917 • *Rhodes Billie* • USA
AND AN ANGEL CAME • 1913 • *Edison* • USA
...AND AROUND HIM WAS DEATH see **...E INTORNO A LUI FU MORTE** • 1967

AND AT LAST see **ABASHESHEY** • 1962
AND BABY MAKES SIX • 1979 • Hussein Waris • TVM • USA
AND BABY MAKES THREE • 1949 • Levin Henry • USA
AND BY THESE DEEDS • 1915 • Physioc Wray • USA
AND COMES THE DAWN.. BUT COLORED RED see **NELLA STRETTA MORSA DEL RAGNO** • 1971
AND DIE OF PLEASURE see **ET MOURIR DE PLAISIR** • 1960
AND FIVE MAKES JASON • 1969 • Stagg William • USA
...AND FOR A ROOF A SKY FULL OF STARS see **...E PER TETTO UN CIELO DI STELLE** • 1968
AND GOD CREATED THE CAFE SINGER see **I BOG STVOTI KAFANSKU PEVACICU** • 1972
AND GOD CREATED WOMAN • 1987 • Vadim Roger • USA
AND GOD CREATED WOMAN (USA) see **ET DIEU CREA LA FEMME** • 1956
AND HE CAME BACK • 1914 • *Essanay* • USA
AND HE CAME STRAIGHT HOME • 1915 • *Atla* • USA
AND HE HAD A LITTLE GUN • 1913 • Wilson Frank? • UKN
AND HE NEVER KNEW • 1915 • *Marshall Boyd* • USA
AND HE WILL RISE AGAIN • 1964 • Tammer Peter • DCS • ASL
AND HIS COAT CAME BACK • 1909 • *Blackton J. Stuart (P)* • ANS • USA
AND HIS COAT CAME BACK • 1909 • *Vitagraph* • USA
AND HIS WIFE CAME BACK • 1913 • Young James • USA
AND HOPE TO DIE see **MAIN A COUPER, LA** • 1974
AND HOPE TO DIE (UKN) see **COURSE DU LIEVRE A TRAVERS LES CHAMPS, LA** • 1972
AND HOW ARE YOU? • 1958 • Fetin Vladimir • SHT • USS
AND I ALONE SURVIVED • 1978 • Graham William A. • TVM • USA
AND IN THE NAME OF LOVE see **AT SA NGALAN NG PAG-IBIG** • 1967
AND IN WALKED UNCLE • 1917 • *Rhodes Billie* • USA
AND JENNY MAKES THREE see **JENNY** • 1970
AND JIMMY WENT TO THE RAINBOW'S END see **UND JIMMY GING ZUM REGENBOGEN** • 1971
...AND JUSTICE FOR ALL • 1979 • Jewison Norman • USA
AND LIFE AND TEARS AND LOVE see **I JIZN', I SLIOZY, I LYUBOV** • 1983
AND LIFE PASSED • 1975 • Salem Atef • EGY
AND LOVE HAS ENDED • 1975 • el Imam Hassan • EGY
AND MILLIONS WILL DIE • 1973 • Martinson Leslie H. • USA
AND NO BIRDS SING • 1969 • Cowie Victor • CND
...AND NO ONE COULD SAVE HER • 1972 • Billington Kevin • MTV • UKN • ALIVE ALIVE O
AND NO ONE ELSE see **I NIKTO DRUGOY** • 1968
AND NO-ONE WOULD BELIEVE HER see **WELCOME TO ARROW BEACH** • 1973
AND NOBODY WAS ASHAMED see **...UND KEINER SCHAMTE SICH** • 1960
AND NONETHELESS I BELIEVE • 1974 • Klimov Elem • USS
...AND NOT YET 16 see **SEX UND NOCH NICHT SECHZEHN** • 1968
AND NOTHING BUT THE TRUTH (USA) see **GIRO CITY** • 1982
AND NOTHING MORE • Sokurov Alexander • DOC • USS
AND NOW FOR SOMETHING COMPLETELY DIFFERENT • 1972 • MacNaughton Ian • UKN
...AND NOW MIGUEL • 1966 • Clark James B. • USA
AND NOW MY LOVE (USA) see **TOUTE UNE VIE** • 1974
AND NOW PASS JUDGEMENT.. see **A TEPYER SUDI..** • 1967
AND NOW THE SCREAMING STARTS! • 1973 • Baker Roy Ward • UKN • I HAVE NO MOUTH BUT I MUST SCREAM ○ FENGRIFFEN
AND NOW THEY REST • 1939 • Salt Brian, Fairthorne Robert • UKN
AND NOW TOMORROW • 1944 • Pichel Irving • USA
AND ON THE EIGHTH DAY • 1968 • Tucker Roger • DOC • UKN
AND ON THE THIRD YEAR, HE ROSE AGAIN see **YAL TERCER ANO, RESUCITO** • 1980
AND ONCE UPON A LOVE see **FANTASIES** • 1981
AND ONCE UPON A TIME • 1975 • Derek John • USA • ONCE UPON A TIME
AND ONE WAS BEAUTIFUL • 1940 • Sinclair Robert B. • USA
AND ONE WAS GOLD • 1966 • Schepisi Fred • DOC • ASL
AND PERCY GOT MARRIED • 1915 • Angeles Bert • USA
AND QUIET FLOWS THE DON see **TIKHII DON** • 1958
AND QUIET ROLLS THE DAWN see **EK DIN PRATIDIN** • 1979
...AND REMEMBER ME TO THE SWALLOWS see **A POZDRAVUJTE VLASTOVKY** • 1972
AND RIDE A TIGER see **STRANGER IN MY ARMS** • 1959
AND SHE NEVER KNEW • 1914 • Physioc Wray • USA
AND SO GOODBYE see **BEYOND TOMORROW** • 1940
AND SO THEY WERE MARRIED • 1936 • Nugent Elliott • USA
AND SO THEY WERE MARRIED see **JOHNNY DOESN'T LIVE HERE ANY MORE** • 1944
AND SO TIBET • 1964 • Kneitel Seymour • ANS • USA
AND SO TO BED (USA) see **GROSSE LIEBESSPIEL, DAS** • 1963
AND SO TO WED • 1936 • Yarbrough Jean • SHT • USA
AND SO TO WORK • 1936 • Massingham Richard • UKN
AND SOON THE DARKNESS • 1970 • Fuest Robert • UKN
AND STILL BREAKS THE DAWN see **EK DIN PRATIDIN** • 1979
AND SUDDEN DEATH • 1936 • Barton Charles T. • USA
...AND SUDDENLY IT'S MURDER (USA) see **CRIMEN** • 1960
AND SUDDENLY ONE DAY.. see **EKDIN ACHANAK** • 1989
AND SUDDENLY YOU RUN (UKN) see **TERROR AT MIDNIGHT** • 1956
AND THAT'S HOW THE ROW BEGAN • 1915 • Birch Cecil • UKN
AND THE ANGELS SING • 1944 • Marshall George • USA
...AND THE BAND PLAYED ON see **SHILLINGBURY BLOWERS, THE** • 1979
AND THE BEST MAN WON • 1915 • Davey Horace • USA
AND THE CHILDREN PAY • 1919 • Tyrol Jacques • USA
AND THE DANCE WENT ON • 1914 • *Kalem* • USA
AND THE DAWNS ARE QUIET HERE.. see **A ZORI ZYDES TIKHIYE..** • 1973
AND THE DAY CAME see **I DOYDE DENYAT** • 1974
AND THE DOG CAME BACK • 1907 • *Lubin* • USA
AND THE EARTH SHALL GIVE BACK LIFE • 1953 • Jurgens • SHT • USA
AND THE EARTH WAS WITHOUT FORM AND VOID • 1959 • Gross Aline, Gross Yoram • SHT • ISR
AND THE FIDDLE FELL SILENT see **I SKRZYPCE PRZESTALY GRAC** • 1988
...AND THE FIFTH RIDER IS FEAR see **...A PATY JEZDEC JE STRACH** • 1964
AND THE FIVE WERE PUNISHED see **KE I PENTE ISAN KOLASMENES** • 1968
AND THE GREATEST OF THESE IS CHARITY • 1912 • *Cruze James* • USA
AND THE GREEN GRASS GREW ALL AROUND • 1931 • Fleischer Dave • ANS • USA
AND THE LAW SAYS • 1916 • *Bennett Richard* • USA
AND THE PARROT SAID..? • 1915 • Metcalfe Earl • USA
AND THE PEOPLE STILL ASK see **MEG KER A NEP** • 1971
AND THE SAME TO YOU • 1960 • Pollock George • UKN
AND THE SHIP SAILS ON (USA) see **E LA NAVE VA** • 1983
...AND THE SKY ABOVE US see **...UND UBER UNS DER HIMMEL** • 1947
AND THE SNOW WAS NO MORE see **ET LA NEIGE N'ETAIT PLUS** • 1965
AND THE VILLAIN STILL PURSUED HER • 1906 • *Vitagraph* • USA • AUTHOR'S DREAM, THE
AND THE VILLAIN STILL PURSUED HER • 1913 • *Nestor* • USA
AND THE VILLAIN STILL PURSUED HER • 1914 • *Roland Ruth* • USA
AND THE VIOLINS STOPPED PLAYING see **I SKRZYPCE PRZESTALY GRAC** • 1988
AND THE WATCH CAME BACK • 1913 • *Kalem* • USA
AND THE WILD, WILD WOMEN (USA) see **NELLA CITTA L'INFERNO** • 1958
AND THE WORLD WAS MADE OF FLESH • 1971 • Marek Dusan • ASL
AND THEN? • 1917 • SAF
AND THEN? • 1985 • Bechard Gorman • USA
AND THEN see **SOREKARA** • 1985
AND THEN HE WOKE UP • 1909 • Aylott Dave • UKN
AND THEN HE WOKE UP • 1915 • Coleby A. E. • UKN
AND THEN IT HAPPENED • 1915 • MacGregor Norval • USA
AND THEN SHE WOKE UP • 1913 • *Summit Films* • UKN
AND THEN THERE WAS LIGHT (UKN) see **ET LA LUMIERE FUT** • 1989
AND THEN THERE WERE NONE • 1945 • Clair Rene • USA • TEN LITTLE NIGGERS (UKN) ○ DIX PETITS INDIENS, LES
AND THEN THERE WERE NONE • 1974 • Collinson Peter • UKN, SPN, FRG • TEN LITTLE INDIANS ○ DEATH IN PERSEPOLIS ○ DIEZ NEGRITOS ○ TEN LITTLE NIGGERS
AND THEN YOU DIE • 1988 • Mankiewicz Francis • CND
AND THERE ARE 365 DAYS • 1971 • Czurko Edward • SHT • PLN
AND THERE CAME A MAN see **E VENNE UN UOMO** • 1964
AND THERE WAS AN EVENING AND A MORNING • 1971 • Saltykov Alexei • USS • THERE WAS EVENING AND THERE WAS MORNING
AND THERE WAS JAZZ see **BYL JAZZ** • 1983
AND THERE WAS LIGHT • 1914 • *Gardner Helen* • USA
AND THERE WAS NO MORE SEA see **EN DE ZEE WAS NIET MEER** • 1956
AND THERE'S DANCING AFTERWARDS see **OG DER ER BAL BAGEFTER** • 1971
AND THEY CALLED HIM HERO • 1915 • Ford Francis • USA
AND THEY CAME see **AT SILA'Y DUMATING** • 1967
AND THIS IS FREE • 1963 • Dayron Norman • USA
AND TO THINK THAT I SAW IT ON MULBERRY STREET • 1944 • Pal George • ANS • USA
AND TOMORROW? see **Y MANANA?** • 1968
AND TOMORROW? see **WA GHADAN..** • 1972
AND TOMORROW THEY'LL BE ADULTS see **Y MANANA SERAN HOMBRES** • 1979
AND VERY NICE TOO • 1913 • Booth W. R.? • UKN
AND VERY NICE TOO • 1914 • Weston Charles? • UKN
AND WHAT IF IT IS LOVE? see **A ESLI ETO LYUBOV?** • 1961
AND WHO BUT I SHOULD BE • 1970 • Roos Jorgen • DNM
AND WOMAN.. WAS CREATED (UKN) see **ET DIEU CREA LA FEMME** • 1956
AND WOMEN MUST WEEP • 1922 • Bruce Robert C. • USA
AND WOMEN SHALL WEEP • 1960 • Lemont John • UKN
AND YET THEY GO ON (USA) see **SHIKAMO KARERA WA YUKU PART I & II** • 1931
AND YET WE LIVE see **DOKKOI IKITEIRU** • 1951
AND YOU WILL WANDER RESTLESS see **UND WANDERN SOLLST DU RUHELOS..** • 1915
AND YOU'LL LIVE IN TERROR! THE BEYOND see **ALDILA, L'** • 1981
AND YOUR NAME IS JONAH • 1979 • Michaels Richard • TVM • USA
ANDA MUCHACHO, SPARA (SPN) see **SOLE SOTTO TERRA, IL** • 1971
ANDADOR, EL • 1967 • Carreras Enrique • ARG • WALK, THE
ANDAHAYLILLAS see **MEMOIRES D'UNE ENFANT DES ANDES** • 1985
ANDALOUSIE • 1950 • Vernay Robert, Lucia Luis • FRN, SPN • SUENO DE ANDALUCIA, EL (SPN)
ANDALUCIA LA BAJA • Chumez Chumy • SHT • SPN
ANDALUSIAN DOG, AN see **CHIEN ANDALOU, UN** • 1930
ANDALUSIAN GIPSIES, THE see **FLAMENCOS, LOS** • 1968
ANDALUSIAN SUPERSTITION • 1912 • *Pathe* • FRN
ANDALUSISCHE NACHTE • 1938 • Maisch Herbert • FRG, SPN • NIGHTS IN ANDALUSIA (USA)
ANDANZAS DEL CANGURO BOXY • 1966 • Delgado Cruz • SHT • SPN
ANDARZI MUDAR • 1972 • Halil Abdul Khaliq • AFG • MOTHER'S ADVICE
ANDAZ • 1949 • Khan Mehboob • IND
ANDECHSER GEFUHL, DAS • 1974 • Achternbusch Herbert • FRG
ANDEL S DABLEM V TELE • 1983 • Matejka Vaclav • CZC • ANGEL-DEVIL, THE
ANDELSKY KABAT • 1948 • Hofman Eduard • CZC • COAT FROM HEAVEN (USA) ○ ANGEL'S COAT, THE
ANDEN, EL • 1952 • Manzanos Eduardo • SPN
ANDER AND YUL see **ANDER ETA YUL** • 1988
ANDER ETA YUL • 1988 • Diez Ana • SPN • ANDER AND YUL
ANDERE, DER • 1913 • Mack Max • FRG • OTHER, THE
ANDERE, DER • 1930 • Wiene Robert • FRG • MAN WITHIN, THE (USA) ○ OTHER, THE ○ DR. HALLERS
ANDERE, DIE • 1924 • Lamprecht Gerhard • FRG • OTHER, THE
ANDERE, DIE • 1949 • Sistig Alfred E. • FRG • OTHER, THE
ANDERE ICH, DAS • 1918 • Freisler Fritz • AUS • OTHER SELF, THE
ANDERE ICH, DAS • 1941 • Liebeneiner Wolfgang • FRG • OTHER SELF, THE
ANDERE LACHELN, DAS • 1978 • van Ackeren Robert • FRG • OTHER SMILE, THE
ANDERE SEITE, DIE • 1931 • Paul Heinz • FRG
ANDERE WELT • 1937 • Stoger Alfred, Allegret Marc • FRG
ANDERE WELT, DIE • 1920 • Batz Lorenz • FRG
ANDERS • 1969 • Breien Anja • NRW
ANDERS ALS DIE ANDERN • 1919 • Oswald Richard • FRG • DIFFERENT FROM THE OTHERS ○ PARAGRAPH 175
ANDERS ALS DU UND ICH • 1957 • Harlan Veit • FRG • THIRD SEX, THE (USA) ○ DRITTE GESCHLECHT, DAS
ANDERSEN HOS FOTOGRAFEN • 1975 • Roos Jorgen • DOC • DNM
ANDERSEN MONOGATARI • 1968 • Yabuki Kimio • ANM • JPN • FABLES FROM HANS CHRISTIAN ANDERSEN
ANDERSENS HEMMELIGHED • 1971 • Roos Jorgen • DOC • DNM
ANDERSEN'S RUN see **PLASTPOSEN** • 1987
ANDERSON, PETTERSSON OCH LUNDSTROM • 1923 • Barcklind Carl • SWD
ANDERSON PLATOON, THE see **PATROUILLE ANDERSON, LA** • 1967
ANDERSON TAPES, THE • 1972 • Lumet Sidney • USA
ANDERSON'S ANGELS see **CHESTY ANDERSON, USN** • 1976
ANDERSONVILLE TRIAL, THE • 1970 • Scott George C. • TVM • USA
ANDERSSON FAMILY, THE see **FAMILJEN ANDERSSON** • 1937
ANDERSSONSKANS KALLE • 1922 • Wallen Sigurd • SWD • MRS. ANDERSSON'S CHARLIE
ANDERSSONSKANS KALLE • 1934 • Wallen Sigurd • SWD • MRS. ANDERSSON'S CHARLIE
ANDERSSONSKANS KALLE • 1950 • Husberg Rolf • SWD • MRS. ANDERSSON'S CHARLIE
ANDERSSONSKANS KALLE • 1972 • Stivell Arne • SWD
ANDERSSONSKANS KALLE I BUSFORM • 1973 • Stivell Arne • SWD
ANDERSSONSKANS KALLE PA NYA UPPTAG • 1923 • Wallen Sigurd • SWD • MRS. ANDERSSON'S CHARLIE AND HIS NEW PRANKS
ANDESU NO HANAYOME • 1966 • Hani Susumu • JPN • BRIDE OF THE ANDES (UKN)
ANDHA DIGANTA • 1988 • Mohapatra Manmohan • IND • BLIND HORIZON
ANDHI • 1940 • *Sircar B. N. (P)* • IND
ANDHI GALLI • 1984 • Dasgupta Buddhadeb • IND • BLIND ALLEY
ANDI • 1952 • Agradoot • IND
ANDJEO CUVAR • 1986 • Paskaljevic Goran • YGS • GUARDIAN ANGEL
ANDO VOLANDO BAJO • 1957 • Gonzalez Rogelio A. • MXC
ANDORRA OU LES HOMMES D'AIRAIN • 1941 • Couzinet Emile • FRN
ANDRA DANSEN • 1983 • Oskarsson Larus • SWD • SECOND DANCE, THE
ANDRE CHENIER • 1909 • Perret Leonce • FRN
ANDRE CHENIER • 1911 • Feuillade Louis • FRN
ANDRE CORNELIS • 1918 • Kemm Jean • FRN
ANDRE CORNELIS • 1927 • Kemm Jean • FRN • SINS OF DESIRE
ANDRE FOLKS BORN • 1958 • Lichtenberg Nicolai • DNM • OTHER PEOPLE'S CHILDREN
ANDRE GIDE see **AVEC ANDRE GIDE** • 1951
ANDRE MASSON ET LES QUATRE ELEMENTS • 1958 • Gremillon Jean • SHT • FRN
ANDRE-MODESTE GRETRY • 1955 • Deroisy Lucien • BLG
ANDRE SKIFTET, DET • 1978 • Glomm Lasse • NRW • SECOND SHIFT, THE
ANDRE UND URSULA • 1955 • Jacobs Werner • FRG
ANDREA • 1975 • Glaeser Henri • FRN
ANDREA • 1979 • Pomes Leopold
ANDREA CHENIER • 1955 • Fracassi Clemente • FRN, ITL • SOUFFLE DE LA LIBERTE, LE
ANDREA DORIA • 1970 • Vailati Bruno • ITL
ANDREA (USA) see **ANDREA -WIE EIN BLATT AUF NACKTER HAUT** • 1968
ANDREA -WIE EIN BLATT AUF NACKTER HAUT • 1968 • Schott-Schobinger Hans • FRG • ANDREA (USA) ○ NYMPHO, THE (UKN)
ANDREAS • 1988 • Lindenmaier Patrick • DOC • SWT
ANDREAS HOFER • 1909 • Biebrach Rudolf • FRG
ANDREAS HOFER • 1914 • Froelich Carl • FRG
ANDREAS HOFER • 1929 • Prechtl Hanns • FRG
ANDREAS SCHLUTER • 1942 • Maisch Herbert • FRG
ANDREES LUFTFARD see **INGENJOR ANDREES LUFTFARD** • 1983
ANDREI KOZHUKHOV • 1917 • Protazanov Yakov • USS
ANDREI RUBLEV (UKN) see **STRASTI PO ANDREYU** • 1966
ANDREI RUBLIOV see **STRASTI PO ANDREYU** • 1966
ANDREIKA • 1958 • Vasiliev Sergei • USS
ANDREINA • 1917 • Serena Gustavo • ITL
ANDREMO IN CITTA • 1966 • Risi Nelo • ITL
ANDRES BELLO • 1974 • de Pedro Manuel • DCS • VNZ
ANDRES DHEN LIYIZOUN POTE, I • 1968 • Andritsos Kostas • GRC • STRONG MEN, THE ○ MEN NEVER BEND
ANDRE'S GRAND TOUR • Munro Grant, MacKay Jim • ANM • CND
ANDREW JACKSON • 1913 • Dwan Allan • USA
ANDREW'S RAIDER see **GREAT LOCOMOTIVE CHASE, THE** • 1956
ANDRIENNE LECOUVREUR see **DREAM OF LOVE** • 1928
ANDRIESH • 1954 • Paradjanov Sergei • USS
ANDRINA • 1981 • Forsyth Bill • TVM • UKN
ANDROCLES • 1912 • Feuillade Louis • FRN • ANDROCLES AND THE LION (USA)
ANDROCLES AND THE LION • 1952 • Erskine Chester, Ray Nicholas (U/c) • USA

ANDROCLES AND THE LION (USA) see **ANDROCLES** • 1912

ANDROID • 1982 • Lipstadt Aaron • USA

ANDROMAQUE OU L'IRREPARABLE • 1977 • Koleva Maria • DCS • FRN

ANDROMEDA NEBULA, THE (USA) see **TUMONNOCT ANDROMED** • 1967

ANDROMEDA STRAIN, THE • 1971 • Wise Robert • USA

ANDROMEDA THE MYSTERIOUS see **TUMONNOCT ANDROMED** • 1967

ANDRU KANDA MUGAM • 1968 • Ramakrishnan G. • IND • FACE THAT I RECOGNISE, THE

ANDY • 1965 • Sarafian Richard C. • USA

ANDY • 1970 • Bryant Peter • SHT • CND

ANDY AND MIN AT THE THEATRE • 1920 • *Celebrated Players* • SHT • USA

ANDY AND THE HYPNOTIST • 1914 • France Charles H. • USA

ANDY AND THE REDSKINS • 1914 • France Charles H. • USA

ANDY CLYDE GETS SPRING CHICKEN • 1939 • White Jules • SHT • USA

ANDY COLBY'S INCREDIBLE ADVENTURE • 1988 • Brock Deborah • USA

ANDY FALLS IN LOVE • 1914 • France Charles H. • USA

ANDY GETS A JOB • 1913 • France Charles H. • USA

ANDY GOES A-PIRATING • 1914 • France Charles H. • USA

ANDY GOES ON THE STAGE • 1914 • France Charles H. • USA

ANDY GOES WILD • 1956 • White Jules • SHT • USA

ANDY HARDY COMES HOME • 1958 • Koch Howard W. • USA

ANDY HARDY GETS SPRING FEVER • 1939 • Van Dyke W. S. • USA

ANDY HARDY MEETS DEBUTANTE • 1940 • Seitz George B. • USA

ANDY HARDY'S BLONDE TROUBLE • 1944 • Seitz George B. • USA

ANDY HARDY'S DOUBLE LIFE • 1942 • Seitz George B. • USA

ANDY HARDY'S PRIVATE SECRETARY • 1940 • Seitz George B. • USA

ANDY HAS A TOOTHACHE • 1914 • France Charles H. • USA

ANDY LEARNS TO SWIM • 1914 • France Charles H. • USA

ANDY OF THE ROYAL MOUNTED • 1915 • *Anderson Broncho Billy* • USA

ANDY ON A DIET • 1920 • *Celebrated Players* • SHT • USA

ANDY ON SKATES • 1920 • *Celebrated Players* • SHT • USA

ANDY PANDA GOES FISHING • 1939 • Gillett Burt • ANS • USA

ANDY PANDA IN CROW CRAZY • 1945 • Lundy Dick • ANS • USA

ANDY PANDA'S CRAZY HOUSE • 1940 • Lantz Walter • ANS • USA

ANDY PANDA'S POP • 1941 • Lovy Alex • ANS • USA

ANDY PANDA'S VICTORY GARDEN • 1942 • Lovy Alex • ANS • USA

ANDY PLAYS CUPID • 1914 • France Charles H. • USA

ANDY PLAYS GOLF • 1920 • *Celebrated Players* • SHT • USA

ANDY PLAYS HERO • 1914 • France Charles H. • USA

ANDY PLAYS HOOKY • 1946 • Bernds Edward • SHT • USA

ANDY SPENDS A QUIET DAY AT HOME • 1920 • *Celebrated Players* • SHT • USA

ANDY, THE ACTOR • 1914 • France Charles H. • USA

ANDY VISITS HIS MAMMA-IN-LAW • 1920 • *Celebrated Players* • SHT • USA

ANDY VISITS THE OSTEOPATH • 1920 • *Celebrated Players* • SHT • USA

ANDY WARHOL • 1965 • Menken Marie • SHT • USA

ANDY WARHOL AND HIS CLAN • 1971 • Koetter Bert • DOC • FRG

ANDY WARHOL AND HIS WORK • Jokel Lana • DOC

ANDY WARHOL FILMS JACK SMITH FILMING NORMAL LOVE • 1963 • Warhol Andy • USA

ANDY WARHOL'S BAD • 1977 • Johnson Jed • USA • BAD

ANDY WARHOL'S DRACULA • 1974 • Morrissey Paul, Margheriti Antonio • ITL, FRN • DRACULA VUOLE VIVERE: CERCA SANGUE DI VERGINE (ITL) ○ BLOOD FOR DRACULA (UKN) ○ DRACULA ○ DRACULA CERCA SANGUE DI VERGINE E.. MORI DI SETE! ○ YOUNG DRACULA

ANDY WARHOL'S FRANKENSTEIN • 1974 • Morrissey Paul, Margheriti Antonio • ITL, FRN, FRG • DE LA CHAIR POUR FRANKENSTEIN (FRN) ○ FLESH FOR FRANKENSTEIN (UKN) ○ FRANKENSTEIN EXPERIMENT, THE ○ CARNE PER FRANKENSTEIN (ITL) ○ MOSTRO E IN TAVOLA.. BARON FRANKENSTEIN

ANDY WARHOL'S RESTAURANT see **NUDE RESTAURANT, THE** • 1967

ANDY WARHOL'S WOMEN • 1971 • Morrissey Paul • USA • WOMEN IN REVOLT ○ SEX

ANDY'S DANCING LESSON • 1920 • *Celebrated Players* • SHT • USA

ANDY'S MOTHER-IN-LAW PAYS HIM A VISIT • 1920 • *Celebrated Players* • SHT • USA

ANDY'S NIGHT OUT • 1920 • *Celebrated Players* • SHT • USA

ANDY'S WASHDAY • 1920 • *Celebrated Players* • SHT • USA

ANDY'S WHITE HOLES • 1965 • *Levine Charles (P)* • SHT • USA

ANE DE BURIDAN, L' • 1932 • Ryder Alexandre • FRN

ANE DE JACQUEMENT, L' • 1947-49 • Canolle Jean • SHT • FRN

ANE IMOUTI see **KOTO YUSHU: ANE IMOUTO** • 1967

ANE JALOUX, L' • 1912 • Linder Max • FRN

ANELLO DI SIVA, L' • 1914 • Genina Augusto • ITL

ANELLO MATRIMONIALE, L' • 1979 • Ivaldi Mauro O. • ITL

ANEMA E CORE • 1952 • Mattoli Mario • ITL

ANEMIC • 1987 • Kotetishvili Tato • USS

ANEMONE • 1966 • Garrel Philippe • FRN

ANEMOS TOU MISSOUS, O • 1958 • Tsiforos M. • GRC • WIND OF HATE (USA)

ANESTHESIA • 1938 • Jason Will • SHT • USA

ANFISA • 1912 • Protazanov Yakov • USS

ANFITEATRO FLAVIO • 1947 • Bava Mario • SHT • ITL

ANFUN WA THALATH UYUN • 1972 • Kamal Hussein • EGY • NEZ ET TROIS YEUX, UN

ANG LIMBAS AT ANG LAWIN • 1967 • Santiago Cirio H. • PHL • FAST ONE AND THE HAWK, THE

ANG: LONE see **ANGAENDE LONE** • 1970

ANG MAGKAIBANG DAIDIGNI JUANITA BANANA see **JUANITA BANANA** • 1968

ANG MAGPAKAILANMAN • Red Raymond • SHT • PHL

ANGAENDE LONE • 1970 • Ernst Franz • DNM • CONCERNING LONE ○ RE: LONE ○ ANG: LONE

ANGAREY • 1954 • *Burman S. D. (M)* • IND

ANGE, L' • 1982 • Bokanowski Patrick • FRN

ANGE AU PARADIS, UN • 1973 • Blanc Jean-Pierre • FRN

ANGE DE LA MAISON, L' • 1913 • Perret Leonce • FRN

ANGE DE LA NUIT, L' • 1942 • Berthomieu Andre • FRN

ANGE DE NOEL, L' • 1904 • Melies Georges • FRN • CHRISTMAS ANGEL, THE (USA) ○ DETRESSE ET CHARITE ○ BEGGAR MAIDEN, THE

ANGE DU FOYER, L' • 1936 • Mathot Leon • FRN

ANGE ET DEMON see **MALAKUN WA SHAITAN** • 1960

ANGE ET LA FEMME, L' • 1977 • Carle Gilles • CND, FRN • ANGEL AND THE WOMAN, THE

ANGE GARDIEN, L' • 1933 • Choux Jean • FRN • MARIN CHANTANT, LE

ANGE GARDIEN, L' • 1942 • de Casembroot Jacques • FRN

ANGE GARDIEN, L' • 1978 • Fournier Jacques • FRN, CND

ANGE PASSE, UN • 1975 • Garrel Philippe • FRN

ANGE QUE J'AI VENDU, L' • 1938 • Bernheim Michel • FRN

ANGE QU'ON M'A DONNE, L' • 1945 • Choux Jean • FRN

ANGE ROUGE, L' • 1948 • Daniel-Norman Jacques • FRN • RED ANGEL, THE

ANGEKLAGT NACH PARAGRAPH 218 see **ARZT STELLT FEST... DER** • 1966

ANGEKLAGTE HAT DAS WORT, DER see **MARESI** • 1948

ANGEL • 1937 • Lubitsch Ernst • USA

ANGEL • 1966 • May Derek • SHT • CND

ANGEL • 1967 • Smirnov Andrei • USS

ANGEL • 1983 • Jordan Neil • UKN • DANNY BOY (USA)

ANGEL • 1983 • O'Neil Robert Vincent • USA

ANGEL • 1984 • Howard Sandy • USA

ANGEL • 1990 • Larsson Stig • SWD

ANGEL see **ANGEL CLOUD** • 1975

ANGEL see **ANGELOS** • 1982

ANGEL 3: THE FINAL CHAPTER see **ANGEL III: THE FINAL CHAPTER** • 1988

ANGEL, EL • 1969 • Escriva Vicente • SPN

ANGEL, THE • 1911 • *Reliance* • USA

ANGEL, THE • 1957 • Li Han-Hsiang • HKG

ANGEL ABOVE AND DEVIL BELOW • 1975 • USA

ANGEL ABOVE, DEVIL BELOW • Bolla Dominic • USA

ANGEL AND MAN see **CZLOWIEK I ANIOL** • 1966

ANGEL AND SINNER (USA) see **BOULE-DE-SUIF** • 1945

ANGEL AND THE BAD MAN • 1947 • Grant James Edward • USA

ANGEL AND THE STRANDED TROUPE, THE • 1912 • *Mcdermott Marc* • USA

ANGEL AND THE WOMAN, THE see **ANGE ET LA FEMME, L'** • 1977

ANGEL, ANGEL, DOWN WE GO • 1969 • Thom Robert • USA • CULT OF THE DAMNED

ANGEL AT MY TABLE, AN • 1990 • Campion Jane • NZL

ANGEL BABY • 1961 • Wendkos Paul, Cornfield Hubert • USA

ANGEL BABY (USA) see **ENGELCHEN -ODER DIE JUNGFRAU VON BAMBERG** • 1968

ANGEL CAIDO, EL • 1948 • Ortega Juan J. • MXC, CUB

ANGEL CAIDO, EL • 1971 • *Prod. Escorpion* • MXC

ANGEL CAKE AND AXLE GREASE • 1913 • *Ne Moyer Frances* • USA

ANGEL CERCADA, EL • 1965 • Buchs Julio • SPN

ANGEL CHILD • 1918 • Otto Henry • USA

ANGEL CHILD, THE • 1908 • Porter Edwin S. • USA

ANGEL CITIZENS • 1922 • Ford Francis • USA

ANGEL CITY • 1977 • Jost Jon • USA

ANGEL CITY • 1980 • Leacock Philip?, Carver Steve? • TVM • USA

ANGEL CLOUD • 1975 • ANM • USA • FLOWER ANGEL, THE ○ ANGEL

ANGEL COMES TO BROOKLYN, AN • 1945 • Goodwins Leslie • USA

ANGEL DE LA CALLE, UN • 1966 • Gomez Urquiza Zacarias • CLM, MXC • STREET ANGEL, A

ANGEL DE MAL GENIO, UN • 1964 • Cardona Rene Jr. • MXC

ANGEL DE TRAPO, EL • 1940 • *Lolito Salvador* • ARG

ANGEL DEL INFIERNO • 1958 • Cardona Rene • MXC • HEREDE EL INFIERNO

ANGEL-DEVIL, THE see **ANDEL S DABLEM V TELE** • 1983

ANGEL DOWN FROM HEAVEN, AN see **BAJO UN ANGEL DEL CIELO** • 1942

ANGEL DUST see **POUSSIERE D'ANGE** • 1986

ANGEL DUSTED • 1981 • Lowry Dick • TVM • USA

ANGEL EN EL FANGO, UN • 1970 • *Peliculas Rodriguez* • MXC

ANGEL ESQUIRE • 1919 • Kellino W. P. • UKN

ANGEL ESTA EN LA CUMBRE, EL • 1958 • Pascual Jesus • SPN • ANGEL IS ON THE TOP, THE

ANGEL EXTERMINADOR, EL • 1962 • Bunuel Luis • MXC • EXTERMINATING ANGEL, THE (USA)

ANGEL EYES • 1928 • Lamont Charles • SHT • USA

ANGEL FACE • 1953 • Preminger Otto • USA

ANGEL FACTORY, THE • 1917 • McGill Lawrence • USA

ANGEL FOR SATAN, AN (UKN) see **ANGELO PER SATANA, UN** • 1966

ANGEL FROM H.E.A.T. see **ANGEL OF H.E.A.T. -THE PROTECTORS: BOOK #1** • 1982

ANGEL FROM MUNICH, AN • 1971 • ANS • FRG

ANGEL FROM TEXAS, AN • 1940 • Enright Ray • USA

ANGEL GRIS, EL • 1947 • Iquino Ignacio F. • SPN

ANGEL HAS COME TO BROOKLYN, AN see **ANGELO E SCESO A BROOKLYN, UN** • 1957

ANGEL HEART • 1987 • Parker Alan • USA

ANGEL III: THE FINAL CHAPTER • 1988 • Desimone Tom • USA • ANGEL 3: THE FINAL CHAPTER

ANGEL IN A SKULLCAP see **ANGEL V TIUBETEIKE** • 1970

ANGEL IN A TAXI (USA) see **BALLERINA E BUON DIO** • 1959

ANGEL IN EXILE • 1948 • Dwan Allan, Ford Philip • USA • BLUE LADY, THE

ANGEL IN GREEN • 1987 • Chomsky Marvin • TVM • USA

ANGEL IN MY POCKET • 1969 • Rafkin Alan • USA

ANGEL IN THE CUPBOARD see **ANIOL W SZAFIE** • 1988

ANGEL IN THE HOUSE • 1979 • Jackson Jane • UKN

ANGEL IN THE MASK, THE • 1915 • *Marshall Boyd* • USA

ANGEL IS ON THE TOP, THE see **ANGEL ESTA EN LA CUMBRE, EL** • 1958

ANGEL LEVINE, THE • 1970 • Kadar Jan • USA

ANGEL MINE • 1979 • Blyth David • NZL

ANGEL NEGRO • 1977 • Demicheli Tulio • SPN

ANGEL NEGRO, EL • 1942 • Bustillo Oro Juan • MXC

ANGEL NO.9 • 1975 • Findlay Roberta • USA

ANGEL O DEMONIO • 1947 • Urruchua Victor • MXC

ANGEL OF BROADWAY, THE • 1927 • Weber Lois • USA

ANGEL OF CONTENTION, THE • 1914 • O'Brien John B. • USA

ANGEL OF CROOKED STREET, THE • 1922 • Smith David • USA

ANGEL OF DAWSON'S CLAIM, THE • 1910 • *Lubin* • USA

ANGEL OF DEATH • 1986 • White A. Frank Drew • USA

ANGEL OF DEATH • 1987 • Frank A. M.

ANGEL OF DEATH, THE • 1913 • Brenon Herbert • USA

ANGEL OF DELIVERANCE, THE • 1914 • Buckland Warwick? • UKN

ANGEL OF H.E.A.T. see **ANGEL OF H.E.A.T. -THE PROTECTORS: BOOK #1** • 1982

ANGEL OF H.E.A.T. -THE PROTECTORS: BOOK #1 • 1982 • Schreibman Myrl A. • USA • ANGEL OF H.E.A.T. ○ ANGEL FROM H.E.A.T.

ANGEL OF HIS DREAMS, THE • 1915 • *Guilford Ada* • ASL

ANGEL OF LOVE, AN see **ANGLE OF LOVE, AN** • 1968

ANGEL OF LUST see **VERWUNDBAREN, DIE** • 1967

ANGEL OF MERCIFUL DEATH, THE • 1966 • Skalsky Stepan • CZC

ANGEL OF MERCY • 1939 • Cahn Edward L. • SHT • USA

ANGEL OF MERCY, THE see **MALAK EL RAHMA** • 1947

ANGEL OF MONS, THE • 1915 • Paul Fred, MacBean L. C. • UKN

ANGEL OF PARADISE RANCH, THE • 1911 • Dwan Allan • USA • GIRL OF THE RANCH, THE

ANGEL OF PIETY FLAT, THE • 1916 • *Malatesta Mary* • USA

ANGEL OF POVERTY ROAD, THE • 1917 • Campbell Colin • SHT • USA

ANGEL OF SATURDAY, AN see **DOYOBI NO TENSHI** • 1954

ANGEL OF SPRING, THE • 1915 • Oliver Guy • USA

ANGEL OF THE ATTIC, THE • 1916 • Grandon Francis J. • SHT • USA

ANGEL OF THE BOWERY • 1911 • *Yankee* • USA

ANGEL OF THE CAMP, THE • 1914 • *Maison Edna* • USA

ANGEL OF THE CANYONS • 1913 • Dwan Allan • USA

ANGEL OF THE DESERT, THE • 1913 • Sturgeon Rollin S. • USA

ANGEL OF THE GULCH, THE • 1914 • *Reliance* • USA

ANGEL OF THE HOUSE, THE • 1914 • *Gaumont* • USA

ANGEL OF THE SLUMS, THE • 1911 • Golden Joseph A. • USA

ANGEL OF THE SLUMS, THE • 1913 • Carleton Lloyd B. • USA

ANGEL OF THE STUDIO, THE • 1912 • Salter Harry • USA

ANGEL OF THE WARD, THE • 1915 • Watts Tom • UKN

ANGEL OF VENGEANCE • 1980 • Ferrara Abel • USA • MS.45

ANGEL OF VENGEANCE • 1987 • Mikels Ted V. • USA • WAR CAT

ANGEL OF VENGEANCE -THE FEMALE HAMLET, THE see **INTIKAM MELEGI -KADIN HAMLET** • 1977

ANGEL ON EARTH (USA) see **ENGEL AUF ERDEN, EIN** • 1959

ANGEL ON MY SHOULDER • 1946 • Mayo Archie • USA

ANGEL ON MY SHOULDER • 1980 • Berry John • TVM • USA

ANGEL ON THE AMAZON • 1948 • Auer John H. • USA • DRUMS ALONG THE AMAZON (UKN)

ANGEL ON WHEELS, AN see **ENGEL AUF ERDEN, EIN** • 1959

ANGEL PARADISE • 1914 • Farnum Marshall • USA

ANGEL PASO POR BROOKLYN, UN (SPN) see **ANGELO E SCESO A BROOKLYN, UN** • 1957

ANGEL PASSED OVER BROOKLYN, AN see **ANGELO E SCESO A BROOKLYN, UN** • 1957

ANGEL PUSS • 1944 • Jones Charles M. • ANS • USA

ANGEL RIVER • 1986 • Greene Sergio Olhovich • USA

ANGEL SIN PANTALONES UN • 1947 • Cahen Enrique • ARG

ANGEL STREET (USA) see **GASLIGHT** • 1940

ANGEL TOWN • 1989 • Karson Eric • USA

ANGEL TUVO LA CULPA, UN • 1959 • Lucia Luis • SPN

ANGEL UNAWARE, AN • 1914 • *Stonehouse Ruth* • USA

ANGEL UNAWARES, AN see **HER WONDERFUL SECRET** • 1916

ANGEL UNCHAINED • 1970 • Madden Lee • USA

ANGEL V TIUBETEIKE • 1970 • Aimanov Shaken • USS • ANGEL IN A SKULLCAP

ANGEL WARRIORS • 1971 • Viola Joe • USA

ANGEL WAS A DEVIL, THE • 1971 • Gez Moshe • ISR

ANGEL WHO PAWNED HER HARP, THE • 1954 • Bromly Alan • UKN

ANGEL WITH A SCAR • 1959 • Ritelis Viktors • ASL

ANGEL WITH A TRUMPET see **ANGEL WITH THE TRUMPET, THE** • 1950

ANGEL WITH ONE WING, AN see **KATAYOKU DAKE NO TENSHI** • 1985

ANGEL WITH THE TRUMPET, THE • 1950 • Bushell Anthony • UKN • ANGEL WITH A TRUMPET

ANGEL WITH THE TRUMPET, THE (UKN) see **ENGEL MIT DER POSAUNE, DER** • 1948

ANGEL WORE RED, THE • 1960 • Johnson Nunnally, Russo Mario L. F. (Itl Version) • USA, ITL • SPOSA BELLA, LA (ITL)

ANGEL Y YO, EL • 1966 • Martinez Solares Gilberto • MXC

ANGELA • 1949 • von Borsody Eduard • AUS • BERGWASSER ○ WEISSES GOLD

ANGELA • 1954 • Anton Edoardo, O'Keefe Dennis (Usa Version) • ITL, USA

ANGELA • 1977 • Sagal Boris • CND

ANGELA see **THIS IS THE LIFE** • 1944

ANGELA see **ONOREVOLE ANGELINA, L'** • 1947

ANGELA see **LOVE COMES QUIETLY** • 1973

ANGELA DAVIS ET L'ENCHAINEMENT • 1978 • Simon Jean-Daniel • FRN • ANGELA DAVIS, L'ENCHAINEMENT ○ ANGELA DAVIS -THE WEB ○ ENCHAINEMENT, L'

ANGELA DAVIS, L'ENCHAINEMENT see **ANGELA DAVIS ET L'ENCHAINEMENT** • 1978

ANGELA DAVIS -THE WEB see **ANGELA DAVIS ET L'ENCHAINEMENT** • 1978

ANGELA MORANTE, CRIMEN O SUICIDIO • 1978 • Estrada Jose • MXC

ANGELA -PORTRAIT OF A REVOLUTIONARY • 1971 • du Luart Yolande • DOC • USA
ANGELAN SOTA • 1983 • Bergholm Eija-Elina • FNL • ANGELA'S WAR
ANGELA'S RETURN • 1985 • Wynne Cordell • MTV • CND
ANGELA'S WAR see **ANGELAN SOTA** • 1983
ANGELE • 1934 • Pagnol Marcel • FRN • HEARTBEAT
ANGELE • 1968 • Yersin Yves • DOC • SWT
ANGELES DE LA CALLE • 1953 • Delgado Agustin P. • MXC, CUB
ANGELES DE PUEBLA, LOS • 1966 • del Villar Francisco • MXC
ANGELES DEL ARRABAL • 1949 • de Anda Raul • MXC
ANGELES DEL VOLANTE, LOS • 1957 • Iquino Ignacio F. • SPN
ANGELES GORDOS • 1980 • Summers Manuel • SPN, USA • FAT ANGELS (USA)
ANGELES TERRIBLES, LOS • 1978 • Chalbaud Roman • VNZ
ANGELES Y QUERUBINES • 1971 • Corkidi Rafael • MXC • ANGELS AND CHERUBIM
ANGELI BIANCHI.. ANGELI NERI • 1969 • Scattini Luigi • DOC • ITL • WITCHCRAFT '70 (USA) ○ SATANISTS, THE (UKN) ○ WHITE ANGEL.. BLACK ANGEL
ANGELI CUSTODI, GLI • 1920 • D'Ambra Lucio • ITL
ANGELI DALLE MANI BENDATE, GLI • 1975 • Brazzi Oscar • ITL
ANGELI DEL DUEMILA, GLI • 1969 • Ranieri Honil • ITL
ANGELI DEL QUARTIERE, GLI • 1952 • Borghesio Carlo • ITL
ANGELI SENZA PARADISO • 1970 • Fizzarotti Ettore Maria • ITL
ANGELIC ATTITUDE, AN • 1916 • Mix Tom • SHT • USA
ANGELIC CONVERSATION, THE • 1985 • Jarman Derek • UKN
ANGELIC GREETING see **ANGYALI UDVOZLET** • 1985
ANGELIC ORGASM see **TENSHI NO KOUKOTSU** • 1973
ANGELIC SERVANT, AN (USA) see **PERLE DES SERVANTES, LA** • 1908
ANGELICA • 1939 • Choux Jean • FRN, ITL • ROSA DI SANGUE (ITL) ○ ROSE DE SANG, LA
ANGELICA • 1951 • Crevenna Alfredo B. • MXC • DIA DE LLUVIA, UN
ANGELICA AVVENTURIERA (ITL) see **SOLEIL NOIR** • 1966
ANGELICA E IL GRAN SULTANO (ITL) see **ANGELIQUE ET LE SULTAN** • 1968
ANGELIKA • 1940 • von Alten Jurgen • FRG
ANGELIKA URBAN • 1970 • Sanders Helma • FRG
ANGELIKA (USA) see **DOKTOR HOLL** • 1951
ANGELINA, M.P. see **ONOREVOLE ANGELINA, L'** • 1947
ANGELINA'S BIRTHDAY PRESENT • 1909 • Rosenthal Joe • UKN
ANGELIQUE see **ANGELIQUE IN BLACK LEATHER** • 1968
ANGELIQUE AND IBRAHIM THE CRAZY see **ANJELIK VE DELI IBRAHIM** • 1968
ANGELIQUE AT THE OTTOMAN COURT see **ANJELIK OSMANLI SARAYLARINDA** • 1967
ANGELIQUE ET LE ROI • 1965 • Borderie Bernard • FRN, ITL, FRG • ANGELIQUE UND DER KONIG (FRG)
ANGELIQUE ET LE SULTAN • 1968 • Borderie Bernard • FRN, FRG, ITL • ANGELICA E IL GRAN SULTANO (ITL) ○ ANGELIQUE UND DER SULTAN (FRG)
ANGELIQUE IN BLACK LEATHER • 1968 • Bouchet Angelique • USA • ANGELIQUE
ANGELIQUE, MARQUISE DES ANGES • 1964 • Borderie Bernard • FRN, ITL, FRG • ANGELIQUE (UKN)
ANGELIQUE -THE ROAD TO VERSAILLES (UKN) see **MERVEILLEUSE ANGELIQUE** • 1964
ANGELIQUE (UKN) see **ANGELIQUE, MARQUISE DES ANGES** • 1964
ANGELIQUE UND DER KONIG (FRG) see **ANGELIQUE ET LE ROI** • 1965
ANGELIQUE UND DER SULTAN (FRG) see **ANGELIQUE ET LE SULTAN** • 1968
ANGELITA • 1935 • King Louis • USA • LITTLE ANGEL
ANGELITO • 1960 • Ruiz-Castillo Arturo • SPN
ANGELITO ALMIRANTE • 1962 • Pachin Lucas, Pachin Gallardo • SPN
ANGELITOS DEL TRAPECIO • 1958 • Delgado Agustin P. • MXC
ANGELITOS NEGROS • 1948 • Rodriguez Joselito • MXC
ANGELMAN • Bainbridge Jonathan • SHT • USA
ANGELO BIANCO • 1955 • Matarazzo Raffaello • ITL
ANGELO BIANCO, L' • 1943 • Antamoro Giulio, Sinibaldi Federico • ITL
ANGELO CUSTODE, L' • 1958 • Tomei Giuliano • ITL
ANGELO DEL CRESPUSCOLO, L' • 1942 • Pons Gianni • ITL
ANGELO DEL MIRACOLO, L' • 1945 • Ballerini Piero • ITL
ANGELO DEL PECCATO, L' • 1952 • De Mitri Leonardo • ITL
ANGELO DELLE ALPI, L' • 1957 • Campogalliani Carlo • ITL
ANGELO DI ASSISI, L' see **TRAGICA NOTTE DI ASSISI, LA** • 1961
ANGELO E IL DIAVOLO • 1947 • Camerini Mario • ITL
ANGELO E SCESO A BROOKLYN, UN • 1957 • Vajda Ladislao • ITL, SPN • ANGEL PASO POR BROOKLYN, UN (SPN) ○ ANGEL PASSED OVER BROOKLYN, AN ○ MAN WHO WAGGED HIS TAIL, THE (UKN) ○ ANGEL HAS COME TO BROOKLYN, AN
ANGELO MY LOVE • 1983 • Duvall Robert • USA
ANGELO PER RIBOT, UN • 1963 • Capriata Carlo • ITL
ANGELO PER SATANA, UN • 1966 • Mastrocinque Camillo • ITL • ANGEL FOR SATAN, AN (UKN)
ANGELO TRA LA FOLLA • 1950 • De Mitri Leonardo • ITL
ANGELO, TYRANT OF PADUA see **TIRANNO DI PADOVA, IL** • 1947
ANGELOS • 1982 • Katakouzinos George • GRC • ANGEL
ANGELS • 1976 • *Schiavelli Vincent*
ANGELS • 1979 • Yolles Edie • CND
ANGELS • 1986 • Williams Joe • USA • COMING OF ANGELS: THE SEQUEL, A
ANGELS see **DEVA KANYA** • 1968
ANGELS see **ANGES, LES** • 1989
ANGELS' ALLEY • 1947 • Beaudine William • USA
ANGELS AND CHERUBIM see **ANGELES Y QUERUBINES** • 1971
ANGELS AND DEMONS see **ANJOS E DEMONIOS** • 1970
ANGELS AND PIRATES (USA) see **ANGELS IN THE OUTFIELD** • 1951
ANGELS AND THE PIRATES see **ANGELS IN THE OUTFIELD** • 1951
ANGELS AS HARD AS THEY COME (UKN) see **ANGELS HARD AS THEY COME** • 1971
ANGELS BEHIND BARS • 1986 • Logan Bruce • USA • VENDETTA
ANGELS BRIGADE • 1979 • Clark Greydon • USA
ANGEL'S COAT, THE see **ANDELSKY KABAT** • 1948
ANGELS DIE HARD • 1970 • Compton Richard • USA • ROUGH BOYS
ANGELS DON'T FLY see **REI DAS BERLENGAS, O** • 1977
ANGELS' DOOR • 1971 • Brakhage Stan • USA
ANGEL'S FACE, THE see **TWARZ ANIOLA** • 1970
ANGELS FROM HELL • 1968 • Kessler Bruce • USA
ANGELS HARD AS THEY COME • 1971 • Viola Joe • USA • ANGELS AS HARD AS THEY COME (UKN)
ANGEL'S HOLIDAY • 1937 • Tinling James • USA
ANGELS IN DISGUISE • 1949 • Yarbrough Jean • USA
ANGELS IN HELL see **MALIKA FI GEHENNAM** • 1947
ANGELS IN HELL see **HUGHES AND HARLOW: ANGELS IN HELL** • 1978
ANGELS IN LOVE see **NAR ENGLE ELSKER** • 1985
ANGELS IN PURGATORY see **ENGEL IM FEGEFEUER** • 1964
ANGELS IN THE OUTFIELD • 1951 • Brown Clarence • USA • ANGELS AND PIRATES (USA) ○ ANGELS AND THE PIRATES
ANGELS IN THE SNOW see **ENGLER I SNEEN** • 1982
ANGELS IN VEGAS • 1978 • Kelljan Bob • USA
ANGEL'S LEAP see **SAUT DE L'ANGE, LE** • 1971
ANGEL'S LOVER see **KAMISAMA NO KOIBITO** • 1968
ANGELS NEVER SLEEP see **IN THE AFTERMATH: ANGELS NEVER SLEEP** • 1987
ANGELS OF DARKNESS (USA) see **DONNE PROIBITE** • 1953
ANGELS OF THE STREET (UKN) see **ENGEL VON ST. PAULI, DIE** • 1969
ANGELS OF THE STREETS (USA) see **ANGES DU PECHES, LES** • 1943
ANGELS OF WAR • 1982 • Pike Andrew • DOC • ASL
ANGELS ONE FIVE • 1952 • O'Ferrall George M. • UKN
ANGELS OVER BROADWAY • 1940 • Garmes Lee, Hecht Ben • USA
ANGEL'S PIT, THE see **FOSSA DEGLI ANGELI, LA** • 1937
ANGEL'S TEMPTATION, AN see **TENSHI NO YUWAKU** • 1968
ANGELS UNAWARE • 1912 • Porter Edwin S. • USA
ANGELS UNAWARES • 1916 • *Stonehouse Ruth* • SHT • USA
ANGELS WASH THEIR FACES • 1939 • Enright Ray • USA • BATTLE OF CITY HALL, THE
ANGELS, WE CALL THEM MOTHERS DOWN HERE • 1922 • *Parkinson H. B. (P)* • SHT • UKN
ANGELS WITH BROKEN WINGS • 1941 • Vorhaus Bernard • USA
ANGELS WITH DIRTY FACES • 1938 • Curtiz Michael • USA
ANGELUS, L' • 1899-00 • Blache Alice • FRN
ANGELUS, THE • 1910 • *Selig* • USA
ANGELUS, THE • 1913 • *Rex* • USA
ANGELUS, THE • 1937 • Bentley Thomas • UKN • WHO KILLED FEN MARKHAM?
ANGELUS BELL, THE • 1911 • *Yankee* • USA
ANGELUS BELL, THE (exp.vers.) • 1911 • *Yankee* • USA
ANGELUS DE LA VICTOIRE, L' • 1915 • Perret Leonce • FRN
ANGEMAEUL • 1983 • Lim Kwon-Taek • SKR • VILLAGE IN THE MIST ○ VILLAGE OF MIST, THE ○ MISTY VILLAGE
ANGER • 1980 • Seiler Alexander J. • MTV • SWT
ANGER AQUARIAN ARCANUM • 1965 • Anger Kenneth • SHT • USA
ANGER IN HIS EYES (UKN) see **CON LA RABBIA AGLI OCCHI** • 1976
ANGES, LES • 1972 • Desvilles Jean • FRN
ANGES, LES • 1989 • Berger Jacob • SWT, FRN, SPN • ANGELS
ANGES AUX MAINS NOIRES, LES (FRN) see **LADRA, LA** • 1955
ANGES DU PECHES, LES • 1943 • Bresson Robert • FRN • ANGELS OF THE STREETS (USA) ○ GRANDE CLARTE, LA ○ FILLES DE L'EXIL
ANGES GARDIENS • 1964 • Vetusto A., Reichenbach Francois • SHT • FRN
ANGES NOIRS, LES • 1937 • Rozier Willy • FRN
ANGESTELLTE, DER • 1972 • Sanders Helma • FRG
ANGHAM HABIBY • 1959 • Salman Mohammed • LBN • CHANTS DE MON AMOUR, LES
ANGI VERA • 1979 • Gabor Pal • HNG • EDUCATION OF VERA, THE ○ VERA'S TRAINING
ANGKARA • 1971 • Rojik Omar • MLY • VENDETTA
ANGKOR • 1937 • Merrick George M. • USA
ANGKOR • 1982 • Kitiparaporn Lek, Randall R. • KAMPUCHEA EXPRESS
ANGKOR see **GRANDE CITE, LA** • 1954
ANGKOR, PAROLE D'UN EMPIRE QUI FUT see **ANGKOR, THE LOST CITY** • 1961
ANGKOR, THE LOST CITY • 1961 • Blais Roger • DCS • CND • ANGKOR, PAROLE D'UN EMPIRE QUI FUT
ANGKOR -THE LOST CITY • 1961 • Parker Morten • DOC • CND
ANGLAIS TEL QUE MAX LE PARLE • 1914 • Linder Max • FRN
ANGLAIS TEL QU'ON LE PARLE, L' • 1930 • Boudrioz Robert • FRN
ANGLAIS TEL QU'ON LE PARLE, L' • 1952 • Tedesco Jean • SHT • FRN
ANGLAISE ROMANTIQUE, UNE • 1974 • Losey Joseph • FRN, UKN • ROMANTIC ENGLISHWOMAN, THE (UKN)
ANGLAR, FINNS DOM? • 1961 • Lindgren Lars-Magnus • SWD • DO YOU BELIVE IN ANGELS? (UKN) ○ LOVE MATES (USA)
ANGLE OF LOVE, AN • 1968 • Hennigar William K. • USA • ANGEL OF LOVE, AN
ANGLE SHOOTER see **BACK IN CIRCULATION** • 1937
ANGLERS, THE • 1914 • Parrott Charles • USA
ANGLER'S DREAM, THE • 1906 • Williamson James • UKN
ANGLER'S DREAM, THE • 1910 • *Gaumont* • FRN
ANGLER'S NIGHTMARE, THE (USA) see **CAUCHEMAR DU PECHEUR, LE** • 1905
ANGOIS AVENTURE, L' • 1921 • Protazanov Yakov • FRN
ANGOISSANTE AVENTURE, L' • 1919 • Protazanov Yakov • USS • AGONIZING ADVENTURE
ANGOISSE see **MENACES** • 1939
ANGOISSE, L' • 1913 • Feuillade Louis • FRN
ANGOISSE, L' • 1918 • Hugon Andre • FRN
ANGOISSE AU FOYER, L' • 1915 • Feuillade Louis • FRN
ANGOIXA • 1986 • Luna Bigas • SPN • ANGUISH
ANGOLA • 1961 • Fraga Augusto • SHT • PRT
ANGOLA A UMA NOVA LUSITANIA • 1945 • Ribeiro Antonio Lopes • DOC • PRT
ANGOLA FILE, THE • 1977 • SAF
ANGOLA NA GUERRA E NO PROGRESSO • 1972 • Simoes Quirino • PRT
ANGOLA-PULLMANN • 1932 • Ginet Rene • DOC • FRN
ANGORA LOVE • 1929 • Foster Lewis R. • SHT • USA
ANGRY BOY • 1950 • Hammid Alexander • USA
ANGRY BREED, THE • 1969 • Commons David • USA
ANGRY DRAGON, THE • 1976 • Chiang Hung • HKG
ANGRY FIST, THE • Tien Han • HKG
ANGRY GHOST, THE see **YUREI OOINI IKARU** • 1943
ANGRY GIRL, THE see **KORITSI TIS ORGIS, TO** • 1967
ANGRY GOD, THE • 1948 • Heilner Van Campel • USA, MXC
ANGRY GUEST, THE • 1972 • Chang Ch'Eh • HKG
ANGRY HARVEST • 1985 • Holland Agnieszka • PLN
ANGRY HILLS, THE • 1959 • Aldrich Robert • UKN, USA
ANGRY JOE BASS • 1976 • Reeves Thomas G. • USA • WILD JOE BASS
ANGRY JOURNEY • 1961 • Korabov Nicolai • BUL
ANGRY MAN, THE see **KIZGIN ADAM** • 1968
ANGRY RED PLANET, THE • 1959 • Melchior Ib, Pink Sidney • USA • JOURNEY TO THE 4TH PLANET ○ INVASION OF MARS
ANGRY RIVER • 1970 • Huang Feng • HKG
ANGRY SEA see **CHINOHATE NI IKIRU MONO** • 1960
ANGRY SEA, THE see **IKARI NO UMI** • 1944
ANGRY SILENCE, THE • 1960 • Green Guy • UKN
ANGRY STREET, THE see **IKARI NO MACHI** • 1950
ANGRY YOUNG MEN, THE see **ZORNIGEN JUNGEN MANNER, DIE** • 1960
ANGST.. DIE TRAGODIE DES HAUSES GARRICK see **MORD.. DIE TRAGODIE DES HAUSES GARRICK** • 1920
ANGST • 1928 • Steinhoff Hans • FRG
ANGST • 1976 • Tuhus Oddvar Bull • NRW • TERROR
ANGST • 1983 • Kargl Gerald • AUS • FEAR
ANGST, DIE • 1918 • Mendel Georg Victor • FRG • AUS ANGST
ANGST DES TORMANNS BIEN ELFMETER • 1971 • Wenders Wim • FRG • GOALIE'S ANXIETY AT THE PENALTY KICK, THE (USA) ○ GOALKEEPER'S FEAR OF THE PENALTY, THE (UKN) ○ ANXIETY OF THE GOALKEEPER AT THE PENALTY KICK, THE
ANGST ESSEN SEELE AUF • 1973 • Fassbinder R. W. • FRG • FEAR EATS THE SOUL (UKN) ○ ALI: FEAR EATS THE SOUL ○ ALI
ANGST (FRG) see **PAURA, LA** • 1954
ANGST HABEN UND ANGST MACHEN • 1976 • Zobus Wolfram • FRG • TO BE AFRAID AND MAKE OTHERS AFRAID
ANGST VOR DER ANGST • 1975 • Fassbinder R. W. • FRG • FEAR OF FEAR
ANGUILLA DA 300 MILIONI, UN • 1971 • Samperi Salvatore • ITL
ANGUISH see **TORMENTO** • 1974
ANGUISH see **ANGOIXA** • 1986
ANGUISHED HOURS • 1912 • *Pathe* • USA
ANGULIMAAL • 1960 • *Biswas Anil (M)* • IND
ANGUSTIA • 1947 • Nieves Conde Jose Antonio • SPN
ANGUSTIA PARA O JANTAR • 1975 • Silva Jaime • PRT
ANGYALFOLDI FIATOLOK • 1955 • Jancso Miklos • SHT • HNG • YOUTH OF "THE LAND OF ANGELS", THE ○ CHILDREN OF ANGYALFOLD
ANGYALI UDVOZLET • 1985 • Jeles Andras • HNG • ANGELIC GREETING
ANGYALOK FOLDJE • 1962 • Revesz Gyorgy • HNG • LAND OF ANGELS, THE
ANHOLT -THE PLACE, THE JOURNEY • 1988 • Johansson Lars • DOC • DNM
ANHONEE • 1952 • Abbas Khwaya Ahmad • IND
ANI IMOTO • 1953 • Naruse Mikio • JPN • OLDER BROTHER, YOUNGER SISTER
ANI IMOTO • 1977 • Imai Tadashi • JPN • OLDER BROTHER AND YOUNGER SISTER ○ MON AND INO ○ HIS YOUNGER SISTER
ANI OHEV OTACH ROSA • 1971 • Mizrahi Moshe • ISR • I LOVE YOU ROSA (UKN)
ANI TO SONO IMOTO • 1939 • Shimazu Yasujiro • JPN • BROTHER AND HIS YOUNGER SISTER, A
ANI TO SONO IMOTO • 1956 • Shimazu Yasujiro • JPN • BROTHER AND SISTER
ANI YERUSHALMI • 1971 • Gaon Yehoram • ISR • I WAS BORN IN JERUSALEM
ANIAKCHAK, THE STORY OF HELL ON EARTH • 1933 • Hubbard Bernard R. • USA
ANIHTI EPISOLI • 1969 • Stamboulopoulos George • GRC • OPEN LETTER ○ ANIKTI EPISTOLI
ANIJAM • 1986 • Newland Marvin • ANS • CND
ANIKI-BOBO • 1942 • de Oliveira Manoel • PRT
ANIKI NO KOIBITO • 1968 • Moritani Shiro • JPN • MY BROTHER, MY LOVE
ANIKINA VREMENA • 1954 • Pogacic Vladimir • YGS • LEGENDS ABOUT ANIKA
ANIKTI EPISTOLI see **ANIHTI EPISOLI** • 1969
ANILLO DE COMPROMISO • 1951 • Gomez Muriel Emilio • MXC
ANIMA ALLEGRA • 1918 • Roberti Roberto Leone • ITL
ANIMA DEL DEMI-MONDE, L' • 1913 • Negroni Baldassare • ITL
ANIMA MUNDI • 1969 • Johansson Erling • SHT • SWD
ANIMA NERA • 1962 • Rossellini Roberto • ITL
ANIMA PERSA • 1976 • Risi Dino • ITL • LOST SOUL
ANIMA -SYMPHONIE PHANTASTIQUE • 1981 • Leber Titus • AUS
ANIMA TORMENTATA • 1919 • Caserini Mario • ITL

ANIMACION EN LA SALA DE ESPERA • 1981 • Coronado J. Manuel, Sanz Carlos Rodriguez • SPN
ANIMAL, L' • 1977 • Zidi Claude • FRN
ANIMAL, THE • 1913 • Dwan Allan • USA
ANIMAL, THE • 1968 • Frost R. L. • USA
ANIMAL BEHAVIOR • 1985 • Bowen Jenny • USA
ANIMAL CRACKER CIRCUS • 1938 • Harrison Ben • ANS • USA
ANIMAL CRACKERS • 1930 • Heerman Victor • USA
ANIMAL DOUE DE DERAISON, UN • 1976 • Kast Pierre • FRN, BRZ
ANIMAL FAIR, THE • 1931 • Foster John, Davis Mannie • ANS • USA
ANIMAL FAIR, THE • 1959 • Kneitel Seymour • ANS • USA
ANIMAL FARM • 1955 • Halas John, Batchelor Joy • ANM • UKN
ANIMAL HOUSE see **NATIONAL LAMPOON'S ANIMAL HOUSE** • 1978
ANIMAL IMITATIONS • 1906 • Gilbert Arthur • UKN
ANIMAL KINGDOM, THE • 1932 • Griffith Edward H., Cukor George (U/c) • USA • WOMAN IN HIS HOUSE, THE (UKN)
ANIMAL KINGDOM, THE see **ONE MORE TOMORROW** • 1946
ANIMAL LOVE • 1969 • Kenny • USA
ANIMAL MOVIE, THE • 1966 • Munro Grant, Tunis Ron • ANS • CND • ANIMAUX EN MARCHE, LES
ANIMAL VEGETABLE MINERAL • 1955 • Halas John • ANS • UKN
ANIMAL WITHIN, THE • 1912 • Dwan Allan • USA
ANIMAL WORLD, THE • 1956 • Allen Irwin • USA
ANIMALE CHIAMATO UOMO, UN • 1972 • Mauri Roberto • ITL
ANIMALI PAZZI • 1939 • Bragaglia Carlo Ludovico • ITL • BELLA FACCIA IL CUOR L'ALLACCIA ○ VICINO A TE COL CUORE ○ IO MUOIO DISPERATA ○ FIORI D'ARANCIO
ANIMALS • 1973 • *Halas John (P)* • ANS • UKN
ANIMALS, THE • 1971 • Joy Ron • USA • FIVE SAVAGE MEN
ANIMALS, THE see **ANIMAUX, LES** • 1959
ANIMALS AND BRIGANDS see **ZVIRATKA A PETROVSTI** • 1946
ANIMALS AND THE BRIGANDS, THE see **ZVIRATKA A PETROVSTI** • 1946
ANIMALS ARE BEAUTIFUL PEOPLE see **BEAUTIFUL PEOPLE** • 1974
ANIMALS ARE PEOPLE TOO (USA) see **BEAUTIFUL PEOPLE** • 1974
ANIMALS FILM, THE • 1982 • Schonfeld Victor, Alaux Myriam • DOC • UKN, USA
ANIMALS IN ACTION • 1955 • *Smith Pete* • SHT • USA
ANIMALS IN MOTION • 1968 • Straiton John S. • SHT • CND
ANIMALS IN THE CITY see **ZVIRATA VE MESTE** • 1988
ANIMALS OF EDEN AND AFTER, THE • 1970 • Brakhage Stan • USA
ANIMALS OF THE ARENA, THE see **ZWIERZETA ARENY** • 1966
ANIMALS OF THE ORCHESTRA, THE • 1971 • Cooper Don • ANS • USA
ANIMALYMPICS • 1979 • Lisberger Steven • ANM • USA
ANIMARATHON • 1984 • Garcia-Sanz Raul • ANS • SPN
ANIMAS TRUJANO, EL HOMBRE IMPORTANTE • 1961 • Rodriguez Ismael • MXC • IMPORTANT MAN, THE (USA) ○ HOMBRE IMPORTANTE, EL ○ MAYORDOMO, EL
ANIMATED BATHTUB, THE • 1912 • *Quirk Billy* • USA
ANIMATED CARTOONS: THE TOY THAT GREW UP • Leenhardt Roger • USA
ANIMATED CLOWN PORTRAIT • 1898 • Smith G. A. • UKN
ANIMATED COSTUMES, THE (USA) see **COSTUMES ANIMES, LES** • 1904
ANIMATED COTTON • 1909 • Booth W. R. • UKN
ANIMATED DOLL, AN • 1908 • *Essanay* • USA
ANIMATED DRESS STAND, THE • 1906 • Green Tom? • UKN
ANIMATED FAN, THE see **EVENTAIL ANIME, L'** • 1909
ANIMATED FOREST, THE see **BOSQUE ANIMADO, EL** • 1988
ANIMATED GENESIS • 1951 • Foldes Joan, Foldes Peter • ANS • UKN
ANIMATED GROUCH CHASERS • 1915-16 • Barre Raoul • ANS • USA
ANIMATED JOURNAL, THE see **JOURNAL ANIME, LE** • 1908
ANIMATED LUNCHEON, THE • 1900 • Porter Edwin S. • USA
ANIMATED MATCHES • 1908 • Cooper Arthur • UKN
ANIMATED MATCHES, THE see **ALLUMETTES ANIMEES, LES** • 1908
ANIMATED MOTION • 1977 • McLaren Norman, Munro Grant • ASS • CND • MOUVEMENT IMAGE PAR IMAGE, LE
ANIMATED PAINTING • 1904 • Porter Edwin S.? • USA
ANIMATED PAINTING • Wein Jeff • ANS • USA
ANIMATED PICTURE STUDIO • 1903 • *Biograph* • USA
ANIMATED PILLAR BOX, THE see **OUR NEW PILLAR BOX** • 1907
ANIMATED POSTER, THE • 1903 • Porter Edwin S. • USA
ANIMATED POSTERS • 1949 • Hofman Eduard • ANS • CZC
ANIMATED POSTERS, THE (USA) see **AFFICHES ANIMEES, LES** • 1908
ANIMATED PUTTY • 1911 • Booth W. R. • UKN
ANIMATED SCARECROW, THE • 1910 • *Atlas* • USA
ANIMATED SNOWBALLS • 1908 • Porter Edwin S. • USA
ANIMATED STATUE, THE • 1903 • *Warwick Trading Co* • UKN
ANIMATED STATUES, THE see **STATUES ANIMEES, LES** • 1906
ANIMATED TOYS • 1912 • Booth W. R. • UKN
ANIMATED WEEKLY • 1912-14 • Cohl Emile • ASS • USA
ANIMATION FOR LIVE ACTION • 1978 • Neubauer Vera • UKN
ANIMATION IN THE NETHERLANDS see **CINEMA D'ANIMATION AUX PAY-BAS, LE** • 1987
ANIMATION POWDERS • 1910 • *Atlas* • USA
ANIMATO • 1988 • Bogdanov Pencho • ANM • BUL
ANIMATRICE POUR COUPLES DEFICIENTS • 1980 • Gregory Gerard • FRN
ANIMAUX, LES • 1959 • Rossif Frederic • DOC • FRN • ANIMALS, THE
ANIMAUX DOMESTIQUES, LES • 1916-24 • Lortac • ANS • FRN
ANIMAUX EN MARCHE, LES see **ANIMAL MOVIE, THE** • 1966
ANIME BUIE • 1915 • Ghione Emilio • ITL
ANIME ERRANTI see **ULTIMO ADDIO, L'** • 1942
ANIME IN CATENA see **TEMPESTA D'ANIME** • 1946
ANIME IN TUMULTO • 1942 • Del Torre Giulio • ITL
ANINO NI SISA • 1968 • Pacheco Lauro • PHL • SHADOW OF SISA, THE
ANIOL W SZAFIE • 1988 • Rozewicz Stanislaw • PLN • ANGEL IN THE CUPBOARD
ANISSA HANAFI, AL- • 1954 • Wahab Fatin Abdel • EGY • MLLE HANAFI
ANITA • 1967 • Khosla Raj • IND
ANITA • 1969 • *Distripix* • USA
ANITA • 1973 • Wickman Torgny • SWD
ANITA CAMACHO • 1987 • Anzola Alfredo J. • VNZ
ANITA -DANCES OF THE DEVIL see **ANITA -TANZE DES LASTERS** • 1988
ANITA ELLIS: FOR THE RECORD • 1980 • Silver Tony • SHT • USA
ANITA GARIBALDI see **CAMICIE ROSSE** • 1952
ANITA JO • 1919 • Buchowetzki Dimitri • FRG
ANITA NEEDS ME • 1963 • Kuchar George • SHT • USA
ANITA -TANZE DES LASTERS • 1988 • von Praunheim Rosa • FRG • ANITA -DANCES OF THE DEVIL
ANITA (USA) see **TRANCE** • 1920
ANITA'S BUTTERFLY • 1915 • Dillon John Francis • USA
ANITRA AL'ARANCIA, L' • 1975 • Salce Luciano • ITL • DUCK IN ORANGE SAUCE (USA)
ANITRA'S DANCE • 1938 • Bute Mary Ellen • SHT • USA
ANIUTA • 1960 • Andjaparidze Marija • USS
ANIVERSARIO DEL FALLECIMIENTO DE LA SUEGRA DE ENHART, EL • 1913 • *Alva Brothers* • MXC
ANJA • 1927 • Preobrazhenskaya Olga • USS
ANJALA, THE DANCER (UKN) see **BALETTPRIMADONNAN** • 1916
ANJAM • 1968 • Kumar Shiv • IND
ANJANGARB • 1948 • Roy Bimal • IND
ANJELIK OSMANLI SARAYLARINDA • 1967 • Erakalin Ulku • TRK • ANGELIQUE AT THE OTTOMAN COURT
ANJELIK VE DELI IBRAHIM • 1968 • Dogan Suha • TRK • ANGELIQUE AND IBRAHIM THE CRAZY
ANJING-ANJING GELADAK • 1972 • Prijono Ami • INN
ANJINHOS NAO VOAM, OS see **REI DAS BERLENGAS, O** • 1977
ANJO ASSASSINO, O • 1967 • Azevedo Dionisio • BRZ • MURDERING ANGEL, THE
ANJO DA NOITE, O • 1974 • Khouri Walter Hugo • BRZ • NIGHT ANGEL, THE
ANJO-KE NO BUTOKAI • 1947 • Yoshimura Kozaburo • JPN • BALL AT THE ANJO HOUSE, A ○ BALL OF THE ANJO FAMILY, THE
ANJO MAU, UM • 1972 • Santos Roberto • BRZ
ANJO NASCEU, UM • 1970 • Bressane Julio • BRZ
ANJOS DA NOITE • 1988 • Barros Wilson • BRZ • NIGHT ANGELS
ANJOS DO ARRABALDE • 1986 • Reicembach Carlos Oscar • BRZ • SUBURBAN ANGELS
ANJOS E DEMONIOS • 1970 • Christensen Carlos Hugo • BRZ • ANGELS AND DEMONS
ANJOU • 1977 • Leenhardt Roger • DCS • FRN
ANJU TO ZUSHIO-MARU • 1961 • Yabushita Taiji, Arikawa Yugo • ANM • JPN • LITTLEST WARRIOR, THE (USA) ○ ORPHAN BROTHER, THE
ANKARA -HEART OF TURKEY see **ANKARA -SERDCHE TURKIYE** • 1934
ANKARA POSTASSI • 1929 • Muhssin Ertugrul • TRK • COURIER OF ANGORA, THE (USA)
ANKARA -SERDCHE TURKIYE • 1934 • Yutkevich Sergei, Arnstam Leo • DOC • USS • ANKARA -HEART OF TURKEY
ANKEMAN JARL • 1945 • Wallen Sigurd • SWD • JARL THE WIDOWER
ANKHEN • 1968 • Sagar Ramanand • IND • EYES
ANKHIN DEKHI • 1976 • Bedi Rajendra Singh • IND
ANKLES AWAY • 1938 • Parrott Charles • SHT • USA
ANKLES PREFERRED • 1927 • Blystone John G. • USA
ANKO KUGAI • 1956 • Yamamoto Kajiro • JPN • UNDERWORLD, THE
ANKOKUGAI NO BIJO • 1957 • Suzuki Seijun • JPN
ANKOKUGAI-NO DANKON • 1960 • Okamoto Kihachi • JPN • BLUEPRINT FOR MURDER
ANKOKUGAI NO KAOYAKU • 1959 • Okamoto Kihachi • JPN • BIG BOSS
ANKOKUGAI NO TAIKETSU • 1960 • Okamoto Kihachi • JPN • LAST GUNFIGHT
ANKOKUGAI SAIGO NO HI • 1962 • Inoue Umeji • JPN • HELL'S KITCHEN
ANKUR • 1974 • Benegal Shyam • IND • SEEDLING, THE (UKN)
ANMELDUNG see **AANMELDING** • 1964
ANN • 1913 • Edwin Walter • USA
ANN AND EVE see **ANN OCH EVE -DE EROTISKA** • 1969
ANN AND THE VAMPIRE see **ANNA I WAMPIR** • 1981
ANN CARVER'S PROFESSION • 1933 • Buzzell Edward • USA
ANN JILLIAN STORY, THE • 1988 • Allen Corey • TVM • USA
ANN KARENINA see **ANNA KARYENINA** • 1968
ANN OCH EVE -DE EROTISKA • 1969 • Mattsson Arne • SWD • ANYBODY'S (UKN) ○ ANN AND EVE
ANN OF THE TRAILS • 1913 • Bowman William J. • USA
ANN THE BLACKSMITH • 1914 • Davis Ulysses • USA
ANN VICKERS • 1933 • Cromwell John • USA
ANNA • 1918 • Edwards Henry • UKN
ANNA • 1936 • Piryof I.
ANNA • 1951 • Lattuada Alberto • ITL
ANNA • 1967 • Koralnik Pierre • SWT, FRN
ANNA • 1969 • Trzos-Rastawiecki Andrzej • DOC • PLN
ANNA • 1970 • Donner Jorn • FNL
ANNA • 1973 • Grifi Alberto • ITL
ANNA • 1981 • Meszaros Marta • HNG
ANNA • 1987 • Bogayevicz Yurek • USA
ANNA see **EDES ANNA** • 1958
ANNA AND COMMANDORE • 1974 • Khrinyuk Yevgyeni • USS
ANNA AND ELIZABETH (USA) see **ANNA UND ELIZABETH** • 1933
ANNA AND GABRIEL see **ANA Y GABRIEL** • 1978
ANNA AND THE KING OF SIAM • 1946 • Cromwell John • USA
ANNA AND THE WOLVES (USA) see **ANA Y LOS LOBOS** • 1972
ANNA AND TOTO • 1977 • Petersen Wolfgang • FRG
ANNA ASCENDS • 1922 • Fleming Victor • USA
ANNA-BALL see **FUREDI ANNA-BAL** • 1973
ANNA & BELLA • 1986 • Ring Borge • ANM • NTH
ANNA BOLEYN • 1921 • Lubitsch Ernst • FRG • DECEPTION (USA) ○ ANNE BOLEYN (UKN)
ANNA, CHILD OF THE DAFFODILS see **KIND VAN DE ZON** • 1975
ANNA CHRISTIE • 1923 • Wray John Griffith • USA
ANNA CHRISTIE • 1929 • Brown Clarence • USA
ANNA CHRISTIE • 1930 • Feyder Jacques • FRG
ANNA CHRISTIE see **KIRI NO MINATO** • 1923
ANNA-CLARA AND HER BROTHERS see **ANNA-CLARA OCH HENNES BRODER** • 1923
ANNA-CLARA OCH HENNES BRODER • 1923 • Lindberg Per • SWD • ANNA-CLARA AND HER BROTHERS
ANNA CROSS, THE • 1954 • Annensky Isider • USS
ANNA CUISSES ENTROUVERTES • 1979 • Benazeraf Jose • FRN • ANNA LES CUISSES ENTROVERTES
ANNA DE BOLEYN A LA TOUR DE LONDRES see **TOUR DE LONDRES: OU, LES DERNIER MOMENTS D'ANNE DE BOLEYN, LA** • 1905
ANNA DI BROOKLYN • 1958 • Lastricati Carlo, Denham Reginald • ITL, USA • FAST AND SEXY (USA) ○ ANNA OF BROOKLYN
ANNA FAVETTI • 1938 • Waschneck Erich • FRG
ANNA GARIBALDI • 1910 • Caserini Mario • ITL
ANNA GOLDIN -LETZTE HEXE • 1989 • Pinkus Gertrud, Portmann Stephan • SWT, FRG, FRN • ANNA GOLDIN -THE LAST WITCH
ANNA GOLDIN -THE LAST WITCH see **ANNA GOLDIN -LETZTE HEXE** • 1989
ANNA I WAMPIR • 1981 • Kidawa Janusz • PLN • ANN AND THE VAMPIRE
ANNA KARAMOZOV • 1990 • Khamdamov Rustam • USS
ANNA KARENINA • 1914 • Gardin Vladimir • USS
ANNA KARENINA • 1915 • Edwards J. Gordon • USA
ANNA KARENINA • 1920 • Zelnik Friedrich • FRG
ANNA KARENINA • 1927 • Buchowetzki Dimitri • USA
ANNA KARENINA • 1935 • Brown Clarence • USA
ANNA KARENINA • 1948 • Duvivier Julien • UKN
ANNA KARENINA • 1985 • Langton Simon • TVM • USA
ANNA KARENINA see **ANNA KARYENINA** • 1975
ANNA KARENINA (UKN) see **LOVE** • 1927
ANNA KARYENINA • 1968 • Zarkhi Alexander • USS • ANN KARENINA
ANNA KARYENINA • 1975 • Pilikhina Margarita • USS • ANNA KARENINA
ANNA LA BONNE • 1958 • Kurnel Harry • SHT • BLG
ANNA LA BONNE • 1963 • Jutra Claude • SHT • FRN
ANNA LANS • 1943 • Carlsten Rune • SWD
ANNA LES CUISSES ENTROVERTES see **ANNA CUISSES ENTROUVERTES** • 1979
ANNA LIZZA • 1967 • Villaflor Romy • PHL
ANNA LUCASTA • 1949 • Rapper Irving • USA
ANNA LUCASTA • 1958 • Laven Arnold • USA
ANNA MAGNANI: UN FILM D'AMOUR see **IO SONO ANNA MAGNANI** • 1979
ANNA MAKOSSA • 1979 • Beni Alphonse • FRN, CND
ANNA MARIA • 1920 • *Transatlantic Film Co* • FRG
ANNA, MY DARLING (USA) see **SOMMARAVENTYR, ETT** • 1965
ANNA NO AJI • 1967 • Okuwaki Toshio • JPN • TASTE OF WOMEN
ANNA OBSESSED • Martin • USA
ANNA OF BROOKLYN see **ANNA DI BROOKLYN** • 1958
ANNA OF RHODES • 1950 • Philippou John, Gazlades Michael
ANNA PAVLOVA • 1954 • Brinson Peter • UKN
ANNA PAVLOVA see **ANNA PAVLOVA: A WOMAN FOR ALL TIME** • 1985
ANNA PAVLOVA: A WOMAN FOR ALL TIME • 1985 • Lotyanu Emil • USS, UKN • ANNA PAVLOVA
ANNA, PERDONAMI! • 1953 • Boccia Tanio • ITL
ANNA PETROVNA • 1916 • Lolli Alberto Carlo • ITL
ANNA PROLETARKA • 1952 • Stekly Karel • CZC • ANNA THE PROLETARIAN
ANNA QUEL PARTICOLARE PIACERE • 1973 • Carnimeo Giuliano • ITL • ANNA: THE PLEASURE, THE TORMENT (USA) ○ SECRETS OF A CALL GIRL (UKN)
ANNA SUSANNA • 1952 • Nicholas Richard • GDR
ANNA SZABO see **SZABONE** • 1949
ANNA THE ADVENTURESS • 1920 • Hepworth Cecil M. • UKN
ANNA: THE PLEASURE, THE TORMENT (USA) see **ANNA QUEL PARTICOLARE PIACERE** • 1973
ANNA THE PROLETARIAN see **ANNA PROLETARKA** • 1952
ANNA TO THE INFINITE POWER • 1982 • Wiemer Robert • USA • GENETIC CONTACT
ANNA UND ELIZABETH • 1933 • Wisbar Frank • FRG • ANNA AND ELIZABETH (USA)
ANNA WENT WRONG see **HERLOCK SHOLMES IN BE-A-LIVE CROOK** • 1930
ANNABEL LEE • *Spring Robert (P)* • SHT • USA
ANNABEL LEE • 1921 • Scully William J. • USA
ANNABEL TAKES A TOUR • 1938 • Landers Lew • USA
ANNABELLA • 1969 • Thome Rudolf • FRG
ANNABELLE LEE • 1972 • Daniels Harold • USA, PRU
ANNABELLE THE DANCER see **SERPENTINE DANCE -ANNABELLE** • 1897
ANNABELLE'S AFFAIRS • 1931 • Werker Alfred L. • USA
ANNABEL'S ROMANCE • 1916 • Gasnier Louis J. • USA
ANNANACKS, LES see **ANNANACKS, THE** • 1962
ANNANACKS, THE • 1962 • Bonniere Rene • DCS • CND • ANNANACKS, LES
ANNAPOLI see **PUITS EN FLAMMES** • 1936
ANNAPOLIS • 1928 • Cabanne W. Christy • USA • BRANDED A COWARD (UKN)
ANNAPOLIS FAREWELL • 1935 • Hall Alexander • USA • GENTLEMEN OF THE NAVY (UKN)
ANNAPOLIS SALUTE • 1937 • Cabanne W. Christy • USA • SALUTE TO ROMANCE (UKN)
ANNAPOLIS STORY, AN • 1955 • Siegel Don • USA • BLUE AND THE GOLD, THE (UKN)
ANNAPURNA (USA) see **VICTOIRE SUR L'ANNAPURNA** • 1953
ANNA'S HAPPINESS • 1971 • Rogov Yu. • USS
ANNA'S MOTHER see **ANNA'S MUTTER** • 1984
ANNA'S MUTTER • 1984 • Driest Burkhard • FRG • ANNA'S MOTHER
ANNA'S SIN see **PECCATO DI ANNA, IL** • 1953
ANNE AGAINST THE WORLD • 1929 • Worne Duke • USA

ANNE AND MURIEL see **DEUX ANGLAISES ET LE CONTINENT, LES** • 1971
ANNE BOLEYN (UKN) see **ANNA BOLEYN** • 1921
ANNE DEVLIN • 1984 • Murphy Pat • IRL
ANNE-LIESE VON DESSAU, DIE • 1925 • Bauer James • FRG
ANNE-MARIE • 1936 • Bernard Raymond • FRN
ANNE OF AVONLEA • 1987 • Sullivan Kevin • TVM • CND • ANNE OF GREEN GABLES: THE SEQUEL
ANNE OF GREEN GABLES • 1919 • Taylor William D. • USA
ANNE OF GREEN GABLES • 1934 • Nicholls George Jr. • USA
ANNE OF GREEN GABLES • 1985 • Sullivan Kevin • TVM • CND
ANNE OF GREEN GABLES: THE SEQUEL see **ANNE OF AVONLEA** • 1987
ANNE OF LITTLE SMOKY • 1921 • Connor Edward • USA
ANNE OF THE GOLDEN HEART • 1914 • Davis Ulysses • USA
ANNE OF THE INDIES • 1951 • Tourneur Jacques • USA
ANNE OF THE MINES • 1914 • Davis Ulysses • USA
ANNE OF THE THOUSAND DAYS • 1970 • Jarrott Charles • UKN
ANNE OF WINDY POPLARS • 1940 • Hively Jack • USA • ANNE OF WINDY WILLOWS (UKN)
ANNE OF WINDY WILLOWS (UKN) see **ANNE OF WINDY POPLARS** • 1940
ANNE ONE HUNDRED • 1933 • Edwards Henry • UKN
ANNE OU LA MORT D'UN PILOTE • 1974 • Doniol-Valcroze Jacques • FRN
ANNE TRISTER • 1986 • Pool Lea • CND
ANNEAU FATAL, L' • 1912 • Feuillade Louis • FRN
ANNEE 1863, L' • 1922 • Puchalski Eduard • PLN
ANNEE A VAUCLUSE, UNE • 1964 • Garceau Raymond • DCS • CND
ANNEE DE JACCO, L' • 1979 • Bal Walter • BLG, FRN
ANNEE DE TREIZE LUNES, L' • 1988 • Theubet Bertrand • SWT
ANNEE DERNIERE A MARIENBAD, L' • 1961 • Resnais Alain • FRN, ITL • ANNO SCORSO A MARIENBAD ,L' (ITL) ○ LAST YEAR AT MARIENBAD (USA) ○ LAST YEAR IN MARIENBAD (UKN)
ANNEE DES MEDUSES, L' • 1984 • Frank Christopher • FRN
ANNEE DU BAC, L' • 1963 • Delbez Maurice, Lacour Jose-Andre • FRN
ANNEE PROCHRAINE SI TOUT VA BIEN • 1981 • Hubert Jean-Loup • FRN
ANNEE SAINTE, L' • 1976 • Girault Jean • FRN, ITL • HOLY SAINT, THE (USA)
ANNEE SE MEURT, UNE • 1951 • Loew Jacques • SHT • FRN
ANNEES 25, LES • 1966 • Kaplan Nelly • FRN
ANNEES 60: CHERCHEZ L'IDOLE, LES • Boisrond Michel • FRN
ANNEES 80, LES • 1983 • Akerman Chantal • BLG, FRN • GOLDEN EIGHTIES
ANNEES DE REVES, LES • 1982 • Labrecque Jean-Claude • CND • YEARS OF DREAMS AND REVOLTS
ANNEES DECLIC, LES • 1983 • Depardon Raymond • FRN
ANNEES FOLLES, LES • 1960 • Torrent Henri, Alexandresco Mirea • FRN
ANNEES LUMIERE, LES • 1972 • Chapot Jean • FRN, SWT
ANNEES LUMIERE, LES (FRN) see **LIGHT YEARS AWAY** • 1981
ANNEES SANDWICHES, LES • 1988 • Boutron Pierre • FRN
ANNELIE • 1941 • von Baky Josef • FRG • GESCHICHTE EINES LEBENS, DIE
ANNEMARIE • 1936 • Buch Fritz Peter • FRG • GESCHICHTE EINER JUNGEN LIEBE, DIE
ANNEMARIE, DIE BRAUT DER KOMPAGNIE • 1932 • Boese Carl • FRG
ANNEMARIE UND IHR ULAN • 1926 • Eriksen Erich • FRG
ANNEMIEK • 1966 • van Gelder Arend • NTH
ANNETTE see **NOCHE DE TORMENTA** • 1952
ANNETTE ET LA DAME BLONDE • 1941 • Dreville Jean • FRN
ANNETTE IM PARADIES • 1934 • Obal Max • FRG • KUSS NACH LADENSCHLUSS, EIN
ANNETTE MESSAGER, REINE DE LA NUIT • 1986 • Demontaut Philippe • FRN
ANNEX, THE • 1984 • Saltzman Deepa Mehta • MTV • CND
ANNEXING BILL • 1918 • Parker Albert • USA
ANNI CHE NON RITORNANO, GLI (ITL) see **MEILLEURE PART, LA** • 1956
ANNI DIFFICILI • 1948 • Zampa Luigi • ITL • DIFFICULT YEARS (USA) ○ LITTLE MAN, THE (UKN)
ANNI DURI • 1979 • Baldi Gian Vittorio • MTV • ITL • MEMORIA E GLI ANNI, LA
ANNI FACILI • 1953 • Zampa Luigi • ITL • EASY YEARS
ANNI RUGGENTI • 1962 • Zampa Luigi • ITL • ROARING YEARS, THE
ANNI STRUGGENTI, GLI see **CONCORRENTE, IL** • 1979
ANNI TAHTOO AIDIN • 1988 • Manttari Anssi • FNL • MOTHER WANTED
ANNIBALE • 1959 • Bragaglia Carlo Ludovico, Ulmer Edgar G. • ITL • HANNIBAL
ANNIE • 1910 • *Imp* • USA
ANNIE • 1948 • Neufeld Max • FRG, AUS
ANNIE • 1982 • Huston John • USA
ANNIE BELL see **MORKE PUNKT, DET** • 1911
ANNIE CAT • 1967 • Balling Erik • DNM
ANNIE CRAWLS UPSTAIRS • 1912 • *Coughlin Helen* • USA
ANNIE DOESN'T LIVE HERE (UKN) see **SWEEPSTAKE ANNIE** • 1935
ANNIE-FOR-SPITE • 1917 • Kirkwood James • USA
ANNIE GET YOUR GUN • 1950 • Sidney George • USA
ANNIE HALL • 1977 • Allen Woody • USA
ANNIE, LA JIERGE DE SAINT TROPEZ • 1975 • Sulistrowski Zygmunt • FRN • VIRGIN OF THE BEACHES
ANNIE LAURIE • 1913 • McGill Lawrence • USA
ANNIE LAURIE • 1916 • Hepworth Cecil M. • UKN
ANNIE LAURIE • 1924-26 • Fleischer Dave • ANS • USA
ANNIE LAURIE • 1927 • Robertson John S. • USA
ANNIE LAURIE • 1936 • Tennyson Walter • UKN
ANNIE, LEAVE THE ROOM! • 1935 • Hiscott Leslie • UKN
ANNIE MAE: BRAVE-HEARTED WOMAN • 1979 • Ritz Lan Brooks • DOC • USA
ANNIE MOVED AWAY • 1934 • Lantz Walter, Nolan William • ANS • USA
ANNIE OAKLEY • 1935 • Stevens George • USA
ANNIE ROWLEY'S FORTUNE • 1913 • Johnson Arthur • USA
ANNIE WAS A WONDER • 1949 • Cahn Edward L. • SHT • USA
ANNIE'S COMING OUT • 1984 • Brealey Gil • ASL • TEST OF LOVE, A (USA)
ANNIHILATION OF BERLIN, THE see **ZAGLADA BERLIN** • 1945
ANNIHILATOR • 1986 • Chapman Michael • TVM • USA
ANNIHILATORS, THE • 1985 • Sellier Charles E. Jr. • USA
ANNIVERSAIRE, L' • 1972 • Minot Gilbert • GUN
ANNIVERSARY, THE • 1965 • Gedris Marionas Vintzo • SHT • USS
ANNIVERSARY, THE • 1967 • Baker Roy Ward • UKN
ANNIVERSARY, THE see **ROCZNICA** • 1969
ANNIVERSARY, THE (UKN) see **HEUREUX ANNIVERSAIRE** • 1962
ANNIVERSARY OF THE REVOLUTION see **GODOVSHCHINA REVOLYUTSII** • 1919
ANNIVERSARY TROUBLE • 1935 • Meins Gus • SHT • USA
ANNO 79 DOPO CRISTO see **ANNO 79, LA DISTRUZIONE DI ERCOLANO** • 1963
ANNO 79, LA DISTRUZIONE DI ERCOLANO • 1963 • Parolini Gianfranco • ITL, FRN • DERNIERS JOURS D'HERCULANUM, LES (FRN) ○ 79 A.D. (USA) ○ ANNO 79 DOPO CRISTO ○ DESTRUCTION OF HERCULANEUM, THE ○ 79 A.D.-THE DESTRUCTION OF HERCULANEUM
ANNO 3003 • 1962 • Lehpamer Ivo • ANM • YGS
ANNO DEI GATTI, I • 1979 • Damiani Amasi • ITL • RAGAZZI DELLA DISCOTECA, I
ANNO DI SCUOLA, UN • 1977 • Giraldi Franco • MTV • ITL • YEAR OF SCHOOL, A
ANNO DOMINO 1573 see **SELJACKA BUNA 1573** • 1975
ANNO SCORSO A MARIENBAD ,L' (ITL) see **ANNEE DERNIERE A MARIENBAD, L'** • 1961
ANNO SULL'ALTIPIANO, UN see **UOMINI CONTRO** • 1970
ANNO TREMILA LA MORTE BIANCA • 1977 • Ricci Sergio • ITL
ANNO UNO • 1974 • Rossellini Roberto • ITL • ITALY: YEAR ONE (UKN) ○ YEAR ONE (USA)
ANNO ZERO GUERRA NELLO SPAZIO • 1977 • Brescia Alfonso • ITL
ANNONCIATION, L' • 1963 • Durand Philippe • FRN
ANNONSERA • 1936 • Henrikson Anders • SWD • IT PAYS TO ADVERTISE
ANNOUCHKA see **ANNUSHKA** • 1959
ANNOUNCING TO THE WORLD • 1950 • DOC • NKR
ANN'S FINISH • 1918 • Ingraham Lloyd • USA
ANNUAL ECLIPSE see **KINKAN-SHOKU** • 1975
ANNUAL TRIP OF THE MOTHERS' MEETING, THE • 1905 • Fitzhamon Lewin • UKN
ANNULAR ECLIPSE see **KINKAN-SHOKU** • 1975
ANNUNCIADOR -O HOMEM DAS TORMENTAS, O • 1971 • Martins Paulo Bastos • BRZ
ANNUNCIATION • 1964 • *Meyer Andrew (P)* • SHT • USA
ANNUSHKA • 1959 • Barnet Boris • USS • ANNOUCHKA
ANNY -STORY OF A PROSTITUTE • 1912 • Eriksen Adam • NRW
ANNYAYA • 1990 • Ghimiray Tulshi • NPL
ANO • Sevcik Igor • ANM • CZC • YES
ANO DE LA PESTE, EL • 1978 • Cazals Felipe • MXC • YEAR OF THE PLAGUE, THE
ANO DE LAS LUCES, EL • 1986 • Trueba Fernando • SPN • YEAR OF AWAKENING, THE
ANO HATA O UTE • 1944 • Abe Yutaka • JPN • FIRE THE FLAG!
ANO NAMI NO HATEMADE I • 1961 • Yagi Mitsuo • JPN • FAR BEYOND THE WAVES
ANO NAMI NO HATEMADE II • 1961 • Yagi Mitsuo • JPN • PEARL IN THE WAVES
ANO NAMI NO HATEMADE III • 1962 • Yagi Mitsuo • JPN • HER LAST PEARL
ANO SHISOSHA O NERAE • 1967 • Mori Kazuo • JPN • SPY ON THE MASKED CAR
ANO SIETE • 1966 • Alvarez Santiago • DOC • CUB
ANO UNO • 1972 • Gomez Sara • DOC • CUB
ANOKH RAAT • 1969 • Sen Asit • IND
ANOKHA PYAR • 1948 • *Biswas Anil (M)* • IND
ANOMALIES see **ANOMALIES -A WORLD OF DREAMS** • 1970
ANOMALIES -A WORLD OF DREAMS • 1970 • *Fine Gerald/ Jackson Jerry (P)* • USA • ANOMALIES ○ ANOMALY
ANOMALY see **ANOMALIES -A WORLD OF DREAMS** • 1970
ANOMIE • 1973 • Castravelli Claude • CND
ANONA'S BAPTISM • 1912 • *Wilbur Crane* • USA
ANONIMA COCOTTES • 1960 • Mastrocinque Camillo • ITL, FRN • CALL GIRL BUSINESS
ANONIMA DE ASESINATOS • 1965 • de Orduna Juan • SPN
ANONIMA ROYLOTT, L' • 1936 • Matarazzo Raffaello • ITL
ANONIMO, EL • 1932 • de Fuentes Fernando • MXC • ANONYMOUS ONE, THE
ANONIMO, EL • 1956 • Ochoa Jose • SPN
ANONIMO VENEZIANO • 1970 • Salerno Enrico Maria • ITL • ANONYMOUS VENETIAN, THE (USA) ○ VENETIAN ANONYMOUS, THE
ANONYME • 1957 • Alexeieff Alexandre • SHT • FRN
ANONYME BRIEFE • 1949 • Rabenalt Arthur M. • FRG
ANONYMOUS AVENGER • 1975 • *Nero Franco*
ANONYMOUS AVENGER see **CITTADINO SI RIBELLA, IL** • 1974
ANONYMOUS LETTER, THE • 1911 • *Walthall William* • USA
ANONYMOUS LOVE • 1913 • *Essanay* • USA
ANONYMOUS ONE, THE see **ANONIMO, EL** • 1932
ANONYMOUS VENETIAN, THE (USA) see **ANONIMO VENEZIANO** • 1970
ANOOP AND THE ELEPHANT see **ANOUP AND THE ELEPHANT** • 1972
ANOS HAN PASADA, LOS • 1945 • Delgado Agustin P. • MXC
ANOS INFAMES, LOS • 1975 • Doria Alejandro • ARG • INFAMOUS YEARS, THE
ANOS VERDES, LOS • 1966 • Salvador Jaime • MXC
ANOTE KONOTE • 1952 • Ichikawa Kon • JPN • THIS WAY THAT WAY
ANOTE KONOTE • 1968 • Shinagawa Shoji • JPN • ALL THE TRICKS
ANOTHER 24 HOURS • 1990 • Hill Walter • USA
ANOTHER AIR see **JINY VZDUCH** • 1939
ANOTHER BOTTLE, DOCTOR • 1926 • Fleischer Dave • SHT • USA
ANOTHER CASE OF POISONING • 1949 • Waterhouse John • UKN
ANOTHER CHANCE • 1914 • Crisp Donald • USA
ANOTHER CHANCE • 1987 • Vint Jesse • USA
ANOTHER CHANCE see **WOMEN OF TWILIGHT** • 1952
ANOTHER COUNTRY • 1984 • Kanievska Marek • UKN
ANOTHER DAWN • 1937 • Dieterle William • USA
ANOTHER DAY • 1932 • Thatcher Leslie • USA
ANOTHER DAY • 1978 • Hadad Saheb • IRQ
ANOTHER DAY, ANOTHER DOORMAT • 1959 • Kouzel Al • ANS • USA
ANOTHER DAY, ANOTHER MAN • 1966 • Wishman Doris • USA
ANOTHER EXPERIENCE see **ERLEBNIS GEHT WEITER, DAS** • 1940
ANOTHER FACE • 1935 • Cabanne W. Christy • USA • IT HAPPENED IN HOLLYWOOD (UKN) ○ TWO FACES
ANOTHER FINE MESS • 1930 • Parrott James • SHT • USA
ANOTHER FOOLISH VIRGIN • 1918 • Hopper E. Mason • USA
ANOTHER JOB FOR THE UNDERTAKER • 1901 • Porter Edwin S. • USA
ANOTHER KIND OF MUSIC • 1977 • Yates Rebecca, Salzman Glen • CND
ANOTHER LANGUAGE • 1933 • Griffith Edward H. • USA
ANOTHER LITTLE RED RIDING HOOD see **ALTA SCHUFITA ROSIE** • 1969
ANOTHER LOVE STORY see **YESHCHYO RAZ PRO LYUBOV** • 1968
ANOTHER LOVE STORY see **OTRA HISTORIA DE AMOR** • 1986
ANOTHER MAGIC BULLET • 1972 • Anderson Robert • DOC • CND
ANOTHER MAN, ANOTHER CHANCE • 1977 • Lelouch Claude • USA, FRN • AUTRE HOMME, UNE AUTRE CHANCE, UN (FRN) ○ ANOTHER MAN, ANOTHER WOMAN
ANOTHER MAN, ANOTHER WOMAN see **ANOTHER MAN, ANOTHER CHANCE** • 1977
ANOTHER MAN'S BOOTS • 1922 • Craft William James • USA
ANOTHER MAN'S POISON • 1951 • Rapper Irving • USA
ANOTHER MAN'S SHOES • 1922 • Conway Jack • USA
ANOTHER MAN'S WIFE • 1913 • Dwan Allan • USA
ANOTHER MAN'S WIFE • 1915 • Weston Harold • UKN
ANOTHER MAN'S WIFE • 1924 • Mitchell Bruce • USA
ANOTHER MAN'S WOMAN see **MUJER DE OTRO, LA** • 1967
ANOTHER MORNING FOR BILLY THE KID see **BILLY THE KID NO ATARASHII YOAKE** • 1987
ANOTHER PART OF THE FOREST • 1948 • Gordon Michael • USA
ANOTHER RAZOR TURN • 1978 • Burns Tim • SHT • ASL
ANOTHER SCANDAL • 1924 • Griffith Edward H. • USA • I WILL REPAY
ANOTHER SHADE OF GREEN • 1915 • *Lubin* • USA
ANOTHER SHORE • 1948 • Crichton Charles • UKN
ANOTHER SHORE see **DRUGI BRZEG** • 1962
ANOTHER SKY • 1960 • Lambert Gavin • USA
ANOTHER SMITH FOR PARADISE • 1972 • Shandel Thomas • CND
ANOTHER TALE • 1914 • *Lubin* • ANM • USA
ANOTHER THIN MAN • 1939 • Van Dyke W. S. • USA
ANOTHER TIME, ANOTHER PLACE • 1958 • Allen Lewis • UKN
ANOTHER TIME, ANOTHER PLACE • 1983 • Radford Michael • UKN
ANOTHER TO CONQUER • 1941 • Ulmer Edgar G. • DCS • USA
ANOTHER WAY see **EGYMASRA NEZVE** • 1983
ANOTHER WAY OF LIFE see **O NECEM JINEM** • 1963
ANOTHER WAY TO LOVE • 1976 • Reichenbach Francois • USA
ANOTHER WILD IDEA • 1934 • Parrott Charles, Dunn Eddie • SHT • USA
ANOTHER WOMAN • 1989 • Allen Woody • USA
ANOTHER WOMAN, ANOTHER DAY see **LOVE MERCHANT, THE** • 1966
ANOTHER WOMAN'S CHILD • 1982 • Erman John • TVM • USA
ANOTHER WORLD see **VERDEN TIL FORSKEL, EN** • 1989
ANOTHER'S GHOST • 1910 • FRN
ANOTHER'S LETTER see **CARTA AJENA** • 1975
ANOTHER'S WIFE AND HUSBAND see **CUDZA ZONA I MAZ POD LOZKIEM** • 1962
ANOTIMPURI • 1963 • Stiopul Savel • RMN • SEASONS
ANOUL BANAT • 1973 • Mizrahi Moshe • ISR • ABOU EL BANAT ○ DAUGHTERS! DAUGHTERS!
ANOUP AND THE ELEPHANT • 1972 • Eady David • UKN • ANOOP AND THE ELEPHANT
AN'S VATERLAND, AN'S TEURE.. • 1915 • Nischwitz-Lisson Heinrich • FRG
ANSATSU • 1964 • Shinoda Masahiro • JPN • ASSASSINATION ○ ASSASSIN, THE
ANSCHLAG AUF BAKU • 1942 • Kirchhoff Fritz • FRG
ANSCHLAG AUF SCHWEDA • 1935 • Martin Karl Heinz • FRG
ANSCHLUSS UM MITTERNACHT • 1929 • Bonnard Mario • FRG
ANSE-AUX-BASQUES • 1958-60 • Bonniere Rene • DCS • CND
ANSE TABATIERE, L' • 1958-60 • Bonniere Rene • DCS • CND
ANSELMO LEE • 1915 • Handworth Harry • USA
ANSHITSU • 1984 • Urayama Kirio • JPN • DARK ROOM
ANSI-PHIA • 1974 • Blanco Javier • DOC • VNZ
ANSICHTEN EINES CLOWNS • 1975 • Jasny Vojtech • FRG • CLOWN, THE (USA)
ANSIEDAD • 1952 • Zacarias Miguel • MXC
ANSIGT TIL ANSIGT • 1987 • Wivel Anne • DOC • DNM • FACE TO FACE
ANSIGTET see **STJAALNE ANSIGT, DET** • 1914
ANSIGTET I FLODEN • 1917 • Davidsen Hjalmar • DNM
ANSIKTE MOT ANSIKTE • 1976 • Bergman Ingmar • MTV • SWD • FACE TO FACE (USA)
ANSIKTEN I SKUGGA • 1956 • Weiss Peter, Stromholm Christer • SHT • SWD • FACES IN THE SHADOWS
ANSIKTET • 1958 • Bergman Ingmar • SWD • MAGICIAN, THE (USA) ○ FACE, THE (UKN)

ANSTALT, DIE • 1978 • Minow Hans-Rudiger • FRG • INSTITUTION, THE
ANSTANDIGE FRAU, EINE see **INSEL DER TRAUME, DIE** • 1925
ANSTANDIGE FRAUEN • 1920 • Wilhelm Carl • FRG
ANSTANDIGT LIV, ETT • 1979 • Jarl Stefan • SWD • RESPECTABLE LIFE, A ○ DECENT LIFE, A
ANSVAR • 1956 • Werner Gosta • SHT • SWD
ANSWER, THE • 1915 • *Myles Norbert A.* • USA
ANSWER, THE • 1916 • *Fairbanks Marion* • USA
ANSWER, THE • 1916 • West Walter • UKN
ANSWER, THE • 1917 • Hopper E. Mason • USA
ANSWER, THE • Lee Spike • USA
ANSWER, THE see **ODPOWIEDZ** • 1961
ANSWER, THE see **HANDS OF A STRANGER** • 1962
ANSWER, THE see **RESPUESTA, LA** • 1969
ANSWER MAN • 1946 • Brecken Jules • SHT • USA
ANSWER OF THE ROSES • 1911 • *Turner Florence* • USA
ANSWER OF THE SEA see **UNDINE** • 1915
ANSWER THE CALL • 1915 • MacBean L. C. • UKN
ANSWER TO VIOLENCE see **ZAMACH** • 1958
ANSWERED PRAYER • 1909 • *Phoenix* • USA
ANSWERED PRAYER, THE • 1913 • *Lawrence Adelaide* • USA
ANSWERING THE CALL • 1914 • Batley Ethyle • UKN
ANSWER'S IN THE WIND, THE see **ANTWORT KENNT NUR DER WIND, DIE** • 1975
ANT AND THE AARDVARK • 1968 • Freleng Friz • ASS • USA
ANT AND THE AARDVARK, THE • 1968 • Freleng Friz • ANS • USA
ANT FROM U.N.C.L.E., THE • 1968 • Gordon George • ANS • USA
ANT-HILL, THE • Renc Ivan • ANS • CZC
ANT PASTED • 1953 • Freleng Friz • ANS • USA
ANTAGONISM • Calinescu Bob • ANM • RMN
ANTAGONISTS, THE • 1916 • Payne John M. • UKN
ANTAGONISTS, THE (UKN) see **MASADA** • 1980
ANTAR, MOUTON DE L'AID • 1964 • Khalifa Omar • SHT • TNS
ANTARA DUA DARJAT • Ramlee P. • MLY • BETWEEN TWO CLASSES
ANTARA DUA HATI • 1988 • Jamil Rosenani • MLY
ANTARA IN ROMANIA • 1976 • Gousini Samir • SYR
ANTARCTIC CROSSING • 1958 • Lowe George, Wright Derek • DOC • UKN
ANTARCTIC STORY see **NANKYOKU MONOGATARI** • 1984
ANTARCTICA (USA) see **NANKYOKU MONOGATARI** • 1984
ANTARJALLI YATRA • 1988 • Ghose Goutam • IND • LAST RITES
ANTE • 1977 • Skauge Arvid, Utsi Nil • MTV • NRW • ONE YEAR IN THE LIFE OF A LAPPLAND BOY
ANTE EL CADAVER DE UN LIDER • 1973 • Galindo Alejandro • MXC • BEFORE THE CORPSE OF A LEADER
ANTE I DROMPOJKEN see **DROMPOJKEN** • 1964
ANTEFATTO, L' see **REAZIONE A CATENA** • 1971
ANTEK'S LUCK see **SZCZESCIE ANTKA** • 1937
ANTENATO, L' • 1922 • Campogalliani Carlo • ITL
ANTENATO, L' • 1936 • Brignone Guido • ITL • ANCESTOR, THE
ANTENNA • 1970 • Ditvoorst Adriaan • NTH
ANTES A MORTE QUE TAL SORTE • 1976 • Silva Joao De Matos • PRT • DEATH RATHER THAN A CHANCE LIKE THAT
ANTES DE ANOCHECER • 1968 • Lorente German • SPN • BEFORE EVENING
ANTES DO ADEUS • 1977 • Ceitil Rogerio • PRT
ANTES LLEGA LA MUERTE • 1964 • Romero-Marchent Joaquin Luis • SPN
ANTES, O VERAO • 1968 • Tavares Gerson • BRZ • BEFORE THE SUMMER ○ SUMMER BEFORE, THE ○ FIRST, THE SUMMER
ANTESALA DE LA MUERTE, LA see **SINDICATO DE LA MUERTE, EL** • 1953
ANTESALA DE LA SILLA ELECTRICA • 1966 • Orol Juan • MXC, PRC
ANTHAR L'INVINCIBILE • 1965 • Margheriti Antonio • ITL, FRN, SPN • DEVIL OF THE DESERT AGAINST THE SON OF HERCULES (USA) ○ MARCHANDS D'ESCLAVES (FRN) ○ MERCANTE DI SCHIAVE, IL ○ SLAVE MERCHANTS, THE
ANTHEM OF LEUTHEN, THE see **CHORAL VON LEUTHEN, DER** • 1933
ANTHOLOGIE DU VICE • 1976 • Maillet Jean-Claude • FRN
ANTHOLOGIE LESBOS • Baudricourt Michel • FRN
ANTHONY ADVERSE • 1936 • LeRoy Mervyn • USA
ANTHONY AND CLEOPATRA • 1981 • Miller Jonathan • MTV • UKN
ANTHONY BURGESS • Scheidsteger Klaus, Filliard Thierry • DOC
ANTHONY BURGESS' ROME • 1978 • Chapman Christopher • DOC • CND
ANTHONY'S BROKEN MIRROR see **ANTONIJEVO RAZBIJENO OGLEDALO** • 1957
ANTHONY'S CHANCE see **ANTONYHO SANCE** • 1987
ANTHRACITE • 1979 • Niermans Edouard • FRN
ANTHRACITE see **ANTRATSIT** • 1972
ANTHRAX see **ANTRAX** • 1990
ANTHROPO-CYNICAL FARCE • 1970 • Kawamoto Kihachiro • ANM • JPN
ANTHROPOPHAGOUS • 1980 • D'Amato Joe • ITL • ANTHROPOPHAGOUS THE BEAST ○ ANTHROPOPHAGOUS BEAST, THE ○ GRIM REAPER, THE ○ MAN EATER
ANTHROPOPHAGOUS 2 • 1981 • D'Amato Joe • ITL • ABSURD
ANTHROPOPHAGOUS BEAST, THE see **ANTHROPOPHAGOUS** • 1980
ANTHROPOPHAGOUS THE BEAST see **ANTHROPOPHAGOUS** • 1980
ANTHROPOS KAI TO TANK, O • 1978 • Georgiadis Vassilis • GRC • MAN AND THE TANK, THE
ANTHROPOS POU HATHIKE, O • 1976 • Maketaki Tonia • GRC • LOST MAN, THE
ANTI-CATS • 1950 • Davis Mannie • ANS • USA
ANTI-CINE • 1976 • Aguirre Javier • SPN
ANTI-CORRUPTION • Ng See Yuen • HKG
ANTI-DARWIN see **CO ZIZALA NETUSILA** • 1969
ANTI-HAIR POWDER, THE • 1908 • *Pathe* • FRN
ANTICASANOVA • 1985 • Tadej Vladimir • YGS, UKN
ANTICHRIST, THE see **ANTICRISTO, L'** • 1974
ANTICHRISTO see **ANTICRISTO, L'** • 1974
ANTICIPATED DAY, THE (USA) see **DZIEN UPRAGNIONY** • 1939
ANTICIPATION OF THE NIGHT • 1957 • Brakhage Stan • USA
ANTICLIMAX • 1970 • Gas Gelsen • MXC
ANTICLOCK • 1980 • Arden Jane, Bond Jack • UKN
ANTICRISTO, L' • 1974 • De Martino Alberto • ITL • ANTICHRIST, THE ○ TEMPTER, THE ○ ANTICHRISTO
ANTICS OF ANN, THE • 1917 • Dillon Eddie • USA
ANTIDOGMIN • 1976 • Jovanovic Zoran • SHT • YGS
ANTIDOTE, THE • 1927 • Bentley Thomas • UKN
ANTIDOTE FOR SUICIDE • 1914 • Hotaling Arthur D. • USA
ANTIGONE • 1911 • Caserini Mario • ITL
ANTIGONE • 1961 • Tzavellas Georges • GRC
ANTIGONE • 1964 • Hobl Pavel • CZC
ANTIMIRACOLO, L' • 1965 • Piccon Elio • ITL
ANTINEA, L'AMANTE DELLA CITTA SEPOLTA • 1961 • Ulmer Edgar G., Masini Giuseppe • ITL • JOURNEY BENEATH THE DESERT (USA) ○ ATLANTIS, THE LOST CONTINENT ○ ATLANTIDE, L' (FRN) ○ LOST KINGDOM, THE
ANTIPOLIS • 1952 • Mariaud Robert • SHT • FRN • RENDEZ-VOUS A ANTIBES-JUAN-LES-PINS
ANTIQUAR VON STRASSBURG, DER • 1917 • Mendel Georg Victor • USA
ANTIQUE ANTICS • 1933 • *Mintz Charles (P)* • ANS • USA
ANTIQUE BROOCH, THE • 1913 • Brabin Charles J. • USA, UKN
ANTIQUE DEALER, THE • 1915 • Knoles Harley • USA
ANTIQUE ENGAGEMENT RING, THE • 1914 • Marston Theodore • USA
ANTIQUE RING, AN • 1912 • *Johnson Arthur* • USA
ANTIQUE VASE, THE • 1913 • Martinek H. O. • UKN
ANTIQUES • 1977 • Wojciechowski Krzysztof • PLN
ANTIQUES AT AUCTION • 1970 • Spencer Ronald • UKN
ANTIQUITES DE L'ASIE OCCIDENTALE, LES • 1943 • Membrin • SHT • FRN
ANTISEMITEN • 1920 • Oswald Richard • FRG
ANTISEPTICS IN HOSPITAL • 1970 • Rawson Peter • DCS • UKN
ANTISTRROPHI METRISI • 1984 • Papakyriakopoulos Panos • GRC • WRONG TIMING
ANTLIGEN! • 1983 • Dahl Christer • SWD • AT LAST
ANTOINE AND ANTOINETTE (USA) see **ANTOINE ET ANTOINETTE** • 1946
ANTOINE DE SAINT-EXUPERY • 1958 • Languepin Jean-Jacques • FRN
ANTOINE ET ANTOINETTE • 1946 • Becker Jacques • FRN • ANTOINE AND ANTOINETTE (USA)
ANTOINE ET SEBASTIEN • 1973 • Perier Jean-Marie • FRN
ANTOINE ET SES ANGES • 1981 • Castravelli Claude • CND
ANTOINETTE see **CONDUISEZ-MOI, MADAME** • 1932
ANTOINETTE SABRIER • 1927 • Dulac Germaine • FRN
ANTOLOGIA UNIVERSALE DELL'AMORE see **IO AMO, TU AMI** • 1960
ANTON • 1973 • Blom Per • NRW
ANTON DER LETZTE • 1939 • Emo E. W. • FRG
ANTON IVANOVIC SERDITSYA • 1941 • Ivanovsky Alexander • USS • ANTON IVANOVICH IS ANGRY ○ ANTON IVANOVICH GETS MAD
ANTON IVANOVICH GETS MAD see **ANTON IVANOVIC SERDITSYA** • 1941
ANTON IVANOVICH IS ANGRY see **ANTON IVANOVIC SERDITSYA** • 1941
ANTON SPELEC, OSTROSTRELEC • 1932 • Fric Martin • CZC • ANTON SPELEC, THE THROWER
ANTON SPELEC, THE THROWER see **ANTON SPELEC, OSTROSTRELEC** • 1932
ANTON THE MAGICIAN • 1978 • Reisch Gunter • GDR
ANTON THE MUSICIAN • 1967 • Ratz Gunter • ANM • GDR
ANTON THE TERRIBLE • 1916 • De Mille William C. • USA
ANTONIA: A PORTRAIT OF A WOMAN • 1974 • Collins Judy, Godmilow Jill • DOC • USA
ANTONIA, ROMANCE HONGROISE • 1934 • Boyer Jean, Neufeld Max • FRN
ANTONIETA • 1982 • Saura Carlos • SPN, MXC, FRN
ANTONIJEVO RAZBIJENO OGLEDALO • 1957 • Makavejev Dusan • SHT • YGS • ANTHONY'S BROKEN MIRROR
ANTONIO • 1966 • Ianzelo Tony • DOC • CND
ANTONIO • 1973 • Guzman Claudio • CHL
ANTONIO AND THE MAYOR • 1975 • Thorpe Jerry • TVM • USA
ANTONIO DA PADOVA • 1949 • Francisci Pietro • ITL • ANTONY OF PADUA (USA)
ANTONIO DAS MORTES • 1969 • Rocha Glauber • BRZ • DRAGAO DA MALDADE CONTRA O SANTO GUERREIRO, O
ANTONIO DI PADOVA • 1931 • Antamoro Giulio • ITL
ANTONIO DUARTE • 1969 • Guimaraes Manuel • SHT • PRT
ANTONIO GAUDI • 1961 • Russell Ken • MTV • UKN
ANTONIO GAUDI • 1985 • Teshigahara Hiroshi • JPN
ANTONIO GRAMSCI I GIORNI DEL CARCERE • 1977 • Del Fra Lino • ITL
ANTONIO MEUCCI • 1940 • Guazzoni Enrico • ITL
ANTONIO SAURA • 1955 • Saura Carlos • SHT • SPN
ANTONIO Y EL ALCADE • 1974 • *I.p.a.* • MXC
ANTONITO see **DAY, THE** • 1961
ANTONKA • 1969 • Nosyryev L. • ANS • USS
ANTONY AND CLEOPATRA • 1908 • Kent Charles • USA
ANTONY AND CLEOPATRA • 1973 • Heston Charlton • UKN, SPN, SWT
ANTONY OF PADUA (USA) see **ANTONIO DA PADOVA** • 1949
ANTONY PHIRINGI • 1967 • Banerjee Sunil • IND • ANTONY THE ANGLO-INDIAN
ANTONY THE ANGLO-INDIAN see **ANTONY PHIRINGI** • 1967
ANTONYHO SANCE • 1987 • Olmer Vit • CZC • ANTHONY'S CHANCE
ANTOSHA RYBKIN • 1942 • Yudin Konstantin • USS
ANTRATSIT • 1972 • Surin Alexander • USS • ANTHRACITE
ANTRAX • 1990 • Kalcheva Stanislava • BUL • ANTHRAX
ANTRE DES ESPRITS, L' • 1901 • Melies Georges • FRN • MAGICIAN'S CAVERN, THE (USA) ○ DEN OF SPIRITS ○ HOUSE OF MYSTERY, THE
ANTRE INFERNALE, L' • 1905 • Velle Gaston • FRN • INFERNAL LAIR, THE
ANTS see **PANIC AT LAKEWOOD MANOR** • 1977
ANTS, THE see **MROWCZE SZLAKI** • 1956
ANTS BRING DEATH see **MRAVENCI NESOU SMRT** • 1985
ANTS IN MY PANTS • 1970 • *M.j. Productions* • USA
ANTS IN THE PANTRY • 1936 • Black Preston • SHT • USA
ANTS IN THE PLANTS • 1940 • Fleischer Dave • ANS • USA
ANTS IN YOUR PANTRY • 1945 • Davis Mannie • ANS • USA
ANT'S JOURNEY, THE • Nazarov Eduard • ANM • USS
ANT'S NEST see **HANGYABOLY** • 1971
ANTS: PANIC AT LAKEWOOD MANOR see **PANIC AT LAKEWOOD MANOR** • 1977
ANTTI PUUHAARA • 1976 • Partanen Heikki • FNL • ANTTI TREEBRANCH
ANTTI TREEBRANCH see **ANTTI PUUHAARA** • 1976
ANTWERP KILLERS, THE • 1984 • Veldman Luc • BLG
ANTWERP STORY, THE • 1945 • Sparling Gordon • CND
ANTWORT KENNT NUR DER WIND, DIE • 1975 • Vohrer Alfred • FRG, FRN • SEUL LE VENT CONNAIT LA RESPONSE (FRN) ○ ANSWER'S IN THE WIND, THE
ANUBAVI RAJA ANUBAVI • 1967 • Balachandar K. • IND • EXPERIENCE, MY BOY!
ANUBHAV • 1972 • Bhattacharya Basu • IND • FEELING
ANUBHAVAM PUDUMAI • 1967 • Rajendran C. V. • IND • TRUTH IS STRANGER THAN FICTION
ANUGHARAM see **KONDURA** • 1977
ANUPAMA • 1955 • Agradoot • IND
ANURAAG • 1972 • *Burman S. D. (M)* • IND
ANURADHA • 1960 • Mukherjee • IND
ANURDOPA • 1977 • Lankesh P. • IND
ANUSCHKA • 1942 • Kautner Helmut • FRG
ANUSH (USA) see **ANUSHIA** • 1931
ANUSHIA • 1931 • Perestiani Ivan • USS • ANUSH (USA)
ANUSHKA, MODEL AND WOMAN see **ANUSKA, MANEQUIM E MUHLER** • 1968
ANUSKA, MANEQUIM E MUHLER • 1968 • Ramalho Francisco Jr. • BRZ • ANUSHKA, MODEL AND WOMAN
ANVESHANE • 1978 • Nagabharana T. S. • IND • SEARCH, THE
ANVESHICHU KANDETHIYILLA • 1967 • Bhaskaran P. • IND • SEARCHED IN VAIN
ANVIL AND ACTORS • 1916 • *Pokes & Jabs* • USA
ANVIL CHORUS, THE • 1922 • Roach Hal • SHT • USA
ANVIL CHORUS GIRL • 1944 • Sparber I. • ANS • USA
ANVIL OR HAMMER see **NAKOVAINA ILLI TCHOUK** • 1972
ANWALT DES HERZENS, DER • 1927 • Thiele Wilhelm • FRG • LETZTEN NACHTE DER MRS. ORCHARD, DIE
ANXIETIES OF A MARRIED WOMAN see **INQUIETACOES DE UMA MULHER CASADA** • 1980
ANXIETY see **ENDISE** • 1975
ANXIETY OF THE GOALKEEPER AT THE PENALTY KICK, THE see **ANGST DES TORMANNS BIEN ELFMETER** • 1971
ANXIOUS DAY FOR MOTHER, AN • 1907 • Stow Percy • UKN
ANXIOUS MORNING, THE see **TREVOZHNOYE UTRO** • 1967
ANXIOUS YEARS, THE see **DARK JOURNEY** • 1937
ANY AMOUNT OF COAL see **JEDE MENGE KOHLE** • 1982
ANY BODY.. ANY WAY • 1968 • Romine Charles • USA • ANYBODY, ANYWHERE ○ ANYBODY'S ANYWAY ○ ANYBODY, ANYWAY
ANY FRIEND OF NICHOLAS NICKLEBY IS A FRIEND OF MINE • 1981 • Rosenblum Ralph • USA
ANY GIRL'S SAFE • 1917 • Ransom Charles • USA
ANY GUN CAN PLAY (USA) see **VADO.. L'AMMAZZO E TORNO** • 1967
ANY LITTLE GIRL THAT'S A NICE LITTLE GIRL • 1931 • Fleischer Dave • ANS • USA
ANY MAN'S DEATH • 1988 • Clegg Tom • UKN
ANY MAN'S WIFE see **MICHAEL O'HALLORAN** • 1937
ANY MAN'S WOMAN see **PIEGE, LE** • 1958
ANY NIGHT • 1922 • Beck Martin • USA
ANY NUMBER CAN PLAY • 1949 • LeRoy Mervyn • USA
ANY NUMBER CAN WIN (USA) see **MELODIE EN SOUS-SOL** • 1962
ANY OL' CLOTHES? • 1912 • *Pathe* • USA
ANY OLD DUKE'LL DO • 1916 • Hartigan P. C. • USA
ANY OLD PORT • 1920 • Goulding Alf, Roach Hal • SHT • USA
ANY OLD PORT • 1932 • Horne James W. • SHT • USA
ANY PORT IN A STORM • 1913 • Bowman William J. • USA
ANY RAGS • 1932 • Fleischer Dave • ANS • USA
ANY SECOND NOW • 1969 • Levitt Gene • TVM • USA
ANY SPECIAL WAY (UKN) see **WAT ZIEN IK** • 1971
ANY TIME ANYWHERE (UKN) see **CLAUDE ET GRETA** • 1970
ANY TIME ANYWHERE (UKN) see **LIAISONS PARTICULIERES, LES** • 1974
ANY WEDNESDAY • 1966 • Miller Robert Ellis • USA • BACHELOR GIRL APARTMENT (UKN)
ANY WHICH WAY YOU CAN • 1980 • Van Horn Buddy • USA
ANY WIFE • 1922 • Brenon Herbert • USA
ANY WOMAN • 1925 • King Henry • USA
ANY WOMAN see **HERHANGI BIR KADIN** • 1982
ANY WOMAN'S CHOICE • 1914 • *Bushman Francis X.* • USA
ANY WOMAN'S MAN see **WOMEN MEN LIKE** • 1928
ANY YOUTH • 1916 • Holubar Allen • SHT • USA
ANYA ES LEANYA • 1981 • Meszaros Marta • HNG, FRN • MERE, UNE FILLE, UNE (FRN) ○ MOTHER AND DAUGHTER
ANYA KORO • 1959 • Toyoda Shiro • JPN • PILGRIMAGE AT NIGHT
ANYANYA • 1971 • D'Aix Alain (c/d) • DOC • CND
ANYASAG • 1974 • Grunwalsky Ferenc • SHT • HNG • MOTHER, A
ANYBODY, ANYWAY see **ANY BODY.. ANY WAY** • 1968
ANYBODY, ANYWHERE see **ANY BODY.. ANY WAY** • 1968
ANYBODY HERE SEEN KELLY? • 1928 • Wyler William • USA • HAS ANYBODY HERE SEEN KELLY? (UKN)
ANYBODY'S ANYWAY see **ANY BODY.. ANY WAY** • 1968
ANYBODY'S BLONDE • 1931 • Strayer Frank • USA • WHEN BLONDE MEETS BLONDE (UKN)
ANYBODY'S GOAT • 1932 • Arbuckle Roscoe • USA
ANYBODY'S MONEY • 1918 • *Jaxon* • USA
ANYBODY'S (UKN) see **ANN OCH EVE -DE EROTISKA** • 1969
ANYBODY'S WAR • 1930 • Wallace Richard • USA • TWO BLACK CROWS IN THE A.E.F.

ANYBODY'S WIDOW • 1919 • *Devore Dorothy* • USA
ANYBODY'S WOMAN • 1930 • Arzner Dorothy • USA
ANYONE BUT MY HUSBAND • 1975 • Norman Robert • USA
ANYONE CAN KILL ME (UKN) see **TOUS PEUVENT ME TUER** • 1957
ANYONE CAN PLAY see **DOLCI SIGNORE, LE** • 1967
ANYONE FOR DENIS? • 1982 • Clement Dick • MTV • UKN
ANYONE FOR VENICE? see **HONEY POT, THE** • 1967
ANYTHING see **CUALQUIER COSA** • 1980
ANYTHING CAN HAPPEN • 1952 • Seaton George • USA
ANYTHING FOR A SONG • 1947 • Rugiani Carlo
ANYTHING FOR A THRILL • 1937 • Goodwins Leslie • USA
ANYTHING FOR LOVE see **11 HARROWHOUSE** • 1974
ANYTHING FOR MONEY • 1967 • Sarno Joe • USA
ANYTHING FOR PEACE AND QUIETNESS • 1906 • *Warwick Trading Co* • UKN
ANYTHING GOES • 1936 • Milestone Lewis • USA • TOPS IS THE LIMIT
ANYTHING GOES • 1956 • Lewis Robert* • USA
ANYTHING MIGHT HAPPEN • 1934 • Cooper George A. • UKN
ANYTHING ONCE • 1917 • De Grasse Joseph • USA
ANYTHING ONCE • 1925 • McHenry James?, McCloskey Justin H.? • USA
ANYTHING ONCE • 1969 • Place Graham • USA • ANYTHING ONCE, OR TWICE IF I LIKE IT ○ ANYTHING ONCE, OR TWICE
ANYTHING ONCE, OR TWICE see **ANYTHING ONCE** • 1969
ANYTHING ONCE, OR TWICE IF I LIKE IT see **ANYTHING ONCE** • 1969
ANYTHING TO DECLARE? • 1938 • Davis Redd • UKN
ANYTHING WITH GIRLS see **HOW TO DO ANYTHING AT ALL WITH GIRLS** • 1968
ANYUTINA DOROGA • 1968 • Golub L. • USS • LITTLE ANYUTA'S DOG
ANZACS IN OVERALLS • 1942 • Hall Ken G. • DOC • ASL
ANZAC'S V.C.'S • 1916 • ASL
ANZIO see **SBARCO DI ANZIO, LO** • 1968
ANZIO LANDING, THE see **SBARCO DI ANZIO, LO** • 1968
ANZUKKO • 1958 • Naruse Mikio • JPN
AO SUL DO MEU CORPO • 1982 • Saraceni Paulo Cesar • BRZ • SOUTH OF MY BODY
AOBEKA MONOGATARI • 1964 • Kawashima Yuzo • JPN • THIS MADDING CROWD (USA)
AOGEBA TOTOSHI • 1966 • Shibuya Minoru • JPN • ODE TO AN OLD TEACHER
AOI FILM SHINASADAME • 1968 • Mukoi Hiroshi • JPN • BLUE FILM -ESTIMATION
AOI KAIRYU • 1961 • Horiuchi Manao • JPN • BLUE CURRENT
AOI ME • 1956 • Suzuki • JPN • BLUE BUD
AOI SANMYAKU • 1949 • Imai Tadashi • JPN • BLUE MOUNTAINS ○ GREEN MOUNTAINS
AOI SANMYAKU • 1957 • Matsubayashi Shue • JPN • BLUE MOUNTAINS
AOI YAJU • 1960 • Horikawa Hiromichi • JPN • BLUE BEAST, THE
AOIRO KAKUMEI • 1953 • Ichikawa Kon • JPN • BLUE REVOLUTION, THE
AOOM • 1970 • Suarez Gonzalo • SPN
AOS • 1964 • Kuri Yoji • ANS • JPN • A.O.S.
AOURE • 1962 • Allasane Mustapha • NGR
AOUT • 1914 • Leprince Rene • FRN
AOZURA MUSUME • 1957 • Masumura Yasuzo • JPN • CHEERFUL GIRL, A
AOZURA NI NAKU • 1931 • Naruse Mikio • JPN • WEEPING BLUE SKY ○ CRYING TO THE BLUE SKY
APA • 1966 • Szabo Istvan • HNG • FATHER (UKN) ○ MY FATHER
APA CA UN BIVOL NEGRU • 1970 • Pita Dan, Veroiu Mircea • DOC • RMN • WATER AS A BLACK BUFFALO
APACHE • 1925 • Millar Adelqui • UKN
APACHE • 1954 • Aldrich Robert • USA
APACHE, L' • 1919 • De Grasse Joseph • USA
APACHE, THE • 1912 • Plumb Hay • UKN
APACHE, THE • 1928 • Rosen Phil • USA
APACHE, THE see **MAN'S MATE, A** • 1924
APACHE AMBUSH • 1955 • Sears Fred F. • USA
APACHE CHIEF • 1949 • McDonald Frank • USA
APACHE COUNTRY • 1952 • Archainbaud George • USA
APACHE DANCE • 1909 • Yates Frank D. • USA
APACHE DANCE, THE • 1913 • Bamberger Joseph J. • UKN
APACHE DANCER, THE • 1923 • Seeling Charles R. • USA • APACHE LOVE (UKN)
APACHE DRUMS • 1951 • Fregonese Hugo • USA
APACHE FATHER'S VENGEANCE, AN • 1913 • *Darkfeather Mona* • USA
APACHE FURY see **HOMBRE DE LA DILIGENCIA ,EL** • 1963
APACHE GOLD • 1910 • *Lubin* • USA
APACHE GOLD (USA) see **WINNETOU I** • 1963
APACHE KID, THE • 1930 • *Mintz Charles (P)* • ANS • USA
APACHE KID, THE • 1941 • Sherman George • USA
APACHE KID'S ESCAPE, THE • 1930 • Horner Robert J. • USA
APACHE KIND, THE • 1913 • *Larkin Dollie* • USA
APACHE LOVE • 1913 • *Nestor* • USA
APACHE LOVE (UKN) see **APACHE DANCER, THE** • 1923
APACHE MASSACRE see **CRY FOR ME, BILLY** • 1972
APACHE RAIDER, THE • 1928 • Maloney Leo • USA
APACHE RENEGADE, THE • 1912 • *Blackwell Carlyle* • USA
APACHE RIFLES • 1965 • Witney William • USA
APACHE ROSE • 1947 • Witney William • USA
APACHE TERRITORY • 1958 • Nazarro Ray • USA
APACHE TRAIL • 1942 • Thorpe Richard • USA
APACHE UPRISING • 1966 • Springsteen R. G. • USA
APACHE WAR SMOKE • 1952 • Kress Harold F. • USA
APACHE WARRIOR • 1957 • Williams Elmo • USA
APACHE WOMAN • 1954 • Corman Roger • USA
APACHEN • 1973 • Kolditz Gottfried • USS, GDR
APACHEN, DIE • 1919 • Dupont E. A. • FRG • PARIS UNDERWORLD
APACHEN VON PARIS, DIE • 1927 • Malikoff Nikolai • FRG • APACHES OF PARIS (USA)
APACHENLORD, DER • 1920 • Sauer Fred • FRG
APACHENRACHE 3 • 1920 • Neff Wolfgang • FRG • VERSCHWUNDENE MILLION, DIE
APACHENRACHE 4 • 1920 • Neff Wolfgang • FRG • AFFENMENSCH, DER
APACHENTANZ • 1906 • Porten Friedrich • FRG
APACHES, LES • 1904 • Melies Georges • FRN • BURLESQUE HIGHWAY ROBBERY IN "GAY PAREE", A
APACHES, LES • 1913 • Bourgeois Gerard • FRN
APACHES DE PARIS, LES • 1905-10 • Heuze Andre • FRN
APACHE'S GRATITUDE, AN • 1913 • Duncan William • USA
APACHES' LAST BATTLE see **OLD SHATTERHAND** • 1964
APACHES OF ATHENS, THE see **APACHIDES TON ATHINON, I** • 1930
APACHES OF PARIS, THE • 1915 • Ellis Robert • USA
APACHES OF PARIS (USA) see **APACHEN VON PARIS, DIE** • 1927
APACHES PAS VEINARDS, LES • 1902 • Blache Alice • FRN
APACHIDES TON ATHINON, I • 1930 • Gaziadis Dimitrios • GRC • APACHES OF ATHENS, THE
APAGA Y VAMONOS • 1981 • Hernandez Antonio • SPN • WE HAD BETTER CALL IT A DAY
APAM NEHANY BOLDOG EVE • 1978 • Simo Sandor • HNG • MY FATHER'S HAPPY YEARS
APANDO, EL • 1975 • Cazals Felipe • MXC • APANDO (ISOLATION CELL), THE
APANDO (ISOLATION CELL), THE see **APANDO, EL** • 1975
APANJAN • 1968 • Sinha Tapan • IND • NEAR ONES
APARADHI • 1931 • Bose Debaki • IND • CULPRIT, THE
APARADHI KAUN • 1957 • *Roy Bhimal (P)* • IND
APARAJITO • 1956 • Ray Satyajit • IND • UNVANQUISHED, THE
APARANHAM • 1990 • Nair M. P. Sukumaran • IND
APARECIDOS, LOS • 1929 • Buchs Jose • SPN
APARIENCIAS ENGANAN, LAS • 1978 • Hermosillo Jaime Humberto • MXC • THINGS AREN'T ALWAYS WHAT THEY SEEM
APART FROM YOU see **KIMI TO WAKARETE** • 1932
APARTADO DE CORREOS 1.001 • 1950 • Salvador Julio • SPN
APARTAMENTO DE LA TENTACION, EL • 1971 • Buchs Julio • SPN
APARTMENT 23 • 1919 • *Christie* • USA
APARTMENT 29 • 1917 • Scardon Paul • USA
APARTMENT, THE • 1960 • Wilder Billy • USA
APARTMENT ABOVE (USA) see **PIETRO WYZEJ** • 1938
APARTMENT FOR PEGGY • 1948 • Seaton George • USA
APARTMENT HOUSE MYSTERY, THE • 1915 • *Roland Ruth* • USA
APARTMENT IN MOSCOW (USA) see **KONETS STAROY BERYOZOVSKI** • 1961
APARTMENT LIVING • 1988 • Romero George A. • USA
APARTMENT NO.13 • 1912 • *West Billy* • USA
APARTMENT ON THE 13TH FLOOR see **SEMANA DEL ASESINO, LA** • 1972
APARTMENT ZERO • 1989 • Donovan Martin • UKN
APARTMENTHAUS, DAS • 1970 • Weidenmann Alfred • FRG
APARUPA • 1982 • Barua Jahnu • IND
APASIONADA • 1952 • Crevenna Alfredo B. • MXC
APASIONADAMENTE • 1944 • Amadori Luis Cesar • ARG
APASSIONATA FANTASY see **APPASSIONATA FANTASY**
A*P*E • 1976 • Leder Paul • USA, SKR • APE (NOT TO BE CONFUSED WITH KING KONG) ○ APE ○ ATTACK OF THE GIANT HORNY GORILLA
APE see **A*P*E** • 1976
APE, THE • 1928 • Rule Beverly C. • USA
APE, THE • 1940 • Nigh William • USA
APE, THE see **MONKEY, THE** • 1959
APE AND SUPERAPE see **BIJ DE BEESTEN AF** • 1973
APE MAN, THE • 1943 • Beaudine William • USA • LOCK YOUR DOORS (UKN) ○ LOCK UP YOUR DAUGHTERS
APE MAN ISLAND see **BALI THE UNKNOWN: OR APE MAN ISLAND** • 1921
APE MAN OF THE JUNGLE (USA) see **TARZAK CONTRO GLI UOMINI LEOPARDO** • 1964
APE (NOT TO BE CONFUSED WITH KING KONG) see **A*P*E** • 1976
APE REGINA, L' see **STORIA MODERNA -L'APE REGINA, UNA** • 1963
APE TERROR, THE • 1961 • Junge Winifried • DOC • GDR
APE WOMAN, THE (USA) see **DONNA SCIMMIA, LA** • 1964
APEA • Kamba Sebastien • SHT • CNG
APEL • 1971 • Czekala Ryszard • ANS • PLN • ROLL-CALL ○ ROLL CALL
APEL POLEGLYCH • 1957 • Poreba Bohdan • DOC • PLN • ROLL-CALL FOR THE DEAD
APEN FRAMTID • 1983 • Wam Svend, Vennerod Petter • NRW • OPEN FUTURE ○ ON MY WAY
APENA UN DELINCUENTE • 1947 • Fregonese Hugo • ARG • HARDLY A CRIMINAL ○ LIVE IN FEAR
APENBARINGEN • 1976 • Lokkeberg Vibeke • SHT • NRW
APENBARINGEN • 1977 • Lokkeberg Vibeke • NRW • REVELATION, THE
APE'S DEVOTION, AN • 1913 • Stow Percy • UKN
APES OF WRATH • 1959 • Freleng Friz • ANS • USA
APFEL IST AB, DER • 1948 • Kautner Helmut • FRG • ORIGINAL SIN, THE (USA) ○ APPLE HAS BEEN EATEN, THE ○ FALLEN APPLE
APHRODESIANS, THE • 1970 • *Stacey Distributors* • USA
APHRODISIAC TRAIL, THE • 1983 • Keir John • NZL
APHRODITE • 1916 • *Carmi Maria* • FRG
APHRODITE • 1982 • Fuest Robert • FRN, SWT
APHRODITE see **AFRODHITI** • 1968
APHRODITE DEESSE DE L'AMOUR (FRN) see **VENERE DI CHERONEA, LA** • 1957
APHRODITE, GODDESS OF LOVE (USA) see **AFRODITE, DEA DELL'AMORE** • 1958
APHROUSA • 1971 • Joannides Evangelos • SHT • UKN
APICULTEUR, L' (FRN) see **MELISSOKOMOS, O** • 1986
APICULTURA: A TECNICA DO APIARIO • 1937 • Coelho Jose Adolfo • SHT • PRT
APINAN VUONNA • 1983 • Kuusi Janne • FNL • IN THE YEAR OF THE APE
APISH TRICK, AN • 1909 • *Pathe* • FRN
APNA HAATH JAGANATH • 1960 • *Burman S. D. (M)* • IND
APNA PARAYA • 1942 • *Biswas Anil (M)* • IND
APNAGAR • 1941 • Bose Debaki • IND
APO LAHTARA SE LAHTARA • 1967 • Melissinos Vangelis • GRC • MR. GOOSE GOES HUNTING ○ FROM WORRY TO WORRY
APO POU PANE TIS HAVOUZA • 1979 • Marangos Thodoros • GRC • WHICH WAY TO THE RUBBISH DUMP
APO TA JEROSOLIMA ME AGAPI • 1967 • Papakostas Giorgos • GRC • FROM JERUSALEM WITH LOVE
APOCALISSE, L' • 1947 • Scotese Giuseppe Maria • ITL
APOCALISSE DOMANI • 1980 • Margheriti Antonio • ITL, SPN • INVASION OF THE FLESH EATERS ○ CANNIBALS ARE IN THE STREETS ○ SLAUGHTERERS ○ CANNIBAL APOCALYPSE ○ LAST HUNTER ○ CANNIBAL APOCALIPSIS
APOCALISSE SUL FIUME GIALLO • 1960 • Merusi Renzo • ITL, FRN • DAM ON THE YELLOW RIVER
APOCALISSE SULL FIUME GIALLO see **MISTERO DEI TREI CONTINENTI, IL** • 1959
APOCALYPSE 3:16 • 1964 • Charlot Martin • USA
APOCALYPSE 2024 • 1983 • Jones L. Q. • USA
APOCALYPSE, L' • 1939 • Tedesco Jean • SHT • FRN
APOCALYPSE, L' • 1969 • See Jean-Claude • FRN
APOCALYPSE DES ANIMAUX, L' • 1973 • Rossif Frederic • DOC • FRN
APOCALYPSE MERCENARIES • Dawson John R. • USA
APOCALYPSE NOW • 1979 • Coppola Francis Ford • USA
APOKAL • 1971 • Anczykowski Paul • FRG
APOKALYPSE • 1918 • Gliese Rochus • FRG
APOLINAR • 1971 • *Zohar* • MXC
APOLITICO, EL • 1977 • Ozores Mariano • SPN
APOLLO FRED BECOMES A HOMESEEKER • 1914 • *Mace Fred* • USA
APOLLO FRED SEE THE POINT • 1914 • *Mace Fred* • USA
APOLLO GOES ON HOLIDAY see **EPIHIRISIS APOLLON** • 1968
APOLLON -UNA FABRICA OCCUPATA • 1969 • Gregoretti Ugo • ITL
APOLOGO, UM • 1939 • Mauro-Humberto • SHT • BRZ
APOLOGY • 1986 • Bierman Robert • TVM • USA • APOLOGY: FOR MURDER
APOLOGY FOR MURDER • 1945 • Newfield Sam • USA
APOLOGY: FOR MURDER see **APOLOGY** • 1986
APOORVA PIRAVIGAL • 1967 • Vishwanathan G. • IND • UNUSUAL BIRTH
APOSTASY • 1979 • Friedrichs Zbigniew • ASL
APOSTASY see **HAKAI** • 1948
APOSTATE • 1987 • Rubinchik Valeri • USS, AUS, FRG
APOSTLE, THE • 1965 • Ratz Gunter • ANM • GDR
APOSTLE OF VENGEANCE, THE • 1916 • Hart William S., Smith Cliff • USA
APOSTLES, THE • 1977 • Shariliev Borislav • BUL
APOSTOL, EL • 1917 • Valle Don Frederico • ANM • ARG
APOSTOLI THANATOU • 1968 • Retsinas Marios • GRC • MISSION OF DEATH
APOTHECARY, THE see **MEDIKUS, A** • 1916
APOTHEKE DES TEUFELS, DIE • 1921 • Eichgrun Bruno • FRG
APOTHEOSE • 1895 • Skladanowsky Max, Skladanowsky Emil • FRG
APOTHEOSE PORNO • Xavier Robert • FRN
APPALOOSA, THE • 1966 • Furie Sidney J. • USA • SOUTHWEST TO SONORA (UKN)
APPARATUS • 1989 • Cohen Larry • USA
APPARE ISSHIN TASUKE • 1945 • Saeki Kiyoshi • JPN • BRAVO TASUKE ISSHIN
APPARENCE FEMININE • 1979 • Rein Richard • DOC • FRN
APPARENCES • 1964 • Kupissonoff Jacques • SHT • BLG • APPEARANCES (USA)
APPARITION, L' • 1972 • Cardinal Roger • CND
APPARITION, THE (USA) see **REVENANT, LE** • 1903
APPARITIONS FANTOMATIQUES see **ROI DES MEDIUMS, LE** • 1910
APPARITIONS FUGITIVES • 1904 • Melies Georges • FRN • FUGITIVE APPARITIONS, THE
APPARIZIONE • 1944 • de Limur Jean • ITL
APPARTEMENT DES FILLES, L' • 1963 • Deville Michel • FRN, FRG, ITL • APPARTEMENTO DELLE RAGAZZE, L' (ITL)
APPARTEMENTO DELLE RAGAZZE, L' (ITL) see **APPARTEMENT DES FILLES, L'** • 1963
APPARTENANCE • 1984 • Macina Michael • MTV • CND
APPASSIONATA • 1944 • Molander Olof • SWD
APPASSIONATA • 1950 • Meyer Johannes • FRG
APPASSIONATA • 1974 • Calderoni Gian Luigi • ITL
APPASSIONATA see **TAKOVA LASKA** • 1959
APPASSIONATA, L' • 1929 • Mathot Leon • FRN
APPASSIONATA, L' • 1988 • Mingozzi Gianfranco • ITL
APPASSIONATA FANTASY • Rogers Roger Bruce • SHT • USA • APASSIONATA FANTASY
APPASSIONATAMENTE • 1954 • Gentilomo Giacomo • ITL
APPAT, L' (FRN) see **ZERSCHOSSENE TRAUME** • 1976
APPEAL, THE • 1913 • *Brunette Fritzie* • USA
APPEAL, THE see **MOLBA** • 1969
APPEAL FROM THE OPPRESSED • 1977 • el Imam Hassan • EGY
APPEAL OF THE PRAIRIE, THE • 1910 • *Pathe* • USA
APPEARANCE see **WIDZIADLO** • 1984
APPEARANCE OF EVIL, THE • 1918 • Windom Lawrence C. • USA
APPEARANCE OF SUPER GIANT • 1956 • JPN
APPEARANCES • 1921 • Crisp Donald • USA, UKN
APPEARANCES see **MAZAHER, EL** • 1945
APPEARANCES (USA) see **APPARENCES** • 1964
APPEL, L' • 1972 • Thamar Tilda • FRN
APPEL DE LA NUIT, L' see **VOIX DU METAL, LA** • 1933
APPEL DE LA VIE, L' • 1937 • Neveux Georges • FRN
APPEL DU BLED, L' • 1942 • Gleize Maurice • FRN • FEMMES DE BONNE VOLANTE
APPEL DU COEUR, L' see **TOUTE SA VIE** • 1930
APPEL DU COURLIS, L' see **DU'A'AL-KARAWAN** • 1959
APPEL DU DESTIN, L' • 1952 • Lacombe Georges • FRN
APPEL DU SANG, L' • 1919 • Mercanton Louis • FRN • CALL OF THE BLOOD
APPEL DU SILENCE, L' • 1936 • Poirier Leon • FRN • CALL, THE (USA)
APPELEZ-MOI MAITRE see **MONSIEUR LE PRESIDENT-DIRECTEUR GENERAL** • 1966
APPELEZ-MOI MATHILDE • 1970 • Mondy Pierre • FRN

APPELKRIGET • 1973 • Danielsson Tage • SWD • APPLE WAR, THE (USA)
APPETIT D'OISEAU • 1964 • Foldes Peter • SHT • FRN • BIRD'S APPETITE, A
APPETITE see **SHITANAMEZURI** • 1968
APPETITE AND LOVE • 1914 • Sandberg Anders W. • DNM
APPLAUDISSEMENTS, LES see **CHIROKROTIMATA, TA** • 1943
APPLAUSE • 1929 • Mamoulian Rouben • USA
APPLAUSE see **CHIROKROTIMATA, TA** • 1943
APPLE • 1964 • Warhol Andy • USA
APPLE, THE • 1914 • Marston Theodore • USA
APPLE, THE • 1962 • Dunning George • ANS • UKN
APPLE, THE • 1980 • Golan Menahem • UKN, USA • STAR-ROCK
APPLE, THE see **JABALKATA** • 1963
APPLE A DAY, AN • 1931 • Edwards Harry J. • SHT • USA
APPLE ANDY • 1946 • Lundy Dick • ANS • USA
APPLE BUTTER • 1916 • Smith Sidney • SHT • USA
APPLE DUMPLING GANG, THE • 1975 • Tokar Norman • USA
APPLE DUMPLING GANG RIDES AGAIN, THE • 1979 • McEveety Vincent • USA
APPLE GAME, THE see **HRA O JABLKO** • 1976
APPLE HAS BEEN EATEN, THE see **APFEL IST AB, DER** • 1948
APPLE IN HIS EYE, AN • 1941 • D'Arcy Harry • SHT • USA
APPLE OF DISCORD • 1959 • Barfod Bent • ANS • DNM
APPLE OF DISCORD, THE • 1907 • Booth W. R. • UKN
APPLE OF DISCORD, THE • 1963 • Pluchek V. • USS
APPLE OF LOVE • 1962 • Vunak Dragutin • ANS • YGS
APPLE THIEVES, THE • Foky Otto • ANS • HNG
APPLE-TREE GIRL, THE • 1917 • Crosland Alan • USA
APPLE TREE MAIDEN, THE see **JABLONOVA PANNA** • 1974
APPLE TREE WITH GOLDEN APPLES, THE see **JABLUNKA SE ZLATYMI JABLKY** • 1952
APPLE WAR, THE (USA) see **APPELKRIGET** • 1973
APPLE WOMAN, THE • 1904 • Collins Alf • UKN
APPLEJOY'S GHOST (UKN) see **FANTASY** • 1927
APPLES • 1909 • *Urban Trading Co* • UKN
APPLES AND DESTINY • 1911 • *Powers* • USA
APPLES AND ORANGES • 1962 • Bass Saul • SHT • USA
APPLES HARVESTED IN 1941, THE • Batyrov Ravil • USS
APPLES OF SODOM • 1913 • Lessey George A. • USA
APPLES TO YOU • 1932 • Jason Leigh • SHT • USA
APPLEYARD ROMANCE see **AISHU NO RINGOEN** • 1957
APPLICATION see **AANMELDING** • 1964
APPLIED ROMANCE • 1915 • MacMackin Archer • USA
APPLY TO JANITOR • 1913 • *Eclair* • USA
APPOINTED, THE • 1989 • Waxman Daniel • ISR
APPOINTED HOUR, THE • 1912 • *Walthall Henry B.* • USA
APPOINTMENT, THE • 1969 • Lumet Sidney • USA, ITL
APPOINTMENT, THE • 1971 • Vincent Chuck • USA
APPOINTMENT, THE • 1982 • Vickers Lindsey C. • UKN
APPOINTMENT AT THE MILL see **DOSTAVENICKO VE MLYNICI** • 1898
APPOINTMENT BY TELEPHONE • 1902 • Porter Edwin S. • USA
APPOINTMENT FOR LOVE • 1941 • Seiter William A. • USA
APPOINTMENT IN BEIRUT see **REBUS** • 1968
APPOINTMENT IN BERLIN • 1943 • Green Alfred E. • USA
APPOINTMENT IN HONDURAS • 1953 • Tourneur Jacques • USA
APPOINTMENT IN LONDON • 1953 • Leacock Philip • UKN
APPOINTMENT IN PERSIA see **TEHERAN** • 1947
APPOINTMENT IN TOKYO • 1945 • Hively Jack • USA
APPOINTMENT IN TRIESTE • 1988 • Mattei Bruno • ITL
APPOINTMENT REMINDER • 1971 • McCarty Greg • SHT • USA
APPOINTMENT WITH A SHADOW • 1958 • Carlson Richard • USA • BIG STORY, THE (UKN)
APPOINTMENT WITH A SHADOW (UKN) see **MIDNIGHT STORY, THE** • 1956
APPOINTMENT WITH AGONY • Davian Joe • USA
APPOINTMENT WITH AN UNKNOWN WOMAN see **RANDEVOU ME MIAN AGNOSTI** • 1968
APPOINTMENT WITH CRIME • 1946 • Harlow John • UKN
APPOINTMENT WITH DANGER • 1951 • Allen Lewis • USA
APPOINTMENT WITH DARKNESS • 1950-53 • Vickrey Robert • SHT • USA
APPOINTMENT WITH DEATH • 1987 • Winner Michael • USA
APPOINTMENT WITH FEAR • 1946 • Haines Ronald • SER • UKN
APPOINTMENT WITH FEAR • 1985 • Thomas Ramzi • USA
APPOINTMENT WITH LUST • Summers Walter
APPOINTMENT WITH MURDER • 1948 • Bernhard Jack • USA
APPOINTMENT WITH THE PRESIDENT see **MAWED MAA EL RAIS** • 1989
APPOINTMENT WITH VENUS • 1951 • Thomas Ralph • UKN • ISLAND RESCUE (USA)
APPREHENSION • 1982 • Warneke Lothar • GDR
APPRENEZ A SOULEVER UNE CHARGE • 1949 • Decae Henri • SHT • FRN
APPRENEZ-MOI L'AMOUR see **ALLIMUNI AL-HUBB** • 1957
APPRENTI-ARCHITECTE, L' • 1908 • *Deed Andre* • FRN
APPRENTI SALAUD, L' • 1977 • Deville Michel • FRN
APPRENTICE, THE • 1973 • Leergaard Lars • DNM
APPRENTICE, THE see **FLEUR BLEUE** • 1970
APPRENTICE TO MURDER • 1988 • Thomas Ralph L. • USA • LONG LOST FRIEND, THE
APPRENTICESHIP see **UCENIE** • 1965
APPRENTICESHIP OF DUDDY KRAVITZ, THE • 1974 • Kotcheff Ted • CND • APPRENTISSAGE DE DUDDY KRAVITZ, L'
APPRENTIE, L' • 1914 • Chautard Emile • FRN
APPRENTIS, LES • 1964 • Tanner Alain • DOC • SWT
APPRENTIS MILITAIRES, LES • 1897 • Melies Georges • FRN • MILITARY APPRENTICES
APPRENTIS SORCIERS, LES • 1977 • Cozarinsky Edgardo • FRN, FRG
APPRENTISSAGE DE DUDDY KRAVITZ, L' see **APPRENTICESHIP OF DUDDY KRAVITZ, THE** • 1974
APPRENTISSAGE DU SENS DES MOTS, L' • 1972 • Lamothe Arthur • DCS • CND
APPRENTISSAGE ET MOUVEMENTS • 1971 • Moreau Michel • DCS • CND
APPRENTISSAGES DE BOIREAU, LES • 1905-10 • Heuze Andre • FRN
APPRENTISSAGES DE BOIREAU, LES • 1907 • Capellani Albert • FRN
APPREZZATO PROFESSIONISTA DI SICURO AVVENIRE, UN • 1972 • De Santis Giuseppe • ITL
APPROACH: INNOCENCE • 1969 • *Saarinnen Eric (P)* • SHT • USA
APPROACH OF AUTUMN, THE see **AKI TACHINU** • 1960
APPROACH TO ART TEACHING • 1961 • Otton Malcolm • ASL
APPROACH TO SCIENCE • 1946 • Mason Bill • DOC • UKN
APPROACHING ZERO, 000 see **LYCKLIGA INGENJORERNA** • 1988
APPROCHE GLOBALE see **TOTAL APPROACH** • 1971
APPROVED EXAM • 1987 • Garcia Agraz Jose Luis • MXC
APPUNTAMENTO, L' • 1956 • Biagetti Giuliano • ITL
APPUNTAMENTO A ISCHIA • 1960 • Mattoli Mario • ITL
APPUNTAMENTO COL DISONORE • 1970 • Bolzoni Adriano • ITL
APPUNTAMENTO CON IL DELITTO (ITL) see **TEMOIN DANS LA VILLE, UN** • 1959
APPUNTAMENTO CON L'ASSASSINO (ITL) see **AGRESSION, L'** • 1974
APPUNTAMENTO IN PARADISO • 1960 • Rolando Giuseppe • ITL
APPUNTAMENTO IN RIVIERA • 1962 • Mattoli Mario • ITL
APPUNTI PER UN FILM SULJAZZ • 1965 • Amico Gianni • ITL • NOTES FOR A FILM ON JAZZ
APPUNTI PER UN FILM SULL'INDIA • 1968 • Pasolini Pier Paolo • DCS • ITL
APPUNTI PER UN ORESTIADE AFRICANA • 1970 • Pasolini Pier Paolo • DCS • ITL • NOTES FOR AN AFRICAN ORESTEIA
APPUNTI SU UN FATTO DI CRONACA • 1951 • Visconti Luchino • DCS • ITL
APRADHI KAUN? • 1958 • Sen Asit • IND • WHO IS GUILTY?
APRE LUTTE, L' • 1917 • Boudrioz Robert • FRN
APRENDA A COMER • 1945 • Coelho Jose Adolfo • SHT • PRT
APRENDIENDO A MORIR • 1962 • Lazaga Pedro • SPN
APRENDIZ DE MALO, EL • 1957 • Lazaga Pedro • SPN
APRES COURS, L' • 1984 • Belanger Fernand • MTV • CND
APRES LA GUERRE • 1989 • Hubert Jean-Loup • FRN
APRES LA PHASE FINALE • 1968 • Celis Louis • BLG
APRES LA VIE see **AFTERLIFE** • 1978
APRES L'AMOUR • 1924 • Champreux Maurice • FRN
APRES L'AMOUR • 1931 • Perret Leonce • FRN
APRES L'AMOUR • 1947 • Tourneur Maurice • FRN
APRES L'AMOUR see **NA DE LIEFDE** • 1983
APRES LE BAL • 1897 • Melies Georges • FRN • BAIN DE LA PARISIENNE, LE ○ TUB, LE ○ AFTER THE BALL
APRES LE SILENCE • 1970 • Goldman Les, Clark John* • ANS • USA
APRES LE VENT DES SABLES • 1976 • Zaccai Claude • BLG, UKN • TRAME, LA ○ WEB, THE
APRES L'ORAGE • 1941 • Ducis Pierre-Jean • FRN • RETOUR
APRES "MEIN KAMPF" MES CRIMES • 1940 • Ryder Alexandre • FRN
APRES-MIDI D'UNE BOURGEOISE EN CHALEUR, LES • 1980 • Roy Jean-Claude • FRN
APRES-SKI • 1971 • Cardinal Roger • CND • SEX IN THE SNOW (USA)
APRES TOUT CE QU'ON A FAIT POUR TOI • Fansten Jacques • FRN
APRES VOUS, DUCHESSE • 1954 • de Nesle Robert • FRN
APRIL • 1916 • MacDonald Donald • USA
APRIL • 1961 • Ioseliani Otar • SHT • USS • APRIL (STORIES ABOUT THINGS)
APRIL 1, 2000 (USA) see **1 APRIL 2000** • 1952
APRIL 1ST, BRAZIL see **1' DE ABRIL, BRASIL** • 1988
APRIL '80 • 1980 • SAF
APRIL, APRIL • 1935 • Sirk Douglas • FRG
APRIL, APRIL • 1969 • Hoffmann Horst • FRG
APRIL CLOUDS see **BOLOND APRILIS** • 1957
APRIL FOLLY • 1920 • Leonard Robert Z. • USA
APRIL FOOL • 1911 • *Selig* • USA
APRIL FOOL • 1911 • *Edison* • USA
APRIL FOOL • 1918 • Holbrook John K. • USA
APRIL FOOL • 1920 • *Hamilton Lloyd* • USA
APRIL FOOL • 1924 • Parrott Charles • SHT • USA
APRIL FOOL • 1926 • Ross Nat • USA
APRIL FOOL see **KILLER PARTY** • 1986
APRIL FOOL JOKE, AN • 1903 • *Biograph* • USA
APRIL FOOLS, THE • 1969 • Rosenberg Stuart • USA
APRIL FOOL'S DAY • 1985 • Dugdale George, Ezra Mark, Litten Peter • USA • SLAUGHTER HIGH
APRIL FOOL'S DAY • 1986 • Walton Fred • USA
APRIL FROM CARIBE see **ABRIL DEL CARIBE** • 1982
APRIL IN PARIS • 1952 • Butler David • USA
APRIL IS HERE • Davidson William • USA
APRIL IS THE CRUELLEST MONTH • 1983 • Manttari Anssi • FNL
APRIL JOURNEY see **PUTESHESTVIE APRELY** • 1963
APRIL LOVE • 1957 • Levin Henry • USA
APRIL MORNING • 1988 • Mann Delbert • TVM • USA
APRIL ROMANCE (USA) see **BLOSSOM TIME** • 1934
APRIL SHOWERS • 1923 • Forman Tom • USA
APRIL SHOWERS • 1948 • Kern James V. • USA
APRIL (STORIES ABOUT THINGS) see **APRIL** • 1961
APROAPE DE SOARE • 1960 • Stiopul Savel • RMN • CLOSE TO THE SUN
APRON FOOLS • 1936 • Newman Widgey R. • UKN
APT PUPIL • 1988 • Bridges Alan • UKN
APTENODYTES FORSTERI • 1953 • Marret Mario • FRN • EMPEROR PENGUINS, THE
APU SANSAR • 1958 • Ray Satyajit • IND • WORLD OF APU, THE
APUNTE SOBRE ANA • 1971 • Galan • SPN • MEMORANDUM ON ANA
APUNTES • 1971 • Villafuerte Santiago • DOC • CUB
APUROS DE CLAUDINA, LOS • 1940 • Paz Miguel Caronatto • CLAUDINA'S TROUBLES (USA)
APUROS DE DOS GALLOS, LOS • 1962 • Gomez Muriel Emilio • MXC
APUROS DE MI AHIJADA, LOS • 1950 • Mendez Fernando • MXC
APUROS DE NARCISO, LOS • 1939 • Herrera Enrique • MXC
AQUA ANTICS • 1942 • Lewyn Louis • SHT • USA
AQUA DI ROMA • 1973 • Smit Boud • DOC • NTH
AQUA DUCK • 1963 • McKimson Robert • ANS • USA
AQUA SEX, THE see **MERMAIDS OF TIBERON, THE** • 1962
AQUAMANIA • 1961 • Reitherman Wolfgang • ANS • USA
AQUARELLE • 1965 • Delouche Dominique • SHT • FRN
AQUARIANS, THE • 1970 • McDougall Don • TVM • USA
AQUARIEN • 1974 • Brakhage Stan • USA
AQUARIUM • 1895 • Lumiere Louis • FRN
AQUARIUM • 1954 • Kollanyi Agoston • HNG
AQUARIUM • 1956 • Pintoff Ernest • ANS • USA
AQUARIUS see **STAGE FRIGHT** • 1986
AQUATIC ARTISTRY • 1936 • Miller David • SHT • USA
AQUATIC KIDS • 1953 • *Smith Pete* • SHT • USA
AQUEDUTOS PORTUGUESES • 1976 • Marques Carlos • SHT • PRT
AQUEL SABADO.. SABADETE • 1977 • Samso Roberto • SPN
AQUEL VIEJO MOLINO • 1946 • Iquino Ignacio F. • SPN
AQUELLA JOVEN DE BLANCO • 1965 • Klimovsky Leon • SPN • THAT GIRL IN WHITE
AQUELLA LARGA NOCHE • 1979 • Pineda Enrique • CUB • THAT LONG NIGHT
AQUELLA ROSITA ALVIREZ • 1965 • Cardona Rene? • MXC
AQUELLOS ANOS • 1972 • Cazals Felipe • MXC • THOSE YEARS
AQUELLOS OJOS VERDES • 1951 • Gomez Urquiza Zacarias • MXC
AQUELLOS TIEMPOS DEL CUPLE • 1959 • Cano Mateo, Merino Jose Luis • SPN
AQUI ESTA HERACLIO BERNAL • 1957 • Gavaldon Roberto • MXC
AQUI ESTA JUAN COLORADO • 1946 • Aguilar Rolando • MXC
AQUI ESTA TU ENAMORADO • 1962 • Salvador Jaime • MXC
AQUI ESTAN LAS VICETIPLES • 1960 • Fernandez Ramon • SPN
AQUI ESTAN LOS AGUILARES • 1955 • Salvador Jaime • MXC
AQUI ESTAN LOS VILLALOBOS • 1959 • Zambrano Enrique • MXC, CUB • REGRESO DE LOS VILLALOBOS, EL
AQUI HA FANTASMAS • 1963 • Martins Pedro • PRT
AQUI HAY PETROLEO • 1955 • Salvia Rafael J. • SPN
AQUI HUELE A MUERTO • 1989 • SPN
AQUI LLEGO EL VALENTON • 1938 • Rivero Fernando A. • MXC • FANFARRON, EL
AQUI MANDO YO • 1966 • Romero-Marchent Rafael • SPN
AQUI NO HA PASADO NADA • 1974 • Cortez Cesar • VNZ • NOTHING HAS HAPPENED HERE
AQUI PORTUGAL • 1948 • Miranda Armando • PRT
AQUILA • 1981 • Romero Eddie • PHL • EAGLE, THE
AQUILA NERA • 1946 • Freda Riccardo • ITL • BLACK EAGLE, THE
AQUILEO VENGANZA • 1968 • Duran Ciro • VNZ, CLM • VENGEANCE OF AQUILLES, THE ○ AQUILEO'S VENGEANCE
AQUILEO'S VENGEANCE see **AQUILEO VENGANZA** • 1968
AR, AGUA E LUZ • 1955 • Garcia Fernando • SHT • PRT
AR DU INTE RIKTIGT KLOK? • 1964 • Gamlin Yngve • SWD • YOU MUST BE CRAZY DARLING!
AR MED HENRY, ET • 1967 • Roos Jorgen • DOC • DNM
ARA IS, AL- • 1959 • Saleh Tewfik • SHT • EGY • MARIONNETTES, LES
ARAB, THE • 1915 • De Mille Cecil B. • USA
ARAB, THE • 1924 • Ingram Rex • USA
ARAB GIRL'S LOVE, THE • 1912 • *Art Films* • UKN
ARAB ISRAELI DIALOGUE • 1974 • Rogosin Lionel • SHT • USA
ARABA: THE VILLAGE STORY • 1967 • Sutherland Efua • GHN
ARABAT AL SHAITAN • 1962 • Qa'l Georges • LBN • DEVIL'S CHARIOT, THE
ARABELLA • 1916 • Hertz Aleksander • PLN
ARABELLA • 1924 • Grune Karl • FRG • ROMAN EINES PFERDES, DER
ARABELLA • 1967 • Bolognini Mauro • ITL, USA
ARABELLA 252104 see **PIACERI DEL SABATO NOTTE, I** • 1960
ARABELLA AND THE SOFT SOAP • 1915 • Read James • UKN • ARABELLA SELLS SOFT SOAP
ARABELLA AND THE WIZARD • 1913 • *Lux* • FRN
ARABELLA IN SOCIETY • 1915 • Read James • SHT • UKN
ARABELLA MEETS RAFFLES • 1915 • Read James • SHT • UKN
ARABELLA OUT OF A JOB • 1915 • Read James • SHT • UKN
ARABELLA SELLS SOFT SOAP see **ARABELLA AND THE SOFT SOAP** • 1915
ARABELLA SPIES SPIES see **PATRIOTIC ARABELLA** • 1915
ARABELLA THE LADY SLAVEY • 1915 • Read James • SHT • UKN
ARABELLA VS. LYNXEYE • 1915 • Read James • SHT • UKN
ARABELLA'S ANTICS • 1915 • Read James • SHT • UKN
ARABELLA'S FRIGHTFULNESS • 1915 • Read James • SHT • UKN
ARABELLA'S MOTOR CAR • 1915 • Read James • SHT • UKN
ARABELLA'S PRINCE • 1916 • *Barnes Justus* • USA
ARABELLA'S ROMANCE • 1914 • *Crystal* • USA
ARABELLA'S UNCLE • 1912 • *Nestor* • USA
ARABESK • 1988 • Egilmez Ertem • TRK
ARABESQUE • 1966 • Donen Stanley • USA, UKN
ARABESQUE see **ETUDE CINEMATOGRAPHIQUE SUR UNE ARABESQUE** • 1928
ARABESQUE FOR KENNETH ANGER • 1961 • Menken Marie • SHT • USA
ARABESQUES ON PIROSMANI • 1986 • Paradjanov Sergei • SHT • USS
ARABIA • 1922 • Reynolds Lynn • USA • TOM MIX IN ARABIA ○ DRUMS OF ARABY
ARABIA AND THE BAY • 1913 • Eagle Oscar • USA
ARABIA INCIDENT, THE • 1978 • Stoneman John • MTV • CND
ARABIA TAKES THE HEALTH CURE • 1913 • Eagle Oscar • USA
ARABIA, THE EQUINE DETECTIVE • 1913 • Eagle Oscar • USA
ARABIAN ADVENTURE, AN • 1979 • Connor Kevin • UKN

ARABIAN BAZAAR • 1937-40 • *Cardiff Jack (Ph)* • DCS • UKN
ARABIAN DESERT OUTLAWS see **OUTLAWS OF THE DESERT** • 1941
ARABIAN DUET • 1922 • Leventhal J. F.
ARABIAN HORSES see **ARABY** • 1964
ARABIAN JEWISH DANCE • 1903 • Porter Edwin S. • USA
ARABIAN KNIGHT, AN • 1920 • Swickard Charles • USA
ARABIAN KNIGHTS • 1931 • Roberts Stephen • SHT • USA
ARABIAN LOVE • 1922 • Storm Jerome • USA
ARABIAN MAGICIAN • 1906 • *Pathe* • FRN
ARABIAN NIGHT, AN • 1929 • Jeffrey R. E. • UKN
ARABIAN NIGHTS • 1926 • IND
ARABIAN NIGHTS • 1942 • Rawlins John • USA
ARABIAN NIGHTS see **POHADKY TISICE A JEDNE NOCI** • 1972
ARABIAN NIGHTS see **FIORE DELLE MILLE E UNA NOTTE, IL** • 1974
ARABIAN NIGHTS CARTOONS • 1923-24 • *Harman Hugh/ Ising Rudolf (P)* • ASS • USA
ARABIAN TIGHTS • 1933 • Roach Hal • SHT • USA
ARABIAN TRAGEDY, AN • 1912 • Olcott Sidney • USA
ARABICS 1,2,3,4,5,6,7,8,9,0,10,11,12,13,14,15,16,17,18,19 • 1980-81 • Brakhage Stan • SER • USA
ARABIE INCONNUE see **ARABIE INTERDITE** • 1937
ARABIE INTERDITE • 1937 • Clement Rene • DOC • FRN • ARABIE INCONNUE
ARABS see **ARABY** • 1964
ARAB'S BRIDE, THE • 1912 • *La Badie Florence* • USA
ARAB'S CURSE, THE • 1915 • Kiralfy A.? • UKN
ARAB'S VENGEANCE, THE • 1915 • Davis Ulysses • USA
ARABS WITH DIRTY FEZZES • 1939 • Lovy Alex • ANS • USA
ARABU NO ARASHI • 1961 • Nakahira Ko • JPN • STORM OVER ARABIA
ARABY • 1964 • Raplewski Zbigniew • DOC • PLN • ARABS ○ ARABIAN HORSES
ARACHIDE DE SANCHIRA, L' • 1966 • Alassane Moustapha • NGR
ARACHNOPHOBIA • 1990 • Marshall Frank* • USA
ARACHVEULEBRIVI GAMOPENA see **NEOBYKNOVENNAIA VYSTAVKA** • 1968
ARADHANA • 1969 • *Burman S. D. (M)* • IND
ARAGO X001 • 1972-73 • Image Jean • ASS • FRN
ARAGOSTE A COLAZIONE • 1979 • Capitani Giorgio • ITL, FRN • LANGOUSTE AU PETIT DEJEUNER, UNE (FRN)
ARAGOUZE, EL • 1988 • Lachine Hani • EGY • PUPPET PLAYER, THE
ARAIGNEE D'EAU, L' • 1969 • Verhaegue Jean-Daniel • FRN • WATER SPIDER, THE
ARAIGNEE VERTE, L' • 1916 • Volkov Alexander • USS
ARAIGNEES ROUGES, LES • 1955 • Tadie, Lacoste • SHT • FRN
ARAIGNELEPHANT • 1969 • Kamler Piotr • ANS • FRN
ARAKURE • 1957 • Naruse Mikio • JPN • UNTAMED WOMAN ○ UNTAMED ○ BRAWNY
ARAMUTES • 1978 • Bacso Peter • HNG • ELECTRIC SHOCK
ARAN • 1973 • Combe Georges • DOC • FRN
ARAN, GREAT ROCK, LITTLE CLAY see **MORCHID CLOCH IS GANNCHUID CRE** • 1988
ARANAS INFERNALES • 1966 • Curiel Federico • MXC • CEREBROS DIABOLICOS ○ HELLISH SPIDERS
ARANKA UND ARAUKA • 1918 • Hanus Emerich? • FRG
ARANYAK • 1963 • *Ghatak Ritwik* • IND
ARANYASO • 1914 • Curtiz Michael • HNG • GOLDEN SHOVEL, THE
ARANYE DINRATRI • 1969 • Ray Satyajit • IND • DAYS AND NIGHTS IN THE FOREST ○ ARANYER DIN RAATRI
ARANYEMBER • 1937 • Gaal Bela • HNG
ARANYEMBER, AZ • 1917 • Korda Alexander • HNG • MAN WITH THE GOLDEN TOUCH, THE ○ GOLDEN MAN
ARANYEMBER, AZ • 1962 • Gertler Viktor • HNG • MAN WITH THE GOLDEN TOUCH, THE
ARANYER DIN RAATRI see **ARANYE DINRATRI** • 1969
ARANYKESZTYU LOVAGJAI, AZ • 1968 • Keleti Marton • HNG • KNIGHTS OF GOLDEN GLOVE, THE
ARANYKOR • 1963 • Gabor Pal • HNG • GOLDEN YEARS
ARANYMETSZES • 1962 • Takacs Gabor • DOC • HNG • GOLDEN SECTION, THE
ARANYSARKANY • 1966 • Ranody Laszlo • HNG • GOLDEN KITE, THE ○ GOLDEN CAGE, THE
ARAPPOINOWA GOMENDAZE • 1967 • Segawa Masaharu • JPN • KILLER COMES BACK, THE
ARASA KATTALAI • 1967 • Chakrapani M. G. • IND • KING'S ORDERS
ARASHI • 1956 • Inagaki Hiroshi • JPN • STORM, THE
ARASHI GA OKA • 1988 • Yoshida Yoshishige • JPN • WUTHERING HEIGHTS
ARASHI KITARI SARU • 1967 • Masuda Toshio • JPN • STORM CAME AND WENT
ARASHI NI TATSU • 1968 • Hase Kazuo • JPN • MAN IN THE STORM
ARASHI NO HATASHIJO • 1968 • Matsuo Akinori • JPN • DUEL IN THE STORM, THE
ARASHI NO KUDOKEN • 1958 • Edagawa Hiroshi • JPN • JUDO CHAMP
ARASHI NO NAKA NO OTOKO • 1957 • Taniguchi Senkichi • JPN • MAN IN THE STORM
ARASHI NO NAKA O TSUPPASHIRE • 1958 • Kurahara Koreyoshi • JPN • SHOWDOWN IN THE STORM
ARASHI O TSUKKIRU JETTOKI • 1961 • Kurahara Koreyoshi • JPN • BREAKING THE STORM BARRIER
ARASHI O YOBU JUHACHI-NIN • 1963 • Yoshida Yoshishige • JPN • EIGHTEEN ROUGHS
ARASHI O YOBU OTOKO • 1957 • Inoue Umeji • JPN • STORMY MAN
ARAT AZ OROSHAZI DOZSA • 1953 • Jancso Miklos • SHT • HNG • HARVEST IN THE COOPERATIVE DOSZA
ARAUCANA, LA • 1970 • Coll Julio • SPN, ITL • ARAUCANA MASSACRO DEGLI DEI, L' (ITL)
ARAUCANA MASSACRO DEGLI DEI, L' (ITL) see **ARAUCANA, LA** • 1970
ARAUMI NO OJA • 1959 • Taguchi Tetsu • JPN
ARAW-ARAW • 1989 • PHL
ARAYA • 1958 • Benacerraf Margot • DOC • VNZ
ARBEIT MACHT FREI (FRG) see **ACCIAIO** • 1933
ARBEJDET ADLER • 1914 • Blom August • DNM
ARBEJDET KALDER • 1941 • Henning-Jensen Bjarne • DOC • DNM
ARBELETE, L' • 1984 • Gobbi Sergio • FRN
ARBITRO, L' • 1974 • D'Amico Luigi Filippo • ITL • FOOTBALL CRAZY
ARBOLES DE BUENOS AIRES, LOS • 1957 • Torre-Nilsson Leopoldo • SHT • ARG
ARBOR DAY • 1936 • Newmeyer Fred • SHT • USA
ARBORIZACAO DAS SERRAS, A • 1947 • Coelho Jose Adolfo • SHT • PRT
ARBRE, L' • 1961 • Mayo Nine • FRN
ARBRE DE GUERNICA, L' • 1975 • Arrabal Fernando • FRN, ITL • GUERNICA
ARBRE DE NOEL, L' • 1969 • Young Terence • FRN, ITL • ALBERO DI NATALE, L' (ITL) ○ CHRISTMAS TREE, THE (USA) ○ WHEN WOLVES CRY
ARBRES • 1935 • Gopax Robert • BLG
ARBRES AUX CHAMPIGNONS • 1951 • Markopoulos Gregory J. • USA
ARBRES ET BETES • 1942-43 • Tessier Albert • DCS • CND
ARBUTUS • 1911 • *Gardner Helen* • USA
ARC • 1970 • Zolnay Pal • HNG • FACE, THE
ARC, THE (USA) see **ARCHE, DIE** • 1919
ARCADE • 1969 • Sharman Jim • SHT • ASL
ARCADE • 1970 • Sinden Tony • UKN
ARCADIA REVISITED • 1919 • Miller Frank • SHT • UKN
ARCADIAN MAID, AN • 1910 • Griffith D. W. • USA
ARCADIAN SPRING SONG • 1935 • Sparling Gordon • DCS • CND
ARCADIANS, THE • 1927 • Saville Victor • UKN • LAND OF HEART'S DESIRE
ARCANA • 1972 • Questi Giulio • ITL
ARCANGELI, GLI • 1963 • Battaglia Enzo • ITL • ARCHANGELS, THE (USA)
ARCANGELO, L' • 1969 • Capitani Giorgio • ITL
ARCANUM • 1916 • Heiland Heinz Karl • FRG
ARCH, THE see **TUNG FU-JEN** • 1969
ARCH CRIMINALS OF PARIS, THE see **VAMPIRES, LES** • 1915-16
ARCH OF TRIUMPH • 1948 • Milestone Lewis • USA
ARCH OF TRIUMPH • 1985 • Hussein Waris • TVM • USA
ARCHA PANA SERVADACA see **NA KOMETE** • 1970
ARCHAEOLOGIST, THE • 1914 • *American* • USA
ARCHAEOLOGY see **ARCHEOLOGIA** • 1968
ARCHANDEL GABRIEL A PANI HUSA • 1965 • Trnka Jiri • ANM • CZC • ARCHANGEL GABRIEL AND MISTRESS GOOSE, THE (USA) ○ ARCHANGEL GABRIEL AND MOTHER GOOSE, THE ○ ARCHANGEL GABRIEL AND MRS. GOOSE, THE
ARCHANGEL • 1966 • Gruen Victor • SHT • USA
ARCHANGEL • 1990 • Maddin Guy • CND
ARCHANGEL GABRIEL AND MISTRESS GOOSE, THE (USA) see **ARCHANDEL GABRIEL A PANI HUSA** • 1965
ARCHANGEL GABRIEL AND MOTHER GOOSE, THE see **ARCHANDEL GABRIEL A PANI HUSA** • 1965
ARCHANGEL GABRIEL AND MRS. GOOSE, THE see **ARCHANDEL GABRIEL A PANI HUSA** • 1965
ARCHANGELS, THE (USA) see **ARCANGELI, GLI** • 1963
ARCHE, DIE • 1919 • Oswald Richard • FRG • ARC, THE (USA)
ARCHE DE NOE, L' • 1946 • Henry-Jacques • FRN • NOAH'S ARK (USA)
ARCHE DE NOE, L' • 1966 • Laguionie Jean-Francois • ANS • FRN • NOAH'S ARK
ARCHE NORA • 1948 • Klinger Werner • FRG
ARCHEOLOGIA • 1968 • Brzozowski Andrzej • DOC • PLN • ARCHAEOLOGY
ARCHER see **ARCHER'S ADVENTURE** • 1987
ARCHER, THE see **JOUSIAMPUJA** • 1983
ARCHER AND THE SORCERESS, THE • 1980 • Corea Nick • MTV • USA • ARCHER: FUGITIVE FROM THE EMPIRE ○ FUGITIVE OF THE EMPIRE
ARCHER: FUGITIVE FROM THE EMPIRE see **ARCHER AND THE SORCERESS, THE** • 1980
ARCHER'S ADVENTURE • 1987 • Lawrence Denny • ASL • ARCHER
ARCHIBALD APPLIES FOR A SITUATION AS A CHAUFFEUR-GARDENER • 1913 • *Summit* • UKN
ARCHIBALD IN A TANGLE • 1914 • Evans Joe? • UKN
ARCHIBALD, THE HERO • 1911 • *Reynolds Noah* • USA
ARCHIBALDO see **ENSAYO DE UN CRIMEN** • 1955
ARCHIBALD'S EGG DIET • 1914 • Evans Joe? • UKN
ARCHIE AND THE BELL-BOY • 1913 • Williams C. Jay • USA
ARCHIE GOES SHOPPING WITH THE GIRLS • 1908 • *Warwick Trading Co* • UKN
ARCHIE SHEPP CHEZ LES TAUREGS • 1970 • Bendeddouche Ghaouti • DCS • ALG
ARCHIE SHEPP CHEZ LES TOUAREGS • 1971 • Robichet Theo • SHT • FRN
ARCHIE SHEPP: JE SUIS JAZZ.. C'EST MA VIE • 1984 • Cassenti Frank • FRN
ARCHIE THE ANT • 1925 • *Smith Frank Percy (P)* • ASS • UKN • BEDTIME STORIES OF ARCHIE THE ANT ○ BERTIE BEETLE
ARCHIE'S ARCHERY • 1910 • *Lubin* • USA
ARCHIMEDE see **ASSEDIO DI SIRACUSA, L'** • 1960
ARCHIMEDE, LE CLOCHARD • 1959 • Grangier Gilles • FRN, ITL • MAGNIFICENT TRAMP, THE (USA) ○ ARCHIMEDE THE TRAMP ○ TRAMP
ARCHIMEDE THE TRAMP see **ARCHIMEDE, LE CLOCHARD** • 1959
ARCHIPEL DE MINGAN, L' • 1978 • Kinsey Nicholas • DOC • CND
ARCHIPEL DE MINGAN, L' • 1981 • Lesaunier Daniel • MTV • CND
ARCHISEXE, L' • 1972 • Rhomm Patrice • FRN, BLG
ARCHITECT OF ONE'S OWN FUTURE see **ENVAR SIN EGEN LYCKAS SMED** • 1917
ARCHITECTURAL MILLINERY • 1954 • Peterson Sidney • USA
ARCHITECTURE -A PERFORMING ART • 1979 • Robertson Michael • DOC • ASL
ARCHITECTURE, ART DE L'ESPACE • 1960 • Haesaerts Paul • BLG • ART OF SPACE, THE
ARCHITECTURE DU M'ZAB • Kerzabi Ahmed • ALG
ARCHITECTURE ET CHAUFFAGE D'AUJOURD'HUI • 1960 • Berr • SHT • FRN
ARCHITECTURE ET LUMIERE • 1953 • Colpi Henri, Ganancia J.-P. • SHT • FRN
ARCHITECTURE OF ENTERTAINMENT • 1960 • Russell Ken • MTV • UKN
ARCHIVES SECRETES DE MAISONS CLOSES, LES • 1976 • Joyeux Philippe • FRN
ARCHY AND MEHITABEL see **SHINBONE ALLEY** • 1971
ARCIDIAVOLO, L' • 1940 • Frenguelli Tony • ITL
ARCIDIAVOLO, L' • 1966 • Scola Ettore • ITL • DEVIL IN LOVE, THE (USA) ○ DIAVOLO INNAMORATO, IL
ARCIERE DELLA FORESTA NERA, L' see **GUGLIELMO TELL** • 1949
ARCIERE DELLE MILLE E UNA NOTTE, L' see **FRECCIA D'ORO, LA** • 1962
ARCIERE DI FUOCO, L' • 1971 • Ferroni Giorgio • ITL, FRN, SPN • GRANDE CHEVAUCHEE DE ROBIN DES BOIS, LA (FRN) ○ ARQUERO DE SHERWOOD, L'
ARCIERE NERO, L' • 1959 • Pierotti Piero • ITL
ARCIPELAGO DI FUOCO • 1957 • Andrei Marcello • DOC • ITL
ARCOBALENO • 1943 • Ferroni Giorgio, Abel Gustavo • ITL
ARCOLAIO DI BARBERINA, L' • 1918 • D'Ambra Lucio • ITL
ARCTIC • 1967 • Pearson Peter • DOC • CND
ARCTIC ANTICS • 1930 • Iwerks Ub • ANS • USA
ARCTIC CIRCLE • 1961 • Bairstow David • SER • CND
ARCTIC DOG TEAM • Wilkinson Douglas • DCS • CND
ARCTIC FLIGHT • 1952 • Landers Lew • USA
ARCTIC FURY • 1949 • Dawn Norman, Feitshans Fred R. Jr. • USA
ARCTIC GIANT, THE • 1942 • Fleischer Dave • ANS • USA
ARCTIC HARVEST • 1946 • Gilbert Lewis* • DCS • UKN
ARCTIC HEAT • 1985 • Harlin Renny • USA • BORN AMERICAN
ARCTIC LABORATORY • 1952 • Blanchard Guy • DOC • UKN
ARCTIC LINE, THE see **ARKTINEN VIIVA** • 1988
ARCTIC MANHUNT • 1949 • Scott Ewing • USA
ARCTIC PATROL, THE • 1929 • Finnie Richard S. • USA
ARCTIC RIVALS • 1954 • Davis Mannie • ANS • USA
ARCTIC SAFARI • 1964 • Hayes Ron • USA
ARCTIC SEA IS CALLING, THE see **EISMEER RUFT, DAS**
ARCTIC SPIRITS • 1982 • Raymont Peter • DOC • CND • NEW SHAMANS, THE
ARD', AL- see **ARD, EL** • 1969
ARD, EL • 1969 • Shahin Youssef • EGY • ARD', AL- ○ TERRE, LA ○ EARTH, THE ○ LAND, THE
ARD' AL-AHLAM • 1957 • el Sheikh Kamal • EGY • TERRE DE REVE
ARD AL MAHROUKA, AL • 1970 • Siam Ali • JRD • BURNING EARTH
ARD' AS-SALAM • 1957 • el Sheikh Kamal • EGY • TERRE DE PAIX
ARD EL NEFAK • 1968 • Wahab Fatin Abdel • EGY • LAND OF LIARS ○ ARDHU AN-NIFAQ
ARDENT HEART, THE see **HOROUCI SRDCE** • 1962
ARDENT PATIENCE see **ARDIENTE PACIENCIA**
ARDH SATYA • 1983 • Nihalani Govind • IND • HALF-TRUTH
ARDHU AN-NIFAQ see **ARD EL NEFAK** • 1968
ARDIENTE PACIENCIA • Skarmeta Antonio • FRG • ARDENT PATIENCE
ARDITI CIVILI • 1940 • Gambino Domenico M. • ITL
ARDOISE, L' • 1969 • Bernard-Aubert Claude • FRN, ITL
ARE ACTORS PEOPLE? • 1917 • *Pokes & Jabs* • USA
ARE ALL MEN ALIKE? • 1920 • Rosen Phil • USA
ARE BLOND MEN BASHFUL? • 1924 • Roach Hal • SHT • USA
ARE BRIDES HAPPY? • 1920 • *Christie* • USA
ARE BRUNETTES FALSE? • 1918 • *Strand* • USA
ARE BRUNETTES SAFE? • 1927 • Roach Hal • SHT • USA
ARE CHILDREN TO BLAME? • 1922 • Price Paul • USA • ARE THE CHILDREN TO BLAME?
ARE CROOKS DISHONEST? • 1918 • Roach Hal • SHT • USA
ARE ERA • 1962 • Landow George • SHT • USA
ARE FLIRTS FOOLISH? • 1919 • *Gayety Comedies* • USA
ARE FLOORWALKERS FICKLE? • 1920 • *Gayety Comedies* • USA
ARE GA MINATO NO HIKARI DA • 1961 • Imai Tadashi • JPN • PAN CHOPALI ○ THAT IS THE PORT LIGHT
ARE HUSBANDS HUMAN? • 1925 • Roach Hal • SHT • USA
ARE HUSBANDS NECESSARY? • 1942 • Taurog Norman • USA • MR. AND MRS. CUGAT
ARE HUSBANDS NECESSARY? see **HONEYMOON IN BALI** • 1939
ARE MARRIED POLICEMAN SAFE? • 1918 • Jones F. Richard • SHT • USA
ARE PARENTS PEOPLE? • 1925 • St. Clair Malcolm • USA
ARE PARENTS PICKLES? • 1925 • Roach Hal • SHT • USA
ARE PEOPLE SHEEP? • 1956 • Biggs Julian • CND
ARE SECOND MARRIAGES HAPPY? • 1918 • *Belasco Jay* • USA
ARE THE BLACKBERRIES RIPE? see **KIZILCIKLAR OLDU MU?** • 1967
ARE THE CHILDREN TO BLAME? see **ARE CHILDREN TO BLAME?** • 1922
ARE THESE OUR CHILDREN? • 1931 • Ruggles Wesley • USA
ARE THESE OUR CHILDREN? see **YOUTH RUNS WILD** • 1944
ARE THESE OUR CHILDREN? (UKN) see **AGE OF CONSENT** • 1932
ARE THESE OUR PARENTS? • 1944 • Nigh William • USA • THEY ARE GUILY (UKN)
ARE THEY BORN OR MADE? • 1915 • *Warners Features* • USA
ARE WAITRESSES SAFE? • 1917 • Heerman Victor • USA
ARE WE? see **SOMOS?** • 1982
ARE WE ALL MURDERERS? (UKN) see **NOUS SOMMES TOUS DES ASSASSINS** • 1952
ARE WE ALONE IN THE UNIVERSE? • 1978 • Gale George • USA
ARE WE CIVILIZED? • 1934 • Carewe Edwin • USA
ARE WE MARRIED? see **A VI GIFTA?** • 1936
ARE WIVES UNREASONABLE? • 1918 • *Brady Ed* • SHT • USA
ARE WORKING GIRLS SAFE? • 1918 • *Ebony* • SHT • USA
ARE YOU A FAILURE? • 1923 • Forman Tom • USA

ARE YOU A MASON? • 1915 • Heffron Thomas N. • USA
ARE YOU A MASON? • 1934 • Edwards Henry • UKN
ARE YOU AFRAID? see **ER I BANGE?** • 1971
ARE YOU ALONE TONIGHT? see **MIND OVER MURDER** • 1979
ARE YOU AMONG THEM? see **CZY JESTES WSROD NICH?** • 1954
ARE YOU AMONGST THEM? see **CZY JESTES WSROD NICH?** • 1954
ARE YOU AN ELK? • 1916 • Webster Harry Mcrae • USA
ARE YOU BEING SERVED? • 1977 • Kellett Bob • UKN
ARE YOU BORED WITH MEN? see **DARLING, ARE YOU BORED WITH MEN?** • 1968
ARE YOU DYING, YOUNG MAN? see **BEAST IN THE CELLAR, THE** • 1970
ARE YOU GOING UP OR DOWN? see **SUBES O BAJAS?** • 1970
ARE YOU IN THE HOUSE ALONE? • 1978 • Grauman Walter • TVM • USA
ARE YOU JOHN BROWN? • 1910 • Fitzhamon Lewin? • UKN
ARE YOU JOKING? • 1973 • Koshelev N., Morozov V. • USS
ARE YOU LEGALLY MARRIED? • 1919 • Thornby Robert T. • USA
ARE YOU LISTENING? • 1932 • Beaumont Harry • USA
ARE YOU POSITIVE? • 1957 • Porter Eric • DOC • USA
ARE YOU SINCERE? • 1907 • Gilbert Arthur • UKN
ARE YOU SINCERE? • 1909 • *Warwick Trading Co* • UKN
ARE YOU THE MAN? • 1909 • *Lubin* • USA
ARE YOU THERE? • 1901 • Williamson James • UKN
ARE YOU THERE? • 1930 • MacFadden Hamilton • USA • EXIT LAUGHING
ARE YOU WITH IT? • 1948 • Hively Jack • USA
AREIA MAR, MAR AREIA • 1972 • Guimaraes Manuel • SHT • PRT
AREJAO • 1951 • Mastrocinque Camillo • SPN
ARENA • 1953 • Fleischer Richard • USA
ARENA • 1969 • Vas Judit • SHT • HNG
ARENA • 1979 • Siegel Lois • ANS • CND
ARENA • 1988 • Manoogian Peter • USA
ARENA see **ARYENA** • 1967
ARENA 61 • 1965 • Perling P. • SHT • FRG
ARENA, THE • 1974 • Carver Steve • USA
ARENA OF FEAR see **GELIEBTE BESTIE** • 1959
ARENA,L' • 1919 • Mari Febo • ITL
ARENDAS ZSIDO, AZ • 1917 • Curtiz Michael • HNG • JOHN, THE TENANT
ARENES JOYEUSES • 1935 • Anton Karl • FRN
ARENES JOYEUSES • 1957 • de Canonge Maurice • FRN
ARENES SANGLANTES • 1917 • Diamant-Berger Henri • FRN
AREN'T MEN BEASTS? • 1937 • Cutts Graham • UKN
AREN'T WE ALL? • 1932 • Lachman Harry • UKN
AREN'T WE WONDERFUL? see **WIR WUNDERKINDER** • 1958
ARENTINO'S BLUE STORIES • 1973 • Bomba Enrico • ITL
ARES CONTRE ATLAS • 1967 • Otero Manuel • ANS • FRN
ARETINO NEI SUOI RAGIONAMENTI.. SULLE CORTIGIANE, LE MARITATE E I CORNUTI CONTENTI, L' • 1972 • Bomba Enrico • ITL
ARETINO'S STORIES OF THE THREE LUSTFUL DAUGHTERS (UKN) see **SI SALVO SOLO L'ARETINO PIETRO CON UNA MANO AVANTI E L'ALTRA DIETRO** • 1972
ARGENT, L' • 1928 • L'Herbier Marcel • FRN • MONEY
ARGENT, L' • 1936 • Billon Pierre • FRN
ARGENT, L' • 1974 • Dansereau Fernand, Rossignol Yolande • SHT • CND
ARGENT, L' • 1983 • Bresson Robert • FRN, SWT • MONEY
ARGENT DE LA BANQUE, L' see **SILENT PARTNER, THE** • 1978
ARGENT DE POCHE, L' • 1976 • Truffaut Francois • FRN • SMALL CHANGE (USA) ○ POCKET MONEY ○ SPENDING MONEY
ARGENT DES AUTRES, L' • 1979 • de Chalonge Christian • FRN • OTHER PEOPLE'S MONEY
ARGENT ET LES FEMMES, L' see **MALUN WA NISA'** • 1960
ARGENT QUI TUE, L' • 1919 • Denola Georges • FRN
ARGENTINA see **LAW OF THE PAMPAS** • 1939
ARGENTINA HASTA LA MUERTE • 1968 • Ayala Fernando • ARG
ARGENTINE LOVE • 1924 • Dwan Allan • USA
ARGENTINE NIGHTS • 1940 • Rogell Albert S. • USA
ARGENTINE SOCCER see **FUTBOL ARGENTINO** • 1990
ARGENTINE TANGO AND OTHER DANCES, THE • 1913 • *Grossmith George* • UKN
ARGENTINIAN TILL I DIE see **ARGENTINO HASTA LA MUERTE** • 1972
ARGENTINISIMA • 1972 • Ayala Fernando, Olivera Hector • ARG
ARGENTINO HASTA LA MUERTE • 1972 • Ayala Fernando • ARG • ARGENTINIAN TILL I DIE
ARGILA • 1940 • Mauro-Humberto • BRZ • CLAY
ARGINE, L' • 1938 • D'Errico Corrado • ITL
ARGIRO, I PRODHOMENI TSELIGOPOULA • 1968 • Konstantinou Panayotis • GRC • ARGIRO, THE BETRAYED
ARGIRO, THE BETRAYED see **ARGIRO, I PRODHOMENI TSELIGOPOULA** • 1968
ARGOMAN SUPERDIABOLICO see **COME RUBARE LA CORONA D'INGHILTERRA** • 1967
ARGOMAN THE FANTASTIC SUPERMAN see **COME RUBARE LA CORONA D'INGHILTERRA** • 1967
ARGONAUTI, GLI see **GIGANTI DELLA TESSAGLIA, I** • 1960
ARGONAUTS, THE • 1911 • *Selig* • USA
ARGONAUTS, THE • 1956 • Bare Richard L. • MTV • USA
ARGONAUTS, THE see **GIGANTI DELLA TESSAGLIA, I** • 1960
ARGONAUTS OF CALIFORNIA • 1916 • Kabierske Henry • USA
ARGUMENT, THE see **EVIDENCE** • 1918
ARGUS X • 1918 • Larsen Viggo • FRG
ARGYLE CASE, THE • 1917 • Ince Ralph • USA
ARGYLE CASE, THE • 1929 • Bretherton Howard • USA
ARGYLE SECRETS, THE • 1948 • Endfield Cy • USA
ARHONTES • 1976 • Manousakis Manousos • GRC • RULERS, THE ○ POWER
ARHONTISA KE O ALITIS, I • 1968 • Dimopoulos Dinos • GRC • LADY AND THE PAUPER, THE
ARHUS BY NIGHT • 1988 • Malmros Nils • DNM
ARI NO MACHI NO MARIA • 1958 • Gosho Heinosuke • JPN • MARIA OF THE ANT VILLAGE ○ MARIA OF THE STREET OF ANTS
ARIA • 1987 • Altman Robert, Beresford Bruce, Bryden Bill, Jarman Derek, Godard Jean-Luc, Roddam Franc, Roeg Nicolas, Sturridge Charles, Temple Julien, Russell Ken • UKN
ARIA DEL CONTINENTE, L' • 1935 • Righelli Gennaro • ITL • CONTINENTAL ATMOSPHERE (USA)
ARIA DI PAESE • 1933 • De Liguoro Eugenio • ITL • IN CAMPAGNA, CHE PASSIONE!
ARIA DI PARIGI (ITL) see **AIR DE PARIS, L'** • 1954
ARIA DLA ATLETY • 1978 • Bajon Filip • PLN • ARIA FOR AN ATHLETE
ARIA FOR AN ATHLETE see **ARIA DLA ATLETY** • 1978
ARIADNE IN HOPPEGARTEN • 1928 • Dinesen Robert • FRG
ARIANE • 1931 • Czinner Paul • UKN, FRG
ARIANE, JEUNE FILLE RUSSE • 1931 • Czinner Paul • FRN
ARIANE (USA) see **LOVES OF ARIANE, THE** • 1931
ARIANNA • 1970 • Obadiah George • ISR
ARIBA LAS MUJERES • 1964 • Salvador Julio • SPN
ARIBARA TO YONJUPIKINO TOZOKU • 1971 • *Toei* • ANM • JPN • ALIBABA AND THE FORTY THIEVES (USA)
ARIE HANGGARA • 1986 • INN
ARIE PRERIE • 1949 • Trnka Jiri • ANM • CZC • SONG OF THE PRAIRIE
ARIEL • 1988 • Kaurismaki Aki • FNL
ARIF FROM BALAT see **BALATLI ARIF** • 1967
ARIGATOSAN • 1937 • Shimizu Hiroshi • JPN
ARINI • Sophiaan Sophan • INN
ARIRANG • 1926 • Ra Un-Gya • KOR
ARIS EL THANI, EL • 1967 • el Saifi Hassan • EGY • SECOND GROOM, THE
ARIS VELOUCHIOTIS –DILEMMA see **ARIS VELOUCHIOTIS – DILIMA** • 1981
ARIS VELOUCHIOTIS –DILIMA • 1981 • Lambrinos Fotos • GRC • ARIS VELOUCHIOTIS –DILEMMA
ARISAN NO KYOJI • 1927 • Tasaka Tomotaka • JPN
ARISE MY LOVE • 1940 • Leisen Mitchell • USA
ARISTIDE MAILLOL, SCULPTEUR • 1943 • Lods Jean • DCS • FRN
ARISTO, L' • 1934 • Berthomieu Andre • FRN
ARISTO CAT, THE • 1943 • Jones Charles M. • ANS • USA
ARISTOCATS, THE • 1970 • Reitherman Wolfgang • ANM • USA
ARISTOCRACY • 1914 • Heffron Thomas N. • USA
ARISTOCRATES, LES • 1955 • de La Patelliere Denys • FRN • ARISTOCRATS, THE
ARISTOCRATS, THE see **ARISTOCRATES, LES** • 1955
ARISTOCRAT'S STAIRS see **KIZOKU NO KAIDAN** • 1959
ARISTOTLE see **JAK SE MOUDRY ARISTOTELES STAL JESTE MOUDREJSIM** • 1970
ARITHMETIQUE, L' • 1951 • Kast Pierre • SHT • FRN
ARIZONA • 1913 • McGill Lawrence • USA
ARIZONA • 1918 • Fairbanks Douglas, Parker Albert • USA
ARIZONA • 1931 • Seitz George B. • USA • VIRTUOUS WIFE, THE (UKN) ○ MEN ARE LIKE THAT
ARIZONA • 1941 • Ruggles Wesley • USA
ARIZONA AMES see **THUNDER TRAIL** • 1937
ARIZONA BAD MAN • 1935 • Luby S. Roy • USA
ARIZONA BILL • 1909 • Durand Jean • SER • FRN
ARIZONA BILL • 1911 • Vignola Robert G., Melford George • USA
ARIZONA BILL see **STRADA PER FORT ALAMO, LA** • 1965
ARIZONA BILL L'ATTAQUE D'UN TRAIN • 1909 • Durand Jean • FRN
ARIZONA BOUND • 1927 • Waters John • USA
ARIZONA BOUND • 1941 • Bennet Spencer Gordon • USA
ARIZONA BUSHWHACKERS • 1968 • Selander Lesley • USA
ARIZONA CATCLAW • 1919 • Bertram William • USA
ARIZONA COLT • 1966 • Lupo Michele • ITL, SPN, FRN • MAN FROM NOWHERE, THE (USA)
ARIZONA COWBOY • 1950 • Springsteen R. G. • USA
ARIZONA CYCLONE • 1928 • Lewis Edgar • USA
ARIZONA CYCLONE • 1934 • Tansey Robert • USA
ARIZONA CYCLONE • 1941 • Taylor Ray, Lewis Joseph H. • USA
ARIZONA DAYS • 1928 • McGowan J. P. • USA
ARIZONA DAYS • 1937 • English John • USA
ARIZONA EPISODE, AN • 1912 • *Essanay* • USA
ARIZONA EXPRESS, THE • 1924 • Buckingham Thomas • USA
ARIZONA FRONTIER • 1940 • Herman Al • USA
ARIZONA GANG BUSTERS • 1940 • Newfield Sam • USA
ARIZONA GUNFIGHTER • 1937 • Newfield Sam • USA
ARIZONA HEAT • 1987 • Thomas John G. • USA
ARIZONA KID, THE • 1929 • Carpenter Horace B. • USA
ARIZONA KID, THE • 1930 • Santell Alfred • USA
ARIZONA KID, THE • 1939 • Kane Joseph • USA
ARIZONA LAND SWINDLE, THE • 1912 • *Bison* • USA
ARIZONA LEGION • 1939 • Howard David • USA
ARIZONA MAHONEY • 1937 • Hogan James P. • USA • ARIZONA THUNDERBOLT
ARIZONA MANHUNT • 1951 • Brannon Fred C. • USA
ARIZONA MISSION • 1956 • McLaglen Andrew V. • USA • GUN THE MAN DOWN
ARIZONA NIGHTS • 1927 • Ingraham Lloyd • USA
ARIZONA NIGHTS • 1934 • Ray Bernard B. • USA
ARIZONA OUTPOST see **DEVIL'S CANYON** • 1953
ARIZONA RAIDERS • 1936 • Hogan James P. • USA • BAD MEN OF ARIZONA
ARIZONA RAIDERS • 1965 • Witney William • USA
ARIZONA RANGER, THE • 1948 • Rawlins John • USA
ARIZONA RIPPER, THE see **BRIDGE ACROSS TIME** • 1985
ARIZONA ROMANCE, AN • 1910 • *Pathe* • USA
ARIZONA ROMANCE, AN • 1911 • *American* • USA
ARIZONA ROMEO, THE • 1925 • Mortimer Edmund • USA
ARIZONA ROUNDUP • 1942 • Tansey Robert • USA
ARIZONA SHEEPDOG • 1955 • Lansburgh Larry • USA
ARIZONA SI SCATENO.. E LI FECE FUORI TUTTI • 1970 • Martino Sergio • ITL
ARIZONA SPEED • 1928 • Horner Robert J. • USA
ARIZONA STAGECOACH • 1942 • Luby S. Roy • USA
ARIZONA STORY • 1944 • Beaudine William • USA
ARIZONA STREAK, THE • 1926 • De Lacy Robert • USA
ARIZONA SWEEPSTAKES, THE • 1926 • Smith Cliff • USA
ARIZONA TERRITORY • 1950 • Fox Wallace • USA
ARIZONA TERROR • 1931 • Rosen Phil • USA
ARIZONA TERROR • 1942 • Sherman George • USA • ARIZONA TERRORS
ARIZONA TERRORS see **ARIZONA TERROR** • 1942
ARIZONA THUNDERBOLT see **ARIZONA MAHONEY** • 1937
ARIZONA TO BROADWAY • 1933 • Tinling James • USA
ARIZONA TRAIL • 1934 • Adamson Victor • USA
ARIZONA TRAIL • 1943 • Keays Vernon • USA
ARIZONA TRAILS • 1935 • James Alan • USA
ARIZONA WHIRLWIND • 1944 • Tansey Robert • USA
ARIZONA WHIRLWIND, THE • 1927 • Craft William James • USA
ARIZONA WILDCAT • 1938 • Leeds Herbert I. • USA
ARIZONA WILDCAT, THE • 1927 • Neill R. William • USA
ARIZONA WOOING, AN • 1915 • Mix Tom • USA
ARIZONIAN, THE • 1935 • Vidor Charles • USA
ARJUN FIGHT see **KRISHNARJUN YUDDHA** • 1945
ARJUN PANDIT • 1976 • *Burman S. D. (M)* • IND
ARJUN SARDAR • 1958 • *Ghatak Ritwik* • IND
ARK • 1970 • Forsberg Rolf • SHT • USA
ARK OF FOOLS see **PAVILON C.6** • 1969
ARK OF THE SUN GOD, THE see **ARK OF THE SUN GOD.. TEMPLE OF HELL, THE** • 1984
ARK OF THE SUN GOD.. TEMPLE OF HELL, THE • 1984 • Margheriti Antonio • ITL • ARK OF THE SUN GOD, THE
ARKADAS • 1975 • Guney Yilmaz • TRK • FRIEND
ARKADASIM SEYTAN • 1988 • Yilmaz Atif • TRK • MY FRIEND THE DEVIL
ARKADASIMIN ASKI • 1968 • Inanoglu Turker • TRK • YOU BELONG TO MY FRIEND
ARKADI RAYKIN • 1968 • Katanyan Vasili • USS
ARKANSAS JUDGE • 1941 • McDonald Frank • USA • FALSE WITNESS (UKN)
ARKANSAS SWING, THE • 1948 • Nazarro Ray • USA • WRONG NUMBER (UKN)
ARKANSAS TRAVELER, THE • 1938 • Santell Alfred • USA
ARKEN • 1965 • Husberg Rolf • SWD
ARKTINEN VIIVA • 1988 • Lehmuskallio Markku • DOC • FNL • ARCTIC LINE, THE
ARLBERG-EXPRESS • 1948 • von Borsody Eduard • AUS
ARLEKIN • 1960 • Kijowicz Miroslaw • ANS • PLN • HARLEQUIN, THE
ARLEKIN • 1969 • Kijowicz Miroslaw • ANS • PLN • HARLEQUIN, THE
ARLEQUIN ET CHARBONNIER • 1897 • Melies Georges • FRN • CHARCOAL MAN'S RECEPTION, THE
ARLES • 1951 • Vilardebo Carlos • SHT • FRN
ARLESIENNE, L' • 1909 • Calmettes Andre • FRN
ARLESIENNE, L' • 1909 • Capellani Albert • FRN
ARLESIENNE, L' • 1912 • Capellani Albert • FRN
ARLESIENNE, L' • 1922 • Antoine Andre • FRN
ARLESIENNE, L' • 1930 • de Baroncelli Jacques • FRN
ARLESIENNE, L' • 1941 • Allegret Marc • FRN
ARLETTE EROBERT PARIS • 1953 • Tourjansky Victor • FRG
ARLETTE ET L'AMOUR • 1943 • Vernay Robert • FRN • ATOUT COEUR
ARLETTE ET SES PAPAS • 1934 • Roussell Henry • FRN • AVRIL
ARLINE'S CHAUFFEUR • 1915 • Morgan George • USA
ARM, THE see **BIG TOWN, THE** • 1987
ARM GOTTES, DER • 1922 • Osten Franz • FRG
ARM OF FIRE see **COLOSSO DI ROMA, IL** • 1964
ARM OF SOCIETY see **BISIG NG LIPUNAN** • 1967
ARM OF THE LAW • 1932 • King Louis • USA
ARM OF THE LAW, THE • 1910 • *Atlas* • USA
ARM OF THE LAW, THE • 1915 • Golden Joseph A.? • USA
ARM OF THE LAW, THE see **SHIELD OF HONOR, THE** • 1927
ARM OF VENGEANCE, THE • 1914 • *Essanay* • USA
ARMA, L' • 1978 • Squitieri Pasquale • ITL
ARMA BIANCA • 1936 • Poggioli Ferdinando M. • ITL
ARMA DE DOS FILOS, UN (MXC) see **SHARK!** • 1969
ARMA, L'ORA, IL MOVENTE, L' • 1972 • Mazzei Francesco • ITL
ARMADALE • 1916 • Garrick Richard • SHT • USA
ARMAGEDDON • 1923 • Woolfe H. Bruce • UKN
ARMAGEDDON • 1963-64 • Fournier Claude • DCS • CND
ARMAGEDDON • 1986 • Rosma Juha, Parviainen Jussi • FNL
ARMAGEDDON (USA) see **ARMAGUEDON** • 1977
ARMAGUEDON • 1977 • Jessua Alain • FRN, ITL • ARMAGEDDON (USA)
ARMALITE COMMANDOS • 1968 • Cruz Abraham • PHL
ARMAN • 1953 • *Burman S. D. (M)* • IND
ARMAND AND MICHAELA DENIS AMONG THE HEADHUNTERS see **AMONG THE HEADHUNTERS** • 1955
ARMAND AND MICHAELA DENIS ON THE BARRIER REEF • 1955 • Denis Armand • DOC • UKN
ARMAND AND MICHAELA DENIS UNDER THE SOUTHERN CROSS • 1954 • Denis Armand • DOC • UKN • UNDER THE SOUTHERN CROSS
ARMAND FELX, FAISEUR DE VIOLONS • 1973 • Plamondon Leo • DOC • CND
ARMANDUS, QUICK CHANGE ARTISTE • 1902 • *Warwick Trading Co* • UKN
ARMARIO DEL TIEMPO, EL • 1971 • Vara Rafael • SPN
ARMAS, AS • 1968 • de Araujo Benedito Astolfo • BRZ • GUNS, THE
ARMAS CONTRA LA LEY • 1961 • Blasco Ricardo • SPN, ITL • ARMI CONTRO LA LEGGE (ITL)
ARMAS E O POVO, AS • 1975 • *De Almeida Acacio (Ph)* • DOC • PRT
ARMATA AZZURRA, L' • 1932 • Righelli Gennaro • ITL • BLUE FLEET, THE (USA) ○ AVIAZIONE
ARMATA BRANCALEONE, L' • 1966 • Monicelli Mario • ITL
ARMATA DEGLI EROI, L' (ITL) see **ARMEE DES OMBRES, L'** • 1969
ARMCHAIR, THE see **FOTEL** • 1963
ARMCHAIR DETECTIVE, THE • 1952 • Stafford Brendan J. • UKN
ARME A GAUCHE, L' • 1965 • Sautet Claude • FRN, ITL, SPN • GUNS FOR THE DICTATOR (UKN) ○ DICTATOR'S GUNS, THE (USA) ○ CORPO A CORPO (ITL)
ARME DRENTHE • 1929 • Ivens Joris • SHT • NTH
ARME EVA • 1914 • Wiene Robert, Berger A. • FRG • FRAUMONT JNR., REISLER SEN. ○ FRAU EVA ○ DEAR EVA

ARME EVA MARIA • 1916 • May Joe • FRG
ARME JENNY, DIE • 1912 • Gad Urban • DNM, FRG • PROLETARPIGEN
ARME JONATHAN, DER see **GELD MUSS MAN HABEN** • 1945
ARME KLEINE COLOMBINE • 1927 • Seitz Franz • FRG
ARME KLEINE EVA • 1918 • *Dagny Alice* • FRG
ARME, KLEINE EVA • 1931 • Heuberger Edmund • FRG
ARME, KLEINE EVA 2 • 1921 • Bach Rudi • FRG
ARME, KLEINE HEDWIG see **HAUS DER LUGE, DAS** • 1925
ARME KLEINE HELGA • 1918 • *Kolberg Ally* • FRG
ARME KLEINE SIF • 1927 • Bergen Arthur • FRG • SIF, DAS WEIB, DAS DEN MORD BEGING
ARME LENA • 1918 • *Orla Ressel* • FRG
ARME LEUTE • 1963 • Kristl Vlado • FRG
ARME MARGARET, DIE • 1920 • Frey Karl • FRG
ARME MARIE • 1914 • Mack Max • FRG
ARME MILLIONAR, DER • 1939 • Stockel Joe • FRG • POOR MILLIONAIRE, THE (USA)
ARME SUNDERIN • 1923 • Gariazzo P. A. • FRG
ARME SYNDIGE MENNESKE • 1978 • Kolsto Egil • NRW • POOR WRETCHED SINNER
ARME THEA • 1919 • Froelich Carl • FRG
ARME VIOLETTA • 1920 • Stein Paul L. • FRG • RED PEACOCK, THE (USA)
ARME WIE EINE KIRCHENMAUS • 1931 • Oswald Richard • FRG
ARMED AND DANGEROUS • 1980 • Weinstock Vladimir • USS
ARMED AND DANGEROUS • 1986 • Lester Mark L. • USA
ARMED FORCES see **RECLUTA -FUERZAS ARMADAS** • 1972
ARMED INTERVENTION • 1913 • Ricketts Thomas • USA
ARMED NATION, AN see **PUEBLOS EN ARMAS** • 1961
ARMED PEOPLE, AN (USA) see **PUEBLOS EN ARMAS** • 1961
ARMED RESPONSE • 1986 • Ray Fred Olen • USA • JADE JUNGLE
ARMEE D'AGENOR, L' see **ECOLE DU SOLDAT, L'** • 1909
ARMEE DES OMBRES, L' • 1969 • Melville Jean-Pierre • FRN, ITL • ARMATA DEGLI EROI, L' (ITL) ○ ARMY IN THE SHADOWS, THE (UKN) ○ SHADOW ARMY ○ ARMY OF THE SHADOWS
ARMEE GRETCHEN, EINE • 1973 • Dietrich Erwin C. • FRG, SWT • FRAULEINS IN UNIFORM (UKN) ○ GRETCHEN IN UNIFORM ○ ARMY GIRL
ARMEE POPULAIRE ARME LE PEUPLE, L' • 1969 • Ivens Joris (c/d) • DOC • FRN
ARMEES DU SOLEIL, LES see **JUYUSHI ASH-SHAMS** • 1975
ARMEN REICHEN, DIE • 1915 • Schmidthassler Walter • FRG
ARMER KLEINER PIERROT • 1920 • Bolten-Baeckers Heinrich • FRG
ARMES A FEU AU CANADA, 400 ANS D'HISTOIRE, LES • 1981 • Beaudry Diane • DOC • CND
ARMES DE LA COLERE, LES • 1969 • Calef Henri • FRN
ARMES DE LA PAIX, LES • 1954 • de Poligny Serge • FRN
ARMES KLEINES MADCHEN • 1924 • Kayser Ulrich • FRG • MADCHEN MIT DEN SCHWEFELHOLZCHEN, DAS
ARMI CONTRO LA LEGGE (ITL) see **ARMAS CONTRA LA LEY** • 1961
ARMI DELLA VENDETTA, LE (ITL) see **HARDI! PARDAILLAN** • 1963
ARMI E GLI AMORI, LE • 1983 • Battiato Giacomo • ITL • PALADINI, STORIA D'ARMI E D'AMORI, I ○ HEARTS AND ARMOUR (USA) ○ PALADINI, I ○ PEERS, THE ○ ARMS AND LOVES ○ PALADINS, A STORY OF LOVE AND WAR, THE ○ HEARTS IN ARMOUR
ARMIAMOCI E PARTITE • 1971 • Cicero Nando • ITL
ARMIDA, IL DRAMMA DI UNA SPOSA • 1970 • Mattei Bruno • ITL
ARMINIUS THE TERRIBLE see **MASSACRO DELLA FORESTA NERA, IL** • 1966
ARMISTICE • 1929 • Saville Victor • UKN
ARMLESS DENTIST, THE • 1943 • *O'Brien Joseph/ Mead Thomas (P)* • SHT • USA
ARMOIRE DES FRERES DAVENPORT, L' • 1902 • Melies Georges • FRN • CABINET TRICK OF THE DAVENPORT BROTHERS (USA) ○ MYSTERIOUS CABINET, THE ○ FRERES DAVENPORT, LES
ARMOIRE VOLANTE, L' • 1948 • Carlo-Rim • FRN • CUPBOARD WAS BARE, THE (USA) ○ MONSIEUR PUC AUX ENFERS
ARMONICA MISTERIOSA • 1906 • Velle Gaston • ITL
ARMONIE PUCCINIANE • 1938 • *Fusco Giovanni (M)* • SHT • ITL
ARMORED CAR • 1937 • Foster Lewis R. • USA
ARMORED CAR ROBBERY • 1950 • Fleischer Richard • USA
ARMORED COMMAND • 1961 • Haskin Byron • USA
ARMORER'S DAUGHTER, THE • 1910 • *Leonard Marion* • USA
ARMOUR OF GOD see **LONGXIONG HUDI** • 1987
ARMOUR OF GOD 2: OPERATION EAGLE, THE see **LUNGHING FUDAI TSUKTSAP** • 1990
ARMOURED ATTACK see **NORTH STAR** • 1943
ARMOURED VAULT, THE see **PANZERGEWOLBE, DAS** • 1914
ARMOURED VAULT, THE see **PANZERGEWOLBE, DAS** • 1926
ARMS AND LOVES see **ARMI E GLI AMORI, LE** • 1983
ARMS AND THE GIRL • 1917 • Kaufman Joseph • USA
ARMS AND THE GIRL, THE see **HEART RAIDER, THE** • 1923
ARMS AND THE GIRL (UKN) see **RED SALUTE** • 1935
ARMS AND THE GRINGO • 1914 • Cabanne W. Christy • USA
ARMS AND THE MAN • 1932 • Lewis Cecil • UKN
ARMS AND THE MAN (USA) see **HELDEN** • 1958
ARMS AND THE WOMAN • 1910 • Merwin Bannister • USA
ARMS AND THE WOMAN • 1916 • Fitzmaurice George • USA
ARMS AND THE WOMAN (UKN) see **MR. WINKLE GOES TO WAR** • 1944
ARMS IN YOUR HANDS see **MED VAPEN I HAND** • 1913
ARMSTRONG'S TRICK WAR INCIDENTS • 1915 • Armstrong Charles • UKN
ARMSTRONG'S WIFE • 1915 • Melford George • USA
ARMY, THE see **RIKUGUN** • 1944
ARMY AIR FORCE BAND, THE • 1942 • Negulesco Jean • SHT • USA
ARMY BOUND • 1952 • Landres Paul • USA
ARMY BRAT see **LITTLE MR. JIM** • 1946
ARMY BRATS • 1984 • van Hemert Ruud • NTH
ARMY BRATS • 1988 • Davidson Boaz • USA
ARMY CAPERS (UKN) see **WAC FROM WALLA WALLA, THE** • 1951
ARMY CHAMPIONS • 1941 • Vogel Paul • SHT • USA
ARMY GAME, THE (USA) see **TIRE-AU-FLANC 1962** • 1961
ARMY GIRL • 1938 • Nicholls George Jr. • USA
ARMY GIRL see **ARMEE GRETCHEN, EINE** • 1973
ARMY IN THE SHADOWS, THE (UKN) see **ARMEE DES OMBRES, L'** • 1969
ARMY IN VILLA ANTA, THE see **EJERCITO EN VILLA ANTA, EL** • 1980
ARMY INTELLIGENCE 33 see **RIKUGUN CHOHO 33** • 1968
ARMY LIFE: OR, HOW SOLDIERS ARE MADE • 1900 • Paul Robert William • SER • UKN
ARMY MASCOT, THE • 1942 • Geronimi Clyde • ANS • USA
ARMY OF HEWN STONE, AN see **LEGER VAN GEHOUWEN STEEN, EEN** • 1957
ARMY OF LOVERS • 1979 • von Praunheim Rosa • DOC • USA
ARMY OF THE SHADOWS see **ARMEE DES OMBRES, L'** • 1969
ARMY OF TWO • 1908 • Porter Edwin S. • USA
ARMY SHOW, THE • 1943 • Negulesco Jean • SHT • USA
ARMY SURGEON • 1942 • Sutherland A. Edward • USA
ARMY SURGEON, THE • 1912 • Ford Francis • USA
ARMY WIVES • 1944 • Rosen Phil • USA
ARMY WIVES • 1988 • Lawrence Denny • ASL
ARNAUD, LES • 1967 • Joannon Leo • FRN, ITL • VOGLIO VIVERE LA MIA VITA (ITL)
ARNE DOMNERUS SPILLER • 1951 • Dahlgren Sten • SHT • SWD
ARNELO AFFAIR, THE • 1947 • Oboler Arch • USA
ARNIS DE MANO AND JUDO KARATE • 1967 • Martinez Tony Blade • PHL
ARNOLD • 1973 • Fenady George • USA
ARNOLD BOCKLIN • 1988 • Raith Bernhard • SWT
ARNOLD ZWEIG • 1962 • Huisken Joop • DOC • GDR
ARNULF RAINER • 1958 • Kubelka Peter • SHT • AUS
ARNYEK A HAVON • 1990 • Janisch Attila • HNG • SHADOW ON THE SNOW
AROHAN • 1981 • Benegal Shyam • IND • ASCENT, THE ○ ASCENDING SCALE
AROMA OF THE SOUTH SEAS • 1931 • Kellino W. P. • UKN
AROUND A STAR see **VIAGGIO DI UNA STELLA, IL** • 1906
AROUND BATTLE TREE • 1913 • Eagle Oscar • USA
AROUND IS AROUND • 1951 • McLaren Norman • ANS • CND
AROUND PERCEPTION see **AUTOUR DE LA PERCEPTION** • 1968
AROUND THE BOREE LOG • 1925 • Walsh Phil K. • ASL
AROUND THE CORNER • 1915 • Le Viness Carl M. • USA
AROUND THE CORNER • 1930 • Glennon Bert • USA
AROUND THE EQUATOR ON ROLLER SKATES • 1932 • De Mond Albert • SHT • USA
AROUND THE MATTER see **WOKOL SPRAWY** • 1963
AROUND THE TOWN • 1938 • Smith Herbert • UKN
AROUND THE VILLAGE GREEN • 1937 • Cherry Evelyn Spice, Grierson Marion • UKN • VILLAGE HARVEST
AROUND THE WOLRD IN EIGHTEEN DAYS • 1923 • Eason B. Reeves, Hill Robert F. • SRL • USA
AROUND THE WORLD • 1916 • Fahrney Milton • USA
AROUND THE WORLD • 1931 • *Terry Paul/ Moser Frank (P)* • ANS • USA
AROUND THE WORLD • 1943 • Dwan Allan • USA
AROUND THE WORLD • 1967 • Pachi • IND
AROUND THE WORLD IN 18 MINUTES • 1932 • De Mond Albert • SHT • USA
AROUND THE WORLD IN 80 DAYS • 1956 • Anderson Michael • USA
AROUND THE WORLD IN 80 MINUTES • 1931 • Fairbanks Douglas, Fleming Victor • DOC • USA • AROUND THE WORLD IN 80 MINUTES WITH DOUGLAS FAIRBANKS
AROUND THE WORLD IN 80 MINUTES see **TOUR DU MONDE EN 80 MINUTES**
AROUND THE WORLD IN 80 MINUTES WITH DOUGLAS FAIRBANKS see **AROUND THE WORLD IN 80 MINUTES** • 1931
AROUND THE WORLD IN 80 WAYS! • 1969 • Goetz Tommy • USA
AROUND THE WORLD IN 80 WAYS • 1986 • Maclean Stephen • ASL
AROUND THE WORLD IN EIGHTY DAYS • 1988 • Kulik Buzz • TVM • USA
AROUND THE WORLD IN THE SPEEJACKS • 1923 • *Famous Players-Lasky* • DOC • USA
AROUND THE WORLD UNDER THE SEA • 1966 • Marton Andrew • USA
AROUND THE WORLD VIA GRAF ZEPPELIN • 1929 • *Mgm* • DOC • USA
AROUND THE WORLD WITH BOLEK AND LOLEK • 1977 • Nehrebecki Wladyslaw, Dulz Stanislaw • ANM • PLN
AROUND THE WORLD WITH BURTON HOLMES • 1922 • *Holmes Burton* • DOC • USA
AROUND THE WORLD WITH DOT see **DOT AND SANTA CLAUS** • 1982
AROUND THE WORLD WITH FANNY HILL see **JORDEN RUNT MED FANNY HILL** • 1973
AROUND THE WORLD WITH NOTHING ON • 1963 • Knight Arthur • USA • SEARCH FOR VENUS AROUND THE WORLD ○ SEARCHING FOR VENUS ○ TRIP AROUND THE WORLD, A
AROUND THE WORLD WITH NOTHING ON see **LUST FOR THE SUN** • 1958
AROUS-E-TEHRAN • 1967 • Najeebzadeh Ahmad • IRN • BRIDE OF TEHRAN, THE
AROUS KODUME? • 1960 • Ghaffary Farrokh • IRN • WHO IS THE BRIDE?
AROUSE AND BEWARE (UKN) see **MAN FROM DAKOTA, THE** • 1940
AROUSED • 1966 • Holden Anton • USA
AROUSERS, THE • 1971 • Hanson Curtis • USA • SWEET KILL (UKN) ○ KISS FROM EDDIE, A ○ SWEETKILL
AROUSS EL NIL • 1963 • Wahab Fatin Abdel • EGY • ARUSS AN-NIL ○ FIANCEE DU NIL, LA
AROUSSET EL BAHR • 1947 • Kamel Abbas • EGY • MERMAID, THE
ARP STATUE, THE • 1971 • Sekers Alan • UKN
ARPA-COLA • 1981 • Perakis Nikos • GRC • PATCHWORK-COLA
ARPAN • 1986 • Sujata • BNG
ARPAYI TIS PERSEFONIS, I • 1956 • Grigoriou Grigoris • GRC • ENLEVEMENT DE PERSEPHONE
ARPENTEURS, LES • 1972 • Soutter Michel • SWT
ARQUERO DE SHERWOOD, L' see **ARCIERE DI FUOCO, L'** • 1971
ARRABALERA • 1950 • Demicheli Tulio • ARG
ARRABALERA • 1950 • Pardave Joaquin • MXC
ARRACHE-COEUR, L' • 1980 • Dansereau Mireille • CND • HEARTBREAK
ARRAH-NA-POGUE • 1911 • Olcott Sidney • USA
ARRANGEMENT, THE • 1969 • Kazan Elia • USA
ARRANGEMENT, THE see **ARREGLO, EL** • 1982
ARRANGEMENT, THE see **ARREGLO, EL** • 1983
ARRANGEMENT WITH FATE, AN • 1915 • Lloyd Frank • USA
ARRANGIATEVI! • 1959 • Bolognini Mauro • ITL
ARRASTAO, LES AMANTS DE LA MER • 1967 • d'Ormesson Antoine • FRN
ARRAU TORTOISE, THE see **TORTUGA ARRAU, LA** • 1979
ARRAYED WITH THE ENEMY • 1917 • Hurst Paul C. • SHT • USA
ARREBATO • 1980 • Zulueta Ivan • SPN • RAPTURE
ARREGLO, EL • 1982 • Ayala Fernando • ARG • ARRANGEMENT, THE
ARREGLO, EL • 1983 • Zorrilla Jose Antonio • SPN • ARRANGEMENT, THE
ARREST AT SUNDOWN (UKN) see **TRAILS OF THE WILD** • 1935
ARREST BULLDOG DRUMMOND • 1939 • Hogan James P. • USA
ARREST NORMA MACGREGOR • 1921 • *Moore Joe* • USA
ARREST OF A BOOKMAKER • 1896 • *Paul R. W.* • UKN
ARREST OF A DESERTER, THE • 1902 • Paul Robert William • UKN
ARREST OF A PICKPOCKET, THE • 1896 • Acres Birt • UKN
ARRESTING FATHER • 1912 • *Majestic* • USA
ARRET AU MILIEU, L' • 1978 • Sentier Jean-Pierre • FRN
ARRET-CAR • 1974 • Ba N'Gaido • SHT • SNL
ARRETE DE RAMER, T'ATTAQUES LA FALAISE see **QU'IL EST JOLI GARCON L'ASSASSIN DE PAPA** • 1978
ARRETE DE RAMER, T'ES SUR LE SABLE see **MEATBALLS** • 1979
ARRETE TON CHAR!!! BIDASSE • 1977 • Gerard Michel • FRN
ARRETE TON CINEMA • Jelot-Blanc Jean-Jacques • FRN
ARRETEZ LE MASSACRE! • 1959 • Hunebelle Andre • FRN
ARRETEZ LES TAMBOURS • 1961 • Lautner Georges • FRN • WOMEN AND WAR (USA) ○ WOMEN IN WAR
ARRIBA EL NORTE! • 1948 • Gomez Muriel Emilio • MXC
ARRIBA ESPANA • 1937 • FRG
ARRIBA HAZANA! • 1977 • Gutierrez Santos Jose Maria • SPN • UP WITH HAZANA!
ARRIBA LAS MUJERES • 1943 • Orellana Carlos • MXC
ARRIBA TEPITO QUE ES MI BARRIO • 1971 • *Cima* • MXC
ARRIBADA FORZOSA • 1943 • Arevalo Carlos • SPN
ARRIERE SAISON • 1950 • Kirsanoff Dimitri • SHT • FRN
ARRIERO DE YACANTO, EL • 1924 • Ferreyra Jose • ARG
'ARRIET'S BABY • 1913 • *Talmadge Norma* • USA
ARRIVA DORELLIK • 1967 • Steno • ITL • DORELLIK (USA) ○ DORELLIK ARRIVES ○ HOW TO KILL 400 DUPONTS
ARRIVA DURANGO, PAGA O MUORI • 1971 • Montero Roberto Bianchi • ITL
ARRIVA LA BANDA • 1959 • Boccia Tanio • ITL
ARRIVA LA ZIA D'AMERICA • 1957 • Montero Roberto Bianchi • ITL
ARRIVA SABATA • 1970 • Demicheli Tulio • ITL, SPN
ARRIVAL OF A TRAIN AT VICENNES STATION see **ARRIVEE D'UN TRAIN (GARE DE VICENNES)** • 1896
ARRIVAL OF A TRAIN (JOINVILLE STATION) see **ARRIVEE D'UN TRAIN (GARE DE JOINVILLE)** • 1896
ARRIVAL OF H.M.S. POWERFUL • 1900 • Hepworth Cecil M. • UKN
ARRIVAL OF JOSE, THE • 1914 • Beggs Lee • USA
ARRIVAL OF PERPETUA, THE • 1915 • Chautard Emile • USA
ARRIVAL OF THE GOVERNMENT OF NATIONAL UNITY IN WARSAW, THE see **PRZYJAZD RZADU JEDNOSCI NARODOWEJ DO WARSZAWY** • 1945
ARRIVANI I DOLLARI • 1957 • Costa Mario • ITL
ARRIVANO DJANGO E SARTANA.. E LA FINE • 1970 • Fidani Demofilo • ITL
ARRIVANO I NOSTRI • 1951 • Mattoli Mario • ITL
ARRIVANO I PUTI POTI • 1969 • Fagarazzi Daniele, Peroni Carlo • SHT • ITL
ARRIVANO I TITANI (ITL) see **TITANS, LES** • 1962
ARRIVANO JOE E MARGHERITO • 1974 • Colizzi Giuseppe • ITL • JOE E MARGHERITO
ARRIVEDERCI, BABY (USA) see **DROP DEAD, DARLING** • 1966
ARRIVEDERCI COWBOY • 1967 • Nazarro Ray • ITL
ARRIVEDERCI FIRENZE • 1958 • Furlan Rate • ITL • GOOD-BYE FIRENZE!
ARRIVEDERCI PAPA! • 1948 • Mastrocinque Camillo • ITL
ARRIVEDERCI ROMA (ITL) see **SEVEN HILLS OF ROME, THE** • 1957
ARRIVEE DES CONGRESSISTES A NEUVILLE-SUR-SAONE see **DEBARQUEMENT** • 1895
ARRIVEE D'UN BATEAU A VAPEUR • 1896-97 • Lumiere Louis • FRN
ARRIVEE D'UN TRAIN EN GARE DE LA CIOTAT, L' • 1895 • Lumiere Louis • FRN
ARRIVEE D'UN TRAIN (GARE DE JOINVILLE) • 1896 • Melies Georges • FRN • ARRIVAL OF A TRAIN (JOINVILLE STATION)
ARRIVEE D'UN TRAIN (GARE DE VICENNES) • 1896 • Melies Georges • FRN • ARRIVAL OF A TRAIN AT VICENNES STATION
ARRIVERDERCI DIMAS • 1957 • Berlanga Luis Garcia • SPN, ITL
ARRIVIAMO NOI! • 1940 • Palermi Amleto • ITL • AMICO PUBBLICO N.1, L' ○ VITA DI LUNA-PARK
ARRIVING TUESDAY • 1985 • Riddiford Richard • NZL
ARRIVISTE, L' • 1914 • Leprieur Gaston • FRN
ARRIVISTE, L' • 1924 • Hugon Andre • FRN
ARRIVISTE, L' • 1977 • Pavel Samy • BLG

ARRIVISTES, LES • 1960 • Daquin Louis • FRN • RABOUILLEUSE, LA
ARRIVISTES, LES (FRN) see **TRUBE WASSER** • 1960
ARRIVO DEL TRENO STAZIONE DI MILANO • 1896 • Pacchioni Italo • ITL
ARROGANCE see **ORGUEIL, L'** • 1907
ARROGANT, THE see **SYLVIA KRISTEL'S DESIRES** • 1987
ARROSEUR, L' • 1896 • Melies Georges • FRN • WATERING THE FLOWERS
ARROSEUR ARROSE, L' • 1895 • Lumiere Louis • FRN • JARDINIER ET LE PETIT ESPIEGLE, LE ○ GARDENER, THE ○ JARDINIER, LE ○ PRACTICAL JOKE ON THE GARDENER, A
ARROSEUR ARROSE, L' • 1897-98 • Blache Alice • FRN
ARROSEUR ARROSE, L' • 1974 • Le Grice Malcolm • UKN
ARROW, THE • 1969 • Calman Mel • UKN
ARROW, THE see **FRECCIA NEL FIANCO, LA** • 1943
ARROW HEAD, THE • 1911 • *Lubin* • USA
ARROW IN THE DUST • 1954 • Selander Lesley • USA
ARROW IN THE DUST (UKN) see **TRAIL OF THE ARROW** • 1953
ARROW MAIDEN, THE • 1915 • Powers Francis • USA
ARROW MAKER'S DAUGHTER, THE • 1914 • Miller Charles? • USA
ARROW OF DEFIANCE, THE • 1912 • *Pathe* • USA
ARROW OF THE AVENGER (UKN) see **GOLIATH E LA SCHIAVA RIBELLE** • 1963
ARROWFEATHER see **GAS-S-S-SI** • 1970
ARROWHEAD • 1953 • Warren Charles Marquis • USA
ARROWHEAD ROMANCE, AN • 1914 • *Leonard Robert* • USA
ARROWMAKER'S DAUGHTER, THE • 1912 • *White Pearl* • USA
ARROW'S TONGUE, THE • 1914 • Farnum Martin • USA
ARROWSMITH • 1931 • Ford John • USA
ARRRIBA LAS MUJERES!! • 1967 • Salvador Julio • SPN • LONG LIVE ALL WOMEN!!
ARRULLO DE DIOS • 1966 • Blake Alfonso Corona • MXC
ARRUZA • 1968 • Boetticher Budd • DOC • USA
'ARRY AND 'ARRIET'S EVENING OUT • 1909 • Williamson James? • UKN
'ARRY ON THE STEAMBOAT • 1901 • Booth W. R.? • UKN
ARS • 1959 • Demy Jacques • SHT • FRN
ARS AMANDI (ITL) see **ART D'AIMER, L'** • 1983
ARS GRATIA ARTIS • 1971 • Vukotic Dusan • ANS • YGS
ARSEN see **ARSEN OF MARABDA** • 1937
ARSEN DZHORGIASHVILI see **ARSEN GEORGIASHVILI** • 1921
ARSEN GEORGIASHVILI • 1921 • Perestiani Ivan • USS • ARSEN DZHORGIASHVILI
ARSEN LUPIN UTOLSO KALANDJA • 1921 • Fejos Paul • HNG • LAST ADVENTURE OF ARSEN LUPIN, THE ○ ARSEN LUPIN'S LAST ADVENTURE
ARSEN LUPIN'S LAST ADVENTURE see **ARSEN LUPIN UTOLSO KALANDJA** • 1921
ARSEN OF MARABDA • 1937 • Chiaureli Mikhail • USS • ARSEN
ARSENAL • 1928 • Dovzhenko Alexander • USS • JANUARY UPRISING IN KIEV IN 1918 (UKN)
ARSENAL • 1976 • Godbout Jacques • CND
ARSENAL OF MIGHT • 1942 • *O'Brien Joseph/ Meads Thomas (P)* • SHT • USA
ARSENAL STADIUM MYSTERY, THE • 1939 • Dickinson Thorold • UKN
ARSENE LUPIN • 1916 • Tucker George Loane • UKN
ARSENE LUPIN • 1917 • Scardon Paul • USA
ARSENE LUPIN • 1932 • Conway Jack • USA
ARSENE LUPIN CONTRE ARSENE LUPIN • 1962 • Molinaro Edouard • FRN, ITL • ARSENIO LUPIN CONTRO ARSENIO LUPIN (ITL)
ARSENE LUPIN, DETECTIVE • 1937 • Diamant-Berger Henri • FRN
ARSENE LUPIN RETURNS • 1937 • Fitzmaurice George • USA
ARSENIC AND OLD LACE • 1944 • Capra Frank • USA
ARSENIO LUPIN • 1945 • Peon Ramon • MXC
ARSENIO LUPIN CONTRO ARSENIO LUPIN (ITL) see **ARSENE LUPIN CONTRE ARSENE LUPIN** • 1962
ARSHIN MAL-ALAN • 1967 • Taghizade Tofic • USS
ARSON FOR HIRE • 1959 • Brooks Thor L. • USA
ARSON GANG BUSTERS • 1938 • Kane Joseph • USA
ARSON INC. • 1949 • Berke William • USA
ARSON RACKET SQUAD • 1938 • Kane Joseph • USA • FIRE FIGHTERS (UKN)
ARSON SQUAD • 1945 • Landers Lew • USA
ARSONIST'S DAUGHTER, THE see **PALICOVA DCERA** • 1941
ARSULE see **REGAIN** • 1937
ART • 1973 • Petty Bruce • ANS • ASL
ART. 519 CODICE PENALE • 1952 • Cortese Leonardo • ITL
ART ACHES • 1917 • Beaudine William • SHT • USA
ART AND ARCHITECTURE OF CEYLON • Hettiarachi P. • DOC • SLN
ART AND ARTHUR • 1916 • Walsh Phil • USA
ART AND CULTURE see **ARTE Y CULTURA** • 1974
ART AND HONOR • 1913 • *Myers Harry* • USA
ART AND LOVE • 1913 • *Champion* • USA
ART AND PAINT • 1917 • *Vim* • USA
ART AND THE LEGACY • 1910 • *Lubin* • USA
ART D'AIMER, L' • 1983 • Borowczyk Walerian • FRN, ITL • ARS AMANDI (ITL) ○ ART OF LOVE
ART DE LA CONVERSATION, L' • 1977 • Bokor Pierre • RMN
ART DE TOURNER EN ROND, L' • 1988 • Bulbulian Maurice • DOC • CND • ART OF GOING AROUND IN CIRCLES, THE
ART DES PAYSANS, L' • 1967 • Tilmissani Abdel-Qadir At- • SHT • EGY
ART D'ETRE COURTIER, L' • 1947-51 • Verneuil Henri • SHT • FRN
ART DU CINEMA D'ANIMATION, L' • 1982 • Desbiens Francine • ANS • CND
ART DU LUTHIER, L' • 1942 • Delacroix Rene • DCS • FRN
ART FOR A HEART • 1914 • North Wilfred, Van Wally • USA
ART FOR ART'S SAKE • 1916 • Lyons Eddie, Moran Lee • SHT • USA
ART FOR ART'S SAKE • 1934 • Stallings George • ANS • USA
ART FOR ART'S SAKE • 1960 • *Halas John (P)* • ANS • UKN
ART GALLERY • 1939 • Harman Hugh • ANS • USA
ART HAUT-RHENAN, L' • 1951 • Gibaud Marcel • SHT • FRN
ART IN REVOLUTION • 1972 • Becker Lutz • DOC • UKN
ART IN THE RAW • 1933 • Sweet Harry • SHT • USA
ART JAPONAIS CONTEMPORAIN • 1983 • Payer Roch Christophe • DOC • CND
ART JARRETT • 1932 • Brice Monte • SHT • USA
ART LOVERS, THE • 1960 • *Halas John (P)* • ANS • UKN
ART LUND - TEX BENEKE - LES BROWN • 1948 • Scholl Jack • SHT • USA
ART OF CLAUDE LORRAIN, THE • 1970 • Ashton Dudley Shaw • UKN
ART OF CRIME, THE • 1975 • Irving Richard • TVM • USA
ART OF EATING, THE • 1976 • Jackson Douglas • DOC • CND
ART OF GENTLE PERSUASION, THE • 1970 • White Sanford • USA • GENTLE PERSUASION
ART OF GETTING ALONG, THE (USA) see **ARTE DI ARRANGIARSI, L'** • 1955
ART OF GOING AROUND IN CIRCLES, THE see **ART DE TOURNER EN ROND, L'** • 1988
ART OF LIVING, THE see **ARTE DE VIVIR, EL** • 1968
ART OF LOVE see **KONSTEN ATT ALSKA** • 1947
ART OF LOVE see **ART D'AIMER, L'** • 1983
ART OF LOVE, THE • 1925 • Greenwood Edwin, Kellino W. P. • SER • UKN
ART OF LOVE, THE • 1965 • Jewison Norman • USA
ART OF LOVE, THE see **PRINZESSIN OLALA** • 1928
ART OF LOVE, THE see **SZTUKA KOCHANIA** • 1989
ART OF MARRIAGE, THE • 1970 • DOC • USA
ART OF MIRRORS, THE • 1974 • Jarman Derek • SER • UKN
ART OF POLITICS: THE NATIVE WHO CAUSED ALL THE TROUBLE, THE • 1989 • Van Rensburg Manie • SAF • NATIVE WHO CAUSED ALL THE TROUBLE, THE
ART OF REVIVAL, THE see **ELADAS MUVESZETE, AZ** • 1960
ART OF SALESMANSHIP, THE see **ELADAS MUVESZETE, AZ** • 1960
ART OF SELF DEFENSE, THE • 1941 • Kinney Jack • ANS • USA
ART OF SKIIING, THE • 1941 • Kinney Jack • ANS • USA
ART OF SPACE, THE see **ARCHITECTURE, ART DE L'ESPACE** • 1960
ART OF SWORDSMITH, THE see **NIPPONTO MONOGATARI** • 1957
ART OF THE ENGLISH CRAFTSMAN • 1933 • Flaherty Robert • DCS • UKN
ART OF THE PEOPLE, THE see **ARTE DEL PUEBLO** • 1974
ART OF THE POSSIBLE, THE • 1978 • Raymont Peter • DOC • CND
ART OF THE YOUNG see **SZTUKA MLODYCH** • 1949
ART OF VISION, THE • 1965 • Brakhage Stan • USA
ART OF WORLDLY WISDOM, THE • 1979 • Elder Bruce • CND
ART OF YOUTH, THE see **SZTUKA MLODYCH** • 1949
ART POPULAIRE, L' • 1976 • Dansereau Fernand, Rossignol Yolande • DCS • CND
ART POUR L'ART (ART FOR ART'S SAKE), L' • 1966 • Godfrey Bob • UKN
ART PRECOLOMBIEN MEXICAIN • 1956 • Fulchignoni Enrico • FRN
ART SACRE AU TIBET, L' • 1955 • Sassy Jean-Paul • SHT • FRN
ART STUDIO IN THE VILLAGE • 1973 • Tilmissani Abdel-Qadir At- • SHT • EGY
ART SURGEON • 1969 • Diggle Lynton • DCS • NZL
ART VS. MUSIC • 1911 • Salter Harry • USA
ART WORKS 1: ACADEMIC STILL LIFE • 1977 • Le Grice Malcolm • UKN • CEZANNE
ART WORKS 2: TIME AND MOTION STUDY • 1977 • Le Grice Malcolm • UKN
ARTAMANOV AFFAIR, THE see **DELO ARTAMANOVICH** • 1941
ARTE COBODA • 1954 • Barreto Victor • BRZ
ARTE DE CASARSE, EL • 1966 • Feliu Jordi, Font Espina Jose Maria • SPN
ARTE DE ENGANAR, EL • 1970 • *Cine Prod. Int.* • MXC
ARTE DE NO CASARSE, EL • 1966 • Feliu Jordi, Font Espina Jose Maria • SPN
ARTE DE VIVIR, EL • 1968 • Diamante Julio • SPN • ART OF LIVING, THE
ARTE DEL PUEBLO • 1974 • Valdes Oscar • CUB • ART OF THE PEOPLE, THE
ARTE DEL TOBACO, EL • 1974 • Alea Tomas Gutierrez • CUB
ARTE DI ARRANGIARSI, L' • 1955 • Zampa Luigi • ITL • ART OF GETTING ALONG, THE (USA)
ARTE E OFICIO DE OURIVES • 1966 • Santos Alberto Seixas • SHT • PRT
ARTE E REALTA • 1950 • Giovannini, Mayer • SHT • ITL
ARTE IN SICILIA • 1948 • Rivalta Giorgio • SHT • ITL
ARTE POPULAR PORTUGUESA • 1954 • Mendes Joao • SHT • PRT
ARTE PORTUGUESA EM LONDRES • 1956 • Ribeiro Antonio Lopes • SHT • PRT
ARTE SACRA • 1954 • Mendes Joao • SHT • PRT
ARTE Y CULTURA • 1974 • de Pedro Manuel • VNZ • ART AND CULTURE
ARTERES DE FRANCE • 1939 • Epstein Jean • FRN
ARTES A LO LARGO DEL MAR • 1979 • Silberman Michel • DOC • VNZ • COASTAL ARTS
ARTESANIA EN EL TIEMPO • 1964 • Aguirre Javier • SHT • SPN
ARTESANIA POPULAR • 1966 • Guzman Patricio • SHT • CHL • POPULAR CRAFTS
ARTFUL ARTIST, AN • 1915 • Hotaling Arthur D. • USA
ARTFUL ARTISTS • 1916 • Beaudine William • USA
ARTFUL ATHLETICS • 1913 • Booth W. R. • UKN
ARTFUL BURGLAR, THE • 1910 • Rains Fred • UKN
ARTFUL CURE, THE • 1912 • *Majestic* • USA
ARTFUL DODGE, AN • 1905 • Collins Alf? • UKN
ARTFUL DODGE, AN • 1916 • *Parsons Bill* • SHT • USA
ARTFUL DODGER, THE • 1906 • Stow Percy • UKN
ARTFUL DODGER, THE • 1908 • Fitzhamon Lewin • UKN
ARTFUL DODGER, THE • 1916 • Millarde Harry • USA
ARTFUL DODGERS • 1949 • Capes Renault • UKN
ARTFUL KATE • 1911 • Ince Thomas H. • USA
ARTFUL LOVERS, THE • 1907 • Fitzhamon Lewin • UKN
ARTFUL, NOT 'ALF • 1915 • Birch Cecil • UKN
ARTFUL PENETRATION, THE see **NERO SU BIANCO** • 1969
ARTFUL PENETRATION OF BARBARA, THE see **NERO SU BIANCO** • 1969
ARTFUL TRAMPS • 1908 • Mottershaw Frank • UKN
ARTFUL WIDOW, THE • 1912 • *Cosmopolitan* • UKN
ARTFUL YOUNG TRUANT, AN • 1904 • *Paul R. W.* • UKN
ARTH • 1983 • Bhatt Mahesh • IND • MEANING, THE
ARTHUR • 1930 • Perret Leonce • FRN • CULTE DE LA BEAUTE, LE
ARTHUR • 1981 • Gordon Steve • USA
ARTHUR 2: ON THE ROCKS • 1988 • Yorkin Bud • USA
ARTHUR, ARTHUR • *Aubier Pascal (P)* • FRN
ARTHUR ARTHUR • 1969 • Gallu Samuel • UKN
ARTHUR CLEARS THE AIR • 1961 • Bryant Gerard • UKN
ARTHUR ET CIE • 1914 • Protazanov Yakov • USS
ARTHUR GETS MARRIED see **ARTUR SE ZENI** • 1910
ARTHUR HAILEY'S THE MONEYCHANGERS see **MONEYCHANGERS, THE** • 1976
ARTHUR HONEGGER • 1955 • Rouquier Georges • SHT • FRN
ARTHUR IMHOFF • 1915 • von Woringen Paul • FRG
ARTHUR IS FANTASTIC • 1971 • Mich Ludo • BLG
ARTHUR MILLER ON HOME GROUND • 1979 • Rasky Harry • USA
ARTHUR PENN, 1922- : THEMES AND VARIANTS • 1970 • Hughes Robert • DOC • USA
ARTHUR PENN -THE DIRECTOR • 1970 • Erwitt Elliott • DOC • USA
ARTHUR RIMBAUD, A BIOGRAPHY see **ARTHUR RIMBAUD, UNE BIOGRAPHIE** • 1989
ARTHUR RIMBAUD, UNE BIOGRAPHIE • 1989 • Dindo Richard • DOC • SWT • ARTHUR RIMBAUD, A BIOGRAPHY
ARTHUR ROBERTS • 1927 • Phillips Bertram • UKN
ARTHUR ROBERTS SKETCH • 1927 • Cooper George A. • UKN
ARTHUR RUBINSTEIN • 1979 • Reichenbach Francois • SER • FRN
ARTHUR RUBINSTEIN -THE LOVE OF LIFE see **ARTUR RUBINSTEIN: L'AMOUR DE LA VIE** • 1970
ARTHUR TAKES OVER • 1948 • St. Clair Malcolm • USA
ARTHUR THE KING • 1983 • Donner Clive • TVM • UKN, USA • MERLIN AND THE SWORD
ARTHUR TRUMAN'S WARD • 1914 • North Wilfred • USA
ARTHUR'S DESPERATE RESOLVE • 1916 • Garwood William • SHT • USA
ARTHUR'S HALLOWED GROUND • 1983 • Young Frederick • UKN
ARTHUR'S LAST FLING • 1916 • Julian Rupert • SHT • USA
ARTICLE 47, L' • 1913 • *Bateman Miss* • USA
ARTICLE 177 OF THE CRIMINAL LAW see **KEIHO 177 JO-FUJO KYOHAKU BOKOZAI** • 1968
ARTICLE 188 OF THE PENAL CODE • Ljubic Milan • DOC • YGS
ARTICLE 330, L' • 1934 • Pagnol Marcel • FRN
ARTIE AND MARTY ROSENBLATT'S BABY PICTURES • 1941 • Jacobs Ken • SHT • USA
ARTIE SHAW AND HIS ORCHESTRA • 1939 • Mack Roy • SHT • USA
ARTIE SHAW AND HIS ORCHESTRA IN SYMPHONY OF SWING • 1939 • Henabery Joseph • SHT • USA
ARTIE SHAW: TIME IS ALL YOU'VE GOT • 1986 • Berman Brigitte • DOC • CND
ARTIE SHAW'S CLASS IN SWING • 1939 • Roush Leslie • SHT • USA
ARTIFICES • 1963 • Reichenbach Francois • SHT • FRN
ARTIFICIAL LIGHT • 1969 • Frampton Hollis • USA
ARTIFICIAL PARADISE see **UMETNI RAJ** • 1990
ARTIFICIAL PNEUMOTHORAX • 1945 • Hudson Claud • DOC • UKN
ARTIGIANI DI SICILIA • 1951 • Carpignano Vittorio • ITL
ARTIK SEVMIYECEGIM • 1968 • Aslan Muzaffer • TRK • I'LL NEVER LOVE AGAIN
ARTISAN, THE • 1989 • Brandauer Klaus Maria • USA
ARTISANAT FAMILIAL • 1939-42 • Tessier Albert • DCS • CND
ARTISANS DU FER • 1951 • Palardy Jean • DCS • CND
ARTISCHOCKE • 1982 • Cook John • AUS
ARTIST, THE • 1918 • Gillstrom Arvid E. • SHT • USA
ARTIST, THE • 1923 • Summerville Slim • SHT • USA
ARTIST, THE • 1989 • Grimas Jonas • SHT • SWD
ARTIST ALEXANDER OTERO, THE see **INTEGRAL VIBRANTE DE ALEJANDRO OTERO** • 1973
ARTIST AND HIS MODEL, THE • 1913 • Batley Ethyle? • UKN
ARTIST AND MUSICIAN • 1904 • Collins Alf? • UKN
ARTIST AND THE BRAIN SPECIALIST, THE • 1912 • *Furniss Harry* • USA
ARTIST AND THE BRUTE, THE • 1913 • *Williams Kathlyn* • USA
ARTIST AND THE FLOWER GIRL, THE • 1901 • *Paul R. W.* • UKN
ARTIST AND THE GIRL, THE • 1909 • *Kalem* • USA
ARTIST AND THE GIRL, THE • 1914 • *Kineto* • UKN
ARTIST AND THE MANNIKIN, THE (USA) see **ARTISTE ET LE MANNEQUIN, L'** • 1900
ARTIST AND THE VENGEFUL ONE, THE • 1915 • Myers Harry • USA
ARTIST FINANCIER, THE • 1911 • Porter Edwin S. • USA
ARTIST NUDE SECRETS see **ARTIST'S STUDIO SECRETS** • 1964
ARTIST WITH THE LADIES (USA) see **COIFFEUR POUR DAMES** • 1931
ARTISTA ANG AKING ASAWA • 1968 • Borlaza Emmanuel • PHL • MY WIFE IS AN ACTRESS
ARTISTE • 1918 • Perret Leonce • FRN
ARTISTE, L' • 1976 • Bokor Pierre • MTV • RMN
ARTISTE ET LE MANNEQUIN, L' • 1900 • Melies Georges • FRN • ARTIST AND THE MANNIKIN, THE (USA)
ARTISTEN • 1928 • von Bolvary Geza • FRG
ARTISTEN • 1935 • Piel Harry • FRG
ARTISTEN IN DER ZIRKUSKUPPEL, RATLOS, DIE • 1968 • Kluge Alexander • FRG • ARTISTES AT THE TOP OF THE BIG TOP: DISORIENTATED ○ ARTISTS UNDER THE BIG TOP: PERPLEXED
ARTISTENBLUT • 1949 • Wehrum Wolfgang • FRG
ARTISTENTREUE • 1919 • Lund Erik • FRG

ARTISTES ANVERSOIS, LEURS MONUMENTS ET LEURS OEUVRES, LES • 1955 • Haesaerts Paul • BLG • ARTISTS OF ANTWERP
ARTISTES AT THE TOP OF THE BIG TOP: DISORIENTATED see **ARTISTEN IN DER ZIRKUSKUPPEL, RATLOS, DIE** • 1968
ARTISTES PRIMITIFS D'HAITI • 1949 • Benoit Real • DOC • CND
ARTISTIC AND PANORAMIC VIEWS OF TURIN see **TORINO ARTISTICA** • 1910
ARTISTIC ATMOSPHERE • 1916 • *Plump And Runt* • SHT • USA
ARTISTIC CREATION • 1901 • Booth W. R.? • UKN
ARTISTIC ENEMIES • 1920 • Goldaine Mark • SHT • USA
ARTISTIC INTERFERENCE • 1916 • Henderson Lucius • SHT • USA
ARTISTIC RAGPICKERS • 1907 • *Pathe* • FRN
ARTISTIC TEMPER • 1932 • *Etting Ruth* • SHT • USA
ARTISTIC TEMPERAMENT • 1920 • *Supreme Comedies* • USA
ARTISTIC TEMPERAMENT, THE • 1919 • Goodwins Fred • UKN • HER GREATER GIFT
ARTISTRY IN RHYTHM • 1944 • Collins Lewis D. • SHT • USA
ARTISTS • 1969 • Perry Margaret • DOC • CND
ARTISTS see **TROLOS** • 1913
ARTISTS AND MODELS • 1937 • Walsh Raoul • USA
ARTISTS AND MODELS • 1955 • Tashlin Frank • USA
ARTISTS AND MODELS ABROAD • 1937 • Leisen Mitchell • USA • STRANDED IN PARIS (UKN)
ARTIST'S ANTICS • 1946 • *Mead Thomas (P)* • SHT • USA
ARTIST'S DILEMMA, THE • 1901 • Porter Edwin S. • USA
ARTIST'S DILEMMA, THE • 1904 • *Warwick Trading Co* • UKN
ARTIST'S DREAM, AN • 1900 • Porter Edwin S. • USA
ARTIST'S DREAM, THE • 1903 • *Biograph* • USA
ARTIST'S DREAM, THE • 1906 • *Pathe* • FRN
ARTIST'S DREAM, THE • 1910 • Bray John R. • USA • DACHSHUND, THE
ARTIST'S DREAM, THE • 1913 • Bray John R. • USA
ARTIST'S DREAM, THE (USA) see **REVE D'ARTISTE** • 1898
ARTIST'S GREAT MADONNA, THE • 1913 • Brooke Van Dyke • USA
ARTIST'S HOAX, THE see **ARTIST'S RUSE, THE** • 1910
ARTIST'S IMPRESSION, AN • 1916 • SAF
ARTISTS IN MONTREAL • 1953-54 • Devlin Bernard • DCS • CND
ARTISTS IN THE COMMUNITY • 1983 • Friedrichs Zbigniew, McLennan Don • DOC • ASL
ARTIST'S INTRIGUE, AN • 1917 • *American* • USA
ARTIST'S JOKE, THE • 1912 • *Furniss Harry* • USA
ARTIST'S MODEL, THE • 1897 • *Prestwich Mfg. Co* • UKN
ARTIST'S MODEL, THE • 1907 • Fitzhamon Lewin • UKN
ARTIST'S MODEL, THE • 1915 • Spencer Richard V. • USA
ARTIST'S MODEL, THE • 1916 • *Pokes & Jabs* • USA
ARTIST'S MODELS see **INTIMATE DIARY OF ARTISTS' MODELS** • 1964
ARTIST'S MUDDLE, AN • 1920 • Smith Noel • SHT • USA
ARTISTS MUDDLES • 1933 • Edwards Harry J. • SHT • USA
ARTISTS OF ANTWERP see **ARTISTES ANVERSOIS, LEURS MONUMENTS ET LEURS OEUVRES, LES** • 1955
ARTISTS ON FIRE • 1988 • Armatage Kay • DOC • CND
ARTIST'S REVENGE, THE • 1909 • Brooke Van Dyke • USA
ARTIST'S ROMANCE, THE • 1913 • Johnson Arthur • USA
ARTIST'S RUSE, THE • 1910 • Martinek H. O. • UKN • ARTIST'S HOAX, THE
ARTIST'S SACRIFICE, THE • 1913 • *Joyce Alice* • USA
ARTIST'S SONS, THE • 1911 • Boggs Frank • USA
ARTIST'S STUDIO SECRETS • 1964 • *Box Office International F. d.* • USA • STORY OF AN ARTIST'S STUDIO SECRETS, THE ○ ARTIST NUDE SECRETS
ARTIST'S TRICK, THE • 1913 • *Wilbur Crane* • USA
ARTISTS UNDER THE BIG TOP: PERPLEXED see **ARTISTEN IN DER ZIRKUSKUPPEL, RATLOS, DIE** • 1968
ARTIST'S WIFE, THE • 1915 • Walsh Raoul • USA
ARTISTS' WORKSHOP, THE • 1964 • Kohanyi Julius • CND
ARTS AND FLOWERS • 1956 • Smith Paul J. • ANS • USA
ARTS AND FLOWERS see **RODENDANSKA PRICA** • 1969
ARTS CUBA • 1977 • Jutra Claude • CND
ARTS ET ARBRES • 1978 • Reichenbach Francois • MTV • FRN
ARTS IN CUBA • 1962 • Macartney-Filgate Terence • DOC • USA
ARTS OF VILLAGE INDIA • 1970 • Beresford Bruce • DCS • UKN
ARTUR RUBINSTEIN: L'AMOUR DE LA VIE • 1970 • Reichenbach Francois, Patris Gerard • FRN • ARTHUR RUBINSTEIN –THE LOVE OF LIFE ○ LOVE OF LIFE (UKN)
ARTUR SE ZENI • 1910 • Pech Antonin • CZC • ARTHUR GETS MARRIED
ARTURO'S ISLAND see **ISOLA DI ARTURO, L'** • 1962
ARTY THE ARTIST • 1914 • *Forsythe Vic* • USA
ARU EIGAKANTOKU NO SHOGAI see **ARU EIGAKANTOKU NO SHOGAI: MIZOGUCHI KENJI NO KIROKU** • 1974
ARU EIGAKANTOKU NO SHOGAI: MIZOGUCHI KENJI NO KIROKU • 1974 • Shindo Kaneto • DOC • JPN • LIFE OF THE FILM DIRECTOR, A ○ ARU EIGAKANTOKU NO SHOGAI ○ LIFE OF A FILM DIRECTOR:RECORD OF KENJI MIZOGUCHI
ARU JOSHI KOKOI NO KIROKU NINSHIN • 1968 • Yuge Taro • JPN • PREGNANCY
ARU JOSHIKOKOI NO KIROKU HATSUTAIKEN • 1968 • Obimori Yoshihiko • JPN • FIRST EXPERIENCE, THE
ARU KENGO NO SHOGAI • 1959 • Inagaki Hiroshi • JPN • LIFE STORY OF A CERTAIN SWORDSMAN, THE ○ SAMURAI SAGA
ARU KOROSHIYA • 1967 • Masumura Yasuzo • JPN • CERTAIN KILLER, A ○ MURDERER, A
ARU KOROSHIYA NO KAGI • 1967 • Mori Issei • JPN • KILLER'S KEY, A
ARU KYOHAKU • 1960 • Kurahara Koreyoshi • JPN • BLACKMAIL
ARU MITTSU • 1967 • Mukoi Kan, Yamamoto Shinya, Wakamatsu Koji • JPN • CERTAIN ADULTERY, A
ARU NINSHIN • 1968 • Yamashita Osamu • JPN • CERTAIN PREGNANCY, A
ARU ONNA • 1942 • Shibuya Minoru • JPN • CERTAIN WOMAN, A ○ THAT WOMAN
ARU ONNA • 1954 • Toyoda Shiro • JPN • CERTAIN WOMAN, A ○ THAT WOMAN
ARU OSAKA NO ONNA • 1962 • Sugawa Eizo • JPN • AYAKO (USA) ○ TWENTY-THREE STEPS TO BED ○ THAT WOMAN FROM OSAKA
ARU OTAKU NA BAAI • 1966 • Tsukioka Sadao • ANS • JPN
ARU RAKUJITSU • 1959 • Ohba Hideo • JPN • SETTING SUN
ARU SEX DOCTOR NO KIROKU • 1968 • Yuge Taro • JPN • DIARY OF A SEX COUNSELLOR, THE
ARU SHOJO NO KOKUHAKU –JUNKETSU • 1968 • Morinaga Kenjiro • JPN • CONFESSION OF A YOUNG GIRL – VIRGINITY
ARU SONAN • 1961 • Sugie Toshio • JPN • DEATH ON THE MOUNTAIN
ARU YO FUTATABI • 1956 • Gosho Heinosuke • JPN • TWICE ON A CERTAIN NIGHT ○ AGAIN ONE NIGHT
ARU YO NO SEPPUN • 1946 • Chiba Yasuki • JPN • CERTAIN NIGHT'S KISS, A
ARU YO NO TONOSAMA • 1946 • Kinugasa Teinosuke • JPN • LORD FOR A NIGHT
ARUBA, BONAIRE, CURAZAO see **A.B.C.** • 1958
ARUHI WATASHI WA • 1959 • Okamoto • JPN • ONE DAY, I..
ARUNATA PERA • 1981 • Jayatilaka Amarnath • SLN • BEFORE THE DAWN
ARUNDHUTI • 1967 • Gupta Prafulla Sen • IND
ARUNODHAYA • 1968 • Srinivasan C. • IND • SUNRISE
ARUNODOYER AGNISHAKHI • 1972 • Dutta Subhash • BNG • IN THE FLAMES OF SUNRISE
ARUPUSU NO WADADAISHO • 1966 • Furusawa Kengo • JPN • IT STARTED IN THE ALPS (USA) ○ ALPS NO WAKADAISHO
ARUPUSU TAISHO • 1934 • Yamamoto Kajiro • JPN • ALPINE VICTORY
ARUSS AN-NIL see **AROUSS EL NIL** • 1963
ARVACSKA • 1976 • Ranody Laszlo • HNG • NO MAN'S DAUGHTER
ARVEN • 1979 • Breien Anja • NRW • NEXT OF KIN ○ HERITAGE
ARVIND DESAI KI AJEEB KAHANI • 1977 • Mirza Saeed • IND • STRANGE FATE OF AJEEB KAHANI, THE
ARVOTTOMAT • 1982 • Kaurismaki Mika • FNL • WORTHLESS, THE
ARWA HAIMA • 1949 • Barakat Kamal • EGY • WANDERING SOULS
ARYAN, THE • 1916 • Barker Reginald • USA
ARYAN, THE • 1916 • Hart William S., Smith Cliff • USA
ARYENA • 1967 • Samsonov Samson • USS • ARENA
ARZOBISPO NO HA MUERTO, EL • 1956 • Portas Rafael E. • MXC
ARZOO • Sagar Ramanand • IND
ARZOO • 1950 • *Biswas Anil (M)* • IND
ARZT AUS HALBERSTADT, EIN • 1969 • Kluge Alexander • SHT • FRG • DOCTOR FROM HALBERSTADT, A
ARZT AUS LEIDENSCHAFT • 1936 • Zerlett Hans H. • FRG
ARZT AUS LEIDENSCHAFT • 1959 • Klinger Werner • FRG
ARZT –DOCTOR WITHOUT A CONSCIENCE see **ARZT OHNE GEWISSEN** • 1959
ARZT OHNE GEWISSEN • 1959 • Harnack Falk • FRG • DOCTOR WITHOUT SCRUPLES (USA) ○ PRIVAT KLINIK PROFESSOR LUND ○ LETZTE GEHEIMNIS, DAS ○ ARZT – DOCTOR WITHOUT A CONSCIENCE ○ PRIVATE CLINIC OF PROFESSOR LUND, THE
ARZT STELLT FEST... DER • 1966 • Ford Aleksander • FRG, SWT • DOCTOR SAYS, THE (USA) ○ ANGEKLAGT NACH PARAGRAPH 218 ○ DOCTOR SPEAKS OUT, THE
ARZT VON BOTHENOW, DER • 1961 • Knittel Johannes • GDR
ARZT VON ST. PAULI, DER • 1968 • Olsen Rolf • FRG • STREET OF SIN (UKN) ○ DOCTOR OF ST. PAULI, THE
ARZT VON STALINGRAD, DAS • 1958 • von Radvanyi Geza • FRG
ARZTRINNEN • 1983 • Seemann Horst • GDR • LADY DOCTORS ○ WOMEN DOCTORS
AS A BOY DREAMS • 1911 • *Imp* • USA
AS A FATHER SPARETH HIS SON • 1913 • Huntley Fred W. • USA
AS A MAN DESIRES • 1925 • Cummings Irving • USA
AS A MAN LIVES • 1923 • Dawley J. Searle • USA • HEARTS AND FACES
AS A MAN SOWS: OR, AN ANGEL OF THE SLUMS • 1914 • Haldane Bert? • UKN
AS A MAN THINKETH • 1914 • Cooley Frank • USA
AS A MAN THINKETH see **WHILE JUSTICE WAITS** • 1922
AS A MAN THINKS • 1919 • Irving George • USA
AS A WIFE, AS A WOMAN see **TSUMA TOSHITE ONNA TOSHITE** • 1961
AS A WOMAN SOWS • 1916 • Haddock William F. • USA
AS ASPERA AD ASTRA • 1969 • Dragic Nedeljko • ANS • YGS • PER ASPERA AD ASTRA
AS BLUE AS THE BLACK SEA see **NIEBIESKIE JAK MORZE CZARNE** • 1972
AS DE OROS • 1968 • Urueta Chano • MXC • ACE OF GOLD
AS DE PIC see **OPERAZIONE CONTROSPIONAGGIO** • 1965
AS DE PIQUE, LES • 1972 • Gagne Jacques • DCS • CND
AS DES AS, L' • 1982 • Oury Gerard • FRN, FRG
AS DU TURF, LES • 1932 • de Poligny Serge • FRN
AS FATE DECIDES • 1916 • Julian Rupert • SHT • USA
AS FATE ORDAINED (UKN) see **ENOCH ARDEN** • 1915
AS FATE WILLED • 1914 • *Victor* • USA
AS FATE WILLS • 1913 • *Frontier* • USA
AS FATE WOULD HAVE IT • 1912 • *Vitagraph* • USA
AS FATE WOULD HAVE IT • 1912 • *Powers* • USA
AS FOR ALL THESE WOMEN see **FOR ATT INTE TALA OM ALLA DESSA KVINNOR** • 1964
AS GOD MADE HER • 1920 • Doxat-Pratt B. E. • UKN • JUST AS I AM
AS GOD MADE HER see **ZOOALS IK BEN** • 1920
AS GOOD AS MARRIED • 1937 • Buzzell Edward • USA
AS GOOD AS NEW • 1933 • Cutts Graham • UKN
AS HE BLEW HE BLEW • 1915 • *Mina* • USA
AS HE WAS BORN • 1919 • Noy Wilfred • UKN
AS HUSBANDS GO • 1934 • MacFadden Hamilton • USA
AS I RODE DOWN TO LAREDO see **RETURN OF THE GUNFIGHTER** • 1966
AS IF IT WERE RAINING (USA) see **COMME S'IL EN PLEUVAIT** • 1963
AS IF IT WERE YESTERDAY see **COMME SI C'ETAIT HIER** • 1980
AS IN A DREAM • 1916 • Le Viness Carl M. • SHT • USA
AS IN A LOOKING GLASS • 1911 • Griffith D. W. • USA
AS IN A LOOKING GLASS • 1913 • *Leonard Marion* • USA
AS IN A LOOKING GLASS • 1916 • Crane Frank H. • USA
AS IN DAYS OF OLD • 1915 • Powers Francis • USA
AS IN DAYS OF YORE • 1917 • Sandground Maurice • UKN
AS IN DREAMS see **SOM I DROMMAR** • 1954
AS IS • 1986 • Lindsay-Hogg Michael • TVM • USA
AS IT HAPPENED • 1915 • O'Sullivan Tony • USA
AS IT IS IN LIFE • 1910 • Griffith D. W. • USA
AS IT MIGHT HAVE BEEN • 1914 • Henderson Dell • USA
AS IT WAS BEFORE see **THIS LOVE OF OURS** • 1945
AS IT WAS IN THE BEGINNING • 1912 • *La Badie Florence* • USA
AS LONG AS I CAN WALK • 1971 • Dodds Peter (c/d) • DOC • ASL
AS LONG AS I LIVE see **SOLANGE LEBEN IN MIR IST** • 1965
AS LONG AS I LIVE see **MIENTRAS ME DURE LA VIDA** • 1981
AS LONG AS THE HEART BEATS see **SO LANGE DAS HERZ SCHLAGT** • 1958
AS LONG AS THERE IS LIFE IN ME see **SOLANGE LEBEN IN MIR IST** • 1965
AS LONG AS THEY'RE HAPPY • 1955 • Thompson J. Lee • UKN
AS LONG AS WE LIVE see **INOCHI ARU KAGIRI** • 1947
AS LONG AS YOU LIVE see **SOLANGE DU LEBST** • 1955
AS LONG AS YOU'RE HEALTHY (UKN) see **TANT QU'ON A LA SANTE** • 1965
AS LONG AS YOU'RE NEAR ME (USA) see **SOLANGE DU DA BIST** • 1953
AS LUCK WOULD HAVE IT • 1917 • Christie Al • SHT • USA
AS MAN MADE HER • 1917 • Archainbaud George • USA • HER HIGHER DESTINY
AS ME KRINOUN I YINEKES • 1968 • Tempos Antonis • GRC • LET WOMEN JUDGE ME ○ WOMEN IN LOVE
AS MEN LOVE • 1917 • Hopper E. Mason • USA
AS NATURE INTENDED (USA) see **NAKED AS NATURE INTENDED** • 1961
AS NEGRO • 1953 • Mendez Fernando • MXC
AS NEGRO, EL • 1943 • Cardona Rene • MXC • BLACK ACE, THE
AS NO MAN HAS LOVED see **MAN WITHOUT A COUNTRY, THE** • 1925
AS OF TOMORROW WE'LL BE RICH AND HONEST see **AB MORGEN SIND WIR REICH UND EHRLICH** • 1977
AS OLD AS THE CENTURY see **ROVESNIK VEKA** • 1960
AS OLD AS THE HILLS • 1950 • Crick Alan, Privett Bob • ANS • UKN
AS ONS TWEE GETROUD IS • 1962 • SAF
AS OTHERS SEE US • 1912 • *Thanhouser* • USA
AS OTHERS SEE US • 1917 • Drew Sidney, Drew Sidney Mrs. • USA
AS PALAVRAS E OS FIOS • 1962 • Lopes Fernando • SHT • PRT
AS PEDRAS E O TEMPO • 1961 • Lopes Fernando • SHT • PRT
AS PRESCRIBED BY THE DOCTOR • 1910 • Aylott Dave? • UKN
AS PUPILAS DO SENHOR REITOR • 1935 • de Barros Jose Leitao • PRT
AS PUPILAS DO SENHOR REITOR • 1960 • Queiroga Perdigao • PRT
AS PURE AS A LILY see **COME UNA ROSA AL NASO** • 1976
AS RUINAS NO INTERIOR • 1976 • Caetano Jose De Sa • PRT
AS SEEN THROUGH THE TELESCOPE • 1900 • Smith G. A. • UKN
AS SPARROWS SEE US • 1905 • Collins Alf? • UKN
AS SUMMER DIES • 1986 • Tramont Jean-Claude • TVM • USA
AS TEARS GO BY see **MONGKOK KAMUN** • 1988
AS THE BEAST DIETH see **EINS OG SKEPNAN DEYR** • 1986
AS THE BELL RINGS • 1913 • *Solax* • USA
AS THE BELLS RANG OUT • 1910 • Griffith D. W. • USA
AS THE CANDLE BURNED • 1916 • Le Brandt Joseph • SHT • USA
AS THE CLOUDS SCATTER see **KUMO GA CHIGIRERU TOKI** • 1961
AS THE CROW FLIES • 1962 • Holly Martin • CZC
AS THE CROW LIES • 1951 • Kneitel Seymour • ANS • USA
AS THE DEVIL COMMANDS • 1933 • Neill R. William • USA
AS THE DOCTOR ORDERED • 1912 • *Imp* • USA
AS THE EARTH TURNS • 1934 • Green Alfred E. • USA
AS THE FATES DECREE • 1912 • *Williams Kathlyn* • USA
AS THE FLY FLIES • 1944 • Swift Howard • ANS • USA
AS THE HEART COMMANDS see **KAK VELIT SYERDTSYE** • 1968
AS THE MASTER ORDERS • 1911 • *Reliance* • USA
AS THE NAKED WIND FROM THE SEA see **SOM HAVETS NAKNA VIND** • 1968
AS THE SEA RAGES (USA) see **RAUBFISCHER IN HELLAS** • 1959
AS THE SHADOWS FALL • 1915 • Worthington William • USA
AS THE SPARKS FLY UPWARDS • 1913 • Plumb Hay • UKN
AS THE SUN WENT DOWN • 1915 • Wilson Frank • UKN
AS THE SUN WENT DOWN • 1918 • Hopper E. Mason • USA
AS THE TOOTH CAME OUT • 1913 • Williams C. Jay • USA
AS THE TWIG IS BENT • 1915 • Melville Wilbert • USA
AS THE WIND BLOWS • 1912 • *Powers* • USA
AS THE WIND BLOWS • 1914 • Lloyd Frank • USA
AS THE WORLD ROLLS ON • 1921 • *Johnson Jack* • USA
AS THINGS USED TO BE • 1911 • *Champion* • USA
AS THOUSANDS CHEER see **THOUSANDS CHEER** • 1943
AS TIME GOES BY • 1987 • Peak Barry • ASL
AS TIME GOES BY see **CLOSE TO MY HEART** • 1951
AS TIME ROLLED ON • 1914 • *Selig* • USA
AS TOLD BY PRINCESS BESS • 1912 • *Red Wing* • USA
AS USUAL see **SANS DEVANT DERRIERE** • 1974
AS USUAL, UNKNOWN see **SOLITI IGNOTI, I** • 1958
...AS WE ARE • 1973 • Gross Marty • CND
AS WE FORGIVE see **BREAKERS AHEAD** • 1938
AS WE FORGIVE THOSE • 1914 • Smiley Joseph • USA

AS WE JOURNEY THROUGH LIFE • 1914 • *Mcquarrie Mudock* • USA
AS WE LIE • 1927 • Mander Miles • UKN • LOST ONE WIFE
AS WE WERE see **GANITO KAMI NOON, PAANO KAYO NGAYON?** • 1977
AS WHITE AS HER HEART, AS RED AS HER LIPS see **SEPUTIH HATINYA SEMERAH BIBIRNYA** • 1981
AS YE REPENT • 1915 • Trimble Larry • UKN • REDEEMED (USA)
AS YE SOW • 1911 • Porter Edwin S. • USA
AS YE SOW • 1913 • *Swayne Marian* • USA
AS YE SOW • 1914 • Crane Frank H. • USA
AS YE SOW see **SO SHALL YE REAP** • 1916
AS YE SOW, SO SHALL YE REAP • 1911 • *Rex* • USA
AS YOU DESIRE ME • 1932 • Fitzmaurice George • USA
AS YOU LIKE IT • 1908 • Buel Kenean • USA
AS YOU LIKE IT • 1912 • Blackton J. Stuart, Young James • USA
AS YOU LIKE IT • 1936 • Czinner Paul • UKN
AS YOU LIKE IT • 1978 • Coleman Basil • MTV • UKN
AS YOU LIKE ME see **SOM DU VILL HA MEJ** • 1943
AS YOU MAKE YOUR BED see **SOM MAN BADDAR** • 1957
AS YOU WERE • 1919 • Santell Alfred • SHT • USA
AS YOU WERE • 1951 • Guiol Fred • USA
AS-YOU-WISH see **RUYI** • 1983
AS YOUNG AS WE ARE • 1958 • Girard Bernard • USA
AS YOUNG AS YOU FEEL • 1951 • Jones Harmon • USA
AS YOUR HAIR GROWS WHITER • 1911 • *Powers* • USA
ASA BRANCA -UM SONHO BRASILEIRO • 1982 • Batista Djalma Limongi • BRZ • WHITE WING -A BRAZILIAN DREAM
ASA-HANNA • 1946 • Henrikson Anders • SWD
ASA-NISSE • 1946 • Frisk Ragnar • SWD
ASA-NISSE AND THE GREAT TUMULT see **ASA-NISSE OCH DEN STORA KALABALIKEN** • 1968
ASA-NISSE AS AN AGENT see **ASA-NISSE I AGENTFORM** • 1967
ASA-NISSE BLAND GREVAR OCH BARONER • 1961 • Frisk Ragnar • SWD
ASA-NISSE FLYGER I LUFTEN • 1956 • Frisk Ragnar • SWD
ASA-NISSE I AGENTFORM • 1967 • Stivell Arne • SWD • ASA-NISSE AS AN AGENT
ASA-NISSE I FULL FART • 1957 • Frisk Ragnar • SWD
ASA-NISSE I KRONANS KLADER • 1958 • Frisk Ragnar • SWD
ASA-NISSE I POPFORM • 1964 • Larsson Borje • SWD
ASA-NISSE I RAKETFORM • 1966 • Frisk Ragnar • SWD
ASA-NISSE JUBILERAR • 1959 • Frisk Ragnar • SWD
ASA-NISSE OCH DEN STORA KALABALIKEN • 1968 • Stivell Arne • SWD • ASA-NISSE AND THE GREAT TUMULT
ASA-NISSE OCH TJOCKA SLAKTEN • 1963 • Larsson Borje • SWD
ASA-NISSE ON MALLORCA see **ASA-NISSE PA MALLORCA** • 1962
ASA-NISSE ORDNAR ALLT • 1955 • Frisk Ragnar • SWD
ASA-NISSE PA HAL IS • 1954 • Frisk Ragnar • SWD
ASA-NISSE PA JAKTSTIGEN • 1950 • Frisk Ragnar • SWD
ASA-NISSE PA MALLORCA • 1962 • Larsson Borje • SWD • ASA-NISSE ON MALLORCA
ASA-NISSE PA NYA AVENTYR • 1952 • Frisk Ragnar • SWD
ASA-NISSE PA SEMESTER • 1953 • Frisk Ragnar • SWD
ASA-NISSE SLAR TILL • 1965 • Palm Bengt • SWD
ASA-NISSE SOM POLIS • 1960 • Frisk Ragnar • SWD
ASA NO HAMON • 1952 • Gosho Heinosuke • JPN • MORNING CONFLICTS ○ TROUBLE IN THE MORNING
ASA NO NAMIKI-MICHI • 1936 • Naruse Mikio • JPN • DAWN IN THE BOULEVARD ○ MORNING'S TREE-LINED STREET
ASADHYUDU • 1968 • Ramachandra Rao V. • IND • UNCHALLENGEABLE
ASAGIRI TOGE • 1936 • Ito Daisuke • JPN • PASS OF MORNING MIST
ASAHI WA KAGAYAKU • 1929 • Mizoguchi Kenji (c/d) • JPN • MORNING SUN SHINES, THE (USA) ○ RISING SUN IS SHINING, THE
ASAKI YUMEMISHI • 1974 • Jissoji Akio • JPN • IT WAS A FAINT DREAM
ASAKUSA KURENAI DAN • 1952 • Hisamatsu Seiji • JPN • RED GROUP OF ASAKUSA
ASAKUSA MONOGATARI • 1953 • Shima Koji • JPN
ASAKUSA NO HADA • 1950 • Kimura Keigo • JPN • SONG OF ASAKUSA
ASAKUSA NO HI • 1937 • Shimazu Yasujiro • JPN • LIGHTS OF ASAKUSA, THE ○ LIGHT OF ASAKUSA, THE ○ LIGHT ON ASAKUSA
ASALTACAMINOS, EL • 1958 • Urueta Chano • MXC
ASALTO • 1969 • Alvarez Carlos • CLM
ASALTO, EL • 1964 • Salvador Jaime? • MXC
ASALTO A LA CIUDAD • 1968 • Cores Carlos • ARG • ASSAULT ON THE CITY
ASALTO AL CASTILLO DE LA MONCLOA, EL • 1978 • Lara Polop Francisco • SPN
ASAMA NO ABARENBO • 1958 • Kono Juichi • JPN • THUNDER KID
ASAMBLEA GENERAL • 1960 • Alea Tomas Gutierrez • DOC • CUB • GENERAL ASSEMBLY
ASANI SANKET see **ASHANI SANKET** • 1973
ASAYAKE NO UTA • 1973 • Kumai Kei • JPN • RISE, FAIR SUN
ASBESTOS HAZARD CONTROL • 1982 • von Puttkamer Peter • DOC • CND
ASCENDANCY • 1983 • Bennett Edward • UKN
ASCENDING SCALE see **AROHAN** • 1981
ASCENSAO E QUEDA DE UM PAQUERA • 1970 • Di Mello Victor • BRZ
ASCENSEUR POUR L'ECHAFAUD, L' • 1957 • Malle Louis • FRN • LIFT TO THE SCAFFOLD (UKN) ○ FRANTIC (USA) ○ ELEVATOR TO THE GALLOWS
ASCENSION AND THE FALL, THE • 1978 • el Sheikh Kamal • EGY
ASCENSION BAY see **WNIEBOWSTAPIENIE** • 1969
ASCENSION DE LA ROSIERE, L' • 1908 • Melies Georges • FRN • ASCENSION OF THE ROSE-QUEEN, THE
ASCENSION DE MONSIEUR LANGE, L' see **CRIME DE MONSIEUR LANGE, LE** • 1935
ASCENSION D'UN BALLON, L' • 1897 • Melies Georges • FRN • BALLOON ASCENSION, A
ASCENSION OF THE ROSE-QUEEN, THE see **ASCENSION DE LA ROSIERE, L'** • 1908
ASCENT see **AAROHI** • 1965
ASCENT see **KODIVETTAM** • 1977
ASCENT, THE see **VOSKHOZHDYENIYE** • 1977
ASCENT, THE see **AROHAN** • 1981
ASCENT DE HIMALAYA, L' see **DRAME A LA NANDA DEVI** • 1951
ASCENT OF MONT BLANC, THE • 1915 • UKN
ASCENT TO HEAVEN see **SUBIDA AL CIELO** • 1951
ASCHENBRODEL • 1914 • Gad Urban • FRG, DNM • CINDERELLA (USA) ○ ASKEPOT (DNM)
ASCHENBRODEL • 1915 • Oberlander Hans • FRG
ASCHENBRODELCHEN • 1915 • *Weixler Dorrit* • FRG
ASCHENBROEDEL • 1916 • Wilson Ben • SHT • USA • MARRIAGE BROKER, THE
ASCHENPUTTEL • 1922 • Reiniger Lotte • ANS • FRG • CINDERELLA (USA)
ASCHENPUTTEL • 1955 • Genschow Fritz • FRG • CINDERELLA (USA)
ASCHERMITTWOCH • 1921 • Rippert Otto • FRG • ASCHERMITTWOCH -EIN SPIEL VON KABALE UND LIEBE
ASCHERMITTWOCH • 1925 • Neff Wolfgang • FRG
ASCHERMITTWOCH • 1930 • Meyer Johannes • FRG • ASH WEDNESDAY (USA)
ASCHERMITTWOCH -EIN SPIEL VON KABALE UND LIEBE see **ASCHERMITTWOCH** • 1921
ASCOLTAMI • 1957 • Campogalliani Carlo • ITL, FRG • LIED VON NEAPEL, DAS (FRG)
ASE • 1929 • Uchida Tomu • JPN • SWEAT
ASEGURA A SU MUJER • 1935 • Seiler Lewis • USA • INSURE YOUR WIFE
ASES BUSCAN LA PAZ, LOS • 1954 • Ruiz-Castillo Arturo • SPN
ASESINATO DE TROTSKY • 1971 • *Internacional Alesandra* • MXC
ASESINATO EN EL COMITE CENTRAL • 1982 • Aranda Vicente • SPN • MURDER IN THE CENTRAL COMMITTEE
ASESINATO EN EL SENADO DE LA NACION • 1984 • Jusid Juan Jose • ARG • MURDER IN THE SENATE
ASESINATO EN LOS ESTUDIOS • 1944 • Sevilla Raphael J. • MXC
ASESINO DE MUNECAS, EL • 1974 • Skaife Michael • SPN
ASESINO DE PEDRALBES, EL • 1978 • Herralde Gonzalo • SPN • MURDERER OF PEDRALBES, THE
ASESINO DE TONTOS, EL (MXC) see **FOOL KILLER, THE** • 1963
ASESINO ESTA ENTRE LOS TRECE, EL • 1973 • Aguirre Javier • SPN
ASESINO ESTA SOLO • 1973 • Garcia de Duenas Jesus • SPN • BLOOD ON THE SHEETS
ASESINO INVISIBLE, EL • 1964 • Cardona Rene • MXC • ENMASCARADO DE ORO CONTRA EL ASESINO INVISIBLE, EL ○ INVISIBLE ASSASSIN, THE ○ MAN IN THE GOLDEN MASK VS. THE INVISIBLE ASSASSIN
ASESINO LOCO Y EL SEXO, EL see **LUCHADORAS CONTRA EL ROBOT ASESINO, LAS** • 1969
ASESINO SE EMBARCA • 1966 • Delgado Miguel M. • MXC
ASESINO X, EL • 1954 • Bustillo Oro Juan • MXC
ASESINOS DE LA LUCHA LIBRE • 1961 • Munoz Manuel • MXC
ASESINOS DE OTROS MUNDOS • 1971 • Galindo Ruben • MXC • MURDERERS FROM OTHER WORLDS
ASESINOS EN LA NOCHE • 1955 • Delgado Miguel M. • MXC
ASESINOS, LOS • 1968 • Salvador Jaime • MXC • MURDERERS, THE
ASESINOS, S.A. • 1956 • Fernandez Bustamente Adolfo • MXC
ASFALTO CHE SCOTTIA (ITL) see **CLASSE TOUS RISQUES** • 1959
ASFALTO SELVAGEM • 1964 • Tanko J. B. • BRZ • LOLLIPOP (USA) ○ FORBIDDEN LOVE AFFAIR
ASFALTTILAMPAAT • 1968 • Niskanen Mikko • FNL • ASPHALT LAMBS, THE
ASFOUR, EL • 1973 • Shahin Youssef • EGY, ALG • USFUR, AL- ○ MOINEAU, LE ○ SPARROW, THE
ASGEIR • 1983 • Vikingsson Vidar • ICL
ASH-CAN ALLEY • 1918 • Smith Dick • SHT • USA
ASH-CAN FLEET, THE • 1939 • Zinnemann Fred • SHT • USA
ASH CAN OR LITTLE DICK'S FIRST ADVENTURE • 1915 • Franklin Sidney A., Franklin Chester M. • USA • LITTLE DICK'S FIRST ADVENTURE
ASH OF DEATH • 1954 • Fueki Juzabure • JPN
ASH WEDNESDAY • 1974 • Peerce Larry • ITL, USA
ASH WEDNESDAY CONFESSION see **FASTNACHTSBEICHTE, DIE** • 1960
ASH WEDNESDAY (USA) see **ASCHERMITTWOCH** • 1930
ASHA NIRASHA • 1985 • Rosy • BNG
ASHAD KA EK DIN • 1972 • Kaul Mani • IND
ASHAMED OF HIS WIFE • 1913 • *All-British Films* • UKN
ASHAMED OF PARENTS • 1921 • Plympton Horace G. • USA
ASHAMED OF THE OLD FOLKS • 1916 • Moore Matt • SHT • USA
ASHANI SANKET • 1973 • Ray Satyajit • IND • DISTANT THUNDER (USA) ○ ASANI SANKET
ASHANTI • 1979 • Fleischer Richard • USA, SWT
ASHES • 1910 • *Edison* • USA
ASHES • 1913 • Apfel Oscar, Lewis Edgar • USA
ASHES • 1916 • Hill Robert F. • SHT • USA
ASHES • 1916 • Wolbert William • SHT • USA
ASHES • 1922 • Anderson G. M. • USA
ASHES • 1930 • Birch Frank • UKN
ASHES • 1975 • Barclay Barry • DOC • NZL
ASHES see **KAIJIN** • 1929
ASHES see **POPIOLY** • 1966
ASHES see **ASKE** • 1973
ASHES OF ZWEBA, THE • 1977 • Darkany Mostafa • MRC
ASHES AND DIAMONDS (UKN) see **POPIOL I DIAMENT** • 1958
ASHES OF DESIRE • 1919 • Borzage Frank • USA
ASHES OF DOOM • Munro Grant • CND
ASHES OF DREAMS • 1915 • *Pathe Exchange* • USA
ASHES OF EMBERS • 1916 • Kaufman Joseph • USA
ASHES OF GOLD • 1915 • Le Saint Edward J. • USA
ASHES OF HOPE • 1912 • *Rex* • USA
ASHES OF HOPE • 1914 • *Bushman Francis X.* • USA
ASHES OF HOPE • 1917 • Edwards Walter • USA
ASHES OF INSPIRATION • 1915 • MacDonald J. Farrell • USA
ASHES OF LOVE • 1918 • Abramson Ivan • USA
ASHES OF REMEMBRANCE • 1916 • Holubar Allen • SHT • USA
ASHES OF REVENGE, THE • 1915 • Shaw Harold • UKN
ASHES OF THE PAST • 1914 • Kirkwood James • USA
ASHES OF THREE • 1913 • Dwan Allan • USA
ASHES OF VENGEANCE • 1923 • Lloyd Frank • USA • PURPLE PRIDE
ASHES ON THE HEARTHSTONE • 1917 • Calvert E. H. • USA
ASHGAA RAGEL FIL ALAM • 1968 • el Saifi Hassan • EGY • BRAVEST MAN IN THE WORLD, THE
ASHGHALDOUNI • 1973 • Mehrjui Dariush • IRN • JUNK HOUSE
ASHI, AL • 1986 • Fanari Mohammed Mounir • IRQ • LOVER, THE
ASHI NI SAWATTA KOUN • 1930 • Ozu Yasujiro • JPN • LUCK TOUCHED MY LEGS ○ LOST LUCK
ASHI NI SAWATTA ONNA • 1952 • Ichikawa Kon • JPN • WOMAN WHO TOUCHED THE LEGS, THE
ASHI NI SAWATTA ONNA • 1960 • Masumura Yasuzo • JPN • WOMAN WHO TOUCHED THE LEGS, THE
ASHIBI • 1928 • *Tsuburaya Eiji (Ph)* • JPN
ASHIK KERIB • 1987 • Paradjanov Sergei • USS • HOARY LEGENDS OF THE CAUCASUS, THE
ASHIRWAD • 1969 • Mukherjee Fishi • IND
ASHITA ARU KAGIRI see **ASU ARU KAGIRI** • 1962
ASHITA HARERUKA • 1960 • Nakahira Ko • JPN • WAIT FOR TOMORROW
ASHITA NO ODORIKO • 1939 • Yoshimura Kozaburo • JPN • TOMORROW'S DANCERS ○ ASU NO ODORIKO ○ DANCERS OF TOMORROW
ASHITA WA ASHITA NO KAZE GA FUKU • 1958 • Inoue Umeji • JPN • TOMORROW IS ANOTHER DAY
ASHIYA KARA NO HIKO (JPN) see **FLIGHT FROM ASHIYA** • 1964
ASHIYANE KHORSHID • 1967 • Kamyar Saeid • IRN • SUN'S HOME, THE
ASHIZURI MISAKI • 1954 • Yoshimura Kozaburo • JPN • CAPE ASHIZURI
ASHLEY GREEN GOES TO SCHOOL • 1943 • Eldridge John • DOC • UKN
ASHOKA THE GREAT • 1978 • Ralhan O. P. • IND
ASHRAM • 1981 • Dobrowolny Wolfgang
ASHRIDGE CASTLE -THE MONMOUTH REBELLION • 1926 • Calvert Charles • UKN • MONMOUTH REBELLION
ASHTON AND RAWSON • 1928 • *De Forest Phonofilm* • UKN
ASHYANA • 1971 • Baker Diane • DOC • USA
ASI AMARON NUESTROS PADRES • 1964 • Bustillo Oro Juan • MXC
ASI ERA PANCHO VILLA • 1957 • Rodriguez Roberto • MXC
ASI ES GALICIA • 1964 • Nunez Santos • SPN
ASI ES LA MUJER • 1936 • Bohr Jose
ASI ES LA VIDA • 1930 • Crone George J. • USA
ASI ES LA VIDA • 1940 • Mujica Francisco • ARG • SUCH IS LIFE (USA)
ASI ES LA VIDA • 1977 • Carreras Enrique • ARG • SUCH IS LIFE
ASI ES MADRID • 1953 • Marquina Luis • SPN
ASI ES MI MEXICO • 1962 • Martinez Arturo • MXC
ASI ES MI TIERRA • 1937 • Boytler Arcady • MXC • SUCH IS MY COUNTRY (USA)
ASI SE QUIERE EN JALISCO • 1942 • de Fuentes Fernando • MXC • THAT'S HOW THEY LOVE IN JALISCO
ASI SON ELLAS • 1943 • Martinez Solares Gilberto • MXC
ASIA • 1928 • Ivanovsky Alexander • USS
ASIA CALLING see **SAKEBU AZIA** • 1932
ASIAN CATHAY PACIFIC BOWLS CHAMPIONSHIP • 1969 • Bourke Terry • DOC • HKG
ASIAN CRESCENT • 1964 • Hopkinson Peter • UKN
ASIAN HEART • 1987 • Trier Bodil, Ravn Malene • DCS • DNM
ASIAN SUN, THE see **SONNE ASIENS, DIE** • 1920
ASIAPOL SECRET SERVICE see **AJIA HIMITSU KEISATSU** • 1966
ASIGNATURA APROBADA • 1987 • Garci Jose Luis • SPN • COURSE COMPLETED
ASIGNATURA PENDIENTE • 1977 • Garci Jose Luis • SPN • PENDING EXAM
ASILACAK KADIN • 1985 • Sabuncu Basar • TRK • WOMAN TO BE HANGED, A
ASILO MUITO LOUCO, UM see **AZYLO MUITO LOUCO** • 1970
ASINO D'ORO: PROCESSO PER FATTI STRANI CONTRO LUCIUS APULEIO CITTADINO ROMANO, L' • 1970 • Spina Sergio • ITL, ALG • GOLDEN ASS -THE TRIAL OF LUCIUS APULEIUS FOR WITCHCRAFT, THE
ASINUS • 1964 • Mirchev Vassil • BUL • DONKEY, THE
ASIREI HACHOFESH • 1968 • Zarecki Yona • ISR • PRISONERS OF FREEDOM
ASIYA • 1960 • Lohani Fateh • BNG
ASIYE NASIL KURTULUR? • 1987 • Yilmaz Atif • TRK • CAN ASIYE BE SAVED?
ASK A POLICEMAN • 1939 • Varnel Marcel • UKN
ASK ANY GIRL • 1959 • Walters Charles • USA
ASK BECCLES • 1973 • Davis Redd • UKN
ASK DAD • 1927 • Newfield Sam • SHT • USA
ASK ESKI BIR YALAN • 1968 • Engin Ilhan • TRK • LOVE, THAT OLD LIE
ASK FATHER • 1919 • Roach Hal • SHT • USA
ASK FOR MY LOVE see **ZISE VIA TIN AGAPI MAS** • 1968
ASK GOD FOR FORGIVENESS ..NOT ME see **CHIEDI PERDONO A DIO -NON A ME** • 1968
ASK GRANDMA • 1925 • Roach Hal • SHT • USA
ASK NO QUARTER • 1974 • Rowley Christopher • SAF
ASK THE C.A.B. • 1942 • Cass Henry • DCS • UKN
ASK THE DEAD THE PRICE OF DEATH see **TSENU SMERTI SPROSI U MYORTVYKH** • 1980
ASKA TOVBE • 1968 • Inanoglu Turker • TRK • LOVE NO MORE
ASKE • 1973 • Udnaes Sverre • NRW • ASHES
ASKELADD • Caprino Ivo • ANM • NRW
ASKEPOT (DNM) see **ASCHENBRODEL** • 1914

ASKIM GUNAHIMDIR • 1968 • Gorec Ertem • TRK • MY LOVE IS A SIN

ASKIN MERHAMETI YOKTUR • 1967 • Turyan Hasim • TRK • LOVE KNOWS NO PITY

ASKING FOR TROUBLE • 1914 • Collins Edwin J.? • UKN

ASKING FOR TROUBLE • 1942 • Mitchell Oswald • UKN

ASKING FOR TROUBLE see **CRY FREEDOM** • 1987

ASKING FOR TROUBLE (UKN) see **HEADIN' FOR DANGER** • 1928

ASKINLA DIVANEYIM • 1967 • Dinler Mehmet • TRK • LOVE CRAZY

ASKLARIN EN GUZELI • 1968 • Gulgen Melih • TRK • BEST OF LOVES, THE

ASKNDRIE.. LIE? see **ISKINDIRIA.. LEH?** • 1978

ASLAN ARKADASIM see **KUDUZ RECEP** • 1967

ASLAN BEY see **ASLANBEY** • 1968

ASLAN YUREKLI KABADAYI • 1967 • Un Memduh • TRK • LION-HEARTED BRAVE, THE

ASLAN YUREKLI RESAT • 1967 • Aslan Mehmet • TRK • LION-HEARTED RESAT

ASLANBEY • 1968 • Yalinkilic Yavuz • TRK • ASLAN BEY

ASLANLARIN DONUSU • 1966 • Atadeniz Yilmaz • TRK • RETURN OF THE HEROES

ASLEEP AT THE SWITCH • 1923 • Del Ruth Roy • SHT • USA

ASLEEP IN THE FLEET • 1933 • Meins Gus • SHT • USA

ASMARA KIRANA • 1970 • Achnas Naz • MLY • WHITE BRIDE, THE

ASPALATHUS FLOWER see **ZAHRAT AL QANDUL** • 1985

ASPASIA'S DOLLARS see **DHOLLARIATIS ASPASIAS, TA** • 1967

ASPECTOS DE MOCAMBIQUE • 1941 • Ribeiro Antonio Lopes • SHT • PRT

ASPECTS MEDICAUX DE L'ARME ATOMIQUE • 1955 • Lanoe Henri • SHT • FRN

ASPEN • 1977 • Heyes Douglas • TVM • USA • INNOCENT AND THE DAMNED, THE ◦ ASPEN MURDER, THE

ASPEN MURDER, THE see **ASPEN** • 1977

ASPERN • 1981 • de Gregorio Eduardo • FRN, PRT

ASPHALT • 1929 • Rittau Gunther, May Joe • FRG • TEMPTATION

ASPHALT • 1951 • Robbeling Harald • AUS

ASPHALT FLOWERS, THE see **FLEURS DE MACADAM, LES** • 1969

ASPHALT JUNGLE, THE • 1950 • Huston John • USA

ASPHALT LAMBS, THE see **ASFALTTILAMPAAT** • 1968

ASPHALT WARRIORS • 1985 • Millet Patrick • FRN

ASPHALTE • 1958 • Bromberger Herve • FRN

ASPHALTE • 1980 • Amar Denis • FRN

ASPHALTIC BITUMEN • 1950 • Armitage Philip • UKN

ASPHALTROSE, DIE • 1921 • Lowenbein Richard • FRG

ASPHYX, THE • 1972 • Newbrook Peter • UKN • SPIRIT OF THE DEAD (USA) ◦ HORROR OF DEATH, THE

ASPHYXIA see **KICMA** • 1976

ASPIRATIONS OF GERALD AND PERCY, THE • 1910 • *Imp* • USA

ASQUITH: THE TAX SCANDAL see **SECRET LIVES OF THE BRITISH PRIME MINISTERS: ASQUITH, THE** • 1983

ASQUITHS, THE see **SECRET LIVES OF THE BRITISH PRIME MINISTERS: ASQUITH, THE** • 1983

ASS • 1971 • *U.c.l.a.* • SHT • USA

ASS AND THE STICK, THE • 1974 • Batchelor Joy • ANS • UKN

ASSA! • 1987 • Soloviev Sergei • USS

ASSA 1 • 1967 • Copin Claude • FRN

ASSALTO, O • 1970 • Lima Walter Jr. • BRZ

ASSALTO AL CENTRO NUCLEARE • 1967 • Caiano Mario • ITL, SPN • PER PIACERE, NON SPARATE COL CANNONE (SPN) ◦ PLEASE, DON'T FIRE THE CANNON ◦ PER FAVORE NON SPARATE COL CANNONE

ASSALTO AL TESORO DI STATO • 1967 • Stanley Peter E. • ITL • ATTACK ON THE STATE TREASURE

ASSALTO AO TREMO PAGADOR • 1962 • Farias Roberto • BRZ • TRAIN ROBBERY CONFIDENTIAL (USA) ◦ TRAIN ROBBERS, THE (UKN) ◦ TIAO MEDONHO

ASSAM GARDEN ,THE • 1985 • McMurray Mary • UKN

ASSASSIN • 1973 • Crane Peter • UKN • ASSASSINATION

ASSASSIN • 1986 • Stern Sandor • TVM • USA

ASSASSIN see **TZ'U-K'O** • 1977

ASSASSIN, L' see **DESSOUS DES CARTES, LE** • 1947

ASSASSIN, THE • 1967 • Garcia Eddie • PHL

ASSASSIN, THE • Chan Hong Man • HKG

ASSASSIN, THE see **ASSASSINO, L'** • 1961

ASSASSIN, THE see **ANSATSU** • 1964

ASSASSIN, THE (UKN) see **GUNFIGHTERS** • 1947

ASSASSIN, THE (USA) see **VENETIAN BIRD** • 1952

ASSASSIN A PEUR LA NUIT, L' • 1942 • Delannoy Jean • FRN

ASSASSIN CHANTAIT, L' see **SEUL DANS LA NUIT** • 1945

ASSASSIN CONNAIT LA MUSIQUE, L' • 1963 • Chenal Pierre • FRN

ASSASSIN EST A L'ECOUTE, L' • 1948 • Andre Raoul • FRN

ASSASSIN EST DANS L'ANNUAIRE, L' • 1961 • Joannon Leo • FRN

ASSASSIN FOR HIRE • 1951 • McCarthy Michael • UKN

ASSASSIN FRAPPE A L'AUBE, L' • Simenon Marc • FRN

ASSASSIN HABITE AU 21, L' • 1942 • Clouzot Henri-Georges • FRN • MURDERER LIVES AT NUMBER 21, THE (USA)

ASSASSIN, L' (FRN) see **ASSASSINO, L'** • 1961

ASSASSIN MUSICIEN, L' • 1976 • Jacquot Benoit • FRN

ASSASSIN N'EST PAS COUPABLE, L' • 1945 • Delacroix Rene • FRN

ASSASSIN N'EST PAS L'ANTIQUAIRE, L' see **VECES ETAIENT FERMES DE L'INTERIEUR, LES** • 1976

ASSASSIN OF YOUTH • 1936 • Clifton Elmer • USA • MARIJUANA

ASSASSIN QUI PASSE, UN • 1977 • Vianey Michel • FRN

ASSASSIN VIENDRA CE SOIR, L' • 1962 • Maley Jean • FRN

ASSASSINA, L' • 1989 • Kuert Beat • SWT

ASSASSINA DEL PONTE SAINT-MARTIN, L' • 1913 • Roberti Roberto Leone • ITL

ASSASSINAT DE LA RUE DU TEMPLE, L' see **CRIME DE LA RUE DU TEMPLE, LE** • 1904

ASSASSINAT DE MACKINLEY, L' • 1902 • Zecca Ferdinand • FRN

ASSASSINAT DE TROTSKY, L'(FRN) see **ASSASSINIO DI TROTSKY, L'** • 1972

ASSASSINAT D'HENRI III • 1912 • Desfontaines Henri • FRN

ASSASSINAT DU COURRIER DU LYON, L' • 1904 • Blache Alice • FRN

ASSASSINAT DU DUC DE GUISE, L' • 1908 • Calmettes Andre, Le Bargy Charles • FRN • ASSASSINATION OF THE DUKE DE GUISE

ASSASSINAT DU PERE NOEL, L' • 1941 • Christian-Jaque • FRN • KILLING OF SANTA CLAUS, THE (UKN) ◦ WHO KILLED SANTA CLAUS? (USA) ◦ MURDER OF FATHER CHRISTMAS, THE

ASSASSINATION • Warhol Andy • USA

ASSASSINATION • 1967 • Miraglia Emilio Paolo • ITL

ASSASSINATION • 1987 • Hunt Peter • USA • PRESIDENT'S WIFE, THE

ASSASSINATION see **ANSATSU** • 1964

ASSASSINATION see **ATENTAT** • 1964

ASSASSINATION see **ASSASSIN** • 1973

ASSASSINATION see **SARAJEVSKI ATENTAT** • 1975

ASSASSINATION, THE see **TOD EINES FREMDEN, DER** • 1972

ASSASSINATION AT SARAJEVO see **SARAJEVSKI ATENTAT** • 1968

ASSASSINATION AT SARAJEVO see **SARAJEVSKI ATENTAT** • 1975

ASSASSINATION BUREAU, THE • 1969 • Dearden Basil • UKN

ASSASSINATION IN DAVOS (UKN) see **KONFRONTATION** • 1975

ASSASSINATION IN ROME see **ASSASSINIO MADE IN ITALY** • 1963

ASSASSINATION IN SARAJEVO see **SARAJEVSKI ATENTAT** • 1975

ASSASSINATION OF A BRITISH SENTRY, THE • 1900 • *Mitchell & Kenyon* • UKN

ASSASSINATION OF CROWN PRINCE FERDINAND see **SARAJEVSKI ATENTAT** • 1968

ASSASSINATION OF RYOMA see **RYOMA ANSATSU** • 1974

ASSASSINATION OF THE DUKE DE GUISE see **ASSASSINAT DU DUC DE GUISE, L'** • 1908

ASSASSINATION OF THE KING AND QUEEN OF SERVIA, THE • 1903 • Winslow Dicky? • UKN

ASSASSINATION OF TROTSKY, THE (UKN) see **ASSASSINIO DI TROTSKY, L'** • 1972

ASSASSINATION RUN, THE • 1984 • Hannam Ken • MTV • UKN • TREACHERY GAME, THE

ASSASSINATION TEAM, THE see **WARDOG: THE KILLING MACHINE** • 1986

ASSASSINI SONO NOSTRI OSPITI, GLI • 1974 • Rigo Vincenzo • ITL

ASSASSINIO COL BOTTO see **ADORABILI E BUGIARDE** • 1959

ASSASSINIO DI TROTSKY, L' • 1972 • Losey Joseph • ITL, FRN, UKN • ASSASSINATION OF TROTSKY, THE (UKN) ◦ ASSASSINAT DE TROTSKY, L'(FRN)

ASSASSINIO MADE IN ITALY • 1963 • Amadio Silvio • ITL, FRN, SPN • SEGRETO DEL VESTITO ROSSO, IL ◦ ASSASSINATION IN ROME ◦ SECRETO DE BILL NORTH, EL

ASSASSINIO SUL TEVERE • 1979 • Corbucci Bruno • ITL • MURDER ON THE TIBER

ASSASSINO, L' • 1961 • Petri Elio • ITL, FRN • LADY KILLER OF ROME, THE (USA) ◦ ASSASSIN, L' (FRN) ◦ ASSASSIN, THE ◦ MURDER, THE

ASSASSINO E AL TELEFONO, L' • 1972 • De Martino Alberto • ITL • KILLERS ON THE PHONE, THE (UKN) ◦ SCENES FROM A MURDER (USA)

ASSASSINO E COSTRETTO AD UCCIDERE ANCORA, L' • 1975 • Cozzi Luigi • ITL

ASSASSINO FANTASMA • 1969 • Seto Javier • ITL

ASSASSINO HA RISERVATO 9 POLTRONE, L' • 1974 • Bennati Giuseppe • ITL

ASSASSINO SENZA VOLTO • 1968 • Morrison R. • ITL

ASSASSINO SIN CHIAMA POMPEO, L' • 1962 • Girolami Marino • ITL

ASSASSINOS see **MAOS SANGRENTAS** • 1954

ASSASSINS, LES see **QATALA, AL-** • 1971

ASSASSINS DE L'ORDRE, LES • 1970 • Carne Marcel • FRN, ITL • INCHIESTA SU UN DELITTO DELLA POLIZIA (ITL)

ASSASSINS D'EAU DOUCE • 1946 • Painleve Jean • SHT • FRN

ASSASSINS DU DIMANCHE, LES • 1956 • Joffe Alex • FRN • EVERY SECOND COUNTS (USA) ◦ CHAQUE MINUTE COMPTE ◦ EVERY MINUTE COUNTS

ASSASSINS ET VOLEURS • 1957 • Guitry Sacha • FRN • LOVERS AND THIEVES (USA)

ASSASSINS IN THE SUN see **MAOS SANGRENTAS** • 1954

ASSASSINS OF ROME (USA) see **GIROLIMONI -IL MOSTRO DI ROMA** • 1972

ASSAULT • 1971 • Hayers Sidney • UKN • IN THE DEVIL'S GARDEN (USA) ◦ TOWER OF TERROR

ASSAULT, THE see **MISSHANDLINGEN** • 1970

ASSAULT, THE see **AANSLAG, DE** • 1986

ASSAULT AND BATTERY see **UBERFALL, DER** • 1928

ASSAULT AND FLATTERY • 1956 • Sparber I. • ANS • USA

ASSAULT AND MATRIMONY • 1987 • Frawley James • TVM • USA

ASSAULT AND PEPPERED • 1965 • McKimson Robert • ANS • USA

ASSAULT FORCE see **NORTH SEA HIJACK** • 1980

ASSAULT FROM HELL see **ODEN JIGOKU** • 1960

ASSAULT IN BROAD DAYLIGHT see **ES GESCHAH AM HELLICHTEN TAG** • 1958

ASSAULT IN THE PARK • 1959 • Wieland Joyce (c/d) • CND

ASSAULT OF THE KILLER BIMBOS • 1988 • Bechard Gorman?, Rosenberg Anita? • USA • SCUMBUSTERS ◦ HACK 'EM HIGH

ASSAULT OF THE PARTY NERDS • 1989 • Gabai Richard • USA

ASSAULT OF THE REBEL GIRLS see **CUBAN REBEL GIRLS** • 1959

ASSAULT ON A QUEEN • 1966 • Donohue Jack • USA

ASSAULT ON AGATHON • 1975 • Benedek Laslo • UKN, GRC

ASSAULT ON PARADISE see **MANIAC** • 1977

ASSAULT ON PRECINCT 13 • 1976 • Carpenter John • USA

ASSAULT ON THE CITY see **ASALTO A LA CIUDAD** • 1968

ASSAULT ON THE WAYNE • 1970 • Chomsky Marvin • TVM • USA

ASSAUT, L' • 1936 • Ducis Pierre-Jean • FRN

ASSAUT ANTI-CHAR • 1968 • Nasser George • SHT • LBN

ASSAUT DE HIMALAYA, L' see **DRAME A LA NANDA DEVI** • 1951

ASSAUT DE LA TERRE, L' • 1913 • Jasset Victorin • FRN

ASSAUT D'ESCRIME (ECOLE DE JOINVILLE) • 1898 • Melies Georges • FRN • FENCING AT THE JOINVILLE SCHOOL

ASSAYER OF LOVE GAP, THE • 1915 • Eason B. Reeves • USA

ASSEDIO DELL'ALCAZAR, L' • 1940 • Genina Augusto • ITL • SIEGE OF ALCAZAR

ASSEDIO DI SIRACUSA, L' • 1960 • Francisci Pietro • ITL, FRN • SIEGE DE SYRACUSE, LE (FRN) ◦ SIEGE OF SYRACUSE (USA) ◦ ARCHIMEDE

ASSENZA INGIUSTIFICATA • 1939 • Neufeld Max • ITL

ASSEZ DE TRISTESSE see **KIFAYA YA IN** • 1955

ASSI ALLA RIBALTA • 1959 • Baldi Ferdinando • ITL

ASSI DELLA RISATA, GLI • 1943 • *Riento Virgilio* • ITL

ASSICURASI VERGINE • 1967 • Bianchi Giorgio • ITL • GUARANTEED VIRGIN

ASSIETTES LOGIQUES, LES • 1970 • Moreau Michel • DCS • CND

ASSIETTES TOURNANTES • 1895 • Lumiere Louis • FRN

ASSIFAT AL-AOURAS • 1967 • Hamina Mohamed Lakhdar • ALG • ORACLE WINDS, THE ◦ WIND FROM AURES ◦ VENT DES AURES, LE

ASSIGNATION, THE • 1953 • Harrington Curtis • SHT • USA

ASSIGNATION, THE see **MIKKAI** • 1960

ASSIGNED SERVANT, THE see **ASSIGNED TO HIS WIFE** • 1911

ASSIGNED TO DANGER • 1948 • Boetticher Budd • USA

ASSIGNED TO HIS WIFE • 1911 • Gavin John F. • ASL • ASSIGNED SERVANT, THE

ASSIGNED TO TREASURY see **TO THE ENDS OF THE EARTH** • 1948

ASSIGNMENT, THE • 1977 • Bisset George • SWD

ASSIGNMENT, THE • 1986 • Arehn Mats • SWD

ASSIGNMENT, THE see **UPPDRAGET** • 1977

ASSIGNMENT ABROAD • 1955 • *Alda Robert* • MTV • USA

ASSIGNMENT CHILDREN • 1955 • *Kaye Danny* • DOC • USA

ASSIGNMENT DRAGON NO.3 see **RIKUGUN NAKANO GAKKO -RYO SANGO SHIREI** • 1967

ASSIGNMENT -FEMALE • 1966 • Phelan Raymond A. • USA

ASSIGNMENT IN BRITTANY • 1943 • Conway Jack • USA

ASSIGNMENT IN CHINA (UKN) see **STATE DEPARTMENT FILE -649** • 1949

ASSIGNMENT: INSTANBUL see **CASTLE OF FU MANCHU, THE** • 1968

ASSIGNMENT K • 1967 • Guest Val • UKN

ASSIGNMENT: KILL CASTRO see **CUBA CROSSING** • 1980

ASSIGNMENT: MUNICH • 1972 • Rich David Lowell • TVM • USA

ASSIGNMENT -OUTER SPACE see **SPACE MEN** • 1960

ASSIGNMENT -PARIS! • 1952 • Parrish Robert, Sherman Vincent (U/c) • USA • ASSIGNMENT PARIS

ASSIGNMENT PARIS see **ASSIGNMENT -PARIS!** • 1952

ASSIGNMENT REDHEAD • 1956 • Rogers Maclean • UKN • MILLION DOLLAR MANHUNT (USA) ◦ UNDERCOVER GIRL

ASSIGNMENT SKYBOLT see **KATASKOPI STO SARONIKO** • 1968

ASSIGNMENT TERROR see **HOMBRE QUE VINO DEL UMMO, EL** • 1970

ASSIGNMENT TO KILL • 1969 • Reynolds Sheldon • USA

ASSIM E MATOSINHOS • 1948 • Mendes Joao • SHT • PRT

ASSIM NEM A CAMA AGUENTA • 1970 • Di Mello Victor • BRZ

ASSISI • 1932 • Blasetti Alessandro • DOC • ITL

ASSISI UNDERGROUND, THE • 1984 • Ramati Alexander • USA

ASSISTANCE see **JOEMBER** • 1970

ASSISTANCE: INDIA -PEOPLE TO PEOPLE • 1967 • Murray John B. • DOC • ASL

ASSISTANT, THE • 1969 • Dooley John • UKN

ASSISTANT, THE see **GEHULFE, DER** • 1976

ASSISTANT, THE see **POMOCNIK** • 1982

ASSISTANT TO HIS HIGHNESS see **POPBOCNIK JEHO VYSOSTI** • 1933

ASSISTANT WIVES • 1927 • Parrott James • SHT • USA

ASSISTED ELOPEMENT, AN • 1910 • *Thanhauser* • USA

ASSISTED ELOPEMENT, AN • 1912 • *Selig* • USA

ASSISTED ELOPEMENT, AN • 1912 • Dwan Allan • *American* • USA

ASSISTED PROPOSAL, AN • 1913 • *American* • USA

ASSMANNS, DIE • 1925 • Bergen Arthur • FRG

ASSO • 1981 • Castellano, Pipolo • ITL

ASSO DI PICCHE OPERAZIONE CONTROSPIONAGGIO see **OPERAZIONE CONTROSPIONAGGIO** • 1965

ASSO DI PICHE see **OPERAZIONE CONTROSPIONAGGIO** • 1965

ASSO PIGLIA TUTTO see **QUATTRO DELL'AVE MARIA, I** • 1968

ASSOCIATE, THE see **ASSOCIE, L'** • 1979

ASSOCIATION, THE • 1975 • *Byong Yu* • CHN

ASSOCIATION DE MALFAITEURS • 1986 • Zidi Claude • FRN

ASSOCIE, L' • 1979 • Gainville Rene • FRN, FRG • ASSOCIATE, THE

ASSOIFFES, LES see **D'AMI'UM, AD-** • 1972

ASSOLUTO NATURALE, L' • 1969 • Bolognini Mauro • ITL • SHE AND HE (UKN) ◦ HE AND SHE

ASSOMMOIR, L' • 1908 • Nonguet Lucien • FRN

ASSOMMOIR, L' • 1909 • Capellani Albert • FRN

ASSOMMOIR, L' • 1921 • Maudru Charles • FRN

ASSOMMOIR, L' • 1933 • Roudes Gaston • FRN

ASSOUFARA see **SUFARA', AS-** • 1975

ASSUMED NAME: SCHLIER see **DECKNAME SCHLIER** • 1985

ASSUNTA SPINA • 1915 • Serena Gustavo • ITL

ASSUNTA SPINA • 1916 • Martoglio Nino • ITL

ASSUNTA SPINA • 1928 • Roberti Roberto Leone • ITL

ASSUNTA SPINA • 1948 • Mattoli Mario • ITL

ASSUNTA SPINA • 1979 • Ippolito Ciro • ITL

ASSUNTINA DAS AMERIKAS • 1974 • Filho Luis Rosemberg • BRZ

ASSUNTO MUITO PARTICULAR, UM • 1984 • de Rossi Nello • BRZ • VERY PRIVATE MATTER, A

ASSURANCE-VIE DESJARDINS, L' • 1983 • Beaudry Michel • MTV • CND
ASSY-TACHI NO MACHI • 1981 • Yamamoto Satsuo • JPN • TOWN FOR ASSEMBLY WORKERS, A
ASSZONY A TELEPEN • 1962 • Feher Imre • HNG • WOMAN AT THE HELM
ASTA MEIN ENGELCHEN • 1980 • Oehme Roland • GDR • ASTA MY ANGEL
ASTA MY ANGEL see **ASTA MEIN ENGELCHEN** • 1980
ASTENICHESKY SINDROM • 1989 • Muratova Kira • USS • ASTHENIC SYNDROME, THE
ASTEPTIND UN TREN • 1982 • Veroiu Mircea • RMN • WAITING FOR A TRAIN
ASTERIE, L' • 1958 • Painleve Jean • SHT • FRN
ASTERIX AND CLEOPATRA (UKN) see **ASTERIX ET CLEOPATRE** • 1968
ASTERIX ET CLEOPATRE • 1968 • Goscinny Rene, Uderzo Albert • ANM • FRN, BLG • ASTERIX AND CLEOPATRA (UKN)
ASTERIX ET LA SURPRISE DE CESAR • 1985 • Brizzi Paul, Brizzi Gaetan • ANM • FRN
ASTERIX LE GAULOIS • 1967 • Goscinny Rene, Uderzo Albert • ANM • FRN • ASTERIX THE GAUL (UKN)
ASTERIX -OPERATION FINKLESTEIN • 1989 • ANM • FRG, FRN
ASTERIX -THE BIG FIGHT • 1989 • Grimond Philippe • ANM • FRG
ASTERIX THE GAUL 2: THE TWELVE TASKS OF ASTERIX see **DOUZE TRAVAUX D'ASTERIX, LES** • 1976
ASTERIX THE GAUL (UKN) see **ASTERIX LE GAULOIS** • 1967
ASTHENIC SYNDROME, THE see **ASTENICHESKY SINDROM** • 1989
ASTHORE • 1917 • Noy Wilfred • UKN
ASTIC • 1956 • Kalla S. P. • IND
ASTONISHED • 1988 • Kahn Jeff • USA
ASTONISHED HEART, THE • 1950 • Darnborough Anthony, Fisher Terence • UKN
ASTONISHING FRAME, THE (USA) see **CADRE AUX SURPRISES, LE** • 1904
ASTOUNDING SHE-MONSTER, THE • 1958 • Ashcroft Ronnie • USA • MYSTERIOUS INVADER (UKN)
ASTRAGALE, L' • 1968 • Casaril Guy • FRN, FRG
ASTRAKAN COAT, THE see **CAPPOTTO DI ASTRAKAN, IL** • 1979
ASTRAL FACTOR • 1976 • Florea John • USA • INVISIBLE STRANGER ○ SILENT KILL
ASTRAL MAN • 1958 • Vanderbeek Stan • ANS • USA
ASTRAPOGIANUS • 1969 • *Kouzkoulos Nikos* • GRC
ASTRAY FROM THE STEERAGE see **AWAY FROM THE STEERAGE** • 1921
ASTRIDE THE TIGRESS see **A CAVALLO DELLA TIGRE** • 1961
ASTRO ZOMBIES see **ASTRO-ZOMBIES, THE** • 1968
ASTRO-ZOMBIES, THE • 1968 • Mikels Ted V. • USA • ASTRO ZOMBIES ○ SPACE VAMPIRES
ASTROBOY see **TETSUWAN ATOM** • 1960
ASTRODUCK • 1966 • McKimson Robert • ANS • USA
ASTROLOGER, THE • 1908 • *Gaumont* • FRN
ASTROLOGER, THE • 1975 • Denny Craig • USA
ASTROLOGER, THE • 1977 • Glickenhaus James • USA • SUICIDE CULT
ASTROLOGIE • 1952 • Gremillon Jean • FRN • ASTROLOGIE OU LE MIROIR DE LA VIE ○ MIROIR DE LA VIE, LE
ASTROLOGIE OU LE MIROIR DE LA VIE see **ASTROLOGIE** • 1952
ASTROMUTI • 1963 • Vukotic Dusan • ANS • YGS • ASTROMUTS
ASTROMUTS see **ASTROMUTI** • 1963
ASTRONAUT, THE • Kaminski Zygmunt, Osadca Marek • PLN
ASTRONAUT, THE • 1972 • Lewis Robert Michael • TVM • USA
ASTRONAUTA, EL • 1970 • Aguirre Javier • SPN
ASTRONAUTAS, LOS • 1960 • Zacarias Miguel • MXC • TURISTAS INTERPLANETARIOS ○ DOS VIAJEROS DEL ESPACIO ○ ASTRONAUTS, THE ○ INTERPLANETARY TOURISTS
ASTRONAUTES, LES • 1959 • Borowczyk Walerian, Marker Chris • ANS • FRN • ASTRONAUTS, THE
ASTRONAUTES ENSEMBLISTES, LES • 1970 • Moreau Michel • DCS • CND
ASTRONAUTS, THE see **ASTRONAUTES, LES** • 1959
ASTRONAUTS, THE see **ASTRONAUTAS, LOS** • 1960
ASTRONOMERS AND ABORIGINES • 1922 • *United Theatres & Films* • ASL • SOLAR ECLIPSE EXPEDITION AT WALLAL
ASTRONOMER'S DREAM, THE (UKN) see **HOMME DANS LA LUNE, L'** • 1898
ASTRONUT • 1963 • Rasinski Connie • ANS • USA
ASTRONUT WOODY • 1966 • Smith Paul J. • ANS • USA
ASTUTO BARONE, L' • 1948 • Freda Riccardo • SHT • ITL • EREDITA CONTESA, L'
ASU ARU KAGIRI • 1962 • Toyoda Shiro • JPN • TILL TOMORROW COMES (USA) ○ ASHITA ARU KAGIRI
ASU ENO SEISO • 1959 • Nakamura Noboru • JPN • MARRY A MILLIONAIRE ○ TOMORROW'S COSTUME
ASU KARA OTANA DA • 1960 • Harada Hasuo • JPN
ASU NO ODORIKO see **ASHITA NO ODORIKO** • 1939
ASU NO TAIYO • 1959 • Oshima Nagisa • SHT • JPN
ASU O TSUKURU HITOBITO • 1946 • Kurosawa Akira, Yamamoto Kajiro, Sekigawa Hideo • JPN • THOSE WHO MAKE TOMORROW
ASU WA NICHIYOBI • 1953 • Saeki Kozo • JPN • TOMORROW WILL BE A SUNDAY
ASUMINEN JA LUONTO • 1966 • Jarva Risto • SHT • FNL • HOUSING AND NATURE
ASUNARI MONOGATARI • 1955 • Horikawa Hiromichi • JPN • STORY OF FAST-GROWING WEEDS, THE
ASUNTO TERMINADO! • 1953 • Land Kurt • ARG
ASWAMEDHER GHORA • 1981 • Bhattacharya Shankar • IND • SACRIFICIAL HORSE
ASWAR, AL- • 1979 • Jamil Mohammed Shoukry • IRQ • WALLS, THE
ASWATHAMA • 1979 • Mohanan K. R. • IND • WANDERING SOUL, THE
ASYA • 1978 • Heifitz Josif • USS
ASYA'S HAPPINESS see **ISTORIA ASI KHYACHINOI, KOTORAYA LYUBILA, DANE VYSHLA ZAMUKH** • 1966
ASYLUM • 1972 • Baker Roy Ward • UKN • HOUSE OF CRAZIES (USA)
ASYLUM • 1972 • Robinson Peter • DOC • UKN
ASYLUM EROTICA see **BESTIA UCCIDE A SANGUE FREDDO, LA** • 1971
ASYLUM FOR A SPY see **MEMORANDUM FOR A SPY** • 1965
ASYLUM OF HORROR see **STUDENT VON PRAG, DER** • 1913
ASYLUM OF HORROR see **HISTOIRES EXTRAORDINAIRES** • 1949
ASYLUM OF SATAN • 1971 • Girdler William • USA
ASYLUM OF THE INSANE • 1971 • Davison Donn • USA
ASYLUM OF THE INSANE see **FLESH AND BLOOD SHOW, THE** • 1972
ASYMVIVASTOS • 1979 • Thomopoulos Andreas • GRC • EASY ROAD
AT • 1982 • Ozzenturk Ali • TRK • HORSE, MY HORSE
AT 3.25 see **PARIS QUI DORT** • 1924
AT 5:40 see **OT ORA 40** • 1939
AT 6 P.M. AFTER THE WAR see **V SHEST CHASOV VECHERA POSLE VOINY** • 1944
AT 11.15 -THE STORY OF THE ROYAL CASTLE IN WARSAW see **GODZINA 11.15 -OPOWIESC O ZAMKU KROLEWSKIM W WARSZAWIE** • 1971
AT 99: A PORTRAIT OF LOUISE TANDY MURCH • 1974 • Saltzman Deepa Mehta • DOC • CND, USA
AT A HIGH COST see **DOROGOI TSENOI** • 1957
AT A HIGH PRICE see **DOROGOI TSENOI** • 1957
AT A PREMIUM • 1916 • Drew Sidney • SHT • USA
AT A QUARTER OF TWO • 1911 • *Pickford Mary* • USA
AT A RICH LADY'S HOUSE see **V DOME BOGATOI GOSPOZHI** • 1970
AT A STONE IN THE HEATHER • 1975 • Henson Laurence • DOC • UKN
AT ANY COST see **AD OGNI COSTO** • 1967
AT ANY PRICE see **A QUALSIASI PREZZO** • 1968
AT AVRAT SILAH • 1966 • Guney Yilmaz, Kazankaya Hasan • TRK • HORSE, THE WOMAN AND THE GUN, THE
AT BACHELOR'S ROOST • 1916 • Beaudine William • SHT • USA
AT BAR U RANCH • 1911 • *Bison* • USA
AT BAY • 1915 • Fitzmaurice George • USA
AT BAY see **ROAD TO PARADISE, THE** • 1931
AT BAY FOR A DAY • 1914 • *Royal* • USA
AT BEAR TRACK GULCH • 1913 • *West William* • USA
AT BREAKNECK SPEED (FALL RIVER, MASS.) • 1900 • *Bitzer Billy (Ph)* • USA
AT CEDAR RIDGE • 1911 • *Nestor* • USA
AT CLOSE RANGE • 1985 • Foley James • USA
AT CONEY ISLAND • 1912 • Sennett Mack • USA
AT CRIPPLE CREEK • 1912 • Reid Hal • USA
AT CROSS PURPOSES • 1913 • *Selig* • USA
AT DAISY FARM • 1911 • *Yankee* • USA
AT DANSE BOURNONVILLE • 1979 • Leth Jorgen • DOC • DNM • DANCING BOURNONVILLE
AT DAWN • 1914 • Crisp Donald • USA
AT DAWN see **NAD RANEM** • 1928
AT DAWN IT'S QUIET HERE see **A ZORI ZYDES TIKHIYE..** • 1973
AT DAWN WE DIE (USA) see **TOMORROW WE LIVE** • 1942
AT DERE TOR! • 1980 • Glomm Lasse • NRW • STOP IT
AT DEVIL'S GORGE • 1923 • Dearholt Ashton • USA
AT DOUBLE CROSS RANCH • 1910 • *Nestor* • USA
AT EASE • 1927 • Taurog Norman • SHT • USA
AT EDGE OF WORLD (USA) see **AM RANDE DER WELT** • 1927
AT ELTHAM • 1973 • Cantrill Arthur, Cantrill Corinne • ASL
AT EYE LEVEL • 1965 • van Nie Rene • SHT • NTH
AT FIRST SIGHT • 1917 • Leonard Robert Z. • USA
AT FIRST SIGHT • 1923 • Roach Hal • SHT • USA
AT FIRST SIGHT (UKN) see **COUP DE FOUDRE** • 1983
AT FIVE O'CLOCK IN THE AFTERNOON see **A LAS CINCO DE LA TARDE** • 1960
AT GOOD OLD SIWASH see **THOSE WERE THE DAYS** • 1940
AT GRANDPARENTS' see **LA BUNICI** • 1988
AT GREAT COST see **DOROGOI TSENOI** • 1957
AT GUNPOINT • 1955 • Werker Alfred L. • USA • GUNPOINT! (UKN) ○ GUN POINT
AT GUNPOINT see **BAJO LA METRALLA** • 1982
AT HEADQUARTERS see **PAAMAJASSA** • 1970
AT HIRSIZI BANU • 1967 • Conturk Remzi • TRK • BANU, THE HORSE THIEF
AT HIS EXPENSE • 1914 • *Lubin* • USA
AT HIS OWN TERMS • 1915 • Giblyn Charles • USA
AT HOME • 1934 • Karmen Roman • DOC • USS
AT HOME • 1968 • Lavut Martin • SHT • CND
AT HOME AMONG STRANGERS see **SVOI SREDI CHUZHIGH, CHUZHOI SREDI SVOIKH** • 1974
AT HOME IN MAY • 1966 • Gass Karl • DOC • GDR
AT HOME WITH JAZZ • Chaudhri Amin • USA
AT HOME WITH THE HARDWICKES • 1952 • *British Movietonews* • SER • UKN
AT HUNDRED MILES PER HOUR see **STO PIECDZIESIAT NA GODZINE** • 1971
AT IT AGAIN • 1912 • Sennett Mack • USA
AT IT AGAIN • 1920 • Goldaine Mark • SHT • USA
AT IT AGAIN • 1928 • Taurog Norman • SHT • USA
AT IT AGAIN see **CAUGHT IN THE RAIN** • 1914
AT JONE'S FERRY • 1911 • *Sutton Charles* • USA
AT LAND • 1944 • Deren Maya • SHT • USA
AT LAST see **ANTLIGEN!** • 1983
AT LAST ALONE.. WITH SOMEONE ELSE see **ENFIM SOS.. COM O OUTRO** • 1968
AT LAST! THAT AWFUL TOOTH • 1902 • Smith G. A. • UKN • OH! THAT AWFUL TOOTH
AT LAST THEY EAT • 1914 • *Brennan John E.* • USA
AT LAST WE ARE ALONE • 1914 • MacGregor Norval • USA
AT LIBERTY -GOOD PRESS AGENT • 1912 • *Thanhauser* • USA
AT LIL'S PLACE see **ORGY AT LIL'S PLACE, THE** • 1963
AT LONG LAST COME see **ACABEMOS DE UNA VEZ** • 1975
AT LONG LAST LOVE • 1975 • Bogdanovich Peter • USA
AT LUST'S END see **SHIKIYOKU NO HATE** • 1968
AT MEALTIME • 1972 • Hadzismajlovic Vefik • SHT • YGS
AT MEXICO'S MERCY • 1914 • *Kerrigan J. Warren* • USA
AT MIDDLE AGE see **REN DAO ZHONGNIAN** • 1983
AT MIDNIGHT • 1913 • *American* • USA
AT MIDNIGHT • 1913 • France Charles H. • *Edison* • USA
AT MIDNIGHT • 1913 • Lucas Wilfred • *Rex* • USA
AT MIDNIGHT IN THE GRAVEYARD (USA) see **V POLNOCH NA KLADBISCHE** • 1909
AT MOTHER'S REQUEST • 1987 • Tuchner Michael • TVM • USA
AT NIGHT ALL CATS ARE GRAY see **NUIT, TOUS LES CHATS SONT GRIS, LA** • 1977
AT OLD FORT DEARBORN OR CHICAGO IN 1812 • 1912 • Morty Frank • USA
AT PANTHER CREEK • 1911 • *Nestor* • USA
AT PERRY'S RANCH • 1911 • *Nestor* • USA
AT PINEY RIDGE • 1916 • Daly William Robert • USA
AT ROLLING FORKS • 1912 • *Forde Victoria* • USA
AT "ROZA" FROM 6 TO 11 see **U "ROZY" OD 6-TEJ DO 11-TEJ** • 1963
AT SA NGALAN NG PAG-IBIG • 1967 • Crisostomo Fely • PHL • AND IN THE NAME OF LOVE
AT SANTA BARBARA • 1929 • Aylott Dave, Symmons E. F. • SHT • UKN
AT SCROGGINSES' CORNER • 1912 • Reid Hal • USA
AT SEA ASHORE • 1936 • Terhune William • SHT • USA
AT SHILOH • 1913 • *Bison* • USA
AT SILA'Y DUMATING • 1967 • Santos Teodorico C. • PHL • AND THEY CAME
AT STALLING SPEED see **KUNST & VLIEGWERK** • 1989
AT SUNSET RANCH • 1911 • *Mersereau Violet* • USA
AT SWORD'S POINT • 1918 • Santell Alfred • SHT • USA
AT SWORD'S POINT • 1951 • Allen Lewis • USA • SONS OF THE MUSKETEERS (UKN)
AT SWORD'S POINT (USA) see **A FIL DI SPADA** • 1953
AT SWORDS POINTS • 1911 • *Reliance* • USA
AT THE 11TH HOUR see **HVEM VAR FORBRYDEREN?** • 1912
AT THE AGE OF LOVE see **LA VIRSTA DRAGOSTEI** • 1963
AT THE ALTAR • 1909 • Griffith D. W. • USA
AT THE BANQUET TABLE • 1915 • Lessey George A. • USA
AT THE BASKET PICNIC • 1912 • Henderson Dell • USA
AT THE BEACH see **HAITAN** • 1985
AT THE BEACH INCOGNITO • 1915 • Curtis Allen • USA
AT THE BEGINNING OF THE CENTURY see **NAR SEKLET VAR UNGT** • 1944
AT THE BINGVILLE BARBECUE • 1915 • Curtis Allen • USA
AT THE BOTTOM OF THINGS • 1915 • *Reliance* • USA
AT THE BREAK OF DAWN • 1911 • *Essanay* • USA
AT THE BRINK • 1986 • Raymont Peter • MTV • USA, JPN
AT THE BURGLAR'S COMMAND • 1912 • *Pate Gwendolyn* • USA
AT THE CINEMA PALACE • 1984 • Black Donald Taylor • DOC • IRL
AT THE CIRCUS • 1939 • Buzzell Edward • USA • MARX BROTHERS AT THE CIRCUS
AT THE CIRCUS • 1944 • Donnelly Eddie • ANS • USA
AT THE CIRCUS see **W CYRKU** • 1954
AT THE CLOSE OF THE NIGHT • 1987 • Nakhapetov Rodion • USS
AT THE CLUB see **W KLUBIE** • 1963
AT THE COUNT OF TEN • 1916 • *Drew Sidney* • SHT • USA
AT THE COURT OF PRINCE MAKE-BELIEVE • 1914 • *Eclair* • FRN
AT THE CROSSING • 1914 • *Tennant Barbara* • USA
AT THE CROSSROADS • 1922 • *Owen Seena* • USA
AT THE CROSSROADS • 1976 • Stouffer Mark, Stouffer Marty • USA
AT THE CROSSROADS • 1985 • Dodd Thomas • MTV • CND
AT THE CROSSROADS OF LIFE • 1908 • McCutcheon Wallace • USA
AT THE CRUCIAL MOMENT • 1914 • *Eclair* • USA
AT THE DOORS OF DOOM • 1916 • Kent Leon D. • SHT • USA
AT THE DOUBLE TROUBLE RANCH • 1911 • *Champion* • USA
AT THE DUKE'S COMMAND • 1911 • *Pickford Mary* • USA
AT THE EARTH'S CORE • 1976 • Connor Kevin • UKN
AT THE EDGE OF A PALM GROVE (USA) see **A LA ORILLA DE UN PALMAR** • 1937
AT THE EDGE OF THE AQUEDUCT • 1916 • *Thanhouser* • SHT • USA
AT THE EDGE OF THE WORLD see **AM RANDE DER WELT** • 1927
AT THE EDGE OF THE WORLD see **AM ENDE DER WELT** • 1943
AT THE EDGE OF THINGS • 1915 • MacMackin Archer • USA
AT THE ELEVENTH HOUR • 1910 • *Edison* • USA
AT THE ELEVENTH HOUR • 1912 • Buckland Warwick • UKN
AT THE ELEVENTH HOUR • 1912 • Ranous William V. • USA
AT THE ELEVENTH HOUR • 1914 • *Selig* • USA
AT THE ELEVENTH HOUR see **I ELFTE TIMMEN** • 1916
AT THE END OF A PERFECT DAY • 1914 • Ricketts Thomas • USA
AT THE END OF A PERFECT DAY • 1915 • *Holmes Gerda* • USA
AT THE END OF HIS ROPE • 1916 • *Miller Rube* • USA
AT THE END OF THE LINE • 1983 • Tanase Dinu • RMN
AT THE END OF THE RAINBOW see **PRINCESS AND THE MAGIC FROG, THE** • 1965
AT THE END OF THE ROAD • 1966 • Wang Chou-Tchez • ANM • CHN
AT THE END OF THE ROAD see **VEGUL** • 1974
AT THE END OF THE ROPE • 1914 • *Darkfeather Mona* • USA
AT THE END OF THE TRAIL • 1912 • *Essanay* • USA
AT THE END OF THE TRAIL • 1912 • *Vitagraph* • USA
AT THE END OF THE WORLD • 1921 • Stanlaws Penrhyn • USA
AT THE FLOOD TIDE • 1915 • Oliver Guy • USA
AT THE FOOT OF THE HILL • 1914 • *Commerford Thomas* • USA
AT THE FOOT OF THE LADDER • 1912 • *Thanhouser* • USA
AT THE FOOT OF THE SCAFFOLD • 1913 • Buckland Warwick? • UKN
AT THE FOOT OF THE STAIRS • 1914 • *Leonard Robert* • USA
AT THE FOUNTAINHEAD • 1980 • Kennedy Anthea, Burton Nick • UKN

AT THE FRENCH BALL • 1908 • McCutcheon Wallace • USA
AT THE FRONTIER • 1937 • MNG
AT THE GATES OF THE EARTH see **LA PORTILE PAMINTULUI** • 1966
AT THE GREY HOUSE see **ZUR CHRONIK VON GRIESHUUS "UM DAS ERBE VON GRIESHUUS"** • 1925
AT THE GRINGO MINE • 1911 • Melies Gaston • USA
AT THE HALF BREED'S MERCY • 1913 • *American* • USA
AT THE HAVANA • 1940 • Mishiku Richard • UKN
AT THE HEIGHT OF SUMMER see **W SRODKU LATA** • 1975
AT THE HOTEL MIX-UP • 1908 • Melies Georges • FRN
AT THE HOUR OF ELEVEN • 1915 • *Reliance* • USA
AT THE HOUR OF THREE • 1912 • Noy Wilfred • UKN
AT THE LADY'S SERVICE see **FRUN TILLHANDA** • 1939
AT THE LAKE see **V OZERA** • 1969
AT THE LARIAT'S END • 1913 • *Carney Augustus* • USA
AT THE LORINC SPINNERY see **LORINCI FONOBAN, A** • 1971
AT THE MARKET-PLACE see **HATE BAJARE** • 1967
AT THE MASK BALL • 1915 • MacGregor Norval • USA
AT THE MASQUERADE BALL • 1912 • Miller Ashley • USA
AT THE MEETING WITH JOYOUS DEATH see **AU RENDEZ-VOUS DE LA MORT JOYEUSE** • 1972
AT THE MERCY OF HIS WIFE • 1925 • Butler Alexander • UKN
AT THE MERCY OF MEN • 1918 • Miller Charles • USA
AT THE MERCY OF THE TIDE • 1910 • Aylott Dave? • UKN
AT THE MERCY OF THE WAVES • 1914 • *Melies* • USA
AT THE MERCY OF TIBERIUS • 1920 • Granville Fred Leroy • UKN • PRICE OF SILENCE, THE
AT THE MIKE • 1934 • Schwarzwald Milton • SHT • USA
AT THE MOMENT OF TRIAL see **I PROVNINGENS STUND** • 1915
AT THE MONKEY HOUSE • 1906 • *Bitzer Billy (Ph)* • USA
AT THE OLD CROSSED ROADS • 1914 • Dear Frank L. • USA
AT THE OLD MAID'S CALL • 1913 • *Beery Wallace* • USA
AT THE OLD STAGE DOOR • 1919 • Roach Hal • SHT • USA
AT THE OTHER SIDE OF THE WINDOW see **Z TAMTEJ STRONY OKIENKA** • 1963
AT THE OUTSKIRTS • 1961 • Lysenko Vadim • USS
AT THE PATRICIAN'S CLUB • 1915 • *Howard Ernest* • USA
AT THE PHONE • 1912 • Blache Alice • USA
AT THE PHOTOGRAPHER'S see **KOD FOTOGRAFA** • 1959
AT THE PLANT'S BALL see **AU BAL DE FLORE** • 1900
AT THE POINT OF A GUN • 1919 • Kull Edward • SHT • USA
AT THE POINT OF THE SWORD • 1912 • *Randall William* • USA
AT THE POST OF SHAME see **U POZERNOVO STOLBA** • 1924
AT THE POSTERN GATE • 1915 • Ingraham Lloyd • USA
AT THE POTTER'S WHEEL • 1914 • *American* • USA
AT THE PROMPTING OF THE DEVIL see **EVIL GENIUS, THE** • 1913
AT THE QUIET PIER • 1959 • Meliava Tamaz • USS
AT THE RAINBOW'S END • 1912 • *August Edwin* • USA
AT THE RINGSIDE • 1921 • Roach Hal • SHT • USA
AT THE RISK OF HER LIFE • 1914 • Santschi Thomas • USA
AT THE RISK OF HIS LIFE • 1913 • *International Feature Film Co* • USA
AT THE RISK OF MY LIFE see **INOCHI BONIFURO** • 1970
AT THE RIVER GALGA see **GALGA MENTEN** • 1954
AT THE ROAD'S END • 1915 • Morgan George • USA
AT THE SERVICE OF THE SPANISH LADY see **AL SERVICIO DE LA MUJER ESPANOLA** • 1978
AT THE SIDE OF DEATH see **A UM PULO DA MORTE** • 1969
AT THE SIGN • 1934 • Nobel Jack • USA
AT THE SIGN OF THE JACK O'LANTERN • 1922 • Ingraham Lloyd • USA
AT THE SIGN OF THE KANGAROO • 1917 • Hurst Paul C. • SHT • USA
AT THE SIGN OF THE LOST ANGEL • 1913 • Sturgeon Rollin S. • USA
AT THE SILVER GLOBE see **NA SREBRNYM GLOBIE** • 1977
AT THE SLAVE AUCTION • 1917 • Chapin Benjamin • SHT • USA
AT THE STAGE DOOR • 1921 • Cabanne W. Christy • USA
AT THE STATION see **NA STACJI** • 1968
AT THE STRASSBURG (USA) see **ZU STRASSBURG AUD DER SCHANZ** • 1934
AT THE STROKE OF NINE • 1957 • Comfort Lance • UKN
AT THE STROKE OF NINE (UKN) see **MURDER ON THE CAMPUS** • 1934
AT THE STROKE OF THE ANGELUS • 1915 • *Clary Charles* • USA
AT THE STROKE OF TWELVE • 1911 • *Essanay* • USA
AT THE STROKE OF TWELVE • 1941 • Negulesco Jean • SHT • USA
AT THE TELEPHONE • 1913 • *Lubin* • USA
AT THE TERMINAL STATION see **TAM NA KONECNE** • 1957
AT THE THRESHOLD OF LIFE • 1911 • *Fuller Mary* • USA
AT THE TIP OF THE TONGUE see **DU BOUT DES LEVRES** • 1976
AT THE TORRENT'S MERCY • 1915 • Martinek H. O. • UKN
AT THE TRAIL'S END • 1911 • *Champion* • USA
AT THE TRANSFER CORNER • 1914 • MacGregor Norval • USA
AT THE VILLA FALCONER see **VILLA FALCONIERI** • 1928
AT THE VILLA ROSE • 1920 • Elvey Maurice • UKN
AT THE VILLA ROSE • 1929 • Hiscott Leslie • UKN • MYSTERY AT THE VILLA ROSE (USA)
AT THE VILLA ROSE • 1939 • Summers Walter • UKN • HOUSE OF MYSTERY (USA)
AT THE WHITE MAN'S DOOR • 1911 • *Vitagraph* • USA
AT THE WINDOW • 1911 • *Powers* • USA
AT THREE O'CLOCK • 1914 • Kirkland David • USA
AT TRINITY CHURCH I MET MY DOOM • 1922 • *Parkinson H. B. (P)* • SHT • UKN
AT TWELVE MIDNIGHT (UKN) see **MYSTIC HOUR, THE** • 1933
AT TWELVE O'CLOCK • 1913 • Sennett Mack • USA
AT TWELVE O'CLOCK • 1915 • *Church Frederick* • USA
AT TWELVE O'CLOCK • 1916 • *Church Frederick* • SHT • USA
AT ULURU • 1977 • Cantrill Arthur, Cantrill Corinne • ASL
AT WAR WITH THE ARMY • 1950 • Walker Hal • USA
AT WEMBLEY STADIUM • 1957 • Grigorov Roumen • DOC • BUL
AT WHOSE DOOR? • 1952 • Anderson Max • SHT • UKN
AT YALE see **HOLD 'EM YALE!** • 1928
AT YOUR DOORSTEP • 1963 • Ordynsky Vassily • USS
AT YOUR ORDERS, MADAME (USA) see **AI VOSTRI ORDINA, SIGNORA!** • 1939
AT YOUR SERVICE • 1935 • *Lantz Walter (P)* • ANS • USA
AT YOUR SERVICE see **LOVE IN WAITING** • 1948
AT YOUR SERVICE, MADAME • 1936 • Freleng Friz • ANS • USA
AT ZIJE NEBOZTIK! • 1935 • Fric Martin • CZC • LONG LIVE THE LOVED ONE! ○ LONG LIVE KINDNESS ○ LONG LIVE THE DECEASED
AT ZIJE REPUBLIKA! • 1965 • Kachyna Karel • CZC • LONG LIVE THE REPUBLIC!
AT ZIJI DUCHOVE • 1976 • Lipsky Oldrich • CZC • LONG LIVE THE GHOSTS! ○ LONG LIVE GHOSTS!
ATABOY • 1967 • Chartrand Alain • SHT • CND
ATACAN LAS BRUJAS see **SANTO ATACA LAS BRUJAS** • 1964
ATACANDO EL PELIGRO • 1957 • Gascon Jose • SPN
ATAHUALPA'S TREASURE see **TESORO DE ATAHUALPA, EL** • 1966
ATAKKU NANBA WAN-NAMIDANO FUSHICHO • 1971 • *Toho* • ANM • JPN
ATALA • 1912 • *Bosworth Hobart* • USA
ATALANTE, L' • 1934 • Vigo Jean • FRN • CHALAND QUI PASSE, LE
ATAMAN KODR • Ulitskaya Olga (c/d) • USS
ATAME • 1989 • Almodovar Pedro • SPN • TIE ME UP, TIE ME DOWN
ATAQUE DE LOS MUERTOS SIN OJOS, EL see **ATAUD DE LOS MUERTOS SIN OJOS, EL** • 1973
ATAQUE DE LOS ZOMBIES ATOMICOS see **NIGHTMARE CITY** • 1980
ATARASHII KOMEISUKURI • 1963 • JPN • NEW METHOD OF RICE PRODUCTION
ATARASHIKI KAZOKU • 1939 • Shibuya Minoru • JPN • NEW FAMILY, THE
ATARASHIKI TSUCHI • 1937 • Itami Mansaku, Fanck Arnold • JPN • DAUGHTER OF THE SAMURAI, A ○ NEW EARTH, THE
ATARIYA TAISHO • 1962 • Nakahira Ko • JPN • CAPTAIN BY CHANCE
ATAUD DE LOS MUERTOS SIN OJOS, EL • 1973 • de Ossorio Amando • SPN, PRT • RETURN OF THE BLIND DEAD (USA) ○ RETURN OF THE EVIL DEAD ○ ATAQUE DE LOS MUERTOS SIN OJOS, EL
ATAUD DEL VAMPIRO, EL • 1957 • Mendez Fernando, Nagle Paul • MXC • VAMPIRE'S COFFIN (USA)
ATAUD INFERNAL, EL • 1958 • Fernandez Fernando • MXC
ATAVISM see **ATAVISMO** • 1923
ATAVISM OF JOHN TOM LITTLE BEAR, THE • 1917 • Smith David • SHT • USA
ATAVISMO • 1923 • Contreras Torres Miguel • MXC • ATAVISM
ATAWENI PUDUMAYA • 1968 • Mastan S. • SLN • EIGHTH WONDER, THE
ATCHI WA KOTCHI • 1962 • Kuri Yoji • ANS • JPN • HERE AND THERE
ATE QUE O CASAMENTO NOS SEPARE • 1968 • Tambellini Flavio • ARG • UNTIL MARRIAGE SEPARATES US ○ TILL MARRIAGE DOES US APART
ATEL EINTERIOR • 1956 • Weiss Peter • SHT • SWD • STUDIO OF DR. FAUSTUS, THE
ATELIER D'ARTISTE, FARCE DE MODELES • 1898 • Melies Georges • FRN • PAINTER'S STUDIO, THE
ATELIER DE FERNAND LEGER • 1954 • Borowczyk Walerian • SHT • FRN
ATELIER DE TRAVAIL SUR LA GESTION SCOLAIRE I • 1971 • Lavoie Richard • SHT • CND
ATELIER DE TRAVAIL SUR LA GESTION SCOLAIRE II • 1971 • Lavoie Richard • SHT • CND
ATELIERS DE LA CIOTAT • 1895 • Lumiere Louis • FRN
ATEMLOS VOR LIEBE • 1970 • Krausser Dietrich • FRG • YEARNING FOR LOVE
ATENCINGO • 1973 • Maldonado Eduardo • MXC
ATENCION PRE NATAL • 1971 • Gomez Sara • DOC • CUB
ATENTADO, EL • 1986 • Urguelles Thaelman • VNZ • ATTEMPT, THE
ATENTAT • 1964 • Sequens Jiri • CZC • ASSASSINATION
ATENTAT U SARAJEVU see **SARAJEVSKI ATENTAT** • 1975
ATHALIAH • 1911 • *Pathe* • FRN
ATHALIE • 1910 • Capellani Albert • FRN
ATHALIE • 1910 • Carre Michel • FRN
ATHANOR, L' • 1972 • Garrel Philippe • SHT • FRN
ATHEIST, THE • 1913 • *Moore Tom* • USA
ATHENA • 1954 • Thorpe Richard • USA
ATHENS AFTER MIDNIGHT see **ATHINA META TA MESANIHTA, I** • 1968
ATHENS, GA • 1987 • Gayton Tony • DOC • USA
ATHENS, THE STADIOU STREET ROBBERY see **ATHINA, KLOPI TIS ODHOU STADHIOU** • 1968
ATHEY KANGAL • 1967 • Thirulokachander A. C. • IND • AUNT'S DAUGHTER
ATHINA, KLOPI TIS ODHOU STADHIOU • 1968 • Bibelas Nasos • GRC • ATHENS, THE STADIOU STREET ROBBERY
ATHINA META TA MESANIHTA, I • 1968 • Fuchs Aristidis Karidis • GRC • ATHENS AFTER MIDNIGHT
ATHLETE, THE • 1932 • Lantz Walter, Nolan William • ANS • USA
ATHLETE AUX MAINS NUES, L' • 1952 • Garand Marcel • FRN
ATHLETE INCOMPLET, L' • 1932 • Autant-Lara Claude • FRN • ATHLETE MAIGRE LUI, L' ○ OLYMPIC 13 GAGNANT ○ LOVE IS A RACKET
ATHLETE MAIGRE LUI, L' see **ATHLETE INCOMPLET, L'** • 1932
ATHLETEN • 1925 • Zelnik Friedrich • FRG
ATHLETIC AMBITIONS • 1915 • Mix Tom • USA
ATHLETIC DAZE • 1932 • McCarey Ray • SHT • USA
ATHLETIC FAMILY, THE • 1914 • Stratton Edmund F. • USA
ATHLETIC GIRL AND BURGLAR • 1905 • *Bitzer Billy (Ph)* • USA
ATHLETIC INSTRUCTOR, AN • 1910 • *Defender* • USA
ATHLETIQUIZ • 1947 • Barclay David • SHT • USA
ATITHI • 1966 • Sinha Tapan • IND • RUNAWAY, THE (UKN)
ATIVIDADES POLITICAS EM SAO PAULO • 1950 • dos Santos Nelson Pereira • SHT • BRZ
ATLANTA CHILD MURDERS, THE • 1985 • Erman John • TVM • USA
ATLANTAVENTYRET • 1934 • Marmstedt Lorens • SWD • ATLANTIC ADVENTURE, THE
ATLANTEAN • 1984 • Quinn Bob • IRL
ATLANTIC • 1929 • Dupont E. A. • UKN
ATLANTIC, THE • 1972 • Kelly Ron • CND
ATLANTIC ADVENTURE • 1935 • Rogell Albert S. • USA
ATLANTIC ADVENTURE • 1961 • *Inter-Tv Films* • DOC • CND
ATLANTIC ADVENTURE, THE see **ATLANTAVENTYRET** • 1934
ATLANTIC CITY • 1944 • McCarey Ray • USA • ATLANTIC CITY HONEYMOON
ATLANTIC CITY HONEYMOON see **ATLANTIC CITY** • 1944
ATLANTIC CITY ROMANCE (UKN) see **CONVENTION GIRL** • 1934
ATLANTIC CITY U.S.A. • 1980 • Malle Louis • CND, USA, FRN • ATLANTIC CITY (UKN)
ATLANTIC CITY (UKN) see **ATLANTIC CITY U.S.A.** • 1980
ATLANTIC CONVOY • 1942 • Landers Lew • USA
ATLANTIC CROSSROADS • 1945 • Daly Tom • DOC • CND
ATLANTIC EPISODE see **CATCH AS CATCH CAN** • 1937
ATLANTIC FERRY • 1941 • Forde Walter • UKN • SONS OF THE SEA (USA)
ATLANTIC FLIGHT • 1937 • Nigh William • USA
ATLANTIC PATROL • 1940 • Legg Stuart • DCS • CND
ATLANTIC REGION, THE • 1957 • Fraser Donald • DOC • CND
ATLANTIC RHAPSODY • 1989 • Ottarsdottir Katrin • DNM
ATLANTIC STORY, AN see **OPOWIESC ATLANTYCKA** • 1954
ATLANTIDE, L' • 1921 • Feyder Jacques • FRN • LOST ATLANTIS ○ MISSING HUSBANDS
ATLANTIDE, L' • 1932 • Pabst G. W. • FRN
ATLANTIDE, L' (FRN) see **ANTINEA, L'AMANTE DELLA CITTA SEPOLTA** • 1961
ATLANTIKSCHWIMMER, DIE • 1975 • Achternbusch Herbert • FRG
ATLANTIS • 1913 • Blom August • DNM
ATLANTIS • 1930 • Kemm Jean, Dupont E. A. • FRN
ATLANTIS see **SIREN OF ATLANTIS** • 1949
ATLANTIS INTERCEPTORS • 1984 • Deodato Ruggero • ITL • RAIDERS OF ATLANTIS
ATLANTIS, THE LOST CONTINENT • 1961 • Pal George, Borzage Frank (U/c) • USA
ATLANTIS THE LOST CONTINENT see **SIREN OF ATLANTIS** • 1949
ATLANTIS, THE LOST CONTINENT see **ANTINEA, L'AMANTE DELLA CITTA SEPOLTA** • 1961
ATLANTYDA • 1972 • Szpakowicz Piotr • PLN
ATLAS • 1960 • Corman Roger • USA
ATLAS AGAINST THE CYCLOPS (USA) see **MACISTE NELLA TERRA DEI CICLOPI** • 1961
ATLAS AGAINST THE CZAR see **MACISTE ALLA CORTE DELLO ZAR** • 1964
ATLAS IN THE LAND OF THE CYCLOPS see **MACISTE NELLA TERRA DEI CICLOPI** • 1961
ATLAS MAGIQUE, L' • 1935 • Pal George • ANS • NTH • MAGIC ATLAS, THE
ATLAS VS. THE CYCLOPS see **MACISTE NELLA TERRA DEI CICLOPI** • 1961
ATLETA DI CRISTALLO, L' • 1947 • Del Fante Mario • ITL
ATLI KARINCA DONUYOR • 1968 • Gultekin Sirri • TRK • MERRY-GO-ROUND, THE
ATM • 1951 • Rodriguez Ismael • MXC • A TODA MAQUINA
ATMA TARANG • 1937 • Modi Sohrab • IND
ATMOS • 1979 • Low Colin • CND
ATMOSFIELDS • 1971 • Stevens Graham • UKN
ATO DE VIOLENCIA • 1981 • Escorel Eduardo • BRZ • ACT OF VIOLENCE
ATOLL K • 1952 • Joannon Leo • FRN, ITL • ROBINSON CRUSOELAND (UKN) ○ UTOPIA (USA) ○ ESCAPADE ○ ATOLLO K
ATOLLO K see **ATOLL K** • 1952
ATOM, THE • 1918 • Dowlan William C. • USA
ATOM AGE VAMPIRE (USA) see **SEDDOK, L'EREDE DI SATANA** • 1961
ATOM BOMBED CHILDREN see **GENBAKU NO KO** • 1952
ATOM-MAN VS. MARTIAN INVADERS • 1967 • *Glut Don (P)* • SHT • USA
ATOM MAN VS. SUPERMAN • 1950 • Bennet Spencer Gordon • SRL • USA
ATOM NA ROZCESTI • 1947 • Duba Cenek • ANS • CZC
ATOME, L' • 1955 • Dornes Yvonne • SHT • FRN
ATOME AU SERVICE DE L'HOMME, L' see **CANADA'S ATOM GOES TO WORK** • 1952
ATOME QUE VOUS VEUT DE BIEN, UN • 1959 • Gruel Henri • ANS • FRN
ATOMERNAS VINTERGATA • 1962 • Barfod Bent • ANS • DNM
ATOMIC AGENT (USA) see **NATHALIE AGENT SECRET** • 1959
ATOMIC BALLAD see **BALLADE ATOMIQUE** • 1948
ATOMIC BRAIN, THE see **MONSTROSITY** • 1964
ATOMIC CAFE, THE • 1982 • Rafferty Kevin, Loader Jayne, Rafferty Pierre • DOC • USA
ATOMIC CATHEDRAL, AN see **ATOMOVA KATEDRALA** • 1985
ATOMIC CITY, THE • 1952 • Hopper Jerry • USA
ATOMIC KID, THE • 1954 • Martinson Leslie H. • USA
ATOMIC MAN, THE (USA) see **TIMESLIP** • 1955
ATOMIC MONSTER, THE see **MAN MADE MONSTER** • 1941
ATOMIC NO OBON, ONNA OYABUN TAIKETSU NO MAKI • 1961 • Saeki Kozo • JPN • OBON'S DIPPING CONTEST (USA)
ATOMIC PHYSICS, PART 1: THE ATOMIC THEORY • 1947 • Mayne Derek • DOC • UKN • ATOMIC THEORY, THE
ATOMIC RULERS OF THE WORLD • 1964 • Ishii Teruo • JPN • ATTACK OF THE FLYING SAUCERS ○ INVADERS FROM SPACE ○ INVINCIBLE SPACEMAN ○ EARTH IN DANGER, THE
ATOMIC STATION, THE see **ATOMSTODIN** • 1983
ATOMIC SUBMARINE, THE • 1959 • Bennet Spencer Gordon • USA
ATOMIC THEORY, THE see **ATOMIC PHYSICS, PART 1: THE ATOMIC THEORY** • 1947
ATOMIC WAR BRIDE (USA) see **RAT** • 1960

ATOMIQUE MONSIEUR PLACIDO, L' • 1949 • Hennion Robert • FRN • DEMOISELLE DES FOLIES, LA ○ TROUS DE BALLES

ATOMIZATION • 1948 • Mason Bill • UKN

ATOMOVA KATEDRALA • 1985 • Balik Jaroslav • CZC • ATOMIC CATHEDRAL, AN

ATOMS FOR PEACE • 1956 • Bogolepov Dimitriy • USS

ATOMSTODIN • 1983 • Jonsson Thorsteinn • ICL • ATOMIC STATION, THE

ATONEMENT • 1914 • *Majestic* • USA

ATONEMENT • 1916 • Sloman Edward • SHT • USA

ATONEMENT • 1920 • Humphrey William • USA

ATONEMENT • 1972 • McKennirey Mike • CND

ATONEMENT, THE • 1911 • *Essanay* • USA

ATONEMENT, THE • 1914 • *Valdez Reina* • USA

ATONEMENT OF GOSTA BERLING, THE (UKN) see **GOSTA BERLINGS SAGA** • 1924

ATOR L'INVINCIBILE • 1983 • D'Amato Joe • ITL • BLADE MASTER, THE (USA) ○ ATOR THE INVINCIBLE

ATOR: THE FIGHTING EAGLE • 1983 • D'Amato Joe • ITL

ATOR THE INVINCIBLE see **ATOR L'INVINCIBILE** • 1983

ATORAGON see **KAITEI GUNKAN** • 1963

ATORAGON, THE FLYING SUPERSUB see **KAITEI GUNKAN** • 1963

ATOSKI VRTOVI • 1989 • Stojcic Stojan • YGS • GARDENS OF ATOS, THE

ATOUT-COEUR • 1931 • Roussell Henry • FRN

ATOUT COEUR see **ARLETTE ET L'AMOUR** • 1943

ATOUT COEUR A TOKYO POUR OSS 117 • 1966 • Boisrond Michel • FRN, ITL • OSS 177 A TOKIO SI MUORE (ITL) ○ MISSION TO TOKYO (UKN) ○ TERROR IN TOKYO ○ HEART TRUMP IN TOKYO FOR OSS 117

ATOUT SEXE • 1971 • Pontiac Jean-Marie • FRN

ATOUTS DE M. WENS, LES • 1946 • de Meyst E. G. • FRN, BLG • CINQ ATOUTS DE M. WENS, LES

ATRACADORES, LOS • 1961 • Rovira Beleta Francisco • SPN • ROBBERS ○ STREET THIEVES

ATRACO A LAS TRES • 1962 • Forque Jose Maria • SPN

ATRACO AL HAMPA (SPN) see **VICOMTE REGLE SES COMPTES, LE** • 1967

ATRACO DE IDA Y VUELTA, UN (SPN) see **SEI SIMPATICHE CAROGNE** • 1968

ATRACO EN EL COSTA AZUL • 1973 • Lorente German • SPN

ATRAGON THE FLYING SUB see **KAITEI GUNKAN** • 1963

ATRAS DE LAS NUBES • 1961 • Gazcon Gilberto • MXC

ATRE, L' • 1922 • Boudrioz Robert • FRN

ATRIE, THE MILLIONAIRE • 1916 • Handworth Harry • USA

ATROCE MENACE • 1934 • Christian-Jaque • FRN

ATROCITIES see **ATYACHAR** • 1983

ATROGON (USA) see **KAITEI GUNKAN** • 1963

ATROPHY OF THE HEART see **ZANIK SERCA** • 1970

ATSALUT PADER • 1979 • Cavara Paolo • ITL

ATSAY • 1978 • *Aunor Nora* • PHL

ATSUI HANKO • 1968 • Sasaki Moto • JPN • HOT CRIME, A

ATSUI SUNA • 1960 • Mizuko Harumi • JPN

ATSUI YORU • 1969 • Yoshimura Kozaburo • JPN • HOT NIGHT, A

ATT ALSKA • 1964 • Donner Jorn • SWD • TO LOVE

ATT ANGORA EN BRYGGA • 1965 • Danielsson Tage • SWD • TO GO ASHORE

ATT DODA ETT BARN • 1952 • Werner Gosta • SWD • TO KILL A CHILD

ATT SEGLA AR NODVANDIGT • 1938 • Fejos Paul (c/d) • DCS • SWD • TO SAIL IS NECESSARY

ATTA BABY • 1927 • Lamont Charles • SHT • USA

ATTA BOY! • 1926 • Griffith Edward H. • USA

ATTA BOY'S LAST RACE • 1916 • Siegmann George • USA • BEST BET, THE

ATTACHED BALLOON, THE see **PRIVARZANIAT BALON** • 1967

ATTACHMENT OF A VIRGIN see **SHOJO MIREN** • 1967

ATTACK! • 1956 • Aldrich Robert • USA

ATTACK see **AKCIJA** • 1960

ATTACK, THE • 1909 • *Powhatan* • USA

ATTACK AND RETREAT (USA) see **ITALIANO, BRAVA GENTE** • 1964

ATTACK AT ROCKY PASS • 1913 • Melford George • USA

ATTACK BY NIGHT see **FIRST COMES COURAGE** • 1943

ATTACK FORCE NORMANDY see **HELL'S BRIGADE** • 1980

ATTACK FORCE Z • 1981 • Burstall Tim • ASL, TWN • Z-TZU T'E KUNG TUI (TWN) ○ Z MEN

ATTACK FROM OUTER SPACE see **MUTINY IN OUTER SPACE** • 1965

ATTACK FROM SPACE • 1964 • Ishii Teruo • JPN • SUPER GIANT AGAINST THE SATELLITES ○ INVADERS FROM SPACE

ATTACK IN THE REAR • 1906 • Hough Harold • UKN

ATTACK OF THE 50 FOOT WOMAN • 1958 • Juran Nathan • USA

ATTACK OF THE BLOOD-LEECHES see **ATTACK OF THE GIANT LEECHES** • 1958

ATTACK OF THE CRAB MONSTERS • 1957 • Corman Roger • USA

ATTACK OF THE ENEMY PLANES, AN see **TEKKI KUSHU** • 1943

ATTACK OF THE FLYING SAUCERS see **ATOMIC RULERS OF THE WORLD** • 1964

ATTACK OF THE GIANT HORNY GORILLA see **A*P*E** • 1976

ATTACK OF THE GIANT LEECHES • 1958 • Kowalski Bernard • USA • DEMONS OF THE SWAMP (UKN) ○ ATTACK OF THE BLOOD-LEECHES ○ GIANT LEECHES, THE

ATTACK OF THE GOLD ESCORT, THE • 1911 • ASL

ATTACK OF THE KILLER TOMATOES! • 1978 • De Bello John • USA

ATTACK OF THE MARCHING MONSTERS see **KAIJU SOSHINGEKI** • 1968

ATTACK OF THE MAYAN MUMMY • 1963 • Warren Jerry • USA, MXC

ATTACK OF THE MONSTERS see **GAMERA TAI GURON** • 1969

ATTACK OF THE MOORS (USA) see **REALI DI FRANCIA, I** • 1960

ATTACK OF THE MUSHROOM PEOPLE (USA) see **MATANGO** • 1963

ATTACK OF THE NORMANS see **NORMANNI, I** • 1962

ATTACK OF THE PHANTOMS see **KISS MEETS THE PHANTOM** • 1978

ATTACK OF THE PUPPET PEOPLE • 1958 • Gordon Bert I. • USA • SIX INCHES TALL (UKN) ○ FANTASTIC PUPPET PEOPLE, THE

ATTACK OF THE ROBOTS (USA) see **CARTAS BOCA ARRIBA** • 1962

ATTACK OF THE SWAMP CREATURE • 1985 • Stevens Arnold • USA

ATTACK ON A CHINESE MISSION -BLUE JACKET TO THE RESCUE • 1900 • Williamson James • UKN

ATTACK ON A JAPANESE CONVOY • 1904 • Mottershaw Frank • UKN

ATTACK ON A MISSION STATION • 1900 • *Mitchell & Kenyon* • UKN

ATTACK ON A PIQUET see **SURPRISING A PICKET** • 1899

ATTACK ON A RUSSIAN OUTPOST • 1904 • *Gaumont* • UKN

ATTACK ON AN ENGLISH BLOCKHOUSE see **ATTAQUE D'UN POSTE ANGLAIS** • 1897

ATTACK ON FEAR • 1984 • Damski Mel • TVM • USA

ATTACK ON FORT RIDGELY • 1910 • *Kalem* • USA

ATTACK ON SINGAPORE see **SHINGAPORU SOKOGEKI** • 1943

ATTACK ON TERROR • 1975 • Chomsky Marvin • TVM • USA • ATTACK ON TERROR: THE F.B.I. VS. THE KU KLUX KLAN

ATTACK ON TERROR: THE F.B.I. VS. THE KU KLUX KLAN see **ATTACK ON TERROR** • 1975

ATTACK ON THE AGENT, THE • 1906 • Green Tom • UKN

ATTACK ON THE IRON COAST • 1968 • Wendkos Paul • UKN, USA

ATTACK ON THE MILL, THE • 1910 • Porter Edwin S. • USA

ATTACK ON THE STATE TREASURE see **ASSALTO AL TESORO DI STATO** • 1967

ATTACK POINT OF WOMEN see **SEIEN, SHISHOGIRI** • 1968

ATTACK SQUADRON see **TAIHEIYO NO TSUBASA** • 1963

ATTACK! THE BATTLE OF NEW BRITAIN • 1944 • Presnell Robert • USA

ATTACKED BY ARAPAHOES • 1910 • *Kalem* • USA

ATTACO ALLA PIOURA • 1985 • Damiani Damiano • ITL • SICILIAN CONNECTION, THE ○ AMORE A PALERMO ○ PIZZA CONNECTION

ATTANASIO, CAVALLO VANESIO • 1953 • Mastrocinque Camillo • ITL

ATTAQUE D'UN DILIGENCE, L' • 1904 • Blache Alice • FRN

ATTAQUE D'UN POSTE ANGLAIS • 1897 • Melies Georges • FRN • ATTACK ON AN ENGLISH BLOCKHOUSE

ATTAQUE NOCTURNE • 1931 • Allegret Marc • FRN

ATTE GONDUKALA SOSE GONDUKALA • 1968 • Swamy Y. R. • IND • EACH DOG HAS HIS DAY

ATTEMPT, THE see **ATENTADO, EL** • 1986

ATTEMPT AT FLIGHT see **FLUCHTVERSUCH** • 1976

ATTEMPT ON THE THREE GREAT POWERS see **ATTENTATO AI TRE GRANDI** • 1967

ATTEMPT TO KILL • 1961 • Morley Royston • UKN

ATTEMPT TO SMASH A BANK, AN • 1909 • Bouwmeester Theo? • UKN

ATTEMPTED CAPTURE OF AN ENGLISH NURSE AND CHILDREN • 1900 • *Mitchell & Kenyon* • UKN

ATTEMPTED DUET, AN • 1928 • *De Forest Phonofilms* • SHT • UKN

ATTEMPTED ELOPEMENT, AN • 1910 • *Defender* • USA

ATTEMPTED ESCAPE see **FLUCHTVERSUCH** • 1976

ATTEMPTED MURDER see **POKUS O VRAZDU** • 1973

ATTEMPTED MURDER IN A RAILWAY TRAIN • 1904 • Stow Percy • UKN

ATTEMPTED NOBBLING OF THE DERBY FAVOURITE • 1905 • Green Tom? • UKN

ATTENDANCE COMPULSORY see **ERSCHEINEN PFLICHT** • 1984

ATTENDENTI, GLI • 1961 • Bianchi Giorgio • ITL

ATTENDING PHYSICIAN • 1986 • Tosheva Nevena • DOC • BUL

ATTENTAT • 1981 • Christensen Bent • DNM

ATTENTAT, DAS • 1921 • *Gura Sascha* • FRG

ATTENTAT, L' • 1966 • Davy Jean-Francois • FRN

ATTENTAT, L' • 1972 • Boisset Yves • FRN, ITL, FRG • FRENCH CONSPIRACY, THE (USA) ○ ATTENTATO, L' (ITL) ○ PLOT (UKN)

ATTENTAT CONTRE Me LABORE • 1899 • Melies Georges • FRN

ATTENTATO, L' (ITL) see **ATTENTAT, L'** • 1972

ATTENTATO AI TRE GRANDI • 1967 • Lenzi Umberto • ITL, FRN, FRG • CHIENS VERTS DU DESERT, LES (FRN) ○ FUNF GEGEN CASABLANCA (FRG) ○ ATTEMPT ON THE THREE GREAT POWERS ○ FIVE FOR CASABLANCA ○ DESERT COMMAND

ATTENTES, LES • 1986 • Leduc Jacques • MTV • CND

ATTENTI AL BUFFONE • 1975 • Bevilacqua Alberto • ITL

ATTENTI.. ARRIVANO LE COLLEGIALI! • 1975 • Mille Giorgio • ITL

ATTENTI RAGAZZI, CHI ROMPE.. PAGA! • 1976 • Ferroni Giorgio • ITL

ATTENTION! see **UWAGA!** • 1958

ATTENTION! see **POZOR!** • 1959

ATTENTION A LA PEINTURE • 1898 • Melies Georges • FRN

ATTENTION ATTENTION • 1974 • Brault Francois, Gauvreau J. • SHT • CND

ATTENTION AU PINGOUIN • 1952 • Masson Jean • SHT • FRN

ATTENTION BANDIT • 1987 • Lelouch Claude • FRN

ATTENTION HOOLIGANS see **UWAGA CHULIGANI!** • 1955

ATTENTION LES ENFANTS REGARDENT • 1977 • Leroy Serge • FRN • CAREFUL, THE CHILDREN ARE WATCHING

ATTENTION LES YEUX • 1975 • Pires Gerard • FRN • LET'S MAKE A DIRTY MOVIE ○ WATCH FOR THE EYES

ATTENTION PAINTING see **UWAGA MALARSTWO** • 1958

ATTENTION RED LIGHT • 1970 • Peronski Konstantin • ANS • BUL

ATTENTION SUCKERS • 1934 • Cummings Jack • SHT • USA

ATTENTION, THE DEVIL • Wasilewski Zenon • ANS • PLN

ATTENTION TORTOISE! see **VNIMANIE CHEREPAKHA** • 1969

ATTENTION! UNE FEMME PEUT EN CACHER UNE AUTRE • 1983 • Lautner Georges • FRN • MY OTHER HUSBAND (USA)

ATTENTION, WET PAINT see **VIGYAZAT, MAZOLVA** • 1961

ATTENTO GRINGO.. E TORNATO SABATA • 1972 • Bragan A. • ITL

ATTI ATROCISSIMA DE AMORE E DI VENDETTA • 1979 • Corbucci Sergio • ITL

ATTI DEGLI APOSTOLI • 1969 • Rossellini Roberto • MTV • ITL • ACTS OF THE APOSTLES (USA)

ATTI IMPURI ALL'ITALIANO • 1977 • Brazzi Fabrizio • ITL

ATTIC, THE • 1979 • Edwards George • USA

ATTIC, THE • 1988 • Adams Doug • USA • BLACKOUT

ATTIC, THE see **ATTICO, L'** • 1963

ATTIC OF FELIX BAVU, THE see **BAVU** • 1923

ATTIC PRINCESS, THE • 1916 • Cochrane George • SHT • USA

ATTIC: THE HIDING OF ANNE FRANK, THE • 1988 • Erman John • TVM • USA

ATTICA • 1973 • Firestone Cinda • DOC • USA

ATTICA • 1980 • Chomsky Marvin • TVM • USA

ATTICK ABOVE, THE • 1914 • *Otto Henry* • USA

ATTICO, L' • 1963 • Puccini Gianni • ITL • ATTIC, THE

ATTILA 74 • 1975 • Cacoyannis Michael • DOC • GRC • ATTILA 74: THE RAPE OF CYPRUS

ATTILA 74: THE RAPE OF CYPRUS see **ATTILA 74** • 1975

ATTILA FLAGELLO DI DIO • 1955 • Francisci Pietro • ITL, FRN • ATTILA FLEAU DE DIEU (FRN) ○ ATTILA (USA) ○ ATTILA THE HUN ○ ATTILA THE SCOURGE OF GOD

ATTILA FLAGELLO DI DIO • 1983 • Castellano, Pipolo • ITL • ATTILA THE SCOURGE OF GOD

ATTILA FLEAU DE DIEU (FRN) see **ATTILA FLAGELLO DI DIO** • 1955

ATTILA THE HUN see **ATTILA FLAGELLO DI DIO** • 1955

ATTILA THE SCOURGE OF GOD see **ATTILA FLAGELLO DI DIO** • 1955

ATTILA THE SCOURGE OF GOD see **ATTILA FLAGELLO DI DIO** • 1983

ATTILA (USA) see **ATTILA FLAGELLO DI DIO** • 1955

ATTITUDE NEERLANDAISE, L' • 1972 • Regnier Michel • DCS • CND

ATTITUDINAL BEHAVIOUR • 1980 • Hicks Scott • DOC • ASL

ATTIUK • 1958-60 • Bonniere Rene • DCS • CND

ATTO DI ACCUSA • 1950 • Gentilomo Giacomo • ITL

ATTONDE DAGEN, DET • 1979 • Gronroos Anders • SWD • EIGHTH DAY, THE

ATTONG see **YOUNG AND THE BRAVE, THE** • 1963

ATTORE SCOMPARSO, L' • 1941 • Zampa Luigi • ITL • ATTORE SI DIVERTE, UN

ATTORE SI DIVERTE, UN see **ATTORE SCOMPARSO, L'** • 1941

ATTORNEY FOR THE DEFENCE • 1913 • *Joyce Alice* • USA

ATTORNEY FOR THE DEFENCE • 1915 • *Lubin* • USA

ATTORNEY FOR THE DEFENCE (UKN) see **SILENT WITNESS** • 1942

ATTORNEY FOR THE DEFENSE • 1932 • Cummings Irving • USA

ATTORNEY FOR THE DEFENSE, THE (USA) see **AVVOCATO DIFENSORE, L'** • 1934

ATTORNEY'S AFFAIR, THE • 1917 • *Sparkle Comedy* • SHT • USA

ATTORNEY'S DECISION, THE • 1914 • Myers Harry • USA

ATTORNEY'S DILEMMA, THE (UKN) see **FALSE FACES** • 1943

ATTRACTA • 1983 • Hickey Kieran • IRL

ATTRACTION • Topouzanov Christo, Donev Donyo • ANS • BUL

ATTRACTION (UKN) see **NERO SU BIANCO** • 1969

ATTRACTIVE CATCH, AN • 1908 • Fitzhamon Lewin • UKN

ATTRAIT DU BOUGE, L' • 1912 • Feuillade Louis • FRN

ATVALTOZAS • 1984 • Darday Istvan • HNG • POINT OF DEPARTURE

ATVALTOZASOK • 1964 • Kovasznai Gyorgy • ANS • HNG • DOUBLE PORTRAIT

ATYACHAR • 1983 • Chandavarkar Bhaskar • IND • ATROCITIES

AU BAGNE • 1905-10 • Heuze Andre • FRN

AU BAL DE FLORE • 1900 • Blache Alice • FRN • AT THE PLANT'S BALL

AU BOIS PIGET • 1956 • Dewever Jean • FRN

AU BONHEUR DES DAMES • 1929 • Duvivier Julien • FRN

AU BONHEUR DES DAMES • 1943 • Cayatte Andre • FRN • SHOP-GIRLS OF PARIS (USA)

AU BONHEUR DES DAMES • 1979 • Kaplan Nelly • FRN

AU BORD DE L'ETANG • Moinet Monique • SHT • BLG

AU BORD DU GOUFFRE • 1911 • Jasset Victorin • FRN

AU BOUT DE MA RUE • 1958 • Carrier Louis-Georges • DCS • CND • STREET TO THE WORLD

AU BOUT DE MON AGE • 1975 • Dufaux Georges • DOC • CND

AU BOUT DES FUSILS • 1972 • Graham Peter • DCS • FRN • GUNPOINT

AU BOUT DU BOUT DU BANC • 1978 • Kassovitz Peter • FRN

AU BOUT DU DOUTE • 1978 • Bonin Laurier • MTV • CND

AU BOUT DU FIL • 1974 • Driessen Paul • ANM • CND • CAT'S CRADLE

AU BOUT DU MONDE • 1933 • Chomette Henri, Ucicky Gustav • FRN • FUGITIFS, LES

AU BOUT DU PRINTEMPS • 1976 • Dubois Bernard • FRN

AU BOUTT' • 1973 • Laliberte Roger • CND

AU CABARET • 1899-00 • Blache Alice • FRN

AU CANADA • 1964 • Portugais Louis • CND

AU CARREFOUR DE LA VIE • 1949 • Storck Henri • DOC • BLG • CROSSROADS OF LIFE

AU CEGEP • 1975 • Brault Francois • DCS • CND

AU CENTRE DE L'AMERIQUE DU SUD INCONNU • 1925 • de Wavrin Marquis Robert • BLG

AU CLAIR DE LA LUNE • 1971-72 • Image Jean • ASS • FRN

AU CLAIR DE LA LUNE • 1982 • Forcier Andre • CND • MOONSHINE

AU CLAIR DE LA LUNE see **AU CLAIR DE LA LUNE OU PIERROT MALHEUREUX** • 1904

AU CLAIR DE LA LUNE OU PIERROT MALHEUREUX • 1904 • Melies Georges • FRN • MOONLIGHT SERENADE OR THE MISER PUNISHED, A ○ AU CLAIR DE LA LUNE ○ PIERROT'S GRIEF ○ PIERROT MALHEUREUX

AU COEUR DE LA CASBAH • 1951 • Cardinal Pierre • FRN

AU COEUR DE LA VIE • 1968 • Enrico Robert • FRN

AU COEUR DE LA VILLE • 1960 • Gautherin Pierre • FRN

AU COEUR DE LA VILLE • 1969 • Jutra Claude • DCS • CND

AU COEUR DE L'ILE-DE-FRANCE • 1954 • Gremillon Jean • SHT • FRN

AU COEUR DE L'ORAGE • 1948 • Le Chanois Jean-Paul • FRN

AU DEBUT DU SIECLE • 1961 • Rybakov Anatoly • USS

AU-DELA DE CETTE LIMITE VOTRE TICKET N'EST PLUS VALABLE see **YOUR TICKET IS NO LONGER VALID** • 1980

AU-DELA DE LA MORT • 1922 • Perojo Benito • SPN • BEYOND DEATH

AU-DELA DE LA PEUR • 1974 • Andrei Yannick • FRN • BEYOND FEAR (USA)

AU-DELA DES GRILLES • 1948 • Clement Rene • FRN, ITL • MURA DI MALAPAGA, LA (ITL) ○ WALLS OF MALAPAGA, THE (USA) ○ MURS DE MALAPAGA, LES ○ TROIS JOURS D'AMOUR

AU-DELA DES LOIS HUMAINES • 1921 • Roudes Gaston, Dumont • FRN

AU-DELA DES MURS • 1968 • Lamothe Arthur • DCS • CND

AU-DELA DU BIEN ET DU MAL see **OLTRE IL BENE E IL MALE** • 1977

AU-DELA DU VISAGE • 1953 • Blais Roger • DCS • CND • AVOCAT DE LA DEFENSE L'

AU-DELA DU VISIBLE • 1943 • Decae Henri • SHT • FRN

AU DESSUS DES LOIS • 1920 • Ravel Gaston • FRN

AU DIABLE LA VERTU • 1952 • Laviron Jean • FRN

AU DIABLE LES ANGES (FRN) see **OPERAZIONE SAN PIETRO** • 1967

AU FEU • 1953 • Masson Jean • SHT • FRN

AU FIL DE L'EAU • 1932 • Matras Christian • SHT • FRN

AU FIL DES ONDES • 1950 • Gautherin Pierre • FRN

AU FIL D'UNE RIVIERE see **A PROPOS D'UNE RIVIERE** • 1955

AU FOU! see **SATSUJINKYO SHIDAI** • 1966

AU GRAND BALCON • 1949 • Decoin Henri • FRN

AU GRAND THEATRE DE QUEBEC • 1972 • Lavoie Richard • DCS • CND

AU GRE DES FLOTS • 1913 • Feuillade Louis • FRN

AU GUADALQUIVIR • 1965 • Puzenat Jean-Loup • SHT • FRN

AU HASARD BALTHAZAR • 1966 • Bresson Robert • FRN, SWD • MIN VAN BALTHAZAR (SWD) ○ BALTHAZAR

AU HASARD DU TEMPS • 1964 • Giraldeau Jacques • DCS • CND

AU LARGE DES COTES TUNISIENNES • 1949 • Cousteau Jacques • FRN

AU LONG DE LA RIVIERE FANGO • 1974 • Sotha • FRN • ALONG THE FANGO RIVER

AU MILIEU DES CRATERES EN FEU • 1951-55 • Tazieff Haroun • SHT • FRN

AU NOM DE LA LOI • 1931 • Tourneur Maurice • FRN

AU NOM DE LA RACE • 1975 • Hillel Marc, Henry Clarissa • DOC • FRN

AU NOM DE TOUS LES MIENS • 1983 • Enrico Robert • FRN, CND • FOR THOSE I LOVED

AU NOM DU FUHRER • 1978 • Chagoll Lydia • BLG • IN THE NAME OF THE FUHRER

AU PAIR GIRL • *Guida Gloria* • ITL

AU PAIR GIRLS • 1972 • Guest Val • UKN

AU PAN COUPE • 1968 • Gilles Guy • FRN

AU PARADIS DES ENFANTS • 1918 • Burguet Charles • FRN

AU PARC LAFONTAINE • 1947 • Petel Pierre • DCS • CND

AU PAYS DE GEORGES SAND • 1926 • Epstein Jean • FRN

AU PAYS DE GUILLAUME LE CONQUERANT • 1954 • Wronecki • SHT • FRN

AU PAYS DE NEUVE FRANCE • 1958-60 • Bonniere Rene • DSS • CND

AU PAYS DE PORGY AND BESS • 1957 • Reichenbach Francois • SHT • FRN

AU PAYS DE TARARANI • 1971 • Ben Halima Hamouda, Ben Milad H., Boughedir Ferid • TNS

AU PAYS DE ZOM • 1983 • Groulx Gilles • CND

AU PAYS DES BASQUES • 1930 • Champreux Maurice • DOC • FRN • PAYS DES BASQUES, LES

AU PAYS DES BELLES FOURRURES • 1957 • Rivard Fernand • DCS • CND

AU PAYS DES BUVEURS DE SANG see **CHEZ LES BUVEURS DE SANG** • 1930

AU PAYS DES CIGALES • 1945 • Cam Maurice • FRN

AU PAYS DES ETANGS CLAIRS • 1950 • Hamman Joe (c/d) • FRN

AU PAYS DES FEES see **ROYAUME DES FEES, LE** • 1903

AU PAYS DES JOUETS see **CONTE DE LA GRAND'MERE ET REVE DE L'ENFANT OU AU PAYS DES JOUETS** • 1908

AU PAYS DES LYONS • 1912 • Feuillade Louis • FRN

AU PAYS DES MAGES NOIR • 1947 • Rouch Jean (c/d) • DCS • FRN

AU PAYS DES PYGMEES • 1946 • Dupont Jacques • SHT • FRN

AU PAYS DES SORCIERS ET DE LA MORT • 1933 • de Wavrin Marquis Robert • DOC • FRN

AU PAYS DES TENEBRES • 1912 • Jasset Victorin • SRL • FRN

AU PAYS DU BLE see **WHEAT COUNTRY** • 1959

AU PAYS DU ROI LEPREUX • 1927 • Chomette Henri, Feyder Jacques • SHT • FRN

AU PAYS DU SCALP • 1930 • de Wavrin Marquis Robert • DOC • BLG, FRN

AU PAYS DU SOLEIL • 1933 • Peguy Robert • FRN

AU PAYS NOIR • 1905 • Nonguet Lucien • FRN • TO THE BLACK LAND

AU PAYS NOIR • 1905 • Zecca Ferdinand • FRN

AU PERIL DE LA MER • 1968 • Roger • SHT • FRN

AU PETIT BONHEUR • 1945 • L'Herbier Marcel • FRN

AU PETIT SUISSE, JOURNAL FILME N.7 • 1982 • Morder Joseph • FRN

AU PIED DE LA LETTRE see **TALE OF MAIL, A** • 1967

AU POISSON COURONNE see **TAVERNE DU POISSON COURONNE, LA** • 1946

AU POULAILLER! • 1905 • Blache Alice • FRN

AU P'TIT ZOUAVE • 1949 • Grangier Gilles • FRN

AU RAVISSEMENT DES DAMES • 1913 • Machin Alfred • NTH

AU REFECTOIRE • 1897-98 • Blache Alice • FRN

AU RENDEZ-VOUS DE LA MORT JOYEUSE • 1972 • Bunuel Juan • FRN, ITL • AT THE MEETING WITH JOYOUS DEATH

AU RENDEZ-VOUS DU DIABLE see **RENDEZ-VOUS DU DIABLE, LES** • 1958

AU REVOIR, A LUNDI • 1980 • Dugowson Maurice • CND, FRN • 'BYE, SEE YOU MONDAY

AU REVOIR ET MERCI see **SALUUT EN DE KOST** • 1974

AU REVOIR LES ENFANTS • 1988 • Malle Louis • FRN, FRG

AU REVOIR, MONSIEUR GROCK • 1949 • Billon Pierre • FRN • MERCI MONSIEUR GROCK

AU ROYAUME DES CIEUX • 1949 • Duvivier Julien • FRN • WOMAN HUNT ○ SINNERS, THE

AU ROYAUME DU CHEVAL see **KINGDOM FOR A HORSE** • 1935

AU ROYAUME DU SAGUENAY • 1956 • Proulx Maurice • DCS • CND

AU RYTHME DE MON COEUR • 1984 • Lefebvre Jean-Pierre • CND • TO THE RHYTHM OF MY HEART

AU RYTHME DU SIECLE • 1953 • Champetier Henri • SHT • FRN

AU SECOURS! • 1923 • Gance Abel • FRN • HAUNTED HOUSE, THE (UKN) ○ HELP!

AU SERVICE DES PRISONNIERS • 1942 • Dekeukeleire Charles • BLG

AU SERVICE DU DIABLE see **PLUS LONGUE NUIT DU DIABLE, LA** • 1971

AU SERVICE DU TSAR • 1936 • Billon Pierre • FRN

AU SEUIL DE L'OPERATOIRE • 1972 • Moreau Michel • DOC • CND

AU SEUIL DU CRIME • 1920 • de Carbonnat Louis • FRN

AU SEUIL DU HAREM • 1922 • Luitz-Morat, Vercourt Alfred • FRN • SANG D'ALLAH, LE

AU SOLEIL DE MARSEILLE • 1937 • Ducis Pierre-Jean • FRN

AU SOMMET DE LA GLOIRE • 1916 • Volkov Alexander • USS

AU SON DES GUITARES • 1936 • Ducis Pierre-Jean • FRN • LOIN DES GUITARES

AU VERRE DE L'AMITIE • 1970 • Makovski Claude • SHT • FRN

AU VOLEUR! • 1960 • Habib Ralph • FRN, FRG

AU VOLEUR! see **ISMIK HARAMI** • 1958

AUANDAR ANAPU • 1974 • Corkidi Rafael • MXC

AUBE see **FAGR** • 1955

AUBE, L' see **FAJR, AL** • 1967

AUBE DE LA CIVILISATION: L'ART DE SUMER, L' see **FAJR AL-HAD'ARA: AL-FANN AS-SUMARY** • 1976

AUBE DE SANG, L' • 1926 • Guarino Joseph • FRN

AUBE DES DAMNES, L' • 1964 • Rachedi Ahmed • ALG • DAWN OF THE DAMNED

AUBE ET CREPUSCULE see **GHURUBUN WA SHUROQ** • 1970

AUBE NOIRE, L' • Djingareye Maiga • NGR • BLACK DAWN

AUBERGE DE L'ABIME, L' • 1942 • Rozier Willy • FRN

AUBERGE DES PLAISIRS, L' • 1969 • Antel Franz • FRN

AUBERGE DU BON REPOS, L' • 1903 • Melies Georges • FRN • INN WHERE NO MAN RESTS, THE (USA) ○ INN OF "GOOD REST", THE

AUBERGE DU PECHE, L' • 1949 • de Marguenat Jean • FRN

AUBERGE DU PETIT DRAGON, L' • 1934 • de Limur Jean • FRN

AUBERGE EN FOLIE, L' see **AUBERGE FLEURIE, L'** • 1956

AUBERGE ENSORCELEE, L' • 1897 • Melies Georges • FRN • BEWITCHED INN, THE (USA)

AUBERGE FLEURIE, L' • 1956 • Chevalier Pierre, Billon Pierre • FRN • AUBERGE EN FOLIE, L'

AUBERGE ROUGE, L' • 1910 • *Gance Abel* • FRN

AUBERGE ROUGE, L' • 1923 • Epstein Jean • FRN • RED INN, THE (USA)

AUBERGE ROUGE, L' • 1950 • Autant-Lara Claude • FRN • RED INN, THE

AUBERGINE EST BIEN FARCIE, L' • Baudricourt Michel • FRN

AUBERVILLIERS • 1945 • Lotar Eli • DOC • FRN

AUBREY'S BIRTHDAY • 1914 • Collins Edwin J.? • UKN

AUBUSSON ET JEAN LURCAT • 1946 • Lods Jean • DCS • FRN

AUCASSIN A NICOLETTA • 1980 • Campulkova Nina • CZC • AUCASSIN AND NICOLETTE

AUCASSIN AND NICOLETTE • 1975 • Reiniger Lotte • ANM • CND

AUCASSIN AND NICOLETTE see **AUCASSIN A NICOLETTA** • 1980

AUCH MANNER SIND KEINE ENGEL • 1958 • Kolm-Veltee H. Walter • AUS

AUCH MIMOSEN WOLLEN BLUHEN • 1976 • Meewes Helmut • FRG • EVEN WALLFLOWERS WANT TO BLOOM

AUCH ZWERGE HABEN KLEIN ANGEFANGEN • 1970 • Herzog Werner • FRG • EVEN DWARFS STARTED SMALL (UKN)

AUCTION, THE • 1919 • Miller Frank • SHT • UKN

AUCTION BLOCK, THE • 1917 • Trimble Larry • USA

AUCTION BLOCK, THE • 1925 • Henley Hobart • USA

AUCTION IN SOULS see **CONSTANT WOMAN, THE** • 1933

AUCTION MART, THE • 1920 • Macrae Duncan • UKN

AUCTION OF SOULS • 1919 • Apfel Oscar • USA • RAVISHED ARMENIA

AUCTION OF VIRTUE, THE • 1917 • Blache Herbert • USA

AUCTION SALE OF RUN-DOWN RANCH, THE • 1915 • Mix Tom • USA

AUCTIONEER, THE • 1927 • Green Alfred E. • USA

AUCUNE INTIMITE LICITE.. see **OSPITE, L'** • 1971

AUDACE COLPI DEI SOLITI IGNOTI • 1959 • Loy Nanni • ITL, FRN • HOLD-UP A LA MILANAISE (FRN) ○ FIASCO IN MILAN

AUDACES DU COEUR, LES • 1913 • Feuillade Louis • FRN

AUDACIOUS MR. SQUIRE, THE • 1923 • Greenwood Edwin • UKN

AUDAZ Y BRAVERO • 1964 • Blake Alfonso Corona • MXC

AUDE NERON VIOLINCELLISTE • 1972-73 • Brault Francois • DCS • CND

AUDIENCE, THE see **UDIENZA, L'** • 1972

AUDIENCE WITH GOD see **HARI DARSHUAN** • 1953

AUDIENCIA PUBLICA • 1946 • Rey Florian • SPN

AUDIENZ IN ISCHL see **KAISERWALZER** • 1932

AUDION, THE • 1922 • Craft E. B. • ANM • USA

AUDIOSCOPIKS • 1935 • *Smith Pete* • SHT • USA

AUDIOVISION NO.17 • 1970 • Moreau Michel • DCS • CND

AUDITION • 1974 • Zwartjes Frans • NTH

AUDITION! • 1980 • Firus Karen • DOC • CND

AUDITION, L' • 1973 • Dion Jean-Francois • SHT • FRN

AUDITION, THE see **KONKURS** • 1963

AUDITIONS • 1980 • Loach Kenneth • MTV • UKN

AUDITORIUM • 1957 • Drach Michel • SHT • FRN

AUDREY • 1916 • Vignola Robert G. • USA

AUDREY ROSE • 1977 • Wise Robert • USA

AUDRY THE RAINMAKER • 1951 • Sparber I. • ANS • USA

AUF BEFEHL DER POMPADOUR • 1924 • Zelnik Friedrich • FRG

AUF DE ALM, DA GIBT'S KO'A SUND • 1930 • *Eschen Hanna* • FRG

AUF DEN BERGEN ROTER MOHN • 1966 • Jung-Alsen Kurt • GDR, UKN • FOUR SOLDIERS

AUF DEN SPUREN DES WEISSEN SKLAVENHANDELS 1 • 1921 • Linke Edmund • FRG

AUF DEN SPUREN DES WEISSEN SKLAVENHANDELS 2 • 1921 • Linke Edmund • FRG

AUF DEN TRUMMERN DES PARADIESES • 1920 • *Ustad-Film* • FRG

AUF DER ALM, DA GIBT'S KA SUND' • 1915 • Biebrach Rudolf • FRG

AUF DER ALM DA GIBT'S KA SUND • 1950 • Antel Franz • AUS

AUF DER GRUNEN WIESE • 1953 • Bottger Fritz • AUS

AUF DER HOHE • 1916 • Fleck Jacob, Fleck Luise • AUS

AUF DER RADRENNBAHN • 1903 • Messter Oskar • FRG

AUF DER REEPERBAHN NACHTS UM HALB EINS • 1929 • Stranz Fred • FRG

AUF DER REEPERBAHN NACHTS UM HALB EINS • 1954 • Liebeneiner Wolfgang • FRG

AUF DER REEPERBAHN NACHTS UM HALB EINS • 1969 • Olsen Rolf • FRG

AUF DER SONNENSEITE • 1962 • Kirsten Ralf • GDR

AUF DES LEBENS RAUFER BAHN • 1918 • Bluen Georg • FRG

AUF ENGEL SCHIESST MAN NICHT • 1960 • Thiele Rolf • FRG

AUF GEFAHRLICHEN SPUREN • 1924 • Piel Harry • FRG • VERWEHTE SPUREN

AUF LEBEN UND TOD • 1929 • Heuberger Edmund • FRG

AUF PROBE GESTELLT • 1917 • Biebrach Rudolf • FRG

AUF UMWEGEN ZUM GLUCK • 1915 • Del Zopp Rudolf • FRG

AUF VERBOTENEN PFADEN • 1920 • *Sohnlin Egon* • FRG

AUF WIEDERSEHEN • 1962 • Philipp Harald • FRG

AUF WIEDERSEHEN AM BODENSEE • 1956 • Albin Hans • FRG

AUF WIEDERSEHEN, FRANZISKA • 1941 • Kautner Helmut • FRG • ADIEU FRANCISKA

AUF WIEDERSEHN • 1957 • Liebeneiner Wolfgang • FRG

AUF WIEDERSEHN, FRANZISKA see **FRANZISKA** • 1957

AUFENTHALT, DIE • 1983 • Beyer Frank • GDR • TURNING POINT

AUFERSTEHUNG • 1923 • Zelnik Friedrich • FRG • KATJUSCHA MASLOVA

AUFERSTEHUNG • 1958 • Hansen Rolf • FRG, ITL, FRN • RESURRECTION ○ RESURREZIONE

AUFFORDERUNG ZUM TANZ • 1935 • van der Noss Rudolf • FRG • INVITATION TO THE DANCE (USA) ○ WEG CARL MARIA VON WEBERS, DER

AUFPASSEN MACHT SCHULE • 1978 • Filmgruppe Demokratische Rechte • SWT

AUFRECHTE GANG, DER • 1976 • Ziewer Christian • FRG • WALKING UPRIGHT

AUFRUHR DER HERZEN • 1944 • Muller Hans • FRG

AUFRUHR DES BLUTES • 1929 • Trivas Victor • FRG

AUFRUHR IM DAMENSTIFT • 1941 • Andam F. D. • FRG

AUFRUHR IM JUNGGESELLENHEIM • 1929 • Noa Manfred • FRG

AUFRUHR IM PARADIES • 1950 • Stockel Joe • FRG

AUFRUHR IN DAMASKUS • 1939 • Ucicky Gustav • FRG • TUMULT IN DAMASCUS (USA)

AUFS EIS GEFUHRT • 1915 • Lubitsch Ernst • FRG

AUFSTAND, DER • 1981 • Lilienthal Peter • FRG • UPRISING, THE

AUFSTAND, DER • 1987 • Patzak Peter • MTV • AUS

AUFSTIEG DER KLEINEN LILIAN • 1924 • Sauer Fred • FRG

AUFTRAG HOGLERS, DER • 1950 • von Wangenheim Gustav • GDR • WESTOSTLICHE HOCHZEIT

AUFZUG, DER see **ABWARTS: DAS DUELL UBER DER TIEFE** • 1984

AUGE DER SPINNE, DER (AUS) see **OCCHIO DEL RAGNO, L'** • 1971

AUGE DES BUDDHA, DAS • 1919 • Mondet Maurice A. • AUS

AUGE DES GOTZEN, DAS • 1919 • Piel Harry • FRG

AUGE DES TOTEN, DAS • 1922 • Boese Carl • FRG

AUGELLIN BEL VERDE, L' • 1975 • Luzzati Emmanuele • ANM • ITL

AUGEN • 1919 • Brenken Arthur • FRG • IM BANNE DER HYPNOSE

AUGEN ALS ANKLAGER, DIE • 1920 • *Eva Evi* • FRG

AUGEN AUS EINEM ANDEREN LAND • 1975 • Kluge Alexander, Reitz Edgar • FRG • EYES FROM ANOTHER COUNTRY

AUGEN DER LIEBE see **ZWISCHEN NACHT UND MORGEN** • 1944

AUGEN DER MASKE, DIE • 1920 • Gerhardt Karl • FRG

AUGEN DER MUMIE MA, DIE • 1918 • Lubitsch Ernst • FRG • EYES OF THE MUMMY MA (USA) ○ EYES OF THE MUMMY, THE (UKN)

AUGEN DER SCHWESTER, DIE • 1918 • Eckstein Franz • FRG

AUGEN DER WELT, DIE • 1920 • Wilhelm Carl • FRG

AUGEN DES OLE BRANDIS, DIE • 1914 • Rye Stellan, Wegener Paul • FRG • OLE BRANDES AUGEN

AUGEN IM WALDE, DIE • 1919 • Guter Johannes • FRG

AUGEN VON JADE, DIE • 1918 • Raffay Iwa • FRG

AUGENBLICK • 1984 • Reichle Franz • SWT

AUGENBLICK DES FRIEDENS (FRG) see **CHWILA POKOJU** • 1965

AUGENBLICK IM PARADIES, EIN • 1919 • Schubert Georg • FRG

AUGH! AUGH! • 1979 • Toniato Marco • ITL

AUGURI E FIGLI MASCHI • 1951 • Simonelli Giorgio C. • ITL

AUGUST • 1972 • Mikhailov V. • USS

AUGUST see **ELOKUU** • 1956

AUGUST 14: ONE DAY IN THE U.S.S.R. • 1948 • Setkina Irina • USS

AUGUST -A MONTH IN THE LIFE OF JERZY T. see **SIERPEN – KRONIKA MIESIACA JERZEGO T.** • 1972
AUGUST AND JULY • 1973 • Markowitz Murray • DOC • CND
AUGUST AND SEPTEMBER • 1905 • *Walterdaw* • UKN
AUGUST DER HALBSTARKE • 1957 • Wolff Hans • AUS
AUGUST DER STARKE • 1936 • Wegener Paul • FRG, PLN
AUGUST DER STARKE see **GALANTE KONIG, DER** • 1920
AUGUST HEAT • 1963 • Zweiback Martin • SHT • USA
AUGUST IN FLACARI • 1973 • Pita Dan • MTV • RMN • AUGUST IN FLAMES
AUGUST IN FLAMES see **AUGUST IN FLACARI** • 1973
AUGUST KARLSSONS ATERKOMST see **SALTSTANK OCH KRUTGUBBAR** • 1946
AUGUST RHAPSODY, AN see **AUGUSTIRAPSODI, EN** • 1939
AUGUST SUNDAY see **SRPNOVA NEDELE** • 1960
AUGUST WEEK-END • 1936 • Lamont Charles • USA • WEEK-END MADNESS (UKN)
AUGUST WITHOUT EMPEROR see **KOTEI NO INAI HACHIGATSU** • 1978
AUGUST WITHOUT THE EMPEROR see **KOTEI NO INAI HACHIGATSU** • 1978
AUGUSTA • 1976 • Wheeler Anne • CND
AUGUSTA KNEADING • 1987 • Varga Csaba • ANM • HNG
AUGUSTAS LILLA FELSTEG • 1933 • Modeen Thor • SWD • AUGUSTA'S LITTLE SHIP
AUGUSTA'S LITTLE SHIP see **AUGUSTAS LILLA FELSTEG** • 1933
AUGUSTE • 1961 • Chevalier Pierre • FRN
AUGUSTE AND BIBB see **AUGUSTE ET BIBB** • 1897
AUGUSTE ET BIBB • 1897 • Melies Georges • FRN • AUGUSTE AND BIBB
AUGUSTINE OF HIPPO (USA) see **AGOSTINO DI IPPONA** • 1972
AUGUSTIRAPSODI, EN • 1939 • Sucksdorff Arne • DCS • SWD • AUGUST RHAPSODY, AN
AULAD • 1968 • Kumar Kundan • IND • SON
AULD LANG SYNE • 1911 • *Turner Florence* • USA
AULD LANG SYNE • 1917 • Morgan Sidney • UKN
AULD LANG SYNE • 1925 • Butler Alexander • UKN
AULD LANG SYNE • 1929 • Pearson George • UKN
AULD LANG SYNE • 1937 • Fitzpatrick James A. • UKN
AULD ROBIN GRAY • 1917 • Milton Meyrick • UKN
AULD ROBIN GREY • 1910 • Trimble Larry • USA
AUNQUE LA HORMONA SE VISTA DE SEDA • 1971 • Escriva Vicente • SPN
AUNT, THE • 1915 • Campbell Colin • USA
AUNT BETTY'S REVENGE • 1913 • *Nestor* • USA
AUNT BILL • 1916 • *Plump & Runt* • USA
AUNT CLARA • 1954 • Kimmins Anthony • UKN
AUNT CLARA • 1977 • Heffner Avram • ISR
AUNT CLARA see **TIA ALEJANDRA, LA** • 1978
AUNT DIANAH'S PLOT • 1912 • *Imp* • USA
AUNT ELIZA RECOVERS HER PET • *Pathe?* • FRN
AUNT ELIZABETH'S GARDEN see **JARDIN DE TIA ISABEL, EL** • 1971
AUNT ELSA'S VISIT • 1913 • Seay Charles M. • USA
AUNT EMMY'S SCRAP BOOK • 1909 • *Lubin* • USA
AUNT FROM CHICAGO, THE • 1960 • Sakellarios Alekos • GRC
AUNT GREEN, AUNT BROWN AND AUNT LILAC see **TANT GRON, TANT BRUN OCH TANT GREDELIN** • 1945
AUNT HANNAH • 1910 • *Powers* • USA
AUNT HETTY'S GOLD FISH • 1912 • *Tennant Barbara* • USA
AUNT HULDA, THE MATCHMAKER • 1911 • *Wiliams Earle* • USA
AUNT JANE'S LEGACY • 1911 • Salter Harry • USA
AUNT JULIA AND THE SCRIPTWRITER • 1990 • Amiel Jon • USA
AUNT KATE'S MISTAKE • 1913 • *Kibby Estelle* • USA
AUNT MARIA'S SUBSTITUTE • 1910 • *Imp* • USA
AUNT MARTHA • Casey Thomas • USA
AUNT MARY • 1915 • Santschi Thomas • USA
AUNT MARY • 1979 • Werner Peter • TVM • USA
AUNT MATILDA OUTWITTED • 1915 • *Farley Dot* • USA
AUNT MATILDA'S NEPHEW • 1929 • *Milne E. A.* • SHT • UKN
AUNT MIRANDA'S CAT • 1912 • *Washburn Alice* • USA
AUNT PEG • 1980 • Brown Wes • USA
AUNT PEG'S FULFILLMENT • 1982 • Brown Wes • USA
AUNT RACHEL • 1920 • Ward Albert • UKN
AUNT SALLIES WONDERFUL BUSTLE • 1901 • Porter Edwin S. • USA
AUNT SALLY • 1933 • Whelan Tim • UKN • ALONG CAME SALLY (USA)
AUNT SELINA • 1900 • *Warwick Trading Co* • UKN
AUNT SUSAN'S WAY • 1914 • Stow Percy • UKN
AUNT TABITHA'S VISIT • 1911 • Coleby A. E. • UKN
AUNT TILLIE'S ELOPEMENT • 1915 • *Banner* • USA
AUNT TULA see **TIA TULA, LA** • 1964
AUNT WITH VIOLETS, THE see **TETKA S FILAKAMI** • 1963
AUNTIE • 1914 • King Burton L. • USA
AUNTIE AND THE COWBOYS • 1911 • Dwan Allan • USA
AUNTIE AT THE BOAT RACE • 1910 • *Vitagraph* • USA
AUNTIE MAME • 1958 • Da Costa Morton • USA
AUNTIE TAKES THE CHILDREN TO THE COUNTRY • 1908 • *Lubin* • USA
AUNTIE WITH VIOLETS see **TETKA S FILAKAMI** • 1963
AUNTIE'S AFFINITY • 1913 • O'Neil Barry • USA
AUNTIE'S ANTE • 1927 • Newfield Sam • SHT • USA
AUNTIE'S ANTICS • 1929 • Gannon Wilfred • UKN
AUNTIE'S CYCLING LESSON • 1905 • Collins Alf? • UKN
AUNTIE'S DILEMMA • 1914 • Collins Edwin J.? • UKN
AUNTIE'S FANTASIES see **TETICKA** • 1941
AUNTIE'S FIRST ATTEMPT AT CYCLING • 1905 • *Paul R. W.* • UKN
AUNTIE'S MISTAKE • 1929 • Lamont Charles • SHT • USA
AUNTIE'S PARROT • 1911 • Aylott Dave • UKN
AUNTIE'S PORTRAIT • 1914 • Baker George D., Young James • USA
AUNTIE'S ROMANCE • 1916 • *Jockey* • USA
AUNTIE'S ROMANTIC ADVENTURES • 1914 • *Crystal* • USA
AUNTIE'S SECRET SORROW • 1913 • Stow Percy • UKN
AUNTIE'S TRIUMPH • 1917 • Perry John D. • SHT • USA
AUNTIE'S WEDDING PRESENT • 1922 • Haldane Bert • UKN
AUNT'S DAUGHTER see **ATHEY KANGAL** • 1967
AUNT'S IN THE PANTS • 1930 • Sandrich Mark • SHT • USA
AUNTS, TOO MANY • 1913 • Dillon Eddie • USA
AUNTY AND THE GIRLS • 1913 • Miller Ashley • USA
AUNTY'S MONEY BAG • 1914 • *Eclair* • USA
AUNTY'S MOTOR BIKE • 1907 • *Walterdaw* • UKN
AUNTY'S ROMANCE • 1912 • Baker George D. • USA
AUORE • 1962 • Alassane Moustapha • ANS • NGR • WEDDING
AUPRES DE MA BLONDE • 1943 • Dunning George • ANM • CND
AUPRES DU PEUPLIER see **MIN QURB AS-SAFSAF** • 1972
AURA • 1923 • Di Domenico Vicente • CLM • VIOLETS, THE
AURA see **STREGA IN AMORE, LA** • 1966
AURA NO.1 • 1930 • West Walter • UKN
AURA NO.2 • 1930 • West Walter • UKN
AURA O LAS VIOLETAS • 1973 • Roa Gustavo Nieto • CLM • AURA OR THE VIOLETS
AURA OR THE VIOLETS see **AURA O LAS VIOLETAS** • 1973
AURAIS DU FAIRE GAFFE, LE CHOC EST TERRIBLE • 1976 • Meunier Jean-Henri • FRN
AURAT • 1939 • Khan Mehboob • IND • WOMAN
AURAT • 1953 • Varma Bhagwandas • IND
AURAT • 1967 • Vasan S. S., Balan S. S. • IND • WOMAN
AURELIA STEINER • 1979 • Duras Marguerite • SER • FRN
AURELIA STEINER -MELBOURNE • 1979 • Duras Marguerite • FRN
AURELIA STEINER -VANCOUVER • 1979 • Duras Marguerite • FRN
AURES 54, AURES 64 • 1964 • Riad Mohamed Slimane • ALG
AURI SACRA FAMES 1 • 1920 • Lasko Leo • FRG • VERFLUCHTE HUNGER NACH GOLD 1, DER ○ AN DER LIEBE NARRENSEIL
AURI SACRA FAMES 2 • 1920 • Lasko Leo • FRG • VERFULCHTE HUNGER NACH GOLD 2, DER ○ TESTAMENT EINES EXZENTRISCHEN, DAS
AURINKOTUULI • 1980 • Linnasalo Timo, Peippo Antti • FNL • SUN WIND ○ SUNWIND
AURORA • 1966 • Reichenbach Francois • SHT • FRN
AURORA • 1984 • Ponzi Maurizio • TVM • USA, ITL • AURORA BY NIGHT ○ QUALCOSA DI BLONDA ○ SOMETHING BLONDE
AURORA BY NIGHT see **AURORA** • 1984
AURORA ENCOUNTER, THE • 1985 • McCullough Jim • USA
AURORA FLOYD • 1912 • Marston Theodore • USA
AURORA FLOYD • 1915 • Vale Travers • USA
AURORA LEIGH • 1915 • *Smalleys* • USA
AURORA OF THE NORTH • 1914 • *Leonard Robert* • USA
AURORA SUL MARE • 1935 • Simonelli Giorgio C. • ITL
AURORE BOREALE, UNE • 1981 • Lucot Rene, Benoit Jacques W. • CND
AURZAURI SALKHINETSHI see **PEREPOLOKH** • 1976
AUS see **GEHEIMNIS DER GELBEN MONCHE, DAS** • 1966
AUS ALLEM RAUS UND MITTEN DRIN • 1988 • Morger Pius • SWT
AUS ANGST see **ANGST, DIE** • 1918
AUS DEM BUCHE DES LEBENS • 1916 • Bolten-Baeckers Heinrich • FRG
AUS DEM JENSEITS KAM..., DIE • 1916 • Heymann Robert • FRG
AUS DEM LABEN EINER SCHULREITERIN • 1919 • *Leux Lori* • FRG
AUS DEM LEBEN DER MARIONETTEN • 1980 • Bergman Ingmar • FRG • FROM THE LIFE OF THE MARIONETTES (USA) ○ LIVES OF THE PUPPETS, THE
AUS DEM LEBEN EINES TAUGENICHTS • 1973 • Bleiweiss Celino • GDR
AUS DEM LEBEN GESTRICHEN • 1916 • Dessauer Siegfried • FRG
AUS DEM LEBEN MEINER ALTEN FREUNDIN • 1918 • Mendel Georg Victor • FRG
AUS DEM SCHWARZBUCH EINES POLIZEIKOMMISSARS 1 • 1921 • Hanus Emerich • FRG • LOGE NR.11
AUS DEM SCHWARZBUCH EINES POLIZEIKOMMISSARS 2 • 1921 • Hanus Emerich, Halm Alfred • FRG • VERBRECHEN AUS LEIDENSCHAFT
AUS DEM TAGEBUCH EINER FRAUENARZTIN see **ERSTE RECHT DES KINDES, DAS** • 1932
AUS DEM TAGEBUCH EINES FRAUENARZTES • 1959 • Klinger Werner • FRG
AUS DEM TAGEBUCH EINES JUNGGESELLEN • 1928 • Schonfelder Erich • FRG
AUS DEM TAGEBUCH EINES SIEBZEHNJAHRIGEN • 1979 • Enz Jurgen • FRG • COME MAKE LOVE WITH ME
AUS DEN AKTEN EINER ANSTANDIGEN FRAU • 1921 • Hofer Franz • FRG
AUS DEN ERINNERUNGEN EINES FRAUENARZTES 1 • 1921 • Lamprecht Gerhard • FRG • AUS DEN GEHEIMAKTEN EINES FRAUENARZTES ○ FLIEHENDE SCHATTEN
AUS DEN ERINNERUNGEN EINES FRAUENARZTES 2 • 1921 • Pick Lupu • FRG • LUGE UND WAHRHEIT
AUS DEN GEHEIMAKTEN EINES FRAUENARZTES see **AUS DEN ERINNERUNGEN EINES FRAUENARZTES 1** • 1921
AUS DEN MEMOIREN EINER FILMSCHAUSPIELERIN • 1921 • Zelnik Friedrich • FRG
AUS DEN TIEFEN DER GROSSTADT see **JENSEITS VON GUT UND BOSE** • 1921
AUS DEN WOLKEN KOMMT DAS GLUCK see **AMPHITRYON** • 1935
AUS DER 12B, DIE • 1962 • Kurz Rudi • FRG
AUS DER FAMILIE DER PANZERECHSEN • 1974 • Wenders Wim • SHT • FRG • FROM THE FAMILY OF THE CROCODILE
AUS DER FERNE SEHE ICH DIESES LAND • 1978 • Ziewer Christian • FRG • FROM AFAR I SEE MY COUNTRY ○ I SEE THIS LAND FROM AFAR
AUS DER HEIMAT DES FREISCHUTZ • 1934 • Gutscher Rudolf, Wild Rudolf • FRG
AUS DER JUGEND KLINGT EIN LIED... • 1924 • Osten Franz • FRG
AUS DER JUGENDZEIT KLINGT EIN LIED • 1918 • Meinert Rudolf • FRG
AUS DES RHEINLANDS SCHICKSALSTAGEN • 1926 • Lackner Helene • FRG • WACHT AM RHEIN, DIE
AUS DEUTSCHLANDS SCHWEREN TAGEN see **GALGENBRAUT, DIE** • 1924
AUS EIGENER KRAFT • 1924 • Zeyn Willy • FRG
AUS EINEM DEUTSCHEN LEBEN • 1978 • Kotulla Theodor • FRG • FROM A GERMAN LIFE ○ DEATH IS MY TRADE
AUS EINER KLEINEN RESIDENZ • 1932 • Schonfelder Erich • FRG
AUS EINES MANNES MADCHENJAHREN • 1919 • Grune Karl • FRG • MAN'S GIRLHOOD
AUS ERSTER EHE • 1940 • Verhoeven Paul • FRG
AUS FRAIS DE LA PRINCESSE • 1969 • Quignon Roland-Jean • FRN
AUS LIEBE GEFEHLT • 1916 • Wolff Carl Heinz • FRG
AUS LIEBE GESUNDIGT • 1919 • Osten Franz • FRG
AUS MANGEL AN BEWEISEN • 1923 • *Lowenberg Albert (P)* • FRG
AUS TAUSEND METER HOHE • 1918 • Arnheim Valy • FRG
AUS UNSEREN TAGEN • 1950 • Bergmann Werner • GDR
AUS VERGESSENEN • 1917 • *Konstantin Leopoldine* • FRG
AUSANTE, EL • 1972 • *Cinema Jalisco* • MXC
AUSCOTT AGRIQUALITY • 1981 • Robertson Michael • DOC • ASL
AUSDATIERTES MATERIAL • 1973 • Hein Wilhelm, Hein Birgit • FRG
AUSGEKOCHTER JUNGE, EIN • 1931 • Schonfelder Erich • FRG
AUSGERECHNET 13 see **KITTY SCHWINDELT SICH INS GLUCK** • 1932
AUSGESCHNITTENE GESICHT, DAS • 1920 • Seitz Franz • FRG
AUSGESPERRTEN, DIE • 1982 • Novotny Franz • AUS • EXCLUDED, THE
AUSGESTOSSENE, DER • 1920 • Seitz Franz • FRG
AUSGESTOSSENEN, DIE • 1927 • Bergen Arthur • FRG
AUSGESTOSSENEN, DIE • 1927 • Berger Martin • FRG
AUSGESTOSSENER, EIN • 1913 • May Joe • FRG
AUSIENTE, LA • 1951 • Bracho Julio • MXC
AUSKLANG see **ALTE FRITZ 2, DER** • 1927
AUSLIEFERUNG, DIE • 1974 • von Gunten Peter • SWT • EXTRADITION, THE ○ NJETSCHAJEV 1869–1972 ○ NECHAYEV 1869–1972
AUSPICIOUS DAY see **MUHOORTHA NAAL** • 1967
AUSSCHWEIFENDE LEBEN DES MARQUIS DE SADE, DAS see **DE SADE** • 1969
AUSSENSEITER, DER • 1935 • Deppe Hans • FRG
AUSSER RAND UND BAND AM WOLFGANGSEE • 1972 • Antel Franz • FRG, AUS • CUTTING LOOSE AT THE WOLFGANGSEE
AUSSERGERICHTLICHE EINIGUNG, EINE see **SCHWEIGEN IM WALDE 2** • 1918
AUSSI LOIN QUE L'AMOUR • 1970 • Rossif Frederic • FRN
AUSSI LONGUE ABSENCE, UNE • 1961 • Colpi Henri • FRN, ITL • INVERNO TI FARA TORNARE, L' (ITL) ○ LONG ABSENCE, THE (USA)
AUSTER UND DIE PERLE, DIE • 1961 • Schnell • MTV • FRG
AUSTERIA • 1983 • Kawalerowicz Jerzy • PLN
AUSTERLITZ • 1960 • Gance Abel, Richebe Roger • FRN, ITL, YGS • NAPOLEONE AD AUSTERLITZ (ITL) ○ BATTLE OF AUSTERLITZ (USA)
AUSTERNKUR, DIE • 1919 • *Doo Loo* • FRG
AUSTERNLILLI, DIE • 1937 • Emo E. W. • FRG
AUSTERNPERLE, DIE • 1915 • Del Zopp Rudolf • FRG
AUSTERNPRINZESSIN ,DIE • 1919 • Lubitsch Ernst • FRG • OYSTER PRINCESS, THE
AUSTRALIA • 1989 • Andrien Jean-Jacques • FRN, BLG, SWD
AUSTRALIA AFTER DARK • 1975 • Lamond John • ASL
AUSTRALIA -AN EMPTY EDEN • 1924 • *Western Australian Government* • ASL
AUSTRALIA AT WAR • 1916 • *Higgins Brothers* • ASL
AUSTRALIA CALLS • 1913 • Longford Raymond • ASL
AUSTRALIA CALLS • 1923 • Longford Raymond • ASL
AUSTRALIA DAY • 1915 • ASL
AUSTRALIA DAY AT PORT ADELAIDE • 1918 • ASL
AUSTRALIA DAY PAGEANT • 1918 • *Krischock H. (Ph)* • ASL
AUSTRALIA DAZE • 1988 • DOC • ASL
AUSTRALIA FELIX • 1963 • Burstall Tim • SHT • ASL
AUSTRALIA IN ACTION • 1917 • *Commonwealth Government Films* • ASL
AUSTRALIA: LAND OF PARADOX • 1970 • Smith Nicol • DOC • USA
AUSTRALIA: LAND OF SUNSHINE • 1923 • Longford Raymond • ASL
AUSTRALIA -LAND WITH A FUTURE • 1960 • Ohlsson Terry • DOC • ASL
AUSTRALIA PREPARED • 1916 • *Australasian Film* • ASL
AUSTRALIA TODAY • 1917 • *Krischock H. (Ph)* • ASL
AUSTRALIA TODAY • 1919 • *Austral Photoplays* • ASL
AUSTRALIA TODAY • 1938-39 • Kathner Rupert • SER • ASL
AUSTRALIAN BEAUTIES IN KINEMACOLOR • 1913 • ASL
AUSTRALIAN BY MARRIAGE • 1923 • Longford Raymond • ASL
AUSTRALIAN DREAM • 1986 • McKimmie Jack • ASL
AUSTRALIAN FLEET AT GLENELG • 1914 • ASL
AUSTRALIAN HERO AND THE RED SPIDER, AN • 1913 • *Mccullagh J. S. (P)* • ASL
AUSTRALIAN MYTHOLOGIES • 1981 • Dawson Jonathan • DOC • ASL
AUSTRALIAN SURFING PHENOMENON see **SURF MOVIES** • 1981
AUSTRALIAN WINE • 1931 • Rotha Paul • DOC • UKN
AUSTRALIAN'S FIGHTING SON IN EGYPT • 1915 • ASL
AUSTRALIANS IN PALESTINE • 1919 • Hurley Frank • DOC • ASL
AUSTRALIA'S FIELDS OF GLORY see **BATTLEFIELDS OF GALLIPOLI** • 1916
AUSTRALIA'S FLAG IN AMERICA • 1912 • ASL
AUSTRALIA'S GOLD COAST • 1958 • Ezard Alex • DOC • ASL
AUSTRALIA'S LAST TRIBUTE TO THE LATE LES DARCY • 1917 • *Higgins Ernest (Ph)* • ASL
AUSTRALIA'S LONELY LANDS • 1924 • ASL
AUSTRALIA'S MILITARY COLLEGE -DUNTROON • 1915 • ASL
AUSTRALIA'S NAVY • 1915 • ASL
AUSTRALIA'S NORTH WEST • 1972 • Howes Oliver • DOC • ASL
AUSTRALIA'S OWN • 1919 • Ward J. E. • ASL
AUSTRALIA'S PERIL • 1917 • Barrett Franklyn • ASL

AUSTRALIA'S QUEEN OF BEAUTY • 1926 • *Fox Films* • ASL
AUSTRALIA'S RESPONSE TO THE EMPIRE'S CALL • 1914 • *Higgins Brothers* • ASL
AUSTRALIA'S WILD NOR' WEST & OCEAN'S TREASURE HOUSE • 1920 • *Jackson W. J. (Ph)* • ASL
AUSTRALIA'S WONDROUS WATERWAYS • 1983 • Benardos Peter • DOC • ASL
AUSTRALIJA, AUSTRALIJA • 1975 • Popov Stole • YGS
AUSTREIBUNG, DIE • 1923 • Murnau F. W. • FRG • DRIVEN FROM HOME ○ EXPULSION
AUSTRIA 1700 see **BRENN, HEXE, BRENN** • 1969
AUSWEG LOS • 1969 • Hauff Reinhard • DOC • FRG
AUTANT EN EMPORTE LE GANG • 1953 • Gast Michel, Moisy Jacques • FRN
AUTANT EN EMPORTE L'HISTOIRE • 1949 • Willemetz Jacques • FRN
AUTARCIE, L' • 1976 • Dansereau Fernand, Rossignol Yolande • DCS • CND
AUTHENTIQUE PROCES DE CARL-EMMANUEL JUNG, L' • 1967 • Hanoun Marcel • FRN
AUTHOR, THE • 1922 • St. John Al • SHT • USA
AUTHOR! AUTHOR! • 1915 • Bertram William • USA
AUTHOR! AUTHOR! • 1982 • Hiller Arthur • USA
AUTHOR IN BABYLAND • 1945 • *O'Brien Joseph/ Mead Thomas (P)* • SHT • USA
AUTHOR OF BELTRAFFIO, THE • 1974 • Scott Anthony • UKN, FRG, FRN
AUTHOR OF THESE WORDS, THE • 1980 • MacGillivray William D. • CND
AUTHORITY see **ADHIKAR** • 1938
AUTHOR'S DREAM, THE see **AND THE VILLAIN STILL PURSUED HER** • 1906
AUTO • 1974 • Boszormenyi Geza • HNG • CAR, THE
AUTO see **AUTO AUTO** • 1962
AUTO ANTICS • 1939 • Cahn Edward L. • SHT • USA
AUTO AUTO • 1962 • Lubtchansky Jean-Claude • SHT • FRN • AUTO
AUTO BOAT ON THE HUDSON • 1904 • *Bitzer Billy (Ph)* • USA
AUTO BUG, THE • 1911 • *Lubin* • USA
AUTO-BUGALOW FRACAS, THE • 1915 • Douglass James • USA
AUTO CHIESE • 1959 • Olmi Ermanno (Spv) • DOC • ITL
AUTO CLINIC, THE • 1938 • *Mintz Charles (P)* • ANS • USA
AUTO HEROINE, THE • 1908 • *Vitagraph* • USA
AUTO-PORTRAIT see **SELF-PORTRAIT** • 1961
AUTO RACE -LAKESIDE see **FIFTY MILE AUTO CONTEST** • 1912
AUTO RACES, ORMONDE, FLA. • 1905 • *Bitzer Billy (Ph)* • USA
AUTO SHOW • 1933 • *Mintz Charles (P)* • ANS • USA
AUTO-STOPPEUSES EN CHALEUR • 1979 • Bernard-Aubert Claude • FRN
AUTO SUGGESTION • 1912 • *Quirk Billy* • USA
AUTO SUR DEUX, UN • 1964 • Portugais Louis • CND
AUTO UND KEIN GELD, EIN • 1931 • Fleck Jacob, Fleck Luise • FRG, HNG
AUTOBAHN • 1979 • Halas John • ANS • UKN
AUTOBANDITEN see **"ACHTUNG! -AUTO-DIEBE!"** • 1930
AUTOBIOGRAPHY OF A FLEA, THE • 1976 • Mitchell Jim, Mitchell Artie • USA
AUTOBIOGRAPHY OF A PRINCESS • 1975 • Ivory James • UKN
AUTOBIOGRAPHY OF MISS JANE PITTMAN, THE • 1974 • Korty John • TVM • USA • FIGHT FOR FREEDOM
AUTOBUS NR.2 • 1929 • Mack Max • FRG
AUTOBUS ODJEZDZA O 6:20 • 1954 • Rybkowski Jan • PLN • BUS LEAVES AT 6:20
AUTOBUS S/MANN KAM NICHT NACH HAUSE, EIN • 1937 • Hille Heinz • FRG
AUTOBUYOGRAPHY • 1934 • Boasberg Al • SHT • USA
AUTOCRAT, THE • 1919 • Watts Tom • UKN
AUTOCRAT OF FLAPJACK JUNCTION, THE • 1913 • Baker George D. • USA
AUTOFAHRT UNTER DER ERDE, DER • 1920 • Kayser Charles Willy • FRG
AUTOGRAPH, THE • 1984 • Lilienthal Peter • FRG
AUTOGRAPH HOUND, THE • 1939 • King Jack • ANS • USA
AUTOGRAPH HUNTER, THE • 1934 • *Mintz Charles (P)* • ANS • USA
AUTOGRIMPEURS, LES • 1962 • Languepin Jean-Jacques • SHT • FRN
AUTOMABOULISME ET AUTORITE • 1899 • Melies Georges • FRN • CLOWN AND THE AUTOMOBILE, THE (USA) ○ CLOWN AND MOTOR CAR, THE
AUTOMANES, LES • 1965 • Arcady • SHT • FRN
AUTOMANIA see **CZAR KOLEK** • 1967
AUTOMANIA 2000 • 1963 • Halas John • ANS • UKN
AUTOMANIACS • 1917 • Blystone John G. • SHT • USA
AUTOMAT NA PRANI • 1967 • Pinkava Josef • CZC, FRN • WISHING MACHINE, THE (USA)
AUTOMATAS DE LA MUERTE, LOS • 1961 • Curiel Federico • MXC • NEUTRON AGAINST THE DEATH ROBOTS (USA) ○ ROBOTS OF DEATH, THE
AUTOMATE, L' • 1908 • Cohl Emile • ANS • FRN
AUTOMATE ACROBATIQUE, L' • 1911 • Cohl Emile • ANS • FRN
AUTOMATIC HOUSE, THE • 1915 • *Empress* • SHT • USA
AUTOMATIC LAUNDRY, THE • 1908 • *Lubin* • USA
AUTOMATIC MACHINE: OR, OH WHAT A SURPRISE • 1901 • *Paul R. W.* • UKN
AUTOMATIC MONKEY, THE see **BEAUX-ARTS DE JOCKO, LES** • 1909
AUTOMATIC MOTORIST, THE • 1911 • Booth W. R. • UKN • AUTOMOBILE MOTORIST, THE
AUTOMATIC MOVING CO., THE see **CHAMBRE ENSORCELEE, LA** • 1911
AUTOMATIC MOVING COMPANY, THE see **MOBILIER FIDELE, LE** • 1910
AUTOMATIC SLOT MACHINE, THE • 1901 • *Warwick Trading Co* • UKN
AUTOMATIC WEATHER PROPHET, THE • 1901 • Porter Edwin S. • USA
AUTOMATION • 1958 • Alexeieff Alexandre • FRN
AUTOMATION • 1973 • Bedrich Vaclav • CZC
AUTOMATION BLUES • 1960 • *Halas John (P)* • ANS • UKN
AUTOMATION OR ACROBAT? • 1910 • *Pathe* • USA
AUTOMNE, L' • 1972 • Hanoun Marcel • FRN
AUTOMOBILE, L' • 1971 • Giannetti Alfredo • ITL • MOTOR CAR
AUTOMOBILE, L' • 1972 • Regnier Michel • DCS • CND
AUTOMOBILE, THE • 1970 • Lenica Jan • ANS • PLN
AUTOMOBILE CHASE, THE (USA) see **RAID PARIS - MONTE CARLO EN 2 HEURES, LE** • 1905
AUTOMOBILE MOTORIST, THE see **AUTOMATIC MOTORIST, THE** • 1911
AUTOMOBILE RACES • 1905 • Barragan Salvador Toscano • MXC
AUTOMOBILE RIDE, THE • 1921 • Fleischer Dave • ANS • USA
AUTOMOBILE THIEVES, THE • 1905 • Blackton J. Stuart • USA
AUTOMOBILES STARTING A RACE see **DEPART DES AUTOMOBILES** • 1896
AUTOMOTIVE STORY, THE • 1953 • Burckhardt Rudy • SHT • USA
AUTOMOVIL GRIS, LA see **BANDA DEL AUTOMOVIL GRIS, LA** • 1919
AUTONUMMER -SEX AUF RADERN, DIE • 1972 • Axel Gabriel • DNM
AUTOPISTA A-2-7 • 1977 • Nunes Jose Maria • SPN
AUTOPORTRAIT • 1969 • Leconte Patrice • FRN
AUTOPORTRAIT D'UN PORNOGRAPHE • 1972 • Swaim Bob • SHT • FRN
AUTOPORTRET • 1988 • Sopterran Marius • RMN
AUTOPSIA • 1973 • Logar Juan • SPN
AUTOPSIA DE UN CRIMINAL • 1962 • Blasco Ricardo • SPN • AUTOPSY OF A CRIMINAL (USA)
AUTOPSIA DE UN FANTASMA • 1966 • Rodriguez Ismael • MXC • AUTOPSY ON A GHOST
AUTOPSIE D'UN MONSTRE see **A CHACUN SON ENFER** • 1977
AUTOPSIE D'UNE EXCLUSION • 1975-77 • Moreau Michel • DCS • CND
AUTOPSY • 1978 • *Farmer Mimsy* • ITL
AUTOPSY see **SEKCJA ZWLOK** • 1973
AUTOPSY OF A CRIMINAL (USA) see **AUTOPSIA DE UN CRIMINAL** • 1962
AUTOPSY ON A GHOST see **AUTOPSIA DE UN FANTASMA** • 1966
AUTORENNEN • 1964 • Kristl Vlado • FRG
AUTORITRATTO • 1979 • Cavedon Giorgio • ITL
AUTOROUTE • Engler Robi • ANS • SWT
AUTOS VOLAGES, LES • 1947 • Martin Marcel • SHT • FRN
AUTOSERIGRAPHIES • 1973 • Plamondon Leo • DCS • CND
AUTOSTOP • 1977 • Festa Campanile Pasquale • ITL • AUTOSTOP ROSSO SANGUE ○ DEATH DRIVE ○ HITCH-HIKE
AUTOSTOP ROSSO SANGUE see **AUTOSTOP** • 1977
AUTOSTRADA • 1969 • Kristo Arild • NRW
AUTOUR DE LA PERCEPTION • 1968 • Hebert Pierre • ANS • CND • AROUND PERCEPTION
AUTOUR DE L'ARGENT • 1928 • Dreville Jean • SHT • FRN
AUTOUR DE RENE MAGRITTE • 1969 • Deroisy Lucien • BLG
AUTOUR DU MYSTERE • 1920 • Desfontaines Henri • FRN
AUTOUR D'UN BERCEAU • 1925 • Monca Georges, Keroul Maurice • FRN
AUTOUR D'UN RECIF • 1949 • Cousteau Jacques • SHT • FRN
AUTOUR D'UNE BAGUE • 1915 • Ravel Gaston • FRN
AUTOUR D'UNE CABINE • 1894 • Reynaud Emile • FRN
AUTOUR D'UNE ENQUETE • 1931 • Chomette Henri, Siodmak Robert • FRN
AUTOUR D'UNE TROMPETTE • 1952 • Neurisse Pierre • DCS • FRN
AUTRE, L' • 1917 • Feuillade Louis • FRN
AUTRE, L' • 1989 • Giraudeau Bernard • FRN
AUTRE AILE, L' • 1924 • Andreani Henri • FRN
AUTRE CRISTOBAL, L' see **OTRO CRISTOBAL, EL** • 1962
AUTRE FEMME, L' • 1963 • Villiers Francois • FRN, ITL, SPN
AUTRE FRANCE, L' • 1975 • Ghalem Ali • ALG
AUTRE HISTOIRE DES PAYS D'EN HAUT, UNE • 1977 • Cornellier Robert • SHT • CND
AUTRE HOMME, UNE AUTRE CHANCE, UN (FRN) see **ANOTHER MAN, ANOTHER CHANCE** • 1977
AUTRE MONDE, L' see **KUESTET-SHESKAMIT** • 1971-77
AUTRE MONDE, UN • 1958 • Vandercam Serge, Kessels Henri • BLG
AUTRE MONDE, UN • 1971 • Baulez Michel • FRN
AUTRE NUIT, L' • 1988 • Limosin Jean-Pierre • FRN
AUTRE PAYS, UN see **DRYLANDERS** • 1963
AUTRE RIVE, L' see **FAR SHORE, THE** • 1976
AUTRE VISAGE, L' • 1916 • Burguet Charles • FRN
AUTRES, LES • 1973 • Santiago Hugo • FRN
AUTRESVILLE D'ART • 1969 • de Gastyne Marco • SHT • FRN
AUTRICHIENNE, L' • 1989 • Granier-Deferre Pierre • FRN
AUTUMN • Khrzhanovsky Andrei • ANM • USS
AUTUMN • 1916 • Lund O. A. C. • USA
AUTUMN • 1930 • Iwerks Ub • ANS • USA
AUTUMN • 1974 • Smirnov Andrei • USS
AUTUMN see **OSEN** • 1940
AUTUMN see **CH'IU** • 1954
AUTUMN see **TOAMNA** • 1961
AUTUMN AFTERNOON, AN see **SAMMA NO AJI** • 1962
AUTUMN CHILD see **REFLECTION OF FEAR, A** • 1973
AUTUMN CROCUS • 1934 • Dean Basil • UKN
AUTUMN DAY, AN see **JESIENNY DZIEN** • 1969
AUTUMN FEVER see **BLONDE FEVER** • 1944
AUTUMN FIRE • 1930 • Weinberg Herman G. • SHT • USA
AUTUMN FIRES • 1977 • Barclay Barry • DOC • NZL
AUTUMN IN BADACSONY see **OSZ BADACSONYBAN** • 1954
AUTUMN IN ROME • 1954 • Menzies William Cameron • SHT • USA
AUTUMN INTERLUDE see **KAZE TACHINU** • 1955
AUTUMN IS BEGINNING see **AKI TACHINU** • 1960
AUTUMN LEAVES • 1956 • Aldrich Robert • USA
AUTUMN LOVE • 1913 • *Warfield Irene* • USA
AUTUMN MARATHON see **OSENNY MARAFON** • 1979
AUTUMN MILK (UKN) see **HERBSTMILCH** • 1988
AUTUMN OF HOPE • 1962 • Lisakovitch Viktor • DOC • USS
AUTUMN OF PRIDE • 1921 • Kellino W. P. • UKN
AUTUMN OF THE KOHAYAGAWA FAMILY, THE see **KOHAYAGAWA-KE NO AKI** • 1961
AUTUMN ROSES • 1912 • Martinek H. O. • UKN
AUTUMN SONATA (USA) see **HERBSTSONATE** • 1978
AUTUMN SPECTRUM • 1958 • Hirsch Hy • SHT • NTH, FRN • AUTUMNUM SPECTRUM
AUTUMN STAR see **ISTEN OSZI CSILLAGA** • 1962
AUTUMN WEDDINGS see **OSYENNIYE SVADBY** • 1968
AUTUMN'S TALE, AN see **QIUTIANDE TONGHUA** • 1987
AUTUMNUM SPECTRUM see **AUTUMN SPECTRUM** • 1958
AUVERGNAT ET L'AUTOBUS, L' • 1968 • Lefranc Guy • FRN
AUVERGNE, L' • 1925 • Gremillon Jean • SHT • FRN
AUX CONFINS D'UNE VILLE • 1952 • Loew Jacques • SHT • FRN
AUX DEUX COLOMBES • 1949 • Guitry Sacha • FRN
AUX FRAIS DE LA PRINCESSE • Leaud Pierre • FRN
AUX FRONTIERES DE L'HOMME • 1953 • Vedres Nicole, Rostand Jean • SHT • FRN • BORDER OF LIFE, THE
AUX JARDINS DE MURCIE • 1923 • Mercanton Louis, Hervil Rene • FRN
AUX JARDINS DE MURCIE • 1935 • Joly Max, Gras Marcel • FRN, SPN
AUX LIONS LES CHRETIENS • 1911 • Feuillade Louis • FRN
AUX PAYS DES GRANDS CAUSSES • 1951 • Mitry Jean • SHT • FRN
AUX PORTES DE LA VILLE see **AUX PORTES DE PARIS** • 1934
AUX PORTES DE PARIS • 1934 • Barrois Charles, de Baroncelli Jacques (U/c) • FRN • AUX PORTES DE LA VILLE
AUX PURS TOUT EST PUR • 1968 • Boisrond Michel • FRN
AUX QUATRE COINS • 1950 • Rivette Jacques • SHT • FRN
AUX URNES, CITOYENS! • 1932 • Hemard Jean • FRN
AUX URNES, CITOYENS.. • 1971 • Bobrowski Edouard • DOC • FRN
AUX YEUX DU SORT ET DES HUMAINS see **FORTUNE AND MEN'S EYES** • 1971
AUX YEUX DU SOUVENIRS • 1948 • Delannoy Jean • FRN • SOUVENIR (USA)
AV HJARTANS LUST • 1960 • Husberg Rolf • SWD • TO ONE'S HEART'S CONTENT
AV ZAMANI • 1987 • Kiral Erden • TRK • HUNTING TIME
AVA AND GABRIEL • 1990 • de Rooy Felix • NTH
AVAETE, A SEED OF VENGEANCE see **AVAETE, A SEMENTE DA VINGANCA** • 1986
AVAETE, A SEMENTE DA VINGANCA • 1986 • Viano Zelito • BRZ • AVAETE, A SEED OF VENGEANCE
AVAILING PRAYER, THE • 1914 • Crisp Donald • USA
AVAL • 1967 • Azeez • IND • SHE
AVALANCHE • 1928 • Brower Otto • USA
AVALANCHE • 1946 • Allen Irving • USA
AVALANCHE • 1950 • Segard Raymond • FRN
AVALANCHE • 1975 • Goode Frederic • UKN
AVALANCHE • 1978 • Allen Corey • USA
AVALANCHE see **HELL'S HOLE** • 1923
AVALANCHE see **LAWINE, DIE** • 1923
AVALANCHE see **STURME UBER DEM MONTBLANC** • 1930
AVALANCHE see **NADARE** • 1937
AVALANCHE see **NADARE** • 1952
AVALANCHE see **NADARE** • 1956
AVALANCHE, THE • 1915 • Davis Will S. • USA
AVALANCHE, THE • 1919 • Fitzmaurice George • USA
AVALANCHE, THE • 1981 • Piskov Hristo, Aktasheva Irina • BUL
AVALANCHE EXPRESS • 1979 • Robson Mark, Hellman Monte (U/c) • USA
AVALANCHES • 1951 • Vilardebo Carlos • SHT • FRN
AVALE-MOTS, L' • 1970 • Lavoie Richard • SHT • CND
AVALON • 1990 • Levinson Barry • USA
AVALON AWAKENING, THE • 1988 • Weeks Stephen • UKN
AVANT LE DELUGE • 1954 • Cayatte Andre • FRN, ITL • PRIMO DEL DILUVIO (ITL)
AVANTA KEMAL TORPIDO YILMAZA KARSI • 1968 • Duru Ugur, Dogan Suha • TRK • AVANTA KEMAL VS. TORPIDO YILMAZ
AVANTA KEMAL VS. TORPIDO YILMAZ see **AVANTA KEMAL TORPIDO YILMAZA KARSI** • 1968
AVANTAZH • 1978 • Dyulgerov Georgi • BUL • ADVANTAGE
AVANTI • 1972 • Wilder Billy • USA
AVANTI A LUI see **DAVANTI A LUI TREMAVA TUTTA ROMA** • 1946
AVANTI C'E POSTO.. • 1942 • Bonnard Mario • ITL
AVANTI POPOLO • 1987 • Bukaee Rafi • ISR
AVANTURE BORIVOJA SURDILOVICA • 1981 • YGS • ADVENTURES OF BORIVOJE SURDILOVIC
AVANZI DI GALERA • 1954 • Cottafavi Vittorio • ITL
AVARE, L' • 1908 • Melies Georges • FRN • MISER, THE (USA)
AVARE, L' • 1910 • Calmettes Andre • FRN
AVARE, L' • 1960 • Blue James, Hermantier R. • FRN
AVARE, L' • 1979 • de Funes Louis, Girault Jean • FRN
AVAREHAYE TEHRAN • 1968 • Bahadori Azizolah • IRN • BEGGARS OF TEHRAN, THE
AVARICE • 1915 • *Payne Edna* • USA
AVARICE • 1917 • Peacocke Leslie T. • SHT • USA
AVARICE see **AVARIZZIA, L'** • 1915
AVARICE see **YOKU** • 1958
AVARICE (UKN) see **SISTERS OF EVE** • 1928
AVARICIOUS MONK, THE • 1912 • Buckland Warwick? • UKN
AVARIZZIA, L' • 1915 • Serena Gustavo • ITL • AVARICE
AVARO, L' • 1990 • Cervi Tonino • ITL, SPN, FRN • MISER, THE
AVARUUSRAKETILLA RAKKAUTEEN see **...UND IMMER RUFT DAS HERZ** • 1958
AVATAR • 1915 • Gallone Carmine • ITL
AVATAR see **AWATAR** • 1965
AVATAR BOTANIQUE DE MLLE FLORA, L' • 1965 • Barbillon Jeanne • SHT • FRN
AVDOTYA PAVLOVNA • 1967 • Muratov Alexander • USS
AVE CAESAR! • 1919 • Korda Alexander • HNG
AVE DA ARRIBACAO • 1943 • Miranda Armando • PRT
AVE DE PASO • 1945 • Gorostiza Celestino • MXC
AVE LUNA • 1973 • Schulz Bob • MTV • CND
AVE MARIA • 1918 • Noy Wilfred • UKN
AVE MARIA • 1928 • Parkinson H. B., Edwards J. Steven • UKN

AVE MARIA • 1936 • Riemann Johannes • FRG
AVE MARIA • 1953 • Braun Alfred • FRG
AVE MARIA • 1984 • Richard Jacques • FRN
AVE MARIA DE SCHUBERT • 1936 • Ophuls Max • SHT • FRN
AVE MARIA (GOUNOD) • 1906 • Gilbert Arthur • UKN
AVE SIN NIDO • 1943 • Urueta Chano • MXC
AVE SIN RUMBO • 1937 • O'Quigley Roberto • MXC • WANDERING BIRD (USA)
AVE VITA • 1971 • Gricaevicius Almantis • USS
AVEC ANDRE GIDE • 1951 • Allegret Marc • FRN • ANDRE GIDE
AVEC-AVEC see **DUFFY** • 1968
AVEC CLAUDE MONET • 1965 • Delouche Dominique • SHT • FRN
AVEC DES SI.. see **AMOUR AVEC DES SI..., L'** • 1963
AVEC DIRK BOUTS see **DIRK BOUTS** • 1976
AVEC LA PEAU DES AUTRES • 1966 • Deray Jacques • FRN, ITL • SCIARADA PER QUATTRO SPIE (ITL) ○ TO SKIN A SPY (UKN)
AVEC L'ASSURANCE • 1932 • Capellani Roger • FRN
AVEC LE 22e EN ALLAMAGNE • 1954-55 • Devlin Bernard • DCS • CND
AVEC LE SANG DES AUTRES • 1974 • Muel Bruno • DOC • FRN
AVEC LE SCEAU DU CANADA see **STAMP OF APPROVAL** • 1951
AVEC LE SOURIRE • 1936 • Tourneur Maurice • FRN • WITH A SMILE
AVEC LES CHEVAUX DE BOIS see **PARADIS DES VOLEURS, LE** • 1939
AVEC LES GENS DU VOYAGE • 1953 • de Gastyne Marco • SHT • FRN
AVEC LES PILOTES DE PORTE-AVIONS • 1953 • Galey • SHT • FRN
AVEC RIYOKAN • 1968 • Yamamoto Shinya • JPN • RENDEZVOUS HOTEL, A
AVEC TAMBOURS ET TROMPETTES • 1967 • Carriere Marcel • DCS • CND
AVEC TOI POUR TOUJOURS see **DA'IMAN MA'AK** • 1953
AVEDIS AHARIAN, LE DERNIER PRESIDENT ARMENIEN • 1947-51 • Verneuil Henri • SHT • FRN
AVEIRO • 1952 • Queiroga Perdigao • SHT • PRT
AVENGED • 1910 • *Thanhouser* • USA
AVENGED • 1914 • *Rex* • USA
AVENGED BY A FISH • 1915 • *Bergman Henry* • USA
AVENGED BY LIONS • 1916 • *Gibson Margaret* • SHT • USA
AVENGED OR THE TWO SISTERS • 1908 • *Vitagraph* • USA
AVENGER, THE • 1916 • Kent Leon D. • SHT • USA
AVENGER, THE • 1924 • Seeling Charles R. • USA
AVENGER, THE • 1931 • Neill R. William • USA
AVENGER, THE • 1933 • Marin Edwin L. • USA
AVENGER, THE • 1938 • Harwood A. R. • ASL
AVENGER, THE • 1973 • Chan-Ho • HKG
AVENGER, THE • 1987 • Barwood Nick • USA
AVENGER, THE • 1987 • Blyth David • USA • NASTY HABITS
AVENGER, THE see **HAMNAREN** • 1915
AVENGER, THE see **MUNTAKEM, EL** • 1947
AVENGER, THE see **MSTITEL** • 1959
AVENGER, THE see **PENDEKAR SAKTI** • 1971
AVENGER, THE (UKN) see **TEXAS ADDIO** • 1966
AVENGER, THE (USA) see **RACHER, DIE** • 1960
AVENGER, THE (USA) see **LEGGENDA DI ENEA, LA** • 1962
AVENGER OF THE SEVEN SEAS (USA) see **GIUSTIZIERE DEI MARE, IL** • 1962
AVENGER OF VENICE (USA) see **PONTE DEI SOSPIRI, IL** • 1964
AVENGERS, THE • 1950 • Auer John H. • USA, ARG
AVENGERS, THE (USA) see **DAY WILL DAWN, THE** • 1942
AVENGERS OF THE REEF • 1973 • McCullough Chris • ASL
AVENGING, THE • 1981 • Dayton Lyman D. • USA
AVENGING ANGEL • 1985 • O'Neil Robert Vincent • USA
AVENGING ANGELS see **MESSENGER OF DEATH** • 1988
AVENGING ARROW, THE • 1921 • Van Dyke W. S., Bowman William J. • SRL • USA
AVENGING BILL • 1915 • Hotaling Arthur D. • USA
AVENGING BOXER • *Chen Peter* • HKG • FEARLESS YOUNG BOXER, THE
AVENGING CONSCIENCE OR THOU SHALT NOT KILL, THE • 1914 • Griffith D. W. • USA
AVENGING DENTIST • 1915 • *Ritchie Billie* • USA
AVENGING EAGLE, THE • Sun Chung • HKG
AVENGING FORCE • 1986 • Firstenberg Sam • USA • NIGHT HUNTER
AVENGING HAND, THE • 1936 • Hanbury Victor • UKN
AVENGING HAND, THE see **WRAITH OF THE TOMB, THE** • 1915
AVENGING RIDER, THE • 1928 • Fox Wallace • USA • PARTNERS (UKN)
AVENGING RIDER, THE • 1943 • Nelson Sam • USA
AVENGING SEA, THE • 1915 • Morgan George • USA
AVENGING SHADOW, THE • 1928 • Taylor Ray • USA
AVENGING SHOT, THE • 1916 • *Sisson Vera* • SHT • USA
AVENGING SPECTER, THE see **SPETTRO VENDICATORE** • 1914
AVENGING STRANGER, THE (UKN) see **GOD'S COUNTRY AND THE MAN** • 1937
AVENGING TRAIL, THE • 1918 • Ford Francis • USA
AVENGING TRAIL, THE • 1920 • *Ridgeway Fritzi* • SHT • USA
AVENGING WATERS • 1936 • Bennet Spencer Gordon • USA
AVENIDA ROMA, 66 • 1956 • Xiol Juan • SPN
AVENIR DE JEREMY, L' • Boiseau Arnold • FRN
AVENIR DE LA MAIN-D'OEUVRE, L' • 1965-66 • Garceau Raymond • DCS • CND
AVENIR D'EMILIE, L' • 1984 • Sanders Helma • FRN, FRG • FUTURE OF EMILY, THE
AVENIR DEVOILE PAR LES LIGNES DES PIEDS, L' • 1917 • Cohl Emile • ANS • FRN
AVENTURA • 1942 • Mihura Jeronimo • SPN
AVENTURA AL CENTRO DE LA TIERRA • 1964 • Crevenna Alfredo B. • MXC • ADVENTURE AT THE CENTRE OF THE EARTH
AVENTURA CALCULADA, A • 1971 • Lopes Fernando • SHT • PRT
AVENTURA DEL CINE, UNA • 1927 • de Orduna Juan • SPN
AVENTURA EN EL PALACIO VIEJO • 1967 • Torres Manuel • SPN
AVENTURA EN LA NOCHE, UNA • 1947 • Aguilar Rolando • MXC • ADVENTURE IN THE NIGHT, AN
AVENTURA EN LAS ISLAS CIES • 1966 • Delgado Luis Maria • SPN
AVENTURA EN PUERTO RICO • 1974 • *Aguila* • MXC
AVENTURA EN RIO • 1952 • Gout Alberto • MXC
AVENTURA PARA DOS (SPN) see **SPANISH AFFAIR** • 1958
AVENTURA PELIGROSA, UNA • 1940 • Peon Ramon • MXC • DANGEROUS ADVENTURE, THE (USA)
AVENTURAS DE CARLOS LACROIX, LAS • 1958 • Gomez Urquiza Zacarias • MXC • CRIMEN PERFECTO, EL
AVENTURAS DE CHUCHO EL ROTO • 1959 • Munoz Manuel • MXC
AVENTURAS DE CUCURUCHITO Y PINOCHO • 1942 • Vejar Carlos Jr. • SRL • MXC • ADVENTURES OF LITTLE CRICKET AND PINOCCHIO
AVENTURAS DE DON JUAN DE MAIRENA • 1947 • Buchs Jose • SPN
AVENTURAS DE JOSELITO EN AMERICA see **AVENTURAS DE JOSELITO Y PULGARCITO** • 1959
AVENTURAS DE JOSELITO Y PULGARCITO • 1959 • Cardona Rene, del Amo Antonio • MXC, SPN • AVENTURAS DE JOSELITO EN AMERICA ○ ADVENTURES OF LITTLE JOE AND TOM THUMB
AVENTURAS DE JUAN LUCAS • 1949 • Gil Rafael • SPN
AVENTURAS DE JUAN QUIN QUIN, LAS • 1967 • Espinosa Julio Garcia • CUB • ADVENTURES OF JUAN QUIN QUIN, THE
AVENTURAS DE LA PANDILLA • 1959 • Porter Julio • MXC
AVENTURAS DE MAR Y SELVA see **CHANOC** • 1966
AVENTURAS DE PITO PEREZ, LAS • 1955 • Bustillo Oro Juan • MXC
AVENTURAS DE ROBINSON CRUSOE, LAS • 1952 • Bunuel Luis • MXC, USA • ADVENTURES OF ROBINSON CRUSOE, THE ○ ROBINSON CRUSOE
AVENTURAS DE TAXI-KEY • 1959 • Fortuny Juan • SPN
AVENTURAS DE UM PARAIBA • 1982 • Altberg Marcos • BRZ • ADVENTURES OF A PARAIBA
AVENTURAS DE UN CABALLO BLANCO • 1973 • *Churubusco Azteca* • MXC
AVENTURAS DE UN NUEVO RICO • 1950 • Aguilar Rolando • MXC
AVENTURAS DEL BARBERO DE SEVILLA • 1954 • Vajda Ladislao • SPN, FRN • ADVENTURER OF SEVILLE, THE (USA) ○ AVENTURIER DE SEVILLE, L'(FRN)
AVENTURAS DEL GUARDIAN, LAS see **YANKO EL GUARDIAN DE LA SELVA** • 1962
AVENTURAS DEL MARQUES DE BRADOMIN see **SONATAS** • 1959
AVENTURAS DEL OESTE • 1964 • Romero-Marchent Joaquin Luis • SPN, ITL, FRG • SETTE ORA DI FUOCO (ITL) ○ SEVEN HOURS OF GUNFIRE
AVENTURAS DEL VIZCONDE, LAS see **VICOMTE REGLE SES COMPTES, LE** • 1967
AVENTURAS DO QUIM E DO MANECAS • 1915 • de Albuquerque Ernesto • SHT • PRT
AVENTURAS DO TENOR ROMAO • 1920 • de Albuquerque Ernesto • PRT
AVENTURE A PARIS • 1936 • Allegret Marc • FRN
AVENTURE A PIGALLE see **MENACE DE MORT** • 1949
AVENTURE AUX SERENADES, L' • 1935 • Masson Jean • SHT • FRN
AVENTURE C'EST L'AVENTURE, L' • 1972 • Lelouch Claude • FRN, ITL • AVVENTURA E L'AVVENTURA, L' (ITL) ○ MONEY, MONEY, MONEY (USA)
AVENTURE COMMENCE DEMAIN, L' • 1947 • Pottier Richard • FRN
AVENTURE DE BILLY THE KID, UNE • 1971 • Mollet Luc • FRN • GIRL IS A GUN, A
AVENTURE DE BOUT DE ZAN, UNE • 1913 • Feuillade Louis • FRN
AVENTURE DE CABASSOU, L' • 1945 • Grangier Gilles • FRN • CABASSOU
AVENTURE DE CURIOSITE, UNE • 1979 • Lavoie Richard • CND
AVENTURE DE GUY, L' • 1936 • Resnais Alain • SHT • FRN
AVENTURE DE M. MOUTONNET, L' see **MOUTONNET** • 1936
AVENTURE DE M. SMITH, L' • 1913-18 • Durand Jean • FRN
AVENTURE DE VAN DYCK, UNE • 1911 • Bourgeois Gerard • FRN
AVENTURE DE VIDOCQ, UN see **CAVALIER DE CROIX-MORT, LE** • 1947
AVENTURE DES MILLION, L' • 1916 • Feuillade Louis • FRN
AVENTURE DU JAZZ, L' • 1970 • Pannasie Louis, Pannasie Claudine • FRN
AVENTURE DU PERE NOEL, L' • 1957 • Image Jean • ANS • FRN • ADVENTURE OF FATHER CHRISTMAS, THE
AVENTURE EN FRANCE, L' • 1962 • N'Gassa Jean-Paul • CMR
AVENTURE EST AU COIN DE LA RUE, L' • 1943 • Daniel-Norman Jacques • FRN
AVENTURE ET SES TERRA-NUEVAS, L' • 1953 • Renaud • SHT • FRN
AVENTURE HAWAIENNE • 1936 • Leboursier Raymond • FRN
AVENTURE MALGACHE • 1944 • Hitchcock Alfred • DCS • UKN • MALAGACHE ADVENTURE, THE
AVENTURE SAUVAGE, L' see **TRAP, THE** • 1966
AVENTURE SUR LA COTE see **SECRET DU FLORIDA, LE** • 1946
AVENTURERA • 1949 • Gout Alberto • MXC
AVENTURERA • 1989 • de la Barra Pablo • VNZ • ADVENTUROUS WOMAN
AVENTURERO, EL • 1957 • Gascon Jose, Hume Kenneth • SPN
AVENTURERO DE GUAYNAS, EL • 1967 • Romero-Marchent Joaquin Luis • SPN
AVENTUREROS, LOS • 1954 • Mendez Fernando • MXC
AVENTURES DANS LA CAPITALE see **PROTEVOUSSIANIKES PERIPETIES** • 1956
AVENTURES D'ARLEQUIN, LES • Image Jean • ANM • FRN
AVENTURES D'ARSENE LUPIN, LES • 1956 • Becker Jacques • FRN, ITL • AVVENTURE DI ARSENIO LUPIN, LE (ITL) ○ ADVENTURES OF ARSENE LUPIN
AVENTURES DE BABAR, LES • de Brunhoff Laurent • ANM • FRN
AVENTURES DE BARON DE CRAC, LES • 1913 • Cohl Emile • ANS • FRN • BARON MUNCHAUSEN (USA) ○ BARON DE CRAC, LE ○ WONDERFUL ADVENTURES OF HERR MUNCHHAUSEN, THE ○ MONSIEUR DE CRAC
AVENTURES DE CASANOVA, LES • 1946 • Boyer Jean • FRN • LOVES OF CASANOVA (USA)
AVENTURES DE CHOUCHOU, LES see **MUGHAMARAT SHUSHU** • 1966
AVENTURES DE CLEMENTINE, LES • 1916 • Cohl Emile (c/d) • ANS • FRN
AVENTURES DE DON QUICHOTTE • 1908 • Melies Georges • FRN • INCIDENT FROM DON QUIXOTE ○ DON QUICHOTTE
AVENTURES DE GIL BLAS DE SANTILLANE, LES • 1955 • Jolivet Rene • FRN, SPN • ADVENTURES OF GIL BLAS (USA) ○ GIL BLAS DE SANTILLANE
AVENTURES DE GUIDON FUTE, LES • 1979 • Durand Jean-Marie • FRN
AVENTURES DE GUILLAUME TELL • 1898 • Melies Georges • FRN • GUILLAUME TELL ET LE CLOWN ○ ADVENTURES OF WILLIAM TELL
AVENTURES DE HOLLY AND WOOD, LES see **ROSE ET LE BLANC, LE** • 1979
AVENTURES DE JOE, LES • 1960 • Image Jean • ANS • FRN
AVENTURES DE LA FAMILLE CARRE, LES • 1964 • Halas John • ASS • UKN
AVENTURES DE LA FAMILLE COEUR DE BOIS, LES see **EXTRAORDINAIRES EXERCICES DE LA FAMILLE COEUR-DE-BUIS, LES** • 1912
AVENTURES DE LAGARDERE, LES • 1911 • Heuze Andre • FRN
AVENTURES DE LAGARDERE, LES see **LAGARDERE** • 1968
AVENTURES DE MALTRACE • 1913 • Cohl Emile • ANS • FRN
AVENTURES DE PINOCCHIO, LES (FRN) see **AVVENTURE DI PINOCCHIO, LE** • 1972
AVENTURES DE RABBI JACOB, LES • 1973 • Oury Gerard • FRN, ITL • FOLLI AVVENTURE DI RABBI JACOB, LE (ITL) ○ ADVENTURES OF RABBI JACOB, THE ○ MAD ADVENTURES OF RABBI JACOB, THE (USA)
AVENTURES DE REINETTE ET MIRABELLE, LES see **QUATRE AVENTURES DE REINETTE ET MIRABELLE** • 1987
AVENTURES DE ROBERT MACAIRE, LES • 1925 • Epstein Jean • FRN • ADVENTURES OF ROBERT MACAIRE, THE (USA)
AVENTURES DE ROBINSON CRUSOE, LES • 1902 • Melies Georges • FRN • ROBINSON CRUSOE
AVENTURES DE ROBINSON CRUSOE, LES • 1923 • Leprieur Gaston • FRN
AVENTURES DE SALAVIN, LES • 1963 • Granier-Deferre Pierre • FRN • CONFESSION DE MINUIT, LA
AVENTURES DE SAMBA GANA, LES • 1962 • Friedman Yona • ANM • FRN
AVENTURES DE SATURNIN FARADOLE, LES • 1915 • Fabre Marcel • FRN
AVENTURES DE TI-KEN, LES • 1960 • Laliberte Roger • CND
AVENTURES DE TILL L'ESPIEGLE, LES • 1956 • Philipe Gerard, Ivens Joris • FRN, FRG • BOLD ADVENTURE, THE (USA) ○ THYL L'ESPIEGLE ○ TILL EULENSPIEGEL (FRG) ○ ADVENTURES OF TILL EULENSPIEGEL, THE ○ ABENTEUER DES TIL ULENSPIEGEL, DIE
AVENTURES DE TROIS PEAUX-ROUGES, LES • 1913 • Durand Jean • FRN
AVENTURES DES HEROS DE LA TOUR DE NESLE • 1947 • Dubout Albert • ANS • FRN • ADVENTURES OF THE HEROES OF THE NESLE TOWER
AVENTURES DES PIED NICKELES, LES • 1917 • Cohl Emile, Rabier Benjamin • ASS • FRN • ADVENTURES OF THE NICKEL-PLATED FEET, THE
AVENTURES DES PIED NICKELES, LES • 1947 • Aboulker Marcel • FRN • PIEDS NICKELES, LES
AVENTURES DU CHEVALIER DE FAUBLAS, LES • 1913 • Pouctal Henri • FRN
AVENTURES DU ROI PAUSOLE, LES • 1933 • Granowsky Alexis • FRN
AVENTURES DU VICOMTE, LES see **VICOMTE REGLE SES COMPTES, LE** • 1967
AVENTURES D'UN BOUT DE PAPIER, LES see **AVENTURES EXTRAORDINAIRES D'UN BOUT DE PAPIER** • 1909
AVENTURES D'UN COW-BOY A PARIS • 1909 • Durand Jean • FRN
AVENTURES D'UN PHOTOGRAPHE, LES • 1960 • Latouche Michel • SHT • FRN
AVENTURES D'UN VOYAGEUR TROP PRESSE, LES • 1902 • Blache Alice • FRN
AVENTURES D'UNE JEUNE VEUVE, LES • 1974 • Fournier Roger • CND
AVENTURES ET LES AMOURS DE CASANOVA, LES (FRN) see **AVVENTURE DI GIACOMO CASANOVA, LE** • 1954
AVENTURES EXTRAORDINAIRES DE CERVANTES, LES (FRN) see **AVVENTURE E GLI AMORI DI MIGUEL CERVANTES, LE** • 1967
AVENTURES EXTRAORDINAIRES DE JULES VERNE • 1952 • Danot Serge • FRN • EXTRAORDINARY ADVENTURES OF JULES VERNE, THE
AVENTURES EXTRAORDINAIRES D'UN BOUT DE PAPIER • 1909 • Cohl Emile • ANS • FRN • AVENTURES D'UN BOUT DE PAPIER, LES
AVENTURIER, L' • 1913 • Bourgeois Gerard • FRN
AVENTURIER, L' • 1923 • Mariaud Maurice • FRN
AVENTURIER, L' • 1934 • L'Herbier Marcel • FRN
AVENTURIER, UN • 1921 • Maudru Charles • FRN
AVENTURIER DE SEVILLE, L'(FRN) see **AVENTURAS DEL BARBERO DE SEVILLA** • 1954
AVENTURIERE, L' • 1912 • Feuillade Louis • FRN
AVENTURIERE DAME DE COMPAGNIE, L' • 1911 • Feuillade Louis • FRN

AVENTURIERE DES CHAMPS-ELYSEES, L' • 1956 • Blanc Roger • FRN • ADVENTURESS OF THE CHAMPS-ELYSEES, THE
AVENTURIERE DU TCHAD, L' • 1953 • Rozier Willy • FRN
AVENTURIERS, LES • 1966 • Enrico Robert • FRN, ITL • TRE AVVENTURIERI, I (ITL) ○ LAST ADVENTURE, THE (UKN)
AVENTURIERS DE L'AIR, LES • 1950 • Jayet Rene • FRN
AVENTURIERS DU MEKONG, LES • 1957 • Bastia Jean • FRN
AVENTURIERS DU TIMBRE PERDU see **TOMMY TRICKER AND THE STAMP TRAVELLER** • 1988
AVENTYR I HAJARNAS HAV see **EXPEDITION RODA HAVET** • 1957
AVENTYR I PYJAMAS • 1935 • Widestedt Ragnar • SWD, DNM
AVENTYR PA HOTELL • 1934 • Rodin Gosta • SWD • HOTEL ADVENTURE
AVENTYR PA STJARNEHOV, ETT see **BROLLOPSNATT PA STJARNEHOV, EN** • 1934
AVENTYRARE, EN • 1942 • Olsson Gunnar • SWD • ADVENTURER
AVENTYRET • 1936 • Branner Per-Axel • SWD • ADVENTURE
AVENTYRET see **HANS BROLLOPSNATT** • 1916
AVENUE O see **MIXED BLOOD** • 1984
AVENUE DE L'OPERA • 1900 • Blache Alice • FRN
AVENUE DES CHAMPS-ELYSEES ET LE PETIT PALAIS, L' • 1900 • Melies Georges • FRN
AVERAGE HUSBAND • 1930 • Sennett Mack • SHT • USA
AVERAGE MAN, AN see **BORGHESE PICCOLO PICCOLO, UN** • 1977
AVERAGE WOMAN, THE • 1924 • Cabanne W. Christy • USA
AVERRE VENT'ANNI • 1978 • Di Leo Fernando • ITL • TO BE TWENTY
AVERTED STEP, THE • 1912 • *Republic* • USA
AVERY'S DREAM • 1911 • *Bison* • USA
AVES COMEN LOS LUNES, LAS • 1978 • San Miguel Santiago • VNZ, SPN • BIRDS EAT ON MONDAYS, THE
AVEU, L' • 1970 • Costa-Gavras • FRN, ITL • CONFESSIONE, LA (ITL) ○ CONFESSION, THE
AVEUGLE, L' • 1897 • Blache Alice • FRN
AVEUGLE, L' • 1899-00 • Blache Alice • FRN
AVEUGLE DE JERUSALEM, L' • 1909 • Feuillade Louis • FRN
AVEUGLES, LES • 1969 • Merbah Lamine • DCS • ALG
AVEUX D'UN MARI, LES see **I'TIRAFATU ZAWJ** • 1964
AVEUX LES PLUS DOUX, LES • 1970 • Molinaro Edouard • FRN, ITL • SWEET TORTURE ○ RICATTO DI UN COMMISSARIO DI POLIZIA A UN GIOVANE INDIZIAT DI REATO (ITL)
AVGORANDET: FLOYD – INGO • 1961 • *Stivell Erne (Edit)* • SWD
AVIACIONNAJA NEDELJA NASEKOMYCH • 1912 • Starevitch Ladislas • ANS • USS • INSECTS, THE (USA) ○ UP TO DATE FLYERS ○ FLYING INSECTS ○ AVIATION WEEK AMONG THE INSECTS
AVIADOR FENOMENO, EL • 1960 • Cortes Fernando • MXC
AVIA'S SUMMER • 1988 • Cohen Eli • ISR
AVIATEUR, L' • 1931 • Seiter William A. • FRN
AVIATEUR MASQUE, L' • 1922 • Peguy Robert • FRN
AVIATIKEREN OG JOURNALISTENS HUSTRU see **FLYVEREN OG JOURNALISTE ENS HUSTRU** • 1911
AVIATION • 1966 • Ratz Gunter • ANM • GDR
AVIATION EXPERT –DONALD DOUGLAS • 1944 • *O'Brien Joseph/ Mead Thomas (P)* • SHT • USA
AVIATION HAS ITS SURPRISES • 1909 • *Pathe* • FRN
AVIATION VACATION • 1941 • Avery Tex • ANS • USA
AVIATION WEEK AMONG THE INSECTS see **AVIACIONNAJA NEDELJA NASEKOMYCH** • 1912
AVIATOR, THE • 1929 • Del Ruth Roy • USA
AVIATOR, THE • 1984 • Miller George* • YGS, USA
AVIATOR, THE see **FLIEGER, DER** • 1987
AVIATOR AND THE JOURNALIST'S WIFE, THE see **FLYVEREN OG JOURNALISTE ENS HUSTRU** • 1911
AVIATOR SPY, THE (USA) see **HIS COUNTRY'S HONOUR** • 1914
AVIATOR TRAITOR, THE • 1914 • *Bunkhorn* • USA
AVIATOR'S AND ARTIST'S RACE FOR A BRIDE • 1912 • *Hammond Lee* • USA
AVIATORS OF HUDSON STRAIT, THE • 1973 • Weintraub William • CND
AVIATOR'S SUCCESS, AN • 1912 • *Scott Blanche* • USA
AVIATOR'S WIFE, THE (UKN) see **FEMME DE L'AVIATEUR, LA** • 1980
AVIAZIONE see **ARMATA AZZURRA, L'** • 1932
AVICENNA • 1957 • Yarmatov Kamil • USS
AVIGNON • 1957 • Kelly Ron • DOC • CND
AVIO MARCH see **AVIO-MARS** • 1934
AVIO-MARS • 1934 • Kaufman Mikhail • USS • AIR MARCH ○ AVIO MARCH
AVION BLANC, L' see **BLEUS DU CIEL, LES** • 1933
AVION DE MINUIT, L' • 1938 • Kirsanoff Dimitri • FRN
AVIONS A REACTIONS see **SCREAMING JETS** • 1951
AVISA A CURRO JIMENEZ • 1978 • Romero-Marchent Rafael • SPN
AVISEN • 1954 • Roos Jorgen • DOC • DNM
AVISHKAR • 1974 • Bhattacharya Basu • IND
AVISPERO, EL • 1973 • Barco Ramon • SPN
AVIVATO see **REY DE LOS VIVOS, EL** • 1949
AVOCADA • 1965 • Vehr Bill • SHT • USA
AVOCAT, L' • 1925 • Ravel Gaston • FRN
AVOCAT DE LA DEFENSE L' see **AU-DELA DU VISAGE** • 1953
AVOCATE D'AMOUR • 1938 • Ploquin Raoul • FRN
AVOIR 16 ANS see **AVOIR SEIZE ANS** • 1979
AVOIR 20 ANS DANS LES AURES • 1972 • Vautier Rene • FRN
AVOIR SEIZE ANS • 1979 • Lefebvre Jean-Pierre • CND • TO BE 16 ○ AVOIR 16 ANS
AVON INC. • 1986 • Amini Stephen • DOC • CND
AVONDEN, DE • 1989 • van den Berg Rudolf • NTH • EVENINGS
AVONTUREN VAN ALLEDAAGSE HELD • 1975 • van der Velde L. • BLG • ADVENTURES OF AN EVERYDAY HERO
AVORTEMENT CLANDESTIN • 1972 • Chevalier Pierre • FRN
AVRIANOS POLEMISTIS • 1981 • Papas Michael • CYP • TOMORROW'S WARRIOR
AVRIGNY TROUPE OF JUGGLERS, THE • 1902 • *Warwick Trading Co* • UKN
AVRIL see **ARLETTE ET SES PAPAS** • 1934
AVSKEDET • 1980 • Niskanen Tuija-Maija • FNL, SWD • FAREWELL, THE ○ JAAHYVAISET
AVTAAR • 1983 • Kumar Mohan • IND
AVVENTURA, L' • 1960 • Antonioni Michelangelo • ITL, FRN • ADVENTURE, THE
AVVENTURA A CAPRI • 1959 • Lipartiti Giuseppe • ITL
AVVENTURA A MONTECARLO see **TERZO CANALE** • 1970
AVVENTURA A MOTEL • 1963 • Polselli Renato • ITL
AVVENTURA AD ALGERI see **MAN FROM CAIRO, THE** • 1953
AVVENTURA DEL GRANDE NORD, L' see **JACK LONDON LA MIA GRANDE AVVENTURA** • 1973
AVVENTURA DEL POLO SUD • 1961 • Tomei Giuliano, Romena Luigi • ITL
AVVENTURA DI ANNABELLA, L' • 1943 • Menardi Leo • ITL
AVVENTURA DI DIO, L' • 1920 • Genina Augusto • ITL
AVVENTURA DI GIACOMO CASANOVA • 1938 • Bassoli Carlo J. • ITL
AVVENTURA DI SALVATOR ROSA, UN • 1940 • Blasetti Alessandro • ITL • ADVENTURE OF SALVATOR ROSA, AN (USA) ○ SALVATOR ROSA
AVVENTURA DI UN ITALIANO IN CINA, L' (ITL) see **MARCO POLO** • 1962
AVVENTURA E L'AVVENTURA, L' (ITL) see **AVENTURE C'EST L'AVENTURE, L'** • 1972
AVVENTURE A CAVALLO • 1967 • Zane Angio • ITL
AVVENTURE DEI TRE MOSCHETTIERI, LE • 1957 • Lerner Joseph • ITL
AVVENTURE DEL BARONE DI MUNCHAUSEN • 1914 • *Psiche* • ITL • ADVENTURE OF BARON MUNCHAUSEN (USA)
AVVENTURE DI ARSENIO LUPIN, LE (ITL) see **AVENTURES D'ARSENE LUPIN, LES** • 1956
AVVENTURE DI BIJOU, LE • 1920 • Genina Augusto • ITL
AVVENTURE DI CARTOUCHE, LE • 1955 • Vernuccio Gianni, Sekely Steve • ITL • CARTOUCHE
AVVENTURE DI DOLORETTA, LE • 1918 • Righelli Gennaro • ITL
AVVENTURE DI DOX, LE see **CACCIA ALL'UOMO** • 1961
AVVENTURE DI ENEA, LE • 1974 • Rossi Franco • ITL
AVVENTURE DI FRACASSA, LE • 1919 • Mari Febo • ITL
AVVENTURE DI GERARD, LE (ITL) see **ADVENTURES OF GERARD, THE** • 1970
AVVENTURE DI GIACOMO CASANOVA, LE • 1954 • Steno • ITL, FRN • AVENTURES ET LES AMOURS DE CASANOVA, LES (FRN) ○ SINS OF CASANOVA ○ CASANOVA (USA)
AVVENTURE DI GOLDEN BOY, LE see **ON A VOLE LA JOCONDE** • 1965
AVVENTURE DI LAURA STORM, LE • 1965 • Mastrocinque Camillo • MTV • ITL
AVVENTURE DI MANDRIN, LE • 1952 • Soldati Mario • ITL, FRN • AFFAIR OF MADAME POMPADOUR, THE (UKN) ○ DON JUAN'S NIGHT OF LOVE ○ ADVENTURES OF MANDRIN, THE (USA) ○ CAPTAIN ADVENTURE ○ MOUNTAIN BRIGAND
AVVENTURE DI MARY READ, LE • 1961 • Lenzi Umberto • ITL • QUEEN OF THE SEAS (USA)
AVVENTURE DI PINOCCHIO, LE • 1936 • Verdini Raoul • ITL
AVVENTURE DI PINOCCHIO, LE • 1947 • Guardone Giannetto • ITL
AVVENTURE DI PINOCCHIO, LE • 1968 • Cenci Giuliano • ANM • ITL • ADVENTURES OF PINOCCHIO, THE ○ PINOCCHIO
AVVENTURE DI PINOCCHIO, LE • 1972 • Comencini Luigi • ITL, FRN • AVENTURES DE PINOCCHIO, LES (FRN)
AVVENTURE DI ROBI E BUCK, LE • 1958 • De Dominicis Gennaro • ITL
AVVENTURE DI SCARAMOUCHE, LE (ITL) see **SCARAMOUCHE** • 1963
AVVENTURE DI TOPO GIGIO, LE • 1961 • Caldura Federico • ANM • ITL • MAGIC WORLD OF TOPO GIGIO (THE ITALIAN MOUSE), THE
AVVENTURE DI ULISSE, LE • 1969 • Rossi Franco • ITL • ADVENTURES OF ULYSSES, THE
AVVENTURE E GLI AMORI DI MIGUEL CERVANTES, LE • 1967 • Sherman Vincent • ITL, FRN, SPN • AVENTURES EXTRAORDINAIRES DE CERVANTES, LES (FRN) ○ YOUNG REBEL, THE (USA) ○ CERVANTES
AVVENTURE E GLI AMORI DI SCARAMOUCHE, LE • 1976 • Castellari Enzo G. • ITL, YGS, MNC • LOVES AND TIMES OF SCARAMOUCHE, THE (USA) ○ SCARAMOUCHE
AVVENTURE IN CITTA • 1960 • Savarese Roberto • ITL • PAISANELLA
AVVENTURE NELL'ARCIPELAGO • 1958 • Partesano Dino • ITL
AVVENTURIERA DEL PIANO DI SOPRA, L' • 1941 • Matarazzo Raffaello • ITL
AVVENTURIERI DEI TROPICI, GLI • 1960 • Bergonzelli Sergio • ITL • SEVEN IN THE SUN (USA)
AVVENTURIERI DELL'URANIO, GLI • 1959 • Zane Angio • ITL • URANIUM ADVENTURES
AVVENTURIERO • 1919 • Mari Febo • ITL
AVVENTURIERO, L' • 1967 • Young Terence • ITL • ROVER, THE
AVVENTURIERO A TAHITI, UN (ITL) see **TENDRE VOYOU** • 1966
AVVENTURIERO DELLA TORTUGA, L' • 1965 • Capuano Luigi • ITL • ADVENTURER OF TORTUGA
AVVENTUROSA FUGA, LA • Doria Enzo • ITL
AVVOCATO DEL DIAVOLO, L' • 1977 • Green Guy • ITL, FRG • DEVIL'S ADVOCATE, THE ○ DES TEUFELS ADVOKAT
AVVOCATO DELLA MALA, L' • 1978 • Marras Alberto • ITL
AVVOCATO DIFENSORE, L' • 1934 • Zambuto Gero • ITL • ATTORNEY FOR THE DEFENSE, THE (USA)
AW, NURSE • 1934 • *Mintz Charles (P)* • ANS • USA
AWADANUKI HENGE SODO • 1958 • Mori Masaki • JPN
AWAITED HOUR, THE • 1915 • *Shay William E.* • USA
AWAITING see **OCZEKIWANIE** • 1962
AWAKE FROM MOURNING • 1981 • Austin Chris • DOC • SAF
AWAKENING see **PRZEBUDZENIE** • 1934
AWAKENING see **PROBUZENI** • 1959
AWAKENING, THE • 1909 • Griffith D. W. • USA
AWAKENING, THE • 1912 • *Eclair* • USA
AWAKENING, THE • 1912 • *Selig* • USA
AWAKENING, THE • 1913 • *Powers* • USA
AWAKENING, THE • 1913 • Pollard Harry • *American* • USA
AWAKENING, THE • 1914 • *Rex* • USA
AWAKENING, THE • 1914 • Taylor William D.? • *Balboa* • USA
AWAKENING, THE • 1915 • Ince Ralph • USA
AWAKENING, THE • 1917 • Archainbaud George • USA
AWAKENING, THE • 1928 • Fleming Victor • USA
AWAKENING, THE • 1938 • Frenguelli Alfonse • UKN
AWAKENING, THE • 1980 • Newell Mike • UKN • WAKING, THE
AWAKENING, THE • 1989 • Russo John • USA
AWAKENING, THE see **SUOR LETIZIA** • 1956
AWAKENING, THE see **YOAKE NO UTA** • 1965
AWAKENING, THE see **PROBUZHDYENIYE** • 1968
AWAKENING AT SNAKEVILLE, THE • 1913 • *Joslin Margaret* • USA
AWAKENING FOR LOVE see **AIJO KAIGAN** • 1967
AWAKENING GIANT –CHINA, THE • 1973 • Bjerre Jens • DOC • DNM
AWAKENING HOUR, THE • 1915 • *Craig Nell* • USA
AWAKENING HOUR, THE • 1957 • Winter Donovan • UKN
AWAKENING LAND, THE • 1978 • Sagal Boris • TVM • USA
AWAKENING OF A MAN, THE • 1913 • Lessey George A. • USA
AWAKENING OF BARBARA DARE, THE • 1914 • North Wilfred • USA
AWAKENING OF BESS, THE • 1909 • Salter Harry • USA
AWAKENING OF BESS MORTON, THE • 1916 • Thayer Otis B. • USA
AWAKENING OF BIANCA, THE • 1912 • Kent Charles • USA
AWAKENING OF CANDRA, THE • 1983 • Wendkos Paul • TVM • USA
AWAKENING OF DONNA ISOLLA, THE • 1914 • Taylor Stanner E. V. • USA
AWAKENING OF EMILY, THE see **EMILY** • 1976
AWAKENING OF GALATEA, THE • 1911 • *Powers* • USA
AWAKENING OF HELENA RICHIE, THE • 1916 • Noble John W. • USA
AWAKENING OF HELENE MINOR, THE • 1917 • Drew Sidney • SHT • USA
AWAKENING OF JIM BURKE, THE • 1935 • Hillyer Lambert • USA • IRON FIST (UKN)
AWAKENING OF JOHN BOND, THE • 1911 • Brabin Charles J. • USA
AWAKENING OF JOHN CLARK, THE • 1911 • *Powers* • USA
AWAKENING OF JONES, THE • 1912 • Trimble Larry • USA
AWAKENING OF KATRINA, THE see **GIRL DOWNSTAIRS, THE** • 1938
AWAKENING OF NORA, THE • 1914 • Trimble Larry • UKN
AWAKENING OF PAPITA, THE • 1913 • *Nestor* • USA
AWAKENING OF PATSY, THE • 1915 • Jaccard Jacques • USA
AWAKENING OF RUTH, THE • 1917 • Griffith Edward H. • USA
AWAKENING OF SPRING, THE see **FRUHLINGS ERWACHEN** • 1929
AWAKENING OF YOUTH, THE see **NAR UNGDOMEN VAKNAR** • 1943
AWAKENINGS • 1990 • Marshall Penny • USA
AWANTURA • 1971 • Marszalek Lechoslaw • ANM • PLN • ROW, THE
AWANTURA O BASIE • 1960 • Kaniewska Maria • PLN • MUCH ADO ABOUT LITTLE BARBARA ○ MUCH ADO ABOUT LITTLE BASIA
AWARA • 1953 • Kapoor Raj • IND • TRAMP, THE (USA) ○ VAGABOND, THE
AWARD OF JUSTICE, THE • 1914 • *Blackwell Carlyle* • USA
AWARD PRESENTATION TO ANDY WARHOL • 1964 • Mekas Jonas • SHT • USA
AWARDS AND DECORATIONS see **NAGRODY I ODZNACZENIA** • 1974
AWATAR • 1965 • Majewski Janusz • PLN • AVATAR
AWAY ALL BOATS • 1956 • Pevney Joseph • USA
AWAY FROM IT ALL • 1981 • Gubenko Nikolai • USS
AWAY FROM THE STEERAGE • 1921 • *Sennett Mack (P)* • SHT • USA • ASTRAY FROM THE STEERAGE
AWAY GOES PRUDENCE • 1920 • Robertson John S. • USA
AWAY IN THE LEAD • 1925 • *Bushman Francis X. Jr.* • USA
AWAY OUT WEST • 1910 • *Anderson Broncho Billy* • USA
AWDA ILA AR-RIF, AL • 1939 • Kamel Morsi Ahmad • EGY • RETOUR A LA TERRE, LE
AWDAT AL-IBN ADH-DHAL see **AWDAT AL IBN AL DAL** • 1976
AWDAT AL IBN AL DAL • 1976 • Shahin Youssef • EGY, ALG • AWDAT AL-IBN ADH-DHAL ○ RETOUR DU FILS PRODIGUE, LE ○ RETURN OF THE PRODIGAL SON
AWDAT MOWATINE • 1987 • Khan Mohamed • EGY • RETURN OF A CITIZEN
AWDET TAKIET EL EKHFAA • 1946 • Jawad Muhammad Abdel • EGY • RETURN OF THE MAGIC HAT
AWDIT EL ROH • 1969 • Abu Saif Salah • EGY • RETURN OF THE SPIRIT, THE
AWDIT HAMIDU • 1974 • Al-Yassiri Fiasal • SYR
AWESOME LOTUS see **AWESOME LOTUS: MISTRESS OF THE MARTIAL ARTS** • 1986
AWESOME LOTUS: MISTRESS OF THE MARTIAL ARTS • 1986 • O'Malley David • USA • AWESOME LOTUS
AWFUL ADVENTURES OF AN AVIATOR, THE • 1915 • MacGregor Norval • USA
AWFUL BACKLASH • 1966-67 • Nelson Robert • SHT • USA
AWFUL DR. ORLOFF, THE (USA) see **GRITOS EN LA NOCHE** • 1962
AWFUL FATE OF MELPOMENUS JONES, THE • 1983 • Potterton Gerald • CND
AWFUL GOOF, THE • 1939 • Lord Del • SHT • USA
AWFUL MOMENT, AN • 1908 • Griffith D. W. • USA
AWFUL ORPHAN • 1949 • Jones Charles M. • ANS • USA
AWFUL RELAPSE, AN • 1913 • *Gaumont* • USA
AWFUL ROMANCE, AN • 1916 • *Heinie & Louie* • USA
AWFUL SCARE, AN • 1913 • *Crystal* • USA
AWFUL SKATE, AN • 1907 • Anderson G. M. • USA
AWFUL SLEUTH, THE • 1951 • Quine Richard • SHT • USA
AWFUL STORY OF THE NUN OF MONZA, THE (UKN) see **MONACA DI MONZA, LA** • 1969
AWFUL TOOTH, THE • 1938 • Watt Nate • SHT • USA
AWFUL TOOTH, THE • 1952 • Kneitel Seymour • ANS • USA

AWFUL TRUTH, THE • 1925 • Powell Paul • USA • JEALOUS SEX
AWFUL TRUTH, THE • 1929 • Neilan Marshall • USA
AWFUL TRUTH, THE • 1937 • McCarey Leo • USA
AWFULLY SAD PRINCESS, THE see **SILENE SMUTNA PRINCEZNA** • 1968
AWHAM AL-HUBB • 1970 • Shukry Mamduh • EGY • ILLUSIONS D'AMOUR
AWKWARD ANARCHISTS • 1915 • Aylott Dave? • UKN
AWKWARD CINDERELLA, AN • 1914 • *Rex* • USA
AWKWARD HORSEMAN, THE • 1905 • Collins Alf? • UKN
AWKWARD MIX-UP, AN • 1913 • *Kinemacolor* • USA
AWKWARD SIGNWRITER, THE see **SIGN WRITER, THE** • 1897
AWKWARD SITUATION, AN • 1907 • Stow Percy • UKN
AWLAD EL EIH • 1988 • Yehia Sherif • EGY • SONS OF ..
AWLAD EL SHAREH • 1951 • Wahby Youssef • EGY • CHILDREN OF THE STREETS
AWLAD EL ZAWAT • 1931 • Wahby Youssef, Karim Muhammed • EGY • SPOILED CHILDREN
AWLADI • 1951 • Gomei Umar • EGY • MES ENFANTS
AWOL • 1989 • Sonnekus Neil • SAF • QUARRY, THE
AXE see **CALIFORNIA AXE MASSACRE** • 1974
AXE AND THE LAMP, THE • 1963 • Halas John • ANS • UKN
AXE FOR THE HONEYMOON, AN see **ROSSO SEGNO DELLA FOLLIA, IL** • 1969
AXE IN THE FOREST, THE • Calinescu Bob • ANM • RMN
AXE ME ANOTHER • 1934 • Fleischer Dave • ANS • USA
AXE OF WANDSBEK, THE see **BEIL VON WANDSBEK, DAS** • 1951
AXEL MUNTHE, DER ARZT VON SAN MICHELE • 1962 • Jugert Rudolf, Capitani Giorgio • FRG, ITL, FRN • DONNE SENZA PARADISO (ITL) ○ STORIA DI SAN MICHELE, LA
AXEL MUNTHE DER ARZT VON SAN MICHELE • 1962 • Marischka Georg • AUS
AXEMAN, THE • 1915 • *Banner* • USA
AXILIAD see **SIEKIEREZADA** • 1986
AXUT • 1976 • Zabalza Jose Maria • SPN
AY AMOR.. COMO ME HAS PUESTO! • 1950 • Martinez Solares Gilberto • MXC
AY.. CALYPSO NO TE RAJES! • 1957 • Salvador Jaime • MXC
AY, CARMELA! • 1989 • Saura Carlos • SPN
AY CHABELA..! • 1960 • Ortega Juan J. • MXC
AY, CHAPARROS, COMO ABUNDAN! • 1955 • Aguilar Rolando • MXC
AY, JALISCO, NO TE RAJES! • 1941 • Rodriguez Joselito • MXC • OH JALISCO, DON'T BACK DOWN!
AY, JALISCO, NO TE RAJES! • 1964 • Morayta Miguel • MXC
AY, PALILLO, NO TE RAJES! • 1948 • Patino Gomez Alfonso • MXC
AY PAYS DU SOLEIL • 1951 • de Canonge Maurice • FRN
AY, QUE RECHULO ES PUEBLA! • 1945 • Cardona Rene • MXC
AY, QUE TIEMPOS, SENOR DON SIMON! • 1941 • Bracho Julio • MXC • OH, WHAT TIMES, MR. DON SIMON
AYA • 1990 • Hoaas Solrun • ASL
AYA NI KANASHIKI • 1956 • Uno Jukichi • JPN • EXTREME SADNESS ○ HOW SORROWFUL
AYA THANG LOKU LAMAYEK • 1974 • Pathirajah Dharmasena • SLN • SHE IS A BIG GIRL NOW
AYADI ARABIYYA • 1975 • Nahhass Hashim An- • SHT • EGY • MAINS ARABES
AYAH'S REVENGE • 1908 • Williamson James? • UKN
AYAKO (USA) see **ARU OSAKA NO ONNA** • 1962
AYAM EL GHADAB • 1988 • Rady Mounir • EGY • DAYS OF ANGER
AYAMONN THE TERRIBLE • 1960 • Coppola Francis Ford • SHT • USA
AYAW NI MAYOR • 1967 • San Juan Luis • PHL • MAYOR OBJECTS, THE
AYD EL SAOUDA, EL • 1937 • Aptekman Elie • EGY • BLACK HAND, THE
AYDI AN-NAIMA, AL- • 1963 • Zulficar Mahmoud • EGY • MAINS DOUCES, LES
AYE, FOLLOW YOUR OWN • 1957 • Biggs Julian • CND
AYER FUE PRIMAVERA • 1954 • Ayala Fernando • ARG
AYER, HOY Y MANANA DEL MISTERIO DE LOS OVNIS, EL • 1977 • Gonzalez Ismael • SPN
AYERS ROCK ROCK • 1970 • Cox Peter • SHT • ASL
AYLWIN • 1920 • Edwards Henry • UKN
AYNA • Kiral Erden • FRG • MIRROR, THE
AYNA AQLI? • 1974 • Salem Atef • EGY • OU EST MA RAISON? ○ WHERE'S MY MIND?
AYNA-O-ABOSHISHTA • 1967 • Dutta Subhash • BNG
AYNI YOLUN YOLCUSU • 1973 • Demirag Turgut • TRK • GOING THE SAME WAY
AYODHYECHA RAJA • 1932 • Shantaram Rajaram • IND • KING OF AYODHYA, THE
AYOREOS, LOS • 1979 • Roncal Hugo • BLV
AYOS NA DARLING • 1968 • Magno Carlo • PHL • ALRIGHT DARLING
AYOUMI • 1977 • Dong Jean-Marie • GBN
AYOUPA • 1957 • Tallas Gregg R. • GRC • BED OF GRASS (USA) ○ AGIOUPA
AYRILIK OLMASAYDI • 1967 • Canturk Husnu • TRK • IF THERE WAS NOT A PARTING
AYRILIK SAATI • 1967 • Wanoglu Turker • TRK • PARTING HOUR, THE
AYRILSAK DA BERABERIZ • 1967 • Aslan Muzaffer • TRK • TOGETHER EVEN IF APART
AYRSHIRE LANG SYNE • 1974 • Alexander Mike • DOC • UKN
AYSA • 1965 • Sanjines Jorge • BLV
AYSECIK, THE POOR PRINCESS • Gorec Ertem • TRK
AYSEM • 1968 • Taydam Nejat • TRK • MY AYSE
AYU DAN AYU • 1988 • Sophiaan Sophan • INN
AYUDAME A VIVIR • 1936 • Ferreyra Jose • ARG
AYUDEME UD, COMPADRE! • 1968 • Becker German • CHL • HELP ME, COMRADE!
AYYAM AL TAWWILA, AL see **AL-AYYAM AL-TAWILLA** • 1980
AYYAM EL HOB • 1968 • Halim Hilmy • EGY • DAYS OF LOVE ○ AYYAM HUBB
AYYAM HUBB see **AYYAM EL HOB** • 1968
AYYAMINA AL-HILWA • 1955 • Halim Hilmy • EGY • NOS BEAUX JOURS
AYYAMUN WA LAYALI • 1955 • Barakat Henry • EGY • JOURS ET NUITS
AZ DO OKONCE • 1985 • Kopriva Antonin • CZC • TILL THE VERY END
AZ JA BUDU VELKY • 1963 • Bedrich Vaclav • ANS • CZC • WHEN I GROW UP
AZ-JANGOZASHTEGAN • 1968 • Vaeziyan Jozeph • IRN • MEN WHO DID NOT FEAR DEATH, THE
AZ PRIJDE KOCOUR • 1963 • Jasny Vojtech • CZC • WHEN THE CAT COMES (USA) ○ ONE DAY A CAT.. ○ THAT CAT ○ CASSANDRA CAT
AZA BY THE SEA see **AZA NAD MORZEM** • 1963
AZA NA SPACERZE • 1963 • Laskowski Jan • ANS • PLN • AZA ON A WALK
AZA NAD MORZEM • 1963 • Laskowski Jan • ANS • PLN • AZA BY THE SEA
AZA ON A WALK see **AZA NA SPACERZE** • 1963
AZADI-KE-DIVANE • 1934 • *Ajanta* • IND
AZAHARES PARA TU BODA • 1950 • Soler Julian • MXC
AZAHARES ROJOS • 1960 • Crevenna Alfredo B. • MXC
AZAIS • 1931 • Hervil Rene • FRN
AZALEA MOUNTAIN • 1974 • CHN
AZAR SE DIVIERTE, EL • 1957 • Pascual Jesus • SPN
AZCIJA STADION • 1978 • Vukotic Dusan • YGS • OPERATION STADIUM ○ ACTION STADIUM ○ AKCIJA STADION
AZIMA, EL • 1939 • Salim Kamel • EGY • DETERMINATION ○ WILL, THE
AZIMAT • 1958 • *Shaw Run Run (P)* • SNG • SEAL OF SOLOMON, THE
AZIT THE PARATROOPER DOG • 1972 • Davidson Boaz • ISR
AZIZA • 1980 • Ben Ammar Abdel Latif • TNS
AZIZE • 1968 • Kan Kemal • TRK
AZONOSITAS • 1976 • Lugossy Laszlo • HNG • IDENTIFICATION ○ MAN WITHOUT A NAME
AZRAIL BENIM • 1968 • Ucanoglu Yucel • TRK • I'M THE ANGEL OF DEATH ○ EXECUTIONER, THE
AZTEC MUMMY, THE (USA) see **MOMIA AZTECA, LA** • 1957
AZTEC ROBOT VS. THE HUMAN ROBOT, THE see **ROBOT HUMANO, EL** • 1959
AZTEC SACRIFICE, THE • 1910 • Olcott Sidney • USA
AZTEC TREASURE, THE • 1914 • *Frazer Robert W.* • USA
AZTECAS, LOS • 1976 • Boudou • MTV • MXC
AZUCAR, EL • 1965 • Villafuerte Santiago • DOC • CUB
AZUL • 1971 • *Cesar* • MXC
AZUL • 1972 • Carrera Gustavo L. • VNZ • BLUE
AZUL, AZUL • 1983 • Caetano Jose De Sa • PRT
AZUL CELESTE • 1990 • Novaro Maria • MXC • SKY BLUE
AZULEJOS DE PORTUGAL • 1958 • Rosa Baptista • SHT • PRT
AZUREXPRESS • 1938 • Balazs Bela • HNG
AZYA', AL • 1974 • Al-Rawi Abdel-Hadi • SHT • IRQ
AZYL • 1978 • Zaluski Roman • PLN • SANCTUARY
AZYLO MUITO LOUCO • 1970 • dos Santos Nelson Pereira • BRZ • ASILO MUITO LOUCO, UM ○ ALIENISTE, L'
AZZEL • 1979 • Cote Guy-L. • CND

B

B.A. BA • 1971 • Segal Abraham • DOC • FRN
B.A.D. CATS, THE • 1980 • Kowalski Bernard • TVM • USA
B.B.C. -DROITWICH • 1934 • Watt Harry, Anstey Edgar • DCS • UKN
B.B.C. MUSICALS • 1936 • Shepherd Horace • SER • UKN
B.B.C. -THE VOICE OF BRITAIN • 1934 • Legg Stuart • DOC • UKN
B.C. AT EXPO 85 • 1985J • Jubenvill Ken • SHT • CND
B.F.'S DAUGHTER • 1948 • Leonard Robert Z. • USA • POLLY FULTON (UKN)
B.G. ARU 19 SAI NO NIKKI AGETE YOKKATA • 1968 • Tanno Yuji • JPN • LOST VIRGIN
B.G. REMEMBERS (UKN) see **BENGURION REMEMBERS** • 1972
B GIRLS, THE see **FICHERAS, LAS** • 1976
B.J. LANG PRESENTS see **B.J. PRESENTS** • 1971
B.J. PRESENTS • 1971 • Yablonsky Yablo • USA • MANIPULATOR, THE ○ B.J. LANG PRESENTS
B.L. STRYKER: THE DANCER'S TOUCH see **DANCER'S TOUCH, THE** • 1988
B LICENSE • 1978 • Gunnarsson Sturla • DOC • CND
B MUST DIE see **HAY QUE MATAR A B** • 1974
"B" MUST BE KILLED see **HAY QUE MATAR A B** • 1974
B-O-I-N-N-G! • 1962 • Lewis Herschell G. • USA
B.R.A.T. PATROL, THE • 1986 • Miller Mollie • USA • BRAT PATROL, THE
B.S. I LOVE YOU • 1967 • Stern Steven Hilliard • CND
B.U.D. • 1988 • Irving David • USA • C.H.U.D. II ○ C.H.U.D. 2: BUD THE CHUD
BAA BAA BLACKSHEEP see **FLYING MISFITS** • 1976
BAAG KI JYOTI • 1953 • *Biswas Anil (M)* • IND
BAAJI • 1951 • *Burman S. D. (M)* • IND
BAAL • 1969 • Schlondorff Volker • MTV • FRG
BAAL BABYLONE • 1971 • Ben Ammar Abdul Latif • SHT • TNS
BAAL CHACHALOMOT • 1959 • Gross Yoram • ISR • JOSEPH THE DREAMER
BAALBEK FESTIVAL 1960, THE • 1960 • MacDonald David • DOC • UKN
BAAN • 1986 • Kopjit Cherd • THL • HOUSE
BAAP BETI • 1950 • Roy Bimal • IND
BAARA • 1979 • Cisse Souleymane • MLI • TRAVAIL, LE ○ WORK ○ JOB, A ○ PORTER, THE
BAAT EK RAAT KI • 1962 • *Burman S. D. (M)* • IND
BAATH OMAR • 1965 • Ruspoli Mario • TNS • REBIRTH OF A NATION
BAAZ see **BAAZI** • 1951
BAAZI • 1951 • Dutt Guru • IND • BAAZ
BAAZI • 1968 • Bhattacharjee Moni • IND • BET
BAB AL-HADID see **BAB EL HADID** • 1957
BAB EL HADID • 1957 • Shahin Youssef • EGY • CAIRO STATION ○ IRON GATE ○ BAB AL-HADID ○ CAIRO: CENTRAL STATION ○ GARE CENTRALE
BAB THE FIXER • 1917 • MacDonald Sherwood • USA
BABA • 1971 • Guney Yilmaz • TRK • FATHER, THE
BABA ALI • Colson-Malleville Marie • DOC • FRN
BABA-ALI • 1952 • Colson-Malleville Marie • SHT • FRN
BABA AMINE • 1950 • Shahin Youssef • EGY • FATHER AMINE
BABA AYEZ KEDA • 1968 • Mustafa Niazi • EGY • DADDY WANTS IT THAT WAY
BABA YAGA • 1973 • Farina Corrado • ITL, FRN • BABA YAGA -DEVIL WITCH ○ DEVIL WITCH, THE
BABA YAGA -DEVIL WITCH see **BABA YAGA** • 1973
BABADOU'S VOYAGE see **VOYAGE DE BADABOU, LE** • 1956
BABAING KIDLAT • 1964 • Cayado Tony • PHL • LIGHTNING WOMAN
BABAR THE ELEPHANT • 1968 • Melendez Bill • ANM • USA
BABAR THE MOVIE • 1990 • Bunce Alan • ANM • CND
BABATUNDE GOES TO SCHOOL • 1955 • UKN
BABBELKOUS EN BRUIDEGOM • 1974 • Roets Koos • SAF
BABBITT • 1924 • Beaumont Harry • USA
BABBITT • 1934 • Keighley William • USA
BABBLING BOOK, THE • 1933 • Scotto Aubrey • SHT • USA
BABBLING TONGUES • 1915 • MacQuarrie Murdock • USA
BABBLING TONGUES • 1917 • Humphrey William • USA
BABE • 1965 • Vas Judit • DOC • HNG
BABE • 1975 • Kulik Buzz • TVM • USA
BABE! • 1980 • Zielinski Rafal • CND • HEY BABE!
BABE • 1981 • Christopher John • USA
BABE AND PUPPIES • 1904 • Porter Edwin S. • USA
BABE COMES HOME • 1927 • Wilde Ted • USA
BABE RUTH STORY, THE • 1948 • Del Ruth Roy • USA
BABEL see **BABYLONIA** • 1970
BABEL OPERA, OU LA REPETITION DE DON JUAN • 1985 • Delvaux Andre • BLG
BABES AND BOOBS • 1918 • Semon Larry • SHT • USA
BABES AT SEA • 1934 • *Mintz Charles (P)* • ANS • USA
BABES IN ARMS • 1939 • Berkeley Busby • USA
BABES IN BAGDAD • 1952 • Ulmer Edgar G., Mihura Jeronimo • USA, SPN • MUCHACHAS DE BAGDAD (SPN) ○ BABES OF BAGDAD
BABES IN SWING STREET • 1944 • Lilley Edward • USA
BABES IN THE GOODS • 1934 • Meins Gus • SHT • USA
BABES IN THE WOOD • 1905 • Fitzhamon Lewin • UKN
BABES IN THE WOOD see **PERNIKOVA CHALOUPKA** • 1927
BABES IN THE WOODS • 1907 • *Miles Brothers* • USA
BABES IN THE WOODS • 1909 • *Pathe* • FRN
BABES IN THE WOODS • 1911 • Walton Fred* • USA
BABES IN THE WOODS • 1913 • *Pathe* • FRN
BABES IN THE WOODS • 1917 • Franklin Chester M., Franklin Sidney A. • USA
BABES IN THE WOODS • 1925 • *Fbo* • ANM • USA
BABES IN THE WOODS • 1932 • Gillett Burt • ANS • USA
BABES IN THE WOODS • 1933 • *Disney Walt (P)* • ANS • USA
BABES IN THE WOODS • 1962 • *Bolin Pat* • USA
BABES IN TOYLAND • 1934 • Rogers Charles, Meins Gus • USA • MARCH OF THE WOODEN SOLDIERS ○ LAUREL AND HARDY IN TOYLAND ○ MARCH OF THE TOYS ○ REVENGE IS SWEET
BABES IN TOYLAND • 1961 • Donohue Jack • USA
BABES IN TOYLAND • 1986 • Donner Clive • TVM • USA
BABES OF BAGDAD see **BABES IN BAGDAD** • 1952
BABES ON BROADWAY • 1941 • Berkeley Busby • USA
BABE'S SCHOOL DAYS • 1915 • Louis Will • USA
BABETTE • 1912 • *Navarro Mary* • USA
BABETTE • 1917 • Brabin Charles J. • USA
BABETTE see **BABETTE IN RETURN OF THE SECRET SOCIETY** • 1968
BABETTE GOES TO WAR (USA) see **BABETTE S'EN VA-T-EN GUERRE** • 1959
BABETTE IN RETURN OF THE SECRET SOCIETY • 1968 • *Cheer Claudia* • USA • RETURN OF THE SECRET SOCIETY ○ BABETTE
BABETTE OF THE BALLY HOO • 1916 • *Equitable* • USA
BABETTE S'EN VA-T-EN GUERRE • 1959 • Christian-Jaque • FRN • BABETTE GOES TO WAR (USA)
BABETTE'S FEAST (UKN) see **BABETTES GAESTEBUD** • 1987
BABETTES GAESTEBUD • 1987 • Axel Gabriel • DNM • BABETTE'S FEAST (UKN)
BABI RIAZANSKIE • 1927 • Preobrazhenskaya Olga • USS • VILLAGE OF SIN, THE ○ WOMEN OF RYAZAN ○ BABI RYAN-SKYE ○ DEVIL'S PLAYTHING, THE ○ PEASANT WOMEN OF RIAZAN
BABI RYAN-SKYE see **BABI RIAZANSKIE** • 1927
BABICKA • 1920 • Cervenkova Thea • CZC • GRANDMOTHER
BABICKA • 1940 • Cap Frantisek • CZC • GRANNY, THE ○ GRANDMOTHER
BABIES' DOLL, THE • 1914 • *Smalley Phillips* • USA
BABIES FOR SALE • 1940 • Barton Charles T. • USA
BABIES IS BABIES • 1919 • Santell Alfred • SHT • USA
BABIES PROHIBITED • 1913 • *Chester Lila* • USA
BABIES ROLLING EGGS • 1902 • Porter Edwin S. • USA
BABIES THREE • 1912 • *Fritzie Miss* • USA
BABIOLE • 1975 • Labonte Francois • MTV • CND
BABLA • 1951 • Agradoot • IND
BABO 73 • 1964 • Downey Robert • USA
BABOONA • 1935 • Johnson Martin E. • DOC • USA
BABR MAZANDARAN • 1968 • Khachikian Samouel • IRN • TIGER OF MAZANDARAN, THE
BAB'S BURGLAR • 1917 • Dawley J. Searle • USA
BAB'S CANDIDATE • 1920 • Griffith Edward H. • USA
BAB'S DIARY • 1917 • Dawley J. Searle • USA
BAB'S MATINEE IDOL • 1917 • Dawley J. Searle • USA
BABU AL-MAFTUH, AL- • 1963 • Barakat Henry • EGY • PORTE OUVERTE, LA
BABUSKIN ZONTIK • 1969 • Milchin L. • ANS • USS • GRANDMOTHER'S UMBRELLA (USA)
BABUTA • 1976 • Rouch Jean • FRN, NGR • BABUTA, LES TROIS CONSEILS ○ TROIS CONSEILS, LES
BABUTA, LES TROIS CONSEILS see **BABUTA** • 1976
BABY • 1920 • *Republic* • USA
BABY • 1932 • Billon Pierre, Lamac Carl • FRN
BABY • 1932 • Lamac Carl • FRG

BABY • 1984 • Norton B. W. L. • USA • BABY.. SECRET OF THE LOST LEGEND
BABY, THE • 1912 • *Edison* • USA
BABY, THE • 1913 • Thornton F. Martin • UKN • POTTED PLAYS NO.2
BABY, THE • 1914 • *Billington Francelia* • USA
BABY, THE • 1915 • Myers Harry • USA
BABY, THE • 1973 • Post Ted • USA
BABY, THE see UNGEN • 1974
BABY, THE see I DON'T WANT TO BE BORN • 1975
BABY, THE see BEBEK • 1979
BABY AND THE APE, THE • 1903 • Smith G. A. • UKN
BABY AND THE BATTLESHIP, THE • 1956 • Lewis Jay • UKN
BABY AND THE BOSS, THE • 1915 • *Marshall Boyd* • USA
BABY AND THE BOTTLE • 1958 • Bilcock David Sr. • DOC • ASL
BABY AND THE COP, THE • 1912 • *Rice Herbert* • USA
BABY AND THE LEOPARD, THE • 1915 • Santschi Thomas • USA
BABY AND THE STORK, THE • 1911 • Griffith D. W. • USA
BABY AND YOUNG GIRLS see BEBE ET FILLETTES • 1896
BABY BE GOOD • 1925 • Lamont Charles • SHT • USA
BABY BE GOOD • 1935 • Fleischer Dave • ANS • USA
BABY BE GOOD (UKN) see BROTHER RAT AND A BABY • 1940
BABY BENEFACTOR, THE • 1915 • *Thanhouser* • USA
BABY BET • 1910 • *Urban Trading Co* • UKN
BABY BETTY • 1912 • *Selig* • USA
BABY BLOOD • 1989 • Robak Alain • FRN
BABY BLUE • 1969 • Dalva Robert • USA
BABY BLUE • Welborn Robert • USA
BABY BLUE MARINE • 1976 • Hancock John • USA
BABY BLUES • 1941 • Cahn Edward L. • USA
BABY BOOGIE • 1955 • Julian Paul • ANS • USA
BABY BOOM • 1987 • Shyer Charles • USA
BABY BOTTLENECK • 1946 • Clampett Robert • ANS • USA
BABY BRIDE, THE • 1912 • *Eline Marie* • USA
BABY BUGGY BUNNY • 1954 • Jones Charles M. • ANS • USA
BABY BUNNY, THE see KOUSAGI MONOGATARI • 1954
BABY BUTCH • 1954 • Hanna William, Barbera Joseph • ANS • USA
BABY CAKES • 1982 • Chinn Robert C. • USA
BABY CARRIAGE see UBAGURUMA • 1956
BABY CARRIAGE, THE see BARNVAGNEN • 1963
BABY CART AT THE RIVER STYX see KOZURE OHKAMI • 1973
BABY CART AT THE RIVER STYX see SHOGUN ASSASSIN • 1980
BABY CART IN HELL see KOZURE OHKAMI • 1973
BABY CAT • 1983 • Unia Pierre • FRN
BABY CLASS AT LUNCH • 1903 • Porter Edwin S. • USA
BABY CLOTHES • 1926 • McGowan Robert • SHT • USA
BABY COMES HOME • 1980 • Hussein Waris • TVM • USA
BABY CYCLONE, THE • 1928 • Sutherland A. Edward • USA
BABY DAY • 1913 • Sennett Mack • USA
BABY DAZE • 1939 • Roberts Charles E. • SHT • USA
BABY DID IT, A • 1914 • Christie Al • USA
BABY DOLL • 1916 • *Plump & Runt* • USA
BABY DOLL • 1956 • Kazan Elia • USA
BABY DOLL • 1988 • Carlsen Jon Bang • DNM
BABY DOLL BANDIT, THE • 1920 • Fishback Fred C. • SHT • USA
BABY ELEPHANT STORY see KOZOU MONOGATARI • 1987
BABY FACE • 1933 • Green Alfred E. • USA
BABY FACE • 1977 • De Renzy Alex • USA
BABY FACE see BABY-FACE HARRINGTON • 1935
BABY-FACE HARRINGTON • 1935 • Walsh Raoul • USA • BABY FACE
BABY FACE MORGAN • 1942 • Dreifuss Arthur • USA
BABY FACE NELSON • 1957 • Siegel Don • USA
BABY FACTORY (UKN) see WILBUR AND THE BABY FACTORY • 1970
BABY FINGERS • 1912 • *Gem* • USA
BABY GAME, THE • 1973 • Hughes Harry* • SAF
BABY GIRL see EMBRACERS, THE • 1963
BABY GIRL SCOTT • 1987 • Korty John • TVM • USA
BABY GIVEN BY GOD, A see KAMISAMA NO KURETA AKAMBO • 1979
BABY GRAND, A • 1916 • *Vogue* • USA
BABY GRAND, A • 1916 • Ellis Robert • *Kalem* • USA
BABY HANDS • 1912 • *Thanhouser* • USA
BABY IN DE BOOM, DE • 1970 • van Brakel Nouchka • SHT • NTH • BABY IN THE TREE, THE
BABY IN THE CASE, THE • 1916 • *Gayety* • USA
BABY IN THE ICE BOX, THE see SHE MADE HER BED • 1934
BABY IN THE TREE, THE see BABY IN DE BOOM, DE • 1970
BABY INCUBATOR, THE • 1910 • *Gaumont* • UKN
BABY INDISPOSED • 1913 • Henderson Dell • USA
BABY IT'S YOU • 1983 • Sayles John • USA
BABY JOHN DOE • 1986 • Gerretsen Peter • CND • KIDNAPPING OF BABY JOHN DOE, THE ○ KIDNAPPING OF BABY JOHN, THE
BABY KITTENS • 1938 • Lovy Alex • ANS • USA
BABY KONG • 1977 • Bava Mario • ITL
BABY, LIGHT MY FIRE • 1970 • Campa Lou • USA • COME ON BABY, LIGHT MY FIRE ○ C'MON BABY, LIGHT MY FIRE
BABY LOVE • 1968 • Reid Alastair • UKN
BABY LOVE • 1974 • Treyens Jacques • FRN
BABY LOVE • 1977 • Di Silvestro Rino • ITL
BABY LOVE -LEMON POPSICLE V • 1983 • Wolman Dan • ISR, FRG • LEMON POPSICLE 5 ○ ROMAN ZAIR
BABY MAKER, THE • 1970 • Bridges James • USA
BABY MAKES TWO • 1952 • *Lamb Gil* • SHT • USA
BABY MARIE'S ROUND-UP • 1919 • Bertram William • SHT • USA
BABY MINE • 1917 • Robertson John S., Ballin Hugo • USA
BABY MINE • 1927 • Leonard Robert Z. • USA
BABY MOTHER, THE see NO BABIES WANTED • 1928
BABY NEEDS MEDICINE • 1911 • *Solax* • USA
BABY OF THE BOARDING HOUSE, THE • 1911 • *Clarke Edwin* • USA
BABY OF THE BOARDING HOUSE, THE • 1912 • *Essanay* • USA
BABY ON THE BARGE, THE • 1915 • Hepworth Cecil M. • UKN
BABY PUSS • 1943 • Hanna William, Barbera Joseph • ANS • USA
BABY QUESTION, THE • 1913 • *Crystal* • USA
BABY REVIEW, THE • 1903 • Porter Edwin S. • USA
BABY ROSEMARIE • 1976 • Perkins Harold • USA • BABY ROSEMARY
BABY ROSEMARY see BABY ROSEMARIE • 1976
BABY SEAL, THE • 1941 • Rasinski Connie • ANS • USA
BABY.. SECRET OF THE LOST LEGEND see BABY • 1984
BABY SHERLOCK • 1912 • *Early Baby* • USA
BABY SHOW, THE • 1911 • Wilson Frank? • UKN
BABY SISTER • 1982 • Stern Steven Hilliard • TVM • USA
BABY SITTER, THE • 1947 • Kneitel Seymour • ANS • USA
BABY SITTER: UN MALEDETTO PASTICCIO see BABYSITTER, LA • 1975
BABY SITTERS JITTERS • 1951 • White Jules • SHT • USA
BABY SNAKES • 1979 • Zappa Frank • USA
BABY SPY, THE • 1914 • Le Saint Edward J. • USA
BABY STORY • 1978 • Bozzetto Bruno • ANM • ITL
BABY, TAKE A BOW • 1934 • Lachman Harry • USA
BABY, THE BOY AND THE TEDDY-BEAR, THE • 1910 • Martinek H. O. • UKN
BABY THE PEACEMAKER • 1910 • *Walturdaw* • UKN
BABY, THE RAIN MUST FALL • 1965 • Mulligan Robert • USA
BABY TRAMP see BUTTERFLY • 1975
BABY TRAMP, THE • 1912 • *Lubin* • USA
BABY VANISHES, THE (UKN) see BROADWAY LIMITED • 1941
BABY VICKIE • 1969 • Perkins Harold • USA
BABY WANTS A BATTLE • 1953 • Kneitel Seymour • ANS • USA
BABY WANTS A BOTTLESHIP • 1942 • Fleischer Dave • ANS • USA
BABY WANTS SPINACH • 1950 • Kneitel Seymour • ANS • USA
BABY WOES see ADIK MANJA • 1979
BABYA TZARSTVO see BABYE TSARSTVO • 1968
BABYE TSARSTVO • 1968 • Saltykov Alexei • USS • WOMEN'S KINGDOM ○ KINGDOM OF WOMEN, THE ○ BABYA TZARSTVO
BABYLAS • 1911 • Machin Alfred • SER • FRN
BABYLAS HABITE UNE MAISON TRANQUILLE • 1911 • Machin Alfred • FRN
BABYLAS VA SE MARIER • 1912 • Machin Alfred • FRN
BABYLON • 1981 • Rosso Franco • UKN
BABYLON PINK • 1979 • Pickard Henri • USA
BABYLONIA • 1970 • Dizikirikis George • GRC • BABEL
BABY'S ADVENTURES • 1912 • *Champion* • USA
BABY'S BIRTHDAY • 1929 • *Sennett Mack (P)* • SHT • USA
BABY'S BREAKFAST see DEJEUNER DE BEBE, LE • 1895
BABY'S CHOICE • 1911 • *Solax* • USA
BABY'S CHUM • 1909 • Raymond Charles? • UKN
BABY'S FAULT, THE • 1915 • Christie Al • USA
BABY'S JOY RIDE • 1913 • *Thanhouser* • USA
BABY'S NEW PIN • 1913 • *Lubin* • USA
BABY'S PERIL • 1906 • *Urban Trading Co* • UKN
BABY'S PETS • 1926 • *Sennett Mack (P)* • SHT • USA
BABY'S PHOTOGRAPH • 1913 • Kellino W. P. • UKN
BABY'S PLAYMATE • 1908 • Fitzhamon Lewin • UKN
BABY'S POWER, A • 1910 • Fitzhamon Lewin? • UKN
BABY'S RATTLE • 1911 • *Solax* • USA
BABY'S REVENGE • 1909 • McDowell J. B.? • UKN
BABY'S RIDE, THE • 1915 • Beranger George A. • USA
BABY'S SHOE, A • 1909 • Griffith D. W. • USA
BABY'S SHOE, A • 1912 • *Edwin Walter* • USA
BABY'S SHOES, THE • 1912 • *Republic* • USA
BABY'S TOOFS • 1916 • Myers Harry • SHT • USA
BABY'S TRUMPET • 1915 • *Pathe Exchange* • USA
BABYSITTER, LA • 1975 • Clement Rene • FRN, ITL, FRG • JEUNE FILLE LIBRE LE SOIR ○ WANTED: BABY-SITTER ○ BABY SITTER: UN MALEDETTO PASTICCIO ○ GANZ GROSSE DING, DAS ○ BABYSITTER, THE
BABYSITTER, THE • 1969 • Henderson Don • USA
BABYSITTER, THE • 1980 • Medak Peter • TVM • CND
BABYSITTER, THE see BABYSITTER, LA • 1975
BABYSITTER-BOOGIE see ADIEU, LEBWOHL, GOODBYE • 1961
BACALL TO ARMS • 1946 • Clampett Robert • ANS • USA
BACANALES ROMANAS • 1982 • Most Jacob • SPN • MY NIGHTS WITH MESSALINA ○ NIGHT WITH MESSALINA, A
BACARA • 1955 • Land Kurt • ARG
BACAROLE • 1934 • Lamprecht Gerhard • FRG
BACCANALI DI TIBERIO, I • 1959 • Simonelli Giorgio C. • ITL
BACCANTI, LE • 1961 • Ferroni Giorgio • ITL, FRN • BACCHANTES, THE (USA)
BACCARA • 1935 • Mirande Yves, Moguy Leonide • FRN
BACCHANAL DES TODES ODER DAS OPFER EINER GROSSEN LIEBE • 1917 • Eichberg Richard • FRG
BACCHANALE • 1970 • Amero John, Amero Lem • USA
BACCHANALES 69 • 1969 • Benazeraf Jose • CMP • FRN
BACCHANALES 73 • 1973 • Benazeraf Jose • CMP • FRN
BACCHANTES, THE (USA) see BACCANTI, LE • 1961
BACCHANTIN, DIE • 1924 • Karfiol William • FRG
BACH AND BROCCOLI see BACH ET BOTTINE • 1986
BACH DETECTIVE • 1936 • Pujol Rene • FRN
BACH EN CORRECTIONNELLE • 1939 • Wulschleger Henry • FRN
BACH ET BOTTINE • 1986 • Melancon Andre • CND • BACH AND BROCCOLI
BACH MILLIONNAIRE • 1933 • Wulschleger Henry • FRN • PAPILLON DIT LYONNAIS LE JUSTE
BACH TO BACH • 1967 • Leaf Caroline • SHT • USA
BACHELIERES EN CHALEUR • Doroy Jean-Jacques • FRN
BACHELIERS DE LA CINQUIEME, LES • 1962 • Seguillon Francois, Perron Clement • DCS • CND
BACHELOR see SHAGIRD • 1967
BACHELOR, THE • 1910 • *Selig* • USA
BACHELOR, THE see SCAPOLO, LO • 1956
BACHELOR, THE see SOLTERO, EL • 1977
BACHELOR AND THE BABY, THE • 1910 • *Vitagraph* • USA
BACHELOR AND THE BABY, THE • 1912 • Ricketts Thomas • USA
BACHELOR AND THE BOBBYSOXER, THE • 1946 • Reis Irving • USA • BACHELOR KNIGHT (UKN)
BACHELOR APARTMENT • 1931 • Sherman Lowell • USA
BACHELOR APARTMENT • 1937 • Buzzell Edward • USA
BACHELOR APARTMENTS • 1920 • Walker Johnny • USA
BACHELOR BABIES • 1926 • Lamont Charles • SHT • USA
BACHELOR BAIT • 1934 • Stevens George • USA
BACHELOR BAIT (UKN) see ADVENTURE IN BALTIMORE • 1949
BACHELOR BILL'S BIRTHDAY PRESENT • 1913 • *August Edwin* • USA
BACHELOR BLUES • 1948 • Goodwins Leslie • SHT • USA
BACHELOR BRIDES • 1926 • Howard William K. • USA • BACHELOR'S BRIDES
BACHELOR BUTT-IN, A • 1926 • *Sennett Mack (P)* • SHT • USA
BACHELOR BUTTONS • 1912 • Baker George D.?, Trimble Larry? • USA
BACHELOR CLUB see CLUB DE SOLTEROS • 1967
BACHELOR DADDY • 1941 • Young Harold • USA
BACHELOR DADDY, THE • 1922 • Green Alfred E. • USA
BACHELOR FATHER see UNGKARLSPAPPAN • 1934
BACHELOR FATHER, THE • 1931 • Leonard Robert Z. • USA
BACHELOR FATHER (USA) see PAPA SOLTERO • 1939
BACHELOR FLAT • 1962 • Tashlin Frank • USA
BACHELOR GIRL • 1968 • USA
BACHELOR GIRL see GARCONNE, LA • 1956
BACHELOR GIRL, THE • 1929 • Thorpe Richard • USA
BACHELOR GIRL APARTMENT (UKN) see ANY WEDNESDAY • 1966
BACHELOR GIRLS (UKN) see BACHELOR'S DAUGHTERS, THE • 1946
BACHELOR HUSBAND, A • 1920 • Foss Kenelm • UKN
BACHELOR IN PARADISE • 1961 • Arnold Jack • USA
BACHELOR IN PARIS (USA) see SONG OF PARIS • 1952
BACHELOR KNIGHT (UKN) see BACHELOR AND THE BOBBYSOXER, THE • 1946
BACHELOR MOTHER • 1932 • Hutchison Charles • USA
BACHELOR MOTHER • 1939 • Kanin Garson • USA • LITTLE MOTHER
BACHELOR OF ARTS • 1934 • King Louis • USA
BACHELOR OF ARTS • 1969 • Booth Harry • UKN
BACHELOR OF HEARTS • 1958 • Rilla Wolf • UKN
BACHELOR PARTY • 1984 • Israel Neal • USA
BACHELOR PARTY, THE • 1957 • Mann Delbert • USA
BACHELOR TOM AND HIS BIKINI PLAYMATES see BACHELOR TOM PEEPING • 1962
BACHELOR TOM PEEPING • 1962 • Castagnoli Joe, Dewar William, Jackson Jerry • USA • BACHELOR TOM AND HIS BIKINI PLAYMATES ○ BIKINI PLAYMATES
BACHELOR VISIT, THE • 1909 • *Selig* • USA
BACHELOR'S AFFAIRS • 1932 • Werker Alfred L. • USA
BACHELOR'S ALLIANCE, THE • 1916 • *Teare Ethel* • SHT • USA
BACHELORS' BABIES see STORK PAYS OFF, THE • 1941
BACHELOR'S BABIES, A • 1915 • Birch Cecil • UKN
BACHELOR'S BABY • 1932 • Hughes Harry • UKN
BACHELOR'S BABY, A • 1922 • Rooke Arthur • UKN
BACHELOR'S BABY, THE • 1915 • *Anderson Broncho Billy* • USA
BACHELOR'S BABY, THE • 1927 • Strayer Frank • USA • WANTED -BABY
BACHELOR'S BABY OR HOW IT ALL HAPPENED, THE • 1913 • Brooke Van Dyke • USA
BACHELORS BEWARE see DOKUSHIN-SHA GOYOJIN • 1930
BACHELOR'S BRIDE, THE • 1912 • *Coxen Ed* • USA
BACHELOR'S BRIDES see BACHELOR BRIDES • 1926
BACHELOR'S BURGLAR, THE • 1915 • *Anderson Broncho Billy* • USA
BACHELOR'S CHILDREN, A • 1918 • Scardon Paul • USA
BACHELOR'S CHRISTMAS, THE • 1912 • Wilson Ben • USA
BACHELORS' CLUB, THE • 1912 • *Quirk Billy* • USA
BACHELORS' CLUB, THE • 1921 • Bramble A. V. • UKN
BACHELOR'S CLUB, THE • 1929 • Smith Noel • USA
BACHELOR'S DAUGHTERS, THE • 1946 • Stone Andrew L. • USA • BACHELOR GIRLS (UKN)
BACHELOR'S DREAM • 1967 • Stephen A. C. • USA
BACHELOR'S DREAM, THE • 1909 • *Phoenix* • USA
BACHELOR'S DREAM, THE see SEN STAREHO MLADENCE • 1910
BACHELOR'S FINISH, A • 1910 • *Powers* • USA
BACHELOR'S FINISH, A • 1917 • *Dillon Jack* • USA
BACHELOR'S FINISH, THE • 1913 • *Crystal* • USA
BACHELOR'S FOLLY (USA) see CALENDAR, THE • 1931
BACHELORS GIRLS' CLUB • 1913 • *Grandon Ethel* • USA
BACHELORS' HOUSEKEEPER, THE • 1913 • *Solax* • USA
BACHELOR'S HOUSEKEEPER, THE • 1914 • *De Forrest Charles* • USA
BACHELOR'S LOVE, A • 1910 • *Imp* • USA
BACHELOR'S LOVE AFFAIR, A • 1909 • *Essanay* • USA
BACHELOR'S LOVE STORY, A • 1914 • Tucker George Loane • UKN
BACHELOR'S OLD MAID, THE • 1911 • *Champion* • USA
BACHELOR'S PARADISE • 1928 • Archainbaud George • USA
BACHELOR'S PARADISE, THE (USA) see CHEZ LA SORCIERE • 1901
BACHELOR'S PARADISE (USA) see PARADIES DER JUNGGESELLEN • 1939
BACHELOR'S PERSISTENCE, A • 1909 • *Urban-Eclipse* • USA
BACHELOR'S PIECE OF WEDDING CAKE, THE • 1907 • Collins Alf? • UKN
BACHELOR'S PUDDING, THE • 1909 • *Anglo-American Films* • UKN
BACHELOR'S ROMANCE, A • 1912 • *Comet* • USA
BACHELOR'S ROMANCE, THE • 1915 • *Emerson John* • USA
BACHELOR'S ROOM see BEKAR ODASI • 1967
BACHELOR'S SUPPER, A • 1909 • *Edison* • USA
BACHELOR'S WARD, THE • 1912 • Buckland Warwick? • UKN
BACHELOR'S WATERLOO, A • 1912 • *Lubin* • USA
BACHELOR'S WATERLOO, THE • 1912 • *Edison* • USA
BACHELOR'S WIFE, A • 1919 • Flynn Emmett J. • USA • MARY O'ROURKE
BACHELOR'S WIFE, THE • 1909 • *Essanay* • USA
BACHER • Tholen Tom • NTH
BACH'S FANTASY IN G MINOR see JOHANN SEBASTIAN BACH: FANTASIA G-MOLL • 1965
BACIAMO LE MANI • 1973 • Schiraldi Vittorio • ITL

BACIO, IL • 1974 • Lanfranchi Mario • ITL

BACIO A FIOR D'ACQUA, UN • 1936 • Guarino Joseph • ITL • AMORE AD ALTA VELOCITA

BACIO DEL SOLE, IL • 1961 • Marcellini Siro • ITL, FRG • DON VESUVIO

BACIO DELL'AURORA, IL see **FRANCOIS IL CONTRABBANDIERE** • 1954

BACIO DI CIRANO, IL • 1913 • Gallone Carmine • ITL

BACIO DI CYRANO, IL • 1920 • Gallone Carmine • ITL

BACIO DI UNA MORTA, IL • 1949 • Brignone Guido • ITL • DEAD WOMAN'S KISS, A (USA)

BACIO DI UNA MORTA, IL • 1974 • Infascelli Carlo • ITL

BACK • 1976 • Dunkley-Smith John • UKN

BACK ALLEY OPROAR • 1948 • Freleng Friz • ANS • USA

BACK ALLEY PRINCES • 1972 • Lo Wei • HKG

BACK AMONG THE OLD FOLKS • 1910 • *Selig* • USA

‡—×(BACK AND FORTH) • 1969 • Snow Michael • CND • DOUBLE-HEADED ARROW, THE

BACK AT THE FRONT • 1952 • Sherman George • USA • WILLIE AND JOE BACK AT THE FRONT ○ WILLIE AND JOE IN TOKYO (UKN)

BACK AT THREE • 1912 • Rains Fred • UKN

BACK-BREAKING LEAF, THE • 1959 • Macartney-Filgate Terence • DCS • CND • FEUILLE QUI BRISE LES REINS, LA

BACK COMES THE TURNIP • 1960 • CHN

BACK DOOR TO HEAVEN • 1939 • Howard William K. • USA

BACK DOOR TO HELL • 1965 • Hellman Monte • USA

BACK FIELD see **BAND PLAYS ON, THE** • 1934

BACK FIRE • 1920 • MacDonald J. Farrell • SHT • USA

BACK FIRE • 1922 • Neitz Alvin J. • USA

BACK FROM ETERNITY • 1956 • Farrow John • USA

BACK FROM SHANGHAI • 1929 • Smith Noel • USA

BACK FROM SPACE see **UCHU KARA NO KIKAN** • 1985

BACK FROM THE DEAD • 1957 • Warren Charles Marquis • USA

BACK FROM THE FRONT • 1943 • White Jules • SHT • USA

BACK FROM THE FRONT see **PRISHOL SOLDAT S FRONTA** • 1972

BACK HOME • 1960 • Abramov A. • USS

BACK HOME • 1989 • Haggard Piers • TVM • UKN

BACK HOME see **TUTTI A CASA** • 1960

BACK HOME AND BROKE • 1922 • Green Alfred E. • USA

BACK IN '14 • 1934 • Sparling Gordon • DCS • CND

BACK IN '22 • 1932 • Sparling Gordon • DCS • CND

BACK IN '23 • 1933 • Sparling Gordon • DCS • CND

BACK IN BEDFORD • 1976 • Dunkley-Smith John • UKN

BACK IN CIRCULATION • 1937 • Enright Ray • USA • ANGLE SHOOTER

BACK IN THE COUNTRY (USA) see **DAHINTEN IN DER HEIDE** • 1936

BACK IN THE MOUNTAINS • 1910 • *Nestor* • USA

BACK IN THE SADDLE • 1941 • Landers Lew • USA

BACK OF BEYOND, THE • 1954 • Heyer John • DOC • ASL

BACK OF THE MAN • 1917 • Barker Reginald • USA

BACK OF THE SHADOWS • 1915 • Daly William Robert • USA

BACK OF THE SUN • 1960 • Kelly Ron • UKN

BACK ON BROADWAY see **SHE'S BACK ON BROADWAY** • 1953

BACK ON THE FARM • 1920 • *Cohn Productions* • USA

BACK PAGE • 1933 • Lorenze Anton • USA

BACK PAGE, THE • 1931 • Arbuckle Roscoe • USA

BACK PAY • 1922 • Borzage Frank • USA

BACK PAY • 1930 • Seiter William A. • USA

BACK PORCH see **IT'S A GIFT** • 1934

BACK ROADS • 1981 • Ritt Martin • USA

BACK ROOM BOY • 1942 • Mason Herbert • UKN

BACK SEAT CABBIE • 1969 • Walsh C. • USA

BACK STAGE • 1917 • Gillstrom Arvid E. • SHT • USA

BACK STAGE • 1919 • Arbuckle Roscoe • SHT • USA

BACK STAGE • 1923 • Roach Hal • SHT • USA

BACK STREET • 1932 • Stahl John M. • USA

BACK STREET • 1941 • Stevenson Robert • USA

BACK STREET • 1961 • Miller David • USA

BACK STREETS OF BEYOGLU, THE see **BEYOGLU'NUN ARKA YAKASI** • 1987

BACK STREETS OF PARIS (USA) see **MACADAM** • 1946

BACK TO BACK • 1989 • Kincade John • USA

BACK TO BATAAN • 1945 • Dmytryk Edward • USA

BACK TO BOARDING • 1919 • *Lubin* • USA

BACK TO BROADWAY • 1914 • Ince Ralph • USA

BACK TO EARTH • 1923 • Herman Al • SHT • USA

BACK TO EDEN • 1913 • Thornby Robert T. • USA

BACK TO GOD'S COUNTRY • 1919 • Hartford David M. • CND, USA

BACK TO GOD'S COUNTRY • 1927 • Shipman Nell • USA

BACK TO GOD'S COUNTRY • 1927 • Willat Irvin V. • USA

BACK TO GOD'S COUNTRY • 1953 • Pevney Joseph • USA

BACK TO HER OWN • 1912 • *Gem* • USA

BACK TO HIS HOME TOWN • 1912 • *Imp* • USA

BACK TO JOBS • 1945 • Balla Nicholas • DCS • CND

BACK TO KAMPUCHEA see **ON L'APPELAIT CAMBODGE** • 1982

BACK TO LIBERTY • 1927 • McEveety Bernard F. • USA

BACK TO LIFE • 1913 • Dwan Allan • USA

BACK TO LIFE • 1925 • Bennett Whitman • USA

BACK TO LIFE see **HAYATA DONUS** • 1967

BACK TO LIFE AFTER 2000 YEARS • 1910 • *Pathe* • FRN • ROMAN'S AWAKENING, THE

BACK TO MY VILLAGE see **DROSO I ARHONTOPOULA** • 1968

BACK TO NATURE • 1910 • *Vitagraph* • USA

BACK TO NATURE • 1911 • *Eline Marie* • USA

BACK TO NATURE • 1919 • *Pioneer Films* • SHT • USA

BACK TO NATURE • 1936 • Tinling James • USA

BACK TO NATURE GIRLS • 1919 • Blystone John G. • SHT • USA

BACK TO OEGSTGEEST see **TERUG NAAR OEGSTGEEST** • 1987

BACK TO OLD VIRGINIA • 1923 • *Jordan Judith* • USA

BACK TO PRIMITIVE • 1913 • *Holland Joseph* • USA

BACK TO SCHOOL • 1986 • Metter Alan • USA

BACK TO SCHOOL DAYS • 1915 • *Asher Max* • USA

BACK TO THE BEACH • 1987 • Hobbs Lyndall • USA

BACK TO THE FARM • 1914 • Louis Will • USA

BACK TO THE FARM • 1915 • Levering Joseph • USA

BACK TO THE FUTURE • 1985 • Zemeckis Robert • USA

BACK TO THE FUTURE II • 1989 • Zemeckis Robert • USA

BACK TO THE FUTURE III • 1990 • Zemeckis Robert • USA

BACK TO THE ISLAND see **TERUG NAAR HET EILAND** • 1950

BACK TO THE KITCHEN • 1912 • *Mackenzie Donald* • USA

BACK TO THE KITCHEN • 1914 • O'Brien Jack • USA

BACK TO THE KITCHEN • 1917 • Curtis Allen • SHT • USA

BACK TO THE KITCHEN • 1919 • Morris Reggie • SHT • USA

BACK TO THE OLD FARM • 1912 • *Bailey William* • USA

BACK TO THE PLANET OF THE APES • 1974 • Weis Don, Laven Arnold • TVM • USA • NEW PLANET OF THE APES

BACK TO THE PRIMITIVE • 1911 • Turner Otis • USA

BACK TO THE PRIMITIVE • 1915 • Drew Sidney • USA

BACK TO THE SIMPLE LIFE • 1914 • Miller Ashley • USA

BACK TO THE SOIL • 1911 • *Pickford Mary* • USA

BACK TO THE SOIL • 1941 • Donnelly Eddie • ANS • USA

BACK TO THE STARS (USA) see **ERINNERUNGEN AUS DER ZUKUNFT** • 1969

BACK TO THE TREES • 1926 • Greenwood Edwin • UKN

BACK TO THE WALL see **DOS AU MUR** • 1958

BACK TO THE WOODS • 1918 • Irving George • USA

BACK TO THE WOODS • 1919 • Roach Hal • SHT • USA

BACK TO THE WOODS • 1937 • Black Preston • SHT • USA

BACK TO YELLOW JACKET • 1922 • Wilson Ben • USA

BACK TRAIL • 1948 • Cabanne W. Christy • USA

BACK TRAIL, THE • 1924 • Smith Cliff • USA

BACK WINDOW, THE • 1912 • *Myers Harry* • USA

BACK YARD, THE • 1920 • Robbins Jess • SHT • USA

BACK YARD THEATRE, A • 1914 • Thornby Robert T. • USA

BACKBITERS see **VIE SANS JOIE, UNE** • 1924

BACKBONE • 1923 • Sloman Edward • USA

BACKBONE see **KICMA** • 1976

BACKFIELD PAY • 1931 • Kelley Albert • SHT • USA

BACKFIRE • 1950 • Sherman Vincent • USA • SOMEWHERE IN THE CITY

BACKFIRE! • 1962 • Almond Paul • UKN

BACKFIRE • 1987 • Cates Gilbert • USA

BACKFIRE (UKN) see **LAW COMES TO GUNSIGHT, THE** • 1947

BACKFIRE (USA) see **ECHAPPEMENT LIBRE** • 1964

BACKGROUND • 1953 • Birt Daniel • UKN • EDGE OF DIVORCE (USA)

BACKGROUND TO DANGER • 1943 • Walsh Raoul • USA

BACKLASH • 1947 • Forde Eugene J. • USA

BACKLASH • 1956 • Sturges John • USA

BACKLASH • 1986 • Bennett Bill • ASL

BACKROADS • 1977 • Noyce Phil • ASL

BACKROOM, THE see **TRASTIENDA, LA** • 1975

BACKS TO NATURE • 1933 • Meins Gus • SHT • USA

BACKSLIDER, THE • 1914 • Morrisey Edward • USA

BACKSTAGE • 1927 • Stone Phil • USA

BACKSTAGE • 1986 • Hardy Jonathan • ASL

BACKSTAGE see **LIMELIGHT** • 1936

BACKSTAGE AT A NURSERY RHYME • 1983 • Sens Al • ANS • CND

BACKSTAGE AT THE KIROV • 1983 • Hart Derek • USA

BACKSTAGE BLUES see **WHY BRING THAT UP?** • 1929

BACKSTAGE FOLLIES • 1948 • Yates Hal • SHT • USA

BACKSTAIRS see **HINTERTREPPE, DIE** • 1921

BACKSTRETCH • 1983 • Trent John • SER • CND

BACKTRACK • 1969 • Bellamy Earl • MTV • USA

BACKTRACK • 1989 • Hopper Dennis • USA

BACKWARD SONS AND FORWARD DAUGHTERS • 1917 • Dunham Phil • SHT • USA

BACKWOODS see **GEEK** • 1987

BACKWOODS BUNNY • 1959 • McKimson Robert • ANS • USA

BACKWOODS MASSACRE see **MIDNIGHT** • 1981

BACKWOODSMAN'S SUSPICION, THE • 1911 • *Essanay* • USA

BACKYARD see **TVA TRAPPOR OVER GARDEN** • 1950

BACKYARD, THE • 1980 • Mehrjui Dariush • IRN

BACKYARD FRONT, THE • 1940 • Buchanan Andrew • UKN

BACKYARD OF LOVE see **HINTERHOEFE DER LIEBE** • 1968

BACO DA SETA, IL • 1974 • Sequi Mario • ITL

BACON GRABBERS • 1929 • Foster Lewis R. • SHT • USA

BAD see **ANDY WARHOL'S BAD** • 1977

BAD, THE see **EIB, EL** • 1967

BAD AND THE BEAUTIFUL, THE • 1952 • Minnelli Vincente • USA

BAD AUF DER TENNE, DAS • 1943 • von Collande Volker • FRG

BAD AUF DER TENNE, DAS • 1956 • Martin Paul • AUS

BAD BARBARA • 1972 • Gerber Paul • USA

BAD BASCOMB • 1945 • Simon S. Sylvan • USA

BAD BIRDS AND GOOD BIRDS see **UCCELLACCI E UCCELLINI** • 1966

BAD BLONDE (USA) see **FLANAGAN BOY, THE** • 1953

BAD BLOOD • 1935 • Mason Herbert • UKN

BAD BLOOD • 1980 • Newell Mike • NZL, UKN • GRAHAM MURDERS, THE ○ SHOOTING, THE

BAD BLOOD • 1989 • Vincent Chuck • USA • SON

BAD BLOOD see **FIRST OFFENCE** • 1936

BAD BOY • 1917 • Withey Chet • USA

BAD BOY • 1925 • McCarey Leo • SHT • USA

BAD BOY • 1935 • Blystone John G. • USA

BAD BOY • 1938 • Huntington Lawrence • UKN • BRANDED

BAD BOY • 1939 • Meyer Herbert • USA • PERILOUS JOURNEY (UKN)

BAD BOY • 1949 • Neumann Kurt • USA

BAD BOY, THE see **ZLY CHLOPIEC** • 1950

BAD BOY BILLY • 1915 • Weston Charles • UKN

BAD BOYS • 1983 • Rosenthal Rick • USA

BAD BOYS' JOKE ON THE NURSE • 1901 • Porter Edwin S. • USA

BAD BOYS (USA) see **FURYO SHONEN** • 1961

BAD BUCK OF SANTA YNEZ, THE • 1915 • Hart William S. • USA

BAD BUNCH, THE • 1976 • Clark Greydon • USA

BAD CASE OF MADNESS, A • 1974 • Maunder Paul • NZL

BAD CHARLESTON CHARLIE • 1973 • Nagy Ivan • USA

BAD CIGAR, A • 1900 • Smith G. A. • UKN

BAD COMPANIONS, THE • 1932 • Orton John • UKN

BAD COMPANY • 1925 • Griffith Edward H. • USA

BAD COMPANY • 1931 • Garnett Tay • USA

BAD COMPANY • 1945 • Barralet Paul • UKN

BAD COMPANY • 1972 • Benton Robert • USA

BAD COMPANY • 1972 • Emerson Wesley • USA

BAD COMPANY • 1985 • SAF

BAD COMPANY see **PERE NOEL A LES YEUX BLEUS, LE** • 1966

BAD COMPANY (USA) see **MAUVAISES FREQUENTATIONS, LES** • 1967

BAD DAUGHTER see **FURYO SHOJO** • 1949

BAD DAY AT BLACK ROCK • 1954 • Sturges John • USA

BAD DAY AT CAT ROCK • 1965 • Jones Charles M. • ANS • USA

BAD DAY FOR LEVINSKY, A • 1909 • Gobbett T. J.? • UKN

BAD DEAL • 1987 • Berry John • USA

BAD DIANE see **DIANA CAZADORA, LA** • 1956

BAD DREAMS • 1988 • Fleming Andrew • USA

BAD EGG, A • 1911 • *Solax* • USA

BAD EGG, A • 1914 • *Powers* • USA

BAD EGGS see **ROTAGG** • 1946

BAD FLOWER, THE see **AHKEA KKOTS** • 1961

BAD FOR EACH OTHER • 1953 • Rapper Irving • USA • SCALPEL

BAD GAME, A • 1913 • Sennett Mack • USA

BAD GENIUS, THE • 1932 • *Mintz Charles (P)* • ANS • USA

BAD GEORGIA ROAD • 1976 • Broderick John • USA

BAD GIRL • 1931 • Borzage Frank • USA

BAD GIRL see **MY TEENAGE DAUGHTER** • 1956

BAD GIRL see **PALOMILLA BRAVA** • 1973

BAD GIRL, THE see **FURYO SHOJO** • 1949

BAD GIRLS DO CRY • 1963 • Melton Sid • USA

BAD GIRLS DON'T CRY see **NOTTE BRAVA, LA** • 1959

BAD GIRLS' DORMITORY • 1985 • Kincaid Tim • USA

BAD GIRLS FOR THE BOYS • 1966 • McGaha William • USA

BAD GIRLS GO TO HELL • 1965 • *Wishman Doris* • USA

BAD GO TO HEAVEN, THE see **CATTIVI VANNO IN PARADISO, I** • 1958

BAD GOODY, A see **PLOKHOY KHOROSHYI CHELOVEK** • 1974

BAD GUY • 1937 • Cahn Edward L. • USA

BAD GUYS • 1985 • Silberg Joel • USA

BAD GUYS see **ROSSZEMEBEREK** • 1979

BAD HALF-DOLLAR, THE • 1911 • *Nestor* • USA

BAD HATS • 1982 • Ortega Pascal • TVM • UKN

BAD HOUSEKEEPING • 1937 • Goodwins Leslie • SHT • USA

BAD INFLUENCE • 1990 • Hanson Curtis • USA

BAD INVESTMENT, A • 1912 • Dwan Allan • USA

BAD JOKE see **SKVENEI ANEKDOT** • 1965

BAD LANDS • 1939 • Landers Lew • USA

BAD LANDS, THE • 1925 • Henderson Dell • USA

BAD LITTLE ANGEL • 1939 • Thiele Wilhelm • USA

BAD LITTLE FOX, THE • 1951 • Wasilewski Zenon • ANM • PLN

BAD LITTLE GOOD MAN, A • 1917 • Beaudine William • SHT • USA

BAD LITTLE SOW GIRL see **NAUGHTY** • 1927

BAD LORD BYRON, THE • 1949 • MacDonald David • UKN

BAD LOVE see **MAL AMADO, O** • 1974

BAD LUCK see **FUUN** • 1934

BAD LUCK see **NODLANDING** • 1952

BAD LUCK see **ZEZOWATE SZCZESCIE** • 1960

BAD LUCK BLACKIE • 1949 • Avery Tex • ANS • USA

BAD MAN, A • 1911 • *Bison* • USA

BAD MAN, THE • 1923 • Carewe Edwin • USA

BAD MAN, THE • 1930 • Badger Clarence • USA

BAD MAN, THE • 1941 • Thorpe Richard • USA • TWO-GUN CUPID (UKN)

BAD MAN AND OTHERS, A • 1915 • Walsh Raoul • USA

BAD MAN AND THE PREACHER, THE • 1910 • *Essanay* • USA

BAD MAN AND THE RANGER, THE • 1912 • Dwan Allan • USA

BAD MAN BOBBS • 1915 • Mix Tom • USA

BAD MAN FROM BIG BEND see **SWING, COWBOY, SWING** • 1944

BAD MAN FROM BODIE • 1925 • *Williams Big Bill* • USA

BAD MAN FROM CHEYENNE, THE • 1917 • Kelsey Fred A. • SHT • USA

BAD MAN FROM RED BUTTE • 1940 • Taylor Ray • USA

BAD MAN FROM THE EAST, THE • 1914 • *Komic* • USA

BAD MAN MASON • 1914 • *Crawford Florence* • USA

BAD MAN OF BRIMSTONE, THE • 1937 • Ruben J. Walter • USA

BAD MAN OF DEADWOOD • 1941 • Kane Joseph • USA

BAD MAN OF WYOMING (UKN) see **WYOMING** • 1940

BAD MANNERS • 1984 • Houston Bobby • CND • GROWING PAINS

BAD MAN'S BLUFF • 1926 • Neitz Alvin J. • USA

BAD MAN'S CHRISTMAS GIFT, THE • 1910 • *Anderson Broncho Billy* • USA

BAD MAN'S DOWNFALL, THE • 1911 • *Anderson Broncho Billy* • USA

BAD MAN'S FIRST PRAYER, THE • 1911 • *Essanay* • USA

BAD MAN'S LAST DEED, THE • 1910 • *Anderson Broncho Billy* • USA

BAD MAN'S MONEY see **BAD MEN'S MONEY** • 1929

BAD MAN'S RIVER (USA) see **...E CONTINUAVANO A FREGARSI IL MILIONE DI DOLLARI** • 1971

BAD MEDICINE • 1936 • Yarbrough Jean • SHT • USA

BAD MEDICINE • 1985 • Miller Harvey • USA

BAD MEN OF ARIZONA see **ARIZONA RAIDERS** • 1936

BAD MEN OF MARYSVILLE • 1955 • Landers Lew • MTV • USA

BAD MEN OF MISSOURI • 1941 • Enright Ray • USA

BAD MEN OF THE BORDER • 1945 • Fox Wallace • USA

BAD MEN OF THE HILLS • 1942 • Berke William • USA • WRONGLY ACCUSED (UKN)

BAD MEN OF THUNDER GAP • 1943 • Herman Al • USA

BAD MEN OF TOMBSTONE, THE • 1949 • Neumann Kurt • USA

BAD MEN'S MONEY • 1929 • McGowan J. P. • USA • BAD MAN'S MONEY

BAD MONEY • 1915 • Coyle Walter • USA

BAD MUSICIAN, THE • Ericsson Alvar • ANM • SWD

BAD NAME see **AKUMYO** • 1961

BAD NAMES' BREAKING OF TERRITORIES see **AKUMYO NAWABARI ARASHI** • 1974

BAD NAMES' CHERRY BLOSSOM see **AKUMYO ZAKURA** • 1966
BAD NEWS • 1918 • Edwards Harry J. • SHT • USA
BAD NEWS BANANAS • 1984 • Siegel Lois • CND
BAD NEWS BEARS, THE • 1976 • Ritchie Michael • USA
BAD NEWS BEARS GO TO JAPAN, THE • 1978 • Berry John • USA
BAD NEWS BEARS IN BREAKING TRAINING, THE • 1977 • Pressman Michael • USA
BAD OL' PUTTY TAT • 1949 • Freleng Friz • ANS • USA
BAD ONE, THE • 1930 • Fitzmaurice George • USA
BAD ONE, THE (UKN) see **SORORITY GIRL** • 1957
BAD PENNY • 1979 • Vincent Chuck • USA
BAD PETE'S GRATITUDE • 1912 • *American* • USA
BAD RABBIT'S MAD NIGHT, THE see **NOTTE PAZZA DEL CONIGLIACCIO, LA** • 1967
BAD REFERENCE see **WILCZY BILET** • 1964
BAD ROAD, THE see **VIACCIA, LA** • 1961
BAD SAMARITAN, THE • 1916 • *Myles Norbert* • SHT • USA
BAD SEED, THE • 1956 • LeRoy Mervyn • USA
BAD SEED, THE • 1964 • Pecen Nevzat • TRK
BAD SEED, THE • 1985 • Wendkos Paul • TVM • USA
BAD SIR BRIAN BOTANY • 1928 • Miller Frank • UKN
BAD SISTER • 1931 • Henley Hobart • USA
BAD SISTER (USA) see **WHITE UNICORN, THE** • 1947
BAD SIXPENCE, THE • 1907 • Cooper Arthur • UKN
BAD SLEEP WELL, THE (USA) see **WARUI YATSU HODO YOKU NEMURU** • 1960
BAD SON, A see **MAUVAIS FILS, UN** • 1981
BAD TANGLE, A • 1912 • *Imp* • USA
BAD TASTE • 1988 • Jackson Peter • NZL
BAD TASTE see **SAL GORDA** • 1983
BAD THIEF, THE see **LADRONE, IL** • 1979
BAD TIMBER see **CARNIVAL BOAT** • 1932
BAD TIMING • 1980 • Roeg Nicolas • UKN • BAD TIMING: A SENSUAL OBSESSION (USA) ○ ILLUSIONS
BAD TIMING: A SENSUAL OBSESSION (USA) see **BAD TIMING** • 1980
BADA ALLA TUA PELLE SPIRITO SANTO • 1972 • Mauri Roberto • ITL
BADAI-PASTI BERLALU • 1977 • Karya Teguh • INN • WHEN THE STORM IS OVER
BADAL • 1967 • Aspi • IND • CLOUDS
BADANG • Noor S. Roomai • MLY
BADARINII • 1960 • Naghi Gheorghe, Alexandrescu Sica • RMN • BOORS, THE
BADARNA • 1968 • Gamlin Yngve • SWD • BATHERS, THE ○ I, A VIRGIN
BADAWIYYA FI RUMA • 1965 • Salman Mohammed • LBN • BEDOUINE A ROME, UNE
BADAWWIYYA FI BARIZ • 1964 • Salman Mohammed • LBN • BEDOUINE A PARIS, UNE
BADDEGAMA see **BEDDEGAMA** • 1980
BADDESLEY MANOR -THE PHANTOM GAMBLER • 1926 • Elvey Maurice • UKN
BADDEST DADDY IN THE WHOLE WORLD, THE see **MOHAMED ALI** • 1971
BADEGATTE, DER • 1919 • Werner Alfred • FRG
BADEK LANG BVANA • 1979 • Lokman Z. • MLY • FIGHTER, THE
BADEKONIGIN, DIE • 1918 • Schmidthassler Walter • FRG
BADEMAUS, DIE • 1919 • Albes Emil • FRG
BADEMEISTER REPORT • 1974 • Casstner Guy • FRG • HOT AND SEXY (UKN)
BADEMEISTER SPAGEL • 1956 • Lehner Alfred • AUS
BADEN-POWELL JUNIOR • 1911 • Stow Percy • UKN
BADESSA DI CASTRO, LA • 1974 • Crispino Armando • ITL
BADGE 373 • 1973 • Koch Howard W. • USA
BADGE OF BRAVERY, THE • 1930 • Levigard Josef • SHT • USA
BADGE OF COURAGE see **DITO NELLA PIAGA, IL** • 1969
BADGE OF COURAGE, THE • 1911 • *Kalem* • USA
BADGE OF COURAGE, THE see **TURN BACK THE HOURS** • 1928
BADGE OF HONOR • 1934 • Bennet Spencer Gordon • USA
BADGE OF HONOR, THE • 1913 • *Kerrigan J. Warren* • USA
BADGE OF MARSHALL BRENNAN, THE • 1957 • Gannaway Albert C. • USA
BADGE OF OFFICE, THE • 1914 • *Reliance* • USA
BADGE OF POLICEMAN O'ROON, THE • 1913 • *Eclair* • USA
BADGE OF SHAME, THE • 1917 • August Edwin • USA
BADGE OF THE ASSASSIN • 1985 • Damski Mel • TVM • USA
BADGE OR THE CROSS, THE see **SARGE** • 1970
BADGER GENERAL see **TANUKI NO TAISHO** • 1965
BADGER PALACE, THE see **OHATARI TANKUI GOTEN** • 1958
BADGERED • 1916 • Heffron Thomas N. • USA
BADGERS, THE • 1910 • *Centaur* • USA
BADGER'S GREEN • 1934 • Brunel Adrian • UKN
BADGER'S GREEN • 1949 • Irwin John • UKN
BADGER'S HOLIDAY see **TANUKI NO KYUJITSU** • 1967
BADHU BIDESHINI • 1980 • Samad Abdus • BNG • CRY NO MORE
BADI BAHU • 1951 • *Biswas Anil (P)* • IND
BADI DIDI • 1939 • *Roy Bimal (Ph)* • IND
BADIDI AAKASH • *Rnfc* • NPL • CHANGING SKY, THE
BADJAO • 1957 • Avellana Lamberto V. • PHL
BADLANDERS, THE • 1958 • Daves Delmer • USA
BADLANDS • 1973 • Malick Terence • USA
BADLANDS see **SERGEANTS THREE** • 1962
BADLANDS OF DAKOTA • 1941 • Green Alfred E. • USA
BADLANDS OF MONTANA • 1957 • Ullman Daniel B. • USA
BADLINDO AAKASH • 1982 • Sharma Laxmi Nath • NPL • CHANGING HORIZON
BADLY-DRAWN HEN see **GALLINA VOGELBIRDAE** • 1963
BADLY-MADE PUPPET, THE see **NEPOVODENY PANACEK** • 1951
BADLY MANAGED HOTEL, A see **HOTEL EMPOISONNE L'** • 1897
BADLY WANTED • 1913 • *Lubin* • USA
BADMAN'S COUNTRY • 1958 • Sears Fred F. • USA
BADMAN'S GOLD • 1951 • Tansey Robert • USA
BADMAN'S TERRITORY • 1946 • Whelan Tim • USA
BADMINTON • 1945 • Anderson Philip • SHT • USA
BADNAM • 1969 • Shahzad Iqbal • PKS • SCANDAL
BADNAM BASTI • Kapoor Prem • IND
BADNESS OF BURGLAR BILL, THE • 1913 • Wilson Frank? • UKN
BADONG BALDADO • 1967 • Gallardo Cesar Chat • PHL • BADONG THE HANDICAPPED
BADONG THE HANDICAPPED see **BADONG BALDADO** • 1967
BADOU BOY, THE • 1970 • Diop Djibril • SNL
BADSHAH DAMPATI • 1953 • Chakrabarty Amiya • IND • HUNCHBACK OF NOTRE DAME, THE
BAENG • 1980 • SAF
BAFFLED • 1924 • McGowan J. P. • USA
BAFFLED • 1972 • Leacock Philip • TVM • UKN
BAFFLED BURGLAR, THE • 1907 • Booth W. R.? • UKN
BAFFLED, NOT BEATEN • 1913 • *Kalem* • USA
BAFFLES, GENTLEMAN BURGLAR • 1914 • Sterling Ford • USA
BAFFLING BUNNIES • 1956 • Rasinski Connie • ANS • USA
BAG AND BAGGAGE • 1923 • Fox Finis • USA
BAG DE ENS FASADER • 1961 • Weiss Peter • SHT • DNM • BEHIND UNIFORM FACADES
BAG OF FLEAS, A (UKN) see **PYTEL BLECH** • 1962
BAG OF GOLD, A • 1915 • Soutar Andrew • USA
BAG OF GOLD, THE • 1912 • *Kalem* • USA
BAG OF MARBLES, A see **SAC DE BILLES, UN** • 1976
BAG OF MONKEY NUTS, A • 1911 • Coleby A. E. • UKN • MAD MONKEY, THE (USA)
BAG OF TROUBLE, A • 1916 • *Burns Robert* • USA
BAGARRE ENTRE JOURNALISTES • 1899 • Melies Georges • FRN
BAGARRES • 1948 • Calef Henri • FRN • WENCH, THE (USA)
BAGATELLE FOR WILLARD MAAS • 1962 • Menken Marie • SHT • USA
BAGDAD • 1949 • Lamont Charles • USA
BAGDAD • 1951 • Thakur Anant • IND
BAGDAD CAFE • 1988 • Adlon Percy • FRG, USA • OUT OF ROSENHEIM
BAGDAD DADDY • 1941 • Ceballos Larry • SHT • USA
BAGDAD GAJA DONGA • 1968 • Yoganand D. • IND • THIEF OF BAGDAD
BAGDAD ON THE SUBWAY see **O. HENRY'S FULL HOUSE** • 1952
BAGDAT HIRSIZI • 1968 • Gorec Ertem • TRK • THIEF OF BAGDAD, THE
BAGDAT YOLU • 1968 • Kan Kemal • TRK • ROAD TO BAGDAD, THE
BAGGAGE BUSTER • 1941 • Kinney Jack • ANS • USA
BAGGAGE MAN, THE • 1917 • *Pokes & Jabs* • SHT • USA
BAGGAGE SMASHER, THE • 1910 • *Lubin* • USA
BAGGAGE SMASHER, THE • 1914 • Wright Walter • USA
BAGGAGE SMASHERS, THE • 1916 • *Hamilton Lloyd V.* • USA
BAGGED • 1912 • Aylott Dave? • UKN
BAGGED • 1934 • Harlow John • UKN
BAGGER • 1968 • Tholen Tom • SHT • NTH
BAGGIN' THE DRAGON • 1966 • Post Howard • ANS • USA
BAGH BAHADUR • 1989 • Dasgupta Buddhadeb • IND • TIGER MAN
BAGHDAD • 1951 • Wadia Homi • IND
BAGHDAD THIRUDAN • 1960 • Sundaram T. P. • IND • THIEF OF BAGHDAD
BAGHE SANGUI • 1975 • Kimiavi Parviz • IRN • STONE GARDEN, THE ○ GARDEN OF STONES
BAGHINI • 1968 • Bose Bijoy • IND • TIGRESS
BAGNAIA, PAESE ITALIANO • 1949 • Maselli Francesco • DOC • ITL
BAGNARD, LE • 1950 • Rozier Willy • FRN
BAGNARDS DE CAYENNE, LES • 1939 • Mejat Raymond • DOC • FRN
BAGNE DE FEMMES see **ZU NEUEN UFERN** • 1937
BAGNES D'ENFANTS • 1914 • Chautard Emile • FRN
BAGNES D'ENFANTS • 1933 • Gauthier Georges • FRN • GOSSES DE MISERE
BAGNOLO -DORF ZWISCHEN SCHWARZ UND ROT • 1964 • Jori Bruno • DOC • ITL, FRG • BAGNOLO (UKN)
BAGNOLO (UKN) see **BAGNOLO -DORF ZWISCHEN SCHWARZ UND ROT** • 1964
BAGNOSTRAFLING, DER • 1921 • Berger Josef • FRG
BAGNOSTRAFLING, DER • 1949 • Frohlich Gustav • FRG
BAGPIPER OF STRAKONICE, THE see **STRAKONICKY DUDAK** • 1955
BAGPIPES • 1960 • Halas John • ANS • UKN
BAGS OF GOLD • 1915 • *Huff Justina* • USA
BAGS (USA) see **WOREK** • 1967
BAGTHORPE SAGA, THE • 1983 • Stone Paul • MTV • UKN
BAGUE, LA • 1908 • Perret Leonce • FRN
BAGUE, LA • 1948 • Resnais Alain • DCS • FRN
BAGUE DU ROI KODA, LA • 1962 • Alassane Moustapha • ANS • NGR • KING KODA'S WEDDING
BAGUE QUI TUE, LA • 1915 • Feuillade Louis • FRN
BAH WILDERNESS • 1943 • Ising Rudolf • ANS • USA
BAHAMA PASSAGE • 1941 • Griffith Edward H. • USA
BAHAR • 1951 • *Burman S. D. (M)* • IND
BAHARDA SOLAN CICEK • 1968 • Utku Umit • TRK • FLOWER THAT WITHERED IN SPRING, THE
BAHARON KE SAPNE • 1967 • Husain Nasir • IND • DREAMS OF SPRING
BAHARON KI MANZIL • 1968 • Rizvi Yakub Hasan • IND • DESTINATION SPRING
BAHAY KUBO KAHIT MUNTI • 1968 • de Villa Jose • PHL • NIPA HUT, THOUGH SMALL, A
BAHEN • 1942 • Khan Mehboob • IND
BAHIA • 1978 • Camus Marcel • PRT
BAHIA DE PALMA • 1962 • Bosch Juan • SPN
BAHNO PRAHY • 1927 • Krnansky M. J. • CZC • BOG OF PRAGUE, THE
BAHRAM SHIRDEL • 1968 • Amin-E-Amini • IRN • BRAVE BAHRAM
BAHU BEGUM • 1967 • Sadiq M. • IND • ADORED WIFE
BAHUT DIN HUWE • 1954 • Vasan S. S. • IND • MANY DAYS HAVE PASSED
BAHUT VA CRAQUER, LE • 1981 • Nerval Michel • FRN
BAI MEE BHOLI • 1967 • Patil Krishna • IND
BAI MOTHI BHAGYACHI • 1968 • Keshev Datta • IND
BAIANO FANTASMA, O • 1984 • de Oliveira Denoy • BRZ • PHANTOM BAIANO, THE
BAID AN AL-WATAN • 1969 • Zubaydi Qays Al- • IRQ • LOIN DE LA PATRIE
BAIE-COMEAU • 1938 • Tessier Albert • DCS • CND
BAIE DES ANGES, LA • 1963 • Demy Jacques • FRN • BAY OF THE ANGELS (USA) ○ BAY OF ANGELS
BAIE D'HUDSON • 1950 • Tessier Albert • DCS • CND
BAIE DU DESIR, LA • 1964 • Pecas Max • FRN • EROTIC TOUCH OF HOT SKIN, THE (USA) ○ EROTIC TOUCH, THE ○ TOUCH OF SKIN
BAIGNADE, LA see **BAINS EN MER** • 1896-97
BAIGNADE DANS LA TORRENT • 1897 • Blache Alice • FRN
BAIGNADE EN MER • 1895 • Lumiere Louis • FRN
BAIGNADE EN MER • 1896-97 • Lumiere Louis • FRN
BAIGNADE EN MER • 1896 • Melies Georges • FRN • SEA BATHING
BAIGNADE IMPOSSIBLE, LA • 1901 • Zecca Ferdinand • FRN
BAIGNOIRE, LA • 1912-14 • Cohl Emile • ANS • USA
BAIJU BAVRA • 1949 • *Chitravani* • IND
BAIL BOND STORY, THE see **DANGEROUS PROFESSION, A** • 1949
BAIL JUMPER • 1990 • Faber Christian • USA
BAIL OUT AT 43.000 • 1957 • Lyon Francis D. • USA • BALE OUT AT 43.000 (UKN) ○ BAILOUT AT 43.000
BAIL UP see **KELLY GANG, THE** • 1910
BAILA MI AMOR • 1962 • Martinez Arturo • MXC
BAILANDO AO SOL • 1928 • Ribeiro Antonio Lopes • SHT • PRT
BAILANDO CHA CHA CHA • 1955 • Salvador Jaime • MXC
BAILANDO EN LAS NUBES • 1945 • Ojeda Manuel R. • MXC
BAILARIN Y EL TRABAJADOR • 1936 • Marquina Luis • SPN
BAILE, EL • 1959 • Neville Edgar • SPN
BAILE DE GRADUACION • 1961 • Toussaint Carlos • MXC
BAILE MI REY • 1951 • Rodriguez Roberto • MXC
BAILES DE GALICIA • 1960 • Castellon Alfredo • SHT • SPN
BAILEY BRIDGE • 1945 • Barnes Arthur W. • UKN
BAILIFF, THE • 1912 • *Cosmopolitan* • UKN
BAILIFF, THE see **SANSHO DAYU** • 1954
BAILIFF AND THE DRESSMAKERS, THE • 1909 • Bouwmeester Theo? • UKN
BAILIFFS, THE • 1932 • Cadman Frank • UKN
BAILIFF'S LITTLE WEAKNESS, THE • 1911 • Fitzhamon Lewin? • UKN
BAILLONNEE, LA • 1921 • Burguet Charles • FRN
BAILOUT AT 43.000 see **BAIL OUT AT 43.000** • 1957
BAIN DE LA PARISIENNE, LE see **APRES LE BAL** • 1897
BAIN D'X • 1956 • Alexeieff Alexandre • SHT • FRN • BENDIX
BAINA AS-SAMA' WA AL-ARDH see **BAYN EL SAMAA WA EL ARD** • 1959
BAINA AYDIK see **BAYEN IDEK** • 1959
BAINS DE DIANE A MILAN, LES • 1896 • Lumiere Louis • FRN
BAINS DE MALATILI, LES see **HAMMAN EL MALATIHI** • 1973
BAINS EN MER • 1896-97 • Lumiere Louis • FRN • BAIGNADE, LA ○ SEA BATHING
BAIQUEN DAIFU • 1964 • Zhang Junxiang • CHN • DOCTOR BETHUNE
BAIROLETTO • 1986 • Polverini Atilio • ARG
BAISAKHI MEGH • 1981 • Dutt Utpal • IND • STORM CLOUD
BAISANO JALIL, EL • 1942 • Pardave Joaquin • MXC
BAISE-MOI PARTOUT • Benazeraf Jose • FRN
BAISE UPRISING, THE • 1989 • CHN
BAISER, LE • 1929 • Feyder Jacques • FRN • KISS, THE
BAISER DE JUDAS, LE • 1909 • Bour Armand
BAISER DE L'EMPEREUR, LE • 1913 • Machin Alfred • NTH
BAISER QUI TUE, LE • 1927 • Choux Jean • FRN
BAISERS • Vallois Philippe • FRN
BAISERS, LES • 1964 • Berri Claude, Bitsch Charles L., Toublanc-Michel Bernard, Tavernier Bertrand, Hauduroy Jean-Francois • FRN, ITL • VOGLIA MATTA DI DONNA (ITL)
BAISERS DE SECOURS, LES • 1989 • Garrel Philippe • FRN
BAISERS VOLES, LES • 1968 • Truffaut Francois • FRN • STOLEN KISSES
BAISEZ MOI! • 1978 • Reinhard Pierre B. • FRN
BAISHEY SHRAVANA • 1960 • Sen Mrinal • IND • WEDDING DAY
BAISSEZ-MOI PARTOUT • 1979 • Benazeraf Jose • FRN
BAIT • 1950 • Richardson Frank • UKN
BAIT • 1954 • Haas Hugo • USA
BAIT • 1973 • Schiess Mario • SAF
BAIT • 1986 • Barr Denis • USA
BAIT, THE • 1916 • Bowman William J. • USA
BAIT, THE • 1921 • Tourneur Maurice • USA • HUMAN BAIT
BAIT, THE • 1973 • Horn Leonard • TVM • USA
BAIT, THE see **ZERSCHOSSENE TRAUME** • 1976
BAITA • 1967 • Seki Koji • JPN • WHORE, A
BAITAUN MIN RIMAL • 1972 • Arafa Saad • EGY • MAISON DE SABLE, UNE
BAITED TRAP • 1926 • Paton Stuart • USA
BAITED TRAP, THE • 1914 • *Baggot King* • USA
BAITED TRAP, THE (UKN) see **TRAP, THE** • 1958
BAITING THE BOBBY • 1909 • Fitzhamon Lewin • UKN
BAIXO GAVEA • 1986 • Barbosa Haroldo Martinho • BRZ • GAVEA GIRLS
BAIYYA AL-KHAWATIM • 1965 • Shahin Youssef • LBN • VENDEUR DE BAGUES, LE ○ BAYA EL KHAWATIM ○ RING SELLER, THE
BAJA OKLAHOMA • 1988 • Roth Bobby • TVM • USA
BAJADERENS HAEVN see **TEMPELDANSERINDENS ELSKOV** • 1914
BAJADSER • 1918 • Magnussen Fritz • DNM
BAJAJA • 1950 • Trnka Jiri • ANM • CZC • PRINCE BAYAYA ○ BAYAYA
BAJAZZO see **SEHNSUCHT** • 1920
BAJAZZO, DER • 1968 • von Karajan Herbert • SWT, FRG, AUS
BAJECNI MUZI S KLIKOU • 1979 • Menzel Jiri • CZC • THOSE WONDERFUL MOVIE CRANKS (UKN) ○ WONDERFUL MOVIE MEN ○ THOSE WONDERFUL MOVIE MEN WITH A CRANK ○ WONDERFUL MOVIE CRANKS ○ MAGICIANS OF THE SILVER SCREEN
BAJI DESHPANDE • 1927 • *Maharashtra* • IND • VALLEY OF IMMORTALS, THE
BAJKA • 1970 • Kuziemski Ryszard • ANS • PLN • FAIRY STORY, THE ○ TALE, A

BAJKA KNOMPRMISNI • 1959 • Hofman Eduard • ANS • PLN • COMPROMISING FABLE

BAJKA O SMOKU • 1962 • Kijowicz Miroslaw • ANS • PLN • STORY OF A DRAGON, THE ○ DRAGON, THE ○ TALES OF A DRAGON

BAJKA W URSUSIE see **POEMAT SYMFONICZNY "BAJKA" STANISLAWA MONIUSZKO** • 1952

BAJO EL CIELO ANDALUZ • 1959 • Ruiz-Castillo Arturo • SPN

BAJO EL CIELO DE MEXICO • 1937 • de Fuentes Fernando • MXC • BENEATH THE SKY OF MEXICO (USA)

BAJO EL CIELO DE MEXICO • 1957 • Baledon Rafael • MXC

BAJO EL CIELO DE SONORA • 1947 • Aguilar Rolando • MXC

BAJO EL IMPERIO DEL HAMPA • 1968 • Delgado Miguel M. • MXC • UNDER GANGSTER RULE

BAJO EL MANTO DE LA NOCHE • 1962 • Orol Juan • MXC • DESTINO DE TRES VIDAS

BAJO EN CIELO DE ASTURIAS • 1950 • Delgras Gonzalo • SPN

BAJO LA INFLUENCIA DEL MIEDO • 1954 • Orol Juan • MXC

BAJO LA METRALLA • 1982 • Cazals Felipe • MXC • AT GUNPOINT

BAJO PRESION • 1989 • Casaus Victor • CUB • UNDER PRESSURE

BAJO UN ANGEL DEL CIELO • 1942 • Amadori Luis Cesar • ARG • ANGEL DOWN FROM HEAVEN, AN

BAK SJU HAV • 1989 • Thorstenson Espen • NRW • BEYOND THE SEVEN SEAS

BAKAI PASTURE see **NEBO NASHEGO DETSTVA** • 1967

BAKALOGATOS, O • 1968 • Melissinos Vangelis • GRC • GROCERY BOY, THE

BAKARUHABAN • 1957 • Feher Imre • HNG • SUNDAY ROMANCE, A

BAKASIN MO SA GUNITA • 1968 • de Guzman Armando • PHL • REMINISCENCE

BAKED POTATO FESTIVAL, THE • 1977 • Ilyenko Yury • USS

BAKENEKO GOYODA • 1958 • Tanaka Tokuzo • JPN

BAKER AND BOY • 1902 • Collins Alf? • UKN

BAKER AND THE SWEEP, THE • 1898 • Smith G. A. • UKN

BAKER COUNTY U.S.A. • 1981 • Fruet William • CND • TRAPPED ○ KILLER INSTINCT, THE

BAKER OF VALORGUE, THE see **BOULANGER DE VALORGUE, LE** • 1952

BAKER STREET BOYS, THE • 1984 • Fox Marilyn • MTV • UKN

BAKER'S BREAD see **BROT DES BACKERS, DAS** • 1977

BAKER'S EMPEROR, THE see **PEKARUV CISAR** • 1951

BAKER'S HAWK • 1976 • Dayton Lyman D. • USA

BAKERS IN TROUBLE (USA) see **BOULANGERIE MODELE, LA** • 1907

BAKER'S WIFE, THE (USA) see **FEMME DU BOULANGER, LA** • 1938

BAKERY, THE • 1921 • Taurog Norman, Semon Larry • SHT • USA

BAKHTIARI MIGRATION, THE • 1975 • Howard Anthony • DOC • USA • PEOPLE OF THE WIND

BAKINTSY • 1938 • Turin Victor • USS • MEN OF BAKU

BAKIT BUGHAW ANG LANGIT? • 1981 • O'Hara Mario • PHL • WHY IS THE SKY BLUE?

BAKIT KITA INIBIG? • 1968 • Recio Teddy C. • PHL • WHY DID I LOVE YOU?

BAKO, L'AUTRE RIVE • 1978 • Champreux Jacques • FRN, SNL

BAKOM JALOUSIN • 1983 • Bjorkman Stig • SWD, DNM • BEHIND THE SHUTTERS

BAKONJA FRA BRNE • 1951 • Hanzekovic Fedor • YGS

BAKS • Thiam Momar • SNL

BAKSMALLA • 1973 • Donner Jorn • SWD • HANGOVER ○ LOVELIER THAN LOVE ○ SEXIER THAN SEX ○ TENDERNESS

BAKU WA TOUKICHIROH • 1955 • Mori Kazuo • JPN • I AM TOKICHIRO

BAKUCHIUCHI • 1967 • Ozawa Shigehiro • JPN • GAMBLER, THE

BAKUCHIUCHI: FUJIMI NO SHOBU • 1967 • Ozawa Shigehiro • JPN • GAMBLERS: INVINCIBLE GAME

BAKUCHIUCHI IPPIKIRYU • 1967 • Ozawa Shigehiro • JPN • DRAGON TATTOO, THE

BAKUCHIUCHI NAGURIKOMI • 1968 • Ozawa Shigehiro • JPN • RAID, THE

BAKUCHIUCHI: SOCHO TOBAKU • 1968 • Yamashita Kosaku • JPN • GAMBLER SERIES: THE GREAT CASINO

BAKUDAN-JI • 1925 • Yamamoto Kajiro • JPN • BOMB HOUR

BAKUDAN-OTOKO TO IWARERU AITSU • 1967 • Hasebe Yasuharu • JPN • SINGING GUNMAN, THE

BAKUHA SANBYO MAE • 1967 • Ida Tan • JPN • THREE SECONDS TO ZERO HOUR

BAKUMATSU • 1970 • Ito Daisuke • JPN • AMBITIOUS, THE

BAKUMATSU see **BAKUMATSU TAIYODEN** • 1958

BAKUMATSU TAIYODEN • 1958 • Kawashima Yuzo • JPN • SUN LEGEND OF THE SHOGUNATE'S LAST DAYS ○ SAHEIJI FINDS A WAY ○ BAKUMATSU

BAKUMATSU TENAMONYA OSODO • 1967 • Furusawa Kengo • JPN • TENAMONYA CONFUSION IN THE LAST DAYS OF THE TOKUGAWA REGIME

BAKUON • 1939 • Tasaka Tomotaka • JPN • AIRPLANE DRONE

BAKUON TO DAICHI • 1957 • Sekigawa Hideo • JPN • ROAR AND EARTH

BAKURO ICHIDAI • 1951 • Kimura Keigo • JPN • LIFE OF A HORSE TRADER ○ LIFE OF A HORSE DEALER

BAKURO ICHIDAI • 1963 • Segawa Masaji • JPN • HORSEMAN

BAKUSHOYARO DAIJIKEN • 1967 • Suzuki Hideo • JPN • GREAT INCIDENTS

BAKUSHU • 1951 • Ozu Yasujiro • JPN • EARLY SUMMER

BAKUSO see **INDI RACE: BAKUSO** • 1967

BAKUTO GAIJIN BUTAI • 1971 • Fukasaku Kinji • JPN • GAMBLERS IN OKINAWA

BAKUTO KAISAN SHIKI • 1968 • Fukasaku Kinji • JPN • GAMBLER'S DISPERSION

BAKUTO RETSUDEN • 1968 • Ozawa Shigehiro • JPN • GAMBLER BIOGRAPHY

BAL, LE • 1931 • Thiele Wilhelm • FRN

BAL, LE • 1983 • Scola Ettore • ITL, FRN, ALG • BALLANDO BALLANDO

BAL A SAVOYBAN see **BAL IM SAVOY** • 1934

BAL CUPIDON • 1948 • Sauvajon Marc-Gilbert • FRN

BAL DE L'HORREUR, LE see **PROM NIGHT** • 1980

BAL DE NUIT • 1959 • Cloche Maurice • FRN

BAL D'ENFANTS • 1896-97 • Lumiere Louis • FRN

BAL DES ESPIONS, LE • 1960 • Clement Michel • FRN, ITL • DANGER IN THE MIDDLE EAST (USA)

BAL DES PASSANTS, LE • 1943 • Radot Guillaume • FRN • CAMELIA BLANC, LE

BAL DES POMPIERS, LE • 1948 • Berthomieu Andre • FRN

BAL DES VOYOUS, LE • 1968 • Dague Jean-Claude, Soulanes Louis • FRN, ITL • KARIN UN CORPO CHE BRUCIA (ITL) ○ PLAYMATES (USA) ○ FEMMES, LES ○ SIN, SUN AND SEX

BAL DU COMTE D'ORGEL, LE • 1969 • Allegret Marc • FRN

BAL DU GOUVERNEUR, LE • 1989 • Pisier Marie-France • FRN

BAL IM SAVOY • 1934 • Sekely Steve • FRG, HNG • BAL A SAVOYBAN ○ BALL AT THE SAVOY

BAL NOIR, LE • 1909 • Carre Michel • FRN

BAL PARE • 1940 • Ritter Karl • FRG • MUNCHNER G'SCHICHTEN

BAL POUSSIERE • 1989 • Duparc Henri • IVC

BAL TABARIN • 1952 • Ford Philip • USA

BALA • 1976 • Ray Satyajit • DOC • IND

BALA DE PLATA • 1959 • Delgado Miguel M. • MXC

BALA DE PLATA EN EL PUEBLO MALDITO • 1959 • Delgado Miguel M. • MXC

BALA ES MI TESTIGO, UNA • 1959 • Urueta Chano • MXC

BALA MARCADA, UNA • 1971 • Bosch Juan • SPN

BALA PERDIDA • 1959 • Urueta Chano • MXC

BALABLOK • 1972 • Pojar Bretislav • ANM • CZC

BALACLAVA • 1928 • Elvey Maurice, Rosmer Milton • SIL • UKN • JAWS OF HELL (USA)

BALACLAVA • 1930 • Elvey Maurice, Rosmer Milton • SND • UKN • JAWS OF HELL (USA)

BALADA • 1958 • Vrbanic Ivo • YGS • BALLAD

BALADA DA PRAIA DOS CAES • 1986 • Costa Jose Fonseca • PRT

BALADA DE JOHNNY RINGO, LA • 1966 • Madrid Jose Luis • SPN, FRG • 5000 DOLLAR FUR DEN KOPF VON JONNY R. (FRG)

BALADA DEL REGRESO, LA • 1974 • Finn Oscar Barney • ARG • HOMECOMING BALLAD, THE

BALADA O SVIREPOM • 1972 • Djukic Radivoje-Lola • YGS • BALLAD OF THE CRUEL ONE, THE

BALADA O TRUBI I OBLAKU • 1961 • Stiglic France • YGS • BALLAD OF A TRUMPET AND A CLOUD ○ BALLAD ABOUT A TRUMPET AND A CLOUD

BALADA O UHERSKEM KRALI • 1980 • Trlica Karel • CZC • BALLAD OF THE HUNGARIAN KING

BALAJI • 1939 • Pulliah P. • IND

BALAJU • 1943 • Aguilar Rolando • MXC

BALALAIKA • 1939 • De Toth Andre • HNG

BALALAIKA • 1939 • Schunzel Reinhold • USA

BALANCE • 1983 • Kirkov Lyudmil • BUL

BALANCE, LA • 1982 • Swaim Bob • FRN

BALANCE, THE • 1915 • Belmont Joseph • USA

BALANCE, THE see **BILANS KWARTALNY** • 1975

BALANCE OF POWER, THE • 1914 • *Princess* • USA

BALANCE OF TERROR • 1962 • Fox Beryl, Leiterman Douglas • DOC • CND

BALANDRA ISABEL LLEGO ESTA TARDE • 1949 • Christensen Carlos Hugo • ARG

BALAOO OU DES PAS AU PLAFOND • 1913 • Jasset Victorin • SRL • FRN • BALAOO (USA)

BALAOO (USA) see **BALAOO OU DES PAS AU PLAFOND** • 1913

BALARRASA • 1950 • Nieves Conde Jose Antonio • SPN

BALAS PARA UN SHERIFF • 1971 • *Rosas Priego* • MXC

BALAST • 1969 • Zeman Bronislaw • ANS • PLN • BALLAST

BALATA DE MAIPO • 1911 • Gallo Mario • ARG

BALATLI ARIF • 1967 • Yilmaz Atif • TRK • ARIF FROM BALAT

BALATUM • 1938 • Alexeieff Alexandre • SHT • FRN

BALAYEUR, LA • 1961 • Desvilles • SHT • FRN

BALBOA • 1983 • Polakoff James • USA • BALBOA: MILLIONAIRE'S PARADISE

BALBOA: MILLIONAIRE'S PARADISE see **BALBOA** • 1983

BALCON DE LA LUNA, EL • 1961 • Saslavsky Luis • SPN

BALCON DE LA MORT, LE • 1917 • Leprieur Gaston • FRN

BALCON EN FORET, UN • 1979 • Mitrani Michel • FRN

BALCON SOBRE EL INFIERNO, UN (SPN) see **CONSTANCE AUX ENFERS** • 1964

BALCONY, THE • 1963 • Strick Joseph • USA

BALCONY, THE see **BALKON** • 1989

BALD DOG see **KOPASZKUTYA** • 1981

BALD HEAD FOR BALD HEAD • Bacso Peter • HNG

BALD LIE, A • 1916 • *Jockey* • USA

BALD STORY, A • 1912 • Stow Percy • UKN

BALDEVINS BROLLOP • 1938 • Wahlberg Gideon, Lingheim Emil A. • SWD • BALDWIN'S WEDDING (USA) ○ BALDEVIN'S WEDDING

BALDEVINS BRYLLUP • 1926 • Schneevoigt George • DNM

BALDEVIN'S WEDDING see **BALDEVINS BROLLOP** • 1938

BALDHEADED AGENT AND THE LAND OF DESTRUCTION MISSION, THE see **THOU VOU FALAKROS PRAKTOR EPIHIRISSIS GIS MADIAM** • 1969

BALDHEADED CLUB, THE • 1913 • *Horner Violet* • USA

BALDORIA NEI CARAIBI • 1956 • Ragona Ubaldo, Zavala Jose Luis • DOC • ITL, SPN • FIESTA EN EL CARIBE (SPN)

BALDWIN'S WEDDING (USA) see **BALDEVINS BROLLOP** • 1938

BALDY BELMONT ALMOST A HERO • 1914 • *Crystal* • USA

BALDY BELMONT AND THE OLD MAID • 1913 • *Crystal* • USA

BALDY BELMONT AS A ROMAN GLADIATOR • 1913 • *Belmont Claude* • USA

BALDY BELMONT BREAKS OUT • 1914 • *Crystal* • USA

BALDY BELMONT LANDS A SOCIETY JOB • 1913 • *Belmont Claude* • USA

BALDY BELMONT PICKS A PEACH • 1914 • *Belmont Claude* • USA

BALDY BELMONT WANTS A WIFE • 1913 • *Belmont Claude* • USA

BALDY BELMONT WINS A PRIZE • 1913 • *Belmont Claude* • USA

BALDY BELMONT'S BUMPS • 1914 • *Crystal* • USA

BALDY IS A WISE OLD BIRD • 1913 • *Crystal* • USA

BALE OUT AT 43.000 (UKN) see **BAIL OUT AT 43.000** • 1957

BALEARI OPERAZIONE ORO • 1966 • Forque Jose Maria • ITL, FRN • BARBOUZE CHERIE (FRN)

BALEINE QUI AVAIT MAL AUX DENTS • 1973 • Bral Jacques • FRN

BALERINA • 1947 • Ivanovsky Alexander • USS • RUSSIAN BALLERINA ○ BALLERINA

BALERINA NA KORABLE • 1969 • Atamanov Lev • ANS • USS • BALLERINA ON A SHIP

BALETE DRIVE HORROR STORY see **HIWAGA SA BALETE DRIVE** • 1988

BALETTPRIMADONNAN • 1916 • Stiller Mauritz • SWD • ANJALA, THE DANCER (UKN) ○ BALLET PRIMADONNA, THE ○ BALLERINA, THE ○ WOLO

BALEYDIER • 1931 • Mamy Jean • FRN

BALGOSPODEN • 1919 • Tourjansky Victor • USS

BALI • 1970 • Liberatore Ugo • ITL

BALI • 1979 • Noyce Phil • DOC • ASL

BALI RAJA see **WAMAN AVATAR** • 1921

BALI THE UNKNOWN: OR APE MAN ISLAND • 1921 • Horton Harold H. • USA • APE MAN ISLAND

BALIDAAN • 1963 • *Ghatak Ritwik* • IND

BALIKA BADHU • 1967 • Mazumdar Tarun • IND • CHILD BRIDE

BALINT FABIAN MEETS GOD see **FABIAN BALINT TALALKOZASA ISTENNEL** • 1981

BALISEURS DU DESERT, LES (FRN) see **HAIMOUNE, EL** • 1984

BALJE LJETO • 1971 • Tanhofer Nikola • YGS • INDIAN SUMMER

BALKAN EKSPRES • 1983 • Baletic Branko • YGS • BALKAN EXPRESS

BALKAN EKSPRES II • 1989 • Djordjevic Aleksandar, Antonijevic Predrag, Radovic Milos • YGS • BALKAN EXPRESS II

BALKAN EXPRESS see **BALKAN EKSPRES** • 1983

BALKAN EXPRESS II see **BALKAN EKSPRES II** • 1989

BALKED AT THE ALTAR • 1908 • Griffith D. W. • USA

BALKON • 1989 • Salykov Klykbek • USS • BALCONY, THE

BALL, DER • 1931 • Thiele Wilhelm • FRG

BALL, THE see **KLUPKO** • 1972

BALL AT SAVOY • 1936 • Hanbury Victor • UKN

BALL AT THE ANJO HOUSE, A see **ANJO-KE NO BUTOKAI** • 1947

BALL AT THE SAVOY see **BAL IM SAVOY** • 1934

BALL DER NATIONEN • 1954 • Ritter Karl • FRG

BALL GAME • 1980 • Perry Ann • USA

BALL GAME, THE • 1932 • Foster John, Rufle George • ANS • USA

BALL GAME, THE see **ULAMA, EL** • 1985

BALL IM METROPOL • 1937 • Wisbar Frank • FRG

BALL IM SAVOY • 1955 • Martin Paul • FRG

BALL IN FLIGHT see **BALLON VOLE** • 1960

BALL IS IN YOUR COURT, THE see **USTEDES TIENEN LA PALABRA** • 1974

BALL OF BURR see **TAKIAISPALLO** • 1970

BALL OF FIRE • 1941 • Hawks Howard • USA

BALL OF FORTUNE, THE • 1926 • Croise Hugh • UKN

BALL OF SUET, A (USA) see **PYSHKA** • 1934

BALL OF THE ANJO FAMILY, THE see **ANJO-KE NO BUTOKAI** • 1947

BALL PLAYER AND THE BANDIT, THE • 1912 • Ford Francis • USA

BALL-TRAP ON THE COTE SAUVAGE • 1989 • Gold Jack • UKN

BALLAD • 1968 • Agren Gosta • SWD

BALLAD see **BALADA** • 1958

BALLAD, THE see **DUMKA** • 1964

BALLAD, THE see **CIPRIAN PORUMBESCU** • 1972

BALLAD ABOUT A DENTIST see **BALLADA O DENTYSCIE** • 1965

BALLAD ABOUT A TRUMPET AND A CLOUD see **BALADA O TRUBI I OBLAKU** • 1961

BALLAD AUX SOURCES • 1965 • Hondo Abib Med • DCS • MRT

BALLAD FOR A CRACK-SHOT see **BALLATA PER UN PISTOLERO** • 1967

BALLAD FOR A GUNFIGHTER see **BALLATA PER UN PISTOLERO** • 1967

BALLAD FOR A MACHINE GUN see **BALLATA PER UN PEZZ DA 90** • 1966

BALLAD FOR MARIUCA, A • 1969 • Neagu Constantin, Constantinescu Titel • RMN

BALLAD IN BLUE • 1964 • Henreid Paul • UKN • BLUES FOR LOVERS (USA)

BALLAD OF A GUNFIGHTER • 1963 • Ward Bill • USA

BALLAD OF A HUSSAR, THE (USA) see **GUSARSKAYA BALLADA** • 1962

BALLAD OF A MAN see **WAJAH SEORANG LAKI-LAKI** • 1971

BALLAD OF A ROOSTER • 1965 • Berkovic Zvonimir • YGS

BALLAD OF A SOLDIER (USA) see **BALLADA O SOLDATE** • 1959

BALLAD OF A TRUMPET AND A CLOUD see **BALADA O TRUBI I OBLAKU** • 1961

BALLAD OF A WITCH see **BALLATA DI UNA STREGA** • 1909

BALLAD OF A WORKMAN see **FUTARI DE ARUITA IKUSHUNJU** • 1962

BALLAD OF ANDY CROCKER, THE • 1973 • McCowan George • TVM • USA

BALLAD OF ANICETO AND FRANCISCA, THE see **ROMANCE DEL ANICETO Y LA FRANCISCA** • 1967

BALLAD OF BERING AND HIS FRIENDS, THE • 1971 • Shvyrev Yuri • USS

BALLAD OF BERLIN, THE see **BERLINER BALLADE** • 1948

BALLAD OF CABLE HOGUE, THE • 1970 • Peckinpah Sam • USA

BALLAD OF CARL-HENNING see **BALLADEN OM CARL-HENNING** • 1969

BALLAD OF COSSACK GLOOTA, THE • 1937 • Savchenko Igor • USS

BALLAD OF CROW-FOOT, THE • 1968 • Dunn Willie • SHT • CND

BALLAD OF DEATH VALLEY see **PISTOLA PER RINGO, UNA** • 1965
BALLAD OF ESKIMO NELL • 1975 • Jean Jacques (c/d) • CND, ASL
BALLAD OF FURNACE CREEK, THE see **FURY AT FURNACE CREEK** • 1948
BALLAD OF GAVILAN • 1968 • Jugo William J. • USA
BALLAD OF GENKAI-SEA see **GENKAI TSUREZURE BUSHI** • 1985
BALLAD OF GREGORIO CORTEZ, THE • 1982 • Young Robert Malcolm • TVM • USA
BALLAD OF HAYACHINE, THE • 1983 • Haneda Sumiko • DOC • JPN
BALLAD OF HILLBILLY JOHN, THE see **LEGEND OF HILLBILLY JOHN, THE** • 1972
BALLAD OF JOE HILL, THE see **JOE HILL** • 1971
BALLAD OF JOSIE, THE • 1967 • McLaglen Andrew V. • USA
BALLAD OF KHEVSUR see **KHEVSURSKAYA BALLADA** • 1965
BALLAD OF LINDA, THE see **THORVALD OG LINDA** • 1982
BALLAD OF LOVE, A (USA) see **DVOYE** • 1965
BALLAD OF MURDER see **GOKUAKU BOZU HITOKIRI KAZOE UTA** • 1968
BALLAD OF NARAYAMA, THE see **NARAYAMA-BUSHI KO** • 1983
BALLAD OF NARAYAMA (USA) see **NARAYAMA BUSHI-KO** • 1958
BALLAD OF OLE HOYLAND, THE see **BALLADEN OM OLE HOYLAND** • 1970
BALLAD OF ORIN, THE see **HANARE GOZE, ORIN** • 1978
BALLAD OF PADUCAH JAIL, THE • 1934 • Roach Hal • SHT • USA
BALLAD OF PONY see **HARUKOMA NO UTA** • 1985
BALLAD OF SILK TREE see **NEMU NO KI NO UTA** • 1973
BALLAD OF SILK TREE, PART 2 see **NEMU NO KI NO UTA GA KIKOERU** • 1976
BALLAD OF SPLENDID SILENCE, A • 1913 • *Williams Eric* • UKN
BALLAD OF TAM-LIN, THE see **TAMLIN** • 1972
BALLAD OF TARA, THE see **TCHERIKE-YE TARA** • 1979
BALLAD OF THE CRUEL ONE, THE see **BALADA O SVIREPOM** • 1972
BALLAD OF THE HUNGARIAN KING see **BALADA O UHERSKEM KRALI** • 1980
BALLAD OF THE MAESTROS, THE • Calinescu Bob • ANM • RMN
BALLAD OF THE NARAYAMA, THE see **NARAYAMA BUSHI-KO** • 1958
BALLAD OF THE SOUTH SEAS, A • 1913 • Melies Gaston • USA
BALLAD OF THE TOP HAT, THE see **BALLADE VAN DEN HOOGEN HOED, DE** • 1936
BALLAD OF WRETCHES, A see **KARA PLNA BOLESTI** • 1985
BALLADA O DENTYSCIE • 1965 • Laskowski Jan • SRL • PLN • BALLAD ABOUT A DENTIST
BALLADA O SOLDATE • 1959 • Chukhrai Grigori • USS • BALLAD OF A SOLDIER (USA)
BALLADE • 1938 • Hagen Peter, Krause Willi • FRG • PRINZESSIN KEHRT HEIM, DIE
BALLADE • 1952 • Brealey Gil • SHT • ASL
BALLADE A BLANC • 1981 • Gauthier Bertrand • FRN
BALLADE ATOMIQUE • 1948 • Image Jean • ANS • FRN • ATOMIC BALLAD
BALLADE CHROMO • 1957 • Jabely Jean • ANS • FRN
BALLADE DE LA FECONDUCTRICE • 1978 • Boutonnat Laurent • FRN
BALLADE D'EMILE, LA • 1966 • Otero Manuel • ANS • FRN
BALLADE DES AMANTS MAUDITS, LE • 1967 • Lethem Roland • BLG • SONG OF THE ACCURSED LOVERS, THE
BALLADE DES DALTON, LA • 1978 • Goscinny Rene, Morris • ANM • FRN, BLG • LUCKY LUKE: BALLAD OF THE DALTONS ○ LUCKY LUKE AND THE DALTON GANG
BALLADE DU GENDARME, LA see **GENDARME EN BALLADE, LE** • 1970
BALLADE PA BULLERBORG • 1959 • Methling Sven • SWD
BALLADE PA CHRISTIANSHAVN • 1971 • Balling Erik • DNM • OUR HOME IS OUR CASTLE
BALLADE PARISIENNE • 1954 • Gibaud Marcel • SHT • FRN
BALLADE POUR UN CHIEN • 1968 • Vergez Gerard • FRN
BALLADE POUR UN VOYOU • 1962 • Bonnardot Jean-Claude • FRN
BALLADE VAN DEN HOOGEN HOED, DE • 1936 • de Haas Max • NTH • BALLAD OF THE TOP HAT, THE ○ BALLET OF THE TOP HAT
BALLADEN OM CARL-HENNING • 1969 • Gronlykke Lene, Gronlykke Sven • DNM • BALLAD OF CARL-HENNING ○ WINDMILLS, THE
BALLADEN OM OLE HOYLAND • 1970 • Andersen Knut • NRW • BALLAD OF OLE HOYLAND, THE
BALLADS AND BOLOGNA • 1917 • Jackson Harry • SHT • USA
BALLAGAS • 1981 • Almasi Tamas • HNG • GRADUATION
BALLAGO IDO • 1975 • Fejer Tamas • HNG • SECRET OF THE ATTIC
BALLANDO BALLANDO see **BAL, LE** • 1983
BALLAST see **BALAST** • 1969
BALLATA DA UN MILIARDO • 1967 • Puccini Gianni • ITL
BALLATA DEI MARITI, LA • 1963 • Taglioni Fabrizio • ITL, SPN
BALLATA DEL BOIA, LA (ITL) see **VERDUGO, EL** • 1964
BALLATA DI UNA STREGA • 1909 • *Ambrosio* • ITL • BALLAD OF A WITCH
BALLATA PER UN PEZZ DA 90 • 1966 • Gomas Guido • ANM • ITL • BALLAD FOR A MACHINE GUN
BALLATA PER UN PISTOLERO • 1967 • Caltabiano Alfio • ITL, FRG • BALLAD FOR A GUNFIGHTER ○ BALLAD FOR A CRACK-SHOT
BALLATA SPAGNOLA • 1958 • Rocco Gian Andrea, Serpi Pino • DOC • ITL • CAROSELLO SPAGNOLA
BALLATA TRAGICA • 1955 • Capuano Luigi • ITL
BALLE AU COEUR, UNE • 1965 • Pollet Jean-Daniel • FRN, GRC • DEVIL AT MY HEELS (USA)
BALLE DANS LE CANON, UNE • 1958 • Deville Michel, Gerard Charles • FRN • SLUG IN THE HEATER, A
BALLE SUFFIT, UNE • 1954 • Sacha Jean • FRN, SPN
BALLERINA • 1949 • Berger Ludwig • FRN • DREAM BALLERINA (USA)
BALLERINA • 1963 • Kaczender George • CND
BALLERINA • 1965 • Campbell Norman • USA, DNM
BALLERINA see **BALERINA** • 1947
BALLERINA see **ROSEN FUR BETTINA** • 1956
BALLERINA, THE • 1970 • Derbenev Vadim • USS
BALLERINA, THE see **BALETTPRIMADONNAN** • 1916
BALLERINA AND THE GOOD GOD see **BALLERINA E BUON DIO** • 1959
BALLERINA E BUON DIO • 1959 • Leonviola Antonio • ITL • ANGEL IN A TAXI (USA) ○ BALLERINA AND THE GOOD GOD
BALLERINA ON A SHIP see **BALERINA NA KORABLE** • 1969
BALLERINA (USA) see **MORT DU CYGNE, LA** • 1937
BALLERINE • 1918 • D'Ambra Lucio • ITL
BALLERINE • 1936 • Machaty Gustav • ITL • FANNY, BALLERINA DELLA SCALA
BALLERS, THE • 1969 • Glick Wizard • USA • CALLERS, THE ○ LISA AND BALLERS
BALLERUP BOULEVARD • 1986 • Wendel Linda • DNM
BALLES PERDUES • 1982 • Comolli Jean-Louis • FRN
BALLET ADAGIO • 1972 • McLaren Norman • DCS • CND
BALLET-BALLADE • 1963 • Barfod Bent • SHT • DNM
BALLET BLACK • 1987 • Dwoskin Stephen • UKN
BALLET DANCER, THE see **BALLETDANSERINDEN** • 1911
BALLET DE FRANCE • 1955 • Blareau Richard • FRN
BALLET DE SINGE see **VERITE SUR L'HOMME-SINGE, LA** • 1907
BALLET DES ONDINES, LES see **BALLET OF THE MERMAIDS** • 1938
BALLET DES SANTONS, LE • 1946 • Martin Marcel • SHT • FRN
BALLET DO BRASIL • 1962 • dos Santos Nelson Pereira • SHT • BRZ
BALLET FESTIVAL • 1949 • Blais Roger • DCS • CND • FESTIVAL DE BALLET
BALLET GIRL see **BALLETBORN** • 1955
BALLET GIRL, THE • 1916 • Irving George • USA
BALLET IN JAZZ • 1960 • Reinhard Hans • SHT • FRG
BALLET JAPONAIS • 1900 • Blache Alice • SER • FRN
BALLET LIBELLA • 1897 • Blache Alice • FRN
BALLET MASTER'S DREAM, THE see **REVE DU MAITRE DE BALLET, LE** • 1903
BALLET MECANIQUE, LE • 1924 • Murphy Dudley, Leger Fernand • SHT • FRN • MECHANICAL BALLET, THE
BALLET OF HANDS see **HANDE** • 1928
BALLET OF OTHELLO see **VENETSIANSKIY MAVR** • 1961
BALLET OF ROMEO AND JULIET, THE see **ROMEO I DZULETTA** • 1955
BALLET OF THE MERMAIDS • 1938 • Sparling Gordon • DCS • CND • BALLET DES ONDINES, LES
BALLET OF THE TOP HAT see **BALLADE VAN DEN HOOGEN HOED, DE** • 1936
BALLET-OOPS • 1954 • Cannon Robert • ANS • USA
BALLET PRIMADONNA, THE see **BALETTPRIMADONNAN** • 1916
BALLET TALES • 1956 • Managadze Shota • USS
BALLETBORN • 1955 • Henning-Jensen Astrid • DOC • DNM • BALLETTENS BORN ○ BALLET GIRL
BALLETDANSERINDEN • 1911 • Blom August, Gad Urban • DNM • BALLET DANCER, THE
BALLETEN DANSER • 1938 • Gade Svend • DNM
BALLETTENS BORN see **BALLETBORN** • 1955
BALLETTENS DATTER • 1913 • Holger-Madsen • DNM • UNJUSTLY ACCUSED ○ DANSERINDEN
BALLETTERHERZOG, DER see **K.U.K. BALLETTMADEL, DAS** • 1926
BALLETTMADELS • 1926 • Steinhoff Hans • FRG
BALLETTRATTEN • 1925 • *A.-G. Films* • FRG
BALLHAUS GOLDENER ENGEL • 1932 • Klaren Georg C. • FRG
BALLMAYER INTERVIEW, THE see **WYWIDD Z BALLMAYEREM** • 1962
BALLNICHT, EINE see **...UND DAS IST DIE HAUPTSACHE** • 1931
BALLO AL CASTELLO • 1939 • Neufeld Max • ITL
BALLON, LE • 1973 • Djingareye Maiga • SHT • NGR
BALLON ROUGE, LE • 1956 • Lamorisse Albert • FRN • RED BALLOON, THE
BALLON VOLE • 1960 • Dasque Jean • SHT • FRN • BALL IN FLIGHT
BALLONEKSPLOSIONEN • 1913 • *Dreyer Carl T.(Sc)* • DNM • BALLOON EXPLOSION, THE
BALLONGEN • 1946 • Poppe Nils • SWD • BALLOON, THE
BALLOON • 1960 • Pennebaker D. A. • USA
BALLOON, THE see **BALLONGEN** • 1946
BALLOON, THE see **FUSEN** • 1956
BALLOON ASCENSCION, MARIONETTES • 1898 • *Edison* • USA
BALLOON ASCENSION, A see **ASCENSION D'UN BALLON, L'** • 1897
BALLOON EXPLOSION, THE see **BALLONEKSPLOSIONEN** • 1913
BALLOON GOES UP, THE • 1942 • Davis Redd • UKN
BALLOON SITE 568 • 1942 • Moffat Ivan • UKN
BALLOON VENDOR, THE see **VENDITORE DI PALLONCINI, IL** • 1974
BALLOON VOYAGE, THE see **VOYAGE EN BALLON, LE** • 1960
BALLOONATIC, THE • 1923 • Cline Eddie, Keaton Buster • SHT • USA • BALLOONATICS
BALLOONATICS • 1917 • Blystone John G. • SHT • USA
BALLOONATICS see **BALLOONATIC, THE** • 1923
BALLOONIST'S MISHAP, THE (USA) see **MESAVENTURES D'UN AERONAUTE** • 1901
BALLOONLAND • 1935 • *Iwerks Ub (P)* • ANS • USA • PINCUSHION MAN, THE
BALLOONS • 1923 • Fleischer Dave • ANS • USA
BALLOONS, THE • 1967 • Buchvarova Radka • BUL
BALLOT BOX BUNNY • 1951 • Freleng Friz • ANS • USA
BALLROOM, THE see **FESTIVITETSSALONGEN** • 1965
BALLROOM HEROES • 1986 • Mulryans Peter • IRL
BALLROOM OF ROMANCE, THE • 1983 • O'Connor Pat • IRL
BALLROOM TRAGEDY • 1905 • *Bitzer Billy (Ph)* • USA
BALL'S BLUFF • 1962 • Downey Robert • USA
BALLSKANDAL • 1919 • von Cserepy Arzen • FRG
BALLYHOO BUSTER, THE • 1928 • Thorpe Richard • USA
BALLYHOOEY • 1960 • Lovy Alex • ANS • USA
BALLYHOO'S STORY, THE • 1913 • Sturgeon Rollin S. • USA
BALLYMUN • 1969 • Laoghaire Colm O. • DOC • IRL
BALMY KNIGHT, A • 1966 • Culhane Shamus • ANS • USA
BALMY SWAMI, A • 1949 • Sparber I. • ANS • USA
BALOCCHI E PROFUMI • 1953 • Montillo Natale, De Bernardi F. M. • ITL
BALRAM, SRIKRISHNA • 1968 • Chandrakant • IND
BALSAMUS L'UOMO DI SANTANA • 1970 • Avati Pupi • ITL • BLOOD RELATIONS (USA)
BALTAZARA KOBERA PRZYPADKI MILOSNE • 1988 • Has Wojciech J. • PLN, FRN • BALTHAZAR KOBER'S LOVE ACCIDENTS
BALTES A LA RECHERCHE D'UN PAYS, LES • 1980 • Dansereau Mireille • CND
BALTHASSAR'S FEAST OR MY NIGHT WITH STALIN see **PIRY VALTASARA ILI NOCH SO STALINIM** • 1989
BALTHAZAR • 1937 • Colombier Piere • FRN
BALTHAZAR see **AU HASARD BALTHAZAR** • 1966
BALTHAZAR KOBER'S LOVE ACCIDENTS see **BALTAZARA KOBERA PRZYPADKI MILOSNE** • 1988
BALTIC DEPUTY (USA) see **DEPUTAT BALTIKI** • 1937
BALTIC EXPRESS see **POCIAG** • 1959
BALTIC RHAPSODY see **RAPSODIA BALTYKU** • 1935
BALTIC SKY see **BALTIYSKOE NEBO** • 1961
BALTIC TRAGEDY, A see **BALTUTLAMNINGEN** • 1970
BALTIMORE BULLET, THE • 1980 • Miller Robert Ellis • USA
BALTIMORE ESCAPADE see **ADVENTURE IN BALTIMORE** • 1949
BALTIYSKOE NEBO • 1961 • Vengerov Vladimir • USS • BALTIC SKY
BALTUTLAMNINGEN • 1970 • Bergenstrahle Johan • SWD • BALTIC TRAGEDY, A
BALUCH • 1972 • Kimiyaei Massoud • IRN
BALUCHARI • 1968 • Ganguly Ajit • IND • SANDY LAND
BALUCHET, ROI DES DETECTIVES • 1922 • Leprieur Gaston • FRN
BALUL DE SIMBATA SEARA • 1968 • Saizescu Geo • RMN • SATURDAY NIGHT DANCE, THE
BALUN CANAN • 1976 • Alazraki Benito • MXC
BALWEG • 1987 • PHL
BALYAKALA SAKHI • 1967 • Sasikumar B. A. • IND • CHILDHOOD FRIEND
BALZAMINOV'S MARRIAGE see **ZHENITBA BALZAMINOVA** • 1965
BAMA THIT • Loon Pe • BRM
BAMA VIJAYAM • 1967 • Pullaiya C. • IND • VICTORY OF SATYAVAMA
BAMAN AVATAR • 1939 • Bhanja Hari • IND
BAMBA • 1948 • Contreras Torres Miguel • MXC
BAMBA, LA see **LA BAMBA** • 1987
BAMBALINAS • 1956 • Demicheli Tulio • MXC
BAMBARU AWITH • 1976 • Pathirajah Dharmasena • SLN
BAMBER KASHER • 1974 • el Imam Hassan • EGY
BAMBI • 1942 • Hand David • ANM • USA
BAMBI MEETS GODZILLA • 1969 • Newland Marvin • ANS • USA
BAMBINA see **FARO DA PADRE, LE** • 1974
BAMBINGER • 1984 • Shaffer Beverly • DOC • CND
BAMBINI CI AMANO, I • 1954 • Della Santa Enzo • ITL
BAMBINI CI GUARDANO, I • 1944 • De Sica Vittorio • ITL • CHILDREN ARE WATCHING US, THE
BAMBINI E NOI, I • 1970 • Comencini Luigi • MTV • ITL
BAMBINI IN CITTA • 1946 • Comencini Luigi • ITL • CHILDREN IN CITIES
BAMBINO see **TAXI DI NOTTE** • 1950
BAMBINO E IL POLIZIOTTO, IL • 1990 • Verdone Carlo • ITL • CHILD AND THE COP, THE
BAMBO • 1968 • MLI
BAMBOLA DI SATANA, LA • 1969 • Casapinta Ferruccio • ITL
BAMBOLE! see **BAMBOLE, LE** • 1964
BAMBOLE, LE • 1964 • Risi Dino, Comencini Luigi, Rossi Franco, Bolognini Mauro • ITL, FRN • POUPEES, LES (FRN) ○ BAMBOLE! ○ DOLLS, THE ○ FOUR KINDS OF LOVE
BAMBOLONA, LA • 1968 • Giraldi Franco • ITL • BIG DOLL, THE
BAMBOO BLONDE, THE • 1946 • Mann Anthony • USA
BAMBOO BROTHERHOOD, THE • *Yuo Tien Lung* • HKG
BAMBOO CROSS, THE • 1955 • Ford John • MTV • USA
BAMBOO DOLL, THE see **ECHIZEN TAKENINGYO** • 1963
BAMBOO DOLL OF ECHIZEN see **ECHIZEN TAKENINGYO** • 1963
BAMBOO DOLLS HOUSE see **WOMEN IN CAGES** • 1971
BAMBOO GODS AND IRON MEN • 1974 • Gallardo Cesar Chat • PHL, USA
BAMBOO HOUSE OF DOLLS, THE • 1973 • Kuei Chih-Hung • HKG
BAMBOO LEAF FLUTE OF NO RETURN see **KAERANU SASABUE** • 1926
BAMBOO PRISON, THE • 1954 • Seiler Lewis • USA • I WAS A PRISONER IN KOREA
BAMBOO SAUCER, THE • 1968 • Telford Frank • USA • COLLISION COURSE
BAMBOOZLED • 1919 • Rains Fred • UKN
BAMBOOZLERS, THE see **KAMO TO NEGI** • 1968
BAMBU • 1945 • Saenz De Heredia Jose Luis • SPN
BAMBUALDERN PA MENTAWEI • 1938 • Fejos Paul • DCS • SWD • AGE OF BAMBOO AT MENTAWEI, THE
BAMBULE • 1979 • Modugno Marco • ITL
BAMEUI YEOLGI SOGEURO • 1985 • Jang Gil-Su • SKR • STREET REVENGE
BAMSE • 1969 • Mattsson Arne • SWD • MY FATHER'S MISTRESS ○ TEDDY BEAR
BANA KURSUN ISLEMEZ • 1967 • Perveroglu Alaaddin • TRK • I'M BULLET-PROOF
BANACEK: DETOUR TO NOWHERE • 1972 • Smight Jack • TVM • USA
BANACEK: HORSE OF A SLIGHTLY DIFFERENT COLOR • 1974 • Daugherty Herschel • TVM • USA
BANACEK: LET'S HEAR IT FOR A LIVING LEGEND • 1972 • Smight Jack • TVM • USA

BANACEK: NO SIGN OF THE CROSS • 1972 • Duke Daryl • TVM • USA
BANACEK: NO STONE UNTURNED • 1973 • Heffron Richard T. • TVM • USA
BANACEK: NOW YOU SEE ME –NOW YOU DON'T • 1974 • McEveety Bernard • TVM • USA
BANACEK: PROJECT PHOENIX • 1972 • Heffron Richard T. • TVM • USA
BANACEK: THE GREATEST COLLECTION OF THEM ALL • 1973 • McCowan George • TVM • USA
BANACEK: THE TWO MILLION CLAMS OF CAP'N JACK • 1973 • Heffron Richard T. • TVM • USA
BANACEK: THE VANISHING CHALICE • 1974 • Kowalski Bernard • TVM • USA
BANACEK: TO STEAL A KING • 1972 • Antonio Lou • TVM • USA
BANADIQ AL-HURIA • 1962 • Chanderli Jamal • ALG • FUSILS DE LA LIBERTE, LES ○ FUSILS POUR LA LIBERTE, LES ○ GUNS FOR LIBERTY
BANAKIE MAIDEN, A • 1915 • Mackley Arthur • USA
BANAL, GANID, AT ANG PUSAKAL, ANG • 1968 • Villaflor Romy • PHL • SACRED, THE SELFISH AND THE VAGABOND, THE
BANAME MI AMOR • 1966 • Gomez Muriel Emilio • MXC
BANANA see **BANANAS** • 1960
BANANA BEACH • 1970 • Millin David • SAF
BANANA COP • 1984 • Liang Puzhi • HKG
BANANA GANG, THE • 1984 • SAF
BANANA JOE • 1982 • Steno • ITL, FRG
BANANA MONSTER, THE see **SCHLOCK** • 1972
BANANA PARADISE see **HSIANG-CHIAO T'IEN-T'ANG** • 1989
BANANA PEEL (USA) see **PEAU DE BANANE** • 1964
BANANA PLANTER'S PERIL, THE • 1911 • *Yankee* • USA
BANANA REPUBLIC • 1979 • Fabbri Ottavio • ITL
BANANA RIDGE • 1941 • Mycroft Walter C. • UKN
BANANA SKIN WALTZ, THE see **BANANHEJKERINGO** • 1986
BANANA SKINS • 1908 • Mottershaw Frank • UKN
BANANA SPLIT see **GANG'S ALL HERE, THE** • 1943
BANANAS • 1960 • Shibuya Minoru • JPN • BANANA
BANANAS • 1971 • Allen Woody • USA
BANANAS ARE COMING BACK AGAIN • 1929 • Aylott Dave, Symmons E. F. • SHT • UKN
BANANAS BOAT, THE (USA) see **WHAT CHANGED CHARLEY FARTHING** • 1974
BANANERA LIBERTAD • 1970 • von Gunten Peter • SWT
BANANES MECANIQUES • 1973 • Davy Jean-Francois • FRN, FRG • MECHANICAL BANANAS (UKN) ○ CLOCKWORK BANANA
BANANHEJKERINGO • 1986 • Bacso Peter • HNG • BANANA SKIN WALTZ, THE
BANAT EL RIF • 1945 • Wahby Youssef • EGY • COUNTRY GIRLS, THE
BANAT LAZIM TITZAWWIG, AL- • 1973 • Ridha Ali • EGY • FILLES DOIVENT SE MARIER, LES
BANAT WA AC-CAIF, AL- • 1960 • Wahab Fatin Abdel, Abu Saif Salah • EGY • FILLES ET L'ETE, LES
BANATUN FI AL-GAMI'A • 1969 • Salem Atef • EGY • JEUNES FILLES A L'UNIVERSITE
BANC DE LA DESOLATION, LE see **DE GRAY –LE BANC DE DESOLATION** • 1973
BANCA DI MONATE, LA • 1976 • Massaro Francesco • ITL
BANCALS, LES • 1982 • Lievre Herve • FRN
BANCHO SARA YASHIKI –OKIKU TO HARIMA • 1954 • Ito Daisuke • JPN • SAMURAI'S LOVE
BANCO, EL • 1973 • *Hanna Barbera* • MXC
BANCO A BANGKOK • 1964 • Hunebelle Andre • FRN, ITL • OSS 117 MINACCIA BANGKOK (ITL) ○ SHADOW OF EVIL (USA) ○ BANCO A BANGKOK POUR OSS 117 ○ JACKPOT IN BANGKOK FOR OSS 117
BANCO A BANGKOK POUR OSS 117 see **BANCO A BANGKOK** • 1964
BANCO DE PRINCE • 1950 • Dulud Michel • FRN • DAUPHIN SUR LA PLAGE, LE
BANCO PORTUGUES DO ATLANTICO • 1963 • Ribeiro Antonio Lopes • SHT • PRT
BANCRUPCY OF BOGGS AND SCHULTZ, THE • 1916 • *Griffith Ray* • SHT • USA
BAND A PART • 1964 • Godard Jean-Luc • FRN • BAND OF OUTSIDERS (USA) ○ OUTSIDERS, THE (UKN)
BAND CONCERT, THE • 1935 • Jackson Wilfred • ANS • USA
BAND LEADER, THE • 1914 • Stratton Edmund F. • USA
BAND MASTER, THE • 1917 • Gillstrom Arvid E. • SHT • USA
BAND MASTER, THE • 1930 • *Mintz Charles (P)* • ANS • USA
BAND MASTER, THE • 1931 • Lantz Walter, Nolan William • ANS • USA
BAND MASTER, THE • 1947 • Lundy Dick • ANS • USA
BAND OF ANGELS • 1957 • Walsh Raoul • USA
BAND OF ASSASSINS, A see **SHINOBI NO MONO** • 1963
BAND OF ASSASSINS (USA) see **SHINSENGUMI** • 1970
BAND OF NINJA see **NINJA BUGEICHO** • 1967
BAND OF OUTSIDERS (USA) see **BAND A PART** • 1964
BAND OF THE HAND • 1986 • Glaser Paul Michael • USA
BAND OF THIEVES • 1962 • Bezencenet Peter • UKN
BAND PARADE see **CHOO CHOO SWING** • 1943
BAND PLAYS ON, THE • 1934 • Mack Russell • USA • BACK FIELD ○ KID FROM COLLEGE
BAND WAGGON • 1940 • Varnel Marcel • UKN
BAND WAGON, THE • 1953 • Minnelli Vincente • USA
BANDA • 1965 • Kuzminski Zbigniew • PLN • GANG, THE
BANDA, LA see **BANDA J.S. CRONACA CRIMINALE DEL FAR WEST, LA** • 1972
BANDA BONNOT, LA (ITL) see **BANDE A BONNOT, LA** • 1969
BANDA CASAROLI, LA • 1962 • Vancini Florestano • ITL • CASAROLI GANG, THE
BANDA DE JAIDER, LA • 1974 • Vogeler Volker • SPN, FRG • JAIDER'S GANG
BANDA DE LOS OCHO, LA • 1962 • Demicheli Tulio • SPN
BANDA DE LOS PANCHITOS, LA • 1985 • Velazco Arturo • MXC • PANCHITOS GANG, THE
BANDA DE LOS TRES CRISANTEMOS, LA • 1969 • Iquino Ignacio F. • SPN
BANDA DEGLI ONESTI, LA • 1956 • Mastrocinque Camillo • ITL
BANDA DEL AUTOMOVIL A LA DAMA ENLUTADA, LA • 1919 • Vollrath Ernesto • MXC
BANDA DEL AUTOMOVIL GRIS, LA • 1919 • Rosas Enrique, Coss Joaquin • MXC • AUTOMOVIL GRIS, LA ○ GREY MOTOR CAR, THE ○ GREY CAR GANG, THE
BANDA DEL BUCO, LA • 1960 • Amendola Mario • ITL
BANDA DEL CINCO DE OROS, LA • 1926 • Urriola Eduardo • MXC
BANDA DEL FANTASMA, LA • 1963 • Salvador Jaime • MXC
BANDA DEL FANTASMA NEGRO, LA • *Clasa-Mohme* • MXC • BLACK GHOST'S BAND, THE
BANDA DEL GOBBO, LA • 1977 • Lenzi Umberto • ITL
BANDA DEL PECAS, LA • 1965 • Pascual Jesus • SPN
BANDA DEL TRUCIDO, LA • 1977 • Massi Stelvio • ITL
BANDA DELLE CIFRE, LA • 1915 • Ghione Emilio • SRL • ITL
BANDA J.S. CRONACA CRIMINALE DEL FAR WEST, LA • 1972 • Corbucci Sergio • ITL, SPN, FRG • J. AND S. – HISTORIA CRIMINAL DEL FAR WEST (SPN) ○ SONNY AND JED (USA) ○ J. AND S. – STORIA CRIMINALE DEL FAR WEST ○ HIJOS DEL DIA Y DE LA NOCHE, LOS ○ BANDA, LA
BANDA NAGARAYATA PEMINEEMA • 1953 • SLN
BANDA VALLANZASCA, LA • 1977 • Bianchi Mario • ITL
BANDAGE BAIT • 1951 • Barclay David • SHT • USA
BANDANA • 1968 • de Guzman Armando • PHL • SCARF
BANDARGAH-E-ESHGH • 1967 • Gorji • IRN • LOVE'S PORT
BANDBOX, THE • 1919 • Neill R. William • USA
BANDE A BOBO, LA • 1963 • Saytor Tony • FRN
BANDE A BONNOT, LA • 1969 • Fourastie Philippe • FRN, ITL • BANDA BONNOT, LA (ITL) ○ ANARCHISTES, LES ○ ANARCHISTES OU LA BANDE A BONNOT, LES
BANDE A BOUBOULE, LA • 1931 • Mathot Leon • FRN
BANDE A PAPA, LA • 1955 • Lefranc Guy • FRN
BANDE DE CONS! • 1970 • Lethem Roland • BLG
BANDE DE L'AUTO GRISE, LA • 1912 • Jasset Victorin • FRN
BANDE DES QUATRE, LA • 1988 • Rivette Jacques • FRN, SWT • GANG OF FOUR, THE (UKN)
BANDE DES SCHRECKENS, DIE • 1960 • Reinl Harald • FRG • TERRIBLE PEOPLE, THE (USA) ○ HAND OF THE GALLOWS
BANDE DU REX, LA • 1980 • Meunier Jean-Henri • FRN
BANDE VON HOHENECK, DIE • 1934 • Wilhelm Hans F. • FRG
BANDEAU SUR LES YEUX, LE • 1917 • Feuillade Louis • FRN
BANDEIRANTES • 1940 • Mauro-Humberto • SHT • BRZ
BANDEIRANTES, OS • 1959 • Camus Marcel • FRN, ITL
BANDERA, LA • 1935 • Duvivier Julien • FRN • ESCAPE FROM YESTERDAY (UKN) ○ GRANDE RELEVE, LA
BANDERA ARGENTINA, LA • 1897 • Py Eugenio • ARG
BANDERA NEGRA • 1985 • Olea Pedro • SPN • BLACK BANNER
BANDERA NEGRA, LA • 1956 • de Ossorio Amando • SPN
BANDERA ROTA • 1979 • Retes Gabriel • MXC • TORN FLAG
BANDERAS DEL AMANECER, LAS • 1984 • Sanjines Jorge • BLV
BANDHAVYALU • 1968 • Ranga Rao S. V. • IND • RELATIONS
BANDIDA see **VIVA MARIA!** • 1966
BANDIDA, LA • 1948 • Delgado Agustin P. • MXC
BANDIDA, LA • 1962 • Rodriguez Roberto • MXC
BANDIDO • 1956 • Fleischer Richard • USA
BANDIDO DE LA SIERRA, EL • 1926 • Ardavin Eusebio F. • SPN
BANDIDO GENEROSO, EL • 1954 • Elorrieta Jose Maria • SPN
BANDIDOS • 1967 • Dallamano Massimo • ITL, SPN • CREPA TU.. CHE VIVO IO ○ YOU DIE.. BUT I LIVE
BANDIDOS DE RIO FRIO, LOS • 1954 • Gonzalez Rogelio A. • MXC
BANDIDOS, LOS (MXC) see **BANDITS, THE** • 1966
BANDINI • 1963 • Roy Bimal • IND
BANDINI • 1988 • Deruddere Dominique • BLG, USA • WAIT UNTIL SPRING, BANDINI (USA)
BANDISH • Islam Nazaral • PKS
BANDIT, A • 1913 • Lehrman Henry • USA
BANDIT, THE see **BANDITO, IL** • 1946
BANDIT, THE see **CANGACEIRO, O** • 1953
BANDIT, THE see **CUCARACHA, LA** • 1959
BANDIT, THE see **JAGGA DAKU** • 1960
BANDIT, THE see **SAKAFLIAS, O** • 1967
BANDIT, THE see **AMANTE DI GRAMIGNA, L'** • 1968
BANDIT AND THE BABY, THE • 1915 • *Perley Charles* • USA
BANDIT AND THE PREACHER, THE see **ON THE NIGHT STAGE** • 1915
BANDIT AND THE PRINCESS, THE • 1964 • Antel Franz • FRG
BANDIT BUSTER, THE • 1926 • Thorpe Richard • USA
BANDIT GENERAL, THE (UKN) see **DEL ODIO NACIO EL AMOR** • 1949
BANDIT ISLAND OF KARABEI see **RETURN TO TREASURE ISLAND** • 1954
BANDIT KING, THE • 1907 • Anderson G. M. • USA
BANDIT KING OF TEXAS • 1949 • Brannon Fred C. • USA
BANDIT MAKES GOOD, THE • 1907 • Anderson G. M. • USA
BANDIT OF HELL'S GAP, THE • 1920 • *Ridgeway Fritzi* • SHT • USA
BANDIT OF POINT LOMA, THE • 1912 • Dwan Allan • USA
BANDIT OF SHERWOOD FORST, THE • 1946 • Sherman George, Levin Henry • USA
BANDIT OF THE BLUE MOUNTAIN see **NEELAMALI THIRUDAN** • 1957
BANDIT OF TROPICO, THE • 1912 • *Nestor* • USA
BANDIT OF ZHOBE, THE • 1959 • Gilling John • UKN
BANDIT PAR AMOUR • 1912 • Linder Max • FRN
BANDIT QUEEN, THE • 1950 • Berke William • USA
BANDIT RANGER • 1942 • Selander Lesley • USA
BANDIT TAMER, THE • 1925 • *Farnum Franklin* • USA
BANDIT TRAIL, THE • 1941 • Killy Edward • USA
BANDITEN DER AUTOBAHN • 1955 • von Cziffra Geza • FRG
BANDITEN VOM RIO GRANDE, DIE • 1965 • Backhaus Helmuth M. • FRG
BANDITEN VON ASNIERES, DIE • 1920 • Muller-Hagen Carl • FRG
BANDITENNEST AUF DEM ADLERSTEIN, DAS see **JAPANISCHE MASKE 1, DIE** • 1922
BANDITI A MILANO • 1968 • Lizzani Carlo • ITL • VIOLENT FOUR, THE (USA) ○ BANDITS IN MILAN
BANDITI A ORGOSOLO • 1961 • De Seta Vittorio • ITL • BANDITS OF ORGOSOLO (USA) ○ BANDITS AT ORGOSOLO
BANDITI A ROMA see **ROMA COME CHICAGO** • 1968
BANDITO • 1976 • Celentino Luciano • ITL
BANDITO, IL • 1946 • Lattuada Alberto • ITL • BANDIT, THE
BANDITO CALABRESE, IL see **CAMPANE DI POMPEI** • 1952
BANDITO DAGLI OCCHI AZZURI, IL • 1980 • Giannetti Alfredo • ITL • BANDITO DAGLI OCCHI BLU, IL ○ BLUE-EYED BANDITS, THE
BANDITO DAGLI OCCHI BLU, IL see **BANDITO DAGLI OCCHI AZZURI, IL** • 1980
BANDITO DELLA 11, IL (ITL) see **PIERROT LE FOU** • 1965
BANDITO SI.. MA D'ONORE • 1968 • Cherasco J. • ITL
BANDITS, THE • 1966 • Conrad Robert, Zacarias Alfredo • USA, MXC • BANDIDOS, LOS (MXC)
BANDITS, THE see **BAZOKU YAKUZA** • 1968
BANDITS AND BALLADS • 1939 • Brock Lou • USA
BANDITS AT ORGOSOLO see **BANDITI A ORGOSOLO** • 1961
BANDIT'S BABY, THE • 1925 • Hogan James P. • USA
BANDITS, BEWARE • 1917 • Santell Alfred • USA
BANDIT'S BRIDE, THE • 1911 • *Pathe* • USA
BANDIT'S BRIDE, THE • 1916 • *Utah* • USA
BANDIT'S CHILD, THE • 1912 • *Anderson Broncho Billy* • USA
BANDIT'S CHILD, THE • 1913 • *Kalem* • USA
BANDIT'S DAUGHTER, THE • 1912 • Collins Edwin J. • UKN
BANDIT'S DOUBLE, THE • 1917 • *Vitagraph* • USA
BANDITS EN AUTOMOBILE, LES • 1912 • Jasset Victorin • FRN
BANDITS FROM SHANTUNG • 1971 • Wang Feng?, Chang Yi? • HKG
BANDIT'S GOLD • 1920 • *Jennings Al* • SHT • USA
BANDIT'S GRATITUDE, THE • 1912 • *101 Bison* • USA
BANDITS IN MILAN see **BANDITI A MILANO** • 1968
BANDITS IN ROME see **ROMA COME CHICAGO** • 1968
BANDITS IN SARDINIA see **BARBAGIA** • 1969
BANDIT'S MASK, THE • 1912 • *Selig* • USA
BANDITS OF CORSICA, THE • 1953 • Nazarro Ray • USA • RETURN OF THE CORSICAN BROTHERS (UKN)
BANDITS OF DARK CANYON • 1947 • Ford Philip • USA
BANDITS OF ELDORADO • 1949 • Nazarro Ray • USA • TRICKED (UKN)
BANDITS OF LAMPIAO see **CANGACEIROS DE LAMPIAO** • 1967
BANDITS OF LONE PINE • 1916 • *Utah* • USA
BANDITS OF MACARONI MOUNTAIN, THE • 1915 • *Duncan Bud* • USA
BANDITS OF ORGOSOLO (USA) see **BANDITI A ORGOSOLO** • 1961
BANDITS OF THE AIR • 1925 • *Macdowell Melbourne* • USA
BANDITS OF THE BADLANDS • 1945 • Carr Thomas • USA
BANDITS OF THE BORDER MINE • 1914 • *Marnell David* • USA
BANDITS OF THE WEST • 1953 • Keller Harry • USA
BANDITS ON THE WIND (USA) see **YATO KAZE NO NAKA O HASHIRU** • 1961
BANDIT'S REDEMPTION, THE • 1913 • *Frontier* • USA
BANDIT'S SON, THE • 1927 • Fox Wallace • USA
BANDIT'S SPUR, THE • 1912 • *Pathe* • USA
BANDIT'S SURPRISE, THE • 1911 • *Powers* • USA
BANDITS VS. SAMURAI SQUADRON • 1980 • Gosha Hideo • JPN
BANDIT'S WAGER, THE • 1916 • Ford Francis • SHT • USA
BANDIT'S WATERLOO, THE • 1908 • Griffith D. W. • USA
BANDIT'S WIFE, THE • 1910 • *Anderson Broncho Billy* • USA
BANDOLA Y EL REY, LA • 1979 • Gadivia F. • VNZ • PANDORA AND THE KING, THE
BANDOLERO! • 1968 • McLaglen Andrew V. • USA
BANDOLERO, THE • 1924 • Terriss Tom • USA
BANDOLERO STANCO, IL • 1952 • Cerchio Fernando • ITL
BANDOLEROS DELLA DODICESIMA ORA, I • 1972 • Bragan A. • ITL
BANDWAGON • 1958 • Hopkinson Peter • SHT • UKN
BANDWIDTH • 1960 • Jodoin Rene • ANS • CND
BANFF TO LAKE LOUISE • 1939 • Oliver Bill • DOC • CND
BANG • 1967 • Godfrey Bob • SHT • UKN
BANG • 1975 • Troell Jan • SWD
BANG BANG • 1967 • Piollet Serge • FRN, ITL • O L'AMMAZZO O LA SPOSO (ITL)
BANG BANG • 1968 • Praeger Stanley?, Lelli Luciano • SPN, ITL, USA • BANG BANG KID, THE
BANG BANG • 1970 • Tokunow Alvin, Kaplan Bill • USA
BANG BANG • 1976 • Vincent Chuck • USA • PORN FLAKES ○ BANG, BANG, YOU'VE GOT IT!
BANG BANG GAME, THE see **BANG BANG GANG, THE** • 1970
BANG BANG GANG, THE • 1970 • Guylder Van • USA • KISS KISS BANG BANG ○ BANG BANG GAME, THE
BANG BANG KID, THE see **BANG BANG** • 1968
BANG! BANG! YOU'RE DEAD (USA) see **OUR MAN IN MARRAKESH** • 1966
BANG, BANG, YOU'VE GOT IT! see **BANG BANG** • 1976
BANG-SHANG-A-LANG • 1968 • Osorio Consuelo P. • PHL
BANG THE DRUM SLOWLY • 1973 • Hancock John • USA
BANG YOU'RE DEAD • 1954 • Comfort Lance • UKN • GAME OF DANGER
BANG YOU'RE DEAD see **BERLINO, APPUNTAMENTO PER LE SPIE** • 1965
BANGALORE MAIL • 1968 • Satyam Lanka • IND
BANGARU PICHIKA • 1968 • Babu • IND • GOLDEN SPARROW, THE
BANGARU SANKELLU • 1968 • Ramaneedu • IND • GOLDEN HANDCUFFS, THE
BANGIKU • 1954 • Naruse Mikio • JPN • LATE CHRYSANTHEMUMS
BANGKANG PAPEL SA DAGAT NG APOY • 1984 • Reyes Edgardo • PHL • PAPER BOAT IN A SEA OF FIRE
BANGKOK KEY CHOR • 1986 • PKS • THIEVES OF BANGKOK
BANGKOK NO YORU • 1965 • Chiba Yasuki • JPN • NIGHT IN BANGKOK ○ BANKOKKU NO YORU
BANGOKU NO ISSHO • 1932 • Yamanaka Sadao • JPN • LIFE OF BANGOKU
BANG'S BURGLAR ALARM • 1912 • *Powers* • USA
BANG'S BURGLAR ALARM • 1914 • *Warner'S Features* • USA
BANGS RENIGS • 1917 • *Mason Dan* • SHT • USA

BANGUNNYA NYI LORO KIDUL • 1986 • INN
BANGVILLE POLICE, THE • 1913 • Sennett Mack • USA
BANISHED FROM PARADISE • 1964 • el Wahab Fatin Abdul • UAR
BANISHED ORIN see **HANARE GOZE, ORIN** • 1978
BANISHED (USA) see **HANARE GOZE, ORIN** • 1978
BANJO • 1947 • Fleischer Richard • USA
BANJO HACKETT • 1976 • McLaglen Andrew V. • TVM • USA
BANJO HACKETT: ROAMIN' FREE • 1976 • McLaglen Andrew V. • TVM • USA
BANJO MAN • 1978 • Vinikow Joseph, Chodosh Reuben • USA
BANJO ON MY KNEE • 1936 • Cromwell John • USA
BANJOMAN • 1975 • Abramson Richard G., Varhol Michael C. • DOC • USA
BANK, AL- • 1965 • Salman Mohammed • LBN • BANQUE, LA
BANK, THE • 1915 • Chaplin Charles • USA
BANK, THE see **MARGEM, A** • 1967
BANK, THE see **BEREG** • 1983
BANK ALARM • 1937 • Gasnier Louis J. • USA
BANK BAN • 1914 • Curtiz Michael • HNG
BANK BOOK, THE see **VILDLEDT ELSKOV** • 1911
BANK BREAKER, THE see **KALEIDOSCOPE** • 1966
BANK BURGLAR'S FATE, THE • 1914 • *Reliance* • USA
BANK BUSTERS • 1984 • SAF
BANK CASHIER, THE • 1912 • *Lubin* • USA
BANK DETECTIVE, THE (UKN) see **BANK DICK, THE** • 1940
BANK DICK, THE • 1940 • Cline Eddie • USA • BANK DETECTIVE, THE (UKN)
BANK DIRECTOR, THE see **KARNEVAL** • 1908
BANK HOLIDAY • 1938 • Reed Carol • UKN • THREE ON A WEEKEND
BANK HOLIDAY AT THE DYKE • 1899 • Williamson James • UKN
BANK HOLIDAY LUCK • 1947 • Honri Baynham • UKN
BANK JOB see **DISORGANISED CRIME** • 1989
BANK MESSENGER, THE • 1913 • *Gaumont* • USA
BANK MESSENGER MYSTERY, THE • 1936 • Huntington Lawrence • UKN
BANK NOTE, THE • 1915 • *Joker* • USA
BANK NOTES • 1939 • Schwarzwald Milton • SHT • USA
BANK OF DEPARTURE • 1956 • Shindo Kaneto • JPN
BANK OF DEPARTURE see **RYURI NO KISHI** • 1956
BANK PRESIDENT'S SON, THE • 1912 • *Lessey George* • USA
BANK RAIDERS, THE • 1958 • Munden Maxwell • UKN
BANK ROBBERY, THE • 1908 • Tilghman William • USA
BANK ROBBERY (UKN) see **RENEGADES OF THE RIO GRANDE** • 1945
BANK SHOT, THE • 1974 • Champion Gower • USA
BANKA • 1957 • Gosho Heinosuke • JPN • ELEGY OF THE NORTH ○ ELEGY, AN
BANKA • 1975 • Kawasaki Yoshisuke • JPN • ELEGY
BANKE SEPAHI • 1938 • Vaidya Ramnik D. • IND
BANKER, THE • 1989 • Webb William • USA
BANKER AND THE THIEF, THE • 1915 • *Rea Isabel* • USA
BANKERL UNTERM BIRNBAUM see **MANN GEHORT INS HAUS, EIN** • 1945
BANKER'S DAUGHTER, THE • 1912 • *Kalem* • USA
BANKER'S DAUGHTER, THE • 1913 • *Eclair* • USA
BANKER'S DAUGHTER, THE • 1914 • Roskam Edward M., Haddock William F. • USA
BANKER'S DAUGHTER, THE • 1927 • Disney Walt • ANS • USA
BANKER'S DAUGHTER, THE • 1933 • *Terry Paul/ Moser Frank (P)* • ANS • USA
BANKER'S DAUGHTERS, THE • 1910 • Griffith D. W. • USA
BANKER'S DOUBLE, THE • 1915 • West Langdon • USA
BANKER'S SONS, THE • 1913 • *Billington Francelia* • USA
BANKER'S TREACHERY, THE • 1920 • *Jennings Al* • SHT • USA
BANKETT DEER SCHMUGGLER, DAS (FRG) see **BANQUET DES FRAUDEURS, LES** • 1951
BANKETTEN • 1948 • Ekman Hasse • SWD • BANQUET, THE
BANKHURST MYSTERY, THE • 1915 • *Sears A. D.* • USA
BANKKRACH UNTER DEN LINDEN, DER • 1925 • Merzbach Paul • FRG
BANKNOTENFALSCHER, DIE see **HILFERUF, DER** • 1916
BANKOKKU NO YORU see **BANGKOK NO YORU** • 1965
BANKOMATT • 1988 • Herman Villi • SWT
BANKRAUB IN DER RUE LATOUR • 1961 • Jurgens Curd • FRG
BANKROWER, DIE • 1973 • Van Rensburg Manie • SAF
BANKRUN, ET see **PRESSENS MAGT** • 1913
BANK'S INTERESTS CANNOT BE THOSE OF LINA BRAAKE see **LINA BRAAKE** • 1975
BANK'S MESSENGER, THE • 1913 • Duncan William • USA
BANKS OF THE WABASH see **ON THE BANKS OF THE WABASH** • 1923
BANKTRESOR 713 • 1957 • Klinger Werner • FRG
BANLIEUE SUD-EST • 1967 • Robin Jacques • FRN
BANLIEUE SUD-EST • 1978 • Grangier Gilles • FRN
BANNED • 1966 • *Adler Judy* • USA
BANNED FROM HEAVEN see **PORTTIKIELTO TAIVAASEEN** • 1989
BANNELING, DIE • 1971 • SAF
BANNER, THE see **SZTANDAR** • 1965
BANNER FILM • 1972 • Winkler Donald • CND
BANNER IN THE SKY see **THIRD MAN ON THE MOUNTAIN** • 1959
BANNER OF YOUTH see **SZTANDAR MLODYCH** • 1957
BANNERLINE • 1951 • Weis Don • USA
BANNING • 1967 • Winston Ron • USA
BANNIS IMAGINAIRES, LES see **FEELING OF REJECTION, THE** • 1947
BANO DE AFRODITA, EL • 1949 • Davison Tito • MXC
BANOVIC STRAHINJA • 1983 • Mimica Vatroslav • YGS, ITL, FRG
BANQUE, LA • 1955 • Vilardebo Carlos • SHT • FRN
BANQUE, LA see **BANK, AL-** • 1965
BANQUE NEMO, LA • 1934 • Viel Marguerite • FRN
BANQUET see **KYOEN** • 1929
BANQUET, LE • 1972 • Kollatos Dimitris • FRN
BANQUET, THE • Gazdag Gyula • DOC • HNG
BANQUET, THE see **BANKETTEN** • 1948
BANQUET BUSTERS • 1948 • Lundy Dick • ANS • USA
BANQUET DES FRAUDEURS, LES • 1951 • Storck Henri • BLG, FRN, FRG • BANKETT DEER SCHMUGGLER, DAS (FRG)
BANQUET OF MELODY • 1946 • Cowan Will • SHT • USA
BANQUIERE, LA • 1980 • Girod Francis • FRN
BANSARI BALA • 1938 • *Par* • IND
BANSARIBALA • 1935 • IND • FAIRY OF THE FLUTE (USA)
BANSHEE, THE • 1913 • *Sherry J. Barney* • USA
BANSHEES, THE • 1967 • Straiton John S. • ANS • CND
BANSHUN • 1949 • Ozu Yasujiro • JPN • LATE SPRING
BANSURI • 1979 • Ghimiray Tulshi • NPL
BANTAM COWBOY, THE • 1928 • King Louis • USA
BANTY RAIDS • 1963 • McKimson Robert • ANS • USA
BANTY TIM • 1913 • *Lubin* • USA
BANU, THE HORSE THIEF see **AT HIRSIZI BANU** • 1967
BANWARA • 1950 • *Kapoor Raj* • IND
BANWARE NAYAN • 1950 • *Kapoor Raj* • IND
BANYA see **BENJA** • 1962
BANYE GESHENG • 1985 • Yang Yanjin • CHN • PHANTOM OF THE OPERA
BANYON • 1971 • Day Robert • TVM • USA • WALK UP AND DIE
BANZAI • 1913 • Giblyn Charles • USA
BANZAI • 1918 • *Hayakawa Sessue* • SHT • USA
BANZAI • 1982 • Zidi Claude • FRN
BANZAI RUNNER • 1986 • Thomas John G. • USA
BAO AND HIS SON see **BAOSHI FUZI** • 1983
BAO GIO CHO DEN THANG MUOI • 1984 • Minh Dang Nhat • VTN • WHEN THE TENTH MONTH COMES
BAO GIO CHO TOI • Minh Dang Nhat • VTN • OCTOBER WON'T RETURN
BAOFENG-ZHOUYU • 1961 • Xie Tieli • CHN • HURRICANE
BAOSHI FUZI • 1983 • Xie Tieli • CHN • BAO AND HIS SON
BAPTEME DE CALINO, LE • 1910 • Durand Jean • FRN
BAPTISM see **KERESZTELO** • 1968
BAPTISM BY FIRE see **TUZKERESZTSEG** • 1951
BAPTISM OF FIRE see **GLORY BRIGADE, THE** • 1953
BAPTIZING • 1975 • King Allan • CND
BAQI ZIDI • 1988 • Li Han-Hsiang • HKG, CHN • SNUFF BOTTLE
BAQIAN LI LU YUN HE YUE • 1947 • Shi Dongshan • CHN • 8000 LI OF CLOUD AND MOON
BAQUET DE MESMER, LE • 1905 • Melies Georges • FRN • MESMERIAN EXPERIMENT, A (USA)
BAR 20 • 1943 • Selander Lesley • USA
BAR 20 JUSTICE • 1938 • Selander Lesley • USA
BAR 20 RIDES AGAIN • 1935 • Bretherton Howard • USA
BAR 51 • 1985 • Guttman Amos • ISR
BAR, THE see **SOME OF MY BEST FRIENDS ARE..** • 1971
BAR ASMAN NEYESHTE • 1968 • Yasami Siyamak • IRN • WRITTEN ON THE SKY
BAR BUCKAROOS • 1940 • French Lloyd • USA
BAR-C MYSTERY, THE • 1926 • Hill Robert F. • SRL • USA
BAR CROSS LIAR, THE • 1914 • *Eclair* • USA
BAR DE LA FOURCHE, LE • 1972 • Levent Alain • FRN
BAR DI GIGI, IL • 1961 • Baldi Gian Vittorio • ITL
BAR DU SAINT-LAURENT, LE • 1960 • Proulx Maurice • DCS • CND
BAR DU SOLEIL, LE see **ADRIEN** • 1943
BAR DU SUD • 1938 • Fescourt Henri • FRN
BAR DU TELEPHONE, LE • 1980 • Barrois Claude • FRN
BAR-EL-MANACH • 1920 • Sarnow Heinz • FRG
BAR ESPERANCA -O ULTIMO QUE FECHA • 1982 • Carvana Hugo • BRZ • HOPE BAR -THE LAST TO CLOSE
BAR FLY, THE • 1924 • Roach Hal • SHT • USA
BAR GIRLS see **BARLUDER** • 1983
BAR-K FOREMAN • 1912 • *Jones Edgar* • USA
BAR L RANCH • 1930 • Webb Harry S. • USA
BAR MAID • 1970 • *Kirt Films International* • USA
BAR MITZVAH BOY • 1976 • Tuchner Michael • TVM • UKN
BAR NOTHIN' • 1921 • Sedgwick Edward • USA
BAR-RAC'S NIGHT OUT • 1937 • Frank Earl • SHT • USA
BAR ROOM SCENE • 1894 • Dickson W. K. L. • USA
BAR SALON • 1973 • Forcier Andre • CND
BAR SINISTER, THE • 1917 • Lewis Edgar • USA
BAR SINISTER, THE see **IT'S A DOG'S LIFE** • 1955
BAR VON BASKERVILLE, DER • 1915 • Piel Harry • FRG
BAR Z BAD MEN • 1937 • Newfield Sam • USA
BAR Z'S NEW COOK • 1911 • *Grandin Ethel* • USA
BARA • 1979 • Sathyu M. S. • IND • FAMINE, THE
BARA EN DANSERSKA • 1927 • Molander Olof • SWD • ONLY A DANCING GIRL
BARA EN KVINNA • 1941 • Henrikson Anders • SWD • ONLY A WOMAN
BARA EN KYPARE • 1960 • Kjellin Alf • SWD • ONLY A WAITER
BARA EN MOR • 1949 • Sjoberg Alf • SWD • ONLY A MOTHER (USA)
BARA EN TRUMPETARE • 1938 • Henrikson Anders • SWD • ONLY A TRUMPETER
BARA-GASSEN • 1950 • Naruse Mikio • JPN • BATTLE OF ROSES, THE
BARA IKUTABI • 1955 • Kinugasa Teinosuke • JPN • GIRL ISN'T ALLOWED TO LOVE, A
BARA NO KI NI BARA NO HANA • 1959 • Edagawa Hiroshi • JPN • TIME OF ROSES AND BLOSSOMING FLOWERS
BARA NO SORETSU • 1970 • Matsumoto Toshio • JPN • FUNERAL OF ROSES ○ FUNERAL PARADE OF ROSES
BARA PER LO SCERIFFO, UNA (ITL) see **TUMBA PARA EL SHERIFF, UNA** • 1967
BARA ROLIGT I BULLERBYN • 1961 • Hellbom Olle • SWD • ONLY FUN AT BULLERBYN
BARA VARSHE 6 MAHINE 3 DIWAS • 1967 • Painter Vasant • IND
BARABAS • 1971 • Cosmi Carlo • VNZ • LIFE OF A MINER, THE
BARABBA • 1961 • Fleischer Richard • ITL • BARABBAS (USA)
BARABBAS • 1953 • Sjoberg Alf • SWD
BARABBAS THE ROBBER (USA) see **WHICH WILL YOU HAVE?** • 1949
BARABBAS (USA) see **BARABBA** • 1961
BARACCA E BURATTINI • 1954 • Corbucci Sergio • ITL
BARAIRO NO FUTARI • 1967 • Sakurai Hideo • JPN • FALLEN ROSEBUD
BARAJ • 1978 • Aksoy Orhan • TRK • DAM, THE
BARAJA DE LA MUERTE, LA • 1916 • Giambastiane Salvador • CHL
BARAJAS, AEROPUERTO INTERNACIONAL • 1950 • Bardem Juan Antonio • SHT • SPN • AEROPUERTO
BARAKA, LA • 1982 • Valere Jean • FRN
BARAKA SUR X 13 • 1965 • Cloche Maurice • FRN, ITL, SPN
BARAKO • 1967 • Castillo Celso Ad. • PHL • HE-MAN
BARANDE HAV • 1951 • Mattsson Arne • SWD • ROLLING SEA
BARAO OLAVO see **BARAO OLAVO, O TERRIVEL** • 1970
BARAO OLAVO, O TERRIVEL • 1970 • Bressane Julio • BRZ • BARAO OLAVO
BARAO OTELO NO BARATO DOS BILHOES • 1972 • Borges Miguel • BRZ
BARAQUE No.1 • 1945 • de Meyst E. G. • FRN
BARATIN • 1957 • Stelli Jean • FRN
BARATINEUR, LE see **CA FAIT TILT** • 1977
BARATINEURS, LES • 1965 • Rigaud Francis • FRN
BARB WIRE • 1922 • Grandon Francis J. • USA • BARBED WIRE
BARB WIRE (THE RAWHIDE HALO) see **RAWHIDE HALO, THE** • 1960
BARBA ZVANE • 1949 • Afric Vjekoslav • YGS
BARBABLU • 1941 • Bragaglia Carlo Ludovico • ITL
BARBABLU, BARBABLU • 1989 • Carpi Fabio • ITL • BLUE BEARD, BLUE BEARD
BARBABLU (ITL) see **BARBE-BLEUE** • 1972
BARBACKA • 1946 • Ekerot Bengt • SWD • BAREBACK
BARBADOS QUEST • 1955 • Knowles Bernard • UKN • MURDER ON APPROVAL (USA)
BARBAGIA • 1969 • Lizzani Carlo • ITL • BANDITS IN SARDINIA ○ SOCIETA DEL MALESSERE
BARBARA • 1961 • Wisbar Frank • FRG
BARBARA • 1970 • Burns Walter • USA
BARBARA • 1972 • Soler Julian • MXC, VNZ
BARBARA • 1980 • Tropa Alfredo • PRT
BARBARA AND JAN see **BARBARA I JAN** • 1965
BARBARA ATOMICA • 1952 • Saraceni Julio • ARG
BARBARA BROADCAST • 1977 • Metzger Radley H. • USA
BARBARA DANES AMERIKA • 1983 • Lonnbro Anders, Martensson Bodil • SWD
BARBARA E BARBERINA see **PAURA D'AMARE** • 1942
BARBARA ELOPES • 1921 • Paul Fred, Raymond Jack • UKN
BARBARA FRIETCHIE • 1908 • Blackton J. Stuart • USA
BARBARA FRIETCHIE • 1915 • Harris Clarence J., Blache Alice • USA
BARBARA FRIETCHIE • 1924 • Hillyer Lambert • USA • LOVE OF A PATRIOT
BARBARA FRITCHIE • 1911 • *Champion* • USA
BARBARA HEPWORTH AT THE TATE • 1968 • Beresford Bruce • DCS • UKN
BARBARA I JAN • 1965 • Ziarnik Jerzy (c/d) • SER • PLN • BARBARA AND JAN
BARBARA IN AMERICA (USA) see **BORCSA AMERIKABEN** • 1939
BARBARA IS A VISION OF LOVELINESS • 1976 • Elder Bruce • CND
BARBARA'S BLINDNESS • 1967 • Wieland Joyce • USA
BARBARE, LA • 1989 • Darc Mireille • FRN
BARBARELLA • 1968 • Vadim Roger • FRN, ITL • BARBARELLA, QUEEN OF THE GALAXY
BARBARELLA, QUEEN OF THE GALAXY see **BARBARELLA** • 1968
BARBARIAN, THE • 1921 • Crisp Donald • USA
BARBARIAN, THE • 1933 • Wood Sam • USA • NIGHT IN CAIRO, A (UKN)
BARBARIAN, THE see **REVAK, LO SCHIAVO DI CARTAGINE** • 1960
BARBARIAN AND THE GEISHA, THE • 1958 • Huston John • USA
BARBARIAN -INGOMAR, THE • 1908 • Griffith D. W. • USA
BARBARIAN KING, THE • 1964 • *Stoichev Victor* • BUL
BARBARIAN MASTER • 1983 • Prosperi Franco • ITL
BARBARIAN QUEEN • 1985 • Olivera Hector • USA, ARG • REINA BARBARA, LA ○ QUEEN OF THE NAKED STEEL ○ REINA SALVAJE
BARBARIAN REVENGE • Brescia Alfonso • ITL, HKG
BARBARIANS, THE • 1953 • Lukov Leonid • USS
BARBARIANS, THE see **SACCO DI ROMA, IL** • 1954
BARBARIANS, THE see **REVAK, LO SCHIAVO DI CARTAGINE** • 1960
BARBARIANS, THE see **BARBARIANS & CO, THE** • 1987
BARBARIANS & CO, THE • 1987 • Deodato Ruggero • ITL, USA • BARBARIANS, THE
BARBARIC BEAST OF BOGGY CREEK, PART II, THE • 1985 • Pierce Charles B. • USA • BOGGY CREEK II: AND THE LEGEND CONTINUES ○ BOGGY CREEK II
BARBARINA see **TANZERIN VON SANSSOUCI, DIE** • 1932
BARBARO CRISTOBAL • 1968 • Santiago Pablo • PHL
BARBARO DEL RITMO, EL • 1963 • Alvarez Santiago • DOC • CUB • RHYTHM BARBARIAN, THE
BARBARO RIVAS • Guedez Jesus Enrique • VNZ
BARBAROS DEL NORTE, LOS • 1961 • Diaz Morales Jose • MXC
BARBAROSA • 1982 • Schepisi Fred • USA
BARBAROUS PLOTS • 1918 • Kerr Robert?, Davis James? • SHT • USA
BARBARY COAST • 1935 • Hawks Howard • USA • PORT OF WICKEDNESS
BARBARY COAST, THE • 1974 • Bixby Bill • TVM • USA
BARBARY COAST BUNNY • 1956 • Jones Charles M. • ANS • USA
BARBARY COAST GENT • 1944 • Del Ruth Roy • USA
BARBARY PIRATE • 1949 • Landers Lew • USA
BARBARY SHEEP • 1917 • Tourneur Maurice • USA
BARBE BLEUE • 1898 • Lumiere Louis • FRN • BLUE BEARD (USA)
BARBE BLEUE • 1901 • Melies Georges • FRN • BLUE BEARD (USA) ○ BARBE-BLEUE
BARBE BLEUE • 1907 • *Pathe* • FRN • BLUEBEARD (USA)
BARBE BLEUE • 1910 • *Pathe* • FRN • BLUEBEARD (USA)

BARBE BLEUE • 1936 • Painleve Jean, Bertrand Rene • ANS • FRN • BLUEBEARD (USA)
BARBE BLEUE • 1951 • Christian-Jaque • FRN, FRG • BLAUBART (FRG) ○ BLUEBEARD (USA)
BARBE-BLEUE • 1972 • Dmytryk Edward, Sacripanti Luciano • FRN, ITL, FRG • BARBABLU (ITL) ○ BLUEBEARD (USA)
BARBE-BLEUE see **BARBE BLEUE** • 1901
BARBECUE BRAWL • 1956 • Hanna William, Barbera Joseph • ANS • USA
BARBECUED TACOS see **TACOS AL CARBON** • 1971
BARBED WIRE • 1927 • Stiller Mauritz, Lee Rowland V. • USA
BARBED WIRE • 1952 • Archainbaud George • USA • FALSE NEWS (UKN)
BARBED WIRE • 1969 • *Welles Orson (N)* • DOC • USA
BARBED WIRE see **BARB WIRE** • 1922
BARBED WIRE (UKN) see **COW TOWN** • 1950
BARBEE-CUES • 1942 • Jason Will • SHT • USA
BARBER, THE • 1918 • Gillstrom Arvid E. • SHT • USA
BARBER AND THE FARMER, THE see **FIGARO ET L'AUVERGNAT** • 1897
BARBER CURE, A • 1913 • Dillon Eddie • USA
BARBER JOHN'S BOY see **MAN TO MAN** • 1921
BARBER JOHN'S BOY see **STREET GIRL** • 1929
BARBER JOHN'S BOY see **MAN TO MAN** • 1931
BARBER OF SEVILLA, OR THE USELESS PRECAUTION, THE see **BARBIER DE SEVILLE, LE** • 1904
BARBER OF SEVILLE, THE • 1944 • Culhane James • ANS • USA
BARBER OF SEVILLE, THE • 1956 • *Gobbi Tito* • ITL
BARBER OF SEVILLE, THE • 1973 • *Prey Bermann* • FRG, FRN
BARBER OF SEVILLE, THE (USA) see **BARBIERE DI SIVIGLIA, IL** • 1946
BARBER OF SEVILLE, THE (USA) see **BARBIER DE SEVILLE, LE** • 1947
BARBER OF STAMFORD HILL, THE • 1962 • Wrede Caspar • UKN
BARBER OF THE POOR QUARTER see **HALLAQ DARB AL FUQHRA'** • 1987
BARBER-OUS AFFAIR, A • 1915 • *La Pearl Harry* • USA
BARBER SHOP, THE • 1933 • Ripley Arthur • SHT • USA
BARBER SHOP BLUES • 1933 • Henabery Joseph • SHT • USA
BARBER SHOP FEUD, A • 1914 • *Crystal* • USA
BARBER SHOP GOSSIP • 1920 • *Moranti Milburn* • SHT • USA
BARBERINA, DIE TANZERIN VON SANSSOUCI see **TANZERIN VON SANSSOUCI, DIE** • 1932
BARBERO DE NAPOLEON, EL • 1930 • Lanfield Sidney • USA
BARBERO PRODIGIOSO, EL • 1941 • Soler Fernando • MXC
BARBEROUSSE • 1916 • Gance Abel • FRN
BARBER'S DAUGHTER, THE • 1929 • Sennett Mack • SHT • USA
BARBERS OF SICILY, THE see **BARBIERI DI SICILIA, I** • 1967
BARBER'S QUEER CUSTOMER, THE • 1902 • *Biograph* • USA
BARBER'S SHOP, THE • 1939 • Llewellyn Richard • UKN
BARBI • 1989 • PHL
BARBIER DE SEVILLE, LE • 1904 • Melies Georges • FRN • BARBER OF SEVILLA, OR THE USELESS PRECAUTION, THE
BARBIER DE SEVILLE, LE • 1933 • Bourlon Hubert, Kemm Jean • FRN
BARBIER DE SEVILLE, LE • 1947 • Loubignac Jean • FRN • BARBER OF SEVILLE, THE (USA)
BARBIER VON FILMERSDORF, DER • 1915 • Wilhelm Carl • FRG
BARBIERE DI SIVIGLIA, IL • 1912 • Maggi Luigi • ITL
BARBIERE DI SIVIGLIA, IL • 1946 • Costa Mario • ITL • BARBER OF SEVILLE, THE (USA)
BARBIERI DI SICILIA, I • 1967 • Ciorciolini Marcello • ITL • BARBERS OF SICILY, THE
BARBIE'S FANTASIES • 1974 • Goddard Claude • USA
BARBIE'S HOSPITAL AFFAIR • 1970 • Roberts Arnold • USA
BARBO FOLLIES • 1967 • Landow George • USA
BARBONI • 1946 • Risi Dino • DOC • ITL
BARBORA HLAVSOVA • 1942 • Fric Martin • CZC
BARBOS, THE DOG AND A CROSS-COUNTRY RUN • 1961 • Gaidai Leonid • USS • DOG BARBOSS AND THE UNUSUAL CROSS, THE
BARBOUILLE OU LA MORT GAIE, LE • 1977 • Koleva Maria • DOC • FRN
BARBOUZE CHERIE (FRN) see **BALEARI OPERAZIONE ORO** • 1966
BARBOUZES, LES • 1964 • Lautner Georges • FRN, ITL, FRG • IN FAMIGLIA SI SPARA (ITL) ○ GREAT SPY CHASE, THE (USA)
BARCA, 75 ANOS DE HISTORIA DEL F.C. BARCELONA • 1974 • Feliu Jordi • SPN
BARCA DE ORO, LA • 1947 • Pardave Joaquin • MXC
BARCA SIN PESCADOR, LA • 1964 • Forn Josep Maria • SPN • BOAT WITHOUT THE FISHERMAN, THE
BARCAIOLO DEL DANUBIO, IL • 1914 • Roberti Roberto Leone • ITL
BARCAIOLO DI AMALFI, IL • 1958 • Roli Mino • ITL
BARCAROLE see **BRAND IN DER OPER** • 1930
BARCAROLLE • 1935 • Le Bon Roger, Lamprecht Gerhard • FRN
BARCAROLLE D'AMOUR • 1930 • Roussell Henry, Froelich Carl • FRN
BARCELONA • 1927 • Edwards J. Steven • UKN
BARCELONA CONNECTION • 1988 • Bonn Miguel Iglesias • SPN
BARCELONA KILL, THE • 1972 • de la Fuente Jose Antonio • SPN
BARCELONA SOUTH see **BARCELONA SUR** • 1981
BARCELONA SUR • 1981 • Cadena Jordi • SPN • BARCELONA SOUTH
BARCELOS • 1961 • Guimaraes Manuel • SHT • PRT
BARCHANTE NEGUIB, EL • 1945 • Pardave Joaquin • MXC
BARCO SIN RUMBO • 1951 • Elorrieta Jose Maria • SPN
BARDAME • 1922 • Guter Johannes • FRG
BARDASHT • 1988 • Chaudhry Haider • PKS
BARDELYS THE MAGNIFICENT • 1926 • Vidor King • USA
BARDIDI • 1939 • *Sircar B. N. (P)* • IND
BARDO FOLLIES • *Landow George (P)* • USA
BARDZO STARY OBOJE • 1967 • Rybkowski Jan • PLN • BOTH VERY OLD
BARE AND THE SHAPELY, THE see **RUINED BRUIN, THE** • 1961
BARE BEHIND BARS • 1987 • de Oliveira Oswaldo • BRZ
BARE CONSCIENCE see **GOLA SUVEST** • 1970
BARE ESCAPE, A • 1916 • *Unicorn* • USA
BARE ESSENCE • 1982 • Grauman Walter • TVM • USA
BARE ET LIV -HISTORIEN OM FRIDTJOF NANSEN • 1968 • Mikailyan Sergei • USS, NRW • ONLY ONE LIFE -THE STORY OF FRIDTJOF NANSEN ○ IN JUST ONE LIFETIME ○ VSEGO ODNA ZHIZN ○ JUST ONE LIFE
BARE FACED FLATFOOT • 1951 • Burness Pete • ANS • USA • BAREFACED FLATFOOT
BARE FEET see **PABERAHNEHA** • 1968
BARE-FISTED GALLAGHER • 1919 • Franz Joseph J. • USA
BARE FISTS • 1919 • Ford John • USA
BARE HEAD, THE see **HIS FAVORITE PASTIME** • 1914
BARE HUNT; OR MY GUN IS JAMMED • 1963 • *August Films* • USA • BEAR HUNT, THE ○ MY GUN IS JAMMED
BARE IS HIS BACK WHO HAS NO BROTHER • 1979 • Pringle Ian • DOC • ASL
BARE KNEES • 1928 • Kenton Erle C. • USA • SHORT SKIRTS (UKN)
BARE KNEES • 1930 • Fraser Harry L. • USA
BARE KNUCKLES • 1921 • Hogan James P. • USA
BARE KNUCKLES • 1976 • Edmonds Don • USA
BARE LADY, BARE WORLD see **MY BARE LADY** • 1962
BARE LIVING, A • 1917 • Curtis Allen • SHT • USA
BARE WITH ME see **CHERRY'S HOUSE OF NUDES** • 1964
BAREBACK see **BARBACKA** • 1946
BAREE, SON OF KAZAN • 1918 • Smith David • USA
BAREE, SON OF KAZAN • 1925 • Smith David • USA
BAREFACED FLATFOOT see **BARE FACED FLATFOOT** • 1951
BAREFOOT ADVENTURE • 1961 • Brown Bruce • USA
BAREFOOT AND HATLESS • 1964 • Bottcher Jurgen • DOC • GDR
BAREFOOT BATTALION see **XIPOLITO TAGMA** • 1954
BAREFOOT BOY • 1912 • *Kalem* • USA
BAREFOOT BOY • 1914 • Vignola Robert G. • USA
BAREFOOT BOY • 1938 • Brown Karl • USA
BAREFOOT BOY, THE • 1923 • Kirkland David • USA
BAREFOOT CONTESSA, THE • 1954 • Mankiewicz Joseph L. • USA, ITL • CONTESSA SCALZA, LA (ITL)
BAREFOOT EAGLE, THE see **AGUILA DESCLAZA, EL**
BAREFOOT EXECUTIVE, THE • 1977 • Butler Robert • USA
BAREFOOT IN THE PARK • 1967 • Saks Gene • USA
BAREFOOT JUDGE, THE • 1944 • *O'Brien Joseph/ Mead Thomas (P)* • SHT • USA
BAREFOOT MAILMAN, THE • 1951 • McEvoy Earl • USA
BAREFOOT ON A GOLDEN BRIDGE • 1977 • Salem Atef • EGY
BAREFOOT SAVAGE, THE (USA) see **SENSUALITA** • 1952
BARENBURGER SCHNURRE • 1957 • Kirsten Ralf • GDR
BAREST HEIRESS, THE see **SHAMELESS, THE** • 1962
BARFLY • 1987 • Schroeder Barbet • USA
BARFLY, THE • 1916 • Chaudet Louis W. • SHT • USA
BARFUSSELE • 1924 • Lisson Heinrich • FRG
BARGAIN, $37.60, A • 1917 • *Price Kate* • SHT • USA
BARGAIN, THE • 1912 • Porter Edwin S. • USA
BARGAIN, THE • 1914 • Barker Reginald • USA
BARGAIN, THE • 1921 • Edwards Henry • UKN
BARGAIN, THE • 1931 • Milton Robert • USA • YOU AND I
BARGAIN AUTOMOBILE, A • 1914 • *Lubin* • USA
BARGAIN BASEMENT • 1935 • Hiscott Leslie • UKN • DEPARTMENT STORE
BARGAIN BASEMENT • 1976 • Smith John* • CND
BARGAIN COUNTER ATTACK • 1946 • Sparber I. • ANS • USA
BARGAIN DAYS • 1931 • McGowan Robert • SHT • USA
BARGAIN DAZE • 1953 • Davis Mannie • ANS • USA
BARGAIN HUNT, THE • 1928 • *Sennett Mack (P)* • SHT • USA
BARGAIN HUNTERS, THE • 1914 • *Beery Wallace* • USA
BARGAIN IN BRIDES, A • 1915 • *Teare Ethel* • USA
BARGAIN MATINEE • 1937 • Schwarzwald Milton • SHT • USA
BARGAIN OF THE CENTURY, THE • 1933 • Parrott Charles • SHT • USA
BARGAIN TABLE CLOTH, A • 1914 • Murphy J. A. • USA
BARGAIN WITH SATAN, A(?) see **STUDENT VON PRAG, DER** • 1913
BARGAINS • 1923 • *Burr Nickle* • USA
BARGE, THE • 1932 • Rodakiewicz Henwar • USA
BARGE-KEEPER'S DAUGHTER, THE see **EDUCATION DE PRINCE** • 1938
BARGEE, THE • 1964 • Wood Duncan • UKN
BARGEE'S DAUGHTER, THE • 1911 • Kinder Stuart? • UKN
BARGEE'S DAUGHTER, THE • 1915 • Batley Ethyle • UKN
BARGEE'S REVENGE, THE • 1912 • Growcott Frank R.? • UKN
BARGEMAN OF OLD HOLLAND, THE • 1910 • *Bosworth Hobart* • USA
BARGEMEN, THE see **FLISACY** • 1963
BARI THEKEY PALIYE • 1959 • Ghatak Ritwik • IND • VAGRANTS, THE ○ RUNWAY, THE ○ RUNAWAY BOY, THE
BARIERA • 1966 • Skolimowski Jerzy • PLN • BARRIER
BARIERATA • 1979 • Hristov Hristo • BUL • BARRIER, THE
BARIL AT ROSARIO • 1968 • Garces Armando • PHL • GUN & ROSARY
BARILOCHE • 1939 • Fregonese Hugo • SHT • ARG
BARIOLE • 1932 • Vigny Benno • FRN
BARIRI • 1958 • Olmi Ermanno (Spv) • DOC • ITL
BARK RIND • 1977 • Winkler Paul • ASL
BARKER, THE • 1917 • Richmond J. A. • USA
BARKER, THE • 1928 • Fitzmaurice George • USA
BARKING DOG • 1973 • Borsos Philip • SHT • CND
BARKING DOGS • 1933 • Davis Mannie • ANS • USA
BARKING DOGS DON'T FITE • 1949 • Sparber I. • ANS • USA
BARKING-DONKEY SONICHI see **SHIRIBOE SONICHI** • 1969
BARKLEYS OF BROADWAY, THE • 1949 • Walters Charles • USA
BARLUDER • 1983 • Corfixen Lizzie • DOC • DNM • BAR GIRLS
BARMA LIMPA CARNIVAL see **CARNAVAL BARRA LIMPA** • 1967
BARMAH BOY • 1974 • Bilcock David Jr. • SHT • ASL
BARMHERZIGE LUGE, DIE • 1939 • Klinger Werner • FRG
BARN BURNER see **BARN BURNING** • 1980
BARN BURNING • 1980 • Werner Peter • MTV • USA • BARN BURNER
BARN DANCE, THE • 1928 • Disney Walt, Iwerks Ub • ANS • USA
BARN OF THE NAKED DEAD see **TERROR CIRCUS** • 1973
BARNA FRAN BLASJOFJALLET • 1980 • Sima Jonas • SWD • CHILDREN FROM BLUE LAKE MOUNTAIN, THE
BARNABE • 1938 • Esway Alexander • FRN
BARNABY • 1919 • Denton Jack • UKN
BARNABY AND ME • 1977 • Panama Norman • USA
BARNABY -FATHER DEAR FATHER • 1962 • Halas John • ANS • UKN
BARNABY -OVERDUE DUES BLUES • 1962 • Halas John • ANS • UKN
BARNABY RUDGE • 1911 • Kent Charles • USA
BARNABY RUDGE • 1915 • Bentley Thomas • UKN
BARNACLE BILL • 1918 • *Ebony* • SHT • USA
BARNACLE BILL • 1930 • Fleischer Dave • ANS • USA
BARNACLE BILL • 1935 • Hughes Harry • UKN
BARNACLE BILL • 1941 • Thorpe Richard • USA
BARNACLE BILL • 1957 • Frend Charles • UKN • ALL AT SEA (USA)
BARNACLE BILL see **WHY SAILORS LEAVE HOME** • 1930
BARNDOMMENS GADE • 1987 • Henning-Jensen Astrid • DNM • STREET OF MY CHILDHOOD ○ EARLY SPRING
BARNEN FRAN FROSTMOFJALLET • 1945 • Husberg Rolf • SWD • CHILDREN FROM FROSTMA MOUNTAIN
BARNENS O • 1980 • Pollak Kay • SWD • CHILDREN'S ISLAND
BARNET • 1909 • *Blom August* • DNM • CHILD'S LOVE, A
BARNET • 1913 • Stiller Mauritz • SWD • CHILD, THE
BARNET • 1940 • Christensen Benjamin • DNM • CHILD, THE
BARNET see **BARNETS MAGT** • 1914
BARNET MURDER CASE, THE see **CONSPIRATORS, THE** • 1924
BARNETS MAGT • 1914 • Holger-Madsen • DNM • BARNET ○ CHILD, THE
BARNEY • 1976 • Waddington David S. • ASL, USA
BARNEY BEAR • 1939-54 • Ising Rudolf(c/d) • ASS • USA
BARNEY BEAR'S POLAR PEST • 1944 • Gordon George • ANS • USA
BARNEY BEAR'S VICTORY GARDEN • 1942 • Ising Rudolf • ANS • USA
BARNEY KESSEL TRIO • 1962 • Binder Steve • SHT • USA
BARNEY OLDFIELD'S RACE FOR A LIFE • 1913 • Sennett Mack • USA
BARNEY ROSS STORY, THE see **MONKEY ON MY BACK** • 1957
BARNEY'S HUNGRY COUSIN • 1953 • Lundy Dick • ANS • USA
BARNFORBJUDET • 1979 • Bergenstrahle Marie-Louise De Geer • SWD • ELEPHANT WALK ○ FOR ADULTS ONLY
BARNSTORMER, THE • 1922 • Ray Charles • USA
BARNSTORMERS • 1905 • *Bitzer Billy (Ph)* • USA
BARNSTORMERS, THE • 1914 • *Powers* • USA
BARNSTORMERS, THE • 1915 • Haldane Bert • UKN
BARNSTORMERS, THE • 1915 • Horne James W. • USA
BARNSTORMERS, THE • 1979 • Eadie Douglas • UKN
BARNUM • 1986 • Philips Lee • TVM • USA
BARNUM see **FREAKS** • 1932
BARNUM AND RINGLING, INC. • 1928 • McGowan Robert • SHT • USA
BARNUM WAS RIGHT • 1929 • Lord Del • USA
BARNUM WAS WRONG • 1930 • Sandrich Mark • SHT • USA
BARNUM'S VALISE see **VALISE DE BARNUM, LA** • 1904
BARNVAGNEN • 1963 • Widerberg Bo • SWD • BABY CARRIAGE, THE ○ PRAM, THE
BARNYARD, THE • 1923 • Semon Larry • SHT • USA
BARNYARD ACTOR • 1955 • Rasinski Connie • ANS • USA
BARNYARD AMATEURS • 1936 • *Terry Paul/ Moser Frank (P)* • ANS • USA
BARNYARD BABIES • 1935 • Ising Rudolf • ANS • USA
BARNYARD BABIES • 1940 • *Mintz Charles (P)* • ANS • USA
BARNYARD BASEBALL • 1939 • Davis Mannie • ANS • USA
BARNYARD BATTLE, THE • 1928 • Disney Walt, Iwerks Ub • ANS • USA
BARNYARD BLACKOUT • 1943 • Davis Mannie • ANS • USA
BARNYARD BOSS, THE • 1937 • Rasinski Connie • ANS • USA
BARNYARD BRAT • 1939 • Fleischer Dave • ANS • USA
BARNYARD BROADCAST, THE • 1931 • Gillett Burt • ANS • USA
BARNYARD BUNK • 1932 • Foster John, Rufle George • ANS • USA
BARNYARD CAVALIER, A • 1922 • Christie Al • USA
BARNYARD CONCERT, THE • 1930 • Disney Walt • ANS • USA
BARNYARD EGGCITEMENT • 1939 • Rasinski Connie • ANS • USA
BARNYARD FIVE, THE • 1936 • *Lantz Walter (P)* • ANS • USA
BARNYARD FLIRTATIONS • 1914 • Dillon Eddie • USA
BARNYARD FOLLIES • 1940 • McDonald Frank • USA
BARNYARD FROLICS • 1917 • *Pokes & Jabs* • SHT • USA
BARNYARD MELODY • 1929 • Foster John • ANS • USA
BARNYARD MIX-UP, A • 1915 • *Lubin* • ANM • USA
BARNYARD OLYMPICS • 1932 • Jackson Wilfred • ANS • USA
BARNYARD ROMANCE, A • 1919 • Robbins Jess • USA
BARNYARD ROMEO • 1938 • *Lantz Walter (P)* • ANS • USA
BARNYARD WAAC • 1942 • Donnelly Eddie • ANS • USA
BARO, IL (ITL) see **GRANDS CHEMINS, LES** • 1963
BAROCCO • 1926 • Burguet Charles • FRN
BAROCCO • 1976 • Techine Andre • FRN
BARON, THE • 1911 • Sennett Mack, Henderson Dell • USA
BARON, THE see **SLAEGTEN** • 1978
BARON, THE see **BARON AND THE KID, THE** • 1984
BARON AND THE KID, THE • 1984 • Nelson Gary • TVM • USA • BARON, THE
BARON AND THE ROSE, THE • 1940 • Wrangell Basil • SHT • USA • BLACK AND WHITE ○ RED ROSE, THE
BARON BLINK'S BRIDE • 1913 • *Imp* • USA

BARON BLOOD (USA) see **ORRORI DEL CASTELLO DI NORIMBERGA, GLI** • 1972

BARON BRAKOLA, EL see **SANTO CONTRA EL BARON BRAKOLA** • 1965

BARON BUNNYS ERLEBNISSE 1 • 1921 • Fiedler-Spies Ernst • FRG • MEISTERDIEB, DER

BARON DE CRAC, LE • 1910 • Cohl Emile • FRN • ADVENTURES OF BARON CRAC

BARON DE CRAC, LE see **AVENTURES DE BARON DE CRAC, LES** • 1913

BARON DE L'ECLUSE, LE • 1959 • Delannoy Jean • FRN, ITL

BARON DEL TERROR, EL • 1961 • Urueta Chano • MXC • BRAINIAC, THE (USA) ○ BARON OF TERROR

BARON FANTOME, LE • 1942 • de Poligny Serge • FRN • PHANTOM BARON, THE (USA) ○ MA SOEUR ANNE

BARON MUNCHAUSEN • 1948 • Low Colin • ANS • CND

BARON MUNCHAUSEN (UKN) see **BARON PRASIL** • 1962

BARON MUNCHAUSEN (USA) see **AVENTURES DE BARON DE CRAC, LES** • 1913

BARON MUNCHAUSEN (USA) see **BARON PRASIL** • 1940

BARON OF ARIZONA, THE • 1950 • Fuller Samuel • USA

BARON OF TERROR see **BARON DEL TERROR, EL** • 1961

BARON OLSSON • 1919 • Petschler Eric A. • SWD

BARON PRASIL • 1940 • Fric Martin • CZC • BARON MUNCHAUSEN (USA)

BARON PRASIL • 1962 • Zeman Karel • CZC • FABULOUS BARON MUNCHAUSEN, THE (USA) ○ BARON MUNCHAUSEN (UKN)

BARON TZIGANE, LE • 1935 • Chomette Henri, Hartl Karl • FRN

BARON VON GO-GO • 1967 • Bakshi Ralph • ANS • USA

BARON X see **X-PARONI** • 1964

BARONCHEN AUF URLAUB • 1917 • Leckband M. • FRG

BARONE CARLO MAZZA, IL • 1948 • Brignone Guido • ITL

BARONE DI CORBO, IL • 1939 • Righelli Gennaro • ITL

BARONESS AND THE BUTLER, THE • 1938 • Lang Walter • USA

BARONESSCHEN AUF STRAFURLAUB • 1918 • Rippert Otto • FRG

BARONI, I • 1975 • Lomi Gian Paolo • ITL

BARONIN KAMMERJUNGFER • 1917 • Peukert Leo • FRG

BARON'S AFRICAN WAR, THE • 1943 • Bennet Spencer Gordon • USA

BARON'S BEAR ESCAPE, THE • 1914 • *Bergman Henry* • USA

BAROOD • 1976 • *Burman S. D. (M)* • IND

BAROOD KI CHAON MEY • 1989 • Islam Nazaral • PKS • BENEATH THE ANGER

BAROUD • 1931 • Ingram Rex • UKN • LOVE IN MOROCCO (USA)

BAROUD • 1931 • Jaeger-Schmidt Andre, Terry Alice, Ingram Rex • FRN • HOMMES BLEUS, LES

BAROUDEURS, LES see **JERK A ISTAMBUL** • 1967

BARQUE EN MER • 1896-97 • Lumiere Louis • FRN

BARQUE EST PLEINE, LA see **BOOT IST VOLL, DAS** • 1981

BARQUE SORTANT DU PORT • 1895 • Lumiere Louis • FRN • SORTIE DU PORT, LA

BARQUE SORTANT DU PORT DE TROUVILLE • 1896 • Melies Georges • FRN • BOAT LEAVING THE HARBOUR OF TROUVILLE

BARQUEIROS DO DOURO • 1959 • Duarte Arthur • SHT • PRT

BARQUERO • 1970 • Douglas Gordon • USA

BARQUES DU SOLEIL, LES • 1961 • Shawqi Khalil • SHT • EGY

BARRA • 1979 • Sathyu M. S. • IND • DROUGHT

BARRABAS • 1919 • Feuillade Louis • SRL • FRN

BARRACA, LA • 1944 • Gavaldon Roberto • MXC • COTTAGE, THE

BARRACKS ARE FULL TODAY, THE see **KISLALAR DOLDU BUGUN** • 1968

BARRACUDA • 1978 • Kerwin Harry E. • TVM • USA • LUCIFER PROJECT, THE

BARRAGE CONTRE LE PACIFIQUE • 1958 • Clement Rene • FRN, USA, ITL • DIGA SUL PACIFICO, LA (ITL) ○ THIS ANGRY AGE (USA) ○ SEA WALL, THE

BARRAGE DE L'AIGLE, LE • 1946 • Leenhardt Roger • DCS • FRN

BARRAGE DU CHALELOT • 1953 • Colson-Malleville Marie • SHT • FRN

BARRAGENS • 1959 • Queiroga Perdigao • SHT • PRT

BARRAGENS DO ZEZERE • 1961 • Esteves Constantino • SHT • PRT

BARRAGENS PORTUGUESAS DO DOURO INTERNACIONAL • 1958 • Esteves Constantino • SHT • PRT

BARRANCA DE LA MUERTE, LA • 1954 • Salvador Jaime • MXC

BARRANCA SANGRIENTA, LA • 1961 • Curiel Federico • MXC

BARRANCA TRAGICA • 1917 • Sierra Santiago • MXC

BARRANCO, LTD. • 1932 • Berthomieu Andre • FRN

BARRANDOV NOCTURNE, OR HOW FILMS DANCE AND SING see **BARRANDOVSKE NOCTURNO, ANEB JAK FILM TANCIL A ZPIVAL** • 1984

BARRANDOVSKE NOCTURNO, ANEB JAK FILM TANCIL A ZPIVAL • 1984 • Sis • CZC • BARRANDOV NOCTURNE, OR HOW FILMS DANCE AND SING

BARRAS HEUTE • 1963 • May Paul • FRG

BARRAVENTO • 1961 • Rocha Glauber • BRZ • TURNING WIND, THE ○ TEMPEST

BARRED FROM THE BAR • 1917 • Beaudine William • SHT • USA

BARRED FROM THE MAILS • 1913 • *Thanhouser* • USA

BARRED ROAD, THE see **TARIK EL MASDUD, EL** • 1958

BARREL FULL OF DOLLARS, A see **PER UNA BARA PIENA DI DOLLARI** • 1971

BARREL ORGAN, THE • 1914 • Stratton Edmund F. • USA

BARREL-ORGAN, THE • 1960 • Kotowski Jerzy • ANM • PLN

BARREL-ORGAN, THE • 1965 • Haupe Wlodzimierz, Bielinska Halina • ANM • PLN

BARRELA • 1989 • Cury Marco Antonio • BRZ

BARRELED • 1914 • *De Forrest Charles* • USA

BARREN DESIRE see **FUMO NO AIYOKU** • 1967

BARREN DREAMS see **PUSTI SNOVI** • 1968

BARREN GAIN, THE • 1915 • Eason B. Reeves • USA

BARREN GROUND, THE • 1977 • Yamamoto Satsuo • JPN

BARREN LIVES see **VIDAS SECAS** • 1963

BARREN LOVE see **AA KIMI GA AI** • 1967

BARRERA, LA • 1965 • Herrero Pedro Mario • SPN

BARRETTS OF WIMPOLE STREET, THE • 1934 • Franklin Sidney A. • USA • FORBIDDEN ALLIANCE

BARRETTS OF WIMPOLE STREET, THE • 1957 • Franklin Sidney A. • UKN, USA

BARRICADE • 1939 • Ratoff Gregory • USA • BY THE DAWN'S EARLY LIGHT

BARRICADE • 1950 • Godfrey Peter • USA

BARRICADE, THE • 1917 • Carewe Edwin • USA

BARRICADE, THE • 1921 • Cabanne W. Christy • USA

BARRICADE DU POINT DU JOUR, LA • 1977 • Richon Rene • FRN

BARRIDOS Y REGADOS • 1961 • Salvador Jaime • MXC

BARRIER see **BARIERA** • 1966

BARRIER, THE • 1913 • Barker Reginald? • USA

BARRIER, THE • 1917 • Lewis Edgar • USA

BARRIER, THE • 1926 • Hill George W. • USA

BARRIER, THE • 1937 • Selander Lesley • USA

BARRIER, THE • 1976 • Bugajski Ryszard • MTV • PLN

BARRIER, THE see **BARIERATA** • 1979

BARRIER BETWEEN, THE • 1915 • Morgan George • USA

BARRIER OF BARS, THE • 1913 • *Kerrigan J. Warren* • USA

BARRIER OF BLOOD, THE • 1913 • *Ammex* • USA

BARRIER OF FAITH, THE • 1915 • Brooke Van Dyke • USA

BARRIER OF FLAMES, THE • 1914 • Harvey John • USA

BARRIER OF IGNORANCE, THE • 1914 • *Melford George* • USA

BARRIER OF RACE, THE • 1916 • *Buffalo* • USA

BARRIER OF THE LAW see **BARRIERA DELLE LEGGE, LA** • 1953

BARRIER ROYAL, A • 1914 • Swickard Charles? • USA

BARRIER THAT WAS BURNED, THE • 1912 • *Storey Edith* • USA

BARRIERA A SETTENTRIONE • 1950 • Trenker Luis • ITL

BARRIERA DELLE LEGGE, LA • 1953 • Costa Piero • ITL • BARRIER OF THE LAW

BARRIERE, LA • 1915 • Feuillade Louis • FRN

BARRIERE, LA see **HAGIZ, AL-** • 1972

BARRIERES • 1949 • Christian-Jaque • SHT • FRN

BARRIERES ARCHITECTURALES • 1973 • Cardinal Roger • DCS • CND

BARRIERS • Young Robert • DOC • UKN

BARRIERS AFLAME see **WHY WOMEN LOVE** • 1925

BARRIERS BURNED AWAY • 1911 • *Vitagraph* • USA

BARRIERS BURNED AWAY • 1925 • Van Dyke W. S. • USA • CHICAGO FIRE, THE (UKN)

BARRIERS OF FOLLY • 1922 • Kull Edward • USA

BARRIERS OF PREJUDICE • 1915 • Davis Ulysses • USA

BARRIERS OF SOCIETY • 1916 • Carleton Lloyd B. • USA

BARRIERS OF THE LAW • 1925 • McGowan J. P. • USA

BARRIERS SWEPT ASIDE • 1915 • Vignola Robert G. • USA

BARRINGS, DIE • 1955 • Thiele Rolf • FRG

BARRIO • 1947 • Vajda Ladislao • PRT

BARRIO BAJO • 1950 • Mendez Fernando • MXC

BARRIO DE PASIONES • 1947 • Fernandez Bustamente Adolfo • MXC

BARRIO GRIS • 1954 • Soffici Mario • ARG

BARRISTER, THE • 1928 • Croise Hugh • UKN

BARRO, O • 1972 • Faria Antonio • SHT • PRT

BARRO HUMANO, EL • 1955 • Amadori Luis Cesar • ARG • HUMAN CLAY, THE

BARRY • 1948 • Pottier Richard • FRN

BARRY BRICKELL: POTTER • 1969 • DCS • NZL

BARRY BUTTS IN • 1919 • Smith Beaumont • ASL

BARRY HUMPHRIES STAGE SHOW FILM • 1975 • Beresford Bruce • DOC • ASL

BARRY LYNDON • 1975 • Kubrick Stanley • UKN • LUCK OF BARRY LYNDON, THE

BARRY MCKENZIE HOLDS HIS OWN • 1974 • Beresford Bruce • ASL

BARRY MCKENZIE HOLDS HIS OWN PROMOTIONAL FILM • 1974 • Beresford Bruce • SHT • ASL

BARRY'S BREAKING IN • 1913 • Miller Ashley • USA

BARS AND STRIPES • 1931 • *Mintz Charles (P) A* • ANS • USA

BARS AND STRIPES FOREVER • 1939 • Hardaway Ben, Dalton Cal • ANS • USA

BARS OF HATE • 1936 • Herman Al • USA

BARS OF IRON • 1920 • Thornton F. Martin • UKN

BARSAAT • 1947 • Kapoor Raj • IND

BART SALAMANCA • 1968 • Dlz • PHL

BARTEK LE VAINQUEUR • 1923 • Puchalski Eduard • PLN

BARTER OF LOUISA, THE • 1913 • *Essanay* • USA

BARTERED BRIDE, THE see **PRODANA NEVESTA** • 1913

BARTERED BRIDE, THE see **VERKAUFTE BRAUT, DIE** • 1932

BARTERED BRIDE, THE see **PRODANA NEVESTA** • 1933

BARTERED CROWN, THE • 1914 • *Ab* • USA

BARTERED CROWN, THE • 1914 • Marston Theodore • USA

BARTERED YOUTH • 1917 • Mong William V. • SHT • USA

BARTHOLOMEW VERSUS THE WHEEL • 1964 • McKimson Robert • ANS • USA

BARTLEBY • 1970 • Friedmann Anthony • UKN

BARTLEBY • 1977 • Ronet Maurice • FRN

BARTLETTS, THE • 1986 • Battle Murray • CND

BARTOK • 1964 • Russell Ken • MTV • UKN

BARTOK BELA: AZ EJSZAKA ZENEJE • 1971 • Gaal Istvan • SHT • HNG • BARTOK BELA: THE MUSIC OF THE NIGHT ○ NIGHT MUSIC, THE

BARTOK BELA: THE MUSIC OF THE NIGHT see **BARTOK BELA: AZ EJSZAKA ZENEJE** • 1971

BARTOLO TOCA LA FLAUTA • 1944 • Contreras Torres Miguel • MXC

BARTON MYSTERY, THE • 1920 • Roberts Harry • UKN

BARTON MYSTERY, THE • 1932 • Edwards Henry • UKN

BARU, EL HOMBRE DE LA SELVA • 1958 • Orona Vicente • MXC • BARU, MAN OF THE JUNGLE

BARU, MAN OF THE JUNGLE see **BARU, EL HOMBRE DE LA SELVA** • 1958

BARUCH see **ALTE GESETZ, DAS** • 1923

BARUFFE CHIOZZOTTE, LE see **PAESE SENZA PACE, IL** • 1943

BARUTEN BUKVAR • 1977 • Dinov Todor • BUL

BARWY ORCHRONNE • 1976 • Zanussi Krzysztof • PLN • CAMOUFLAGE

BARWY WALKI • 1965 • Passendorfer Jerzy • PLN • SCENES OF BATTLE

BARYSHNIKOV • 1974 • Rasky Harry • CND

BARYSHNYA I CHULIGAN see **POET NA EKRANE** • 1973

BAS BELASI • 1977 • Yilmaz Atif • TRK • TROUBLE

BAS DE LAINE OU LE TRESOR, LE • 1911 • Feuillade Louis • FRN • TRESOR, LE

BAS DE SOIE NOIRE, LE • 1976 • Bernard-Aubert Claude • FRN

BAS-FONDS, LES • 1936 • Renoir Jean • FRN • LOWER DEPTHS, THE ○ UNDERWORLD

BAS YA BAHR • 1971 • Siddik Khalid • KWT • CRUEL SEA, THE ○ MER CRUELLE, LA

BASAETTELSE • 1944 • Ipsen Bodil • DNM

BASANT • 1943 • *Biswas Anil (M)* • IND

BASATRHAYE JODAGANE • 1968 • Ghaderi Iraj • IRN • SEPARATE BEDS

BASCO D'AMORE • 1981 • Bevilacqua Alberto • ITL

BASE BRAWL • 1948 • *Paramount* • ANS • USA

BASE DECEIVERS, THE • 1918 • Sandground Maurice • UKN

BASEBALL see **BEISBOL, EL** • 1977

BASEBALL, A GRAND OLD GAME • 1914 • *Ab* • USA

BASEBALL AND BLOOMERS • 1911 • *Garwood William* • USA

BASEBALL AND BLOOMERS • 1919 • MacFadden Barnar • SHT • USA

BASEBALL AND TROUBLE • 1915 • *Lubin* • USA

BASEBALL AT MUDVILLE • 1917 • MacGregor Norval • SHT • USA

BASEBALL BILL, PART 1 • 1916 • Mason Billy • SHT • USA

BASEBALL BILL, PART 2: FLIRTING WITH MARRIAGE • 1916 • Mason Billy • SHT • USA

BASEBALL BUG, THE • 1911 • *Noble John W.* • USA

BASEBALL BUGS • 1946 • Freleng Friz • ANS • USA

BASEBALL FAN, THE • 1908 • Anderson G. M. • USA

BASEBALL FAN, THE • 1914 • *Powers* • USA

BASEBALL FANS OF FANVILLE • 1914 • *Franey William* • USA

BASEBALL MADNESS • 1917 • Mason Billy • SHT • USA

BASEBALL STAR FROM BINGO, THE • 1911 • *Essanay* • USA

BASEBALL, THAT'S ALL! • 1910 • *Melies* • USA

BASEBALL UMPIRE, THE • 1913 • *Majestic* • USA

BASEBALL'S PEERLESS LEADER • 1913 • *Chance Frank* • USA

BASHFUL • 1917 • Roach Hal • SHT • USA

BASHFUL BACHELOR, THE • 1942 • St. Clair Malcolm • USA

BASHFUL BACHELOR BILL • 1913 • *Majestic* • USA

BASHFUL BEN • 1914 • *Crystal* • USA

BASHFUL BILLIE • 1915 • Metcalfe Earl • USA

BASHFUL BOY, THE • 1913 • *Solax* • USA

BASHFUL BUCCANEER • 1925 • Brown Harry J. • USA

BASHFUL BUCK BAILEY • 1918 • *Rancho* • SHT • USA

BASHFUL BUZZARD, THE • 1945 • Clampett Robert • ANS • USA

BASHFUL CHARLEY'S PROPOSAL • 1916 • Curtis Allen • SHT • USA

BASHFUL ELEPHANT, THE • 1962 • McGowan Dorrell, McGowan Stuart E. • USA, FRG

BASHFUL GLEN • 1915 • Adolfi John G. • USA

BASHFUL HERO see **GREAT MR. NOBODY, THE** • 1941

BASHFUL JIM • 1925 • Cline Eddie • SHT • USA

BASHFUL ROMEO, THE see **DOUBLING FOR ROMEO** • 1922

BASHFUL SON, A • 1911 • *Reliance* • USA

BASHFUL SUITOR, A • 1921 • Blache Herbert • SHT • USA

BASHTATA NA YAITSETO • 1990 • Koulev Henri • BUL • FATHER OF THE EGG, THE

BASHU, THE LITTLE STRANGER • 1989 • Beyzai Bahram • IRN

BASIC PRINCIPLES OF LUBRICATION, THE • 1952 • Tambling Richard • DOC • UKN

BASIC TRAINING • 1971 • Wiseman Frederick • DOC • USA

BASIC TRAINING • 1985 • Sugerman Andrew • USA • UP THE PENTAGON ○ UP THE MILITARY

BASIE • 1961 • SAF

BASILEUS QUARTET • 1982 • Carpi Fabio • FRN, ITL • QUATUOR BASILEUS

BASILISCHI, I • 1963 • Wertmuller Lina • ITL • LIZARDS ○ BASILISKS, THE

BASILISK, THE • 1914 • Hepworth Cecil M. • UKN

BASILISK, THE see **BAZYLISZEK** • 1961

BASILISKS, THE see **BASILISCHI, I** • 1963

BASIN STREET REVUE • 1955 • Kohn Joseph • USA

BASINGSTOKE, RUNCORN, VILLES NOUVELLES BRITANNIQUES • 1974 • Regnier Michel • DOC • CND

BASIS • 1914 • *Rex* • USA

BASIS, THE see **FUNDAMENTY** • 1972

BASKERVILLE CURSE, THE see **SHERLOCK HOLMES: THE BASKERVILLE CURSE** • 1983

BASKET CASE • 1982 • Henenlotter Frank • USA

BASKET CASE II • 1989 • Henenlotter Frank • USA

BASKET HABIT, THE • 1914 • Williams C. Jay • USA

BASKET-MAKER AND THE MIRACLE, THE see **TEJEDOR DE MILAGROS, EL** • 1961

BASKET WITH LICHEN see **KOKEZARU NO TSUBO** • 1954

BASKETBALL • 1967 • Shebib Donald • CND

BASKETBALL FIX, THE • 1951 • Feist Felix E. • USA • BIG DECISION, THE (UKN)

BASKETBALL TACTICS AND PLAYS • 1931 • Kelley Albert • SHT • USA

BASKETBALL TECHNIQUE • 1935 • McCarey Ray • SHT • USA

BASNA • 1979 • Petricic Neven • YGS • FABLE, A ○ BRSNA

BASQUINES VERGELTUNG see **MEMOIREN EINES KAMMERDIENERS 2** • 1921

BASSARI • 1960 • Jaworski Tadeusz • DOC • PLN

BASSE-COUR see **QUE LES "GROS SALAIRES" LEVENT LE DOIGT!** • 1982

BASTA • 1970 • Eguino Antonio • BLV

BASTA CHE NON SI SAPPIA IN GIRO • 1976 • Magni Luigi, Comencini Luigi, Loy Nanni • ITL

BASTA CON LA GUERRA, FACCIAMO L'AMORE • 1974 • Bianchi Andrea • ITL

BASTA GUARDARLA • 1970 • Salce Luciano • ITL

BASTARD see **VILDMARKENS SANG** • 1940

BASTARD, DER • 1919 • Delmont Joseph • FRG

BASTARD, DER • 1925 • Righelli Gennaro • FRG

BASTARD, THE • Ch'U Yuan • HKG
BASTARD, THE • 1978 • Katzin Lee H. • TVM • USA • KENT CHRONICLES, THE
BASTARD, THE see **BASTARDI, I** • 1968
BASTARD, THE (USA) see **KUNDELEK** • 1969
BASTARD, DER (FRG) see **BASTARDI, I** • 1968
BASTARD WENCH FROM CHICAGO, THE see **FABULOUS BASTARD FROM CHICAGO, THE** • 1969
BASTARDI, I • 1968 • Tessari Duccio • ITL, FRN, FRG • BATARD, LE (FRN) ○ BASTARD, DER (FRG) ○ SONS OF SATAN ○ BASTARDS, THE ○ CATS, THE ○ BASTARD, THE
BASTARDI, I (ITL) see **NE DE PERE INCONNU** • 1950
BASTARDO, EL • 1937 • Peon Ramon • MXC
BASTARDO, EL • 1965 • Martinez Arturo • MXC
BASTARDO.. VAMOS A MATAR • 1971 • Mangini Gino • ITL
BASTARDS, THE see **BASTARDI, I** • 1968
BASTIEN, BASTIENNE • 1979 • Andrieu Michel • FRN
BASTILLE • 1984 • van den Berg Rudolf • NTH
BASUDEV • 1984 • Shah Neer • NPL • LECTURER, A
BAT 21 • 1988 • Markle Peter • USA • BAT.21
BAT.21 see **BAT 21** • 1988
BAT, THE • 1926 • West Roland • USA
BAT, THE • 1959 • Wilbur Crane • USA
BAT, THE (USA) see **FLEDERMAUS, DIE** • 1945
BAT LEUNG KAM • 1989 • Zhang Wanting • HKG • EIGHT TAELS OF GOLD
BAT PEOPLE, THE • 1974 • Jameson Jerry • USA • IT LIVES BY NIGHT
BAT WHISPERS, THE • 1930 • West Roland • USA
BAT WOMAN, THE see **MUJER MURCIELAGO, LA** • 1968
BATAAN • 1943 • Garnett Tay • USA
BATACLAN MEXICANO • 1955 • de Anda Raul • MXC
BATAILLE, LA • 1923 • Violet Edouard-Emile • FRN
BATAILLE, LA • 1933 • Farkas Nicolas • FRN
BATAILLE A COMMENCE A LANDEREAU, LA • 1978 • Mordillat Gerard, Philibert Nicolas • DOC • FRN
BATAILLE D'AUSTERLITZ, LA • 1909 • Cohl Emile • ANS • FRN • BATTLE OF AUSTERLITZ, THE
BATAILLE DE BOULES DE NEIGE • 1899-00 • Blache Alice • FRN
BATAILLE DE CHICKAMAUGA, LA • 1956-62 • Enrico Robert • SHT • FRN
BATAILLE DE CONFETTIS • 1897 • Melies Georges • FRN • BATTLE WITH CONFETTI
BATAILLE DE CORINTHE, LA (FRN) see **CONQUISTATORE DI CORINTO, IL** • 1962
BATAILLE DE FRANCE, LA • 1964 • Aurel Jean • DOC • FRN
BATAILLE DE LA CHATEAUGUAY, LA • 1978 • Carriere Marcel • CND
BATAILLE DE LA VIE, LA • 1950 • Daquin Louis • FRN
BATAILLE DE L'EAU LOURDE, LA • 1947 • Dreville Jean, Vibe-Muller Titus • FRN, NRW • OPERATION SWALLOW ○ KAMPEN OM TUNGTVANNET
BATAILLE DE QUEBEC, LA • 1974 • Danis Aime • DOC • CND
BATAILLE DE SAN SEBASTIAN, LA (FRN) see **CANONES DE SAN SEBASTIAN, LOS** • 1967
BATAILLE DE WATERLOO, LA • 1913 • Machin Alfred • NTH
BATAILLE DE YORKTOWN, LA • 1976 • Danis Aime • DOC • CND
BATAILLE DES DIX MILLIONS, LA • 1969 • Marker Chris • FRN, BLG • CUBA: BATTLE OF THE 10,000,000 (USA) ○ CUBA: LA BATAILLE DES DIX MILLIONS
BATAILLE DES MAROULLES, LA • 1970 • Manuel Pierre, Peche Jean-Jacques • BLG
BATAILLE D'OREILLERS • 1899-00 • Blache Alice • FRN
BATAILLE DU CLOCHER, LA • 1955 • Delacroix Rene • FRN
BATAILLE DU FEU, LA • 1948 • de Canonge Maurice • FRN • JOYEUX CONSCRIT, LES
BATAILLE DU RAIL, LA • 1945 • Clement Rene • FRN • BATTLE OF THE RAILS (USA)
BATAILLE SILENCIEUSE, LA • 1937 • Billon Pierre • FRN • POISSON CHINOIS, LE
BATAILLE SUR LA MONTAGNE see **SIRAUN FI AL-GABAL** • 1960
BATAILLE SUR LE GRAND FLEUVE • 1951 • Rouch Jean • FRN • CHASSE A L'HIPPOPOTAME
BATAILLES DE LA VIE, LES • 1912 • Jasset Victorin • SRL • FRN
BATAILLES DE L'ARGENT, LES see **TRUST, LE** • 1911
BATAILLON DE LA SOMBRAS, EL • 1956 • Mur Oti • SPN
BATAILLON DU CIEL, LE • 1945 • Esway Alexander • FRN
BATAILLON ELASTIQUE, LE • 1902 • Melies Georges • FRN • ELASTIC BATTALION, THE (USA)
BATAILLON EN FOLIE • 1976 • Samperi Salvatore • ITL, FRN
BATALIA DIN UMBRA • 1988 • Blaier Andrei • RMN • BATTLE IN THE SHADOWS
BATALION • 1927 • Prazsky Premysl • CZC • AMAZING BATTALION, THE
BATALION • 1937 • Cikan Miroslav • CZC
BATALLA DE CHILE: LA LUCHA DE UN PUEBLO SIN ARMAS, LA • 1974-79 • Guzman Patricio • CHL, CUB • BATTLE OF CHILE, THE ○ BATTLE OF CHILE: THE STRUGGLE OF AN UNARMED PEOPLE, THE
BATALLA DE CHILE: PART 1 • 1974 • Guzman Patricio • CHL, CUB • INSURRECCION DE LA BURGUESIA, LA ○ INSURRECTION OF THE BOURGEOISE
BATALLA DE CHILE: PART 2 • 1976 • Guzman Patricio • CHL, CUB • GOLPE DE ESTADO, EL ○ COUP D'ETAT
BATALLA DE CHILE: PART 3, LA • 1979 • Guzman Patricio • CUB • PODER POPULAR, EL ○ POPULAR POWER, THE ○ POWER OF THE PEOPLE, THE
BATALLA DE LOS PASTELES, LA • 1966 • Delgado Agustin P. • MXC
BATALLA DEL DOMINGO, LA • 1962 • Marquina Luis • SPN
BATALLA DEL PORRO, LA • 1982 • Minguell Joan • SPN • JOINT'S BATTLE, THE
BATALLA DEL ULTIMO PANZER, LA • 1968 • Merino Jose Luis • SPN, ITL • BATTAGLIA DELL'ULTIMO PANZER, LA (ITL) ○ BATTLE OF THE LAST PANZER, THE
BATALLA NAVAL DE MARACAIBO, LA • 1974 • Scheuren Bruno • DOC • VNZ • SEA-BATTLE OF MARACAIBO, THE
BATALLA RITUAL • 1975 • Nisiyama Eulogio, Vignati Jorge • DOC • PRU
BATALLAS EN EL DESIERTO, LAS • 1986 • Isaac Alberto • MXC • BATTLES IN THE DESERT
BATANAGAR • 1936 • Moylan William • DOC • UKN
BATANGAS see **MISSION BATANGAS** • 1967
BATARD, LE • 1982 • Van Effenterre Bertrand • FRN
BATARD, LE (FRN) see **BASTARDI, I** • 1968
BATARDE, LA see **MARIAGE DE VERENA, LE** • 1938
BATAVERNAS TROHETSED • 1957 • Derkert • SHT • SWD • BATAVIAN'S OATH OF FIDELITY, THE
BATAVIAN'S OATH OF FIDELITY, THE see **BATAVERNAS TROHETSED** • 1957
BATCH '81 • 1981 • De Leon Mike • PHL
BATEAU A SOUPE, LE • 1946 • Gleize Maurice • FRN
BATEAU D'EMILE, LE • 1962 • de La Patelliere Denys • FRN
BATEAU-MOUCHE SUR LA SEINE • 1896 • Melies Georges • FRN • STEAMBOATS ON RIVER SEINE
BATEAU SUR L'HERBE, LE • 1970 • Brach Gerard • FRN
BATELIERS DE LA VOLGA, LES • 1936 • von Strischewski Wladimir • FRN
BATEN • 1961 • Troell Jan • DOC • SWD • SHIP, THE
BATE'S CAR • 1974 • Ianzelo Tony • DOC • CND
BATES MOTEL • 1987 • Rothstein Richard • TVM • USA
BATH see **BENJA** • 1962
BATH BETWEEN, THE • 1929 • Stoloff Ben • USA
BATH DAY • 1946 • Nichols Charles • ANS • USA
BATH DUB, THE • 1920 • *Franey William* • USA
BATH HAREM, THE see **UKIYO BURO** • 1929
BATH HOUSE, THE see **BENJA** • 1962
BATH HOUSE BLONDE, A • 1916 • Henderson Dell • USA
BATH HOUSE SCANDAL, THE • 1918 • Beery Wallace • SHT • USA
BATH HOUSE TANGLE, A • 1917 • Edwards Harry J. • SHT • USA
BATH HOUSE TRAGEDY, THE • 1915 • Lehrman Henry, Frazee Edwin • USA
BATH OF THE TRANSITORY WORLD see **UKIYO BURO** • 1929
BATH TUB BANDIT • 1917 • Santell Alfred • USA
BATH TUB ELOPEMENT, A • 1916 • *Perez Tweedledum* • SHT • USA
BATH TUB MARRIAGE, A • 1917 • Ray John • SHT • USA
BATHERS, THE • 1900 • Hepworth Cecil M. • UKN
BATHERS, THE see **BADARNA** • 1968
BATHER'S DIFFICULTIES, A • 1906 • Green Tom? • UKN
BATHERS DISTURBED: OR, THE LOVER'S SURPRISE, THE • 1899 • *Wolff Philipp* • UKN
BATHER'S REVENGE, THE • 1904 • Haggar William • UKN
BATHERS WILL BE PROSECUTED • 1905 • Fitzhamon Lewin? • UKN
BATHHOUSE BLUNDER, A • 1916 • Henderson Dell • SHT • USA
BATHING BEAUTIES AND BIG BOOBS see **BIG BOOBS AND BATHING BEAUTIES** • 1918
BATHING BEAUTY • 1944 • Sidney George • USA • MR. CO-ED
BATHING BEAUTY, A • 1914 • Sennett Mack • USA
BATHING BUDDIES • 1946 • Lundy Dick • ANS • USA
BATHING NOT ALLOWED • 1905 • Haggar William • UKN
BATHING OR CHARLIE AND MARY IN THE COUNTRY • 1908 • *Vitagraph* • USA
BATHING PROHIBITED • 1908 • *Tyler Walter* • UKN
BATHROOM, THE • 1970 • Kuri Yoji • ANS • JPN
BATHROOM PROBLEM, A • 1913 • Evans Fred, Evans Joe • UKN
BATHTUB MYSTERY, A • 1916 • McKim Edwin • SHT • USA
BATHTUB PERILS • 1916 • Frazee Edwin • SHT • USA
BATIDA DE RAPOSAS • 1976 • Serrano Carlos • SPN
BATIKHA, EL • 1972 • Khan Mohamed • SHT • EGY • WATERMELON, THE
BATIR A NOTRE AGE • 1958 • Leenhardt Roger • DCS • FRN
BATISSEURS, LES • 1938 • Epstein Jean • FRN
BATISSEURS, LES • 1977 • Haudiquet Philippe • DOC • FRN • LARZAC 75-77
BATITO THE UNEMPLOYED • 1988 • *Revach Zeev* • ISR
BATMAN • 1964 • Warhol Andy • USA
BATMAN • 1966 • Martinson Leslie H. • USA
BATMAN • 1989 • Burton Tim • USA
BATMAN see **BATMAN, THE** • 1943
BATMAN, THE • 1943 • Hillyer Lambert • SRL • USA • BATMAN
BATMAN AND ROBIN • 1949 • Bennet Spencer Gordon • SRL • USA • NEW ADVENTURES OF BATMAN AND ROBIN, THE ○ RETURN OF BATMAN, THE
BATMAN AND ROBIN • 1964 • Glut Don • SHT • USA
BATMAN DRACULA • 1964 • Warhol Andy • USA
BATMAN FIGHTS DRACULA • 1967 • Diaz Leody M. • PHL
BATMEN OF AFRICA • 1936 • Eason B. Reeves, Kane Joseph • USA
BATO SA BATO • 1967 • de Jesus Ding M. • PHL • STONE ON STONE
BATON, LE • 1946 • Gibaud Marcel • SHT • FRN
BATON BUNNY • 1959 • Jones Charles M. • ANS • USA
BATON ROUGE • 1988 • Moleon Rafael • SPN
BATOUK • 1967 • Manigot Jean-Jacques • DOC • FRN
BATS IN THE BELFRY • 1942 • Brewer Jerry • ANS • USA
BATS IN THE BELFRY • 1960 • Smith Paul J. • ANS • USA
BATS IN THE BELFRY see **BUBE U GLAVI** • 1971
BATS WITH BABY FACES see **SKY WEST AND CROOKED** • 1965
BATTACHERJEE • 1943 • Roy Bimal • IND
BATTAGLIA, LA • 1942 • Orioli Giuseppe • ITL • QUATTRO DI BIR EL GOBI, I
BATTAGLIA DALL'ASTICO AL PIAVE • 1917 • Rosa Silvio Laurenti • ITL
BATTAGLIA DE FORT APACHE, LA (ITL) see **OLD SHATTERHAND** • 1964
BATTAGLIA DEI MODS, LA • 1966 • Montemurro Francesco • ITL, FRG • BATTLE OF THE MODS, THE (USA) ○ SIEBZEHN JAHR, BLONDES HAAR ○ SEVENTEEN AND FAIR OF HAIR ○ CRAZY BABY
BATTAGLIA DEL DESERTO, LA • 1969 • Loy Mino • ITL, FRN • SEPT HOMMES POUR TOBROUK (FRN) ○ DESERT BATTLE (UKN) ○ DESERT ASSAULT
BATTAGLIA DEL SINAI, LA • 1968 • Lucidi Maurizio • ITL, ISR • BATTLE OF SINAI, THE
BATTAGLIA DELLA NERETVA, LA (ITL) see **BITKA NA NERETVI** • 1969
BATTAGLIA DELL'ULTIMO PANZER, LA (ITL) see **BATALLA DEL ULTIMO PANZER, LA** • 1968
BATTAGLIA DI ALGERI, LA • 1965 • Pontecorvo Gillo • ITL, ALG • BATTLE OF ALGIERS, THE (UKN) ○ MAARAKAT MADINAT AL JAZAER ○ MAARAKAT ALGER
BATTAGLIA DI EL ALAMEIN, LA • 1969 • Ferroni Giorgio • ITL, FRN • DESERT TANKS (UKN) ○ BATTLE OF EL ALAMEIN, THE
BATTAGLIA DI MARATONA, LA • 1959 • Vailati Bruno, Tourneur Jacques • ITL • GIANT OF MARATHON, THE (UKN) ○ BATTLE OF MARATHON, THE
BATTAGLIA DI NAPOLI, LA see **QUATTRO GIORNATE DI NAPOLI, LE** • 1962
BATTAGLIA D'INGHILTERRA, LA • 1969 • Castellari Enzo G. • ITL, SPN, FRN • BATTAGLIA SOBRE BRITANA, LA (USA) ○ LARGO DIA DEL AGUILA, EL (SPN) ○ BATTLE SQUADRON (UKN) ○ BATTLE COMMAND ○ BATTLE OF THE EAGLES ○ EAGLES OVER LONDON ○ EAGLES OVER BRITAIN
BATTAGLIA SOBRE BRITANA, LA (USA) see **BATTAGLIA D'INGHILTERRA, LA** • 1969
BATTAGLIE NEGLI SPAZI STELLARI • 1978 • Brescia Alfonso • ITL • BATTLE OF THE STARS
BATTAGLIE SUI MARI • 1961 • Savarese Roberto • DOC • ITL
BATTALION DES VA-NU-PIEDS, LE see **XIPOLITO TAGMA** • 1954
BATTALION SHOT, THE • 1912 • Martinek H. O. • UKN
BATTANT, LE • 1982 • Delon Alain • FRN
BATTELLIERI DEL VOLGA, I • 1959 • Tourjansky Victor • ITL, FRN • PRISONER OF THE VOLGA (USA) ○ BOATMEN, THE (UKN)
BATTEMENT DE COEUR • 1939 • Decoin Henri • FRN
BATTEMENTS DE COEUR see **NABADHATU QALB** • 1971
BATTER UP • 1927 • Roberts Stephen • SHT • USA
BATTERED • 1978 • Werner Peter • TVM • USA
BATTERED see **INTIMATE STRANGERS** • 1977
BATTERED BRIDEGROOM, THE • 1916 • Ellis Robert • SHT • USA
BATTERED BRIDEGROOMS, THE • 1911 • *American* • USA
BATTERIES NOT INCLUDED • 1987 • Robbins Matthew • USA
BATTEUSE A VAPEUR • 1896 • Melies Georges • FRN • THRESHING MACHINES WORKED BY POWER
BATTICUORE • 1939 • Camerini Mario • ITL
BATTITO D'ALI DOPO LA STRAGE, UN (ITL) see **FILS, LE** • 1973
BATTLE, THE • 1911 • Griffith D. W. • USA
BATTLE, THE • 1914 • *Sterling* • USA
BATTLE, THE • 1923 • Fleischer Dave • ANS • USA
BATTLE, THE • 1934 • Farkas Nicolas • UKN • THUNDER IN THE EAST (USA) ○ HARA-KIRI
BATTLE, THE see **DANGER LINE, THE** • 1924
BATTLE ABOARD THE DEFIANT see **H.M.S. DEFIANT** • 1962
BATTLE AT APACHE PASS, THE • 1952 • Sherman George • USA • BATTLE OF APACHE PASS, THE
BATTLE AT BLOODY BEACH • 1961 • Coleman Herbert • USA • BATTLE ON THE BEACH (UKN) ○ BATTLE OF BLOODY BEACH, THE
BATTLE AT ELDERBUSH GULCH, THE • 1914 • Griffith D. W. • USA • BATTLE OF ELDERBUSH GULCH, THE
BATTLE AT FORT LARAMIE, THE • 1913 • *Kalem* • USA
BATTLE AT KAWANAKAJIMA see **KAWANAKAJIMA KASSEN** • 1941
BATTLE BENEATH THE EARTH • 1968 • Tully Montgomery • UKN • BATTLE BENEATH THE SEA
BATTLE BENEATH THE SEA see **BATTLE BENEATH THE EARTH** • 1968
BATTLE BEYOND THE STARS • 1980 • Murakami Jimmy T. • USA
BATTLE BEYOND THE STARS see **GAMMA SANGO UCHU DAISAKUSEN** • 1968
BATTLE BEYOND THE SUN • 1963 • Colchart Thomas • USA
BATTLE BEYOND THE SUN see **NEBO ZOVYOT** • 1959
BATTLE CIRCUS • 1952 • Brooks Richard • USA
BATTLE COMMAND see **BATTAGLIA D'INGHILTERRA, LA** • 1969
BATTLE CREEK BRAWL • 1980 • Clouse Robert • USA, HKG • SHA-SHOU HAO (HKG) ○ BIG BRAWL, THE (UKN)
BATTLE CRY • 1955 • Walsh Raoul • USA
BATTLE CRY OF PEACE, THE • 1915 • Blackton J. Stuart, North Wilfred • USA • CALL TO ARMS AGAINST WAR, A
BATTLE DUST see **SENJIN** • 1935
BATTLE FLAME • 1959 • Springsteen R. G. • USA
BATTLE FOR A BOTTLE • 1942 • Tashlin Frank • ANS • USA
BATTLE FOR ANZIO, THE see **SBARCO DI ANZIO, LO** • 1968
BATTLE FOR BERLIN • 1971 • Ozerov Yury • USS • BATTLE OF BERLIN
BATTLE FOR CHINA • 1953 • Varlamov Leonid • USS
BATTLE FOR FREEDOM, THE • 1913 • Melford George • USA
BATTLE FOR HIS HEART, THE see **KAMPEN OM HANS HJARTA** • 1916
BATTLE FOR MUSIC • 1943 • Taylor Donald • UKN
BATTLE FOR OUR SOVIET UKRAINE, THE see **BITVA ZA NASHA SOVIETSKAYA UKRAINU** • 1943
BATTLE FOR ROME see **KAMPF UM ROM, TEIL 1: KOMM NUR, MEIN LIEBSTES VOGELEIN** • 1969
BATTLE FOR THE PLANET OF THE APES • 1973 • Thompson J. Lee • USA
BATTLE FOR TSARITSIN see **BOI POD TSARITSYNOM** • 1919
BATTLE FORCE see **GRANDE ATTACCO, IL** • 1978
BATTLE-GROUND, THE • 1912 • Dwan Allan • USA
BATTLE HELL (USA) see **YANGTSE INCIDENT** • 1957
BATTLE HYMN • 1956 • Sirk Douglas • USA
BATTLE HYMN OF THE REPUBLIC, THE • 1911 • Trimble Larry • USA
BATTLE IN OUTER SPACE (USA) see **UCHU DAISENSO** • 1959
BATTLE IN PEACE see **UTKOZET BEKEBEN** • 1951
BATTLE IN THE CLOUDS, THE (USA) see **AIRSHIP DESTROYER, THE** • 1909
BATTLE IN THE DARK, A • 1916 • Ritchie Robert Welles • SHT • USA

BATTLE IN THE SHADOWS see **BATALIA DIN UMBRA** • 1988
BATTLE IN THE VIRGINIA HILLS • 1912 • *Cooper Miriam* • USA
BATTLE INFERNO see **HUNDE! WOLLT IHR EWIG LEBEN?** • 1959
BATTLE OF ALGIERS, THE (UKN) see **BATTAGLIA DI ALGERI, LA** • 1965
BATTLE OF AMBROSE AND WALRUS, THE • 1915 • Wright Walter • USA
BATTLE OF APACHE PASS, THE see **BATTLE AT APACHE PASS, THE** • 1952
BATTLE OF AUSTERLITZ, THE see **BATAILLE D'AUSTERLITZ, LA** • 1909
BATTLE OF AUSTERLITZ (USA) see **AUSTERLITZ** • 1960
BATTLE OF BALLOTS, THE • 1915 • Coigne Frank B. • USA
BATTLE OF BERLIN see **BATTLE FOR BERLIN** • 1971
BATTLE OF BERLIN, THE (USA) see **SCHLACT UM BERLIN** • 1973
BATTLE OF BILLY'S POND, THE • 1976 • Cokliss Harley • USA
BATTLE OF BLOOD ISLAND • 1960 • Rapp Joel • USA
BATTLE OF BLOODY BEACH, THE see **BATTLE AT BLOODY BEACH** • 1961
BATTLE OF BLOODY FORD, THE • 1913 • Melford George • USA
BATTLE OF BRITAIN • 1969 • Hamilton Guy • UKN
BATTLE OF BRITAIN, THE • 1943 • Veiller Anthony, Capra Frank • DOC • USA • WHY WE FIGHT (PART 4): THE BATTLE OF BRITAIN
BATTLE OF BROADWAY • 1937 • Marshall George • USA
BATTLE OF BULL CON, THE • 1913 • *Lyons Eddie* • USA
BATTLE OF BULL RUN, THE • 1913 • *Cunard Grace* • USA
BATTLE OF BUNKER HILL, THE • 1911 • Dawley J. Searle • USA
BATTLE OF CAULIFLOWERS, A • 1905 • Fitzhamon Lewin • UKN
BATTLE OF CHAMPIONS • 1968 • Herrera Armando A. • PHL
BATTLE OF CHILE, THE see **BATALLA DE CHILE: LA LUCHA DE UN PUEBLO SIN ARMAS, LA** • 1974-79
BATTLE OF CHILE CON CARNE, THE • 1916 • Chaudet Louis W. • SHT • USA
BATTLE OF CHILE: THE STRUGGLE OF AN UNARMED PEOPLE, THE see **BATALLA DE CHILE: LA LUCHA DE UN PUEBLO SIN ARMAS, LA** • 1974-79
BATTLE OF CHILI AND BEANS, THE • 1914 • *Mace Fred* • USA
BATTLE OF CHINA, THE • 1944 • Litvak Anatole, Capra Frank • DOC • USA • WHY WE FIGHT (PART 6): THE BATTLE OF CHINA
BATTLE OF CITY HALL, THE see **ANGELS WASH THEIR FACES** • 1939
BATTLE OF CRETE, THE • 1970 • Georgiadis Vassilis • GRC, SPN, ITL
BATTLE OF CULLODEN, THE • 1964 • Watkins Peter • UKN • CULLODEN
BATTLE OF CUPIDOVICH, THE • 1916 • MacMackin Archer • SHT • USA
BATTLE OF EL ALAMEIN, THE see **BATTAGLIA DI EL ALAMEIN, LA** • 1969
BATTLE OF ELDERBUSH GULCH, THE see **BATTLE AT ELDERBUSH GULCH, THE** • 1914
BATTLE OF FRENCHMAN'S RUN, THE • 1915 • Marston Theodore • USA
BATTLE OF GALLIPOLI (USA) see **TELL ENGLAND** • 1931
BATTLE OF GETTYSBURG, THE • 1914 • Ince Thomas H., Giblyn Charles • USA
BATTLE OF GETTYSOWNBACK, THE • 1914 • Evans Fred, Evans Joe • UKN
BATTLE OF GLENCOE, THE • 1899 • Ashe Robert • UKN
BATTLE OF GREED • 1937 • Higgin Howard • USA
BATTLE OF HAWAII see **HAWAI-MAREI-OKI KAISEN** • 1942
BATTLE OF HEARTS • 1916 • Apfel Oscar • USA
BATTLE OF JUTLAND, THE • 1921 • Woolfe H. Bruce • UKN
BATTLE OF KAWANAKAJIMA, THE see **KAWANAKAJIMA KASSEN** • 1941
BATTLE OF KOLBERG, THE see **BITWA O KOLOBRZEG** • 1945
BATTLE OF KOLOBRZEG, THE see **BITWA O KOLOBRZEG** • 1945
BATTLE OF KOSOVO, THE see **BOJ NA KOSOVU** • 1989
BATTLE OF LA PEROUSE • 1910 • ASL
BATTLE OF 'LET'S GO', THE • 1917 • Hutchinson Craig • SHT • USA
BATTLE OF LIFE, THE • 1916 • Vincent James • USA
BATTLE OF LOVE, THE • 1914 • *Bushman Francis X.* • USA
BATTLE OF LOVE, THE • 1923 • Bentley Thomas • UKN
BATTLE OF LOVE'S RETURN, THE • 1971 • Kaufman Lloyd • USA
BATTLE OF MANCHURIA, THE see **SENSO TO NINGEN** • 1970
BATTLE OF MANILA, THE • 1913 • Ford Francis • USA
BATTLE OF MARATHON, THE see **BATTAGLIA DI MARATONA, LA** • 1959
BATTLE OF MICE AND FROGS, THE • 1978 • Hartman Rivka • SHT • ASL
BATTLE OF MIDWAY, THE • 1942 • Ford John, Litvak Anatole • DOC • USA
BATTLE OF MIDWAY (UKN) see **MIDWAY** • 1976
BATTLE OF MONMOUTH • 1908 • *Lubin* • USA
BATTLE OF MONS, THE see **MONS** • 1926
BATTLE OF MOSCOW, THE • 1986 • Ozerov Yury • USS, CZC, GDR
BATTLE OF NERETVA, THE (USA) see **BITKA NA NERETVI** • 1969
BATTLE OF NEW ORLEANS, THE • 1960 • Godfrey Bob • SHT • UKN
BATTLE OF NOT YET, THE • 1915 • *Atla* • USA
BATTLE OF OKINAWA see **OKINAWA KESSEN** • 1971
BATTLE OF OREL, THE see **ORLOVSKAYA BITVA** • 1943
BATTLE OF PARIS, THE • 1929 • Florey Robert • USA • GAY LADY, THE
BATTLE OF POTTSBURG BRIDGE • 1912 • *Cooper Marian* • USA
BATTLE OF POWDER RIVER, THE (UKN) see **TOMAHAWK** • 1951
BATTLE OF POZIRALNIK, THE see **BOJ NA POZIRALNIKU** • 1983
BATTLE OF ROGUE RIVER • 1954 • Castle William • USA
BATTLE OF ROSES, THE see **BARA-GASSEN** • 1950
BATTLE OF RUNNING BULL, THE • 1915 • *Gould Dot* • USA
BATTLE OF RUSSIA, THE • 1943 • Litvak Anatole • DOC • USA • WHY WE FIGHT (PART 5): THE BATTLE OF RUSSIA
BATTLE OF SAN JUAN HILL, THE • 1913 • *Bison* • USA
BATTLE OF SAN PASQUALE, THE see **CAVALRY COMMAND** • 1963
BATTLE OF SAN PIETRO, THE • 1944 • Huston John • DOC • USA • SAN PIETRO
BATTLE OF SHANGHAI • 1959 • Wang Ping • CHN
BATTLE OF SHILOH, THE • 1914 • Ince John • USA
BATTLE OF SINAI, THE see **BATTAGLIA DEL SINAI, LA** • 1968
BATTLE OF SNAKEVILLE, THE • 1915 • *Essanay* • USA
BATTLE OF SOKOL, THE • 1942 • Rasumny Alexander • USS
BATTLE OF STALINGRAD, THE see **STALINGRADSKAYA BITVA** • 1950
BATTLE OF STALINGRAD, THE see **STALINGRADSKAYA BITVA** • 1970
BATTLE OF THE ACES see **VON RICHTOFEN AND BROWN** • 1971
BATTLE OF THE ANTILLES see **QUEMADA!** • 1969
BATTLE OF THE ASTROS see **KAIJU DAISENSO** • 1965
BATTLE OF THE BARN • 1932 • *Mintz Charles (P)* • ANS • USA
BATTLE OF THE BOOKS, THE • 1941 • Chambers Jack • DOC • UKN
BATTLE OF THE BULGE • 1965 • Annakin Ken • USA
BATTLE OF THE CENTURY, THE • 1927 • Bruckman Clyde • SHT • USA
BATTLE OF THE CHIEFS, THE see **HAKANLARIN SAVASI** • 1968
BATTLE OF THE COMMANDOS (USA) see **LEGIONE DEI DANNATI, LA** • 1969
BATTLE OF THE CORAL SEA • 1959 • Wendkos Paul • USA
BATTLE OF THE CORONEL AND FALKLAND ISLANDS, THE • 1927 • Summers Walter • UKN • DEEDS MEN DO, THE
BATTLE OF THE DAMNED see **QUELLA DANNATA PATTUGLIA** • 1969
BATTLE OF THE EAGLES see **BATTAGLIA D'INGHILTERRA, LA** • 1969
BATTLE OF THE FLOWERS AND THE STUPID FATHER, THE see **OYABAKA HANAGASSEN** • 1953
BATTLE OF THE GIANTS see **BORBA GIGANTOV** • 1926
BATTLE OF THE GIANTS see **ONE MILLION B.C.** • 1940
BATTLE OF THE JAPAN SEA see **NIHONKAI DAIKAISEN** • 1969
BATTLE OF THE LADIES see **DEVIL MAY CARE** • 1929
BATTLE OF THE LAST PANZER, THE see **BATALLA DEL ULTIMO PANZER, LA** • 1968
BATTLE OF THE LONG SAULT, THE • 1913 • Crane Frank H. • CND • DOLLARD DES ORMEAUX
BATTLE OF THE MARETHLINE see **GRANDE ATTACCO, IL** • 1978
BATTLE OF THE MODS, THE (USA) see **BATTAGLIA DEI MODS, LA** • 1966
BATTLE OF THE NATIONS, THE • 1914 • *Joker* • USA
BATTLE OF THE RAILS (USA) see **BATAILLE DU RAIL, LA** • 1945
BATTLE OF THE RED MEN, THE • 1912 • Ince Thomas H. • USA
BATTLE OF THE RIVER PLATE • 1956 • Powell Michael, Pressburger Emeric • UKN • PURSUIT OF THE GRAF SPREE (USA)
BATTLE OF THE SEXES, THE • 1914 • Griffith D. W. • USA
BATTLE OF THE SEXES, THE • 1928 • Griffith D. W. • USA
BATTLE OF THE SEXES, THE • 1959 • Crichton Charles • UKN
BATTLE OF THE SOMME • 1916 • *Woolfe H. Bruce (P)* • UKN
BATTLE OF THE SPARTANS see **BRENNO IL NEMICO DI ROMA** • 1964
BATTLE OF THE STARS see **BATTAGLIE NEGLI SPAZI STELLARI** • 1978
BATTLE OF THE V 1 • 1958 • Sewell Vernon • UKN • UNSEEN HEROES (USA) ○ MISSILES FROM HELL ○ V 1
BATTLE OF THE VILLA FIORITA, THE • 1965 • Daves Delmer • USA, UKN • AFFAIR AT THE VILLA FIORITA, THE
BATTLE OF THE WEAK, THE • 1914 • Marston Theodore • USA
BATTLE OF THE WILLS • 1911 • *Shay William* • USA
BATTLE OF THE WORLDS (USA) see **PIANETA DEGLI UOMINI SPENTI, IL** • 1961
BATTLE OF TRAFALGAR, THE • 1911 • Dawley J. Searle • USA
BATTLE OF TRUTH, THE • 1916 • MacDonald J. Farrell • SHT • USA
BATTLE OF TSARITSIN see **BOI POD TSARITSYNOM** • 1919
BATTLE OF WANGAPORE, THE • 1955 • Daborn John • ANS • UKN
BATTLE OF WATERLOO, THE • 1913 • Weston Charles • UKN
BATTLE OF WHO RUN, THE • 1913 • Sennett Mack • USA
BATTLE OF WILLS, THE • 1913 • Dwan Allan • USA
BATTLE OF WITS, A • 1912 • *Joyce Alice* • USA
BATTLE ON THE BEACH (UKN) see **BATTLE AT BLOODY BEACH** • 1961
BATTLE ON THE RIVER NERETVA see **BITKA NA NERETVI** • 1969
BATTLE ON THE ROAD see **BITVA V PUTI** • 1961
BATTLE RAGE see **MISSING IN ACTION 2: THE BEGINNING** • 1985
BATTLE ROYAL • 1918 • Jones F. Richard • SHT • USA
BATTLE ROYAL, A • 1908 • *Essanay* • USA
BATTLE ROYAL, A • 1936 • Davis Mannie, Gordon George • ANS • USA
BATTLE ROYAL, THE • 1916 • *Plump & Runt* • USA
BATTLE SHOCK see **WOMAN'S DEVOTION, A** • 1956
BATTLE SQUADRON (UKN) see **BATTAGLIA D'INGHILTERRA, LA** • 1969
BATTLE STATIONS • 1956 • Seiler Lewis • USA
BATTLE STRIPE see **MEN, THE** • 1950
BATTLE TAXI • 1955 • Strock Herbert L. • USA
BATTLE UNDER THE WALLS OF KERCHENETZ • 1971 • Ivanov-Vano Ivan, Norshtein Yuri • ANM • USS
BATTLE WITH CONFETTI see **BATAILLE DE CONFETTIS** • 1897
BATTLE WITHOUT ARMS, THE see **BUKI NAKI TATAKI** • 1960
BATTLE ZONE • 1952 • Selander Lesley • USA
BATTLEAXE, THE • 1962 • Grayson Godfrey • UKN
BATTLEFIELDS OF GALLIPOLI • 1916 • ASL • AUSTRALIA'S FIELDS OF GLORY
BATTLEGROUND • 1949 • Wellman William A. • USA
BATTLER, THE • 1916 • Semon Larry • SHT • USA
BATTLER, THE • 1919 • Reicher Frank • USA
BATTLER, THE • 1925 • Bradbury Robert North • USA
BATTLER VS. THE BOTTLER, THE • 1920 • *Selznick* • SHT • USA
BATTLES IN THE DESERT see **BATALLAS EN EL DESIERTO, LAS** • 1986
BATTLES IN THE SHADOWS see **LOTTE NELL'OMBRA** • 1939
BATTLES OF CHIEF PONTIAC, THE • 1952 • Feist Felix E. • USA
BATTLES OF HAWAII AND MALAY OFF SHORE, THE see **HAWAI-MAREI-OKI KAISEN** • 1942
BATTLES OF IVAN, THE see **IVAN THE TERRIBLE PART 3** • 1947
BATTLES OF THE GLADIATORS see **GLADIATORE DI ROMA, IL** • 1962
BATTLESHIP POTEMKIN see **BRONENOSETS POTYOMKIN** • 1925
BATTLESHIP POTEMKIN, THE see **EVENEMENTS D'ODESSA, LES** • 1905
BATTLESHIPS • 1911 • Dwan Allan • USA
BATTLESTAR GALACTICA • 1978 • Colla Richard A., Levi Alan J. (U/c) • USA • STAR WORLDS
BATTLETRUCK • 1983 • Cokliss Harley • NZL, USA • WARLORDS OF THE 21ST CENTURY
BATTLIN' BILL • 1927 • *Carter Dick* • USA
BATTLIN' BUCKAROO • 1924 • *Paton Bill* • USA
BATTLING BATES • 1923 • Cullison Webster • USA
BATTLING BELLBOY, THE • 1917 • Beaudine William • SHT • USA
BATTLING BELLHOP see **KID GALAHAD** • 1937
BATTLING BLUEFINS • 1947 • Perry Margaret • DOC • CND
BATTLING BOOKWORM • 1928 • *Barrymore William* • USA
BATTLING BOSKO • 1931-32 • Harman Hugh • ANS • USA
BATTLING BREWSTER • 1924 • Henderson Dell • SRL • USA
BATTLING BRITISH, THE (USA) see **BLACK-EYED SUSAN** • 1914
BATTLING BROWN OF BIRMINGHAM • 1914 • Weston Charles • UKN
BATTLING BRUISERS • 1925 • Brunel Adrian • UKN
BATTLING BUCKAROO • 1932 • Schaefer Armand • USA • HIS LAST ADVENTURE (UKN)
BATTLING BUDDY • 1924 • Thorpe Richard • SHT • USA
BATTLING BUNYON • 1925 • Hurst Paul C. • USA
BATTLING BURKE • 1928 • *Hoxie Al* • USA
BATTLING BUTLER • 1926 • Keaton Buster • USA
BATTLING CHARLIE see **CHAMPION, THE** • 1915
BATTLING FOOL, THE • 1924 • Van Dyke W. S. • USA
BATTLING HEARTS see **VERGODO SZIVEK** • 1916
BATTLING HOOFER see **SOMETHING TO SING ABOUT** • 1937
BATTLING JANE • 1918 • Clifton Elmer • USA
BATTLING KELLY • 1912 • Coleby A. E. • UKN
BATTLING KID • 1926 • Hurst Paul C. • USA
BATTLING KID, THE • 1930 • Nelson Jack • SHT • USA
BATTLING KING • 1922 • Sargent P. D. • USA
BATTLING MARSHAL • 1950 • Drake Oliver • USA
BATTLING MASON • 1924 • Nelson Jack?, Craft William James? • USA
BATTLING ORIOLES, THE • 1924 • Wilde Ted, Guiol Fred • USA • HOW ARE ALL THE BOYS?
BATTLING WITH BUFFALO BILL • 1931 • Taylor Ray • SRL • USA
BATTON STORY see **IMPIEGATE STRADALI, L'** • 1976
BATTUTMATDIK YAN • 1989 • Chen You • HKG • FISHY STORY, A
BATTY BASEBALL • 1944 • Avery Tex • ANS • USA
BATTY BILL ALMOST MARRIED • 1914 • *Melies* • USA
BATTY BILL AND THE SUICIDE CLUB • 1914 • *Melies* • USA
BATTY BILL, MONKEY AND PELICAN • 1914 • *Melies* • USA
BATTY BILL'S HONEYMOON • 1914 • *Melies* • USA
BATU BELAH BATU BERTANGKUP • 1959 • Sulong Jamil • MLY • DEVOURING ROCK, THE
BATULA • 1952 • *Louis G. Cowan Inc.* • SHT • USA • FEARLESS FOSDICK IN BATULA
BATWOMAN (USA) see **MUJER MURCIELAGO, LA** • 1968
BAUDELARIAN CAPERS see **BAUDELERIAN CAPERS** • 1962
BAUDELERIAN CAPERS • 1962 • Jacobs Ken • SHT • USA • BAUDELARIAN CAPERS
BAUER ALS MILLIONAR, DER • 1961 • Stoger Alfred • AUS
BAUER VON BRUCKNERHOF, DER • 1956 • Deppe Hans • FRG • MEIN BRUDER JOSUA
BAUERNDOKTOR VON BAYRISCHZELL • 1957 • Schott-Schobinger Hans • FRG
BAUERNEHRE • 1918 • Burghardt Georg • FRG
BAUHAUS, LE • Fournier Jean-Louis • FRN
BAUHUTTE '63 • 1963 • Hart Wolf • FRG • CATHEDRAL OPERATION 1963
BAUL MACABRO, EL • 1936 • Zacarias Miguel • MXC • MACABRE TRUNK, THE (USA)
BAULE LES PINS, LA • 1990 • Kurys Diane • FRN
BAUTIZO, EL • 1966 • Fandino Roberto • CUB
BAVU • 1923 • Paton Stuart • USA • ATTIC OF FELIX BAVU, THE ○ THUNDERING DAWN
BAWALAH AKU PERGI • 1981 • Risyaf M. T. • INN • TAKE ME AWAY
BAWANG BIE JI • 1988 • Guan Jinpeng • HKG
BAWANG PUTEH, BAWANG MERAH • 1958 • Noor S. Roomai • MLY • WHITE ONION, RED ONION
BAWAT KANTO BASAGULO • 1968 • Rizaldy • PHL • TROUBLE AT EVERY CORNER
BAWBS O' BLUE RIDGE • 1916 • Miller Charles • USA
BAWDY ADVENTURES OF TOM JONES, THE • 1975 • Owen Cliff • UKN • ADVENTURES OF TOM JONES, THE ○ BAWDY TALES OF TOM JONES, THE
BAWDY TALES OF TOM JONES, THE see **BAWDY ADVENTURES OF TOM JONES, THE** • 1975
BAWDY TALES (USA) see **STORIE SCELLERATE** • 1973
BAWLED OUT • 1918 • Davis James • SHT • USA
BAWLEROUT, THE • 1913 • Apfel Oscar • USA

BAXTER! • 1973 • Jeffries Lionel • UKN
BAXTER • 1989 • Boivin Jerome • FRN
BAXTER EARNS HIS WINGS • 1982 • Arioli Don • ANS • CND
BAXTER MILLIONS, THE (UKN) see **THREE KIDS AND A QUEEN** • 1935
BAXTER MILLIONS, THE (UKN) see **LITTLE MISS BIG** • 1946
BAXTER, VERA BAXTER • 1976 • Duras Marguerite • FRN • VERA BAXTER OU LES PLAGES DE L'ATLANTIQUE ○ VERA BAXTER
BAXTER'S BUSY DAY • 1913 • *Powers* • USA
BAY BOY, THE • 1984 • Petrie Daniel • CND, FRN • PRINTEMPS SOUS LA NEIGE, LE
BAY COVE see **BAY COVEN** • 1987
BAY COVEN • 1987 • Schenkel Carl • TVM • USA • BAY COVE
BAY OF ANGELS see **BAIE DES ANGES, LA** • 1963
BAY OF BISCAY see **GOLFO DE VIZCAYA** • 1985
BAY OF BLOOD see **REAZIONE A CATENA** • 1971
BAY OF GOLD see **DOBRODRUZSTVI NA ZLATE ZATOCE** • 1955
BAY OF ST. MICHEL, THE • 1963 • Ainsworth John • UKN • PATTERN FOR PLUNDER (USA) ○ OPERATION MERMAID
BAY OF SEVEN ISLES, THE • 1915 • Lloyd Frank • USA
BAY OF THE ANGELS (USA) see **BAIE DES ANGES, LA** • 1963
BAY THE MOON see **HIGH COST OF LOVING, THE** • 1958
BAYA EL KHAWATIM see **BAIYYA AL-KHAWATIM** • 1965
BAYADERE'S REVENGE, THE see **TEMPELDANSERINDENS ELSKOV** • 1914
BAYAN KO -KAPIT SA PATALIM • 1984 • Brocka Lino • PHL • BAYAN KO: MY OWN COUNTRY
BAYAN KO: MY OWN COUNTRY see **BAYAN KO -KAPIT SA PATALIM** • 1984
BAYAYA see **BAJAJA** • 1950
BAYEN IDEK • 1959 • Shahin Youssef • EGY • BETWEEN YOUR HANDS ○ BAINA AYDIK
BAYER TAPI NYICIL • 1989 • *Petet Didi* • INN
BAYERISCHE HIASEL, DER • 1920 • Seitz Franz? • FRG
BAYN AL-QASRAYN • Al Imam Hassan • EGY • ENTRE LES DEUX PALAIS
BAYN EL SAMAA WA EL ARD • 1959 • Abu Saif Salah • EGY • BETWEEN HEAVEN AND EARTH ○ BETWEEN HEAVEN AND HELL ○ BAINA AS-SAMA' WA AL-ARDH
BAYO • 1985 • Ransen Mort • CND
BAYOU • 1957 • Daniels Harold • USA • POOR WHITE TRASH
BAYT AL-'ACHBAH' see **BEIT AL ASHBAH** • 1952
BAYTEKIN FEZADA CARPISANLAR • 1967 • Ozonuk Sinasi • TRK • FLASH GORDON'S BATTLE IN SPACE
BAZA LUDZI UMARLYCH • 1958 • Petelski Czeslaw • PLN • DAMNED ROADS
BAZAN • 1960 • Tamayo Ramiro • ARG
BAZAR DELLE IDEE, IL • 1941 • Albani Marcello • ITL
BAZAR-E-HUSN • 1988 • Fazil Javed • PKS • MARKET
BAZOKU YAKUZA • 1968 • Ozawa Shigehiro • JPN • BANDITS, THE
BAZU TALAEI • 1967 • Ekhart Robert • IRN • GOLDEN ARMS
BAZY-E-SHANCE • 1968 • Ajrame Farough • IRN • GAME OF LUCK, THE
BAZYLISZEK • 1961 • Serafinowicz Leokadia, Wieczorkieloica W. • ANM • PLN • ENCOUNTER WITH THE BASILISK ○ BASILISK, THE
BBONG • 1985 • I Du-Yong • SKR • MULBERRY LEAVES ○ MULBERRY TREE ○ BHONG
BE A GOOD BOY, FATHER see **PATERA KATSE FRONIMA** • 1967
BE A LITTLE SPORT • 1919 • Dunlap Scott R. • USA
BE A MAN -SELL OUT • 1969 • Fox Beryl • DOC • CND
BE ATTRACTIVE • 1971 • McElroy Hal • DOC • ASL
BE BEAUTIFUL AND SHUT UP (USA) see **SOIS BELLE ET TAIS-TOI** • 1958
BE BEAUTIFUL BUT SHUT UP see **DES GENS SANS IMPORTANCE** • 1955
BE BIG • 1930 • Parrott James • SHT • USA
BE BLESSED • 1978 • Obreshkov Alexander • BUL
BE CAREFUL • 1925 • Beaudine Harold • SHT • USA
BE CAREFUL see **HANSOM CABMAN, THE** • 1924
BE CAREFUL BOYS • 1964 • Linnecar Vera, Hanna Nancy, Learner Keith • UKN
BE CAREFUL HOW YOU WISH see **INCREDIBLE MR. LIMPET, THE** • 1964
BE CAREFUL MR. SMITH • 1935 • Mack Max • USA • SINGING THROUGH
BE CAREFUL RED RIDING HOOD see **AKUZUKINCHAN KIOTSUKETE** • 1970
BE CAREFUL WITH THE LADIES see **CUIDADO CON LAS SENORAS** • 1968
BE GENTLE, PENGUIN see **SEI ZARTLICH, PINGUIN** • 1982
BE GLAD FOR THE SONG HAS NO ENDING • 1970 • Neal Peter • DOC • UKN • BE GLAD.. (USA)
BE GLAD.. (USA) see **BE GLAD FOR THE SONG HAS NO ENDING** • 1970
BE GOOD FOREVER see **LEGY JO MINDHALALIG** • 1960
BE GOOD UNTIL DEATH see **LEGY JO MINDHALALIG** • 1960
BE GREAT! see **ERAKU NARE** • 1932
BE HAPPY see **EXO PTOCHIA** • 1932
BE HONEST • 1923 • Roach Hal • SHT • USA
BE HUMAN • 1936 • Fleischer Dave • ANS • USA
BE IT EVER SO HUMBLE • 1913 • *Nestor* • USA
BE IT EVER SO HUMBLE see **HI, BEAUTIFUL!** • 1944
BE KIND TO ANIMALS • 1935 • Fleischer Dave • ANS • USA
BE MINE ALONE see **MAGING AKIN KA LAMANG** • 1988
BE MINE TONIGHT (USA) see **TELL ME TONIGHT** • 1932
BE MY BEST MAN • 1917 • Wright Fred E. • SHT • USA
BE MY GUEST • 1965 • Comfort Lance • UKN
BE MY LOVELY CHILD AGAIN see **CH'I-TAI NI CHANG-TA** • 1988
BE MY VALENTINE, OR ELSE.. see **X-RAY** • 1981
BE MY WIFE • 1919 • Roach Hal • SHT • USA
BE MY WIFE • 1921 • Linder Max • USA
BE NEUTRAL • 1914 • Ford Francis • USA
BE NOT AFRAID • 1938 • Newman Widgey R. • UKN
BE PATIENT, PATIENT • 1944 • Wickersham Bob • ANS • USA
BE PREPARED see **TROOP BEVERLY HILLS** • 1989
BE REASONABLE • 1921 • Del Ruth Roy • SHT • USA
BE SAFE OR BE SORRY • 1955 • Peries Lester James • SHT • SLN
BE SICK.. IT'S FREE see **MEDICO DELLA MUTUA, IL** • 1968
BE SKILFUL, MAN! see **TORD MAGAD, OREG** • 1971
BE SURE AND INSURE • 1913 • Stow Percy • UKN
BE SURE AND SEND ME POSTCARDS see **TU M'ENVERRAS DES CARTES POSTALES**
BE SURE YOUR SINS • 1915 • Hepworth Cecil M. • UKN • CANKER OF JEALOUSY, THE
BE SURE YOU'RE RIGHT • 1917 • Fahrney Milton • USA
BE TOUGH, VICTOR see **TALPRA, GYOZO!** • 1983
BE TRUE UNTIL DEATH see **LEGY JO MINDHALALIG** • 1936
BE UNFAITHFUL AND DON'T CARE WITH WHOM see **SE INFIEL Y NO MIRES CON QUIEN** • 1985
BE UP TO DATE • 1938 • Fleischer Dave • ANS • USA
BE WANTON AND TREAD NO SHAME see **SE INFIEL Y NO MIRES CON QUIEN** • 1985
BE YOUR AGE • 1926 • McCarey Leo • SHT • USA
BE YOUR AGE see **MONKEY BUSINESS** • 1952
BE YOURSELF • 1924 • St. John Al • SHT • USA
BE YOURSELF! • 1930 • Freeland Thornton • USA • CHAMP, THE
BE YOURSELF see **GOOD MORNING, JUDGE** • 1928
BEACH see **PLAZA** • 1964
BEACH, THE see **SPIAGGIA, LA** • 1954
BEACH AND PIER AT TROUVILLE PART 2 see **JETEE ET PLAGE DE TROUVILLE (2e PARTIE)** • 1896
BEACH AND PIER AT TROUVILLE PART ONE see **JETTE ET PLAGE DE TROUVILLE 1er PARTIE** • 1896
BEACH AT VILLIERS IN A GALE, THE see **PLAGE DE VILLIERS PAR GROS TEMPS, LA** • 1896
BEACH BALL • 1965 • Weinrib Lennie • USA
BEACH BALLS • 1988 • Ritter Joe • USA • SUMMERTIME FUN
BEACH BIRDS • 1915 • Mann Hank • USA
BEACH BIRDS • 1917 • Seiter William A. • SHT • USA
BEACH BLANKET BINGO • 1965 • Asher William • USA
BEACH BOYS: AN AMERICAN BAND, THE • 1984 • Leo Malcolm • USA
BEACH BUNNIES • 1977 • Stephen A. C. • USA • RED, HOT AND SEXY
BEACH CALLED DESIRE, A see **PLAYA LLAMADO DESEO, UNA** • 1977
BEACH CASANOVA (USA) see **DONGIOVANNI DELLA COSTA AZZURRA, I** • 1963
BEACH CLUB, THE • 1928 • Edwards Harry J. • SHT • USA
BEACH COMBER, THE see **UNDER CRIMSON SKIES** • 1920
BEACH COMBERS • 1936 • *Lantz Walter (P)* • ANS • USA
BEACH COMBERS, THE • 1912 • *Melies* • USA
BEACH GIRLS see **GIRLS ON THE BEACH, THE** • 1965
BEACH GIRLS, THE • 1982 • Townsend Pat • USA
BEACH GIRLS AND THE MONSTER, THE • 1965 • Hall Jon • USA • MONSTER FROM THE SURF ○ SURF TERROR
BEACH GUARD IN WINTER see **CUVAR PLAZE U ZIMSKOM PERIODU** • 1977
BEACH HOUSE • 1982 • Gallagher John A. • USA • DOWN THE SHORE
BEACH HUT, THE (USA) see **CASOTTO, IL** • 1977
BEACH KEEPER IN WINTERTIME see **CUVAR PLAZE U ZIMSKOM PERIODU** • 1977
BEACH NUT, A • 1919 • Beery Wallace • SHT • USA
BEACH NUT, THE • 1944 • Culhane James • ANS • USA
BEACH NUTS • 1917 • Fahrney Milton • *Cub* • USA
BEACH NUTS • 1917 • Smith Noel • *L-Ko* • SHT • USA
BEACH NUTS • 1918 • Roach Hal • SHT • USA
BEACH OF DREAMS • 1921 • Parke William • USA
BEACH OF THE WAR GODS see **ZHAN SHEN TAN** • 1972
BEACH OF WAR GODS see **ZHAN SHEN TAN** • 1972
BEACH PAJAMAS • 1931 • Arbuckle Roscoe • USA
BEACH PARTY • 1931 • Gillett Burt • ANS • USA
BEACH PARTY • 1963 • Asher William • USA
BEACH PARTY IN A HAUNTED HOUSE see **GHOST IN THE INVISIBLE BIKINI, THE** • 1966
BEACH PARTY ITALIAN STYLE see **DICIOTTENNI AL SOLE** • 1962
BEACH PATROL • 1979 • Kelljan Bob • TVM • USA
BEACH PEACH • 1950 • Kneitel Seymour • ANS • USA
BEACH PICNIC • 1939 • Geronimi Clyde • ANS • USA
BEACH RECOVERY • 1946 • Hughes Ken • DCS • UKN
BEACH RED • 1967 • Wilde Cornel • USA
BEACH SABRAS • 1971 • Dahlen Armin • ISR
BEACHCOMBER, THE • 1915 • *Bosworth* • USA
BEACHCOMBER, THE • 1916 • Windom Lawrence C. • SHT • USA
BEACHCOMBER, THE • 1954 • Box Muriel • UKN
BEACHCOMBER, THE (USA) see **VESSEL OF WRATH** • 1938
BEACHCOMBERS, THE • 1912 • *Gray Betty* • USA
BEACHCOMBERS, THE • 1971-75 • Keatley Philip (c/d) • SER • CND
BEACHED AND BLEACHED • 1915 • Chaudet Louis W. • USA
BEACHES • 1988 • Marshall Garry • USA • FRIENDS
BEACHES AND PEACHES • 1918 • Mayo Archie • SHT • USA
BEACHHEAD • 1954 • Heisler Stuart • USA
BEACON see **LEUCHTFEHER** • 1954
BEACON, THE see **MAYAK** • 1942
BEAD GAME, THE • 1977 • Patel Ishu • ANS • CND • HISTOIRE DE PERLES
BEADED BUCKSKIN BAG, THE • 1913 • Martin E. A. • USA
BEADS OF ONE ROSARY, THE see **PACIORKI JEDNEGO ROZANCA** • 1979
BEAKS TO THE GRINDSTONE • 1985 • Godfrey Bob • ANS • UKN
BEALE STREET • 1979 • Krasilovsky Alexis • USA
BEALE STREET MAMA • 1946 • Williams Spencer • USA
BEANED BY A BEANSHOOTER • 1916 • Marston Theodore • SHT • USA
BEANED ON THE BOARDER • 1920 • *Bletcher Billy* • USA
BEANS • 1914 • *Essanay* • USA
BEANS • 1918 • Dillon John Francis • USA
BEANS AND BULLETS • 1916 • Beaudine William • SHT • USA
BEANS FOR TWO • 1918 • Sidney Scott • SHT • USA
BEANSTALK BUNNY • 1955 • Jones Charles M. • ANS • USA
BEANSTALK JACK • 1933 • *Terry Paul/ Moser Frank (P)* • ANS • USA
BEANSTALK JACK • 1946 • Donnelly Eddie • ANS • USA
BEAR, THE • 1984 • Sarafian Richard C. • USA
BEAR, THE • 1989 • Annaud Jean-Jacques • FRN
BEAR, THE see **LOKIS** • 1926
BEAR, THE see **OURS, L'** • 1960
BEAR, THE see **MEDVED** • 1961
BEAR, THE (USA) see **LOKIS** • 1969
BEAR AFFAIR, THE • 1915 • *Fazenda Louise* • USA
BEAR AND THE BEAN, THE • 1948 • Lah Michael, Blair Preston • ANS • USA
BEAR AND THE BEAVERS, THE • 1942 • Ising Rudolf • ANS • USA
BEAR AND THE DOLL, THE see **OURS ET LA POUPEE, L'** • 1970
BEAR AND THE HARE, THE • 1948 • Lah Michael, Blair Preston • ANS • USA
BEAR AND THE MOUSE, THE • 1966 • Rubbo Michael • SHT • CND
BEAR CAGE, THE see **CAGE AUX OURS, LA** • 1974
BEAR CATS • 1926 • Lamont Charles • SHT • USA
BEAR COUNTRY • 1953 • Algar James • DOC • USA
BEAR ESCAPE, A • 1912 • Sennett Mack • USA
BEAR ESCAPE, A • 1913 • *Gebhardt George* • USA
BEAR ESCAPE, A • 1914 • *Sterling* • USA
BEAR EYE'S CURSE, THE see **OCHI DE URS** • 1983
BEAR FACT, A • 1917 • Richmond J. A. • SHT • USA
BEAR FACTS • 1938 • Douglas Gordon • SHT • USA
'BEAR' FACTS, THE • 1914 • Johnson Tefft • USA
BEAR FEAT • 1949 • Jones Charles M. • ANS • USA
BEAR FOR PUNISHMENT, A • 1951 • Jones Charles M. • ANS • USA
BEAR HUG • 1963 • Hanna William, Barbera Joseph • ANS • USA
BEAR HUNT, THE see **BARE HUNT; OR MY GUN IS JAMMED** • 1963
BEAR HUNT IN THE ROCKIES • 1910 • *Dickens Frank* • USA
BEAR HUNT ROMANCE • 1911 • *Pathe* • USA
BEAR HUNTER, THE • 1913 • *Gebhardt George* • USA
BEAR ISLAND • 1979 • Sharp Don • UKN, CND
BEAR KNEES • 1928 • Sandrich Mark • SHT • USA
BEAR KNUCKLES • 1963 • Hanna William, Barbera Joseph • ANS • USA
BEAR OF A STORY, A • 1916 • Mix Tom • SHT • USA
BEAR RAID WARDEN • 1944 • Gordon George • ANS • USA
BEAR SCARE, THE • 1911 • *Urban Trading Co* • UKN
BEAR SHOOTERS • 1930 • McGowan Robert • SHT • USA
BEAR SKINNED BEAUTIES • 1920 • Windermere Fred • SHT • USA
BEAR TAKEN IN BY THE FOX, THE • 1957 • Sibianu Gheorghe • ANM • RMN
BEAR THAT COULDN'T SLEEP, THE • 1939 • Ising Rudolf • ANS • USA
BEAR THAT WASN'T, THE • 1967 • Jones Charles M. • ANS • USA
BEAR TRAP, THE • 1912 • *Pathe* • USA
BEAR TRAP, THE see **EXCUSE MY DUST** • 1920
BEAR UP • 1963 • Hanna William, Barbera Joseph • ANS • USA
BEAR YE ONE ANOTHER'S BURDENS • 1910 • Salter Harry • USA
BEAR YE ONE ANOTHER'S BURDENS see **EINER TRAGE DES ANDEREN LAST** • 1987
BEARCAT, THE • 1922 • Sedgwick Edward • USA
BEARD OF STRENGTH see **HIGE NO CHIKARA** • 1931
BEARDED BANDIT, THE • 1910 • *Anderson Broncho Billy* • USA
BEARDED FISHERMAN, THE • 1917 • *American* • USA
BEARDED GENERAL see **CHANGGUN UI SUYUM** • 1968
BEARDED LADY, THE see **DONNA SCIMMIA, LA** • 1964
BEARDED YOUTH • 1911 • Lehrman Henry, Sennett Mack (Spv) • USA
BEARDLESS WARRIORS, THE see **YOUNG WARRIORS, THE** • 1967
BEARER OF BURDENS, THE • 1913 • *Baggot King* • USA
BEARHEART OF THE GREAT NORTHWEST • 1964 • Brooks Rand • USA • LEGEND OF THE NORTHWEST ○ BEARTOOTH
BEARLY ABLE • 1962 • Hanna William, Barbera Joseph • ANS • USA
BEARLY ASLEEP • 1955 • Hannah Jack • ANS • USA
BEARN • 1983 • Chavarri Jaime • SPN
BEARS AND BAD MEN • 1918 • Semon Larry • USA
BEARS AND BULLETS • 1916 • *Vitagraph* • SHT • USA
BEARS AND I, THE • 1974 • McEveety Bernard • USA
BEARS AND THE BEES • 1961 • Hannah Jack • ANS • USA
BEARS AND THE BEES, THE • 1932 • Jackson Wilfred • ANS • USA
BEAR'S TALE, THE • 1940 • Avery Tex • ANS • USA
BEARS VERSUS YUDENICH, THE see **MISHKI PROTIV YUDENICHA** • 1925
BEAR'S WEDDING, THE see **LOKIS** • 1926
BEARSKIN, THE • 1989 • Guedes Eduardo, Guedes Ann • UKN • BEARSKIN AN URBAN FAIRYTALE
BEARSKIN AN URBAN FAIRYTALE see **BEARSKIN, THE** • 1989
BEARTOOTH see **BEARHEART OF THE GREAT NORTHWEST** • 1964
BEAST, THE • 1914 • Buel Kenean • USA
BEAST, THE • 1915 • Hertz Aleksander • PLN
BEAST, THE • 1915 • Jones Edgar • USA
BEAST, THE • 1916 • Stanton Richard • USA
BEAST, THE • 1988 • Reynolds Kevin • USA • BEAST OF WAR, THE
BEAST, THE see **WOLF MAN, THE** • 1924
BEAST, THE see **EQUINOX** • 1970
BEAST, THE see **BESTIA, LA** • 1978
BEAST, THE see **BESTIJE** • 1978
BEAST, THE see **SHAN KOU** • 1981
BEAST, THE see **EINS OG SKEPNAN DEYR** • 1986
BEAST, THE (UKN) see **BETE, LA** • 1975
BEAST ALLEY (USA) see **KEMONOMICHI** • 1965
BEAST AND THE BODY see **BEAUTY AND THE BODY** • 1963
BEAST AT BAY, A • 1912 • Griffith D. W. • USA
BEAST CALLED MAN, THE see **KOKOKARA HAJIMARU** • 1965

BEAST FROM 20,000 FATHOMS, THE • 1953 • Lourie Eugene • USA
BEAST FROM HAUNTED CAVE, THE • 1959 • Hellman Monte • USA
BEAST IN HEAT, THE see **BETE, LA** • 1975
BEAST IN THE CELLAR, THE • 1970 • Kelly James • UKN • ARE YOU DYING, YOUNG MAN?
BEAST KILLS IN COLD BLOOD, THE see **BESTIA UCCIDE A SANGUE FREDDO, LA** • 1971
BEAST MUST DIE, THE • 1974 • Annett Paul • UKN
BEAST MUST DIE, THE see **BESTIA DEBE MORIR, LA** • 1952
BEAST OF BABYLON AGAINST THE SON OF HERCULES, THE (USA) see **EROE DI BABILONIA, L'** • 1963
BEAST OF BLOOD • 1970 • Romero Eddie • USA, PHL • BLOOD DEVILS (UKN) ○ BEAST OF THE DEAD ○ RETURN TO THE HORRORS OF BLOOD ISLAND
BEAST OF BORNEO • 1935 • Garson Harry • USA
BEAST OF BUDAPEST, THE • 1958 • Jones Harmon • USA
BEAST OF HOLLOW MOUNTAIN, THE • 1956 • Rodriguez Ismael, Nassour Edward • USA, MXC • MONSTRUO DE LA MONTANA HUECA, EL (MXC) ○ BESTIA DE LA MONTANA, LA
BEAST OF MOROCCO see **HAND OF NIGHT, THE** • 1966
BEAST OF PARADISE ISLE see **PORT SINISTER** • 1953
BEAST OF SOCIETY, A • 1916 • Vale Travers • SHT • USA
BEAST OF THE CITY, THE • 1932 • Brabin Charles J. • USA • CITY SENTINEL, THE
BEAST OF THE DEAD see **BEAST OF BLOOD** • 1970
BEAST OF THE HIMALAYAS (UKN) see **DAEMON DER BERGE, DER** • 1934
BEAST OF THE YELLOW NIGHT • 1970 • Romero Eddie • USA, PHL
BEAST OF WAR, THE see **BEAST, THE** • 1988
BEAST OF YUCCA FLATS, THE • 1961 • Francis Coleman • USA
BEAST SHALL DIE, THE see **YAJU SHISUBESHI** • 1959
BEAST THAT KILLED WOMEN, THE • 1965 • Mahon Barry • USA • BEAST THAT MOLESTED WOMEN, THE ○ BEAST THAT RUINED WOMEN, THE
BEAST THAT MOLESTED WOMEN, THE see **BEAST THAT KILLED WOMEN, THE** • 1965
BEAST THAT RUINED WOMEN, THE see **BEAST THAT KILLED WOMEN, THE** • 1965
BEAST WITH A MILLION EYES, THE • 1956 • Kramarsky David • USA
BEAST WITH FIVE FINGERS, THE • 1946 • Florey Robert • USA
BEAST WITHIN, THE • 1915 • *Reliance* • USA
BEAST WITHIN, THE • 1982 • Mora Philippe • USA
BEASTLY TREATMENT • 1980 • Foulk Bill • UKN
BEASTLY VACATION, A see **VACANZA BESTIALE, UNA** • 1980
BEASTMASTER, THE • 1980 • Coscarelli Don • USA
BEASTS • 1983 • Hawks Don • USA
BEASTS, THE see **BESTIJE** • 1978
BEASTS ARE IN THE STREETS, THE • 1977 • Hunt Peter • TVM • USA
BEASTS IN THE JUNGLE • 1920 • Darling Roy • DOC • IND
BEASTS OF BERLIN see **GOOSE STEP** • 1939
BEASTS OF MARSEILLES, THE (USA) see **SEVEN THUNDERS** • 1957
BEASTS OF PARADISE • 1923 • Craft William James • SRL • USA
BEASTS OF PREY see **DRAVCI** • 1948
BEASTS OF PREY see **DRAPIEZCY** • 1990
BEASTS-OF-PREY BUILDING see **PAVILON SELIEM** • 1982
BEASTS OF TERROR, THE see **BESTIAS DE TERROR, LAS** • 1972
BEASTS OF THE JUNGLE • 1913 • Warren Edward • USA
BEAST'S PASSAGE see **KEDAMONO NO TORU MICHI** • 1959
BEAT • MacLaine Christopher • SHT • USA
BEAT • 1975 • Blanchard Andre • CND
BEAT 13 see **TRINACTY REVIR** • 1945
BEAT, THE • 1987 • Mones Paul • USA • CONJUROR
BEAT AT HIS OWN GAME • 1912 • *Lewis Grace* • USA
BEAT GENERATION, THE • 1959 • Haas Charles • USA • THIS REBEL AGE
BEAT GIRL • 1959 • Greville Edmond T. • UKN • WILD FOR KICKS (USA)
BEAT IT • 1918 • Roach Hal • SHT • USA
BEAT IT • 1966 • Langestraat Bob • SHT • NTH
BEAT IT see **FAR OCH FLYG** • 1955
BEAT ME DADDY, EIGHT TO THE BAR • 1940 • Ceballos Larry • SHT • USA
BEAT OF THE YEAR, THE • 1914 • *Pallette Eugene* • USA
BEAT STREET • 1984 • Lathan Stan • USA
BEAT THE BAND • 1947 • Auer John H. • USA
BEAT THE DEVIL • 1953 • Huston John • USA, ITL, UKN • TESORO DELL'AFRICA, IL (ITL)
BEAT THE DRUM see **BEI BARABAN** • 1962
BEATA • 1965 • Sokolowska Anna • HNG
BEATE • 1948 • Boese Carl • FRG
BEATEN • 1924 • Moody H. G. • USA
BEATEN AT THE BATH • 1916 • *Gilroy Barbara* • SHT • USA
BEATEN PATH, THE • 1913 • Lund O. A. C. • USA
BEATER, THE see **NAGANIACZ** • 1963
BEATES FLITTERWOCHEN • 1940 • May Paul • FRG
BEATI I RICCHI • 1972 • Samperi Salvatore • ITL
BEATI PAOLI, I see **CAVALIERI DALLA MASCHERA NERA, I** • 1948
BEATIFICATION DE MERE D'YOUVILLE • 1960 • Proulx Maurice • DCS • CND
BEATING BACK • 1914 • Fleming Carroll • USA
BEATING CHEATERS • 1920 • Parrott Charles • USA
BEATING FATHER TO IT • 1915 • De Gray Sidney • USA
BEATING HE NEEDED, THE • 1912 • Sennett Mack • USA
BEATING HEARTS AND CARPETS • 1915 • Frazee Edwin • USA
BEATING HIM TO IT • 1918 • *Jaxon* • USA
BEATING MOTHER TO IT • 1913 • *Lubin* • USA
BEATING THE BOOK • 1926 • West Walter • UKN
BEATING THE BURGLAR • 1914 • *Lubin* • USA
BEATING THE GAME • 1921 • Schertzinger Victor • USA
BEATING THE LIMITED • 1918 • *Hart Neal* • SHT • USA
BEATING THE ODDS • 1919 • Scardon Paul • USA
BEATING THEIR BOARD BILL • 1914 • *Ab* • USA
BEATLEMANIA • 1981 • Manduke Joe • USA • BEATLEMANIA, THE MOVIE
BEATLEMANIA, THE MOVIE see **BEATLEMANIA** • 1981
BEATLES, THE • 1966 • Dunning George • ASS • UKN
BEATLES: A HARD DAY'S NIGHT see **HARD DAY'S NIGHT, A** • 1964
BEATLES ELECTRONIQUES • *Yalkut Jud/ Paik Nam June (P)* • SHT
BEATLES: YELLOW SUBMARINE see **YELLOW SUBMARINE** • 1968
BEATNIK ET LE MINET, LE • 1967 • Leenhardt Roger • DCS • FRN
BEATNIKS, THE • 1958 • Frees Paul • USA
BEATO FRA LE DONNE (ITL) see **HOMME-ORCHESTRE, L'** • 1969
BEATRICE • 1920 • Brenon Herbert
BEATRICE • 1959 • Delouche Dominique • SHT • FRN
BEATRICE CENCI • 1909 • Caserini Mario • ITL
BEATRICE CENCI • 1910 • Falena Ugo • ITL
BEATRICE CENCI • 1926 • Negroni Baldassare • ITL • TRAGIC HOUR, THE
BEATRICE CENCI • 1941 • Brignone Guido • ITL
BEATRICE CENCI • 1956 • Freda Riccardo • ITL • MALEDETTI, I
BEATRICE CENCI • 1969 • Fulci Lucio • ITL
BEATRICE DEVANT LE DESIR • 1943 • de Marguenat Jean • FRN
BEATRICE ET CAROLINE • Lewis James H. • FRN
BEATRICE FAIRFAX • 1916 • Wharton Theodore, Wharton Leopold, Golden Joseph A. • SRL • USA
BEATRICE (USA) see **PASSION BEATRICE, LA** • 1988
BEATRIX • 1963 • Degelin Emile • BLG
BEATRIX DE BRUID • 1966 • Buis Piet • NTH
BEATRIZ • 1976 • Suarez Gonzalo • SPN
BEATS: AN EXISTENTIAL COMEDY, THE • 1976 • Long Philomene • USA
BEAU AND ARROWS • 1932 • Lantz Walter, Nolan William • ANS • USA
BEAU AND HOBO • 1914 • *Joker* • USA
BEAU BANDIT • 1930 • Hillyer Lambert • USA
BEAU BASHFUL • 1934 • Horne James W. • SHT • USA
BEAU BEST • 1933 • Lantz Walter, Nolan William • ANS • USA
BEAU BOSKO • 1933 • Freleng Friz • ANS • USA
BEAU BROADWAY • 1928 • St. Clair Malcolm • USA
BEAU BROCADE • 1916 • Bentley Thomas • UKN
BEAU BRUMMEL • 1913 • Young James • USA
BEAU BRUMMEL see **BEAU BRUMMELL** • 1924
BEAU BRUMMELL • 1924 • Beaumont Harry • USA • BEAU BRUMMEL
BEAU BRUMMELL • 1954 • Bernhardt Curtis • UKN, USA
BEAU CHUMPS (UKN) see **BEAU HUNKS** • 1931
BEAU CRUMMEL AND HIS BRIDE • 1913 • Williams C. Jay • USA
BEAU FIXE • 1953 • Loew Jacques • SHT • FRN
BEAU GESTE • 1926 • Brenon Herbert • USA
BEAU GESTE • 1939 • Wellman William A. • USA
BEAU GESTE • 1966 • Heyes Douglas • USA
BEAU HUNKS • 1931 • Horne James W. • SHT • USA • BEAU CHUMPS (UKN)
BEAU IDEAL • 1931 • Brenon Herbert • USA
BEAU JAMES • 1957 • Shavelson Melville • USA
BEAU MARIAGE, UN • 1981 • Rohmer Eric • FRN • GOOD MARRIAGE, A (USA) ○ PERFECT MARRIAGE, THE
BEAU MASQUE • 1972 • Paul Bernard • FRN, ITL
BEAU MEC, LE • 1978 • Potts Wallace • FRN
BEAU MILITAIRE, LE • 1968 • Lambert Pierre • SHT • FRN
BEAU MONSTRE, UN (FRN) see **BEL MOSTRO, IL** • 1971
BEAU NOT WANTED • 1911 • *Powers* • USA
BEAU-PERE • 1981 • Blier Bertrand • FRN • STEPFATHER
BEAU PLAISIR, LE • 1968 • Gosselin Bernard, Brault Michel, Perrault Pierre • DCS • CND
BEAU POMPIER • 1914 • Burguet Charles • FRN
BEAU REVEL • 1921 • Wray John Griffith • USA
BEAU SABREUR • 1928 • Waters John • USA
BEAU SAVOIR, LE • 1974 • Dansereau Fernand, Rossignol Yolande • SHT • CND
BEAU SERGE, LE • 1958 • Chabrol Claude • FRN • BITTER REUNION (USA) ○ HANSOME SERGE
BEAU TIES • 1945 • Kneitel Seymour • ANS • USA
BEAU VOYAGE, LE • 1946 • Cuny Louis • FRN
BEAUBOURG • 1977 • Rossellini Roberto • DOC • FRN
BEAUCOUP TROP POUR UN SEUL HOMME (FRN) see **IMMORALE, L'** • 1967
BEAUJOLAIS NOUVEAU EST ARRIVE, LE • 1977 • Voulfow Jean-Luc • FRN
BEAUS WILL BE BEAUS • 1955 • Sparber I. • ANS • USA
BEAUT FROM BUTTE, THE • 1913 • *Lubin* • USA
BEAUTE DE L'EFFORT, LA • 1953 • de Gastyne Marco • SHT • FRN
BEAUTE DU DIABLE, LA • 1950 • Clair Rene • FRN, ITL • BELLEZZA DEL DIAVOLO, LA (ITL) ○ BEAUTY AND THE DEVIL (USA) ○ BEAUTY AND THE BEAST (UKN)
BEAUTE MEME, LA • 1964 • Fortier Monique • DOC • CND
BEAUTE QUI MUERT, LA • 1915 • Bernard-Deschamps • FRN
BEAUTIES AND BOMBS • 1917 • Seiter William A. • SHT • USA
BEAUTIES BEWARE • 1929 • Roberts Stephen • SHT • USA
BEAUTIES IN DISTRESS • 1920 • *West Billy* • USA
BEAUTIES OF THE NIGHT (USA) see **BELLES DE NUITS, LES** • 1952
BEAUTIFUL see **RIGHT TO ROMANCE, THE** • 1933
BEAUTIFUL ADVENTURE, A • 1917 • Henderson Dell • USA
BEAUTIFUL ADVENTURE, THE see **SCHONE ABENTEUER, DAS** • 1959
BEAUTIFUL AND DAMNED, THE • 1922 • Seiter William A. • USA
BEAUTIFUL AND THE BLOODY, THE see **BEAUTIFUL, THE BLOODY, AND THE BARE, THE** • 1964
BEAUTIFUL AND WILD ON IBIZA see **SCHONEN WILDEN VON IBIZA, DIE**
BEAUTIFUL BANFF AND LAKE LOUISE • 1935 • Sharpe • SHT • USA
BEAUTIFUL BELINDA • 1915 • Martin E. A. • USA
BEAUTIFUL BISMARCK • 1913 • *Garwood William* • USA
BEAUTIFUL BLONDE FROM BASHFUL BEND, THE • 1949 • Sturges Preston • USA
BEAUTIFUL BORDERS see **CHULAS FRONTERAS** • 1976
BEAUTIFUL BUDAPEST • 1938 • Fitzpatrick James • SHT • USA
BEAUTIFUL BUT BROKE • 1944 • Barton Charles T. • USA
BEAUTIFUL BUT DANGEROUS • 1955 • Leonard Robert Z. • USA
BEAUTIFUL BUT DANGEROUS (UKN) see **SHE COULDN'T SAY NO** • 1954
BEAUTIFUL BUT DANGEROUS (USA) see **DONNA PIU BELLA DEL MONDO, LA** • 1955
BEAUTIFUL BUT DEADLY see **DON IS DEAD, THE** • 1973
BEAUTIFUL BUT DUMB • 1928 • Clifton Elmer • USA
BEAUTIFUL BUT DUMB see **ALMOST HUMAN** • 1927
BEAUTIFUL BUT POOR see **BELLE MA POVERE** • 1957
BEAUTIFUL CARP SPIRIT, THE (USA) see **YU MEI-JEN**
BEAUTIFUL CHEAT, THE • 1926 • Sloman Edward • USA
BEAUTIFUL CHEAT, THE • 1945 • Barton Charles T. • USA • WHAT A WOMAN! (UKN)
BEAUTIFUL CHEAT, THE (UKN) see **WHAT A WOMAN!** • 1943
BEAUTIFUL CITY, THE • 1925 • Webb Kenneth • USA
BEAUTIFUL COFFEE-SELLER, THE see **KAHVECI GUZELI** • 1968
BEAUTIFUL DAYS see **URUWASHIKI SAIGETSU** • 1955
BEAUTIFUL DREAMER see **BELLE CEREBRALE, LA** • 1968
BEAUTIFUL DREAMER, THE see **BELLO DURMIENTE, EL** • 1952
BEAUTIFUL DREAMERS • 1990 • Harrison John Kent • CND
BEAUTIFUL FEELING see **KIMI URUWASHIKU** • 1956
BEAUTIFUL FRAUD, THE (UKN) see **AMERICAN BEAUTY** • 1927
BEAUTIFUL GAMBLER, THE • 1921 • Worthington William • USA
BEAUTIFUL GARDEN OF ROSES, A • 1914 • Cooper Toby? • UKN
BEAUTIFUL GHOST (USA) see **KUEI-WU LI-JEN** • 1969
BEAUTIFUL GIPSY, THE see **CINGENE GUZELI** • 1968
BEAUTIFUL GIRL see **KHUBSURAT BALA** • 1934
BEAUTIFUL GIRL, THE see **KARSAVITSA** • 1969
BEAUTIFUL GIRL FROM ABROAD, A see **OREA EGIOTISA** • 1968
BEAUTIFUL HAWK see **UTSUKUSHIKI TAKA** • 1937
BEAUTIFUL HERO, THE see **KHOSHGELE GHAHRAMAN** • 1967
BEAUTIFUL IMAGE, THE see **BELLE IMAGE, LA** • 1950
BEAUTIFUL IMPOSTOR, THE • 1917 • Henderson Lucius • SHT • USA
BEAUTIFUL JIM • 1914 • Elvey Maurice • UKN • PRICE OF JUSTICE, THE (USA)
BEAUTIFUL KITTY • 1923 • West Walter • UKN
BEAUTIFUL LADY, THE • 1915 • *Ehfe William* • USA
BEAUTIFUL LEADING LADY, THE • 1914 • Williams C. Jay • USA
BEAUTIFUL LENNARD ISLAND • 1977 • Shaffer Beverly • DOC • CND
BEAUTIFUL LEUKANIDA, THE • 1912 • Starevitch Ladislas • USS
BEAUTIFUL LIAR, THE • 1921 • Worsley Wallace • USA
BEAUTIFUL LIE, THE • 1917 • Noble John W. • USA
BEAUTIFUL LIER, THE • 1918 • Wilson Ben • SHT • USA
BEAUTIFUL LOVE • 1915 • *Tincher Fay* • USA
BEAUTIFUL LUCANIDAE (USA) see **PREKRASNAJA LJUKANIDA** • 1912
BEAUTIFUL MARGARET, THE see **TOUT PETIT FAUST, LE** • 1910
BEAUTIFUL MEMORY see **KAUNIS MUISTO** • 1977
BEAUTIFUL MRS. REYNOLDS, THE • 1918 • Ashley Arthur • USA
BEAUTIFUL PEOPLE • 1974 • Uys Jamie • DOC • SAF • ANIMALS ARE PEOPLE TOO (USA) ○ ANIMALS ARE BEAUTIFUL PEOPLE
BEAUTIFUL PEOPLE, THE (UKN) see **YORU NO HENRIN** • 1964
BEAUTIFUL PERSON see **UTSUKUSHII HITO** • 1954
BEAUTIFUL PRINCESS, THE • 1951 • ANM • USS
BEAUTIFUL REBEL, THE see **JANICE MEREDITH** • 1924
BEAUTIFUL SINNER, THE • 1924 • Van Dyke W. S. • USA
BEAUTIFUL SINNER, THE see **UND WANDERN SOLLST DU RUHELOS..** • 1915
BEAUTIFUL SNOW, THE • 1910 • *Vitagraph* • USA
BEAUTIFUL SPY, THE (UKN) see **CHARGE OF THE GAUCHOS, THE** • 1928
BEAUTIFUL STAG BEETLE see **PREKRASNAJA LJUKANIDA** • 1912
BEAUTIFUL START see **URUWASHIKI SHUPPATSU** • 1939
BEAUTIFUL STRANGER, THE • 1954 • Miller David • UKN • TWIST OF FATE (USA) ○ LIFELINE
BEAUTIFUL SUSAN AND THE OLD MEN see **SKONA SUSANNA OCH GUBBARNA** • 1959
BEAUTIFUL SWINDLERS, THE see **PLUS BELLES ESCROQUERIES DU MONDE, LES** • 1963
BEAUTIFUL, THE BLOODY, AND THE BARE, THE • 1964 • Johnsen S. N. • USA • BEAUTIFUL AND THE BLOODY, THE ○ BLOODY, BARE, AND BEAUTIFUL
BEAUTIFUL THOUGHTS • 1915 • Drew Sidney • USA
BEAUTIFUL TROUBLES • 1976 • Dayan Assaf • ISR
BEAUTIFUL UNKNOWN, THE • 1914 • *Moore Matt* • USA
BEAUTIFUL VOICE, THE • 1911 • Sennett Mack • USA
BEAUTIFUL WOMAN AND THE HYDROGEN MAN, THE see **BIYO TO EKITAININGEN** • 1958
BEAUTIFUL WOMEN WALKING AROUND • 1986 • Zilnik Zelimir • YGS
BEAUTIFUL YEARS, THE see **URUWASHIKI SAIGETSU** • 1955
BEAUTIFULLY TRIMMED • 1920 • De Sano Marcel • USA
BEAUTY • 1970 • van der Keuken Johan • NTH
BEAUTY see **REIJIN** • 1946
BEAUTY #2 • 1965 • Warhol Andy • USA • BEAUTY NUMBER TWO
BEAUTY 420 see **HASINA 420** • 1988
BEAUTY, A see **KARSAVITSA** • 1969
BEAUTY AND BOOTY • 1919 • Howe J. A. • SHT • USA
BEAUTY AND BULLETS • 1928 • Taylor Ray • USA
BEAUTY AND DENISE • 1988 • Israel Neal • USA
BEAUTY AND THE BAD MAN • 1925 • Worthington William • USA
BEAUTY AND THE BANDIT, THE • 1946 • Nigh William • USA

BEAUTY AND THE BARGE • 1914 • Shaw Harold • UKN
BEAUTY AND THE BARGE • 1937 • Edwards Henry • UKN
BEAUTY AND THE BEAST • *Radio & Tv Packagers Inc.* • ANM • USA
BEAUTY AND THE BEAST • 1903 • *Lubin* • USA
BEAUTY AND THE BEAST • 1905 • Stow Percy • UKN
BEAUTY AND THE BEAST • 1912 • *Rex* • USA
BEAUTY AND THE BEAST • 1913 • Matthews H. C. • USA
BEAUTY AND THE BEAST • 1916 • Hancock H. E. • USA
BEAUTY AND THE BEAST • 1922 • Newall Guy • UKN
BEAUTY AND THE BEAST • 1934 • Freleng Friz • ANS • USA
BEAUTY AND THE BEAST • 1962 • Cahn Edward L. • USA
BEAUTY AND THE BEAST • 1966 • *Rose Dik (Art Dir.)* • USA
BEAUTY AND THE BEAST • 1974 • Cook Fielder • TVM • USA
BEAUTY AND THE BEAST • 1983 • Vadim Roger • TVM • USA
BEAUTY AND THE BEAST • 1987 • Marner Eugene • USA
BEAUTY AND THE BEAST see **BELLA Y LA BESTIA, LA**
BEAUTY AND THE BEAST see **BIJO TO TOZOKU** • 1952
BEAUTY AND THE BEAST see **SKONHEDEN OG UDYRET** • 1983
BEAUTY AND THE BEAST (UKN) see **BEAUTE DU DIABLE, LA** • 1950
BEAUTY AND THE BEAST (USA) see **BELLE ET LA BETE, LA** • 1899
BEAUTY AND THE BEAST (USA) see **BELLE ET LA BETE, LA** • 1908
BEAUTY AND THE BEAST (USA) see **BELLE ET LA BETE, LA** • 1945
BEAUTY AND THE BEAST (USA) see **PANNA A NETVOR** • 1978
BEAUTY AND THE BLADE • 1948 • Sparling Gordon • DCS • CND
BEAUTY AND THE BOAT • 1913 • Fitzhamon Lewin? • UKN
BEAUTY AND THE BODY • 1963 • Mart Paul • USA • BEAST AND THE BODY
BEAUTY AND THE BOLSHEVIK see **KOMBRIG IVANOV** • 1923
BEAUTY AND THE BOOB • 1919 • *Howell Alice* • SHT • USA
BEAUTY AND THE BOSS • 1932 • Del Ruth Roy • USA • CHURCH MOUSE
BEAUTY AND THE BULLFIGHTER see **SANG ET LUMIERES** • 1954
BEAUTY AND THE BUS • 1933 • Meins Gus • SHT • USA
BEAUTY AND THE DEVIL (USA) see **BEAUTE DU DIABLE, LA** • 1950
BEAUTY AND THE DRAGON, THE see **BIJO TO KAIRYU** • 1955
BEAUTY AND THE ROBOT see **SEX KITTENS GO TO COLLEGE** • 1960
BEAUTY AND THE ROGUE • 1918 • King Henry • USA
BEAUTY AND THE UGLY ONE, THE • 1913 • *Nestor* • USA
BEAUTY BUNGLERS, THE • 1915 • Avery Charles • USA
BEAUTY CAPITAL see **BIBOU NO MIYAKO** • 1957
BEAUTY CARE IN THE JUNGLE see **SKONHETSVARD I DJUNGELN** • 1936
BEAUTY COMPETITION, THE • 1908 • Fitzhamon Lewin • UKN
BEAUTY CONTEST see **BEAUTY PRIZE, THE** • 1924
BEAUTY DOCTOR, THE • 1917 • Steppling John • SHT • USA
BEAUTY DOCTOR, THE • 1936 • Beaumont L. C. • USA
BEAUTY ENVIRONMENT OF THE YEAR 2065 • Vehr Bill • USA
BEAUTY FOR SALE • 1933 • Boleslawski Richard • USA • BEAUTY! (UKN)
BEAUTY FOR THE ASKING • 1939 • Tryon Glenn • USA
BEAUTY FROM NIVERNAISE, THE see **BELLE NIVERNAISE, LA** • 1923
BEAUTY HUNTERS, THE • 1916 • Daly William Robert • SHT • USA
BEAUTY IN CHAINS • 1918 • Wilson Elsie Jane • USA
BEAUTY IN DISTRESS • 1915 • *Vokes Harry* • USA
BEAUTY IN THE SEASHELL • 1913 • *Thanhouser* • USA
BEAUTY IS WITH US • 1960 • Stiopul Savel • RMN
BEAUTY JUNGLE, THE • 1964 • Guest Val • UKN • CONTEST GIRL (USA)
BEAUTY KNOWS NO PAIN • 1972 • Erwitt Elliott • DCS • USA
BEAUTY MARKET, THE • 1920 • Campbell Colin • USA
BEAUTY NUMBER TWO see **BEAUTY #2** • 1965
BEAUTY OF COUNTRY LIFE, THE see **LEPO JE ZIVETI NA DEZELI** • 1974
BEAUTY OF LODI, THE see **BELLA DI LODI, LA** • 1963
BEAUTY OF THE BARBARIANS see **AMAZZONI DONNE D'AMORE E DI GUERRA** • 1973
BEAUTY OF THE PUSTA see **PUSZTAI SZEL** • 1938
BEAUTY OF THE SLEEPING FOREST, THE see **BELLE AU BOIS DORMANT, LA** • 1935
BEAUTY OF THE WORLD see **ALAM ARA** • 1931
BEAUTY ON BROADWAY • 1933 • Brice Monte • SHT • USA
BEAUTY ON PARADE • 1950 • Landers Lew • USA
BEAUTY ON THE BEACH • 1950 • Rasinski Connie • ANS • USA
BEAUTY PARADE, THE • 1930 • Newfield Sam • SHT • USA
BEAUTY PARLOR • 1932 • Thorpe Richard • USA
BEAUTY PARLOR GRADUATE, A • 1913 • *Thanhouser* • USA
BEAUTY PARLOR OF STONE GULCH, THE • 1912 • *Roland Ruth* • USA
BEAUTY PRIZE, THE • 1924 • Ingraham Lloyd • USA • BEAUTY CONTEST
BEAUTY PROOF • 1919 • Scardon Paul • USA
BEAUTY QUEEN see **LADY GODIVA RIDES AGAIN** • 1951
BEAUTY SECRET, THE • 1955 • Ordynsky Vassily • USS
BEAUTY SHOP, THE • 1922 • Dillon Eddie • USA
BEAUTY SHOP, THE • 1950 • Donnelly Eddie • ANS • USA
BEAUTY SHOPPE • 1936 • Lantz Walter • ANS • USA
BEAUTY SHOPPE • 1938 • Schwarzwald Milton • SHT • USA
BEAUTY SHOPPERS • 1927 • Gasnier Louis J. • USA
BEAUTY TAKES A TRAMP • 1912 • *Nestor* • USA
BEAUTY TREATMENT • 1960 • *Halas John (P)* • ANS • UKN
BEAUTY! (UKN) see **BEAUTY FOR SALE** • 1933
BEAUTY UNADORNED • 1913 • Lytton L. Rogers, Young James • USA
BEAUTY'S DAUGHTER see **NAVY WIFE** • 1935
BEAUTY'S SORROWS, THE see **BIJIN AISHU** • 1931
BEAUTY'S TORTURE, A see **BIJO GOMON** • 1931
BEAUTY'S WORTH • 1922 • Vignola Robert G. • USA
BEAUX AND ERRORS • 1938 • Roberts Charles E. • SHT • USA
BEAUX-ARTS DE JOCKO, LES • 1909 • Cohl Emile • ANS • FRN • FINE ARTS OF JOCKO, THE ○ AUTOMATIC MONKEY, THE ○ JACKO THE ARTIST
BEAUX-ARTS MYSTERIEUX, LES • 1910 • Cohl Emile • ANS • FRN • MYSTERIOUS FINE ARTS, THE
BEAUX BECS DU QUEBEC • 1978 • Menard Robert • MTV • CND
BEAUX JOURS, LES • 1935 • Allegret Marc • FRN
BEAUX JOURS D'ARANJUEZ, LES see **ADIEU LES BEAUX JOURS** • 1933
BEAUX JOURS DU ROI MURAT, LES • 1946 • Pathe Theophile • FRN, ITL • ECO DELLA GLORIA, L' (ITL)
BEAUX SOUVENIRS, LES • 1982 • Mankiewicz Francis • CND • OLD MEMORIES, THE
BEAVER BOYS, THE • 1969 • USA
BEAVER COAT, THE see **BIBERPELZ, DER** • 1928
BEAVER COAT, THE see **BIBERPELZ, DER** • 1937
BEAVER DAM • 1956 • Crawley Budge • DOC • CND
BEAVER TROUBLE • 1951 • Rasinski Connie • ANS • USA
BEAVER VALLEY • 1950 • Algar James • DOC • USA
BEAVER'S TRACE see **BIBERSPUR**
BEAZLEYHOPPERS, THE • 1914 • *Miller'S 101 Ranch* • USA
BEBE • 1910-13 • Feuillade Louis • SER • FRN
BEBE A LA BEGUIN • 1911 • Feuillade Louis • FRN
BEBE A LA FERME • 1911 • Feuillade Louis • FRN
BEBE A LA PESTE • 1912 • Feuillade Louis • FRN
BEBE A LU LA FABLE • 1911 • Feuillade Louis • FRN
BEBE ADOPTE UN PETIT FRERE • 1912 • Feuillade Louis • FRN
BEBE AGENT D'ASSURANCES • 1911 • Feuillade Louis • FRN
BEBE APACHE • 1910 • Feuillade Louis • FRN
BEBE, BOUT DE ZAN ET LE VOLEUR • 1912 • Feuillade Louis • FRN
BEBE CANDIDAT AU MARIAGE • 1911 • Feuillade Louis • FRN
BEBE CHEMINEAU • 1911 • Feuillade Louis • FRN
BEBE CHEZ LE PHARMACIEN • 1912 • Feuillade Louis • FRN
BEBE COLLE LES TIMBRES • 1912 • Feuillade Louis • FRN
BEBE CORRIGE SON FRERE • 1911 • Feuillade Louis • FRN
BEBE COURT APRES SA MONTRE • 1911 • Feuillade Louis • FRN
BEBE DE L'ESCADRON, LE • 1935 • Sti Rene • FRN • QUAND LA VIE ETAIT BELLE
BEBE DEVIENT FEMINISTE • 1912 • Feuillade Louis • FRN
BEBE EMBARRASSANT, LE • 1905 • Blache Alice • FRN
BEBE EN VACANCES • 1913 • Feuillade Louis • FRN
BEBE EST ANGE GARDIEN • 1912 • Feuillade Louis • FRN
BEBE EST AU SILENCE • 1911 • Feuillade Louis • FRN
BEBE EST MYOPE • 1912 • Feuillade Louis • FRN
BEBE EST NEURASTHENIQUE • 1911 • Feuillade Louis • FRN
BEBE EST PERPLEXE • 1912 • Feuillade Louis • FRN
BEBE EST SOCIALISTE • 1911 • Feuillade Louis • FRN
BEBE EST SOURD • 1911 • Feuillade Louis • FRN
BEBE ET FILLETTES • 1896 • Melies Georges • FRN • BABY AND YOUNG GIRLS
BEBE ET LA DANSEUSE • 1911 • Feuillade Louis • FRN
BEBE ET LA GOUVERNANTE • 1912 • Feuillade Louis • FRN
BEBE ET LA LETTRE ANONYME • 1912 • Feuillade Louis • FRN
BEBE ET LE FINANCIER • 1912 • Feuillade Louis • FRN
BEBE ET LE SATYRE • 1912 • Feuillade Louis • FRN
BEBE ET LE VIEUX MARCHEUR • 1912 • Feuillade Louis • FRN
BEBE ET SA PROPRIETAIRE • 1911 • Feuillade Louis • FRN
BEBE ET SES GRANDS-PARENTS • 1912 • Feuillade Louis • FRN
BEBE ET SON ANE • 1911 • Feuillade Louis • FRN
BEBE FAIT CHANTER SA BONNE • 1911 • Feuillade Louis • FRN
BEBE FAIT DE L'HYPNOTISME • 1911 • Feuillade Louis • FRN
BEBE FAIT DU SPIRITISME • 1912 • Feuillade Louis • FRN
BEBE FAIT SON PROBLEME • 1911 • Feuillade Louis • FRN
BEBE FLIRTE • 1911 • Feuillade Louis • FRN
BEBE FUME • 1910 • Feuillade Louis • FRN
BEBE HERCULE • 1911 • Feuillade Louis • FRN
BEBE JARDINIER • 1912 • Feuillade Louis • FRN
BEBE LA TERREUR • 1911 • Feuillade Louis • FRN
BEBE MARCHAND DES QUATRE-SAISONS • 1911 • Feuillade Louis • FRN
BEBE MARIE SA BONNE • 1912 • Feuillade Louis • FRN
BEBE MARIE SON ONCLE • 1911 • Feuillade Louis • FRN
BEBE MILLIONNAIRE • 1911 • Feuillade Louis • FRN
BEBE MORALISTE • 1911 • Feuillade Louis • FRN
BEBE NEGRE • 1911 • Feuillade Louis • FRN
BEBE PACIFICATEUR • 1912 • Feuillade Louis • FRN
BEBE PECHEUR • 1910 • Feuillade Louis • FRN
BEBE PERSECUTE SA BONNE • 1912 • Feuillade Louis • FRN
BEBE PHILANTHROPE • 1911 • Feuillade Louis • FRN
BEBE PRATIQUE LE JIU-JITSU • 1911 • Feuillade Louis • FRN
BEBE PRESTIDIGITATEUR • 1911 • Feuillade Louis • FRN
BEBE PROTEGE SA SOEUR • 1911 • Feuillade Louis • FRN
BEBE RECALCITRANT • 1913 • Durand Jean • FRN
BEBE ROI • 1911 • Feuillade Louis • FRN
BEBE SE NOIE • 1912 • Feuillade Louis • FRN
BEBE SONAMBULE • 1912 • Feuillade Louis • FRN
BEBE SUR LA CANEBIERE • 1911 • Feuillade Louis • FRN
BEBE TIRE A LA CIBLE • 1912 • Feuillade Louis • FRN
BEBE TOUT NEUF, UN • 1982 • Girard Helene • MTV • CND
BEBEK • 1979 • Yuce Ihsan • TRK • BABY, THE
BEBEL, GAROTA • 1968 • Capovilla Maurice • BRZ • BEBEL, PROPAGANDA GIRL
BEBEL, PROPAGANDA GIRL see **BEBEL, GAROTA** • 1968
BEBERT AND THE TRAIN see **BEBERT ET L'OMNIBUS** • 1963
BEBERT ET L'OMNIBUS • 1963 • Robert Yves • FRN • HOLY TERROR, THE ○ BEBERT AND THE TRAIN
BEBES A GOGO • 1956 • Mesnier Paul • FRN
BEBO'S GIRL (USA) see **RAGAZZA DI BUBE, LA** • 1963
BECANCOUR, QUEBEC • 1974 • Audy Michel • DCS • CND
BECARAC • 1966 • Bourek Zlatko • ANS • YGS • DANCING SONGS
BECASSINE • 1939 • Caron Pierre • FRN
BECASSOTTE • 1920-24 • O'Galop Marius • ASS • FRN
BECAUSE • 1909 • *Warwick Trading Co* • UKN
BECAUSE • 1918 • Morgan Sidney • UKN
BECAUSE • 1929 • Aylott Dave, Symmons E. F. • SHT • UKN
BECAUSE see **LAUNDRY GIRL, THE** • 1919
BECAUSE HE LOVED HER • 1916 • Henderson Dell • SHT • USA
BECAUSE HE'S MY FRIEND • 1978 • Nelson Ralph • TVM • ASL
BECAUSE I AM KING • 1982 • Mackinnon Stuart • UKN
BECAUSE I AM THE EMPEROR see **CAR JE SUIS L'EMPEREUR**
BECAUSE I LOVE see **SUKI NAREBA KOSO** • 1928
BECAUSE I LOVE see **AISUREBAKOSO** • 1955
BECAUSE I LOVE YOU • 1927 • Edwards J. Steven • UKN
BECAUSE I LOVED YOU • Walther-Fein Rudolf • FRG
BECAUSE I'M IN LOVE • 1974 • Dobrolyubov Igor • USS
BECAUSE I'M UGLY see **SAPAGKA'T AKO'Y PANGIT LAMANG** • 1968
BECAUSE OF A FLOWER see **DAHIL SA ISANG BULAKLAK** • 1967
BECAUSE OF A HAT • 1914 • Dillon Eddie • USA
BECAUSE OF A WOMAN see **BECAUSE OF THE WOMAN** • 1917
BECAUSE OF BOBBIE • 1912 • *Tennant Barbara* • USA
BECAUSE OF HER LOVE see **FOR SIN KARLEKS SKULL** • 1914
BECAUSE OF HIM • 1946 • Wallace Richard • USA
BECAUSE OF LOVE see **FOR SIN KARLEKS SKULL** • 1914
BECAUSE OF LOVE see **EVERYTHING IN LIFE** • 1936
BECAUSE OF MOTHER BECAUSE OF WOMAN see **HANAREBA ONNANAREBA** • 1952
BECAUSE OF MY HOT YOUTH see **FOR MIN HETA UNGDOMS SKULL** • 1952
BECAUSE OF THAT WAR • 1988 • Dor-Niv Orna Ben • DOC • ISR
BECAUSE OF THE CATS (UKN) see **NIET VOOR DE POEZEN** • 1972
BECAUSE OF THE WOMAN • 1917 • Conway Jack • USA • BECAUSE OF A WOMAN
BECAUSE OF YOU • 1952 • Pevney Joseph • USA
BECAUSE SHE LOVED HIM • 1914 • *Victor* • USA
BECAUSE THAT ROAD IS TRODDEN • 1969 • King Tim • UKN
BECAUSE THESE ARE EVIL DAYS see **FOR DAGENE ER ONDE** • 1990
BECAUSE THEY ARE IN LOVE • 1972 • Iacob Mihai • RMN
BECAUSE THEY'RE YOUNG • 1960 • Wendkos Paul • USA
BECAUSE YOU'RE MINE • 1952 • Hall Alexander • USA
BECERRADA, LA • 1962 • Forque Jose Maria • SPN
BECKET • 1910 • *Vitagraph* • USA
BECKET • 1923 • Ridgwell George • UKN
BECKET • 1964 • Glenville Peter • UKN
BECKET AFFAIR, THE (USA) see **AFFARE BECKET, L'** • 1966
BECKONING FLAME, THE • 1916 • Edwards Walter? • USA
BECKONING ROADS • 1920 • Hickman Howard • USA
BECKONING TRAIL, THE • 1916 • Conway Jack • USA
BECKWITH'S GUN • 1910 • *Barker Will (P)* • UKN
BECKY • 1927 • McCarthy John P. • USA
BECKY BECKY • 1913 • *Gardner Helen* • USA
BECKY GETS A HUSBAND • 1912 • *Lubin* • USA
BECKY SHARP • 1935 • Mamoulian Rouben • USA
BECKY STRIKES OUT • 1920 • *Supreme Comedies* • USA
BECOMING • 1955 • Davis James* • SHT • USA
BECOMING LAURA • 1982 • Lavut Martin • MTV • CND
BECOMING MIDDLE-CLASS see **DO PANSKEHO STAVU** • 1925
BECSAPOTT UJSAPIRO, A • 1914 • Korda Alexander, Zilahi Gyula • HNG • DUPED JOURNALIST, THE
BECSULET ES DICSOSEG • 1951 • Gertler Viktor • HNG • HONOUR AND GLORY
BED, THE • 1966 • Warhol Andy • USA
BED, THE • 1968 • Broughton James • USA
BED, THE see **CAMA, LA** • 1968
BED, THE see **LIT, LE** • 1981
BED, THE (USA) see **SECRETS D'ALCOVE** • 1954
BED AND BOARD (USA) see **DOMICILE CONJUGALE** • 1970
BED AND BREAKFAST • 1930 • Forde Walter • UKN
BED AND BREAKFAST • 1936 • West Walter • UKN
BED AND BREAKFAST TWO SHILLINGS • 1904 • Collins Alf? • UKN
BED AND HOW TO MAKE IT!, THE • 1966 • Sarno Joe • USA
BED AND SOFA • 1979 • Armatage Kay • CND
BED AND SOFA see **TRETYA MESHCHANSKAYA** • 1927
BED AND THE BEAUTIFUL, THE see **CARGO OF LOVE** • 1968
BED BUG, THE • 1931 • Ptushko Alexander • ANM • USS
BED DANCE • 1967 • Okuwaki Toshio • JPN
BED FOR BROTHER AND SISTER see **SYSKONBADD 1782** • 1965
BED OF A THOUSAND PLEASURES see **FINALMENTE LE MILLE E UNA NOTTE** • 1972
BED OF FIRE see **GLASS CAGE, THE** • 1964
BED OF GRASS (USA) see **AYOUPA** • 1957
BED OF ROSES • 1933 • La Cava Gregory • USA
BED OF ROSES, A • 1922 • Roach Hal • SHT • USA
BED OF VIOLENCE • 1967 • Sarno Joe • USA
BED PARTNERS see **MACHE ALLES** • 1971
BED SITTING ROOM, THE • 1969 • Lester Richard • UKN
BED STORY see **NEMONOGATARI** • 1967
BED WITHOUT BREAKFAST see **NATLOGI BETALT** • 1957
BEDA WA ELHAGAR, EL • 1989 • Khalik Ali Abdel • EGY • SWINDLER, THE
BEDAYA, EL • 1986 • Abu Saif Salah • EGY • EMPIRE OF SATAN, THE ○ BEGINNING, THE
BEDAYA WA NEHAYAT • 1960 • Abu Saif Salah • EGY • BEGINNING AND THE END, THE ○ BIDAYA WA NIHAYA
BEDAZZLED • 1967 • Donen Stanley • UKN
BEDDEGAMA • 1980 • Peries Lester James • SLN • VILLAGE IN THE JUNGLE, THE ○ BADDEGAMA
BEDEAU, LE • 1952 • Garceau Raymond • DCS • CND
BEDELIA • 1930 • Fleischer Dave • ANS • USA
BEDELIA • 1946 • Comfort Lance • UKN
BEDELIA AND HER NEIGHBOR • 1912 • *Reliance* • USA
BEDELIA AND MRS. BUSYBODY • 1912 • *Reliance* • USA
BEDELIA AND THE NEWLYWEDS • 1912 • *Reliance* • USA
BEDELIA AND THE SUFFRAGETTE • 1912 • *Reliance* • USA
BEDELIA AS A MOTHER-IN-LAW • 1912 • *Fearnley Jane* • USA
BEDELIA BECOMES A LADY • 1913 • *Charleson Mary* • USA
BEDELIA HAS A TOOTHACHE • 1912 • *Reliance* • USA
BEDELIA'S "AT HOME" • 1912 • *Reliance* • USA
BEDELIA'S BLUFF • 1916 • *Tincher Fay* • SHT • USA

BEDELIA'S BUSY MORNING • 1912 • *Reliance* • USA
BEDEVILLED • 1955 • Leisen Mitchell • USA
BEDEVILLED RABBIT • 1957 • McKimson Robert • ANS • USA
BEDFELLOWS • 1979 • Pringle Julian • MTV • ASL
BEDFORD • 1976 • Dunkley-Smith John • UKN
BEDFORD INCIDENT, THE • 1965 • Harris James B. • UKN, USA
BEDFORD'S BACK • 1976 • Dunkley-Smith John • UKN
BEDINGUNG: KEIN ANHUNG • 1913 • Rye Stellan • FRG
BEDKNOBS AND BROOMSTICKS • 1971 • Stevenson Robert • USA
BEDLAM • 1946 • Robson Mark • USA
BEDLAM IN PARADISE • 1955 • White Jules • SHT • USA
BEDLAM OF BEARDS • 1934 • Holmes Ben • USA
BEDMANIA see **LIT, LE** • 1974
BEDNATA ULITSA • 1963 • Piskov Hristo • BUL • POOR MAN'S STREET
BEDOUINE A PARIS, UNE see **BADAWWIYYA FI BARIZ** • 1964
BEDOUINE A ROME, UNE see **BADAWIYYA FI RUMA** • 1965
BEDOUIN'S LOVE SONG • 1907 • Gilbert Arthur • UKN
BEDOUIN'S SACRIFICE, THE • 1915 • Beaumont Harry • USA
BEDOUR • 1974 • Galal Nader • EGY
BEDRANA • 1974 • Duru Sureyya • TRK
BEDROCK • 1930 • Blackwell Carlyle • UKN
BEDROOM • 1971 • Gidal Peter • UKN
BEDROOM, THE see **QUARTO, O** • 1969
BEDROOM BLUNDER, A • 1917 • Cline Eddie • SHT • USA • ROOM 23
BEDROOM EYES • 1986 • Fruet William • USA
BEDROOM EYES 2 • 1988 • Vincent Chuck • USA
BEDROOM MAZURKA (UKN) see **MAZURKA PA SENGEKANTEN** • 1970
BEDROOM VENDETTA see **JUMENT VERTE, LA** • 1959
BEDROOM WINDOW, THE • 1924 • De Mille William C. • USA
BEDROOM WINDOW, THE • 1987 • Hanson Curtis • USA
BEDS, BATHS AND BEDLAM • 1917 • Leigh J. L. V. • UKN
BEDSIDE • 1934 • Florey Robert • USA
BEDSIDE DENTIST see **TANDLAEGE PA SENGEKANTEN** • 1971
BEDSIDE HEAD see **REKTOR PA SENGEKANTEN** • 1972
BEDSIDE MANNER see **HER FAVORITE PATIENT** • 1945
BEDSIDE ROMANCE see **ROMANTIK PA SENGEKANTEN** • 1973
BEDSPREAD, THE • 1969 • *Kirk Films International* • USA
BEDSTEMODERS VUGGEVISE see **OPERABRANDEN** • 1912
BEDTIME • 1923 • Fleischer Dave • ANS • USA
BEDTIME • 1968 • Irvin John • SHT • UKN
BEDTIME AT THE ZOO • 1929 • Woods Arthur • DOC • UKN
BEDTIME BEDLAM • 1955 • Smith Paul J. • ANS • USA
BEDTIME FOR BONZO • 1951 • De Cordova Frederick • USA
BEDTIME FOR SNIFFLES • 1940 • Jones Charles M. • ANS • USA
BEDTIME STORIES OF ARCHIE THE ANT see **ARCHIE THE ANT** • 1925
BEDTIME STORY • 1933 • Taurog Norman • USA
BEDTIME STORY • 1938 • Pedelty Donovan • UKN
BEDTIME STORY • 1941 • Hall Alexander • USA
BEDTIME STORY • 1964 • Levy Ralph • USA • KING OF THE MOUNTAIN
BEDTIME WITH ROSIE • 1974 • Rilla Wolf • UKN
BEDTIME WORRIES • 1933 • McGowan Robert • SHT • USA
BEDZIE LEPIEJ • 1937 • Waszynski Michael • PLN
BEE AND THE DOVE, THE see **ALBINA SI PORUMBELUL** • 1951
BEE AND THE ROSE, THE • 1908 • *Pathe* • SHT • FRN
BEE AT THE BEACH • 1950 • Hannah Jack • ANS • USA
BEE BOPPED • 1959 • Hannah Jack • ANS • USA
BEE CALLED MAJA, A see **BIENE MAJA, DIE** • 1977
BEE-DEVILED BRUIN, THE • 1949 • Jones Charles M. • ANS • USA
BEE-EATER, THE • 1986 • Ogilvie George • ASL
BEE GEES, THE • 1968 • *Associated London* • SHT • UKN
BEE-HIVE, THE see **COLMENA, LA** • 1983
BEE MILLENIUM, THE see **TISICROCNA VCELA** • 1983
BEE ON GUARD • 1951 • Hannah Jack • ANS • USA
BEECHWOOD GHOST, THE • 1910 • *Powers* • USA
BEEF • 1963 • Weintraub William • DOC • CND
BEEF AND THE BANANA, THE see **BIFFEN OCH BANANEN** • 1951
BEEF-FOR AND AFTER • 1962 • Hanna William, Barbera Joseph • ANS • USA
BEEHIVE see **KANDOO** • 1974
BEEKEEPER, THE see **MELISSOKOMOS, O** • 1986
BEEKEEPER'S SCRAPBOOK see **SLIKOVNICA PCELARA** • 1958
BEELD VAN EEN KIND • 1989 • Vanderwildt Albert • DOC • NTH
BEELZEBUB'S DAUGHTERS (USA) see **FILLES DU DIABLE, LES** • 1903
BEEN DOWN SO LONG IT LOOKS LIKE UP TO ME • 1971 • Young Jeffrey • USA
BEEP BEEP • 1952 • Jones Charles M. • ANS • USA
BEEP PREPARED • 1961 • Jones Charles M. • ANS • USA
BEER • 1985 • Kelly Patrick • USA • SELLING OF AMERICA, THE
BEER see **PIWO** • 1965
BEER AND PYJAMAS • 1914 • Cooper Toby? • UKN
BEER BARON, THE see **SONG OF THE EAGLE** • 1933
BEER BARREL POLECATS • 1946 • White Jules • SHT • USA
BEER INDUSTRY, THE • 1915 • ASL
BEER MUST GO DOWN • 1916 • Lyons Eddie, Moran Lee • SHT • USA
BEER PARADE, THE • 1933 • *Mintz Charles (P)* • ANS • USA
BEER TWOPENCE A GLASS • 1906 • Stow Percy • UKN
BEES, THE • 1978 • Zacarias Alfredo • USA, MXC
BEES AND BEE SKEPS • 1984 • Shaw-Smith David • DOC • IRL
BEE'S BUZZ, THE • 1929 • Sennett Mack • SHT • USA
BEES IN HIS BONNET • 1918 • Roach Hal • SHT • USA
BEES IN PARADISE • 1944 • Guest Val • UKN
BEEST, HET • 1981 • Collet Paul • BLG • BETE, LA
BEETHOVEN • 1927 • Kowenstein Hans O. • AUS • STUDENT LOVE
BEETHOVEN 3RD SYMPHONY -EROICA (UKN) see **SYMPHONIE NR.3 IN ES-DUR, OPUS 55 "EROICA" VON LUDWIG VON BEETHOVEN** • 1967
BEETHOVEN AND ALL THAT JAZZ • 1964 • Tammer Peter • DOC • ASL
BEETHOVEN CONCERTO • 1937 • Schmidthof V., Gavronsky M.
BEETHOVEN -DAYS FROM A LIFE see **BEETHOVEN -TAGE AUS EINEM LEBEN** • 1976
BEETHOVEN FIDELIO • 1977 • Jourdan Pierre • FRN • FIDELIO
BEETHOVEN PIANO CONCERTO NO.4 (UKN) see **KLAVIERKONZERT NR.4 IN G -DUR LUDWIG VAN BEETHOVEN** • 1967
BEETHOVEN -TAGE AUS EINEM LEBEN • 1976 • Seemann Horst • GDR • BEETHOVEN -DAYS FROM A LIFE
BEETHOVEN (UKN) see **GRAND AMOUR DE BEETHOVEN, UN** • 1936
BEETHOVENS LEBENSROMAN see **MARTHYRER SEINES HERZENS** • 1918
BEETHOVEN'S NEPHEW (USA) see **NEUVEU DE BEETHOVEN, LE** • 1985
BEETLE, THE • 1919 • Butler Alexander • UKN
BEETLE GOES FLAT OUT, A see **KAFER GIBT VOLLGAS, EIN** • 1972
BEETLE IN OVERDRIVE, A see **KAFER AUF EXTRATOUR, EIN** • 1973
BEETLEJUICE • 1988 • Burton Tim • USA
BEEZY BEAR • 1955 • Hannah Jack • ANS • USA
BEFEHL IST BEFEHL • 1936 • Elling Alwin • FRG
BEFEHL ZUR EHE, DER • 1930 • Neufeld Max • AUS
BEFFE, LICENZE E AMORI DEL DECAMERONE SEGRETO • 1973 • Pisani Walter • ITL • LOVE, PASSION AND PLEASURE
BEFORE A JOURNEY see **PRZED PODROZA** • 1960
BEFORE AND AFTER • 1914 • *Simon Louis* • USA
BEFORE AND AFTER • 1979 • Friedman Kim • TVM • USA
BEFORE AND AFTER SEX see **PRIMA E DOPO L'AMORE.. UN GRIDO D'ALLARME** • 1972
BEFORE AND AFTER TAKING • 1918 • Drew Sidney, Drew Sidney Mrs. • SHT • USA
BEFORE BREAKFAST • 1919 • Roach Hal • SHT • USA
BEFORE DAWN • 1933 • Pichel Irving • USA • DEATH WATCH, THE
BEFORE DAWN • 1961 • Melik-Avekyan G. • USS
BEFORE DAWN see **REIMEI IZEN** • 1931
BEFORE DAWN (USA) see **YOAKE MAE** • 1953
BEFORE ELECTION see **VALASZTAS ELOTT** • 1953
BEFORE EVENING see **ANTES DE ANOCHECER** • 1968
BEFORE GOD see **PRIVATE TUTOR** • 1988
BEFORE GOD AND MAN see **ISTEN ES EMBER ELOTT** • 1968
BEFORE HIM ALL ROME TREMBLED see **DAVANTI A LUI TREMAVA TUTTA ROMA** • 1946
BEFORE HINDSIGHT • 1977 • Lewis Jonathan, Taylor-Mead Elizabeth • UKN
BEFORE I DIE see **TARGETS** • 1968
BEFORE I HANG • 1940 • Grinde Nick • USA • WIZARD OF DEATH
BEFORE I WAKE • 1954 • Rogell Albert S. • UKN • SHADOW OF FEAR (USA)
BEFORE IT'S TOO LATE see **POKA .NE. POZDNO** • 1958
BEFORE ME, YESTERDAY • 1971 • O'Kelly Jeffrey • UKN
BEFORE MIDNIGHT • 1925 • Adolfi John G. • USA
BEFORE MIDNIGHT • 1933 • Hillyer Lambert • USA
BEFORE MORNING • 1933 • Hoerl Arthur • USA
BEFORE MY EYES • 1988 • Kaul Mani • DOC • IND
BEFORE OCTOBER see **PERED OKTYABRE** • 1965
BEFORE SPRING • 1958 • Ivens Joris • SHT • CHN • LETTERS FROM CHINA ○ EARLY SPRING
BEFORE STONEWALL • 1985 • Schiller Greta, Rosenberg Robert • DOC • USA
BEFORE THE BAT'S FLIGHT IS DONE see **MIELOTT BEFEJEZI ROPTET A DENEVER** • 1988
BEFORE THE CIRCUS • 1919 • Kellette John William • SHT • USA
BEFORE THE CORPSE OF A LEADER see **ANTE EL CADAVER DE UN LIDER** • 1973
BEFORE THE DAWN • 1909 • *Lubin* • USA
BEFORE THE DAWN see **YOAKE MAE** • 1953
BEFORE THE DAWN see **ARUNATA PERA** • 1981
BEFORE THE ELECTION see **PRZED WYBORAMI** • 1963
BEFORE THE END OF THE BAT'S FLIGHT see **MIELOTT BEFEJEZI ROPTET A DENEVER** • 1988
BEFORE THE FACT see **SUSPICION** • 1941
BEFORE THE GREAT TRIP see **PRZED PODROZA** • 1960
BEFORE THE GUESTS ARRIVE see **FOR GOESTERNE KOMMER** • 1987
BEFORE THE JUDGMENT OF HISTORY see **PERED SUDOM ISTORII** • 1966
BEFORE THE LAST LEAVES FALL • 1913 • Jones Edgar • USA
BEFORE THE LEAVES FALL see **ZANIM OPADNA LISCIE** • 1963
BEFORE THE MAST • 1909 • *Selig* • USA
BEFORE THE MATRICULATION see **PRED MATURITOU** • 1932
BEFORE THE PUBLIC • 1922 • Roach Hal • SHT • USA
BEFORE THE RAID • 1943 • Weiss Jiri • DOC • UKN
BEFORE THE REVOLUTION (USA) see **PRIMA DELLA RIVOLUZIONE** • 1964
BEFORE THE SHOW • 1917 • *Pokes & Jabs* • SHT • USA • PROPERTY MAN, THE
BEFORE THE STORM • 1925 • Mardzhanishvili Kote • USS
BEFORE THE SUMMER see **ANTES, O VERAO** • 1968
BEFORE THE TIME COMES see **TEMPS DE L'AVANT, LE** • 1975
BEFORE THE TOURNAMENT see **PRZED TURNIEJEM** • 1966
BEFORE THE TRUTH see **PRE ISTINE** • 1968
BEFORE THE WAR • 1966 • Babic Vuk • YGS
BEFORE THE WHITE MAN CAME • 1912 • *Bison* • USA
BEFORE THE WHITE MAN CAME • 1912 • Turner Otis • *Reliance* • USA
BEFORE THE WHITE MAN CAME • 1920 • Maple John E. • USA
BEFORE THEY ARE SIX • 1943 • Parker Gudrun • CND
BEFORE THIS NIGHT IS OVER see **KYM SA SKONCI TATO NOC** • 1965
BEFORE TOMORROW • 1968 • Geyra Ellida • ISR • DAYS BEFORE TOMORROW, THE
BEFORE TONIGHT IS OVER see **KYM SA SKONCI TATO NOC** • 1965
BEFORE WE WAKE UP • Corfixen Lizzie • DNM
BEFORE WINTER COMES • 1969 • Thompson J. Lee • UKN
BEFORE YORKTOWN • 1911 • *Cunard Grace* • USA
BEFRAGUNG DER FREIHEITSTATUE see **C'EST LA VIE RROSE -EIN JUNGGESELLENSPIEL** • 1977
BEFREITE HANDE • 1939 • Schweikart Hans • FRG • FREED HANDS (USA)
BEFRISTETER AUFENTHALT • 1987 • Madeja Georg • MTV • AUS
BEG • 1971 • Alov Alexander, Naumov Vladimir • USS • FLIGHT, THE
BEG, BORROW OR STEAL • 1937 • Thiele Wilhelm • USA • MATTER OF PRIDE, A
BEG, BORROW OR STEAL • 1973 • Rich David Lowell • TVM • USA
BEG STEAL OR BORROW • 1980 • Lofven Chris • DOC • ASL
BEG TO REPORT see **POSLUSNE HLASIM** • 1957
BEGAR • 1946 • Adolphson Edvin • SWD • DESIRE
BEGEBENHEIT: DAS GRAB OHNE TOTEN see **FRAU MIT DEN ZEHN MASKEN 1, DIE** • 1921
BEGEBENHEIT: DAS SCHATTEN DES GEHENKTEN see **FRAU MIT DEN ZEHN MASKEN 2, DIE** • 1921
BEGEBENHEIT: TOTE, DIE LEBEN see **FRAU MIT DEN ZEHN MASKEN 3, DIE** • 1922
BEGEGNUNG IM ZWIELICHT see **SPOTKANIA W MROKU** • 1960
BEGEGNUNG IN ROM • 1954 • Kobler Erich • FRG, ITL
BEGEGNUNG IN SALZBURG • 1964 • Friedmann Max • FRG, FRN
BEGEGNUNG MIT WERTHER • 1949 • Stroux Karl H. • FRG • WERTHER UND LOTTE
BEGGAR, THE see **ACCATTONE!** • 1961
BEGGAR AND HIS CHILD, THE • 1916 • *Hamilton Lloyd V.* • USA
BEGGAR AND THE CLOWN, THE • 1913 • *Imp* • USA
BEGGAR AND THE RICKSHAW MAN, THE • 1979 • Umboh Wim • INN
BEGGAR CHILD, THE • 1914 • Taylor William D. • USA
BEGGAR GIRL'S WEDDING, THE • 1915 • Bantock Leedham • UKN
BEGGAR IN PURPLE, A • 1920 • Lewis Edgar • USA
BEGGAR KING, THE • 1916 • Melville Wilbert • SHT • USA
BEGGAR LIFE, THE see **SVET, KDE SE ZEBRA** • 1938
BEGGAR MAID, THE • 1921 • Blache Herbert • SHT • USA
BEGGAR MAIDEN, THE see **ANGE DE NOEL, L'** • 1904
BEGGAR MAN OF PARIS, THE see **SMIL** • 1916
BEGGAR OF CAWNPORE, THE • 1916 • Swickard Charles • USA
BEGGAR ON HORSEBACK • 1925 • Cruze James • USA
BEGGAR PRINCE, THE • 1920 • Worthington William • USA
BEGGAR PRINCE OF INDIA, A • 1914 • Warren Edward • USA
BEGGAR PRINCESS, THE see **GREVINDE HJERTELOS** • 1915
BEGGAR STUDENT, THE • 1931 • Harvel John, Hanbury Victor • UKN
BEGGAR STUDENT, THE see **BETTELSTUDENT, DER** • 1936
BEGGAR STUDENT, THE (USA) see **BETTELSTUDENT, DER** • 1956
BEGGARMAN, THIEF • 1979 • Chaffey Don, Doheny Lawrence • TVM • USA
BEGGARS AND HUMILIATED • 1989 • el Brakry Asma • EGY, FRN
BEGGAR'S DECEIT, THE • 1900 • Hepworth Cecil M. • UKN
BEGGAR'S DREAM, THE (USA) see **REVE DU PAUVRE** • 1898
BEGGAR'S HOLIDAY • 1934 • Newfield Sam • USA
BEGGARS IN ERMINE • 1934 • Rosen Phil • USA
BEGGARS OF LIFE • 1928 • Wellman William A. • USA
BEGGARS OF LOVE see **SECRET HOUR, THE** • 1928
BEGGARS OF TEHRAN, THE see **AVAREHAYE TEHRAN** • 1968
BEGGAR'S OPERA, THE • 1953 • Brook Peter • UKN
BEGGAR'S OPERA, THE see **DREIGROSCHENOPER, DIE** • 1930
BEGGARS' STRIKE, THE see **EDRAB AL SHAHATIN** • 1967
BEGGAR'S TOWN • 1978 • Cheyaroon Permpol • THL
BEGGAR'S TRIO • 1988 • Shomov Vlado • ANM • BUL
BEGGAR'S UPROAR, THE • 1960 • *Halas John (P)* • ANS • UKN
BEGGERSTUDENT, THE • 1932 • Vajda Ladislao • UKN
BEGGING THE RING • 1978 • Gregg Colin • UKN
BEGIERDE • 1920 • Hofer Franz • FRG • ABENTEUER DER KATJA NASTJENKO, DAS
BEGIERDE see **ABWEGE** • 1928
BEGIN THE BEGUINE • 1981 • Garci Jose Luis • SPN
BEGINNER'S LUCK • 1935 • Meins Gus • SHT • USA
BEGINNER'S LUCK • 1983 • Mouris Frank, Mouris Caroline Ahlfors • USA
BEGINNER'S LUCK (UKN) see **TWO DOLLAR BETTOR** • 1951
BEGINNERS THREE, THE see **FIRST TIME, THE** • 1968
BEGINNING • 1964 • Doukov Stoyan • ANM • BUL
BEGINNING, THE • 1973 • *Dullea Keir* • MTV • USA
BEGINNING, THE see **NACHALO** • 1971
BEGINNING, THE see **PRINCIPIO, EL** • 1972
BEGINNING, THE see **BEDAYA, EL** • 1986
BEGINNING AND THE END, THE see **BEDAYA WA NEHAYAT** • 1960
BEGINNING AT THE END • 1915 • *Larkin George* • USA
BEGINNING OF A HOLIDAY, THE see **NACIALOTO NA EDNA VACANZIA** • 1966
BEGINNING OF A STORY, THE see **BEGYNNELSEN PA EN HISTORIE** • 1986
BEGINNING OF ETERNITY see **SIMULANG WALANG HANGGAN** • 1968
BEGINNING OF HISTORY, THE • 1946 • Wallace Graham • UKN
BEGINNING OF LIFE, THE • 1950 • Schneiderov Vladimir • DOC • USS
BEGINNING OF THE END • 1957 • Gordon Bert I. • USA
BEGINNING OF THE GAME OF DIABLO • 1908 • *Pathe* • FRN
BEGINNING OF THE SERPENTINE, THE • 1909 • *Pathe* • FRN
BEGINNING OF WISDOM, THE see **PRINCIPIO DA SABEDORIO, O** • 1975
BEGINNING OR THE END, THE • 1946 • Taurog Norman • USA
BEGINNING OR THE END?, THE see **KONIEC CZY POCZATEK?** • 1956
BEGINNING WAS SIN, THE (USA) see **AM ANFANG WAR ES SUNDE** • 1954

BEGINNINGS see **PREMIERS JOURS** • 1980
BEGINNINGS OF A LEGEND • 1976 • Grigoryev Boris • USS
BEGONE DULL CARE • 1949 • McLaren Norman, Lambart Evelyn • ANS • CND • CAPRICE EN COULEURS
BEGONIA see **SHUKAIDO** • 1949
BEGRABENE ICH, DAS • 1921 • Lasko Leo • FRG
BEGRABNIS, DAS • 1960 • Houwer Rob • FRG
BEGRIJPT U NU WAAROM IK HUIL? • 1970 • van Gasteren Louis A. • NTH • DO YOU GET IT NOW, WHY I'M CRYING? ○ NOW DO YOU GET IT WHY I'M CRYING
BEGSTVO PUANKARE • 1932 • Ptushko Alexander • ANS • USS • FLIGHT OF POINCARE, THE
BEGUILED, THE • 1971 • Siegel Don • USA
BEGUIN DE LA GARNISON, LE • 1932 • Weill Pierre, Vernay Robert • FRN
BEGUINES, THE (UKN) see **REMPART DES BEGUINES, LE** • 1972
BEGUNEC • 1974 • Kavcic Jane • YGS • FUGITIVE, A
BEGUSHCHAYA PO VOLNAM • 1967 • Lyubimov Pavel • USS, BUL • SHIMMERING OVER THE WAVES ○ RUNNING ACROSS THE WAVES ○ HURRYING ON THE WAVES ○ RUNNING THROUGH THE WAVES
BEGYNNELSEN PA EN HISTORIE • 1986 • Robsahm Margrete • NRW • BEGINNING OF A STORY, THE
BEHAVE YOURSELF! • 1951 • Beck George • USA
BEHAVE YOURSELF • 1962 • Winner Michael • UKN
BEHEADING PLACE see **KUBI NO ZA** • 1929
BEHEMOTH, THE SEA MONSTER • 1959 • Hickox Douglas, Lourie Eugene • UKN • GIANT BEHEMOTH, THE (USA)
BEHEST OF THE INCA, THE • 1966 • BUL, FRG, PRU
BEHEXTE NEPTUN, DER • 1925 • Achsel Willy • FRG
BEHIND CITY LIGHTS • 1945 • English John • USA
BEHIND CLOSED DOORS • 1929 • Neill R. William • USA
BEHIND CLOSED DOORS see **LOVE'S CROSS ROADS** • 1916
BEHIND CLOSED DOORS see **A PORTE CHIUSE** • 1961
BEHIND CLOSED DOORS (UKN) see **ONE MYSTERIOUS NIGHT** • 1944
BEHIND CLOSED SHUTTERS (USA) see **PERSIANE CHIUSE** • 1952
BEHIND CONVENT WALLS (UKN) see **INTERNO DI UN CONVENTO** • 1977
BEHIND ENEMY LINES • 1985 • Larry Sheldon • TVM • USA
BEHIND ENEMY LINES • 1988 • Santiago Cirio H. • USA • KILLER INSTINCT
BEHIND ENEMY LINES see **P.O.W. THE ESCAPE** • 1986
BEHIND GLASS • 1981 • van Ieperen Ab • NTH
BEHIND GREEN LIGHTS • 1946 • Brower Otto • USA
BEHIND JURY DOORS • 1933 • Eason B. Reeves • USA
BEHIND LIFE'S STAGE • 1916 • Holubar Allen • SHT • USA
BEHIND LOCKED DOORS • 1948 • Boetticher Budd • USA
BEHIND LOCKED DOORS • 1976 • Romine Charles • SAF
BEHIND LOCKED DOORS see **HINTER VERSCHLOSSENEN TUREN** • 1989
BEHIND MASKS • 1921 • Reicher Frank • USA • JEANNE OF THE MARSHES (UKN)
BEHIND OFFICE DOORS • 1931 • Brown Melville • USA • PRIVATE SECRETARY
BEHIND PRISON BARS see **OUTER GATE, THE** • 1937
BEHIND PRISON GATES • 1939 • Barton Charles T. • USA
BEHIND PRISON WALLS • 1943 • Sekely Steve • USA • YOUTH TAKES A HAND (UKN)
BEHIND RED CURTAINS see **ONE HOUR BEFORE DAWN** • 1920
BEHIND SOUTHERN LINES • 1952 • Carr Thomas • MTV • USA
BEHIND STONE WALLS • 1932 • Strayer Frank • USA
BEHIND THAT CURTAIN • 1929 • Cummings Irving • USA
BEHIND THE AIRLINE • 1950 • Coffey Frank • DOC • ASL
BEHIND THE ALTAR see **GEHEIMNIS DES ABBE X, DAS** • 1927
BEHIND THE BADGE see **KILLING AFFAIR, A** • 1977
BEHIND THE BARS see **PARMAKLILAR ARKASINDA** • 1967
BEHIND THE BARS see **RACS** • 1970
BEHIND THE BLACKTHORN BUSH see **ZA TRNKOVYM KEREM** • 1981
BEHIND THE BRICK WALL see **TEGLAFAL MOGOTT** • 1980
BEHIND THE CONVENT WALLS see **INTERNO DI UN CONVENTO** • 1977
BEHIND THE COUNTER (UKN) see **DARING DAUGHTERS** • 1933
BEHIND THE CRIMINAL • 1937 • Bucquet Harold S. • SHT • USA
BEHIND THE CURTAIN • 1915 • Wilson Frank • UKN • CURTAIN'S SECRET, THE
BEHIND THE CURTAIN • 1916 • Otto Henry • SHT • USA
BEHIND THE CURTAIN • 1924 • Franklin Chester M. • USA
BEHIND THE CURTAIN see **WARRA' EL SETAR** • 1937
BEHIND THE CURTAIN see **DIBELAKANG TABIR** • 1970
BEHIND THE CURTAIN OF DEATH • 1923 • Futurista Ferenc • CZC
BEHIND THE DOOR • 1920 • Willat Irvin V. • USA
BEHIND THE DOOR see **CHI SEI?** • 1974
BEHIND THE DOOR see **OLTRE LA PORTA** • 1983
BEHIND THE DOOR (UKN) see **MAN WITH NINE LIVES, THE** • 1940
BEHIND THE EIGHT BALL • 1942 • Cline Eddie • USA • OFF THE BEATEN TRACK (UKN)
BEHIND THE ENEMY LINES • 1941 • Shneider E. • USS
BEHIND THE EVIDENCE • 1934 • Hillyer Lambert • USA
BEHIND THE FOOTLIGHTS • 1914 • *Briscoe Lottie* • USA
BEHIND THE FOOTLIGHTS • 1916 • *Pokes & Jabs* • USA
BEHIND THE FRONT • 1919 • *Mack Hughie* • SHT • USA
BEHIND THE FRONT • 1926 • Sutherland A. Edward • USA
BEHIND THE GLASS see **TRAS EL CRISTAL** • 1985
BEHIND THE GREAT WALL see **MURAGLIA CINESE, LA** • 1958
BEHIND THE GREEN DOOR • 1972 • Mitchell Jim, Mitchell Artie • USA
BEHIND THE GREEN LIGHTS • 1935 • Cabanne W. Christy • USA
BEHIND THE GUN • 1913 • *Nestor* • USA
BEHIND THE GUNS • 1940 • Tully Montgomery • DCS • UKN
BEHIND THE HEADLINES • 1936 • Cahn Edward L. • SHT • USA
BEHIND THE HEADLINES • 1937 • Rosson Richard • USA • TOMORROW'S HEADLINES
BEHIND THE HEADLINES • 1953 • Rogers Maclean • UKN
BEHIND THE HEADLINES • 1956 • Saunders Charles • UKN
BEHIND THE HIGH WALL • 1956 • Biberman Abner • USA
BEHIND THE IRON CURTAIN see **IRON CURTAIN, THE** • 1948
BEHIND THE LINE • Dickenson Margaret • DOC
BEHIND THE LINES • 1916 • McRae Henry • USA
BEHIND THE MAKE-UP • 1930 • Milton Robert, Arzner Dorothy • USA
BEHIND THE MAP • 1917 • Beaudine William • SHT • USA
BEHIND THE MASK • 1915 • Morgan George • USA
BEHIND THE MASK • 1917 • Blache Alice • USA
BEHIND THE MASK • 1932 • Dillon John Francis • USA
BEHIND THE MASK • 1946 • Karlson Phil • USA
BEHIND THE MASK • 1958 • Hurst Brian Desmond • UKN • PACK, THE
BEHIND THE MASK see **HIS MAJESTY DICK TURPIN** • 1916
BEHIND THE MASK OF ZORRO (USA) see **ZORRO CABALGA OTRA VEZ, EL** • 1965
BEHIND THE MASKS see **FOUR MASKED MEN** • 1934
BEHIND THE MEAT BALL • 1945 • Tashlin Frank • ANS • USA
BEHIND THE MIKE • 1937 • Salkow Sidney • USA
BEHIND THE MOSQUITO NET see **DIBALIK KELAMBU** • 1983
BEHIND THE NEWS • 1940 • Santley Joseph • USA
BEHIND THE NUDIST CURTAIN • 1964 • Wishman Doris • USA • NATURE GIRLS UNLIMITED
BEHIND THE RENT STRIKE • 1973 • Broomfield Nicholas • DOC • UKN
BEHIND THE RISING SUN • 1943 • Dmytryk Edward • USA
BEHIND THE SCENES • 1910 • Haldane Bert? • UKN
BEHIND THE SCENES • 1913 • Noy Wilfred • UKN
BEHIND THE SCENES • 1914 • Kirkwood James • USA
BEHIND THE SCENES see **DANS LES COULISSES** • 1897
BEHIND THE SCENES see **HIGH HAT** • 1927
BEHIND THE SCENES OF AN ADULT MOVIE • 1981 • Sherman Joe • USA • BEHIND THE SCENES OF AN X-RATED MOVIE
BEHIND THE SCENES OF AN X-RATED MOVIE see **BEHIND THE SCENES OF AN ADULT MOVIE** • 1981
BEHIND THE SCENES: OR, ALGY'S MISHAP • 1904 • Collins Alf • UKN
BEHIND THE SCENES: WHERE ALL IS NOT GOLD THAT GLITTERS • 1908 • Griffith D. W. • USA
BEHIND THE SCREEN • 1915 • Christie Al • USA
BEHIND THE SCREEN • 1916 • Chaplin Charles • SHT • USA
BEHIND THE SCREEN see **SHUI LIAN TING ZHENG** • 1983
BEHIND THE SECRET PANEL • 1916 • Ridgwell George • SHT • USA
BEHIND THE SHOP WINDOWS see **ZA VITRINOI UNIVERMAGA** • 1955
BEHIND THE SHUTTERS see **CORRUPCION DE CHRIS MILLER, LA** • 1972
BEHIND THE SHUTTERS see **BAKOM JALOUSIN** • 1983
BEHIND THE SPANISH LINES • 1938 • Dickinson Thorold, Cole Sidney • DCS • UKN
BEHIND THE STOCKADE • 1911 • Ince Thomas H., Tucker George Loane • USA
BEHIND THE STREET MIRROR see **KATUPEILIN TAKANA** • 1948
BEHIND THE TABS • 1938 • Hopwood R. A. • UKN
BEHIND THE TIMES • 1911 • *Imp* • USA
BEHIND THE TIMES • 1913 • *Powers* • USA
BEHIND THE VEIL • 1914 • Weber Lois, Smalley Phillips • USA
BEHIND THE VEIL • 1916 • Henderson Lucius • SHT • USA
BEHIND THE WALL (USA) see **ZA SCIANA** • 1971
BEHIND THESE WALLS see **JERICHO** • 1945
BEHIND THIS MASK see **IN A LONELY PLACE** • 1950
BEHIND TWO GUNS • 1924 • Bradbury Robert North • USA
BEHIND UNIFORM FACADES see **BAG DE ENS FASADER** • 1961
BEHIND YOUR BACK • 1937 • Pedelty Donovan • UKN
BEHIND YOUR WALLS • 1970 • Zwartjes Frans • SHT • NTH
BEHINDERT • 1973 • Dwoskin Stephen, Regnier Carola • FRG, UKN • HINDERED
BEHINDERTE LIEBE see **AMOUR HANDICAPE, L'** • 1979
BEHINDERTE ZUKUNFT • 1971 • Herzog Werner • DOC • FRG • HANDICAPPED FUTURE ○ FRUSTRATED FUTURE
BEHLIVAN • 1985 • Okten Zeki • TRK • WRESTLER, THE
BEHOLD A PALE HORSE • 1964 • Zinnemann Fred • USA
BEHOLD MY WIFE! • 1920 • Melford George • USA • TRANSLATION OF A SAVAGE, THE
BEHOLD MY WIFE • 1935 • Leisen Mitchell • USA
BEHOLD THE MAN • 1921 • Bennet Spencer Gordon • USA
BEHOLD THE MAN see **GOLGOTHA** • 1935
BEHOLD THIS MOTHER see **KONO HAHA O MIYO** • 1930
BEHOLD THIS WOMAN • 1924 • Blackton J. Stuart • USA
BEHOLD THY SON see **KIIROI KARASU** • 1957
BEHOLD WE LIVE (UKN) see **IF I WERE FREE** • 1933
BEHULI • 1989 • Pradhan Shambhu • NPL • BRIDE
BEI AIQING YIWANGDE JIAOLUO • 1981 • Zhang Qi, Li Yalin • CHN • LOVE-FORSAKEN CORNER, A
BEI BARABAN • 1962 • Saltykov Alexei • USS • BEAT THE DRUM ○ DRUMBEATS
BEI DER BLONDEN KATHREIN • 1934 • Seitz Franz • FRG
BEI DER BLONDEN KATHREIN • 1959 • Quest Hans • FRG
BEI DIR WAR ES IMMER SO SCHON • 1954 • Wolff Hans • FRG
BEI PICHLER STIMMT DIE KASSE NICHT • 1961 • Quest Hans • FRG
BEI VOLLMOND MORD (AUS) see **LYCANTHROPUS** • 1962
BEICHTE DER AUSGESTOSSENEN, DIE see **FRAUENBEICHTE 1** • 1921
BEICHTE DER KRANKENSCHWESTER, DIE see **FRAUENBEICHTE 3** • 1921
BEICHTE DER MORDERIN, DIE see **FRAUENBEICHTE 2** • 1921
BEICHTE DES MONCHS, DIE • 1918 • Leffler Robert • FRG
BEICHTE EINER GEFALLEN, DIE • 1921 • Hofer Franz • FRG
BEICHTE EINER TOTEN, DIE • 1920 • *Krauss Werner* • FRG
BEICHTE EINER VERURTEILTEN, DIE • 1915 • Del Zopp Rudolf • FRG
BEICHTGEHEIMNIS • 1956 • Tourjansky Victor • FRG
BEIDEN FRAUEN DES HERZOGS VON PORTA, DIE • 1922 • Seitz Franz • FRG
BEIDEN GATTEN DER FRAU RUTH, DIE • 1919 • Biebrach Rudolf • FRG
BEIDEN RIVALEN, DIE • 1914 • Etievant Henri • FRG
BEIDEN SCHWESTERN, DIE • 1943 • Waschneck Erich • FRG
BEIDEN SEEHUNDE, DIE • 1928 • Neufeld Max • AUS
BEIDEN SEEHUNDE, DIE • 1934 • Sauer Fred • FRG • SEINE HOHEIT DER DIENSTMANN
BEIJING • 1990 • Obayashi Nobuhiko • JPN
BEIJING, NI ZAO • 1990 • Zhang Nuanxin • CHN
BEIJO 23480/72 • 1989 • Rogerio Walter • BRZ • KISS 23480/72
BEIJO DE VIDA, O • 1976 • de Fonseca Teixeira • PRT • REVOLUCAO ESCUTURAL ○ ESCULTERAL REVOLUTION ○ KISS OF LIFE
BEIL VON WANDSBEK, DAS • 1951 • Harnack Falk • GDR • AXE OF WANDSBEK, THE
BEIM JODELN JUCKT DIE LEDERHOSEN • 1974 • Brummer Alois • FRG
BEIM NACHSTEN MANN WIRD ALLES ANDERS • 1989 • FRG • WITH THE NEXT MAN EVERYTHING WILL BE DIFFERENT
BEIM NERVENATZ • 1936 • Valentin Karl • FRG
BEIM RECHTSANWALT • 1936 • Valentin Karl • FRG
BEINE MAJA • 1926 • Junghans Karl • CZC
BEINE VON DOLORES, DIE • 1957 • von Cziffra Geza • FRG
BEING • 1972 • Perris Anthony • CND
BEING, THE • 1983 • Kong Jackie • USA • EASTER SUNDAY
BEING DIFFERENT • 1981 • Rasky Harry • DOC • CND
BEING IN LIFE -BE IN IT • 1979 • Stitt Alexander • SHT • ASL
BEING RESPECTABLE • 1924 • Rosen Phil • USA
BEING THERE • 1979 • Ashby Hal • USA
BEING TWO ISN'T EASY (UKN) see **WATASHI WA NISAI** • 1962
BEIRUT, AL LIQA • 1983 • Alawiya Burhan • LBN • BEIRUT, THE ENCOUNTER ○ BEIRUT, THE MEETING
BEIRUT CONTRACT see **HONEYBABY, HONEYBABY** • 1974
BEIRUT, MADINATI • 1983 • Saab Jocelyne • LBN • BEIRUT, MY CITY
BEIRUT, MY CITY see **BEIRUT, MADINATI** • 1983
BEIRUT, THE ENCOUNTER see **BEIRUT, AL LIQA** • 1983
BEIRUT, THE MEETING see **BEIRUT, AL LIQA** • 1983
BEISBOL, EL • 1977 • Anzola Alfredo J. • DOC • VNZ • BASEBALL
BEISPIELLOSE VERTEIDIGUNG DER FESTUNG DEUTSCHKREUTZ, DIE • 1966 • Herzog Werner • SHT • FRG • UNPRECEDENTED DEFENCE OF THE FORTRESS DEUTSCHKREUTZ, THE
BEISS MICH, LIEBLING • 1970 • Fornbacher Helmut • FRG • BITE ME, DARLING
BEIT AL ASHBAH • 1952 • Wahab Fatin Abdel • EGY • HOUSE OF GHOSTS ○ BAYT AL-'ACHBAH'
BEIT EL TALIBAT • 1967 • Eddin Ahmed Dia • EGY • GIRL STUDENT'S HOME, THE
BEJARANA, LA • 1925 • Ardavin Eusebio F. • SPN
BEJLEREN -EN JYSK ROVERHISTORIE • 1975 • Thomsen Knud Leif • DNM
BEKAR ODASI • 1967 • Inanoglu Turker • TRK • BACHELOR'S ROOM
BEKCI • 1985 • Ozzenturk Ali • TRK • GUARD, THE
BEKE UTJA, A • 1917 • Curtiz Michael • HNG • ROAD TO PEACE, THE
BEKEIDO • 1980 • Vitezy Laszlo • HNG • PEACETIME
BEKENNTNIS DER INA KAHR, DAS • 1954 • Pabst G. W. • FRG • CONFESSIONS OF INA KAHR, THE (USA) ○ AFRAID TO LOVE ○ AFRAID TO LIVE
BEKENNTNISSE see **FUND IM NEUBAU 2, DER** • 1915
BEKENNTNISSE DES HOCHSTAPLERS FELIX KRULL, DIE • 1957 • Hoffmann Kurt • FRG • CONFESSIONS OF FELIX KRULL (USA)
BEKEVAR JUBILEE • 1977 • Kish Albert • DOC • CND
BEKOTOTT SZEMMEL • 1974 • Kovacs Andras • HNG • BLINDFOLD
BEKSTVA • 1968 • Novakovic Rados • YGS • ESCAPES
BEL AGE, LE • 1958 • Kast Pierre • FRN • LOVE IS WHEN YOU MAKE IT ○ GOOD AGE, THE
BEL AMI • 1919 • Genina Augusto • ITL
BEL AMI • 1939 • Forst Willi • FRG • LIEBLING SCHONER FRAUEN, DER
BEL AMI • 1946 • Momplet Antonio • MXC • BUEN MOZO, EL
BEL AMI • 1955 • Daquin Louis • FRN, AUS
BEL AMI • 1975 • Ahlberg Mac • SWD • FOR MEN ONLY
BEL AMI 2000 ODER: WIE VERFUHRT MAN EINEN PLAYBOY? • 1966 • Pfleghar Michael • FRN, AUS, ITL • 100 RAGAZZE PER UN PLAYBOY (ITL) ○ HOW TO SEDUCE A PLAYBOY (USA) ○ CENTO RAGAZZE PER UN PLAYBOY
BEL AMOUR • 1950 • Campaux Francois • FRN
BEL ANTONIO see **BELL'ANTONIO, IL** • 1960
BEL INDIFFERENT, LE • 1957 • Demy Jacques • SHT • FRN
BEL MOSTRO, IL • 1971 • Gobbi Sergio • ITL, FRN • STRANGE LOVE AFFAIR, A (UKN) ○ BEAU MONSTRE, UN (FRN)
BEL ORDURE • 1973 • Marboeuf Jean • FRN
BEL OUVRAGE • 1943 • Cloche Maurice • SHT • FRN
BELA • 1967 • Rostotsky Stanislav • USS
BELA BARTOK • 1955 • Takacs Gabor • DOC • HNG
BELA LUGOSI MEETS A BROOKLYN GORILLA • 1952 • Beaudine William • USA • MONSTER MEETS THE GORILLA, THE (UKN) ○ BOYS FROM BROOKLYN, THE
BELALI BESLER • 1968 • Okcugil Nejat • TRK • TROUBLESOME FIVE, THE
BELALI HAYAT • 1968 • Gorec Ertem • TRK • LIFE OF TROUBLE, A
BELANG PERTENDA • 1971 • Sudarmadji S. • MLY • TREACHERY
BELANGER • 1961 • Regnier Michel, Rivard Fernand • DCS • CND
BELANIN YEDI TURLUSU • 1969 • Ergun Nuri • TRK • SEVEN KINDS OF TROUBLE
BELARMINO • 1964 • Lopes Fernando • PRT
BELARUS FILE, THE see **KOJAK: THE BELARUS FILE** • 1985
BELATED BRIDEGROOM, THE • 1911 • *Lubin* • USA
BELATED FLOWERS (USA) see **CHVETI ZAPOZDALIE** • 1972
BELATED HONEYMOON, THE • 1915 • *Lubin* • USA
BELAYA VORONA • 1941 • Yutkevich Sergei • USS • WHITE RAVEN, THE
BELCANTO ODER DARF EINE NUTTE SCHLUCHZEN? • 1977 • van Ackeren Robert • FRG

BELE TRAVE • 1977 • Hladnik Bostjan • YGS • WHITE GRASS
BELEPOK • 1990 • Stojanovic Nikola • YGS • BELLE EPOQUE
BELFAST ASSASSIN • 1982 • Clark Lawrence Gordon • MTV • UKN • HARRY'S GAME: THE MOVIE ○ HARRY'S GAME
BELGES ET LA MER, LES • 1954 • Storck Henri • DOC • BLG
BELGIAN, THE • 1917 • Olcott Sidney • USA
BELGIAN GIRL'S HONOUR, A • 1915 • *Gordon Olive* • UKN
BELGIAN GRAND PRIX • 1955 • Hughes • DOC • NTH
BELGIQUE MEURTRIE • 1920 • Flon Paul • BLG
BELGIQUE NOUVELLE, LA • 1937 • Storck Henri • DOC • BLG
BELGIQUE PROFONDE, LA • 1980 • Reichenbach Francois • MTV • FRN
BELGISCHE FOLKLORE, DE • 1970 • Storck Henri • DOC • BLG
BELI BIM-CHORNOYE UKHO • 1977 • Rostotsky Stanislav • USS • WHITE BIM THE BLACK EAR ○ WHITE BIM WITH A BLACK EAR
BELI DJAVO (YGS) see **AGI MURAD, IL DIAVOLO BIANCO** • 1959
BELIEFS see **CROYANCES**
BELIEVE IN ME • 1971 • Hagmann Stuart • USA • SPEED IS OF THE ESSENCE
BELIEVE IN ME, PEOPLE • 1965 • Gurin Ilya, Berenshtein V. • USS
BELIEVE IT OR ELSE • 1939 • Avery Tex • ANS • USA
BELIEVE ME, IF ALL THOSE ENDEARING YOUNG CHARMS • 1912 • *Sawyer Laura* • USA
BELIEVE ME, XANTIPPE • 1918 • Crisp Donald • USA
BELIEVED VIOLENT • 1989 • Lautner Georges • FRN
BELIEVER IN DREAMS, A • 1914 • Smiley Joseph • USA
BELIEVERS, THE • 1987 • Schlesinger John • USA
BELINDA • 1972 • Franklin Richard • ASL
BELINDA • 1987 • Gibbons Pamela • ASL • MIDNIGHT DANCER (USA)
BELINDA AND THE EGGS • 1915 • Batley Ethyle? • UKN
BELINDA MAKES A BLOOMER • 1915 • Batley Ernest G.? • UKN
BELINDA, THE SLAVEY • 1913 • *Talmadge Norma* • USA
BELINDA'S BRIDAL BREAKFAST • 1916 • *Gilroy Barbara* • USA
BELINDA'S DREAM • 1913 • Kinder Stuart? • UKN
BELINDA'S ELOPEMENT • 1913 • Aylott Dave? • UKN
BELINSKI • 1953 • Kozintsev Grigori • USS
BELIYE NOCHI • 1960 • Pyriev Ivan • USS • WHITE NIGHTS ○ BELYE NOCHI
BELIZAIRE THE CAJUN see **BELLIZAIRE THE CAJUN** • 1986
BELL, THE • 1967 • Aoshima Yukio • JPN
BELL, THE see **CLOCHE, LA** • 1964
BELL, BARE AND BEAUTIFUL • 1963 • Lewis Herschell G. • USA
BELL, BOOK AND CANDLE • 1958 • Quine Richard • USA
BELL-BOTTOM GEORGE • 1943 • Varnel Marcel • UKN
BELL BOY 13 • 1923 • Seiter William A. • USA
BELL BOY, THE • 1918 • Arbuckle Roscoe • SHT • USA
BELL BOYS, THE • 1914 • *Royal* • USA
BELL DE MONTPARNASSE, LA • 1937 • Cammage Maurice • FRN
BELL FOR ADANO, A • 1945 • King Henry • USA
BELL FOR PHILADELPHIA, A • 1963 • Kuwahara Bob • ANS • USA
BELL FROM HELL (USA) see **CAMPANA DEL INFIERNO, LA** • 1973
BELL HOP, THE • 1915 • *Turpin Ben* • USA
BELL HOP, THE • 1921 • Taurog Norman, Semon Larry • SHT • USA
BELL HOPPY • 1954 • McKimson Robert • ANS • USA
BELL JAR, THE • 1979 • Peerce Larry • USA
BELL OF EMILLE, THE see **EMILLE JONG** • 1961
BELL OF HELL, THE see **CAMPANA DEL INFIERNO, LA** • 1973
BELL OF JUSTICE, THE • 1911 • *Vitagraph* • USA
BELL OF PENANCE, THE • 1912 • Blackwell Carlyle • USA
BELL OF SAYAT see **KOLOKOL SAYATA** • 1967
BELL TOLLS, THE see **CAMPANADA, LA** • 1979
BELLA • 1974 • Kubelka Alexander • USA
BELLA ADDORMENTATA, LA • 1942 • Chiarini Luigi • ITL • SLEEPING BEAUTY (USA)
BELLA ANTONIA PRIMA MONICA E POI DIMONIA • 1972 • Laurenti Mariano • ITL • NAUGHTY NUN (UKN)
BELLA DE CADIZ, LA • 1953 • Ardavin Eusebio F., Bernard Raymond • SPN, FRN • BELLE DE CADIX, LA (FRN)
BELLA DEL ALHAMBRA, LA • 1989 • Barnet Enrique Pineda • CUB, SPN • BELLE OF THE ALHAMBRA, THE
BELLA DES BELLES, LA (FRN) see **DONNA PIU BELLA DEL MONDO, LA** • 1955
BELLA DI GIORNO (ITL) see **BELLE DE JOUR** • 1967
BELLA DI GIORNO MOGLIE DI NOTTE • 1971 • Rossati Nello • ITL • WIFE BY NIGHT (UKN)
BELLA DI LODI, LA • 1963 • Missiroli Mario • ITL • BEAUTY OF LODI, THE
BELLA DI ROMA, LA • 1955 • Comencini Luigi • ITL • ROMAN SIGNORINA
BELLA DONNA • 1915 • Porter Edwin S., Ford Hugh • USA
BELLA DONNA • 1923 • Fitzmaurice George • USA
BELLA DONNA • 1934 • Milton Robert • UKN
BELLA DONNA see **TEMPTATION** • 1946
BELLA E LA BESTIA, LA • 1977 • Russo Luigi • ITL
BELLA FACCIA IL CUOR L'ALLACCIA see **ANIMALI PAZZI** • 1939
BELLA FIORAIA, LA • 1958 • Amadori Luis Cesar • ITL, SPN
BELLA GOVERNANTE DI COLORE, UNA • 1977 • Russo Luigi • ITL
BELLA GRINTA, UNA • 1965 • Montaldo Giuliano • ITL
BELLA LA SALVAJE • 1952 • Medina Raul, Rey Roberto • SPN
BELLA LOLA, LA • 1962 • Balcazar Alfonso • SPN
BELLA MIMI, LA • 1960 • Elorrieta Jose Maria • SPN
BELLA MUGNAIA, LA • 1955 • Camerini Mario • ITL • MILLER'S BEAUTIFUL WIFE, THE (USA) ○ MILLER'S WIFE, THE
BELLA, NON PIANGERE! • 1955 • Carbonari David • ITL
BELLA OTERA, LA (ITL) see **BELLE OTERO, LA** • 1955
BELLA RICCA LIEVE DIFETTO FISICO CERCA ANIMA GEMELLA • 1973 • Cicero Nando • ITL
BELLA Y LA BESTIA, LA • Quiroga Marcelo • BRZ • BEAUTY AND THE BEAST
BELLADONNA see **KANASHIMI NO BELLADONNA** • 1973
BELLAMY THE MAGNIFICENT see **CERTAIN YOUNG MAN, A** • 1926
BELLAMY TRIAL, THE • 1928 • Bell Monta • USA
BELL'ANTONIO, IL • 1960 • Bolognini Mauro • ITL, FRN • BEL ANTONIO ○ HANDSOME ANTONIO
BELLA'S BEAUS • 1912 • Smalley Phillips • USA
BELLAS DE NOCHE • 1974 • *Cinema Calderon* • MXC
BELLA'S ELOPEMENT • 1914 • Costello Maurice, Gaillord Robert • USA
BELLBOY, THE • 1960 • Lewis Jerry • USA
BELLBOY AND THE PLAYGIRLS, THE see **MIT EVA FING DIE SUNDE AN** • 1958
BELLBOY DONALD • 1942 • King Jack • ANS • USA
BELLE • 1973 • Delvaux Andre • BLG, FRN
BELLE AFFAIRE, LA • 1972 • Besnard Jacques • FRN
BELLE AMERICAINE, LA • 1961 • Dhery Robert, Tchernia Pierre • FRN
BELLE AND THE BELLHOP, THE • 1916 • Clements Roy • SHT • USA
BELLE AND THE BILL, THE • 1920 • Davey Horace • SHT • USA
BELLE APPARENCE, LA • 1979 • Benoit Denyse • CND
BELLE AU BOIS DORMANT, LA • Lenoir Claudine • SHT • FRN • SLEEPING BEAUTY
BELLE AU BOIS DORMANT, LA • 1902 • Zecca Ferdinand • FRN • SLEEPING BEAUTY (USA)
BELLE AU BOIS DORMANT, LA • 1908 • Velle Gaston • FRN • SLEEPING BEAUTY (USA)
BELLE AU BOIS DORMANT, LA • 1915 • Bernard-Deschamps • FRN • SLEEPING BEAUTY
BELLE AU BOIS DORMANT, LA • 1935 • Alexeieff Alexandre • ANS • FRN • BEAUTY OF THE SLEEPING FOREST, THE ○ SLEEPING BEAUTY
BELLE AU BOIS DORMANT, LA see **SPYASHCHAYA KRASAVITSA** • 1930
BELLE AUX CHEVEUX D'OR, LA • 1916 • Perret Leonce • FRN
BELLE AVENTURE, LA • 1932 • Le Bon Roger, Schunzel Reinhold • FRN
BELLE AVENTURE, LA • 1942 • Allegret Marc • FRN • TWILIGHT (USA)
BELLE BORDELAISE, LA see **INTRIGANTE, L'** • 1939
BELLE BOYD -A CONFEDERATE SPY • 1913 • Eagle Oscar • USA
BELLE BOYS • 1953 • Patterson Don • ANS • USA
BELLE CAPTIVE, LA • 1983 • Robbe-Grillet Alain • FRN
BELLE CEREBRALE, LA • 1968 • Foldes Peter • ANM • FRN • BEAUTIFUL DREAMER
BELLE COMME LA MORT • 1914 • Volkov Alexander • USS
BELLE DAME SANS MERCI, LA • 1921 • Dulac Germaine • FRN
BELLE D'AMORE • 1971 • De Agostini Fabio • ITL
BELLE DE CADIX, LA (FRN) see **BELLA DE CADIZ, LA** • 1953
BELLE DE JOUR • 1967 • Bunuel Luis • FRN, ITL • BELLA DI GIORNO (ITL)
BELLE DE NUIT • 1933 • Valray Louis • FRN
BELLE DELLA NOTTE, LE (ITL) see **BELLES DE NUITS, LES** • 1952
BELLE DELL'ARIA, LE • 1958 • Costa Mario • ITL, SPN
BELLE EMMERDEUSE, LA see **ON PEUT LE DIRE SANS SE FACHER!** • 1978
BELLE ENSORCELEUSE see **FLAME OF NEW ORLEANS, THE** • 1941
BELLE EPOQUE see **BELEPOK** • 1990
BELLE EQUIPE, LA • 1936 • Duvivier Julien • FRN • THEY WERE FIVE (USA) ○ JOUR DE PAQUES
BELLE ET LA BETE, LA • 1899 • *Pathe* • FRN • BEAUTY AND THE BEAST (USA)
BELLE ET LA BETE, LA • 1908 • *Pathe* • FRN • BEAUTY AND THE BEAST (USA)
BELLE ET LA BETE, LA • 1945 • Clement Rene, Cocteau Jean • FRN • BEAUTY AND THE BEAST (USA)
BELLE ET LE CAVALIER, LA (FRN) see **C'ERA UNA VOLTA** • 1967
BELLE ET LE TZIGANE, LA • 1957 • Dreville Jean, Keleti Marton • FRN, HNG
BELLE ETOILE • 1938 • de Baroncelli Jacques • FRN
BELLE ETOILE, LA see **LUCKY STAR, THE** • 1980
BELLE FAMIGLIE, LE • 1965 • Gregoretti Ugo • ITL, FRN
BELLE FAMILLE • 1978 • Tremblay Robert • CND
BELLE FILLE COMME MOI, UNE • 1972 • Truffaut Francois • FRN • SUCH A GORGEOUS KID LIKE ME (USA) ○ GORGEOUS BIRD LIKE ME, A (UKN)
BELLE GARCE, UNE • 1930 • de Gastyne Marco • FRN
BELLE GARCE, UNE • 1947 • Daroy Jacques • FRN
BELLE HELENE, LA • 1957 • Reiniger Lotte, Koch Carl • ANS • UKN • HELENE LA BELLE
BELLE HUMEUR • 1921-22 • Feuillade Louis • SER • FRN
BELLE IMAGE, LA • 1950 • Heymann Claude • FRN • BEAUTIFUL IMAGE, THE
BELLE JOURNEE, UNE • 1972 • Tacchella Jean-Charles • SHT • FRN
BELLE LE GRAND • 1951 • Dwan Allan • USA
BELLE MA POVERE • 1957 • Risi Dino • ITL • BEAUTIFUL BUT POOR ○ IRRESISTIBLE
BELLE MADAME MOYSE, LA • 1931 • Greville Edmond T. • SHT • FRN
BELLE-MAMAN BAT LES RECORDS • 1908 • Durand Jean • FRN
BELLE MARINIERE, LA • 1932 • Lachman Harry • FRN
BELLE MENTALITE • 1952 • Berthomieu Andre • FRN
BELLE MEUNIERE, LA • 1948 • Pagnol Marcel, de Rieux Max • FRN
BELLE NIVERNAISE, LA • 1923 • Epstein Jean • FRN • BEAUTY FROM NIVERNAISE, THE
BELLE O BRUTTE SI SPOSAN TUTTE.. • 1939 • Bragaglia Carlo Ludovico • ITL • SE SEI BRUTTA NON TI SPOSA
BELLE OF ALASKA • 1922 • Bennett Chester • USA
BELLE OF BAR Z RANCH, THE • 1912 • Ricketts Thomas • USA
BELLE OF BARNEGAT • 1915 • Greene Clay M. • USA
BELLE OF BETTWS-Y-COED, THE • 1912 • Northcote Sidney • UKN • BELLE OF NORTH WALES, THE (USA)
BELLE OF BREWERYVILLE, THE • 1914 • *Lubin* • USA
BELLE OF BROADWAY, THE • 1926 • Hoyt Harry O. • USA • DARLING OF PARIS, THE
BELLE OF CRYSTAL PALACE, THE • 1914 • Youngdeer James • UKN
BELLE OF NEW ORLEANS, THE • 1912 • *Moore Tom* • USA
BELLE OF NEW YORK, THE • 1919 • Steger Julius • USA
BELLE OF NEW YORK, THE • 1951 • Walters Charles • USA
BELLE OF NORTH WALES, THE • 1913 • *Kalem* • USA
BELLE OF NORTH WALES, THE (USA) see **BELLE OF BETTWS-Y-COED, THE** • 1912
BELLE OF OLD MEXICO • 1950 • Springsteen R. G. • USA
BELLE OF SAMOA • 1929 • Silver Marcel • USA
BELLE OF SCHOOL, THE • 1914 • *Marshall Boyd* • USA
BELLE OF SISKIYOU, THE • 1913 • *Clayton Marguerite* • USA
BELLE OF THE ALHAMBRA, THE see **BELLA DEL ALHAMBRA, LA** • 1989
BELLE OF THE BEACH, THE • 1912 • *Roland Ruth* • USA
BELLE OF THE BOWERY see **SUNBONNET SUE** • 1945
BELLE OF THE GAMBLING DEN • 1921 • Parkinson H. B. • UKN
BELLE OF THE NINETIES • 1934 • McCarey Leo • USA • IT AIN'T NO SIN
BELLE OF THE SEASON, THE • 1919 • Drew Sidney • USA
BELLE OF THE YUKON • 1944 • Seiter William A. • USA
BELLE OF YORKTOWN, THE • 1913 • Ford Francis • USA
BELLE OTERO, LA • 1955 • Pottier Richard • FRN, ITL • BELLA OTERA, LA (ITL)
"BELLE" OUVRAGE, LA • 1947 • Palardy Jean • DCS • CND
BELLE OUVRAGE, LA • 1977-80 • Gosselin Bernard, Plamondon Leo • SER • CND
BELLE PEUR, UNE • 1958 • Rouquier Georges • DCS • FRN
BELLE QUE VOILA, LA • 1949 • Le Chanois Jean-Paul • FRN
BELLE REVANCHE, LA • 1938 • Mesnier Paul • FRN
BELLE RUSSE, LA • 1914 • *Russell Evelyn* • USA
BELLE RUSSE, LA • 1919 • Brabin Charles J. • USA
BELLE SOMMERS • 1962 • Silverstein Elliot • USA
BELLE STARR • 1941 • Cummings Irving • USA
BELLE STARR • 1980 • Alonzo John A. • TVM • USA
BELLE STARR see **BELLE STARR STORY, THE** • 1968
BELLE STARR STORY, THE • 1968 • Wertmuller Lina • ITL • MIO CORPO PER UN POKER, IL ○ QUEEN OF DIAMONDS ○ BELLE STARR
BELLE STARR'S DAUGHTER • 1948 • Selander Lesley • USA
BELLE VASSILISSA, LA • 1940 • Rou Aleksandr • USS
BELLE VIE, LA • 1962 • Enrico Robert • FRN • GOOD LIFE, THE (UKN)
BELLE VIE, LA see **A FORCE ON S'HABITUE** • 1979
BELLE WHO TALKS, THE • 1909 • Wormald S.? • UKN
BELLES AND BALLETS • 1960 • *Bejart Maurice* • FRN
BELLES, BLONDES ET BRONZEES • 1981 • Pecas Max • FRN, SPN, FRG
BELLES CONDUITES, LES see **BONNE OCCASE, LA** • 1964
BELLES DAMES, VILAINS MESSIEURS see **SIGNORE E SIGNORI** • 1966
BELLES DE NUITS, LES • 1952 • Clair Rene • FRN, ITL • BELLE DELLA NOTTE, LE (ITL) ○ BEAUTIES OF THE NIGHT (USA) ○ NIGHT BEAUTIES (UKN)
BELLES MANIERES, LES • 1975 • Manuel Pierre • BLG
BELLES MANIERES, LES • 1978 • Guiguet Jean-Claude • FRN • FINE MANNERS
BELLES OF LIBERTY, THE • 1918 • Davis James • SHT • USA
BELLES OF ST. CLEMENTS, THE • 1936 • Campbell Ivar • UKN
BELLES OF ST. TRINIANS, THE • 1954 • Launder Frank • UKN
BELLES ON THEIR TOES • 1952 • Levin Henry • USA
BELLES SALOPES • Antony Michel • FRN
BELLES SOEURS, LES • 1977 • Corey Sam • FRN
BELLEZZA DEL DIAVOLO, LA (ITL) see **BEAUTE DU DIABLE, LA** • 1950
BELLEZZA DEL MONDO, LA • 1926 • Almirante Mario • ITL
BELLEZZA DI IPPOLITA, LA • 1962 • Zagni Giancarlo • ITL • SHE GOT WHAT SHE ASKED FOR
BELLEZZE A CAPRI • 1952 • Bianchi Adelchi • ITL
BELLEZZE IN BICICLETTA • 1951 • Campogalliani Carlo • ITL
BELLEZZE IN MOTOSCOOTER • 1953 • Campogalliani Carlo • ITL
BELLEZZE SULLA SPIAGGIA • 1961 • Guerrieri Romolo • ITL
BELLI E BRUTI RIDONO TUTTI • 1979 • Paolella Domenico • ITL
BELLIGERENT BENJAMIN • 1912 • *Scardon Paul* • USA
BELLIGERENT BETTIE • 1920 • Murray Grace Mel • USA
BELLISSIMA • 1951 • Visconti Luchino • ITL
BELLISSIMA ESTATE, LA • 1974 • Martino Sergio • ITL
BELLISSIME GAMBE DI SABRINA, LE • 1958 • Mastrocinque Camillo • ITL, FRG • SCHONEN BEINE DER SABRINA, DIE (FRG) ○ SABRINA'S WONDERFUL LEGS
BELLISSIMO NOVEMBRE, UN • 1968 • Bolognini Mauro • ITL, FRN • THAT SPLENDID NOVEMBER (USA) ○ WONDERFUL NOVEMBER, A ○ MERVEILLEUX AUTOMNE, UN
BELLIZAIRE THE CAJUN • 1986 • Pitre Glen • USA • BELIZAIRE THE CAJUN
BELLMAN, THE (USA) see **SORTILEGES** • 1944
BELLMAN AND TRUE • 1988 • Loncraine Richard • UKN
BELLO AMANECER • 1964 • Martinez Tony • MXC, PRC
BELLO COME UN ARCANGELO • 1974 • Giannetti Alfredo • ITL
BELLO DURMIENTE, EL • 1952 • Martinez Solares Gilberto • MXC • BEAUTIFUL DREAMER, THE
BELLO, IL BRUTO, IL CRETINO, IL • 1967 • Grimaldi Gianni • ITL, FRG • HANDSOME, THE UGLY, THE STUPID, THE
BELLO MA DANNATO • 1979 • Festa Campanile Pasquale • ITL
BELLO MIO BELLEZZA MIA • 1982 • Corbucci Sergio • ITL • MY HANDSOME MY BEAUTIFUL ○ MY DARLING, MY DEAREST
BELLO, ONESTO, EMIGRATO AUSTRALIA SPOSEREBBE COMPAESANA ILLIBATA • 1971 • Zampa Luigi • ITL, ASL • GIRL IN AUSTRALIA
BELLO RECUERDO • 1962 • del Amo Antonio • MXC
BELLRINGER'S DAUGHTER, THE • 1910 • *Edison* • USA
BELLS • 1981 • Anderson Michael • CND • MURDER BY PHONE ○ CALLING, THE
BELLS, THE • 1911 • Lincoln W. J. • ASL
BELLS, THE • 1913 • Apfel Oscar • *Reliance* • USA

BELLS, THE • 1913 • Lessey George A. • *Edison* • USA
BELLS, THE • 1914 • *Sawyer's Features* • USA
BELLS, THE • 1914 • *Irving H. B.* • UKN
BELLS, THE • 1918 • Warde Ernest C. • USA
BELLS, THE • 1923 • Greenwood Edwin • UKN
BELLS, THE • 1926 • Young James • USA
BELLS, THE • 1931 • Templeman Harcourt, Werndorff O. M. • UKN, FRG
BELLS AND BELLES • 1916 • Myll Louis • SHT • USA
BELLS ARE RINGING, THE • 1960 • Minnelli Vincente • USA
BELLS GO DOWN, THE • 1943 • Dearden Basil • UKN
BELLS HAVE GONE TO ROME, THE see **HARANGOK ROMABA MENTEK, A** • 1958
BELLS OF ATLANTIS • 1952 • Hugo Ian • SHT • USA
BELLS OF AUSTI, THE • 1914 • West Raymond B. • USA
BELLS OF CAPISTRANO • 1942 • Morgan William • USA
BELLS OF CORONADO • 1950 • Witney William • USA
BELLS OF DEATH, THE see **LOCENG MAUT** • 1976
BELLS OF EVENING, THE • 1986 • Zafranovic Lordan • YGS
BELLS OF RHEIMS, THE • 1914 • Elvey Maurice • UKN
BELLS OF ROSARITA • 1945 • McDonald Frank • USA
BELLS OF ST. MARY'S, THE • 1928 • Davis Redd • UKN
BELLS OF ST. MARY'S, THE • 1937 • Fitzpatrick James A. • UKN
BELLS OF ST. MARY'S, THE • 1945 • McCarey Leo • USA
BELLS OF SAN ANGELO • 1947 • Witney William • USA
BELLS OF SAN FERNANDO • 1947 • Morse Terry O. • USA
BELLS OF SAN JUAN • 1922 • Dunlap Scott R. • USA
BELLS OF THE OLD TOWN see **KLOCKORNA I GAMLA STAN** • 1946
BELLY OF AN ARCHITECT, THE • 1987 • Greenaway Peter • UKN
BELLY OF THE WHALE, THE • 1984 • Dorrie Doris • FRG
BELMONT BUTTS IN • 1914 • *Crystal* • USA
BELMONT STUNG • 1913 • *Belmont Joe* • USA
BELOE SOLNTSE PUOSTINI • 1971 • Motyl Vladimir • USS • WHITE SUN OVER THE DESERT ∘ WHITE SUN OF THE DESERT, THE ∘ BYELOE SOLNTSE PUOSTINI
BELOFTES VAN MORE • 1981 • Retief Daan • SAF • PROMISES FROM TOMORROW
BELONGING • 1922 • Thornton F. Martin • UKN
BELONNINGEN • 1981 • Lien Bjorn • NRW • REWARD, THE
BELOVED • 1929 • Aylott Dave, Symmons E. F. • SHT • UKN
BELOVED • 1934 • Schertzinger Victor • USA
BELOVED see **DEL ODIO NACIO EL AMOR** • 1949
BELOVED see **RAKAS** • 1961
BELOVED see **MAYULA** • 1986
BELOVED see **MAYAPRITI** • 1989
BELOVED, THE • 1971 • Cosmatos George Pan • GRC, UKN • RESTLESS ∘ SIN
BELOVED, THE see **GELIEBTE, DIE** • 1927
BELOVED, THE see **BIEN-AIMEE, LA** • 1980
BELOVED, THE see **AMANTE, L'** • 1989
BELOVED ADVENTURER, THE • 1914 • Smiley Joseph, Ince John • SRL • USA
BELOVED ADVENTURESS, THE • 1917 • Cowl George • USA
BELOVED BACHELOR, THE • 1931 • Corrigan Lloyd • USA
BELOVED BLACKMAILER, THE • 1918 • Henderson Dell • USA
BELOVED BOZO, THE • 1925 • Cline Eddie • SHT • USA
BELOVED BRAT, THE • 1938 • Lubin Arthur • USA • DANGEROUS AGE, A (UKN)
BELOVED BRUTE, THE • 1924 • Blackton J. Stuart • USA
BELOVED CHEATER, THE • 1919 • Gasnier Louis J. • USA
BELOVED CHEATER, THE • 1920 • Cabanne W. Christy • USA
BELOVED ENEMY • 1936 • Potter H. C. • USA • LOVE UNDER FIRE
BELOVED FISH, THE • 1954 • Sparling Gordon • DCS • CND
BELOVED GAME, THE see **KARA LEKEN, DEN** • 1959
BELOVED IMPOSTOR • 1936 • Hanbury Victor • UKN
BELOVED IMPOSTOR, THE • 1918 • Gleason Joseph • USA
BELOVED INFIDEL • 1959 • King Henry • USA
BELOVED JIM • 1917 • Paton Stuart • USA
BELOVED LIAR, THE • 1916 • Cochrane George • USA
BELOVED LOVE see **LJUBAVNI ZIVOT BUDIMIRA TRAJKOVICA** • 1978
BELOVED MILENA see **GELIEBTE MILENA** • 1990
BELOVED MOTHER see **MATER AMATISIMA** • 1980
BELOVED OF MY SOUL see **NIANIVIL NINDRAVAL** • 1967
BELOVED PARIS see **PARIGI O CARA** • 1962
BELOVED ROGUE, THE • 1927 • Crosland Alan • USA • RAGGED LOVER, THE
BELOVED ROGUES • 1917 • Santell Alfred • USA
BELOVED TRAITOR, THE • 1918 • Worthington William • USA
BELOVED VAGABOND, THE • 1912 • Jose Edward • USA
BELOVED VAGABOND, THE • 1923 • Granville Fred Leroy • UKN
BELOVED VAGABOND, THE • 1936 • Bernhardt Curtis • UKN
BELOVED VAMPIRE, THE • 1917 • *Knickerbocker Star* • SHT • USA
BELOW STAIRS • 1913 • Lucas Wilfred • USA
BELOW THE BELT • 1971 • *Tull John* • USA
BELOW THE BELT • 1980 • Fowler Robert • USA • TO SMITHEREENS
BELOW THE BELT see **COLPI BASSI, I** • 1972
BELOW THE BORDER • 1942 • Bretherton Howard • USA
BELOW THE DEAD LINE • 1920 • McGowan J. P. • USA
BELOW THE DEADLINE • 1913 • *Reliance* • USA
BELOW THE DEADLINE • 1929 • McGowan J. P. • USA
BELOW THE DEADLINE • 1936 • Lamont Charles • USA
BELOW THE DEADLINE • 1946 • Beaudine William • USA
BELOW THE LINE • 1925 • Raymaker Herman C. • USA
BELOW THE RIO GRANDE • 1923 • Hart Neal • USA
BELOW THE SAHARA • 1953 • Denis Armand • DOC • USA
BELOW THE SEA • 1933 • Rogell Albert S. • USA • HELL'S CARGO
BELOW THE SURFACE • 1920 • Willat Irvin V. • USA
BELOW THE SURFACE • 1938 • Kathner Rupert • ASL
BELOW ZERO • 1918 • Townley Robin H. • USA
BELOW ZERO • 1925 • Taurog Norman • SHT • USA
BELOW ZERO • 1930 • Parrott James • SHT • USA
BELOW ZERO • 1971 • Regnier Michel • CND
BELOW ZERO • 1989 • Awad Adel • EGY
BELPAESE, IL • 1977 • Salce Luciano • ITL
BELPHEGOR • 1926 • Desfontaines Henri • FRN
BELPHEGOR THE MOUNTEBANK • 1921 • Wynne Bert • UKN
BELSHAZZAR'S FEAST • 1905 • *Pathe* • FRN
BELSTONE FOX, THE • 1973 • Hill James • UKN • FREE SPIRIT (USA)
BELT AND SUSPENDERS MAN, THE • 1970 • Levy Donald J. • USA
BELT GIRLS AND THE PLAYBOY, THE • 1960 • Coppola Francis Ford • USA
BELVA, LA • 1970 • Costa Mario • ITL
BELVA COL MITRA, LA • 1977 • Grieco Sergio • ITL
BELVA DI SAIGON, LA • 1964 • Montero Roberto Bianchi, Roland Jurgen • ITL, FRG
BELVE, LE • 1971 • Grimaldi Gianni • ITL
BELYE NOCHI see **BELIYE NOCHI** • 1960
BELYI KARAVAN • 1964 • Shengelaya Eldar, Meliava Tamaz • USS • WHITE CARAVAN, THE ∘ BELYI KARAVAN
BELYI KARAVAN see **BELYI KARAVAN** • 1964
BELYI PAROKHOD see **BYELI PAROKHOD** • 1976
BEMOOSTE HAUPT, DAS • 1918 • Neuss Alwin • FRG
BEN • Cabouat Patrick • FRN
BEN • 1972 • Karlson Phil • USA
BEN ALI BEY • 1913 • Piel Harry • FRG
BEN AND ME • 1953 • Luske Hamilton • ANS • USA
BEN BLAIR • 1916 • Taylor William D. • USA
BEN BOLT • 1913 • Blache Alice • USA
BEN ET BENEDICT • 1977 • Delsol Paula • FRN
BEN GETS A DUCK AND IS DUCKED • 1907 • *Turpin Ben* • USA
BEN-GURION STORY, THE see **42:6 (BEN GURION)** • 1969
BEN HALL AND HIS GANG • 1911 • Gavin John F. • ASL
BEN HALL -THE NOTORIOUS BUSHRANGER • 1911 • Mervale Gaston • ASL
BEN-HUR • 1907 • Olcott Sidney, Rose Frank Oakes • USA
BEN-HUR • 1924 • Niblo Fred • USA
BEN-HUR • 1959 • Wyler William • USA
BEN-HUR • 1987 • ANM • USA
BEN KABARA, DER JAPANISCHE MESSERWERFER • 1918 • Dessauer Siegfried • FRG
BEN MING NIAN • 1989 • Xie Fei • CHN • BLACK SNOW
BEN OLDUKCE YASARIM • 1965 • Sagiroglu Duygu • TRK
BEN POLLACK AND HIS ORCHESTRA • 1934 • Henabery Joseph • SHT • USA
BEN POLLACK AND HIS PICK-A-RIB BOYS • 1962 • Binder Steve • SHT • USA
BEN, THE SAILOR • 1916 • Taylor R. F., Wheatley W. W. • SHT • USA
BEN THE STOWAWAY • 1913 • *Hall Ben* • USA
BEN TRUMAN 'OPENING TIME' see **WATCHMAKER** • 1980
BEN WEBSTER IN EUROPE see **BIG BEN** • 1967
BENAZIR • 1961 • *Roy Bhimal (P)* • IND
BENAZIR • 1964 • *Burman S. D. (M)* • IND
BENCH, THE • 1967 • Atamanov Lev • ANM • USS
BENCH OF DESOLATION, THE see **DE GRAY -LE BANC DE DESOLATION** • 1973
BEND OF THE RIVER • 1952 • Mann Anthony • USA • WHERE THE RIVER BENDS (UKN)
BENDIO ENTRE LAS MUJERES • 1958 • Delgado Miguel M. • MXC
BENDIX see **BAIN D'X** • 1956
BENEATH A STONY SKY see **UNDER EN STEINHIMMEL** • 1974
BENEATH THE 12 MILE REEF • 1953 • Webb Robert D. • USA
BENEATH THE ANGER see **BAROOD KI CHAON MEY** • 1989
BENEATH THE ANGKA: THE STORY OF THE KHMER ROUGE • 1982 • Ackerman Justin • DOC • USA
BENEATH THE COAT OF A BUTLER • 1915 • *De Carlton Grace* • USA
BENEATH THE CZAR • 1914 • Blache Alice • USA
BENEATH THE GLACIER • 1989 • Halldorsdottir Gudny • ICL, FRG
BENEATH THE LAW • 1929 • Sweet Harry • USA
BENEATH THE MASK • 1914 • *Grandin Ethel* • USA
BENEATH THE MASK • 1915 • Haldane Bert? • UKN
BENEATH THE PLANET OF THE APES • 1970 • Post Ted • USA • PLANET OF THE APES REVISITED ∘ PLANET OF THE MEN
BENEATH THE SEA • 1915 • *Fowler Charles* • USA
BENEATH THE SKY see **ZIR-E-GONBAD-E-KABOUD** • 1967
BENEATH THE SKY OF MEXICO (USA) see **BAJO EL CIELO DE MEXICO** • 1937
BENEATH THE STARRY SKIES (UKN) see **COWBOY BLUES** • 1946
BENEATH THE SURFACE, STRICKEN BY ANOMALOUS PASSION see **SOTTO.. SOTTO, STRAPAZZATO DA ANOMALA PASSIONE** • 1984
BENEATH THE TOWER RUINS • 1911 • *Urban-Eclipse* • UKN
BENEATH THE VALLEY OF THE ULTRAVIXENS • 1979 • Meyer Russ • USA
BENEATH THE VEIL • 1911 • *Thanhouser* • USA
BENEATH WESTERN SKIES • 1912 • *Nestor* • USA
BENEATH WESTERN SKIES • 1944 • Bennet Spencer Gordon • USA
BENEDICT ARNOLD • 1909 • Blackton J. Stuart (Spv) • USA
BENEFACTOR, THE • 1913 • *Johnson Arthur* • USA
BENEFIT OF THE DOUBT • 1967 • Whitehead Peter • UKN • US
BENEFITS FORGOT see **OF HUMAN HEARTS** • 1938
BENEFIZ -VORSTELLUNG DER VIER TEUFEL, DIE • 1920 • Sandberg Anders W. • FRG
BENEVOLENCE OF CONDUCTOR 786, THE • 1914 • *Chamberlin Riley* • USA
BENEVOLENT EMPLOYER • 1909 • *Urban-Eclipse* • UKN
BENGADOR GUSTICIERO Y SU PASTELERA MADRE, EL • 1976 • Forges • SPN
BENGAL BRIGADE • 1954 • Benedek Laslo • USA • BENGAL RIFLES (UKN)
BENGAL FAMINE • 1943 • Roy Bimal • SHT • IND
BENGAL RIFLES (UKN) see **BENGAL BRIGADE** • 1954
BENGAL TIGER • 1934 • May Joe • USA
BENGAL TIGER • 1936 • King Louis • USA
BENGAL TIGER, THE • 1972 • Martin Richard • DOC • USA
BENGALI VII see **GAIETES DE LA FINANCE, LES** • 1935
BENGASI • 1942 • Genina Augusto • ITL
BENGAZI • 1955 • Brahm John • USA
BENGELCHEN HAT'S WIRKLICH SCHWER see **BENGELCHEN LIEBT KREUZ UND QUER** • 1968
BENGELCHEN LIEBT KREUZ UND QUER • 1968 • Gosov Marran • FRG • SEX ADVENTURES OF A SINGLE MAN, THE (UKN) ∘ 24-HOUR LOVER (USA) ∘ CRUNCH ∘ BENGELCHEN HAT'S WIRKLICH SCHWER ∘ LITTLE RASCAL LOVES CRISS-CROSS
BENGT'S NEW LOVE see **BENGTS NYA KARLEK** • 1916
BENGTS NYA KARLEK • 1916 • Klercker Georg • SWD • BENGT'S NEW LOVE
BENGURION REMEMBERS • 1972 • Hesera Simon • DOC • ISR • B.G. REMEMBERS (UKN)
BENI-HENDEL • 1976 • Merbah Lamine • ALG • DERACINES, LES
BENI KATIL ETTILER • 1967 • Hancer Nisan • TRK • THEY MADE ME A KILLER
BENI KOMORI • 1931 • *Tsuburaya Eiji (Ph)* • JPN • RED BAT
BENI KOMORI • 1951 • Kinugasa Teinosuke • JPN
BENI-KUJAKO • 1955 • JPN • RED PEACOCK
BENIGNO, HERMANO MIO • 1963 • Gonzalez Arturo • SPN
BENILDE OR THE VIRGIN MOTHER see **BENILDE OU A VIRGEM MAE** • 1975
BENILDE OU A VIRGEM MAE • 1975 • de Oliveira Manoel • PRT • BENILDE OR THE VIRGIN MOTHER ∘ BENILDE: VIRGIN AND MOTHER
BENILDE: VIRGIN AND MOTHER see **BENILDE OU A VIRGEM MAE** • 1975
BENIM ADIM KERIM • 1967 • Guney Yilmaz • TRK • MY NAME IS KERIM
BENIM SINEMALARIM • 1989 • Karamustafa Gulsun, Furuzan • TRK
BENIMDE KALBIM VAR • 1968 • Inanoglu Turker • TRK • I TOO HAVE A HEART
BENIMERITO, EL • 1974 • de Pedro Manuel • VNZ
BENIMLE EVLENIRMISIN? • 1968 • Gulyuz Aram • TRK • WILL YOU MARRY ME?
BENISSEZ LE SEIGNEUR • 1937 • Tessier Albert • DCS • CND
BENITO CERENO • 1968 • Roullet Serge • FRN, ITL, BRZ
BENITO MUSSOLINI • 1962 • Rossellini Roberto, Prunas Pasquale • DOC • ITL • BLOOD ON THE BALCONY
BENITO MUSSOLINI: ANATOMIA DI UN DITTATORE • 1961 • Loy Mino, Baracco Adriano • DOC • ITL
BENJA • 1962 • Yutkevich Sergei, Karanovich Anatoli • ANM • USS • BATH HOUSE, THE ∘ BANYA ∘ BATH
BENJAMIN see **BENJAMIN OU LES MEMOIRES D'UN PUCEAU** • 1968
BENJAMIN ARGUMEDO • 1978 • Estrada Jose • MXC
BENJAMIN BUNTER, BOOK-AGENT • 1915 • Van Deusen Courtlandt • USA
BENJAMIN DISRAELI see **SECRET LIVES OF THE BRITISH PRIME MINISTERS: DISRAELI, THE** • 1981
BENJAMIN FRANKLIN, JR. • 1943 • Glazer Herbert • SHT • USA
BENJAMIN, OR THE DIARY OF AN INNOCENT YOUNG MAN see **BENJAMIN OU LES MEMOIRES D'UN PUCEAU** • 1968
BENJAMIN OU LES MEMOIRES D'UN PUCEAU • 1968 • Deville Michel • FRN • BENJAMIN: THE DIARY OF AN INNOCENT BOY ∘ BENJAMIN ∘ BENJAMIN, OR THE DIARY OF AN INNOCENT YOUNG MAN
BENJAMIN: THE DIARY OF AN INNOCENT BOY see **BENJAMIN OU LES MEMOIRES D'UN PUCEAU** • 1968
BENJI • 1974 • Camp Joe • USA
BENJI THE HUNTED • 1987 • Camp Joe • USA
BENJY • 1951 • Zinnemann Fred • DOC • USA
BENNIE-BOET • 1967 • Botha Kappie • SAF
BENNO SCHOTZ • 1973 • McConnell Edward • DOC • UKN
BENNO STEHKRAGEN • 1927 • Santen Trude • FRG
BENNY AND BARNEY: LAS VEGAS UNDERCOVER • 1977 • Satlof Ron • TVM • USA
BENNY AND BUFORD see **GHOST FEVER** • 1984
BENNY FROM PANAMA • 1934 • Parrott James • SHT • USA
BENNY GOODMAN STORY, THE • 1955 • Davies Valentine • USA
BENNYS BADEKAR • 1971 • Hastrup Jannik, Quist-Moller Fleming • ANM • DNM • BENNY'S BATHTUB
BENNY'S BATHTUB see **BENNYS BADEKAR** • 1971
BENNY'S PLACE • 1982 • Schultz Michael • TVM • USA
BENOIT • 1965 • Jackson Douglas • CND
BENOIT • 1978 • Shaffer Beverly • DOC • CND
BEN'S KID • 1909 • *Arbuckle Roscoe* • USA
BENSAA SUONISSA • 1971 • Jarva Risto • FNL • GAS IN THE VEINS ∘ RALLY
BENSON MURDER CASE, THE • 1930 • Tuttle Frank • USA
BENT GUN, THE • 1915 • *Deer* • USA
BENTEN BOY see **BENTEN KOZO** • 1958
BENTEN KOZO • 1928 • Kinugasa Teinosuke • JPN • GAY MASQUERADE
BENTEN KOZO • 1958 • Ito Daisuke • JPN • GAY MASQUERADE ∘ BENTEN BOY
BENTLEY ACADEMY, THE see **PRETTY SMART** • 1987
BENTLEY'S CONSCIENCE • 1922 • Clift Denison • UKN
BENVENUTA • 1983 • Delvaux Andre • BLG, FRN, ITL
BENVENUTO CELLINI • 1910 • Feuillade Louis • FRN
BENVENUTO CELLINI OR A CURIOUS EVASION see **BENVENUTO CELLINI OU UNE CURIEUSE EVASION** • 1904
BENVENUTO CELLINI OU UNE CURIEUSE EVASION • 1904 • Melies Georges • FRN • BENVENUTO CELLINI OR A CURIOUS EVASION ∘ CURIEUSE EVASION, UNE ∘ CURIOUS EVASION, A
BENVENUTO ONOREVOLE see **GENTE FELICE** • 1957
BENVENUTO REVERENDO! • 1950 • Fabrizi Aldo • ITL
BEOWULF • 1976 • Fairservice Don • UKN
BEPPIE • 1965 • van der Keuken Johan • NTH
BEPPO • 1914 • Otto Henry • USA
BEPPO, THE BARBER • 1915 • Dillon Eddie • USA
BEQASOOR • 1950 • *Biswas Anil (M)* • IND
BEQUEST TO THE NATION, A • 1973 • Jones James Cellan • UKN • NELSON AFFAIR, THE
BERANAK DALAM KUBUR • 1972 • Prijono Ami • INN
BERCAIL, LE • 1919 • L'Herbier Marcel • SHT • FRN
BERCANDA DALAM DUKA • 1981 • Subardjo Ismail • INN • HIDDEN TRUTH, THE
BERCEAU DE CRISTAL, LE • 1976 • Garrel Philippe • FRN

BERCEAU DE DIEU, LE • 1926 • Granville Fred Leroy • FRN • CRADLE OF GOD, THE
BERCEAUX, LES • 1932 • Epstein Jean • FRN
BERCEAUX, LES • 1935 • Kirsanoff Dimitri • SHT • FRN
BERCEUSE • 1948 • Tyrlova Hermina • ANM • CZC
BERCHTESGADEN UBER SALZBURG • 1938 • Riefenstahl Leni • FRG
BERDUGO NG MGA HARI • 1967 • Sun Leo • PHL • PROFESSIONAL KILLER
BEREDSKAPSPOJKAR • 1941 • Wallen Sigurd • SWD • OUR BOYS IN UNIFORM
BEREG • 1983 • Alov Alexander, Naumov Vladimir • USS • BANK, THE
BEREGIS AVTOMOBILYA! • 1966 • Ryazanov Eldar • USS • WATCH OUT FOR THE AUTOMOBILE (USA) ○ LOOK OUT FOR THE CARS ○ BEWARE THE CAR! ○ UNCOMMON THIEF, AN ○ WATCH YOUR CAR
BEREKETLI TOPRAKLAR UZERINDE • 1980 • Kiral Erden • TRK • ON FERTILE LANDS
BERENICE • 1954 • Rohmer Eric • SHT • FRN
BERENICE • 1967 • Jolivet Pierre-Alain • FRN
BERENSTAIN BEARS MEET BIG PAW, THE • 1980 • ANM • USA
BERESFORD OF THE BABOONS • 1919 • Harrison Saul • SHT • USA
BERG, DER • 1989 • Imhoof Markus • SWT • MOUNTAIN, THE
BERG DES SCHICKSALS, DER • 1924 • Fanck Arnold • FRG • PEAK OF DESTINY ○ PEAK OF FATE ○ PEAKS OF DESTINY
BERG-EJVIND OCH HANS HUSTRU • 1918 • Sjostrom Victor • SWD • LOVE THE ONLY LAW (UKN) ○ OUTLAW AND HIS WIFE, THE ○ YOU AND I (USA)
BERG IN FLAMMEN • 1931 • Trenker Luis, Hartl Karl • FRG • DOOMED BATTALION
BERG RUFT, DER • 1937 • Trenker Luis • FRG
BERGADLER, DER (FRG) see **MOUNTAIN EAGLE, THE** • 1926
BERGBLUME • 1919 • von Woringen Paul • FRG
BERGERE ET LE RAMONEUR, LA • 1953 • Grimault Paul • ANM • FRN • CURIOUS ADVENTURES OF MR. WONDERBIRD (USA) ○ ADVENTURES OF MR. WONDERBIRD ○ SHEPHERDESS AND THE CHIMNEY SWEEP, THE ○ MR. WONDERBIRD
BERGET PA MANENS BAKSIDA • 1983 • Hjulstrom Lennart • SWD • HILL ON THE DARK SIDE OF THE MOON, A
BERGFUHRER, DER • 1917 • Bienz Eduard • SWT
BERGHOFBAUER, DER see **ULLI UND MAREI** • 1945
BERGKATZE, DIE • 1921 • Lubitsch Ernst • FRG • MOUNTAIN CAT, THE ○ WILDCAT, THE (USA)
BERGKRISTALL • 1949 • Reinl Harald • AUS
BERGSLAGSFOLKEN • 1937 • Olsson Gunnar • SWD • PEOPLE OF BERGSLAGEN
BERGSUNDEN • 1919 • Batz Lorenz • FRG
BERGWASSER see **ANGELA** • 1949
BERK, THE see **THURSDAY'S GAME** • 1974
BERKELEY SQUARE • 1933 • Lloyd Frank • USA
BERLIN • 1945 • Raizman Yuli, Svilova Elizaveta • DOC • USS • FALL OF BERLIN, THE
BERLIN see **BERLIN -DIE SYMPHONIE DER GROSSTADT** • 1927
BERLIN AFFAIR • 1970 • Rich David Lowell • TVM • USA
BERLIN AFFAIR see **INTERNO BERLINESE** • 1985
BERLIN-ALEXANDERPLATZ • 1931 • Jutzi Phil • FRG
BERLIN ALEXANDERPLATZ • 1979 • Fassbinder R. W. • MTV • FRG
BERLIN, APPOINTMENT FOR THE SPIES see **BERLINO, APPUNTAMENTO PER LE SPIE** • 1965
BERLIN BLUES • 1988 • Franco Ricardo • SPN
BERLIN CHAMISSOPLATZ • 1980 • Thome Rudolf • FRG
BERLIN CONFERENCE, THE • 1945 • Gerasimov Sergei, Kopalin Ilya • USS
BERLIN CORRESPONDENT • 1942 • Forde Eugene J. • USA
BERLIN, DE L'AUBE A LA NUIT • 1981 • Leroy Annick • BLG, FRG
BERLIN -DIE SYMPHONIE DER GROSSTADT • 1927 • Ruttmann Walter • DOC • FRG • BERLIN, SYMPHONY OF A GREAT CITY (USA) ○ BERLIN
BERLIN -ECKE SCHONHAUSER • 1957 • Klein Gerhard • GDR • BERLIN SCHOENHAUSER CORNER
BERLIN EXPRESS • 1948 • Tourneur Jacques • USA
BERLIN FROBELSTRASSE. IM ASYL FUR OBDACHLOSE see **GEHEIMNISSE VON BERLIN 4, DIE** • 1922
BERLIN HORSE • 1970 • Le Grice Malcolm • UKN
BERLIN INTERIOR see **INTERNO BERLINESE** • 1985
BERLIN IST EINE SUNDE WELT • 1966 • Tremper Will • FRG • THAT WOMAN (USA) ○ PLAYGIRL
BERLIN JERUSALEM • 1989 • Gitai Amos • FRN, ISR
BERLIN KAPUTT • 1982 • Milosevic Mica • YGS
BERLIN-MOABIT. HINTER GITTERFENSTERN see **GEHEIMNISSE VON BERLIN 3, DIE** • 1921
BERLIN N. DIE DUNKLE GROSSTADT see **GEHEIMNISSE VON BERLIN 1, DIE** • 1921
BERLIN OLYMPIAD (UKN) see **OLYMPISCHE SPIELE 1936** • 1938
BERLIN ROMANCE see **BERLINER ROMANZE** • 1956
BERLIN SCHOENHAUSER CORNER see **BERLIN -ECKE SCHONHAUSER** • 1957
BERLIN, SYMPHONY OF A GREAT CITY (USA) see **BERLIN -DIE SYMPHONIE DER GROSSTADT** • 1927
BERLIN TUNNEL 21 • 1981 • Michaels Richard • TVM • USA
BERLIN VIA AMERICA • 1918 • Ford Francis • USA
BERLIN W • 1920 • Noa Manfred • FRG
BERLIN W. DIE GROSSTADT IN GLANZ UND LICHT see **GEHEIMNISSE VON BERLIN 2, DIE** • 1921
BERLIN WALL, THE see **SCHAUT AUF DIESE STADT** • 1962
BERLIN WALL, THE see **MUR DE BERLIN, LE** • 1988
BERLINER, THE • 1948 • *Morgan Henry (Nar)* • FRG
BERLINER, THE see **BERLINER BALLADE** • 1948
BERLINER BALLADE • 1948 • Stemmle R. A. • FRG • BALLAD OF BERLIN, THE ○ BERLINER, THE
BERLINER KOMODIE • 1988 • Levy Dani • SWT
BERLINER RANGE, DIE • 1920 • Hagen Carl • FRG • STREICH: LOTTE ALS SCHULSCHRECK
BERLINER ROMANZE • 1956 • Klein Gerhard • GDR • BERLIN ROMANCE
BERLINFRESSER, DER • 1971 • Heyde Friedhelm • SHT • FRG
BERLINGER • 1976 • Sinkel Bernard, Brustellin Alf • FRG • OUTSIDER, THE
BERLINGOT ET CIE • 1939 • Rivers Fernand • FRN
BERLINGUER TI VOGLIO BENE • 1977 • Bertolucci Giuseppe • ITL
BERLINO, APPUNTAMENTO PER LE SPIE • 1965 • Sala Vittorio • ITL • SPY IN YOUR EYE (USA) ○ EPITAPH FOR A SPY ○ BANG YOU'RE DEAD ○ CULT OF VIOLENCE, THE ○ BERLIN, APPOINTMENT FOR THE SPIES
BERLONGOT • 1932 • Greville Edmond T. • SHT • FRN
BERMONDSEY KID, THE • 1933 • Dawson Ralph • UKN
BERMUDA AFFAIR • 1957 • Sutherland A. Edward • USA
BERMUDA DEPTHS, THE • 1978 • Kotani Tom • TVM • USA
BERMUDA MYSTERY • 1944 • Stoloff Ben • USA • MURDER IN BERMUDA
BERMUDA TRIANGLE, THE • 1978 • Friedenberg Richard • DOC • USA
BERMUDA TRIANGLE, THE see **DIABOLICO TRIANGULO DE LA BERMUDAS, EL** • 1977
BERMUDE: LA FOSSA MALEDETTA see **FOSSA MALEDETTA, LA** • 1978
BERNADETTE • 1988 • Delannoy Jean • FRN
BERNADETTE DE LOURDES see **IL SUFFIT D'AIMER** • 1960
BERNADETTE OF LOURDES (USA) see **IL SUFFIT D'AIMER** • 1960
BERNAL BLUES • 1970 • Agins Jack • UKN
BERNARD AND BIANCA • 1976 • Reitherman Wolfgang • ANM • USA
BERNARD FRANK EST INSUPPORTABLE • 1981 • Jaeggi Danielle, Sorin Raphael • FRN
BERNARD LE BUCHERON • 1907 • Melies Georges • FRN • FORESTER MADE KING, A (USA) ○ MIRACLE DE SAINT HUBERT, THE
BERNARD-L'HERMITE, LE • 1930 • Painleve Jean • SHT • FRN
BERNARD MILES ON GUN DOGS • 1948 • Wright Basil • DOC • UKN
BERNARDINE • 1957 • Levin Henry • USA
BERNARDO'S CONFESSION • 1914 • Vernon Charles • UKN
BERNICE BOBS HER HAIR • 1976 • Silver Joan Micklin • USA • RITES OF PASSAGE
BERNSTEIN IN ISRAEL • 1958 • Leacock Richard • DOC • USA
BERNSTEIN IN MOSCOW • 1959 • Leacock Richard • DOC • USA
BERORINGEN • 1970 • Bergman Ingmar • SWD, USA • TOUCH, THE (USA)
BERRE, CITE DU PETROLE • 1953 • Champetier Henri • SHT • FRN
BERRY GORDY'S THE LAST DRAGON see **LAST DRAGON, THR** • 1985
BERSAGLIERE'S GIRL, THE see **RAGAZZA DEL BERSAGLIERE, LA** • 1967
BERSAGLIERI DELLA SIGNORA • 1945 • Risi Dino • DOC • ITL
BERSAGLIO • 1979 • Zurli Guido • ITL
BERSAGLIO MOBILE • 1967 • Corbucci Sergio • ITL • MOVING TARGET ○ DEATH ON THE RUN
BERSEMI DI LEMBAH TIDAR • 1983 • Rorimpandey Frank • INN • BLOSSOMING IN THE TIDAR VALLEY
BERSERK! • 1967 • O'Connolly Jim • UKN, USA • CIRCUS OF BLOOD
BERSERKER • 1987 • Richard Jefferson • USA • BERSERKER: THE NORDIC CURSE
BERSERKER: THE NORDIC CURSE see **BERSERKER** • 1987
BERT RIGBY, YOU'RE A FOOL • 1989 • Reiner Carl • USA
BERT, THE KARATE FIGHTER see **BERTONG KARATE** • 1967
BERTA OF THE MARKET see **BERTANG PALENGKE** • 1967
BERTANG PALENGKE • 1967 • Orian Monic • PHL • BERTA OF THE MARKET
BERTA'S MOTIVES see **MOTIVOS DE BERTA, LOS** • 1985
BERTA'S REASONS see **MOTIVOS DE BERTA, LOS** • 1985
BERTH CONTROL • 1918 • Lyons Eddie, Moran Lee • SHT • USA
BERTH MARK • 1926 • Fleischer Dave • ANS • USA
BERTH MARKS • 1929 • Foster Lewis R. • SHT • USA
BERTH QUAKES • 1938 • Yarbrough Jean • SHT • USA
BERTHA • 1969 • Sclater Michael • UKN
BERTHA, THE BUTTON-HOLE MAKER • 1914 • Henderson Dell • USA
BERTHA THE SEWING MACHINE GIRL • 1926 • Cummings Irving • USA
BERTHA'S MISSION • 1911 • *Vitagraph* • USA
BERTHE • 1977 • Ledoux Patrick • BLG
BERTHE AUX GRANDS PIEDS • Bettiol Bruno, Lonati, Bettiol Guido • ANS • FRN • BIG FOOTED BERTHA (USA)
BERTIE AND THE TRAMP • 1905 • *Cricks & Sharp* • UKN
BERTIE AT THE GYMNASIUM see **INQUISITIVE BERTIE** • 1906
BERTIE AT THE LADIES' COLLEGE • 1914 • *Eclair* • UKN
BERTIE BEETLE see **ARCHIE THE ANT** • 1925
BERTIE BUYS A BULLDOG • 1909 • Coleby A. E. • UKN
BERTIE BUYS A CARETAKER • 1914 • Collins Edwin J.? • UKN
BERTIE'S BABY • 1914 • Kellino W. P. • UKN
BERTIE'S BANDIT • 1911 • *American* • USA
BERTIE'S BID FOR BLISS • 1911 • Aylott Dave • UKN
BERTIE'S BIKE: OR, THE MERRY MADCAPS • 1899 • *Paul R. W.* • UKN
BERTIE'S BOOK OF MAGIC • 1912 • Wilson Frank? • UKN
BERTIE'S BRAINSTORM • 1911 • *Thanhouser* • USA
BERTIE'S COURTSHIP • 1904 • Mottershaw Frank • UKN
BERTIE'S ELOPEMENT • 1910 • *Selig* • USA
BERTIE'S HOLIDAY • 1915 • *Wright Bertie* • UKN
BERTIE'S LOVE LETTER • 1907 • Green Tom? • UKN
BERTIE'S REFORMATION • 1911 • *Kalem* • USA
BERTIE'S STRATAGEM • 1915 • Beggs Lee • USA
BERTOLDO, BERTOLDINO E CACASENNO • 1936 • Simonelli Giorgio C. • ITL
BERTOLDO, BERTOLDINO E CACASENNO • 1954 • Amendola Mario, Maccari Ruggero • ITL
BERTOLDO, BERTOLDINO E CACASENNO • 1984 • Monicelli Mario • ITL
BERTOLUCCI SECONDO IL CINEMA • 1976 • Amelio Gianni • MTV • ITL
BERTONG KARATE • 1967 • Gaudite Solano • PHL • BERT, THE KARATE FIGHTER
BERTRAND, COEUR DE LION • 1950 • Dhery Robert • FRN
BERU AT CES DAMES • 1968 • Lefranc Guy • FRN
BERUHMTE FRAU, DIE • 1927 • Wiene Robert • FRG • DANCER OF BARCELONA, THE
BERUHRTE, DIE • 1981 • Sanders Helma • FRG • NO MERCY NO FUTURE
BERUSAIYU NO BARA • 1978 • Demy Jacques • JPN, FRN • ROSE OF VERSAILLES, THE ○ LADY OSCAR ○ LADY'O ○ VERSAILLES NO BARA
BERYGTEDE HUS, DET see **HVIDE SLAVEHANDEL III, DEN** • 1912
BERYL CORONET, THE • 1912 • Treville Georges • UKN
BERYL CORONET, THE • 1913 • *Union* • USA
BERYL CORONET, THE • 1921 • Elvey Maurice • UKN
BES ASI ADAM • 1968 • Ziyal Tolgay • TRK • FIVE REBELLIOUS MEN
BES ATESLI KADIN • 1968 • Tiryaki Seyfettin • TRK • FIVE HOT WOMEN
BES NASLOVA • 1964 • Dovnikovic Borivoj • ANS • YGS • NO CREDITS ○ WITHOUT TITLE
BES SVIDETELEY see **BEZ SVIDETELEI** • 1983
BES UZUN SAAT • 1967 • Engin Ilhan • TRK • FIVE ENDLESS HOURS
BESAME, MONSTRUO • 1968 • Franco Jesus • SPN, FRG • KISS ME MONSTER (USA) ○ CASTLE OF THE DOOMED
BESAME MUCHO • 1944 • Ugarte Eduardo • MXC
BESAME MUCHO • 1986 • Ramalho Francisco Jr. • BRZ
BESATZUNG DORA • 1943 • Ritter Karl • FRG
BESCHREIBUNG EINER INSEL • 1979 • Thome Rudolf, Beatt Cynthia • FRG • STUDY OF AN ISLAND ○ DESCRIPTION OF AN ISLAND
BESCHREIBUNG EINES SOMMERS • 1963 • Kirsten Ralf • GDR
BESESSEN -DAS LOCH IN DER WAND • 1969 • de la Parra Pim • FRG, NTH • BEZETEN -HET GAT IN DE MUUR ○ OBSESSIONS
BESESSENE ODER DAS FRAULEIN VON SCUDERI, DER • 1920 • Hacker Gottfried • FRG
BESIDE A MOONLIT STREAM • 1938 • Fleischer Dave • ANS • USA
BESIDE THE BONNIE BRIER BUSH • 1921 • Crisp Donald • UKN, USA • BONNIE BRIAR BUSH, THE ○ BONNIE BRIER BUSH, THE
BESIDE THE RAILWAY LINE see **PRZY TORZE KOLEJOWYM**
BESIEGED see **AMORE BREVE, L'** • 1969
BESITO A PAPA • 1960 • Diaz Morales Jose • MXC
BESITZ BURGERIN, JAHRGANG 1908 • 1973 • Kluge Alexander • SHT • FRG • WOMAN FROM THE PROPERTY-OWNING MIDDLE CLASS, BORN 1908
BESMRTNA MLADOST • 1948 • Nanovic Vojislav • YGS • IMMORTAL YOUTH
BESO ANTES DE ESCONDERME, UN • 1975 • Camus Mario • SPN
BESO DE JUDAS, EL • 1953 • Gil Rafael • SPN
BESO DE ULTRATUMBA, EL • 1962 • Toussaint Carlos • MXC • KISS FROM BEYOND THE GRAVE, THE
BESO EN EL PUERTO, UN • 1965 • Torrado Ramon • SPN
BESO EN LA NOCHE, UN • 1944 • Martinez Solares Gilberto • MXC
BESO MORTAL, EL • 1938 • Rivero Fernando A. • MXC • FATAL KISS, THE (USA)
BESOEKER, DIE see **GUEST, THE** • 1976
BESOEKET • 1966 • Bechrendtz Nils Erik • SHT • SWD • VISIT
BESOINS CACHES • 1975 • Moreau Michel • DCS • CND
BESOINS FONDAMENTAUX AUX DE L'HOMME • 1977 • Beaudry Michel • SHS • CND
BESONDERE KENNZEICHEN • 1929 • Heuberger Edmund • FRG
BESONDERE KENNZEICHEN: KEINE • 1956 • Kunert Joachim • GDR • SPECIAL PECULIARITIES -NONE ○ SPECIAL MARKS -NONE
BESOS A UN CADAVER • 1968 • Madrid Jose Luis • SPN
BESOS BRUJOS • 1937 • Ferreyra Jose • ARG • BEWITCHING KISSES (USA)
BESOS DE ARENA • 1957 • Martinez Solares Gilberto • MXC
BESOS PROHIBIDOS • 1956 • Baledon Rafael • MXC
BESPECTACLED, THE see **SZEMUVEGESEK** • 1969
BESPOKE OVERCOAT, THE • 1955 • Clayton Jack • UKN
BESPRIDANNITSA • 1936 • Protazanov Yakov • USS • WITHOUT DOWRY ○ WITHOUT A DOWRY
BESS OF THE FOREST • 1911 • *Lubin* • USA
BESS THE DETECTIVE'S DAUGHTER see **TO SAVE HER DAD** • 1913
BESS THE DETECTRESS IN TICK, TICK, TICK • 1914 • *Meredyth Bess* • USA
BESS THE DETECTRESS OR THE DOG WATCH • 1914 • *Meredyth Bess* • USA
BESS THE DETECTRESS OR THE OLD MILL AT MIDNIGHT • 1914 • *Meredyth Bess* • USA
BESS, THE OUTCAST • 1914 • Pollard Harry • USA
BESSERER HERR, EIN • 1928 • Ucicky Gustav • FRG
BESSIE SMITH • 1969 • Levine Charles I. • SHT • USA
BESSIE'S BACHELOR BOOBS • 1915 • *Lane Winfred* • USA
BESSIE'S DREAM • 1912 • *Eyton Bessie* • USA
BESSIE'S RIDE • 1911 • Melies Gaston • USA
BESSIE'S SUITORS • 1912 • *Quirk Billy* • USA
BESSMERTNYI GARNIZON • 1956 • Tisse Eduard, Agranenko Zakhar • USS • IMMORTAL GARRISON, THE (USA) ○ BIESSMIERTNYI GARNISON
BEST, THE • 1979 • Guerin M.
BEST, THE see **NAJBOLJI** • 1989
BEST AGE, THE see **NEJKRASNEJSI VEK** • 1968
BEST BAD MAN, THE • 1919 • Kull Edward • SHT • USA
BEST BAD MAN, THE • 1925 • Blystone John G. • USA
BEST BET, THE see **ATTA BOY'S LAST RACE** • 1916
BEST BIT OF CRUMPET IN DENMARK, THE see **BORDELLET** • 1972
BEST BOUZOUKI-PLAYER, THE see **PIO LAMBRO BOUZOUKI, TO** • 1968

BEST BOY • 1979 • Wohl Ira • DOC • USA
BEST DAMN FIDDLER FROM CALABOGIE TO KALADAR, THE • 1968 • Pearson Peter • CND
BEST DEFENSE • 1984 • Huyck Willard • USA
BEST FOOT FORWARD • 1943 • Buzzell Edward • USA
BEST FRIEND see **NAJLEPSZY KOLEGA** • 1970
BEST FRIENDS • 1973 • Nosseck Noel • USA
BEST FRIENDS • 1982 • Jewison Norman • USA
BEST FRIENDS, THE see **CHIH AI-CH'IN P'ENG** • 1977
BEST FRIENDS IN THE LAND OF PLENTY • 1972 • Le Bon Patrick • DOC • BLG
BEST GIRL I EVER HAD, THE see **NEJLEPSI ZENSKA MEHO ZIVOTE** • 1967
BEST GIRL IN THE WORLD, THE see **NEJLEPSI ZENSKA MEHO ZIVOTE** • 1967
BEST HOUSE IN LONDON, THE • 1969 • Saville Philip • UKN
BEST IN THE WEST, THE see **DA BEST IN DA WEST** • 1967
BEST KEPT SECRETS • 1984 • Freedman Jerrold • TVM • USA
BEST LITTLE GIRL IN THE WORLD, THE • 1906 • Fitzhamon Lewin • UKN
BEST LITTLE GIRL IN THE WORLD, THE • 1981 • O'Steen Sam • TVM • USA
BEST LITTLE WHOREHOUSE IN TEXAS, THE • 1982 • Higgins Colin • USA
BEST MAN, THE • 1914 • *Frontier* • USA
BEST MAN, THE • 1914 • Brabin Charles J. • *Edison* • USA
BEST MAN, THE • 1914 • Hotaling Arthur D. • *Lubin* • USA
BEST MAN, THE • 1916 • Jackson Harry • SHT • USA
BEST MAN, THE • 1917 • Bracken Bertram • USA
BEST MAN, THE • 1919 • Heffron Thomas N. • USA
BEST MAN, THE • 1928 • Edwards Harry J. • SHT • USA
BEST MAN, THE • 1964 • Schaffner Franklin J. • USA
BEST MAN, THE • 1986 • McMahon Joe • IRL
BEST MAN WINS • 1948 • Sturges John • USA
BEST MAN WINS, THE • 1909 • *Anderson Broncho Billy* • USA
BEST MAN WINS, THE • 1910 • *Thanhouser* • USA
BEST MAN WINS, THE • 1911 • Ricketts Thomas • USA
BEST MAN WINS, THE • 1912 • *Majestic* • USA
BEST MAN WINS, THE • 1912 • Dwan Allan • *American* • USA
BEST MAN WINS, THE • 1913 • Henderson Dell • USA
BEST MAN WINS, THE • 1935 • Kenton Erle C. • USA
BEST MAN'S BRIDE, THE • 1916 • Worthington William • SHT • USA
BEST OF A BAD BARGAIN, THE • 1918 • *Sparkle* • SHT • USA
BEST OF BENNY HILL, THE • 1974 • Robins John • UKN
BEST OF BOTH WORLDS • 1983 • Williams Douglas • CND
BEST OF CINERAMA, THE • 1963 • USA
BEST OF ENEMIES, THE • 1915 • Griffin Frank C. • USA
BEST OF ENEMIES, THE • 1933 • James Rian • USA • FIVE CENTS A GLASS
BEST OF ENEMIES, THE (UKN) see **DUE NEMICI, I** • 1962
BEST OF EVERYTHING, THE • 1959 • Negulesco Jean • USA
BEST OF FRIENDS see **WHAT'S THE MATTER WITH HELEN?** • 1971
BEST OF FRIENDS, THE • 1927 • Edwards Harry J. • SHT • USA
BEST OF FRIENDS, THE • 1982 • Robertson Michael • ASL
BEST OF LAUREL AND HARDY, THE • 1969 • USA
BEST OF LOVES, THE see **ASKLARIN EN GUZELI** • 1968
BEST OF LUCK, THE • 1920 • Smallwood Ray C. • USA
BEST OF SEX AND VIOLENCE, THE • 1981 • Dixon Ken • USA
BEST OF THE BADMEN • 1951 • Russell William D. • USA
BEST OF THE BEST • 1989 • Radler Bob • USA
BEST OF THE BLUES see **ST. LOUIS BLUES** • 1939
BEST OF THE FESTIVAL OF CLAYMATION, THE • 1987 • Vinton Will • ANM • USA
BEST OF TIMES, THE • 1986 • Spottiswoode Roger • USA
BEST OF W. C. FIELDS, THE • 1969 • *Fields W. C.* • ANT • USA • W.C. FIELDS FILM FESTIVAL ○ ONE HOUR WITH W.C. FIELDS
BEST OF WALT DISNEY'S TRUE-LIFE ADVENTURES • 1975 • Algar James • CMP • USA
BEST ON RECORD, THE • 1969 • Warren Mark • MTV • USA • GRAMMY AWARDS
BEST PAIR OF LEGS IN THE BUSINESS, THE • 1972 • Hodson Christopher • UKN
BEST PEOPLE, THE • 1925 • Olcott Sidney • USA
BEST PEOPLE, THE see **FAST AND LOOSE** • 1930
BEST PLACE TO BE, THE • 1979 • Miller David • TVM • USA
BEST PLAYBOY IN JAPAN, THE see **NIPPON ICHI NO IRO-OTOKO** • 1963
BEST POLICY, THE • 1911 • *Solax* • USA
BEST POLICY, THE • 1912 • Dwan Allan • USA
BEST PUPIL, THE see **PIO KALOS O MATHITIS, O** • 1968
BEST REVENGE (USA) see **MISDEAL** • 1981
BEST SELLER • 1987 • Flynn John • USA • HARD COVER
BEST SHOT (UKN) see **HOOSIERS** • 1987
BEST THINGS IN LIFE ARE FREE, THE • 1956 • Curtiz Michael • USA
BEST TO YOU EACH MORNING, THE • 1971 • Scharf Jim • SHT • USA
BEST WAY, THE see **MEILLEURE FACON DE MARCHER, LA** • 1976
BEST WAY TO WALK, THE see **MEILLEURE FACON DE MARCHER, LA** • 1976
BEST WISHES see **SONHOS DE MENINA MOCA** • 1988
BEST WOMAN IN MY LIFE, THE see **NEJLEPSI ZENSKA MEHO ZIVOTE** • 1967
BEST YEARS, THE see **BESTEN JAHRE, DIE** • 1965
BEST YEARS OF OUR LIVES, THE • 1946 • Wyler William • USA • GLORY FOR ME
BESTED BY A BEARD • 1940 • Roberts Charles E. • SHT • USA
BESTEIGUNG DES CHIMBORAZO, DIE • 1988 • Simon Rainer • GDR • CLIMBING OF CHIMBORAZO, THE
BESTEN JAHRE, DIE • 1965 • Rucker Gunther • GDR • BEST YEARS, THE
BESTIA, LA • 1978 • Castellet Antonio, Canudas Jorge • VNZ • BEAST, THE
BESTIA ACORRALADA, LA • 1974 • *Conacine* • MXC
BESTIA DE LA MONTANA, LA see **BEAST OF HOLLOW MOUNTAIN, THE** • 1956
BESTIA DEBE MORIR, LA • 1952 • Barreto Roman Vinoly • ARG • BEAST MUST DIE, THE
BESTIA DESNUDA, LA • 1968 • Vieyra Emilio • MXC • NUDE BEAST, THE
BESTIA HUMANO, LA • 1964 • *Lynch Ana-Maria* • ARG • HUMAN BEAST, THE (USA)
BESTIA IN CALORE, LA • 1978 • Solvay Paolo • ITL
BESTIA MAGNIFICA, LA • 1952 • Urueta Chano • MXC
BESTIA NEGRA, LA • 1938 • Soria Gabriel • MXC
BESTIA UCCIDE A SANGUE FREDDO, LA • 1971 • Di Leo Fernando • ITL • SLAUGHTER HOTEL (USA) ○ COLD BLOODED BEAST (UKN) ○ ASYLUM EROTICA ○ BEAST KILLS IN COLD BLOOD, THE
BESTIAIRE D'AMOUR, LE • 1965 • Calderon Gerald • DOC • FRN
BESTIALITA • 1977 • Mattei Virgilio • ITL
BESTIARIO • 1970 • Teles Luis Galvao, Jaculewicz Bernard • PRT
BESTIAS DE TERROR, LAS • 1972 • *Cardenas Elsa* • MXC • BEASTS OF TERROR, THE
BESTIAS, LAS • 1970 • Bellmunt Francisco • SHT • SPN
BESTIAS NO SE MIRAN AL ESPEJO, LAS • 1975 • Macian Francisco • SPN
BESTIE, DIE • 1922 • George Burton • FRG
BESTIE IM MENSCHEN, DIE • 1921 • Wolff Ludwig • FRG
BESTIE MENSCH see **FLUCHT, DIE** • 1963
BESTIE VON SAN SILOS, DIE • 1925 • Stockel Joe • FRG
BESTIEN DES ALTEN ROM, DIE • 1923 • *Thea Film* • FRG
BESTIJE • 1978 • Nikolic Zivko • YGS • BEAST, THE ○ BEASTS, THE
BESTIOLES ARTISTES, LES • 1911 • Cohl Emile • ANS • FRN
BESTIONE, IL • 1974 • Corbucci Sergio • ITL, FRN • DEUX GRANDES GUEULES (FRN) ○ 8-WHEEL BEAST, THE
BESUCH, DER • 1964 • Wicki Bernhard • FRG, ITL, FRN • VENDETTA DELLA SIGNORA, LA (ITL) ○ RANCUNE, LA (FRN) ○ VISIT, THE (USA)
BESUCH AM ABEND • 1934 • Jacoby Georg • FRG
BESUCH AUF IMRALI • 1979 • Stempel Hans, Ripkens Martin • DOC • FRG • PORTRAIT OF YILMAZ GUNEY
BESUCH AUS HEITEREM HIMMEL • 1959 • Dorfler Ferdinand • FRG
BESZELNEK A SZINEK • 1953 • Kollanyi Agoston • HNG • COLOURS SPEAK, THE
BESZTERCE OSTROMA • 1948 • Keleti Marton • HNG • SIEGE OF BESZTERCZE, THE
BET see **BAAZI** • 1968
BET FLUGELMAN: PUBLIC SCULPTOR • 1979 • Hicks Scott • SHT • ASL
BET ON FIRE see **FOMOU FUNGWAN** • 1988
BET THAT DIDN'T COME OFF, THE • 1907 • Hough Harold • UKN
BET WITH A NAVEL, A see **OHESO DE SHOBU** • 1967
BET WITH A VENGEANCE, A • 1914 • *Britannia Films* • UKN
BET YOUR LIFE • 1948 • Yates Hal • SHT • USA
BETA SOM see **FINCHE DURA LA TEMPESTA** • 1962
BETE, LA • 1975 • Borowczyk Walerian • FRN • BEAST, THE (UKN) ○ BEAST IN HEAT, THE ○ DEATH'S ECSTACY
BETE, LA see **BEEST, HET** • 1981
BETE A L'AFFUT, LA • 1959 • Chenal Pierre • FRN, ITL
BETE A PLAISIR, LA • 1974 • Matalon Eddy • FRN
BETE AUX SEPT MANTEAUX, LA • 1936 • de Limur Jean • FRN • HOMME A LA CAGOULE NOIRE, L'
BETE D'AMOUR, LA see **TANYA'S ISLAND** • 1980
BETE DU VACCARES, LA • 1963 • Colomb De Daunant Denys • FRN
BETE ERRANTE, LA • 1931 • de Gastyne Marco • FRN
BETE HUMAINE, LA • 1938 • Renoir Jean • FRN • HUMAN BEAST, THE (USA) ○ JUDAS WAS A WOMAN (UKN)
BETE LUMINEUSE, LA • 1983 • Perrault Pierre • CND
BETE MAIS DISCIPLINE • 1978 • Zidi Claude • FRN • DUMB BUT DISCIPLINED
BETE NOIRE, LA • 1958 • Rouquier Georges • DCS • FRN
BETE NOIRE, LA • 1983 • Chaput Patrick • FRN
BETE SEXUELLE, LA • 1979 • Bernard-Aubert Claude • FRN
BETE TRAQUEE, LA • 1921 • Le Somptier Rene • FRN
BETES A JOUIR • 1978 • FRN
BETES COMME LES HOMMES • 1925 • Wulschleger Henry, Machin Alfred • FRN
BETES CURIEUSES, LES see **QUE LES "GROS SALAIRES" LEVENT LE DOIGT!** • 1982
BETHANE • 1971 • Shapiro Nesya • CND
BETHSABEE • 1947 • Moguy Leonide • FRN
BETHUNE • 1965 • Brittain Don?, Demeny John • DOC • CND • BETHUNE -HEROS DE NOTRE TEMPS
BETHUNE • 1977 • Till Eric • CND
BETHUNE see **BETHUNE: THE MAKING OF A HERO** • 1989
BETHUNE -HEROS DE NOTRE TEMPS see **BETHUNE** • 1965
BETHUNE: THE MAKING OF A HERO • 1989 • Borsos Philip • USA • BETHUNE
BETIA, OVVERO NELL'AMORE PER OGNI GAUDENZIA CI VUOLE SOFFERENZA • 1971 • De Bosio Gianfranco • ITL
BETO ROCKEFELLER • 1970 • Perroy Oliver • BRZ
BETON DANS LA VILLE, LA • 1964-69 • Rohmer Eric • MTV • FRN
BETRAGEN UNGENUGEND (FRG) see **KANTOR IDEAL** • 1932
BETRAYAL • 1929 • Milestone Lewis • USA
BETRAYAL • 1932 • Fogwell Reginald • UKN
BETRAYAL • 1948 • Micheaux Oscar • USA
BETRAYAL • 1974 • Hessler Gordon • TVM • USA
BETRAYAL • 1978 • Wendkos Paul • TVM • USA
BETRAYAL • 1983 • Jones David • UKN
BETRAYAL see **KATZENSTEG, DER** • 1927
BETRAYAL see **TARAKANOWA** • 1938
BETRAYAL see **IZMYENA** • 1967
BETRAYAL see **UPTIGHT** • 1968
BETRAYAL see **LOPERJENTEN** • 1983
BETRAYAL, THE • 1958 • Morris Ernest • UKN
BETRAYAL, THE see **BOLIBAR** • 1928
BETRAYAL, THE see **FRAULEIN DOKTOR** • 1969
BETRAYAL, THE see **PETOS** • 1988
BETRAYAL AND REVENGE • 1986 • Zheng Kangyu • CHN
BETRAYAL FROM THE EAST • 1945 • Berke William • USA
BETRAYAL OF AFFAIRS see **URAGIRI NO IROGOTO** • 1968
BETRAYAL OF MAGGIE, THE • 1917 • *Murray Charles* • SHT • USA
BETRAYED! • 1916 • Mitchell Howard M. • USA
BETRAYED • 1917 • Walsh Raoul • USA
BETRAYED • 1926 • Barnett Charles • UKN
BETRAYED • 1954 • Reinhardt Gottfried • USA
BETRAYED • 1988 • Costa-Gavras • USA
BETRAYED see **WHEN STRANGERS MARRY** • 1944
BETRAYED see **VITA E BELLA, LA** • 1980
BETRAYED, THE see **MAKHDU UN, AL-** • 1972
BETRAYED BY A HANDPRINT • 1908 • Griffith D. W. • USA
BETRAYED BY INNOCENCE • 1986 • Silverstein Elliot • TVM • USA
BETRAYED BY THE CAMERA • 1916 • *Sorter Irma* • SHT • USA
BETRAYED WOMEN • 1955 • Cahn Edward L. • USA
BETRAYER, THE • 1921 • Smith Beaumont • ASL • 'NEATH THE SOUTHERN CROSS ○ OUR BIT OF THE WORLD ○ MAID OF MAORILAND, A
BETRAYER, THE (USA) see **VANINA VANINI** • 1961
BETROGEN BIS ZUM JUNGSTEN TAG • 1957 • Jung-Alsen Kurt • GDR • DUPED TILL DOOMSDAY
BETROTHAL, THE see **KIHLAUS** • 1955
BETROTHED see **NAGASUGITA HARU** • 1957
BETRUGER DES VOLKES • 1921 • Schunzel Reinhold • FRG
BETRUGER DES VOLKES see **GELD AUF DER STRASSE, DAS** • 1922
BETRUGERISCHE MEDIEN • 1925 • *Vera-Film-Werke* • FRG
BETSURINO UTA • 1960 • Mizuko Harumi • JPN
BETSY • 1983 • Chbib Bachar • CND
BETSY, THE • 1978 • Petrie Daniel • USA • HAROLD ROBBINS' THE BETSY
BETSY ROSS • 1917 • Vale Travers, Cowl George • USA
BETSY'S BURGLAR • 1917 • Powell Paul • USA
BETSY'S LAST CHANCE • 1978 • Zaritsky John • MTV • CND
BETSY'S WEDDING • 1990 • Alda Alan • USA
BETT EINER JUNGFRAU, DAS (ITL) see **VERGINE PER UN BASTARDO** • 1966
BETTA, BETTA • 1971 • Hillman William Byron • USA
BETTA THE GYPSY • 1918 • Raymond Charles • UKN
BETTELGRAFIN, DIE • 1918 • May Joe • FRG
BETTELGRAFIN VOM KURFURSTENDAMM, DIE • 1921 • Eichberg Richard • FRG
BETTELPRINZESSIN, DIE • 1916 • Moest Hubert • FRG
BETTELSTUDENT, DER • 1922 • Steinhoff Hans • FRG
BETTELSTUDENT, DER • 1927 • Fleck Jacob, Fleck Luise • FRG
BETTELSTUDENT, DER • 1931 • Janson Victor • FRG
BETTELSTUDENT, DER • 1936 • Jacoby Georg • FRG • BEGGAR STUDENT, THE
BETTELSTUDENT, DER • 1956 • Jacobs Werner • FRG • BEGGAR STUDENT, THE (USA)
BETTELSTUDENT, DER see **MAZURKA DER LIEBE** • 1957
BETTELSTUDENT ODER: WAS MACH' ICH MIT DEN MADCHEN, DER • 1969 • Verhoeven Michael • FRG
BETTER A WIDOW (USA) see **MEGLIO VEDOVA** • 1967
BETTER BAIT THAN NEVER • 1953 • Kneitel Seymour • ANS • USA
BETTER BET, THE • 1916 • Birch Cecil • UKN
BETTER BUSINESS BUREAU • 1954-55 • Devlin Bernard • DCS • CND
BETTER DAYS • 1913 • Brooke Van Dyke • USA
BETTER DAYS • 1927 • Mattison Frank S. • USA
BETTER DAYS WILL COME see **DIAS MELHORES VIRAO** • 1989
BETTER EDUCATION, JUST NOW see **MEJOR EDUCACION, YA** • 1974
BETTER FATHER, THE • 1913 • *Eclair* • USA
BETTER HALF • 1918 • Gerrard Douglas • USA
BETTER HALF, THE • 1918 • Robertson John S. • USA
BETTER HALVES • 1916 • *Plump & Runt* • SHT • USA
BETTER HOUSING IN B.C. see **COLOMBIE-BRITANNIQUE ET L'HABITATION, LA** • 1967
BETTER INFLUENCE, THE • 1912 • *Majestic* • USA
BETTER INSTINCT, THE • 1916 • Bracken Bertram • SHT • USA
BETTER LATE THAN NEVER • 1914 • Kinder Stuart? • UKN
BETTER LATE THAN NEVER • 1916 • Griffin Frank C., Havez Jean • SHT • USA
BETTER LATE THAN NEVER • 1950 • Donnelly Eddie • ANS • USA
BETTER LATE THAN NEVER • 1979 • Crenna Richard • TVM • USA
BETTER LATE THAN NEVER • 1982 • Forbes Bryan • USA
BETTER LIVING see **BOLJI ZIVOT** • 1989
BETTER MAN, THE • 1911 • Melies Gaston • USA
BETTER MAN, THE • 1912 • *Vitagraph* • USA
BETTER MAN, THE • 1912 • *Reliance* • USA
BETTER MAN, THE • 1914 • Powers Mr. • *Famous Players* • USA
BETTER MAN, THE • 1914 • Smiley Joseph • *Lubin* • USA
BETTER MAN, THE • 1915 • *Majestic* • USA
BETTER MAN, THE • 1915 • Noble John W. • USA • BIGGER MAN, THE
BETTER MAN, THE • 1916 • Hunt Jay • SHT • USA
BETTER MAN, THE • 1921 • Lucas Wilfred • USA
BETTER MAN, THE • 1926 • Dunlap Scott R. • USA
BETTER MAN WINS, THE • 1922 • Perez Marcel, Mattison Frank S. • USA
BETTER MOVIES • 1925 • Roach Hal • SHT • USA
BETTER OFF DEAD • 1985 • Holland Savage Steve • USA
BETTER 'OLE, THE • 1926 • Reisner Charles F. • USA
BETTER 'OLE; OR, THE ROMANCE OF OLD BILL, THE • 1918 • Pearson George • UKN • CARRY ON
BETTER PART, THE • 1912 • *Gem* • USA
BETTER REIGN IN HELL • 1968 • Noyce Phil • SHT • ASL
BETTER SUCCESS, THE • 1913 • *Kinemacolor* • USA
BETTER THAN GOLD • 1912 • *Fischer Marguerita* • USA
BETTER TIMES • 1919 • Vidor King • USA
BETTER TOMORROW see **YINGXIONG BENSE** • 1987
BETTER TOMORROW, A • 1945 • Hammid Alexander • DOC • USA
BETTER TOMORROW III, A see **YINGHUNG BUNSIK III - TSIKYEUNGTSI 90** • 1989

BETTER UNDERSTANDING, A • 1914 • Morrisey Edward • USA
BETTER WAY, THE • 1909 • Griffith D. W. • USA
BETTER WAY, THE • 1911 • *Baggot King* • USA
BETTER WAY, THE • 1913 • Physioc Wray • USA
BETTER WAY, THE • 1914 • *Selig* • USA
BETTER WAY, THE • 1914 • Cabanne W. Christy • *Majestic* • USA
BETTER WAY, THE • 1915 • *Powers* • USA
BETTER WAY, THE • 1926 • Ince Ralph • USA
BETTER WIFE, THE • 1919 • Earle William P. S. • USA
BETTER WOMAN, THE • 1915 • Golden Joseph A. • USA
BETTER WOMAN, THE • 1916 • *Eason Reeves* • SHT • USA
BETTERAVE A SUCRE, LA • 1942 • Proulx Maurice • DCS • CND
BETTINA LOVED A SOLDIER • 1916 • Julian Rupert • USA • ABBE CONSTANTIN, L'
BETTINA'S SUBSTITUTE • 1912 • *Rosson Richard* • USA
BETTKARRIERE • 1971 • von Anutroff Ilja • FRG
BETTLER -G.M.B.H., DIE • 1919 • Neuss Alwin • FRG
BETTLER VOM KOLNER DOM, DER • 1927 • Randolf Rolf • FRG
BETTLER VON ASSISSI, DER • 1920 • Frey Karl • FRG
BETTLER VON SAVERN, DER • 1918 • Hofer Franz • FRG
BETTY AND THE BOYS • 1919 • *Strand* • SHT • USA
BETTY AND THE BUCCANEERS • 1917 • Sturgeon Rollin S. • USA
BETTY AND THE DOCTOR • 1912 • *Buckley May* • USA
BETTY AND THE GAMBLER • 1955 • *Sunset* • SHT • UKN
BETTY AND THE ROSES • 1912 • *White Irving* • USA
BETTY BABY see **HURRAY FOR BETTY BOOP** • 1980
BETTY BE GOOD • 1917 • MacDonald Sherwood • USA
BETTY BECOMES A MAID • 1911 • *Normand Mabel* • USA
BETTY BLOKK-BUSTER FOLLIES • 1976 • Batey Peter • ASL
BETTY BLUE (UKN) see **37'2 LE MATIN** • 1985
BETTY BOOP • 1930-39 • Fleischer Dave • ASS • USA
BETTY BOOP AND GRAMPY • 1935 • Fleischer Dave • ANS • USA
BETTY BOOP AND LITTLE JIMMY • 1936 • Fleischer Dave • ANS • USA
BETTY BOOP AND THE LITTLE KING • 1936 • Fleischer Dave • ANS • USA
BETTY BOOP FOLLIES, THE • 1973 • Fleischer Dave • ANM • USA
BETTY BOOP FOR PRESIDENT • 1932 • Fleischer Dave • ANS • USA
BETTY BOOP LIMITED, THE • 1932 • Fleischer Dave • ANS • USA
BETTY BOOP, M.D. • 1932 • Fleischer Dave • ANS • USA
BETTY BOOP WITH HENRY, THE FUNNIEST LIVING AMERICAN • 1935 • Fleischer Dave • ANS • USA
BETTY BOOP'S BAMBOO ISLE • 1932 • Fleischer Dave • ANS • USA
BETTY BOOP'S BIG BOSS • 1933 • Fleischer Dave • ANS • USA
BETTY BOOP'S BIRTHDAY PARTY • 1933 • Fleischer Dave • ANS • USA
BETTY BOOP'S BIZZY BEE • 1932 • Fleischer Dave • ANS • USA
BETTY BOOP'S CRAZY INVENTIONS • 1933 • Fleischer Dave • ANS • USA
BETTY BOOP'S HALLOWE'EN PARTY • 1933 • Fleischer Dave • ANS • USA
BETTY BOOP'S KER-CHOO • 1933 • Fleischer Dave • ANS • USA
BETTY BOOP'S LIFEGUARD • 1934 • Fleischer Dave • ANS • USA
BETTY BOOP'S LITTLE PAL • 1934 • Fleischer Dave • ANS • USA
BETTY BOOP'S MAY PARTY • 1933 • Fleischer Dave • ANS • USA
BETTY BOOP'S MUSEUM • 1932 • Fleischer Dave • ANS • USA
BETTY BOOP'S PENTHOUSE • 1933 • Fleischer Dave • ANS • USA
BETTY BOOP'S PRIZE SHOW • 1934 • Fleischer Dave • ANS • USA
BETTY BOOP'S RISE TO FAME • 1934 • Fleischer Dave • ANS • USA
BETTY BOOP'S TRIAL • 1934 • Fleischer Dave • ANS • USA
BETTY BOOP'S UPS AND DOWNS • 1932 • Fleischer Dave • ANS • USA
BETTY BURTON AND THE BAD MAN • 1913 • *Lawrence Adelaide* • USA
BETTY BURTON M.D. • 1915 • *Novelty* • USA
BETTY CHESTER • 1926 • *De Forrest Phonofilm* • SHT • UKN
BETTY CO-ED • 1931 • Fleischer Dave • ANS • USA
BETTY CO-ED • 1946 • Dreifuss Arthur • USA • MELTING POT, THE (UKN)
BETTY CO-ED see **SWEETHEART OF THE CAMPUS** • 1941
BETTY FOOLS DEAR OLD DAD • 1912 • *Colwell Goldie* • USA
BETTY FORD STORY, THE • 1987 • Greene David • TVM • USA
BETTY IN BLUNDERLAND • 1934 • Fleischer Dave • ANS • USA
BETTY IN SEARCH OF A THRILL • 1915 • Smalley Phillips? • USA
BETTY IN THE LION'S DEN • 1913 • Thompson Frederick A. • USA
BETTY OF GRAYSTONE • 1916 • Dwan Allan • USA
BETTY SLOW DRAG • 1953 • Borneman Ernest • UKN
BETTY TAKES A HAND • 1918 • Dillon John Francis • USA
BETTY, THE BOY AND THE BIRD • 1916 • Johnson Tefft • SHT • USA
BETTY, THE COXSWAIN • 1912 • *Imp* • USA
BETTY TO THE RESCUE • 1917 • Reicher Frank • USA
BETTY WAKES UP • 1917 • *Compson Betty* • SHT • USA
BETTY'S A LADY see **COUNT OF TEN, THE** • 1928
BETTY'S ADVENTURE • 1918 • *Compson Betty* • SHT • USA
BETTY'S AFFAIR • 1915 • Earle George • SHT • USA
BETTY'S AFFAIR • 1916 • *Vitagraph* • SHT • USA
BETTY'S BABY • 1913 • *Vitagraph* • USA
BETTY'S BACK AGAIN • 1919 • *Strand* • SHT • USA
BETTY'S BANDIT • 1912 • *Nestor* • USA
BETTY'S BANDIT • 1913 • *Frontier* • USA
BETTY'S BIG IDEA • 1917 • *Belasco Jay* • SHT • USA
BETTY'S BIRTHDAY • 1914 • Kellino W. P. • UKN
BETTY'S BOLSHEVIKI • 1919 • *Strand* • SHT • USA
BETTY'S BONDAGE • 1915 • De Grasse Joseph • USA
BETTY'S BUTTONS • 1911 • Merwin Bannister • USA
BETTY'S CHOICE • 1909 • Brooke Van Dyke • USA
BETTY'S DREAM HERO • 1915 • Leonard Robert Z. • USA
BETTY'S ELECTRIC BLANKET • 1910 • *Pathe* • SHT • USA
BETTY'S FIRST SPONGE CAKE • 1915 • MacMackin Archer • USA
BETTY'S HOBO • 1916 • Cochrane R. H. • SHT • USA
BETTY'S NIGHT OUT • 1916 • Noy Wilfred? • UKN
BETTY'S NIGHTMARE • 1912 • Salter Harry • USA
BETWEEN BLOWS AND BOLEROS see **ENTRE GOLPES Y BOLEROS** • 1988
BETWEEN BROTHERS see **BRODER EMALLAN** • 1946
BETWEEN CALAIS AND DOVER see **ENTRE CALAIS ET DOUVRES** • 1897
BETWEEN DANCES • 1913 • *Lubin* • USA
BETWEEN DANGERS • 1927 • Thorpe Richard • USA
BETWEEN ELEVEN AND MIDNIGHT (USA) see **ENTRE ONZE HEURES ET MINUIT** • 1948
BETWEEN EVENING AND MORNING see **ZWISCHEN ABEND UND MORGEN** • 1923
BETWEEN FACING MIRRORS see **INTRE OGLINZI PARALELE** • 1978
BETWEEN FATHER AND SON • 1911 • *Kalem* • USA
BETWEEN FATHER AND SON • 1915 • Vale Travers • USA
BETWEEN FEAR AND DUTY see **IZMEDJU STRAHA I DUZNOSTI** • 1977
BETWEEN FIGHTING MEN • 1932 • Sheldon Forrest • USA
BETWEEN FOUR WINDS see **NA SEMI VETRAKH** • 1962
BETWEEN FRIENDS • 1924 • Blackton J. Stuart • USA
BETWEEN FRIENDS • 1973 • Shebib Donald • CND • ENTRE AMIS
BETWEEN FRIENDS • 1983 • Antonio Lou • TVM • USA
BETWEEN GOD, THE DEVIL AND A WINCHESTER (USA) see **ANCHE NEL WEST, C'ERA UNA VOLTA DIO** • 1968
BETWEEN HALF PAST AND QUARTER TO see **BYLO CTVRT A BUDE PUL** • 1968
BETWEEN HEAVEN AND EARTH • 1957 • Gass Karl • DOC • GDR
BETWEEN HEAVEN AND EARTH • 1958 • Podskalsky Zdenek • CZC
BETWEEN HEAVEN AND EARTH see **BAYN EL SAMAA WA EL ARD** • 1959
BETWEEN HEAVEN AND HELL • 1956 • Fleischer Richard • USA
BETWEEN HEAVEN AND HELL • 1988 • Ernst Franz • DOC • DNM
BETWEEN HEAVEN AND HELL see **BAYN EL SAMAA WA EL ARD** • 1959
BETWEEN HOME AND COUNTRY • 1913 • *Walpole Stanley* • USA
BETWEEN LIFE AND DEATH see **MELLAN LIV OCH DOD** • 1917
BETWEEN LIFE AND DEATH see **YINYANG JIE** • 1988
BETWEEN LIPS AND GLASS see **IZMEDJU USANA I CASE** • 1968
BETWEEN LOVE AND DESIRE (UKN) see **BOIS DES AMANTS, LE** • 1960
BETWEEN LOVE AND DUTY • 1910 • *Kalem* • USA
BETWEEN LOVE AND DUTY see **BOIS DES AMANTS, LE** • 1960
BETWEEN LOVE AND HONOR • 1910 • *Vitagraph* • USA
BETWEEN LOVE AND THE LAW • 1912 • *Duncan William* • USA
BETWEEN MAN AND BEAST • 1917 • Campbell Colin • SHT • USA
BETWEEN MATINEE AND NIGHT • 1915 • *Selig* • USA
BETWEEN MEALS • 1922 • Roach Hal • SHT • USA
BETWEEN MEN • 1915 • Barker Reginald • USA
BETWEEN MEN • 1916 • Hart William S. • USA
BETWEEN MEN • 1935 • Bradbury Robert North • USA
BETWEEN MIDNIGHT • 1916 • De Haven Carter • SHT • USA
BETWEEN MIDNIGHT AND DAWN • 1950 • Douglas Gordon • USA • PROWL CAR
BETWEEN MIRACLES • 1979 • Manfredi Nino • ITL
BETWEEN MOUNTAIN AND SHORE see **MILLI FJALLS OG FJORU** • 1948
BETWEEN ONE AND TWO • 1914 • *Lubin* • USA
BETWEEN ONE AND TWO • 1916 • Drew Sidney • SHT • USA
BETWEEN ONE AND TWO A.M. • 1907 • Cooper Arthur • UKN
BETWEEN OPPOSITE MIRRORS see **INTRE OGLINZI PARALELE** • 1978
BETWEEN ORTON JUNCTION AND FALLONVILLE • 1913 • Seay Charles M. • USA
BETWEEN PARALLEL MIRRORS see **INTRE OGLINZI PARALELE** • 1978
BETWEEN SEPTEMBER AND MAY see **MIEDZY WRZESNIEM A MAJEM** • 1969
BETWEEN SHOWERS • 1914 • Lehrman Henry • USA • CHARLIE AND THE UMBRELLA ○ IN WRONG ○ FLIRTS, THE
BETWEEN TEARS AND SMILES (USA) see **SUN TAI SIL YEN YIN** • 1964
BETWEEN THE ACTS • 1919 • Semon Larry • SHT • USA
BETWEEN THE DANCES • 1905 • *Bitzer Billy (Ph)* • USA
BETWEEN THE DARKNESS AND THE DAWN • 1985 • Levin Peter • TVM • USA
BETWEEN THE GLASS AND THE LIP see **IZMEDJU USANA I CASE** • 1968
BETWEEN THE LINES • 1977 • Silver Joan Micklin • USA
BETWEEN THE NETS see **MORESQUE OBIETTIVO ALLUCINANTE** • 1967
BETWEEN THE RIFLE SIGHTS • 1913 • *Selig* • USA
BETWEEN THE SHEETS • 1984 • Spinelli Anthony • USA • DIARY OF A BED
BETWEEN THE TIDES • 1958 • Keene Ralph • DOC • UKN
BETWEEN THE TWO OF THEM • 1915 • Drew Sidney • USA
BETWEEN THE WORLDS see **BORDERLAND** • 1922
BETWEEN THREE AND FIVE MINUTES • 1972 • Nemec Jan • DOC • CZC
BETWEEN TIME AND ETERNITY(USA) see **ZWISCHEN ZEIT UND EWIGKEIT** • 1956
BETWEEN TWO BROTHERS • 1982 • Lewis Robert • TVM • USA
BETWEEN TWO CLASSES see **ANTARA DUA DARJAT**
BETWEEN TWO FIRES • 1911 • Dawley J. Searle • USA
BETWEEN TWO FIRES • 1912 • *Beggs Lee* • USA
BETWEEN TWO FIRES • 1914 • Jones Edgar • USA
BETWEEN TWO FIRES • 1915 • Van Deusen Courtlandt • USA
BETWEEN TWO HEARTS (USA) see **ZWISCHEN ZWEI HERZEN** • 1934
BETWEEN TWO HUSBANDS • 1922 • *Gabriel Jean* • USA
BETWEEN TWO ROSES see **ENTRE DOS ROSAS** • 1953
BETWEEN TWO SHORES see **MIEDZY BRZEGAMI** • 1962
BETWEEN TWO WARS see **ZWISCHEN ZWEI KRIEGEN** • 1977
BETWEEN TWO WOMEN • 1937 • Seitz George B. • USA • SURROUNDED BY WOMEN
BETWEEN TWO WOMEN • 1944 • Goldbeck Willis • USA • DOCTOR RED ADAMS
BETWEEN TWO WOMEN • 1986 • Avnet Jon • TVM • USA
BETWEEN TWO WOMEN see **ANAMESA SE DHIO YINEKES** • 1967
BETWEEN TWO WORLDS • 1944 • Blatt Edward A. • USA • OUTWARD BOUND
BETWEEN TWO WORLDS • 1952 • Cote Guy-L. • DCS • CND, UKN
BETWEEN TWO WORLDS see **MUDE TOD, DER** • 1921
BETWEEN TWO WORLDS see **BORDERLAND** • 1922
BETWEEN TWO WORLDS see **DELOVAK ATHARA** • 1966
BETWEEN TWO WORLDS see **HADYBBUK** • 1968
BETWEEN TWO WORLDS see **PATESHESTVIE MEZHDU DVA BRYAGA** • 1968
BETWEEN TWO WORLDS (USA) see **LIEBE DES MAHARADSCHA, DIE** • 1936
BETWEEN US see **OKKAR A MILLI** • 1982
BETWEEN US see **COUP DE FOUDRE** • 1983
BETWEEN US BARONS see **OSS BARONER EMELLAN** • 1940
BETWEEN US GIRLS • 1942 • Koster Henry • USA • BOY MEETS BABY ○ LOVE AND KISSES, CAROLINE ○ WHAT HAPPENED, CAROLINE?
BETWEEN US THIEVES see **OSS TJUVAR EMELLAN ELLER EN BURK ANANAS** • 1945
BETWEEN WARS • 1974 • Thornhill Michael • ASL
BETWEEN WIFE AND LADY (USA) see **TSUMA TO ONNA NO AIDA** • 1976
BETWEEN WOMEN AND WIVES (USA) see **TSUMA TO ONNA NO AIDA** • 1976
BETWEEN WORLDS see **MUDE TOD, DER** • 1921
BETWEEN YOUR HANDS see **BAYEN IDEK** • 1959
BETWIXT LOVE AND FIRE see **TWIXT LOVE AND FIRE** • 1913
BETY BOMBA • 1970 • Sganzerla Rogerio • BRZ
BEULAH • 1915 • *Walthall Henry B.* • USA
BEULAH LAND • 1980 • Vogel Virgil W., Falk Harry • TVM • USA
BEUTE, DIE • 1925 • *Convent-Film* • FRG
BEUTE DER ERINNYEN, DIE • 1921 • Rippert Otto • FRG
BEUX DIMANCHES, LES • 1974 • Martin Richard • CND
BEVERLY DE PERALVILLO, LOS • 1971 • *America* • MXC
BEVERLY HILLS BODY SNATCHERS • 1988 • Moston Jon, Soles Titus R. • USA
BEVERLY HILLS BRATS • 1989 • Sotos Jim • USA
BEVERLY HILLS CALL BOYS, THE see **UPSTAIRS ROOM, THE** • 1970
BEVERLY HILLS CONNECTION see **BEVERLY HILLS COWGIRL BLUES** • 1985
BEVERLY HILLS COP • 1984 • Brest Martin • USA
BEVERLY HILLS COP II • 1987 • Scott Anthony • USA
BEVERLY HILLS COWGIRL BLUES • 1985 • Allen Corey • TVM • USA • BEVERLY HILLS CONNECTION
BEVERLY HILLS MADAM • 1986 • Hart Harvey • TVM • USA
BEVERLY HILLS NIGHTMARE see **DIAL RAT FOR TERROR** • 1972
BEVERLY HILLS VAMPIRE • 1989 • Ray Fred Olen • USA
BEVERLY OF GRAUSTARK • 1914 • *Arvidson Linda* • USA
BEVERLY OF GRAUSTARK • 1926 • Franklin Sidney A. • USA
BEVOR DER BLITZ EINSCHLAGT • 1959 • Groschopp Richard • GDR
BEWAFA • 1952 • *Kapoor Raj* • IND
BEWAHRUNGSFRIST see **FREIHEIT IN FESSELN** • 1929
BEWAQOOF • 1960 • *Burman S. D. (M)* • IND
BEWARE • 1919 • Nigh William • USA
BEWARE • 1946 • Pollard Bud • USA
BEWARE MY BRETHREN (USA) see **FIEND, THE** • 1971
BEWARE MY LOVELY • 1952 • Horner Harry • USA • DAY WITHOUT END
BEWARE OF BACHELORS • 1928 • Del Ruth Roy • USA • NO QUESTIONS ASKED
BEWARE OF BARNACLE BILL • 1935 • Fleischer Dave • ANS • USA
BEWARE OF BLONDES • 1928 • Seitz George B. • USA
BEWARE OF BLONDIE • 1950 • Bernds Edward • USA
BEWARE OF BLONDS • 1918 • *Rhodes Billie* • USA
BEWARE OF BOARDERS • 1918 • Fishback Fred C. • SHT • USA
BEWARE OF CHILDREN (USA) see **NO KIDDING** • 1960
BEWARE OF LADIES • 1937 • Pichel Irving • USA
BEWARE OF MARRIED MEN • 1928 • Mayo Archie • USA
BEWARE OF PITY • 1946 • Elvey Maurice • UKN
BEWARE OF REDHEADS • 1945 • Yates Hal • SHT • USA
BEWARE OF STRANGERS • 1918 • Campbell Colin • USA
BEWARE OF THE BRETHREN see **FIEND, THE** • 1971
BEWARE OF THE BRIDE • 1920 • Mitchell Howard M. • USA
BEWARE OF THE BULL see **THREE MAIDEN LADIES AND A BULL**
BEWARE OF THE DOG • 1915 • *World* • USA
BEWARE OF THE DOG • 1923 • La Cava Gregory • SHT • USA
BEWARE OF THE DOG • 1964 • Ford Phil • SRL • UKN
BEWARE OF THE ENEMY see **ETHIRIGAL JAGGIRITHAI** • 1967
BEWARE OF THE HOLY WHORE (USA) see **WARNUNG VOR EINER HEILIGEN NUTTE** • 1970
BEWARE OF THE LAW • 1922 • Douglas W. A. S. • USA • WATERED STOCK
BEWARE OF THE RAFFLED TURKEY • 1905 • Green Tom? • UKN
BEWARE OF THE YETI see **OSTROZNIE YETI** • 1958

BEWARE OF WIDOWS • 1927 • Ruggles Wesley • USA
BEWARE OF WOMEN • 1933 • King George • UKN
BEWARE OF ZEPPELINS • 1915 • *Horseshoe* • USA
BEWARE, SPOOKS! • 1939 • Sedgwick Edward • USA
BEWARE THE BLACK WIDOW • 1968 • Crane Larry • USA
BEWARE! THE BLOB • 1972 • Hagman Larry • USA • SON OF BLOB
BEWARE THE CAR! see **BEREGIS AVTOMOBILYA!** • 1966
BEWARE THE HOLY WHORE see **WARNUNG VOR EINER HEILIGEN NUTTE** • 1970
BEWARE THE WOMAN see **UNTAMED YOUTH** • 1924
BEWILDERED TRAVELLER, A see **TEMPETE DANS UN CHAMBRE A COUCHER, UNE** • 1901
BEWILDERING CABINET, THE (USA) see **PLACARD INFERNAL, LE** • 1907
BEWILDERING TRANSFORMATIONS • 1912 • Booth W. R. • UKN
BEWITCHED • 1910 • *Lux* • FRN
BEWITCHED • 1945 • Oboler Arch • USA • ALTER EGO
BEWITCHED see **EMBRUJO** • 1941
BEWITCHED BOXING GLOVES, THE • 1910 • Bouwmeester Theo? • UKN
BEWITCHED BRETON • 1908 • *Kleine* • FRN
BEWITCHED BUNNY • 1953 • Jones Charles M. • ANS • USA
BEWITCHED BY HOPE see **RONTAS ES REMENYSEG** • 1982
BEWITCHED DUNGEON (USA) see **TOUR MAUDITE, LA** • 1901
BEWITCHED FIANCEE, THE see **FIANCEE ENSORCELEE, LA** • 1903
BEWITCHED HAND, THE see **ENCHANTED HAND, THE** • 1967
BEWITCHED IN THE WHITE MOUNTAINS see **EMBRUJO EN CERROS BLANCOS** • 1955
BEWITCHED INN, THE (USA) see **AUBERGE ENSORCELEE, L'** • 1897
BEWITCHED MANOR HOUSE, THE • 1909 • *Pathe* • FRN
BEWITCHED MATCHES • 1912-14 • Cohl Emile • ANS • USA
BEWITCHED MATCHES • 1913 • *Eclair* • FRN
BEWITCHED MESSENGER, THE • 1910 • *Bat & Brockliss* • USA
BEWITCHED RIDERS, THE see **JINETES DE LA BRUJA, LOS** • 1965
BEWITCHED SON-IN-LAW • 1907 • *Pathe* • FRN
BEWITCHED SPIRITS OF THE CASTLE OF WHITE WAX, THE see **BYAKUROJO NO YOKI** • 1957
BEWITCHED TRAVELER, THE (USA) see **JONAH MAN: OR, THE TRAVELLER BEWITCHED, THE** • 1904
BEWITCHED TRUNK, THE (USA) see **COFFRE ENCHANTE, LE** • 1904
BEWITCHED WINDOW, THE • 1911 • *Pathe* • FRN
BEWITCHING KISSES (USA) see **BESOS BRUJOS** • 1937
BEWITCHING LOVE OF MADAME PAI, THE see **BYAKU FUJIN NO YUREN** • 1956
BEWITCHING OF THE FLESH see **NIKU NO KYOH-EN** • 1968
BEWOONBAAR LAND, EEN • 1968 • Wiegel Jan • SHT • NTH
BEYAZ ATLI ADAM • 1965 • Conturk Remzi • TRK
BEYAZ BISIKLET • 1986 • Yonder Nisan • TRK • WHITE BICYCLE, THE
BEYAZ MENDIL • 1955 • Akat Lutfu • TRK
BEYOGLU CANAVARI • 1968 • Gorec Ertem • TRK • MONSTER OF BEYOGLU, THE
BEYOGLU'NUN ARKA YAKASI • 1987 • Goren Serif • TRK • BACK STREETS OF BEYOGLU, THE
BEYOND • 1921 • Taylor William D. • USA
BEYOND, THE • *Maccoll Katherine*
BEYOND, THE see **ALDILA, L'** • 1981
BEYOND A REASONABLE DOUBT • 1956 • Lang Fritz • USA
BEYOND ADVENTURE see **MAS ALLA DE LA AVENTURA** • 1980
BEYOND ALL IS LOVE • 1915 • Greene Clay M. • USA
BEYOND ALL LAW • 1913 • O'Sullivan Tony • USA
BEYOND ALL LIMITS see **FLOR DE MAYO** • 1957
BEYOND ALL ODDS • 1926 • Neitz Alvin J. • USA
BEYOND ALL REASONABLE DOUBT • 1974 • Haldane Don • CND
BEYOND AND BACK • 1978 • Conway James L. • DOC • USA
BEYOND ATLANTIS • 1974 • Romero Eddie • PHL, USA
BEYOND BELIEF • 1976 • *Geller Uri* • USA
BEYOND BENGAL • 1934 • Schenck Harry
BEYOND CONTROL (USA) see **SOMMERSPROSSEN** • 1968
BEYOND DEATH see **AU-DELA DE LA MORT** • 1922
BEYOND DEATH'S DOOR • 1979 • Schellerup Henning • USA
BEYOND DECAY see **CHORAKU NO KANATA** • 1923
BEYOND DERANGED • 1988 • Vincent Chuck • USA
BEYOND ENDURANCE • 1910 • *Dramagraph* • USA
BEYOND EVIL • 1980 • Freed Herb • USA
BEYOND EVIL see **OLTRE IL BENE E IL MALE** • 1977
BEYOND FEAR (USA) see **AU-DELA DE LA PEUR** • 1974
BEYOND FORTY see **OVER FORTY** • 1982
BEYOND GENOCIDE • 1987 • Bose Tapan K., Mulay Suhasini • DOC • IND
BEYOND GLORY • 1948 • Farrow John • USA • LONG GREY LINE, THE
BEYOND GOOD AND EVIL (UKN) see **OLTRE IL BENE E IL MALE** • 1977
BEYOND HILLS AND MOUNTAINS • 1964 • Mesaros Titus • DOC • RMN
BEYOND HIS FONDEST HOPES • 1915 • *Eclectic* • USA
BEYOND LONDON LIGHTS • 1928 • Terriss Tom • USA • KITTY CARSTAIRS (UKN)
BEYOND LOVE AND EVIL (USA) see **PHILOSOPHIE DANS LE BOUDOIR, LA** • 1969
BEYOND LOVE AND HATE see **AI TO NIKUSHIME NO KANATA** • 1951
BEYOND MOMBASA • 1956 • Marshall George • USA
BEYOND MY REACH • 1990 • Burstall Dan • ASL
BEYOND OBSESSION see **OLTRE LA PORTA** • 1983
BEYOND OUR HORIZON • 1939 • Walker Norman • UKN
BEYOND PRICE • 1921 • Dawley J. Searle • USA
BEYOND PRICE • 1947 • Williamson Cecil H. • UKN
BEYOND REASON • 1970 • Mangiamele Giorgio • ASL
BEYOND REASON • 1977 • Savalas Telly • USA • MATI
BEYOND REASONABLE DOUBT • 1980 • Laing John • NZL
BEYOND RECALL • 1916 • Hansel Howell • SHT • USA
BEYOND REPROACH • 1913 • *Kinemacolor* • USA
BEYOND SEX see **MAS ALLA DEL SEXO** • 1967
BEYOND SILENCE see **MAS ALLA DEL SILENCIO**
BEYOND SING THE WOODS see **UND EWIG SINGEN DIE WALDER** • 1959
BEYOND SORROW, BEYOND PAIN see **SMARTGRANSEN** • 1983
BEYOND TERROR • 1980 • Aznar Tomas • SPN
BEYOND THE AEGEAN • 1989 • Kazan Elia • USA
BEYOND THE BARRICADE see **HAR JEG RET TIL AT TAGE MIT EGET LIV** • 1917
BEYOND THE BERMUDA TRIANGLE • 1975 • Graham William A. • TVM • USA
BEYOND THE BLUE HORIZON • 1942 • Santell Alfred • USA • MALAYA
BEYOND THE BORDER • 1925 • Dunlap Scott R. • USA
BEYOND THE BORDER (UKN) see **HONOR OF THE MOUNTED** • 1932
BEYOND THE BRIDGE see **DINCOLO DE POD** • 1974
BEYOND THE BRIDGE see **TASTE OF SIN, A** • 1983
BEYOND THE CITIES • 1930 • Blackwell Carlyle • UKN
BEYOND THE CITY • 1914 • Pollard Harry? • USA
BEYOND THE CROSS ROADS • 1922 • Carleton Lloyd B. • USA • BEYOND THE CROSSROADS
BEYOND THE CROSSROADS see **BEYOND THE CROSS ROADS** • 1922
BEYOND THE CURTAIN • 1960 • Bennett Compton • UKN
BEYOND THE DARKNESS • 1974 • Walter Michael • FRG
BEYOND THE DARKNESS see **BUIO OMEGA** • 1979
BEYOND THE DOOR 2 see **SHOCK TRANSFERT SUSPENCE HYPNOS** • 1977
BEYOND THE DOOR (USA) see **CHI SEI?** • 1974
BEYOND THE DOOR (USA) see **OLTRE LA PORTA** • 1983
BEYOND THE DREAMS OF AVARICE • 1920 • Bentley Thomas • UKN
BEYOND THE FIRE • 1988 • Ayyari Kianoush • IRN
BEYOND THE FLOATING CLOUD see **KUMO NAGARURU HATENI** • 1953
BEYOND THE FOG see **TOWER OF EVIL** • 1972
BEYOND THE FOREST • 1949 • Vidor King • USA
BEYOND THE FOREST see **TAM ZA LESEM** • 1962
BEYOND THE FORESTS, BEYOND THE WOODS see **ZA BOREM ZA LASEM** • 1961
BEYOND THE FRINGE see **SHIMANA PERIYE** • 1978
BEYOND THE GATE see **HUMAN EXPERIMENTS** • 1979
BEYOND THE GREAT WALL • 1967 • Li Han-Hsiang • HKG
BEYOND THE HORIZON see **OTVAD HORIZONTA** • 1960
BEYOND THE HORIZON (USA) see **VAHAN** • 1937
BEYOND THE LAST FRONTIER • 1943 • Bretherton Howard • USA
BEYOND THE LAST MOUNTAIN • Jabbar Javed • PKS
BEYOND THE LAW • 1911 • Trimble Larry • USA • CODE OF THE HILLS, THE
BEYOND THE LAW • 1913 • *Nestor* • USA
BEYOND THE LAW • 1916 • Oyen Henry • SHT • USA
BEYOND THE LAW • 1918 • Marston Theodore • USA
BEYOND THE LAW • 1930 • McGowan J. P. • USA
BEYOND THE LAW • 1934 • Lederman D. Ross • USA
BEYOND THE LAW • 1968 • Mailer Norman • USA • BEYOND THE LAW -BLUE
BEYOND THE LAW • 1968 • Pennebaker D. A. • USA
BEYOND THE LAW see **FLYING HOOFS** • 1925
BEYOND THE LAW see **SEALED LIPS** • 1941
BEYOND THE LAW see **AL AI LA DELLA LEGGE** • 1968
BEYOND THE LAW see **LAIN ULKOPUOLELLA** • 1988
BEYOND THE LAW -BLUE see **BEYOND THE LAW** • 1968
BEYOND THE LAW (UKN) see **LAW RUSTLERS, THE** • 1923
BEYOND THE LAW (UKN) see **CALIFORNIANS, THE** • 1937
BEYOND THE LIMIT • 1983 • Mackenzie John • UKN • HONORARY CONSUL, THE
BEYOND THE LINE OF DUTY see **MAGISKA CIRKELN, DEN** • 1971
BEYOND THE LIVING see **NURSE SHERRI** • 1978
BEYOND THE LIVING DEAD see **ORGIA DE LOS MUERTOS, LA** • 1972
BEYOND THE MIST • 1985 • Asgari-Nasab Manoochehr • IRN
BEYOND THE MOON • 1954 • *Reed Roland (P)* • MTV • USA
BEYOND THE MOUNTAINS see **MAS ALLA DE LAS MONTANAS** • 1967
BEYOND THE NORTH WIND • 1983 • O'Mara John • IRL
BEYOND THE OCEAN see **OLTRE L'OCEANO** • 1990
BEYOND THE OUTBACK • 1958 • Robinson Lee • DOC • ASL
BEYOND THE PECOS • 1945 • Hillyer Lambert • USA • BEYOND THE SEVEN SEAS (UKN)
BEYOND THE PLAINS WHERE MAN WAS BORN • 1976 • Raeburn Michael • UKN, FRN
BEYOND THE POSEIDON ADVENTURE • 1979 • Allen Irwin • USA
BEYOND THE PURPLE HILLS • 1950 • English John • USA
BEYOND THE RAINBOW • 1922 • Cabanne W. Christy • USA
BEYOND THE REEF • 1981 • Clark Frank C. • USA • SHARK BOY OF BORA BORA ○ SEA KILLER
BEYOND THE RIO GRANDE • 1930 • Webb Harry S. • USA
BEYOND THE RISING MOON • 1988 • Cook Philip • USA
BEYOND THE RIVER see **JENSEITS DES STROMES** • 1922
BEYOND THE RIVER (UKN) see **BOTTOM OF THE BOTTLE, THE** • 1956
BEYOND THE ROCKIES • 1909 • *Centaur* • USA
BEYOND THE ROCKIES • 1926 • Nelson Jack • USA
BEYOND THE ROCKIES • 1932 • Allen Fred • USA • SUNRISE TRAIL
BEYOND THE ROCKS • 1922 • Wood Sam • USA
BEYOND THE SACRAMENTO • 1940 • Hillyer Lambert • USA • POWER OF JUSTICE (UKN)
BEYOND THE SANDS see **DINCOLO DE NISIPURI** • 1973
BEYOND THE SEASONAL WIND see **KISETSUFU NO KANATANI** • 1958
BEYOND THE SEVEN SEAS see **BAK SJU HAV** • 1989
BEYOND THE SEVEN SEAS (UKN) see **BEYOND THE PECOS** • 1945
BEYOND THE SHADOWS • 1918 • McLaughlin J. W. • USA
BEYOND THE SIERRAS • 1928 • Grinde Nick • USA
BEYOND THE SQUARE see **TUL A KALVIN-TEREN** • 1955
BEYOND THE STARS see **UNEARTHLY STRANGER** • 1963
BEYOND THE SUN see **MAS ALLA DEL SOL** • 1975
BEYOND THE SUNSET see **FEIYIT WONGFAN** • 1988
BEYOND THE SWAN-LIKE CLOUDS • 1956 • Armand P. • USS
BEYOND THE TIME BARRIER • 1960 • Ulmer Edgar G. • USA
BEYOND THE TIME OF DUTY • 1942 • Seiler Lewis • USA
BEYOND THE TRAIL • 1915 • *Empire* • USA
BEYOND THE TRAIL • 1916 • Wilson Ben • SHT • USA
BEYOND THE TRAIL • 1926 • Herman Al • USA
BEYOND THE UNIVERSE • 1981 • Emenegger Robert, Sandler Allan • USA
BEYOND THE VALLEY OF THE DOLLS • 1970 • Meyer Russ • USA
BEYOND THE VEIL see **SECRET KINGDOM, THE** • 1925
BEYOND THE WALL see **MUDE TOD, DER** • 1921
BEYOND THE WALLS see **ME'ACHOREI HA'SORAGIM** • 1984
BEYOND THE WHITE GLACIER see **SHIROKI HYOGA NO HATENI** • 1978
BEYOND THE WOOD see **ZA BOREM ZA LASEM** • 1961
BEYOND THE WOOD see **TAM ZA LESEM** • 1962
BEYOND THERAPY • 1987 • Altman Robert • USA
BEYOND THESE WALLS see **ME'ACHOREI HA'SORAGIM** • 1984
BEYOND THESE WORDS • 1983 • Day Subhash • DOC • IND
BEYOND THIS PLACE • 1959 • Cardiff Jack • UKN • WEB OF EVIDENCE (USA)
BEYOND TIME see **NINCS IDO** • 1973
BEYOND TOMORROW • 1940 • Sutherland A. Edward • USA • AND SO GOODBYE
BEYOND YOUTH'S PARADISE • 1914 • *Drew Lillian* • USA
BEYROUTH A DEFAUT D'ETRE MORT • 1983 • Rached Tahani • CND
BEZ BEBEK • 1987 • Ayca Engin • TRK • RAG DOLL
BEZ KONCA see **BEZ KONVA** • 1984
BEZ KONVA • 1984 • Kieslowski Krzysztof • PLN • NO END ○ BEZ KONCA
BEZ MILOSCI • 1980 • Sass Barbara • PLN • WITHOUT LOVE
BEZ STRAKHA UPREKA • 1963 • Mitta Alexander • USS • WITHOUT FEAR OF REPROACH
BEZ SVIDETELEI • 1983 • Mikhalkov Nikita • USS • WITHOUT WITNESSES ○ WITHOUT WITNESS ○ BES SVIDETELEY
BEZ VINI VINOVATIYE • 1945 • Petrov Vladimir • USS • GUILTY THOUGH INNOCENT
BEZ ZNIECZULENIA • 1978 • Wajda Andrzej • PLN • ROUGH TREATMENT ○ WITHOUT ANAESTHETIC ○ WITHOUT ANAESTHESIA
BEZAUBERNDE ARABELLA • 1959 • von Ambesser Axel • FRG
BEZAUBERNDES FRAULEIN see **WER WAGT -GEWINNT!** • 1935
BEZAUBERNDES MADCHEN, EIN • 1963 • Frank Hubert • FRG
BEZETEN -HET GAT IN DE MUUR see **BESESSEN -DAS LOCH IN DER WAND** • 1969
BEZHIN LUG • 1937 • Eisenstein Sergei • USS • BEZHIN MEADOW ○ TIME IN THE SUN
BEZHIN MEADOW see **BEZHIN LUG** • 1937
BEZLUDNA PLANETA • 1962 • Debowski Krzysztof • ANS • PLN • UNINHABITED PLANET
BEZUCELNA PROCHAZKA • 1930 • Hammid Alexander • SHT • CZC • AIMLESS WALK
BGS OF GINZA see **YORU NO NETTAIGYO** • 1965
BHAGWAN SHRI KRISHNA • 1950 • Yagnik Raja • IND • GOD LORD KRISHNA
BHAGYA CHAKRA • 1935 • Bose Nitin • IND • WHEEL OF FATE, THE
BHAGYA CHAKRAMU • 1968 • Reddy K. V. • IND • WHEEL OF FATE
BHAGYADEVATHE • 1968 • Ratnagar D. • IND • GOD OF FORTUNE
BHAKT PRAHLAD • 1934 • Bhave K. P. • IND • DEVOTEE PRAHLAD
BHAKTA DHRUV • 1947 • Kumar Shanti • IND • DHRUV, DEVOTEE TO THE GOD
BHAKTA KABIR • 1935 • *Krishnaih Radha* • IND
BHAKTA-KE-BHAGWAN • 1934 • Gunjal V. M. • IND • DEVOTEE TO THE GOD
BHAKTA PRAHLAD • 1924 • *Hindustan* • IND • PRAHLAD, DEVOTEE TO THE GOD
BHAKTA PRAHLAD • 1924 • *Maharaashtra* • IND • PRAHLAD, DEVOTEE TO THE GOD
BHAKTA PRAHLADA • 1967 • Narayanamoorthy C. H. • IND • SAINT PRAHLADA
BHAKTA RATNA • 1957 • Thakur Ramchandra • IND
BHAKTA SURDAS • 1938 • *Prabhat* • IND • SURDAS, DEVOTEE TO THE GOD
BHAKTA VIDUR • 1919 • *Narayandas Dwarkadas/ Patel Manecklal(P)* • IND • VIRUR, DEVOTEE TO THE GOD
BHAKTARAJ • 1944 • Desai Jayant • IND
BHAKTHA KUCHELA • 1935 • Subrahmanyam K. • IND • KUCHELA, DEVOTEE TO THE GOD
BHAKTHA KUCHELA • 1963 • Subramoniam P. • IND • KUCHELA, DEVOTEE TO THE GOD
BHAKTHA TULASIDAS • 1937 • Sekhar Raja Chandra • IND • TULASIDAS, DEVOTEE TO THE GOD
BHAKTI • 1970 • Bejart Maurice • BLG
BHALE KODALU • 1968 • Balachandar K. • IND • DAUGHTER-IN-LAW
BHALE MONAGADU • 1968 • Vittalachari B. • IND • SHOW-OFF, THE
BHARAT MATA • 1957 • Khan Mehboob • IND • MOTHER INDIA (UKN)
BHARRYA • 1968 • Prakash Rao K. S. • IND • WIFE
BHARTRUHARI • 1945 • Doshi Chaturbhuj • IND
BHASMASUR MOHINI • 1913 • Phalke Dada • IND • LEGEND OF BHASMASUR, THE
BHASMASUR MOHINI see **BHOLA SHANKAR** • 1951
BHAVANA • 1984 • Bhatt Pravin • IND • IDEAL
BHAVANI • 1967 • Ramanna T. R. • IND • GODDESS BHAVANI
BHAVNI BHAVAI • 1980 • Mehta Ketan • IND • FOLK TALE, A
BHEDI TRISHUL • 1938 • Khan A. M. • IND
BHEMA • 1985 • SAF
BHIKKUNI • 1983 • SKR • BUDDHIST NUN'S STORY
BHIM'S VICTORY see **JAI BHIM** • 1949
BHISMA PRATIGYA • 1950 • Painter Vasant • IND
BHOLA SHANKAR • 1951 • Bedekar Vishram • IND • BHASMASUR MOHINI ○ SIMPLE SHANKAR
BHONG see **BBONG** • 1985

BHOO KAILAS • 1938 • Nadkarni Sundarao • IND
BHOOKH • 1947 • *Biswas Anil (M)* • IND
BHOOLOKA RAMBHAI • 1958 • Yoganand D. • IND
BHOOT BUNGLA • 1965 • *Mahmood* • IND • HORROR THAT HORRIFIES
BHOWANI JUNCTION • 1956 • Cukor George • UKN, USA
BHUMIKA • 1976 • Benegal Shyam • IND • ROLE, THE
BHUTIO MAHAL • 1932 • Desai Jayant • IND • HAUNTED HOUSE
BHUVAN SHOME • 1969 • Sen Mrinal • IND • MR. SHOME
BI AMR AL-HUBB • 1965 • Salman Mohammed • LBN • A CAUSE DE L'AMOUR
BI-ENERGIE • 1984 • Payer Roch Christophe (c/d) • DOC • CND
BIALE ZNIWA • 1978 • Domaradzki Jerzy • PLN • WHITE HARVEST
BIALY MURZYN • 1939 • Buczkowski Leonard • PLN • WHITE NEGRO, THE
BIALY NIEDZWIEDZ • 1959 • Zarzycki Jerzy • PLN • WHITE BEAR
BIANCA • 1913 • Thornby Robert T. • USA
BIANCA • 1984 • Moretti Nanni • ITL
BIANCA, DIE HELDIN VON BASSANO • 1923 • *Filmatelier Nymphenburg* • FRG
BIANCA FORGETS • 1915 • *La Badie Florence* • USA
BIANCAVE E I SETTE LADRI • 1949 • Gentilomo Giacomo • ITL
BIANCHENG • 1985 • Ling Zhifeng • CHN • BORDER TOWN
BIANCHI CAVALLI D'AGOSTO • 1975 • Del Balzo Raimondo • ITL • WHITE HORSES OF SUMMER, THE ○ WHITE HORSES IN AUGUST
BIANCHI PASCOLI • 1947 • Emmer Luciano, Gras Enrico • ITL
BIANCO E NERO • 1975 • Pietrangeli Paolo • ITL
BIANCO, IL GIALLO, IL NERO, IL • 1975 • Corbucci Sergio • ITL, FRN, SPN • BLANC, LE JAUNE ET LE NOIR, LE (FRN)
BIANCO, ROSSO E.. • 1972 • Lattuada Alberto • ITL, FRN, SPN • BONNE PLANQUE, LA (FRN) ○ WHITE SISTER (USA) ○ SIN, THE
BIANCO, ROSSO E VERDONE • 1980 • Verdone Carlo • ITL • WHITE, RED AND VERDONE GREEN
BIANCO, ROSSO, GIALLO, ROSA • 1965 • Mida Massimo • ITL • LOVE FACTORY (USA) ○ WHITE, RED, YELLOW AND PINK
BIANCO VESTITO PER MARIALE, UN • 1972 • Scavolini Romano • ITL
BIBBI, ELIN AND CHRISTINA • 1985 • Kolsto Egil • NRW
BIBBIA, LA • 1966 • Huston John • ITL, USA • BIBLE.. IN THE BEGINNING, THE (USA)
BIBERPELZ, DER • 1928 • Schonfelder Erich • FRG • BEAVER COAT, THE
BIBERPELZ, DER • 1937 • von Alten Jurgen • FRG • BEAVER COAT, THE
BIBERPELZ, DER • 1949 • Engel Erich • GDR
BIBERSPUR • Beck Walter • GDR • BEAVER'S TRACE
BIBI FRICOTIN • 1950 • Blistene Marcel • FRN
BIBI LA PUREE • 1925 • Champreux Maurice • FRN
BIBI LA PUREE • 1934 • Joannon Leo • FRN
BIBI -SUNDIG UND SUSS • 1974 • Sarno Joe • FRG, SWD
BIBITTES DE CHROMAGNON, LES • 1971 • Desbiens Francine • ANS • CND
BIBLE! • 1974 • *White Bo* • USA • IN THE BEGINNING
BIBLE, LA • 1976 • Carne Marcel • DOC • FRN
BIBLE, THE • 1921-22 • *Sacred Films* • SHS • USA
BIBLE.. IN THE BEGINNING, THE (USA) see **BIBBIA, LA** • 1966
BIBLE STORIES • 1980 • *Halas John (P)* • ANS • UKN
BIBLIOTEKET ER ABENT • 1948 • Melson Soren • DNM • LIBRARY IS OPEN, THE
BIBLIOTHEQUES, LES • 1963 • Borowczyk Walerian • ANS • FRN
BIBO NI TSUMI ARI • 1959 • Masumura Yasuzo • JPN • SO BEAUTIFUL IT'S A SIN
BIBOU NO MIYAKO • 1957 • Matsubayashi Shue • JPN • BEAUTY CAPITAL
BIBULOUS CLOTHIER, THE • 1899 • *Edison* • USA
BICAZ, THE 563 LEVEL • 1959 • Iliesu Mirel • DOC • RMN
BICE SKORO PROPAST SVETA see **I DODJE PROPAST SVETA** • 1969
BICEP BUILT FOR TWO, A • 1955 • Kneitel Seymour • ANS • USA
BICHES, LES • 1968 • Chabrol Claude • FRN, ITL • GIRLFRIENDS, THE ○ HETEROSEXUAL, THE ○ DOES, THE
BICHO DA SEDA, O • 1934 • do Canto Jorge Brum • SHT • PRT
BICHO DA SERRA DE SINTRA, O • 1927 • Fonseca Joao De Sousa • PRT
BICHON • 1935 • Rivers Fernand • FRN
BICHON • 1947 • Jayet Rene • FRN
BICICLETA, LA • 1973 • Molinari Oscar • VNZ • BICYCLE, THE
BICICLETAS SON PARA EL VERANO, LAS • 1983 • Chavarri Jaime • SPN • BICYCLES ARE FOR THE SUMMER
BICYCLE, THE see **ROWER** • 1957
BICYCLE, THE see **BICICLETA, LA** • 1973
BICYCLE AND THE WITCH see **HEKSEN OG CYKLISTEN** • 1909
BICYCLE BUG'S DREAM, THE • 1911 • *Imp* • USA
BICYCLE FLIRT, THE • 1928 • *Sennett Mack (P)* • SHT • USA
BICYCLE HORA • 1968 • Perera K. A. W. • SLN • BICYCLE THIEF
BICYCLE POUR PIT, UN • 1968 • Chabot Jean • SHT • CND
BICYCLE RACE see **W POGONI ZA ZOLTA KOSZULKA** • 1954
BICYCLE RUN • 1988 • Makhmalbaf Mohsen • IRN • CYCLIST, THE
BICYCLE THIEF see **BICYCLE HORA** • 1968
BICYCLE THIEF, THE • 1904 • *Urban Trading Co* • UKN
BICYCLE THIEF, THE see **LADRI DI BICICLETTE** • 1948
BICYCLE THIEVES (UKN) see **LADRI DI BICICLETTE** • 1948
BICYCLES ARE FOR THE SUMMER see **BICICLETAS SON PARA EL VERANO, LAS** • 1983
BICYCLES REPAIRED • 1908 • Fitzhamon Lewin? • UKN
BICYCLETTES DE BELSIZE, LES • 1968 • Hickox Douglas • UKN
BICZ BOZY • 1967 • Kaniewska Maria • PLN • SCOURGE OF GOD, THE ○ SCOURGE, THE
BID FOR BOUNTY, A • 1915 • Birch Cecil • UKN
BID FOR FORTUNE, A • 1911 • Haldane Bert? • UKN
BID FOR FORTUNE, A • 1917 • Morgan Sidney • UKN
BID IT UP SUCKER • 1944 • MacKay Jim • DCS • CND
BIDASSES AU PENSIONNAT, LES • 1978 • Vocoret Michel • FRN
BIDASSES AUX GRANDES MANOEUVRES, LES • 1981 • Delpard Raphael • FRN
BIDASSES EN CAVALE, LES • 1976 • Clair Philippe • FRN
BIDASSES EN FOLIE, LES • 1971 • Zidi Claude • FRN • FIVE CRAZY BOYS, THE (UKN)
BIDASSES EN VADROUILLE, LES • 1978 • Caza Christian • FRN
BIDASSES S'EN VONT EN GUERRE, LES • 1974 • Zidi Claude • FRN, ITL • CINQUE MATTI VANNO IN GUERRA (ITL)
BIDAYA WA NIHAYA see **BEDAYA WA NEHAYAT** • 1960
BIDDY • 1984 • Edzard Christine • UKN
BIDDY BRADY'S BOY • 1915 • *Chamberlin Riley* • USA
BIDDY ON HER METTLE • 1913 • *Komic* • USA
BIDESIYA • 1968 • Tripathi S. M. • IND • FOREIGNER
BIDON D'OR, LE • 1932 • Christian-Jaque • FRN
BIDONATA, LA • 1978 • Ercoli Luciano • ITL
BIDONE, IL • 1955 • Fellini Federico • ITL, FRN • SWINDLERS, THE (UKN) ○ SWINDLE, THE(USA)
BIDROHI • 1935 • *Burman S. D. (M)* • IND
BIEDRONKA • 1964 • Lorek Leszek • PLN • LADYBUG, THE
BIEG • 1971 • Kosinski Bohdan • PLN • RELAY EVENT, A
BIELLES DES SABLES • 1952 • Huisman Jean-Claude • SHT • FRN
BIEN AIMEE, LA • 1966 • Doniol-Valcroze Jacques • FRN
BIEN-AIMEE, LA • 1980 • Bouchard Michel • CND • BELOVED, THE
BIEN AMADA, LA • 1951 • Fernandez Emilio • MXC
BIEN ET LE MAL, LE see **KHAIR WA ASH-SHARR, AL-** • 1946
BIEN FAIRE ET LES SEDUIRE see **SEXYRELLA** • 1968
BIEN PAGADA, LA • 1934 • Ardavin Eusebio F. • SPN
BIEN PAGADA, LA • 1947 • Gout Alberto • MXC
BIENAVENTURADOS LOS QUE CREEN • 1945 • Pereda Ramon • MXC
BIENE MAJA, DIE • 1977 • Murphy Martin* • ANM • AUS, JPN • BEE CALLED MAJA, A
BIENE MAJA UND IHRE ABENTEUER, DIE • 1926 • Junghans Wolfram • FRG
BIENE MAYA, DIE • 1929 • Bonsels Waldemar • FRG • ADVENTURES OF MAYA (USA)
BIENENSTAAT, DER • 1936 • FRG
BIENFAITEUR, LE • 1942 • Decoin Henri • FRN
BIENFAITS DU CINEMATOGRAPHE, LES • 1904 • Blache Alice • FRN
BIENHEUREUX, LES • 1982 • Payer Roch Christophe • MTV • CND • SAINTS, LES
BIENTOT NOEL see **DAYS BEFORE CHRISTMAS, THE** • 1958
BIENVENIDO, MR. KRIF • 1974 • Demicheli Tulio • SPN
BIENVENIDO, MR. MARSHALL • 1952 • Bardem Juan Antonio, Berlanga Luis Garcia • SPN • WELCOME, MR. MARSHALL
BIENVENIDO, PADRE MURRAY • 1962 • Torrado Ramon • SPN
BIENVENUE A BORD • 1989 • Leconte Jean-Louis • FRN
BIENVENUE A.. DUKE ELLINGTON • 1973 • Job Guy • DOC • FRN
BIENVENUE A L'AMOUR see **MARHABAN AIUHA AL-HUBB** • 1962
BIENVENUE A MONTREAL • 1976 • Cardinal Roger • DCS • CND
BIERE, LA • Cantagrel Marc • DOC • FRN
BIERE, LA • 1924 • Gremillon Jean • SHT • FRN
BIERKAMPF • 1976 • Achternbusch Herbert • FRG
BIESPOKOINAIA • 1956 • Medvedkin Alexander • USS
BIESSMIERTNYI GARNISON see **BESSMERTNYI GARNIZON** • 1956
BIEVRE, LA • 1939 • Clement Rene • DCS • FRN • BIEVRE, FILLE PERDUE, LA
BIEVRE, FILLE PERDUE, LA see **BIEVRE, LA** • 1939
BIFF BANG BUDDY • 1924 • Inghram Frank L. • USA
BIFF! BANG!! WALLOP!!! • 1914 • Aylott Dave? • UKN
BIFFEN AND THE BANANA see **BIFFEN OCH BANANEN** • 1951
BIFFEN OCH BANANEN • 1951 • Husberg Rolf • SWD • BEEF AND THE BANANA, THE ○ BIFFEN AND THE BANANA
BIFFY VISITS THE THEATRE • 1913 • *Barker* • UKN
BIFUR 3 • 1944 • Cam Maurice • FRN
BIG • 1988 • Marshall Penny • USA
BIG see **WIELKA, WIELKA I NAJWIEKSZA** • 1962
BIG ADVENTURE, THE • 1921 • Eason B. Reeves • USA
BIG ADVENTURE, THE • 1987 • Strayer Colin • DCS • CND
BIG ALLIGATOR RIVER see **ALLIGATORS** • 1980
BIG AND SMALL see **VELIKI I MALI** • 1956
BIG AND THE BAD, THE (UKN) see **SI PUO FARE.. AMIGO** • 1972
BIG ATTACK, THE see **GRANDE ASSALTO, O** • 1967
BIG BACKYARD, THE • 1976 • Auzins Igor • SHT • ASL
BIG BAD BOBCAT • 1968 • Anzilotti Cosmo • ANS • USA
BIG BAD JOHN • 1989 • Kennedy Burt • USA
BIG BAD MAMA • 1974 • Carver Steve • USA
BIG BAD MAMA II • 1987 • Wynorski Jim • USA
BIG BAD SINBAD • 1952 • Kneitel Seymour • ANS • USA
BIG BAD SIS • Sun Chung • HKG
BIG BAD WOLF, THE • 1934 • Gillett Burt • ANS • USA
BIG BAD WOLF, THE • *Childhood Prod.* • USA
BIG BAD WOLF (USA) see **WOLF UND DIE SIEBEN JUNGEN GEISSLEIN, DER** • 1957
BIG BANANA FEET • 1976 • Grigor Murray • UKN
BIG BANG see **PANG I BYGGET** • 1966
BIG BANG, THE • 1987 • Picha • ANM • BLG, FRN
BIG BANG, THE • 1990 • Toback James • DOC • USA
BIG BANKROLL, THE (UKN) see **KING OF THE ROARING TWENTIES -THE STORY OF ARNOLD ROTHSTEIN** • 1961
BIG BAZAR see **JOUR, LA FETE, UN** • 1974
BIG BEAT see **MOCNE UDERZENIE** • 1967
BIG BEAT, THE • 1958 • Cowan Will • USA
BIG BEAVER • 1970 • Lavender Semore • USA
BIG BEEF, THE • 1945 • Roberts Charles E. • SHT • USA
BIG BEN • 1967 • van der Keuken Johan • NTH • BEN WEBSTER IN EUROPE
BIG BENEFIT, THE • 1933 • Shores Lynn • SHT • USA
BIG BEN'S DREAM OF GREATNESS • 1912 • Coleby A. E. • UKN
BIG BET, THE • 1986 • Gordon Bert I. • USA
"BIG" BILL BLUES • 1956 • Delire Jean • SHT • BLG
BIG BIRD CAGE, THE • 1972 • Hill Jack • USA
BIG BIRDCAST, THE • 1938 • *Mintz Charles (P)* • ANS • USA
BIG BITE, THE • 1966 • Smith Paul J. • ANS • USA
BIG BLACK PILL, THE • 1981 • Badiyi Reza • TVM • USA • JOE DANCER ○ JOE DANCER VOL.1
BIG BLOCKADE, THE • 1942 • Frend Charles • UKN
BIG BLOND see **ISO VAALEE** • 1983
BIG BLUE, THE (UKN) see **GRAND BLEU, LE** • 1988
BIG BLUFF, THE • 1933 • Denny Reginald • USA • WORTHY DECEIVER (UKN)
BIG BLUFF, THE • 1955 • Wilder W. Lee • USA
BIG BLUFF, THE see **SEIN GROSSTER BLUFF** • 1927
BIG BLUFF, THE (USA) see **GROSSE BLUFF, DER** • 1933
BIG BLUFFS AND BOWLING BALLS • 1917 • Semon Larry • SHT • USA
BIG BOB • 1913 • *Nestor* • USA
BIG BOB JOHNSON AND HIS FANTASTIC SPEED CIRCUS • 1978 • Starrett Jack • USA
BIG BOB WAITS • 1913 • *Vitagraph* • USA
BIG BONANZA, THE • 1944 • Archainbaud George • USA
BIG BOOBS AND BATHING BEAUTIES • 1918 • Semon Larry • SHT • USA • BATHING BEAUTIES AND BIG BOOBS
BIG BOODLE, THE • 1956 • Wilson Richard • USA • NIGHT IN HAVANA (UKN)
BIG BOSS see **ANKOKUGAI NO KAOYAKU** • 1959
BIG BOSS 2 • Cheng Kay Ying • HKG • BRUCE AGAINST THE ODDS
BIG BOSS, THE • 1913 • Sullivan Frederick • USA
BIG BOSS, THE • 1941 • Barton Charles T. • USA • CHAIN GANG
BIG BOSS, THE see **JEFE MAXIMO, EL** • 1940
BIG BOSS, THE see **T'ANG-SHAN TA-HSIUNG** • 1971
BIG BOUNCE, THE • 1969 • March Alex • USA
BIG BOY • 1930 • Crosland Alan • USA
BIG BOY RIDES AGAIN • 1935 • Herman Al • USA
BIG BRAIN, THE • 1933 • Archainbaud George • USA • ENEMIES OF SOCIETY (UKN)
BIG BRAWL, THE (UKN) see **BATTLE CREEK BRAWL** • 1980
BIG BREAK, THE • 1950 • Strick Joseph • DOC • USA
BIG BROADCAST, THE • 1932 • Tuttle Frank • USA
BIG BROADCAST OF 1936, THE • 1935 • Taurog Norman • USA
BIG BROADCAST OF 1937, THE • 1936 • Leisen Mitchell • USA
BIG BROADCAST OF 1938, THE • 1938 • Leisen Mitchell • USA
BIG BROTHER • 1923 • Dwan Allan • USA
BIG BROTHER see **YOUNG DONOVAN'S KID** • 1931
BIG BROTHER, THE • 1915 • McElravy Robert C. • USA
BIG BROTHER, THE • 1916 • *King Henry* • SHT • USA
BIG BROTHER BILL • 1915 • *Badgley Helen* • USA
BIG BROTHER CHENG • Kuei Chih-Hung • HKG
BIG BROWN EYES • 1936 • Walsh Raoul • USA
BIG BUILD-UP, THE • 1942 • Davis Mannie • ANS • USA
BIG BUS, THE • 1976 • Frawley James • USA
BIG BUS GOING TO NASHVILLE • 1971 • Lynch Paul • CND
BIG BUSINESS • 1924 • McGowan Robert • SHT • USA
BIG BUSINESS • 1929 • Horne James W. • SHT • USA
BIG BUSINESS • 1930 • Sheridan Oscar M. • UKN
BIG BUSINESS • 1934 • Gardner Cyril • UKN
BIG BUSINESS • 1937 • Strayer Frank • USA • JONES FAMILY IN BIG BUSINESS, THE
BIG BUSINESS • 1988 • Abrahams Jim • USA
BIG BUSINESS GIRL • 1931 • Seiter William A. • USA
BIG BUSTOUT, THE • 1973 • del Amo Antonio • ITL
BIG CAGE, THE • 1933 • Neumann Kurt • USA
BIG CALIBRE • 1935 • Bradbury Robert North • USA
BIG CAPER, THE • 1957 • Stevens Robert • USA
BIG CARNIVAL, THE • 1951 • Wilder Billy • USA • ACE IN THE HOLE (UKN)
BIG CASINO, THE • 1933 • MacDonald Ballard • SHT • USA
BIG CAT, THE • 1949 • Karlson Phil • USA
BIG CAT, THE see **RETURN OF THE BIG CAT** • 1975
BIG CAT AND THE LITTLE MOUSIE, THE • 1938 • Lovy Alex • ANS • USA
BIG CATCH, THE • 1920 • Maloney Leo • SHT • USA
BIG CATCH, THE • 1968 • Henson Laurence • UKN
BIG CATS AND HOW THEY CAME TO BE, THE • 1976 • Giersz Witold • ANS • PLN
BIG CHANCE, THE • 1933 • Herman Al • USA
BIG CHANCE, THE • 1957 • Scott Peter Graham • UKN
BIG CHEESE ROBBERY, THE see **VELKA SYROVA LOUPEZ** • 1987
BIG CHEEZE, THE • 1930 • Foster John • ANS • USA
BIG CHIEF, THE see **GRAND CHEF, LE** • 1959
BIG CHIEF KO-KO • 1925 • Fleischer Dave • ANS • USA
BIG CHIEF LITTLE PIMPLE • 1914 • Evans Fred, Evans Joe • UKN
BIG CHIEF, NO TREATY • 1962 • Kuwahara Bob • ANS • USA
BIG CHIEF UGH-AMUGH-UGH • 1938 • Fleischer Dave • ANS • USA
BIG CHILL, THE • 1983 • Kasdan Lawrence • USA
BIG CIRCUS, THE • 1959 • Newman Joseph M. • USA
BIG CITY • 1948 • Taurog Norman • USA
BIG CITY see **VILLE, LA** • 1970
BIG CITY, A see **GRAN CIUDAD, UNA** • 1973
BIG CITY, THE • 1928 • Browning Tod • USA
BIG CITY, THE • 1937 • Borzage Frank • USA • SKYSCRAPER WILDERNESS
BIG CITY, THE • 1963 • Dixon Paul Weld • DCS • UKN
BIG CITY, THE see **GRANDE CIDADE, A** • 1966
BIG CITY, THE (UKN) see **MAHANAGAR** • 1963
BIG CITY BLUES • 1932 • LeRoy Mervyn • USA
BIG CITY BLUES • 1962 • van der Linden Charles Huguenot • SHT • USA
BIG CITY JUNGLE see **JUNGLE D'UNE GRAND VILLE** • 1929
BIG CLEAN-UP, THE • 1963 • Tendlar Dave • ANS • USA
BIG CLOCK, THE • 1948 • Farrow John • USA
BIG CLUBS, THE • 1977 • Kreck Joachim • DCS • FRG
BIG COMBO, THE • 1955 • Lewis Joseph H. • USA

BIG COUNTRY see **GREAT OUTDOORS, THE** • 1988
BIG COUNTRY, THE • 1958 • Wyler William • USA
BIG CRASH see **STORA SKRALLEN** • 1943
BIG CUBE, THE • 1969 • Davison Tito • USA, MXC
BIG DAM, THE • 1911 • *Prior Herbert* • USA
BIG DAME HUNTING • 1932 • Marshall George • SHT • USA
BIG DAN • 1923 • Wellman William A. • USA
BIG DAY, THE • 1960 • Scott Peter Graham • UKN
BIG DAY, THE see **JOUR DE FETE** • 1948
BIG DAY IN BOGO • 1958 • Reed N. • SHT • UNN
BIG DEAL • 1985 • Healey Barry • MTV • CND
BIG DEAL see **KOCHAJ ALBO RZUC** • 1977
BIG DEAL, THE see **SOLITI IGNOTI, I** • 1958
BIG DEAL, THE (UKN) see **BLONDIE'S BIG DEAL** • 1949
BIG DEAL AT DODGE CITY (UKN) see **BIG HAND FOR THE LITTLE LADY, A** • 1966
BIG DEAL OF MADONNA STREET, THE (USA) see **SOLITI IGNOTI, I** • 1958
BIG DEAL ON MADONNA STREET TWENTY YEARS AFTER see **SOLITI IGNOTI VENT'ANNI DOPO** • 1985
BIG DECISION see **MEGALI APOFASI** • 1977
BIG DECISION, THE (UKN) see **BASKETBALL FIX, THE** • 1951
BIG DEPARTURE, THE see **GRAND DEPART, LE** • 1972
BIG DIAMOND ROBBERY, THE • 1929 • Forde Eugene J. • USA
BIG DIG, THE • 1969 • Kishon Ephraim • ISR
BIG DOG HOUSE, THE • 1931 • White Jules, Myers Zion • SHT • USA
BIG DOLL, THE see **BAMBOLONA, LA** • 1968
BIG DOLL HOUSE, THE • 1971 • Hill Jack • USA
BIG DRIP, THE • 1949 • Sparber I. • ANS • USA
BIG DRIVE, THE • 1928 • *Harris Jack* • USA
BIG DROP, THE (USA) see **GRAN CAIDA, LA** • 1958
BIG DRUNKEN HERO see **TA TSUI HSIA** • 1966
BIG DUEL IN THE NORTH SEA see **NANKAI NO DAI KETTO** • 1966
BIG DUST-UP, THE see **GROSSE VERHAU, DER** • 1970
BIG EARS • 1931 • McGowan Robert • SHT • USA
BIG EASY, THE • 1987 • McBride Jim • USA • NOTHING BUT THE TRUTH
BIG ENOUGH N' OLD ENOUGH • 1968 • Prieto Joseph G. • USA • SAVAGES FROM HELL
BIG EXECUTIVE • 1933 • Kenton Erle C. • USA
BIG EYES • 1973 • Zohar Uri • ISR
BIG FALL, THE see **UNDER MY SKIN** • 1950
BIG FAMILY, THE see **BOLSHAYA SEMYA** • 1954
BIG FAMILY, THE see **ONORATA FAMIGLIA, UCCIDERE E COSA NOSTRA, L'** • 1973
BIG FELLA • 1937 • Wills J. Elder • UKN
BIG FIBBER, THE • 1933 • Marshall George • SHT • USA
BIG FIGHT, THE • 1930 • Lang Walter • USA
BIG FIGHT, THE see **JOE PALOOKA IN THE BIG FIGHT** • 1949
BIG FISH, THE see **BOY OF GOLD** • 1952
BIG FISH, THE see **DOBRODRUZSTVI NA ZLATE ZATOCE** • 1955
BIG FISHERMAN, THE • 1959 • Borzage Frank • USA
BIG FIX, THE • 1947 • Flood James • USA
BIG FIX, THE • 1978 • Kagan Jeremy Paul • USA
BIG FLAME, THE • 1969 • Loach Kenneth • MTV • UKN
BIG FLAME-UP, THE • 1949 • Sparber I. • ANS • USA
BIG FLASH, THE • 1932 • Gillstrom Arvid E. • SHT • USA
BIG FOOT see **BIGFOOT** • 1970
BIG FOOT, THE • 1978 • Flicker Theodore J. • USA
BIG FOOT AND THE MUSCLE MACHINES • 1987 • ANM • USA
BIG FOOT -MAN OR BEAST • 1975 • Crowley Lawrence • USA
BIG FOOTED BERTHA (USA) see **BERTHE AUX GRANDS PIEDS**
BIG FOREST, THE see **DAI-SHINRIN** • 1930
BIG FOUR IN CONFERENCE, THE see **GROTE VIER, DE** • 1947
BIG FRAME, THE see **UNDERTOW** • 1949
BIG FRAME, THE (USA) see **LOST HOURS, THE** • 1952
BIG FREEZE, THE see **ON THIN ICE** • 1961
BIG FUN CARNIVAL, THE • 1957 • Daniels Marc • USA
BIG GAMBLE, THE • 1931 • Niblo Fred • USA
BIG GAMBLE, THE • 1961 • Fleischer Richard, Williams Elmo • USA
BIG GAME • 1921 • Fitzgerald Dallas M. • USA
BIG GAME • 1921 • Parrott Charles, Roach Hal • SHT • USA
BIG GAME • 1924 • Lamont Charles • SHT • USA
BIG GAME • 1931 • *Van Beuren* • ANS • USA
BIG GAME • 1936 • Nicholls George Jr. • USA
BIG GAME, THE • 1972 • Day Robert • USA, ITL, SAF
BIG GAME FISHING • 1968 • Bartsch Art • ANS • USA
BIG GAME GEORGE • 1927 • Newfield Sam • SHT • USA
BIG GAME HAUNT • 1968 • Lovy Alex • ANS • USA
BIG GAME HUNT, THE • 1937 • Davis Mannie, Gordon George • ANS • USA
BIG GAME HUNTER, THE • 1925 • Marshall George • SHT • USA
BIG GAME HUNTING • 1929 • *Chester Educational* • DOC • USA
BIG GAME OF LIFE, THE • 1935 • Kearton Cherry • UKN
BIG GENERATION • 1977 • Stolen Will • USA
BIG GIRL • 1988 • Yaron-Gronich Nirith • ISR
BIG GIVER, THE • 1988 • Golden John • USA
BIG GRAB, THE see **MELODIE EN SOUS-SOL** • 1962
BIG GRASSHOPPER, THE see **GRANDE SAUTERELLE, LA** • 1967
BIG GRAY-BLUE BIRD, A see **GROSSER GRAU-BLAUER VOGEL, EIN** • 1970
BIG GREEN VALLEY see **BOLSHAYA ZELYONAYA DOLINA** • 1968
BIG GUNDOWN, THE (USA) see **RESA DEI CONTI, LA** • 1967
BIG GUNS (FRN) see **TONY ARZENTA** • 1973
BIG GUSHER, THE • 1951 • Landers Lew • USA
BIG GUY, THE • 1940 • Lubin Arthur • USA
BIG HAIRCUT see **WILD HARVEST** • 1947
BIG HAND FOR EVERYONE, A • 1971 • Petty Bruce • ANS • ASL
BIG HAND FOR THE LITTLE LADY, A • 1966 • Cook Fielder • USA • BIG DEAL AT DODGE CITY (UKN)
BIG HANGOVER, THE • 1950 • Krasna Norman • USA
BIG HAPPINESS • 1920 • Campbell Colin • USA
BIG HATE, THE see **BUYUK KIN** • 1967
BIG-HEAD KID see **PIBE CABEZA, EL** • 1975
BIG HEART, THE (UKN) see **MIRACLE ON 34TH STREET, THE** • 1947
BIG HEARTED BOSKO • 1931-32 • Harman Hugh • ANS • USA
BIG-HEARTED HERBERT • 1934 • Keighley William • USA
BIG HEARTED JIM • 1911 • *Melford George* • USA
BIG-HEARTED JIM • 1913 • *Eclair* • USA
BIG-HEARTED JIM • 1915 • *Alhambra* • USA
BIG HEARTED SIM • 1912 • *Pollard Harry* • USA
BIG HEAT, THE • 1953 • Lang Fritz • USA
BIG HEEL WATHA • 1944 • Avery Tex • ANS • USA
BIG HOLIDAY, THE see **VACANTA CEA MARE** • 1988
BIG HOP, THE • 1928 • Horne James W. • USA
BIG HORN MASSACRE • 1913 • Hurst Paul C. • USA
BIG HOUSE • 1930 • Fejos Paul, Hill George W. • FRN
BIG HOUSE, THE • 1930 • Hill George W. • USA
BIG HOUSE, THE see **CASA GRANDE, LA** • 1975
BIG HOUSE, THE see **DOIN' TIME** • 1984
BIG HOUSE BLUES • 1947 • Swift Howard • ANS • USA
BIG HOUSE BUNNY • 1950 • Freleng Friz • ANS • USA
BIG HOUSE U.S.A. • 1955 • Koch Howard W. • USA
BIG HUG, A see **STORA FAMNEN** • 1940
BIG HUNT, THE • 1969 • Sherwood George • DOC • USA
BIG HUNT, THE see **MERCENARIO, EL** • 1968
BIG HURT, THE • 1986 • Peak Barry • ASL
BIG IDEA, THE • *Three Stooges* • SHT • USA
BIG IDEA, THE • 1918 • Roach Hal • SHT • USA
BIG IDEA, THE • 1919 • *Parsons William* • USA
BIG IDEA, THE • 1923 • Roach Hal • SHT • USA
BIG IDEAS see **SWELL-HEAD, THE** • 1927
BIG JACK • 1949 • Thorpe Richard • USA
BIG JAKE • 1971 • Sherman George • USA
BIG JEWEL CASE, THE • 1930 • Roberts Stephen • SHT • USA
BIG JIM GARRITY • 1916 • Fitzmaurice George • USA
BIG JIM MCLAIN • 1952 • Ludwig Edward • USA
BIG JIM OF THE SIERRAS • 1913 • *Selig* • USA
BIG JIM'S HEART • 1915 • O'Brien John B. • USA
BIG JOB, THE • 1965 • Thomas Gerald • UKN
BIG JOE see **VELI JOZE** • 1980
BIG JOHN see **ELECTRA GLIDE IN BLUE** • 1973
BIG JUMP, THE see **GROSSE SPRUNG, DER** • 1927
BIG KICK, THE • 1925 • Roach Hal • SHT • USA
BIG KICK, THE • 1930 • Doane Warren • SHT • USA
BIG KILLING, THE • 1928 • Jones F. Richard • USA
BIG KNIFE, THE • 1955 • Aldrich Robert • USA
BIG LAND • 1985 • SAF
BIG LAND, THE • 1956 • Douglas Gordon • USA • STAMPEDED (UKN)
BIG LEAGUER • 1953 • Aldrich Robert • USA
BIG LI, YOUNG LI AND OLD LI • 1962 • Xie Jin • CHN
BIG LIFT, THE • 1950 • Seaton George • USA • TWO CORRIDORS EAST
BIG LITTLE PERSON, THE • 1919 • Leonard Robert Z. • USA
BIG LOBBY, THE see **ROSEBUD BEACH HOTEL, THE** • 1985
BIG MAN, THE • 1990 • Leland David • UKN
BIG MAN FROM THE NORTH • 1930 • Harman Hugh, Ising Rudolf • ANS • USA
BIG MAN ON CAMPUS • 1989 • Kagan Jeremy Paul • USA • HUNCHBACK OF UCLA, THE
BIG MEAT EATER • 1982 • Windsor Chris • CND
BIG MEDICINE • 1910 • *Selig* • USA
BIG MESS, THE see **GROSSE VERHAU, DER** • 1970
BIG MILL, THE see **DAMO FANG** • 1989
BIG MILLER • 1962 • Binder Steve • SHT • USA
BIG MO see **MAURIE** • 1973
BIG MOMENTS FROM LITTLE PICTURES • 1924 • Howe J. A. • SHT • USA
BIG MONEY • 1918 • Lorraine Harry • UKN
BIG MONEY • 1930 • Mack Russell • USA • EASY MONEY (UKN)
BIG MONEY • 1936 • Jackson Pat, Watt Harry • DCS • UKN
BIG MONEY, THE • 1956 • Carstairs John Paddy • UKN
BIG MOSQUITOES, THE see **ZANZARONI, I** • 1967
BIG MOUSE-TAKE • 1963 • Hanna William, Barbera Joseph • ANS • USA
BIG MOUTH, THE • 1967 • Lewis Jerry • USA
BIG NEWS • 1929 • La Cava Gregory • USA
BIG NIGHT, THE • 1915 • *Ab* • USA
BIG NIGHT, THE • 1951 • Losey Joseph • USA
BIG NIGHT, THE • 1960 • Salkow Sidney • USA
BIG NIGHT, THE see **HER BIG NIGHT** • 1926
BIG NIGHT, THE see **GRAND SOIR, UN** • 1976
BIG NOISE, THE • 1928 • Dwan Allan • USA • NINE DAYS' WONDER
BIG NOISE, THE • 1936 • Bryce Alex • UKN • MODERN MADNESS
BIG NOISE, THE • 1936 • McDonald Frank • USA
BIG NOISE, THE • 1944 • St. Clair Malcolm • USA
BIG NOISE HANK • 1911 • *Sprague Mr.* • USA
BIG NORTH, THE see **WILD NORTH, THE** • 1951
BIG O, THE • 1958 • D'Avino Carmen • SHT • USA
BIG ONE MONOGATARI • 1977 • Yoshida Yoshishige • JPN
BIG OPERATOR, THE • 1959 • Haas Charles • USA • ANATOMY OF A SYNDICATE
BIG PACK, THE • 1944 • UKN
BIG PAL • 1925 • Adolfi John G. • USA
BIG PALOOKA, THE • 1929 • Sennett Mack • SHT • USA
BIG PARADE, THE • 1925 • Vidor King • USA
BIG PARADE, THE • 1952 • Godfrey Bob • ANS • UKN
BIG PARADE, THE see **DA YUEBING** • 1985
BIG PARADE OF COMEDY • 1964 • Youngson Robert • CMP • USA • MGM'S BIG PARADE OF COMEDY
BIG PARTY, THE • 1930 • Blystone John G. • USA
BIG PARTY, THE (USA) see **GRAN FIESTA, LA** • 1987
BIG PAY-OFF, THE see **PRIDE OF THE LEGION, THE** • 1932
BIG PICTURE, THE • 1989 • Guest Christopher • USA
BIG POND, THE • 1930 • Henley Hobart • USA
BIG POT see **COLPACCIO, IL** • 1976
BIG PREMIERE, THE • 1940 • Cahn Edward L. • SHT • USA
BIG PUNCH, THE • 1921 • Ford John • USA
BIG PUNCH, THE • 1948 • Shourds Sherry • USA
BIG PUSH, THE see **TIMBER TRAMP** • 1973
BIG QUESTION, THE • 1917 • *Facts Films* • USA
BIG RACE, THE • 1934 • Newmeyer Fred • USA • RAISING THE WIND
BIG RACE, THE • 1937 • *Lantz Walter (P)* • ANS • USA
BIG RACE, THE • 1960 • *Halas John (P)* • ANS • UKN
BIG RACE, THE (UKN) see **TEXAN, THE** • 1930
BIG RALLY, A • 1951 • Dovnikovic Borivoj, Vukotic Dusan • ANS • YGS
BIG RASCAL, THE • 1980 • Chi Kuan-Chun • HKG
BIG RED • 1962 • Tokar Norman • USA
BIG RED ONE, THE • 1979 • Fuller Samuel • USA
BIG RED RIDING HOOD • 1925 • McCarey Leo • SHT • USA
BIG RED RIDING HOODS, THE • 1973 • Danis Aime • DCS • CND
BIG RIP-OFF, THE • 1975 • Hargrove Dean • TVM • USA • SHOT, THE
BIG RISK, THE • *Cheung Nick* • HKG
BIG RISK, THE (USA) see **CLASSE TOUS RISQUES** • 1959
BIG ROAD, THE see **BOLSHAIA DOROGA** • 1963
BIG ROCK'S LAST STAND • 1912 • Montgomery Frank E. • USA
BIG ROSE • 1974 • Krasny Paul • TVM • USA • BIG ROSE: DOUBLE TROUBLE
BIG ROSE: DOUBLE TROUBLE see **BIG ROSE** • 1974
BIG SCARE, THE • 1929 • Terry Paul • ANS • USA
BIG SCOOP, THE • 1910 • *August Edwin* • USA
BIG SCORE, THE • 1983 • Williamson Fred • USA
BIG SEARCH, THE see **GRANDE CACCIA, LA** • 1957
BIG SHAKEDOWN, THE • 1934 • Dillon John Francis • USA • SHAKEDOWN, THE
BIG SHAR see **WIELKI SZU** • 1982
BIG SHAVE, THE • 1967 • Scorsese Martin • SHT • USA
BIG SHOT see **MY PALIKARI** • 1982
BIG SHOT, THE • 1931 • Murphy Ralph • USA • OPTIMIST, THE (UKN)
BIG SHOT, THE • 1937 • Killy Edward • USA
BIG SHOT, THE • 1942 • Seiler Lewis • USA • ESCAPE FROM CRIME
BIG SHOT, THE see **DOUGH BOYS, THE** • 1930
BIG SHOT, THE see **OFFICER O'BRIEN** • 1930
BIG SHOTS • 1987 • Mandel Robert • USA
BIG SHOW, THE • 1920 • *Chester* • SHT • USA
BIG SHOW, THE • 1923 • McGowan Robert • SHT • USA
BIG SHOW, THE • 1926 • Terwilliger George W. • USA
BIG SHOW, THE • 1929 • Harman Bobby • UKN
BIG SHOW, THE • 1936 • Wright Mack V. • USA
BIG SHOW, THE • 1961 • Clark James B. • USA
BIG SHOW-OFF, THE • 1945 • Bretherton Howard • USA
BIG SHOWDOWN, THE see **GRANDE DUELLO, IL** • 1973
BIG SIN CITY • 1970 • Tobalina Carlos • USA • NOTORIOUS BIG SIN CITY
BIG SISTER • 1912 • *Thanhouser* • USA
BIG SISTER • 1913 • Tucker George Loane • USA
BIG SISTER, THE • 1916 • O'Brien John B. • USA
BIG SISTER'S CHRISTMAS, THE • 1914 • Turner Otis • USA
BIG SKY, THE • 1952 • Hawks Howard • USA
BIG SLAMMER, THE see **SLAMMER GIRLS** • 1987
BIG SLEEP, THE • 1946 • Hawks Howard • USA
BIG SLEEP, THE • 1978 • Winner Michael • USA, UKN
BIG SNATCH, THE see **MELODIE EN SOUS-SOL** • 1962
BIG SNIT, THE • 1986 • Condie Richard • ANS • CND
BIG SNOOZE, THE • 1946 • Clampett Robert • ANS • USA
BIG SNOOZE, THE • 1957 • Lovy Alex • ANS • USA
BIG SOFTIE, THE see **GRAND DADAIS, LE** • 1967
BIG SOMBRERO, THE • 1949 • McDonald Frank • USA
BIG SPACE MONSTER GUILALA see **UCHU DAIKAIJU GUILALA** • 1967
BIG SPLASH • 1981 • Ohlsson Terry • SHT • ASL
BIG SPLASH, THE • 1935 • Hiscott Leslie • UKN
BIG SPLIT see **MEGALOS DHIHASMOS** • 1968
BIG SQUAWK ,THE • 1929 • Doane Warren • SHT • USA
BIG SQUEAL • 1933 • Lamont Charles • SHT • USA
BIG SQUIRT, THE • 1937 • Lord Del • SHT • USA
BIG STAKES • 1920 • Jaccard Jacques • SHT • USA
BIG STAKES • 1922 • Elfelt Clifford S. • USA
BIG STAMPEDE, THE • 1932 • Wright Tenny • USA
BIG STEAL, THE • 1949 • Siegel Don • USA
BIG STEAL, THE • 1989 • Tass Nadia • ASL
BIG STICK, THE • 1914 • *Luna* • USA
BIG STICKUP AT BRINK'S see **BRINK'S JOB, THE** • 1978
BIG STORE see **GRANDI MAGAZZINI** • 1987
BIG STORE, THE • 1941 • Reisner Charles F. • USA
BIG STORM, THE • 1974 • Wu Sze-Yuan • HKG
BIG STORY, THE (UKN) see **APPOINTMENT WITH A SHADOW** • 1958
BIG STREET, THE • 1942 • Reis Irving • USA
BIG STRONG MAN, THE • 1922 • Cooper George A. • UKN
BIG STUNT • 1925 • *Williams Big Boy* • USA
BIG SURPRISE, THE • 1984 • Battersby Roy • UKN
BIG SWALLOW, THE • 1901 • Williamson James • UKN
BIG SWITCH, THE • 1968 • Walker Pete • UKN • STRIP POKER
BIG T.N.T. SHOW, THE • 1966 • Peerce Larry • USA • THIS COULD BE THE NIGHT
BIG, THE BIGGER AND THE BIGGEST, THE see **WIELKA, WIELKA I NAJWIEKSZA** • 1962
BIG THIEF, THE see **STORTJUVEN** • 1979
BIG THRILL, THE (UKN) see **HIGH GEAR** • 1933
BIG THUMBS • 1977 • Lipton Richard • USA
BIG TIMBER • 1917 • Taylor William D. • USA
BIG TIMBER • 1924 • Craft William James • USA
BIG TIMBER • 1950 • Yarbrough Jean • USA • TALL TIMBER
BIG TIME • 1929 • Hawks Kenneth • USA
BIG TIME see **BIGTIME** • 1976
BIG TIME OPERATORS (USA) see **SMALLEST SHOW ON EARTH, THE** • 1956
BIG TIME OR BUST • 1934 • Newfield Sam • USA • HEAVEN BOUND (UKN)
BIG TIMER, THE • 1932 • Buzzell Edward • USA
BIG TIP-OFF, THE • 1955 • McDonald Frank • USA
BIG TOP, THE • 1938 • Davis Mannie • ANS • USA
BIG TOP, THE see **THREE RING CIRCUS** • 1954
BIG TOP BUNNY • 1951 • McKimson Robert • ANS • USA
BIG TOP PEE-WEE • 1988 • Kleiser Randall • USA
BIG TOWN • 1932 • Hoerl Arthur • USA

BIG TOWN • 1947 • Thomas William C. • USA • GUILTY ASSIGNMENT
BIG TOWN, THE • 1924 • Roach Hal • SHT • USA
BIG TOWN, THE • 1987 • Bolt Ben • USA • ARM, THE
BIG TOWN AFTER DARK • 1947 • Thomas William C. • USA • UNDERWORLD AFTER DARK
BIG TOWN CZAR • 1939 • Lubin Arthur • USA
BIG TOWN GIRL • 1936 • Werker Alfred L. • USA
BIG TOWN GIRL • 1937 • Strayer Frank • USA
BIG TOWN IDEAS • 1921 • Harbaugh Carl • USA
BIG TOWN ROUND-UP • 1921 • Reynolds Lynn • USA
BIG TOWN SCANDAL • 1948 • Thomas William C. • USA • UNDERWORLD SCANDAL
BIG TRAIL, THE • 1930 • Walsh Raoul • USA
BIG TRAIN, THE see **ALCATRAZ EXPRESS** • 1960
BIG TREES, THE • 1952 • Feist Felix E. • USA
BIG TREMAINE • 1916 • Otto Henry • USA
BIG TROUBLE • 1985 • Cassavetes John • USA
BIG TROUBLE IN LITTLE CHINA • 1986 • Carpenter John • USA
BIG TRUCK AND POOR CLARE • 1971 • Miller Robert Ellis • ISR
BIG TYLL • Raamat Rein • ANM • USS
BIG VALLEY, THE • 1965 • Graham William A. • TVM • USA
BIG WASH, THE • 1948 • Geronimi Clyde • ANS • USA
BIG WAVE, THE • 1962 • Danielewski Tad • USA, JPN
BIG WEDNESDAY • 1978 • Milius John • USA
BIG WHEEL, THE • 1949 • Ludwig Edward • USA
BIG WHEELS AND SAILOR • 1979 • Aitken Doug • UKN
BIG WHITE CHIEF, THE • 1912 • *Nestor* • USA
BIG WIND FROM TOKYO (USA) see **ISHINAKA SENSEI GYOJOKI** • 1966
BIG WOOD, THE • 1966 • Jakubowska Wanda • PLN
BIG WORLD OF LITTLE CHILDREN see **WIELKA, WIELKA I NAJWIEKSZA** • 1962
BIG ZAPPER • 1973 • Shonteff Lindsay • UKN
BIGAME, LE (FRN) see **BIGAMO, IL** • 1956
BIGAMIE • 1922 • Walther-Fein Rudolf • FRG
BIGAMIE • 1927 • Speyer Jaap • FRG
BIGAMIST, THE • 1916 • *Wontner Arthur* • UKN
BIGAMIST, THE • 1916 • Brenon Herbert • USA
BIGAMIST, THE • 1921 • Newall Guy • UKN
BIGAMIST, THE • 1953 • Lupino Ida • USA
BIGAMIST, THE see **BIGAMO, IL** • 1956
BIGAMO, IL • 1956 • Emmer Luciano • ITL, FRN • BIGAME, LE (FRN) ○ PLEA FOR PASSION, A ○ BIGAMIST, THE
BIGANE BIYA • 1968 • Kimiyaei Massoud • IRN • COME STRANGER
BIGAT NG KAMAY • 1968 • Garces Armando • PHL • MIGHT OF THE HAND
BIGFELLON CRAINT LES AUTOS • 1916-24 • Lortac • ANS • FRN
BIGFOOT • 1970 • Slatzer Robert F. • USA • BIG FOOT
BIGFOOT • 1987 • Huston Danny • TVM • USA
BIGFOOT AND THE HENDERSONS (UKN) see **HARRY AND THE HENDERSONS** • 1987
BIGFOOT, THE MYSTERIOUS MONSTERS • 1975 • Guenette Robert • DOC • USA • MYSTERIOUS MONSTERS, THE
BIGGER AND BETTER • 1930 • Kennedy Edgar • SHT • USA
BIGGER AND BETTER BLONDES • 1927 • Roach Hal • SHT • USA
BIGGER MAN, THE see **BETTER MAN, THE** • 1915
BIGGER PLAY see **LANCE MAIOR** • 1968
BIGGER SPLASH, A • 1974 • Hazan Jack • DOC • UKN
BIGGER THAN BARNUM'S • 1926 • Ince Ralph • USA
BIGGER THAN LIFE • 1956 • Ray Nicholas • USA • ONE IN A MILLION
BIGGEST AND THE LITTLEST LADY IN THE WORLD, THE • 1918 • *Clark Marguerite* • SHT • USA
BIGGEST BANK ROBBERY, THE • 1980 • Thomas Ralph • TVM • UKN • NIGHTINGALE SANG IN BERKELEY SQUARE, A
BIGGEST BATTLE, THE see **GRANDE ATTACCO, IL** • 1978
BIGGEST BUNDLE OF THEM ALL, THE • 1967 • Annakin Ken • USA
BIGGEST FIGHT ON EARTH, THE see **SANDAI KAIJU CHIKYU SAIDAI NO KESSEN** • 1965
BIGGEST GAME, THE see **STORSTE SPILLET, DET** • 1967
BIGGEST LAZYBONES IN THE WORLD, THE see **POPOLVAR NAJVACSI NA SVETE** • 1982
BIGGEST SHOW ON EARTH, THE • 1918 • Storm Jerome • USA
BIGGEST WISH, THE see **NEJVETSI PRANI** • 1966
BIGGLES • 1985 • Hough John • UKN • BIGGLES: ADVENTURES IN TIME (USA) ○ BIGGLES GETS OF THE GROUND
BIGGLES: ADVENTURES IN TIME (USA) see **BIGGLES** • 1985
BIGGLES GETS OF THE GROUND see **BIGGLES** • 1985
BIGONAHI DAR SHAHR • 1968 • Sadeghpoor Manouchehr • IRN • INNOCENT IN THE CITY, AN
BIGORNE, CAPORAL DE FRANCE, LA • 1957 • Darene Robert • FRN
BIGOT, THE • 1915 • MacDonald Donald • USA
BIGOTE PARA DOS, UN • 1940 • de Lara Antonio, Mihura Miguel • SPN
BIGTIME • 1976 • Georgias Andrew • USA • BIG TIME
BIJ DE BEESTEN AF • 1973 • Haanstra Bert • DOC • NTH, USA • APE AND SUPERAPE
BIJELI MIS • 1961 • Vrbanic Ivo • YGS • WHITE MOUSE, THE
BIJELI TRAGOVI see **GJURME TE BARDHA** • 1981
BIJIN AISHU • 1931 • Ozu Yasujiro • JPN • BEAUTY'S SORROWS, THE
BIJIN GUMO • 1960 • Misumi Kenji • JPN • PURLOINED MAP, THE
BIJO GOMON • 1967 • Komori Haku • JPN • BEAUTY'S TORTURE, A
BIJO TO EKITAI NINGEN see **BIYO TO EKITAININGEN** • 1958
BIJO TO KAIRYU • 1955 • Yoshimura Kozaburo • JPN • BEAUTY AND THE DRAGON, THE ○ LADY AND THE DRAGON, THE
BIJO TO TOZOKU • 1952 • Kimura Keigo • JPN • BEAUTY AND THE BEAST
BIJOMARU SWORD, THE see **MEITO BIJOMARU** • 1945
BIJOMARU, THE NOTED SWORD see **MEITO BIJOMARU** • 1945
BIJOU, LE • 1947 • Lee Francis • SHT • USA • JEWEL, THE
BIJOUTIERS DU CLAIR DE LUNE, LES • 1958 • Vadim Roger • FRN, ITL • AMANTI DEL CHIARO DI LUNA, GLI (ITL) ○ NIGHT HEAVEN FELL, THE (USA) ○ HEAVEN FELL THAT NIGHT (UKN)
BIJOUX D'AMOUR • 1977 • Rhomm Patrice • FRN
BIJOUX DE FAMILLE, LES • 1974 • Laureux Jean-Claude • FRN • MEMBRES DE LA FAMILLE, LES ○ FAMILY JEWELS ○ FRENCH BLUE
BIJOYA • 1935 • *Sircar B. N. (P)* • IND
BIJSTERE LAND VAN VELUWEN, HET • 1948 • van der Horst Herman • NTH • RAPE OF A COUNTRY
BIJUTERII DE FAMILIE • 1958 • Teodorescu Marius • RMN • FAMILY JEWELS, THE
BIKE AND I, THE see **TAN-CH'E YU WO** • 1983
BIKE BOY • 1967 • Warhol Andy • USA
BIKE BUG, THE • 1921 • Roach Hal • SHT • USA
BIKINI see **OPERATION BIKINI** • 1963
BIKINI BEACH • 1965 • Asher William • USA
BIKINI BEACH see **OPERATION BIKINI** • 1963
BIKINI BEACH PARTY • 1967 • Conde Conrado • PHL
BIKINI PARADISE • 1964 • Tallas Gregg R. • USA • MISSION TO PARADISE ○ WHITE SAVAGE
BIKINI PARTY IN A HAUNTED HOUSE see **GHOST IN THE INVISIBLE BIKINI, THE** • 1966
BIKINI PLAYMATES see **BACHELOR TOM PEEPING** • 1962
BIKINI SHOP, THE • 1986 • Wechter David • USA • MALIBU BIKINI SHOP, THE
BIKINIS Y ROCK • 1972 • *Cinema Calderon* • MXC
BIKO INQUEST, THE • 1987 • Finney Albert • MTV • UKN
BIL WALIDAIN IHSANAN • 1976 • Al Imam Hassan • EGY • MERCY ON YOUR PARENTS
BILA JEDNOM JEDNA TOCKA • 1964 • Dejakovic Mladen • ANS • YGS • ONCE UPON A TIME THERE WAS A FULL STOP ○ ONCE UPON A TIME THERE WAS A DOT
BILA NEMOC • 1937 • Haas Hugo • CZC • SKELETON ON HORSEBACK ○ WHITE ILLNESS, THE ○ WHITE DISEASE, THE ○ WHITE SICKNESS, THE
BILA PANI • 1965 • Podskalsky Zdenek • CZC • WHITE LADY, THE
BILA SAATNYA TIBA • 1986 • INN
BILA SPONA • 1960 • Fric Martin • CZC • WHITE SLIDE, THE
BILA TMA • 1948 • Cap Frantisek • CZC • WHITE DARKNESS
BILAKORO • 1988 • De Brahima Traore Issa, Dany Kouyate, Sekou Traore • SHT • BRK
BILAN DE TRAVAIL see **SIJILLUS AMAL** • 1974
BILANS KWARTALNY • 1975 • Zanussi Krzysztof • PLN • WOMAN'S DECISION, A ○ QUARTERLY BALANCE ○ BALANCE, THE
BILAWAL • 1989 • Kaifi • PKS
BILBAO see **BILBAO, UNA HISTORIA DE AMOR** • 1978
BILBAO, UNA HISTORIA DE AMOR • 1978 • Luna Bigas • SPN • BILBAO
BILD DER AHNFRAU, DAS • 1916 • Moest Hubert • FRG
BILD DER GELIEBTEN, DAS • 1920 • Walther-Fein Rudolf • FRG
BILDERBOGEN DER EHE • 1927 • Volcker Hansjurgen • FRG
BILDERBUCH GOTTES • 1960 • Holmann J. A. • AUS
BILDNIS DES DORIAN GRAY, DAS • 1917 • Oswald Richard • FRG • PICTURE OF DORIAN GRAY, THE (USA)
BILDNIS DES DORIAN GRAY, DAS (FRG) see **DIO CHIAMATO DORIAN, IL** • 1970
BILDNIS EINER UNBEKANNTEN • 1954 • Kautner Helmut • FRG • PORTRAIT OF AN UNKNOWN WOMAN (USA)
BILDOD • 1979 • Wam Svend, Vennerod Petter • SHT • NRW • CAR DEATH
BILDSCHNITZER VOM WALSERTAL, DER • 1951 • Greville Edmond T. • FRG
BILET POWROTNY • 1978 • Petelska Ewa, Petelski Czeslaw • PLN
BILIAR • 1961 • Pojar Bretislav • ANS • CZC • BILLIARDS
BILITIS • 1977 • Hamilton David • FRN
BILJETT TILL AVENTYRET see **BOTTE I FARTEN** • 1945
BILJETT TILL PARADISET • 1962 • Mattsson Arne • SWD • TICKET TO PARADISE
BILL • 1913 • Hopper E. Mason • USA
BILL • 1981 • Page Anthony • TVM • USA
BILL AND COO • 1931 • Orton John • UKN
BILL AND COO • 1947 • Riesner Dean • USA
BILL AND ETHEL AT THE BALL • 1914 • *Tincher Fay* • USA
BILL AND SON see **GAOL BREAK** • 1936
BILL AND TED'S EXCELLENT ADVENTURE • 1987 • Hereck Stephen • USA
BILL AND THE BEARDED LADY • 1917 • MacGregor Norval • SHT • USA
BILL APPERTON'S BOY • 1919 • Kirkwood James • USA • BILL APPERTON'S SON
BILL APPERTON'S SON see **BILL APPERTON'S BOY** • 1919
BILL BAILEY'S RETURN • 1904 • Collins Alf? • UKN
BILL BARLOW'S CLAIM see **FIGHTING STRAIN, THE** • 1923
BILL BECOMES MENTALLY DERANGED • 1912 • *Lux* • FRN
BILL BOGGS' WINDFALL • 1912 • Henderson Dell • USA
BILL BRENNAN'S CLAIM • 1917 • Marshall George • SHT • USA
BILL BUMPER'S BARGAIN • 1911 • *Cashman Harry* • USA
BILL BUMPER'S BOY • 1913 • Stow Percy • UKN
BILL BUNKS THE BANDITS • 1915 • *Cunningham Arthur* • USA
BILL CAMPS OUT • 1918 • *Capitol* • USA
BILL COLEMAN FROM BOOGIE TO FUNK • 1961 • Rocamora Pierre-A. • SHT • FRN
BILL COSBY: 49 • 1987 • Lewis David*, Cosby Camille • USA
BILL COSBY HIMSELF • 1983 • Cosby Bill • CND
BILL CRACKS DOWN • 1937 • Nigh William • USA • MEN OF STEEL (UKN)
BILL EVANS • 1968 • Wyler Leland • SHT • USA
BILL EVANS, JAZZ PIANIST -ON THE CREATIVE PROCESS AND SELF-TEACHING • 1966 • Cavrell Louis • USA
BILL FOR DIVORCEMENT, A • 1922 • Clift Denison • UKN
BILL GIVES A SMOKER • 1915 • Dillon Eddie • USA
BILL GOES IN BUSINESS FOR HIMSELF • 1914 • *Komic* • USA
BILL HAS A HUNDRED FACES • 1969 • Imre Istvan • ANM • HNG
BILL HAYWOOD, PRODUCER • 1915 • Mix Tom • USA
BILL HENRY • 1919 • Storm Jerome • USA
BILL IL TACITURNO • 1967 • Pupillo Massimo • ITL
BILL JOHNSON STORY, THE see **GOING FOR THE GOLD: THE BILL JOHNSON STORY** • 1985
BILL JOINS THE W.W.W'S • 1914 • *Komic* • USA
BILL JONES' NEW YEAR RESOLUTIONS • 1908 • *Essanay* • USA
BILL MANAGES A PRIZE FIGHTER • 1914 • *Dillon Eddie* • USA
BILL MASON'S RIDE • 1910 • *Capitol* • USA
BILL MIXES WITH HIS RELATIONS • 1912 • *Carney Augustus* • USA
"BILL" NO.1 • 1914 • *Komic* • USA
BILL OF DIVORCEMENT, A • 1932 • Cukor George • USA
BILL OF DIVORCEMENT, A • 1940 • Farrow John • USA • NOT FOR EACH OTHER ○ NEVER TO LOVE
BILL OF HARE • 1962 • McKimson Robert • ANS • USA
BILL: ON HIS OWN • 1983 • Page Anthony • TVM • USA
BILL ORGANIZES A UNION • 1914 • *Komic* • USA
BILL PETER'S KID • 1916 • Sturgeon Rollin S. • SHT • USA
BILL POSTER, THE • 1899 • Norton C. Goodwin • UKN
BILL POSTER, THE • 1933 • *Mintz Charles (P)* • ANS • USA
BILL POSTERS • 1940 • Geronimi Clyde • ANS • USA
BILL-POSTER'S REVENGE, THE • 1901 • Smith G. A. • UKN
BILL-POSTING • 1914 • *Rigby Freddie* • UKN
BILL REID • 1979 • Long Jack • CND
BILL SAVES THE DAY • 1914 • *Komic* • USA
BILL SETTLES DOWN • 1918 • *Parsons William* • SHT • USA
BILL SPOILS A VACATION • 1914 • *Komic* • USA
BILL-STICKER AND THE SAUSAGE VENDOR, THE see **VYSTAVNI PARKAR A LEPIC PLAKATU** • 1898
BILL STINGERS' POEMS • 1919 • SHS • USA
BILL SYKES UP TO DATE • 1903 • Cooper Arthur • UKN
BILL TAKES A HOLIDAY see **TONIGHT'S THE NIGHT** • 1932
BILL TAKES A LADY OUT TO LUNCH -NEVER AGAIN! • 1914 • *Browning Tod* • USA
BILL TELL, PAWNBROKER • 1914 • MacDonald J. Farrell • USA
BILL THE CONQUEROR see **MR. BILL THE CONQUEROR** • 1932
BILL TURNS VALET • 1915 • *Tincher Fay* • USA
BILL WALLACE OF CHINA • 1967 • Green Douglas • USA
BILL WANTS BRITISH WASHING • 1914 • *Bertho Paul* • UKN
BILL WILSON'S GAL • 1912 • Sturgeon Rollin S. • USA
BILLABONG • 1968 • Hindle Will • SHT • USA
BILLARD CASSE, LE • 1916 • Feyder Jacques • FRN
BILLBOARD FROLICS • 1936 • Freleng Friz • ANS • USA
BILLBOARD GIRL, THE • 1932 • *Sennett Mack (P)* • SHT • USA
BILLE DE CLOWN • 1950 • Wall Jean • FRN
BILLET DE BANQUE, LE • 1906 • Feuillade Louis • FRN
BILLET DE FAVEUR, LE • 1906 • Heuze Andre • FRN
BILLET DE LOGEMENT, LE • 1932 • Tavano Charles-Felix • FRN
BILLET DE MILLE, LE • 1934 • Didier Marc • FRN
BILLET DOUX, LE see **MAX ET LE BILLET DOUX** • 1913
BILLETED see **MISLEADING WIDOW, THE** • 1919
BILLETERO, EL • 1951 • Sevilla Raphael J. • MXC
BILLETS • 1925 • Hiscott Leslie • UKN
BILLIARD ROOM, THE • 1972 • Weir Peter • SHT • ASL
BILLIARD TABLE see **PANO VERDE** • 1972
BILLIARDS see **BILIAR** • 1961
BILLIARDS MAD • 1912 • Wilson Frank? • UKN
BILLIE • 1912 • *Shelby Margaret* • USA
BILLIE • 1965 • Weis Don • USA
BILLIE BARNES • 1929 • *B.s.f.p.* • SHT • UKN
BILLIE BARNES • 1930 • *Balcon Michael (P)* • SHT • UKN
BILLIE "BOW-WOW" • 1915 • Moore Rowland • UKN
BILLIE BROWN OF LONDON TOWN • 1908 • *Walturdaw* • UKN
BILLIE JOINS THE NAVY • 1915 • Hotaling Arthur D. • USA
BILLIE, THE HILL BILLY • 1915 • MacMackin Archer • USA
BILLIE'S BABY • 1915 • Lloyd Frank • USA
BILLIE'S DEBUT • 1915 • *Reeves Billie* • USA
BILLIE'S DOUBLE • 1916 • Metcalfe Earl • SHT • USA
BILLIE'S FIND • 1916 • *Jockey* • USA
BILLIE'S HEADACHE • 1916 • Metcalfe Earl • SHT • USA
BILLIE'S HEIRESS • 1915 • *Reeves Billie* • USA
BILLIE'S LUCKY BILL • 1916 • Metcalfe Earl • SHT • USA
BILLIE'S MOTHER • 1916 • Belmore Lionel • SHT • USA
BILLIE'S NEW WATCH • 1913 • *Majestic* • USA
BILLIE'S RESCUE • 1915 • *Reliance* • USA
BILLIE'S REVENGE • 1916 • Metcalfe Earl • SHT • USA
BILLIE'S ROSE • 1922 • Sanderson Challis • UKN
BILLIE'S WATERLOO • 1916 • *Ritchie Billie* • USA
BILLIKEN REVOLTS • 1913 • Aylott Dave? • UKN
BILLIKIN • 1909 • *Lubin* • USA
BILLION-DOLLAR BONER • 1960 • Lovy Alex • ANS • USA
BILLION DOLLAR BOY'S CLUB see **BILLIONAIRE BOY'S CLUB** • 1987
BILLION DOLLAR BRAIN • 1967 • Russell Ken • UKN, USA
BILLION DOLLAR CAPER, THE see **MONEY JUNGLE, THE** • 1968
BILLION DOLLAR HOBO, THE • 1978 • McGowan Stuart E. • USA
BILLION DOLLAR LIMITED • 1942 • Fleischer Dave • ANS • USA
BILLION DOLLAR SCANDAL, THE • 1933 • Brown Harry J. • USA
BILLION DOLLAR THREAT, THE • 1979 • Shear Barry • USA
BILLION FOR BORIS, A • 1985 • Grasshoff Alex • USA
BILLIONAIRE, A see **OKUMAN CHOJA** • 1954
BILLIONAIRE, THE • 1914 • Kirkwood James • USA
BILLIONAIRE, THE • 1955 • *Halas John (P)* • ANS • UKN
BILLIONAIRE BOY'S CLUB • 1987 • Chomsky Marvin • TVM • USA • BILLION DOLLAR BOY'S CLUB
BILLIONAIRE LORD, THE • 1915 • Barber La Verne • USA
BILLIONS • 1920 • Smallwood Ray C. • USA
BILLPOSTER'S TRIALS • 1909 • *Pathe* • FRN
BILL'S ANNIVERSARY • 1919 • Clements Roy • SHT • USA
BILL'S BABY • 1918 • *Parsons Bill* • SHT • USA
BILL'S BILLS • 1912 • *Pathe* • USA
BILL'S BIRTHDAY PRESENT • 1913 • Duncan William • USA
BILL'S BLIGHTED CAREER • 1915 • *Ritchie Billie* • USA
BILL'S BOARD BILL • 1913 • *Roland Ruth* • USA
BILL'S BOY • 1914 • Mainhall Harry • USA

BILL'S CAREER AS BUTLER • 1913 • *Prior Herbert* • USA
BILL'S FINISH • 1919 • Clements Roy • SHT • USA
BILL'S FLUTE • 1911 • Harting P. C. • USA
BILL'S HAT • 1967 • Wieland Joyce • USA
BILL'S LEGACY • 1931 • Revier Harry • UKN
BILL'S MONICKER • 1915 • Kellino W. P. • UKN
BILL'S NARROW ESCAPE • 1916 • *Ritchie Billie* • SHT • USA
BILL'S NEW PAL • 1915 • *Ritchie Billie* • USA
BILL'S OPPORTUNITY • 1918 • *Parsons "smiling Bill"* • SHT • USA
BILL'S PLUMBER AND PLUMBER'S BILL • 1915 • *Mason Billy* • USA
BILL'S REFORMATION • 1912 • Haldane Bert? • UKN
BILL'S RETURN TO PICTURES • 1914 • *Bertho Paul* • UKN
BILL'S RISE IN THE WORLD • 1914 • Nash Percy? • UKN
BILL'S RIVAL • 1914 • Taylor William D. • USA
BILL'S SURRENDER • 1912 • *Powers* • USA
BILL'S SWEETIE • 1918 • *Parsons William* • SHT • USA
BILL'S TEMPTATION • 1912 • Haldane Bert? • UKN
BILL'S WARD • 1911 • *Lubin* • USA
BILL'S WIDOW • 1911 • *Champion* • USA
BILL'S WIFE • 1916 • Reynolds Lynn • SHT • USA
BILL'S WIFE • 1920 • *Wilson Ben* • SHT • USA
BILLY AND HIS PAL • 1911 • Melies Gaston • USA
BILLY AND PERCY • 1972 • Power John • MTV • ASL
BILLY AND THE BIG STICK • 1917 • Griffith Edward H. • USA
BILLY AND THE BUTLER • 1912 • *Bushman Francis X.* • USA
BILLY BLAZES, ESQ. • 1919 • Roach Hal • SHT • USA
BILLY BORNTIRED • 1908 • Coleby A. E. • UKN
BILLY BOY • 1912 • *Solax* • USA
BILLY BOY • 1914 • *Neptune* • ASS • UKN
BILLY BOY • 1954 • Avery Tex • ANS • USA
BILLY BOY • 1978 • SAF
BILLY BRIGHT see **COMIC, THE** • 1969
BILLY BUDD • 1962 • Ustinov Peter • UKN
BILLY BUNGLER THE SILENT BURGLAR • 1912 • Aylott Dave? • UKN
BILLY BUNGLE'S FIRST DAY ON THE FORCE • 1913 • *Sun Films* • UKN
BILLY BUNGLE'S LUCK • 1913 • *Sun Film Co* • UKN
BILLY CHANGES HIS MIND • 1912 • *Steppling John* • USA
BILLY CONVINCING FATHER • 1915 • *Santa Barbara* • USA
BILLY DODGES BILL • 1913 • Avery Charles • USA
BILLY FOOLS DAD • 1913 • *Quirk Billy* • USA
BILLY GALVIN • 1986 • Gray John • USA
BILLY GETS ARRESTED • 1913 • *Quirk Billy* • USA
BILLY GOAT • 1915 • *Majestic* • USA
BILLY GOAT WHISKERS, THE • 1937 • Foster John • ANS • USA
BILLY IN ARMOR • 1913 • *Quirk Billy* • USA
BILLY IN HARNESS • 1918 • *Highgrade Films* • SHT • USA
BILLY IN SOCIETY • 1918 • *West Billy* • SHT • USA
BILLY IN THE LOWLANDS • 1979 • Egleson Jan • USA
BILLY JACK • 1972 • Laughlin Tom • USA
BILLY JACK GOES TO WASHINGTON • 1977 • Laughlin Tom • USA
BILLY JIM • 1922 • Borzage Frank • USA
BILLY JOINS THE BAND • 1913 • Quirk William • USA
BILLY JONES OF NEW YORK • 1912 • *Champion* • USA
BILLY LIARI • 1963 • Schlesinger John • UKN
BILLY MAKES A BLUFF • 1915 • *Santa Barbara* • USA
BILLY MAY AND HIS ORCHESTRA • 1952 • Cowan Will • SHT • USA
BILLY MAYERL ENTERTAINS • 1951 • *Church Gilbert (P)* • SHS • UKN
BILLY MCGRATH OF BROADWAY • 1913 • *Steppling John* • USA
BILLY MCGRATH'S ART CAREER • 1912 • *Essanay* • USA
BILLY MCGRATH'S LOVE LETTERS • 1912 • *Steppling John* • USA
BILLY MERSON • 1926 • *Deforest Phonofilms* • SHT • UKN
BILLY MOUSE'S AWKAKADE • 1940 • Donnelly Eddie • ANS • USA
BILLY NOW A MEDICO • 1915 • *Mica* • USA
BILLY PLAYS POKER • 1913 • *Quirk Billy* • USA
BILLY: PORTRAIT OF A STREET KID • 1977 • Gethers Steve • TVM • USA
BILLY PUTS ONE OVER • 1915 • *Santa Barbara* • USA
BILLY ROSE'S CASA MANANA REVUE • 1938 • Sidney George • SHT • USA
BILLY ROSE'S DIAMOND HORSESHOE see **DIAMOND HORSESHOE** • 1945
BILLY ROSE'S JUMBO • 1962 • Walters Charles • USA • JUMBO
BILLY SMOKE • 1917 • Wolbert William • SHT • USA
BILLY STRIKES OIL • 1917 • Kellino W. P. • UKN
BILLY STUDIES MUSIC • 1915 • *Santa Barbara* • USA
BILLY THE BANDIT • 1916 • Steppling John • SHT • USA
BILLY, THE BEAR TAMER • 1915 • Beggs Lee • USA
BILLY, THE DETECTIVE • 1912 • *Quirk Billy* • USA
BILLY THE JANITOR • 1918 • *Ebony* • SHT • USA
BILLY THE KID • 1911 • Trimble Larry • USA
BILLY THE KID • 1930 • Vidor King • USA • HIGHWAYMAN RIDES, THE
BILLY THE KID • 1941 • Miller David • USA
BILLY THE KID • 1988 • Graham William A. • USA • GORE VIDAL'S BILLY THE KID
BILLY THE KID see **FUERA DE LA LEY** • 1962
BILLY THE KID AND THE GREEN BAIZE VAMPIRE • 1986 • Clarke Alan • UKN
BILLY THE KID IN SANTA FE • 1941 • Newfield Sam • USA
BILLY THE KID IN TEXAS • 1940 • Newfield Sam • USA
BILLY THE KID NO ATARASHII YOAKE • 1987 • Yamakawa Naoto • JPN • ANOTHER MORNING FOR BILLY THE KID
BILLY THE KID OUTLAWED • 1940 • Newfield Sam • USA
BILLY THE KID RETURNS • 1938 • Kane Joseph • USA
BILLY THE KID, SHERIFF OF SAGE VALLEY see **SHERIFF OF SAGE VALLEY** • 1942
BILLY THE KID TRAPPED • 1942 • Newfield Sam • USA
BILLY THE KID VS. DRACULA • 1966 • Beaudine William • USA
BILLY THE KID WANTED • 1941 • Newfield Sam • USA
BILLY THE KID'S FIGHTING PALS • 1941 • Newfield Sam • USA
BILLY THE KID'S GUN JUSTICE • 1940 • Newfield Sam • USA
BILLY THE KID'S LAW AND ORDER see **LAW AND ORDER** • 1942
BILLY THE KID'S RANGE WAR • 1941 • Newfield Sam • USA
BILLY THE KID'S ROUNDUP • 1941 • Newfield Sam • USA
BILLY THE KID'S SMOKING GUNS • 1942 • Newfield Sam • USA • SMOKING GUNS (UKN)
BILLY THE SUFFRAGETTE see **SHAM SUFFRAGETTE, THE** • 1913
BILLY THE TRUTHFUL • 1917 • Kellino W. P. • UKN
BILLY, THE WISE GUY • 1913 • *Gem* • USA
BILLY TURNS BURGLAR • 1913 • *Gem* • USA
BILLY TWO HATS • 1974 • Kotcheff Ted • USA, UKN • LADY AND THE OUTLAW, THE
BILLY VAN DEUSEN AND THE MERRY WIDOW • 1915 • MacMackin Archer • USA
BILLY VAN DEUSEN AND THE VAMPIRE • 1916 • MacMackin Archer • USA
BILLY VAN DEUSEN, MASQUERADER • 1916 • MacMackin Archer • USA
BILLY VAN DEUSEN, THE CAVE MAN • 1916 • MacMackin Archer • SHT • USA
BILLY VAN DEUSEN'S ANCESTRY • 1916 • MacMackin Archer • USA
BILLY VAN DEUSEN'S CAMPAIGN • 1915 • MacMackin Archer • USA
BILLY VAN DEUSEN'S FIANCEE • 1916 • MacMackin Archer • USA
BILLY VAN DEUSEN'S MUDDLE • 1916 • MacMackin Archer • USA
BILLY VAN DEUSEN'S OPERATION • 1916 • MacMackin Archer? • USA
BILLY VAN DEUSEN'S SHADOW • 1916 • MacMackin Archer? • USA
BILLY VAN DEUSEN'S WEDDING EVE • 1916 • MacMackin Archer • USA
BILLY WAS A RIGHT SMART BOY • 1915 • *Sterling* • USA
BILLY WEST • 1982 • Gulpilil David (c/d) • ASL
BILLY WHISKERS • 1920 • *Commonwealth* • USA
BILLY WILDER see **PORTRAIT D'UN HOMME 60% PARFAIT** • 1980
BILLY WINS • 1913 • *Quirk Billy* • USA
BILLY'S ADVENTURE • 1913 • *Quirk Billy* • USA
BILLY'S BABIES • 1914 • *Favourite Films* • UKN
BILLY'S BIBLE • 1911 • Aylott Dave • UKN
BILLY'S BIOSCOPE • 1914 • *Captain Kettle Films* • UKN
BILLY'S BOARD BILL • 1913 • *Quirk Billy* • USA
BILLY'S BOOK ON BOOKING • 1911 • Martinek H. O. • UKN
BILLY'S BOXING GLOVES • 1913 • Aylott Dave? • UKN
BILLY'S BUGLE • 1908 • Aylott Dave? • UKN
BILLY'S BULLDOG • 1910 • Coleby A. E. • UKN
BILLY'S BURGLAR • 1912 • Brooke Van Dyke • USA
BILLY'S CHARGE • 1914 • *Sterling* • USA
BILLY'S COLLEGE JOB • 1915 • Goldin Sidney M. • USA
BILLY'S CUPIDITY see **LITTLE MR. FIXER** • 1915
BILLY'S DOUBLE • 1913 • *Quirk Billy* • USA
BILLY'S DOUBLE CAPTURE • 1913 • *Rex* • USA
BILLY'S FIRST COURTSHIP • 1913 • *Gerrard Films* • UKN
BILLY'S FIRST QUARREL • 1913 • *Gem* • USA
BILLY'S FORTUNE • 1918 • *Parsons William* • SHT • USA
BILLY'S HAT • 1919 • Clements Roy • SHT • USA
BILLY'S HONEYMOON • 1913 • *Quirk Billy* • USA
BILLY'S INSOMNIA • 1912 • *Quirk Billy* • USA
BILLY'S LETTERS • 1911 • *Comet* • USA
BILLY'S LOVE MAKING • 1915 • Garwood William • USA
BILLY'S MELODRAMA • 1916 • Currier Frank • SHT • USA
BILLY'S MISTAKEN OVERCOAT • 1913 • *Quirk Billy* • USA
BILLY'S NEW WATCH • 1913 • *Majestic* • USA
BILLY'S NURSE • 1912 • *Quirk Billy* • USA
BILLY'S NURSE • 1915 • *Genung Eddie* • USA
BILLY'S PIPE DREAM • 1912 • *Vitagraph* • USA
BILLY'S PREDICAMENT • 1918 • *Parsons William* • SHT • USA
BILLY'S REFORMATION • 1916 • *Ritchie Billy* • SHT • USA
BILLY'S RIOT • 1914 • *Sterling* • USA
BILLY'S RUSE • 1914 • *Princess* • USA
BILLY'S SCOOP • 1915 • *Fisher Harry Jr.* • USA
BILLY'S SERVICE • 1911 • *Imp* • USA
BILLY'S SHOES • 1912 • *Quirk Billy* • USA
BILLY'S SISTER • 1910 • *Melies* • USA
BILLY'S SPANISH LOVE SPASM • 1915 • Kellino W. P. • UKN
BILLY'S STORMY COURTSHIP • 1916 • Kellino W. P. • UKN
BILLY'S STRATAGEM • 1912 • Griffith D. W. • USA
BILLY'S STRATAGEM • 1915 • Mitchell Bruce • USA
BILLY'S STRATEGY • 1913 • *Quirk Billy* • USA
BILLY'S SUICIDE • 1913 • *Gem* • USA
BILLY'S SURRENDER • 1912 • *Powers* • USA
BILLY'S SWEETHEART • 1913 • *Ayres Sidney* • USA
BILLY'S TROUBLE • 1913 • *Gem* • USA
BILLY'S TROUBLESOME GRIP • 1912 • *Quirk Billy* • USA
BILLY'S VACATION • 1914 • *Sterling* • USA
BILLY'S VALENTINE • 1911 • *Vitagraph* • USA
BILLY'S WAGER • 1915 • Beggs Lee • USA
BILLY'S WAR BRIDES • 1916 • Garwood William • SHT • USA
BILLY'S WATERLOO • 1915 • *Santa Barbara* • USA
BILLY'S WATERLOO • 1916 • *Rogers Gene* • SHT • USA
BILOCATION • 1973 • Cornu • SHT • UKN • WITHIN HAIL
BILOXI BLUES • 1987 • Nichols Mike • USA
BILTMORE DIAMOND, THE • 1914 • *Melies* • USA
BILWAMANGAL • 1919 • *Madan J. F. (P)* • IND
BILWAMANGAL • 1955 • Madhok D. N. • IND
BILY RAJ • 1924 • Lamac Carl • CZC • WHITE PARADISE, THE
BILY VAN DEUSEN'S EGG-SPENSIVE ADVENTURE • 1916 • MacMackin Archer • USA
BIM • 1949 • Lamorisse Albert • FRN • BIM, LE PETIT ANE
BIM • 1976 • Robertson Hugh A. • USA, T&T
BIM, BAM, BUM see **BIM-BUM** • 1972
BIM-BUM • 1972 • Grgic Zlatko • ANS • YGS • BIM, BAM, BUM
BIM BUM BAM • 1979 • Chiesa Aurelio • ITL
BIM, LE PETIT ANE see **BIM** • 1949
BIMBERG'S LOVE AFFAIR • 1914 • *Crystal* • USA
BIMBI LONTANI • 1920 • Negroni Baldassare • ITL
BIMBO • Hammer Erich • ANM • GDR
BIMBO • 1931 • Fleischer Dave • ASS • USA
BIMBO THE GREAT (USA) see **RIVALEN DER MANEGE** • 1958
BIMBO'S EXPRESS • 1931 • Fleischer Dave • ANS • USA
BIMBO'S INITIATION • 1931 • Fleischer Dave • ANS • USA
BIMI • 1931 • Eason B. Reeves, Thorpe Richard • USA
BIMINI CODE • 1984 • Clark Barry • USA
BIN AL-ATLAL • 1948 • Zulficar Izzeddine • EGY • ENTRE LES RUINES
BIN BADAL BARSAAT • 1963 • Swaroop Jyoti • IND
BIN DEFA OLURUM • 1969 • Aslan Mehmet • TRK
BIN YILLIK YOL • 1968 • Duru Yilmaz • TRK • TWO THOUSAND YEARS' ROAD, THE
BINAN-JO • 1959 • Sasaki Yasushi • JPN • FORBIDDEN CASTLE
BINAN KAIMASU • 1960 • Magatani Morehei • JPN
BINAN O NEGURU JUNIN NO ONNA • 1960 • Magatani Morehei • JPN
BINARY see **PURSUIT** • 1972
BINARY BIT PATTERNS • 1969 • *Whitney Michael (P)* • ANS • USA
BINBASI TAYFUN • 1968 • Ziyal Tolgay • TRK • CAPTAIN HURRICANE
BINDING SENTIMENTS see **HOLDUDVAR, A** • 1969
BINDING SHOT, THE • 1910 • *American* • USA
BINDING TIES see **HOLDUDVAR, A** • 1969
BINDLE • 1926 • Parkinson H. B. • SHS • UKN
BINDLE AT THE PARTY • 1926 • Parkinson H. B. • SHT • UKN
BINDLE IN CHARGE • 1926 • Parkinson H. B. • SHT • UKN
BINDLE INTRODUCED • 1926 • Parkinson H. B. • SHT • UKN
BINDLE, MATCHMAKER • 1926 • Parkinson H. B. • SHT • UKN
BINDLE, MILLIONAIRE • 1926 • Parkinson H. B. • SHT • UKN
BINDLE (ONE OF THEM DAYS) • 1966 • Saunders Peter • UKN
BINDLE'S COCKTAIL • 1926 • Parkinson H. B. • SHT • UKN
BINDU THEKEY BRITTA • 1970 • Rebecca • PKS • CIRCLE FROM A DOT
BINETTOSCOPE, LE • 1910 • Cohl Emile • ANS • FRN • COMEDY-GRAPH, THE
BING! BANG! • 1917 • Parrott Charles • SHT • USA
BING, BANG, BIFF • 1915 • *Pathe Exchange* • USA
BING BANG BOOM • 1922 • Butler Fred J. • USA
BING BANG BOOM • 1970 • Henson Joan • SHT • CND
BING-BANG BROTHERS • 1915 • *Lehnberg John* • USA
BING PRESENTS ORESTE • 1955 • Dmytryk Edward • SHT • USA
BINGE see **PARRANDA** • 1977
BINGLE AT THE PAPER CHASE • 1921 • *Payne Gilbert* • SHT • UKN
BINGLES AND THE CABARET • 1913 • Thompson Frederick A. • USA
BINGLES MENDS THE CLOCK • 1913 • Thompson Frederick A. • USA
BINGLES' NIGHTMARE • 1913 • Ince Ralph • USA
BINGO • 1973 • Lord Jean-Claude • CND
BINGO • 1989 • Imboden Markus • SWT
BINGO BONGO • 1983 • Festa Campanile Pasquale • ITL
BINGO, BRIDESMAIDS AND BRACES • 1988 • Armstrong Gillian • DOC • ASL
BINGO CROSBYANA • 1936 • Freleng Friz • ANS • USA
BINGO LONG TRAVELING ALL-STARS AND MOTOR KINGS, THE • 1976 • Badham John • USA
BINGVILLE FIRE DEPARTMENT, THE • 1914 • *Kalem* • USA
BINKS ADVERTISES FOR A WIFE • 1913 • *Imp* • USA
BINKS AND JINKS, ATTORNEYS AT LAW • 1912 • *Benner Yale* • USA
BINKS AND THE BATHING GIRLS • 1913 • *De Forrest Charles* • USA
BINKS DID IT • 1913 • *Imp* • USA
BINKS ELEVATES THE STAGE • 1913 • *Imp* • USA
BINKS ENDS THE WAR • 1913 • *Imp* • USA
BINKS' GOUTY FOOT • 1913 • *Imp* • USA
BINK'S PLAYS CUPID • 1913 • *Imp* • USA
BINKS THE BLACK HAND • 1913 • *Imp* • USA
BINKS, THE HAWKSHAW • 1913 • *De Forrest George* • USA
BINKS, THE STRIKEBREAKER • 1913 • *Imp* • USA
BINKS, THE TERRIBLE TURK • 1913 • *Imp* • USA
BINKS THE TIGHTWAD • 1913 • *Imp* • USA
BINK'S VACATION • 1913 • Dillon Eddie • USA
BINK'S WIFE'S UNCLE • 1913 • Haldane Bert? • UKN
BINNING STREET • 1984 • Coote Gilly • DOC • ASL
BINO FABULE • 1988 • Taillon Rejeane, Roussil Andre, Lombaerts Robert • CND
BINT AL-H'ARIS • 1968 • Barakat Henry • LBN • FILLE DU GARDIEN, LA
BINT AL-YUM • 1956 • Barakat Henry • EGY • JEUNES FILLES MODERNES
BINT EL HAWA • 1953 • Wahby Youssef • EGY • DAUGHTER OF LOVE
BINT EL NIL • 1929 • *Amir Aziza* • EGY • DAUGHTER OF THE NILE
BINT MIN EL BANAT • 1968 • Al Imam Hassan • EGY • STORY OF A GIRL
BINT SABATASHAR • 1959 • Abu Saif Salah • EGY • GIRL OF SEVENTEEN, A
BINT SHAKIEH • 1967 • Mustafa Hassam Eddin • EGY • LOVELY GIRL
BINTANG PUJAAN • 1979 • Dom Shahrom • MLY • SUPERSTAR
BIO-GRAPHY see **VIO-GRAFIA** • 1975
BIO WOMAN • 1981 • Godfrey Bob • ANS • UKN
BIOGRAPH DRAMATISED SONGS • 1902 • Moss Hugh • SER • UKN
BIOGRAPH'S IMPROVED INCUBATOR • 1902 • *Biograph* • USA
BIOGRAPHY OF A BACHELOR GIRL • 1934 • Griffith Edward H. • USA
BIOHAZARD • 1984 • Ray Fred Olen • USA
BIOHAZARD see **WARNING SIGN** • 1985
BIOMBO DE CAGLIOSTRO, EL • 1910 • de Chomon Segundo • SHT • SPN • CAGLIOSTRO'S FOLDING SCREEN
BIONDA DI PECHINO, LA (ITL) see **BLONDE DE PEKIN, LA** • 1968
BIONDA SOTTOCHIAVE • 1939 • Mastrocinque Camillo • ITL
BIONDINA, LA • 1919 • Palermi Amleto • ITL

BIONIC BOY • 1977 • Diaz Leody M. • PHL, HKG
BIONIC NINJA • 1986 • Ashby Tim • USA
BIOSCOPE • 1983 • Moretti Pierre • CND
BIOTAXIA • 1967 • Nunes Jose Maria • SPN
BIP GOES TO TOWN • 1941 • Ivens Joris • USA
BIQUEFARRE • 1983 • Rouquier Georges • FRN
BI'R AL-HIRMAN • 1969 • el Sheikh Kamal • EGY • PUITS DE LA PRIVATION, LES
BIR ANENIN GOZ YASLARI MUHUR GOZLUM • 1967 • Erakalin Ulku • TRK • TEARS OF A MOTHER, THE
BIR AVUC CENNET • 1985 • Ozer Muammer • TRK • HANDFUL OF PARADISE, A
BIR AVUC GOKYUZU • 1987 • Elci Umit • TRK • HANDFUL OF SKY, A
BIR CIRKIN ADAM • 1969 • Guney Yilmaz • TRK • UGLY MAN, AN
BIR DAG MASALI • 1967 • Demirag Turgut • TRK • STORY OF A MOUNTAIN, THE ◦ TALE OF A MOUNTAIN
BIR DAMAT ARANIYOR • 1968 • Saner Hulki • TRK • LOOKING FOR A BRIDEGROOM
BIR GUN MUTLAKA • 1976 • Olgac Bilge • TRK • ONE DAY SURELY ◦ ONE DAY CERTAINLY
BIR GUNUN HIKAYYESI • 1982 • Cetin Sinan • TRK • STORY OF A DAY, THE
BIR KATIL SEVDIM • 1967 • Erakalin Ulku • TRK • I'VE LOVED A MURDERER
BIR KIRIK BEBEK • 1987 • Yonder Nisan • TRK • BROKEN DOLL, A
BIR MAHKUM KACTI • 1968 • Hancer Nisan • TRK • CONVICT HAS ESCAPED, A
BIR SOFORUN GIZLI DEFTERI • 1967 • Conturk Remzi • TRK • CABMAN'S SECRET DIARY, A
BIR TURK'E GONUL VERDIM • 1969 • Refig Halit • TRK • I GAVE MY HEART TO A TURK ◦ EVA LOVED A TURK
BIR UDUM SEVGI • 1985 • Yilmaz Atif • TRK • SIP OF LOVE, A
BIRAGHIN • 1946 • Gallone Carmine • ITL
BIRAJ BAHU • 1954 • Roy Bimal • IND
BIRAJ BOU • 1946 • *Sircar B. N. (P)* • IND
BIRAKIN YASIYALIM • 1967 • Gultekin Sirri • TRK • LET US LIVE
BIRCH INTERVAL • 1977 • Mann Delbert • USA
BIRCH STREET see **ULICA BRZOZOWA** • 1947
BIRCH TREE, THE see **BREZA** • 1967
BIRCH WOOD, THE see **BRZEZINA** • 1971
BIRCHWOOD see **BRZEZINA** • 1971
BIRD • 1978 • Brakhage Stan • SHT • USA
BIRD • 1988 • Eastwood Clint • USA
BIRD, THE • 1965 • Murakami Jimmy T. • ANS • USA
BIRD, THE • 1965 • Wolf Fred • ANS • USA
BIRD, THE see **OISEAU, L'** • 1965
BIRD, THE see **PTAK** • 1968
BIRD AND ANIMAL • 1963 • Burstall Tim • SHT • ASL
BIRD AND THE WORM, THE see **PTICA I CRVEK** • 1977
BIRD BOY • 1984 • SAF
BIRD-BRAIN DOG • 1954 • Lundy Dick • ANS • USA
BIRD BUILT OF NEWSPAPER, A • ANS • FRN
BIRD CAME C.O.D., THE • 1942 • Jones Charles M. • ANS • USA
BIRD FANCIER, THE • 1920 • Goldin Sidney M. • UKN
BIRD FANCIER, THE see **HOMME AUX OISEAUX, L'** • 1952
BIRD FROM AFRICA, THE see **AFRICA NO TORI** • 1975
BIRD IN A BONNET, A • 1958 • Freleng Friz • ANS • USA
BIRD IN A CAGE see **PINJRE KE PANCHHI** • 1968
BIRD IN A GILDED CAGE, A • 1909 • Porter Edwin S. • USA
BIRD IN A GUILTY CAGE • 1952 • Freleng Friz • ANS • USA
BIRD IN THE HAND, A • 1911 • *Essanay* • USA
BIRD IN THE HAND, A see **GOURMANDINES, LES** • 1973
BIRD IN THE HEAD, A • 1946 • Bernds Edward • SHT • USA
BIRD IN THE HOUSE • 1973 • King Allan • CND
BIRD IS GOOD, THE • 1963 • Carpi Cioni • ANS • USA
BIRD MAN, THE • 1935 • *Mintz Charles (P)* • ANS • USA
BIRD MAN, THE see **LINTUMIES** • 1977
BIRD MANOR • 1925 • *Weisman T. Walter* • DOC • USA
BIRD MISSING SPRING, THE see **SEKISHUN-CHO** • 1959
BIRD OF BAGDAD, A • 1918 • Webb Kenneth • SHT • USA
BIRD OF BLOOD, THE see **OISEAU DE SANG, L'**
BIRD OF FREEDOM, A • 1908 • Raymond Charles? • UKN
BIRD OF NEWSPAPER, A see **OISEAU EN PAPIER JOURNAL, UN** • 1962
BIRD OF PARADISE • 1932 • Vidor King • USA
BIRD OF PARADISE • 1951 • Daves Delmer • USA
BIRD OF PARADISE see **PARADISFAGELN** • 1916
BIRD OF PARADISE, THE see **OISEAU DE PARADIS, L'** • 1962
BIRD OF PASSAGE • 1960 • Defalco Martin • DOC • CND
BIRD OF PREY see **EPERVIER, L'** • 1933
BIRD OF PREY, A • 1916 • Nowland Eugene • USA • THIEF IN THE NIGHT, A
BIRD OF PREY, THE • 1918 • Le Saint Edward J. • USA
BIRD OF SPRINGS PAST, THE see **SEKISHUN-CHO** • 1959
BIRD OF WISDOM (USA) see **OISEAU DE LA SAGESSE, L'** • 1966
BIRD ON A WIRE • 1989 • Badham John • USA
BIRD ON NELLIE'S HAT, THE • 1939 • Lovy Alex • ANS • USA
BIRD SCOUTS • 1935 • Gillett Burt, Palmer Tom • ANS • USA
BIRD STORE, THE • 1932 • Jackson Wilfred • ANS • USA
BIRD STUFFER, THE • 1936 • *Mintz Charles (P)* • ANS • USA
BIRD SYMPHONY • 1955 • Rasinski Connie • ANS • USA
BIRD, THE FOX AND THE FULL MOON, THE see **HORNERO, EL ZORRO Y LA LUNA LLENA, EL** • 1977
BIRD TOWER, THE • 1941 • Davis Mannie • ANS • USA
BIRD WHO CAME TO DINNER, THE • 1961 • Hannah Jack • ANS • USA
BIRD WITH THE CRYSTAL PLUMAGE, THE (USA) see **UCCELLO DALLE PIUME DE CRISTALLO, L'** • 1970
BIRD WITH THE GLASS FEATHERS, THE see **UCCELLO DALLE PIUME DE CRISTALLO, L'** • 1970
BIRDIE AND THE BEAST • 1944 • Clampett Robert • ANS • USA
BIRDIE IN SEARCH OF A HUSBAND • 1909 • *Anglo-American* • UKN
BIRDIES see **MADARKAK** • 1971
BIRDLAND • 1935 • *Terry Paul/ Moser Frank (P)* • ANS • USA
BIRDMAN OF ALCATRAZ • 1962 • Frankenheimer John • USA
BIRDMEN, THE • 1971 • Leacock Philip • USA • ESCAPE OF THE BIRDMEN ◦ OPERATION BRAINDRAIN
BIRDS • 1965 • Becker Harold • SHT • USA
BIRDS • 1969 • Zwartjes Frans • SHT • NTH
BIRDS, THE • 1963 • Hitchcock Alfred • USA
BIRDS, THE • 1963 • Joseph Stanley • DCS • UKN
BIRDS, THE see **PTAKI** • 1963
BIRD'S A BIRD, A • 1915 • Frazee Edwin • USA
BIRDS AND GREYHOUNDS see **PTITSI I HRUTKI** • 1968
BIRDS AND THE BEES, THE • 1956 • Taurog Norman • USA • LADY EVE, THE
BIRDS AND THE BEES, THE see **THREE DARING DAUGHTERS** • 1947
BIRDS ANONYMOUS • 1957 • Freleng Friz • ANS • USA
BIRD'S APPETITE, A see **APPETIT D'OISEAU** • 1964
BIRDS AT SUNRISE • 1985 • Wieland Joyce • CND
BIRDS BEES AND STORKS • 1964 • Halas John • ANS • UKN
BIRDS' CHRISTMAS CAROL, THE • 1917 • Warrenton Lule • USA • BIT O' HEAVEN, A
BIRDS COME FLYING TO US • 1971 • Zhandov Zahari • BUL
BIRDS COME TO DIE IN PERU, THE (UKN) see **OISEAUX VONT MOURIR AU PEROU, LES** • 1968
BIRDS DO IT • 1966 • Marton Andrew • USA
BIRDS DO IT.. BEES DO IT.. • 1974 • Noxon Nicolas • DOC • USA
BIRDS EAT ON MONDAYS, THE see **AVES COMEN LOS LUNES, LAS** • 1978
BIRD'S-EYE VIEW OF ST. HELIER (JERSEY) see **PANORAMA DU PORT DE SAINT-HELIER** • 1899
BIRDS IN LOVE • 1936 • *Mintz Charles (P)* • ANS • USA
BIRDS IN PERU (USA) see **OISEAUX VONT MOURIR AU PEROU, LES** • 1968
BIRDS IN THE SPRING • 1973 • Hand David • ANS • USA
BIRDS IN THEIR LITTLE NESTS • 1905 • *Urban Trading Co* • UKN
BIRDS OF A FATHER • 1961 • McKimson Robert • ANS • USA
BIRDS OF A FEATHER • 1911 • *Neason Hazel* • USA
BIRDS OF A FEATHER • 1916 • Mong William V. • SHT • USA
BIRDS OF A FEATHER • 1917 • Roach Hal • SHT • USA
BIRDS OF A FEATHER • 1918 • *Parsons William* • SHT • USA
BIRDS OF A FEATHER • 1931 • Gillett Burt • ANS • USA
BIRDS OF A FEATHER • 1931 • Hart Ben R. • UKN
BIRDS OF A FEATHER • 1935 • Baxter John • UKN
BIRDS OF A FEATHER • 1965 • Marcus Sid • ANS • USA
BIRDS OF A FEATHER see **CAGE AUX FOLLES, LA** • 1978
BIRDS OF A FEATHER.. FLOCKING TOGETHER see **WILD FEMALES, THE** • 1968
BIRDS OF A FEATHER PLOT TOGETHER • 1914 • Birch Cecil • UKN
BIRDS OF BADEN-BADEN, THE see **PAJAROS DE BADEN-BADEN, LOS** • 1974
BIRDS OF OUR HOPES, THE • 1977 • Ishmukhamedov Elyor • USS
BIRDS OF PARADISE • 1981 • SAF
BIRDS OF PASSAGE • 1914 • *Eclair* • USA
BIRDS OF PASSAGE see **TAZNI PTACI** • 1961
BIRDS OF PREY • 1913 • *Kalem* • USA
BIRDS OF PREY • 1917 • Terwilliger George W. • SHT • USA
BIRDS OF PREY • 1927 • Craft William James • USA
BIRDS OF PREY • 1930 • Dean Basil • UKN • PERFECT ALIBI, THE (USA)
BIRDS OF PREY • 1973 • Graham William A. • TVM • USA • TURBO BLADE
BIRDS OF PREY • 1984 • Montesi Jorge • CND • TRAPPED
BIRDS OF PREY • 1986 • Weston Eric • USA
BIRDS OF PREY see **RAPACE, LA** • 1968
BIRDS OF PREY (UKN) see **ACE OF ACES, THE** • 1938
BIRDS, ORPHANS AND FOOLS see **VTACKOVIA, SIROTY A BLAZNI** • 1969
BIRDS OVER THE CITY • 1974 • Nikolenko S. • USS
BIRDS, THE BEES AND THE ITALIANS, THE (USA) see **SIGNORE E SIGNORI** • 1966
BIRDSNESTING • 1898 • *Paul R. W.* • UKN
BIRDSVILLE • 1986 • Schultz Carl • ASL
BIRDY • 1984 • Parker Alan • USA
BIRGIT HAAS MUST BE KILLED (USA) see **IL FAUT TUER BIRGITT HAAS** • 1981
BIRIBI • 1922 • Steinhoff Hans • AUS
BIRIBI • 1970 • Moosmann Daniel • FRN, TNS
BIRICHINO DI PAPA, IL • 1943 • Matarazzo Raffaello • ITL
BIRJUK see **BIRYUK** • 1979
BIRMINGHAM GIRL'S LAST HOPE, A • 1917 • Haldane Bert • UKN • LAST HOPE, THE
BIRTH see **BREATH** • 1975
BIRTH see **NAISSANCE** • 1982
BIRTH AND ADVENTURES OF A FOUNTAIN PEN see **MAGIC FOUNTAIN PEN, THE** • 1907
BIRTH CERTIFICATE, THE see **SWIATDECTWO URODZENIA** • 1961
BIRTH CONTROL • 1917 • *Sanger Margaret* • USA
BIRTH MARK, THE • 1911 • *Yankee* • USA
BIRTH OF A BABY • 1938 • Christie Al • USA
BIRTH OF A BAND • 1955 • Cowan Will • SHT • USA
BIRTH OF A FILM, THE • 1946 • Grey Richard M. • DOC • UKN
BIRTH OF A FLIVVER • 1915 • O'Brien Willis • ANS • USA
BIRTH OF A FLOWER • 1910 • Smith Percy • UKN
BIRTH OF A LEGEND • 1973 • Kemp Matty • DOC
BIRTH OF A MAN, THE • 1916 • *Walthall Henry B.* • USA
BIRTH OF A MILL • 1968 • Murray John B. • DOC • ASL
BIRTH OF A MOUNTAIN, THE • 1973 • Cohen Einan • ANS • NTH
BIRTH OF A NATION, THE • 1915 • Griffith D. W. • USA • CLANSMAN, THE
BIRTH OF A NOTION • 1947 • McKimson Robert • ANS • USA
BIRTH OF A RACE • 1919 • Noble John W. • USA
BIRTH OF A ROBOT • 1934 • Lye Len, Jennings Humphrey • ANS • UKN • BIRTH OF THE ROBOT, THE
BIRTH OF A SCULPTURE see **GIPS-ROMANCA** • 1960
BIRTH OF A SHIP, THE see **NARODZINY STATKU** • 1961
BIRTH OF A SOUL, THE • 1920 • Hollywood Edwin L. • USA
BIRTH OF A TANKER see **NAISSANCE D'UN PETROLIER** • 1958
BIRTH OF A TOOTHPICK • 1939 • Gillett Burt • ANS • USA
BIRTH OF A TOWN • 1959 • Lomnicki Jan • DOC • PLN
BIRTH OF A YOUNG HERO see **WAKAOYABUN TANJO** • 1967
BIRTH OF APHRODITE, THE • 1971 • Auslender Leland • SHT • USA
BIRTH OF ASHTANNI see **JANMASHTAMI** • 1950
BIRTH OF CHARACTER, THE • 1916 • Hopper E. Mason? • USA
BIRTH OF CINEMA, THE see **NAISSANCE DU CINEMA, LA** • 1960
BIRTH OF EMOTION • 1915 • Otto Henry • USA
BIRTH OF FRANKENSTEIN see **CURSE OF FRANKENSTEIN, THE** • 1957
BIRTH OF HANUMAN see **HANUMAN JANMAN** • 1925
BIRTH OF HANUMAN see **HANUMAN JANMAN** • 1953
BIRTH OF JAPAN see **NIPPON TANJO** • 1959
BIRTH OF JAZZ • 1932 • *Mintz Charles (P)* • ANS • USA
BIRTH OF JESUS, THE • 1909 • *Pathe* • FRN
BIRTH OF JUDO, THE see **YAWARA SEMPU** • 1965
BIRTH OF LORD KRISHNA, THE see **SHRI KRISHNA JANMA** • 1918
BIRTH OF MENYHERT SIMON, THE see **SIMON MENYHERT SZULTESE** • 1954
BIRTH OF NANDINI see **JANAK NANDINI** • 1938
BIRTH OF NEW CHINA, THE • 1989 • CHN
BIRTH OF NEW ZEALAND • 1922 • NZL
BIRTH OF OUR SAVIOUR, THE • 1914 • Brabin Charles J. • USA
BIRTH OF PATRIOTISM, THE • 1917 • Ingleton E. Magnus • USA
BIRTH OF THE AMERICAN FLAG • 1965 • Vanderbeek Stan • USA
BIRTH OF THE BEATLES • 1979 • Marquand Richard • TVM • USA, UKN
BIRTH OF THE BLUES, THE • 1941 • Schertzinger Victor • USA
BIRTH OF THE HOSTS OF THE FOREST, THE see **ROZDESTVO OBITATELEJ LESA** • 1912
BIRTH OF THE LOTUS BLOSSOM, THE • 1912 • *Takagi Taku* • USA
BIRTH OF THE ROBOT, THE see **BIRTH OF A ROBOT** • 1934
BIRTH OF THE STAR-SPANGLED BANNER, THE • 1914 • Lessey George A. • USA
BIRTH OF THE YEAR • 1938 • Cherry Evelyn Spice • UKN
BIRTH OF TRIPLETS • 1964 • *Alexander Claude (P)* • DOC • USA • WONDROUS STORY OF BIRTH, THE ◦ STORY OF BIRTH, THE
BIRTH OF WHITE AUSTRALIA, THE • 1928 • Walsh Phil K. • ASL
BIRTH SCANDAL, A • 1917 • *Dillon Jack* • SHT • USA
BIRTHDAY • 1922 • Fleischer Dave • ANS • USA
BIRTHDAY • 1942 • Cooper Budge • DOC • UKN
BIRTHDAY see **SYNTYMAPAIVA** • 1973
BIRTHDAY see **DYEN ROZHDYENIYA** • 1978
BIRTHDAY AFFAIR, A • 1909 • *Essanay* • USA
BIRTHDAY BLUES • 1932 • McGowan Robert • SHT • USA
BIRTHDAY BLUES • 1945 • Yates Hal • SHT • USA
BIRTHDAY BLUNDER, A • 1917 • *Triangle* • USA
BIRTHDAY CAKE, THE • 1913 • *Cummings Irving* • USA
BIRTHDAY CAKE, THE • 1960 • Halas John • ANS • UKN
BIRTHDAY CIGARS • 1910 • Melies Gaston • USA
BIRTHDAY CLOCK, THE • 1970 • McConnell Edward • SHT • UKN
BIRTHDAY GIFT, THE • 1913 • Kent Charles • USA
BIRTHDAY GIFT, THE • 1916 • *Supreme* • USA
BIRTHDAY GIFT, THE see **FODSELSDAGSGAVEN** • 1912
BIRTHDAY OF A STOOGE see **FUGITIVES FOR A NIGHT** • 1938
BIRTHDAY OF THE YOUNG INHABITANTS OF WARSAW see **URODZINY MLODEGO WARSZAWIAKA** • 1980
BIRTHDAY PARTY • 1937 • *Lantz Walter (P)* • ANS • USA
BIRTHDAY PARTY • 1944 • Sparber I. • ANS • USA
BIRTHDAY PARTY • 1970 • *Xis* • USA
BIRTHDAY PARTY • 1977 • USA, DNM
BIRTHDAY PARTY, THE • 1913 • *Komic* • USA
BIRTHDAY PARTY, THE • 1931 • Gillett Burt • ANS • USA
BIRTHDAY PARTY, THE • 1970 • Friedkin William • UKN
BIRTHDAY PRESENT see **FODELSEDAGSPRESENTEN** • 1914
BIRTHDAY PRESENT, A • 1914 • *Komic* • USA
BIRTHDAY PRESENT, THE • 1912 • *Reliance* • USA
BIRTHDAY PRESENT, THE • 1957 • Jackson Pat • UKN
BIRTHDAY RING, THE • 1913 • *Ab* • USA
BIRTHDAY TANGLE, A • 1920 • Davis James • SHT • USA
BIRTHDAY THAT MATTERED, THE • 1912 • Haldane Bert? • UKN
BIRTHDAY TODAY • 1966 • Milsin Lev • ANS • USS
BIRTHDAY TOWN • 1988 • Papayiannidis Takis • GRC
BIRTHDAY TREAT • 1960 • *Halas John (P)* • ANS • UKN
BIRTHDAY UMBRELLA, A • 1905 • Collins Alf • UKN • UNLUCKY UMBRELLA, THE
BIRTHMARK, THE • 1911 • *Reliance* • USA
BIRTHMARK, THE • 1913 • *Lubin* • USA
BIRTHMARK, THE • 1915 • *Clayton Marguerite* • USA
BIRTHPLACE • 1975 • Blagg Linda • SHT • ASL
BIRTHPLACE OF A NATION • 1967 • Kelly Ron • CND
BIRTHPLACE OF THE HOOTENANNY see **GREENWICH VILLAGE STORY** • 1963
BIRTHRIGHT • 1920 • Hemmer Edward L. • USA
BIRTHRIGHT • 1924 • Micheaux Oscar • USA
BIRTHRIGHT • 1939 • Micheaux Oscar • USA
BIRTHRIGHT • 1952 • Clifford Bill • USA
BIRTLES THE OVERLANDER • 1912 • *Gaumont* • ASL
BIRUMA NO TATEGOTO • 1956 • Ichikawa Kon • JPN • BURMESE HARP, THE (UKN) ◦ HARP OF BURMA, THE
BIRUNI • 1974 • Abbasov Shukhrat • USS
BIRYUK • 1979 • Balayan Roman • USS • BIRJUK ◦ LONE WOLF, THE
BIS ANS ENDE DER WELT • 1989 • Wenders Wim • FRG, ASL • TO THE END OF THE WORLD ◦ UNTIL THE END OF THE WORLD
BIS DAS DER TOD EUCH SCHEIDET • Carow Heiner • GDR • UNTIL DEATH DO YOU PART
BIS DAS GELD EUCH SCHEIDET • 1960 • Vohrer Alfred • FRG
BIS FRUH UM FUNFE • 1919 • Bolten-Baeckers Heinrich • FRG
BIS INS DRITTE UND VIERTE GLIED • 1983 • Sander Helke • FRG
BIS WIR UNS WIEDERSEHEN • 1952 • Ucicky Gustav • FRG

BIS ZUM ENDE ALLER TAGE • 1961 • Wirth Franz Peter • FRG • GIRL FROM HONG KONG (USA)
BIS ZUR BITTEREN NEIGE • 1975 • Oswald Gerd • AUS, FRG • TO THE BITTER END (USA)
BISARCA, LA • 1950 • Simonelli Giorgio C. • ITL
BISBETICA DOMATA, LA • 1942 • Poggioli Ferdinando M. • ITL
BISBETICA DOMATA, LA (ITL) see **TAMING OF THE SHREW, THE** • 1967
BISBETICO DOMATO, IL • 1981 • Castellano, Pipolo • ITL
BISCADERA • 1972 • Al-Rawi Abdel-Hadi • SHT • IRQ
BISCOT SE TROMPE D'ETAGE • 1916 • Feyder Jacques • FRN
BISCOTDSING • 1973 • Walton Lloyd A. • DOC • CND
BISCOTIN • 1920 • Feuillade Louis • SER • FRN
BISCOTIN CANDIDAT • 1920 • Feuillade Louis • FRN
BISCOTIN NEURASTHENIQUE • 1920 • Feuillade Louis • FRN
"BISCOTS-NEGRES" VOS COUSINS, LES • 1974 • Hondo Abib Med • FRN, MRT
BISCUIT EATER, THE • 1940 • Heisler Stuart • USA • GOD GAVE HIM A DOG (UKN)
BISCUIT EATER, THE • 1972 • McEveety Vincent • USA
BISEXUAL (UKN) see **ONZE MILLE VIERGES, LES** • 1975
BISHOP MISBEHAVES, THE • 1935 • Dupont E. A. • USA • BISHOP'S MISADVENTURES, THE (UKN)
BISHOP MURDER CASE, THE • 1929 • Grinde Nick, Burton David • USA
BISHOP OF THE OZARKS, THE • 1923 • Fox Finis • USA
BISHOP'S BATHE, THE • 1912 • Plumb Hay • UKN
BISHOP'S BEDROOM, THE see **STANZA DEL VESCOVO, LA** • 1977
BISHOP'S CANDLESTICKS, THE • 1913 • Brenon Herbert • USA
BISHOP'S EMERALDS, THE • 1919 • O'Brien John B. • USA
BISHOP'S MISADVENTURES, THE (UKN) see **BISHOP MISBEHAVES, THE** • 1935
BISHOP'S ROOM, THE see **STANZA DEL VESCOVO, LA** • 1977
BISHOP'S SECRETS, THE • 1916 • *Unity Sales* • USA
BISHOP'S SILENCE, THE • 1914 • Weston Charles • UKN
BISHOP'S SILENCE, THE • 1915 • *Regent Company* • ASL
BISHOP'S WIFE, THE • 1947 • Koster Henry • USA • CARY AND THE BISHOP'S WIFE
BISIG NG LIPUNAN • 1967 • Cruz Abraham • PHL • ARM OF SOCIETY
BISMARCK • 1925 • Paul Heinz • FRG
BISMARCK • 1925 • Wendt Ernst • FRG
BISMARCK • 1940 • Liebeneiner Wolfgang • FRG
BISMARCK 1862-1898 • 1926 • Blachnitzky Curt • FRG
BISMARCK'S DISMISSAL (UKN) see **ENTLASSUNG, DIE** • 1942
BISON HUNTERS, THE see **LOWCY BIZONOW** • 1970
BISSCHEN LIEBE FUR DICH, EIN • 1932 • Neufeld Max • FRG • ZWEI GLUCKLICHE HERZEN
BISTURI, LA MAFIA BIANCA • 1973 • Zampa Luigi • ITL • HOSPITALS, THE WHITE MAFIA
BIT O' HEAVEN, A • 1915 • *Eclair* • USA
BIT O' HEAVEN, A see **BIRDS' CHRISTMAS CAROL, THE** • 1917
BIT OF BARK, A • 1959 • Kelly Ron • CND
BIT OF BENT WIRE, A • 1916 • Smith David • SHT • USA
BIT OF BLACK STUFF, A • 1921 • Paul Fred • UKN
BIT OF BLARNEY, A • 1946 • Moore Harold James • SHT • USA
BIT OF BLUE RIBBON, A • 1912 • Sturgeon Rollin S. • USA
BIT OF HEAVEN, A • 1928 • Wheeler Cliff • USA • LITTLE BIT OF HEAVEN
BIT OF HUMAN DRIFTWOOD, A • 1914 • Vale Travers • USA
BIT OF IMMORTALITY, A (USA) see **TIZ DEKA HALHATATLANSAG** • 1967
BIT OF JADE, A • 1918 • Sloman Edward • USA
BIT OF KINDLING, A • 1917 • MacDonald Sherwood • USA • STICKS
BIT OF LACE, A • 1915 • *Mayo Edna* • USA
BIT OF LIFE, A • 1917 • *Goldin Features* • SHT • USA
BIT OF LOVE, A • 1919 • Terwilliger George W. • USA
BIT OF OULDE IRELAND, A • 1910 • *London Cinematograph Co.* • UKN
BIT PARTS • 1988 • Rojas Guillermo Orlando • CUB
BIT PLAYER, THE see **SALUT L'ARTISTE** • 1973
BITA • 1973 • Daryoush Hagir • IRN
BITCH • 1965 • Warhol Andy • USA
BITCH, THE • 1979 • O'Hara Gerry • UKN
BITCH, THE see **PERRA, LA** • 1967
BITCH WANTS BLOOD, THE • *Vitti Monica* • FRN
BITCHIN' SORORITY BABES • 1987 • Decoteau David • USA
BITE, THE • 1965 • Mukoi Kan • JPN
BITE AND RUN (USA) see **MORDI E FUGGI** • 1973
BITE ME, DARLING see **BEISS MICH, LIEBLING** • 1970
BITE OF A SNAKE, THE • 1913 • Henderson Dell • USA
BITE OF THE GORILLA, THE see **GORILLE A MORDU L'ARCHEVEQUE, LE** • 1962
BITE THE BULLET • 1975 • Brooks Richard • USA
BITE TO EAT, A see **SOUSTO** • 1960
BITER BIT, A • 1899 • *Riley Brothers* • UKN
BITER BIT, THE • 1909 • Coleby A. E. • UKN
BITER BIT, THE • 1914 • *Crusade* • UKN
BITER BIT, THE • 1920 • Vanderlyn S. • UKN
BITER BIT, THE • 1943 • UKN
BITER BIT, THE see **CALLING ALL MA'S** • 1937
BITER BITTEN, THE • 1904 • Haggar William • UKN
BITER BITTEN, THE • 1912 • *Essanay* • USA
BITER BITTEN, THE • 1913 • *Lyman Laura* • USA
BITING BUSINESS, A • 1911 • *Imp* • USA
BITING HUSBAND (USA) see **HARAPOS FERJ** • 1939
BITKA NA NERETVI • 1969 • Bulajic Velko • YGS, ITL, FRG • BATTAGLIA DELLA NERETVA, LA (ITL) ◦ BATTLE OF NERETVA, THE (USA) ◦ BATTLE ON THE RIVER NERETVA ◦ SCHLACHT AN DEN NERETVA, DIE
BITOKU NO YOROMEKI • 1957 • Nakahira Ko • JPN • FLESH IS WEAK, THE
BITS OF BROADWAY • 1930 • Grinde Nick • SHT • USA
BITS OF LIFE • 1921 • Neilan Marshall • USA
BITS OF OUR AIRCRAFT ARE MISSING • 1943 • Catling Darrell • UKN
BITTEN BITER, THE • 1920 • Mannering Cecil • UKN
BITTER APPLES • 1927 • Hoyt Harry O. • USA
BITTER ASH • 1963 • Kent Larry • CND
BITTER BREAD see **PIKRO PSOMI, TO** • 1951
BITTER CHANCE, THE see **PRICE OF GREED, THE** • 1955
BITTER COFFEE see **SECANGKIR KOPI PAHIT** • 1985
BITTER CREEK • 1954 • Carr Thomas • USA
BITTER CUP, THE • 1915 • *Ramona* • USA
BITTER DAYS see **ACI GUNLER** • 1967
BITTER DAYS, SWEET DAYS see **YOM MUR, YON HELW** • 1987
BITTER DOSE, A • 1913 • *Powers* • USA
BITTER DREGS, THE • 1915 • *Alhambra* • USA
BITTER END OF SWEET NIGHT see **AMAI YORU NO HATE** • 1961
BITTER FAITH see **ACI INANC** • 1968
BITTER FRUIT • 1920 • Bradley William • USA
BITTER FRUIT see **FRUITS AMERS** • 1967
BITTER GRAIN see **GORKIYE ZYORNA** • 1967
BITTER GRAINS see **GORKIYE ZYORNA** • 1967
BITTER GRASS, THE see **GORKE TRAVE** • 1965
BITTER HARVEST • 1963 • Scott Peter Graham • UKN
BITTER HARVEST • 1981 • Young Roger • TVM • USA
BITTER HERBS see **GORKE TRAVE** • 1965
BITTER HONEYMOON (USA) see **KESERU MEZESHETEK** • 1939
BITTER LESSON, A • 1909 • *Lubin* • USA
BITTER MEDICINE • 1983 • Shandel Thomas • MTV • CND
BITTER MEMORIES see **ACI HATIRALAR** • 1978
BITTER MORSEL see **NEEM ANAPURNA** • 1979
BITTER MOVIE see **DELERIUM** • 1984
BITTER RAGE see **KARA OFKE** • 1968
BITTER REUNION (USA) see **BEAU SERGE, LE** • 1958
BITTER REVENGE see **ACI INTIKAM** • 1968
BITTER RICE (UKN) see **RISO AMARO** • 1949
BITTER SONG see **ACI TURKU** • 1967
BITTER SPEARS • 1956 • Gatti Attilio
BITTER SPIRIT see **EIEN NO HITO** • 1961
BITTER SPRINGS • 1950 • Smart Ralph • UKN, ASL
BITTER-SWEET • 1910 • *Essanay* • USA
BITTER SWEET • 1916 • Conway Jack • USA
BITTER SWEET • 1933 • Wilcox Herbert • UKN
BITTER SWEET • 1940 • Van Dyke W. S. • USA
BITTER SWEETS • 1914 • *Balboa* • USA
BITTER SWEETS • 1928 • Hutchison Charles • USA • SECOND SHOT, THE (UKN)
BITTER SWEETS see **PALACES** • 1927
BITTER TASTE IN THE MORNING see **MANANA DE COBRE** • 1985
BITTER TEA OF GENERAL YEN • 1933 • Capra Frank • USA
BITTER TEARS OF PETRA VON KANT, THE (USA) see **BITTEREN TRANEN DER PETRA VON KANT, DIE** • 1972
BITTER TRUTH • 1917 • Buel Kenean • USA
BITTER TRUTH see **KESERU IGAZSAG** • 1956
BITTER VICTORY see **PAID IN FULL** • 1950
BITTER VICTORY (UKN) see **AMERE VICTOIRE** • 1957
BITTER YEARS see **ACI YILLAR** • 1968
BITTER YEARS, THE see **ZESTOKE GODINE** • 1980
BITTEREKRAUTER (FRG) see **GORKE TRAVE** • 1965
BITTEREN TRANEN DER PETRA VON KANT, DIE • 1972 • Fassbinder R. W. • FRG • BITTER TEARS OF PETRA VON KANT, THE (USA)
BITTERNESS see **GORYCZ** • 1962
BITTERNESS OF SWEETS, THE see **LOOK YOUR BEST** • 1923
BITTERNESS OF THE JEWISH SCAPEGOAT, THE see **IOANNIS O VIEOS** • 1972
BITTERSWEET • 1916 • Sturgeon Rollin S. • SHT • USA
BITTERSWEET see **SHOCK, THE** • 1923
BITTERSWEET LOVE • 1977 • Miller David • USA
BITTESCHON - DANKESCHON • 1975 • Panayotopoulos Nikos • GRC
BITVA V PUTI • 1961 • Basov Vladimir • USS • BATTLE ON THE ROAD
BITVA ZA NASHA SOVIETSKAYA UKRAINU • 1943 • Andeyenko Y., Solntseva Yulia • USS • BATTLE FOR OUR SOVIET UKRAINE, THE ◦ UKRAINE IN FLAMES ◦ FIGHT FOR OUR SOVIET UKRAINE, THE ◦ BYTVA ZA NASHU RADYANSKU UKRAYINU
BITWA O KOLOBRZEG • 1945 • Bossak Jerzy, Ford Aleksander • PLN • BATTLE OF KOLOBRZEG, THE ◦ BATTLE OF KOLBERG, THE
BIUTSE, NEI HOU YE! • 1990 • Chang Chien-T'Ing • HKG
BIVIO, IL • 1952 • Cerchio Fernando • ITL
BIVOUAC, LE • 1896 • Melies Georges • FRN • BIVOUAC, THE
BIVOUAC, THE see **BIVOUAC, LE** • 1896
BIWI O BIWI • 1981 • *Kapoor Raj (P)* • IND
BIX: "AIN'T NONE OF THEM PLAY LIKE HIM YET" • 1981 • Berman Brigitte • DOC • CND
BIXBY'S DILEMMA • 1915 • Stratton Edmund F. • SHT • USA
BIYAKKO NO TETSU • 1968 • Yamashita Kosaku • JPN • THREE OUTLAWS AND THEIR AFFECTION FOR ONE ANOTHER
BIYAKU NO WANA • 1967 • Seki Koji • JPN • TRAP OF A LOVE POTION
BIYO TO EKITAININGEN • 1958 • Honda Inoshiro • JPN • H-MAN, THE (USA) ◦ BIJO TO EKITAI NINGEN ◦ BEAUTIFUL WOMAN AND THE HYDROGEN MAN, THE
BIZA IZINTOMBI • 1980 • SAF
BIZALOM • 1980 • Szabo Istvan • HNG • CONFIDENCE
BIZANSI TITRETEN ADAM • 1967 • Gurses Muharrem • TRK • MAN WHO MADE BYZANTIUM TREMBLE, THE
BIZANSLI ZORBA • 1967 • Yalaz Suat • TRK • BYZANTINE VILLAIN, THE
BIZANT DUPA BIZANT • Petringenaru Adrian • ANM • RMN
BIZARRE BIZARRE (USA) see **DROLE DE DRAME** • 1937
BIZARRE NIGHT STORY OF SEXUAL DESIRE see **RYOKI SHIKIJO YAWA** • 1968
BIZARRE ONES, THE • 1968 • Sullivan Ron • USA
BIZARRE (USA) see **SECRETS OF SEX** • 1969
BIZENESS see **BUSINESS** • 1959
BIZET'S CARMEN see **CARMEN** • 1983
BIZIM AILE • 1976 • Orbey Ergin • TRK • OUR FAMILY
BIZONYOS JOSLATOK • 1968 • Toth Janus • ANS • HNG • CERTAIN PROPHESIES
BJ AND THE BEAR • 1978 • Peyser John • TVM • USA
BJORCK FAMILY, THE see **FAMILJEN BJORCK** • 1940
BJORGUNARAFREKID VID LATRABJARG • 1946 • Gislason Oskar • DOC • ICL • RESCUE AT LATRABJARG
BJORN BORG • 1983 • Zaritsky John • MTV • CND
BJORNETAEMMEREN • 1912 • Lind Alfred • DNM
BJORN'S INFERNO • 1964 • King Allan • CND
BLA DRENGE, DE • 1933 • Schneevoigt George • DNM
BLA HIMMEL • 1955 • Arlin Georg • SWD • BLUE SKY
BLA UNDULATER, DE • 1965 • Henning-Jensen Astrid • DNM
BLAA NATVIOL, DEN • 1911 • Blom August • DNM • DAUGHTER OF THE FORTUNE TELLER, THE
BLAAVAND MELDER STORM • 1937 • Lauritzen Lau Jr. • DNM
BLACK see **ITIM** • 1977
BLACK 13 • 1953 • Hughes Ken • UKN
BLACK ABBOT, THE • 1934 • Cooper George A. • UKN
BLACK ABBOT, THE (USA) see **SCHWARZE ABT, DER** • 1963
BLACK ACE, THE • 1928 • Maloney Leo • USA
BLACK ACE, THE see **TOMORROW AT SEVEN** • 1933
BLACK ACE, THE see **AS NEGRO, EL** • 1943
BLACK ACES • 1937 • Jones Buck • USA
BLACK ACES • 1937 • Selander Lesley • USA
BLACK ADVERTISING see **CAROSELLO NERO** • 1973
BLACK ALLEYCATS, THE • 1974 • Schellerup Henning • USA
BLACK AND BLUE • 1980 • Dubin Jay • USA
BLACK AND BLUE • 1989 • Pierson Frank R. • USA
BLACK AND BLUE MARKET see **COCKY BANTAM, THE** • 1943
BLACK AND SILVER • 1982 • Raban William, Raban Marilyn • UKN
BLACK AND TAN • 1929 • Murphy Dudley • SHT • USA
BLACK AND TAN MIX-UP, A • 1918 • *Ebony* • SHT • USA
BLACK AND WHITE • 1910 • *Barker Will (P)* • UKN
BLACK AND WHITE • 1913 • *Crystal* • USA
BLACK AND WHITE • 1913 • Cabanne W. Christy • *Ab* • USA
BLACK AND WHITE • 1913 • Kinder Stuart • UKN
BLACK AND WHITE • 1915 • *La Pearl Harry* • USA
BLACK AND WHITE • 1929 • Jeffrey R. E. • UKN
BLACK AND WHITE • 1929 • Machin Alfred • FRN
BLACK AND WHITE • 1930 • Oumansky Alexander • UKN
BLACK AND WHITE • 1932 • Amalrik Leonid, Ivanov-Vano Ivan • ANM • USS
BLACK AND WHITE • 1971 • Haanstra Rimko • ANS • NTH
BLACK AND WHITE see **FANTASMAGORIE** • 1908
BLACK AND WHITE see **ROBINSON JUNIOR** • 1931
BLACK AND WHITE see **BARON AND THE ROSE, THE** • 1940
BLACK AND WHITE see **NOIR ET BLANC** • 1961
BLACK AND WHITE BURLESQUE • 1960 • Preston Richard • SHT • USA
BLACK AND WHITE CINEMA • 1984 • Sokolov Stanislav • ANM • USS • BLACK AND WHITE MOVIE
BLACK AND WHITE IN COLOR (USA) see **NOIRS ET BLANCS EN COULEURS** • 1976
BLACK AND WHITE LIKE DAY AND NIGHT see **SCHWARZ UND WEISS WIE TAGE UND NACHTE** • 1978
BLACK AND WHITE MOVIE see **BLACK AND WHITE CINEMA** • 1984
BLACK AND WHITE PEACOCK, THE • 1962 • Linder Carl • SHT • USA
BLACK AND WHITE SNOWBALL, THE • 1915 • Johnson Tefft • USA • WHITE AND BLACK SNOWBALL, THE
BLACK AND WHITE (UKN) see **MUSTAA VALKOISELLA** • 1968
BLACK ANGEL • 1946 • Neill R. William • USA
BLACK ANGEL see **SCHWARZE ENGEL, DER** • 1973
BLACK ANGELS • 1970 • Merrick Laurence • USA
BLACK ANGELS see **CHERNITE ANGELI** • 1970
BLACK APHRODITE • 1977 • Sangiorgi Daniele • ITL • NEL MIRINO DI BLACK APHRODITE
BLACK ARROW • 1944 • Eason B. Reeves • SRL • USA
BLACK ARROW • 1985 • Hough John • TVM • USA
BLACK ARROW, THE • 1911 • Apfel Oscar • USA
BLACK ARROW, THE • 1948 • Douglas Gordon • USA • BLACK ARROW STRIKES, THE (UKN)
BLACK ARROW, THE • 1973 • ANM • ASL
BLACK ARROW STRIKES, THE (UKN) see **BLACK ARROW, THE** • 1948
BLACK ART • 1915 • *Edwards John* • USA
BLACK ART (USA) see **MAGIE DIABOLIQUE** • 1898
BLACK BAG, THE • 1922 • Paton Stuart • USA
BLACK BANDIT • 1938 • Waggner George • USA
BLACK BANNER see **BANDERA NEGRA** • 1985
BLACK BART • 1948 • Sherman George • USA • BLACK BART, HIGHWAYMAN (UKN)
BLACK BART, HIGHWAYMAN (UKN) see **BLACK BART** • 1948
BLACK BATTALION • 1958 • Cech Vladimir • CZC
BLACK BEACH see **LOVE FLOWER, THE** • 1920
BLACK BEAUTY • 1906 • Fitzhamon Lewin • UKN
BLACK BEAUTY • 1910 • Fitzhamon Lewin • UKN
BLACK BEAUTY • 1912 • *Pathe* • USA
BLACK BEAUTY • 1913 • *Lubin* • USA
BLACK BEAUTY • 1921 • Smith David • USA
BLACK BEAUTY • 1933 • Rosen Phil • USA
BLACK BEAUTY • 1946 • Nosseck Max • USA
BLACK BEAUTY • 1971 • Hill James • UKN, FRG, SPN
BLACK BEAUTY • 1978 • ANM • USA
BLACK BEAUTY • 1978 • Haller Daniel • TVM • USA
BLACK BEAUTY • 1988 • ANM
BLACK BELLY OF THE TARANTULA, THE (UKN) see **TARANTOLA DAL VENTRE NERO, LA** • 1971
BLACK BELT HISTORY OF THREE COUNTRIES see **KUROOBI SANGOKUSHI** • 1956
BLACK BELT JONES • 1974 • Clouse Robert • USA
BLACK BELT PHANTOM • 1967 • Gaudite Solano • PHL
BLACK BIRCH, THE see **CHYORNAYA BERYOZA** • 1977
BLACK BIRD, THE • 1925 • Browning Tod • USA • MOCKING BIRD, THE
BLACK BIRD, THE • 1975 • Giler David • USA
BLACK BIRDS see **CRNE PTICE** • 1967
BLACK BOOK, THE • 1925 • *Clifford William H. (P)* • USA
BLACK BOOK, THE • 1929 • Bennet Spencer Gordon, Storey Thomas L. • SRL • USA
BLACK BOOK, THE see **REIGN OF TERROR** • 1949
BLACK BOOK, THE see **KUROI GOSHO** • 1960
BLACK BORDERED LETTER, THE • 1911 • *Edison* • USA
BLACK BOUNTY KILLER (UKN) see **BOSS NIGGER** • 1975
BLACK BOX, THE • 1915 • Turner Otis • SRL • USA
BLACK BOX AFFAIR IL MONDO TREMA • 1966 • Ciorciolini Marcello • ITL
BLACK BROOD see **CAMADA NEGRA** • 1977
BLACK BUCCANEER, THE see **GORDON, IL PIRATO NERO** • 1961

BLACK BUFFALO WATER • 1970 • Veroiu Mircea (c/d) • DOC • RMN
BLACK BUNCH, THE • 1972 • Schellerup Henning • USA • JUNGLE SEX
BLACK BUTTERFLIES • 1928 • Horne James W. • USA • BUTTERFLIES (UKN)
BLACK BUTTERFLIES see **MARIPOSAS NEGRAS** • 1953
BLACK BUTTERFLY, THE • 1916 • King Burton L. • USA
BLACK CAESAR • 1973 • Cohen Larry • USA • GODFATHER OF HARLEM (UKN)
BLACK CAMEL, THE • 1931 • MacFadden Hamilton • USA
BLACK CANNON AFFAIR, THE see **HEI PAO SHIJIAN** • 1985
BLACK CANNON INCIDENT, THE see **HEI PAO SHIJIAN** • 1985
BLACK CAPTAIN, THE see **FEKETE KAPITANY** • 1920
BLACK CARRION • 1984 • Hough John • UKN
BLACK CASTLE, THE • 1952 • Juran Nathan • USA
BLACK CAT • 1959 • Ansari N. A. • IND
BLACK CAT see **YABU NO NAKA NO KURONEKO** • 1968
BLACK CAT, THE • 1934 • Ulmer Edgar G. • USA • HOUSE OF DOOM (UKN) ◦ VANISHING BODY, THE
BLACK CAT, THE • 1941 • Rogell Albert S. • USA
BLACK CAT, THE • 1956 • Jersey William C. • SHT • USA
BLACK CAT, THE • 1960 • Marvel Frank • ANM • USA
BLACK CAT, THE • 1966 • Hoffman Harold • USA
BLACK CAT, THE see **GATTO NERO, IL** • 1981
BLACK CAT AND DINNER FOR TWO, THE • 1899 • *Mutoscope & Biograph* • UKN
BLACK CAT IN THE BUSH see **YABU NO NAKA NO KURONEKO** • 1968
BLACK CAT MANSION (USA) see **BOREI KAIBYO YASHIKI** • 1958
BLACK CATS, THE see **GATOS NEGROS, LOS** • 1964
BLACK CAULDRON, THE • 1985 • Berman Ted, Rich Richard • ANM • USA
BLACK CHALLENGER, THE see **YARO NI KOKKYO WA NAI** • 1965
BLACK CHAMBER see **RENDEZVOUS** • 1935
BLACK CHANCELLOR, THE see **SORTE KANSLER, DEN** • 1912
BLACK CHANNEL see **KUROI KAIKYO** • 1964
BLACK CHAPEL, THE (USA) see **GEHEIMAKTION SCHWARZE KAPELLE** • 1960
BLACK CHARIOT • 1971 • Goodwin Robert L. • USA
BLACK CHASM, THE • 1911 • *Case Miss* • USA
BLACK CHRISTMAS • 1975 • Clark Bob • CND • SILENT NIGHT, EVIL NIGHT ◦ STRANGER IN THE HOUSE
BLACK CHRISTMAS see **TRE VOLTI DELLA PAURA, I** • 1963
BLACK CHRONICLE • 1990 • Traikova Eldora • BUL
BLACK CIRCLE, THE • 1917 • Ellis Robert • SHT • USA
BLACK CIRCLE, THE • 1919 • Reicher Frank • USA
BLACK CIRCLE, THE see **HIDDEN DANGERS** • 1920
BLACK CIRCLE GANG, THE • 1916 • Batley Ernest G. • UKN
BLACK CLAW OF IRON, THE see **GARRA NEGRA DE HIERRO, LA** • 1978
BLACK CLOAK, THE see **DARK INTRUDER, THE** • 1965
BLACK CLOUD'S DEATH • 1911 • *Powers* • USA
BLACK COATED BRIGANDS • 1909 • *Powhatan* • USA
BLACK COBRA see **EVA NERA** • 1976
BLACK COBRA, THE • 1987 • Massi Stelvio • USA
BLACK COBRA, THE (USA) see **SCHWARZE KOBRA, DIE** • 1963
BLACK COFFEE • 1931 • Hiscott Leslie • UKN
BLACK COIN, THE • 1936 • Herman Al • SRL • USA
BLACK CONSPIRACY, A • 1913 • Edwards Walter • USA
BLACK CORSAIR, THE (USA) see **CORSARO NERO, IL** • 1936
BLACK CREEK • 1972 • Ondaatje Kim • DCS • CND
BLACK CROOK, THE • 1915 • *Sullivan E. P.* • USA
BLACK CROOK, THE • 1916 • Vignola Robert G. • USA
BLACK CROSS GANG, THE • 1914 • Youngdeer James • UKN
BLACK CROSS (USA) see **KRZYZACY** • 1960
BLACK CROWN, THE see **CORONA NEGRA, LA** • 1950
BLACK CROWS see **SVARTE FUGLER** • 1983
BLACK CURTAIN, THE see **STREET OF CHANCE** • 1942
BLACK CYCLONE • 1925 • Jackman Fred • USA
BLACK DAKOTAS, THE • 1954 • Nazarro Ray • USA
BLACK DAVUT see **KARA DAVUT** • 1967
BLACK DAWN see **AUBE NOIRE, L'**
BLACK DAWN see **SVART GRYNING** • 1988
BLACK DECAMERON (UKN) see **DECAMERONE NERO, IL** • 1972
BLACK DEEP THROAT see **GOLA PROFONDA NERA** • 1977
BLACK DEVILS OF KALI, THE see **MISTERI DELLA GIUNGLA NERA, I** • 1954
BLACK DIAMOND see **FEKETE GYEMANTOK** • 1977
BLACK DIAMOND, THE • 1915 • Le Saint Edward J. • USA
BLACK DIAMOND, THE (USA) see **CERNY DEMANT** • 1956
BLACK DIAMOND EXPRESS • 1896 • USA
BLACK DIAMOND EXPRESS, THE • 1917 • Bretherton Howard • USA
BLACK DIAMONDS • 1904 • *Mitchell & Kenyon* • UKN
BLACK DIAMONDS • 1932 • Hanmer Charles • UKN
BLACK DIAMONDS • 1940 • Cabanne W. Christy • USA
BLACK DIAMONDS • 1944 • Annakin Ken • DCS • UKN
BLACK DOLL, THE • 1937 • Garrett Otis • USA
BLACK DOLPHIN CAMP • 1966 • Bielik Palo • CZC
BLACK DOMINO, THE see **BROADWAY MADONNA, THE** • 1922
BLACK DOOR, THE • 1917 • Terwilliger George W. • SHT • USA
BLACK DOOR, THE see **BRAIN THAT WOULDN'T DIE, THE** • 1962
BLACK DOOR, THE see **PUERTA NEGRA, LA** • 1989
BLACK DRAGON, THE • 1974 • Lo Gio • HKG
BLACK DRAGON, THE • 1974 • Lu Chun • HKG
BLACK DRAGON AVENGES THE DEATH OF BRUCE LEE, THE • 1975 • Lu Chun • HKG
BLACK DRAGON OF MANZANAR • 1943 • Witney William • USA
BLACK DRAGONS • 1942 • Nigh William • USA
BLACK DREAM, THE see **SCHWARZE TRAUM, DER** • 1911
BLACK DRESS, THE see **CZARNA SUKNIA** • 1967
BLACK DUKE, THE (USA) see **DUCA NERO, IL** • 1963
BLACK DYNASTY, THE • 1962 • Skalsky Stepan • CZC
BLACK EAGLE • 1915 • *Prussing Margaret* • USA
BLACK EAGLE • 1948 • Gordon Robert • USA
BLACK EAGLE • 1988 • Karson Eric • USA
BLACK EAGLE, THE see **AQUILA NERA** • 1946
BLACK EAGLE, THE see **KARA KARTAL** • 1967
BLACK EAGLE OF SANTA FE (UKN) see **SCHWARZEN ADLER VON SANTA FE, DIE** • 1962
BLACK EAGLES OF SANTA FE see **SCHWARZEN ADLER VON SANTA FE, DIE** • 1962
BLACK EAR OF CORN, THE see **MAVRO STAHI, TO** • 1968
BLACK ELIMINATOR, THE see **DEATH DIMENSION** • 1978
BLACK EMMANUELLE see **EMANUELLE NERA** • 1975
BLACK EMMANUELLE 2 see **EMANUELLE NERA N.2** • 1975
BLACK EMMANUELLE GOES EAST see **EMANUELLE NERA ORIENT REPORTAGE** • 1976
BLACK EMMANUELLE IN BANGKOK see **EMANUELLE NERA ORIENT REPORTAGE** • 1976
BLACK EMMANUELLE, WHITE EMMANUELLE see **VELLUTO NERO** • 1976
BLACK EVIDENCE • 1917 • McDermott John • SHT • USA
BLACK EYE • 1974 • Arnold Jack • USA
BLACK-EYED SUSAN • 1908 • *Gaumont* • UKN
BLACK-EYED SUSAN • 1913 • Nash Percy • UKN
BLACK-EYED SUSAN • 1914 • Elvey Maurice • UKN • BATTLING BRITISH, THE (USA) ◦ IN THE DAYS OF TRAFALGAR
BLACK EYES • 1915 • Louis Will • USA
BLACK EYES • 1939 • Brenon Herbert • UKN
BLACK EYES • 1989 • Potter Dennis • MTV • UKN
BLACK EYES see **THREE BLACK EYES** • 1919
BLACK EYES see **YEUX NOIRS, LES** • 1935
BLACK EYES see **OCI CIORNIE** • 1988
BLACK FANTASY • 1972 • Rogosin Lionel • USA
BLACK FEAR • 1915 • Noble John W. • USA
BLACK FEATHER • 1928 • Ince John • USA
BLACK FILM • 1971 • Zilnik Zelimir • SHT • YGS
BLACK FIST • 1976 • Galfas Timothy, Kaye Richard • USA • BLACK STREETFIGHTER, THE ◦ FIST
BLACK FIVE • 1968 • Barnes Paul • UKN
BLACK FLAME, THE see **CERNY PLAMEN** • 1930
BLACK FLASH, THE see **PRINCE OF PEP, THE** • 1925
BLACK FLOWERS FOR THE BRIDE see **SOMETHING FOR EVERYONE** • 1970
BLACK FOREST, THE • 1954 • Martel Gene • USA
BLACK FOX, THE • 1962 • Stoumen Louis Clyde • DOC • USA
BLACK FRANKENSTEIN, THE see **BLACKENSTEIN** • 1973
BLACK FREIGHT see **SCHWARZE FRACHT** • 1956
BLACK FRIDAY • 1916 • Carleton Lloyd B. • USA
BLACK FRIDAY • 1940 • Lubin Arthur • USA
BLACK FURY • 1935 • Curtiz Michael • USA
BLACK FURY see **MITSUYUSEN** • 1954
BLACK FUTURE • 1977 • O'Brien James • UKN
BLACK GALLEON, THE see **SCHWARZE GALEERE, DIE** • 1962
BLACK GAMBLER, THE see **KUROI TOBAKUSHI** • 1965
BLACK GATE, THE • 1919 • Marston Theodore • USA
BLACK GENERATION • 1979 • Lommel Ulli • USA
BLACK GENESIS: THE ART OF TRIBAL AFRICA • 1970 • *Moss Carlton* • DOC • USA
BLACK GESTAPO • 1975 • Frost Lee • USA • GHETTO WARRIORS
BLACK GHOST see **LAST FRONTIER, THE** • 1932
BLACK GHOST BANDIT, THE • 1915 • *American* • USA
BLACK GHOST'S BAND, THE see **BANDA DEL FANTASMA NEGRO, LA**
BLACK GIRL • 1972 • Davis Ossie • USA
BLACK GIRL see **NOIRE DE..., LA** • 1967
BLACK GLOVE, THE (USA) see **FACE THE MUSIC** • 1954
BLACK GOD AND THE BLOND DEVIL, THE see **DEUS E O DIABO NA TERRA DO SOL** • 1964
BLACK GOD AND THE WHITE DEVIL, THE see **DEUS E O DIABO NA TERRA DO SOL** • 1964
BLACK GOD, WHITE DEVIL (UKN) see **DEUS E O DIABO NA TERRA DO SOL** • 1964
BLACK GODDESS see **DEUSA NEGRA, A** • 1980
BLACK GODFATHER, THE • 1974 • Evans John, Fanaka Jamaa • USA • STREET WAR
BLACK GOLD • 1924 • Sheldon Forrest • USA
BLACK GOLD • 1928 • *Corman Lawrence* • USA
BLACK GOLD • 1947 • Karlson Phil • USA
BLACK GOLD • 1963 • Martinson Leslie H. • USA
BLACK GOLD-DAYS see **DIAS DEL ORO NEGRO, LOS** • 1971
BLACK GRAVEL see **SCHWARZER KIES** • 1961
BLACK GREEN see **CZARNE ZIELONE** • 1971
BLACK GUNN • 1972 • Hartford-Davis Robert • USA
BLACK HAND • 1906 • *Bitzer Billy (Ph)* • USA
BLACK HAND • 1949 • Thorpe Richard • USA • KNIFE, THE
BLACK HAND see **KALKA** • 1988
BLACK HAND, A • 1914 • *Royal* • USA
BLACK HAND, THE • 1912 • *Stuart Julia* • USA
BLACK HAND, THE • 1913 • *Brennan John* • USA
BLACK HAND, THE • 1917 • Quirk William • SHT • USA
BLACK HAND, THE see **AYD EL SAOUDA, EL** • 1937
BLACK HAND, THE see **MANO NERA, LA** • 1973
BLACK HAND, THE see **MANO NEGRA, LA** • 1980
BLACK HAND BLUES • 1925 • Roach Hal • SHT • USA
BLACK HAND CONSPIRACY • 1914 • *Mace Fred* • USA
BLACK HAND ELOPEMENT, A • 1913 • *Hayward Lillian* • USA
BLACK HAND GANG, THE • 1930 • Banks Monty • UKN
BLACK HANDS • 1914 • *Sterling* • USA
BLACK HANDS AND DIRTY MONEY • 1914 • *Frontier* • USA
BLACK HANDS AND SOAPSUDS • 1917 • Christie Al • SHT • USA
BLACK HARVEST OF COUNTESS DRACULA, THE see **NACHT DER VAMPIRE** • 1970
BLACK HARVEST OF COUNTESS DRACULA, THE see **RETORNO DE WALPURGIS, EL** • 1973
BLACK HAWK see **KUROTAKA-MARU** • 1927
BLACK HAWK, THE see **KARA ATMACA** • 1967
BLACK HEAD see **KARA KAFA** • 1980
BLACK HEART • 1911 • *Powers* • USA
BLACK HEART, THE • 1915 • *Lindblom E. O.* • USA
BLACK HEAT • 1981 • Adamson Al • USA • MURDER GANG, THE
BLACK HEN, THE see **CHERNAYA KURITSA** • 1983
BLACK HILLS • 1947 • Taylor Ray • USA
BLACK HILLS AMBUSH • 1952 • Keller Harry • USA
BLACK HILLS EXPRESS • 1943 • English John • USA
BLACK HOLE, THE • 1979 • Nelson Gary • USA
BLACK HOLIDAY (USA) see **VILLEGGIATURA, LA** • 1973
BLACK HOOKER • 1974 • Roberson Arthur • USA
BLACK HORDE, THE • 1919 • Protazanov Yakov • USS
BLACK HORIZONS see **SVARTA HORISONTER** • 1936
BLACK HORSE BANDIT, THE • 1919 • Harvey Harry • SHT • USA
BLACK HORSE CANYON • 1954 • Hibbs Jesse • USA
BLACK HUMOR see **UMORISMO NERO** • 1965
BLACK HUNTER, THE • 1919 • Binovec Vaclav • CZC
BLACK HUSSAR see **SCHWARZE HUSAR, DER** • 1932
BLACK ICE • 1980 • Shatalow Peter • CND
BLACK ICE, THE • 1957 • Grayson Godfrey • UKN
BLACK IMP, THE (USA) see **DIABLE NOIR, LE** • 1905
BLACK IN THE FACE • 1955 • Irwin John • UKN
BLACK INFERNO • Brzezinski Tony • SHT • USA
BLACK INN • Yeh Yung-Tsu • HKG
BLACK INVADERS, THE • 1960 • *De Metz Danielle* • ITL
BLACK IS • 1969 • Tamellini Aldo • SHT • USA
BLACK IS BEAUTIFUL • 1970 • *Institute For Adult Education* • DOC • USA • AFRICANUS SEXUALIS
BLACK IS WHITE • 1920 • Giblyn Charles • USA
BLACK ISLAND • 1979 • Bolt Ben • UKN
BLACK ISLAND, THE see **TINTIN: THE BLACK ISLAND** • 1987
BLACK JACK • 1927 • Dull Orville O. • USA
BLACK JACK • 1949 • Duvivier Julien, Nieves Conde Jose Antonio • FRN, SPN, USA • CAPTAIN BLACK JACK (USA) ◦ JACK EL NEGRO (SPN)
BLACK JACK • 1968 • Baldanello Gianfranco • ITL
BLACK JACK • 1980 • Loach Kenneth • UKN
BLACK JACK see **WILD IN THE SKY** • 1972
BLACK JACK'S ATONEMENT • 1913 • *Pollard Harry* • USA
BLACK JACK'S TREASURE see **SKARB CZARNEGO JACKA** • 1961
BLACK JESUS see **SEDUTO ALLA SUA DESTRA** • 1968
BLACK JOURNAL (USA) see **SIGNORA DEGLI ORRORI, LA** • 1977
BLACK JOURNEY see **CROISIERE NOIRE, LA** • 1927
BLACK JOY • 1977 • Simmons Anthony • UKN
BLACK KILLER • 1971 • Croccolo Carlo • ITL
BLACK KING, THE • 1932 • Pollard Bud • USA
BLACK KING, THE • 1962 • Kotowski Jerzy • ANM • PLN
BLACK KITTEN, THE • 1910 • Fitzhamon Lewin • UKN
BLACK KLANSMAN, THE • 1966 • Mikels Ted V. • USA • I CROSSED THE COLOR LINE
BLACK KNIGHT, THE • 1916 • Weston Harold • UKN
BLACK KNIGHT, THE • 1954 • Garnett Tay • UKN
BLACK LASH, THE • 1952 • Ormond Ron • USA
BLACK LEGEND • 1948 • Schlesinger John, Cooke Alan • UKN
BLACK LEGION • 1937 • Mayo Archie • USA
BLACK LEOPARD, THE • 1915 • Chaudet Louis W. • USA
BLACK LIGHTNING • 1924 • Hogan James P. • USA
BLACK LIKE ME • 1964 • Lerner Carl • USA • NO MAN WALKS ALONE
BLACK LIMELIGHT • 1938 • Stein Paul L. • UKN
BLACK LIST, THE see **BLACKLIST** • 1916
BLACK LITTER see **CAMADA NEGRA** • 1977
BLACK LIZARD see **KURO TOKAGE** • 1962
BLACK LIZARD see **HEI HSI-YI** • 1981
BLACK LIZARD (USA) see **KUROTOKAGE** • 1968
BLACK LOVE • 1972 • Lewis Herschell G. • USA
BLACK LOVE • 1974 • Benazeraf Jose • FRN • HOMME QUI VOULAIT VIOLER LE MONDE ENTIER, L'
BLACK LOVE see **MUSTA RAKKAUS** • 1957
BLACK LOVE AND WHITE (USA) see **AMOUR NOIR ET AMOUR BLANC** • 1927
BLACK LOVE -WHITE LOVE see **SWEET LOVE, BITTER** • 1967
BLACK MAGIC • 1916 • Horne James W. • SHT • USA
BLACK MAGIC • 1917 • *Victor* • SHT • USA
BLACK MAGIC • 1929 • Seitz George B. • USA
BLACK MAGIC • 1932 • Micheaux Oscar • USA
BLACK MAGIC • 1949 • Ratoff Gregory • USA
BLACK MAGIC • 1985 • SAF
BLACK MAGIC see **MAGICIEN, LE** • 1898
BLACK MAGIC see **INSEL DER DAMONEN, DIE** • 1933
BLACK MAGIC see **WAJAN (SON OF A WITCH)** • 1934
BLACK MAGIC see **CHARLIE CHAN IN BLACK MAGIC** • 1944
BLACK MAMA, WHITE MAMA • 1973 • Romero Eddie • PHL, USA • HOT, HARD AND MEAN ◦ CHAINED WOMEN ◦ CHAINS OF HATE
BLACK MAN see **SORTEPER** • 1979
BLACK MAN AND HIS BRIDE, THE • 1960 • Burstall Tim • SHT • ASL
BLACK MAN WITH A SAX see **NEGRE AMB UN SAXO, UN** • 1988
BLACK MANTILLA, THE • 1917 • Baldwin Ruth Ann • SHT • USA
BLACK MARBLE, THE • 1980 • Becker Harold • USA
BLACK MARK, THE • 1916 • *Judy* • USA
BLACK MARKET • 1967 • Singh S. R. • IND
BLACK MARKET BABIES • 1945 • Beaudine William • USA
BLACK MARKET BABY • 1977 • Day Robert • TVM • USA • DON'T STEAL MY BABY ◦ DANGEROUS LOVE, A
BLACK MARKET RUSTLERS • 1943 • Luby S. Roy • USA • LAND AND THE LAW (UKN)
BLACK MASK • 1935 • Ince Ralph • UKN
BLACK MASK, THE • 1906 • Larsen Viggo • DNM
BLACK MASK, THE • 1916 • *Rancho* • USA
BLACK-MASKED NEUTRON see **NEUTRON, EL ENMASCARADO NEGRO** • 1960
BLACK MASKS, THE • 1913 • *Ford Francis* • USA • DIAMOND CUT DIAMOND
BLACK MASKS, THE see **SVARTA MASKERNA, DE** • 1912
BLACK MEMORY • 1947 • Mitchell Oswald • UKN
BLACK MIC-MAC • 1985 • Gilou Thomas • FRN
BLACK MIDNIGHT • 1949 • Boetticher Budd • USA
BLACK MINUTE, A • 1970 • Medved Jozef • CZC
BLACK MIRROR • 1981 • Jolivet Pierre-Alain • CND
BLACK MONDAY • 1914 • *Captain Kettle* • UKN
BLACK MONOCLE, THE (USA) see **MONOCLE NOIR, LE** • 1961
BLACK MOON • 1934 • Neill R. William • USA
BLACK MOON • 1975 • Malle Louis • FRN, FRG, ITL
BLACK MOON RISING • 1986 • Cokliss Harley • USA
BLACK MOUNTAIN see **CHERNAYA GORA** • 1971

BLACK MUSIC IN AMERICA -FROM THEN TILL NOW • 1971 • Robertson Hugh A. • DCS • USA
BLACK NARCISSUS • 1947 • Powell Michael, Pressburger Emeric • UKN
BLACK NARCISSUS OF DESIRE see **JOYOKU NO KUROZUISEN** • 1967
BLACK NETS see **KINDAN NO SUNA** • 1957
BLACK NETWORK, THE • 1936 • Mack Roy • SHT • USA
BLACK NINE, THE • 1917 • Mason Billy • USA
BLACK NINJA see **MABOROSHI KUROZUKIN: YAMI NI TOBU KAGE** • 1967
BLACK NOON • 1971 • Kowalski Bernard • TVM • USA
BLACK NYLONS see **SPIKED HEELS AND BLACK NYLONS** • 1967
BLACK OAK CONSPIRACY • 1977 • Kelljan Bob • USA • CONSPIRACY
BLACK ON WHITE (USA) see **MUSTAA VALKOISELLA** • 1968
BLACK ON WHITE (USA) see **NERO SU BIANCO** • 1969
BLACK ONE FROM.., THE see **NOIRE DE.., LA** • 1967
BLACK OPAL, THE • 1913 • *Ramo* • USA
BLACK ORCHID • 1953 • Saunders Charles • UKN
BLACK ORCHID, THE • 1916 • Heffron Thomas N. • SHT • USA
BLACK ORCHID, THE • 1959 • Ritt Martin • USA
BLACK ORCHIDS • 1916 • Ingram Rex • USA • FATAL ORCHIDS, THE (UKN)
BLACK ORPHEUS (USA) see **ORFEU NEGRO** • 1958
BLACK OUT • 1970 • Roy Jean-Louis • SWT
BLACK OXEN • 1924 • Lloyd Frank • USA
BLACK OXFORDS • 1924 • *Sennett Mack (P)* • SHT • USA
BLACK PAGE, THE • 1915 • Baldwin Ruth Ann • USA
BLACK PALACE see **PALACIO NEGRO** • 1976
BLACK PALM see **SVARTA PALMKRONOR** • 1968
BLACK PALM TREES see **SVARTA PALMKRONOR** • 1968
BLACK PANTHER see **ELDRIDGE CLEAVER, BLACK PANTHER** • 1969
BLACK PANTHER, THE • 1977 • Merrick Ian • UKN
BLACK PANTHER OF RATANA (USA) see **SCHWARZE PANTHER VON RATANA, DER** • 1963
BLACK PANTHERS • 1968 • Varda Agnes • DCS • USA • HUEY
BLACK PANTHER'S CUB, THE • 1921 • Chautard Emile • USA
BLACK PARACHUTE, THE • 1944 • Landers Lew • USA
BLACK PARADISE • 1926 • Neill R. William • USA
BLACK PATCH • 1957 • Miner Allen H. • USA
BLACK PAWL see **GODLESS MEN** • 1921
BLACK PEARL, THE • 1915 • Paton Stuart • USA
BLACK PEARL, THE • 1928 • Pembroke Scott • USA
BLACK PEARL, THE • 1977 • Swimmer Saul • USA
BLACK PEARLS • 1914 • *Melies* • USA
BLACK PEARLS see **CRNI BISERI** • 1958
BLACK PETER • 1922 • Ridgwell George • UKN
BLACK PETER (USA) see **CERNY PETR** • 1963
BLACK PETE'S REFORMATION • 1910 • *Bison* • USA
BLACK PIRATE, THE • 1926 • Parker Albert • USA
BLACK PIRATE, THE see **GORDON, IL PIRATO NERO** • 1961
BLACK PIRATE, THE see **CORSARO NERO, IL** • 1971
BLACK PIRATE, THE (USA) see **PIRATA NEGRA, EL** • 1954
BLACK PIRATES, THE • 1954 • Miner Allen H. • USA, MXC
BLACK PIT OF DR. M., THE (USA) see **MISTERIOS DE ULTRATUMBA** • 1958
BLACK POWER see **PODER NEGRO** • 1974
BLACK PRINCE, THE • 1912 • *Crystal* • USA
BLACK PRINCE, THE • 1973 • Bobrovsky Anatoli • USS
BLACK PROCESSION, THE • 1964 • Zhebrunas Arunas • DOC • USS
BLACK RAIN • 1989 • Scott Ridley • USA
BLACK RAIN see **KUROI AME** • 1989
BLACK RAINBOW • 1966 • Zuckerman Michael T. • USA
BLACK RAINBOW • 1989 • Hodges Mike • UKN
BLACK RAINBOW, THE see **FEKETE SZIVARVANY, A** • 1916
BLACK RAVEN, THE • 1943 • Newfield Sam • USA
BLACK REPORT see **KURO NO HOKOKUSHU** • 1963
BLACK REVENGE see **SCORPIO '70** • 1970
BLACK RIBBON FOR DEBORAH, A see **FIOCCO NERO PER DEBORAH, UN** • 1974
BLACK RIDER, THE • 1954 • Rilla Wolf • UKN
BLACK RIDER, THE • 1983 • Verstappen Wim • NTH
BLACK RIDER, THE see **JOSHUA** • 1977
BLACK RIDER OF TASAJARA, THE • 1917 • Horne James W. • SHT • USA
BLACK RING, THE • 1915 • *Moore Tom* • USA
BLACK RIVER see **KUROI KAWA** • 1957
BLACK RIVER see **RIO NEGRO** • 1977
BLACK RIVER see **RIO NEGRO** • 1989
BLACK ROAD, THE see **SORTE VEJ, DEN** • 1987
BLACK ROBE, THE see **STRANGERS IN LOVE** • 1932
BLACK ROBE, THE see **SECRETS OF CHINATOWN** • 1934
BLACK RODEO • 1972 • Kanew Jeff • DOC • USA
BLACK RODERICK THE POACHER • 1914 • Martinek H. O. • UKN
BLACK ROOM, THE • 1935 • Neill R. William • USA • BLACK ROOM MYSTERY, THE
BLACK ROOM, THE • 1981 • Kenner Elly, Vane Norman Thaddeus • USA
BLACK ROOM MYSTERY, THE see **BLACK ROOM, THE** • 1935
BLACK ROOTS • 1970 • Rogosin Lionel • DOC • USA
BLACK ROSE • 1935 • Wadia Jamshed • IND
BLACK ROSE see **KUROBARA NO YAKATA** • 1969
BLACK ROSE, THE • 1950 • Hathaway Henry • UKN, USA
BLACK ROSE INN, THE see **KUROBARA NO YAKATA** • 1969
BLACK ROSES • 1921 • Campbell Colin • USA
BLACK ROSES • 1988 • Fasano John • USA
BLACK ROSES see **SVARTA ROSOR** • 1932
BLACK ROSES see **DID I BETRAY?** • 1936
BLACK ROSES see **SVARTA ROSOR** • 1945
BLACK RUDOLF see **SVARTE RUDOLF** • 1928
BLACK RUSKS see **CHORNYYE SUKHARI** • 1972
BLACK SABBATH (USA) see **TRE VOLTI DELLA PAURA, I** • 1963
BLACK SAIL, THE see **CHYORNI PARUS** • 1929
BLACK SAMOURAI • Santiago Cirio H.
BLACK SAMSON • 1974 • Bail Chuck • USA
BLACK SAMURAI • 1976 • Adamson Al • USA
BLACK SATURDAY • 1969 • Calotescu Virgil • RMN
BLACK SCARLET • 1974 • Munger Chris • USA
BLACK SCORPION, THE • 1957 • Ludwig Edward • USA
BLACK SEA FIGHTERS • 1943 • Beleyev Vassili • USS
BLACK SEAGULL, THE • 1962 • Koltunov G. • USS
BLACK SECRET, THE • 1920 • Seitz George B. • SRL • USA
BLACK SEED, THE see **CRNO SEME** • 1972
BLACK SHACK ALLEY see **RUE CASES-NEGRES** • 1983
BLACK SHADOW, THE (UKN) see **VENGEANCE OF THE WEST** • 1942
BLACK SHADOWS • 1920 • Mitchell Howard M. • USA
BLACK SHADOWS • 1923 • Salisbury Edward A. • DOC • USA
BLACK SHADOWS see **EQUATEUR AUX CENT VISAGES, L'** • 1948
BLACK SHADOWS ON THE SILVER SCREEN • 1975 • York Steven • DOC • USA
BLACK SHAMPOO • 1976 • Clark Greydon • USA
BLACK SHEEP • 1912 • *Solax* • USA
BLACK SHEEP • 1912 • Griffith D. W. • *Ab* • USA
BLACK SHEEP • 1913 • *Ray Charles* • USA
BLACK SHEEP • 1921 • Hurst Paul C. • USA
BLACK SHEEP • 1935 • Dwan Allan • USA • STAR FOR A NIGHT
BLACK SHEEP, A • 1915 • Heffron Thomas N. • *Selig* • USA
BLACK SHEEP, THE • 1909 • *Anderson Broncho Billy* • USA
BLACK SHEEP, THE • 1912 • *Vitagraph* • USA
BLACK SHEEP, THE • 1912 • *Eclair* • USA
BLACK SHEEP, THE • 1914 • Moore Tom • USA
BLACK SHEEP, THE • 1915 • Belmont Joseph • *Reliance* • USA
BLACK SHEEP, THE • 1915 • MacDonald J. Farrell • *Ab* • USA
BLACK SHEEP, THE • 1920 • Morgan Sidney • UKN
BLACK SHEEP, THE • 1932 • *Mintz Charles (P)* • ANS • USA
BLACK SHEEP, THE • 1934 • *Terry Paul/ Moser Frank (P)* • ANS • USA
BLACK SHEEP, THE see **SEISHUN NO UMI** • 1967
BLACK SHEEP, THE see **PECORA NERA, LA** • 1968
BLACK SHEEP, THE see **OVEJA NEGRA, LA** • 1987
BLACK SHEEP BLACKSMITH • 1967 • Post Howard • ANS • USA
BLACK SHEEP OF THE FAMILY, THE • 1916 • Hunt Jay • USA
BLACK SHEEP OF WHITEHALL • 1941 • Hay Will, Dearden Basil • UKN
BLACK SHEEP'S WOOL • 1912 • *Republic* • USA
BLACK SHERLOCK HOLMES, A • 1918 • Phillips R. W. • SHT • USA
BLACK SHIELD OF FALWORTH, THE • 1954 • Mate Rudolph • USA
BLACK SHIP see **CZARNA ONCA** • 1971
BLACK SIGNAL, THE • 1914 • *Essanay* • USA
BLACK SILK STOCKINGS • Thornberg Billy • USA
BLACK SIN • 1989 • Straub Jean-Marie, Huillet Daniele • FRG
BLACK SISTER'S REVENGE see **EMMA MAE** • 1977
BLACK SIX, THE • 1974 • Cimber Matt • USA
BLACK SKULL, THE • 1934 • Greenwood Edwin • UKN
BLACK SKULL, THE see **CALAVERA NEGRA, LA** • 1959
BLACK SLEEP, THE • 1956 • Le Borg Reginald • USA • DR. CADMAN'S SECRET
BLACK SMALL POX SCARE, THE • 1913 • *Powers* • USA
BLACK SNOW see **BEN MING NIAN** • 1989
BLACK SNOW WHITE see **MUSTA LUMIKKI** • 1971
BLACK SPIDER, THE • 1920 • Humphrey William J. • UKN
BLACK SPIDER, THE • 1931 • *Terry Paul/ Moser Frank (P)* • ANS • USA
BLACK SPIDER, THE see **SCHWARZE SPINNE, DIE** • 1984
BLACK SPOT, THE • 1914 • Tucker George Loane • UKN
BLACK SPURS • 1964 • Springsteen R. G. • USA
BLACK SQUARE (UKN) see **CHIORNY KVADRAT** • 1988
BLACK STALLION, THE • 1979 • Ballard Carroll • USA
BLACK STALLION RETURNS, THE • 1983 • Dalva Robert • USA
BLACK STALLION (UKN) see **RETURN OF WILDFIRE, THE** • 1948
BLACK STATUE, THE • 1915 • *Starlight* • USA
BLACK STORK, THE • 1917 • *Haiseld Harry J.* • USA
BLACK STORY • 1971 • Lazaga Pedro • SPN
BLACK STREETFIGHTER, THE see **BLACK FIST** • 1976
BLACK STUFF, THE • 1984 • Goddard Jim • UKN
BLACK SUN see **SOLEIL NOIR** • 1966
BLACK SUN see **CHORNOYE SOLNTSYE** • 1972
BLACK SUN see **CERNE SLUNCE** • 1978
BLACK SUN, THE see **KUROI TAIYO** • 1964
BLACK SUNDAY • 1977 • Frankenheimer John • USA
BLACK SUNDAY (USA) see **MASCHERA DEL DEMONIO, LA** • 1960
BLACK SWAN, THE • 1942 • King Henry • USA
BLACK SWAN, THE • 1952 • Reeve Leonard • UKN
BLACK SWAN, THE see **DARK SWAN, THE** • 1924
BLACK TEARS • 1927 • Gorman John • USA • WHITE LIES (UKN)
BLACK TENT, THE • 1956 • Hurst Brian Desmond • UKN
BLACK TERROR, THE • 1916 • *Curran Thomas* • SHT • USA
BLACK TEST CAR, THE see **KURO NO SHISOSHA** • 1962
BLACK THUNDERBOLT, THE • 1922 • *Johnson Jack* • USA
BLACK THURSDAY (USA) see **GUICHETS DU LOUVRE, LES** • 1974
BLACK TIDE see **KUROI USHIO** • 1954
BLACK TIDE (USA) see **STORMY CROSSING** • 1958
BLACK TIGHTS (USA) see **UN, DEUX, TROIS, QUATRE!** • 1960
BLACK TORMENT, THE • 1964 • Hartford-Davis Robert • UKN • ESTATE OF INSANITY
BLACK TORPEDOES see **PEAU DE TORPEDO, LA** • 1970
BLACK TRACKERS, THE • 1913 • Melies Gaston • USA
BLACK TRASH see **DEATH OF A SNOWMAN** • 1976
BLACK TRIANGLES, THE • 1916 • Stow Percy? • UKN
BLACK TRUNK, THE see **PASSENGER TO LONDON** • 1937
BLACK TUESDAY • 1955 • Fregonese Hugo • USA
BLACK TULIP, THE • 1920 • Binger Maurits H., Richardson Frank • NTH
BLACK TULIP, THE • 1921 • Richardson Frank • UKN
BLACK TULIP, THE • 1937 • Bryce Alex • UKN
BLACK TULIP, THE see **TULIPE NOIRE, LA** • 1963
BLACK TURIN see **TORINO NERA** • 1972
BLACK UHURU: TEAR IT UP -LIVE • 1982 • Rowe Annie • UKN
BLACK VAMPIRE, THE see **VAMPIRO NEGRO, EL** • 1953
BLACK VEIL, THE • 1990 • Warner Glenn • SHT • CND
BLACK VEIL FOR LISA, A (USA) see **MORTE NON HA SESSO, LA** • 1968
BLACK VEILED BRIDE, THE see **KARA DUVAKLI GELIN** • 1967
BLACK VELVET see **RED CANYON** • 1949
BLACK VELVET see **SCHWARZER SAMT** • 1964
BLACK VENUS • 1983 • Mulot Claude • USA
BLACK VICTORY see **NOIRS ET BLANCS EN COULEURS** • 1976
BLACK VIPER, THE • 1908 • Griffith D. W. • USA
BLACK VISION • 1965 • Brakhage Stan • SHT • USA
BLACK WALL, THE • 1912 • *De Garde Adele* • USA
BLACK WALLET, THE • 1915 • Davis Ulysses • USA
BLACK WATCH, THE • 1929 • Ford John • USA • KING OF THE KHYBER RIFLES (UKN)
BLACK WATER GOLD • 1969 • Landsburg Alan • TVM • USA
BLACK WATERS • 1929 • Neilan Marshall • UKN
BLACK WATERS • 1955 • Sremec Rudolf • SHT • YGS
BLACK WHIP, THE • 1956 • Warren Charles Marquis • USA
BLACK - WHITE • 1974 • Rentzis Thanasis, Zervos Nikos • GRC
BLACK, WHITE AND BLUES • 1971 • Guest Revel, Guest Robert • USA
BLACK WIDOW • 1951 • Sewell Vernon • UKN
BLACK WIDOW • 1954 • Johnson Nunnally • USA
BLACK WIDOW • 1986 • Rafelson Bob • USA
BLACK WIDOW see **BODY DISAPPEARS, THE** • 1942
BLACK WIDOW, THE • 1947 • Bennet Spencer Gordon, Brannon Fred C. • SRL • USA
BLACK WINDMILL, THE • 1974 • Siegel Don • UKN
BLACK WINGS see **CZARNE SKRZYDLA** • 1963
BLACK WITCH, THE • 1907 • *Pathe* • FRN
BLACK WITHOUT SUGAR • 1985 • Konermann Lutz • FRG, ICL
BLACK WOLF, THE • 1916 • Reicher Frank • USA
BLACK YOGA • 1967 • Legarda Johnny • PHL
BLACK ZOO • 1963 • Gordon Robert • USA • HORRORS OF THE BLACK ZOO
BLACKAMOORS see **MORIANERNA** • 1965
BLACKBEARD • 1911 • *Bosworth Hobart* • USA
BLACKBEARD THE PIRATE • 1952 • Walsh Raoul • USA
BLACKBEARD'S GHOST • 1968 • Stevenson Robert • USA
BLACKBELTER, THE • 1968 • Garces Armando • PHL
BLACKBIRD, THE see **MERLE, LE** • 1958
BLACKBIRD DESCENDING • 1977 • Le Grice Malcolm • UKN • TENSE ALIGNMENT
BLACKBIRDS • 1915 • Dawley J. Searle? • USA
BLACKBIRDS • 1920 • Dillon John Francis • USA
BLACKBOARD • 1985 • Shindo Kaneto • JPN
BLACKBOARD AND BLACKMAIL • 1917 • Moore Vin • SHT • USA
BLACKBOARD BUNGLE • 1972 • Michalak Richard • SHT • ASL
BLACKBOARD JUMBLE • 1957 • Lah Michael • ANS • USA
BLACKBOARD JUNGLE, THE • 1955 • Brooks Richard • USA
BLACKBOARD MASSACRE (UKN) see **MASSACRE AT CENTRAL HIGH** • 1976
BLACKBOARD REVUE • 1940 • Iwerks Ub • ANS • USA
BLACKENED HILLS • 1912 • Dwan Allan • USA
BLACKENSTEIN • 1973 • Levey William A. • USA • BLACK FRANKENSTEIN, THE
BLACKFOOT HALF-BREED, THE • 1911 • *Melford George* • USA
BLACKFOOT'S CONSPIRACY • 1912 • *Darkfeather Mona* • USA
BLACKGUARD, THE • 1925 • Cutts Graham • UKN
BLACKHAWK • 1952 • Bennet Spencer Gordon, Sears Fred F. • SRL • USA
BLACKHAWK COMMANDOS • 1968 • Batista Butch • PHL
BLACKHEAD • Topaldgikov Stefan • BUL
BLACKIE AND THE LAW (UKN) see **BOSTON BLACKIE AND THE LAW** • 1946
BLACKIE GOES HOLLYWOOD (UKN) see **BOSTON BLACKIE GOES HOLLYWOOD** • 1942
BLACKIE THE PIRATE (USA) see **CORSARO NERO, IL** • 1971
BLACKIE'S REDEMPTION • 1919 • Ince John • USA
BLACKIE'S RENDEZVOUS (UKN) see **BOSTON BLACKIE'S RENDEZVOUS** • 1945
BLACKJACK BARGAINER, A • *Wadsworth William* • SHT • USA
BLACKJACK KETCHUM, DESPERADO • 1956 • Bellamy Earl • USA
BLACKJACKETS see **RAGGARE** • 1959
BLACKLIST • 1916 • De Mille William C. • USA • BLACK LIST, THE
BLACKMAIL • 1912 • Collins Edwin J. • UKN
BLACKMAIL • 1917 • Drew Sidney • SHT • USA
BLACKMAIL • 1920 • Fitzgerald Dallas M. • USA
BLACKMAIL • 1929 • Hitchcock Alfred • UKN
BLACKMAIL • 1939 • Potter H. C. • USA
BLACKMAIL • 1947 • Selander Lesley • USA
BLACKMAIL • 1971 • van Nie Rene • NTH
BLACKMAIL see **WHISPERED NAME, THE** • 1924
BLACKMAIL see **ARU KYOHAKU** • 1960
BLACKMAIL see **SANTAJ** • 1981
BLACKMAIL IN A HOSPITAL • 1915 • *Griffith Ray* • USA
BLACKMAIL IS MY LIFE see **KYOKATSU KOSO WAGA JINSEI** • 1968
BLACKMAILED • 1951 • Allegret Marc • UKN
BLACKMAILED WIVES • 1968 • Clay Adam • USA
BLACKMAILER • 1936 • Wiles Gordon • USA
BLACKMAILER, THE • 1907 • Mottershaw Frank • UKN
BLACKMAILER, THE • 1912 • *Nestor* • USA
BLACKMAILER, THE • 1916 • Julian Rupert • SHT • USA
BLACKMAILER, THE • 1919 • Carlton Frank • UKN
BLACKMAILERS, THE • 1915 • *Terriss Tom* • USA
BLACKMAILERS, THE • 1915 • Coleby A. E. • UKN
BLACKMAILERS, THE • 1963 • Gil Rafael • SPN
BLACKOUT • 1950 • Baker Robert S., Gilling John (U/c) • UKN
BLACKOUT • 1977 • Mordacq Philippe • FRN • NAUFRAGEUR, LE
BLACKOUT • 1985 • Gustavson Erik F. • NRW

BLACKOUT • 1985 • Hickox Douglas • TVM • USA
BLACKOUT see **CONTRABAND SPAIN** • 1955
BLACKOUT see **BROWNOUT** • 1969
BLACKOUT see **NEW YORK NE REPOND PAS** • 1977
BLACKOUT see **ATTIC, THE** • 1988
BLACKOUT NIGHTS • 1989 • Kurcenli Yusuf • TRK
BLACKOUT TIME • 1939 • Byass Nigel • UKN
BLACKOUT (USA) see **CONTRABAND** • 1940
BLACKOUT (USA) see **MURDER BY PROXY** • 1955
BLACKS AND WHITES, DAYS AND NIGHTS • 1960 • Vanderbeek Stan • ANS • USA
BLACKS BRITANNICA • 1978 • Koff David • DOC • USA
BLACK'S FUNERAL • 1909 • *Powhatan* • USA
BLACK'S MYSTERIOUS BOX • 1915 • Barre Raoul • USA
BLACKSMITH, THE • 1912 • *Gibson Frances* • USA
BLACKSMITH, THE • 1920 • *Mann Hank* • USA
BLACKSMITH, THE • 1922 • Keaton Buster, St. Clair Malcolm • SHT • USA
BLACKSMITH, THE see **SONG OF THE FORGE** • 1937
BLACKSMITH, THE see **ELDSMIDURINN** • 1981
BLACKSMITH BEN • 1914 • Reehm George E. • USA
BLACKSMITH IN HIS WORKSHOP see **FORGERONS, LES** • 1896
BLACKSMITH'S APPRENTICE, THE see **KOVACEV SEGRT** • 1961
BLACKSMITHS AT WORK • 1899 • Williamson James • UKN
BLACKSMITH'S DAUGHTER, A • 1909 • *Centaur* • USA
BLACKSMITH'S DAUGHTER, THE • 1904 • *Gaumont* • UKN
BLACKSMITH'S DAUGHTER, THE • 1914 • *Frontier* • USA
BLACKSMITH'S LOVE, THE • 1911 • *Santschi Tom* • USA
BLACKSMITH'S STORY, THE • 1913 • Vale Travers • USA
BLACKSMITH'S WIFE, THE • 1909 • *Bison* • USA
BLACKSNAKE! • 1973 • Meyer Russ • USA • SLAVES (UKN) ○ SWEET SUZY
BLACKSNAKE'S TREACHERY • 1911 • *Bison* • USA
BLACKSTAR • 1981 • ANM • USA
BLACKTOP • 1950 • Eames Charles, Eames Ray • SHT • USA
BLACKWELL STORY, THE • 1957 • Neilson James • TVM • USA
BLACKWELL'S ISLAND • 1939 • McGann William • USA
BLACKWOOD • 1976 • Ianzelo Tony, Thomson Andy • DOC • CND
BLACULA • 1972 • Crain William • USA
BLACULA II see **SCREAM BLACULA SCREAM** • 1973
BLADE • 1973 • Pintoff Ernest • USA
BLADE AF SATANS BOG • 1919 • Dreyer Carl T. • DNM • LEAVES FROM SATAN'S BOOK
BLADE IN HONG KONG • 1985 • Badiyi Reza • TVM • USA
BLADE IN THE BODY, THE see **LAMA NEL CORPO, LA** • 1966
BLADE IN THE DARK, A (USA) see **CASA CON LA SCALA NEL BUIO, LA** • 1983
BLADE MASTER, THE (USA) see **ATOR L'INVINCIBILE** • 1983
BLADE O' GRASS • 1915 • George Burton • USA
BLADE RIDER: ATTACK OF THE INDIAN NATION • 1965 • Harris Harry, Reisner Allen, McEveety Bernard • MTV • USA • RIDE TO GLORY ○ CALL TO GLORY
BLADE RUNNER • 1982 • Scott Ridley • USA
BLADES AND BRASS • 1967 • Canning William • CND • LAMES ET CUIVRES
BLADES OF COURAGE see **BLADES OF STEEL** • 1987
BLADES OF STEEL • 1987 • Bradshaw Randy • CND • BLADES OF COURAGE ○ SKATE
BLADESTORM see **NORMANNI, I** • 1962
BLADYS OF THE STEWPONY • 1919 • MacBean L. C. • UKN
BLAGO U SREBRNOM JEZERU (YGS) see **SCHATZ IM SILBERSEE, DER** • 1962
BLAGUE DANS LE COIN • 1963 • Labro Maurice • FRN
BLAHO LASKY • 1966 • Brdecka Jiri • ANM • CZC • BLISS OF LOVE, THE ○ JOY OF LOVE, THE ○ SHE AND HE
BLAISE PASCAL • 1972 • Rossellini Roberto • MTV • ITL • PASCAL (USA)
BLAJACKOR • 1945 • Husberg Rolf • SWD • BLUE-JACKETS
BLAJACKOR • 1964 • Mattsson Arne • SWD • BLUE BOYS
BLAKE • 1969 • Mason William • DCS • CND
BLAKE MURDER MYSTERY, THE (UKN) see **HAUNTED HOUSE** • 1940
BLAKE OF SCOTLAND YARD • 1927 • Hill Robert F. • SRL • USA
BLAKE OF SCOTLAND YARD • 1937 • Hill Robert F. • SRL • USA
BLAKE -THE GAMBLER see **SEXTON BLAKE, GAMBLER** • 1928
BLAKE THE LAWBREAKER • 1928 • Cooper George A. • UKN
BLAKE'S MARAUDERS • 1980 • *Burns Ed* • USA
BLAKE'S SEVEN: ORAC • 1978 • Briant Michael E., Lorrimer Vere • MTV • UKN
BLAKE'S SEVEN: THE BEGINNING • 1978 • Nation Terry • MTV • UKN
BLAKE'S SEVEN: THE DUEL • 1978 • Briant Michael E. • MTV • UKN
BLAKES SLEPT HERE, THE • 1954 • Massingham Richard, Brunius Jacques-Bernard • UKN • FAMILY ALBUM
BLAME IT ON RIO • 1983 • Donen Stanley • USA • ONLY IN RIO
BLAME IT ON THE NIGHT • 1984 • Taft Gene • USA
BLAME IT ON THE SAMBA • 1948 • Geronimi Clyde • ANS • USA
BLAME THE TAILOR • 1914 • *Ab* • USA
BLAME THE WIFE • 1913 • O'Sullivan Tony • USA
BLAME THE WOMAN (USA) see **DIAMOND CUT DIAMOND** • 1932
BLAMING THE DUCK OR DUCKING THE BLAME • 1915 • Metcalfe Earl • USA
BLANANDE HAV • 1956 • Skoglund Gunnar • SWD • BLUE SEA
BLANC COMME NEIGE • 1931 • Elias Francisco, Lemoine Camille, Choux Jean • FRN • SOURIS BLONDE, LA
BLANC COMME NEIGE • 1947 • Berthomieu Andre • FRN
BLANC ET LE NOIR, LE • 1930 • Florey Robert, Allegret Marc • FRN
BLANC ET LE NOIR, LE see **ABIADH WA AL-ASWAD, AL-** • 1970
BLANC, LE JAUNE ET LE NOIR, LE (FRN) see **BIANCO, IL GIALLO, IL NERO, IL** • 1975
BLANCA • 1955 • Iacob Mihai • RMN
BLANCA POR FUERA, ROSA POR DENTRO • 1971 • Lazaga Pedro • SPN
BLANCA'S WEDDING see **BODAS DE BLANCA, LA** • 1976
BLANCHE • 1971 • Borowczyk Walerian • FRN
BLANCHE COMME NEIGE • 1908 • Cohl Emile • ANS • FRN
BLANCHE ET CLAIRE • 1976 • Cote Guy-L. • DCS • CND
BLANCHE ET MARIE • 1984 • Renard Jacques • FRN
BLANCHE FESSE ET LES SEPT NAINS • Baudricourt Michel • FRN
BLANCHE FURY • 1948 • Allegret Marc • UKN
BLANCHETTE • 1912 • Pouctal Henri • FRN
BLANCHETTE • 1921 • Hervil Rene • FRN
BLANCHETTE • 1936 • Caron Pierre • FRN
BLANCHEVILLE MONSTER, THE (USA) see **HORROR** • 1963
BLANCHISSERIE AMERICAINE, LA • 1915 • Cohl Emile • ANS • FRN
BLANCHISSEUSES, LES • 1896 • Melies Georges • FRN • WASHERWOMEN, THE
BLANCO SOBRE BLANCO • 1974 • Artero Antonio • SHT • SPN
BLANCO VERTICAL • 1968 • Aguirre Javier • SHT • SPN
BLAND SUNAR OCH MODS see **HEJA ROLAND!** • 1966
BLANDT BYENS BORN • 1925 • Lauritzen Lau • DNM
BLANDT MENNESKEAEDERE PA NY GUINEA • 1954 • Bjerre Jens • DNM • LAST CANNIBALS, THE
BLANK CHECK, A • 1909 • *Lubin* • USA
BLANK GENERATION, THE • 1976 • Poe Amos, Kral Ivan • USA
BLANK NOTE, THE • 1915 • *Joker* • USA
BLANK PAGE, THE • 1915 • Henderson Lucius • USA
BLANK WALL, THE see **RECKLESS MOMENT, THE** • 1949
BLANKE SLAVIN, DE • 1969 • Daalder Renee • NTH • WHITE SLAVE, THE
BLARNEY • 1917 • Kerrigan J. M. • UKN
BLARNEY • 1926 • De Sano Marcel • USA • IN PRAISE OF JAMES CARABINE
BLARNEY • 1938 • O'Donovan Harry • UKN • IRELAND'S BORDER LINE (USA)
BLARNEY COCK, THE • 1975 • *Lang Jennings* • MXC
BLARNEY KISS, THE (USA) see **BLARNEY STONE, THE** • 1933
BLARNEY STONE, THE • 1933 • Walls Tom • UKN • BLARNEY KISS, THE (USA)
BLASON, LE • 1915 • Feuillade Louis • FRN
BLASPHEMER, THE • 1921 • Goebel O. E. • USA
BLASSE ALBERT, DER • 1919 • Rex Eugen • FRG
BLAST • 1975 • Grigor Murray • DOC • UKN
BLAST • 1976 • Wilson Frank Arthur • USA
BLAST see **FINAL COMEDOWN, THE** • 1972
BLAST OF SCIENCE • 1961 • Baron Allen • USA
BLAST OFF • 1954 • *Reed Roland (P)* • MTV • USA
BLAST OFF! see **JULES VERNE'S ROCKET TO THE MOON** • 1967
BLAST-OFF GIRLS • 1967 • Lewis Herschell G. • USA
BLASTED EVENT, A • 1934 • Goulding Alf • SHT • USA
BLASTED HOPES • 1910 • *Selig* • USA
BLASTED HOPES • 1924 • Rosson Arthur • USA
BLASTFIGHTER • 1984 • Bava Lamberto • ITL
BLATT PAPIER, EIN • 1916 • May Joe • FRG
BLAU WUNDER, DAS • Fischer-Kosen Kaskeline, Fischer-Kosen Hans • ANM • FRG • BLUE WONDER, THE
BLAUAUGIG • 1988 • Hauff Reinhard • FRG • BLUE-EYED
BLAUBART (FRG) see **BARBE BLEUE** • 1951
BLAUE DIAMANT, DER • 1935 • Blachnitzky Curt • FRG
BLAUE DRACHEN, DER • 1919 • Piel Harry • FRG
BLAUE ENGEL, DER • 1930 • von Sternberg Josef • FRG • BLUE ANGEL, THE
BLAUE HAND, DIE • 1967 • Vohrer Alfred • FRG • CREATURE WITH THE BLUE HAND (USA) ○ BLUE HAND, THE
BLAUE JUNGS • 1957 • Schleif Wolfgang • FRG
BLAUE JUNGS VON DER MARINE see **KORVETTENKAPITAN, DER** • 1930
BLAUE LATERNE, DIE • 1918 • Biebrach Rudolf • FRG
BLAUE LICHT, DAS • 1932 • Riefenstahl Leni, Balazs Bela • FRG • BLUE LIGHT, THE
BLAUE MARITIUS, DIE • 1918 • Larsen Viggo • FRG
BLAUE MAUS, DIE • 1912 • Mack Max • FRG
BLAUE MAUS, DIE • 1915 • Mack Max • FRG
BLAUE MAUS, DIE • 1928 • Guter Johannes • FRG • BLUE MOUSE, THE
BLAUE MEER UND DU, DAS • 1959 • Engel Thomas • FRG
BLAUE MOND, DER • 1989 • Schmitt Monika • FRG • BLUE MOON, THE
BLAUE NACHTFALTER, DER • 1959 • Schleif Wolfgang • FRG
BLAUE STERN DES SUDENS, DER • 1951 • Liebeneiner Wolfgang • AUS
BLAUE STROHUT, DER • 1949 • Tourjansky Victor • FRG
BLAUE STUNDE, DIE • 1953 • Harlan Veit • FRG
BLAUE VOM HIMMEL, DAS • 1932 • Janson Victor • FRG
BLAUE WASSER see **GESPENSTERUHR, DIE** • 1915
BLAUEN SCHWERTER, DIE • 1949 • Schleif Wolfgang • FRG
BLAUFUCHS, DER • 1938 • Tourjansky Victor • FRG • BLUE FOX (USA)
BLAUVOGEL • Weiss Ulrich • GDR • BLUEBIRD
BLAUW LICHT • 1966 • van der Heyden Jef • NTH
BLAZE • 1989 • Shelton Ron • USA
BLAZE AWAY • 1922 • Curran William Hughes • USA
BLAZE AWAY • 1922 • Roach Hal • SHT • USA
BLAZE BUSTERS • 1951 • Youngson Robert • DOC • USA
BLAZE O' GLORY • 1929 • Hoffman Renaud, Crone George J. • USA
BLAZE OF GLORY • 1963 • Lynn Robert • UKN
BLAZE OF GLORY (UKN) see **BOY FROM INDIANA, THE** • 1950
BLAZE OF NOON • 1947 • Farrow John • USA
BLAZE STARR GOES BACK TO NATURE see **BLAZE STARR GOES NUDIST** • 1962
BLAZE STARR GOES NUDIST • 1962 • Wishman Doris • USA • BLAZE STARR GOES BACK TO NATURE ○ BUSTING OUT
BLAZED TRAIL • 1921 • Apfel Oscar • USA
BLAZED TRAIL, THE • 1910 • *Nestor* • USA
BLAZES • 1961 • Breer Robert • SHT • USA
BLAZING A TRAIL TO THE STARS see **DOROGA K ZVEZDAM** • 1957
BLAZING ACROSS THE PECOS • 1948 • Nazarro Ray • USA • UNDER ARREST (UKN)
BLAZING ARROWS • 1922 • McCarty Henry • USA • SKYFIRE
BLAZING ARROWS see **FIGHTING CARAVANS** • 1930
BLAZING AWAY • 1928 • Taurog Norman • SHT • USA
BLAZING BARRIERS see **JACQUELINE, OR BLAZING BARRIERS** • 1923
BLAZING BULLETS • 1951 • Fox Wallace • USA
BLAZING CARAVAN, THE • 1954 • Hughes Ken • UKN
BLAZING CONTINENT see **MOERU TAIRIKU** • 1968
BLAZING DAYS • 1927 • Wyler William • USA
BLAZING FLOWERS • 1978 • Zappulla Griseppe • ITL
BLAZING FOREST, THE • 1952 • Ludwig Edward • USA
BLAZING FRONTIER • 1943 • Newfield Sam • USA
BLAZING GUNS • 1935 • Heinz Ray • USA
BLAZING GUNS • 1943 • Tansey Robert • USA
BLAZING GUNS see **MARSHAL OF HELDORADO** • 1950
BLAZING HILLS, THE see **BLAZING SUN, THE** • 1950
BLAZING JUSTICE • 1936 • Herman Al • USA
BLAZING LOVE • 1916 • Buel Kenean • USA
BLAZING MAGNUM • 1977 • De Martino Alberto • CND, ITL • MAGNUM SPECIAL PER TONY SAITTA, UNA (ITL) ○ SPECIAL MAGNUM ○ STRANGE SHADOWS IN AN EMPTY ROOM (USA) ○ SHADOWS IN A ROOM ○ BLAZING MAGNUMS
BLAZING MAGNUMS see **BLAZING MAGNUM** • 1977
BLAZING NINJA, THE • 1985 • Ho Godfrey • HKG
BLAZING SADDLES • 1974 • Brooks Mel • USA
BLAZING SAND • 1960 • Nussbaum Raphael • ISR, FRG
BLAZING SECRET, THE • 1917 • *Baggot King* • SHT • USA
BLAZING SIX SHOOTERS • 1940 • Lewis Joseph H. • USA • STOLEN WEALTH (UKN)
BLAZING SIXES • 1937 • Smith Noel • USA
BLAZING STEWARDESSES • 1975 • Adamson Al • USA
BLAZING SUN, THE • 1950 • English John • USA • BLAZING HILLS, THE
BLAZING SUN, THE see **SERAA FIL WADA** • 1953
BLAZING SUN, THE see **DDAENG BYEOT** • 1985
BLAZING SUN(UKN) see **PLEIN SOLEIL** • 1960
BLAZING THE OVERLAND TRAIL • 1956 • Bennet Spencer Gordon • SRL • USA
BLAZING THE TRAIL • 1912 • *Bison* • USA
BLAZING THE TRAIL • 1915 • *Premier* • USA
BLAZING THE WAY • 1920 • Webster George H. • SHT • USA
BLAZING THE WESTERN TRAIL • 1945 • Keays Vernon • USA • WHO KILLED WARING? (UKN)
BLAZING TRAIL • 1921 • Thornby Robert T. • USA
BLAZING TRAIL, THE • 1949 • Nazarro Ray • USA • FORGED WILL, THE (UKN)
BLAZING WINTER see **RASCOALA** • 1965
BLAZNI, VODNICI, A PODVODNICI • 1980 • Svoboda Jiri • CZC • FOOLS, WATER SPRITES, AND IMPOSTERS
BLAZNOVA KRONIKA • 1964 • Zeman Karel • CZC • JESTER'S TALE, THE ○ DUA MOSKETYRI ○ INSANE CHRONICLE ○ TWO MUSKETEERS
BLE EN HERBE, LE • 1953 • Autant-Lara Claude • FRN • GAME OF LOVE, THE (USA) ○ RIPENING SEED, THE
BLEAK HOUSE • 1920 • Elvey Maurice • UKN
BLEAK HOUSE • 1922 • Parkinson H. B. • UKN
BLEAK HOUSE • 1985 • Devenish Ross • MTV • UKN
BLEAK MOMENTS • 1971 • Leigh Mike • UKN
BLEAK MORNING see **KHMUROE UTRO** • 1959
BLEARY-OH! THE VILLAGE AVIATOR • 1909 • *Gaumont* • FRN
BLECHTROMMEL, DIE • 1979 • Schlondorff Volker • FRG, FRN • TAMBOUR, LE (FRN) ○ TIN DRUM ,THE (UKN)
BLED, LE • 1929 • Renoir Jean • FRN
BLEEDING EARTH see **MATOMENI YI** • 1967
BLEEDING HEARTS OR JEWISH FREEDOM UNDER KING CASIMER OF POLAND • 1913 • *Wallace Irene* • USA
BLEEDING WOUND, THE see **KANAYAN YARA** • 1968
BLEEKE BET • 1934 • Benno Alex, Oswald Richard • NTH • PALE BETTY
BLEEP • 1971 • Erdman Richard • USA
BLEIB SAUBER, LIEBLING! • 1971 • Thiele Rolf • FRG
BLEICHE RENATE, DIE • 1916 • *Morena Erna* • FRG
BLEIERNE ZEIT, DIE • 1981 • von Trotta Margarethe • FRG • LEADEN TIME ○ MARIANNE AND JULIANNE ○ GERMAN SISTERS, THE
BLEKA GREVEN • 1937 • Rodin Gosta • SWD
BLEKITNY KRZYZ • 1956 • Munk Andrzej • PLN • MEN OF THE BLUE CROSS ○ MANNER VOM BLAUEN KREUZ, DIE ○ BLUE CROSS ○ HOMMES DE LA CROIX BLEUE, LES
BLEKITNY POKOJ • 1965 • Majewski Janusz • PLN • BLUE ROOM
BLESS 'EM ALL • 1949 • Hill Robert Jordan • UKN
BLESS 'EM ALL see **ACT, THE** • 1983
BLESS THE BEASTS AND CHILDREN • 1972 • Kramer Stanley • USA
BLESS THE LADIES • 1931 • Edwards Harry J. • SHT • USA
BLESS THIS HOUSE • 1972 • Thomas Gerald • UKN
BLESSED EVENT • 1932 • Del Ruth Roy • USA
BLESSED EVENTS see **LORSQUE L'ENFANT PARAIT** • 1956
BLESSED MADNESS see **SIUNATTI HULLUUS** • 1975
BLESSED MIRACLE, THE • 1915 • *Clayton Ethel* • USA
BLESSING OF THE FLEET, THE • 1980 • Hill Robert • DOC • ASL
BLESSING ON THE WOODS • 1966 • Perry Margaret • DOC • CND
BLESSURE • 1921 • Roberti Roberto Leone • ITL
BLESSURE, LA • 1926 • de Gastyne Marco • FRN
BLEU DE ORIGINES, LE • 1979 • Garrel Philippe • FRN
BLEU NUIT • 1979 • Reusser Francis • SWT
BLEU PERDU, LE • 1972 • Driessen Paul • ANM • CND
BLEUE BRUME • 1982 • Sauriol Brigitte • CND
BLEUS DE LA MARINE, LES • 1934 • Cammage Maurice • FRN
BLEUS DE L'AMOUR, LES • 1919 • Desfontaines Henri • FRN
BLEUS DE L'AMOUR, LES • 1932 • de Marguenat Jean • FRN
BLEUS DU CIEL, LES • 1933 • Decoin Henri • FRN • OISEAU BLANC, L' ○ AVION BLANC, L'
BLEUS.. LA NUIT.., LES • 1980 • Rancourt Daniel • SHT • CND
BLICK IN DEN ABGRUND, DER • 1919 • *Haack Kate* • FRG
BLICK UND DIE LIEBE BRICHT AUS, EIN • 1987 • Bruckner Jutta • FRG

BLICK ZURUCK, EIN • 1944 • Menzel Gerhard • FRG • AM VORABEND
BLICK ZURUCK UND DANN.., EIN see **LOCKENDE ZIEL, DAS** • 1930
BLIGGS FAMILY AT THE ZOO, THE • 1912 • Martinek H. O. • UKN
BLIGGS ON THE BRINY • 1913 • Raymond Charles • UKN
BLIGHT, THE • 1913 • *Carlyle Francis* • UKN
BLIGHT OF GREED, THE • 1915 • *Empire* • USA
BLIGHT OF SIN, THE • 1909 • *Selig* • USA
BLIGHT OF WEALTH, THE • 1913 • *Thanhouser* • USA
BLIGHTED LIVES • 1912 • *Greenleaf Mace* • USA
BLIGHTED SON, THE • 1912 • *Pathe* • USA
BLIGHTED SPANIARD, THE • 1914 • *L-Ko* • USA
BLIGHTY • 1927 • Brunel Adrian • UKN
BLIJFT ZOEKEN, HET • 1972 • van Brakel Nouchka • DCS • NTH
BLIND • 1912 • *Champion* • USA
BLIND • 1930 • Kalatozov Mikhail • USS
BLIND ADVENTURE • 1933 • Schoedsack Ernest B. • USA • IN THE FOG
BLIND ADVENTURE, THE • 1918 • Ruggles Wesley • USA • AGONY COLUMN, THE
BLIND ALIBI • 1938 • Landers Lew • USA
BLIND ALLEY • 1939 • Vidor Charles • USA
BLIND ALLEY see **IN GEFAHR UND GROSSTER NOT BRINGT DER MITTELWEG DEN TOD** • 1975
BLIND ALLEY see **ANDHI GALLI** • 1984
BLIND ALLEY see **PERFECT STRANGERS** • 1984
BLIND ALLEYS • 1927 • Tuttle Frank • USA
BLIND AMBITION • 1984 • Schaefer George • TVM • USA
BLIND BARGAIN, A • 1922 • Worsley Wallace • USA • OCTAVE OF CLAUDIUS, THE
BLIND BASKET WEAVER, THE • 1913 • *Hollister Alice* • USA
BLIND BEAST, THE (USA) see **MOJU** • 1969
BLIND BIRD, THE • 1962 • Dolin Boris • DOC • USS
BLIND BOY, THE • 1900 • Gibbons Walter • UKN
BLIND BOY, THE • 1917 • Collins Edwin J., Clare Jack • UKN
BLIND BUDDY see **BLIND MAKKER** • 1976
BLIND BUSINESS, A • 1914 • *Lubin* • USA
BLIND CATTLE KING, THE • 1912 • *Lubin* • USA
BLIND CHANCE • 1920 • Kull Edward • SHT • USA
BLIND CHANCE see **PRZYPADEK** • 1982
BLIND CHESS • 1988 • *Reynolds Burt* • TVM • USA
BLIND CHILD see **BLIND KIND** • 1964
BLIND CIRCUMSTANCES • 1922 • Morante Milburn • USA
BLIND COMPOSER'S DILEMMA, THE • 1913 • *Compton Dixie* • USA
BLIND COOK, THE • Shepitko Larissa • USS
BLIND CORNER • 1963 • Comfort Lance • UKN • MAN IN THE DARK (USA)
BLIND DATE • 1934 • Neill R. William • USA • HER SACRIFICE (UKN)
BLIND DATE • 1954 • Donnelly Eddie • ANS • USA
BLIND DATE • 1959 • Losey Joseph • UKN • CHANCE MEETING (USA)
BLIND DATE • 1983 • Mastorakis Nico • USA, GRC
BLIND DATE • 1987 • Edwards Blake • USA
BLIND DEAD, THE see **NOCHE DEL TERROR CIEGO, LA** • 1972
BLIND DECEPTION, A • 1911 • Salter Harry • USA
BLIND DESIRE (USA) see **PART DE L'OMBRAGE, LA** • 1945
BLIND ENDEAVOUR see **VAKVILAGBAN** • 1986
BLIND FAITH • 1982 • Trent John • MTV • CND
BLIND FATE • 1914 • Hepworth Cecil M. • UKN
BLIND FATE see **LOTTERISEDDEL NO.22152** • 1915
BLIND FEAR • 1989 • Berry Thomas • USA • LONG DARK NIGHT, A
BLIND FIDDLER, THE • 1914 • Ridgely Richard • USA
BLIND FOLLY • 1939 • Denham Reginald • UKN
BLIND FURY • 1916 • Kent Leon D. • USA
BLIND FURY • 1989 • Noyce Phil • USA
BLIND GARY DAVIS • 1964 • Becker Harold • DCS • USA
BLIND GIRL OF CASTLE GUILLE, THE • 1913 • *Patheplay* • USA
BLIND GODDESS, THE • 1926 • Fleming Victor • USA
BLIND GODDESS, THE • 1948 • French Harold • UKN
BLIND GYPSY, THE • 1913 • *Gebhardt George* • USA
BLIND HEARTS • 1921 • Lee Rowland V. • USA
BLIND HEROINE, THE • 1912 • Haldane Bert • UKN
BLIND HORIZON see **ANDHA DIGANTA** • 1988
BLIND HUSBANDS • 1918 • von Stroheim Erich • USA • PINNACLE
BLIND IS BEAUTIFUL see **BLIND MAKKER** • 1976
BLIND JUSTICE • 1915 • Windom Lawrence C. • USA
BLIND JUSTICE • 1917 • *Vitagraph* • USA
BLIND JUSTICE • 1934 • Vorhaus Bernard • UKN
BLIND JUSTICE • 1961 • *Van Eyck Peter* • FRG • WHOLE TRUTH, THE
BLIND JUSTICE • 1986 • Holcomb Rod • TVM • USA
BLIND JUSTICE see **HAEVNENS NAT** • 1915
BLIND JUSTICE see **LAST HOUR, THE** • 1923
BLIND KIND • 1964 • van der Keuken Johan • DOC • NTH • BLIND CHILD
BLIND KIND 2 • 1966 • van der Keuken Johan • DOC • NTH • HERMAN SLOBBE
BLIND LOVE • 1910 • *Centaur* • USA
BLIND LOVE • 1912 • Lucas Wilfred • USA
BLIND LOVE • 1988 • Legrand Michel • FRN
BLIND LOVE, THE • 1920 • Bailey Oliver D. • USA
BLIND MAKKER • 1976 • Kristensen Hans • DNM • BLIND BUDDY ○ BLIND IS BEAUTIFUL ○ DUMMY PARTNER
BLIND MAN, THE • 1909 • Bouwmeester Theo? • UKN
BLIND MAN OF JERUSALEM • 1909 • *Gaumont* • FRN
BLIND MAN OF VERDUN, THE • 1916 • Bramble A. V. • UKN
BLIND MAN'S BLUFF • 1903 • Cooper Arthur • UKN
BLIND MAN'S BLUFF • 1905 • Stow Percy • UKN
BLIND MAN'S BLUFF • 1912 • *Nestor* • USA
BLIND MAN'S BLUFF • 1914 • *Essanay* • USA
BLIND MAN'S BLUFF • 1916 • Moore Matt • SHT • USA
BLIND MAN'S BLUFF • 1936 • Parker Albert • UKN
BLIND MAN'S BLUFF • 1952 • Saunders Charles • UKN
BLIND MAN'S BLUFF • 1976 • O'Hara Gerry • UKN
BLIND MAN'S BLUFF (USA) see **COLECCIONISTA DE CADAVERES, EL** • 1967
BLIND MAN'S CHILD, THE • 1905 • Collins Alf? • UKN
BLIND MAN'S DOG, THE • 1912 • Fitzhamon Lewin • UKN
BLIND MAN'S EYES • 1919 • Ince John • USA
BLIND MAN'S HOLIDAY • 1917 • Justice Martin • USA
BLIND MAN'S LUCK • 1917 • Fitzmaurice George • USA
BLIND MAN'S TACT, THE • 1910 • Salter Harry • USA
BLIND MARRIAGE • 1914 • *Melies* • USA
BLIND MATADOR, THE see **BULAG NA MATADOR** • 1968
BLIND MINER, THE • 1912 • *Morey Harry T.* • USA
BLIND MOTHERS (UKN) see **PASSIONATE YOUTH** • 1925
BLIND MUSIC MASTER, THE • 1915 • *Hill Lee* • USA
BLIND MUSICIAN, THE • 1909 • *Lubin* • USA
BLIND MUSICIAN, THE • 1912 • *Prescott Vivian* • USA
BLIND ONE, THE see **BLINDE, DER** • 1989
BLIND OWL, THE see **BOOFE-KOUR** • 1975
BLIND OWL, THE see **BLINDE EULE, DIE** • 1979
BLIND PHOTOGRAPHER, THE see **BLINDE FOTOGRAAF, DE** • 1972
BLIND PIG, A • 1918 • Davis James • SHT • USA
BLIND PLANET, THE see **PLANETA CIEGO, EL** • 1975
BLIND PRINCESS AND THE POET, THE • 1911 • Griffith D. W. • USA
BLIND RAGE • 1978 • Pinon Efren C. • PHL
BLIND RAGE see **BOYS NEXT DOOR, THE** • 1985
BLIND RAGE see **SURROGATE, THE** • 1985
BLIND SATURDAY • 1987 • Panayotov Panayot • BUL
BLIND SPOT • 1932 • Daumery John • UKN
BLIND SPOT • 1947 • Gordon Robert • USA
BLIND SPOT • 1958 • Maxwell Peter • UKN
BLIND SPOT see **SECRET FURY, THE** • 1950
BLIND SPOT see **WHISPERING DEATH** • 1975
BLIND SPOT see **BLINDGANGERS** • 1976
BLIND SPOT, THE see **TAXI!** • 1931
BLIND SPOT UNDER THE SUN see **HAKUCHO NO SHIKAKU** • 1978
BLIND SWORDSMAN see **ZATO ICHI MONOGATARI** • 1962
BLIND SWORDSMAN AND THE FUGITIVES, THE see **ZATOICHI HATASHIJO** • 1968
BLIND SWORDSMAN SAMARITAN, THE see **ZATO ICHI KENKA-DAIKO** • 1968
BLIND SWORDSMAN'S CANE SWORD, THE see **ZATO-ICHI TEKKA-TABI** • 1967
BLIND SWORDSMAN'S RESCUE, THE see **ZATO ICHI RO-YABURI** • 1967
BLIND SWORDSMAN'S VENGEANCE, THE see **ZATO ICHI NO UTA GA KIKOERU** • 1966
BLIND TERROR • 1971 • Fleischer Richard • UKN • SEE NO EVIL (USA)
BLIND TRAIL • 1926 • Maloney Leo • USA
BLIND VIOLINIST, THE • 1907 • Gilbert Arthur • UKN
BLIND WARRIOR, THE see **SI BUTA** • 1974
BLIND WHITE DURATION • 1967 • Le Grice Malcolm • UKN
BLIND WIVES • 1920 • Brabin Charles J. • USA • MY LADY'S DRESS
BLIND WIVES see **FREE LOVE** • 1930
BLIND WIVES (UKN) see **LADY SURRENDERS, A** • 1930
BLIND WOMAN'S CURSE, THE (USA) see **KAIDAN NOBORIRYU** • 1970
BLIND YOUTH • 1920 • Sloman Edward • USA
BLINDE, DER • 1989 • Kuster Diethard • FRG • BLIND ONE, THE
BLINDE, DIE • 1911 • Stark Kurt • FRG
BLINDE EULE, DIE • 1979 • Mandavi Mansur • AUS • BLIND OWL, THE
BLINDE FOTOGRAAF, DE • 1972 • Ditvoorst Adriaan • NTH • BLIND PHOTOGRAPHER, THE
BLINDE GLUCK, DAS • 1922 • Raffay Iwa • FRG
BLINDE KUH • 1914 • Lubitsch Ernst • FRG
BLINDE PASSAGIER • 1937 • Sauer Fred • FRG • STOWAWAYS (USA)
BLINDE PASSAGIER, DER • 1922 • Janson Victor • FRG
BLINDE SKAEBNE, DEN see **LOTTERISEDDEL NO.22152** • 1915
BLINDED BY THE LIGHT • 1980 • Alonzo John A. • TVM • USA
BLINDED HEART, THE • 1914 • Johnson Arthur • USA
BLINDFOLD • 1928 • Klein Charles • USA
BLINDFOLD • 1966 • Dunne Philip • USA
BLINDFOLD see **BEKOTOTT SZEMMEL** • 1974
BLINDFOLD see **OJOS VENDADOS, LOS** • 1978
BLINDFOLDED • 1915 • *Travers Richard C.* • USA
BLINDFOLDED • 1918 • West Raymond B. • USA
BLINDFOLDED EYES see **OJOS VENDADOS, LOS** • 1978
BLINDGANGERS • 1976 • de Jong Ate • NTH • BLINDSPOT ○ BLIND SPOT
BLINDING TRAIL, THE • 1919 • Powell Paul • USA
BLINDMAN • 1972 • Baldi Ferdinando • ITL, USA • CIECO, IL
BLINDNESS • 1964 • Parker Morten • DOC • CND
BLINDNESS, THE • 1916 • Le Viness Carl M. • SHT • USA
BLINDNESS OF COURAGE OR BETWEEN TWO LOVES, THE • 1913 • *White Glen* • USA
BLINDNESS OF DEVOTION, THE • 1915 • Edwards J. Gordon • USA
BLINDNESS OF DIVORCE, THE • 1918 • Lloyd Frank • USA
BLINDNESS OF FORTUNE, THE • 1917 • Wilson Frank • UKN
BLINDNESS OF JEALOUSY, THE • 1916 • *Lily* • USA
BLINDNESS OF LOVE, THE • 1916 • Horan Charles • USA
BLINDNESS OF VIRTUE, THE • 1915 • Totten Joseph Byron • USA
BLINDNESS OF YOUTH, THE • 1919 • *Garsson Murray W.* • USA
BLINDSIDE • 1988 • Greene Don Fox • USA • FROM FATHER TO SON
BLINDSIDE • 1988 • Lynch Paul • CND, USA
BLINDSPOT see **BLINDGANGERS** • 1976
BLINK STEFAANS • 1981 • Rautenbach Jans • SAF
BLINKENDE FENSTER, DAS • 1919 • Jutzi Phil • FRG
BLINKER CIKO see **MRKACEK CIKO** • 1982
BLINKER'S SPY-SPOTTER • 1971 • Stephens Jack • UKN
BLINKEYES • 1926 • Pearson George • UKN
BLINKITY BLANK • 1954 • McLaren Norman • ANS • CND
BLINKY • 1923 • Sedgwick Edward • USA
BLISS • 1917 • *Lloyd Harold* • SHT • USA
BLISS • 1967 • Markopoulos Gregory J. • USA
BLISS • 1985 • Lawrence Ray • ASL
BLISS OF IGNORANCE, THE • 1915 • *King Henry* • USA
BLISS OF LOVE, THE see **BLAHO LASKY** • 1966
BLISS OF MRS. BLOSSOM, THE • 1968 • McGrath Joseph • UKN
BLISS ON EARTH, A see **NAMIDA** • 1957
BLISSFUL BLUNDER, A • 1952 • White Jules • SHT • USA
BLISSFUL CALAMITY, A • 1917 • Heffron Thomas N. • SHT • USA
BLISSVILLE THE BEAUTIFUL • 1909 • *Lubin* • USA
BLITHE SPIRIT • 1945 • Lean David • UKN
BLITZ KISS, THE • *Brendel El* • SHT • USA
BLITZ ON BRITAIN • 1960 • Booth Harry • DOC • UKN
BLITZ ON THE FRITZ • 1943 • White Jules • SHT • USA
BLITZ WOLF, THE • 1942 • Avery Tex • ANS • USA
BLITZKRIEG -THE WAR FOR RUSSIA • 1958 • DOC • FRG
BLITZMADELS AN DIE FRONT • 1958 • Klinger Werner • FRG
BLITZZENTRALE, DIE • 1921 • Arnheim Valy • FRG • HOCHSPANNUNG 100.000 VOLT!
BLITZZUG DER LIEBE • 1925 • Guter Johannes • FRG • EXPRESS TRAIN OF LOVE
BLIXT OCH DUNDER • 1938 • Henrikson Anders • SWD • THUNDER AND LIGHTNING
BLIZNA • 1976 • Kieslowski Krzysztof • PLN • SCAR, A
BLIZZARD, THE • 1964 • Basov Vladimir • USS
BLIZZARD, THE (USA) see **GUNNAR HEDES SAGA** • 1923
BLIZZARD PASS see **FUBUKITOGE** • 1929
BLOB, THE • 1958 • Yeaworth Irvin S. Jr. • USA
BLOB, THE • 1989 • Russell Chuck • USA
BLOCK 15 see **BLOK 15** • 1959
BLOCK, THE • 1964 • Orlando Tony • USA
BLOCK, THE • 1972 • *Watson Paul (P)* • UKN
BLOCK AND TACKLE • 1932 • *Mgm* • SHT • USA
BLOCK BUSTERS • 1944 • Fox Wallace • USA
BLOCK HEAD, THE see **LOVE AND DOUGHNUTS** • 1921
BLOCK-NOTES DI UN REGISTA see **FELLINI -A DIRECTOR'S NOTEBOOK** • 1968
BLOCK SIGNAL, THE • 1926 • O'Connor Frank • USA
BLOCKADE • 1928 • Seitz George B. • USA
BLOCKADE • 1938 • Dieterle William • USA
BLOCKADE • 1975 • Ershov Mikhail • USS
BLOCKADE see **Q-SHIPS** • 1928
BLOCKADE, THE see **BLOKO** • 1965
BLOCKED RAILS see **BLOCKERAT SPAR** • 1955
BLOCKED TRAIL, THE • 1943 • Clifton Elmer • USA
BLOCKERAT SPAR • 1955 • Wickman Torgny • SWD • BLOCKED RAILS
BLOCKHEADS • 1938 • Blystone John G. • USA
BLOCKHOUSE, THE • 1973 • Rees Clive • UKN
BLOCKHOUSE DE ALTA LUZ, EL • 1919 • Berra Fernando Orozco • MXC
BLOCKIERTE SIGNALE • 1948 • Meyer Johannes • FRG
BLOD OCH ELD • 1945 • Henrikson Anders • SWD • BLOOD AND FIRE
BLODETS ROST • 1913 • Sjostrom Victor • SWD • VOICE OF BLOOD, THE ○ VOICE OF THE BLOOD
BLODIGA TIDEN, DEN • 1960 • Leiser Erwin • SWD • MEIN KAMPF (USA)
BLODRAUTT SOLARLAG • 1978 • Gunnlaugsson Hrafn • MTV • ICL • CRIMSON SUNSET
BLODVEIEN see **KRVAVI PUT** • 1955
BLOED • 1973 • Grasveld Fons • DOC • NTH • BLOOD
BLOEDROOI PAPAWER • 1960 • SAF
BLOEDVERWANTEN • 1976 • Lindner Wim • NTH, FRN • BLOOD RELATIONS
BLOK 15 • 1959 • Schorm Evald • CZC • BLOCK 15
BLOKO • 1965 • Kyrou Ado • GRC • BLOCKADE, THE
BLOMKVIST THE MASTER DETECTIVE see **MASTERDETEKTIVEN BLOMKVIST** • 1947
BLOMMOR AT GUDARNA • 1957 • Lundqvist Jagmastare Eric • SWD • FLOWERS FOR THE GODS
BLOMSTERTID, DEN • 1940 • Sjoberg Alf • SWD • BLOSSOM TIME ○ FLOWERING TIME
BLOMSTRANDE TIDER • 1979 • Olsson John • SWD • PROSPEROUS TIMES
BLOND CAPTIVE, THE see **BLONDE CAPTIVE, THE** • 1932
BLOND DREAM, A see **BLONDER TRAUM, EIN** • 1932
BLOND! -GEFAHR! see **FLUCHT VOR BLOND** • 1928
BLOND GORILLA see **WHITE PONGO** • 1945
BLOND ICE • 1948 • Bernhard Jack • USA
BLOND MUSS MAN SEIN AUF CAPRI • 1961 • Schleif Wolfgang • FRG
BLOND WIFE, THE see **OGGI DOMANI DOPODOMANI** • 1965
BLONDE ALIBI • 1946 • Jason Will • USA
BLONDE AMBITION • 1980 • Amero John, Amero Lem • USA • CAN I COME AGAIN? ○ CAN I COME TOO?
BLONDE AND GROOM • 1943 • Edwards Harry J. • SHT • USA
BLONDE AND THE BLACK PUSSYCAT, THE (UKN) see **ALLE KATZCHEN NASCHEN GERN** • 1969
BLONDE ATOM BOMB • 1951 • White Jules • SHT • USA
BLONDE BAIT • 1956 • Williams Elmo • USA
BLONDE BAIT (USA) see **WOMEN WITHOUT MEN** • 1956
BLONDE BANDIT, THE • 1950 • Keller Harry • USA
BLONDE BLACKMAILER (USA) see **STOLEN TIME** • 1955
BLONDE BOMBSHELL (UKN) see **BOMBSHELL** • 1933
BLONDE CAPTIVE, THE • 1932 • Withington Paul, Childs Clinton • DOC • USA • BLOND CAPTIVE, THE
BLONDE CARMEN, DIE • 1935 • Janson Victor • FRG
BLONDE CHAUFFEUR, DER • 1915 • Schmidthassler Walter • FRG
BLONDE CHEAT • 1938 • Santley Joseph • USA • MUDDLED DEAL
BLONDE CHRISTEL, DIE • 1933 • Seitz Franz • FRG
BLONDE COBRA • 1959-62 • Smith Jack**, Jacobs Ken • SHT • USA
BLONDE COMET, THE • 1941 • Beaudine William • USA
BLONDE COMME CA!, UNE see **MISS SHUMWAY JETTE UN SORT** • 1962
BLONDE CRAZY • 1931 • Del Ruth Roy • USA • LARCENY LANE (UKN)
BLONDE DE PEKIN, LA • 1968 • Gessner Nicolas • FRN, ITL, FRG • BLONDE VON PEKING, DIE (FRG) ○ PEKING BLONDE (USA) ○ BIONDA DI PECHINO, LA (ITL) ○ PROFESSIONAL BLONDE ○ BLONDE FROM PEKING, THE
BLONDE DES TROPIQUES, LA • 1957 • Roy Andre • FRN

BLONDE DYNAMITE • 1950 • Beaudine William • USA
BLONDE DYNAMITE see **SOME BLONDES ARE DANGEROUS** • 1937
BLONDE ENGEL SIND NICHT BILLING • 1969 • FRG
BLONDE FEVER • 1944 • Whorf Richard • USA • AUTUMN FEVER
BLONDE FIRE • 1979 • Chinn Robert C. • USA
BLONDE FOR A DAY • 1946 • Newfield Sam • USA
BLONDE FOR A NIGHT, A • 1928 • Hopper E. Mason • USA
BLONDE FOR DANGER (UKN) see **SOIS BELLE ET TAIS-TOI** • 1958
BLONDE FOR DANGER (USA) see **FLAMINGO AFFAIR, THE** • 1948
BLONDE FRAU DES MAHARADSCHA, DIE • 1962 • Harlan Veit • FRG
BLONDE FROM BROOKLYN • 1945 • Lord Del • USA
BLONDE FROM PEKING, THE see **BLONDE DE PEKIN, LA** • 1968
BLONDE FROM SINGAPORE, THE • 1941 • Dmytryk Edward • USA • HOT PEARLS (UKN)
BLONDE GEISHA, DIE • 1923 • Czerny Ludwig • FRG
BLONDE GIFT, DAS • 1923 • Neufeld Max • FRG
BLONDE GIRL AT THE BAR see **ROSSA DEL BAR, LA** • 1985
BLONDE GODDESS, THE • 1982 • Eagle Bill • USA
BLONDE HANNELE, DAS • 1924 • Seitz Franz • FRG
BLONDE IN A WHITE CAR see **TOI LE VENIN** • 1958
BLONDE IN BONDAGE see **BLONDIN I FARA** • 1958
BLONDE IN LOVE, A (UKN) see **LASKY JEDNE PLAVOVLASKY** • 1965
BLONDE IN THE BAR see **ROSSA DEL BAR, LA** • 1985
BLONDE IN THE BLUE MOVIE, THE see **VICHINGO VENUTO DAL SUD, IL** • 1971
BLONDE INSPIRATION • 1940 • Berkeley Busby • USA • FOOLS RUSH IN ◦ FOUR CENTS A WORD
BLONDE KODER FUR DEN MORDER • 1970 • Philipp Harald • FRG
BLONDE LADY, THE • 1912 • *Crystal* • USA
BLONDE LOO, DIE • 1919 • Coenen Josef • FRG
BLONDE NACHTIGALL, DIE • 1930 • Meyer Johannes • FRG
BLONDE NEXT DOOR, THE • 1981 • Sherman Joe • USA
BLONDE ON A BUM RAP see **BLONDE ON A BUM TRIP** • 1968
BLONDE ON A BUM TRIP • 1968 • Mauro Ralph • USA • BLONDE ON A BUM RAP
BLONDE OR BRUNETTE • 1927 • Rosson Richard • USA
BLONDE PRESSURE • 1931 • Buzzell Edward • SHT • USA
BLONDE RANSOM • 1945 • Beaudine William • USA
BLONDE REPORTER, THE (UKN) see **SOB SISTER** • 1931
BLONDE SAINT, THE • 1926 • Gade Svend • USA
BLONDE SAVAGE • 1947 • Sekely Steve • USA
BLONDE SINNER (USA) see **YIELD TO THE NIGHT** • 1956
BLONDE STAYED ON, THE • 1946 • Edwards Harry J. • SHT • USA
BLONDE TROUBLE • 1937 • Archainbaud George • USA
BLONDE VAMPIRE, THE • 1922 • Physioc Wray • USA
BLONDE VELVET • 1978 • Antonero Luis F. • USA
BLONDE VENUS • 1932 • von Sternberg Josef • USA
BLONDE VERGNUGEN, DAS • 1918 • Kaden Danny • FRG
BLONDE VERHANGNIS, DAS • 1922 • Speyer Jaap • FRG
BLONDE VON PEKING, DIE (FRG) see **BLONDE DE PEKIN, LA** • 1968
BLONDE WITCH see **HAXAN** • 1955
BLONDEN MADELS VOM LINDENHOF, DIE • 1918 • Bolten-Baeckers Heinrich • FRG
BLONDER TRAUM, EIN • 1932 • Martin Paul • FRG • BLONDE'S DREAM, A (USA) ◦ BLOND DREAM, A
BLONDES AND BONDS (UKN) see **STOCKS AND BLONDES** • 1928
BLONDES AT WORK • 1938 • McDonald Frank • USA
BLONDES AWAY • 1947 • Yates Hal • SHT • USA
BLONDES BEWARE • 1928 • Taurog Norman • SHT • USA
BLONDE'S DREAM, A (USA) see **BLONDER TRAUM, EIN** • 1932
BLONDES FOR DANGER • 1938 • Raymond Jack • UKN
BLONDES GIFT • 1919 • Moest Hubert • FRG
BLONDES HAVE MORE FUN • 1981 • Seeman John • USA
BLONDES LIKE IT HOT • 1986 • *Olinka* • FRG
BLONDES PREFER BONDS • 1931 • Foster Lewis R. • SHT • USA
BLONDES PREFER BOXERS see **BOXERBRAUT, DIE** • 1926
BLONDE'S REVENGE, A • 1926 • Cline Eddie • SHT • USA
BLONDIE • 1938 • Strayer Frank • USA
BLONDIE see **BLONDY** • 1975
BLONDIE BIFFEN OCH BANANEN • 1952 • Kjellgren Lars-Eric • SWD • BLONDIE, THE BEEF AND THE BANANA
BLONDIE BRINGS UP BABY • 1939 • Strayer Frank • USA
BLONDIE FOR VICTORY • 1942 • Strayer Frank • USA • TROUBLES THROUGH BILLETS (UKN)
BLONDIE GOES LATIN • 1941 • Strayer Frank • USA • CONGA SWING (UKN)
BLONDIE GOES TO COLLEGE • 1942 • Strayer Frank • USA • BOSS SAID "NO", THE
BLONDIE HAS SERVANT TROUBLE • 1940 • Strayer Frank • USA
BLONDIE HITS THE JACKPOT • 1949 • Bernds Edward • USA • HITTING THE JACKPOT (UKN)
BLONDIE IN SOCIETY • 1941 • Strayer Frank • USA • HENPECKED (UKN) ◦ SOCIETY WOMAN
BLONDIE IN THE DOUGH • 1947 • Berlin Abby • USA
BLONDIE JOHNSON • 1933 • Enright Ray • USA
BLONDIE KNOWS BEST • 1946 • Berlin Abby • USA
BLONDIE MEETS THE BOSS • 1939 • Strayer Frank • USA
BLONDIE OF THE FOLLIES • 1932 • Goulding Edmund • USA
BLONDIE ON A BUDGET • 1940 • Strayer Frank • USA
BLONDIE PLAYS CUPID • 1940 • Strayer Frank • USA
BLONDIE TAKES A VACATION • 1939 • Strayer Frank • USA
BLONDIE, THE BEEF AND THE BANANA see **BLONDIE BIFFEN OCH BANANEN** • 1952
BLONDIE'S ANNIVERSARY • 1947 • Berlin Abby • USA
BLONDIE'S BIG DEAL • 1949 • Bernds Edward • USA • BIG DEAL, THE (UKN)
BLONDIE'S BIG MOMENT • 1947 • Berlin Abby • USA
BLONDIE'S BLESSED EVENT • 1942 • Strayer Frank • USA • BUNDLE OF TROUBLE, A (UKN)
BLONDIE'S HERO • 1950 • Bernds Edward • USA
BLONDIE'S HOLIDAY • 1947 • Berlin Abby • USA
BLONDIE'S LUCKY DAY • 1946 • Berlin Abby • USA
BLONDIE'S REWARD • 1948 • Berlin Abby • USA
BLONDIE'S SECRET • 1948 • Bernds Edward • USA
BLONDIN I FARA • 1958 • Brandt Robert • SWD • NOTHIN' BUT BLONDES ◦ BLONDE IN BONDAGE
BLONDINE • 1943 • Mahe Henri • FRN
BLONDY • 1975 • Gobbi Sergio • FRN, FRG • VORTEX (USA) ◦ BLONDIE
BLOOD! • 1973 • *Stansbury Hope* • USA
BLOOD • 1973 • Milligan Andy • USA
BLOOD see **BLOED** • 1973
BLOOD see **RAKHTO** • 1973
BLOOD, THE see **HSI-HSUEH JEN-MO** • 1976
BLOOD, THE see **KAN** • 1985
BLOOD ALLEY • 1955 • Wellman William A. • USA
BLOOD AND BLACK LACE (USA) see **SEI DONNE PER L'ASSASSINO** • 1964
BLOOD AND BOSH • 1913 • Plumb Hay? • UKN
BLOOD AND BULLETS see **PADRONI DELLA CITTA, I** • 1977
BLOOD AND DEFIANCE (USA) see **SANGUE E LA SFIDA, IL** • 1962
BLOOD AND FIRE • 1958 • Macartney-Filgate Terence • DOC • CND
BLOOD AND FIRE see **BLOD OCH ELD** • 1945
BLOOD AND FIRE see **SANGRE Y FUEGO** • 1983
BLOOD AND FLESH • NKR
BLOOD AND GUNS see **TEPEPA** • 1969
BLOOD AND GUTS • 1978 • Lynch Paul • CND • HEAVY THUNDER
BLOOD AND HONOUR • 1982 • Fischerauer Bernd • FRG
BLOOD AND LACE • 1972 • Gilbert Philip • USA
BLOOD AND ORCHIDS see **BLOOD & ORCHIDS** • 1986
BLOOD AND ROSES (USA) see **ET MOURIR DE PLAISIR** • 1960
BLOOD AND SAND • 1922 • Niblo Fred • USA
BLOOD AND SAND • 1941 • Mamoulian Rouben • USA
BLOOD AND SAND see **SANGRE Y ARENA** • 1988
BLOOD AND SOUL (USA) see **CHI TO REI** • 1922
BLOOD AND STEEL • 1925 • McGowan J. P. • USA
BLOOD AND STEEL • 1959 • Kowalski Bernard • USA
BLOOD AND THUNDER • 1931 • Stevens George • SHT • USA
BLOOD AND WATER • 1913 • Blache Alice • USA
BLOOD AND WINE see **EQUALISER: BLOOD AND WINE, THE** • 1987
BLOOD ARROW • 1958 • Warren Charles Marquis • USA
BLOOD AT SUNDOWN • 1972 • Cardone Alberto • ITL
BLOOD BARON, THE see **ORRORI DEL CASTELLO DI NORIMBERGA, GLI** • 1972
BLOOD BARRIER see **BORDER, THE** • 1981
BLOOD BARRIER, THE • 1920 • Blackton J. Stuart • USA
BLOOD BATH • 1966 • Hill Jack, Rothman Stephanie • USA • TRACK OF THE VAMPIRE
BLOOD BATH • 1975 • Reed Joel M. • USA
BLOOD BATH see **REAZIONE A CATENA** • 1971
BLOOD BATH AT THE HOUSE OF DEATH • 1983 • Cameron Ray • USA
BLOOD BEACH • 1980 • Bloom Jeffrey • USA
BLOOD BEAST FROM HELL see **BLOOD BEAST TERROR, THE** • 1968
BLOOD BEAST FROM OUTER SPACE (USA) see **NIGHT CALLER, THE** • 1966
BLOOD BEAST TERROR, THE • 1968 • Sewell Vernon • UKN • VAMPIRE-BEAST CRAVES BLOOD, THE (USA) ◦ BLOOD BEAST FROM HELL ◦ DEATHSHEAD VAMPIRE
BLOOD BEAT see **BLOODBEAT** • 1985
BLOOD BOND see **STIMMES DES BLUTES** • 1937
BLOOD BOND, THE • 1925 • *Maloney Leo* • USA
BLOOD BRIDE • 1980 • Avrech Robert J. • USA
BLOOD BRIDES see **BRIDES OF BLOOD** • 1968
BLOOD BRIDES (UKN) see **ROSSO SEGNO DELLA FOLLIA, IL** • 1969
BLOOD BROTHER, THE (UKN) see **TEXAS PIONEERS** • 1932
BLOOD BROTHER TO THE PINES see **MAGNIFICENT BRUTE, THE** • 1921
BLOOD BROTHERHOOD, THE • 1913 • Weber Lois • USA
BLOOD BROTHERS • 1953 • Snyder Robert • USA
BLOOD BROTHERS see **GUAPPI, I** • 1974
BLOOD BROTHERS see **BLOODBROTHERS** • 1978
BLOOD BROTHERS see **VERSZERZODES** • 1983
BLOOD BROTHERS, THE see **CHINESE VENGEANCE** • 1973
BLOOD BROTHERS (UKN) see **BROTHERS** • 1930
BLOOD CALLS BLOOD see **SANGUE CHIAMA SANGUE** • 1968
BLOOD CASTLE see **IVANNA** • 1970
BLOOD CEREMONY see **CEREMONIA SANGRIETA** • 1972
BLOOD CIRCUS • 1985 • Harris Bob • USA
BLOOD COUPLE see **GANJA AND HESS** • 1973
BLOOD CREATURE see **TERROR IS A MAN** • 1959
BLOOD CROWD, THE see **MCMASTERS, THE** • 1970
BLOOD CRYSTAL, THE • 1990 • Andlibi Jamshid • IRN
BLOOD CULT • 1985 • Lewis Christopher • USA
BLOOD DEBT see **HUTANG DARAH** • 1971
BLOOD DEMON • 1969 • Romero Eddie • USA
BLOOD DEMON, THE (UKN) see **SCHLANGENGRUBE UND DAS PENDEL, DIE** • 1967
BLOOD DEVILS (UKN) see **BEAST OF BLOOD** • 1970
BLOOD DINER • 1987 • Kong Jackie • USA
BLOOD DOCTOR see **MAD DOCTOR OF BLOOD ISLAND** • 1969
BLOOD DRINKERS, THE • 1966 • De Leon Gerardo • USA, PHL • VAMPIRE PEOPLE
BLOOD EVIL see **DEMONS OF THE MIND** • 1971
BLOOD FARMERS see **INVASION OF THE BLOOD FARMERS** • 1971
BLOOD FEAST • 1963 • Lewis Herschell G. • USA • FEAST OF FLESH
BLOOD FEAST see **FIN DE FIESTA** • 1960
BLOOD FEAST OF THE BLIND DEAD see **NOCHE DE LAS GAVIOTAS, LA** • 1975
BLOOD FEUD • 1935 • *Sircar B. N. (P)* • IND
BLOOD FEUD • 1973 • Wendkos Paul • TVM • USA
BLOOD FEUD • 1982 • Newell Mike • TVM • USA
BLOOD FEUD see **UMIR KRVI** • 1971
BLOOD FEUD (USA) see **FATTO DI SANGUE FRA DUE UOMINI PER CAUSA DI UNA VEDOVA (SI SOSPETTANO MOVENTI POLITICI)** • 1978
BLOOD FIEND see **SEDDOK, L'EREDE DI SATANA** • 1961
BLOOD FIEND see **THEATRE OF DEATH** • 1967
BLOOD FOR A SILVER DOLLAR see **DOLLARO BUCATO, UN** • 1965
BLOOD FOR BLOOD • 1927 • *United Pictures* • IND • HAMLET
BLOOD FOR BLOOD see **KHOON-KA-KHOON** • 1935
BLOOD FOR BLOOD, DEATH FOR DEATH see **KROV ZA KROV, SMERT ZA SMERT** • 1941
BLOOD FOR DRACULA (UKN) see **ANDY WARHOL'S DRACULA** • 1974
BLOOD FROM THE MUMMY'S TOMB • 1972 • Holt Seth, Carreras Michael • UKN • CURSE OF THE MUMMY
BLOOD GROUPIE see **GROUPIE GIRL** • 1970
BLOOD HARVEST • 1987 • Rebane Bill • USA
BLOOD HERITAGE • 1915 • Shaw Brinsley • USA
BLOOD HONEYMOON see **ORS AL-DAM** • 1977
BLOOD HOOK • 1986 • Mallon James • USA
BLOOD HUNT • 1985 • Barber-Fleming Peter • TVM • UKN
BLOOD IN THE STREETS (USA) see **REVOLVER** • 1973
BLOOD IS LIFE • 1957 • Simmons Anthony • UKN
BLOOD IS MY HERITAGE (UKN) see **BLOOD OF DRACULA** • 1957
BLOOD IS THICKER THAN WATER • 1912 • *Baggot King* • USA
BLOOD IS THICKER THAN WATER see **MATIMBANG ANG DUGO SA TUBIG** • 1967
BLOOD KIN see **LAST OF THE MOBILE HOT-SHOTS, THE** • 1970
BLOOD LEGACY • 1971 • Monson Carl • USA • LEGACY OF BLOOD ◦ WILL TO DIE
BLOOD LINK • 1983 • De Martino Alberto • ITL • LINK, THE
BLOOD MANIA • 1970 • O'Neil Robert Vincent • USA
BLOOD MONEY • 1917 • Kelsey Fred A. • SHT • USA
BLOOD MONEY • 1921 • Goodwins Fred • UKN
BLOOD MONEY • 1933 • Brown Rowland • USA
BLOOD MONEY • 1982 • SAF
BLOOD MONEY • 1988 • Schatzberg Jerry • USA • BLOOD MONEY: THE STORY OF CLINTON AND NADINE ◦ CLINTON AND NADINE
BLOOD MONEY see **SNATCH** • 1980
BLOOD MONEY: THE STORY OF CLINTON AND NADINE see **BLOOD MONEY** • 1988
BLOOD MONEY (UKN) see **REQUIEM FOR A HEAVYWEIGHT** • 1962
BLOOD MONEY (UKN) see **LA DOVE NON BATTE IL SOLE** • 1975
BLOOD MONSTER see **BLOOD SHACK** • 1981
BLOOD NEED NOT BE SPILLED see **NE NADO KROVI** • 1917
BLOOD OATH • 1989 • Wallace Stephen • ASL
BLOOD OF A DEGENERATE • 1966 • Wakamatsu Koji • JPN
BLOOD OF A POET, THE (USA) see **SANG D'UN POETE, LE** • 1930
BLOOD OF A WARRIOR see **DARAH PENGLIMA** • 1971
BLOOD OF BEASTS, THE see **SANG DES BETES, LE** • 1949
BLOOD OF BROTHERS see **SANGRE HERMANA** • 1914
BLOOD OF DR. JEKYLL, THE see **DOCTEUR JEKYLL ET LES FEMMES** • 1981
BLOOD OF DRACULA • 1957 • Strock Herbert L. • USA • BLOOD IS MY HERITAGE (UKN) ◦ BLOOD OF THE DEMON
BLOOD OF DRACULA'S CASTLE • 1969 • Adamson Al • USA • DRACULA'S CASTLE
BLOOD OF FRANKENSTEIN see **DRACULA VS. FRANKENSTEIN** • 1971
BLOOD OF FU MANCHU, THE (GBR) see **TODESKUSS DES DR. FU MAN CHU, DER** • 1968
BLOOD OF GHASTLY HORROR • 1972 • Adamson Al • USA • MAN WITH THE SYNTHETIC BRAIN, THE ◦ PSYCHO A GO-GO! ◦ FIEND WITH THE ATOMIC BRAIN, THE ◦ LOVE MANIAC, THE ◦ FIEND WITH THE ELECTRONIC BRAIN, THE
BLOOD OF HIS BROTHER, THE • 1915 • McRae Henry • USA
BLOOD OF HIS FATHERS • 1917 • Ingraham Harrish • USA
BLOOD OF HUSSAIN, THE • 1980 • Dehlavi Jamil • PKS, UKN
BLOOD OF JESUS • 1941 • Williams Spencer • USA
BLOOD OF MINAS see **SANGUE MINEIRO** • 1929
BLOOD OF NOSTRADAMUS, THE (USA) see **SANGRE DE NOSTRADAMUS, LA** • 1960
BLOOD OF OTHERS, THE see **CHEMINS DE LA VIOLENCE, LES** • 1972
BLOOD OF OTHERS, THE see **SANG DES AUTRES, LE** • 1983
BLOOD OF OUR BROTHERS, THE • 1915 • Maude Arthur • USA
BLOOD OF THE BEASTS see **SANG DES BETES, LE** • 1949
BLOOD OF THE CHILDREN, THE • 1915 • McRae Henry • USA
BLOOD OF THE CONDOR (UKN) see **YAWAR MALLKU** • 1969
BLOOD OF THE DEMON see **BLOOD OF DRACULA** • 1957
BLOOD OF THE DRAGON see **DESPERATE CHASE, THE** • 1974
BLOOD OF THE DRAGON PERIL • Mann Rocky • HKG
BLOOD OF THE IRON MAIDEN see **IS YOUR TRIP REALLY NECESSARY?** • 1969
BLOOD OF THE MAN BEAST see **HOUSE OF THE BLACK DEATH** • 1965
BLOOD OF THE MAN-DEVIL see **HOUSE OF THE BLACK DEATH** • 1965
BLOOD OF THE PARIAS, THE see **SANG DES PARIAS, LE** • 1973
BLOOD OF THE POOR, THE • 1911 • Davis Ulysses • USA
BLOOD OF THE TREVORS see **HEREDITY** • 1918
BLOOD OF THE UNDEAD see **SCHIZO** • 1976
BLOOD OF THE VAMPIRE • 1958 • Cass Henry • UKN
BLOOD OF THE VIRGINS see **SANGRE DE VIRGENES** • 1967
BLOOD OF THE WALSUNGS see **WALSUNGENBLUT** • 1964
BLOOD OF THE WEREWOLF see **I WAS A TEENAGE WEREWOLF** • 1957
BLOOD ON EASTER SUNDAY see **NON C'E PACE TRA GLI ULIVI** • 1950
BLOOD ON HER LIPS see **ROUGE AUX LEVRES, LE** • 1970
BLOOD ON HIS LIPS (UKN) see **HIDEOUS SUN DEMON, THE** • 1959
BLOOD ON HIS SWORD (USA) see **MIRACLE DES LOUPS, LE** • 1961
BLOOD ON MY HANDS (UKN) see **KISS THE BLOOD OFF MY HANDS** • 1948
BLOOD ON MY HANDS (UKN) see **CONDE, UN** • 1970

BLOOD ON SAND see **DUGO SA BUHANGIN** • 1967
BLOOD ON SATAN'S CLAW (USA) see **SATAN'S SKIN** • 1970
BLOOD ON THE ARROW • 1964 • Salkow Sidney • USA
BLOOD ON THE BALCONY see **BENITO MUSSOLINI** • 1962
BLOOD ON THE LAND see **HOMA VAFTIKE KOKKINO, TO** • 1965
BLOOD ON THE MOON • 1948 • Wise Robert • USA
BLOOD ON THE MOON see **COP** • 1987
BLOOD ON THE SHEETS see **ASESINO ESTA SOLO** • 1973
BLOOD ON THE STREETS (UKN) see **BORSALINO E CIE** • 1974
BLOOD ON THE SUN • 1945 • Lloyd Frank • USA
BLOOD ORANGE • 1953 • Fisher Terence • UKN
BLOOD & ORCHIDS • 1986 • Thorpe Jerry • TVM • USA • BLOOD AND ORCHIDS
BLOOD ORGY see **GORE-GORE GIRLS, THE** • 1972
BLOOD ORGY OF THE SHE-DEVILS • 1973 • Mikels Ted V. • USA
BLOOD PACT see **PACTO DE SANGRE** • 1989
BLOOD PIE see **PASTEL DE SANGRE** • 1971
BLOOD PUDDING see **PASTEL DE SANGRE** • 1971
BLOOD QUEEN see **LITTLE MOTHER** • 1972
BLOOD RED • 1987 • Masterson Peter • USA
BLOOD RED TAPE OF CHARITY, THE • 1913 • *August Edwin* • USA
BLOOD REINCARNATION • 1974 • Ting Shan-Hsi • HKG
BLOOD RELATIONS • 1988 • Campbell Graeme • CND
BLOOD RELATIONS see **BLOEDVERWANTEN** • 1976
BLOOD RELATIONS (USA) see **BALSAMUS L'UOMO DI SANTANA** • 1970
BLOOD RELATIVES (USA) see **LIENS DE SANG, LES** • 1978
BLOOD RIVER • 1968 • Breakston George • USA
BLOOD RIVER • 1971 • Baldanello Gianfranco • ITL
BLOOD RIVER see **UND DER AMAZONAS SCHWEIGT** • 1963
BLOOD RIVER see **DIO PERDONA.. IO NO!** • 1967
BLOOD ROSE, THE see **ROSE ECORCHEE, LA** • 1970
BLOOD RUBY, THE • 1914 • Costello Maurice, Gaillord Robert • USA
BLOOD SABBATH • 1972 • Murphy Brianna • USA
BLOOD SEEDLING, THE • 1915 • Santschi Thomas • USA
BLOOD SEEKERS, THE see **CAIN'S WAY** • 1970
BLOOD SEEKERS, THE see **DRACULA VS. FRANKENSTEIN** • 1971
BLOOD SHACK • 1981 • Steckler Ray Dennis • USA • BLOOD MONSTER ○ CHOOPER, THE
BLOOD SHIP, THE • 1927 • Seitz George B. • USA
BLOOD SIMPLE • 1985 • Coen Joel • USA
BLOOD SISTERS • 1986 • Findlay Roberta • USA
BLOOD SISTERS see **SISTERS** • 1973
BLOOD SONG • 1982 • Levi Alan J., Angus Robert • USA
BLOOD-SPATTERED BRIDE, THE (USA) see **NOVIA ENSANGRENTADA, LA** • 1972
BLOOD SPELL • 1987 • Warren Deryn • USA • BOY FROM HELL, THE ○ BLOODSPELL
BLOOD SPLATTERED BRIDE, THE see **NOVIA ENSANGRENTADA, LA** • 1972
BLOOD SPORT • 1986 • McEveety Vincent • TVM • USA
BLOOD STAIN, THE • 1912 • Blache Alice • USA • BLOODSTAIN, THE
BLOOD STAIN, THE see **MANCHA DE SANGRE, LA** • 1937
BLOOD-STAINED HAND, THE • 1917 • *Moore Matt* • SHT • USA
BLOOD-STAINED LADY, THE see **KRVAVA PANI**
BLOOD STORY • 1972 • Damiani Amasi • ITL
BLOOD SUCKERS, THE see **RETURN FROM THE PAST** • 1967
BLOOD, SWEAT AND FEAR (USA) see **MARK IL POLIZIOTTO** • 1975
BLOOD TAINT, THE • 1915 • *Grandin* • USA
BLOOD TELLS: OR, THE ANTI-FRIVOLITY LEAGUE • 1916 • Collins Edwin J. • UKN
BLOOD TEST • 1923 • Maquis Don • USA
BLOOD TEST, THE • 1914 • Baggot King • USA
BLOOD THAT HAD TO BE SHED • 1984 • Ghiaurov Sergei • BUL
BLOOD THIRST • 1965 • Arnold Newt • USA, PHL • HORROR FROM BEYOND, THE
BLOOD TIDE see **BLOODTIDE** • 1984
BLOOD TIES see **RODNAYA KROV** • 1964
BLOOD TIES see **CUGINO AMERICANO, IL** • 1986
BLOOD TRACKS • 1986 • Jackson Michael • USA, SWD
BLOOD TRANSFUSION • 1941 • Nieter Hans M. • DOC • UKN
BLOOD VENGEANCE • 1911 • *Ambrosio* • ITL
BLOOD VENGEANCE • *Eastman George* • ITL
BLOOD VIRGIN, THE see **SYMPTOMS** • 1974
BLOOD VOWS • 1986 • Wendkos Paul • USA • BLOOD VOWS: THE STORY OF A MAFIA WIFE
BLOOD VOWS: THE STORY OF A MAFIA WIFE see **BLOOD VOWS** • 1986
BLOOD VOYAGE • 1976 • Mitchell Frank • USA • NIGHTMARE VOYAGE
BLOOD WATERS OF DR. Z, THE see **ZAAT** • 1972
BLOOD WEDDING see **ORS AL-DAM** • 1977
BLOOD WEDDING see **BODAS DE SANGRE** • 1981
BLOOD WEDDING see **HE KNOWS YOU'RE ALONE** • 1981
BLOOD WEDDING (USA) see **NOCES ROUGES, LES** • 1972
BLOOD WILL HAVE BLOOD see **DEMONS OF THE MIND** • 1971
BLOOD WILL TELL • 1912 • Edwards Walter • USA
BLOOD WILL TELL • 1913 • *Shay William* • USA
BLOOD WILL TELL • 1914 • Wharton Theodore • USA
BLOOD WILL TELL • 1917 • *Kb* • USA
BLOOD WILL TELL • 1917 • Quirk William • *Rolma* • USA
BLOOD WILL TELL • 1927 • Flynn Ray • USA
BLOOD YOKE, THE • 1915 • Le Saint Edward J. • USA
BLOODBATH see **MARTA** • 1971
BLOODBATH see **SKY IS FALLING, THE** • 1973
BLOODBATH BAY OF DEATH see **REAZIONE A CATENA** • 1971
BLOODBATH OF DR. JEKYLL see **DOCTEUR JEKYLL ET LES FEMMES** • 1981
BLOODBEAT • 1985 • Zaphiratos Fabrice A. • USA • BLOOD BEAT
BLOODBROTHERS • 1978 • Mulligan Robert • USA • BLOOD BROTHERS ○ FATHER'S LOVE, A
BLOODEATERS • 1980 • McCrann Chuck • USA • TOXIC ZOMBIES ○ FOREST OF FEAR
BLOODFIGHT see **OPPONENT, THE** • 1987
BLOODHOUND, THE • 1925 • Craft William James • USA
BLOODHOUNDS OF BROADWAY • 1952 • Jones Harmon • USA
BLOODHOUNDS OF BROADWAY • 1989 • Brookner Howard • USA
BLOODHOUNDS OF THE NORTH • 1913 • Dwan Allan • USA
BLOODHOUNDS OF THE NORTH • 1917 • *Macquarrie Murdock J.* • USA
BLOODHOUNDS TRACKING A CONVICT • 1903 • Paul Robert William • UKN • TRAILED BY BLOODHOUNDS (USA)
BLOODLINE see **SIDNEY SHELDON'S BLOODLINE** • 1979
BLOODLINE see **SECRET LIVES OF THE BRITISH PRIME MINISTERS: PITT, THE** • 1983
BLOODLUST • 1961 • Brooke Ralph • USA
BLOODLUST see **MOSQUITO DER SCHANDER** • 1976
BLOODMOON • 1989 • Mills Alec • ASL
BLOODRAGE • 1979 • Bigwood Joseph • USA
BLOODSCAPE • 1989 • Jones Brian Thomas • USA • INFERNO IN SAFEHAVEN
BLOODSHED ON THE WEDDING see **MAKEDONSKA KRVAVA SVADBA** • 1968
BLOODSIPPERS see **KRVOPIJCI** • 1989
BLOODSPELL see **BLOOD SPELL** • 1987
BLOODSPORT • 1973 • Freedman Jerrold • TVM • USA
BLOODSPORT • 1987 • Arnold Newt • USA
BLOODSTAIN, THE see **BLOOD STAIN, THE** • 1912
BLOODSTAINED SHADOW • Bido Antonio • ITL
BLOODSTAINED SHOE, THE • 1914 • *Urban Trading Co.* • UKN
BLOODSTONE • 1988 • Little Dwight H. • USA
BLOODSTONE, THE • 1908 • *Lubin* • USA
BLOODSUCKER see **INCENSE FOR THE DAMNED** • 1970
BLOODSUCKERS, THE (UKN) see **GEHEIMNIS DER TODESINSEL, DAS** • 1967
BLOODSUCKERS FROM OUTER SPACE • 1985 • USA
BLOODSUCKERS (USA) see **INCENSE FOR THE DAMNED** • 1970
BLOODSUCKING FREAKS see **INCREDIBLE TORTURE SHOW, THE** • 1977
BLOODTHIRSTY BUTCHERS • 1970 • Milligan Andy • USA
BLOODTHIRSTY EYES see **CHIOSU ME** • 1971
BLOODTHIRSTY FAIRY, THE see **FEE SANGUINAIRE, LA** • 1968
BLOODTIDE • 1984 • Jeffries Richard • USA • BLOOD TIDE ○ RED TIDE, THE
BLOODY AMBITION see **AMBICION SANGRIENTA** • 1968
BLOODY, BARE, AND BEAUTIFUL see **BEAUTIFUL, THE BLOODY, AND THE BARE, THE** • 1964
BLOODY BIRTHDAY • 1980 • Hunt Ed • USA • BLOODY SUNDAY
BLOODY BRIDE, THE see **NOVIA ENSANGRENTADA, LA** • 1972
BLOODY BROOD, THE • 1962 • Roffman Julian • CND
BLOODY BUSHIDO BLADE, THE see **BUSHIDO BLADE, THE** • 1979
BLOODY CAMP, THE see **KANLI OBA** • 1968
BLOODY CEREMONY see **CEREMONIA SANGRIETA** • 1972
BLOODY CHASE, THE see **KANLI TAKIP** • 1967
BLOODY CHE CONTRA see **CHE GUEVARA, EL** • 1968
BLOODY FAIRY, THE see **FEE SANGUINAIRE, LA** • 1968
BLOODY FIANCEE see **NOVIA ENSANGRENTADA, LA** • 1972
BLOODY FIST, THE see **DANG KOU-TAN** • 1969
BLOODY FISTS, THE see **DANG KOU-TAN** • 1969
BLOODY FRIDAY see **BLUTIGER FREITAG** • 1972
BLOODY GHOST see **ERATHA PEY** • 1968
BLOODY HANDS OF THE LAW see **MANO SPIETATO DELLE LEGGE, LA** • 1973
BLOODY HELL, DAD! see **JO, PAPA** • 1975
BLOODY HEROES, THE • 1977 • Chi Yiu Cheung • HKG
BLOODY INN, THE see **POSADA SANGRIETA, LA** • 1941
BLOODY JUDGE, THE (UKN) see **PROCESO DE LAS BRUJAS, EL** • 1970
BLOODY KIDS • 1980 • Frears Stephen • TVM • UKN • RED SATURDAY
BLOODY KILLER, THE see **CANGACEIRO SANGUINARIO, O** • 1969
BLOODY LIFE see **KANLI HAYAT** • 1967
BLOODY MACEDONIAN WEDDING, THE see **MAKEDONSKA KRVAVA SVADBA** • 1968
BLOODY MAMA • 1970 • Corman Roger • USA
BLOODY MARY • 1989 • Hodi Jeno • USA
BLOODY MARY see **RENACER** • 1980
BLOODY MISSION • *Liu Yung* • HKG
BLOODY MOON • *Pascal Olivia*
BLOODY MOON see **SAGE DES TODES, DIE** • 1981
BLOODY NEW YEAR • 1987 • Warren Norman J. • UKN • TIME WARP TERROR
BLOODY NIGAR see **KANTI NIGAR** • 1968
BLOODY PARROT see **HSUEH YING-WU** • 1980
BLOODY PIT OF HORROR (USA) see **BOIA SCARLATTO, IL** • 1965
BLOODY PLEASURE see **PLACER SANGRIENTO** • 1967
BLOODY POM POMS see **CHEERLEADER CAMP** • 1988
BLOODY ROAD, THE see **KRVAVI PUT** • 1955
BLOODY SALTPETRE see **CALICHE SANGRIENTO** • 1969
BLOODY SCREAM OF DRACULA, THE see **DRACULA -PRINCE OF DARKNESS** • 1965
BLOODY SEA • 1965 • MXC
BLOODY SHIRT, THE see **KRVAVA KOSULJA** • 1957
BLOODY SPEAR AT MOUNT FUJI, A see **CHIYARI FUJI** • 1955
BLOODY SPEAR ON MOUNT FUJI, A see **CHIYARI FUJI** • 1955
BLOODY SUNDAY • *Cordell Melinda*
BLOODY SUNDAY see **SUNDAY, BLOODY SUNDAY** • 1971
BLOODY SUNDAY see **BLOODY BIRTHDAY** • 1980
BLOODY TALE see **KRVAVA BAJKA** • 1971
BLOODY TRAIL • 1972 • Robinson Richard • USA
BLOODY TWILIGHT see **MATOMENA HELIOVASILEMA** • 1959
BLOODY VAMPIRE, THE (USA) see **VAMPIRO SANGRIENTO, EL** • 1962
BLOODY VIOLATION see **CHI NO BOHKOH** • 1968
BLOODY VIRGIN • 1976 • Andritsos Kostas • GRC
BLOODY WEDNESDAY • 1985 • Gilhuis Mark G. • USA
BLOOM OF VOLUPTUOUSNESS see **IROKEZAKARI** • 1968
BLOOMER AND THE EGG POWDER see **KRI-KRI MANGIA I GAMBERI** • 1913
BLOOMFIELD • 1969 • Harris Richard • UKN, ISR • HERO, THE
BLOOMING ANGEL, THE • 1920 • Schertzinger Victor • USA
BLOOMING AT NIGHT see **YORU HIRAKU** • 1931
BLOOMSBURY BURGLARS, THE • 1912 • Coleby A. E. • UKN
BLOSSOM see **HANA** • 1941
BLOSSOM TIME • 1934 • Stein Paul L. • UKN • APRIL ROMANCE (USA)
BLOSSOM TIME see **BLOMSTERTID, DEN** • 1940
BLOSSOMING IN THE TIDAR VALLEY see **BERSEMI DI LEMBAH TIDAR** • 1983
BLOSSOMING PORT, THE see **HANA SAKU MINATO** • 1943
BLOSSOMS IN AUTUMN see **CVIJECE U JESEN** • 1974
BLOSSOMS IN THE DUST • 1941 • LeRoy Mervyn • USA
BLOSSOMS OF BROADWAY • 1937 • Wallace Richard • USA
BLOSSOMS OF LOVE see **AJISAI NO UTA** • 1960
BLOT, THE • 1921 • Weber Lois • USA
BLOT FROM THE SKY • 1915 • *Balboa* • USA
BLOT IN THE FAIRY-TALE, A see **KANKA DO POHADKY** • 1981
BLOT IN THE 'SCUTCHEON, A • 1912 • Griffith D. W. • USA
BLOT ON THE SHIELD, A • 1915 • Eason B. Reeves • USA
BLOTT EN DROM • 1911 • Hoffman-Uddgren Anna • SWD • ONLY A DREAM
BLOTTED BRAND, THE • 1911 • Dwan Allan • USA
BLOTTED OUT • 1914 • Forman Tom • USA
BLOTTED PAGE, THE • 1914 • *Billington Francelia* • USA
BLOTTO • 1930 • Parrott James • SHT • USA
BLOUDENI • 1965 • Masa Antonin, Curik Jan • CZC • WANDERING
BLOUDENI ORIENTACNIHO BEZCE • 1985 • Matula Julius • CZC • GOING ASTRAY ON AN ORIENTATION COURSE
BLOUSE KING, THE see **BLUSENKONIG, DER** • 1917
BLOUSES BLANCHES, LES • 1912 • Perret Leonce • FRN
BLOW-BALL see **BOBITA** • 1964
BLOW BUGLES BLOW • 1936 • Messell Rudolf • USA
BLOW BY BLOW • 1928 • McCarey Leo, Parrott James • SHT • USA
BLOW 'EM UP • 1922 • Roach Hal • SHT • USA
BLOW FOR BLOW • 1915 • *Butler W. J.* • USA
BLOW FOR BLOW see **COUP POUR COUP** • 1971
BLOW JOB • 1964 • Warhol Andy • SHT • USA
BLOW JOB • 1978 • Martin Susan • SHT • USA
BLOW, LOVE WIND see **FUKEYO KOIKAZE** • 1935
BLOW ME DOWN • 1933 • Fleischer Dave • ANS • USA
BLOW OUT • 1981 • De Palma Brian • USA
BLOW-OUT, THE • 1936 • Avery Tex • ANS • USA
BLOW OUT, THE see **CAMPANADA, LA** • 1979
BLOW OUT IN THE NORTH SEA see **HALTENBANKEN** • 1986
BLOW-OUT (UKN) see **GRANDE ABBUFFATA, LA** • 1973
BLOW SOME MY WAY • Davian Joe • USA
BLOW SPRING BREEZE • 1953 • Taniguchi Senkichi • JPN
BLOW THAT KILLED FATHER, THE • 1920 • Williamson Robin E. • SHT • USA
BLOW THE MAN DOWN • 1968 • Dupree Hayes • USA
BLOW TO THE HEART see **COLPIRE AL CUORE** • 1983
BLOW-UP • 1967 • Antonioni Michelangelo • UKN
BLOW YOUR HORN • 1916 • Myll Louis • SHT • USA
BLOW YOUR OWN HORN • 1923 • Horne James W. • USA
BLOW YOUR OWN TRUMPET • 1958 • Musk Cecil • UKN
BLOWING HOT AND GOLD • 1988 • Graoic Marc • ASL
BLOWING UP OF THE MAINE IN HAVANA HARBOUR, THE see **GUERRE DE CUBA ET L'EXPLOSION DU MAINE A LA HAVANE** • 1898
BLOWING UP THE POWDER MAGAZINE • 1901 • *Mitchell & Kenyon* • UKN
BLOWING WILD • 1953 • Fregonese Hugo • USA
BLOWN INTO CUSTODY • 1915 • *Ab* • USA
BLOWN UPON • 1915 • Frank Alexander F. • USA
BLOWOUT AT SANTA BANANA, A • 1914 • *American* • USA
BLU GANG • 1973 • Bazzoni Camillo • ITL
BLUCHER • 1988 • Tuhus Oddvar Bull • NRW
BLUDGEON, THE • 1915 • *Osterman Kathryn* • USA
BLUDICKA • 1921 • Cervenkova Thea • CZC • THIEF, THE
BLUDSOE'S DILEMMA • 1912 • *American* • USA
BLUE • 1968 • Narizzano Silvio • USA
BLUE see **AZUL** • 1972
BLUE 9, THE see **PLAVI 9** • 1950
BLUE AND ORANGE • 1977 • Lipsett Arthur, Ballantyne Tanya • CND
BLUE AND THE GOLD, THE (UKN) see **ANNAPOLIS STORY, AN** • 1955
BLUE AND THE GRAY, THE • 1982 • McLaglen Andrew V. • TVM • USA
BLUE AND THE GRAY, THE DAYS OF '61, THE • 1908 • Porter Edwin S. • USA
BLUE AND THE GREY, THE • 1908 • *Edison* • USA
BLUE ANGEL, THE • 1959 • Dmytryk Edward • USA
BLUE ANGEL, THE • 1988 • D'Amato Joe • ITL
BLUE ANGEL, THE see **BLAUE ENGEL, DER** • 1930
BLUE APRON • Hutecka K. • ANS • CZC
BLUE BALL, THE see **NIEBIESKA KULA** • 1968
BLUE BANDANA, THE • 1919 • Franz Joseph J. • USA
BLUE BEADS FROM GREECE see **THALASSEIES I HANDRES, I** • 1967
BLUE BEARD, BLUE BEARD see **BARBABLU, BARBABLU** • 1989
BLUE BEARD (USA) see **BARBE BLEUE** • 1898
BLUE BEARD (USA) see **BARBE BLEUE** • 1901
BLUE BEAST, THE see **AOI YAJU** • 1960
BLUE BELLE (UKN) see **FINE DELL'INNOCENZA, LA** • 1976
BLUE BIRD, THE • 1908 • *Pathe* • FRN
BLUE BIRD, THE • 1910 • *Gilmer Pauline* • UKN
BLUE BIRD, THE • 1940 • Lang Walter • USA
BLUE BIRD, THE see **BLUEBIRD, THE** • 1918
BLUE BIRD, THE (USA) see **SINYAYA PTITSA** • 1975
BLUE BIRD OF A FAIR WIND see **POPUTNOVO VYETRA "SINYAYA PTITSA"** • 1967
BLUE BLACKBIRDS • 1933 • Lamont Charles • SHT • USA
BLUE BLAZES • 1922 • Kelly Robert?, Mack Charles W.? • USA
BLUE BLAZES • 1926 • Franz Joseph J. • USA
BLUE BLAZES • 1936 • *Keaton Buster* • SHT • USA
BLUE BLAZES see **RACING YOUTH** • 1932
BLUE BLAZES RAWDEN • 1918 • Hart William S. • USA
BLUE BLOOD • 1918 • Howe Eliot • USA
BLUE BLOOD • 1922 • *Calhoun Alice* • USA
BLUE BLOOD • 1925 • Dunlap Scott R. • USA

BLUE BLOOD • 1951 • Landers Lew • USA
BLUE BLOOD • 1973 • Sinclair Andrew • UKN
BLUE BLOOD AND BEVO • 1919 • *West Billy* • SHT • USA
BLUE BLOOD AND BLACK SKIN • 1916 • *Russell Dan* • SHT • USA
BLUE BLOOD AND RED • 1914 • *Loveridge Margaret* • USA
BLUE BLOOD AND RED • 1916 • Walsh Raoul • USA
BLUE BLOOD AND YELLOW • 1915 • *King Henry* • USA
BLUE BLOOD AND YELOW BACKS • 1915 • *Gribbon Harry* • USA
BLUE BONNET, THE • 1908 • *Selig* • USA
BLUE BONNET, THE • 1920 • Chaudet Louis W. • USA
BLUE BOYS see **BLAJACKOR** • 1964
BLUE BOYS NO.1, THE • 1930 • *Balcon Michael (P)* • SHT • UKN
BLUE BOYS NO.2, THE • 1930 • *Balcon Michael (P)* • SHT • UKN
BLUE BUD see **AOI ME** • 1956
BLUE CAMELLIA, THE • 1954 • Sekely Steve • USA
BLUE CANADIAN ROCKIES • 1952 • Archainbaud George • USA
BLUE CARBUNCLE, THE • 1923 • Ridgwell George • UKN
BLUE CAT, THE • 1959 • Lehky Vladimir • ANS • CZC
BLUE CAT BLUES • 1956 • Hanna William, Barbera Joseph • ANS • USA
BLUE CHRISTMAS • 1978 • Okamoto Kihachi • JPN
BLUE CITY • 1986 • Manning Michelle • USA
BLUE CITY SLAMMERS • 1988 • Shatalow Peter • CND
BLUE CLAY (UKN) see **SON OF DAVY CROCKETT, THE** • 1942
BLUE CLIFF, THE • 1943 • Braun Vladimir • USS
BLUE COLLAR • 1978 • Schrader Paul • USA
BLUE COLLAR AMERICA • 1980 • Ribbsjo Anders, Marklund Inger • SWD
BLUE CONTINENT see **SESTO CONTINENTE** • 1954
BLUE COUNTRY, THE (USA) see **PAYS BLEU, LE** • 1977
BLUE COYOTE CHERRY CROP, THE • 1914 • Miller Ashley • USA
BLUE CROSS see **BLEKITNY KRZYZ** • 1956
BLUE CURRENT see **AOI KAIRYU** • 1961
BLUE DAHLIA, THE • 1946 • Marshall George • USA
BLUE DANUBE, THE • 1928 • Sloane Paul • USA • HONOUR ABOVE ALL (UKN)
BLUE DANUBE, THE • 1932 • Wilcox Herbert • UKN • RHAPSODY
BLUE DANUBE, THE • 1939 • Harman Hugh • ANS • USA
BLUE DE VILLE see **BLUE DEVILLE** • 1986
BLUE DEMON, THE see **DEMONIO AZUL, EL** • 1964
BLUE DEMON AGAINST THE BRAINS OF HELL see **BLUE DEMON CONTRA CEREBROS INFERNALES** • 1968
BLUE DEMON AGAINST THE DEVIL GIRLS see **BLUE DEMON CONTRA LAS DIABOLICAS** • 1968
BLUE DEMON AND THE SEDUCTRESSES see **BLUE DEMON Y LAS SEDUCTORAS** • 1968
BLUE DEMON CONTRA CEREBROS INFERNALES • 1968 • Urueta Chano • MXC • BLUE DEMON AGAINST THE BRAINS OF HELL ○ BLUE DEMON VS. EL CRIMEN ○ CEREBRO INFERNAL ○ BLUE DEMON VERSUS THE INFERNAL BRAINS ○ HELLISH BRAIN, THE
BLUE DEMON CONTRA EL PODER SATANICO • 1964 • Urueta Chano • MXC • BLUE DEMON VS. THE SATANICAL POWER ○ PODER SATANICO, EL
BLUE DEMON CONTRA LAS DIABOLICAS • 1968 • Urueta Chano • MXC • BLUE DEMON AGAINST THE DEVIL GIRLS ○ BLUE DEMON VS. THE DIABOLICAL WOMEN
BLUE DEMON DESTRUCTOR DE ESPIAS • 1968 • Gomez Muriel Emilio • MXC • BLUE DEMON THE DESTROYER OF SPIES ○ BLUE DEMON, SPY DESTROYER
BLUE DEMON EN PASAPORTE A LA MUERTE • 1968 • Crevenna Alfredo B. • MXC • BLUE DEMON IN PASSPORT TO DEATH ○ BLUE DEMON PASSPORT TO DEATH
BLUE DEMON IN PASSPORT TO DEATH see **BLUE DEMON EN PASAPORTE A LA MUERTE** • 1968
BLUE DEMON PASSPORT TO DEATH see **BLUE DEMON EN PASAPORTE A LA MUERTE** • 1968
BLUE DEMON, SPY DESTROYER see **BLUE DEMON DESTRUCTOR DE ESPIAS** • 1968
BLUE DEMON THE DESTROYER OF SPIES see **BLUE DEMON DESTRUCTOR DE ESPIAS** • 1968
BLUE DEMON VERSUS THE INFERNAL BRAINS see **BLUE DEMON CONTRA CEREBROS INFERNALES** • 1968
BLUE DEMON VS. EL CRIMEN see **BLUE DEMON CONTRA CEREBROS INFERNALES** • 1968
BLUE DEMON VS. THE DIABOLICAL WOMEN see **BLUE DEMON CONTRA LAS DIABOLICAS** • 1968
BLUE DEMON VS. THE SATANICAL POWER see **BLUE DEMON CONTRA EL PODER SATANICO** • 1964
BLUE DEMON Y LAS SEDUCTORAS • 1968 • Martinez Solares Gilberto • MXC • BLUE DEMON AND THE SEDUCTRESSES
BLUE DENIM • 1959 • Dunne Philip • USA • BLUE JEANS (UKN)
BLUE DEVILLE • 1986 • Johnson Jim • TVM • USA • BLUE DE VILLE
BLUE DUCKLING, THE • 1967 • Dembinski Lucjan • ANM • PLN
BLUE EAGLE, THE • 1926 • Ford John • USA
BLUE ECSTASY • 1976 • Mulot Claude • FRN
BLUE ENVELOPE MYSTERY, THE • 1916 • North Wilfred • USA
BLUE EXPRESS, THE see **GOLUBOI EKSPRESS** • 1929
BLUE EYE, THE see **OEIL BLEU, L'** • 1968
BLUE-EYED see **BLAUAUGIG** • 1988
BLUE-EYED BANDITS, THE see **BANDITO DAGLI OCCHI AZZURI, IL** • 1980
BLUE-EYED MARY • 1918 • Millarde Harry • USA
BLUE EYES OF DEATH see **PARAPSYCHICS** • 1974
BLUE EYES OF THE BROKEN DOLL, THE see **OJOS AZULES DE LA MUNECA ROTA, LOS** • 1973
BLUE FANTASIES see **SCHULMADCHEN-REPORT 12** • 1978
BLUE FIELD DURATION • 1972 • Le Grice Malcolm • UKN
BLUE FILM -ESTIMATION see **AOI FILM SHINASADAME** • 1968
BLUE FIN • 1978 • Schultz Carl • ASL • SEA QUEST
BLUE FIRE LADY • 1977 • Dimsey Ross • ASL • BLUE FYRE LADY
BLUE FLAME, THE • 1914 • Le Saint Edward J. • USA
BLUE FLEET, THE (USA) see **ARMATA AZZURRA, L'** • 1932
BLUE FOR WATERLOO see **WATERLOO ROAD** • 1945
BLUE FOX (USA) see **BLAUFUCHS, DER** • 1938
BLUE FROM HEAVEN see **MODRE Z NEBE** • 1962
BLUE FROM HEAVEN see **MODRE Z NEBE** • 1983
BLUE FYRE LADY see **BLUE FIRE LADY** • 1977
BLUE GARDENIA, THE • 1953 • Lang Fritz • USA
BLUE GARTER • 1909 • *Lubin* • USA
BLUE GATES OF THE CITY, THE see **PORTILE ALBASTRE ALE ORASULUI** • 1973
BLUE GRASS • 1915 • Seay Charles M. • USA
BLUE GRASS see **BLUEGRASS** • 1988
BLUE GRASS OF KENTUCKY • 1950 • Beaudine William • USA
BLUE GUM ROMANCE, A • 1913 • Barrett Franklyn • ASL
BLUE HAND, THE see **BLAUE HAND, DIE** • 1967
BLUE HARES • 1973 • Aksenov V. • USS
BLUE HAWAII • 1950 • Kneitel Seymour • ANS • USA
BLUE HAWAII • 1961 • Taurog Norman • USA • HAWAII BEACH BOY
BLUE HEAVEN • 1984 • Dowdey Kathleen • USA
BLUE HOLOCAUST see **BUIO OMEGA** • 1979
BLUE HORSE MINE • 1910 • *Myers Harry* • USA
BLUE HOTEL • 1987 • Cohen Rob • USA • PRIVATE EYE: BLUE HOTEL ○ BLUE HOTEL: PRIVATE EYE
BLUE HOTEL: PRIVATE EYE see **BLUE HOTEL** • 1987
BLUE ICE see **GOLUBOI LIED** • 1970
BLUE IDOL, THE see **KEK BALVANY, A** • 1931
BLUE IGUANA, THE • 1987 • Lafia John • USA
BLUE ISLAND • Rosso Luigi • ITL • CASTAWAYS: A LOVE STORY
BLUE-JACKETS see **BLAJACKOR** • 1945
BLUE JEAN COP see **SHAKEDOWN** • 1988
BLUE JEANS • 1917 • Collins John H. • USA
BLUE JEANS • 1958 • Rozier Jacques • SHT • FRN
BLUE JEANS • 1975 • Imperoli Mario • ITL
BLUE JEANS • 1977 • Burin Des Roziers Hugues • FRN • DU BUERRE AUX ALLEMANDS
BLUE JEANS (UKN) see **BLUE DENIM** • 1959
BLUE KNIGHT, THE • 1973 • Butler Robert • TVM • USA
BLUE KNIGHT, THE • 1975 • Thompson J. Lee • TVM • USA
BLUE KNOT, KING OF POLO • 1914 • Ricketts Thomas • USA
BLUE LADY, THE see **ANGEL IN EXILE** • 1948
BLUE LAGOON, THE • 1923 • Cruickshanks Dick, Bowden W. • SAF
BLUE LAGOON, THE • 1949 • Launder Frank • UKN
BLUE LAGOON, THE • 1980 • Kleiser Randall • USA
BLUE LAMP, THE • 1950 • Dearden Basil • UKN
BLUE LIGHT, THE see **BLAUE LICHT, DAS** • 1932
BLUE LIGHTNING, THE • 1986 • Philips Lee • TVM • ASL
BLUE LOTUS see **NEEL KAMAL** • 1968
BLUE MAGIC • 1981 • Revene Larry • USA
BLUE MAMMY • 1986 • Lehmuskallio Markku • FNL
BLUE MAN, THE • 1986 • Mihalka George • CND • ETERNAL EVIL
BLUE MARGARITA see **MARGARITA AZUL** • 1974
BLUE MAX, THE • 1966 • Guillermin John • UKN, USA
BLUE MEN, THE • 1959 • Frankenheimer John • MTV • USA
BLUE MONDAY • 1938 • Hanna William • ANS • USA
BLUE MONEY • 1984 • Bucksey Colin • TVM • UKN
BLUE MONKEY • 1987 • Fruet William • USA • INVASION OF THE BODYSUCKERS ○ GREEN MONKEY ○ INSECT
BLUE MONTANA SKIES • 1939 • Eason B. Reeves • USA
BLUE MOON, THE • 1920 • Cox George L. • USA
BLUE MOON, THE see **BLAUE MOND, DER** • 1989
BLUE MOON MURDER CASE, THE • 1932 • Florey Robert • USA
BLUE MOSES • 1962 • Brakhage Stan • SHT • USA
BLUE MOUNTAIN MYSTERY, THE see **BLUE MOUNTAINS MYSTERY, THE** • 1922
BLUE MOUNTAINS see **AOI SANMYAKU** • 1949
BLUE MOUNTAINS see **AOI SANMYAKU** • 1957
BLUE MOUNTAINS see **GOLUBYE GORY ELY NEPRAVDOPODOBNAYA** • 1983
BLUE MOUNTAINS MYSTERY, THE • 1922 • Longford Raymond, Lyell Lottie • ASL • BLUE MOUNTAIN MYSTERY, THE
BLUE MOUSE, THE see **BLAUE MAUS, DIE** • 1928
BLUE MOVIE • 1969 • Warhol Andy • USA • FUCK ○ F**K ○ VIVA AND LOUIS
BLUE MOVIE • 1970 • Rimmer David • CND
BLUE MOVIE • 1971 • Verstappen Wim • NTH, FRG
BLUE MOVIE • 1978 • Cavallone Alberto • ITL
BLUE MOVIE BLACKMAIL (UKN) see **SI PUO ESSERE PIU BASTARDI DELL'ISPETTORE CLIFF?** • 1973
BLUE MOVIE STAR see **CONFESSIONS OF A BLUE MOVIE STAR** • 1982
BLUE MOVIES • 1988 • Fitzgerald Ed • USA
BLUE MURDER AT ST. TRINIANS • 1957 • Launder Frank • UKN
BLUE NEON see **SAKARIBA BLUES** • 1968
BLUE NOTEBOOK, THE see **SINYAYA TETRAD** • 1963
BLUE NOTTE • 1989 • Serafini Giorgio • FRG • DIRTY NIGHT
BLUE NUDE • 1978 • Scattini Luigi • ITL
BLUE OF THE NIGHT • 1933 • Pearce A. Leslie • SHT • USA
BLUE-ONE IN HIGH SOCIETY, THE see **EFKARLI SOSYETEDE** • 1968
BLUE OR THE GRAY, THE • 1913 • Cabanne W. Christy • USA
BLUE PARROT, THE • 1953 • Harlow John • UKN
BLUE PEARL, THE • 1920 • Irving George • USA
BLUE PEARL, THE • Honda Inoshiro • JPN
BLUE PETER • 1958 • Ferno John • SHT • UKN
BLUE PETER, THE • 1928 • Rooke Arthur • UKN
BLUE PETER, THE • 1954 • Sharp Don, Rilla Wolf • UKN • NAVY HEROES (USA)
BLUE PETE'S ESCAPE • 1914 • *De Grasse Sam* • USA
BLUE PINAFORE, THE • 1965 • Tyrlova Hermina • ANM • CZC
BLUE PLANET, THE see **PIANETA AZZURRO, IL** • 1983
BLUE PLATE SYMPHONY • 1954 • Rasinski Connie • ANS • USA
BLUE PULLMAN • 1960 • Ritchie James • UKN
BLUE REVOLUTION, THE see **AOIRO KAKUMEI** • 1953
BLUE RHYTHM • 1931 • Gillett Burt • ANS • USA
BLUE RIBBON MUTT, A • 1920 • Reisner Charles F. • SHT • USA
BLUE RIDGE FOLKS • 1912 • *Champion* • USA
BLUE RIDGE ROMANCE, A • 1912 • *Republic* • USA
BLUE RITA • 1977 • Franco Jesus • FRN
BLUE ROOM see **BLEKITNY POKOJ** • 1965
BLUE ROSE, THE • 1913 • Brooke Van Dyke • USA
BLUE SCAR • 1949 • Craigie Jill • UKN
BLUE SEA see **BLANANDE HAV** • 1956
BLUE SEAGULL, THE see **SINJI GALEB** • 1953
BLUE SEX PARTY • Thierry Alain • FRN
BLUE SEXTET • 1971 • Durston David E. • USA
BLUE SIERRA • 1946 • Wilcox Fred M. • USA
BLUE SKIES • 1929 • Werker Alfred L. • USA
BLUE SKIES • 1946 • Heisler Stuart • USA
BLUE SKIES AGAIN • 1983 • Michaels Richard • USA
BLUE SKY see **BLA HIMMEL** • 1955
BLUE SLEIGH, THE see **SANIA ALBASTRA** • 1987
BLUE SMILE, THE see **SOURIRE BLEU, LE** • 1968
BLUE SMOKE • 1935 • Ince Ralph • UKN
BLUE SQUADRON, THE • 1934 • King George • UKN
BLUE STADIUM, THE • 1957 • Stoyanov Yuli • DOC • BUL
BLUE STAR see **KYI PYAR** • 1980
BLUE STEEL • 1934 • Bradbury Robert North • USA
BLUE STEEL • 1990 • Bigelow Kathryn • USA
BLUE STORY, THE • 1971 • Peranne Antti • ANS • FNL
BLUE STREAK, THE • 1917 • Nigh William • USA
BLUE STREAK, THE • 1926 • Smith Noel • USA
BLUE STREAK, THE (UKN) see **KENTUCKY BLUE STREAK** • 1935
BLUE STREAK MCCOY • 1920 • Eason B. Reeves • USA
BLUE STREAK O'NEIL • 1926 • Hurst Paul C. • USA
BLUE SUEDE SHOES • 1980 • Clark Curtis • DOC • UKN
BLUE SUMMER • 1971 • Vincent Chuck • USA
BLUE SUNDAY • 1921 • Parrott Charles • USA
BLUE SUNSHINE • 1976 • Lieberman Jeff • USA
BLUE SURFARI see **SURFARI** • 1967
BLUE THUNDER • 1982 • Badham John • USA
BLUE TUNES • 1960 • Henryson Robert • SHT • USA
BLUE VANGUARD • 1957 • McNeill • UNN
BLUE VEIL, THE • 1951 • Bernhardt Curtis • USA
BLUE VEIL, THE (USA) see **VOILE BLEU, LE** • 1942
BLUE VELVET • 1986 • Lynch David • USA
BLUE VULTURES • 1985 • SAF
BLUE WATER • 1923 • *Shipman Ernest G. (P)* • CND
BLUE WATER, WHITE DEATH • 1971 • Gimbel Peter, Lipscombe Jim • DOC • USA
BLUE WEEK see **SININEN VIIKKO** • 1954
BLUE, WHITE AND PERFECT • 1941 • Leeds Herbert I. • USA
BLUE WINGS, THE see **TSUBASA**
BLUE WINTER see **HIVER BLEU, L'** • 1980
BLUE WONDER, THE see **BLAU WUNDER, DAS**
BLUE YONDER, THE • 1985 • Rosman Mark • USA • TIME FLYER
BLUEBEARD • 1902 • *Warwick Trading Co.* • UKN
BLUEBEARD • 1909 • Dawley J. Searle • USA
BLUEBEARD • 1944 • Ulmer Edgar G. • USA
BLUEBEARD see **LANDRU** • 1962
BLUEBEARD, JR. • 1922 • Dunlap Scott R. • USA
BLUEBEARD THE SECOND • 1914 • *Ab* • USA
BLUEBEARD (USA) see **BARBE BLEUE** • 1907
BLUEBEARD (USA) see **BARBE BLEUE** • 1910
BLUEBEARD (USA) see **BARBE BLEUE** • 1936
BLUEBEARD (USA) see **BARBE BLEUE** • 1951
BLUEBEARD (USA) see **BARBE-BLEUE** • 1972
BLUEBEARD'S BROTHER • 1932 • *Terry Paul/ Moser Frank (P)* • ANS • USA
BLUEBEARD'S CASTLE • 1964 • Powell Michael
BLUEBEARD'S EIGHTH WIFE • 1922 • Wood Sam • USA
BLUEBEARD'S EIGHTH WIFE • 1938 • Lubitsch Ernst • USA
BLUEBEARD'S LAST WIFE • 1966 • Stoddart John • SHT • UKN
BLUEBEARD'S SEVEN WIVES • 1926 • Santell Alfred • USA
BLUEBEARD'S TEN HONEYMOONS • 1960 • Wilder W. Lee • USA
BLUEBERRY HILL • 1988 • de Hert Robbe • BLG
BLUEBERRY HILL • 1988 • Hamilton Strathford • USA
BLUEBIRD see **BLAUVOGEL**
BLUEBIRD, THE • 1918 • Tourneur Maurice • USA • BLUE BIRD, THE
BLUEBIRD'S BABY • 1938 • *Mintz Charles (P)* • ANS • USA
BLUEBOTTLES • 1928 • Montagu Ivor • UKN
BLUEFIN FURY see **CONTADINI DEL MARE** • 1955
BLUEFIN RODEO • 1960 • Perry Margaret • DOC • CND
BLUEGRASS • 1988 • Wincer Simon • TVM • USA • BLUE GRASS
BLUEGRASS ROMANCE, A • 1913 • Giblyn Charles • USA
BLUENOSE SHORE • 1969 • Perry Margaret • DOC • CND
BLUEPRINT FOR MURDER • 1953 • Stone Andrew L. • USA
BLUEPRINT FOR MURDER see **WALLET, THE** • 1952
BLUEPRINT FOR MURDER see **ANKOKUGAI-NO DANKON** • 1960
BLUEPRINT FOR ROBBERY • 1961 • Hopper Jerry • USA
BLUEPRINT MYSTERY, THE • 1917 • *Baggot King* • SHT • USA
BLUES • 1931 • *Terry Paul/ Moser Frank (P)* • ANS • USA
BLUES see **INSPECTEUR CONNAIT LA MUSIQUE, L'** • 1955
BLUES, THE • 1962 • Charters Samuel • SHT • USA
BLUES, THE • 1962 • Wawrzyn Dietrich, Wawrzyn Anne Maria • SHT • USA
BLUES ACCORDIN' TO LIGHTNIN' HOPKINS • 1968 • Blank Les, Gerson Skip • DOC • USA
BLUES AND GOSPEL TRAIN • 1964 • Casson Philip • UKN
BLUES BAND, THE • 1982 • Sykes Peter • DOC • UKN
BLUES BETWEEN THE TEETH see **BLUES ENTRE LES DENTS, LE** • 1972
BLUES, BLANC, ROUGE • 1976 • Brisson Jean-Claude, Cavalier Jean-Louis, Dumont Bernard, Rea Robert • DOC • FRN
BLUES BROTHERS, THE • 1980 • Landis John • USA
BLUES BUSTERS • 1950 • Beaudine William • USA
BLUES DELLA DOMENICA, IL • 1952 • Zurlini Valerio • SHT • ITL

BLUES ENTRE LES DENTS, LE • 1972 • Manthoulis Robert • FRN • BLUES UNDER THE SKIN (UKN) ○ BLUES BETWEEN THE TEETH
BLUES FOR A JUNKMAN • 1962 • Gist Robert, Peyser John • MTV • USA • MURDER MEN, THE
BLUES FOR LOVERS (USA) see **BALLAD IN BLUE** • 1964
BLUES FROM THE JUNGLE • 1966 • Burstall Tim • DOC • USA
BLUES HAHOFESH HAGADOL • 1987 • Schorr Renen • ISR • LATE SUMMER BLUES
BLUES IN THE NIGHT • 1941 • Litvak Anatole • USA • HOT NOCTURNE ○ NEW ORLEANS BLUES
BLUES LIKE SHOWERS OF RAIN • 1970 • Jeremy John • SHT • UKN
BLUES MAKER • 1969 • Garrison Christian • SHT • USA
BLUES PATTERN • 1956 • Pintoff Ernest, Whitney John • ANS • USA
BLUES UNDER THE SKIN (UKN) see **BLUES ENTRE LES DENTS, LE** • 1972
BLUFF • 1915 • Backner Arthur • UKN
BLUFF • 1916 • *Kolb C. William* • USA
BLUFF • 1921 • Malins Geoffrey H. • UKN
BLUFF • 1924 • Wood Sam • USA • FOUR FLUSHER, THE
BLUFF • 1969 • Georgiadis Vassilis • GRC
BLUFF • 1982 • Bensoussan Philippe • SHT • FRN • MEME LES MOULES ONT DU VAGUE A L'AME
BLUFF see **BLUFF STORIA DI TRUFFE E DI IMBROGLIONI** • 1976
BLUFF, LE • 1916 • Feyder Jacques • FRN
BLUFF STOP! • 1977 • Cornell Jonas • SWD
BLUFF STORIA DI TRUFFE E DI IMBROGLIONI • 1976 • Corbucci Sergio • ITL • CON ARTISTS, THE (USA) ○ CON MEN, THE ○ BLUFF
BLUFFER • 1917 • *Rhodes Billie* • SHT • USA
BLUFFER, THE • 1919 • Vale Travers • USA
BLUFFER, THE • 1930 • Sennett Mack • SHT • USA
BLUFFERS, THE • 1915 • Eason B. Reeves • USA
BLUFFEUR, LE • 1932 • Luguet Andre, Blanke Henry • FRN
BLUFFEUR, LE • 1963 • Gobbi Sergio • FRN
BLUFFING IT • 1987 • Sadwith James • TVM • USA
BLUM AFFAIR, THE see **AFFARE BLUM** • 1948
BLUME IN LOVE • 1973 • Mazursky Paul • USA
BLUME VON HAWAII, DIE • 1933 • Oswald Richard • FRG
BLUMEN AUS NIZZA • 1936 • Genina Augusto • AUS • FLOWERS FROM NICE
BLUMEN FUR DEN MANN IM MOND • 1975 • Losansky Rolf • GDR • FLOWERS FOR THE MAN IN THE MOON
BLUMENFRAU VOM POTSDAMER PLATZ, DIE • 1925 • Speyer Jaap • FRG
BLUMENFRAU VON LINDENAU, DIE • 1931 • Jacoby Georg • FRG, AUS • STURM IM WASSERGLAS
BLUMENMADCHEN VOM GRAND-HOTEL, DAS • 1934 • Boese Carl • FRG, ITL • LISETTA (ITL)
BLUMENWUNDER, DAS • 1926 • *Solveg Maria* • FRG
BLUNDEN HARBOR • 1952 • Peterson Sidney • USA
BLUNDER BELOW • 1942 • Fleischer Dave • ANS • USA
BLUNDER BOYS • 1955 • White Jules • SHT • USA
BLUNDERBALL • 1966 • Thoms Albie • SHT • ASL
BLUNDERER, THE • 1910 • *Lubin* • USA
BLUNDERER'S MARK, THE • 1914 • *Stanley R.* • USA
BLUNDERING BLACKSMITHS, THE • 1917 • *Hamilton Lloyd V.* • SHT • USA
BLUNDERING BOOB, THE see **NEW JANITOR, THE** • 1914
BLUNDERING BOOBS • 1917 • *Pokes & Jabbs* • USA
BLUNDERLAND OF BIG GAME, THE • 1925 • Brunel Adrian • UKN
BLUNDERS OF MR. BUTTERBUN: TRIPS AND TRIBUNALS, THE • 1918 • Rains Fred • SHT • UKN
BLUNDERS OF MR. BUTTERBUN: UNEXPECTED TREASURE, THE • 1918 • Rains Fred • SHT • UKN
BLUSENKONIG, DER • 1917 • Lubitsch Ernst • FRG • BLOUSE KING, THE
BLUSHING BRIDE, THE • 1921 • Furthman Jules G. • USA
BLUSHING CHARLIE (UKN) see **LYCKLIGA SKITAR** • 1970
BLUT, DAS • 1921 • Legband Paul • FRG
BLUT AN DEN LIPPEN see **ROUGE AUX LEVRES, LE** • 1970
BLUT DER AHNEN, DAS • 1920 • Gerhardt Karl • FRG
BLUT DER SCHWESTER, DAS • 1922 • Barth Otto Wilhelm • FRG
BLUT DES BOSEN, DIE • 1979 • Anders Christian • FRG, SPN • ROOTS OF EVIL
BLUT UND BODEN • 1933 • Ruttmann Walter • FRG
BLUTEN, GAUNER UND DIE NACHT VON NIZZA (FRG) see **JARDINIER D'ARGENTEUIL, LE** • 1966
BLUTIGE SEIDE (FRG) see **SEI DONNE PER L'ASSASSINO** • 1964
BLUTIGE SPUREN • 1921 • Beck Hanns • FRG
BLUTIGEN GEIER VON ALASKA, DIE • 1973 • Reinl Harald • FRG, YGS • HELLHOUNDS OF ALASKA (UKN) ○ KRVAVI JASTREBOVI ALJASKE
BLUTIGER FREITAG • 1972 • Olsen Rolf • FRG • BLOODY FRIDAY
BLUTJUNGE VERFUHRERINNEN • 1971 • Dietrich Erwin C. • FRG, SWT
BLUTO • 1967 • Thoms Albie • SHT • ASL
BLUTRACHE see **VENDETTA** • 1919
BLUTSBRUDER • 1935 • Hubler-Kahla J. A. • FRG • BOSNIAKEN
BLUTSBRUDERSCHAFT • 1940 • Mayring Philipp L. • FRG
BLYGE ANTON • 1940 • Lingheim Emil A. • SWD • SHY ANTON
BMX BANDITS • 1983 • Trenchard-Smith Brian • ASL
BO WIDERBERG • 1980 • Wedel Karsten • SWD
BOADICEA • 1926 • Hill Sinclair • UKN
BOARD AND ROOM see **LAUGH AND GET RICH** • 1931
BOARD-BILL DODGERS, THE • 1915 • *Heinie & Louie* • USA
BOARDED WINDOW, THE see **OKNO ZABITE DESKAMI** • 1972
BOARDER, THE see **SEVENTH SIGN, THE** • 1988
BOARDER BUSTERS • 1917 • *Rolin* • SHT • USA
BOARDER PARSON, THE • 1912 • *Nestor* • USA
BOARDERS AND BOMBS • 1913 • Dillon Eddie • USA
BOARDERS AND BOMBS • 1916 • *West Billy* • SHT • USA
BOARDER'S MISHAP, A • 1914 • *Joker* • USA
BOARDING HOUSE • 1982 • Wintergate John • USA
BOARDING HOUSE BATTLE, A • 1917 • *Marks Lou* • USA
BOARDING HOUSE BLUES • 1948 • Binney Josh • USA
BOARDING HOUSE FEUD, THE • 1915 • Beggs Lee • USA
BOARDING HOUSE FOR BACHELORS see **PENSION PRO SVOBODNE PANY** • 1967
BOARDING HOUSE FOR GENTLEMEN see **PENSION PRO SVOBODNE PANY** • 1967
BOARDING HOUSE FOR SINGLE GENTLEMEN see **PENSION PRO SVOBODNE PANY** • 1967
BOARDING HOUSE HAM, A • 1916 • Pearson Thomas • SHT • USA
BOARDING HOUSE HEIRESS, THE • 1912 • *Quirk Billy* • USA
BOARDING HOUSE MYSTERY, A • 1912 • Porter Edwin S. • USA
BOARDING HOUSE ROMANCE, A • 1912 • *Lubin* • USA
BOARDING HOUSE ROMANCE, A • 1914 • France Charles H. • USA
BOARDING HOUSE SCANDAL, A • 1916 • Evans Joe • UKN
BOARDING HOUSE SCRAMBLE, A • 1914 • *Essanay* • USA
BOARDING SCHOOL see **LEIDENSCHAFTLICHE BLUMCHEN** • 1978
BOARDING SCHOOL, THE see **RESIDENCIA, LA** • 1969
BOARDING SCHOOL GIRLS, THE • 1905 • Porter Edwin S. • USA
BOARDING SCHOOL ROMANCE, A • 1910 • *Vitagraph* • USA
BOARDWALK • 1979 • Verona Stephen F. • USA
BOARDWALK • 1988 • Larry Sheldon • USA
BOASTER, THE • 1907 • Fitzhamon Lewin? • UKN
BOASTER, THE • 1926 • Worne Duke • USA
BOASTFUL KNIGHT, THE • 1955 • Sturlis Edward • ANM • PLN
BOASTS AND BOLDNESS • 1917 • Semon Larry • SHT • USA
BOAT, THE • 1921 • Cline Eddie, Keaton Buster • SHT • USA
BOAT, THE • 1975 • Henson Laurence • UKN
BOAT, THE see **RYURI NO KISHI** • 1956
BOAT, THE (UKN) see **BOOT, DAS** • 1981
BOAT BUILDERS • 1938 • Sharpsteen Ben • ANS • USA
BOAT BUILDING • 1972 • Weir Peter • SHT • ASL
BOAT FROM SHANGHAI (USA) see **CHIN CHIN CHINAMAN** • 1931
BOAT HOUSE • 1985 • Scherberger Aiken • CND
BOAT IS FULL, THE (USA) see **BOOT IST VOLL, DAS** • 1981
BOAT LEAVING THE HARBOUR OF TROUVILLE see **BARQUE SORTANT DU PORT DE TROUVILLE** • 1896
BOAT PEOPLE see **T'OU-PEN NU-HAI** • 1983
BOAT RACE MYSTERY, THE • 1915 • *Britannia* • UKN
BOAT WITHOUT THE FISHERMAN, THE see **BARCA SIN PESCADOR, LA** • 1964
BOATING INCIDENT, A • 1905 • Haggar William • UKN
BOATMEN, THE (UKN) see **BATTELLIERI DEL VOLGA, I** • 1959
BOATNIKS, THE • 1970 • Tokar Norman • USA
BOATS UNDER OARS • 1901 • *Bitzer Billy (Ph)* • USA
BOATSMAN ON AN ICE-FLOE • 1964 • Krausse Werner • ANM • GDR
BOATSWAIN'S DAUGHTER, THE • 1913 • Coleby A. E.? • UKN
BOATSWAIN'S MATE, THE • 1924 • Haynes Manning • UKN
BOB AND ROWDY • 1911 • *Boss Yale* • USA
BOB AND SALLY see **STORY OF BOB AND SALLY, THE** • 1948
BOB ARMSTRONG'S REWARD • 1916 • *Hiawatha* • USA
BOB BUILDS A BOAT • 1913 • *Lubin* • USA
BOB BUILDS A CHICKEN HOUSE • 1913 • *Lubin* • USA
BOB BUYS AN AUTO • 1913 • *Lubin* • USA
BOB & CAROL & TED & ALICE • 1969 • Mazursky Paul • USA
BOB CRAY • 1916 • Schubert Georg • FRG
BOB CROSBY AND HIS ORCHESTRA • 1938 • Roush Leslie • SHT • USA
BOB DOWNE'S SCHOOLDAYS • 1916 • Aylott Dave • UKN
BOB HAMPTON OF PLACER • 1921 • Neilan Marshall • USA • CUSTER'S LAST STAND
BOB HOPE VIETNAM CHRISTMAS SHOW, THE • 1966 • Lachman Mort • DOC • USA
BOB KICK, L'ENFANT TERRIBLE • 1903 • Melies Georges • FRN • BOB KICK, THE MISCHEVIOUS KID (USA)
BOB KICK, THE MISCHEVIOUS KID (USA) see **BOB KICK, L'ENFANT TERRIBLE** • 1903
BOB LE FLAMBEUR • 1955 • Melville Jean-Pierre • FRN • FEVER HEAT (USA) ○ BOB THE GAMBLER
BOB MARLEY AND THE WAILERS LIVE! • 1978 • Macmillan Keith • UKN
BOB MATHIAS STORY, THE • 1954 • Lyon Francis D. • USA • FLAMING TORCH, THE (UKN)
BOB, SON OF BATTLE (UKN) see **THUNDER IN THE VALLEY** • 1947
BOB STOKES -THE COURAGEOUS see **VIRTUOUS MEN** • 1919
BOB THE COSTER'S PONY • 1912 • Coleby A. E. • UKN
BOB THE GAMBLER see **BOB LE FLAMBEUR** • 1955
BOB UND MARY • 1923 • Glass Max • FRG
BOB UND MARY see **FAHRT INS GLUCK, DIE** • 1923
BOB WILLS AND HIS TEXAS PLAYBOYS • 1944 • Prinz Leroy • USA
BOBBED HAIR • 1922 • Heffron Thomas N. • USA
BOBBED HAIR • 1925 • Crosland Alan • USA
BOBBED SQUAD, THE see **ALL DOLLED UP** • 1921
BOBBIE AND THE HELPING HAND • 1917 • Seay Charles M. • SHT • USA
BOBBIE JO AND THE OUTLAW • 1976 • Lester Mark L. • USA • BOBBIE JOE AND THE OUTLAW ○ BOBBY JOE AND THE OUTLAW
BOBBIE JOE AND THE OUTLAW see **BOBBIE JO AND THE OUTLAW** • 1976
BOBBIE OF THE BALLET • 1916 • De Grasse Joseph • USA
BOBBIE'S LONG TROUSERS • 1913 • *Edison* • USA
BOBBIKINS • 1959 • Day Robert • UKN
BOBBIKINS AND THE BATHING BELLES • 1916 • Aylott Dave? • UKN
BOBBY • 1974 • Kapoor Raj • IND
BOBBY • 1974 • Schadt Fritz G. • INN
BOBBY AND COMPANY • 1917 • Ridgwell George • SHT • USA
BOBBY AND HIS FAMILY • 1906 • *Pathe* • FRN
BOBBY AND THE BANKER • 1914 • *Melies* • USA
BOBBY AND THE BOB, THE • 1906 • *Walturdaw* • UKN
BOBBY AND THE FAIRY • 1917 • Ridgwell George • SHT • USA
BOBBY, BOY SCOUT • 1917 • Kennedy J. Raymond • SHT • USA
BOBBY COMES MARCHING HOME • 1919 • *Christie* • USA
BOBBY DEERFIELD • 1977 • Pollack Sydney • USA
BOBBY, DER BENZINJUNGE • 1929 • Boese Carl • FRG
BOBBY DODD GREIFT, EIN • 1959 • von Cziffra Geza • FRG
BOBBY GEHT LOS • 1931 • Piel Harry • FRG
BOBBY HACKETT • 1961 • Rubin Bernard • SHT • USA
BOBBY JOE AND THE OUTLAW see **BOBBIE JO AND THE OUTLAW** • 1976
BOBBY, MAYOR OF KID CITY • 1917 • Seay Charles M. • SHT • USA
BOBBY, MOVIE DIRECTOR • 1917 • Ruggles Wesley • SHT • USA
BOBBY OF THE HOME DEFENDERS • 1917 • *Connelly Bobby* • SHT • USA
BOBBY, PHILANTHROPIST • 1917 • Ruggles Wesley • SHT • USA
BOBBY TAKES A WIFE • 1917 • Ridgwell George • SHT • USA
BOBBY THE BOY SCOUT: OR, THE BOY DETECTIVE • 1909 • Stow Percy • UKN
BOBBY THE COWARD • 1911 • Griffith D. W. • USA
BOBBY, THE MAGICIAN • 1917 • Ridgwell George • SHT • USA
BOBBY, THE PACIFIST • 1917 • Ruggles Wesley • SHT • USA
BOBBY THE TAMER • 1912 • *Cosmopolitan* • UKN
BOBBY TO THE RESCUE • 1917 • Ridgwell George • SHT • USA
BOBBY WARE IS MISSING • 1955 • Carr Thomas • USA
BOBBY WHITE IN WONDERLAND • 1908 • *Selig* • USA
BOBBY WIDEAWAKE • 1909 • Booth W. R. • UKN
BOBBY'S BABY • 1913 • Smalley Phillips, Weber Lois • USA
BOBBY'S BABY • 1920 • *Christie* • SHT • USA
BOBBY'S BANDIT • 1915 • Kelsey Fred A. • USA
BOBBY'S BARGAIN • 1915 • Morrisey Edward • USA
BOBBY'S BIRTHDAY • 1907 • Williamson James? • UKN
BOBBY'S BOB, THE • 1914 • *Phoenix Film Agency* • UKN
BOBBY'S BRAVERY • 1917 • Ruggles Wesley • SHT • USA
BOBBY'S BUM BOMB • 1913 • *Punch* • USA
BOBBY'S COUNTRY ADVENTURE • 1917 • Ridgwell George • SHT • USA
BOBBY'S DOWNFALL, THE • 1904 • Mottershaw Frank • UKN
BOBBY'S DREAM • 1912 • *Edison* • USA
BOBBY'S DREAM OF BATTLE • 1907 • *Warwick Trading Co.* • UKN
BOBBY'S FAIRY • 1917 • Ridgwell George • SHT • USA
BOBBY'S FATHER • 1912 • *Vitagraph* • USA
BOBBY'S KODAK • 1908 • *Bitzer Billy (Ph)* • USA
BOBBYS KRIG • 1973 • Berg Arnljot • NRW • BOBBY'S WAR
BOBBY'S LETTER • 1912 • Coleby A. E.? • UKN
BOBBY'S MAGIC NICKEL • 1913 • Pollard Harry • USA
BOBBY'S MEDAL • 1914 • *Feuhrer Bobby* • USA
BOBBY'S NIGHTMARE, THE • 1905 • Collins Alf? • UKN
BOBBY'S SECRET • 1917 • Seay Charles M. • SHT • USA
BOBBY'S WAR see **BOBBYS KRIG** • 1973
BOBE MO MOTSENG • 1984 • SAF
BOBITA • 1964 • Meszaros Marta • SHT • HNG • BLOW-BALL
BOBO see **WALK LIKE A MAN** • 1987
BOBO, THE • 1967 • Parrish Robert • UKN
BOBO, JACCO • 1979 • Bal Walter • BLG, FRN, PLN
BOBOSSE • 1958 • Perier Etienne • FRN
BOBS • 1928 • Gremillon Jean • SHT • FRN
BOB'S BABY • 1913 • *Gem* • USA
BOB'S DECEPTION • 1912 • *Rex* • USA
BOB'S ELECTRIC THEATRE • 1909 • *Pathe* • FRN
BOB'S LOVE AFFAIR • 1915 • Coyle Walter • USA
BOB'S NEW SCHEME • 1911 • *Lubin* • USA
BOB'S NIGHTMARE • 1912 • *Mono Film* • USA
BOB'S YOUR UNCLE • 1941 • Mitchell Oswald • UKN
BOCA DE OURO, O • 1962 • dos Santos Nelson Pereira • BRZ
BOCA DEL LOBO, LA • 1988 • Lombardi Francisco • PRU, SPN • LION'S DEN, THE
BOCAGE • 1936 • de Barros Jose Leitao • PRT
BOCAL AUX POISSONS-ROUGES • 1895 • Lumiere Louis • FRN
BOCCA SULLA STRADA, LA • 1941 • Roberti Roberto Leone • ITL
BOCCACCIO • 1920 • Curtiz Michael • ITL
BOCCACCIO • 1936 • Maisch Herbert • FRG
BOCCACCIO • 1940 • Albani Marcello • ITL
BOCCACCIO • 1972 • Corbucci Bruno • ITL
BOCCACCIO '70 • 1962 • Fellini Federico, Visconti Luchino, De Sica Vittorio, Monicelli Mario • ITL, FRN • BOCCACE 70
BOCCACCIO MIO STATTE ZITTO see **DECAMERON PROIBITISSIMO** • 1972
BOCCACCIOS LIEBESABENTEUER • 1920 • Bruck Reinhard • FRG
BOCCACE 70 see **BOCCACCIO '70** • 1962
BOCCHAN SHAIN SEISHUN DE TSUPPASHIRE! • 1967 • Matsumori Takashi • JPN • YOUNG WHITE COLLAR: LET'S RUN
BOCCHAN SHAIN: SEISHUN WA ORE NO MONODA • 1967 • Matsumori Takashi • JPN • YOUTH BELONGS TO US!
BOCCHE CUCITE • 1970 • Tosini Pino • ITL
BOCCONCINO, IL • 1976 • Scandariato Romano • ITL
BOCHORNO • 1962 • de Orduna Juan • SPN
BOCK I ORTAGARD • 1958 • Folke Gosta • SWD • SQUARE PEG IN A ROUND HOLE, A
BOCKBIERFEST • 1930 • Boese Carl • FRG • WER NIEMALS EINEN RAUSCH GEHABT..
BOCKERER, DER • 1981 • Antel Franz • AUS, FRG • OBSTINATE MAN, THE
BOCKSHORN • Beyer Frank • GDR • TAKEN FOR A RIDE
BODA, LA • 1986 • Urguelles Thaelman • VNZ • WEDDING, THE
BODA ACCIDENTADA • 1942 • Iquino Ignacio F. • SPN
BODA DE QUINITA FLORES • 1943 • Delgras Gonzalo • SPN
BODA DE ROSARIO, LA • 1925 • Saenz De Sicilia Gustavo • MXC
BODA DEL ACORDEONISTA, LA • 1985 • Bottia Luis Fernando • CLM
BODA EN EL INFIERNO • 1941 • Roman Antonio • SPN • WEDDING IN HELL

BODA ERA A LAS DOCE, LA • 1962 • Salvador Julio • SPN
BODA O LA VIDA, LA • 1972 • Romero-Marchent Rafael • SPN
BODA SECRETA • 1988 • Agresti Alejandro • ARG • SECRET WEDDING
BODAKUNGEN • 1920 • Molander Gustaf • SWD • KING OF BODA
BODAS DE BLANCA, LA • 1976 • Regueiro Francisco • SPN • BLANCA'S WEDDING
BODAS DE CAMACHO, LAS • 1977 • Fenollar Augusto • SPN
BODAS DE FUEGO • 1949 • Aurelio Galindo Marco • MXC
BODAS DE ORO • 1955 • Davison Tito • MXC
BODAS DE PAPEL • 1979 • Chalbaud Roman • VNZ
BODAS DE SANGRE • 1981 • Saura Carlos • SPN, FRN • NOCES DE SANG (FRN) ○ BLOOD WEDDING
BODAS TRAGICAS • 1946 • Martinez Solares Gilberto • MXC
BODEGA, LA • 1930 • Perojo Benito • FRN
BODEGA BOHEMIA • 1962 • Schamoni Peter • SHT • FRG
BODEGA VON LOS CUERROS, DIE • 1919 • Lund Erik • FRG
BODEN'S BOY • 1923 • Edwards Henry • UKN
BODENSEE see **JEZIORO BODENSKI** • 1985
BODES DER FOR, DET see **HAEVNET** • 1911
BODIAM CASTLE AND ERIC THE SLENDER • 1926 • Bramble A. V. • UKN
BODIES BEAR TRACES OF CARNAL VIOLENCE, THE see **CORPI PRESENTANO TRACCE DI VIOLENZA CARNALE, I** • 1973
BODRIK THE DOG • Renc Ivan • ANS • CZC
BODRUM HAKIMI • 1977 • Soray Turkan • TRK • JUDGE OF BODRUM, THE
BODY, THE • 1970 • Battersby Roy • DOC • UKN
BODY, THE see **TIJELO** • 1966
BODY, THE see **CORPO, IL** • 1974
BODY, THE see **STAND BY ME** • 1986
BODY, THE see **CORPO, O** • 1989
BODY, THE (USA) see **RATAI** • 1962
BODY AND SOUL • 1915 • *Rockwell Florence* • USA
BODY AND SOUL • 1920 • Swickard Charles • USA
BODY AND SOUL • 1925 • Micheaux Oscar • USA
BODY AND SOUL • 1927 • Barker Reginald • USA • BRANDING IRON, THE
BODY AND SOUL • 1931 • Santell Alfred • USA
BODY AND SOUL • 1947 • Rossen Robert • USA
BODY AND SOUL • 1981 • Bowers George • USA
BODY AND SOUL see **PRIDE OF THE MARINES** • 1945
BODY AND SOUL (PARTS I & II) • 1966 • Daalder Renee • NTH
BODY AND THE WHIP, THE see **FRUSTA E IL CORPO, LA** • 1963
BODY BEAT see **DANCE ACADEMY** • 1988
BODY BEAUTIFUL • 1953 • Nosseck Max • USA
BODY BEAUTIFUL see **NIKUTAIBI** • 1928
BODY BENEATH, THE • 1970 • Milligan Andy • USA
BODY COUNT • 1986 • Deodato Ruggero • ITL
BODY COUNT • 1988 • Leder Paul • USA
BODY DISAPPEARS, THE • 1942 • Lederman D. Ross • USA • BLACK WIDOW
BODY DOUBLE • 1984 • De Palma Brian • USA
BODY FEVER • 1972 • Steckler Ray Dennis • USA • LAST ORIGINAL B-MOVIE, THE ○ SUPER COOL
BODY HEAT • 1981 • Kasdan Lawrence • USA
BODY HUMAN, THE • 1979 • Kelman Alfred R. • SER • USA
BODY IN THE TRUNK, THE • 1914 • O'Brien John B. • USA
BODY IN THE WEB see **TOTER HING IM NETZ, EIN** • 1960
BODY IS A SHELL, THE • 1956 • Ballbusch Peter • USA
BODY IS MISSING, THE see **BRICOLEURS, LES** • 1962
BODY LIKE MINE • 1955 • *Faro Films* • SHT • UKN
BODY LOVE • 1977 • Hunderte Alberto • FRG
BODY LUST see **TALE OF TIFFANY LUST, THE** • 1981
BODY MAGIC • 1982 • Conrad Sven • USA
BODY OF A FEMALE • 1965 • Ellsworth J., Findlay Michael • USA
BODY OF DIANA, THE see **TELO DIANA** • 1969
BODY OF EVIDENCE • 1988 • Campanella Roy Ii • TVM • USA
BODY POLITIC • 1989 • Bomberg Betzy • USA
BODY PUNCH, THE • 1929 • Jason Leigh • USA
BODY ROCK • 1984 • Epstein Marcelo • USA
BODY SAID NO!, THE • 1950 • Guest Val • UKN
BODY SCENT see **ZADAH TELA** • 1984
BODY SLAM • 1987 • Needham Hal • USA
BODY SNATCHER, THE • 1945 • Wise Robert • USA
BODY SNATCHERS see **LADRON DE CADAVERES** • 1956
BODY SNATCHERS, THE see **HORROR STAR** • 1981
BODY STEALERS, THE • 1969 • Levy Gerry • UKN, USA • INVASION OF THE BODY STEALERS (USA) ○ THIN AIR
BODY TALK: THE LANGUAGE OF LOVE • 1982 • Sweet Pedie • USA
BODY VANISHES, THE • 1939 • Tennyson Walter • UKN
BODY WORK • 1988 • Caesar David • DOC • ASL
BODYBUILDING • 1966 • Schmidt Ernst • AUS
BODYGUARD • 1948 • Fleischer Richard • USA
BODYGUARD, THE • Alexander Mike • SHT • UKN
BODYGUARD, THE • 1944 • Hanna William, Barbera Joseph • ANS • USA
BODYGUARD, THE • 1976 • Nuchtern Simon • USA
BODYGUARD, THE • 1981 • Khamraev Ali • USS
BODYGUARD, THE see **YOJIMBO** • 1961
BODYGUARD OF HELL see **JIGOKU NO YOJIMBO** • 1955
BODYHOLD • 1949 • Friedman Seymour • USA
BODYLINE • 1984 • Marinos Lex, Lawrence Denny • TVM • ASL
BODY'S LITTLE THEATRE, THE see **TOPOS** • 1985
BODY'S LUST see **TUAH BADAN** • 1970
BOEF JE • 1938 • Sirk Douglas • SAF • WILTON'S ZOO (USA)
BOEING BOEING • 1965 • Rich John • USA
BOEMERANG 11.15 • 1972 • SAF
BOER BOERSON JR. • 1939 • Sandoe Toralf
BOER PIETERSEN SCHIET IN DE ROOS • 1949 • Brusse Kees • NTH • BULL'S EYE FOR FARMER PIETERSEN
BOER WAR, THE • 1914 • Melford George • USA
BOERBOEL DE WET • 1961 • SAF
BOERS BRINGING IN BRITISH PRISONERS • 1900 • Porter Edwin S. • USA
BOESMAN AND LENA • 1973 • Devenish Ross • SAF
BOETIE GAAN BORDER TOE • 1984 • SAF • BROTHER GOES TO THE BORDER
BOETIE OP MANOEUVRES • 1985 • SAF • BROTHER ON MANOEUVRES
BOEUF GRAS see **CORTEGE DU BOEUF GRAS PASSANT PLACE DE LA CONCORDE** • 1897
BOEUF SUR LA LANGUE, LA • 1933 • Christian-Jaque • FRN
BOEUFS DE LABOUR, LES • 1977 • Gosselin Bernard, Plamondon Leo • DCS • CND
BOEVOI KINOSBORNIK 9 • 1942 • Savchenko Igor, Braun Vladimir, Donskoi Mark • USS • FIGHTING FILM ALBUM NO.9
BOF see **BOF! -ANATOMIE D'UN LIVREUR** • 1971
BOF! -ANATOMIE D'UN LIVREUR • 1971 • Faraldo Claude • FRN • BOF
BOFORS GUN, THE • 1968 • Gold Jack • UKN
BOG • 1978 • Keeslar Don • USA
BOG OF PRAGUE, THE see **BAHNO PRAHY** • 1927
BOGARD • 1975 • Galfas Timothy • USA
BOGATYR BOUND FOR MARTEAU, THE • 1954 • Bryunchugin Yevgeniy, Navrotsky S. • USS
BOGDAN KHMELNITSKY • 1941 • Savchenko Igor • USS • BOHDAN KHMELNYTSKY
BOGDAN STIMOFF • 1916 • Jacoby Georg • FRG
BOGEY MAN, THE see **KUMMATY** • 1978
BOGEY MAN, THE see **BOOGEYMAN, THE** • 1980
BOGEY WOMAN, THE • 1909 • *Pathe* • FRN
BOGGS' PREDICAMENT • 1913 • *Brennan John* • USA
BOGGY CREEK II see **BARBARIC BEAST OF BOGGY CREEK, PART II, THE** • 1985
BOGGY CREEK II: AND THE LEGEND CONTINUES see **BARBARIC BEAST OF BOGGY CREEK, PART II, THE** • 1985
BOGIE • 1980 • Sherman Vincent • TVM • USA • BOGIE: THE LAST HERO
BOGIE: THE LAST HERO see **BOGIE** • 1980
BOGOTAYA NEVESTA • 1937 • Pyriev Ivan • USS • COUNTRY BRIDE ○ RICH BRIDE, THE
BOGUMIE I BARBARA see **NOCE I DNIE** • 1974
BOGUS BANDIT, A • 1915 • *Victor* • USA
BOGUS BANDITS see **DEVIL'S BROTHER, THE** • 1933
BOGUS BARON, A • 1914 • *Sterling Ford* • USA
BOGUS BOOKING AGENTS, THE • 1916 • *Hamilton Lloyd V.* • SHT • USA
BOGUS BRIDE, THE • 1917 • *Ham & Bud* • SHT • USA
BOGUS EARL, THE • 1915 • Arlington Paul • USA
BOGUS GHOST, THE • 1916 • Millarde Harry • SHT • USA
BOGUS HOUSE AGENT, THE • 1926 • Engholm F. W. • UKN
BOGUS LORD, THE • 1908 • *Lubin* • USA
BOGUS MARRIAGE • 1988 • Buzaglo Haim • ISR
BOGUS MOTOR ELOPEMENT, THE • 1909 • Booth W. R. • UKN
BOGUS NAPOLEON, THE • 1912 • Humphrey William • USA
BOGUS POLICEMAN, THE see **NISE KEIJI** • 1967
BOGUS UNCLE, THE • 1918 • *Pixley Gus* • USA
BOHATER ROKU • 1986 • Falk Feliks • PLN • HERO OF THE YEAR
BOHATERSTWO POLSKIEGO SKAVTO • 1919 • Boleslawski Richard • PLN
BOHDAN KHMELNYTSKY see **BOGDAN KHMELNITSKY** • 1941
BOHEME • 1923 • Righelli Gennaro • FRG
BOHEME, LA • 1917 • D'Ambra Lucio • ITL
BOHEME, LA • 1917 • Palermi Amleto • ITL
BOHEME, LA • 1926 • Vidor King • USA
BOHEME, LA • 1965 • Zeffirelli Franco • SWT
BOHEME, LA • 1987 • Comencini Luigi • ITL, FRN
BOHEME, LA see **VIE DE BOHEME, LA** • 1916
BOHEME, LA see **MIMI** • 1935
BOHEME, LA see **ADDIO, MIMI** • 1947
BOHEME, LA (ITL) see **VIE DE BOHEME, LA** • 1942
BOHEME, LA (FRG) see **VIE DE BOHEME, LA** • 1923
BOHEMES 64 • 1963-64 • Fournier Claude, Portugais Louis • DCS • CND
BOHEMIA see **ETERNAL SAPHO, THE** • 1916
BOHEMIAN GIRL, THE • 1912 • *Republic* • USA
BOHEMIAN GIRL, THE • 1922 • Knoles Harley • UKN
BOHEMIAN GIRL, THE • 1927 • Parkinson H. B. • UKN
BOHEMIAN GIRL, THE • 1936 • Horne James W., Rogers Charles • USA
BOHEMIAN LIGHTS see **LUCES DE BOHEMIA** • 1985
BOHEMIAN LOVE see **FEMME NUE, LA** • 1926
BOHEMIAN RAPTURE • 1948 • Krska Vaclav • CZC
BOHEMIANS see **BOHEMIOS** • 1934
BOHEMIOS • 1934 • Portas Rafael E. • MXC • BOHEMIANS
BOHEMIOS • 1937 • Elias Francisco • SPN
BOHOC A FALON • 1968 • Sandor Pal • HNG • CLOWNS ON THE WALL
BOHUS BATALJON • 1949 • Spjuth Arthur, Cederstrand Solve • SWD • BOHUS BATTALION
BOHUS BATTALION see **BOHUS BATALJON** • 1949
BOHUSLAV MARTINU • 1980 • Jires Jaromil • MTV • CZC
BOI DE PRATA • 1982 • Ribeiro Augusto Jr. • BRZ • SILVER OX
BOI POD TSARITSYNOM • 1919 • Vertov Dziga • USS • FIGHTING NEAR TSARITSIN ○ BATTLE OF TSARITSIN ○ BATTLE FOR TSARITSIN
BOIA DI LILLA, IL • 1953 • Cottafavi Vittorio • ITL • MILADY AND THE MUSKETEERS (USA) ○ VITA AVVENTUROSA DI MILADY, LA
BOIA DI VENEZIA, IL • 1964 • Capuano Luigi • ITL • EXECUTIONER OF VENICE, THE ○ EXECUTIONER, THE ○ HANGMAN OF VENICE, THE
BOIA SCARLATTO, IL • 1965 • Pupillo Massimo • ITL, USA • BLOODY PIT OF HORROR (USA) ○ CASTELLO DI ARTENA, IL ○ RED HANGMAN, THE ○ CRIMSON EXECUTIONER, THE ○ CASTLE OF ARTENA, THE ○ SCARLET EXECUTIONER, THE
BOILED BIRDS see **PIECZONE GOLABKI** • 1966
BOILED EGG (USA) see **OEUF A LA COQUE, L'** • 1963
BOILER-MAKER'S DAY OF REST, THE • 1914 • *Ab* • USA
BOILESK • 1933 • Fleischer Dave • ANS • USA
BOILING POINT • 1983 • Levis Paul • USA
BOILING POINT, THE • 1932 • Melford George • USA
BOINA BLANCA • 1941 • Barth-Moglia Luis • ARG
BOIPHETETSO • 1984 • SAF
BOIREAU • 1905-10 • Heuze Andre • SER • FRN
BOIREAU A MANGE DE L'AIL • 1908 • *Deed Andre* • FRN
BOIREAU CUIRASSIER • 1913 • *Deed Andre* • FRN
BOIREAU DEMENAGE • 1905 • Heuze Andre • FRN
BOIREAU DOMESTIQUE • 1913 • *Deed Andre* • FRN
BOIREAU FAIT LA NOCE • 1908 • *Deed Andre* • FRN
BOIREAU LUTTEUR • 1907 • *Deed Andre* • FRN
BOIS DE BOULOGNE (PORTE DE MADRID) • 1896 • Melies Georges • FRN
BOIS DE BOULOGNE (TOURING-CLUB) • 1896 • Melies Georges • FRN
BOIS DES AMANTS, LE • 1960 • Autant-Lara Claude • FRN, ITL • BETWEEN LOVE AND DESIRE (UKN) ○ BETWEEN LOVE AND DUTY
BOIS ET CUIVRES • 1958 • Leduc • SHT • FRN
BOIS-FRANCS • 1966 • Carriere Marcel • DCS • CND
BOIS NOIRS, LES • 1989 • Deray Jacques • FRN • DARK WOODS (UKN)
BOIS SACRE, LE • 1939 • Mathot Leon, Bibal Robert • FRN
BOISSIERE • 1937 • Rivers Fernand • FRN
BOITE A MALICE, LA • 1903 • Melies Georges • FRN • MYSTERIOUS BOX, THE (USA) ○ SHALLOW BOX TRICK, THE
BOITE A MUSIQUE • 1961 • Borowczyk Walerian, Lenica Jan • SHT • FRN
BOITE A SOLEIL, LA • 1988 • Lefebvre Jean-Pierre • CND • BOX OF SUN, THE
BOITE AUX REVES, LA • 1943 • Allegret Yves, Choux Jean (U/c) • FRN • CE QUE FEMME VEUT ○ BOX OF DREAMS
BOITE DE NUIT • 1951 • Rode Alfred • FRN • HOTBED OF SIN (USA)
BOITE DIABOLIQUE, LA • 1911 • Cohl Emile • ANS • FRN
BOITEUSE, LA • 1909 • Jasset Victorin • FRN
BOJ NA KOSOVU • 1989 • Sotra Zdravko • YGS • BATTLE OF KOSOVO, THE
BOJ NA POZIRALNIKU • 1983 • Drozg Janez • YGS • BATTLE OF POZIRALNIK, THE ○ BOJ NA PROZDRLJIVCU
BOJ NA PROZDRLJIVCU see **BOJ NA POZIRALNIKU** • 1983
BOJE SANJAJU • 1958 • Makavejev Dusan • SHT • YGS • COLORS ARE DREAMING
BOJO NO HITO • 1961 • Maruyama Seiji • JPN • LOVE AND FASCINATION
BOKEN, BOKEN, MATA BOKEN • 1968 • Wada Yoshinori • JPN • ADVENTURE, ADVENTURE
BOKHANDLAREN SOM SLUTADE BARA • 1969 • Kulle Jarl • SWD • BOOKSELLER WHO GAVE UP BATHING, THE
BOKO SHOJO NIKK-MESU • 1968 • Mukoi Hiroshi • JPN • DIARY OF A VIOLATED VIRGIN -FEMALE
BOKOHAN • 1968 • Yamamoto Shinya • JPN • VIOLATOR, A
BOKS • 1963 • Skolimowski Jerzy • PLN • BOXING ○ BOXER
BOKSER • 1967 • Dziedzina Julian • PLN • BOXER, THE (UKN) ○ PRIZE FIGHTER, THE
BOKSERI IDU U RAJ • 1967 • Celovic Brana • YGS • FIGHTERS GO TO PARADISE ○ BOXERS GO TO PARADISE
BOKU NO MARUMAGE • 1933 • Naruse Mikio • JPN • MAN WITH A MARRIED WOMAN'S HAIRDO, A
BOKU WA NAICHICHI • 1960 • Horiiki Kiyoshi • JPN
BOKUL • 1954 • *Sircar B. N. (P)* • IND
"BOKUL" FLOWER, THE see **THALIRUKAL** • 1967
BOKURA NO KASAN • 1959 • Itaya Norijuki • JPN
BOKUTO KIDAN • 1960 • Toyoda Shiro • JPN • TWILIGHT STORY, THE
BOKYAKU NO HANABIRA • 1957 • *Tsukasa Yoko* • JPN • FORSAKEN PEDALS
BOKYO see **SANDAKAN HACHIBAN SHOKAN, BOHKYO** • 1975
BOLA AO CENTRO • 1947 • Moreira Joao • PRT
BOLAND • 1974 • Retief Bertrand • SAF
BOLCHAIA SEMIA see **BOLSHAYA SEMYA** • 1954
BOLD ADVENTURE, A • 1912 • Buckland Warwick? • UKN
BOLD ADVENTURE, THE (USA) see **AVENTURES DE TILL L'ESPIEGLE, LES** • 1956
BOLD ADVENTURESS, THE • 1915 • West Walter • UKN
BOLD AND THE BRAVE, THE • 1956 • Foster Lewis R. • USA
BOLD, BAD BOYS • 1915 • *Starlight* • USA
BOLD BAD BREEZE, A • 1916 • *Ritchie Billy* • SHT • USA
BOLD, BAD BURGLAR, A • 1915 • *Kalem* • USA
BOLD, BAD BURGLAR, THE • 1916 • Matthews H. C. • SHT • USA
BOLD, BAD KNIGHT, A • 1917 • Christie Al • SHT • USA
BOLD BAD PIRATE, A • 1920 • *Reelcraft* • USA
BOLD BANDITTI AND THE RAH RAH BOY, THE • 1914 • *Hamilton Lloyd V.* • USA
BOLD BANK ROBBERY • 1904 • Lubin Sigmund • USA
BOLD CABALLERO, THE • 1936 • Root Wells • USA • BOLD CAVALIER, THE (UKN)
BOLD CAVALIER, THE (UKN) see **BOLD CABALLERO, THE** • 1936
BOLD DRAGOON, THE • 1954 • *Woolley Monty* • SHT • USA
BOLD EMMETT, IRELAND'S MARTYR • 1915 • Olcott Sidney • USA
BOLD FRONTIERSMAN, THE • 1948 • Ford Philip • USA
BOLD IMPERSONATION, A • 1915 • Kelsey Fred A. • USA
BOLD KING COLE • 1936 • Gillett Burt • ANS • USA
BOLD NEW APPROACH • 1966 • Jacoby Irving • DOC • USA
BOLD SEVEN, THE see **SEMERO SMELYKH** • 1936
BOLDEST JOB IN THE WEST, THE see **MAS FABULOSO GOLPE DE FAR-WEST, EL** • 1971
BOLDOG SZULETESNAPOT MARILYN! • 1981 • Szoreny Rezso • HNG • HAPPY BIRTHDAY, MARILYN!
BOLDOGTALAN KALAP • 1981 • Sos Maria • HNG • UNHAPPY HAT, THE
BOLDYN • 1981 • Petelski Czeslaw, Petelska Ewa • PLN
BOLEK AND LOLEK IN THE WILD WEST • 1970 • Nehrebecki Wladyslaw • ANS • PLN
BOLEK AND LOLEK SET OUT TO SEE THE WORLD see **BOLEK I LOLEK WYRUSZAJA W SWIAT** • 1969
BOLEK I LOLEK WYRUSZAJA W SWIAT • 1969 • Nehrebecki Wladyslaw • ASS • PLN • BOLEK AND LOLEK SET OUT TO SEE THE WORLD
BOLERO • 1934 • Ruggles Wesley • USA
BOLERO • 1941 • Boyer Jean • FRN
BOLERO • 1967 • Thoms Albie • SHT • ASL

BOLERO • 1984 • Derek John • USA
BOLERO see **BOLERO INMORTAL** • 1958
BOLERO see **UNS ET LES AUTRES, LES** • 1981
BOLERO DE RAQUEL, EL • 1956 • Delgado Miguel M. • MXC
BOLERO INMORTAL • 1958 • Portillo Rafael • MXC • BOLERO
BOLESLAUS THE COURAGEOUS see **BOLESLAW SMIALY** • 1970
BOLESLAW SMIALY • 1970 • Lesiewicz Witold • PLN • BOLESLAUS THE COURAGEOUS ○ KING BOLESLAUS THE BOLD
BOLETTES BRUDFAERD • Viby Margaret, Gregers Emanuel • DNM
BOLIBAR • 1928 • Summers Walter • UKN • BETRAYAL, THE
BOLICHE • 1933 • Elias Francisco • SPN
BOLIDES AU MANS • 1957 • Champetier Henri, Vilardebo Carlos • FRN • WEEKEND AT LE MANS
BOLIDI SULL'ASFALTO A TUTTA BIRRA • 1970 • Corbucci Bruno • ITL • A TUTTA BIRRA
BOLIVAR, A TROPICAL SYMPHONY see **BOLIVAR, SINFONIA TROPICAL** • 1980
BOLIVAR, SINFONIA TROPICAL • 1980 • Risquez Diego • VNZ • BOLIVAR, UNA SINFONIA TROPIKAL ○ BOLIVAR, A TROPICAL SYMPHONY
BOLIVAR, UNA SINFONIA TROPIKAL see **BOLIVAR, SINFONIA TROPICAL** • 1980
BOLIVAR'S HOUSE see **CASA DE BOLIVAR, LA** • 1975
BOLIVIA '70 • 1973 • Zecca Adriano, Zecca Damiano, Condal Elias • ITL
BOLJI ZIVOT • 1989 • Vukobratovic Mihailo • YGS • BETTER LIVING
BOLLY • 1968 • Batchelor Joy • ANS • UKN
BOLO-MOLA LAND • 1939 • Lovy Alex • ANS • USA
BOLOGNE, UNE VILLE ANCIENNE POUR UNE SOCIETE NOUVELLE • 1974 • Regnier Michel • DOC • CND
BOLOGNESE, LA • 1976 • Rizzo Alfredo • ITL
BOLOND APRILIS • 1957 • Fabri Zoltan • CZC • APRIL CLOUDS ○ SUMMER CLOUDS
BOLONDOS VAKACIO • 1968 • Makk Karoly • HNG, RMN • CRAZY HOLIDAYS ○ SUMMER CLOUD
BOLSHAIA DOROGA • 1963 • Ozerov Yury • USS, CZC • GREAT ROAD, THE ○ BIG ROAD, THE
BOLSHAYA RUDA • 1964 • Ordynsky Vassily • USS • GREAT ORE, THE ○ RICH VEIN
BOLSHAYA SEMYA • 1954 • Heifitz Josif • USS • BOLCHAIA SEMIA ○ BIG FAMILY, THE
BOLSHAYA ZELYONAYA DOLINA • 1968 • Kokochashvili Merab • USS • WIDE GREEN VALLEY, THE ○ BIG GREEN VALLEY
BOLSHAYA ZEMLYA • 1944 • Gerasimov Sergei • USS • MAINLAND ○ GREAT EARTH, THE ○ GREAT LAND, THE
BOLSHAYA ZHIZN • 1940 • Lukov Leonid • USS • GREAT LIFE, A
BOLSHEVISM ON TRIAL • 1919 • Knoles Harley • USA
BOLSHIYE KHLOPOTY IZ-ZA MALENKOVO MALCHIKA • 1968 • Muratov Alexander, Vasilkovski V. • USS • MUCH WORRY ABOUT A LITTLE BOY
BOLSHOI BALLET 67 (USA) see **SEKRET USPEKHA** • 1965
BOLSHOI BALLET, THE • 1957 • Czinner Paul • UKN
BOLSHOI KONCERT • 1951 • Stroyeva Vera • USS • GRAND CONCERT, THE ○ GREAT CONCERT
BOLSTER FIGHT • 1897 • *Chard'S Vitagraph* • UKN
BOLT FROM THE BLUE, A • 1910 • Aylott Dave? • UKN
BOLT FROM THE SKY, A • 1913 • *Joyce Alice* • USA
BOLT FROM THE SKY, A • 1915 • *Saunders Jackie* • USA
BOLTED DOOR, THE • 1911 • *Melford George* • USA
BOLTED DOOR, THE • 1914 • *Kerrigan J. Warren* • USA
BOLTED DOOR, THE • 1923 • Worthington William • USA
BOLWIESER • 1977 • Fassbinder R. W. • FRG
BOM DIA, SENHORA PROFESSORA • 1953 • Garcia Fernando • SHT • PRT
BOM POVO PORTUGUES • 1981 • Simoes Rui • DOC • PRT • PORTUGAL'S GOOD PEOPLE
BOM -THE CUSTOMS OFFICER see **TULL-BOM** • 1951
BOMAN FAR SNURREN • 1949 • Soderblom Ake • SWD • BOMAN GETS CRAZY
BOMAN GETS CRAZY see **BOMAN FAR SNURREN** • 1949
BOMAN'S BOY see **BOMANS POJKE** • 1933
BOMANS POJKE • 1933 • Johansson Ivar • SWD • BOMAN'S BOY
BOMARZO • 1949 • Antonioni Michelangelo • DCS • ITL • ROMARZO
BOMB see **BOMBEN** • 1920
BOMB, THE • 1914 • Smiley Joseph • USA
BOMB, THE • 1957 • Balik Jaroslav • CZC
BOMB, THE see **BOMBA, LA** • 1974
BOMB AT 10.10, THE see **BOMBA U 10,10** • 1967
BOMB AT RANDOM, A see **BOMBE PAR HASARD, UNE** • 1969
BOMB BOY, THE • 1914 • Fitzmaurice George • USA
BOMB BY ACCIDENT, A see **BOMBE PAR HASARD, UNE** • 1969
BOMB FOR THE DICTATOR, A (USA) see **FANATIQUES, LES** • 1957
BOMB HOUR see **BAKUDAN-JI** • 1925
BOMB IN THE HIGH STREET, A • 1961 • Bishop Terry, Bezencenet Peter • UKN
BOMB MANIA see **BOMBOMANIE** • 1959
BOMB OF LAUGHTER see **SKRATTBOMBEN** • 1954
BOMB THROWERS, THE • 1915 • *August Edwin* • USA
BOMB THROWERS, THE see **BOMBASI** • 1974
BOMB WAS STOLEN, A see **S-A FURAT O BOMBA** • 1961
BOMBA, LA • 1974 • Marmol Julio Cesar • VNZ • BOMB, THE
BOMBA AND THE AFRICAN TREASURE (UKN) see **AFRICAN TREASURE** • 1952
BOMBA AND THE ELEPHANT STAMPEDE (UKN) see **ELEPHANT STAMPEDE** • 1951
BOMBA AND THE HIDDEN CITY • 1950 • Beebe Ford • USA
BOMBA AND THE JUNGLE GIRL • 1952 • Beebe Ford • USA • JUNGLE GIRL
BOMBA AND THE LION HUNTERS (UKN) see **LION HUNTERS, THE** • 1951
BOMBA AND THE SAFARI DRUMS (UKN) see **SAFARI DRUMS** • 1953
BOMBA KEMAL • 1967 • Kurthan Nazif • TRK • KEMAL THE BOMB
BOMBA ON PANTHER ISLAND • 1949 • Beebe Ford • USA
BOMBA THE JUNGLE BOY • 1949 • Beebe Ford • USA
BOMBA U 10,10 • 1967 • Damjanovic Caslav • YGS, USA • BOMB AT 10.10, THE
BOMBADIER • 1943 • Wallace Richard • USA
BOMBAI KA BABU • 1960 • *Burman S. D. (M)* • IND
BOMBAI RAAT KI BAHON MEIN • 1967 • Abbas Khwaya Ahmad • IND • IN THE ARMS OF THE BOMBAY NIGHT
BOMBALERA • 1945 • Madison Noel • USA
BOMBARDED • 1914 • Jackson Harry • USA
BOMBARDEO • 1974 • Padron Alejandro • SHT • VNZ • BOMBARDMENT
BOMBARDMENT see **BOMBARDEO** • 1974
BOMBARDMENT OF MAFEKING, THE • 1899 • Ashe Robert • UKN
BOMBARDMENT OF PORT ARTHUR, THE • 1904 • Hough Harold? • UKN
BOMBARDONE, LE • 1968 • Szulzinger Boris • SHT • BLG
BOMBAS PARA LA PAZ • 1958 • Roman Antonio • SPN • BOMBS FOR PEACE
BOMBASI • 1974 • Golubovic Predrag • YGS • BOMB THROWERS, THE
BOMBAY BUDDHA, THE • 1915 • Paton Stuart • USA
BOMBAY CLIPPER • 1942 • Rawlins John • USA
BOMBAY MAIL • 1934 • Marin Edwin L. • USA
BOMBAY OUR CITY see **HAMARA SHAHER** • 1985
BOMBAY TALKIE • 1970 • Ivory James • IND
BOMBE, LA • 1966 • de Hert Robbe • BLG
BOMBE PAR HASARD, UNE • 1969 • Laguionie Jean-Francois • ANS • FRN • BOMB AT RANDOM, A ○ ACCIDENTAL BOMB, AN ○ BOMB BY ACCIDENT, A
BOMBE SUR MONTE CARLO, UN see **CAPITAINE CRADDOCK, LE** • 1931
BOMBEN • 1920 • Carlsten Rune • SWD • BOMB
BOMBEN AUF MONTE CARLO • 1931 • Schwarz Hanns • FRG
BOMBEN AUF MONTE CARLO • 1960 • Jacoby Georg • FRG
BOMBER • 1982 • Lupo Michele • ITL
BOMBERO ATOMICA, EL • 1950 • Delgado Miguel M. • MXC
BOMBERPILOT, DER • 1970 • Schroeter Werner • FRG
BOMBERS B-52 • 1957 • Douglas Gordon • USA • NO SLEEP TILL DAWN (UKN)
BOMBER'S MOON • 1943 • Fuhr Charles, Florey Robert (U/c) • USA
BOMBER'S MOON • 1958 • Frankenheimer John • MTV • USA
BOMBI BITT OCH JAG • 1936 • Rodin Gosta • SWD
BOMBOMANIE • 1959 • Pojar Bretislav • ANS • CZC • BOMB MANIA
BOMBS • 1916 • Griffin Frank C. • SHT • USA
BOMBS AND BANDITS • 1917 • Jaeschke A. • SHT • USA
BOMBS AND BANGS • 1914 • *Keystone* • USA
BOMBS AND BANKNOTES • 1917 • Beery Wallace • SHT • USA
BOMBS AND BLUNDERS • 1917 • Semon Larry • SHT • USA
BOMBS AND BULL • 1918 • *Highgrade Films* • SHT • USA
BOMBS AWAY • 1985 • Wilson Bruce • USA
BOMBS FOR PEACE see **BOMBAS PARA LA PAZ** • 1958
BOMBS OVER BURMA • 1942 • Lewis Joseph H. • USA
BOMBS OVER CHINA see **HONG KONG** • 1951
BOMBS OVER JAPAN see **WILD BLUE YONDER, THE** • 1951
BOMBS OVER LONDON (USA) see **MIDNIGHT MENACE** • 1937
BOMBSHELL • 1933 • Fleming Victor • USA • BLONDE BOMBSHELL (UKN)
BOMBSHELL, THE see **ISO VAALEE** • 1983
BOMBSIGHT STOLEN (USA) see **COTTAGE TO LET** • 1941
BOMBSKY AND THE BOMBS • 1914 • *Royal* • USA
BOMEI KI • 1955 • Nomura Yoshitaro • JPN • REFUGEE
BOMMALATTAM • 1968 • Srinivasan V. • IND • PUPPETRY
BOMSALVA • 1977 • Molin Lars • SWD • MISFIRE
BOMZH • 1989 • Skuibin Nikolai • USS • NO PERMANENT RESIDENCE ○ FOOTLOOSE
BON APPETIT • 1969 • Gross Yoram • ANS • ASL
BON APPETIT • 1981 • Vincent Chuck • USA
BON BAISERS DE BANGKOK • 1964 • Malle Louis • DOC • FRN
BON BAISERS DE DINARD • 1949 • Loew Jacques • SHT • FRN
BON BAISERS DE HONG-KONG • 1975 • Chiffre Yvan • FRN
BON BON PARADE • 1935 • *Mintz Charles (P)* • ANS • USA
BON-BON RIOT, A • 1917 • Mann Hank • SHT • USA
BON DIEU SANS CONFESSION, LE • 1953 • Autant-Lara Claude • FRN
BON ET LES MECHANTS, LE • 1976 • Lelouch Claude • FRN • GOOD AND THE BAD, THE
BON LIT, UN • 1899 • Melies Georges • FRN • MIDNIGHT EPISODE, A (USA) ○ GOOD BED, A
BON PASTEUR A QUEBEC, LE • 1949 • Lavoie Hermenegilde • DOC • CND
BON PETIT DIABLE, UN • 1924 • Leprince Rene • FRN
BON PETIT DIABLE, UN • 1983 • Brialy Jean-Claude • FRN
BON PLAISIR, LE • 1983 • Girod Francis • FRN
BON POUR LA VIE CIVILE see **CHEMINS DE LA MAUVAISE ROUTE, LES** • 1962
BON PROPRIETAIRE, LE • 1913 • Feuillade Louis • FRN
BON ROI DAGOBERT, LE • 1963 • Chevalier Pierre • FRN, ITL • GOOD KING DAGOBERT, THE
BON ROI DAGOBERT, LE (FRN) see **DAGOBERT** • 1984
BON SAMARITAIN, LE • 1910 • Perret Leonce • FRN
BON VOYAGE • 1932 • Sweet Harry • SHT • USA
BON VOYAGE • 1944 • Hitchcock Alfred • DOC • UKN
BON VOYAGE! • 1962 • Neilson James • USA
BON VOYAGE • 1985 • Vardy Mike • MTV • UKN
BON VOYAGE see **CE SACRE AMEDEE** • 1955
BON VOYAGE, CHARLIE BROWN • 1979 • Melendez Bill • ANM • USA • BON VOYAGE, CHARLIE BROWN (AND DON'T COME BACK!)
BON VOYAGE, CHARLIE BROWN (AND DON'T COME BACK!) see **BON VOYAGE, CHARLIE BROWN** • 1979
BON VOYAGE, SIM see **VOYAGE DE SIM, LA** • 1966
BONA • 1981 • Brocka Lino • PHL
BONA MANZI • 1984 • SAF
BONANZA BUCKAROO, THE • 1926 • Thorpe Richard • USA
BONANZA BUNNY • 1959 • McKimson Robert • ANS • USA
BONANZA & COMPANHIA • 1969 • Martins Pedro • PRT
BONANZA KING, THE • 1911 • *American* • USA
BONANZA: THE NEXT GENERATION • 1988 • Claxton William F. • TVM • USA
BONANZA TOWN • 1951 • Sears Fred F. • USA • TWO-FISTED AGENT (UKN)
BONAPARTE ET LA REVOLUTION • 1971 • Gance Abel • FRN
BONAVENTURE (UKN) see **THUNDER ON THE HILL** • 1951
BONBAST • 1975 • Sayyad Parviz • IRN • DEAD END
BONCHI • 1960 • Ichikawa Kon • JPN • YOUNG LORD ○ SON, THE
BOND, THE • 1918 • Chaplin Charles • SHT • USA • CHARLES CHAPLIN IN A LIBERTY BOND APPEAL
BOND AND WORD • 1918 • SAF
BOND BETWEEN, THE • 1915 • *House Raymond* • USA
BOND BETWEEN, THE • 1917 • Crisp Donald • USA
BOND BOY, THE • 1922 • King Henry • USA
BOND ETERNAL, THE • 1914 • Melford George • USA
BOND OF BLOOD, THE • 1916 • Brooke Van Dyke • SHT • USA
BOND OF FEAR • 1956 • Cass Henry • UKN
BOND OF FEAR, THE • 1917 • Conway Jack • USA
BOND OF FRIENDSHIP, THE • 1915 • MacDonald Donald • USA
BOND OF LOVE, THE • 1914 • *Selig* • USA
BOND OF LOVE, THE • 1914 • *Eclectic* • USA
BOND OF MUSIC • 1912 • *Williams Earle* • USA
BOND OF THE RING, THE see **THUNDERING DAWN** • 1923
BOND OF WOMANHOOD, THE • 1914 • Smiley Joseph • USA
BOND SINISTER, THE • 1914 • O'Sullivan Tony • USA
BOND STREET • 1948 • Parry Gordon • UKN
BOND THAT BINDS, THE • 1913 • *Frontier* • USA
BOND WITHIN, THE • 1916 • Sloman Edward • SHT • USA
BONDAGE • 1917 • Park Ida May • USA
BONDAGE • 1933 • Santell Alfred • USA • HOUSE OF REFUGE
BONDAGE see **LEIBEIGENEN, DIE** • 1927
BONDAGE see **KOTELEK** • 1968
BONDAGE OF BARBARA, THE • 1919 • Flynn Emmett J. • USA
BONDAGE OF FEAR, THE • 1914 • *Howley Irene* • USA
BONDAGE OF FEAR, THE • 1917 • Vale Travers • USA
BONDAGE OF THE BUSH, THE • 1913 • Woods Charles • ASL
BONDED WOMAN, THE • 1922 • Rosen Phil • USA
BONDESGARDEN • 1949 • Lichtenberg Nicolai • DNM • FARM, THE
BONDI • 1978 • Jonsson Thorsteinn • DOC • ICL • FARMER
BONDITIS • 1967 • Suter Karl • SWT • GRAUSIGEN UND SCHRECKLICHEN ABENTEUER EINES BEINAHE NORMALEN MENSCHEN, DIE
BONDMAN, THE • 1916 • Lewis Edgar • USA
BONDMAN, THE • 1929 • Wilcox Herbert • UKN
BONDS AND BANNERS • 1918 • Howe J. A. • SHT • USA
BONDS OF DECEPTION • 1916 • Ricketts Thomas • SHT • USA
BONDS OF HATE see **PROMETHEUS** • 1919
BONDS OF HONOR • 1919 • Worthington William • USA
BONDS OF HONOUR (UKN) see **NO RANSOM** • 1934
BONDS OF LOVE • 1919 • Barker Reginald • USA
BONDS THAT CHAFE (UKN) see **EROTIKON** • 1920
BONDS THAT TIE, THE • 1918 • *Farrar Geraldine* • SHT • USA
BONDSMAN, THE • 1913 • *Ray Charles* • USA
BONDWOMAN, THE • 1915 • Buel Kenean • USA
BONDWOMEN • 1915 • August Edwin • USA
BONE see **DIAL RAT FOR TERROR** • 1972
BONE, THE see **HUESO, EL** • 1968
BONE BANDIT • 1948 • Nichols Charles • ANS • USA
BONE CRUSHERS • 1933 • Wing Ward • SHT • USA
BONE DRY • 1920 • *West Billy* • SHT • USA
BONE DRY • 1922 • Roach Hal • SHT • USA
BONE FOR A BONE, A • 1951 • Freleng Friz • ANS • USA
BONE, O HOMEM VIRGEM • 1972 • Serkeis George Michil • BRZ
BONE OF CONTENTION, THE see **MANZANA DE LA DISCORDIA, LA** • 1968
BONE RANGER, THE • 1957 • Rasinski Connie • ANS • USA
BONE, SWEET BONE • 1948 • Davis Arthur • ANS • USA
BONE TROUBLE • 1940 • Kinney Jack • ANS • USA
BONEKA PERMATA • 1974 • Azman Tony • MLY • DIAMOND DOLL, THE
BONES • 1984 • Goddard Jim • UKN
BONES see **PARKER** • 1985
BONFIRE OF THE VANITIES • 1990 • De Palma Brian • USA
BONGO • 1947 • Kinney Jack • ANS • USA
BONGO FUEGO - FORMS - PETIT MATIN • 1967 • Foldes Peter • ANM • FRN
BONGO PUNCH, THE • 1957 • Lovy Alex • ANS • USA
BONGO WOLF'S REVENGE • 1970 • Baker Tom • DOC • USA
BONGOLO • 1952 • Cauvin Andre • BLG
BONHEUR, LE • 1935 • L'Herbier Marcel • FRN
BONHEUR, LE • 1964 • Varda Agnes • FRN • HAPPINESS (USA)
BONHEUR A ENCORE FRAPPE, LE • 1985 • Trotignon Jean-Luc • FRN
BONHEUR CONJUGAL, LE • 1922 • Saidreau Robert • FRN
BONHEUR D'ANDROUSS, LE • 1955 • Rappaport Herbert • USS
BONHEUR DANS 20 ANS, LE • 1971 • Knobler Albert • DOC • FRN • HAPPINESS IN TWENTY YEARS (UKN)
BONHEUR DES AUTRES, LE • 1918 • Dulac Germaine • FRN
BONHEUR D'ETRE AIMEE, LE • 1962 • Storck Henri • DOC • BLG
BONHEUR D'OCCASION • 1983 • Fournier Claude • CND • TIN FLUTE, THE
BONHEUR EN LOCATION • 1948 • Wall Jean • FRN • ESPRIT DE FAMILLE, L'
BONHEUR EST POUR DEMAIN, LE • 1962 • Fabiani Henri • FRN
BONHEUR PERDU, LE • 1912 • Fescourt Henri • FRN
BONHOMME, LE • 1972 • Maheu Pierre • DOC • CND
BONHOMME DE NEIGE • 1917 • Monca Georges • FRN
BONHOMME DE NEIGE, LE see **STATUE DE NEIGE, LA** • 1899
BONIFACE SOMNAMBULE • 1950 • Labro Maurice • FRN • SLEEPWALKER, THE
BONIFACE'S HOLIDAY • 1965 • Hitruck Fedor • ANM • USS
BONITA OF EL CAJON • 1911 • Dwan Allan • USA

BONITAS LA TAPATIAS • 1960 • Gomez Landero Humberto • MXC
BONITINHA, MAS ORDINARIA • 1963 • de Carvalho J. P. • BRZ • PRETTY BUT WICKED (USA)
BONIVUR'S HEART • 1971 • Orlov M. • USS
BONJOUR see **NAHARIK SA'ID** • 1954
BONJOUR A CELLE QUE J'AIME see **SALAM ALA AL-HABAIB** • 1958
BONJOUR BALTHAZAR • 1972 • Mebale Louis • SHT • GBN
BONJOUR BALWYN • 1971 • Buesst Nigel • ASL
BONJOUR CAPITALISTE.. • 1982 • Grusch Werner • DOC • AUS • HELLO, CAPITALIST!
BONJOUR CINEMA • 1955 • Guillon Jacques • SHT • FRN
BONJOUR JEUNESSE • 1956 • Cam Maurice • FRN
BONJOUR KATHRIN • 1955 • Anton Karl • FRG
BONJOUR LA CHANCE • 1954 • Lefranc Guy • FRN, SPN
BONJOUR MA FEMME CHERIE! see **SABAH AL-KHAYR YA ZAWGATI**
BONJOUR, MONSIEUR LA BRUYERE • 1956 • Doniol-Valcroze Jacques • SHT • FRN
BONJOUR MONSIEUR LE MAITRE • 1971 • Manuel Pierre, Peche Jean-Jacques • BLG
BONJOUR MONSIEUR TURGEON • 1970 • Moreau Michel • DCS • CND
BONJOUR NEW YORK! • 1928 • Florey Robert • SHT • USA
BONJOUR PARIS • 1953 • Image Jean • ANM • FRN • GOOD MORNING PARIS
BONJOUR SOURIRE • 1955 • Sautet Claude • FRN • SOURIRE AUX LEVRES
BONJOUR TOUBIB • 1956 • Cuny Louis • FRN
BONJOUR TRISTESSE • 1958 • Preminger Otto • UKN
BONNE, LA • 1985 • Samperi Salvatore • ITL, FRN
BONNE ABSINTHE, LA • 1899-00 • Blache Alice • FRN
BONNE ALBERGE, LA • 1977 • Benazeraf Jose • FRN
BONNE ANNEE • 1913 • Feuillade Louis • FRN
BONNE ANNEE • 1916 • Cohl Emile • ANS • FRN
BONNE ANNEE, LA • 1973 • Lelouch Claude • FRN, ITL • DONNA E UNA CANAGLIA, UNA (ITL) ○ HAPPY NEW YEAR (USA) ○ HAPPY NEW YEAR CAPER, THE
BONNE AVENTURE, LA • 1932 • Diamant-Berger Henri • FRN
BONNE BERGERE ET LA MAUVAISE PRINCESSE, LA see **BONNE BERGERE ET LA MECHANTE PRINCESSE, LA** • 1908
BONNE BERGERE ET LA MECHANTE PRINCESSE, LA • 1908 • Melies Georges • FRN • GOOD SHEPHERDESS AND THE EVIL PRINCESS, THE ○ BONNE BERGERE ET LA MAUVAISE PRINCESSE, LA
BONNE CHANCE • 1935 • Guitry Sacha, Rivers Fernand • FRN
BONNE CHANCE, CHARLIE • 1962 • Richard Jean-Louis • FRN
BONNE CHANCE, INSPECTOR! • 1983 • Donev Peter • BUL
BONNE ETOILE, LA • 1942 • Boyer Jean • FRN
BONNE FARCE, UNE • 1896 • Melies Georges • FRN • CHIFFONIER, LE ○ RAG-PICKER, THE ○ GOOD JOKE, A
BONNE FARCE AVEC MA TETE, UNE see **PRETE POUR UN RENDU: OU, UNE BONNE FARCE AVEC MA TETE, UN** • 1904
BONNE HOTESSE, LA • 1912 • Perret Leonce • FRN
BONNE NOUVELLE, LA • 1975 • Weinfeld Andre • FRN
BONNE OCCASE, LA • 1964 • Drach Michel • FRN • BELLES CONDUITES, LES
BONNE PLANQUE, LA (FRN) see **BIANCO, ROSSO E..** • 1972
BONNE SOUPE, LA • 1964 • Thomas Robert • FRN, ITL • PAPPA REALE, LA (ITL) ○ CARELESS LOVE
BONNE SURPRISE, UNE see **INVITES DE M. LATOURTE, LES** • 1904
BONNE TISANE, LA • 1957 • Bromberger Herve • FRN • KILL OR CURE
BONNE VIE, LA see **QUAND ON EST BELLE** • 1931
BONNES A TUER • 1954 • Decoin Henri • FRN, ITL • QUATTRO DONNE NELLA NOTTE (ITL) ○ ONE STEP TO ETERNITY (USA)
BONNES CAUSES, LES • 1963 • Christian-Jaque • FRN, ITL • DELITTO DU PRE, IL (ITL) ○ DON'T TEMPT THE DEVIL (USA)
BONNES FAMILLES, LES • 1973 • Damardji Jaffar • ALG
BONNES FEMMES, LES • 1960 • Chabrol Claude • FRN, ITL • DONNE FACILI, LE (ITL) ○ GIRLS, THE ○ GIRLS.. GIRLS!!
BONNES MANIERES, LES • 1951 • Robert Yves • SHT • FRN
BONNET PLUME • 1982 • Raymont Peter • DOC • CND
BONNIE AND CLYDE • 1967 • Penn Arthur • USA
BONNIE AND CLYDE ITALIAN STYLE see **BONNIE E CLYDE ALL'ITALIANA** • 1983
BONNIE ANNIE LAURIE • 1918 • Millarde Harry • USA
BONNIE BANKS OF LOCH LOMOND, THE • 1921 • *Parkinson H. B. (P)* • SHT • UKN
BONNIE, BONNIE BANKS O' LOCH LOMOND, THE • 1912 • *Tennant Barbara* • USA
BONNIE, BONNIE LASSIE • 1919 • Browning Tod • USA
BONNIE BRIAR BUSH, THE see **BESIDE THE BONNIE BRIER BUSH** • 1921
BONNIE BRIER BUSH, THE see **BESIDE THE BONNIE BRIER BUSH** • 1921
BONNIE E CLYDE ALL'ITALIANA • 1983 • Steno • ITL • BONNIE AND CLYDE ITALIAN STYLE
BONNIE MARY • 1918 • Bramble A. V. • UKN
BONNIE MAY • 1920 • De Grasse Joseph, Park Ida May • USA
BONNIE OF THE HILLS • 1911 • *Champion* • USA
BONNIE OF THE HILLS • 1913 • *Clayton Marguerite* • USA
BONNIE PARKER STORY, THE • 1958 • Witney William • USA
BONNIE PRINCE CHARLIE • 1923 • Calvert Charles • UKN
BONNIE PRINCE CHARLIE • 1948 • Kimmins Anthony • UKN
BONNIE SCOTLAND • 1935 • Horne James W. • USA • HEROES OF THE REGIMENT
BONNIE'S KIDS • 1973 • Marks Arthur • USA
BONNY ET LAFONT • 1972 • Coutard Raoul • FRN
BONS AMIS, LES • 1958 • Lucot Rene • FRN
BONS BAISERS A LUNDI • 1974 • Audiard Michel • FRN
BONS DEBARRAS, LES • 1980 • Mankiewicz Francis • CND • GOOD RIDDANCE (USA)
BONS VIVANTS, LES • 1966 • Grangier Gilles, Lautner Georges • FRN, ITL • HOW TO KEEP THE RED LAMP BURNING (USA) ○ GRAND SEIGNEUR, UN ○ PER FAVORE CHIUDETE LE PERSIANE (ITL)
BONSOIR MESDAMES, BONSOIR MESSIEURS • 1943 • Tual Roland • FRN
BONSOIR MONSIEUR CHAMPAGNE • 1964 • Blais Roger • DCS • CND
BONSOIR PARIS, BONJOUR L'AMOUR • 1956 • Baum Ralph • FRN
BONSOIRS • 1910 • Cohl Emile • ANS • FRN
BONSOIRS RUSSES • 1910 • Cohl Emile • ANS • FRN
BONTA NO KEKKON YA • 1968 • Chino Koji • JPN • WEDDING SALESMAN, THE
BONUS, THE see **PREMIA** • 1975
BONY A KLID • 1987 • Olmer Vit • CZC • EASY MONEY
BONZA • 1989 • Swann David • SHT • ASL
BONZE MAGICIAN, THE see **YOSO** • 1963
BONZESSE, LA • 1975 • Jouffa Francois • FRN
BONZO • 1924-25 • *Ward W. A. (P)* • ASS • UKN
BONZO • 1924-26 • Studdy George E. • ASS • USA
BONZO BROADCASTED see **BONZOLINO** • 1924
BONZO GOES TO COLLEGE • 1952 • De Cordova Frederick • USA
BONZOLINO • 1924 • *Ward W. A. (P)* • ANM • UKN • BONZO BROADCASTED
BOO • 1932 • De Mond Albert • SHT • USA
BOO, BOO, THEME SONG • 1933 • Fleischer Dave • ANS • USA
BOO BOP • 1957 • Kneitel Seymour • ANS • USA
BOO-HOO • 1974 • Munro Grant • ANS • CND
BOO-HOO BABY • 1951 • Kneitel Seymour • ANS • USA
BOO KIND TO ANIMALS • 1955 • Sparber I. • ANS • USA
BOO MOON • 1954 • Kneitel Seymour • ANS • USA
BOO RIBBON WINNER • 1954 • Sparber I. • ANS • USA
BOO SCOUT • 1951 • Sparber I. • ANS • USA
BOOB, THE • 1912 • *Cuneo Lester* • USA
BOOB, THE • 1913 • *Leonard Robert* • USA
BOOB, THE • 1917 • Thayer Otis B. • SHT • USA
BOOB, THE • 1926 • Wellman William A. • USA • YOKEL, THE (UKN) ○ I'LL TELL THE WORLD
BOOB AND THE BAKER, THE • 1915 • *Powell Russell* • USA
BOOB AND THE MAGICIAN, THE • 1915 • *Ab* • USA
BOOB DETECTIVE, THE see **SHERLOCK BOOB, THE** • 1914
BOOB FOR LUCK • 1915 • *Kalem* • USA
BOOB FOR LUCK, A • 1917 • Beaudine William • SHT • USA
BOOB INCOGNITO, A • 1914 • *Leonard Robert* • USA
BOOB THERE WAS, A • 1914 • *Leonard Robert* • USA
BOOB TUBE, THE • 1974 • Odin Christopher • USA
BOOB WEEKLY, THE • 1916 • Goldberg Rube • SHS • USA
BOOBLEY'S BABY • 1915 • Drew Sidney • USA
BOOBS AND BRICKS • 1913 • Dwan Allan • USA
BOOBS AND BUMPS • 1919 • Donovan Frank P. • SHT • USA
BOOB'S DREAM GIRL • 1913 • *Leonard Robert* • USA
BOOB'S ELEMENT, THE • 1915 • *Moore Frank* • USA
BOOB'S HONEYMOON, THE • 1914 • Leonard Robert Z. • USA
BOOBS IN ARMS • 1940 • White Jules • SHT • USA
BOOBS IN THE WOODS • 1925 • Edwards Harry J. • SHT • USA
BOOBS IN THE WOODS • 1940 • Lord Del • SHT • USA
BOOBS IN THE WOODS • 1950 • McKimson Robert • ANS • USA
BOOB'S INHERITANCE, THE • 1913 • *De Forrest Claude* • USA
BOOB'S LEGACY, THE • 1914 • *Leonard Robert* • USA
BOOB'S NEMESIS, THE • 1914 • *Leonard Robert* • USA
BOOB'S RACING CAREER, THE • 1915 • Mitchell Bruce • USA
BOOB'S ROMANCE, A • 1915 • Leonard Robert Z. • USA
BOOB'S VICTORY, THE • 1916 • Leonard Robert Z. • SHT • USA
BOOBY, THE see **BOUFOS, O** • 1968
BOOBY DUPES • 1945 • Lord Del • SHT • USA
BOOBY HATCHED • 1944 • Tashlin Frank • ANS • USA
BOOBY SOCKS • 1945 • Swift Howard, Wickersham Bob • ANS • USA
BOOBY TRACK • 1957 • Cass Henry • UKN
BOOBY TRAP see **HOT, FAST AND LOOSE** • 1973
BOOBY TRAP see **WIRED TO KILL** • 1986
BOODLE AND BANDITS • 1918 • Semon Larry • SHT • USA
BOOFE-KOUR • 1975 • Derambakhs Kioomars • IRN • BLIND OWL, THE
BOOGALOO • 1967 • Wenceslao Jose Pepe • PHL
BOOGENS, THE • 1980 • Conway James L. • USA
BOOGEYMAN 2, THE • 1983 • Star Bruce • USA
BOOGEYMAN, THE • 1980 • Lommel Ulli • USA • BOGEY MAN, THE
BOOGIE DOODLE • 1939-41 • McLaren Norman • ANS • USA
BOOGIE MAN WILL GET YOU, THE • 1942 • Landers Lew • USA
BOOGIE WOOGIE • 1945 • Madison Noel • SHT • USA
BOOGIE WOOGIE • 1958 • Barfod Bent • ANS • DNM
BOOGIE WOOGIE BUGLE BOY OF COMPANY B • 1941 • Lantz Walter • ANS • USA
BOOGIE WOOGIE DREAM • 1941 • Burger Hans • SHT • USA
BOOGIE WOOGIE MAN • 1943 • Culhane James • ANS • USA
BOOGIE WOOGIE SIOUX • 1942 • Lovy Alex • ANS • USA
BOOGSCHUTTER, EEN • 1966 • van der Heyde Nikolai • SHT • NTH
BOOK, THE • 1913 • Buckland Warwick? • UKN
BOOK AGENT, THE • 1915 • *Novelty* • USA
BOOK AGENT, THE • 1917 • Turner Otis • USA
BOOK AGENT'S ROMANCE, THE • 1916 • *Anderson G. M.* • SHT • USA
BOOK AND THE SWORD, THE see **SHU JIAN EN CHOU LU** • 1988
BOOK BARGAIN • 1936 • McLaren Norman, Jackson Pat • DCS • UKN
BOOK IN THE COUNTRY see **KNIGA V DEREVNE** • 1929
BOOK OF ESTHER, THE see **ESZTERKONYV** • 1989
BOOK OF GOOD LOVE, THE see **LIBRO DE BUEN AMOR I, EL** • 1974
BOOK OF JOB, THE • 1954 • *Jacobs Lewis* • SHT • USA
BOOK OF KINGS, THE see **SIAVASH IN PERSEPOLIS** • 1966
BOOK OF NUMBERS, THE • 1972 • St. Jacques Raymond • USA
BOOK OF PSALMS, THE • 1927 • Barnett Charles • SER • UKN
BOOK OF VERSES, A • 1913 • *Rex* • USA
BOOK REVUE • 1945 • Clampett Robert • ANS • USA
BOOK SHOP, THE • 1937 • Davis Mannie, Gordon George • ANS • USA
BOOK TAUGHT HYPNOTISM • 1909 • *Pathe* • FRN
BOOK TO BURN, A see **YAKILACAK KITAP** • 1968
BOOKED ON SUSPICION (UKN) see **BOSTON BLACKIE BOOKED ON SUSPICION** • 1945
BOOKMAKER, THE • 1907 • Martin J. H.? • UKN
BOOKMAKER'S PROGRESS • 1979 • Winkler Donald • MTV • CND
BOOKS AND CROOKS • 1920 • Ross Jack • UKN
BOOKS AND PEOPLE: THE WEALTH WITHIN • 1947 • Kopel Hal • USA
BOOKSELLER WHO GAVE UP BATHING, THE see **BOKHANDLAREN SOM SLUTADE BARA** • 1969
BOOKWORM, THE • 1939 • Freleng Friz • ANS • USA
BOOKWORM TURNS, THE • 1917 • *Depp Harry* • SHT • USA
BOOKWORMS • 1920 • Brunel Adrian • UKN
BOOKWORM'S BLESSED BLUNDERS, THE • 1916 • Walsh Phil • USA
BOOLEAN PROCEDURE • 1979 • Bruce Nichola, Coulson Michael • UKN
BOOLOO • 1938 • Elliott Clyde E. • USA
BOOM! • 1968 • Losey Joseph • UKN
BOOM • 1968 • Okeyev Tolomush • SHT • USS
BOOM • 1979 • Pojar Bretislav • ANS • CZC • BUM
BOOM see **BOOM, IL** • 1963
BOOM, IL • 1963 • De Sica Vittorio • ITL • BOOM
BOOM BABIES • 1988 • Twomey Siobhan • IRL
BOOM, BOOM • 1936 • King Jack • ANS • USA
BOOM GOES THE GROOM • 1939 • Parrott Charles • SHT • USA
BOOM IN THE MOON (USA) see **MODERNO BARBA AZUL, EL** • 1946
BOOM TOWN • 1940 • Conway Jack • USA
BOOM TOWN (USA) see **UZAVRELI GRAD** • 1961
BOOMERANG • 1934 • Maude Arthur • UKN
BOOMERANG! • 1947 • Kazan Elia • USA
BOOMERANG • 1968 • Campani Paul • ANS • ITL
BOOMERANG • 1979 • Nichev Ivan • BUL
BOOMERANG see **BUMERANG** • 1962
BOOMERANG, A • 1916 • *Selig* • SHT • USA
BOOMERANG, THE • 1912 • *Davis Howard* • USA
BOOMERANG, THE • 1913 • *Kalem* • USA
BOOMERANG, THE • 1913 • *Thanhouser* • USA
BOOMERANG, THE • 1913 • Ince Thomas H. • *Kb* • USA
BOOMERANG, THE • 1913 • Webster Harry Mcrae • *Essanay* • USA
BOOMERANG, THE • 1919 • Bracken Bertram • USA
BOOMERANG, THE • 1925 • Gasnier Louis J. • USA • LOVE DOCTOR, THE
BOOMERANG BILL • 1922 • Terriss Tom • USA
BOOMERANG FRAME-UP, A • 1917 • *Triangle* • USA
BOOMERANG GOLD BRICK, A • 1916 • Humphrey Orral • USA
BOOMERANG JOKE, A • 1912 • *Pathe* • USA
BOOMERANG JUSTICE • 1922 • Sedgwick Edward • USA
BOOMERANG OF BLOOD, A • 1915 • *Essanay* • USA
BOOMERANG SWINDLE, A • 1914 • Smiley Joseph • USA
BOOMING BUSINESS • 1910 • *Thanhouser* • USA
BOOMING FIFI • 1915 • *Atla* • USA
BOOMING THE BOXING BUSINESS • 1916 • *Mcnish Frank E.* • SHT • USA
BOOMING TRIXIE • 1915 • *Mina* • USA
BOOMSVILLE • 1968 • Mallette Yvon • ANS • CND
BOON, THE see **KONDURA** • 1977
BOOND JO BAN GAYE MOTI • 1968 • Shantaram Victor • IND • DROP THAT TURNED INTO A PEARL, THE
BOONER BILL • 1917 • Sullivan Pat • ASS • USA
BOONTON AFFAIR, THE • 1917 • Baggot King • SHT • USA
BOOP-OOP-A-DOOP • 1932 • Fleischer Dave • ANS • USA
BOORS, THE see **BADARINII** • 1960
BOOS AND ARROWS • 1954 • Kneitel Seymour • ANS • USA
BOOS AND SADDLES • 1953 • Sparber I. • ANS • USA
BOOS IN THE NIGHT • 1950 • Sparber I. • ANS • USA
BOO'S UPS AND DOWNS • 1962 • Fellbom Claes • SHT • SWD
BOOST • 1988 • Becker Harold • USA
BOOSTER, THE • 1928 • Yates Hal • SHT • USA
BOOSTING BUSINESS • 1913 • *Steppling John* • USA
BOOT, DAS • 1981 • Petersen Wolfgang • FRG • BOAT, THE (UKN)
BOOT AND THE LOOT, THE • 1917 • Santell Alfred • SHT • USA
BOOT BUSINESS, THE • 1915 • *Wright Bertie* • UKN
BOOT HILL BANDITS • 1942 • Luby S. Roy • USA
BOOT HILL (USA) see **COLLINA DEGLI STIVALI, LA** • 1969
BOOT IST VOLL, DAS • 1981 • Imhoof Markus • SWT • BOAT IS FULL, THE (USA) ○ BARQUE EST PLEINE, LA ○ FULL HOUSE
BOOT POLISH • 1954 • Arora Prakash • IND • 1c
BOOTED BABE, BUSTED BOSS see **HYAPPATSU HYAKUCHU** • 1968
BOOTHILL BRIGADE • 1937 • Newfield Sam • USA
BOOTLE BEETLE • 1947 • Hannah Jack • ANS • USA
BOOTLEGGER, THE • 1911 • *Selig* • USA
BOOTLEGGERS • 1974 • Pierce Charles B. • USA • BOOTLEGGERS' ANGEL
BOOTLEGGERS see **SAMOGONSHCHIKI** • 1961
BOOTLEGGERS, THE • 1922 • Sheldon Roy • USA
BOOTLEGGERS' ANGEL see **BOOTLEGGERS** • 1974
BOOTLEGGER'S DAUGHTER, THE • 1922 • Schertzinger Victor • USA
BOOTLE'S BABY • 1910 • *Edison* • USA
BOOTLE'S BABY • 1914 • Miller Ashley • USA
BOOTLE'S BABY • 1914 • Shaw Harold • UKN
BOOTMAKER'S TEN POUND NOTE, THE • 1910 • *Walturdaw* • UKN
BOOTS • 1919 • Clifton Elmer • USA
BOOTS see **BUTY** • 1965
BOOTS AND SADDLES • 1909 • Boggs Frank • USA
BOOTS AND SADDLES • 1916 • *Grey R. Henry* • USA
BOOTS AND SADDLES • 1937 • Kane Joseph • USA
BOOTS AT MIDNIGHT see **DOPE** • 1968
BOOTS! BOOTS! • 1934 • Tracy Bert • UKN
BOOTS FROM BOOTLE • 1916 • Collins Edwin J.? • UKN

BOOTS HE COULDN'T LOSE, THE • 1909 • *Edison* • USA
BOOTS MALONE • 1952 • Dieterle William • USA
BOOTS? NOT 'ARF! • 1915 • Collins Edwin J. • UKN
BOOTS OF DESTINY • 1937 • Rosson Arthur • USA
BOOTY AND THE BEAST • 1953 • White Jules • SHT • USA
BOOZE HANGS HIGH, THE • 1930 • Harman Hugh, Ising Rudolf • ANS • USA
BOP GIRL • 1983 • Armstrong Gillian • SHT • ASL
BOP GIRL see **BOP GIRL GOES CALYPSO** • 1957
BOP GIRL GOES CALYPSO • 1957 • Koch Howard W. • USA • BOP GIRL
BOP SCOTCH • 1953 • Belson Jordan • ANS • USA
BOPIN' HOOD • 1961 • Kneitel Seymour • ANS • USA
BOQUITAS PINTADAS • 1974 • Torre-Nilsson Leopoldo • ARG • PAINTED LIPS
BOR BORSON • 1973 • During Jan Erik • NRW
BOR BORSON II • 1976 • Bull Stein Roger • NRW
BORA BORA • 1968 • Liberatore Ugo • ITL, FRN
BORBA GIGANTOV • 1926 • Turin Victor • USS • BATTLE OF THE GIANTS
BORBOLETAS TAMBEM AMAM, AS • 1980 • Tanko J. B. • BRZ • BUTTERFLIES ALSO LOVE
BORBURATA • 1977 • Enriquez Cesar • VNZ
BORCSA AMERIKABEN • 1939 • Keleti Marton • HNG • BARBARA IN AMERICA (USA)
BORDEL, LE • 1974 • Benazeraf Jose • FRN
BORDEL POUR FEMMES • 1980 • Kikoine Gerard • FRN
BORDEL SS • 1978 • Benazeraf Jose • FRN
BORDELLA • 1976 • Avati Pupi • ITL
BORDELLE, SCULPTEUR MONUMENTAL • 1962 • Navarra • SHT • FRN
BORDELLET • 1972 • Ege Ole • DNM • BEST BIT OF CRUMPET IN DENMARK, THE ◦ BORDELLO ◦ BORDELLET: EN GLAEDESPIGES ERINDRINGER
BORDELLET: EN GLAEDESPIGES ERINDRINGER see **BORDELLET** • 1972
BORDELLO • 1985 • Koundouros Nikos • GRC
BORDELLO see **BORDELLET** • 1972
BORDER, THE • 1981 • Leitch Christopher • USA • BORDER, USA, THE ◦ BLOOD BARRIER
BORDER, THE • 1982 • Richardson Tony • USA
BORDER, THE see **FRONTIER, THE** • 1935
BORDER, THE see **GRANICA** • 1967
BORDER, THE see **MARGEM, A** • 1967
BORDER, THE see **GRANICA** • 1989
BORDER BADMEN • 1945 • Newfield Sam • USA
BORDER BANDITS • 1946 • Hillyer Lambert • USA
BORDER BLACKBIRDS • 1927 • Maloney Leo • USA
BORDER BRIGANDS • 1935 • Grinde Nick • USA
BORDER BUCKAROOS • 1943 • Drake Oliver • USA
BORDER CABALLERO • 1936 • Newfield Sam • USA
BORDER CAFE • 1937 • Landers Lew • USA • MEXICAN QUARTER
BORDER CAVALIER, THE • 1927 • Wyler William • USA
BORDER CITY RUSTLERS • 1953 • McDonald Frank • MTV • USA
BORDER DETECTIVE, THE • 1912 • *D'Orsay Lawrence* • USA
BORDER DEVILS • 1932 • Nigh William • USA
BORDER FENCE • 1951 • Sheldo Norman, Kier H. W. • USA
BORDER FEUD • 1947 • Taylor Ray • USA
BORDER FEUD, THE see **GRANSFOLKEN** • 1914
BORDER FLIGHT • 1936 • Lovering Otho • USA
BORDER G-MAN • 1938 • Howard David • USA
BORDER GUNS • 1934 • Nelson Jack • USA
BORDER HEAT • 1988 • Gaudioz Tony • USA
BORDER INCIDENT • 1949 • Mann Anthony • USA
BORDER INTRIGUE • 1925 • McGowan J. P. • USA
BORDER JUSTICE • 1925 • Eason B. Reeves • USA
BORDER LAW • 1922 • Maloney Leo, Beebe Ford • USA
BORDER LAW • 1931 • King Louis • USA
BORDER LEGION, THE • 1919 • *Bosworth Hobart* • USA
BORDER LEGION, THE • 1924 • Howard William K. • USA
BORDER LEGION, THE • 1930 • Brower Otto, Knopf Edwin H. • USA
BORDER LEGION, THE • 1940 • Kane Joseph • USA
BORDER LEGION, THE see **LAST ROUND-UP, THE** • 1934
BORDER LINE, THE • 1916 • Windom Lawrence C. • SHT • USA
BORDER MENACE, THE • 1934 • Nelson Jack • USA
BORDER OF LIFE, THE see **AUX FRONTIERES DE L'HOMME** • 1953
BORDER OUTLAWS • 1950 • Talmadge Richard • USA • PHANTOM HORSEMAN, THE (UKN)
BORDER PATROL • 1935 • Clifton Elmer • USA
BORDER PATROL • 1943 • Selander Lesley • USA
BORDER PATROL, THE • 1928 • Hogan James P. • USA
BORDER PATROL, THE (UKN) see **LAWLESS BORDERS** • 1935
BORDER PATROLMAN, THE • 1936 • Howard David • USA
BORDER PHANTOM • 1937 • Luby S. Roy • USA
BORDER PLOT, THE see **GRANSLOTS** • 1990
BORDER RAIDERS, THE • 1918 • Paton Stuart • USA
BORDER RAIDERS, THE • 1921 • *Hill Ben* • USA
BORDER RANGER, THE • 1911 • *Anderson Broncho Billy* • USA
BORDER RANGERS • 1950 • Berke William • USA
BORDER RENEGADE see **LIGHT OF WESTERN STARS, THE** • 1940
BORDER RIDER, THE • 1924 • Reel Frederick Jr. • USA
BORDER RIVER • 1954 • Sherman George • USA
BORDER RIVER, THE • 1919 • *Brent Evelyn* • SHT • USA
BORDER ROMANCE • 1930 • Thorpe Richard • USA
BORDER ROUNDUP (UKN) see **LONE RIDER IN BORDER ROUNDUP** • 1943
BORDER RUNNER, THE • 1915 • *Navajo* • USA
BORDER SADDLEMATES • 1952 • Witney William • USA
BORDER SCOURGE, THE • 1917 • SAF
BORDER SCOUTS, THE • 1922 • Hall Bert • USA
BORDER SHERIFF, THE • 1926 • Bradbury Robert North • USA
BORDER SHOWDOWN • 1956 • Bare Richard L. • MTV • USA
BORDER STREET (UKN) see **ULICA GRANICZNA** • 1948
BORDER TERROR, THE • 1919 • Harvey Harry • SHT • USA
BORDER-TOWN • 1935 • Mayo Archie • USA
BORDER TOWN see **BIANCHENG** • 1985
BORDER TRAILS • 1931 • Oliver Bill • DOC • CND
BORDER TREASURE • 1950 • Archainbaud George • USA
BORDER, USA, THE see **BORDER, THE** • 1981
BORDER VENGEANCE • 1925 • Webb Harry S. • USA
BORDER VENGEANCE • 1935 • Heinz Ray • USA
BORDER VIGILANTES • 1941 • Abrahams Derwin • USA
BORDER WEAVE • 1942 • Curthoys • DCS • UKN
BORDER WHIRLWIND, THE • 1926 • McCarthy John P. • USA
BORDER WILDCAT, THE • 1929 • Taylor Ray • USA
BORDER WIRELESS, THE • 1918 • Hart William S., Ince Thomas H. (Spv) • USA
BORDER WOLVES • 1916 • Horne James W. • SHT • USA
BORDER WOLVES • 1917 • Marshall George • SHT • USA
BORDER WOLVES • 1938 • Lewis Joseph H. • USA
BORDER WOMEN • 1924 • Neitz Alvin J. • USA
BORDERLAND • 1922 • Powell Paul • USA • BETWEEN TWO WORLDS ◦ BETWEEN THE WORLDS
BORDERLAND • 1937 • Watt Nate • USA
BORDERLINE • 1930 • Macpherson Kenneth • USA
BORDERLINE • 1950 • Seiter William A. • USA
BORDERLINE • 1980 • Freedman Jerrold • USA
BORDERLINE see **OKRAINA** • 1933
BORDERLINE CASES • 1949 • Sparling Gordon • DCS • CND
BORDERLINE -GUILTY see **BORDERLINE -SCHULDIG?** • 1987
BORDERLINE -SCHULDIG? • 1987 • Allahyari Houchang • AUS • BORDERLINE -GUILTY
BORDERLINES (UKN) see **CARETAKERS, THE** • 1963
BORDERS see **HUDUD** • 1984
BORDERS AND BOMBS • 1916 • *West Billy* • SHT • USA
BORDERS: WHERE SCOTLAND AND ENGLAND MEET • 1970 • Pavett Michael • DOC • UKN
BORDERTOWN GUNFIGHTERS • 1943 • Bretherton Howard • USA
BORDERTOWN TRAIL • 1944 • Selander Lesley • USA
BORDON Y LA ESTRELLA, EL • 1966 • Klimovsky Leon • SPN
BORE OF A BOY, A • 1913 • Fitzhamon Lewin • UKN
BORED • 1916 • Buss Harry? • SHT • UKN
BORED CUCKOO, THE • 1948 • Tytla Bill • ANS • USA
BORED OF EDUCATION • 1936 • Douglas Gordon • SHT • USA
BORED OF EDUCATION • 1946 • Tytla Bill • ANS • USA
BOREDOM • 1970 • Salamuni Samy • EGY • ENNUI, L'
BOREDOM • 1976 • Siegel Lois • CND
BOREI KAIBYO YASHIKI • 1958 • Nakagawa Nobuo • JPN • BLACK CAT MANSION (USA) ◦ GHOST CAT MANSION
BORETS I KLOUN • 1957 • Barnet Boris, Yudin Konstantin • USS • WRESTLER AND THE CLOWN, THE (USA)
BORGES, LES • 1979 • Mallet Marilu • CND
BORGES FOR MILLIONS see **BORGES PARA MILLONES** • 1978
BORGES PARA MILLONES • 1978 • Wulicher Ricardo • ARG • BORGES FOR MILLIONS
BORGHESE PICCOLO PICCOLO, UN • 1977 • Monicelli Mario • ITL • AVERAGE MAN, AN
BORGIA • 1920 • Caramba Luigi • ITL
BORGIA STICK, THE • 1967 • Rich David Lowell • TVM • USA
BORGNE, LE • 1981 • Ruiz Raul • FRN • ONE-EYED MAN, THE
BORGO A MOZZANO • 1958 • Gandin Michele • ITL • AGRICULTURAL EXPERIMENT IN ITALY, AN
BORINAGE • 1933 • Ivens Joris, Storck Henri • SHT • BLG • MISERE AU BORINAGE
BORING AFTERNOON, A see **FADNI ODPOLENE** • 1965
BORIS AND NATASHA • 1989 • Smith Charles Martin • USA • BORIS AND NATASHA IN OUR BOY BADENOV
BORIS AND NATASHA IN OUR BOY BADENOV see **BORIS AND NATASHA** • 1989
BORIS GODOUNOV • 1986 • Bondarchuk Sergei • USS
BORIS GODOUNOV • 1989 • Zulawski Andrzej • FRN
BORIS GODUNOV • 1955 • Stroyeva Vera • USS
BORIS GUDONOV • 1907 • Drankov A. O. • USS
BORIS I • 1982 • Shariliev Borislav • BUL
BORMAN • 1966 • Paolinelli Bruno • ITL
BORN 1921 see **ROCNIK JEDENADVACET** • 1957
BORN 1944 see **URODZENI W 44** • 1965
BORN: A DAUGHTER see **DOTTER FODD, EN** • 1944
BORN A NINJA • 1988 • *L'Argent Patrick* • HKG
BORN AGAIN • 1914 • *Booking K. C.* • USA
BORN AGAIN • 1978 • Rapper Irving • USA
BORN AMERICAN see **ARCTIC HEAT** • 1985
BORN APRIL FIRST • 1934 • Horne James W. • SHT • USA
BORN BEAUTIFUL • 1982 • Hart Harvey • TVM • USA
BORN BLACK (UKN) see **VERLOGENE AKT, DER** • 1969
BORN ERECT • Sanderson Jon • USA
BORN FOR GLORY (USA) see **BROWN ON RESOLUTION** • 1935
BORN FOR HELL see **NE POUR L'ENFER** • 1976
BORN FOR TROUBLE see **MURDER IN THE BIG HOUSE** • 1942
BORN FREE • 1965 • Hill James • UKN
BORN HUSTLER • 1972 • Shebib Donald • CND
BORN IN 44 see **URODZENI W 44** • 1965
BORN IN 1921 see **ROCNIK JEDENADVACET** • 1957
BORN IN EAST L.A. • 1987 • Marin Cheech • USA
BORN IN FLAMES • 1983 • Borden Lizzie • USA
BORN IN MARCH see **NATA DI MARZO** • 1958
BORN IN SIN (USA) see **KAWANO HOTORIDE** • 1963
BORN IN THE SUN • 1946 • Heyer John • DOC • ASL
BORN INNOCENT • 1974 • Wrye Donald • TVM • USA
BORN LOSERS • 1967 • Laughlin Tom • USA
BORN LUCKY • 1932 • Powell Michael • UKN
BORN MAKER TO THE WORLD • 1969 • Dalen Zale R. • CND
BORN OF FIRE • 1987 • Dehlavi Jamil • PKS
BORN OF MAN AND WOMAN • 1954 • Nourse Alan • SHT • USA
BORN OF THE AMERICAS • 1972 • Alvarez Santiago • CUB
BORN OF THE CYCLONE see **UNTAMED YOUTH** • 1924
BORN OF THE PEOPLE • 1916 • Ford Francis • SHT • USA
BORN OF THE SEA • 1949 • Mavrogordato Anthony • UKN
BORN OF THE WIND • 1961 • Kuchar Mike, Kuchar George • SHT • USA
BORN ON SUNDAY see **URODZENI W NIEDZIELE** • 1967
BORN ON THE FOURTH OF JULY • 1989 • Stone Oliver • USA
BORN RECKLESS • 1930 • Ford John • USA
BORN RECKLESS • 1937 • Machaty Gustav • USA
BORN RECKLESS • 1937 • St. Clair Malcolm • USA
BORN RECKLESS • 1959 • Koch Howard W. • USA
BORN RICH • 1924 • Nigh William • USA
BORN THAT WAY • 1936 • Faye Randall • UKN
BORN TO BATTLE • 1926 • De Lacy Robert • *R-C Pictures* • USA
BORN TO BATTLE • 1927 • Neitz Alvin J. • *Bill Cody Productions* • USA
BORN TO BATTLE • 1935 • Webb Harry S. • USA
BORN TO BE BAD • 1934 • Sherman Lowell • USA
BORN TO BE BAD • 1950 • Ray Nicholas • USA
BORN TO BE COPS see **CARABINIERI SI NASCE** • 1985
BORN TO BE LOVED • 1959 • Haas Hugo • USA
BORN TO BE SOLD • 1981 • Brinckerhoff Burt • TVM • USA
BORN TO BE WILD • 1938 • Kane Joseph • USA
BORN TO BOOGIE • 1972 • Starr Ringo • DOC • UKN
BORN TO BUCK • 1968 • Tibbs Casey • DOC • USA
BORN TO DANCE • 1936 • Del Ruth Roy • USA
BORN TO FIGHT • 1936 • Hutchison Charles • USA
BORN TO GAMBLE • 1935 • Rosen Phil • USA
BORN TO KILL • 1947 • Wise Robert • USA • LADY OF DECEIT (UKN)
BORN TO KILL • 1988 • Prior David A. • USA
BORN TO KILL see **NATO PER UCCIDERE** • 1967
BORN TO KILL see **COCKFIGHTER** • 1974
BORN TO LOVE • 1931 • Stein Paul L. • USA
BORN TO PECK • 1952 • Lantz Walter • ANS • USA
BORN TO RACE • 1988 • Fargo James • USA
BORN TO RUN (USA) see **HARNESS FEVER** • 1976
BORN TO SING • 1941 • Ludwig Edward • USA
BORN TO SING (UKN) see **ALMOST ANGELS** • 1962
BORN TO SPEED • 1947 • Cahn Edward L. • USA
BORN TO SUCCEED see **TI KI AN GENNITHIKA FTOHOS** • 1968
BORN TO SWING • 1973 • Jeremy John • UKN
BORN TO THE SADDLE • 1929 • Levigard Josef • USA
BORN TO THE SADDLE • 1953 • Beaudine William • USA
BORN TO THE WEST • 1926 • Waters John • USA
BORN TO THE WEST • 1938 • Barton Charles T. • USA • HERITAGE OF THE PLAINS ◦ HELL TOWN
BORN TO TROUBLE • 1932 • Hillyer Lambert • USA
BORN TO WIN • 1971 • Passer Ivan • USA • SCRAPING BOTTOM
BORN TO WIN • 1983 • Kaplan Jonathan • USA • HEART LIKE A WHEEL
BORN TOUGH see **HE COULDN'T TAKE IT** • 1933
BORN WILD see **YOUNG ANIMALS, THE** • 1968
BORN YESTERDAY • 1950 • Cukor George • USA
BORNENES SYND • 1916 • Holger-Madsen • DNM • SINS OF THE CHILDREN, THE
BORNEO • 1937 • Johnson Martin E., Talley Truman • DOC • USA
BORNEO • 1954 • Bourguignon Serge • FRN
BORNEVENNERNE • 1914 • Holger-Madsen • DNM • MARRIAGE OF CONVENIENCE, A
BORO NO KESSHITAI • 1943 • Imai Tadashi • JPN • SUICIDE TROOPS OF THE WATCH TOWER ◦ DEATH COMMAND OF THE TOWER
BOROKA UR SZORONGASAI • 1972 • Bacso Peter • HNG • MR. BOROKA'S ANGUISH
BOROM SARRET • 1963 • Sembene Ousmane • SHT • FRN, SNL
BORORO • 1954 • Brandt Henry • SWT
BOROTALCO • 1982 • Verdone Carlo • ITL • TALCUM POWDER
BOROUGH, THE see **PODGRODZIE** • 1959
BOROYA NO SHUNJU • 1958 • Nakamura Noboru • JPN
BORRAH MINEVITCH AND HIS HARMONICA SCHOOL • 1945 • Negulesco Jean • SHT • USA
BORRASCA • 1977 • Rivas Miguel Angel • SPN
BORRASCA DE CELOS • 1946 • Iquino Ignacio F. • SPN
BORRASCA EN LAS ALMAS • 1953 • Rodriguez Ismael • MXC
BORRASCA HUMANA • 1939 • Bohr Jose • MXC
BORROMINI • 1974 • Grottesi Marcello • ITL
BORROW A MILLION • 1934 • Denham Reginald • UKN
BORROWED BABIES see **KOLCSONKERT CSECSEMOK, A** • 1914
BORROWED BABY, THE • 1910 • *Kalem* • USA
BORROWED BABY, THE • 1911 • Wilson Frank? • UKN
BORROWED BABY, THE • 1918 • Curtis Allen • SHT • USA
BORROWED BLONDE • 1947 • Yates Hal • SHT • USA
BORROWED BOOK, THE • 1914 • Reehm George E. • USA
BORROWED CASTLE, THE see **KOLCSONKERT KASTELY, A** • 1935
BORROWED CLOTHES • 1909 • Brooke Van Dyke • USA
BORROWED CLOTHES • 1918 • Weber Lois, Smalley Phillips • USA
BORROWED CLOTHES • 1934 • Maude Arthur • UKN
BORROWED ENGINE, THE • 1917 • Morton Walter • USA
BORROWED FACE, THE see **ZTRACENA TVAR** • 1965
BORROWED FINERY • 1916 • *Gayety* • SHT • USA
BORROWED FINERY • 1925 • Apfel Oscar • USA
BORROWED FINERY, THE • 1914 • *West William* • USA
BORROWED FLAT, THE • 1911 • *American* • USA
BORROWED GOLD • 1913 • King Burton L.? • USA
BORROWED HERO • 1941 • Collins Lewis D. • USA
BORROWED HUSBANDS • 1924 • Smith David • USA
BORROWED IDENTITY • 1913 • *Clayton Marguerite* • USA
BORROWED LADDER, THE • 1907 • *Walturdaw* • UKN
BORROWED NECKLACE, THE • 1915 • O'Sullivan Tony • USA
BORROWED PLUMAGE • 1917 • West Raymond B. • USA
BORROWED PLUMES • 1916 • Beery Wallace • *Universal* • SHT • USA
BORROWED PLUMES • 1916 • Wilson Ben • *Rex* • SHT • USA
BORROWED PLUMES (UKN) see **IN BORROWED PLUMES** • 1926
BORROWED SUNSHINE • 1916 • Windom Lawrence C. • SHT • USA
BORROWED TIME see **YOU CAN'T BUY LUCK** • 1937
BORROWED TROUBLE • 1948 • Archainbaud George • USA
BORROWED UMBRELLA, THE • 1912 • *Selig* • USA
BORROWED WIVES • 1930 • Strayer Frank, De Cordova Leander • USA
BORROWER, THE • 1988 • McNaughton John • USA
BORROWERS, THE • 1973 • Miller Walter C. • USA
BORROWING HOGAN • 1915 • *Kromann Ann* • USA

BORROWING SIMP, THE • 1912 • *Republic* • USA
BORROWING TROUBLE • 1913 • France Charles H. • USA
BORROWING TROUBLE • 1916 • Drew Sidney • SHT • USA
BORROWING TROUBLE • 1937 • Strayer Frank • USA
BORSALINI, LES • 1979 • Nerval Michel • FRN
BORSALINO • 1970 • Deray Jacques • FRN, ITL
BORSALINO AND CO. see **BORSALINO E CIE** • 1974
BORSALINO E CIE • 1974 • Deray Jacques • FRN, FRG, ITL • BLOOD ON THE STREETS (UKN) ○ BORSALINO AND CO.
BORSE UND ADEL • 1917 • Basch Felix • FRG
BORSENKONIGIN, DIE • 1916 • Edel Edmund • FRG
BORSOS MIKLOS • 1966 • Meszaros Marta • DCS • HNG • MIKLOS BORSOS
BORTREIST PA UBESTEMT TID • 1973 • Bang-Hansen Pal • NRW • DEPARTED FOR EVER
BORYOKU • 1952 • Yoshimura Kozaburo • JPN • VIOLENCE
BORYOKU NO MACHI • 1950 • Yamamoto Satsuo • JPN • STREET OF VIOLENCE
BORZA • 1935 • von Wangenheim Gustav • FRG • STRUGGLE, THE
BOSAMBO (USA) see **SANDERS OF THE RIVER** • 1935
BOSATSU, SHIMOYAMA JIKEN • 1982 • Kumai Kei • JPN • MURDER CASE SHIMOYAMA
BOSCH see **PARADISO PERDUTO, IL** • 1948
BOSCHPLAAT, DE • 1972 • Gols Albert • DOC • NTH
BOSCOMBE VALLEY MYSTERY, THE • 1922 • Ridgwell George • UKN
BOSE GEIST LUMPACI VAGABUNDUS, DER • 1922 • Wilhelm Carl • FRG • LUMPACI VAGABUNDUS ○ LUMPACI THE VAGABOND
BOSE LUST, DIE see **DIKTATUR DER LIEBE 1, DIE** • 1921
BOSEN BUBEN, DIE • 1915 • Lowenbein Richard • FRG
BOSHI • 1915 • Collins Edwin J.? • UKN
BOSHI ZO • 1956 • *Yamada Isuzu* • JPN • STATUE OF MOTHER AND CHILD
BOSHUNDHARA • 1977 • Dutta Subhash • BNG • MOTHER EARTH
BOSKO • 1929-33 • *Harman-Ising* • ASS • USA
BOSKO AND BRUNO • 1931-32 • Harman Hugh • ANS • USA
BOSKO AND HONEY • 1931-32 • Harman Hugh • ANS • USA
BOSKO AND THE CANNIBALS • 1937 • Harman Hugh • ANS • USA
BOSKO AND THE PIRATES • 1937 • Harman Hugh • ANS • USA
BOSKO AT THE BEACH • 1931-32 • Harman Hugh • ANS • USA
BOSKO BUHA • 1979 • Bauer Branko • YGS
BOSKO IN BAGDAD • 1938 • Harman Hugh • ANS • USA
BOSKO IN DUTCH • 1933 • Freleng Friz • ANS • USA
BOSKO IN PERSON • 1933 • Freleng Friz • ANS • USA
BOSKO SHIPWRECKED • 1930 • Harman Hugh, Ising Rudolf • ANS • USA
BOSKO THE DOUGHBOY • 1931-32 • Harman Hugh • ANS • USA
BOSKO THE DRAWBACK • 1933 • Harman Hugh • ANS • USA
BOSKO THE LUMBERJACK • 1931-32 • Harman Hugh • ANS • USA
BOSKO THE MUSKETEER • 1933 • Harman Hugh • ANS • USA
BOSKO THE SHEPHERDER • 1933 • Harman Hugh • ANS • USA
BOSKO THE SPEED KING • 1933 • Harman Hugh • ANS • USA
BOSKO'S DIZZY DATE • 1933 • Harman Hugh • ANS • USA
BOSKO'S DOG RACE • 1931-32 • Harman Hugh • ANS • USA
BOSKO'S EASTER EGGS • 1937 • Harman Hugh • ANS • USA
BOSKO'S FOX HUNT • 1931-32 • Harman Hugh • ANS • USA
BOSKO'S HOLIDAY • 1930 • Harman Hugh, Ising Rudolf • ANS • USA
BOSKO'S KNIGHT-MARE • 1933 • Harman Hugh • ANS • USA
BOSKO'S MECHANICAL MAN • 1933 • Harman Hugh • ANS • USA
BOSKO'S PARLOR PRANKS • 1934 • Harman Hugh • ANS • USA
BOSKO'S PARTY • 1931-32 • Harman Hugh • ANS • USA
BOSKO'S PICTURE SHOW • 1933 • Freleng Friz • ANS • USA
BOSKO'S SODA FOUNTAIN • 1931-32 • Harman Hugh • ANS • USA
BOSKO'S STORE • 1931-32 • Harman Hugh • ANS • USA
BOSKO'S WOODLAND DAZE • 1933 • Harman Hugh • ANS • USA
BOSKO'S ZOO • 1931-32 • Harman Hugh • ANS • USA
BOSNIAKEN see **BLUTSBRUDER** • 1935
BOSOM FRIEND, THE • 1982 • NTH
BOSQUE ALOJAMIENTO see **VILLA CARINO** • 1967
BOSQUE ANIMADO, EL • 1988 • Cuerda Jose Luis • SPN • ANIMATED FOREST, THE
BOSQUE DE ANCINES, EL • 1969 • Olea Pedro • SPN • WOLFMAN OF GALICIA, THE ○ BOSQUE DEL LOBO, EL ○ ANCINES WOODS, THE ○ WOLF FOREST, THE
BOSQUE DEL LOBO, EL see **BOSQUE DE ANCINES, EL** • 1969
BOSS • 1970 • Krolikiewicz Grzegorz • DOC • PLN
BOSS see **BOSS, IL** • 1973
BOSS see **BOSS NIGGER** • 1975
BOSS, IL • 1973 • Di Leo Fernando • ITL • MURDER INFERNO (UKN) ○ NEW MAFIA, THE (USA) ○ WIPEOUT! ○ BOSS
BOSS, THE • 1915 • Chautard Emile • USA
BOSS, THE • 1956 • Haskin Byron • USA
BOSS, THE see **KAOYAKU** • 1957
BOSS, THE see **JEFE, EL** • 1958
BOSS ARRIVES AT MIDDAY, THE see **12 UHR MITTAGS KOMMT DER BOSS** • 1968
BOSS COWBOY • 1934 • Adamson Victor • USA
BOSS DIDN'T SAY GOOD MORNING, THE • 1937 • Tourneur Jacques • SHT • USA
BOSS IN JAIL see **GOKUCHO NO KAOYAKU** • 1968
BOSS IS ALWAYS RIGHT, THE • 1960 • Kneitel Seymour • ANS • USA
BOSS NIGGER • 1975 • Arnold Jack • USA • BLACK BOUNTY KILLER (UKN) ○ BOSS
BOSS OF BIG TOWN, THE • 1942 • Dreifuss Arthur • USA
BOSS OF BOOM TOWN • 1945 • Taylor Ray • USA
BOSS OF BULLION CITY • 1941 • Taylor Ray • USA
BOSS OF CAMP 4, THE • 1922 • Van Dyke W. S. • USA
BOSS OF CIRCLE E RANCH, THE • 1910 • *Nestor* • USA
BOSS OF COPPERHEAD, THE • 1920 • Feeney Edward • SHT • USA
BOSS OF GUN CREEK, THE see **BOSS RIDER OF GUN CREEK, THE** • 1936
BOSS OF HANGTOWN MESA, THE • 1942 • Lewis Joseph H. • USA
BOSS OF JAPAN, A see **NIHON NO DON** • 1976
BOSS OF LITTLE ARCADY, THE see **HEAD MAN, THE** • 1928
BOSS OF LONE VALLEY see **BOSS OF LONELY VALLEY** • 1937
BOSS OF LONELY VALLEY • 1937 • Taylor Ray • USA • BOSS OF LONE VALLEY
BOSS OF LUCKY RANCH, THE • 1911 • *American* • USA
BOSS OF LUMBER CAMP NO.4, THE • 1912 • Apfel Oscar • USA
BOSS OF RAWHIDE • 1943 • Clifton Elmer • USA
BOSS OF RUSTLER'S ROOST, THE • 1928 • Maloney Leo • USA
BOSS OF THE EIGHTH, THE • 1914 • *Broncho* • USA
BOSS OF THE FAMILY, THE • 1917 • Beaudine William • SHT • USA
BOSS OF THE FLYING H • 1922 • Holt George • USA
BOSS OF THE KATY MINE, THE • 1912 • *Shaw Brinsley* • USA
BOSS OF THE LAZY Y, THE • 1918 • Smith Cliff • USA
BOSS OF THE RANCH • 1913 • *Ammex* • USA
BOSS RIDER OF GUN CREEK, THE • 1936 • Selander Lesley • USA • BOSS OF GUN CREEK, THE
BOSS SAID "NO", THE see **BLONDIE GOES TO COLLEGE** • 1942
BOSS' WIFE, THE see **BOSS'S WIFE, THE** • 1986
BOSSA NOVA • 1964 • Christensen Carlos Hugo • ARG
BOSS'S SON, THE • 1978 • Roth Bobby • USA
BOSS'S WIFE, THE • 1986 • Steinberg Ziggy • USA • BOSS' WIFE, THE
BOSSU, LE • Decourt Jean-Pierre • FRN
BOSSU, LE • 1914 • Heuze Andre • FRN
BOSSU, LE • 1922 • *Merelle Claude* • FRN
BOSSU, LE • 1925 • Kemm Jean • FRN
BOSSU, LE • 1934 • Sti Rene • FRN
BOSSU, LE • 1944 • Delannoy Jean • FRN
BOSSU, LE • 1959 • Hunebelle Andre • FRN, ITL
BOSSU DE ROME, LE (FRN) see **GOBBO, IL** • 1960
BOSTON AND KILBRIDE: THE CHINESE TYPEWRITER • 1979 • Antonio Lou • TVM • USA • CHINESE TYPEWRITER, THE
BOSTON BEANY • 1947 • Marcus Sid • ANS • USA
BOSTON BLACKIE • 1923 • Dunlap Scott R. • USA
BOSTON BLACKIE AND THE LAW • 1946 • Lederman D. Ross • USA • BLACKIE AND THE LAW (UKN)
BOSTON BLACKIE BOOKED ON SUSPICION • 1945 • Dreifuss Arthur • USA • BOOKED ON SUSPICION (UKN)
BOSTON BLACKIE GOES HOLLYWOOD • 1942 • Gordon Michael • USA • BLACKIE GOES HOLLYWOOD (UKN)
BOSTON BLACKIE'S CHINESE VENTURE • 1949 • Friedman Seymour • USA • CHINESE VENTURE (UKN)
BOSTON BLACKIE'S LITTLE PAL • 1918 • Hopper E. Mason • USA
BOSTON BLACKIE'S RENDEZVOUS • 1945 • Dreifuss Arthur • USA • BLACKIE'S RENDEZVOUS (UKN)
BOSTON NORMAL SCHOOL PAGEANT see **PAGEANT, DEDICATION, FESTIVAL** • 1908
BOSTON QUACKIE • 1957 • McKimson Robert • ANS • USA
BOSTON STRANGLER, THE • 1968 • Fleischer Richard • USA
BOSTON TEA PARTY, THE • 1908 • Porter Edwin S. • USA
BOSTON TEA PARTY, THE • 1915 • Nowland Eugene • USA
BOSTON WARRIORS see **HELL'S BELLES** • 1970
BOSTONIANS, THE • 1983 • Ivory James • UKN
BOSU WA ORE NO KENJU DE • 1966 • Murayama Shinji • JPN
BOSUN'S MATE, THE • 1914 • Shaw Harold • UKN
BOSUN'S MATE, THE • 1953 • Warren Richard • UKN
BOSUN'S WATCH, THE • 1911 • *O'Connor Edward* • USA
BOSUN'S YARN, THE • 1915 • *Excel* • UKN
BOSVELDER, DIE • 1958 • SAF
BOSVELDHOTEL • 1982 • SAF
BOSWELL SISTERS • 1933 • Brice Monte • SHT • USA
BOSZORKANYSZOMBAT • 1984 • Rozsa Janos • HNG • WITCHES' SABBATH
BOTAN • 1963 • Kuri Yoji • ANS • JPN • BUTTON, THE
BOTAN-DORO • 1955 • Nobuchi Akira • JPN • PEONIES AND STONE LANTERNS
BOTAN DORO see **KAIDAN BOTAN DORO** • 1968
BOTANDORO see **KAIDAN BOTAN DORO** • 1968
BOTANY BAY • 1953 • Farrow John • USA
BOTCHAN • 1935 • Yamamoto Kajiro • JPN
BOTCHAN JUYAKU • 1952 • Mizuko Harumi • JPN • BOY DIRECTOR
BOTCHAN SHAIN • 1954 • Yamamoto Kajiro • JPN • MR. VALIANT
BOTH ALONE see **SOLO LOS DOS** • 1968
BOTH BARRELS BLAZING • 1945 • Abrahams Derwin • USA • YELLOW STREAK, THE (UKN)
BOTH ENDS OF THE CANDLE (UKN) see **HELEN MORGAN STORY, THE** • 1957
BOTH SIDES OF LIFE • 1915 • Leonard Robert Z., Reynolds Lynn • USA
BOTH SIDES OF SEX see **SEI NO URAOMOTE** • 1968
BOTH SIDES OF THE LAW (USA) see **STREET CORNER** • 1953
BOTH VERY OLD see **BARDZO STARY OBOJE** • 1967
BOTH WITH NO MASTERS see **KAPWA WALANG PANGINOON** • 1968
BOTH YOU AND I see **ORE MO OMAE MO** • 1946
BOTHER ABOUT A BOMB, A • 1914 • Plumb Hay? • UKN
BOTHERED BATHERS, THE • 1907 • Martin J. H.? • UKN
BOTHERED BY A BEARD • 1946 • Emmett E. V. H. • UKN
BOTON DE ANCLA • 1947 • Torrado Ramon • SPN
BOTON DE ANCLA EN COLOR • 1960 • Lluch Miguel • SPN
BOTSCHAFTERIN, DIE • 1960 • Braun Harald • FRG
BOTSOTSO • 1979 • SAF
BOTSOTSO II • 1980 • SAF
BOTSOTSO III • 1983 • SAF
BOTTA DI VITA, UNA • 1988 • Oldoini Enrico • ITL • TASTE OF LIFE, A
BOTTA E RISPOSTA • 1951 • Soldati Mario • ITL
BOTTE I FARTEN • 1945 • Rodin Gosta • SWD, FNL • MATKALLA SEIKKAILUUN (FNL) ○ BILJETT TILL AVENTYRET
BOTTICELLI see **ALLEGORIA DI PRIMAVERA** • 1949
BOTTLE, THE • 1915 • Hepworth Cecil M. • UKN
BOTTLE, THE see **FLASKEN** • 1987
BOTTLE BABIES • 1924 • Roach Hal • SHT • USA
BOTTLE IMP, THE • 1917 • Neilan Marshall • USA
BOTTLE IMP, THE • 1952 • ANM • FRG
BOTTLE OF MUSK, A • 1913 • *Walters William* • USA
BOTTLE PARTY • 1936 • Hopwood R. A. • UKN
BOTTLED COURAGE • 1913 • Melford Mark? • UKN
BOTTLED ROMANCE, A • 1914 • *Kalem* • USA
BOTTLED SPIDER, THE • 1914 • *Darkfeather Mona* • USA
BOTTLED SUN see **SOL EN BOTELLITAS, EL** • 1986
BOTTLED UP • 1909 • *Pathe* • FRN
BOTTLENECK • 1979 • Comencini Luigi • ITL, FRN, FRG • GRAND EMBOUTEILLAGE, LE (FRN) ○ TRAFFIC JAM ○ INGORGO, UNA STORIA IMPOSSIBILE, L' ○ INGORGO, L' ○ STAU
BOTTLES • 1912 • *Beggs Lee* • USA
BOTTLES • 1936 • Harman Hugh • ANS • USA
BOTTOM LINE • 1989 • Gold Jeffrey • USA
BOTTOM LINE, THE (USA) see **ON AURA TOUT VU** • 1976
BOTTOM OF THE BOTTLE, THE • 1956 • Hathaway Henry • USA • BEYOND THE RIVER (UKN)
BOTTOM OF THE SEA, THE • 1914 • *Lubin* • ANM • USA
BOTTOM OF THE WELL, THE • 1917 • Robertson John S. • USA
BOTTOMLESS PIT • 1915 • *Hamilton Shorty* • USA
BOTTOMS see **YOKO ONO FILM NO.4** • 1967
BOTTOMS UP • 1934 • Butler David • USA
BOTTOMS UP! • 1960 • Zampi Mario • UKN
BOTTOMS UP • 1978 • Hoffman Sonia • SHT • ASL
BOTTOMS UP see **WHAT A WAY TO GO**
BOTTOMS UP see **CON EL CULO AL AIRE** • 1980
BOU VAN 'N NASIE, DIE • 1939 • Albrecht Joseph, Pienaar A. A. • SAF • THEY BUILT A NATION ○ BUILDING A NATION ○ SALUTE TO PIONEERS
BOUASSA, EL • 1944 • Salim Kamel • EGY • LES MISERABLES
BOUBA • 1988 • *Revach Zeev* • ISR
BOUBOU-CRAVATE • 1973 • Kamwa Daniel • SHT • CND
BOUBOUF • 1914 • Burguet Charles • FRN
BOUBOULE 1ER, ROI NEGRE • 1933 • Mathot Leon • FRN
BOUBOUROCHE • 1911 • Monca Georges • FRN
BOUBOUROCHE • 1922 • Diamant-Berger Henri • FRN
BOUCANIERS DES CARAIBES, LES see **BUCANEROS DEL CARIBE, LOS** • 1960
BOUCHE A BOUCHE • Depierre Charles • FRN
BOUCHE COUSUE • 1960 • Boyer Jean • FRN
BOUCHE-TROU, LE • 1976 • Roy Jean-Claude • FRN
BOUCHER, LE • 1969 • Chabrol Claude • FRN, ITL • TAGLIAGOLE, IL (ITL) ○ BUTCHER, THE (USA)
BOUCHER, LA STAR ET L'ORPHELINE, LE • 1973 • Savary Jerome • FRN
BOUCHES LASCIVES • Xavier Robert • FRN
BOUCLES see **LOOPS** • 1940
BOUCLETTE • 1918 • Mercanton Louis, Hervil Rene • FRN
BOUCLIER, LE • 1960 • Rouquier Georges • DCS • FRN
BOUDDI • 1970 • Cantrill Arthur, Cantrill Corinne • ASL
BOUDI • 1968 • Bose Dilip • IND • ELDER BROTHER'S WIFE
BOUDOIR BROTHERS, THE • 1932 • *Sennett Mack (P)* • SHT • USA
BOUDOIR BUTLER, THE • 1932 • Pearce A. Leslie • SHT • USA
BOUDOIR DIPLOMAT, THE • 1930 • St. Clair Malcolm • USA
BOUDOIR SECRETS • 1902 • Collins Alf? • UKN
BOUDOUKOU AN II • 1973 • Vodio N'Dabian • SHT • IVC
BOUDU SAUVE DES EAUX • 1932 • Renoir Jean • FRN • BOUDU SAVED FROM DROWNING (USA)
BOUDU SAVED FROM DROWNING (USA) see **BOUDU SAUVE DES EAUX** • 1932
BOUFFON, LE • 1909 • Jasset Victorin • FRN
BOUFOS, O • 1968 • Laskos Orestis • GRC • BOOBY, THE
BOUGHT • 1912 • *Majestic* • USA
BOUGHT • 1915 • O'Neil Barry • USA
BOUGHT • 1931 • Mayo Archie • USA
BOUGHT AND FOUGHT FOR • 1920 • Murphy Martin • SHT • USA
BOUGHT AND PAID FOR • 1916 • Knoles Harley • USA • FAUN, THE (UKN)
BOUGHT AND PAID FOR • 1922 • De Mille William C. • USA
BOUGNATS, LES • 1966 • Otero Manuel • SHT • FRN
BOUGNOUL, LE • 1974 • Moosmann Daniel • FRN • LIGNE 12, LA
BOUIF ERRANT, LE • 1926 • Hervil Rene • FRN
BOUJOU' SOLEIL • 1958 • Forest Leonard • DCS • CND
BOUKA • 1988 • M'Bala Gnoan • IVC
BOULANGER DE VALORGUE, LE • 1952 • Verneuil Henri • FRN, ITL • ME LI MANGIO VIVI! (ITL) ○ WILD OAT, THE (USA) ○ BAKER OF VALORGUE, THE
BOULANGERE DE MONCEAU, LA • 1962 • Rohmer Eric • SHT • FRN
BOULANGERIE MODELE, LA • 1907 • Melies Georges • FRN • BAKERS IN TROUBLE (USA)
BOULDER DAM • 1936 • McDonald Frank • USA
BOULDER WHAM • 1965 • Larriva Rudy • ANS • USA
BOULE DE GOMME • 1931 • Lacombe Georges • FRN
BOULE-DE-SUIF • 1945 • Christian-Jaque • FRN • ANGEL AND SINNER (USA)
BOULE DE SUIF see **PYSHKA** • 1934
BOULEVARD • 1960 • Duvivier Julien • FRN
BOULEVARD DES ASSASSINS • 1982 • Tioulong Boramy • FRN
BOULEVARD DES ITALIENS • 1896 • Melies Georges • FRN
BOULEVARD DU CRIME • 1955 • Gaveau Rene • FRN
BOULEVARD DU RHUM • 1971 • Enrico Robert • FRN, ITL, SPN • VIA DEL RHUM, LA (ITL) ○ WINNER TAKES ALL ○ RUM RUNNER
BOULEVARD DU RUN • 1971 • *Gaumont International* • MXC
BOULEVARD IN CANADA, THE • 1987 • May Derek • DOC • CND, NTH
BOULEVARD NIGHTS • 1979 • Pressman Michael • USA

BOULEVARD OF BROKEN DREAMS • 1988 • Amenta Pino • ASL
BOULEVARD SAINT-LAURENT MONTREAL see **MONTREAL MAIN** • 1973
BOULEVARD SPEED HOUNDS, THE • 1917 • George Burton • SHT • USA
BOULEVARDIER FROM THE BRONX, THE • 1936 • Freleng Friz • ANS • USA
BOULOT AVIATEUR • 1937 • de Canonge Maurice • FRN • FRIPONS, VOLEURS ET CIE
BOUM 2, LA • 1982 • Pinoteau Claude • FRN
BOUM, LA • 1980 • Pinoteau Claude • FRN • PARTY, THE (USA)
BOUM SUR PARIS! • 1953 • de Canonge Maurice • FRN
BOUNA • 1975 • Tsancov Villy • BUL • RIOT, THE
BOUNCER, THE • 1925 • Roach Hal • SHT • USA
BOUNCER BREAKS UP • 1953 • Chaffey Don • UKN
BOUNCING BABIES • 1929 • McGowan Robert • SHT • USA
BOUNCING BEAUTY see **PETIT BAIGNEUR, LE** • 1967
BOUNCING BUNNY • 1960 • Kneitel Seymour • ANS • USA
BOUND AND GAGGED • 1919 • Seitz George B. • SRL • USA
BOUND BY THE LEOPARD'S LOVE • 1915 • Chaudet Louis W. • USA
BOUND FOR CAIRO (USA) see **RUMBO AL CAIRO** • 1935
BOUND FOR GLORY • 1976 • Ashby Hal • USA
BOUND IN MOROCCO • 1918 • Dwan Allan • USA
BOUND ON THE WHEEL • 1915 • De Grasse Joseph • USA
BOUND TO BE HEARD • 1972 • Baker Baldwin Jr. • DOC • USA • CRUSADE FOR JAZZ
BOUND TO OCCUR • 1913 • Hopper E. Mason • USA
BOUND TO WIN • 1925 • *Taylor Leslie* • USA
BOUNDARIES OF THE HEART • 1988 • Marinos Lex • ASL
BOUNDARY HOUSE • 1918 • Hepworth Cecil M. • UKN
BOUNDARY LINE, THE • 1915 • Mackley Arthur • USA
BOUNDARY LINES • 1947 • Forrell Gene • ANS • USA
BOUNDARY RIDER, THE • 1914 • Wharton Leopold • USA
BOUNDER • 1912 • *Harte Betty* • USA
BOUNDING BERTIE'S BUNGALOW • 1913 • Plumb Hay? • UKN
BOUNTIFUL SUMMER (USA) see **SCHEDROYE LETO** • 1951
BOUNTY, THE see **MUTINY ON THE BOUNTY** • 1983
BOUNTY HUNTER, THE • 1954 • De Toth Andre • USA
BOUNTY HUNTERS, THE (UKN) see **INDIO BLACK, SAI CHE TI DICO: SEI UN GRAN FIGLIO DI..** • 1970
BOUNTY KILLER, THE • 1965 • Bennet Spencer Gordon • USA • BOUNTY KILLERS
BOUNTY KILLER, THE see **PRECIO DE UN HOMBRE, EL** • 1966
BOUNTY KILLER A TRINITA, UN • 1972 • Santaniello Oscar • ITL
BOUNTY KILLERS see **BOUNTY KILLER, THE** • 1965
BOUNTY MAN, THE • 1972 • Moxey John Llewellyn • TVM • USA
BOUQUET, THE • 1910 • *Essanay* • USA
BOUQUET, THE • 1915 • *Beery Wallace* • USA
BOUQUET DE JOIE • 1951 • Cam Maurice • FRN
BOUQUET D'ILLUSIONS • 1901 • Melies Georges • FRN • TRIPLE-HEADED LADY, THE (USA)
BOUQUET OF BARBED WIRE, A • 1976 • Wharmby Tony • MTV • UKN
BOUQUET OF STARS, A • Buchvarova Radka • ANS • BUL
BOUQUETIERE DE MONTMARTRE, LA • 1913 • Jasset Victorin • FRN
BOUQUETS FROM NICHOLAS (USA) see **INNOCENT, L'** • 1937
BOURBON ST. SHADOWS • 1962 • Parker Ben • USA
BOURBON STREET see **PASSION STREET, U.S.A.** • 1964
BOURBON STREET BLUES • 1978 • Sirk Douglas • SHT • FRG
BOURBON STREET SHADOWS see **INVISIBLE AVENGER** • 1958
BOURDELLE • 1950 • Lucot Rene • SHT • FRN
BOURE NAD TATRAMI • 1932 • *Stallich Jan (Ph)* • CZC • STORM IN TATRA
BOURGAULT, LES • 1940 • Tessier Albert • DCS • CND
BOURGEOIS GENTIL MEC, LE • 1969 • Andre Raoul • FRN
BOURGEOIS GENTILHOMME, LE • 1958 • Meyer Jean • FRN • WOULD-BE GENTLEMAN, THE (USA)
BOURGEOIS GENTILHOMME, LE • 1982 • Coggio Roger • FRN
BOURGEOIS SCANDAL, A see **SCANDALO PERBENE, UNO** • 1984
BOURGEOISE, LA • 1979 • Granier-Deferre Pierre • FRN
BOURGEOISE ET LE LOUBARD, LA • 1977 • Daniel Jean-Louis • FRN • TROTTOIR DES ALLONGES, LE
BOURGEOISE ET.. PUTE! • Kikoine Gerard • FRN
BOURGOGNE, LA • 1936 • Epstein Jean • FRN
BOURNE IDENTITY, THE • 1988 • Young Roger • MTV • USA
BOURNEVILLE STORY • 1952 • Reeve Leonard • DOC • UKN
BOURRACHON • 1935 • Guissart Rene • FRN
BOURRASQUE • 1935 • Billon Pierre • FRN • MOGHREB
BOURRASQUE see **WEST WIND: THE STORY OF TOM THOMPSON** • 1942
BOURRASQUE, LA • 1920 • Maudru Charles • FRN
BOURRASQUES see **MON AMI TIM** • 1932
BOURREAU, LE see **TETE DE TURC** • 1935
BOURREAU ATTENDRA, LE • 1960 • Vernay Robert • FRN
BOURREAU DES COEURS, LE • 1983 • Gion Christian • FRN
BOURREAU TURC, LE • 1904 • Melies Georges • FRN • TERRIBLE TURKISH EXECUTIONER, THE (USA) ○ TURKISH EXECUTIONER, THE ○ TERRIBLE TURKISH EXECUTIONER, OR IT SERVED HIM RIGHT, THE
BOURREAUX D'ENFANTS see **CLARA ET LES MECHANTS** • 1957
BOURSE, LA see **VALISE DIPLOMATIQUE, LA** • 1909
BOURSE ET LA VIE, LA • 1965 • Dansereau Jean • DOC • CND
BOURSE ET LA VIE, LA • 1965 • Mocky Jean-Pierre • FRN, ITL, FRG • YOUR MONEY OR YOUR LIFE (UKN) ○ GELD ODER LEBEN (FRG) ○ MONEY OR YOUR LIFE
BOURSE OU LA VIE, LA see **ADIEU LEONARD** • 1943
BOUSTAGUY, AL • 1968 • Kamal Hussein • EGY • POSTMAN, THE ○ BUST'AGI, AL-
BOUT, THE • Paul Robert William • UKN
BOUT DE CHOU • 1935 • Wulschleger Henry • FRN
BOUT DE LA ROUTE, LE • 1948 • Couzinet Emile • FRN
BOUT DE ZAN • 1912-16 • Feuillade Louis • SER • FRN
BOUT DE ZAN A LA GALE • 1914 • Feuillade Louis • FRN
BOUT DE ZAN A LE VER SOLITAIRE • 1914 • Feuillade Louis • FRN
BOUT DE ZAN AU BAL MASQUE • 1913 • Feuillade Louis • FRN
BOUT DE ZAN CHANTEUR AMBULANT • 1913 • Feuillade Louis • FRN
BOUT DE ZAN ECRIT SES MAXIMES • 1914 • Feuillade Louis • FRN
BOUT DE ZAN EN VACANCES • 1913 • Feuillade Louis • FRN
BOUT DE ZAN EN VILLEGIATURE • 1914 • Feuillade Louis • FRN
BOUT DE ZAN EPICIER • 1914 • Feuillade Louis • FRN
BOUT DE ZAN EST PATRIOTE • 1916 • Feuillade Louis • FRN
BOUT DE ZAN ET LA GAMINE • 1916 • Feuillade Louis • FRN
BOUT DE ZAN ET LA TORPILLE • 1916 • Feuillade Louis • FRN
BOUT DE ZAN ET LE CHEMINEAU • 1913 • Feuillade Louis • FRN
BOUT DE ZAN ET LE CHIEN DE POLICE • 1913 • Feuillade Louis • FRN
BOUT DE ZAN ET LE CIGARE • 1913 • Feuillade Louis • FRN
BOUT DE ZAN ET LE CRIME AU TELEPHONE • 1914 • Feuillade Louis • FRN
BOUT DE ZAN ET LE CROCODILE • 1913 • Feuillade Louis • FRN
BOUT DE ZAN ET LE FANTOME • 1915 • Feuillade Louis • FRN
BOUT DE ZAN ET LE LION • 1913 • Feuillade Louis • FRN
BOUT DE ZAN ET LE MANNEQUIN • 1913 • Feuillade Louis • FRN
BOUT DE ZAN ET LE PECHEUR • 1913 • Feuillade Louis • FRN
BOUT DE ZAN ET LE RAMONEUR • 1914 • Feuillade Louis • FRN
BOUT DE ZAN ET LE SAC DE NOIX • 1914 • Feuillade Louis • FRN
BOUT DE ZAN ET L'ESPION • 1914 • Feuillade Louis • FRN
BOUT DE ZAN ET SA PETITE AMIE • 1913 • Feuillade Louis • FRN
BOUT DE ZAN FAIT LES COMMISSIONS • 1913 • Feuillade Louis • FRN
BOUT DE ZAN FAIT UNE ENQUETE • 1913 • Feuillade Louis • FRN
BOUT DE ZAN LE CHIEN RATIER • 1913 • Feuillade Louis • FRN
BOUT DE ZAN PACIFISTE • 1914 • Feuillade Louis • FRN
BOUT DE ZAN PUGILISTE • 1914 • Feuillade Louis • FRN
BOUT DE ZAN REGARDE PAR LA FENETRE • 1913 • Feuillade Louis • FRN
BOUT DE ZAN REVIENT DU CIRQUE • 1912 • Feuillade Louis • FRN
BOUT DE ZAN S'AMUSE • 1913 • Feuillade Louis • FRN
BOUT DE ZAN SE VENGE • 1916 • Feuillade Louis • FRN
BOUT DE ZAN VAUDEVILLISTE • 1914 • Feuillade Louis • FRN
BOUT DE ZAN VEUT S'ENGAGER • 1916 • Feuillade Louis • FRN
BOUT DE ZAN VOLE UN ELEPHANT • 1913 • Feuillade Louis • FRN
BOUT DU LAC, LE • 1984 • Lagrange Jean-Jacques • SWT, FRN
BOUT WITH A TROUT, A • 1947 • Sparber I. • ANS • USA
BOUTIQUE, LA see **PIRANAS, LAS** • 1967
BOUTIQUE AUX ILLUSIONS, LA • 1939 • Severac Jacques • FRN
BOUTIQUE DES MIRACLES, LA see **TENDA DOS MILAGRES** • 1978
BOUTON D'OR • 1936 • Kapps Walter • FRN
BOUWSPELEMENT • 1963 • van der Linden Charles Huguenot • NTH • BUILDING GAME, THE
BOW BELLS • 1954 • Simmons Anthony • UKN
BOW OF QUEEN DOROTHY, THE see **LUK KRALOVNY DOROTKY** • 1970
BOW TO FIRE see **PAY TRIBUTE TO THE FIRE** • 1972
BOW WOW • 1922 • Jackman Fred • SHT • USA
BOW WOW see **VAU-VAU** • 1964
BOW WOWS, THE • 1922 • Roach Hal • SHT • USA
BOWERY, THE • 1933 • Walsh Raoul • USA
BOWERY AT MIDNIGHT • 1942 • Fox Wallace • USA
BOWERY BATTALION • 1951 • Beaudine William • USA
BOWERY BIMBOS • 1930 • Lantz Walter, Nolan William • ANS • USA
BOWERY BISHOP, THE • 1924 • Campbell Colin • USA
BOWERY BLITZKRIEG • 1941 • Fox Wallace • USA • STAND AND DELIVER (UKN)
BOWERY BLOODHOUNDS see **PRIVATE EYES** • 1953
BOWERY BOMBSHELL • 1946 • Karlson Phil • USA
BOWERY BOY • 1941 • Morgan William • USA
BOWERY BOYS • 1914 • Thornby Robert T. • USA
BOWERY BOYS see **HIGH SOCIETY** • 1955
BOWERY BOYS MEET THE MONSTERS • 1954 • Bernds Edward • USA
BOWERY BUCKAROOS • 1947 • Beaudine William • USA
BOWERY BUGS • 1949 • Davis Arthur • ANS • USA
BOWERY CHAMPS • 1944 • Beaudine William • USA
BOWERY CINDERELLA, A • 1927 • King Burton L. • USA • BOWERY ROSE (UKN)
BOWERY DAZE • 1934 • *Mintz Charles (P)* • ANS • USA
BOWERY KNIGHTS see **LOOSE IN LONDON** • 1953
BOWERY PEARL FISHERS, THE • 1912 • *Majestic* • USA
BOWERY ROSE (UKN) see **BOWERY CINDERELLA, A** • 1927
BOWERY TO BAGDAD • 1955 • Bernds Edward • USA
BOWERY TO BROADWAY • 1944 • Lamont Charles • USA
BOWL BEARER, THE • 1915 • *Burke Peggy* • USA
BOWL OF ROSES, A • 1914 • *Leonard Robert* • USA
BOWLED OVER • 1923 • Roach Hal • SHT • USA
BOWLER HAT, THE • 1960 • Lopes Fernando • SHT • UKN
BOWLING ALLEY, THE • 1963 • van der Heyde Nikolai • SHT • NTH • SKITTLE ALLEY, THE
BOWLING ALLEY CAT, THE • 1942 • Hanna William, Barbera Joseph • ANS • USA
BOWLING MATCH, THE • 1913 • Nicholls George, Sennett Mack (Spv) • USA
BOWLING TRICKS • 1948 • Barclay David • SHT • USA
BOX • 1971 • Hill Robert • SHT • ASL
BOX, THE • 1967 • Wolf Fred • ANS • JPN
BOX, THE • 1975 • Eddy Paul • ASL
BOX, THE see **LADAN** • 1968
BOX AND COX • 1913 • *Crystal* • USA
BOX BOY, THE • 1970 • *Xerxes Productions* • USA
BOX CAR BABY, THE • 1912 • *Wade Lillian* • USA
BOX CAR BANDIT • 1957 • Smith Paul J. • ANS • USA
BOX CAR BERTHA • 1972 • Scorsese Martin • USA • BOXCAR BERTHA
BOX CAR BLUES • 1930 • Harman Hugh, Ising Rudolf • ANS • USA
BOX CAR BRIDE, THE • 1914 • *Kalem* • USA
BOX COUCH, THE • 1914 • *Baggot King* • USA
BOX OF BANDITS, A • 1915 • *Victor* • USA
BOX OF CHOCOLATES, A • 1915 • O'Sullivan Tony • USA
BOX OF DELIGHTS, THE • 1984 • Rye Renny • MTV • UKN
BOX OF DREAMS see **BOITE AUX REVES, LA** • 1943
BOX OF MATCHES, A • 1914 • *Humpty Dumpty Films* • UKN
BOX OF REAL TURKISH, A • 1914 • Aylott Dave • UKN
BOX OF SUN, THE see **BOITE A SOLEIL, LA** • 1988
BOX OF TRICKS, A • 1917 • Steppling John • SHT • USA
BOX OFFICE • 1981 • Bogdanovich Josef • USA
BOXCAR BERTHA see **BOX CAR BERTHA** • 1972
BOXEADOR, EL • 1957 • Gazcon Gilberto • MXC
BOXER • 1977 • Terayama Shuji • JPN • BOXER, THE
BOXER see **BOKS** • 1963
BOXER, THE • 1976 • SAF
BOXER, THE see **UOMO DALLA PELLE DURA, UN** • 1972
BOXER, THE see **BOXER** • 1977
BOXER, THE (UKN) see **BOKSER** • 1967
BOXER A SMRT • 1962 • Solan Peter • CZC • BOXER AND DEATH, THE
BOXER ADVENTURE see **BOXER'S ADVENTURE, THE**
BOXER AND DEATH, THE see **BOXER A SMRT** • 1962
BOXER FROM SHANTUNG, THE • 1972 • Chang Ch'Eh, Pao Houeh-Li • HKG
BOXER REBELLION see **PA KUO LIEN-CHUN** • 1975
BOXERBRAUT, DIE • 1926 • Guter Johannes • FRG • BLONDES PREFER BOXERS
BOXER'S ADVENTURE, THE • *Pai Ying* • HKG • BOXER ADVENTURE
BOXERS GO TO PARADISE see **BOKSERI IDU U RAJ** • 1967
BOXERS SACKING A MISSION STATION • 1900 • *Harrison* • UKN
BOXES see **KUTIJE** • 1967
BOXES AND BOXERS • 1914 • *Prescott Vivian* • USA
BOXEUR PAR AMOUR see **MAX BOXEUR PAR AMOUR** • 1912
BOXIGANGA • 1967 • O'Horgan Tom, Gress Elsa • DNM
BOXING see **BOKS** • 1963
BOXING CATS • 1894 • *Edison* • USA
BOXING FEVER • 1909 • Coleby A. E. • UKN
BOXING FILM • 1900 • Barrett Franklyn • DOC • NZL
BOXING GLOVES • 1929 • Mack Anthony, McGowan Robert • SHT • USA
BOXING KANGAROO, THE • 1896 • Acres Birt • UKN
BOXING KANGAROO, THE • 1920 • Fleischer Dave • ANS • USA
BOXING MATCH see **MATCH DE BOXE (ECOLE DE JOINVILLE)** • 1897
BOXING MATCH: OR, GLOVE CONTEST • 1896 • Acres Birt • UKN
BOXING RING, THE • 1959 • Kostelac Nikola • ANM • YGS • RING, THE
BOXING WAITER, THE • 1909 • Collins Alf? • UKN
BOXY • 1967 • Delgado Cruz • ASS • SPN
BOXY CAMPEON DEL TORTAZO • 1967 • Delgado Cruz • SHT • SPN
BOXY, REY DEL K.O. • 1970 • Delgado Cruz • ANS • SPN
BOY • 1914 • *Jackson Charles* • USA
BOY • 1924 • Perojo Benito • SPN
BOY see **SHONEN** • 1969
BOY, THE see **NINO, EL** • 1968
BOY.. A GIRL, A • 1969 • Derek John • USA • SUN IS UP, THE
BOY, A GIRL AND A BIKE, A • 1949 • Smart Ralph • UKN
BOY, A GIRL AND A DOG, A • 1946 • Kline Herbert • USA • LUCKY (UKN)
BOY, A GUN AND BIRDS, A • 1940 • Harrison Ben • ANS • USA
BOY AGUILA • 1967 • Gallardo Cesar Chat • PHL • EAGLE BOY
BOY AND A BALL, A see **DJECAK I LOPTA** • 1960
BOY AND A CAMEL, A see **HAGAMAL VEHAYELED** • 1968
BOY AND A GIRL, A see **RAGAZZO E UNA RAGAZZA, UN** • 1984
BOY AND A PIGEON, A see **MALCHIK I GOLUB** • 1958
BOY AND HIS DOG, A • 1936 • *Mintz Charles (P)* • ANS • USA
BOY AND HIS DOG, A • 1975 • Jones L. Q. • USA
BOY AND HIS KITE, THE • 1909 • Fitzhamon Lewin • UKN
BOY AND ONE STRAW, A • 1967 • Watanabe Kuzohiko • ANS • JPN
BOY AND THE BALL see **DJECAK I LOPTA** • 1960
BOY AND THE BRIDGE, THE • 1959 • McClory Kevin • UKN
BOY AND THE CHEESE, THE • 1914 • Bramble A. V. • UKN
BOY AND THE CONVICT, THE • 1909 • Aylott Dave? • UKN
BOY AND THE GIRL, THE • 1912 • *Edison* • USA
BOY AND THE GIRL FROM NORTH AND SOUTH CAROLINA, THE • 1946 • Crouch William Forest • SHT • USA
BOY AND THE KITE, THE see **POJKEN OCH DRACKEN** • 1961
BOY AND THE LAUGHING DOG, THE see **GOODBYE, MY LADY** • 1956
BOY AND THE LAW, THE • 1914 • Stahl John M. • USA
BOY AND THE PELICAN, THE • 1964 • Gurrin Geoffrey • UKN
BOY AND THE PHYSIC, THE • 1910 • Rains Fred • UKN
BOY AND THE PIGEON, THE see **MALCHIK I GOLUB** • 1958
BOY AND THE PIRATES, THE • 1960 • Gordon Bert I. • USA
BOY AND THE PURSE, THE • 1909 • Fitzhamon Lewin • UKN
BOY AND THE SNOW GOOSE, THE • 1984 • Thomas Gayle • CND
BOY AND THE VIOLIN, THE see **DECAK I VIOLINA** • 1976
BOY AND THE WAVES, THE • 1962 • Slesicki Wladyslaw • DOC • PLN
BOY AND THE WIND, THE see **MENINO E O VENTO, O** • 1967
BOY AND THE WOLF, THE • 1943 • Ising Rudolf • ANS • USA

BOY AND THREE MOTHERS, A see **HAHA SANNIN** • 1958
BOY AND WAVES see **PLYNA TRATWY** • 1962
BOY BANDITS, THE • 1907 • *Paul R. W.* • UKN
BOY BUILT CITY, A • 1918 • *Boy City Film* • SHT • USA
BOY CALLED CHARLIE BROWN, A (UKN) see **BOY NAMED CHARLIE BROWN, A** • 1969
BOY CALLED THIRD BASE, THE see **SADO** • 1977
BOY CRAZY • 1922 • Seiter William A. • USA
BOY CRIED MURDER, THE • 1966 • Breakston George • UKN, FRG, YGS • DECAK JE VIKAO UBISTVO (YGS) ○ JUNGE SCHRIE MORD, EIN (FRG)
BOY DETECTIVE • 1908 • *Bitzer Billy (Ph)* • USA
BOY DETECTIVES, THE see **CHIISANA TANEI TACHI** • 1956
BOY DETECTIVES, THE see **SHONEN TANTEIDAN** • 1959
BOY, DID I GET A WRONG NUMBER! • 1966 • Marshall George • USA
BOY DIRECTOR see **BOTCHAN JUYAKU** • 1952
BOY-DOLL see **DOCKPOJKEN** • 1990
BOY FRIEND • 1939 • Tinling James • USA
BOY FRIEND, THE • 1926 • Bell Monta • USA
BOY FRIEND, THE • 1928 • Guiol Fred • SHT • USA
BOY FRIEND, THE • 1971 • Russell Ken • UKN
BOY FROM.., THE see **GARCON SAVOYARD, LE** • 1967
BOY FROM BARNARDO'S, THE see **LORD JEFF** • 1938
BOY FROM CALABRIA, A see **RAGAZZO DI CALABRIA, UN** • 1988
BOY FROM HELL, THE see **BLOOD SPELL** • 1987
BOY FROM INDIANA, THE • 1950 • Rawlins John • USA • BLAZE OF GLORY (UKN)
BOY FROM OKLAHOMA, THE • 1954 • Curtiz Michael • USA
BOY FROM STALINGRAD, THE • 1943 • Salkow Sidney • USA
BOY FROM THE GILDED EAST, THE • 1916 • Chaudet Louis W. • USA
BOY FROM THE NAVY, THE see **KAIKOKO DANJI** • 1926
BOY FROM THE PLANTATIONS, THE see **MENINO DE ENGENHO** • 1966
BOY FROM THE POORHOUSE, THE see **THAT BOY FROM THE POORHOUSE** • 1914
BOY GIRL, THE • 1917 • Stevens Edwin • USA
BOY GOES TO BISKRA, THE • 1924 • Brunel Adrian • SHT • UKN
BOY IN BLUE, THE • 1985 • Jarrott Charles • CND
BOY IN BLUE, THE see **KNABE IN BLAU, DER** • 1919
BOY IN THE BARREL • 1903 • *Bitzer Billy (Ph)* • USA
BOY IN THE PLASTIC BUBBLE, THE • 1976 • Kleiser Randall • TVM • USA
BOY IN THE TREE, THE see **POJKEN I TRADET** • 1961
BOY INTO MAN • 1970 • Eden Mark • USA
BOY IS TEN FEET TALL, A see **SAMMY GOING SOUTH** • 1963
BOY KUMASENU • 1951 • Graham Sean • GHN
BOY LIKE ME, A see **MUCHACHO COMO YO, UN** • 1968
BOY LIKE THAT, A see **ZHIVET TAKOI PAREN** • 1964
BOY MEETS BABY see **BETWEEN US GIRLS** • 1942
BOY MEETS GIRL • 1938 • Bacon Lloyd • USA
BOY MEETS GIRL • 1983 • Carax Leos • FRN
BOY MEETS GIRL see **KILLE OCH EN TJEJ, EN** • 1974
BOY MEETS JOY • 1939 • Staub Ralph • USA
BOY MESSENGER, THE • 1920 • Sandground Maurice • UKN
BOY MILLIONAIRE, THE • 1936 • Sandberg Anders W. • DNM
BOY NAMED CHARLIE BROWN, A • 1969 • Melendez Bill • ANM • USA • BOY CALLED CHARLIE BROWN, A (UKN)
BOY NEXT DOOR, THE see **TO FIND A MAN** • 1972
BOY OF FLANDERS, A • 1924 • Schertzinger Victor • USA
BOY OF GOLD • 1952 • Pojar Bretislav • CZC • BIG FISH, THE
BOY OF GRANITE • 1978 • Peippo Antti • FNL
BOY OF IRELAND • 1971 • Hickey Kieran • DOC • IRL
BOY OF MINE • 1923 • Beaudine William • USA
BOY OF THE DARDANELLES • 1923 • Darling Roy • ASL
BOY OF THE DISTRICT, THE see **EBN EL HETTA** • 1968
BOY OF THE MUDDY SHORE • 1982 • Chang Hyong-Il • MTV • SKR
BOY OF THE REVOLUTION, A • 1911 • *Cruze James* • USA
BOY OF THE STREETS • 1938 • Nigh William • USA
BOY OF THE STREETS, A • 1927 • Hunt Charles J. • USA
BOY OF THE WORLD see **PAW** • 1959
BOY OF TWO WORLDS see **PAW** • 1959
BOY, OH, BOY • 1932 • Edwards Harry J. • SHT • USA
BOY ON A DOLPHIN • 1957 • Negulesco Jean • USA
BOY OR GIRL? • 1966 • Tyrlova Hermina • ANM • CZC • BOY OR THE GIRL, THE
BOY OR THE GIRL, THE see **BOY OR GIRL?** • 1966
BOY PARTISANS • 1951 • NKR
BOY RANGERS, THE • 1912 • *Edison* • USA
BOY RENTS GIRL see **CAN'T BUY ME LOVE** • 1987
BOY RIDER, THE • 1927 • King Louis • USA
BOY SCOUT • 1921 • Dyer Anson • ANM • UKN
BOY SCOUT DETECTIVE, THE • 1914 • *Conqueror Films* • UKN
BOY SCOUTS • 1916 • *Unicorn* • USA
BOY SCOUTS • 1922 • Dudley Bernard • UKN
BOY SCOUTS BE PREPARED • 1917 • Nash Percy • UKN • BOY SCOUTS TO THE RESCUE (USA)
BOY SCOUT'S DREAM: OR, HOW BILLIE CAPTURED THE KAISER, THE • 1917 • *Brum Films* • SHT • UKN
BOY SCOUTS TO THE RESCUE • 1918 • SER • USA
BOY SCOUTS TO THE RESCUE, THE • 1911 • *Champion* • USA
BOY SCOUTS TO THE RESCUE, THE • 1913 • *Nestor* • USA
BOY SCOUTS TO THE RESCUE (USA) see **BOY SCOUTS BE PREPARED** • 1917
BOY SLAVES • 1939 • Wolfson P. J. • USA • PURE IN MIND, THE
BOY SOLDIER • 1987 • Francis Karl • UKN
BOY TAKES GIRL • 1983 • Bat-Adam Michal • ISR
BOY TEN FEET TALL, A (USA) see **SAMMY GOING SOUTH** • 1963
BOY, THE GIRL AND THE AUTO, THE • 1916 • Davey Horace • SHT • USA
BOY TROUBLE • 1938 • Archainbaud George • USA • PARENTS ON PROBATION
BOY TURNS MAN, THE • Kirkov Lyudmil • BUL
BOY WANTED • 1913 • Williams C. Jay • USA
BOY! WHAT A GIRL • 1947 • Leonard Arthur • USA
BOY WHO BECOMES AN ORPHAN, THE see **GODHULI** • 1978
BOY WHO CAME BACK, THE see **FUMIHAZUSHITA HARU** • 1958
BOY WHO CAUGHT A CROOK, THE • 1961 • Cahn Edward L. • USA
BOY WHO COULD FLY, THE • 1986 • Castle Nick • USA
BOY WHO CRIED WEREWOLF, THE • 1973 • Juran Nathan • USA
BOY WHO CRIED WOLF, THE • 1917 • Griffith Edward H. • USA
BOY WHO DISAPPEARED, THE see **DRENGEN DER FORSVANT** • 1984
BOY WHO DRANK TOO MUCH, THE • 1980 • Freedman Jerrold • TVM • USA
BOY WHO FOLLOWED THE SUN, THE see **DJECAK JE ISAO ZA SUNCEM** • 1983
BOY WHO HAD EVERYTHING, THE • 1984 • Wallace Stephen • ASL
BOY WHO LEFT HOME TO FIND OUT ABOUT THE SHIVERS, THE • 1985 • Clifford Graeme • USA
BOY WHO LOVED HORSES, THE see **HVIDE HINGST, DEN** • 1962
BOY WHO NEVER WAS, THE • 1979 • Godwin Frank • UKN
BOY WHO SAW THROUGH, THE • 1958 • Bute Mary Ellen • SHT • USA
BOY WHO STOLE A MILLION, THE • 1961 • Crichton Charles • UKN
BOY WHO STOLE AN ELEPHANT, THE • Caffey Michael
BOY WHO STOPPED NIAGARA, THE • 1946 • McFarlane Leslie • CND
BOY WHO TALKED TO BADGERS, THE • 1975 • Nelson Gary • TVM • USA
BOY WHO TURNED YELLOW, THE • 1972 • Powell Michael • UKN
BOY WHO WANTED TO LEARN FEAR • 1935 • *Gebruder Diehl* • ANS • FRG
BOY WITH A FLUTE • 1964 • Tully Montgomery • UKN
BOY WITH A FUTURE, A see **GARCON PLEIN D'AVENIR, UN** • 1965
BOY WITH GREEN HAIR, THE • 1948 • Losey Joseph • USA
BOY WITH THE BLACK HORSE, THE see **KUROUMA NO DANSHICHI** • 1948
BOY WITH THE DRUM, THE see **NINO DEL TAMBOR, EL** • 1981
BOY WITH TWO HEADS, THE • 1974 • Ingrams Jonathan • UKN
BOY WOODBURN • 1922 • Newall Guy • UKN
BOYANA MASTER, THE • 1956 • Topouzanov Christo • ANM • BUL
BOYARS' PLOT, THE see **IVAN THE TERRIBLE PART 2** • 1946
BOYCOTT • 1985 • Baaf Mohsen Makhmal • IRN
BOYCOTTED BABY, THE • 1917 • *Hardy Babe* • SHT • USA
BOYD RAEBURN AND HIS ORCHESTRA • 1947 • *Columbia* • SHT • USA
BOYD'S SHOP • 1960 • Cass Henry • UKN
BOYEVOYE KINOSBORNIK N.1 • 1941 • Gerasimov Sergei • USS • FIGHTING FILM ALBUM NO.1 ○ WAR NEWSREEL NO.1
BOYFRIENDS AND GIRLFRIENDS (USA) see **AMI DE MON AMIE, L'** • 1987
BOYHOOD DAZE • 1957 • Jones Charles M. • ANS • USA
BOYHOOD HE FORGOT, THE • 1917 • Weber Lois, Smalley Phillips • SHT • USA
BOYHOOD OF AN AGRICULTURAL PIONEER see **NINOMIYA SONTOKU NO SHONENJIDAI** • 1957
BOYHOOD OF DR. NOGUCHI, THE see **NOGUCHI HIDEYO NO SHONEN JIDAI** • 1956
BOYHOOD OF THE JUDO CHAMPION see **YAMASHITA SHONEN MONOGATARI** • 1985
BOYICHI AND THE SUPERMONSTER see **GAMERA TAI GYAOS** • 1967
BOYKOTT • 1930 • Land Robert • FRG • PRIMANEREHRE
BOYOKU NO SHIKIBUTON • 1967 • Watanabe Yuzuru • JPN • COLOURFUL BED OF VIOLENT DESIRE
BOYS • 1912 • *Majestic* • USA
BOYS • 1972 • Stashevskaya Ye. • USS
BOYS see **DRENGE** • 1976
BOYS, THE • 1962 • Furie Sidney J. • UKN
BOYS, THE • 1970 • Shakhmalieva A. • USS
BOYS, THE see **CHICOS, LOS** • 1959
BOYS, THE see **POJAT** • 1962
BOYS AND GIRLS • 1969 • Ne'Eman Yehuda • ISR
BOYS AND GIRLS • 1983 • McBrearty Don • SHT • CND
BOYS AND GIRLS TOGETHER • 1979 • Marsden Ralph • UKN
BOYS' BASEBALL TEAM OF SETOUCHI see **SETOUCHI SHONEN YAKYUDAN** • 1984
BOY'S BEST FRIEND, A • 1911 • *Imp* • USA
BOYS FROM BEVERLY HILLS, THE see **UPSTAIRS ROOM, THE** • 1970
BOYS FROM BRAZIL, THE • 1978 • Schaffner Franklin J. • USA, UKN
BOYS FROM BROOKLYN, THE see **BELA LUGOSI MEETS A BROOKLYN GORILLA** • 1952
BOYS FROM FENGKUEI, THE see **FENG-KUEI-LAI-TE JEN** • 1983
BOYS FROM LENINGRAD, THE • 1955 • Timoshenko S. • USS
BOYS FROM OUR COURTYARD see **REBYATA S NASHEGO DVORA** • 1959
BOYS FROM SYRACUSE, THE • 1940 • Sutherland A. Edward • USA
BOYS FROM THE LAKE OF CRANES, THE see **JUNGEN VOM KRANICHSEE, DIE** • 1950
BOYS FROM THE SEA, THE see **KAIKOKO DANJI** • 1926
BOYS FROM THE SOUTH OF STOCKHOLM see **SODERPOJKAR** • 1941
BOYS FROM THE SQUARE see **FIUK A TERROL** • 1968
BOYS FROM THE WEST COAST see **VESTERHAVSDRENGE** • 1950
BOY'S HALF HOLIDAY, THE • 1907 • Cooper Arthur • UKN
BOYS IN BLUE, THE • 1983 • Guest Val • UKN
BOYS IN BROWN • 1949 • Tully Montgomery • UKN
BOYS IN CHAINS • 1969 • USA
BOYS IN COMPANY C, THE • 1978 • Furie Sidney J. • USA, HKG
BOYS IN THE BAND, THE • 1970 • Friedkin William • USA
BOYS IN THE DARK see **DRENGE** • 1976
BOYS IN THE ISLAND • 1988 • Bennett Geoffrey • ASL
BOYS IN THE STREETS see **FIUK A TERROL** • 1968
BOYS IN UNIFORM see **KADETTEN** • 1931
BOY'S LIFE see **STAYING THE SAME** • 1989
BOYS NEXT DOOR, THE • 1985 • Spheeris Penelope • USA • NO APPARENT MOTIVE ○ BLIND RAGE ○ KILLERS
BOYS' NIGHT OUT • 1962 • Gordon Michael • USA
BOYS OF I.O.U., THE • 1914 • North Wilfred, Van Wally • USA
BOYS OF PAUL STREET, THE • 1969 • Fabri Zoltan • USA, HNG • PAL UTCAI FIUK, A (HNG)
BOYS OF STORHOLMEN, THE see **POJKARNA PA STORHOLMEN** • 1932
BOYS OF THE CITY • 1940 • Lewis Joseph H. • USA • GHOST CREEPS, THE
BOYS OF THE OLD BRIGADE • 1945 • Williamson A. Stanley • UKN
BOYS OF THE OLD BRIGADE, THE • 1916 • Batley Ernest G. • UKN
BOYS OF THE OTTER PATROL • 1918 • Nash Percy • UKN
BOYS OF TOPSY-TURVY RANCH, THE • 1910 • *Nestor* • USA
BOYS OF VIA PANISPERNA, THE see **RAGAZZI DI VIA PANISPERNA, I** • 1988
BOYS' RANCH • 1946 • Rowland Roy • USA
BOY'S REFORMATORY • 1939 • Bretherton Howard • USA
BOYS' SCHOOL (USA) see **DISPARUS DE SAINT-AGIL, LES** • 1938
BOYS TO BOARD • 1923 • McNamara Tom • SHT • USA
BOYS TOWN • 1938 • Taurog Norman • USA
BOY'S VILLAGE • 1963 • Kelly Ron • CND
BOYS WILL BE BOYS • 1904 • Mottershaw Frank • UKN
BOYS WILL BE BOYS • 1909 • *Lubin* • USA
BOYS WILL BE BOYS • 1911 • Bouwmeester Theo • UKN
BOYS WILL BE BOYS • 1915 • Totten Joseph Byron • USA
BOYS WILL BE BOYS • 1921 • Badger Clarence • USA
BOYS WILL BE BOYS • 1932 • Stevens George • SHT • USA
BOYS WILL BE BOYS • 1935 • Beaudine William • UKN • NARKOVER
BOYS WILL BE BOYS see **DEAR BOYS HOME FOR THE HOLIDAYS, THE** • 1903
BOYS WILL BE GIRLS • 1937 • Pratt Gilbert • UKN
BOYS WILL BE JOYS • 1925 • Roach Hal • SHT • USA
BOYS WITH THE GIRLS, THE see **CHICOS CON LAS CHICAS, LOS** • 1967
BOZARTS • 1969 • Giraldeau Jacques • DOC • CND
BOZKIRLAR SAHINI TARGAN • 1968 • Aslan Mehmet • TRK • TARGAN, THE FALCON OF THE STEPPES
BOZKURTLAR GELIYOR • 1967 • Yoruklu Cavit • TRK • BOZKURTS ARE COMING, THE
BOZKURTLARIN INTIKAMI • 1967 • Yoruklu Cavit • TRK • VENGEANCE OF THE BOZKURTS, THE
BOZKURTS ARE COMING, THE see **BOZKURTLAR GELIYOR** • 1967
BOZO AND BIMBO • 1984 • SAF
BOZO ARRIVES • 1913 • *Gebhardt George* • USA
BOZSKA EMA • 1983 • Krejcik Jiri • CZC • DIVINE EMMA, THE (USA)
BRA FLICKA REDER SIG SJALV • 1913 • Sjostrom Victor • SWD • GOOD GIRL SHOULD SOLVE HER OWN PROBLEMS, A ○ CLEVER GIRL TAKES CARE OF HERSELF, A
BRA MANNINSKOR • 1937 • Sinding Leif • NRW
BRACCIA APERTE, LE • 1922 • Gallone Carmine • ITL
BRACCIA SI, UOMINI NO • 1971 • Ammann Peter, Burri Rene • SWT
BRACCIO VIOLENTO DELLA MALA, IL • 1979 • Garrone Sergio • ITL
BRACE UP • 1918 • Clifton Elmer • USA
BRACELET -2 see **BRASLYET -2** • 1968
BRACELET, THE • 1913 • *Reliance* • USA
BRACELET, THE • 1914 • *Balboa* • USA
BRACELET DE BRONZE, LE • 1974 • Aw Tidiane • SNL
BRACELET DE LA MARQUISE, LE • 1911 • Feuillade Louis • FRN
BRACELETS • 1931 • Collins Sewell • UKN
BRACERO DE ANO, EL • 1963 • Baledon Rafael • MXC
BRACONNIER DE DIEU, LE • 1982 • Darras Jean-Pierre • FRN
BRACONNIERS, LES • 1903 • Blache Alice • FRN
BRACOS DE SOLOGNE • 1933 • Aurenche Jean (c/d) • SHT • FRN
BRAD • 1977 • Noyce Phil • DCS • ASL
BRADDOCK: MISSING IN ACTION III • 1988 • Norris Aaron • USA • MISSING IN ACTION 3
BRADFORD'S DREAM • 1910 • Porter Edwin S. • USA
BRADLEY MASEN STORY, THE see **UNKNOWN MAN, THE** • 1951
BRADMAN ERA, THE • 1983 • Thoms Albie • DOC • ASL
BRADO RETUMBANTE • 1968 • Diegues Carlos • BRZ • RESOUNDING CRY, THE
BRADY GIRLS GET MARRIED, THE • 1981 • Baldwin Peter • TVM • USA
BRADY'S ESCAPE see **LONG RIDE, THE** • 1983
BRAENDENDE SPORGSMAL, DET • 1943 • O'Fredericks Alice • DNM
BRAGA'S DOUBLE • 1915 • *Lewis Sheldon* • USA
BRAGGART, OR WHAT HE SAID HE WOULD DO AND WHAT HE REALLY DID, THE • 1908 • *Vitagraph* • USA
BRAGG'S LITTLE POKER GAME • 1917 • *Sparkle* • USA
BRAGG'S NEW SUIT • 1913 • Seay Charles M. • USA
BRAGHE DEL PADRONE, LE • 1978 • Mogherini Flavio • ITL
BRAHMA DIAMOND, THE • 1909 • Griffith D. W. • USA
BRAHMACHARI • 1968 • Sonie Bhappi • IND • CELIBATE
BRAHMANE ET LE PAPILLON, LE see **CHRYSALIDE ET LE PAPILLON D'OR, LA** • 1901
BRAHMARATHAM • 1949 • *Agasthya Sree* • IND • NAGUSHACHARITA
BRAHMIN AND THE BUTTERFLY, THE (USA) see **CHRYSALIDE ET LE PAPILLON D'OR, LA** • 1901
BRAHMIN'S MIRACLE, THE • 1908 • *Pathe* • FRN
BRAHM'S HUNGARIAN DANCE • 1931 • Fischinger Oskar • ANS • FRG • STUDIE 9
BRAID, THE • 1912 • *Comet* • USA
BRAIDS see **PLETENICE** • 1974
BRAIN 17 • 1985 • USA
BRAIN, THE • 1988 • Hunt Ed • CND, USA

BRAIN, THE see **CERVEAU, LE** • 1968
BRAIN, THE see **BRAIN OF BLOOD** • 1971
BRAIN, THE (USA) see **VENGEANCE** • 1962
BRAIN CREATURE see **MIND KILLER** • 1987
BRAIN DAMAGE • 1988 • Henenlotter Frank • USA
BRAIN DAMAGE see **DEATH WARMED UP** • 1984
BRAIN DEAD • 1989 • Jackson Peter • NZL
BRAIN EATERS, THE • 1958 • Ve Sota Bruno • USA • KEEPERS OF THE EARTH, THE ○ KEEPERS, THE
BRAIN FROM PLANET AROUS, THE • 1958 • Juran Nathan • USA
BRAIN INSPECTOR, THE see **RETAPEUR DE CERVELLE, LE** • 1911
BRAIN MACHINE, THE • 1955 • Hughes Ken • UKN
BRAIN MACHINE, THE • 1972 • Houck Joy N. Jr. • USA • GRAY MATTER ○ MIND MACHINE ○ MIND WARP ○ GREY MATTER
BRAIN OF BLOOD • 1971 • Adamson Al • USA • CREATURE'S REVENGE, THE ○ BRAIN, THE
BRAIN OF FRANKENSTEIN, THE see **ABBOTT AND COSTELLO MEET FRANKENSTEIN** • 1948
BRAIN STORM • 1927 • Roberts Stephen • SHT • USA
BRAIN-STORM see **HIRNBRENNEN** • 1982
BRAIN THAT WOULDN'T DIE, THE • 1962 • Green Joseph • USA • HEAD THAT WOULDN'T DIE, THE ○ BLACK DOOR, THE
BRAIN TRANSPLANT see **CRYSTALBRAIN L'UOMO DAL CERVELLO DI CRISTALLO** • 1970
BRAINIAC, THE (USA) see **BARON DEL TERROR, EL** • 1961
BRAINKILL see **QUALCUNO DIETRO LA PORTA** • 1971
BRAINS AND DRAINS • 1912 • *Selig* • USA
BRAINS REPAIRED see **RETAPEUR DE CERVELLE, LE** • 1911
BRAINS VS. BRAWN • 1912 • *Chamberlin Riley* • USA
BRAINSNATCHER(S), THE see **MAN WHO CHANGED HIS MIND, THE** • 1936
BRAINSTORM • 1917 • Edwards Harry J. • SHT • USA
BRAINSTORM • 1965 • Conrad William • USA
BRAINSTORM • 1983 • Trumbull Douglas • USA
BRAINWASH • 1968 • Abalos Ruben • PHL
BRAINWASH • 1972 • Bijlsma Ronald • SHT • NTH
BRAINWASH • 1981 • Roth Bobby • USA • NAKED WEEKEND, THE ○ CIRCLE OF POWER ○ MYSTIQUE
BRAINWASHED see **DROIT D'AIMER, LE** • 1972
BRAINWASHED (USA) see **SCHACHNOVELLE, DIE** • 1960
BRAINWAVES • 1982 • Lommel Ulli • USA • SHADOW OF DEATH
BRAKE FLUID • 1970 • Davies Brian • SHT • ASL
BRAKER • 1985 • Lobl Victor • TVM • USA
BRAKING IN THE SKY • 1989 • Buturlin Victor • USS
BRAM STOKER'S COUNT DRACULA see **CONDE DRACULA, EL** • 1970
BRAMBLE BUSH, THE • 1919 • Terriss Tom • USA
BRAMBLE BUSH, THE • 1960 • Petrie Daniel • USA
BRAMBLE BUSH, THE • 1967 • Hani Susumu • JPN
BRAMY RAJU (YGS) see **VRATA RAJA** • 1967
BRANCALEONE ALLA CRUSADA see **BRANCALEONE ALLE CROCIATE** • 1970
BRANCALEONE ALLE CROCIATE • 1970 • Monicelli Mario • ITL, ALG • BRANCALEONE AT THE CRUSADES ○ BRANCALEONE ALLA CRUSADA
BRANCALEONE AT THE CRUSADES see **BRANCALEONE ALLE CROCIATE** • 1970
BRANCH ET BRANCH • 1974 • Longpre Bernard • SHT • CND
BRANCH NUMBER 37 • 1915 • Beranger George A. • USA
BRANCHE MORTE, LA • 1927 • Guarino Joseph • FRN
BRANCHES • 1970 • Emshwiller Ed • USA
BRANCHES A SAINT-TROPEZ, LES • 1983 • Pecas Max • FRN • DESSOUS DE RAMATUELLE, LES
BRANCO DI VIGLIACCHI, UN • 1962 • Taglioni Fabrizio • ITL, FRN
BRAND, THE • 1912 • Dwan Allan • USA
BRAND, THE • 1914 • Buel Kenean • USA
BRAND, THE • 1919 • Barker Reginald • USA
BRAND, THE see **BRAND OF SHAME** • 1968
BRAND BLOTTER, THE • 1912 • Stedman Marshall • USA
BRAND BLOTTER, THE • 1920 • *Gibson Hoot* • SHT • USA
BRAND BLOTTERS • 1915 • *Payne Edna* • USA
BRAND-BORGE RYKKER UD • 1975 • Mossin Ib • DNM
BRAND FROM THE BURNING, A • 1912 • *Republic* • USA
BRAND FROM THE BURNING, A • 1913 • *Frontier* • USA
BRAND IM OZEAN • 1939 • Rittau Gunther • FRG
BRAND IN DER OPER • 1930 • Froelich Carl • FRG • FIRE IN THE OPERA HOUSE ○ BARCAROLE ○ LOVE DUET, THE
BRAND NEW HERO, A • 1914 • Arbuckle Roscoe, Dillon Eddie • USA
BRAND NEW LIFE, A • 1972 • O'Steen Sam • TVM • USA
BRAND OF BARS, THE • 1914 • *P.w.s. Film* • USA
BRAND OF CAIN • 1914 • Giblyn George • USA
BRAND OF CAIN, THE • 1915 • Nowland Eugene • USA • SCAR OF CONSCIENCE, THE
BRAND OF CAIN, THE • 1916 • Campbell Colin • SHT • USA
BRAND OF COWARDICE • 1925 • McCarthy John P. • USA
BRAND OF COWARDICE, THE • 1916 • Noble John W. • USA
BRAND OF DEATH • 1917 • *Reid Wallace* • SHT • USA
BRAND OF EVIL see **AKU NO MONSHO** • 1964
BRAND OF EVIL, THE • 1913 • Webster Harry Mcrae • SHT • USA
BRAND OF FEAR • 1949 • Drake Oliver • USA
BRAND OF FEAR, THE • 1911 • Dwan Allan • USA
BRAND OF FEAR, THE • 1916 • *Sunset* • SHT • USA
BRAND OF HATE • 1935 • Collins Lewis D. • USA
BRAND OF HATE, THE • 1917 • Stevens Edwin • SHT • USA
BRAND OF HIS TRIBE, THE • 1914 • McRae Henry • USA
BRAND OF JUDAS, THE • 1919 • *Howarth Lillian* • USA
BRAND OF LOPEZ, THE • 1920 • De Grasse Joseph • USA
BRAND OF MAN, THE see **NEMESIS, THE** • 1915
BRAND OF SATAN, THE • 1917 • Archainbaud George • USA
BRAND OF SHAME • 1968 • Elliott B. Ron • USA • BRAND, THE
BRAND OF SHAME, THE • 1916 • *Sunset* • USA
BRAND OF THE DEVIL • 1944 • Fraser Harry L. • USA
BRAND OF THE OUTLAWS • 1936 • Bradbury Robert North • USA
BRAND X • 1970 • Chamberlain Win • USA
BRANDE MONDE, LE • 1990 • Simard Marcel • DOC • CND
BRANDED • 1920 • Calvert Charles • UKN
BRANDED • 1931 • Lederman D. Ross • USA
BRANDED • 1950 • Mate Rudolph • USA
BRANDED see **BAD BOY** • 1938
BRANDED A BANDIT • 1924 • Hurst Paul C. • USA
BRANDED A COWARD • 1935 • Newfield Sam • USA
BRANDED A COWARD (UKN) see **ANNAPOLIS** • 1928
BRANDED A THIEF • 1924 • Hart Neal • USA
BRANDED ARM, THE • 1912 • *Gebhardt George* • USA
BRANDED BY HIS BROTHER'S CRIME • 1913 • *Frontier* • USA
BRANDED FOR LIFE see **MARCADOS PARA VIVER** • 1976
BRANDED FOUR, THE • 1920 • Worne Duke • SRL • USA
BRANDED GIRL, THE see **KIZ KOLUNDA DAMGA VAR** • 1967
BRANDED INDIAN, A • 1911 • *Powers* • USA
BRANDED MAN • 1922 • *Waggoner George* • USA
BRANDED MAN • 1928 • Pembroke Scott • USA
BRANDED MAN, THE • 1910 • *Bison* • USA
BRANDED MAN, THE • 1918 • *Gibson Hoot* • SHT • USA
BRANDED MEN • 1931 • Rosen Phil • USA
BRANDED SHOULDER, THE • 1911 • *Joyce Alice* • USA
BRANDED SIX-SHOOTER, THE • 1913 • *Frontier* • USA
BRANDED SOMBRERO, THE • 1928 • Hillyer Lambert • USA
BRANDED SOUL, A • 1917 • Bracken Bertram • USA
BRANDED SOUL, THE (USA) see **IRON STAIR, THE** • 1920
BRANDED TO KILL see **KOROSHI NO RAKUIN** • 1967
BRANDED WOMAN, THE • 1920 • Parker Albert • USA
BRANDENDE LIEFDE • 1983 • de Jong Ate • NTH • BURNING LOVE
BRANDENDE STRAAL, DE • 1911 • Ivens Joris • SHT • NTH • FLAMING ARROW, THE (USA) ○ WIGWAM, DE
BRANDENDE VRAAG, EEN • van der Heyden Jef • NTH
BRANDHERD see **VERLOGENE MORAL** • 1921
BRANDING • 1929 • Ivens Joris, Franken Mannus • SHT • NTH • BREAKERS
BRANDING A BAD MAN see **BRANDISHING A BAD MAN** • 1911
BRANDING A THIEF • 1910 • *Melies* • USA
BRANDING BROADWAY • 1918 • Hart William S., Ince Thomas H. (Spv) • USA
BRANDING FIRE • 1930 • *Cheyenne Bill* • USA
BRANDING IRON, THE • 1920 • Barker Reginald • USA
BRANDING IRON, THE see **BODY AND SOUL** • 1927
BRANDING THE INNOCENT see **LOST PARADISE, THE** • 1916
BRANDING THE THIEF • 1910-12 • Melies Gaston • USA
BRANDISHING A BAD MAN • 1911 • Dwan Allan • USA • BRANDING A BAD MAN
BRANDMAL DER VERGANGENHEIT, DAS • 1921 • Baron Erwin • FRG
BRANDON'S LAST RIDE • 1914 • Davis Ulysses • USA
BRANDOS COSTUMES • 1975 • Santos Alberto Seixas • PRT • SWEET COSTUMES ○ GENTLE HABITS
BRAND'S DAUGHTER • 1917 • Harvey Harry • USA
BRANDS HATCH BEAT • 1964 • Gibson Brian • SHT • UKN
BRANDSOLDATEN • 1916 • Englind Arvid • SWD • FIREMAN
BRANDSTIFTER, DIE • 1969 • Lemke Klaus • FRG
BRANDSTIFTER EUROPAS, DIE • 1926 • Neufeld Max • FRG • OBERST REDLS ERBEN ○ COLONEL REDL'S LEGACY ○ INCENDIARY OF EUROPE, THE
BRANDUNG • 1915 • Colani Ludwig, Nischwitz-Lisson Heinrich • FRG
BRANDY see **BRANDY, EL SHERIFF DE LOSATUMBA** • 1963
BRANDY ALEXANDER • 1976 • Siegel Lois, Vais Marco • ANS • CND
BRANDY ASHORE see **GREEN GROW THE RUSHES** • 1951
BRANDY, EL SHERIFF DE LOSATUMBA • 1963 • Borau Jose Luis • SPN • BRANDY, THE SHERIFF OF LOSATUMBA ○ BRANDY
BRANDY FOR THE PARSON • 1952 • Eldridge John • UKN
BRANDY IN THE WILDERNESS • 1969 • Kaye Stanton • USA
BRANDY, THE SHERIFF OF LOSATUMBA see **BRANDY, EL SHERIFF DE LOSATUMBA** • 1963
BRANKAR BYDLI V NASI ULICI • 1957 • Duba Cenek • CZC • GOALKEEPER LIVES IN OUR STREET, THE
BRANLE-BAS DE COMBAT see **ACTION STATIONS!** • 1943
BRANNEN • 1973 • Sandoy Hakon • NRW • FIRE, THE
BRANNIGAN • 1975 • Hickox Douglas • UKN, USA • JOE BATTLE
BRANNIGAN'S BAND • 1914 • Murphy J. A. • USA
BRANNIGAN'S PROMOTION • 1912 • *Nestor* • USA
BRANNINGAR • 1935 • Johansson Ivar • SWD • BREAKERS
BRANNINGAR, ELLER STULEN LYCKA • 1912 • Malmberg Eric • SWD • BREAKERS, OR STOLEN HAPPINESS
BRANQUIGNOL • 1949 • Dhery Robert • FRN
BRANSCOMBE'S PAL • 1914 • Shaw Harold • UKN
BRANSFORD IN ARCADIA OR THE LITTLE EOHIPPUS • 1914 • *Johnson J. W.* • USA
BRANSFORD OF RAINBOW RIDGE see **SURE FIRE** • 1921
BRANT BARN • 1967 • Abramson Hans • SWD • SINNING URGE, THE (UKN) ○ BURNT CHILD
BRANTOME 81, VIE DE DAMES GALANTES • 1982 • Benazeraf Jose • FRN
BRAS CUBAS • 1986 • Bressane Julio • BRZ
BRAS DE LA NUIT, LES • 1961 • Guymont Jacques • FRN
BRAS DE LA SEINE, LES • 1955 • Bonnardot Jean-Claude • SHT • FRN
BRAS DE LEVIER ET LA RIVIERE, LE • 1973 • Brault Michel • DCS • CND
BRASA ADORMECIDA • 1988 • Batista Djalma Limongi • BRZ • SMOULDERING EMBERS
BRASHER DOUBLOON, THE • 1947 • Brahm John • USA • HIGH WINDOW, THE (UKN)
BRASIER, LE • 1989 • Barbier Eric • FRN
BRASIER ARDENT, LE • 1922 • Mosjoukine Ivan • FRN • GLOWING BRASIER, THE ○ BURNING BRASIER, THE
BRASIL ANNO 2000 • 1969 • Lima Walter Jr. • BRZ • BRAZIL YEAR 2000
BRASIL NA SEGUNDA GUERRA • 1989 • Back Silvio • DOC • BRZ • BRAZIL IN THE SECOND WORLD WAR
BRASIL VERDADE • 1968 • Gimenez Manuel Horacio, Sarno Geraldo, Capovilla Maurice, Soares Paulo Gil • BRZ • TRUE BRAZIL
BRASILEIRO CHAMADO ROSAFLEUR, UM • 1980 • Miranda Geraldo • BRZ • BRAZILIAN CALLED ROSAFLOR, A
BRASLYET -2 • 1968 • Tsutsulkovski Lev, Shamkovich Mikhail • USS • BRACELET -2
BRASONG BAKAL • 1968 • Callardo Cesar Chat • PHL • IRON ARM
BRASS • 1923 • Franklin Sidney A. • USA
BRASS • 1985 • Allen Corey • TVM • USA
BRASS BOTTLE, THE • 1914 • *World* • USA
BRASS BOTTLE, THE • 1914 • Morgan Sidney • UKN
BRASS BOTTLE, THE • 1923 • Tourneur Maurice • USA
BRASS BOTTLE, THE • 1964 • Keller Harry • USA
BRASS BOWL, THE • 1914 • *Wilson Ben* • USA
BRASS BOWL, THE • 1924 • Storm Jerome • USA
BRASS BULLET, THE • 1918 • Wilson Ben • SRL • USA
BRASS BUTTON, A • 1911 • *Reliance* • USA
BRASS-BUTTONED ROMANCE, A • 1916 • *Compson Betty* • SHT • USA
BRASS BUTTONS • 1913 • *Lyman Laura* • USA
BRASS BUTTONS • 1914 • *Rich Vivian* • USA
BRASS BUTTONS • 1919 • King Henry • USA
BRASS CHECK, THE • 1918 • Davis Will S. • USA
BRASS COMMANDMENTS • 1923 • Reynolds Lynn • USA
BRASS GIRL, THE • 1917 • Moore Matt • USA
BRASS KNUCKLES • 1927 • Bacon Lloyd • USA
BRASS LEGEND, THE • 1956 • Oswald Gerd • USA
BRASS MONKEY, A • 1917 • Richmond J. A. • SHT • USA
BRASS MONKEY, THE • 1948 • Freeland Thornton • UKN • LUCKY MASCOT
BRASS PICKERS, THE see **DANGAN TAISHO** • 1960
BRASS RING, THE • 1975 • Beck Martin* • USA
BRASS TARGET • 1978 • Hough John • USA
BRAT, THE • 1919 • Blache Herbert • USA
BRAT, THE • 1931 • Ford John • USA
BRAT, THE • *Summers Jamie* • USA
BRAT, THE see **NIPPER, THE** • 1930
BRAT, THE (UKN) see **SONS OF NEW MEXICO** • 1950
BRAT DOKTORA HOMERA • 1968 • Mitrovic Zika • YGS • DOCTOR HOMER'S BROTHER
BRAT GEROYA • 1940 • Vasilchikov Yu. • USS • BROTHER OF A HERO ○ HERO'S BROTHER, THE
BRAT PATROL, THE see **B.R.A.T. PATROL, THE** • 1986
BRATISHKA • 1926 • Kozintsev Grigori, Trauberg Leonid • USS • BUDDY ○ LITTLE BROTHER
BRAT'JA KARAMAZOVY • 1914 • Tourjansky Victor • USS • BROTHERS KARAMAZOV, THE
BRATS • 1930 • Parrott James • SHT • USA
BRATUSHKA • 1975 • Dobrolyubov Igor • USS, BUL • SOLDIER OF THE TRANSPORT UNIT, THE ○ VOINIKUT OT OBOZA ○ BUDDY
BRATYA KARAMAZOVY • 1968 • Pyriev Ivan • USS • MURDER OF DIMITRI KARAMAZOV, THE ○ BROTHERS KARAMAZOV, THE
BRAUT AUF 24 STUNDEN, DIE • 1922 • Karfiol William • FRG
BRAUT DES COWBOY, DIE • 1921 • Seefeld Eddie F. • FRG
BRAUT DES ENTMUNDIGTEN, DIE • 1919 • Lund Erik • FRG
BRAUT DES RESERVELEUTNANTS ODER DIE MISSION DER GRAFIN CERUTTI, DIE • 1916 • Jacoby Georg • FRG
BRAUT DES SATANS, DIE (FRG) see **TO THE DEVIL A DAUGHTER** • 1976
BRAUTIGAM AUF AKTIEN • 1918 • Larsen Viggo • FRG
BRAUTIGAM AUF KREDIT • 1921 • Steinhoff Hans • FRG
BRAUTIGAM DIE KOMODIANTIN UND DER ZUHALTER, DER • 1968 • Straub Jean-Marie • SHT • FRG • BRIDEGROOM, THE COMEDIENNE AND THE PIMP, THE
BRAUTIGAME DER BABETTE BOMBERLING • 1927 • Janson Victor • FRG
BRAUTIGAMSWITWE • 1931 • Eichberg Richard • FRG
BRAVADE LEGENDAIRE, LA see **ECLIPSE SUR UN ANCIEN CHEMIN VERS COMPOSTELLE** • 1978
BRAVADOS • 1967 • Santiago Cirio H. • PHL
BRAVADOS, THE • 1958 • King Henry • USA
BRAVATA, LA • 1977 • Montero Roberto Bianchi • ITL
BRAVE AND BOLD • 1912 • Sennett Mack • USA
BRAVE AND BOLD • 1915 • *Tincher Fay* • USA
BRAVE AND BOLD • 1918 • Harbaugh Carl • USA
BRAVE AND THE BEAUTIFUL, THE (UKN) see **MAGNIFICENT MATADOR, THE** • 1955
BRAVE ARCHER AND HIS MATE see **SHEN-TIAO** • 1981
BRAVE ARCHERS, THE see **SHE TIAO YING-HSIUNG CH'UAN** • 1977
BRAVE BAHRAM see **BAHRAM SHIRDEL** • 1968
BRAVE BLACKSMITH, THE see **STATECNEM KOVARI, O** • 1983
BRAVE BOYS IN UNIFORM see **KRONANS KACKA GOSSAR** • 1940
BRAVE, BRAVER AND BRAVEST • 1912 • *Lubin* • USA
BRAVE BULLS, THE • 1951 • Rossen Robert • USA
BRAVE BUNCH, THE see **GENNEI TOU VORRA, I** • 1969
BRAVE CHICKEN, THE see **STATECNE KURATKO** • 1960
BRAVE CHILDREN: OR, THE LITTLE THIEF CATCHERS, THE • 1908 • Coleby A. E. • UKN
BRAVE COWARDS • 1927 • Sandrich Mark • SHT • USA
BRAVE DESERVE THE FAIR, THE • 1910 • *Lubin* • USA
BRAVE DESERVE THE FAIR, THE • 1915 • Mix Tom • USA
BRAVE DOG, THE • 1951 • Macskassy Gyula • ANS • HNG
BRAVE DON'T CRY, THE • 1952 • Leacock Philip • UKN
BRAVE FELLOWS see **JUNACY** • 1967
BRAVE FROG: A VERY FROGGY AFFAIR, THE • 1985 • Reynolds Michael • ANM • USA
BRAVE FROG: GREATEST ADVENTURE, THE • Reynolds Michael • ANM • USA • BRAVE FROG'S GREATEST ADVENTURES, THE
BRAVE FROG'S GREATEST ADVENTURES, THE see **BRAVE FROG: GREATEST ADVENTURE, THE**
BRAVE GIRL ON THE FIFTEENTH FLOOR, THE • 1909 • *Phoenix* • USA
BRAVE HANS • Georgi Katja, Georgi Klaus • ANM • GDR • VALIANT HANS
BRAVE HARE, THE • 1955 • Ivanov-Vano Ivan • ANM • USS
BRAVE HEARTS • 1910 • *Kalem* • USA
BRAVE HEART'S HIDDEN LOVE • 1912 • *Pathe* • USA
BRAVE HUNTER, THE • 1912 • Sennett Mack • USA
BRAVE IRISH LASS, THE • 1909 • Blackton J. Stuart (Spv) • USA
BRAVE LAD'S REWARD, THE • 1907 • *Warwick Trading Co* • UKN

BRAVE LION, THE • Ng Fei Chien • HKG

BRAVE LITTLE BAT, THE • 1941 • Jones Charles M. • ANS • USA

BRAVE LITTLE BRAVE, THE • 1956 • Davis Mannie • ANS • USA

BRAVE LITTLE INDIAN, A • 1912 • *Panzer Paul* • USA

BRAVE LITTLE MAN see **MODIGA MINDRE MAN** • 1968

BRAVE LITTLE TAILOR, THE • 1938 • Gillett Burt • ANS • USA

BRAVE LITTLE TAILOR, THE • 1964 • Brumberg Valentina, Brumberg Zinaida • ANS • USS

BRAVE LITTLE TAILOR, THE • 1969 • *Childhood Prod.* • FRG

BRAVE LITTLE TAILOR, THE see **TAPFERE SCHNEIDERLEIN, DAS** • 1956

BRAVE LITTLE TOASTER, THE • 1987 • Rees Jerry • ANM • USA

BRAVE LITTLE WALDO • 1917 • *Voss Fatty* • SHT • USA

BRAVE LITTLE WOMAN, A • 1912 • Ricketts Thomas • USA

BRAVE MARCO see **YUNAK MARKO** • 1953

BRAVE MEN, THE see **SMELYE LYUDI** • 1950

BRAVE MEN, THE see **IKISI DE CESURDU** • 1963

BRAVE NEW WORLD • 1980 • Brinckerhoff Burt • TVM • USA

BRAVE OLD BILL • 1912 • *Brennan John E.* • USA

BRAVE ONE, THE • 1956 • Rapper Irving • USA

BRAVE ONES, THE • 1916 • *Plump & Runt* • USA

BRAVE SCHOOL TRUANT, THE see **TAPFERE SCHULSCHWANZER, DER** • 1967

BRAVE SEVEN, THE see **SEMERO SMELYKH** • 1936

BRAVE SOLDAT SCHWEJK, DER • 1960 • von Ambesser Axel • FRG • GOOD SOLDIER SCHWEIK, THE (USA)

BRAVE SOLDIER AT DAWN, A see **AKATSUKI NO YUSHI** • 1927

BRAVE STRANGER, THE see **CESUR YABANCI** • 1968

BRAVE SUNDER, DER • 1931 • Kortner Fritz • FRG • UPRIGHT SINNER, THE (USA)

BRAVE SWIFT EAGLE'S PERIL • 1911 • *Bison* • USA

BRAVE, THE ROUGH AND THE RAW, THE • 1973 • SAF

BRAVE, THE RUTHLESS, THE TRAITOR, THE see **CORAGGIOSO, LO SPIETATO, IL TRADITORE, IL** • 1967

BRAVE TIN SOLDIER, THE • 1934 • Iwerks Ub • ANS • USA

BRAVE TRUANTS, THE see **TAPFERE SCHULSCHWANZER, DER** • 1967

BRAVE WARRIOR • 1952 • Bennet Spencer Gordon • USA

BRAVE WARRIOR, THE see **BRAVO GUERREIRO, O** • 1968

BRAVE WESTERN GIRL, A • 1910 • *Bison* • USA

BRAVE WOMEN OF '76 • 1909 • *Lubin* • USA

BRAVEHEART • 1925 • Hale Alan • USA

BRAVER THAN THE BRAVEST • 1916 • Roach Hal • *Sht* • USA

BRAVERY • 1966 • Makhnach Leonid • DOC • USS

BRAVERY IN THE FIELD • 1978 • Walker Giles • MTV • CND

BRAVERY OF DORA, THE • 1912 • *Payne Edna* • USA

BRAVES GENS, LES • 1912 • Feuillade Louis • FRN

BRAVES PETITS SOLDATS DE PLOMB, LES • 1915 • Cohl Emile • ANS • FRN

BRAVEST FISHMONGER see **ISSHIN TASUKE –OTOKO NO NAKA NO OTOKO IPPIKI** • 1959

BRAVEST GIRL IN CALIFORNIA, THE • 1913 • *Kalem* • USA

BRAVEST GIRL IN THE SOUTH • 1910 • Olcott Sidney • USA

BRAVEST MAN, THE • 1913 • *Majestic* • USA

BRAVEST MAN IN THE WORLD, THE see **ASHGAA RAGEL FIL ALAM** • 1968

BRAVEST OF THE BRAVE • 1915 • Curtis Allen • USA

BRAVEST WAY, THE • 1918 • Melford George • USA

BRAVESTARR see **BRAVESTARR: THE LEGEND** • 1986

BRAVESTARR: THE LEGEND • 1986 • Tatarnowicz Tom • ANM • USA • MARSHAL BRAVESTARR ○ BRAVESTARR

BRAVING BLAZES • 1917 • Richmond J. A. • USA

BRAVISSIMO! • 1955 • D'Amico Luigi Filippo • ITL

BRAVO • Chung Jin-Woo • SKR

BRAVO, THE • 1928 • Malins Geoffrey H. • UKN

BRAVO ALPHA • 1957 • Venard Jean • SHT • FRN

BRAVO! BRAVO! • 1979 • Skagen Solve, Wadman Malte • DOC • NRW

BRAVO DI VENEZIA, IL • 1941 • Campogalliani Carlo • ITL

BRAVO FOR BILLY • 1979 • *Halas John (P)* • ANS • UKN

BRAVO GUERREIRO, O • 1968 • Dahl Gustavo • BRZ • BRAVE WARRIOR, THE

BRAVO KILTIES! • 1914 • Thornton F. Martin? • UKN

BRAVO MAESTRO • 1978 • Grlic Rajko • YGS

BRAVO MR. STRAUSS • 1943 • Pal George • ANS • USA

BRAVO –MY BROTHER see **SABASH THAMBI** • 1967

BRAVO PORTUGAL • 1970 • Chickerling Lisa, Porterfield Jean • DOC • USA

BRAVO TASUKE ISSHIN see **APPARE ISSHIN TASUKE** • 1945

BRAVO TERRITORIALS • 1909 • *Warwick Trading Co.* • UKN

BRAVO, YOUNG GUY (USA) see **BURABO! YANGU GAI** • 1970

BRAVOS, THE • 1971 • Post Ted • USA

BRAVOS DE CALIFORNIA, LOS • 1962 • Marin Jesus • MXC

BRAVUCONAS, LAS • 1962 • Ortega Juan J. • MXC

BRAWN OF THE NORTH • 1922 • Trimble Larry • USA

BRAWNY see **ARAKURE** • 1957

BRAZA DORMIDA • 1928 • Mauro-Humberto • BRZ • EXTINGUISHED CINDERS ○ SLEEPING EMBER

BRAZEN see **FATAL LADY** • 1936

BRAZEN BEAUTY • 1918 • Browning Tod • USA

BRAZEN BELL, THE • 1963 • Sheldon James • MTV • USA

BRAZEN WOMEN OF BALZAC, THE (USA) see **TOLLDREISTEN GESCHICHTEN DES HONORE DE BALZAC** • 1969

BRAZIL • 1944 • Santley Joseph • USA

BRAZIL • 1984 • Gilliam Terry • UKN

BRAZIL: A REPORT ON TORTURE • 1971 • Wexler Haskell, Landau Saul • DOC • USA

BRAZIL IN THE SECOND WORLD WAR see **BRASIL NA SEGUNDA GUERRA** • 1989

BRAZIL SYMPHONY (USA) see **SINFONIA AMAZONICA** • 1952

BRAZIL YEAR 2000 see **BRASIL ANNO 2000** • 1969

BRAZILIAN CALLED ROSAFLOR, A see **BRASILEIRO CHAMADO ROSAFLEUR, UM** • 1980

BRAZO FUERTE, EL • 1958 • Korporaal Giovanni • MXC

BRAZZA • 1954 • Quilici Folco • SHT • ITL

BRAZZA OU L'EPOPEE DU CONGO • 1939 • Poirier Leon • FRN

BREACH, THE see **PRULOM** • 1946

BREACH IN BREECHES, A • 1912 • Stow Percy • UKN

BREACH OF CONTRACT • 1984 • Guttfreund Andre

BREACH OF FAITH, A • 1911 • *Weber Lois* • USA

BREACH OF PROMISE • 1912 • *Prescott Vivian* • USA

BREACH OF PROMISE • 1932 • Stein Paul L. • USA

BREACH OF PROMISE • 1941 • Huth Harold, Pertwee Roland • UKN • ADVENTURE IN BLACKMAIL (USA)

BREACH OF PROMISE CASE, A • 1908 • McDowell J. B.? • UKN

BREAD • 1918 • Park Ida May • USA

BREAD • 1924 • Schertzinger Victor • USA

BREAD • 1971 • Long Stanley • UKN

BREAD • 1972 • *Shopov Naoum (P)* • BUL

BREAD • 1983 • Kish Albert • DOC • CND

BREAD see **KHLEB** • 1918

BREAD see **ROTI** • 1941

BREAD see **PAO, O** • 1959

BREAD AND CHEESES, AND KISSES • 1969 • Boulting John • UKN

BREAD AND CHOCOLATE (USA) see **PANE E CIOCCOLATA** • 1974

BREAD AND ROSES see **KHLEB I ROZI** • 1960

BREAD AND ROSES see **BROT UND ROSEN** • 1967

BREAD AND SALT • 1970 • Makarenko M., Kokhan G. • USS

BREAD AND STONES see **BROT UND STEINE** • 1979

BREAD CAST UPON THE WATERS • 1912 • *King Charles E.* • USA

BREAD CAST UPON THE WATERS • 1913 • Ince Thomas H. • USA

BREAD FOR A FUGITIVE see **PSOMI YIA ENA DHRAPETI** • 1967

BREAD IS ALWAYS BORN see **ZAWSZE RODZI SIE CHLEB** • 1969

BREAD LINE, THE • 1915 • Grandon Francis J. • USA

BREAD, LOVE AND.. see **PANE, AMORE E..** • 1955

BREAD, LOVE AND DREAMS (USA) see **PANE, AMORE E FANTASIA** • 1953

BREAD, LOVE AND JEALOUSY see **PANE AMORE E GELOSIA** • 1954

BREAD OF LOVE, THE see **KARLEKENS BROD** • 1953

BREAD OF OUR EARLY YEARS, THE see **BROT DER FRUHEN JAHRE, DAS** • 1962

BREAD ON THE WATERS • 1913 • Merwin Bannister • USA

BREAD PEDDLER, THE (USA) see **PORTEUSE DE PAIN, LA** • 1963

BREAD UPON THE WATERS • 1912 • Eagle Oscar • USA

BREAD UPON THE WATERS • 1913 • *Essanay* • USA

BREAD UPON THE WATERS • 1913 • *Princess* • USA

BREAD UPON THE WATERS • 1914 • North Wilfred • USA

BREADALBANE • 1983 • Mason William • DOC • CND

BREADWINNER, THE • 1898 • *Paul R. W.* • UKN

BREADWINNER, THE • 1932 • Sparling Gordon • CND

BREAK, THE • 1962 • Comfort Lance • UKN

BREAK, THE • 1966 • Adrien Pierre • BLG

BREAK, THE see **RUPTURE** • 1961

BREAK, THE see **BRUCH, DER** • 1988

BREAK, BREAK, BREAK • 1914 • Pollard Harry • USA

BREAK FOR FREEDOM, A • 1913 • *Patheplay* • USA

BREAK IN THE CIRCLE • 1955 • Guest Val • UKN

BREAK IN THE ICE, A • 1975 • Jubenvill Ken • MTV • CND

BREAK LOOSE see **PARADES** • 1972

BREAK OF DAY • 1976 • Hannam Ken • ASL

BREAK OF HEARTS • 1935 • Moeller Philip • USA

BREAK OUT • 1984 • Godwin Frank • UKN

BREAK STREET • 1984 • Silberg Joel • USA

BREAK THE CHAINS see **SPRINGT DIE KETTEN** • 1930

BREAK THE NEWS • 1938 • Clair Rene • UKN • FAUSSES NOUVELLES

BREAK THE NEWS TO MOTHER • 1919 • *Shepard Pearl* • USA

BREAK-THROUGH, THE • 1968 • Ozerov Yury • USS

BREAK TO FREEDOM • 1955 • McGuire Don • USA

BREAK TO FREEDOM (USA) see **ALBERT R.N.** • 1953

BREAK-UP • 1975 • Wallace Stephen • SHT • ASL

BREAK UP see **UOMO DAI PALLONCINI, L'** • 1964

BREAK-UP see **NOUS NE VIEILLIRONS PAS ENSEMBLE** • 1972

BREAK UP, THE • 1930 • Robertson Jack • USA

BREAK-UP, THE • 1930 • Zamkovoy L.

BREAK-UP, THE see **KAISANSHIKI** • 1967

BREAK UP THE DANCE see **ROZBIJEMY ZABAWA** • 1957

BREAK UP THE PARTY see **ROZBIJEMY ZABAWA** • 1957

BREAKAWAY • 1956 • Cass Henry • UKN

BREAKAWAY • 1967 • Conner Bruce • SHT • USA

BREAKAWAY • Skaaren Warren • USA

BREAKAWAY • 1990 • McLennan Don • ASL

BREAKDANCE 2: ELECTRIC BOOGALOO see **BREAKIN' 2 ELECTRIC BOOGALOO** • 1984

BREAKDANCE: THE MOVIE see **BREAKIN'** • 1984

BREAKDOWN • 1951 • Anderson Robert • DOC • CND

BREAKDOWN • 1952 • Angelo Edmund • USA

BREAKDOWN see **KVAR** • 1977

BREAKDOWN see **LOVELESS, THE** • 1983

BREAKDOWN see **FREEWAY MANIAC, THE** • 1987

BREAKDOWN, THE • 1912 • *Baggot King* • USA

BREAKDOWN OF THE AEROMOBILES, THE see **PANNA DEGLI AEROMOBILI, LA** • 1915

BREAKDOWN (USA) see **SI J'ETAIS UN ESPION** • 1966

BREAKER, THE • Nyby Christian • USA

BREAKER, THE • 1916 • Wright Fred E. • USA

BREAKER, THE • 1973 • Shields Frank • DOC • ASL

BREAKER, THE see **BREAKER MORANT** • 1979

BREAKER! BREAKER! • 1977 • Hulette Donald • USA

BREAKER MORANT • 1979 • Beresford Bruce • ASL • BREAKER, THE

BREAKERS see **BRANDING** • 1929

BREAKERS see **BRANNINGAR** • 1935

BREAKERS AHEAD • 1918 • Brabin Charles J. • USA

BREAKERS AHEAD • 1935 • Gilkison Anthony • UKN

BREAKERS AHEAD • 1938 • Sewell Vernon • UKN • AS WE FORGIVE

BREAKERS, OR STOLEN HAPPINESS see **BRANNINGAR, ELLER STULEN LYCKA** • 1912

BREAKFAST • 1967 • Sach William • SHT • UKN

BREAKFAST • 1968 • Zwartjes Frans • SHT • NTH

BREAKFAST • 1976 • Snow Michael • CND

BREAKFAST AT MANCHESTER MORGUE see **FIN DE SEMANA PARA LOS MUERTOS** • 1974

BREAKFAST AT SUNRISE • 1927 • St. Clair Malcolm • USA

BREAKFAST AT THE MANCHESTER MORGUE see **FIN DE SEMANA PARA LOS MUERTOS** • 1974

BREAKFAST AT TIFFANY'S • 1961 • Edwards Blake • USA

BREAKFAST CLUB, THE • 1984 • Hughes John • USA

BREAKFAST FOR TWO • 1937 • Santell Alfred • USA • LOVE LIKE THAT, A

BREAKFAST IN BED • 1977 • *Sullivan Jenny* • USA

BREAKFAST IN BED (USA) see **FRUHSTUCK IM DOPPELBETT** • 1963

BREAKFAST IN HOLLYWOOD • 1946 • Schuster Harold • USA • TOM BRENEMAN'S BREAKFAST IN HOLLYWOOD ○ MAD HATTER, THE

BREAKFAST IN PARADISE • 1982 • Lamond John • ASL • BREAKFAST IN PARIS

BREAKFAST IN PARIS see **BREAKFAST IN PARADISE** • 1982

BREAKFAST OF CHAMPIONS • 1989 • Golding Paul • USA

BREAKFAST WITH THE DEVIL see **DORUCAK SA DAVOLOM** • 1972

BREAKHEART PASS • 1976 • Gries Tom • USA

BREAKIN' • 1984 • Silberg Joel • USA • BREAKDANCE: THE MOVIE

BREAKIN' 2 ELECTRIC BOOGALOO • 1984 • Firstenberg Sam • USA • BREAKDANCE 2: ELECTRIC BOOGALOO

BREAKIN' AND ENTERIN' • 1985 • Carew Topper • USA

BREAKIN' IT DOWN • 1946 • Collins Lewis D. • USA

BREAKING • 1985 • Nesher Avi • ISR

BREAKING ALL THE RULES • 1985 • Orr James • CND • BREAKING THE RULES ○ FUN PARK

BREAKING AWAY • 1979 • Yates Peter • USA

BREAKING BRANCHES IS FORBIDDEN see **HANAORI** • 1968

BREAKING GLASS • 1980 • Gibson Brian • UKN

BREAKING HOME TIES • 1910 • *Columbia* • USA

BREAKING HOME TIES • 1922 • Seltzer Frank N., Rolands George K. • USA

BREAKING IN • 1915 • North Wilfred • USA

BREAKING IN • 1917 • *Pokes & Jabs* • SHT • USA

BREAKING IN • 1989 • Forsyth Bill • USA

BREAKING INTO JAIL • 1914 • *Selig* • USA

BREAKING INTO SOCIETY • 1915 • *Santa Barbara* • USA

BREAKING INTO SOCIETY • 1916 • Beery Wallace • SHT • USA

BREAKING INTO SOCIETY • 1923 • Stromberg Hunt • USA

BREAKING INTO THE BIG LEAGUE • 1913 • *Millarde Harry* • USA

BREAKING INTO THE MOVIES see **SHOW PEOPLE** • 1928

BREAKING IT UP see **A TOUT CASSER** • 1968

BREAKING LOOSE • 1988 • Hay Rod • ASL

BREAKING OF BRANCHES IS FORBIDDEN see **HANAORI** • 1968

BREAKING OF BUMBO, THE • 1969 • Sinclair Andrew • UKN

BREAKING OF THE DROUGHT, THE • 1920 • Barrett Franklyn • ASL

BREAKING OUT • 1982 • Manatis Janine • CND

BREAKING OUT see **AIDANKAATAJAT** • 1983

BREAKING POINT • 1976 • Clark Bob • CND

BREAKING POINT • 1989 • Markle Peter • USA

BREAKING POINT, THE • 1914 • Wilson Frank • UKN

BREAKING POINT, THE • 1921 • Scardon Paul • USA

BREAKING POINT, THE • 1924 • Brenon Herbert • USA

BREAKING POINT, THE • 1950 • Curtiz Michael • USA

BREAKING POINT, THE • 1961 • Comfort Lance • UKN • GREAT ARMORED CAR SWINDLE, THE (USA)

BREAKING THE FAMILY STRIKE • 1917 • Moore Matt • SHT • USA

BREAKING THE HABIT • 1964 • Korty John • ANM • USA

BREAKING THE ICE • 1925 • Bacon Lloyd • SHT • USA

BREAKING THE ICE • 1938 • Cline Eddie • USA

BREAKING THE LANGUAGE BARRIER • 1965 • Schepisi Fred • SHT • ASL

BREAKING THE NEWS • 1912 • Lincoln W. J. • ASL

BREAKING THE NEWS • 1939 • *Calloway Cab* • SHT • USA

BREAKING THE NEWS see **FOUNTAIN, THE** • 1934

BREAKING THE PARTY see **ROZBIJEMY ZABAWA** • 1957

BREAKING THE RULES see **BREAKING ALL THE RULES** • 1985

BREAKING THE SEVENTH COMMANDMENT • 1911 • *Imp* • USA

BREAKING THE SHACKLES • 1915 • King Carleton S. • USA

BREAKING THE SILENCE • 1986 • Shaffer Beverly • DOC • CND

BREAKING THE SOUND BARRIER (USA) see **SOUND BARRIER, THE** • 1952

BREAKING THE STORM BARRIER see **ARASHI O TSUKKIRU JETTOKI** • 1961

BREAKING THROUGH • 1921 • Ensminger Robert • USA

BREAKING THROUGH THE SOUND BARRIER see **SOUND BARRIER, THE** • 1952

BREAKING UP • 1978 • Mann Delbert • TVM • USA

BREAKING UP IS HARD TO DO • 1979 • Antonio Lou • TVM • USA

BREAKING UP OF THE TERRITORIAL ARMY see **LIBERATION DES TERRITORIAUX** • 1896

BREAKING UP THE DANCE see **ROZBIJEMY ZABAWA** • 1957

BREAKING UP THE HAPPY HOME • 1902 • *Warwick Trading Co.* • UKN

BREAKING UP THE PARTY see **ROZBIJEMY ZABAWA** • 1957

BREAKING WAVES • 1901 • Hepworth Cecil M. • UKN

BREAKING WITH OLD IDEAS • 1975 • CHN

BREAKOUT • 1959 • Scott Peter Graham • UKN

BREAKOUT • 1970 • Irving Richard • TVM • USA

BREAKOUT • 1975 • Gries Tom • USA, SPN, FRN

BREAKOUT, THE see **DATSUGOKUSHA** • 1967

BREAKOUT ON PRISON PLANET see **SPACE RAGE** • 1985

BREAKOUT (USA) see **DANGER WITHIN** • 1959

BREAKS see **. . .** • 1972

BREAKS OF THE GAME, THE • 1915 • Nowland Eugene • USA

BREAKTHROUGH • 1944 • Beveridge James • DCS • CND

BREAKTHROUGH • 1950 • Seiler Lewis • USA

BREAKTHROUGH • 1978 • McLaglen Andrew V. • FRG • SERGEANT STEINER ○ STEINER, DAS EISERNE KRUZ II ○ CROSS OF IRON II

BREAKTHROUGH • 1981 • Kuusisto Janne • FNL

BREAKTHROUGH, THE see **DURCHBRUCH LOK 234** • 1963
BREAKTHROUGH, THE see **TOLPAR** • 1978
BREAKUP see **RASLOM** • 1971
BREAKUP, THE (USA) see **RUPTURE, LA** • 1970
BREAKWATER • 1932 • Seibert Mike • USA
BREAST OF RUSS MEYER, THE • 1983 • Meyer Russ • USA
BREATH • 1967 • Murakami Jimmy T. • USA
BREATH • 1975 • Elder Bruce • CND • LIGHT ○ BIRTH
BREATH OF AIR, A see **DIH/DAH** • 1984
BREATH OF ARABY, THE • 1915 • Gaskill Charles L. • USA
BREATH OF LIFE • 1962 • Piperno J. Henry • UKN
BREATH OF SCANDAL see **HIS GLORIOUS NIGHT** • 1929
BREATH OF SCANDAL, A • 1960 • Curtiz Michael • USA, ITL, AUS • OLYMPIA (ITL)
BREATH OF SCANDAL, THE • 1913 • *Coombs Guy* • USA
BREATH OF SCANDAL, THE • 1924 • Gasnier Louis J. • USA
BREATH OF SUMMER, A • 1915 • Siegmann George • USA
BREATH OF THE GODS, THE • 1920 • Sturgeon Rollin S. • USA
BREATHDEATH • 1964 • Vanderbeek Stan • SHT • USA
BREATHE, LITTLE MAN! • 1980 • Gerinska Vesselina • BUL
BREATHING • 1963 • Breer Robert • ANS • USA
BREATHING TOGETHER: REVOLUTION OF THE ELECTRIC FAMILY • 1971 • Markson Morley • CND • VIVRE ENSEMBLE: LA REVOLUTION DE LA FAMILLE ELECTRIQUE
BREATHLESS • 1983 • McBride Jim • USA
BREATHLESS MOMENT, THE • 1924 • Hill Robert F. • USA • SENTENCED TO SOFT LABOR
BREATHLESS MOMENTS • 1938 • Ford Charles E. • SHT • USA
BREATHLESS (USA) see **A BOUT DE SOUFFLE** • 1960
BREATHWORLD • 1964 • *Delta S.f. Film Group* • UKN
BRED IN OLD KENTUCKY • 1926 • Dillon Eddie • USA
BRED IN THE BONE • 1913 • Lucas Wilfred • USA
BRED IN THE BONE • 1915 • Powell Paul • USA
BREED APART, A • 1984 • Mora Philippe • USA
BREED O' THE MOUNTAINS • 1914 • Reid Wallace • USA
BREED O' THE NORTH • 1914 • Edwards Walter • USA
BREED OF COURAGE • 1927 • Mitchell Howard M. • USA
BREED OF MEN • 1919 • Hart William S., Hillyer Lambert • USA
BREED OF THE BORDER • 1933 • Bradbury Robert North • USA • SPEED BRENT WINS (UKN)
BREED OF THE BORDER, THE • 1924 • Garson Harry • USA
BREED OF THE NORTH • 1913 • *Jones Edgar* • USA
BREED OF THE SEA • 1926 • Ince Ralph • USA
BREED OF THE SUNSETS • 1928 • Fox Wallace • USA
BREED OF THE TRESHAMS, THE • 1920 • Foss Kenelm • UKN
BREED OF THE WEST • 1913 • *Von Schiller Carl* • USA
BREED OF THE WEST • 1930 • Neitz Alvin J. • USA
BREEDERS • 1986 • Kincaid Tim • USA
BREEDING see **SHIIKU** • 1961
BREEDING OF THE FLESH see **NIKU NO SHIIKU** • 1968
BREEKPUNT • 1971 • SAF
BREEZE OF LOVE see **KOIKAZE DOCHU** • 1957
BREEZES OF LOVE see **FUKEYO KOIKAZE** • 1935
BREEZING ALONG • 1927 • Taurog Norman • SHT • USA
BREEZING ALONG • 1933 • Sparling Gordon • DCS • CND
BREEZING HOME • 1937 • Carruth Milton • USA • I HATE HORSES
BREEZY • 1973 • Eastwood Clint • USA
BREEZY BILL • 1930 • McGowan J. P. • USA
BREEZY BILL, OUTCAST • 1915 • MacDonald Donald • USA
BREEZY JIM • 1919 • Johnston Lorimer • USA
BREEZY MORNING, A • 1911 • *Solax* • USA
BREITE WEG, DER • 1917 • Gad Urban • FRG
BREITNER • 1976 • Smit Boud • SHT • NTH
BREL • 1982 • Rossif Frederic • FRN
BRELAN D'AS • 1952 • Verneuil Henri • FRN
BREMEN TOWN MUSICIANS • 1935 • *Iwerks Ub (P)* • ANS • USA
BREMEN TOWN MUSICIANS, THE (USA) see **BREMER STADTMUSIKANTEN, DIE** • 1954
BREMEN TOWN MUSICIANS, THE (USA) see **BREMER STADTMUSIKANTEN, DIE** • 1959
BREMEN TOWN MUSICIANS, THE (USA) see **BREMENSKIE MUSIKANTI** • 1969
BREMENSKIE MUSIKANTI • 1969 • Kovalevskaia I. • ANS • USS • BREMEN TOWN MUSICIANS, THE (USA)
BREMER FREEDOM see **BREMER FREIHEIT** • 1972
BREMER FREIHEIT • 1972 • Fassbinder R. W. (c/d) • MTV • FRG • BREMER FREEDOM
BREMER MUSICIANS, THE see **CUATRO MUSICOS DE BREMEN, LAS** • 1988
BREMER STADTMUSIKANTEN, DIE • 1954 • Bottge Bruno J. • ANS • GDR • BREMEN TOWN MUSICIANS, THE (USA)
BREMER STADTMUSIKANTEN, DIE • 1959 • Geis Rainer • FRG • BREMEN TOWN MUSICIANS, THE (USA)
BRENDA OF THE BARGE • 1920 • Rooke Arthur • UKN
BRENDA STARR • 1976 • Stuart Mel • TVM • USA
BRENDA STARR • 1987 • Miller Robert Ellis • USA
BRENDA STARR, REPORTER • 1945 • Fox Wallace • SRL • USA
BRENDAN BEHAN'S DUBLIN • 1966 • Cohen Norman • DOC • IRL
BRENN, HEXE, BRENN • 1969 • Armstrong Michael, Hoven Adrian • FRG, UKN • BURN, WITCH, BURN (UKN) ○ MARK OF THE DEVIL (USA) ○ HEXEN BIS AUFS BLUT GEQUALT ○ MARK OF THE WITCH ○ SATAN ○ AUSTRIA 1700
BRENNAN OF THE MOOR • 1913 • Warren Edward • USA
BRENNENDE ACKER, DER • 1913 • *Nielson Asta* • FRG
BRENNENDE ACKER, DER • 1922 • Murnau F. W. • FRG • BURNING ACRE, THE ○ BURNING SOIL ○ BURNING EARTH, THE
BRENNENDE AKROBATIN, DIE see **EHE DER HEDDA OLSEN ODER DIE BRENNENDE AKROBATIN, DIE** • 1921
BRENNENDE BERG, DER • 1921 • Piel Harry • FRG
BRENNENDE BLOMSTER • 1985 • Dahr Eva, Isaksen Eva • NRW • BURNING FLOWERS
BRENNENDE GEHEIMNIS, DAS see **MUTTER, DEIN KIND RUFT** • 1923
BRENNENDE GERICHT, DAS (FRG) see **CHAMBRE ARDENTE, LA** • 1961
BRENNENDE GRENZE • 1926 • Waschneck Erich • FRG • AFTERMATH (USA)
BRENNENDE HERZ, DAS • 1929 • Berger Ludwig • FRG • BURNING HEART, THE (USA)
BRENNENDE KUGEL, DIE • 1923 • Rippert Otto • FRG • DEATH CHEAT, THE
BRENNENDE SCHIFF, DAS • 1927 • David Constantin J. • FRG
BRENNENDES GEHEIMNIS • 1933 • Siodmak Robert • FRG • BURNING SECRET, THE
BRENNENDES LAND • 1921 • Herald Heinz • FRG
BRENNENDES MEER see **STERBENDE VOLKER 2** • 1922
BRENNER I NATT, DET • 1955 • Skouen Arne • NRW
BRENNO IL NEMICO DI ROMA • 1964 • Gentilomo Giacomo • ITL • BATTLE OF THE SPARTANS ○ BRENNUS, ENEMY OF ROME
BRENNON O' THE MOOR • 1916 • Ford Francis • SHT • USA
BRENNUS, ENEMY OF ROME see **BRENNO IL NEMICO DI ROMA** • 1964
BRENT JORD • 1971 • Andersen Knut • NRW • SCORCHED EARTH
BRERA MUSEO VIVENTE • 1955 • Heusch Paolo • DOC • ITL
BRESAGLIO UMANO • 1922 • Campogalliani Carlo • ITL
BRESIL: ETAT DE FORCE • 1977 • Bertolino Daniel • DOC • CND
BRESIL: LA TRANSAMAZONIE • 1973 • Floquet Francois • DOC • CND
BRETAGNE, LA • 1936 • Epstein Jean • FRN
BRETELLES, LES • 1913 • Perret Leonce • FRN
BRETHREN • 1977 • Zahoruk Denis • CND
BRETHREN see **HARAKARA** • 1975
BRETHREN OF THE SACRED FISH • 1913 • *Thanhouser* • USA
BREV TILL PARADISET • 1990 • Wistrom Mikael • SWD • LETTER TO PARADISE
BREVE STAGIONE, UNA • 1969 • Castellani Renato • ITL • BRIEF SEASON, A
BREVE VACANZA, UNA • 1973 • De Sica Vittorio • ITL • BRIEF VACATION, A (USA)
BREVE VISION DE TOKYO • 1967 • Comeron Luis Jose • SHT • SPN
BREVET 95-75 • 1934 • Lequim Pierre • FRN
BREVET DE PILOTE NO.1: BLERIOT • 1960 • Galey • SHT • FRN
BREVI AMORE A PALMA DI MAJORCA • 1959 • Bianchi Giorgio • ITL, SPN • ISLAND AFFAIR
BREWER'S DAUGHTER, THE see **BRYGGERENS DATTER** • 1912
BREWERY-TOWN ROMANCE, A • 1914 • *Lubin* • USA
BREWSTER MCCLOUD • 1970 • Altman Robert • USA
BREWSTER TRIO, THE • 1902 • *Warwick Trading Co.* • UKN
BREWSTER TRIO OF HIGH KICKERS AND DANCERS, THE • 1902 • *Warwick Trading Co.* • UKN
BREWSTER'S MILLIONS • 1914 • Apfel Oscar, De Mille Cecil B. • USA
BREWSTER'S MILLIONS • 1921 • Henabery Joseph • USA
BREWSTER'S MILLIONS • 1935 • Freeland Thornton • UKN
BREWSTER'S MILLIONS • 1945 • Dwan Allan • USA
BREWSTER'S MILLIONS • 1985 • Hill Walter • USA
BREZA • 1967 • Babaja Ante • YGS • BIRCH TREE, THE
BREZAIA • Petringenaru Adrian • ANM • RMN
BREZJE • Ljubic Milan • DOC • YGS
BRIAN WALKER, PLEASE CALL HOME see **INTO THIN AIR** • 1985
BRIAN'S SONG • 1970 • Kulik Buzz • TVM • USA
BRIBE, THE • 1913 • Vignola Robert G. • USA
BRIBE, THE • 1915 • *Ogle Charles* • USA
BRIBE, THE • 1948 • Leonard Robert Z. • USA
BRICK-A-BRAC • 1935 • White Sam • SHT • USA
BRICK BRADFORD • 1947 • Bennet Spencer Gordon, Carr Thomas • SRL • USA
BRICK DOLLHOUSE, THE • 1967 • Martinez Tony • USA • HOUSE OF THE BRICK DOLLS, THE ○ DOLL HOUSE, THE
BRICK TOP • 1916 • McDermott John • SHT • USA
BRICKLAYER AND HIS MATE: OR, A JEALOUS MAN'S CRIME, THE • 1899 • *Paul R. W.* • UKN
BRICKLAYERS, THE see **ALBANILES, LOS** • 1976
BRICOLAGE • 1984 • Rimmer David • CND
BRICOLEURS, LES • 1962 • Girault Jean • FRN • WHO STOLE THE BODY (USA) ○ BODY IS MISSING, THE
BRIDAL BAIL • 1934 • Stevens George • SHT • USA
BRIDAL BOUQUET, THE • 1915 • *Anderson Mignon* • USA
BRIDAL CHAIR, THE • 1919 • Samuelson G. B. • UKN
BRIDAL COUPLE DODGING THE CAMERAS • 1908 • Porter Edwin S. • USA
BRIDAL GARLAND, THE see **MORSIUSSEPPELE** • 1954
BRIDAL PATH, THE • 1959 • Launder Frank • UKN
BRIDAL PATH, THE see **ALL'S FAIR IN LOVE** • 1921
BRIDAL ROOM, THE • 1912 • Daly William Robert • USA
BRIDAL SHOWER, THE • 1971 • Wilson Sandra • CND
BRIDAL SUITE • 1939 • Thiele Wilhelm • USA • MAIDEN VOYAGE
BRIDAL TRAIL, THE • 1911 • *Nestor* • USA
BRIDE see **BEHULI** • 1989
BRIDE 13 • 1920 • Stanton Richard • SRL • USA
BRIDE 68 see **TERRA SENZA DONNE** • 1929
BRIDE, THE • 1929 • Croise Hugh • UKN
BRIDE, THE • 1973 • Pelissie Jean-Marie • USA • HOUSE THAT CRIED MURDER, THE ○ HERE COMES THE BRIDE ○ NO WAY OUT
BRIDE, THE • 1985 • Roddam Franc • USA
BRIDE, THE see **OLD MAN'S BRIDE, THE** • 1967
BRIDE, THE see **NEVESTA** • 1970
BRIDE, THE see **GELIN** • 1973
BRIDE, THE see **SPOSINA, LA** • 1976
BRIDE AND GLOOM • 1917 • *Rhodes Billie* • SHT • USA
BRIDE AND GLOOM • 1918 • Roach Hal • SHT • USA
BRIDE AND GLOOM • 1954 • Sparber I. • ANS • USA
BRIDE AND GLOOMY • 1931 • Pearce A. Leslie • USA
BRIDE AND GROOM • 1956 • Daborn John, Potterton Gerald • SHT • UKN
BRIDE AND GROOM'S VISIT TO THE NEW YORK ZOOLOGICAL GARDENS, A • 1909 • *Edison* • USA
BRIDE AND THE BEAST, THE • 1958 • Weiss Adrian • USA • QUEEN OF THE GORILLAS
BRIDE AND THE BEASTS, THE • 1969 • Donne John
BRIDE BY MISTAKE • 1944 • Wallace Richard • USA
BRIDE CAME C.O.D., THE • 1941 • Keighley William • USA
BRIDE CAME THROUGH THE CEILING, THE see **BRUDEN KOM GENOM TAKET** • 1947
BRIDE COMES HOME, THE • 1935 • Ruggles Wesley • USA
BRIDE COULDN'T WAIT, THE see **SPOSA NON PUO ATTENDERE, LA** • 1950
BRIDE FOR A KNIGHT, A • 1923 • *Hull Henry* • USA
BRIDE FOR A SINGLE NIGHT see **DULHAN EK RAAT KI** • 1967
BRIDE FOR ALL REASONS, A • 1984 • Wallace Stephen • TVM • ASL
BRIDE FOR BRENDA, A • 1969 • Goetz Tommy • USA
BRIDE FOR FRANK, A (USA) see **MOGLIE E BUOI..** • 1956
BRIDE FOR HENRY, A • 1937 • Nigh William • USA
BRIDE FOR SALE • 1949 • Russell William D., Skirball Jack H. • USA
BRIDE FROM HADES, THE see **KAIDAN BOTAN DORO** • 1968
BRIDE FROM HELL, THE see **KAIDAN BOTAN DORO** • 1968
BRIDE FROM JAPAN, THE see **HANAYOME-SAN WA SEKAI ICHI** • 1959
BRIDE FROM THE SEA, A • 1913 • *Robinson Gertrude* • USA
BRIDE FROM THE TRAIN, THE see **MIREASA DIN TREN** • 1980
BRIDE GOES WILD, THE • 1948 • Taurog Norman • USA • VIRTUOUS
BRIDE HAS A MOTHER, THE see **UM AL-ARUSSA** • 1963
BRIDE IN A BATHING SUIT see **MIZUGI NO HANAYOME** • 1954
BRIDE IN DISTRESS, A see **NIMFIOS ANIMFEFTOS** • 1967
BRIDE IS MUCH TOO BEAUTIFUL, THE (USA) see **MARIEE EST TROP BELLE, LA** • 1956
BRIDE IS TOO BEAUTIFUL, THE (UKN) see **MARIEE EST TROP BELLE, LA** • 1956
BRIDE OF BOOGEDY • 1987 • Scott Oz • TVM • USA
BRIDE OF DEATH, A see **DODENS BRUD** • 1911
BRIDE OF FEAR, THE • 1918 • Franklin Sidney A. • USA
BRIDE OF FRANKENSTEIN • 1935 • Whale James • USA • FRANKENSTEIN LIVES AGAIN ○ RETURN OF FRANKENSTEIN, THE
BRIDE OF GLOMDAL, THE see **GLOMDALSBRUDEN** • 1925
BRIDE OF GLOMSDALE, THE see **GLOMDALSBRUDEN** • 1925
BRIDE OF GUADELOUPE, THE • 1915 • *Storm Jerome* • USA
BRIDE OF HATE, THE • 1917 • Edwards Walter • USA
BRIDE OF LAMMERMOOR • 1914 • *Kennedy Pictures* • USA
BRIDE OF LAMMERMOOR, THE • 1909 • Blackton J. Stuart • USA
BRIDE OF LAMMERMOOR, THE • 1922 • Sanderson Challis • UKN
BRIDE OF MARBLE HEAD, THE • 1914 • *Myers Harry* • USA
BRIDE OF MYSTERY, THE • 1914 • Ford Francis • USA
BRIDE OF TEHRAN, THE see **AROUS-E-TEHRAN** • 1967
BRIDE OF THE ANDES (UKN) see **ANDESU NO HANAYOME** • 1966
BRIDE OF THE ATOM see **BRIDE OF THE MONSTER** • 1956
BRIDE OF THE COLORADO • 1927 • Bray John R. • USA
BRIDE OF THE DESERT • 1929 • Worne Duke • USA
BRIDE OF, THE EARTH see **SEYYIT KHAN** • 1968
BRIDE OF THE GODS see **SHATTERED IDOLS** • 1922
BRIDE OF THE GORILLA • 1951 • Siodmak Curt • USA • QUEEN OF THE GORILLAS
BRIDE OF THE HAUNTED CASTLE, THE • 1910 • *Artistic* • USA
BRIDE OF THE LAKE, THE (USA) see **LILY OF KILLARNEY** • 1934
BRIDE OF THE LUMBERJACK, THE see **TUKKIPOJAN MORSIAN** • 1931
BRIDE OF THE MONSTER • 1956 • Wood Edward D. Jr. • USA • BRIDE OF THE ATOM
BRIDE OF THE NANCY LEE, THE • 1915 • Reynolds Lynn • USA
BRIDE OF THE REGIMENT • 1930 • Dillon John Francis • USA • LADY OF THE ROSE (UKN)
BRIDE OF THE SEA, THE • 1913 • *Dragon* • USA
BRIDE OF THE SEA, THE • 1915 • Powers Francis • USA
BRIDE OF THE STORM • 1926 • Blackton J. Stuart • USA
BRIDE OF VENGEANCE • 1923 • *Richter Ellen* • USA
BRIDE OF VENGEANCE • 1949 • Leisen Mitchell • USA
BRIDE SIXTY-SIX see **LOTTERY BRIDE, THE** • 1930
BRIDE SUR LE COU, LA • 1961 • Vadim Roger, Aurel Jean (U/c) • FRN, ITL • A BRIGLIA SCIOLTA (ITL) ○ PLEASE, NOT NOW! (USA)
BRIDE TALKS IN HER SLEEP, THE see **HANAYOME NO NEGOTO** • 1933
BRIDE TO BE see **PEPITA JIMENEZ** • 1975
BRIDE-TO-BE, THE • 1922 • Roach Hal • SHT • USA
BRIDE TO ORDER, A • 1916 • *Gayety* • USA
BRIDE WALKS OUT, THE • 1936 • Jason Leigh • USA
BRIDE WAS RADIANT, THE see **MENYASSZONY GYONYORU, A** • 1987
BRIDE WASN'T WILLING, THE (UKN) see **FRONTIER GAL** • 1945
BRIDE WITH A DOWRY • 1954 • Lukashevich Tatyana • USS
BRIDE WITH A DOWRY • 1954 • Ravenskikh B.
BRIDE WON BY BRAVERY, A • 1909 • *Lubin* • USA
BRIDE WORE BLACK, THE (UKN) see **MARIEE ETAIT EN NOIR, LA** • 1968
BRIDE WORE BOOTS, THE • 1946 • Pichel Irving • USA
BRIDE WORE CRUTCHES, THE • 1941 • Traube Shepard • USA
BRIDE WORE RED, THE • 1937 • Arzner Dorothy • USA
BRIDEGROOM 68 see **NOVIOS 68** • 1967
BRIDEGROOM FOR TWO SISTERS, A see **NOVIO PARA DOS HERMANAS, UN** • 1967
BRIDEGROOM FOR TWO (USA) see **LET'S LOVE AND LAUGH** • 1931
BRIDEGROOM FROM LONDON, THE see **GAMBROS APO TO LONDHINO, O** • 1967
BRIDEGROOM FROM THE OTHER WORLD see **ZHENIKH S TOGO SVETA** • 1958
BRIDEGROOM OF HAPPINESS see **HELLE FOR LYKKE** • 1969
BRIDEGROOM TALKS IN HIS SLEEP, A see **HANAMUKO NO NEGOTO** • 1934
BRIDEGROOM, THE COMEDIENNE AND THE PIMP, THE see **BRAUTIGAM DIE KOMODIANTIN UND DER ZUHALTER, DER** • 1968

BRIDEGROOMS AND THE KNIVES, THE • 1964 • Vasiliev V. • USS
BRIDEGROOMS BEWARE • 1913 • Elvey Maurice • UKN
BRIDEGROOM'S DILEMMA, THE • 1909 • *Edison* • USA
BRIDEGROOM'S DILEMMA, THE • 1911 • *Vitagraph* • USA
BRIDEGROOM'S DILEMMA, THE see **COUCHER DE LA MARIEE, LE** • 1899
BRIDEGROOM'S JOKE, THE • 1909 • *Vitagraph* • USA
BRIDEGROOM'S MISHAPS, A • 1910 • *Defender* • USA
BRIDEGROOM'S TROUBLES, A • 1912 • *Powers* • USA
BRIDEGROOMS WANTED • 1935 • Bhavnani Mohan Dayaram • IND
BRIDEGROOM'S WIDOW, THE see **LET'S LOVE AND LAUGH** • 1931
BRIDELESS GROOM • 1947 • Bernds Edward • SHT • USA
BRIDENAPPING see **HUA T'IEN-T'SO** • 1961
BRIDES AND BRIDLES • 1912 • *Nestor* • USA
BRIDES ARE LIKE THAT • 1936 • McGann William • USA
BRIDE'S AWAKENING, THE • 1918 • Leonard Robert Z. • USA
BRIDE'S BEREAVEMENT: OR, SNAKE IN THE GRASS, THE • 1932 • *Ray Charles* • SHT • USA
BRIDE'S CONFESSION, THE • 1921 • Abramson Ivan • USA
BRIDE'S FIRST NIGHT, THE • 1898 • *Haydon & Urry* • UKN
BRIDES FOR TWO • 1919 • Beaudine William • SHT • USA
BRIDE'S HISTORY, THE • 1913 • Ford Francis • USA
BRIDE'S MISTAKE, THE • 1931 • Rodney Earle • SHT • USA
BRIDE'S MOTHER, THE see **UM AL-ARUSSA** • 1963
BRIDES OF BLOOD • 1968 • Romero Eddie, De Leon Gerardo • USA • TERROR ON BLOOD ISLAND ○ ISLAND OF LIVING HORROR • BLOOD BRIDES ○ BRIDES OF DEATH ○ GRAVE DESIRES
BRIDES OF DEATH see **BRIDES OF BLOOD** • 1968
BRIDES OF DRACULA, THE • 1960 • Fisher Terence • UKN
BRIDES OF FU MANCHU, THE • 1966 • Sharp Don • UKN
BRIDE'S PLAY, THE • 1921 • Terwilliger George W. • USA
BRIDE'S RELATIONS, THE • 1929 • Sennett Mack • SHT • USA
BRIDE'S SILENCE, THE • 1917 • King Henry • USA
BRIDE'S THIEF see **JHOMAR CHOR** • 1986
BRIDES TO BE • 1934 • Denham Reginald • UKN
BRIDESHEAD REVISITED • 1981 • Sturridge Charles, Lindsay-Hogg Michael • MTV • UKN
BRIDESMAID'S SECRET, THE • 1916 • Brabin Charles J. • SHT • USA
BRIDGE • 1969 • Krvavac Hajrudin • YGS
BRIDGE, A • Makinen Aito • DOC • FNL
BRIDGE, THE • 1918 • SAF
BRIDGE, THE • 1932 • Vidor Charles • SHT • USA • SPY, THE
BRIDGE, THE • 1942 • Van Dyke Willard, Maddow Ben • DOC • USA
BRIDGE, THE • 1946 • Chambers Jack • UKN
BRIDGE, THE • 1987 • Poster Piak • THL
BRIDGE, THE see **BRUG, DE** • 1928
BRIDGE, THE see **MOST** • 1946
BRIDGE, THE see **BRUCKE, DIE** • 1949
BRIDGE, THE see **GIRL ON THE BRIDGE, THE** • 1951
BRIDGE, THE see **BRUCKE, DIE** • 1959
BRIDGE, THE see **KOPRU** • 1976
BRIDGE, THE see **PUENTE, EL** • 1977
BRIDGE, THE see **PUENTE, EL** • 1985
BRIDGE ACROSS, THE • 1915 • *Drumier Jack* • USA
BRIDGE ACROSS NO RIVER see **HASHI NO NAI KAWA** • 1969
BRIDGE ACROSS THE SEA see **SETU BANDHAN** • 1932
BRIDGE ACROSS TIME • 1985 • Swackhamer E. W. • TVM • USA • ARIZONA RIPPER, THE ○ TERROR AT LONDON BRIDGE
BRIDGE AHOY • 1936 • Fleischer Dave • ANS • USA
BRIDGE AT REMAGEN, THE • 1969 • Guillermin John • USA
BRIDGE BEYOND, THE see **CHANGBAGGE JAMSUGYOGA BOINDA** • 1985
BRIDGE CANNOT BE CROSSED, THE see **MOST PEREYTI NELIEYA** • 1960
BRIDGE CHAT • 1933 • Sparling Gordon • DCS • CND
BRIDGE DESTROYER, THE • 1914 • Wilson Frank? • UKN
BRIDGE GROWS IN BROOKLYN, A • 1967 • Harriton Chuck • ANS • USA
BRIDGE HIGH • 1979 • Kirchheimer Manny • SHT • USA
BRIDGE IN THE JUNGLE, THE • 1970 • Kohner Pancho • MXC, USA
BRIDGE OF FANCY, A • 1917 • Windom Lawrence C. • SHT • USA
BRIDGE OF JAPAN see **NIHONBASHI** • 1956
BRIDGE OF SAN LUIS REY, THE • 1929 • Brabin Charles J. • USA
BRIDGE OF SAN LUIS REY, THE • 1944 • Lee Rowland V. • USA
BRIDGE OF SHADOWS, THE • 1913 • Huntley Fred W. • USA
BRIDGE OF SIGHS, THE • 1908 • Merwin Bannister • USA
BRIDGE OF SIGHS, THE • 1915 • *Broadway* • USA
BRIDGE OF SIGHS, THE • 1915 • Bracken Bertram • *Lubin* • USA
BRIDGE OF SIGHS, THE • 1925 • Rosen Phil • USA
BRIDGE OF SIGHS, THE • 1936 • Rosen Phil • USA
BRIDGE OF SIGHTS • 1908 • Porter Edwin S. • USA
BRIDGE OF STORSTROM, THE see **STORSSTROEMBROEN** • 1949
BRIDGE OF THE GODS, THE • 1914 • Ferris Mabel • USA
BRIDGE OF TIME, THE • 1915 • Beal Frank • USA
BRIDGE OF TIME, THE • 1952 • Eady David • DOC • UKN
BRIDGE OF WITCHES, THE see **PONTE DELLE STREGHE, IL** • 1909
BRIDGE ON THE RIVER KWAI, THE • 1957 • Lean David • UKN, USA
BRIDGE THAT GAP • 1965 • De Palma Brian • SHT • USA
BRIDGE TO HELL • 1986 • Ciccarese Luis, Lenzi Umberto • ITL
BRIDGE TO INDONESIA, THE • 1988 • Willanto Willy, Markowitz Robert • INN, USA
BRIDGE TO NOWHERE, THE • 1985 • Mune Ian • NZL
BRIDGE TO SILENCE • 1989 • Arthur Karen • USA
BRIDGE TO THE SUN • 1961 • Perier Etienne • USA, FRN • PONT VERS LE SOLEIL, LE (FRN)
BRIDGE TO THE SUN see **GUNESE KOPRU** • 1985
BRIDGE TOO FAR, A • 1977 • Attenborough Richard • UKN
BRIDGE UNDER THE OCEAN • 1957 • Garceau Raymond • DCS • CND • PONT SOUS L'OCEAN, UN
BRIDGE WIVES • 1932 • Arbuckle Roscoe • USA
BRIDGEHEAD • Parkes Roger • UKN
BRIDGEHEAD FOR EIGHT RUTHLESS MEN see **TESTA DI SBARCO PER OTTO IMPLACABILI** • 1968
BRIDGER • 1975 • Rich David Lowell • TVM • USA • BRIDGER –THE FORTIETH DAY
BRIDGER –THE FORTIETH DAY see **BRIDGER** • 1975
BRIDGES AT TOKO-RI, THE • 1954 • Robson Mark • USA
BRIDGES BURNED • 1917 • Vekroff Perry N. • USA
BRIDGES-GO-ROUND • 1958 • Clarke Shirley • SHT • USA
BRIDGES OF HOLLAND • 1968 • Haanstra Bert • DCS • NTH
BRIDGET AND THE EGG • 1911 • *Lubin* • USA
BRIDGET BRIDGES IT • 1914 • *Boulder Robert* • USA
BRIDGET'S BLUNDER • 1916 • *U.s.m.p.* • SHT • USA
BRIDGET'S EXPLANATION • 1912 • *Lubin* • USA
BRIDGET'S SUDDEN WEALTH • 1912 • *O'Connor Edward* • USA
BRIDGING OF LANKA, THE see **SETU BANDHAN** • 1932
BRIEF, DER • 1966 • Kristl Vlado • FRG
BRIEF AFFAIR, A • 1981 • Lewis Louie • USA
BRIEF AUTHORITY • 1914 • Buckland Warwick? • UKN
BRIEF DEBUT OF TILDY, THE • 1918 • Ridgwell George • SHT • USA
BRIEF ECSTASY • 1937 • Greville Edmond T. • UKN
BRIEF EINEN TOTEN, DER • 1917 • Freisler Fritz • AUS
BRIEF ENCOUNTER • 1945 • Lean David • UKN
BRIEF ENCOUNTER • 1975 • Bridges Alan • TVM • UKN
BRIEF ENCOUNTER see **CHHOTISI MULAQAT** • 1967
BRIEF ENCOUNTERS see **KOROTKIYE VSTRYECHI** • 1968
BRIEF HISTORY see **SCURTA ISTORIE** • 1956
BRIEF MOMENT • 1933 • Burton David • USA
BRIEF RAPTURE (USA) see **LEBBRA BIANCA** • 1951
BRIEF SEASON, A see **BREVE STAGIONE, UNA** • 1969
BRIEF SUMMER see **KORTE SOMMER, DEN** • 1975
BRIEF VACATION, A (USA) see **BREVE VACANZA, UNA** • 1973
BRIEFE, DIE IHN NICHT ERREICHTEN • 1925 • Zelnik Friedrich • FRG
BRIEFE EINER UNBEKANNTEN see **NARKOSE** • 1929
BRIEFOFFNER, DER • 1916 • Gartner Adolf • FRG
BRIEFTRAGER MULLER • 1953 • Ruhmann Heinz • FRG
BRIERE, LA • 1924 • Poirier Leon • FRN
BRIG, THE • Sato Jason • USA
BRIG, THE • 1965 • Mekas Jonas, Mekas Adolfas • USA
BRIG "THREE LILIES", THE see **BRIGGEN TRE LILJOR** • 1961
BRIGA DE FOICE • 1980 • Salva Alberto • BRZ • SICKLE FIGHT
BRIGAD see **PAN PROKOUK JEDE NA BRIGADU** • 1947
BRIGADA CRIMINAL • 1950 • Iquino Ignacio F. • SPN
BRIGADE, LA • 1974 • Gilson Rene • FRN
BRIGADE ANTI-GANGS • 1966 • Borderie Bernard • FRN, ITL • PATTUGLIA ANTI-GANG (ITL)
BRIGADE ANTI-SEX • 1971 • Rental J. W. • BLG
BRIGADE CRIMINELLE • 1947 • Gil Gilbert • FRN
BRIGADE CRIMINELLE • 1980 • Blorovich Elie • FRN • INTERNATIONAL PROSTITUTION
BRIGADE DES MOEURS • 1958 • Boutel Maurice • FRN
BRIGADE EN DENTELLES, LA see **BRIGADE EN JUPONS, LA** • 1936
BRIGADE EN FOLIE, LA • 1972 • Clair Philippe • FRN
BRIGADE EN JUPONS, LA • 1936 • de Limur Jean • FRN • BRIGADE EN DENTELLES, LA
BRIGADE MISCELLANEOUS IN THE MOUNTAINS AND AT THE SEASIDE • 1970 • Dragan Mircea • RMN
BRIGADE MISCELLANEOUS ON ALERT • 1970 • Dragan Mircea • RMN
BRIGADE MISCELLANEOUS STEPS IN • 1970 • Dragan Mircea • RMN
BRIGADE MONDAINE • 1978 • Scandelari Jacques • FRN
BRIGADE MONDAINE II • Scandelari Jacques • FRN
BRIGADE MONDAINE: LA SECTE DE MARRAKECH • 1979 • Matalon Eddy • FRN • SECTE DE MARRAKECH, LA
BRIGADE MONDAINE: VAUDOU AUX CARAIBES • 1980 • Monnier Philippe • FRN, FRG
BRIGADE OF LEAD, THE see **OLOVNA BRIGADA** • 1981
BRIGADE SAUVAGE, LA • 1939 • Dreville Jean, L'Herbier Marcel • FRN
BRIGADEN I SVERIGE • 1945 • Henning-Jensen Bjarne • DNM • DANISH BRIGADE IN SWEDEN
BRIGADIER GERARD • 1915 • Haldane Bert • UKN
BRIGADIER GERARD see **FIGHTING EAGLE, THE** • 1927
BRIGADIERE PASQUALE ZACARIA AMA LA MAMMA E LA POLIZIA • 1973 • Forges Davanzati Maria • ITL
BRIGADISTA, EL • 1978 • Cortazar Octavio • CUB • TEACHER, THE
BRIGADOON • 1954 • Minnelli Vincente • USA
BRIGADY see **PAN PROKOUK JEDE NA BRIGADU** • 1947
BRIGAND, THE • 1952 • Karlson Phil • USA
BRIGAND, THE see **LOUPEZNIK** • 1931
BRIGAND, THE see **BRIGANTE, IL** • 1961
BRIGAND GENTILHOMME, LE • 1942 • Couzinet Emile • FRN
BRIGAND OF KANDAHAR, THE • 1965 • Gilling John • UKN
BRIGANDAGE MODERNE • 1905 • Zecca Ferdinand • FRN • MODERN BRIGANDAGE
BRIGANDS, THE • 1906 • Fitzhamon Lewin • UKN
BRIGAND'S BLOOD see **ESKIYA KANI** • 1968
BRIGAND'S DAUGHTER, THE • 1907 • Williamson James? • UKN
BRIGAND'S REVENGE, THE • 1911 • Coleby A. E. • UKN
BRIGAND'S WOOING, A • 1913 • Collins Edwin J.? • UKN
BRIGANTE, IL • 1961 • Castellani Renato • ITL • BRIGAND, THE
BRIGANTE DI TACCA DEL LUPO, IL • 1952 • Germi Pietro • ITL
BRIGANTE MUSOLINO, IL • 1950 • Camerini Mario • ITL • FUGITIVE
BRIGANTENLIEBE • 1920 • Hartwig Martin • FRG
BRIGANTENRACHE • 1920 • Bruck Reinhard • FRG
BRIGANTI ITALIANI, I • 1961 • Camerini Mario • ITL, FRN • SEDUCTION OF THE SOUTH (USA) ○ GUERILLEROS, LES (FRN)
BRIGANTIN VON COSTILIZA, DIE • 1920 • Attenberger Toni • FRG
BRIGANTIN VON NEW YORK, DIE • 1924 • Werckmeister Hans • FRG
BRIGATA DELLA SPERANZA, LA • 1953 • Pisu Mario • ITL
BRIGGEN TRE LILJOR • 1961 • Abramson Hans • SWD • BRIG "THREE LILIES", THE
BRIGGS FAMILY, THE • 1940 • Mason Herbert • UKN
BRIGHAM YOUNG –FRONTIERSMAN • 1940 • Hathaway Henry • USA • BRIGHAM YOUNG (UKN)
BRIGHAM YOUNG (UKN) see **BRIGHAM YOUNG – FRONTIERSMAN** • 1940
BRIGHT AND BREEZY • 1956 • Cowan Will • SHT • USA
BRIGHT AND EARLY • 1918 • Parrott Charles • SHT • USA
BRIGHT ANGEL • 1990 • Fields Michael • USA
BRIGHT, BRIGHT DAY, A see **BYELY, BYELY DYEN** • 1974
BRIGHT DAY OF MY LIFE, THE see **WAGA SHOGAI NO KAGAYAKERU HI** • 1948
BRIGHT EYES • 1922 • St. Clair Malcolm • SHT • USA
BRIGHT EYES • 1934 • Butler David • USA
BRIGHT EYES see **CHAMPAGNER** • 1929
BRIGHT GEM AT NIGHT see **GOHAR-E-SHABCHERAGH** • 1967
BRIGHT LEAF • 1950 • Curtiz Michael • USA
BRIGHT LIGHTS • 1924 • Christie Al • USA
BRIGHT LIGHTS • 1925 • Leonard Robert Z. • USA • LITTLE BIT OF BROADWAY, A
BRIGHT LIGHTS • 1928 • Disney Walt • ANS • USA
BRIGHT LIGHTS • 1930 • Curtiz Michael • USA
BRIGHT LIGHTS • 1935 • Berkeley Busby • USA • FUNNY FACE (UKN)
BRIGHT LIGHTS, THE • 1916 • Arbuckle Roscoe • SHT • USA • LURE OF BROADWAY, THE
BRIGHT LIGHTS, BIG CITY • 1988 • Bridges James • USA
BRIGHT LIGHTS DIMMED, THE • 1918 • Drew Sidney, Drew Sidney Mrs. • USA
BRIGHT LIGHTS OF BROADWAY • 1923 • Campbell Webster • USA
BRIGHT LIGHTS OF LONDON see **THAT NIGHT IN LONDON** • 1932
BRIGHT PATH see **SVETYLI PUT** • 1940
BRIGHT PATH, THE • 1939 • Sparling Gordon • CND
BRIGHT PROSPECTS see **LJUSNANDE FRAMTID, DEN** • 1941
BRIGHT ROAD • 1953 • Mayer Gerald • USA • SEE HOW THEY RUN
BRIGHT SEA see **HIKARU UMI** • 1963
BRIGHT SHAWL, THE • 1923 • Robertson John S. • USA
BRIGHT SKIES • 1920 • Kolker Henry • USA
BRIGHT STAR AT THE STAKE, A see **CSILLAG A MAGLYAN** • 1979
BRIGHT TOWN, THE see **SVETLYI GOROD** • 1928
BRIGHT VICTORY • 1951 • Robson Mark • USA • LIGHTS OUT (UKN)
BRIGHT YOUNG THINGS • 1927 • Dewhurst George • UKN
BRIGHTENED SUNSETS • 1913 • *Walters George W. (Mrs.)* • USA
BRIGHTEST STAR, THE see **PIO LAMBRO ASTERI, TO** • 1967
BRIGHTHAVEN EXPRESS (USA) see **SALUTE THE TOFF** • 1952
BRIGHTNESS see **YEELEN** • 1987
BRIGHTNESS AND DARKNESS see **MEIRAN** • 1929
BRIGHTON BEACH MEMOIRS • 1987 • Saks Gene • USA
BRIGHTON MYSTERY, THE • 1924 • Croise Hugh • UKN
BRIGHTON ROCK • 1947 • Boulting John • UKN • YOUNG SCARFACE (UKN)
BRIGHTON STORY, THE • 1956 • Bower Dallas • SHT • UKN
BRIGHTON STRANGLER, THE • 1945 • Nosseck Max • USA
BRIGHTY OF GRAND CANYON see **BRIGHTY OF THE GRAND CANYON** • 1967
BRIGHTY OF THE GRAND CANYON • 1967 • Foster Norman • USA • BRIGHTY (UKN) ○ BRIGHTY OF GRAND CANYON
BRIGHTY (UKN) see **BRIGHTY OF THE GRAND CANYON** • 1967
BRIGITTA • 1967 • *Cole Elke*
BRIGITTE ET BRIGITTE • 1967 • Mollet Luc • FRN
BRIGITTE HORNEY • 1977 • Zanussi Krzysztof • FRG
BRIGITTE, LAURA, URSULA...E SOFIA LE CHIAMO TUTTE.. ANIMA MIA • 1974 • Ivaldi Mauro O. • ITL
BRIGLIADORO • 1959 • Zane Angio • ITL
BRILANTINA ROCK • 1979 • Tarantini Michele Massimo • ITL
BRILLANCES SUR DEUX SAXOS • 1981 • Soussigne Jean-Pierre • FRN
BRILLANTE PORVENIR • 1964 • Aranda Vicente, Gubern Ramon • SPN • BRILLIANT FUTURE
BRILLANTEN • 1937 • von Borsody Eduard • FRG
BRILLANTENMARDER see **SCHATZKAMMER IM SEE 1, DIE** • 1921
BRILLANTENMIEZE 1, DIE • 1921 • Neff Wolfgang • FRG
BRILLANTENMIEZE 2, DIE • 1921 • Neff Wolfgang • FRG
BRILLANTSTJERNEN • 1912 • Blom August • DNM • FOR HER SISTER'S SAKE
BRILLIANT COLLECTOR, A see **TORITATE NO KAGAYAKI** • 1982
BRILLIANT FUTURE see **BRILLANTE PORVENIR** • 1964
BRILLIANT MARRIAGE • 1936 • Rosen Phil • USA
BRILLIANT MURDER see **KENRANTARU SATSUJIN** • 1951
BRILLIANT SHOWA PERIOD, THE see **KAGAYAKU SHOWA** • 1928
BRILLIANT WOMAN, THE see **HIKARU ONNA** • 1988
BRILLIANTEN SCHIFF, DAS see **SPINNEN PART 2, DIE** • 1920
BRILLIANTOVAYA RUKA • 1968 • Gaidai Leonid • USS • DIAMOND HAND, THE ○ DIAMOND ARM
BRIMADE DANS UNE CASERNE see **SAUT A LA COUVERTURE** • 1895
BRIMSTONE • 1949 • Kane Joseph • USA
BRIMSTONE & TREACLE • 1981 • Loncraine Richard • UKN
BRINDAMORE ISLAND CONSPIRACY, THE • 1988 • Hussein Waris • USA
BRINDIS A MANOLETE • 1948 • Rey Florian • SPN
BRINDIS AL CIELO • 1953 • Buchs Jose • SPN
BRING 'EM BACK A LIE • 1935 • Goulding Alf • SHT • USA
BRING 'EM BACK A WIFE • 1933 • Lord Del • USA
BRING 'EM BACK ALIVE • 1932 • Elliott Clyde E. • DOC • USA
BRING 'EM BACK HALF-SHOT • 1932 • Foster John, Davis Mannie • ANS • USA
BRING 'EM BACK SOBER • 1932 • *Sennett Mack (P)* • SHT • USA
BRING HIM IN • 1921 • Williams Earle, Ensminger Bert • USA

BRING HIMSELF BACK ALIVE • 1940 • Fleischer Dave • ANS • USA
BRING HOME THE TURKEY • 1927 • Roach Hal • SHT • USA
BRING ME THE HEAD OF ALFREDO GARCIA • 1973 • Peckinpah Sam • USA, MXC • TRAIGANME LA CABEZA DE ALFREDO GARCIA (MXC)
BRING ME THE HEAD OF DOBIE GILLIS • 1988 • Cherry Stanley Z. • TVM • USA
BRING ME THE VAMPIRE (USA) see **ECHENME AL VAMPIRO** • 1961
BRING ON THE GIRLS • 1946 • Lanfield Sidney • USA
BRING ON THE NIGHT • 1985 • Apted Michael • DOC • UKN
BRING OUT A BRITON • 1957 • Robinson Lee • DCS • ASL
BRING WHISKY AND A SMILE • 1974 • Fruet William • CND
BRING YOUR SMILE ALONG • 1955 • Edwards Blake • USA
BRING'EM ON • 1982 • Pyke Roger • CND
BRINGIN' HOME THE BACON • 1924 • Thorpe Richard • USA • WINTON WAKES UP
BRINGING FATHER AROUND • 1912 • *Steppling John* • USA
BRINGING HOME FATHER • 1917 • Worthington William • USA
BRINGING HOME THE BACON • 1941 • Davis Mannie • ANS • USA
BRINGING HOME THE PUP • 1912 • *Edison* • USA
BRINGING IN THE LAW • 1914 • *West Josphine* • USA
BRINGING IT ALL BACK HOME • 1972 • May David • UKN
BRINGING IT HOME • 1940 • Lewis J. E. • UKN
BRINGING IT HOME TO HIM • 1914 • Cooper Toby • UKN
BRINGING OUT OF PAPA, THE • 1913 • *Vitagraph* • USA
BRINGING UP BABY • 1938 • Hawks Howard • USA
BRINGING UP BETTY • 1919 • Apfel Oscar • USA
BRINGING UP FATHER • 1916 • Moser Frank • ANM • USA
BRINGING UP FATHER • 1928 • Conway Jack • USA
BRINGING UP FATHER • 1946 • Cline Eddie • USA
BRINGING UP HUBBY • 1914 • *Selig* • USA
BRINGING UP HUSBANDS see **DANSEI SHIIKU-HO** • 1959
BRINGING UP MOTHER • 1954 • Hurtz William • ANS • USA
BRINGING UP THE CHILDREN see **KOSODATE GOKKO** • 1978
BRINK, THE • 1915 • Edwards Walter? • USA
BRINK, THE • 1916 • Reynolds Lynn • SHT • USA
BRINK OF HELL (UKN) see **TOWARD THE UNKNOWN** • 1956
BRINK OF LIFE (USA) see **NARA LIVET** • 1958
BRINK'S JOB, THE • 1978 • Friedkin William • USA • BIG STICKUP AT BRINK'S
BRINK'S: THE GREAT ROBBERY • 1976 • Chomsky Marvin • TVM • USA
BRIONES, YOU'RE MAD see **TU ESTORS LOCO, BRIONES** • 1980
BRISBANE BOTANICAL GARDENS • 1914 • ASL
BRISBANE CUP 1922 • 1922 • ASL
BRISCOLA see **RICCHI E POVERI** • 1949
BRISEUR DE CHAINES, LE • 1941 • Daniel-Norman Jacques • FRN • MAMOURET
BRISTET LYKKE • 1913 • Blom August • DNM • PARADISE LOST, A
BRISTLE FACE • Sweeney Bob • USA
BRISTOL TYPE 170 • 1945-52 • Napier-Bell J. B. • DOC • UKN
BRITA I GROSSHANDLARHUSET • 1946 • Ohberg Ake • SWD • BRITA IN THE WHOLESALER'S HOUSE
BRITA IN THE WHOLESALER'S HOUSE see **BRITA I GROSSHANDLARHUSET** • 1946
BRITAIN AT BAY • 1940 • Watt Harry • DOC • UKN
BRITAIN CAN MAKE IT NO.1 • 1946 • Gysin Francis • DOC • UKN
BRITAIN CAN MAKE IT NO.7 • 1946 • Hill James • DOC • UKN
BRITAIN NOW • 1973 • *Halas John (P)* • ASS • UKN
BRITAIN'S COMET • 1952 • Hill James • DCS • UKN
BRITAIN'S EFFORT • 1918 • Dyer Anson • ANM • UKN
BRITAIN'S NAVAL SECRET • 1915 • Moran Percy • UKN
BRITAIN'S SECRET TREATY • 1914 • Raymond Charles • UKN
BRITAIN'S TRIBUTE TO HER SONS • 1901 • Booth W. R.? • UKN
BRITAIN'S WELCOME TO HER SONS • 1900 • Booth W. R. • UKN
BRITANNIA HOSPITAL • 1982 • Anderson Lindsay • UKN
BRITANNIA MEWS • 1948 • Negulesco Jean • UKN • FORBIDDEN STREET (USA) ○ AFFAIRS OF ADELAIDE, THE
BRITANNIA OF BILLINGSGATE • 1933 • Hill Sinclair • UKN
BRITANNICUS • 1912 • de Morlhon Camille • FRN
BRITISH AGENT • 1934 • Curtiz Michael • USA
BRITISH AIRCRAFT REVIEW 1948 • 1948 • Hughes Geoffrey • DOC • UKN
BRITISH -ARE THEY ARTISTIC?, THE • 1947 • UKN • THIS MODERN AGE NO.16
BRITISH ARMY, THE • 1900 • Hepworth Cecil M. • UKN
BRITISH BULLDOG CONQUERS, A see **SCALES OF JUSTICE, THE** • 1914
BRITISH CAPTURING A MAXIM GUN • 1899 • Ashe Robert • UKN
BRITISH FAMILY IN PEACE AND WAR, A • 1940 • Pearson George • DCS • UKN
BRITISH INTELLIGENCE • 1940 • Morse Terry O. • USA • ENEMY AGENT (UKN)
BRITISH LION VARIETIES NOS.1-9 • 1936 • Smith Herbert • SER • UKN
BRITISH MADE • 1939 • Pearson George • DCS • UKN
BRITISH NAVY, THE • 1900 • Hepworth Cecil M. • UKN
BRITISH SOUNDS • 1969 • Godard Jean-Luc • UKN • SEE YOU AT MAO
BRITISH WORKERS, THE • 1959 • Kelly Ron • DOC • CND
BRITISH YOUTH • 1941 • Pearson George • DCS • UKN
BRITON AND BOER • 1909 • *Selig* • USA
BRITON V. BOER • 1900 • *Acres Bert* • UKN
BRITON VS. BOER • 1900 • Fitzhamon Lewin • UKN
BRITONS AWAKE! • 1915 • Kinder Stuart? • UKN
BRITTLE WEATHER JOURNEY • 1973 • Wallace Stephen • SHT • ASL
BRITTON OF THE SEVENTH • 1916 • Belmore Lionel • USA
BRIVIDO • 1941 • Gentilomo Giacomo • ITL • TRIANGOLO MAGICO, IL
BRIVIDO DI PIACERE, UN • 1978 • Ausino Carlo • ITL
BRIVIDO FATALE • 1912 • De Liguoro Giuseppe • ITL
BRIVIDO SULLA PELLE, UN • 1966 • Damiani Amasi • ITL • SHIVER ON THE SKIN, A
BRNO TRAIL, THE see **TANA A DVA PISTOLNICI** • 1967
BROAD ARROW, THE • 1911 • Haldane Bert • UKN
BROAD COALITION, THE • 1972 • Nuchtern Simon • USA
BROAD DAYLIGHT • 1922 • Cummings Irving • USA • IN BROAD DAYLIGHT (UKN)
BROAD HIGHWAY see **SZEROKA DROGA** • 1949
BROAD HORIZONS see **HORIZONTE TE HAPURA** • 1968
BROAD-MINDED • 1931 • LeRoy Mervyn • USA
BROAD ROAD, THE • 1923 • Mortimer Edmund • USA
BROADBACK • 1974 • Valcour Pierre • DCS • CND
BROADCAST see **EKPOMBI, I** • 1968
BROADCAST NEWS • 1987 • Brooks James L. • USA
BROADCASTING • 1922 • USA
BROADCASTING • 1926 • Sanderson Challis, Newman Widgey R. • UKN
BROADCASTING • 1929 • Berthomieu Andre • FRN
BROADCLOTH AND BUCKSKIN • 1915 • Cooley Frank • USA
BROADWAY • 1929 • Fejos Paul • USA
BROADWAY • 1942 • Seiter William A. • USA
BROADWAY AFTER DARK • 1924 • Bell Monta • USA
BROADWAY AFTER MIDNIGHT • 1927 • Windermere Fred • USA • GANGSTERS ON BROADWAY (UKN)
BROADWAY AHEAD (UKN) see **SWEETHEART OF THE CAMPUS** • 1941
BROADWAY AND HOME • 1920 • Crosland Alan • USA
BROADWAY, ARIZONA • 1917 • Reynolds Lynn • USA
BROADWAY BABIES • 1929 • LeRoy Mervyn • USA • BROADWAY DADDIES (UKN)
BROADWAY BAD • 1933 • Lanfield Sidney • USA • HER REPUTATION (UKN)
BROADWAY BIG SHOT, THE • 1942 • Beaudine William • USA
BROADWAY BILL • 1918 • Balshofer Fred J. • USA
BROADWAY BILL • 1934 • Capra Frank • USA • STRICTLY CONFIDENTIAL (UKN)
BROADWAY BILLY • 1926 • Brown Harry J. • USA
BROADWAY BLUES • 1929 • Sennett Mack • USA
BROADWAY BLUES see **SYNCOPATING SUE** • 1926
BROADWAY BOOB, THE • 1926 • Henabery Joseph • USA
BROADWAY BOW WOWS • 1954 • Patterson Ray • ANS • USA
BROADWAY BRIDE, A (UKN) see **GIRL HE DIDN'T BUY, THE** • 1928
BROADWAY BROKE • 1923 • Dawley J. Searle • USA
BROADWAY BUBBLE, THE • 1920 • Sargent George L. • USA
BROADWAY BUCKAROO • 1921 • *Fairbanks William* • USA
BROADWAY BUTTERFLY, A • 1925 • Beaudine William • USA
BROADWAY BY LIGHT • 1958 • Klein William • SHT • USA
BROADWAY COWBOY, A • 1920 • Franz Joseph J. • USA
BROADWAY DADDIES • 1928 • Windermere Fred • USA • GIRL OF THE NIGHT (UKN)
BROADWAY DADDIES see **SHE HAS WHAT IT TAKES** • 1943
BROADWAY DADDIES (UKN) see **BROADWAY BABIES** • 1929
BROADWAY DANCER, THE see **SOUTH SEA LOVE** • 1923
BROADWAY DANNY ROSE • 1983 • Allen Woody • USA
BROADWAY DRIFTER, THE • 1927 • McEveety Bernard F. • USA
BROADWAY FARMER • 1945 • *O'Brien Joseph/ Mead Thomas (P)* • SHT • USA
BROADWAY FEVER • 1929 • Cline Eddie • USA
BROADWAY FOLLY • 1930 • Lantz Walter, Nolan William • ANS • USA
BROADWAY GALLANT, THE • 1926 • Smith Noel • USA
BROADWAY GOLD • 1923 • Dillon Eddie, Cooper J. Gordon • USA • VIRTUOUS FOOL, A
BROADWAY GONDOLIER • 1935 • Bacon Lloyd • USA
BROADWAY HIGHLIGHTS • 1935 • *Hopkins Claude* • SHT • USA
BROADWAY HOOFER, THE • 1929 • Archainbaud George • USA • DANCING FEET (UKN)
BROADWAY HOSTESS • 1935 • McDonald Frank • USA
BROADWAY HOSTESS, THE see **PAINTED ANGEL, THE** • 1929
BROADWAY JAMBOREE see **YOU'RE A SWEETHEART** • 1937
BROADWAY JONES • 1917 • Kaufman Joseph • USA
BROADWAY KID, THE (UKN) see **GINSBERG THE GREAT** • 1927
BROADWAY LADY • 1925 • Ruggles Wesley • USA
BROADWAY LIMITED • 1941 • Douglas Gordon • USA • BABY VANISHES, THE (UKN)
BROADWAY LOVE • 1918 • Park Ida May • USA
BROADWAY MADNESS • 1927 • King Burton L. • USA
BROADWAY MADONNA, THE • 1922 • Revier Harry • USA • MOTHERS OF MEN ○ BLACK DOMINO, THE
BROADWAY MALADY, THE • 1933 • *Mintz Charles (P)* • ANS • USA
BROADWAY MELODY, THE • 1929 • Beaumont Harry • USA
BROADWAY MELODY OF 1936 • 1935 • Del Ruth Roy • USA
BROADWAY MELODY OF 1938 • 1937 • Del Ruth Roy • USA
BROADWAY MELODY OF 1940 • 1940 • Taurog Norman • USA
BROADWAY MUSKETEERS • 1938 • Farrow John • USA • THREE GIRLS ON BROADWAY
BROADWAY NIGHTS • 1927 • Boyle Joseph C. • USA
BROADWAY OR BUST • 1924 • Sedgwick Edward • USA
BROADWAY PEACOCK, THE • 1922 • Brabin Charles J. • USA
BROADWAY PIN-UP HONEYS see **NUDES, INC.** • 1964
BROADWAY RHYTHM • 1943 • Del Ruth Roy • USA
BROADWAY ROSE • 1922 • Leonard Robert Z. • USA
BROADWAY SAINT, A • 1919 • Hoyt Harry O. • USA
BROADWAY SCANDAL • 1918 • De Grasse Joseph • USA
BROADWAY SCANDALS • 1929 • Archainbaud George • USA
BROADWAY SERENADE • 1939 • Leonard Robert Z. • USA • SERENADE (UKN)
BROADWAY SINGER (UKN) see **TORCH SINGER** • 1933
BROADWAY SPORT, THE • 1917 • Harbaugh Carl • USA
BROADWAY THRU A KEYHOLE • 1933 • Sherman Lowell • USA
BROADWAY TO CHEYENNE (UKN) see **FROM BROADWAY TO CHEYENNE** • 1932
BROADWAY TO HOLLYWOOD • 1933 • Mack Willard • USA • RING UP THE CURTAIN (UKN) ○ MARCH OF TIME, THE ○ SHOW WORLD
BROADWAY VARIETIES • 1934 • Schwarzwald Milton • SHT • USA
BROCELIANDE • 1969 • Hacquard • SHT • FRN
BROCK'S LAST CASE • 1972 • Rich David Lowell • TVM • USA
BRODER CARL • 1971 • Sontag Susan • SWD • BROTHER CARL
BRODER EMALLAN • 1946 • Larsson Borje • SWD • BETWEEN BROTHERS
BRODERNA • 1914 • Stiller Mauritz • SWD • BROTHERS, THE
BRODERNA KARLSSON • 1974 • Sjoman Vilgot • SHT • SWD • KARLSSON BROTHERS, THE
BRODERNA LEJONHJARTA • 1977 • Hellbom Olle • SWD • BROTHERS LIONHEART, THE
BRODERNA MOZART • 1986 • Osten Suzanne • SWD • MOZART BROTHERS, THE
BRODERNA OSTERMANS BRAVADER • 1956 • Frisk Ragnar • SWD
BRODERNA OSTERMANS HUSKORS • 1925 • Larsson William • SWD • VIRAGO OF THE OSTERMAN BROTHERS
BRODERNA OSTERMANS HUSKORS • 1932 • Alfe Thure • SWD • VIRAGO OF THE OSTERMAN BROTHERS
BRODERNA OSTERMANS HUSKORS • 1945 • Johansson Ivar • SWD
BRODERNAS KVINNA • 1943 • Cederlund Gosta • SWD • BROTHER'S WOMAN, THE
BRODRENE PA UGLEGARDEN • 1967 • O'Fredericks Alice, Mossin Ib • DNM • BROTHERS OF THE "UGLEGARD", THE
BROER MATIE • 1984 • Rautenbach Jans • SAF • BROTHER MATE
BROGLIACCIO D'AMORE • 1976 • Silla Decio • ITL
BROILED SQUABS see **PIECZONE GOLABKI** • 1966
BROKE, BUT AMBITIOUS • 1916 • Chaudet Louis W. • SHT • USA
BROKE IN CHINA • 1927 • *Sennett Mack (P)* • SHT • USA
BROKE OR HOW TIMOTHY ESCAPED • 1911 • *Imp* • USA
BROKEN ANGEL • 1988 • Heffron Richard T. • TVM • USA
BROKEN ARROW • 1950 • Daves Delmer • USA
BROKEN BADGE, THE • 1978 • Katzin Lee H. • TVM • USA
BROKEN BARRIER • 1917 • Bellamy George • UKN • QUICKSANDS
BROKEN BARRIER • 1952 • Mirams Roger, O'Shea John • NZL
BROKEN BARRIER, THE • 1914 • *Reliance* • USA
BROKEN BARRIER, THE • 1914 • Ricketts Thomas • *American* • USA
BROKEN BARRIER, THE see **ISLE OF CONQUEST, THE** • 1919
BROKEN BARRIERS • 1919 • Davenport Charles E. • USA
BROKEN BARRIERS • 1924 • Barker Reginald • USA
BROKEN BARRIERS • 1928 • King Burton L. • USA
BROKEN BARRIERS, THE • 1914 • *Frontier* • USA
BROKEN BLOSSOMS • 1919 • Griffith D. W. • USA
BROKEN BLOSSOMS • 1936 • Brahm John • UKN
BROKEN BOTTLE, THE • 1914 • *Marsh Mae* • USA
BROKEN BOTTLES • 1920 • Henson Leslie • UKN
BROKEN BRIDGE, THE see **ZERWANY MOST** • 1962
BROKEN BROOM, THE • 1904 • Stow Percy • UKN • KISS AND A TUMBLE, A (USA)
BROKEN BUBBLES • 1920 • *Mann Hank* • SHT • USA
BROKEN BUTTERFLY see **BUTTERFLY** • 1975
BROKEN BUTTERFLY, THE • 1919 • Tourneur Maurice • USA
BROKEN CHAINS • 1913 • Barker Reginald • USA
BROKEN CHAINS • 1916 • Thornby Robert T. • USA
BROKEN CHAINS • 1922 • Holubar Allen • USA
BROKEN CHAINS see **YEVO PRIZYV** • 1925
BROKEN CHISEL, THE • 1913 • Weston Charles • UKN • ESCAPE FROM BROADMOOR (USA)
BROKEN CLOUD, A • 1915 • Eason B. Reeves • USA
BROKEN COIN, THE • 1911 • *Reliance* • USA
BROKEN COIN, THE • 1915 • Ford Francis, Cunard Grace • SRL • USA
BROKEN COMEDY see **COMEDIA ROTA** • 1978
BROKEN COMMANDMENT, THE see **HAKAI** • 1961
BROKEN COMMANDMENTS • 1919 • Beal Frank • USA
BROKEN CONTRACT, A • 1920 • Kellino W. P. • UKN
BROKEN CROSS, THE • 1911 • Griffith D. W. • USA
BROKEN CROSS, THE • 1916 • Ricketts Thomas • SHT • USA
BROKEN DIKES see **GEBROKEN DIJKEN** • 1945
BROKEN DISHES see **TOO YOUNG TO MARRY** • 1931
BROKEN DOLL • 1959 • Barclay Robert • SHT • CND
BROKEN DOLL, A • 1921 • Dwan Allan • USA
BROKEN DOLL, A see **BIR KIRIK BEBEK** • 1987
BROKEN DOLL, THE • 1910 • Griffith D. W. • USA
BROKEN DOLL, THE • 1914 • *Sterling* • USA
BROKEN DREAMS • 1933 • Vignola Robert G. • USA
BROKEN DREAMS see **WASHINGTON MISTRESS** • 1982
BROKEN DRUM, THE see **YABURE-DAIKO** • 1949
BROKEN EARTH • 1934 • Freulich Roman, Muse Clarence • USA
BROKEN ECSTASY see **KUZURETA KANNO** • 1968
BROKEN ENGLISH • 1981 • Gleason Michie • USA
BROKEN ENGLISH: THREE SONGS BY MARIANNE FAITHFULL • 1980 • Jarman Derek • SHT • UKN
BROKEN FAITH • 1912 • Aylott Dave • UKN
BROKEN FAMILY see **TSUMIKI KUZUSHI** • 1984
BROKEN FETTERS • 1916 • *Knickerbocker Star* • SHT • USA
BROKEN FETTERS • 1916 • Ingram Rex • *Bluebird* • USA
BROKEN GATE, THE • 1920 • Scardon Paul • USA
BROKEN GATE, THE • 1927 • McKay James C. • USA
BROKEN GENIUS, A • 1916 • Ricketts Thomas • SHT • USA
BROKEN GLASS, THE • 1915 • Daly William Robert • USA
BROKEN HEADS see **CABEZAS CORTADAS** • 1970
BROKEN HEART, A • 1909 • *Lubin* • USA
BROKEN HEART, THE • 1913 • *Gaumont* • USA
BROKEN HEART, THE • 1913 • Webster Harry Mcrae • *Essanay* • USA
BROKEN-HEARTED • 1917 • *Shay William* • SHT • USA
BROKEN HEARTED • 1929 • Mattison Frank S. • USA
BROKEN HEARTED LOVE STORY, A see **KIRIK BIR ASK HIKAYESI** • 1982
BROKEN HEARTS • 1912 • *Pathe* • USA
BROKEN HEARTS • 1916 • *Buffalo* • USA
BROKEN HEARTS • 1926 • Schwartz Maurice • USA • SOULS IN EXILE (UKN)
BROKEN HEARTS see **SUTCH-DELAN** • 1978
BROKEN HEARTS AND NOSES see **CRIMEWAVE** • 1986

BROKEN HEARTS AND PLEDGES • 1915 • *Mann Hank* • USA
BROKEN HEARTS OF BROADWAY • 1923 • Cummings Irving • USA
BROKEN HEARTS OF HOLLYWOOD • 1926 • Bacon Lloyd • USA
BROKEN HILL NEW YEAR'S DAY MASSACRE • 1915 • ASL
BROKEN HILL TRAGEDY • 1915 • ASL
BROKEN HOME, THE see **YIKILAN YUVA** • 1967
BROKEN HOMES • 1926 • Dierker Hugh • USA
BROKEN HORSESHOE, THE • 1953 • Webster Martyn C. • UKN
BROKEN HORSESHOE, THE • 1973 • Aranovich S. • USS
BROKEN IDYL, THE • 1913 • *Pathe* • USA
BROKEN IMAGES see **LIL HOB KESSA AKHIRA** • 1986
BROKEN IN THE WARS • 1919 • Hepworth Cecil M. • UKN
BROKEN JOURNEY • 1948 • Annakin Ken • UKN • RESCUE
BROKEN JUG, THE see **ZERBROCHENE KRUG, DER** • 1937
BROKEN LANCE • 1954 • Dmytryk Edward • USA
BROKEN LAND, THE • 1962 • Bushelman John • USA • VANISHING FRONTIER
BROKEN LARIAT, THE see **WILD WESTERNERS, THE** • 1962
BROKEN LAW, THE • 1915 • Apfel Oscar • USA
BROKEN LAW, THE • 1924 • Russell Bernard (Spvn) • USA
BROKEN LAW, THE • 1926 • *Meehan Jack* • USA
BROKEN LAWS • 1924 • Neill R. William • USA
BROKEN LEASE, THE • 1912 • *Cumpson John* • USA
BROKEN LEGHORN, A • 1959 • McKimson Robert • ANS • USA
BROKEN LIFE, A • 1913 • Collins Edwin J.? • UKN
BROKEN LINKS (UKN) see **LEFTOVER LADIES** • 1931
BROKEN LIVES • 1914 • *Cummings Irving* • USA
BROKEN LIVES • 1916 • *Pathe* • USA
BROKEN LOCKET, THE • 1909 • Griffith D. W. • USA
BROKEN LULLABY • 1932 • Lubitsch Ernst • USA • MAN I KILLED, THE (UKN)
BROKEN LULLABY, THE • 1915 • *Majestic* • USA
BROKEN MARRIAGE • 1983 • Bernal Ishmael • PHL
BROKEN MASK, THE • 1928 • Hogan James P. • USA
BROKEN MELODY, A • 1909 • *Phoenix* • USA
BROKEN MELODY, A • 1913 • Thornby Robert T. • USA
BROKEN MELODY, THE • 1896 • Collings Esme • UKN
BROKEN MELODY, THE • 1907 • Gilbert Arthur • UKN
BROKEN MELODY, THE • 1912 • Fitzhamon Lewin • UKN
BROKEN MELODY, THE • 1916 • Morton Cavendish • UKN
BROKEN MELODY, THE • 1920 • Earle William P. S. • USA
BROKEN MELODY, THE • 1929 • Paul Fred • UKN
BROKEN MELODY, THE • 1934 • Vorhaus Bernard • UKN • VAGABOND VIOLINIST
BROKEN MELODY, THE • 1938 • Hall Ken G. • ASL • VAGABOND VIOLINIST, THE
BROKEN MIRRORS see **GEBROKEN SPIEGELS** • 1984
BROKEN NOSE BAILEY • 1914 • *Pallette Eugene* • USA
BROKEN OATH, THE • 1910 • Salter Harry • USA
BROKEN OATH, THE • 1913 • Buckland Warwick • UKN
BROKEN OATHS • 1912 • *Solax* • USA
BROKEN PAROLE, THE • 1913 • *Church Fred* • USA
BROKEN PLEDGE, THE • 1915 • *Beery Wallace* • USA
BROKEN PRIDE see **YIKILAN GURUR** • 1967
BROKEN PROMISE • 1981 • Taylor Don • TVM • USA
BROKEN PROMISE • 1983 • Tung Sandy • USA • MARRIAGE, A
BROKEN PROMISE, THE • 1916 • *Drew Ann* • SHT • USA
BROKEN RAINBOW • 1985 • Florio Maria, Mudd Victoria • DOC • USA
BROKEN RING, THE • 1912 • *Rex* • USA
BROKEN ROAD, THE • 1921 • Plaissetty Rene • UKN
BROKEN ROMANCE, A • 1929 • Edwards J. Steven • UKN
BROKEN ROSARY, THE • 1934 • Hughes Harry • UKN
BROKEN ROSE, THE • 1914 • *Ab* • USA
BROKEN SABER • 1965 • McEveety Bernard • USA
BROKEN SAINTS, THE see **SANTOS ROTOS, LOS** • 1971
BROKEN SAND see **LOVERS IN ARABY** • 1924
BROKEN SHOES • 1934 • Barskaya Margarita • TORN SHOES
BROKEN SILENCE, THE • 1922 • Henderson Dell • USA
BROKEN SIXPENCE, THE • 1913 • Wilson Frank? • UKN
BROKEN SKY see **BRUSTEN HIMMEL** • 1981
BROKEN SPELL, A • 1910 • *Vitagraph* • USA
BROKEN SPELL, THE • 1913 • Smalley Phillips • USA
BROKEN SPUR, A • 1912 • *Selig* • USA
BROKEN SPUR, THE • 1916 • Wilson Ben • SHT • USA
BROKEN SPUR, THE • 1921 • Wilson Ben • USA
BROKEN STAR, THE • 1956 • Selander Lesley • USA
BROKEN STRINGS • 1940 • Ray Bernard B. • USA
BROKEN SWORDS see **HIKEN YABURI** • 1969
BROKEN SYMPHONY, A • 1910 • *Vitagraph* • USA
BROKEN THREAD, THE • 1913 • Edwards Walter? • USA
BROKEN THREADS • 1917 • Edwards Henry • UKN
BROKEN THREADS • 1919 • *Barriscale Bessie* • USA
BROKEN THREADS UNITED • 1913 • *Commerford Thomas* • USA
BROKEN TIES • 1918 • Ashley Arthur • USA • ALIBI, THE
BROKEN TIES, THE • 1912 • Dwan Allan • USA
BROKEN TOY, THE • 1915 • Henderson Lucius • USA
BROKEN TOYS • 1935 • Sharpsteen Ben • ANS • USA
BROKEN TRAIL, THE • 1911 • *Kalem* • USA
BROKEN TRAP, THE • 1911 • *Bison* • USA
BROKEN TREATIES • 1941 • Fennell Paul • ANS • USA
BROKEN TREATY AT BATTLE MOUNTAIN • 1974 • Freedman Joel L. • DOC • USA
BROKEN VASE, THE • 1913 • Kirkland Hardee • USA
BROKEN VIOLIN, THE • 1923 • Dillon John Francis • USA
BROKEN VIOLIN, THE • 1927 • Micheaux Oscar • USA
BROKEN VIOLIN, THE see **LULLI OU LE VIOLON BRISE** • 1908
BROKEN VOW, THE see **SENKETSU NO TOBA** • 1968
BROKEN VOWS • 1911 • *Reliance* • USA
BROKEN VOWS • 1914 • *Wallace Irene* • USA
BROKEN VOWS • 1915 • *Wayne Justina* • USA
BROKEN VOWS • 1986 • Taylor Jud • TVM • USA
BROKEN WAYS • 1913 • Griffith D. W. • USA
BROKEN WEDDING BELLS • 1930 • Foster Lewis R. • SHT • USA
BROKEN WINDOW, THE • 1915 • Otto Henry • USA
BROKEN WING, THE • 1923 • Forman Tom • USA
BROKEN WING, THE • 1932 • Corrigan Lloyd • USA
BROKEN WING, THE see **YABURE-DAIKO** • 1949
BROKEN WINGS see **PODRANKI** • 1977
BROKEN WINGS, THE see **LAL AGHNIHAT ELMOUTAKASRA** • 1964
BROKEN WORD, THE • 1915 • McGlynn Frank • USA
BROKEN WRIST, THE • 1915 • Reehm George E. • USA
BROKEN "X", THE • 1914 • Le Saint Edward J. • USA
BROKERS, THE • 1984 • Raymont Peter • CND
BROKER'S DAUGHTER, THE • 1910 • *Yankee* • USA
BROKIGA BLAD • 1931 • Adolphson Edvin, Dahlquist Valdemar • SWD
BROLLOPET I BRANNA • 1927 • Petschler Eric A. • SWD • WEDDING AT BRANNA
BROLLOPET PA SOLO • 1946 • Johansson Ivar • SWD • WEDDING AT SOLO
BROLLOPET PA ULFASA • 1910 • Engdahl Carl • SWD • WEDDING AT ULFASA
BROLLOPSBESVAR • 1964 • Falck Ake • SWD • SWEDISH WEDDING NIGHT (USA) ○ WEDDING –SWEDISH STYLE (UKN)
BROLLOPSDAGEN • 1960 • Fant Kenne • SWD • WEDDING DAY
BROLLOPSNATT, EN • 1959 • Blomberg Erik • SWD, FNL, PLN • NOC POSLUBNA (PLN) ○ HAAYO (FNL) ○ WEDDING NIGHT
BROLLOPSNATT PA STJARNEHOV, EN • 1934 • Lundqvist Torsten • SWD • WEDDING NIGHT AT STJARNEHOV ○ AVENTYR PA STJARNEHOV, ETT
BROLLOPSNATTEN • 1947 • Ipsen Bodil • SWD • WEDDING NIGHT
BROLLOPSRESAN • 1936 • Molander Gustaf • SWD • HONEYMOON TRIP, THE
BROLLY, THE see **PARAPLICKO** • 1956
BROMAS, S.A. • 1966 • Mariscal Alberto • MXC, PRU
BROMISTA, EL • 1980 • David Mario • ARG • JOKER, THE
BROMLEY CASE, THE • 1920 • Collins Tom • USA
BROMO AND JULIET • 1926 • McCarey Leo • SHT • USA
BRONBEEK BIJVOORBEELD • 1969 • van Nie Rene • NTH • BRONBEEK FOR EXAMPLE
BRONBEEK FOR EXAMPLE see **BRONBEEK BIJVOORBEELD** • 1969
BRONC RIDER • 1986 • Falcon P. • USA
BRONC STOMPER, THE • 1928 • Maloney Leo • USA
BRONCE Y LUNA • 1952 • Seto Javier • SPN
BRONCHO AND THE INDIAN MAID • 1912 • *Anderson Broncho Billy* • USA
BRONCHO BILL WELL REPAYED • 1915 • *Anderson Broncho Billy* • USA
BRONCHO BILL'S LAST SPREE • 1911 • *Anderson Broncho Billy* • USA
BRONCHO BILL'S LOVE AFFAIR • 1912 • *Bison* • USA
BRONCHO BILLY, A FRIEND IN NEED • 1914 • Anderson G. M. • USA
BRONCHO BILLY AND THE BABY • 1915 • *Anderson Broncho Billy* • USA
BRONCHO BILLY AND THE BAD MAN • 1914 • *Anderson Broncho Billy* • USA
BRONCHO BILLY AND THE BANDITS • 1912 • *Anderson Broncho Billy* • USA
BRONCHO BILLY AND THE CARD SHARP • 1915 • *Anderson Broncho Billy* • USA
BRONCHO BILLY AND THE CLAIM JUMPERS • 1915 • *Anderson Broncho Billy* • USA
BRONCHO BILLY AND THE ESCAPED BANDIT • 1914 • Anderson G. M. • USA
BRONCHO BILLY AND THE EXPRESS RIDER • 1913 • *Anderson Broncho Billy* • USA
BRONCHO BILLY AND THE FALSE NOTE • 1915 • *Anderson Broncho Billy* • USA
BRONCHO BILLY AND THE GAMBLER • 1914 • *Anderson Broncho Billy* • USA
BRONCHO BILLY AND THE GIRL • 1912 • *Anderson Broncho Billy* • USA
BRONCHO BILLY AND THE GREASER • 1914 • *Anderson Broncho Billy* • USA
BRONCHO BILLY AND THE LAND GRABBER • 1915 • *Anderson Broncho Billy* • USA
BRONCHO BILLY AND THE LUMBER KING • 1915 • *Anderson Broncho Billy* • USA
BRONCHO BILLY AND THE MAID • 1912 • *Anderson Broncho Billy* • USA
BRONCHO BILLY AND THE MINE SHARK • 1914 • *Anderson Broncho Billy* • USA
BRONCHO BILLY AND THE NAVAJO MAID • 1913 • *Anderson Broncho Billy* • USA
BRONCHO BILLY AND THE OUTLAW'S MOTHER • 1913 • *Anderson Broncho Billy* • USA
BRONCHO BILLY AND THE PARSON • 1915 • *Anderson Broncho Billy* • USA
BRONCHO BILLY AND THE POSSE • 1915 • *Anderson Broncho Billy* • USA
BRONCHO BILLY AND THE RATTLER • 1914 • *Anderson Broncho Billy* • USA
BRONCHO BILLY AND THE RED MAN • 1914 • Anderson G. M. • USA • BRONCHO BILLY AND THE REDSKIN
BRONCHO BILLY AND THE REDSKIN see **BRONCHO BILLY AND THE RED MAN** • 1914
BRONCHO BILLY AND THE RUSTLER'S CHILD • 1913 • *Anderson Broncho Billy* • USA
BRONCHO BILLY AND THE SCHOOLMAM'S SWEETHEART • 1913 • *Anderson Broncho Billy* • USA
BRONCHO BILLY AND THE SCHOOLMISTRESS • 1912 • *Anderson Broncho Billy* • USA
BRONCHO BILLY AND THE SETTLER'S DAUGHTER • 1914 • *Anderson Broncho Billy* • USA
BRONCHO BILLY AND THE SHERIFF • 1914 • *Anderson Broncho Billy* • USA
BRONCHO BILLY AND THE SHERIFF'S KID • 1913 • Anderson G. M. • USA
BRONCHO BILLY AND THE SHERIFF'S OFFICE • 1914 • *Anderson Broncho Billy* • USA
BRONCHO BILLY AND THE SISTERS • 1915 • *Anderson Broncho Billy* • USA
BRONCHO BILLY AND THE SQUATTER'S DAUGHTER • 1913 • *Anderson Broncho Billy* • USA
BRONCHO BILLY AND THE STEP-SISTERS • 1913 • *Anderson Broncho Billy* • USA
BRONCHO BILLY AND THE VIGILANTE • 1915 • *Anderson Broncho Billy* • USA
BRONCHO BILLY AND THE WESTERN GIRLS • 1913 • *Anderson Broncho Billy* • USA
BRONCHO BILLY BEGINS LIFE ANEW • 1915 • *Anderson Broncho Billy* • USA
BRONCHO BILLY BUTTS IN • 1914 • Anderson G. M. • USA
BRONCHO BILLY EVENS MATTERS • 1915 • *Anderson Broncho Billy* • USA
BRONCHO BILLY –FAVORITE • 1914 • *Anderson Broncho Billy* • USA
BRONCHO BILLY FOR SHERIFF • 1912 • Anderson G. M. • USA
BRONCHO BILLY GETS SQUARE • 1913 • *Anderson Broncho Billy* • USA
BRONCHO BILLY –GUARDIAN • 1914 • *Anderson Broncho Billy* • USA
BRONCHO BILLY –GUNMAN • 1914 • *Anderson Broncho Billy* • USA
BRONCHO BILLY MISLAID • 1915 • *Anderson Broncho Billy* • USA
BRONCHO BILLY –OUTLAW • 1914 • *Anderson Broncho Billy* • USA
BRONCHO BILLY OUTWITTED • 1912 • *Anderson Broncho Billy* • USA
BRONCHO BILLY PUTS ONE OVER • 1914 • *Anderson Broncho Billy* • USA
BRONCHO BILLY REFORMS • 1913 • *Anderson Broncho Billy* • USA
BRONCHO BILLY REWARDED • 1914 • *Anderson Broncho Billy* • USA
BRONCHO BILLY, SHEEPMAN • 1915 • *Anderson Broncho Billy* • USA
BRONCHO BILLY STEPS IN • 1915 • *Anderson Broncho Billy* • USA
BRONCHO BILLY, THE VAGABOND • 1914 • *Anderson Broncho Billy* • USA
BRONCHO BILLY TRAPPED • 1914 • *Anderson Broncho Billy* • USA
BRONCHO BILLY WELL REPAID • 1915 • *Anderson Broncho Billy* • USA
BRONCHO BILLY WINS OUT • 1914 • *Anderson Broncho Billy* • USA
BRONCHO BILLY'S ADVENTURE • 1911 • Barker Reginald • USA
BRONCHO BILLY'S BIBLE • 1912 • Barker Reginald • USA
BRONCHO BILLY'S BROTHER • 1913 • *Anderson Broncho Billy* • USA
BRONCHO BILLY'S BROTHER • 1915 • *Anderson Broncho Billy* • USA
BRONCHO BILLY'S CAPTURE • 1913 • Anderson G. M. • USA
BRONCHO BILLY'S CHRISTMAS DEED • 1913 • *Anderson Broncho Billy* • USA
BRONCHO BILLY'S CHRISTMAS DINNER • 1911 • *Anderson Broncho Billy* • USA
BRONCHO BILLY'S CHRISTMAS SPIRIT • 1914 • *Anderson Broncho Billy* • USA
BRONCHO BILLY'S CLOSE CALL • 1914 • *Anderson Broncho Billy* • USA
BRONCHO BILLY'S CONSCIENCE • 1913 • *Anderson Broncho Billy* • USA
BRONCHO BILLY'S COWARDLY BROTHER • 1915 • *Anderson Broncho Billy* • USA
BRONCHO BILLY'S CUNNING • 1914 • *Anderson Broncho Billy* • USA
BRONCHO BILLY'S DAD • 1914 • *Anderson Broncho Billy* • USA
BRONCHO BILLY'S DECISION • 1914 • *Anderson Broncho Billy* • USA
BRONCHO BILLY'S DOUBLE ESCAPE • 1914 • *Anderson Broncho Billy* • USA
BRONCHO BILLY'S DUTY • 1914 • *Anderson Broncho Billy* • USA
BRONCHO BILLY'S ELOPEMENT • 1913 • *Anderson Broncho Billy* • USA
BRONCHO BILLY'S ESCAPADE • 1912 • *Anderson Broncho Billy* • USA
BRONCHO BILLY'S FATAL JOKE • 1912 • *Anderson Broncho Billy* • USA
BRONCHO BILLY'S FIRST ARREST • 1913 • *Anderson Broncho Billy* • USA
BRONCHO BILLY'S GRATEFULNESS • 1913 • *Anderson Broncho Billy* • USA
BRONCHO BILLY'S GRATITUDE • 1912 • *Anderson Broncho Billy* • USA
BRONCHO BILLY'S GREASER DEPUTY • 1915 • *Anderson Broncho Billy* • USA
BRONCHO BILLY'S GRIT • 1913 • *Anderson Broncho Billy* • USA
BRONCHO BILLY'S GUN-PLAY • 1913 • *Anderson Broncho Billy* • USA
BRONCHO BILLY'S HEART • 1912 • *Anderson Broncho Billy* • USA
BRONCHO BILLY'S INDIAN ROMANCE • 1914 • Anderson G. M. • USA
BRONCHO BILLY'S JEALOUSY • 1914 • *Anderson Broncho Billy* • USA
BRONCHO BILLY'S JUDGEMENT • 1914 • *Anderson Broncho Billy* • USA
BRONCHO BILLY'S LAST DEED • 1913 • *Anderson Broncho Billy* • USA
BRONCHO BILLY'S LAST HOLD-UP • 1912 • *Anderson Broncho Billy* • USA
BRONCHO BILLY'S LEAP • 1914 • *Anderson Broncho Billy* • USA
BRONCHO BILLY'S LOVE AFFAIR • 1912 • Anderson G. M. • USA
BRONCHO BILLY'S LOVE AFFAIR • 1915 • *Anderson Broncho Billy* • USA
BRONCHO BILLY'S MARRIAGE • 1915 • *Anderson Broncho Billy* • USA

BRONCHO BILLY'S MARRIAGE • 1915 • *Anderson Broncho Billy* • USA
BRONCHO BILLY'S MEXICAN WIFE • 1912 • *Anderson Broncho Billy* • USA
BRONCHO BILLY'S MISSION • 1914 • *Anderson Broncho Billy* • USA
BRONCHO BILLY'S MISTAKE • 1913 • *Anderson Broncho Billy* • USA
BRONCHO BILLY'S MOTHER • 1914 • *Anderson Broncho Billy* • USA
BRONCHO BILLY'S NARROW ESCAPE • 1912 • Anderson G. M. • USA
BRONCHO BILLY'S OATH • 1913 • Anderson G. M. • USA
BRONCHO BILLY'S PAL • 1912 • *Anderson Broncho Billy* • USA
BRONCHO BILLY'S PARENTS • 1915 • *Anderson Broncho Billy* • USA
BRONCHO BILLY'S PROMISE • 1912 • *Anderson Broncho Billy* • USA
BRONCHO BILLY'S PROTEGE • 1915 • *Anderson Broncho Billy* • USA
BRONCHO BILLY'S PUNISHMENT • 1914 • *Anderson Broncho Billy* • USA
BRONCHO BILLY'S REASON • 1913 • *Anderson Broncho Billy* • USA
BRONCHO BILLY'S REDEMPTION • 1910 • *Anderson Broncho Billy* • USA
BRONCHO BILLY'S SCHEME • 1914 • *Anderson Broncho Billy* • USA
BRONCHO BILLY'S SECRET • 1913 • *Anderson Broncho Billy* • USA
BRONCHO BILLY'S SENTENCE • 1915 • *Anderson Broncho Billy* • USA
BRONCHO BILLY'S SERMON • 1914 • *Andreson Broncho Billy* • USA
BRONCHO BILLY'S SISTER • 1913 • *Anderson Broncho Billy* • USA
BRONCHO BILLY'S SQUARENESS • 1913 • *Anderson Broncho Billy* • USA
BRONCHO BILLY'S STRATEGY • 1913 • *Anderson Broncho Billy* • USA
BRONCHO BILLY'S TEACHINGS • 1915 • *Anderson Broncho Billy* • USA
BRONCHO BILLY'S TRUE LOVE • 1914 • *Anderson Broncho Billy* • USA
BRONCHO BILLY'S VENGEANCE • 1915 • *Anderson Broncho Billy* • USA
BRONCHO BILLY'S WARD • 1913 • *Anderson Broncho Billy* • USA
BRONCHO BILLY'S WAY • 1913 • *Anderson Broncho Billy* • USA
BRONCHO BILLY'S WILD RIDE • 1914 • *Anderson Broncho Billy* • USA
BRONCHO BILLY'S WORD OF HONOR • 1915 • *Anderson Broncho Billy* • USA
BRONCHO BUSTER, THE • 1927 • Laemmle Ernst • USA
BRONCHO BUSTER'S BRIDE, THE • 1911 • Dwan Allan • USA
BRONCHO BUSTER'S RIVAL, THE • 1911 • *Bison* • USA
BRONCHO BUSTING FOR FLYING A PICTURES • 1912 • Dwan Allan • USA • BUCKING HORSES
BRONCHO KID, A • 1920 • Wright Mack V. • SHT • USA
BRONCHO PIMPLE • 1914 • Evans Fred, Evans Joe • UKN
BRONCHO TWISTER, THE • 1927 • Dull Orville O. • USA
BRONCHOGRAPHY • 1945 • Hudson Claud • DOC • UKN
BRONCHO'S SURRENDER • 1915 • *Anderson Broncho Billy* • USA
BRONCO BILLY • 1980 • Eastwood Clint • USA
BRONCO BULLFROG • 1970 • Platt-Mills Barney • UKN
BRONCO BUSTER • 1935 • *Lantz Walter (P)* • ANS • USA
BRONCO BUSTER • 1952 • Boetticher Budd • USA
BRONCO BUSTERS see **GONE WITH THE WEST** • 1969
BRONCO REYNOSA, EL • 1960 • Delgado Miguel M. • MXC
BRONENOSETS POTYOMKIN • 1925 • Eisenstein Sergei • USS • POTEMKIN (USA) ○ BATTLESHIP POTEMKIN ○ CRUISER POTEMKIN
BRONK • 1975 • Donner Richard • TVM • USA
BRONSON LEE, CHAMPION • 1978 • Noda Yukio • HKG
BRONSTEIN'S CHILDREN see **BRONSTEINS KINDER** • 1990
BRONSTEINS KINDER • 1990 • Kawalerowicz Jerzy • FRG • BRONSTEIN'S CHILDREN
BRONTE • 1983 • Mann Delbert • USA, IRL
BRONTE: CRONACA DI UN MASSACRO CHE I LIBRI DI STORIA NON HANNO RACCONTATO • 1972 • Vancini Florestano • ITL • FATTI DI BRONTE, I ○ LIBERTY ○ BRONTE: STORY OF A MASSACRE IGNORED BY THE HISTORY BOOKS
BRONTE SISTERS, THE see **SOEURS BRONTE, LES** • 1979
BRONTE: STORY OF A MASSACRE IGNORED BY THE HISTORY BOOKS see **BRONTE: CRONACA DI UN MASSACRO CHE I LIBRI DI STORIA NON HANNO RACCONTATO** • 1972
BRONTOSAURUS • 1978 • Plivova-Simkova Vera • CZC
BRONX COCKTAIL, A • 1912 • *Imp* • USA
BRONX MORNING • 1932 • Leyda Jay • USA
BRONX WARRIORS see **1990: I GUERRIERI DEL BRONX** • 1982
BRONX WARRIORS 2: THE BATTLE OF MANHATTAN see **FUGA DAL BRONX** • 1984
BRONZE • 1970 • Moretti Pierre • CND
BRONZE BELL, THE • 1921 • Horne James W. • USA
BRONZE BRIDE, THE • 1917 • McRae Henry • USA
BRONZE BUCKAROO, THE • 1939 • Kahn Richard C. • USA
BRONZE GIRLS OF SHAOLIN see **EIGHTEEN BRONZE GIRLS OF SHAOLIN, THE** • 1983
BRONZE IDOL, THE • 1914 • Wilson Frank • UKN
BRONZE VENUS see **DUKE IS TOPS, THE** • 1938
BRONZES, LES • 1978 • Leconte Patrice • FRN
BRONZES FONT DU SKI, LES • 1979 • Leconte Patrice • FRN
BROOBA • 1955 • Suzuki Jukichi • JPN
BROOD, THE • 1979 • Cronenberg David • CND • CLINIQUE DE LA TERREUR, LA ○ CHROMOSOME 3
BROOD EN SPELEN • 1971 • Le Bon Patrick • BLG
BROOD HEN AND HER GOLDEN CHICKS, THE • Bostan Elisabeta • SHT • RMN
BROODING EYES • 1926 • Le Saint Edward J. • USA
BROODING HEART, THE • 1915 • Morgan George • USA
BROOK, THE • 1917 • *Edison* • SHT • USA
BROOKFIELD RECREATION CENTER, THE • 1964 • Baillie Bruce • USA
BROOKLYN BRIDGE • 1981 • Burns Ken • USA
BROOKLYN BUCKAROOS • 1950 • Goodwins Leslie • SHT • USA
BROOKLYN ORCHID • 1942 • Neumann Kurt • USA
BROOM, THE see **METLA** • 1972
BROOMS AND DUSTPANS • 1912 • *Eclair* • USA
BROOMSTICK BUNNY • 1956 • Jones Charles M. • ANS • USA
BROR MIN OCH JAG • 1954 • Frisk Ragnar • SWD
BROSSE, LA • 1974 • Ba N'Gaido • SHT • SNL
BROSSINGS SIND GEADELT • 1916 • Trautmann Ludwig • FRG
BROSTA STIN AGHONI (MIA SFERA YIA MENA) • 1968 • Asimakopoulos Kostas • GRC • IN FRONT OF THE GALLOWS
BROT! • 1915 • Del Zopp Rudolf • FRG
BROT DER FRUHEN JAHRE, DAS • 1962 • Vesely Herbert • FRG • BREAD OF OUR EARLY YEARS, THE
BROT DES BACKERS, DAS • 1977 • Keusch Erwin • FRG, SWT • BAKER'S BREAD
BROT UND ROSEN • 1967 • Thiel Heinz, Brandt Horst E. • GDR • BREAD AND ROSES
BROT UND STEINE • 1979 • Rissi Mark M. • SWT, BLG • BREAD AND STONES
BROTH OF A BOY • 1915 • King Carleton S. • USA
BROTH OF A BOY • 1959 • Pollock George • UKN
BROTHEL • 1966 • Vehr Bill • USA
BROTHEL, THE • 1971 • Arnfred Morten • DNM
BROTHEL NO.8 see **SANDAKAN HACHIBAN SHOKAN, BOHKYO** • 1975
BROTHER AGAINST BROTHER • 1909 • *Selig* • USA
BROTHER ALFRED • 1932 • Edwards Henry • UKN
BROTHER AND HIS YOUNGER SISTER, A see **ANI TO SONO IMOTO** • 1939
BROTHER AND SISTER • 1913 • *Victor* • USA
BROTHER AND SISTER see **ANI TO SONO IMOTO** • 1956
BROTHER ANDRE see **FRERE ANDRE, LE** • 1988
BROTHER BAT • 1967 • Culhane Shamus • ANS • USA
BROTHER BILL • 1913 • *Storey Edith* • USA
BROTHER BOB'S BABY • 1911 • *Thanhouser* • USA
BROTHER BRAT • 1944 • Tashlin Frank • ANS • USA
BROTHER, CAN YOU SPARE A DIME? • 1975 • Mora Philippe • DOC • UKN
BROTHER CARL see **BRODER CARL** • 1971
BROTHER, CRY FOR ME • 1970 • White William • USA
BROTHER FOR BROTHER • 1914 • *Frontier* • USA
BROTHER FOR SALE • 1930 • Beaudine William • SHT • USA
BROTHER FROM ANOTHER PLANET, THE • 1984 • Sayles John • USA
BROTHER FROM OUTER SPACE • 1964 • Rasinski Connie • ANS • USA
BROTHER GOES TO THE BORDER see **BOETIE GAAN BORDER TOE** • 1984
BROTHER IN ARMS, A • 1911 • *Pathe* • USA
BROTHER JIM • 1916 • *Jefferson Thomas* • SHT • USA
BROTHER JOHN • 1950 • Cowan Will • ANS • USA
BROTHER JOHN • 1972 • Goldstone James • USA • KANE
BROTHER JONATHAN see **MY BROTHER JONATHAN** • 1948
BROTHER KNOWS BEST • 1948 • Yates Hal • SHT • USA
BROTHER LOVE • 1913 • *American* • USA
BROTHER MAN • 1910 • *Vitagraph* • USA
BROTHER MATE see **BROER MATIE** • 1984
BROTHER, MY SONG • 1976 • Cain Christopher • USA
BROTHER OF A HERO see **BRAT GEROYA** • 1940
BROTHER OF THE "BAT", THE • 1912 • *Reliance* • USA
BROTHER OF THE WIND • 1972 • Robinson Richard • USA, CND
BROTHER OFFICERS • 1915 • Shaw Harold • UKN
BROTHER OFFICERS see **SOLDIER'S HONOUR, A** • 1914
BROTHER ON MANOEUVRES see **BOETIE OP MANOEUVRES** • 1985
BROTHER ON THE RUN • 1973 • Strock Herbert L. • USA
BROTHER ORCHID • 1940 • Bacon Lloyd • USA
BROTHER RAT • 1938 • Keighley William • USA
BROTHER RAT AND A BABY • 1940 • Enright Ray • USA • BABY BE GOOD (UKN)
BROTHER SUN, SISTER MOON (UKN) see **FRATELLO SOLE, SORELLA LUNA** • 1972
BROTHER, THE SISTER AND THE COWPUNCHER, THE • 1910 • *Essanay* • USA
BROTHERHOOD • 1967 • Sens Al • ANS • CND
BROTHERHOOD, THE • 1926 • West Walter • UKN
BROTHERHOOD, THE • 1968 • Ritt Martin • USA
BROTHERHOOD OF DEATH • 1976 • Berry Bill • USA
BROTHERHOOD OF JUSTICE, THE • 1986 • Braverman Charles • TVM • USA
BROTHERHOOD OF MAN, THE • 1912 • *Duncan William* • USA
BROTHERHOOD OF MAN, THE • 1946 • Cannon Robert • ANS • USA
BROTHERHOOD OF SATAN • 1970 • McEveety Bernard • USA • COME IN, CHILDREN
BROTHERHOOD OF THE BELL • 1970 • Wendkos Paul • TVM • USA
BROTHERHOOD OF THE YAKUZA see **YAKUZA, THE** • 1974
BROTHERLY FEUD see **KARDES KAVGASI** • 1967
BROTHERLY LOVE • 1910 • *Great Western* • USA
BROTHERLY LOVE • 1911 • *Reliance* • USA
BROTHERLY LOVE • 1928 • Reisner Charles F. • USA
BROTHERLY LOVE • 1936 • Fleischer Dave • ANS • USA
BROTHERLY LOVE • 1985 • Bleckner Jeff • TVM • USA
BROTHERLY LOVE see **NIISAN NO AIJO** • 1955
BROTHERLY LOVE (USA) see **COUNTRY DANCE** • 1969
BROTHERS • 1910 • *Atlas* • USA
BROTHERS • 1910 • *Lubin* • USA
BROTHERS • 1912 • Field George • USA
BROTHERS • 1913 • Griffith D. W. • *Ab* • USA
BROTHERS • 1915 • *Premier* • USA
BROTHERS • 1929 • Pembroke Scott • USA • TWO SONS (UKN)
BROTHERS • 1930 • Lang Walter • USA • BLOOD BROTHERS (UKN)
BROTHERS • 1961 • Lettrich Andrej • CZC
BROTHERS • 1971 • Krolikiewicz Grzegorz • DOC • PLN
BROTHERS • 1977 • Barron Arthur • USA
BROTHERS • 1983 • Bourke Terry • ASL • HOUNDS OF WAR
BROTHERS • 1989 • Allen Woody • USA
BROTHERS see **BRUDER** • 1929
BROTHERS see **TWINS** • 1988
BROTHERS, THE • 1909 • *Essanay* • USA
BROTHERS, THE • 1910 • Bouwmeester Theo? • UKN
BROTHERS, THE • 1911 • Smiley Joseph, Tucker George Loane • USA
BROTHERS, THE • 1913 • *Nestor* • USA
BROTHERS, THE • 1913 • Dwan Allan • *American* • USA
BROTHERS, THE • 1914 • Wilson Frank? • UKN
BROTHERS, THE • 1915 • Batley Ethyle • UKN
BROTHERS, THE • 1947 • MacDonald David • UKN
BROTHERS, THE • 1958 • Mangiamele Giorgio • SHT • ASL
BROTHERS, THE • 1970 • Moldovan Mircea, Gheorghe Gica • RMN
BROTHERS, THE • 1976 • Michalak Richard • SHT • ASL
BROTHERS, THE see **HERMANOS, LOS**
BROTHERS, THE see **BRODERNA** • 1914
BROTHERS, THE see **KESYTTOMAT VELJEKSET** • 1970
BROTHERS, THE see **BRUDER, DIE** • 1976
BROTHERS ALL • 1913 • *Excelsior* • USA
BROTHERS AND RELATIONS • 1988 • VTN
BROTHERS AND SISTERS • 1963 • Heynowski Walter • DOC • GDR
BROTHERS AND SISTERS • 1980 • Wooley Richard • UKN
BROTHERS AND SISTERS see **RYOOK NAM-MAI** • 1960
BROTHERS AND SISTERS IN CONCERT see **SAVE THE CHILDREN** • 1973
BROTHERS AND SISTERS OF THE TODA FAMILY, THE see **TODA-KE NO KYODAI** • 1941
BROTHER'S ATONEMENT, A • 1914 • Haldane Bert? • UKN
BROTHERS.. BUT ENEMIES • 1974 • Mustafa Hassam Eddin • EGY
BROTHERS CARRY-MOUSE-OFF, THE • 1965 • Pabian Jim • ANS • USA
BROTHERS CARTAGENA, THE see **HERMANOS CARTAGENA, LOS** • 1985
BROTHERS' CODE –THE BACK RELATION see **KYODAI JINGI GYAKUEN NO SAKAZUKI** • 1968
BROTHER'S DEVOTION, A • 1910 • *Vitagraph* • USA
BROTHERS DIVIDED • 1919 • Keenan Frank • USA
BROTHERS DYNAMITE, THE see **FRATELLI DINAMITE, I** • 1950
BROTHERS EQUAL • 1916 • *Gilroy Barbara* • SHT • USA
BROTHER'S ERROR, A • 1912 • *Essanay* • USA
BROTHER'S FEUD, THE • 1910 • *Imp* • USA
BROTHERS FOR HIRE • 1968 • Buenaventura Augusto • PHL
BROTHERS IN ARMS • 1909 • *Edison* • USA
BROTHERS IN ARMS • 1988 • Bloom George Jay Iii • USA
BROTHERS IN LAW • 1957 • Boulting Roy • UKN
BROTHERS-IN-LAW • 1985 • Swackhamer E. W. • TVM • USA
BROTHERS IN THE SADDLE • 1949 • Selander Lesley • USA
BROTHERS KARAMAZOV, THE • 1957 • Brooks Richard • USA
BROTHERS KARAMAZOV, THE see **BRAT'JA KARAMAZOVY** • 1914
BROTHERS KARAMAZOV, THE see **BRUDER KARAMASOFF, DIE** • 1920
BROTHERS KARAMAZOV, THE see **MORDER DIMITRI KARAMASOFF, DER** • 1931
BROTHERS KARAMAZOV, THE see **BRATYA KARAMAZOVY** • 1968
BROTHERS LIONHEART, THE see **BRODERNA LEJONHJARTA** • 1977
BROTHER'S LOYALTY, A • 1913 • *Bushman Francis X.* • USA
BROTHER'S LOYALTY, A • 1916 • *Essanay* • SHT • USA
BROTHER'S MISTAKE, THE • 1914 • *Gaumont* • UKN
BROTHERS OF THE "UGLEGARD", THE see **BRODRENE PA UGLEGARDEN** • 1967
BROTHERS OF THE WEST • 1937 • Katzman Sam • USA
BROTHERS OF THE WILDERNESS • 1984 • Hillman David Michael • USA
BROTHERS O'TOOLE, THE • 1973 • Erdman Richard • USA • DOUBLE TROUBLE
BROTHER'S REDEMPTION, A • 1911 • *Lubin* • USA
BROTHER'S REDEMPTION, A • 1915 • *Beal Scott* • USA
BROTHER'S REQUITAL, A • 1912 • *Reliance* • USA
BROTHERS RICO, THE • 1956 • Karlson Phil • USA
BROTHER'S SACRIFICE, A • 1912 • Haldane Bert? • UKN
BROTHER'S SACRIFICE, A • 1917 • Grandon Francis J. • SHT • USA
BROTHERS SPAGHETTI, THE see **GALUCCI BROTHERS** • 1988
BROTHERS UNDER THE CHIN • 1924 • Ceder Ralph • SHT • USA
BROTHERS UNDER THE SKIN • 1912 • *Dion Hector* • USA
BROTHERS UNDER THE SKIN • 1922 • Hopper E. Mason • USA
BROTHER'S WOMAN, THE see **BRODERNAS KVINNA** • 1943
BROTHERS WOOD see **FRERES BOUTDEBOIS, LES** • 1908
BROTHER'S WRONG, A • 1909 • Olcott Sidney • USA
BROTT, ETT • 1940 • Henrikson Anders • SWD • CRIME, A
BROTT I PARADISET • 1959 • Kjellgren Lars-Eric • SWD • CRIME IN PARADISE
BROTT I SOL • 1947 • Gentele Goran • SWD • CRIME IN THE SUN
BROTT OCH STRAFF • 1945 • Faustman Erik • SWD • CRIME AND PUNISHMENT
BROTTMALSDOMAREN • 1917 • Klercker Georg • SWD • CRIMINAL COURT JUDGE, THE
BROUGHT HOME • 1915 • Windom Lawrence C. • USA
BROUGHT TO BAY • 1913 • McGowan J. P. • USA
BROUGHT TO JUSTICE • 1914 • *Kalem* • USA
BROUGHT TO JUSTICE (UKN) see **YELLOWBACK, THE** • 1929
BROUGHT TO TERMS • 1909 • *Selig* • USA
BROWN ALE WITH GERTIE • 1975 • Brown Alan • UKN
BROWN BEWITCHED • 1911 • Coleby A. E. • UKN
BROWN BREAD SANDWICHES • 1990 • Liconti Carlo • CND
BROWN DERBY, THE • 1926 • Hines Charles • USA
BROWN EYE EVIL EYE see **SMEDE OKO SLO OKO** • 1967
BROWN EYES AND BANK NOTES • 1919 • Davis James • SHT • USA
BROWN GOLD • 1952 • Noman Theo Van Haren, van Gasteren Louis A. • DOC • NTH
BROWN MOVES TO TOWN • 1912 • *Imp* • USA

BROWN OF CULVER see **TOM BROWN OF CULVER** • 1932

BROWN OF HARVARD • 1911 • Campbell Colin • USA

BROWN OF HARVARD • 1918 • Beaumont Harry • SHT • USA

BROWN OF HARVARD • 1926 • Conway Jack • USA

BROWN ON RESOLUTION • 1935 • Forde Walter, Asquith Anthony • UKN • BORN FOR GLORY (USA) ○ FOREVER ENGLAND

BROWN ON RESOLUTION see **SINGLE-HANDED** • 1953

BROWN ROT • 1950 • Durden J. V. • UKN • PLANT PESTS AND DISEASES -BROWN ROT

BROWN SUGAR • 1922 • Paul Fred • UKN

BROWN SUGAR • 1931 • Hiscott Leslie • UKN

BROWN WALLET, THE • 1936 • Powell Michael • UKN

BROWN WOLF • 1971 • Kaczender George • CND

BROWNED OFF • 1944 • Taylor Donald • UKN

BROWNIE see **HEINZELMANNCHEN** • 1956

BROWNIE BUCKS THE JUNGLE see **MILD CARGO** • 1934

BROWNIE THE PEACE MAKER • 1920 • Taylor W. • SHT • USA

BROWNIE'S BABY DOLL • 1921 • Goulding Alf • SHT • USA

BROWNIE'S BUSY DAY • 1920 • Howe J. A. • SHT • USA • BROWNIE'S TAKING WAYS

BROWNIE'S DOG GONE TRICKS • 1919 • Moore Vin • SHT • USA

BROWNIE'S TAKING WAYS see **BROWNIE'S BUSY DAY** • 1920

BROWNIE'S VICTORY GARDEN see **HOW'S CROPS?** • 1934

BROWNING, LE • 1913 • Feuillade Louis • FRN

BROWNING VERSION, THE • 1951 • Asquith Anthony • UKN

BROWNOUT • 1969 • Abalos Ruben, Tecson A., Conde Conrado, De Leon Gerardo • PHL • BLACKOUT

BROWN'S BACHELOR SUPPER • 1914 • *Ab* • USA

BROWN'S BIG BUTLER • 1914 • *Lubin* • USA

BROWN'S BIRTHDAY PRESENT • 1915 • *Gaumont* • USA

BROWN'S COOK • 1914 • *Lubin* • USA

BROWN'S DAY OFF • 1912 • Collins Edwin J.? • UKN

BROWN'S FISHING(?) EXCURSION • 1906 • Martin J. H.? • UKN

BROWNS HAD VISITORS, THE • 1912 • *Essanay* • USA

BROWN'S HALF HOLIDAY • 1905 • Williamson James • UKN

BROWN'S NEW MONETARY STANDARD • 1913 • Kirkland Hardee • USA

BROWN'S PUDDING • 1904 • Collins Alf • UKN • WHEN FATHER MAKES A PUDDING

BROWN'S SEANCE • 1912 • Sennett Mack • USA

BROWNS SEE THE FAIR, THE • 1916 • Davey Horace • SHT • USA

BROWNS STUDY ASTROLOGY, THE • 1913 • *Essanay* • USA

BROWN'S SUMMER BOARDERS • 1915 • Ridgwell George • USA

BROYEUSE DE COEUR, LA • 1913 • de Morlhon Camille • FRN

BRRR.. see **UNCANNY, THE** • 1977

BRSNA see **BASNA** • 1979

BRUBAKER • 1979 • Rosenberg Stuart • USA

BRUCE AGAINST IRON HAND • Tu Lu-Po • HKG

BRUCE AGAINST THE ODDS see **BIG BOSS 2**

BRUCE AND SHAOLIN KUNG FU 1 • Nam James • HKG

BRUCE AND SHAOLIN KUNG FU 2 • Nam James • HKG

BRUCE AND THE SHAOLIN BRONZEMEN • Kong Joseph • HKG • BRUCE AND THE SHAOLIN BRONZEMEN MASTER

BRUCE AND THE SHAOLIN BRONZEMEN MASTER see **BRUCE AND THE SHAOLIN BRONZEMEN**

BRUCE CONTRE-ATTAQUE • 1982 • Koob Andre • FRN, HKG

BRUCE GENTRY -DAREDEVIL OF THE SKIES • 1949 • Bennet Spencer Gordon, Carr Thomas • SRL • USA

BRUCE LEE AGAINST SUPERMEN • 1976 • Wu Chia-Chun • HKG

BRUCE LEE AND I • 1976 • Lo Mar • HKG

BRUCE LEE IN NEW GUINEA • 1980 • Yang C. Y. • HKG

BRUCE LEE STORY, THE • 1974 • Hop Sin Su?, Kong Hung? • HKG

BRUCE LEE STORY, THE • 1974 • Shih Ti • TWN, USA • DRAGON STORY, A ○ SUPERDRAGON

BRUCE LEE THE INVINCIBLE • 1980 • *Li Bruce* • HKG • BRUCE LI: THE INVINCIBLE ○ INVINCIBLE, THE

BRUCE LEE: THE MAN – THE MYTH • 1976 • Ng See Yuen • HKG • LI HSIAO-LUNG CH'UAN-CHI ○ BRUCE LEE: THE TRUE STORY

BRUCE LEE: THE TRUE STORY see **BRUCE LEE: THE MAN – THE MYTH** • 1976

BRUCE LEE, WE MISS YOU see **CHIN-SE TAI YANG** • 1976

BRUCE LEE'S DEADLY KUNG FU • 1981 • Chin Wah • HKG

BRUCE LEE'S GAME OF DEATH (UKN) see **SZU-WAN YU-HSI** • 1978

BRUCE LEE'S GREATEST REVENGE • 1978 • Tu Lu-Po • HKG • BRUCE LI'S GREATEST REVENGE ○ DRAGON'S GREATEST REVENGE

BRUCE LI: THE INVINCIBLE see **BRUCE LEE THE INVINCIBLE** • 1980

BRUCE LI'S GREATEST REVENGE see **BRUCE LEE'S GREATEST REVENGE** • 1978

BRUCE PARTINGTON PLANS, THE • 1922 • Ridgwell George • UKN

BRUCE THE KING OF KUNG FU • 1984 • Huang Kin Lung • HKG

BRUCE THE SUPERHERO • 1984 • Huang Kin Lung • HKG

BRUCELOSE, A • 1947 • Coelho Jose Adolfo • SHT • PRT

BRUCE'S DEADLY FINGERS see **BRUCE'S FINGERS**

BRUCE'S FINGERS • Kong Joseph • HKG • BRUCE'S DEADLY FINGERS

BRUCH, DER • 1988 • Beyer Frank • GDR, FRG • BREAK, THE

BRUCIA, AMORE, BRUCIA • 1969 • Di Leo Fernando • ITL • AMARSI MALE

BRUCIA, RAGAZZO, BRUCIA • 1969 • Di Leo Fernando • ITL • WOMAN ON FIRE, A (USA) ○ BURN, BOY, BURN (UKN)

BRUCIATI DA COCENTE PASSIONE • 1976 • Capitani Giorgio • ITL

BRUCKE, DIE • 1949 • Pohl Arthur • GDR • BRIDGE, THE

BRUCKE, DIE • 1959 • Wicki Bernhard • FRG • BRIDGE, THE

BRUCKE DES SCHICKSALS • 1960 • FRG

BRUDAR OCH BOLLAR • 1955 • Jarrel Bengt • SWD • DOLLS AND BALLS

BRUDASEK • 1951 • Nasfeter Janusz • SHT • PLN • DIRTY LITTLE BOY, THE

BRUDEN KOM GENOM TAKET • 1947 • Palm Bengt • SWD • BRIDE CAME THROUGH THE CEILING, THE

BRUDER • 1919 • Mack Max • FRG

BRUDER • 1923 • Gliese Rochus • FRG • ZWISCHEN HIMMEL UND ERDE

BRUDER • 1929 • Hochbaum Werner • FRG • BROTHERS

BRUDER, DIE • 1917 • Kehlmann Michael • FRG

BRUDER, DIE • 1976 • Gremm Wolfgang • FRG • BROTHERS, THE

BRUDER BERNARD • 1929 • Seitz Franz • FRG

BRUDER IN NOT. OSTPREUSSEN UND SEIN HINDENBERG see **OSTPREUSSEN UND SEIN HINDENBURG** • 1915

BRUDER KARAMASOFF, DIE • 1920 • Buchowetzki Dimitri, Froelich Carl • FRG • BROTHERS KARAMAZOV, THE

BRUDER MARTIN see **UND DER HIMMEL LACHT DAZU** • 1954

BRUDER NOLTENIUS, DIE • 1945 • Lamprecht Gerhard • FRG

BRUDER SCHELLENBERG, DIE • 1926 • Grune Karl • FRG • TWO BROTHERS

BRUDER VAN ZAARDEN, DIE • 1918 • Wauer William • FRG

BRUDER VON ST. PARASITUS, DIE • 1919 • Obal Max • FRG

BRUDERHERZEN • 1915 • Haase Magnus • FRG

BRUDERLEIN FEIN • 1942 • Thimig Hans • FRG

BRUDERMORD • 1922 • Neff Wolfgang • FRG

BRUEGEL • 1969 • Haesaerts Paul • BLG

BRUG, DE • 1928 • Ivens Joris • NTH • BRIDGE, THE

BRUGES • 1954 • Degelin Emile, de Boe Gerard • BLG

BRUGES-LA-MORTE see **BRUGGE-DIE-STILLE** • 1981

BRUGGE-DIE-STILLE • 1981 • Verhavert Roland • BLG • BRUGES-LA-MORTE

BRUIN TROUBLE • 1918 • *Nestor* • SHT • USA

BRUISER, THE • 1916 • Bartlett Charles • USA

BRUIT, LE • 1955 • Leenhardt Roger • DCS • FRN

BRUIT QUI COURT, UN • 1983 • Laloux Daniel, Sentier Jean-Pierre • FRN

BRUJA, LA • 1954 • Urueta Chano • MXC • WITCH, THE

BRUJA, MAS QUE BRUJA • 1976 • Fernan-Gomez Fernando • SPN

BRUJA SIN ESCOBA, UNA • 1966 • Elorrieta Jose Maria • SPN, USA • WITCH WITHOUT A BROOM, A (USA)

BRUJITA, LA • 1966 • Bartolome Cecilia • SHT • SPN

BRUJO DESAPARECIENDO, EL • 1898 • Casasus Jose E. • CUB

BRUK • 1971 • Kudla Zdzislaw • PLN • PAVEMENT, THE

BRULER LES PLANCHES • 1983 • Garran Gabriel • FRN

BRULERE DE MILLE SOLEILS, LA • 1964 • Kast Pierre • FRN • RADIANCE OF A THOUSAND SUNS, THE ○ FIRE OF A THOUSAND SUNS, THE ○ BURNING OF A THOUSAND SUNS, THE

BRULES, LES • 1958 • Devlin Bernard • CND • PROMISED LAND, THE

BRULURES D'HERBE, LES see **MAUVAISES HERBES** • 1896

BRUMES see **DERNIER CHOC, LE** • 1932

BRUMES D'AUTOMNE • 1929 • Kirsanoff Dimitri • SHT • FRN • MISTS OF AUTUMN

BRUMES DE PARIS • 1932 • Sollin Maurice • FRN

BRUN BITTER • 1988 • Skagen Solve • NRW • HAIR OF THE DOG

BRUNA FORMOSA CERCA SUPERDOTATO • 1974 • Cardone Alberto • ITL

BRUNA INDIAVOLATA, UNA • 1952 • Bragaglia Carlo Ludovico • ITL

BRUNE ET MOI, LA • 1979 • Puicouyoul Philippe • FRN

BRUNE QUI VOILA, LA • 1960 • Regamey Maurice, Lamoureux Robert • FRN

BRUNET WIECZOROWA PORA • 1976 • Bareja Stanislaw • PLN

BRUNETTES PREFER GENTLEMEN • 1927 • Lamont Charles • SHT • USA

BRUNKEL • 1943 • Henning-Jensen Bjarne • DNM

BRUNNEN DES WAHNSINNS, DER • 1921 • Ostermayr Ottmar • FRG

BRUNO DER SCHWARZE, ES BLIES EIN JAGER WOHL IN SEIN HORN • 1972 • Eisholz Lutz • FRG

BRUNO, L'ENFANT DU DIMANCHE • 1968 • Grospierre Louis • FRN, BLG • BRUNO -SUNDAY'S CHILD (UKN) ○ BRUNO OU LES ENFANTS DU DIMANCHE

BRUNO OU LES ENFANTS DU DIMANCHE see **BRUNO, L'ENFANT DU DIMANCHE** • 1968

BRUNO -SUNDAY'S CHILD (UKN) see **BRUNO, L'ENFANT DU DIMANCHE** • 1968

BRUSH BETWEEN COWBOYS AND INDIANS • 1904 • Porter Edwin S. • USA

BRUSHFIRE! • 1962 • Warner Jack Jr. • USA

BRUSSELS 1958 • 1958 • Grigoriev Roman • DOC • USS

BRUSSELS BY NIGHT • 1984 • Didden Marc • BLG

BRUSSELS FILM LOOPS • 1958 • Pennebaker D. A. • USA

BRUSSELS LOOPS see **LOOPS** • 1958

BRUSSELS-TRANSIT see **BRUXELLES-TRANSIT** • 1981

BRUSTEN HIMMEL • 1981 • Thulin Ingrid • SWD • BROKEN SKY

BRUTAL • 1981 • Diaz-Abaya Marilou • PHL

BRUTAL BURGLAR, THE • 1900 • *Paul R. W.* • UKN

BRUTAL GLORY • 1988 • Roets Koos • SAF

BRUTAL MASTER, A • 1909 • Fitzhamon Lewin • UKN

BRUTALISATION OF FRANK BLUM, THE see **VERROHUNG DES FRANZ BLUM, DIE** • 1975

BRUTALITAT IN STEIN • 1960 • Kluge Alexander, Schamoni Peter • SHT • FRG • EWIGKEIT VON GESTERN ○ BRUTALITY IN STONE ○ YESTERDAY GOES ON FOR EVER

BRUTALITY • 1912 • Griffith D. W. • USA

BRUTALITY IN STONE see **BRUTALITAT IN STEIN** • 1960

BRUTALITY REWARDED • 1904 • Haggar William • UKN

BRUTE, THE • 1912 • Davis Ulysses • USA

BRUTE, THE • 1913 • *Frontier* • USA

BRUTE, THE • 1914 • Kirkland Hardee • *Vitagraph* • USA

BRUTE, THE • 1914 • Olcott Sidney • USA

BRUTE, THE • 1925 • Micheaux Oscar • USA

BRUTE, THE • 1927 • Cummings Irving • USA

BRUTE, THE • 1976 • O'Hara Gerry • UKN

BRUTE, THE see **BRUTO, EL** • 1952

BRUTE, THE see **DUVAD** • 1959

BRUTE, THE see **YAJU NO SEISHUN** • 1963

BRUTE AND THE BEAST, THE see **TEMPO DI MASSACRO** • 1966

BRUTE BREAKER, THE • 1919 • Reynolds Lynn • USA

BRUTE CORPS • 1971 • Jameson Jerry • USA

BRUTE FORCE • 1913 • Griffith D. W. • USA • WARS OF THE PRIMEVAL TRIBES ○ PRIMITIVE MAN, THE ○ IN PREHISTORIC DAYS

BRUTE FORCE • 1917 • Rice A. W. • SHT • USA

BRUTE FORCE • 1947 • Dassin Jules • USA

BRUTE HUMAINE, UNE • 1914 • de Morlhon Camille • FRN

BRUTE MAN • 1946 • Yarbrough Jean • USA

BRUTE MASTER, THE • 1920 • Kyson Charles H. • USA

BRUTE'S REVENGE, A • 1912 • Coleby A. E.? • UKN

BRUTO, EL • 1952 • Bunuel Luis • MXC • BRUTE, THE

BRUTO, EL CHULO Y LA CAMARERA, EL • 1975 • Ozores Mariano • SPN

BRUTO II • 1911 • De Liguoro Giuseppe • ITL

BRUTO PARA PARTICIA, UN • 1960 • Klimovsky Leon • SPN

BRUTTI DI NOTTE • 1968 • Grimaldi Gianni • ITL • UGLY ONES BY NIGHT

BRUTTI, SPORCHI E CATTIVI • 1976 • Scola Ettore • ITL • UGLY, DIRTY AND MEAN ○ DOWN AND DIRTY ○ UGLY, DIRTY AND BAD

BRUTUS • 1910 • Guazzoni Enrico • ITL

BRUTUS AND CASSIUS • 1918 • Moore Marshall • UKN

BRUXELLES, RENDEZ-VOUS DES NATIONS • 1958 • Haesaerts Paul • BLG

BRUXELLES-TRANSIT • 1981 • Szlingerbaum Samy • BLG • BRUSSELS-TRANSIT

BRYGGERENS DATTER • 1912 • Ottesen • DNM • BREWER'S DAUGHTER, THE

BRYLLUPSFESTEN • 1989 • Wam Svend, Vennerod Petter • NRW • WEDDING PARTY, THE

BRZEZINA • 1971 • Wajda Andrzej • MTV • PLN • BIRCH WOOD, THE ○ BIRCHWOOD

BRZINA, ALI OPREZ • 1968 • Vunak Dragutin • ANM • YGS • FAST, BUT CAREFUL

BU HUO YINGXIONG • 1985 • Liang Puzhi • HKG • TIME TRAVELLER

BU-SU • 1988 • Ichikawa Jun • JPN

BU VATANIN COCUKLARI • 1958 • Yilmaz Atif • TRK • CHILDREN OF THIS COUNTRY, THE

BUBASINTER • 1972 • Jelic Milan • YGS • BUG KILLER

BUBBLE, THE • 1967 • Oboler Arch • USA • FANTASTIC INVASION OF PLANET EARTH

BUBBLE, THE • 1976 • Charyev Mejek • ANM • USS

BUBBLE BEE • 1949 • Nichols Charles • ANS • USA

BUBBLE OF LOVE, THE • 1917 • Gerrard Douglas • SHT • USA

BUBBLE TROUBLE • 1953 • White Jules • SHT • USA

BUBBLES • 1916 • Brenon Herbert • SHT • USA

BUBBLES • 1920 • Mack Wayne • USA

BUBBLES • 1922 • Fleischer Dave • ANS • USA

BUBBLES AND THE BARBER, THE • 1916 • Watt Nate • SHT • USA

BUBBLES AND TROUBLES • 1933 • Davis Mannie • ANS • USA

BUBBLES IN THE GLASS, THE • 1915 • *Huling Lorraine* • USA

BUBBLES IN THE GLASS, THE • 1916 • Warde Ernest C. • SHT • USA

BUBBLES OF SONG • 1951 • Cowan Will • SHT • USA

BUBBLES OF TROUBLE • 1916 • Cline Eddie • SHT • USA

BUBBLES SCHROEDER STORIE, DIE • 1961 • SAF

BUBBLING OVER • 1921 • Roach Hal • SHT • USA

BUBBLING OVER • 1932 • Jason Leigh • SHT • USA

BUBBLING TROUBLE • 1940 • Cahn Edward L. • SHT • USA

BUBBLING WATER • 1915 • Mackley Arthur • USA

BUBCHEN • 1968 • Klick Roland • FRG • KLEINE VAMPIR, DER ○ LITTLE VAMPIRE, THE ○ LADDIE ○ LITTLE BOY LOST

BUBE U GLAVI • 1971 • Radivojevic Milos • YGS • BATS IN THE BELFRY

BUBI, DER TAUSENSASSA • 1918 • Henning Hanna • FRG

BUBU • 1971 • Bolognini Mauro • ITL

BUCANEROS DEL CARIBE, LOS • 1960 • Martin Eugenio • SPN, FRN • BOUCANIERS DES CARAIBES, LES

BUCCANEER see **MY MARRIAGE** • 1935

BUCCANEER, THE • 1938 • De Mille Cecil B. • USA

BUCCANEER, THE • 1958 • Quinn Anthony • USA

BUCCANEER BUNNY • 1948 • Freleng Friz • ANS • USA

BUCCANEER WOODPECKER • 1953 • Patterson Don • ANS • USA

BUCCANEERS, THE • 1911 • *Selig* • USA

BUCCANEERS, THE • 1913 • Turner Otis • USA

BUCCANEERS, THE • 1924 • Roach Hal • SHT • USA

BUCCANEERS, THE see **PIRATES, THE** • 1904

BUCCANEER'S GIRL • 1950 • De Cordova Frederick • USA

BUCCIA DI BANANA see **PEAU DE BANANE** • 1964

BUCH DES LASTER, DAS • 1917 • Rippert Otto • FRG

BUCH ESTHER, DAS • 1919 • Reicher Ernst, Krafft Uwe Jens • FRG

BUCHAMUKURE DAIHAKKEN • 1969 • Furusawa Kengo • JPN • COMPUTER FREE-FOR-ALL (USA)

BUCHANAN RIDES ALONE • 1958 • Boetticher Budd • USA

BUCHANAN'S WIFE • 1918 • Brabin Charles J. • USA

BUCHAREST IDENTITY CARD • 1983 • Calotescu Virgil • RMN

BUCHAREST MEMORIES see **AMINTIRI BUCURESTENE** • 1970

BUCHAREST, THE CITY IN BLOSSOM • 1955 • Stiopul Savel • RMN

BUCHERONS DE LA MANOUANE • 1962 • Lamothe Arthur • DCS • CND • MANOUANE RIVER LUMBERJACKS

BUCHHALTERIN, DIE • 1918 • von Woringen Paul • FRG

BUCHSE DER PANDORA, DIE • 1929 • Pabst G. W. • FRG • PANDORA'S BOX ○ LULU

BUCK AND THE PREACHER • 1972 • Poitier Sidney • USA

BUCK BENNY RIDES AGAIN • 1940 • Sandrich Mark • USA

BUCK CLAYTON AND HIS ALL STARS • 1961 • Bruynoghe Yannick • BLG

BUCK, EL PREDICAR • 1971 • *Columbia* • MXC

BUCK PARVIN AND THE MOVIES • 1915 • *Acord Arthur* • USA

BUCK PRIVATES • 1928 • Brown Melville • USA

BUCK PRIVATES • 1941 • Lubin Arthur • USA • ROOKIES (UKN)

BUCK PRIVATES COME HOME • 1947 • Barton Charles T. • USA • ROOKIES COME HOME (UKN)
BUCK RICHARDS' BRIDE • 1913 • Huntley Fred W. • USA
BUCK ROGERS • 1939 • Beebe Ford, Goodkind Saul • SRL • USA • BUCK ROGERS CONQUERS THE UNIVERSE
BUCK ROGERS see **BUCK ROGERS IN THE 25TH CENTURY** • 1979
BUCK ROGERS CONQUERS THE UNIVERSE see **BUCK ROGERS** • 1939
BUCK ROGERS: FLIGHT OF THE WAR WITCH • 1979 • Stewart Larry • USA
BUCK ROGERS IN THE 25TH CENTURY • 1979 • Haller Daniel • USA • BUCK ROGERS
BUCK ROGERS: PLANET OUTLAWS • 1939 • Beebe Ford, Goodkind Saul • USA
BUCK SIMMONS, PUNCHER • 1916 • Kent Leon D. • SHT • USA
BUCKAROO • 1967 • Bianchi Adelchi • ITL • WINCHESTER CHE NON PERDONA, IL
BUCKAROO BANZAI see **ADVENTURES OF BUCKAROO BANZAI, THE** • 1984
BUCKAROO BROADCAST, A • 1938 • Yarbrough Jean • SHT • USA
BUCKAROO BUGS • 1944 • Clampett Robert • ANS • USA
BUCKAROO FROM POWDER RIVER • 1947 • Nazarro Ray • USA
BUCKAROO KID, THE • 1926 • Reynolds Lynn • USA
BUCKAROO SHERIFF OF TEXAS • 1951 • Ford Philip • USA
BUCKET OF BLOOD, A • 1960 • Corman Roger • USA
BUCKET OF BLOOD (USA) see **TELL-TALE HEART, THE** • 1934
BUCKET SHARPERS • 1914 • *Joker* • USA
BUCKEYE AND BLUE • 1988 • Compton J. C. • USA
BUCKIN' THE WEST • 1924 • *Sheldon Forrest (Scen)* • USA
BUCKING BROADWAY • 1918 • Ford John • USA • SLUMBERING FIRES (UKN)
BUCKING BROADWAY • 1922 • Christie Al • USA
BUCKING BRONCHO, THE • 1910 • *Nestor* • USA
BUCKING BRONCOS • 1904 • Porter Edwin S. • USA
BUCKING HORSES see **BRONCHO BUSTING FOR FLYING A PICTURES** • 1912
BUCKING SOCIETY • 1916 • Williams Harry, Campbell William • SHT • USA
BUCKING THE BARRIER • 1923 • Campbell Colin • USA
BUCKING THE LINE • 1921 • Harbaugh Carl • USA
BUCKING THE TIGER • 1917 • Williamson Robin E. • SHT • USA
BUCKING THE TIGER • 1921 • Kolker Henry • USA
BUCKING THE TRUTH • 1926 • Morante Milburn • USA
BUCKLIGE UND DIE TANZERIN, DER • 1920 • Murnau F. W. • FRG • HUNCHBACK AND THE DANCER, THE
BUCKLIGE VON SOHO, DER • 1966 • Vohrer Alfred • FRG
BUCK'S LADY FRIEND • 1915 • Bertram William • USA
BUCK'S ROMANCE • 1912 • Duncan William • USA
BUCKSHOT FEUD, THE • 1916 • McKim Edwin • SHT • USA
BUCKSHOT JOHN • 1915 • Bosworth Hobart • USA
BUCKSKIN • 1968 • Moore Michael • USA • FRONTIERSMAN, THE
BUCKSKIN COAT, THE • 1913 • *Kalem* • USA
BUCKSKIN COUNTY PRISON • 1978 • Huston Jimmy • USA
BUCKSKIN FRONTIER • 1943 • Selander Lesley • USA • IRON ROAD, THE (UKN)
BUCKSKIN JACK THE EARL OF GLENMORE • 1911 • *Prior Herbert* • USA
BUCKSKIN LADY, THE • 1957 • Hittelman Carl K. • USA
BUCKSKIN SHIRT, THE • 1915 • *Ab* • USA
BUCKSKIN SHIRT, THE • 1915 • Physioc Wray • USA
BUCKTOWN • 1975 • Marks Arthur • USA
BUCKTOWN ROMANCE, A • 1912 • *Errol Eileen* • USA
BUCO, IL (ITL) see **TROU, LE** • 1960
BUCO IN FRONTE, UN • 1968 • Vari Giuseppe • ITL • HOLE IN THE FOREHEAD, A
BUD AND LOU • 1978 • Thompson Robert C. • TVM • USA
BUD, BILL AND THE WAITER • 1914 • Neilan Marshall • USA
BUD BLOSSOM • 1915 • *Thanhouser Kidlet* • USA
BUD NEVINS -BAD MAN • 1911 • *American* • USA
BUD TILDEN, MAIL THIEF • 1913 • *Reliance* • USA
BUDAI CUKRASZDA • 1936 • Gaal Bela • HNG
BUDAK NAFSU • 1984 • Syumanjaya • INN • PREY OF PASSIONS ○ FATIMA
BUDAPEST, AMIERT SZERETEM • 1971 • Szabo Istvan • SHS • HNG • BUDAPEST, WHY I LOVE IT
BUDAPEST -CITY OF SPORTS • 1967 • Csoke Jozsef • DOC • HNG
BUDAPEST TALES see **BUDAPESTI MESEK** • 1976
BUDAPEST TAVASZ • 1955 • Mariassy Felix • HNG • SPRING IN BUDAPEST
BUDAPEST, WHY I LOVE IT see **BUDAPEST, AMIERT SZERETEM** • 1971
BUDAPESTI MESEK • 1976 • Szabo Istvan • HNG • TALES OF BUDAPEST ○ BUDAPEST TALES
BUDAWANNY • 1987 • Quinn Bob • IRL
BUDD DOBLE COMES BACK • 1913 • Campbell Colin • USA
BUDDA'S CURSE, THE • 1910 • *Lux* • FRN
BUDDENBROOKS, DIE • 1923 • Lamprecht Gerhard • FRG
BUDDENBROOKS, DIE • 1959 • Weidenmann Alfred • FRG
BUDDHA see **SHAKA** • 1962
BUDDHA'S LOCK see **TIAN PUSA** • 1987
BUDDHIST NUN'S STORY see **BHIKKUNI** • 1983
BUDDHIST PRIESTESS, THE • 1911 • *Thanhouser* • USA
BUDDIES • 1984 • Nicholson Arch • ASL
BUDDIES • 1985 • Bresson Arthur Jr. • USA
BUDDIES see **POLARE** • 1976
BUDDIES THICKER THAN WATER • 1962 • Deitch Gene • ANS • USA
BUDDING OF LOVE see **SHIROI AKUMA** • 1958
BUDDY see **BRATISHKA** • 1926
BUDDY see **BRATUSHKA** • 1975
BUDDY AND HIS DOG • 1912 • *Solax* • USA
BUDDY AND TOWSER • 1934 • Freleng Friz • ANS • USA
BUDDY, BUDDY • 1981 • Wilder Billy • USA
BUDDY GOES WEST see **OCCHIO ALLA PENNA** • 1981
BUDDY HOLLY STORY, THE • 1978 • Rash Steve • USA
BUDDY IN AFRICA • 1935 • Hardaway Ben • ANS • USA
BUDDY OF THE APES • 1934 • Hardaway Ben • ANS • USA
BUDDY OF THE LEGION • 1935 • Hardaway Ben • ANS • USA
BUDDY RICH AND HIS ORCHESTRA • 1948 • Cowan Will • SHT • USA
BUDDY STEPS OUT • 1935 • King Jack • ANS • USA
BUDDY SYSTEM, THE • 1984 • Jordan Glenn • USA
BUDDY THE DENTIST • 1935 • Hardaway Ben • ANS • USA
BUDDY THE DETECTIVE • 1934 • King Jack • ANS • USA
BUDDY THE GEE MAN • 1935 • King Jack • ANS • USA
BUDDY THE GOB • 1934 • Freleng Friz • ANS • USA
BUDDY THE LITTLE GUARDIAN • 1911 • *Selig* • USA
BUDDY THE WOODSMAN • 1934 • King Jack • ANS • USA
BUDDY'S ADVENTURES • 1935 • Hardaway Ben • ANS • USA
BUDDY'S BEARCATS • 1934 • King Jack • ANS • USA
BUDDY'S BEER GARDEN • 1933 • Duval Earl • ANS • USA
BUDDY'S BIG HUNT • 1935 • King Jack • ANS • USA
BUDDY'S CHRISTMAS • 1916 • *Lincoln E. K.* • SHT • USA
BUDDY'S CIRCUS • 1934 • King Jack • ANS • USA
BUDDY'S DAY OUT • 1933 • King Jack • ANS • USA
BUDDY'S DOWNFALL • 1914 • Johnson Tefft • USA
BUDDY'S FIRST CALL • 1914 • Johnson Tefft • USA
BUDDY'S GARAGE • 1934 • Duval Earl • ANS • USA
BUDDY'S LOST WORLD • 1935 • King Jack • ANS • USA
BUDDY'S PONY EXPRESS • 1935 • Hardaway Ben • ANS • USA
BUDDY'S SHOWBOAT • 1933 • King Jack • ANS • USA
BUDDY'S SONG • 1990 • Whatham Claude • UKN
BUDDY'S THEATRE • 1935 • Hardaway Ben • ANS • USA
BUDDY'S TROLLEY TROUBLES • 1934 • Freleng Friz • ANS • USA
BUDENJE PACOVA • 1967 • Pavlovic Zivojin • YGS • RATS WAKE UP, THE ○ RATS AWAKE, THE ○ BUDJENJE PACOVA
BUDJENJE PACOVA see **BUDENJE PACOVA** • 1967
BUDOSVIZ • 1966 • Ban Frigyes • HNG • HEALING WATER, THE
BUD'S RECRUIT • 1918 • Vidor King • SHT • USA
BUD'S TRIUMPH • 1910 • *Bison* • USA
BUDSKAB TIL NAPOLEON PAA ELBA, ET • 1909 • *Blom August* • DNM • MESSAGE TO NAPOLEON, A
BUDUJEMY • 1934 • Jakubowska Wanda, Cekalski Eugeniusz • DCS • PLN • WE ARE BUILDING ○ WE BUILD
BUDUJEMY NOWE WSIE • 1946 • Jakubowska Wanda • DCS • PLN • WE ARE BUILDERS OF THE COUNTRY ○ WE ARE BUILDING NEW VILLAGES
BUDULINEK AND THE FOXES • Zykmund V., Vesela A. • ANM • CZC
BUEK! • 1979 • Szoreny Rezso • HNG • HAPPY NEW YEAR!
BUEN AMOR, EL • 1963 • Regueiro Francisco • SPN
BUEN CAMINO, POR • 1936 • Morera Eduardo
BUEN LADRON, EL • 1955 • de la Serna Mauricio • MXC
BUEN MOZO, EL see **BEL AMI** • 1946
BUENA SUERTE, EL • 1960 • Gonzalez Rogelio A. • MXC
BUENAS NOCHES, ANO NUEVO • 1964 • Soler Julian • MXC
BUENAS NOCHES MI AMOR • 1950 • Rivero Fernando A. • MXC
BUENAS NOTICIAS • 1953 • Manzanos Eduardo • SPN
BUENAVENTURA, LA • 1934 • McGann William • USA
BUENAVENTURA, LA • 1934 • Reachi Manuel • MXC
BUENOS AIRES • 1922 • Ferreyra Jose • ARG
BUENOS AIRES: LA TERCERA FUNDACION • 1980 • Zapettini Clara • ARG • BUENOS AIRES: THE THIRD FOUNDATION
BUENOS AIRES ROCK 82 • 1982 • Olivera Hector • ARG
BUENOS AIRES: THE THIRD FOUNDATION see **BUENOS AIRES: LA TERCERA FUNDACION** • 1980
BUENOS DIAS ACAPULCO • 1962 • Delgado Agustin P. • MXC
BUENOS DIAS, AMOR (SPN) see **AMORE A PRIMA VISTA** • 1958
BUENOS DIAS, BUENOS AIRES • 1960 • Birri Fernando • SHT • ARG
BUENOS DIAS CONDESITA • 1967 • Amadori Luis Cesar • SPN • GOOD MORNING, LITTLE COUNTESS
BUENOS DIAS, LOS • 1931 • Rey Florian • FRN
BUENOS DIAS PERDIDOS, LOS • 1975 • Gil Rafael • SPN
BUFERE • 1953 • Brignone Guido • ITL • DANGEROUS WOMAN ○ FILLE DANGEREUSE
BUFFALO BILL • 1944 • Wellman William A. • USA
BUFFALO BILL see **BUFFALO BILL, L'EROE DEL FAR WEST** • 1965
BUFFALO BILL see **BUFFALO BILL AND THE INDIANS OR SITTING BULL'S HISTORY LESSON** • 1976
BUFFALO BILL A ROMA • 1953 • Accatino Giuseppe • ITL
BUFFALO BILL AND THE INDIANS OR SITTING BULL'S HISTORY LESSON • 1976 • Altman Robert • USA • BUFFALO BILL
BUFFALO-BILL ET LA BERGERE • 1949 • Ciampi Yves • FRN
BUFFALO BILL, HERO OF THE FAR WEST see **BUFFALO BILL, L'EROE DEL FAR WEST** • 1965
BUFFALO BILL IN TOMAHAWK TERRITORY • 1952 • Ray Bernard B. • USA
BUFFALO BILL, L'EROE DEL FAR WEST • 1965 • Costa Mario • ITL, FRN, FRG • DAS WAR BUFFALO BILL (FRG) ○ BUFFALO BILL ○ BUFFALO BILL, HERO OF THE FAR WEST
BUFFALO BILL ON THE BRAIN • 1911 • Bouwmeester Theo • UKN
BUFFALO BILL ON THE U.P. TRAIL • 1926 • Mattison Frank S. • USA • WITH BUFFALO BILL ON THE U.P. TRAIL
BUFFALO BILL RIDES AGAIN • 1947 • Ray Bernard B. • USA
BUFFALO GUN • 1961 • Gannaway Albert C. • USA
BUFFALO HUNT • 1912 • *Bison* • USA
BUFFALO JIM • 1914 • *Vitagraph* • USA
BUFFALO STAMPEDE see **THUNDERING HERD, THE** • 1933
BUFFER, THE • 1913 • *Reliance* • USA
BUFFER, THE • 1914 • *Holmes Rapley* • USA
BUFFER ZONE see **CSEREPEK** • 1981
BUFFERIN • 1966 • Warhol Andy • USA • GERARD MALANGA READS POETRY
BUFFET FROID • 1979 • Blier Bertrand • FRN • COLD CUTS (USA)
BUG • 1975 • Szwarc Jeannot • USA • HEPHAESTUS PLAGUE, THE
BUG AND THE COUNT, THE • 1912 • *Reliance* • USA
BUG BAND, THE • 1917 • McCay Winsor • ANS • USA
BUG BOY OF LANCASHIRE, THE • 1914 • Weston Charles • UKN
BUG CARNIVAL • 1937 • Davis Mannie, Gordon George • ANS • USA
BUG HOUSE COLLEGE DAYS • 1929 • Terry Paul • ANS • USA
BUG KILLER see **BUBASINTER** • 1972
BUG PARADE, THE • 1941 • Avery Tex • ANS • USA
BUG PROFESSOR, THE • 1913 • *Pilot* • USA
BUG VAUDEVILLE • 1917 • McCay Winsor • ANS • USA
BUGAMBILIA • 1944 • Fernandez Emilio • MXC
BUGAROOS • 1970 • *Jessel Paul (P)* • ANS • USA
BUGAWAN SOLO • 1951 • Ichikawa Kon • JPN • RIVER SOLO FLOWS
BUGGED BY A BEE • 1969 • McKimson Robert • ANS • USA
BUGGED BY A BUG • 1967 • Bakshi Ralph • ANS • USA
BUGGED IN A RUG • 1968 • Smith Paul J. • ANS • USA
BUGHOUSE BELL HOPS • 1915 • Roach Hal • USA
BUGIARDA, LA • 1965 • Comencini Luigi • ITL, FRN, SPN • MENTIROSA, LA (SPN) ○ SIX DAYS A WEEK (USA) ○ PARTAGE DE CATHERINE, LE (FRN)
BUGIE BIANCHE • 1979 • Rolla Stefano • ITL
BUGLARIOUS BILLY • 1915 • Beggs Lee • USA
BUGLE CALL, THE • 1909 • *Vitagraph* • USA
BUGLE CALL, THE • 1912 • *101 Bison* • USA
BUGLE CALL, THE • 1915 • Martin E. A. • USA
BUGLE CALL, THE • 1916 • Barker Reginald • USA
BUGLE CALL, THE • 1927 • Sedgwick Edward • USA
BUGLE SOUNDS, THE • 1941 • Simon S. Sylvan • USA • STEEL CAVALRY
BUGLER, THE • 1917 • *Big U* • SHT • USA
BUGLER OF ALGIERS, THE • 1916 • Julian Rupert • USA • COMRADES (UKN) ○ WE ARE FRENCH
BUGLER OF BATTERY B, THE • 1912 • Melford George • USA
BUGLER OF COMPANY B, THE • 1913 • *Bison* • USA
BUGLES IN THE AFTERNOON • 1952 • Rowland Roy • USA
BUGS AND BOOKS • 1932 • Foster John, Davis Mannie • ANS • USA
BUGS AND BUGLES • 1916 • MacMackin Archer • USA
BUGS AND THUGS • 1954 • Freleng Friz • ANS • USA
BUGS BEETLE AND HIS ORCHESTRA • 1938 • Foster John • ANS • USA
BUGS BONNET • 1956 • Jones Charles M. • ANS • USA
BUGS BUNNY AND THE THREE BEARS • 1944 • Jones Charles M. • ANS • USA
BUGS BUNNY GETS THE BOID • 1942 • Clampett Robert • ANS • USA
BUGS BUNNY NIPS THE NIP • 1944 • Freleng Friz • ANS • USA
BUGS BUNNY RIDES AGAIN • 1948 • Freleng Friz • ANS • USA
BUGS BUNNY / ROAD RUNNER MOVIE, THE • 1979 • Jones Charles M., Monroe Phil • ANM • USA
BUGS BUNNY, SUPERSTAR • 1975 • Jackson Larry • ANM • USA
BUGS IN LOVE • 1932 • Gillett Burt • ANS • USA
BUGSY AND MUGSY • 1957 • Freleng Friz • ANS • USA
BUGSY MALONE • 1976 • Parker Alan • UKN
BUHAY ARTISTA • 1967 • Carlos Luciano B. • PHL • LIFE OF AN ARTIST
BUHAY BOMBERO • 1968 • Wenceslao Jose Pepe • PHL • FIREMAN'S LIFE, A
BUHAY MARINO • 1967 • Garces Armando • PHL • SAILOR'S LIFE
BUHNE FREI FUR MARIKA • 1958 • Jacoby Georg • FRG • STAGE IS CLEARED FOR MARIKA, THE
BUHO, EL • 1974 • Kamin Bernardo • ARG • OWL, THE
BUICK AND THE MONUMENT, THE see **BUICKEN OG REISVERKET** • 1990
BUICKEN OG REISVERKET • 1990 • Nicolayssen Hans Otto • NRW • BUICK AND THE MONUMENT, THE
BUILD MY GALLOWS HIGH (UKN) see **OUT OF THE PAST** • 1947
BUILD THY HOUSE • 1920 • Goodwins Fred • UKN
BUILD-UP, THE • 1970 • Bryant Gerard • UKN
BUILD-UP, THE see **KYOJIN TO GANGU** • 1958
BUILDER OF BRIDGES • 1915 • Irving Henry George • USA
BUILDER OF THE CATHEDRAL, THE see **STAVITEL CHRAMU** • 1919
BUILDERS • 1942 • Jackson Pat • DCS • UKN
BUILDERS, THE • 1954 • Altman Robert • USA
BUILDERS, THE • 1960 • Sprager Hart • USA
BUILDERS LABOURERS MURAL • 1978 • Patterson Garry • DOC • ASL
BUILDERS OF CASTLES • 1917 • Turbett Ben • USA
BUILDING A BUILDING • 1933 • Hand David • ANS • USA
BUILDING A CHICKEN HOUSE • 1914 • Lyndhurst F. L. • UKN
BUILDING A FIRE • 1914 • *Lubin* • USA
BUILDING A NATION see **BOU VAN 'N NASIE, DIE** • 1939
BUILDING A TRUST • 1913 • Hotaling Arthur D. • USA
BUILDING CHILDREN'S PERSONALITIES WITH CREATIVE DANCING • 1953 • Goldsmith Frank • USA
BUILDING EACH DAY, COMPANERO see **CONSTRUCTOR CADA DIA, COMPANERO** • 1982
BUILDING FOR DEMOCRACY • 1918 • *Stevens Emily* • SHT • USA
BUILDING GAME, THE see **BOUWSPELEMENT** • 1963
BUILDING THE BRIDGE • 1966 • Yefremov O. • USS
BUILDING THE GREAT LOS ANGELES AQUEDUCT • 1912 • Dwan Allan • DOC • USA
BUILDING THE NEW LINE • 1911 • *Kalem* • USA
BUILDING THE SOLDIER • 1919 • *Miller-Hodkinson* • SHT • USA
BUILT FOR RUNNING • 1924 • *Maloney Leo* • USA
BUILT FOR THE JOB • 1949 • Brownrigg Rosanne • UKN
BUILT ON A BLUFF • 1924 • Lamont Charles • SHT • USA
BUIO IN SALA • 1950 • Risi Dino • SHT • ITL
BUIO OMEGA • 1979 • D'Amato Joe • ITL • BLUE HOLOCAUST ○ BEYOND THE DARKNESS
BUISSON ARDENT • 1986 • Perrin Laurent • FRN
BUISSON ARDENT, LE • 1955 • Alexeieff Alexandre • SHT • FRN
BUITRE, EL • 1925 • Garcia Moreno Gabriel • MXC

BUITRES CAVARAN TU FOSA, LOS • 1971 • Bosch Juan • SPN
BUITRES SOBRE EL TEJADO, LOS • 1945 • Gout Alberto • MXC
BUKAN SALAH ASUHAN • 1975 • Sasakul Ismail • MLY
BUKAN SANDIWARA • 1981 • Jaya Syuman • INN
BUKHTA SMERTI • 1926 • Room Abram • USS • DEATH BAY
BUKI NAKI TATAKI • 1960 • Yamamoto Satsuo • JPN • BATTLE WITHOUT ARMS, THE
BUKIT KEPONG • 1981 • Shamsuddin Jins • MLY
BUKOD KANG PINAGPALA • 1967 • Torres Mar S. • PHL
BUKOVYNA–ZEMLYA UKRAYINSKA • 1940 • Solntseva Yulia • USS
BULAG NA MATADOR • 1968 • Gaudite Solano • PHL • BLIND MATADOR, THE
BULAN • 1989 • Wedel Karsten • SWD • BUMP, THE
BULANDRA AND THE DEVIL • 1959 • Zitzman Jerzy • ANS • PLN
BULAT BATYR • 1927 • Tarich Yuri • USS • REVOLT OVER KASAN
BULBULE–PARISTAN • 1934 • *Gulab* • IND
BULDOCI A TRESNE • 1981 • Herz Juraj • CZC • BULLDOGS AND CHERRIES
BULGANIN • 1946 • Grigoriev Roman • DOC • USS
BULGAR IS A GENTLEMAN, THE see **BULGARIAN IS A GALLANT MAN, THE** • 1915
BULGARIA, LAND, PEOPLE, SUN • 1966 • Tosheva Nevena • DOC • BUL
BULGARIAN IS A GALLANT MAN, THE • 1915 • Gendov Vassil • BUL • BULGAR IS A GENTLEMAN, THE
BULGARIAN STATE RAILWAYS • 1971 • Zahariev Edward • DOC • BUL
BULGARIAN SUMMER • 1966 • Grigorov Roumen • DOC • BUL
BULGARIANS ARE GALLANT • 1910 • Gendov Vassil • BUL
BULGE OF FIRE, THE • 1968 • Ozerov Yury • USS
BULISS AS–SIRRI, AL– • 1958 • Wahab Fatin Abdel • EGY • POLICE SECRETE
BULL, THE • 1985 • Uusberg Valter • ANM • USS
BULL, THE see **TORO, EL** • 1962
BULL, THE see **TAUREAU** • 1973
BULL AND SAND • 1924 • *Sennett Mack (P)* • SHT • USA
BULL AND THE PICKNICKERS • 1902 • Porter Edwin S. • USA
BULL DOG • 1937 • *Biswas Anil (M)* • IND
BULL DOGGER, THE • 1922 • *Pickett Bill* • USA
BULL DURHAM • 1988 • Shelton Ron • USA
BULL–ERO • 1932 • *Terry Paul/ Moser Frank (P)* • ANS • USA
BULL FIGHT • 1959 • King Allan • CND
BULL FIGHTER, THE • 1920 • *Franey William* • USA
BULL FIGHTER, THE • 1927 • Cline Eddie, Rodney Earle • SHT • USA • BULLFIGHTERS, THE
BULL FRIGHT • 1955 • Kneitel Seymour • ANS • USA
BULL OF THE CAMPUS see **DAIGAKU NO WAKADAISHO** • 1962
BULL OF THE WEST, THE • 1971 • Stanley Paul, Hopper Jerry • MTV • USA
BULL RUSHES • 1931 • Kellino W. P. • UKN
BULL THROWER, THE • 1920 • Howe J. A. • SHT • USA
BULLAMAKANKA • 1983 • Heath Simon • ASL
BULLDANCE • 1989 • Barron Zelda • UKN • FORBIDDEN SUN
BULLDANCE, THE • 1981 • Hardy Robin • UKN
BULLDOG AND THE BABY, THE • 1942 • Geiss Alec • ANS • USA
BULLDOG AND THE FLAG, THE • 1911 • *Walturdaw* • UKN
BULLDOG BREED, THE • 1960 • Asher Robert • UKN
BULLDOG COURAGE • 1922 • Kull Edward • USA
BULLDOG COURAGE • 1935 • Newfield Sam • USA
BULLDOG DRUMMOND • 1923 • Apfel Oscar • UKN
BULLDOG DRUMMOND • 1929 • Jones F. Richard • USA
BULLDOG DRUMMOND AT BAY • 1937 • Lee Norman • UKN
BULLDOG DRUMMOND AT BAY • 1947 • Salkow Sidney • USA
BULLDOG DRUMMOND COMES BACK • 1937 • King Louis • USA
BULLDOG DRUMMOND ESCAPES • 1937 • Hogan James P. • USA
BULLDOG DRUMMOND IN AFRICA • 1938 • King Louis • USA
BULLDOG DRUMMOND STRIKES BACK • 1934 • Del Ruth Roy • USA
BULLDOG DRUMMOND STRIKES BACK • 1947 • McDonald Frank • USA
BULLDOG DRUMMOND'S BRIDE • 1939 • Hogan James P. • USA
BULLDOG DRUMMOND'S PERIL • 1938 • Hogan James P. • USA
BULLDOG DRUMMOND'S REVENGE • 1937 • King Louis • USA
BULLDOG DRUMMOND'S SECRET POLICE • 1939 • Hogan James P. • USA
BULLDOG DRUMMOND'S THIRD ROUND • 1925 • Morgan Sidney • UKN • THIRD ROUND, THE
BULLDOG EDITION • 1936 • Lamont Charles • USA • LADY REPORTER (UKN)
BULLDOG GRIT • 1915 • Batley Ethyle • UKN
BULLDOG JACK • 1935 • Forde Walter • UKN • ALIAS BULLDOG DRUMMOND (USA)
BULLDOG PLUCK • 1927 • Nelson Jack • USA
BULLDOG SEES IT THROUGH • 1940 • Huth Harold • UKN
BULLDOGS AND CHERRIES see **BULDOCI A TRESNE** • 1981
BULLDOGS OF THE TRAIL, THE • 1915 • MacDougall Kenneth • USA
BULLDOZER • 1973 • Harel Pierre • CND
BULLDOZER see **LO CHIAMAVANO BULLDOZER** • 1978
BULLDOZING THE BULL • 1938 • Fleischer Dave • ANS • USA
BULLDOZING THE BULL • 1951 • Rasinski Connie • ANS • USA
BULLE UND DAS MADCHEN, DER • 1985 • Keglevic Peter • AUS, FRG • COP AND THE GIRL, THE
BULLES DE SAVON see **SEIFENBLASEN** • 1933
BULLES DE SAVON ANIMEES, LES • 1906 • Melies Georges • FRN • SOAP BUBBLES (USA)
BULLET, A • 1973 • Wojciechowski Krzysztof • DOC • PLN
BULLET CODE • 1940 • Howard David • USA
BULLET FOR A BADMAN • 1964 • Springsteen R. G. • USA • RENEGADE POSSE
BULLET FOR BERLIN, A • 1918 • Hart William S. • SHT • USA
BULLET FOR BILLY THE KID • 1963 • Baledon Rafael • MXC
BULLET FOR JOEY, A • 1955 • Allen Lewis • USA
BULLET FOR PRETTY BOY, A • 1970 • Buchanan Larry • USA
BULLET FOR ROMMEL, A see **HORA CERO: OPERACION ROMMEL** • 1968
BULLET FOR SANDOVAL, A (USA) see **QUEI DISPERATI CHE PUZZANO DI SUDORE E DI MORTE** • 1970
BULLET FOR STEFANO, A (USA) see **PASSATORE, IL** • 1947
BULLET FOR THE GENERAL, A (USA) see **QUIEN SABE?** • 1966
BULLET FROM THE PAST • 1957 • Hume Kenneth • UKN
BULLET IS STILL IN MY POCKET, THE • 1974 • Mustafa Hassam Eddin • EGY
BULLET IS WAITING, A • 1954 • Farrow John • USA
BULLET MARK, THE • 1928 • Paton Stuart • USA
BULLET ON THE RUN • 1982 • SAF
BULLET PROOF • 1920 • Reynolds Lynn • USA
BULLET–PROOF COAT, THE • 1912 • *Imp* • USA
BULLET ROAD see **KURSUN YOLU** • 1968
BULLET SCARS • 1942 • Lederman D. Ross • USA
BULLET TRAIN, THE see **SHINKANSEN DAIBABUHA** • 1975
BULLET WOUND see **DANKON** • 1969
BULLETEERS, THE • 1942 • Fleischer Dave • ANS • USA
BULLETPROOF • 1988 • Carver Steve • USA
BULLETS AND BALLADS • 1940 • Ceballos Larry • SHT • USA
BULLETS AND BROWN EYES • 1916 • Sidney Scott • USA
BULLETS AND JUSTICE • 1929 • *Acord Art* • USA
BULLETS AND SADDLES • 1943 • Marshall Anthony • USA • VENGEANCE IN THE SADDLE (UKN)
BULLETS DO NOT TURN BACK see **SFERES DHEN YIRIZOUN PISO, I** • 1967
BULLETS FOR BANDITS • 1942 • Fox Wallace • USA
BULLETS FOR O'HARA • 1941 • Howard William K. • USA
BULLETS FOR RUSTLERS • 1940 • Nelson Sam • USA • ON SPECIAL DUTY (UKN)
BULLET'S MARK, THE • 1913 • *Patheplay* • USA
BULLETS OR BALLOTS • 1936 • Keighley William • USA
BULLETS OR BONEHEADS • 1917 • Hutchinson Craig • SHT • USA
BULLETS STRIKE LIKE HAILSTONES see **PEFTOUN I SFAIRES SAN TO HALAZI** • 1977
BULLFIGHT • 1955 • Clarke Shirley • SHT • USA
BULLFIGHT see **COURSE DE TAUREAUX, LA** • 1951
BULLFIGHT, THE • 1935 • *Terry Paul/ Moser Frank (P)* • ANS • USA
BULLFIGHT AT MALAGA • 1958 • *Leacock Richard (Ph)* • DOC • USA
BULLFIGHT BY FUENTES • 1905 • Barragan Salvador Toscano • MXC
BULLFIGHTER see **MATADOR** • 1985
BULLFIGHTER AND THE LADY, THE • 1951 • Boetticher Budd • USA • TORERO
BULLFIGHTERS, THE • 1945 • St. Clair Malcolm • USA
BULLFIGHTERS, THE see **BULL FIGHTER, THE** • 1927
BULLIES • 1986 • Lynch Paul • CND
BULLIES AND BULLETS • 1916 • Semon Larry • SHT • USA
BULLIN THE BOLSHEVIKI • 1919 • Donovan Frank P. • USA
BULLITT • 1968 • Yates Peter • USA
BULLONEY • 1933 • *Iwerks Ub (P)* • ANS • USA
BULLS • 1974 • Noonan Chris • SHT • ASL
BULLS AND BEARS • 1930 • Sennett Mack • SHT • USA
BULL'S EYE, THE • 1918 • Horne James W. • SRL • USA
BULL'S EYE FOR FARMER PIETERSEN see **BOER PIETERSEN SCHIET IN DE ROOS** • 1949
BULLS–EYE FOR LOVE see **OSHIDORI KAGO** • 1958
BULLS OF HIDALGO, THE • 1959 • Gass Karl • DOC • GDR
BULLS OR BULLETS • 1917 • Santell Alfred • SHT • USA
BULLSEYE • 1987 • Schultz Carl • ASL
BULLSEYE • 1990 • Winner Michael • UKN, USA
BULLSHEVIKS, THE • 1919 • Lyons Eddie, Moran Lee • SHT • USA
BULLSHOT! • 1983 • Clement Dick • UKN • BULLSHOT CRUMMOND (USA)
BULLSHOT CRUMMOND (USA) see **BULLSHOT!** • 1983
BULLTRAINER'S REVENGE, THE • 1914 • *Melies* • USA
BULLWHIP • 1958 • Jones Harmon • USA
BULLY • 1978 • Hunt Peter H. • USA
BULLY, THE • 1910 • Bouwmeester Theo • UKN
BULLY, THE • 1913 • *Kb* • USA
BULLY, THE • 1918 • *Robinson Sam* • SHT • USA
BULLY, THE • 1932 • *Iwerks Ub (P)* • ANS • USA
BULLY, THE see **KABADAYI** • 1968
BULLY AFFAIR, A • 1915 • Douglass James • USA
BULLY AND THE RECRUIT, THE • 1908 • Chart Jack • UKN
BULLY AND THE SHRIMP, THE • 1912 • *Reliance* • USA
BULLY BEEF • 1930 • *Terry Paul/ Moser Frank (P)* • ANS • USA
BULLY FOR BUGS • 1953 • Jones Charles M. • ANS • USA
BULLY FROG, A • 1936 • Davis Mannie, Gordon George • ANS • USA
BULLY OF BINGO GULCH, THE • 1911 • *Stedman Myrtle* • USA
BULLY ROMANCE, A • 1939 • Donnelly Eddie • ANS • USA
BULLY'S DOOM, THE • 1914 • Hotaling Arthur D. • USA
BULLY'S END, THE • 1933 • Bailey Harry • ANS • USA
BUM see **BOOM** • 1979
BUM AND A BOMB, A • 1911 • *Solax* • USA
BUM AND THE BOMB, THE • 1910 • *Vitagraph* • USA
BUM AND THE BOMB, THE • 1912 • *Champion* • USA
BUM BANDIT, THE • 1931 • Fleischer Dave • ANS • USA
BUM BOMB, A • 1918 • McDermott John • SHT • USA
BUM–BUM–BUM • 1917 • *Essanay* • SHT • USA
BUM MISTAKE, A • 1914 • *Princess* • USA
BUM STEER, A • 1916 • *Vogue* • USA
BUM STEER, A • 1957 • Davis Mannie • ANS • USA
BUM VOYAGE • 1934 • Grinde Nick • SHT • USA
BUMAZHNIYE GLAZA PRISHVINA • 1989 • Ogorodnikov Valery • USS • PRISHVIN'S PAPER EYES
BUMBLEBIRD • *Weiner Peter (P)* • ANS • USA
BUMBLES AND THE BASS • 1913 • Kellino W. P. • UKN
BUMBLES' APPETITE • 1914 • Kellino W. P. • UKN
BUMBLES BECOMES A CROOK • 1913 • Kellino W. P. • UKN
BUMBLE'S BLUNDER • 1915 • Birch Cecil • UKN
BUMBLES' DIMINISHER • 1913 • Kellino W. P. • UKN
BUMBLES' ELECTRIC BELT • 1913 • Kellino W. P. • UKN
BUMBLES GOES BUTTERFLYING • 1914 • Kellino W. P. • UKN
BUMBLES' GOOSE • 1913 • Kellino W. P. • UKN
BUMBLES' HOLIDAY • 1913 • Kellino W. P. • UKN
BUMBLE'S JOB • 1916 • *Humphrey Orral* • USA
BUMBLES, PHOTOGRAPHER • 1913 • Kellino W. P. • UKN
BUMBLES' RADIUM MINSTRELS • 1913 • Kellino W. P. • UKN
BUMBLES' WALK TO BRIGHTON • 1913 • Kellino W. P. • UKN
BUMERANG • 1960 • Weidenmann Alfred • FRG • CRY DOUBLE CROSS (UKN)
BUMERANG • 1962 • Kolar Boris • ANM • YGS • BOOMERANG
BUMKE DISCOVERS THE TURNING MICROBE • 1913 • *Elite* • USA
BUMMELLOTTE • 1922 • Neff Wolfgang • FRG
BUMMELSTUNDENTEN • 1917 • Biebrach Rudolf • FRG
BUMMER • 1973 • Castleman William Allen • USA • SADIST, THE
BUMP, THE • 1920 • Brunel Adrian • UKN
BUMP, THE see **BULAN** • 1989
BUMPED FOR FAIR • 1915 • *Superba* • USA
BUMPING INTO BROADWAY • 1919 • Roach Hal • SHT • USA
BUMPING THE BUMPS • 1916 • *Hamilton Lloyd V.* • USA
BUMPKIN OF TOKYO, A see **KIGEKI TOKYO NO INAKAPPE** • 1967
BUMPKIN'S PATENT SPYOPTICON • 1910 • Coleby A. E. • UKN
BUMPS • 1912 • *Casey Kenneth* • USA
BUMPS see **UKHABY ZHIZNI** • 1928
BUMPS AND BOARDERS • 1918 • Pratt Gilbert • SHT • USA
BUMPS AND WILLIE • 1913 • Huntley Fred W. • USA • ELOPEMENT, THE
BUMPSTONE see **BUTNSKALA** • 1985
BUMPTIOUS AS A FIREMAN • 1910 • *Edison* • USA
BUMPTIOUS AS ROMEO • 1911 • *Compson John* • USA
BUMPTIOUS PLAYS BASEBALL • 1910 • *Edison* • USA
BUMPTIOUS TAKES UP AUTOMOBILING • 1910 • *Edison* • USA
BUM'S HALLOWEEN, THE • 1913 • *Champion* • USA
BUMSFIDELEN MADCHEN VON BIRKENHOF, DIE • 1974 • Dietrich Erwin C. • SWT • RANCH OF THE NYMPHOMANIAC GIRLS ○ RANCH OF THE NYMPHOMANIACS
BUN NGO TSONG TINNGAI • 1989 • Lam Ringo • HKG • WILD SEARCH
BUNA DIMINEATA POVESTE • 1969 • Cazacu Luminita • ANS • RMN • GOOD MORNING TALES
BUNBEN • 1968 • Shindo Takae • JPN • IN LABOUR
BUNBUKU CHAGAMA • 1958 • *Dentsu* • SHT • JPN • GRATEFUL BADGER, THE (USA)
BUNBURY see **LIEBE, SCHERZ UND ERNST** • 1932
BUNCH OF FLIVVERS, A • 1916 • *Hamilton Lloyd V.* • USA
BUNCH OF FLOWERS, A • 1914 • Henderson Dell • USA
BUNCH OF KEYS, A • 1915 • Baker Richard Foster • USA
BUNCH OF MATCHES, A • 1915 • *Turpin Ben* • USA
BUNCH OF VIOLETS, A • 1912 • *Phillips E. R.* • USA
BUNCH OF VIOLETS, A • 1916 • Wilson Frank • UKN
BUNCO • 1985 • Singer Alexander • TVM • USA
BUNCO BILL'S VISIT • 1914 • Baker George D. • USA
BUNCO BILLY • 1918 • *Highgrade Films* • SHT • USA
BUNCO BUSTERS • 1955 • Smith Paul J. • ANS • USA
BUNCO GAME AT LIZARDHEAD, THE • 1911 • *Essanay* • USA
BUNCO SQUAD • 1950 • Leeds Herbert I. • USA
BUNCOED • 1912 • *Trunnelle Mabel* • USA
BUNCOED STAGE JOHNNIE • 1908 • Melies Georges • FRN
BUND DER DREI, DER • 1929 • Behrendt Hans • FRG
BUNDFALD • 1957 • Kjaerulff-Schmidt Palle, Saaskin Robert • DNM • SIN ALLEY (USA) ○ GENTLE SEX, THE ○ DREGS
BUNDLE OF BLISS, A • 1940 • White Jules • SHT • USA
BUNDLE OF BLUES • 1933 • *Ellington Duke* • SHT • USA
BUNDLE OF JOY • 1957 • Taurog Norman • USA
BUNDLE OF LOVE see **AI NO NIMOTSU** • 1956
BUNDLE OF TROUBLE, A • 1917 • Chaudet Louis W. • SHT • USA
BUNDLE OF TROUBLE, A (UKN) see **BLONDIE'S BLESSED EVENT** • 1942
BUNGA BANGSA • 1983 • Sophiaan Sophan • INN • FLOWER OF THE NATION
BUNGA MAS • 1972 • Achnas Naz • MLY • FLOWER OF GOLD
BUNGA PADI BERDAUN LALANG • 1974 • Hassan Hussein Abu • MLY
BUNGALA BOYS • 1961 • Jeffrey Jim • UKN, ASL
BUNGALOW 13 • 1948 • Cahn Edward L. • USA
BUNGALOW BOOBS • 1924 • McCarey Leo • SHT • USA
BUNGALOW BUNGLE • 1920 • *Moranti Milburn* • SHT • USA
BUNGALOW BURGLARS, THE • 1911 • *Imp* • USA
BUNGALOW CRAZE, THE • 1911 • *American* • USA
BUNGALOW TROUBLES • 1920 • Austin Albert • SHT • USA
BUNGALOWING • 1917 • Jackson Harry • SHT • USA
BUNGLE UNCLE • 1961 • Hanna William, Barbera Joseph • ANS • USA
BUNGLED BUNGALOW • 1950 • Burness Pete • ANS • USA
BUNGLED BUNGALOWS • 1920 • Lyons Eddie, Moran Lee • SHT • USA
BUNGLED BURGLARY • 1915 • *Wright Bertie* • UKN
BUNGLES' ELOPEMENT • 1916 • Stull Walter, Burns Bobby • USA
BUNGLES ENFORCES THE LAW • 1916 • Stull Walter, Burns Bobby • USA
BUNGLES LANDS A JOB • 1916 • Stull Walter, Burns Bobby • USA
BUNGLES' RAINY DAY • 1916 • Stull Walter, Burns Bobby • USA
BUNGLING BILL, BURGLAR • 1916 • Dillon John Francis • SHT • USA
BUNGLING BILL, DETECTIVE • 1916 • Dillon John Francis • USA
BUNGLING BILL, DOCTOR • 1916 • Dillon John Francis • USA
BUNGLING BILL'S BOW–WOW • 1916 • *Mcquire Paddy* • SHT • USA
BUNGLING BILL'S DREAM • 1916 • Dillon John Francis • USA
BUNGLING BILL'S DRESS SUIT • 1916 • Dillon John Francis • USA

BUNGLING BILL'S PEEPING WAYS • 1916 • Dillon John Francis • SHT • USA
BUNGLING BUILDER, THE • 1970 • Smith Paul J. • ANS • USA
BUNGLING BUNK'S BUNCO • 1914 • *Eclectic* • USA
BUNGLING BURGLARS • 1912 • Wilson Frank? • UKN
BUNGLING BURGLARS BURGLE • 1915 • *Heinie & Louie* • USA
BUNGS AND BUNGLERS • 1919 • Smith Noel • SHT • USA
BUNKER, THE • 1981 • Schaefer George • TVM • USA • ADOLF HITLER: THE BUNKER
BUNKER BEAN • 1936 • Hamilton William, Killy Edward • USA • HIS MAJESTY BUNKER BEAN (UKN)
BUNKER HILL BUNNY • 1950 • Freleng Friz • ANS • USA
BUNKER PALACE HOTEL • 1989 • Bilal Enki • FRN
BUNKERED • 1919 • Drew Sidney Mrs. • SHT • USA
BUNKERED • 1929 • Davis Redd • UKN
BUNKER'S PATENT BELLOWS • 1910 • Aylott Dave? • UKN
BUNKIE • 1912 • *Bosworth Hobart* • USA
BUNKS BUNKED • 1915 • *La Pearl Harry* • USA
BUNNIES ABUNDANT • 1962 • Hanna William, Barbera Joseph • ANS • USA
BUNNIES AND BONNETS • 1933 • *Mintz Charles (P)* • ANS • USA
BUNNY ALL AT SEA • 1912 • Baker George D.?, Trimble Larry? • USA
BUNNY AND CLAUDE • 1968 • McKimson Robert • ANS • USA
BUNNY AND THE DOGS • 1912 • Baker George D.?, Trimble Larry? • USA
BUNNY AND THE TWINS • 1912 • *Bunny John* • USA
BUNNY AS A REPORTER • 1913 • North Wilfred • USA
BUNNY AT THE DERBY • 1912 • Trimble Larry • UKN
BUNNY BACKSLIDES • 1914 • Baker George D. • USA
BUNNY BLARNEYED: OR, THE BLARNEY STONE • 1913 • Trimble Larry • UKN
BUNNY BLOSSOM FOR PRESIDENT • 1970 • *Topar Productions* • USA
BUNNY BUYS A HAREM • 1914 • Baker George D. • USA
BUNNY BUYS A HAT FOR HIS BRIDE • 1914 • *Bunny John* • USA
BUNNY CAPER, THE (USA) see **GAMES GIRLS PLAY** • 1974
BUNNY & CLOD • 1970 • *Poore Robert A. (P)* • USA
BUNNY FOR THE CAUSE • 1913 • North Wilfred • USA
BUNNY HUGGED • 1951 • Jones Charles M. • ANS • USA
BUNNY IN BUNNYLAND • 1915 • Baker George D.? • USA
BUNNY IN DISGUISE • 1914 • Baker George D. • USA
BUNNY LAKE IS MISSING • 1965 • Preminger Otto • UKN
BUNNY MOONING • 1937 • Fleischer Dave • ANS • USA
BUNNY O'HARE • 1972 • Oswald Gerd • USA • BUNNY O'HARE MOB, THE
BUNNY O'HARE MOB, THE see **BUNNY O'HARE** • 1972
BUNNY PICNIC, THE see **TALE OF THE BUNNY PARK, THE**
BUNNY TAKES A DIP INTO SOCIETY OR BUNNY AND THE BUNNY HUG • 1913 • North Wilfred • USA
BUNNY VERSUS CUTEY • 1913 • North Wilfred • USA
BUNNY YEAGER'S NUDE CAMERA • 1963 • Mahon Barry • USA • NUDE CAMERA
BUNNY YEAGER'S NUDE LAS VEGAS • 1964 • Mahon Barry • USA • NUDE LAS VEGAS
BUNNY'S BIRTHDAY • 1914 • Baker George D. • USA
BUNNY'S BIRTHDAY SURPRISE • 1913 • North Wilfred • USA
BUNNY'S DILEMMA • 1913 • North Wilfred • USA
BUNNY'S HONEYMOON • 1913 • North Wilfred • USA
BUNNY'S LITTLE BROTHER • 1914 • Baker George D. • USA
BUNNY'S MISTAKE • 1914 • Baker George D. • USA
BUNNY'S SCHEME • 1914 • Baker George D. • USA
BUNNY'S SUICIDE • 1912 • Trimble Larry • USA
BUNNY'S SWELL AFFAIR • 1914 • Beggs Lee • USA
BUNNY'S TALE, A • 1985 • Arthur Karen • TVM • USA
BUNTE TRAUM, DER • 1952 • von Cziffra Geza • FRG
BUNTER REIGEN • 1942 • Jacoby Georg • FRG
BUNTER'S PATENT BELLOWS • 1910 • *Cricks & Martin* • UKN
BUNTING'S BLINK • 1915 • Nash Percy? • UKN
BUNTKARIERTEN, DIE • 1949 • Maetzig Kurt • GDR
BUNTY PULLS THE STRINGS • 1921 • Barker Reginald • USA
BUNTY WINS A PUP • 1953 • Gover Victor M. • UKN
BUNZLI'S GROSSTADTABENTEUER • 1930 • Wohlmuth Robert • SWT
BUON APPETITO • 1956 • Saraceni Fausto • SHT • ITL
BUON FUNERALE AMIGOS.. PARA SARTANA • 1970 • Carnimeo Giuliano • ITL
BUON NATALE, BUON ANNO • 1989 • Comencini Luigi • ITL • MERRY CHRISTMAS, HAPPY NEW YEAR
BUON RAGAZZO, UN see **ULTIMA AVVENTURA, L'** • 1932
BUON SOLDATO, IL • 1982 • Brusati Franco • ITL • GOOD SOLDIER, THE
BUON VIAGGIO POVER'UOMO • 1951 • Pastina Giorgio • ITL • JOURNEY OF LOVE (USA)
BUON VIAJE, PABLO • 1959 • Iquino Ignacio F. • SPN
BUONA FORTUNA, LA • 1944 • Cerchio Fernando • ITL
BUONA PARTE DI PAOLINA • 1973 • Rossati Nello • ITL
BUONA SERA, MRS. CAMPBELL • 1969 • Frank Melvin • USA
BUONANOTTE AVVOCATO! • 1955 • Bianchi Giorgio • ITL
BUONE NOTIZIE, LE see **STANZA DELLE BUONE NOTIZE** • 1979
BUONGIORNO ELEFANTE • 1952 • Franciolini Gianni • ITL • HELLO ELEPHANT (USA) ○ SABU PRINCIPE LADRO ○ PARDON MY TRUNK ○ HULLO ELEPHANT
BUONGIORNO, MADRID! (ITL) see **MADRID DE MIS SUENOS** • 1942
BUONGIORNO NATURA • 1955 • Olmi Ermanno • DOC • ITL
BUONGIORNO PRIMO AMORE • 1957 • Girolami Marino • ITL
BUONO, IL BRUTO, IL CATTIVO • 1967 • Leone Sergio • ITL • GOOD, THE BAD AND THE UGLY, THE (UKN)
BUQUE FANTASMA, EL • 1969 • Delgado Cruz • ANS • SPN
BUQUE MALDITO, EL • 1974 • de Ossorio Amando • SPN • HORROR OF THE ZOMBIES (USA) ○ SHIP OF ZOMBIES
BURABO! YANGU GAI • 1970 • Iwauchi Katsumi • JPN • BRAVO, YOUNG GUY (USA)
BURAI HITOKIRI GORO • 1968 • Ozawa Keiichi • JPN • KILLER GORO
BURAI KURODOSU • 1968 • Ozawa Keiichi • JPN • BURAI –THE BLACK KNIFE
BURAI –THE BLACK KNIFE see **BURAI KURODOSU** • 1968
BURAIKAN • 1970 • Shinoda Masahiro • JPN • SCANDALOUS ADVENTURES OF BURAIKAN, THE (USA) ○ OUTLAWS
BURAQ, AL- • 1972 • Rechiche Majid • MRC
BURARI BURABURA MONOGATARI • 1960 • Matsuyama Zenzo • JPN • MY HOBO
BURATTINO DI NOME PINOCCHIO, UN • 1972 • Cenci Giuliano • ITL
BURBERO, IL • 1987 • Castellano, Pipolo • ITL • GRUMP, THE
BURBRIDGE'S AFRICAN GORILLA HUNT see **GORILLA HUNT, THE** • 1926
'BURBS, THE • 1989 • Dante Joe • USA • BURBS, THE
BURBS, THE see **'BURBS, THE** • 1989
BURCAK TARLASI • 1966 • Utku Umit • TRK
BURDEN • 1973 • Babic Vuk • YGS
BURDEN, THE • 1914 • Adolfi John G. • USA
BURDEN, THE • 1988 • Breaud • SHT • FRN
BURDEN BEARER, THE • 1913 • *Rex* • USA
BURDEN BEARER, THE • 1913 • Johnson Arthur • *Lubin* • USA
BURDEN BEARER, THE • 1915 • King Burton L. • USA
BURDEN OF DEATH, THE • 1909 • USA
BURDEN OF DREAMS, THE • 1983 • Blank Les • DOC • USA
BURDEN OF LIFE see **JINSEI NO ONIMOTSU** • 1935
BURDEN OF PROOF, THE • 1918 • Steger Julius • USA
BURDEN OF RACE, THE • 1921 • *Verwayen Percy* • USA
BURDEN THEY CARRY, THE • 1970 • Ransen Mort • CND
BURDUS • 1971 • Popovic Mica • YGS
BUREAU DES MARIAGES, LE • 1962 • Bellon Yannick • SHT • FRN
BUREAU OF MISSING PERSONS • 1933 • Del Ruth Roy • USA
BUREAU OF MISSING PERSONS • 1953-54 • Devlin Bernard • DCS • CND
BUREAUCRACY, THE • 1974 • Sens Al • ANS • CND
BUREAUCRATIE, LE • 1972 • Bendeddouche Jamal • ALG
BURGERMEISTER ANNA • 1950 • Muller Hans • GDR
BURGESS, PHILBY AND MACLEAN: SPY SCANDAL OF THE CENTURY see **PHILBY, BURGESS AND MACLEAN** • 1977
BURGIS • 1981 • Brocka Lino • PHL
BURGLAR • 1987 • Wilson Hugh • USA
BURGLAR see **VZLOMSHCHIK** • 1987
BURGLAR, THE • 1916 • Hartigan P. C. • SHT • USA
BURGLAR, THE • 1917 • Knoles Harley • USA
BURGLAR, THE • 1924 • Marshall George • SHT • USA
BURGLAR, THE • 1928 • Capra Frank • SHT • USA • SMITH'S BURGLAR
BURGLAR, THE • 1957 • Wendkos Paul • USA
BURGLAR, THE see **INBREKER, DE** • 1972
BURGLAR ALARM, THE • 1914 • *Melies* • USA
BURGLAR ALARM MAT, THE • 1912 • *Majestic* • USA
BURGLAR AND LITTLE PHYLLIS, THE • 1910 • Fitzhamon Lewin • UKN
BURGLAR AND THE BABY, THE • 1910 • *Powers* • USA
BURGLAR AND THE BABY, THE • 1913 • *Kalem* • USA
BURGLAR AND THE CAT, THE • 1906 • Fitzhamon Lewin • UKN
BURGLAR AND THE CHILD, THE • 1909 • Bouwmeester Theo? • UKN
BURGLAR AND THE CLOCK, THE • 1908 • Fitzhamon Lewin • UKN
BURGLAR AND THE GIRL, THE • 1928 • Croise Hugh • UKN
BURGLAR AND THE GIRLS, THE • 1904 • Stow Percy • UKN
BURGLAR AND THE JUDGE, THE • 1906 • Fitzhamon Lewin • UKN
BURGLAR AND THE LADY, THE see **LADY AND THE BURGLAR, THE** • 1915
BURGLAR AND THE MOUSE, THE • 1915 • Smallwood Ray C. • USA
BURGLAR AND THE ROSE, THE • 1912 • *August Edwin* • USA
BURGLAR AS FATHER CHRISTMAS, THE • 1911 • Bouwmeester Theo • UKN
BURGLAR AT THE BALL, THE • 1913 • Plumb Hay? • UKN
BURGLAR BILL • 1916 • Gilbert Lewis, Frenguelli Alfonse • UKN
BURGLAR BURGLED, THE • 1912 • *Cosmopolitan* • USA
BURGLAR BY PROXY • 1919 • Dillon John Francis • USA
BURGLAR BY REQUEST • 1917 • Chaudet Louis W. • SHT • USA
BURGLAR CATCHER • 1960 • *Halas John (P)* • ANS • UKN
BURGLAR CUPID, A • 1909 • Porter Edwin S. • USA
BURGLAR EXPECTED, THE • 1910 • Stow Percy • UKN
BURGLAR FOR A NIGHT, A • 1911 • Haldane Bert • UKN
BURGLAR FOR A NIGHT, A • 1918 • Warde Ernest C. • USA
BURGLAR HELPED, THE • 1912 • Plumb Hay? • UKN
BURGLAR LOVER, THE • 1905 • Collins Alf? • UKN
BURGLAR ON THE ROOF, THE • 1898 • Blackton J. Stuart • USA
BURGLAR: OR, THE HUE AND CRY, THE • 1905 • Collins Alf? • UKN
BURGLAR-PROOF • 1920 • Campbell Maurice • USA
BURGLAR STORY, THE see **NIPPON DOROBO MONOGATARI** • 1965
BURGLAR TO THE RESCUE, A • 1931 • Cochrane George • SHT • USA
BURGLAR WHO ROBBED DEATH, THE • 1913 • Parker Lem B. • USA
BURGLARIZED BURGLAR, THE • 1911 • Baker R. E. • USA
BURGLARIZING BILLY • 1913 • *Quirk Billy* • USA
BURGLARS • 1918 • *Rhodes Billie* • SHT • USA
BURGLARS • 1919 • Kellette John William • SHT • USA
BURGLARS see **EINBRECHER** • 1930
BURGLARS, THE (USA) see **CASSE, LE** • 1971
BURGLARS AND THE OTTOMAN, THE • 1909 • *Empire Films* • UKN
BURGLARS AT THE BALL • 1907 • Fitzhamon Lewin • UKN
BURGLAR'S BABY, THE • 1915 • *Edwards Walter* • USA
BURGLARS BOLD • 1921 • Roach Hal • SHT • USA
BURGLAR'S BOY, THE • 1905 • Fitzhamon Lewin • UKN
BURGLAR'S BRIDE, A • 1917 • Curtis Allen • SHT • USA
BURGLARS BY REQUEST • 1915 • *Royal* • USA
BURGLAR'S CHILD, THE • 1913 • Nash Percy • UKN
BURGLAR'S DAUGHTER, THE • 1912 • Fitzhamon Lewin? • UKN
BURGLAR'S DILEMMA, THE • 1905 • *Cricks & Sharp* • UKN
BURGLAR'S DILEMMA, THE • 1912 • Griffith D. W. • USA
BURGLAR'S GODFATHER, THE • 1915 • *Anderson Broncho Billy* • USA
BURGLARS IN THE HOUSE • 1911 • *Urban Trading Co.* • UKN
BURGLARS IN THE WINE CELLAR, THE see **PIQUEURS DE FUTS, LES** • 1901
BURGLAR'S JOKE WITH THE AUTOMATIC DOLL, THE • 1908 • Collins Alf? • UKN
BURGLAR'S MISFORTUNE, THE • 1910 • Rains Fred • UKN
BURGLAR'S MISTAKE, A • 1909 • Griffith D. W. • USA
BURGLAR'S PICNIC, THE • 1916 • Parke William • SHT • USA
BURGLAR'S REFORMATION, THE • 1912 • *Walthall Henry B.* • USA
BURGLAR'S SACRIFICE, THE • 1914 • *Ab* • USA
BURGLAR'S SLIDE FROM LIFE • 1905 • Porter Edwin S. • USA
BURGLAR'S SURPRISE, THE • 1907 • Martin J. H.? • UKN
BURGLARY BY AIRSHIP • 1910 • *Gaumont* • FRN
BURGOMASTER OF STILEMONDE, THE • 1928 • Banfield George J. • UKN
BURGOMEISTER, THE • 1935 • Southwell Harry • ASL
BURGOS • Eguiluz Enrique L. • SHT • SPN
BURGOS TRIAL, THE see **PROCESO DE BURGOS, EL** • 1980
BURGSCHAFT FUER EIN JAHR • 1980 • Zschoche Hermann • GDR • WARRANTY FOR ONE YEAR ○ GUARANTOR FOR ONE YEAR
BURGTHEATER • 1936 • Forst Willi • AUS • VIENNA BURGTHEATER
BURIAL GROUND • 1985 • Bianchi Andrea • ITL
BURIAL PATH • 1978 • Brakhage Stan • SHT • USA
BURIALS IN BAN NADI • 1982 • King Del • NZL
BURIDAN • 1924 • Marodon Pierre • FRN
BURIDAN, HEROS DE LA TOUR DE NESLE • 1951 • Couzinet Emile • FRN
BURIED ALIVE • 1908 • Brooke Van Dyke • USA
BURIED ALIVE • 1909 • *Selig* • USA
BURIED ALIVE • 1917 • *Reid Wallace* • SHT • USA
BURIED ALIVE • 1940 • Halperin Victor Hugo • USA
BURIED ALIVE • 1980 • D'Amato Joe • ITL
BURIED ALIVE see **DR. RENAULT'S SECRET** • 1942
BURIED ALIVE see **SEPOLTA VIVA, LA** • 1949
BURIED ALIVE see **PLANQUE, LA** • 1961
BURIED CITY, THE • 1921 • SAF
BURIED CRIME, THE • 1914 • *Melies* • USA
BURIED GOLD • 1926 • McGowan J. P. • USA
BURIED HAND, THE • 1915 • Walsh Raoul • USA
BURIED IN MY HEART see **SENI KALBIME GONDUM** • 1982
BURIED LOOT • 1935 • Seitz George B. • SHT • USA
BURIED PAST, A • 1911 • Porter Edwin S. • USA
BURIED PAST, THE • 1913 • *Ray Charles* • USA
BURIED SECRET, A • 1909 • *Lubin* • USA
BURIED SECRET, THE see **UNGE BLOD, DET** • 1915
BURIED TREASURE • La Cava Gregory? • ANS • USA
BURIED TREASURE • 1921 • Baker George D. • USA
BURIED TREASURE • 1926 • Roach Hal • SHT • USA
BURIED TREASURE • 1938 • Allen Robert • ANS • USA
BURIED TREASURE, A • 1913 • *Melies* • USA
BURIED TREASURE, THE • 1915 • *Reliance* • USA
BURIED TREASURE, THE • 1919 • Webb Kenneth • SHT • USA
BURIED TREASURE OF COBRE, THE • 1916 • Beal Frank • SHT • USA
BURKE AND HARE • 1971 • Sewell Vernon • UKN • HORRORS OF BURKE AND HARE, THE (USA)
BURKE AND WILLS • 1986 • Clifford Graeme • ASL
BURKINO FASO: LAND OF THE PEOPLE OF DIGNITY • 1987 • Ford Abiyi • BRK, USA
BURLA, LA • 1912 • De Liguoro Giuseppe • ITL
BURLADA • 1950 • Rivero Fernando A. • MXC
BURLESK QUEEN • 1977 • Castillo Celso Ad. • PHL • BURLESQUE QUEEN
BURLESQUE • 1932 • *Terry Paul/ Moser Frank (P)* • ANS • USA
BURLESQUE see **DANCE OF LIFE, THE** • 1929
BURLESQUE see **WHEN MY BABY SMILES AT ME** • 1948
BURLESQUE ATTACK ON A SETTLER'S CABIN • 1900 • *Leno Dan* • UKN
BURLESQUE BLACKMAILERS, THE • 1917 • Smith David • SHT • USA • FOOTLIGHT LURE, THE
BURLESQUE FOX HUNT • 1900 • *Warwick Trading Co.* • UKN
BURLESQUE HIGHWAY ROBBERY IN "GAY PAREE", A see **APACHES, LES** • 1904
BURLESQUE NAVAL GUN DRILL • 1903 • *Warwick Trading Co.* • UKN
BURLESQUE OF POPULAR COMPOSERS • 1902 • Williamson James • UKN
BURLESQUE QUEEN see **BURLESK QUEEN** • 1977
BURLESQUE QUEEN, THE • 1910 • *Powers* • USA
BURLESQUE SHOW, THE • 1916 • *Tweedledum* • USA
BURLESQUE SUICIDE • 1902 • Porter Edwin S. • USA
BURLY BILL • 1910 • *Essanay* • USA
BURMA CONVOY • 1941 • Smith Noel • USA
BURMA VICTORY • 1941-45 • MacDonald David • DOC • UKN
BURMA VICTORY • 1945 • Boulting Roy • DOC • UKN
BURMESE HARP, THE • 1985 • Ichikawa Kon • MTV • JPN
BURMESE HARP, THE (UKN) see **BIRUMA NO TATEGOTO** • 1956
BURN! see **QUEMADA!** • 1969
BURN, BABY, BURN see **CAROLYN LIMA STORY, THE** • 1966
BURN, BOY, BURN (UKN) see **BRUCIA, RAGAZZO, BRUCIA** • 1969
BURN 'EM UP BARNES • 1921 • Beranger George A., Hines Johnny • USA
BURN 'EM UP BARNES • 1934 • Clark Colbert, Schaefer Armand • USA • DEVIL ON WHEELS (UKN)
BURN 'EM UP BARNES • 1934 • Clark Colbert, Schaefer Armand • SRL • USA
BURN 'EM UP O'CONNOR • 1938 • Sedgwick Edward • USA
BURN, WITCH, BURN (UKN) see **BRENN, HEXE, BRENN** • 1969
BURN, WITCH, BURN (USA) see **NIGHT OF THE EAGLE** • 1962
BURNED BRIDGE see **VERBRANDE BRUG** • 1975
BURNED CITY, THE see **CIUTAT CREMADA, LA** • 1976
BURNED HAND, THE • 1915 • Browning Tod • USA
BURNED MAP, THE see **MOETSUKITA CHIZU** • 1968
BURNIN' LOVE see **LOVE AT STAKE** • 1988

BURNING see USIJANJE • 1979
BURNING, THE • 1968 • Frears Stephen • SHT • UKN
BURNING, THE • 1981 • Maylam Tony • USA
BURNING, THE see DON'T GO IN THE HOUSE • 1980
BURNING ACRE, THE see BRENNENDE ACKER, DER • 1922
BURNING AN ILLUSION • 1982 • Shabazz Menelik • UKN
BURNING ANGEL, THE see PALAVA ENKELI • 1983
BURNING ARROWS (UKN) see CAPTAIN JOHN SMITH AND POCAHONTAS • 1953
BURNING AUTUMN see MOERU AKI • 1978
BURNING BAND, THE • 1916 • Calvert E. H. • SHT • USA
BURNING BED, THE • 1985 • Greenwald Robert • TVM • USA
BURNING BLOOD see HEISSES BLUT • 1911
BURNING BODY see JALTE BADAN • 1973
BURNING BODY, THE see CORPO ARDENTE, O • 1967
BURNING BRAND, THE • 1912 • Broncho • USA
BURNING BRASIER, THE see BRASIER ARDENT, LE • 1922
BURNING BRIDGES • 1928 • Hogan James P. • USA
BURNING CLOUDS see MOERU KUMO • 1967
BURNING COURT, THE see CHAMBRE ARDENTE, LA • 1961
BURNING CROSS, THE • 1947 • Colmes Walter • USA
BURNING CROSS, THE see KLANSMAN, THE • 1974
BURNING DAYLIGHT • 1914 • Bosworth Hobart • USA
BURNING DAYLIGHT • 1920 • Sloman Edward • USA
BURNING DAYLIGHT • 1928 • Brabin Charles J. • USA
BURNING EARTH see ARD AL MAHROUKA, AL • 1970
BURNING EARTH, THE see BRENNENDE ACKER, DER • 1922
BURNING FLOWERS see BRENNENDE BLOMSTER • 1985
BURNING FOX • 1966 • Larkin Ryan • ANS • CND
BURNING GOLD • 1927 • Noble Jack • USA
BURNING GOLD • 1936 • Newfield Sam • USA
BURNING HEART, THE see HOROUCI SRDCE • 1962
BURNING HEART, THE (USA) see BRENNENDE HERZ, DAS • 1929
BURNING HILLS, THE • 1956 • Heisler Stuart • USA
BURNING HOME, THE • 1909 • Smith Jack ? • UKN
BURNING LAND see ADAMA HAMA • 1984
BURNING LARIAT, THE • 1913 • Frontier • USA
BURNING LOVE see BRANDENDE LIEFDE • 1983
BURNING MAN, THE see CAROLYN LIMA STORY, THE • 1966
BURNING MAN, THE see DANGEROUS SUMMER • 1982
BURNING MEMORIES • 1988 • Somer Yossi • ISR
BURNING NATURE see HANA O KUU MUSHI • 1967
BURNING OF A THOUSAND SUNS, THE see BRULERE DE MILLE SOLEILS, LA • 1964
BURNING OF CEYLON see LANKA DAHAN • 1935
BURNING OF CEYLON, THE see LANKADAHAN • 1933
BURNING OF DAHAN see LANKA DAHAN • 1935
BURNING OF DAHAN, THE see LANKA DAHAN • 1918
BURNING OF DAHAN, THE see LANKADAHAN • 1933
BURNING OF JUDAS, THE see QUEMA DE JUDAS, LA • 1974
BURNING OF LANKA, THE see LANKA DAHAN • 1918
BURNING OF THE IMPERIAL PALACE see HUOSHAO YUANMINGYUAN • 1983
BURNING OF THE RED LOTUS TEMPLE, THE • 1928-31 • CHN
BURNING OF YUANMINGYUAN, THE see HUOSHAO YUANMINGYUAN • 1983
BURNING PYRAMIDS • 1973 • Jarman Derek • UKN
BURNING QUESTION, THE • 1919 • Edgington Ida • USA
BURNING QUESTION, THE • 1940 • Gasnier Louis J. • USA • TELL YOUR CHILDREN ○ REEFER MADNESS ○ DOPE ADDICT ○ DOPED YOUTH ○ LOVE MADNESS
BURNING QUESTION, THE • 1945 • Hughes Ken • DCS • UKN
BURNING RAGE • 1984 • Cates Gilbert • TVM • USA
BURNING RIVET, THE • 1913 • Lubin • USA
BURNING RUBBER • 1980 • SAF
BURNING SANDS • 1922 • Melford George • USA • DWELLER IN THE DESERT, THE
BURNING SECRET • 1989 • Birkin Andrew • UKN, USA, FRG
BURNING SECRET, THE see BRENNENDES GEHEIMNIS • 1933
BURNING SHADOWS • 1967 • de Hadeln Moritz • DOC • SWT
BURNING SILENCE, THE • 1917 • Rice A. W. • SHT • USA
BURNING SKY, THE see MOERU OZORA • 1940
BURNING SOIL see BRENNENDE ACKER, DER • 1922
BURNING STABLE, THE • 1896 • USA
BURNING STABLE, THE • 1900 • Hepworth Cecil M. • UKN
BURNING SUN, THE see MOERO TAIYO • 1967
BURNING THE CANDLE • 1917 • Beaumont Harry • USA
BURNING THE WIND • 1929 • McRae Henry, Blache Herbert • USA
BURNING TRAIL, THE • 1925 • Rosson Arthur • USA
BURNING TRAIN, THE • 1978 • Chopra B. R. • IND
BURNING UP • 1930 • Sutherland A. Edward • USA
BURNING UP BROADWAY • 1928 • Rosen Phil • USA
BURNING WORDS • 1923 • Paton Stuart • USA
BURNING YEARS, THE see CONCORRENTE, IL • 1979
BURNING YOUTH see YAMA NO SANKA: MOYURU WAKAMONO-TACHI • 1962
BURNOUT • 1979 • Meech-Burkestone Graham • USA
BURNS AND ALLEN IN LAMB CHOPS • 1929 • Burns George • USA
BURNS-JOHNSON FIGHT, THE • 1908 • Longford Raymond • DOC • ASL
BURNT BRIDGE see VERBRANDE BRUG • 1975
BURNT CHILD see BRANT BARN • 1967
BURNT CORK • 1912 • Vitagraph • USA
BURNT CORK, A • 1912 • Lubin • USA
BURNT EVIDENCE • 1954 • Birt Daniel • UKN
BURNT FINGERS • 1927 • Campbell Maurice • USA
BURNT IN • 1920 • Macrae Duncan • UKN
BURNT LAND see TIERRA QUEMADA • 1968
BURNT OFFERING (UKN) see PASSPORT TO HELL, A • 1932
BURNT OFFERINGS • 1976 • Curtis Dan • USA
BURNT SKIN see PIEL QUEMADA, LA • 1968
BURNT WINGS • 1916 • West Walter • UKN
BURNT WINGS • 1920 • Cabanne W. Christy • USA • PRIMROSE PATH, THE
BURSCHENLIED AUS HEIDELBERG, EIN • 1930 • Hartl Karl • FRG
BURST CITY • 1982 • Ishii Sogo • JPN
BURSTUP HOLMES, DETECTIVE • 1913 • Solax • USA
BURSTUP HOLMES' MURDER CASE • 1913 • Karr Darwin • USA
BURT GILLETT'S RAINBOW PARADE • 1934-35 • Gillett Burt, Palmer Tom • ASS • USA
BURY ME AN ANGEL • 1971 • Peeters Barbara • USA
BURY ME DEAD • 1947 • Vorhaus Bernard • USA
BURY ME NOT ON THE LONE PRAIRIE • 1941 • Taylor Ray • USA
BURY THEM DEEP (UKN) see ALL'ULTIMO SANGUE • 1968
BURYAN • 1967 • Bukoveski Anatoli • USS • WILD GRASS ○ WEEDS
BURYING THE POTATO see POGRZEB KARTOFLA • 1990
BUS, THE • 1965 • Wexler Haskell • DOC • USA
BUS, THE • 1985 • Samadi Yadollah • IRN
BUS, THE see OTOBUS • 1976
BUS ACTION, THE see ACTIUNEA AUTOBUZUL • 1978
BUS DRIVER • el Tayeb Atif • EGY
BUS IS COMING, THE • 1971 • Franklin Wendell James • USA
BUS LEAVES AT 6:20 see AUTOBUS ODJEZDZA O 6:20 • 1954
BUS NUMBER THREE see XIAOZI BEI • 1980
BUS PESTS • 1945 • Reisner Charles F. • SHT • USA
BUS RILEY'S BACK IN TOWN • 1965 • Hart Harvey • USA
BUS STOP • 1956 • Logan Joshua • USA • WRONG KIND OF GIRL, THE
BUS STOP • 1967 • Torres Mar S. • PHL
BUS STOP • 1978 • Dunkley-Smith John • ASL
BUS TERMINAL see FLORENCE 13.30 • 1957
BUS WAY TO TRAVEL, THE • 1964 • Kneitel Seymour • ANS • USA
BUSCA, LA • 1967 • Fons Angelino • SPN • SEARCH, THE
BUSCABULLAS, EL • 1974 • Cine Vision • MXC
BUSCH SINGT • Wolf Konrad (c/d) • DOC • GDR
BUSCO TONTA PARA FIN DE SEMANA • 1972 • Iquino Ignacio F. • SPN
BUSCON, EL • 1974 • Berriatua Luciano • SPN
BUSH CHRISTMAS • 1947 • Smart Ralph • UKN, ASL
BUSH CHRISTMAS • 1983 • Safran Henri • ASL
BUSH LEAGUER, THE • 1917 • MacGregor Norval • SHT • USA
BUSH LEAGUER, THE • 1927 • Bretherton Howard • USA
BUSH MAMA • 1979 • Gerima Haile • USA
BUSH OF LOVE FOOLERY, A see JOCHI NO SHIGEMI • 1968
BUSH PILOT • 1947 • Campbell Sterling
BUSH POLICEMAN • 1953 • Robinson Lee • DOC • ASL
BUSH SHRINK • 1988 • Hall Ivan • SAF
BUSH WHACKER, THE see BUSHWHACKER, THE • 1968
BUSHBABY, THE • 1970 • Trent John • UKN
BUSHER, THE • 1919 • Storm Jerome • USA
BUSHFIRE see DANGEROUS SUMMER • 1980
BUSHFIRE BRIGADE • 1949 • Thompson Eric* • ASL
BUSHFIRE MOON • 1987 • Miller George* • TVM • USA • CHRISTMAS VISITOR, THE (USA)
BUSHIDO • 1970 • Agustsson Agust • SHT • USA • WAY OF THE WARRIOR, THE
BUSHIDO see BUSHIDO ZANKOKU MONOGATARI • 1963
BUSHIDO BLADE, THE • 1979 • Kotani Tom • JPN • BLOODY BUSHIDO BLADE, THE
BUSHIDO, DAS EISERNE GESETZ • 1926 • Heiland Heinz Karl, Kako Zamnu • FRG
BUSHIDO-SAMURAI SAGA see BUSHIDO ZANKOKU MONOGATARI • 1963
BUSHIDO ZANKOKU MONOGATARI • 1963 • Imai Tadashi • JPN • CRUEL STORY OF THE SAMURAI'S WAY ○ CRUEL TALES OF BUSHIDO ○ BUSHIDO-SAMURAI SAGA ○ OATH OF OBEDIENCE, THE ○ BUSHIDO
BUSHLAND SYMPHONY • 1952 • Hall Ken G. • DOC • ASL
BUSHLEAGUER'S DREAM, THE • 1913 • Russell William • USA
BUSHMAN • 1971 • Schickele David • USA
BUSHMAN, THE • 1927 • Cadle C. Ernest • DOC • USA
BUSHMAN'S BRIDE, THE • 1912 • Spencer Australian Co. • ASL
BUSHRANGER, THE • 1928 • Withey Chet • USA
BUSHRANGER'S BRIDE, THE • 1914 • Sawyer'S Features • USA
BUSHRANGER'S RANSOM, A • 1911 • Pathe Freres • ASL • RIDE FOR LIFE, A
BUSHRANGER'S STRATEGY, A • 1917 • Hurst Paul C. • SHT • USA
BUSHWACKER, THE see BUSHWHACKER, THE • 1968
BUSHWACKERS see BUSHWHACKER, THE • 1968
BUSHWHACKER, THE • 1968 • Elliott B. Ron • USA • BUSH WHACKER, THE ○ BUSHWACKER, THE ○ BUSHWACKERS
BUSHWHACKERS, THE • 1925 • Longford Raymond • ASL
BUSHWHACKERS, THE • 1951 • Amateau Rod • USA • REBEL, THE (UKN)
BUSHY HARE • 1950 • McKimson Robert • ANS • USA
BUSINESS • 1959 • Boutel Maurice • FRN • BIZENESS
BUSINESS see PRINCE BABOULE • 1938
BUSINESS AND LOVE • 1914 • Hotaling Arthur D. • USA
BUSINESS AND PLEASURE • 1931 • Butler David • USA • PLUTOCRAT
BUSINESS AS USUAL • 1987 • Barrett Lezli-An • UKN
BUSINESS AS USUAL DURING ALTERATIONS • 1913 • Stow Percy • UKN • OPEN DURING ALTERATIONS
BUSINESS BEFORE HONESTY • 1918 • Parrott Charles • SHT • USA
BUSINESS BUCCANEER, A • 1912 • Joyce Alice • USA
BUSINESS IS BUSINESS • 1912 • Noy Wilfred • UKN
BUSINESS IS BUSINESS • 1915 • United Film Services • USA
BUSINESS IS BUSINESS • 1915 • Turner Otis • Universal • USA
BUSINESS IS BUSINESS • 1921 • Kenton Erle C. • SHT • USA
BUSINESS IS BUSINESS see WAT ZIEN IK • 1971
BUSINESS MAN'S LUNCH, THE see MID-DAY MISTRESS • 1968
BUSINESS MUST NOT INTERFERE • 1913 • Cohl Emile • ANS • USA
BUSINESS OF LIFE, THE • 1918 • Terriss Tom • USA
BUSINESS OF LOVE, THE • 1925 • Reis Irving, Robbins Jess • USA • CRASH, THE
BUSINESS RIVALS • 1915 • Lewis Sheldon • USA
BUSINESS TRIP, A • 1962 • Yegorov Yuri • USS
BUSINESS VS. LOVE • 1914 • Ayres Sydney • USA
BUSINESS WITHOUT PLEASURE • 1919 • Perez Marcel • USA
BUSINESS WOMAN, A • 1913 • Marston Lawrence (Mrs.) • USA
BUSINESSMAN, THE see DELOVYE LYUDI • 1963
BUSKER'S REVENGE, THE • 1914 • Storrie Kelly • UKN
BUSMAN'S HOLIDAY • 1936 • Rogers Maclean • UKN
BUSMAN'S HOLIDAY • 1961 • Smith Paul J. • ANS • USA
BUSMAN'S HONEYMOON • 1940 • Woods Arthur • UKN • HAUNTED HONEYMOON (USA)
BUSQUEDA, LA • 1972 • Blanco Javier • SHT • VNZ • SEARCH, THE
BUSQUEME A ESA CHICA • 1964 • Palacios Fernando • SPN
BUSSE RHYTHM • 1938 • Roush Leslie • SHT • USA
BUSSENDE MAGDALENA, DIE • 1914-18 • Zelnik Friedrich • FRG
BUSSENDE MAGDALENA, DIE • 1915 • Albes Emil • FRG
BUSSES ROAR • 1942 • Lederman D. Ross • USA
BUST'AGI, AL- see BOUSTAGUY, AL • 1968
BUSTED BLOOMS • 1934 • Terry Paul/ Moser Frank (P) • ANS • USA
BUSTED BUT BENEVOLENT • 1915 • Cunningham Arthur • USA
BUSTED FLUSH, A • 1915 • Zenith Films • USA
BUSTED HEARTS • 1916 • Stull Walter, Burns Bobby • SHT • USA
BUSTED HEARTS see THOSE LOVE PANGS • 1914
BUSTED HEARTS AND BUTTERMILK • 1918 • Christie Al • SHT • USA
BUSTED HONEYMOON, A • 1916 • Howell Alice • SHT • USA
BUSTED JOHNNY, A see MAKING A LIVING • 1914
BUSTED RIVALS see THOSE LOVE PANGS • 1914
BUSTED ROMANCE • 1918 • Ebony • SHT • USA
BUSTED UP • 1986 • Palmisano Conrad E. • CND
BUSTER • 1988 • Green David • UKN
BUSTER, THE • 1923 • Campbell Colin • USA
BUSTER AND BILLIE • 1974 • Petrie Daniel • USA
BUSTER AND HIS GOAT • 1914 • France Charles H. • USA
BUSTER AND SUNSHINE • 1913 • Eyton Bessie • USA
BUSTER AND THE CANNIBALS • 1912 • Lubin • USA
BUSTER AND THE GYPSIES • 1912 • Lubin • USA
BUSTER AND THE PIRATES • 1912 • Lubin • USA
BUSTER BROWN • 1904 • Porter Edwin S. • SER • USA
BUSTER BROWN • 1914 • France Charles H. • SER • USA
BUSTER BROWN AND THE GERMAN BAND • 1914 • France Charles H. • USA
BUSTER BROWN CAUSES A COMMOTION • 1914 • France Charles H. • USA
BUSTER BROWN GETS THE WORST OF IT • 1914 • Edison • USA
BUSTER BROWN ON THE CARE AND TREATMENT OF GOATS • 1914 • France Charles H. • USA
BUSTER BROWN PICKS OUT THE COSTUMES • 1914 • France Charles H. • USA
BUSTER BROWN'S EDUCATION • 1914 • France Charles H. • USA
BUSTER BROWN'S UNCLE • 1914 • Edison • USA
BUSTER IN NODLAND • 1912 • Lubin • USA
BUSTER KEATON RIDES AGAIN • 1965 • Spotton John • CND
BUSTER KEATON STORY, THE • 1957 • Sheldon Sidney • USA
BUSTER MINDS THE BABY • 1928 • Newfield Sam • SHT • USA
BUSTER SE MARIE • 1931 • Brothy William, Autant-Lara Claude • FRN
BUSTER TO THE RESCUE • 1912 • Pathe • USA
BUSTER TRAINS UP • 1928 • Newfield Sam • SHT • USA
BUSTER'S DREAM • 1912 • Lubin • USA
BUSTER'S JOKE ON PAPA • 1903 • Porter Edwin S. • USA
BUSTER'S LAST STAND • 1970 • Smith Paul J. • ANS • USA
BUSTER'S LITTLE GAME • 1913 • Duncan William • USA
BUSTER'S NIGHTMARE • 1912 • Pathe • USA
BUSTER'S SPOOKS • 1928 • Newfield Sam • SHT • USA
BUSTER'S WORLD see WORLD OF BUSTER, THE • 1984
BUSTIN' LOOSE • 1981 • Scott Oz • USA
BUSTIN' OUT see COONSKIN • 1975
BUSTIN' THRU • 1925 • Smith Cliff • USA
BUSTING • 1973 • Hyams Peter • USA
BUSTING BUSTER • 1928 • Newfield Sam • SHT • USA
BUSTING IN AND OUT OF SOCIETY • 1916 • Whiting Ralph • SHT • USA
BUSTING INTO SOCIETY • 1917 • Curtis Allen • SHT • USA
BUSTING OUT see BLAZE STARR GOES NUDIST • 1962
BUSTING THE BEANERY • 1916 • Roach Hal • SHT • USA
BUSTY BROWN see ADVENTURES OF BUSTY BROWN, THE • 1964
BUSY BAKERS • 1940 • Hardaway Ben, Dalton Cal • ANS • USA
BUSY BARBER, THE • 1932 • Lantz Walter, Nolan William • ANS • USA
BUSY BEAVERS, THE • 1931 • Jackson Wilfred • ANS • USA
BUSY BEE, THE • 1916 • Gayety • USA
BUSY BEE, THE • 1936 • Terry Paul/ Moser Frank (P) • ANS • USA
BUSY BEES • 1922 • Roach Hal • SHT • USA
BUSY BELL BOY, THE • 1915 • Rooney Pat • USA
BUSY BODIES • 1933 • French Lloyd • SHT • USA
BUSY BODY see ISOGASHII NIKUTAI • 1967
BUSY BODY, THE • 1967 • Castle William • USA
BUSY BUDDIES • 1944 • Lord Del • SHT • USA
BUSY BUDDIES • 1956 • Hanna William, Barbera Joseph • ANS • USA
BUSY BUS • 1934 • Mintz Charles (P) • ANS • USA
BUSY CUPID, A • 1911 • Gaumont • FRN
BUSY DAY, A • 1914 • Chaplin Charles • USA • MILITANT SUFFRAGETTE ○ LADY CHARLIE
BUSY DAY IN THE JUNGLE, A • 1912 • Neilan Marshall • USA
BUSY IZZY • 1915 • Sidney George • USA
BUSY KIND OF BLOKE, A • 1978 • Armstrong Gillian • DOC • ASL
BUSY LITTLE BEARS • 1939 • Haeseler John A. • ANS • USA
BUSY MAN, THE • 1907 • Fitzhamon Lewin • UKN
BUSY MAN, THE • 1914 • Royal • USA
BUSY NIGHT, A • 1909 • Anglo-American Films • UKN
BUSYBODY see MORDSKAB • 1969
BUSYBODY, THE • 1923 • La Cava Gregory • SHT • USA
BUSYBODY BEAR • 1952 • Lundy Dick • ANS • USA
BUSYBODY (UKN) see KIBITZER, THE • 1930
BUSYBODY'S BUSY DAY, A • 1915 • Pathe Exchange • USA
BUT • 1959 • Haupe Wlodzimierz, Bielinska Halina • PLN
BUT • 1966 • Delouche Dominique • SHT • FRN

BUT A BUTLER • 1922 • Santell Alfred • SHT • USA
BUT DE SA VIE, LE • 1958 • Rybakov Anatoly • USS
BUT DO NOT DELIVER US FROM EVIL see **MAIS NE NOUS DELIVREZ PAS DU MAL** • 1970
BUT I DON'T WANT TO GET MARRIED • 1970 • Paris Jerry • TVM • USA
BUT IT'S NOTHING SERIOUS (USA) see **MA NON E UNA COSA SERIA** • 1936
BUT NOT FOR ME • 1959 • Lang Walter • USA
BUT NOT GOODBYE see **COCKEYED MIRACLE, THE** • 1946
BUT NOT IN VAIN • 1948 • Greville Edmond T. • UKN, NTH • NEIT TEVERGEEFS (NTH)
BUT THE FLESH IS WEAK • 1932 • Conway Jack • USA • TRUTH GAME, THE
BUT THE MONSTERS WERE MUZZLED see **...MAIS LES MONSTRES ETAIENT MUSELES** • 1956
BUT THE PEOPLE ARE BEAUTIFUL • 1972 • Armstrong John • UKN
BUT THEN, SHE'S BETTY CARTER • 1980 • Parkerson Michelle D. • USA
BUT WHAT DO THEY WANT? see **MAIS QUEST'CE QU'ELLES VEULENT?** • 1977
BUT WHERE IS DANIEL VAX? (USA) see **LE'AM NE'ELAN DANIEL WAKS** • 1972
BUT YOU WERE DEAD (UKN) see **LUNGA NOTTE DI VERONIQUE, LA** • 1966
BUTA TO GUNKAN • 1961 • Imamura Shohei • JPN • FLESH IS HOT, THE (USA) ○ HOGS AND WARSHIPS ○ PIGS AND BATTLESHIPS ○ DIRTY GIRLS, THE
BUTASAGOM TORTENETE • 1966 • Keleti Marton • HNG • STORY OF MY STUPIDITY, THE
BUTCH AND SUNDANCE: THE EARLY DAYS • 1979 • Lester Richard • USA
BUTCH CASSIDY AND THE SUNDANCE KID • 1969 • Hill George Roy • USA
BUTCH MINDS THE BABY • 1942 • Rogell Albert S. • USA
BUTCHER, THE see **KOSHAI** • 1980
BUTCHER, THE see **PSYCHO FROM TEXAS** • 1982
BUTCHER, THE (USA) see **BOUCHER, LE** • 1969
BUTCHER AND THE TRAMP, THE • 1899 • *Norton C. Goodwin* • UKN
BUTCHER, BAKER, NIGHTMARE MAKER see **NIGHT WARNING** • 1982
BUTCHER BOY, THE • 1917 • Arbuckle Roscoe • SHT • USA
BUTCHER BOY, THE • 1932 • Lantz Walter, Nolan William • ANS • USA
BUTCHER OF BURQUITLAM • 1981 • Windsor Chris • CND
BUTCHER OF SEVILLE, THE • 1944 • Donnelly Eddie • ANS • USA
BUTCHER'S BOY AND THE PENNY DREADFUL, THE • 1909 • Coleby A. E. • UKN
BUTCHER'S BRIDE, THE • 1915 • *L-Ko* • USA
BUTCHER'S DREAM, THE • 1909 • *Lux* • FRN
BUTCHER'S NIGHTMARE, THE • 1917 • Williamson Robin E. • SHT • USA
BUTCHER'S WIFE, THE see **MUJER DEL CARNICERO, LA** • 1968
BUTHISALIGAL • 1968 • Arun • IND • CLEVER ONES
BUTLER, THE • 1915 • Ridgwell George • USA
BUTLER, THE • 1916 • McKim Edwin • SHT • USA
BUTLER BUST-UP, A • 1918 • *Triangle* • SHT • USA
BUTLER'S BABY, THE • 1915 • *Joker* • USA
BUTLER'S BLUNDER, THE • 1918 • Curtis Allen • SHT • USA
BUTLER'S BUSTED ROMANCE, THE • 1915 • *Shields Ernest* • USA
BUTLER'S DILEMMA, THE • 1943 • Hiscott Leslie • UKN
BUTLER'S MILLIONS, THE see **MONEY MEANS NOTHING** • 1932
BUTLER'S REVENGE, THE • 1910 • Martinek H. O. • UKN
BUTLER'S SECRET, THE • 1913 • Humphrey William • USA
BUTLEY • 1974 • Pinter Harold • UKN
BUTNSKALA • 1985 • Slak Franci • YGS • BUMPSTONE
BUTOKEN MOKO GEKISATSUI • 1976 • Yamaguchi Kazuhiko • JPN
BUTT-ING IN • 1914 • Hotaling Arthur D. • USA
BUTTER AGAIN • 1918 • Curtis Allen • SHT • USA
BUTTER AND EGG MAN, THE • 1928 • Wallace Richard • USA • ACTRESS AND ANGEL (UKN)
BUTTER FINGERS • 1925 • *Sennett Mack (P)* • SHT • USA
BUTTER-IN-YEGGMAN, A • 1931 • Lehrman Henry • SHT • USA
BUTTERCUP CHAIN, THE • 1970 • Miller Robert Ellis • UKN
BUTTERCUP P.C. • 1913 • Kinder Stuart? • UKN
BUTTERCUP P.C., DETECTIVE • 1913 • Kinder Stuart? • UKN
BUTTERCUPS • 1913 • Thompson Frederick A. • USA
BUTTERFIELD 8 • 1960 • Mann Daniel • USA
BUTTERFLIES • 1908 • *Cines* • ITL
BUTTERFLIES • 1978 • Gwenlan Gareth • MTV • UKN
BUTTERFLIES • 1987 • Zimonovic Kresimir • ANM • YGS
BUTTERFLIES see **MOTYLE** • 1973
BUTTERFLIES ALSO LOVE see **BORBOLETAS TAMBEM AMAM, AS** • 1980
BUTTERFLIES AND ORANGE BLOSSOMS • 1914 • Physioc Wray • USA
BUTTERFLIES ARE FREE • 1972 • Katselas Milton • USA
BUTTERFLIES DO NOT LIVE HERE see **MOTYLI TADY NEZIJI** • 1958
BUTTERFLIES DON'T CRY see **SCHMETTERLINGE WEINEN NICHT** • 1970
BUTTERFLIES IN THE RAIN • 1926 • Sloman Edward • USA
BUTTERFLIES WITH WINGS • 1985 • Kool Allen • CND
BUTTERFLY • 1924 • Brown Clarence • USA
BUTTERFLY • 1971 • Theirmann Eric • SHT • USA
BUTTERFLY • 1975 • Sarno Joe • SWT • BROKEN BUTTERFLY ○ BABY TRAMP
BUTTERFLY • 1981 • Cimber Matt • USA, CND
BUTTERFLY, THE • 1910 • Paul Robert William • UKN
BUTTERFLY, THE • 1912 • Goodman Robert • USA
BUTTERFLY, THE • 1914 • Gaskill Charles L. • *Vitagraph* • USA
BUTTERFLY, THE • 1914 • Ricketts Thomas • *American* • USA
BUTTERFLY, THE • 1915 • *Estabrook Howard* • USA
BUTTERFLY, THE • 1917 • Baldwin Ruth Ann • USA
BUTTERFLY, THE see **MOONLIGHT FOLLIES** • 1921
BUTTERFLY AFFAIR, THE (USA) see **POPSY POP** • 1970
BUTTERFLY AND FLOWERS see **PEESUA LAE DOKMAI** • 1985
BUTTERFLY AND THE FLAME, THE see **FJARILEN OCH LJUSLAGAN** • 1954
BUTTERFLY AUTUMN see **SOMMERFUGLER** • 1972
BUTTERFLY BALL • 1976 • Klinger Tony • ANS • UKN
BUTTERFLY BOMB • 1943 • Birt Daniel • DOC • UKN
BUTTERFLY BUG, THE • 1914 • *Blakemore Harry* • USA
BUTTERFLY CLOUD see **LEPTIROV OBLAK** • 1977
BUTTERFLY GIRL, THE • 1917 • Otto Henry • USA
BUTTERFLY GIRL, THE • 1921 • Gorman John • USA
BUTTERFLY IN THE NIGHT, A see **MARIPOSA EN LA NOCHE, UNE** • 1976
BUTTERFLY MAN, THE • 1920 • Park Ida May • USA
BUTTERFLY MAN, THE • 1925 • Seiler Lewis • SHT • USA
BUTTERFLY MURDERS see **TIEH PIEN** • 1980
BUTTERFLY NET, THE • 1912 • *Bushman Francis X.* • USA
BUTTERFLY OF NIGHT see **YORU NO CHO** • 1957
BUTTERFLY ON THE SHOULDER see **PAPILLON SUR L'EPAULE, UN** • 1978
BUTTERFLY ON THE WHEEL, A • 1915 • Tourneur Maurice • *Shubert* • USA
BUTTERFLY ON THE WHEEL, THE • 1915 • *Box Office Attractions* • USA
BUTTERFLY ON THE WHEEL, THE see **FRAU AUF DER FOLTER, DIE** • 1928
BUTTERFLY RANCH see **BUTTERFLY RANGE** • 1922
BUTTERFLY RANGE • 1922 • Hart Neal • USA • BUTTERFLY RANCH
BUTTERFLY REVOLUTION, THE see **SUMMER CAMP NIGHTMARE** • 1987
BUTTERFLY'S DREAM • 1986 • Kurkvaara Maunu • FNL
BUTTERFLY'S LESSON, THE • 1915 • Humphrey William • USA
BUTTERFLY'S WING, THE • 1978 • Alexander Mike • UKN
BUTTERFLY'S WINGS, THE • 1914 • Santschi Thomas • USA
BUTTERSCOTCH AND SODA • 1948 • *Litte Audry* • ANS • USA
BUTTIGLIONE DIVENTA CAPO DEL SERVIZIO SEGRETO • 1975 • Guerrini Mino • ITL
BUTTING IN ON BABY • 1920 • Lyons Eddie, Moran Lee • SHT • USA
BUTTLERFLIES (UKN) see **BLACK BUTTERFLIES** • 1928
BUTTON, THE see **BOTAN** • 1963
BUTTON, THE see **GUZIK** • 1965
BUTTON MY BACK • 1929 • *Sennett Mack (P)* • SHT • USA
BUTTONS • 1915 • Pearson George • UKN
BUTTONS • 1927 • Hill George W. • USA
BUTTONS • 1934 • *Sound City* • SHT • UKN
BUTTS CASEY, CROOK • 1916 • *Knickerbocker Star* • SHT • USA
BUTTSUKE HONBAN • 1958 • Saeki Kozo • JPN • GO AND GET IT
BUTY • 1965 • Petelska Ewa, Petelski Czeslaw • MTV • PLN • BOOTS
BUVOS SZEK • 1952 • Gertler Viktor • HNG • MAGIC CHAIR, THE
BUWANA TOSHI NO UTA • 1965 • Hani Susumu • JPN • BWANA TOSHI (USA) ○ SONG OF BWANA TOSHI, THE
BUXOM COUNTRY LASS, THE • 1914 • Williams C. Jay • USA
BUY AND CELL • 1988 • Boris Robert • USA
BUY-BUY BABY • 1915 • *Farley Dot* • USA
BUY LIBERTY BONDS see **LIBERTY LOAN BOND SHORT** • 1918
BUY ME THAT TOWN • 1941 • Forde Eugene J. • USA
BUY ONE TAKE ONE • 1968 • Villaflor Romy • PHL
BUY WOOL • 1914 • *Ab* • USA
BUY YOUR OWN CHERRIES • 1904 • *Paul R. W.* • UKN
BUYANG-BUYANG KELABU • 1979 • Prijono Ami • INN
BUYER BEWARE • 1940 • Newman Joseph M. • SHT • USA
BUYER FROM CACTUS CITY, THE • 1918 • Miller Ashley • SHT • USA
BUYING A HORSE • 1914 • *Rigby Freddie* • UKN
BUYING A TITLE • 1908 • Porter Edwin S. • USA
BUYING MANHATTAN • 1909 • *Edison* • USA
BUYING TIME • 1988 • Gabourie Mitchell • CND
BUYUK CELLATLAR see **SEYTANIN OGLU** • 1967
BUYUK GUNAH • 1968 • Dogan Suha • TRK • GREAT SIN, THE
BUYUK KIN • 1967 • Basaran Tunc • TRK • BIG HATE, THE
BUYUK YEMIN • 1967 • Duru Yilmaz • TRK • GREAT OATH, THE
BUZAVIRAG • 1935 • Sekely Steve • HNG • CORNFLOWER
BUZDUGANUL CU TREI PECETI • 1976 • Vaeni Constantin • RMN
BUZY BUDDIES • 1960 • Kneitel Seymour • ANS • USA
BUZZARD, THE • 1976 • Cain Christopher • USA
BUZZARDS OVER BAGHDAD • 1951-56 • Smith Jack** • USA
BUZZARD'S PREY • 1916 • *Imp* • SHT • USA
BUZZARD'S SHADOW, THE • 1915 • Ricketts Thomas • USA
BUZZIN' AROUND • 1933 • Goulding Alf • SHT • USA
BUZZY AND THE PHANTOM PINTO • 1941 • Kahn Richard C. • USA
BUZZY BOOP • 1938 • Fleischer Dave • ANS • USA
BUZZY BOOP AT THE CONCERT • 1938 • Fleischer Dave • ANS • USA
BUZZY RIDES THE RANGE • 1940 • Kahn Richard C. • USA • WESTERN TERROR
BWANA DEVIL • 1952 • Oboler Arch • USA
BWANA KIKOTO • 1955 • Cauvin Andre • BLG
BWANA MAGOO • 1959 • McDonald Tom • ANS • USA
BWANA TOSHI (USA) see **BUWANA TOSHI NO UTA** • 1965
BY A BROTHER'S HAND see **BY THE HAND OF A BROTHER** • 1915
BY A STRANGE ROAD • 1915 • *Essanay* • USA
BY A WOMAN'S WIT • 1908 • *Vitagraph* • USA
BY A WOMAN'S WIT • 1911 • *Kalem* • USA
BY AEROPLANE TO PYGMYLAND • 1927 • *Sterling Matthew W.* • DOC • USA • ADVENTURES IN PYGMYLAND
BY AN AFRICAN CAMP FIRE • 1956 • SAF
BY APPOINTMENT ONLY • 1933 • Strayer Frank • USA
BY BERWIN BANKS • 1920 • Morgan Sidney • UKN
BY BOAT see **EN BATEAU** • 1952
BY CANDLELIGHT • 1933 • Whale James • USA
BY CONSCIENCE'S EYE • 1916 • Cochrane George • SHT • USA
BY DECREE OF FATE • 1911 • *Champion* • USA
BY DESIGN • 1981 • Jutra Claude • CND
BY DESIGN OF HEAVEN • 1913 • *Grandais Susanne* • FRN
BY DIVINE RIGHT • 1924 • Neill R. William • USA • WAY MEN LOVE, THE
BY FAIR MEANS OF FOUL • 1915 • *Tincher Fay* • USA
BY FATE'S DECREE • 1913 • *Leonard Robert* • USA
BY FIRE AND WATER • 1913 • Miller Ashley • USA
BY FOOT, BY HORSE AND BY SPUTNIK see **A PIED, A CHEVAL ET EN SPOUTNIK** • 1958
BY FOWL MEANS • 1918 • *Strand* • USA
BY GOLLY • 1920 • Murray Charles • SHT • USA
BY-GONE DAYS • 1913 • *Mitchell Harry* • USA
BY HECK! • 1922 • Del Ruth Roy • SHT • USA
BY HECK, I'LL SAVE HER • 1918 • Curtis Allen • SHT • USA
BY HIS FATHER'S ORDERS • 1914 • Haldane Bert? • UKN
BY HIS OWN HANDS • 1910 • *Bison* • USA
BY HOOK OR BY CROOK (UKN) see **I DOOD IT** • 1943
BY HOOK OR CROOK • 1918 • Henderson Dell • USA
BY IMPULSE • 1913 • *Balboa* • USA
BY INDIAN POST • 1919 • Ford John • SHT • USA
BY INJUNCTION • 1918 • Smith David • SHT • USA
BY LEAPS AND BOUNDS • 1951 • Sparber I. • ANS • USA
BY LOVE.. BY MAGIC see **PER AMORE.. PER MAGIA** • 1967
BY LOVE POSSESSED • 1961 • Sturges John • USA
BY LOVE REDEEMED • 1916 • Williams C. Jay • SHT • USA
BY MAN'S LAW • 1913 • Cabanne W. Christy • USA
BY MIGHT OF HIS RIGHT • 1915 • Drew Sidney • USA
BY MUTUAL ARRANGEMENT • 1913 • Seay Charles M. • USA
BY MY PISTOLS (USA) see **POR MIS PISTOLAS** • 1939
BY ORANGE AID • 1918 • *Vernon Bobby* • USA
BY PARCEL POST • 1913 • *Rice Herbert* • USA
BY PARCEL POST • 1914 • France Charles H. • USA
BY PASS • 1970 • Nicholson Arch • SHT • ASL
BY-PASS TO HAPPINESS • 1934 • Kimmins Anthony • UKN
BY PROXY • 1918 • Smith Cliff • USA
BY RADIUM'S RAYS • 1914 • Turner Otis • USA
BY REASON OF INSANITY • 1982 • Shebib Donald • TVM • CND
BY REGISTERED MAIL • 1911 • *Balfour Sue* • USA
BY REQUEST • 1935 • Mack Roy • SHT • USA
BY RETURN MALE • 1915 • Clements Roy • USA
BY RIGHT OF BIRTH • 1921 • *Brooks Clarence* • USA
BY RIGHT OF CONQUEST see **ISLE OF CONQUEST, THE** • 1919
BY RIGHT OF LOVE • 1916 • Kent Leon D. • SHT • USA
BY RIGHT OF POSSESSION • 1917 • Wolbert William • USA
BY RIGHT OF PURCHASE • 1918 • Miller Charles • USA
BY ROCKET TO THE MOON (UKN) see **FRAU IM MOND, DIE** • 1929
BY ST. ANTHONY see **U SVETEHO ANTONICKA** • 1933
BY ST. MATTHIAS see **U SV. MATEJE** • 1928
BY SEA AND LAND • 1944 • Lee Jack • DOC • UKN
BY SECRET COMMAND see **SECRET COMMAND, THE** • 1944
BY SPESHUL DELIVERY • 1917 • Sargent George L. • SHT • USA
BY STORK DELIVERY • 1916 • Fishback Fred C. • SHT • USA
BY SUPER STRATEGY • 1917 • Gaye Howard • USA
BY TAXI TO FORTUNE • 1914 • *Melies* • USA
BY THE AID OF THE LARIAT • 1911 • *Kalem* • USA
BY THE ARAX see **POTU STORONU ARAKSA** • 1947
BY THE BEAUTIFUL SEA • 1931 • Fleischer Dave • ANS • USA
BY THE BLOOD OF OTHERS see **PAR LE SANG DES AUTRES** • 1973
BY THE BLUEST OF SEAS see **U SAMOVA SINEVO MORYA** • 1936
...BY THE CAMP FIRE'S FLICKER • 1911 • *Vitagraph* • USA
BY THE CURATE'S AID • 1913 • *Mecca* • USA
BY THE DAWN'S EARLY LIGHT see **BARRICADE** • 1939
BY THE FAITH OF A CHILD • 1910 • *Vitagraph* • USA
BY THE FLIP OF A COIN • 1915 • Sloman Edward • USA
BY THE GOVERNOR'S ORDER • 1914 • Gaillord Robert, Costello Maurice • USA
BY THE HAND OF A BROTHER • 1915 • West Walter • UKN • BY A BROTHER'S HAND
BY THE HAND OF A CHILD • 1912 • *Solax* • USA
BY THE HOUSE THAT JACK BUILT • 1911 • *Imp* • USA
BY THE KAISER'S ORDERS • 1914 • Thornton F. Martin • UKN
BY THE LAKE see **V OZERA** • 1969
BY THE LAW see **PO ZAKONU** • 1926
BY THE LIGHT OF THE MOON • 1911 • Porter Edwin S. • USA
BY THE LIGHT OF THE SILVERY MOON • 1927 • Fleischer Dave • ANS • USA
BY THE LIGHT OF THE SILVERY MOON • 1931 • Fleischer Dave • ANS • USA
BY THE LIGHT OF THE SILVERY MOON • 1953 • Butler David • USA
BY THE OLD DEAD TREE • 1914 • O'Sullivan Tony • USA
BY THE OLD MILL SCREAM • 1953 • Kneitel Seymour • ANS • USA
BY THE PALE LIGHT OF THE MOON see **A LA PALIDA LUZ DE LA LUNA** • 1985
BY THE SAD SEA WAVES • 1914 • Kinder Stuart? • UKN
BY THE SAD SEA WAVES • 1916 • Christie Al • SHT • USA
BY THE SAD SEA WAVES • 1917 • Roach Hal • SHT • USA
BY THE SEA • 1912 • *Lubin* • USA
BY THE SEA • 1913 • *Manners Mercy* • UKN
BY THE SEA • 1915 • Chaplin Charles • USA • CHARLIE'S DAY OUT
BY THE SEA • 1931 • *Terry Paul/ Moser Frank (P)* • ANS • USA
BY THE SHORTEST OF HEADS • 1915 • Haldane Bert • UKN
BY THE SUN'S RAYS • 1914 • *Mcquarrie Murdock* • USA
BY THE TWO OAK TREES • 1913 • *Gebhardt George* • USA
BY THE WORLD FORGOT • 1918 • Smith David • USA
BY THEIR OWN STRENGTH • 1940 • Cherry Evelyn Spice • CND
BY UNSEEN HAND • 1914 • Duncan William • USA
BY VED NAVN KOBENHAVN, EN • 1960 • Roos Jorgen • DOC • DNM • CITY CALLED COPENHAGEN, A ○ COPENHAGUE ○ COPENHAGEN

BY WAY OF MRS. BROWNING • 1911 • *Williams Earle* • USA
BY-WAY OF PROSTITUTION see **SEITENSTRASSE DER PROSTITUTION** • 1967
BY-WAYS OF JASPER • 1937 • Oliver Bill • DOC • CND
BY WHOSE HAND? • 1914 • Terwilliger George W. • USA
BY WHOSE HAND? • 1915 • *Kalem* • USA
BY WHOSE HAND • 1915 • Otto Henry • *American* • USA
BY WHOSE HAND? • 1916 • Durkin James • USA
BY WHOSE HAND? • 1927 • Lang Walter • USA
BY WHOSE HAND? • 1932 • Stoloff Ben • USA
BY WHOSE HAND? see **MYSTERY OF MR. MARKS, THE** • 1914
BY WHOSE HAND? (UKN) see **RUSTLERS OF THE BADLANDS** • 1945
BY WOMAN'S WIT • 1911 • *Vitagraph* • USA
BY WORD OR MOUSE • 1954 • Freleng Friz • ANS • USA
BY YOUR LEAVE • 1935 • Corrigan Lloyd • USA
BYAGSTVO V ROPOTAMO • 1973 • Vulchanov Rangel • BUL • FLIGHT TO THE ROPOTAMO ○ FLIGHT TO ROPOTAMO
BYAKKO NITORYU • 1958 • Kato Tai • JPN • SWORDS OF MYSTERY
BYAKU FUJIN NO YUREN • 1956 • Toyoda Shiro • JPN • BEWITCHING LOVE OF MADAME PAI, THE ○ WHITE SERPENT, THE ○ MADAME WHITE SNAKE
BYAKU-YA NO SHIRABE • 1975 • *Kurahara Komaki* • JPN, USS • LENINGRAD - KYOTO
BYAKURAN NO UTA • 1939 • Watanabe Kunio • JPN • SONG OF THE WHITE ORCHID
BYAKUROJO NO YOKI • 1957 • *Shintoho* • JPN • BEWITCHED SPIRITS OF THE CASTLE OF WHITE WAX, THE
BYAKUYA NO YOJO • 1958 • Takizawa Eisuke • JPN • TEMPTRESS AND THE MONK, THE (USA) ○ DEATH BY WITCHCRAFT ○ TEMPTRESS, THE ○ ENCHANTRESS, THE
BYALATA STAYA • 1968 • Andonov Metodi • BUL • WHITE ROOM, THE
BYC • 1967 • Marzynski Marian • DOC • PLN • TO BE
BYE BYE BABY • 1989 • Oldoini Enrico • ITL
BYE BYE BARBARA • 1968 • Deville Michel • FRN
BYE BYE BIRDIE • 1963 • Sidney George • USA
BYE BYE BLACKBIRD • 1972 • Smith Paul J. • ANS • USA
BYE, BYE BLUEBEARD • 1949 • Davis Arthur • ANS • USA
BYE BYE BLUES • 1989 • Wheeler Anne • CND
BYE BYE BRASIL • 1980 • Diegues Carlos • BRZ • BYE BYE BRAZIL
BYE BYE BRAVERMAN • 1968 • Lumet Sidney • USA
BYE BYE BRAZIL see **BYE BYE BRASIL** • 1980
BYE-BYE BUDDY • 1929 • Mattison Frank S. • USA
BYE BYE BUNTING • 1933 • Fryer Bryant • ANS • CND
BYE BYE CHAPERON ROUGE • 1988 • Meszaros Marta • CND, HNG • PIROSKA ES A FARKAS (HNG) ○ BYE BYE RED RIDING HOOD
BYE BYE MONKEY see **REVE DE SINGE** • 1978
BYE BYE RED RIDING HOOD see **BYE BYE CHAPERON ROUGE** • 1988
BYE BYE SUI GENERIS see **ADIOS SUI GENERIS** • 1976
BYE, BYE, SWEETIE • 1977 • Salem Atef • EGY
'BYE, SEE YOU MONDAY see **AU REVOIR, A LUNDI** • 1980
BYEG INOKHODTSA see **PRASHNAI GULSARA** • 1970
BYELAYA PTITSA S CHORNOY OTMYETINOY • 1972 • Ilyenko Yury • USS • WHITE BIRD WITH THE BLACK MARK, THE ○ WHITE BIRD WITH A BLACK SPOT, THE ○ WHITE BIRD WITH A BLACK MARKING, A
BYELEYET PARUS ODINOKY • 1937 • Legoshin Vladimir • USS • LONE WHITE SAIL, THE ○ LONELY WHITE SAIL
BYELI OREL • 1928 • Protazanov Yakov • USS • LASH OF THE CZAR, THE ○ WHITE EAGLE, THE
BYELI PAROKHOD • 1976 • Shamshiev Bolotbek • USS • WHITE STEAMER, THE ○ WHITE SHIP, THE ○ BELYI PAROKHOD ○ WHITE BOAT, THE
BYELOE SOLNTSE PUOSTINI see **BELOE SOLNTSE PUOSTINI** • 1971
BYELORUSSIAN RAILWAY STATION, THE see **BYELORUSSKI VOKZAL** • 1972
BYELORUSSIAN STATION, THE see **BYELORUSSKI VOKZAL** • 1972
BYELORUSSKI VOKZAL • 1972 • Smirnov Andrei • USS • BYELORUSSIAN RAILWAY STATION, THE ○ BYELORUSSIAN STATION, THE
BYELY, BYELY DYEN • 1974 • Tarkovsky Andrei • USS • WHITE, WHITE DAY, THE ○ BRIGHT, BRIGHT DAY, A
BYELYYE, BYELYYE AISTY • 1967 • Khamraev Ali • USS • WHITE, WHITE STORKS
BYENS HERKULEN • 1918 • Lauritzen Lau • DNM
BYEREG NADYEZHDY • 1967 • Vingranovski Nikolai • USS • SHORES OF HOPE, THE
BYEWAYS OF FATE, THE • 1917 • Kerrigan J. M. • UKN
BYGONES see **VROEGER IS DOOD** • 1987
BYKOWI CHWALA • 1971 • Papuzinski Andrzej • SHT • PLN • GLORY TO THE BULL
BYL JAZZ • 1983 • Falk Feliks • PLN • THAT'S JAZZ ○ AND THERE WAS JAZZ
BYL SOBIE RAZ • 1957 • Borowczyk Walerian, Lenica Jan • ANS • PLN • ONCE UPON A TIME (UKN) ○ ONCE THERE WAS (USA)
BYLEM KAPO • 1965 • Jaworski Tadeusz • DOC • PLN • I WAS A KAPO ○ I WAS KAPO
BYLETH • 1971 • Savona Leopoldo • ITL • DEMONE DELL'INCESTO, IL
BYLI JSME TO MY? • 1990 • Masa Antonin • CZC • WERE WE REALLY LIKE THIS?
BYLO CTVRT A BUDE PUL • 1968 • Cech Vladimir • CZC • IT WAS A QUARTER AND WILL SOON BE HALF PAST ○ BETWEEN HALF PAST AND QUARTER TO
BYLO NAS DESET • 1963 • Kachlik Antonin • CZC • THERE WERE TEN OF US ○ WE WERE TEN
BYLO TO V MAJI • 1951 • Fric Martin, Berdych Vaclav • CZC • MAY EVENTS
BYLO WESELE.. • 1968 • Halladin Danuta • DOC • PLN • WEDDING TOOK PLACE.., A
BYN VID DEN TRIVSAMME BRUNNEN • 1938 • Fejos Paul • DCS • SWD • VILLAGE NEAR THE PLEASANT FOUNTAIN, THE
BYPASS • 1975 • Martin Susan • USA
BYRD IN THE ANDES -A JAZZ ODYSSEY • 1976 • Grofe Ferde Jr. • SHT • USA
BYT • 1968 • Svankmajer Jan • SHT • CZC • FLAT, THE
BYT LISHNIM • 1977 • Brench Alois • USS • TO BE SUPERFLUOUS
BYTVA ZA NASHU RADYANSKU UKRAYINU see **BITVA ZA NASHA SOVIETSKAYA UKRAINU** • 1943
BYZANCE • 1964 • Pialat Maurice • SHT • FRN
BYZANTINE MERCHANT'S TREASURE, THE • 1967 • Novak Ivo • CZC
BYZANTINE RHAPSODY (IMPERIALE), A see **VIZANTINI RAPSODHIA (IMPERIALE)** • 1968
BYZANTINE VILLAIN, THE see **BIZANSLI ZORBA** • 1967
BZ-MAXE & CO. • 1916 • Rippert Otto • FRG

C

"C" • 1959 • *Lateef Ahmed (P)* • SHT • IND • CALICLOTH
C. A. K. POLNI MARSALEK • 1930 • Lamac Carl • CZC • HIS MAJESTY'S FIELD MARSHALL
C.A.S.H. (UKN) see **WHIFFS** • 1975
C.A.T. SQUAD • 1986 • Friedkin William • TVM • USA
C.A.T. SQUAD 2: OPERATION PYTHON WOLF • 1988 • Friedkin William • TVM • USA
C.B. HUSTLERS • 1976 • Segall Stuart • USA
C.C. AND COMPANY • 1970 • Robbie Seymour • USA
C.C.C.I. • 1971 • Chambers Jack* • DOC • CND
C.D. • 1914 • Le Saint Edward J. • USA
C.D.E. • 1922 • Petersen Rolf • FRG • CLUB DER ENTGLEISTEN
C.H.O.M.P.S. • 1979 • Chaffey Don • USA
C.H.U.D. • 1984 • Cheek Douglas • USA
C.H.U.D. 2: BUD THE CHUD see **B.U.D.** • 1988
C.H.U.D. II see **B.U.D.** • 1988
C.I.D.999 FROM GOA see **GOA DALLI C.I.D.999** • 1968
C.I.D. AGENT 302 • 1968 • Azim S. • IND
C.I.V'S MARCHING ABOARD S.S. GARTH CASTLE • 1900 • Hepworth Cecil M. • UKN
C-MAN • 1949 • Lerner Irving • USA
C.O.D. • 1915 • Johnson Tefft • USA
C.O.D. • 1932 • Powell Michael • UKN
C.O.D. • 1982 • Vincent Chuck • USA • SNAP
C.O.P.S. • 1989 • Prior David A. • USA • FUTURE FORCE
C OF C • 1942 • Cooper Budge • DOC • UKN
C.P. -A DAY AT A TIME • 1986 • von Puttkamer Peter • DOC • CND
C.Q.D. • 1909 • *Vitagraph* • USA
C.R.I.A. • 1970 • Whitney Michael • ANS • USA
CA AIDE BEAUCOUP • 1980 • Strong Mike • FRN
CA C'EST DU CINEMA • 1951 • Accursi Claude, Bardonnet Raymond • CMP • FRN
CA C'EST DU SPORT! • 1938 • Pujol Rene • FRN
CA COLLE • 1933 • Christian-Jaque • FRN
CA DEVAIT ARRIVER see **CHRISTINE SE MARIE** • 1945
CA FAIT DU BIEN • 1982 • Pierson Claude • FRN
CA FAIT TILT • 1977 • Hunebelle Andre • FRN • BARATINEUR, LE
CA FREMIT DANS L'ENTRECUISSE • 1980 • Turbay Max, Lirkin Mark • FRN
CA GLISSE PAR LES DEUX TROUS • 1980 • Baudricourt Michel • FRN
CA IRA, IL FIUME DELLA RIVOLTA • 1965 • Brass Tinto • DOC • ITL • TELL IT LIKE IT IS
CA MARCHE • 1970 • Leduc Jacques, Gelbart Arnie • DCS • CND
CA ME TROTTE DANS LA TETE • 1986 • Shekter Louise • CND
CA N'ARRIVE QU'AUX AUTRES • 1971 • Trintignant Nadine • FRN, ITL • IT ONLY HAPPENS TO OTHERS (USA) ○ TEMPO D'AMORE (ITL) ○ VIE EST UNE FETE, LA
CA N'ARRIVE QU'AUX VIVANTS • 1958 • Saytor Tony • FRN
CA N'EST PAS LE TEMPS DES ROMANS • 1967 • Dansereau Fernand • SHT • CND • THIS IS NOT THE TIME FOR ROMANCE
CA PEUT PAS ETRE L'HIVER, ON N'A MEME PAS EU ETE • 1980 • Carre Louis • CND
CA ROULE.. see **AH! QUELLE GARE!** • 1932
CA S'EST PASSE A ROME (FRN) see **GIORNATA BALORDA, LA** • 1960
CA VA BARDER • 1954 • Berry John • FRN, ITL • SILENZIO.. SI SPARA (ITL) ○ THERE GOES BARDER (USA) ○ GIVE 'EM HELL
CA VA, CA VIENT • 1970 • Barouh Pierre • FRN
CA VA ETRE TA FETE • 1960 • Montazel Pierre • FRN
CA VA FAIRE MAL! • 1982 • Davy Jean-Francois • FRN
CA VA PAS ETRE TRISTE! • 1982 • Sisser Pierre • FRN
CA VA PAS LA TETE!? • 1977 • Delpard Raphael • FRN
CAB, THE • 1926 • Elliott William J. • UKN
CAB CALLOWAY'S HI-DE-HO • 1934 • Waller Fred • SHT • USA
CAB CALLOWAY'S JITTERBUG PARTY • 1935 • Waller Fred • SHT • USA
CAB NO.519 see **DROSKE 519** • 1909
CAB WAITING • 1931 • Taurog Norman • SHT • USA
CABALE, LA • 1980 • Cornellier Robert • SHT • CND
CABALGANDO A LA LUNA • 1972 • *Estudios America* • MXC
CABALGANDO HACIA LA MUERTE • 1962 • Romero-Marchent Joaquin Luis • SPN, ITL • SHADOW OF ZORRO, THE (USA) ○ OMBRA DI ZORRO
CABALLA SALVAJE • 1982 • Cortes Joaquin • VNZ
CABALLERIA DEL IMPERIO • 1942 • Contreras Torres Miguel • MXC
CABALLERO A LA MEDIDA • 1953 • Delgado Miguel M. • MXC
CABALLERO ANDALUZ, UN • 1954 • Lucia Luis • SPN
CABALLERO DE FRAC, UN • 1932 • San Martin Conrado • SPN
CABALLERO DE MAX, EL • 1930 • San-Andrews Jaime • CUB
CABALLERO DROOPY • 1952 • Lundy Dick • ANS • USA
CABALLERO FAMOSO, UN • 1942 • Buchs Jose • SPN
CABALLEROS see **SNAPPY CABALLERO, THE** • 1931
CABALLEROS DE LA ANTORCHA, LOS • 1966 • Cervera Pascual • SPN
CABALLEROS DEL BOTON DE ANCLA, LOS • 1972 • Torrado Ramon • SPN
CABALLERO'S WAY, THE • 1914 • *Johnston J. W.* • USA
CABALLITO VOLADOR, EL • 1982 • Joscowicz Alfredo • MXC • LITTLE FLYING HORSE, THE
CABALLO A CABALLO • 1939 • Bustillo Oro Juan • MXC
CABALLO BAYO, EL • 1966 • Cardona Rene • MXC
CABALLO BLANCO, EL • 1961 • Baledon Rafael • MXC, SPN • WHITE HORSE, THE
CABALLO DEL PUEBLO, EL • 1935 • Romero Manuel
CABALLO DIABLO, EL • 1974 • *Cima* • MXC
CABALLO PRIETO AZABACHE • 1965 • Cardona Rene • MXC • TUMBA DE VILLA, LA
CABALLO QUE CANTA, EL • 1963 • Soler Julian • MXC • PAR DE SINVERGUENZAS, UN
CABALLO TORERO, EL • 1972 • *Panorama* • MXC
CABANE, LA • 1973 • Lavoie Richard • CND
CABANE AUX SOUVENIRS, LA • 1946 • Stelli Jean • FRN • HOMME PERDU, UN
CABANE D'AMOUR, LA • 1927 • Bruno-Ruby Jane • FRN • CABIN OF LOVE
CABARET • 1927 • Vignola Robert G. • USA
CABARET • 1945 • Richardson Frank • UKN
CABARET • 1952 • Manzanos Eduardo • SPN
CABARET • 1972 • Fosse Bob • USA
CABARET see **KABARET** • 1964
CABARET, THE • 1918 • Knoles Harley • USA
CABARET DANCER, THE • 1914 • Vignola Robert G. • USA
CABARET DU GRAND LARGE, LE • 1946 • Jayet Rene • FRN
CABARET GIRL, THE • 1919 • Gerrard Douglas • USA
CABARET NIGHTS NOS.1-7 • 1936 • SER • UKN
CABARET SCRATCH, THE • 1917 • Hutchinson Craig • SHT • USA
CABARET SHANGAY see **CABARET SHANGHAI** • 1949
CABARET SHANGHAI • 1949 • Orol Juan • MXC • CABARET SHANGAY
CABARET SINGER, THE • 1913 • Smalley Phillips • USA
CABARET SINGER, THE • 1915 • Moore Tom • USA
CABARET TRAGICO • 1957 • Blake Alfonso Corona • MXC
CABARET (USA) see **DIESES LIED BLIEBT BEI DIR** • 1954
CABARETING UNDER DIFFICULTIES • 1920 • *Katterjohn Comedy* • USA
CABASCABO • 1967 • Ganda Oumarou • NGR
CABASSOU see **AVENTURE DE CABASSOU, L'** • 1945
CABBAGE FAIRY, THE see **FEE AUX CHOUX, LA** • 1896
CABBAGE QUEEN, THE • 1918 • *Howell Alice* • SHT • USA
CABBAGES AND KINGS • 1938 • Alderson John • UKN
CABBY AND THE DEMON • 1913 • *Majestic* • USA
CABBY'S DREAM, THE • 1906 • Raymond Charles? • UKN
CABBY'S NIGHTMARE • 1914 • Melies Georges • FRN
CABBY'S SWEETHEART • 1908 • Fitzhamon Lewin • UKN
CABECAS CORTADAS (BRZ) see **CABEZAS CORTADAS** • 1970
CABELLERA BLANCA • 1950 • Diaz Morales Jose • MXC
CABEZA DE HIERRO • 1944 • Iquino Ignacio F. • SPN
CABEZA DE PANCHO VILLA, LA • 1955 • Urueta Chano • MXC • HEAD OF PANCHO VILLA, THE
CABEZA VIVIENTE, LA • 1961 • Urueta Chano • MXC • LIVING HEAD, THE (USA) ○ OJO DE LA MUERTE, EL
CABEZAS CORTADAS • 1970 • Rocha Glauber • SPN, BRZ • CABECAS CORTADAS (BRZ) ○ CABEZAS ROTAS ○ BROKEN HEADS ○ CUTTING HEADS ○ HEADS THAT ARE CUT ○ SEVERED HEADS
CABEZAS ROTAS see **CABEZAS CORTADAS** • 1970
CABILDO DE NA ROMUALDA • 1908 • Quesada Enrique Diaz • CUB
CABIN BOY, THE • 1911 • Hunt Jay • USA
CABIN IN THE COTTON • 1932 • Curtiz Michael, Keighley William • USA
CABIN IN THE SKY • 1942 • Minnelli Vincente • USA
CABIN OF LOVE see **CABANE D'AMOUR, LA** • 1927
CABINA, LA • 1973 • Bozzetto Bruno • ANM • ITL
CABINET DE MEPHISTOPHELE, LE • 1897 • Melies Georges • FRN • LABORATORY OF MEPHISTOPHELES (USA)
CABINET DES DR. CALIGARI, DAS see **KABINETT DES DR. CALIGARI, DAS** • 1919
CABINET MINISTER, A see **AMATHIKAMA** • 1968
CABINET OF CALIGARI, THE • 1962 • Kay Roger • USA
CABINET OF DR. CALIGARI, THE (USA) see **KABINETT DES DR. CALIGARI, DAS** • 1919
CABINET OF DR. SEGATO, THE see **KABINETT DES DR. SEGATO, DAS** • 1923
CABINET PARTICULIER, UN • 1902 • Blache Alice • FRN • PECULIAR CABINET, A ○ SCENE EN CABINET PARTICULIER VUE A TRAVERS LE TROU DE LA SERRURE, UNE
CABINET TRICK OF THE DAVENPORT BROTHERS (USA) see **ARMOIRE DES FRERES DAVENPORT, L'** • 1902
CABINETS DE PHYSIQUE AU XVIIIeme SIECLE, LES • 1964-69 • Rohmer Eric • MTV • FRN
CABIRIA • 1914 • Pastrone Giovanni • ITL
CABIRIA (UKN) see **NOTTI DI CABIRIA, LE** • 1957
CABITO, EL • 1977 • Oropeza Daniel • VNZ • SMALL ONE, THE
CABLE CAR MURDER, THE see **CROSSCURRENT** • 1971
CABLE SHIP • 1933 • Legg Stuart, Shaw Alexander • UKN
CABMAN KATE • 1915 • Williams C. Jay • USA
CABMAN NO.13 • 1937 • Pekalski Aleksander
CABMAN'S DELUSION • 1907 • *Pathe* • FRN
CABMAN'S GOOD FAIRY, THE • 1909 • Fitzhamon Lewin • UKN
CABMAN'S SECRET DIARY, A see **BIR SOFORUN GIZLI DEFTERI** • 1967
CABO DE HORNOS • 1955 • Davison Tito • MXC, SPN, CHL
CABO DE VARA • 1977 • Artigot Raul • SPN
CABO VERDE DE RELANCE • 1960 • Spiguel Miguel • SHT • PRT
CABOBLANCO • 1979 • Thompson J. Lee • USA
CABOS BLANCOS • 1954 • Van Dyke Willard, Rivera Angel • DOC • USA
CABRA, LA (MXC) see **CHEVRE, LA** • 1981

CABRIOLA see **EVERY DAY IS A HOLIDAY** • 1966

CACA, A • 1963 • de Oliveira Manoel • PRT • HUNT, THE

CACADA DO MALHADEIRO, A • 1968 • Simoes Quirino • PRT • HAMMERER'S CHASE, THE

CACADOR DE ESMERALDAS, O • 1980 • de Oliveira Carlos • BRZ • EMERALD HUNTER, THE

CACCIA AI VIOLENTI (ITL) see **ONE STEP TO HELL** • 1968

CACCIA AL MARITO • 1960 • Girolami Marino • ITL

CACCIA AL MASCHIIO (ITL) see **CHASSE A L'HOMME, LA** • 1964

CACCIA ALLA VOLPE • 1938 • Blasetti Alessandro • DOC • ITL

CACCIA ALLA VOLPE • 1965 • De Sica Vittorio • ITL, UKN • AFTER THE FOX (UKN)

CACCIA ALL'UOMO • 1961 • Freda Riccardo • ITL • DOX, CACCIA ALL'UOMO ○ AVVENTURE DI DOX, LE

CACCIA IN BRUGHIERA • 1949 • Risi Dino • SHT • ITL

CACCIA TRAGICA • 1947 • De Santis Giuseppe • ITL • TRAGIC PURSUIT, THE ○ TRAGIC HUNT (USA) ○ PURSUIT

CACCIATORE 2 • 1981 • Margheriti Antonio • ITL • LAST HUNTER, THE

CACCIATORE DE SQUALI, IL • 1979 • Castellari Enzo G. • ITL, SPN • SHARK HUNTER, THE

CACCIATORI DEL COBRA D'ORO, I see **PREDATORI DEL COBRA D'ORO, I** • 1982

CACCIATORI DI DOTE • 1961 • Amendola Mario • ITL

CACHENCO • Puccio Carlos • DCS • FRG

CACHIVACHE • 1958 • Dawidowicz Enrique • ARG

CACHORRO, EL • 1965 • Martinez Arturo • MXC

CACHORROS, LOS • 1971 • Fons Jorge • MXC

CACIQUES DE SAN CRISPIN, LOS • 1973 • *Cinetelmex* • MXC

CACOULHA DO BARULHO, O • 1949 • Freda Riccardo • ITL

CACTUS • 1960 • Dembinski Lucjan • ANM • PLN

CACTUS • 1986 • Cox Paul • ASL

CACTUS see **GARGA M'BOSE** • 1974

CACTUS ARTIST • 1943 • *O'Brien Joseph/ Mead Thomas (P)* • SHT • USA

CACTUS AT FORTY-FIVE, A • 1913 • *Frontier* • USA

CACTUS BLOSSOM, THE • 1915 • Chatterton Thomas • USA

CACTUS CAPERS • 1942 • Roberts Charles E. • USA

CACTUS CARAVAN • 1950 • Cowan Will • USA

CACTUS COUNTY LAWYER • 1912 • *Gebhardt George* • USA

CACTUS CRANDALL • 1918 • Smith Cliff • USA • CACTUS RANDALL

CACTUS CURE, THE • 1925 • Hayes Ward • USA

CACTUS CUT-UP • 1949 • Roberts Charles E. • SHT • USA

CACTUS FLOWER • 1969 • Saks Gene • USA

CACTUS IN THE SNOW see **YOU CAN'T HAVE EVERYTHING** • 1970

CACTUS JACK (UKN) see **VILLAIN, THE** • 1979

CACTUS JAKE, HEART-BREAKER • 1914 • Mix Tom • USA

CACTUS JIM'S SHOP GIRL • 1915 • *Mix Tom* • USA

CACTUS KID, THE • 1930 • Disney Walt • ANS • USA

CACTUS KID, THE • 1934 • Webb Harry S. • USA

CACTUS KING • 1934 • Stallings George • ANS • USA

CACTUS MAKES PERFECT • 1942 • Lord Del • SHT • USA

CACTUS MY PAL • 1917 • Ford John • USA

CACTUS NELL • 1917 • Fishback Fred C. • SHT • USA

CACTUS RANDALL see **CACTUS CRANDALL** • 1918

CACTUS TRAILS • 1925 • Webb Harry S. • USA

CACTUS TRAILS • 1927 • Pembroke Percy • USA

CAD, A • 1916 • Wilson Ben • USA

CAD AND CADDY • 1947 • Sparber I. • ANS • USA

CADA HIJO UNA CRUZ • 1957 • Bustillo Oro Juan • MXC

CADA LOCO CON SU TEMA • 1938 • Bustillo Oro Juan • MXC

CADA OVEJA CON SU PAREJA • 1964 • Crevenna Alfredo B. • MXC

CADA QUIEN SU LUCHA • 1965 • Martinez Solares Gilberto • MXC

CADA QUIEN SU MUSICA • 1958 • de la Serna Mauricio • MXC

CADA QUIEN SU VIDA • 1959 • Bracho Julio • MXC

CADA VEZ MAS LEJOS see **TARAHUMARA** • 1964

CADA VEZ QUE.. • 1968 • Duran Carlos • SPN • EVERY TIME THAT.. ○ WHENEVER

CADA VOZ LLEVA SU ANGUSTIA • 1964 • Bracho Julio • MXC, CLM

CADANS • 1987 • van Reijen Jan Wouter • SHT • NTH

CADAVER EXQUISITO, EL see **CRUELES, LAS** • 1969

CADAVER IN THE CLUTTER, THE • 1977 • Pevney Joseph • TVM • USA

CADAVERE A SPASSO • 1965 • Masi Marco • ITL

CADAVERE DAGLI ARTIGLI D'ACCIAIO, IL (ITL) see **QUI?** • 1970

CADAVERE DI TROPPO, UN (ITL) see **MAIN A COUPER, LA** • 1974

CADAVERE PER SIGNORA • 1964 • Mattoli Mario • ITL

CADAVERI ECCELLENTI • 1976 • Rosi Francesco • ITL, FRN • CADAVRES EXQUIS (FRN) ○ ILLUSTRIOUS CORPSES ○ CONTESTO, IL ○ CONTEXT, THE

CADAVRES EN VACANCES • 1961 • Audry Jacqueline • FRN • CORPSES ON HOLIDAY

CADAVRES EXQUIS (FRN) see **CADAVERI ECCELLENTI** • 1976

CADDIE • 1976 • Crombie Donald • ASL

CADDIES, THE • 1960 • *Halas John (P)* • ANS • UKN

CADDO LAKE • 1989 • Franklin Carl • USA

CADDY, THE • 1953 • Taurog Norman • USA

CADDY'S DREAM, THE • 1911 • *Majestic* • USA

CADDYSHACK • 1980 • Ramis Harold • USA

CADDYSHACK II • 1988 • Arkush Allan • USA

CADEAU, LE • 1961 • Roberts Richard, Vausseur Jacques • ANS • FRN • PRESENT, THE ○ GIFT, THE

CADEAU, LE • 1982 • Lang Michel • FRN, ITL • GIFT, THE

CADEAU D'OSCAR, LE • 1965 • Coignon Jean • ANS • BLG • GIFT OF OSCAR, THE ○ OSCAR'S GIFT

CADEAU PRECIEUX, UN • 1956 • Rou Aleksandr • USS

CADENA DE AMOR • 1971 • Brocka Lino • PHL

CADENA DE MENTIRAS • 1955 • Fernandez Bustamente Adolfo • MXC

CADENA PERPETUA • 1978 • Ripstein Arturo • MXC • IN FOR LIFE

CADET GIRL • 1941 • McCarey Ray • USA

CADET ROUSSELLE • 1947 • Dunning George, Low Colin • ANS • CND

CADET-ROUSSELLE • 1954 • Hunebelle Andre • FRN • CADET ROUSSELLE

CADET ROUSSELLE see **CADET-ROUSSELLE** • 1954

CADETES DE LA NAVAL • 1944 • Palacios Fernando • MXC

CADETES DE SAN MARTIN • 1939 • Soffici Mario • ARG

CADETS • 1990 • Shopova Kristina • BUL

CADETS DE L'OCEAN • 1942 • Dreville Jean • FRN

CADETS DU CONSERVATOIRE, LES • 1946 • Ciampi Yves • FRN

CADET'S HONOR, A • 1913 • *Excelsior* • USA

CADETS ON PARADE • 1942 • Landers Lew • USA

CADETS ON PARADE (UKN) see **JUNIOR ARMY** • 1942

CADETTE • 1913 • Poirier Leon • FRN

CADETTI DI GUASCOGNA, I • 1950 • Mattoli Mario • ITL

CADEUSE DE MATELAS, LA • 1906 • Melies Georges • FRN • TRAMP AND THE MATTRESS MAKER, THE (USA)

CADIA, EL see **QADIA 68** • 1968

CADILLAC • 1974 • Borsos Philip • SHT • CND

CADOUDAL • 1911 • Bourgeois Gerard • FRN

CADRAN, LE see **CAFE DE CADRAN, LE** • 1946

CADRE AUX SURPRISES, LE • 1904 • Melies Georges • FRN • ASTONISHING FRAME, THE (USA)

CADRES FLEURIS • 1910 • Cohl Emile • ANS • FRN • FLORAL STUDIES

CADRO DE JACK • 1968 • Buenaventura Augusto • PHL

CADUTA DEGLI DEI, LA • 1968 • Visconti Luchino • ITL, FRG • GOTTERDAMMERUNG (FRG) ○ DAMNED, THE (UKN) ○ FALL OF THE GODS, THE

CADUTA DI TROIA, LA • 1910 • Pastrone Giovanni • ITL • FALL OF TROY, THE

CAESAR AGAINST THE PIRATES (USA) see **GIULIO CESARE CONTRO I PIRATI** • 1962

CAESAR AND CLEOPATRA • 1946 • Pascal Gabriel, Hurst Brian Desmond • UKN

CAESAR AND THE DETECTIVES see **CEZAR A DETEKTIVI** • 1967

CAESAR THE CONQUEROR see **GIULIO CESARE IL CONQUISTATORE DELLE GALLIE** • 1963

CAESARIAN -AN OPERETTA see **KAISERSCHNITT -EINE OPERETTE** • 1978

CAESAR'S GHOST • 1922 • *Universal* • SHT • USA

CAFAJESTES, OS • 1962 • Guerra Ruy • BRZ • UNSCRUPULOUS ONES, THE ○ PLAGE DU DESIR, LA

CAFE BAR • 1975 • De Vere Alison • UKN

CAFE BOHEME • 1939 • Schwarzwald Milton • SHT • USA

CAFE CANTANTE • 1951 • Momplet Antonio • MXC

CAFE CHANTANT • 1954 • Mastrocinque Camillo • ITL

CAFE COLETTE • 1937 • Stein Paul L. • UKN • DANGER IN PARIS (USA)

CAFE COLON • 1958 • Alazraki Benito • MXC

CAFE CONCORDIA • 1939 • Gout Alberto • MXC

CAFE DE ANGOLA • 1957 • Spiguel Miguel • SHT • PRT

CAFE DE ANGOLA • 1973 • Mendes Joao • SHT • PRT

CAFE DE CADRAN, LE • 1946 • Gehret Jean, Decoin Henri (U/c) • FRN • CADRAN, LE

CAFE DE CHINITAS • 1960 • Delgras Gonzalo • SPN

CAFE DE CHINOS • 1949 • Rodriguez Joselito • MXC

CAFE DE L'EGYPTE, THE see **CAFE L'EGYPTE, THE** • 1924

CAFE DE L'UNION • 1990 • Probst Dominikus • FRG

CAFE DE PARIS • 1938 • Mirande Yves, Lacombe Georges, Vernay Robert • FRN

CAFE DE PARIS • 1943 • Neville Edgar • SPN

CAFE DES JULES, LE • 1988 • Vecchiali Paul, Nolot Jacques • FRN

CAFE DU PORT, LE • 1939 • Choux Jean • FRN

CAFE ELECTRIC • 1927 • Ucicky Gustav • AUS, FRG • WENN EIN WEIB DEN WEG VERLIERT ○ LIEBESBORSE, DIE

CAFE EXPRESS (USA) see **CAFFE ESPRESSO** • 1979

CAFE FLESH • 1986 • Dream Rinse, Pope F. X. • USA

CAFE FROM THE PAST see **SPOTKANIE W "BAJCE"** • 1962

CAFE HOSTESS • 1940 • Salkow Sidney • USA • STREETS OF MISSING WOMEN

CAFE IN CAIRO, A • 1924 • Withey Chet • USA

CAFE IN PLIUSHIHA STREET see **TRI TOPOLYA NA PLYUSHCHIKHYE** • 1968

CAFE IN THE MAIN STREETS • 1953 • Hubacek Miroslav • CZC

CAFE L'EGYPTE, THE • 1924 • Paul Fred • UKN • CAFE DE L'EGYPTE, THE

CAFE LUNCHRASTEN • 1954 • Faustman Erik • SWD • LUNCHBREAK CAFE, THE

CAFE MASCOT • 1936 • Huntington Lawrence • UKN

CAFE METROPOLE • 1937 • Griffith Edward H. • USA

CAFE MOSCOW see **CAFE MOSZKA** • 1936

CAFE MOSZKA • 1936 • Sekely Steve • HNG • CAFE MOSCOW

CAFE OF SEVEN SINNERS (UKN) see **SEVEN SINNERS** • 1940

CAFE ORIENTAL • 1922 • Schundler Rudolf • FRG

CAFE PARADIS • 1950 • Ipsen Bodil, Lauritzen Lau Jr. • DNM

CAFE SOCIETY • 1939 • Griffith Edward H. • USA

CAFE WAITER'S DREAM see **SONGE D'UN GARCON DE CAFE, LE** • 1910

CAFETAL ADENTRO • 1989 • Malave Carlos • PRC • INSIDE THE COFFEE PLANTATION

CAFFE ASTORIA see **KAVARNA ASTORIA** • 1989

CAFFE DEL PORTO, IL (ITL) see **TOURNANT DANGEREUX, LE** • 1955

CAFFE E UN PIACERE.. SE NON E BUONO CHE PIACERE E?, IL see **CAFFE ESPRESSO** • 1979

CAFFE ESPRESSO • 1979 • Loy Nanni • ITL • CAFE EXPRESS (USA) ○ CAFFE E UN PIACERE.. SE NON E BUONO CHE PIACERE E?, IL

CAFFE ITALIA, MONTREAL • 1986 • Tana Paul • DOC • CND

CAGASOTTO, I see **TERRIBILI SETTE, I** • 1964

CAGE, LA • 1910 • Jasset Victorin • FRN

CAGE, LA • 1975 • Granier-Deferre Pierre • FRN

CAGE, LA see **MAMY WATTA** • 1962

CAGE, THE • 1914 • Tucker George Loane • UKN

CAGE, THE • 1947 • Peterson Sidney • SHT • USA

CAGE, THE • 1989 • Lang Elliott • USA

CAGE, THE see **MAMY WATTA** • 1962

CAGE, THE see **STAR TREK -THE CAGE** • 1964

CAGE, THE see **MAFU CAGE, THE** • 1978

CAGE, THE see **GABBIA, LA** • 1985

CAGE AUX FILLES, LA • 1949 • Cloche Maurice • FRN • CAGE OF GIRLS

CAGE AUX FOLLES 3: ELLE SE MARIENT see **CAGE AUX FOLLES III, LA** • 1986

CAGE AUX FOLLES, LA • 1978 • Molinaro Edouard • FRN, ITL • CAGE AUX FOLLES -BIRDS OF A FEATHER, LA (USA) ○ BIRDS OF A FEATHER

CAGE AUX FOLLES -BIRDS OF A FEATHER, LA (USA) see **CAGE AUX FOLLES, LA** • 1978

CAGE AUX FOLLES II, LA • 1980 • Molinaro Edouard • FRN, ITL

CAGE AUX FOLLES III, LA • 1986 • Lautner Georges • FRN • CAGE AUX FOLLES III: THE WEDDING, LA (USA) ○ CAGE AUX FOLLES 3: ELLE SE MARIENT

CAGE AUX FOLLES III: THE WEDDING, LA (USA) see **CAGE AUX FOLLES III, LA** • 1986

CAGE AUX OURS, LA • 1974 • Handwerker Marian • BLG • BEAR CAGE, THE

CAGE AUX ROSSIGNOLS, LA • 1943 • Dreville Jean • FRN • CAGE OF NIGHTINGALES, A (USA)

CAGE AUX SOURIS, LA • 1954 • Gourguet Jean • FRN

CAGE DE PIERRE, LA • Zucca Pierre • FRN

CAGE DE VERRE, LA • 1964 • Arthuys Philippe, Levi-Alvares Jean-Louis • FRN, ISR • GLASS CAGE, THE (UKN)

CAGE FOR HUSBANDS see **OTTOBI KAGO** • 1952

CAGE FOR TWO, A see **KLEC PRO DVA** • 1967

CAGE FRIGHT • 1952 • Kneitel Seymour • ANS • USA

CAGE MAN, THE • 1916 • Jaccard Jacques • SHT • USA

CAGE OF DOOM (UKN) see **TERROR FROM THE YEAR 5000** • 1958

CAGE OF EVIL • 1960 • Cahn Edward L. • USA

CAGE OF GIRLS see **CAGE AUX FILLES, LA** • 1949

CAGE OF GOLD • 1950 • Dearden Basil • UKN

CAGE OF NIGHTINGALES, A (USA) see **CAGE AUX ROSSIGNOLS, LA** • 1943

CAGE WITHOUT A KEY • 1975 • Kulik Buzz • TVM • USA

CAGED • 1950 • Cromwell John • USA • LOCKED IN

CAGED see **NELLA CITTA L'INFERNO** • 1958

CAGED BIRD, THE • 1913 • *Snow Marguerite* • USA

CAGED DESIRES • 1970 • Davis Don • USA

CAGED FURY • 1948 • Berke William • USA

CAGED FURY • 1984 • Santiago Cirio H. • USA

CAGED HEART, THE see **ADDITION, L'** • 1984

CAGED HEAT • 1974 • Demme Jonathan • USA • RENEGADE GIRLS

CAGED VAMPIRES see **VIERGES ET VAMPIRES** • 1972

CAGED VIRGINS see **VIERGES ET VAMPIRES** • 1972

CAGED WOMEN • 1970 • *Cosmos Films* • USA

CAGED WOMEN see **EMANUELLE REPORTAGE DA UN CARCERE FEMMINILE** • 1982

CAGES • 1983 • Pal Deep • DOC • IND

CAGES see **KLATKI** • 1967

CAGEY BIRD • 1946 • Swift Howard • ANS • USA

CAGEY BUSINESS • 1965 • Post Howard • ANS • USA

CAGEY CANARY, THE • 1941 • Avery Tex • ANS • USA

CAGLIOSTRO • 1910 • *Du Montel Helene* • FRN • CAGLIOSTRO AND THE SEERESS

CAGLIOSTRO • 1928 • *De Liguoro Rino* • ITL

CAGLIOSTRO • 1928 • Oswald Richard • FRN

CAGLIOSTRO • 1975 • Pettinari Daniele • ITL

CAGLIOSTRO AND THE SEERESS see **CAGLIOSTRO** • 1910

CAGLIOSTRO (USA) see **GRAF VON CAGLIOSTRO, DER** • 1920

CAGLIOSTRO'S DEAD HAND see **CAGLIOSTROS TOTENHAND** • 1919

CAGLIOSTRO'S FOLDING SCREEN see **BIOMBO DE CAGLIOSTRO, EL** • 1910

CAGLIOSTRO'S MIRROR (USA) see **MIROIR DE CAGLIOSTRO, LE** • 1899

CAGLIOSTROS TOTENHAND • 1919 • Chrisander Nils • FRG • CAGLIOSTRO'S DEAD HAND

CAGNA, LA • 1972 • Ferreri Marco • ITL, FRN • LOVE TO ETERNITY (UKN) ○ MELAMPO ○ LIZA

CAGNEY & LACEY • 1981 • Post Ted • TVM • USA

CAGNEY & LACEY: A FAIR SHAKE • 1988 • Badiyi Reza • TVM • USA

CAGNEY & LACEY: TURN, TURN, TURN • 1987 • Miller Sharron • TVM • USA

CAGOULE, LA • 1970 • Tolbi Abdelaziz • ALG

CAHIBU AL-JALALA • 1963 • Wahab Fatin Abdel • EGY • SA MAJESTE

CAHILL see **CAHILL -U.S. MARSHAL** • 1973

CAHILL -U.S. MARSHAL • 1973 • McLaglen Andrew V. • USA • CAHILL -UNITED STATES MARSHAL ○ CAHILL ○ WEDNESDAY MORNING

CAHILL -UNITED STATES MARSHAL see **CAHILL -U.S. MARSHAL** • 1973

CAICARA • 1950 • Cavalcanti Alberto (U/c), Celi Adolfo • BRZ • LOAFER

CAID, LE • 1960 • Borderie Bernard • FRN

CAID, LE see **DERNIERE CHEVAUCHEE, LA** • 1946

CAID DE CHAMPIGNOL, LE • 1965 • Bastia Jean • FRN

CAIDA, LA • 1959 • Torre-Nilsson Leopoldo • ARG • FALL, THE

CAIDA DEL CONDOR, LA • 1982 • Alarcon Sebastian • FALL OF THE CONDOR, THE

CAIDOS EN EL INFIERNO • 1954 • Amadori Luis Cesar • ARG • FALLEN IN HELL, THE

CAIDS, LES • 1968 • Santiago Hugo • ARG

CAIDS, LES • 1972 • Enrico Robert • FRN • HELL BELOW, THE (UKN)

CAIFANES, LOS • 1966 • Ibanez Juan • MXC

CAILLAUX CASE, THE • 1918 • Stanton Richard • USA

CAILLE, LA see **ON N'AIME QU-UNE FOIS** • 1949

CAILLES SUR CANAPE • Korber Serge • FRN

CAIMAN DEL ORINOCO, EL • 1979 • Sole Jorge • DOC • VNZ • ORINOCO CAYMAN, THE

CAIMANO DEL PIAVE, IL • 1950 • Bianchi Giorgio • ITL

CAIN • 1965 • Patry Pierre • CND

CAIN 18TH • 1963 • Kosheverova Nadezhda, Shapiro Mikhail • USS

CAIN ADOLESCENTE • 1959 • Chalbaud Roman • VNZ • ADOLESCENT CAIN

CAIN AND ABEL • 1911 • *Vitagraph* • USA

CAIN AND ABEL see **CAIN ET ABEL** • 1911

CAIN AND ARTEM • 1930 • Petrov-Bytov P. • USS
CAIN AND MABEL • 1936 • Bacon Lloyd • USA
CAIN AND MABEL see **GREAT WHITE WAY, THE** • 1924
CAIN AT ABEL • 1982 • Brocka Lino • PHL
CAIN, AVENTURES DES MERS EXOTIQUES • 1930 • Poirier Leon • FRN
CAIN DE NULLE PART • 1969 • Daert Daniel • FRN • VOYAGE POUR L'ENFER DES PASSIONS
CAIN ET ABEL • 1911 • Andreani Henri • FRN • CAIN AND ABEL
CAIN Y ABEL • 1954 • Cardona Rene • MXC
CAINE see **SHARK!** • 1969
CAINE MUTINY, THE • 1954 • Dmytryk Edward • USA
CAINE MUTINY COURT MARTIAL, THE • 1987 • Altman Robert • TVM • USA
CAINGANGUE • 1973 • Christensen Carlos Hugo • ARG
CAINO E ABELE • 1973 • Vernuccio Gianni • ITL
CAIN'S CUTTHROATS see **CAIN'S WAY** • 1970
CAIN'S RETRIBUTION • 1911 • *Ambrosio* • USA
CAIN'S WAY • 1970 • Osborne Kent, Dell Budd • USA • BLOOD SEEKERS, THE ○ CAIN'S CUTTHROATS
CAIRE '30, LE see **CAIRO 30** • 1966
CAIRE 1830, LE see **QAHIR 1830, AL-** • 1969
CAIRO • 1942 • Van Dyke W. S. • USA
CAIRO • 1963 • Rilla Wolf • UKN
CAIRO 30 • 1966 • Abu Saif Salah • EGY • AL-QAHIRA THALATHIN ○ CAIRE '30, LE
CAIRO: CENTRAL STATION see **BAB EL HADID** • 1957
CAIRO ROAD • 1950 • MacDonald David • UKN • POISON ROAD
CAIRO STATION see **BAB EL HADID** • 1957
CAIS DO SOBRE • 1946 • Perla Alejandro • PRT
CAISSES POPULAIRES DESJARDINS, LES • 1945 • Palardy Jean • DCS • CND
CAISSONBOUW ROTTERDAM • 1929 • Ivens Joris • SHT • NTH
CAIUS JULIUS CAESAR • 1914 • Guazzoni Enrico • ITL
CAKE, THE • Richly Zsolt • ANS • HNG
CAKE EATER, THE • 1924 • Howe J. A. • SHT • USA
CAKE IN THE SKY (USA) see **TORTA IN CIELO, UNA** • 1970
CAKE-WALK DE LA PENDULE, LE • 1904 • Blache Alice • FRN
CAKE-WALK INFERNAL, LE • 1903 • Melies Georges • FRN • CAKE WALK INFERNAL, THE (USA) ○ INFERNAL CAKEWALK, THE
CAKE WALK INFERNAL, THE (USA) see **CAKE-WALK INFERNAL, LE** • 1903
CAKES OF KHANDIPORE, THE • 1915 • Aylott Dave • UKN
CAKEWALK, THE • 1902 • Smith G. A. • UKN
CAL • 1984 • O'Connor Pat • UKN
CAL MARVIN'S WIFE • 1915 • Davis Ulysses • USA
CAL TJADER QUINTET • 1962 • Binder Steve • SHT • USA
CALA NAPRZOD • 1967 • Lenartowicz Stanislaw • PLN • FULL STEAM AHEAD ○ FULL AHEAD ○ FORWARD
CALABACITAS TIERNAS • 1948 • Martinez Solares Gilberto • MXC • TENDER LITTLE PUMPKINS
CALABOOSE • 1943 • Roach Hal Jr. • USA
CALABOOSE • 1943 • Tryon Glenn • USA
CALABUCH (SPN) see **CALABUIG** • 1956
CALABUIG • 1956 • Berlanga Luis Garcia • SPN, ITL • ROCKET FROM CALABUCH (USA) ○ CALABUCH (SPN)
CALAFURIA • 1943 • Calzavara Flavio • ITL
CALAIS – DOUVRES • 1931 • Boyer Jean, Litvak Anatole • FRN
CALAMARI UNION • 1985 • Kaurismaki Aki • FNL
CALAMITA D'ORO • 1949 • Fizzarotti Armando • ITL
CALAMITOUS ELOPEMENT, A • 1908 • Griffith D. W. • USA
CALAMITY see **KALAMITA** • 1978
CALAMITY ANN, GUARDIAN • 1916 • *Lester Louise* • USA
CALAMITY ANNE, DETECTIVE • 1913 • Dwan Allan • USA
CALAMITY ANNE, HEROINE • 1913 • *Lester Louise* • USA
CALAMITY ANNE IN SOCIETY • 1914 • *Lester Louise* • USA
CALAMITY ANNE PARCEL POST • 1913 • Dwan Allan • USA
CALAMITY ANNE TAKES A TRIP • 1913 • *Lester Louise* • USA
CALAMITY ANNE'S BEAUTY • 1913 • Dwan Allan • USA
CALAMITY ANNE'S DREAM • 1913 • *Lester Louise* • USA
CALAMITY ANNE'S INHERITANCE • 1913 • Dwan Allan • USA
CALAMITY ANNE'S LEGACY • 1917 • *American* • SHT • USA
CALAMITY ANNE'S LOVE AFFAIR • 1914 • Ricketts Thomas • USA
CALAMITY ANNE'S NEW JOB • 1917 • *Lester Louise* • SHT • USA
CALAMITY ANNE'S PROTEGE • 1917 • *Lester Louise* • SHT • USA
CALAMITY ANNE'S SACRIFICE • 1913 • *Lester Louise* • USA
CALAMITY ANNE'S TRUST • 1913 • Dwan Allan • USA
CALAMITY ANNE'S VANITY • 1913 • Dwan Allan • USA
CALAMITY ANNE'S WARD • 1912 • Dwan Allan • USA
CALAMITY JANE • 1953 • Butler David • USA
CALAMITY JANE • 1984 • Goldstone James • TVM • USA
CALAMITY JANE AND SAM BASS • 1949 • Sherman George • USA
CALAMITY THE COW • 1967 • Eastman David • UKN
CALAMO • 1976 • Pirri Massimo • ITL
CALANDA • 1966 • Bunuel Juan • DOC • FRN
CALANDRIA, LA • 1933 • de Fuentes Fernando • MXC
CALANDRIA, LA • 1972 • Festa Campanile Pasquale • ITL
CALAVERA, LA • 1954 • Borcosque Carlos • ARG • SKULL, THE
CALAVERA NEGRA, LA • 1959 • Rodriguez Joselito • MXC • BLACK SKULL, THE
CALAVERAS • 1969 • Colombat Jacques • ANM • FRN
CALAVERAS DEL TERROR, LAS • 1943 • Mendez Fernando • SRL • MXC
CALCULATED RISK • 1963 • Harrison Norman, Spiro Julian • UKN
CALCULUS AFFAIR, THE see **TINTIN: THE CALCULUS AFFAIR**
CALCUTTA • 1947 • Farrow John • USA
CALCUTTA • 1968 • Malle Louis • FRN
CALCUTTA • 1970 • Cox Paul • SHT • ASL
CALCUTTA '71 • 1972 • Sen Mrinal • IND
CALCUTTA CRUEL CITY see **DO BIGHA ZAMIN** • 1953
CALDA NOTTE DI EMANUELLE, LA • 1979 • Vari Giuseppe • ITL
CALDA PELLE, LA (ITL) see **DE L'AMOUR** • 1964
CALDA PREDA, LA (ITL) see **CUREE, LA** • 1966
CALDA VITA, LA • 1963 • Vancini Florestano • ITL, FRN
CALDE LABBRA • 1976 • Fidani Demofilo • ITL • EXCITATION
CALDE NOTTE DEL DECAMERON, LE • 1972 • Callegari Gian Paolo • ITL
CALDE NOTTI DI DON GIOVANNI, LE • 1971 • Brescia Alfonso • ITL • NIGHTS AND LOVES OF DON JUAN, THE
CALDE NOTTI DI LADY HAMILTON, LE (ITL) see **LADY HAMILTON ZWISCHEN SCHMACH UND LIEBE** • 1968
CALDE NOTTI DI POPPEA, LE • 1969 • Malatesta Guido • ITL
CALDI AMORE DI UNA MINORENNE, I • 1969 • Buchs Julio • ITL, SPN • AGAIN (UKN) ○ PERVERSION STORY
CALDONIA • 1945 • Crouch William Forest • SHT • USA
CALEB PIPER'S GIRL • 1919 • Traxler Ernest • USA
CALEB WEST • 1912 • *Sullivan E. P.* • USA
CALEB WEST, MASTER DIVER see **DEEP WATERS** • 1920
CALEIDOSCOPE • 1968 • Wiertsema Jan • SHT • NTH
CALENDAR, THE • 1931 • Hunter T. Hayes • UKN • BACHELOR'S FOLLY (USA)
CALENDAR, THE • 1948 • Crabtree Arthur • UKN
CALENDAR GIRL • 1947 • Dwan Allan • USA
CALENDAR GIRL, THE • 1917 • Sturgeon Rollin S. • USA
CALENDAR OF THE YEAR • 1937 • Cherry Evelyn Spice • DOC • UKN
CALENDAR OF WOMEN see **ONNA NO KOYOMI** • 1954
CALENDAR PIN-UP GIRLS • 1966 • Roscoe John • USA • CALENDAR PIN-UPS
CALENDAR PIN-UPS see **CALENDAR PIN-UP GIRLS** • 1966
CALETA OLVIDIDA, LA • 1958 • Gebel Bruno • CHL • FORGOTTEN COVE, THE ○ FORGOTTEN CREEK, THE
CALF SKIN • 1963 • Weintraub William • DOC • CND
CALGARY STAMPEDE, THE • 1925 • Blache Herbert • USA
CALHOUN see **NIGHTSTICK** • 1987
CALI: TOWN OF AMERICA • 1974 • Giraldo Diego Leon • SHT • CLM
CALIBRE 9 see **MILANO CALIBRO 9** • 1972
CALIBRE 38 • 1919 • Lewis Edgar • USA
CALIBRE 44 • 1959 • Soler Julian • MXC
CALIBRE 45 • 1924 • McGowan J. P.?, Nelson Jack? • USA
CALIBRE .357 • 1982 • Nicart Eddie • PHL
CALIBRO 38 (ITL) see **HOMME QUI TRAHIT LA MAFIA, L'** • 1967
CALICHE SANGRIENTO • 1969 • Soto Helvio • CHL • BLOODY SALTPETRE
CALICLOTH see **"C"** • 1959
CALICO CAT, THE • 1914 • *Edison* • USA
CALICO DRAGON, THE • 1935 • Ising Rudolf • ANS • USA
CALICO PONY, THE see **COUNT THREE AND PRAY** • 1955
CALICO QUEEN, THE see **HANGING OF JAKE ELLIS, THE** • 1969
CALICO SHERIFF, THE see **SECOND TIME AROUND, THE** • 1961
CALICO VAMPIRE, THE • 1916 • *Tincher Fay* • SHT • USA
CALICOWANI • 1913 • *Crystal* • USA
CALIDO VERANO DEL SENOR RODRIGUEZ, EL • 1963 • Lazaga Pedro • SPN
CALIENTE LOVE • 1933 • Marshall George • SHT • USA
CALIFAR'S MILL • 1985 • Marinescu Serban • RMN
CALIFFA, LA • 1970 • Bevilacqua Alberto • ITL, FRN
CALIFORNIA • 1927 • Van Dyke W. S. • USA
CALIFORNIA • 1946 • Farrow John • USA
CALIFORNIA • 1963 • Petroff Hamil • TVM • USA
CALIFORNIA • 1977 • Lupo Michele • ITL
CALIFORNIA ADDIO • 1977 • Lupo Michele • ITL
CALIFORNIA AXE MASSACRE • 1974 • Friedel Frederick R. • USA • LISA, LISA ○ AXE
CALIFORNIA BULLS • 1987 • *Burke Delta* • USA
CALIFORNIA CONQUEST • 1952 • Landers Lew • USA
CALIFORNIA DOLLS, THE (UKN) see **ALL THE MARBLES** • 1981
CALIFORNIA DREAMING • 1979 • Hancock John • USA
CALIFORNIA DREAMING • 1989 • Wilson Sandra • USA
CALIFORNIA DRIVE-IN GIRLS see **CARHOPS** • 1980
CALIFORNIA FIREBRAND • 1948 • Ford Philip • USA
CALIFORNIA FRONTIER • 1939 • Clifton Elmer • USA
CALIFORNIA GIRLS • 1982 • Webb William • USA
CALIFORNIA GIRLS • 1985 • Wallace Rick • TVM • USA
CALIFORNIA GOLD RUSH • 1946 • Springsteen R. G. • USA
CALIFORNIA GOLD RUSH • 1981 • Hively Jack • TVM • USA
CALIFORNIA HOLIDAY (UKN) see **SPINOUT** • 1966
CALIFORNIA IN '49 • 1924 • Jaccard Jacques • USA
CALIFORNIA IN 1878 see **FIGHTING THRU: OR, CALIFORNIA IN 1878** • 1930
CALIFORNIA JOE • 1944 • Bennet Spencer Gordon • USA
CALIFORNIA JUNIOR SYMPHONY • 1942 • Negulesco Jean • SHT • USA
CALIFORNIA KID, THE • 1974 • Heffron Richard T. • TVM • USA
CALIFORNIA LOVE STORY, A • 1911 • *American* • USA
CALIFORNIA MAIL, THE • 1929 • Rogell Albert S. • USA
CALIFORNIA MAIL, THE • 1937 • Smith Noel • USA
CALIFORNIA MOVIE • 1971 • Burke Martyn • CND
CALIFORNIA OIL CROOKS • 1913 • *Sais Marin* • USA
CALIFORNIA OR BUST • 1917 • Rosen Phil • USA
CALIFORNIA OR BUST • 1923 • Roach Hal • SHT • USA
CALIFORNIA OR BUST • 1927 • Rosen Phil • USA
CALIFORNIA OR BUST • 1941 • French Lloyd • SHT • USA
CALIFORNIA OUTPOST see **OLD LOS ANGELES** • 1948
CALIFORNIA PASSAGE • 1950 • Kane Joseph • USA
CALIFORNIA REICH, THE • 1976 • Parkes Walter, Critchlow Keith F. • DOC • USA
CALIFORNIA REVOLUTION OF 1846, THE • 1911 • *Kalem* • USA
CALIFORNIA ROMANCE, A • 1922 • Storm Jerome • USA • ACROSS THE BORDER
CALIFORNIA SNIPE HUNT, A • 1912 • *Kalem* • USA
CALIFORNIA SPLIT • 1974 • Altman Robert • USA
CALIFORNIA STRAIGHT AHEAD • 1925 • Pollard Harry • USA
CALIFORNIA STRAIGHT AHEAD • 1937 • Lubin Arthur • USA
CALIFORNIA SUITE • 1978 • Ross Herbert • USA
CALIFORNIA TRAIL, THE • 1933 • Hillyer Lambert • USA
CALIFORNIAN, THE see **CALIFORNIANS, THE** • 1937
CALIFORNIANS, THE • 1937 • Meins Gus • USA • BEYOND THE LAW (UKN) ○ GENTLEMAN FROM CALIFORNIA, THE ○ CALIFORNIAN, THE
CALIFORNY 'ER BUST • 1945 • Kinney Jack • ANS • USA
CALIGOLA • 1977 • Brass Tinto • ITL, USA • CALIGULA (USA)
CALIGULA • 1916 • Guazzoni Enrico • ITL
CALIGULA AND MESSALINA see **CALIGULA E MESSALINA** • 1982
CALIGULA E MESSALINA • 1982 • Passalia Antonio • ITL, FRN • FALL AND RISE OF THE ROMAN EMPIRE, THE ○ CALIGULA ET MESSALINA ○ CALIGULA AND MESSALINA
CALIGULA EROTICA • 1977 • Montero Roberto Bianchi • ITL • CALIGULA'S HOT NIGHTS
CALIGULA ET MESSALINA see **CALIGULA E MESSALINA** • 1982
CALIGULA: THE UNTOLD STORY • D'Amato Joe • ITL, USA • EMPEROR CALIGULA: THE UNTOLD STORY
CALIGULA (USA) see **CALIGOLA** • 1977
CALIGULA'S HOT NIGHTS see **CALIGULA EROTICA** • 1977
CALINO • 1910 • Durand Jean • SER • FRN
CALINO AMONG THE CANNIBALS • 1909 • Durand Jean • FRN
CALINO COURTIER EN PARATONNERRES • 1910 • Durand Jean • FRN
CALINO GARDIEN DE PRISON • 1910 • Durand Jean • FRN
CALINO'S NEW INVENTION • 1912 • Durand Jean • FRN
CALIPH OF THE NEW BAGDAD, A • 1916 • Brooke Van Dyke • SHT • USA
CALIPH STORK • 1954 • Reiniger Lotte • ANS • UKN
CALIPH'S ADVENTURES, THE • 1909 • *Nordisk* • DNM
CALL, THE • 1910 • Griffith D. W. • USA
CALL, THE • 1913 • Ince Ralph • *Vitagraph* • USA
CALL, THE • 1913 • Smalley Phillips • *Rex* • USA
CALL, THE • 1914 • Hepworth Cecil M. • UKN • HIS COUNTRY'S BIDDING
CALL, THE see **RUF, DER** • 1949
CALL, THE see **LLAMADA, LA** • 1965
CALL, THE see **WEZWANIE** • 1971
CALL, THE (USA) see **APPEL DU SILENCE, L'** • 1936
CALL A COP • 1921 • St. Clair Malcolm • SHT • USA
CALL A COP! • 1931 • Stevens George • SHT • USA
CALL A MESSENGER • 1939 • Lubin Arthur • USA
CALL A TAXI • 1920 • Roach Hal • SHT • USA
CALL BACK, THE • 1914 • *Victor* • USA
CALL BACK YESTERDAY • 1960 • *Williams Derek* • SHT • UKN
CALL DETROIT 9000 (UKN) see **DETROIT 9000** • 1973
CALL FOR ARMS, A • 1940 • Hurst Brian Desmond • UKN
CALL FOR HELP, THE • 1917 • McRae Henry • SHT • USA
CALL FOR MR. CAVE MAN • 1919 • Roach Hal • SHT • USA
CALL FROM HOME, A • 1913 • Smalley Phillips • USA
CALL FROM THE DEAD, A • 1915 • *Cook Ethyle* • USA
CALL FROM THE HILLS, THE • 1911 • *Powers* • USA
CALL FROM THE PAST, A • 1915 • Wilson Frank? • UKN
CALL FROM THE WILD, THE • 1921 • James Wharton • USA
CALL GIRL • Myler Elias • FRN
CALL-GIRL • 1976 • Martin Eugenio • SPN • VIDA PRIVADA DE UNA SENORITA BIEN
CALL GIRL see **MODELS INC.** • 1952
CALL GIRL 777 see **SURFTIDE 77** • 1962
CALL GIRL BUSINESS see **ANONIMA COCOTTES** • 1960
CALL GIRLS, THE • Lung Kong • HKG
CALL GIRLS OF COPENHAGEN see **VILLA VENNELY** • 1964
CALL GIRLS OF FRANKFURT (USA) see **IN FRANKFURT SIND DIE NACHTE HEISS** • 1966
CALL HARRY CROWN (UKN) see **99 AND 44/100% DEAD** • 1974
CALL HER MOM • 1971 • Paris Jerry • TVM • USA
CALL HER SAUSAGE • 1927 • *Blue Ben* • SHT • USA
CALL HER SAVAGE • 1932 • Dillon John Francis • USA
CALL HIM MR. SHATTER • 1975 • Carreras Michael, Hellman Monte, Hessler Gordon (U/c) • UKN, CHN • MISTER SHATTER ○ SHATTER
CALL HIM WHISKERS • 1913 • *Gem* • USA
CALL IT A DAY • 1937 • Mayo Archie • USA
CALL IT LUCK • 1934 • Tinling James • USA
CALL IT MURDER see **MIDNIGHT** • 1934
CALL LOAN, THE • 1920 • Smith David • SHT • USA
CALL ME • 1988 • Mitchell Sollace • USA
CALL ME A CAB • 1963 • Thomas Gerald • UKN • CARRY ON CABBY
CALL ME A TAXI • 1964 • Kneitel Seymour • ANS • USA
CALL ME BAD (USA) see **DIANA CAZADORA, LA** • 1956
CALL ME BWANA • 1963 • Douglas Gordon • UKN
CALL ME GENIUS (USA) see **REBEL, THE** • 1960
CALL ME LUCKY • 1973 • Van Der Watt Keith • SAF • JUST CALL ME LUCKY
CALL ME MADAM • 1953 • Lang Walter • USA
CALL ME MAME • 1933 • Daumery John • UKN
CALL ME MISTER • 1951 • Bacon Lloyd • USA
CALL ME ROBERT • Ungvald-Hilkevich George • USS • FORMULA OF THE RAINBOW, THE ○ ITS NAME WAS ROBERT
CALL ME ROBERT see **YEVO ZOVUT ROBERT** • 1967
CALL ME ROCKEFELLER see **MOW MI ROCKEFELLER** • 1990
CALL ME SAVAGE (UKN) see **SAUVAGE, LE** • 1975
CALL NORTHSIDE 777 • 1948 • Hathaway Henry • USA • CALLING NORTHSIDE 777
CALL OF A SONG, THE • 1915 • *Browne H. A.* • UKN
CALL OF BOB WHITE, THE • 1919 • *Guinan Texas* • USA
CALL OF COURAGE, THE • 1925 • Smith Cliff • USA
CALL OF FLESH, THE see **JOTAI** • 1964
CALL OF GOD, THE • 1927 • *Amir Aziza* • EGY • LAILA
CALL OF HEARTS, THE • 1917 • Stahl John M. • USA
CALL OF HER CHILD, THE • 1915 • Reehm George E. • USA
CALL OF HER HEART, THE • 1913 • Nicholls George • USA
CALL OF HER PEOPLE, THE • 1917 • Noble John W. • USA
CALL OF HIS PEOPLE, THE • 1922 • *Brown George Edward* • USA
CALL OF HOME • 1922 • Gasnier Louis J. • USA
CALL OF JUSTICE, THE (UKN) see **OUTLAWS OF THE RANGE** • 1936
CALL OF MEXICO, THE see **MEKISHIKO MUSHUKU** • 1962
CALL OF MOTHERHOOD, THE • 1915 • *Wilbur Crane* • USA
CALL OF SIVA, THE • 1923 • Coleby A. E. • UKN
CALL OF SPRING • 1918 • *Pyramid* • SHT • USA
CALL OF SPRING, THE see **PRIZIVANJE PROLJECA** • 1979

CALL OF THE ANGELUS • 1913 • *Frontier* • USA
CALL OF THE BLOOD • 1948 • Clements John, Vajda Ladislao • UKN
CALL OF THE BLOOD see **APPEL DU SANG, L'** • 1919
CALL OF THE BLOOD, THE • 1910 • *Lanning Frank* • USA
CALL OF THE BLOOD, THE • 1912 • *Lehr Anna* • USA
CALL OF THE BLOOD, THE • 1913 • *Patheplay* • USA
CALL OF THE CANYON, THE • 1923 • Fleming Victor • USA
CALL OF THE CANYON, THE • 1942 • Santley Joseph • USA
CALL OF THE CIRCUS, THE • 1910 • Salter Harry • USA
CALL OF THE CIRCUS, THE • 1930 • O'Connor Frank • USA
CALL OF THE CITY, THE • 1915 • Beaumont Harry • USA
CALL OF THE CUCKOO, THE • 1927 • Bruckman Clyde • SHT • USA
CALL OF THE CUMBERLANDS, THE • 1915 • Lloyd Frank • USA
CALL OF THE CUMBERLANDS, THE • 1916 • Ivers Julia Crawford • USA
CALL OF THE DANCE, THE • 1915 • Sargent George L. • USA
CALL OF THE DEMONS, THE see **VOLANIE DEMONOV** • 1967
CALL OF THE DESERT • 1930 • McGowan J. P. • USA
CALL OF THE DESERT ,THE • 1912 • *Nestor* • USA
CALL OF THE DESERT, THE • 1916 • *Hiawatha* • USA
CALL OF THE DRUM • 1912 • *Fischer Marguerite* • USA
CALL OF THE DRUM, THE • 1914 • Weston Harold • UKN
CALL OF THE EAST, THE • 1917 • Melford George • USA
CALL OF THE EAST, THE • 1922 • Wynne Bert • UKN • HIS SUPREME SACRIFICE
CALL OF THE FLESH • 1930 • Brabin Charles J. • USA • SINGER OF SEVILLE, THE
CALL OF THE FOOTLIGHTS • 1914 • France Charles H. • USA
CALL OF THE FOREST • 1949 • Link John F. • USA
CALL OF THE FRONT, THE • 1983 • Van Long • VTN
CALL OF THE HEART • 1915 • *Balboa* • USA
CALL OF THE HEART • 1928 • Ford Francis • USA
CALL OF THE HEART see **HER CODE OF HONOR** • 1919
CALL OF THE HEART, THE • 1909 • *Lubin* • USA
CALL OF THE HEART, THE • 1910 • *Vitagraph* • USA
CALL OF THE HEART, THE • 1911 • *Powers* • USA
CALL OF THE HEART, THE • 1916 • *Supreme* • SHT • USA
CALL OF THE HEART, THE see **DIL NE PUKARA** • 1967
CALL OF THE HILLS, THE • 1923 • Hornby Fred • USA
CALL OF THE HOUR, THE see **LLAMADO DE LA HORA, EL** • 1970
CALL OF THE JUNGLE • 1944 • Rosen Phil • USA
CALL OF THE KLONDIKE • 1950 • McDonald Frank • USA
CALL OF THE KLONDIKE, THE • 1926 • Apfel Oscar • USA
CALL OF THE MATE • 1924 • Neitz Alvin J. • USA
CALL OF THE MOTHERLAND, THE • 1915 • Thornton F. Martin • UKN
CALL OF THE MOUNTAIN see **KITAHODAKA ZESSHO** • 1968
CALL OF THE NIGHT • 1926 • *Truart Film Corp.* • USA
CALL OF THE NIGHTINGALE see **DOA EL-KARAWAN** • 1959
CALL OF THE NORTH • 1970 • Thompson Darrell • DOC • USA
CALL OF THE NORTH, THE • 1914 • De Mille Cecil B., Apfel Oscar • USA
CALL OF THE NORTH, THE • 1921 • Henabery Joseph • USA • CONJUROR'S HOUSE, THE (UKN)
CALL OF THE OPEN RANGE, THE • 1911 • Dwan Allan • USA
CALL OF THE PAST, THE • 1916 • Lowery William, Mack Charles W. • SHT • USA
CALL OF THE PIPES, THE • 1917 • Watts Tom • UKN
CALL OF THE PLAINS, THE • 1913 • *Mackley Arthur* • USA
CALL OF THE PRAIRIE • 1936 • Bretherton Howard • USA
CALL OF THE RING, THE (UKN) see **DUKE COMES BACK, THE** • 1937
CALL OF THE ROAD, THE • 1913 • *Logan Mr.* • USA
CALL OF THE ROAD, THE • 1920 • Coleby A. E. • UKN
CALL OF THE ROCKIES • 1931 • Johnston Raymond K. • USA
CALL OF THE ROCKIES • 1938 • James Alan • USA
CALL OF THE ROCKIES • 1944 • Selander Lesley • USA
CALL OF THE ROSE, THE • 1912 • *Solax* • USA
CALL OF THE SAVAGE • 1935 • Taylor Ray • USA
CALL OF THE SAVAGE, THE • 1935 • Landers Lew • SRL • USA
CALL OF THE SEA, THE • 1915 • Otto Henry • *Monty* • USA
CALL OF THE SEA, THE • 1915 • Totten Joseph Byron • *Essanay* • USA
CALL OF THE SEA, THE • 1915 • Waller Wallett • UKN
CALL OF THE SEA, THE • 1919 • *Muir Stella* • UKN
CALL OF THE SEA, THE • 1927 • *Colorart* • SHT • USA
CALL OF THE SEA, THE • 1930 • Hiscott Leslie • UKN
CALL OF THE SEA, THE • 1990 • Rezaie Rahman • IRN
CALL OF THE SONG, THE • 1911 • *Pickford Mary* • USA
CALL OF THE SOUL, THE • 1919 • Le Saint Edward J. • USA
CALL OF THE SOUTH SEAS • 1944 • English John • USA
CALL OF THE TRAUMEREL, THE • 1914 • Johnston Lorimer • USA
CALL OF THE TRIBE, THE • 1914 • *Darkfeather Mona* • USA
CALL OF THE UNBORN, THE • 1916 • Wilson Millard K. • USA
CALL OF THE WAVES, THE • 1914 • *Ford Francis* • USA
CALL OF THE WEST • 1912 • *Champion* • USA
CALL OF THE WEST • 1930 • Ray Albert • USA
CALL OF THE WEST, THE • 1910 • *Nestor* • USA
CALL OF THE WILD • 1972 • Annakin Ken • UKN, FRG, ITL • RICHIAMO DELLA FORESTA, IL (ITL) ○ RUF DER WILDNIS (FRG)
CALL OF THE WILD • 1976 • Jameson Jerry • TVM • USA
CALL OF THE WILD, THE • 1908 • Griffith D. W. • USA
CALL OF THE WILD, THE • 1914 • *Lasky* • USA
CALL OF THE WILD, THE • 1923 • Jackman Fred • USA
CALL OF THE WILD, THE • 1935 • Wellman William A. • USA
CALL OF THE WILDERNESS • 1911 • Melies Gaston • USA
CALL OF THE WILDERNESS, THE • 1926 • Nelson Jack • USA
CALL OF THE WOLF see **RICHIAMO DEL LUPO, IL** • 1975
CALL OF THE YUKON • 1938 • Eason B. Reeves, Coyle John T. (U/c) • USA
CALL OF YESTERDAY, THE • 1915 • *Essanay* • USA
CALL OF YOUTH, THE • 1920 • Ford Hugh • UKN
CALL ON THE PRESIDENT, A see **JOE AND ETHEL TURP CALL ON THE PRESIDENT** • 1939
CALL OUT THE MARINES • 1942 • Ryan Frank, Hamilton William • USA
CALL SURFSIDE 77 see **SURFTIDE 77** • 1962
CALL THE COPS • 1919 • Le Brandt Joseph • SHT • USA
CALL THE MESQUITEERS • 1938 • English John • USA • OUTLAWS OF THE WEST (UKN)
CALL THE WITNESS • 1921 • Roach Hal • SHT • USA
CALL TO ARMS • 1917 • Chapin Benjamin • SHT • USA
CALL TO ARMS • 1937 • Macheret Alexander • USS
CALL TO ARMS, A • 1918 • *Chapin* • USA
CALL TO ARMS, THE • 1902 • Hepworth Cecil M. • UKN
CALL TO ARMS, THE • 1910 • Griffith D. W. • USA
CALL TO ARMS, THE see **IN LOVE AND WAR** • 1913
CALL TO ARMS AGAINST WAR, A see **BATTLE CRY OF PEACE, THE** • 1915
CALL TO DANGER • 1973 • Gries Tom • TVM • USA
CALL TO GLORY • 1984 • Carter Thomas • TVM • USA
CALL TO GLORY see **BLADE RIDER: ATTACK OF THE INDIAN NATION** • 1965
CALL TO GLORY: JFK • 1985 • Levin Peter • TVM • USA
CALL-UP, THE see **REPMANAD** • 1979
CALL YOUR SHOTS • 1928 • Roberts Stephen • SHT • USA
CALLAGHAN REMET CA • 1960 • Rozier Willy • FRN
CALLAHANS AND THE MURPHYS, THE • 1927 • Hill George W. • USA
CALLALOO • 1937 • Montagu Brian, Nicholson Irene • USA, T&T • DOC
CALLAN • 1974 • Sharp Don • UKN • THIS IS CALLAN
CALLAWAY WENT THATAWAY • 1951 • Panama Norman, Frank Melvin • USA • STAR SAID NO, THE (UKN)
CALLE DE LOS AMORES, LA • 1953 • Sevilla Raphael J. • MXC
CALLE ENTRE TU Y YO, UNA • 1952 • Rodriguez Roberto • MXC
CALLE GRITA, LA • 1947 • Demare Lucas • ARG
CALLE MAYOR • 1955 • Bardem Juan Antonio • SPN, FRN • GRAND-RUE (FRN) ○ LOVEMAKER, THE (USA) ○ MAIN STREET
CALLE OG PALLE see **HJALTAR MOT SIN VILJA** • 1948
CALLE P • 1965 • Brandt Robert • SWD
CALLE SIN SOL, LA • 1948 • Gil Rafael • SPN
CALLE SOM MILJONAR • 1916 • Klercker Georg • SWD • CHARLIE AS A MILLIONAIRE
CALLED BACK • 1911 • Lincoln W. J. • ASL
CALLED BACK • 1911 • Porter Edwin S. • USA
CALLED BACK • 1912 • *Barrett Franklyn (P)* • ASL
CALLED BACK • 1912 • *Cruze James* • USA
CALLED BACK • 1914 • Tucker George Loane • UKN
CALLED BACK • 1914 • Turner Otis • USA
CALLED BACK • 1933 • Denham Reginald, Harris Jack • UKN
CALLED TO THE FRONT • 1914 • Weston Charles • UKN
CALLEJERA • 1949 • Cortazar Ernesto • MXC
CALLEJON SIN SALIDA, UN • 1964 • Baledon Rafael • MXC
CALLER, THE • 1987 • Seidelman Arthur Allan • USA
CALLER HEERING • 1909 • *Warwick Trading Co.* • UKN
CALLERS, THE see **BALLERS, THE** • 1969
CALLES DE BUENOS AIRES • 1934 • Ferreyra Jose • ARG
CALLES NYA (UNDER)KLADER • 1916 • Klercker Georg • SWD • CHARLIE'S NEW UNDERWEAR
CALLIE & SON • 1981 • Hussein Waris • TVM • USA
CALLIGRAPHIE ARABE, LA • 1974 • Tilmissani Abdel-Qadir At- • SHT • EGY
CALLIGRAPHIE JAPONAISE • 1961 • Alechinsky Pierre • FRN
CALLING, THE see **BELLS** • 1981
CALLING ALL CARS • 1935 • Bennet Spencer Gordon • USA
CALLING ALL CARS • 1954 • Rogers Maclean • UKN
CALLING ALL CATS see **6.5 SPECIAL** • 1958
CALLING ALL CROOKS • 1938 • Black George • UKN
CALLING ALL CUCKOOS • 1956 • Smith Paul J. • ANS • USA
CALLING ALL CURS • 1939 • White Jules • SHT • USA
CALLING ALL DOCTORS • 1937 • Lamont Charles • SHT • USA
CALLING ALL DRIVERS • Cripps Erik • DOC • UKN
CALLING ALL HUSBANDS • 1940 • Smith Noel • USA
CALLING ALL KIDS • 1943 • Baerwitz Sam • SHT • USA
CALLING ALL MARINES • 1939 • Auer John H. • USA
CALLING ALL MA'S • 1937 • Davis Redd • UKN • BITER BIT, THE
CALLING ALL PAS • 1942 • Jason Will • SHT • USA
CALLING ALL STARS • 1937 • Smith Herbert • UKN
CALLING ALL STARS see **STARS ON PARADE** • 1944
CALLING BULLDOG DRUMMOND • 1951 • Saville Victor • UKN, USA
CALLING DR. DEATH • 1943 • Le Borg Reginald • USA
CALLING DR. GILLESPIE • 1942 • Bucquet Harold S. • USA
CALLING DR. KILDARE • 1939 • Bucquet Harold S. • USA
CALLING DR. MAGOO • 1956 • Burness Pete • ANS • USA
CALLING DR. PORKY • 1940 • Freleng Friz • ANS • USA
CALLING DR. WOODPECKER • 1963 • Smith Paul J. • ANS • USA
CALLING HOMICIDE • 1956 • Bernds Edward • USA
CALLING HUBBY'S BLUFF • 1929 • *Sennett Mack (P)* • SHT • USA
CALLING NORTHSIDE 777 see **CALL NORTHSIDE 777** • 1948
CALLING OF DAN MATTHEWS, THE • 1935 • Rosen Phil • USA
CALLING OF JIM BARTON, THE • 1914 • *Anderson Broncho Billy* • USA
CALLING OF LOUIS MONA, THE • 1913 • *August Edwin* • USA
CALLING PAUL TEMPLE • 1948 • Rogers Maclean • UKN • PAUL TEMPLE AND THE CANTERBURY CASE
CALLING PHILO VANCE • 1940 • Clemens William • USA
CALLING THE SHOTS • 1988 • Cole Janis, Dale Holly • CND
CALLING THE TUNE • 1936 • Denham Reginald • UKN
CALLING WILD BILL ELLIOTT • 1943 • Bennet Spencer Gordon • USA
CALLIOPE • 1971 • Cimber Matt • USA
CALLISTO • 1943 • Marty • SHT • FRN
CALLY'S COMET • 1911 • *Garwood William* • USA
CALM • 1975 • Kieslowski Krzysztof • MTV • PLN
CALM YOURSELF • 1935 • Seitz George B. • USA
CALMA RAGAZZO, OGGI MI SPOSO (ITL) see **GENDARME SE MARIE, LE** • 1968
CALMOS • 1976 • Blier Bertrand • FRN • FEMMES FATALES
CALOMNIA COLOMNIEI • 1969 • Calinescu Bob • ANS • RMN • CALUMNY OF CALUMNY, THE
CALOMNIEE • 1913 • de Morlhon Camille • FRN
CALOOLA • 1911 • Rolfe Alfred • ASL • ADVENTURES OF A JACKAROO, THE
CALOR DE LA LLAMA, EL • 1977 • Romero-Marchent Rafael • SPN
CALORE IN PROVINCIA • 1975 • Montero Roberto Bianchi • ITL
CALTIKI IL MOSTRO IMMORTALE • 1959 • Freda Riccardo, Kresel Lee • ITL, USA • CALTIKI, THE IMMORTAL MONSTER (USA) ○ IMMORTAL MONSTER, THE
CALTIKI, THE IMMORTAL MONSTER (USA) see **CALTIKI IL MOSTRO IMMORTALE** • 1959
CALTZONZIN INSPECTOR • 1972 • Arau Alfonso • MXC • CALTZONZIN THE INSPECTOR ○ CALZONZIN INSPECTOR ○ INSPECTOR, EL
CALTZONZIN THE INSPECTOR see **CALTZONZIN INSPECTOR** • 1972
CALUMET, THE see **LULA MIRA** • 1962
CALUMET "K" • 1912 • *Edison* • USA
CALUMNIA • 1938 • Elias Francisco • MXC
CALUMNIADA, LA • 1949 • Delgado Fernando • SPN
CALUMNY OF CALUMNY, THE see **CALOMNIA COLOMNIEI** • 1969
CALUNIA, A • 1926 • Vieira Manuel Luis • PRT
CALUNNIATORI, I • 1956 • Cirino Franco, Volpe Mario • ITL
CALVAIRE, LA • 1914 • Feuillade Louis • FRN
CALVAIRE D'AMOUR • 1923 • Tourjansky Victor • FRN
CALVAIRE DE CIMIEZ, LE • 1934 • de Baroncelli Jacques, Dalliere Rene • FRN
CALVAIRE DU MOUSSE, LE • 1912 • Machin Alfred • FRN
CALVAIRE D'UNE FEMME, LE • 1919 • Protazanov Yakov • USS
CALVAIRE D'UNE MERE, LE • 1913 • Leprince Rene • FRN
CALVARIO DE UNA ESPOSA, EL • 1936 • Orol Juan • MXC
CALVARY • 1920 • Collins Edwin J. • UKN
CALVARY see **PAMIATKA Z KALWARII** • 1958
CALVARY see **KALVARIA** • 1960
CALVARY OF A CHILD • 1950 • O'Fredericks Alice • DNM
CALVERT'S FOLLY (UKN) see **CALVERT'S VALLEY** • 1922
CALVERT'S VALLEY • 1922 • Dillon John Francis • USA • CALVERT'S FOLLY (UKN)
CALYPSO • 1958 • Moser Giorgio • ITL
CALYPSO • 1959 • Rossi Franco, Colonna Golfiero, Benvenuti Leo • DOC • ITL, FRN • CALYPSOS
CALYPSO CAT • 1962 • Deitch Gene • ANS • USA
CALYPSO HEAT WAVE • 1957 • Sears Fred F. • USA
CALYPSO JOE • 1957 • Dein Edward • USA
CALYPSO (UKN) see **MANFISH** • 1955
CALYPSOS see **CALYPSO** • 1959
CALZONAZOS, EL • 1974 • Ozores Mariano • SPN
CALZONZIN INSPECTOR see **CALTZONZIN INSPECTOR** • 1972
CAMA, LA • 1968 • Gomez Muriel Emilio • MXC, ARG • BED, THE
CAMA DE PIEDRA, LA • 1957 • Cardona Rene • MXC
CAMACCHIO • 1942 • Cerchio Fernando • SHT • ITL
CAMADA NEGRA • 1977 • Gutierrez Aragon Manuel • SPN • BLACK LITTER ○ BLACK BROOD
CAMARADES • 1970 • Karmitz Marin • FRN
CAMARADES, LES (FRN) see **COMPAGNI, I** • 1963
CAMARERAS, LAS • 1976 • Coll Joaquin • SPN
CAMAROTE DE LUJO • 1957 • Gil Rafael • SPN
CAMBIALE, LA • 1959 • Mastrocinque Camillo • ITL
CAMBIO, EL • 1971 • Joscowicz Alfredo • MXC • CHANGE, THE
CAMBIO DE SEXO • 1977 • Aranda Vicente • SPN • I WANT TO BE A WOMAN (UKN) ○ CHANGE OF SEX ○ SEX CHANGE ○ FORBIDDEN LOVE
CAMBIO DELLA GUARDIA, IL • 1962 • Bianchi Giorgio • ITL
CAMBODIAN IDYL, A • 1913 • Melies Gaston • USA
CAMBRIC MASK, THE • 1919 • Terriss Tom • USA
CAMBRIDGE • 1932 • Legg Stuart, Noxon G. F. • DOC • UKN
CAMBRIDGE • 1944 • Massingham Richard • UKN
CAMBRIDGE DIARY • 1966 • Malanga Gerard • USA
CAMBRIDGE STEAM ENGINE • 1968 • Jenkins Charles, Edelmann Heinz • ANS • UKN
CAMBRIOLEUR, LE see **FLAG DELIT** • 1930
CAMBRIOLEUR ET AGENT • 1904 • Blache Alice • FRN
CAMBRIOLEURS, LES • 1897-98 • Blache Alice • FRN
CAMBRIOLEURS DE PARIS, LES • 1904 • Blache Alice • FRN
CAMDEN TOWN BOY see **TALL GUY, THE** • 1988
CAME A HOT FRIDAY • 1985 • Mune Ian • NZL
CAME THE BRAWN • 1938 • Douglas Gordon • SHT • USA
CAME THE DAWN • 1928 • Heath Arch B. • SHT • USA
CAME THE HERO see **VIOLENT ENEMY, THE** • 1969
CAMEE, LE • 1913 • Tourneur Maurice • FRN
CAMEL BOY • 1984 • Gross Yoram • ANM • ASL
CAMEL THROUGH THE NEEDLE'S EYE see **VELBLOUD UCHEM JEHLY** • 1926
CAMEL THROUGH THE NEEDLE'S EYE see **VELBLOUD UCHEM JEHLY** • 1936
CAMELEON • 1984 • Noel Jean-Guy • CND
CAMELEONS, LES • 1967 • Hella Patrick • BLG
CAMELIA • 1947 • Vernuccio Gianni • EGY
CAMELIA • 1953 • Gavaldon Roberto • MXC, SPN
CAMELIA BLANC, LE see **BAL DES PASSANTS, LE** • 1943
CAMELOT • 1967 • Logan Joshua • USA
CAMELS, THE see **CAMMELLI, I** • 1988
CAMELS ARE COMING, THE • 1934 • Whelan Tim • UKN
CAMELS WEST (UKN) see **SOUTHWEST PASSAGE** • 1954
CAMEO KIRBY • 1915 • Apfel Oscar • USA
CAMEO KIRBY • 1923 • Ford John • USA
CAMEO KIRBY • 1930 • Cummings Irving • USA
CAMEO OF YELLOWSTONE • 1914 • Ayres Sydney • USA
CAMEO OPERAS • 1927 • SER • UKN
CAMEO RING, THE • 1915 • Giblyn Charles • USA
CAMERA ALBA • 1964 • Calotescu Virgil • RMN • WHITE ROOM, THE
CAMERA AND THE SONG, THE • 1975 • Fiks Henri, Hanley J. • SER • CND
CAMERA AT SCHOOL, THE • 1974 • Alexander Mike • DCS • UKN
CAMERA BUFF see **AMATOR** • 1979
CAMERA CAUGHT IT, THE • 1954 • *Pete Smith Speciality* • SHT • USA

CAMERA COCKTALES see **NERVO AND KNOX** • 1926
CAMERA COCKTALES see **THAT BRUTE SIMMONS** • 1928
CAMERA COCKTALES NO.1 see **MEDEVEDEFF'S BALALAIKA ORCHESTRA** • 1929
CAMERA COCKTALES NO.2 see **GORNO MARIONETTES, THE** • 1928
CAMERA COCKTALES NO.3 see **DIMPLES AND TEARS** • 1929
CAMERA COCKTALES NO.3 see **GENTLEMEN THE CHORUS NO.1** • 1929
CAMERA COCKTALES NO.6 -VISIT TO A CINEMA ON AMATEUR NIGHT • 1932 • Vorhaus Bernard • SHT • UKN
CAMERA COCKTALES NOS.1-6 • 1932 • Vorhaus Bernard • SER • UKN
CAMERA CORNER • 1964-66 • Schepisi Fred • SHS • ASL
CAMERA CURE, THE • 1917 • *Binns George H.* • USA
CAMERA D'ALBERGO • 1980 • Monicelli Mario • ITL, FRN • CHAMBRE D'HOTEL (FRN) ○ HOTEL ROOM
CAMERA DEL TERROR, LA see **FEAR CHAMBER, THE** • 1968
CAMERA EYE see **KINO-GLAZ** • 1924
CAMERA FIEND, THE • 1913 • Wilson Frank • UKN
CAMERA IN THE CLOUDS, THE • 1912 • *Higgins Ernest (Ph)* • ASL
CAMERA MAKES WHOOPEE • 1935 • McLaren Norman • ANS • UKN
CAMERA MAN, THE • 1920 • *Franey William* • USA
CAMERA REFLECTIONS • 1945 • Woolf Julia • UKN
CAMERA REPORTERS ON THE LINE OF FIRE see **NA LINII OGNYA -OPERATORY KINOKHRONIKI** • 1941
CAMERA SLEUTH • 1951 • Barclay David • SHT • USA
CAMERA SUTRA OF DE BLEEKGEZICHTEN • 1973 • de Hert Robbe • BLG
CAMERA THRILLS • 1935 • *Universal* • SHT • USA
CAMERAMAN, THE • 1928 • Sedgwick Edward, Keaton Buster (U/c) • USA
CAMERAMAN'S REVENGE, THE see **MEST' KINEMATOGRAFICESKOGO OPERATORA** • 1912
CAMERAMEN AT WAR • 1944 • Lye Len • DCS • UKN
CAMERA'S TESTIMONY, THE • 1913 • Melville Wilbert • USA
CAMERE SEPARATE • 1918 • Righelli Gennaro • ITL
CAMERIERA, LA • 1975 • Montero Roberto Bianchi • ITL
CAMERIERA BELLA PRESENZA OFFRESI • 1951 • Pastina Giorgio • ITL • POSITION WANTED (USA)
CAMERIERA NERA, LA • 1976 • Bianchi Mario • ITL
CAMERIERE, LE • 1958 • Bragaglia Carlo Ludovico, Grieco Sergio • ITL
CAMERINO SIN BIOMBO • 1967 • Zabalza Jose Maria • SPN • CAMERINO WITHOUT A FOLDING SCREEN
CAMERINO WITHOUT A FOLDING SCREEN see **CAMERINO SIN BIOMBO** • 1967
CAMERON OF THE ROYAL MOUNTED • 1922 • McRae Henry • CND
CAMERONS, THE • 1974 • Wilson Frederick • UKN
CAMERON'S CLOSET • 1988 • Mastroianni Armand • USA
CAMICIA NERA • 1933 • Forzano Giovacchino • ITL
CAMICIA NERA see **EROE DEL NOSTRO TEMPO, UN** • 1960
CAMICIE ROSSE • 1952 • Alessandrini Goffredo, Rosi Francesco, Rosi Francesco • ITL, FRN • CHEMISES ROUGES, LES (FRN) ○ ANITA GARIBALDI ○ RED SHIRTS
CAMILA • 1984 • Bemberg Maria Luisa • ARG, SPN • CAMILLE
CAMILLA • 1954 • Emmer Luciano • ITL
CAMILLA AND THE THIEF see **KAMILLA OG TYVEN** • 1988
CAMILLE • 1907 • Larsen Viggo • DNM
CAMILLE • 1912 • Brenon Herbert • USA
CAMILLE • 1916 • Capellani Albert • USA
CAMILLE • 1917 • Edwards J. Gordon • USA
CAMILLE • 1921 • Smallwood Ray C. • USA
CAMILLE • 1927 • Niblo Fred • USA
CAMILLE • 1936 • Cukor George • USA
CAMILLE • 1984 • Davis Desmond • TVM • UKN
CAMILLE see **DAME AUX CAMELIAS, LA** • 1910
CAMILLE see **CAMILA** • 1984
CAMILLE 2000 • 1969 • Metzger Radley H. • ITL, USA
CAMILLE, AS SHE NEVER WAS • 1914 • *Superba* • USA
CAMILLE CLAUDEL • 1989 • Nuytten Bruno • FRN
CAMILLE DESMOULINS • 1911 • Calmettes Andre • FRN
CAMILLE DESMOULINS • 1911 • Pouctal Henri • FRN
CAMILLE OF THE BARBARY COAST • 1925 • Dierker Hugh • USA • FALLEN ANGEL, THE
CAMILLE (USA) see **SIGNORA DALLE CAMELIE, LA** • 1909
CAMILLE WITHOUT CAMELIAS (USA) see **SIGNORA SENZA CAMILIE, LA** • 1953
CAMILO EL CURA GUERILLERO • 1973 • Norden Francisco • CLM • CAMILO THE GUERILLA PRIEST
CAMILO THE GUERILLA PRIEST see **CAMILO EL CURA GUERILLERO** • 1973
CAMILO TORRES • 1969 • Ginaldo D. Leon • CLM
CAMINANDO PASOS.. CAMINANDO • 1976 • Weingartshofer A. Federico • MXC • WALKING ON.. WALKING
CAMINHO DE MADRID, A • 1936 • Contreiras Anibal • SHT • PRT
CAMINHOS LONGOS • 1955 • Ferreira Eurico • PRT
CAMINHOS PARA A ANGUSTIA • 1963 • de Almeida Manuel Faria • SHT • PRT • STREETS OF EARLY SORROW
CAMINITO ALEGRE • 1943 • Morayta Miguel • MXC
CAMINITO DE GLORIA • 1939 • Amadori Luis Cesar • ARG
CAMINITO DE GLORIA • 1939 • Barth-Moglia Luis • ARG
CAMINO, EL • 1963 • Mariscal Ana • SPN
CAMINO, UN • 1972 • *Churubusco Azteca* • MXC
CAMINO AL CIELO, UN • 1974 • *Potosi* • MXC
CAMINO CORTADO • 1955 • Iquino Ignacio F. • SPN
CAMINO DE BABEL, EL • 1944 • Mihura Jeronimo • SPN
CAMINO DE GUANAJUATO • 1955 • Baledon Rafael • MXC
CAMINO DE LA HORCA • 1961 • Urueta Chano • MXC
CAMINO DE LA VERDAD • 1968 • Navarro Agustin • SPN
CAMINO DE LA VIDA, EL • 1955 • Blake Alfonso Corona • MXC
CAMINO DE LOS ESPANTOS, EL • 1965 • Martinez Solares Gilberto • MXC
CAMINO DE LOS GATOS, EL • 1943 • Urueta Chano • MXC
CAMINO DE SACRAMENTO • 1945 • Urueta Chano • MXC
CAMINO DEL INFIERNO • 1946 • Saslavsky Luis • ARG
CAMINO DEL INFIERNO • 1950 • Morayta Miguel • MXC
CAMINO DEL MAL • 1955 • Delgado Miguel M. • MXC
CAMINO DEL ROCIO • 1966 • Gil Rafael • SPN
CAMINO DEL SUR • 1964 • Romero-Marchent Joaquin Luis • SPN
CAMINO DEL SUR, EL • 1987 • Stagnaro Juan Bautista • ARG • HEADING SOUTH
CAMINO HACIA LA MUERTE DEL VIEJO REALES, EL • Vallejo Gerardo • ARG • ROAD TO DEATH OF OLD REALES, THE
CAMINO HACIA LAS ESTRELLAS • 1963 • Merino Jose Luis • SPN
CAMINO LARGO A TIJUANA • 1988 • Estrada Luis • MXC • LONG ROAD TO TIJUANA
CAMINO PARA EUROPA, UN • 1965 • Suarez De Lozo Luis • SPN
CAMINOS DE AYER • 1938 • Michelena Quirino • MXC
CAMINOS DE SANGRE • 1945 • Aguilar Rolando • MXC
CAMION, LE • 1977 • Duras Marguerite • FRN • LORRY, THE (UKN) ○ TRUCK, THE
CAMION BLANC, LE • 1942 • Joannon Leo • FRN • WHITE WAGON, THE
CAMIONETA GRIS, LA • 1990 • Urquieta Jose Luis • MXC • GREY VAN, THE
CAMISARDS, LES • 1971 • Allio Rene • FRN
CAMMELLI, I • 1988 • Bertolucci Giuseppe • ITL • CAMELS, THE
CAMMINACAMMINA • 1983 • Olmi Ermanno • ITL • KEEP ON WALKING ○ KEEP WALKING ○ WALKING WALKING
CAMMINO DELLA SPERANZA, IL • 1950 • Germi Pietro • ITL • PATH OF HOPE, THE ○ ROAD TO HOPE, THE
CAMOENS see **CAMOES** • 1946
CAMOES • 1946 • de Barros Jose Leitao • PRT • CAMOENS
CAMOES • 1966 • de Almeida Manuel Faria • SHT • PRT
CAMOKANIN DONUSU • 1968 • Yalaz Suat • TRK • RETURN OF DJAMOKA, THE
CAMOMILLE • 1988 • Charef Mehdi • FRN
CAMORRA • 1972 • Squitieri Pasquale • ITL
CAMORRA see **AMORE E SANGUE** • 1951
CAMORRA see **SCHATTEN UBER NEAPEL** • 1951
CAMORRA see **COMPLICATO INTRIGO DI DONNE, VICOLI E DELITTI, UN** • 1985
CAMORRA MAN, THE see **CAMORRISTA, IL** • 1986
CAMORRA MEMBER, THE see **CAMORRISTA, IL** • 1986
CAMORRA: THE NAPLES CONNECTION see **COMPLICATO INTRIGO DI DONNE, VICOLI E DELITTI, UN** • 1985
CAMORRISTA, IL • 1986 • Tornatore Giuseppe • ITL • CAMORRA MEMBER, THE ○ PROFESSOR, THE ○ CAMORRA MAN, THE
CAMOUFLAGE • 1918 • *Tweede Dan* • SHT • USA
CAMOUFLAGE • 1943 • Donnelly Eddie • ANS • USA
CAMOUFLAGE see **BARWY ORCHRONNE** • 1976
CAMOUFLAGE BALL • 1918 • *Pyramid* • SHT • USA
CAMOUFLAGE KISS, A • 1918 • Millarde Harry • USA
CAMOUFLAGED BABY, THE • 1918 • *Vera Lillian* • USA
CAMP • 1965 • Warhol Andy • USA
CAMP • 1966 • Pearson Peter • DOC • CND
CAMP 708 • 1977 • Cohen Dan • ISR, USA • MADMAN
CAMP, THE • 1990 • Dyulgerov Georgi • BUL
CAMP AT PRZEMYSLOWA STREET, THE see **OBOZ NA PRZEMYSLOWEJ** • 1970
CAMP CLOBBER • 1958 • Tendlar Dave • ANS • USA
CAMP DE JEUNES FILLES, LE see **MOASKAR EL BANAT** • 1967
CAMP DE THIARROYE • 1988 • Sembene Ousmane, Sow Thierno Faty • SNL
CAMP DES HOMMES PERDUS, LE see **FUGITIF, LE** • 1946
CAMP DOG • 1950 • Nichols Charles • ANS • USA
CAMP-FIRE GIRLS • 1984 • Schellerup Henning • USA
CAMP FOLLOWERS, THE (USA) see **SOLDATESSE, LE** • 1965
CAMP FORESTIER DE SAINT-MATHIEU, LE • 1939 • Tessier Albert • DCS • CND
CAMP MEETIN' • 1936 • Goodwins Leslie • SHT • USA
CAMP NUTS see **TRAMP, TRAMP, TRAMP** • 1942
CAMP ON BLOOD ISLAND, THE • 1958 • Guest Val • UKN
CAMP VOLANT • 1932 • Reichmann Max • FRN, FRG • MARCO, DER CLOWN (FRG)
CAMPA CAROGNA.. LA TAGLIA CRESCE • 1973 • Rosati Giuseppe • ITL, SPN
CAMPAGNE DE CICERON, LA • 1989 • Davila Jacques, Hairet Michel, Frot-Coutaz Gerard • FRN
CAMPAGNE DE FRANCE 1814 • 1916 • Cohl Emile • ANS • FRN
CAMPAGNE DE FRANCE, UNE • 1955 • Masson Jean • SHT • FRN
CAMPAGNE DE L'ARBRE, LA • 1964 • Rachedi Ahmed • SHT • ALG
CAMPAGNE ROMAINE • 1956 • Ruspoli Mario • SHT • FRN
CAMPAGNOLA BELLA • 1976 • Siciliano Mario • ITL
CAMPAIGN BURMA see **NEVER SO FEW** • 1959
CAMPAIGNERS, THE • 1964 • Brittain Don • CND
CAMPAIGNING MANAGERESS, THE • 1913 • *Thanhouser* • USA
CAMPAIGNING WITH CUSTER • 1913 • *Bison* • USA
CAMPANA DEL INFIERNO, LA • 1973 • Guerin Claudio • SPN, FRN • CAMPANAS DEL INFIERNO, LAS ○ HELL'S BELLS ○ BELL FROM HELL (USA) ○ BELL OF HELL, THE
CAMPANA DI SAN GUSTO, LA • 1954 • Amendola Mario, Maccari Ruggero • ITL
CAMPANA NUEVA, LA • 1950 • Barth-Moglia Luis • ARG
CAMPANADA, LA • 1979 • Camino Jaime • SPN • BELL TOLLS, THE ○ TEARING AWAY ○ BLOW OUT, THE
CAMPANADAS A MEDIANOCHE • 1966 • Welles Orson • SPN, SWT • FALSTAFF (UKN) ○ CHIMES AT MIDNIGHT
CAMPANAS DE AMANECER see **GUERRILLEROS, LOS** • 1962
CAMPANAS DEL INFIERNO, LAS see **CAMPANA DEL INFIERNO, LA** • 1973
CAMPANAS ROJAS see **KRASNYE KOLOKOLA** • 1981
CAMPANE A MARTELLO • 1949 • Zampa Luigi • ITL • CHILDREN OF CHANGE
CAMPANE DI POMPEI • 1952 • Lombardi Giuseppe • ITL • BANDITO CALABRESE, IL
CAMPANHA DO TRIGO, A • 1929 • Coelho Jose Adolfo • SHT • PRT
CAMPANILE D'ORO, IL • 1956 • Simonelli Giorgio C. • ITL
CAMPBELLS ARE COMING, THE • 1915 • Ford Francis, Cunard Grace • USA
CAMPBELL'S KINGDOM • 1957 • Thomas Ralph • UKN
CAMPBELLS SOUPS • 1912 • Cohl Emile • ANS • FRN
CAMPEMENT 13 • 1939 • Constant Jacques • FRN
CAMPEMENT DE BOHEMIENS • 1896 • Melies Georges • FRN • GIPSIES AT HOME
CAMPEOES DO MUNDO • 1950 • Campos Henrique • SHT • PRT
CAMPEON CICLISTA, EL • 1956 • Cortes Fernando • MXC
CAMPEON DEL BARRIO • 1964 • Baledon Rafael • MXC
CAMPEON SIN CORONA • 1945 • Galindo Alejandro • MXC
CAMPEONES • 1942 • Torrado Ramon • SPN
CAMPEONES JUSTICIEROS, LOS • 1970 • *Grovas* • MXC
CAMPER IN TROUBLE, A see **CAMPISTA EM APUROS, UM** • 1968
CAMPESINOS • 1976 • Rodriguez Martha, Silva Jorge • DOC • CLM • PEASANTS
CAMPHOR see **KARPURAM** • 1967
CAMPI SPERIMENTALI • 1957 • Olmi Ermanno (Spv) • DOC • ITL
CAMPING • 1917 • De Vonde Chester M. • USA
CAMPING • 1958 • Zeffirelli Franco • ITL
CAMPING • 1978 • Chanowski Thijs • NTH
CAMPING BY PROXY • 1920 • *Pioneer Film* • SHT • USA
CAMPING OUT • 1912 • *Rex* • USA
CAMPING OUT • 1918 • *Capitol* • SHT • USA
CAMPING OUT • 1918 • Lyons Eddie, Moran Lee • *Star* • SHT • USA
CAMPING OUT • 1919 • Arbuckle Roscoe • SHT • USA
CAMPING OUT • 1931 • Sweet Harry • SHT • USA
CAMPING OUT • 1934 • Hand David • ANS • USA
CAMPINOS • 1932 • Lopes Antonio Luis • PRT
CAMPION DE CAMPIONES • 1981 • Darino Eduardo • DCS • URG
CAMPIONATA MONDIALE DI CALCIO • 1950 • Canzio Stefano • ITL
CAMPIONE, IL • 1943 • Borghesio Carlo • ITL
CAMPISTA EM APUROS, UM • 1968 • Peyroteo Herlander • PRT • CAMPER IN TROUBLE, A
CAMPO AJUERA • 1919 • Ferreyra Jose • ARG
CAMPO ARADO • 1959 • Fleider Leo • ARG
CAMPO BRAVO • 1949 • Lazaga Pedro • SPN
CAMPO DE' FIORI • 1943 • Bonnard Mario • ITL • PEDDLER AND THE LADY, THE (USA) ○ C'E PRIMA LA SIGNORA
CAMPO DI MAGGIO • 1935 • Forzano Giovacchino • ITL
CAMPSITE MASSACRE see **FINAL TERROR, THE** • 1981
CAMPTOWN RACES • 1948 • Kneitel Seymour • ANS • USA
CAMPUS A GO-GO (USA) see **EREKI NO WAKADAISHO** • 1966
CAMPUS CAPERS • 1941 • Le Borg Reginald • SHT • USA
CAMPUS CAPERS • 1949 • Tytla Bill • ANS • USA
CAMPUS CARMEN, THE • 1928 • *Sennett Mack (P)* • SHT • USA
CAMPUS CHAMPS • 1931 • Guiol Fred • SHT • USA
CAMPUS CHRISTI • 1969 • *Jones D. B./ Jenning J. K. (P)* • SHT • USA
CAMPUS CONFESSIONS • 1938 • Archainbaud George • USA • FAST PLAY (UKN)
CAMPUS CONFIDENTIAL • 1968 • Edwards Charles • USA
CAMPUS CORPSE, THE see **HAZING, THE** • 1978
CAMPUS CRUSHES • 1930 • Sennett Mack • SHT • USA
CAMPUS FLIRT, THE • 1926 • Badger Clarence • USA • COLLEGE FLIRT, THE (UKN)
CAMPUS GIRLS • 1973 • D'Antoni Richard • USA
CAMPUS HEAT • 1969 • Rich Tom • USA
CAMPUS HONEYMOON • 1948 • Sale Richard • USA
CAMPUS IN FRONT OF A STATION see **KIGEKI EKIMAE GAKUEN** • 1967
CAMPUS KILLINGS see **SPLATTER UNIVERSITY** • 1985
CAMPUS KNIGHTS • 1929 • Kelley Albert • USA
CAMPUS MAN • 1987 • Casden Ron • USA
CAMPUS RHYTHM • 1943 • Dreifuss Arthur • USA
CAMPUS SLEUTH • 1948 • Jason Will • USA
CAMPUS VAMP, THE • 1928 • Edwards Harry J. • SHT • USA
CAMUS • Dayan Josee • DOC • FRN
CAN A JEALOUS WIFE BE CURED? • 1915 • *Kelly Jack* • USA
CAN A MAN FOOL HIS WIFE? • 1915 • *Mason Dan* • USA
CAN A WOMAN LOVE TWICE? • 1923 • Horne James W. • USA
CAN AM TRAVELS • 1974 • Siegel Lois, Passet Jean-Pol, Rixon Mike • CND
CAN ASIYE BE SAVED? see **ASIYE NASIL KURTULUR?** • 1987
CAN BE DONE AMIGO see **SI PUO FARE.. AMIGO** • 1972
CAN-CAN • 1960 • Lang Walter • USA
CAN ELLEN BE SAVED? • 1974 • Hart Harvey • TVM • USA
CAN HEIRONYMUS MERKIN EVER FORGET MERCY HUMPPE AND FIND TRUE HAPPINESS? • 1969 • Newley Anthony • UKN
CAN HORSES SING? • 1971 • Sussex • SHT • UKN
CAN I COME AGAIN? see **BLONDE AMBITION** • 1980
CAN I COME TOO? see **BLONDE AMBITION** • 1980
CAN I COUNT YOU IN? • 1972 • King Allan • CND
CAN I DO IT 'TIL I NEED GLASSES? • 1980 • Levy I. Robert • USA
CAN I HELP YOU? • 1966 • Fletcher John • SHT • UKN
CAN LOVE GROWN COLD BE REVIVED? • 1915 • *Evans Millicent* • USA
CAN OF BAKED BEANS, A • 1914 • *Turner Twins* • USA
CAN PAZARI • 1968 • Gorec Ertem • TRK
CAN PRIMITIVE PEOPLE SURVIVE? • 1975 • Leiterman Richard • DOC • CND
CAN SHE BAKE A CHERRY PIE? • 1983 • Jaglom Henry • USA
CAN THE AVANT-GARDE ARTIST BE WHOLED see **ON THE MARRIAGE BROKER JOKE AS CITED BY CLEMENT FREUD IN WIT AND ITS RELATION TO THE UNCONSCIOUS** • 1979
CAN THIS BE DIXIE? • 1936 • Marshall George • USA
CAN THIS BE TRUE? • 1935 • Fryer Bryant • ANS • CND
CAN WE BE RICH? • 1946 • Musk Cecil • DOC • UKN
CAN WE ESCAPE see **HAR JEG RET TIL AT TAGE MIT EGET LIV** • 1917
CAN WIVES BE TRUSTED? • 1919 • Christie Al • USA
CAN YOU BEAT IT? • 1919 • Perez Marcel • USA

CAN YOU COME DOCTOR? see **KAN DOKTORN KOMMA?** • 1942
CAN YOU DO THIS? • 1915 • Booth W. R.? • UKN
CAN YOU FEEL ME DANCING? • 1986 • Miller Michael • TVM • USA
CAN YOU HEAR ME? • 1966 • Babaja Ante • SHT • YGS
CAN YOU HEAR ME MOTHER? • 1935 • Pearce A. Leslie • UKN
CAN YOU HEAR THE LAUGHTER? –THE STORY OF FREDDIE PRINZE • 1979 • Brinckerhoff Burt • TVM • USA
CAN YOU KEEP IT UP FOR A WEEK? • 1974 • Atkinson Jim • UKN
CAN YOU TAKE IT • 1934 • Fleischer Dave • ANS • USA
CANA BRAVA • 1965 • Pereda Ramon • MXC, PRC
CANABUS • *Kimball John (P)* • ANS • USA
CANADA • 1973 • Chapman Christopher • DOC • CND
CANADA '67 • 1965 • Barclay Robert • SHT • CND
CANADA AT 8:30 • 1970 • Vaitiekunas Vince • CND
CANADA AT WAR • 1962 • Brittain Don • SER • CND
CANADA INDUSTRIEL, LE see **INDUSTRIAL CANADA** • 1957
CANADA IS MY PIANO • 1967 • Dunning George • ANS • CND • CONFEDERATION
CANADA MOVES NORTH • 1939 • Finnie Richard S. • DOC • CND
CANADA ON STAGE • 1960 • Howe John • DOC • CND
CANADA –PAYS VASTE see **PAYS VASTE** • 1968
CANADA TODAY • 1967 • Fournier Claude • SHT • CND
CANADA VIGNETTES: WESTERLIES ANTHEM • 1980 • Mills Michael • CND
CANADA'S ATOM GOES TO WORK • 1952 • Blais Roger • DCS • CND • ATOME AU SERVICE DE L'HOMME, L'
CANADA'S NATIVE PEOPLE –A QUESTION OF SURVIVAL • 1974 • Richardson Boyce • DOC • CND
CANADA'S NUCLEAR EDGE • 1983 • Burton Robert H. • CND
CANADA'S SWEETHEART: THE SAGA OF HAL C. BANKS • 1986 • Brittain Don • CND
CANADA'S WORK FOR WOUNDED SOLDIERS • 1918 • Craft William James • DOC • CND
CANADIAN, THE • 1926 • Beaudine William • USA
CANADIAN BUSINESSMAN, THE • 1963 • Koenig Wolf, Kroitor Roman • CND • CANADIAN BUSINESSMEN
CANADIAN BUSINESSMEN see **CANADIAN BUSINESSMAN, THE** • 1963
CANADIAN CAMEO • 1932-54 • Sparling Gordon • SHS • CND
CANADIAN CAPER, THE see **ESCAPE FROM IRAN** • 1982
CANADIAN CAPERS • 1931 • *Terry Paul/ Moser Frank (P)* • ANS • USA
CANADIAN COAST GUARD • 1986 • Reusch Peter • CND
CANADIAN CONNECTION • 1985 • Pyke Roger • MTV • CND
CANADIAN FURNITURE • 1963 • Weintraub William • DOC • CND
CANADIAN HEADLINES OF 1948 • 1948 • Sparling Gordon • DCS • CND
CANADIAN HEADLINES OF 1949 • 1949 • Sparling Gordon • DCS • CND
CANADIAN HEADLINES OF 1950 • 1950 • Sparling Gordon • DCS • CND
CANADIAN HEADLINES OF 1952 • 1952 • Sparling Gordon • DCS • CND
CANADIAN INFANTRYMAN, THE • 1956 • Macartney-Filgate Terence • DOC • CND
CANADIAN LANDSCAPE • 1941 • Crawley Budge, Crawley Judith • DOC • CND
CANADIAN MOONSHINERS, THE • 1910 • Olcott Sidney • USA
CANADIAN MOUNTIES VS. ATOMIC INVADERS • 1953 • Adreon Franklin • SRL • USA
CANADIAN NOTEBOOK see **NOTATNIK KANADYJSKI** • 1961
CANADIAN OFFICERS IN THE MAKING • 1917 • Pearson George • DCS • UKN
CANADIAN PACIFIC • 1949 • Marin Edwin L. • USA
CANADIAN PACIFIC • 1974 • Rimmer David • CND
CANADIAN PACIFIC II • 1975 • Rimmer David • CND
CANADIAN PACIFIC RAILROAD SHOTS • 1899 • *Bitzer Billy (Ph)* • USA
CANADIAN POWER • 1940 • Crawley Budge, Crawley Judith • DOC • CND
CANADIAN SOLUTIONS • 1985 • Skagen Peter • DOC • CND
CANADIAN SOLUTIONS • 1986 • Nicolle Douglas • DOC • CND
CANADIANS, THE • 1959 • Daly Tom • DOC • CND
CANADIANS, THE • 1961 • Kennedy Burt • USA, UKN, CND
CANADIANS, THE • 1986 • Gunnarsson Sturla • MTV • CND
CANADIANS CAN DANCE • 1967 • Howe John • DOC • CND
CANADIENS, LES • 1986 • McKeown Robert • DOC • CND
CANADIENSES, LOS • 1975 • Kish Albert • DOC • CND
CANAGLIE, LE (ITL) see **CANAILLES, LES** • 1959
CANAILLES, LES • 1959 • Labro Maurice • FRN, ITL • CANAGLIE, LE (ITL) ○ TAKE ME AS I AM (UKN) ○ RIFF-RAFF (USA) ○ RUFFIANS, THE
CANAIMA • 1945 • Bustillo Oro Juan • MXC
CANAIMA • 1973 • Blanco Javier • DOC • VNZ
CANAL, THE see **KANAL** • 1979
CANAL GRANDE • 1943 • Robilant Andrea • ITL
CANAL ZONE • 1942 • Landers Lew • USA
CANAL ZONE • 1977 • Wiseman Frederick • DOC • USA
CANALE, IL • 1967 • Bertolucci Bernardo • ITL
CANALE DEGLI ANGELI, IL • 1934 • Pasinetti Francesco • ITL
CANALE DI PANAMA, IL see **PONTE DELL'UNIVERSO, IL** • 1958
CANALE GRANDE • 1983 • Pezold Friederike • AUS, FRG
CANALETTO, PAINTER OF WARSAW see **WARSZAWA W OBRASACH CANALETTA** • 1955
CANALLAS, LOS • 1968 • Curiel Federico • MXC • DESPICABLE ONES, THE ○ SCOUNDRELS, THE ○ INFERNAL ANGELS
CANALLITA Y LA DAMA, EL • 1939 • Amadori Luis Cesar • ARG • NEWSIE AND THE LADY, THE (USA)
CANANEA • 1976 • Violante Marcela Fernandez • MXC
CANARD EN FER BLANC, LE • 1967 • Poitrenaud Jacques • FRN, SPN • OLD TIN CAN, THE
CANARD PRESSE, LE • 1965 • ANS • BLG • PRESSED DUCK, THE
CANARIES SOMETIMES SING • 1930 • Walls Tom • UKN
CANARIS • 1954 • Weidenmann Alfred • FRG • DEADLY DECISION (USA) ○ CANARIS MASTER SPY (UKN)
CANARIS MASTER SPY (UKN) see **CANARIS** • 1954
CANARY • 1964 • *Askew Maurice/ Cosgrove Brian (P)* • ANS • UKN
CANARY, THE • 1975 • Shebib Donald • CND
CANARY BANANAS see **CANARY ISLAND BANANAS** • 1935
CANARY BIRD, THE see **KANARIFUGLEN** • 1973
CANARY ISLAND BANANAS • 1935 • Leacock Richard • DOC • USA • CANARY BANANAS
CANARY MURDER CASE, THE • 1929 • St. Clair Malcolm • USA
CANARY ROW • 1950 • Freleng Friz • ANS • USA
CANARY YELLOW • 1989 • Bani-Etemad Rakhshan • IRN
CANAS AL AIRE • 1949 • Sevilla Raphael J. • MXC
CANAS Y BARRO • 1954 • de Orduna Juan • SPN
CANASTA DE CUENTOS MEXICANOS • 1955 • Bracho Julio • MXC
CANASTA URUGUAYA • 1951 • Cardona Rene • MXC
CANBERRA • 1968 • Crombie Donald • DOC • ASL
CANBERRA POLLUTION • 1970 • Michalak Richard • SHT • ASL
CANBYHILL OUTLAWS, THE • 1916 • Mix Tom • SHT • USA
CANCAO DA SAUDADE, A • 1964 • Campos Henrique • PRT
CANCAO DA TERRA, A • 1938 • do Canto Jorge Brum • PRT
CANCAO DE LISBOA, A • 1933 • Telmo Cottinelli • PRT • SONG OF LISBON, THE
CANCAO DO BERCO, A • 1930 • Cavalcanti Alberto • PRT
CANCEL MY RESERVATION • 1972 • Bogart Paul • USA
CANCELED • 1915 • *Eclair* • USA
CANCELLED DEBT, THE • 1927 • Rosen Phil • USA
CANCELLED MORTGAGE, THE • 1915 • O'Sullivan Tony • USA
CANCER • 1977 • Friel Deirdre • MTV • IRL
CANCER, LE • 1940 • Ciampi Yves • FRN
CANCER RISING • 1975 • Curiel Herbert • NTH
CANCHA VASCA • 1954 • Hurtado Alfredo, Plaza Aselo • SPN
CANCION A LA VIRGEN, UNA • 1949 • Cardona Rene • MXC
CANCION DE AIXA, LA • 1939 • Rey Florian • SPN, FRG
CANCION DE ARRABAL • Carreras Miguel • SPN
CANCION DE CUNA • 1952 • de Fuentes Fernando • MXC
CANCION DE CUNA • 1961 • Elorrieta Jose Maria • SPN
CANCION DE JEAN RICHEPIN, LA • 1957 • Toussaint Carlos • SHT • MXC • POEM OF JEAN RICHEPIN, THE (USA)
CANCION DE JUVENTUD • 1962 • Lucia Luis • SPN
CANCION DE LA MALIBRAN, LA • 1951 • Escobar Luis • SPN
CANCION DE LOS BARRIOS, LA • 1941 • Amadori Luis Cesar • ARG
CANCION DE MEDIANOCHE • 1947 • de Lara Antonio • SPN
CANCION DE MEXICO, LA • 1944 • Fitzpatrick James • MXC • SONG OF MEXICO
CANCION DEL ALMA • 1937 • Urueta Chano • MXC • SONG OF THE SOUL (USA)
CANCION DEL ALMA • 1963 • Davison Tito • MXC
CANCION DEL DIA, LA • 1933 • Samuelson G. B. • SPN
CANCION DEL GAUCHO, LA • 1930 • Ferreyra Jose • ARG
CANCION DEL HUERFANO, LA • 1939 • Ojeda Manuel R. • MXC
CANCION DEL MILAGRO, LA • 1940 • Aguilar Rolando • MXC • MIRACLE SONG, THE (USA)
CANCION DEL PENAL, LA • 1954 • Llado Juan, Sacha Jean • SPN
CANCION DEL PLATEADO, LA • 1941 • Elias Francisco • MXC
CANCION DEL REGRESO, LA • 1940 • Miro Sergio • HOME-COMING SONG (USA)
CANCION EN LA NOCHE, UNA • 1945 • Cardona Rene • MXC
CANCION MANSA PARA UN PUEBLO BRAVO • 1977 • Carrer Giancarlo • VNZ • TAME SONG FOR A BRAVE PEOPLE, A
CANCION MORTAL • 1948 • Iquino Ignacio F. • SPN
CANCION PARA RECORDAR, UNA • 1958 • Bracho Julio • MXC
CANCION VA CONMIGO, LA • 1964 • Mariscal Ana • SPN
CANCIONES DE NUESTRA VIDA • 1975 • Manzanos Eduardo • SPN • SONGS OF OUR LIFE
CANCIONES PARA DESPUES DE UNA GUERRA • 1971 • Patino Basilio Martin • SPN • SONGS FOR AFTER A WAR
CANCIONES UNIDAS, LAS • 1959 • Patino Gomez Alfonso, Davison Tito, Urueta Chano • MXC
CANCIONES Y RECUERDOS • 1947 • Rivero Fernando A. • MXC
CANDI GIRL • 1977 • Christopher John • USA • JET SEX
CANDICE CANDY • 1975 • Unia Pierre • FRN • FRENCH NYMPHO
CANDID CAMERA, THE • 1932 • *Sennett Mack (P)* • SHT • USA
CANDID CAMERAMANIACS • 1937 • Yates Hal • SHT • USA
CANDID CANDIDATE, THE • 1937 • Fleischer Dave • ANS • USA
CANDIDAT COCO LA FLEUR, LE see **COCO LA FLEUR** • 1978
CANDIDAT GOUVERNEUR, MILTON SHAPP see **SHAPP FOR GOVERNOR** • 1966
CANDIDATE see **HOUBU DUIYUAN** • 1983
CANDIDATE, THE • 1964 • Angus Robert • USA • PARTY GIRLS FOR THE CANDIDATE
CANDIDATE, THE • 1972 • Ritchie Michael • USA
CANDIDATE, THE see **KANDIDAAT, DIE** • 1968
CANDIDATE, THE see **GOOD, THE BAD AND THE BEAUTIFUL, THE** • 1970
CANDIDATE, THE see **KANDIDAT, DER** • 1980
CANDIDATE FOR A KILLING (USA) see **CANDIDATO PER UN ASSASSINO** • 1969
CANDIDATE FOR MAYOR, A • 1914 • *Whitman Velma* • USA
CANDIDATE FOR MURDER • 1962 • Villiers David • UKN
CANDIDATES, THE • 1918 • Townley Robin H. • USA
CANDIDATE'S PAST, THE • 1915 • Reehm George E. • USA
CANDIDATO, EL • 1959 • Ayala Fernando • ARG
CANDIDATO PER UN ASSASSINO • 1969 • Elorrieta Jose Maria • SPN, ITL, USA • CANDIDATE FOR A KILLING (USA) ○ SUDARIO A LA MEDIA, UN
CANDIDE • 1973 • McTaggart James • TVM • UKN
CANDIDE see **CANDIDE, OU L'OPTIMISME AU XXEME SIECLE** • 1960
CANDIDE, OU L'OPTIMISME AU XXEME SIECLE • 1960 • Carbonnaux Norbert • FRN • CANDIDE
CANDIDINHA • 1975 • de Macedo Antonio • PRT
CANDIDO EROTICA • 1978 • De Molinis Claudio • ITL • COPENHAGEN NIGHTS ○ CANDIDO EROTICO
CANDIDO EROTICO see **CANDIDO EROTICA** • 1978
CANDLE, THE • 1916 • Kent Leon D. • SHT • USA
CANDLE AND THE MOTH, THE see **EVANGELIEMANDENS LIV** • 1914
CANDLE FOR THE DEVIL, A see **VELA PARA EL DIABLO, UNA** • 1973
CANDLE IN THE WIND, A see **FUZEN NO TOMOSHIBI** • 1957
CANDLELIGHT IN ALGERIA • 1943 • King George • UKN
CANDLELIGHT MURDER, THE • 1953 • Hughes Ken • UKN
CANDLEMAKER, THE • 1956 • Halas John, Batchelor Joy • ANS • UKN
CANDLES AT NINE • 1944 • Harlow John • UKN
CANDLESHOE • 1977 • Tokar Norman • USA
CANDOMBLE ET MACUMBA see **DRAPEAU BLANC D'OXALA, LE** • 1969
CANDY • 1968 • Marquand Christian, Zagni Giancarlo • USA, FRN, ITL • CANDY E IL SUO PAZZO MONDO (ITL)
CANDY see **CANDY BABY** • 1969
CANDY BABY • 1969 • Dial B. H. • USA • DREAMY LOVE BED ○ CANDY
CANDY CABARET • 1954 • Tendlar Dave • ANS • USA
CANDY CANDY • ANM • USA
CANDY COOK, THE • 1916 • *Trembly Lem* • USA
CANDY E IL SUO PAZZO MONDO (ITL) see **CANDY** • 1968
CANDY GIRL, THE • 1912 • *Imp* • USA
CANDY GIRL, THE • 1917 • Moore W. Eugene • USA
CANDY GOES TO HOLLYWOOD • 1979 • Palmer Gail • USA
CANDY HOUSE, THE • 1934 • Lantz Walter, Nolan William • ANS • USA
CANDY JAG, A • 1917 • Ray John • USA
CANDY KID, THE • 1917 • Gillstrom Arvid E. • SHT • USA
CANDY KID, THE • 1928 • Kirkland David • USA
CANDY MAN, THE • 1969 • Leder Herbert J. • USA
CANDY MOUNTAIN • 1987 • Frank Robert, Wurlitzer Rudy • CND, FRN, SWT
CANDY REGENTAG • 1987 • Ricketson James • ASL • KISS THE NIGHT
CANDY STRIPE NURSES • 1975 • Holleb Alan • USA
CANDY STRIPPERS • 1978 • Chinn Robert C. • USA
CANDY TANGERINE MAN, THE • 1975 • Cimber Matt • USA • TANGERINE MAN, THE
CANDY TRAIL, THE • 1916 • *Plump & Runt* • USA
CANDY WEB, THE see **THIRTEEN FRIGHTENED GIRLS** • 1963
CANDYLAND • 1935 • *Lantz Walter (P)* • ANS • USA
CANDY'S LUSTFUL NATURE • 1967 • Millard Nicholas • USA • CANDY'S NATURE
CANDY'S NATURE see **CANDY'S LUSTFUL NATURE** • 1967
CANDYTUFT, I MEAN VERONICA • 1921 • Richardson Frank • UKN
CANE AND ABLE • 1961 • Kneitel Seymour • ANS • USA
CANE E GATTO • 1983 • Corbucci Bruno • ITL • DOG AND CAT
CANE TOADS • 1987 • Lewis Mark • DOC • ASL
CANECUTTERS, THE • 1947 • Heyer John • DOC • ASL
CANELITA EN RAMA • 1942 • Maroto Eduardo G. • SPN
CANGACEIRO, O • 1953 • Barreto Victor • BRZ • CANGACEIRO –THE STORY OF AN OUTLAW BANDIT ○ BANDIT, THE
CANGACEIRO SANGUINARIO, O • 1969 • de Oliveira Oswaldo • BRZ • BLOODY KILLER, THE
CANGACEIRO –THE STORY OF AN OUTLAW BANDIT see **CANGACEIRO, O** • 1953
CANGACEIROS DE LAMPIAO • 1967 • Coimbra Carlos • BRZ • BANDITS OF LAMPIAO
CANGO OLUM SUVARISI • 1967 • Conturk Remzi • TRK • DJANGO, RIDER OF DEATH
CANH DONG MA • 1940 • VTN
CANHAMO, SUA CULTURA E APLICACOES INDUSTRIAIS, O • 1939 • Coelho Jose Adolfo • SHT • PRT
CANI • 1976 • Straub Jean-Marie, Huillet Daniele • FRG, FRN, ITL • CANI DEL SINAI, I (ITL) ○ FORTINI
CANI DEL SINAI, I (ITL) see **CANI** • 1976
CANI E GATTI • 1952 • De Mitri Leonardo • ITL
CANI PERDUTI SENZA COLLARE (ITL) see **CHIENS PERDUS SANS COLLIER** • 1955
CANIBAIS, OS • 1988 • de Oliveira Manoel • PRT • CANNIBALS, THE
CANICHE • 1979 • Luna Bigas • SPN • POODLE
CANICULE • 1983 • Boisset Yves • FRN • DOG DAY (USA) ○ DOGSDAY
CANILER KRALI KILLING • 1967 • Atadeniz Yilmaz • TRK • KILLING, KING OF CRIMINALS
CANIM ANNEM • 1967 • Gulyuz Aram • TRK • MY BELOVED MOTHER
CANIM KARDESIM • 1973 • Egilmez Ertem • TRK • MY BELOVED BROTHER
CANIMATED NOOZ PICTORIAL • 1915-17 • Carlson Wallace A. • ASS • USA
CANINABUS • 1979 • Pindal Kaj • ANS • CND • JUNKIE DOG
CANINE CADDY • 1941 • Geronimi Clyde • ANS • USA
CANINE CAPERS • 1937 • *Mintz Charles (P)* • ANS • USA
CANINE CASANOVA • 1945 • Nichols Charles • ANS • USA
CANINE COMMANDOS • 1943 • Lovy Alex • ANS • USA
CANINE CRIMEBUSTERS • 1952 • Sparling Gordon • DCS • CND
CANINE DETECTIVE, A • 1911 • *Walturdaw* • UKN
CANINE MATCHMAKER, A • 1913 • Duncan William • USA
CANINE PATROL • 1945 • Nichols Charles • ANS • USA
CANINE RIVAL, A • 1914 • *Wadsworth William* • USA
CANINE RIVALS • 1912 • *Solax* • USA
CANINE SHERLOCK HOLMES, A • 1912 • Kinder Stuart • UKN
CANKER OF JEALOUSY, THE see **BE SURE YOUR SINS** • 1915
CANNABIS • 1969 • Koralnik Pierre • FRN, ITL
CANNE A PECHE, LA • 1959 • Dansereau Fernand • SHT • CND
CANNE A SUCRE, LA • 1971 • Al-Rawi Abdel-Hadi • SHT • IRQ
CANNE MOZZE • 1977 • Imperoli Mario • ITL
CANNED CURIOSITY • 1916 • *August Edwin* • SHT • USA
CANNED DOG FEUD • 1965 • Smith Paul J. • ANS • USA
CANNED FEUD • 1951 • Freleng Friz • ANS • USA
CANNED FISHING • 1938 • Douglas Gordon • SHT • USA

CANNED HARMONY • 1912 • *Beggs Lee* • USA
CANNED MUSIC • 1929 • *Mintz Charles (P)* • ANS • USA
CANNERIES, THE • 1988 • Devlin Bonni • DOC • CND
CANNERY RODENT • 1967 • Jones Charles M. • ANS • USA
CANNERY ROW • 1982 • Ward David S. • USA
CANNERY WOE • 1961 • Freleng Friz • ANS • USA
CANNIBAL see **ULTIMO MONDO CANNIBALE** • 1977
CANNIBAL APOCALIPSIS see **APOCALISSE DOMANI** • 1980
CANNIBAL APOCALYPSE see **APOCALISSE DOMANI** • 1980
CANNIBAL ATTACK • 1954 • Sholem Lee • USA
CANNIBAL CAPERS • 1930 • Gillett Burt • ANS • USA
CANNIBAL COUNTRY see **IN THE COUNTRY OF THE CANNIBALS** • 1958
CANNIBAL FEROX • 1980 • Lenzi Umberto • ITL • MAKE THEM DIE SLOWLY
CANNIBAL GIRLS • 1973 • Reitman Ivan • CND
CANNIBAL HOLOCAUST • 1980 • Deodato Ruggero • ITL • JUNGLE HOLOCAUST
CANNIBAL HOOKERS • 1987 • Farmer Dan • USA
CANNIBAL KING • 1915 • *Hardy Oliver* • USA
CANNIBAL MAN, THE see **SEMANA DEL ASESINO, LA** • 1972
CANNIBAL ORGY, OR THE MADDEST STORY EVER TOLD see **SPIDER BABY** • 1964
CANNIBAL TERROR • Steeve Allan W. • FRN
CANNIBAL TOURS • 1988 • O'Rourke Dennis • DOC • ASL
CANNIBAL WOMEN IN THE AVOCADO JUNGLE OF DEATH see **PIRANHA WOMEN** • 1988
CANNIBALI, I • 1970 • Cavani Liliana • ITL • YEAR OF THE CANNIBALS, THE (USA) ○ CANNIBALS AMONG US, THE ○ CANNIBALS, THE
CANNIBALS see **MANGIATI VIVI DAI CANNIBALI** • 1980
CANNIBALS, THE see **CANNIBALI, I** • 1970
CANNIBALS, THE see **CANIBAIS, OS** • 1988
CANNIBALS AMONG US, THE see **CANNIBALI, I** • 1970
CANNIBALS AND CARNIVALS • 1918 • Moore Vin • SHT • USA • CARNIVALS AND CANNIBALS
CANNIBALS ARE IN THE STREETS see **APOCALISSE DOMANI** • 1980
CANNIBALS OF THE SOUTH SEAS • 1912 • Johnson Martin E. • USA • HEAD HUNTERS OF MALEKULA
CANNING THE CANNIBAL KING • 1917 • Beaudine William • SHT • USA
CANNON • 1970 • McCowan George • TVM • USA
CANNON see **KARAMBOLAGE** • 1983
CANNON BALL, THE • 1915 • Parrott Charles • USA
CANNON BALL EXPRESS, THE • 1924 • *Sennett Mack (P)* • SHT • USA
CANNON BALL JUGGLING • 1901 • *Warwick Trading Co* • UKN
CANNON FOR CORDOBA • 1970 • Wendkos Paul • USA, SPN • DRAGON MASTER
CANNON: HE WHO DIGS A GRAVE • 1973 • Donner Richard • TVM • USA
CANNON MOVIE TALES: RED RIDING HOOD see **LITTLE RED RIDING HOOD** • 1987
CANNON MOVIE TALES: SLEEPING BEAUTY see **SLEEPING BEAUTY** • 1987
CANNON MOVIE TALES: SNOW WHITE see **SNOW WHITE** • 1987
CANNON MOVIE TALES: THE EMPEROR'S NEW CLOTHES see **EMPEROR'S NEW CLOTHES, THE** • 1987
CANNON SMOKE AND RAIN OF SHELLS see **HOEN DANU** • 1927
CANNONADE see **KANONADA** • 1964
CANNONBALL • 1976 • Bartel Paul • USA, HKG • CARQUAKE (UKN)
CANNONBALL, THE • 1931 • Lord Del • SHT • USA
CANNONBALL, THE see **ORGANCHIK** • 1946
CANNONBALL ADDERLEY SEXTET • 1962 • Binder Steve • SHT • USA
CANNONBALL EXPRESS, THE • 1932 • Fox Wallace • USA
CANNONBALL RUN, THE • 1981 • Needham Hal • USA
CANNONBALL RUN II • 1984 • Needham Hal • USA
CANNONI DI SAN SEBASTIAN, I (ITL) see **CANONES DE SAN SEBASTIAN, LOS** • 1967
CANNONI TUONANO ANCORA, I • 1975 • Colasanti Sergio • ITL
CANNONS OR TRACTORS see **SEGODNYA** • 1930
CANOA • 1975 • Cazals Felipe • MXC
CANOL • 1944 • Finnie Richard S. • DOC • CND
CANON • 1964 • McLaren Norman, Munro Grant • ANS • CND
CANON CITY • 1948 • Wilbur Crane • USA • CANYON CITY
CANONES DE SAN SEBASTIAN, LOS • 1967 • Verneuil Henri • FRN, ITL, MXC • BATAILLE DE SAN SEBASTIAN, LA (FRN) ○ GUNS FOR SAN SEBASTIAN (USA) ○ CANNONI DI SAN SEBASTIAN, I (ITL)
CANOODLING • 1928 • *De Forest Films* • SHT • UKN
CANOTS DE GLACE, LES • 1969 • Labrecque Jean-Claude • DCS • CND
CAN'T BUY ME LOVE • 1987 • Rash Steve • USA • BOY RENTS GIRL
CAN'T HELP LOVING DAT MAN • 1929 • Aylott Dave, Symmons E. F. • SHT • UKN
CAN'T HELP SINGING • 1944 • Ryan Frank • USA
CAN'T STOP THE MUSIC • 1980 • Walker Nancy • USA
CAN'T STOP THE WAR • 1983 • Yu K'An-P'Ing • TWN
CAN'T YOU HEAR THE DOGS BARKING? see **NO OYES LADRAR A LOS PERROS?** • 1974
CANTA MI CORAZON • 1964 • Gomez Muriel Emilio • MXC
CANTA Y NO LLORES • 1949 • Patino Gomez Alfonso • MXC
CANTACLARO • 1945 • Bracho Julio • MXC
CANTAGALLO • 1969 • Inman Jeff • DCS • UKN
CANTAMI: BUONGIORNO TRISTEZZA! • 1956 • Pastina Giorgio • ITL
CANTANDO A LA VIDA • 1968 • Fons Angelino • SPN
CANTANDO LLEGO EL AMOR • 1938 • Bauer James • ARG
CANTANDO NACE EL AMOR • 1953 • Delgado Miguel M. • MXC
CANTANDO SOTTO LE STELLE • 1956 • Girolami Marino • ITL
CANTANTE CON ME! • 1940 • Brignone Guido • ITL
CANTANTE DE NAPOLES, EL • 1935 • Bretherton Howard • MXC • SINGER OF NAPLES, THE (USA)
CANTANTE DELL'OPERA, LA • 1932 • Malasomma Nunzio • ITL
CANTANTE MISTERIOSO, IL • 1955 • Girolami Marino • ITL
CANTAR DI MI CIUDAD, EL • 1930 • Ferreyra Jose • ARG
CANTATA DE CHILE • 1977 • Solas Humberto • CUB • CANTATA OF CHILE
CANTATA OF CHILE see **CANTATA DE CHILE** • 1977
CANTATA (UKN) see **OLDAS ES KOTES** • 1963
CANTATE CON ME! • 1940 • Brignone Guido • ITL • LASCIATEMI CANTARE!
CANTATE CON NOI • 1956 • Montero Roberto Bianchi • ITL
CANTE-MIRACLE see **MILAGRO DEL CANTE, EL** • 1967
CANTERBURY N.2, NUOVE STORIE D'AMORE DEL '300 • 1973 • Shadow John • ITL
CANTERBURY PROIBITO • 1972 • Alfaro Italo • ITL
CANTERBURY TALE, A • 1944 • Powell Michael, Pressburger Emeric • UKN
CANTERBURY TALES, THE (UKN) see **RACCONTI DI CANTERBURY, I** • 1972
CANTERVILLE GHOST, THE • 1944 • Dassin Jules • USA
CANTERVILLE GHOST, THE • 1954 • *Woolley Monty* • SHT • USA
CANTERVILLE GHOST, THE • 1986 • Bogart Paul • TVM • USA
CANTERVILLE GHOST, THE see **DUCH Z CANTERVILLE** • 1967
CANTICO see **CHICAS DE CLUB** • 1970
CANTICO DELLA TERRA • 1935 • Ramponi Salvatore F. • ITL • CAPANNA DELL'AMORE, LA
CANTICO DELLE CREATURE • 1943 • Emmer Luciano, Gras Enrico • ITL
CANTICO FINAL • 1976 • Guimaraes Manuel, Guimaraes Dordio • PRT • LAST SONG, THE
CANTIERE D'INVERNO • 1955 • Olmi Ermanno • DOC • ITL
CANTIERI DELL'ADRIATICO, I • 1933 • Barbaro Umberto • SHT • ITL • SHIPYARD AT THE ADRIATIC SEA
CANTIGA DA RUA • 1949 • Campos Henrique • PRT
CANTIGAMENTE • 1976 • Ceitil Rogerio, de Sousa Ernesto, Vasconcelos Antonio-Pedro • PRT
CANTINAS ESCOLARES • 1950 • Garcia Fernando • SHT • PRT
CANTINIER DE LA COLONIALE, LE • 1937 • Wulschleger Henry • FRN • UN DE LA COLONIALE
CANTIQUE DE LA CREATION • 1942 • Tessier Albert • DCS • CND
CANTIQUE DES PIERRES • 1989 • Khleifi Michel • BLG
CANTIQUE DU SOLEIL • 1935 • Tessier Albert • DCS • CND
CANTO A LA ESPERANZA • 1964 • Aguirre Javier • SHT • SPN
CANTO A LAS AMERICAS • 1942 • Pereda Ramon • MXC
CANTO A MI TIERRA • 1938 • Bohr Jose • MXC • MEXICO CANTA
CANTO DA SAUDADE, O • 1952 • Mauro-Humberto • BRZ • SONG OF SADNESS, THE
CANTO D'ADDIO see **VIVERE!** • 1937
CANTO DE LA SIRENA, EL • 1946 • Foster Norman • MXC • SONG OF THE SIREN (UKN)
CANTO DEL GALLO, EL • 1955 • Gil Rafael • SPN
CANTO DELLA VITA, IL • 1945 • Gallone Carmine • ITL
CANTO DELL'AMORE, IL see **IN CERCA DI FELICITA** • 1943
CANTO DELL'EMIGRANTE, IL • 1956 • Forzano Andrea • ITL
CANTO DI CIRCE, IL • 1920 • De Liguoro Giuseppe • ITL
CANTO DO MAR, O • 1954 • Cavalcanti Alberto • BRZ • SONG OF THE SEA
CANTO LIBRE • 1979 • Sapiain Claudio • MTV • SWD • FREE SONG
CANTO LIVRE, O • 1968 • Barreto Luis Carlos • BRZ • FREE SONG, THE
CANTO, MA SOTTOVOCE • 1946 • Brignone Guido • ITL
CANTO NEL DESERTO, UN • 1960 • Girolami Marino • ITL
CANTO PARATI • 1958 • Almeida Sebastian • SPN
CANTO PER TE • 1956 • Girolami Marino • ITL
CANTON IRON KUNG FU • Li Chao • HKG • IRON FIST OF KWANGTUNG ○ CANTONEN IRON KUNG FU ○ CANTONESE IRON KUNG FU
CANTONEN IRON KUNG FU see **CANTON IRON KUNG FU**
CANTONESE IRON KUNG FU see **CANTON IRON KUNG FU**
CANTOR DE BUENOS AIRES, EL • 1940 • Irigoyen Julio • ARG
CANTOR E A BAILARINA, O • 1959 • Miranda Armando • PRT
CANTORIA D'ANGELI • 1949 • Hamza D. A. • SHT • ITL
CANTOR'S SON, THE • 1937 • Motylef Ilya
CANTRELL'S MADONNA • 1916 • Mills Thomas R. • SHT • USA
CANUDOS • 1980 • Pontes Ipojuca • BRZ
CANVAS KISSER, THE • 1925 • Worne Duke • USA
CANVASBACK DUCK • 1953 • Hannah Jack • ANS • USA
CANYON AMBUSH • 1953 • Collins Lewis D. • USA
CANYON CITY • 1943 • Bennet Spencer Gordon • USA
CANYON CITY see **CANON CITY** • 1948
CANYON CROSSROADS • 1955 • Werker Alfred L. • USA
CANYON DWELLER, THE • 1912 • Dwan Allan • USA
CANYON HAWKS • 1930 • Neitz Alvin J. • USA
CANYON HOLD-UP, THE • 1918 • Bradbury Robert North • USA
CANYON MYSTERY, THE • 1919 • Harvey Harry • SHT • USA
CANYON OF ADVENTURE, THE • 1928 • Rogell Albert S. • USA
CANYON OF LIGHT, THE • 1926 • Stoloff Ben • USA
CANYON OF MISSING MEN, THE • 1930 • McGowan J. P. • USA
CANYON OF THE FOOLS • 1923 • Paul Val • USA
CANYON PASS (UKN) see **RATON PASS** • 1951
CANYON PASSAGE • 1946 • Tourneur Jacques • USA
CANYON RAIDERS • 1951 • Collins Lewis D. • USA
CANYON RIVER • 1956 • Jones Harmon • USA
CANYON RUSTLERS • 1925 • Webb Harry S. • USA
CANZONE APPASSIONATA • 1954 • Simonelli Giorgio C. • ITL
CANZONE D'AMORE • 1954 • Simonelli Giorgio C. • ITL
CANZONE DEL CUORE, LA • 1955 • Campogalliani Carlo • ITL
CANZONE DEL DESTINO • 1958 • Girolami Marino • ITL
CANZONE DEL SOLE, LA • 1933 • Neufeld Max • ITL
CANZONE DELL'AMORE, LA • 1930 • Righelli Gennaro • ITL • SILENZIO
CANZONE DI PRIMAVERA • 1950 • Costa Mario • ITL
CANZONE PIU BELLA, LA • 1957 • Bertolini Ottorino Franco • ITL
CANZONE PROIBITA • 1956 • Calzavara Flavio • ITL
CANZONE RUBATA, LA • 1941 • Neufeld Max • ITL • VALZER DELLA FELICITA, IL
CANZONI A DUE VOCI • 1954 • Vernuccio Gianni • ITL
CANZONI A TEMPO DI TWIST • 1962 • Canzio Stefano • ITL
CANZONI, BULLI E PUPE • 1964 • Infascelli Carlo • ITL
CANZONI, CANZONI, CANZONI • 1953 • Paolella Domenico • ITL • CAVALCADE OF SONG (USA)
CANZONI DI IERI, CANZONI DI OGGI, CANZONI DI DOMANI • 1962 • Paolella Domenico • ITL
CANZONI DI MEZZO SECOLO • 1952 • Paolella Domenico • ITL • HALF A CENTURY OF SONGS (USA)
CANZONI DI TUTTI ITALIA • 1956 • Paolella Domenico • ITL
CANZONI IN.. BIKINI • 1963 • Vari Giuseppe • ITL
CANZONI NEL MONDO • 1963 • Sala Vittorio • ITL • 38 – 24 – 36 (USA)
CANZONI PER LE STRADE • 1951 • Landi Mario • ITL
CAO-XA • 1972 • Herrero Pedro Mario • SPN
CAP, THE see **KAPA** • 1971
CAP AU LARGE • 1942 • Paulin Jean-Paul • FRN • VENT DEBOUT
CAP CANAILLE • 1982 • Roger Jean-Henri, Berto Juliet • FRN, BLG
CAP DE L'ESPERANCE, LE • 1951 • Bernard Raymond • FRN, ITL • NOSTRA PELLE, LA (ITL)
CAP D'ESPOIR • 1970 • Leduc Jacques • CND
CAP DU SUD • 1935 • Storck Henri • DOC • BLG
CAP HORN • 1977 • Hussenot Yves • FRN
CAP NAPPING • 1951 • Hanna William, Barbera Joseph • ANS • USA
CAP NIPPED • 1932 • Lantz Walter, Nolan William • ANS • USA
CAP OF DESTINY, THE • 1913 • Smalley Phillips, Weber Lois • USA
CAP OF FORTUNE, THE • 1909 • *Edison* • USA
CAP OF INVISIBILITY, THE • 1911 • Bouwmeester Theo?, Booth W. R.? • UKN
CAP PERDU, LE • 1931 • Dupont E. A. • FRN
CAPABLE LADY COOK, A • 1916 • Beery Wallace • SHT • USA
CAPABLES D'ETRE UN PEU FOUS.. • 1973 • Favreau Robert • DCS • CND
CAPAILL • 1969 • Marcus Louis • DOC • IRL
CAPALLOLOGY • 1974 • Marcus Louis • SHT • IRL • HORSE LAUGHS
CAPANNA DELL'AMORE, LA see **CANTICO DELLA TERRA** • 1935
CAPAS NEGRAS • 1947 • Miranda Armando • PRT
CAPCANA • 1973 • Marcus Manole • RMN • SINGLE-HANDED
CAPE ASHIZURI see **ASHIZURI MISAKI** • 1954
CAPE CANAVERAL MONSTERS, THE • 1960 • Tucker Phil • USA
CAPE FEAR • 1961 • Thompson J. Lee • USA
CAPE FORLORN • 1930 • Dupont E. A. • UKN • LOVE STORMS (USA) ○ LOVE STORM, THE
CAPE ISLANDER, THE • 1962 • Perry Margaret • DOC • CND
CAPE KIDNAVERAL • 1961 • Kneitel Seymour • ANS • USA
CAPE OF THE NORTH see **KITA NO MISAKI** • 1975
CAPE TOWN AFFAIR, THE see **ESCAPE ROUTE CAPE TOWN** • 1967
CAPEDIMONTE • 1957 • Sala Vittorio • DOC • ITL
CAPEK'S TALES (USA) see **CAPKOVY POVIDKY** • 1947
CAPER OF THE GOLDEN BULLS, THE • 1966 • Rouse Russell • USA • CARNIVAL OF THIEVES (UKN)
CAPERS see **HOW COME NOBODY'S ON OUR SIDE** • 1975
CAPERS AND CROOKS • 1918 • Howe J. A. • SHT • USA
CAPERS OF COLLEGE CHAPS • 1915 • *Chamberlin Riley* • USA
CAPERS OF CUPID, THE • 1913 • *Vitagraph* • USA
CAPERUCITA ROJA, LA • 1960 • Rodriguez Roberto • MXC • LITTLE RED RIDING HOOD (USA)
CAPERUCITA Y PULGARCITO CONTRA LOS MONSTRUOS • 1960 • Rodriguez Roberto • MXC • LITTLE RED RIDING HOOD AND THE MONSTERS (USA) ○ LITTLE RED RIDING HOOD AND TOM THUMB VS. THE MONSTERS
CAPERUCITA Y ROJA • 1976 • Goiricelaya Aitor, Revenga Luis • SPN • RIDING HOOD AND RED
CAPERUCITA Y SUS TRE AMIGOS • 1960 • Rodriguez Roberto • MXC • LITTLE RED RIDING HOOD AND HER FRIENDS (USA) ○ LITTLE RED RIDING HOOD AND HER THREE FRIENDS
CAPINERA DEL MULINO, LA • 1957 • Zane Angio • ITL
CAPITAINE ARDANT • 1951 • Zwobada Andre • FRN
CAPITAINE BENOIT, LE • 1938 • de Canonge Maurice • FRN
CAPITAINE BLOMET • 1947 • Feix Andree • FRN • N'ECRIVEZ JAMAIS
CAPITAINE CORSAIRE see **MOLLENARD** • 1937
CAPITAINE CRADDOCK, LE • 1931 • de Vaucorbeil Max, Schwarz Hanns • FRN • BOMBE SUR MONTE CARLO, UN ○ CROISSEUR EN FOLIE, LE
CAPITAINE DE 15 ANS, UN • 1972 • Franco Jesus
CAPITAINE FRACASSE, LE • 1909 • Jasset Victorin • FRN
CAPITAINE FRACASSE, LE • 1929 • Cavalcanti Alberto • FRN
CAPITAINE FRACASSE, LE • 1942 • Gance Abel • FRN, ITL • MASCHERA SUL CUORE, LA (ITL)
CAPITAINE FRACASSE, LE • 1960 • Gaspard-Huit Pierre • FRN, ITL
CAPITAINE FUOCO (FRN) see **CAPITAN FUOCO** • 1959
CAPITAINE H, LE • 1960 • Languepin Jean-Jacques • UKN
CAPITAINE JAUNE, LE • 1930 • Sandberg Anders W. • FRN
CAPITAINE MOLLENARD see **MOLLENARD** • 1937
CAPITAINE MORGAN (FRN) see **MORGAN IL PIRATA** • 1960
CAPITAINE NOIR, LE • 1916 • Bourgeois Gerard • FRN
CAPITAINE PANTOUFLE • 1953 • Lefranc Guy • FRN
CAPITAINE RASCASSE, LE • 1927 • Desfontaines Henri • FRN
CAPITAINE SABORD APPAREILLE, LE • 1943 • Rigal Andre • ANS • FRN
CAPITAINE SINGRID • 1967 • Leduc Jean • FRN, ITL, PRT • MERCENARI MUOIONO ALL'ALBA, I (ITL) ○ CAPTAIN SINGRID (UKN)
CAPITAL • 1980 • Kroeker Allan • CND
CAPITAL OFFENSE see **HOT SUMMER NIGHT** • 1956
CAPITAL PRIZE, THE • 1916 • Stevens Edwin • SHT • USA
CAPITAL PUNISHMENT • 1915 • Levering Joseph • USA
CAPITAL PUNISHMENT • 1925 • Hogan James P. • USA

CAPITAL STORY • 1945 • Rodakiewicz Henwar • SHT • USA
CAPITAL VS. LABOR • 1910 • Brooke Van Dyke • USA
CAPITALE DE L'OR see **CITY OF GOLD** • 1957
CAPITALI DI NOTTE N.2 • 1978 • Bernabei Claudio • ITL
CAPITAN, LE • 1945 • Vernay Robert • FRN • CHEVALIER DU ROI, LE ○ FLAMBERGE AU VENT ○ KING'S KNIGHT, THE
CAPITAN, LE • 1960 • Hunebelle Andre • FRN, ITL • CAPITANO DEL RE, IL (ITL) ○ CAPTAIN BLOOD (USA)
CAPITAN AVENTURERO, EL • 1938 • Boytler Arcady • MXC • ADVENTUROUS CAPTAIN, THE (USA) ○ DON GIL DE ALCALA
CAPITAN BIANCO • 1914 • Martoglio Nino • ITL
CAPITAN CASANOVA, EL (MXC) see **ADVENTURES OF CASANOVA** • 1947
CAPITAN CENTELLAS, EL • 1941 • Pereda Ramon • MXC
CAPITAN DE LOYOLA, EL • 1948 • Diaz Morales Jose • SPN • LOYOLA, THE SOLDIER SAINT
CAPITAN DE RURALES • 1950 • Galindo Alejandro • MXC
CAPITAN DEMONIO • 1951 • Borghesio Carlo • ITL
CAPITAN FANTASMA • 1954 • Zeglio Primo • ITL • CAPTAIN GHOST
CAPITAN FRACASSA • 1909 • Pasquali Ernesto Maria • ITL
CAPITAN FRACASSA • 1917 • Caserini Mario • ITL
CAPITAN FRACASSA • 1919 • Guazzoni Enrico • ITL
CAPITAN FRACASSA • 1940 • Coletti Duilio • ITL
CAPITAN FUOCO • 1959 • Campogalliani Carlo • ITL, FRN • CAPITAINE FUOCO (FRN) ○ CAPTAIN FALCON -ADVENTURER
CAPITAN MALACARA, EL • 1944 • Orellana Carlos • MXC
CAPITAN MIRANDA • 1981 • Sola Raul • URG
CAPITAN PEREZ • 1946 • Cahen Enrique • ARG
CAPITAN TEMPESTA • 1942 • D'Errico Corrado • ITL
CAPITAN VENENO, EL • 1950 • Marquina Luis • SPN
CAPITANAL ET SASSAMASKIN • 1943-44 • Tessier Albert • DCS • CND
CAPITANI DI VENTURA • 1961 • Dorigo Angelo • ITL
CAPITANO DEGLI USSARI, IL • 1941 • Szlatinay Alessandro • ITL
CAPITANO DEL RE, IL (ITL) see **CAPITAN, LE** • 1960
CAPITANO DELLA LEGIONE, IL (ITL) see **SENECHAL LE MAGNIFIQUE** • 1957
CAPITANO DI FERRO, IL • 1963 • Grieco Sergio • ITL
CAPITANO DI VENEZIA, IL • 1954 • Puccini Gianni • ITL
CAPITANO NERO, IL • 1951 • Pozzetti Alberto, Ansoldi Giorgio • ITL
CAPITOL, THE • 1920 • Irving George • USA
CAPITOL HELL • 1987 • Jameson Jerry • USA
CAPITOL SONG CYCLE see **MASTER SONG SCENAS** • 1922
CAPITU • 1968 • Saraceni Paulo Cesar • BRZ
CAPITULATION OF THE MAJOR, THE • 1915 • North Wilfred • USA
CAPKOVY POVIDKY • 1947 • Fric Martin • CZC • CAPEK'S TALES (USA) ○ TALES FROM CAPEK ○ TALES OF CAPEK ○ TALES BY CAPEK ○ KAREL CAPEK'S TALES
CAP'N ABE'S NIECE see **CAPTAIN'S CAPTAIN, THE** • 1918
CAP'N JERICHO (UKN) see **HELL AND HIGH WATER** • 1933
CAPODANNO 2000 • Comencini Luigi • ITL • NEW YEAR'S DAY 2000
CAPONE • 1975 • Carver Steve • USA
CAPONE • 1988 • Milius John • USA
CAPONE'S ENFORCER see **NITTI** • 1988
CAPORAL, EL • 1921 • Abitia Jesus B., Zatarain Rafael Bermudez • MXC
CAPORAL, EL see **GABINO BARRERA** • 1964
CAPORAL EPINGLE, LE • 1961 • Renoir Jean • FRN • VANISHING CORPORAL, THE (UKN) ○ ELUSIVE CORPORAL, THE (USA)
CAPORALE DI GIORNATA • 1958 • Bragaglia Carlo Ludovico • ITL • SOLDIER ON DUTY
CAPPELLA SISTINA, LA • 1920 • Lolli Alberto Carlo • DOC • ITL
CAPPELLO A TRE PUNTE, IL • 1935 • Camerini Mario • ITL
CAPPELLO DA PRETE, IL • 1944 • Poggioli Ferdinando M. • ITL • CASTIGO
CAPPOTTO, IL • 1952 • Lattuada Alberto • ITL • OVERCOAT, THE
CAPPOTTO DI ASTRAKAN, IL • 1979 • Vicario Marco • ITL • ASTRAKAN COAT, THE
CAPPOTTO DI LEGNO • 1979 • Manera Gianni • ITL
CAPPUCINO • 1988 • Bowman Anthony • ASL
CAPPY RICKS • 1921 • Forman Tom • USA
CAPPY RICKS RETURNS • 1935 • Wright Mack V. • USA
CAPRELLES ET PANTOPODES • 1930 • Painleve Jean • SHT • FRN
CAPRICCI • 1969 • Bene Carmelo • ITL
CAPRICCIO • 1938 • Ritter Karl • FRG
CAPRICCIO • Huszarik Zoltan • SHT • HNG
CAPRICCIO • 1987 • Brass Tinto • ITL • LETTER FROM CAPRI ○ CAPRICE
CAPRICCIO ALL'ITALIANA • 1968 • Zac Pino, Steno, Monicelli Mario, Bolognini Mauro, Pasolini Pier Paolo • ITL • CAPRICE ITALIAN STYLE
CAPRICE • 1913 • Dawley J. Searle • USA
CAPRICE • 1967 • Tashlin Frank • USA
CAPRICE • 1987 • Hogg Joanna • USA
CAPRICE • 1989 • Marr Leon G. • CND
CAPRICE see **CAPRICCIO** • 1987
CAPRICE DE CAROLINE CHERIE, UN • 1952 • Devaivre Jean • FRN • CAPRICE OF "DEAR CAROLINE" (USA) ○ CAPRICE OF CAROLINE
CAPRICE DE LA POMPADOUR, UN • 1930 • Hamman Joe, Wolff Willi • FRN
CAPRICE DE NOEL see **CHRISTMAS CRACKER** • 1964
CAPRICE DE PRINCESSE • 1933 • Clouzot Henri-Georges, Hartl Karl • FRN
CAPRICE EN COULEURS see **BEGONE DULL CARE** • 1949
CAPRICE ESPAGNOL see **DEVIL IS A WOMAN, THE** • 1935
CAPRICE ITALIAN STYLE see **CAPRICCIO ALL'ITALIANA** • 1968
CAPRICE OF CAROLINE see **CAPRICE DE CAROLINE CHERIE, UN** • 1952
CAPRICE OF "DEAR CAROLINE" (USA) see **CAPRICE DE CAROLINE CHERIE, UN** • 1952
CAPRICE OF THE MOUNTAINS • 1916 • Adolfi John G. • USA
CAPRICES • 1941 • Joannon Leo • FRN
CAPRICES DE MARIANNE, LES see **REGLE DU JEU, LA** • 1939
CAPRICES DE MARIE, LES • 1969 • de Broca Philippe • FRN, ITL • PORTAMI QUELLO CHE HAI E PRENDITI QUELLO CHE VUOI (ITL) ○ GIVE HER THE MOON (USA) ○ FIGURANTS DU NOUVEAU MONDE, LES
CAPRICES DE MICHELINE, LES see **LECON DE CONDUITE** • 1945
CAPRICES D'UNE SOURI, LES • Reinhard Pierre B. • FRN
CAPRICES OF FORTUNE • 1912 • *Johnstone Lamar* • USA
CAPRICES OF KITTY, THE • 1915 • Smalley Phillips • USA
CAPRICES OF LOVE, THE see **ROZMARY LASKY** • 1970
CAPRICHOSA Y MILLONARIA • 1940 • Discepolo Enrique Santos • ARG
CAPRICIOUS SUMMER see **ROZMARNE LETO** • 1967
CAPRICORN ONE • 1978 • Hyams Peter • USA
CAPRIOLEN • 1937 • Grundgens Gustaf • FRG
CAPRIOLEN • 1939 • Forst Willi • FRG
CAPSHEAF BALLAD, A see **CHOCOLOWA BALLADA** • 1961
CAPTAIN • Weiler Kurt • ANM • GDR
CAPTAIN, THE • 1954 • Braun Vladimir • USS
CAPTAIN ADVENTURE see **AVVENTURE DI MANDRIN, LE** • 1952
CAPTAIN ALVAREZ • 1914 • Sturgeon Rollin S. • USA
CAPTAIN AMERICA • 1944 • Clifton Elmer, English John • SRL • USA • RETURN OF CAPTAIN AMERICA, THE
CAPTAIN AMERICA • 1979 • Holcomb Rod • TVM • USA
CAPTAIN AMERICA BATTLES THE RED SKULL • 1964 • *Glut Don (P)* • SHT • USA
CAPTAIN AMERICA II • 1970 • Nagy Ivan • TVM • USA • CAPTAIN AMERICAN II: DEATH TOO SOON
CAPTAIN AMERICA VS. THE MUTANT • 1964 • *Glut Don (P)* • SHT • USA
CAPTAIN AMERICAN II: DEATH TOO SOON see **CAPTAIN AMERICA II** • 1970
CAPTAIN APACHE • 1971 • Singer Alexander • USA, UKN, SPN • GUN OF APRIL MORNING, THE
CAPTAIN APPLEJACK • 1931 • Henley Hobart • USA
CAPTAIN APPLEJACK see **STRANGERS OF THE NIGHT** • 1923
CAPTAIN ARBANAS MARKO see **KAPETAN ARBANAS MARKO** • 1968
CAPTAIN ATOM • Brzezinski Tony • SHT • USA
CAPTAIN AVENGER • 1979 • *Ritter John* • USA
CAPTAIN BARNACLE, DIPLOMAT • 1911 • *Costello Maurice* • USA
CAPTAIN BARNACLE, REFORMER • 1912 • Brooke Van Dyke • USA
CAPTAIN BARNACLE'S BABY • 1911 • *Vitagraph* • USA
CAPTAIN BARNACLE'S CHAPERONE • 1910 • *Vitagraph* • USA
CAPTAIN BARNACLE'S COURTSHIP • 1911 • Baker George D. • USA
CAPTAIN BARNACLE'S LEGACY • 1912 • *Brooke Van Dyke* • USA
CAPTAIN BARNACLE'S MESSMATE • 1912 • *Bunny John* • USA
CAPTAIN BARNACLE'S WAIF • 1912 • Brooke Van Dyke • USA
CAPTAIN BEN'S YARN • 1912 • *Prior Herbert* • USA
CAPTAIN BILL • 1935 • Ceder Ralph • UKN
CAPTAIN BILL'S WARM RECEPTION • 1914 • *Moran Lee* • USA
CAPTAIN BILLY'S MATE • 1913 • *Cunard Grace* • USA
CAPTAIN BLACK JACK (USA) see **BLACK JACK** • 1949
CAPTAIN BLACKBIRD see **LOST AND FOUND ON A SOUTH SEA ISLAND** • 1923
CAPTAIN BLOOD • 1924 • Smith David • USA
CAPTAIN BLOOD • 1935 • Curtiz Michael • USA
CAPTAIN BLOOD, FUGITIVE (UKN) see **CAPTAIN PIRATE** • 1952
CAPTAIN BLOOD (USA) see **CAPITAN, LE** • 1960
CAPTAIN BOBBY OF THE HOME DEFENDERS • 1917 • Ridgwell George • SHT • USA
CAPTAIN BOYCOTT • 1947 • Launder Frank • UKN
CAPTAIN BRAND'S WIFE • 1911 • *Ayres Sydney* • USA
CAPTAIN BUSBY • 1967 • Wolff Ann • UKN
CAPTAIN BY CHANCE see **ATARIYA TAISHO** • 1962
CAPTAIN CALAMITY • 1936 • Reinhardt John • USA
CAPTAIN CARELESS • 1928 • Storm Jerome • USA
CAPTAIN CAREY, U.S.A. • 1950 • Leisen Mitchell • USA • AFTER MIDNIGHT (UKN)
CAPTAIN CAUTION • 1940 • Wallace Richard • USA
CAPTAIN CHINA • 1949 • Foster Lewis R. • USA
CAPTAIN CLEGG • 1962 • Scott Peter Graham • UKN • NIGHT CREATURES (USA) ○ DR. SYN
CAPTAIN COURTESY • 1915 • Bosworth Hobart • USA
CAPTAIN COWBOY • 1929 • McGowan J. P. • USA
CAPTAIN CUFF'S NEIGHBOURS • 1912 • Aylott Dave? • UKN
CAPTAIN DABAC see **KAPITAN DABAC** • 1959
CAPTAIN DANDY, BUSHRANGER • 1912 • Aylott Dave? • UKN
CAPTAIN DIEPPE (UKN) see **ADVENTURE IN HEARTS, AN** • 1920
CAPTAIN EDDIE • 1944 • Bacon Lloyd • USA • FIRST, LAST AND ALWAYS
CAPTAIN ENRICO'S WATCH see **CHASY KAPITANA ENRIKO** • 1968
CAPTAIN ERI • 1915 • Lessey George A. • USA
CAPTAIN FALCON -ADVENTURER see **CAPITAN FUOCO** • 1959
CAPTAIN FANTIS see **KAPETAN FANTIS BASTOUNIS, O** • 1968
CAPTAIN FLORIAN OF THE MILL see **HAUPTMANN FLORIAN VON DER MUHLE** • 1968
CAPTAIN FLY-BY-NIGHT • 1922 • Howard William K. • USA
CAPTAIN FRACASSE • 1915 • *Smith Vola* • USA
CAPTAIN FROM CASTILE • 1947 • King Henry • USA
CAPTAIN FROM KOPENICK, THE (USA) see **HAUPTMANN VON KOPENICK, ER** • 1956
CAPTAIN FROM TOLEDO (UKN) see **HOMBRE DE TOLEDO, EL** • 1966
CAPTAIN FURY • 1939 • Roach Hal • USA
CAPTAIN FUTURE: SPECIAL AGENTS AND ALIEN CUT-THROATS • 1985 • Barron Robert • ANM • USA
CAPTAIN GHOST see **CAPITAN FANTASMA** • 1954
CAPTAIN GOODVIBES -HOT TO TROT • 1977 • Elfick David • SHT • ASL
CAPTAIN GRANT'S CHILDREN see **DETI KAPITANA GRANTA** • 1936
CAPTAIN HAREBLOWER • 1954 • Freleng Friz • ANS • USA
CAPTAIN HARLOCK VOL.1 • 1977 • ANM • JPN
CAPTAIN HATES THE SEA, THE • 1934 • Milestone Lewis • USA
CAPTAIN HITS THE CEILING, THE • 1935 • Lamont Charles • SHT • USA
CAPTAIN HORATIO HORNBLOWER R.N. • 1951 • Walsh Raoul • UKN • CAPTAIN HORATIO HORNBLOWER (USA) ○ HORATIO HORNBLOWER
CAPTAIN HORATIO HORNBLOWER (USA) see **CAPTAIN HORATIO HORNBLOWER R.N.** • 1951
CAPTAIN HURRICANE • 1935 • Robertson John S. • USA
CAPTAIN HURRICANE see **BINBASI TAYFUN** • 1968
CAPTAIN IS A LADY, THE • 1940 • Sinclair Robert B. • USA • OLD LADY THIRTY-ONE
CAPTAIN JACK • 1973 • Neretniece E. • USS
CAPTAIN JACK V.C. • 1913 • Plumb Hay • UKN
CAPTAIN JANUARY • 1924 • Cline Eddie • USA
CAPTAIN JANUARY • 1936 • Butler David • USA
CAPTAIN JENKS' DILEMMA • 1912 • *Bunny John* • USA
CAPTAIN JENKS' DIPLOMACY • 1912 • Brooke Van Dyke • USA
CAPTAIN JENNY, S.A. • 1914 • Turner Otis • USA
CAPTAIN JINKS' ALIBI • 1917 • Brooke Van Dyke • SHT • USA
CAPTAIN JINKS AND HIMSELF • 1917 • Bertsch Marguerite • SHT • USA
CAPTAIN JINKS' BETTER HALF • 1917 • *Vitagraph* • USA
CAPTAIN JINKS' CURE • 1917 • Brooke Van Dyke • SHT • USA
CAPTAIN JINKS' EVOLUTION • 1916 • Ellery Arthur • SHT • USA
CAPTAIN JINKS' EXPLOSIVE TEMPER • 1917 • Brooke Van Dyke • SHT • USA
CAPTAIN JINKS' GETAWAY • 1916 • Brooke Van Dyke • SHT • USA
CAPTAIN JINKS' GREAT EXPECTATIONS • 1917 • Brooke Van Dyke • SHT • USA
CAPTAIN JINKS' HIDDEN TREASURE • 1916 • Dickson Charles • SHT • USA
CAPTAIN JINKS' IN AND OUT • 1917 • Ruggles Wesley • SHT • USA
CAPTAIN JINKS' KIDS • 1917 • Brooke Van Dyke • SHT • USA
CAPTAIN JINKS' LOVE INSURANCE • 1917 • Brooke Van Dyke • SHT • USA
CAPTAIN JINKS' LOVE LETTERS • 1917 • Brooke Van Dyke • SHT • USA
CAPTAIN JINKS OF THE HORSE MARINES • 1916 • Wright Fred E. • USA
CAPTAIN JINKS' PARTNER • 1917 • *Vitagraph* • USA
CAPTAIN JINKS SHOULD WORRY • 1916 • Ellery Arthur • SHT • USA
CAPTAIN JINKS' SPRAINED ANKLE • 1916 • Ellery Arthur • SHT • USA
CAPTAIN JINKS' STINGY SPIRIT • 1917 • *Vitagraph* • USA
CAPTAIN JINKS, THE COBBLER • 1916 • Brooke Van Dyke • SHT • USA
CAPTAIN JINKS, THE PLUMBER • 1917 • Brooke Van Dyke • SHT • USA
CAPTAIN JINKS' TRIAL BALANCE • 1917 • *Vitagraph* • USA
CAPTAIN JINKS' WIFE'S HUSBAND • 1917 • Brooke Van Dyke • SHT • USA
CAPTAIN JOHN SMITH AND POCAHONTAS • 1953 • Landers Lew • USA • BURNING ARROWS (UKN)
CAPTAIN JOLLY'S CHRISTMAS • 1915 • *Pyramid* • UKN
CAPTAIN JUNIOR • 1914 • Hamilton G. P.? • USA
CAPTAIN KATE • 1911 • Boggs Frank • USA
CAPTAIN KEMAL see **YUZBASI KEMAL** • 1967
CAPTAIN KHORSHEED • 1987 • Taghvai Nasser • IRN
CAPTAIN KID AND HIS PIRATES • 1906 • *Urban Trading Co.* • UKN
CAPTAIN KIDD • 1913 • Turner Otis • USA
CAPTAIN KIDD • 1945 • Lee Rowland V. • USA
CAPTAIN KIDD AND DITTO • 1915 • Hotaling Arthur D. • USA
CAPTAIN KIDD AND THE SLAVE GIRL • 1954 • Landers Lew • USA • SLAVE GIRL, THE
CAPTAIN KIDD, JR. • 1919 • Taylor William D. • USA
CAPTAIN KIDD, THE BOLD • 1914 • *Ab* • USA
CAPTAIN KIDDO • 1917 • Moore W. Eugene • USA
CAPTAIN KIDD'S KIDS • 1919 • Roach Hal • SHT • USA
CAPTAIN KIDD'S PRICELESS TREASURE • 1914 • *Joker* • USA
CAPTAIN KIDD'S TREASURE • 1938 • Fenton Leslie • SHT • USA
CAPTAIN KING'S RESCUE • 1912 • *Lubin* • USA
CAPTAIN KLEINSCHMIDT'S ADVENTURES IN THE FAR NORTH see **ADVENTURES IN THE FAR NORTH** • 1923
CAPTAIN KORDA see **KAPITAN KORDA** • 1979
CAPTAIN KRONOS -VAMPIRE HUNTER • 1972 • Clemens Brian • UKN • KRONOS (USA)
CAPTAIN LASH • 1929 • Blystone John G. • USA
CAPTAIN LESI see **KAPETAN LESI** • 1960
CAPTAIN LIGHTFOOT • 1955 • Sirk Douglas • USA
CAPTAIN LOY'S DREAM see **TRAUM DES HAUPTMANN LOY, DER** • 1961
CAPTAIN LUST • 1977 • Buchanan Beau • USA • CAPTAIN LUST AND THE PIRATE WOMEN
CAPTAIN LUST AND THE PIRATE WOMEN see **CAPTAIN LUST** • 1977
CAPTAIN MACKLIN • 1915 • O'Brien John B., Conway Jack • USA
CAPTAIN MARIA see **KAPTEIN MARIA** • 1978
CAPTAIN MARJORIE'S ADVENTURE • 1917 • *Big U* • SHT • USA
CAPTAIN MARTENS BROTHERS, THE see **FRATII JDERI** • 1973
CAPTAIN MARTEN'S TREASURE see **SKARB KAPITANA MARTENSA** • 1957
CAPTAIN MARVEL • 1962 • *Glut Don (P)* • SHT • USA
CAPTAIN MARY BROWN • 1913 • *Vitagraph* • USA

CAPTAIN MEPHISTO AND THE TRANSFORMATION MACHINE* • 1945 • Canutt Yakima, Bennet Spencer Gordon, Grissell Wallace A. • USA
CAPTAIN MIDNIGHT • 1942 • Horne James W. • SRL • USA
CAPTAIN MIDNIGHT see **ON THE AIR LIVE WITH CAPTAIN MIDNIGHT** • 1979
CAPTAIN MIDNIGHT -THE BUSH KING • 1911 • Rolfe Alfred • ASL
CAPTAIN MILKSHAKE • 1970 • Crawford Richard • USA
CAPTAIN MOLLY • 1908 • *Lubin* • USA
CAPTAIN MOONLIGHT (USA) see **D'YE KEN JOHN PEEL?** • 1935
CAPTAIN MOONLITE see **MOONLITE -KING OF THE ROAD** • 1910
CAPTAIN NELL • 1911 • Porter Edwin S. • USA
CAPTAIN NEMO AND THE FLOATING CITY see **CAPTAIN NEMO AND THE UNDERWATER CITY** • 1969
CAPTAIN NEMO AND THE UNDERWATER CITY • 1969 • Hill James • UKN, USA • CAPTAIN NEMO AND THE FLOATING CITY
CAPTAIN NEWMAN M.D. • 1963 • Miller David • USA
CAPTAIN NIGHTHAWK • 1914 • Lawrence Gerald • UKN
CAPTAIN OF COLOGNE, THE see **HAUPTMANN VON KOLN, DER** • 1956
CAPTAIN OF HIS SOUL • 1918 • Hamilton G. P. • USA
CAPTAIN OF KOEPENICK • 1942 • Oswald Richard • USA • I WAS A CRIMINAL
CAPTAIN OF KOPENICK, THE see **HAUPTMANN VON KOPENICK, DER** • 1926
CAPTAIN OF KOPENICK, THE see **HAUPTMANN VON KOPENICK, DER** • 1931
CAPTAIN OF THE GRAY HORSE TROOP, THE • 1917 • Wolbert William • USA
CAPTAIN OF THE GUARD • 1930 • Robertson John S., Fejos Paul (U/c) • USA • MARSEILLAISE, LA
CAPTAIN OF THE GUARDS see **KRYLYA** • 1966
CAPTAIN OF THE HURRICANE, THE see **STORMY WATERS** • 1928
CAPTAIN OF THE LUCKY SUBMARINE SHCHUKA, THE • 1973 • Volchek B. • USS
CAPTAIN OF THE NANCY LEE, THE • 1912 • *Selig* • USA
CAPTAIN OF THE PINAFORE • 1906 • Gilbert Arthur • UKN
CAPTAIN OF THE TYPHOON, THE • 1916 • Webster Harry Mcrae • SHT • USA
CAPTAIN OF VILLANY, THE • 1915 • *Kerrigan J. Warren* • USA
CAPTAIN PIRATE • 1952 • Murphy Ralph • USA • CAPTAIN BLOOD, FUGITIVE (UKN)
CAPTAIN "POSTMAN" BLAKE, V.C. • 1914 • *Captain Kettle Films* • UKN
CAPTAIN RIVERA'S REWARD • 1912 • *Kalem* • USA
CAPTAIN SALVATION • 1927 • Robertson John S. • USA
CAPTAIN SCARFACE • 1953 • Guilfoyle Paul • USA
CAPTAIN SCARLET • 1953 • Carr Thomas • USA
CAPTAIN SINBAD see **CAPTAIN SINDBAD** • 1963
CAPTAIN SINDBAD • 1963 • Haskin Byron • USA, FRG • CAPTAIN SINBAD
CAPTAIN SINGRID (UKN) see **CAPITAINE SINGRID** • 1967
CAPTAIN SIROCCO see **PIRATI DI CAPRI, I** • 1949
CAPTAIN SPANKY'S SHOW BOAT • 1939 • Cahn Edward L. • SHT • USA
CAPTAIN STARLIGHT -GENTLEMAN OF THE ROAD • 1911 • Rolfe Alfred • ASL • GENTLEMAN OF THE ROAD -CAPTAIN STARLIGHT
CAPTAIN SWAGGER • 1928 • Griffith Edward H. • USA
CAPTAIN SWIFT • 1914 • Lewis Edgar • USA
CAPTAIN SWIFT • 1920 • Terriss Tom • USA
CAPTAIN THUNDER • 1930 • Crosland Alan • USA • GAY CABALLERO, THE
CAPTAIN THUNDERBOLT • 1953 • Holmes Cecil • ASL
CAPTAIN TUGBOAT ANNIE • 1945 • Rosen Phil • USA
CAPTAIN ULTRA • 1967 • Takemoto Koichi • JPN
CAPTAIN VIDEO • 1951 • Bennet Spencer Gordon, Grissell Wallace A. • SRL • USA
CAPTAIN YANKEE AND THE JUNGLE RAIDERS • 1984 • Margheriti Antonio • ITL • JUNGLE RAIDERS
CAPTAINS AND THE KINGS • 1976 • Heyes Douglas, Reisner Allen • TVM • USA
CAPTAIN'S BIRTHDAY, HE • 1901 • Booth W. R. • UKN
CAPTAIN'S BRIDE, THE • 1910 • *Edison* • USA
CAPTAIN'S CAPTAIN, THE • 1918 • Terriss Tom • USA • CAP'N ABE'S NIECE
CAPTAIN'S CHAIR, THE • 1914 • Martin E. A. • USA
CAPTAIN'S CHRISTMAS, THE • 1938 • *Captain And The Kids* • ANS • USA
CAPTAIN'S COURAGE, A • 1926 • Chaudet Louis W. • USA
CAPTAINS COURAGEOUS • 1937 • Fleming Victor • USA
CAPTAINS COURAGEOUS • 1977 • Hart Harvey • TVM • USA
CAPTAIN'S DAUGHTER, THE see **KAPITANSKAIA DOTSHKA** • 1958
CAPTAIN'S DAUGHTER, THE see **YUBASININ KIZI** • 1968
CAPTAIN'S DAUGHTER, THE (USA) see **FIGLIA DEL CAPITANO, LA** • 1947
CAPTAINS DO NOT LEAVE THE SHIP see **KAPITANE BLEIBEN AN BORD** • 1959
CAPTAIN'S HONOUR, THE • 1909 • *Tyler Walter* • UKN
CAPTAIN'S KID, THE • 1937 • Grinde Nick • USA
CAPTAINS OF THE CLOUDS • 1942 • Curtiz Michael • USA
CAPTAIN'S ORDERS • 1937 • Campbell Ivar • UKN
CAPTAINS OUTRAGEOUS • 1952 • Burness Pete • ANS • USA
CAPTAIN'S PARADISE, THE • 1953 • Kimmins Anthony • UKN • GOLDEN KEY, THE ○ PARADISE
CAPTAIN'S PUP • 1938 • Allen Robert • ANS • USA
CAPTAIN'S TABLE, THE • 1936 • Marmont Percy • UKN
CAPTAIN'S TABLE, THE • 1959 • Lee Jack • UKN
CAPTAIN'S WIVES, THE • 1908 • Stow Percy • UKN
CAPTIF, LE • 1957 • Labro Maurice • FRN • ESCAPE FROM SAIGON (USA) ○ HOMME A VENDRE, UN
CAPTIVATED BY A VOICE see **FANGAD AV EN ROST** • 1943
CAPTIVATING CAPTIVE, THE • 1920 • *Christie* • USA
CAPTIVATING MARY CARSTAIRS • 1915 • Mitchell Bruce • USA
CAPTIVATING WIDOW, THE • 1913 • *Roland Ruth* • USA
CAPTIVATION • 1931 • Harvel John • UKN
CAPTIVE • 1980 • Sandler Allan, Emenegger Robert • USA
CAPTIVE • 1985 • Mayersberg Paul • UKN, FRN • HEROINE
CAPTIVE, THE • 1915 • De Mille Cecil B. • USA
CAPTIVE, THE see **PRISONNIERE, LA**
CAPTIVE, THE see **VACANCES EN ENFER** • 1960
CAPTIVE BALLOON, THE see **PRIVARZANIAT BALON** • 1967
CAPTIVE BRIDE, THE • 1919 • Hoyt George • SHT • USA
CAPTIVE CITY see **CITTA PRIGIONERA, LA** • 1962
CAPTIVE CITY, THE • 1952 • Wise Robert • USA
CAPTIVE DU DESERT, LA • 1989 • Depardon Raymond • FRN
CAPTIVE GIRL • 1950 • Berke William • USA
CAPTIVE GIRL OF THE CAUCASUS OR NEW ADVENTURES OF SHURIK see **KAKAZSKAYA PLENNITZA** • 1967
CAPTIVE GOD, THE • 1916 • Swickard Charles • USA
CAPTIVE HEART, THE • 1946 • Dearden Basil • UKN • LOVERS' MEETING
CAPTIVE HEARTS • 1987 • Almond Paul • USA • FATE OF THE HUNTER
CAPTIVE HEARTS see **FIRE WITH FIRE** • 1986
CAPTIVE MINDS: HYPNOSIS AND BEYOND • 1984 • Lasry Pierre • CND • PRISONS DE L'ESPRIT, LES
CAPTIVE OF BILLY THE KID • 1952 • Brannon Fred C. • USA
CAPTIVE OF THE JUNGLE see **CAUTIVA DE LA SELVA, LA** • 1968
CAPTIVE PLANET • 1986 • Brescia Alfonso • ITL
CAPTIVE RAGE • 1988 • Sundstrom Cedric • SAF
CAPTIVE RIVER, THE • 1960 • Dalrymple J. Blake • ZIM
CAPTIVE SOUL see **RABLELEK** • 1913
CAPTIVE WILD WOMAN • 1943 • Dmytryk Edward • USA
CAPTIVE WOMEN • 1952 • Gilmore Stuart • USA • 3000 A.D. (UKN) ○ 1000 YEARS FROM NOW
CAPTIVE WOMEN see **TERRIFYING CONFESSIONS OF CAPTIVE WOMEN** • 1977
CAPTIVES, THE • 1970 • Borch Carl • DNM
CAPTIVES, THE see **FLUCHT NACH BERLIN** • 1961
CAPTIVE'S ISLAND see **SHOKEI NO SHIMA** • 1966
CAPTIVES OF A NIGHT DANCE see **GECE DANSI TUTSAKLARI** • 1988
CAPTIVES OF CARE • 1981 • Wallace Stephen • SHT • ASL
CAPTURA DE CHUCHO EL ROTO, LA • 1959 • Munoz Manuel • MXC
CAPTURE • 1932 • *Sound City* • SHT • UKN
CAPTURE • 1969 • Gosselin Bernard • DCS • CND
CAPTURE, THE • 1913 • Hopper E. Mason • USA
CAPTURE, THE • 1950 • Sturges John • USA
CAPTURE, THE • 1955 • Brownlow Kevin • UKN • PRISONNIERS, LES
CAPTURE AND EXECUTION AS SPIES OF TWO JAPANESE OFFICERS, THE • 1904 • *Paul R. W.* • UKN
CAPTURE OF A RUSSIAN SPY BY THE JAPANESE, THE • 1904 • *Cricks & Sharp* • UKN
CAPTURE OF AGUINALDO, THE • 1913 • *Bison* • USA
CAPTURE OF BAD BROWN, THE • 1913 • Duncan William • USA
CAPTURE OF BIGFOOT, THE • 1979 • Rebane Bill • USA
CAPTURE OF BOER BATTERY BY THE BRITISH • 1900 • Porter Edwin S. • USA
CAPTURE OF FORT TICONDEROGA, THE • 1911 • Dawley J. Searle • USA
CAPTURE OF RATTLESNAKE IKE, THE • 1916 • *Kerrigan J. Warren* • USA
CAPTURE OF TARZAN, THE see **TARZAN ESCAPES!** • 1936
CAPTURE OF THE BIDDLE BROTHERS • 1902 • Porter Edwin S. • USA
CAPTURE OF THE DRAGON, THE see **DRAGENS FANGE** • 1984
CAPTURE OF YEGG BANK BURGLARS • 1904 • Porter Edwin S. • USA
CAPTURE THAT CAPSULE! • 1961 • Zens Will • USA • SPY SQUAD
CAPTURED • 1933 • Del Ruth Roy • USA
CAPTURED • 1981 • Kotcheff Ted • USA • SPLIT IMAGE
CAPTURED ALIVE • 1918 • Harvey Harry • SHT • USA
CAPTURED BY ABORIGINALS • 1913 • *Melies* • USA
CAPTURED BY BEDOUINS • 1912 • Olcott Sidney • USA
CAPTURED BY BOOMERANG THROWERS • 1913 • Melies Gaston • USA
CAPTURED BY BOY SCOUTS • 1909 • *London Cinematograph Co.* • UKN
CAPTURED BY CONSENT • 1914 • Kinder Stuart? • UKN
CAPTURED BY MEXICANS • 1914 • *Ridgeley Don* • USA
CAPTURED BY REDSKINS • 1914 • *Belmont* • USA
CAPTURED BY STRATEGY • 1913 • *Cooper Marian* • USA
CAPTURED BY WIRELESS • 1910 • *Yankee* • USA
CAPTURED IN CHINATOWN • 1935 • Clifton Elmer • USA
CAPTURED SQUADRON see **PLENENO YATO** • 1962
CAPTURING BAD BILL • 1915 • Louis Will • USA
CAPTURING OF DAVID DUNNE, THE • 1913 • *Hale Alan* • USA
CAPTURING STELLA • 1915 • *Ck* • USA
CAPTURING THE COOK • 1915 • *Clayton Ethel* • USA
CAPTURING THE NORTH POLE • 1909 • *Urban-Eclipse* • UKN
CAPULETTI ET PINTOS • 1953 • Vilardebo Carlos (c/d) • SHT • FRN
CAPULINA CHISME CALIENTE • 1975 • *Panorama* • MXC
CAPULINA ENTRE LAS MOMIAS • 1972 • *Panorama* • MXC
CAPULINA VS. LOS MONSTRUOS • 1973 • *Panorama* • MXC
CAPULLITO DE ADHELI • 1944 • Soler Fernando • MXC
CAR, THE • 1977 • Silverstein Elliot • USA
CAR, THE see **AUTO** • 1974
CAR, A VIOLIN AND KLYASKA DOG, A • 1975 • *Bykov Rolan* • USS
CAR CRASH • 1981 • Margheriti Antonio • ITL, MXC, SPN
CAR CRAZY see **KAR A KENZINERT** • 1964
CAR DEATH see **BILDOD** • 1979
CAR IS BORN, A • 1946 • Stafford Brendan J. • DOC • UKN
CAR JE SUIS L'EMPEREUR • Misonne Claude • ANS • BLG • BECAUSE I AM THE EMPEROR
CAR NAPPING • 1980 • Wicker Wigbert • FRG • FORTUNE IS STANDING AROUND IN THE STREETS, A ○ ESCAPADE
CAR NO.99 • 1935 • Barton Charles T. • USA
CAR OF CHANCE, THE • 1917 • Worthington William • USA
CAR OF DEATH, THE • 1914 • McGowan J. P. • USA
CAR OF DREAMS • 1935 • Cutts Graham, Melford Austin • UKN
CAR OF TOMORROW • 1951 • Avery Tex • ANS • USA
CAR-RAZY DRIVERS • 1955 • Kneitel Seymour • ANS • USA
CAR RIDE • 1903 • Cooper Arthur • UKN
CAR THIEF see **JIDOSHA DOROBO** • 1964
CAR TROUBLE • 1985 • Green David • UKN
CAR-TUNE PORTRAIT, A • 1937 • Fleischer Dave • ANS • USA
CAR WASH • 1976 • Schultz Michael • USA
CARA A CARA • 1968 • Bressane Julio • BRZ • FACE TO FACE
CARA AL SOL QUE MAS CALIENTA • 1977 • Yague Jesus • SPN
CARA DE ANGEL • 1955 • Morayta Miguel • MXC
CARA DE FOGO • 1960 • Garcia Gallileu • BRZ
CARA DE GOMA • 1957 • Buchs Jose • SPN
CARA DEL TERROR, LA • 1962 • Ferry Isidoro Martinez, Hole William Jr. • SPN • FACE OF TERROR (USA) ○ FACE OF FEAR
CARA DOLCE NIPOTE • 1977 • Bianchi Andrea • ITL
CARA PARCHADA, EL • 1960 • Diaz Morales Jose • MXC
CARA SPOSA • 1977 • Festa Campanile Pasquale • ITL
CARABAS see **GRAF VON CARABAS, DER** • 1935
CARABINA 30-30 • 1958 • Delgado Miguel M. • MXC
CARABINA PER SCHUT, UNA • 1966 • Siodmak Robert • ITL
CARABINIERE, IL • 1911 • Pasquali Ernesto Maria • ITL
CARABINIERE A CAVALLO, IL • 1961 • Lizzani Carlo • ITL
CARABINIERI SI NASCE • 1985 • Laurenti Mariano • ITL • BORN TO BE COPS
CARABINIERS, LES • 1962 • Godard Jean-Luc • FRN, ITL • RIFLEMEN, THE (USA) ○ SOLDIERS, THE
CARACAS • 1972 • Arevalo Eduardo • DOC • VNZ
CARACAS • 1988 • Schottenberg Michael • AUS
CARACAS CLAVE TRES • 1974 • *Otolina Renny* • VNZ, SPN, ITL
CARACAS CONTACT, THE see **CONTACTO EN CARACAS** • 1990
CARAMBOL see **KARAMBOL** • 1966
CARAMBOLA • 1974 • Baldi Ferdinando • ITL
CARAMBOLA, FILOTTO, TUTTI IN BUCA • 1975 • Baldi Ferdinando • ITL
CARAMBOLAGES • 1963 • Bluwal Marcel • FRN
CARAMELLE DA UNO SCONOCIUTO • 1987 • Ferrini Franco • ITL • SWEETS FROM A STRANGER
CARANCHOS DE LA FLORIDA, LOS • 1938 • de Zavalia Alberto • ARG
CARAPATE, LA • 1978 • Oury Gerard • FRN
CARAQUE BLONDE, LA • 1952 • Audry Jacqueline • FRN
CARAS NUEVAS • 1955 • de la Serna Mauricio • MXC
CARAVAGGIO • 1986 • Jarman Derek • UKN
CARAVAGGIO (IL PITTORE MALEDOTTO) • 1941 • Alessandrini Goffredo • ITL
CARAVAN • 1934 • Charell Erik • USA
CARAVAN • 1946 • Crabtree Arthur • UKN
CARAVAN • 1952 • Belson Jordan • ANS • USA
CARAVAN, THE • 1916 • Wells Raymond • SHT • USA
CARAVAN, THE see **KARAWANA** • 1964
CARAVAN DE LA LUMIERE, LA • 1947 • Colson-Malleville Marie • SHT • FRN
CARAVAN FOR YOUTH, A • 1985 • von Puttkamer Peter • DOC • CND
CARAVAN OF COURAGE see **CARAVAN OF COURAGE: AN EWOK ADVENTURE** • 1984
CARAVAN OF COURAGE: AN EWOK ADVENTURE • 1984 • Korty John • USA • EWOK ADVENTURE, AN ○ CARAVAN OF COURAGE
CARAVAN OF DEATH (USA) see **TODESKARAWANE, DIE** • 1920
CARAVAN PARK • 1973 • Noyce Phil • SHT • ASL
CARAVAN PETROL • 1960 • Amendola Mario • ITL
CARAVAN SERAI • 1987 • Psarras Tasos • GRC
CARAVAN TO VACCARES • 1974 • Reeve Geoffrey • UKN, FRN
CARAVAN TRAIL, THE • 1946 • Tansey Robert • USA
CARAVANA DE ESCLAVOS • 1958 • Torrado Ramon • SPN
CARAVANE • 1934 • Charell Erik • FRN
CARAVANE D'AMOUR, LA (FRN) see **MEDICINE BALL CARAVAN** • 1971
CARAVANE D'ASIE • 1946 • Philippe Anne • SHT • BLG
CARAVANE POUR ZAGORA see **TRESOR DES HOMMES BLEUS, LE** • 1960
CARAVANS • 1978 • Fargo James • USA, IRN
CARAVANS WEST see **WAGON WHEELS** • 1934
CARAVELLE • 1959 • Languepin Jean-Jacques • FRN
CARAY, QUE PALIZAS • 1974 • de Ossorio Amando • SPN
CARBANICA • 1982 • Stefankovicova Eva • CZC • SCRIBBLE, THE
CARBIDE AND SORREL see **KARBID UND SAUERAMPFER** • 1963
CARBINE WILLIAMS • 1952 • Thorpe Richard • USA
CARBON • 1968 • De Normanville Peter • UKN
CARBON ARC PROJECTION • 1947 • Wright • SHT • USA
CARBON COPY • 1981 • Schultz Michael • USA
CARBON COPY see **TEMPS DES LOUPS -TEMPO DI VIOLENZA, LE** • 1970
CARBON COPY, THE • 1914 • *American* • USA
CARBONE, LA • 1982 • Gallotte Jean-Francois, Malberg Joelle • DOC • FRN
CARBUNARA • 1955-59 • Taviani Paolo, Taviani Vittorio • DCS • ITL
CARCACHITA, LA • 1966 • Fernandez Raul • MXC
CARCAJOU ET LE PERIL BLANC • 1971-77 • Lamothe Arthur • SER • CND • KAUAPISHIT MIAM KUAKUATSHEU ETENTAKUESS
CARCASSE ET LE TORD-COU, LA • 1947 • Chanas Rene • FRN
CARCASSE, L'IMMORTEL • 1945 • Rou Aleksandr • USS
CARCEL DE CANANEA, LA • 1960 • Gazcon Gilberto • MXC
CARCEL DE CRISTAL, LA • 1956 • Coll Julio • SPN
CARCEL DE MUJERES • 1951 • Delgado Miguel M. • MXC
CARCELERAS • 1922 • Buchs Jose • SPN
CARCELERAS • 1932 • Buchs Jose • SPN
CARCERATO • 1951 • Zorri Armando • ITL
CARCINOMA OF THE BREAST TREATED WITH RADIUM • 1929 • Keynes Geoffrey • UKN
CARD, THE • 1922 • Bramble A. V. • UKN
CARD, THE • 1952 • Neame Ronald • UKN • PROMOTER, THE (USA)

CARD GAME, A see **PARTIE D'ECARTE** • 1895
CARD GAME, THE see **POKER** • 1920
CARD-INDEX, THE see **KARTOTEKA** • 1966
CARD MANIAC, THE • 1924 • *Jupiter* • ANS • FRN
CARD MANIAC, THE • 1930 • Teschner Richard • ANM • AUS
CARD MANIPULATIONS • 1912 • Booth W. R. • UKN
CARD OF FATE (UKN) see **GRAND JEU, LE** • 1954
CARD OF INTRODUCTION, A • 1911 • *Edison* • USA
CARD OF MYSTERY, THE • 1914 • Hotaling Arthur D. • USA
CARD PARTY see **PARTIE D'ECARTE** • 1895
CARD PARTY, THE • 1910 • *Powers* • USA
CARD PLAYERS, THE • 1915 • Garrick Richard • USA
CARD SHARPS, THE • 1914 • *Ray Charles* • USA
CARDAMOM TOWN see **FOLK OG ROVERE I KARDEMOMME BY** • 1988
CARDBOARD BABY, THE • 1909 • Olcott Sidney • USA
CARDBOARD BOX, THE • 1923 • Ridgwell George • UKN
CARDBOARD CAVALIER • 1949 • Forde Walter • UKN
CARDBOARD CITY see **CIUDAD DE CARTON, LA** • 1934
CARDBOARD LOVER, THE • 1928 • Leonard Robert Z. • USA • HER CARDBOARD LOVER
CARDBOARD LOVER, THE see **PASSIONATE PLUMBER, THE** • 1932
CARDENAL, EL • 1951 • Delgado Miguel M., Bennett Charles • MXC • PRINCIPE DE LA IGLESIA, UN
CARDIAC ARREST • 1980 • Mintz Murray • USA
CARDIGAN • 1922 • Noble John W. • USA
CARDIGAN'S LAST CASE (UKN) see **STATE'S ATTORNEY** • 1932
CARDILLAC • 1969 • Reitz Edgar • FRG
CARDIN IN AUSTRALIA • 1967 • Thompson Peter • DOC • ASL
CARDINAL, THE • 1936 • Hill Sinclair • UKN
CARDINAL, THE • 1963 • Preminger Otto • USA
CARDINAL RICHELIEU • 1936 • Lee Rowland V. • USA
CARDINAL RICHELIEU'S WARD • 1914 • *Cruze James* • USA
CARDINAL WOLSEY • 1912 • Blackton J. Stuart, Trimble Larry • USA
CARDINALE LAMBERTINI, IL • 1934 • Bassi Parsifal • ITL
CARDINALE LAMBERTINI, IL • 1955 • Pastina Giorgio • ITL
CARDINAL'S CONSPIRACY, THE • 1909 • Griffith D. W., Powell Frank • USA • RICHELIEU
CARDINAL'S EDICT, THE • 1911 • *Edison* • USA
CARDINAL'S VISIT, THE • 1981 • Baillie Bruce • USA
CARDIOGRAM • 1971 • Zaluski Roman • PLN
CARDS • 1913 • Davis Will S. • USA
CARDS AND CUPID • 1920 • Davey Horace • SHT • USA
CARDS ARE MY LIFE see **HANAFUDA TOSEI** • 1967
CARDS FACE UP see **CARTAS BOCA ARRIBA** • 1962
CARDS NEVER LIE • 1915 • *Myers Harry* • USA
CARDS ON THE TABLE see **CARTAS BOCA ARRIBA** • 1962
CARDS ON THE TABLE see **CARTAS NA MESA** • 1975
CARDS WILL TELL see **TEKKABA NO KAZE** • 1960
CARDSHARPERS, THE • 1910 • Fitzhamon Lewin • UKN
CARE AND AFFECTION see **SZERETET** • 1963
CARE BEARS -ADVENTURES IN WONDERLAND, THE • 1988 • Jafelife Raymond • ANM • CND
CARE BEARS MOVIE, THE • 1985 • Selznick Arna • ANM • CND • CARE BEARS MOVIE: LAND WITHOUT FEELING, THE
CARE BEARS MOVIE II • 1986 • Schott Dale • ANM • CND • CARE BEARS MOVIE II: A NEW GENERATION
CARE BEARS MOVIE II: A NEW GENERATION see **CARE BEARS MOVIE II** • 1986
CARE BEARS MOVIE: LAND WITHOUT FEELING, THE see **CARE BEARS MOVIE, THE** • 1985
CARE OF ST. CHRISTOPHERS • 1959 • Ritchie James • UKN
CAREER • 1939 • Jason Leigh • USA
CAREER • 1960 • Anthony Joseph • USA
CAREER see **KARRIAR** • 1938
CAREER see **KARRIERE** • 1966
CAREER, THE see **KARIERA** • 1948
CAREER, THE see **KARIERA** • 1955
CAREER BED • 1969 • Reed Joel M. • USA
CAREER GIRL • 1943 • Fox Wallace • USA
CAREER GIRL • 1959 • David Harold • USA
CAREER OF A CHAMBERMAID, THE (USA) see **TELEFONI BIANCHI** • 1976
CAREER OF CATHERINE BUSH, THE see **CAREER OF KATHERINE BUSH, THE** • 1919
CAREER OF DIMA see **DIMA GORINA** • 1961
CAREER OF KATHERINE BUSH, THE • 1919 • Neill R. William • USA • CAREER OF CATHERINE BUSH, THE
CAREER OF WATERLOO PETERSON, THE • 1914 • Smalley Phillips • USA
CAREER OPPORTUNITIES • 1990 • Gordon Bryan • USA
CAREER WOMAN • 1936 • Seiler Lewis • USA
CAREERS • 1929 • Dillon John Francis • USA
CAREERS FOR EVERYONE • 1977 • Greenwald Barry • DOC • CND
CAREERS FOR THE YOUNG AUSTRALIANS • 1952 • Holmes Cecil • DOC • ASL
CAREFREE • 1938 • Sandrich Mark • USA
CAREFUL -BANALITY! • Klimov Elem • SHT • USS
CAREFUL, HE MIGHT HEAR YOU • 1983 • Schultz Carl • ASL
CAREFUL KATE • 1919 • *Strand* • SHT • USA
CAREFUL LITTLE ANGEL, THE • 1956 • Dinov Todor • ANS • BUL • LITTLE GUARDIAN ANGEL, THE
CAREFUL NURSING • 1912 • *Rex* • USA
CAREFUL PLEASE • 1926 • Taurog Norman • SHT • USA
CAREFUL SERVANT, A • 1915 • *Gaumont* • USA
CAREFUL SOFT SHOULDER • 1942 • Garrett Oliver H. P. • USA
CAREFUL, THE CHILDREN ARE WATCHING see **ATTENTION LES ENFANTS REGARDENT** • 1977
CAREL VISSER -SCULPTOR • 1972 • Severijn Jonne • SHT • NTH
CARELESS see **PROFESSIONAL SWEETHEART** • 1933
CARELESS see **SOHO** • 1933
CARELESS see **SLIGHTLY DANGEROUS** • 1943
CARELESS AGE, THE • 1929 • Wray John Griffith • USA
CARELESS ANARCHIST, THE • 1915 • Murphy J. A. • USA
CARELESS CARETAKER • 1962 • Smith Paul J. • ANS • USA
CARELESS COP, THE • 1917 • Beaudine William • SHT • USA
CARELESS HOD CARRIER, THE • 1904 • *Urban Trading Co.* • UKN
CARELESS HUBBY • 1927 • Sandrich Mark • SHT • USA
CARELESS LADY • 1932 • MacKenna Kenneth • USA
CARELESS LOVE see **BONNE SOUPE, LA** • 1964
CARELESS WOMAN, THE • 1922 • *Exclusive Features* • USA
CARELESS YEARS, THE • 1957 • Hiller Arthur • USA
CARESS see **AIBU** • 1933
CARESSED see **SWEET SUBSTITUTE** • 1964
CARESSES INAVOUABLES • 1978 • Bernard-Aubert Claude • FRN
CARESSES PERVERSES • 1976 • Hustaix Lucien • FRN
CARESSEUSES, LES • 1974 • Hustaix Lucien • FRN
CARETAKER, THE • 1912 • *Lubin* • USA
CARETAKER, THE • 1963 • Donner Clive • UKN • GUEST, THE (USA)
CARETAKERS, THE • 1963 • Bartlett Hall • USA • BORDERLINES (UKN)
CARETAKER'S DAUGHTER, THE • 1925 • McCarey Leo • SHT • USA
CARETAKER'S DAUGHTER, THE • 1934 • French Lloyd • SHT • USA
CARETAKER'S DAUGHTER, THE (USA) see **LOVE'S A LUXURY** • 1952
CARETAKER'S DILEMMA, THE • 1915 • *Duncan Bud* • USA
CAREVO NOVO RUHO • 1961 • Babaja Ante • YGS • EMPEROR'S NEW CLOTHES, THE
CAREW AND SON • 1916 • Davenport Harry • SHT • USA
CAREY TREATMENT, THE • 1972 • Edwards Blake • USA • EMERGENCY WARD
CARGA, LA • 1972 • de la Cerda Clemente, Odreman Mauricio • VNZ • CARGO, THE
CARGA DE LA POLICIA MONTADA, LA • 1964 • Torrado Ramon • SPN
CARGA PARA ESCAPAR, UNA • 1963 • Gordon Robert • MXC, USA
CARGADOR, EL • Figueroa Luis • SHT • PRU
CARGAISON BLANCHE • 1957 • Lacombe Georges • FRN • ILLEGAL CARGO (USA)
CARGAISON BLANCHE see **CHEMIN DE RIO, LE** • 1936
CARGAISON CLANDESTINE • 1947 • Rode Alfred • FRN
CARGAMENTO PROHIBIDO • 1965 • Delgado Miguel M. • MXC
CARGANDO EL MUERTO • 1964 • Gomez Urquiza Zacarias • MXC
CARGO • 1981 • Dubor Serge • FRN
CARGO, THE see **CARGA, LA** • 1972
CARGO FOR ARDROSSAN • 1939 • Grierson Ruby I. • UKN
CARGO FROM JAMAICA • 1934 • Wright Basil • DOC • UKN
CARGO OF INNOCENTS (UKN) see **STAND BY FOR ACTION** • 1942
CARGO OF LOVE • 1968 • Holden Anton • USA • BED AND THE BEAUTIFUL, THE
CARGO TO CAPETOWN • 1950 • McEvoy Earl • USA
CARHOPS • 1980 • Locke Peter • USA • CALIFORNIA DRIVE-IN GIRLS ○ KITTY CAN'T HELP IT
CARI GENITORI • 1973 • Salerno Enrico Maria • ITL
CARI MOSTRI DEL MARE • 1977 • Vailati Bruno • ITL
CARIB GOLD • 1957 • *Waters Ethel* • USA
CARIBBEAN • 1951 • Wallace Graham • UKN
CARIBBEAN • 1952 • Ludwig Edward • USA • CARIBBEAN GOLD (UKN)
CARIBBEAN CRISIS, THE • 1989 • Dinkevitsh Arkadi • FNL
CARIBBEAN GOLD (UKN) see **CARIBBEAN** • 1952
CARIBBEAN HAWK (USA) see **SPARVIERO DEI CARAIBI, LO** • 1963
CARIBBEAN HOLIDAY see **ONE NIGHT IN THE TROPICS** • 1940
CARIBBEAN MYSTERY, A • 1983 • Lewis Robert • TVM • USA • AGATHA CHRISTIE'S A CARIBBEAN MYSTERY
CARIBBEAN MYSTERY, THE • 1945 • Webb Robert D. • USA
CARIBBEAN, STAR AND EAGLE, THE see **CARIBE, ESTRELLA Y AGUILA** • 1975
CARIBE • 1972 • Gibson Bill • USA, VNZ
CARIBE • 1988 • Kennedy Michael • CND
CARIBE, ESTRELLA Y AGUILA • 1975 • Arau Alfonso • DOC • MXC, CUB • CARIBBEAN, STAR AND EAGLE, THE
CARIBENA • 1952 • Baviera Jose • MXC, GTM
CARIBOO COUNTRY • 1963-65 • Keatley Philip • SER • CND
CARIBOO TRAIL, THE • 1950 • Marin Edwin L. • USA
CARIBOU HUNTERS • 1951 • Blais Roger • DCS • CND • CHASSEURS DE CARIBOUS
CARIBOUS, LES • 1970 • Gagne Jacques • CND
CARICA DEGLI EROI, LA • 1943 • Majano Anton Giulio, Biancoli Oreste • ITL
CARICA DELLE PATATE, LA • 1979 • Santesso Walter • ITL
CARICA EROICA • 1952 • De Robertis Francesco • ITL
CARICATURE OF A FACE, A • 1912 • *Francis Evelyn* • USA
CARIDAD! • 1919 • MXC
CARILLON DE MINUIT, LE • 1922 • de Baroncelli Jacques • FRN
CARILLONS, LES • 1936 • Storck Henri • DOC • BLG
CARILLONS SANS JOIE • 1962 • Brabant Charles • FRN, ITL
CARINE see **INHIBITION** • 1976
CARING FOR CHRYSLER • 1977-80 • Zaritsky John • MTV • CND
CARINO MIO • 1961 • Gil Rafael • SPN
CARINOSAS, LAS • 1953 • Cortes Fernando • MXC
CARINOSO, EL • 1958 • Baledon Rafael • MXC
CARIOCA SERENADERS • 1941 • Negulesco Jean • SHT • USA
CARIOCA TIGRE • 1977 • Carnimeo Giuliano • ITL
CARITA, EL • 1973 • *Panorama* • MXC
CARITA DE CIELO • 1946 • Diaz Morales Jose • MXC
CARL DREYER • 1964-69 • Rohmer Eric • MTV • FRN
CARL GUSTAV AND HIS GANG see **CARL GUSTAV OG GJENGEN** • 1981
CARL GUSTAV OG GJENGEN • 1981 • Solum Ola • NRW • CARL GUSTAV AND HIS GANG
CARL HOFF AND HIS BAND • 1942 • Negulesco Jean • SHT • USA
CARL MICHAEL ZIEHRER, DER LETZTE WALZERKONIG • 1922 • *Thiele Wilhelm* • AUS
CARL MICHAEL ZIEHRERS MARCHEN AUS ALT-WIEN see **MARCHEN AUS ALT-WIEN** • 1923
CARL NIELSEN 1865-1931 • 1978 • Roos Jorgen • DCS • DNM
CARL PETERS • 1941 • Selpin Herbert • FRG
CARL SANDBURG -ECHOES AND SILENCES • 1982 • Adato Perry Miller • TVM • USA
CARL TH. DREYER • 1966 • Roos Jorgen • DOC • DNM
CARL UND CARLA • 1915 • Wilhelm Carl • FRG
CARL VAN GORDON'S FAMILY • 1912 • *Nestor* • USA
CARL XII: S KURIR • 1924 • Anthoni Rudolf • SWD • COURIER OF CHARLES XII
CARLA'S BED see **CARLA'S THING** • 1970
CARLA'S THING • 1970 • *Stacey Dist.* • USA • CARLA'S BED
CARLIN AT CARNEGIE • 1983 • Santos Steven J. • USA
CARLO GORBACIOV • 1988 • Lizzani Carlo • ITL • DEAR GORBACHOV
CARLO PISACANE • 1955-59 • Taviani Paolo, Taviani Vittorio • DCS • ITL
CARLOS • 1970 • *Chaplin Geraldine* • ISR
CARLOS • 1971 • Geissendorfer Hans W. • FRG
CARLOS CRUZ DIEZ • 1972 • Roche Luis Armando • VNZ
CARLOS CRUZ, UN GUANACASTECO • 1978 • Trigueros Edgar • DOC • CRC
CARLOS EL TERRORISTA • 1977 • Cardona Rene • MXC
CARLOS MARIGHELA • 1970 • Marker Chris • FRN
CARLOS MOLINA AND HIS ORCHESTRA • 1948 • Cowan Will • SHT • USA
CARLOS MONZON • 1973 • Reichenbach Francois • DOC • ARG
CARLOS UND ELISABETH • 1924 • Oswald Richard • FRG • DON CARLOS AND ELIZABETH
CARLOTA • 1959 • Cahen Enrique • SPN
CARLOTTA • 1981 • Rolla Stefano • ITL
CARLOTTA THE BEAN STRINGER • 1914 • Dwan Allan • USA • MENACE OF CARLOTTA, THE
CARLOTTA, THE MAD EMPRESS (UKN) see **MAD EMPRESS, THE** • 1939
CARLTON-BROWNE OF THE F.O. • 1958 • Boulting Roy, Dell Jeffrey • UKN • MAN IN A COCKED HAT (USA)
CARLY'S WEB • 1987 • Inch Kevin • TVM • USA
CARMA • 1916 • Harvey John • USA
CARMELA • 1942 • Calzavara Flavio • ITL
CARMELA • 1981 • Love John • FRN
CARMELA E UNA BAMBOLA • 1958 • Puccini Gianni • ITL
CARMELITA'S REVENGE • 1914 • MacGregor Norval • USA
CARMELITES, THE (UKN) see **DIALOGUE DES CARMELITES, LE** • 1959
CARMEN • 1900-07 • Blache Alice • FRN
CARMEN • 1907 • Gilbert Arthur • UKN
CARMEN • 1909 • Falena Ugo • ITL
CARMEN • 1910 • Calmettes Andre • FRN
CARMEN • 1913 • *Monopol* • USA
CARMEN • 1913 • Marston Theodore • *Thanhouser* • USA
CARMEN • 1914 • Cabanne W. Christy • USA
CARMEN • 1915 • De Mille Cecil B. • *Lasky* • USA
CARMEN • 1915 • Walsh Raoul • *Fox* • USA
CARMEN • 1918 • Lubitsch Ernst • FRG • GYPSY BLOOD (USA) ○ GYPSY LOVE
CARMEN • 1920 • Vollrath Ernesto • MXC
CARMEN • 1922 • Wynn George • UKN
CARMEN • 1926 • Feyder Jacques, Rosay Francoise • FRN
CARMEN • 1927 • Parkinson H. B. • UKN
CARMEN • 1933 • Reiniger Lotte • ANS • FRG
CARMEN • 1936 • Dyer Anson • ANM • UKN
CARMEN • 1943 • Amadori Luis Cesar • ARG
CARMEN • 1943 • Christian-Jaque • FRN, ITL
CARMEN • 1960 • Vanzi Luigi • ITL
CARMEN • 1967 • von Karajan Herbert • SWT
CARMEN • 1983 • Rosi Francesco • ITL, FRN • BIZET'S CARMEN
CARMEN • 1983 • Saura Carlos • SPN
CARMEN see **CHARLIE CHAPLIN'S BURLESQUE ON CARMEN** • 1914
CARMEN 63 (FRN) see **CARMEN DI TRASTEVERE** • 1962
CARMEN, LA • 1975 • Diamante Julio • SPN
CARMEN BABY • 1967 • Metzger Radley H. • USA, YGS, FRG
CARMEN BOOM • 1962 • Iquino Ignacio F. • SPN
CARMEN COMES HOME see **KARUMEN KOKYO NI KAERU** • 1951
CARMEN DE CARABANCHEL • 1965 • Bartolome Cecilia • SHT • SPN
CARMEN DI TRASTEVERE • 1962 • Gallone Carmine • FRN, ITL • CARMEN 63 (FRN)
CARMEN FRA I ROSSI • 1939 • Neville Edgar • ITL
CARMEN GET IT • 1962 • Deitch Gene • ANS • USA
CARMEN JONES • 1954 • Preminger Otto • USA
CARMEN, JR. • 1923 • USA
CARMEN, LA DE RONDA • 1959 • Demicheli Tulio • SPN • DEVIL MADE A WOMAN, THE (USA) ○ GIRL AGAINST NAPOLEON, A
CARMEN, LA DE TRIANA • 1938 • Rey Florian • SPN, FRG
CARMEN LA QUE CONTABA 16 ANOS • 1978 • Chalbaud Roman • VNZ • CARMEN WHEN SHE WAS ONLY 16 YEARS OLD
CARMEN NEJEN PODLE BIZETA • 1967 • Schorm Evald • CZC • CARMEN -NOT ONLY BY BIZET ○ CARMEN NOT ACCORDING TO BIZET
CARMEN NOT ACCORDING TO BIZET see **CARMEN NEJEN PODLE BIZETA** • 1967
CARMEN -NOT ONLY BY BIZET see **CARMEN NEJEN PODLE BIZETA** • 1967
CARMEN NUE • 1984 • Lopez Albert • FRN, ITL, SPN
CARMEN OF THE ISLES • 1912 • *Eyton Bessie* • USA
CARMEN OF THE KLONDIKE • 1918 • Barker Reginald • USA
CARMEN OF THE NORTH • 1920 • Binger Maurits H. • USA
CARMEN ON ICE • 1989 • Hohlfeld Horant • FRG
CARMEN PROIBITA • 1953 • Scotese Giuseppe Maria • ITL
CARMEN (USA) see **GYPSY BLOOD** • 1931
CARMEN VON ST. PAULI, DIE • 1928 • Waschneck Erich • FRG • WATER RAT, THE
CARMEN WHEN SHE WAS ONLY 16 YEARS OLD see **CARMEN LA QUE CONTABA 16 ANOS** • 1978
CARMENA • 1929 • Aylott Dave, Symmons E. F. • SHT • UKN
CARMENITA, THE FAITHFUL • 1911 • *Anderson Broncho Billy* • USA

CARMEN'S PURE LOVE see **KARUMEN JUNJOSU** • 1952
CARMEN'S ROMANCE • 1914 • *Sterling* • USA
CARMEN'S VERANDA • 1944 • Davis Mannie • ANS • USA
CARMEN'S WASH DAY • 1914 • *Sterling* • USA
CARMILLA • 1968 • Fellbom Claes • SWD • SWEDISH LOVE PLAY (UKN) ○ WHAT NEXT? (USA) ○ INCEST
CARMINELLA • 1910 • Merwin Bannister • USA
CARNABY M.D. (USA) see **DOCTOR IN CLOVER** • 1966
CARNAGE • 1969 • *Craig Ray (P)* • USA
CARNAGE • 1977 • Burns Tim • ASL
CARNAGE • 1984 • Milligan Andy • USA
CARNAGE (USA) see **REAZIONE A CATENA** • 1971
CARNAL DESIRE see **NIKUTAI NO YOKKYU** • 1968
CARNAL GAMES • Lander Ralph • USA
CARNAL KNOWLEDGE • 1970 • *Cosmos Films* • USA
CARNAL KNOWLEDGE • 1970 • Nichols Mike • USA
CARNAL PUNISHMENT see **NIKUKEI** • 1967
CARNALITA • 1974 • Rizzo Alfredo • ITL • EROTIC REVENGE ○ HOT PLAYMATES
CARNAP • 1967 • Pajarillo Sim • PHL
CARNATION FRANK • 1961 • Haynes Stanley • FRG
CARNATION KID, THE • 1929 • Hopper E. Mason • USA
CARNAVAL • 1953 • Verneuil Henri • FRN
CARNAVAL A LA NOUVELLE ORLEANS • 1957 • Reichenbach Francois • SHT • FRN
CARNAVAL BARRA LIMPA • 1967 • Tanko J. B. • BRZ • BARMA LIMPA CARNIVAL
CARNAVAL DE MALEMORT, LE see **FILLES DE MALEMORT, LES** • 1973
CARNAVAL DE QUEBEC • 1957 • Palardy Jean • DCS • CND
CARNAVAL DE QUEBEC see **CARNIVAL IN QUEBEC** • 1956
CARNAVAL DES BARBOUZES, LE (FRN) see **GERN HAB' ICH DIE FRAUEN GEKILLT** • 1966
CARNAVAL DES VERITIES, LE • 1919 • L'Herbier Marcel • FRN
CARNAVAL D'HIVER see **WINTER CARNIVAL** • 1949
CARNAVAL EN CHUTE LIBRE • 1965 • Bouchard Guy • CND
CARNAVAL EN EL TROPICO • 1941 • Villatoro Carlos • MXC
CARNAVAL EN MI BARRIO • 1960 • Cardona Rene • MXC
CARNAVAL TRAGICO • 1921 • Abitia Jesus B. • MXC
CARNAVALS • 1950 • Storck Henri • DOC • BLG
CARNE • 1968 • Bo Armando • ARG • FLESH
CARNE, LA see **SLACHTVEE** • 1980
CARNE APALEADA • 1977 • Aguirre Javier • SPN
CARNE DE CABARET • 1931 • Cabanne W. Christy • USA
CARNE DE CABARET • 1939 • Patino Gomez Alfonso • MXC • ROSA LA TERCIOPELO
CARNE DE HORCA • 1953 • Vajda Ladislao • SPN, ITL • TERRORE DELL'ANDALUSIA, IL
CARNE DE HORCA • 1972 • *Churubusco Azteca* • MXC
CARNE DE PRESIDIO • 1951 • Gomez Muriel Emilio • MXC
CARNE E L'ANIMA, LA • 1943 • von Strischewski Wladimir • ITL
CARNE INQUIETA • 1952 • Prestifilippo Silvestro • ITL
CARNE MANDA, LA • 1947 • Urueta Chano • MXC
CARNE PER FRANKENSTEIN (ITL) see **ANDY WARHOL'S FRANKENSTEIN** • 1974
CARNE Y DEMONIO see **SUSANA** • 1950
CARNEGIE HALL • 1947 • Ulmer Edgar G. • USA
CARNET DE BAL, UN • 1937 • Duvivier Julien • FRN • LIFE DANCES ON (USA) ○ CHRISTINE (UKN) ○ DANCE PROGRAMME, THE
CARNET DE PLONGEE • 1950 • Cousteau Jacques • FRN
CARNET DE VIAJE • 1961 • Ivens Joris • SHT • CUB • TRAVEL NOTEBOOK (USA)
CARNET PER UN MORTO (ITL) see **JUDOKA AGENT SECRET** • 1966
CARNETS DU MAJOR THOMPSON, LES • 1955 • Sturges Preston • FRN • DIARY OF MAJOR THOMPSON, THE (UKN) ○ FRENCH THEY ARE A FUNNY RACE, THE
CARNEVAL • 1919 • *De Rheidt Celly* • FRG
CARNEVALE DEI PAZZI, IL • 1920 • Lolli Alberto Carlo • ITL
CARNEVALE DI VENEZIA, IL • 1927 • Almirante Mario • ITL • CARNIVAL OF VENICE
CARNEVALE DI VENEZIA, IL • 1940 • Adami Giuseppe, Gentilomo Giacomo • ITL
CARNEVALESCA • 1918 • Palermi Amleto • ITL
CARNIVAL • 1921 • Knoles Harley • UKN
CARNIVAL • 1931 • Wilcox Herbert • UKN • VENETIAN NIGHTS (USA)
CARNIVAL • 1935 • Lang Walter • USA • CARNIVAL NIGHTS (UKN) ○ WORLD'S FAIR
CARNIVAL • 1946 • Haynes Stanley • UKN
CARNIVAL • 1950-53 • Vickrey Robert • SHT • USA
CARNIVAL • 1955 • Biggs Julian • CND
CARNIVAL see **KARNEVAL** • 1908
CARNIVAL see **DANCE PRETTY LADY** • 1932
CARNIVAL see **IMMENSEE** • 1943
CARNIVAL see **KARNEVAL** • 1961
CARNIVAL see **SUMMER WISHES, WINTER DREAMS** • 1973
CARNIVAL, THE • 1911 • Olcott Sidney • USA
CARNIVAL, THE • 1990 • Grubcheva Ivanka • BUL
CARNIVAL, ANGEL AND DUST see **KARNEVAL, ANDEO I PRAH** • 1990
CARNIVAL BOAT • 1932 • Rogell Albert S. • USA • BAD TIMBER
CARNIVAL CAPERS • 1932 • Lantz Walter, Nolan William • ANS • USA
CARNIVAL COURAGE • 1945 • Swift Howard • ANS • USA
CARNIVAL CRIME, THE • 1929 • Wolff Willi • FRG
CARNIVAL DRESS • Weiler Kurt • ANM • GDR
CARNIVAL GIRL see **YOUNG DESIRE** • 1930
CARNIVAL GIRL, THE • 1926 • Tate Cullen • USA
CARNIVAL IN CARACAS • 1909 • Vidal Augusto Gonzalez, Gonham M. A. • VNZ
CARNIVAL IN COSTA RICO • 1947 • Ratoff Gregory • USA
CARNIVAL IN FLANDERS (UKN) see **KERMESSE HEROIQUE, LA** • 1935
CARNIVAL IN MOSCOW (USA) see **KARNAVALNAYA NOCH** • 1956
CARNIVAL IN QUEBEC • 1956 • Blais Roger • DCS • CND • CARNAVAL DE QUEBEC
CARNIVAL IN THE CLOTHES CUPBOARD • 1940 • Halas John, Batchelor Joy • ANS • UKN
CARNIVAL LADY • 1933 • Higgin Howard • USA
CARNIVAL LADY see **SHADOW, THE** • 1937
CARNIVAL MAGIC • 1982 • Adamson Al • USA
CARNIVAL NIGHT see **KARNAVALNAYA NOCH** • 1956
CARNIVAL NIGHTS (UKN) see **CARNIVAL** • 1935
CARNIVAL OF BLOOD • 1971 • Kirtman Leonard • USA • DEATH RIDES A CAROUSEL
CARNIVAL OF BLOOD see **CHIMATSURI** • 1929
CARNIVAL OF CRIME • 1961 • Cahan George M. • USA
CARNIVAL OF HERETICS see **SPALOVAC MRTVOL** • 1968
CARNIVAL OF LOWICZ, THE see **KARUZELA LOWICKA** • 1958
CARNIVAL OF SINNERS see **MAIN DU DIABLE, LA** • 1942
CARNIVAL OF SOULS • 1962 • Harvey Herk • USA
CARNIVAL OF TERROR see **FUNHOUSE, THE** • 1981
CARNIVAL OF THIEVES (UKN) see **CAPER OF THE GOLDEN BULLS, THE** • 1966
CARNIVAL OF THRILLS • 1980 • Moder Dick • TVM • USA
CARNIVAL OF VENICE see **CARNEVALE DI VENEZIA, IL** • 1927
CARNIVAL ON SKATES • 1933 • Sparling Gordon • DCS • CND
CARNIVAL QUEEN, THE • 1937 • Watt Nate • USA
CARNIVAL ROCK • 1958 • Corman Roger • USA
CARNIVAL STORY • 1954 • Neumann Kurt • USA
CARNIVAL TIME • 1936 • Schwarzwald Milton • SHT • USA
CARNIVAL WEEK • 1927 • *Terry Paul* • ANS • USA
CARNIVALS • 1972 • Burke Martyn • CND
CARNIVALS AND CANNIBALS see **CANNIBALS AND CARNIVALS** • 1918
CARNY • 1980 • Kaylor Robert • USA
CARNY GIRL • 1970 • Garto Frank • USA
CARO MICHELE • 1976 • Monicelli Mario • ITL • DEAR MICHAEL
CARO PAPA • 1979 • Risi Dino • ITL, FRN, CND • CHER PAPA (FRN) ○ DEAR FATHER ○ DEAR PAPA
CAROBNI ZVUCI • 1957 • Vukotic Dusan • YGS • CHARMING SOUNDS ○ MAGIC SOUNDS, THE
CARODEJUV UCEN • 1977 • Zeman Karel • ANM • CZC, FRG • MAGICIAN'S APPRENTICE, THE ○ KRABAT CARODEJUV UCEN
CAROGNE SI NASCE • 1968 • Brescia Alfonso • ITL • ONE IS BORN A SWINE
CAROL • 1970 • Emshwiller Ed • USA
CAROL FOR ANOTHER CHRISTMAS • 1964 • Mankiewicz Joseph L. • TVM • USA
CAROLA DE DIA, CAROLA DE NOCHE • 1969 • de Arminan Jaime • SPN
CAROLA LAMBERTI -EINE VOM ZIRKUS • 1954 • Muller Hans • GDR • WOMAN OF THE CIRCUS
CAROLANN • 1989 • Wharmby Tony • TVM • USA
CAROLINA • 1934 • King Henry • USA • HOUSE OF CONNELLY, THE (UKN)
CAROLINA BLUES • 1944 • Jason Leigh • USA
CAROLINA CANNONBALL • 1955 • Lamont Charles • USA
CAROLINA MOON • 1940 • McDonald Frank • USA
CAROLINA REDIVIVA • 1920 • Hedqvist Ivan • SWD
CAROLINE • 1964 • Dufaux Georges, Perron Clement • SHT • CND
CAROLINE AU PAYS NATAL • 1951 • de Gastyne Marco • SHT • FRN
CAROLINE CHERIE • 1950 • Pottier Richard • FRN • DEAR CAROLINE (USA)
CAROLINE CHERIE • 1967 • de La Patelliere Denys • FRN, FRG, ITL • SCHON WIE DIE SUNDE (FRG)
CAROLINE DU SUD • 1952 • de Gastyne Marco • SHT • FRN
CAROLINE UND DIE MANNER UBER VIERZIG (FRG) see **MOI ET LES HOMMES DE QUARANTE ANS** • 1964
CAROLYN CARLSON • Cloue Eric • DOC
CAROLYN LIMA STORY, THE • 1966 • Rowe John • USA • BURN, BABY, BURN ○ BURNING MAN, THE
CAROLYN OF THE CORNER • 1919 • Thornby Robert T. • USA
CARONI • 1978 • de Pedro Manuel • DCS • VNZ
CAROSELLO DI CANZONI • 1958 • Capuano Luigi • ITL
CAROSELLO DI NOTTE • 1964 • Balletti Elio • DOC • ITL • SEX SERVICE (UKN) ○ SEXY SHOW (USA)
CAROSELLO DI VARIETA • 1955 • Bonaldi Aldo, Quinti Aldo
CAROSELLO NAPOLETANO • 1954 • Giannini Ettore • ITL • NEAPOLITAN CAROUSEL (USA) ○ NEAPOLITAN FANTASY
CAROSELLO NERO • 1973 • Gandin Michele • ITL • BLACK ADVERTISING
CAROSELLO SPAGNOLA see **BALLATA SPAGNOLA** • 1958
CAROTTES SONT CUITES, LES • 1956 • Vernay Robert • FRN
CAROUSALS • 1979 • Diego Constante • DOC • CUB • PARRANDAS
CAROUSEL • 1956 • King Henry • USA
CAROUSEL • 1969 • *Grenier Louie (P)* • ANS • USA
CAROUSEL • 1978 • Darino Eduardo • ANM • URG
CAROUSEL see **KARUSEL** • 1971
CAROUSELLA • 1965 • Irvin John • DCS • UKN
CAROVANA see **SIGNORA DELL'OVEST, UNA** • 1942
CAROVANA DEL PECCATO, LA • 1953 • Mercanti Pino • ITL
CAROVANA DI CANZONI • 1955 • Corbucci Sergio • ITL
CAROVANE see **SIGNORA DELL'OVEST, UNA** • 1942
CAROVNE DEDICTVI • 1985 • Zelenka Zdenek • CZC • ENCHANTED HERITAGE
CARPATHIAN CASTLE, THE • 1957 • Cavalcanti Alberto • RMN • CASTLE IN THE CARPATHIANS (USA)
CARPATHIAN EAGLE • 1982 • Megahy Francis • MTV • UKN
CARPENTER, THE • 1911 • *Vitagraph* • USA
CARPENTER, THE • 1913 • North Wilfred • USA
CARPENTER, THE • 1932 • Petrov Vladimir • USS
CARPENTER, THE • 1988 • Wellington David • CND, USA
CARPENTER AND CHILDREN, A see **CHIISAKOBE** • 1962
CARPENTER AND THE COOK, THE • 1900 • *Warwick Trading Co.* • UKN
CARPENTERS, THE • 1941 • Fennell Paul • ANS • USA
CARPET FROM BAGDAD, THE • 1915 • Campbell Colin • USA
CARPET OF HORROR, THE (USA) see **TEPPICH DES GRAUENS** • 1962
CARPETBAGGERS, THE • 1964 • Dmytryk Edward • USA
CARPOCAPSE DES POMMES, LE • 1955 • Tadie, Lacoste • SHT • FRN
CARPOOL • 1983 • Swackhamer E. W. • TVM • USA
CARQUAKE (UKN) see **CANNONBALL** • 1976
CARQUENEZ WOODS, THE see **HALF BREED, THE** • 1916
CARRARA • 1950 • Lomazi • SHT • ITL
CARRASCOS ESTAO ENTRE NOS • 1968 • Chadler C. Adolpho • BRZ • KILLERS ARE AMONG US, THE
CARRE DE DAMES POUR LEYTON see **CARRE DE DAMES POUR UN AS** • 1966
CARRE DE DAMES POUR UN AS • 1966 • Poitrenaud Jacques • FRN, SPN, ITL • LAYTON.. BAMBOLE E KARATE (ITL) ○ CARRE DE DAMES POUR LEYTON
CARRE DE VALETS • 1947 • Berthomieu Andre • FRN
CARREFOUR • 1938 • Bernhardt Curtis • FRN • CROSSROADS (USA) ○ HOMME DE LA NUIT, L'
CARREFOUR DE L'OPERA • 1898 • Melies Georges • FRN • PLACE DE L'OPERA 3RD VIEW
CARREFOUR DES ENFANTS PERDUS, LE • 1943 • Joannon Leo • FRN • CHILDREN OF CHAOS (USA)
CARREFOUR DES PASSIONS • 1947 • Giannini Ettore, Calef Henri (U/c) • FRN, ITL
CARREFOUR DU CRIME • 1947 • Sacha Jean • FRN • J'AI TUE
CARRERA -DAS GEHEIMNIS DER BLONDEN KATZE (FRG) see **MAGNIFICO TONY CARRERAS, EL** • 1968
CARRERA DE CICLISMO EN EL VELODROME DE ARROYO SECO • 1898 • Oliver Felix • URG
CARRERA DEL MILLON, LA • 1971 • *Filmadora Chapultepel* • MXC
CARRERA -THE SECRET OF THE BLONDE CAT see **MAGNIFICO TONY CARRERAS, EL** • 1968
CARRETERA GENERAL • 1956 • Elorrieta Jose Maria • SPN
CARRIAGE • 1935 • Field Mary • UKN
CARRIAGE ENTRANCE see **MY FORBIDDEN PAST** • 1951
CARRIAGE OF DEATH, THE • 1916 • *Swayne Marion* • SHT • USA
CARRIAGE TO VIENNA see **KOCAR DO VIDNE** • 1966
CARRIE • 1952 • Wyler William • USA
CARRIE • 1976 • De Palma Brian • USA
CARRIE FROM LANCASHEER • 1928 • *De Forest Phonofilm* • SHT • UKN
CARRIER • 1987 • White Nathan J. • USA
CARRIER PIGEON, THE • 1911 • *Kalem* • USA
CARRIERE • 1921 • Feher Friedrich, Heil Heinz • FRG
CARRIERE DE SUZANNE, LA • 1963 • Rohmer Eric • FRN • SUZANNE'S PROFESSION
CARRINGFORD SCHOOL MYSTERY, THE • 1958 • Hammond William C. • SRL • UKN
CARRINGTON V.C. • 1954 • Asquith Anthony • UKN • COURT MARTIAL (USA)
CARRO ARMATO DELL'8 SEPTEMBRE, IL • 1960 • Puccini Gianni • ITL
CARRONA • 1975 • *Cine Vision* • MXC
CARROSSE D'OR, LE • 1952 • Renoir Jean • FRN, ITL • CARROZZA D'ORO, LA (ITL) ○ GOLDEN CARRIAGE, THE ○ GOLDEN COACH, THE
CARROT NOSE • 1959 • Weiler Kurt • ANM • GDR
CARROTS • 1917 • Wilson Frank • UKN
CARROTS & PEAS • 1969 • Frampton Hollis • USA
CARROUSEL see **EVASION DES CARROUSELS, L'** • 1968
CARROUSSEL • 1968 • Ignatov Avram • SHT • BUL
CARROUSSEL BOREAL • 1959 • Starevitch Ladislas • ANS • FRN
CARROZZA D'ORO, LA (ITL) see **CARROSSE D'OR, LE** • 1952
CARR'S REGENERATION • 1911 • *Phillips E. R.* • USA
CARRUSEL NOCTURNO • 1963 • Madruga Esteban • SPN
CARRY GREENHAM HOME • 1984 • Kidron Beeban, Richardson Amanda • UKN
CARRY HARRY • 1942 • Edwards Harry J. • SHT • USA
CARRY IT ON • 1970 • Coyne James, Jones Robert C., Knight Christopher • USA • JOAN (UKN)
CARRY ME BACK • 1982 • Reid John • NZL
CARRY ON • 1927 • Shurey Dinah, Peers Victor • UKN
CARRY ON • 1931 • Kelley Albert • SHT • USA
CARRY ON • 1944-45 • Jodoin Rene • ANS • CND
CARRY ON see **BETTER 'OLE; OR, THE ROMANCE OF OLD BILL, THE** • 1918
CARRY ON ABROAD • 1972 • Thomas Gerald • UKN
CARRY ON ADMIRAL • 1957 • Guest Val • UKN • SHIP WAS LOADED, THE (USA)
CARRY ON AGAIN, DOCTOR • 1969 • Thomas Gerald • UKN
CARRY ON AT YOUR CONVENIENCE • 1971 • Thomas Gerald • UKN
CARRY ON BEHIND • 1975 • Thomas Gerald • UKN
CARRY ON CABBY see **CALL ME A CAB** • 1963
CARRY ON CAMPING • 1969 • Thomas Gerald • UKN
CARRY ON CLEO • 1964 • Thomas Gerald • UKN
CARRY ON CONSTABLE • 1960 • Thomas Gerald • UKN
CARRY ON COWBOY • 1965 • Thomas Gerald • UKN
CARRY ON CRUISING • 1962 • Thomas Gerald • UKN
CARRY ON DICK • 1974 • Thomas Gerald • UKN
CARRY ON DOCTOR • 1967 • Thomas Gerald • UKN
CARRY ON DON'T LOSE YOUR HEAD see **DON'T LOSE YOUR HEAD** • 1966
CARRY ON EMMANNUELLE • 1978 • Thomas Gerald • UKN
CARRY ON ENGLAND • 1976 • Thomas Gerald • UKN
CARRY ON FOLLOW THAT CAMEL see **FOLLOW THAT CAMEL** • 1967
CARRY ON GIRLS • 1973 • Thomas Gerald • UKN
CARRY ON HENRY • 1970 • Thomas Gerald • UKN • CARRY ON HENRY VIII (USA)
CARRY ON HENRY VIII (USA) see **CARRY ON HENRY** • 1970
CARRY ON JACK • 1963 • Thomas Gerald • UKN • CARRY ON VENUS (USA)
CARRY ON LONDON • 1937 • Frazer D. R. • UKN
CARRY ON LOVING • 1970 • Thomas Gerald • UKN
CARRY ON MATRON • 1972 • Thomas Gerald • UKN
CARRY ON MILKMAIDS • 1974 • Batchelor Joy • ANS • UKN
CARRY ON NURSE • 1959 • Thomas Gerald • UKN
CARRY ON REGARDLESS • 1961 • Thomas Gerald • UKN
CARRY ON SCREAMING • 1966 • Thomas Gerald • UKN
CARRY ON SERGEANT • 1927 • Bairnsfather Bruce • CND
CARRY ON SERGEANT • 1958 • Thomas Gerald • UKN
CARRY ON SPYING • 1964 • Thomas Gerald • UKN
CARRY ON TEACHER • 1959 • Thomas Gerald • UKN
CARRY ON TV (USA) see **DENTIST ON THE JOB** • 1961
CARRY ON UP THE JUNGLE • 1970 • Thomas Gerald • UKN
CARRY ON.. UP THE KHYBER • 1968 • Thomas Gerald • UKN

CARRY ON VENUS (USA) see **CARRY ON JACK** • 1963
CARRYING OUT THE SNAKES • 1901 • Porter Edwin S. • USA
CARRYING THE MAIL • 1934 • Tansey Robert • SHT • USA
CARS, CARS AND MORE CARS • 1976 • Mason Bill • DOC • UKN
CARS IN YOUR LIFE, THE see **ONE THIRD DOWN AND 24 MONTHS TO PAY** • 1959
CARS THAT ATE PARIS, THE • 1974 • Weir Peter • ASL • CARS THAT EAT PEOPLE, THE
CARS THAT EAT PEOPLE, THE see **CARS THAT ATE PARIS, THE** • 1974
CARSON CITY • 1952 • De Toth Andre • USA
CARSON CITY CYCLONE • 1943 • Bretherton Howard • USA
CARSON CITY KID, THE • 1940 • Kane Joseph • USA
CARSON CITY RAIDERS • 1948 • Canutt Yakima • USA
CART, THE see **WOZEK** • 1966
CARTA, LA • 1930 • Millar Adelqui • SPN
CARTA A MESTRE DORDIO GOMES • 1971 • Guimaraes Manuel • SHT • PRT
CARTA A NADIE • 1964 • Cano Manuel • SPN
CARTA A SARA • 1956 • Manzanos Eduardo, Bercovici Ludovico • SPN, ITL
CARTA A UNA MUJER • 1961 • Iglesias Miguel • SPN
CARTA AJENA • 1975 • Giraldo Diego Leon • SHT • CLM • ANOTHER'S LETTER
CARTA AL CIELO • 1958 • Ruiz-Castillo Arturo • SPN
CARTA BRAVA • 1948 • Delgado Agustin P. • MXC
CARTA DE AMOR, UNA • 1943 • Zacarias Miguel • MXC
CARTA DE AMOR DE DUERME, MI AMOR • 1971 • Regueiro Francisco • SPN
CARTA DE AMOR DE UN ASESINO • 1972 • Regueiro Francisco • SPN • LOVE LETTER FROM A MURDERER
CARTA DE CARACAS • 1973 • Figueroa Alberto Vazquez • VNZ • LETTER FROM CARACAS, A
CARTACALHA, REINE DES GITANS • 1941 • Mathot Leon • FRN
CARTAGINE IN FIAMME • 1959 • Gallone Carmine • ITL, FRN • CARTHAGE EN FLAMMES (FRN) ○ CARTHAGE IN FLAMES
CARTAS A MAMA • 1961 • Antin Manuel • ARG
CARTAS A UFEMIA • 1952 • Diaz Morales Jose • MXC
CARTAS A UN PEREGRINO • 1964 • Ardavin Cesar • SHT • SPN
CARTAS BOCA ARRIBA • 1962 • Franco Jesus • SPN, FRN • ATTACK OF THE ROBOTS (USA) ○ CARTES SUR TABLE (FRN) ○ CARDS ON THE TABLE ○ CARDS FACE UP
CARTAS DE AMOR • 1951 • Lugones Mario C. • ARG
CARTAS DE AMOR DE UNA MONJA • 1978 • Grau Jorge • SPN
CARTAS DEL JAPON • 1972 • MXC • LETTERS FROM JAPAN
CARTAS DESDE CULLERA • 1966 • Briz Jose • SHT • SPN
CARTAS MARCADAS • 1947 • Cardona Rene • MXC
CARTAS NA MESA • 1975 • Ceitil Rogerio • PRT • CARDS ON THE TABLE
CARTE AMERICAINE • 1912-14 • Cohl Emile • ANS • USA
CARTE DE CREDIT, LA • 1973 • Lavoie Richard • SHT • CND
CARTER CASE, THE • 1919 • Mackenzie Donald • SRL • USA
CARTER CASE, THE (UKN) see **MR. DISTRICT ATTORNEY IN THE CARTER CASE** • 1941
CARTER'S ARMY • 1969 • McCowan George • TVM • USA
CARTERS OF GREENWOOD, THE • 1964 • Halas John • ASS • UKN
CARTER'S TERRIBLE TASK • 1908 • *Paul R. W.* • UKN
CARTES SUR TABLE (FRN) see **CARTAS BOCA ARRIBA** • 1962
CARTES TRANSPARENTES, LES • 1904 • Velle Gaston • FRN • TRANSPARENT CARDS, THE
CARTES VIVANTES, LES • 1905 • Melies Georges • FRN • LIVING PLAYING CARDS, THE (USA)
CARTESIUS • 1974 • Rossellini Roberto • MTV • ITL
CARTHAGE EN FLAMMES (FRN) see **CARTAGINE IN FIAMME** • 1959
CARTHAGE IN FLAMES see **CARTAGINE IN FIAMME** • 1959
CARTHUSIAN, THE see **KARTHAUZI, A** • 1916
CARTIER AFFAIR, THE • 1984 • Holcomb Rod • TVM • USA
CARTOGRAFIA, ARTE E CIENCIA • 1970 • Rosa Baptista • SHT • PRT
CARTOGRAPHER AND THE WAITER, THE • 1977 • Pringle Ian • SHT • ASL
CARTON FANTASTIQUE, LE • 1907 • Melies Georges • FRN • MISCHEVIOUS SKETCH, A (USA)
CARTOON CRUSADE • 1946 • *Mead Thomas (P)* • SHT • USA
CARTOON FACTORY • 1925 • Fleischer Dave • ANS • USA
CARTOONIST'S NIGHTMARE, A • 1935 • King Jack • ANS • USA
CARTOONLAND • 1921 • Fleischer Dave • ANS • USA
CARTOONS AIN'T HUMAN • 1943 • Kneitel Seymour • ANS • USA
CARTOONS BY HY MAYER • 1913 • Mayer Henry • ANM • USA
CARTOONS IN THE COUNTRY • 1915 • Barre Raoul • USA
CARTOONS IN THE HOTEL • 1915 • Barre Raoul • ANS • USA
CARTOONS IN THE KITCHEN • 1916 • Barre Raoul • SHT • USA
CARTOONS IN THE PARLOR • 1915 • Barre Raoul • USA
CARTOONS ON TOUR • 1915 • Barre Raoul • USA
CARTOUCHE • 1934 • Daroy Jacques • FRN
CARTOUCHE • 1962 • de Broca Philippe • FRN, ITL • SWORDS OF BLOOD (UKN)
CARTOUCHE see **AVVENTURE DI CARTOUCHE, LE** • 1955
CARTOUCHE, ROI DE PARIS • 1948 • Radot Guillaume • FRN
CARUGA • 1990 • Grlic Rajko • YGS • CHARUGA
CARUSO PASCOSKI (DI PADRE POLACCO) • 1988 • Nuti Francesco • ITL • CARUSO PASCOSKI (SON OF A POLE)
CARUSO PASCOSKI (SON OF A POLE) see **CARUSO PASCOSKI (DI PADRE POLACCO)** • 1988
CARVALHO • 1969 • Mejia Alberto • CLM
CARVAO VEGETAL • 1943 • Coelho Jose Adolfo • SHT • PRT
CARVE HER NAME WITH PRIDE • 1958 • Gilbert Lewis* • UKN
CARVED IN IVORY • 1974 • Gill Michael • SHT • UKN
CARVING THE CHRISTMAS TURKEY • 1905 • Green Tom? • UKN
CARY AND THE BISHOP'S WIFE see **BISHOP'S WIFE, THE** • 1947
CARYL CHESSMAN STORY, THE • 1977 • Kulik Buzz • TVM • USA • KILL ME IF YOU CAN (UKN)
CARYL OF THE MOUNTAINS • 1914 • Santschi Thomas • USA
CARYL OF THE MOUNTAINS • 1936 • Ray Bernard B. • USA • GET THAT GIRL (UKN)
CAS DE CONSCIENCE • 1939 • Kapps Walter • FRN • CREANCIER, LE
CAS DE CONSCIENCE • 1957 • Devlin Bernard • SHT • CND
CAS DU DOCTEUR BRENNER, LE • 1932 • Daumery John • FRN
CAS DU DOCTEUR GALLOY, LE • 1949 • Boutel Maurice • FRN • MAL DES SIECLES, LE
CAS DU DR. LAURENT, LE • 1956 • Le Chanois Jean-Paul • FRN • CASE OF DR. LAURENT, THE
CAS DU PROCUREUR LESMIN, LE • 1918 • de Baroncelli Jacques • FRN
CAS JE NEUPROSNY • 1978 • Chytilova Vera • CZC • TIME IS MERCILESS
CAS LEBRECQUE, LE • 1957 • Devlin Bernard • SHT • CND
CASA, LA • 1974 • Fons Angelino • SPN • HOUSE, THE
CASA AI CONFINI DEL PARCO, LA • 1980 • Deodato Ruggero • ITL • HOUSE ON THE EDGE OF THE PARK, THE ○ CASA SPERDUTA DEL PARCO, LA ○ CASA NEL PARCO, LA ○ HOUSE AT THE EDGE OF THE PARK, THE
CASA ASSASSINADA, A • 1972 • Saraceni Paulo Cesar • BRZ
CASA CHICA, LA • 1949 • Gavaldon Roberto • MXC
CASA COLORADA, LA • 1947 • Morayta Miguel • MXC
CASA CON LA SCALA NEL BUIO, LA • 1983 • Bava Lamberto • ITL • HOUSE WITH THE DARK STAIRCASE, THE ○ BLADE IN THE DARK, A (USA) ○ HOUSE OF THE DARK STAIRWAY ○ QUELLA CASA CON LA AL BUIO
CASA D LAS MUJERES QUE VIVIERON HASTA EL FINAL DEL DIA, LA • 1965 • Revenga Luis • SPN
CASA DALLE FINESTRE CHE RIDONO, LA • 1976 • Avati Pupi • ITL
CASA D'APPUNTAMENTO • 1972 • Merighi Ferdinando • ITL
CASA DE BERNARDA ALBA, LA • 1987 • Camus Mario • SPN • HOUSE OF BERNARDA ALBA, THE
CASA DE BOLIVAR, LA • 1975 • Dennis John • SHT • CLM • BOLIVAR'S HOUSE
CASA DE CRISTAL, LA • 1967 • Alcoriza Luis • MXC
CASA DE LA CHICAS, LA • 1971 • Klimovsky Leon • SPN
CASA DE LA LLUVIA, LA • 1943 • Roman Antonio • SPN
CASA DE LA TROYA, LA • 1947 • Orellana Carlos • MXC
CASA DE LA TROYA, LA • 1959 • Gil Rafael • SPN
CASA DE LA ZORRO, LA • 1945 • Ortega Juan J. • MXC
CASA DE LAS MIL MUNECAS, LA (SPN) see **HAUS DER TAUSEND FREUDEN, DAS** • 1967
CASA DE LAS MUERTAS VIVIENTES, LA • 1972 • Balcazar Alfonso • SPN • NOCHE DE UNA MUERTO QUE VIVIO, LA ○ NIGHT OF A DEAD WOMAN WHO LIVED, THE
CASA DE LAS PALOMAS, LA • 1971 • Guerin Claudio • SPN • HOUSE OF THE DOVES, THE
CASA DE LAS SIETE TUMBAS, LA • 1982 • Stocki Pedro • ARG • HOUSE OF THE SEVEN TOMBS, THE
CASA DE LAS SOMBRAS, LA • 1976 • Wulicher Ricardo • ARG • HOUSE OF SHADOWS ○ MECHA ORTIZ GERMAN KRAUSS
CASA DE LOS CUERVOS, LA • 1941 • Borcosque Carlos • ARG • HOUSE OF THE RAVENS, THE
CASA DE LOS ESPANTOS, LA • 1961 • Crevenna Alfredo B. • MXC • HOUSE OF THE FRIGHTS ○ SPOOK HOUSE
CASA DE LOS MARTINEZ, LA • 1971 • Navarro Agustin, Villalba Romano (U/c) • SPN
CASA DE MADAME LULU, LA • 1968 • Porter Julio • ARG • HOUSE OF MADAME LULU, THE
CASA DE MUJERES • 1942 • Soria Gabriel • MXC
CASA DE MUJERES • 1966 • Soler Julian • MXC
CASA DE MUJERES • 1977 • Cordido Enver • VNZ • HOUSE FOR WOMEN, A
CASA DE MUNECAS • 1953 • Crevenna Alfredo B. • MXC
CASA DE ORATES, A • 1972 • Semedo Artur • MTV • PRT
CASA DE PERDICION • 1954 • Pereda Ramon • MXC • HOUSE OF PERDITION (USA)
CASA DE QUIROS, LA • 1937 • Barth-Moglia Luis • ARG
CASA DE VECINDAD • 1950 • Bustillo Oro Juan • MXC
CASA DEI PULCINI, LA • 1924 • Camerini Mario • ITL
CASA DEL ANGEL, LA • 1957 • Torre-Nilsson Leopoldo • ARG • HOUSE OF THE ANGEL, THE ○ END OF INNOCENCE
CASA DEL OGRO, LA • 1938 • de Fuentes Fernando • MXC • HOUSE OF THE OGRE, THE ○ OGRE'S HOUSE, THE
CASA DEL PARAISO, LA • 1981 • San Miguel Santiago • SPN, VNZ • HOUSE OF PARADISE, THE
CASA DEL PECCATO, LA • 1939 • Neufeld Max • ITL
CASA DEL PELICANO, LA • 1977 • Vejar • MXC
CASA DEL RECUERDO, LA • 1940 • Saslavsky Luis • ARG
CASA DEL RENCOR, LA • 1941 • Martinez Solares Gilberto • MXC
CASA DEL SUR, LA • 1974 • Olhovich Sergio • MXC • HOUSE IN THE SOUTH, THE
CASA DEL TAPPETO GIALLO, LA • 1983 • Lizzani Carlo • ITL • HOUSE WITH THE YELLOW CARPET, THE
CASA DEL TERROR, LA • 1959 • Martinez Solares Gilberto, Warren Jerry • MXC • FACE OF THE SCREAMING WEREWOLF (USA) ○ HOUSE OF TERROR, THE
CASA DELLA PAURA, LA • 1919 • Campogalliani Carlo • ITL
CASA DELL'AMORE LA POLIZIA INTERVIENE • 1979 • Polselli Renato • ITL
CASA DELLE BAMBOLE CRUDELI, LA (ITL) see **MAISON DES FILLES PERDUES, LA** • 1974
CASA DELLE DEMI-VIERGES, LA • 1970 • Weiss Helmut • ITL
CASA DELLE MELE MATURE, LA • 1971 • Tosini Pino • ITL
CASA DELLE VEDOVE, LA • 1960 • Baldi Gian Vittorio • ITL • WIDOW'S HOME, THE
CASA DELL'EXORCISMO, LA • 1975 • Bava Mario • ITL • HOUSE OF EXORCISM, THE ○ LISA E IL DIAVOLO ○ LISA AND THE DEVIL ○ DEVIL IN THE HOUSE OF EXORCISM, THE ○ DIABOLO SE LLEVA A LOS MUERTOS
CASA DI BAMBOLA • 1919 • Mari Febo • ITL
CASA DI VETRO, LA • 1919 • Righelli Gennaro • ITL
CASA DINTRE CIMPURI • 1980 • Tatos Alexandru • RMN • HOUSE IN THE FIELDS, THE
CASA EMBRUJADA, LA • 1944 • Rivero Fernando A. • MXC
CASA EMBRUJADA, LA see **MALDICION DE LA LLORONA, LA** • 1961
CASA ESTA VACIA, LA • 1944 • Schliepper Carlos • CHL
CASA FLORA • 1972 • Fernandez Ramon • SPN
CASA FUNDADA EN 1940 • 1975 • Forque Jose Maria • SPN
CASA GRANDE, LA • 1975 • Rodriguez Francisco • SPN • BIG HOUSE, THE ○ GREAT HOUSE, THE
CASA LONTANA • 1940 • Meyer Johannes • ITL
CASA MANANA • 1951 • Yarbrough Jean • USA
CASA MUERTE • 1974 • Cosmi Carlo • VNZ • DEAD HOUSE
CASA NEL PARCO, LA see **CASA AI CONFINI DEL PARCO, LA** • 1980
CASA NETERMINATA • 1964 • Blaier Andrei • RMN • UNFINISHED HOUSE, THE
CASA PRIVATA PER LE S(CHULTZ) S(TAFFELN) • 1977 • Mattei Bruno • ITL
CASA RICORDI • 1954 • Gallone Carmine • ITL, FRN • HOUSE OF RICORDI (USA) ○ MAISON DU SOUVENIR, LA
CASA SENZA TEMPO, LA • 1943 • Sabbia Andrea Della • ITL • IL MISTERIO DEL 2o PIANO
CASA SIN FRONTERAS, LA • 1971 • Olea Pedro • SPN • HOUSE WITHOUT FRONTIERS, THE (USA) ○ HOUSE WITHOUT BOUNDARIES, THE
CASA SOTTO LA NEVE, LA • 1922 • Righelli Gennaro • ITL
CASA SPERDUTA DEL PARCO, LA see **CASA AI CONFINI DEL PARCO, LA** • 1980
CASA SUL FIUME, LA see **DUE CUORI** • 1943
CASA SUL LAGO, LA • 1977 • Leoni Guido • ITL
CASA SULLA FUNGAIA, LA see **CRIMINE A DUE** • 1965
CASABIANCA • 1950 • Peclet Georges • FRN • CASABLANCA
CASABLAN • 1964 • Frisch Larry • GRC
CASABLANCA • 1942 • Curtiz Michael • USA
CASABLANCA • 1961 • Solas Humberto • CUB
CASABLANCA see **CASABIANCA** • 1950
CASABLANCA CIRCUS, THE see **CIRKUS CASABLANCA** • 1981
CASABLANCA, NID D'ESPIONS • 1963 • Decoin Henri • FRN, ITL • SPIONAGGIO A CASABLANCA (ITL)
CASADAS ENGANAN DE 4 A 6, LAS • 1945 • Cortes Fernando • MXC
CASADO CASA QUIERE, EL • 1947 • Martinez Solares Gilberto • MXC
CASADOS Y LA MENOR • 1975 • Coll Joaquin • SPN
CASAMENTO, O • 1975 • Jabor Arnaldo • BRZ
CASAMIENTO DE CHICHILO, EL • 1938 • Navarro Isidoro • ARG
CASAMIENTO DE LAUCHA, EL • 1977 • Dawi Enrique • ARG • LAUCHA'S WEDDING
CASANOVA • 1919 • *Lugosi Bela* • FRG
CASANOVA • 1927 • Volkov Alexander • FRN • LOVES OF CASANOVA, THE ○ PRINCE OF ADVENTURERS
CASANOVA • 1933 • Barberis Rene • FRN • AMOURS DE CASANOVA, LES
CASANOVA • 1976 • Fellini Federico • ITL • CASANOVA DE FELLINI (FRN) ○ FELLINI'S CASANOVA ○ CASANOVA DI FEDERICO FELLINI, IL
CASANOVA • 1987 • Langton Simon, Russell Ken • TVM • UKN
CASANOVA see **CASANOVA '70** • 1965
CASANOVA see **INFANZIA, VOCAZIONE E PRIMA ESPERIENZE DI GIACOMO CASANOVA, VENEZIANO** • 1969
CASANOVA '70 • 1965 • Monicelli Mario • ITL, FRN • CASANOVA
CASANOVA BROWN • 1944 • Wood Sam • USA
CASANOVA CAT • 1951 • Hanna William, Barbera Joseph • ANS • USA
CASANOVA & CO. see **CASANOVA E COMPAGNI** • 1978
CASANOVA DE FELLINI (FRN) see **CASANOVA** • 1976
CASANOVA DI FEDERICO FELLINI, IL see **CASANOVA** • 1976
CASANOVA E COMPAGNI • 1978 • Antel Franz • ITL, FRN, FRG • RISE AND RISE OF CASANOVA, THE (UKN) ○ 13 FEMMES POUR CASANOVA (FRN) ○ SOME LIKE IT COOL (USA) ○ CASANOVA & CO.
CASANOVA FAREBBE COSI! • 1942 • Bragaglia Carlo Ludovico • ITL
CASANOVA HEIRATAT • 1940 • de Kowa Viktor • FRG
CASANOVA IN BURLESQUE • 1944 • Goodwins Leslie • USA
CASANOVA OF SWEDEN see **RASKENSTAM** • 1983
CASANOVA: PART 2 • 1982 • Tobalina Carlos • USA
CASANOVA (USA) see **AVVENTURE DI GIACOMO CASANOVA, LE** • 1954
CASANOVA WIDER WILLEN • 1931 • Brophy Edward • FRG
CASANOVA'S BIG NIGHT • 1954 • McLeod Norman Z. • USA
CASANOVAS ERBE • 1928 • Noa Manfred • FRG
CASANOVAS ERSTE UND LETZTE LIEBE • 1920 • Szoreghi Julius • AUS
CASANOVA'S LAST ROSE see **POSLEDNI RUZE OD CASANOVY** • 1966
CASAROLI GANG, THE see **BANDA CASAROLI, LA** • 1962
CASAS GRANDES: AN APPROACH TO THE GREAT CHICHIMECA see **CASAS GRANDES: UNA APROXIMACION A LA GRAN CHICHIMECA** • 1990
CASAS GRANDES: UNA APROXIMACION A LA GRAN CHICHIMECA • 1990 • Montero Rafael • MXC • CASAS GRANDES: AN APPROACH TO THE GREAT CHICHIMECA
CASATE Y VERAS • 1946 • Orellana Carlos • MXC
CASBAH • 1948 • Berry John • USA
CASBAH see **PEPE LE MOKO** • 1936
CASCABEL • 1976 • Arraiza Raul • MXC
CASCABELITO • 1961 • Salvador Jaime • MXC
CASCADE DE FEU, LA • 1904 • Melies Georges • FRN • FIREFALL, THE (USA)
CASCADEUR, LE (FRN) see **STUNTMAN** • 1968
CASCADEURS, LES see **STUNT FAMILY, THE** • 1978
CASCARRABIAS • 1930 • *Vilches Ernesto* • USA
CASCO BLANCO, EL • 1959 • Balana Pedro, Saitor Tony • SPN
CASE 33: ANTWERP • 1965 • *Hoven Adrian* • FRG
CASE 68 see **QADIA 68** • 1968
CASE AGAINST BROOKLYN, THE • 1958 • Wendkos Paul • USA
CASE AGAINST CALVIN COOKE see **ACT OF MURDER, AN** • 1948
CASE AGAINST FERRO, THE (USA) see **POLICE PYTHON 357** • 1976

CASE AGAINST MRS. AMES, THE • 1936 • Seiter William A. • USA
CASE AGAINST PAUL RYKER, THE see **SERGEANT RYKER** • 1967
CASE AT LAW, A • 1917 • Rosson Arthur • USA
CASE CLOSED • 1988 • Lowry Dick • TVM • USA
CASE DE L'ONCLE TOM, LA (FRN) see **ONKEL TOMS HUTTE** • 1965
CASE FOR A YOUNG HANGMAN, A see **PRIPAD PRO ZACINAJICIHO KATA** • 1969
CASE FOR P.C.49, A • 1951 • Searle Francis • UKN
CASE FOR SHERLOCK HOLMES, A • 1911 • Coleby A. E. • UKN
CASE FOR SOLOMON, A see **MOTHERHOOD OR POLITICS** • 1913
CASE FOR THE BARRISTER, A • 1964 • Holly Martin • CZC
CASE FOR THE CROWN, THE • 1934 • Cooper George A. • UKN
CASE FOR THE JURY, A see **DOCK BRIEF, THE** • 1962
CASE FOR THE NEW HANGMAN, A see **PRIPAD PRO ZACINAJICIHO KATA** • 1969
CASE IS CLOSED, THE see **KHARIJ** • 1983
CASE IS NOT CLOSED, THE see **PRIPAD JESTE REKONCI** • 1957
CASE NO.205/1913 • 1983 • Kolarov Keran • BUL
CASE OF A DOPED ACTRESS, THE • 1919 • Carlton Wilfred • UKN
CASE OF A PACKING CASE, THE • 1921 • Gordon Edward R. • UKN
CASE OF ARSON, A • 1913 • Coleby A. E. • UKN
CASE OF BARNABAS KOS, THE see **PRIPAD BARNABAS KOS** • 1964
CASE OF BEANS, A • 1915 • Daly William Robert • USA
CASE OF BECKY, THE • 1915 • Reicher Frank • USA
CASE OF BECKY, THE • 1921 • Franklin Chester M. • USA
CASE OF BENNY, THE • 1918 • *Boy City Film* • SHT • USA
CASE OF BURGLARS, A • 1912 • Wilson Frank? • UKN
CASE OF CHARLES PEACE, THE • 1949 • Lee Norman • UKN
CASE OF CHARLIE GORDON, THE • 1939 • Legg Stuart • DCS • CND
CASE OF CHERRY PURCELLE, THE • 1914 • *Adair Belle* • USA
CASE OF COMFORT, A • 1918 • Rains Fred • UKN
CASE OF CONSCIENCE, A • 1958 • Haldane Don • CND
CASE OF DEADLY FORCE, A • 1986 • Miller Michael • TVM • USA
CASE OF DR. KOVARE, THE see **PRIPAD DR. KOVARE** • 1949
CASE OF DR. LAURENT, THE see **CAS DU DR. LAURENT, LE** • 1956
CASE OF DR. STANDING, THE • 1917 • Weston C. H. • SHT • USA
CASE OF DYNAMITE, A • 1912 • *Cumpson John* • USA
CASE OF EGGS, A • 1974 • Devlin Bernard • CND
CASE OF EUGENICS, A • 1915 • Drew Sidney • USA
CASE OF EXPLOSIVES, A • 1912 • Fitzhamon Lewin • UKN • MUNITION WORKERS
CASE OF GABRIEL PERRY, THE • 1935 • De Courville Albert • UKN
CASE OF HIGH TREASON, A • 1911 • *Edison* • USA
CASE OF HIGH TREASON, A see **KONSERTO YIA POLIVOLA** • 1967
CASE OF HONOR, A • 1989 • Romero Eddie • PHL, USA
CASE OF HONOUR, A see **SEIGIHA** • 1957
CASE OF IDENTITY, A • 1910 • *Edison* • USA
CASE OF IDENTITY, A • 1921 • Elvey Maurice • UKN
CASE OF IMAGINATION, A • 1914 • *Melies* • USA
CASE OF JONATHAN DREW, THE (USA) see **LODGER: A STORY OF THE LONDON FOG, THE** • 1926
CASE OF KURT CLAUSEWITZ, THE • 1963 • Panfilov Gleb • SHT • USS
CASE OF LADY BROOKES, THE see **THAT DANGEROUS AGE** • 1949
CASE OF LADY CAMBER, THE • 1920 • West Walter • UKN
CASE OF LADY CAMBER, THE see **LORD CAMBER'S LADIES** • 1932
CASE OF LENA SMITH, THE • 1929 • von Sternberg Josef • USA
CASE OF LIBEL • 1967 • Jarrott Charles • MTV • UKN
CASE OF LIBEL, A • 1984 • Till Eric • TVM • USA, CND
CASE OF LIMBURGER, A • 1915 • *Mina* • USA
CASE OF LONE, THE • 1970 • Strandgaard Charlotte • DNM
CASE OF MARCEL DUCHAMP, THE • 1983 • Rowan • USA
CASE OF MRS. LORING, THE (USA) see **QUESTION OF ADULTERY, A** • 1958
CASE OF MRS. PEMBROKE, THE (UKN) see **TWO AGAINST THE WORLD** • 1936
CASE OF PATTI SMITH, THE • 1962 • Handel Leo A. • USA • SHAME OF PATTI SMITH, THE
CASE OF PILOT MARESZ, THE (USA) see **SPRAWA PILOTA MARESZA** • 1956
CASE OF PIT NO.8, THE see **SLUCHAI NA SHAKHTE 8** • 1957
CASE OF POISON, A • 1915 • *Glaum Louise* • USA
CASE OF POISONS, THE (USA) see **AFFAIRE DES POISONS, L'** • 1955
CASE OF RAPE, A • 1974 • Sagal Boris • TVM • USA
CASE OF SERGEANT GRISCHA, THE • 1930 • Brenon Herbert • USA
CASE OF SMALLPOX, A • 1912 • *Imp* • USA
CASE OF SOHO RED, THE • 1953 • Crabtree Arthur • UKN
CASE OF SPIRITS, A • 1909 • *Vitagraph* • USA • ALL'S WELL THAT ENDS WELL
CASE OF THE 44'S, THE • 1964 • McGowan Tom • UKN, DNM
CASE OF THE BABYSITTER, THE • 1947 • Hillyer Lambert • USA
CASE OF THE BLACK CAT, THE • 1936 • McGann William • USA
CASE OF THE BLACK PARROT, THE • 1941 • Smith Noel • USA
CASE OF THE BOGUS COUNT, THE • 1954 • Krish John • UKN
CASE OF THE BROTHER NAVES, THE see **CASO DOS IRMAOS NAVES, O** • 1967
CASE OF THE COCKEYED CANARY, THE • 1952 • Kneitel Seymour • ANS • USA
CASE OF THE COLD-STORAGE YEGG • 1963 • Smith Paul J. • ANS • USA
CASE OF THE CONSTANT GOD see **LOVE LETTERS OF A STAR** • 1936
CASE OF THE CURIOUS BRIDE, THE • 1935 • Curtiz Michael • USA
CASE OF THE ELEPHANT'S TRUNK, THE • 1965 • Smith Paul J. • ANS • USA
CASE OF THE EVIL MOUSE, THE see **CASE OF THE MISSING MOUSE, THE** • 1961
CASE OF THE EXCITING WIVES, THE see **CASE OF THE STRIPPING WIVES, THE** • 1966
CASE OF THE FRIGHTENED LADY, THE • 1940 • King George • UKN • FRIGHTENED LADY, THE (USA)
CASE OF THE FULL MOON MURDERS • 1971 • Cunningham Sean S. • USA • SEX ON THE GROOVE TUBE
CASE OF THE HILLSIDE STRANGLERS, THE • 1988 • Gethers Steve • USA • HILLSIDE STRANGLERS, THE
CASE OF THE HOWLING DOG, THE • 1934 • Crosland Alan • USA
CASE OF THE INVESTIGATING MAGISTRATE, THE • 1984 • Spassov Krassimir • BUL
CASE OF THE LOST SHEEP, THE • 1935 • Lantz Walter, McLeod Victor • ANS • USA
CASE OF THE LUCKY LEGS, THE • 1935 • Mayo Archie • USA
CASE OF THE MALTESE CHICKEN, THE • 1964 • *Lantz Walter (P)* • ANS • USA
CASE OF THE MISSING BLONDE, THE (UKN) see **LADY IN THE MORGUE** • 1938
CASE OF THE MISSING BRIDES, THE (UKN) see **CORPSE VANISHES, THE** • 1942
CASE OF THE MISSING CLERK, THE see **FORSVUNDNE FULDMAEGTIG, DEN** • 1972
CASE OF THE MISSING GIRL, THE • 1913 • *Solax* • USA
CASE OF THE MISSING HARE • 1942 • Jones Charles M. • ANS • USA
CASE OF THE MISSING HEIR, THE • 1910 • *Yankee* • USA
CASE OF THE MISSING MAN, THE • 1935 • Lederman D. Ross • USA
CASE OF THE MISSING MOUSE, THE • 1961 • Dovnikovic Borivoj • ANS • YGS • CASE OF THE EVIL MOUSE, THE
CASE OF THE MISSING SCENE, THE • 1951 • Chaffey Don • UKN
CASE OF THE MUKKINESE BATTLEHORN, THE • 1956 • Stirling Joseph • UKN
CASE OF THE OLD ROPE MAN, THE • 1952 • Catling Darrell • UKN
CASE OF THE RED-EYED RUBY • 1961 • Smith Paul J. • ANS • USA
CASE OF THE RED MONKEY, THE (USA) see **LITTLE RED MONKEY** • 1953
CASE OF THE RIVER MORGUE, THE • 1956 • Tully Montgomery • UKN
CASE OF THE SCREAMING BISHOP, THE • 1944 • *Mintz Charles (P)* • ANS • USA
CASE OF THE SLEEPY BOXER, THE see **SLUCAJ POSPANOG BOKSERA** • 1961
CASE OF THE SMILING STIFF, THE • 1974 • Cunningham Sean S., Talbot Brud • USA
CASE OF THE SMILING WIDOW, THE • 1957 • Tully Montgomery • UKN
CASE OF THE STRIPPING WIVES, THE • 1966 • Conde Manuel S.?, Maury Maria D.? • USA • CASE OF THE EXCITING WIVES, THE ○ STRIPPING WIVES ○ EXCITING WIVES
CASE OF THE STUTTERING BISHOP, THE • 1937 • Clemens William • USA
CASE OF THE STUTTERING PIG, THE • 1937 • Tashlin Frank • ANS • USA
CASE OF THE TWO BEAUTIES, THE see **CASO DE LAS DOS BELLEZAS, EL** • 1968
CASE OF THE VANISHED BONDS, THE • 1914 • West Langdon • USA
CASE OF THE VELVET CLAWS, THE • 1936 • Clemens William • USA
CASE OF THE WITCH WHO WASN'T, THE see **PAS DE REIT POUR MELANIE** • 1990
CASE OF TOMATOES, A • 1909 • *Essanay* • USA
CASE ON THE DOCTOR, A • 1914 • *Glaum Louise* • USA
CASELLO N.3 • 1945 • Ferroni Giorgio • ITL
CASERNE EN FOLIE, LA • 1934 • Cammage Maurice • FRN
CASEY • 1970 • Haydon Tom • DOC • ASL
CASEY AND HIS NEIGHBOR'S GOAT • 1903 • Porter Edwin S. • USA
CASEY AT THE BAT • 1912 • Young James • USA
CASEY AT THE BAT • 1916 • Ingraham Lloyd • USA
CASEY AT THE BAT • 1927 • Brice Monte • USA
CASEY AT THE BAT • 1946 • Geronimi Clyde • ANS • USA
CASEY AT THE BAT • 1986 • Steinberg David • USA
CASEY BATS AGAIN • 1954 • Kinney Jack • ANS • USA
CASEY GOES SHOPPING • 1916 • Fitzgerald J. A.?, McEvoy Tom? • SHT • USA
CASEY IN A PAWNSHOP • 1916 • *Ray Johnnie* • SHT • USA
CASEY IN MEXICO • 1916 • Fitzgerald J. A.?, McEvoy Tom? • SHT • USA
CASEY IN THE GRANDSTAND • 1916 • Fitzgerald J. A.?, McEvoy Tom? • SHT • USA
CASEY JONES • 1927 • Hunt Charles J. • USA
CASEY OF THE COAST GUARD • 1926 • Nigh William • SRL • USA
CASEY THE BANDMASTER • 1917 • Fitzgerald J. A.?, McEvoy Tom? • SHT • USA
CASEY THE DETECTIVE • 1916 • Fitzgerald J. A.?, McEvoy Tom? • SHT • USA
CASEY THE FIREMAN • 1917 • Fitzgerald J. A.?, McEvoy Tom? • SHT • USA
CASEY THE MILLIONAIRE • 1916 • Fitzgerald J. A.?, McEvoy Tom? • SHT • USA
CASEY THE WIZARD • 1916 • Fitzgerald J. A.?, McEvoy Tom? • SHT • USA
CASEY'S BIRTHDAY • 1914 • *Lubin* • USA
CASEY'S BORDER RAID • 1917 • Marshall George • SHT • USA
CASEY'S DREAM • 1916 • Fitzgerald J. A.?, McEvoy Tom? • SHT • USA
CASEY'S FIGHTFUL DREAM • 1904 • Porter Edwin S. • USA
CASEY'S JUMPING TOOTHACHE • 1909 • USA
CASEY'S KIDS • 1916 • Fitzgerald J. A.?, McEvoy Tom? • SHT • USA
CASEY'S MILLIONS • 1922 • MacDonagh John • IRL
CASEY'S SERVANTS • 1916 • Fitzgerald J. A.?, McEvoy Tom? • SHT • USA
CASEY'S SHADOW • 1977 • Ritt Martin • USA
CASEY'S TRIBULATIONS • 1915 • *Royal* • USA
CASEY'S VENDETTA • 1914 • Dillon Eddie • USA
CASH • 1933 • Korda Zoltan • UKN • FOR LOVE OR MONEY (USA)
CASH AND CARRY • 1937 • Lord Del • SHT • USA
CASH AND CARRY (UKN) see **RINGSIDE MAISIE** • 1941
CASH AND MARRY • 1930 • Foster Lewis R. • SHT • USA
CASH CALLS HELL see **GOHIKI NO SHINSHI** • 1966
CASH? CASH! • 1968 • Collet Paul • BLG
CASH CUSTOMERS • 1920 • Goulding Alf, Roach Hal • SHT • USA
CASH MCCALL • 1960 • Pevney Joseph • USA
CASH ON DELIVERY • 1910 • *Capitol* • USA
CASH ON DELIVERY • 1926 • Rosmer Milton • UKN
CASH ON DELIVERY (USA) see **TO DOROTHY, A SON** • 1954
CASH ON DEMAND • 1961 • Lawrence Quentin • UKN
CASH PARRISH'S PAL • 1915 • Hart William S., Smith Cliff • USA • DOUBLE CROSSED
CASH -POLITICAL FAIRY TALE • 1989 • Kuckelmann Norbert • FRG
CASH STASHERS • 1953 • Barclay David • SHT • USA
CASHEL BYRON'S PROFESSION see **ROMAN BOXERA** • 1921
CASHIER, THE see **KASSIERE, DE** • 1989
CASHIER'S ORDEAL, THE • 1912 • *Champion* • USA
CASHIER'S ORDEAL, THE • 1916 • *Supreme* • USA
CASI CASADOS • 1961 • Delgado Miguel M. • MXC
CASI JUGANDO • 1969 • Enciso Luis S. • SPN
CASI UN CABALLERO • 1964 • Forque Jose Maria • SPN
CASIMIR • 1950 • Pottier Richard • FRN
CASINO • 1980 • Chaffey Don • TVM • USA
CASINO, THE • 1973 • Chang Tseng Chai • HKG
CASINO DE PAREE (UKN) see **GO INTO YOUR DANCE** • 1935
CASINO DE PARIS • 1957 • Hunebelle Andre • FRN, ITL, FRG
CASINO MURDER CASE, THE • 1935 • Marin Edwin L. • USA
CASINO OF GOLD see **CLEOPATRA JONES AND THE CASINO OF GOLD** • 1975
CASINO RAIDERS • 1989 • Wong Ching • HKG
CASINO ROYALE • 1967 • Huston John, Hughes Ken, Guest Val, Parrish Robert, McGrath Joseph, Talmadge Richard, Squire Anthony • UKN
CASK OF AMONTILLADO, THE • 1954 • *Woolley Monty* • SHT • USA
CASKET FOR LIVING, A see **TOSEI TAMATEBAKO** • 1925
CASO ALMERIA, EL • 1984 • Muste Pedro Costa • SPN • ALMERIA AFFAIR, THE
CASO APPARENTEMENTE FACILE, UN • 1968 • Serra Gianni • ITL
CASO DE LA MUJER ASESINADITA, EL • 1954 • Davison Tito • MXC
CASO DE LAS DOS BELLEZAS, EL • 1968 • Franco Jesus • SPN, FRG • CASE OF THE TWO BEAUTIES, THE
CASO DE UNA ADOLESCENTE, EL • 1957 • Gomez Muriel Emilio • MXC
CASO DEFREGGER, IL see **QUEL GIORNO DIO NON C'ERA** • 1970
CASO DEL GIUDICE HALLER, IL see **CASO HALLER, IL** • 1933
CASO DI COSCIENZA, UN • 1970 • Grimaldi Gianni • ITL
CASO DIFFICILE DEL COMMISSARIO MAIGRET, IL (ITL) see **MAIGRET UND SEIN GROSSTER FALL** • 1966
CASO DOS IRMAOS NAVES, O • 1967 • Person Luis Sergio • BRZ • CASE OF THE BROTHER NAVES, THE
CASO HALLER, IL • 1933 • Blasetti Alessandro • ITL • CASO DEL GIUDICE HALLER, IL ○ GIUDICE HALLER, IL
CASO HUAYANAY: TESTIMONIO DE PART • 1980 • Garcia Federico • PRU
CASO MATTEI, IL • 1972 • Rosi Francesco • ITL • MATTEI AFFAIR, THE (UKN)
CASO MAURITIUS, IL (ITL) see **AFFAIRE MAURIZIUS, L'** • 1953
CASO MORO, IL • 1987 • Ferrara Giuseppe • ITL • MORO AFFAIR, THE
CASO PISCIOTTA, IL • 1972 • Visconti Eriprando • ITL
CASO RAOUL, IL • 1975 • Ponzi Maurizio • ITL
CASO SAVOLTA, EL see **VERDAD SOBRE EL CASO SAVOLTA, LA** • 1980
CASO SCORPIO: STERMINATE QUELLI DELLA CALIBRO 38 • 1978 • Montero Roberto Bianchi • ITL
CASO TAYRONA, EL • 1975 • Giraldo Diego Leon • SHT • CLM • TAYRONA CASE, THE
CASO VENERE PRIVATA, IL (ITL) see **CRAN D'ARRET** • 1970
CASO VOLPI GEROSI, IL • 1973 • Sabatini Mario • ITL
CASOTTO, IL • 1977 • Citti Sergio • ITL • BEACH HUT, THE (USA)
CASPAR DAVID FRIEDRICH • 1987 • Schamoni Peter • FRG
CASPER • 1950 • ASS • USA
CASPER COMES TO CLOWN • 1951 • Sparber I. • ANS • USA
CASPER GENIE • 1954 • Kneitel Seymour • ANS • USA
CASPER TAKES A BOW-WOW • 1951 • Sparber I. • ANS • USA
CASPER'S BIRTHDAY PARTY • 1959 • Kneitel Seymour • ANS • USA
CASPER'S FIRST CHRISTMAS • 1987 • Urbano Carl • ANS • USA
CASPER'S SPREE UNDER THE SEA • 1950 • Tytla Bill • ANS • USA
CASPIAN OIL WORKERS see **POVEST O NEFTYANIKAKH KASPIYA** • 1953
CASPIAN STORY see **POVEST O NEFTYANIKAKH KASPIYA** • 1953
CASQUE D'OR • 1952 • Becker Jacques • FRN • GOLDEN HELMET (USA) ○ GIRL WITH GOLDEN HAIR, THE ○ GOLDEN MARIE (UKN) ○ MARIE
CASS • 1979 • Noonan Chris • TVM • ASL
CASS TIMBERLANE • 1947 • Sidney George • USA
CASSANDRA • 1987 • Eggleston Colin • ASL
CASSANDRA CAT see **AZ PRIJDE KOCOUR** • 1963

CASSANDRA CROSSING, THE • 1977 • Cosmatos George Pan • UKN, FRG, ITL
CASSE, LE • 1971 • Verneuil Henri • FRN, ITL • SCASSINATORI, GLI (ITL) ○ BURGLARS, THE (USA)
CASSE-COU MADEMOISELLE • 1954 • Stengel Christian • FRN • AH! QUEL COUREUR!
CASSE-PIEDS, LES • 1948 • Dreville Jean • FRN • SPICE OF LIFE, THE (USA) ○ FACHEUX MODERNES, LES ○ PARADE DU TEMPS PERDU
CASSE-TETE CHINOIS POUR LE JUDOKA • 1968 • Labro Maurice • FRN, ITL, FRG • CHINESE PUZZLE FOR JUDOKA
CASSETTE DE L'EMIGREE, LA • 1912 • Feuillade Louis • FRN
CASSETTE LOVE AFFAIRS see **KASSETTENLIEBE** • 1982
CASSIDY • 1917 • Rosson Arthur • USA
CASSIDY OF BAR 20 • 1938 • Selander Lesley • USA
CASSINO TO KOREA • 1950 • Genock Edward • DOC • USA
CASSIODORO IL PIU DORO DEL PRETORIO • 1978 • Coltellacci Oreste • ITL
CASSIS • 1964 • Mekas Jonas • USA
CASSIS COLANK • 1958-59 • Breer Robert • USA
CASSIUS LE GRAND • 1964 • Klein William • FRN
CASSOWARY see **HIKUIDORI** • 1927
CASSURE, LA • 1981 • Munoz Ramon • FRN
CASSY JONES, O MAGNIFICO SEDUTOR • 1973 • Person Luis Sergio • BRZ
CAST, THE • 1915 • *Santa Barbara* • USA
CAST A DARK SHADOW • 1955 • Gilbert Lewis* • UKN
CAST A GIANT SHADOW • 1966 • Shavelson Melville • USA • EVASIVE PEACE
CAST A LONG SHADOW • 1959 • Carr Thomas • USA
CAST ADRIFT • 1917 • Sandground Maurice • UKN
CAST ADRIFT IN THE SOUTH SEAS • 1914 • McRae Henry • USA
CAST AMID BOOMERANG THROWERS • 1913 • *Melies* • USA
CAST-IRON • 1964 • Ioseliani Otar • SHT • USS • CAST IRON
CAST IRON see **CAST-IRON** • 1964
CAST IRON (UKN) see **VIRTUOUS SIN, THE** • 1930
CAST OF NIGHT see **YORU NON HAIYAKU** • 1959
CAST OF THE DIE, THE • 1914 • *Church Fred* • USA
CAST-OFF, THE • 1918 • West Raymond B. • USA
CAST-OFF, THE see **HANRAN** • 1959
CAST THY BREAD UPON THE WATER • 1910 • *Atlas* • USA
CAST THY BREAD UPON THE WATERS • 1910 • Haldane Bert? • UKN
CAST UP BY THE DEEP • 1911 • *Vitagraph* • USA
CAST UP BY THE SEA • 1915 • Buel Kenean • USA
CAST US NOT OUT • 1969 • Bigham Richard • UKN
CASTA DIVA • 1935 • Gallone Carmine • ITL
CASTA DIVA • 1955 • Gallone Carmine • ITL, FRN
CASTA DIVA • 1983 • de Kuyper Eric • NTH
CASTA DIVINA, LA • 1976 • Pastor Julian • MXC • DIVINE CASTE, THE
CASTA SUSANA, LA • 1944 • Perojo Benito • ARG
CASTA SUSANA, LA • 1962 • Amadori Luis Cesar • SPN
CASTAGNE SONO BUONE, LE • 1970 • Germi Pietro • ITL • TILL DIVORCE DO YOU PART (USA)
CASTAGNINO, DIARIO ROMANO • 1966 • Birri Fernando • SHT • ITL
CASTANUELAS • 1945 • Torrado Ramon • SPN
CASTAWAY • 1912 • *Baggot King* • USA
CASTAWAY • 1975 • Pallant Clive • UKN
CASTAWAY • 1987 • Roeg Nicolas • UKN
CASTAWAY, THE • 1912 • *Melies* • USA
CASTAWAY, THE • 1931 • Jackson Wilfred • ANS • USA
CASTAWAY, THE see **CHEATERS, THE** • 1945
CASTAWAY COWBOY, THE • 1975 • McEveety Vincent • USA
CASTAWAYS • Ljubic Milan, Giersz Witold • ANS • YGS
CASTAWAYS, THE • 1909 • Blackton J. Stuart • USA
CASTAWAYS, THE • 1910 • *Kalem* • USA
CASTAWAYS, THE • 1915 • Malins Geoffrey H. • UKN
CASTAWAYS, THE see **IN SEARCH OF THE CASTAWAYS** • 1961
CASTAWAYS, THE see **ROZBITKOWIE** • 1969
CASTAWAYS: A LOVE STORY see **BLUE ISLAND**
CASTAWAYS ON GILLIGAN'S ISLAND, THE • 1979 • Bellamy Earl • TVM • USA
CASTE • 1913 • Williams C. Jay • USA
CASTE • 1917 • Trimble Larry • USA, UKN
CASTE • 1930 • Gullan Campbell • UKN
CASTEL SANT'ANGELO • 1946 • Blasetti Alessandro • DOC • ITL
CASTELA DAS BERLENGAS, A • 1930 • Leitao Antonio • PRT
CASTELLANA DEL LIBANO, LA (ITL) see **CHATELAINE DU LIBAN, LA** • 1956
CASTELLI IN ARIA • 1939 • Genina Augusto • ITL, FRG • INS BLAUE LEBEN (FRG) ○ TRE GIORNI IN PARADISO
CASTELLO DALLE PORTE DI FUOCO, IL • 1970 • Merino Jose Luis • ITL, SPN • CASTLE WITH THE FIREY GATES, THE (USA)
CASTELLO DEI MORTI VIVI, IL • 1964 • Ricci Luciano • ITL, FRN • CHATEAU DES MORTS VIVANTS, LE (FRN) ○ CASTLE OF THE LIVING DEAD(USA)
CASTELLO DEL DIAVOLO, IL • 1913 • *Ambrosio* • ITL • DEVIL'S CASTLE, THE
CASTELLO DELLA MALINCONIA, IL • 1920 • Genina Augusto • ITL
CASTELLO DELLA PAURA, IL see **CASTELLO DELLE DONNE MALEDETTE, IL** • 1973
CASTELLO DELLE DONNE MALEDETTE, IL • 1973 • Oliver Robert H. • ITL • DOCTOR FRANKENSTEIN'S CASTLE OF FREAKS ○ MONSTERS OF FRANKENSTEIN ○ DR. FRANKENSTEIN'S CASTLE OF FREAKS ○ HOUSE OF FREAKS ○ TERROR CASTLE ○ CASTELLO DELLA PAURA, IL ○ TERROR
CASTELLO DELL'URAGANO, IL • 1920 • Maggi Luigi • ITL
CASTELLO DI ARTENA, IL see **BOIA SCARLATTO, IL** • 1965
CASTELLO DI CARTE • 1962 • Luzzati Emmanuele • ANM • ITL
CASTELLO IN SVEZIA, IL (ITL) see **CHATEAU EN SUEDE** • 1963
CASTELO DE CHOCOLATE, O • 1923 • Duarte Arthur • PRT
CASTELOS PORTUGUESES • 1959 • Garcia Fernando • SHT • PRT
CASTIGADOR, EL • 1965 • Bosch Juan • SPN
CASTIGADORES, LOS • 1960 • Balcazar Alfonso • SPN
CASTIGAT RIDENDO MORES • 1974 • Ecare Desire • IVC
CASTIGLIONE, LA • 1953 • Combret Georges • FRN, ITL • CONTESSA DI CASTIGLIONE, LA (ITL) ○ MISSION SECRETE: LA CASTIGLIONE
CASTIGO see **CAPPELLO DA PRETE, IL** • 1944
CASTIGO AL TRAIDOR • 1966 • Antin Manuel • ARG
CASTILIAN, THE (USA) see **VALLE DE LAS ESPADAS, EL** • 1963
CASTILLO DE FU MANCHU, EL(SPN) see **CASTLE OF FU MANCHU, THE** • 1968
CASTILLO DE LA PUREZA, EL • 1972 • Ripstein Arturo • MXC • CASTLE OF PURITY, THE (USA)
CASTILLO DE LAS BOFETADAS, EL • 1945 • de Orzal J. • SPN • CASTLE OF THE SLAPS IN THE FACE, THE
CASTILLO DE LOS MONSTRUOS, EL • 1957 • Soler Julian • MXC • CASTLE OF THE MONSTERS, THE (USA) ○ NOCHE DE TERROR
CASTILLO DE NAIPES • 1943 • Mihura Jeronimo • SPN
CASTILLO DE ROCHAL, EL • 1946 • Xiol Juan • SPN
CASTILLOS DE CASTILLA, LOS • Chumez Chumy • SHT • SPN
CASTILLOS EN EL AIRE • 1938 • Salvador Jaime • MXC • CASTLES IN THE AIR (USA)
CASTINET DANCE • 1898 • *Cinematograph Co.* • UKN
CASTING CALL • 1970 • Stewart Ken • USA
CASTING COUCH, THE • 1970 • *Stacey Dist.* • USA
CASTLE 1 • 1966 • Le Grice Malcolm • UKN
CASTLE 2 • 1968 • Le Grice Malcolm • UKN
CASTLE, THE • 1987 • Pakkasvirta Jaakko • FNL
CASTLE, THE (USA) see **SCHLOSS, DAS** • 1968
CASTLE AND CAPITAL • 1978 • Alexander Mike • DOC • UKN
CASTLE AND COUNTRY -A VIEW OF SCOTLAND • 1964 • Cobham Shirley • DOC • UKN
CASTLE CALLED WOMAN see **ONNA TOYO SHIRO** • 1953
CASTLE IN FLANDERS, A see **SCHLOSS IN FLANDERN, DAS** • 1936
CASTLE IN GREECE • 1960 • Meritzis T.
CASTLE IN SWEDEN see **CHATEAU EN SUEDE** • 1963
CASTLE IN THE AIR • 1952 • Cass Henry • UKN
CASTLE IN THE AIR see **RAINBOW 'ROUND MY SHOULDER** • 1952
CASTLE IN THE AIR see **DROMMESLOTTET** • 1984
CASTLE IN THE CARPATHIANS, THE • 1981 • Gulea Stere • RMN
CASTLE IN THE CARPATHIANS (USA) see **CARPATHIAN CASTLE, THE** • 1957
CASTLE IN THE DESERT • 1942 • Lachman Harry • USA
CASTLE IN THE FOREST, THE see **ZAMEK W LESIE** • 1971
CASTLE IN THE SAND see **PESCENI GRAD** • 1962
CASTLE IN THE SKY AND RHINESTONES see **WOLKENBAU UND FLIMMERSTERN** • 1919
CASTLE KEEP • 1969 • Pollack Sydney • USA
CASTLE OF ARTENA, THE see **BOIA SCARLATTO, IL** • 1965
CASTLE OF BLOOD (USA) see **DANZA MACABRA** • 1964
CASTLE OF CRIMES see **HOUSE OF THE ARROW, THE** • 1940
CASTLE OF DESPAIR, THE • 1916 • Wilson Ben • SHT • USA
CASTLE OF DOOM see **VAMPYR** • 1931
CASTLE OF DRACULA • 1968 • *Delta* • SHT • UKN
CASTLE OF DREAMS • 1919 • Noy Wilfred • UKN
CASTLE OF DREAMS see **PILVILINNA** • 1970
CASTLE OF EVIL • 1966 • Lyon Francis D. • USA • HAUNTING OF CASTLE MONTEGO, THE
CASTLE OF FU MANCHU, THE • 1968 • Franco Jesus • UKN, SPN, FRG • FOLTERKAMMER DES DR. FU MAN CHU, DIE (FRG) ○ CASTILLO DE FU MANCHU, EL(SPN) ○ ASSIGNMENT: INSTANBUL ○ TORTURE CHAMBER OF DR. FU MANCHU, THE
CASTLE OF LUST (USA) see **IM SCHLOSS DER BLUTIGEN BEGIERDE** • 1968
CASTLE OF OTRANTO, THE see **OTRANSKY ZAMEK** • 1977
CASTLE OF POT see **PILVILINNA** • 1970
CASTLE OF PURITY, THE (USA) see **CASTILLO DE LA PUREZA, EL** • 1972
CASTLE OF SAND, THE see **SUNA NO UTSUWA** • 1974
CASTLE OF TERROR (UKN) see **VERGINE DI NORIMBERGA, LA** • 1963
CASTLE OF TERRORS • 1964 • *Marks Aub* • SHT • UKN
CASTLE OF THE DOOMED see **BESAME, MONSTRUO** • 1968
CASTLE OF THE DOOMED, THE • 1969 • Iacob Mihai • RMN
CASTLE OF THE LIVING DEAD(USA) see **CASTELLO DEI MORTI VIVI, IL** • 1964
CASTLE OF THE MONSTERS, THE (USA) see **CASTILLO DE LOS MONSTRUOS, EL** • 1957
CASTLE OF THE SLAPS IN THE FACE, THE see **CASTILLO DE LAS BOFETADAS, EL** • 1945
CASTLE OF THE SPIDER'S WEB, THE see **KUMONOSU-JO** • 1957
CASTLE OF THE TERRIFIED see **GEHEIMNIS DER SCHWARZEN KOFFER, DAS** • 1962
CASTLE ON THE HUDSON • 1940 • Litvak Anatole • USA • YEARS WITHOUT DAYS (UKN)
CASTLE RANCH, THE • 1915 • Otto Henry • USA
CASTLE SINISTER • 1932 • Newman Widgey R. • UKN
CASTLE SINISTER • 1948 • Burn Oscar • UKN
CASTLE VOGELOD see **SCHLOSS VOGELOD** • 1921
CASTLE WITH THE FIREY GATES, THE (USA) see **CASTELLO DALLE PORTE DI FUOCO, IL** • 1970
CASTLE WITHIN A CASTLE see **SLOT I ET SLOT, ET** • 1955
CASTLES, THE see **STORY OF VERNON AND IRENE CASTLE, THE** • 1939
CASTLES AND COTTAGES see **SCHLOSSER UND KATEN** • 1957
CASTLES FOR TWO • 1917 • Reicher Frank • USA
CASTLES IN SPAIN • 1920 • Lucoque H. Lisle • UKN
CASTLES IN SPAIN (USA) see **CHATEAUX EN ESPAGNE** • 1953
CASTLES IN THE AIR • 1911 • Porter Edwin S. • USA
CASTLES IN THE AIR • 1914 • MacGregor Norval • USA
CASTLES IN THE AIR • 1919 • Baker George D. • USA
CASTLES IN THE AIR • 1981 • Bittman Roman • MTV • CND
CASTLES IN THE AIR see **LET'S PRETEND** • 1922
CASTLES IN THE AIR (USA) see **CASTILLOS EN EL AIRE** • 1938
CASTO SUSANO, EL • 1952 • Pardave Joaquin • MXC
CASTO VARON SPANOL, UN • 1973 • de Arminan Jaime • SPN
CASTOR AND POLLUX • 1974 • Noyce Phil • DOC • ASL
CASTRATI, I see **VOCI BIANCHE, LE** • 1964
CASTRITO Y LA LAMPARA DE ALADINO • 1954 • Barth-Moglia Luis • ARG
CASTRO ALVES • 1948 • de Barros Jose Leitao • PRT
CASTRO, CUBA AND COMMUNISM • 1962 • *Mel O'Dee Productions* • USA • DANGER ON OUR DOORSTEP
CASTRO STREET • 1966 • Baillie Bruce • SHT • USA
CASTRO'S FIRST YEAR OF POWER • 1959 • Watson Patrick • DOC • CND
CASUAL RELATIONS • 1973 • Rappaport Mark • USA
CASUAL RELATIONS see **FLUCHTIGE BEZIEHUNGEN** • 1982
CASUAL SEX? • 1988 • Robert Genevieve • USA
CASUALTIES OF WAR • 1989 • De Palma Brian • USA
CASUS KIRAN • 1968 • Atadeniz Yilmaz • TRK • SPY BREAKER, THE
CAT! • 1966 • Kadison Ellison • USA
CAT, THE see **CHAT, LE** • 1971
CAT, THE see **MACKA** • 1971
CAT, THE (USA) see **CHATTE, LA** • 1958
CAT, THE (USA) see **GATTO, IL** • 1978
CAT, A MOUSE AND A BELL, A • 1935 • *Mintz Charles (P)* • ANS • USA
CAT ABOVE, THE MOUSE BELOW, THE • 1964 • Jones Charles M. • ANS • USA
CAT ALARM • 1961 • Rasinski Connie • ANS • USA
CAT AND DOG • 1950-54 • Hofman Eduard • ASS • CZC • STORIES ABOUT A DOGGY AND A PUSSY
CAT AND DRIED BONITO see **NEKO TO KATSUOBUSHI** • 1961
CAT AND DUPLICAT • 1967 • Jones Charles M. • ANS • USA
CAT AND MERMOUSE • 1949 • Hanna William, Barbera Joseph • ANS • USA • CAT AND THE MERMOUSE, THE
CAT AND MOUSE • 1958 • Rotha Paul • UKN • DESPERATE MEN, THE
CAT AND MOUSE (UKN) see **MOUSEY** • 1974
CAT AND MOUSE (USA) see **KATZ UND MAUS** • 1967
CAT AND MOUSE (USA) see **CHAT ET LA SOURIS, LE** • 1975
CAT AND THE BELL, THE • 1938 • Lovy Alex • ANS • USA
CAT AND THE BONNET, THE • 1913 • *Kalem* • USA
CAT AND THE CANARY, THE • 1912 • *Weed Frank* • USA
CAT AND THE CANARY, THE • 1927 • Leni Paul • USA
CAT AND THE CANARY, THE • 1939 • Nugent Elliott • USA
CAT AND THE CANARY, THE • 1972 • Pine Phillip • USA
CAT AND THE CANARY, THE • 1978 • Metzger Radley H. • UKN
CAT AND THE CHESTNUTS, THE • 1913 • Buckland Warwick? • UKN
CAT AND THE FIDDLE, THE • 1933 • Howard William K. • USA
CAT AND THE MERMOUSE, THE see **CAT AND MERMOUSE** • 1949
CAT AND THE MOUSE, THE see **MYSZKA I KOTEK** • 1958
CAT AND THE SPHINX, THE • 1969 • Bunin Louis • ANM • USA
CAT AND TWO WOMEN, A see **NEKO TO SHOZO TO FUTARI NO ONNA** • 1956
CAT-ASTROPHE • 1916 • *Terry Paul* • ANS • USA
CAT BALLOU • 1965 • Silverstein Elliot • USA
CAT BLUES • 1968 • Rossif Frederic • SHT • FRN
CAT BURGLAR, THE • 1961 • Witney William • USA
CAT CAME BACK, THE • 1909 • Fitzhamon Lewin • UKN
CAT CAME BACK, THE • 1910 • *Atlas* • USA
CAT CAME BACK, THE • 1911 • *Essanay* • USA
CAT CAME BACK, THE • 1936 • Freleng Friz • ANS • USA
CAT CAME BACK, THE • 1944 • Rasinski Connie • ANS • USA
CAT CAME BACK, THE • 1987 • Barker Cordell • ANS • CND
CAT CARSON RIDES AGAIN • 1952 • Kneitel Seymour • ANS • USA
CAT CHASER • 1989 • Ferrara Abel • USA
CAT-CHOO • 1951 • Kneitel Seymour • ANS • USA
CAT CITY • 1987 • ANM • USA
CAT COLLEGE • 1940 • Newman Joseph M. • SHT • USA
CAT CONCERTO, THE • 1947 • Hanna William, Barbera Joseph • ANS • USA
CAT CREATURE, THE • 1973 • Harrington Curtis • TVM • USA
CAT CREEPS, THE • 1930 • Julian Rupert • USA
CAT CREEPS, THE • 1946 • Kenton Erle C. • USA
CAT, DOG & CO. • 1929 • Mack Anthony • SHT • USA
CAT FEUD • 1958 • Jones Charles M. • ANS • USA
CAT FISHIN' • 1947 • Hanna William, Barbera Joseph • ANS • USA
CAT FROM OUTER SPACE, THE • 1978 • Tokar Norman • USA
CAT GANG, THE • 1959 • Catling Darrell • UKN
CAT GIRL • 1957 • Shaughnessy Alfred • UKN
CAT HAPPY • 1950 • Rasinski Connie • ANS • USA
CAT HERE AND THERE, THE • 1962 • Carpi Cioni • ANS • USA
CAT HOUSE, THE see **PAVILON SELIEM** • 1982
CAT IN A CAGE • 1983 • Zarindast Tony • USA • CAT IN THE CAGE
CAT IN THE ACT • 1957 • Tendlar Dave • ANS • USA
CAT IN THE BAG, THE see **CHAT DANS LE SAC, LE** • 1964
CAT IN THE CAGE see **CAT IN A CAGE** • 1983
CAT IN THE SACK, THE (USA) see **CHAT DANS LE SAC, LE** • 1964
CAT MEETS MOUSE • 1942 • Davis Mannie • ANS • USA
CAT NAP PLUTO • 1948 • Nichols Charles • ANS • USA
CAT O' NINE TAILS, THE (UKN) see **GATTO A NOVE CODE, IL** • 1971
CAT OF THE NIGHT see **YORU NO MESUNEKO** • 1928
CAT ON A HOT TIN ROOF • 1958 • Brooks Richard • USA
CAT ON A HOT TIN ROOF • 1985 • Hofsiss Jack • USA
CAT ON A HOT TIN ROOF see **CAT ON FIRE, A** • 1977
CAT ON FIRE, A • 1977 • Sayf Samir • EGY • CAT ON A HOT TIN ROOF
CAT O'NINE TAILS • 1948 • Kneitel Seymour • ANS • USA
CAT PEOPLE • 1942 • Tourneur Jacques • USA
CAT PEOPLE • 1982 • Schrader Paul • USA
CAT SHOWS HER CLAWS, THE (UKN) see **CHATTE SORT SES GRIFFES, LA** • 1960
CAT, SHOZO AND TWO WOMEN, A see **NEKO TO SHOZO TO FUTARI NO ONNA** • 1956
CAT-TAILS FOR TWO • 1953 • McKimson Robert • ANS • USA

CAT TAMALE • 1951 • Kneitel Seymour • ANS • USA
CAT TANGO see **TANGO DES CHATS** • 1930
CAT-TASTROPHY • 1949 • Marcus Sid • ANS • USA
CAT THAT CHANGED INTO A WOMAN, THE (USA) see **CHATTE METAMORPHOSEE EN FEMME, LA** • 1909
CAT THAT HATED PEOPLE, THE • 1948 • Avery Tex • ANS • USA
CAT, THE WEASEL AND THE LITTLE RABBIT, THE see **CHAT, LE BELETTE ET LE PETIT LAPIN, LE**
CAT, THE WEASEL AND THE RABBIT, THE • 1969 • Stefanescu Horia • ANS • FRN
CAT TROUBLE • 1947 • Rasinski Connie • ANS • USA
CAT WITHOUT BOOTS, THE see **GATO SIN BOTAS, EL** • 1956
CAT WOMEN OF THE MOON • 1953 • Hilton Arthur • USA • ROCKET TO THE MOON ○ MISSILE TO THE MOON
CATACLYSM • 1972 • Tallas Gregg R., Marshak Philip, McGowan Tom • USA • NIGHTMARE NEVER ENDS, THE ○ SATAN'S SUPPER ○ CATALYSM
CATACLYSM, THE • 1934 • Lenard Andrew J. • SHT • HNG
CATACOMBS • 1964 • Hessler Gordon • UKN • WOMAN WHO WOULDN'T DIE, THE (USA)
CATACOMBS • 1988 • Schmoeller David • USA
CATACOMBS see **KATAKOMBY** • 1940
CATALINA CAPER • 1967 • Sholem Lee • USA • NEVER STEAL ANYTHING WET
CATALINA DE INGLATERRA • 1951 • Ruiz-Castillo Arturo • SPN
CATALINA, HERE I COME • 1927 • *Sennett Mack (P)* • SHT • USA
CATALINA INTERLUDE • 1945 • Ganzer Alvin • SHT • USA
CATALINA ROWBOAT RACE see **SMITH'S CATALINA ROWBOAT RACE** • 1928
CATALLI KOY • 1968 • Erakalin Ulku • TRK • VILLAGE OF CATALLI, THE
CATALOGUE • 1961 • Whitney John • ANS • USA
CATALOGUE OF LOVE • 1988 • Leth Jorgen • DNM
CATALYSM see **CATACLYSM** • 1972
CATALYTIC REFORMING PART I: THE REFORMING ACTION • 1958 • Cons David • DOC • UKN
CATALYTIC REFORMING PART II: THE REFORMING UNIT • 1958 • Cons David • DOC • UKN
CATAMARAN • 1970 • Lavoie Richard • DCS • CND
CATAMARCA LA TIERRA DE LA VIRGEN DEL VALLE • 1941 • Catrani Catrano • DOC • ARG
CATAMOUNT, THE see **FIGHTING GRIN, THE** • 1918
CATAMOUNT KILLING, THE • 1974 • Zanussi Krzysztof • FRG, USA
CATAPAULT AND THE KITE, THE see **PRAK A DRAK** • 1960
CATAPHOTE • 1964 • Lapoujade Robert • ANS • FRN
CATAPULT • 1973 • Paterson Tony • SHT • ASL
CATASTROFE EN EL MAR, UNA • 1927 • Urriola Eduardo • MXC
CATASTROPHE 1999 see **NOSTRADAMUS NO DAIYOGEN** • 1974
CATASTROPHE, THE see **HALODHIA CHORAYA BAODHAN KHAI** • 1988
CATASTROPHE DE LA MARTINIQUE, LA • 1902 • Zecca Ferdinand • FRN
CATASTROPHE DU BALLON "LE PAX" • 1902 • Melies Georges • FRN • CATASTROPHE OF THE BALLOON "LE PAX", THE
CATASTROPHE OF THE BALLOON "LE PAX", THE see **CATASTROPHE DU BALLON "LE PAX"** • 1902
CATATAN SI BOY • 1989 • INN
CATCH-22 • 1970 • Nichols Mike • USA
CATCH 69 • 1970 • *Kirt Films International* • USA
CATCH, THE • 1971 • Gosselin Bernard • SHT • CND
CATCH, THE • 1980 • Kroeker Allan • CND
CATCH, THE see **SHIIKU** • 1961
CATCH A PEBBLE • 1970 • Collier James F. • USA
CATCH-AS-CATCH-CAN • 1927 • Hutchison Charles • USA
CATCH AS CATCH CAN • 1931 • Neilan Marshall • SHT • USA • CATCH-AS-CATCH-CAN
CATCH AS CATCH CAN • 1937 • Kellino Roy • UKN • ATLANTIC EPISODE
CATCH-AS-CATCH-CAN see **CATCH AS CATCH CAN** • 1931
CATCH AS CATCH CAN (USA) see **SCATENATO, LO** • 1967
CATCH AS CATS CAN • 1947 • Davis Mannie • ANS • USA
CATCH ME A SPY • 1971 • Clement Dick • UKN, USA, FRN • DOIGTS CROISES, LES (FRN) ○ TO CATCH A SPY (USA) ○ KEEP YOUR FINGERS CROSSED
CATCH ME IF YOU CAN • 1989 • Sommers Stephen • USA
CATCH ME WHEN I FALL • 1970 • USA
CATCH MEOW • 1961 • Hanna William, Barbera Joseph • ANS • USA
CATCH MY SMOKE • 1922 • Beaudine William • USA
CATCH MY SOUL • 1974 • McGoohan Patrick • USA • SANTA FE SATAN
CATCH OF THE SEASON, THE • 1905 • *Cricks & Sharp* • UKN
CATCH OF THE SEASON, THE • 1906 • Collins Alf? • UKN
CATCH OF THE SEASON, THE • 1914 • *Lubin* • USA
CATCH OF THE SEASON, THE • 1914 • Reed Langford • UKN
CATCH THE HEAT • 1987 • Silberg Joel • USA • FEEL THE HEAT
CATCH THE KID • 1907 • Collins Alf • UKN
CATCH US IF YOU CAN • 1965 • Boorman John • UKN • HAVING A WILD WEEKEND (USA) ○ DAVE CLARK FIVE RUNS WILD, THE
CATCH YOUR OWN FISH • 1907 • Booth W. R. • UKN
CATCHER, THE • 1971 • Miner Allen H. • TVM • USA
CATCHING A BURGLAR • 1908 • Fitzhamon Lewin • UKN
CATCHING A COON • 1921 • Roach Hal • SHT • USA
CATCHING A SPEEDER • 1915 • *Punchinello* • USA
CATCHING A TARTAR • 1905 • Raymond Charles? • UKN
CATCHING A TARTAR • 1908 • Fitzhamon Lewin • UKN
CATCHING STORY, A • 1906 • Cooper Arthur • UKN
CATCHING THAT BURGLAR • 1916 • *Lynne Ethel* • USA
CATCHING THE MILK THIEF • 1899 • *Riley Brothers* • UKN
CATEGORIES DE DETENUS see **TYPES OF INMATES** • 1965
CATEMBE • 1965 • de Almeida Manuel Faria • PRT
CATENA, LA see **TENEBRE** • 1934
CATENA DELL'ODIO, LA • 1955 • Costa Piero • ITL
CATENE • 1950 • Matarazzo Raffaello • ITL
CATENE • 1974 • Amadio Silvio • ITL
CATENE see **TENEBRE** • 1934
CATENE INVISIBILI • 1942 • Mattoli Mario • ITL
CATERED AFFAIR, THE • 1956 • Brooks Richard • USA • WEDDING BREAKFAST (UKN)
CATERINA DA SIENA • 1948 • Palella Oreste • ITL
CATERINA DI RUSSIA • 1962 • Lenzi Umberto • ITL, FRN, FRG • CATHERINE DE RUSSIE (FRN) ○ CATHERINE OF RUSSIA (USA)
CATERINA SFORZA, LEONESSA DI ROMAGNA • 1959 • Chili Giorgio W. • ITL
CATERPILLAR AND THE WILD ANIMALS, THE • 1969 • Baldwin Gerard H. • ANS • USA
CATETO A BABOR • 1971 • Fernandez Ramon • SPN
CATFISH ROMANCE • 1932 • Foster John, Davis Mannie • ANS • USA
CATFOOD • 1968 • Wieland Joyce • SHT • CND
CATHARSIS see **SFIDA AL DIAVOLO** • 1965
CATHEDRAL BUILDER, THE see **STAVITEL CHRAMU** • 1919
CATHEDRAL CITY • 1949 • Chaffey Don • DOC • UKN
CATHEDRAL DE CHARTRES, LE see **CHARTRES** • 1923
CATHEDRAL OPERATION 1963 see **BAUHUTTE '63** • 1963
CATHERINE • 1964 • Loach Kenneth • MTV • UKN
CATHERINE see **VIE SANS JOIE, UNE** • 1924
CATHERINE see **CATHERINE, IL SUFFIT D'UN AMOUR** • 1968
CATHERINE see **CATHERINE CHERIE** • 1982
CATHERINE AND HER DAUGHTERS see **KATARINA A JEJI DETI** • 1970
CATHERINE CHERIE • 1982 • Frank Hubert • FRG, SPN • CATHERINE
CATHERINE & CO. see **CATHERINE ET CIE** • 1975
CATHERINE DE RUSSIE (FRN) see **CATERINA DI RUSSIA** • 1962
CATHERINE –EIN LEBEN FUR DIE LIEBE (FRG) see **CATHERINE, IL SUFFIT D'UN AMOUR** • 1968
CATHERINE ET CIE • 1975 • Boisrond Michel • FRN, ITL • CATHERINE & CO.
CATHERINE GRAFIN VON ARMAGNAC • 1922 • Vollmoller Karl • FRG
CATHERINE, IL SUFFIT D'UN AMOUR • 1968 • Borderie Bernard • FRN, ITL, FRG • CATHERINE, UN SOLO IMPOSSIBILE AMORE (ITL) ○ CATHERINE ○ CATHERINE –EIN LEBEN FUR DIE LIEBE (FRG)
CATHERINE OF RUSSIA (USA) see **CATERINA DI RUSSIA** • 1962
CATHERINE THE GREAT • 1934 • Czinner Paul • UKN • RISE OF CATHERINE THE GREAT, THE
CATHERINE THE LAST see **KATHARINA DIE LETZTE** • 1935
CATHERINE, UN SOLO IMPOSSIBILE AMORE (ITL) see **CATHERINE, IL SUFFIT D'UN AMOUR** • 1968
CATHERINE'S MARRIAGE see **KIS KATALIN HAZASSAGA** • 1949
CATHIE'S CHILD see **CATHY'S CHILD** • 1979
CATHODE RAY OSCILLOGRAPH, THE • 1934 • Holmes J. B. • DOC • UKN
CATHOLIC BOYS (UKN) see **HEAVEN HELP US** • 1985
CATHOLIC CENTENNIAL CELEBRATION, THE • 1908 • Melies Gaston • USA
CATHOLICS • 1973 • Gold Jack • TVM • USA • CONFLICT, THE
CATHOLICS IN BRITAIN • 1944 • Cass Henry • DCS • UKN
CATHY • 1984 • Rautenbach Jans • SAF
CATHY see **KATKA** • 1949
CATHY COMES HOME • 1966 • Loach Kenneth • MTV • UKN
CATHY FILLE SOUMISE • Sanders Bob W. • FRN
CATHY TIPPEL see **KEETJE TIPPEL** • 1975
CATHY'S CHILD • 1979 • Crombie Donald • ASL • CATHIE'S CHILD
CATHY'S CURSE • 1976 • Matalon Eddy, Boisvert Nicole Mathieu • CND, FRN • CAUCHEMARS
CATI –THE GIRL see **ELTAVOZOTT NAP** • 1968
CATILINA • 1910 • Caserini Mario • ITL
CATLOW • 1971 • Wanamaker Sam • USA, UKN
CATMAN OF PARIS, THE • 1946 • Selander Lesley • USA
CATNIP CAPERS • 1940 • Davis Mannie • ANS • USA
CATNIP GANG, THE • 1949 • Donnelly Eddie • ANS • USA
CATNIPPED • 1946 • Wickersham Bob • ANS • USA
CATS • 1915 • MacGregor Norval • USA
CATS • 1925 • Hiscott Leslie • UKN
CATS • 1956 • Breer Robert • SHT • USA
CATS, THE see **KATTORNA** • 1965
CATS, THE see **BASTARDI, I** • 1968
CATS, THE (UKN) see **FELINES, LES** • 1973
CATS A-WEIGH • 1953 • McKimson Robert • ANS • USA
CATS AND BRUISES • 1965 • Freleng Friz • ANS • USA
CATS AND DOGS • 1932 • Lantz Walter, Nolan William • ANS • USA
CATS AND KITTENS • 1965 • Wilkosz Tadeusz • ANM • PLN
CAT'S BAH, THE • 1954 • Jones Charles M. • ANS • USA
CAT'S CANARY, THE • 1932 • Foster John, Davis Mannie • ANS • USA
CATS, CASH AND A COOK BOOK • 1915 • Dillon John Francis • USA
CAT'S CRADLE • 1959 • Brakhage Stan • SHT • USA
CAT'S CRADLE see **AU BOUT DU FIL** • 1974
CATS' CUP FINAL, THE • 1912 • Cooper Arthur • UKN
CAT'S EYE • 1985 • Teague Lewis • USA • STEPHEN KING'S CAT'S EYE
CAT'S GAME see **MACSKAJATEK** • 1974
CATS IN THE BAG • 1936 • Davis Mannie, Gordon George • ANS • USA
CAT'S ME-OUCH, THE • 1965 • Jones Charles M. • ANS • USA
CAT'S MEOW • 1957 • Avery Tex • ANS • USA
CAT'S MEOW, THE • 1924 • Del Ruth Roy • SHT • USA
CAT'S MEOW, THE • 1930 • *Mintz Charles (P)* • ANS • USA
CAT'S NIGHTMARE, THE see **CAT'S OUT, THE** • 1931
CAT'S NINE LIVES • 1927 • Lantz Walter • ANS • USA
CAT'S NINE LIVES, THE • 1910 • *Empire Films* • UKN
CATS OF HAMRA, THE • Ghoseini Samir • LBN
CAT'S OUT, THE • 1931 • Jackson Wilfred • ANS • USA • CAT'S NIGHTMARE, THE
CAT'S PATH, THE see **KATZENSTEG, DER** • 1937
CAT'S PAW • 1959 • McKimson Robert • ANS • USA
CAT'S PAW, THE • 1912 • *Essanay* • USA
CAT'S PAW, THE • 1914 • *Cruze James* • USA
CAT'S PAW, THE • 1931 • Edwards Harry J. • SHT • USA
CAT'S PAW, THE • 1934 • Taylor Sam • USA
CAT'S PYJAMAS, THE • 1926 • Wellman William A. • USA
CAT'S REVENGE • 1954 • Davis Mannie • ANS • USA
CAT'S REVENGE, THE • 1908 • *Lux* • FRN
CAT'S SEVEN LIVES, THE see **SIETE VIDAS DEL GATO, LAS** • 1970
CAT'S SOUP • 1974 • Jordan Richard • FRN
CAT'S TAIL, THE • 1941 • Freleng Friz • ANS • USA
CAT'S TALE, A • 1951 • Davis Mannie • ANS • USA
CAT'S WHISKERS • 1923 • *Terry Paul* • ANS • USA
CAT'S WHISKERS • 1926 • Lantz Walter • ANS • USA
CAT'S WORD OF HONOR, A see **KOCICI SLOVO** • 1960
CATSKINNER COUNTRY • 1974 • Brittain Don • DOC • CND
CATSPAW, THE • 1916 • Wright George A. • USA
CATSPAW, THE • 1918 • Ritchey Will M. • SHT • USA
CATSPLAY (USA) see **MACSKAJATEK** • 1974
CATTIVA EVASIONE see **ELOPEMENT** • 1923
CATTIVI PENSIERI • 1976 • Tognazzi Ugo • ITL • WHO MISLAID MY WIFE? ○ EVIL THOUGHTS
CATTIVI VANNO IN PARADISO, I • 1958 • Horne Dionisio, Mazzetti Lorenza • ITL • BAD GO TO HEAVEN, THE
CATTIVO SOGGETTO, UN • 1933 • Bragaglia Carlo Ludovico • ITL • TRAGEDIA DELLA CERNIERA, LA ○ VENERE BRUNA ○ PAPA PAGA
CATTLE • 1914 • *Frontier* • USA
CATTLE ANNIE AND LITTLE BRITCHES • 1979 • Johnson Lamont • USA
CATTLE BARON'S DAUGHTER, THE • 1910 • *Bison* • USA
CATTLE CALL • 1944 • Abrahams Derwin • USA
CATTLE CARTERS, THE • 1962 • Williams Derek • UKN
CATTLE DRIVE • 1951 • Neumann Kurt • USA
CATTLE EMPIRE • 1958 • Warren Charles Marquis • USA
CATTLE, GOLD AND OIL • 1911 • Dwan Allan • USA
CATTLE HERDER'S ROMANCE, A • 1911 • *Kalem* • USA
CATTLE KATE see **REDHEAD FROM WYOMING, THE** • 1952
CATTLE KING • 1963 • Garnett Tay • USA • GUNS OF WYOMING
CATTLE KING OF ARIZONA, THE • 1911 • *Powers* • USA
CATTLE KING'S DAUGHTER, THE • 1912 • *Essanay* • USA
CATTLE QUEEN • 1950 • *El* • USA • QUEEN OF THE WEST
CATTLE QUEEN OF MONTANA • 1954 • Dwan Allan • USA
CATTLE QUEEN RANCHER • 1915 • *Kriterion* • USA
CATTLE QUEEN'S ROMANCE, A • 1915 • *Acord Art* • USA
CATTLE RAIDERS • 1938 • Nelson Sam • USA
CATTLE RANCH • 1961 • Cote Guy-L. • DCS • CND • TETES BLANCHES
CATTLE RUSTLERS, THE • 1908 • *Selig* • USA
CATTLE RUSTLERS, THE • 1912 • *Duncan William* • USA
CATTLE RUSTLER'S DAUGHTER, A • 1910 • *Bison* • USA
CATTLE RUSTLER'S END, THE • 1911 • Dwan Allan • USA
CATTLE RUSTLER'S FATHER, THE • 1911 • *Essanay* • USA
CATTLE STAMPEDE • 1943 • Newfield Sam • USA
CATTLE STATION see **PHANTOM STOCKMAN** • 1953
CATTLE THIEF, THE • 1936 • Bennet Spencer Gordon • USA
CATTLE THIEF'S BRAND, THE • 1911 • Dwan Allan • USA
CATTLE THIEF'S ESCAPE, THE • 1913 • Duncan William • USA
CATTLE THIEF'S REVENGE, THE • 1910 • *Defender* • USA
CATTLE THIEVES, THE • 1909 • Olcott Sidney • USA
CATTLE TOWN • 1952 • Smith Noel • USA
CATTLE WAR, THE • 1917 • Ford John • USA
CATTLEMAN'S DAUGHTER, THE • 1911 • *Essanay* • USA
CATTLEMEN'S FEUD, THE • 1910 • *Columbia* • USA
CATTLEMEN'S WAR, THE • 1911 • *Bison* • USA
CATTURA, LA • 1969 • Cavara Paolo • ITL, YGS, USA • RAVINE, THE (USA)
CATTY CORNERED • 1953 • Freleng Friz • ANS • USA
CATTY CORNERED • 1966 • Levitow Abe • ANS • USA
CATUOR • 1970 • Klein Judith • SHT • CND
CAUCASIAN CAPTIVE see **KAKAZSKAYA PLENNITZA** • 1967
CAUCASIAN GHOST see **KAIDAN IJIN YUREI** • 1963
CAUCASIAN LOVE see **ELISO** • 1928
CAUCASIAN PRISONER • 1930 • Ivanovsky Alexander • USS
CAUCASIAN PRISONER, THE see **KAKAZSKAYA PLENNITZA** • 1967
CAUCHEMAR • 1980 • Simsolo Noel • FRN
CAUCHEMAR, LE • 1897 • Melies Georges • FRN • NIGHTMARE, A (USA)
CAUCHEMAR DU FANTOCHE, LE • 1908 • Cohl Emile • ANS • FRN • FANTOCHE'S NIGHTMARE ○ PUPPET'S NIGHTMARE, THE ○ LIVING BLACKBOARD
CAUCHEMAR DU PECHEUR, LE • 1905 • Melies Georges • FRN • ANGLER'S NIGHTMARE, THE (USA) ○ POLICEMAN'S TROUBLES, A ○ ESCARPOLETTE FANTASTIQUE, L'
CAUCHEMAR ET DOUX REVE • 1908 • de Chomon Segundo • FRN • NIGHTMARE AND SWEET DREAM
CAUCHEMARS see **CATHY'S CURSE** • 1976
CAUCHEMARS VIENNENT LA NUIT • 1970 • Franco Jesus
CAUDILLO • 1976 • Patino Basilio Martin • SPN • LEADER
CAUDILLO, EL • 1957 • Aguilar Rolando • MXC
CAUDILLO, EL • 1968 • Mariscal Alberto • MXC • LEADER, THE
CAUGHT • 1912 • Aylott Dave? • UKN
CAUGHT • 1915 • *Washburn Bryant* • USA
CAUGHT • 1931 • Sloman Edward • USA • ROPED IN
CAUGHT • 1949 • Ophuls Max • USA
CAUGHT • 1987 • Collier James F. • USA
CAUGHT AT HIS OWN GAME • 1913 • *Frontier* • USA
CAUGHT AT LAST • 1909 • Brooke Van Dyke • USA
CAUGHT BENDING • 1914 • *Hepworth* • UKN
CAUGHT BETWEEN, THE ENGLISH IN QUEBEC • 1978 • Bittman Roman • DOC • CND
CAUGHT BLUFFING • 1912 • *Mortimer Dorothy* • USA
CAUGHT BLUFFING • 1922 • Hillyer Lambert • USA
CAUGHT BY A CHILD • 1910 • *Walturdaw* • UKN
CAUGHT BY A THREAD • 1915 • Christie Al • USA
CAUGHT BY COWBOYS • 1910 • *Champion* • USA
CAUGHT BY TELEVISION (UKN) see **TRAPPED BY TELEVISION** • 1936
CAUGHT BY THE CAMERA • 1910 • *Lubin* • USA
CAUGHT BY THE COUPON CRAZE • 1909 • *Edison* • USA
CAUGHT BY THE HANDLE • 1915 • Dillon Eddie • USA

CAUGHT BY THE LEG • 1915 • *Horseshoe* • UKN
CAUGHT BY THE NIGHT see **ZASIHLA ME NOC** • 1985
CAUGHT BY THE TIDE • 1906 • Stow Percy • UKN
CAUGHT BY WIRELESS • 1908 • *Bitzer Billy (Ph)* • USA
CAUGHT CHEATING • 1931 • Strayer Frank • USA
CAUGHT COURTING • 1913 • Costello Maurice, North Wilfred • USA
CAUGHT FLIRTING • 1899 • *Paul R. W.* • UKN
CAUGHT IN A CABARET • 1914 • Chaplin Charles, Normand Mabel • USA • JAZZING WITH SOCIETY ○ JAZZ WAITER ○ WAITER, THE ○ FAKING WITH SOCIETY
CAUGHT IN A FLASH • 1912 • *Baggot King* • USA
CAUGHT IN A FLUE • 1914 • Wright Walter • USA
CAUGHT IN A JAM • 1916 • Roach Hal • SHT • USA
CAUGHT IN A KILT • 1915 • Kellino W. P. • UKN
CAUGHT IN A PARK • 1915 • Griffin Frank C. • USA
CAUGHT IN A TAXI • 1929 • *Sennett Mack (P)* • SHT • USA
CAUGHT IN A TIGHT PINCH • 1914 • *Fischer Marguerite* • USA
CAUGHT IN HER OWN PLOT see **KIMI GA SEISHUN NO TOKI** • 1967
CAUGHT IN HER OWN TRAP • 1911 • Kinder Stuart? • UKN
CAUGHT IN HIS OWN NET • 1912 • Collins Edwin J.? • UKN
CAUGHT IN HIS OWN NET • 1913 • *Komic* • USA
CAUGHT IN HIS OWN TRAP • 1910 • *Vitagraph* • USA
CAUGHT IN HIS OWN TRAP see **MEDBEJLERENS HAEVN** • 1910
CAUGHT IN HIS OWN TRAP see **DIREKTORENS DATTER** • 1912
CAUGHT IN THE ACT • 1904 • *Cricks & Sharp* • UKN
CAUGHT IN THE ACT • 1911 • *Selig* • USA
CAUGHT IN THE ACT • 1913 • Smalley Phillips • USA
CAUGHT IN THE ACT • 1915 • Griffin Frank C. • USA
CAUGHT IN THE ACT • 1917 • Heffron Thomas N. • SHT • USA
CAUGHT IN THE ACT • 1918 • Millarde Harry • USA
CAUGHT IN THE ACT • 1936 • Lord Del • SHT • USA
CAUGHT IN THE ACT • 1941 • Yarbrough Jean • USA
CAUGHT IN THE ACT! • 1966 • Nehemiah J. • USA • CAUGHT IN THE ACT –NAKED
CAUGHT IN THE ACT • 1981 • Brocka Lino • PHL
CAUGHT IN THE ACT –NAKED see **CAUGHT IN THE ACT!** • 1966
CAUGHT IN THE CAN • 1970 • *Stacey Dist.* • USA
CAUGHT IN THE DRAFT • 1917 • Hutchison Charles • SHT • USA
CAUGHT IN THE DRAFT • 1941 • Butler David • USA
CAUGHT IN THE END • 1917 • *Triangle* • USA
CAUGHT IN THE END • 1917 • Williamson Robin E. • *Vogue* • SHT • USA
CAUGHT IN THE END • 1920 • Lyons Eddie, Moran Lee • USA • CREEPING FLAMES
CAUGHT IN THE FOG • 1928 • Bretherton Howard • USA
CAUGHT IN THE KITCHEN • 1928 • *Sennett Mack (P)* • SHT • USA
CAUGHT IN THE MESH see **FLAMES OF PASSION** • 1922
CAUGHT IN THE MOVIES • 1916 • *Judy* • SHT • USA
CAUGHT IN THE NET • 1928 • *Marshall Vaughn C. (P)* • ASL
CAUGHT IN THE NET • 1960 • Haggarty John • UKN
CAUGHT IN THE RAIN • 1910 • *Selig* • USA
CAUGHT IN THE RAIN • 1912 • *Costello Maurice* • USA
CAUGHT IN THE RAIN • 1914 • Chaplin Charles • USA • AT IT AGAIN ○ WHO GOT STUNG?
CAUGHT IN THE TOILS • 1912 • *Kalem* • USA
CAUGHT IN THE TOILS see **HVIDE DJOEVEL, DEN** • 1916
CAUGHT IN THE WEB • 1908 • *Kalem* • USA
CAUGHT IN THE WEB • 1914 • *Reliance* • USA
CAUGHT IN THE WEB see **LADY IN LACE, THE** • 1925
CAUGHT IN TIGHTS • 1914 • Henderson Dell • USA
CAUGHT NAPPING • 1910 • Rains Fred • UKN
CAUGHT NAPPING • 1913 • Calvert Charles? • UKN
CAUGHT ON A SKYSCRAPER • 1916 • *Gribbon Harry* • SHT • USA
CAUGHT ON THE CLIFFS • 1909 • *Urban-Eclipse* • USA
CAUGHT ON THE HOP • 1904 • *Cricks & Sharp* • UKN
CAUGHT PLASTERED • 1931 • Seiter William A. • USA
CAUGHT SHORT • 1930 • Reisner Charles F. • USA
CAUGHT WITH THE GOODS • 1911 • *Essanay* • USA
CAUGHT WITH THE GOODS • 1911 • Sennett Mack • *Ab* • USA
CAUGHT WITH THE GOODS • 1914 • Finley Ned • USA
CAUGHT WITH THE GOODS • 1915 • *Lubin* • USA
CAUGHT WITH THE GOODS • 1915 • *L-Ko* • USA
CAUGHT WITH THE GOODS • 1916 • *Mina* • USA
CAUGHT WITH THE GOODS • 1916 • Lyons Eddie, Moran Lee • *Nestor* • USA
CAUGHT WITH THE GOODS • 1917 • *Triangle* • USA
CAULDRON OF BLOOD (UKN) see **COLECCIONISTA DE CADAVERES, EL** • 1967
CAULDRON OF DEATH, THE • 1979 • Demicheli Tulio • ITL
CAUSA DI DIVORZIO • 1972 • Fondato Marcello • ITL
CAUSA KAISER • 1932 • Wenzler Franz • FRG • KAISER CASE, THE (USA)
CAUSA KRALIK • 1979 • Jires Jaromil • CZC • RABBIT CASE, THE
CAUSA PERDUTA • 1977 • Donev Donyo • ANS • BUL
CAUSE, THE • 1913 • *Nestor* • USA
CAUSE CIVIL, UN see **CAUSE EN CIVIL, UN** • 1973
CAUSE COMMUNE, LA • 1940 • Cavalcanti Alberto • DOC • UKN • FACTORY FRONT
CAUSE EN CIVIL, UN • 1973 • Mankiewicz Francis • SHT • CND • CAUSE CIVIL, UN
CAUSE FOR ALARM • 1950 • Garnett Tay • USA
CAUSE FOR ALARM see **FIRECHASERS, THE** • 1970
CAUSE FOR DIVORCE • 1923 • Dierker Hugh • USA
CAUSE FOR THANKFULNESS, A • 1913 • *Conway Lizzie* • USA
CAUSE FOR THANKSGIVING • 1914 • Johnson Tefft • USA
CAUSE OF ALL THE TROUBLE, THE • 1923 • Roberts Edward D. • UKN
CAUSE OF IT ALL, THE • 1915 • *Kalem* • USA
CAUSE OF THE GREAT EUROPEAN WAR, THE • 1914 • Pearson George • UKN
CAUSE TOUJOURS, MON LAPIN! • 1961 • Lefranc Guy • FRN
CAUSE TOUJOURS, TU M'INTERESSES • 1978 • Molinaro Edouard • FRN
CAUSED BY A CLOCK • 1913 • *Komic* • USA
CAUTION DANGER see **PROSOCHI KINDINOS** • 1983
CAUTIVA DE LA SELVA, LA • 1968 • Fleider Leo • ARG • SENSUAL JUNGLE (UKN) ○ CAPTIVE OF THE JUNGLE
CAUTIVAS, LAS • 1971 • *Cima* • MXC
CAVALCA E UCCIDI • 1963 • Borau Jose Luis • ITL, SPN, FRN • RIDE AND KILL (UKN)
CAVALCADE • 1933 • Lloyd Frank • USA
CAVALCADE • 1955 • Allen Lewis • MTV • USA
CAVALCADE D'AMOUR • 1939 • Bernard Raymond • FRN
CAVALCADE DES HEURES, LA • 1943 • Noe Yvan • FRN
CAVALCADE OF AVIATION • 1942 • *O'Brien Joseph/ Mead Thomas (P)* • SHT • USA
CAVALCADE OF LAUGHS, THE • 1963 • USA
CAVALCADE OF RUSSIAN BALLET AND DANCE • 1965 • CMP • USS
CAVALCADE OF SONG (USA) see **CANZONI, CANZONI, CANZONI** • 1953
CAVALCADE OF THE DANCE • 1943 • Negulesco Jean • SHT • USA
CAVALCADE OF THE MOVIES see **FILM PARADE, THE** • 1933
CAVALCADE OF THE STARS • 1938 • Benstead Geoffrey • UKN
CAVALCADE OF THE WEST • 1935 • Fraser Harry L. • USA
CAVALCADE OF VARIETY • 1940 • Bentley Thomas • UKN
CAVALCATA ARDENTE • 1915 • Gallone Carmine • ITL
CAVALCATA ARDENTE • 1929 • Gallone Carmine • ITL
CAVALCATA ARDENTE, LA • 1923 • Gallone Carmine • ITL
CAVALCATA D'EROI • 1951 • Costa Mario • ITL
CAVALCATA DI MEZZO SECOLO • 1951 • Emmer Luciano • ITL
CAVALCATA SELVAGGIA • 1960 • Pierotti Piero • ITL
CAVALE, LA • 1971 • Mitrani Michel • FRN
CAVALERIE LEGERE • 1935 • Vitrac Roger, Hochbaum Werner • FRN
CAVALEUR, LE • 1979 • de Broca Philippe • FRN • PRACTICE MAKES PERFECT (USA)
CAVALIER, THE • 1928 • Willat Irvin V. • USA
CAVALIER COSTANTE NICOSIA DEMONIACO OVVERO DRACULA IN BRIANZA, IL • 1975 • Fulci Lucio • ITL
CAVALIER DE CROIX-MORT, LE • 1947 • Gasnier-Raymond Lucien • FRN • AVENTURE DE VIDOCQ, UN
CAVALIER DE RIOUCLARE, LE see **SORTILEGES** • 1944
CAVALIER IN DEVIL'S CASTLE (USA) see **CAVALIERE DEL CASTELLO MALEDETTO, IL** • 1959
CAVALIER LAFLEUR, LE • 1934 • Ducis Pierre-Jean • FRN
CAVALIER NOIR, LE • 1944 • Grangier Gilles • FRN
CAVALIER OF THE GOLD STAR see **KAVALER ZOLOTOI ZVEZDY** • 1950
CAVALIER OF THE STREETS, THE • 1937 • French Harold • UKN
CAVALIER OF THE WEST • 1931 • McCarthy John P. • USA
CAVALIERE DAI CENTO VOLTI, IL • 1960 • Mercanti Pino • ITL
CAVALIERE DALLA SPADA NERA, IL • 1958 • Kish Ladislao • ITL
CAVALIERE DEL CASTELLO MALEDETTO, IL • 1959 • Costa Mario • ITL • CAVALIER IN DEVIL'S CASTLE (USA) ○ KNIGHT OF THE CURSED CASTLE
CAVALIERE DEL SOGNO, IL • 1946 • Mastrocinque Camillo • ITL • LIFE OF DONIZETTI, THE (USA) ○ VITA DI DONIZETTI, LA ○ DONIZETTI
CAVALIERE DI FERRO, IL see **CONTE UGOLINO, IL** • 1950
CAVALIERE DI KRUJA, IL • 1940 • Campogalliani Carlo • ITL • ALBANIA
CAVALIERE DI MAISON ROUGE, IL • 1953 • Cottafavi Vittorio • ITL
CAVALIERE DI SAN MARCO, IL • 1939 • Righelli Gennaro • ITL
CAVALIERE E LA CZARINA, IL see **SECRET DU CHEVALIER D'EON, LE** • 1960
CAVALIERE INESISTENTE, IL • 1970 • Zac Pino • ITL • NON-EXISTENT KNIGHT, THE ○ IMAGINARY KNIGHT, THE
CAVALIERE MISTERIOSO, IL • 1948 • Freda Riccardo • ITL • CENTO DONNE DI CASANOVA, LE ○ MYSTERIOUS RIDER, THE (USA)
CAVALIERE SENZA NOME, IL • 1941 • Cerio Ferruccio • ITL
CAVALIERE SENZA TERRA, IL • 1958 • Gentilomo Giacomo • ITL
CAVALIERI DALLA MASCHERA NERA, I • 1948 • Mercanti Pino • ITL • BEATI PAOLI, I
CAVALIERI DEL DESERTO, I • 1942 • Talamo Gino, Valenti Osvaldo • ITL • PREDONI DEL DESERTO, I ○ ULTIMI TAUREG, GLI ○ PREDONI DEL SAHARA, I
CAVALIERI DEL DIAVOLO, I • 1959 • Marcellini Siro • ITL • DEVIL'S CAVALIERS, THE (USA)
CAVALIERI DELLA MONTAGNA • 1951 • Casara Severino • ITL
CAVALIERI DELLA REGINA, I • 1955 • Bolognini Mauro • ITL
CAVALIERI DELL'ILLUSIONE, I • 1956 • Allegret Marc • ITL, FRN
CAVALIERI DI MALTA, I • 1971 • De Sica Vittorio • ITL
CAVALIERI DI RODI, I • 1912 • Caserini Mario • ITL
CAVALIERI, I • 1912 • Oxilia Nino • ITL
CAVALIERS DE LA TERREUR, LES (FRN) see **TERRORE DEI MANTELLI ROSSI, IL** • 1963
CAVALIERS DE L'ORAGE, LES • 1983 • Vergez Gerard • FRN, YGS
CAVALIER'S DREAM, THE • 1898 • Porter Edwin S. • USA
CAVALIERS ROUGES, LES (FRN) see **OLD SHATTERHAND** • 1964
CAVALIER'S WIFE, THE • 1908 • Stow Percy • UKN
CAVALLA TUTTA NUDA, UNA • 1972 • Rossetti Franco • ITL
CAVALLERIA • 1936 • Alessandrini Goffredo • ITL
CAVALLERIA COMMANDOS see **CAVALRY COMMAND** • 1963
CAVALLERIA RUSTICANA • 1917 • Falena Ugo • ITL
CAVALLERIA RUSTICANA • 1939 • Palermi Amleto • ITL
CAVALLERIA RUSTICANA • 1953 • *Rhodes Marion*
CAVALLERIA RUSTICANA • 1953 • Gallone Carmine • ITL • FATAL DESIRE
CAVALLERIA RUSTICANA • 1968 • Falck Ake • SWT, AUS, FRG
CAVALLI SI NASCE • 1988 • Staino Sergio • ITL • HORSES ARE BORN SUCH
CAVALLINA BRETTONE, LA • 1908 • Lolli Alberto Carlo • ITL
CAVALLINA STORNA, LA • 1956 • Morelli Giulio • ITL
CAVALO DE OXUMAIRE, O • 1961 • Guerra Ruy • BRZ • HORSE OF OXUMAIRE, THE
CAVALRY • 1936 • Bradbury Robert North • USA
CAVALRY CHARGE see **LAST OUTPOST, THE** • 1951
CAVALRY COMMAND • 1963 • Romero Eddie • USA, PHL • CAVALLERIA COMMANDOS ○ BATTLE OF SAN PASQUALE, THE
CAVALRY SCHOOL AT SAUMUR, THE • 1897 • DOC • FRN
CAVALRY SCOUT • 1951 • Selander Lesley • USA
CAVANAUGH OF THE FOREST RANGERS • 1918 • Wolbert William • USA
CAVAR UN FOSO • 1966 • Torre-Nilsson Leopoldo • ARG • TO DIG A PIT
CAVE, THE see **CAVE OF OUTLAWS** • 1951
CAVE, UN • 1971 • Grangier Gilles • FRN
CAVE AND BASIN • 1985 • Battle Murray • SHT • CND
CAVE DWELLERS • 1913 • *Bison* • USA • CAVE DWELLER'S ROMANCE, THE
CAVE DWELLERS, THE • 1914 • Johnson Tefft • USA
CAVE DWELLERS, THE see **ONE MILLION B.C.** • 1940
CAVE DWELLER'S ROMANCE, THE see **CAVE DWELLERS** • 1913
CAVE GIRL • 1985 • Oliver David • USA • CAVEGIRL
CAVE GIRL, THE • 1921 • Franz Joseph J. • USA
CAVE-INI • 1983 • Fenady George • TVM • USA
CAVE-IN, THE (UKN) see **DRAEGERMAN COURAGE** • 1937
CAVE MAN see **ONE MILLION B.C.** • 1940
CAVE MAN, THE • 1912 • *Johnson Tefft* • USA
CAVE MAN, THE • 1915 • Marston Theodore • USA
CAVE MAN, THE • 1934 • *Iwerks Ub (P)* • ANS • USA
CAVE MAN STUFF • 1918 • Curtis Allen • SHT • USA
CAVE MAN WOOING, A • 1912 • *Baggot King* • USA
CAVE MAN'S WAR, THE • 1913 • *Kalem* • USA
CAVE OF ALI BABA, THE see **CUEVA DE ALI BABA, LA** • 1954
CAVE OF DEATH, THE • 1914 • *Darkfeather Mona* • USA
CAVE OF DESIRE, THE see **LO-SHAN FENG** • 1988
CAVE OF DIAMONDS see **SFIDA VIENE DA BANGKOK, LA** • 1965
CAVE OF OUTLAWS • 1951 • Castle William • USA • CAVE, THE
CAVE OF THE BLUE DRAGON see **SEIRYU NA DOKUTSU**
CAVE OF THE DEMONS, THE (USA) see **CAVERNE MAUDITE, LA** • 1898
CAVE OF THE LIVING DEAD (UKN) see **FLUCH DER GRUNEN AUGEN, DER** • 1964
CAVE OF THE SHARKS see **FOSSA MALEDETTA, LA** • 1978
CAVE ON THUNDER CLOUD, THE • 1915 • *D'Arcy Camille* • USA
CAVE SE REBIFFE, LE • 1961 • Grangier Gilles • FRN, ITL • COUNTERFEITERS OF PARIS, THE (USA) ○ RE DEI FALSARI, IL (ITL) ○ COUNTERFEITERS, THE (UKN) ○ MONEY, MONEY, MONEY
CAVEGIRL see **CAVE GIRL** • 1985
CAVELL CASE, THE see **WOMAN THE GERMANS SHOT** • 1918
CAVEMAN • 1980 • Gottlieb Carl • USA
CAVEMAN, THE • 1926 • Milestone Lewis • USA
CAVEMAN, THE see **HIS PREHISTORIC PAST** • 1914
CAVEMAN INKI • 1950 • Jones Charles M. • ANS • USA
CAVEMAN'S BLUFF • 1917 • Drew Sidney • SHT • USA
CAVENDISH COUNTRY • 1974 • Brittain Don • DOC • CND
CAVERN, THE (USA) see **SETTE CONTRO LA MORTE** • 1965
CAVERN DEEP • Dalgleish Ian
CAVERN SPIDER, THE • 1924 • Bentley Thomas • UKN
CAVERNE MAUDITE, LA • 1898 • Melies Georges • FRN • CAVE OF THE DEMONS, THE (USA)
CAVERNS OF VICE see **NACHTLOKAL ZUM SILBERMOND, DAS** • 1959
CAVES AND COQUETTES • 1919 • Pratt Gilbert • SHT • USA
CAVES, CAVERNS AND A PARK see **CUEVAS, CAVERNAS Y UN PARQUE** • 1988
CAVES DU MAJESTIC, LES • 1944 • Pottier Richard • FRN
CAVES OF EROLA, THE • 1913 • Phalke Dada • SHT • IND
CAVES OF LA JOLLA • 1911 • Dwan Allan • DOC • USA
CAVES OF PERIGORD, THE • 1939 • Lucas Caroline Byng • UKN
CAVES OF STEEL • 1967 • Taylor Eric?, Sasdy Peter? • UKN
CAVIAR • 1930 • *Terry Paul/ Moser Frank (P)* • ANS • USA
CAVIAR-MAUSCHEN, DAS • 1922 • *Lloyd Kinofilm* • FRG
CAVIAR ROUGE, LE • 1985 • Hossein Robert • FRN, SWT
CAVO OLIO FLUDIO 220,000 VOLT • 1959 • Olmi Ermanno (Spv) • DOC • ITL
CAXAMBU • 1967 • *Larsen Keith*
CAYO DE LA GLORIA EL DIABLO • 1971 • Estrada Jose • MXC
CAZA, LA • 1965 • Saura Carlos • SPN • HUNT, THE ○ CHASE, THE
CAZA DEL ORO, LA • 1973 • Bosch Juan • SPN
CAZADOR DE LA MUERTE, EL • 1982 • Sbardellati Jim • ARG • DEATHSTALKER (USA) ○ DEATH STALKER
CAZADORA INCONSCIENTE, LA see **HOMENAJE A TARZAN** • 1970
CAZADORES DE ASESINOS see **DUELO DE VALIENTES** • 1962
CAZADORES DE CABEZAS • 1960 • Curiel Federico • MXC • HEAD HUNTERS
CAZADORES, LOS (SPN) see **OPEN SEASON** • 1974
CAZAR UN GATO NEGRO • 1977 • Romero-Marchent Rafael • SPN
CE BON LA FONTAINE • 1914 • Ravel Gaston • FRN
CE BON MONSIEUR NICOT • 1976 • Danblon Paul, Deconinck Jean-Marie • BLG
CE CHER VICTOR • 1975 • Davis Robin • FRN
CE COCHON DE MORIN • 1924 • Tourjansky Victor • FRN
CE COCHON DE MORIN • 1932 • Lacombe Georges • FRN
CE COCHON DE MORIN see **TERREUR DE DAMES, LA** • 1956
CE COQUIN D'ANATOLE • 1951 • Couzinet Emile • FRN
CE CORPS TANT DESIRE • 1958 • Saslavsky Luis • FRN • WAY OF THE WICKED
CE DIVANE • 1968 • Moghadam Jalal • IRN • THREE STUPID MEN
CE DONT ON NE PARLE PAS • 1924 • Puchalski Eduard • PLN
CE GAMIN, LA • 1975 • Victor Renaud • FRN
CE JOLI MONDE • 1957 • Carlo-Rim • FRN

CE MONDE BANAL • 1960 • Wagner • SHT • FRN
CE N'EST PAS MOI • 1941 • de Baroncelli Jacques • FRN
CE PAUVRE CHERI • 1924 • Kemm Jean • FRN
C'E PRIMA LA SIGNORA see **CAMPO DE' FIORI** • 1943
CE QUE FEMME VEUT see **BOITE AUX REVES, LA** • 1943
CE QUE JE VOIS DANS MON TELESCOPE • 1902 • Zecca Ferdinand • FRN • THAT WHICH I SEE IN MY TELESCOPE
CE QUE LES FLOTS RACONTENT • 1916 • Gance Abel • FRN
CE QUE L'ON VOIT DE SON SIXIEME • 1901 • Zecca Ferdinand • FRN
CE QUE SAVAIT MORGAN • 1974 • Beraud Luc • FRN
CE QUE TU VERRAS ICI TU NE LE VERRAS PAS AILLEURS • 1978 • Lesaunier Daniel • MTV • CND
CE QUI RESTE DE CE QU'ON NOUS A DONNE • 1984 • Colmant Jean-Louis • BLG
CE REPONDEUR NE PREND PAS DE MESSAGES • 1979 • Cavalier Alain • FRN
CE SACRE AMEDEE • 1955 • Felix Louis • FRN • BON VOYAGE
CE SACRE GRAND-PERE • 1968 • Poitrenaud Jacques • FRN • MARRIAGE CAME TUMBLING DOWN, THE (USA)
C'E SARTANA.. VENDI LA PISTOLA E COMPRATI LA BARA • 1970 • Carnimeo Giuliano • ITL
C'E SEMPRE UN MA! • 1943 • Zampa Luigi • ITL • FELICITA IN PERICOLO
CE SIECLE A CINQUANTE ANS • 1949 • Tual Denise R., Tual Roland • FRN • DAYS OF OUR YEARS (USA) ○ CENTURY IS FIFTY, THE
CE SOIR-LA GILLES VIGNEAULT • 1967 • Lamothe Arthur • DOC • CND
CE SOIR.. LE CIRQUE • 1951 • Gerard • SHT • FRN
CE SOIR LES JUPONS VOLENT • 1956 • Kirsanoff Dimitri • FRN
CE SOIR ON JOUE MACBETH see **RIDEAU ROUGE, LE** • 1952
CE SOIR OU JAMAIS • 1960 • Deville Michel • FRN • TONIGHT OR NEVER
C'E UN FANTASMA NEL CASTELLO • 1942 • Simonelli Giorgio C. • ITL
C'E UN SENTIERO NEL CIELO • 1957 • Girolami Marino • ITL
C'E UNA SPIA NEL MIO LETTO • 1976 • Petrini Luigi • ITL
CE VIEUX PAYS OU RIMBAUD EST MORT see **VIEUX PAYS OU RIMBAUD EST MORT, LE** • 1977
CEASE FIRE • 1953 • Crump Owen • USA
CEASE FIRE • 1985 • Nutter David • USA • IN COUNTRY
CEASE FIRING (USA) see **CESSEZ LE FEU** • 1934
CEBO PARA UNA ADOLESCENTE • 1973 • Lara Polop Francisco • SPN
CECELIA, LA • 1975 • Comolli Jean-Louis • FRN, ITL
CECH PANEN KUTNOHORSKYCH • 1938 • Vavra Otakar • CZC • GUILD OF THE MAIDENS OF KUTNA HORA ○ GUILD OF THE VIRGINS OF KUTNA ○ GUILD OF THE KUTNA HORA VIRGINS ○ MERRY WIVES, THE ○ VIRGIN'S GUILD OF KUTNA HORA
CECI EST MON CORPS • 1986 • Melancon Andre • MTV • CND
CECI EST UN MESSAGE ENREGISTRE • 1973 • Bedard Jean-Thomas • CND • THIS IS A RECORDED MESSAGE
CECIL TAYLOR AND ALLEN GINSBERG • 1968 • Pennebaker D. A. • SHT • USA
CECILE AIME CA • 1981 • Warren Ken • FRN
CECILE EST MORTE • 1943 • Tourneur Maurice • FRN
CECILIA • 1982 • Solas Humberto • CUB, SPN • CECILIA VALDES
CECILIA, A MOORLAND TRAGEDY • 1972 • Thomsen Knud Leif • DNM
CECILIA OF THE PINK ROSES • 1918 • Steger Julius • USA
CECILIA VALDES see **CECILIA** • 1982
CECROPIA MOTH, THE • 1916 • *Edison* • USA
CEDAR MADONNA, THE see **MADONA DE CEDRO, A** • 1968
CEDARBROOK FARM • 1920 • *Damfool Twins* • SHT • USA
CEDDO • 1977 • Sembene Ousmane • SNL, NGR • PEOPLE , THE ○ OUTSIDERS
CEDRIC SHARPE AND HIS SEXTETTE • 1936 • Shepherd Horace • UKN
CEHENNEMDE BOS YER YOK • 1968 • Figenli Yavuz • TRK • NO PLACE IN HELL
CEIFA, A • 1931 • Coelho Jose Adolfo • SHT • PRT
CEILING see **STROP** • 1962
CEILING HERO • 1940 • Avery Tex • ANS • USA
CEILING WHACKS • 1934 • Horne James W. • SHT • USA
CEILING ZERO • 1936 • Hawks Howard • USA
CEINTURE ELECTRIQUE, LA • 1907 • Rosetti Romeo • FRN • WONDERFUL ELECTRIC BELT, THE
CEINTURE ELECTRIQUE, LA • 1912 • *Cosmopolitan* • FRN • ELECTRIC BELT, THE
CEKANI NA DEST • 1978 • Kachyna Karel • CZC • WAITING FOR THE RAIN ○ WAITING FOR RAIN
CEKANI NA GODOTA • 1966 • Jakubisko Juraj • SHT • CZC • WAITING FOR GODOT
CEKANKY • 1940 • Borsky Vladimir • CZC • WAITING GIRLS, THE
CELA S'APPELLE L'AURORE • 1955 • Bunuel Luis • FRN, ITL • AMANTI DI DOMANI, GLI (ITL) ○ THAT IS CALLED DAWN
CELEBRATED CASE, A • 1914 • Melford George • USA
CELEBRATED CASE, THE • 1910 • *Phoenix* • USA
CELEBRATED CASE, THE • 1912 • Nicholls George • USA
CELEBRATED MOUNTAIN CLIMBERS, THE • 1909 • *Urban-Eclipse* • USA
CELEBRATED SCANDAL, A • 1915 • Edwards J. Gordon • USA
CELEBRATED STIELOW CASE, THE • 1916 • Weber Lois, Smalley Phillips • USA
CELEBRATION • 1966 • Tasker Rex, Weintraub William • DCS • CND
CELEBRATION see **STRIPPER, THE** • 1963
CELEBRATION see **CELEBRATION AT BIG SUR** • 1971
CELEBRATION AT BIG SUR • 1971 • Bryant Baird, Demetrakis Johanna • DOC • USA • CELEBRATION
CELEBRATION IN THE SPRINGTIME see **PRIZIVANJE PROLJECA** • 1979
CELEBRATIONS, LES • 1978 • Simoneau Yves • CND
CELEBRITY • 1928 • Garnett Tay • USA
CELEBRITY • 1984 • Wendkos Paul • TVM • USA
CELEDONIO Y YO SOMOS ASI • 1976 • Ozores Mariano • SPN
CELERY STALKS AT MIDNIGHT • 1957 • Whitney John • SHT • USA
CELESTE • 1915 • *Ostriche Muriel* • USA
CELESTE • 1916 • Coyle Walter • SHT • USA
CELESTE • 1970 • Gast Michel • FRN, ITL
CELESTE • 1981 • Adlon Percy • FRG
CELESTE OF THE AMBULANCE CORPS • 1916 • George Burton • SHT • USA
CELESTIAL BODIES see **CORPUS CELESTES** • 1976
CELESTIAL CITY, THE • 1929 • Orton John • UKN
CELESTIAL CODE, THE • 1915 • Walsh Raoul • USA
CELESTIAL CREATURE, THE • Obratsa Natason • ANM • USS
CELESTIAL PALACE, THE • 1966 • Abbas Khwaya Ahmad • IND
CELESTIAL VENGEANCE • 1910 • *Lubin* • USA
CELESTINA see **SOLE NEGLI OCCHI, IL** • 1953
CELESTINA, LA • 1968 • Ardavin Cesar • SPN • WANTON OF SPAIN -LA CELESTINA, THE ○ WANTON OF SPAIN, THE (UKN)
CELESTINA, LA • 1973 • *Cineprod Selene* • MXC
CELESTINA P.. R.., LA • 1965 • Lizzani Carlo • ITL
CELESTINE see **CELESTINE, BONNE A TOUT FAIRE** • 1974
CELESTINE, BONNE A TOUT FAIRE • 1974 • Franco Jesus • FRN • CELESTINE, MAID AT YOUR SERVICE ○ CELESTINE
CELESTINE, MAID AT YOUR SERVICE see **CELESTINE, BONNE A TOUT FAIRE** • 1974
CELIA • 1949 • Searle Francis • UKN
CELIA • 1988 • Turner Ann* • ASL
CELIBATE see **BRAHMACHARI** • 1968
CELIK BILEK • 1967 • Inanc Cetin • TRK • STEEL-WRIST
CELIMENE -LA POUPEE DE MONTMARTRE (FRN) see **SPIELZEUG VON PARIS, DAS** • 1925
CELINA'S CRY see **GRITO DE CELINA, EL** • 1975
CELINE AND JULIE GO BOATING (UKN) see **CELINE ET JULIE VONT EN BATEAU** • 1974
CELINE ET JULIE VONT EN BATEAU • 1974 • Rivette Jacques • FRN • CELINE AND JULIE GO BOATING (UKN)
CELL 16 • 1971 • Duckworth Martin • DOC • CND
CELL 2455, DEATH ROW • 1955 • Sears Fred F. • USA
CELL, THE see **ZELLE, DIE** • 1971
CELL NO.501 see **501 NUMARALI HUCRE** • 1967
CELLAR, THE • 1989 • Tenney Kevin S. • USA
CELLAR, THE see **DO SKLEPA**
CELLAR DWELLER • 1987 • Buechler John • USA
CELLAR OF DEATH, THE • 1914 • *l.s.p.* • USA
CELLAR OF DEATH, THE • 1916 • Calvert Charles • UKN
CELLAR SPY • 1915 • Hotaling Arthur D. • USA
CELLBOUND • 1955 • Avery Tex, Lah Michael • ANS • USA
CELLE QUE J'AIME see **JO LA ROMANCE** • 1948
CELLE QUI DOMINE • 1927 • Gallone Carmine • FRN
CELLE QUI N'ETAIT PLUS • 1957 • Gerard • SHT • FRN
CELLES QU'ON N'A PAS EUES • 1980 • Thomas Pascal • FRN
CELLIST, THE • 1985 • Marchand Robert • SHT • ASL
CELLO • 1977 • Keenan Haydn • DOC • ASL
CELLO CHAMPION, THE • 1915 • Hotaling Arthur D. • USA
CELLOVOLDE • 1989 • Sopsits Arpad • HNG • SHOOTING RANGE
CELLULE, LA • 1967 • Bouamari Mohamed • SHT • ALG
CELLULOID ET LA MARBRE, LE • 1965 • Rohmer Eric • MTV • FRN
CELLULOSE see **CELULOZA** • 1953
CELLY AND FRIENDS • 1984 • Muller John • MTV • CND
CELOS • 1935 • Boytler Arcady • MXC
CELOS • 1947 • Soffici Mario • ARG
CELOS, AMOR Y MERCADO COMUN • 1973 • Paso Alfonso • SPN
CELOS Y EL DUENDE, LOS • 1966 • Balbuena Silvio F. • SPN
CELOVEK ANFIBJAN see **CHELOVEK AMPHIBIA** • 1962
CELSO AND CORA • 1982 • Kildea Gary • DOC • ASL
CELTIC TRILOGY, A • 1981 • Dowdey Kathleen • DOC • USA
CELUI QUI DOIT MOURIR • 1956 • Dassin Jules • FRN, ITL • COLUI CHE DEVE MORIRE (ITL) ○ HE WHO MUST DIE (USA)
CELUI QUI ESPERE LA PROSPERITE see **CHAYF KHIR** • 1964
CELUI QUI RESTE • 1915 • Feuillade Louis • FRN
CELULOZA • 1953 • Kawalerowicz Jerzy • PLN • NIGHT OF REMEMBRANCE, A ○ CELLULOSE
CEM ANOS DE ABOLICAO • 1989 • Coutinho Eduardo • DOC • BRZ • EMANCIPATION CENTENNIAL, THE
CEMENT see **TSEMYENT** • 1975
CEMENTERY OF REMU, THE see **CMENTARZ REMUCH** • 1962
CEMENTHEAD • 1979 • Thomas Ralph L. • TVM • CND
CEMETARIO DE LAS AGUILAS, EL • 1938 • Lezama Luis • MXC • EAGLE'S CEMETERY, THE (USA)
CEMETERY GIRLS see **VELVET VAMPIRE, THE** • 1971
CEMETERY GIRLS see **GRAN AMOR DEL CONDE DRACULA, EL** • 1972
CEMETERY NIGHT see **NUIT DU CIMITIERE, LA** • 1973
CEMETERY OF TERROR • 1984 • Galindo Ruben Jr. • MXC
CEMETERY OF THE LIVING DEAD see **CINQUE TOMBE PER UN MEDIUM** • 1966
CEMILE • 1968 • Yilmaz Atif • TRK • DJEMILE
CEMO • 1973 • Yilmaz Atif • TRK
CENA DE MATRIMONIOS • 1962 • Balcazar Alfonso • SPN
CENA DEI BORGIA, LA • 1910 • De Liguoro Giuseppe • ITL
CENA DELLE BEFFE, LA • 1941 • Blasetti Alessandro • ITL
CENA GRADA • 1971 • Georgievski Ljubisa • YGS • PRICE OF A TOWN, THE
CENAS DE CACA NO BAIXO ALENTEJO • 1973 • de Macedo Antonio • SHT • PRT
CENDRILLON • 1899 • Melies Georges • FRN • CINDERELLA (USA)
CENDRILLON • 1907 • Capellani Albert • FRN • CINDERELLA (USA)
CENDRILLON • 1912 • Melies Georges • FRN • CINDERELLA OR THE GLASS SLIPPER (USA) ○ PANTOUFLE MYSTERIEUSE, LA ○ MAGIC SLIPPERS, THE
CENDRILLON A PARIS • 1930 • Roussell Henry • FRN
CENDRILLON DE PARIS • 1930 • Hemard Jean • FRN
CENERE • 1916 • Ambrosio Arturo, Mari Febo • ITL
CENERENTOLA • 1919 • Falena Ugo • ITL
CENERENTOLA • 1949 • Cerchio Fernando • ITL • CINDERELLA (USA)
CENERENTOLA 80 • 1984 • Malenotti Roberto • ITL, FRN • CINDERELLA 80
CENERENTOLA E IL SIGNOR BONAVENTURA • 1942 • Tofano Sergio • ITL • REGINA IN BERLINA, CON BONAVENTURA E CENERENTOLA
CENERENTOLA E LA PRINCIPESSA SUL PISELLO • 1974 • Regnoli Piero • ITL
CENERI DELLA MEMORIA, LE • 1961 • Caldana Alberto • ITL
CENERI E VAMPE • 1916 • Falena Ugo • ITL
CENGKAMAN MAUT • 1971 • Sudarmadji S. • MLY • GRIP OF DEATH, THE
CENICIENTA Y ERNESTO, LA • 1957 • Ramirez Pedro L. • SPN
CENICIENTO, EL • 1951 • Martinez Solares Gilberto • MXC
CENICIENTO, EL • 1955 • Llado Juan • SPN
CENIZA AL VIENTO • 1942 • Saslavsky Luis • ARG
CENIZAS DEL DIPUTADO, LAS • 1976 • *Conacite 1* • MXC
CENPA • 1939 • Alexeieff Alexandre • SHT • FRN
CENSORED • 1965 • Mahon Barry • CMP • USA • THIS PICTURE IS CENSORED
CENSORED • 1966 • Frost R. L. • USA
CENSORSHIP IN DENMARK: A NEW APPROACH see **PORNOGRAPHY IN DENMARK: A NEW APPROACH** • 1970
CENSUS OF HARES, THE see **PREBROYVANE NA DIVITE ZAITSI** • 1973
CENSUS TAKER • 1984 • Cook Bruce • USA
CENT ANS DE GLOIRE • 1952 • de Poligny Serge • FRN
CENT ANS DEJA • 1967 • Heroux Denis • DCS • CND
CENT BRIQUES ET DES TUILES • 1965 • Grimblat Pierre • FRN, ITL • HOW NOT TO ROB A DEPARTMENT STORE (USA) ○ COLPO GROSSO A PARIGI (ITL)
CENT DOLLARS MORT OU VIF • 1912 • Durand Jean • FRN • MORT OU VIF
CENT FRANCS L'AMOUR • 1985 • Richard Jacques • USA
CENT FRANCS PAR SECONDE • 1951 • Boyer Jean • FRN
CENT MILLE DOLLARS AU SOLEIL • 1963 • Verneuil Henri • FRN, ITL • CENTOMILA DOLLARI AL SOLE (ITL) ○ GREED IN THE SUN (USA)
CENT MILLE FRANCS POUR UN BAISER • 1933 • Bourlon Hubert, Delance Georges • FRN • POURQUOI PAS?
CENT MILLIONS DE JEUNE • 1968 • Danis Aime • DSS • CND
CENT POUR CENT • 1957 • Alexeieff Alexandre • FRN
CENT VINGT-DEUX RUE DE PROVENCE see **ONE TWO TWO: 122 RUE DE PROVENCE** • 1978
CENTAURO DEL NORTE, EL • 1960 • Pereda Ramon • MXC
CENTAURO NEGRO, EL • 1975 • *Peliculas Latinoamericanos* • MXC
CENTAUROS • 1962 • Camino Jaime • SHT • SPN
CENTAURS, THE • 1916 • McCay Winsor • ANS • USA
CENTAURS, THE see **KENTAUROK** • 1979
CENTENAIRE 1934 • 1934 • Tessier Albert • DCS • CND
CENTENAIRE, LE • 1934 • Ducis Pierre-Jean • FRN
CENTENAIRE DE V.I. LENINE • 1970 • Cherif Hachemi • SHT • ALG
CENTENAIRE DU SAGUENAY, LE • 1938 • Imbault Thomas-Louis, Joron Paul • DOC • CND
CENTENARIO, O • 1922 • Ferreira Lino • PRT
CENTENARIO DOS CAMINHOS DE FERRO • 1956 • Mendes Joao • SHT • PRT
CENTENNIAL CLIPS • 1964 • Potterton Gerald • CND
CENTENNIAL EXPOSITION • 1964 • Jordan Larry • SHT • USA
CENTENNIAL SUMMER • 1946 • Preminger Otto • USA
CENTENNIAL TRAVELLERS • 1966 • Kelly Ron • CND
CENTER FIELDER, EL • 1986 • Deshon Lacayo • NCR
CENTER OF THE WEB, THE • 1914 • *Kroell Claire* • USA
CENTERFOLD FEVER • 1981 • Milner Richard • USA
CENTERFOLD GIRLS • 1974 • Peyser John • USA
CENTINELLA ALERTA! • 1935 • Gremillon Jean, Bunuel Luis (U/c) • SPN
CENTO ANNI D'AMORE • 1954 • De Felice Lionello • ITL
CENTO CAVALIERI, I • 1965 • Cottafavi Vittorio • ITL, SPN • CIEN CABALLEROS, LOS (SPN) ○ HUNDRED HORSEMEN, THE
CENTO CHILOMETRI, LA • 1959 • Petroni Giulio • ITL
CENTO DI QUESTI GIORNI • 1933 • Camerini Mario, Camerini Augusto • ITL • GIOCATTOLO DEE'AMORE, IL
CENTO DOLLARI D'ODIO (ITL) see **ONKEL TOMS HUTTE** • 1965
CENTO DONNE DI CASANOVA, LE see **CAVALIERE MISTERIOSO, IL** • 1948
CENTO GIORNI A PALERMO • 1984 • Ferrera Giuseppe • ITL, FRN • ONE HUNDRED DAYS IN PALERMO
CENTO HP • 1916 • Genina Augusto • ITL
CENTO LETTERE D'AMORE • 1940 • Neufeld Max • ITL • LETTERE D'AMORE DI SUA ECCELLENZA
CENTO MILIONI PER MORIRE (ITL) see **JERK A ISTAMBUL** • 1967
CENTO PICCOLE MADRI see **CENTO PICCOLE MAMME** • 1952
CENTO PICCOLE MAMME • 1952 • Morelli Giulio • ITL • FIGLIO DI UN ALTRO, IL ○ CENTO PICCOLE MADRI
CENTO RAGAZZE PER UN PLAYBOY see **BEL AMI 2000 ODER: WIE VERFUHRT MAN EINEN PLAYBOY?** • 1966
CENTO SERENATE • 1954 • Majano Anton Giulio • ITL
CENTOMILA DOLLARI • 1940 • Camerini Mario • ITL
CENTOMILA DOLLARI AL SOLE (ITL) see **CENT MILLE DOLLARS AU SOLEIL** • 1963
CENTRAL AIRPORT • 1933 • Wellman William A. • USA
CENTRAL AMERICAN ROMANCE, A • 1910 • *Edison* • USA
CENTRAL BAZAAR • 1973 • Dwoskin Stephen • UKN • PUPPET PEOPLE
CENTRAL HOTEL, THE • 1983 • Branev Vesselin • BUL
CENTRAL PARK • 1932 • Adolfi John G. • USA
CENTRAL PARK • 1972 • Amico Gianni • ITL
CENTRAL REGION, THE see **REGION CENTRALE, LA** • 1971
CENTRAL STATION see **ESTACION CENTRAL** • 1988
CENTRALES DE LA MINE, LES • 1958 • Gillet • SHT • FRN
CENTRALISED CONTROL OF FLOW OF PRODUCTION see **SCENTRALIZOWANA KONTROLA PRZEBIEGU PRODUKCJI** • 1951
CENTRE • 1978 • Brakhage Stan • SHT • USA
CENTRE EPIC, LE • 1975 • Brault Francois • DCS • CND
CENTRE FORWARD DIED AT DAWN, THE see **CENTROFORWARD MUREO AL AMANECER, EL** • 1961

CENTRE GEORGES POMPIDOU, LE • 1977 • Rossellini Roberto • MTV • FRN

CENTRE OF ATTENTION -FARMING see **IM BLICKPUNKT - LANDWIRTSCHAFT** • 1967

CENTRE OF THE NATION • 1990 • Yukol Prince Chatri • THL

CENTRE SPREAD see **CENTRESPREAD** • 1982

CENTRE-VILLE ET PIETONS • 1974 • Regnier Michel • DOC • CND

CENTREPOINT • 1990 • Haggard Piers • UKN

CENTRESPREAD • 1982 • Paterson Tony • ASL • CENTRE SPREAD

CENTRESPREAD GIRLS • 1982 • McCallum Robert • USA

CENTROFORWARD MUREO AL AMANECER, EL • 1961 • Mujica Rene • ARG • CENTRE FORWARD DIED AT DAWN, THE

CENTURION • *Mohner Carl* • ITL

CENTURION, THE (USA) see **CONQUISTATORE DI CORINTO, IL** • 1962

CENTURIONS, THE see **LOST COMMAND** • 1966

CENTURY IS FIFTY, THE see **CE SIECLE A CINQUANTE ANS** • 1949

CENTURY OF CANADIAN MEDICINE, A • 1966 • Barclay Robert • DOC • CND

CENTURY OF CEYLON TEA ,A • 1969 • Hettiarachi P. • DOC • SLN

CENTURY OF THE BUSES, A • 1957 • Thompson Tony • DOC • UKN

CENTURY TURNS, THE • 1971 • Petrie Daniel • TVM • USA • HEC RAMSEY

CEOUR NEUF POUR UN VIEUX, UN • 1956-57 • Devlin Bernard, Lenauer Jean • DCS • CND

C'ERA UNA VOLTA • 1917 • Righelli Gennaro • ITL

C'ERA UNA VOLTA • 1967 • Rosi Francesco • ITL, FRN • BELLE ET LE CAVALIER, LA (FRN) ○ MORE THAN A MIRACLE (USA) ○ HAPPILY EVER AFTER ○ ONCE UPON A TIME ○ CINDERELLA, ITALIAN STYLE

C'ERA UNA VOLTA ANGELO MUSCO • 1953 • Chili Giorgio W. • ITL

C'ERA UNA VOLTA IL WEST • 1969 • Leone Sergio • ITL • ONCE UPON A TIME IN THE WEST (UKN)

C'ERA UNA VOLTA IN AMERICA see **ONCE UPON A TIME IN AMERICA** • 1983

C'ERA UNA VOLTA UN COMMISSARIO (ITL) see **IL ETAIT UNE FOIS UN FLIC** • 1972

C'ERA UNA VOLTA UN GANGSTER • 1969 • Masi Marco • ITL

CERA VIRGEN, LA • 1971 • Forque Jose Maria • SPN

CERAMIKA ILZECKA • 1951 • Wajda Andrzej • DOC • PLN • POTTERY AT ILZA, THE ○ ILZA CERAMICS ○ POTTERY OF ILZECKA, THE

CERAMIQUE see **FEUX ET COULEURS** • 1959

CERASELLA • 1960 • Matarazzo Raffaello • ITL

C'ERAVAMO TANTO AMATI • 1974 • Scola Ettore • ITL • WE ALL LOVED EACH OTHER SO MUCH

CERCA DE LA CIUDAD • 1952 • Lucia Luis • SPN

CERCA DE LAS ESTRELLAS • 1961 • Ardavin Cesar • SPN

CERCA DEL CIELO • 1951 • Viladomat Domingo • SPN

CERCA DI CAPIRMI • 1970 • Laurenti Mariano • ITL

CERCASI BIONDA BELLA PRESENZA • 1942 • Renzi Pina • ITL

CERCASI GESU • 1982 • Comencini Luigi • ITL • JESUS WANTED

CERCASI MARITO see **TRE RAGAZZE CERCANO MARITO** • 1944

CERCASI MODELLA • 1932 • Emo E. W. • ITL

CERCATI UN POSTO PER MORIRE see **JOE, CERCATI UN POSTO PER MORIRE** • 1968

CERCEAU MAGIQUE, LA • 1908 • Cohl Emile • ANS • FRN • MAGIC HOOP, THE

CERCLE DES PASSIONS, LE • 1983 • d'Anna Claude • FRN, ITL, SPN

CERCLE ENCHANTEE, LE • 1955 • de Gastyne Marco • SHT • FRN

CERCLE ROUGE, LE • 1970 • Melville Jean-Pierre • FRN, ITL • SENZA NOME, I (ITL) ○ RED CIRCLE, THE (UKN)

CERCLE VICIEUX, LE • 1959 • Pecas Max • FRN

CERCLE VICIEUX, LE see **RIEN QUE DES MENSONGES** • 1932

CERCO, EL • 1955 • Iglesias Miguel • SPN

CERCO, O • 1969 • Teles Antonio Da Cunha • PRT • CIRCLE, THE

CERCO DE FORAJIDOS • 1965 • del Amo Antonio • SPN

CERCO DE IRA • 1949 • Serrano De Osma Carlos • SPN

CERCO DE TERROR • 1971 • Marquina Luis • SPN

CERCO DEL DIABLO, EL • 1950 • Castillo Ruiz, Gomez Bascuas Enrique, Elorrieta Jose Maria, Nieves Conde Jose Antonio, del Amo Antonio, Neville Edgar • SPN

CERCUEIL DE VERRE, LE • 1912 • Jasset Victorin • FRN

CERCUL • Veroiu Mircea • SHT • RMN • CIRCLE, THE

CEREAMICA DE ONTEM E DE HOJE • 1967 • Tropa Alfredo • SHT • PRT

CEREBRO INFERNAL see **BLUE DEMON CONTRA CEREBROS INFERNALES** • 1968

CEREBROS DIABOLICOS see **ARANAS INFERNALES** • 1966

CEREBRUL 702 • 1962 • Iacob Mihai • RMN • FAMOUS 702, THE

CEREMONIA, LA (SPN) see **CEREMONY, THE** • 1963

CEREMONIA SANGRIETA • 1972 • Grau Jorge • SPN • LEGEND OF BLOOD CASTLE ○ BLOODY CEREMONY ○ FEMALE BUTCHER ○ BLOOD CEREMONY ○ COUNTESS DRACULA ○ LADY DRACULA ○ VERGINI CAVALCANO LA MORTE, LE

CEREMONIAL TURQUOISE, THE • 1915 • *Hunt Irene* • USA

CEREMONIE D'AMOUR • 1988 • Borowczyk Walerian • FRN

CEREMONIES OF INNOCENCE • 1980 • Paakspuu Kalli • DOC • CND

CEREMONIJA • 1965 • Dovnikovic Borivoj • ANS • YGS • CEREMONY, THE

CEREMONY, THE • 1963 • Harvey Laurence • USA, SPN • CEREMONIA, LA (SPN)

CEREMONY, THE see **CEREMONIJA** • 1965

CEREMONY, THE see **GISHIKI** • 1971

CERFVOLANT DU BOUT DU MONDE, LE • 1957 • Pigaut Roger • FRN, CHN • KITE FROM THE END OF THE WORLD, THE ○ MAGIC OF THE KITE, THE (USA) ○ KITE FROM ACROSS THE WORLD, THE ○ WISHING MACHINE, THE

CERIMONIA DEI SENSI, LA • 1979 • D'Agostino Antonio • ITL

CERISES DE BOUT DE ZAN, LES • 1913 • Feuillade Louis • FRN

CERITAKU CERITAMU • 1979 • Saadiah • MLY • MY STORY'S YOUR STORY

CERNE SLUNCE • 1978 • Vavra Otakar • CZC • BLACK SUN

CERNY DEMANT • 1956 • *Zeman Karel (Sc)* • CZC • BLACK DIAMOND, THE (USA)

CERNY PETR • 1963 • Forman Milos • CZC • BLACK PETER (USA) ○ PETER AND PAVLA ○ PETER AND PAULA

CERNY PLAMEN • 1930 • Krnansky M. J. • CZC • BLACK FLAME, THE

CERRADO POR ASESINATO • 1962 • Gamboa Jose Luis • SPN

CERRO CORA • 1978 • Gonzalez Ladislao • PRG

CERRO DE LOS LOCOS, EL • 1960 • Navarro Agustin • SPN

CERRO DOS ENFORCADOS, O • 1954 • Garcia Fernando • PRT

CERRO PELADO • 1966 • Alvarez Santiago • DOC • CUB

CERTAIN ADULTERY, A see **ARU MITTSU** • 1967

CERTAIN CIRCUMSTANCE, A see **CIRCOSTANZA, LA** • 1974

CERTAIN DAY, A see **CERTO GIORNO, UN** • 1968

CERTAIN DESIRE, A see **FLAGRANT DESIR** • 1985

CERTAIN FURY • 1985 • Gyllenhaal Stephen • USA

CERTAIN HEAT see **SPOOK WHO SAT BY THE DOOR, THE** • 1973

CERTAIN JOSETTE BAUER, UNE • 1986 • Meier Uli, Gujer Elisabeth • DOC • SWT

CERTAIN KILLER, A see **ARU KOROSHIYA** • 1967

CERTAIN KIND OF HAPPINESS, A • 1973 • Constantinescu Mihai • RMN

CERTAIN KIND OF LOOK, A see **OLELKEZO TEKINTETEK** • 1982

CERTAIN M. GRANT, UN • 1933 • Le Bon Roger, Lamprecht Gerhard • FRN

CERTAIN MONSIEUR, UN • 1949 • Ciampi Yves • FRN

CERTAIN MONSIEUR JO, UN • 1957 • Jolivet Rene • FRN

CERTAIN NIGHT'S KISS, A see **ARU YO NO SEPPUN** • 1946

CERTAIN PRACTICES • 1979 • Lavut Martin • MTV • CND

CERTAIN PREGNANCY, A see **ARU NINSHIN** • 1968

CERTAIN PROPHESIES see **BIZONYOS JOSLATOK** • 1968

CERTAIN RICH MAN, A • 1920 • Masi Philip W. • SHT • USA

CERTAIN RICH MAN, A • 1921 • Hickman Howard • USA

CERTAIN SACRIFICE, A • 1985 • Lewicki Stephen Jon • USA

CERTAIN SMILE, A • 1958 • Negulesco Jean • USA

CERTAIN WOMAN, A see **ARU ONNA** • 1942

CERTAIN WOMAN, A see **ARU ONNA** • 1954

CERTAIN YOUNG MAN, A • 1926 • Henley Hobart • USA • BELLAMY THE MAGNIFICENT

CERTAINE DOULEUR, UNE see **SHAI'UN MINA AL-ADHAB** • 1969

CERTAINES NOUVELLES • 1979 • Davila Jacques • FRN

CERTAINS L'AIMENT FROIDE! • 1959 • Bastia Jean • FRN

CERTAINS L'APPELLENT FRANCOIS... • Aubree Patrick • DOC • FRN

CERTAINTY OF MAN, THE • 1914 • *American* • USA

CERTIFICADO, EL • 1968 • Lluch Vicente • SPN

CERTIFICAT, LE • 1979 • Aw Tidiane • SNL

CERTIFICAT D'INDIGENCE, LE • 1981 • Bathily Moussa • SHT • SNL

CERTIFICATE OF VIRGINITY see **SHOJO SHOMEISHO** • 1967

CERTIFIED CORRECT see **ISPAVLENNOMU VERIT** • 1959

CERTO CAPITAO RODRIGO, UM • 1970 • Duarte Anselmo • BRZ

CERTO, CERTISSIMO, ANZI.. PROBABILE • 1969 • Fondato Marcello • ITL

CERTO GIORNO, UN • 1968 • Olmi Ermanno • ITL • ONE FINE DAY (UKN) ○ CERTAIN DAY, A

CERTOSA DI PARMA, LA • 1947 • Christian-Jaque • ITL, FRN • CHARTREUSE DE PARME, LA (FRN)

CERTUV MLYN • 1951 • Trnka Jiri • ANM • CZC • DEVIL'S MILL, THE (USA)

CERUL INCEPE LA ETAJUL III • 1967 • Munteanu Francisc • RMN • SKY BEGINS ON THE 3RD FLOOR, THE

CERUL N-ARE GRATII • 1962 • Munteanu Francisc • RMN • SKY HAS NO BARS, THE

CERUZA ES RADIR • 1960 • Macskassy Gyula • ANS • HNG • CRAYON AND THE ERASER, THE ○ PENCIL AND INDIA RUBBER ○ PENCIL AND RUBBER

CERVANTES see **AVVENTURE E GLI AMORI DI MIGUEL CERVANTES, LE** • 1967

CERVANTES FROM A SMALL TOWN see **SERVANTES IZ MALOGA MISTA** • 1983

CERVEAU, LE • 1968 • Oury Gerard • FRN, ITL • CERVELLO, IL (ITL) ○ BRAIN, THE

CERVEAU GELE • 1969 • Moretti Pierre • ANS • CND • FROZEN BRAIN, THE (USA)

CERVELLO, IL (ITL) see **CERVEAU, LE** • 1968

CERVENA AEROVKA • 1960 • Hofman Eduard • ANS • PLN • OLD RED CAR, THE

CERVENA KULNA • 1968 • Hanibal Jiri • CZC • RED SHED, THE

CES CHERS PETITS see **DROLES DE PHENOMENES** • 1958

CES DAMES AUX CHAPEAUX VERTS • 1929 • Berthomieu Andre • FRN

CES DAMES AUX CHAPEAUX VERTS • 1937 • Cloche Maurice • FRN • LADIES IN THE GREEN HATS, THE (USA)

CES DAMES AUX CHAPEAUX VERTS • 1948 • Rivers Fernand • FRN

CES DAMES PREFERENT LE MAMBO • 1957 • Borderie Bernard • FRN, ITL • SIGNORE PREFERISCONO IL MAMBO, LE (ITL) ○ DISHONORABLE DISCHARGE (USA)

CES DAMES S'EN MELENT • 1964 • Andre Raoul • FRN, ITL • JEFF GORDON SPACCA TUTTO (ITL)

CES FLICS ETRANGES VENUS D'AILLEURS • 1979 • Clair Philippe • FRN

CES GENS ET LE NIL see **NASSU WA AN-NIL, AN-** • 1968

CES MALADES QUI NOUS GOUVERNENT • 1980 • Vajda Claude • FRN

CES MESSIEURS DAMES see **SIGNORE E SIGNORI** • 1966

CES MESSIEURS DE LA FAMILLE • 1968 • Andre Raoul • FRN

CES MESSIEURS DE LA GACHETTE • 1969 • Andre Raoul • FRN

CES MESSIEURS DE LA SANTE • 1933 • Colombier Piere • FRN

CES SACREES VACANCES • 1955 • Vernay Robert • FRN

CES TROTTOIRS DE SATURNE • 1986 • Santiago Hugo • FRN

CES VOYOUS D'HOMMES • 1954 • Boyer Jean • FRN, ITL

CESAR • 1936 • Pagnol Marcel • FRN

CESAR AND ROSALIE (UKN) see **CESAR ET ROSALIE** • 1972

CESAR BIROTTEAU • 1911 • Chautard Emile • FRN

CESAR CHEZ LES GAULOIS • 1931 • Clement Rene • ANS • FRN

CESAR ET ROSALIE • 1972 • Sautet Claude • FRN, FRG, ITL • E SIMPATICO MA GLI ROMPEREI IL MUSO (ITL) ○ CESAR AND ROSALIE (UKN)

CESAR ET SON CANOT D'ECORCE • 1971 • Gosselin Bernard • DOC • CND

CESAR GRANDBLAISE • 1970 • Dewever Jean • FRN, ITL • WEEK END PROIBITO DI UNA FAMIGLIA QUASI PER BENE (ITL) ○ JAMBES EN L'AIR, LES ○ CESAR GRANDBLAISE OU LES JAMBES EN L'AIR

CESAR GRANDBLAISE OU LES JAMBES EN L'AIR see **CESAR GRANDBLAISE** • 1970

CESAREE • 1978 • Duras Marguerite • SHT • FRN

CESARIN JOUE LES ETROITS MOUSQUETAIRES • 1962 • Couzinet Emile • FRN

CESKE NEBE • 1918 • Palous Jan A. • CZC • CZECH HEAVEN

CESKOSLOVENSKY JEZISEK • 1918 • Branald Richard F. • CZC • SMALL CZECHOSLOVAK ICON

CESSEZ LE FEU • 1934 • de Baroncelli Jacques • FRN • CEASE FIRING (USA) ○ AMIS COMME AUTREFOIS

CEST A SLAVA • 1968 • Bocan Hynek • CZC • HONOUR AND GLORY

C'EST ARRIVE A 36 CHANDELLES • 1957 • Diamant-Berger Henri • FRN

C'EST ARRIVE A ADEN • 1956 • Boisrond Michel • FRN • IT HAPPENED IN ADEN

C'EST ARRIVE A PARIS • 1952 • Berry John (U/c), Lavorel Henri • FRN • IT HAPPENED IN PARIS (USA)

C'EST ARRIVE DEMAIN see **IT HAPPENED TOMORROW** • 1943

C'EST ARRIVE UNE CERTAIN NUIT see **HADAT'HA D'ATA LAYLA** • 1954

C'EST BEBE QUI BOIT LE MUSCAT • 1912 • Feuillade Louis • FRN

C'EST BEN BEAU L'AMOUR • 1971 • Daigle Marc • DOC • CND

C'EST BIEN MA VEINE see **MA LIHHYA ZAHR** • 1948

C'EST CA, L'AMOUR! see **HAZA HOWA EL HOB** • 1958

C'EST CRIMINAL see **IT'S A CRIME** • 1957

C'EST DANGEREUX ICI • 1978 • Lamothe Arthur • DOC • CND

C'EST DINGUE.. MAIS ON Y VA! • 1978 • Gerard Michel • FRN, ITL

C'EST DUR POUR TOUT LE MONDE • 1975 • Gion Christian • FRN

C'EST ENCORE LOIN D'AMERIQUE • 1979 • Coggio Roger • FRN

C'EST FACILE ET CA PEUT RAPPORTER.. VINGT ANS! • 1983 • Luret Jean • FRN

C'EST FINI see **A BANNA** • 1980

C'EST JEUNE ET CA SAIT TOUT! • 1974 • Mulot Claude • FRN, CND • EDUCATRICE, L'

C'EST LA FAUTE D'ADAM • 1957 • Audry Jacqueline • FRN • IT'S ALL ADAM'S FAULT ○ IT'S ADAM'S FAULT

C'EST LA FAUTE DE L'ABBE MOURET see **FAUTE DE L'ABBE MOURET, LA** • 1970

C'EST LA VIE • 1981 • Vecchiali Paul • CND

C'EST LA VIE see **A NOUS DEUX, MADAME LA VIE** • 1936

C'EST LA VIE PARISIENNE • 1953 • Rode Alfred • FRN

C'EST LA VIE RROSE -EIN JUNGGESELLENSPIEL • 1977 • Stenzel Hans Christof • FRG • INTERROGATION OF THE STATUE OF LIBERTY ○ BEFRAGUNG DER FREIHEITSTATUE

C'EST L'AVIRON • 1945 • McLaren Norman • ANS • CND

C'EST L'AVIRON QUI NOUS MENE • 1942 • Tessier Albert • DCS • CND

C'EST L'AVIRON QUI NOUS MENE • 1959 • Brault Francois • DCS • CND

C'EST LE PRINTEMPS • 1916 • Feuillade Louis • FRN

C'EST PAPA QUI PREND LA PURGE • 1906 • Feuillade Louis • FRN

C'EST PAS CHINOIS • 1974 • Hebert Pierre, Gascon Gilles • DCS • CND • PIECE OF CAKE, A

C'EST PAS LA FAUTE A JACQUES CARTIER • 1967 • Dufaux Georges, Perron Clement • CND

C'EST PAS L'ARGENT QUI MANQUE • 1972 • Favreau Robert • DOC • CND

C'EST PAS MOI, C'EST L'AUTRE • 1962 • Boyer Jean • FRN

C'EST PAS MOI, C'EST L'AUTRE • 1983 • Letourneau Diane • CND

C'EST PAS MOI, C'EST LUI • 1980 • Richard Pierre • FRN

C'EST PAS PARCE QU'ON EST PETIT QU'ON PEUT PAS ETRE GRAND • 1987 • Jasny Vojtech • CND, CZC • GREAT LAND OF SMALL, THE

C'EST PAS PARCE QU'ON N'A RIEN A DIRE QU'IL FAUT FERMER SA GUEULE • 1974 • Besnard Jacques • FRN

C'EST PLUS FACILE DE GARDER LA BOUCHE OUVERTE • 1973 • Barney Jacques-Paul • FRN

C'EST PU COMME CA ANYMORE • 1976-77 • Brault Michel, Gladu Andre • DCS • CND

C'EST QUOI UN METIER • 1973 • Beaudry Michel • CND

C'EST ROULANT • 1906 • Nonguet Lucien • FRN

C'EST ROULANT • 1911 • Cohl Emile • ANS • FRN

C'EST SURTOUT PAS DE L'AMOUR see **NOT A LOVE STORY: A FILM ABOUT PORNOGRAPHY** • 1981

C'EST TOI QUE J'AIME see **JE N'AIME QUE TOI** • 1949

C'EST UN MYSTERE see **HERITIER DES MONDESIR, L'** • 1939

C'EST UN VRAI PARADIS • Gaudard Lucette • FRN • IT'S A REAL PARADISE

C'EST UNE FILLE DE PANAME • 1957 • Lepage Henri • FRN

"C'EST VOTRE PLUS BEAU TEMPS" • 1973 • Dostie Alain • DOC • CND

C'EST VOUS SEULE QUE J'AIME see **VOUS SEULE QUE J'AIME** • 1939

CESTA, LA • 1963 • Salvia Rafael J. • SPN

CESTA DO HUBIN STUDAKOVY DUSE • 1939 • Fric Martin • CZC • SEARCHING THE HEARTS OF STUDENTS

CESTA DO PRAHY VINCENCE MOSTEK A SIMONA PESLA Z VLCNOZA L.P.1969 • 1969 • Jires Jaromil (c/d) • CZC • JOURNEY OF VINCENC MOSTEK AND SIMON PESL OF VLCNOV TO PRAGUE 1969 A.D., THE
CESTA DO PRAVEKU • 1955 • Zeman Karel • CZC • JOURNEY TO THE BEGINNING OF TIME (USA) ○ JOURNEY TO PRIMEVAL TIMES, A ○ JOURNEY TO A PRIMEVAL AGE ○ JOURNEY INTO PREHISTORY, A ○ JOURNEY INTO PRIMEVAL TIMES, A
CESTA DUGA GODINU DANA (YGS) see **STRADA LUNGA UN ANNO, LA** • 1958
CESTA K BARIKADAM • 1946 • Vavra Otakar • DOC • CZC • ROAD TO THE BARRICADES, THE
CESTA ZPATKY • 1945 • Makovec Milos • DOC • CZC
CESTA ZPATKY • 1958 • Krska Vaclav • CZC • ROAD BACK, THE ○ WAY BACK, THE
CESTY MUZU • 1972 • Toman Ivo • CZC • ROADS OF MEN, THE
CESUR YABANCI • 1968 • Hekimoglu Yucel • TRK • BRAVE STRANGER, THE
CET AGE EST SANS PITIE • 1950 • Blistene Marcel • FRN
CET HOMME EST DANGEREUX • 1953 • Sacha Jean • FRN • DANGEROUS AGENT (USA) ○ THIS MAN IS DANGEROUS
CET OBSCUR OBJET DU DESIR • 1977 • Bunuel Luis • FRN, SPN • THAT OBSCURE OBJECT OF DESIRE (USA)
C'ETAIT HIER L'ETE • 1970 • Boisrond Michel • FRN
C'ETAIT IL Y A 4 ANS • 1955 • Vieyra Paulin • SNL
C'ETAIT LA PLUS BELLE FILLE DANS LA VILLE • 1981 • Ferreri Marco • FRN, ITL
C'ETAIT MOI see **RAPHAEL LE TATOUE** • 1938
C'ETAIT UN MUSICIEN • 1933 • Gleize Maurice, Zelnik Friedrich • FRN
C'ETAIT UN QUEBECOIS EN BRETAGNE, MADAME • 1977 • Perrault Pierre • CND
CETIRI DANA DO SMRTI • 1977 • Jokic Miroslav • YGS • FOUR DAYS TILL DEATH ○ LAST FOUR DAYS, THE
CETIRI KILOMETRA NA SAT • 1958 • Stojanovic Velimir • YGS • FOUR KILOMETRES PER HOUR
CETTE ANCIENNE CITE, BYBLOS • 1962 • Nasser George • SHT • LBN
CETTE NUIT-LA • 1933 • Sorkin Marc • FRN
CETTE NUIT-LA • 1958 • Cazeneuve Maurice • FRN • NIGHT HEAT (UKN)
CETTE PETITE EST PARFAITE see **JEUNESSE D'ABORD** • 1935
CETTE SACREE GAMINE • 1955 • Boisrond Michel • FRN • THAT NAUGHTY GIRL (USA) ○ MAM'ZELLE PIGALLE ○ MADEMOISELLE PIGALLE ○ NAUGHTY GIRL
CETTE VIEILLE CANAILLE • 1933 • Litvak Anatole • FRN
CETVRTI SUPUTNIK • 1967 • Bauer Branko • YGS • FOURTH TRAVELLING COMPANION, THE ○ FOURTH PARTY, THE
CETYRE CORTA • 1913 • Starevitch Ladislas • ANM • USS • FLYING FROGS, THE (USA)
CEU ABERTO • 1986 • de Andrade Joao Batista • DOC • BRZ • OPEN SKIES
CEUX DE CHEZ NOUS • 1919 • Guitry Sacha • DOC • FRN
CEUX DE DEMAIN • 1938 • Millar Adelqui, Pallu Georges • FRN • ENFANT DE TROUPE, L'
CEUX DE LA DOUANE see **FRAUDEUR, LE** • 1937
CEUX DE LA MONDAINE see **POLICE MONDAINE** • 1937
CEUX DE VIKING • 1931 • Ginet Rene, Frissell Varick • FRN
CEUX DU BALLON ROND • 1948 • Griboff • SHT • FRN
CEUX DU CIEL • 1940 • Noe Yvan • FRN
CEUX DU RAIL • 1942 • Clement Rene • DCS • FRN
CEUX DU RIVAGE • 1943 • Severac Jacques • FRN • VENT DE NOROIT
CEUX QUI FOUILLENT LES ENTRAILLES DU SOL see **RIJALUM YAH'FURUNA A'MAKIN FI AL-ARD** • 1971
CEYLON, LAND SHORT OF PEOPLE • 1945 • Hornby Clifford • DOC • UKN
CEZANNE see **ART WORKS 1: ACADEMIC STILL LIFE** • 1977
CEZAR A DETEKTIVI • 1967 • Plichta Dimitrij • CZC • CAESAR AND THE DETECTIVES
CHA CHA • 1980 • Curiel Herbert • NTH
CHA-CHA-CHA • 1983 • Kovacsi Janos • HNG
CHA CHA CHA • 1989 • Kaurismaki Mika • FNL
CHA-CHA-CHA BOOM • 1956 • Sears Fred F. • USA
CHAALCHITRA • 1981 • Sen Mrinal • IND • KALEIDOSCOPE, THE
CHAAN PARDESSE • 1981 • Singh Chitrartha • IND • HANDSOME STRANGER
CHABAB EMRAA • 1956 • Abu Saif Salah • EGY • WOMAN'S YOUTH, A ○ SHABAB IMRA'A
CHABAN, THE • 1966 • Shamshiev Bolotbek • USS
CHABICHOU • 1934 • Wulschleger Henry • FRN, ALG
CHABUKWALI • 1937 • *Mohan* • IND
CHAC • 1974 • Klein Rolando • MXC
CHACAL DE NAHUELTORO, EL • 1969 • Littin Miguel • CHL • JACKAL OF NAHUELTORO, THE (UKN)
CHACAL TRAQUE LES FILLES, LE • 1967 • Rankovitch Jean-Michel • FRN
CHACALES DE LA ISLA VERDE, LOS see **DIOSA DE TAHITI, LA** • 1952
CHACALES, LOS • 1963 • Urueta Chano • MXC
CHACITA LA DE TRIANA • 1947 • Rodriguez Ismael • MXC
CHACUN DE NOUS • 1971 • Buyens Frans • BLG
CHACUN PORTE SA CROIX • 1929 • Choux Jean • FRN
CHACUN POUR TOUS • 1945 • Palardy Jean • DCS • CND
CHACUN SA CHANCE • 1930 • Pujol Rene, Steinhoff Hans • FRN • CHUTE DANS LE BONHEUR, LA
CHACUN SA VIE • 1931 • de La Falaise Henri • FRN
CHACUN SON ALIBI (FRN) see **CRIMEN** • 1960
CHACUN SON TOUR • 1951 • Berthomieu Andre • FRN
CHAD HANNA • 1940 • King Henry • USA
CHADFORD DIAMONDS, THE • 1915 • Reehm George E. • USA
CHADWICK FAMILY, THE • 1974 • Rich David Lowell • TVM • USA
CHAFARICA, A • 1970 • Faria Antonio • SHT • PRT
CHAFED ELBOWS • 1967 • Downey Robert • USA
CHAFIKA AND MEATBALLS • 1978 • Badrakhan Ali • EGY
CHAGALL • 1955 • Hessens Robert • FRN
CHAGALL • 1966 • Campos Antonio • SHT • PRT
CHAGRIN D'AMOUR • 1901 • Zecca Ferdinand • FRN
CHAGRIN ET LA PITIE, LE • 1970 • Ophuls Marcel • DOC • FRN, SWT, FRG • SORROW AND THE PITY, THE (USA)
CHAHADAT AT'FAL FI ZAMAN AL-HARB • 1972 • Zubaydi Qays Al- • IRQ • TEMOIGNAGE DES ENFANTS PALESTINIENS EN TEMPS DE GUERRE
CHAHAR DARVISH • 1968 • Amin-E-Amini • IRN • FOUR HUMBLE MEN
CHAHAR KHAHAR • 1967 • Najeebzadeh Ahmad • IRN • FOUR SISTERS
CHAHR ASSAL BIDOUN EZAAG • 1968 • Shukry Abdel Moneim • EGY • HONEYMOON WITHOUT TROUBLES
CHAI • 1924 • Viskovski Vyacheslav • USS • MAYBE
CHAIKA • 1971 • Karasik Yuli • USS • SEAGULL, THE (UKN)
CHAIKAGAI 24-JIKAN see **CHIKAGAI NIJUYO-JIKAN** • 1947
CHAIKOVSKI see **TCAIKOVSKI** • 1969
CHAIMITE • 1953 • do Canto Jorge Brum • PRT
CHAIN see **SANGAL** • 1987
CHAIN, THE • 1985 • Gold Jack • UKN
CHAIN, THE see **VERIGATA** • 1964
CHAIN, THE see **DAISY CHAIN, THE** • 1969
CHAIN, THE see **RETEZ** • 1981
CHAIN, THE see **ZANGIR** • 1986
CHAIN GANG • 1950 • Landers Lew • USA
CHAIN GANG • 1984 • Keeter Worth • USA
CHAIN GANG see **BIG BOSS, THE** • 1941
CHAIN GANG, THE • 1930 • Gillett Burt • ANS • USA
CHAIN GANG WOMEN • 1971 • Frost Lee • USA
CHAIN INVISIBLE, THE • 1916 • Powell Frank • USA
CHAIN IS BROKEN, THE • 1951 • Strbac Milenko • YGS
CHAIN LETTER DIMES • 1935 • Ray Albert • SHT • USA
CHAIN LETTERS • 1935 • *Terry Paul/ Moser Frank (P)* • ANS • USA
CHAIN LETTERS • 1985 • Rappaport Mark • USA
CHAIN LIGHTNING • 1922 • Wilson Ben • USA
CHAIN LIGHTNING • 1927 • Hillyer Lambert • USA
CHAIN LIGHTNING • 1950 • Heisler Stuart • USA
CHAIN OF CIRCUMSTANCE • 1951 • Jason Will • USA
CHAIN OF EVENTS • 1958 • Thomas Gerald • UKN
CHAIN OF EVIDENCE • 1957 • Landres Paul • USA
CHAIN OF EVIDENCE, THE • 1916 • Coyle Walter • SHT • USA
CHAIN REACTION • 1971 • Dinov Todor • ANS • BUL
CHAIN REACTION • 1979 • Barry Ian, Miller George • USA
CHAIN REACTION see **SILKWOOD** • 1983
CHAIN REACTION see **STATE OF EMERGENCY, A** • 1986
CHAINED • 1934 • Brown Clarence • USA • SACRED AND PROFANE LOVE
CHAINED FOR LIFE • 1959 • Fraser Harry L. • USA
CHAINED GIRLS • 1965 • Mawra Joseph P. • USA
CHAINED HEAT • 1983 • Nicolas Paul • USA, FRG
CHAINED TIGER see **PANCHA INDERA HARIMAU BERANTAI** • 1970
CHAINED TO THE ENEMY • 1914 • Thornton F. Martin • UKN
CHAINED TO YESTERDAY see **LIMBO** • 1972
CHAINED (USA) see **MICHAEL** • 1924
CHAINED WOMEN see **BLACK MAMA, WHITE MAMA** • 1973
CHAINES see **GESCHLECHT IN FESSELN** • 1928
CHAINES, LES • 1910 • Cohl Emile • ANS • FRN
CHAINES DE SOIE see **SALASIL MIN HARIR** • 1962
CHAINGANG GIRLS see **SWEET SUGAR** • 1972
CHAINON MANQUANT, LE • 1981 • Picha • ANM • BLG, FRN • MISSING LINK, THE
CHAINS • 1912 • *Stonehouse Ruth* • USA
CHAINS OF AN OATH, THE • 1913 • *Vitagraph* • USA
CHAINS OF BONDAGE • 1914 • *Travers Richard C.* • USA
CHAINS OF BONDAGE • 1916 • Coleby A. E. • UKN
CHAINS OF EVIDENCE • 1920 • Brenon Herbert • USA
CHAINS OF EVIDENCE • 1920 • Fitzgerald Dallas M. • USA
CHAINS OF GOLD • 1990 • Holcomb Rod • USA
CHAINS OF HATE see **BLACK MAMA, WHITE MAMA** • 1973
CHAINS (UKN) see **FISKEBYN** • 1920
CHAINWORK LOVE see **AMOUR A LA CHAINE, L'** • 1965
CHAIR, THE • 1962 • Leacock Richard, Pennebaker D. A., Lipscombe Jim • DOC • USA
CHAIR, THE • 1967 • Dunning George • ANS • UKN
CHAIR, THE • 1987 • Korzeniowsky Waldemar • USA
CHAIR, THE see **ISU** • 1962
CHAIR, THE see **FOTEL** • 1963
CHAIR ARDENTE • 1932 • Plaissetty Rene • FRN
CHAIR DE L'ORCHIDEE, LA • 1974 • Chereau Patrice • FRN, ITL, FRG • ORCHIDEA ROSSO SANGUE, UN' (ITL)
CHAIR DE POULE • 1964 • Duvivier Julien • FRN, ITL • HIGHWAY PICKUP (USA)
CHAIR ET LE DIABLE, LA • 1953 • Josipovici Jean • FRN, ITL • FUOCO NELLE VENE, IL (ITL) ○ FLESH AND DESIRE (USA)
CHAIR FOR SOMEBODY, A see **DARE NO ISU?** • 1968
CHAIRMAN, THE • 1969 • Thompson J. Lee • USA, UKN • MOST DANGEROUS MAN IN THE WORLD, THE (UKN)
CHAIRMAN, THE see **PREDSEDATEL** • 1965
CHAIRMAN: A PORTRAIT OF PAUL DESMARAIS, THE • 1981 • Pearson Peter • MTV • CND
CHAIRMAN, OUR CHAIRMAN • 1988 • Om Chong-Sun • SKR
CHAIRMEN see **AGE DE CHAISE, L'** • 1979
CHAIRY TALE, A • 1957 • McLaren Norman, Jutra Claude • ANS • CND • HISTOIRE D'UNE CHAISE ○ IL ETAIT UN CHAISE
CHAISE A PORTEURS ENCHANTEE, LA • 1905 • Melies Georges • FRN • ENCHANTED SEDAN-CHAIR, THE (USA)
CHAISE VIDE, LA • 1975 • Jallaud Pierre • FRN • EMPTY CHAIR, THE
CHAISES ROULANTES, LES • 1977 • Moreau Michel • DCS • CND
CHAITANYA MAHAPRABHU • 1953 • Bhatt Vijay • IND
CHAKHMATNAIA GORIATCHKA see **SHAKHMATNAYA GORYACHKA** • 1925
CHAKHTIERY • 1936 • Yutkevich Sergei • USS • MINERS ○ SHACHTERY
CHAKKARAM • 1968 • Kasilingam A. • IND • WHEEL
CHAKRA • 1979 • Dharmaraj Rabindra • IND • WHEEL
CHAKU-JUDO AIKIDO • 1968 • Capistrano Johnny F. • PHL
CHAL, BOMBAY, CHAL • 1988 • Nair Mira • IND • SALAAM, BOMBAY!
CHALAND QUI PASSE, LE see **ATALANTE, L'** • 1934
CHALET DE LOS CHALADOS, EL • 1969 • Merino Fernando • SPN
CHALEUR see **CHALEURS** • 1970
CHALEUR DE MINUIT, LA see **ESPIONS A L'AFFUT** • 1966
CHALEUR DU SEIN, LA • 1938 • Boyer Jean • FRN
CHALEURS • 1970 • Daert Daniel • FRN • S FOR SEX (UKN) ○ FEMME CREA L'AMANT, LA ○ CHALEUR ○ VOYAGEUR, LE ○ HOT AND ADOLESCENTS
CHALEURS D'ETE • 1959 • Felix Louis • FRN • HEAT OF THE SUMMER (USA)
CHALIAPIN • 1970 • Donskoi Mark • USS
CHALICE OF COURAGE, THE • 1915 • Sturgeon Rollin S. • USA
CHALICE OF REMORSE, THE (UKN) see **CHALICE OF SORROW, THE** • 1916
CHALICE OF SORROW, THE • 1916 • Ingram Rex • USA • CHALICE OF REMORSE, THE (UKN)
CHALIS BABA EK CHOR • 1954 • *Burman S. D. (M)* • IND
CHALIYA • 1960 • *Kapoor Raj* • IND
CHALK GARDEN, THE • 1963 • Neame Ronald • UKN
CHALK LINE, THE • 1916 • *Myers Harry* • USA
CHALK MARKS • 1924 • Adolfi John G. • USA
CHALK UP • 1932 • Myers Zion • SHT • USA
CHALLANI NEEDA • 1968 • Rama Rao T. • IND • COOL SHED, THE
CHALLENGE • 1974 • Beck Martin* • USA
CHALLENGE, THE • 1916 • Mackenzie Donald • USA
CHALLENGE, THE • 1922 • Fleischer Dave • ANS • USA
CHALLENGE, THE • 1922 • Terriss Tom • USA
CHALLENGE, THE • 1938 • Rosmer Milton, Trenker Luis • UKN
CHALLENGE, THE • 1948 • Yarbrough Jean • USA
CHALLENGE, THE • 1951 • Arnold Jack • DOC • USA
CHALLENGE, THE • 1960 • Gilling John • UKN • IT TAKES A THIEF
CHALLENGE, THE • 1970 • Smithee Alan • TVM • USA • SURROGATE, THE
CHALLENGE, THE • 1982 • Frankenheimer John • USA
CHALLENGE, THE see **SFIDA, LA** • 1958
CHALLENGE, THE see **WEZWANIE** • 1971
CHALLENGE, THE (UKN) see **WOMAN HUNGRY** • 1931
CHALLENGE, THE (UKN) see **ACROSS THE BADLANDS** • 1950
CHALLENGE.. A TRIBUTE TO MODERN ART, THE • 1974 • Kline Herbert • DOC • USA • CHALLENGE OF GREATNESS, THE
CHALLENGE ACCEPTED, THE • 1918 • Hollywood Edwin L. • USA
CHALLENGE AT MIDNIGHT see **SHINYA NO CHOSEN** • 1959
CHALLENGE FOR GLORY see **EIKO ENO CHOSEN** • 1966
CHALLENGE FOR ROBIN HOOD, A • 1967 • Pennington-Richards C. M. • UKN
CHALLENGE IN THE SNOW (UKN) see **13 JOURS EN FRANCE** • 1968
CHALLENGE OF A LIFETIME • 1985 • Mayberry Russ • TVM • USA
CHALLENGE OF CHANCE, THE • 1919 • Revier Harry • USA
CHALLENGE OF DEATH • 1979 • *Wang Tao* • HKG
CHALLENGE OF GREATNESS, THE see **CHALLENGE.. A TRIBUTE TO MODERN ART, THE** • 1974
CHALLENGE OF RIN TIN TIN, THE • 1958 • Landers Lew • USA
CHALLENGE OF THE FRONTIER see **MAN OF THE FOREST** • 1933
CHALLENGE OF THE GIANT, THE see **SFIDA DEI GIGANTI, LA** • 1965
CHALLENGE OF THE GLADIATOR (USA) see **GLADIATORE CHE SFIDO L'IMPERO** • 1965
CHALLENGE OF THE GOBOTS: INVASION FROM THE 21ST LEVEL • 1985 • Hanna William, Barbera Joseph • ANM • USA
CHALLENGE OF THE GOBOTS: THE GOBOTRON SAGA • 1985 • Hanna William, Barbera Joseph • ANM • USA
CHALLENGE OF THE LAW, THE • 1920 • Dunlap Scott R. • USA
CHALLENGE OF THE MASTERS • 1981 • Chang Hsin-Yi • HKG
CHALLENGE OF THE MASTERS, THE see **HUANG FEI-HUNG YU LU A-TS'AI** • 1978
CHALLENGE OF THE MCKENNAS, THE see **SFIDA DEI MACKENNA, LA** • 1970
CHALLENGE OF THE RANGE • 1949 • Nazarro Ray • USA • MOONLIGHT RAID (UKN)
CHALLENGE OF THE TIGER see **DRAGON BRUCE LEE**
CHALLENGE OF THE WILD • 1954 • Graham Frank • DOC • USA
CHALLENGE OF YOUNG BRUCE LEE • HKG
CHALLENGE: SCIENCE AGAINST CANCER • 1950 • Parker Morten • DOC • CND
CHALLENGE: THE CANADIAN ROCKIES • 1981 • Shatalow Peter • CND
CHALLENGE THE NINJA • 1986 • Ho Godfrey • HKG
CHALLENGE TO BE FREE • 1972 • Garnett Tay, Beebe Ford • USA • MAD TRAPPER OF THE YUKON ○ MAD TRAPPER, THE
CHALLENGE TO LASSIE • 1949 • Thorpe Richard • USA
CHALLENGE TO LIVE see **AI TO HONOHO TO** • 1961
CHALLENGE TO SURVIVE see **LAND OF NO RETURN, THE** • 1975
CHALLENGE TO THE LOGIC OF THINGS • Ogorodnikov Valery • USS
CHALLENGER, THE see **LADY AND GENT** • 1932
CHALLENGERS, THE • 1969 • Martinson Leslie H. • TVM • USA
CHALLENGERS, THE • 1978 • Pearson Peter • DSS • CND
CHALLENGING GHOST, THE see **GEKKO KAMEN** • 1959
CHALTI KA NAAM GADDI • 1958 • *Burman S. D. (M)* • IND
CHALUMEAU • 1920 • Saidreau Robert • SER • FRN
CHALUMEAU SERRURIER PAR AMOUR • 1922 • Monca Georges • FRN
CHALUTZIM see **SABRA** • 1934
CHAMADE, LA • 1968 • Cavalier Alain • FRN, ITL • HEARTBEAT
CHAMAK CHANDNI • 1959 • Vyas Manibhai • IND
CHAMALEON, DAS • 1920 • Muller-Hagen Carl • FRG

CHAMAS NO CAFEZAL • 1954 • Burle Jose Carlos • BRZ • FLAMES OVER THE CAFEZAL
CHAMBER HARMONY see **KOMORNI HARMONIE** • 1963
CHAMBER MYSTERY, THE • 1920 • Schomer Abraham S. • USA
CHAMBER OF FEAR see **FEAR CHAMBER, THE** • 1968
CHAMBER OF FORGETFULNESS • 1912 • *Francis Alec B.* • USA
CHAMBER OF HORROR (USA) see **DOOR WITH SEVEN LOCKS, THE** • 1940
CHAMBER OF HORRORS • *Bowers Charles (P)* • ANS • USA
CHAMBER OF HORRORS • 1929 • Summers Walter • UKN
CHAMBER OF HORRORS • 1966 • Averback Hy • USA
CHAMBER OF HORRORS see **HOUSE OF FRANKENSTEIN** • 1945
CHAMBER OF TORTURES, THE see **ORRORI DEL CASTELLO DI NORIMBERGA, GLI** • 1972
CHAMBERLAIN, THE see **KAMMARJUNKAREN** • 1914
CHAMBERS, TRACKS AND GESTURES (1931-78) • 1982 • Walker John • DOC • CND
CHAMBRE 13 • 1940 • Hugon Andre • FRN
CHAMBRE 17 • Ducrest Philippe • FRN
CHAMBRE, LA • 1966 • Antoine Jean • ANS • BLG • ROOM, THE
CHAMBRE, LA • 1972 • Akerman Chantal • BLG
CHAMBRE A PART • 1989 • Cukier Jackie • FRN
CHAMBRE ARDENTE, LA • 1961 • Duvivier Julien • FRN, ITL, FRG • PECCATORI DELLA FORESTA NERA, I (ITL) ○ BRENNENDE GERICHT, DAS (FRG) ○ CURSE AND THE COFFIN, THE (UKN) ○ BURNING COURT, THE
CHAMBRE BLANCHE, LA • 1969 • Lefebvre Jean-Pierre • CND • HOUSE OF LIGHT, THE
CHAMBRE DES PHANTASMES, LA • 1979 • Senecal Jean-Michel • FRN
CHAMBRE D'HOTEL (FRN) see **CAMERA D'ALBERGO** • 1980
CHAMBRE EN VILLE, UNE • 1982 • Demy Jacques • FRN • ROOM IN TOWN, A
CHAMBRE ENSORCELEE, LA • 1911 • Cohl Emile • ANS • FRN • AUTOMATIC MOVING CO., THE
CHAMBRE OBSCURE, LA (FRN) see **LAUGHTER IN THE DARK** • 1969
CHAMBRE ROUGE, LA • 1973 • Berckmans Jean-Pierre • BLG
CHAMBRE VERTE, LA • 1978 • Truffaut Francois • FRN • GREEN ROOM, THE (USA)
CHAMELEON • 1960 • Heyer John • SHT • ASL
CHAMELEON • 1978 • Jost Jon • USA
CHAMELEON MAN, THE see **HOMME PROTEE, L'** • 1899
CHAMELEONS, THE see **KAMELEONTERNA** • 1970
CHAMP, THE • 1931 • *Terry Paul/ Moser Frank (P)* • ANS • USA
CHAMP, THE • 1931 • Vidor King • USA
CHAMP, THE • 1974 • Bedel Jean-Pierre • MTV • USA
CHAMP, THE • 1979 • Zeffirelli Franco • USA
CHAMP, THE see **BE YOURSELF!** • 1930
CHAMP D'ACTION • 1965 • Lavoie Richard • DCS • CND
CHAMP DE LIN, LE see **VLASCHAARD, DE** • 1983
CHAMP D'HONNEUR • 1987 • Denis Jean-Pierre • FRN
CHAMP DU POSSIBLE, LE • 1962 • Toublanc-Michel Bernard • SHT • FRN
CHAMP FOR A DAY • 1953 • Seiter William A. • USA
CHAMP MAUDIT, LE see **ESPOIRS** • 1940
CHAMPAGNE • 1928 • Hitchcock Alfred • UKN
CHAMPAGNE CHARLIE • 1936 • Tinling James • USA
CHAMPAGNE CHARLIE • 1944 • Cavalcanti Alberto • UKN
CHAMPAGNE CHARLIE see **NIGHT OUT, A** • 1915
CHAMPAGNE DETECTIVE, THE • 1914 • *De Forrest Charles* • USA
CHAMPAGNE FOR BREAKFAST • 1935 • Brown Melville • USA
CHAMPAGNE FOR BREAKFAST see **TALK NAUGHTY TO ME** • 1981
CHAMPAGNE FOR CAESAR • 1950 • Whorf Richard • USA
CHAMPAGNE FOR TWO see **SHADES OF LOVE: CHAMPAGNE FOR TWO** • 1987
CHAMPAGNE MURDERS, THE (USA) see **SCANDALE, LE** • 1966
CHAMPAGNE MUSIC • 1946 • Cowan Will • SHT • USA
CHAMPAGNE MUSIC OF LAWRENCE WELK AND HIS ORCHESTRA • 1949 • Cowan Will • SHT • USA
CHAMPAGNE ROSE IS DEAD • 1970 • Floyd Calvin • SWD, NTH, UKN
CHAMPAGNE WALTZ • 1937 • Sutherland A. Edward • USA
CHAMPAGNEGALOPPEN • 1938 • Schneevoigt George • DNM
CHAMPAGNEGALOPPEN • 1974 • Becker Vernon P. • SWD, DNM, UKN
CHAMPAGNER • 1929 • von Bolvary Geza • AUS, UKN • BRIGHT EYES
CHAMPEEN, THE • 1922 • McGowan Robert • SHT • USA
CHAMPI-TORTU • 1918 • de Baroncelli Jacques • FRN
CHAMPIGNOL MAIGRE LUI • 1913 • *Aubrey Madeleine* • FRN
CHAMPIGNOL MAIGRE LUI • 1933 • Ellis Fred • FRN
CHAMPIGNON, LE • 1970 • Simenon Marc • FRN
CHAMPION • 1949 • Robson Mark • USA
CHAMPION • 1972 • Chien Lung • HKG
CHAMPION see **SHORISHA** • 1957
CHAMPION, THE • 1913 • Lehrman Henry • USA
CHAMPION, THE • 1915 • Chaplin Charles • USA • CHAMPION CHARLIE ○ BATTLING CHARLIE
CHAMPION, THE • 1990 • Bostan Elisabeta • RMN, CND
CHAMPION, THE see **CHINURARETA OJA** • 1968
CHAMPION BABY • 1917 • *Mckee Raymond* • USA
CHAMPION BEAR SLAYER, THE • 1914 • Martin E. A. • USA
CHAMPION CHARLIE see **CHAMPION, THE** • 1915
CHAMPION CHUMP • 1966 • Kuwahara Bob • ANS • USA
CHAMPION DU JEU A LA MODE, LE • 1910 • Cohl Emile • ANS • FRN • SOLVING THE PUZZLE
CHAMPION DU REGIMENT, LE • 1932 • Wulschleger Henry • FRN
CHAMPION LASSO THROWER • 1894 • *Edison* • USA
CHAMPION LIER, THE • 1920 • Gibson Ed Hoot • SHT • USA
CHAMPION LOSER, A • 1920 • Reisner Charles F. • SHT • USA
CHAMPION OF BOXERS, THE • 1975 • Aloni R. H. • HKG
CHAMPION OF DEATH • 1976 • Yamaguchi Kazuhiko • JPN
CHAMPION OF JUSTICE, THE • 1944 • Davis Mannie • ANS • USA
CHAMPION OF LOST CAUSES • 1925 • Bennett Chester • USA
CHAMPION OF THE LAW, A • 1917 • *Boardman True* • SHT • USA
CHAMPION OF THE RACE, THE • 1910 • *Pathe* • USA
CHAMPION ON FIRE see **NINJA OPERATION 8: CHAMPION ON FIRE** • 1988
CHAMPION PROCESS SERVER, THE • 1915 • Ransom Charles • USA
CHAMPION WOMAN GAMBLER, THE see **ONNA TOBAKUSHI ZETSUENJO** • 1968
CHAMPIONNAT DE SKI NAUTIQUE A BEYROUTH • 1956 • Nasser George • SHT • LBN
CHAMPIONS • 1983 • Irvin John • UKN
CHAMPIONS, THE • 1978 • Brittain Don • CND
CHAMPIONS: A LOVE STORY • 1979 • Alonzo John A. • TVM • USA
CHAMPIONS DE FRANCE • 1938 • Rozier Willy • FRN
CHAMPIONS JUNIORS • 1950 • Blondy Pierre • SHT • FRN
CHAMPIONS OF JUSTICE RETURN, THE see **VUELVEN LOS CAMPEONES JUSTICIEROS** • 1972
CHAMPIONSHIP SEASON, THE see **THAT CHAMPIONSHIP SEASON** • 1982
CHAMPIONSHIP WRESTLING • 1932 • Sparling Gordon • DCS • CND
CHAMPLAIN • 1963 • Arcand Denys • SHT • CND
CHAMPS D'HONNEUR see **FIELDS OF SACRIFICE** • 1963
CHAMPS-ELYSEES • 1928 • Lods Jean • SHT • FRN
CHAMS • 1985 • Sefraoui Najib • MRC
CHAM'S BLOW see **DARBET CHAMS** • 1978
CHAMUNDESWARI • 1937 • Roy Drupad • IND • GODDESS DURGA
CHAN IS MISSING • 1982 • Wang Wayne • USA
CHAN MAHI • 1957 • Pasha A. K. • PKS
CHANBARA FUFU • 1930 • Naruse Mikio • JPN • MR. AND MRS. SWORDPLAY
CHANCE see **CHANS** • 1962
CHANCE, A see **SZANSA** • 1970
CHANCE, LA • 1931 • Guissart Rene • FRN
CHANCE, THE • 1979 • Falk Feliks • PLN
CHANCE, THE see **SZANSA** • 1980
CHANCE, THE see **PRZYPADEK** • 1982
CHANCE AT HEAVEN • 1933 • Seiter William A. • USA
CHANCE AT HEAVEN see **KEY TO HARMONY** • 1935
CHANCE DECEPTION, A • 1913 • Cabanne W. Christy • USA
CHANCE D'ETRE FEMME, LA (FRN) see **FORTUNA DI ESSERE DONNA, LA** • 1956
CHANCE ET L'AMOUR, LA • 1964 • Berri Claude, Bitsch Charles L., Chabrol Claude, Tavernier Bertrand, Schlumberger Eric • FRN, ITL
CHANCE IN A MILLION (UKN) see **ONE CHANCE IN A MILLION** • 1927
CHANCE IN LIFE, A • 1914 • *Lubin* • USA
CHANCE MARKET, THE • 1916 • Baggot King • SHT • USA
CHANCE MEETING • 1936 • Savchenko Igor • USS
CHANCE MEETING see **YURAKUCHO DE AIMASHO** • 1958
CHANCE MEETING see **PRVNI DEN MEHO SYNA** • 1964
CHANCE MEETING see **YOUNG LOVERS, THE** • 1964
CHANCE MEETING (USA) see **YOUNG LOVERS, THE** • 1954
CHANCE MEETING (USA) see **BLIND DATE** • 1959
CHANCE OF A LIFETIME • 1950 • Miles Bernard, Osbiston Alan • UKN
CHANCE OF A LIFETIME, THE • 1916 • Phillips Bertram • UKN
CHANCE OF A LIFETIME, THE • 1943 • Castle William • USA
CHANCE OF A NIGHT TIME, THE • 1931 • Wilcox Herbert, Lynn Ralph • UKN
CHANCE SHOT, A • 1911 • Hartigan P. C. • USA
CHANCE SHOT, THE • 1912 • Salter Harry • USA
CHANCE THE IDOL see **SPIELERIN, DIE** • 1927
CHANCE TO LIVE, A • 1978 • Allen Corey • TVM • USA
CHANCES • 1931 • Dwan Allan • USA
CHANCES ARE • 1988 • Ardolino Emile • USA • LIFE AFTER LIFE
'CHAND D'HABITS • 1897 • Alexandre M. • BLG
CHAND PAR CHADAYEE • 1967 • Sundaram T. P. • IND • TRIP TO THE MOON
CHAND-SADAGAR • 1934 • Roy Prafulla • IND
CHANDAMARUTHA • 1976 • Reddy Pattabhi Rama, Cowan Tom • IND • WILD WIND
CHANDAN KA PALNA • 1967 • Memon Ismail • IND • SANDALWOOD CRADLE
CHANDI SONA • 1977 • *Kapoor Raj* • IND
CHANDIDAS • 1932 • Bose Debaki • IND
CHANDIGARH see **VIE A CHANDIGARH, LA** • 1966
CHANDLER • 1971 • Magwood Paul • USA
CHANDNI • 1989 • Chopra Yash • IND
CHANDNI CHOWK • 1955 • Chopra B. R. • IND
CHANDRA KESHAR • 1947 • Bose Debaki • IND
CHANDRA SENA • 1935 • Shantaram Victor • IND
CHANDRAHA • 1915 • Phalke Dada • IND
CHANDRASENA • 1959 • Mistry Babhubhai • IND
CHANDU • 1939 • *Malayan Films Inc.* • MLY
CHANDU AND THE MAGIC ISLE see **CHANDU ON THE MAGIC ISLAND** • 1935
CHANDU ON THE MAGIC ISLAND • 1935 • Taylor Ray • USA • CHANDU AND THE MAGIC ISLE
CHANDU THE MAGICIAN • 1932 • Menzies William Cameron, Varnel Marcel • USA
CHANEL SOLITAIRE • 1981 • Kaczender George • USA, FRN
CHANG • 1927 • Cooper Merian C., Schoedsack Ernest B. • USA
CHANG AND THE LAW • 1920 • Harbaugh Carl • USA
CHANG-JEN MEN • 1983 • Liu Chia-Liang • HKG • LADY IS THE BOSS, THE
CHANG-PEI • 1981 • Liu Chia-Liang • HKG • MY YOUNG AUNTIE ○ MY AUNTIE
CHANGBAGGE JAMSUGYOGA BOINDA • 1985 • Song Yeong-Su • SKR • BRIDGE BEYOND, THE
CHANGE, THE see **CAMBIO, EL** • 1971
CHANGE FOR A SOVEREIGN • 1937 • Elvey Maurice • UKN
CHANGE FOR THE BETTER, A • 1915 • Louis Will • USA
CHANGE HEART, A • 1910 • *Lubin* • USA
CHANGE IN ADMINISTRATION, A • 1913 • Kirkland David • USA
CHANGE IN BAGGAGE CHECKS, A • 1914 • Baker George D. • USA
CHANGE IN LIFE, A see **MUDAR DE VIDA** • 1967
CHANGE IN LOVERS, A • 1915 • Blystone John G. • USA
CHANGE IN THE MARITIMES, A • 1966 • Spry Robin • DOC • CND
CHANGE OF BUSINESS, A • 1914 • Seay Charles M. • USA
CHANGE OF COMPLEXION • 1909 • *Powers* • USA
CHANGE OF COMPLEXION • 1914 • *Crystal* • USA
CHANGE OF DESTINY • 1987 • Muratova Kira • USS
CHANGE OF HABIT • 1969 • Graham William A. • USA
CHANGE OF HEART • 1934 • Blystone John G. • USA
CHANGE OF HEART • 1938 • Tinling James • USA • HEADLINE HUNTRESS
CHANGE OF HEART • 1951 • Whale Peter • UKN
CHANGE OF HEART • 1984 • Wheeler Anne • MTV • CND
CHANGE OF HEART see **HIT PARADE OF 1943** • 1943
CHANGE OF HEART, A • 1909 • Griffith D. W. • USA
CHANGE OF HEART, A • 1914 • *Bergen Thurlow* • USA
CHANGE OF HEART, A • 1916 • *Pathe* • USA
CHANGE OF HEART, A • 1916 • Kent Leon D. • *Lubin* • SHT • USA
CHANGE OF HEART, A • 1982 • Taylor Don • TVM • USA
CHANGE OF HEART, A see **TWO AND TWO MAKE SIX** • 1962
CHANGE OF LUCK, A • 1915 • *Ovey George* • USA
CHANGE OF MIND • 1969 • Stevens Robert • USA, CND
CHANGE OF SEASONS, A • 1980 • Black Noel, Lang Richard • USA
CHANGE OF SEX see **CAMBIO DE SEXO** • 1977
CHANGE OF SPIRIT, A • 1912 • Griffith D. W. • USA
CHANGE OF STRIPES, A • 1912 • *Pollard Harry* • USA
CHANGE PARTNERS • 1965 • Lynn Robert • UKN
CHANGE PAS DE MAIN • 1975 • Vecchiali Paul • FRN
CHANGE THE NEEDLE • 1925 • Roach Hal • SHT • USA
CHANGED IDENTITY • 1941 • Rowland Roy • SHT • USA
CHANGED LIVES • 1915 • Turner Otis • USA
CHANGEFUL REVENGE see **ADAUCHI SOMATO** • 1927
CHANGELING 2: THE REVENGE • 1988 • Bava Lamberto
CHANGELING, THE • 1913 • *Thanhouser Kid* • USA
CHANGELING, THE • 1914 • Terwilliger George W. • USA
CHANGELING, THE • 1928 • Malins Geoffrey H. • UKN
CHANGELING, THE • 1980 • Medak Peter • CND
CHANGEMENTS? PARLONS-EN see **CHANGES, LET'S TALK ABOUT THEM** • 1971
CHANGES • 1969 • Bartlett Hall • USA
CHANGES • 1970 • Damiano Gerard • USA
CHANGES • 1971 • Owen Don • CND
CHANGES see **PREMENY** • 1966
CHANGES, THE see **PARIVARTAN**
CHANGES, CHANGES • 1974 • Deitch Gene • USA, CZC
CHANGES IN THE FRANCHISE • 1937 • Jones Andrew Miller • UKN
CHANGES IN THE VILLAGE see **GAMPERILAYA** • 1964
CHANGES, LET'S TALK ABOUT THEM • 1971 • Blais Roger • DOC • CND • CHANGEMENTS? PARLONS-EN
CHANGGUN UI SUYUM • 1968 • Lee Sungkoo • SKR • BEARDED GENERAL
CHANGING CLOUDS see **VALTOZO FELHOZET** • 1967
CHANGING COOKS • 1911 • Melies Gaston • USA
CHANGING COUNTRYSIDE, THE see **GAMPERILAYA** • 1964
CHANGING EARTH, THE see **AARDOLIE** • 1953
CHANGING HARVEST, THE • 1954 • Swingler Humphrey • UKN
CHANGING HORIZON see **BADLINDO AAKASH** • 1982
CHANGING HUSBANDS • 1924 • Urson Frank, Iribe Paul • USA
CHANGING LIFE see **MUDAR DE VIDA** • 1967
CHANGING OF SILAS WARNER, THE • 1911 • *Vitagraph* • USA
CHANGING OF THE GUARD see **ZMIANA WARTY** • 1958
CHANGING SKY, THE see **BADIDI AAKASH**
CHANGING SKYLINE, THE • 1964 • Dayan Michael Shah • SHT • UKN
CHANGING THE NEEDLE • 1982 • Ansara Martha • DOC • ASL
CHANGING TIME see **VALTOZO IDOK** • 1978
CHANGING TRAINS see **OMBYTE AV TAG** • 1943
CHANGING VILLAGE PART 2 see **KALIYUGAYA** • 1982
CHANGING WHEATBELT, THE • 1968 • Koenig Joseph • CND
CHANGING WOMAN, THE • 1918 • Smith David • USA
CHANGING YEAR, THE • 1932 • Field Mary • UKN
CHANGING YEARS, THE • 1958 • Sharp Don • DOC • UKN
CHANGLE, EL • 1980 • MXC
CHANLER RAO, CRIMINAL EXPERT • 1914 • Finley Ned • USA
CHANNEL CROSSING • 1933 • Rosmer Milton • UKN
CHANNEL INCIDENT • 1940 • Asquith Anthony • UKN
CHANNEL ONE • 1988 • Alix Steve, Brady David • USA
CHANNING OF THE NORTHWEST • 1922 • Ince Ralph • USA
CHANNINGS, THE • 1920 • Collins Edwin J. • UKN
CHANOC • 1966 • Gonzalez Rogelio A. • MXC • AVENTURAS DE MAR Y SELVA
CHANOC CONTRA EL TIGRE Y EL VAMPIRO • 1971 • Martinez Solares Gilberto • MXC • CHANOC VS. THE TIGER AND THE VAMPIRE
CHANOC EN EL FOSO DE LAS SERPIENTES • 1974 • *Cinema Ra* • MXC
CHANOC VS. LOS DEVORADORES DE HOMBRES • 1971 • *Tele Talia* • MXC
CHANOC VS. THE TIGER AND THE VAMPIRE see **CHANOC CONTRA EL TIGRE Y EL VAMPIRO** • 1971
CHANOINE LIONEL GROULX, HISTORIEN #1 & 2 • 1959 • Patry Pierre • DCS • CND
CHANS • 1962 • Hellstrom Gunnar • SWD • JUST ONCE MORE ○ CHANCE
CHANSON D'AMOUR • 1934 • Epstein Jean • FRN
CHANSON DE LA MORT • 1973 • Marzouk Said • SHT • EGY • SONG OF DEATH
CHANSON DE L'ADIEU, LA • 1934 • Valentin Albert, von Bolvary Geza • FRN • AMOUR DE FREDERIC CHOPIN, UN ○ VALSE DE L'ADIEU, LA
CHANSON DE L'AMOUR, LA see **DERNIERE BERCEUSE, LA** • 1930
CHANSON DE ROLAND, LA • 1959 • Clarence Michel • FRN
CHANSON DE ROLAND, LA • 1979 • Cassenti Frank • FRN
CHANSON DE RUE • 1945 • Sevestre • SHT • FRN

CHANSON DES NATIONS, LA • 1930 • Gleize Maurice, Meinert Rudolf • FRN
CHANSON DES PEUPLIERS, LA • 1931 • Epstein Jean • FRN
CHANSON DU FEU, LA • 1918 • Monca Georges • FRN
CHANSON DU JARDINIER FOU, LA • 1960 • Lepeuve Monique • ANM • FRN • MAD GARDENER'S SONG, THE
CHANSON DU JARDINIER FOU, LA • 1962 • Lecat & Espagne • ANS • FRN
CHANSON DU LIN, LA • 1931 • Monca Georges • FRN
CHANSON DU MAL AIME, LA (FRN) see **PISEN NEMILOVA-NEHO** • 1982
CHANSON DU PAVE, LA • 1951 • Gerard • SHT • FRN
CHANSON DU SOUVENIR, LA • 1936 • de Poligny Serge, Sirk Douglas • FRN • CONCERT A LA COUR ○ SONG OF REMEMBRANCE
CHANSON DU VOYAGEUR, LA • 1958 • Cauvin Andre • BLG
CHANSON D'UNE NUIT, LA • 1932 • Litvak Anatole • FRN
CHANSON POUR JULIE • 1976 • Vallee Jacques • CND
CHANSON POUR TOI, UNE see **TOUT POUR L'AMOUR** • 1933
CHANSON QUI TUE, LA see **SOMBRE DIMANCHE** • 1948
CHANSON SUR LE PASSAGE see **UGHNIA 'ALA AL-MAMARR** • 1972
CHANSON TRISTE • 1917 • Tallroth Konrad • SWD
CHANSONS CREOLES see **TROPICAL LAMENT** • 1950
CHANSONS DE PARIS • 1934 • de Baroncelli Jacques • FRN
CHANSONS SANS PAROLES • 1958 • Gross Aline, Gross Yoram • ANS • ISR • SONGS WITHOUT WORDS
CHANSONS S'ENVOLENT, LES • 1947-51 • Verneuil Henri • SHT • FRN
CHANT D'AMOUR, UN • 1950 • Genet Jean • FRN
CHANT DE LA FORET, LE see **CRY OF THE WILD** • 1972
CHANT DE LA MINE ET DU FEU, LE • 1931 • Benoit-Levy Jean • FRN
CHANT DE L'AMOUR, LE • 1935 • Roudes Gaston • FRN • FEMMES DEVANT L'AMOUR, LES
CHANT DE L'AMOUR TRIOMPHANT, LE • 1923 • Tourjansky Victor • FRN
CHANT DE L'EXILE, LE • 1942 • Hugon Andre • FRN
CHANT DES ONDES, LE • 1943 • Leenhardt Roger • DCS • FRN
CHANT DES SIRENES, LE see **I'VE HEARD THE MERMAIDS SINGING** • 1987
CHANT DU DEPART, LE • 1975 • Aubier Pascal • FRN
CHANT DU DESTIN, LE • 1933 • Legrand Jean-Rene • FRN
CHANT DU MARIN, LE • 1931 • Gallone Carmine • FRN
CHANT DU MONDE, LE • 1965 • Camus Marcel • FRN
CHANT DU STYRENE, LE • 1958 • Resnais Alain • SHT • FRN
CHANT IMMORTEL see **LAH NAL-KHULUD** • 1952
CHANT OF JIMMY BLACKSMITH, THE • 1978 • Schepisi Fred • ASL
CHANTAGE • 1955 • Lefranc Guy • FRN • LOWEST CRIME, THE
CHANTAGE see **LAN ATARIF** • 1961
CHANTAJE • 1945 • Obregon Antonio • SPN
CHANTAJE A UN ASESINO • 1966 • Eguiluz Enrique L. • SPN
CHANTAJE A UN TORERO • 1963 • Gil Rafael • SPN
CHANTAL • 1968 • Lindus Allan • USA
CHANTAL EN VRAC • 1967 • Leduc Jacques • DOC • CND
CHANTAS, LOS • 1975 • Suarez Jose Martinez • ARG • PHONIES, THE
CHANTE ET DANSE • 1944 • Tessier Albert • DCS • CND • FOLK-LORE
CHANTE JEUNESSE • 1948 • Blais Roger • DCS • CND
CHANTECOQ • 1916 • Pouctal Henri • FRN • COEUR DE FRANCAISE
CHANTELOUVE • 1922 • Monca Georges (c/d) • FRN
CHANTEUR DE MEXICO, LE • 1956 • Pottier Richard • FRN, SPN
CHANTEUR DE MINUIT, LE • 1937 • Joannon Leo • FRN
CHANTEUR DE SEVILLE, LE • 1930 • Noe Yvan, Novarro Ramon • FRN • SEVILLE DE MES AMOURS
CHANTEUR INCONNU, LE • 1931 • Tourjansky Victor • FRN
CHANTEUR INCONNU, LE • 1946 • Cayatte Andre • FRN
CHANTEUSE, THE see **SCIANTOSA, LA** • 1970
CHANTICLER HAT, A • 1910 • Fitzhamon Lewin? • UKN
CHANTIER • 1954 • Bail Rene • CND
CHANTIER • 1957-67 • Bail Rene • CND
CHANTIER COOPERATIF • 1955 • Palardy Jean • DCS • CND
CHANTIER EN RUINES, LE • 1945 • Leenhardt Roger • DCS • FRN
CHANTONS MAINTENANT • 1956 • Jutra Claude • DCS • CND
CHANTONS NOEL • 1948 • Ladouceur Jean-Paul • ANS • CND
CHANTONS QUAND MEME • 1939 • Caron Pierre • FRN
CHANTONS SOUS L'OCCUPATION • 1976 • Halimi Andre • DOC • FRN
CHANTS • 1975 • Winkler Paul • ASL
CHANTS CORPORELS • 1973 • Chabot Jean • DCS • FRN
CHANTS DE MON AMOUR, LES see **ANGHAM HABIBY** • 1959
CHANTS ET DANSES DU MONDE ANIME -LE METRO see **SONGS AND DANCES OF THE INANIMATE WORLD -THE SUBWAY** • 1986
CHANTS RETROUVES, LES • 1948 • Breteuil • SHT • FRN
CHAO AMOR • 1968 • Santillan Diego • ARG, CHL
CHAO BRUTO • 1959 • de Azevedo Dionizio • BRZ
CH'AO-CHI SHIH-MIN • 1985 • Wan Jen • TWN • SUPER CITIZEN
CHAOCHOW GUY • 1972 • Tie Hang • HKG
CHAOS AM GOTTHARD • 1988 • Egger Urs • SWT
CHAOS BY DESIGN see **LIAN'AI MIYU** • 1987
CHAP' LA • 1978 • Lara Christian • FRN
CHAPAGUA (FRN) see **ORO DEI BRAVADOS, L'** • 1970
CHAPAYEV • 1935 • Vasiliev Sergei, Vasiliev Georgi • USS
CHAPAYEV IS WITH US • 1941 • Petrov Vladimir • USS
CHAPEAU, LE • 1965 • Chabot Jean • SHT • CND
CHAPEAU, LE • 1975 • M'Bala Gnoan • IVC
CHAPEAU A SURPRISES, LE • 1901 • Melies Georges • FRN • HAT WITH MANY SURPRISES, THE (USA)
CHAPEAU DE MAX, LE • 1913 • Linder Max • FRN
CHAPEAU DE PAILLE D'ITALIE, UN • 1927 • Clair Rene • FRN • ITALIAN STRAW HAT, THE ○ HORSE ATE THE HAT, THE
CHAPEAU DE PAILLE D'ITALIE, UN • 1940 • Cammage Maurice • FRN
CHAPEAU MAGIQUE, LE • 1903 • Velle Gaston • FRN • MAGIC HAT, THE (USA)
CHAPEAUX A TRANSFORMATIONS • 1895 • Lumiere Louis • FRN • TREWEY: UNDER THE HAT
CHAPEAUX DES BELLES DAMES, LES • 1909 • Cohl Emile • ANS • FRN
CHAPEL, THE see **CHAPPELLE, LA** • 1980
CHAPERON, THE • 1912 • *Reeves Edith* • USA
CHAPERON, THE • 1916 • Berthelet Arthur • USA
CHAPERON GETS A DUCKING, THE • 1912 • *Brennan John E.* • USA
CHAPERONE, THE • 1909 • *Essanay* • USA
CHAPERONE, THE • 1912 • Kinder Stuart? • UKN
CHAPERONES, THE • 1912 • *Champion* • USA
CHAPERONS • 1929 • Newfield Sam • SHT • USA
CHAPITEAU • 1984 • Flutsch Johannes • SWT
CHAPLET OF PEARLS, THE • 1913 • Martinek H. O. • UKN
CHAPLIE CHARLIN SPECIAL CONSTABLE • 1915 • *Hatton Leslie* • UKN
CHAPLIN REVUE, THE • 1960 • Chaplin Charles • CMP • USA
CHAPLINESQUE, MY LIFE AND HARD TIMES • 1972 • Hurwitz Harry • USA
CHAPLIN'S ART OF COMEDY • 1966 • *Sherman Samuel M. (P)* • CMP • USA
CHAPMAN REPORT, THE • 1962 • Cukor George • USA
CHAPPAQUA • 1967 • Rooks Conrad • USA
CHAPPELLE, LA • 1980 • Tchissoukou Jean-Michel • CNG • CHAPEL, THE
CHAPPIE AT THE WELL, THE • 1904 • *Paul R. W.* • UKN
CHAPPIE THE CHAPERONE • 1912 • *Cumpson John* • USA
CHAPPIE'S CODE • 1913 • *Fraser Harry* • USA
CHAPPY -THAT'S ALL • 1924 • Bentley Thomas • UKN
CHAPTER AND VERSE • 1936 • Hawes Stanley • UKN
CHAPTER IN HER LIFE, A • 1923 • Weber Lois • USA • JEWEL
CHAPTER TWO • 1979 • Moore Robert • USA
CHAPTERS ABOUT THE HUMAN BRAIN • 1966 • Somlo Tamas • SHT • HNG
CHAQUE JOUR A SON SECRET • 1958 • Boissol Claude • FRN
CHAQUE MINUTE COMPTE • 1959 • Bibal Robert • FRN
CHAQUE MINUTE COMPTE see **ASSASSINS DU DIMANCHE, LES** • 1956
CHAR ANKHEN • 1944 • *Biswas Anil (M)* • IND
CHAR CERVESH • 1964 • Wadia Homi • IND
CHAR DIL CHAR RAHEN • 1959 • Abbas Khwaya Ahmad • IND • FOUR FACES OF INDIA (UKN)
CHAR DOST • 1956 • Bose Nitin • IND • FOUR FRIENDS
CHARACTER RETRIEVED, A • 1905 • *Gaumont* • UKN
CHARACTER WOMAN, THE • 1914 • *Stuart Julia* • USA
CHARADE • 1952 • Kellino Roy • USA
CHARADE • 1963 • Donen Stanley • USA
CHARADE • 1983 • Minnis Jon • ANM • CND
CHARADE see **SZARADA** • 1977
CHARADE CHINOISE • 1986 • Leduc Jacques • MTV • CND
CHARAN KAVI MUKUNDADAS • 1968 • Choudhury Nirmal • IND • POET MUKUNDADAS, THE
CHARANDAS CHOR • 1975 • Benegal Shyam • IND • CHARANDAS THE THIEF
CHARANDAS THE THIEF see **CHARANDAS CHOR** • 1975
CHARBONNIER, LE see **FAHHAM, AL-** • 1972
CHARCOAL DIGGER, THE • 1956 • Espinosa Julio Garcia • CUB
CHARCOAL MAN'S RECEPTION, THE see **ARLEQUIN ET CHARBONNIER** • 1897
CHARCOAL SKETCHES see **SZKICE WEGLEM** • 1957
CHARCUTERIE MECANIQUE • 1895 • Lumiere Louis • FRN • MECHANICAL BUTCHER, THE
CHARCUTIER DE MACHONVILLE, LE • 1946 • Ivernel Vicky • FRN
CHARDONS DU BARAGAN, LES (FRN) see **CIULINII BARAGANULUI** • 1957
CHARGE AT FEATHER RIVER, THE • 1953 • Douglas Gordon • USA
CHARGE IS MURDER, THE (UKN) see **TWILIGHT OF HONOR** • 1963
CHARGE IT • 1921 • Garson Harry • USA
CHARGE IT TO ME • 1919 • Neill R. William • USA
CHARGE OF BOER CAVALRY • 1900 • Porter Edwin S. • USA
CHARGE OF THE BLACK LANCERS (USA) see **LANCIERI NERI, I** • 1963
CHARGE OF THE GAUCHOS, THE • 1928 • Kelley Albert • USA • BEAUTIFUL SPY, THE (UKN)
CHARGE OF THE LANCERS • 1953 • Castle William • USA
CHARGE OF THE LIGHT BRIGADE, THE • 1912 • Dawley J. Searle • USA
CHARGE OF THE LIGHT BRIGADE, THE • 1914 • *Williams Eric* • UKN
CHARGE OF THE LIGHT BRIGADE, THE • 1936 • Curtiz Michael • USA
CHARGE OF THE LIGHT BRIGADE, THE • 1968 • Richardson Tony • UKN
CHARGE OF THE MODEL Ts, THE • 1979 • McCullough Jim • USA
CHARGE OF THE SNOW BRIGADE, THE • 1970 • Potterton Gerald • CND
CHARGE OF THE UHLANS IN THE TEMPLEHOF FELDT - BERLIN • 1895 • Acres Birt • UKN
CHARING CROSS ROAD • 1935 • De Courville Albert • UKN
CHARIOT DE THESPIS, LE • 1941 • Canolle Jean • SHT • FRN
CHARIOTS OF FIRE • 1981 • Hudson Hugh • UKN
CHARIOTS OF THE GODS (UKN) see **ERINNERUNGEN AUS DER ZUKUNFT** • 1969
CHARITABLE DECEPTION, A • 1913 • *Kinemacolor* • USA
CHARITE DU PRESTIDIGITEUR, LA • 1905 • Blache Alice • FRN
CHARITY? • 1916 • Powell Frank • USA
CHARITY • 1919 • Wilson Rex • UKN • SOME ARTIST
CHARITY ANN • 1915 • Elvey Maurice • UKN
CHARITY BALL, THE • 1914 • *Ritchie Franklin* • USA
CHARITY BALL, THE • 1978 • *True Andrea* • USA
CHARITY BEGINS AT HOME • 1916 • *Myers Harry* • USA
CHARITY BEGINS AT HOME • 1977-80 • Zaritsky John • MTV • CND
CHARITY CASTLE • 1917 • Ingraham Lloyd • USA
CHARITY COVERS A MULTITUDE OF SINS • 1905 • Fitzhamon Lewin? • UKN
CHARITY OF THE POOR • 1911 • *Thanhouser* • USA
CHARKH-E-BAZIGAR • 1968 • Khani • IRN • DESTINY
CHARKHI-O-FALAK • 1967 • Rahbar Saber • IRN • SUN AND PLANET WHEEL
CHARLATAN, LE • 1901 • Melies Georges • FRN • PAINLESS DENTISTRY
CHARLATAN, LE see **SAHHAR, AS-** • 1969
CHARLATAN, THE • 1916 • Morgan Sidney • UKN
CHARLATAN, THE • 1929 • Melford George • USA
CHARLATAN, THE see **KURUZSLO, A** • 1917
CHARLATAN, THE see **CHARLATANOS, O** • 1973
CHARLATANOS, O • 1973 • Thalassinos Errikos • GRC • CHARLATAN, THE
CHARLEBOIS • 1970 • Bonniere Rene • DCS • CND
CHARLEMAGNE • 1933 • Colombier Piere • FRN
CHARLENE'S INJUSTICE • 1969 • *Chancellor Films* • USA
CHARLES AND FRANCOIS • 1987 • Hoedeman Co • ANM • CND
CHARLES AND LUCIE (USA) see **CHARLES ET LUCIE** • 1979
CHARLES AUGUSTUS MILVERTON • 1922 • Ridgwell George • UKN
CHARLES CHAPLIN IN A LIBERTY BOND APPEAL see **BOND, THE** • 1918
CHARLES DARWIN • 1960 • Schneiderov Vladimir • DOC • USS
CHARLES, DEAD OR ALIVE (USA) see **CHARLES MORT OU VIE** • 1969
CHARLES & DIANA: A ROYAL LOVE STORY • 1982 • Goldstone James • TVM • USA
CHARLES ET LUCIE • 1979 • Kaplan Nelly • FRN • CHARLES AND LUCIE (USA)
CHARLES FOREST, CURE FONDATEUR • 1959 • Palardy Jean • DCS • CND
CHARLES GAGNON • 1970 • Melancon Andre • DOC • CND
CHARLES LLOYD -JOURNEY WITHIN • 1968 • Sherman Eric • DOC • USA
CHARLES MORT OU VIE • 1969 • Tanner Alain • FRN, SWT • CHARLES, DEAD OR ALIVE (USA)
CHARLES PEACE • 1905 • Haggar William • UKN • LIFE OF CHARLES PEACE, THE
CHARLES PEACE, KING OF CRIMINALS • 1914 • Batley Ernest G. • UKN
CHARLES PERKINS • 1967 • Hannam Ken • DOC • ASL
CHARLES RAY IN A LIBERTY BOND PLEA • 1918 • *Par.* • SHT • USA
CHARLES ROGERS IN THE MOVIE MAN • 1928 • Mayo Archie • SHT • USA
CHARLES TRENET • Ertaud Jacques, Bouteiller Pierre • DOC • FRN
CHARLES XII see **KARL XII** • 1925
CHARLESTON • 1959 • Demicheli Tulio • SPN, MXC
CHARLESTON • 1977 • Fondato Marcello • ITL
CHARLESTON • 1979 • Arthur Karen • TVM • USA
CHARLESTON CHAIN-GANG • 1902 • Porter Edwin S. • USA
CHARLESTON DANCE • 1927 • Johnson S. H. • UKN
CHARLESTON-PARADE see **SUR UN AIR DE CHARLESTON** • 1926
CHARLESTON (USA) see **SUR UN AIR DE CHARLESTON** • 1926
CHARLESTON Y BESOS • 1922 • Barth-Moglia Luis • ARG
CHARLEVOIX ROUTE DES SIECLES • Lavoie Hermenegilde • DCS • CND
CHARLEY • 1918-19 • Sullivan Pat • ASS • USA
CHARLEY • 1946-47 • Halas John, Batchelor Joy • ASS • UKN
CHARLEY • 1964 • Dunning George • ANS • USA
CHARLEY • 1965 • Murakami Jimmy T. • ANS • USA
CHARLEY AND THE ANGEL • 1973 • McEveety Vincent • USA
CHARLEY BUTT see **KARLI KIPPE** • 1962
CHARLEY HANNAH • 1986 • Hunt Peter H. • TVM • USA • CHARLEY HANNAH'S WAR
CHARLEY HANNAH'S WAR see **CHARLEY HANNAH** • 1986
CHARLEY IN THE NEW MINES • 1946-47 • Halas John, Batchelor Joy • ANS • UKN
CHARLEY IN THE NEW SCHOOLS • 1946-47 • Halas John, Batchelor Joy • ANS • UKN
CHARLEY IN THE NEW TOWNS • 1946-47 • Halas John, Batchelor Joy • ANS • UKN • NEW TOWN
CHARLEY IN "YOUR VERY GOOD HEALTH" • 1946-47 • Halas John, Batchelor Joy • ANS • UKN • YOUR VERY GOOD HEALTH
CHARLEY JUNIOR'S SCHOOLDAYS • 1946-47 • Halas John, Batchelor Joy • ANS • UKN
CHARLEY MOON • 1956 • Hamilton Guy • UKN
CHARLEY MY BOY • 1926 • McCarey Leo • SHT • USA
CHARLEY ONE-EYE • 1973 • Chaffey Don • USA, UKN, SPN
CHARLEY SMILER COMPETES IN A CYCLE RACE • 1911 • Aylott Dave • UKN
CHARLEY SMILER IS ROBBED • 1911 • Aylott Dave • UKN • CHARLEY SMILER LOSES HIS WATCH (USA)
CHARLEY SMILER IS STAGE STRUCK • 1911 • Coleby A. E. • UKN • SMILER HAS STAGE FEVER (USA)
CHARLEY SMILER JOINS THE BOY SCOUTS • 1911 • Aylott Dave • UKN
CHARLEY SMILER LOSES HIS WATCH (USA) see **CHARLEY SMILER IS ROBBED** • 1911
CHARLEY SMILER TAKES UP JU-JITSU • 1911 • Aylott Dave • USA
CHARLEY VARRICK • 1973 • Siegel Don • USA
CHARLEY'S AMERICAN AUNT (UKN) see **CHARLEY'S AUNT** • 1941
CHARLEY'S AUNT • 1925 • Sidney Scott • USA, UKN
CHARLEY'S AUNT • 1930 • Christie Al • USA
CHARLEY'S AUNT • 1941 • Mayo Archie • USA • CHARLEY'S AMERICAN AUNT (UKN)
CHARLEY'S AUNT • 1977 • Muir Graeme • MTV • UKN
CHARLEY'S AUNT see **CHARLEYS TANT** • 1926
CHARLEY'S AUNT DRESSED IN A MINI-SKIRT see **TIA DE CARLOS EN MINIFALDA, LA** • 1967
CHARLEY'S (BIG HEARTED) AUNT • 1940 • Forde Walter • UKN
CHARLEY'S HOLIDAY • 1912 • *Eclair* • USA

CHARLEY'S MARCH OF TIME • 1946-47 • Halas John, Batchelor Joy • ANS • UKN
CHARLEYS NICHTEN • 1974 • Boos Walter • FRG • CONFESSIONS OF A WINDOW CLEANER
CHARLEY'S ONKEL • 1969 • Jacobs Werner • FRG • CHARLEY'S UNCLE
CHARLEYS TANT • 1926 • Ellis Elis • SWD • CHARLEY'S AUNT
CHARLEYS TANTE • 1934 • Stemmle R. A. • FRG
CHARLEY'S TANTE • 1956 • Quest Hans • FRG
CHARLEY'S TANTE • 1963 • von Cziffra Geza • FRG
CHARLEY'S TANTE NACKT • 1969 • Terry Norbert • SWT • SEXY DOZEN, THE
CHARLEY'S UNCLE see **CHARLEY'S ONKEL** • 1969
CHARLEY'S WEB • 1986 • Heath Simon • ASL
CHARLIE • 1969 • Lynch Paul • CND
CHARLIE AND A DOG • 1914 • *De Forrest Charles* • USA
CHARLIE AND A HALF • 1973 • Davidson Boaz • ISR
CHARLIE AND CO. • 1964 • Bottcher Jurgen • DOC • GDR
CHARLIE AND THE GREAT BALLOON CHASE • 1981 • Elikann Larry • TVM • USA • CHARLIE'S BALLOON
CHARLIE AND THE HOOKER • 1979 • Summers Emmanuele
CHARLIE AND THE PERFECT LADY see **WOMAN, A** • 1915
CHARLIE AND THE SAUSAGES see **MABEL'S BUSY DAY** • 1914
CHARLIE AND THE TALKING BUZZARD • 1979 • *Penn Christopher* • USA
CHARLIE AND THE UMBRELLA see **BETWEEN SHOWERS** • 1914
CHARLIE AS A MILLIONAIRE see **CALLE SOM MILJONAR** • 1916
CHARLIE AT THE RACES see **GENTLEMEN OF NERVE** • 1914
CHARLIE AT THE SHOW see **NIGHT IN THE SHOW, A** • 1915
CHARLIE AT THE STUDIO see **FILM JOHNNIE, A** • 1914
CHARLIE AT THE SYDNEY SHOW • 1916 • Gavin John F. • SHT • ASL
CHARLIE BARNET AND HIS BAND • 1949 • Skinner Charles • SHT • USA
CHARLIE BARNET AND HIS ORCHASTRA • 1947 • Cowan Will • SHT • USA
CHARLIE BARNET AND HIS ORCHESTRA IN REDSKIN RHUMBA • 1948 • Cowan Will • SHT • USA
CHARLIE BOY • 1982 • Young Robert • UKN
CHARLIE BRAVO • 1980 • Bernard-Aubert Claude • FRN
CHARLIE BUBBLES • 1967 • Finney Albert • UKN
CHARLIE CHAN AND BLACK MAGIC see **CHARLIE CHAN IN BLACK MAGIC** • 1944
CHARLIE CHAN AND THE CURSE OF THE DRAGON QUEEN • 1981 • Donner Clive • USA
CHARLIE CHAN AND THE JADE MASK see **JADE MASK, THE** • 1945
CHARLIE CHAN AND THE SCARLET CLUE see **SCARLET CLUE, THE** • 1945
CHARLIE CHAN AT MONTE CARLO • 1937 • Forde Eugene J. • USA
CHARLIE CHAN AT THE CIRCUS • 1936 • Lachman Harry • USA
CHARLIE CHAN AT THE OLYMPICS • 1937 • Humberstone H. Bruce • USA
CHARLIE CHAN AT THE OPERA • 1936 • Humberstone H. Bruce • USA
CHARLIE CHAN AT THE RACE TRACK • 1936 • Humberstone H. Bruce • USA
CHARLIE CHAN AT THE WAX MUSEUM • 1940 • Shores Lynn • USA
CHARLIE CHAN AT TREASURE ISLAND • 1939 • Foster Norman • USA
CHARLIE CHAN CARRIES ON • 1931 • MacFadden Hamilton • USA
CHARLIE CHAN (HAPPINESS IS A WARM CLUE) • 1971 • Martinson Leslie H. • TVM • USA • RETURN OF CHARLIE CHAN
CHARLIE CHAN IN BLACK MAGIC • 1944 • Rosen Phil • USA • CHARLIE CHAN IN THE MURDER CHAMBER ○ MEETING AT MIDNIGHT ○ BLACK MAGIC ○ MURDER CHAMBER, THE ○ CHARLIE CHAN AND BLACK MAGIC
CHARLIE CHAN IN CITY IN DARKNESS • 1939 • Leeds Herbert I. • USA • CITY IN DARKNESS
CHARLIE CHAN IN EGYPT • 1935 • King Louis • USA
CHARLIE CHAN IN HONOLULU • 1938 • Humberstone H. Bruce • USA
CHARLIE CHAN IN LONDON • 1934 • Forde Eugene J. • USA
CHARLIE CHAN IN MURDER OVER NEW YORK see **MURDER OVER NEW YORK** • 1940
CHARLIE CHAN IN PANAMA • 1940 • Foster Norman • USA
CHARLIE CHAN IN PARIS • 1935 • Seiler Lewis • USA
CHARLIE CHAN IN RENO • 1939 • Foster Norman • USA
CHARLIE CHAN IN RIO • 1941 • Lachman Harry • USA
CHARLIE CHAN IN SECRET SERVICE • 1944 • Rosen Phil • USA
CHARLIE CHAN IN SHANGHAI • 1935 • Tinling James • USA
CHARLIE CHAN IN THE CHINESE CAT see **CHINESE CAT, THE** • 1944
CHARLIE CHAN IN THE MURDER CHAMBER see **CHARLIE CHAN IN BLACK MAGIC** • 1944
CHARLIE CHAN IN THE SHANGHAI COBRA see **SHANGHAI COBRA, THE** • 1945
CHARLIE CHAN ON BROADWAY • 1937 • Forde Eugene J. • USA
CHARLIE CHAN'S CHANCE • 1932 • Blystone John G. • USA
CHARLIE CHAN'S COURAGE • 1934 • Hadden George, Forde Eugene J. • USA
CHARLIE CHAN'S GREATEST CASE • 1933 • MacFadden Hamilton • USA
CHARLIE CHAN'S MURDER CRUISE • 1940 • Forde Eugene J. • USA
CHARLIE CHAN'S SECRET • 1936 • Wiles Gordon • USA
CHARLIE CHAPLIN CARNIVAL • 1938 • Chaplin Charles • CMP • USA
CHARLIE CHAPLIN CAVALCADE • 1938 • Chaplin Charles • CMP • USA
CHARLIE CHAPLIN FESTIVAL • 1938 • Chaplin Charles • CMP • USA
CHARLIE CHAPLIN'S BURLESQUE ON CARMEN • 1914 • Chaplin Charles • USA • CARMEN
CHARLIE COBB: NICE NIGHT FOR A HANGING • 1977 • Michaels Richard • TVM • USA
CHARLIE CUCKOO • 1939 • Perkins Elmer • ANS • USA
CHARLIE ET SES DEUX NENETTES • 1974 • Seria Joel • FRN
CHARLIE GETS A JOB • 1920 • Robbins Jess • SHT • USA
CHARLIE GRANT'S WAR • 1984 • Lavut Martin • CND
CHARLIE IN HOT WATER • 1970 • Smith Paul J. • ANS • USA
CHARLIE IN TURKEY • 1919 • *Universal* • SHT • USA
CHARLIE IS MY DARLING • 1965 • Whitehead Peter • DOC • UKN
CHARLIE MCCARTHY AND MORTIMER SNERD IN SWEDEN • 1950 • *Bergen Edgar* • SHT • USA
CHARLIE MCCARTHY, DETECTIVE • 1939 • Tuttle Frank • USA
CHARLIE MUFFIN • 1979 • Gold Jack • TVM • UKN
CHARLIE ON THE OCEAN see **SHANGHAIED** • 1915
CHARLIE ON THE SPREE see **IN THE PARK** • 1915
CHARLIE RIVEL • 1978 • Abrahamsen Svend • SHT • DNM
CHARLIE SMILER ASKS PAPA • 1912 • Aylott Dave • UKN
CHARLIE SMILER AT THE PICNIC • 1912 • Aylott Dave • UKN
CHARLIE SMILER CATCHES A TARTAR • 1912 • Aylott Dave • UKN
CHARLIE SMILER TAKES BRAIN FOOD • 1911 • Aylott Dave • UKN
CHARLIE SMILER'S LOVE AFFAIR • 1912 • Aylott Dave • UKN
CHARLIE, SON OF THE GODS • 1917 • USA
CHARLIE SPIVAK AND HIS ORCHESTRA • 1947 • Cowan Will • SHT • USA
CHARLIE STEEL • 1984 • SAF
CHARLIE THE BURGLAR see **POLICE!** • 1916
CHARLIE THE HERO • 1919 • Goulding Alf • SHT • USA
CHARLIE THE HOBO see **TRAMP, THE** • 1915
CHARLIE, THE LITTLE DAREDEVIL • 1919 • *L-Ko* • SHT • USA
CHARLIE, THE LONESOME COUGAR • 1967 • Hibler Winston • USA
CHARLIE THE RAINMAKER • 1971 • Smith Paul J. • ANS • USA
CHARLIE THE SAILOR see **SHANGHAIED** • 1915
CHARLIE WOOS VIVIAN • 1914 • *Crystal* • USA
CHARLIE WORD 'N STER • 1979 • SAF
CHARLIE'S ANGELS • 1976 • Moxey John Llewellyn • TVM • USA
CHARLIE'S BALLOON see **CHARLIE AND THE GREAT BALLOON CHASE** • 1981
CHARLIE'S BIG ROMANCE see **TILLIE'S PUNCTURED ROMANCE** • 1914
CHARLIE'S BUTTE • 1911 • *Champion* • USA
CHARLIE'S CAMPOUT • 1969 • Smith Paul J. • ANS • USA
CHARLIE'S DAY • 1965 • Defalco Martin • DOC • CND
CHARLIE'S DAY OUT see **BY THE SEA** • 1915
CHARLIE'S GOLF CLASSIC • 1970 • Smith Paul J. • ANS • USA
CHARLIE'S KIDS • 1989 • Stewart Douglas Day • USA • MISMATCH
CHARLIE'S LITTLE JOKE • 1913 • *Crystal* • USA
CHARLIE'S MOTHER-IN-LAW • 1963 • Smith Paul J. • ANS • USA
CHARLIE'S NEW SUIT • 1914 • *Crystal* • USA
CHARLIE'S NEW UNDERWEAR see **CALLES NYA (UNDER) KLADER** • 1916
CHARLIE'S RECREATION see **TANGO TANGLES** • 1914
CHARLIE'S REFORM • 1912 • *Edison* • USA
CHARLIE'S RIVAL • 1914 • *Crystal* • USA
CHARLIE'S SMOKE • 1914 • *Crystal* • USA
CHARLIE'S TOOTHACHE • 1914 • *Crystal* • USA
CHARLIE'S TWIN SISTER • 1915 • *Novelty* • USA
CHARLIE'S WATERLOO • 1914 • *Crystal* • USA
CHARLOTS CONNECTION • 1983 • Couturier Jean • FRN
CHARLOTS CONTRE DRACULA, LES • 1980 • Desagnat Jean-Pierre • FRN
CHARLOTS EN DELIRE, LES • 1979 • Basnier Alain • FRN
CHARLOTS FONT L'ESPAGNE, LES • 1972 • Girault Jean • FRN, SPN
CHARLOTT ETWAS VERRUCKT • 1928 • Licho Adolf Edgar • FRG
CHARLOTTE • 1917 • Eagle Oscar • USA
CHARLOTTE • 1981 • Weisz Frans • NTH
CHARLOTTE see **JEUNE FILLE ASSASSINEE, LA** • 1974
CHARLOTTE: A GIRL MURDERED see **JEUNE FILLE ASSASSINEE, LA** • 1974
CHARLOTTE AND HER STEAK see **PRESENTATION OU CHARLOTTE ET SON STEAK** • 1951
CHARLOTTE CORDAY • 1919 • Zelnik Friedrich • FRG
CHARLOTTE ET SON JULES • 1958 • Godard Jean-Luc • SHT • FRN
CHARLOTTE ET VERONIQUE see **TOUS LES GARCONS S'APPELLENT PATRICK** • 1957
CHARLOTTE FORTEN'S MISSION: EXPERIMENT IN FREEDOM • 1985 • Crane Barry • TVM • USA
CHARLOTTE LOWENSKJOLD see **CHARLOTTE LOWENSKOLD** • 1930
CHARLOTTE LOWENSKOLD • 1930 • Molander Gustaf • SWD • CHARLOTTE LOWENSKJOLD
CHARLOTTE LOWENSKOLD • 1979 • Soderman Jackie • MTV • SWD
CHARLOTTE, MOVILLE TA CULOTTE • 1980 • Leroi Francis • FRN
CHARLOTTE'S WEB • 1973 • Takamoto Iwao, Nichols Charles • ANM • USA • E.B. WHITE'S CHARLOTTE'S WEB
CHARLY • 1968 • Nelson Ralph • USA
CHARLY AND STEFFEN see **CHARLY OG STEFFEN** • 1979
CHARLY BILL • 1919 • Bauer Leopold • FRG
CHARLY, DER WUNDERAFFE • 1915 • May Joe • AUS
CHARLY OG STEFFEN • 1979 • Kristiansen Henning • DNM • CHARLY AND STEFFEN
CHARM, THE see **FETICHE** • 1933
CHARM BRACELET, THE • 1939 • *Mintz Charles (P)* • ANS • USA
CHARM OF CHILDREN'S DRAWINGS, THE see **JAK SI DETI MALUJI** • 1958
CHARM OF DYNAMITE, THE see **ABEL GANCE -THE CHARM OF DYNAMITE** • 1968
CHARM OF LA BOHEME, THE (USA) see **ZAUBER DER BOHEME** • 1937
CHARM SCHOOL, THE • 1921 • Cruze James • USA
CHARM SCHOOL, THE (UKN) see **COLLEGIATE** • 1936
CHARM THAT CHARMED, THE • 1915 • Aylott Dave • UKN
CHARMAINE • 1928 • *De Forest Phonofilm* • SHT • UKN
CHARMANT FROU-FROU • 1901 • Blache Alice • FRN
CHARMANT VOYAGE DE NOCES • 1899 • Melies Georges • FRN • INTERRUPTED HONEYMOON, THE ○ CHARMING WEDDING TRIP, A
CHARMANTS GARCONS • 1957 • Decoin Henri • FRN • TOO MANY LOVERS (USA)
CHARME DES FLEURS, LA • 1910 • Velle Gaston • FRN • SPELL OF THE FLOWERS, THE
CHARME DISCRET DE LA BOURGEOISIE, LE • 1972 • Bunuel Luis • FRN, ITL, SPN • FASCINO DISCRETO DELLA BORGHESIA, IL (ITL) ○ DISCREET CHARM OF THE BOURGEOISIE, THE (UKN)
CHARMED ARROW, THE • 1914 • Huntley Fred W. • USA
CHARMED SWORD • 1907 • *Pathe* • FRN
CHARMER, THE • 1917 • Conway Jack • USA
CHARMER, THE • 1925 • Olcott Sidney • USA
CHARMER, THE • 1986 • Gibson Alan • MTV • UKN
CHARMER, THE see **MOONLIGHT SONATA** • 1937
CHARMER, THE see **GOISSA** • 1967
CHARMERS AT SEA see **SJOCHARMORER** • 1939
CHARMES DE L'EXISTENCE, LES • 1949 • Gremillon Jean, Kast Pierre • SHT • FRN • CHARMS OF LIFE, THE (UKN)
CHARMIDES • 1948 • Markopoulos Gregory J. • SHT • USA
CHARMING DECEIVER, THE • 1921 • Sargent George L. • USA
CHARMING DECEIVER, THE (USA) see **HEADS WE GO** • 1933
CHARMING FAMILY, A see **REMENYKEDOK** • 1971
CHARMING MAN, A see **ROZTOMILY CLOVEK** • 1941
CHARMING MATT SAXON, THE see **SAXON CHARM, THE** • 1948
CHARMING MRS. CHASE, THE • 1920 • Drew Sidney Mrs. • SHT • USA
CHARMING SINNERS • 1929 • Milton Robert, Arzner Dorothy • USA • CONSTANT WIFE, THE (UKN)
CHARMING SOUNDS see **CAROBNI ZVUCI** • 1957
CHARMING VILLAIN, A • 1916 • Steppling John • SHT • USA
CHARMING WEDDING TRIP, A see **CHARMANT VOYAGE DE NOCES** • 1899
CHARMS OF LIFE, THE (UKN) see **CHARMES DE L'EXISTENCE, LES** • 1949
CHARNELLES, LES • 1975 • Mulot Claude • FRN • SEX WITHOUT LOVE (UKN)
CHARNO KI DASI • 1959 • Vyas Ramesh • IND • WOMAN DEDICATED TO GOD
CHARPENTIER DU CIEL see **HIGH STEEL** • 1965
CHARRETIER DE LA MORT, LE see **CHARRETTE FANTOME, LA** • 1939
CHARRETTE FANTOME, LA • 1939 • Duvivier Julien • FRN • PHANTOM WAGON, THE (USA) ○ CHARRETIER DE LA MORT, LE
CHARRO! • 1969 • Warren Charles Marquis • USA
CHARRO A LA FUERZA • 1948 • Morayta Miguel • MXC
CHARRO DE LAS CALAVERAS, EL • 1965 • Salazar Alfredo • MXC • RIDER OF THE SKULLS, THE
CHARRO DEL ARRABAL, EL • 1948 • Orol Juan • MXC
CHARRO DEL CRISTO, EL • 1949 • Cardona Rene • MXC
CHARRO IMMORTAL, EL • 1955 • Portas Rafael E. • MXC
CHARRO NEGRO, EL • 1940 • de Anda Raul • MXC
CHARRO NEGRO CONTRA LA BANDA DE LOS CUERVOS, EL • 1962 • Martinez Arturo • MXC
CHARRO NEGRO EN EL NORTE, EL • 1949 • de Anda Raul • MXC
CHARRO Y LA DAMA, EL • 1949 • Cortes Fernando • MXC
CHARRON, LE • 1943 • Rouquier Georges • SHT • FRN
CHARRON AVEC EMILE ASSELIN FORGERON-CHARRON • 1975 • Plamondon Leo • DCS • CND
CHARROS YUYUYUY • 1938 • Diaz Morales Jose • SHT • MXC
CHARTER FLIGHT NO... • 1976 • Papic Krsto • SHT • YGS
CHARTER PILOT • 1940 • Forde Eugene J. • USA
CHARTER TRIP, THE see **SALLSKAPSRESAN** • 1980
CHARTRES • 1923 • Gremillon Jean • SHT • FRN • CATHEDRAL DE CHARTRES, LE
CHARTRES • 1989 • Butler Heinz • SWT
CHARTREUSE DE PARME, LA (FRN) see **CERTOSA DI PARMA, LA** • 1947
CHARTROOSE CABOOSE • 1960 • Reynolds William Red • USA
CHARUGA see **CARUGA** • 1990
CHARULATA • 1964 • Ray Satyajit • IND • LONELY WIFE, THE (UKN) ○ LONELY WOMAN, THE
CHARWOMAN, THE see **FEMME DE MENAGE, LA** • 1954
CHAS POLNOLUNIYA • 1989 • Zhebrunas Arunas • USS • HOUR OF THE FULL MOON, THE
CHASE • 1985 • Holcomb Rod • TVM • USA
CHASE, THE • 1913 • Dwan Allan • USA
CHASE, THE • 1946 • *Crockwell Douglas (P)* • SHT • USA
CHASE, THE • 1946 • Ripley Arthur • USA
CHASE, THE • 1966 • Penn Arthur • USA
CHASE, THE see **HARIKOMI** • 1958
CHASE, THE see **CHERCHEZ L'IDOLE** • 1964
CHASE, THE see **CAZA, LA** • 1965
CHASE, THE see **HAJKA** • 1978
CHASE A CROOKED SHADOW • 1958 • Anderson Michael • UKN
CHASE ACROSS THE CONTINENT, A • 1912 • *Reigel Charles* • USA
CHASE AFTER ADAM see **W POGONI ZA ADAMEM** • 1969
CHASE AFTER OPIUM DEALERS, THE see **SHIROI KONA NO KYOFU** • 1960
CHASE BY MOONLIGHT, A • 1915 • *Tincher Fay* • USA
CHASE FOR MILLIONS, THE see **JAGD NACH DER MILLION, DIE** • 1930
CHASE FOR THE GOLDEN NEEDLES, THE see **GOLDEN NEEDLES** • 1974
CHASE ME • 1920 • Del Ruth Roy • SHT • USA
CHASE ME CHARLIE • 1917 • Reed Langford • UKN
CHASE ME CHARLIE • 1932 • Chaplin Charles • CMP • USA

CHASE OF A LIFETIME, THE • 1969 • *Murphy Kenton G. (P)* • USA
CHASE OF DEATH, THE • 1914 • Brett B. Harold • UKN
CHASE STEP BY STEP • 1978 • Woo Min Shiong • HKG
CHASE THAT DREAM • 1980 • Cameron Ken • SHT • ASL
CHASED BRIDE, THE • 1923 • Christie Al • USA
CHASED BY BLOODHOUNDS • 1912 • Trimble Larry • USA
CHASED BY DOGS • 1904 • Collins Alf? • UKN
CHASED BY THE DEVIL see **VOM TEUFEL GEJAGT** • 1950
CHASED INTO LOVE • 1917 • Parrott Charles • SHT • USA
CHASER, THE • 1914 • *Luna* • USA
CHASER, THE • 1928 • Langdon Harry • USA
CHASER, THE • 1938 • Marin Edwin L. • USA
CHASER, THE • 1980 • Kagan Jeremy Paul • USA
CHASER, THE see **LA KAM LOK** • 1983
CHASER CHASED, THE • 1906 • Hough Harold • UKN
CHASER CHASED, THE • 1916 • *Miller Rube* • USA
CHASER ON THE ROCKS • 1965 • Larriva Rudy • ANS • USA
CHASERS, THE (USA) see **DRAGUEURS, LES** • 1959
CHASES OF PIMPLE STREET, THE • 1934 • Parrott Charles • SHT • USA
CHASHAR MEYE • 1931 • *Sircar B. N. (P)* • IND
CHASING A FORTUNE see **PUTTING ONE OVER** • 1919
CHASING A RAINBOW • 1911 • Porter Edwin S. • USA
CHASING ADAM see **W POGONI ZA ADAMEM** • 1969
CHASING DANGER • 1939 • Cortez Ricardo • USA
CHASING DE WET • 1901 • *Mitchell & Kenyon* • UKN
CHASING 'EM OUT IN THE OPEN • 1916 • *Heinie & Louie* • USA
CHASING GAME, THE see **CHUI CH'IU CHUI CH'IU** • 1976
CHASING GLOOM • 1914 • *Komic* • USA
CHASING HER FUTURE • 1919 • Fishback Fred C. • SHT • USA
CHASING RAIN-BEAUX • 1919 • *Capitol* • SHT • USA
CHASING RAINBOWS • 1919 • Beal Frank • USA
CHASING RAINBOWS • 1930 • Reisner Charles F. • USA • ROAD SHOW, THE ○ HAPPY DAYS ARE HERE AGAIN
CHASING RAINBOWS • 1988 • Blandford Mark • CND
CHASING THE BALL • 1909 • UKN
CHASING THE BLUES • 1942 • Le Borg Reginald • SHT • USA
CHASING THE BLUES • 1947 • Chambers Jack, Ellitt Jack • SHT • UKN
CHASING THE CHASER • 1925 • Roach Hal • SHT • USA
CHASING THE LIMITED • 1915 • McRae Henry • USA
CHASING THE MOON • 1922 • Sedgwick Edward • USA
CHASING THE RAINBOW • 1911 • *Anderson Helen* • USA
CHASING THE SHADOWS • 1990 • Hatami Alishah • IRN
CHASING THE SMUGGLERS • 1914 • Blackwell Carlyle • USA
CHASING THROUGH EUROPE • 1929 • Butler David, Werker Alfred L. • USA
CHASING TROUBLE • 1926 • Morante Milburn • USA
CHASING TROUBLE • 1931 • Guiol Fred • SHT • USA
CHASING TROUBLE • 1940 • Bretherton Howard • USA
CHASING YESTERDAY • 1935 • Nicholls George Jr. • USA
CHASKANAWI, LA • 1976 • Cuellar Urizar • BLV
CHASM, THE • 1914 • *Thanhouser* • USA
CHASM, THE • 1914 • *Essanay* • USA
CHASME BUDDHOOR • 1981 • Paranjpye Sai • IND • NO EVIL EYE!
CHASSE A COURRE, UNE • 1951 • Kirsanoff Dimitri • SHT • FRN • MORT DU CERF, LA ○ MORT D'UN CERF
CHASSE A LA PANTHERE • 1909 • Machin Alfred • FRN
CHASSE A LA PIEVRE see **OCTOPUS HUNT, THE** • 1965
CHASSE A L'HIPPOPOTAME • 1946 • Rouch Jean • DCS • FRN
CHASSE A L'HIPPOPOTAME see **BATAILLE SUR LE GRAND FLEUVE** • 1951
CHASSE A L'HIPPOPOTAME SUR LE NIL BLEU • 1908 • Machin Alfred • FRN
CHASSE A L'HOMME, LA • 1914 • Durand Jean • FRN
CHASSE A L'HOMME, LA • 1953 • Kast Pierre • SHT • FRN
CHASSE A L'HOMME, LA • 1964 • Molinaro Edouard • FRN, ITL • CACCIA AL MASCHIIO (ITL) ○ GENTLE ART OF SEDUCTION, THE ○ MALE HUNT (USA)
CHASSE AU CAMBRIOLEUR, LA • 1903-04 • Blache Alice • FRN
CHASSE AU LION A L'ARC, LA • 1967 • Rouch Jean • DOC • FRN • LION HUNTERS, THE
CHASSE AUX IMAGE, LA • 1936 • Tessier Albert • DCS • CND
CHASSE AUX MONTAGNAIS, LA • 1974 • Lamothe Arthur • DCS • CND
CHASSE-CROISE • 1932 • Diamant-Berger Henri • FRN
CHASSE-CROISE • 1981 • Dombasle Arielle • FRN
CHASSE DES TOUCHES • 1959 • Hirsch Hy • SHT • FRN
CHASSE EN SOLOGNE, LA see **REGLE DU JEU, LA** • 1939
CHASSE ROYALE, LA • 1969 • Leterrier Francois • FRN, CZC • KRALOVSKA POLOVACKA (CZC) ○ ROYAL HUNTING, THE
CHASSEPIERE • 1953 • Haesaerts Paul • BLG
CHASSES DE NEPTUNE • 1949 • Este Philippe • FRN
CHASSEUR, LE • 1971 • Reichenbach Francois • SHT • FRN
CHASSEUR DE CHEZ MAXIM'S, LE • 1927 • Lion Roger, Rimsky Nicolas • FRN
CHASSEUR DE CHEZ MAXIM'S, LE • 1932 • Anton Karl • FRN
CHASSEUR DE CHEZ MAXIM'S, LE • 1939 • Cammage Maurice • FRN
CHASSEUR DE CHEZ MAXIM'S, LE • 1953 • Diamant-Berger Henri • FRN
CHASSEUR DE CHEZ MAXIM'S, LE • 1976 • Vital Claude • FRN
CHASSEURS CRIS DE MISTASSINI see **CREE HUNTERS OF MISTASSINI** • 1974
CHASSEURS DE CARIBOUS see **CARIBOU HUNTERS** • 1951
CHASSEURS DE LIONS, LES • 1913 • Feuillade Louis • FRN
CHASSEURS D'ETOILES • 1989 • Garcia Nicole • FRN
CHASTE SUSANNE see **KEUSCHE SUSANNE, DIE** • 1926
CHASTE SUZANNE, LA • 1937 • Berthomieu Andre • FRN
CHASTEL • 1960 • Lapoujade Robert • ANS • FRN
CHASTISER, THE • 1969 • Zakharias Manos • USS
CHASTITY • 1923 • Schertzinger Victor • USA
CHASTITY • 1969 • De Paola Alessio • USA
CHASTITY BELT, THE (UKN) see **CINTURA DI CASTITA, LA** • 1967
CHASTNAYA ZHIZN • 1983 • Raizman Yuli • USS • PRIVATE LIFE
CHASTNYI SLUCHAI • 1934 • Trauberg Ilya • USS • UNUSUAL CASE, AN
CHASY KAPITANA ENRIKO • 1968 • Lacis Eriks, Streics Janis • USS • CAPTAIN ENRICO'S WATCH
CHAT, LE • 1971 • Granier-Deferre Pierre • FRN, ITL • CHAT – L'IMPLACABILE UOMO DI SAINT GERMAIN, LE (ITL) ○ CAT, THE
CHAT BOTTE • 1902 • Nonguet Lucien, Zecca Ferdinand • SHT • FRN • PUSS IN BOOTS (USA)
CHAT BOTTE, LE • 1908 • Capellani Albert • FRN • PUSS 'N BOOTS (USA)
CHAT DANS LE SAC, LE • 1964 • Groulx Gilles • CND • CAT IN THE SACK, THE (USA) ○ CAT IN THE BAG, THE
CHAT EST MORT DE FAIM, LE • 1968 • Sanchez-Ariza Jose • PLN
CHAT ET LA SOURIS, LE • 1975 • Lelouch Claude • FRN • SEVEN SUSPECTS FOR MURDER (UKN) ○ CAT AND MOUSE (USA)
CHAT, LE BELETTE ET LE PETIT LAPIN, LE • Tourane Jean • SHT • FRN • CAT, THE WEASEL AND THE LITTLE RABBIT, THE
CHAT –L'IMPLACABILE UOMO DI SAINT GERMAIN, LE (ITL) see **CHAT, LE** • 1971
CHAT SIU FUK • 1988 • Law Kai-Yui • HKG • PAINTED FACES
CHATEAU DANS LE MIDI, UN see **CHATEAU DE REVE** • 1933
CHATEAU DE CARTES • 1956 • Portugais Louis • SHT • CND
CHATEAU DE CARTES • 1980 • Labonte Francois • CND
CHATEAU DE CARTES, LE • 1908 • Cohl Emile • ANS • FRN
CHATEAU DE LA DERNIERE CHANCE, LE • 1946 • Paulin Jean-Paul • FRN • COBAYES, LES
CHATEAU DE LA PEUR, LE • 1912 • Feuillade Louis • FRN
CHATEAU DE LA TERREUR, LE see **QUELQU'UN A TUE** • 1933
CHATEAU DE NEIGE, LE see **GUERRE DES TUQUES, LA** • 1985
CHATEAU DE POINTILLY, LE • 1971 • Arrieta Adolfo • FRN
CHATEAU DE REVE • 1933 • Clouzot Henri-Georges, von Bolvary Geza • FRN • CHATEAU DANS LE MIDI, UN
CHATEAU DE SABLE, LE • 1977 • Hoedeman Co • ANS • CND • SAND CASTLE, THE
CHATEAU DE VERRE, LE • 1950 • Clement Rene • FRN, ITL • AMANTE DI UNA NOTTE, L' (ITL)
CHATEAU DES FANTOMES, LE • 1923 • Marodon Pierre • FRN
CHATEAU DES MORTS VIVANTS, LE (FRN) see **CASTELLO DEI MORTI VIVI, IL** • 1964
CHATEAU DES QUATRE OBESES, LE • 1939 • Noe Yvan • FRN
CHATEAU DU PASSE, LE • 1958 • de Gastyne Marco • SHT • FRN
CHATEAU EN SUEDE • 1963 • Vadim Roger • FRN, ITL • CASTELLO IN SVEZIA, IL (ITL) ○ NUTTY, NAUGHTY CHATEAU (USA) ○ CASTLE IN SWEDEN
CHATEAU HANTE, LE • 1897 • Melies Georges • FRN • DEVIL'S CASTLE, THE (USA) ○ HAUNTED CHATEAU, THE ○ HAUNTED CASTLE, THE
CHATEAU HISTORIQUE • 1923 • Desfontaines Henri • FRN
CHATEAUX DE FRANCE • 1949 • Resnais Alain • DCS • FRN
CHATEAUX DE LA LOIRE, LES • 1909 • Cohl Emile • ANS • FRN
CHATEAUX DE LA LOIRE, LES • 1916 • Desfontaines Henri • FRN
CHATEAUX EN ESPAGNE • 1953 • Wheeler Rene • FRN, ITL, SPN • CASTLES IN SPAIN (USA) ○ TORERO, EL
CHATEAUX STOP.. SUR LA LOIRE • 1962 • Desvilles, Vernick • SHT • FRN
CHATEI EL MARAH • 1967 • Mustafa Hassam Eddin • EGY • FUN ON THE BEACH
CHATELAINE DU LIBAN, LA • 1925 • de Gastyne Marco • FRN
CHATELAINE DU LIBAN, LA • 1933 • Epstein Jean • FRN
CHATELAINE DU LIBAN, LA • 1956 • Pottier Richard • FRN, ITL • CASTELLANA DEL LIBANO, LA (ITL) ○ WOMAN FROM LEBANON, THE ○ LEBANESE MISSION, THE (USA) ○ LADY OF LEBANON ○ DESERT RETOUR
CHATIMENT, LE • 1975 • Ramoulian Charles • FRN
CHATOLLETS HEMMELIGHED • 1913 • Davidsen Hjalmar • DNM • SECRET OF THE OLD WRITING DESK, THE ○ GAMLE CHATOL, DET ○ OLD WRITING DESK, THE
CHATO'S LAND • 1972 • Winner Michael • UKN, SPN
CHATOUILLEUSES, LES • 1974 • Franco Jesus • FRN
CHATS BOTTES, LES • 1971 • Fournier Claude • CND
CHATTAHOOCHEE • 1989 • Johnson Mick • USA
CHATTANOOGA CHOO CHOO • 1984 • Bilson Bruce • USA
CHATTE, LA • 1958 • Decoin Henri • FRN • CAT, THE (USA) ○ FACE OF THE CAT, THE
CHATTE METAMORPHOSEE EN FEMME, LA • 1909 • Feuillade Louis • FRN • CAT THAT CHANGED INTO A WOMAN, THE (USA)
CHATTE SANS PUDEUR, LA • 1974 • Matalon Eddy • FRN
CHATTE SORT SES GRIFFES, LA • 1960 • Decoin Henri • FRN • CAT SHOWS HER CLAWS, THE (UKN)
CHATTE SUR UN DOIGT BRULANT, LA • 1974 • Chardon Cyril • FRN
CHATTEL, THE • 1916 • Thompson Frederick A. • USA
CHATTERBOX • 1936 • Nicholls George Jr. • USA
CHATTERBOX • 1943 • Santley Joseph • USA
CHATTERBOX • 1977 • Desimone Tom • USA
CHATTES EN CHALEUR • 1978 • Bernard-Aubert Claude • FRN
CHATWILL'S VERDICT • 1981 • Fruet William • CND
CHAUD LAPIN, LE • 1975 • Thomas Pascal • FRN
CHAUD LES SECRETS see **GEHEIMNISSE IN GOLDENEN NYLONS** • 1966
CHAUDE ET PERVERSE EMILIA • Renato Lazlo • FRN
CHAUDES ADOLESCENTES • 1980 • Kikoine Gerard • FRN
CHAUDIERE, LA see **WAYWARD RIVER** • 1961
CHAUDRON INFERNAL, LE • 1903 • Melies Georges • FRN • INFERNAL CAULDRON AND THE PHANTASMAL VAPOURS, THE ○ INFERNAL CAULDRON, THE
CHAUDRONNIER, LE • 1949 • Rouquier Georges • SHT • FRN
CHAUFFEUR, THE • 1919 • Parrott Charles • SHT • USA
CHAUFFEUR ANTOINETTE • 1931 • Selpin Herbert • FRG
CHAUFFEUR DE MADEMOISELLE, LE • 1927 • Chomette Henri • FRN
CHAUFFEUR DE TAXI, LE • 1954 • Portugais Louis • DCS • CND
CHAUFFEUR, THE GIRL AND THE COP, THE • 1912 • *Essanay* • USA
CHAUFFEUR'S DREAM, THE • 1908 • Booth W. R. • UKN
CHAUFFEUR'S DREAM, THE • 1912 • *Kalem* • USA
CHAUNCEY EXPLAINS • 1905 • *Bitzer Billy (Ph)* • USA
CHAUSETTE-SURPRISE • 1978 • Davy Jean-Francois • FRN
CHAUSSEE DES GEANTS, LA • 1926 • Durand Jean • FRN
CHAUSSETTE, LA • 1906 • Blache Alice • FRN
CHAUSSURES MATRIMONIALES • 1909 • Cohl Emile • ANS • FRN
CHAUTAUQUA see **TROUBLE WITH GIRLS, THE** • 1969
CHAUVE-SOURIS, LA • 1931 • Billon Pierre, Lamac Carl • FRN
CHAVAL • 1971 • Ruspoli Mario • SHT • FRN
CHAVALA, LA • 1925 • Rey Florian • SPN
CHAYF KHIR • 1964 • Jamil Mohammed Shoukry • IRQ • CELUI QUI ESPERE LA PROSPERITE
CHCIALBYM SIE OGOLIC • 1967 • Kondratiuk Andrzej • PLN • I'D LIKE TO SHAVE ○ I'D LIKE A SHAVE ○ SHAVE, PLEASE
CHDY I INNI • 1967 • Kluba Henryk • PLN • THIN AND THE OTHERS, THE ○ SLIM AND THE OTHERS ○ SKINNY AND OTHERS
CHE! • 1969 • Fleischer Richard • USA
CHE? • 1972 • Polanski Roman • ITL, FRN, FRG • QUOI? (FRN) ○ DIARY OF FORBIDDEN DREAMS ○ WHAT? (USA)
CHE, BUENOS AIRES • 1962 • Birri Fernando • DOC • ARG
CHE C'ENTRIAMO NOI CON LA RIVOLUZIONE? • 1972 • Corbucci Sergio • ITL • WHAT ARE WE DOING IN THE MIDDLE OF THE REVOLUTION?
CHE, COMANDANTE AMIGO • 1979 • Hernandez Bernabe • DOC • CUB • CHE, FRIEND COMMANDER
CHE DISTINTA FAMIGLIA! • 1943 • Bonnard Mario • ITL
CHE DOTTORESSA RAGAZZI! • 1977 • Baldanello Gianfranco • ITL
CHE FANNO I NOSTRI SUPERMEN TRA LE VERGINI DELLA GIUNGLA • 1970 • Albertini Bitto • ITL, SPN • LOS TRE SUPERMEN EN LA SELVA (SPN) ○ SUPERMEN ○ THREE SUPERMEN IN THE JUNGLE, THE
CHE FEMMINA.. E CHE DOLLARI! • 1961 • Simonelli Giorgio C. • ITL
CHE FINE HA FATTO TOTO BABY? • 1964 • Heusch Paolo, Alessi Ottavio • ITL
CHE, FRIEND COMMANDER see **CHE, COMANDANTE AMIGO** • 1979
CHE GIOIA VIVERE (ITL) see **QUELLE JOIE DE VIVRE** • 1961
CHE GUEVARA, EL • 1968 • Heusch Paolo • ITL • REBEL WITH A CAUSE (UKN) ○ MUERTE DEL CHE GUEVARA, LA ○ BLOODY CHE CONTRA
CHE IS ALIVE see **DIALOGO CON CHE** • 1969
CHE NOTTE QUELLA NOTTE! • 1977 • De Chiara Ghigo • ITL
CHE NOTTE RAGAZZI! • 1966 • Capitani Giorgio • ITL
CHE O.V.N.I. • 1968 • Uset Anibal E. • ARG
CHE ORA E • 1989 • Scola Ettore • ITL, FRN • WHAT TIME IS IT (UKN)
CHE POR-SETARE BOOD SHABAM • 1977 • Gholam-Rezai Nasser • IRN • HOW STARRY WAS MY NIGHT
CHE, QUE LOCO! • 1952 • Torrado Ramon • SPN
CHE TEMPI! • 1948 • Bianchi Giorgio • ITL
CHEAP BEER • 1907 • Collins Alf? • UKN
CHEAP BOOT STORE, A • 1904 • Fitzhamon Lewin • UKN
CHEAP DETECTIVE, THE • 1978 • Moore Robert • USA
CHEAP KISSES • 1924 • Ince John, Tate Cullen • USA
CHEAP REMOVAL, A • 1909 • Fitzhamon Lewin? • UKN
CHEAP REMOVAL, A • 1910 • Martinek H. O. • UKN
CHEAP SKATES • 1925 • Taurog Norman • SHT • USA
CHEAP SWEET AND A KID see **KASHI TO KODOMO** • 1962
CHEAP TRANSPORTATION • 1914 • *Lubin* • USA
CHEAP VACATION, A • 1916 • Hugon P. D. • SHT • USA
CHEAPER BY THE DOZEN • 1950 • Lang Walter • USA
CHEAPER TO KEEP HER • 1980 • Annakin Ken • USA
CHEAPER TO MARRY • 1924 • Leonard Robert Z. • USA
CHEAPEST WAY, THE • 1913 • *Panzer Paul* • USA
CHEAT, THE • 1912 • Rolfe Alfred • ASL
CHEAT, THE • 1915 • De Mille Cecil B. • USA
CHEAT, THE • 1923 • Fitzmaurice George • USA
CHEAT, THE • 1931 • Abbott George • USA
CHEAT, THE see **FORFAITURE** • 1937
CHEAT, THE (UKN) see **ROMAN D'UN TRICHEUR, LE** • 1936
CHEAT, THE (UKN) see **LONE HAND TEXAN, THE** • 1947
CHEAT, THE (USA) see **MANEGES** • 1949
CHEATED, THE see **MAKHDU UN, AL-** • 1972
CHEATED BY THE WINDS see **HABANERA, LA** • 1937
CHEATED HEARTS • 1921 • Henley Hobart • USA
CHEATED LOVE • 1921 • Baggot King • USA
CHEATED VENGEANCE • 1918 • Balk Maurice E. • UKN
CHEATER, THE • 1920 • Otto Henry • USA • JUDAH
CHEATER REFORMED, THE • 1921 • Dunlap Scott R. • USA
CHEATERS • 1916 • Henderson Lucius • SHT • USA
CHEATERS • 1927 • Apfel Oscar • USA
CHEATERS • 1934 • Rosen Phil • USA
CHEATERS, THE • 1930 • McDonagh Paulette • ASL
CHEATERS, THE • 1945 • Kane Joseph • USA • CASTAWAY, THE
CHEATERS, THE (USA) see **TRICHEURS, LES** • 1958
CHEATERS AT PLAY • 1932 • MacFadden Hamilton • USA
CHEATERS CHEATED, THE • 1907 • Martin J. H.? • UKN
CHEATING • 1913 • *Powers* • USA
CHEATING BLONDES • 1933 • Levering Joseph • USA • HOUSE OF CHANCE (UKN)
CHEATING CHEATERS • 1919 • Dwan Allan • USA
CHEATING CHEATERS • 1927 • Laemmle Edward • USA • LAW'S THE LAW, THE
CHEATING CHEATERS • 1934 • Thorpe Richard • USA
CHEATING HERSELF • 1919 • Lawrence Edmund • USA
CHEATING IN GAMBLING • 1949 • Cohen Arthur • DCS • USA
CHEATING ITALIAN STYLE see **OLTRAGGIO AL PUDORE** • 1965
CHEATING LOVE see **YORU NO MESU-INU** • 1966
CHEATING THE PUBLIC • 1918 • Stanton Richard • USA
CHEATING THE SWEEP • 1907 • Williamson James • UKN
CHEATING THE WIFE • 1917 • *Ray Johnnie* • SHT • USA
CHEAT'S LAST THROW, THE (UKN) see **HEADIN' WEST** • 1946
CHECHAHCOS, THE • 1924 • Moomaw Lewis H. • USA

CHECHEMENI-GO NO BOKEN • 1976 • Kadota Ryutaro • JPN • ADVENTURE OF CHECHEMENI
CHECK AND DOUBLE CHECK • 1930 • Brown Melville • USA
CHECK AND RUBBER CHECK • 1931 • Buzzell Edward • SHT • USA
CHECK IS IN THE MAIL, THE • 1986 • Darling Joan • USA • CHEQUE IS IN THE POST, THE (UKN)
CHECK NO. 130 • 1915 • *Ostriche Muriel* • USA
CHECK POINT • 1967 • Cacas Nick C. • PHL
CHECK TO SONG • 1951 • Halas John • ANS • UKN
CHECK TO THE QUEEN see **SCACCO ALLA REGINA** • 1969
CHECK YOUR BAGGAGE • 1918 • Roach Hal • SHT • USA
CHECK YOUR GUNS • 1948 • Taylor Ray • USA
CHECK YOUR HAT, SIR? • 1918 • Hotaling Arthur D. • SHT • USA
CHECKED THROUGH • 1915 • *Royal* • USA
CHECKERBOARD see **TRIPES AU SOLEIL, LES** • 1959
CHECKERED COAT, THE • 1948 • Cahn Edward L. • USA • CHEQUERED COAT, THE
CHECKERED FLAG, THE • 1926 • Adolfi John G. • USA
CHECKERED FLAG, THE • 1963 • Grefe William • USA
CHECKERED FLAG OR CRASH • 1977 • Gibson Alan • USA
CHECKERS • 1913 • *Ross Thomas W.* • USA
CHECKERS • 1919 • Stanton Richard • USA
CHECKERS • 1937 • Humberstone H. Bruce • USA
CHECKING CHARLIE'S CHILD • 1915 • *Marlo George* • USA
CHECKING OUT • 1988 • Leland David • UKN, USA
CHECKMATE • 1911 • *Garwood William* • USA
CHECKMATE • 1912 • Dwan Allan • USA
CHECKMATE • 1915 • *Majestic* • USA
CHECKMATE • 1917 • Le Saint Edward J. • *Selig* • SHT • USA
CHECKMATE • 1917 • MacDonald Sherwood • *Horkheimer* • USA
CHECKMATE • 1935 • Pearson George • UKN
CHECKMATE (UKN) see **DESERT HORSEMAN, THE** • 1946
CHECKMATED • 1910 • Bouwmeester Theo? • UKN
CHECKMATED • 1913 • Trimble Larry • USA
CHECKPOINT • 1956 • Thomas Ralph • UKN
CHECKPOINT • 1972 • Haldane Don • CND
CHECKPOINT • 1986 • Gherman Alexei • USS
CHEECH AND CHONG: THINGS ARE TOUGH ALL OVER see **THINGS ARE TOUGH ALL OVER** • 1982
CHEECH AND CHONG'S UP IN SMOKE see **UP IN SMOKE** • 1978
CHEECH & CHONG'S NEXT MOVIE • 1980 • Chong Thomas • USA
CHEECH & CHONG'S NICE DREAMS • 1981 • Chong Thomas • USA • NICE DREAMS
CHEECH & CHONG'S STILL SMOKIN' • 1983 • Chong Thomas • USA • STILL SMOKIN'
CHEECH & CHONG'S THE CORSICAN BROTHERS • 1984 • Chong Thomas • USA • CORSICAN BROTHERS, THE
CHEECHAKO TALE OF ALASKA • 1954 • Camp Jack • USA
CHEEK • 1969 • Zwartjes Frans • SHT • NTH
CHEEKIEST MAN ON EARTH, THE • 1908 • McDowell J. B.? • UKN
CHEER BOYS CHEER • 1939 • Forde Walter • UKN
CHEER HARAN • 1935 • IND
CHEER LEADER, THE • 1928 • Neitz Alvin J. • USA • PLAYING THE GAME (UKN)
CHEER THE BRAVE • 1951 • Hume Kenneth • UKN
CHEER UP • 1924 • Roberts Stephen • SHT • USA
CHEER UP! • 1936 • Mittler Leo • UKN
CHEER UP! see **NE GORIUY!** • 1970
CHEER UP AND SMILE • 1930 • Lanfield Sidney • USA
CHEERFUL ALLEY see **YOKI NO URAMACHI** • 1939
CHEERFUL CANARY, THE see **VESSIOLAIA KANAREIKA** • 1929
CHEERFUL FRAUD, THE • 1927 • Seiter William A. • USA
CHEERFUL GIRL, A see **AOZURA MUSUME** • 1957
CHEERFUL GIVERS • 1917 • Powell Paul • USA
CHEERFUL LAD, THE see **MUCHACHO ALEGRE, EL** • 1947
CHEERFUL LIAR, A • 1919 • *Devore Dorothy* • USA
CHEERFUL LIARS • 1918 • De Barge C. R. • SHT • USA
CHEERING MR. GOODHEART see **CURING MR. GOODHEART** • 1914
CHEERING SECTION see **CRAZY CAMPUS** • 1977
CHEERING TOWN see **KANKO NO MACHI** • 1944
CHEERIO! • 1935 • *Fidelity Films* • SHT • UKN
CHEERLEADER CAMP • 1988 • Quinn John • USA • BLOODY POM POMS
CHEERLEADERS, THE • 1973 • Glicker Paul • USA • 18 YEARS OLD SCHOOLGIRLS, THE (UKN)
CHEERLEADERS' BEACH PARTY • 1978 • Goitein Alex E. • USA
CHEERLEADER'S WILD WEEKEND • 1979 • Werner Jeff • USA
CHEERLESS LANE see **FREUDLOSE GASSE, DIE** • 1925
CHEERS! BYUNG TAE • 1981 • Kim Soo-Yong • SKR
CHEERS FOR MISS BISHOP • 1941 • Garnett Tay • USA
CHEERS OF THE CROWD • 1935 • Moore Vin • USA
CHEERS ON THE UNKNOWN SOLDIERS see **EIREI-TACHI NO OENKA** • 1979
CHEESE • 1976 • West Alan • USA
CHEESE BURGLAR • 1946 • Sparber I. • ANS • USA
CHEESE CHASERS • 1951 • Jones Charles M. • ANS • USA
CHEESE IT, THE CAT • 1957 • McKimson Robert • ANS • USA
CHEESE MINING • 1914 • France Charles H. • USA
CHEESE MITES • 1903 • Duncan F. Martin • UKN
CHEESE MITES: OR, LILLIPUTIANS IN A LONDON RESTAURANT, THE • 1901 • Booth W. R.? • UKN
CHEESE NAPPERS • 1938 • Lovy Alex • ANS • USA
CHEESE OF POLICE, THE • 1914 • *Mace Fred* • USA
CHEESE SPECIAL, THE • 1913 • Curtis Allen • USA
CHEESEVILLE COPS, THE • 1914 • *Ab* • USA
CHEETAH, THE see **GUEPARDO, EL** • 1971
CHEF, THE • 1918 • *Hardy Oliver* • SHT • USA
CHEF, THE see **ON THE FIRE** • 1919
CHEF AT CIRCLE G, THE • 1915 • Mix Tom • USA
CHEF DONALD • 1941 • King Jack • ANS • USA
CHEF-LIEU DE CANTON, LE • 1911 • Feuillade Louis • FRN
CHEF SCHICKT SEINEN BESTEN MANN, DER • 1966 • Sollima Sergio • FRG, ITL, SPN • REQUIEM PER UN AGENTE SEGRETO (ITL) ○ REQUIEM FOR A SECRET AGENT ○ CONSIGNA: TANGER 67
CHEF WUNSCHT KEINE ZEUGEN, DER • 1963 • Albin Hans, Berneis Peter • FRG • NO SURVIVORS, PLEASE (USA) ○ CHIEF WANTS NO SURVIVORS, THE
CHEFS DE DEMAIN • 1944 • Clement Rene • DCS • FRN
CHEFS D'OEUVRES DE BEBE, LES • 1910 • Cohl Emile • ANS • FRN
CHEF'S DOWNFALL, THE • 1912 • *Imp* • USA
CHEF'S REVENGE, THE • 1907 • Martin J. H.? • UKN
CHEF'S REVENGE, THE • 1914 • *Sterling* • USA
CHEIK ROUGE, LE (FRN) see **SCEICCO ROSSO, LO** • 1962
CHEKA COMMISSAR, THE see **CHREZVICHAINI KOMMISSAR** • 1971
CHEKHOV • 1954 • Leoniv A.
CHEKLA PAIKHRABADA • 1989 • Singh M. A. • IND • WHEN THE BIRD FLEW AWAY
CHELKASH • 1957 • Filippov Fyodor • USS
CHELLELI KOSAM • 1968 • Rao Mallikarjuna • IND • FOR THE YOUNGER SISTER
CHELOVEK AMPHIBIA • 1962 • Kazansky Gennadi, Chebotaryov Vladimir • USS • AMPHIBIAN MAN, THE (USA) ○ HUMAN AMPHIBIAN, THE ○ CELOVEK ANFIBJAN ○ AMPHIBIOUS MAN, THE
CHELOVEK BEZ PASPORTA • 1966 • Bobrovsky Anatoli • USS • MAN WITHOUT A PASSPORT
CHELOVEK IDYOT ZA SOLNTSEM • 1962 • Kalik Mikhail • USS • SANDU FOLLOWS THE SUN (USA) ○ MAN FOLLOWING THE SUN ○ FOLLOWING THE SUN
CHELOVEK IZ RESTARANA • 1927 • Protazanov Yakov • USS • MAN FROM THE RESTAURANT, THE ○ TCHILAVIEK IZ RESTARANA
CHELOVEK KOTOROGO YA LYUBLYU • 1966 • Karasik Yuli • USS • MAN I LOVE, THE
CHELOVEK NIOTKUDA • 1961 • Ryazanov Eldar • USS • MAN FROM NOWHERE
CHELOVEK NO.217 • 1944 • Romm Mikhail • USS • GIRL NO. 217
CHELOVEK S DRUGOI STORONI (USS) see **MANNEN FRAN ANDRA SIDEN** • 1971
CHELOVEK S KINOAPPARATOM • 1928 • Vertov Dziga, Svilova Elizaveta • USS • LIVING RUSSIA OR THE MAN WITH A CAMERA ○ MAN WITH A MOVIE CAMERA, THE ○ MAN WITH THE CAMERA ○ MOSCOW TODAY
CHELOVEK S PLANETA ZEMLYA • 1959 • Buneyev Boris • USS • MAN FROM PLANET EARTH
CHELOVEK S RUZHYOM • 1938 • Yutkevich Sergei • USS • MAN WITH A RIFLE, THE ○ MAN WITH THE GUN, THE ○ MAN WITH A GUN, THE
CHELOVIEKU CHELOVIEK • 1958 • Alexandrov Grigori • USS • FROM MAN TO MAN
CHELOVYEK BROSAYET YAKOR • 1968 • Babayev Arif • USS • MAN CASTS ANCHOR, A
CHELSEA 7750 • 1913 • *Dixey Henry E.* • USA
CHELSEA GIRLS, THE • 1966 • Warhol Andy • USA
CHELSEA LIFE • 1933 • Morgan Sidney • UKN
CHELSEA NIGHTS • 1929 • Jeffrey R. E. • UKN
CHELSEA STORY • 1951 • Saunders Charles • UKN
CHELY • 1976 • Fernandez Ramon • SPN • HISTORIA ESTRICTAMENTE INMORAL, UNA
CHEMI BEBIA • 1929 • Mikaberidze Kote • USS • MY GRANDMOTHER
CHEMICAL KO-KO • 1929 • Fleischer Dave • ANS • USA
CHEMICAL PORTRAITURE • 1909 • Smith F. Percy • UKN
CHEMIE UND LIEBE • 1948 • Rabenalt Arthur M. • GDR • CHEMISTRY AND LOVE
CHEMIN DE DAMAS, LE • 1952 • Glass Max • FRN
CHEMIN DE LA DROGUE, LE • 1951 • Licot Louis-S. • FRN
CHEMIN DE LA GLOIRE, LE • 1927 • Roudes Gaston • FRN
CHEMIN DE LA GLOIRE, LE • 1949 • Rybakov Anatoly • USS
CHEMIN DE LA TERRE, LE • 1962 • Menegoz Robert • SHT • FRN
CHEMIN DE L'HONNEUR, LE • 1929 • Paulin Jean-Paul • FRN
CHEMIN DE LUMIERE, LE • 1937 • Mesnier Paul • FRN
CHEMIN DE RIO, LE • 1936 • Siodmak Robert • FRN • TRAFFIC IN SOULS (USA) ○ WOMEN RACKET (UKN) ○ FRENCH WHITE CARGO ○ CARGAISON BLANCHE
CHEMIN DE RONCES, UN see **NAH'NU LA NAZRA ASH-SHUK** • 1970
CHEMIN DE ROSELAND, LE • 1924 • Gleize Maurice • FRN
CHEMIN D'ERNOA, L' see **AMERICAIN OU LE CHEMIN D'ERNOA, L'** • 1920
CHEMIN DES ECOLIERS, LE • 1959 • Boisrond Michel • FRN, ITL • FURORE DI VIVERE (ITL) ○ WAY OF YOUTH, THE (USA)
CHEMIN DES LARMES, LE see **T'ARIQ AD-DUMU** • 1961
CHEMIN DU BONHEUR, LE • 1933 • Mamy Jean • FRN
CHEMIN DU BONHEUR, LE see **PARIS-MEDITERRANEE** • 1931
CHEMIN DU COEUR, LE • 1913 • Jasset Victorin • FRN
CHEMIN DU PARADIS, LE • 1930 • de Vaucorbeil Max, Thiele Wilhelm • FRN
CHEMIN DU VRAI BONHEUR, LE see **AMOUR QU'IL FAUT AUX FEMMES, L'** • 1933
CHEMIN PERDU, LE • 1980 • Moraz Patricia • SWT, FRN, BLG • LOST WAY, THE
CHEMIN SOLITAIRE, LE • 1974 • Franco Jesus
CHEMINEAU, LE • 1917 • Krauss Henry (c/d) • FRN
CHEMINEAU, LE • 1926 • Monca Georges, Keroul Maurice • FRN
CHEMINEAU, LE • 1935 • Rivers Fernand • FRN • OPEN ROAD, THE (USA)
CHEMINEMENTS PERVERS • Lewis James H. • FRN
CHEMINOT, LE • 1968 • FRN • CHEMINOTS EN GREVE, LES
CHEMINOTS, LES see **RAILROADERS, THE** • 1958
CHEMINOTS EN GREVE, LES see **CHEMINOT, LE** • 1968
CHEMINS DE KATMANDOU, LES • 1969 • Cayatte Andre • FRN, ITL • ROAD TO KATMANDU, THE (UKN) ○ KATMANDU (ITL)
CHEMINS DE LA MAUVAISE ROUTE, LES • 1962 • Herman Jean • DOC • FRN • BON POUR LA VIE CIVILE
CHEMINS DE LA VIOLENCE, LES • 1972 • Ruder Ken • FRN • LIPS OF BLOOD (UKN) ○ SANG DES AUTRES, LE ○ BLOOD OF OTHERS, THE ○ OTHERS' BLOOD, THE ○ PATHS OF VIOLENCE, THE
CHEMINS DE L'EXIL, OU LES DERNIERES ANNEES DE JEAN-JACQUES ROUSEAU, LES • 1978 • Goretta Claude • SWT, FRN • ROADS OF EXILE, THE (UKN)
CHEMINS DE LUMIERE • 1958 • Lucot Rene • DCS • FRN
CHEMINS DE SAINT-PAUL DE VENCE, LES • Carre Cesar • FRN
CHEMINS SANS LOI • 1946 • Radot Guillaume • FRN
CHEMISES ROUGES, LES (FRN) see **CAMICIE ROSSE** • 1952
CHEMIST, THE • 1936 • *Christie Al (P)* • SHT • USA
CHEMIST REPOPULATOR, THE see **CHIMISTE REPOPULATEUR, LE** • 1901
CHEMISTRY AND LOVE see **CHEMIE UND LIEBE** • 1948
CHEMISTRY OF OIL • 1954 • Crosfield Michael • DOC • UKN
CHEMPAKA BIRU • Rao B. N. • SNG
CHEMPION MIRA • 1954 • Gonchukov V. • USS • WORLD CHAMPION
CHENE D'ALLOUVILLE, LE • 1980 • Penard Serge • FRN • ILS SONT FOUS CES NORMANDS
CHENG-KWAN • 1968 • Lee Chih-San • HKG • TEMPTATION (USA) ○ OBSTACLE OF AFFECTION, AN
CH'ENG-SHIH-CHIH KUANG • 1984 • Chang Chien-T'ing • HKG • FAMILY LIGHT AFFAIR
CHENGJI SIHAN • 1985 • Zhan Xiangchi • CHN • GENGHIS KHAN
CHEQUE AU PORTEUR • 1941 • Boyer Jean • FRN
CHEQUE IS IN THE POST, THE (UKN) see **CHECK IS IN THE MAIL, THE** • 1986
CHEQUERED COAT, THE see **CHECKERED COAT, THE** • 1948
CHER FRANGIN • 1989 • *Thuiller Luc* • FRN
CHER PAPA (FRN) see **CARO PAPA** • 1979
CHER THEO • 1975 • Beaudin Jean • CND
CHER VIEUX PARIS! • 1950 • de Gastyne Marco • SHT • FRN
CHERCHEURS DE LA MER • 1945 • Palardy Jean • DCS • CND
CHERCHEURS D'OR DE L'ARKANSAS, LES (FRN) see **GOLDSUCHER VON ARKANSAS, DIE** • 1964
CHERCHEZ LA FEMME • 1921 • Curtiz Michael • AUS
CHERCHEZ LA FEMME! • 1955 • Andre Raoul • FRN
CHERCHEZ LA FEMME • 1968 • Berkovic Zvonimir • YGS
CHERCHEZ L'ERREUR • 1980 • Korber Serge • FRN
CHERCHEZ L'IDOLE • 1964 • Boisrond Michel • FRN, ITL • CHASE, THE
CHERE INCONNUE • 1980 • Mizrahi Moshe • FRN • I SENT A LETTER TO MY LOVE (USA) ○ JE T'AI ECRIT UNE LETTRE D'AMOUR
CHERE LOUISE • 1971 • de Broca Philippe • FRN, ITL • LUNGA NOTTE DI LOUISE, LA (ITL) ○ LOUISE (UKN)
CHERE MARTINIQUE • 1949 • Leherissey Jean • SHT • FRN
CHERE PE CHERA • 1978 • Tilak Raj • IND
CHEREMUSHKI see **CHERYOMUSHKI** • 1963
CHERES IMAGES, LES • 1920 • Hugon Andre • FRN
CHERES VIEILLES CHOSES • 1957 • Vogel Raymond • SHT • FRN
CHEREVICHKI • 1945 • Kasheverova Nadezhda, Shapiro Mikhail • USS • CHRISTMAS SLIPPERS (USA) ○ SILVER SLIPPERS
CHEREZ TERNII K ZVEZDAM • 1981 • Viktorov Richard • USS • THORNY WAY TO THE STARS, THE ○ PER ASPERA AD ASTRA ○ HUMANOID WOMAN ○ TO THE STARS
CHERGUI, EL • 1978 • Smihi Moumen • MRC • VIOLENT SILENCE, THE
CHERI • 1950 • Billon Pierre • FRN
CHERI-BIBI • 1937 • Mathot Leon • FRN
CHERI-BIBI • 1954 • Pagliero Marcello • FRN, ITL • FORZATO DELLA GUIANA, IL (ITL)
CHERI-BIBI see **PHANTOM OF PARIS, THE** • 1931
CHERI DE SA CONCIERGE, LE • 1934 • Guarino Joseph • FRN
CHERI DE SA CONCIERGE, LE • 1951 • Jayet Rene • FRN
CHERI FAIS-MOI PEUR • 1958 • Pinoteau Jack • FRN
CHERIA, TA • 1962 • Contes John G. • GRC • HANDS, THE
CHERIE • 1930 • Mercanton Louis • FRN
CHERITH • 1987 • Barrett Shirley • ASL
CHERNAYA GORA • 1971 • Zguridi Alexander • USS, IND • BLACK MOUNTAIN
CHERNAYA KURITSA • 1983 • Gres Victor • USS • BLACK HEN, THE
CHERNITE ANGELI • 1970 • Radev Vulo • BUL • BLACK ANGELS
CHERNOBYL: CHRONICLE OF TOUGH WEEKS • 1987 • Shevchenko V. • DOC • USS
CHERNOBYL WARNING BELL, THE • 1987 • Sergienko R. • DOC • USS
CHERNUSHKA see **CHYERNUSHKA** • 1967
CHEROKEE FLASH, THE • 1944 • Carr Thomas • USA
CHEROKEE KID, THE • 1927 • De Lacy Robert • USA • STRANGER, THE (UKN)
CHEROKEE STRIP • 1937 • Smith Noel • USA • STRANGE LAWS (UKN)
CHEROKEE STRIP • 1940 • Selander Lesley • USA • FIGHTING MARSHAL, THE (UKN)
CHEROKEE STRIP, THE • 1925 • *Bethew Herbert* • USA
CHEROKEE UPRISING • 1950 • Collins Lewis D. • USA
CHERRY • 1914 • Young James • USA
CHERRY 2000 • 1987 • De Jarnatt Steve • USA
CHERRY BLOSSOM • 1975 • Middleton Joseph • USA
CHERRY BLOSSOM CHORUS see **SAKURA ONDO** • 1934
CHERRY BLOSSOM FESTIVAL • 1963 • Kuwahara Bob • ANS • USA
CHERRY BLOSSOMS • 1911 • *Morrison James* • USA
CHERRY BLOSSOMS • 1972 • Brocka Lino • PHL
CHERRY COUNTRY see **SAKURA NO KUNI** • 1941
CHERRY, HARRY AND RAQUEL • 1969 • Meyer Russ • USA • THREE WAYS TO LOVE
CHERRY HILL HIGH • 1976 • Goitein Alex E. • USA • VIRGIN CONFESSIONS
CHERRY IN A PARK, A see **VISNJA NA TASMAJDANU** • 1968
CHERRY ORCHARD • 1979 • Andonov Ivan • BUL
CHERRY PICKER, THE • 1973 • Curran Peter • UKN
CHERRY PICKERS, THE • 1914 • *Eyton Bessie* • USA
CHERRY RIPE • 1921 • Foss Kenelm • UKN
CHERRY TREE GATE see **SAKURADA-MON** • 1961
CHERRY'S HOUSE see **CHERRY'S HOUSE OF NUDES** • 1964

CHERRY'S HOUSE OF NUDES • 1964 • Williams Wade • USA • SHERRY'S HOUSE OF NUDES ○ CHERRY'S HOUSE ○ BARE WITH ME
CHERT A KACHA • 1955 • Bedrich Vaclav • ANS • CZC • DEVIL AND KACHA, THE
CHERTE DES VIVRES, LA • 1911 • Machin Alfred • FRN
CHERYL HANSON: COVER GIRL see **COVER GIRL** • 1981
CHERYOMUSHKI • 1963 • Rappaport Herbert • USS • SONG OVER MOSCOW (USA) ○ WILD CHERRY TREES ○ CHEREMUSHKI
CHESS see **ROKH** • 1975
CHESS CLUB see **KLUB SZACHISTOW** • 1967
CHESS DISPUTE, A • 1903 • Paul Robert William • UKN
CHESS FEVER see **SHAKHMATNAYA GORYACHKA** • 1925
CHESS KING see **QI WANG** • 1988
CHESS KING see **QI WANG** • 1988
CHESS KING, THE see **OOSHO** • 1948
CHESS MASTER, THE see **OOSHO** • 1948
CHESS NUTS • 1932 • Fleischer Dave • ANS • USA
CHESS OF WIND, THE see **SHATRANJE BAAD** • 1975
CHESS PLAYER, THE (USA) see **JOUEUR D'ECHECS, LE** • 1926
CHESS PLAYER, THE (USA) see **JOUEUR D'ECHECS, LE** • 1938
CHESS PLAYERS, THE (USA) see **SHATRANJ KE KHILARI** • 1977
CHESS QUEEN, THE • 1916 • *Bray J. R. (P)* • USA
CHESSCETERA • 1957 • Richter Hans • SWT • PASSIONATE PASTIME
CHESSGAME: ENTER HASSAN see **ALAMUT AMBUSH, THE** • 1983
CHEST OF FORTUNE, THE • 1914 • *Kalem* • USA
CHESTER FORGETS HIMSELF • 1924 • Wilson Andrew P. • UKN
CHESTERFIELD CELEBRITIES • 1931 • USA
CHESTY • 1970 • Ford John • DOC • USA
CHESTY ANDERSON, U.S.NAVY see **CHESTY ANDERSON, USN** • 1976
CHESTY ANDERSON, USN • 1976 • Forsyth Ed • USA • ANDERSON'S ANGELS ○ CHESTY ANDERSON, U.S.NAVY
CHETAN, INDIAN BOY see **TSCHETAN, DER INDIANERJUNGE** • 1972
CHETICAMP • 1962 • Garceau Raymond • DCS • CND
CHETIRE STRANITZ ODNOI MOLODOI ZHIZHNI see **CHYETYRYE STRANITSY ODNOY MOLODY ZHIZNI** • 1968
CHETNA • 1971 • Ishara B. R. • IND
CHETNICKS THE FIGHTING GUERRILLAS see **CHETNIKS!** • 1943
CHETNIKS! • 1943 • King Louis • USA • CHETNICKS THE FIGHTING GUERRILLAS ○ UNDERGROUND GUERILLAS (UKN)
CHET'S ROMANCE • 1988 • Fevre Bertrand • FRN
CHETVERO • 1957 • Ordynsky Vassily • USS • FOUR, THE
CHETVERTAYA KOMNATA • 1974 • Khrabrovitsky Daniil • USS • FOURTH ROOM, THE
CHEVAL DE BOUE • 1970 • Abnudi Atiat Al- • SHT • EGY
CHEVAL DE FER, LE • 1974 • Glenn Pierre-William • DOC • FRN
CHEVAL D'ORGEUIL, LE • 1980 • Chabrol Claude • FRN • PROUD ONES, THE (UKN)
CHEVAL ET L'ENFANT, LE • Doria Enzo • FRN
CHEVAL MYSTERY, THE • 1915 • Myers Harry • USA
CHEVAL POUR DEUX, UN • 1961 • Thibault Jean-Marc • FRN
CHEVAL SAUVAGE see **CRIN BLANC** • 1953
CHEVALIER DE GABY, LE • 1921 • Burguet Charles • FRN
CHEVALIER DE LA NUIT, LE • 1954 • Darene Robert • FRN • KNIGHT OF THE NIGHT, THE
CHEVALIER DE MAISON-ROUGE, LE • 1963 • Barma Claude • FRN
CHEVALIER DE MAUPIN, LE (FRN) see **MADAMIGELLA DI MAUPIN** • 1966
CHEVALIER DE MENILMONTANT • 1954 • Baratier Jacques • FRN
CHEVALIER DE PARDAILLAN, LE • 1962 • Borderie Bernard • FRN • CLASH OF STEEL (USA)
CHEVALIER DEMONTABLE, LE • 1905 • Melies Georges • FRN • COLLAPSIBLE KNIGHT, THE
CHEVALIER DEMONTABLE ET LE GENERAL BOUM, LE • 1901 • Melies Georges • FRN • FIERCE CHARGER AND THE KNIGHT, THE (UKN) ○ GOOD TRICK, A (USA)
CHEVALIER DES NEIGES, LE • 1912 • Melies Georges • FRN • KNIGHT OF THE SNOWS, THE (USA)
CHEVALIER DU ROI, LE see **CAPITAN, LE** • 1945
CHEVALIER MYSTERE, LE • 1899 • Melies Georges • FRN • MYSTERIOUS KNIGHT, THE (USA)
CHEVALIER MYSTERE, LE • 1907 • de Chomon Segundo • FRN • KNIGHT MYSTERY, THE
CHEVALIER MYSTERE, LE • 1907 • Velle Gaston • FRN • MYSTERIOUS KNIGHT
CHEVALIER SANS ARMURE, LE (FRN) see **KNIGHT WITHOUT ARMOUR** • 1937
CHEVALIERS DE LA MONTAGNE, LES • 1930 • Bonnard Mario • FRN
CHEVALIERS DE L'AMOUR, LES • *Stanford Pamela* • FRN
CHEVALIERS DU CHLOROFORME, LES • 1905 • Melies Georges • FRN • CHLOROFORM FIENDS, THE (USA)
CHEVAUCHEE, LA • 1964 • Bourguignon Serge • FRN
CHEVAUX D'ACIER, LES • 1983 • Goulet Stella (c/d) • MTV • CND
CHEVAUX DE BOIS, LES • 1896 • Melies Georges • FRN • MERRY-GO-ROUND, A
CHEVAUX DE VAUGIRARD, LES • 1961 • Grospierre Louis • SHT • FRN
CHEVAUX DE VERCORS, LES • 1943 • Audry Jacqueline • FRN • HORSES OF THE VERCORS, THE
CHEVAUX D'HOLLYWOOD, LES • 1964 • Reichenbach Francois • DOC • FRN • HOLLYWOOD THROUGH A KEYHOLE
CHEVAUX ONT-ILS DES AILES?, LES • 1975 • Carle Gilles • DCS • CND
CHEVELURE, LA • 1960 • Kyrou Ado • SHT • FRN
CHEVRE, LA • 1961 • Grospierre Louis • SHT • FRN
CHEVRE, LA • 1981 • Veber Francis • FRN, MXC • CABRA, LA (MXC) ○ GOAT, THE
CHEVRE AUX PIEDS D'OR, LA see **DANSEUSE ROUGE, LA** • 1937
CHEVRE D'OR, LA • 1942 • Barberis Rene • FRN
CHEVRES • 1954 • Brault Michel, Sylvestre Claude • SHT • CND
CHEW-CHEW BABY • 1945 • Culhane James • ANS • USA
CHEW CHEW BABY • 1958 • Sparber I. • ANS • USA
CHEW CHEW LAND • 1910 • *De Garde Adele* • USA
CHEWIN' BRUIN, THE • 1940 • Clampett Robert • ANS • USA
CHEYENNE • 1929 • Rogell Albert S. • USA
CHEYENNE see **WYOMING KID, THE** • 1947
CHEYENNE AUTUMN • 1964 • Ford John • USA
CHEYENNE BRAVE, A • 1910 • Youngdeer James • USA
CHEYENNE COWBOY • 1949 • Watt Nate • SHT • USA
CHEYENNE CYCLONE • 1932 • Schaefer Armand • USA • SMASHING THROUGH (UKN)
CHEYENNE KID • 1933 • Hill Robert F. • USA
CHEYENNE KID, THE • 1930 • Jaccard Jacques • USA • FIGHTING TEST, THE (UKN)
CHEYENNE KID, THE • 1940 • Johnston Raymond K. • USA
CHEYENNE LOVE FOR A SIOUX • 1910 • *Bison* • USA
CHEYENNE MASSACRE, THE • 1913 • *Blackwell Carlyle* • USA
CHEYENNE MEDICINE MAN, THE • 1911 • *Bison* • USA
CHEYENNE RAIDERS, OR KIT CARSON ON THE SANTA FE TRAIL, THE • 1910 • *Kalem* • USA
CHEYENNE RIDES AGAIN • 1937 • Hill Robert F. • USA
CHEYENNE ROUNDUP • 1943 • Taylor Ray • USA
CHEYENNE SOCIAL CLUB, THE • 1970 • Kelly Gene • USA
CHEYENNE TAKES OVER • 1947 • Taylor Ray • USA
CHEYENNE TORNADO • 1935 • O'Connor William A. • USA
CHEYENNE TRAILS • 1928 • Horner Robert J. • USA
CHEYENNE WILDCAT • 1944 • Selander Lesley • USA
CHEYENNE'S BRIDE, THE • 1911 • *Pathe* • USA
CHEYENNE'S COURTSHIP, A • 1911 • *Bison* • USA
CHEYENNE'S PAL • 1917 • Ford John • SHT • USA
CHEZ LA SORCIERE • 1901 • Melies Georges • FRN • BACHELOR'S PARADISE, THE (USA)
CHEZ LE DENTISTE • 1903 • Zecca Ferdinand • FRN
CHEZ LE MAGNETISEUR • 1897-98 • Blache Alice • FRN
CHEZ LE MARECHAL-FERRANT • 1899-00 • Blache Alice • FRN
CHEZ LE PHOTOGRAPHE • 1900 • Blache Alice • FRN
CHEZ LES BUVEURS DE SANG • 1930 • Gourgaud Baron • DOC • FRN • VRAI VISAGE DE L'AFRIQUE, LE ○ AU PAYS DES BUVEURS DE SANG
CHEZ LES MANGEURS D'HOMMES • 1928 • Antoine Andre, Lugeon Robert • FRN • LAND OF THE CANNIBALS, THE
CHEZ NOUS • 1978 • Halldoff Jan • SWD
CHEZ NOUS, C'EST CHEZ NOUS • 1973 • Carriere Marcel • DOC • CND
CHEZ PORKY see **PORKY'S** • 1982
CHEZ PORKY II, LE LENDEMAIN see **PORKY'S II, THE NEXT DAY** • 1983
CHHAND PRITICHA • 1968 • Bhoite Madhav • IND
CHHATRABHANG • 1976 • Shivdasani Nina • IND • DIVINE PLAN, THE
CHHOTA BHAI • 1949 • *Sircar B. N. (P)* • IND
CHHOTI CHHOTI BATEN • 1965 • *Biswas Anil (M)* • IND
CHHOTISI MULAQAT • 1967 • Sircar Alo • IND • BRIEF ENCOUNTER
CHHOTTO JIJNASA • 1968 • Chatterjee Jagannath • IND • TINY QUESTION, A
CHHOU DANCE OF PURALIA • 1970 • *Ghatak Ritwik* • DOC • IND
CHHUPA RUSTAM • 1973 • *Burman S. D. (M)* • IND
CHHUTI • 1967 • Devi Arundhuti • IND • HOLIDAY ○ VACATION
CHI DE CHI O ARAU • 1924 • Ito Daisuke • JPN
CHI DICE DONNA DICE DONNA • 1976 • Cervi Tonino • ITL
CHI E MR. KLEIN? (ITL) see **MONSIEUR KLEIN** • 1976
CHI E PIU FELICE DI ME? • 1938 • Brignone Guido • ITL • WHO IS HAPPIER THAN I? (USA)
CHI E SENZA PECCATO.. • 1953 • Matarazzo Raffaello • ITL
CH'I-HSIEN NU • *Ling-Po Ivy* • HKG • SEVENTH FAIRY, THE ○ SEVENTH FAIRY SISTER, THE
CHI ILLUMINA LA GRANDE NOTTE? • 1981 • Petri Elio • ITL
CHI LAVORI E PERDUTO • 1963 • Brass Tinto • FRN, ITL • IN CAPO AL MONDO ○ WHO WORKS IS LOST
CHI L'HA VISTA MORIRE? • 1972 • Lado Aldo • ITL
CHI L'HA VISTO? • 1943 • Alessandrini Goffredo • ITL
CH'I-MOU-MIAO CHI WU FU-HSING • 1984 • Hong Jinbao • HKG • WINNERS AND SINNERS
CHI NO BOHKOH • 1968 • Higashimoto Kaoru • JPN • BLOODY VIOLATION
CHI NO MURE • 1970 • Kumai Kei • JPN • THRONGS OF THE EARTH, THE
CHI O SUU NINGYO • 1970 • Yamamoto Michio • JPN • VAMPIRE DOLL, THE (USA)
CH'I-PAI-WAN TA CHIEH-AN • 1976 • Wu Sze-Yuan • HKG • MILLION DOLLARS SNATCH
CHI SEI? • 1974 • Hellman Oliver, D'Ettore Piazzoli Roberto • ITL, USA • DEVIL WITHIN HER, THE (UKN) ○ BEYOND THE DOOR (USA) ○ BEHIND THE DOOR
CHI SEI TU? • 1939 • Valori Gino • ITL
CHI SI DICE A ROMA • 1979 • Scola Ettore • ITL
CHI SI FERMA E PERDUTO • 1961 • Corbucci Sergio • ITL
CH'I-SOU SHIN ERH TAO • 1982 • Cheng Yu-Wen • HKG • DYNAMITE TRIO
CH'I-TAI NI CHANG-TA • 1988 • Liao Ch'Ing-Sung • TWN • BE MY LOVELY CHILD AGAIN
CHI TO REI • 1922 • Mizoguchi Kenji • JPN • BLOOD AND SOUL (USA)
CHI TO SUNA • 1965 • Okamoto Kihachi • JPN • FORT GRAVEYARD
CHI TROVA UN AMICO TROVA UN TESORO • 1979 • Corbucci Sergio • ITL • WHO FINDS A FRIEND FINDS A TREASURE
CHI VUOL DORMIRE NEL MIO LETTO? (ITL) see **MEFIEZ-VOUS, MESDAMES!** • 1963
CHI WA KAWAITEIRU • 1960 • Yoshida Yoshishige • JPN • DRY EARTH
CHIA • 1953 • Wa Hui • HKG • FAMILY
CHIA-CHUANG YI-NIU-CH'E • 1983 • Chang Mei-Chun • TWN • OXCART DIARY, AN
CHIA-JU WO SHIH CHEN-TE • 1981 • Wang T'Ung • TWN • IF I WERE FOR REAL
CHIA TAO KUNG-LI-TE NAN-JEN • 1990 • Pai Ching-Jui • TWN
CHIA TSAI HSIANG-KANG • 1984 • Ching Hai-Lin • HKG • HOME AT HONG KONG
CHIAMATE 22-22 TENENTE SHERIDAN • 1960 • Bianchi Giorgio • ITL
CHIAMAVAN CAPINERA, LA • 1957 • Regnoli Piero • ITL
CHIAMAVANO MEZZOGIORNO, LO (ITL) see **MAN CALLED NOON, THE** • 1973
CHIAMAVANO SPIRITO SANTO, LO see **UOMO AVVISATO MEZZO AMMAZZATO.. PAROLA DI SPIRITO SANTO** • 1972
CHIANG-HU HAN-TZU • 1976 • Chang Ch'Eh • HKG • HEROIC EVENTS, THE
CH'IANG-NEI CH'IANG-WAI • 1980 • Yu Jen-T'Ai, Ch'En Hsin-Chien • HKG • SERVANTS, THE
CHIANG SHAN MEI JEN • 1959 • *Dai Lin* • JPN • KINGDOM AND THE BEAUTY, THE (USA)
CHIARAJE, BATALLA RITUAL • 1977 • Figueroa Luis • PRU
CHIAVE, LA • 1984 • Brass Tinto • ITL • KEY, THE
CHIBIKKO REMI TO MEIKEN KAPI • 1970 • Serikawa Yugo, Flocker Jim • ANM • JPN • NOBODY'S BOY
CHIBIKURO SAMBO NO TORA TAIJI • 1957 • Mochinaga Tadahito • ANS • JPN • LITTLE BLACK SAMBO HUNTS THE TIGER
CHIBOUGAMAU • 1956 • Rivard Fernand • DCS • CND
CHIBUSA NO KAORI • 1967 • Kawashima Satomi • JPN • FRAGRANCE OF BREASTS
CHIBUSA NO KAORI • 1968 • Ure Hajime • JPN • ODOUR OF THE BREAST
CHIBUSA NO MITSURYOH • 1968 • Sawa Kensuke • JPN • POACHING OF BREASTS
CHIBUSA O DAKU MUSUMETACHI • 1962 • Yamamoto Satsuo • JPN
CHIBUSA YO EIEN NARE • 1955 • Tanaka Kinuyo • JPN • ETERNAL HEART, THE
CHICA CASI DECENTE, UNA • 1971 • Lorente German • SPN
CHICA DE CHICAGO, UNA • 1958 • Mur Oti • SPN
CHICA DE LOS ANUNCIOS, LA • 1968 • Lazaga Pedro • SPN • ADVERTISEMENT GIRL, THE
CHICA DE VIA CONDOTTI, LA • 1973 • Lorente German • SPN, ITL • RAGAZZA DI VIA CONDOTTI, LA (ITL)
CHICA DEL AUTO-STOP, LA • 1964 • Lluch Miguel • SPN
CHICA DEL BARRIO, LA • 1955 • Nunez Ricardo • SPN
CHICA DEL GATO, LA • 1962 • Pamplona Clemente • SPN
CHICA DEL LUNES, LA • 1967 • Torre-Nilsson Leopoldo, Kennedy Burt • ARG • MONDAY'S CHILD (USA)
CHICA DEL MOLINO ROJO, LA • 1973 • Martin Eugenio • SPN
CHICA DELLA CALLE FLORIDA, LA • 1921 • Ferreyra Jose • ARG
CHICA PARA DOS, UNA • 1965 • Klimovsky Leon • SPN
CHICA PARA TODO • 1962 • Ozores Mariano • SPN
CHICA Y UN SENOR, UNA • 1973 • Maso Pedro • SPN
CHICAGO • 1927 • Urson Frank • USA
CHICAGO 70 • 1970 • Feltham Kerry B. • USA, CND • GREAT CHICAGO CONSPIRACY CIRCUS, THE ○ CONSPIRACY CIRCUS -CHICAGO '70
CHICAGO AFTER MIDNIGHT • 1928 • Ince Ralph • USA
CHICAGO BLUES • 1970 • Cokliss Harley • UKN
CHICAGO CALLING • 1951 • Reinhardt John • USA
CHICAGO, CHICAGO (UKN) see **GAILY, GAILY** • 1969
CHICAGO CONFIDENTIAL • 1957 • Salkow Sidney • USA
CHICAGO DEADLINE • 1949 • Allen Lewis • USA
CHICAGO DIGEST • 1951 • Paviot Paul • SHT • FRN • DU SANG DANS LA SCIURE
CHICAGO FIRE, THE (UKN) see **BARRIERS BURNED AWAY** • 1925
CHICAGO JOE AND THE SHOWGIRL • 1989 • Rose Bernard • UKN
CHICAGO KID, THE • 1945 • McDonald Frank • USA
CHICAGO KID, THE see **FABULOUS BASTARD FROM CHICAGO, THE** • 1969
CHICAGO MASQUERADE (UKN) see **LITTLE EGYPT** • 1951
CHICAGO MATERNITY CENTER STORY, THE • 1977 • Blumenthal Jerry, Davenport Suzanne, Karp Sharon, Quinn Gordon • USA
CHICAGO MAY THE MODERN ADVENTURESS • 1909 • *Anglo-American Films* • UKN
CHICAGO MUSEUM OF SCIENCE AND INDUSTRY • 1986 • Chapman Christopher • DOC • CND
CHICAGO SAL see **ENVIRONMENT** • 1922
CHICAGO SEVEN, THE • 1970 • Ray Nicholas • DOC • USA
CHICAGO STORY, THE • 1981 • London Jerry • TVM • USA
CHICAGO SYNDICATE • 1955 • Sears Fred F. • USA
CHICANO • 1975 • Casillas Jaime • MXC
CHICANO GRUESO CALIBRE • 1975 • *Peliculas Rodriguez* • MXC • CHICANO HEAVY CALIBRE
CHICANO HEAVY CALIBRE see **CHICANO GRUESO CALIBRE** • 1975
CHICANO JUSTICIERO, EL • 1974 • *Cima* • MXC
CHICAS CASADERAS • 1959 • Crevenna Alfredo B. • MXC
CHICAS DE ALQUILER • 1973 • Iquino Ignacio F. • SPN • GIRLS FOR HIRE
CHICAS DE CLUB • 1970 • Grau Jorge • SPN • CANTICO
CHICAS DE LA CRUZ ROJA, LAS • 1958 • Salvia Rafael J. • SPN
CHICHI • 1924 • Shimazu Yasujiro • JPN • FATHER
CHICHI • 1988 • Kinoshita Keisuke • JPN • FATHER
CHICHI ARIKI • 1942 • Ozu Yasujiro • JPN • THERE WAS A FATHER ○ THERE IS A FATHER
CHICHI TO KO • 1983 • Hosaka Nobuhiko • JPN • FATHER AND SON
CHICHI TO KO see **ZOKU NAMONAKU MAZUSHIKU UTUSUKUSHIKU: CHICHI TO KO** • 1967
CHICHIBU SUIKODEN: KAGE O KIRU KEN • 1967 • Ida Tan • JPN • LIVING BY THE SWORD
CHICHICHETTE ET CIE • 1921 • Desfontaines Henri • FRN
CHICHIKO GUSA • 1966 • Maruyama Seiji • JPN • GREEN LIGHT TO JOY (USA)
CHICHO O MIENTRAS EL CUERPO AGUANTE • 1983 • Trueba Fernando • DOC • SPN • CHICO OR AS LONG AS THE BODY CAN STAND IT
CHICK • 1928 • Bramble A. V. • UKN
CHICK • 1936 • Hankinson Michael • UKN

CHICK AND DOUBLE CHICK • 1946 • Kneitel Seymour • ANS • USA
CHICK CARTER, DETECTIVE • 1946 • Abrahams Derwin • SRL • USA
CHICK THAT WAS NOT EGGS-TINCT, THE • 1914 • Plumb Hay? • UKN
CHICKEN! • 1914 • *Selig* • USA
CHICKEN, THE • 1928 • *Sennett Mack (P)* • SHT • USA
CHICKEN, THE see **TOWN SCANDAL, THE** • 1923
CHICKEN, THE (USA) see **POULET, LE** • 1963
CHICKEN A LA CABARET • 1920 • Heerman Victor • SHT • USA
CHICKEN A LA KING • 1919 • *Lyons Eddie* • USA
CHICKEN A LA KING • 1928 • Lehrman Henry • USA • GAY DECEIVER, THE
CHICKEN A LA KING • 1937 • Fleischer Dave • ANS • USA
CHICKEN AND DUCK TALK see **GAITUNGAP GONG** • 1988
CHICKEN CASEY • 1917 • West Raymond B. • USA
CHICKEN CHASED AND HENPECKED • 1917 • Moore Vin • SHT • USA
CHICKEN CHASER • 1914 • Lehrman Henry • USA
CHICKEN CHASERS, THE • 1914 • *Joker* • USA
CHICKEN CHRONICLES, THE • 1977 • Simon Francis • CND
CHICKEN COOP see **LUL** • 1988
CHICKEN EVERY SUNDAY • 1949 • Seaton George • USA
CHICKEN FEED • 1927 • Roach Hal • SHT • USA
CHICKEN FRACAS-SEE • 1962 • Hanna William, Barbera Joseph • ANS • USA
CHICKEN HEARTED • 1915 • Nash Percy? • UKN
CHICKEN-HEARTED JIM • 1916 • Ford Francis • SHT • USA
CHICKEN-HEARTED WOLF • 1962 • Hanna William, Barbera Joseph • ANS • USA
CHICKEN HUNTERS, THE • 1919 • *National Film Corp. Of America* • SHT • USA
CHICKEN IN THE CASE, THE • 1921 • Heerman Victor • USA • LEND ME YOUR WIFE
CHICKEN IN THE ROUGH • 1951 • Hannah Jack • ANS • USA
CHICKEN INSPECTOR, THE • 1914 • Van Wally, North Wilfred • USA
CHICKEN JITTERS • 1939 • Clampett Robert • ANS • USA
CHICKEN LITTLE • 1943 • Geronimi Clyde • ANS • USA
CHICKEN PARADE, THE • 1922 • Smith John P., Peebles Mort • USA
CHICKEN RANCH • 1983 • Broomfield Nicholas, Sissell Sandi • DOC • USA
CHICKEN REEL • 1933 • Lantz Walter, Nolan William • ANS • USA
CHICKEN THAT CAME HOME TO ROOST, THE see **TOWN SCANDAL, THE** • 1923
CHICKEN THAT LAID GOLDEN EGGS, THE see **POULE AUX OEUFS D'OR, LA** • 1906
CHICKEN THIEF • 1904 • *Bitzer Billy (Ph)* • USA
CHICKEN WAGON FAMILY • 1939 • Leeds Herbert I. • USA
CHICKENHAWKS, THE • 1974 • Steckler Ray Dennis • USA
CHICKENS • 1916 • Stull Walter, Burns Bobby • USA
CHICKENS • 1921 • Nelson Jack • USA
CHICKENS COME HOME • 1931 • Horne James W. • SHT • USA
CHICKENS IN TURKEY • 1919 • *Tweede Dan* • USA
CHICKIE • 1925 • Dillon John Francis • USA
CHICKIE see **CHICKIE TETTRAZZINI** • 1975
CHICKIE TETTRAZZINI • 1975 • Dodgson Charles • USA • CHICKIE
CHICKS TO ORDER see **STRICTLY FRESH EGGS** • 1903
CHICO-CHICA-BOOM • 1968 • Bosch Juan • SPN
CHICO FININHO, O • 1982 • Fernandes Serio • PRT
CHICO O CHICA? • 1962 • del Amo Antonio • SPN
CHICO OR AS LONG AS THE BODY CAN STAND IT see **CHICHO O MIENTRAS EL CUERPO AGUANTE** • 1983
CHICO VALIENTE, UN • 1958 • de la Serna Mauricio • MXC
CHICOASEN • 1978 • Baledon Rafael • MXC
CHICOS CON LAS CHICAS, LOS • 1967 • Aguirre Javier • SPN • BOYS WITH THE GIRLS, THE
CHICOS DE LA ESCUELA, LOS • 1925 • Rey Florian • SPN
CHICOS DE LA GUERRA, LOS • 1984 • Kamin Bebe • ARG • WAR KIDS, THE
CHICOS DE LA PRENSA, LOS • 1921 • Noriega Hope Carlos • MXC
CHICOS DE LA PRENSA, LOS • 1936 • Peon Ramon • MXC • NEWSPAPER BOYS, THE (USA)
CHICOS DEL PREU, LOS • 1967 • Lazaga Pedro • SPN
CHICOS, LOS • 1959 • Ferreri Marco • SPN • BOYS, THE
CHICOT, DENTISTE AMERICAIN • 1896 • Melies Georges • FRN • UP-TO-DATE DENTIST, AN ○ DENTISTE DIABOLIQUE, LA
CHIDAMBARAN • 1985 • Aravindan G. • IND
CHIDIAKHANA • 1967 • Ray Satyajit • IND • ZOO
CHIEDI PERDONO A DIO -NON A ME • 1968 • Musolino Vincenzo • ITL • ASK GOD FOR FORGIVENESS ..NOT ME
CHIEDO ASILO • 1979 • Ferreri Marco • ITL, FRN • PIPICACADODO (FRN) ○ NO CHILD'S LAND ○ MY ASYLUM ○ PIPI, CACA, DODO
CHIEF, THE • 1933 • Reisner Charles F. • USA • MY OLD MAN'S A FIREMAN (UKN) ○ FIRE CHIEF, THE
CHIEF, THE • 1964 • Fox Beryl, Leiterman Douglas • DOC • CND
CHIEF, THE see **JEFE, EL** • 1958
CHIEF BLACKFOOT'S VINDICATION • 1910 • *Kalem* • USA
CHIEF CHARLIE HORSE • 1956 • Smith Paul J. • ANS • USA
CHIEF COOK, THE • 1917 • Gillstrom Arvid E. • SHT • USA
CHIEF CRAZY HORSE • 1955 • Sherman George • USA • VALLEY OF FURY (UKN)
CHIEF FIRE EYE'S GAME • 1911 • *Champion* • USA
CHIEF FROM GOINGE, THE see **GOINGEHOVDINGEN** • 1953
CHIEF INSPECTOR, THE • 1915 • MacDonald J. Farrell • USA
CHIEF LO GATTO see **COMMISSARIO LO GATTO, IL** • 1987
CHIEF OF CHUKOTKA see **NACHALNIK CHUKOTKI** • 1967
CHIEF OF POLICE, THE • 1914 • *Kalem* • USA
CHIEF OF THE HORSE FARM, THE see **MENESGAZDA** • 1978
CHIEF OF THE SOULS' DEPARTMENT, THE see **SEFUL SECTORULUI SUFLETE** • 1967
CHIEF WANTS NO SURVIVORS, THE see **CHEF WUNSCHT KEINE ZEUGEN, DER** • 1963
CHIEF WHITE EAGLE • 1912 • Fielding Romaine • USA
CHIEFLY CONCERNING MALES • 1915 • Johnson Tefft • USA
CHIEFS • 1969 • Leacock Richard • DOC • USA
CHIEFS • 1985 • London Jerry • TVM • USA • ONCE UPON A MURDER
CHIEF'S BLANKET, THE • 1912 • Lucas Wilfred? • USA
CHIEF'S DAUGHTER, THE • 1911 • *Selig* • USA
CHIEF'S DAUGHTER, THE • 1911 • Griffith D. W. • *Ab* • USA
CHIEF'S GOAT, THE • 1915 • Van Wally • USA
CHIEF'S LOVE AFFAIR, THE • 1914 • *Ab* • USA
CHIEF'S PREDICAMENT, THE • 1913 • Nicholls George, Sennett Mack (Spv) • USA
CHIEF'S SON IS DEAD, THE see **HOVDINGENS SON AR DOD** • 1938
CHIEFTAIN, THE see **HOVDINGEN** • 1984
CHIEFTAIN KODR • 1958 • Kalik Mikhail, Rytsarev Boris • USS
CHIEFTAIN'S REVENGE OR A TRAGEDY IN THE HIGHLANDS OF SCOTLAND, THE • 1908 • *Vitagraph* • USA
CHIEFTAIN'S SONS, THE • 1913 • Cabanne W. Christy • USA
CHIEH-CH'UAN-TAO • 1976 • Wang Hsing-Lei • HKG • JEET-KUNE-DO - THE KILLER PUNCH OF BRUCE LEE
CHIEKO-SHO • 1957 • Kumagai Hisatora • JPN • CHIEKO STORY
CHIEKO-SHO • 1967 • Nakamura Noboru • JPN • PORTRAIT OF CHIEKO
CHIEKO STORY see **CHIEKO-SHO** • 1957
CHIEMI NO HAIHIIRU • 1956 • Suzuki • JPN • CHIEMI'S HIGH HEELED SHOES
CHIEMI'S HIGH HEELED SHOES see **CHIEMI NO HAIHIIRU** • 1956
CHIEN, LE • 1984 • Gallotte Jean-Francois • FRN
CHIEN ANDALOU, UN • 1930 • Bunuel Luis, Dali Salvador • FRN • ANDALUSIAN DOG, AN
CH'IEN CHIANG YU SHUI CH'IEN CHIANG MING • 1982 • Li Hsing • TWN
CHIEN DANS UN JEU DE QUILLES, UN • 1962 • Collin Fabien • FRN, ITL
CHIEN DANS UN JEU DE QUILLES, UN • 1982 • Guillou Bernard • FRN
CHIEN DE BASKERVILLE, LE • 1914 • *Pathe* • FRN • HOUND OF THE BASKERVILLES, THE (USA)
CHIEN DE PIQUE, LE • 1961 • Allegret Yves • FRN
CHIEN ET LA PIPE, LE • 1903 • Zecca Ferdinand • FRN
CHIEN FOU, LE • 1966 • Matalon Eddy • FRN, CND • MAD DOG, THE ○ LOSER
CHIEN JAUNE, LE • 1932 • Tarride Jean • FRN
CHIEN JOUANT A LA BALLE • 1905 • Blache Alice • FRN
CH'IEN LUNG HUANG-TI • 1977 • Li Han-Hsiang • HKG • EMPEROR CHIEN LUNG PART II
CH'IEN LUNG HUANG YU KU-NIANG • 1980 • Li Han-Hsiang • HKG • EMPEROR CHIEN LUNG AND THE BEAUTY ○ KINGDOM AND THE BEAUTY, THE
CHIEN MELOMANE, LE • 1973 • Grimault Paul • ANM • FRN
CHIEN-NU YU-HU • 1970 • *Ching Li* • HKG • MISSION IMPOSSIBLE (USA) ○ SOUL OF A SWORDSMAN
CH'IEN-NU YU-HUN • 1959 • Li Han-Hsiang • HKG • ENCHANTING SHADOW ○ CHIN NU YU HUN
CHIEN QUI RAPPORTE, UN • 1931 • Choux Jean • FRN
CH'IEN TSO KUAI • 1980 • Wu Yusen • HKG
CHIENNE, LA • 1931 • Renoir Jean • FRN • ISN'T LIFE A BITCH?
CHIENNES, LES • 1972 • Lemoine Michel • FRN
CHIENNES DE SOLEDOR, LES see **CINQ FILLES EN FURIE** • 1964
CHIENS, LES • 1971 • Cherif Hachemi • ALG
CHIENS, LES • 1979 • Jessua Alain • FRN • DOGS, THE (USA)
CHIENS-CHAUDS, LES see **HOT DOGS** • 1980
CHIENS CONTREBANDIERS, LES • 1906 • Heuze Andre • FRN
CHIENS DANS LA NUIT, LES • 1965 • Rozier Willy • FRN, GRC • GIRL CAN'T STOP, THE (USA)
CHIENS PERDUS SANS COLLIER • 1955 • Delannoy Jean • FRN, ITL • CANI PERDUTI SENZA COLLARE (ITL) ○ LITTLE REBELS, THE (USA)
CHIENS SAVANTS, LES • 1902 • Blache Alice • FRN
CHIENS VERTS DU DESERT, LES (FRN) see **ATTENTATO AI TRE GRANDI** • 1967
CHIESA, LA • 1988 • Soavi Michele • ITL • CHURCH, THE
CHIFFONIER, LE • 1899-00 • Blache Alice • FRN
CHIFFONIER, LE see **BONNE FARCE, UNE** • 1896
CHIFFONIERS D'EMMAUS, LES • 1955 • Darene Robert • FRN
CHIFFY KIDS (2ND SERIES), THE • 1978 • Bracknell David • UKN
CHIFFY KIDS, THE • 1976 • Bracknell David • SRL • UKN
CHIFLADOS DEL ROCK'N ROLL, LOS • 1956 • Diaz Morales Jose • MXC
CHIFUBUKI SHIMODA-KAIDO • 1959 • Mori Issei • JPN
CHIGO NO KEMPO • 1927 • Otsuka • JPN • CHILDISH SWORD MASTER ○ SWORD OF THE CHILD
CHIH AI-CH'IN P'ENG • 1977 • Ch'En-Feng • DOC • HKG • BEST FRIENDS, THE
CHIH TAO HUANG LUNG • 1975 • Wang Yu, Trenchard-Smith Brian • HKG • MAN FROM HONGKONG, THE ○ DRAGON FLIES, THE
CHIHEISEN • 1984 • Shindo Kaneto • JPN • HORIZON, THE
CHIISAKOBE • 1962 • Tasaka Tomotaka • JPN • CARPENTER AND CHILDREN, A
CHIISANA BOKEN RYOKO • 1963 • Oshima Nagisa • JPN • SMALL CHILD'S FIRST ADVENTURE, A ○ CHILD'S FIRST ADVENTURE, A ○ SMALL ADVENTURE, A
CHIISANA KUKAN • 1964 • Kuri Yoji • ANS • JPN • SMALL SPACE
CHIISANA SASAYAKI • 1966 • Kuri Yoji • ANS • JPN • LITTLE MURMUR
CHIISANA SNACK see **CHIISANA SUNAKKA** • 1968
CHIISANA SUNAKKA • 1968 • Saito Koichi • JPN • WE MET AT THE SNACK BAR ○ CHIISANA SNACK
CHIISANA TANEI TACHI • 1956 • Wakasughi Mitsuo • JPN • BOY DETECTIVES, THE
CHIISANA TOBOSHA • 1967 • Kinugasa Teinosuke • JPN, USS • LITTLE RUNAWAY, THE
CHIJIN NO AI • 1949 • Kimura Keigo • JPN • FOOL'S LOVE
CHIJIN NO AI • 1960 • Kimura Keigo • JPN • IDIOT IN LOVE, AN
CHIJIN NO AI • 1967 • Masumura Yasuzo • JPN • IDIOT IN LOVE, AN
CHIJO • 1957 • Yoshimura Kozaburo • JPN • ON THIS EARTH ○ ON THE EARTH
CHIKAGAI NIJUYO-JIKAN • 1947 • Sekigawa Hideo, Imai Tadashi • JPN • TWENTY FOUR HOURS OF A SECRET LIFE ○ TWENTY FOUR HOURS OF THE UNDERGROUND STREET ○ 24 HOURS IN AN UNDERGROUND MARKET ○ CHAIKAGAI 24-JIKAN
CHIKAMATSU MONOGATARI • 1954 • Mizoguchi Kenji • JPN • STORY FROM CHIKAMATSU, A (USA) ○ CRUCIFIED LOVERS, THE
CHIKAN NO KISETSU • 1968 • Yamamoto Shinya • JPN • SEASON OF SEX CRIMINALS, THE
CHIKEMURI TAKADA NO BABA • 1928 • Ito Daisuke • JPN
CHIKIYU KOGERI MEIREI see **GOJIRA TAI GAIGAN** • 1972
CHIKUMAGAWA ZESSHO • 1967 • Toyoda Shiro • JPN • RIVER OF FOREVER
CHIKUZAN HITORI TABI • 1976 • Shindo Kaneto • JPN • LONELY JOURNEY OF CHIKUZAN ○ CHIKUZAN TRAVELS ALONE ○ LIFE OF CHIKUZAN, THE ○ LIFE OF CHIKUZAN, TSUGARU GAMISEN PLAYER
CHIKUZAN TRAVELS ALONE see **CHIKUZAN HITORI TABI** • 1976
CHIKWEMBO • 1953 • Marques Carlos • PRT
CHIKYU BOEIGUN • 1957 • Honda Inoshiro • JPN • MYSTERIANS, THE (USA) ○ EARTH DEFENCE FORCE ○ EARTH DEFENSE FORCES
CHIKYU WA MAWARU • 1928 • Tasaka Tomotaka • JPN • SPINNING EARTH 1-11
CHIL-SU AND MAN-SU • 1988 • Park Gwang-Su • SKR
CHILAM BALAM • 1955 • de Martino Inigo • MXC
CHILD • 1948 • Zils Paul • IND
CHILD, THE • 1954 • Mason James • SHT • USA
CHILD, THE • 1977 • Voskanian Robert • USA • KILL AND GO HIDE ○ ZOMBIE CHILD
CHILD, THE see **BARNET** • 1913
CHILD, THE see **BARNETS MAGT** • 1914
CHILD, THE see **BARNET** • 1940
CHILD, A DOG, A VAGABOND, A see **KEIN, EIN HUND, EIN VAGABUND, EIN** • 1934
CHILD, A WAND AND A WISH, A • 1912 • Martinek H. O. • UKN
CHILD ACCUSER, THE • 1907 • Hough Harold • UKN
CHILD AND THE BALL, THE see **DECAP I LOPTA** • 1960
CHILD AND THE COP, THE see **BAMBINO E IL POLIZIOTTO, IL** • 1990
CHILD AND THE FIDDLER, THE • 1910 • Bouwmeester Theo? • UKN
CHILD AND THE FIDDLER, THE • 1917 • Haldane Bert • UKN
CHILD AND THE KILLER, THE • 1959 • Varnel Max • UKN
CHILD AND THE TRAMP, THE • 1911 • Merwin Bannister • USA
CHILD BRIDE • 1938 • Revier Harry • USA
CHILD BRIDE see **BALIKA BADHU** • 1967
CHILD BRIDE AT SHORT CREEK • 1981 • Lewis Robert Michael • TVM • USA • CHILD BRIDE OF SHORT CREEK, THE
CHILD BRIDE OF SHORT CREEK, THE see **CHILD BRIDE AT SHORT CREEK** • 1981
CHILD CRUSOES, THE • 1911 • Brooke Van Dyke • USA
CHILD DETECTIVE, THE • 1912 • Haldane Bert? • UKN
CHILD DETECTIVE, OR SHADOWS OF LIFE, THE • 1913 • *Belmont* • USA
CHILD DEVELOPMENT • 1950 • Crawley Judith • SER • CND
CHILD FOR SALE, A • 1920 • Abramson Ivan • USA
CHILD FROM NGATCH, THE see **DOOMI NGACC** • 1979
CHILD IN JUDGEMENT, A • 1915 • King Carleton S. • USA
CHILD IN PAWN, A • 1921 • *D.w.d. Film Corp.* • USA
CHILD IN THE HOUSE • 1956 • Endfield Cy, De La Tour Charles • UKN
CHILD IS BORN, A • 1940 • Bacon Lloyd • USA • GIVE ME A CHILD
CHILD IS WAITING, A • 1963 • Cassavetes John • USA
CHILD LABOR • 1913 • *Hodges Runa* • USA
CHILD MOTHER, THE see **LITTLE MOTHER, THE** • 1913
CHILD NEEDED A MOTHER, THE • 1915 • *Mann Hank* • USA
CHILD O' MY HEART • 1914 • Shaw Harold • UKN
CHILD OF A SUFFRAGETTE, THE • 1913 • Thornton F. Martin? • UKN
CHILD OF CIRCUMSTANCES, A • 1916 • *Robbins Marc* • SHT • USA
CHILD OF DESTINY, THE • 1916 • Nigh William • USA
CHILD OF DIVORCE • 1946 • Fleischer Richard • USA
CHILD OF FATE, THE see **MIGNON** • 1912
CHILD OF FORTUNE, A • 1916 • *Mayo Frank* • SHT • USA
CHILD OF GOD, A • 1915 • Adolfi John G. • USA
CHILD OF LOVE see **CHILD UNDER A LEAF** • 1974
CHILD OF MANHATTAN • 1933 • Buzzell Edward • USA
CHILD OF M'SIEU, THE • 1917 • King Henry • USA
CHILD OF M'SIEU, THE • 1919 • Ingraham Lloyd • USA
CHILD OF MYSTERY, A • 1916 • Henley Hobart • USA
CHILD OF PARIS see **CHILD OF THE PARIS STREETS, A** • 1916
CHILD OF THE BIG CITY see **DITYA BOLSHOVA GORODA** • 1914
CHILD OF THE COMMUNITY, A see **OPSTINSKO DETE** • 1951
CHILD OF THE DAFFODILS see **KIND VAN DE ZON** • 1975
CHILD OF THE DESERT, A • 1914 • *Rich Vivian* • USA
CHILD OF THE FOREST, A • 1909 • Porter Edwin S. • USA
CHILD OF THE GHETTO, A • 1910 • Griffith D. W. • USA
CHILD OF THE HILLS, A • 1913 • *Pilot* • USA
CHILD OF THE NIGHT see **NIGHT HAIR CHILD** • 1971
CHILD OF THE NORTH, A • 1915 • Sturgeon Rollin S. • USA
CHILD OF THE PARIS STREETS, A • 1916 • Ingraham Lloyd • USA • CHILD OF PARIS
CHILD OF THE PRAIRIE, A • 1915 • Mix Tom • USA
CHILD OF THE PRAIRIE, A • 1925 • Mix Tom • USA
CHILD OF THE PRAIRIE, THE • 1913 • *Selig* • USA
CHILD OF THE PURPLE SAGE, A • 1912 • *Anderson Broncho Billy* • USA
CHILD OF THE RANCHO, A • 1911 • *Bison* • USA
CHILD OF THE REGIMENT, A • 1910 • *Motograph* • USA
CHILD OF THE SEA, A • 1909 • *Kalem* • USA
CHILD OF THE SEA, A • 1910 • *Lubin* • USA
CHILD OF THE SEA, A • 1915 • Wilson Frank? • UKN
CHILD OF THE SEA, THE • 1913 • Parker Lem B. • USA
CHILD OF THE STREETS, A • 1915 • Batley Ernest G. • UKN

CHILD OF THE STREETS, A • 1967 • Benegal Shyam • DCS • IND
CHILD OF THE SURF, A • 1915 • *Sampson Teddy* • USA
CHILD OF THE TENEMENTS, A • 1912 • *Cornwall Blanche* • USA
CHILD OF THE WEST, A • 1910 • *Bison* • USA
CHILD OF THE WEST, A • 1911 • *Essanay* • USA
CHILD OF THE WEST, THE • 1916 • *Saunders Jackie* • SHT • USA
CHILD OF THE WILD, A • 1917 • Adolfi John G. • USA
CHILD OF THE WILDERNESS, A • 1912 • *Wade Frankie* • USA
CHILD OF WAR, A • 1913 • Conway Jack? • USA
CHILD PSYKOLOJIKY • 1941 • Fleischer Dave • ANS • USA
CHILD SAVER, THE • 1988 • Lathan Stan • TVM • USA
CHILD SOCK-OLOGY • 1961 • Hanna William, Barbera Joseph • ANS • USA
CHILD SOCKOLOGY • 1953 • Sparber I. • ANS • USA
CHILD STEALER, THE • 1979 • Damski Mel • TVM • USA
CHILD STEALERS OF PARIS, THE • 1913 • Brenon Herbert • USA
CHILD, THE DOG AND THE VILLAIN, THE • 1915 • Mix Tom • USA
CHILD THOU GAVEST ME, THE • 1914 • O'Sullivan Tony • USA
CHILD THOU GAVEST ME, THE • 1921 • Stahl John M. • USA • RETRIBUTION
CHILD UNDER A LEAF • 1974 • Bloomfield George • CND • LOVE CHILD (UKN) ○ CHILD OF LOVE ○ ADULTERESS, THE
CHILD WENT FORTH, A • 1941 • Losey Joseph • SHT • USA
CHILD WRITERS see **TSUZURIKATA KYODAI** • 1958
CHILDE JOHN see **JANOS VITEZ** • 1973
CHILDHOOD • 1987 • Kuhn Siegfried • GDR
CHILDHOOD DAYS • 1943 • Negulesco Jean • SHT • USA
CHILDHOOD FRIEND see **BALYAKALA SAKHI** • 1967
CHILDHOOD OF GORKY see **DETSTVO GORKOVO** • 1938
CHILDHOOD OF IVAN see **IVANOVO DETSTVO** • 1962
CHILDHOOD OF JACK HARKAWAY, THE • 1910 • *Thanhouser* • USA
CHILDHOOD OF KRISHNA, THE see **KALYA MARDAN** • 1919
CHILDHOOD OF MAXIM GORKI, THE see **DETSTVO GORKOVO** • 1938
CHILDHOOD'S HAPPY DAYS • 1916 • *Drew Sidney* • SHT • USA
CHILDHOOD'S VOWS • 1900 • *Bitzer Billy (Ph)* • USA
CHILDISH SWORD MASTER see **CHIGO NO KEMPO** • 1927
CHILDISH THINGS see **TALE OF THE COCK** • 1966
CHILDREN • 1976 • Davies Terence • UKN
CHILDREN see **NINOS** • 1972
CHILDREN, THE • 1980 • Kalmanowicz Max • USA • CHILDREN OF RAVENSBACK
CHILDREN, THE see **MARRIAGE PLAYGROUND, THE** • 1929
CHILDREN ACCUSE see **DZIECI OSKARZAJA** • 1956
CHILDREN ADRIFT see **ENFANTS DES COURANTS D'AIR, LES** • 1959
CHILDREN AND CARS • 1971 • Halas John • ANS • UKN
CHILDREN AND THE LIONS, THE • 1900 • Green George • UKN
CHILDREN AND THE STATUE OF BUDDHA, THE • 1952 • Shimizu Hiroshi • JPN
CHILDREN ARE SINGING, THE • 1960 • Takacs Gabor • DOC • HNG
CHILDREN ARE WATCHING US, THE see **BAMBINI CI GUARDANO, I** • 1944
CHILDREN AT SCHOOL • 1937 • Wright Basil • DOC • UKN
CHILDREN AT TABLE see **TWIN'S TEA PARTY, THE** • 1896
CHILDREN AT WORK see **PAISTI AG OBAIR** • 1973
CHILDREN BATHING • 1901 • Porter Edwin S. • USA
CHILDREN, BOOKS see **GYERMEKEK, KONYVEK** • 1962
CHILDREN CARE, THE • 1986 • Arsenault Ray • MTV • CND
CHILDREN DANCING • 1897 • Norton C. Goodwin • UKN
CHILDREN FEEDING DUCKLINGS • 1899 • *Bitzer Billy (Ph)* • USA
CHILDREN FROM BLUE LAKE MOUNTAIN, THE see **BARNA FRAN BLASJOFJALLET** • 1980
CHILDREN FROM FROSTMA MOUNTAIN see **BARNEN FRAN FROSTMOFJALLET** • 1945
CHILDREN FROM NUMBER 67, THE see **KINDER AUS NR.67 ODER HEIL HITLER, ICH HATT GERN 'N PAAR PFERDEAPPEL..** • 1980
CHILDREN GALORE • 1954 • Fisher Terence • UKN
CHILDREN GROWING UP WITH OTHER PEOPLE • 1947 • Thomson Margaret • UKN
CHILDREN HAND IN HAND see **TE O TSUNAGU KORA** • 1947
CHILDREN HAND IN HAND (USA) see **TE O TSUNAGU KORA** • 1962
CHILDREN IN CITIES see **BAMBINI IN CITTA** • 1946
CHILDREN IN CONFLICT • 1967 • King Allan • SER • CND
CHILDREN IN NEED • 1956 • Sturt George • SLN
CHILDREN IN PARADISE (USA) see **ENFANTS DU PARADIS, LES** • 1944
CHILDREN IN THE CLASSROOM see **KYOSHITSU NO KODOMOTACHI** • 1954
CHILDREN IN THE CROSSFIRE • 1984 • Schaefer George • TVM • USA • SUMMERTIME YANKS
CHILDREN IN THE HOUSE, THE • 1916 • Franklin Sidney A., Franklin Chester M. • USA
CHILDREN IN THE LIMELIGHT see **DZIECI Z RAMPY** • 1963
CHILDREN IN THE NURSERY • 1896 • *Paul R. W.* • UKN
CHILDREN IN THE SURF • 1904 • *Bitzer Billy (Ph)* • USA
CHILDREN IN THE WAR see **KINDER IM KRIEG** • 1986
CHILDREN IN THE WIND see **KAZE NO NAKA NO KODOMOTACHI** • 1937
CHILDREN IN TORMENT • 1938 • Shimizu Hiroshi • JPN
CHILDREN IN TRAFFIC see **DJEVA U SAOBRACAJU** • 1968
CHILDREN IN UNIFORM see **MADCHEN IN UNIFORM** • 1958
CHILDREN LEARN FROM FILMSTRIPS • 1963 • Jackson Stanley R. • DOC • CND
CHILDREN LEARNING BY EXPERIENCE • 1947 • Thomson Margaret • UKN
CHILDREN MAKING CARTOONS • 1973 • *Halas John (P)* • UKN
CHILDREN, MOTHERS AND A GENERAL see **KINDER, MUTTER UND EIN GENERAL** • 1955
CHILDREN MUST LAUGH see **DROGA MLODYCH** • 1935
CHILDREN MUST LEARN, THE • 1941 • Van Dyke Willard • DOC • USA
CHILDREN MUSTN'T SMOKE • 1911 • Fitzhamon Lewin • UKN
CHILDREN NOBODY WANTED, THE • 1981 • Michaels Richard • TVM • USA
CHILDREN NOT WANTED • 1920 • Scardon Paul • USA
CHILDREN OF A LESSER GOD • 1986 • Haines Randa • USA
CHILDREN OF AN LAC, THE • 1980 • Moxey John Llewellyn • TVM • USA
CHILDREN OF ANGYALFOLD see **ANGYALFOLDI FIATOLOK** • 1955
CHILDREN OF BANISHMENT • 1919 • MacGregor Norval • USA
CHILDREN OF BLOOD see **COLECCIONISTA DE CADAVERES, EL** • 1967
CHILDREN OF BULLERBY VILLAGE, THE see **ALLA VI BARN I BULLERBYN** • 1986
CHILDREN OF CHANCE • 1915 • *Rex* • USA
CHILDREN OF CHANCE • 1930 • Esway Alexander • UKN
CHILDREN OF CHANCE • 1949 • Zampa Luigi • UKN
CHILDREN OF CHANGE see **CAMPANE A MARTELLO** • 1949
CHILDREN OF CHAOS (UKN) see **ENFANTS DU DESORDRE, LES** • 1989
CHILDREN OF CHAOS (USA) see **CARREFOUR DES ENFANTS PERDUS, LE** • 1943
CHILDREN OF COMMANDER SCHMIDT, THE see **DECA VOJVODE SMITA** • 1967
CHILDREN OF COURAGE see **FROGGY'S LITTLE BROTHER** • 1921
CHILDREN OF DARKNESS see **KINDER DER FINSTERNIS 1** • 1921
CHILDREN OF DESTINY • 1914 • Vale Travers • USA
CHILDREN OF DESTINY • 1920 • Irving George • USA
CHILDREN OF DIVORCE • 1927 • Lloyd Frank, von Sternberg Josef (U/c) • USA
CHILDREN OF DIVORCE • 1980 • Lee Joanna • TVM • USA
CHILDREN OF DIVORCE • 1989 • Milani Tahmineh • IRN
CHILDREN OF DIVORCE see **HIJOS DEL DIVORCIO, LOS** • 1957
CHILDREN OF DIVORCE, THE see **SKILSMISSENS BORN** • 1939
CHILDREN OF DIVORCE (UKN) see **WHAT BECOMES OF THE CHILDREN?** • 1935
CHILDREN OF DON QUIXOTE, THE see **DETI DON QUIXOTE** • 1966
CHILDREN OF DREAMS • 1931 • Crosland Alan • USA
CHILDREN OF DUST • 1923 • Borzage Frank • USA
CHILDREN OF EVE, THE • 1915 • Collins John H. • USA
CHILDREN OF FATALITY • 1914 • *Melies* • USA
CHILDREN OF FATE • 1914 • Reid Wallace • USA • LOVE'S WESTERN FLIGHT
CHILDREN OF FATE • 1926 • *Schoengold Joseph* • USA
CHILDREN OF FATE • 1928 • *Henderson Harry* • USA
CHILDREN OF GIBEON, THE • 1920 • Morgan Sidney • UKN
CHILDREN OF HIROSHIMA see **GENBAKU NO KO** • 1952
CHILDREN OF JAZZ • 1923 • Storm Jerome • USA
CHILDREN OF LONELINESS • 1934 • Kahn Richard C. • USA
CHILDREN OF LOVE see **ENFANTS DE L'AMOUR, LES** • 1953
CHILDREN OF MATA HARI see **PEAU DE TORPEDO, LA** • 1970
CHILDREN OF MIKE AND MEYER ELOPE, THE • 1915 • *World* • USA
CHILDREN OF NO IMPORTANCE (USA) see **UNEHELICHEN, DIE** • 1926
CHILDREN OF PAIN see **SMERTENS BORN** • 1977
CHILDREN OF PEACE • 1962 • Barclay Robert • MTV • CND
CHILDREN OF PLEASURE • 1930 • Beaumont Harry • USA • SONG WRITER, THE
CHILDREN OF RAGE • 1975 • Seidelman Arthur Allan • UKN, ISR
CHILDREN OF RAVENSBACK see **CHILDREN, THE** • 1980
CHILDREN OF ST. ANNE, THE • 1913 • McGill Lawrence • USA
CHILDREN OF SANCHEZ, THE • 1978 • Bartlett Hall • USA, MXC
CHILDREN OF THE ATOM BOMB see **GENBAKU NO KO** • 1952
CHILDREN OF THE BEEHIVE see **SONOGONO HACHINOSU NO KODOMOTACHI** • 1948
CHILDREN OF THE CITY • 1944 • Cooper Budge • DOC • UKN
CHILDREN OF THE CITY • 1945 • Rotha Paul • DOC • UKN
CHILDREN OF THE CORN • 1984 • Kiersch Fritz • USA
CHILDREN OF THE DAMNED • 1963 • Leader Anton M. • UKN • HORROR!
CHILDREN OF THE DARKNESS see **KINDER DER FINSTERNIS 1** • 1921
CHILDREN OF THE EARTH see **DHARTI KE LAL** • 1946
CHILDREN OF THE EARTH see **SOSKEN PA GUDS JORD** • 1983
CHILDREN OF THE FEUD • 1914 • Finley Ned • USA
CHILDREN OF THE FEUD • 1916 • Henabery Joseph • USA
CHILDREN OF THE FOG • 1935 • Jessner Leopold, Quin John • UKN
CHILDREN OF THE FOREST • 1912 • Fitzhamon Lewin • UKN
CHILDREN OF THE FOREST • 1913 • Kirkland David • USA
CHILDREN OF THE FULL MOON • 1982 • Clegg Tom • TVM • UKN
CHILDREN OF THE FUTURE see **FREMTIDENS BORN** • 1984
CHILDREN OF THE GHETTO, THE • 1915 • Powell Frank • USA
CHILDREN OF THE GOOD EARTH see **TA-TI NU-ERH** • 1967
CHILDREN OF THE JUNGLE • 1914 • *E & R Jungle Film* • USA
CHILDREN OF THE LOTUS EATERS see **PSYCHIATRIST: GOD BLESS THE CHILDREN, THE** • 1970
CHILDREN OF THE MOON • 1974 • Weis Bob • ASL
CHILDREN OF THE NEW DAY • 1930 • Petrov Vladimir • USS
CHILDREN OF THE NIGHT • 1921 • Dillon John Francis • USA
CHILDREN OF THE NIGHT • 1985 • Markowitz Robert • TVM • USA
CHILDREN OF THE NIGHT see **NATTENS BARN** • 1916
CHILDREN OF THE NIGHT see **NATTBARN** • 1956
CHILDREN OF THE NIGHT NO.1 • 1925 • Calvert Charles • UKN
CHILDREN OF THE NIGHT NO.2 • 1925 • Calvert Charles • UKN
CHILDREN OF THE NORTH WOODS see **IN SEARCH OF A GOLDEN SKY** • 1983
CHILDREN OF THE PLAINS • 1909 • *Vitagraph* • USA
CHILDREN OF THE REVOLUTION • 1936 • Maslyukov Alexei
CHILDREN OF THE REVOLUTION, THE see **REVOLUTIONENS BORN** • 1981
CHILDREN OF THE RITZ • 1929 • Dillon John Francis • USA
CHILDREN OF THE SEA • 1909 • *Lubin* • USA
CHILDREN OF THE SEA • 1915 • *Clary Charles* • USA
CHILDREN OF THE SEA (USA) see **KAIKOKO DANJI** • 1926
CHILDREN OF THE SILVER SCREEN see **AADI HAQEEQAT AADHA FASANA** • 1990
CHILDREN OF THE SOVIET ARCTIC see **ROMANTIKI** • 1941
CHILDREN OF THE STONES • 1977 • Scott Peter Graham • MTV • UKN
CHILDREN OF THE STORM see **DETI BURI** • 1926
CHILDREN OF THE STORM see **STORMENS BARN** • 1928
CHILDREN OF THE STREET see **GATANS BARN** • 1914
CHILDREN OF THE STREETS see **AWLAD EL SHAREH** • 1951
CHILDREN OF THE SUN • 1917 • Sandberg Anders W. • DNM
CHILDREN OF THE SUN • 1960 • Hubley John • ANS • USA
CHILDREN OF THE SWALLOW, THE • 1988 • *Chronopoulou Mary* • GRC
CHILDREN OF THE TAIGA • 1941 • Preobrazhenskaya Olga, Pravov Ivan • USS
CHILDREN OF THE WEST • 1914 • *Warner's Features* • USA
CHILDREN OF THE WHIRLWIND • 1925 • Bennett Whitman • USA
CHILDREN OF THE WILD (UKN) see **TOPA TOPA** • 1938
CHILDREN OF THEATRE STREET, THE • 1978 • Dornhelm Robert • DOC • USS
CHILDREN OF THIS COUNTRY, THE see **BU VATANIN COCUKLARI** • 1958
CHILDREN OF TIMES SQUARE, THE • 1986 • Hanson Curtis • TVM • USA
CHILDREN OF TWO COUNTRIES • 1984 • Ohlsson Terry • DOC • ASL
CHILDREN OF UNDERDEVELOPMENT see **HIJOS DEL SUBDESARROLLO, LOS** • 1975
CHILDREN ON TRIAL • 1946 • Lee Jack • DOC • UKN
CHILDREN PADDLING AT THE SEASIDE • 1897 • Smith G. A. • UKN
CHILDREN PAY, THE • 1916 • Ingraham Lloyd • USA
CHILDREN PLAYING ON THE BEACH see **ENFANTS JOUANT SUR LA PLAGE** • 1896
CHILDREN SEE IT THROUGH, THE • 1941 • Fletcher Yvonne • DOC • UKN • CHILDREN SEE IT THRU, THE
CHILDREN SEE IT THRU, THE see **CHILDREN SEE IT THROUGH, THE** • 1941
CHILDREN SHALL PAY, THE • 1916 • *Laemmle* • USA
CHILDREN SHOULDN'T PLAY WITH DEAD THINGS! • 1972 • Clark Benjamin • USA
CHILDREN UPSTAIRS, THE • 1955 • Anderson Lindsay • DCS • UKN
CHILDREN VS. EARTHQUAKES -EARTHQUAKES PREFERRED • 1905 • Fitzhamon Lewin • UKN
CHILDREN WERE WATCHING, THE • 1961 • Leacock Richard (c/d) • DOC • USA
CHILDREN WHO DRAW PICTURES see **EO KAKU KODOMOTACHI** • 1956
CHILDREN WHO LABOR • 1912 • *West William* • USA
CHILDREN'S CABARET • 1954 • Negus Olive • UKN
CHILDREN'S CHARTER • 1945 • Bryant Gerard • UKN
CHILDREN'S CONCERT • 1949 • Parker Gudrun • DOC • CND
CHILDREN'S CONSPIRACY, THE • 1913 • *Thanhouser Kid* • USA
CHILDREN'S CORNER • 1939 • L'Herbier Marcel • SHT • FRN
CHILDREN'S CORNER • 1956 • Lassally Walter (c/d) • SHT • UKN • DAY NURSING
CHILDREN'S CRUSADE, THE • 1984 • Brittain Don • CND
CHILDREN'S DENTAL LEAGUE, THE • 1912 • UKN
CHILDREN'S DREAMS • 1960 • Stanzl Karl • ANS • AUS
CHILDREN'S EYES see **KODOMO NO ME** • 1955
CHILDREN'S FESTIVAL see **FESTIVAL DEL NINO** • 1973
CHILDREN'S FILM FESTIVAL • 1968 • *National Film Board Of Canada* • CMP • CND
CHILDREN'S FRIEND, THE • 1909 • Griffith D. W. • USA
CHILDREN'S HOME, THE • 1921 • Rowden W. C. • SHT • UKN
CHILDREN'S HOUR see **HORA DE LOS NINOS, LA** • 1969
CHILDREN'S HOUR, THE • 1913 • *Thanhouser* • USA
CHILDREN'S HOUR, THE • 1961 • Wyler William • USA • LOUDEST WHISPER, THE (UKN)
CHILDREN'S ISLAND see **BARNENS O** • 1980
CHILDREN'S PLAYGROUND • Proskurin S. • USS
CHILDREN'S REVOLT, THE • 1910 • *Vitagraph* • USA
CHILDREN'S SPORTS see **FOUNDLING HOSPITAL SPORTS DAY** • 1897
CHILDREN'S STORY, THE • 1938 • Shaw Alexander • UKN
CHILDREN'S TESTIMONY IN WARTIME • Al-Yassiri Fiasal • DOC • IRQ
CHILDREN'S THEATRE • 1961 • Bagnall Frank, Morris John, Fraser Lilian, Hawes Stanley • ASL
CHILDREN'S THEATRE • 1965 • Bottcher Jurgen • DOC • GDR
CHILDREN'S THEATRE OF JOHN DONAHUE, THE • 1971 • Pennebaker D. A. • DOC • USA
CHILDREN'S THOUGHTS FOR THE FUTURE • 1912 • Thornton F. Martin • UKN • AMBITIOUS CHILDREN
CHILDREN'S WAR, THE see **WAR AND LOVE** • 1985
CHILD'S CHARITY, A • 1911 • *Walturdaw* • UKN
CHILD'S CONCEPTION OF AGE, THE • 1979 • Paakspuu Kalli • DOC • CND
CHILD'S CRY • 1986 • Cates Gilbert • TVM • USA
CHILD'S DEBT, A • 1908 • *Urban-Eclipse* • USA
CHILD'S DEVOTION, A • 1912 • *Johnson Arthur* • USA
CHILD'S DREAM • *Contemporary* • ANS • USA
CHILD'S DREAM, THE see **REVE D'ENFANT** • 1910
CHILD'S DREAM OF CHRISTMAS, A • 1912 • Southwell Gilbert • UKN
CHILD'S FAITH, A • 1910 • Griffith D. W. • USA
CHILD'S FIRST ADVENTURE, A see **CHIISANA BOKEN RYOKO** • 1963
CHILD'S FIRST LOVE, A • 1912 • *Fearnley Jane* • USA

CHILD'S GUIDE TO BLOWING UP A CAR, A • 1965 • Spencer Ronald • UKN
CHILD'S HAND, A • 1913 • *Aldridge Wallace* • UKN
CHILD'S HAND, THE • 1954 • Jordan Larry • USA
CHILD'S HANDS, A • 1945 • Makarczynski Tadeusz • DOC • PLN
CHILD'S IMPULSE, A • 1910 • Griffith D. W. • USA
CHILD'S INFLUENCE, A • 1912 • *Baggot King* • USA
CHILD'S INFLUENCE, A • 1913 • Smalley Phillips • USA
CHILD'S INTRODUCTION TO THE COSMOS, A • 1964 • Barwood Hal • ANS • USA
CHILD'S INTUITION, A • 1913 • *Karr Darwin* • USA
CHILD'S JUDGEMENT, A • 1910 • *Imp* • USA
CHILD'S LOVE, A see **BARNET** • 1909
CHILD'S MESSAGE TO HEAVEN, A • 1910 • Gobbett T. J. • UKN
CHILD'S PLAY • 1954 • Thomson Margaret • UKN
CHILD'S PLAY • 1972 • Lumet Sidney • USA
CHILD'S PLAY • 1988 • Holland Tom • USA
CHILD'S PLAY II • 1990 • Lafia John • USA
CHILD'S PLEA, A • 1909 • *Phoenix* • USA
CHILD'S PLEA, A • 1912 • *Eclair* • USA
CHILD'S PRAYER, A • 1906 • *Walturdaw* • UKN
CHILD'S PRAYER, A • 1909 • Porter Edwin S. • USA
CHILD'S PRAYER, A • 1910 • Stow Percy • UKN
CHILD'S PRAYER, A • 1912 • *Lubin* • USA
CHILD'S PRECAUTION, A • 1913 • *Essanay* • USA
CHILD'S REMORSE, A • 1912 • Griffith D. W. • USA
CHILD'S SACRIFICE, A • 1910 • *Solax* • USA
CHILD'S SACRIFICE, A see **DOLL, THE** • 1911
CHILD'S STRATAGEM, A • 1910 • Griffith D. W. • USA
CHILD'S STRATEGY, A • 1912 • Batley Ernest G. • UKN
CHILD'S VOICE, A • 1978 • Hickey Kieran • SHT • IRL
CHILD'S WORLD, A • Young Robert • DOC • UKN
CHILE, DONDE COMIENZA EL DOLOR • 1982 • Lubbert Orlando • DOC • FRG • CHILE, WHERE PAIN BEGINS
CHILE FIGHTS • 1978 • Patterson Garry • DOC • ASL
CHILE -HAPPENINGS • 1973 • Karmen Roman
CHILE: HASTA CUANDO? • 1986 • Bradbury David • DOC • ASL
CHILE, I DON'T EVOKE YOUR NAME IN VAIN see **CHILE, NO INVOCO TU NOMBRE EN VANO**
CHILE, LAND OF CHARM • 1937 • Fitzpatrick James • SHT • USA
CHILE, NO INVOCO TU NOMBRE EN VANO • Colectivo Cine-Ojo • DOC • FRN, CHL • CHILE, I DON'T EVOKE YOUR NAME IN VAIN
CHILE NO SE RINDE CARAJO • 1976 • DOC • CLM
CHILE, WHERE PAIN BEGINS see **CHILE, DONDE COMIENZA EL DOLOR** • 1982
CHILI-CHALA, THE MAGICIAN see **VARAZSLO, A** • 1970
CHILI CON CARDIN • 1972 • Bonniere Rene • DCS • CND
CHILI CON CARMEN • 1930 • Lantz Walter, Nolan William • ANS • USA
CHILI CON CORNY • 1965 • McKimson Robert • ANS • USA
CHILI CON CORNY • 1972 • Smith Paul J. • ANS • USA
CHILI: VOLVEREMOS • 1976 • Bertolino Daniel • DOC • CND
CHILI WEATHER • 1963 • Freleng Friz • ANS • USA
CHILL FACTOR, THE see **COLD NIGHT'S DEATH, A** • 1973
CHILLER • 1985 • Craven Wes • TVM • USA
CHILLER DILLERS • 1968 • Smith Paul J. • ANS • USA
CHILLI AND HAM see **HOPE FOR TOMORROW** • 1990
CHILLI BOUQUET see **MIRCH MASALA** • 1985
CHILLING, THE see **NIGHT OF THE ZOMBIES** • 1981
CHILLS AND CHICKENS • 1915 • Curtis Allen • USA
CHILLY AND THE LOONEY GOONEY • 1969 • Smith Paul J. • ANS • USA
CHILLY AND THE WOODCHOPPER • 1967 • Smith Paul J. • ANS • USA
CHILLY CHUMS • 1967 • Smith Paul J. • ANS • USA
CHILLY DAYS • 1928 • Lamont Charles • SHT • USA
CHILLY NIGHT see **HANYE** • 1983
CHILLY RECEPTION, A • 1958 • Lovy Alex • ANS • USA
CHILLY SCENES OF WINTER see **HEAD OVER HEELS** • 1979
CHILLY WILLY • 1953 • Lovy Alex • ANS • USA
CHILLY WILLY see **I'M COLD** • 1954
CHILLY'S COLD WAR • 1970 • Smith Paul J. • ANS • USA
CHILLY'S HIDE-AWAY • 1971 • Smith Paul J. • ANS • USA
CHILLY'S ICE FOLLY • 1970 • Smith Paul J. • ANS • USA
CHILTERN COUNTRY, THE • 1938 • Cavalcanti Alberto • DCS • UKN
CHILTERN HUNDREDS, THE • 1949 • Carstairs John Paddy • UKN • AMAZING MR. BEECHAM, THE (USA)
CHIMATA NI AME NO FURU GOTOKU • 1941 • Yamamoto Kajiro • JPN
CHIMATSURI • 1929 • *Tsuburaya Eiji (Ph)* • JPN • CARNIVAL OF BLOOD
CHIMBELLA • 1939 • Ferreyra Jose • ARG
CHIMERA • 1968 • Fizzarotti Ettore Maria • ITL
CHIMERA NA POLNEJ DRODZE • 1970 • Mucha Kazimierz • SHT • PLN • ILLUSION ON THE FIELD ROAD, THE
CHIMERE • 1920 • Negroni Baldassare • ITL
CHIMERE • 1989 • Devers Claire • FRN
CHIMES, THE • 1914 • Bentley Thomas • UKN
CHIMES, THE • 1914 • Terriss Tom • USA
CHIMES AT MIDNIGHT see **CAMPANADAS A MEDIANOCHE** • 1966
CHIMIE ET LA POMME DE TERRE, LA • 1949 • Proulx Maurice • DCS • CND
CHIMIMORYO • 1971 • Shindo Kaneto • JPN
CHIMIMORYO -A SOUL OF DEMONS see **YAMI NO NAKA NO CHIMIMORYO** • 1971
CHIMISTE REPOPULATEUR, LE • 1901 • Melies Georges • FRN • MAIDEN'S PARADISE, A (USA) ○ CHEMIST REPOPULATOR, THE
CHIMMIE FADDEN • 1915 • De Mille Cecil B. • USA
CHIMMIE FADDEN OUT WEST • 1915 • De Mille Cecil B. • USA
CHIMNEY SWEEP see **KLEINE SCHORNSTEINFEGER, DAS** • 1935
CHIMNEY SWEEP, THE • 1916 • Windom Lawrence C. • SHT • USA
CHIMNEY SWEEP, THE • 1954 • Reiniger Lotte • ANS • UKN
CHIMNEY SWEEP, THE (USA) see **PERAK A SS** • 1946
CHIMNEY SWEEP (USA) see **JACK LE RAMONEUR** • 1906
CHIMNEY-SWEEPER, THE see **KOMINIARCZYK** • 1960
CHIMNEY SWEEPS, THE • 1963 • Birch Dudley • UKN
CHIMNEY THIEF, THE see **VOLEUR DE PARATONNERRES, LE** • 1946
CHIMNEY'S SECRET, THE • 1915 • Chaney Lon • USA
CHIMP, THE • 1932 • Parrott James • SHT • USA
CHIMP AND ZEE • 1968 • Lovy Alex • ANS • USA
CHIMPMATES • 1975 • Orton Harold • UKN
CHIMPMATES -SERIES 2 • 1976 • Orton Harold • SER • UKN
CHIMUKALA PAHUNA • 1967 • Balsawar Shubba • IND
CHIN CHIH YU YEH • 1980 • Kung Min • TWN
CHIN CHIN CHINAMAN • 1931 • Newall Guy • UKN • BOAT FROM SHANGHAI (USA)
CHIN-CHIN EL TEPOROCHO • 1975 • Retes Gabriel • MXC • CHIN-CHIN THE DRUNKARD
CHIN-CHIN THE DRUNKARD see **CHIN-CHIN EL TEPOROCHO** • 1975
CHIN FEN SHEN-HSIEN SHOU • 1975 • Lo Wei • HKG • GIRL WITH THE DEXTEROUS TOUCH, THE
CHIN NU YU HUN see **CH'IEN-NU YU-HUN** • 1959
CHIN-P'ING-MEI • 1969 • Wakamatsu Koji • JPN • NOTORIOUS CONCUBINES, THE ○ CONCUBINES, THE ○ KINPEIBEI
CHIN-SE TAI YANG • 1976 • Lee Koon-Cheng • HKG • BRUCE LEE, WE MISS YOU ○ DRAGON DIES HARD, THE
CHIN-SHUI SHEN • 1988 • Ch'Ing-Chieh Lin • TWN • SONS OF THE SEA
CHINA • 1931 • *Terry Paul/ Moser Frank (P)* • ANS • USA
CHINA • 1942 • Cooper Budge • DOC • UKN
CHINA • 1943 • Farrow John • USA
CHINA! • 1965 • Greene Felix • DOC • UKN
CHINA • 1970 • Bjerre Jens • DOC • DNM
CHINA see **CHUNG-KUO** • 1972
CHINA 9 LIBERTY 37 • 1978 • Hellman Monte • ITL • CLAYTON AND CATHERINE (USA) ○ AMORE, PIOMBO E FURORE
CHINA: A LAND TRANSFORMED • 1980 • Ianzelo Tony, Richardson Boyce • DOC • CND
CHINA AFLAME • 1925 • USS
CHINA ARMED ESCORT see **PAO-PIAO** • 1977
CHINA BEHIND see **ZAIJIAN ZHONGGUO** • 1974
CHINA -BETWEEN TODAY AND TOMORROW • 1956 • Huisken Joop • DOC • GDR
CHINA BOUND • 1929 • Reisner Charles F. • USA
CHINA BOUND see **ACROSS TO SINGAPORE** • 1928
CHINA CARAVAN (UKN) see **YANK ON THE BURMA ROAD, A** • 1941
CHINA CAT, THE • 1977 • Chinn Robert C. • USA
CHINA CLIPPER • 1936 • Enright Ray • USA
CHINA CORSAIR • 1951 • Nazarro Ray • USA
CHINA DEFENDS HERSELF • 1939 • Karmen Roman • DOC • USS
CHINA DOLL • 1958 • Borzage Frank • USA
CHINA EXPRESS see **GOLUBOI EKSPRESS** • 1929
CHINA GATE • 1957 • Fuller Samuel • USA
CHINA GIRL • 1942 • Hathaway Henry • USA
CHINA GIRL • 1976 • Uccelo Paolo • USA • EMBODIMENT OF FORBIDDEN PLEASURE, THE
CHINA GIRL • 1987 • Ferrara Abel • USA
CHINA HILARIA, LA • 1938 • Curwood Robert • MXC
CHINA HISTORY • 1978 • Ianzelo Tony, Richardson Boyce • DOC • CND
CHINA IS NEAR see **CINA E VICINA, LA** • 1967
CHINA JONES • 1959 • McKimson Robert • ANS • USA
CHINA NIGHT see **SHINA NO YORU** • 1940
CHINA O'BRIEN • 1989 • Clouse Robert • USA
CHINA PASSAGE • 1937 • Killy Edward • USA
CHINA PERIL, THE • 1924 • Quiribet Gaston • UKN
CHINA PLATE, THE • 1931 • Jackson Wilfred • ANS • USA
CHINA ROARS • 1934 • Elliott Clyde E. • USA
CHINA ROSE • 1983 • Day Robert • TVM • USA
CHINA SEAS • 1935 • Garnett Tay • USA
CHINA SHOP, THE • 1934 • Jackson Wilfred • ANS • USA
CHINA SKY • 1945 • Enright Ray • USA
CHINA SLAVER • 1929 • Mattison Frank S. • USA
CHINA STORY see **SATAN NEVER SLEEPS** • 1962
CHINA STORY: ONE-FOURTH OF HUMANITY, THE • 1968 • Snow Edgar • DOC • UKN • ONE FOURTH OF HUMANITY: THE CHINA STORY
CHINA STRIKES BACK • 1937 • USA
CHINA SYNDROME, THE • 1979 • Bridges James • USA
CHINA TEA • 1966 • Le Grice Malcolm • UKN
CHINA: THE CULTURAL REVOLUTION • 1981 • Rodgers Bob • DOC • CND
CHINA VENTURE • 1953 • Siegel Don • USA
CHINA VERSUS ALLIED POWERS see **CONGRES DES NATIONS EN CHINE** • 1901
CHINAMAN, THE • 1920 • Fleischer Dave • ANS • USA
CHINAMAN'S CHANCE, A • 1933 • *Iwerks Ub (P)* • ANS • USA
CHINAMAN'S FIRST DAY IN LONDON, A • 1912 • *Gaumont* • UKN
CHINARA NA SKALYE • 1967 • Khojikov Sultan • USS • PLANE TREE ON A ROCK
CHINA'S FOUR HUNDRED MILLION see **400 MILLION, THE** • 1939
CHINA'S LITTLE DEVILS • 1945 • Bell Monta • USA
CHINATOWN • 1974 • Polanski Roman • USA
CHINATOWN AFTER DARK • 1931 • Paton Stuart • USA
CHINATOWN AT MIDNIGHT • 1949 • Friedman Seymour • USA
CHINATOWN CHARLIE • 1928 • Hines Charles • USA
CHINATOWN CHUMPS • 1954 • Yates Hal • SHT • USA
CHINATOWN KID see **T'ANG-JEN-CHIEH HSAIO-TZU** • 1977
CHINATOWN, MY CHINATOWN • 1929 • Fleischer Dave • ANS • USA
CHINATOWN MYSTERY • 1932 • *Mintz Charles (P)* • ANS • USA
CHINATOWN MYSTERY, THE • 1915 • Barker Reginald • USA
CHINATOWN MYSTERY, THE • 1928 • McGowan J. P. • SRL • USA
CHINATOWN NIGHTS • 1929 • Wellman William A. • USA • TONG WAR
CHINATOWN NIGHTS • 1938 • Frenguelli Tony • UKN
CHINATOWN SLAVERY • 1909 • *Selig* • USA
CHINATOWN SQUAD • 1935 • Roth Murray • USA • FRISCO LADY
CHINATOWN VILLAINS • 1916 • Dillon John Francis • USA
CHINCHERO see **LAST MOVIE, THE** • 1971
CHINE MA DOULEUR • 1988 • Si-Jie Dai • FRN
CHINESE, DER • 1979 • Gloor Kurt • MTV • SWT, FRG • CHINESE, THE
CHINESE, THE see **CHINESE, DER** • 1979
CHINESE ADVENTURES IN CHINA see **TRIBULATIONS D'UN CHINOIS EN CHINE, LES** • 1965
CHINESE AND MINI-SKIRTS see **CHINOS Y MINIFALDAS** • 1968
CHINESE BOXER, THE see **LUNG HU TOU** • 1969
CHINESE BOXES • 1984 • Petit Christopher • UKN
CHINESE BUNGALOW, THE • 1926 • Hill Sinclair • UKN
CHINESE BUNGALOW, THE • 1930 • Williams J. B., Barnes Arthur W. • UKN
CHINESE BUNGALOW, THE • 1940 • King George • UKN • CHINESE DEN, THE (USA)
CHINESE CABARET • 1936 • Harris Buddy • UKN
CHINESE CAT, THE • 1944 • Rosen Phil • USA • CHARLIE CHAN IN THE CHINESE CAT
CHINESE CHECKERS • 1965 • Dwoskin Stephen • USA, UKN
CHINESE CONNECTION, THE (USA) see **CHING-WU MEN** • 1972
CHINESE DEATH THORN, THE • 1913 • Melford George • USA
CHINESE DEN, THE (USA) see **CHINESE BUNGALOW, THE** • 1940
CHINESE DOCUMENT, A see **SHANGHAISKY DOKUMENT** • 1928
CHINESE DRAGON • Chang I • HKG
CHINESE DRAGON, THE • *Man Ting* • HKG
CHINESE FAN, THE • 1914 • Edwin Walter • USA
CHINESE FIREDRILL • 1964 • Hindle Will • SHT • USA
CHINESE FUNERAL, A • 1913 • Melies Gaston • DOC • USA
CHINESE GHOST STORY, A see **QIANNU YOUHAN** • 1988
CHINESE GHOST STORY II, A see **RENJIAN DAO** • 1988
CHINESE GIRL, THE see **CHINOISE, LA** • 1967
CHINESE GOLD see **GENERAL DIED AT DAWN, THE** • 1936
CHINESE HERCULES • 1973 • Choy Tak?, Liu Ching? • HKG • FROM CHINA WITH DEATH
CHINESE JUNKS • 1932 • Foster John, Davis Mannie • ANS • USA
CHINESE LOTTERY, THE • 1915 • *Reliance* • USA
CHINESE MAGIC • 1900 • Booth W. R. • UKN • YELLOW PERIL
CHINESE MOON • 1927 • Edwards J. Steven • UKN
CHINESE MOON, A • 1928 • Freund Karl • UKN
CHINESE MUSKETEER, THE • 1918 • De Barge C. R. • SHT • USA
CHINESE NIGHTINGALE, THE • 1935 • Ising Rudolf • ANS • USA
CHINESE NIGHTINGALE, THE see **CHINESISCHE NACHTIGALL, DIE** • 1927
CHINESE NIGHTINGALE, THE see **CHINESISCHE NACHTIGALL, DIE** • 1964
CHINESE PARROT, THE • 1927 • Leni Paul • USA
CHINESE PUZZLE, A • 1913 • Henderson Dell • USA
CHINESE PUZZLE, THE • 1919 • Goodwins Fred • UKN
CHINESE PUZZLE, THE • 1932 • Newall Guy • UKN
CHINESE PUZZLE FOR JUDOKA see **CASSE-TETE CHINOIS POUR LE JUDOKA** • 1968
CHINESE RING, THE • 1947 • Beaudine William • USA • RED HORNET, THE
CHINESE ROOM, THE • 1966 • Zugsmith Albert • USA, MXC • CUARTO CHINO, EL (MXC)
CHINESE ROULETTE (UKN) see **CHINESISCHES ROULETT** • 1976
CHINESE RUBBERNECKS, THE • 1903 • *Biograph* • USA
CHINESE SHADOW PLAY • *Weng Wango (P)* • USA • WHITE SNAKE LADY, THE
CHINESE SHADOWS see **OMBRES CHINOISES, LES** • 1982
CHINESE SHADOWS, THE see **OMBRES CHINOISES, LES** • 1907
CHINESE SHAVING SCENE • 1902 • Porter Edwin S. • USA
CHINESE SHOE, THE see **ZAPATO CHINO, EL** • 1979
CHINESE SMUGGLERS • 1912 • *Bison* • USA
CHINESE STUNTMEN • *Li Bruce* • HKG
CHINESE TYPEWRITER, THE see **BOSTON AND KILBRIDE: THE CHINESE TYPEWRITER** • 1979
CHINESE VASE, THE see **VASENS HEMMELIGHED** • 1913
CHINESE VENGEANCE • 1973 • Chang Ch'Eh • HKG • BLOOD BROTHERS, THE
CHINESE VENGEANCE, A • 1914 • *Phoenix Film Agency* • UKN
CHINESE VENTURE (UKN) see **BOSTON BLACKIE'S CHINESE VENTURE** • 1949
CHINESE WALL, THE see **MURAGLIA CINESE, LA** • 1958
CHINESE WEB, THE see **SPIDERMAN: THE DRAGON'S CHALLENGE** • 1979
CHINESISCHE GOTZE, DER • 1916 • Oswald Richard • FRG • UNHEIMLICHE HAUS 3, DAS
CHINESISCHE NACHTIGALL, DIE • 1927 • Reiniger Lotte • ANS • FRG • CHINESE NIGHTINGALE, THE
CHINESISCHE NACHTIGALL, DIE • 1964 • Arnz • FRG, NTH • CHINESE NIGHTINGALE, THE
CHINESISCHES ROULETT • 1976 • Fassbinder R. W. • FRG, FRN • CHINESE ROULETTE (UKN) ○ ROULETTE CHINOISE (FRN)
CH'ING-CH'ENG-CHIH LIEN • 1984 • Hsu An-Hua • HKG • REIGNING BEAUTY, THE
CHING, CHING, CHINAMAN see **SHADOWS** • 1922
CHING-CHING'S REVENGE • 1910 • *Walturdaw* • UKN
CH'ING KUO CH'ING CH'ENG • 1975 • Li Han-Hsiang • HKG • EMPRESS DOWAGER, THE
CHING LING FOO OUTDONE • 1900 • Porter Edwin S. • USA
CH'ING T'IEH • 1981 • Sun Chung • HKG • RENDEZVOUS WITH DEATH
CHING-WU MEN • 1972 • Lo Wei • HKG • CHINESE CONNECTION, THE (USA) ○ FIST OF FURY
CHING-WU MEN SU-TSI • 1976 • Lee Tso Nam • HKG • FIST OF FURY, PART 2 ○ FISTS OF FURY 2
CHINGACHGOCK -DIE GROSSE SCHLANGE • 1967 • Groschopp Richard • GDR • CHINGACHGOCK -THE BIG SNAKE

CHINGACHGOCK -THE BIG SNAKE see **CHINGACHGOCK -DIE GROSSE SCHLANGE** • 1967

CHINK, THE • 1921 • Roach Hal • SHT • USA

CHINKASAI • 1960 • Mizuko Harumi • JPN • SO LIKE THE FLOWERS

CHINKS AND CHICKENS • 1915 • Ransom Charles • USA

CHINMEN NU • 1941 • *Lee Bruce* • HKG • TEARS OF SAN FRANCISCO ○ GOLDEN GATE TEARS

CHINMOKU • 1972 • Shinoda Masahiro • JPN • SILENCE (USA)

CHINNARI PUTTANNA • 1968 • Panthalu B. R. • IND

CHINO (USA) see **VALDEZ IL MEZZOSANGUE** • 1974

CHINOHATE NI IKIRU MONO • 1960 • Hisamatsu Seiji • JPN • ANGRY SEA

CHINOIS A PARIS, LES • 1974 • Yanne Jean • FRN, ITL

CHINOIS ENCORE UN EFFORT see **CHINOIS, ENCORE UN EFFORT POUR ETRE REVOLUTIONNAIRES** • 1976

CHINOIS, ENCORE UN EFFORT POUR ETRE REVOLUTIONNAIRES • 1976 • Vienet Rene • DOC • FRN • CHINOIS ENCORE UN EFFORT

CHINOISE, LA • 1967 • Godard Jean-Luc • FRN • CHINOISE, OU PLUTOT A LA CHINOISE, LA ○ CHINESE GIRL, THE

CHINOISE, OU PLUTOT A LA CHINOISE, LA see **CHINOISE, LA** • 1967

CHINOS Y MINIFALDAS • 1968 • Comas Ramon • SPN, FRG, ITL • CHINESE AND MINI-SKIRTS

CHINPINDO • 1960 • Toyoda Shiro • JPN • CURIO MASTER, THE

CHINTAMANS see **CINTAMANI A PODVODNIK** • 1965

CHINTAMANS AND MARRIAGE SWINDLER see **CINTAMANI A PODVODNIK** • 1965

CHINTAO YOSAI BAKUGEKI MEIREI • 1963 • Furusawa Kengo • JPN • SIEGE OF FORT BISMARCK (USA)

CHINURARETA OJA • 1968 • Noda Sachio • DOC • JPN • CHAMPION, THE

CHINY I LIUDI • 1929 • Protazanov Yakov • USS • HOUR WITH CHEKHOV, AN ○ RANKS AND PEOPLE

CHIO SU BARA • 1975 • *Kishida Mori* • JPN • EVIL OF DRACULA

CHIORNY KVADRAT • 1988 • Pasternak • USS • BLACK SQUARE (UKN)

CHIOSU ME • 1971 • Yamamoto Michio • JPN • LAKE OF DRACULA (USA) ○ DRACULA'S LUST FOR BLOOD ○ BLOODTHIRSTY EYES

CHIP 'N' DALE • 1947 • Hannah Jack • ANS • USA

CHIP OF THE EMPIRE, A see **OBLOMOK IMPERII** • 1929

CHIP OF THE FLYING "U" • 1914 • Campbell Colin • USA

CHIP OF THE FLYING U • 1926 • Reynolds Lynn • USA

CHIP OF THE FLYING U • 1939 • Staub Ralph • USA

CHIP OFF THE OLD BLOCK • 1944 • Lamont Charles • USA

CHIP OFF THE OLD BLOCK • 1971 • Bonniere Rene • SHT • CND

CHIP OFF THE OLD BLOCK ,A • 1913 • Lehrman Henry • USA

CHIP OFF THE OLD BLOCK, A • 1915 • Aylott Dave • *Martin* • UKN

CHIP OFF THE OLD BLOCK, A • 1915 • Birch Cecil • *Bamforth* • UKN

CHIP OFF THE OLD BLOCK, A • 1915 • Castle James W. • USA

CHIP OFF THE OLD BLOCK, A • 1916 • Fitzpatrick James A.* • SHT • USA

CHIP THE PLUMBER • 1916 • *Juvenile Film* • USA

CHIPEE • 1937 • Goupillieres Roger • FRN • COUP DE FOUDRE

CHIPMUNK ADVENTURE, THE • 1987 • Karman Janice • ANM • USA

CHIPS • 1938 • Godal Edward • UKN

CHIPS AHOY • 1956 • Kinney Jack • ANS • USA

CHIPS ARE DOWN, THE (USA) see **JEUX SONT FAIT, LES** • 1947

CHIP'S BACKYARD BARN STORMERS • 1916 • Fitzpatrick James A.*? • SHT • USA

CHIP'S CARMEN • 1916 • Fitzpatrick James A.* • SHT • USA

CHIP'S ELOPEMENT • 1916 • Fitzpatrick James A.* • SHT • USA

CHIP'S MOVIE COMPANY • 1916 • Fitzpatrick James A.* • SHT • USA

CHIPS OFF THE OLD BLOCK • 1912 • *Kalem* • USA

CHIPS OFF THE OLD BLOCK • 1942 • Allen Robert • ANS • USA

CHIP'S RIVAL • 1916 • Fitzpatrick James A.*? • SHT • USA

CHIQITO PERO PICOSO see **SUPERFLACO, EL** • 1957

CHIQUE • 1930 • Colombier Piere • FRN

CHIQUITA THE DANCER • 1912 • Hamilton G. P. • USA

CHIRA KUMAR SABHA • 1932 • *Sircar B. N. (P)* • IND

CHIRAG-E-CHIN • 1955 • IND

CHIRCALES • 1975 • Rodriguez Martha, Silva Jorge • SHT • CLM

CHIRGWIN IN HIS HUMOROUS BUSINESS • 1896 • *Paul R. W.* • UKN

CHIRGWIN PLAYS A SCOTCH REEL • 1896 • *Paul R. W.* • UKN

CHIROKROTIMATA, TA • 1943 • Tzavellas Georges • GRC • APPLAUSE ○ APPLAUDISSEMENTS, LES

CHIROMANTE, IL • 1941 • Biancoli Oreste • ITL

CHIRRUPPING OF A BIRD, THE see **TIRIRIT NG MAYA, TIRIRIT NG IBON** • 1968

CHIRUCA • 1946 • Perojo Benito • ARG

CHIRURGIE CORRECTRICE, LA • 1958 • Painleve Jean • SHT • FRN

CHIRURGIE DE L'AVENIR, LA • 1901 • Melies Georges • FRN • TWENTIETH CENTURY SURGERY (USA)

CHIRURGIE FIN DE SIECLE • 1900 • Blache Alice • FRN

CHIRURGIEN AMERICAIN • 1897 • Melies Georges • FRN • TWENTIETH CENTURY SURGEON, A (USA)

CHIRURGIEN DISTRAIT, LE • 1909 • Cohl Emile • ANS • FRN • ABSENT-MINDED SURGEON, THE

CHIRURGO OPERA, IL • 1964 • Pasinetti Francesco, Lamperti Piero • DOC • ITL

CHISAI TOBASHA (JPN) see **MALENKI BEGLYETS** • 1967

CHISELER, THE • 1931 • Sennett Mack • SHT • USA

CHISELERS OF HOLLYWOOD • 1930 • O'Connor William A. • USA

CHISHOLMS, THE • 1978 • Stuart Mel • MTV • USA

CHISMOSO DE LA VENTANA, EL • 1955 • Martinez Solares Gilberto • MXC

CHISSA PERCHE CAPITANO TUTTO A ME see **NUOVE AVVENTURE DEL SCERIFFO EXTRA-TERRESTRE, LE** • 1980

CHISSA PERSCHE.. CAPITANO TUTTO A ME see **SCERIFFO EXTRATERRESTRE.. POCO EXTRA E MOLTO TERRESTRE, UNO** • 1979

CHISSIBI -LA MORT D'UN FLEUVE • 1973 • Richardson Boyce, Fournier Jean-Pierre • DOC • CND

CHISTE, EL • 1977 • Manzanos Eduardo • SPN

CHISTOIE NEBO • 1961 • Chukhrai Grigori • USS • CLEAR SKIES ○ CLEAR SKY, A

CHISTOPHE COLOMB • 1973 • Gagne Jean • SHT • CND

CHISUM • 1970 • McLaglen Andrew V. • USA

CHIT IN DANGER • Calinescu Bob • ANM • RMN

CHIT THU WAING WAING LAI • 1982 • Nyunt Win • BRM • ADMIRERS GALORE

CHITEI NO UTA • 1956 • Noguchi Hiroshi • JPN

CHITHOD VIJAY • 1947 • *Kapoor Raj* • IND

CHITRA MELA • 1967 • Muthiah T. S. • IND • EXHIBITION OF PAINTINGS

CHITRANGADAH • 1939 • Chandrasekhar Raja • IND

CHITTOR VIJAY • 1947 • *Burman S. D. (M)* • IND

CHITTY CHITTY BANG BANG • 1968 • Hughes Ken • UKN

CH'IU • 1954 • Ch'In Chien • HKG • AUTUMN

CHIU-CH'ING MIEN-MIEN • 1988 • Yeh Hung-Wei • TWN • NEVER-ENDING MEMORY

CH'IU CHUEH • 1971 • Li Hsing • TWN • EXECUTION IN AUTUMN

CHIU-SHIH-CHE • 1981 • Yu Jen-T'Ai • HKG • SAVIOUR, THE

CHIUZOI PIDZAK • 1927 • Schpiss • USS

CHIVALROUS CHARLEY • 1921 • Ellis Robert • USA

CHIVALROUS DAYS • 1913 • *Powers* • USA

CHIVALROUS HUNCHBACK, THE see **SATRIA** • 1971

CHIVALROUS LIFE, THE see **KYOKOTSU ICHIDAI** • 1967

CHIVALROUS STORY IN JAPAN -THE STORM, A see **NIPPON KYOKAKUDEN-KIRIKOMI** • 1967

CHIVALROUS STORY OF JAPAN see **NIHON KYOKYAKU DEN ZETSUENJO** • 1968

CHIVALROUS STRANGER, THE • 1910 • *Vitagraph* • USA

CHIVAS RAYADOS, LAS • 1962 • Munoz Manuel • MXC

CHIVATO • 1961 • Gannaway Albert C. • USA • REBELLION IN CUBA

CHIYARI FUJI • 1955 • Uchida Tomu • JPN • BLOODY SPEAR AT MOUNT FUJI, A ○ BLOODY SPEAR ON MOUNT FUJI, A ○ ON THE TRAIL

CHIZU NO NAI MACHI • 1960 • Nakahira Ko • JPN • JUNGLE BLOCK

CHLAP JAKO HORA • 1960 • Makovec Milos • CZC

CHLAPI PRECE NEPLACOU • 1980 • Pinkava Josef • CZC • MEN NEVER CRY

CHLEN PRAVITELSTAVA • 1940 • Heifitz Josif, Zarkhi Alexander • USS • MEMBER OF THE GOVERNMENT ○ GREAT BEGINNING, THE

CHLOE • 1929 • Aylott Dave, Symmons E. F. • SHT • UKN

CHLOE • 1934 • Neilan Marshall • USA

CHLOE IN THE AFTERNOON (USA) see **AMOUR L'APRES-MIDI, L'** • 1972

CHLOE, L'OBSEDEE SEXUELLE • Baudricourt Michel • FRN

CHLOPI • 1974 • Rybkowski Jan • PLN • PEASANTS

CHLOROFORM FIENDS, THE (USA) see **CHEVALIERS DU CHLOROFORME, LES** • 1905

CHNOUF -TO TAKE IT IS DEADLY see **RAZZIA SUR LA CHNOUF** • 1954

CHO-CHIEN CH'U-SHIH • 1976 • Li Han-Hsiang • HKG • THAT'S ADULTERY

CHOBIZENESSE • 1975 • Yanne Jean • FRN

CHOC, LE • 1982 • Davis Robin • FRN

CHOC EN RETOUR • 1937 • Monca Georges, Keroul Maurice • FRN

CHOCA, LA • 1973 • Fernandez Emilio • MXC

CHOCKY • 1984 • Hughes Vic, Hodson Christopher • MTV • UKN

CHOCOLAT • 1988 • Denis Claire • FRN, FRG

CHOCOLATE BUNNY, FROOTSIE & CONTENDER, THE • 1975 • Hadley Jack, Levin Arnold • USA

CHOCOLATE COPS, THE • 1986 • Menzel Jiri • FRG

CHOCOLATE DYNAMITE • 1914 • Dillon Eddie • USA

CHOCOLATE FACTORY • 1952 • Peterson Sidney • USA

CHOCOLATE GIRL see **CHOKOREITU GAARU** • 1932

CHOCOLATE KILLER, THE • 1986 • Adrien Michael • USA • LIFE AND TIMES OF THE CHOCOLATE KILLER, THE

CHOCOLATE OF THE GANG • 1918 • Vidor King • SHT • USA

CHOCOLATE REVOLVER, THE • 1912 • *Vitagraph* • USA

CHOCOLATE SOLDIER, THE • 1915 • Morton Walter • USA

CHOCOLATE SOLDIER, THE • 1941 • Del Ruth Roy • USA

CHOCOLATE WAR, THE • 1988 • Gordon Keith • USA

CHOCOLATES IN THE SUN • 1975 • Kent Larry • MTV • CND

CHOCOLOWA BALLADA • 1961 • Laskowski Jan • ANS • PLN • CAPSHEAF BALLAD, A

CHOE HAK-SIN • NKR

CHOEKI JUHACHINEN • 1967 • Kato Tai • JPN • EIGHTEEN YEARS' IMPRISONMENT

CHOEKI JUHACHINEN: KARI SHUTSUGOKU • 1967 • Furuhata Yasuo • JPN • EIGHTEEN YEARS' IMPRISONMENT: PAROLE

CHOGOLISA, THE BRIDE'S PEAK see **HANAYOME NO MINE, CHOGOLISA** • 1959

CHOHICHIRO MATSUDAIRA • 1930 • *Tsuburaya Eiji (Ph)* • JPN

CHOICE, THE • 1914 • Davis Ulysses • USA

CHOICE, THE • 1918 • *Joyce Alice* • SHT • USA

CHOICE, THE • 1925 • Butler Alexander • UKN

CHOICE, THE • 1961 • Barclay Robert • SHT • CND

CHOICE, THE • 1971 • Crombie Donald • SHT • ASL

CHOICE, THE • Bondarev Yuri, Naumov Vladimir • USS

CHOICE, THE • 1981 • Greene David • TVM • USA

CHOICE, THE see **EKHTIAR, AL** • 1970

CHOICE, THE see **CHOIX, LE** • 1975

CHOICE, THE see **YAM DAABO** • 1986

CHOICE BY ACCIDENT, A • 1912 • *Larkin George* • USA

CHOICE CHANCE WOMEN DANCE • 1971 • Emshwiller Ed • USA

CHOICE IS YOURS, THE • 1971 • Ohlsson Terry • DOC • ASL

CHOICE KILL see **DANGEROUSLY CLOSE** • 1986

CHOICE OF A GOAL, THE see **VYBOR TSELI** • 1974

CHOICE OF ARMS, THE (USA) see **CHOIX DES ARMES, LE** • 1981

CHOICE OF GOAL see **VYBOR TSELI** • 1974

CHOICE OF THE PEOPLE, THE see **CHOIX D'UN PEUPLE, LE** • 1986

CHOICE OF TWO, A • 1981 • Howe John • CND

CHOICE OF WEAPONS, A see **TRIAL BY COMBAT** • 1976

CHOICE SILVER see **SEN GIN** • 1935

CHOICES • 1981 • Narizzano Silvio • USA • DILEMMA ○ TOUCHDOWN

CHOICES • 1986 • Rich David Lowell • TVM • USA

CHOICES OF THE HEART • 1983 • Sargent Joseph • TVM • USA • IN DECEMBER THE ROSES WILL BLOOM AGAIN

CHOIR BOYS, THE • 1915 • *Reliance* • USA

CHOIR OF DENSMORE, THE • 1912 • *Hawley Ormi* • USA

CHOIR PRACTICE see **VALLEY OF SONG** • 1953

CHOIRBOYS, THE • 1977 • Aldrich Robert • USA

CHOIX, LE • 1975 • Faber Jacques • BLG, FRN • CHOICE, THE

CHOIX, LE see **EKHTIAR, AL** • 1970

CHOIX D'ASSASSINS, UN • 1967 • Fourastie Philippe • FRN, ITL

CHOIX DES ARMES, LE • 1981 • Corneau Alain • FRN • CHOICE OF ARMS, THE (USA)

CHOIX D'UN PEUPLE, LE • 1986 • Mignault Hugues • DOC • CND • CHOICE OF THE PEOPLE, THE

CHOJI, A TAVERN MASTER see **IZAKAYA CHOJI** • 1984

CHOKE • 1974 • Nicolaou Panos • UKN

CHOKE CANYON • 1986 • Bail Chuck • USA • ON DANGEROUS GROUNDS

CHOKON • 1926 • Ito Daisuke • JPN

CHOKON YASHA • 1928 • Kinugasa Teinosuke • JPN • FEMALE DEMON

CHOKOREITU GAARU • 1932 • Naruse Mikio • JPN • CHOCOLATE GIRL

CHOKOSO NO AKEBONO • 1969 • Sekigawa Hideo • JPN • SKYSCRAPER STORY, THE ○ SKY SCRAPER!

CHOLERA IN PRAGUE see **CHOLERA V PRAZE** • 1913

CHOLERA ON THE PLAINS • 1912 • *Pathe* • USA

CHOLERA V PRAZE • 1913 • Jalovec Alois • CZC • CHOLERA IN PRAGUE

CHOLLY POLLY • 1942 • Geiss Alec • ANS • USA

CHOLPON see **CHOLPON -UTRENNYAYA ZVEZDA** • 1960

CHOLPON -UTRENNYAYA ZVEZDA • 1960 • Tikhomirov Roman • USS • MORNING STAR (USA) ○ CHOLPON

CHOMANA DHUDI • 1975 • Karanth B. V. • IND • CHOMANA'S DRUM

CHOMANA'S DRUM see **CHOMANA DHUDI** • 1975

CHOMEUR DE CLOCHEMERLE, LE • 1957 • Boyer Jean • FRN • EASIEST PROFESSION, THE (USA)

CHOO CHOO • 1932 • McGowan Robert • SHT • USA • CHOO-CHOO

CHOO-CHOO see **CHOO CHOO** • 1932

CHOO CHOO LOVE • 1918 • Blystone John G. • SHT • USA

CHOO CHOO SWING • 1943 • Berne Josef • USA • BAND PARADE

CHOO CHOO SWING • 1948 • Cowan Will • SHT • USA

CHOOPER, THE see **BLOOD SHACK** • 1981

CHOOSE LIFE see **WAHLE DAS LEBEN** • 1962

CHOOSE ME • 1984 • Rudolph Alan • USA

CHOOSE YOUR EXIT • 1918 • Parrott Charles • SHT • USA

CHOOSE YOUR PARTNERS • 1935 • Lamont Charles • SHT • USA

CHOOSE YOUR PARTNERS (UKN) see **TWO GIRLS ON BROADWAY** • 1940

CHOOSE YOUR WEPPINS • 1935 • Fleischer Dave • ANS • USA

CHOOSING A HUSBAND • 1909 • Griffith D. W. • USA

CHOOSING THE WALLPAPER • 1909 • Smith G. A. • UKN

CHOP SUEY • 1930 • *Terry Paul/ Moser Frank (P)* • ANS • USA

CHOP SUEY & CO. • 1919 • Roach Hal • SHT • USA

CHOPIN • 1919 • Boese Carl • FRG

CHOPIN • 1957 • Mitry Jean • SHT • FRN

CHOPIN MAZURKAS • 1949 • Makarczynski Tadeusz • DOC • PLN

CHOPIN NOCTURNE, A • 1913 • Protazanov Yakov • USS

CHOPIN RECITAL AT THE DUSZNIKI FESTIVAL • 1947 • Makarczynski Tadeusz • DOC • PLN

CHOPIN'S BIRTH PLACE • 1967 • Kidawa Janusz • DOC • PLN

CHOPIN'S FUNERAL MARCH BURLESQUED (USA) see **MARCHE FUNEBRE DE CHOPIN, LA** • 1907

CHOPIN'S YOUTH see **MLODOSC CHOPINA** • 1952

CHOPPERS, THE • 1961 • Jason Leigh • USA

CHOPPING MALL • 1986 • Wynorski Jim • USA • KILL-BOTS ○ R.O.B.O.T.

CHOPPY AND THE PRINCESS • 1984 • ANM • USA • ADVENTURES OF CHOPPY AND THE PRINCESS, THE ○ SECRET OF THE PHANTOM KNIGHT

CHOR KANTA • 1931 • *Sircar B. N. (P)* • IND

CHORAKU NO KANATA • 1923 • Kinugasa Teinosuke • JPN • BEYOND DECAY

CHORAL CAMEO • 1930 • Jeffrey R. E. • UKN

CHORAL VON LEUTHEN, DER • 1933 • Froelich Carl, von Cserepy Arzen • FRG • ANTHEM OF LEUTHEN, THE

CHORAR O ENTRUDO • 1975 • Teles Luis Galvao • PRT

CHORD OF DEATH see **AKORD SMRTI** • 1919

CHOREOGRAPHY FOR CAMERA see **STUDY IN CHOREOGRAPHY FOR CAMERA, A** • 1945

CHORI CHORI • 1956 • *Kapoor Raj* • IND

CHORMANN • 1983 • Strebel Lukas • SWT

CHORNOYE SOLNTSYE • 1972 • Speshnev Alexei • USS • BLACK SUN

CHORNYI PARUS see **CHYORNI PARUS** • 1929

CHORNYYE SUKHARI • 1972 • Rappaport Herbert • USS, GDR • SCHWARZER ZWIEBACK ○ BLACK RUSKS

CHORON KA BADSHAH • 1988 • Mohammad Jan • PKS • THIEVES

CHORUS • 1974 • Sen Mrinal • IND

CHORUS AND PRINCIPALS ON STAGE PLEASE • 1976 • Howes Oliver • SHT • ASL

CHORUS AT DAWN • 1965 • *Takarada Akira* • JPN
CHORUS CALL • 1979 • Shepherd Antonio • USA
CHORUS, GENTLEMEN! • 1906 • Gilbert Arthur • UKN
CHORUS GIRL • 1948 • Tomson Randolph • UKN
CHORUS GIRL, THE • 1912 • Smalley Phillips • USA
CHORUS GIRL AND THE KID, THE • 1916 • *Empress Marie* • SHT • USA
CHORUS GIRL'S ROMANCE, A • 1913 • *Gaumont* • USA
CHORUS GIRL'S ROMANCE, A • 1920 • Dowlan William C. • USA
CHORUS GIRL'S THANKSGIVING, THE • 1914 • Lloyd Frank • USA
CHORUS KID, THE • 1928 • Bretherton Howard • USA • HER GREAT AMBITION (UKN)
CHORUS LADY, THE • 1915 • Reicher Frank • USA
CHORUS LADY, THE • 1924 • Ince Ralph • USA
CHORUS LINE, A • 1985 • Attenborough Richard • USA
CHORUS MAID • 1928 • Bretherton Howard • USA
CHORUS OF DISAPPROVAL, A • 1989 • Winner Michael • UKN
CHORUS OF TOKYO, THE see **TOKYO NO GASSHO** • 1931
CHOSEN, THE • 1981 • Kagan Jeremy Paul • USA
CHOSEN, THE see **HOLOCAUST 2000** • 1978
CHOSEN CHILDREN • 1954 • Devlin Bernard • DCS • CND
CHOSEN ONE, THE • 1974 • Jabbour Souheil • SYR, LBN
CHOSEN PATH, THE • 1919 • *Leslie Margaret* • USA
CHOSEN PRINCE, THE • 1917 • *Alexander Edward* • USA • FRIENDSHIP OF DAVID AND JONATHAN, THE
CHOSEN SURVIVORS • 1974 • Roley Sutton • USA, MXC
CHOSES DE LA VIE, LES • 1970 • Sautet Claude • FRN, ITL, SWT • THINGS OF LIFE, THE (USA) ○ AMANTE, L' (ITL) ○ THESE THINGS HAPPEN
CHOTARD ET CIE • 1932 • Renoir Jean • FRN
CH'OU WEN • 1975 • Li Han-Hsiang • HKG • SCANDAL
CHOU YEN LI CHUAN • 1977 • Liu Chia-Ch'Ang • TWN • LEGENDARY HEROES OF CHEN CHOW, THE
CHOUAN, UN • 1914 • Pouctal Henri • FRN
CHOUANS, LES • 1946 • Calef Henri • FRN • COURRIER DU ROI, LE
CHOUCHOU DE L'ASILE, LE see **COMMENT SE FAIRE VIRER DE L'HOSTO** • 1977
CHOUCHOU POIDS PLUME • 1925 • Ravel Gaston • FRN
CHOUCHOU POIDS PLUME • 1932 • Bibal Robert • FRN
CHOUPINET • 1946 • Boucquey Omer • ANS • FRN
CHOUPINET AUX ENFERS • 1945 • Boucquey Omer • FRN
CHOUQUETTE ET SON AS • 1921 • Monca Georges • FRN
CHOURINETTE • 1933 • Hugon Andre • FRN • JEUNE HOMME QUI SE TUE, UN
CHOVEKAT V SYANKA • 1967 • Yakimov Yakim • BUL • MAN IN THE SHADE, THE
CHOW HOUND • 1951 • Jones Charles M. • ANS • USA
CHOWRINGHEE • 1968 • Mukherjee Pinaki • IND • CROSSROADS
CHR.IV SOM BYGHERRE see **CHRISTIAN IV SOM BYGMESTER** • 1941
CHREZVICHAINI KOMMISSAR • 1971 • Khamraev Ali • USS • COMMISSAR EXTRAORDINARY ○ CHEKA COMMISSAR, THE
CHRIS AND THE WONDERFUL LAMP • 1917 • Crosland Alan • USA
CHRIS BARBER BANDSTAND • 1962 • Gomelsky Giorgio • SHT • UKN
CHRIS BARBER'S JAZZ BAND • 1956 • Gomelsky Giorgio • SHT • UKN
CHRIS COLUMBO • 1938 • Donnelly Eddie • ANS • USA
CHRIS COLUMBUS, JR. • 1934 • Lantz Walter • ANS • USA
CHRISMOSA, LA • 1940 • Susini Enrique T. • GOSSIPER, THE (USA)
CHRISS-CROSSED • 1931 • Buzzell Edward • SHT • USA
CHRIS'S MRS. • 1929 • Gannon Wilfred • UKN
CHRISSY AND ME • 1980 • Sobel Mark • MTV • USA
CHRIST EN CROIX, LE • 1910 • Feuillade Louis • FRN
CHRIST IN BRONZE see **SEIDO NO KIRISUTO** • 1955
CHRIST IS RISEN • 1976 • Canning William • CND
CHRIST MARCHANT SUR LES FLOTS, LE • 1899 • Melies Georges • FRN • CHRIST WALKING ON WATER (USA)
CHRIST OF THE OCEAN, THE see **CRISTO DEL OCEANO, EL** • 1970
CHRIST STOPPED AT EBOLI see **CRISTO SI E FERMATO A EBOLI** • 1979
CHRIST WALKING ON WATER (USA) see **CHRIST MARCHANT SUR LES FLOTS, LE** • 1899
CHRISTA • 1971 • O'Connell Jack • USA, DNM • SWEDISH FLY GIRLS
CHRISTA, FOLLE DE SON SEXE • 1979 • Berkowitch Michel • FRN
CHRISTA HARTUNGEN • 1917 • Biebrach Rudolf • FRG
CHRISTALOT HANSON • 1966 • Shebib Donald • CND
CHRISTEL VON DER POST, DIE • 1956 • Anton Karl • FRG
CHRISTENED BY FIRE see **SKAPANI W OGNIU** • 1963
CHRISTENING PARTY see **KERESZTELO** • 1968
CHRISTENING PARTY, THE see **KRTINY** • 1981
CHRISTIAN • 1989 • Axel Gabriel • DNM
CHRISTIAN, THE • 1911 • Barrett Franklyn • ASL
CHRISTIAN, THE • 1913 • *Moore Tom* • USA
CHRISTIAN, THE • 1914 • Thompson Frederick A. • USA
CHRISTIAN, THE • 1915 • Tucker George Loane • UKN
CHRISTIAN, THE • 1923 • Tourneur Maurice • USA
CHRISTIAN AND MOOR • 1911 • *Gordon James* • USA
CHRISTIAN DIOR • 1969 • Reichenbach Francois • SHT • FRN
CHRISTIAN IV: MASTER BUILDER see **CHRISTIAN IV SOM BYGMESTER** • 1941
CHRISTIAN IV SOM BYGMESTER • 1941 • Henning-Jensen Bjarne • DNM • CHRISTIAN IV: MASTER BUILDER ○ CHR. IV SOM BYGHERRE
CHRISTIAN LICORICE STORE, THE • 1971 • Frawley James • USA
CHRISTIAN MARTYRS, THE • 1909 • Turner Otis • USA
CHRISTIAN THE LION • 1976 • Hill James, Travers Bill • UKN
CHRISTIAN (USA) see **KRISTIAN** • 1939
CHRISTIAN WAHNSCHAFFE 1 see **WELTBRAND** • 1920
CHRISTIAN WAHNSCHAFFE 2 • 1921 • Gad Urban • FRG • FLUCHT AUS DEM GOLDENEN KERKER, DIE
CHRISTIANE F. (UKN) see **CHRISTIANE F. WIR KINDER VOM BAHNHOF ZOO** • 1981
CHRISTIANE F. WIR KINDER VOM BAHNHOF ZOO • 1981 • Edel Ulrich • FRG • WE CHILDREN FROM BAHNHOF ZOO (USA) ○ CHRISTIANE F. (UKN)
CHRISTIANIA • 1975 • Nyholm Ove, Colstrup Flemming • DNM
CHRISTIANS AWAKE! • 1907 • Gilbert Arthur • UKN
CHRISTIE JOHNSTONE • 1921 • MacDonald Norman • UKN
CHRISTINA • 1929 • Howard William K. • USA
CHRISTINA • 1953 • Eichler Fritz • FRG
CHRISTINA • 1974 • Krasny Paul • CND
CHRISTINA AND SEXUAL RETRAINING see **CHRISTINA Y LA RECONVERSION SEXUAL** • 1984
CHRISTINA MCNAB see **FORTUNE OF CHRISTINA MCNAB** • 1921
CHRISTINA (USA) see **MADCHEN CHRISTINE, DAS** • 1949
CHRISTINA Y LA RECONVERSION SEXUAL • 1984 • Lara Paco • SPN, USA • CHRISTINA AND SEXUAL RETRAINING
CHRISTINE • 1916 • Tsutsunava Alexander • USS
CHRISTINE • 1959 • Gaspard-Huit Pierre • FRN, ITL • AMANTE PURA, L' (ITL)
CHRISTINE • 1963 • Dudow Slatan • FRG
CHRISTINE • 1983 • Carpenter John • USA
CHRISTINE see **CHRISTINE JORGENSEN STORY, THE** • 1970
CHRISTINE ET SA NUIT see **KRYSTYNA ET SA NUIT** • 1977
CHRISTINE JORGENSEN STORY, THE • 1970 • Rapper Irving • USA • CHRISTINE
CHRISTINE KEELER AFFAIR, THE • 1964 • Spafford Robert B. • UKN • KEELER AFFAIR, THE ○ SCANDAL '64
CHRISTINE OF THE BIG TOPS • 1926 • Mayo Archie • USA
CHRISTINE OF THE HUNGRY HEART • 1924 • Archainbaud George • USA
CHRISTINE OF THE YOUNG HEART see **HIGH HEELS** • 1921
CHRISTINE SE MARIE • 1945 • Le Henaff Rene • FRN • CA DEVAIT ARRIVER
CHRISTINE (UKN) see **CARNET DE BAL, UN** • 1937
CHRISTINE UND DIE STORCHE • 1962 • Jahn Jiri • GDR
CHRISTMAS • 1922 • St. Clair Malcolm • SHT • USA
CHRISTMAS see **XMAS** • 1962
CHRISTMAS ACCIDENT, A • 1912 • Merwin Bannister • USA
CHRISTMAS ADVENTURE, A • 1912 • Stow Percy • UKN
CHRISTMAS ANGEL, THE (USA) see **ANGE DE NOEL, L'** • 1904
CHRISTMAS AT LONESOME GULCH • 1915 • *Frontier* • USA
CHRISTMAS AT THE BROTHEL see **NATALE IN CASA D'APPUNTAMENTO** • 1976
CHRISTMAS AT THE FOX'S BOARDING HOUSE see **ROZDESTVO OBITATELEJ LESA** • 1912
CHRISTMAS AT THE MOOSE FACTORY • 1971 • Obomsawin Alanis • CND
CHRISTMAS BURGLARS, THE • 1908 • Griffith D. W. • USA
CHRISTMAS CARD: OR, THE STORY OF THREE HOMES, A • 1905 • Martin J. H.? • UKN
CHRISTMAS CAROL, A • 1908 • *Ricketts Thomas* • USA
CHRISTMAS CAROL, A • 1910 • Miller Ashley • UKN
CHRISTMAS CAROL, A • 1911 • Collins John H., Dawley J. Searle (Spv) • *Edison* • USA
CHRISTMAS CAROL, A • 1911 • Kent Charles • USA
CHRISTMAS CAROL, A • 1914 • Shaw Harold • UKN
CHRISTMAS CAROL, A • 1938 • Marin Edwin L. • USA
CHRISTMAS CAROL, A • 1940 • Markopoulos Gregory J. • SHT • USA
CHRISTMAS CAROL, A • 1956 • Levy Ralph • USA
CHRISTMAS CAROL, A • 1960 • Hartford-Davis Robert • UKN
CHRISTMAS CAROL, A • 1971 • Williams Richard • ANM • UKN, USA
CHRISTMAS CAROL, A • 1979 • ANM • ASL
CHRISTMAS CAROL, A • 1984 • Donner Clive • TVM • USA
CHRISTMAS CAROL, A see **RIGHT TO BE HAPPY, THE** • 1916
CHRISTMAS CAROL, A (USA) see **SCROOGE** • 1951
CHRISTMAS CIRCUS see **GINGER NUTT'S CHRISTMAS** • 1949
CHRISTMAS COAL MINE MIRACLE, THE see **CHRISTMAS MIRACLE IN CAUFIELD** • 1977
CHRISTMAS COMES BUT ONCE A YEAR • 1936 • Fleischer Dave • ANS • USA
CHRISTMAS COMES TO WILLOW CREEK • 1987 • Lang Richard • TVM • USA
CHRISTMAS CRACKER • 1963 • Munro Grant • ANS • CND
CHRISTMAS CRACKER • 1964 • McLaren Norman, Hale Jeffrey, Potterton Gerald • SHT • CND • CAPRICE DE NOEL
CHRISTMAS DAY IN THE WORKHOUSE • 1914 • Pearson George • UKN
CHRISTMAS DREAM • 1928 • Silver Marcel • SHT • USA
CHRISTMAS DREAM see **SOGNO DI NATALE** • 1910
CHRISTMAS DREAM, A see **VANOCNI SEN** • 1945
CHRISTMAS DREAM, THE (USA) see **REVE DE NOEL, LE** • 1900
CHRISTMAS EVE • 1915 • Frenguelli Alfonse • UKN
CHRISTMAS EVE • 1947 • Marin Edwin L. • USA • SINNER'S HOLIDAY
CHRISTMAS EVE • 1986 • Oper Stuart • TVM • USA
CHRISTMAS EVE see **ROZDESTVO OBITATELEJ LESA** • 1912
CHRISTMAS EVE see **WIECZOR WIGILIJNY** • 1946
CHRISTMAS EVE see **PRZEDSWIATECZNY WIECZOR** • 1966
CHRISTMAS EVE AT PILOT BUTTE see **DESPERATE TRAILS** • 1921
CHRISTMAS EVE AT SUNSET • 1908 • *Lubin* • USA
CHRISTMAS EVIL • 1980 • Jackson Lewis • USA • YOU BETTER WATCH OUT ○ TERROR IN TOYLAND
CHRISTMAS FEAST • 1974 • Halas John • ANS • UKN
CHRISTMAS GIFT, A • 1980 • Vinton Will • ANS • USA
CHRISTMAS GIFT, THE • 1986 • Pressman Michael • TVM • USA
CHRISTMAS HOLIDAY • 1944 • Siodmak Robert • USA
CHRISTMAS HOLIDAYS see **VACANZE DI NATALE** • 1984
CHRISTMAS IN CONNECTICUT • 1945 • Godfrey Peter • USA • INDISCRETION (UKN)
CHRISTMAS IN JULY • 1940 • Sturges Preston • USA • NEW YORKERS, THE
CHRISTMAS IN VIGALA • 1980 • Soosar Mark • USS
CHRISTMAS KID, THE (USA) see **JOE NAVIDAD** • 1966
CHRISTMAS LACE • 1978 • Mendeluk George • MTV • CND
CHRISTMAS LILIES OF THE FIELD • 1979 • Nelson Ralph • TVM • USA
CHRISTMAS MARTIAN, THE (USA) see **MARTIEN DE NOEL, LE** • 1970
CHRISTMAS MEMORIES • 1915 • Leonard Robert Z. • USA
CHRISTMAS MIRACLE, THE • 1912 • *C.g.p.c. Films* • FRN
CHRISTMAS MIRACLE IN CAUFIELD • 1977 • Taylor Jud • TVM • USA • CHRISTMAS COAL MINE MIRACLE, THE
CHRISTMAS MORN see **JULOTTA** • 1937
CHRISTMAS MORNING • 1978 • MacBride Tiernan • SHT • IRL
CHRISTMAS MOUNTAIN • 1980 • Moro Pierre • USA
CHRISTMAS NIGHT see **ROZDESTVO OBITATELEJ LESA** • 1912
CHRISTMAS NIGHT see **PALS** • 1933
CHRISTMAS OF THE FOREST'S INHABITANTS (USA) see **ROZDESTVO OBITATELEJ LESA** • 1912
CHRISTMAS ON EARTH • Rubin Barbara • USA
CHRISTMAS PARTY • 1928 • *British Sound Film Prod.* • SHT • UKN
CHRISTMAS PARTY, THE see **JACKIE COOPER'S CHRISTMAS** • 1931
CHRISTMAS PRESENT • 1985 • Bicat Tony • TVM • UKN
CHRISTMAS PRESENT see **REGALO DE NAVIDAD** • 1967
CHRISTMAS PRESENT see **REGALO DI NATALE** • 1987
CHRISTMAS PRESENTS • 1912 • *Solax* • USA
CHRISTMAS RAFFLE, A • 1908 • Collins Alf • UKN • FATHER WINS A TURKEY
CHRISTMAS REFORMATION, A • 1915 • *Vanguard* • USA
CHRISTMAS REVENGE, A • 1915 • *Anderson Broncho Billy* • USA
CHRISTMAS SLIPPERS (USA) see **CHEREVICHKI** • 1945
CHRISTMAS SONNET • 1968 • Tyrlova Hermina • ANM • CZC
CHRISTMAS SPIRIT, THE • 1914 • *Mcquarrie Murdock* • USA
CHRISTMAS STAR, THE • 1986 • Shapiro Alan • TVM • USA
CHRISTMAS STORY, A • 1913 • Castle James W., Johnson Tefft • USA
CHRISTMAS STORY, A • 1918 • *Williams Eric* • SHT • UKN
CHRISTMAS STORY, A • 1984 • Clark Bob • CND
CHRISTMAS STRIKE, THE see **FOR SUCH IS THE KINGDOM OF HEAVEN** • 1913
CHRISTMAS THAT ALMOST WASN'T, THE (USA) see **NATALE CHE QUASI NON FU, IL** • 1965
CHRISTMAS TIME IN A BROTHEL see **NATALE IN CASA D'APPUNTAMENTO** • 1976
CHRISTMAS TO REMEMBER, A • 1978 • Englund George • TVM • USA
CHRISTMAS TREE • 1967 • Tyrlova Hermina • ANM • CZC
CHRISTMAS TREE • 1973 • Mendeluk George • MTV • CND
CHRISTMAS TREE, THE • 1966 • Clark Jim • UKN
CHRISTMAS TREE, THE (USA) see **ARBRE DE NOEL, L'** • 1969
CHRISTMAS UNDER FIRE • 1941 • Watt Harry • DOC • UKN
CHRISTMAS UNDER FIRE • 1942 • Hasse Charles • DOC • UKN
CHRISTMAS VISITOR, THE • 1958 • Halas John • ANS • UKN
CHRISTMAS VISITOR, THE (USA) see **BUSHFIRE MOON** • 1987
CHRISTMAS WAITS: OR, HIGH LIFE BELOW STAIRS • 1903 • Collins Alf? • UKN
CHRISTMAS WEEKEND see **THIS MAN IS MINE** • 1946
CHRISTMAS WITH ELIZABETH see **VANOCE S ALZBETOU** • 1968
CHRISTMAS WITHOUT DADDY • 1914 • Batley Ernest G. • UKN
CHRISTMAS WITHOUT SNOW, A • 1980 • Korty John • TVM • USA
CHRISTOPH COLUMBUS • 1922 • Garas Martin • FRG
CHRISTOPHE COLOMB • 1917 • Bourgeois Gerard • FRN
CHRISTOPHE COLOMB • 1939 • Gance Abel • FRN
CHRISTOPHER BEAN • 1933 • Wood Sam • USA • LATE CHRISTOPHER BEAN, THE ○ HER SWEETHEART
CHRISTOPHER BEAN • 1955 • Allen Lewis • MTV • USA
CHRISTOPHER BLAKE see **DECISION OF CHRISTOPHER BLAKE, THE** • 1948
CHRISTOPHER COLUMBUS • 1949 • MacDonald David • UKN
CHRISTOPHER COLUMBUS see **CRISTOFORO COLOMBO** • 1984
CHRISTOPHER CRUMPET • 1953 • Cannon Robert • ANS • USA
CHRISTOPHER CRUMPET'S PLAYMATE • 1955 • Cannon Robert • ANS • USA
CHRISTOPHER PLUMMER • 1964 • King Allan • CND
CHRISTOPHER PLUMMER • 1967 • Macartney-Filgate Terence • DOC • CND
CHRISTOPHER STRONG • 1933 • Arzner Dorothy • USA • GREAT DESIRE, THE
CHRISTOPHER WOTAN see **YOUNG SINNER, THE** • 1965
CHRISTOPHER'S HOUSE see **KRISTOFFERS HUS** • 1979
CHRISTOPHER'S MOVIE MATINEE • 1967 • Ransen Mort • CND
CHRISTOPHOROS • 1986 • Mlakar Andrej • YGS
CHRISTO'S VALLEY CURTAIN • 1972 • Maysles Albert, Maysles David • USA
CHRISTUS • 1916 • Antamoro Giulio • ITL
CHRISTUS VON OBERAMMERGAU, DER • 1920 • Seitz Franz? • FRG
CHRISTY • 1975 • Harris Steve • USA
CHROMATA TIS IRIDOS, TA • 1973 • Panayotopoulos Nikos • GRC • COLOURS OF THE RAINBOW, THE ○ HROMATA TIS IRIDOS, TA ○ COLOURS OF IRIS, THE
CHROME AND HOT LEATHER • 1971 • Frost Lee • USA
CHROMOFOBIA see **CHROMOPHOBIA** • 1965
CHROMOPHOBIA • 1965 • Servais Raoul • ANS • BLG • CHROMOFOBIA
CHROMOSOME 3 see **BROOD, THE** • 1979
CHRONIC PROBLEM, A • 1985 • Scott Cynthia • MTV • CND
CHRONICLE see **KRONIKA** • 1968
CHRONICLE INNOCENCE, THE see **KRONISKE USKYLD, DEN** • 1985
CHRONICLE OF A CRIME see **KRONIKA JEDNOG ZLOCINA** • 1974
CHRONICLE OF A DEATH FORETOLD (UKN) see **CRONACA DI UNA MORTE ANNUNCIATA** • 1987
CHRONICLE OF A GREAT CONSTRUCTION, THE see **KRONIKA WIELKIEJ BUDOWY** • 1961
CHRONICLE OF A HOT SUMMER see **KRONIKA ZHAVEHO LETA** • 1972
CHRONICLE OF A LADY see **CRONICA DE UNA SENORA** • 1972
CHRONICLE OF A LATIN-AMERICAN SUBVERTER see **CRONICA DE UN SUBVERSIVO LATINOAMERICANO** • 1974
CHRONICLE OF A LOVE see **CRONACA DI UN AMORE** • 1950

CHRONICLE OF A LOVE AFFAIR see **KRONIKA WYPADKOW MILOSNYCH** • 1985
CHRONICLE OF A SINGLE DAY see **KHRONIKA ODNOGO DNIA** • 1963
CHRONICLE OF A SUMMER (USA) see **CHRONIQUE D'UN ETE** • 1961
CHRONICLE OF AMOROUS INCIDENTS, A see **KRONIKA WYPADKOW MILOSNYCH** • 1985
CHRONICLE OF AN INDUSTRIAL see **CRONICA DE UM INDUSTRIAL** • 1980
CHRONICLE OF ANNA MAGDALENA BACH, THE (USA) see **CHRONIK DER ANNA MAGDALENA BACH** • 1967
CHRONICLE OF DAWN see **CRONICA DEL ALBA** • 1983
CHRONICLE OF FEELINGS, A • 1962 • Sharlandgiev Ljobomir • BUL
CHRONICLE OF FLAMING YEARS see **POVEST PLAMENNYKH LET** • 1960
CHRONICLE OF FOUR YEARS see **KRONIKA CZTERECH LAT** • 1965
CHRONICLE OF JAPANESE OUTLAWS: A TOAST TO SWORDS see **NIHON KYOKAKUDEN: SHIRAHA NON SAKAZUKI** • 1967
CHRONICLE OF KOSZALIN see **KRONIKA KOSZALINA** • 1960
CHRONICLE OF ONE DAY see **KHRONIKA ODNOGO DNIA** • 1963
CHRONICLE OF POOR LOVERS see **CRONACHE DI POVERI AMANTI** • 1954
CHRONICLE OF THE BAREFOOT EMPERORS see **MINIA** • 1978
CHRONICLE OF THE HOT YEARS see **AHDAT SANAWOUACH EL-DJAMR** • 1975
CHRONICLE OF THE MAY RAIN (USA) see **SAMIDARE ZOSHI** • 1924
CHRONICLE OF THE YEARS OF EMBERS see **AHDAT SANAWOUACH EL-DJAMR** • 1975
CHRONICLE OF THE YEARS OF THE BRAZIER see **AHDAT SANAWOUACH EL-DJAMR** • 1975
CHRONICLE WITHOUT SENSATION • 1966 • Lisakovitch Viktor • DOC • USS
CHRONICLES OF BLOOM CENTER, THE • 1915 • Neilan Marshall • SER • USA
CHRONICLES OF BLOOM CENTER, THE see **SPOOKS** • 1915
CHRONICLES OF THE GRAY HOUSE, THE (USA) see **ZUR CHRONIK VON GRIESHUUS "UM DAS ERBE VON GRIESHUUS"** • 1925
CHRONICLES OF THE GREY HOUSE, THE (UKN) see **ZUR CHRONIK VON GRIESHUUS "UM DAS ERBE VON GRIESHUUS"** • 1925
CHRONIK DER ANNA MAGDALENA BACH • 1967 • Straub Jean-Marie • FRG, ITL • CRONACA DI ANNA MAGDALENA BACH (ITL) ○ CHRONICLE OF ANNA MAGDALENA BACH, THE (USA)
CHRONIK EINES MORDES • 1965 • Hasler Joachim • FRG
CHRONIK VON GRIESHUUS see **ZUR CHRONIK VON GRIESHUUS "UM DAS ERBE VON GRIESHUUS"** • 1925
CHRONIK VON GRIESHUUS, DIE see **ZUR CHRONIK VON GRIESHUUS "UM DAS ERBE VON GRIESHUUS"** • 1925
CHRONIK VON PRUGIASCO • 1978 • Legnazzi Remo • DOC • SWT
CHRONIQUE 1909 • 1983 • Brizzi Paul, Brizzi Gaetan • ANS • FRN
CHRONIQUE ALBANAISE, UNE • 1977 • Bertolino Jean, Krausse Edith, Landau Olivier • FRN, ALB
CHRONIQUE DE LA VIE QUOTIDIENNE • 1978 • Leduc Jacques • SER • CND
CHRONIQUE DES ANNEES DE BRAISE see **AHDAT SANAWOUACH EL-DJAMR** • 1975
CHRONIQUE DES SAISONS D'ACIER • 1981 • Michel Thierry, Pireaux Christine • BLG
CHRONIQUE DU TEMPS SEC • 1977 • Billon Yves • DOC • FRN
CHRONIQUE D'UN ETE • 1961 • Rouch Jean, Morin Edgar • DOC • FRN • CHRONICLE OF A SUMMER (USA)
CHRONIQUE D'UN TEMPS FLOU • 1988 • Groulx Sylvie • DOC • CND
CHRONIQUE D'UNE OBSERVATION • 1971 • Moreau Michel • DCS • CND
CHRONIQUE D'UNE PASSION • 1971 • Verhavert Roland • BLG
CHRONIQUE INDIENNE • 1981 • Mazauric Bernard, Sabarros Antoine • FRN
CHRONIQUE PROVINCIALE • 1958 • Rappeneau Jean-Paul • SHT • FRN
CHRONIQUES DE FRANCE, LES • 1965 • Pialat Maurice • SHT • FRN
CHRONIQUES LABRADORIENNES • 1967 • Forcier Andre • SHT • CND
CHRONOGRAMS • 1961 • Carpi Cioni • ANS • CND
CHRONOPOLIS • 1982 • Kamler Piotr • ANM • FRN
CHRONOS CHILDREN, THE • 1985 • Korras Giorgos • GRC
CHROUSSOUSIS, O • 1952 • Tzavellas Georges • GRC • SUSCEPTIBLE, THE
CHRYSALIDE ET LE PAPILLON D'OR, LA • 1901 • Melies Georges • FRN • BRAHMIN AND THE BUTTERFLY, THE (USA) ○ BRAHMANE ET LE PAPILLON, LE
CHRYSALIS • 1973 • Emshwiller Ed, Nikolais Alwin • USA
CHRYSANTHEME • 1918 • *Toelle Carola* • FRG
CHRYSANTHEME ROUGE, LE • 1911 • Perret Leonce • FRN
CHRYSANTHEMUMS • 1914 • Chardynin Pyotr • USS
CHRYSANTHEMUMS FOR A BUNCH OF SWINE see **CRISANTEMI PER UN BRANCO DI CAROGNE** • 1968
CHTO DELAT' • 1928 • Ptushko Alexander • ANS • USS • WHAT TO DO
CHU-CHIEN SHAO-NIEN • 1983 • Chang Yi • TWN • KENDO KIDS
CHU CHIN CHOW • 1923 • Wilcox Herbert • UKN
CHU CHIN CHOW • 1934 • Forde Walter • UKN
CHU CHU AND THE PHILLY FLASH • 1981 • Rich David Lowell • USA
CH'U LIU-HSIANG • 1977 • Ch'U Yuan • HKG • CLANS OF INTRIGUE
CHUANG TAO CHENG • 1981 • Hsu An-Hua • HKG • SPOOKY BUNCH, THE
CHUANG TAPESTRY, A • 1959 • CHN
CHUBASCO • 1968 • Miner Allen H. • USA
CHUBBY INHERITS A HAREM • 1917 • De La Parelle M. • SHT • USA
CHUBBY TAKES A HAND • 1917 • Mong William V. • SHT • USA
CHUCHO AND THE LATIN-AMERICANS see **INSOLITA Y ESPECTACULAR MARCHA DE CHUCHO EL ESENIO Y SU COMBO LATINO-AMERICANOS** • 1972
CHUCHO EL REMENDADO • 1951 • Martinez Solares Gilberto • MXC
CHUCHO EL ROTO • 1934 • Soria Gabriel • MXC
CHUCHO EL ROTO • 1954 • Delgado Miguel M. • MXC
CHUCHO EL ROTO • 1959 • Munoz Manuel • MXC
CHUCK BERRY HAIL! HAIL! ROCK 'N' ROLL • 1987 • Hackford Taylor • USA • HAIL! HAIL! ROCK 'N' ROLL
CHUCK MOOL see **CIAK MULL -L'UOMO DELLA VENDETTA** • 1970
CHUCKWAGON • 1964 • Barclay Robert • SHT • CND
CHUDA HOLKA • 1929 • Fric Martin, Lamac Carl • CZC • POOR GIRL
CHUDAKI • 1974 • Shengelaya Eldar • USS • ODDBALLS, THE ○ ECCENTRICS, THE
CHUDESNITSA see **TCHOUDESNITSA** • 1936
CHUDI LIDE • 1939 • Klos Elmar • CZC • POOR PEOPLE
CHUDOTVORETS • 1960 • Skuibin Vladimir • USS • MIRACLE WORKER, THE
CHUEH-TAI SHUANG CHIAO • 1979 • Ch'U Yuan • HKG
CHUEH-TOU LAO-HU CHUANG • 1973 • Pao Houeh-Li • HKG • TOUGH GUYS ○ TOUGH GUY ○ KUNG FU -THE HEADCRUSHER
CHUI CH'IU CHUI CH'IU • 1976 • Ch'En Yao-Ch'I • HKG • CHASING GAME, THE
CH'UI KU-CH'UI • 1988 • Li Tao-Ming • TWN
CHUI LIAN TING ZHENG • 1983 • Li Han-Hsiang • CHN • REIGN BEHIND A CURTAIN
CHUJI KUNISADA • 1933 • Inagaki Hiroshi • JPN • KUNISADA CHUJI
CHUJI TABINIKKI • 1927 • Ito Daisuke • JPN • DIARY OF CHUJI'S TRAVELS, A
CHUK AND GEK see **CHUK I GEK** • 1953
CHUK I GEK • 1953 • Lubinsky Ivan • USS • CHUK AND GEK
CHUKA • 1967 • Douglas Gordon • USA
CHULAS FRONTERAS • 1976 • Blank Les • USA • BEAUTIFUL BORDERS
CHULO, EL • 1973 • Lazaga Pedro • SPN
CHUMLUM • 1964 • Rice Ron • SHT • USA
CHUMP AT OXFORD, A • 1940 • Goulding Alf • USA
CHUMP CHAMP, THE • 1950 • Avery Tex • ANS • USA
CHUMP TAKES A BUMP, THE • 1939 • Lord Del • SHT • USA
CHUMPS • 1912 • Baker George D. • USA
CHUMPS, THE • 1930 • Sennett Mack • SHT • USA
CHUMPS AND CHANCES • 1917 • Semon Larry • SHT • USA
CHUMPS AND COPS • 1918 • Howe J. A. • SHT • USA
CHUMS • 1914 • Kellino W. P. • UKN
CHUMS see **DVA DRUGA** • 1955
CHUM'S TRAGEDY, A • 1910 • Haldane Bert? • UKN
CHUMS (UKN) see **FURY OF THE WILD** • 1929
CH'UN • 1953 • Li Ch'En-Feng • HKG • SPRING
CH'UN-CH'IU CH'A-SHIH • 1988 • Ch'En K'Un-Hou • TWN • MY MOTHER'S TEAHOUSE
CHUN HYANG-JON • 1939 • Yi Pil-U, Yi Miong-U • KOR
CHUN TAO • 1988 • Ling Zhifeng • CHN
CHUNDOU FONGTSI • 1990 • Fong Eddie • HKG
CHUNG-KUO • 1972 • Antonioni Michelangelo • DOC • ITL • CHINA ○ CINA, LA
CHUNG-KUO K'AI-KUO CH'I-TAN • 1982 • Wang Chu-Chin • TWN
CHUNG LIEH T'U • 1975 • Hu King • HKG • PATRIOTS, THE ○ VALIANT ONES, THE ○ PORTRAIT OF THE PATRIOTIC HEROES
CH'UNG P'O see **CH'UNG P'O SZU-WANG HSIEN** • 1981
CH'UNG P'O SZU-WANG HSIEN • 1981 • Hua Yi-Hung • HKG • STRUGGLE TO SURVIVE ○ CH'UNG P'O
CHUNG-SHEN TA SHIH • 1981 • Hu King • HKG • JUVENIZER, THE ○ REJUVENATOR, THE
CHUNGKUO T'I T'AN CH'UN YING HUI • 1976 • Fu Ch'I • DOC • HKG • NATIONAL GAMES, THE
CHUO GIL • 1974 • Guerra • VNZ
CHUPKE CHUPKE • 1975 • *Burman S. D. (M)* • IND
CHUQUIAGO see **HISTORIAS DEL CHUQUIAGO** • 1976
CHURCH, THE see **CHIESA, LA** • 1988
CHURCH ACROSS THE WAY, THE • 1912 • *Williams Earle* • USA
CHURCH AND COUNTRY • 1912 • *Edison* • USA
CHURCH AND STAGE • 1912 • Buckland Warwick? • UKN
CHURCH AND THE WOMAN, THE • 1917 • Longford Raymond • ASL
CHURCH MOUSE see **BEAUTY AND THE BOSS** • 1932
CHURCH MOUSE, THE • 1934 • Banks Monty • UKN
CHURCH PARADE FROM "THE CATCH OF THE SEASON" • 1907 • Morland John • UKN
CHURCH WITH AN OVERSHOT WHEEL, THE • 1919 • Totten Joseph Byron • SHT • USA
CHURCHILL AND THE GENERALS • 1979 • Gibson Alan • MTV • UKN
CHURCHILL RIVER DIVERSION • 1973 • Rodgers Bob • MTV • CND
CHURCHILL THE MAN • 1973 • Lambert Peter • UKN
CHURCHILL'S ISLAND • 1941 • Legg Stuart • DCS • CND • FORTERESSE DE CHURCHILL, LA
CHURCHILL'S LEOPARDS see **LEOPARDI DI CHURCHILL, I** • 1970
CHURNING, THE see **MANTHAN** • 1976
CHUSHINGURA • 1932 • Kinugasa Teinosuke • JPN • VENGEANCE OF THE FORTY-SEVEN RONIN, THE ○ LOYAL FORTY-SEVEN RONIN, THE
CHUSHINGURA • 1934 • Ito Daisuke • JPN • LOYAL FORTY-SEVEN RONIN, THE
CHUSHINGURA • 1939 • Yamamoto Kajiro • JPN • LOYAL FORTY-SEVEN RONIN, THE
CHUSHINGURA • 1954 • Osone Tatsuo • JPN • LOYAL FORTY-SEVEN RONIN, THE
CHUSHINGURA • 1958 • Watanabe Kunio • JPN • LOYAL FORTY-SEVEN RONIN, THE
CHUSHINGURA • 1962 • Inagaki Hiroshi • JPN • LOYAL FORTY-SEVEN RONIN, THE ○ FAITHFUL 47, THE ○ 47 RONIN, THE ○ 47 SAMURAI
CHUT.. • 1971 • Gagne Jacques • DCS • CND
CHUT • 1971 • Marangos Thodoros • ANS • GRC
CHUT! • 1971 • Mocky Jean-Pierre • FRN
CHUT, ORPHAN OF THE WILDERNESS see **ORPHAN OF THE WILDERNESS** • 1936
CHUTE, LA • 1971 • Dopff Paul • FRN
CHUTE DANS LE BONHEUR, LA see **CHACUN SA CHANCE** • 1930
CHUTE DE CINQ ETAGES, UNE • 1906 • Melies Georges • FRN • MIX-UP IN THE GALLERY, A
CHUTE DE LA MAISON USHER, LA • Astruc Alexandre • FRN
CHUTE DE LA MAISON USHER, LA • 1928 • Epstein Jean • FRN • FALL OF THE HOUSE OF USHER, THE
CHUTE DE L'EMPIRE ROMAIN, LA • 1967 • Kast Pierre • MTV • FRN
CHUTE D'UN CORPS, LA • 1973 • Polac Michel • FRN
CHUTES, LES see **FALLS** • 1946
CHUTES DE PIERRES • 1958-59 • Breer Robert • USA
CHUVAS DE VERAO • 1977 • Diegues Carlos • BRZ • SUMMER SHOWERS ○ SUMMER RAIN
CHUVSTVA • 1971 • Gricaevicius Almantis, Dousa A. • USS • FEELINGS
CHUZHIE DETI • 1959 • Abuladze Tengiz, Dzhaparidze R. • USS • STEPCHILDREN (USA) ○ SOMEONE ELSE'S CHILDREN
CHUZHOI BEREG • 1930 • Donskoi Mark • USS • OTHER SHORE, THE ○ ALIEN SHORE
CHUZHOY PIDZHAK • 1927 • Ships Boris • USS
CHVENI EZO see **NASH DVOR** • 1956
CHVETI ZAPOZDALIE • 1972 • Room Abram • USS • BELATED FLOWERS (USA)
CHWILA CISZY • 1965 • Slesicki Wladyslaw • DOC • PLN • MOMENT OF QUIET, A
CHWILA POKOJU • 1965 • Konwicki Tadeusz (c/d) • MTV • PLN, FRG, FRN • AUGENBLICK DES FRIEDENS (FRG) ○ MOMENT OF PEACE, A
CHWILA WSPOMNIEN 1958-64 • 1965 • Lomnicki Jan • DOC • PLN • MOMENT OF REMINISCENCE 1958-1964, A
CHWILA WSPOMNIEN: ROK 1944/45 • 1964 • Perski Ludwik • DOC • PLN • MOMENT OF REMINISCENCE: 1944/45, A
CHWILA WSPOMNIEN: ROK 1945/46 • 1964 • Bossak Jerzy • DOC • PLN • MOMENT OF REMINISCENCE: THE YEAR 1945/46
CHWILA WSPOMNIEN: ROK 1947 • 1964 • Bossak Jerzy (c/d) • DOC • PLN • MOMENT OF REMINISCENCE 1947, A
CHWILA WSPOMNIEN: ROK 1956/57 • 1964 • Hoffman Jerzy • DCS • PLN • MOMENT OF REMINISCENCE 1956/57, A
CHYERNUSHKA • 1967 • Shabanov Rufat, Makmudbekov Shamil • USS • CHERNUSHKA
CHYETYRYE STRANITSY ODNOY MOLODY ZHIZNI • 1968 • Esadze Rezo • USS • CHETIRE STRANITZ ODNOI MOLODOI ZHIZHNI ○ FOUR PAGES OF A YOUNG LIFE ○ FOUR PAGES FROM A YOUNG LIFE
CHYLE POLA • 1970 • Slesicki Wladyslaw • DOC • PLN • HILLY FIELDS
CHYORNAYA BERYOZA • 1977 • Chetverikov Vitali • USS • BLACK BIRCH, THE
CHYORNI PARUS • 1929 • Yutkevich Sergei • USS • BLACK SAIL, THE ○ CHORNYI PARUS
CHYORT S PORTFYELEM • 1968 • Gerasimov Vladimir • USS • DEVIL WITH A BRIEFCASE, THE
CHYORTOVO KOLESO • 1926 • Kozintsev Grigori, Trauberg Leonid • USS • DEVIL'S WHEEL, THE
CI RISIAMO VERA PROVVIDENZA? • 1973 • De Martino Alberto • ITL
CI SPOSEREMO A CAPRI • 1956 • Marcellini Siro • ITL
CI TROVIAMO IN GALLERIA • 1953 • Bolognini Mauro • ITL
CIAK MULL -L'UOMO DELLA VENDETTA • 1970 • Clucher E. B. • ITL • UNHOLY FOUR, THE (UKN) ○ CHUCK MOOL
CIAK SI MUORE! • 1974 • Moroni Mario • ITL
CIAO • 1967 • Tucker David • USA
CIAO, CIALTRONI • 1979 • Rossini Danilo M. • ITL
CIAO CIAO BAMBIMA • 1959 • Grieco Sergio • ITL
CIAO, FEDERICO! • 1970 • Bachmann Gideon • DOC • USA, SWD
CIAO GULLIVER • 1970 • Tuzii Carlo • ITL
CIAO, LES MECS! • 1979 • Gobbi Sergio • FRN
CIAO MALE see **REVE DE SINGE** • 1978
CIAO! MANHATTAN • 1973 • Palmer John, Weisman David • DOC • USA
CIAO MARIA • 1963 • Kelly Ron • CND
CIAO MASCHIO (ITL) see **REVE DE SINGE** • 1978
CIAO NI! • 1979 • Poeti Paolo • ITL
CIAO NOVOLA • 1956 • Roli Mino • ITL
CIAO, PAIS.. • 1956 • Langini Osvaldo • ITL
CIAO SCIMMIA see **REVE DE SINGE** • 1978
CIBERNETIC 5.3 • 1969 • Stehura John • ANS • USA • CYBERNETIC 5.3
CIBLE, LA • 1979 • FRN
CIBLE HUMAINE • 1904 • Blache Alice • FRN
CIBLES VIVANTES • 1960 • Rovira Beleta Francisco • SPN, FRN • HAUTES VARIETES (FRN)
CIBO CIRE, UN • 1983 • Cornellier Robert • MTV • CND
CIBOULETTE • 1933 • Autant-Lara Claude • FRN • VALSE MIRACULEUSE, LA
CICA TOMINA KOLIBA (YGS) see **ONKEL TOMS HUTTE** • 1965
CICADA IS NOT AN INSECT, THE see **CIGARRA NO ES UN BICHO, LA** • 1963
CICALA, LA • 1980 • Lattuada Alberto • ITL • CRICKET, THE
CICATRICE INTERIEURE, LA • 1971 • Garrel Philippe • FRN • INNER SCAR (USA)
CICATRICES, LAS • 1966 • Lazaga Pedro • SPN
CICATRICES, LAS • 1967 • Torrado Ramon • SPN
CICCIO FORGIVES.. NOT I! see **CICCIO PERDONA.. IO NO!** • 1968
CICCIO PERDONA.. IO NO! • 1968 • Ciorciolini Marcello • ITL • CICCIO FORGIVES.. NOT I!
CICCIOLINA AMORE MIO • 1979 • Damiani Amasi, Mattei Bruno • ITL
CICEK ABBAS • 1982 • Cetin Sinan • TRK • ABBAS THE FLOWER
CICERUACCHIO • 1915 • Ghione Emilio • ITL

CICHA NOC • 1978 • Chmielewski Tadeusz • PLN • SILENT NIGHT
CICI GELIN • 1967 • Ergun Nuri • TRK • NICE BRIDE
CICLON • 1963 • Alvarez Santiago • DOC • CUB • CYCLONE ○ HURRICANE
CICLON • 1977 • Cardona Rene Jr. • MXC • CYCLONE
CICLON, EL • 1957 • Martinez Solares Gilberto • MXC
CICLON DE JALISCO, EL • 1963 • Urueta Chano • MXC • YO SOY CHARRO DONDEQUIERA
CICLON DEL CARIBE, EL • 1950 • Pereda Ramon • MXC
CICY • 1976 • Popescu-Gopo Ion • RMN
CID, IL • 1910 • Caserini Mario • ITL
CIDADE, A • 1968 • Costa Jose Fonseca • SHT • PRT
CIDADE AMEACADA • 1959 • Farias Roberto • BRZ • THREATENED CITY, THE
CIDADE DE TOMAR • 1915 • de Albuquerque Ernesto • SHT • PRT
CIDADE DO NOME DE DEUS, O • 1969 • Keele Latif • JPN • OMOON OR THE CITY IN THE NAME OF GOD (USA) ○ CITY OF THE NAME OF GOD, THE
CIDADE MULHER • 1936 • Mauro-Humberto • BRZ
CIDADE OCULTA • 1986 • Botelho Chico • BRZ • HIDDEN CITY
CIECA DI SORRENTO, LA • 1934 • Malasomma Nunzio • ITL
CIECA DI SORRENTO, LA • 1952 • Gentilomo Giacomo • ITL
CIECA DI SORRENTO, LA • 1965 • Iquino Ignacio F. • ITL • VENDETTA DEL CAVALIERE NERO, LA
CIECO, IL see **BLINDMAN** • 1972
CIEGUITA DE LA AVENIDA ALVEAR, LA • 1939 • Irigoyen Julio • ARG
CIEL, LE see **OURANOS** • 1963
CIEL BLEU • 1971 • Leroy Serge • FRN
CIEL DES HOMMES, LE • 1956 • Dornes Yvonne • SHT • FRN
CIEL EST A VOUS, LE • 1943 • Gremillon Jean • FRN • WOMAN WHO DARED, THE (USA)
CIEL EST PAR DESSUS LE TOIT, LE • 1956 • Decourt Jean-Pierre • SHT • FRN
CIEL ET LA BOUE, LE • 1961 • Gaisseau Pierre-Dominique • DOC • FRN, BLG, NTH • SKY ABOVE, THE MUD BELOW, THE
CIEL ET SES AFFAIRES, LE • 1967 • Bouamari Mohamed • ALG • HEAVEN AND ITS AFFAIRS
CIEL, LA TERRE, LE • 1965 • Ivens Joris • FRN, VTN • THREATENING SKY, THE (UKN) ○ SKY, THE EARTH, THE
CIEL SUR LA TETE, LE • 1964 • Ciampi Yves • FRN, ITL • ALLARME DAL CIELO (ITL) ○ SKY ABOVE HEAVEN (USA) ○ STADE ZERO ○ SKY BEYOND HEAVEN ○ CIELO SULLA TESTA, IL ○ SKIES ABOVE ○ ITL ○ HEAVEN ON ONE'S HEAD
CIELITO LINDO • 1936 • O'Quigley Roberto • MXC
CIELITO LINDO • 1956 • Delgado Miguel M. • MXC
CIELO BRUCIA, IL • 1958 • Masini Giuseppe • ITL
CIELO DENTRO DE CASA, EL • 1960 • Demicheli Tulio • SPN
CIELO E ROSSO, IL • 1950 • Gora Claudio • ITL
CIELO ES DE LOS PORRES, EL see **AMOR NO ES PECADO, EL** • 1964
CIELO NEGRO • 1951 • Mur Oti • SPN
CIELO PIANGE, IL • 1962 • Della Santa Enzo • ITL
CIELO ROJO • 1961 • Gazcon Gilberto • MXC
CIELO SULLA PALUDE • 1949 • Genina Augusto • ITL • HEAVEN OVER THE MARSHES
CIELO SULLA TESTA, IL see **CIEL SUR LA TETE, LE** • 1964
CIELO Y LA TIERRA, EL • 1962 • Blake Alfonso Corona • MXC
CIELO Y TU, EL • 1970 • *Brooks* • MXC
CIELO Y TU, EL • 1970 • *Avant* • MXC
CIELOS DE LA MUERTE, LOS • 1977 • Marmol Julio Cesar • VNZ, MXC • SKIES OF DEATH, THE
CIEMNA RZEKA • 1974 • Szyszko Sylwester • PLN • DARK RIVER, THE
CIEN • 1956 • Kawalerowicz Jerzy • PLN • SHADOW, THE
CIEN CABALLEROS, LOS (SPN) see **CENTO CAVALIERI, I** • 1965
CIEN GRITOS DE TERROR • 1964 • Obon Ramon • MXC • 100 CRIES OF TERROR (USA) ○ ONE HUNDRED CRIES OF TERROR
CIEN JUZ NIEDALCKO • 1984 • Karabasz Kazimierz • PLN • LOOMING SHADOW, A
CIEN METROS CON CHARLOT • 1967 • Guzman Patricio • SHT • SPN • 100 METERS WITH CHAPLIN
CIEN MIL LADRONES • 1970 • Lorente German • SPN
CIEN NINOS ESPERANDO UN TREN • 1988 • Aguero Ignacio • CHL, UKN • 100 KIDS WAITING FOR A TRAIN
CIEN VECES NO DEBO • 1988 • Doria Alejandro • ARG • ONE HUNDRED TIMES I SHOULDN'T
CIFRA IMPAR, LA • 1961 • Antin Manuel • ARG • ODD NUMBER, THE
CIFRADO ESPECIAL (SPN) see **CIFRATO SPECIALE** • 1966
CIFRATO SPECIALE • 1966 • Mercanti Pino • ITL, SPN • CIFRADO ESPECIAL (SPN) ○ SPECIAL CIPHER
CIFTE TABANCALI DAMAT • 1967 • Ergun Nuri • TRK • TWO-FISTED BRIDEGROOM, THE
CIFTE TABANCALI KABADAYI • 1969 • Aslan Mehmet • TRK
CIFTE YUREKLI • 1970 • Evin Semih • TRK
CIGALE, LA • 1913 • Neame Elwin • UKN
CIGALE ET LA FOURMI, LA • 1897 • Melies Georges • FRN • GRASSHOPPER AND THE ANT (USA)
CIGALE ET LA FOURMI, LA • 1909 • Feuillade Louis • FRN • GRASSHOPPER AND THE ANT, THE
CIGALE ET LA FOURMI, LA • 1916-24 • Lortac • ANS • FRN • GRASSHOPPER AND THE ANT, THE
CIGALE ET LA FOURMI, LA • 1955 • Image Jean • ANS • FRN • GRASSHOPPER AND THE ANT, THE
CIGALON • 1935 • Pagnol Marcel • FRN
CIGANYOK • 1962 • Sara Sandor • SHT • HNG • GYPSIES
CIGAR, THE see **CIGARA** • 1975
CIGAR BUTTS • 1914 • *Majestic* • USA
CIGARA • 1975 • Grgic Zlatko • ANS • YGS • CIGAR, THE
CIGARETPIGEN • 1915 • Holger-Madsen • DNM • CIGARETTE MAKER, THE
CIGARETTE, LA • 1919 • Dulac Germaine • FRN
CIGARETTE CHARLIE see **KARLI KIPPE** • 1962
CIGARETTE GIRL • 1947 • Fritsch Gunther V. • USA
CIGARETTE GIRL, THE • 1917 • Parke William • USA
CIGARETTE-GIRL FROM MOSSELPROM, THE see **PAPIROSNITSA OT MOSSELPROMA** • 1924
CIGARETTE MAKER, THE see **CIGARETPIGEN** • 1915
CIGARETTE-MAKER'S ROMANCE, A • 1913 • Wilson Frank? • UKN
CIGARETTE MAKER'S ROMANCE, A • 1920 • Watts Tom • UKN
CIGARETTE: PARLONS-EN?, LA • 1965 • Blais Roger • DCS • CND
CIGARETTE POUR UN INGENU, UNE • 1968 • Grangier Gilles • FRN
CIGARETTE TESTS • 1934 • Fischinger Oskar • ANS • FRG
CIGARETTE -THAT'S ALL, A • 1915 • Smalley Phillips • USA
CIGARETTES BASTOS, LES • 1938 • Alexeieff Alexandre • SHT • FRN
CIGARETTES DAVRO, LES • 1938 • Alexeieff Alexandre • SHT • FRN
CIGARETTES, WHISKEY AND WILD WOMEN (USA) see **CIGARETTES, WHISKY ET P'TITES PEPEES** • 1958
CIGARETTES, WHISKY ET P'TITES PEPEES • 1958 • Regamey Maurice • FRN, ITL • CIGARETTES, WHISKEY AND WILD WOMEN (USA)
CIGARRA, LA • 1948 • Rey Florian • SPN
CIGARRA ESTA QUE ARDE, LA • 1967 • Demare Lucas • ARG • CIGARRA IS ON FIRE, THE
CIGARRA IS ON FIRE, THE see **CIGARRA ESTA QUE ARDE, LA** • 1967
CIGARRA NO ES UN BICHO, LA • 1963 • Tinayre Daniel • ARG • GAMES MEN PLAY, THE (USA) ○ CICADA IS NOT AN INSECT, THE ○ HOTEL, THE
CIGARRA SI ES UN BICHO, LA • 1971 • *America* • MXC
CIGARS OR NUTS • 1911 • Wilson Frank? • UKN
CIGOGNES N'EN FONT QU'A LEUR TETE • 1989 • Kaminka Didier • FRN
CIGUENA DIJO SI, LA • 1958 • Baledon Rafael • MXC
CIGUENA DISTRAIDA, LA • 1964 • Gomez Muriel Emilio • MXC
CIKANI • 1921 • Anton Karl • CZC • GIPSIES, THE ○ GYPSY
CIKLAMEN • 1916 • Korda Alexander • HNG • CYCLAMEN
CIKO THE BLINKER see **MRKACEK CIKO** • 1982
CIL HOROZ • 1987 • Duru Sureyya • TRK • COCK, THE
CILDIRAN KADIN • 1948 • Gelenbevi Baha • TRK • WOMAN WHO BECAME MAD, THE
CILDIRTAN ARZU see **ADEM ILE HAVVA** • 1967
CILDIRTAN DARBE • 1967 • Evin Semih • TRK • MADDENING BLOW, THE
CILDIRTAN DUDAKLAR • 1967 • Alyanak Arsavir • TRK • MADDENING LIPS
CILLY GOOSE • 1944 • Kneitel Seymour • ANS • USA
CIMARRON • 1931 • Ruggles Wesley • USA
CIMARRON • 1960 • Mann Anthony, Walters Charles • USA
CIMARRON • 1967 • Giral Sergio • SHT • CUB
CIMARRON KID, THE • 1951 • Boetticher Budd • USA
CIMARRONES • 1982 • Ferrand Carlos • CND, PRU
CIMBO • 1927 • Johnson Martin E. • USA
CIMEGO see **SAN MASSENZA** • 1955
CIMENTO, O • 1933 • Vieira Manuel Luis • SHT • PRT
CIMES ET MERVEILLES • 1951 • Samivel • FRN
CIMETIERE DE VOITURES, LE • 1982 • Arrabal Fernando • FRN
CIMETIERES DANS LA FALAISE • 1950 • Rouch Jean • DCS • FRN
CIMITERO SENZA CROCI (ITL) see **CORDE.. UN COLT, UNE** • 1968
CIMZETT ISMERETLEN • 1935 • Sekely Steve • HNG
CIMZETT ISMERETLEN • 1936 • Gaal Bela • HNG
CIN.. CIN.. CIANURO • 1968 • Gastaldi Ernesto • ITL
CINA, LA see **CHUNG-KUO** • 1972
CINA E VICINA, LA • 1967 • Bellocchio Marco • ITL • CHINA IS NEAR
CINCINNATI KID, THE • 1965 • Jewison Norman • USA
CINCO ADVERTENCIAS DE SATANAS, LAS • 1938 • Socias I. • SPN • SATAN'S FIVE WARNINGS
CINCO ADVERTENCIAS DE SATANAS, LAS • 1945 • Soler Julian • MXC • SATAN'S FIVE WARNINGS
CINCO ADVERTENCIAS DE SATANAS, LAS • 1969 • Merino Jose Luis • SPN, PRT • SATAN'S FIVE WARNINGS
CINCO ALMOHADAS PARA UNA NOCHE • 1973 • Lazaga Pedro • SPN
CINCO ASESINOS ESPERAN • 1964 • Urueta Chano • MXC
CINCO BESOS • 1946 • Saslavsky Luis • ARG
CINCO DE CHOCOLATE Y UNO DE FRESA • 1968 • Velo Carlos • MXC • FIVE CHOCOLATE AND ONE STRAWBERRY ICE CREAM
CINCO EN LA CARCEL • 1968 • Gomez Muriel Emilio • MXC • FIVE IN JAIL
CINCO FUERON ESCOGIDOS • 1942 • Kline Herbert • MXC
CINCO HALCONES, LOS • 1960 • Delgado Miguel M. • MXC
CINCO LOBITAS • 1972 • de Arminan Jaime • SPN • FIVE LITTLE WOLVES
CINCO LOBITOS • 1945 • Vajda Ladislao • SPN
CINCO MIL DOLARES AL SOL • 1973 • Balcazar Alfonso • SPN
CINCO MINUTOS DE AMOR • 1941 • Patino Gomez Alfonso • MXC
CINCO NOCHES DE ADAN, LAS • 1942 • Martinez Solares Gilberto • MXC
CINCO PISTOLAS DE TEXAS • 1961 • Xiol Juan • SPN
CINCO ROSTROS DE MUJER • 1946 • Martinez Solares Gilberto • MXC
CINCO TEMAS PARA REFINARIA E QUARTETO • 1971 • de Macedo Antonio • SHT • PRT
CINCO VEZES FAVELA • 1962 • Diegues Carlos (c/d) • BRZ
CINCO VIDAS Y UN DESTINO • 1956 • Baviera Jose • MXC, SLV
CINCUENTICINCO HERMANOS • 1979 • Diaz Jesus • CUB • FIFTY-FIVE BROTHERS
CIND PRIMAVARA E FIERBINTE • 1961 • Saucan Mircea • RMN • WHEN SPRING IS HOT
CINDER ALLEY • 1934 • *Mintz Charles (P)* • ANS • USA
CINDER-ELFRED • 1914 • Plumb Hay? • UKN
CINDERBALLER • 1970 • *Stacey Dist.* • USA
CINDERELLA • 1898 • Smith G. A. • UKN
CINDERELLA • 1905 • *Pathe* • FRN
CINDERELLA • 1907 • Fitzhamon Lewin • UKN
CINDERELLA • 1911 • Campbell Colin • *Selig* • USA
CINDERELLA • 1911 • Marston Theodore • *Thanhouser* • USA
CINDERELLA • 1912 • Cooper Arthur • UKN
CINDERELLA • 1913 • Ambrosio Arturo • ITL
CINDERELLA • 1913 • Buss Harry • UKN
CINDERELLA • 1915 • Kirkwood James • USA
CINDERELLA • 1922 • Disney Walt • ANS • USA
CINDERELLA • 1925 • Lantz Walter • ANS • USA
CINDERELLA • *Maglin Kiddies* • SHT • USA
CINDERELLA • 1930 • *Mintz Charles (P)* • ANS • USA
CINDERELLA • 1933 • *Terry Paul/ Moser Frank (P)* • ANS • USA
CINDERELLA • 1937 • Caron Pierre • FRN • SEDUCTION
CINDERELLA • 1947 • SHT • ASL
CINDERELLA • 1947 • Kosheverova Nadezhda, Shapiro Mikhail • USS
CINDERELLA • 1949 • Jackson Wilfred, Luske Hamilton, Geronimi Clyde • ANM • USA
CINDERELLA • 1954 • *Reiniger Lotte (P)* • ANS • UKN
CINDERELLA • 1958 • Gernert Bill • SHT • USA
CINDERELLA • *National Film Board Of Canada* • ANS • CND
CINDERELLA • 1963 • *Alberti Walter (P)* • ITL
CINDERELLA • 1963 • Just Erika • GDR
CINDERELLA • 1963 • Reiniger Lotte • ANS • UKN
CINDERELLA • *Childhood Prod.* • FRG
CINDERELLA • 1977 • Kimiavi Parviz • IRN
CINDERELLA • 1977 • Pataki Michael, Long Stanley • USA • OTHER CINDERELLA, THE
CINDERELLA • 1985 • Cullingham Mark • MTV • USA
CINDERELLA see **PEPELJUGA** • 1979
CINDERELLA 80 see **CENERENTOLA 80** • 1984
CINDERELLA 2000 • 1977 • Adamson Al • USA
CINDERELLA A-GO-GO • 1967 • Torres Mar S., Conde Conrado • PHL
CINDERELLA AND THE BOOB • 1913 • Henderson Dell • USA
CINDERELLA AND THE FAIRY GODMOTHER • 1898 • Smith G. A. • UKN
CINDERELLA AND THE GOLDEN —— see **SINDERELLA AND THE GOLDEN BRA** • 1964
CINDERELLA AND THE GOLDEN DRESS see **SINDERELLA AND THE GOLDEN BRA** • 1964
CINDERELLA AND THE MAGIC SLIPPER • 1917 • *Wholesome Films* • USA
CINDERELLA BLUES • 1931 • Foster John, Bailey Harry • ANS • USA
CINDERELLA GOES TO A PARTY • 1942 • Tashlin Frank • ANS • USA
CINDERELLA HUSBAND • 1917 • De Vonde Chester M. • SHT • USA
CINDERELLA, ITALIAN STYLE see **C'ERA UNA VOLTA** • 1967
CINDERELLA JONES • 1946 • Berkeley Busby • USA
CINDERELLA LIBERTY • 1973 • Rydell Mark • USA
CINDERELLA MAN, THE • 1918 • Tucker George Loane • USA
CINDERELLA MEETS FELLA • 1938 • Avery Tex • ANS • USA
CINDERELLA OF CRIPPLE CREEK • 1915 • Davis Ulysses • SHT • USA
CINDERELLA OF THE FARMS • 1931 • French John McLean • CND
CINDERELLA OF THE HILLS • 1921 • Mitchell Howard M. • USA
CINDERELLA OR THE GLASS SLIPPER (USA) see **CENDRILLON** • 1912
CINDERELLA SWINGS IT • 1943 • Cabanne W. Christy • USA • SCATTERGOOD SWINGS IT
CINDERELLA UP-TO-DATE • 1909 • Melies Georges • FRN
CINDERELLA (USA) see **CENDRILLON** • 1899
CINDERELLA (USA) see **CENDRILLON** • 1907
CINDERELLA (USA) see **ASCHENBRODEL** • 1914
CINDERELLA (USA) see **ASCHENPUTTEL** • 1922
CINDERELLA (USA) see **VERLORENE SCHUH, DER** • 1923
CINDERELLA (USA) see **CENERENTOLA** • 1949
CINDERELLA (USA) see **ASCHENPUTTEL** • 1955
CINDERELLA (USA) see **KHRUSTALNYY BASHMACHOK** • 1961
CINDERELLA'S FELLER • 1940 • McGann William • SHT • USA
CINDERELLA'S GLOVES • 1913 • *Hennessy Ruth* • USA
CINDERELLA'S SHOES • 1969 • Georgescu Jean • RMN
CINDERELLA'S SLIPPER • 1913 • *Walker Lillian* • USA
CINDERELLA'S TWIN • 1920 • Fitzgerald Dallas M. • USA
CINDERELLA'S WONDERLAND see **CINDERELLA'S WONDERWORLD** • 1980
CINDERELLA'S WONDERWORLD • 1980 • ANM • USA • CINDERELLA'S WONDERLAND
CINDERELLER AND HER FELLER see **RINDERCELLA** • 1970
CINDERFELLA • 1960 • Tashlin Frank • USA
CINDERS • 1913 • *Stanley George* • USA
CINDERS • 1916 • Hill Robert F. • SHT • USA
CINDERS • 1920 • Laemmle Edward • SHT • USA
CINDERS • 1926 • Mercanton Louis • UKN, FRN
CINDERS OF LOVE • 1916 • Wright Walter • SHT • USA
CINDY • 1978 • Graham William A. • TVM • USA
CINDY AND DONNA • 1970 • Anderson Robert J. • USA
CINDY AND HER GOLDEN DRESS see **SINDERELLA AND THE GOLDEN BRA** • 1964
CINDY'S LOVE GAMES see **AMANTI MIEI** • 1979
CINE ALAMEDA see **VIDAS ERRANTES** • 1984
CINE BALLETS DE PARIS • 1959 • Cuny Louis • FRN
CINE-BOUM • 1964 • Jutra Claude, Russell Robert • CND
CINE-CRIME • 1968 • Blackburn Maurice • SHT • CND
CINE FOLLIES • 1976 • Collin Philippe • FRN
CINE-GIRL • 1968 • Leroi Francis • FRN
CINE JAZZ see **MAX ROACH** • 1967
CINE-MAFFIA • 1980 • Storck Henri • BLG
CINE SOMOS NOSOSTROS, EL • 1979 • Agusti Andres • DOC • VNZ • WE ARE THE CINEMA
CINE SOY YO, EL • 1977 • Roche Luis Armando • VNZ, FRN • MOVING PICTURE MAN, THE
CINE VA DESCHIDE USA? • 1967 • Naghi Gheorghe • RMN • WHO IS GOING TO OPEN THE DOOR?
CINE WEEKLY see **KONO NEDELYA** • 1919
CINEMA • 1972 • Schroeder Sebastian C. • SWT
CINEMA • 1979 • Avati Pupi • MTV • ITL
CINEMA see **ENTR'ACTE** • 1924

CINEMA AU SERVICE DE L'HISTOIRE, LE • 1927 • Dulac Germaine • FRN
CINEMA, CHE PASSIONE! • 1935 • Petrucci Antonio • ITL
CINEMA CINEMA • 1980 • Shah Krishna • IND
CINEMA CIRCUS • 1937 • Rowland Roy • SHT • USA
CINEMA D'ALTRI TEMPI • 1953 • Steno • FRN, ITL
CINEMA D'ANIMATION AUX PAY-BAS, LE • 1987 • Crama Nico • DCS • NTH • ANIMATION IN THE NETHERLANDS
CINEMA DE L'AMOUR, LE see **PAYSAGES DE FLORENCE** • 1981
CINEMA DE PAPA, LE • 1970 • Berri Claude • FRN • PAPA'S CINEMA
CINEMA EN QUESTION -TRAVELLING BLUES, LE • 1972 • Chabot Jean • DCS • CND
CINEMA ET REALITE • 1967 • Dufaux Georges, Perron Clement • DOC • CND
CINEMA EYE see **KINO-GLAZ** • 1924
CINEMA GIRL'S ROMANCE, A • 1915 • Pearson George • UKN
CINEMA IN THE COUNTRY see **KINO V DEREVNE** • 1930
CINEMA MACHINE, THE (USA) see **MACCHINA CINEMA, LA** • 1978
CINEMA MORT OU VIF? • 1978 • Graf Urs • DOC • SWT
CINEMA MURDER, THE • 1920 • Baker George D. • USA
CINEMA OF RAYMOND FARK, THE • 1970 • Beresford Bruce • SHT • UKN
CINEMA PAS MORT, MISTER GODARD • 1978 • Dehayes-Bee John • FRN, USA
CINEMA-SALSA POUR GOLDMAN see **AINAMA** • 1980
CINEMA STRUCK • 1915 • *Horseshoe* • UKN
CINEMA-TRUTH see **KINO PRAVDA** • 1922-25
CINEMA VERITE • 1968 • Lindus Allan • USA
CINEMATHEQUE FRANCAISE, LA • 1962 • Herman Jean • FRN
CINEMATOGRAPHE, LE • 1969 • Baulez Michel • FRN
CINEMATOGRAPHIE • 1966 • Goldschmidt D., Meppiel Jacqueline • SHT • FRN
CINEMATON • 1978 • Courant Gerard • FRN
CINEPAMPHLET • 1958-71 • Medvedkin Alexander • SER • USS
CINERAMA HOLIDAY • 1955 • Bendick Robert, De Lacey Philippe • USA
CINERAMA -SOUTH SEAS ADVENTURE • 1958 • Thompson Walter, Wrangell Basil, Lyon Francis D. • USA • SOUTH SEAS ADVENTURE
CINERAMA'S RUSSIAN ADVENTURE • 1966 • *Frankel J. Jay (P)* • DOC • USS, USA • RUSSIAN ADVENTURE
CINESOUND VARIETIES • 1934 • Hall Ken G. • SHT • ASL
CINETRACTS • 1968 • Godard Jean-Luc • FRN
CINETUDE • 1969 • Rodan Keith • ANS • CND
CINGENE GUZELI • 1968 • Pekmezoglu Oksal • TRK • BEAUTIFUL GIPSY, THE
CINICO, L'INFAME, IL VIOLENTO, IL • 1977 • Lenzi Umberto • ITL • CYNIC, THE RAT AND THE FIST, THE
CINOFRENIC • 1980 • Sutherland Joseph • CND
CINOPOLIS • 1930 • Elias Francisco • FRN
CINQ ATOUTS DE M. WENS, LES see **ATOUTS DE M. WENS, LES** • 1946
CINQ DERNIERES MINUTES, LES (FRN) see **ULTIMI CINQUE MINUTI, GLI** • 1955
CINQ ET LA PEAU • 1982 • Rissient Pierre • FRN, PHL • FIVE AND THE SKIN
CINQ FILLES EN FURIE • 1964 • Pecas Max • FRN • FIVE WILD GIRLS (USA) ○ CHIENNES DE SOLEDOR, LES ○ FIVE WILD KIDS
CINQ GARS POUR SINGAPOUR • 1967 • Toublanc-Michel Bernard • FRN, ITL • CINQUE MARINES PER SINGAPORE (ITL) ○ SINGAPORE, SINGAPORE (USA) ○ FIVE ASHORE IN SINGAPORE
CINQ GENTLEMEN MAUDITS, LES • 1920 • Regnier Pierre, Luitz-Morat • FRN • FIVE ACCURSED GENTLEMEN, THE ○ FIVE DOOMED GENTLEMEN
CINQ GENTLEMEN MAUDITS, LES • 1931 • Duvivier Julien • FRN
CINQ JOURS D'ANGOISSE • 1944 • Greville Edmond T. • FRN
CINQ JOURS D'ANGOISSE see **MENACES** • 1939
CINQ JOURS D'UNE VIE • 1971 • Cisse Souleymane • SHT • MLI • FIVE DAYS OF A LIFE
CINQ JOURS EN JUIN • 1989 • Legrand Michel • FRN
CINQ LECONS DE THEATRE D'ANTOINE VITEZ • 1977 • Koleva Maria • SER • FRN
CINQ MILLIONS COMPTANT • 1956 • Berthomieu Andre • FRN
CINQ MINUTES DE CINEMA PUR • 1926 • Chomette Henri • SHT • FRN • FIVE MINUTES OF PURE CINEMA
CINQ POUR CENT DE RISQUES • 1979 • Pourtale Jean • FRN, BLG • 5% DE RISQUE
CINQ SOUS DE LAVAREDE, LES • 1928 • Champreux Maurice • FRN
CINQ SOUS DE LAVAREDE, LES • 1939 • Cammage Maurice • FRN
CINQ TULIPS ROUGES • 1948 • Stelli Jean • FRN
CINQUANT'ANNI DI EMOZIONI • 1954 • Ferronetti Ignazio • ITL
CINQUANTE BRIQUES POUR JO • 1967 • Maley Jean • FRN • HOLD-UP POUR LAURA
CINQUANTENAIRE DES CAISSES POPULAIRES, LE • 1957 • Proulx Maurice • DCS • CND
CINQUE A ZERO • 1932 • Bonnard Mario • ITL
CINQUE BAMBOLE PER LA LUNA DI AGOSTO • 1970 • Bava Mario • ITL • FIVE DOLLS FOR AN AUGUST MOON
CINQUE CAINI, I • 1919 • D'Ambra Lucio • ITL
CINQUE DELLA VENDETTA, I • 1966 • Florio Aldo • ITL, SPN • FIVE GIANTS FROM TEXAS
CINQUE DELL'ADAMELLO, I • 1955 • Mercanti Pino • ITL
CINQUE DOLLARI PER L'ASSASSINO • 1975 • Massi Stelvio • ITL
CINQUE DOLLARI PER RINGO • 1966 • Iquino Ignacio F. • ITL
CINQUE FIGLI DI CANE • 1968 • Caltabiano Alfio • ITL, SPN • FIVE SONS-OF-BITCHES
CINQUE FURBASTRI E UN FURBACCHIONE • 1977 • De Caro Lucio • ITL • COME TI RAPISCO IL PUPO
CINQUE GIORNATE, LE • 1973 • Argento Dario • ITL
CINQUE LEONI UN SOLDO • 1961 • Casadio Aglauco • ITL
CINQUE MARINES PER CENTO RAGAZZE • 1961 • Mattoli Mario • ITL
CINQUE MARINES PER SINGAPORE (ITL) see **CINQ GARS POUR SINGAPOUR** • 1967
CINQUE MATTI VANNO IN GUERRA (ITL) see **BIDASSES S'EN VONT EN GUERRE, LES** • 1974
CINQUE ORE IN CONTANTI (ITL) see **FIVE GOLDEN HOURS** • 1961
CINQUE PER L'INFERNO • 1969 • Parolini Gianfranco • ITL • FIVE FOR HELL (UKN)
CINQUE POVERI IN AUTOMOBILE • 1952 • Mattoli Mario • ITL
CINQUE TOMBE PER UN MEDIUM • 1966 • Pupillo Massimo • ITL, USA • TERROR-CREATURES FROM THE GRAVE (USA) ○ CEMETERY OF THE LIVING DEAD ○ TOMB OF HORROR ○ FIVE GRAVES FOR THE MEDIUM
CINQUIEME EMPREINTE, LA • 1934 • Anton Karl • FRN • LILAS BLANC
CINQUIEME SOLEIL, LE • 1965 • Reichenbach Francois (c/d) • SHT • FRN
CINTA DAN LAGU • 1975 • Sulong Jamil • MLY • LOVE AND SONGS
CINTA PERTAMA • 1973 • Karya Teguh • INN • FIRST LOVE
CINTAMANI A PODVODNIK • 1965 • Krejcik Jiri • CZC • CHINTAMANS AND MARRIAGE SWINDLER ○ ORIENTAL CARPET, THE ○ CHINTAMANS
CINTURA DI CASTITA • 1950 • Mastrocinque Camillo • ITL
CINTURA DI CASTITA, LA • 1967 • Festa Campanile Pasquale • ITL, USA • ON MY WAY TO THE CRUSADES, I MET A GIRL WHO.. (USA) ○ CHASTITY BELT, THE (UKN)
CIOCIARA, LA • 1961 • De Sica Vittorio • ITL • TWO WOMEN (USA)
CIPELICE NA ASFALTU • 1956 • Vucinic Bosko, Randic Zdravko, Radicevic Ljubomir • YGS • TINY SHOES
CIPHER BUREAU • 1938 • Lamont Charles • USA
CIPHER KEYS, THE • 1915 • Terwilliger George W. • USA
CIPHER MESSAGE, THE • 1913 • Grandon Francis J. • USA
CIPHERS see **CISLICE** • 1966
CIPLAK VATANDAS • 1985 • Sabuncu Basar • TRK • NAKED CITIZEN, THE
CIPOLLA COLT • 1975 • Castellari Enzo G. • ITL, SPN, FRG • CRY ONION (UKN)
CIPOTE DE ARCHIDONA, EL • 1979 • Fernandez Ramon • SPN • DONG OF ARCHIDONA, THE
CIPRIAN PORUMBESCU • 1972 • Vitandis Gheorghe • RMN • BALLAD, THE
CIRANO DE BERGERAC • 1909 • Pasquali Ernesto Maria • ITL
CIRANO DE BERGERAC see **CYRANO DE BERGERAC** • 1923
CIRCADIAN RHYTHMS • 1965 • Vas Judit • DOC • HNG
CIRCARC GEAR, THE • 1964 • McNaughton Richard Q. • SHT • UKN
CIRCE • 1963 • Antin Manuel • ARG
CIRCE THE ENCHANTRESS • 1924 • Leonard Robert Z. • USA
CIRCLE • 1969 • Chambers Jack* • CND
CIRCLE see **KREISE** • 1933
CIRCLE 17 • 1914 • Turner Otis • USA
CIRCLE, THE • 1925 • Borzage Frank • USA
CIRCLE, THE • 1967 • Ransen Mort • CND
CIRCLE, THE • 1973 • Rappaport Herbert • USS
CIRCLE, THE see **RING, THE** • 1927
CIRCLE, THE see **STRICTLY UNCONVENTIONAL** • 1930
CIRCLE, THE see **KRUH** • 1959
CIRCLE, THE see **CERCUL**
CIRCLE, THE see **CERCO, O** • 1969
CIRCLE, THE (USA) see **VICIOUS CIRCLE, THE** • 1957
CIRCLE BED • 1981 • Perol Guy
CIRCLE C RANCH'S WEDDING PRESENT • 1910 • *Essanay* • USA
CIRCLE CANYON • 1934 • Adamson Victor • USA
CIRCLE C'S NEW BOSS • 1911 • *Champion* • USA
CIRCLE FROM A DOT see **BINDU THEKEY BRITTA** • 1970
CIRCLE MAN • 1988 • Lee Damian • CND • CIRCLEMAN
CIRCLE OF CHILDREN, A • 1977 • Taylor Don • TVM • USA
CIRCLE OF DANGER • 1951 • Tourneur Jacques • UKN • WHITE HEATHER
CIRCLE OF DEATH • 1955 • Crevenna Alfredo B. • MXC
CIRCLE OF DEATH, THE • 1916 • *Darkfeather Mona* • SHT • USA
CIRCLE OF DEATH, THE • 1935 • Glendon J. Frank • USA
CIRCLE OF DECEIT (UKN) see **FALSCHUNG, DIE** • 1981
CIRCLE OF DECEPTION • 1960 • Lee Jack • UKN
CIRCLE OF FATE • 1914 • *Kb* • USA
CIRCLE OF FATE, THE • 1913 • *Kalem* • USA
CIRCLE OF FEAR (UKN) see **RAIDERS OF TOMAHAWK CREEK** • 1950
CIRCLE OF FIRE see **CIRCULO DE FOGO** • 1989
CIRCLE OF FOUR, A see **CTYRI V KRUHU** • 1967
CIRCLE OF GOLD, A • 1914 • *Frontier* • USA
CIRCLE OF IRON • 1978 • Moore Richard • USA • SILENT FLUTE, THE (UKN)
CIRCLE OF LOVE (USA) see **RONDE, LA** • 1964
CIRCLE OF POWER see **BRAINWASH** • 1981
CIRCLE OF THE SUN • 1961 • Low Colin • DCS • CND • SOLEIL PERDU, LE
CIRCLE OF TWO • 1980 • Dassin Jules • CND
CIRCLE OF VIOLENCE: A FAMILY DRAMA, A • 1986 • Greene David • TVM • USA
CIRCLEMAN see **CIRCLE MAN** • 1988
CIRCLES • 1967 • Levi Ricardo • SPN
CIRCLES see **MA'AGALIM** • 1980
CIRCLES see **SHAKKAR** • 1988
CIRCLE'S END, THE • 1913 • *Fielding Romaine* • USA
CIRCLES IN A FOREST • 1989 • Van Der Bergh Regardt • SAF
CIRCLES OF LOVE • 1971 • Ilinchev Kiril • BUL
CIRCO, EL • 1942 • Delgado Miguel M. • MXC
CIRCO, EL • 1949 • Berlanga Luis Garcia • SPN
CIRCO, O • 1965 • Jabor Arnaldo • SHT • BRZ
CIRCO EQUESTRE ZA-BUM • 1944 • Mattoli Mario • ITL
CIRCO MAGICO, EL • 1977 • Guedez Jesus Enrique • VNZ • MAGIC CIRCUS, THE
CIRCO MAS PEQUENO DEL MUNDO, EL • 1963 • Ivens Joris • CHL, FRN • LITTLE CIRCUS, THE
CIRCO TRAGICO, EL • 1938 • Ojeda Manuel R. • MXC • TRAGIC CIRCUS, THE (USA)
CIRCONCISION, LA • 1949 • Rouch Jean • DCS • FRN
CIRCONSTANCES ATTENUANTES • 1939 • Boyer Jean • FRN
CIRCONSTANCES ATTENUANTES • 1946 • Boyer Jean • FRN • EXTENUATING CIRCUMSTANCES (USA)
CIRCOSTANZA, LA • 1974 • Olmi Ermanno • ITL • CERTAIN CIRCUMSTANCE, A ○ CIRCUMSTANCE, THE
CIRCUIT DE L'ALCOOL, LE • 1912 • O'Galop Marius • ANM • FRN
CIRCUIT DE MINUIT • 1956 • Govar Yvan • BLG
CIRCUIT RIDER OF THE HILLS, THE • 1913 • *Frontier* • USA
CIRCUITO CHIUSO • 1977 • Montaldo Giuliano • MTV • ITL • CLOSED CIRCUIT
CIRCULAR FENCE, THE • 1911 • Dwan Allan • USA
CIRCULAR PANORAMA OF THE ELECTRIC TOWER • 1901 • Porter Edwin S. • USA
CIRCULAR PATH, THE • 1915 • Calvert E .h. • USA
CIRCULAR ROOM, THE • 1916 • Wilson Ben • SHT • USA
CIRCULAR STAIRCASE, THE • 1915 • Le Saint Edward J. • USA
CIRCULAR TENSIONS see **NUMBER 5** • 1950
CIRCULAR TRIANGLE, THE (USA) see **GRAIN DE SABLE, LE** • 1964
CIRCULEZ! • 1931 • de Limur Jean • FRN
CIRCULEZ, Y'A RIEN A VOIR • 1982 • Leconte Patrice • FRN
CIRCULO DE FOGO • 1989 • Moraes Geraldo • BRZ • CIRCLE OF FIRE
CIRCUMCISION see **TIYABU BIRU** • 1978
CIRCUMSTANCE • 1922 • Harris Lawson • ASL
CIRCUMSTANCE see **SITUM** • 1984
CIRCUMSTANCE, THE see **CIRCOSTANZA, LA** • 1974
CIRCUMSTANCES ALTER FACES • 1913 • *Bull'S Eye* • UKN
CIRCUMSTANCES MAKE HEROES • 1913 • *Learn Bessie* • USA
CIRCUMSTANCES OF A VERY NORMAL EVENT • 1978 • Hakki Haitham • MTV • SYR
CIRCUMSTANCIAL EVIDENCE • 1920 • Micheaux Oscar • USA
CIRCUMSTANTIAL EVIDENCE • 1910 • Haldane Bert? • UKN
CIRCUMSTANTIAL EVIDENCE • 1911 • *Champion* • USA
CIRCUMSTANTIAL EVIDENCE • 1912 • Thayer Otis B. • USA
CIRCUMSTANTIAL EVIDENCE • 1914 • *Melies* • USA
CIRCUMSTANTIAL EVIDENCE • 1918 • Christie Al • USA
CIRCUMSTANTIAL EVIDENCE • 1919 • *Capitol* • SHT • USA
CIRCUMSTANTIAL EVIDENCE • 1920 • Collins Tom • USA
CIRCUMSTANTIAL EVIDENCE • 1929 • Noy Wilfred • USA
CIRCUMSTANTIAL EVIDENCE • 1935 • Lamont Charles • USA
CIRCUMSTANTIAL EVIDENCE • 1945 • Larkin John • USA
CIRCUMSTANTIAL EVIDENCE • 1952 • Birt Daniel • UKN
CIRCUMSTANTIAL GUILT • 1916 • Cochrane George • SHT • USA
CIRCUMSTANTIAL HERO, A • 1913 • Dillon Eddie • USA
CIRCUMSTANTIAL HERO, A • 1916 • *Hippo* • USA
CIRCUMSTANTIAL JUSTICE • 1916 • Kelsey Fred A. • SHT • USA
CIRCUMSTANTIAL NURSE, A • 1914 • *Princess* • USA
CIRCUMSTANTIAL SCANDAL, A • 1915 • Davey Horace • USA
CIRCUS • 1932 • *Iwerks Ub (P)* • ANS • USA
CIRCUS see **CIRK** • 1936
CIRCUS see **VESELY CIRKUS** • 1951
CIRCUS, THE • 1914 • *Sterling* • USA
CIRCUS, THE • 1915 • Matthews H. C. • USA
CIRCUS, THE • 1920 • Fleischer Dave • ANS • USA
CIRCUS, THE • 1928 • Chaplin Charles • USA
CIRCUS, THE • 1962 • Donev Donyo • ANS • BUL
CIRCUS, THE see **CYRK** • 1954
CIRCUS, THE see **CIRK, AL** • 1968
CIRCUS ACE, THE • 1927 • Stoloff Ben • USA
CIRCUS AND THE BOY, THE • 1914 • Johnson Tefft • USA
CIRCUS ARRIVES see **DANSERINDENS HAEVN** • 1915
CIRCUS BLUES • 1928 • Lamont Charles • SHT • USA
CIRCUS BOY • 1947 • Musk Cecil • UKN
CIRCUS CAPERS • 1930 • Foster John, Bailey Harry • ANS • USA
CIRCUS CLOWN, THE • 1934 • Enright Ray • USA
CIRCUS COMES TO CLOWN, THE • 1947 • Sparber I. • ANS • USA
CIRCUS COMES TO TOWN, THE (UKN) see **UNDER THE BIG TOP** • 1938
CIRCUS COWBOY, THE • 1924 • Wellman William A. • USA
CIRCUS CYCLONE, THE • 1917 • Miller Rube • SHT • USA
CIRCUS CYCLONE, THE • 1925 • Rogell Albert S. • USA
CIRCUS DAREDEVILS • 1953 • Ozerov Yury • USS • DARING CIRCUS YOUTH (USA)
CIRCUS DAYS • 1919 • Kellette John William • SHT • USA
CIRCUS DAYS • 1920 • *Roubert Matty* • USA
CIRCUS DAYS • 1923 • Cline Eddie • USA
CIRCUS DAYS • 1935 • *Terry Paul/ Moser Frank (P)* • ANS • USA
CIRCUS DAZE • 1937 • Harman Hugh • ANS • USA
CIRCUS DRAWINGS • 1964 • Williams Richard • ANS • UKN
CIRCUS FANDANGO see **SIRKUS FANDANGO** • 1954
CIRCUS-FARM • 1956 • Carlsen Henning • SHT • DNM
CIRCUS FEVER • 1925 • Roach Hal • SHT • USA
CIRCUS FRIENDS • 1956 • Thomas Gerald • UKN
CIRCUS GIRL • 1937 • Auer John H. • USA
CIRCUS GIRL, THE • 1912 • *Feature Photoplay* • USA
CIRCUS GIRL, THE • 1916 • Wright Walter • USA • HER CIRCUS KNIGHT
CIRCUS GIRL'S ROMANCE, THE • 1915 • McRae Henry • USA • PATSY OF THE CIRCUS
CIRCUS HOODOO • 1934 • Gillstrom Arvid E. • SHT • USA
CIRCUS IMPS, THE • 1920 • *Lee Jane* • SHT • USA
CIRCUS IN A CIRCUS see **CIRKUS V CIRKUSE** • 1977
CIRCUS IS COMING, THE see **CIRKUS JEDE** • 1960
CIRCUS JIM • 1921 • Doxat-Pratt B. E. • UKN
CIRCUS JOYS • 1923 • *Joy Gloria* • USA
CIRCUS KID, THE • 1928 • Seitz George B. • USA
CIRCUS LURE • 1924 • Mattison Frank S. • USA
CIRCUS MAN, THE • 1914 • Apfel Oscar • USA
CIRCUS MARY • 1915 • Henderson Lucius • USA
CIRCUS MAXIMUS • 1981 • von Radvanyi Geza • FRG, HNG
CIRCUS NOTEBOOK, THE see **NOTES ON THE CIRCUS** • 1966
CIRCUS OF BLOOD see **BERSERK!** • 1967
CIRCUS OF FEAR • 1966 • Moxey John Llewellyn • UKN • PSYCHO-CIRCUS (USA)
CIRCUS OF HORROR • 1960 • Hayers Sidney • UKN
CIRCUS OF LIFE, THE • 1917 • Julian Rupert • USA

CIRCUS OF LIFE, THE see **FLUCHT IN DEN ZIRKUS, DIE** • 1926
CIRCUS OF LOVE see **RUMMELPLATZ DER LIEBE** • 1954
CIRCUS OF SIN, THE see **SALTO MORTALE** • 1931
CIRCUS ON ICE • 1953 • Sparling Gordon • DCS • CND
CIRCUS OZ • 1977 • Patterson Garry • DOC • ASL
CIRCUS PALS • 1923 • Seiler Lewis, Stoloff Ben • SHT • USA
CIRCUS QUEEN MURDER, THE • 1933 • Neill R. William • USA
CIRCUS REVUE, THE see **CIRKUSREVYEN** • 1967
CIRCUS REX • Bourek Zlatko • CZC
CIRCUS ROMANCE • 1932 • Foster John, Bailey Harry • ANS • USA
CIRCUS ROMANCE, A • 1914 • *Princess* • USA
CIRCUS ROMANCE, A • 1914 • *Melies* • USA
CIRCUS ROMANCE, A • 1916 • Seay Charles M. • USA
CIRCUS ROOKIES • 1928 • Sedgwick Edward • USA • MONKEY BUSINESS
CIRCUS ROYALE • 1977 • Patterson Garry • DOC • ASL
CIRCUS SARAH • 1917 • Curtis Allen • SHT • USA
CIRCUS SAVAGE, THE • 1961 • Jordan Larry • USA
CIRCUS SHADOW, THE (UKN) see **SHADOW, THE** • 1937
CIRCUS SHADOWS • 1935 • Hutchison Charles • USA
CIRCUS SHOW-UP, THE • 1932 • Seiler Lewis • SHT • USA
CIRCUS STAR • 1960 • Halas John • ANS • UKN
CIRCUS STARS • 1958 • Kristi Leonid • DOC • USS
CIRCUS STOWAWAY, A • 1911 • *Thanhouser* • USA
CIRCUS TENT, THE see **THAMPU** • 1978
CIRCUS TIME IN TOYLAND • 1914 • *Lubin* • USA
CIRCUS TODAY • 1926 • Bacon Lloyd • SHT • USA
CIRCUS TODAY • 1940 • Avery Tex • ANS • USA
CIRCUS UNDER THE STARS see **CYRK** • 1962
CIRCUS UNDER THE STARS, THE • 1960 • Bielinska Halina • HNG
CIRCUS WORLD • 1963 • Hathaway Henry • USA • MAGNIFICENT SHOWMAN, THE (UKN)
CIRCUS WORLD • 1974 • Kroitor Roman • CND
CIRCUSMANIA (UKN) see **ZIRKUSKONIG, DER** • 1924
CIRK • 1936 • Alexandrov Grigori • USS • CIRCUS
CIRK, AL • 1968 • Salem Atef • EGY • CIRCUS, THE ◦ SIRK, AS- ◦ CIRQUE, LE
CIRKIN KIRAL • 1966 • Atadeniz Yilmaz • TRK
CIRKIN KIRAL AFFETMEZ see **CIRKIN KRAL AFFETMEZ** • 1967
CIRKIN KRAL AFFETMEZ • 1967 • Atadeniz Yilmaz • TRK • UGLY KING DOES NOT FORGIVE, THE ◦ CIRKIN KIRAL AFFETMEZ
CIRKIN VE CESUR • 1971 • Ozer Nazmi • TRK
CIRKINLER DE SEVER • 1982 • Cetin Sinan • TRK • UGLIES CAN LOVE TOO
CIRKUS • 1939 • Schneevoigt George • DNM, SWD
CIRKUS BUDE • 1954 • Lipsky Oldrich • CZC • SHOW IS ON, THE
CIRKUS BUSTER • 1961 • Balling Erik • DNM
CIRKUS CASABLANCA • 1981 • Clausen Erik • DNM • CASABLANCA CIRCUS, THE
CIRKUS HUMBERTO • 1978 • Lipsky Oldrich • CZC • HUMBERTO CIRCUS, THE
CIRKUS HURVINEK • 1955 • Trnka Jiri • ANM • CZC • HURVINEK CIRCUS, THE ◦ HURVINEK'S CIRCUS
CIRKUS JEDE • 1960 • Lipsky Oldrich • DOC • CZC • CIRCUS IS COMING, THE
CIRKUS V CIRKUSE • 1977 • Lipsky Oldrich • CZC • CIRCUS IN A CIRCUS
CIRKUS WOLFONS SIDSTE GALLAFORESTILLING • 1916 • Lind Alfred • DNM
CIRKUSREVYEN • 1967 • Kaas Preben • DNM • CIRCUS REVUE, THE
CIRQUE, LE see **CIRK, AL** • 1968
CIRQUE DE LA MORT, LE • 1916 • Lind Alfred • ITL
CISARUV PEKAR • 1951 • Fric Martin • CZC • EMPEROR AND THE GOLEM, THE (USA) ◦ EMPEROR'S BAKER, THE ◦ RETURN OF THE GOLEM, THE
CISARUV SLAVIK • 1948 • Makovec Milos • DOC • CZC
CISARUV SLAVIK • 1948 • Trnka Jiri • ANM • CZC • EMPEROR AND THE NIGHTINGALE, THE ◦ EMPEROR'S NIGHTINGALE, THE
CISCO AND THE ANGEL see **RIDING THE CALIFORNIA TRAIL** • 1947
CISCO KID, THE • 1931 • Cummings Irving • USA
CISCO KID AGAIN see **CISCO KID RETURNS, THE** • 1945
CISCO KID AND THE LADY, THE • 1940 • Leeds Herbert I. • USA
CISCO KID COMES THROUGH, THE see **CISCO KID RETURNS, THE** • 1945
CISCO KID IN OLD NEW MEXICO, THE (UKN) see **IN OLD NEW MEXICO** • 1945
CISCO KID RETURNS, THE • 1945 • McCarthy John P. • USA • CISCO KID COMES THROUGH, THE ◦ CISCO KID AGAIN
CISCO PIKE • 1972 • Norton B. W. L. • USA
CISEAU ET LE PINCEAU, LE • 1932 • Bohdziewicz Antoni • SHT • FRN
CISKA BARNA, DIE ZIGEUNERIN • 1921 • *Reinach Gerda* • FRG
CISKE -A CHILD WANTS LOVE see **CISKE, EIN KIND BRAUCHT LIEBE** • 1955
CISKE DE RAT see **CISKE, EIN KIND BRAUCHT LIEBE** • 1955
CISKE, EIN KIND BRAUCHT LIEBE • 1955 • Staudte Wolfgang • FRG, NTH • CISKE (USA) ◦ CISKE DE RAT ◦ CISKE THE RAT ◦ CISKE -A CHILD WANTS LOVE
CISKE THE RAT see **CISKE, EIN KIND BRAUCHT LIEBE** • 1955
CISKE (USA) see **CISKE, EIN KIND BRAUCHT LIEBE** • 1955
CISLICE • 1966 • Prochazka Pavel • ANM • CZC • CIPHERS
CISSIN.. 5 ANS PLUS TARD • 1982 • Bulbulian Maurice, Kola Djim Mamadou • DOC • CND
CISSY'S INNOCENT WINK • 1915 • Middleton Edwin • USA
CISSY'S MONEY BOX • 1910 • *Empire Films* • UKN
CITA CON LA MUERTE • 1948 • Salvador Jaime • MXC
CITA CON LA VIDA, UNA • 1957 • del Carril Hugo • ARG
CITA CON MARILIN • 1968 • Kaps Arturo • ANS • SPN • DATE WITH MARILIN
CITA DE AMOR, UNA • 1956 • Fernandez Emilio • MXC • REBEL, THE
CITA IMPOSIBLE • 1953 • Santillan Antonio • SPN
CITADEL, THE • 1938 • Vidor King • USA, UKN
CITADEL, THE (UKN) see **KALAA, EL** • 1988
CITADEL OF CRIME • 1941 • Sherman George • USA • OUTSIDE THE LAW (UKN)
CITADEL OF CRIME (UKN) see **MAN BETRAYED, A** • 1937
CITADEL OF SILENCE, THE (USA) see **CITADELLE DU SILENCE, LA** • 1937
CITADEL OF WARSAW, THE see **WARSCHAUER ZITADELLE, DIE** • 1930
CITADELA SFARIMATA • 1957 • Maurette Marc • RMN • CRUMBLING CITADEL, THE
CITADELLE, LA see **HISN, AL-** • 1977
CITADELLE DU SILENCE, LA • 1937 • L'Herbier Marcel • FRN • CITADEL OF SILENCE, THE (USA)
CITE D'ARGENT, LA • 1955 • Galey • SHT • FRN
CITE DE LA VIOLENCE (FRN) see **CITTA VIOLENTA** • 1970
CITE DE L'ESPERANCE • 1948 • Stelli Jean • FRN
CITE DE L'INDICIBLE PEUR, LA see **GRANDE FROUSSE, LA** • 1964
CITE DE NOTRE-DAME, LA • 1942 • Paquette Vincent • DCS • CND
CITE DES LUMIERES, LA • 1938 • de Limur Jean • FRN
CITE DU MIDI • 1952 • Baratier Jacques • SHT • FRN • FLYING TRAPEZE, THE
CITE FANTOME, LA • Des Vallieres Jean • SHT • FRN
CITE FOUDROYEE, LA • 1923 • Luitz-Morat • FRN • CITY DESTROYED, THE ◦ DESTROYED CITY, THE
CITE LUMINEUSE, LA see **SVETLYI GOROD** • 1928
CITE MAGIQUE, LA see **MAYIKI POLIS, I** • 1955
CITE MORTE, LA see **NEKRI POLITIA** • 1951
CITE RADIEUSE, LA • 1952 • Sacha Jean • SHT • FRN
CITE SAVANTE see **ESSAY ON SCIENCE, AN** • 1962
CITE UNIVERSITAIRE DE PARIS, LA • 1933 • Deslaw Eugene • FRN
CITES DU CIEL • 1959 • See Jean-Claude • SHT • FRN
CITIES AND TIMES see **GORODA I GODY** • 1973
CITIES AND YEARS • 1931 • Tcherviakov Evgeni
CITIES OF CHEMISTRY, THE • Muresan Mircea • RMN
CITIES OF LIGHTS see **VILLES-LUMIERES** • 1959
CITIES OF THE DESERT • 1934 • Glover T. A. • UKN
CITIES OF THE EMPIRE • 1931-32 • Thring F. W. • SER • ASL
CITIES WE BUILD, THE • 1974 • Richardson Boyce • DOC • CND
CITIZEN, THE see **NAGARIK** • 1952
CITIZEN BRYCH see **OBCAN BRYCH** • 1958
CITIZEN HAROLD • 1971 • Foulds Hugh • CND
CITIZEN IM5 see **GRADANIM IM5** • 1962
CITIZEN IN THE MAKING, A • 1912 • *Duncan William* • USA
CITIZEN KANE • 1941 • Welles Orson • USA
CITIZEN KAREL HAVLICEK see **OBCAN KAREL HAVLICEK** • 1966
CITIZEN NEEDS SELF PROTECTION, THE • 1975 • *Conte Richard*
CITIZEN P. see **OBYWATEL PISZCYK** • 1988
CITIZEN REBELS, THE (USA) see **CITTADINO SI RIBELLA, IL** • 1974
CITIZEN SAINT • 1948 • Young Harold • USA
CITIZEN URBAN • Bevc Joze • DOC • YGS
CITIZENS ALL • 1916 • *Coxen Edward* • SHT • USA
CITIZEN'S ARMY see **HOME GUARD, THE** • 1941
CITIZEN'S BAND • 1977 • Demme Jonathan • USA • HANDLE WITH CARE
CITIZEN'S BAND see **FM** • 1978
CITIZEN'S MEDICINE • 1970 • Klein Bonnie • DOC • CND • CLINIQUE DES CITOYENS
CITIZENS OF THE FUTURE • 1935 • Taylor Donald • UKN
CITLIVA MISTA • 1987 • Drha Vladimir • CZC • SENSITIVE SPOT
CITTA APERTA see **ROMA, CITTA APERTA** • 1945
CITTA BIANCA • 1942 • Pasinetti Francesco • ITL
CITTA CANORA, LA • 1952 • Costa Mario • ITL • SINGING CITY
CITTA DEI TRAFFICI, LA • 1949 • Risi Dino • SHT • ITL
CITTA DEL MONDO, LA • 1975 • Risi Nelo • MTV • ITL
CITTA DEL SOLE, LA • 1973 • Amelio Gianni • ITL • CITY OF SUN, THE
CITTA DELL'AMORE, LA • 1934 • Franchini Mario, Gentilomo Giacomo • ITL
CITTA DELLE DONNE, LA • 1979 • Fellini Federico • ITL, FRN • CITY OF WOMEN (UKN)
CITTA DELL'ULTIMA PAURA, LA • 1975 • Ausino Carlo • ITL
CITTA DI NOTTE • 1958 • Trieste Leopoldo • ITL
CITTA DOLENTE • 1949 • Bonnard Mario • ITL
CITTA GIOCA D'AZZARDO, LA • 1975 • Martino Sergio • ITL
CITTA PRIGIONERA, LA • 1962 • Anthony Joseph • ITL • CONQUERED CITY (USA) ◦ CAPTIVE CITY
CITTA PROIBITE, LE • 1963 • Scotese Giuseppe Maria • DOC • ITL • MONDO SI RIVELA, UN
CITTA SCONVOLTA: CACCIA SPIETATA AI RAPITORI, LA • 1975 • Di Leo Fernando • ITL
CITTA SI DEFENDE, LA • 1951 • Germi Pietro • ITL • FOUR WAYS OUT (USA) ◦ PASSPORT TO HELL
CITTA VIOLENTA • 1970 • Sollima Sergio • ITL, FRN • CITE DE LA VIOLENCE (FRN) ◦ VIOLENT CITY (UKN) ◦ FAMILY, THE
CITTADINO SI RIBELLA, IL • 1974 • Castellari Enzo G. • ITL • CITIZEN REBELS, THE (USA) ◦ ANONYMOUS AVENGER
CITY, A see **MADINA, AL-** • 1971
CITY, THE • 1911 • *Reliance* • USA
CITY, THE • 1914 • West Raymond B. • USA
CITY, THE • 1916 • Wharton Theodore • USA
CITY, THE • 1926 • Neill R. William • USA
CITY, THE • 1939 • Elton Arthur • DOC • UKN
CITY, THE • 1939 • Van Dyke Willard, Steiner Ralph • DOC • USA
CITY, THE • 1959 • Ramsbott Wolfgang • SHT • FRG
CITY, THE • 1970 • Pindal Kaj • ANS • CND
CITY, THE • 1971 • Petrie Daniel • TVM • USA
CITY, THE • 1977 • Hart Harvey • TVM • USA
CITY, THE see **CIUDAD, LA** • 1971
CITY ACROSS THE RIVER • 1949 • Shane Maxwell • USA • AMBOY DUKES, THE
CITY AFTER DARK • 1981 • Bernal Ishmael • PHL • MANILA BY NIGHT
CITY AFTER MIDNIGHT (USA) see **THAT WOMAN OPPOSITE** • 1957
CITY AND THE DREAM, THE see **SHEHAR AUR SAPNA** • 1963
CITY AT CHANDIGARH, A (UKN) see **VIE A CHANDIGARH, LA** • 1966
CITY AT NIGHT see **MESTO V NOCI** • 1960
CITY AWAKENS EARLY, THE see **GOROD PROSYPAYETSYA RANO** • 1968
CITY BEAUTIFUL, A • 1914 • Cabanne W. Christy • USA
CITY BENEATH THE SEA • 1953 • Boetticher Budd • USA
CITY BENEATH THE SEA • 1970 • Allen Irwin • TVM • USA • ONE HOUR TO DOOMSDAY (UKN)
CITY BRIDE, THE see **NOIVA DA CIDADE, A** • 1980
CITY-BUILDERS, THE see **LYUBIT CHELOVYEKA** • 1972
CITY BY NIGHT, THE see **KILLER BY NIGHT** • 1971
CITY CALLED COPENHAGEN, A see **BY VED NAVN KOBENHAVN, EN** • 1960
CITY CALLED DRAGON, A (USA) see **LUNG-CH'ANG SHIH-JIH** • 1969
CITY CHAP, THE • 1922 • St. John Al • SHT • USA
CITY DESTROYED, THE see **CITE FOUDROYEE, LA** • 1923
CITY DUDE, THE • 1919 • *Briggs* • SHT • USA
CITY-DWELLERS • 1975 • Rogovoi Vladimir • USS
CITY FAMILY, THE • 1972 • McGill Chris • DOC • ASL
CITY FARM • 1980 • Davies John, Smith Robert • UKN
CITY FELLER, THE see **WATCH YOUR STEP** • 1922
CITY FELLOW, THE • 1913 • Ball Eustace Hale • USA
CITY FOR CONQUEST • 1940 • Litvak Anatole • USA
CITY GIRL • 1930 • Murnau F. W., Erickson A. F. • USA • OUR DAILY BREAD
CITY GIRL • 1937 • Werker Alfred L. • USA
CITY GIRL • 1984 • Coolidge Martha • USA
CITY GONE WILD, THE • 1927 • Cruze James • USA
CITY HALL SCANDAL see **NIGHT CLUB SCANDAL** • 1937
CITY HALL TO HARLEM IN 15 SECONDS VIA THE SUBWAY ROUTE • 1904 • Porter Edwin S. • USA
CITY HAS YOUR FACE, THE see **MESTOMA SVOU TVAR** • 1958
CITY HEAT • 1984 • Benjamin Richard • USA
CITY IN DARKNESS see **CHARLIE CHAN IN CITY IN DARKNESS** • 1939
CITY IN FEAR • 1980 • Taylor Jud • TVM • USA • PANIC ON PAGE ONE
CITY IN FEAR see **PLACE CALLED TODAY, A** • 1972
CITY IN HISTORY, A • 1967 • Chowdhury Shanti P. • DOC • IND
CITY IN TERROR see **MAN WHO DARED, THE** • 1939
CITY IN THE SEA see **CITY UNDER THE SEA, THE** • 1965
CITY IS DARK, THE (UKN) see **CRIME WAVE** • 1954
CITY JUNGLE, THE (UKN) see **YOUNG PHILADELPHIANS, THE** • 1958
CITY KILLER • 1984 • Lewis Robert • TVM • USA
CITY KITTY • 1952 • Sparber I. • ANS • USA
CITY LIFE • 1989 • van Leeuwaarden Mildren, Rijneke Dick, Kieslowski Krzysztof, Agresti Alejandro, Guerin Jose Luis, Altorjag Gabor, Klopfenstein Clemens, Reichenbach Carlos, Kotetishvili Tato, Pennell Eagle, Mbaye Ousmane William, Tarr Bela, Sen Mrinal • NTH
CITY LIGHTS • 1931 • Chaplin Charles • USA
CITY LIMITS • 1934 • Nigh William • USA
CITY LIMITS • 1984 • Lipstadt Aaron • USA
CITY LIMITS see **FATHER STEPS OUT** • 1941
CITY MAN'S BUSY DAY, A • 1905 • *Urban Trading Co.* • UKN
CITY MAP see **VAROSTERKEP** • 1977
CITY MOUSE, THE • 1913 • *Thanhouser* • USA
CITY NEWS • 1983 • Fishelson David, Zinman Zoe • USA
CITY OF ASHES • 1990 • Hedayat Hassan • IRN
CITY OF BADMEN • 1953 • Jones Harmon • USA
CITY OF BEAUTIFUL NONSENSE, THE • 1919 • Edwards Henry • UKN
CITY OF BEAUTIFUL NONSENSE, THE • 1935 • Brunel Adrian • UKN
CITY OF BELLS, THE see **HARANGOK VAROSA -VESZPREM** • 1966
CITY OF BLOOD • 1987 • Roodt Darrell • SAF
CITY OF CHANCE • 1940 • Cortez Ricardo • USA
CITY OF CHILDREN • 1949 • *Mgm* • SHT • USA
CITY OF COMRADES, THE • 1919 • Beaumont Harry • USA
CITY OF CONTRAST • 1952 • Hartford-Davis Robert • DOC • UKN
CITY OF CONTRASTS • 1972 • Browning Irving • USA
CITY OF DARKNESS, THE • 1914 • Barker Reginald • USA
CITY OF DESIRE see **JOEN NO CHIMATA** • 1922
CITY OF DIM FACES, THE • 1918 • Melford George • USA
CITY OF DREAMS see **TRAUMSTADT** • 1973
CITY OF FAILING LIGHT, THE • 1916 • Terwilliger George W. • USA
CITY OF FEAR • 1959 • Lerner Irving • USA
CITY OF FEAR • 1966 • Bezencenet Peter • UKN
CITY OF GOLD • 1957 • Low Colin, Koenig Wolf • DCS • CND • CAPITALE DE L'OR
CITY OF GREAT DESTINY • 1960 • Kopalin Ilya • DOC • USS
CITY OF HER DREAMS, THE • 1910 • *Thanhouser* • USA
CITY OF HISTROS, THE • 1956 • Bostan Ion • DOC • RMN
CITY OF ILLUSION, THE • 1916 • Abramson Ivan • USA
CITY OF JAMES JOYCE • 1962 • St. Leger Bill • IRL
CITY OF LITTLE MEN, THE • 1948 • Loud Harry • SHT • USA
CITY OF LIVE WATER see **MESTO ZIVE VODY** • 1934
CITY OF LONDON, THE • 1951 • Baylis Peter, Bradford Peter • DOC • UKN
CITY OF LOST MEN • 1935 • Revier Harry • USA
CITY OF LOVE see **AIJO NO MIYAKO** • 1958
CITY OF MASKS, THE • 1920 • Heffron Thomas N. • USA
CITY OF MEN see **OTOKO TO OTOKO NO IKARU MACHI** • 1962
CITY OF MICE, THE • 1985 • Boroomand M., Talebi Ali • ANM • IRN
CITY OF MISSING GIRLS, THE • 1941 • Clifton Elmer • USA
CITY OF MY DREAMS see **MINA DROMMARS STAD** • 1976
CITY OF NIGHT see **CITY OF SHADOWS** • 1986
CITY OF PARIS • 1967 • Reichenbach Francois • SHT • FRN
CITY OF PIRATES see **VILLE DES PIRATES, LA** • 1983
CITY OF PLAY • 1929 • Clift Denison • UKN
CITY OF PROMISE, THE • 1914 • *Loftus Cecilia* • USA
CITY OF PURPLE DREAMS • 1928 • Worne Duke • USA
CITY OF PURPLE DREAMS, THE • 1918 • Campbell Colin • USA

CITY OF SADNESS, A (UKN) see **PEI-CH'ING CH'ENG-SHIH** • 1989
CITY OF SECRETS (USA) see **STADT IST VOLLER GEHEIMNISSE, DIE** • 1955
CITY OF SHADOWS • 1955 • Witney William • USA
CITY OF SHADOWS • 1986 • Mitchell David • USA • CITY OF NIGHT ○ NIGHTMARE CITY
CITY OF SHADOWS see **NIGHT PATROL, THE** • 1929
CITY OF SILENT MEN • 1919 • De Mille William C. • USA
CITY OF SILENT MEN • 1921 • Forman Tom • USA
CITY OF SILENT MEN • 1942 • Nigh William • USA
CITY OF SIN see **SCAVENGERS, THE** • 1959
CITY OF SONG, THE • 1930 • Gallone Carmine • UKN • FAREWELL TO LOVE (USA)
CITY OF SUN, THE see **CITTA DEL SOLE, LA** • 1973
CITY OF TALES see **SHAHRE GHESSEH** • 1973
CITY OF TEARS, THE • 1918 • Wilson Elsie Jane • USA
CITY OF TEMPTATION, THE see **STADT DER VERSUCHUNG, DIE** • 1925
CITY OF TERRIBLE NIGHT, THE • 1915 • Lessey George A. • USA
CITY OF THE BEES • 1962 • USA
CITY OF THE DEAD • 1960 • Moxey John Llewellyn • UKN • HORROR HOTEL (USA)
CITY OF THE DEAD see **FORBIDDEN ADVENTURE, THE** • 1915
CITY OF THE LIVING DEAD see **PAURA, LA** • 1980
CITY OF THE NAME OF GOD, THE see **CIDADE DO NOME DE DEUS, O** • 1969
CITY OF THE WALKING DEAD see **NIGHTMARE CITY** • 1980
CITY OF TORMENT (USA) see **...UND UBER UNS DER HIMMEL** • 1947
CITY OF TOWERS • 1935 • Sparling Gordon • DCS • CND
CITY OF VIOLENCE see **AMORE E SANGUE** • 1951
CITY OF WOMEN (UKN) see **CITTA DELLE DONNE, LA** • 1979
CITY OF YOUTH see **KOMSOMOLSK** • 1938
CITY OF YOUTH, THE • 1928 • Calvert Charles • UKN
CITY ON A HUNT • 1953 • Bennett Charles • USA • NO ESCAPE
CITY ON ANGELS see **NOVEMBER PLAN, THE** • 1976
CITY ON FIRE • 1979 • Rakoff Alvin • CND
CITY ON FIRE see **LONGHU FENGYUN** • 1987
CITY ON TRIAL see **PROCESSO ALLA CITTA** • 1952
CITY OUT OF TIME • 1959 • Low Colin • DOC • CND
CITY OUT OF WILDERNESS • 1973 • *Hammid Alexander (Ph)* • USA
CITY PARK • 1934 • Thorpe Richard • USA
CITY PREPARES, A see **FIRST DAYS, THE** • 1939
CITY RAT AND THE COUNTRY RAT, THE see **RAT DE VILLE ET LE RAT DES CHAMPS, LE** • 1926
CITY RATS see **RATAS DE LA CIUDAD**
CITY REBORN, A • 1945 • Eldridge John • DOC • UKN
CITY RUBE, A • 1915 • Davis Ulysses • USA
CITY SCENE • 1963 • Kaczender George • CND
CITY SENTINEL, THE see **BEAST OF THE CITY, THE** • 1932
CITY SHADOWS see **CITY STREETS** • 1938
CITY SINGS, A see **LISTEN TO THE PRAIRIES** • 1945
CITY SLICKER • 1952 • Davis Mannie • ANS • USA
CITY SLICKER, THE • 1918 • Roach Hal • SHT • USA
CITY SLICKER, THE • 1938 • *Mintz Charles (P)* • ANS • USA
CITY SPARROW, THE • 1920 • Wood Sam • USA
CITY SPEAKS, A • 1947 • Gysin Francis • UKN
CITY STANDS TRIAL, THE (USA) see **PROCESSO ALLA CITTA** • 1952
CITY STORIES: SOMEONE'S COMING see **HISTORIAS DE CIUDAD: ALGUIEN SE ACERCA** • 1990
CITY STORY • 1954 • Beaudine William • USA
CITY STREETS • 1931 • Mamoulian Rouben • USA
CITY STREETS • 1938 • Rogell Albert S. • USA • CITY SHADOWS
CITY SYMPHONY see **TOKAI KOKYOGAKU** • 1929
CITY SYMPHONY, A • 1931 • Weinberg Herman G. • USA
CITY THAT NEVER SLEEPS, THE • 1924 • Cruze James • USA
CITY THAT NEVER SLEEPS, THE • 1953 • Auer John H. • USA
CITY THAT STOPPED HITLER: HEROIC STALINGRAD, THE • 1943 • DOC • USS
CITY TIGRESS, THE • 1915 • Johnston Lorimer • SHT • USA
CITY TRAMP, THE see **STADTSTREICHER** • 1966
CITY TWILIGHT • 1955 • Werner Gosta • SHT • SWD
CITY UNDER THE SEA, THE • 1965 • Tourneur Jacques • UKN, USA • WAR-GODS OF THE DEEP (USA) ○ CITY IN THE SEA
CITY WITHOUT JEWS, THE • 1928 • von Santer Carl
CITY WITHOUT MEN • 1943 • Salkow Sidney • USA
CITY WOLF, A • 1911 • *Atlas* • USA
CITY'S CHILD, A • 1971 • Kavanagh Brian • ASL
CITY'S EDGE, THE • 1983 • Quinnell Ken • ASL • EDGE OF THE CITY ○ RUNNING MAN, THE
CITYSCAPE • 1965 • Larkin Ryan • ANS • CND
CITYSCAPE • 1969 • Kamnitzer Peter • ANS • USA
CIUDAD, LA • 1971 • Posani Clara • VNZ • CITY, THE
CIUDAD DE CARTON, LA • 1934 • King Louis • USA • CARDBOARD CITY
CIUDAD DE ENSUENO • 1922 • Ferreyra Jose • ARG
CIUDAD DE LOS MUNECOS, LA • 1946 • Elorrieta Jose Maria • SPN
CIUDAD DE LOS NINOS, LA • 1956 • Martinez Solares Gilberto • MXC
CIUDAD DE LOS PIRATOS, LA (PRT) see **VILLE DES PIRATES, LA** • 1983
CIUDAD DE LOS SUENOS, LA • 1954 • Gomez Bascuas Enrique • SPN
CIUDAD NO ES PARA MI, LA • 1966 • Lazaga Pedro • SPN
CIUDAD PERDIDA, LA • 1950 • Delgado Agustin P. • MXC
CIUDAD PERDIDA, LA • 1954 • Aleixandre Margarita, Torrecilla Rafael • SPN
CIUDAD QUEMADA, LA see **CIUTAT CREMADA, LA** • 1976
CIUDAD SAGRADA, LA • 1959 • Rodriguez Ismael • MXC, USA
CIUDAD SIN HOMBRES, LA see **SUMURU** • 1968
CIUDAD Y LOS PERROS, LA • 1985 • Lombardi Francisco • PRU
CIUDADO CON LAS PERSONAS FORMALES • 1961 • Navarro Agustin • SPN
CIUJYE PISMA • 1976 • Averbach Ilya • USS • STRANGE LETTERS ○ OTHER PEOPLE'S LETTERS
CIULEANDRA (RMN) see **VERKLUNGENE TRAUME** • 1930
CIULINII BARAGANULUI • 1957 • Daquin Louis • RMN, FRN • CHARDONS DU BARAGAN, LES (FRN) ○ THISTLES OF BARAGAN, THE ○ THISTLES OF THE BARAGAN, THE
CIUTAT CREMADA, LA • 1976 • Ribas Antoni • SPN • CIUDAD QUEMADA, LA ○ BURNED CITY, THE
CIVIL ENGINEERING • 1946 • Eldridge John (c/d) • SHT • UKN
CIVIL SERVANT, THE • 1990 • Detwiler John • SHT • CND
CIVIL SPEECH • 1980 • Leventakos Diamantis • DOC • GRC
CIVILFORSVARET • 1950 • Carlsen Henning • SHT • DNM
CIVILIAN, THE • 1912 • Balshofer Fred J. • USA
CIVILIAN CLOTHES • 1920 • Ford Hugh • USA
CIVILISATION A TRAVERS LES AGES, LA • 1907 • Melies Georges • FRN • HUMANITY THROUGH THE AGES (USA) ○ CIVILISATION ACROSS THE AGES
CIVILISATION ACROSS THE AGES see **CIVILISATION A TRAVERS LES AGES, LA** • 1907
CIVILISATION DU BOIS, LA • 1976 • Dansereau Fernand, Rossignol Yolande • DCS • CND
CIVILISATION: GRANDEUR AND OBEDIENCE • 1969 • Montagnon Peter • UKN
CIVILISATION: MAN -THE MEASURE OF THINGS • 1969 • Turner Ann • UKN
CIVILISATION: PROTEST AND COMMUNICATION • 1969 • Montagnon Peter • UKN
CIVILISATION: ROMANCE AND REALITY • 1969 • Gill Michael • UKN
CIVILISATION; THE GREAT THAW • 1969 • Montagnon Peter • UKN
CIVILISATION: THE HERO AS ARTIST • 1969 • Gill Michael • UKN
CIVILISATION: THE LIGHT OF EXPERIENCE • 1969 • Gill Michael • UKN
CIVILISATION: THE PURSUIT OF HAPPINESS • 1969 • Montagnon Peter • UKN
CIVILISATION: THE SKIN OF OUR TEETH • 1969 • Gill Michael • UKN
CIVILISATION; THE SMILE OF REASON • 1969 • Gill Michael • UKN
CIVILISATION: THE WORSHIP OF NATURE • 1969 • Gill Michael, Turner Ann • UKN
CIVILIZACION ESTA HACIENDO MASA Y NO DEJA OIR, LA • 1973 • Ludueña Julio • ARG
CIVILIZATION • 1911 • *Powers* • USA
CIVILIZATION • 1916 • Ince Thomas H., Barker Reginald, West Raymond B. • USA
CIVILIZATION AND ITS DISCONTENTS • 1964 • Morrissey Paul • USA
CIVILIZATION'S CHILD • 1916 • Giblyn Charles • USA
CIVILIZED AND SAVAGE • 1913 • *Weber Lois* • USA
CJAMANGO • 1967 • Mulargia Edoardo • ITL
CLAIM 36 see **SILBERKONIG 3, DER** • 1921
CLAIM, THE • 1918 • Reicher Frank • USA
CLAIM AGENT'S MIS-ADVENTURE, THE • 1911 • Dwan Allan • USA • MISADVENTURES OF A CLAIM AGENT, THE
CLAIM JUMPER, THE • 1912 • *Republic* • USA
CLAIM JUMPER, THE • 1913 • Morty Frank • USA
CLAIM JUMPERS, THE • 1911 • Dwan Allan • USA • RANGE SQUATTER, THE
CLAIM NUMBER THREE • 1914 • *Lubin* • USA
CLAIM OF HONOR, THE • 1915 • Reehm George E. • USA
CLAIR DE FEMME • 1979 • Costa-Gavras • FRN, FRG, ITL
CLAIR DE LUNE • 1932 • Diamant-Berger Henri • FRN
CLAIR DE LUNE A MAUBEUGE, UN • 1962 • Cherasse Jean-A. • FRN
CLAIR DE LUNE SOUS RICHELIEU, UN • 1911 • Capellani Albert • FRN
CLAIR DE TERRE • 1969 • Gilles Guy • FRN
CLAIR OBSCUR • 1963 • Sluizer George • SHT • NTH
CLAIR OBSCUR • 1988 • Chbib Bachar • CND
CLAIRE • 1924 • Dinesen Robert • FRG • GESCHICHTE EINES JUNGEN MADCHENS, DIE
CLAIRE.. CETTE NUIT ET DEMAIN • 1986 • Castillo Nardo • CND
CLAIRE DE LUNE ESPAGNOL • 1909 • Cohl Emile, Arnaud • ANS • FRN • MOON-STRUCK MATADOR, THE ○ MAN IN THE MOON, THE
CLAIRE'S KNEE (UKN) see **GENOU DE CLAIRE, LE** • 1971
CLAIRE'S WISH • 1979 • Marr Leon G. • MTV • CND
CLAIRVOYANT, THE • 1935 • Elvey Maurice • UKN • EVIL MIND, THE
CLAIRVOYANT, THE see **VOYANTE, LA** • 1923
CLAIRVOYANT, THE see **MEIN HERZ SEHNT SICH NACH LIEBE** • 1931
CLAIRVOYANT, THE see **KILLING HOUR, THE** • 1984
CLAIRVOYANT SWINDLERS, THE • 1915 • *Sais Marin* • USA
CLAM-SHELL SUFFRAGETTES, THE • 1915 • MacGregor Norval • USA
CLAMBAKE • 1967 • Nadel Arthur H. • USA
CLAMOR DEL SILENCIO, EL • Ruiz Jorge • DOC • BLV
CLAN, THE • 1984 • Kaurismaki Mika • FNL
CLAN DE LOS INMORALES, EL • 1973 • Gutierrez Maesso Jose • SPN • ORDER TO KILL (USA)
CLAN DE LOS NAZARENOS, EL • 1976 • Romero-Marchent Joaquin Luis • SPN
CLAN DEGLI UOMINI VIOLENTI, IL (ITL) see **HORSE, LA** • 1969
CLAN DEI DUE BORSALINI, IL • 1971 • Orlandini Giuseppe • ITL
CLAN DEI MARSIGLIESI, IL (ITL) see **SCOUMOUNE, LA** • 1973
CLAN DEL QUARTIERE LATINO, IL • 1974 • Cantillon B. • ITL
CLAN DES SICILIENS, LE • 1969 • Verneuil Henri • FRN • SICILIAN CLAN, THE (UKN)
CLAN OF AMAZONS see **HSIU-HUA TA TAO** • 1978
CLAN OF THE CAVE BEAR, THE • 1985 • Chapman Michael • USA
CLAN OF THE WHITE LOTUS see **HUNG WEN-TING SAN P'O PAI LIEN CHIAO** • 1980
CLANCARTY • 1914 • Shaw Harold • UKN
CLANCY • 1910 • *Vitagraph* • USA
CLANCY • 1974 • Brakhage Stan • USA
CLANCY AT THE BAT • 1929 • Rodney Earle • SHT • USA
CLANCY IN WALL STREET • 1930 • Wilde Ted • USA
CLANCY OF THE MOUNTED • 1933 • Taylor Ray • SRL • USA
CLANCY STREET BOYS • 1943 • Beaudine William • USA
CLANCY, THE MODEL • 1913 • *Crystal* • USA
CLANCY'S KOSHER WEDDING • 1927 • Gillstrom Arvid E. • USA
CLANDESTINE • 1967 • Abalos Ruben • PHL
CLANDESTINE DESTINATION see **CLANDESTINO DESTINO** • 1987
CLANDESTINES, LES • 1954 • Andre Raoul • FRN • VICE DOLLS (USA)
CLANDESTINO A TRIESTE • 1952 • Salvini Guido • ITL
CLANDESTINO DESTINO • 1987 • Hermosillo Jaime Humberto • MXC • CLANDESTINE DESTINATION
CLANDESTINS, LES • 1945 • Chotin Andre • FRN • DANGER DE MORT
CLANS OF INTRIGUE see **CH'U LIU-HSIANG** • 1977
CLANSMAN, THE see **BIRTH OF A NATION, THE** • 1915
CLAP HANDS • 1935 • Dormand Frank • UKN
CLAP VOCALISM see **NINGEN DOBUTSUEN** • 1961
CLAP YOUR HANDS • 1949 • Cowan Will • SHT • USA
CLAPHAM AND DWYER NO.1 • 1929 • *B.s.f.p.* • SHT • UKN • MUSICAL MEDLEY NO.5
CLAPHAM AND DWYER NO.2 • 1929 • *B.s.f.p.* • SHT • UKN
CLARA AND HER MYSTERIOUS TOYS • 1912-14 • Cohl Emile • ANS • USA
CLARA AND NORA • 1975 • *Koscina Sylvia*
CLARA CLEANS HER TEETH • 1926 • Disney Walt • ANS • USA
CLARA DE MONTARGIS • 1950 • Decoin Henri • FRN
CLARA DEANE see **STRANGE CASE OF CLARA DEANE, THE** • 1932
CLARA ES EL PRECIO • 1974 • Aranda Vicente • SPN • PRICE IS CLARA, THE ○ CLARA IS THE PRICE
CLARA ET LES CHICS TYPES • 1981 • Monnet Jacques • FRN
CLARA ET LES MECHANTS • 1957 • Andre Raoul • FRN • BOURREAUX D'ENFANTS
CLARA GIBBINGS • 1934 • Thring F. W. (c/d) • ASL
CLARA IS THE PRICE see **CLARA ES EL PRECIO** • 1974
CLARA'S HEART • 1988 • Mulligan Robert • USA
CLARA'S MYSTERIOUS TOYS • 1913 • *Horton Clara* • USA
CLARENCE • 1922 • De Mille William C. • USA
CLARENCE • 1937 • Archainbaud George • USA
CLARENCE AND ANGEL • 1980 • Gardner Robert • USA
CLARENCE AND PERCY'S SAILING PARTY • 1914 • *Edison* • USA
CLARENCE CHEATS AT CROQUET • 1915 • *Chamberlin Riley* • USA
CLARENCE, CROOKS AND CHIVALRY • 1919 • *Lane Lupino* • SHT • UKN
CLARENCE, THE COWBOY • 1913 • *Patheplay* • USA
CLARENCE THE COWBOY • 1916 • *Jockey* • USA
CLARENCE, THE CROSS-EYED LION • 1965 • Marton Andrew • USA
CLARENDON SPEAKING PICTURES • 1913 • Noy Wilfred • SER • UKN
CLARETTA • 1984 • Squitieri Pasquale • ITL
CLARINES DEL MIEDO, LOS • 1958 • Roman Antonio • SPN
CLARINES Y CAMPANAS • 1966 • Torrado Ramon • SPN
CLARION, THE • 1916 • Durkin James • USA
CLARION CALL, THE • 1918 • Miller Ashley • SHT • USA
CLARISSA • 1941 • Lamprecht Gerhard • FRG
CLARISSA • *Lahaye Brigitte* • FRN • CLARISSE
CLARISSA see **GAMBIER'S ADVOCATE** • 1915
CLARISSA'S CHARMING CALF • 1915 • *Cunningham Arthur* • USA
CLARISSE see **CLARISSA**
CLARK • 1977 • Martinsen Poul • DNM
CLARK AND MCCULLOUGH IN THE HONOR SYSTEM • 1928 • *Fox* • USA
CLARK AND MCCULLOUGH IN THE INTERVIEW • 1928 • *Fox* • USA
CLARK CITY • 1978 • Lesaunier Daniel • MTV • CND
CLARK HARRISON'S REVENGE see **VENGANZA DE CLARK HARRISON, LA** • 1968
CLARK'S CAPTURE OF KASKASKIA • 1911 • *Champion* • USA
CLARO • 1975 • Rocha Glauber • ITL
CLARO DE LUNA • 1942 • Amadori Luis Cesar • ARG
CLAROS MOTIVOS DEL DESEO, LOS • 1977 • Picazo Miguel • SPN
CLASE APARTE • 1971 • Lugo Alfredo • VNZ • SPECIAL QUALITY
CLASH • 1983 • Delpard Raphael • FRN, YGS
CLASH, THE • 1973 • Puchinyan S. • USS
CLASH AND CARRY • 1961 • Hannah Jack • ANS • USA
CLASH BY NIGHT • 1952 • Lang Fritz • USA
CLASH BY NIGHT • 1957 • Frankenheimer John • MTV • USA
CLASH BY NIGHT • 1963 • Tully Montgomery • UKN • ESCAPE BY NIGHT (USA)
CLASH OF STEEL • 1917 • Howard George Bronson • SHT • USA
CLASH OF STEEL (USA) see **CHEVALIER DE PARDAILLAN, LE** • 1962
CLASH OF THE ASH, THE • 1987 • Tighe Fergus • IRL
CLASH OF THE SWORDS • 1984 • Weeks Stephen • UKN
CLASH OF THE TITANS • 1981 • Davis Desmond • UKN
CLASH OF THE WARLORDS • *Williams Will* • ITL
CLASH OF THE WOLVES • 1925 • Smith Noel • USA
CLASH OF VIRTUES, A • 1914 • *Essanay* • USA
CLASHING LOYALTIES see **MAS'ALA AL KUBRA, AL** • 1983
CLASS • 1983 • Carlino Lewis John • USA
CLASS, THE • 1961 • Schlesinger John • DCS • UKN
CLASS ACTION • 1990 • Apted Michael • USA
CLASS AND NO CLASS • 1921 • Kellino W. P. • UKN
CLASS CERTIFICATE see **ZALICZENIE** • 1968
CLASS CONDITIONS see **KLASSENVERHALTNISSE** • 1984
CLASS ENEMY • 1983 • Stein Peter • FRG
CLASS IN SWING • 1940 • Ceballos Larry • SHT • USA
CLASS MATES see **KLASSKAMRATER** • 1952
CLASS OF '44 • 1973 • Bogart Paul • USA
CLASS OF '63 • 1973 • Korty John • TVM • USA
CLASS OF 69 • 1970 • *Janus Ii Productions* • USA
CLASS OF '74 • 1972 • Bing Mack, Marks Arthur • USA • GIRLS MOST LIKELY TO, THE (UKN)
CLASS OF 1984, THE • 1981 • Lester Mark L. • USA
CLASS OF 1999 • 1989 • Lester Mark L. • USA

CLASS OF MISS MACMICHAEL, THE • 1978 • Narizzano Silvio • UKN
CLASS OF NUKE 'EM HIGH • 1986 • Haines Richard W., Weil Samuel • USA • NUKE 'EM HIGH
CLASS ONE see **PIERWSZA KLASA** • 1959
CLASS RELATIONS see **KLASSENVERHALTNISSE** • 1984
CLASS REUNION see **NATIONAL LAMPOON'S CLASS REUNION** • 1982
CLASS REUNION, THE • 1911 • *Imp* • USA
CLASS REUNION MASSACRE • 1977 • USA
CLASS STRUGGLE: FILM FROM THE CLYDE see **FILM FROM THE CLYDE** • 1977
CLASSE DES FINISSANTES, LA • 1968 • Dansereau Fernand • DCS • CND
CLASSE DI FERRO • 1957 • Vasile Turi • ITL
CLASSE D'OPERA, LA see **OPERA SCHOOL** • 1951
CLASSE DU SEXE, LA • 1972 • Terry Norbert • FRN
CLASSE MISTA • 1976 • Laurenti Mariano • ITL
CLASSE OPERAIA VA IN PARADISO, LA • 1971 • Petri Elio • ITL • WORKING CLASS GOES TO HEAVEN, THE ○ LULU THE TOOL (USA) ○ WORKING CLASS GOES TO PARADISE, THE
CLASSE SANS ECOLE, UNE • 1980 • Beaudry Jean • CND
CLASSE TOUS RISQUES • 1959 • Sautet Claude • FRN, ITL • ASFALTO CHE SCOTTIA (ITL) ○ BIG RISK, THE (USA)
CLASSES • 1979 • Bugajski Ryszard • MTV • PLN
CLASSIC EGG, THE • 1986 • Arsenault Ray • DOC • CND
CLASSIC FAIRY TALES • 1966 • Batchelor Joy • ASS • UKN
CLASSIC V JAZZ • 1930 • Oumansky Alexander • UKN
CLASSIFICATION DES PLANTES, LA • 1982 • Ruiz Raul • SHT • FRN • CLASSIFICATION OF PLANTS, THE
CLASSIFICATION OF PLANTS, THE see **CLASSIFICATION DES PLANTES, LA** • 1982
CLASSIFIED • 1925 • Santell Alfred • USA
CLASSIFIED LOVE • 1986 • Taylor Don • TVM • USA
CLASSMATES • 1908 • *Bitzer Billy (Ph)* • USA
CLASSMATES • 1913 • *Ryno* • USA
CLASSMATES • 1914 • Kirkwood James • USA
CLASSMATES • 1924 • Robertson John S. • USA • WINNING THROUGH (UKN)
CLASSMATE'S FROLIC, THE • 1913 • Ince Ralph • USA
CLASSROOM JUNGLE see **HIKO SHONEN** • 1964
CLAUDE • 1965 • McLaughlin Dan • ANS • USA
CLAUDE see **VIEIL HOMME ET L'ENFANT, LE** • 1967
CLAUDE DEPUTISES • 1930 • Jeffrey R. E. • UKN
CLAUDE DUVAL • 1924 • Cooper George A. • UKN
CLAUDE ET GRETA • 1970 • Pecas Max • FRN • HER AND SHE AND HIM (USA) ○ ANY TIME ANYWHERE (UKN) ○ LIAISONS PARTICULIERES, LES
CLAUDE ET HUMIDE NATACHA • Baudricourt Michel • FRN
CLAUDE FRANCOIS, LE FILM DE SA VIE • 1979 • Pavel Samy • DOC • FRN, BLG
CLAUDE GAVREAU POETE • 1974 • Labrecque Jean-Claude • DOC • CND
CLAUDE-NICHOLAS LEDOUX, ARCHITECTE MAUDIT • 1954 • Kast Pierre • SHT • FRN
CLAUDE ST. DENIS • 1966 • Bonniere Rene • DCS • CND
CLAUDE THORNHILL AND HIS ORCHESTRA • 1947 • *Columbia* • SHT • USA
CLAUDE THORNHILL AND HIS ORCHESTRA • 1950 • Cowan Will • SHT • USA
CLAUDELLE INGLISH • 1961 • Douglas Gordon • USA • YOUNG AND EAGER (UKN)
CLAUDE'S WIFE see **DANGER WOMAN** • 1946
CLAUDI VOM GEISERHOF, DIE • 1917 • Biebrach Rudolf • FRG
CLAUDIA • 1916 • Hill Robert F. • SHT • USA
CLAUDIA • 1943 • Goulding Edmund • USA
CLAUDIA • 1971 • *Cima* • MXC
CLAUDIA • 1985 • Kawadri Anwar • UKN • CLAUDIA'S STORY ○ DINNER DATE
CLAUDIA AND DAVID • 1946 • Lang Walter • USA
CLAUDIA'S STORY see **CLAUDIA** • 1985
CLAUDINA'S TROUBLES (USA) see **APUROS DE CLAUDINA, LOS** • 1940
CLAUDINE • 1913 • Pouctal Henri • FRN
CLAUDINE • 1974 • Berry John • USA
CLAUDINE A L'ECOLE • 1937 • de Poligny Serge • FRN
CLAUSE IN THE CONSTITUTION, THE • 1915 • Le Saint Edward J. • USA
CLAUSE IN THE WILL, A • 1910 • *Defender* • USA
CLAVELES DE LA VIRGEN, LOS • 1928 • Rey Florian • SPN
CLAVELES, LOS • 1935 • Ardavin Eusebio F. • SPN
CLAVELES, LOS • 1960 • Lluch Miguel • SPN
CLAVIGO • 1970 • Ophuls Marcel • MTV • FRG
CLAVILLAZO EN LA LUNA see **CONQUISTADOR DE LA LUNA, EL** • 1960
CLAVO, EL • 1944 • Gil Rafael • SPN
CLAW, THE • 1918 • Vignola Robert G. • USA
CLAW, THE • 1927 • Olcott Sidney • USA
CLAW MONSTERS, THE • 1955 • Adreon Franklin • USA
CLAW STRIKES, THE (UKN) see **LANDRUSH** • 1946
CLAWS • 1977 • Bansbach Richard, Pierson Robert • USA • DEVIL BEAR
CLAWS FOR ALARM • 1954 • Jones Charles M. • ANS • USA
CLAWS IN THE LEASE • 1963 • McKimson Robert • ANS • USA
CLAWS OF GREED, THE • 1914 • *Ramo* • USA
CLAWS OF SATAN, THE see **SATAN NO TSUME** • 1959
CLAWS OF THE HUN, THE • 1918 • Schertzinger Victor, Ince Thomas H. (Spv) • USA
CLAWS OF THE SPIDER, THE see **DANS LES GRIFFES DE L'ARAIGNEE** • 1920
CLAY • 1965 • Mangiamele Giorgio • ASL
CLAY • 1965 • Noyes Eliot • ANS • CND • ORIGIN OF THE SPECIES, THE
CLAY see **KORKARLEN** • 1921
CLAY see **SHATTERED DREAMS** • 1922
CLAY see **ARGILA** • 1940
CLAY BAKER, THE • 1910 • Mong William V. • USA
CLAY DOLLARS • 1921 • Archainbaud George • USA • OUTWITTED
CLAY ELF, THE see **HLINAK** • 1972
CLAY HEART, THE see **GULDETS GIFT** • 1916
CLAY PIGEON • 1971 • Stern Tom, Slate Lane • USA • TRIP TO KILL (UKN)
CLAY PIGEON, THE • 1949 • Fleischer Richard • USA
CLAY PIGEON, THE see **GLINENI GOLUB** • 1966
CLAYDON TREASURE MYSTERY, THE • 1938 • Haynes Manning • UKN
CLAYMATION • 1978 • Vinton Will • ANS • USA
CLAYR FAIT see **LOUVE, LA** • 1948
CLAYTON AND CATHERINE (USA) see **CHINA 9 LIBERTY 37** • 1978
CLE DES CHANTS SURREALISTES, LA • 1966 • Haesaerts Paul • BLG
CLE SUR LA PORTE, LA • 1978 • Boisset Yves • FRN
CLEAN AND SOBER • 1988 • Caron Glenn Gordon • USA
CLEAN BREAK see **KILLING, THE** • 1956
CLEAN FARMING • 1946 • Harper Alan • DOC • UKN
CLEAN GUN, THE • 1917 • Harvey Harry • USA
CLEAN HANDS • 1955 • Lettrich Andrej • CZC
CLEAN HEART, THE • 1924 • Blackton J. Stuart • USA
CLEAN PASTURES • 1937 • Freleng Friz • ANS • USA
CLEAN SHAVEN MAN, A • 1936 • Fleischer Dave • ANS • USA
CLEAN SLATE, A • 1914 • *Lubin* • USA
CLEAN SLATE (UKN) see **COUP DE TORCHON** • 1981
CLEAN SWEEP • 1967 • Harriton Chuck • ANS • USA
CLEAN SWEEP see **KEHRAUS** • 1984
CLEAN SWEEP, A • 1915 • Ransom Charles • USA
CLEAN SWEEP, A • 1918 • *Sterling Merta* • SHT • USA
CLEAN SWEEP, A • 1938 • Roberts Charles E. • SHT • USA
CLEAN SWEEP, A • 1958 • Rogers Maclean • UKN
CLEAN UP, THE • 1913 • *Nestor* • USA
CLEAN-UP, THE • 1915 • Bartlett Charles • USA
CLEAN-UP, THE • 1917 • Worthington William • USA
CLEAN UP, THE • 1922 • *Fairbanks William* • USA
CLEAN-UP, THE • 1923 • Parke William • USA • UPSIDE DOWN
CLEAN-UP, THE • 1929 • McEveety Bernard F. • USA
CLEAN-UP MAN, THE • 1928 • Taylor Ray • USA
CLEAN-UP SQUAD, THE see **HOT DOGS** • 1980
CLEANER, THE • 1928 • *Bard Wilkie* • SHT • UKN
CLEANING HOUSE • 1938 • Allen Robert • ANS • USA
CLEANING TIME • 1915 • Louis Will • USA
CLEANING UP • 1920 • St. John Al • SHT • USA
CLEANING UP • 1926 • Arbuckle Roscoe • USA
CLEANING UP • 1933 • Hiscott Leslie • UKN
CLEANSING OF A DIRTY DOG, THE • 1914 • Reed Langford? • UKN
CLEANSING WATERS • 1915 • *Ramona* • USA
CLEAR ALL WIRES • 1933 • Hill George W. • USA
CLEAR AND PRESENT DANGER, A • 1970 • Goldstone James • TVM • USA
CLEAR DAY OF LIBERTY see **JASNY DZIEN WOLNOSCI** • 1962
CLEAR FOR ACTION see **STAND BY FOR ACTION** • 1942
CLEAR IRON • 1952 • USA
CLEAR PONDS • 1966 • Sakharov Alexei • USS
CLEAR SKIES see **CHISTOIE NEBO** • 1961
CLEAR SKY, A see **CHISTOIE NEBO** • 1961
CLEAR THE DECKS • 1929 • Henabery Joseph • USA
CLEAR THE DECKS FOR ACTION see **KLART TILL DRABBNING** • 1937
CLEAR THE WAY • 1924 • Lamont Charles • SHT • USA
CLEAR WATER see **AGUA CLARA** • 1974
CLEAR WEATHER see **HAREKOSODE** • 1961
CLEARED FOR ACTION (USA) see **KLART TILL DRABBNING** • 1937
CLEARING THE RANGE • 1931 • Brower Otto • USA
CLEARING THE TRAIL • 1928 • Eason B. Reeves • USA
CLEF DE L'ENIGME, LA • 1971 • Tolbi Abdelaziz • ALG
CLEGG • 1969 • Shonteff Lindsay • UKN
CLEMENCEAU CASE, THE • 1915 • Brenon Herbert • USA • INFIDELITY (UKN)
CLEMENCIA • 1934 • Urueta Chano • MXC
CLEMENT MEADMORE • 1963 • Beresford Bruce • DCS
CLEMENT MOREAU • 1978 • Dindo Richard • DOC • SWT
CLEMENTINE see **SONG OF PARIS** • 1952
CLEMENTINE CHERIE • 1963 • Chevalier Pierre • FRN, ITL
CLEMENTINE TANGO • 1982 • Roboh Caroline • FRN
CLEO • 1989 • Vincent Chuck • USA
CLEO DE 5 A 7 • 1961 • Varda Agnes • FRN • CLEO FROM 5 TO 7
CLEO E DANIEL • 1971 • Freire Roberto • BRZ
CLEO FROM 5 TO 7 see **CLEO DE 5 A 7** • 1961
CLEO, ROBES ET MANTEAUX • 1933 • Malasomma Nunzio • ITL
CLEOPAKWAK, THE DUCK THAT LAYS GOLDEN EGGS • 1969 • Pacheco Lauro • PHL
CLEOPATRA • 1913 • Gaskill Charles L. • USA
CLEOPATRA • 1917 • Edwards J. Gordon • USA
CLEOPATRA • 1918 • *Gardner Helen* • USA
CLEOPATRA • 1928 • Neill R. William • SHT • USA
CLEOPATRA • 1934 • De Mille Cecil B. • USA
CLEOPATRA • 1963 • Mankiewicz Joseph L., Mamoulian Rouben (U/c) • USA
CLEOPATRA • 1970 • Yamamoto Eiichi • ANM • JPN
CLEOPATRA JONES • 1973 • Starrett Jack • USA
CLEOPATRA JONES AND THE CASINO OF GOLD • 1975 • Bail Chuck • USA, HKG • CASINO OF GOLD
CLEOPATRA OR A NIGHT OF ENCHANTMENT • 1909 • *Vitagraph* • USA • CLEOPATRA'S LOVER
CLEOPATRA, QUEEN OF SEX • 1971 • Tomita Isa • ANM • JPN
CLEOPATRA WONG see **THEY CALL HER CLEOPATRA WONG** • 1978
CLEOPATRA'S DAUGHTER (USA) see **SEPOLCRO DEI RE, IL** • 1961
CLEOPATRA'S LOVER see **CLEOPATRA OR A NIGHT OF ENCHANTMENT** • 1909
CLEOPATRE • 1899 • Melies Georges • FRN • ROBBING CLEOPATRA'S TOMB (USA)
CLEOPATSY • 1918 • Roach Hal • SHT • USA
CLEOPAZZA • 1964 • Moscovini Carlo • ITL
CLEPSIDRA • 1972 • Popescu-Gopo Ion • RMN
CLERAMBARD • 1969 • Robert Yves • FRN
CLERGYMAN, THE see **PRASTEN** • 1913
CLERGYMAN AND THE WARD, THE • 1910 • *Atlas* • USA
CLERGYMAN FROM THE SUBURBS, THE see **FOORSTADSPRASTEN** • 1917
CLERGYMAN FROM THE WILDS see **ODEMARKSPRASTEN** • 1946
CLERGYMAN FROM UDDARBO, THE see **PRASTEN I UDDARBO** • 1958
CLERK, THE • 1914 • *Nigh William* • USA
CLERK AND THE COAT, THE see **GARM COAT** • 1955
CLERK'S DOWNFALL, THE • 1910 • Raymond Charles • UKN
CLEVER AND COMIC CYCLE ACT • 1900 • Williamson James • UKN
CLEVER BRIGAND, THE see **SURA CHOWRAYA** • 1967
CLEVER COLLIE'S COMEBACK, A • 1916 • *Keyes Francis* • USA
CLEVER CORRESPONDENT, A • 1900 • *Mitchell & Kenyon* • UKN
CLEVER CUBS • 1920 • *Cohn Productions* • SHT • USA
CLEVER DANCES • 1904 • *Paul R. W.* • UKN
CLEVER DICK • 1968 • Baker Ian • SHT • ASL
CLEVER DUMMY, A • 1917 • Raymaker Herman C. • SHT • USA
CLEVER EGG CONJURING • 1912 • Booth W. R. • UKN
CLEVER FRAUD, A • 1911 • *Vitagraph* • USA
CLEVER GIRL see **OKOS LANY** • 1955
CLEVER GIRL TAKES CARE OF HERSELF, A see **BRA FLICKA REDER SIG SJALV** • 1913
CLEVER ILLUSIONS AND HOW TO DO THEM • 1911 • Stow Percy • UKN
CLEVER MRS. CARFAX, THE • 1917 • Crisp Donald • USA • MRS. CARFAX THE CLEVER
CLEVER MRS. CARTER, THE • 1916 • Ridgwell George • SHT • USA
CLEVER ONE, THE • 1914 • Weston Charles • UKN
CLEVER ONES see **BUTHISALIGAL** • 1968
CLEVER RUSE, A • 1910 • *Imp* • USA
CLEVER STORY, A • 1913 • *Carlyle Francis* • USA
CLEVEREST, THE • *Shanghai Students Collective* • CHN
CLICKING HOOFS • 1926 • *Truart Film Corp.* • USA
CLICKING OF CUTHBERT, THE • 1924 • Wilson Andrew P. • SER • UKN
CLICKING OF CUTHBERT, THE • 1924 • Wilson Andrew P. • UKN
CLIENT SERIEUX, UN • 1932 • Autant-Lara Claude • FRN
CLIENTE SEDUCTOR, EL • 1932 • Rey Florian, Blumenthal • SPN, FRN
CLIENTS OF AARON GREEN, THE • 1918 • Sargent George L. • SHT • USA
CLIFF, THE see **GAMPEKI** • 1953
CLIFF, THE see **SHIROI GAKE** • 1960
CLIFF DWELLERS, THE • 1910 • Olcott Sidney • USA
CLIFF EDWARDS AND HIS MUSICAL BUCKAROOS • 1941 • Negulesco Jean • SHT • USA
CLIFF FACE see **TRUT!** • 1944
CLIFF GIRL, THE • 1915 • *Williams William* • USA
CLIFF MONSTER, THE • 1962 • *Golden Eagle Films* • SHT • USA
CLIFF OF ARSHAUL, THE • 1930 • Rondeli David • USS
CLIFF OF SIN, THE • Montero Roberto Bianchi
CLIFF OF THE GHOST GIRL, THE see **ZEPPEKI NO ONI-MUSUME** • 1959
CLIFFS OF MERSA, THE see **TOBRUK** • 1966
CLIFTON HOUSE MYSTERY, THE • 1978 • David Hugh • MTV • UKN
CLIMATES OF LOVE (UKN) see **CLIMATS** • 1962
CLIMATS • 1962 • Lorenzi Stellio • FRN • CLIMATES OF LOVE (UKN)
CLIMATS • 1975 • Gervais Suzanne • ANS • CND
CLIMAX • 1967 • Okuwaki Toshio • JPN
CLIMAX • 1977 • Lara Polop Francisco • SPN
CLIMAX, THE • 1913 • *Solax* • USA
CLIMAX, THE • 1913 • *Patheplay* • USA
CLIMAX, THE • 1930 • Hoffman Renaud • USA
CLIMAX, THE • 1944 • Waggner George • USA
CLIMAX, THE see **MOTHERHOOD** • 1915
CLIMAX, THE (USA) see **IMMORALE, L'** • 1967
CLIMAX (UKN) see **ICH, DAS ABENTEUER HEUTE EINE FRAU ZU SEIN** • 1973
CLIMB, THE • 1986 • Shebib Donald • CND
CLIMB AN ANGRY MOUNTAIN • 1972 • Horn Leonard • TVM • USA
CLIMB UP THE WALL • 1960 • Winner Michael • UKN
CLIMBER, THE • 1917 • King Henry • USA
CLIMBERS, THE • 1915 • O'Neil Barry • USA
CLIMBERS, THE • 1919 • Terriss Tom • USA
CLIMBERS, THE • 1927 • Stein Paul L. • USA
CLIMBERS, THE (USA) see **AMBITIEUSE, L'** • 1959
CLIMBING HIGH • 1938 • Reed Carol • UKN
CLIMBING OF CHIMBORAZO, THE see **BESTEIGUNG DES CHIMBORAZO, DIE** • 1988
CLIMBING ROSES see **SARMASIK GULLERI** • 1968
CLIMBING THE AMERICAN ALPS • 1905 • *Biograph* • USA
CLIMBING THE MATTERHORN • 1947 • Allen Irving • USA
CLIN D'OEIL • 1983 • Amat Jorge • FRN
CLINCH see **KLINCZ** • 1980
CLINGING VINE, THE • 1926 • Sloane Paul • USA
CLINIC • 1987 • Malikov Rashid • USS
CLINIC, THE • 1982 • Stevens David • ASL
CLINIC, THE see **SANITARIUM, THE** • 1910
CLINIC FOR THE STUDY OF STUMBLE • 1948 • Peterson Sidney • SHT • USA • CLINIC OF STUMBLE
CLINIC OF STUMBLE see **CLINIC FOR THE STUDY OF STUMBLE** • 1948
CLINIC XCLUSIVE • 1971 • Chaffey Don • UKN • SEX CLINIC ○ WITH THESE HANDS
CLINICA DEL DOCTOR CURETA, LA • 1987 • Fischermann Alberto • ARG • DR. CURETO'S CLINIC
CLINICA DELL'AMORE, LA • 1977 • Cadueri Renato • ITL
CLINIQUE DE LA TERREUR, LA see **BROOD, THE** • 1979
CLINIQUE DES CITOYENS see **CITIZEN'S MEDICINE** • 1970
CLINK IN THE KLINK • *Vague Vera* • SHT • USA
CLINT CLOBBER'S CAT • 1957 • Rasinski Connie • ANS • USA

CLINT EL SOLITARIO • 1965 • Balcazar Alfonso • SPN, ITL, FRG • CLINT IL SOLITARIO (ITL) ○ LONELY CLINT
CLINT, EL SOLITARIO • 1971 • Ramirez Pedro L. • SPN
CLINT IL SOLITARIO (ITL) see **CLINT EL SOLITARIO** • 1965
CLINTON AND NADINE see **BLOOD MONEY** • 1988
CLIPA • 1979 • Vitandis Gheorghe • RMN • MOMENT, THE
CLIPPED WINGS • 1936 • Paton Stuart • USA
CLIPPED WINGS • 1953 • Bernds Edward • USA
CLIPPED WINGS (UKN) see **HELLO SISTER** • 1933
CLIPPETY CLOBBERED • 1966 • Larriva Rudy • ANS • USA
CLIPPINGS see **POSTRIZINY** • 1980
CLIQUE OF GOLD, THE see **EVIL WOMEN DO, THE** • 1916
CLITO DE CINQ A SEPT • Antony Michel • FRN
CLIVE OF INDIA • 1935 • Boleslawski Richard • USA
CLIVIA • 1954 • Anton Karl • FRG
CLOAK, THE see **SHINEL** • 1926
CLOAK, THE see **SHINEL** • 1960
CLOAK AND DAGGER • 1946 • Lang Fritz • USA
CLOAK AND DAGGER • 1984 • Franklin Richard • USA
CLOAK AND STAGGER • 1956 • Rasinski Connie • ANS • USA
CLOAK OF CHARITY, THE see **MANTEL DER LIEFTE, DER** • 1978
CLOAK OF GUILT, THE • 1913 • *Joyce Alice* • USA
CLOAK WITHOUT DAGGER • 1956 • Stirling Joseph • UKN • OPERATION CONSPIRACY
CLOBBER'S BALLET ACHE • 1959 • Rasinski Connie • ANS • USA
CLOCHARD • 1932 • Peguy Robert • FRN
CLOCHARD MILLIARDAIRE, LE • 1950 • Gomez Leopold • FRN • LUI ET MOI
CLOCHE, LA • 1964 • L'Hote Jean • FRN • BELL, THE
CLOCHEMERLE • 1947 • Chenal Pierre • FRN • SCANDALS OF CLOCHEMERLE, THE (USA)
CLOCHES DE CORNEVILLE, LES • 1917 • Bentley Thomas • UKN
CLOCHES DE PAQUES, LES • 1912 • Feuillade Louis • FRN
CLOCK, THE • 1917 • Worthington William • USA • TIME AND TIDE (UKN)
CLOCK, THE • 1945 • Minnelli Vincente • USA • UNDER THE CLOCK (UKN)
CLOCK, THE see **KHOROOS** • 1973
CLOCK, THE see **KELLO** • 1984
CLOCK AT RONNEBERGA, THE see **KLOCKAN PA RONNEBERGA** • 1944
CLOCK CLEANERS • 1937 • Sharpsteen Ben • ANS • USA
CLOCK GOES ROUND AND ROUND, THE • 1937 • *Mintz Charles (P)* • ANS • USA
CLOCK MAKER'S DREAM, THE (USA) see **REVE DE L'HOROLOGER, LE** • 1904
CLOCK SHOP, THE • 1930 • Brooks Marty • USA
CLOCK STOPPED, THE • 1913 • *Ab* • USA
CLOCK STORE, THE • 1931 • Jackson Wilfred • ANS • USA • IN A CLOCK STORE
CLOCK STRIKES EIGHT, THE • 1946 • Haines Ronald • UKN
CLOCK STRIKES EIGHT, THE • 1958 • Winner Michael • UKN
CLOCK STRIKES EIGHT, THE (UKN) see **COLLEGE SCANDAL** • 1935
CLOCK STRIKES THREE, THE see **WHEN THE CLOCK STRIKES** • 1961
CLOCK STRUCK ONE, THE • 1917 • Windom Lawrence C. • SHT • USA
CLOCK STRUCK TWELVE, THE see **PASSPORT TO SUEZ** • 1943
CLOCK WATCHER, THE • 1945 • King Jack • ANS • USA
CLOCK WENT WRONG, THE • 1914 • Jackson Harry • USA
CLOCK WISE • 1939 • Roberts Charles E. • SHT • USA
CLOCKMAKER, THE see **HORLOGER DE ST. PAUL, L'** • 1973
CLOCKMAKER OF ST. PAUL, THE (USA) see **HORLOGER DE ST. PAUL, L'** • 1973
CLOCKMAKERS DOG • 1956 • Rasinski Connie • ANS • USA
CLOCKMAKER'S SECRET, THE • 1907 • *Pathe* • FRN
CLOCKTIME • 1972 • Pound Stuart • UKN
CLOCKWISE • 1985 • Morahan Christopher • UKN
CLOCKWORK BANANA see **BANANES MECANIQUES** • 1973
CLOCKWORK NYMPHO • 1976 • Pecas Max • FRN
CLOCKWORK ORANGE, A • 1971 • Kubrick Stanley • UKN
CLOCKWORK TERROR • *Mitchum Chris* • USA
CLOD, THE • 1913 • Fielding Romaine • USA
CLODHOPPER, THE • 1917 • Schertzinger Victor • USA
CLODO ET LES VICIEUSES • 1970 • Clair Georges • FRN
CLODOCHE • 1938 • Lamy Raymond, Orval Claude • FRN • SOUS LES PONTS DE PARIS
CLOG DANCING • 1898 • *Paul R. W.* • UKN
CLOISTER AND THE HEARTH, THE • 1913 • Plumb Hay • UKN
CLOISTER AND THE WOMAN, THE • 1913 • *Stuart Eve* • UKN
CLOISTERED • 1936 • Alexandre Robert
CLOISTER'S TOUCH, THE • 1910 • Griffith D. W. • USA
CLONE MASTER • 1978 • Medford Don • TVM • USA
CLONES, THE • 1973 • Hunt Paul, Card Lamar • USA
CLONES OF BRUCE LEE, THE • 1979 • Chiang Hung • HKG
CLONING OF CLIFFORD SWIMMER, THE • 1974 • Swift Lela • USA
CLONK! • 1928 • *De Forest Phonofilm* • SHT • UKN
CLONUS see **CLONUS HORROR, THE** • 1979
CLONUS HORROR, THE • 1979 • Fiveson Robert S. • USA • PARTS: THE CLONUS HORROR ○ CLONUS ○ ALTER EGO
CLOPORTES (USA) see **METAMORPHOSE DES CLOPORTES** • 1965
CLOS PUSTYNI • 1933 • Brodo E.
CLOSE CALL • 1929 • Bailey Harry • ANS • USA
CLOSE CALL • 1975 • Theberge Andre • SHT • CND
CLOSE CALL, A • 1909 • *Centaur* • USA
CLOSE CALL, A • 1911 • *Yankee* • USA
CLOSE CALL, A • 1912 • Sennett Mack • USA
CLOSE CALL, A • 1914 • *Sterling* • USA
CLOSE CALL, A • 1914 • North Wilfred • *Vitagraph* • USA
CLOSE CALL, A • 1916 • Mix Tom • SHT • USA
CLOSE CALL, A (UKN) see **CLOSE CALL FOR ELLERY QUEEN** • 1942
CLOSE CALL FOR BOSTON BLACKIE, A • 1946 • Landers Lew • USA • LADY OF MYSTERY (UKN)
CLOSE CALL FOR ELLERY QUEEN • 1942 • Hogan James P. • USA • CLOSE CALL, A (UKN)
CLOSE-CROPPED CLIPPINGS • 1915 • *Eclectic* • USA
CLOSE ENCOUNTERS OF THE THIRD KIND • 1977 • Spielberg Steven • USA
CLOSE ENCOUNTERS OF THE THIRD KIND SPECIAL EDITION • 1980 • Spielberg Steven • USA
CLOSE FARMONY • 1932 • Scotto Aubrey • SHT • USA
CLOSE FRIENDS see **VERNYE DRUZYA** • 1954
CLOSE FRIENDS see **PRANAMITHRULU** • 1967
CLOSE HARMONY • 1929 • Cromwell John, Sutherland A. Edward • USA
CLOSE HARMONY (UKN) see **COWBOY CANTEEN** • 1944
CLOSE KUNG FU ENCOUNTER, THE • Chin Raymond • HKG
CLOSE OF THE AMERICAN REVOLUTION, THE • 1912 • *Mcdermott Marc* • USA
CLOSE QUARTERS • 1943 • Lee Jack • DOC • UKN • UNDERSEA RAIDER
CLOSE QUARTERS, WITH A NOTION OF THE MOTION OF THE OCEAN • 1902 • Williamson James • UKN
CLOSE RESEMBLANCE, A • 1917 • Drew Sidney, Drew Sidney Mrs. • SHT • USA
CLOSE SEASON FOR FOXES see **SCHONZEIT FUR FUCHSE** • 1966
CLOSE SHAVE • 1981 • Hendrickson Robert • USA
CLOSE SHAVE, A • 1910 • *Essanay* • USA
CLOSE SHAVE, A • 1913 • *Punch* • USA
CLOSE SHAVE, A • 1920 • Pratt Gilbert • USA
CLOSE SHAVE, A • 1929 • Edwards Harry J. • SHT • USA
CLOSE SHAVE, A • 1937 • Davis Mannie • ANS • USA
CLOSE SHAVES • 1926 • Lamont Charles • SHT • USA
CLOSE TIME FOR FOXES see **SCHONZEIT FUR FUCHSE** • 1966
CLOSE TO DANGER see **VAAKSA VAARAA** • 1965
CLOSE TO HOME • 1985 • Beairsto Ric • CND
CLOSE TO MY HEART • 1951 • Keighley William • USA • AS TIME GOES BY
CLOSE TO NATURE • 1917 • *Par.* • USA
CLOSE TO NATURE • 1968 • Benegal Shyam • DCS • IND
CLOSE TO THE SUN see **APROAPE DE SOARE** • 1960
CLOSE TO THE WIND (UKN) see **OSS EMELLAN** • 1969
CLOSE TO YOU • 1967 • Feleo Ben • PHL
CLOSE-UP • 1948 • Donohue Jack • USA
CLOSE UP • 1984 • Gidal Peter • UKN
CLOSE-UP • 1989 • Kia-Rostami Abbas • IRN
CLOSE-UP OF THE MAN IN THE ORCHESTRA see **PROXIMACION AL HOMBRE ORQUESTA** • 1973
CLOSE-UP PLEASE! see **ZAOSTRIT PROSIM** • 1956
CLOSE UP: THE BLOOD see **KOZELROL: A VER** • 1966
CLOSE YOUR EYES AND PRAY see **HIDE AND GO SHRIEK** • 1987
CLOSED AREA, THE see **OBSZAR ZAMKNIETY** • 1973
CLOSED AT TEN • 1914 • *Fischer Marguerita* • USA
CLOSED BECAUSE OF WEALTH see **WEGEN REICHTEN GESCHLOSSEN** • 1968
CLOSED BIBLE, THE • 1912 • *Hendric Anita* • USA
CLOSED CIRCUIT • 1985 • Rezaie Rahman • IRN
CLOSED CIRCUIT see **CIRCUITO CHIUSO** • 1977
CLOSED COUNTRY, OPEN THEATRE see **PAIS CERRADO, TEATRO ABIERTO** • 1990
CLOSED DOOR • 1921 • Seyffertitz G. V. • USA
CLOSED DOOR, THE • 1910 • *Vitagraph* • USA
CLOSED DOOR, THE • 1913 • *Essanay* • USA
CLOSED DOOR, THE • 1913 • Salter Harry • *Victor* • USA
CLOSED DOOR, THE • 1915 • *Sais Marin* • USA
CLOSED DOOR, THE • 1916 • *Jockey* • USA
CLOSED DOOR, THE • 1922 • Phelps Livingstone • FRN
CLOSED DOOR (USA) see **PUERTA CERADA** • 1939
CLOSED DOORS see **S VYLOUCENIM VEREJNOSTI** • 1933
CLOSED EYES, THE see **YEUX FERMES, LES** • 1972
CLOSED GATES • 1914 • Weber Lois, Smalley Phillips • USA
CLOSED GATES • 1927 • Rosen Phil • USA
CLOSED MONDAYS • 1974 • Vinton Will • ANS • USA
CLOSED ON SUNDAY • 1909 • *Edison* • USA
CLOSED ROAD, THE • 1916 • Tourneur Maurice • USA
CLOSED SHUTTERS (USA) see **VOLETS CLOS, LES** • 1972
CLOSED WARD see **LUKKET AVDELING** • 1972
CLOSED WINDOW see **KLISTO PARATHIRO** • 1976
CLOSELY OBSERVED TRAINS (UKN) see **OSTRE SLEDOVANE VLAKY** • 1966
CLOSELY WATCHED TRAINS (USA) see **OSTRE SLEDOVANE VLAKY** • 1966
CLOSER AND CLOSER APART • 1988 • Middleton Steve • ASL
CLOSER TO THE BONE THE SWEETER THE MEAT • 1969 • Findlay Michael • USA
CLOSERIE DES GENETS, LA • 1928 • Liabel Andre • FRN
CLOSEST OF KIN, THE see **ALL THE LOVIN' KINFOLK** • 1970
CLOSET, THE • 1965 • Warhol Andy • USA
CLOSET CASANOVA, THE • 1979 • Roter Ted • USA
CLOSET CHILDREN, THE (UKN) see **ENFANTS DU PLACARD, LES** • 1977
CLOSEUPS OF CHINA • 1927 • *Holmes Burton* • DOC • USA
CLOSIN' IN • 1918 • McLaughlin J. W. • USA
CLOSING CHAPTER, THE • 1915 • MacQuarrie Murdock • USA
CLOSING HOUR, THE see **POLICEJNI HODINA** • 1960
CLOSING HOURS AT VIBERT'S PERFUME FACTORY see **SORTIE DES ATELIERS VIBERT** • 1896
CLOSING NET, THE • 1915 • Jose Edward • USA
CLOSING OF THE CIRCUIT, THE • 1915 • Davenport Harry • USA
CLOSING TIME see **OPBRUD** • 1987
CLOSING WEB, THE • 1914 • Vale Travers • USA
CLOTHES • 1920 • Sittenham Fred • USA
CLOTHES • 1924 • *O'Leary James* • USA
CLOTHES AND THE MAN • 1917 • *Rhodes Billie* • USA
CLOTHES AND THE WOMAN • 1937 • De Courville Albert • UKN
CLOTHES AND THE WOMAN see **ON YOUR BACK** • 1930
CLOTHES COUNT • 1915 • Hotaling Arthur D. • USA
CLOTHES LINE QUARREL, THE • 1913 • *Thanhouser* • USA
CLOTHES MAKE MAN see **SATY DELAJI CLOVECKA** • 1912
CLOTHES MAKE PEOPLE see **KLEIDER MACHEN LEUTE** • 1940
CLOTHES MAKE THE MAN • 1910 • *Vitagraph* • USA
CLOTHES MAKE THE MAN • 1915 • Louis Will • USA
CLOTHES MAKE THE MAN see **KLEIDER MACHEN LEUTE** • 1940
CLOTHES MAKE THE PIRATE • 1925 • Tourneur Maurice • USA
CLOTHES MAKE THE WOMAN • 1928 • Terriss Tom • USA
CLOTHES OF DECEPTION see **ITSUWARERU SEISO** • 1951
CLOTHS • 1914 • Powers Francis • USA
CLOUD, THE • 1917 • Davis Will S. • USA
CLOUD AND CLEAR see **OBLACNA PRICA** • 1972
CLOUD-CAPPED STAR, THE see **MEGHEY DHAAKA TAARA** • 1959
CLOUD DANCER • 1980 • Brown Barry • USA
CLOUD DODGER, THE • 1928 • Mitchell Bruce • USA
CLOUD HAS MANY COLOURS, THE see **MEGHER ANEK RANG** • 1977
CLOUD IN LOVE, THE see **KARA SEVDALI BULUT** • 1987
CLOUD IN THE SKY • 1940 • Ulmer Edgar G. • DCS • USA
CLOUD OF ANDROMEDA see **TUMONNOCT ANDROMED** • 1967
CLOUD OVER PARADISE • 1964 • Joseph Stanley • SHT • UKN
CLOUD PUNCHER, THE • 1917 • Parrott Charles • SHT • USA
CLOUD RIDER, THE • 1925 • Mitchell Bruce • USA
CLOUD SHEEP, THE • Georgi Katja • ANM • GDR
CLOUD WALTZER see **CLOUD WALTZING** • 1987
CLOUD WALTZING • 1987 • Flemyng Gordon • TVM • USA • CLOUD WALTZER
CLOUDBURST • 1922 • *Wells Billy* • USA
CLOUDBURST • 1951 • Searle Francis • UKN
CLOUDBURST see **DOSHABURI** • 1957
CLOUDBURST, THE see **WINGS OF FIRE** • 1967
CLOUDED CRYSTAL, THE • 1948 • Cullimore Alan J. • UKN
CLOUDED CRYSTAL, THE • 1985 • Rodgers Bob • DOC • CND
CLOUDED MIND, A see **CLOUDED NAME, A** • 1923
CLOUDED NAME, A • 1923 • Hohn Austin O. • USA • CLOUDED MIND, A
CLOUDED NAME, THE • 1919 • Fleming Caryl S. • USA • MAN WITHOUT A NAME, THE
CLOUDED YELLOW, THE • 1950 • Thomas Ralph • UKN
CLOUDS see **BADAL** • 1967
CLOUDS, THE • 1973 • Stepanov Boris • USS
CLOUDS AND SUNSHINE • 1911 • *Reliance* • USA
CLOUDS AT SUNSET see **AKANEGUMO** • 1967
CLOUDS AT TWILIGHT see **YUYAKE-KUMO** • 1956
CLOUDS IN SUNSHINE VALLEY • 1916 • *Clifford William* • SHT • USA
CLOUDS OF GLORY • 1978 • Russell Ken • MTV • UKN
CLOUDS OVER BORSK • 1961 • Ordynsky Vassily • USS
CLOUDS OVER EUROPE (USA) see **Q PLANES** • 1939
CLOUDS OVER HELLESTA see **MOLN OVER HELLESTA** • 1956
CLOUDS OVER ISRAEL (USA) see **SINAIA** • 1962
CLOUDS WILL ROLL AWAY, THE see **NENI STALE ZAMRACENO** • 1950
CLOUDY ROMANCE, A • 1925 • Seiler Lewis • SHT • USA
CLOUDY SKIES see **SINEFIASMENOI ORIZONTES** • 1968
CLOUZOT & C. CONTRO BORSALINO & C. • 1973 • Pinzauti Mario • ITL
CLOVEK JE TVOR SPOLECENSKY • 1960 • Kabrt Josef • ANS • CZC • MAN IS A SOCIAL BEING
CLOVEK, KI GA JE TREBA UBITI see **COVJEK KOGA TREBA UBITI** • 1979
CLOVEK POD VODOU • 1961 • Brdecka Jiri • ANS • CZC • MAN UNDER THE SEA ○ MAN UNDER WATER
CLOVEN HORIZON • 1965 • Rathod Kantilal • SHT • IND
CLOVER'S REBELLION • 1917 • North Wilfred • USA
CLOWN • Cortes Luis • SPN
CLOWN see **KLOVNEN** • 1926
CLOWN, THE • 1916 • De Mille William C. • USA
CLOWN, THE • 1927 • Craft William James • USA
CLOWN, THE • 1931 • *Universal* • SHT • USA
CLOWN, THE • 1950 • Williamson Cecil H. • UKN
CLOWN, THE • 1952 • Leonard Robert Z. • USA
CLOWN, THE (USA) see **ANSICHTEN EINES CLOWNS** • 1975
CLOWN AND HIS BEST PERFORMANCES, THE • 1911 • *Bunny John* • USA
CLOWN AND HIS DOG, THE see **PAJACYK I PIKUS** • 1959
CLOWN AND HIS DONKEY, THE • 1910 • Armstrong Charles • UKN
CLOWN AND MOTOR CAR, THE see **AUTOMABOULISME ET AUTORITE** • 1899
CLOWN AND POLICEMAN • 1900 • Hepworth Cecil M. • UKN
CLOWN AND THE ALCHEMIST • 1900 • Porter Edwin S. • USA
CLOWN AND THE AUTOMATON see **GUGUSSE ET L'AUTOMATON** • 1897
CLOWN AND THE AUTOMOBILE, THE (USA) see **AUTOMABOULISME ET AUTORITE** • 1899
CLOWN AND THE ENCHANTED CRADLE, THE • 1900 • *Warwick Trading Co.* • UKN
CLOWN AND THE KID, THE • 1962 • Cahn Edward L. • USA
CLOWN AND THE KIDS, THE • 1968 • Brown Mende • USA, BUL • SVIRACHUT (BUL) ○ PIED PIPER, THE
CLOWN AND THE LITTLE DOG, THE see **PAJACYK I PIKUS** • 1959
CLOWN AND THE LITTLE DOG AND THE FLAME, THE see **PAJACYK, PIESEK I PLOMIEN** • 1959
CLOWN AND THE MINISTER, THE • 1910 • *Lubin* • USA
CLOWN AND THE PRIMA DONNA, THE • 1913 • Costello Maurice, North Wilfred • USA
CLOWN AUS LIEBE see **ZIRKUSKONIG, DER** • 1924
CLOWN BARBER, THE • 1898 • Williamson James • UKN
CLOWN BUX, LE • 1935 • Natanson Jacques • FRN
CLOWN CHARLY • 1918 • Neuss Alwin • FRG
CLOWN EN SAC • 1904 • Blache Alice • FRN
CLOWN FERDINAND AND THE ROCKET see **KLAUN FERDINAND A RAKETA** • 1962
CLOWN GEORGE • 1932 • Soloviev Alexander
CLOWN HERO, THE • 1913 • *Champion* • USA
CLOWN MURDERS, THE • 1975 • Burke Martyn • CND
CLOWN MUST LAUGH, A (USA) see **PAGLIACCI** • 1936
CLOWN OF THE JUNGLE • 1947 • Hannah Jack • ANS • USA
CLOWN ON THE FARM • 1952 • Kneitel Seymour • ANS • USA
CLOWN, PANTALOON AND BOBBY • 1902 • Collins Alf? • UKN
CLOWN PRINCES • 1939 • Sidney George • SHT • USA
CLOWN VS. SATAN, THE (USA) see **GUGUSTE ET BELZEBUTH** • 1901

CLOWNESSE FANTOME, LA • 1902 • Melies Georges • FRN • SHADOW GIRL, THE (USA) ○ TWENTIETH CENTURY CONJURING
CLOWNING • 1931 • *Terry Paul/ Moser Frank (P)* • ANS • USA
CLOWNLAND • 1912 • *Imp* • USA
CLOWNS, LES • 1902 • Blache Alice • FRN
CLOWNS, THE see **PALIATSOS, O** • 1968
CLOWNS, THE see **CLOWNS, I** • 1970
CLOWNS, THE see **SALTIMBANCHI** • 1981
CLOWNS AND MONSTERS • 1971 • Steed Judy • SHT • CND
CLOWN'S BABY, THE • 1911 • *Kahn Eleanor* • USA
CLOWN'S BIG MOMENT, THE • 1910 • *Actophone* • USA
CLOWN'S CRIME, A • 1910 • Coleby A. E. • UKN
CLOWN'S DAUGHTER, THE • 1913 • *Mills Thomas R.* • USA
CLOWNS FOR CHRISTMAS • 1980 • Yalden-Tomson Peter • MTV • CND
CLOWNS, I • 1970 • Fellini Federico • ITL, FRG, FRN • CLOWNS, THE
CLOWN'S LITTLE BROTHER, THE • 1920 • Fleischer Dave • ANS • USA
CLOWNS OF EUROPE, THE • 1914 • Evans Fred, Evans Joe • UKN
CLOWNS ON THE WALL see **BOHOC A FALON** • 1968
CLOWN'S PUP, THE • 1919 • Fleischer Dave • ANS • USA
CLOWN'S TELEGRAM, THE • 1904 • Williamson James • UKN
CLOWN'S TRIUMPH, THE • 1912 • Brenon Herbert • USA
CLUB, THE • 1980 • Beresford Bruce • ASL • PLAYERS
CLUB CURE, THE • 1913 • Henderson Dell • USA
CLUB DE FEMMES • 1936 • Deval Jacques • FRN
CLUB DE FEMMES • 1957 • Habib Ralph • FRN, ITL • CLUB DI RAGAZZE (ITL)
CLUB DE SENORITAS • 1955 • Martinez Solares Gilberto • MXC
CLUB DE SOLTEROS • 1967 • Herrero Pedro Mario • SPN • BACHELOR CLUB
CLUB DER ENTGLEISTEN see **C.D.E.** • 1922
CLUB DER HAZARDEURE, DER • 1920 • Hartt Hanns Heinz • FRG
CLUB DER TODGEWEIHTEN, DER • 1924 • *Bayer F. Wilhelm* • FRG
CLUB DER ZWOLF, DER see **SCHATZKAMMER IM SEE 2, DIE** • 1921
CLUB DES 400 COUPS, LE • 1952 • Daroy Jacques • FRN
CLUB DES ARISTOCRATES, LE • 1937 • Colombier Piere • FRN
CLUB DES FADAS, LE • 1939 • Couzinet Emile • FRN
CLUB DES SOUPIRANTS, LE • 1941 • Gleize Maurice • FRN
CLUB DES SUICIDES, LE • 1909 • Jasset Victorin • FRN
CLUB DI RAGAZZE (ITL) see **CLUB DE FEMMES** • 1957
CLUB EARTH see **GALACTIC GIGOLO** • 1988
CLUB HAVANA • 1945 • Ulmer Edgar G. • USA
CLUB-HOUSE PARTY • 1935 • Schwarzwald Milton • SHT • USA
CLUB-LAW OF FREEDOM see **FAUSTRECHT DER FREIHEIT** • 1975
CLUB LIFE • 1987 • Vane Norman Thaddeus • USA • KING OF THE CITY
CLUB LIFE IN STONE AGE • 1940 • Davis Mannie • ANS • USA
CLUB MAN, THE • 1915 • Hotaling Arthur D. • USA
CLUB-MAN AND THE CROOK, THE • 1912 • Henderson Dell • USA
CLUB MED • 1986 • Giraldi Bob • TVM • USA
CLUB MEDITERRANEE • 1976 • Reichenbach Francois • DOC • FRN
CLUB OF PHAROS, THE • 1915 • Aylott Dave • UKN
CLUB OF THE BIG DEED, THE see **S.V.D.** • 1927
CLUB OF THE BIG IDEAS, THE see **S.V.D.** • 1927
CLUB PARADISE • 1986 • Ramis Harold • USA
CLUB PARTY AND POLICE • 1898 • *Cinematograph Co.* • UKN
CLUB PEST, THE • 1915 • *Ab* • USA
CLUB PRIVE • 1973 • Pecas Max • FRN • CLUB PRIVE (POUR COUPLES AVERTIS) ○ PRIVATE CLUB (UKN)
CLUB PRIVE (POUR COUPLES AVERTIS) see **CLUB PRIVE** • 1973
CLUB RAID, THE • 1898 • *Cinematograph Co.* • UKN
CLUB SANDWICH • 1931 • *Terry Paul/ Moser Frank (P)* • ANS • USA • DANCING MICE
CLUB SANDWICH see **LAST RESORT, THE** • 1985
CLUB VERDE • 1944 • Aguilar Rolando • MXC
CLUBMAN AND THE TRAMP, THE • 1908 • Griffith D. W. • USA
CLUBMAN'S WAGER, THE • 1915 • *Bowman William* • USA
CLUBS ARE TRUMPS • 1917 • Roach Hal • SHT • USA
CLUE • 1985 • Lynn Jonathan • USA
CLUE, THE • 1912 • *Essanay* • USA
CLUE, THE • 1913 • *Rex* • USA
CLUE, THE • 1913 • Kirkland Hardee • *Selig* • USA
CLUE, THE • 1915 • Neill James • USA
CLUE, THE (UKN) see **OUTCAST OF BLACK MESA** • 1950
CLUE ACCORDING TO SHERLOCK HOLMES, THE • 1980 • Golden Murray • MTV • UKN
CLUE IN THE DUST, THE • 1912 • Weston C. H. • USA
CLUE OF THE CIGAR BAND, THE • 1915 • Martinek H. O. • UKN
CLUE OF THE MISSING APE, THE see **GIBRALTAR ADVENTURE** • 1953
CLUE OF THE NEW PIN, THE • 1929 • Maude Arthur • UKN
CLUE OF THE NEW PIN, THE • 1961 • Davis Allan • UKN
CLUE OF THE OAK LEAF, THE • 1926 • Coleby A. E. • UKN
CLUE OF THE PIGTAIL, THE • 1923 • Coleby A. E. • UKN
CLUE OF THE PORTRAIT, THE • 1915 • *Eclair* • USA
CLUE OF THE SECOND GOBLET, THE • 1928 • Cooper George A. • UKN
CLUE OF THE SILVER KEY • 1961 • Glaister Gerald • UKN
CLUE OF THE TWISTED CANDLE • 1960 • Davis Allan • UKN
CLUES TO ADVENTURE • 1949 • *John Nesbitt'S Passing Parade* • SHT • USA
CLUM PERDESI • 1960 • Yilmaz Atif • TRK • SCREEN OF DEATH, THE
CLUMSY LITTLE ELEPHANT, THE see **UNLUCKY LITTLE ELEPHANT, THE** • 1959
CLUMSY MASON, A see **MACON MALADROIT, LE** • 1898
CLUMSY PAPA see **PAPAI TRAPLAHAO** • 1968
CLUNKED ON THE CORNER • 1929 • Edwards Henry • SHT • USA
CLUNY BROWN • 1946 • Lubitsch Ernst • USA
CLUTCH OF CIRCUMSTANCE, THE • 1915 • Calvert E. H. • USA
CLUTCH OF CIRCUMSTANCE, THE • 1918 • Houry Henri • USA
CLUTCH OF CONSCIENCE, THE • 1913 • *Pathe* • USA
CLUTCH OF THE EMPEROR, THE • 1915 • Wilson Ben • USA
CLUTCHING HAND, THE • 1936 • Herman Al • SRL • USA
CLUTCHING HAND, THE see **HIRAM NA KAMAY**
CLYDESCOPE • 1974 • Grigor Murray • SAF
CMA • 1980 • Zygadlo Tomasz • PLN • MOTH, THE
CMENTARZ REMUCH • 1962 • Etler Edward • DOC • PLN • REMUCH CEMETERY, THE ○ CEMENTERY OF REMU, THE
C'MON BABY, LIGHT MY FIRE see **BABY, LIGHT MY FIRE** • 1970
C'MON LET'S LIVE A LITTLE • 1967 • Butler David • USA
CO-ED PROFESSOR, THE • 1911 • Daly William Robert • USA
CO HOEDEMAN, ANIMATOR • 1980 • Crama Nico • DOC • CND, NTH
CO JSME UDELALI SLEPICIM • 1977 • Hekrdla Josef, Jiranek Vladimir • CZC • WHAT HAVE WE DONE TO THE HENS ○ WHAT DID WE DO TO HENS
CO OKO NEVIDI • 1987 • Koutsky Pavel • ANM • CZC • WHAT THE EYE DOES NOT SEE
CO-OPERATIVE RESEARCH IN INDUSTRY • 1949 • Arthur Noel • DOC • UKN
CO-OPTIMISTS, THE • 1929 • Greenwood Edwin, Cliff Laddie • UKN
CO-ORDINATES OF DEATH • 1989 • Tyen Nguyen Shang • VTN
CO REKNE ZENA • 1957 • Mach Jaroslav • CZC, PLN • WHAT WILL MY WIFE SAY
CO-RESPONDENT, THE • 1917 • Ince Ralph • USA
CO-RESPONDENT, THE see **WHISPERED NAME, THE** • 1924
CO SE SEPTA • 1938 • Haas Hugo • HNG
CO SJEM PRINCI NEREKLA • 1975 • Brdecka Jiri • ANM • CZC • WHAT I DIDN'T SAY TO THE PRINCE
CO TO BOUCHLO • 1970 • Pojar Bretislav • ANM • CZC • WHAT EXPLODED?
CO TO JEST "DUDEK" • 1967 • Ziarnik Jerzy • DOC • PLN • WHAT IS "DUDEK"
CO ZIZALA NETUSILA • 1969 • Pojar Bretislav • ANM • CZC • ANTI-DARWIN
COACH • 1978 • Townsend Bud • USA
COACH, THE see **TRENER** • 1979
COACH HOLDUP IN DICK TURPIN'S DAY, A see **ROBBERY OF THE MAIL COACH** • 1903
COACH OF DREAMS, THE see **DILIZANSA SNOVA** • 1960
COACH OF THE YEAR • 1980 • Medford Don, Sidaris Andy • TVM • USA
COACH TO VIENNA, THE see **KOCAR DO VIDNE** • 1966
COAL • 1940 • DOC • UKN
COAL see **MINE, THE** • 1936
COAL AT THE CROSSROADS • 1956 • Haldane Don, Lenauer Jean • CND
COAL BLACK AND DE SEBBEN DWARFS • 1942 • Clampett Robert • ANS • USA
COAL CRISIS • 1947 • DOC • UKN • THIS MODERN AGE NO.7
COAL FACE see **COALFACE** • 1935
COAL FACE CANADA • 1943 • Edmunds Robert • SHT • CND
COAL KING, THE • 1915 • Nash Percy • UKN
COAL MAN, THE • 1977 • Boammery Ahmad • ALG
COAL MINER, THE • 1955 • Dimond Peter • DOC • ASL
COAL-MINERS, THE • 1978 • Demetriou Alinda • DOC • GRC
COAL MINER'S DAUGHTER, THE • 1979 • Apted Michael • USA • NASHVILLE LADY
COAL PILES • 1962 • Kidawa Janusz • DOC • PLN
COAL SHORTAGE • 1920 • Miller Frank • UKN
COALFACE • 1935 • Wright Basil, Cavalcanti Alberto • DOC • UKN • COAL FACE
COALING A BATTLESHIP AT NAGASAKI • 1904 • Hepworth Cecil M. • UKN
COALS FOR THE FIRE • 1918 • Baker Graham • SHT • USA
COALS OF FIRE • 1910 • Haldane Bert? • UKN
COALS OF FIRE • 1911 • *Atlas* • USA
COALS OF FIRE • 1911 • *Selig* • USA
COALS OF FIRE • 1914 • *Benham Harry* • USA
COALS OF FIRE • 1915 • *American* • USA
COALS OF FIRE • 1918 • Schertzinger Victor • USA
COALVILLE STORY, THE • 1965 • Healy Mike • SHT • UKN
COARTADA EN DISCO ROJO • 1972 • Demicheli Tulio • SPN
COAST GUARD • 1939 • Ludwig Edward • USA
COAST GUARD, THE • 1910 • *Essanay* • USA
COAST GUARD PATROL, THE • 1919 • Shipman Nell • USA
COAST GUARD'S BRIDE, THE • 1914 • *Wallace Irene* • USA
COAST GUARD'S SISTER, THE • 1913 • Brabin Charles J. • USA • COASTGUARD'S SISTER, THE
COAST OF CHANCE, THE • 1913 • Eagle Oscar • USA
COAST OF FOLLY, THE • 1925 • Dwan Allan • USA
COAST OF OPPORTUNITY, THE • 1920 • Warde Ernest C. • USA
COAST OF SKELETONS • 1964 • Lynn Robert • UKN, SAF • SANDERS
COAST PATROL, THE • 1925 • Barsky Bud • USA
COAST TO COAST • 1980 • Sargent Joseph • USA
COAST TO COAST • 1988 • Bennett Bill • ASL
COASTAL ARTS see **ARTES A LO LARGO DEL MAR** • 1979
COASTAL COMMAND • 1942 • Holmes J. B. • DOC • UKN
COASTAL SEA HOMES • 1984 • Arnold Jeffrey • DOC • CND
COASTER • 1981 • Cloutier Jon Craig • DOC • USA
COASTER, THE • 1947 • Holmes Cecil • DOC • NZL
COASTGUARD'S HAUL, THE see **REUB'S LITTLE GIRL** • 1913
COASTGUARD'S SISTER, THE see **COAST GUARD'S SISTER, THE** • 1913
COAST'S HAPPY CAVALIERS, THE (USA) see **KUSTENS GLADA KAVALJERER** • 1938
COASTS OF CLYDE, THE • 1958 • Ritchie James • UKN
COAT FROM HEAVEN (USA) see **ANDELSKY KABAT** • 1948
COAT TALE, A • 1915 • *Essanay* • USA
COAT THAT CAME BACK, THE • 1913 • *Solax* • USA
COAT'S A COAT, A • 1915 • Lyons Eddie • USA
COAT'S TALE, A • 1914 • Wright Walter • USA
COAX ME • 1919 • Hamilton G. P. • USA • TANGLED ROMANCE, A
COBARDE, EL • 1938 • Cardona Rene • MXC
COBARDE, LA • 1952 • Bracho Julio • MXC
COBAYES, LES • 1965 • Lavoie Richard • DCS • CND
COBAYES, LES see **CHATEAU DE LA DERNIERE CHANCE, LE** • 1946
COBBLER, THE • 1911 • *Reliance* • USA
COBBLER, THE • 1915 • Coleby A. E. • UKN • FIGHTING COBBLER, THE
COBBLER, THE • 1923 • McNamara Tom • SHT • USA
COBBLER AND THE CALIPH, THE • 1909 • Blackton J. Stuart (Spv) • USA
COBBLER STAY AT YOUR BENCH see **SKOMAKARE BLIV VID DIN LAST** • 1915
COBBLER STICK TO YOUR LAST see **SKOMAKARE BLIV VID DIN LAST** • 1915
COBBLESTONES see **STEADY COMPANY** • 1932
COBRA • 1925 • Henabery Joseph • USA
COBRA • 1980 • Castellari Enzo G. • USA • DAY OF THE COBRA
COBRA • 1986 • Cosmatos George Pan • USA
COBRA see **NAGIN JOGI** • 1989
COBRA, EL • 1968 • Sequi Mario • SPN, ITL • COBRA, IL (ITL) ○ COBRA, THE (USA)
COBRA, IL (ITL) see **COBRA, EL** • 1968
COBRA, THE (USA) see **COBRA, EL** • 1968
COBRA AGAINST NINJA • Lai Joseph • HKG
COBRA CHALLENGES THE JOKERS • 1967 • Saez Nilo • PHL
COBRA GIRL (USA) see **NAAG RANI** • 1962
COBRA MISSION see **OPERATION 'NAM** • 1985
COBRA STRIKES, THE • 1948 • Reisner Charles F. • USA
COBRA (UKN) see **SAUT DE L'ANGE, LE** • 1971
COBRA VERDE • 1987 • Herzog Werner • FRG
COBRA WOMAN • 1944 • Siodmak Robert, Waggner George • USA
COBS AND ROBBERS • 1953 • Lundy Dick • ANS • USA
COBWEB • 1986 • Zaoral Zdenek • CZC
COBWEB see **JADARABALE** • 1968
COBWEB see **POKHALO** • 1973
COBWEB, THE • 1917 • Hepworth Cecil M. • UKN
COBWEB, THE • 1955 • Minnelli Vincente • USA
COBWEB CASTLE see **KUMONOSU-JO** • 1957
COBWEB HOTEL, THE • 1936 • Fleischer Dave • ANS • USA
COBWEB ON A PARACHUTE • 1969 • Marek Dusan • ASL
COCA COLA KID, THE • 1985 • Makavejev Dusan • ASL
COCAGNE • 1960 • Cloche Maurice • FRN
COCAGNE see **PAYS DE COCAGNE** • 1971
COCAIN • 1921 • Schaffers Willy • FRG
COCAINA see **COCAINE WARS** • 1985
COCAINE • 1922 • Cutts Graham • UKN • WHILE LONDON SLEEPS
COCAINE see **MIXED BLOOD** • 1984
COCAINE AND BLUE EYES • 1982 • Swackhamer E. W. • TVM • USA
COCAINE COWBOYS • 1979 • Lommel Ulli • USA
COCAINE FIENDS, THE • 1936 • O'Connor William A. • USA • PACE THAT THRILLS, THE
COCAINE: ONE MAN'S POISON see **COCAINE: ONE MAN'S SEDUCTION** • 1982
COCAINE: ONE MAN'S SEDUCTION • 1982 • Wendkos Paul • TVM • USA • COCAINE: ONE MAN'S POISON
COCAINE WARS • 1985 • Olivera Hector • USA, ARG • FINE WHITE LINE, THE ○ MUERTA BLANCA ○ COCAINA
COCCINELLE ALFRED see **MONSIEUR COCCINELLE** • 1938
COCCO DI MAMMA, IL • 1957 • Morassi Mauro • ITL • MUMMY'S DARLING
COCHE CAMA ALOJAMIENTO • 1968 • Porter Julio • ARG • SLEEPING-CAR DWELLING
COCHECITO, EL • 1960 • Ferreri Marco • SPN • WHEELCHAIR, THE ○ MOTORCART, THE
COCHER, LE • 1953 • Garceau Raymond • DCS • CND
COCHER DE FIACRE ENDORMI, LE • 1897-98 • Blache Alice • FRN
COCHON, LE • 1971 • Eustache Jean, Barjol Jean-Michel • DOC • FRN
COCHONNES, LES • Ayranu Lino • FRN
COCINA MAGNETICA, LA (SPN) see **CUISINE MAGNETIQUE** • 1908
COCINERO DE MI MUJER, EL • 1946 • Peon Ramon • MXC
COCINOR • 1957 • Alexeieff Alexandre • SHT • FRN
COCK, THE • 1966 • Dembinski Lucjan • ANM • PLN
COCK, THE see **CIL HOROZ** • 1987
COCK-A-DOODLE DINO • 1957 • Sparber I. • ANS • USA
COCK-A-DOODLE-DOO • 1910 • Stow Percy • UKN
COCK CROWS AGAIN, THE see **NIWATORI WA FUTATABI NAKU** • 1954
COCK CROWS AT MIDNIGHT, THE • 1966 • Yeou Lei • ANM • CHN
COCK CROWS TWICE, THE see **NIWATORI WA FUTATABI NAKU** • 1954
COCK-EYED WORLD, THE • 1929 • Walsh Raoul • USA
COCK O' THE NORTH • 1935 • Mitchell Oswald, Sanderson Challis • UKN
COCK O' THE WALK • 1915 • Plumb Hay? • UKN
COCK O' THE WALK • 1930 • Neill R. William, Lang Walter • USA
COCK O' THE WALK • 1935 • Sharpsteen Ben • ANS • USA
COCK OF THE AIR • 1932 • Buckingham Thomas • USA
COCK OF THE DAWN see **KOHOUT PLASI SMRT** • 1961
COCK THAT SCARES DEATH see **KOHOUT PLASI SMRT** • 1961
COCKABOODY • 1973 • Hubley John • ANS • USA
COCKADOODLE DOG • 1951 • Avery Tex • ANS • USA
COCKATOOS FOR TWO • 1947 • Wickersham Bob • ANS • USA
COCKEYED CAVALIERS • 1934 • Sandrich Mark • USA
COCKEYED COWBOYS OF CALICO COUNTY, THE • 1970 • Leader Tony • USA • WOMAN FOR CHARLIE, A
COCKEYED CRUISE see **MAD HOLIDAY** • 1936
COCKEYED MIRACLE, THE • 1946 • Simon S. Sylvan • USA • MR. GRIGGS RETURNS (UKN) ○ BUT NOT GOODBYE
COCKFIGHT, THE • 1902 • *Paul R. W.* • UKN

COCKFIGHTER • 1974 • Hellman Monte • USA • BORN TO KILL ○ WILD DRIFTER ○ GAMBLIN' MAN
COCKLESHELL HEROES • 1955 • Ferrer Jose • UKN
COCKNEY SPIRIT IN THE WAR, THE • 1930 • Knight Castleton • SHT • UKN • TOMMY ATKINS ○ COCKNEY WAR STORIES
COCKNEY SPIRIT IN THE WAR NO.2, THE • 1930 • Knight Castleton • SHT • UKN
COCKNEY SPIRIT IN THE WAR NO.3, THE • 1930 • Knight Castleton • SHT • UKN
COCKNEY WAR STORIES see **COCKNEY SPIRIT IN THE WAR, THE** • 1930
COCKROACH, THE • 1927 • Ivanov A., Voinov H. • USS
COCKSUCKER BLUES • 1976 • Frank Robert • USA • CS BLUES
COCKSURE JONES, DETECTIVE • 1915 • King Burton L. • USA
COCKSURE'S CLEVER RUSE • 1910 • Fitzhamon Lewin • UKN • TOO CLEVER FOR ONCE
COCKTAIL • 1936 • Beaumont L. C. • UKN
COCKTAIL • 1937 • *Henning-Jensen Astrid* • DNM
COCKTAIL • 1938 • Joly Max • FRN
COCKTAIL • 1988 • Donaldson Roger • USA
COCKTAIL HOUR, THE • 1933 • Schertzinger Victor • USA
COCKTAIL MAGAZINE NO.1 • 1946 • Petrossian Eddie • SHT • FRN
COCKTAIL MOLOTOV • 1981 • Kurys Diane • FRN
COCKTAIL PARTY • 1937 • Schwarzwald Milton • SHT • USA
COCKTAIL PORNO • 1976 • Payet Alain • FRN
COCKTAIL SPECIAL • 1978 • Franco Jesus • FRN
COCKTAILS • 1928 • Banks Monty • UKN
COCKTAILS IN THE KITCHEN (USA) see **FOR BETTER, FOR WORSE** • 1954
COCKY BANTAM, THE • 1943 • Sommer Paul • ANS • USA • BLACK AND BLUE MARKET
COCKY COCKROACH • 1932 • *Terry Paul/ Moser Frank (P)* • ANS • USA
COCO LA FLEUR • 1978 • Lara Christian • FRN • CANDIDAT COCO LA FLEUR, LE
COCOA FROM THE GOLDCOAST • 1936 • DOC • UKN
COCOANUT, THE see **HINDISTAN CEVIZI** • 1967
COCOANUT FAIR • 1897 • IND
COCOANUT GROVE • 1938 • Santell Alfred • USA
COCOANUTS, THE • 1929 • Florey Robert, Santley Joseph • USA
COCONUTS • 1985 • Novotny Franz • AUS, FRG
COCOON • 1965 • *Oonk Jan (P)* • SHT • NTH
COCOON • 1985 • Howard Ron • USA
COCOON AND THE BUTTERFLY, THE • 1914 • *Van Meter Harry* • USA
COCOON: THE RETURN • 1988 • Petrie Daniel • USA
COCORICO MONSIEUR POULET • 1977 • Rouch Jean • FRN
COCOTIERS, LES • 1963 • Rouch Jean • DCS • FRN
COCU MAGNIFIQUE, LE • 1946 • de Meyst E. G. • FRN, BLG
COCU MAGNIFIQUE, LE (FRN) see **MAGNIFICO CORNUTO, IL** • 1964
CO'D IN HIS HEAD, A • 1914 • Cooper Toby? • UKN
CODA • 1987 • Lahiff Craig • ASL • SYMPHONY OF EVIL
CODA DEL DIAVOLO • 1965 • Rossi Moraldo • ITL
CODA DELLO SCORPIONE, LA • 1971 • Martino Sergio • ITL
CODE 7.. VICTIM 5 (USA) see **VICTIM FIVE** • 1964
CODE 645 • 1948 • Brannon Fred C., Canutt Yakima • USA
CODE, THE see **HEAT WAVE** • 1935
CODE, THE see **SZYFRY** • 1966
CODE, THE see **ADIEU L'AMI** • 1968
CODE CRIMINEL, LE see **CRIMINEL** • 1932
CODE LETTER, THE • 1916 • Ellis Robert • SHT • USA
CODE NAME ACHILLES • 1967 • Mann Gerry • USA, GRC
CODE NAME: COBRA see **SAUT DE L'ANGE, LE** • 1971
CODE NAME COUGAR see **DAIHAO MEIZHOUBAO** • 1988
CODE NAME: DIAMOND HEAD • 1977 • Szwarc Jeannot • TVM • USA
CODE NAME: DORA see **DORA JELENTI** • 1978
CODE NAME: EMERALD • 1985 • Sanger Jonathan • USA • CODENAME EMERALD ○ EMERALD
CODE NAME: FOXFIRE • 1985 • Allen Corey • TVM • USA • CODENAME FOXFIRE –SLAY IT AGAIN SAM ○ CODENAME: FIREFOX
CODE NAME: HERACLITUS • 1967 • Goldstone James • TVM • USA
CODE NAME IS KILL see **LIEBESNACHTE IN DER TAIGA** • 1967
CODE NAME: MINUS ONE see **GEMINI MAN** • 1976
CODE NAME: OPERATION CROSSBOW see **OPERATION CROSSBOW** • 1965
CODE NAME RED ROSES (USA) see **ROSE ROSSE PER IL FUHRER** • 1968
CODE NAME RUNNING JUMP • 1972 • Kroitor Roman • CND
CODE NAME: TIGER (USA) see **TIGRE AIME LA CHAIR FRAICHE, LE** • 1964
CODE NAME: TRIXIE see **CRAZIES, THE** • 1973
CODE NAME: VENGEANCE • 1989 • Winters David • USA
CODE NAME: WESTWARD HO! • 1949 • Beales Mary • UKN
CODE NAME: ZEBRA • 1986 • Tornatore Joe • USA
CODE OF CHIVALRY see **KYOKAKU NO OKITE** • 1967
CODE OF HIS ANCESTORS, THE • 1916 • Schrock Raymond L. • SHT • USA
CODE OF HONOR • 1930 • McGowan J. P. • USA
CODE OF HONOR see **HER CODE OF HONOR** • 1919
CODE OF HONOR, THE • 1911 • *Clark Frank* • USA
CODE OF HONOR, THE • 1916 • Borzage Frank • SHT • USA
CODE OF HONOUR see **KILL SQUAD** • 1981
CODE OF HONOUR, THE see **NIGHT OF MYSTERY, A** • 1928
CODE OF MAN, THE see **OTOKO NO OKITE** • 1968
CODE OF MARCIA GRAY • 1916 • Lloyd Frank • USA
CODE OF SCOTLAND YARD, THE (USA) see **SHOP AT SLY CORNER, THE** • 1947
CODE OF SILENCE • 1985 • Davis Andrew • USA
CODE OF SILENCE see **KILLER'S CAGE** • 1960
CODE OF THE AIR • 1928 • Hogan James P. • USA
CODE OF THE CACTUS • 1939 • Newfield Sam • USA
CODE OF THE COW COUNTRY • 1927 • Apfel Oscar • USA
CODE OF THE FEARLESS • 1939 • Johnston Raymond K. • USA
CODE OF THE HILLS, THE • 1916 • Mayo Melvin • SHT • USA
CODE OF THE HILLS, THE see **BEYOND THE LAW** • 1911
CODE OF THE LAWLESS • 1945 • Fox Wallace • USA • MYSTERIOUS STRANGER, THE (UKN)
CODE OF THE MOUNTAINS, THE see **WOMAN'S POWER, A** • 1916
CODE OF THE MOUNTED • 1916 • Jaccard Jacques • SHT • USA
CODE OF THE MOUNTED • 1935 • Newfield Sam • USA
CODE OF THE NORTH • 1919 • *Lowell John* • SHT • USA
CODE OF THE NORTHWEST • 1926 • Mattison Frank S. • USA
CODE OF THE OUTLAW • 1942 • English John • USA
CODE OF THE PLAINS see **RENEGADE, THE** • 1943
CODE OF THE PRAIRIE • 1944 • Bennet Spencer Gordon • USA
CODE OF THE RANGE • 1927 • Cohn Bennett, Schlank Morris R. • USA
CODE OF THE RANGE • 1936 • Coleman C. C. Jr. • USA
CODE OF THE RANGERS • 1938 • Newfield Sam • USA
CODE OF THE RUTHLESS see **AKUTO SHAIN YUKYO-DEN** • 1968
CODE OF THE SADDLE • 1947 • Carr Thomas • USA
CODE OF THE SCARLET, THE • 1928 • Brown Harry J. • USA
CODE OF THE SEA • 1924 • Fleming Victor • USA
CODE OF THE SECRET SERVICE • 1939 • Smith Noel • USA
CODE OF THE SILVER SAGE • 1950 • Brannon Fred C. • USA
CODE OF THE STREETS • 1939 • Young Harold • USA
CODE OF THE U.S.A., THE • 1913 • *Vale Louis* • USA
CODE OF THE WEST • 1925 • Howard William K. • USA
CODE OF THE WEST • 1929 • McGowan J. P. • USA
CODE OF THE WEST • 1947 • Berke William • USA
CODE OF THE WEST see **HOME ON THE RANGE** • 1935
CODE OF THE WILDERNESS • 1924 • Smith David • USA
CODE OF THE YUKON • 1919 • Bracken Bertram • USA
CODE OF VENGEANCE • 1985 • Rosenthal Rick • TVM • USA
CODE OF WOMEN see **JOKYO** • 1960
CODE RED • 1981 • Thompson J. Lee • TVM • USA
CODE TWO • 1953 • Wilcox Fred M. • USA
CODE, UNE NORME • 1978 • Beaudry Michel • SHS • CND
CODENAME: BLACKFIRE • 1986 • Page Teddy • HKG
CODENAME: COQ ROUGE • 1989 • Berglund Pelle • SWD
CODENAME: DANCER see **HER SECRET LIFE** • 1987
CODENAME EMERALD see **CODE NAME: EMERALD** • 1985
CODENAME: FIREFOX see **CODE NAME: FOXFIRE** • 1985
CODENAME FOXFIRE –SLAY IT AGAIN SAM see **CODE NAME: FOXFIRE** • 1985
CODENAME: ICARUS • 1983 • Fox Marilyn • MTV • UKN
CODENAME: KYRIL • 1988 • Sharp Ian • TVM • UKN
CODENAME: RED DEVIL • Albertini Bitto • ITL
CODENAME: ROBOTECH • 1985 • Barron Robert • ANM • USA
CODENAME: THE SOLDIER see **SOLDIER, THE** • 1982
CODENAME: VENGEANCE • 1987 • Dante Maria • ITL
CODENAME: WILD GEESE • 1986 • Margheriti Antonio • ITL, FRG
CODES OF HONOR • 1914 • Carleton Lloyd B. • USA
CODEX • 1982 • Pound Stuart • UKN
CODFISH AND ALOES • 1915 • Birch Cecil • UKN
CODFISH BALLS • 1930 • *Terry Paul/ Moser Frank (P)* • ANS • USA
CODICE D'AMORE ORIENTALE • 1974 • Vivarelli Piero • ITL
CODICE PRIVATO • 1988 • Maselli Francesco • ITL • PRIVATE CODE
CODICIA • 1955 • Catrani Catrano • ARG
CODICIL, THE • 1912 • Buckland Warwick • UKN
CODIGO PENAL, EL • 1931 • Rosen Phil • USA
CODINE • 1962 • Colpi Henri • FRN, RMN
CODO CON CODO • 1967 • Auz Victor • SPN • HAND IN HAND
CODOU • 1972 • Samb Ababacar • SNL • KODOU
CODY • 1977 • Blackburn William D. • ASL
CODY OF THE PONY EXPRESS • 1950 • Bennet Spencer Gordon • SRL • USA
COEUR, LE • 1975 • Brault Francois • DCS • CND
COEUR A COEUR • 1967 • Benani Hamid • SHT • MRC
COEUR A L'ENVERS, LE • 1980 • Apprederis Franck • FRN
COEUR A SES RAISONS, LE • 1985 • Shekter Louise • CND
COEUR A SES RAISONS, LE see **QALB LAHU WAH'ID, AL-** • 1944
COEUR A SES RAISONS, LE see **QALB LAHU HUKM, AL-** • 1956
COEUR BATTANT, LE • 1960 • Doniol-Valcroze Jacques • FRN • FRENCH GAME, THE (USA)
COEUR BLEU • 1980 • Courant Gerard • FRN
COEUR DE BOHEMIENNE • 1911 • Bourgeois Gerard • FRN
COEUR DE COQ • 1946 • Cloche Maurice • FRN • AFFAIRES DE COEUR
COEUR DE FRANCAISE • 1915 • Leprince Rene • FRN
COEUR DE FRANCAISE see **CHANTECOQ** • 1916
COEUR DE GOSSE see **GOSSE EN OR, UN** • 1938
COEUR DE GUEUX • 1936 • Epstein Jean • FRN, ITL • CUOR DI VAGABONDO (ITL) ○ PER LE STRADE DEL MONDO
COEUR DE LA FRANCE, LE • 1966 • Leenhardt Roger • DCS • FRN
COEUR DE LILAS • 1931 • Litvak Anatole • FRN • LILAC (USA)
COEUR DE MAMAN • 1953 • Delacroix Rene • CND
COEUR DE PARIS • 1931 • Benoit-Levy Jean, Epstein Marie • FRN
COEUR DECOUVERT, LE • 1988 • Laforce Jean-Yves • CND • HEART EXPOSED, THE
COEUR DES GUEUX, LE • 1925 • Machin Alfred • FRN
COEUR DISPOSE, LE • 1936 • Lacombe Georges • FRN
COEUR DU MAL, LE • 1916 • Volkov Alexander • USS
COEUR D'UNE NATION, LE see **UNTEL PERE ET FILS** • 1940
COEUR EBLOUI, LE • 1938 • Vallee Jean • FRN
COEUR EN ECHARPE, LE • 1980 • Viard Philippe • FRN
COEUR ET L'ARGENT, LE • 1912 • Feuillade Louis • FRN
COEUR FIDELE • 1923 • Epstein Jean • FRN • FAITHFUL HEART, THE
COEUR FOU, LE • 1970 • Albicocco Jean-Gabriel • FRN
COEUR FROID, LE • 1977 • Helman Henri • FRN • COLD HEART, THE
COEUR GROS COMME CAI, UN • 1962 • Reichenbach Francois • DOC • FRN • WINNER, THE (USA)
COEUR LEGER • 1923 • Saidreau Robert • FRN
COEUR MAGNIFIQUE, LE • 1922 • Mars Severin (c/d) • FRN
COEUR SUR LA MAIN, LE • 1948 • Berthomieu Andre • FRN
COEUR SUR LA MAIN, LE see **DEFENSE D'AIMER** • 1942
COEUR-SUR-MER • 1950 • Daniel-Norman Jacques • FRN
COEURS BELGES • Navarra Aimee • BLG
COEURS BRULES see **QALBUN YAHTARIQ** • 1959
COEURS FAROUCHES • 1924 • Duvivier Julien • FRN
COEURS FLAMBES see **FLAMBEREDE HJERTER** • 1986
COEURS JOYEUX • 1931 • de Vaucorbeil Max, Schwarz Hanns • FRN
COEURS NEUFS • 1969 • Fournier Claude • DCS • CND • HEARTS
COEURS VERTS, LES • 1966 • Luntz Edouard • FRN • NAKED HEARTS
COEVALS • 1959 • Ordynsky Vassily • USS
COEXISTENCE see **EGYUTTELES** • 1983
COFFEE FORTUNE TELLER, THE see **KAPHETZOU** • 1961
COFFEE GRINDER, THE • 1963 • Zitzman Jerzy • ANS • PLN
COFFEE, TEA OR ME? • 1973 • Panama Norman • USA
COFFIN, THE see **TRAFRACKEN** • 1966
COFFIN, THE see **COUSINES, LES** • 1970
COFFIN AFFAIR, THE see **AFFAIRE COFFIN, L'** • 1980
COFFIN CAME BY POST, THE see **VIOLENTS, LES** • 1957
COFFIN FROM HONG KONG, A (USA) see **SARG AUS HONGKONG, EIN** • 1964
COFFIN OF TERROR see **DANZA MACABRA** • 1964
COFFIN SHIP, THE • 1911 • *Thanhouser* • USA
COFFIN SHOP, THE • 1966 • Svankmajer Jan • ANS • CZC
COFFIN STAYS SHUT TODAY, THE see **SARG BLEIBT HEUTE ZU, DER** • 1967
COFFINS ON WHEELS • 1941 • Newman Joseph M. • SHT • USA
COFFRE ENCHANTE, LE • 1904 • Melies Georges • FRN • BEWITCHED TRUNK, THE (USA)
COFFRE-FORT, LE • 1908 • Cohl Emile • ANS • FRN
COFFRET DE CRISTAL, LE see **PHENIX OU LE COFFRET DE CRISTAL, LE** • 1905
COFFRET DE JADE, LE • 1921 • Poirier Leon • FRN • JADE CASKET, THE
COFFRET DE LAQUE, LE • 1932 • Kemm Jean • FRN
COFFRET DE TOLEDE, LE • 1914 • Feuillade Louis • FRN
COFFY • 1973 • Hill Jack • USA
COFRE DEL PIRATA, EL • 1958 • Mendez Fernando • MXC
COGNASSE • 1932 • Mercanton Louis • FRN
COGNATINA, LA • 1975 • Bergonzelli Sergio • ITL
COHEN AND MURPHY • 1910 • *Powers* • USA
COHEN AND TATE • 1988 • Red Eric • USA
COHEN AT CONEY ISLAND • 1909 • Baker George D. • USA
COHEN COLLECTS A DEBT • 1912 • Sennett Mack • USA
COHEN FORMS A NEW COMPANY • 1929 • Aylott Dave, Symmons E. F. • SHT • UKN
COHEN ON THE TELEPHONE • 1929 • Aylott Dave, Symmons E. F. • SHT • UKN
COHEN SAVES THE FLAG • 1913 • Sennett Mack • USA
COHEN'S ADVERTISING SCHEME • 1904 • Porter Edwin S. • USA
COHENS AND KELLYS, THE see **COHENS AND THE KELLYS, THE** • 1926
COHENS AND KELLYS IN AFRICA, THE • 1930 • Moore Vin • USA
COHENS AND KELLYS IN ATLANTIC CITY, THE • 1929 • Craft William James • USA
COHENS AND KELLYS IN HOLLYWOOD, THE • 1932 • Dillon John Francis • USA
COHENS AND KELLYS IN PARIS, THE • 1928 • Beaudine William • USA
COHENS AND KELLYS IN SCOTLAND, THE • 1930 • Craft William James • USA
COHENS AND KELLYS IN TROUBLE, THE • 1933 • Stevens George • USA
COHENS AND THE KELLYS, THE • 1926 • Pollard Harry • USA • TWO BLOCKS AWAY ○ COHENS AND KELLYS, THE
COHEN'S FIRE SALE • 1907 • Porter Edwin S. • USA
COHEN'S GENEROSITY • 1910 • *Defender* • USA
COHEN'S LUCK • 1915 • Collins John H. • USA
COHEN'S OUTING • 1913 • Sennett Mack • USA
COIFFEUR POUR DAMES • 1931 • Guissart Rene • FRN • ARTIST WITH THE LADIES (USA)
COIFFEUR POUR DAMES • 1951 • Boyer Jean • FRN • FRENCH TOUCH, THE (USA)
COIFFEUR POUR DAMES see **HALA'E AL SAYEDAT** • 1960
COILIN AND PLATONIDA • 1976 • Scott James • UKN
COIMBRA, UMA NOVA UNIVERSIDADE • 1962 • Tropa Alfredo • SHT • PRT
COIN, THE see **MONETA** • 1963
COIN IS A COIN, A see **SLANT AR EN SLANT, INTE SANT?, EN**
COIN-THROWING DETECTIVE, THE see **ZENIGATA HEIJI** • 1967
COIN TRANQUILLE, LE • 1957 • Vernay Robert • FRN
COIN TRANQUILLE A LA CAMPAGNE, UN (FRN) see **TRANQUILLO POSTO DI CAMPAGNA, UN** • 1968
COINCIDENCE • 1915 • Physioc Wray • USA
COINCIDENCE • 1921 • Withey Chet • USA
COINCIDENCES • 1946 • Debecque Serge • FRN
COINCIDENCES ON A TROLLEY • 1975 • Davlopoulos Takis • SHT • GRC
COINCIDENTAL BRIDEGROOM, A • 1914 • *August Edwin* • USA
COINERS, THE • 1904 • Mottershaw Frank • UKN
COINER'S DEN, THE • 1912 • Wilson Frank • UKN
COINER'S GAME, THE • 1915 • *Picture Playhouse* • USA
COISA SEM IMPORTANCIA, UMA • 1946 • Coelho Jose Adolfo • SHT • PRT
COL CUORE IN GOLA • 1967 • Brass Tinto • ITL, FRN • DEADLY SWEET (USA) ○ WITH HEART IN MOUTH ○ WITH BATED BREATH ○ HEART BEAT
COL. E.D. BAKER, 1ST CALIFORNIA • 1911 • *Champion* • USA
COL FERRO E COL FUOCO • 1962 • Cerchio Fernando • FRN, ITL, YGS • PAR LE FER ET PAR LE FEU (FRN) ○ INVASION 1700 (USA) ○ WITH FIRE AND SWORD ○ FIRE AND SWORD ○ DAGGERS OF BLOOD
COL KARTALI SEYH AHMET • 1968 • Canturk Husnu • TRK • SHEIK AHMET, EAGLE OF THE DESERT
COLAGEM • 1967 • Campos Antonio • SHT • PRT

COLD see **NEI-YI-NIEN WO-MEN CH'U KAN HSUEH** • 1988
COLD AND ITS CONSEQUENCES, A • 1909 • Coleby A. E. • UKN
COLD BLADE, THE • 1971 • Ch'U Yuan • HKG
COLD BLOOD • 1984 • SAF
COLD BLOOD • 1988 • Weiss Stephanie • NTH
COLD BLOODED BEAST (UKN) see **BESTIA UCCIDE A SANGUE FREDDO, LA** • 1971
COLD COMFORT • 1957 • Hill James • UKN
COLD COMFORT • 1989 • Sarin Vic • CND
COLD CUTS (USA) see **BUFFET FROID** • 1979
COLD DAYS (UKN) see **HIDEG NAPOK** • 1966
COLD DECK, THE • 1917 • Hart William S. • USA
COLD DOG SOUP • 1989 • Metter Alan • USA, UKN
COLD EYES OF FEAR, THE see **OCCHI FREDDI DELLA PAURA, GLI** • 1971
COLD FEAST, THE • 1930 • Petrov Vladimir • USS
COLD FEET • 1930 • Lantz Walter, Nolan William • ANS • USA
COLD FEET • 1984 • Van Dusen Bruce • USA
COLD FEET • 1989 • Dornhelm Robert • AUS
COLD FEET GETAWAY, THE • 1916 • Williams C. Jay • SHT • USA
COLD FEVER see **KALTES FIEBER** • 1984
COLD FURY • 1925 • *Richardson Jack* • USA
COLD HEART, THE see **KALTE HERZ, DAS** • 1923
COLD HEART, THE see **WIRTSHAUS IM SPESSART, DAS** • 1923
COLD HEART, THE see **KALTE HERZ, DAS** • 1930
COLD HEART, THE see **KALTE HERZ, DAS** • 1950
COLD HEART, THE see **COEUR FROID, LE** • 1977
COLD HEARTS AND HOT FLAMES • 1916 • *Ritchie Billie* • SHT • USA
COLD HEAVEN • 1990 • Roeg Nicolas • USA
COLD IN THE HEAD, A see **RYSKA SNUVAN** • 1937
COLD JOURNEY • 1972 • Defalco Martin • CND
COLD MARCH • Minaiev Igor • USS
COLD NERVE • 1925 • McGowan J. P. • USA
COLD NIGHT'S DEATH, A • 1973 • Freedman Jerrold • TVM • USA • CHILL FACTOR, THE
COLD PIZZA • 1972 • Kent Larry • MTV • CND
COLD RIVER • 1981 • Sullivan Fred G. • USA
COLD ROMANCE • 1949 • Davis Mannie • ANS • USA
COLD ROOM, THE • 1983 • Dearden James • TVM • UKN, USA
COLD ROOM, THE • 1989 • Rader Peter • USA
COLD SHIVERS • 1929 • Roberts Stephen • SHT • USA
COLD STEEL • 1912 • Collins Edwin J. • UKN
COLD STEEL • 1921 • MacDonald Sherwood • USA
COLD STEEL • 1987 • Puzo Dorothy Ann • USA • STILETTO
COLD STEEL see **TRAIL TO RED DOG, THE** • 1921
COLD STORAGE • 1951 • Kinney Jack • ANS • USA
COLD STORAGE EGG, THE • 1913 • *Kalem* • USA
COLD STORAGE RADIATOR, A • 1910 • *Selig* • USA
COLD SUMMER OF 1953 • 1987 • Proskin Alexander • USS
COLD SUN, THE • 1959 • Morse Hollingsworth • USA
COLD SWEAT • 1971 • Young Terence • UKN, FRN, ITL • DE LA PART DES COPAINS (FRN) ○ UOMO DALLE DUE OMBRE, L' (ITL)
COLD TRACKS see **KALDE SPOR** • 1962
COLD TURKEY • 1925 • Cline Eddie • SHT • USA
COLD TURKEY • 1929 • Lantz Walter, Nolan William • ANS • USA
COLD TURKEY • 1940 • Lord Del • SHT • USA
COLD TURKEY • 1951 • Nichols Charles • ANS • USA
COLD TURKEY • 1971 • Lear Norman • USA
COLD WAR • 1951 • Kinney Jack • ANS • USA
COLD WIND FROM HELL, A see **FUEGO** • 1964
COLD WIND IN AUGUST, A • 1961 • Singer Alexander • USA
COLDEST WINTER IN PEKING, THE see **HUANG-T'IEN HOU-T'U** • 1981
COLDITZ STORY, THE • 1955 • Hamilton Guy • UKN
COLE YOUNGER, GUNFIGHTER • 1958 • Springsteen R. G. • USA
COLECCIONISTA DE CADAVERES, EL • 1967 • Alcocer Santos • SPN, USA • BLIND MAN'S BLUFF (USA) ○ MORTE VIENE DEL BUIO, LA ○ CAULDRON OF BLOOD (UKN) ○ DEATH COMES FROM THE DARK ○ CORPSE COLLECTORS, THE ○ CHILDREN OF BLOOD
COLEGAS • 1983 • de la Iglesia Eloy • SPN • PALS ○ MATES
COLEGIALAS, LAS • 1945 • Delgado Miguel M. • MXC
COLEGIALAS LESBIANAS Y EL PLACER DE PERVERTIR • 1982 • Balcazar Alfonso • SPN • SEXUAL DESIRES
COLEGIO DE LA MUERTE, EL • 1974 • Ramirez Pedro L. • SPN
COLEGIO MILITAR • 1971 • *Filmadora Chapultepec* • MXC
COLEI CHE TUTTO SOFFRE • 1914 • Palermi Amleto • ITL
COLEMAN HAWKINS QUARTET • 1962 • Bruynoghe Yannick • BLG
COLERA DEL VIENTO, LA • 1969 • Camus Mario • SPN • COLLERA DEL VENTO, LA (ITL)
COLERE DES DIEUX, LA • 1946 • Lamac Carl • FRN
COLERE FROIDE • 1960 • Sassy Jean-Paul, Haguet Andre • FRN • THUNDER IN THE BLOOD (USA) ○ WARM BODY, THE
COLETTE • 1913 • Pouctal Henri • FRN
COLETTE • 1950 • Bellon Yannick • FRN
COLEURS D'ALGERIE • 1965 • Bendeddouche Ghaouti • DCS • ALG
COLHEITA DA AZEITONA, A • 1939 • Coelho Jose Adolfo • SHT • PRT
COLIBRI • 1924 • Janson Victor • FRG • KOLIBRI
COLIN ROSS MIT DEM KURBELKASTEN UM DIE ERDE • 1924 • *Neumann-Produktion* • FRG • MIT DEM KURBELKASTEN UM DEN ERDBALL
COLINA DE LOS PEQUENOS DIABLOS, LA • 1964 • Klimovsky Leon • SPN
COLINOT, L'ALZASOTTANE (ITL) see **COLINOT TROUSSE CHEMISE** • 1973
COLINOT TROUSSE CHEMISE • 1973 • Companeez Nina • FRN, ITL • COLINOT, L'ALZASOTTANE (ITL) ○ HISTOIRE TRES BONNE ET TRES JOYEUSE DE COLINOT TROUSSE-CHEMISE, L'
COLIS MYSTERIEUX, LE • 1909 • Jasset Victorin • FRN
COLLABORATORS, THE • 1912 • *Powers* • USA
COLLABORATORS, THE • 1973 • Robertson George C. • SER • CND
COLLAGE • 1961 • Hammid Alexander • USA
COLLANTS NOIRS, LES see **UN, DEUX, TROIS, QUATRE!** • 1960
COLLAPSE OF A BOSS see **TOKAI NO KAOYAKU** • 1960
COLLAPSE OF A SWIMMING WOMAN, THE see **TOKAI O OYOGU ONNA** • 1929
COLLAPSE OF THE RUSSIAN MONUMENT IN AYESTAFANOS, THE • 1914 • Uzkinay Fuat • TRK
COLLAPSIBLE KNIGHT, THE see **CHEVALIER DEMONTABLE, LE** • 1905
COLLAR AND THE BRACELET, THE see **FETTERS** • 1987
COLLAR BUTTON see **KARABOTAN** • 1926
COLLAR STUD, THE • 1913 • *Gca* • UKN
COLLARS AND CUFFS • 1923 • Roach Hal • SHT • USA
COLLE UNIVERSELLE, LA • 1907 • Melies Georges • FRN • GOOD GLUE STICKS (USA)
COLLEAGUES see **KOLLEGI** • 1963
COLLECTING POINT, THE see **SABIRNI CENTAR** • 1989
COLLECTING THE BILL • 1913 • Hotaling Arthur D. • USA
COLLECTING THE RENT • 1914 • *Royal* • USA
COLLECTION, THE • 1970 • *Blue Max* • USA
COLLECTION DAY • 1912 • *Lubin* • USA
COLLECTION MENARD, LA • 1943 • Bernard-Roland, Joannon Leo • FRN
COLLECTION OF POSTAGE STAMPS, A • 1908 • *Pathe* • USA
COLLECTION PARTICULIERE, UNE • 1973 • Borowczyk Walerian • DCS • FRN
COLLECTIONNEUSE, LA • 1967 • Rohmer Eric • FRN • COLLECTOR, THE (USA)
COLLECTIONS PRIVEES • 1975 • Borowczyk Walerian, Jaeckin Just • FRN, JPN • PRIVATE COLLECTIONS (USA)
COLLECTOR see **KOLEKCIONAR** • 1971
COLLECTOR, THE • 1965 • Wyler William • UKN, USA
COLLECTOR, THE (USA) see **COLLECTIONNEUSE, LA** • 1967
COLLECTOR OF PEARLS, THE • 1913 • *Leighton Lillian* • USA
COLLECTORS, THE • 1917 • *Pokes & Jabbs* • SHT • USA
COLLEEN • 1927 • O'Connor Frank • USA
COLLEEN • 1936 • Green Alfred E. • USA
COLLEEN BAWN • 1911 • *Yankee* • USA
COLLEEN BAWN • 1911 • Mervale Gaston • ASL
COLLEEN BAWN, THE • 1911 • Olcott Sidney • *Kalem* • USA
COLLEEN BAWN, THE • 1924 • Kellino W. P. • UKN • LOVES OF COLLEEN BAWN, THE
COLLEEN OF THE PINES • 1922 • Bennett Chester • USA
COLLEGE • 1927 • Horne James W., Keaton Buster (U/c) • USA
COLLEGE • 1931 • Lantz Walter, Nolan William • ANS • USA
COLLEGE see **HOHE SCHULE** • 1934
COLLEGE, THE • 1963 • Zimmerman Vernon • DOC • CND
COLLEGE BOOB, THE • 1926 • Garson Harry • USA
COLLEGE BOOMERANG, A • 1916 • Kelley J. Winthrop • SHT • USA
COLLEGE BOYS' SPECIAL, THE • 1917 • Sidney Scott • USA
COLLEGE CAPERS • 1931 • Foster John, Bailey Harry • ANS • USA
COLLEGE CHAPERONE, THE • 1913 • France Charles H. • USA
COLLEGE CHICKEN, A • 1910 • *Essanay* • USA
COLLEGE CHUMS • 1907 • Porter Edwin S. • USA
COLLEGE CHUMS • 1911 • *American* • USA
COLLEGE CHUMS • 1911 • Fitzhamon Lewin? • UKN
COLLEGE CHUMS • 1913 • Smalley Phillips • USA
COLLEGE COACH • 1933 • Wellman William A. • USA • FOOTBALL COACH (UKN)
COLLEGE CONFIDENTIAL • 1960 • Zugsmith Albert • USA
COLLEGE CONTEMPORAIN • 1960 • Patry Pierre • DCS • CND
COLLEGE COQUETTE, THE • 1929 • Archainbaud George • USA
COLLEGE CORRUPTION • 1970 • *Cosmos Films* • USA
COLLEGE CUPID, A • 1913 • *Lubin* • USA
COLLEGE DAYS • 1915 • Sidney Scott • USA
COLLEGE DAYS • 1926 • Thorpe Richard • USA
COLLEGE DAYS see **FRESHMAN, THE** • 1925
COLLEGE DAYS see **SO THIS IS COLLEGE** • 1929
COLLEGE EN FOLIE, LE • 1953 • Lepage Henri • FRN
COLLEGE FLIRT, THE (UKN) see **CAMPUS FLIRT, THE** • 1926
COLLEGE FOLLIES OF 1938 see **START CHEERING** • 1938
COLLEGE FOR MEN see **OTOKO DAIGAKU** • 1955
COLLEGE GIRL, A • 1912 • *Johnson Arthur* • USA
COLLEGE GIRLS • 1968 • Stephen A. C. • USA
COLLEGE GIRLS • *Denessy Sandra* • USA
COLLEGE HERO, THE • 1927 • Lang Walter • USA • PLAYING STRAIGHT
COLLEGE HOLIDAY • 1936 • Tuttle Frank • USA
COLLEGE HUMOR • 1933 • Ruggles Wesley • USA
COLLEGE IS A NICE PLACE see **DAIGAKU YOITOKO** • 1936
COLLEGE IS SUCH A NICE PLACE see **DAIGAKU YOITOKO** • 1936
COLLEGE KIDDO • 1927 • *Sennett Mack (P)* • SHT • USA
COLLEGE LOVE • 1929 • Ross Nat • USA
COLLEGE LOVERS • 1930 • Adolfi John G. • USA
COLLEGE MILITAIRE, LE • 1969 • Cardinal Roger • DCS • CND
COLLEGE ORPHAN, THE • 1915 • Dowlan William C. • USA
COLLEGE RACEHORSE (UKN) see **SILKS AND SADDLES** • 1936
COLLEGE RACKET, A • 1931 • Beaudine Harold • USA
COLLEGE RHYTHM • 1934 • Taurog Norman • USA
COLLEGE RUGGERS see **DAIGAKU NO NIJU-HACHININ SHU** • 1959
COLLEGE SCANDAL • 1935 • Nugent Elliott • USA • CLOCK STRIKES EIGHT, THE (UKN)
COLLEGE SPENDTHRIFT, THE • 1911 • *American* • USA
COLLEGE SPIRIT • 1932 • *Terry Paul/ Moser Frank (P)* • ANS • USA
COLLEGE SWING • 1938 • Walsh Raoul • USA • SWING, TEACHER, SWING (UKN)
COLLEGE SWING see **AMOURS, DELICES ET ORGUES** • 1946
COLLEGE VAMP, THE • 1931 • Beaudine William • SHT • USA
COLLEGE WIDOW, THE • 1915 • O'Neil Barry • USA
COLLEGE WIDOW, THE • 1927 • Mayo Archie • USA
COLLEGIALE, LA • 1975 • Martucci Gianni Antonio • ITL
COLLEGIANS, THE • 1929 • Edwards Harry J., Hill Robert F., Ruggles Wesley, Ross Nat, Fraser Harry L., Holmes Ben • USA
COLLEGIANS IN BUSINESS see **FOURFLUSHER, THE** • 1928
COLLEGIATE • 1926 • Andrews Del • USA
COLLEGIATE • 1936 • Murphy Ralph • USA • CHARM SCHOOL, THE (UKN)
COLLEGIATES, THE • 1974 • Stevens Carter • USA
COLLEGIENNES, LES • 1957 • Hunebelle Andre, Metzger Radley H. • FRN • TWILIGHT GIRLS, THE (USA) ○ TWILITE GIRLS
COLLERA DEL VENTO, LA (ITL) see **COLERA DEL VIENTO, LA** • 1969
COLLETTE ET SON MARI • 1932 • Pellenc Andre • FRN • AMOUREUX DE COLETTE, LES
COLLIDE-OSCOPE • 1966 • Vanderbeek Stan, Knowlton Kenneth • ANS • USA
COLLIE MARKET, THE • 1917 • Blackton J. Stuart • SHT • USA
COLLIER DE CHANVRE, LE • 1940 • Mathot Leon • FRN • MYSTERE DU BOIS BELLEAU, LE
COLLIER DE LA REINE, LE • 1909 • Feuillade Louis • FRN
COLLIER DE LA REINE, LE • 1929 • Ravel Gaston, Lekain Tony • FRN • AFFAIRE DU COLLIER DE LA REINE, L'
COLLIER DE MIMI PINSON, LE • 1911 • Perret Leonce • FRN
COLLIER DE PERLES, LE • 1915 • Feuillade Louis • FRN
COLLIER DE PERLES, LE see **PERLES DE LA COURONNE, LES** • 1937
COLLIER DE RUBIS, LE • 1937 • Reinert Emile Edwin • FRN
COLLIER DU GRAND DUC, LE • 1935 • Peguy Robert • FRN
COLLIER MAGIQUE, LE see **LOON'S NECKLACE, THE** • 1948
COLLIER TRICOLORE, LE • 1921 • de Carbonnat Louis • FRN
COLLIER VIVANT, LE • 1913 • Durand Jean • FRN
COLLINA DEGLI STIVALI, LA • 1969 • Colizzi Giuseppe • ITL • BOOT HILL (USA)
COLLINES DE SION, LES see **SALUT JERUSALEM** • 1972
COLLINGSBY PEARLS, THE • 1915 • *Herberlein Francis* • USA
COLLISION • 1932 • Samuelson G. B. • UKN
COLLISION see **THIEVES' HIGHWAY** • 1949
COLLISION AND SHIPWRECK AT SEA see **COLLISION ET NAUFRAGE EN MER** • 1898
COLLISION COURSE • 1988 • Teague Lewis • USA
COLLISION COURSE see **BAMBOO SAUCER, THE** • 1968
COLLISION ET NAUFRAGE EN MER • 1898 • Melies Georges • FRN • COLLISION AND SHIPWRECK AT SEA
COLLISIONS • 1976 • Emshwiller Ed • USA
COLLISON COURSE • 1975 • Page Anthony • TVM • USA
COLLIT'S INN • 1934 • Thring F. W. • ASL
COLLOIDS • 1969 • Jessop • UKN
COLLOQUE DE CHIENS see **COLOQUIO DE PERROS** • 1977
COLLOQUIUM OF DOGS see **COLOQUIO DE PERROS** • 1977
COLMENA, LA • 1983 • Camus Mario • SPN • BEE-HIVE, THE
COLMILLO DE BUDA, EL • 1949 • Bustillo Oro Juan • MXC
COLOCADAS, LAS • 1972 • Maso Pedro • SPN
COLOMBA • *Vina Victor* • FRN
COLOMBA • 1915 • Vale Travers • USA
COLOMBA • 1918 • von Cserepy Arzen • FRG
COLOMBA • 1933 • Severac Jacques • FRN
COLOMBA • 1947 • Couzinet Emile • FRN
COLOMBA NON DEVE VOLARE, LA • 1970 • Garrone Sergio • ITL
COLOMBES, LES • 1972 • Lord Jean-Claude • CND • DOVES, THE
COLOMBIA • 1976 • Giraldo Diego Leon • DOC • CLM
COLOMBIA '70 see **FEBRERO 28 DE 1970** • 1970
COLOMBIE-BRITANNIQUE ET L'HABITATION, LA • 1967 • Carriere Marcel • DCS • CND • BETTER HOUSING IN B. C.
COLOMBINE • 1920 • Hartwig Martin • FRG
COLOMBINE see **NUR EINE LUGE** • 1915
COLOMBO NIGHT, A see **ONE COLOMBO NIGHT** • 1926
COLOMBO PLAN • 1967 • Batchelor Joy • ANS • UKN
COLOMBUS OF SEX • 1970 • Reitman Ivan • CND • MY SECRET LIFE ○ COLUMBUS OF SEX
COLONEL, THE see **EZREDES, AZ** • 1917
COLONEL AND THE KING, THE • 1911 • *Thanhouser* • USA
COLONEL AND THE WOLFMAN, THE see **CORONEL E O LOBISOMEM, O** • 1980
COLONEL BLIMP (USA) see **LIFE AND DEATH OF COLONEL BLIMP, THE** • 1943
COLONEL BLOOD • 1934 • Lipscomb W. P. • UKN
COLONEL BOGEY • 1948 • Fisher Terence • UKN
COLONEL BONTEMPS, LE • 1915 • Feuillade Louis • FRN
COLONEL CARTER OF CARTERSVILLE • 1915 • Hansel Howell • USA
COLONEL CHABERT, LE • 1911 • Calmettes Andre, Pouctal Henri • FRN
COLONEL CHABERT, LE • 1943 • Le Henaff Rene • FRN
COLONEL CUSTARD'S LAST STAND • 1914 • *Frontier* • USA
COLONEL DELMIRO GOUVEIA see **CORONEL DEMIRO GOUVEIA** • 1979
COLONEL DURAND, LE • 1948 • Chanas Rene • FRN
COLONEL EFFINGHAM'S RAID • 1945 • Pichel Irving • USA • MAN OF THE HOUR (UKN)
COLONEL EN FOLIE, LE • Brega Andrea • FRN
COLONEL EST DE LA REVUE, LE • 1956 • Labro Maurice • FRN
COLONEL HEEZA LIAR • 1913-23 • *Bray John R. (P)* • ASS • USA
COLONEL HEEZA LIAR AND THE GHOST • 1923 • *Bray John R. (P)* • ANS • USA
COLONEL HEEZA LIAR, GHOST BREAKER • 1915 • *Bray John R. (P)* • ANS • USA
COLONEL HEEZA LIAR IN AFRICA • 1913 • *Bray John R. (P)* • ANS • USA
COLONEL HEEZA LIAR IN THE HAUNTED CASTLE • 1915 • *Bray John R. (P)* • ANS • USA
COLONEL HEEZA LIAR'S ANCESTORS • 1924 • Lantz Walter • ANS • USA
COLONEL HEEZA LIAR'S FORBIDDEN FRUIT • 1924 • Lantz Walter • ANS • USA
COLONEL HEEZA LIAR'S KNIGHTHOOD • 1924 • Lantz Walter • ANS • USA

COLONEL HEEZA LIAR'S VACATION • 1924 • Lantz Walter • ANS • USA
COLONEL MARCH INVESTIGATES • 1953 • Endfield Cy • UKN
COLONEL NEWCOME THE PERFECT GENTLEMAN • 1920 • Goodwins Fred • UKN
COLONEL OF THE NUTS, THE • 1914 • *Frontier* • USA
COLONEL OF THE RED HUSSARS, THE • 1914 • Ridgely Richard • USA
COLONEL OF THE SERTAO see **CORONEL DEMIRO GOUVEIA** • 1979
COLONEL REDL (UKN) see **OBERST REDL** • 1985
COLONEL REDL'S LEGACY see **BRANDSTIFTER EUROPAS, DIE** • 1926
COLONEL STEELE, MASTER GAMBLER • 1915 • MacQuarrie Murdock • USA
COLONEL SVEC see **PLUKOVNIK SVEC** • 1929
COLONEL WOLODYJOWSKI (UKN) see **PAN WOLODYJOWSKI** • 1969
COLONEL'S ADOPTED DAUGHTER, THE • 1914 • *Little Anna* • USA
COLONEL'S CUP, THE see **SPORTS DAY** • 1945
COLONEL'S DAUGHTER, THE • 1911 • Porter Edwin S. • USA
COLONEL'S ERRAND, THE • 1910 • *Kalem* • USA
COLONEL'S ESCAPE, THE • 1912 • *Kalem* • USA
COLONEL'S LITTLE LOVE AFFAIR, THE • 1921 • *Hearty Harry* • SHT • USA
COLONEL'S OATH, THE • 1913 • *Reliance* • USA
COLONEL'S ORDERLY, THE • 1914 • Hamilton G. P.? • USA
COLONEL'S PERIL, THE • 1912 • Ince Thomas H. • USA
COLONEL'S SHOWER BATH, THE see **DOUCHE DE COLONEL, LA** • 1901
COLONEL'S SON, THE • 1911 • *Kalem* • USA
COLONEL'S WARD, THE • 1912 • Ince Thomas H. • USA
COLONEL'S WIFE, THE see **PUKOVNIKOVICA** • 1973
COLONIA PENAL, LA • 1971 • Ruiz Raul • CHL • PENAL CAMP ○ PENAL COLONY, THE
COLONIAL BELLE, A • 1910 • *Vignola Robert* • USA
COLONIAL DAYS • 1910 • *Pantograph* • USA
COLONIAL DOLL'S HOUSE, A • 1974 • King John • NZL
COLONIAL ROMANCE, A • 1909 • Brooke Van Dyke • USA
COLONIAL VIRGINIA • 1908 • *Edison* • USA
COLONIALSKANDAL • 1927 • Jacoby Georg • FRG • LIEBE IM RAUSCH ○ KOLONIALSKANDAL
COLONIE SICEDISON • 1958 • Olmi Ermanno (Spv) • DOC • ITL
COLONIZACAO INTERNA • 1947 • Coelho Jose Adolfo • SHT • PRT
COLONNA INFAME, LA • 1973 • Risi Nelo • ITL
COLONNA INFAME, LA see **ROSSETTO, IL** • 1960
COLONNA TRAIANA, LA • 1949 • Emmer Luciano, Gras Enrico • ITL
COLONNE, LA • 1910 • Perret Leonce • FRN
COLONNE DE CENDRES, LA • 1969 • Coutard Raoul • FRN
COLONNE DE FEU, LA see **DANSE DU FEU, LA** • 1899
COLONNELLO BUTTIGLIONE, IL • 1973 • Guerrini Mino • ITL • UFFICIALE NON SI ARRENDE MAI, NEMMENO DI FRONTE ALL'EVIDENZA: FIRMATA COLONNELLO BUTTIGLIONE, UN
COLONNELLO BUTTIGLIONE DIVENTA GENERALE, IL • 1974 • Guerrini Mino • ITL
COLONNELLO GHABERT, IL • 1922 • Gallone Carmine • ITL
COLONY BENEATH THE EARTH see **GYARMAT A FOLD ALATT** • 1951
COLOQUIO DE PERROS • 1977 • Ruiz Raul • ANS • FRN • COLLOQUE DE CHIENS ○ COLLOQUIUM OF DOGS
COLOR AND LIGHT • 1950 • Davis James* • SHT • USA
COLOR BOX, A see **COLOUR BOX** • 1935
COLOR CRY • 1952 • Lye Len • SHT • USA
COLOR DANCES NO.1 • 1952 • Davis James* • SHT • USA
COLOR DE CUBA • 1968 • Hernandez Bernabe • CUB
COLOR DESIGNS #1 • 1948 • Latelin Hugo • SHT • USA
COLOR ESCONDIDO • 1987 • de la Torre Raul • ARG • HIDDEN COLOUR
COLOR FIELDS • 1977 • Vanderbeek Stan • USA
COLOR IDIOMS • 1968 • Kuenstler Frank • SHT • USA
COLOR ME BLOOD RED • 1964 • Lewis Herschell G. • USA
COLOR ME DEAD • 1970 • Davis Eddie • ASL
COLOR MOMMY DEAD see **PICTURE MOMMY DEAD** • 1966
COLOR OF HER SKIN, THE see **NIGHT OF THE QUARTER MOON, THE** • 1959
COLOR OF MONEY, THE • 1987 • Scorsese Martin • USA
COLOR OF RITUAL THE COLOR OF THOUGHT, THE • De Hirsch Storm • SHT • USA
COLOR OF THE DAY • 1955 • USA
COLOR OF THE FORM, THE see **COULEUR DE LA FORME, LA** • 1961
COLOR OF THE POMEGRANATE (USA) see **SAYAT NOVA** • 1969
COLOR POEM • 1938 • Fischinger Oskar • ANS • USA
COLOR PURPLE, THE • 1985 • Spielberg Steven • USA
COLOR RHAPSODY • 1954 • Bute Mary Ellen • ANS • USA
COLOR RHYTHM • 1942 • Fischinger Oskar • ANM • FRG
COLOR SCALES • 1932 • Myers Zion • SHT • USA
COLOR SERGEANT'S HORSE, THE • 1910 • *Vitagraph* • USA
COLORADO • 1915 • MacGregor Norval • USA
COLORADO • 1921 • Eason B. Reeves • USA
COLORADO • 1940 • Kane Joseph • USA
COLORADO see **RUN FOR COVER** • 1955
COLORADO AMBUSH • 1951 • Collins Lewis D. • USA
COLORADO CHARLIE • 1966 • Mauri Roberto • ITL
COLORADO KID, THE • 1937 • Newfield Sam • USA
COLORADO PIONEERS • 1945 • Springsteen R. G. • USA
COLORADO PLUCK • 1921 • Furthman Jules G. • USA
COLORADO RANGER • 1950 • Carr Thomas • USA • GUNS OF JUSTICE
COLORADO SERENADE • 1946 • Tansey Robert • USA
COLORADO STONE see **GOT IT MADE** • 1973
COLORADO SUNDOWN • 1952 • Witney William • USA
COLORADO SUNSET • 1939 • Sherman George • USA
COLORADO TERRITORY • 1949 • Walsh Raoul • USA
COLORADO TRAIL, THE • 1938 • Nelson Sam • USA
COLORADOS, I • 1967 • Witney William • USA • I COLORADOS
COLORATURA see **KOLORATUREN** • 1931
COLORED FOX, THE • Ivanov A. • ANS • USS
COLORED GIRL'S LOVE, A • 1914 • Sennett Mack • USA
COLORED STENOGRAPHER, THE • 1909 • Porter Edwin S. • USA
COLORED VILLAINY • 1915 • Cogley Nick • USA
COLORED YARNS see **TSVETNITE NISCHKI** • 1969
COLORFUL BOMBAY • 1937 • Fitzpatrick James • SHT • USA
COLORFUL CHINA see **SZINFOLTOK KINABOL** • 1957
COLORFUL ISLANDS -MADAGASCAR AND SEYCHELLES • 1936 • Fitzpatrick James • SHT • USA
COLORI DELLA LUCE, I • 1962 • SHT • ITL • COLOURS OF LIGHT, THE
COLORIN, COLORADO • 1976 • Garcia Sanchez Jose Luis • SPN
COLORS • 1988 • Hopper Dennis • USA
COLORS ARE DREAMING see **BOJE SANJAJU** • 1958
COLORS OF CHINA see **SZINFOLTOK KINABOL** • 1957
COLOSO DE MARMOL, EL • 1928 • Ojeda Manuel R. • MXC
COLOSO DE RODAS, EL (SPN) see **COLOSSO DI RODI, IL** • 1961
COLOSSE DE RHODES, LE (FRN) see **COLOSSO DI RODI, IL** • 1961
COLOSSEUM AND JUICY LUCY • 1970 • Palmer Tony, Williams Paul • UKN
COLOSSI, THE see **JABABIRA, AL** • 1965
COLOSSO DI RODI, IL • 1961 • Leone Sergio • ITL, FRN, SPN • COLOSSE DE RHODES, LE (FRN) ○ COLOSSUS OF RHODES, THE (USA) ○ COLOSO DE RODAS, EL (SPN)
COLOSSO DI ROMA, IL • 1964 • McNamara Richard • ITL • HERO OF ROME (USA) ○ MUZIO SCEVOLA ○ ARM OF FIRE
COLOSSUS • 1989 • MacDonald Peter • USA
COLOSSUS 1980 see **FORBIN PROJECT, THE** • 1969
COLOSSUS AND THE AMAZON QUEEN see **REGINA DELLE AMAZZONI, LA** • 1960
COLOSSUS AND THE AMAZONS (USA) see **REGINA DELLE AMAZZONI, LA** • 1960
COLOSSUS AND THE HEADHUNTERS (UKN) see **MACISTE CONTRO I CACCIATORI DI TESTE** • 1962
COLOSSUS AND THE HUNS • 1962 • Montero Roberto Bianchi • ITL
COLOSSUS OF NEW YORK, THE • 1958 • Lourie Eugene • USA
COLOSSUS OF RHODES, THE (USA) see **COLOSSO DI RODI, IL** • 1961
COLOSSUS OF THE ARENA see **MACISTE IL GLADIATORE PIU FORTE DEL MONDO** • 1962
COLOSSUS OF THE STONE AGE(UKN) see **MACISTE CONTRO I MOSTRI** • 1962
COLOSSUS THE FORBIN PROJECT see **FORBIN PROJECT, THE** • 1969
COLOUR • 1975 • Short Anthony • DCS • UKN
COLOUR see **RANG** • 1986
COLOUR BOX • 1935 • Lye Len • ANS • UKN • COLOR BOX, A
COLOUR CAPERS • 1957 • Holland Frank • ANS • UKN
COLOUR COCKTAIL • 1935 • McLaren Norman • ANS • UKN
COLOUR FLIGHT • 1939 • Lye Len • ANS • UKN
COLOUR IN CLAY • 1942 • Catling Darrell • DCS • UKN
COLOUR OF DESTINY, THE see **COR DO SEU DESTINO, A** • 1986
COLOURED HANDKERCHIEF, A see **KUSHUME RUMAL** • 1985
COLOURED LANCES, THE see **LANZAS COLORADAS, LAS** • 1972
COLOURED STOCKINGS see **KOLOROWE PONCZOCHY** • 1960
COLOURFUL BED OF VIOLENT DESIRE see **BOYOKU NO SHIKIBUTON** • 1967
COLOURFUL CHRONICLE see **KOLOROWA KRONIKA** • 1962
COLOURFUL WORLD see **KOLOROWY SWIAT** • 1961
COLOURS • 1972 • Al-Zobidi Kais • SHT • SYR
COLOURS IN PAINTING • 1964 • Takacs Gabor • DOC • HNG
COLOURS OF IRIS, THE see **CHROMATA TIS IRIDOS, TA** • 1973
COLOURS OF LIFE see **KOLORY ZYCIA** • 1975
COLOURS OF LIGHT, THE see **COLORI DELLA LUCE, I** • 1962
COLOURS OF LOVE, THE see **LACHES VIVENT D'ESPOIR, LES** • 1961
COLOURS OF THE RAINBOW, THE see **CHROMATA TIS IRIDOS, TA** • 1973
COLOURS OF VASARHELY, THE see **VASARHELYI SZINEK** • 1961
COLOURS SPEAK, THE see **BESZELNEK A SZINEK** • 1953
COLPA DI GIOVANNI, LA • 1914 • Falena Ugo • ITL
COLPA DI UNA MADRE, LA • 1954 • Duse Carlo • ITL
COLPA ET LA PENA, LA • 1961 • Bellocchio Marco • SHT • ITL
COLPACCIO, IL • 1976 • Paolinelli Bruno • ITL • BIG POT
COLPEVOLI, I • 1957 • Vasile Turi • ITL, FRN • RESPONSABILITE LIMITEE?
COLPI BASSI, I • 1972 • Sabato Mario • ITL • BELOW THE BELT
COLPI DI LUCE • 1985 • Castellari Enzo G. • ITL, USA • LIGHT BLAST ○ RAY OF LIGHT
COLPI DI TIMONE • 1942 • Righelli Gennaro • ITL
COLPIRE AL CUORE • 1983 • Amelio Gianni • ITL • STRIKE AT THE HEART ○ BLOW TO THE HEART
COLPITA DA IMPROVVISO BENESSERE • 1976 • Giraldi Franco • ITL
COLPO DA DUE MILIARDI, UN (ITL) see **SAIT-ON JAMAIS** • 1957
COLPO DA MILLE MILIARDI, UN (ITL) see **GOLPE DE MIL MILLONES, UN** • 1966
COLPO DA RE, UN • 1967 • Dorigo Angelo • ITL
COLPO DI FULMINE • 1985 • Risi Marco • ITL • LOVE AT FIRST SIGHT
COLPO DI PISTOLA, UN • 1942 • Castellani Renato • ITL
COLPO DI SOLE • 1968 • Guerrini Mino • ITL • SUNSTROKE
COLPO DI STATO • 1968 • Salce Luciano • ITL • COUP D'ETAT
COLPO DI VENTO, UN • 1936 • Forzano Giovacchino?, Tavano Charles-Felix? • ITL
COLPO DOPPIO DEL CAMALEONTE D'ORO • 1967 • Stegani Giorgio • ITL
COLPO FALLITO • 1910 • Lolli Alberto Carlo • ITL
COLPO GOBBO ALL'ITALIANA • 1962 • Fulci Lucio • ITL
COLPO GROSSO A GALATA BRIDGE • 1965 • Isasi Antonio • ITL, FRN, SPN • HOMME D'ISTAMBUL, L' (FRN) ○ THAT MAN IN ISTANBUL (USA) ○ ESTAMBUL 65 (SPN) ○ MAN FROM ISTANBUL, THE ○ ISTANBUL 65
COLPO GROSSO A PARIGI (ITL) see **CENT BRIQUES ET DES TUILES** • 1965
COLPO GROSSO AL CASINO (ITL) see **MELODIE EN SOUS-SOL** • 1962
COLPO GROSSO DEGLI UOMINI SQUALO • 1978 • Piccioli Gianfranco • ITL
COLPO GROSSO, GROSSISSIMO, ANZI PROBABILE • 1972 • Ricci Tonino • ITL
COLPO GROSSO MA NON TROPPO (ITL) see **CORNIARD, LE** • 1965
COLPO IN CANNA • 1975 • Di Leo Fernando • ITL • STICK 'EM UP DARLINGS (UKN) ○ LOADED GUNS (USA)
COLPO MAESTRO AL SERVIZIO DI SUA MAESTA BRITANNICA • 1967 • Lupo Michele • ITL, SPN • GREAT DIAMOND ROBBERY, THE ○ GRAN GOPLE AL SERVICIO DE SU MAJESTAD BRITANICA ○ SPN
COLPO ROVENTE • 1970 • Zuffi Piero • ITL
COLPO SEGRETO DI D'ARTAGNAN, IL (ITL) see **SECRET DE D'ARTAGNAN, LE** • 1962
COLPO SENSAZIONALE AL SERVIZIO DEL SIFAR • 1968 • Merino Jose Luis • ITL, SPN • MASTER-STROKE IN THE SERVICE OF SIFAR
COLT '45 (UKN) see **THUNDERCLOUD** • 1950
COLT, THE see **ZHEREBYONOK** • 1960
COLT CANTARONO LA MORTE E FU TEMPO DI MASSACRO, LE see **TEMPO DI MASSACRO** • 1966
COLT, CINQUE DOLLARI, UNA CAROGNA, UNA • 1967 • Chardon Richard • ITL • COLT, FIVE DOLLARS AND CARRION, A
COLT COMMANDO • 1987 • Bolivar Cesar • VNZ
COLT COMRADES • 1943 • Selander Lesley • USA
COLT CONCERT see **TEMPO DI MASSACRO** • 1966
COLT CONTRO TUTTI, UNA see **MAGNIFICO TEXANO, IL** • 1967
COLT E LA MIA LEGGE, LA • 1967 • Brescia Alfonso • ITL
COLT, FIVE DOLLARS AND CARRION, A see **COLT, CINQUE DOLLARI, UNA CAROGNA, UNA** • 1967
COLT IN A DEVIL'S FIST, A see **COLT IN PUGNA AL DIAVOLO, UNA** • 1967
COLT IN MANO AL DIAVOLO, UNA • 1972 • Baldanello Gianfranco • ITL
COLT IN PUGNA AL DIAVOLO, UNA • 1967 • Bergonzelli Sergio • ITL • COLT IN A DEVIL'S FIST, A ○ DEVIL WAS AN ANGEL, THE
COLT IS MY PASSPORT see **COLT WA ORE NO PASSPORT** • 1967
COLT POR CUATRO CIRIOS, UN • 1971 • Iquino Ignacio F. • SPN
COLT WA ORE NO PASSPORT • 1967 • Nomura Takeshi • JPN • COLT IS MY PASSPORT
COLTELLI DEL VENDICATORE, I • 1967 • Bava Mario • ITL • KNIVES OF THE AVENGERS (USA) ○ RAFFICA DI COLTELLI ○ SHOWER OF KNIVES
COLTELLO DI GHIACCIO, IL • 1972 • Lenzi Umberto • ITL
COLTELLO NELLA PIAGA, IL (ITL) see **COUTEAU DANS LA PLAIE, LE** • 1962
COLTER CRAVEN STORY, THE • 1960 • Ford John • MTV • USA
COLTON, U.S.N. • 1915 • Scardon Paul • USA
COLUI CHE DEVE MORIRE (ITL) see **CELUI QUI DOIT MOURIR** • 1956
COLUMBIA CONNECTION, THE • 1982 • Kowalewich Len • CND • DEAD WRONG ○ ENTRAPMENT
COLUMBIA REVOLT, THE • 1968 • Newsreel • DOC • USA
COLUMBIUM • 1966 • Fournier Claude • DCS • CND
COLUMBO: A CASE OF IMMUNITY • 1975 • Post Ted • TVM • USA
COLUMBO: AN EXERCISE IN FATALITY • 1974 • Kowalski Bernard • TVM • USA
COLUMBO: CANDIDATE FOR CRIME • 1973 • Sagal Boris • TVM • USA
COLUMBO: DAGGER OF THE MIND • 1972 • Quine Richard • TVM • USA
COLUMBO: DEAD WEIGHT • 1973 • Smight Jack • TVM • USA
COLUMBO: DEATH LENDS A HAND • 1971 • Kowalski Bernard • TVM • USA
COLUMBO: DOUBLE EXPOSURE • 1973 • Quine Richard • TVM • USA
COLUMBO: DOUBLE SHOCK • 1973 • Butler Robert • TVM • USA
COLUMBO GOES TO THE GUILLOTINE • 1989 • Penn Leo • TVM • USA
COLUMBO: GRAND DECEPTIONS • 1989 • Wanamaker Sam • TVM • USA
COLUMBO: MURDER BY THE BOOK • 1971 • Spielberg Steven • TVM • USA
COLUMBO: MURDER, SMOKE AND SHADOWS • 1988 • Frawley James • TVM • USA • MURDER, SMOKE AND SHADOWS
COLUMBO: REQUIEM FOR A FALLING STAR • 1972 • Quine Richard • TVM • USA
COLUMBO: SEX AND THE MARRIED DETECTIVE • 1989 • Frawley James • TVM • USA • SEX AND THE MARRIED DETECTIVE
COLUMBO: SWAN SONG • 1974 • Colasanto Nicholas • TVM • USA
COLUMBO: THE GREENHOUSE JUNGLE • 1972 • Sagal Boris • TVM • USA
COLUMBO: TROUBLED WATERS • 1975 • Gazzara Ben • TVM • USA
COLUMBUS • 1923 • Hollywood Edwin L. • USA
COLUMBUS DAY CONSPIRACY, A • 1911 • *Thanhouser* • USA
COLUMBUS ENTDECKT KRAHWINKEL • 1954 • Paal Alexander, Erfurth Ulrich • FRG
COLUMBUS OF SEX see **COLOMBUS OF SEX** • 1970
COLUMBUSES, THE see **KOLUMBOWIE** • 1970
COLUMN, THE see **COLUMNA** • 1968
COLUMN OF FIRE, THE see **DANSE DU FEU, LA** • 1899
COLUMN SOUTH • 1953 • De Cordova Frederick • USA

COLUMNA • 1968 • Dragan Mircea • RMN, FRG • COLUMN, THE ○ TRAJAN'S COLUMN ○ TYRANN, DER
COM LICENCA, EU VOU A LUTA • 1986 • Farias Lui • BRZ • I'M STEPPING OUT
COMA • 1978 • Crichton Michael • USA
COMA • 1989 • Adomenaite Nijele, Gorlov Boris • USS
COMADRITA, LA • 1975 • *Diana* • MXC
COMALA • 1976 • Bolanos Jose • MXC
COMANCHE • 1956 • Sherman George • USA
COMANCHE BLANCO • 1967 • Briz Jose • SPN, USA • WHITE COMANCHE (USA)
COMANCHE STATION • 1960 • Boetticher Budd • USA
COMANCHE TERRITORY • 1950 • Sherman George • USA
COMANCHEROS, THE • 1961 • Curtiz Michael • USA
COMANDAMENTI PER UN GANGSTER • 1968 • Caltabiano Alfio • ITL, YGS • COMMANDMENTS FOR A GANGSTER
COMANDANTE, IL • 1963 • Heusch Paolo • ITL
COMANDANTE FURIA, EL • 1965 • Gomez Urquiza Zacarias • MXC
COMANDANTE TIERINA, EL see **PISTOLERO DESCONOCIDO, EL** • 1966
COMANDO AL INFIERNO • 1968 • Merino Jose Luis • SPN, ITL • SETTE EROICHE CAROGNE (ITL)
COMANDO DE ASESINOS • 1968 • Coll Julio • SPN, FRG, PRT • COMMAND OF MURDERERS ○ MURDERER'S COMMAND
COMANDO DES BRAVES, LE • 1976 • Merino Jose Luis • SPN
COMANDO SUICIDA (SPN) see **COMMANDO SUICIDA** • 1968
COMANDO TXIQUIA see **MUERTE DE UN PRESIDENTE** • 1977
COMANDOS COMUNALES • 1972 • Guzman Patricio • CHL • COMMUNAL ORGANIZATION
COMAT AND FAMILY see **KELUARGA SI COMAT** • 1974
COMATA, THE SIOUX • 1909 • Griffith D. W. • USA
COMBAT • 1927 • Hiatt Albert • USA • ISLE OF MYSTERY, THE (UKN)
COMBAT see **COMBATE**
COMBAT, THE • 1916 • Ince Ralph • USA
COMBAT, THE • 1926 • Reynolds Lynn • USA
COMBAT ACADEMY see **COMBAT HIGH** • 1986
COMBAT AVEC L'OMBRE • 1949 • Deroisy Lucien • BLG
COMBAT DANS L'ILE, LE • 1962 • Cavalier Alain • FRN • FIRE AND ICE (USA)
COMBAT DANS UNE RUE AUX INDES • 1897 • Melies Georges • FRN • FIGHTING IN THE STREETS IN INDIA
COMBAT DE BOXE • 1927 • Dekeukeleire Charles • BLG
COMBAT DE CHAMEAUX • 1967 • Ben Aicha Sadok • SHT • TNS
COMBAT DE COQS • 1899 • Melies Georges • FRN • LIVELY COCK-FIGHT, A
COMBAT DE COQS • 1962 • Kyrou Ado • FRN
COMBAT DES SOURDS, LE • 1974 • Moreau Michel • DOC • CND
COMBAT D'ONESIME TREMBLAY, LE • 1985 • Bedard Jean-Thomas • MTV • CND
COMBAT HEROIQUE see **SIRA AL-ABT'AL** • 1961
COMBAT HIGH • 1986 • Israel Neal • TVM • USA • COMBAT ACADEMY
COMBAT KILLERS • 1968 • Loring Ken • PHL
COMBAT NAVAL DEVANT MANILLE • 1898 • Melies Georges • FRN • DEFENDING THE FORT AT MANILA
COMBAT NAVAL EN GRECE • 1897 • Melies Georges • FRN • SEA FIGHTING IN GREECE
COMBAT SHOCK • 1986 • Giovinazzo Buddy • USA • AMERICAN NIGHTMARES
COMBAT SQUAD • 1953 • Roth Cy • USA
COMBAT ZONE • 1982 • Shonteff Lindsay • UKN
COMBAT ZONE see **HOW SLEEP THE BRAVE** • 1981
COMBATE • Quiroga Marcelo • BRZ • COMBAT
COMBATE A PRAGA DOS GAFANHOTOS, O • 1944 • Coelho Jose Adolfo • SHT • PRT
COMBATE DE GIGANTES • 1966 • Capitani Giorgio • ITL, SPN • WAR OF THE GIANTS
COMBATS D'ALSACE see **FILS DE FRANCE** • 1945
COMBATTRE POUR NOS DROITS • 1961 • Buyens Frans • BLG
COMBINARDS, LES • 1964 • Roy Jean-Claude • FRN, SPN, ITL
COMBINATION, THE • 1915 • Drew Sidney • USA
COMBINATION OF THE SAFE, THE • 1912 • *Foxe Earle* • USA
COMBINED CADETS • 1944 • Annakin Ken • DCS • UKN
COMBINED FLEET, THE see **RENGO KANTAI** • 1982
COMBINED OPERATIONS • 1945 • Cutts Graham • DCS • UKN
COMBOURG, VISAGE DE PIERRE • 1948 • de Casembroot Jacques • FRN
COME ACROSS • 1929 • Taylor Ray • USA
COME ACROSS • 1938 • Bucquet Harold S. • SHT • USA
COME AGAIN SMITH • 1919 • Hopper E. Mason • USA
COME ALONG DO! • 1898 • Paul Robert William • UKN
COME ALONG.. FOLLOW ME see **SEGUME.. VENI CONMIGO** • 1973
COME AND GET IT • 1929 • Fox Wallace • USA
COME AND GET IT! • 1936 • Hawks Howard, Wyler William • USA • ROARING TIMBER
COME AND GET ME! • 1922 • Maloney Leo, Beebe Ford • USA
COME AND LAY DOWN • Davis Joan • ITL
COME AND PLAY see **WE ARE NO VIRGINS** • 1974
COME AND PLAY, SIR see **POJDTE, PANE, BUDEME SI HRAT!** • 1965-67
COME AND SEE (UKN) see **IDI I SMOTRI** • 1986
COME AWAY, COME AWAY • 1972 • Schulz Bob • MTV • CND
COME BACK • 1981 • Severijn Jonne • NTH
COME BACK, THE • 1915 • *Premier* • USA
COME-BACK, THE • 1916 • Balshofer Fred J. • USA
COME BACK, AFRICA • 1960 • Rogosin Lionel • DOC • USA, SAF
COME BACK BABY • 1968 • Greene David Allen • USA
COME BACK, CHARLESTON BLUE • 1972 • Warren Mark • USA
COME BACK HOME, DADDY see **YUVANA DON BABA** • 1968
COME BACK, LITTLE SHEBA • 1952 • Mann Daniel • USA
COME BACK, LITTLE SHICKSA • 1949 • Lewis Jerry • SHT • USA
COME BACK, MISS PIPPS • 1941 • Cahn Edward L. • SHT • USA
COME BACK OF PERCY, THE • 1915 • Neilan Marshall • USA
COME BACK PETER • 1952 • Saunders Charles • UKN
COME BACK PETER • 1969 • Winter Donovan • UKN • IMPORTANCE OF BEING SEXY, THE ○ SOME LIKE IT SEXY
COME BACK SEBASTIANA see **VUELVE SEBASTIANA** • 1953
COME BACK TO ERIN • 1911 • *Powers* • USA
COME BACK TO ERIN • 1914 • Olcott Sidney • USA
COME BACK TO HEARING • 1914 • Storrie Kelly • UKN
COME BACK TO ME (UKN) see **DOLL FACE** • 1945
COME BACK TO THE FIVE AND DIME, JIMMY DEAN, JIMMY DEAN • 1982 • Altman Robert • USA
COME BACK TOMORROW • 1963 • Tashkov Yevgyeni • USS
COME BACK WITH A VICTORY see **MY ZHDOM VAS S POBEDOI** • 1941
COME BLOW YOUR HORN • 1963 • Yorkin Bud • USA
COME CAMBIARE MOGLIE • 1970 • Mocky Jean-Pierre • ITL
COME CANO ARRABBIATI • 1976 • Imperoli Mario • ITL
COME CLEAN • 1931 • Horne James W. • SHT • USA
COME CLOSER • 1953 • Hirsch Hy • SHT • USA
COME CLOSER, FOLKS • 1936 • Lederman D. Ross • USA
COME, COME, COME UPWARD see **AJE, AJE, BARA AJE** • 1989
COME, COME TO A HIGHER PLACE see **AJE, AJE, BARA AJE** • 1989
COME DANCE WITH ME • 1950 • Zampi Mario • UKN
COME DANCE WITH ME (USA) see **VOULEZ-VOUS DANSER AVEC MOI** • 1960
COME DOWN UNTO US • 1983 • Lee Chang-Ho • SKR
COME DREAM WITH ME • 1969 • Evans Jack • USA
COME DRINK WITH ME see **TA TSUI HSIA** • 1966
COME FILL THE CUP • 1951 • Douglas Gordon • USA
COME FLY WITH ME • 1963 • Levin Henry • USA, UKN
COME FLY WITH US • 1976 • USA
COME FOR A STROLL • 1938 • Massingham Richard • UKN
COME HAIL OR HIGH WATER see **STAND BY FOR ACTION** • 1942
COME HAVE COFFEE WITH US (USA) see **VENGA A PRENDERE IL CAFFE DA NOI** • 1970
COME HERE, MUKHTAR! • 1964 • Tumanov Semyon • USS • HERE, MUKHTAR!
COME HOME WITH ME see **GAA MED MIG HJEM** • 1941
COME IMPARAI AD AMARE LE DONNE • 1966 • Salce Luciano • ITL, FRG, FRN • GEWISSE ETWAS DER FRAUEN, DAS (FRG) ○ HOW I LEARNED TO LOVE WOMEN
COME IN, CHILDREN see **BROTHERHOOD OF SATAN** • 1970
COME IN, IF YOU PLEASE see **UDI, AKO HOCES** • 1968
COME IN, JUPITER • 1955 • Wallace Ettilie • SHT • USA
COME INGUAIAMMO L'ESERCITO • 1965 • Fulci Lucio • ITL
COME INTO MY BED see **KOM I MIN SANG** • 1968
COME INTO MY PARLOUR • 1932 • Longden John • UKN
COME INTO THE GARDEN, MAUD • 1909 • *Warwick Trading Co.* • UKN
COME INTO THE KITCHEN • 1920 • *Malone Molly* • USA
COME L'AMORE • 1968 • Muzii Enzo • ITL • LIKE LOVE
COME LE FOGLIE • 1934 • Camerini Mario • ITL
COME LE FOGLIE • 1938 • Besozzi Angelo • ITL • LIKE THE LEAVES (USA)
COME LIVE WITH ME • 1940 • Brown Clarence • USA
COME MAKE LOVE WITH ME see **AUS DEM TAGEBUCH EINES SIEBZEHNJAHRIGEN** • 1979
COME MARRY ME see **OYOME IN OIDE** • 1966
COME MY LAD AND BE A SOLDIER • 1908 • Gilbert Arthur • UKN
COME 'N' GET IT see **LUNCH WAGON** • 1981
COME NEXT SPRING • 1956 • Springsteen R. G. • USA
COME NOW, MY DEAR LITTLE BIRD see **KOMM NUR, MEIN LIEBSTES VOGELEIN** • 1968
COME-ON, THE • 1916 • Moore Matt • SHT • USA
COME-ON, THE • 1956 • Birdwell Russell J. • USA
COME ON BABY, LIGHT MY FIRE see **BABY, LIGHT MY FIRE** • 1970
COME ON CHILDREN • 1973 • King Allan • CND
COME ON COWBOYS! • 1924 • Hayes Ward • USA • HIS GLORIOUS ROMANCE (UKN)
COME ON, COWBOYS! • 1937 • Kane Joseph • USA
COME ON DANGER • 1932 • Hill Robert F. • USA
COME ON, DANGER! • 1942 • Killy Edward • USA
COME ON GEORGE • 1939 • Kimmins Anthony • UKN
COME ON IN • 1918 • Emerson John • USA
COME ON LEATHERNECKS • 1938 • Cruze James • USA
COME ON MARINES • 1934 • Hathaway Henry • USA
COME ON OUT • 1962 • Coppola Francis Ford • USA
COME ON OVER • 1922 • Green Alfred E. • USA • DARLIN' (UKN) ○ DARLING
COME ON, PONCIANO (USA) see **ORA PONCIANO!** • 1936
COME ON, RANGERS! • 1938 • Kane Joseph • USA
COME ON STUPID see **VIENI AVANTI CRETINO** • 1982
COME ON, TARZAN • 1932 • James Alan • USA
COME ONE, COME ALL! • 1970 • Vorno Anthony • USA
COME OUT, COME OUT! • 1969 • Yellen Linda • USA
COME OUT FIGHTING • 1945 • Beaudine William • USA
COME OUT FIGHTING • 1973 • Buesst Nigel • ASL
COME OUT OF KITCHEN see **COME OUT OF THE KITCHEN** • 1919
COME OUT OF THE KITCHEN • 1919 • Robertson John S. • USA • COME OUT OF KITCHEN
COME OUT OF THE KITCHEN see **HONEY** • 1930
COME OUT OF THE PANTRY • 1935 • Raymond Jack • UKN
COME OUTSIDE • 1905 • *Warwick Trading Co.* • UKN
COME PARLI, FRATE? • 1974 • Moretti Nanni • ITL
COME PERDERE UNA MOGLIE E TROVARE UN'AMANTE • 1978 • Festa Campanile Pasquale • ITL
COME PERSI LA GUERRA • 1947 • Borghesio Carlo • ITL • HOW I LOST THE WAR
COME PLAY WITH ME • 1968 • Cosentino Nick • USA
COME PLAY WITH ME • 1970 • Fergeson James • USA
COME PLAY WITH ME • 1977 • Marks George Harrison • UKN
COME PLAY WITH ME see **GRAZIE, ZIA** • 1967
COME PLAY WITH ME 2 • 1980 • Dietrich Erwin C. • SWT
COME PLAY WITH ME 3 see **JULCHEN UND JETTCHEN: DIE VERLIEBTEN APOTHEKERSTOCHTER** • 1980
COME, QUANDO, PERCHE • 1968 • Pietrangeli Antonio, Zurlini Valerio • ITL • HOW, WHEN, WHY? ○ HOW, WHEN AND WITH WHOM
COME RE CANDAULE • 1920 • Serena Gustavo • ITL
COME RIDE THE WILD PINK HORSE • 1967 • Sarno Joe • USA
COME 'ROUND AN' TAKE Y'R ELEPHANT AWAY • 1915 • MacGregor Norval • USA
COME RUBAMMO LA BOMBA ATOMICA • 1967 • Fulci Lucio • ITL, EGY • HOW WE STOLE THE ATOMIC BOMB
COME RUBARE LA CORONA D'INGHILTERRA • 1967 • Grieco Sergio • ITL • HOW TO STEAL THE CROWN OF ENGLAND ○ ARGOMAN SUPERDIABOLICO ○ ARGOMAN THE FANTASTIC SUPERMAN ○ FANTASTIC ARGOMAN
COME RUBARE UN QUINTALE DI DIAMANTI IN RUSSIA • 1967 • Malatesta Guido • ITL, SPN • HOW TO STEAL A HUNDRED KILOS OF DIAMONDS IN RUSSIA
COME SATURDAY • 1949 • Reeve Leonard, Davies Jim, Caunter Julian • UKN
COME SCOPERSI L'AMERICA • 1949 • Borghesio Carlo • ITL
COME SEBEN, LEBEN • 1913 • Henderson Dell • USA
COME SEE THE PARADISE • 1990 • Parker Alan • USA
COME SEPTEMBER • 1961 • Mulligan Robert • USA
COME SHARE MY LOVE! see **WHAT A BLONDE** • 1945
COME SHARE MY LOVE see **NEVER A DULL MOMENT** • 1950
COME SI DISTRUGGE LA REPUTAZIONE DEL PIU GRANDE AGENTE SEGRETO DEL MONDO (ITL) see **COMMENT DETRUIRE LA REPUTATION DU PLUS CELEBRE AGENT SECRET DU MONDE** • 1973
COME SI UCCIDE UNA SIGNORA? see **GEHEIMNIS DER GELBEN MONCHE, DAS** • 1966
COME SONO BUONI I BIANCI • 1988 • Ferreri Marco • ITL, SPN, FRN • HOW GOOD THE WHITES ARE!
COME SPY WITH ME • 1967 • Stone Marshall • USA • AGENT 36-24-36 ○ RED OVER RED
COME STRANGER see **BIGANE BIYA** • 1968
COME SVALIGIAMMO LA BANCA D'ITALIA • 1966 • Fulci Lucio • ITL
COME TAKE A TRIP IN MY AIRSHIP • 1924 • Fleischer Dave • ANS • USA
COME TAKE A TRIP IN MY AIRSHIP • 1930 • Fleischer Dave • ANS • USA
COME TE MOVI TE FULMINO • 1958 • Mattoli Mario • ITL
COME THROUGH • 1917 • Conway Jack • USA
COME THURSDAY • 1964 • Davis Robert P. • USA
COME TI CHIAMI, AMORE MIO? • 1970 • Silva Umberto • ITL
COME TI RAPISCO IL PUPO see **CINQUE FURBASTRI E UN FURBACCHIONE** • 1977
COME TO BABY DO • 1946 • Crouch William Forest • SHT • USA
COME TO MY HOUSE • 1927 • Green Alfred E. • USA
COME TO PAPA • 1928 • Lamont Charles • SHT • USA
COME TO THE POINT, TREASURE see **ZUR SACHE SCHATZCHEN** • 1968
COME TO THE STABLE • 1949 • Koster Henry • USA
COME TOGETHER • 1971 • Swimmer Saul • USA
COME UNA ROSA AL NASO • 1976 • Rossi Franco • ITL, UKN • PURE AS A LILY (UKN) ○ AS PURE AS A LILY ○ VIRGINITY ○ VIRGINITA
COME UNTO ME • 1911 • *Reliance* • USA
COME UP SMILING • 1939 • Freshman William • ASL
COME UP SMILING (UKN) see **SING ME A LOVE SONG** • 1936
COME WITH ME MY LOVE see **TAKE TIME TO SMELL THE FLOWERS** • 1977
COME WITH US see **POJDTE NAMI** • 1938
COMEBACK • 1980 • Buschmann Christel • FRG
COMEBACK • 1982 • Bartlett Hall • USA
COMEBACK • 1982 • Vadim Roger
COMEBACK, THE • 1915 • *Majestic* • USA
COMEBACK, THE • 1915 • *Ramona* • USA
COMEBACK, THE • 1917 • Marshall George • SHT • USA
COMEBACK, THE • 1978 • Walker Pete • UKN • DAY THE SCREAMING STOPPED, THE
COMEBACK, THE • 1988 • Freedman Jerrold • USA
COMEBACK, THE see **WOMEN IN HIS LIFE, THE** • 1933
COMEBACK, THE see **DONUS** • 1973
COMEBACK, THE see **LOVE IS FOREVER** • 1982
COMEBACK KID, THE • 1980 • Levin Peter • TVM • USA
COMEBACK OF BARNACLE BILL, THE • 1918 • *Ebony* • SHT • USA
COMEBACK TRAIL, THE • 1974 • Hurwitz Harry • USA
COMEDIA FANTASTICA • 1975 • Popescu-Gopo Ion • RMN • FANTASTIC COMEDY, A
COMEDIA IMMORTAL, LA • 1950 • Demicheli Tulio • ARG
COMEDIA IMMORTAL, LA • 1951 • Catrani Catrano • ARG
COMEDIA ROTA • 1978 • Finn Oscar Barney • ARG • BROKEN COMEDY
COMEDIAN, THE • 1956 • Frankenheimer John • MTV • USA
COMEDIAN, THE • 1983 • Ijas Matti • FNL
COMEDIAN AND THE FLY PAPER, THE • 1902 • Smith G. A. • UKN
COMEDIAN PAULUS SINGING "COQUIN DE PRINTEMPS" see **PAULUS CHANTANT: COQUIN DE PRINTEMPS** • 1897
COMEDIAN PAULUS SINGING "DERRIERE L'OMNIBUS" see **PAULUS CHANTANT: DERRIERE L'OMNIBUS** • 1897
COMEDIAN PAULUS SINGING "DUELLISTE MARSEILLAIS" see **PAULUS CHANTANT: DUELLISTE MARSEILLAIS** • 1897
COMEDIANS see **COMICOS** • 1953
COMEDIANS, THE • 1967 • Glenville Peter • USA, FRN • COMEDIENS, LES (FRN)
COMEDIANS, THE • 1985 • SAF
COMEDIANS, THE see **KOMEDIANTY** • 1961
COMEDIAN'S DOWNFALL, THE • 1913 • France Charles H. • USA
COMEDIAN'S MASK, THE • 1913 • *Baggot King* • USA
COMEDIE • Karmitz Marin • SHT • FRN
COMEDIE • 1987 • Doillon Jacques • FRN
COMEDIE AVANT MOLIERE, LA • 1946 • Tedesco Jean • SHT • FRN
COMEDIE D'AMOUR • 1989 • Rawson Jean-Pierre • FRN
COMEDIE D'ETE • 1989 • Vigne Daniel • FRN
COMEDIE DU BONHEUR, LA • 1940 • L'Herbier Marcel • FRN, ITL • ECCO LA FELICITA! (ITL) ○ COMEDY OF HAPPINESS, THE

COMEDIE DU TRAIN DES PIGNES, LA • 1977 • de Chavannes Francois • FRN
COMEDIE EXOTIQUE • 1984 • Toure Kitia • IVC
COMEDIE FRANCAISE see **SOIREE A LA COMEDIE FRANCAISE, UNE** • 1934
COMEDIEN, LE • 1947 • Guitry Sacha • FRN • PRIVATE LIFE OF AN ACTOR, THE (USA) ○ LUCIEN GUITRY
COMEDIEN SANS PARADOX, LE • 1975 • Lapoujade Robert • FRN
COMEDIENNE'S STRATEGY, THE • 1914 • Myers Harry • USA
COMEDIENS ERRANTS, LES see **VAGABONDS DU REVE, LA** • 1949
COMEDIENS, LES (FRN) see **COMEDIANS, THE** • 1967
COMEDY ABOUT MONEY, A see **KOMEDIE OM GELD** • 1936
COMEDY AND TRAGEDY • 1909 • *Pilar-Morin Mlle.* • USA
COMEDY AND TRAGEDY • 1914 • Edwin Walter • USA
COMEDY AROUND A DOOR HANDLE see **KOMEDIE S KLIKOU** • 1964
COMEDY AT HAGERSKOG see **KOMEDI I HAGERSKOG** • 1968
COMEDY CARTOON • *Urban Charles (P)* • ANM • UKN
COMEDY CARTOONS • 1907 • Booth W. R. • UKN
COMEDY COMPANY, THE • 1978 • Philips Lee • TVM • USA
COMEDY-GRAPH, THE see **BINETTOSCOPE, LE** • 1910
COMEDY, HORSE RACE, SHOT GAMBLING see **KIGEKI KEIBA HISHO-HO IPPATSU SHOBU** • 1968
COMEDY IN BLACK AND WHITE • 1908 • Porter Edwin S. • USA
COMEDY MAN, THE • 1963 • Rakoff Alvin • UKN
COMEDY OF ERRORS see **KOMEDIA POMYLEK** • 1968
COMEDY OF ERRORS, A • 1912 • *Quirk Billy* • USA
COMEDY OF ERRORS, A • 1915 • Birch Cecil • UKN
COMEDY OF HAPPINESS, THE see **COMEDIE DU BONHEUR, LA** • 1940
COMEDY OF TERRORS, THE • 1963 • Tourneur Jacques • USA • GRAVESIDE STORY, THE
COMEDY ON MONEY see **KOMEDIE OM GELD** • 1936
COMEDY TALE OF FANNY HILL, A • 1964 • Goodwins Leslie • SHT • USA
COMEDY TEAM'S STRATEGY, THE • 1913 • *Kalem* • USA
COMEDY TRAIN SERIES: NEW YEAR TRIP see **KIGEKI HATSUMOUDE RESHA** • 1968
COMEMORACOES HENRIQUINAS • 1961 • de Barros Jose Leitao • SHT • PRT
COMES A HORSEMAN • 1978 • Pakula Alan J. • USA • COMES A HORSEMAN WILD AND FREE
COMES A HORSEMAN WILD AND FREE see **COMES A HORSEMAN** • 1978
COMES A TIME see **SILENCE OF THE NORTH** • 1981
COMET • 1986 • Goldsmith Sidney • ANS • CND
COMET, THE • 1910 • *Kalem* • USA
COMET OVER BROADWAY • 1938 • Berkeley Busby • USA
COMET QUEST see **ADVENTURES OF MARK TWAIN, THE** • 1985
COMETES, LES • 1985 • Waucampt Yves, Poulain Evelyne • DOC • FRN
COMETS • 1930 • Geneen Sasha • UKN
COMET'S COME-BACK, THE • 1916 • MacMackin Archer • USA
COMEZON DEL AMOR, LA • 1959 • Salvador Jaime • MXC
COMFORT AND JOY • 1984 • Forsyth Bill • UKN
COMI-COLOR CARTOONS • 1933-34 • Iwerks Ub • ASS • USA
COMIC, THE • 1969 • Reiner Carl • USA • BILLY BRIGHT
COMIC, THE • 1985 • Driscoll Richard • USA
COMIC BARBER see **COMIC SHAVING** • 1897
COMIC BOOK CONFIDENTIAL • 1988 • Mann Ron, Lippincott Charles • DOC • CND, USA
COMIC BOOK LAND • 1950 • Davis Mannie • ANS • USA
COMIC BOXING MATCH • 1899 • *Warwick Trading Co.* • UKN
COMIC CONJURING • 1905 • *Mutoscope & Biograph* • UKN
COMIC COSTUME RACE • 1896 • Paul Robert William • UKN
COMIC DUEL, A • 1906 • Green Tom? • UKN
COMIC FACE • 1897 • Smith G. A. • UKN • MAN DRINKING
COMIC GOLF see **GOLFING** • 1913
COMIC GRIMACER, THE • 1901 • Hepworth Cecil M. • UKN
COMIC HISTORY OF AVIATION, A see **JAK SE CLOVEK NAUCIL LETAT** • 1958
COMIC MAGAZINE • 1987 • Takita Yojiro • JPN
COMIC SHAVING • 1897 • Smith G. A. • UKN • COMIC BARBER
COMIC STORYTELLER: THE GREAT BURGLAR, A see **RAKUGOYARO: ODOROBO** • 1967
COMIC STORYTELLER'S UPROARIOUS LAUGHTER, A see **RAKUGOYARO DAIBAKUSHO** • 1967
COMIC STRIP HERO see **JEU DE MASSACRE** • 1967
COMIC STRIP: MORE BAD NEWS • 1987 • Edmundson Adrian • UKN
COMIC STRIP PRESENTS: DIDN'T YOU KILL MY BROTHER? • 1987 • Spiers Bob • MTV • UKN • DIDN'T YOU KILL MY BROTHER?
COMIC STRIP PRESENTS: MISTER JOLLY LIVES NEXT DOOR • 1987 • Frears Stephen • MTV • UKN • MISTER JOLLY LIVES NEXT DOOR
COMIC STRIP PRESENTS: THE FUNSEEKERS • 1987 • Wright Simon • MTV • UKN • FUNSEEKERS, THE
COMIC STRIP PRESENTS: THE STRIKE • 1988 • Richardson Peter • UKN • STRIKE, THE
COMIC STRIP PRESENTS: THE YOB • 1987 • Emes Ian • MTV • UKN • YOB, THE
COMICAL CONJURING see **JACQUES ET JIM** • 1903
COMICAL SCULPTURE see **JODAI NO CHOKOKU** • 1950
COMICON • 1976 • Lennick Michael • CND, USA
COMICOS • 1953 • Bardem Juan Antonio • SPN • COMEDIANS
COMICOS DE LA LEGUA • 1956 • Cortes Fernando • MXC
COMICOS Y CANCIONES • 1960 • Cortes Fernando • MXC
COMIK SUTRA • 1970 • Schneider Kenny • ANS • USA
COMIN' AT YA! • 1981 • Baldi Ferdinando • USA
COMIN' ROUND THE MOUNTAIN • 1936 • Wright Mack V. • USA
COMIN' ROUND THE MOUNTAIN • 1940 • Archainbaud George • USA
COMIN' ROUND THE MOUNTAIN • 1949 • Sparber I. • ANS • USA
COMIN' ROUND THE MOUNTAIN • 1951 • Lamont Charles • USA
COMIN' THRO' THE RYE • 1916 • Hepworth Cecil M. • UKN
COMIN' THRO' THE RYE • 1923 • Hepworth Cecil M. • UKN
COMIN' THRO' THE RYE • 1947 • Mycroft Walter C. • UKN
COMIN' THROUGH THE RYE • 1926 • Fleischer Dave • ANS • USA
COMINCERA TUTTO UN MATTINO • 1979 • Pannaccio Elo • ITL • IO DONNA, TU DONNA
COMING, THE • 1981 • Gordon Bert I. • USA
COMING ALIVE see **VENIR AL MUNDO** • 1989
COMING AN' GOING • 1926 • Thorpe Richard • USA
COMING APART • 1969 • Ginsberg Milton Moses • USA
COMING ATTRACTIONS • 1971 • Conrad Beverly Grant • USA
COMING ATTRACTIONS • 1976 • Starr Duncan • USA • EROTIC CONFESSIONS
COMING ATTRACTIONS see **LOOSE SHOES** • 1979
COMING AVIATOR'S DREAM, THE • 1910 • *Lux* • FRN
COMING BACK see **VOLVER** • 1982
COMING BACK ALIVE • 1980 • Koenig Wolf, Cowan Paul, Mason William, Shapley Rosemarie • CND
COMING-BACK OF KIT DENVER, THE • 1912 • Buckland Warwick? • UKN
COMING DOWN • 1916 • Myll Louis • SHT • USA
COMING DOWN TO EARTH • 1986 • Petkova Roumyana • BUL
COMING GENERATION, THE • 1912 • *Early Baby* • USA
COMING HOME • 1913 • Noy Wilfred • UKN
COMING HOME • 1914 • *Francis Alec B.* • USA
COMING HOME • 1919 • *Austral Photoplay* • ASL
COMING HOME • 1973 • Reid Bill • CND
COMING HOME • 1978 • Ashby Hal • USA
COMING OF AGE • 1938 • Haynes Manning • UKN
COMING OF AGE, THE see **REIFEZEIT** • 1976
COMING OF AGE IN IBIZA see **RUNNING AWAY BACKWARDS** • 1964
COMING OF ALIENS, THE see **INCONTRI MOLTO.. RAVVICINATI DEL QUARTO TIPO** • 1978
COMING OF AMOS, THE • 1925 • Sloane Paul • USA
COMING OF ANGELO, THE • 1913 • Griffith D. W. • USA
COMING OF ANGELS, A • 1977 • Scott Joel • USA
COMING OF ANGELS: THE SEQUEL, A see **ANGELS** • 1986
COMING OF COLUMBUS, THE • 1912 • Thayer Otis B. • USA
COMING OF FARO NELL, THE • 1918 • Watt Allen • SHT • USA
COMING OF GRETCHEN, THE • 1913 • *Lackeye James* • USA
COMING OF KING OLMOS, THE see **VENIDA DEL REY OLMOS, LA** • 1974
COMING OF LONE WOLF, THE • 1914 • *Kalem* • USA
COMING OF SANTA CLAUS, THE • 1916 • *Walturdaw* • UKN
COMING OF SOPHIE'S MAMA, THE • 1914 • *Potel Victor* • USA
COMING OF SUNBEAM, THE • 1913 • *Karr Darwin* • USA
COMING OF THE DIAL, THE • 1933 • Legg Stuart • DOC • UKN
COMING OF THE LAW, THE • 1919 • Reynolds Lynn • USA
COMING OF THE PADRES, THE • 1914 • *American* • USA
COMING OF THE REAL PRINCE, THE • 1914 • *Treskoff Olga* • USA
COMING OUT ALIVE • 1982 • McBreeny Don • CND
COMING OUT OF MAGGIE, THE • 1917 • Justice Martin • SHT • USA
COMING OUT OF THE ICE • 1982 • Hussein Waris • TVM • USA
COMING-OUT PARTY • 1934 • Blystone John G. • USA
COMING-OUT PARTY • 1963 • Smith Paul J. • ANS • USA
COMING OUT PARTY • 1970 • *Stacey Dist.* • USA
COMING OUT PARTY, A (USA) see **VERY IMPORTANT PERSON** • 1961
COMING OUT PARTY, THE • 1965 • Loach Kenneth • MTV • UKN
COMING POWER, THE • 1914 • Mackey Edward • USA
COMING SOON • 1984 • *Landis John (P)* • CMP • USA
COMING THING, THE • 1970 • Reberg Dave • USA
COMING THROUGH • 1925 • Sutherland A. Edward • USA
COMING THROUGH • 1985 • Barber-Fleming Peter • UKN
COMING TO AMERICA • 1988 • Landis John • USA
COMING TO THE POINT • 1913 • Stow Percy • UKN
COMING UP ROSES • 1987 • Bayley Stephen • UKN
COMIQUE EST NE, UN • 1977 • Polac Michel • FRN
COMISAR ACUZA, UN • 1973 • Nicolaescu Sergiu • RMN • POLICE INSPECTOR ACCUSES, A
COMISARIO DE TRANCO LARGO, EL • 1942 • Torres-Rios Leopoldo • ARG
COMISARIO EN TURNO • 1948 • de Anda Raul • MXC
COMISARIO G. EN EL CASO DEL CABARET, EL • 1973 • Merino Fernando • SPN
COMISSARIO DA POLICIA, O • 1952 • Esteves Constantino • PRT
COMITE DES CHOMEURS, LE • 1968 • Dansereau Fernand • DCS • CND
COMITE D'EXPRESSION POPULAIRE • 1971 • Dansereau Fernand • DOC • CND
COMITES DE GESTION • 1963 • Rachedi Ahmed • SHT • ALG
COMIZI D'AMORE • 1965 • Pasolini Pier Paolo • DOC • ITL
COMMAND 5 • 1985 • Swackhamer E. W. • TVM • USA
COMMAND, THE • 1954 • Butler David • USA • REAR GUARD
COMMAND DECISION • 1948 • Wood Sam • USA
COMMAND FROM GALILEE, THE • 1911 • *Reliance* • USA
COMMAND IN HELL see **ALONE IN THE NEON JUNGLE** • 1988
COMMAND OF MURDERERS see **COMANDO DE ASESINOS** • 1968
COMMAND PERFORMANCE • 1931 • Lang Walter • USA
COMMAND PERFORMANCE • 1937 • *Royston Roy* • SHT • UKN
COMMAND PERFORMANCE • 1937 • Hill Sinclair • UKN
COMMANDANT, LE • 1928 • Puchalski Eduard • USS
COMMANDANT DE L'ILE AUX OISEAUX, LE • 1939 • Pronin Vassily • USS
COMMANDER, THE • 1988 • Margheriti Antonio • ITL
COMMANDER DIMAS see **KUMANDER DIMAS** • 1968
COMMANDER GREAT GUY • 1968 • Bartsch Art • ANS • USA
COMMANDER LAWIN • *Verona Danny* • USA
COMMANDER OF MOLINETTE, THE see **KOMMANDANT VON MOLINETTE, DER** • 1967
COMMANDER OF THE DETACHMENT, THE see **KOMANDIRAT NA OTRIADA** • 1959
COMMANDING OFFICER, THE • 1915 • Dwan Allan • USA
COMMANDMENTS FOR A GANGSTER see **COMANDAMENTI PER UN GANGSTER** • 1968
COMMANDO • 1985 • Lester Mark L. • USA
COMMANDO 52 • 1965 • Heynowski Walter • DOC • GDR
COMMANDO ATTACK see **POSTO ALL'INFERNO, UN** • 1969
COMMANDO CODY, SKY MARSHAL OF THE UNIVERSE • 1953 • Brannon Fred C., Keller Harry, Adreon Franklin • SRL • USA
COMMANDO DES CHAUDS LAPINS, LE • 1973 • Perol Guy • FRN
COMMANDO DUCK • 1944 • King Jack • ANS • USA
COMMANDO LEOPARD see **KOMMANDO LEOPARD** • 1985
COMMANDO POUR UN HOMME SEUL • 1970 • Perier Etienne • FRN
COMMANDO SQUAD • 1987 • Ray Fred Olen • USA
COMMANDO SUICIDA • 1968 • Bazzoni Camillo • ITL, SPN • SUICIDE COMMANDOS (USA) ○ COMANDO SUICIDA (SPN) ○ SUICIDE COMMANDO
COMMANDO THE NINJA see **AMERICAN COMMANDO NINJA** • 1988
COMMANDO (USA) see **MARSCHIER UND KREPIER** • 1962
COMMANDOS • 1968 • Crispino Armando • ITL, FRG • HIMMELFAHRTSKOMMANDO EL ALAMEIN (FRG)
COMMANDOS ARE COMING, THE see **KOMANDOLAR GELIYOR** • 1968
COMMANDOS STRIKE AT DAWN • 1942 • Farrow John • USA
COMMARE SECCA, LA • 1962 • Bertolucci Bernardo • ITL • GRIM REAPER, THE (USA) ○ THIN GOSSIP, THE
COMME EN CALIFORNIE • 1983 • Godbout Jacques • CND
COMME IL EST BON MON FRANCAIS see **COMO ERA GOSTOSO O MEU FRANCES** • 1971
COMME LA LUNE • 1977 • Seria Joel • FRN
COMME LES ANGES DECHUS DE LA PLANETE SAINT-MICHEL • 1978 • Schmidt Jean • DOC • FRN
COMME LES DOIGTS DE LA MAIN • 1978 • Melancon Andre • CND
COMME MARS EN CAREME see **NE JOUEZ PAS AVEC LES MARTIANS** • 1967
COMME ON FAIT SON LIT ON SE COUCHE • 1903-04 • Blache Alice • FRN
COMME SI C'ETAIT HIER • 1980 • Abramowicz Myriam, Hoffenberg Esther • DOC • BLG • AS IF IT WERE YESTERDAY
COMME S'IL EN PLEUVAIT • 1963 • Monter Jose Luis • FRN, SPN • AS IF IT WERE RAINING (USA)
COMME SUR DES ROULETTES • 1977 • Companeez Nina • FRN
COMME UN BATEAU DANS LE CIEL • 1981 • D'Aix Alain • DOC • CND
COMME UN BOOMERANG • 1976 • Giovanni Jose • FRN, ITL • LIKE A BOOMERANG
COMME UN CHEVEU SUR LA SOUPE • 1956 • Regamey Maurice • FRN • HAIR IN THE SOUP, A
COMME UN ECLAIR • 1968 • Dassin Jules • DOC • FRN • ISRAEL, AN 5727 ○ GUERRE AMERE, LA
COMME UN FEMME • 1979 • Dura Christian • FRN
COMME UN POISSON DANS L'EAU • 1961 • Michel Andre • FRN
COMME UN POT DE FRAISES • 1974 • Aurel Jean • FRN
COMME UN REFLET D'OISEAU • 1961 • Jallaud Sylvia • SHT • FRN
COMME UNE AME • 1965 • Bouguermouh Abderrahmane • SHT • ALG
COMME UNE FEUILLE DE CELLOPHANE see **ALA WARAQU SILUFAN** • 1974
COMME UNE LETTRE A LA POSTE • 1938 • Storck Henri • DOC • BLG
COMMEDIA DAL MIO PALKO, LA • 1918 • D'Ambra Lucio • ITL
COMMEDIA DELLA FELICITA, LA see **ECCO LA FELICITA** • 1940
COMMENCEMENT DAY • 1924 • Roach Hal • SHT • USA
COMMENT CA VA • 1976 • Godard Jean-Luc, Mieville Anne-Marie • FRN
COMMENT CA VA LES JEUNESSES? • 1974 • Duceppe Pierre • DCS • CND
COMMENT CONSTRUIRE VOTRE IGLOU see **HOW TO BUILD AN IGLOO** • 1949
COMMENT DETRUIRE LA REPUTATION DU PLUS CELEBRE AGENT SECRET DU MONDE • 1973 • de Broca Philippe • FRN, ITL • MAGNIFIQUE, LE ○ COME SI DISTRUGGE LA REPUTAZIONE DEL PIU GRANDE AGENTE SEGRETO DEL MONDO (ITL) ○ ITL
COMMENT DRAGUER TOUS LES MECS • 1984 • Feuillebois Jean-Paul • FRN
COMMENT DRAGUER TOUTES LES FILLES • 1981 • Vocoret Michel • FRN
COMMENT EPOUSER UN PREMIER MINISTRE • 1964 • Boisrond Michel • FRN, ITL
COMMENT FABIEN DEVIENT ARCHITECTE • 1901 • Zecca Ferdinand • FRN • FABIEN BECOMES AN ARCHITECT
COMMENT FAIRE L'AMOUR AVEC UN NEGRE SANS SE FATIGUER • 1988 • Benoit Jacques W. • CND, FRN • HOW TO MAKE LOVE TO A NEGRO WITHOUT GETTING TIRED
COMMENT FONCTIONNE LE MOTEUR A JET see **INTRODUCTION TO JET ENGINE, AN** • 1959
COMMENT LE DESIR VIENT AUX FILLES see **JE SUIS FRIGIDE.. POURQUOI?** • 1972
COMMENT LES SEDUIRE • 1967 • Roy Jean-Claude • FRN • 1001 WAYS TO LOVE (UKN)
COMMENT MAX FAIT LE TOUR DU MONDE • 1913 • Linder Max • FRN
COMMENT MONSIEUR PREND SON BAIN • 1902 • Blache Alice • FRN
COMMENT NAISSENT LES MEDUSES • 1960 • Painleve Jean • SHT • FRN
COMMENT ON DEVIENT UN ENNEMI DE L'INTERIEUR see **FOLLE DE TOUJANE, LA** • 1975
COMMENT ON DISPERSE LES FOULES • 1903-04 • Blache Alice • FRN
COMMENT ON DORT A PARIS! • 1905 • Blache Alice • FRN

COMMENT PASSER SON PERMIS DE CONDUIRE • 1979 • Derouillat Roger • FRN
COMMENT QU'ELLE EST? • 1960 • Borderie Bernard • FRN • WOMEN ARE LIKE THAT (USA)
COMMENT REUSSIR DANS LA VIE QUAND ON EST CON ET PLEURNICHARD • 1974 • Audiard Michel • FRN • COMMENT REUSSIR QUAND ON EST CON ET PLEURNICHARD
COMMENT REUSSIR EN AMOUR • 1962 • Boisrond Michel • FRN, ITL
COMMENT REUSSIR QUAND ON EST CON ET PLEURNICHARD see **COMMENT REUSSIR DANS LA VIE QUAND ON EST CON ET PLEURNICHARD** • 1974
COMMENT SAVOIR • 1966 • Jutra Claude • DOC • CND • KNOWING TO LEARN
COMMENT SE DIVERTIR QUAND ON EST COCU MAIS INTELLIGENT • 1972 • Garnier Pierre-Claude • FRN
COMMENT SE FAIRE REFORMER • 1977 • Clair Philippe • FRN
COMMENT SE FAIRE VIRER DE L'HOSTO • 1977 • Cachoux Georges • FRN • CHOUCHOU DE L'ASILE, LE ○ ADOLPHO ,FILS DU FUHRER
COMMENT SUPPRIMER SON PROCHAIN • 1963 • Pinoteau Jack • FRN
COMMENT TROUVEZ-VOUS MA SOEUR? • 1963 • Boisrond Michel • FRN
COMMENT VIT LE QUEBECOIS? • 1969 • Dansereau Jean • DCS • CND
COMMENT YUKONG DEPLACA LES MONTAGNES • 1976 • Ivens Joris, Loridan Marceline • FRN • HOW YUKONG MOVED THE MOUNTAINS (UKN) ○ JORIS IVEN'S CHINA
COMMERCIAL, THE • 1963 • Tammer Peter • DOC • ASL
COMMERCIAL MEDLEY • 1933 • Jacobs Lewis • USA
COMMERCIAL PIRATES • 1919 • Holbrook John K. • USA
COMMESSA, LA • 1975 • Garrone Riccardo • ITL
COMMIES ARE COMING, THE COMMIES ARE COMING, THE • 1984 • Waggner George • USA
COMMISSAIRE EST BON ENFANT, LE • 1934 • Becker Jacques, Prevert Pierre • FRN
COMMISSAIRE MENE L'ENQUETE, LE • 1965 • Collin Fabien, Delile Jacques • FRN
COMMISSAIRE SAN ANTONIO • 1966 • Lefranc Guy • FRN • SALE TEMPS POUR LES MOUCHES ○ COMMISSARIO SAN ANTONIO -SALE TEMPS POUR LES MOUCHES
COMMISSAIRE X TRAQUE LES CHIENS VERTS (FRN) see **KOMMISSAR X -DREI GRUNE HUNDE** • 1967
COMMISSAR • 1967 • Askoldov Alexander • USS
COMMISSAR EXTRAORDINARY see **CHREZVICHAINI KOMMISSAR** • 1971
COMMISSAR OF LIGHT, THE see **KOMISARI I DRITES** • 1966
COMMISSARIATO DI NOTTURNA • 1973 • Leoni Guido • ITL
COMMISSARIO, IL • 1962 • Comencini Luigi • ITL
COMMISSARIO DI FERRO, IL • 1978 • Massi Stelvio • ITL
COMMISSARIO LE GUEN E IL CASO GRASSOT, IL (ITL) see **TUEUR, LE** • 1972
COMMISSARIO LO GATTO, IL • 1987 • Risi Dino • ITL • CHIEF LO GATTO ○ INSPECTOR LO GATTO
COMMISSARIO PELLISSIER, IL (ITL) see **MAX ET LES FERRAILLEURS** • 1970
COMMISSARIO PEPE, IL • 1969 • Scola Ettore • ITL
COMMISSARIO SAN ANTONIO -SALE TEMPS POUR LES MOUCHES see **COMMISSAIRE SAN ANTONIO** • 1966
COMMISSARIO VERRAZZANO, IL • 1979 • Prosperi Franco • ITL • DEADLY CHASE
COMMISSIONAIRE • 1915 • *A.a.a.* • UKN
COMMISSIONAIRE • 1933 • Dryhurst Edward • UKN
COMMISSIONER MANAGES THE TOWN HALL, THE see **YA TIENE COMISARIO EL PUEBLO** • 1967
COMMISSIONER X -THREE BLUE PANTHERS see **KOMMISSAR X -DREI BLAUE PANTHER** • 1968
COMMISSIONER X -THREE GREEN DOGS see **KOMMISSAR X -DREI GRUNE HUNDE** • 1967
COMMITMENT, THE • 1976 • Grand Richard • USA
COMMITMENTS, THE • 1990 • Parker Alan • IRL
COMMITTED • 1983 • McLaughlin Sheila • USA
COMMITTED • 1988 • Levey William A. • USA
COMMITTEE, THE • 1968 • Jack Del • USA • SESSION WITH THE COMMITTEE, A
COMMITTEE, THE • 1968 • Sykes Peter • UKN
COMMITTEE OF NINETEEN see **KOMITET DEVYATNADTSATI** • 1972
COMMITTEE OF THE NINETEEN see **KOMITET DEVYATNADTSATI** • 1972
COMMITTEE ON CREDENTIALS, THE • 1916 • Carey Harry • SHT • USA
COMMITTEE ON CREDENTIALS, THE • 1922 • Marshall George • SHT • USA
COMMON AFTERNOON see **DUPAAMIAZA OBISNUITA** • 1968
COMMON CAUSE • 1943 • Cass Henry • DCS • UKN
COMMON CAUSE, THE • 1918 • Blackton J. Stuart • USA
COMMON CLAY • 1919 • Fitzmaurice George • USA
COMMON CLAY • 1930 • Fleming Victor • USA
COMMON ENEMY, THE • 1910 • Turner Otis • USA
COMMON GRAVE see **FOSA COMUN**
COMMON GROUND, THE • 1916 • De Mille William C. • USA
COMMON GROUND, THE (UKN) see **FRISCO JENNY** • 1933
COMMON LAW, THE • 1916 • Capellani Albert • USA
COMMON LAW, THE • 1923 • Archainbaud George • USA
COMMON LAW, THE • 1931 • Stein Paul L. • USA
COMMON-LAW CABIN see **HOW MUCH LOVING DOES A NORMAL COUPLE NEED?** • 1967
COMMON LAW CABIN! see **HOW MUCH LOVING DOES A NORMAL COUPLE NEED?** • 1967
COMMON LAW WIFE • 1963 • Sayers Eric • USA
COMMON LEVEL, A • 1920 • King Burton L. • USA
COMMON MISTAKE, A • 1914 • *Domino* • USA
COMMON PROBLEMS • 1983 • Ranieri Nik • ANS • CND
COMMON PROPERTY • 1919 • Powell Paul, Dowlan William C. • USA
COMMON SCENTS • 1962 • Hanna William, Barbera Joseph • ANS • USA
COMMON SENSE • 1920 • Chaudet Louis W. • USA
COMMON SENSE BRACKETT • 1916 • *Frederick William* • USA
COMMON SIN, THE • 1917 • Gaskill Charles L. • SHT • USA
COMMON SIN, THE • 1920 • King Burton L. • USA
COMMON SPRING see **HABITUAL SPRING, A** • 1962
COMMON TOUCH, THE • 1941 • Baxter John • UKN
COMMONWEALTH, THE • 1967 • Batchelor Joy • ANS • UKN
COMMOTION see **KHATABALA** • 1971
COMMOTION see **PEREPOLOKH** • 1976
COMMOTION ON THE OCEAN • 1956 • White Jules • SHT • USA
COMMUNAL ORGANIZATION see **COMANDOS COMUNALES** • 1972
COMMUNALE, LA • 1965 • L'Hote Jean • FRN
COMMUNAUTE JUIVE DE MONTREAL, LA • 1957 • Dansereau Fernand • DCS • CND
COMMUNE see **GROMADA** • 1950
COMMUNE, A • 1954 • Totwen Ewa, Totwen Olga • ANM • PLN
COMMUNE, LA • 1967 • Desvilles, Darribehaude • SHT • FRN
COMMUNE, LA • 1967 • Rachedi Ahmed • SHT • ALG
COMMUNE, THE • 1970 • *Harry Robert* • USA
COMMUNE DE PARIS, LA • 1951 • Menegoz Robert • SHT • FRN
COMMUNE EFFORT, A • 1953 • Totwen Olga • ANM • PLN
COMMUNICATION • 1970 • Lanitis George • DCS • GRC
COMMUNICATION, LA • 1976 • Godard Jean-Luc • MTV • FRN • 6 x 2: SUR ET SOUS LA COMMUNICATION
COMMUNICATION A 13 ANS • 1970 • Moreau Michel • DCS • CND
COMMUNICATIONS • 1969 • Godard Jean-Luc • FRN
COMMUNICATIONS PRIMER • 1953 • Eames Charles, Eames Ray • SHT • USA
COMMUNION • 1989 • Mora Philippe • UKN
COMMUNION see **ALICE, SWEET ALICE** • 1977
COMMUNION SOLENNELLE, LA • 1977 • Feret Rene • FRN • SOLEMN COMMUNION
COMMUNIQUE, LE • 1970 • Laskri Amar • SHT • ALG
COMMUNIST, THE see **KOMMUNIST** • 1957
COMMUNIST PARTY CONGRESS A ARLES • 1938 • Becker Jacques • DCS • FRN
COMMUNISTS see **KOMMUNISTI** • 1975
COMMUNITY • 1947 • Zils Paul • IND
COMMUNITY, THE see **GROMADA** • 1950
COMMUNITY BUILDER • 1968 • Coward Roger • UKN
COMMUNITY HEALTH REPRESENTATIVE, THE • 1981 • von Puttkamer Peter • DOC • CND
COMMUNITY LIFE • 1936 • Field Mary • UKN
COMMUNITY RESPONSIBILITIES • 1955 • Parker Gudrun • CND
COMMUNITY SING • 1938 • Lamont Charles • SHS • USA
COMMUTED SENTENCE, THE • 1915 • *Cooke Ethyle* • USA
COMMUTER, THE • 1967 • Norland Tom M. • UKN
COMMUTER GAME • 1969 • Kamiel Fred • USA
COMMUTER HUSBANDS • 1972 • Ford Derek • UKN • SEX GAMES
COMMUTER KIND OF LOVE, A see **KJAERLEIKENS FERJEREISER** • 1979
COMMUTING • 1917 • Jackson Harry • SHT • USA
COMMUTORS, THE • 1915 • Fitzmaurice George • USA
COMMUTOR'S CAT, THE • 1913 • *Thanhouser* • USA
COMMUTOR'S WIFE, THE • 1912 • *Cooper Bigelow* • USA
COMMY, THE CANVASSER • 1911 • *Essanay* • USA
COMO A INDIA RECEBE O SEU GOVERNADOR-GERAL • 1958 • Spiguel Miguel • SHT • PRT
COMO CASARSE CON UN MILLONARIO see **ESTRATEGIA MATRIMONIO** • 1966
COMO CASARSE EN SIETE DIAS • 1969 • Fernan-Gomez Fernando • SPN
COMO DESTRUIR AL MAS CELEBRE AGENTE DEL MUNDO • 1973 • *Films Ariane* • MXC
COMO DOS GOTAS DE AGUA • 1963 • Amadori Luis Cesar • SPN
COMO ERA GOSTOSO O MEU FRANCES • 1971 • dos Santos Nelson Pereira • BRZ • HOW TASTY WAS MY LITTLE FRENCHMAN ○ MY FRENCHMAN WAS VERY TASTY ○ COMME IL EST BON MON FRANCAIS ○ QU'IL ETAIT BON MON PETIT FRANCAIS
COMO ESTA EL SERVICIO! • 1968 • Ozores Mariano • SPN • HOW THE SERVICE IS!
COMO HAY GENTE SINVERGUENZA • 1971 • *Prod. Film Re-Al* • MXC
COMO LA PROPRIA TIERRA • 1975 • *Priego Alfonso Rosas* • MXC
COMO LA TIERRA • 1953 • Hurtado Alfredo • SPN
COMO LA VIDA MISMA • 1985 • Casaus Victor • CUB • LIKE LIFE ITSELF
COMO LE FOGLIE • 1916 • Righelli Gennaro • ITL
COMO MATAR A PAPA SIN HACERLE DANO • 1974 • Fernandez Ramon • SPN
COMO MATAR UM PLAY-BOY • 1968 • Christensen Carlos Hugo • BRZ • HOW TO MURDER A PLAYBOY ○ HOW TO KILL A PLAYBOY
COMO MATAR UMA SOGRA • 1980 • Correa Luis De Miranda • BRZ • HOW TO KILL A MOTHER-IN-LAW
COMO MEXICO NO HAY DOS! • 1944 • Orellana Carlos • MXC
COMO NACE UNA FAMILIA? • 1970 • Delgado Cruz • SHT • SPN
COMO OBTER BATATA-SEMENTE • 1947 • Coelho Jose Adolfo • SHT • PRT
COMO PESCAR MARIDO • 1966 • Crevenna Alfredo B. • MXC
COMO, PORQUE Y PARA QUE SE ASESINA A UN GENERAL? • 1971 • Alvarez Santiago • CUB • HOW, WHY AND FOR WHAT IS A GENERAL ASSASSINATED
COMO SE COMBATEM AS PRAGAS DOS LARANJAIS • 1936 • Coelho Jose Adolfo • SHT • PRT
COMO SE HACE UNA MAPA • 1978 • Lovera Lester • DOC • VNZ • HOW A MAP IS MADE
COMO SEDUCIR A UNA MUJER • 1967 • Alventosa Ricardo • ARG • HOW TO SEDUCE A WOMAN
COMO SOIS LA MUJERES • 1968 • Lazaga Pedro • SPN • HOW YOU WOMEN ARE
COMO SUCEDIO • 1974 • Cordido Ivork • DOC • VNZ • HOW IT HAPPENED
COMO TE AMO! • 1966 • Iglesias Miguel • SPN, ITL • DIO COME TI AMO! (ITL)
COMO TODAS LAS MADRES • 1944 • Soler Fernando • MXC
COMO TU LO SONASTE • 1946 • Demare Lucas • ARG
COMO TU NINGUNA • 1946 • Ratti Roberto • MXC
COMO UN PAJARO • 1969 • Settimo M. • ANS • SPN • LIKE A BIRD
COMO YO NO HAY DOS • 1952 • Land Kurt • ARG
COMO YO TE QUERIA • 1944 • Sevilla Raphael J. • MXC
COMOARA DE CA VADIL VECHI • 1963 • Iliu Victor • RMN • TREASURE AT VADUL VECHI, THE
COMPACT, THE • 1912 • Golden Joseph A. • USA
COMPACT OF MATURITY see **CYROGRAF DOJRZALOSCI** • 1967
COMPACT WITH DEATH, A see **DARBUJAN A PANDRHOLA** • 1960
COMPADECE AL DELINCUENTE see **VOLVER A VIVIR** • 1956
COMPADECIDA, A • 1969 • Joanas George • BRZ • OUR LADY OF COMPASSION ○ ROGUE'S TRIAL, THE
COMPADRE MAS PADRE, EL • 1975 • *Filmicas Agrasanchez* • MXC
COMPADRE MENDOZA, EL • 1933 • de Fuentes Fernando • MXC • MY FRIEND MENDOZA ○ GODFATHER MENDOZA
COMPAGNA DI BANCO, LA • 1977 • Laurenti Mariano • ITL
COMPAGNE NUDE • 1978 • Pischiutta Bruno • ITL
COMPAGNES DE LA NUIT, LES • 1953 • Habib Ralph • FRN • COMPANIONS OF THE NIGHT
COMPAGNI DI SCUOLA • 1988 • Verdone Carlo • ITL • SCHOOLMATES
COMPAGNI, I • 1963 • Monicelli Mario • ITL, FRN, YGS • CAMARADES, LES (FRN) ○ ORGANIZER, THE (USA) ○ STRIKERS, THE
COMPAGNIA DEI MATTI, LA • 1928 • Almirante Mario • ITL • COMPAGNIE DES FOUS, LA
COMPAGNIA DEI MATTI, LA see **SE NON SON MATTI NO LI VOGLIAMO** • 1941
COMPAGNIA DELLA TEPPA, LA • 1941 • D'Errico Corrado • ITL
COMPAGNIE DES FOUS, LA see **COMPAGNIA DEI MATTI, LA** • 1928
COMPAGNO DI VIAGGIO • 1976 • Bernardi Romano • ITL
COMPAGNO DON CAMILLO, IL • 1965 • Comencini Luigi • ITL, FRN, FRG • DON CAMILLO EN RUSSIE (FRN)
COMPAGNON INDESIRABLE, LE • 1973 • Enrico Robert • FRN
COMPAGNONS DE LA GLOIRE, LES • 1945 • Ciampi Yves • FRN
COMPAGNONS DE LA MARGUERITE, LES • 1967 • Mocky Jean-Pierre • FRN, ITL • ORDER OF THE DAISY (UKN)
COMPAGNONS DE VOYAGE EMCOMBRANTS • 1903 • Blache Alice • FRN
COMPANERAS AND COMPANEROS • 1970 • Stone David C., Stone Barbara, Mekas Adolfas • DOC • USA
COMPANERO • 1975 • Smith Martin • DOC • UKN
COMPANERO AUGUSTO • 1976 • Cordido Enver • VNZ • COMRADE AUGUSTO
COMPANERO DE VIAJE • 1977 • de la Cerda Clemente • VNZ • TRAVELLING COMPANION
COMPANERO PRESIDENTE • 1971 • Littin Miguel • DOC • CHL, MXC • COMRADE PRESIDENT
COMPANEROS see **VAMOS A MATAR COMPANEROS!** • 1970
COMPANEROS! (USA) see **VAMOS A MATAR COMPANEROS!** • 1970
COMPANION see **SAATHI** • 1968
COMPANION, THE • 1976 • Hood Randall • USA
COMPANIONATE MARRIAGE, THE • 1928 • Kenton Erle C. • USA • JAZZ BRIDE, THE (UKN)
COMPANIONATE SERVICE • 1928 • Lamont Charles • SHT • USA
COMPANIONS IN NIGHTMARE • 1968 • Lloyd Norman • TVM • USA
COMPANIONS OF LOVE see **IRO NO MICHIZURE** • 1967
COMPANIONS OF THE NIGHT see **COMPAGNES DE LA NUIT, LES** • 1953
COMPANY • 1919 • Harvey John Joseph • SHT • USA
COMPANY D TO THE RESCUE • 1910 • *Bison* • USA
COMPANY EXECUTIVES see **SHASO** • 1989
COMPANY LIMITED see **SEEMABADHA** • 1972
COMPANY OF COWARDS see **ADVANCE TO THE REAR** • 1964
COMPANY OF FOOLS • 1966 • Duffell Peter • UKN
COMPANY OF KILLERS • 1968 • Thorpe Jerry • USA • PROTECTORS, THE ○ HIT TEAM, THE
COMPANY OF THE BLACK FEATHER, THE see **DRUZINA CERNEHO PERA** • 1973
COMPANY OF WOLVES, THE • 1984 • Jordan Neil • UKN
COMPANY PARDONS A FIT OF MADNESS, THE see **EMPRESA PERDONA UN MOMENTO DE LOCURA, LA** • 1977
COMPANY SHE KEEPS, THE • 1951 • Cromwell John • USA • WALL OUTSIDE, THE
COMPANYS, PROCES A CATALUNYA • 1979 • Forn Josep Maria • SPN • COMPANYS, TRIAL AT CATALONIA
COMPANYS, TRIAL AT CATALONIA see **COMPANYS, PROCES A CATALUNYA** • 1979
COMPARAISONS: QUATRE FAMILLES • 1959 • Giraldeau Jacques • DCS • CND
COMPARISON OF HEIGHTS see **TAKEKURABE** • 1955
COMPARTIMENT DE DAMES SEULES • 1934 • Christian-Jaque • FRN • LADIES ONLY
COMPARTIMENTS TUEURS • 1965 • Costa-Gavras • FRN • SLEEPING CAR MURDERS, THE
COMPASS ROSE, THE see **ROSA DE LOS VIENTOS, LA** • 1981
COMPASSION • 1927 • Adamson Victor, MacGregor Norval • USA
COMPELLED • 1960 • Herrington Ramsey • UKN
COMPELLED TO BE A MAGICIAN see **MAGO PER FORZA** • 1952
COMPENSATION • 1915 • *Ideal* • USA
COMPERES, LES • 1983 • Veber Francis • FRN
COMPETITION • Damiano Gerard • USA
COMPETITION • 1915 • Eason B. Reeves • USA
COMPETITION • 1963 • Kidawa Janusz • DOC • PLN
COMPETITION see **KONKURS** • 1963
COMPETITION, THE • 1980 • Oliansky Joel • USA
COMPETITORS, THE • 1970 • Mendoza Joe • DCS • UKN
COMPETITORS, THE see **ZAWODNICY** • 1964
COMPLAINT • 1990 • Rossenov Ivan • BUL
COMPLAINT see **AGIT** • 1971
COMPLAINTE DU BELUGA, LA • 1990 • Belhumeur Alain • DOC • CND

COMPLEAT BEATLES, THE • 1982 • Montgomery Patrick • DOC
COMPLEAT 'WEIRD AL' YANKOVIC, THE • 1985 • Levey Jay, Weiss Robert K. • USA
COMPLESSI, I • 1965 • Risi Dino, Rossi Franco, D'Amico Luigi Filippo • ITL, FRN • COMPLEXES, LES (FRN) ○ COMPLEXES
COMPLETE CHANGE, A • 1920 • Mannering Cecil • UKN
COMPLETE STATE OF DEATH see **STONE KILLER, THE** • 1973
COMPLETELY AT SEA see **OUT ALL NIGHT** • 1927
COMPLETELY POGUED • 1989 • Magra • DOC • IRL
COMPLEX see **NIGHTMARE AT SHADOW WOODS** • 1987
COMPLEX PLOT ABOUT WOMEN, ALLEYS AND CRIME, A see **COMPLICATO INTRIGO DI DONNE, VICOLI E DELITTI, UN** • 1985
COMPLEXE • 1964 • Obayashi Nobuhiko • JPN
COMPLEXE D'ARTIX, LE • 1960 • Lanoe Henri • SHT • FRN
COMPLEXES see **COMPLESSI, I** • 1965
COMPLEXES, LES (FRN) see **COMPLESSI, I** • 1965
COMPLICATED CAMPAIGN, A • 1912 • *Myers Harry* • USA
COMPLICATED GIRL, A (UKN) see **RAGAZZA PIUTTOSTA COMPLICATA, UNA** • 1968
COMPLICATED INTRIGUE OF BACK ALLEYS AND CRIME see **COMPLICATO INTRIGO DI DONNE, VICOLI E DELITTI, UN** • 1985
COMPLICATO INTRIGO DI DONNE, VICOLI E DELITTI, UN • 1985 • Wertmuller Lina • ITL • COMPLEX PLOT ABOUT WOMEN, ALLEYS AND CRIME, A ○ CAMORRA: THE NAPLES CONNECTION ○ COMPLICATED INTRIGUE OF BACK ALLEYS AND CRIME ○ CAMORRA ○ MAMA SANTISSIMA ○ NAPLES CONNECTION, THE
COMPLICE, LA • 1920 • Pavanelli Livio • ITL
COMPLICE, LA • 1932 • Guarino Joseph • FRN • ENTRE DEUX FORCES
COMPLICE, LA • 1964 • Cardona Rene Jr. • MXC, ARG
COMPLIMENTS OF MR. FLOW see **MISTER FLOW** • 1936
COMPLIMENTS OF THE SEASON • 1918 • Miller Ashley • SHT • USA
COMPLOT see **MUAMARA** • 1953
COMPLOT, LE • 1972 • Gainville Rene • FRN, ITL, SPN
COMPLOT DELS ANELLS, EL • 1987 • Bellmunt Francisco • SPN • CONSPIRACY OF THE RINGS
COMPLOT MONGOL, EL • 1976 • Eceiza Antonio • MXC • MONGOLIAN CONSPIRACY, THE
COMPLOT PETROLEO: LA CABEZA DE LA HIDRA • 1980 • Leduc Paul • MXC • OIL CONSPIRACY, THE
COMPO • 1988 • Buesst Nigel • ASL
COMPOSERS U.S.A.: THE AVANT GARDE • 1966 • Macartney-Filgate Terence • DOC • USA
COMPOSITEUR TOQUE, LE • 1905 • Melies Georges • FRN • CRAZY COMPOSER, A (USA)
COMPOSITEURS ET CHANSONS DE PARIS • 1947-51 • Verneuil Henri • SHT • FRN
COMPOSITION CLASS see **TSUZURIKATA KYOSHITSU** • 1938
COMPOSITION IN BLUE see **KOMPOSITION IN BLAU** • 1935
COMPOSITION IN PAINTING • 1961 • Takacs Gabor • DOC • HNG
COMPRESSED AIR • 1915 • *Flamingo* • USA
COMPRESSED HARE • 1961 • Jones Charles M. • ANS • USA
COMPROMESSO EROTICO, IL • 1977 • Bergonzelli Sergio • ITL • MENAGE A QUATTRO
COMPROMIS, HET • 1968 • Bregstein Philo • NTH • COMPROMISE, THE ○ WITHIN BOUNDS
COMPROMIS, LE • 1978 • Zerbib Christian • BLG, FRN
COMPROMISE • 1925 • Crosland Alan • USA
COMPROMISE • 1968 • Dansereau Mireille • SHT • UKN
COMPROMISE see **KOMPROMIS** • 1972
COMPROMISE see **COMPROMISSION, LA** • 1986
COMPROMISE, A • 1912 • *Burns Robert* • USA
COMPROMISE, THE see **COMPROMIS, HET** • 1968
COMPROMISE, THE see **COMPROMISO, EL** • 1989
COMPROMISED • 1931 • Adolfi John G. • USA • WE THREE (UKN)
COMPROMISED see **LILY OF THE DUST** • 1924
COMPROMISED BY A KEY • 1910 • Coleby A. E.? • UKN
COMPROMISED (UKN) see **SOPHOMORE, THE** • 1929
COMPROMISED! (USA) see **COMPROMISING DAPHNE** • 1930
COMPROMISING COMPLICATION, A • 1913 • Henderson Dell • USA
COMPROMISING DAPHNE • 1930 • Bentley Thomas • UKN • COMPROMISED! (USA)
COMPROMISING FABLE see **BAJKA KNOMPRMISNI** • 1959
COMPROMISING POSITIONS • 1985 • Perry Frank • USA
COMPROMISO, EL • 1989 • Siso Roberto • VNZ • COMPROMISE, THE
COMPROMISSION, LA • 1986 • Lahalolo Latif • MRC • COMPROMISE
COMPTES A REBOURS • 1970 • Pigaut Roger • FRN, ITL • CONTO ALLA ROVESCIA (ITL)
COMPTESSE DODDY • 1919 • Jacoby Georg • FRG
COMPULSION • 1959 • Fleischer Richard • USA
COMPULSORY HUSBAND, THE • 1930 • Banks Monty, Lachman Harry • UKN
COMPULSORY INSURANCE • 1912 • Coleby A. E. • UKN
COMPULSORY WIFE, THE • 1937 • Woods Arthur • UKN
COMPUTER, THE see **ROBOTER, DER** • 1969
COMPUTER CENTRE, THE • 1972 • Weir Peter • SHT • ASL
COMPUTER FREE-FOR-ALL (USA) see **BUCHAMUKURE DAIHAKKEN** • 1969
COMPUTER GAME • 1960 • *Kirt Films International* • USA
COMPUTER GENERATED BALLET, A • Noll Michael • USA
COMPUTER GENERATION • 1973 • Vanderbeek Stan • USA
COMPUTER GHOSTS • 1987 • Stewart Rob • ASL
COMPUTER GLOSSARY, A • 1967 • Eames Charles, Eames Ray • SHT • USA
COMPUTER KID, THE see **WHERE'S WILLIE?** • 1978
COMPUTER KILLERS (USA) see **HORROR HOSPITAL** • 1973
COMPUTER WIZARD see **WHERE'S WILLIE?** • 1978
COMPUTER WORE TENNIS SHOES, THE • 1970 • Butler Robert • USA
COMPUTERCIDE • 1982 • Lewis Robert Michael • TVM • USA • FINAL EYE, THE
COMPUTERS see **KOMPUTERY** • 1967
COMRADE ABRAM • 1919 • Rasumny Alexander • SHT • USS
COMRADE AUGUSTO see **COMPANERO AUGUSTO** • 1976
COMRADE JOHN • 1915 • Hunter T. Hayes • USA
COMRADE KITTY • 1915 • *Johnson Arthur* • USA
COMRADE PRESIDENT see **COMPANERO PRESIDENTE** • 1971
COMRADE X • 1940 • Vidor King • USA
COMRADES • 1911 • Sennett Mack • USA
COMRADES • 1913 • *Dragon* • USA
COMRADES • 1913 • *Nestor* • USA
COMRADES • 1915 • Sennett Mack • USA
COMRADES • 1916 • *Burns Robert* • USA
COMRADES • 1921 • Wynn George • SHT • UKN
COMRADES • 1928 • Wheeler Cliff • USA
COMRADES • 1987 • Douglas Bill • UKN
COMRADES AT SEA (USA) see **KAMERADEN AUF SEE** • 1938
COMRADES! DON'T PUT UP WITH IT, DON'T ALLOW IT! see **EMBEREK! NE ENGEDJETEK!** • 1954
COMRADES IN ARMS see **COMRADESHIP** • 1919
COMRADES IN UNIFORM see **KAMRATER I VAPENROCKEN** • 1938
COMRADES OF 1918 see **WESTFRONT 1918** • 1930
COMRADES: OR, TWO LADS AND A LASS • 1910 • Aylott Dave • UKN
COMRADES THREE • 1915 • Otto Henry • USA
COMRADE'S TREACHERY, A • 1911 • Martinek H. O. • UKN
COMRADES (UKN) see **BUGLER OF ALGIERS, THE** • 1916
COMRADESHIP • 1919 • Elvey Maurice • UKN • COMRADES IN ARMS
COMRADESHIP see **KAMERADSCHAFT** • 1931
COMTE DE MONTE-CHRISTO, LE see **AMIR AL-INTIQAM** • 1950
COMTE DE MONTE-CRISTO, LE • 1914 • Pouctal Henri • FRN • MONTE CRISTO
COMTE DE MONTE-CRISTO, LE • 1928 • Fescourt Henri • FRN
COMTE DE MONTE-CRISTO, LE • 1942 • Vernay Robert • FRN, ITL • COUNT OF MONTE CRISTO, THE (USA)
COMTE DE MONTE-CRISTO, LE • 1953 • Vernay Robert • FRN, ITL • TESORO DI MONTECRISTO, IL (ITL) ○ COUNT OF MONTE CRISTO, THE
COMTE DE MONTE-CRISTO, LE • 1961 • Autant-Lara Claude • FRN, ITL • STORY OF THE COUNT OF MONTE CRISTO, THE (USA) ○ CONTE DI MONTECRISTO, IL (ITL) ○ STORY OF MONTE CRISTO, THE ○ COUNT OF MONTE CRISTO, THE
COMTE DE MONTE-CRISTO, LE • 1979 • de La Patelliere Denys • MTV • FRN
COMTE OBLIGADO, LE • 1934 • Mathot Leon • FRN
COMTESSE NOIRE, LA • 1912 • Zecca Ferdinand (c/d) • FRN
COMTESSE NOIRE, LA • 1974 • Franco Jesus
COMTESSE PERVERSE, LA • 1973 • Franco Jesus
COMTESSE SARAH • 1912 • Pouctal Henri • FRN
COMTESSE X, LA • 1976 • Rollin Jean • FRN
COMUNE SENSO DEL PUDORE, IL • 1976 • Sordi Alberto • ITL
COMUNIDADE LUSO-BRASILEIRA • 1956 • Ribeiro Antonio Lopes • SHT • PRT
CON ARTISTS, THE (USA) see **BLUFF STORIA DI TRUFFE E DI IMBROGLIONI** • 1976
CON EL CORAZON EN LA MANO • 1988 • Walerstein Mauricio • VNZ • WITH YOUR HEART IN YOUR HAND
CON EL CORAZON SOBRE LA TIERRA • 1985 • Diego Constante • CUB • MY HEART IS THAT LAND
CON EL CULO AL AIRE • 1980 • Mira Carlos • SPN • NAKED BOTTOM ○ BOTTOMS UP
CON EL DEDO EN EL GATILLO • 1940 • Barth-Moglia Luis • ARG
CON EL DEDO EN EL GATILLO • 1958 • Spota Luis • SRL • MXC
CON EL DIABLO EN EL CUERPO • 1954 • de Anda Raul • MXC • IMP IN THE BODY, THE
CON EL VIENTO SOLANO • 1968 • Camus Mario • SPN • WITH THE WIND IN HOT SUNLIGHT
CON ELLA LLEGO EL AMOR • 1969 • Torrado Ramon • SPN
CON.. FUSIONE • 1980 • Natoli Piero • ITL
CON GUSTO A RABIA • 1964 • Ayala Fernando • ARG
"CON" IN ECONOMY, THE • 1919 • Gillstrom Arvid E. • SHT • USA
CON LA DIVISION DEL NORTE see **LOS DE ABAJO** • 1939
CON LA MISMA MONEDA • 1959 • Curiel Federico • MXC
CON LA MORTE ALLE SPALLE (ITL) see **CON LA MUERTE EN LA ESPALDA** • 1967
CON LA MUERTE EN LA ESPALDA • 1967 • Balcazar Alfonso • SPN, ITL • CON LA MORTE ALLE SPALLE (ITL) ○ WITH DEATH ON YOUR BACK
CON LA MUSICA A OTRA PARTE • 1970 • Merino Fernando • SPN
CON LA MUSICA POR DENTRO • 1946 • Gomez Landero Humberto • MXC
CON LA RABBIA AGLI OCCHI • 1976 • Margheriti Antonio • ITL • ANGER IN HIS EYES (UKN) ○ DEATH RAGE ○ INDESIDERABILI, GLI ○ SHADOW OF A KILLER
CON LA SANGRE CALIENTE • 1975 • *Cinema Jalisco* • MXC
CON LA VIDA HICIERON FUEGO • 1957 • Mariscal Ana • SPN
CON LAS MANOS EN LA MASA • 1975 • Coll Joaquin • SPN
CON LAS MUJERES CUBANAS • 1974 • Cortazar Octavio • CUB • WITH THE CUBAN WOMEN
CON LE DONNE NO SI SCHERZA • 1941 • Simonelli Giorgio C. • ITL
CON LOS DORADOS DE VILLA • 1939 • de Anda Raul • MXC
CON LOS HOMBRES AZULES • 1953 • Ardavin Cesar • SHT • SPN
CON LUI CAVALCA LA MORTE • 1967 • Vari Giuseppe • ITL
CON MEN, THE see **BLUFF STORIA DI TRUFFE E DI IMBROGLIONI** • 1976
CON MEN, THE (UKN) see **TEDEUM** • 1972
CON MI MUJER NO PUEDO • 1978 • Dawi Enrique • ARG • WITH MY WIFE I CAN'T
CON MUCHO CARINO • 1977 • Garcia Gerardo • SPN
CON QUALE AMORE, CON QUANTO AMORE • 1970 • Festa Campanile Pasquale • ITL
CON QUIEN ANDAN NUESTRAS HIJAS? • 1955 • Gomez Muriel Emilio • MXC
CON QUIEN ANDAN NUESTROS LOCOS • 1960 • Alazraki Benito • MXC
CON RISPETTO PARLANDO • 1965 • Ciorciolini Marcello • ITL
CON SU AMABLE PERMISO • 1940 • Soler Fernando • MXC
CON, THE CAR CONDUCTOR • 1915 • *Chamberlin Riley* • USA
CON THE SHAUGHRAN • 1912 • *Carbasse Louise* • ASL
CON TODO EL CORAZON • 1951 • Portas Rafael E. • MXC
CON UNAS Y DIENTES • 1977 • Viota Paulino • SPN
CONAN DOYLE • 1967 • Bonniere Rene • DCS • CND
CONAN THE BARBARIAN • 1982 • Milius John • USA
CONAN THE DESTROYER • 1984 • Fleischer Richard • USA
CONCEALED TRUTH, THE • 1915 • Abramson Ivan • USA
CONCEALING A BURGLAR • 1908 • Griffith D. W. • USA
CONCEALMENT (UKN) see **SECRET BRIDE, THE** • 1934
CONCEIT • 1921 • George Burton • USA
CONCEITED STEPHAN • 1957 • Nehrebecki Wladyslaw • ANS • PLN
CONCENTRATE • 1929 • Terry Paul • ANS • USA
CONCENTRATED SHOCK OF WOMEN, A see **ONNA NO TAKOBEYA** • 1968
CONCENTRATIN' KID, THE • 1930 • Rosson Arthur • USA
CONCENTRATION • 1914 • O'Sullivan Tony • USA
CONCENTRATION • 1945 • Hitchcock Alfred • DOC • USA
CONCENTRATION see **JIPNYUM** • 1977
CONCENTRATION, LA • 1968 • Garrel Philippe • FRN
CONCENTRATION CAMP • 1939 • Macheret Alexander • USS
CONCENTRATION CAMP NIS see **LAGER NIS** • 1987
CONCEPT FILMS • 1961-69 • *Halas John (P)* • ASS • UKN
CONCEPTION AND CONTRACEPTION • 1972 • Patel Ishu • ANS • CND
CONCERNING A FIRST COMBAT see **SOBRE UN PRIMER COMBATE** • 1971
CONCERNING LONE see **ANGAENDE LONE** • 1970
CONCERNING LOVE see **DE L'AMOUR** • 1964
CONCERNING MR. MARTIN • 1937 • Kellino Roy • UKN
CONCERT • 1964 • Topouzanov Christo • ANM • BUL
CONCERT see **KONCERT** • 1961
CONCERT, A see **KONSERTTI** • 1963
CONCERT, THE • 1921 • Schertzinger Victor • USA
CONCERT, THE see **KONCERT** • 1962
CONCERT, THE see **KONCERT, A** • 1982
CONCERT A LA COUR see **CHANSON DU SOUVENIR, LA** • 1936
CONCERT AT THE END OF SUMMER see **KONCERT NA KONCI LETA** • 1978
CONCERT FOR BANGLADESH, THE • 1972 • Swimmer Saul • DOC • USA
CONCERT FOR FRYING PAN AND ORCHESTRA • 1976 • Unterberg Hannelore • GDR
CONCERT FOR STUDENTS see **KONCERT PRO STUDENTY** • 1970
CONCERT HALL 62 see **ESTRADA 62** • 1962
CONCERT HALL ROMANCE, A • 1911 • *Powers* • USA
CONCERT KID • 1934 • *Mintz Charles (P)* • ANS • USA
CONCERT MAN, THE • 1982 • Ianzelo Tony • DOC • CND
CONCERT OF INTRIGUE (USA) see **TRADITA** • 1954
CONCERT OF MR. AND MRS. KABAL see **THEATRE DE M. ET MME. KABAL, LE** • 1965
CONCERT OF MONSIEUR AND MADAME KABAL, THE see **THEATRE DE M. ET MME. KABAL, LE** • 1965
CONCERT OF STARS • 1952 • Rappaport Herbert, Ivanovsky Alexander • USS • SONG AND DANCE CONCERT
CONCERT OF THE MASTERS OF UKRAINIAN ART see **KONTSERT MASTEROV UKRAINSKOVO ISKUSSTVA** • 1952
CONCERT OF YOUTH see **ZVENI, NASHA YUNOST!** • 1959
CONCERT PARTY • 1937 • Hopwood R. A. • UKN
CONCERT RESOURCES • 1986 • Skagen Peter • DOC • CND
CONCERT STAGES OF EUROPE, THE • 1984 • Walker Giles • MTV • CND
CONCERT VALSE see **KONSERT-VALS** • 1940
CONCERT WALTZ see **KONSERT-VALS** • 1940
CONCERTISSIMO • Gemes Jozsef • ANM • HNG
CONCERTO • Misonne Claude • ANM • BLG
CONCERTO L. • 1967 • Castanet Alain • FRN
CONCERTO BRANDENBOURGEOIS • 1967 • Reichenbach Francois • SHT • FRN
CONCERTO DE LA PEUR, LA see **DROGUE DU VICE, LA** • 1963
CONCERTO DE L'AUBE • 1960 • Prigent Yves, Ferret Roger • FRN
CONCERTO EROTICA • 1964 • Hastrup Jannik, Quist-Moller Fleming • DNM
CONCERTO FOR AN EXILE see **CONCERTO POUR UN EXILE** • 1968
CONCERTO FOR MACHINE GUN see **KONCERT ZA MASINSKU PUSKU** • 1959
CONCERTO FOR MACHINE-GUNS see **KONSERTO YIA POLIVOLA** • 1967
CONCERTO FOR SUB-MACHINE GUN (USA) see **KONCERT ZA MASINSKU PUSKU** • 1959
CONCERTO FOR THE VIOLIN, A • 1913 • Brabin Charles J. • USA
CONCERTO FOR VIOLIN AND FOUR FEET • 1967 • Vystrcil Frantisek • ANS • CZC
CONCERTO GROSSO • 1964 • Iliesu Mirel • DOC • RMN
CONCERTO IN B-FLAT MINOR • 1942 • Tashlin Frank • ANS • USA
CONCERTO IN X MINOR • 1968 • Kuri Yoji • ANS • JPN
CONCERTO PER MICHELANGELO • 1974 • Rossellini Roberto • MTV • ITL
CONCERTO PER PISTOLA SOLISTA • 1970 • Lupo Michele • ITL • WEEKEND MURDERS, THE (USA)
CONCERTO POUR UN EXILE • 1968 • Ecare Desire • IVC, FRN • CONCERTO FOR AN EXILE
CONCERTO POUR UN HOMME SEUL • 1981 • Nicolas Serge • BLG
CONCERTO POUR VIOLINCELLE • 1962 • Lepeuve Monique • ANM • FRN
CONCERTO (UKN) see **I'VE ALWAYS LOVED YOU** • 1946
CONCHITA • 1954 • Hinrich Hans, Eichhorn Franz • FRG
CONCHITA, THE SPANISH BELLE • 1909 • *Urban-Eclipse* • USA
CONCIERGE, LA • 1900 • Blache Alice • FRN
CONCIERGE, LE • 1973 • Girault Jean • FRN
CONCIERGE REVIENT DE SUITE, LE • 1978 • Wyn Michel • MTV • FRN
CONCIERTO DE BASTON • 1951 • Cahen Enrique • ARG
CONCIERTO EN EL PRADO • 1959 • Lluch Vicente • SPN

CONCIERTO EN LLAMAS • 1971 • Aznar Tomas • SHT • SPN
CONCIERTO MACABRO • Tinayre Daniel • ARG • MACABRE CONCERT
CONCIERTO MAGICO • 1952 • Salvia Rafael J. • SPN
CONCILE D'AMOUR, LE • 1982 • Schroeter Werner • FRG
CONCILIO ECUMENICO VATICANO II • 1963 • Petrucci Antonio • DOC • ITL
CONCITOYENS • 1974 • Heynowski Walter, Scheumann Gerhard • GDR
CONCORDE AFFAIR see **CONCORDE AFFAIRE '79** • 1979
CONCORDE AFFAIRE '79 • 1979 • Deodato Ruggero • ITL • SOS CONCORDE ○ CONCORDE AFFAIR
CONCORDE -AIRPORT '79, THE • 1979 • Rich David Lowell • USA • AIRPORT '80 -THE CONCORDE (UKN)
CONCORDIA I • 1972 • Regnier Michel • DCS • CND
CONCORDIA II • 1972 • Regnier Michel • DCS • CND
CONCORRENTE, IL • 1979 • Sindoni Vittorio • ITL • ANNI STRUGGENTI, GLI ○ BURNING YEARS, THE
CONCOURS DE BEAUTE, UN • 1934 • de Saint-Ogan Alain • ANM • FRN
CONCOURS DE BEBES • 1904 • Blache Alice • FRN
CONCOURS DE BOULES • 1896-97 • Lumiere Louis • FRN
CONCRETE BEAT • 1984 • Butler Robert • TVM • USA
CONCRETE BISQUITS • 1920 • Lyons Eddie, Moran Lee • SHT • USA
CONCRETE COWBOYS, THE • 1979 • Kennedy Burt • TVM • USA
CONCRETE HELL see **TURNING TO STONE** • 1985
CONCRETE JUNGLE • 1988 • Liconti Carlo • CND
CONCRETE JUNGLE, THE • 1983 • Desimone Tom • USA
CONCRETE JUNGLE, THE (USA) see **CRIMINAL, THE** • 1960
CONCRETE PASTURES see **PASLA KONE NA BETONE** • 1982
CONCRETE WILDERNESS see **MEDIUM COOL** • 1969
CONCUBINES, THE see **CHIN-P'ING-MEI** • 1969
CONCURRENCE • 1965 • Georgi Katja • ANM • GDR
CONCURS • 1983 • Pita Dan • RMN • CONTEST
CONCURSA DE BELLEZA • 1957 • Diaz Morales Jose • MXC
CONDAMNE A MORT S'EST ECHAPPE, UN • 1956 • Bresson Robert • FRN • MAN ESCAPED, A (USA) ○ VENT SOUFFLE OU IL VEUT, LE ○ MAN ESCAPED, OR THE WIND BLOWETH WHERE IT LISTETH, A
CONDAMNES, LES • 1947 • Lacombe Georges • FRN • TU M'APPARTIENDRAS TOUJOURS
CONDANNATA SENZA COLPA • 1954 • De Marchi Luigi • ITL • MARIA ZEF
CONDANNETELO! • 1953 • Capuano Luigi • ITL
CONDE, UN • 1970 • Boisset Yves • FRN, ITL • UOMO VENUTO DA CHICAGO, L' (ITL) ○ BLOOD ON MY HANDS (UKN) ○ CONFESSIONS OF A BLOOD COP ○ COP, THE ○ COP, A ○ MURDER GO ROUND ○ PRISON, THE
CONDE DE MARAVILLAS, EL • 1927 • Buchs Jose • SPN
CONDE DE MONTE CRISTO, EL • 1941 • Gavaldon Roberto • MXC
CONDE DE MONTECRISTO, EL • 1941 • Urueta Chano • MXC
CONDE DE MONTECRISTO, EL • 1953 • Klimovsky Leon • SPN
CONDE DRACULA, EL • 1970 • Franco Jesus • SPN, FRG, ITL • COUNT DRACULA (UKN) ○ CONTE DRACULA, IL (ITL) ○ BRAM STOKER'S COUNT DRACULA
CONDE FRANKENHAUSEN, EL see **VAMPIRO SANGRIENTO, EL** • 1962
CONDEMNATION, THE • 1916 • *Karr Darwin* • SHT • USA
CONDEMNATION OF FAUST, THE • 1904 • *Lubin* • USA
CONDEMNATION OF FAUST, THE see **FAUST AUX ENFERS** • 1903
CONDEMNED • 1923 • Rosson Arthur • USA
CONDEMNED • 1929 • Ruggles Wesley • USA • CONDEMNED TO DEVIL'S ISLAND (UKN)
CONDEMNED see **KUNIN NO SHIKEISHU** • 1957
CONDEMNED see **SKAZANY** • 1976
CONDEMNED, THE see **DANSERINDENS KAERLIGHEDSDROM** • 1915
CONDEMNED, THE see **OSUDJENI** • 1987
CONDEMNED BY SOCIETY see **SAMHALLETS DOM** • 1912
CONDEMNED IN ERROR (UKN) see **QUICK ON THE TRIGGER** • 1949
CONDEMNED MEN • 1940 • Beaudine William • USA
CONDEMNED OF ALTONA, THE (USA) see **SEQUESTRATI DI ALTONA, I** • 1962
CONDEMNED TO DEATH • 1911 • *Yankee* • USA
CONDEMNED TO DEATH • 1932 • Forde Walter • UKN • JACK O'LANTERN
CONDEMNED TO DEVIL'S ISLAND (UKN) see **CONDEMNED** • 1929
CONDEMNED TO LIFE see **LIFE FOR RUTH** • 1962
CONDEMNED TO LIVE • 1935 • Strayer Frank • USA
CONDEMNED VILLAGE, THE see **VERURTEILTE DORF, DAS** • 1951
CONDEMNED WOMEN • 1938 • Landers Lew • USA
CONDEMNING CIRCUMSTANCE, THE • 1915 • Reehm George E. • USA
CONDEMNING HAND, THE • 1914 • Vale Travers • USA
CONDENADAS PELO SEXO • 1972 • Porto Ismar • BRZ
CONDENADOS • 1953 • Mur Oti • SPN
CONDENADOS, OS • 1974 • Viano Zelito • BRZ • ALMA
CONDENADOS A MUERTE • 1963 • Portillo Rafael • MXC
CONDENADOS A VIVIR • 1971 • Romero-Marchent Joaquin Luis • SPN
CONDESA MARIA, LA • 1928 • Perojo Benito • SPN
CONDESA MARIA, LA • 1942 • Delgras Gonzalo • SPN
CONDITION OF A FOUNTAIN see **JOTAI NO IZUMI** • 1959
CONDITION OF MAN • 1971 • *Halas John (P)* • ANS • UKN
CONDITION OF MAN, THE • 1971 • *Halas John (P)* • ASS • UKN
CONDITIONED REFLEXES see **MEKHANIKHA GOLOVNOVO MOZGA** • 1926
CONDITIONS DE L'ENSEIGNEMENT A L'ELEMENTAIRE, LES • 1969 • Lamothe Arthur • DCS • CND
CONDITIONS DE L'ENSEIGNEMENT AU SECONDAIRE • 1969 • Lamothe Arthur • SHT • CND
CONDOR • 1986 • Vogel Virgil W. • TVM • USA
CONDOR DE LA LIBERTAD • 1978 • Cosmi Carlo • DOC • VNZ • CONDOR OF LIBERTY
CONDOR OF LIBERTY see **CONDOR DE LA LIBERTAD** • 1978
CONDORES NO ENTIERRAN TODOS LOS DIAS • 1985 • Norden Francisco • CLM • MAN OF PRINCIPLE, A
CONDORMAN • 1981 • Jarrott Charles • UKN
CONDOR'S NEST see **TREASURE OF THE GOLDEN CONDOR** • 1953
CONDOTTIERI • 1937 • Trenker Luis • FRG, ITL • GIOVANNI DE MEDICI -THE LEADER ○ KNIGHTS OF THE BLACK EAGLE
CONDUCT REPORT OF PROFESSOR ISHINAKA see **ISHINAKA SENSEI GYOJOKI** • 1950
CONDUCT REPORT ON PROFESSOR ISHINAWA see **ISHINAKA SENSEI GYOJOKI** • 1950
CONDUCT UNBECOMING • 1975 • Anderson Michael • UKN
CONDUCT UNSATISFACTORY see **KANTOR IDEAL** • 1932
CONDUCTOR 786 • 1912 • *Chamberlin Riley* • USA
CONDUCTOR 1492 • 1924 • Hines Charles, Griffin Frank C. • USA
CONDUCTOR, THE (UKN) see **DYRYGENT** • 1980
CONDUCTOR KATE • 1916 • Stratton Edmund F. • SHT • USA
CONDUCTOR'S CLASSY CHAMPION, THE • 1915 • *Chamberlin Riley* • USA
CONDUCTOR'S COURTSHIP, THE • 1914 • *Kalem* • USA
CONDUISEZ-MOI, MADAME • 1932 • Selpin Herbert • FRN • ANTOINETTE
CONDUITE A GAUCHE • 1961 • Lefranc Guy • FRN
CONE OF SILENCE • 1960 • Frend Charles • UKN • TROUBLE IN THE SKY (USA)
CONEY AS PEACEMAKER • 1913 • Mozart George • UKN
CONEY GETS THE GLAD EYE • 1913 • Mozart George • UKN
CONEY ISLAND • 1905 • Porter Edwin S. • USA
CONEY ISLAND • 1928 • Ince Ralph • USA
CONEY ISLAND • 1943 • Lang Walter • USA
CONEY ISLAND • 1950 • Sherry • SHT • USA
CONEY ISLAND see **FATTY AT CONEY ISLAND** • 1917
CONEY ISLAND NIGHTMARE, A • 1914 • Beggs Lee • USA • JOSIE'S CONEY ISLAND NIGHTMARE
CONEY ISLAND POLICE PATROL • 1904 • *Bitzer Billy (Ph)* • USA
CONEY ISLAND PRINCESS, A • 1916 • Henderson Dell • USA
CONEY, RAGTIMER • 1913 • Mozart George • UKN
CONFECTION • 1962 • Nacif Abdel-Halim • DCS • ALG
CONFEDERACAO, A • 1977 • Teles Luis Galvao • PRT • CONFEDERATION, THE
CONFEDERATE HONEY • 1940 • Freleng Friz • ANS • USA
CONFEDERATE IRONCLAD, THE • 1912 • *Cooper Marian* • USA
CONFEDERATE SPY, THE • 1910 • *Kalem* • USA
CONFEDERATION see **CANADA IS MY PIANO** • 1967
CONFEDERATION, THE see **CONFEDERACAO, A** • 1977
CONFERENCE DE M. JEAN MARCHAND • 1968 • Dansereau Fernand • DCS • CND
CONFERENCE OF ANIMALS • Lind Curt • ANM • FRG
CONFERENCEVILLE • 1982 • Pringle Julian • MTV • ASL
CONFERENCIER DISTRAIT, LE • 1899 • Melies Georges • FRN • ABSENT-MINDED LECTURER (USA)
CONFERENZA CON PROIEZIONI see **IO, IO, IO.. E GLI ALTRI** • 1966
CONFESION • 1940 • Barth-Moglia Luis • ARG
CONFESION TRAGICA • 1918 • Gonzalez Carlos • MXC
CONFESIONAL AMANECER • 1951 • Chenal Pierre • CHL
CONFESS DR. CORDA (USA) see **GESTEHEN SIE DR. CORDA!** • 1958
CONFESSION • 1918 • Franklin Sidney A. • USA
CONFESSION • 1929 • Barrymore Lionel • USA
CONFESSION • 1937 • May Joe • USA • ONE HOUR OF ROMANCE
CONFESSION • 1949 • Gilkison Anthony • UKN
CONFESSION • 1950 • Lehovec Laur • CZC
CONFESSION • 1955 • Hughes Ken • UKN • DEADLIEST SIN, THE (USA)
CONFESSION • 1957 • Leader Anton M. • USA • GRAFT AND CORRUPTION
CONFESSION • 1969 • Yankov Yanko • BUL
CONFESSION, A see **KOKUHAKU** • 1968
CONFESSION, LA see **ITARAF, AL-** • 1964
CONFESSION, THE • 1910 • *Essanay* • USA
CONFESSION, THE • 1915 • Vale Travers • *Ab* • USA
CONFESSION, THE • 1915 • Wilson Frank • UKN
CONFESSION, THE • 1920 • Bracken Bertram • USA
CONFESSION, THE see **QUICK, LET'S GET MARRIED** • 1964
CONFESSION, THE see **AVEU, L'** • 1970
CONFESSION, A CHRONICLE OF ALIENATION • 1988 • Gavrilov Georgy • DOC • USS
CONFESSION A LAURA • 1990 • Osorio Jaime • CLM, CUB, SPN • CONFESSION TO LAURA
CONFESSION AT DEATH'S DOOR, THE see **HOUSE OF MORTAL SIN** • 1975
CONFESSION CORNER see **CONFESSIONS** • 1925
CONFESSION DE MINUIT, LA see **AVENTURES DE SALAVIN, LES** • 1963
CONFESSION OF A YOUNG GIRL -VIRGINITY see **ARU SHOJO NO KOKUHAKU -JUNKETSU** • 1968
CONFESSION OF MADAME BARASTOFF, THE • 1915 • Gaskill Charles L. • USA
CONFESSION TO LAURA see **CONFESSION A LAURA** • 1990
CONFESSIONAL, THE • 1911 • *Champion* • USA
CONFESSIONAL, THE see **HOUSE OF MORTAL SIN** • 1975
CONFESSIONAL MURDERS, THE see **HOUSE OF MORTAL SIN** • 1975
CONFESSIONE • 1942 • Calzavara Flavio • ITL
CONFESSIONE, LA (ITL) see **AVEU, L'** • 1970
CONFESSIONE DI UN COMMISSARIO DI POLIZIA AL PROCURATORE DELLA REPUBBLICA • 1971 • Damiani Damiano • ITL • CONFESSIONS OF A POLICE CAPTAIN (USA) ○ CONFESSIONS OF A POLICE COMMISSIONER TO THE DISTRICT ATTORNEY (UKN)
CONFESSIONI DI UNA DONNA, LE • 1928 • Palermi Amleto • ITL
CONFESSIONI DI WANDA SACHER VON MASOCH, LE see **MASOCH** • 1979
CONFESSIONI SEGRETE DI UN CONVENTO DI CLAUSURA • 1973 • Solvay Paolo • ITL
CONFESSIONS • 1925 • Kellino W. P. • UKN • CONFESSION CORNER
CONFESSIONS FROM A HOLIDAY CAMP • 1977 • Cohen Norman • UKN
CONFESSIONS FROM THE DAVID GALAXY AFFAIR • 1979 • Roe Willy • UKN • SECRETS OF A SEXY GAME ○ STAR SEX
CONFESSIONS OF A BAD GIRL • 1965 • Mahon Barry • USA
CONFESSIONS OF A BIGAMIST see **WARUM HAB ICH BLOSS 2 X JA GESAGT** • 1969
CONFESSIONS OF A BLACK MOTHER SUCCUBA • 1965 • Nelson Robert • SHT • USA
CONFESSIONS OF A BLOOD COP see **CONDE, UN** • 1970
CONFESSIONS OF A BLUE MOVIE STAR • 1982 • Kostenko Andrzej • FRG • BLUE MOVIE STAR
CONFESSIONS OF A CO-ED • 1931 • Murphy Dudley, Burton David • USA • HER DILEMMA (UKN)
CONFESSIONS OF A CONCUBINE see **YUAN WANG AI TA JEN!** • 1976
CONFESSIONS OF A COUNTERSPY (UKN) see **MAN ON A STRING** • 1960
CONFESSIONS OF A DIRTY PAIR see **CONFESSIONS OF A WILD PAIR** • 1967
CONFESSIONS OF A DIVORCEE see **DIVORCEE, THE** • 1969
CONFESSIONS OF A DRIVING INSTRUCTOR • 1976 • Cohen Norman • UKN
CONFESSIONS OF A FRUSTRATED HOUSEWIFE (UKN) see **MOGLIE DI MIO PADRE, LA** • 1976
CONFESSIONS OF A FRUSTRATED WIFE see **MOGLIE DI MIO PADRE, LA** • 1976
CONFESSIONS OF A LADY COP • 1988 • Katzin Lee H. • TVM • USA • POLICE IN ACTION: CONFESSIONS OF A LADY COP
CONFESSIONS OF A LESBOS HONEY • Milonakos Ilias • ITL
CONFESSIONS OF A MALE ESCORT see **OBSZONI TATEN** • 1974
CONFESSIONS OF A MARRIED MAN • 1982 • Gethers Steve • TVM • USA • SUCCESS
CONFESSIONS OF A NAKED VIRGIN see **SCHULMADCHEN-REPORT 11** • 1976
CONFESSIONS OF A NAZI SPY • 1939 • Litvak Anatole • USA
CONFESSIONS OF A POLICE CAPTAIN (USA) see **CONFESSIONE DI UN COMMISSARIO DI POLIZIA AL PROCURATORE DELLA REPUBBLICA** • 1971
CONFESSIONS OF A POLICE COMMISSIONER TO THE DISTRICT ATTORNEY (UKN) see **CONFESSIONE DI UN COMMISSARIO DI POLIZIA AL PROCURATORE DELLA REPUBBLICA** • 1971
CONFESSIONS OF A POP PERFORMER • 1975 • Cohen Norman • UKN
CONFESSIONS OF A PRIVATE SECRETARY • Chen Hao • HKG
CONFESSIONS OF A PROSTITUTE see **IMMORALE, L'** • 1980
CONFESSIONS OF A PSYCHO CAT • 1968 • Stanley Herb • USA
CONFESSIONS OF A QUEEN • 1925 • Sjostrom Victor • USA
CONFESSIONS OF A RIDING MISTRESS • 1977 • Serdaris Vangelis • GRC • LOVE ON A HORSE
CONFESSIONS OF A ROGUE (USA) see **COPIE CONFORME** • 1946
CONFESSIONS OF A SEX KITTEN • 1975 • Sarno Joe • FRG
CONFESSIONS OF A SEX MANIAC • 1975 • Birkinshaw Alan • UKN • MAN WHO COULDN'T GET ENOUGH, THE ○ DESIGN FOR LOVE ○ DESIGN FOR LUST
CONFESSIONS OF A SEX MANIAC (USA) see **RIVELAZIONI DI UN MANIACO SESSUALE AL CAPO DELLA SQUADRA MOBILE** • 1972
CONFESSIONS OF A STARDREAMER • 1978 • Canemaker John • USA
CONFESSIONS OF A STREETWALKER see **DEROBADE, LA** • 1979
CONFESSIONS OF A TEENAGE VIRGIN • 1975 • Hofbauer Ernst • FRG
CONFESSIONS OF A VICE BARON • 1942 • Thew Harvey • USA
CONFESSIONS OF A WAHINE see **MAEVA** • 1961
CONFESSIONS OF A WIFE • 1928 • Kelley Albert • USA
CONFESSIONS OF A WILD PAIR • 1967 • Davis Joe • USA • CONFESSIONS OF A DIRTY PAIR
CONFESSIONS OF A WINDOW CLEANER • 1974 • Guest Val • UKN
CONFESSIONS OF A WINDOW CLEANER see **CHARLEYS NICHTEN** • 1974
CONFESSIONS OF A YOUNG AMERICAN HOUSEWIFE • 1978 • Sarno Joe • FRN, USA • CONFESSIONS OF AN AMERICAN HOUSEWIFE
CONFESSIONS OF AMANS, THE • 1976 • Nava Gregory • USA
CONFESSIONS OF AN AMERICAN HOUSEWIFE see **CONFESSIONS OF A YOUNG AMERICAN HOUSEWIFE** • 1978
CONFESSIONS OF AN ODD-JOB MAN see **UPS AND DOWNS OF A HANDYMAN, THE** • 1975
CONFESSIONS OF AN OPIUM EATER • 1962 • Zugsmith Albert • USA • EVILS OF CHINATOWN (UKN) ○ SECRETS OF A SOUL ○ SOULS FOR SALE
CONFESSIONS OF BOSTON BLACKIE • 1941 • Dmytryk Edward • USA • CONFESSIONS (UKN)
CONFESSIONS OF EMMANUELLE see **EMANUELLE PERCHE VIOLENZA ALLA DONNE?** • 1977
CONFESSIONS OF FELIX KRULL (USA) see **BEKENNTNISSE DES HOCHSTAPLERS FELIX KRULL, DIE** • 1957
CONFESSIONS OF INA KAHR, THE (USA) see **BEKENNTNIS DER INA KAHR, DAS** • 1954
CONFESSIONS OF LOVE • 1985 • Corjos Nicolae • RMN
CONFESSIONS OF LOVING COUPLES see **LIEFDESBEKENTENISSEN** • 1967
CONFESSIONS OF PONGO, THE • 1915 • *Kineto* • UKN
CONFESSIONS OF THE NAUGHTY NYMPHOS see **SEX WITH THE STARS** • 1980
CONFESSIONS OF THE SEX SLAVES see **TANZERINNEN FUR TANGER** • 1977
CONFESSIONS OF TOM HARRIS see **TALE OF THE COCK** • 1966
CONFESSIONS OF WINIFRED WAGNER see **WINIFRED WAGNER UND DIE GESCHICHTEN DES HAUSES WAHNFRIED 1914-75** • 1976

CONFESSIONS, THEORIES, ACTRESSES see **KOKUHAKUTEKI JOYU-RON** • 1971
CONFESSIONS (UKN) see **CONFESSIONS OF BOSTON BLACKIE** • 1941
CONFESSOR • 1973 • Bergman Edward, Soffin Alan • USA
CONFEST BREDBO • 1977 • Patterson Garry • DOC • ASL
CONFETTI • 1927 • Cutts Graham • UKN
CONFETTI see **KONFETTI** • 1936
CONFETTI AL PEPE (ITL) see **DRAGEES AU POIVRE** • 1963
CONFETTI BREAKFAST • 1980 • SAF
CONFIDENCE • 1909 • Griffith D. W. • USA
CONFIDENCE • 1913 • Merwin Bannister • USA
CONFIDENCE • 1922 • Pollard Harry • USA • RAINBOW CHASERS
CONFIDENCE • 1933 • Lantz Walter, Nolan William • ANS • USA
CONFIDENCE • 1989 • Jenkins Michael • ASL, USA
CONFIDENCE see **BIZALOM** • 1980
CONFIDENCE GAME, A • 1915 • *Brockwell Gladys* • USA
CONFIDENCE GIRL • 1952 • Stone Andrew L. • USA
CONFIDENCE MAN, THE • 1924 • Heerman Victor • USA
CONFIDENCE, OR LENIN IN FINLAND see **LUOTTAMUS, ELI LENIN JA SUOMI** • 1975
CONFIDENCE TRICK, THE • 1904 • Fitzhamon Lewin • UKN
CONFIDENCE TRICK, THE • 1926 • Engholm F. W. • UKN
CONFIDENCE TRICKSTERS • 1938 • Delamar Mickey, Kavanagh Denis • UKN
CONFIDENCES • 1955 • Jakubowska Wanda • PLN
CONFIDENCES DE LA NUIT see **AMOUR BLESSE, L'** • 1975
CONFIDENCES DE SANDRA, LES • 1973 • Roy Jean-Claude • FRN
CONFIDENCES D'UN PIANO • 1957 • Leduc • SHT • FRN
CONFIDENCES D'UN TROU MIGNON AU DOCTEUR SEXE • 1981 • Pierson Claude • FRN
CONFIDENCES D'UNE PETITE VICIEUSE • Baudricourt Michel • FRN
CONFIDENCES EROTIQUES D'UN LIT TROP ACCUEILLANT, LES • 1973 • Lemoine Michel • FRN
CONFIDENCES POUR CONFIDENCES • 1978 • Thomas Pascal • FRN • HEART TO HEART (USA)
CONFIDENCES SUR L'OUVRIER • 1978 • Mordillat Gerard, Philibert Nicolas • DOC • FRN
CONFIDENCIAS • 1947 • Mihura Jeronimo • SPN
CONFIDENCIAS • 1982 • Hermosillo Jaime Humberto • MXC • SECRETS
CONFIDENCIAS DE UN MARIDO • 1963 • Prosper Francisco • SPN
CONFIDENCIAS DE UN RULETERO • 1949 • Galindo Alejandro • MXC
CONFIDENCIAS DE UNA SECRETARIA • 1970 • *A.a.mexicanos* • MXC
CONFIDENCIAS MATRIMONIALES • 1958 • Diaz Morales Jose • MXC
CONFIDENT DE CES DAMES, LE • 1959 • Boyer Jean • FRN, ITL • PSICANALISTA PER SIGNORA (ITL)
CONFIDENTIAL • 1935 • Cahn Edward L. • USA
CONFIDENTIAL • 1987 • Pittman Bruce • CND
CONFIDENTIAL AGENT • 1945 • Shumlin Herman • USA
CONFIDENTIAL FILE see **CONFIDENTIAL REPORT** • 1955
CONFIDENTIAL LADIES see **STRICTLY IN CONFIDENCE** • 1933
CONFIDENTIAL LADY • 1939 • Woods Arthur • UKN
CONFIDENTIAL REPORT • 1955 • Welles Orson • UKN, SWT, SPN • MR. ARKADIN ○ CONFIDENTIAL FILE ○ MONSIEUR ARKADIN
CONFIDENTIAL SQUAD see **SLEEPING CITY, THE** ○ 1950
CONFIDENTIALLY CONNIE • 1952 • Buzzell Edward • USA
CONFIDENTIALLY YOURS see **VIVEMENT DIMANCHE** • 1983
CONFIN DE LOS MISERABLES • 1974 • *Churubusco Azteca* • MXC
CONFINES, LOS • 1987 • Valdez Mitl • MXC • LIMITS, THE
CONFIRM OR DENY • 1941 • Mayo Archie, Lang Fritz (U/c) • USA
CONFIRMATION CANDIDATE, THE see **FIRMLING, DER** • 1934
CONFISCATED COUNT, A • 1914 • *Kalem* • USA
CONFISSOES DE FREI ABOBORA, AS • 1970 • Chediak Braz • BRZ
CONFLAGRATION (USA) see **ENJO** • 1958
CONFLICT • 1936 • Howard David • USA
CONFLICT • 1945 • Bernhardt Curtis • USA
CONFLICT • Raizman Yuli • USS
CONFLICT see **WOMAN BETWEEN, THE** • 1931
CONFLICT see **KONFLIKT** • 1937
CONFLICT see **KONFLIKTY** • 1960
CONFLICT see **JUDITH** • 1966
CONFLICT see **SUNGHURSH** • 1968
CONFLICT see **RAZMEDJA** • 1974
CONFLICT, THE • 1911 • *Leonard Marion* • USA
CONFLICT, THE • 1915 • Roach Joseph A. • USA
CONFLICT, THE • 1916 • Daly William Robert • *Selig* • USA
CONFLICT, THE • 1916 • Ince Ralph • *Vitagraph* • USA
CONFLICT, THE • 1921 • Paton Stuart • USA
CONFLICT, THE see **CATHOLICS** • 1973
CONFLICT OF MAGICIANS see **YOJA NO MADEN** • 1956
CONFLICT OF WINGS • 1954 • Eldridge John • UKN • FUSS OVER FEATHERS (USA)
CONFLICT (UKN) see **SWEET MAMA** • 1930
CONFLICTING CONSCIENCE, A • 1916 • Bennett C. D. • SHT • USA
CONFLICTO INESPERADO • 1947 • Gascon Jose • SPN
CONFLICTS • 1967 • Brault Michel • DCS • CND • CONFLITS
CONFLICTS see **KONFLIKTY** • 1960
CONFLICT'S END, THE • 1912 • *Rex* • USA
CONFLIT • 1938 • Moguy Leonide • FRN • SOEURS GARNIER, LES ○ AFFAIR LAFONT, THE
CONFLIT • 1963 • Bouamari Mohamed • SHT • ALG
CONFLIT DALY-MORIN, LE • 1970 • Gagne Jacques • DCS • CND
CONFLITO • 1951 • Padovani Guido • BRZ
CONFLITS see **CONFLICTS** • 1967
CONFLUENCE see **MOHNA** • 1980
CONFORMIST, THE (UKN) see **CONFORMISTA, IL** • 1970
CONFORMISTA, IL • 1970 • Bertolucci Bernardo • ITL, FRN, FRG • CONFORMIST, THE (UKN)
CONFORT ET L'INDIFFERENCE, LE • 1981 • Arcand Denys • CND
CONFRONTATION • 1968 • Dansereau Fernand • DOC • CND
CONFRONTATION • 1970 • Hiller Arthur • SHT • USA
CONFRONTATION, THE (UKN) see **FENYES SZELEK** • 1968
CONFRONTING THE SEA • VTN
CONFUSION see **YASSA MOSSA** • 1953
CONFUSION CONTIDIANA • 1950 • Almendros Nestor, Alea Tomas Gutierrez • SHT • CUB
CONFUSIONS OF A NUTZY SPY • 1942 • McCabe Norman • ANS • USA
CONGA SWING (UKN) see **BLONDIE GOES LATIN** • 1941
CONGAMANIA • 1940 • Ceballos Larry • SHT • USA
CONGIUNTURA, LA • 1965 • Scola Ettore • ITL, FRN
CONGIURA, LA see **INCONFIDENTES, OS** • 1972
CONGIURA DE' PAZZI, LA see **GIULIANO DE' MEDICI** • 1941
CONGIURA DEI BORGIA, LA • 1958 • Racioppi Antonio • ITL
CONGIURA DEI DIECI, LA • 1962 • Bandini Baccio • ITL
CONGIURA DEI FIRSCHI, LA • 1921 • Falena Ugo • ITL
CONGIURA DI SPIE (ITL) see **PEAU D'ESPION** • 1967
CONGO • 1944 • Cauvin Andre • BLG
CONGO BILL • 1948 • Bennet Spencer Gordon, Carr Thomas • SRL • USA
CONGO CROSSING • 1956 • Pevney Joseph • USA
CONGO EXPRESS • 1987 • Gubbels Luk, de Hesselle Armand • BLG
CONGO HELL (UKN) see **SETTE BASCHI ROSSI** • 1968
CONGO JAZZ • 1930 • Harman Hugh, Ising Rudolf • ANS • USA
CONGO MAISIE • 1939 • Potter H. C. • USA
CONGO, TERRE D'EAUX VIVES • 1939 • Cauvin Andre • BLG
CONGO VIVO • 1962 • Bennati Giuseppe • ITL, FRN
CONGOLAISE • 1950 • Dupont Jacques • FRN
CONGORILLA • 1932 • Johnson Martin E. • DOC • USA
CONGRATULATION • 1965 • Ratz Gunter • ANM • GDR
CONGRATULATIONS, IT'S A BOY • 1971 • Graham William A. • TVM • USA
CONGRATULATORY SPEECH see **SHUKUJI** • 1985
CONGREGATION, THE • 1951 • Beaudine William • USA
CONGRES • 1960 • Dansereau Fernand, Dansereau Jean, Dufaux Georges • DOC • CND
CONGRES DES BELLES-MERES, LE • 1954 • Couzinet Emile • FRN
CONGRES DES NATIONS EN CHINE • 1901 • Melies Georges • FRN • CHINA VERSUS ALLIED POWERS
CONGRES DES SOCIETES PHOTOGRAPHIQUES DE FRANCE see **DEBARQUEMENT DU CONGRES DE PHOTOGRAPHIE** • 1895
CONGRES EUCHARISTIQUE DIOCESAIN • 1953 • Pialat Maurice • SHT • FRN
CONGRES EUCHARISTIQUE TRIFLUVIEN • 1941 • Tessier Albert • DCS • CND
CONGRES MARIAL D'OTTAWA • 1950 • Proulx Maurice • DCS • CND
CONGRES QUI DANSE, LE see **CONGRES S'AMUSE, LE** • 1931
CONGRES S'AMUSE, LE • 1931 • Boyer Jean, Charell Erik • FRN • CONGRES QUI DANSE, LE
CONGRES UGET 1964 • 1964 • Khalifa Omar • DCS • TNS
CONGRESO EN SEVILLA • 1955 • Roman Antonio • SPN
CONGRESS DANCES • 1931 • Charell Erik • UKN
CONGRESS DER VAKVEREEINIGINGEN see **NVV CONGRES** • 1929
CONGRESS OF LOVE, THE see **KONGRESS AMUSIERT SICH, DER** • 1966
CONGRESS OF NATIONS • 1900 • Porter Edwin S. • USA
CONIGLIACCIO, LA see **NOTTE PAZZA DEL CONIGLIACCIO, LA** • 1967
CONJUGAL BED, THE (USA) see **STORIA MODERNA -L'APE REGINA, UNA** • 1963
CONJUGAL CABIN see **HOW MUCH LOVING DOES A NORMAL COUPLE NEED?** • 1967
CONJUGAL LOVE • 1972 • Mariani Dacia • ITL
CONJURE WIFE see **NIGHT OF THE EAGLE** • 1962
CONJURE WOMAN, THE • 1926 • Micheaux Oscar • USA
CONJURER see **FOKUSNIK** • 1968
CONJURER, THE • 1900 • Smith G. A. • UKN
CONJURER AND THE BEER, THE • 1900 • Hepworth Cecil M. • UKN
CONJURER MAKING TEN HATS IN SIXTY SECONDS (USA) see **DIX CHAPEAUX EN 60 SECONDES** • 1896
CONJURER WITH A HUNDRED TRICKS, THE (USA) see **HOMME AUX CENT TRUCS, L'** • 1901
CONJURERS, THE • 1922 • Dudley Bernard • UKN
CONJURER'S NEW ASSISTANT, THE • 1915 • *Horseshoe* • UKN
CONJURER'S PUPIL, THE • 1906 • Booth W. R.? • UKN
CONJURER'S RETURN see **KOUZELNIKUV NAVRAT** • 1985
CONJURING A LADY AT ROBERT-HOUDIN'S see **ESCAMOTAGE D'UNE DAME CHEZ ROBERT-HOUDIN** • 1896
CONJURING CLOWN, THE see **PIERROT AND THE DEVIL'S DICE, THE** • 1905
CONJURING COOK, THE • 1915 • *Browne H. A.* • UKN
CONJURING TRAMPS, THE • 1912 • *Cosmopolitan* • UKN
CONJURING TRICKS • 1908 • *Lux* • FRN
CONJURING (USA) see **SEANCE DE PRESTIDIGITATION** • 1896
CONJUROR see **BEAT, THE** • 1987
CONJUROR AND THE BOER, THE • 1900 • *Hepworth Cecil (P)* • UKN
CONJUROR'S HOUSE, THE (UKN) see **CALL OF THE NORTH, THE** • 1921
CONMAN AND THE KUNG FU KID • 1973 • Wu Ma • HKG
CONMAN HARRY AND THE OTHERS • 1979 • Wallace Stephen • SHT • ASL
CONN THE SHAUGHRAUN • 1912 • Mervale Gaston • ASL
CONNAISSANCE DU DESSIN • Calderon Philippe • DCS • FRN
CONNAISSONS-NOUS: BON APPETIT • 1981 • Duckworth Martin • DOC • CND
CONNAISSONS-NOUS: SALUT MONTREAL • 1981 • Duckworth Martin • DOC • CND
CONNECTICUT YANKEE, A • 1931 • Butler David • USA • YANKEE AT KING ARTHUR'S COURT, THE (UKN)
CONNECTICUT YANKEE AT KING ARTHUR'S COURT, A • 1921 • Flynn Emmett J. • USA
CONNECTICUT YANKEE IN KING ARTHUR'S COURT, A • 1948 • Garnett Tay • USA • YANKEE IN KING ARTHUR'S COURT, A (UKN)
CONNECTING BATH, THE • 1916 • *Myers Harry* • USA
CONNECTING LINK, THE • 1915 • Franz Joseph J. • USA
CONNECTING ROOMS • 1969 • Gollings Franklin • UKN
CONNECTION • 1973 • Gries Tom • TVM • USA
CONNECTION, THE • 1962 • Clarke Shirley • USA
CONNECTIONS • 1977 • Burke Martyn • DOC • CND
CONNECTIONS II • 1979 • Burke Martyn • DOC • CND
CONNEE BOSWELL AND ADA LEONARD • 1952 • Cowan Will • SHT • USA
CONNEE BOSWELL AND LES BROWN'S ORCHESTRA • 1950 • Cowan Will • SHT • USA
CONNEMARA AND ITS PONIES • 1971 • Shaw-Smith David • DOC • IRL
CONNEXIONS • 1970 • Curnoe Greg • CND
CONNY UND PETER MACHEN MUSIK • 1960 • Jacobs Werner • FRG
CONOCES LAS SENALES? • 1970 • Delgado Cruz • SHT • SPN
CONOCESA YU MUJER • 1931 • Howard David • USA
CONOZCO A LOS DOS • 1948 • Martinez Solares Gilberto • MXC
CONQUER BY THE CLOCK • 1942 • Vorkapich Slavko • SHT • USA
CONQUERANT DE L'INUTILE, LE • 1967 • Ichac Marcel • DCS • FRN
CONQUERANTS HEROIQUES (FRN) see **LEGGENDA DI ENEA, LA** • 1962
CONQUERANTS SOLITAIRES, LES • 1949 • Vermorel Claude • FRN
CONQUERED CITY (USA) see **CITTA PRIGIONERA, LA** • 1962
CONQUERED DREAM, THE • 1972 • Robinson Richard, McKennirey Mike • CND
CONQUERED HEARTS • 1918 • Grandon Francis J. • USA
CONQUERED PLANET, THE • 1952 • van Gelder Hans, Toonder Marten • ANS • NTH
CONQUERED SEAS see **POKORITELI MORYA** • 1959
CONQUERING CARRIE • 1911 • *Kalem* • USA
CONQUERING CASK, THE • 1910 • Fitzhamon Lewin • UKN
CONQUERING HERO, THE • 1909 • *Lubin* • USA
CONQUERING HERO, THE • 1910 • *Nestor* • USA
CONQUERING HERO, THE • 1916 • Fahrney Milton • USA
CONQUERING HORDE, THE • 1931 • Sloman Edward • USA • STAMPEDE
CONQUERING POWER, THE • 1921 • Ingram Rex • USA
CONQUERING SPACE -THE STORY OF MODERN COMMUNICATIONS • 1934 • Legg Stuart • DOC • UKN
CONQUERING THE WOMAN • 1922 • Vidor King • USA
CONQUERING THE WORLD'S HIGHEST PEAK • 1960 • CHN
CONQUEROR, THE • 1910 • *Vitagraph* • USA
CONQUEROR, THE • 1914 • *Stonehouse Ruth* • USA
CONQUEROR, THE • 1916 • Barker Reginald • USA
CONQUEROR, THE • 1917 • Walsh Raoul • USA
CONQUEROR, THE • 1956 • Powell Dick • USA
CONQUEROR OF ATLANTIS (USA) see **CONQUISTATORE DELL'ATLANTIDA, IL** • 1965
CONQUEROR OF MARACAIBO, THE (UKN) see **CONQUISTATORE DI MARACAIBO, IL** • 1961
CONQUEROR OF OBSCURITY • 1979 • Salem Atef • EGY
CONQUEROR OF THE DESERT (USA) see **FORTUNE CARREE** • 1954
CONQUEROR OF THE ORIENT (USA) see **CONQUISTATORE D'ORIENTE, IL** • 1961
CONQUEROR OF TIME see **KAHER EL ZAMAN** • 1986
CONQUEROR WORM (USA) see **WITCHFINDER GENERAL** • 1968
CONQUERORS, THE • 1932 • Wellman William A. • USA • PIONEER BUILDERS
CONQUERORS OF THE NIGHT • 1933 • Sorokhtin Igor, Minkin Adolph • USS
CONQUERORS OF THE PACIFIC, THE see **CONQUISTADORES DEL PACIFICO, LOS** • 1963
CONQUERORS OF THE PEAKS • 1952 • Rondeli David • USS
CONQUEST • 1928 • Del Ruth Roy • USA
CONQUEST • 1930 • Wright Basil, Grierson John • DOC • UKN
CONQUEST • 1937 • Brown Clarence • USA • MARIE WALEWSKA (UKN)
CONQUEST • 1983 • Fulci Lucio • ITL, SPN
CONQUEST see **AKRAMANA** • 1978
CONQUEST see **SEIHA** • 1983
CONQUEST see **VIJETA** • 1983
CONQUEST, THE see **AKUTO** • 1965
CONQUEST IN THE DRY ZONE see **CONQUEST OF THE DRY ZONE** • 1954
CONQUEST OF A GERM • 1945 • Eldridge John • DOC • UKN
CONQUEST OF A WIFE see **NYOBO SEIFUKU** • 1933
CONQUEST OF ALBANIA, THE see **CONQUISTA DE ALBANIA, LA** • 1983
CONQUEST OF CANAAN, THE • 1916 • *Taliaferro Edith* • USA
CONQUEST OF CANAAN, THE • 1921 • Neill R. William • USA
CONQUEST OF CHEYENNE • 1947 • Springsteen R. G. • USA
CONQUEST OF COCHISE • 1953 • Castle William • USA
CONQUEST OF CONSTANTIA, THE • 1915 • Van Deusen Courtlandt • USA
CONQUEST OF CONSTANTINOPLE • 1954 • Arakon A.
CONQUEST OF EVEREST, THE • 1953 • Stobart Thomas • DOC • UKN
CONQUEST OF LIGHT • 1977 • Marcus Louis • IRL
CONQUEST OF MAN, THE • 1914 • *Valdez Reina* • USA
CONQUEST OF MYCENE (USA) see **ERCOLE CONTRO MOLOCH** • 1964
CONQUEST OF OIL • 1921 • Saville Victor • DOC • UKN
CONQUEST OF PARADISE, THE see **CONQUISTA DEL PARAISO, LA** • 1981
CONQUEST OF SIBERIA • 1908 • Goncharov Vasili M. • USS
CONQUEST OF SPACE • 1955 • Haskin Byron • USA
CONQUEST OF THE AIR • 1936 • Korda Zoltan, Esway Alexander, Taylor Donald, Shaw Alexander, Saunders John M. • UKN
CONQUEST OF THE AIR, THE • 1940 • UKN
CONQUEST OF THE AIR (USA) see **A LA CONQUETE DE L'AIR** • 1901

CONQUEST OF THE AIR (USA) see **A LA CONQUETE DE L'AIR** • 1906
CONQUEST OF THE CITADEL, THE see **EROBERUNG DER ZITADELLE, DIE** • 1976
CONQUEST OF THE DEEPS see **NEPTUNE FACTOR, THE** • 1973
CONQUEST OF THE DRY ZONE • 1954 • Peries Lester James • SHT • SLN • CONQUEST IN THE DRY ZONE
CONQUEST OF THE EARTH • 1980 • Crane Barry, Hayers Sidney, Neufeld Sigmund Jr. • MTV • USA • GALACTICA 3: CONQUEST OF THE EARTH
CONQUEST OF THE MOON see **CONQUISTADOR DE LA LUNA, EL** • 1960
CONQUEST OF THE NORMANS see **NORMANNI, I** • 1962
CONQUEST OF THE PLANET OF THE APES • 1972 • Thompson J. Lee • USA
CONQUEST OF THE POLE, THE see **A LA CONQUETE DU POLE** • 1912
CONQUEST OF THE SOUTH POLE • 1989 • MacKinnon Giles • UKN
CONQUESTS OF MR. ROSE, THE see **EROTIC MR. ROSE, THE** • 1964
CONQUESTS OF PETER THE GREAT, THE see **PYOTR PERVY** • 1937-39
CONQUETE, LA • 1972 • Gagne Jacques • CND
CONQUETE, UNE • 1908 • Linder Max • FRN
CONQUETE CONSTRUCTIVE • 1939 • Tessier Albert • DCS • CND
CONQUETE D'ANGLETERRE, LA • 1935 • Cohl Emile • ANM • FRN
CONQUETE DE L'ANGLETERRE, LA • 1955 • Leenhardt Roger • DCS • FRN
CONQUETE DES GAULES, LA • 1922 • Burel Leonce-Henry • FRN
CONQUETE DU BONHEUR, LA • 1912 • Bourgeois Gerard • FRN
CONQUETE DU POLE, LA see **A LA CONQUETE DU POLE** • 1912
CONQUISTA • 1971 • Syson Michael • UKN
CONQUISTA DE ALBANIA, LA • 1983 • Ungria Alfonso • SPN • CONQUEST OF ALBANIA, THE
CONQUISTA DE EL DORADO, LA • 1965 • Portillo Rafael • MXC
CONQUISTA DEI DIAMANTI • 1916 • Genina Augusto • ITL
CONQUISTA DEL PACIFICO, LA see **CONQUISTADORES DEL PACIFICO, LOS** • 1963
CONQUISTA DEL PARAISO, LA • 1981 • Subiela Eliseo • ARG • CONQUEST OF PARADISE, THE
CONQUISTA DELL'ARIA, LA • 1940 • Marcellini Romolo • ITL
CONQUISTA DELLE GALLIE, LA see **SCHIAVA DI ROMA, LA** • 1961
CONQUISTA DELL'IMPERO, LA • 1973 • Gregoretti Ugo • ITL
CONQUISTADOR, EL • 1946 • Soler Fernando • MXC
CONQUISTADOR DE LA LUNA, EL • 1960 • Gonzalez Rogelio A. • MXC • CLAVILLAZO EN LA LUNA ○ CONQUEST OF THE MOON
CONQUISTADORES, LES • 1975 • Pauly Marco • FRN
CONQUISTADORES DEL PACIFICO, LOS • 1963 • Elorrieta Jose Maria • SPN, ITL • LEGGENDARIO CONQUISTATORE, IL (ITL) ○ CONQUERORS OF THE PACIFIC, THE ○ CONQUISTA DEL PACIFICO, LA
CONQUISTATORE DELL'ATLANTIDA, IL • 1965 • Brescia Alfonso • ITL, EGY • CONQUEROR OF ATLANTIS (USA) ○ KINGDOM OF THE SAND (UKN)
CONQUISTATORE DI CORINTO, IL • 1962 • Costa Mario • ITL, FRN • BATAILLE DE CORINTHE, LA (FRN) ○ CENTURION, THE (USA)
CONQUISTATORE DI MARACAIBO, IL • 1961 • Martin Eugenio • ITL, SPN • CONQUEROR OF MARACAIBO, THE (UKN) ○ CORSARIOS DEL CARIBE, LOS
CONQUISTATORE D'ORIENTE, IL • 1961 • Boccia Tanio • ITL • CONQUEROR OF THE ORIENT (USA)
CONQUISTATORI D'ANIME • 1936 • Chiosso Renzo, Minotti Felice • ITL
CONQUISTATORI, I • 1920 • Maggi Luigi • ITL
CONRACK • 1974 • Ritt Martin • USA
CONRAD IN QUEST OF HIS YOUTH • 1920 • De Mille William C. • USA
CONRAD THE SAILOR • 1942 • Jones Charles M. • ANS • USA
CONSCIENCE • 1905 • *Pathe* • FRN
CONSCIENCE • 1911 • Griffith D. W. • USA
CONSCIENCE • 1913 • *Gem* • USA
CONSCIENCE • 1914 • *Broncho* • USA
CONSCIENCE • 1914 • *Thanhouser* • USA
CONSCIENCE • 1915 • Paton Stuart • USA
CONSCIENCE • 1917 • Bracken Bertram • USA
CONSCIENCE • 1966 • Alexeyev Sergei • USS
CONSCIENCE see **SACHE MIT SCHORRSIEGEL, DIE** • 1928
CONSCIENCE see **SVEDOMI** • 1949
CONSCIENCE AND THE TEMPTRESS • 1914 • MacGregor Norval • USA
CONSCIENCE BAY • 1960 • Vane Norman Thaddeus • UKN
CONSCIENCE DE CHEVAL ROUGE, LA • 1911 • Roudes Gaston • FRN
CONSCIENCE DE PRETRE • 1906 • Blache Alice • FRN
CONSCIENCE FUND, THE • 1913 • Grandon Francis J. • USA
CONSCIENCE OF HASSAN BEY, THE • 1913 • Cabanne W. Christy • USA
CONSCIENCE OF JOHN DAVID, THE • 1916 • *Wilbur Crane* • USA
CONSCIENCE OF JUROR NO.10, THE • 1915 • *Gish Lillian* • USA
CONSCIENCE OR THE BAKER BOY • 1910 • Brooke Van Dyke • USA
CONSCIENCE OR THE CHAMBER OF HORRORS • 1912 • *Tapley Rose* • USA
CONSCIENTIOUS ADOLF see **SAMVETSOMMA ADOLF** • 1936
CONSCIENTIOUS CAROLINE • 1914 • *Edison* • USA
CONSCRIPT, THE see **LOTELING, DE** • 1974
CONSCRIPTION • 1915 • Aylott Dave? • UKN
CONSCRIT, LE • 1918-19 • du Plessis Armand • BLG
CONSCRIT, LE see **LOTELING, DE** • 1974
CONSCRIT DE 1809, LE • 1908 • Bourgeois Gerard • FRN
CONSEGUENZE, LE • 1964 • Capogna Sergio • ITL
CONSEIL D'AMI, UN • 1916 • Feyder Jacques • FRN
CONSEIL DE GUERRE EN SEANCE A RENNES • 1899 • Melies Georges • FRN
CONSEIL DU PIPELET, LE • 1908 • Melies Georges • FRN • TOUR A LA FOIRE, UN ○ UP-TO-DATE CLOTHES CLEANING
CONSENTING ADULTS • 1985 • Cates Gilbert • TVM • USA
CONSEQUENCE, THE see **KONSEQUENZ, DIE** • 1977
CONSEQUENCES • 1918 • Rooke Arthur • UKN
CONSEQUENCES, THE • 1912 • *Brunette Fritzie* • USA
CONSEQUENCES OF JEALOUSY see **SVARTSJUKANS FOLJDER** • 1916
CONSEQUENTLY see **SUTORANG** • 1964
CONSERJE EN CONDIMINIO • 1973 • *Rioma* • MXC
CONSIDER YOUR VERDICT • 1938 • Boulting Roy • UKN
CONSIDERABLE MILK • 1915 • *Heinie & Louie* • USA
CONSIGLIORI, IL • 1973 • De Martino Alberto • ITL, SPN
CONSIGNA: MATAR AL COMDANDANTE EN JEFE • 1972 • Merino Jose Luis • SPN
CONSIGNA: TANGER 67 see **CHEF SCHICKT SEINEN BESTEN MANN, DER** • 1966
CONSOLATION MARRIAGE • 1931 • Sloane Paul • USA • MARRIED IN HASTE (UKN)
CONSOLATION PRIZE • 1979 • Hartman Rivka • SHT • ASL
CONSOLATIONS • 1988 • Elder Bruce • CND
CONSPICUOUS BRAVERY • 1914 • Kellino W. P. • UKN
CONSPIRACION • 1928 • Ojeda Manuel R. • MXC
CONSPIRACY • 1930 • Cabanne W. Christy • USA
CONSPIRACY • 1939 • Landers Lew • USA
CONSPIRACY • 1989 • Barnard Christopher • USA
CONSPIRACY • 1989 • Eggleston Colin • ASL
CONSPIRACY see **BLACK OAK CONSPIRACY** • 1977
CONSPIRACY, A • 1909 • *Tiger* • USA
CONSPIRACY, THE • 1914 • Dwan Allan • USA
CONSPIRACY, THE • 1916 • McRae Henry • USA
CONSPIRACY, THE see **SAZISH** • 1976
CONSPIRACY AGAINST THE KING, A • 1911 • Dawley J. Searle • USA
CONSPIRACY AT THE CHATEAU, THE • 1915 • *Roscoe Albert* • USA
CONSPIRACY CIRCUS -CHICAGO '70 see **CHICAGO 70** • 1970
CONSPIRACY IN TEHERAN see **TEHERAN** • 1947
CONSPIRACY OF HEARTS • 1960 • Thomas Ralph • UKN • ITALY 1943
CONSPIRACY OF LOVE • 1987 • Black Noel • TVM • USA
CONSPIRACY OF PONTIAC, THE • 1910 • Olcott Sidney • USA
CONSPIRACY OF TERROR • 1975 • Moxey John Llewellyn • TVM • USA
CONSPIRACY OF THE AMBASSADORS • 1964 • Barnet Boris • USS
CONSPIRACY OF THE DOOMED see **ZAGOVOR OBRECHENNYKH** • 1950
CONSPIRACY OF THE RINGS see **COMPLOT DELS ANELLS, EL** • 1987
CONSPIRACY: THE TRIAL OF THE CHICAGO 8 • 1987 • Kagan Jeremy Paul • TVM • USA
CONSPIRATION DES DRAPEAUX, LA • 1912 • *Gance Abel* • FRN
CONSPIRATION SOUS HENRI III, UNE • 1906 • Nonguet Lucien • FRN
CONSPIRATOR • 1949 • Saville Victor • UKN, USA
CONSPIRATOR, THE see **HANGYAKUJI** • 1961
CONSPIRATORS, THE • 1909 • Olcott Sidney • USA
CONSPIRATORS, THE • 1914 • *Lockwood Harold* • USA
CONSPIRATORS, THE • 1924 • Hill Sinclair • UKN • BARNET MURDER CASE, THE
CONSPIRATORS, THE • 1944 • Negulesco Jean • USA • GIVE ME THIS WOMAN
CONSPIRATORS, THE see **INCONFIDENTES, OS** • 1972
CONSTABLE, THE • 1940 • Fleischer Dave • ANS • USA
CONSTABLE COPPEM AND THE SPY PERIL • 1914 • Collins Edwin J.? • UKN
CONSTABLE PAULUS'S EASTER BOMB see **POLIS PAULUS PASKASMALL** • 1925
CONSTABLE SMITH AND THE MAGIC BATON • 1912 • Collins Edwin J.? • UKN
CONSTABLE SMITH IN COMMAND • 1912 • Collins Edwin J.? • UKN
CONSTABLE SMITH IN TROUBLE AGAIN • 1912 • Coleby A. E. • UKN
CONSTABLE SMITH ON THE WARPATH • 1912 • Collins Edwin J.? • UKN
CONSTABLE SMITH'S DREAM OF PROMOTION • 1911 • Coleby A. E.? • UKN
CONSTABLE'S CONFUSION, THE • 1911 • Wilson Frank? • UKN
CONSTABLE'S DAUGHTER, THE • 1913 • *Lubin* • USA
CONSTABLE'S DAUGHTER, THE • 1915 • *Harris Joseph* • USA
CONSTABLE'S MOVE, THE • 1923 • Haynes Manning • UKN
CONSTABULE, THE • 1929 • Sennett Mack • SHT • USA
CONSTANCE • 1957 • Alexeieff Alexandre • SHT • FRN
CONSTANCE • 1984 • Morrison Bruce • NZL
CONSTANCE AUX ENFERS • 1964 • Villiers Francois • FRN, SPN • BALCON SOBRE EL INFIERNO, UN (SPN) ○ WEB OF FEAR (USA)
CONSTANS • 1980 • Zanussi Krzysztof • PLN • CONSTANT FACTOR, THE (USA) ○ CONSTANT
CONSTANT see **CONSTANS** • 1980
CONSTANT BEAM see **YONG BUXIOSHI DE DIANBO** • 1958
CONSTANT FACTOR, THE (USA) see **CONSTANS** • 1980
CONSTANT HOT WATER • 1923 • Cooper George A. • UKN
CONSTANT HUSBAND, THE • 1955 • Gilliat Sidney • UKN
CONSTANT NYMPH, THE • 1928 • Brunel Adrian, Dean Basil (U/c) • UKN
CONSTANT NYMPH, THE • 1933 • Dean Basil • UKN
CONSTANT NYMPH, THE • 1943 • Goulding Edmund • USA
CONSTANT WIFE, THE see **FINDEN SIE, DASS CONSTANZE SICH RICHTIG VERHALT?** • 1962
CONSTANT WIFE, THE (UKN) see **CHARMING SINNERS** • 1929
CONSTANT WOMAN, THE • 1933 • Schertzinger Victor • USA • AUCTION IN SOULS
CONSTANTINE AND THE CROSS (USA) see **COSTANTINO IL GRANDE -IN HOC SIGNO VINCES** • 1960
CONSTANTINE THE GREAT see **COSTANTINO IL GRANDE -IN HOC SIGNO VINCES** • 1960
CONSTANTINE THE PHILOSOPHER • 1983 • Stoyanov Georgi • BUL
CONSTANTINO IL GRANDE see **COSTANTINO IL GRANDE -IN HOC SIGNO VINCES** • 1960
CONSTELACIONES • 1980 • Joscowicz Alfredo • MXC • CONSTELLATIONS
CONSTELLATION OF THE VIRGO see **SOUHVEZDI PANNY** • 1966
CONSTELLATION: VIRGO see **SOUHVEZDI PANNY** • 1966
CONSTELLATIONS see **CONSTELACIONES** • 1980
CONSTRUCOES METALICOS • 1954 • Mendes Joao • SHT • PRT
CONSTRUCTION, THE • 1974 • Jakubisko Juraj • CZC
CONSTRUCTION DESIGN see **SZERKEZETTERVEZES** • 1960
CONSTRUCTION DU COMPLEXE OLYMPIQUE • 1976 • Jean Jacques • DOC • CND
CONSTRUCTION GANG • 1970 • *Distripix* • USA
CONSTRUCTOR CADA DIA, COMPANERO • 1982 • Chaskel Pedro • CUB • BUILDING EACH DAY, COMPANERO
CONSTRUIRE EN FEU • 1926 • Autant-Lara Claude • FRN • HOW TO START A FIRE
CONSTRUZIONE MECCHANICHE RIVA • 1956 • Olmi Ermanno • DOC • ITL
CONSUELA see **RIO GUADALQUIVIR** • 1956
CONSUELITA • 1921 • Roberti Roberto Leone • ITL
CONSUELO • 1988 • Vera Luis R. • CHL, SWD
CONSUL AND OTHERS see **KONSUL I INNI** • 1971
CONSUL CROSSES THE ATLANTIC • 1909 • *Urban Trading Co.* • UKN
CONSULTARE A MR. BROWN • 1946 • Ballesteros Pio • SPN
CONSUMER SOCIETY see **KATANALOTIKI KINONIA** • 1971
CONSUMING LOVE • 1911 • *Vitagraph* • USA
CONSUMING PASSIONS • 1988 • Foster Giles • UKN
CONSUMPTION • 1971 • Shapiro Nesya • CND
CONTACT • 1933 • Rotha Paul • DOC • UKN
CONTACT • 1973 • Gaine Michael • USA
CONTACT • 1973 • Halas John, Batchelor Joy • ANS • UKN
CONTACT • 1974 • Zwartjes Frans • SHT • NTH
CONTACT • 1985 • SAF
CONTACT see **CONTRATTO CARNALE** • 1973
CONTACT MAN, THE (UKN) see **ALIAS NICK BEAL** • 1948
CONTACTO EN CARACAS • 1990 • Toledano Philippe • VNZ • CARACAS CONTACT, THE
CONTACTOS • 1984 • Ferreira Leandro • PRT
CONTADINI DEL MARE • 1955 • De Seta Vittorio • ITL • BLUEFIN FURY
CONTADINI MERCANTI E PRINCIPI • 1979 • Giannarelli Ansano • ITL
CONTAGION • 1911 • *Powers* • USA
CONTAGION • 1988 • Zwicky Karl • USA
CONTAGIOUS DISEASE, A • 1911 • Wilson Frank? • UKN
CONTAMINATION see **ALIEN CONTAMINATION** • 1981
CONTE AQUILA, IL • 1956 • Salvini Guido • ITL
CONTE CENTANNI E IL VISCONTE GIOVENTU, IL • 1919 • D'Ambra Lucio • ITL
CONTE DE LA FOLIE ORDINAIRE (FRN) see **STORIE DI ORDINARIA FOLLIA** • 1981
CONTE DE LA GRAND'MERE ET REVE DE L'ENFANT OU AU PAYS DES JOUETS • 1908 • Melies Georges • FRN • GRANDMOTHER'S STORY OR TO THE LAND OF TOYS, A (USA) ○ AU PAYS DES JOUETS
CONTE DE MON VILLAGE • 1946 • Petel Pierre • DCS • CND
CONTE DE NOEL, UN • 1902 • Zecca Ferdinand • FRN • STORY OF CHRISTMAS, A
CONTE DE PRINTEMPS • 1989 • Rohmer Eric • FRN
CONTE DE SUFI, UN see **SUFI TALE, A** • 1977
CONTE DI BRECHARD, IL • 1938 • Bonnard Mario • ITL • COUNT OF BRECHARD, THE (USA)
CONTE DI LUNA, IL • 1943 • Emmer Luciano, Gras Enrico • ITL
CONTE DI MATERA, IL • 1959 • Capuano Luigi • ITL
CONTE DI MONTECRISTO, IL (ITL) see **COMTE DE MONTE-CRISTO, LE** • 1961
CONTE DI SANT'ELMO, IL • 1951 • Brignone Guido • ITL • COUNT OF ST. ELMO, THE (USA)
CONTE DRACULA, IL (ITL) see **CONDE DRACULA, EL** • 1970
CONTE DU VIEUX TALUTE, LE • 1909 • Melies Georges • FRN
CONTE MAX, IL • 1957 • Bianchi Giorgio • ITL, SPN
CONTE TACCHIA, IL • 1983 • Corbucci Sergio • ITL • COUNT TACCHIA
CONTE UGOLINO, IL • 1950 • Freda Riccardo • ITL • IRON SWORDSMAN, THE (USA) ○ CAVALIERE DI FERRO, IL
CONTEBLEU • 1976 • Belanger Fernand • CND
CONTEMPLATIONS, LES • 1964-69 • Rohmer Eric • MTV • FRN
CONTEMPORARIES see **ROWIESNICY** • 1962
CONTEMPORARIES see **ZEITGENOSSEN** • 1983
CONTEMPORARY, THE see **AIKALAINEN** • 1984
CONTEMPORARY DICTIONARY OF LOVE: AGE OF CURIOSITY see **GENDAI AI NO JITEN: SHIRITAI TOSHIGORO** • 1967
CONTEMPORARY HISTORY see **HISTORIA WSPOLCZESNA** • 1961
CONTEMPORARY HORROR see **GENDAI NO KYOGU** • 1967
CONTEMPORARY JEWELRY BOX see **TOSEI TAMATEBAKO** • 1925
CONTEMPORARY MEDICAL SCIENCE ON WOMEN see **GENDAI JOI IGAKU** • 1967
CONTEMPORARY STORY see **HISTORIA WSPOLCZESNA** • 1961
CONTEMPT OF COURT see **NOCE AU VILLAGE, UNE** • 1901
CONTEMPT (USA) see **MEPRIS, LE** • 1963
CONTENDER, THE • 1944 • Newfield Sam • USA
CONTENT • 1920 • Physioc Wray • SHT • USA
CONTENTED WOMAN, A • 1917 • Richmond J. A. • SHT • USA
CONTENTS OF THE SUITCASE, THE • 1913 • *Milford Buss* • USA
CONTES • 1963 • Carlo-Rim • MTV • FRN
CONTES DE LA FONTAINE, LES • 1980 • Benazeraf Jose • FRN • CONTES GALANTS DE JEAN DE LA FONTAINE, LES
CONTES DE L'AMERE LOI, LES • 1975 • Hebert Pierre • ANM • CND

CONTES DES 1000 NEZ, LES • 1986 • Simoneau Guy • MTV • CND
CONTES DES MILLE ET UNE NUITS, LES • 1921 • Tourjansky Victor • FRN • TALES OF A THOUSAND AND ONE NIGHTS, THE (USA)
CONTES GALANTS DE JEAN DE LA FONTAINE, LES see **CONTES DE LA FONTAINE, LES** • 1980
CONTES IMMOREAUX • 1974 • Borowczyk Walerian • FRN • IMMORAL TALES
CONTES PERVERS • 1980 • Deforges Regine • FRN, ITL • TALES OF EROTIC FANTASY ○ PERVERSE TALES ○ EROTIC TALES
CONTESSA AZZURRA, LA • 1960 • Gora Claudio • ITL
CONTESSA CASTIGLIONE, LA • 1942 • Calzavara Flavio • ITL
CONTESSA DI CASTIGLIONE, LA (ITL) see **CASTIGLIONE, LA** • 1953
CONTESSA DI CHALLANT, LA • 1916 • Falena Ugo • ITL
CONTESSA DI PARMA, LA • 1937 • Blasetti Alessandro • ITL • COUNTESS OF PARMA, THE
CONTESSA SARA, LA • 1919 • Roberti Roberto Leone • ITL • COUNTESS SARAH
CONTESSA SCALZA, LA (ITL) see **BAREFOOT CONTESSA, THE** • 1954
CONTEST see **CONCURS** • 1983
CONTEST, THE • 1923 • Fleischer Dave • ANS • USA
CONTEST, THE • 1964 • Mansurov Bulat • USS
CONTEST, THE • 1970 • *Cosmos Films* • USA
CONTEST CRAZY • 1948 • Yates Hal • SHT • USA
CONTEST GIRL (USA) see **BEAUTY JUNGLE, THE** • 1964
CONTESTATION, LA (FRN) see **AMORE E RABBIA** • 1969
CONTESTAZIONE GENERALE • 1970 • Zampa Luigi • ITL
CONTESTO, IL see **CADAVERI ECCELLENTI** • 1976
CONTEXT, THE see **CADAVERI ECCELLENTI** • 1976
CONTIGO A LA DISTANCIA • 1954 • Martinez Solares Gilberto • MXC
CONTINENT IN FLAMES • 1973 • Karmen Roman • DOC • USS
CONTINENTAL ATMOSPHERE (USA) see **ARIA DEL CONTINENTE, L'** • 1935
CONTINENTAL CIRCUS • 1972 • Laperrousaz Jerome • DOC • FRN
CONTINENTAL DIVIDE • 1981 • Apted Michael • USA
CONTINENTAL DRIFT • 1968 • Hoedeman Co • ANS • CND • DERIVE DES CONTINENTS, LES
CONTINENTAL EXPRESS (USA) see **SILENT BATTLE, THE** • 1939
CONTINENTAL GIRL, A • 1915 • Adelman Joseph • USA
CONTINENTAL TWIST, THE see **TWIST ALL NIGHT** • 1962
CONTINENTE DI GHIACCIO, IL • 1975 • Turolla Luigi • ITL • ICE CONTINENT, THE
CONTINENTE PERDUTO • 1955 • Bonzi Leonardo, Craveri Mario, Lavagnino Francesco Angelo, Moser Giorgio, Gras Enrico • DOC • ITL • LOST CONTINENT, THE (USA)
CONTINENTI IN FIAMME • 1956 • Rivelli Cesare • DOC • ITL
CONTINUAR A VIVER • 1977 • Teles Antonio Da Cunha • PRT • GO ON LIVING
CONTINUAVANO A CHIAMARLI.. ER PIU ER MENO • 1972 • Orlandini Giuseppe • ITL
CONTINUAVANO A CHIAMARLI I DUE PILOTI PIU MATTI DEL MONDO • 1972 • Laurenti Mariano • ITL
CONTINUAVANO A CHIAMARLO, TRINITA • 1971 • Clucher E. B. • ITL • TRINITY IS STILL MY NAME (USA) ○ THEY STILL CALL ME TRINITY
CONTINUAVANO A METTERE LO DIAVOLO NE LO INFERNO • 1973 • Albertini Bitto • ITL
CONTINUOUS OBSERVATION • 1955 • Thomson Margaret • SHT • UKN
CONTO ALLA ROVESCIA (ITL) see **COMPTES A REBOURS** • 1970
CONTO E CHIUSO, IL • 1977 • Massi Stelvio • ITL
CONTORTIONIST • 1896 • *Paul R. W.* • UKN
CONTOS EROTICOS • 1980 • Escorel Eduardo, Santos Roberto, de Andrade Joaquim Pedro • BRZ • EROTIC STORIES
CONTOUR CONNECTION, THE • 1983 • Low Colin • DOC • CND
CONTRA LA CORRIENTE • 1936 • Novarro Ramon • MXC
CONTRA LA LEY DE DIOS • 1946 • Fernandez Bustamente Adolfo • MXC
CONTRA LA PARED • 1975 • Fernandez Bernardo • SPN
CONTRA LA RAZON Y POR LA FUERZA • 1973 • Tejeda Carlos Ortiz • MXC • WITHOUT REASON AND BY FORCE
CONTRA VIENTO Y MAREA • 1962 • Gomez Urquiza Zacarias • MXC
CONTRABAND • 1925 • Crosland Alan • USA
CONTRABAND • 1940 • Powell Michael • UKN • BLACKOUT (USA)
CONTRABAND see **LUCK OF A SAILOR, THE** • 1934
CONTRABAND see **FORTY MILLION BUCKS** • 1978
CONTRABAND LOVE • 1931 • Morgan Sidney • UKN
CONTRABAND SPAIN • 1955 • Huntington Lawrence, Salvador Julio • UKN, SPN • CONTRABANDO (SPN) ○ BLACKOUT
CONTRABANDIERI DI SANTA LUCIA, I • 1979 • Brescia Alfonso • ITL
CONTRABANDISTAS DEL CARIBE • 1966 • Orol Juan • MXC, PRC
CONTRABANDO • 1941 • Mendez Fernando • MXC
CONTRABANDO (SPN) see **CONTRABAND SPAIN** • 1955
CONTRACEPTIVE REVOLUTION see **HININ KAKUMEI** • 1967
CONTRACT see **KONTRAKT** • 1980
CONTRACT, THE • 1953 • Mangiamele Giorgio • SHT • ASL
CONTRACT, THE see **SAIGNEE, LA** • 1971
CONTRACT, THE see **MAI-SHEN CH'I** • 1978
CONTRACT, THE (UKN) see **MILANO CALIBRO 9** • 1972
CONTRACT FOR LIFE: THE S.A.D.D. STORY • 1984 • Pevney Joseph • USA
CONTRACT FOR LOVE • 1986 • Wolman Dan • ISR
CONTRACT ON CHERRY STREET • 1977 • Graham William A. • TVM • USA
CONTRACT WITH CUPID, A • 1983 • Noonan Chris • MTV • ASL
CONTRADICTIONS • 1988 • Knaus David • DOC • ASL
CONTRAKT see **KONTRAKT** • 1980
CONTRARY CONDOR • 1944 • King Jack • ANS • USA
CONTRARY SHOES see **CONTREPIED** • 1965
CONTRAS CIRY • 1968 • Diop Djibril • DCS • SNL
CONTRAST see **CONTRASTE** • 1964
CONTRAST, THE • 1926 • Elliott William J. • UKN
CONTRASTE • 1964 • Urchs Wolfgang • ANS • FRG • CONTRAST
CONTRASTES • 1959 • Dewever Jean • FRN
CONTRASTES • 1961 • Camino Jaime • SHT • SPN
CONTRASTS IN RHYTHM • 1948 • Kinney Jack, Luske Hamilton • ANS • USA
CONTRAT, LE • 1973 • Lavoie Richard • SHT • CND
CONTRAT D'AMOUR • 1973 • Dansereau Fernand • SHT • CND
CONTRAT DE TRAVAIL • 1950 • Devlin Bernard • DCS • CND
CONTRATHEMIS • 1941 • Grant Dwinnel • SHT • USA
CONTRATTO, IL • 1970 • Gregoretti Ugo • ITL
CONTRATTO CARNALE • 1973 • Bontempi Giorgio • ITL, GHN • CONTACT
CONTRE CENSURE • 1976 • D'Aix Alain (c/d) • DOC • CND
CONTRE-COEUR • 1978 • Tanner Alain • SWT, FRN
CONTRE COEUR see **MESSIDOR** • 1979
CONTRE-ENQUETE • 1930 • Daumery John • FRN
CONTRE-ENQUETE • 1946 • Faurez Jean • FRN • COUNTER INVESTIGATION (USA)
CONTREBANDIERES, LES • 1968 • Moullet Luc • FRN • SMUGGLERS, THE (USA)
CONTREBANDIERI DEL MARE, I • 1949 • Montero Roberto Bianchi • ITL
CONTREBASSE, LA • 1962 • Fasquel Maurice • SHT • FRN
CONTRECHANT • 1963 • Boissol Claude • SHT • FRN
CONTRECOEUR • 1980 • Noel Jean-Guy • CND
CONTREPIED • 1965 • Otero Manuel • ANS • FRN • CONTRARY SHOES ○ OUT OF STEP
CONTREPOINT • 1964 • Enrico Robert • FRN
CONTRIBUTION see **KONTRYBUCJA** • 1967
CONTRITION • Wurst Charles • SHT • USA
CONTRO LA LEGGE • 1951 • Calzavara Flavio • ITL
CONTRO QUATTRO BANDIERE • 1979 • Lenzi Umberto • ITL
CONTROFIGURA, LA • 1971 • Guerrieri Romolo • ITL
CONTROL • 1920 • Miller Frank • UKN
CONTROL • 1987 • Montaldo Giuliano • TVM • USA, ITL
CONTROL FACTOR • Day Robert • USA
CONTROL OF INMATES • 1964 • Jackson Douglas • DOC • CND
CONTROL ROOM • 1942 • Bell Geoffrey • DOC • UKN
CONTROL YOURSELF • 1925 • Kerr Robert • USA
CONTROLEUR DES CHAMPS-ELYSEES, LE see **RENDEZ-VOUS CHAMPS-ELYSEES** • 1937
CONTROLEUR DES WAGON-LITS, LE (FRN) see **SCHLAFWAGENKONTROLLEUR, DER** • 1935
CONTROLLED HEAT • 1955 • Clarke Douglas, Chambers Jack • UKN
CONTROLLERS, THE • 1920 • Crawford Harold A. • UKN
CONTRONATURA • 1969 • Margheriti Antonio • ITL • UNNATURAL, THE
CONTRONATURA • 1977 • Damiani Amasi • ITL
CONTRORAPINA • 1979 • Margheriti Antonio • ITL, USA • HO TENTATO DI VIVERE ○ SQUEEZE, THE (USA) ○ RIP-OFF, THE
CONTROSESSO • 1964 • Rossi Franco, Ferreri Marco, Castellani Renato • ITL
CONTROTEMPI • 1989 • Soldini Silvio • SWT, ITL
CONTROVERSY see **SOSTYAZANIE** • 1964
CONTROVERSY! see **KONTROVERSIAL** • 1981
CONVALESCENT, THE • 1912 • *Briscoe Lottie* • USA
CONVENIENT BURGLAR, A • 1911 • Sennett Mack • USA
CONVENIENT CIGAR LIGHTER, A • 1900 • *Warwick Trading Co.* • UKN
CONVENT GATE, THE • 1913 • Noy Wilfred • UKN
CONVENTILLO DE LA PALOMA, EL • 1936 • Torres-Rios Leopoldo • ARG
CONVENTION CITY • 1933 • Mayo Archie • USA
CONVENTION CITY see **SONS OF THE DESERT** • 1933
CONVENTION GIRL • 1934 • Reed Luther • USA • ATLANTIC CITY ROMANCE (UKN)
CONVENTION GIRLS • 1978 • Adler Joseph • USA
CONVERGING PATHS • 1916 • King Burton L. • USA
CONVERSA ACABADA • 1982 • Botelho Joao • PRT • OTHER ONE, THE
CONVERSATION, THE • 1974 • Coppola Francis Ford • USA
CONVERSATION, THE see **ROZMOWA** • 1970
CONVERSATION BETWEEN A NAIL AND A STOCKING • 1958 • Adachi Masao • SHT • JPN
CONVERSATION PIECE (USA) see **GRUPPO DI FAMIGLIA IN UN INTERNO** • 1974
CONVERSATION WITH ARNOLD TOYNBEE • 1954 • Hammid Alexander • USA
CONVERSATIONS IN LIMBO • Preston Richard • USA
CONVERSATIONS WITH SHAKEY JAKE • 1972 • Konigsberg Franklin • SHT • USA
CONVERSATIONS WITH WILLARD VAN DYKE • 1981 • Rothschild Amalie • DOC • USA
CONVERSION D'IRMA, LA • 1913 • Feuillade Louis • FRN
CONVERSION OF FERDYS PISTORA, THE see **OBRACENI FERDYSE PISTORY** • 1931
CONVERSION OF FROSTY BLAKE, THE • 1915 • Hart William S., Smith Cliff • USA • GENTLEMAN FROM BLUE GULCH, THE
CONVERSION OF MR. ANTI, THE • 1913 • Newell Willard • USA
CONVERSION OF SMILING TOM, THE • 1915 • Mix Tom • USA
CONVERT, THE • 1911 • *Imp* • USA
CONVERT, THE • 1915 • Barker Reginald • USA
CONVERT, THE • 1923 • Haynes Manning • UKN
CONVERT, THE see **ROUGHNECK, THE** • 1915
CONVERT OF SAN CLEMENTE, THE • 1911 • *Selig* • USA
CONVERT OF THE NORTH, THE • 1917 • *Selig* • SHT • USA
CONVERT TO REVENGE, A • 1924 • Horan Charles • USA
CONVERTED DEACON, THE • 1910 • *Thanhouser* • USA
CONVERTS, THE • 1910 • Griffith D. W. • USA
CONVEYOR OF DEATH, THE see **KONVEYER SMERTI** • 1933
CONVICT 13 • 1920 • Cline Eddie, Keaton Buster • SHT • USA
CONVICT 99 • 1909 • Gilbert Arthur • UKN
CONVICT 99 • 1919 • Samuelson G. B. • UKN
CONVICT 99 • 1938 • Varnel Marcel • UKN
CONVICT 993 • 1918 • Parke William • USA
CONVICT, THE • 1910 • *Thanhouser* • USA
CONVICT AND THE CURATE, THE • 1904 • Stow Percy • UKN • CONVICT'S ESCAPE, THE (USA)
CONVICT AND THE DOVE, THE • 1908 • Collins Alf? • UKN
CONVICT CONCERTO • 1954 • Patterson Don • ANS • USA
CONVICT, COSTUMES AND CONFUSION • 1914 • Beggs Lee • USA
CONVICT GUARDIAN'S NIGHTMARE, THE • *Pathe* • FRN
CONVICT HAS ESCAPED, A see **BIR MAHKUM KACTI** • 1968
CONVICT HERO, THE • 1914 • *Sawyer'S Features* • USA
CONVICT KING, THE • 1915 • Sloman Edward • USA
CONVICT LABOUR see **KATORGA** • 1928
CONVICT MOLLY X see **STORY OF MOLLY X, THE** • 1950
CONVICT NO.113 see **FANGE NR.113** • 1917
CONVICT NO.796 • 1910 • Brooke Van Dyke • USA
CONVICT STAGE • 1965 • Selander Lesley • USA
CONVICTED • 1931 • Cabanne W. Christy • USA
CONVICTED • 1938 • Barsha Leon • USA, CND • FACE WORK
CONVICTED • 1950 • Levin Henry • USA
CONVICTED • 1986 • Rich David Lowell • TVM • USA
CONVICTED: A MOTHER'S STORY • 1987 • Heffron Richard T. • TVM • USA
CONVICTED BY HYPNOTISM • 1912 • *Krauss Charles* • FRN • DOUBLE LIFE, A
CONVICTED FOR MURDER • 1916 • Ricketts Thomas • SHT • USA
CONVICTED WOMAN • 1940 • Grinde Nick • USA
CONVICTS • 1989 • Masterson Peter • USA
CONVICTS AT LARGE • 1938 • Beal Scott R., Friedman David • USA
CONVICT'S CODE • 1939 • Hillyer Lambert • USA
CONVICT'S CODE, THE • 1930 • Revier Harry • USA
CONVICT'S CONSPIRACY • 1915 • *Ideal* • USA
CONVICT'S DARING, A • 1902 • *Paul R. W.* • UKN
CONVICT'S DASH FOR LIBERTY, A • 1908 • Fitzhamon Lewin • UKN
CONVICT'S DAUGHTER, THE • 1906 • Collins Alf? • UKN
CONVICT'S DAUGHTER, THE • 1912 • Buckland Warwick • UKN
CONVICT'S DAUGHTER, THE • 1913 • Smalley Phillips • USA
CONVICT'S DREAM, THE • 1909 • Coleby A. E. • UKN
CONVICT'S DREAM, THE • 1914 • Cornwallis Donald • UKN
CONVICT'S ESCAPE, THE (USA) see **CONVICT AND THE CURATE, THE** • 1904
CONVICT'S ESCAPE FROM PRISON, THE • 1903 • Mottershaw Frank • UKN
CONVICTS FOUR • 1962 • Kaufman Millard • USA • REPRIEVE
CONVICT'S HAPPY BRIDE • 1920 • *Howell Alice* • SHT • USA
CONVICT'S HEART, A • 1911 • *Panzer Paul* • USA
CONVICT'S LAST CHANCE, THE • 1911 • *Yankee* • USA
CONVICTS NO.10 AND NO.13 see **POLITIMESTEREN** • 1911
CONVICT'S PAROLE, THE • 1912 • Porter Edwin S. • USA
CONVICT'S RETURN, THE • 1912 • *Gem* • USA
CONVICT'S SACRIFICE, A • 1909 • Griffith D. W. • USA
CONVICT'S SISTERS, THE • 1911 • Haldane Bert • UKN
CONVICT'S STORY, THE • 1914 • *Blackwell Carlyle* • USA
CONVICT'S THREAT, THE • 1915 • *Anderson Broncho Billy* • USA
CONVIENE FAR BENE L'AMORE • 1975 • Festa Campanile Pasquale • ITL • SEX MACHINE, THE (USA)
CONVOI DE FEMMES • Chevalier Pierre • FRN, USA • CONVOY OF WOMEN
CONVOLUTION OF LUST, A see **WOKUJOH NO UZUMAKI** • 1968
CONVOY • 1927 • Boyle Joseph C., Mendes Lothar (U/c) • USA
CONVOY • 1933 • Lukov Leonid • USS
CONVOY • 1940 • Tennyson Pen • UKN
CONVOY • 1978 • Peckinpah Sam • USA
CONVOY BUSTERS see **POLIZIOTTO SCOMODO, UN** • 1978
CONVOY OF WOMEN see **CONVOI DE FEMMES**
CONWAY THE KERRY DANCER • 1912 • Olcott Sidney • USA
COO COO BIRD, THE • 1947 • Lundy Dick • ANS • USA
COO-COO BIRD DOG • 1949 • Marcus Sid • ANS • USA
COO-COO NUT GROVE • 1936 • Freleng Friz • ANS • USA
COO COO NUTS • 1970 • Smith Paul J. • ANS • USA
COO-COO, THE MAGICIAN • 1933 • *Iwerks Ub (P)* • ANS • USA
COOEE AND THE ECHO • 1912 • Rolfe Alfred • ASL
COOEE FROM HOME, A • 1918 • Woods Charles • ASL
COOGAN'S BLUFF • 1968 • Siegel Don • USA
COOK, THE • 1911 • *Lubin* • USA
COOK, THE • 1918 • Arbuckle Roscoe • SHT • USA
COOK, THE • 1966 • Keosayan Edmond • USS
COOK, THE see **DOUGH AND DYNAMITE** • 1914
COOK, THE see **SOMETHING FOR EVERYONE** • 1970
COOK CAME BACK, THE • 1912 • *Majestic* • USA
COOK IN TROUBLE, THE (USA) see **SORCELLERIE CULINAIRE, LA** • 1904
COOK MAKES MADEIRA SAUCE, THE • 1909 • *Vitagraph* • USA
COOK NEXT DOOR, THE • 1914 • *Lubin* • USA
COOK OF CANYON CAMP, THE • 1917 • Crisp Donald • USA
COOK OF THE RANCH, THE • 1911 • *Champion* • USA
COOK & PEARY: THE RACE TO THE POLE • 1983 • Day Robert • TVM • USA • RACE TO THE POLE, THE ○ ONLY ONE WINNER
COOK QUESTION, THE • 1913 • *Imp* • USA
COOK, THE THIEF, HIS WIFE AND HER LOVER, THE • 1989 • Greenaway Peter • UKN
COOKED GOOSE, A • 1914 • *Gane Nolan* • USA
COOKERY CARNIVAL, THE • 1935 • Sharpsteen Ben • ANS • USA
COOKERY NOOK • 1951 • *Terry-Thomas* • SHT • UKN
COOKIE • 1988 • Seidelman Susan • USA
COOKIE see **STREETWALKIN'** • 1985
COOKING CAVALIER • 1975 • Sherborne Colin • UKN
COOKING FOR TROUBLE • 1913 • *Fraunholz Fraunie* • USA
COOKING HER GOOSE see **RUNAWAY BRIDE, THE** • 1930
COOKING HIS GOOSE • 1916 • Watt Nate • SHT • USA
COOKING WITH GAGS • 1955 • Sparber I. • ANS • USA
COOKS • 1942 • Annakin Ken • DCS • UKN
COOKS AND CROOKS • 1918 • Davis James • SHT • USA
COOKS AND CROOKS • 1942 • James Henry • SHT • USA

COOK'S BID FOR FAME • 1912 • Wilson Frank? • UKN
COOK'S DREAM, THE • 1907 • Martin J. H.? • UKN
COOK'S LOVERS • 1904 • Collins Alf? • UKN
COOK'S MISTAKE, THE • 1915 • Louis Will • USA
COOK'S REVENGE, THE • 1913 • *Patheplay* • USA
COOK'S REVENGE, THE (USA) see **VENGEANCE DU GATE-SAUCE, LA** • 1900
COOKS VERSUS CHEFS • 1916 • *International Film Service* • SHT • USA
COOKY'S ADVENTURE • 1915 • Ward Chance E. • USA
COOL AND GROOVY • 1956 • Cowan Will • SHT • USA
COOL AND THE CRAZY, THE • 1958 • Witney William • USA
COOL BREEZE • 1972 • Pollack Barry • USA
COOL CAT • 1967 • Lovy Alex • ANS • USA
COOL CAT BLUES • 1961 • Kneitel Seymour • ANS • USA
COOL CHANGE • 1986 • Miller George* • ASL
COOL HAND LUKE • 1967 • Rosenberg Stuart • USA
COOL IT CAROL! • 1970 • Walker Pete • UKN • OH, CAROL
COOL IT CHARLIE • 1969 • Smith Paul J. • ANS • USA
COOL MCCOOL • 1966 • Potterton Gerald, Dunning George • ASS • UKN
COOL MIKADO, THE • 1963 • Winner Michael • UKN
COOL MILLION • 1972 • Levitt Gene • TVM • USA • MASK OF MARCELLA
COOL MILLION: ASSAULT ON GRAVALONI • 1972 • Badham John • TVM • USA
COOL ONES, THE • 1967 • Nelson Gene • USA
COOL PROCEEDINGS • 1902 • *Mitchell & Kenyon* • UKN
COOL SHED, THE see **CHALLANI NEEDA** • 1968
COOL SOUND FROM HELL, A • 1957 • Furie Sidney J. • CND
COOL STEADY LOOK AT THE WRAC, A • 1966 • Durst John • SHT • UKN
COOL WORLD, THE • 1964 • Clarke Shirley • USA • ECHOES OF THE JUNGLE ○ HARLEM STORY
COOLANGATTA GOLD, THE see **GOLD AND THE GLORY, THE** • 1989
COOLEY HIGH • 1975 • Schultz Michael • USA
COON TOWN SUFFRAGETTES • 1914 • *Edwards John* • USA
COONSKIN • 1975 • Bakshi Ralph • ANM • USA • BUSTIN' OUT ○ STREET FIGHT
COOP HOUSING: GETTING IT TOGETHER • 1975 • Sky Laura • DOC • CND
COOP HOUSING: THE BEST MOVE WE EVER MADE • 1975 • Sky Laura • DOC • CND
COOPER see **MISSION TERMINATE** • 1987
COOPERAGE • 1976 • Borsos Philip • SHT • CND
COOPERATIVA AGRICOLA TORRE BELA • 1975 • Teles Luis Galvao • PRT
COOPERATIVAS AGRICOLAS • 1960 • Gomez Manuel Octavio • DOC • CUB
COOPERATIVES, LES • 1965-66 • Garceau Raymond • DCS • CND
COORAB IN THE ISLE OF GHOSTS • 1929 • *Birtles Francis (Ph)* • ASL
COP • 1981 • Waxman Albert • MTV • CND
COP • 1987 • Harris James B. • USA • BLOOD ON THE MOON
COP see **STROMER** • 1976
COP, A see **CONDE, UN** • 1970
COP, LE see **RIPOUX, LES** • 1984
COP, THE • 1928 • Crisp Donald • USA
COP, THE see **VIGILE, IL** • 1960
COP, THE see **CONDE, UN** • 1970
COP, THE see **HASHOTER AZULAI** • 1971
COP AND THE ANTHEM, THE • 1917 • Mills Thomas R. • SHT • USA
COP AND THE GIRL, THE see **BULLE UND DAS MADCHEN, DER** • 1985
COP AU VIN see **POULET AU VINAIGRE** • 1984
COP FOOLS THE SERGEANT, THE • 1904 • Porter Edwin S. • USA
COP FROM HELL'S KITCHEN see **MY SON IS GUILTY** • 1940
COP HATER • 1958 • Berke William • USA
COP IN BLUE JEANS, THE (USA) see **SQUADRA ANTISCIPPO** • 1976
COP KILLERS see **ORDER OF DEATH** • 1983
COP KILLERS, THE • Dye Ted • USA
COP OF HONOUR see **PAROLE DE FLIC** • 1986
COP ON THE BEAT • 1975 • Vogel Virgil W. • TVM • USA
COP ON THE BEAT, THE • 1914 • *Selig* • USA
COP-OUT (USA) see **STRANGER IN THE HOUSE** • 1967
COPA DAVIS • 1965 • Camino Jaime • SPN
COPA DE ORO • 1981 • Acosta Walter • URG
COPACABANA • 1947 • Green Alfred E. • USA
COPACABANA • 1985 • Hussein Waris • TVM • USA
COPACABANA MON AMOUR • 1970 • Sganzerla Rogerio • BRZ
COPACABANA PALACE • 1962 • Steno • ITL, FRN, BRZ • SAGA OF THE FLYING HOSTESSES, THE ○ GIRL GAME (USA)
COPAINS, LES • 1964 • Robert Yves • FRN
COPENHAGEN • 1956 • Carlsen Henning • SHT • DNM
COPENHAGEN see **BY VED NAVN KOBENHAVN, EN** • 1960
COPENHAGEN CALL GIRLS see **VILLA VENNELY** • 1964
COPENHAGEN NIGHTS see **CANDIDO EROTICA** • 1978
COPENHAGUE see **BY VED NAVN KOBENHAVN, EN** • 1960
COPIE CONFORME • 1946 • Dreville Jean • FRN • CONFESSIONS OF A ROGUE (USA) ○ MONSIEUR ALIBI ○ DUPLICATA
COPIE MUTILEE, UNE • 1973 • Lemaitre Maurice • FRN
COPKILLER see **ORDER OF DEATH** • 1983
COPLA ANDALUZA, LA • 1959 • Mihura Jeronimo • SPN
COPLA DE LA DOLORES, LA • 1947 • Perojo Benito • ARG • SONG OF DOLORES (USA)
COPLAN, AGENT SECRET FX18 • 1964 • Cloche Maurice • FRN, ITL, SPN • UCCIDETE AGENTE SEGRETO 777-STOP (ITL)
COPLAN FX18 CASSE TOUT • 1965 • Freda Riccardo • FRN, ITL • AGENTE 777 MISSIONE SUPERGAME (ITL) ○ EXTERMINATORS, THE (USA) ○ FX-18 SUPERSPY ○ FERMATI COPLAN
COPLAN OUVRE LE FEU A MEXICO (FRN) see **MORESQUE OBIETTIVO ALLUCINANTE** • 1967
COPLAN PREND DES RISQUES • 1963 • Labro Maurice • FRN, ITL, BLG • AGENTE COPLAN: MISSIONE SPIONAGGIO (ITL) ○ SPY I LOVE, THE (USA)
COPLAN SAUVE SA PEAU • 1967 • Boisset Yves • FRN, ITL • HORROR: L'ASSASSINO HA LE ORE CONTATE (ITL) ○ COPLAN SAVES HIS SKIN (USA) ○ DEVIL'S GARDEN ○ JARDINS DU DIABLE, LES
COPLAN SAVES HIS SKIN (USA) see **COPLAN SAUVE SA PEAU** • 1967
COPLAND PORTRAIT • 1975 • Sanders Terry • USA
COPO DE AGUA, UM • 1926 • Fonseca Joao De Sousa • SHT • PRT
COPPED • 1915 • *Superba* • USA
COPPELIA • 1964 • *Dale Margaret (P)* • MTV • UKN
COPPELIA • 1967 • Branss Truck • AUS
COPPELIA see **FANTASTICO MUNDO DEL DR. COPPELIUS, EL** • 1966
COPPELIA: LA POUPEE ANIMEE • 1900 • Melies Georges • FRN • COPPELIA, THE ANIMATED DOLL (USA)
COPPELIA, THE ANIMATED DOLL (USA) see **COPPELIA: LA POUPEE ANIMEE** • 1900
COPPER • 1915 • *Imp* • USA
COPPER see **STROMER** • 1976
COPPER AND THE CROOK, THE • 1910 • *Yankee* • USA
COPPER BEECHES, THE • 1912 • Treville Georges • UKN
COPPER BEECHES, THE • 1921 • Elvey Maurice • UKN
COPPER CANYON • 1950 • Farrow John • USA
COPPER COIN KING, THE see **DOKA O** • 1926
COPPER CYLINDER, THE • 1926 • Coleby A. E. • UKN
COPPER IN THE COPPER, A • 1910 • *Empire Films* • UKN
COPPER KING, THE see **DOKA O** • 1926
COPPER MASK • 1919 • SAF
COPPER PROOF see **PERFECT CRIME, THE** • 1937
COPPER SKY • 1957 • Warren Charles Marquis • USA
COPPER TOWER, THE see **MEDENA VEZA** • 1970
COPPER WEB • 1937 • Harvey Maurice • DOC • UKN
COPPER WIT • 1911 • *Powers* • USA
COPPERHEAD • 1984 • Payton Leland • USA
COPPERHEAD, THE • 1911 • Davis Ulysses • USA
COPPERHEAD, THE • 1920 • Maigne Charles • USA
COPPERS AND CUTUPS • 1915 • Aylott Dave • UKN
COPPER'S REVENGE, THE • 1912 • Fitzhamon Lewin? • UKN
COPPIA, LA • 1968 • Siciliano Enzo • ITL • COUPLE, THE
COPPIA TRANQUILLA, UNA see **RUBA AL PROSSIMO TUO** • 1968
COPPIE, LE • 1970 • Sordi Alberto, De Sica Vittorio, Monicelli Mario • ITL • COUPLES, THE
COPPING THE COPPERS • 1909 • Aylott Dave? • UKN
COPRNICA ZOFKA • 1989 • Milcinski Matija • ANM • YGS • SOPHIE THE WITCH
COPS • 1922 • Cline Eddie, Keaton Buster • SHT • USA
COPS AND COWBOYS • 1912 • *Nestor* • USA
COPS AND CUSSEDNESS • 1917 • Semon Larry • SHT • USA
COPS AND OTHER LOVERS • 1979 • Fournier Claude • CND
COPS AND ROBBERS • 1973 • Avakian Aram • USA
COPS AND ROBBERS see **GUARDIE E LADRI** • 1951
COPS AND ROBBERS see **TIEN CHIH PING-PING** • 1980
COPS AND ROBIN, THE • 1978 • Reisner Allen • TVM • USA
COPS AND WATCHERS see **TWENTY MINUTES OF LOVE** • 1914
COP'S HONOUR see **PAROLE DE FLIC** • 1986
COPS IS ALWAYS RIGHT • 1938 • Fleischer Dave • ANS • USA
COPS IS TOPS • 1955 • Sparber I. • ANS • USA
COPTER KIDS, THE • 1975 • Spencer Ronald • UKN
COPY CAT • 1941 • Fleischer Dave • ANS • USA
COQ DU REGIMENT, LE • 1933 • Cammage Maurice • FRN
COQ DU VILLAGE, LE see **PAPERBACK HERO** • 1972
COQ EN PATE • 1950 • Tavano Charles-Felix • FRN
COQ EN PATE, LE • 1912 • Perret Leonce • FRN
COQUECIGROLE • 1931 • Berthomieu Andre • FRN
COQUELUCHE • 1970 • Lorente German • SPN
COQUELUCHE, LA • 1968 • Arrighi Christian-Paul • FRN
COQUELUCHE DE CES DAMES, LA • 1935 • Rosca Gabriel • FRN
COQUETA • 1949 • Rivero Fernando A. • MXC
COQUETTE • 1929 • Taylor Sam • USA
COQUETTE, THE • 1910 • *Edison* • USA
COQUETTE, THE • 1911 • *Santschi Tom* • USA
COQUETTE, THE • 1915 • *Martin Rea* • USA
COQUETTE, THE see **DOKHTARE ESHVEGAR** • 1968
COQUETTE'S AWAKENING • 1915 • Beal Frank • USA
COQUILLE ET LE CLERGYMAN, LA • 1928 • Dulac Germaine • FRN • SEASHELL AND THE CLERGYMAN, THE
COQUIN, UN • 1924 • Guarino Joseph • FRN
COQUIN DE PRINTEMPS see **PAULUS CHANTANT: COQUIN DE PRINTEMPS** • 1897
COQUITO, LA • 1977 • Maso Pedro • SPN
COR, LE • 1931 • Epstein Jean • FRN
COR DO SEU DESTINO, A • 1986 • Duran Jorge • BRZ • COLOUR OF DESTINY, THE
CORA • 1915 • Carewe Edwin • USA
CORACAO, O • 1960 • de Oliveira Manoel • SHT • PRT
CORACAO DE LUTO • 1968 • Llorente Eduardo • BRZ • HEART IN MOURNING
CORACAO PARTIDO • Costa Jose Fonseca • PRT
CORAGGIO, IL • 1955 • Paolella Domenico • ITL
CORAGGIOSO, LO SPIETATO, IL TRADITORE, IL • 1967 • Mulargia Edoardo, Xiol Juan • ITL, SPN • VALIENTE, EL DESPIADADO, EL TRAIDOR, EL (SPN) ○ BRAVE, THE RUTHLESS, THE TRAITOR, THE
CORAJE DEL PUEBLO, EL see **NOTTE DI SAN JUAN, LA** • 1971
CORAL • 1915 • McRae Henry • USA
CORAL KINGDOM • 1958 • Monkman Noel • DOC • ASL
CORALIE ET CIE • 1933 • Cavalcanti Alberto • FRN
CORAZON • 1947 • *Salvador Lolito* • MXC
CORAZON AYMARA • 1925 • Sambarino Pedro • BLV • HEART OF AYMARA
CORAZON BANDOLERO • 1934 • Sevilla Raphael J. • MXC
CORAZON BURLADO, UN • 1944 • Benavides Jose Jr. • MXC
CORAZON DE FIERA • 1950 • Cortazar Ernesto • MXC
CORAZON DE LA GLORIA, EL • 1926 • Harvey Harry • MXC
CORAZON DE LA NOCHE, EL • 1983 • Hermosillo Jaime Humberto • MXC • HEART OF THE NIGHT, THE
CORAZON DE MADRE • 1926 • Pierkoff Jorge • MXC
CORAZON DE NINO • 1939 • Galindo Alejandro • MXC • HEART OF A CHILD (USA)
CORAZON DE NINO • 1962 • Bracho Julio • MXC
CORAZON DE PAPEL • 1982 • Bodegas Roberto • SPN • PAPER HEART
CORAZON DEL BOSQUE • 1978 • Gutierrez Aragon Manuel • SPN • IN THE HEART OF THE FOREST ○ HEART OF THE FOREST, THE
CORAZON HECHO GARRAS, EL see **CORAZONES EN DERROTA** • 1933
CORAZON SALVAJE • 1955 • Ortega Juan J. • MXC
CORAZON SALVAJE • 1968 • Davison Tito • MXC • SAVAGE HEART
CORAZON SOLITARIO • 1972 • Betriu Francisco • SPN • LONELY HEART
CORAZON Y LA ESPADA, EL • 1953 • Dein Edward, Vejar Carlos Jr. • MXC • SWORD OF GRANADA, THE (USA)
CORAZONES DE MEXICO • 1945 • Gavaldon Roberto • MXC
CORAZONES EN DERROTA • 1933 • Navarro Ruben C. • MXC • CORAZON HECHO GARRAS, EL
CORAZONES SIN RUMBO • 1928 • Perojo Benito • SPN
CORAZZIERE, IL • 1960 • Mastrocinque Camillo • ITL
CORBARI • 1970 • Orsini Valentino • ITL
CORBATA, LA • 1971 • *Cinema Marte* • MXC
CORBEAU, LE • 1943 • Clouzot Henri-Georges • FRN • RAVEN, THE (USA) ○ MALADIE CONTAGIEUSE ○ LAURA ○ CROW, THE
CORBEAU ET LE RENARD, LE • 1969 • Hebert Pierre, Desbiens Francine, Leduc Andre, Pauze Michele • ANS • CND
CORBEAUX, LES • Ansorge Ernest, Ansorge Giselle • ANS • SWT • CROWS, THE
CORBEDDU • 1975 • van Gasteren Louis A. • NTH
CORBEILLE ENCHANTEE, LA • 1903 • Melies Georges • FRN • ENCHANTED BASKET, THE (USA)
CORBILLARD DE JULES, LE • 1981 • Penard Serge • FRN
CORBUSIER, L'ARCHITECTE DU BONHEUR • 1956 • Kast Pierre • SHT • FRN
CORD, THE see **INTERRUPTED JOURNEY, THE** • 1949
CORD OF LIFE, THE • 1909 • Griffith D. W. • USA
CORDA D'ACCIAIO, LA • 1954 • Borghesio Carlo • ITL
CORDE, LA • 1972 • Cherif Hachemi • ALG
CORDE AU COU, LA • 1926 • Saidreau Robert • FRN
CORDE AU COU, LA • 1964 • Lisbona Joseph • FRN
CORDE AU COU, LA • 1964 • Patry Pierre • CND, FRN • ROPE AROUND THE NECK (USA)
CORDE RAIDE, LA • 1959 • Dudrumet Jean-Charles • FRN • LOVERS ON A TIGHTROPE (USA)
CORDE.. UN COLT, UNE • 1968 • Hossein Robert • FRN, ITL • CIMITERO SENZA CROCI (ITL)
CORDELIA • 1980 • Beaudin Jean • CND
CORDELIA THE MAGNIFICENT • 1923 • Archainbaud George • USA
CORDILLERA see **FLIGHT TO FURY** • 1966
CORDOBA • 1967 • Enciso Luis S. • SHT • SPN
CORDON-BLEU • 1931 • Anton Karl • FRN
CORDULA • 1950 • Ucicky Gustav • AUS
CORE 'NGRATO • 1952 • Brignone Guido • ITL
COREA, LA • 1976 • Olea Pedro • SPN
CORECZKA • 1965 • Petelska Ewa, Petelski Czeslaw • MTV • PLN • LITTLE DAUGHTER, THE
CORETHRE • 1935 • Painleve Jean • SHT • FRN
COREY: FOR THE PEOPLE • 1977 • Kulik Buzz • TVM • USA
CORINNA • 1978 • Heming Antonia, Gerlach Claus • FRG
CORINNA SCHMIDT • 1951 • Pohl Arthur • GDR
CORINNE, COME HERE! see **CORINNE COMES HOME** • 1919
CORINNE COMES HOME • 1919 • Bartlett Charles • SHT • USA • CORINNE, COME HERE!
CORINNE IN DOLLYLAND • 1911 • *Solax* • USA
CORINTHIAN, THE see **CORINTIANO, O** • 1967
CORINTHIAN JACK • 1921 • Rowden W. C. • UKN • FIGHTING JACK
CORINTIANO, O • 1967 • Amaral Milton • BRZ • CORINTHIAN, THE
CORIOLAN • 1950 • Cocteau Jean • FRN
CORIOLANO, EROE SENZA PATRIA • 1965 • Ferroni Giorgio • ITL, FRN • CORIOLANUS: HERO WITHOUT A COUNTRY ○ THUNDER OF BATTLE
CORIOLANUS: HERO WITHOUT A COUNTRY see **CORIOLANO, EROE SENZA PATRIA** • 1965
CORISCO O DIABO LOURO • 1970 • Coimbra Carlos • BRZ
CORISTA, LA • 1960 • Elorrieta Jose Maria • SPN
CORISTA, LA • 1960 • Seto Javier • SPN
CORKSCREW see **KORKOCIAG** • 1970
CORKY • 1971 • Horn Leonard • USA • GOING ALL OUT ○ LOOKIN' GOOD
CORKY • 1979 • Willis Gordon • USA
CORKY OF GASOLINE ALLEY • 1951 • Bernds Edward • USA • CORKY (UKN)
CORKY (UKN) see **CORKY OF GASOLINE ALLEY** • 1951
CORLEONE • 1978 • Squitieri Pasquale • ITL • CORLEONE: FATHER OF THE GODFATHERS
CORLEONE: FATHER OF THE GODFATHERS see **CORLEONE** • 1978
CORLETTO & SON • 1980 • Yates Rebecca, Salzman Glen • CND
CORMACK • *Frederick Lynne* • USA • CORMACK OF THE MOUNTIES
CORMACK OF THE MOUNTIES see **CORMACK**
CORN see **KORN** • 1943
CORN CHIPS • 1951 • Hannah Jack • ANS • USA
CORN IS GREEN, THE • 1945 • Rapper Irving • USA
CORN IS GREEN, THE • 1978 • Cukor George • TVM • USA
CORN ON THE COP • 1965 • Spector Irv • ANS • USA
CORN PLASTERED • 1951 • McKimson Robert • ANS • USA
CORNBREAD, EARL AND ME • 1975 • Manduke Joe • USA
CORNELIUS AND THE WILD MAN • 1915 • *Prescott John* • USA
CORNER, THE • 1916 • Edwards Walter • USA
CORNER, THE • 1987 • Sarin Vic • USA
CORNER, GETTING OFF! see **ESQUINA BAJAN!** • 1948
CORNER GROCER, THE • 1917 • Cowl George • USA
CORNER HOUSE BURGLARY, THE • 1914 • Martinek H. O. • UKN

CORNER IN BABIES, A • 1915 • *Royal* • USA
CORNER IN CATS, A • 1915 • *Fitzgerald Cissy* • USA
CORNER IN COLLEENS, A • 1916 • Miller Charles • USA
CORNER IN COTTON, A • 1916 • Balshofer Fred J., Truesdell Howard • USA
CORNER IN CROOKS, A • 1913 • *Thornby Robert* • USA
CORNER IN HATS, A • 1914 • *Komic* • USA
CORNER IN KISSES, A • 1912 • *Majestic* • USA
CORNER IN SMITHS, A • 1917 • Beaumont Harry • SHT • USA
CORNER IN WATER, A • 1916 • Mix Tom • SHT • USA
CORNER IN WHEAT, A • 1909 • Griffith D. W. • USA
CORNER IN WHISKERS, A • 1912 • *Mason Billy* • USA
CORNER MAN, THE • 1921 • Bruun Einar J. • UKN
CORNER OF ARBAT AND BABULINOS STREET, THE see **ON THE CORNER OF THE ARBAT AND BUBULINOS STREET** • 1973
CORNER OF GREAT TOKYO, A see **DAI-TOKYO NO IKKAKU** • 1930
CORNER OF THE VIRGINS, THE see **RINCON DE LAS VIRGENES, EL** • 1972
CORNER POCKET, THE • 1921 • Roach Hal • SHT • USA
CORNERED • 1924 • Beaudine William • USA
CORNERED • 1933 • Eason B. Reeves • USA
CORNERED • 1945 • Dmytryk Edward • USA
CORNET, DER • 1955 • Reisch Walter • FRG
CORNET, THE • 1915 • Ince John • USA
CORNET AT NIGHT • 1963 • Jackson Stanley R. • DOC • CND
CORNETTI A COLAZIONE • 1978 • Cools Alan W. • ITL • EMMANUELLE IN THE COUNTRY ○ COUNTRY NURSE
CORNFIELDS QUARTETTE • 1900 • Gibbons Walter • UKN
CORNFLOWER see **BUZAVIRAG** • 1935
CORNIARD, LE • 1965 • Oury Gerard • FRN, ITL, SPN • COLPO GROSSO MA NON TROPPO (ITL) ○ SUCKER, THE (USA) ○ SUCKER.. OR HOW TO BE GLAD WHEN YOU'VE BEEN HAD, THE
CORNICHE DU NIL see **KURNICH AN-NIL** • 1956
CORNISH ENGINE, THE • 1948 • UKN
CORNISH GIANT • Cartwright J. A. D. • DOC • UKN
CORNISH IDYLL, A • 1936 • Searle Francis • DCS • UKN
CORNISH ROMANCE, A • 1912 • Northcote Sidney • UKN
CORNSTALKS, THE • 1918 • *Sterry & Haldane* • ASL
CORNWALL • 1949 • Stringer G. Henry • DOC • UKN
CORNY • 1967 • Bentzon Niels Viggo • DNM
CORNY CASANOVAS • 1952 • White Jules • SHT • USA
CORNY CONCERTO, A • 1943 • Clampett Robert • ANS • USA
CORNY CONCERTO, A • 1962 • Hannah Jack • ANS • USA
CORONA DE LAGRIMAS • 1968 • Galindo Alejandro • MXC • CROWN OF TEARS
CORONA DI FERRO, LA • 1941 • Blasetti Alessandro • ITL • IRON CROWN, THE
CORONA NEGRA, LA • 1950 • Saslavsky Luis • SPN, FRN • COURONNE NOIRE, LA (FRN) ○ BLACK CROWN, THE ○ CORONNA NERA, LA
CORONACION • 1975 • Olhovich Sergio • MXC
CORONADO • 1935 • McLeod Norman Z. • USA
CORONADO NEW YEAR'S DAY see **WINTER SPORTS AND PASTIMES OF CORONADO BEACH** • 1912
CORONATION CEREMONIES, THE • 1902 • *Bromhead A. C.* • UKN
CORONATION DEEP 1922 • 1984 • *Rands Jonathan* • SAF • 1922: A MINER'S STRIKE
CORONATION OF A VILLAGE MAIDEN see **COURONNEMENT DE LA ROSIERE** • 1896
CORONATION OF EDWARD VII, THE see **SACRE D'EDOUARD VII, LE** • 1902
CORONATION OF KING EDWARD VII • 1901 • Hepworth Cecil M. • UKN
CORONATION OF QUEEN ELIZABETH II • 1953 • DOC • UKN
CORONATION OF THEIR MAJESTIES KING EDWARD VII AND QUEEN ALEXANDRIA • 1902 • Smith G. A., Melies Georges • UKN
CORONATION PARADE, THE • 1953 • Hathaway Henry • SHT • USA
CORONEL DEMIRO GOUVEIA • 1979 • Sarno Geraldo • BRZ • COLONEL OF THE SERTAO ○ COLONEL DELMIRO GOUVEIA
CORONEL E O LOBISOMEM, O • 1980 • Diniz Alcino • BRZ • COLONEL AND THE WOLFMAN, THE
CORONELAS, LAS • 1954 • Baledon Rafael • MXC
CORONER CREEK • 1948 • Enright Ray • USA • CORONER'S CREEK
CORONER'S CREEK see **CORONER CREEK** • 1948
CORONER'S MISTAKE, THE • 1907 • *Miles Bros* • USA
CORONETS AND HEARTS • 1912 • *Williams Earle* • USA
CORONNA NERA, LA see **CORONA NEGRA, LA** • 1950
COROT • 1965 • Leenhardt Roger • DCS • FRN
COROUNNE D'EPINES, LA • 1969 • Maleh Nabil • SHT • SYR
CORPI PRESENTANO TRACCE DI VIOLENZA CARNALE, I • 1973 • Martino Sergio • ITL • BODIES BEAR TRACES OF CARNAL VIOLENCE, THE ○ TORSO (USA)
CORPO, IL • 1974 • Scattini Luigi • ITL • LOVE SLAVE OF THE ISLANDS ○ TAKE THIS MY BODY ○ BODY, THE ○ LAURA
CORPO, O • 1989 • Garcia Jose Antonio • BRZ • BODY, THE
CORPO A CORPO (ITL) see **ARME A GAUCHE, L'** • 1965
CORPO ARDENTE, O • 1967 • Khouri Walter Hugo • BRZ • BURNING BODY, THE
CORPO CALDO PER L'INFERNO, UN • 1968 • Montemurro Francesco • ITL, FRN • WARM BODY FOR HELL, A
CORPO D'AMORE • 1973 • Carpi Fabio • ITL
CORPO DELLA RAGASSA, IL • 1979 • Festa Campanile Pasquale • ITL • YOUNG GIRL'S BODY, THE
CORPORAL AND THE OTHERS, THE see **TIZEDES MEG A TOBRIEK, A** • 1965
CORPORAL BILLY'S COMEBACK • 1916 • Cochrane George • SHT • USA
CORPORAL DOLAN AWOL see **RENDEZVOUS WITH ANNIE** • 1946
CORPORAL DOLAN GOES A.W.O.L. see **RENDEZVOUS WITH ANNIE** • 1946
CORPORAL KATE • 1926 • Sloane Paul • USA • MILITARY MAIDS (UKN)
CORPORAL TRUMAN'S WAR STORY • 1910 • *Kalem* • USA
CORPORAL'S DAUGHTER, THE • 1915 • West Langdon • USA
CORPORAL'S DREAM, THE see **SUENO DEL CAPORAL, EL** • 1922
CORPORAL'S GUN, THE see **REVOLVER DES CORPORALS, DER** • 1967
CORPORAL'S KIDDIES, THE • 1914 • Buckland Warwick? • UKN
CORPORAL'S REVOLVER, THE see **REVOLVER DES CORPORALS, DER** • 1967
CORPORATE QUEEN, THE • 1970 • Amero John, Amero Lem • USA
CORPORATION AND THE RANCH GIRL, THE • 1911 • *Anderson Broncho Billy* • USA
CORPOREAL • 1983 • Cantrill Arthur, Cantrill Corinne • DOC • ASL
CORPS A COEUR • 1979 • Vecchiali Paul • FRN
CORPS A CORPS • 1976 • Roy Jean-Claude • FRN
CORPS CELESTES, LES • 1973 • Carle Gilles • CND, FRN
CORPS DE DIANE, LE (FRN) see **TELO DIANA** • 1969
CORPS DE MON ENNEMI, LE • 1976 • Verneuil Henri • FRN
CORPS ET AMES • 1972 • Audy Michel • CND
CORPS ET LE FOUET, LE (FRN) see **FRUSTA E IL CORPO, LA** • 1963
CORPS PERDUS (FRN) see **CUERPOS PERDIDOS** • 1988
CORPS, UNE NUIT, UNE • 1969 • Bontempi Giorgio • FRN
CORPSE, THE see **CRUCIBLE OF HORROR** • 1971
CORPSE CAME C.O.D., THE • 1947 • Levin Henry • USA
CORPSE COLLECTORS, THE see **COLECCIONISTA DE CADAVERES, EL** • 1967
CORPSE GRINDERS, THE • 1971 • Mikels Ted V. • USA
CORPSE MAKERS, THE see **TWICE-TOLD TALES** • 1963
CORPSE NO.1346 • 1912 • *Thieman Paul/ Reinhardt F. (P)* • USS
CORPSE OF BEVERLY HILLS, THE (USA) see **TOTE VON BEVERLY HILLS, DIE** • 1964
CORPSE VANISHED, THE (UKN) see **REVENGE OF THE ZOMBIES** • 1943
CORPSE VANISHES, THE • 1942 • Fox Wallace • USA • CASE OF THE MISSING BRIDES, THE (UKN)
CORPSE WHICH DIDN'T WANT TO DIE, THE (USA) see **DAMA ROSSA UCCIDE SETTE VOLTE, LA** • 1972
CORPSES NEVER LIE • 1989 • Harper Max • USA
CORPSES ON HOLIDAY see **CADAVRES EN VACANCES** • 1961
CORPUS • 1978 • Rentzis Thanasis • GRC
CORPUS CELESTES • 1976 • Caetano Jose De Sa • PRT • CELESTIAL BODIES
CORPUS CHRISTI BANDITS • 1945 • Grissell Wallace A. • USA
CORRAL • 1954 • Low Colin • DCS • CND
CORRAL CUTIES • 1954 • Cowan Will • SHT • USA
CORRALEJAS DE SINCELEJO • 1975 • Duran Ciro, Mitrotti Mario • SHT • CLM • FEASTS OF SINCELEJO
CORRALLING A SCHOOL MARM • 1940 • Roberts Charles E. • SHT • USA
CORRECTION PLEASE -OR HOW WE GOT INTO PICTURES • 1980 • Burch Noel • UKN
CORRECTIONAL PROCESS, THE • 1964 • Devlin Bernard • DOC • CND • PROGRAMME DE FORMATION
CORREGIDOR • 1943 • Nigh William • USA
CORRELIEU • 1959 • Palardy Jean • DCS • CND
CORREO DE INDAS • 1942 • Neville Edgar • SPN
CORREO DEL NORTE, EL • 1960 • Gomez Urquiza Zacarias • MXC
CORREO DEL REY, EL • 1950 • Gascon Jose • SPN
CORREO DEL ZAR, EL see **MIGUEL STROGOFF** • 1943
CORRERIAS DEL VIZCONDE ARNAU, LAS • 1973 • Coll Joaquin • SPN
CORREVA L'ANNO DI GRAZIA 1870... • 1971 • Giannetti Alfredo • ITL
CORRI, UOMO, CORRI • 1968 • Sollima Sergio • ITL • RUN, MAN, RUN
CORRIDA • 1964 • Marszalek Lechoslaw • ANM • PLN
CORRIDA, LA see **KORRIDA** • 1983
CORRIDA DEI MARITI, LA • 1956 • Grangier Gilles • FRN, ITL
CORRIDA DI SPOSA, IL • 1962 • Baldi Gian Vittorio • ITL
CORRIDA INTERDITE, LA • 1959 • de Daunant Denys Colomb • FRN
CORRIDA POUR UN ESPION • 1965 • Labro Maurice • FRN, FRG, SPN • SPION, DER IN DIE HOLLE GING, DER (FRG) ○ SPY WHO WENT INTO HELL, THE ○ PERSECUCION A UN ESPIA (SPN)
CORRIDO DE "EL HIJO DESOBEDIENTE", EL • 1968 • Gomez Muriel Emilio • MXC • FOLK SONG "THE DISOBEDIENT SON", THE
CORRIDO DE MARIA PISTOLAS, EL • 1962 • Cardona Rene • MXC
CORRIDOR • 1970 • Lawder Standish D. • USA
CORRIDOR, THE see **KORRIDOREN** • 1968
CORRIDOR OF MIRRORS • 1948 • Young Terence • UKN
CORRIDORS OF BLOOD • 1958 • Day Robert • UKN • DOCTOR FROM SEVEN DIALS, THE
CORRIDORS - PRIS AU PIEGE • 1979 • Favreau Robert • CND
CORRIERE DEL RE, IL • 1948 • Righelli Gennaro • ITL • ROUGE ET LE NOIR, LE
CORRIERE DI FERRO, IL • 1948 • Zavatta Francesco • ITL
CORRINGA see **DIABLESSES, LES** • 1972
CORRISPONDENTI DE GUERRA see **INVIATI SPECIALI** • 1943
CORROMPUS, LES see **SIGILLO DI PECHINO, IL** • 1966
CORROSION see **TADARE** • 1962
CORRUPCION DE CHRIS MILLER, LA • 1972 • Bardem Juan Antonio • SPN • CORRUPTION OF CHRIS MILLER, THE (USA) ○ SISTERS OF CORRUPTION ○ BEHIND THE SHUTTERS
CORRUPT see **ORDER OF DEATH** • 1983
CORRUPT, THE (UKN) see **SYMPHONIE POUR UN MASSACRE** • 1963
CORRUPT ONES, THE (USA) see **SIGILLO DI PECHINO, IL** • 1966
CORRUPTED WOMAN, A see **DARAKU SURU ONNA** • 1967
CORRUPTEURS, LES • 1941 • Ramelot Pierre • FRN
CORRUPTION • 1917 • Gorman John • USA
CORRUPTION • 1933 • Roberts Charles E. • USA • DOUBLE EXPOSURE (UKN)
CORRUPTION • 1968 • Hartford-Davis Robert • UKN
CORRUPTION see **COURRUZIONE, LA** • 1963
CORRUPTION IN THE HALLS OF JUSTICE see **CORRUZIONE AL PALAZZO DI GIUSTIZIA** • 1975
CORRUPTION OF CHRIS MILLER, THE (USA) see **CORRUPCION DE CHRIS MILLER, LA** • 1972
CORRUPTION OF THE DAMNED • 1965 • Kuchar George • USA
CORRUZIONE AL PALAZZO DI GIUSTIZIA • 1975 • Aliprandi Marcello • ITL • CORRUPTION IN THE HALLS OF JUSTICE
CORSA AL TRONO, LA • 1918 • Roberti Roberto Leone • ITL
CORSA DEL SECOLO, LA (ITL) see **CRACKS, LES** • 1968
CORSA DELLE LEPRE ATTRAVERSO I CAMPI, LA (ITL) see **COURSE DU LIEVRE A TRAVERS LES CHAMPS, LA** • 1972
CORSA DI PRIMAVERA • 1990 • Campiotti Giacomo • ITL • SPRINGTIME RACE
CORSAIR • 1931 • West Roland • USA
CORSAIR, THE • 1914 • Jose Edward • USA
CORSAIRE, LE • 1939 • Allegret Marc • FRN
CORSAIRES DU BOIS DE BOULOGNE, LES • 1953 • Carbonnaux Norbert • FRN
CORSARI DELL'ISOLA DEGLI SQUALI, I • 1972 • Merino Jose Luis • ITL, SPN • PIRATES OF BLOOD ISLAND (UKN)
CORSARIO, EL (SPN) see **CORSARO, IL** • 1970
CORSARIO NEGRO, EL • 1944 • Urueta Chano • MXC
CORSARIOS DEL CARIBE, LOS see **CONQUISTATORE DI MARACAIBO, IL** • 1961
CORSARO, IL • 1923 • Gallone Carmine • ITL
CORSARO, IL • 1923 • Genina Augusto • ITL
CORSARO, IL • 1970 • Mollica Nino • ITL, SPN • CORSARIO, EL (SPN)
CORSARO DELLA MEZZA LUNA, IL • 1958 • Scotese Giuseppe Maria • ITL
CORSARO NERO, IL • 1936 • Palermi Amleto • ITL • BLACK CORSAIR, THE (USA)
CORSARO NERO, IL • 1971 • Alberto Juan • ITL, SPN • BLACKIE THE PIRATE (USA) ○ BLACK PIRATE, THE
CORSARO NERO, IL • 1976 • Sollima Sergio • ITL
CORSARO NERO NELL'ISOLA DEGLI SQUALI, IL • 1966 • De Angelis Vertunio • ITL
CORSEAU ROUGE, LE see **CORSO ROUGE, LE** • 1913
CORSICAN BROTHERS, THE • 1898 • Smith G. A. • UKN
CORSICAN BROTHERS, THE • 1902 • Winslow Dicky • UKN
CORSICAN BROTHERS, THE • 1908 • *Cameraphone* • USA
CORSICAN BROTHERS, THE • 1912 • Apfel Oscar, Dawley J. Searle • USA
CORSICAN BROTHERS, THE • 1915 • Lessey George A. • USA
CORSICAN BROTHERS, THE • 1920 • Campbell Colin • USA
CORSICAN BROTHERS, THE • 1941 • Ratoff Gregory • USA
CORSICAN BROTHERS, THE • 1954 • ARG
CORSICAN BROTHERS, THE • 1985 • Sharp Ian • TVM • UKN
CORSICAN BROTHERS, THE see **HERMANOS CORSOS, LOS** • 1955
CORSICAN BROTHERS, THE see **CHEECH & CHONG'S THE CORSICAN BROTHERS** • 1984
CORSICAN BROTHERS, THE (USA) see **FRERES CORSES, LES** • 1917
CORSICAN BROTHERS, THE (USA) see **FRATELLI CORSI, I** • 1961
CORSICAN BROTHERS UP TO DATE, THE • 1915 • *Browning Will* • USA
CORSICAN SISTERS, THE • 1916 • Horne James W. • USA
CORSO ROUGE, LE • 1913 • Tourneur Maurice • FRN • CORSEAU ROUGE, LE
CORTA NOTTE DELLE BAMBOLE DI VETRO, LA • 1971 • Lado Aldo • ITL
CORTA YA, BWANA • 1976 • Vazquez Ricardo • SPN
CORTE D'ASSISE • 1930 • Brignone Guido • ITL
CORTE DE FARAON, LA • 1943 • Bracho Julio • MXC
CORTE DE FARAON, LA • 1985 • Garcia Sanchez Jose Luis • SPN • COURT OF FARAON, THE ○ FARAON'S COURT
CORTEGE DE LA MI-CAREME • 1897 • Melies Georges • FRN • MID-LENT PROCESSION IN PARIS
CORTEGE DU BOEUF GRAS BOULEVARD DES ITALIENS • 1897 • Melies Georges • FRN
CORTEGE DU BOEUF GRAS PASSANT PLACE DE LA CONCORDE • 1897 • Melies Georges • FRN • MARDI GRAS PROCESSION, THE ○ BOEUF GRAS
CORTEGE DU TZAR ALLANT A VERSAILLES • 1896 • Melies Georges • FRN • CZAR AND HIS CORTEGE GOING TO VERSAILLES, THE
CORTEGE DU TZAR AU BOIS DE BOULOGNE • 1896 • Melies Georges • FRN • CZAR'S CORTEGE IN THE BOIS DE BOULOGNE, THE
CORTEJO HISTORICO DE LISBOA • 1947 • Ribeiro Antonio Lopes • SHT • PRT
CORTEJO HISTORICO DE VIATURAS • 1934 • Vieira Manuel Luis • SHT • PRT
CORTEJOS DE OFERENDAS • 1953 • Ribeiro Antonio Lopes • SHT • PRT
CORTESANA • 1947 • Gout Alberto • MXC
CORTIGIANA DI BABILONIA, LA • 1955 • Bragaglia Carlo Ludovico • ITL • QUEEN OF BABYLON, THE ○ SLAVE WOMAN, THE
CORTILE • 1931 • Campogalliani Carlo • ITL
CORTILE • 1956 • Petrucci Antonio • ITL
CORTILE CASCINO • 1957 • Roemer Michael, Young Robert Malcolm • USA
CORTILI • 1947 • Risi Dino • SHT • ITL
CORTINA CONQUEST see **YEAR OF THE CORTINA, THE** • 1964
CORTINA DI CRISTALLO • 1958 • Barlacchi Cesare, Ruiz Henrique • ITL, VNZ • TI AMERO SEMPRE
CORTOCIRCUITO • 1943 • Gentilomo Giacomo • ITL • POLIZIA A VILLABIANCA, LA ○ ORCHIDEA AZZURRA
CORVEE DE QUARTIER ACCIDENTEE • 1898 • Melies Georges • FRN • SOLDIER'S TEDIOUS DUTY, A
CORVETTE K-225 • 1943 • Rosson Richard, Hawks Howard (U/c) • USA • NELSON TOUCH, THE (UKN)
CORVETTE PORT ARTHUR • 1943 • Ivens Joris • DOC • CND
CORVETTE SUMMER • 1978 • Robbins Matthew • USA • HOT ONES, THE (UKN)
CORVI, TI SCAVERANNO LA FOSSA, I • 1971 • Iquino Ignacio F. • ITL

CORVINI INHERITANCE, THE • 1984 • Beaumont Gabrielle • UKN

CORWIN • 1969 • Bonniere Rene • SER • CND

COSA AVETE FATTO A SOLANGE? • 1972 • Dallamano Massimo • ITL, FRG • GEHEIMNIS DER GRUEN STECKNADELN, DAS (FRG) ○ SECRET OF THE GREEN PINS, THE ○ WHAT HAVE YOU DONE TO SOLANGE? (USA)

COSA BUFFA, LA • 1972 • Lado Aldo • ITL

COSA FACIL • 1979 • Gurrola Alfredo • MXC

COSA NOSTRA • 1972 • Young Terence • FRN, ITL • JOE VALACHI: A SEGRETI DI COSA NOSTRA ○ VALACHI PAPERS, THE (UKN) ○ JOE VALACHI (ITL)

COSA NOSTRA -ARCH ENEMY OF THE F.B.I. • 1967 • Medford Don • USA

COSA PROHIBIDAS, LAS • 1958 • Diaz Morales Jose • MXC

COSAS DE MUJER see **PECADO** • 1950

COSAS DEL QUERER, LAS • 1989 • Chavarri Jaime • SPN • FOND THINGS

COSCIENZA • 1923 • Serena Gustavo • ITL

COSE DA PAZZI • 1954 • Pabst G. W. • ITL • DROLL STORIES

COSE DELL'ALTRO MONDO • 1939 • Malasomma Nunzio • ITL

COSE DI COSA NOSTRA • 1971 • Steno • ITL

COSECHA INDIGENA, LA • 1976 • Montana Antonio • DOC • CLM

COSH BOY • 1952 • Gilbert Lewis* • UKN • SLASHER, THE (USA)

COSI BELLO COSI CORROTTO COSI CONTESO • 1973 • Gobbi Sergio • ITL, FRN • VORACES, LES (FRN)

COSI COME SEI • 1978 • Lattuada Alberto • ITL, SPN • STAY AS YOU ARE (USA)

COSI, COSI.. PIU FORTE • 1970 • Petrini Luigi • ITL

COSI DOLCE.. COSI PERVERSA • 1969 • Lenzi Umberto • ITL, FRG, FRN • SI DOUCES, SI PERVERSES (FRN) ○ SO SWEET, SO PERVERSE

COSI FAN TUTTE • 1970 • Kaslik Vaclav • AUS, FRG

COSI SIA • 1972 • Caltabiano Alfio • ITL • THEY CALLED HIM AMEN ○ THEY CALL HIM AMEN

COSMETIC REVOLUTION, THE see **KOSMETIKKREVOLUSJONEN** • 1977

COSMIC ADVENTURES OF ALICE IN WONDERLAND • *Brodax Al (P)* • ANM • USA

COSMIC EYE, THE • 1985 • Hubley Faith • ANM • USA

COSMIC FIRE • 1984 • Burton Robert H. • MTV • CND

COSMIC JOURNEY • 1928 • USS

COSMIC MAN, THE • 1959 • Greene Herbert • USA

COSMIC MAN APPEARS IN TOKYO, THE see **UCHUJIN TOKYO NI ARAWARU** • 1956

COSMIC MONSTER, THE (USA) see **STRANGE WORLD OF PLANET X, THE** • 1958

COSMIC MONSTERS see **STRANGE WORLD OF PLANET X, THE** • 1958

COSMIC PRINCESS • 1976 • Crichton Charles, Medak Peter • MTV • UKN • SPACE 1999: COSMIC PRINCESS

COSMIC RAY #1 • 1961 • Conner Bruce • SHT • USA

COSMIC RAY #2 • 1961 • Conner Bruce • SHT • USA

COSMIC RAY #3 • 1961 • Conner Bruce • SHT • USA

COSMIC VESSEL see **KOSMITCHESKY REIS** • 1935

COSMIC VOYAGE, THE see **KOSMITCHESKY REIS** • 1935

COSMIC ZOOM • 1968 • Szasz Eva • SHT • CND

COSMICAL PASSAGE see **KOSMITCHESKY REIS** • 1935

COSMO 2000: PLANET WITHOUT A NAME see **COSMOS: WAR OF THE PLANETS** • 1977

COSMO JONES -CRIME SMASHER • 1943 • Tinling James • USA • CRIME SMASHER (UKN)

COSMODROME 1999 • 1969 • ANS • CZC

COSMONAUTS ON VENUS see **PLANETA BURG** • 1962

COSMONAUTS STREET • 1963 • Roshal Marianna • USS

COSMOS • 1970 • Belson Jordan • SHT • USA

COSMOS, THE FANTASTIC JOURNEY! • 1964 • Pederson Con, Jackson Ben • ANS • USA

COSMOS: WAR OF THE PLANETS • 1977 • Brescia Alfonso • ITL • COSMO 2000: PLANET WITHOUT A NAME ○ WAR OF THE PLANETS

COSMOSPOLIS • 1919 • Ravel Gaston

COSSACHI, I • 1960 • Tourjansky Victor, Rivalta Giorgio • ITL, FRN • COSSAQUES, LES (FRN) ○ COSSACKS, THE

COSSACK BEYOND THE DANUBE, A • 1954 • Lapoknysh Vasil • USS

COSSACK TRICK RIDERS • 1896 • Fedetsky A. P. • USS

COSSACK WHIP, THE • 1916 • Collins John H. • USA

COSSACKS, THE • 1928 • Hill George W., Brown Clarence (U/c) • USA

COSSACKS, THE see **COSSACHI, I** • 1960

COSSACKS, THE see **KASAKI** • 1961

COSSACKS ACROSS THE DANUBE see **ZAPOROSH SA DUNAYEM** • 1939

COSSACKS IN EXILE see **ZAPOROSH SA DUNAYEM** • 1939

COSSACKS OF THE DON see **TIKHU DON** • 1931

COSSACKS OF THE KUBAN see **KUBANSKIE KAZAKI** • 1949

COSSAQUES, LES (FRN) see **COSSACHI, I** • 1960

COST, THE • 1915 • *West Josephine* • USA

COST, THE • 1920 • Knoles Harley • USA

COST OF A KISS, THE • 1917 • Brunel Adrian • UKN

COST OF BEAUTY, THE • 1924 • Summers Walter • UKN

COST OF DRINK, THE • 1911 • *Champion* • USA

COST OF DYING, THE see **QUANTO COSTA MORIRE** • 1968

COST OF HATRED, THE • 1917 • Melford George • USA

COST OF HIGH LIVING, THE • 1916 • Wolbert William • SHT • USA

COST OF LIVING, THE see **COSTO DE LA VIDA, EL** • 1989

COST OF LOVING see **PROWLER, THE** • 1951

COSTA AZZURRA • 1959 • Sala Vittorio • ITL, FRN • WILD CATS ON THE BEACH (USA) ○ COTE D'AZURE (FRN)

COSTA DE AFRICA, O • 1954 • Mendes Joao • PRT

COSTA DE LA LUZ, LA • 1967 • Enciso Luis S. • SHT • SPN

COSTA DE LA MUERTE, LA • 1945 • Royan Eladio • SPN

COSTA DEL SOL, LA • Chumez Chumy • SHT • SPN

COSTA DO CASTELO, O • 1943 • Duarte Arthur • PRT • COSTA OF THE CASTLE

COSTA OF THE CASTLE see **COSTA DO CASTELO, O** • 1943

COSTANTINO IL GRANDE -IN HOC SIGNO VINCES • 1960 • De Felice Lionello • ITL • CONSTANTINE AND THE CROSS (USA) ○ CONSTANTINO IL GRANDE ○ CONSTANTINE THE GREAT

COSTANZA DELLA RAGIONE, LA • 1964 • Festa Campanile Pasquale • ITL

COSTAUD DES EPINETTES, LE • 1922 • Bernard Raymond • FRN

COSTAUD DES P.T.T., LE • 1931 • Bertin Jean, Mate Rudolph • FRN • ROI DES FACTEURS, LE ○ P.T.T.

COSTELLO CASE, THE • 1930 • Lang Walter • USA • COSTELLO MURDER CASE, THE (UKN)

COSTELLO MURDER CASE, THE (UKN) see **COSTELLO CASE, THE** • 1930

COSTER AND HIS DONKEY, THE • 1902 • Stow Percy • UKN

COSTER BILL • 1912 • Coleby A. E.? • UKN

COSTER BILL OF PARIS (USA) see **CRAINQUEBILLE** • 1922

COSTER BURGLAR AND HIS DOG, THE • 1915 • Green Tom? • UKN

COSTER JOE • 1915 • Frenguelli Alfonse • UKN

COSTER JOE see **COSTER'S WEDDING, THE** • 1913

COSTER'S CHRISTENING, THE • 1905 • Collins Alf? • UKN

COSTER'S HOLIDAY, THE • 1914 • *Captain Kettle Films* • UKN

COSTER'S HONEYMOON, THE • 1912 • Kellino W. P. • UKN

COSTER'S PHANTOM FORTUNE, THE • 1910 • Collins Alf • UKN

COSTER'S REVENGE, THE • 1906 • Stow Percy • UKN

COSTER'S SERENADE, THE • 1906 • Gilbert Arthur • UKN

COSTER'S WEDDING, THE • 1904 • Collins Alf • *Gaumont* • UKN

COSTER'S WEDDING, THE • 1904 • Fitzhamon Lewin • *Hepworth* • UKN

COSTER'S WEDDING, THE • 1910 • Bouwmeester Theo • UKN

COSTER'S WEDDING, THE • 1913 • Stow Percy • UKN • COSTER JOE

COSTLY EXCHANGE, A • 1915 • *Komic* • USA

COSTLY GIFT, A • 1910 • Coleby A. E.? • UKN

COSTLY PLEDGE, A • 1911 • *Solax* • USA

COSTO DE LA VIDA, EL • 1989 • Montero Rafael • MXC • COST OF LIVING, THE

COSTUME MEETING see **KOSTIMIRANI RENDEZ-VOUS** • 1965

COSTUME PIECE, A • 1914 • *Walker Lillian* • USA

COSTUMES ANIMES, LES • 1904 • Melies Georges • FRN • ANIMATED COSTUMES, THE (USA)

COSTUMI E BELLEZZE D'ITALIA • 1948 • Risi Dino • SHT • ITL

COSTUREIRINHA DA SE, A • 1959 • Guimaraes Manuel • PRT

COSY COOL • 1977 • Young Gary • ASL

COSY CORNER GIRL • 1907 • *Walturdaw* • UKN

COSY COTTAGE, A • 1963 • Fejer Tamas • HNG

COTE COEUR, COTE JARDIN • 1953 • Blais Roger • DCS • CND

COTE COEUR, COTE JARDIN • 1984 • Van Effenterre Bertrand • FRN

COTE D'ADAM, LE • 1963 • Sengissen • SHT • FRN

COTE D'AMOUR, LA • 1982 • Dubreuil Charlotte • FRN

COTE D'AZUR • 1931 • Capellani Albert • FRN

COTE D'AZUR, LA • 1948 • Leenhardt Roger • DCS • FRN

COTE D'AZURE (FRN) see **COSTA AZZURRA** • 1959

COTE NORD A L'AUTRE BOUT DU MONDE, LA • 1968 • Brault Francois • DCS • CND

COTO DE CAZA • 1984 • Grau Jorge • SPN • GAME RESERVE

COTOLAY • 1966 • Nieves Conde Jose Antonio • SPN

COTON, LE • 1935 • Storck Henri • DOC • BLG

COTON, LE • 1958 • Shawqi Khalil • SHT • EGY

COTTAGE, THE see **BARRACA, LA** • 1944

COTTAGE BY THE RIVER, A • 1914 • *Melies* • USA

COTTAGE ON DARTMOOR, A • 1929 • Asquith Anthony • UKN, SWD • ESCAPED FROM DARTMOOR (USA) ○ FANGAN 53

COTTAGE PIE see **SOLDIER'S COTTAGE, THE** • 1946

COTTAGE TO LET • 1941 • Asquith Anthony • UKN • BOMBSIGHT STOLEN (USA)

COTTER • 1973 • Stanley Paul • TVM • USA

COTTON AND CATTLE • 1921 • Franchon Leonard • USA

COTTON AND SILK see **IT'S A GREAT LIFE** • 1929

COTTON CANDY • 1978 • Howard Ron • TVM • USA

COTTON CHICKEN see **VATSALA KALYANAM** • 1950

COTTON CHICKEN see **VATSALA KALYANAM** • 1950

COTTON CLUB, THE • 1984 • Coppola Francis Ford • USA

COTTON COMES TO HARLEM • 1970 • Davis Ossie • USA

COTTON KING, THE • 1915 • Eagle Oscar • USA

COTTON QUEEN • 1937 • Vorhaus Bernard • UKN • CRYING OUT LOUD

COTTONPICKIN' CHICKENPICKERS • 1967 • Jackson Larry E. • USA

COTTONTAIL see **HOT CHOCOLATE** • 1941

COUCARACHA see **KOUKARACHA** • 1983

COUCH • 1964 • Warhol Andy • USA

COUCH, THE • 1962 • Crump Owen • USA

COUCH TRIP, THE • 1988 • Ritchie Michael • USA

COUCHE DE LA MARIEE, LE • 1933 • Lion Roger • FRN

COUCHER DE LA MARIEE, LE • 1899 • Melies Georges • FRN • TRISTE NUIT DE NOCES ○ BRIDEGROOM'S DILEMMA, THE

COUCHER D'UNE PARISIENNE • 1900 • Blache Alice • FRN

COUCHER D'YVETTE • 1897 • Blache Alice • FRN

COUCHES CHAUDES • 1942 • Proulx Maurice • DCS • CND

COUCHETTE NO.3 see **SURPRISES DU SLEEPING, LES** • 1933

COUCOU, LE (FRN) see **LUPO E L'AGNELLO, IL** • 1980

COUGAR COUNTRY • 1970 • *Meyer David W.* • DOC • USA

COUGAR, THE KING KILLER • 1933 • *Master Arts* • USA • COUGAR (UKN)

COUGAR (UKN) see **COUGAR, THE KING KILLER** • 1933

COUGHING HIGGINS • 1917 • Ray John • SHT • USA

COUGHING HORROR, THE • 1924 • Paul Fred • UKN

COULD A MAN DO MORE? • 1915 • Broadwell Robert B. • USA

COULD I BUT LIVE see **WARE HITOTSUBU NO MUGI NAREDO** • 1964

COULD IT HAPPEN HERE? • 1969 • Noonan Chris • SHT • ASL

COULD YOU BLAME HER • 1914 • Christie Al • USA

COULD YOU BLAME HIM? • 1911 • *Nestor* • USA

COULD YOU SAVE A LIFE • 1980 • Armstrong Mary • MTV • CND

COULDN'T POSSIBLY HAPPEN (UKN) see **MEN WITH STEEL FACES** • 1940

COULEUR CHAIR • 1977 • Weyergans Francois • BLG, FRN

COULEUR DE FEU see **COULEURS DE FEU** • 1957

COULEUR DE LA FORME, LA • 1961 • Hirsch Hy • SHT • USA • COLOR OF THE FORM, THE

COULEUR ENCERCLEE, LA • 1986 • Gagne Jean, Gagne Serge • CND

COULEURS see **ALWAN** • 1973

COULEURS AU CORPS • 1972 • Smihi Moumen • SHT • MRC

COULEURS DE FEU • 1957 • Storck Henri • DOC • BLG • COULEUR DE FEU

COULISSES, LES • 1971 • Fettar Sid-Ali • ALG

COULISSES DE L'ENTRAIDE • 1984 • Favreau Robert • CND • TOUCH OF HEALING

COULOMB'S LAW • 1959 • Leacock Richard • DOC • USA

COUNCIL BLUFFS TO OMAHA -TRAIN SCENIC • 1900 • *Bitzer Billy (Ph)* • USA

COUNCIL OF THE GODS see **RAT DER GOTTER, DER** • 1950

COUNCIL OF THREE, THE • 1909 • *London Cinematograph Co.* • UKN

COUNSEL FOR CRIME • 1937 • Brahm John • USA

COUNSEL FOR THE DEFENCE • 1912 • Brooke Van Dyke • USA

COUNSEL FOR THE DEFENCE • 1913 • *Theby Rosemary* • USA

COUNSEL FOR THE DEFENCE • 1915 • *Livingston Jack* • USA

COUNSEL FOR THE DEFENSE • 1925 • King Burton L. • USA

COUNSEL FOR THE PROSECUTION HAS THE FLOOR, THE see **PROKURATOR MA GLOS** • 1965

COUNSEL ON DE FENCE • 1934 • Ripley Arthur • SHT • USA

COUNSELITIS • 1935 • Boasberg Al • SHT • USA

COUNSELLOR, THE see **STUDENT CONFIDENTIAL** • 1987

COUNSELLOR AT LAW • 1933 • Wyler William • USA

COUNSELLOR BOBBY • 1913 • Trimble Larry • USA

COUNSEL'S OPINION • 1933 • Dwan Allan • UKN

COUNT, THE • 1916 • Chaplin Charles • SHT • USA

COUNT, THE see **KREIVI** • 1970

COUNT AND THE COWBOYS, THE • 1911 • *Hamilton G. P.* • USA

COUNT AND THE WEDDING GUEST, THE • 1918 • Justice Martin • SHT • USA

COUNT BARBER • 1913 • Angeles Bert • USA

COUNT BASIE SHOW AT THE RIVERBOAT, THE • 1968 • Weaver John • SHT • USA

COUNT CAGLIOSTRO see **GRAF VON CAGLIOSTRO, DER** • 1920

COUNT DOWN CLOWN • 1960 • Hanna William, Barbera Joseph • ANS • USA

COUNT DOWNE see **SON OF DRACULA** • 1974

COUNT DRACULA • 1978 • Saville Philip • TVM • UKN

COUNT DRACULA AND HIS VAMPIRE BRIDE see **SATANIC RITES OF DRACULA, THE** • 1973

COUNT DRACULA (UKN) see **CONDE DRACULA, EL** • 1970

COUNT DRACULA'S GREAT LOVE see **GRAN AMOR DEL CONDE DRACULA, EL** • 1972

COUNT 'EM • 1915 • Ince Ralph • USA

COUNT EROTICA VAMPIRE • 1971 • Teresi Tony • USA

COUNT FIVE AND DIE • 1958 • Vicas Victor • UKN

COUNT FRANKENHAUSEN see **VAMPIRO SANGRIENTO, EL** • 1962

COUNT FROM MUNKBRO see **MUNKBROGREVEN** • 1935

COUNT FROM THE LANE, THE see **GREVEN FRAN GRANDEN** • 1949

COUNT HENRI, THE HUNTER • 1912 • *Quirk Billy* • USA

COUNT IVAN AND THE WAITRESS • 1911 • *Thanhouser* • USA

COUNT MACARONI • 1915 • Louis Will • USA

COUNT ME OUT • 1938 • Hardaway Ben, Dalton Cal • ANS • USA

COUNT ME OUT • 1946 • Crouch William Forest • SHT • USA

COUNT MEOUT • 1916 • *Unicorn* • USA

COUNT OF ARIZONA, THE see **MY AMERICAN WIFE** • 1922

COUNT OF BRAGELONNE, THE see **VICOMTE DE BRAGELONNE, LE** • 1954

COUNT OF BRECHARD, THE (USA) see **CONTE DI BRECHARD, IL** • 1938

COUNT OF CHAROLAIS, THE see **GRAF VON CHAROLAIS, DER** • 1922

COUNT OF DAYS, THE • 1969 • Beavers Robert • USA

COUNT OF LUXEMBOURG, THE • 1926 • Gregor Arthur • USA

COUNT OF MONTE CRISTO, THE • 1908 • Boggs Frank • USA

COUNT OF MONTE CRISTO, THE • 1913 • Porter Edwin S., Golden Joseph A. • USA

COUNT OF MONTE CRISTO, THE • 1934 • Lee Rowland V. • USA

COUNT OF MONTE CRISTO, THE • 1975 • Greene David • TVM • USA, UKN

COUNT OF MONTE CRISTO, THE see **MONTE CRISTO** • 1912

COUNT OF MONTE CRISTO, THE see **COMTE DE MONTE-CRISTO, LE** • 1953

COUNT OF MONTE CRISTO, THE see **COMTE DE MONTE-CRISTO, LE** • 1961

COUNT OF MONTE CRISTO, THE (USA) see **COMTE DE MONTE-CRISTO, LE** • 1942

COUNT OF MONTEBELLO, THE • 1910 • *Imp* • USA

COUNT OF NO ACCOUNT, THE • 1911 • *Solax* • USA

COUNT OF NO-ACCOUNT, THE • 1921 • Dunstall George • UKN

COUNT OF NOACCOUNT, THE • 1910 • *Atlas* • USA

COUNT OF ST. ELMO, THE (USA) see **CONTE DI SANT'ELMO, IL** • 1951

COUNT OF TEN, THE • 1928 • Flood James • USA • BETTY'S A LADY

COUNT OF TWELVE • 1955 • Gerrard Paul • UKN

COUNT ON TROUBLE see **RAKNA MED BRAK** • 1957

COUNT PUSHKIN VODKA see **IMPERIAL GUARD CAVALRY** • 1976

COUNT RETIRES, THE • 1913 • *Imp* • USA

COUNT SVENSSON see **GREVE SVENSSON** • 1951

COUNT TACCHIA see **CONTE TACCHIA, IL** • 1983

COUNT TAKES THE COUNT, THE • 1936 • Parrott Charles, Law Harold • SHT • USA
COUNT THAT COUNTED, THE • 1910 • *Essanay* • USA
COUNT THAT TOOK THE COUNT, THE • 1914 • *Eclectic* • USA
COUNT THE HAPPY MOMENTS ONLY see **RAKNA DE LYCKLIGA STUNDERNA BLOTT** • 1944
COUNT THE HOURS • 1952 • Siegel Don • USA • EVERY MINUTE COUNTS (UKN)
COUNT THE STARS IN THE HEAVENS • 1989 • Perez Elwood • PHL
COUNT THE VOTES • 1919 • *Lloyd Harold* • SHT • USA
COUNT THREE AND PRAY • 1955 • Sherman George • USA • CALICO PONY, THE
COUNT TWENTY • 1915 • Physioc Wray • USA
COUNT VIM'S LAST EXERCISE • 1967 • Weir Peter • SHT • ASL • VIM'S LAST EXERCISE
COUNT YORGA, VAMPIRE • 1970 • Kelljan Bob • USA • LOVES OF COUNT IORGA -VAMPIRE, THE ○ VAMPYRE
COUNT YOUR BLESSINGS • 1959 • Negulesco Jean • USA
COUNT YOUR BLESSINGS see **VAN GELUK GESPROKEN** • 1987
COUNT YOUR BULLETS see **CRY FOR ME, BILLY** • 1972
COUNT YOUR CHANGE • 1919 • Roach Hal • SHT • USA
COUNTDOWN • 1968 • Altman Robert, Conrad William • USA • MOONSHOT
COUNTDOWN see **VISSZASZAMLALAS** • 1985
COUNTDOWN AT KUSINI • 1976 • Davis Ossie • NGR, USA
COUNTDOWN TO DANGER • 1967 • Seabourne Peter • UKN
COUNTDOWN TO LOOKING GLASS • 1984 • Barzyk Fred • TVM • USA
COUNTED OUT see **KNOCK OUT, THE** • 1914
COUNTED OUT (UKN) see **SWELLHEAD, THE** • 1930
COUNTER-ATTACK • 1945 • Korda Zoltan • USA • ONE AGAINST SEVEN (UKN)
COUNTER ATTACK • 1960 • Kneitel Seymour • ANS • USA
COUNTER-ATTACK OF GIRLS see **MUSUME NO GYAKUSHU** • 1947
COUNTER-ESPIONAGE • 1942 • Dmytryk Edward • USA
COUNTER INTRIGUE, THE • 1915 • *Bayne Beverly* • USA
COUNTER INVESTIGATION (USA) see **CONTRE-ENQUETE** • 1946
COUNTER JUMPER, THE • 1922 • Semon Larry • SHT • USA • STORE KEEPER
COUNTER-MELODY, THE • 1914 • *Stonehouse Ruth* • USA
COUNTER PLOT, THE • 1920 • Goldaine Mark • SHT • USA
COUNTER TENORS, THE see **VOCI BIANCHE, LE** • 1964
COUNTERBLAST • 1948 • Stein Paul L. • UKN • DEVIL'S PLOT, THE ○ SO DIED A RAT
COUNTERFEIT • 1919 • Fitzmaurice George • USA
COUNTERFEIT • 1936 • Kenton Erle C. • USA
COUNTERFEIT see **JAAL** • 1967
COUNTERFEIT, THE • 1914 • *Balboa* • USA
COUNTERFEIT, THE • 1915 • *Victor* • USA
COUNTERFEIT CAT • 1949 • Avery Tex • ANS • USA
COUNTERFEIT CLUES • 1918 • *Roland Ruth* • SHT • USA
COUNTERFEIT COIN, THE (USA) see **KALPIKI LIRA, I** • 1955
COUNTERFEIT COMMANDOS see **QUEL MALEDETTO TRENO BLINDATO** • 1978
COUNTERFEIT CONSTABLE, THE (USA) see **ALLEZ FRANCE!** • 1964
COUNTERFEIT COURTSHIP, THE • 1913 • *Victor* • USA
COUNTERFEIT COWBOY, THE • 1915 • Birch Cecil • UKN
COUNTERFEIT EARL, THE • 1916 • Le Viness Carl M. • SHT • USA
COUNTERFEIT HERO • Halling Daniel
COUNTERFEIT KILLER, THE • 1968 • Leytes Joseph, Rosenberg Stuart • USA • CRACKSHOT
COUNTERFEIT LADY • 1937 • Lederman D. Ross • USA
COUNTERFEIT LOVE • 1916 • Miller Rube • USA
COUNTERFEIT LOVE • 1923 • Sheldon Roy, Ince Ralph • USA
COUNTERFEIT PLAN, THE • 1957 • Tully Montgomery • UKN
COUNTERFEIT ROLL, THE • 1911 • *Lubin* • USA
COUNTERFEIT SANTA CLAUS, A • 1912 • Turner Otis • USA
COUNTERFEIT SCENT, A • 1917 • *Triangle* • USA
COUNTERFEIT TRAIL, THE • 1920 • Kull Edward • SHT • USA
COUNTERFEIT TRAITOR, THE • 1962 • Seaton George • USA
COUNTERFEITER, THE • 1913 • West Raymond B. • USA
COUNTERFEITERS • 1914 • Salter Harry • *Victor* • USA
COUNTERFEITERS, THE • 1914 • Kendall Preston • *Edison* • USA
COUNTERFEITERS, THE • 1915 • Raymond Charles • UKN
COUNTERFEITERS, THE • 1917 • Terwilliger George W. • SHT • USA
COUNTERFEITERS, THE • 1948 • Newfield Sam • USA
COUNTERFEITERS, THE (UKN) see **CAVE SE REBIFFE, LE** • 1961
COUNTERFEITER'S CONFEDERATE, THE • 1913 • *Nilsson Anna Q.* • USA
COUNTERFEITER'S DAUGHTER, THE • 1914 • Morrisey Edward • USA
COUNTERFEITER'S FATE, THE • 1913 • Fielding Romaine • USA
COUNTERFEITERS OF PARIS, THE (USA) see **CAVE SE REBIFFE, LE** • 1961
COUNTERFEITER'S PLOT, THE • 1914 • Lawrence Edmund • USA
COUNTERFEITING INVESTIGATION • 1959 • Hani Susumu • DOC • JPN
COUNTERFORCE • 1987 • de la Loma Jose Antonio • MXC
COUNTERPLAN see **VSTRECHNYI** • 1932
COUNTERPLOT • 1959 • Neumann Kurt • USA
COUNTERPOINT • 1959 • Krish John • UKN
COUNTERPOINT • 1968 • Nelson Ralph • USA
COUNTERPOINT IN WHITE • 1964 • Stiopul Savel • RMN
COUNTERSPY • 1953 • Sewell Vernon • UKN • UNDERCOVER AGENT (USA)
COUNTERSPY MEETS SCOTLAND YARD, THE • 1950 • Friedman Seymour • USA
COUNTESS, THE • 1914 • *Bushman Francis X.* • USA
COUNTESS AND THE BURGLAR, THE • 1914 • *Coghlan Gertrude* • USA
COUNTESS ANKARSTROM • 1910 • *Deutsche Bioscop* • FRG
COUNTESS BETTY'S MINE • 1914 • Reid Wallace • USA
COUNTESS CHARMING, THE • 1917 • Crisp Donald • USA
COUNTESS COSEL (UKN) see **HRABINA COSEL** • 1968
COUNTESS DONELLI see **GRAFIN DONELLI** • 1924
COUNTESS DORA see **KONTESA DORA** • 1990
COUNTESS DRACULA • 1970 • Sasdy Peter • UKN
COUNTESS DRACULA see **CEREMONIA SANGRIETA** • 1972
COUNTESS FROM HONGKONG, THE • 1966 • Chaplin Charles • UKN
COUNTESS OF MONTE CRISTO, THE • 1934 • Freund Karl • USA
COUNTESS OF MONTE CRISTO, THE • 1948 • De Cordova Frederick • USA
COUNTESS OF MONTE CRISTO, THE see **GRAFIN VON MONTE CHRISTO, DIE** • 1919
COUNTESS OF MONTE CRISTO, THE see **GRAFIN VON MONTE CHRISTO, DIE** • 1932
COUNTESS OF NEW ORLEANS, THE see **FLAME OF NEW ORLEANS, THE** • 1941
COUNTESS OF PARMA, THE see **CONTESSA DI PARMA, LA** • 1937
COUNTESS OF SUMMACOUNT, THE • 1917 • Wilson Frank • UKN
COUNTESS SARAH see **CONTESSA SARA, LA** • 1919
COUNTESS SWEEDIE • 1914 • *Beery Wallace* • USA
COUNTESS VESCHKI'S JEWELS • 1915 • *Essanay* • USA
COUNTESS VESCHKI'S JEWELS, THE • 1914 • Finley Ned • *Vitagraph* • USA
COUNTESS'S HONOR, THE see **GREVINDENS AERE** • 1918
COUNTING 'EM UP • 1917 • *Pokes & Jabbs* • SHT • USA
COUNTING HOUSE MYSTERY, THE • 1911 • *Yankee* • USA
COUNTING OF TIME, THE • 1912 • *Conway Jack* • USA
COUNTING OUT THE COUNT • 1915 • *Reeves Billie* • USA
COUNTING OUT THE COUNT • 1916 • Beaudine William • USA
COUNTING OUT THE COUNT • 1917 • Dunham Phil • SHT • USA
COUNTING SHEEP • 1982 • Kachyna Karel • MTV • CZC
COUNTLESS COUNT, A • 1915 • *Fries Eddie* • USA
COUNTLESS COUNT, THE • 1914 • *Joker* • USA
COUNTRY • 1984 • Pearce Richard • USA
COUNTRY BEYOND, THE • 1926 • Cummings Irving • USA
COUNTRY BEYOND, THE • 1936 • Forde Eugene J. • USA
COUNTRY BLOOD • 1915 • Johnson Arthur • USA
COUNTRY BLUE • 1980 • Conrad Jack • USA
COUNTRY BOARDER, THE • 1910 • *Imp* • USA
COUNTRY BOSS see **KAMITSUKARETA KAOYAKU** • 1958
COUNTRY BOY • 1935 • Freleng Friz • ANS • USA
COUNTRY BOY see **HERE COMES THE NASHVILLE SOUND** • 1966
COUNTRY BOY, THE • 1912 • *Gray Betty* • USA
COUNTRY BOY, THE • 1915 • Thompson Frederick A. • USA
COUNTRY BRIDE see **BOGOTAYA NEVESTA** • 1937
COUNTRY BUMPKIN (UKN) see **ALL-AMERICAN CHUMP** • 1936
COUNTRY CATTLE SHOW, A • 1897 • Norton C. Goodwin • UKN • AGRICULTURAL SHOW
COUNTRY CHILDREN • 1976 • Petit Christopher • UKN
COUNTRY CIRCUS, THE • 1915 • *Macmillan Violet* • USA
COUNTRY COMES TO TOWN, THE • 1931 • Wright Basil • DOC • UKN
COUNTRY COMFORT • 1981 • Augustus Bob • USA
COUNTRY COURTSHIP • 1905 • *Bitzer Billy (Ph)* • USA
COUNTRY COUSIN, THE • 1913 • *Nestor* • USA
COUNTRY COUSIN, THE • 1919 • Crosland Alan • USA
COUNTRY COUSIN, THE • 1936 • Hand David • ANS • USA
COUNTRY CUPID, A • 1911 • Griffith D. W. • USA
COUNTRY CUZZINS • 1972 • *Bond Rene* • USA
COUNTRY DANCE • 1969 • Thompson J. Lee • UKN, USA • BROTHERLY LOVE (USA) ○ SAME SKIN, THE
COUNTRY DIARY OF AN EDWARDIAN LADY, THE • 1988 • Campbell Dirk • UKN
COUNTRY DOCTOR, THE • 1909 • Griffith D. W. • USA
COUNTRY DOCTOR, THE • 1927 • Julian Rupert • USA
COUNTRY DOCTOR, THE • 1936 • King Henry • USA
COUNTRY DOCTOR, THE see **SELSKII VRACH** • 1952
COUNTRY DOCTOR, THE see **FUNDOSHI ISHA** • 1960
COUNTRY DOCTOR, THE see **POUTA** • 1961
COUNTRY FAIR • 1941 • McDonald Frank • USA
COUNTRY FIRE BRIGADE see **FIRE BRIGADE TURN-OUT IN THE COUNTRY** • 1899
COUNTRY FLAPPER, THE • 1922 • Jones F. Richard • USA • CYNIC EFFECT, A
COUNTRY FOR MY SON, A • 1969 • Wiegel Jan • SHT • NTH
COUNTRY FROLIC see **RENTAK DESA** • 1989
COUNTRY GENTLEMEN • 1937 • Staub Ralph • USA
COUNTRY GIRL • 1968 • Davis Bobby • USA
COUNTRY GIRL, A • 1908 • Fitzhamon Lewin? • UKN
COUNTRY GIRL, A • 1911 • *Reliance* • USA
COUNTRY GIRL, A • 1912 • *Imp* • USA
COUNTRY GIRL, A • 1914 • Jones Edgar • USA
COUNTRY GIRL, THE • 1915 • *Thanhouser* • USA
COUNTRY GIRL, THE • 1915 • Easton Clem • *Imp* • USA
COUNTRY GIRL, THE • 1954 • Seaton George • USA
COUNTRY GIRLS, THE • 1984 • Davis Desmond • UKN
COUNTRY GIRLS, THE see **BANAT EL RIF** • 1945
COUNTRY GIRL'S PERIL, A • 1909 • *Selig* • USA
COUNTRY GIRL'S SEMINARY LIFE AND EXPERIENCES • 1908 • Porter Edwin S. • USA
COUNTRY GOLD • 1982 • Cates Gilbert • TVM • USA
COUNTRY HERO, A • 1917 • Arbuckle Roscoe • SHT • USA
COUNTRY HOLIDAY, A • 1912 • Kinder Stuart • UKN
COUNTRY HUSBAND, THE • 1955 • Neilson James • MTV • USA
COUNTRY IN MY ARMS see **TENKA GOMEN** • 1960
COUNTRY INNOCENCE • 1914 • *Imp* • USA
COUNTRY IS CALM, THE see **ES HERRSCHT RUHE IM LAND** • 1976
COUNTRY JAZZ • 1971 • Kingsbury R. • SHT • ASL
COUNTRY KID, THE • 1923 • Beaudine William • USA
COUNTRY LAD, A • 1915 • *Larkin Dolly* • USA
COUNTRY LASS, A • 1912 • Collins Edwin J.? • UKN
COUNTRY LOVERS, THE • 1911 • Sennett Mack • USA
COUNTRY LTD. see **PAIS, S.A.** • 1975
COUNTRY MAGISTRATE • 1953 • Anderson Robert • DOC • CND
COUNTRY MOUSE, THE • 1914 • Smalley Phillips? • USA
COUNTRY MOUSE, THE • 1935 • Freleng Friz • ANS • USA
COUNTRY MOUSE AND THE CITY MOUSE, THE • 1921 • *Terry Paul* • ANS • USA
COUNTRY MUSIC • 1971 • Vitale Frank, Moyle Allan • CND
COUNTRY MUSIC • 1972 • Hinkle Robert • USA
COUNTRY MUSIC BOY see **COUNTRY MUSIC HOLIDAY** • 1958
COUNTRY MUSIC CARAVAN • 1964 • *Colorama Roadshows* • USA • COUNTRY MUSIC CARNIVAL
COUNTRY MUSIC CARNIVAL see **COUNTRY MUSIC CARAVAN** • 1964
COUNTRY MUSIC DAUGHTER see **NASHVILLE GIRL** • 1976
COUNTRY MUSIC HOLIDAY • 1958 • Ganzer Alvin • USA • COUNTRY MUSIC BOY
COUNTRY MUSIC JAMBOREE • 1970 • Williams Gene • USA
COUNTRY MUSIC MURDERS, THE see **MURDER IN MUSIC CITY** • 1979
COUNTRY MUSIC NITELY • 1979 • Gunnarsson Sturla • CND
COUNTRY MUSIC ON BROADWAY • 1964 • Duncan Victor • USA
COUNTRY NURSE • 1951 • Garceau Raymond • DCS • CND • INFIRMIERE RURALE, L'
COUNTRY NURSE see **CORNETTI A COLAZIONE** • 1978
COUNTRY OF COUNTRIES, THE see **ZEME ZEMI** • 1962
COUNTRY OF THE MARIACHI (USA) see **TIERRA DEL MARIACHI, LA** • 1938
COUNTRY OF THE MIND, A • 1972 • Watson Patricia • CND
COUNTRY OF THE SOVIETS see **STRANA SOVIETOV** • 1937
COUNTRY PARSON, THE • 1915 • *Vale Louise* • USA
COUNTRY PARTY CHIEF SECRETARY, THE • NKR
COUNTRY PEOPLE see **XIANGYIN** • 1983
COUNTRY POLICEMAN • 1946 • Gunn Gilbert • DOC • UKN
COUNTRY SCHOOL • 1931 • Lantz Walter, Nolan William • ANS • USA
COUNTRY SCHOOL TEACHER, THE • 1912 • *Johnson Arthur* • USA
COUNTRY SCHOOLMASTER • 1906 • *Bitzer Billy (Ph)* • USA
COUNTRY SPORTS • 1897 • Norton C. Goodwin • UKN • SPORTS MEETING
COUNTRY STORE • 1937 • *Lantz Walter (P)* • ANS • USA
COUNTRY TEACHERS • Phthum Surasee • THL
COUNTRY THAT GOD FORGOT, THE • 1916 • Neilan Marshall • USA
COUNTRY THRESHING • 1958 • Koenig Wolf • CND
COUNTRY TO COUNTRY see **ZEME ZEMI** • 1962
COUNTRY TOWN • 1971 • Maxwell Peter • ASL
COUNTRY WAITER: OR, THE TALE OF A CRUSHED HAT, THE • 1899 • *Paul R. W.* • UKN
COUNTRY WESTERN HOEDOWN • 1967 • Johnson William R. • USA • PEE WEE KING'S COUNTRY WESTERN HOEDOWN
COUNTRY WITHOUT STARS, THE see **PAYS SANS ETOILES, LE** • 1945
COUNTRYMAN • 1982 • Jobson Dickie • UKN
COUNTRYMAN AND THE CINEMATOGRAPH, THE • 1901 • *Paul R. W.* • UKN
COUNTRYMAN AND THE FLUTE, THE • 1902 • Stow Percy • UKN
COUNTRYMAN'S DAY IN TOWN, A • 1908 • Williamson James? • UKN
COUNTRYMAN'S ROMANCE, A • 1913 • *Majestic* • USA
COUNTRYWOMEN, THE • 1942 • Page John • DOC • UKN
COUNTS, THE • 1912 • Ince Ralph • USA
COUNTS, THE • 1915 • Ince Ralph • USA
COUNTS AND NO ACCOUNTS • 1918 • Howe J. A. • SHT • USA
COUNT'S INFATUATION, THE • 1914 • *Powers* • USA
COUNTS OF SVANSTA, THE see **GREVARNA PA SVANSTA** • 1924
COUNT'S WILL, THE • 1913 • *Handworth Octavia* • USA
COUNT'S WOOING, THE • 1909 • Melies Georges • FRN
COUNTY CHAIRMAN, A • 1914 • Dwan Allan • USA
COUNTY CHAIRMAN, THE • 1935 • Blystone John G. • USA
COUNTY FAIR • 1937 • Bretherton Howard • USA
COUNTY FAIR • 1950 • Beaudine William • USA
COUNTY FAIR see **SONG OF THE PLOUGH** • 1933
COUNTY FAIR, THE • 1910 • *Selig* • USA
COUNTY FAIR, THE • 1912 • *Joyce Alice* • USA
COUNTY FAIR, THE • 1920 • Tourneur Maurice, Mortimer Edmund • USA
COUNTY FAIR, THE • 1932 • King Louis • USA
COUNTY FAIR, THE • 1934 • Lantz Walter, Nolan William • ANS • USA
COUNTY HOSPITAL • 1932 • Parrott James • SHT • USA
COUNTY LINE see **SELLOUT, THE** • 1951
COUNTY SEAT, THE • 1931 • Sandrich Mark • SHT • USA
COUNTY SEAT WAR, THE • 1914 • *Holmes Helen* • USA
COUNTY'S PRIZE BABY, THE • 1912 • *La Badie Florence* • USA
COUP DE BAMBOU • 1962 • Boyer Jean • FRN
COUP DE BOL, LE • 1983 • Colmant Jean-Louis • BLG
COUP DE FEU A L'AUBE • 1932 • de Poligny Serge • FRN • FEMME ET LE DIAMANT, LA
COUP DE FEU DANS LA NUIT • 1925 • Ravel Gaston • FRN
COUP DE FEU DANS LA NUIT • 1942 • Peguy Robert • FRN • UN COUP DE FEU DANS LA NUIT ○ SECRETS DE FAMILLE
COUP DE FOUDRE • 1951 • Daroy Jacques • SHT • FRN
COUP DE FOUDRE • 1978 • Enrico Robert • FRN
COUP DE FOUDRE • 1983 • Kurys Diane • FRN • AT FIRST SIGHT (UKN) ○ ENTRE NOUS (USA) ○ BETWEEN US
COUP DE FOUDRE see **CHIPEE** • 1937
COUP DE GONG A HONG-KONG (FRN) see **LOTOSBLUTEN FUR MISS QUON** • 1966
COUP DE GRACE see **FANGSCHUSS, DER** • 1976
COUP DE GRACE, LE • 1964 • Cayrol Jean, Durand Claude • FRN, CND
COUP DE JARNAC, UN • 1909 • Cohl Emile • ANS • FRN • JARNAC'S TREACHEROUS BLOW
COUP DE MAIN, LE • 1958 • Herman Jean • FRN
COUP DE MAITRE see **DESTIN S'AMUSE, LE** • 1946
COUP DE MISTRAL, UN • 1933 • Roudes Gaston • FRN • MON ONCLE D'ARLES
COUP DE PARAPLUIE, LE • 1980 • Oury Gerard • FRN
COUP DE ROUGE, UN • 1937 • Roudes Gaston • FRN

COUP DE SANG • 1980 • Payer Roch Christophe • MTV • CND
COUP DE SINGE, LE • 1978 • Bitton Ode, Kalfon Jean-Pierre • FRN
COUP DE SIROCCO, LE • 1978 • Arcady Alexandre • FRN
COUP DE TELEPHONE, UN • 1931 • Lacombe Georges • FRN
COUP DE TETE • 1943 • Le Henaff Rene • FRN
COUP DE TETE • 1978 • Annaud Jean-Jacques • FRN • HOTHEAD
COUP DE TORCHON • 1981 • Tavernier Bertrand • FRN • CLEAN SLATE (UKN)
COUP DE TROIS, LE • 1935 • de Limur Jean • FRN
COUP DE VENT • 1935 • Dreville Jean, Forzano Giovacchino • FRN
COUP DE VILLE • 1989 • Roth Joe • USA
COUP D'ETAT see **COLPO DI STATO** • 1968
COUP D'ETAT see **KAIGENREI** • 1972
COUP D'ETAT see **BATALLA DE CHILE: PART 2** • 1976
COUP D'ETAT see **CUARTELAZO** • 1976
COUP D'ETAT see **POWER PLAY** • 1978
COUP D'OEIL BLANC • 1973 • Benoit Denyse • CND
COUP DU BERGER, LE • 1956 • Rivette Jacques • SHT • FRN
COUP DU FAKIR, LE • 1915 • Feuillade Louis • FRN
COUP DUR CHEZ LES MOUS • 1955 • Loubignac Jean • FRN
COUP POUR COUP • 1971 • Karmitz Marin • FRN, FRG • BLOW FOR BLOW
COUP POUR RIEN, UN • 1958 • Lemaire Yvan • BLG
COUPABLE? • 1950 • Noe Yvan • FRN
COUPABLE, LE • 1917 • Antoine Andre • FRN
COUPABLE, LE • 1936 • Bernard Raymond • FRN
COUPE A DIX FRANCS, LA • 1975 • Condroyer Philippe • FRN
COUPE DES ALPES: THE STORY OF THE 1958 ALPINE RALLY • 1958 • Armstrong John • DOC • UKN
COUPE-TOI LES ONGLES, PASSE-MOI LE BUERRE • Baudricourt Michel • FRN
COUPLE, THE see **ZHILI-BILI STARIK SO STARUKHOI** • 1965
COUPLE, THE see **COPPIA, LA** • 1968
COUPLE, UN • 1960 • Mocky Jean-Pierre • FRN • LOVE TRAP, THE
COUPLE CHERCHE ESCLAVE SEXUEL • 1978 • Roy Jean-Claude • FRN
COUPLE IDEAL, LE • 1945 • Bernard-Roland • FRN • VOYAGE AU PAYS DES LOUFOQUES ○ DIAVOLO CONTRE JUSTEX
COUPLE MARIE, UN see **MARRIED COUPLE, A** • 1970
COUPLE NEXT DOOR, THE • 1913 • *Risser Marguerite* • USA
COUPLE OF DOWN AND OUTS, A • 1923 • Summers Walter • UKN
COUPLE OF SIDE-ORDER FABLES, A • 1915 • *Essanay* • USA
COUPLE OF THE WORLD see **FUTARI NO SEKAI** • 1966
COUPLE OF TROUBLE, A • 1969 • *D'Ore Justine* • USA
COUPLE ON THE MOVE, A see **HIKKOSHI FUFU** • 1928
COUPLE, REGARDS, POSITIONS • 1983 • Lehman Boris • BLG
COUPLE TAKES A WIFE, THE • 1972 • Paris Jerry • TVM • USA
COUPLE TEMOIN, LE • 1977 • Klein William • FRN, SWT
COUPLES • 1975 • Goddard Claude • USA
COUPLES, THE see **COPPIE, LE** • 1970
COUPLES COMPLICES • 1977 • Desvilles Jean • FRN
COUPLES, COUPLES, COUPLES see **SANDUI YINGYANG YIZHANG CHUANG** • 1988
COUPLES DU BOIS DE BOULOGNE, LES • 1974 • Legrand Bernard • FRN
COUPLES EN CHALEUR • 1977 • Ayranu Lino • FRN
COUPLES PERVERS • Debest Maxime • FRN
COUPLINGS see **PAARUNGEN** • 1967
COUPON COLLECTORS • 1914 • *Lubin* • USA
COUPON COURTSHIP, A • 1913 • *Roland Ruth* • USA
COUPS DE FEU • 1939 • Barberis Rene • FRN • DUELS
COUPS DE ROULIS • 1931 • de La Cour Jean • FRN
COUPS POUR RIN, LES • 1970 • Lambert Pierre • FRN
COUR DE FERME • 1897 • Melies Georges • FRN • FARM YARD, A
COUR DES MIRACLES, LA • 1902 • Blache Alice • FRN
COURAGE • 1915 • Ingraham Lloyd • USA
COURAGE • 1921 • Franklin Sidney A. • USA
COURAGE • 1924 • McGowan J. P. • USA
COURAGE • 1930 • Mayo Archie • USA
COURAGE • 1984 • Rosen Robert L. • USA • RAW COURAGE
COURAGE • 1986 • Kagan Jeremy Paul • TVM • USA
COURAGE see **LOVERS COURAGEOUS** • 1932
COURAGE see **MUT** • 1939
COURAGE AND THE MAN • 1915 • Jones Edgar • USA
COURAGE AND THE PASSION, THE • 1978 • Moxey John Llewellyn • TVM • USA
COURAGE DES AUTRES, LE • 1982 • Richard Christian • BRK, FRN • COURAGE OF OTHERS, THE
COURAGE FOR EVERY DAY see **KAZDY DEN ODVAHU** • 1964
COURAGE FOR EVERYDAY LIFE see **KAZDY DEN ODVAHU** • 1964
COURAGE FOR TWO • 1919 • Henderson Dell • USA
COURAGE FUYONS • 1979 • Robert Yves • FRN • COURAGE, LET'S RUN
COURAGE! JAPANESE HE-MEN • Ishida • JPN
COURAGE, LET'S RUN see **COURAGE FUYONS** • 1979
COURAGE MOUNTAIN • 1989 • Leitch Christopher • USA
COURAGE OF A COWARD, THE • 1914 • Stannard Eliot • UKN
COURAGE OF BLACK BEAUTY • 1957 • Schuster Harold • USA
COURAGE OF DESPAIR, THE • 1923 • Bentley Thomas • UKN
COURAGE OF KAVIK, THE WOLF DOG, THE • 1980 • Carter Peter • TVM • CND • KAVIK, THE WOLF DOG
COURAGE OF LASSIE • 1946 • Wilcox Fred M. • USA • HOLD HIGH THE TORCH
COURAGE OF MARGE O'DOONE, THE • 1920 • Smith David • USA
COURAGE OF OTHERS, THE see **COURAGE DES AUTRES, LE** • 1982
COURAGE OF SILENCE, THE • 1917 • Earle William P. S. • USA
COURAGE OF SORTS • 1911 • *Vitagraph* • USA
COURAGE OF SORTS • 1913 • *American* • USA
COURAGE OF THE COMMONPLACE • 1913 • Sturgeon Rollin S. • USA
COURAGE OF THE COMMONPLACE • 1917 • Turbett Ben • USA
COURAGE OF THE NORTH • 1935 • Tansey Robert • USA
COURAGE OF THE PEOPLE, THE see **NOTTE DI SAN JUAN, LA** • 1971
COURAGE OF THE WEST • 1937 • Lewis Joseph H. • USA
COURAGE TO LIVE see **MOD ATT LEVA** • 1982
COURAGEOUS ANT, THE see **MOTIG MAUR, EIN** • 1979
COURAGEOUS AVENGER, THE • 1935 • Bradbury Robert North • USA
COURAGEOUS BLOOD • 1913 • *Fielding Romaine* • USA
COURAGEOUS COWARD, A • 1915 • *Trump* • USA
COURAGEOUS COWARD, THE • 1919 • Worthington William • USA
COURAGEOUS COWARD, THE • 1924 • Hurst Paul C. • USA
COURAGEOUS DR. CHRISTIAN, THE • 1940 • Vorhaus Bernard • USA
COURAGEOUS FOOL • 1925 • *Howes Reed* • USA
COURAGEOUS MR. PENN, THE (USA) see **PENN OF PENNSYLVANIA** • 1941
COURAGEOUS OLD MAID, THE see **ODVAZNA SLECNA** • 1969
COURAGEOUS (UKN) see **LOST LADY, A** • 1934
COUREUR, LE see **RUNNER** • 1962
COUREURS DE BROUSSE • 1955 • Dupont Jacques • SHT • FRN
COURIER • Shakhnazarov Karen • USS
COURIER, THE • 1988 • Deasy Frank, Lee Joe • IRL
COURIER OF ANGORA, THE (USA) see **ANKARA POSTASSI** • 1929
COURIER OF CHARLES XII see **CARL XII: S KURIR** • 1924
COURIER OF DEATH • 1985 • Shaw Tom • USA
COURIER OF LYON, THE (USA) see **AFFAIRE DU COURRIER DE LYON, L'** • 1937
COURIER TO THE CZAR, THE see **MICHAEL STROGOFF** • 1914
COURONNE DE ROSES, LA • 1910 • Perret Leonce • FRN
COURONNE NOIRE, LA (FRN) see **CORONA NEGRA, LA** • 1950
COURONNEMENT DE LA ROSIERE • 1896 • Melies Georges • FRN • CORONATION OF A VILLAGE MAIDEN
COURONNEMENT D'EDOUARD VII, LE see **SACRE D'EDOUARD VII, LE** • 1902
COURONNES • 1909 • Cohl Emile • ANS • FRN • LAURELS
COURRIER D'ASIE • 1939 • Gilbert Oscar-Paul, Marcilly Rodolphe • FRN
COURRIER DE LYON, LE • 1904 • Blache Alice • FRN
COURRIER DE LYON, LE • 1911 • Capellani Albert • FRN
COURRIER DE LYON, LE see **AFFAIRE DU COURRIER DE LYON, L'** • 1937
COURRIER DU ROI, LE see **CHOUANS, LES** • 1946
COURRIER-SUD • 1936 • Billon Pierre • FRN
COURRUZIONE, LA • 1963 • Bolognini Mauro • ITL • CORRUPTION
COURS APRES MOI QUE JE T'ATTRAPE • 1976 • Pouret Robert • FRN • RUN AFTER ME UNTIL I CATCH YOU
COURS DU SOIR POUR MESSIEURS SEULS • 1974 • Maryse Jean-Paul • FRN
COURS D'UNE VIE, LE • 1966 • Desvilles, Darribehaude • SHT • FRN
COURSE A LA PERRUQUE, LA • Feuillade Louis • FRN
COURSE A LA PERRUQUE, LA • 1905 • Zecca Ferdinand • FRN
COURSE A LA PERRUQUE, LA • 1906 • Heuze Andre • FRN
COURSE A LA VERTU, LA • 1936 • Gleize Maurice • FRN
COURSE A L'ABIME, LA • 1915 • Feuillade Louis • FRN
COURSE A L'ECHALOTTE, LA • 1975 • Zidi Claude • FRN, FRG • WILD GOOSE CHASE, THE (USA)
COURSE AU FLAMBEAU, LA • 1925 • Luitz-Morat • FRN
COURSE AU PETROLE, LA • 1938 • Leenhardt Roger • DCS • FRN
COURSE AU POTIRON, LA • 1906 • Feuillade Louis • FRN
COURSE AUX MILLIONS, LA • 1912 • Feuillade Louis • FRN
COURSE AUX POTIRONS, LA • 1907 • Cohl Emile • ANS • FRN • COURSE DES POTIRONS, LA ○ PUMPKIN RACE, THE
COURSE AUX TONNEAUX, LA • 1905 • Zecca Ferdinand • FRN
COURSE COMPLETED see **ASIGNATURA APROBADA** • 1987
COURSE DE TAUREAUX, LA • 1951 • Braunberger Pierre, Myriam • CMP • FRN • BULLFIGHT
COURSE DE TAUREAUX A NIMES • 1906 • Blache Alice • FRN
COURSE DE YACHTS, UNE • 1903 • Melies Gaston • FRN • YACHT RACE (RELIANCE-SHAMROCK III), THE ○ YACHT RACE, A
COURSE DES BELLES-MERES, LA • 1905-10 • Heuze Andre • FRN
COURSE DES BELLES-MERES, LA • 1907 • Feuillade Louis • FRN
COURSE DES POTIRONS, LA see **COURSE AUX POTIRONS, LA** • 1907
COURSE DU LIEVRE A TRAVERS LES CHAMPS, LA • 1972 • Clement Rene • FRN, ITL • CORSA DELLE LEPRE ATTRAVERSO I CAMPI, LA (ITL) ○ AND HOPE TO DIE (UKN)
COURSE EN SAC • 1895 • Lumiere Louis • FRN
COURSE EN TETE, LA • 1974 • Santoni Joel • FRN • EDDY MERCKX
COURSE FOR HUSBANDS • 1961 • Lehky Vladimir • ANM • CZC
COURSE FOR WIVES • 1962 • Lehky Vladimir • ANM • CZC
COURSE OF A BIRTH, THE see **FODSELS FORLOB, EN** • 1972
COURSE OF TRUE LOVE, THE • 1910 • Griffith D. W.? • USA
COURSE OF TRUE LOVE, THE • 1911 • Fitzhamon Lewin? • UKN
COURSE OF TRUE LOVE, THE • 1916 • Page Will • UKN
COURSES DES SERGENTS DE VILLE, LA • 1905 • Heuze Andre • FRN
COURSES D'OBSTACLES • 1957 • Berr • SHT • FRN
COURSES SOUS HARNAIS see **SILKS AND SULKIES** • 1950
COURT CIRCUITS see **COURTS-CIRCUITS** • 1980
COURT DANCER, THE see **RAJ NARTIKI** • 1940
COURT HOUSE CROOKS • 1915 • Parrott Charles • USA
COURT INTRIGUE, A see **HOFINTRIGE, EN** • 1912
COURT JESTER, THE • 1956 • Panama Norman, Frank Melvin • USA
COURT-MARTIAL • 1928 • Seitz George B. • USA • COURT MARTIAL
COURT MARTIAL see **COURT-MARTIAL** • 1928
COURT MARTIAL see **PRIJEKI SUD** • 1979
COURT MARTIAL OF BILLY MITCHELL, THE • 1955 • Preminger Otto • USA • ONE MAN MUTINY (UKN)
COURT MARTIAL OF GENERAL GEORGE ARMSTRONG CUSTER, THE • 1978 • Jordan Glenn • TVM • USA
COURT MARTIAL OF MAJOR KELLER, THE • 1961 • Morris Ernest • UKN
COURT MARTIAL OF SGT. RYKER, THE see **SERGEANT RYKER** • 1967
COURT MARTIAL (USA) see **CARRINGTON V.C.** • 1954
COURT MARTIAL (USA) see **KRIEGSGERICHT** • 1959
COURT-MARTIALLED • 1915 • Paton Stuart • USA
COURT-MARTIALLED see **TRAITOR, THE** • 1915
COURT OF FARAON, THE see **CORTE DE FARAON, LA** • 1985
COURT OF HONOR (USA) see **SUD CHESTI** • 1948
COURT SUMMONS JOSHI, THE see **MOHAN JOSHI HAZIR HO** • 1984
COURT WALTZES..., THE see **WALZERKRIEG** • 1933
COURTE ECHELLE • 1899-00 • Blache Alice • FRN
COURTE ECHELLE, LA • 1964 • Giraldeau Jacques • DCS • CND
COURTE TETE • 1956 • Carbonnaux Norbert • FRN • PHOTO FINISH (USA) ○ COURTE-TETE ○ SHORT HEAD
COURTE-TETE see **COURTE TETE** • 1956
COURTESAN, THE • 1916 • Maude Arthur • USA
COURTESY CALL, A • 1973 • Raizman Yuli • USS
COURTIER CAUGHT, THE • 1912 • Melford Mark • UKN
COURTIN' OF CALLIOPE CLEW, THE • 1916 • Borzage Frank • SHT • USA
COURTIN' TROUBLE • 1948 • Beebe Ford • USA
COURTIN' WILDCATS • 1929 • Storm Jerome • USA
COURTING see **NAMLUVY** • 1961
COURTING ACROSS THE COURT • 1911 • *Garwood William* • USA
COURTING AND CAUGHT • 1904 • *Warwick Trading Co.* • UKN
COURTING BETTY'S BEAU • 1914 • Seay Charles M. • USA
COURTING OF MARY, THE • 1911 • Tucker George Loane, Kirkwood James • USA
COURTING OF MISS FORTUNE, THE • 1915 • *Deer* • USA
COURTING OF PRUDENCE, THE • 1914 • Pollard Harry • USA
COURTING OF THE MERRY WIDOW, THE • 1910 • *Vitagraph* • USA
COURTING SONGS • 1955 • Bunin Louis • ANM • USA
COURTING TROUBLE • 1915 • *Empress* • USA
COURTING TROUBLE • 1932 • *Sennett Mack (P)* • SHT • USA
COURTNEY AFFAIR, THE (USA) see **COURTNEYS OF CURZON STREET, THE** • 1947
COURTNEYS OF CURZON STREET, THE • 1947 • Wilcox Herbert • UKN • COURTNEY AFFAIR, THE (USA) ○ KATHY'S LOVE AFFAIR
COURTROOM • 1967 • Warhol Andy • USA
COURTS AND CONVICTS • 1918 • Howe J. A. • SHT • USA
COURTS-CIRCUITS • 1980 • Grandperret Patrick • FRN • COURT CIRCUITS
COURT'S DECREE, THE • 1911 • *Thanhouser* • USA
COURTSHIP • 1989 • Fakhimzadeh Mehdi • IRN
COURTSHIP OF ANDY HARDY, THE • 1941 • Seitz George B. • USA
COURTSHIP OF EDDIE'S FATHER, THE • 1963 • Minnelli Vincente • USA
COURTSHIP OF MILES SANDWICH, THE • 1923 • Parrott Charles, Roach Hal • SHT • USA
COURTSHIP OF MILES STANDISH, THE • 1910 • Turner Otis • USA
COURTSHIP OF MILES STANDISH, THE • 1923 • Sullivan Frederick • USA
COURTSHIP OF MISS TWIGGLES, THE • 1911 • Coleby A. E. • UKN
COURTSHIP OF O SAN, THE see **O MIMI SAN** • 1914
COURTSHIP OF THE COOKS, THE • 1914 • Ransom Charles • USA
COURTSHIP OF THE NEWT, THE • 1938 • Rowland Roy • SHT • USA
COURTSHIP UNDER DIFFICULTIES • 1899 • Williamson James • UKN
COUSIN ANGELICA (USA) see **PRIMA ANGELICA, LA** • 1973
COUSIN BILLY • 1914 • *Simon Louis* • USA
COUSIN CLARA'S COOK BOOK • 1915 • *Howell William* • USA
COUSIN COUSINE • 1975 • Tacchella Jean-Charles • FRN
COUSIN DE CALLAO, LE • 1962 • Pierre • SHT • FRN
COUSIN EBENEEZER • 1920 • Kellino W. P. • UKN
COUSIN FLUFFY • 1915 • *Moore Frank* • USA
COUSIN JANE • 1913 • *Bayne Beverly* • USA
COUSIN KATE • 1920 • Drew Sidney Mrs. • USA
COUSIN KATE'S REVOLUTION • 1912 • *Eclair* • USA
COUSIN PONS • 1914 • Vale Travers • USA
COUSIN WILBUR • 1939 • Sidney George • SHT • USA
COUSINE • 1915 • Hugon Andre • FRN
COUSINE BETTE, LA • 1928 • de Rieux Max • FRN
COUSINE DE FRANCE • 1927 • Roudes Gaston • FRN
COUSINE, JE T'AIME • 1979 • Trueba Fernando • FRN, SPN
COUSINES, LES • 1970 • Soulanes Louis • FRN • FROM EAR TO EAR (USA) ○ FRENCH COUSINS, THE ○ COFFIN, THE
COUSINS • 1912 • *Thanhouser* • USA
COUSINS • 1917 • Perry John D. • SHT • USA
COUSINS • 1988 • Schumacher Joel • USA
COUSINS, LES • 1958 • Chabrol Claude • FRN • COUSINS, THE (USA)
COUSINS, THE (USA) see **COUSINS, LES** • 1958
COUSINS IN LOVE see **TENDRES COUSINES** • 1980
COUSINS OF SHERLOCK HOLMES • 1912 • *Solax* • USA
COUSTAUD DES BATIGNOLLES, LE • 1951 • Lacourt Guy • FRN
COUTE QUE COUTE • 1983 • Girard Helene • CND
COUTEAU DANS LA PLAIE, LE • 1962 • Litvak Anatole • FRN, ITL, USA • FIVE MILES TO MIDNIGHT (USA) ○ COLTELLO NELLA PIAGA, IL (ITL) ○ TERZA DIMENZIONE, LA ○ TROISIEME DIMENSION, LA
COUTEAU SOUS LA GORGE, LE • 1955 • Severac Jacques • FRN
COUTES ZAGHAURA, LES • 1966 • Gruel Henri (c/d) • ANM • FRN
COUTURIER DE CES DAMES, LE • 1956 • Boyer Jean • FRN • FERNANDEL, THE DRESSMAKER (USA)

COUTURIER DE MON COEUR • 1935 • Jayet Rene, de Cesse Raymond • FRN • C'T'AMOUR DE COUTURIER ○ ROI DE LA COUTURE, LE
COUTURIER DES DAMES, LE see **KHAYYAT' AS-SAYYIDAT** • 1970
COUTURIERE DE LUNEVILLE, LA • 1931 • Lachman Harry • FRN
COVARRUBIAS • Eguiluz Enrique L. • SHT • SPN
COVEK I ZVER see **MENSCH UND BESTIE** • 1963
COVEK NIJE TICA see **COVJEK NIJE TICA** • 1965
COVEK OD ZEMLJE see **NJERIU PREJ DHEU** • 1985
COVEK SA CETIRI NOGE • 1984 • Djukic Radivoje-Lola • YGS • FOUR-LEGGED MAN, THE
COVEK SA FOTOGRAFIJE • 1963 • Pogacic Vladimir • YGS • MAN FROM THE PHOTOGRAPHY DEPARTMENT, THE ○ COVJEK SA FOTOGRAFIJE
COVENANT • 1985 • Grauman Walter • TVM • USA
COVENANT WITH DEATH, A • 1966 • Johnson Lamont • USA
COVENTRY CATHEDRAL • 1958 • Ashton Dudley Shaw • DOC • UKN
COVER see **AABROO** • 1968
COVER GIRL • 1944 • Vidor Charles • USA
COVER GIRL • 1967 • Lorente German • SPN
COVER GIRL • 1981 • De Renzy Alex • USA • CHERYL HANSON: COVER GIRL
COVER GIRL KILLER • 1960 • Bishop Terry • UKN
COVER GIRL MODELS • 1975 • Santiago Cirio H. • USA, PHL
COVER GIRLS • 1967 • Carlos Luciano B. • PHL
COVER GIRLS • 1977 • London Jerry • TVM • USA
COVER GIRLS, RAGAZZE DI TUTTI • 1965 • Benazeraf Jose • FRN, ITL • COVER GIRLS (USA)
COVER GIRLS (USA) see **COVER GIRLS, RAGAZZE DI TUTTI** • 1965
COVER KILL see **NOVEMBER PLAN, THE** • 1976
COVER ME BABE • 1970 • Black Noel • USA • RUN SHADOW RUN
COVER TO COVER • 1936 • Shaw Alexander • DOC • UKN • PREFACE TO LIFE
COVER-UP • 1949 • Green Alfred E. • USA
COVER UP • 1984 • Crane Peter • UKN
COVER-UP, THE • 1984 • Roets Koos • SAF
COVERED FLAGON, THE • 1925 • Ruggles Wesley • SHT • USA
COVERED PUSHCART, THE • 1949 • Davis Mannie • ANS • USA
COVERED TRAIL, THE • 1924 • Nelson Jack • USA
COVERED TRAILER, THE • 1939 • Meins Gus • USA
COVERED WAGON, THE • 1923 • Cruze James • USA
COVERED WAGON DAYS • 1940 • Sherman George • USA
COVERED WAGON RAID • 1950 • Springsteen R. G. • USA
COVERED WAGON TRAILS • 1930 • McGowan J. P. • USA
COVERED WAGON TRAILS • 1940 • Johnston Raymond K. • USA
COVERGIRL • 1982 • Lord Jean-Claude • CND • DREAMWORLD ○ COVERGIRLS
COVERGIRLS see **COVERGIRL** • 1982
COVERT ACTION • 1988 • Ingvordsen J. Christian • USA
COVERT ACTION see **SONO STATO UN AGENTE C.I.A.** • 1978
COVETED COAT, THE • 1924 • Quiribet Gaston • UKN
COVETED HERITAGE, THE • 1915 • *Balboa* • USA
COVETED PRIZE, THE • 1913 • Henderson Dell • USA
COVJEK 12 MIRNE ULICE • 1957 • Mimica Vatroslav • YGS • MAN FROM THE QUIET STREETS, THE
COVJEK I SJENA • 1960 • Vunak Dragutin • ANS • YGS • MAN AND HIS SHADOW, THE (USA)
COVJEK KOGA TREBA UBITI • 1979 • Bulajic Velko • YGS • MAN TO DESTROY, THE ○ CLOVEK, KI GA JE TREBA UBITI ○ MAN TO KILL, THE
COVJEK KOJI JE MORAO PJEVATI • 1970 • Blazekovic Milan • ANS • YGS, USA • MAN WHO HAD TO SING, THE (USA)
COVJEK KOJI JE VOLIO SPROVODE • 1989 • Tadic Zoran • YGS • MAN FOND OF FUNERALS, THE
COVJEK NIJE TICA • 1965 • Makavejev Dusan • YGS • MAN IS NOT A BIRD, A ○ COVEK NIJE TICA
COVJEK SA FOTOGRAFIJE see **COVEK SA FOTOGRAFIJE** • 1963
COVO, IL • 1941 • Emmer Luciano, Gras Enrico • ITL
COW, THE see **KOEN** • 1944
COW, THE (UKN) see **GAV** • 1968
COW AND I, THE (UKN) see **VACHE ET LE PRISONNIER, LA** • 1959
COW AND THE MOON, THE see **KRAVA NA MJESECU** • 1959
COW-BOYS FRANCAIS • 1953 • Vaudremont • SHT • FRN
COW-CATCHER'S DAUGHTER, THE • 1931 • Stafford Babe • SHT • USA
COW COUNTRY • 1953 • Selander Lesley, Bishop Curtis • USA
COW COW BOOGIE • 1943 • Lundy Dick • ANS • USA
COW JUMPED OVER THE MOON, THE • 1917 • De Vonde Chester M. • SHT • USA
COW ON THE FRONTIER (USA) see **KRAVA NA GRANICI** • 1964
COW ON THE MOON, THE see **KRAVA NA MJESECU** • 1959
COW PUNCHER'S SWEETHEART, THE • 1910 • *Kalem* • USA
COW THAT.., THE see **KRAVATA, KOIATO..** • 1966
COW TOWN • 1950 • English John • USA • BARBED WIRE (UKN)
COW WHICH.., THE see **KRAVATA, KOIATO..** • 1966
COW WHO.., THE see **KRAVATA, KOIATO..** • 1966
COWARD! • 1915 • Wilson Frank • UKN • THEY CALLED HIM COWARD
COWARD • 1987 • Gossens Anne, Friedrich Gunther • GDR
COWARD see **TOFFLAN -EN LYCKLIG KOMEDI** • 1967
COWARD, A • 1909 • Porter Edwin S. • USA
COWARD, THE • 1911 • *Pathe* • USA
COWARD, THE • 1911 • Noy Wilfred • UKN
COWARD, THE • 1912 • Dwan Allan • USA
COWARD, THE • 1913 • *Ammex* • USA
COWARD, THE • 1914 • *Mortimer Edward* • USA
COWARD, THE • 1914 • Calvert Charles? • UKN
COWARD, THE • 1915 • *Essanay* • USA
COWARD, THE • 1915 • Barker Reginald • *Kb* • USA
COWARD, THE • 1927 • Raboch Alfred • USA
COWARD, THE see **ZBABELEC** • 1961
COWARD AND THE GREAT MAN, THE see **KAPURUSH O MAHAPURUSH** • 1965
COWARD AND THE HOLY MAN, THE (UKN) see **KAPURUSH O MAHAPURUSH** • 1965
COWARD AND THE MAN, THE • 1914 • Miller Ashley • USA
COWARD AND THE SAINT, THE (USA) see **KAPURUSH O MAHAPURUSH** • 1965
COWARD HATER, THE • 1914 • *Rex* • USA
COWARD IN LOVE • 1975 • Youssef Hassan • EGY
COWARD OF THE COUNTY • 1981 • Lowry Dick • TVM • USA
COWARD OR HERO • 1911 • *Vitagraph* • USA
COWARDICE COURT • 1919 • Dowlan William C. • USA
COWARDLY WATCHDOG, THE • 1966 • Kuwahara Bob • ANS • USA
COWARDLY WAY, THE • 1915 • Ince John • USA
COWARDS • 1970 • Nuchtern Simon • USA
COWARD'S ATONEMENT, THE • 1913 • Edwards Walter? • USA
COWARD'S CHARM, THE • 1913 • *Kirkwood James* • USA
COWARD'S CODE, THE • 1916 • McGlynn Frank • SHT • USA
COWARD'S COURAGE, A • 1909 • Bouwmeester Theo? • UKN
COWARD'S COURAGE, A • 1918 • *Triangle* • USA
COWARDS DON'T PRAY see **VIGLIACCHI NON PREGANO, I** • 1968
COWARD'S FLUTE, THE • 1911 • Davis Ulysses • USA
COWARD'S REGENERATION, A • 1911 • *Yankee* • USA
COWBOY • 1958 • Daves Delmer • USA
COWBOY • 1973 • Salamuni Samy • EGY
COWBOY • 1982 • Jameson Jerry • TVM • USA
COWBOY • 1986 • Black Donald • DCS • CND
COWBOY, DER • 1918 • Neuss Alwin • FRG
COWBOY, THE • 1954 • Williams Elmo • DOC • USA
COWBOY, THE • de Arma Jesus • ANS • CUB
COWBOY ACE, THE • 1921 • Franchon Leonard • USA
COWBOY AND A LORD, A • 1911 • *Champion* • USA
COWBOY AND INDIAN • 1972 • Owen Don • DOC • CND
COWBOY AND THE ARTIST, THE • 1911 • Dwan Allan • USA
COWBOY AND THE BABY, THE • 1912 • *Panzer Paul* • USA
COWBOY AND THE BACHELOR GIRL, THE • 1910 • Melies Gaston • USA
COWBOY AND THE BALLERINA, THE • 1984 • Jameson Jerry • TVM • USA
COWBOY AND THE BANDIT, THE • 1935 • Herman Al • USA
COWBOY AND THE BLONDE, THE • 1941 • McCarey Ray • USA
COWBOY AND THE COUNTESS, THE • 1926 • Neill R. William • USA
COWBOY AND THE EASTERNER, THE • 1910 • *Champion* • USA
COWBOY AND THE FLAPPER, THE • 1924 • Neitz Alvin J. • USA • SHERIFF'S LONE HAND, THE
COWBOY AND THE FLUTE, THE • ANS • CHN
COWBOY AND THE GIRL, THE see **LADY TAKES A CHANCE, THE** • 1943
COWBOY AND THE INDIANS, THE • 1949 • English John • USA
COWBOY AND THE KID, THE • 1936 • Taylor Ray • USA
COWBOY AND THE LADY, THE • 1915 • *Kent S. Miller* • USA
COWBOY AND THE LADY, THE • 1922 • Maigne Charles • USA
COWBOY AND THE LADY, THE • 1938 • Potter H. C. • USA
COWBOY AND THE LIEUTENANT, THE • 1910 • *Nestor* • USA
COWBOY AND THE OUTLAW, THE • 1911 • Dwan Allan • USA
COWBOY AND THE OUTLAW, THE • 1929 • McGowan J. P. • USA
COWBOY AND THE PRIZEFIGHTER • 1949 • Collins Lewis D. • USA
COWBOY AND THE SCHOOLMARM, THE • 1908 • Porter Edwin S. • USA
COWBOY AND THE SCHOOLMARM, THE • 1910 • *Bison* • USA
COWBOY AND THE SENORITA, THE • 1944 • Kane Joseph • USA
COWBOY AND THE SHREW, THE • 1911 • *Rawlinson Herbert* • USA
COWBOY AND THE SQUAW, THE • 1910 • *Champion* • USA
COWBOY AND THE SQUAW, THE • 1910 • *Essanay* • USA
COWBOY ARGUMENT, A • 1909 • *Lubin* • USA
COWBOY ARTIST'S JONAH DAY, THE • 1911 • *Kalem* • USA
COWBOY BLUES • 1931 • Foster John, Bailey Harry • ANS • USA
COWBOY BLUES • 1946 • Nazarro Ray • USA • BENEATH THE STARRY SKIES (UKN)
COWBOY CABARET • 1931 • Foster John, Davis Mannie • ANS • USA
COWBOY CANTEEN • 1944 • Landers Lew • USA • CLOSE HARMONY (UKN)
COWBOY CAVALIER • 1929 • *Montana Bill* • USA
COWBOY CAVALIER • 1948 • Abrahams Derwin • USA
COWBOY CAVALIER, THE • 1928 • Thorpe Richard • USA
COWBOY CHIVALRY • 1910 • *Lubin* • USA
COWBOY CLEM • 1915 • Haldane Bert • UKN
COWBOY COMMANDOS • 1943 • Luby S. Roy • USA
COWBOY COP, THE • 1926 • De Lacy Robert • USA
COWBOY COUNSELLOR, THE • 1932 • Melford George • USA
COWBOY COURAGE • 1925 • Horner Robert J. • USA
COWBOY COWARD, THE • 1911 • *Anderson Broncho Billy* • USA
COWBOY DAMON AND PYTHIAS • 1912 • *Schaefer Anne* • USA
COWBOY EDITOR, THE • 1913 • *Selig* • USA
COWBOY FOR A DAY, A • 1911 • *Bison* • USA
COWBOY FOR LOVE, A • 1910 • *Bison* • USA
COWBOY FROM BROOKLYN, THE • 1938 • Bacon Lloyd • USA • ROMANCE AND RHYTHM (UKN)
COWBOY FROM LONESOME RIVER, THE • 1944 • Kline Benjamin • USA • SIGNED JUDGEMENT (UKN)
COWBOY FROM SUNDOWN • 1940 • Bennet Spencer Gordon • USA
COWBOY GIRLS • 1912 • *Pathe* • USA
COWBOY GIRLS, THE • 1910 • *Selig* • USA
COWBOY GRIT • 1925 • Roberts Victor • USA
COWBOY GUARDIANS, THE • 1912 • *Bison* • USA
COWBOY HEIR, THE • 1913 • *American* • USA
COWBOY HOLIDAY • 1934 • Hill Robert F. • USA
COWBOY IN AFRICA see **AFRICA -TEXAS STYLE** • 1967
COWBOY IN MANHATTAN • 1943 • Woodruff Frank • USA
COWBOY IN THE CLOUDS • 1943 • Kline Benjamin • USA
COWBOY JIMMIE see **COWBOY JIMMY** • 1957
COWBOY JIMMY • 1957 • Vukotic Dusan • ANS • YGS • COWBOY JIMMIE
COWBOY KID, THE • 1912 • Melies Gaston • USA
COWBOY KID, THE • 1928 • Carruth Clyde • USA
COWBOY KING, THE • 1922 • Seeling Charles R. • USA
COWBOY KING (UKN) see **KING COWBOY** • 1928
COWBOY MAD • 1912 • *Evans Fred* • UKN
COWBOY MAGNET, THE • 1913 • *Bison* • USA
COWBOY-MILLIARDAR, DER • 1920 • Stockel Joe • FRG
COWBOY MILLIONAIRE, THE • 1909 • *Selig* • USA
COWBOY MILLIONAIRE, THE • 1935 • Cline Eddie • USA
COWBOY MILLIONAIRE, THE see **MILLIONAIRE COWBOY, THE** • 1913
COWBOY MUSKETEER, THE • 1925 • De Lacy Robert • USA • MYSTERY BRACELET, THE
COWBOY NEEDS A HORSE, A • 1956 • Justice Bill • ANS • USA
COWBOY PASTIME, A • 1914 • Fielding Romaine • USA
COWBOY PREACHER, THE • 1910 • *Nestor* • USA
COWBOY PRINCE, THE • 1924 • Ford Francis • USA • MEET THE PRINCE (UKN)
COWBOY PRINCE, THE • 1930 • *Cheyenne Bill* • USA
COWBOY PUGILIST, THE • 1911 • *Nestor* • USA
COWBOY QUARTERBACK, THE • 1939 • Smith Noel • USA
COWBOY ROUND-UP see **RIDE 'EM, COWBOY** • 1936
COWBOY SAMARITAN, THE • 1913 • *Essanay* • USA
COWBOY SERENADE • 1942 • Morgan William • USA • SERENADE OF THE WEST (UKN)
COWBOY SHEIK, THE • 1924 • Howe J. A. • SHT • USA
COWBOY SOCIALIST, THE see **AGITATOR, THE** • 1912
COWBOY STAR, THE • 1936 • Selman David • USA
COWBOY TWIST, THE • 1913 • *Selsior Films* • UKN
COWBOY VILLAGE, THE • 1915 • Leigh J. L. V. • UKN
COWBOY VS. TENDERFOOT • 1912 • Melies Gaston • USA
COWBOYS • 1989 • Geldof Bob • UKN
COWBOYS, THE • 1924 • Seiler Lewis, Stoloff Ben • SHT • USA
COWBOYS, THE • 1972 • Rydell Mark • USA
COWBOY'S ADOPTED CHILD, THE • 1911 • *Selig* • USA
COWBOYS AND THE BACHELOR GIRLS, THE • 1910 • *Melies* • USA
COWBOY'S BABY, THE • 1908 • *Selig* • USA
COWBOY'S BEST GIRL, THE • 1912 • *Selig* • USA
COWBOY'S BRIDE, THE • 1911 • *Kalem* • USA
COWBOY'S CHICKEN DINNER, THE • 1914 • *Reliance* • USA
COWBOY'S CONQUEST, THE • 1915 • *Christy Ivan* • USA
COWBOY'S COURTSHIP, THE • 1910 • *Defender* • USA
COWBOY'S DARING RESCUE, THE • 1910 • *Bison* • USA
COWBOY'S DELIVERANCE, THE • 1911 • Dwan Allan • USA
COWBOY'S DEVOTION, THE • 1910 • *Lubin* • USA
COWBOYS DON'T CRY • 1988 • Wheeler Anne • CND
COWBOYS FROM TEXAS • 1939 • Sherman George • USA
COWBOY'S GENEROSITY, A • 1910 • *Bison* • USA
COWBOY'S HOLIDAY • 1950 • Sparling Gordon • DCS • CND
COWBOY'S HOLIDAY, A • 1949 • *Davis Art* • SHT • USA
COWBOYS' LEAP YEAR, THE • 1912 • *Powers* • USA
COWBOY'S LOVE, A • 1911 • *Lubin* • USA
COWBOY'S LOVE, A • 1916 • *Utah* • USA
COWBOY'S LOYALTY, A • 1911 • *Bison* • USA
COWBOY'S MATRIMONIAL TANGLE • 1910 • *Bison* • USA
COWBOY'S MOTHER, THE • 1912 • *Selig* • USA
COWBOY'S MOTHER-IN-LAW, THE • 1910 • *Anderson Broncho Billy* • USA
COWBOY'S NARROW ESCAPE • 1909 • *Bison* • USA
COWBOYS' PIES, THE • 1911 • *Champion* • USA
COWBOY'S PLEDGE, A • 1910 • *Champion* • USA
COWBOY'S PROPOSAL, A • 1912 • Melies Gaston • USA
COWBOY'S RACE FOR A WIFE, A • 1910 • *Bison* • USA
COWBOY'S REWARD, A • 1910 • *Bison* • USA
COWBOY'S ROMANCE • 1909 • *Centaur* • USA
COWBOY'S RUSE, THE • 1911 • Dwan Allan • USA
COWBOY'S SACRIFICE, A • 1911 • *American* • USA
COWBOY'S SISTER, THE • 1911 • *Pathe* • USA
COWBOY'S STRATAGEM, A • 1912 • Merwin Bannister • USA
COWBOY'S STRATAGEM, THE • 1910 • *Selig* • USA
COWBOY'S SWEETHEART, A • 1909 • *Centaur* • USA
COWBOY'S SWEETHEART, THE • 1910 • *Essanay* • USA
COWBOY'S SWEETHEART, THE • 1915 • *Acord Art* • USA
COWBOY'S SWEETHEART AND THE BANDIT, THE • 1910 • *Pathe* • USA
COWBOYS TO THE RESCUE, THE • 1910 • *Champion* • USA
COWBOY'S VACATION, THE • 1911 • *Bison* • USA
COWBOY'S VINDICATION, THE • 1910 • *Anderson Broncho Billy* • USA
COWBOY'S WAIF, THE • 1911 • *Bison* • USA
COWGIRL AND THE NIGHT, THE • 1913 • *Ammex* • USA
COWGIRL CINDERELLA, A • 1912 • *Oakley Laura* • USA
COWGIRL QUEEN, THE • 1922 • Croise Hugh • UKN
COWGIRLS' PRANKS • 1911 • *Little Anna* • USA
COWHERD AND THE PRINCESS, THE • ANM • CHN
COWING OF ALDERSON CREE, THE • 1920 • *Durning Bernard* • USA
COWPUNCHER, THE • 1911 • *Mersereau Violet* • USA
COWPUNCHER'S GLOVE, THE • 1910 • Porter Edwin S. • USA
COWPUNCHER'S PERIL, THE • 1916 • Mix Tom • SHT • USA
COWPUNCHER'S WARD, THE • 1910 • *Anderson Broncho Billy* • USA
COWS AND CUDDLES • 1927 • Ordell Tal • SHT • ASL
COW'S HUSBAND, THE • 1928 • Sandrich Mark • SHT • USA
COW'S HUSBAND, THE • 1931 • Fleischer Dave • ANS • USA
COW'S KIMONO • 1926 • Roach Hal • SHT • USA
COWSLIPS • 1931 • Sandrich Mark • SHT • USA
COWTOWN REFORMATION, A • 1913 • *Kb* • USA
COY DECOY • 1963 • Marcus Sid • ANS • USA
COY DECOY, A • 1941 • Clampett Robert • ANS • USA
COYOTE, EL • 1954 • Romero-Marchent Joaquin Luis • SPN
COYOTE, THE • 1915 • Oliver Guy • USA
COYOTE CANYON • 1949 • Cowan Will • SHT • USA
COYOTE FANGS • 1924 • Webb Harry S. • USA

COYOTE TRAILS • 1935 • Ray Bernard B. • USA
COZ TAKHLE DAT SI SPENAT? • 1976 • Vorlicek Vaclav, Macourek Milos • CZC • WHAT WOULD YOU SAY TO SOME SPINACH ○ NICE PLATE OF SPINACH, A ○ HAVE SOME SPINACH?
CRAB, THE • 1917 • Edwards Walter • USA
CRAB-CANNING BOAT see **KANIKOSEN** • 1953
CRAB-CANNING SHIP see **KANIKOSEN** • 1953
CRAB WITH GOLDEN CLAWS, THE see **CRABE AUX PINCES D'OR, LE** • 1947
CRAB WITH THE GOLDEN CLAWS,THE see **TINTIN ET LE CRABE AUX PINCES D'OR** • 1987
CRABE AUX PINCES D'OR, LE • 1947 • *Misone Claude (P)* • BLG • CRAB WITH GOLDEN CLAWS, THE
CRABE TAMBOUR, LE • 1977 • Schoendoerffer Pierre • FRN • CRABE-TAMBOUR, LE
CRABE-TAMBOUR, LE see **CRABE TAMBOUR, LE** • 1977
CRABES, LES • 1930 • Painleve Jean • SHT • FRN
CRAC see **MAN WHO PLANTED TREES, THE** • 1987
CRACK • 1988 • Dragoti Stan • USA
CRACK 2 see **CRACK 2, EL** • 1983
CRACK 2, EL • 1983 • Garci Jose Luis • SPN • CRACK 2
CRACK, EL • 1980 • Garci Jose Luis • SPN • CRACK, THE
CRACK, THE see **CRACK, EL** • 1980
CRACK CONNECTION, THE see **SCHIMANSKI 2** • 1987
CRACK DOWN • 1967 • Garces Armando • PHL
CRACK DOWN see **PACE THAT THRILLS, THE** • 1952
CRACK IN THE CURTAINS • 1989 • Dulhunty • SHT • ASL
CRACK IN THE MIRROR • 1960 • Fleischer Richard • USA
CRACK IN THE MIRROR • 1988 • Benson Robby • USA • WHITE HOT ○ DO IT UP
CRACK IN THE WALL, A see **JARHA FI AL-HAIT** • 1977
CRACK IN THE WORLD • 1965 • Marton Andrew • USA
CRACK O' DAWN • 1925 • Rogell Albert S. • USA
CRACK SHOT, THE • 1910 • *Powers* • USA
CRACK SHOWDOWN BOXERS • Wan Yao Hua • HKG
CRACK-UP • 1936 • St. Clair Malcolm • USA
CRACK-UP • 1946 • Reis Irving • USA
CRACK-UP • 1969 • Findlay Michael • USA
CRACK YOUR HEELS • 1919 • Roach Hal • SHT • USA
CRACKDOWN • 1987 • Garwood John • USA
CRACKED • 1985 • Gosha Hideo • JPN
CRACKED ICE • 1924 • Fadman Edwin Miles • ANM • USA
CRACKED ICE • 1938 • Tashlin Frank • ANS • USA
CRACKED ICEMAN, THE • 1934 • Parrott Charles, Dunn Eddie • USA
CRACKED NUT, THE see **WOODY WOODPECKER** • 1941
CRACKED NUTS • 1931 • Cline Eddie • USA
CRACKED NUTS • 1941 • Cline Eddie • USA
CRACKED QUACK • 1952 • Freleng Friz • ANS • USA
CRACKED SHOTS • 1934 • Stevens George • SHT • USA
CRACKED UP • 1987 • Arthur Karen • TVM • USA
CRACKED WEDDING BELLS • 1920 • Roach Hal • SHT • USA
CRACKER FACTORY, THE • 1979 • Brinckerhoff Burt • TVM • USA
CRACKERJACK • 1938 • De Courville Albert • UKN • MAN WITH A HUNDRED FACES, THE (USA) ○ MAN WITH 100 FACES
CRACKERJACK, THE • 1925 • Hines Charles • USA
CRACKERS • 1983 • Malle Louis • USA, FRN
CRACKERS see **STREET GIRLS** • 1973
CRACKER'S BRIDE, THE • 1909 • *Kalem* • USA
CRACKING see **GASOLINE: PART 2: CRACKING** • 1948
CRACKING UP • 1977 • Goren Rowby, Staley Chuck • USA
CRACKING UP see **SMORGASORD** • 1983
CRACKLE OF DEATH • 1974 • Weis Don, Grasshoff Alex • MTV • USA
CRACKPOT CRUISE • 1939 • Lovy Alex • ANS • USA
CRACKPOT KING, THE • 1946 • Donnelly Eddie • ANS • USA
CRACKPOT QUAIL, THE • 1941 • Avery Tex • ANS • USA
CRACKS, LES • 1968 • Joffe Alex • FRN, ITL • CORSA DEL SECOLO, LA (ITL)
CRACKSHOT see **COUNTERFEIT KILLER, THE** • 1968
CRACKSMAN, THE • 1963 • Scott Peter Graham • UKN
CRACKSMAN SANTA CLAUS, THE • 1913 • Reid Wallace, Robards Willis • USA
CRACKSMAN'S DAUGHTER, THE • 1913 • Calvert Charles? • UKN
CRACKSMAN'S GRATITUDE, THE • 1914 • O'Sullivan Tony • USA
CRACKSMAN'S REFORMATION, THE • 1913 • Reid Wallace, Robards Willis • USA
CRACKSMEN AND THE BLACK DIAMONDS, THE • 1908 • Raymond Charles? • UKN
CRACOVIA • 1969 • Bossak Jerzy (c/d) • DOC • PLN
CRACOW IN THE YEAR 1500 see **MINIATURY KODEKSU BEHEMA** • 1953
CRACOW WEDDING see **WESELE KRAKOWSKIE** • 1956
CRADLE, THE • 1922 • Powell Paul • USA
CRADLE BUSTER, THE • 1922 • Tuttle Frank • USA
CRADLE IS ROCKING, THE • 1968 • De Cola Frank • SHT • USA
CRADLE OF COURAGE, THE • 1920 • Hillyer Lambert • USA
CRADLE OF GENIUS • 1959 • Rotha Paul • DOC • UKN
CRADLE OF GOD, THE see **BERCEAU DE DIEU, LE** • 1926
CRADLE OF THE WASHINGTONS, THE • 1922 • *Thompson & Branscombe* • USA
CRADLE ROBBERS • 1924 • Roach Hal • SHT • USA
CRADLE SNATCHERS, THE • 1927 • Hawks Howard • USA
CRADLE SONG • 1933 • Leisen Mitchell, Moise Mina • USA
CRADLE SONG see **KOLYBELNAYA** • 1960
CRADLE WILL FALL, THE • 1983 • Moxey John Llewellyn • TVM • USA
CRADLES • 1957 • Kollanyi Agoston • HNG
CRADLESONG FROM THE EARTH, A see **DAICHI NO KOMORI-UTA** • 1975
CRAFTS OF MY PROVINCE • 1964 • Jackson Douglas • DOC • CND
CRAFTSMEN OF CANADA • 1957 • Bonniere Rene • DCS • CND • MAITRES ARTISANS DU CANADA
CRAFTY SELIM see **TILKI SELIM** • 1966
CRAFTY USURPER AND THE YOUNG KING, THE • 1909 • Stow Percy • UKN
CRAGMIRE TOWER • 1924 • Paul Fred • UKN
CRAIG • 1970 • *Coldwater Clam* • USA
CRAIG KENNEDY INVESTIGATES • 1950 • Weiss Adrian • USA
CRAIG'S WIFE • 1928 • De Mille William C. • USA
CRAIG'S WIFE • 1936 • Arzner Dorothy • USA
CRAINQUEBILLE • 1922 • Feyder Jacques • FRN • COSTER BILL OF PARIS (USA)
CRAINQUEBILLE • 1933 • de Baroncelli Jacques • FRN
CRAINQUEBILLE • 1953 • Habib Ralph • FRN
CRAMMER, THE see **PAUKER, DER** • 1958
CRAMP see **KRC** • 1979
CRAN D'ARRET • 1970 • Boisset Yves • FRN, ITL • CASO VENERE PRIVATA, IL (ITL)
CRANBERRY RANCH • 1953-54 • Devlin Bernard • DCS • CND
CRANE see **TSURU** • 1988
CRANE AND HERON • Norshtein Yuri • ANM • USS • HERON AND THE CRANE, THE
CRANE FIGHTER, THE • *Liu Raymond* • HKG
CRANES ARE FLYING, THE see **LETYAT ZHURAVLI** • 1957
CRANES AT WORK • 1960 • Russell Ken • MTV • UKN
CRANE'S MAGIC GIFT, THE • ANM • JPN
CRANEUR, LE • 1955 • Kirsanoff Dimitri • FRN • VALLEE DU PARADIS, LA
CRANIUM LANDSCAPE see **TOPOS KRANIOU** • 1972
CRAPULAS, LOS • 1981 • Pantano Jorge • ARG • HEELS, THE
CRASH • 1974 • Clemens Rolf • NRW
CRASH! • 1977 • Band Charles • USA • DEATH RIDE
CRASH • 1978 • Shear Barry • TVM • USA
CRASH, THE • 1914 • *Sterling Ford* • USA
CRASH, THE • 1916 • Melville Wilbert • SHT • USA
CRASH, THE • 1928 • Cline Eddie • USA • WRECKING BOSS, THE
CRASH, THE • 1932 • Dieterle William • USA
CRASH, THE see **BUSINESS OF LOVE, THE** • 1925
CRASH AND BURN • 1990 • Band Charles • USA
CRASH CHE BOTTE! • 1973 • Albertini Bitto • ITL • STRIPPO STRAPPO STROPPIO
CRASH COURSE • 1988 • Scott Oz • TVM • USA
CRASH DIVE • 1943 • Mayo Archie • USA
CRASH DIVE • 1959 • Varnel Max • UKN
CRASH DONOVAN • 1936 • Nigh William • USA
CRASH GOES THE HASH • 1944 • White Jules • SHT • USA
CRASH LANDING • 1958 • Sears Fred F. • USA
CRASH OF MOONS • 1954 • *Reed Roland (P)* • MTV • USA
CRASH OF SILENCE (USA) see **MANDY** • 1952
CRASHIN' THROUGH • 1924 • Neitz Alvin J. • USA
CRASHIN' THRU • 1923 • Paul Val • USA • ONE MAN, THE
CRASHIN' THRU • 1939 • Clifton Elmer • USA • RENFREW OF THE ROYAL MOUNTED IN CRASHIN' THRU
CRASHIN' THRU DANGER • 1938 • Newfield Sam • USA
CRASHING BROADWAY • 1933 • McCarthy John P. • USA
CRASHING COURAGE • 1923 • Moody Harry • USA
CRASHING HOLLYWOOD • 1938 • Landers Lew • USA • LIGHTS OUT
CRASHING LAS VEGAS • 1956 • Yarbrough Jean • USA
CRASHING RENO • 1931 • Watson William • USA
CRASHING THE GATE • 1933 • Henabery Joseph • SHT • USA
CRASHING THE MOVIES • 1950 • *Smith Pete* • SHT • USA
CRASHING THROUGH • 1928 • Buckingham Thomas • USA
CRASHING THRU • 1949 • Taylor Ray • USA
CRASHOUT • 1955 • Foster Lewis R. • USA
CRATER LAKE MONSTER, THE • 1977 • Stromberg William R. • USA
CRATERS OF FIRE, THE • 1915 • *Carpozzi Albert* • USA
CRATES • 1970 • Joskowics Alfredo • MXC
CRAVACHE, LA • 1971 • Kalfon Pierre • FRN
CRAVEN, THE • 1912 • *Schaefer Anne* • USA
CRAVEN, THE • 1915 • Cabanne W. Christy • USA
CRAVEN HEART, A • 1911 • *Rawlinson Herbert* • USA
CRAVING, THE • 1916 • Bartlett Charles • USA
CRAVING, THE • 1918 • Ford Francis, Ford John? • USA • DELIRIUM
CRAVING, THE • 1985 • Molina Jacinto • SPN • NIGHT OF THE WEREWOLF
CRAVING FOR LUST, A see **ISLAND OF DEATH** • 1975
CRAWL, RED, CRAWL • 1946 • Crouch William Forest • SHT • USA
CRAWLING EYE, THE (USA) see **TROLLENBERG TERROR, THE** • 1958
CRAWLING HAND, THE • 1963 • Strock Herbert L. • USA • STRIKE ME DEADLY ○ TOMORROW YOU DIE ○ DON'T CRY WOLF
CRAWLING MONSTER, THE see **CREEPING TERROR, THE** • 1964
CRAWLING TERROR, THE see **STRANGE WORLD OF PLANET X, THE** • 1958
CRAWLSPACE • 1971 • Newland John • TVM • USA
CRAWLSPACE • 1986 • Schmoeller David • USA, ITL
CRAYANO • 1907 • *Bitzer Billy (Ph)* • USA
CRAYON AND THE ERASER, THE see **CERUZA ES RADIR** • 1960
CRAZE • 1973 • Francis Freddie • UKN • INFERNAL IDOL, THE
CRAZE, THE see **TANGO MAD** • 1914
CRAZED • 1982 • Cassidy Richard • USA
CRAZED see **I DISMEMBER MAMA** • 1972
CRAZED BY JEALOUSY • 1908 • *Selig* • USA
CRAZED FRUIT see **KURUTTA KAJITSU** • 1956
CRAZED ON CHARLIE • 1915 • *Ward Lily* • UKN
CRAZED VAMPIRE, THE see **VIERGES ET VAMPIRES** • 1972
CRAZIES, THE • 1973 • Romero George A. • USA • CODE NAME: TRIXIE
CRAZINESS OF LOVE see **VERWIRRUNG DER LIEBE** • 1959
CRAZY ADVENTURE see **DAIBOKEN** • 1966
CRAZY, ALL LIFE'S CRAZY see **WAHNSINN, DAS GANZE LEBEN IS WAHNSINN** • 1980
CRAZY AMERICAN GIRL (USA) see **FILLE D'AMERIQUE, LA** • 1974
CRAZY APPLES • 1910 • *Vitagraph* • USA
CRAZY BABY see **BATTAGLIA DEI MODS, LA** • 1966
CRAZY BUGS, THE • 1908 • Melies Georges • FRN • TWO CRAZY BUGS
CRAZY BY PROXY • 1917 • Christie Al • SHT • USA
CRAZY CAMPUS • 1977 • Kerwin Harry E. • USA • CHEERING SECTION
CRAZY CAN-CAN, THE see **SILENY KANKAN** • 1982
CRAZY COMPANIES II, THE • 1989 • Wong Ching • HKG
CRAZY COMPOSER, A (USA) see **COMPOSITEUR TOQUE, LE** • 1905
CRAZY COUNTESS, THE see **TOLLE KOMTESS, DIE** • 1928
CRAZY CRUISE • 1942 • Avery Tex • ANS • USA
CRAZY DANDY (USA) see **LOCO LINDO** • 1938
CRAZY DAY, A see **GIORNATA BALORDA, LA** • 1960
CRAZY DAYO TENKA MUTEKI • 1967 • Tsuboshima Takashi • JPN • INDUSTRIAL SPY FREE-FOR-ALL
CRAZY DAYS • 1962 • Anderson James M. • UKN
CRAZY DAYS see **LUDI DANI** • 1978
CRAZY DESIRE (USA) see **VOGLIA MATTA, LA** • 1962
CRAZY DOPE • 1911 • *Pathe* • FRN
CRAZY FAMILY, THE see **GYAKUFUNSHA KAZOKU** • 1984
CRAZY FAT ETHEL II • 1987 • Phillips Nick • USA
CRAZY FEET • 1929 • Doane Warren • USA
CRAZY FINLAND see **PAHKAHULLA SUOMI** • 1967
CRAZY FOR LOVE (USA) see **TROU NORMAND, LE** • 1952
CRAZY FOR THAT GIRL see **VURULDUM BU KIZA** • 1968
CRAZY FOR YOU see **VISION QUEST** • 1985
CRAZY FROLIC • 1953 • Cowan Will • SHT • USA
CRAZY GULCH • 1911 • *American* • USA
CRAZY HEART, A see **LUDO SRCE** • 1959
CRAZY HOLIDAYS see **BOLONDOS VAKACIO** • 1968
CRAZY HORSE • 1977 • *Lennox John* • FRN
CRAZY HORSE • 1988 • Withrow Stephen • CND • SHE DRIVES ME CRAZY
CRAZY HORSE DE PARIS • 1975 • Bernardin Alain • FRN
CRAZY HOUSE • 1928 • McGowan Robert • SHT • USA
CRAZY HOUSE • 1931 • USA
CRAZY HOUSE • 1940 • Lantz Walter • ANS • USA
CRAZY HOUSE • 1943 • Cline Eddie • USA
CRAZY HOUSE see **HOUSE IN NIGHTMARE PARK, THE** • 1973
CRAZY IN THE NOODLE • 1957 • Regamey Maurice • FRN
CRAZY JACK AND THE BOY see **SILENCE** • 1974
CRAZY JOE • 1974 • Lizzani Carlo • ITL, USA
CRAZY KAMIKAZE, THE • 1980 • GRC
CRAZY KNIGHTS • 1944 • Beaudine William • USA • MURDER IN THE FAMILY ○ GHOST CRAZY
CRAZY LEG see **LUDA NOGA** • 1965
CRAZY LEGS • 1987 • Berry Bill • USA • OF THE MARK
CRAZY LIKE A FOX • 1926 • McCarey Leo • SHT • USA
CRAZY LOVE • 1987 • Deruddere Dominique • BLG • LOVE IS A DOG FROM HELL (USA)
CRAZY MAGICIAN, THE see **TOM WHISKY OU L'ILLUSIONNISTE TOQUE** • 1900
CRAZY MAMA • 1975 • Demme Jonathan • USA
CRAZY MAN WITH BRAINS, A see **TRELLOS TAHI TETRAKOSIS, O** • 1968
CRAZY MAN WITH FOUR HUNDRED, THE see **TRELLOS TAHI TETRAKOSIS, O** • 1968
CRAZY MEXICAN DAISAKUSEN • 1968 • Tsuboshima Takashi • JPN • MEXICAN FREE-FOR-ALL
CRAZY MIXED-UP PUP • 1955 • Avery Tex • ANS • USA
CRAZY MOON • 1986 • Eastman Allan • CND • HUGGERS
CRAZY MUSIC see **5000 FINGERS OF DR.T., THE** • 1952
CRAZY MUSICIAN, THE (USA) see **LOCO SERENATA, EL** • 1940
CRAZY NIGHT see **ZWARIOWANA NOC** • 1967
CRAZY NO KISOUTENGAI • Tsuboshima Takashi • JPN • WHO'S CRAZY NOW?
CRAZY NUT, THE • 1929 • Lamont Charles • SHT • USA
CRAZY OGON SAKUSEN see **KUREIZI OGON SAKUSEN** • 1967
CRAZY ONE, THE see **DELI FISEK** • 1967
CRAZY ONES, THE • 1967 • Haas Hugo • USA
CRAZY OVER HORSES • 1951 • Beaudine William • USA
CRAZY PAGE, A see **KURUTTA IPPEIJI** • 1927
CRAZY PARADISE see **TOSSEDE PARADIS, DET** • 1962
CRAZY PEOPLE • 1934 • Hiscott Leslie • UKN
CRAZY PEOPLE • 1977 • SAF
CRAZY PEOPLE • 1989 • Bill Tony • USA
CRAZY POISON see **LOCO VENENO** • 1988
CRAZY PROSPECTOR, A • 1913 • *Essanay* • USA
CRAZY QUILT • 1966 • Korty John • USA
CRAZY RADIO see **RADIO FOLLA, LA** • 1985
CRAZY RAY, THE (USA) see **PARIS QUI DORT** • 1924
CRAZY RIDICULOUS AMERICAN PEOPLE see **THIS IS AMERICA** • 1977
CRAZY SEX see **NIEN HUA JE TS'AO** • 1976
CRAZY STORY see **PRICA BEZ VEZE** • 1966
CRAZY SWORDSMAN, THE • 1968 • Lo Che • HKG
CRAZY THAT WAY • 1930 • MacFadden Hamilton • USA
CRAZY THUNDERROAD • 1980 • Ishii Sogo • JPN
CRAZY TIMES • 1981 • Philips Lee • TVM • USA
CRAZY TO ACT • 1927 • Rodney Earle • SHT • USA
CRAZY TO KILL (UKN) see **DR. GILLESPIE'S CRIMINAL CASE** • 1943
CRAZY TO MARRY • 1921 • Cruze James • USA
CRAZY TOWN • 1932 • Fleischer Dave • ANS • USA
CRAZY TOWN • 1954 • Sparber I. • ANS • USA
CRAZY UPROAR see **TENYA WANYA** • 1950
CRAZY WILD AND CRAZY • 1965 • Mahon Barry • USA
CRAZY WITH THE HEAT • 1947 • Carlson Bob • ANS • USA
CRAZY WORLD • 1968 • Kuri Yoji • ANS • JPN
CRAZY WORLD, INSANE WORLD see **MONDO CANE N.2** • 1963
CRAZY WORLD OF JULIUS VROODER, THE • 1974 • Hiller Arthur • USA • VROODER'S HOOCH
CRAZY WORLD OF LAUREL AND HARDY, THE • 1967 • *Roach Hal (P)* • CMP • USA
CRAZY YEARS see **LUDE GODINE** • 1979
CRAZY YUSUF see **DELI YUSUF** • 1976
CRAZYLEGS • 1953 • Lyon Francis D. • USA
CREACION, LA • 1968 • Morales Antonio • ANS • SPN • CREATION, THE
CREAKING STAIRS • 1919 • Julian Rupert • USA
CREAM IN MY COFFEE • 1980 • Millar Gavin • TVM • UKN
CREAM OF THE EARTH (UKN) see **RED LIPS** • 1928
CREAM PUFF ROMANCE, A • 1916 • Arbuckle Roscoe • SHT • USA • RECKLESS ROMEO, A ○ HIS ALIBI
CREAM SODA • 1975 • Dale Holly • DOC • CND
CREAM'S FAREWELL CONCERT see **FAREWELL CONCERT OF CREAM, THE** • 1969

CREANCIER, LE see **CAS DE CONSCIENCE** • 1939

CREATED TO KILL see **EMBRYO** • 1976

CREATION • 1922 • Wright Humberston • UKN

CREATION • 1979 • Brakhage Stan • SHT • USA

CREATION, THE • 1966 • Huisken Joop • DOC • GDR

CREATION, THE • 1982 • Vinton Will • ANS • USA

CREATION, THE see **CREACION, LA** • 1968

CREATION D'ULCERES ARTIFICIELS CHEZ LE CHIEN • 1934 • Storck Henri • DOC • BLG

CREATION OF THE HUMANOIDS, THE • 1962 • Barry Wesley E. • USA

CREATION OF THE WORLD, THE (USA) see **STVORENI SVETA** • 1958

CREATION OF WOMAN, THE • *Merchant Ismail (P)* • IND

CREATION'S MORNING • 1920 • *Storyart* • SHT • USA

CREATIONS SPONTANEES • 1898 • Melies Georges • FRN • FANTASTICAL ILLUSIONS (USA) ○ ILLUSIONS FANTASTIQUES

CREATIVE HANDS • 1948 • Crawley Judith • SER • CND

CREATOR • 1985 • Passer Ivan • USA

CREATOR OF "HUNGER", THE • 1914 • *Marshall Boyd* • USA

CREATORS AND CREATIONS • 1968 • Nepp Jozsef • ANS • HNG

CREATURA D'UNA NOTTE see **CREATURE DELLE NOTTE** • 1933

CREATURE see **TITAN FIND** • 1985

CREATURE CALLED MAN, THE see **JAGA WA HASHITTA** • 1970

CREATURE DEL MALE (ITL) see **HOMME ET L'ENFANT, L'** • 1956

CREATURE DELLE NOTTE • 1933 • Palermi Amleto • ITL • CREATURA D'UNA NOTTE

CREATURE FROM ANOTHER WORLD see **TROLLENBERG TERROR, THE** • 1958

CREATURE FROM BLACK LAKE, THE • 1976 • Houck Joy N. Jr. • USA • CREATURE FROM THE BLACK LAKE, THE

CREATURE FROM BLOOD ISLAND see **TERROR IS A MAN** • 1959

CREATURE FROM GALAXY 27, THE see **NIGHT OF THE BLOOD BEAST** • 1958

CREATURE FROM SHADOW LAKE, THE • 1984 • Rebane Bill • USA • RANA: CREATURE FROM SHADOW LAKE ○ RANA ○ RANA: THE LEGEND OF SHADOW LAKE

CREATURE FROM THE BLACK LAGOON, THE • 1954 • Arnold Jack • USA

CREATURE FROM THE BLACK LAKE, THE see **CREATURE FROM BLACK LAKE, THE** • 1976

CREATURE FROM THE HAUNTED SEA • 1961 • Corman Roger • USA

CREATURE MYSTERIEUSE, LA • 1914 • *Astrup Carl* • DNM • MYSTERIOUS CREATURE, THE

CREATURE OF DESTRUCTION • 1967 • Buchanan Larry • USA

CREATURE OF THE DEVIL see **DEAD MEN WALK** • 1943

CREATURE OF THE WALKING DEAD • 1965 • Cortes Fernando • USA

CREATURE WALKS AMONG US, THE • 1956 • Sherwood John • USA

CREATURE WASN'T NICE, THE • 1981 • Kimmel Bruce • USA • SPACESHIP

CREATURE WITH THE ATOM BRAIN • 1955 • Cahn Edward L. • USA • CREATURE WITH THE ATOMIC BRAIN

CREATURE WITH THE ATOMIC BRAIN see **CREATURE WITH THE ATOM BRAIN** • 1955

CREATURE WITH THE BLUE HAND (USA) see **BLAUE HAND, DIE** • 1967

CREATURES, LES • 1966 • Varda Agnes • FRN, SWD • VARELSERNA (SWD) ○ CREATURES, THE

CREATURES, THE see **CREATURES, LES** • 1966

CREATURES FROM ANOTHER WORLD see **STRANGE WORLD OF PLANET X, THE** • 1958

CREATURES FROM BEYOND THE GRAVE see **FROM BEYOND THE GRAVE** • 1973

CREATURES OF CLAY • 1914 • Wilson Frank? • UKN

CREATURES OF DARKNESS • 1969 • Williams Bill • USA

CREATURES OF EVIL (UKN) see **CURSE OF THE VAMPIRES** • 1970

CREATURES OF HABIT • 1914 • Trimble Larry • UKN

CREATURE'S REVENGE, THE see **BRAIN OF BLOOD** • 1971

CREATURES THE WORLD FORGOT • 1971 • Chaffey Don • UKN, SAF

CRECER DE GOLPE • 1977 • Renan Sergio • ARG • TO GROW UP SUDDENLY

CRECHE D'YOUVILLE, LA • 1954-55 • Devlin Bernard • DCS • CND

CREDO • 1923 • Duvivier Julien • FRN • TRAGEDIE DE LOURDES, LA

CREDO DU PAYSAN, LE • 1942 • Tessier Albert • DCS • CND

CREE HUNTERS OF MISTASSINI • 1974 • Ianzelo Tony, Richardson Boyce • DOC • CND • CHASSEURS CRIS DE MISTASSINI

CREE WAY • 1977 • Ianzelo Tony • DOC • CND

CREED OF THE CLAN, THE • 1915 • *Stonehouse Ruth* • USA

CREED THAT WEAKENS, THE see **GALLOPING ACE, THE** • 1924

CREEK CLAIM, THE • 1911 • *Bison* • USA

CREEPER, THE • 1948 • Yarbrough Jean • USA

CREEPER, THE see **RITUALS** • 1976

CREEPER, THE see **DARK SIDE OF MIDNIGHT, THE** • 1986

CREEPERS • 1985 • Argento Dario • ITL • PHENOMENA

CREEPERS, THE see **ISLAND OF TERROR** • 1965

CREEPING FLAME, THE • 1914 • *Nestor* • USA

CREEPING FLAMES see **CAUGHT IN THE END** • 1920

CREEPING FLESH, THE • 1973 • Francis Freddie • UKN

CREEPING SHADOWS • 1931 • Orton John • UKN • LIMPING MAN, THE (USA)

CREEPING TERROR, THE • 1964 • Sherwood John • USA • CRAWLING MONSTER, THE

CREEPING UNKNOWN, THE (USA) see **QUATERMASS EXPERIMENT, THE** • 1955

CREEPOZOIDS • 1987 • Decoteau David • USA

CREEPS • 1926 • Taurog Norman • SHT • USA

CREEPS • 1956 • White Jules • SHT • USA

CREEPS see **DRESZCZE** • 1981

CREEPSHOW • 1982 • Romero George A. • USA

CREEPSHOW 2 • 1987 • Gornick Michael • USA

CREEPY TIME PAL • 1960 • Hanna William, Barbera Joseph • ANS • USA

CREEZY • 1974 • Granier-Deferre Pierre • FRN, ITL

CREMATION, LA • 1899 • Melies Georges • FRN • SPANISH INQUISITION, THE

CREMATOR, THE (USA) see **SPALOVAC MRTVOL** • 1968

CREMATOR OF CORPSES, THE see **SPALOVAC MRTVOL** • 1968

CREMATORS, THE • 1972 • Essex Harry • USA • DUNE ROLLER, THE ○ CREMATORS ARE COMING, THE

CREMATORS ARE COMING, THE see **CREMATORS, THE** • 1972

CREME SIMON, LA • 1936 • Alexeieff Alexandre • SHT • FRN

CREO EN DIOS • 1940 • de Fuentes Fernando • MXC • LABIOS SELLADOS

CREOLE MOON (USA) see **LUNA CRIOLLA** • 1938

CREOLES, LES • 1976-77 • Brault Michel, Gladu Andre • DCS • CND

CREOLE'S LOVE STORY, A • 1913 • Raymond Charles • UKN

CREOSOOT • 1931 • Ivens Joris • NTH • CREOSOTE

CREOSOTE • 1929 • Dreville Jean • SHT • FRN

CREOSOTE see **CREOSOOT** • 1931

CREPA PADRONE TUTTO VA BENE (ITL) see **TOUT VA BIEN** • 1972

CREPA TU.. CHE VIVO IO see **BANDIDOS** • 1967

CREPE BONNET, A • 1913 • *Thanhouser* • USA

CREPUSCOLO • 1961 • Paolucci Alex • ITL

CREPUSCOLO DE UN DIOS • 1968 • Fernandez Emilio • MXC

CREPUSCOLO DI FUOCO • 1970 • Boccia Tanio • ITL

CREPUSCULE D'EPOUVANTE • 1922 • *Francen Victor* • FRN • TWILIGHT OF TERROR

CREPUSCULO • 1944 • Bracho Julio • MXC

CRESCENDO • 1943 • Harrington Curtis • SHT • USA

CRESCENDO • 1969 • Gibson Alan • UKN

CRESCENT MOON see **YUEYAER** • 1988

CRESCENT MOON, THE see **YUMIHARI-ZUKI** • 1955

CRESCETE E MOLTIPLICATEVI • 1973 • Petroni Giulio • ITL

CREST OF MAN, THE • 1965 • *Noshinaga Sayuri* • JPN

CREST OF THE WAVE (USA) see **SEAGULLS OVER SORRENTO** • 1954

CREST OF VON ENDHEIM, THE • 1915 • *Moody Harry* • USA

CRESTED BIRD, THE see **KAKOLI** • 1989

CRESUS • 1917 • Cande Adolphe • FRN

CRESUS • 1960 • Giono Jean • FRN

CRETINETTI AL BALLO • 1909 • *Deed Andre* • ITL

CRETINETTI ALCOOLISTA • 1909 • *Deed Andre* • ITL

CRETINETTI ALLA GUERRA • 1909 • *Deed Andre* • ITL

CRETINETTI CERCA UN DUELLO • 1909 • *Deed Andre* • ITL

CRETINETTI DI SORTITA • 1909 • *Deed Andre* • ITL

CRETINETTI DISTRATTO • 1910 • *Deed Andre* • ITL

CRETINETTI E GLI STIVALI DEL BRASILIANO • 1915 • *Deed Andre* • ITL

CRETINETTI E IL MATRIMONIO • 1909 • *Deed Andre* • ITL

CRETINETTI E LA FIDANZATA • 1909 • *Deed Andre* • ITL

CRETINETTI E LE DONNE • 1907 • Deed Andre • ITL

CRETINETTI EROE • 1909 • *Deed Andre* • ITL

CRETINETTI FACCHINO • 1910 • *Deed Andre* • ITL

CRETINETTI FINTO FRATE • 1910 • *Deed Andre* • ITL

CRETINETTI FRA DUE FUOCHI • 1910 • *Deed Andre* • ITL

CRETINETTI IMPARA IL SALTO MORTALE • 1910 • *Deed Andre* • ITL

CRETINETTI INVENTORE • 1909 • *Deed Andre* • ITL

CRETINETTI LOTTATORE • 1909 • *Deed Andre* • ITL

CRETINETTI MANGIA I GAMBERI • 1909 • *Deed Andre* • ITL

CRETINETTI MANNEQUIN • 1911 • *Deed Andre* • ITL

CRETINETTI PAGA I DEBITI • 1915 • *Deed Andre* • ITL

CRETINETTI RICEVE • 1909 • *Deed Andre* • ITL

CRETINETTI SI BATTE AL CANNONE • 1910 • *Deed Andre* • ITL

CRETINETTI SUICIDA • 1909 • *Deed Andre* • ITL

CRETINETTI SULLE ALPE • 1909 • *Deed Andre* • ITL

CRETINETTI VOLONTARIO ALLA CROLE ROSSA • 1910 • *Deed Andre* • ITL

CRETINETTI VUOL SPOSARE LA FIGLIA DEL PATRONE • 1910 • *Deed Andre* • ITL

CREVE-COEUR • 1952 • Dupont Jacques • FRN

CREVETTES, LES • 1930 • Painleve Jean • SHT • FRN

CREVETTES, LES • 1965-66 • Garceau Raymond • DCS • CND

CREVICE see **KIRETSU** • 1968

CREW, THE see **ZALOGA** • 1952

CREW, THE (UKN) see **EQUIPAGE, L'** • 1927

CREW RACING • 1935 • Miller David • SHT • USA

CRI, UN see **DOCTEUR FRANCOISE GAILLAND** • 1975

CRI-CRI, EL GRILLITO CANTOR • 1963 • Davison Tito • MXC • CRI-CRI, THE SINGING CRICKET ○ CRI CRI, EL GRILLITO CANTOR

CRI CRI, EL GRILLITO CANTOR see **CRI-CRI, EL GRILLITO CANTOR** • 1963

CRI-CRI, THE SINGING CRICKET see **CRI-CRI, EL GRILLITO CANTOR** • 1963

CRI DANS LA NUIT, UN • 1912 • Jasset Victorin • FRN

CRI DANS L'ABIME, UN • 1922 • Carl Renee • FRN • SHOUT FROM THE ABYSS, A

CRI DE LA CHAIR, LE • 1963 • Benazeraf Jose • FRN • SIN ON THE BEACH (USA) ○ ETERNITE POUR NOUS, L' ○ ETERNITY FOR US ○ ROMANCE ON THE BEACH

CRI DU COEUR, LE • 1974 • Lallemand Claude • FRN

CRI DU CORMORAN LE SOIR AU-DESSUS DES JONGES, LE • 1970 • Audiard Michel • FRN • PAUME, LE

CRI DU DESIR, LE • 1976 • Nauroy Alain C. • FRN

CRI DU HIBOU, LE • 1988 • Chabrol Claude • FRN

CRI DU MUEZZIN, LE • 1973 • Vodio N'Dabian • IVC • CRY FROM THE MUEZZIN, THE

CRI ET CONNAISSANCE • 1963 • Haesaerts Paul • BLG

CRIA! see **CRIA CUERVOS** • 1976

CRIA CUERVOS • 1976 • Saura Carlos • SPN • RAISE RAVENS ○ CRIA! ○ REAR RAVENS ○ RAISING RAVENS

CRIADA BIEN CRIADA, LA • 1970 • *America* • MXC

CRIADA E A JUSTICA, A • 1973 • de Macedo Antonio • SHT • PRT

CRIADA MAL CRIADA, LA • 1965 • Martinez Solares Gilberto • MXC, PRC

CRIANDO FONTES DE RIQUEZA • 1960 • Mendes Joao • SHT • PRT

CRIATURA, LA • 1977 • de la Iglesia Eloy • SPN

CRICCA DORATA, LA • 1913 • Ghione Emilio • ITL

CRICKET, THE • 1917 • Wilson Elsie Jane • USA

CRICKET, THE see **CICALA, LA** • 1980

CRICKET IN THE EAR, A • 1976 • Stoyanov Georgi • USS

CRICKET IN TIMES SQUARE, THE • 1971 • Jones Charles M. • ANS • USA

CRICKET ON THE HEARTH see **SVERCHOK NA PECHI** • 1915

CRICKET ON THE HEARTH, THE • 1909 • Griffith D. W. • USA

CRICKET ON THE HEARTH, THE • 1914 • Blache Alice • USA

CRICKET ON THE HEARTH, THE • 1914 • Johnston Lorimer • *American* • USA

CRICKET ON THE HEARTH, THE • 1914 • Marston Lawrence • *Ab* • USA

CRICKET ON THE HEARTH, THE • 1923 • Johnston Lorimer • USA

CRICKET ON THE HEARTH, THE • 1949 • Martin Sobey • SHT • USA

CRICKET ON THE HEARTH, THE • *U.p.a.* • ANM • USA

CRICKET TERMS ILLUSTRATED • 1905 • *Cricks & Sharp* • UKN

CRIES AND WHISPERS (UKN) see **VISKINGAR OCH ROP** • 1972

CRIES IN THE NIGHT • 1980 • Fruet William • CND • FUNERAL HOME

CRIES IN THE NIGHT see **GRITOS EN LA NOCHE** • 1962

CRIES OF DESPAIR see **RATAPAN RINTIHAN** • 1974

CRIES OF LOVE, THE see **PETITES CRUAUTES, LES** • 1984

CRIEZ-LE SUR LES TOITS • 1932 • Anton Karl • FRN • SHOUT IT FROM THE HOUSE TOPS (USA)

CRIME • 1964 • Timar Istvan • DOC • HNG

CRIME, A see **BROTT, ETT** • 1940

CRIME, LA • 1983 • Labro Philippe • FRN

CRIME, THE see **MORDERSTWO** • 1957

CRIME AFLOAT • 1938 • Clifton Elmer • USA

CRIME AGAINST JOE • 1956 • Sholem Lee • USA

CRIME AND PASSION • 1975 • Passer Ivan • USA, UKN, FRG • THERE'S AN ACE UP MY SLEEVE ○ ACE UP YOUR SLEEVE ○ ACE UP MY SLEEVE ○ FRANKENSTEIN'S SPUKSCHLOSS

CRIME AND PUNISHMENT • 1917 • McGill Lawrence • USA

CRIME AND PUNISHMENT • 1935 • von Sternberg Josef • USA

CRIME AND PUNISHMENT see **PRESTUPLENIE I NAKAZANIE** • 1911

CRIME AND PUNISHMENT see **RASKOLNIKOW** • 1923

CRIME AND PUNISHMENT see **BROTT OCH STRAFF** • 1945

CRIME AND PUNISHMENT see **CRIMEN Y CASTIGO** • 1950

CRIME AND PUNISHMENT see **CRIME ET CHATIMENT** • 1956

CRIME AND PUNISHMENT see **PRESTUPLENIE I NAKAZANIE** • 1970

CRIME AND PUNISHMENT see **RIKOS JA RANGAISTUS** • 1983

CRIME AND PUNISHMENT U.S.A. • 1959 • Sanders Denis • USA

CRIME AND PUNISHMENT (USA) see **CRIME ET CHATIMENT** • 1935

CRIME AND THE CRIMINAL • 1912 • Rolfe Alfred • ASL

CRIME AND THE PENALTY • 1916 • West R. Harley • UKN

CRIME AT A GIRLS' SCHOOL see **ZLOCIN V DIVCI SKOLE** • 1965

CRIME AT BLOSSOMS, THE • 1933 • Rogers Maclean • UKN

CRIME AT DAWN see **MERENYLET** • 1958

CRIME AT PORTA ROMANA see **DELITTO A PORTA ROMANA** • 1980

CRIME AT POSILLIPO see **DELITTO A POSILLIPO** • 1967

CRIME AT THE GIRLS' SCHOOL see **ZLOCIN V DIVCI SKOLE** • 1965

CRIME AT THE MILL • 1913 • Kinder Stuart • UKN

CRIME AT THE NIGHT CLUB see **ZLOCIN V SANTANU** • 1968

CRIME AU CONCERT MAYOL • 1954 • Mere Pierre • FRN, ITL • PALACE OF NUDES (USA) ○ PALACE OF SHAME

CRIME AU MUSIC-HALL, UN see **ACCUSEE, LEVEZ-VOUS** • 1930

CRIME BOSS (USA) see **FAMILIARI DELLE VITTIME NON SARANNO AVVERTITI, I** • 1972

CRIME BUSTERS (USA) see **DUE SUPERPIEDI QUASI PIATTI, I** • 1977

CRIME BY NIGHT • 1944 • Clemens William • USA

CRIME CITY see **FORTERESSE, LA** • 1947

CRIME CLUB • 1973 • Rich David Lowell • TVM • USA

CRIME CLUB • 1975 • Szwarc Jeannot • TVM • USA

CRIME CONTROL • 1941 • Roush Leslie • USA

CRIME DA ALDEIA VELHA, O • 1964 • Guimaraes Manuel • PRT

CRIME D'AMOUR • 1982 • Gilles Guy • FRN

CRIME D'ANTOINE, LE • 1989 • *Novembre Tom* • FRN

CRIME DE BOUT DE ZAN, LE • 1913 • Feuillade Louis • FRN

CRIME DE CHEMIN ROUGE, LE • 1932 • Severac Jacques • FRN • MORT D'HOMME

CRIME DE DAVID LEVINSTEIN, LE • 1968 • Charpak Andre • FRN

CRIME DE GRAND-PERE, LE • 1910 • *Gance Abel* • FRN

CRIME DE LA RUE DU CHERCHE-MIDI A 14 HEURES, LE see **CURIOSITE PUNIEE, LA** • 1908

CRIME DE LA RUE DU TEMPLE, LE • 1904 • Blache Alice • FRN • ASSASSINAT DE LA RUE DU TEMPLE, L'

CRIME DE LORD ARTHUR SAVILLE, LE • 1921 • Hervil Rene • FRN • LORD ARTHUR SAVILLE'S CRIME (USA)

CRIME DE MONIQUE, LE • 1924 • Peguy Robert • FRN

CRIME DE MONSIEUR LANGE, LE • 1935 • Renoir Jean • FRN • CRIME OF MONSIEUR LANGE, THE (USA) ○ SUR LA COUR ○ ASCENSION DE MONSIEUR LANGE, L'

CRIME DE SIMAO BOLANDAS, O • 1980 • do Canto Jorge Brum • PRT • SIMAO BOLANDA'S CRIME ○ RAIZES OCULTAS ○ OCCULT ROOTS

CRIME DE SYLVESTRE BONNARD, LE • 1929 • Berthomieu Andre • FRN

CRIME DES HOMMES, LE • 1923 • Roudes Gaston • FRN

CRIME DES JUSTES, LE • 1948 • Gehret Jean • FRN

CRIME DO ZE BIGORNA, O • 1980 • Duarte Anselmo • BRZ • CRIME OF ZE BIGORNA, THE

CRIME DOCTOR • 1943 • Gordon Michael • USA

CRIME DOCTOR, THE • 1934 • Robertson John S. • USA

CRIME DOCTOR'S COURAGE • 1945 • Sherman George • USA • DOCTOR'S COURAGE, THE (UKN)

CRIME DOCTOR'S DIARY • 1949 • Friedman Seymour • USA

CRIME DOCTOR'S GAMBLE • 1947 • Castle William • USA • DOCTOR'S GAMBLE, THE (UKN)
CRIME DOCTOR'S MAN HUNT • 1946 • Castle William • USA
CRIME DOCTOR'S RENDEZVOUS, THE see **SHADOWS IN THE NIGHT** • 1944
CRIME DOCTOR'S STRANGEST CASE • 1943 • Forde Eugene J. • USA • STRANGEST CASE, THE (UKN)
CRIME DOCTOR'S VACATION, THE see **MILLERSON CASE, THE** • 1947
CRIME DOCTOR'S WARNING • 1945 • Castle William • USA • DOCTOR'S WARNING, THE (UKN)
CRIME DOES NOT PAY (USA) see **CRIME NE PAIE PAS, LE** • 1962
CRIME DOESN'T PAY • 1970 • *Anvil* • SHT • UKN
CRIME DOESN'T PAY • 1984 • SAF
CRIME DOS BANHADOS, O • 1913 • Santos Francisco • BRZ
CRIME D'OVIDE PLOUFFE, LE • 1984 • Arcand Denys, Carle Gilles • MTV • CND • CRIME OF OVIDE PLOUFFE, THE ◦ MURDER IN THE FAMILY
CRIME DU BOUIF, LE • 1921 • Pouctal Henri • FRN
CRIME DU BOUIF, LE • 1932 • Berthomieu Andre • FRN
CRIME DU BOUIF, LE • 1951 • Cerf Andre • FRN
CRIME DU DOCTEUR CHARDIN, LE see **HOMMES VEULENT VIVRE!, LES** • 1961
CRIME D'UNE SAINTE, LE • 1923 • Maudru Charles • FRN
CRIME ENSEVELI, LE • 1913 • Fescourt Henri • FRN
CRIME ET CHATIMENT • 1935 • Chenal Pierre • FRN • CRIME AND PUNISHMENT (USA)
CRIME ET CHATIMENT • 1956 • Lampin Georges • FRN • MOST DANGEROUS SIN, THE (USA) ◦ CRIME AND PUNISHMENT
CRIME IN A NIGHT CLUB see **ZLOCIN V SANTANU** • 1968
CRIME IN A PEACEFUL STREET, A see **GARIMA FIL HAY EL HADY** • 1967
CRIME IN PARADISE see **BROTT I PARADISET** • 1959
CRIME IN THE CAFE CHANTAN see **ZLOCIN V SANTANU** • 1968
CRIME IN THE CLOUDS (UKN) see **FLY-AWAY BABY** • 1937
CRIME IN THE GIRLS' SCHOOL see **ZLOCIN V DIVCI SKOLE** • 1965
CRIME IN THE MAGINOT LINE (USA) see **DOUBLE CRIME SUR LA LIGNE MAGINOT** • 1937
CRIME IN THE MIRROR see **DELITTO ALLO SPECCHIO** • 1964
CRIME IN THE MUSEUM OF HORRORS (USA) see **HORRORS OF THE BLACK MUSEUM** • 1959
CRIME IN THE NIGHT CLUB see **ZLOCIN V SANTANU** • 1968
CRIME IN THE STREETS • 1956 • Siegel Don • USA
CRIME IN THE SUN see **BROTT I SOL** • 1947
CRIME INC., GANGS INC. see **PAPER BULLETS** • 1941
CRIME INCORPORATED • 1945 • Landers Lew • USA
CRIME KILLER, THE • 1985 • Pan-Andreas George • USA
CRIME LAB • 1948 • Montagne Edward J. • DOC • USA
CRIME NE PAIE PAS, LE • 1962 • Oury Gerard • FRN, ITL • GENTLE ART OF MURDER, THE (UKN) ◦ DELITTO NON PAGA, IL (ITL) ◦ CRIME DOES NOT PAY (USA)
CRIME NO.. VERAO, UM • 1972 • Pini Americo • BRZ
CRIME NOBODY SAW, THE • 1937 • Barton Charles T. • USA
CRIME OF CAIN, THE • 1914 • Marston Theodore • USA
CRIME OF CARELESSNESS, THE • 1912 • *Cooper Bigelow* • USA
CRIME OF CIRCUMSTANCE, THE • 1916 • *Cody Lewis J.* • SHT • USA
CRIME OF CUENCA, THE see **CRIMEN DE CUENCA, EL** • 1979
CRIME OF DEFEAT see **GOTT MIT UNS** • 1970
CRIME OF DIMITRI KARAMAZOV, THE see **MORDER DIMITRI KARAMASOFF, DER** • 1931
CRIME OF DR. CRESPI, THE • 1935 • Auer John H. • USA • PREMATURE BURIAL, THE
CRIME OF DOCTOR FORBES, THE • 1936 • Marshall George • USA
CRIME OF DR. HALLET, THE • 1938 • Simon S. Sylvan • USA
CRIME OF HELEN STANLEY, THE • 1934 • Lederman D. Ross • USA • MURDER IN THE STUDIO
CRIME OF HONOUR • 1958 • Tully Montgomery • UKN
CRIME OF HONOUR see **SONG FOR EUROPE, A** • 1985
CRIME OF INNOCENCE • 1985 • Miller Michael • TVM • USA
CRIME OF MARY ANDREWS, THE see **TRIAL OF MARY DUGAN, THE** • 1940
CRIME OF MONSIEUR LANGE, THE (USA) see **CRIME DE MONSIEUR LANGE, LE** • 1935
CRIME OF OVIDE PLOUFFE, THE see **CRIME D'OVIDE PLOUFFE, LE** • 1984
CRIME OF PASSION • 1957 • Oswald Gerd • USA
CRIME OF PETER FRAME, THE see **SECOND THOUGHTS** • 1938
CRIME OF SHIRO KAMISAKA, THE see **KAMISAKA SHIRO NO HANZAI** • 1957
CRIME OF THE BLUE STAR see **ZLOCIN V MODRE HVEZDE** • 1973
CRIME OF THE CENTURY • 1946 • Ford Philip • USA
CRIME OF THE CENTURY, THE • 1933 • Beaudine William • USA
CRIME OF THE CENTURY (UKN) see **WALK EAST ON BEACON** • 1952
CRIME OF THE HOUR • 1918 • Ricketts Thomas • USA
CRIME OF THOUGHT, THE • 1915 • *Clifford William* • USA
CRIME OF VOODOO see **DRUMS OF THE JUNGLE** • 1935
CRIME OF WALL STREET, THE • 1913 • *True Features* • USA
CRIME OF ZE BIGORNA, THE see **CRIME DO ZE BIGORNA, O** • 1980
CRIME ON CAT-THE-VENTRILOQUIST STREET, THE • 1962 • Wasilewski Zenon • ANM • PLN
CRIME ON THE HILL • 1933 • Vorhaus Bernard • UKN
CRIME ON THEIR HANDS • 1948 • Bernds Edward • USA
CRIME OVER LONDON • 1936 • Zeisler Alfred • UKN
CRIME PASSIONEL, UN • 1931 • Greville Edmond T. • SHT • FRN
CRIME PASSIONNEL see **GARIMAT HUBB** • 1959
CRIME PATROL, THE • 1936 • Cummings Eugene • USA
CRIME RAVE • 1939 • Yarbrough Jean • USA
CRIME REPORTER • 1947 • Hart Ben R. • UKN
CRIME RING • 1938 • Goodwins Leslie • USA
CRIME SCHOOL • 1938 • Seiler Lewis • USA
CRIME SMASHER (UKN) see **COSMO JONES -CRIME SMASHER** • 1943
CRIME SQUAD (UKN) see **MAN FROM CAIRO, THE** • 1953
CRIME STORY • 1986 • Ferrara Abel • USA
CRIME STORY PART 2: THE MAFIA WAR • 1987 • Ferrara Abel • TVM • USA
CRIME STORY PART 3: BLOOD FEUD • 1987 • Ferrara Abel • TVM • USA
CRIME STORY PART 4: THE VEGAS CONNECTION • 1987 • Ferrara Abel • TVM • USA
CRIME STORY PART 5: LUCA'S FALL • 1987 • Ferrara Abel • TVM • USA
CRIME STORY PART 6: THE FINAL CHAPTER • 1987 • Ferrara Abel • TVM • USA
CRIME TAKES A HOLIDAY • 1938 • Collins Lewis D. • USA
CRIME THIEF, THE see **VOLEUR DE CRIMES, LES** • 1969
CRIME UNLIMITED • 1935 • Ince Ralph • UKN
CRIME WAVE • 1954 • De Toth Andre • USA • CITY IS DARK, THE (UKN)
CRIME WITHOUT PASSION • 1934 • Hecht Ben, MacArthur Charles • USA
CRIME ZONE • 1988 • Llosa Luis • USA, PRU
CRIMEBUSTER, THE • 1968 • Gallardo Cesar Chat • PHL
CRIMEBUSTERS • 1976 • Tarantini Michele Massimo • ITL
CRIMEBUSTERS, THE • 1961 • Sagal Boris • USA
CRIMEN • 1960 • Camerini Mario • FRN, ITL • ...AND SUDDENLY IT'S MURDER (USA) ◦ CHACUN SON ALIBI (FRN) ◦ KILLING AT MONTE CARLO (UKN) ◦ KILLING IN MONTE CARLO
CRIMEN • 1964 • Lluch Miguel • SPN
CRIMEN A LAS TRES • 1935 • Saslavsky Luis • ARG
CRIMEN DE CUENCA, EL • 1979 • Miro Pilar • SPN • MURDER OF CUENCA, THE ◦ CUENCA CRIME, THE ◦ CUENCA'S CRIME ◦ CRIME OF CUENCA, THE
CRIMEN DE DOBLE FILO • 1964 • Borau Jose Luis • SPN • DOUBLE-EDGED CRIME ◦ DOUBLE-EDGED MURDER
CRIMEN DE LA CALLE DE BORDADORES, EL • 1946 • Neville Edgar • SPN
CRIMEN DE LA HACIENDA, EL • 1963 • Orol Juan • MXC, PRC
CRIMEN DE MEDIA NOCHE, EL • 1936 • Ray Bernard B.
CRIMEN DE ORIBE, EL • 1950 • Torre-Nilsson Leopoldo, Torres-Rios Leopoldo • ARG • ORIBE'S CRIME
CRIMEN DEL EXPRESO, EL • 1938 • Noriega Manuel • MXC
CRIMEN DEL EXPRESO DE ANDALUCIA, EL see **AL MARGEN DE LA LEY** • 1935
CRIMEN DEL OTRO, EL • 1919 • Stahl Carlos • MXC
CRIMEN DEL SIGLO, EL • 1971 • *Coop. Prod. Raul Deanda* • MXC
CRIMEN EN LA ALCOBA • 1946 • Gomez Muriel Emilio • MXC
CRIMEN IMPERFECTO • 1970 • Fernan-Gomez Fernando • SPN
CRIMEN IMPOSIBLE • 1953 • Ardavin Cesar • SPN
CRIMEN PARA RECIEN CASADOS • 1959 • Ramirez Pedro L. • SPN
CRIMEN PERFECTO • 1977 • Blanco Javier • VNZ, USA • PERFECT CRIME
CRIMEN PERFECTO, EL see **AVENTURAS DE CARLOS LACROIX, LAS** • 1958
CRIMEN Y CASTIGO • 1950 • de Fuentes Fernando • MXC • CRIME AND PUNISHMENT
CRIMENES DE PETIOT, LOS • 1972 • Madrid Jose Luis • SPN
CRIMES A VENDRE see **FURET, LE** • 1949
CRIMES AND MISDEMEANOURS • 1990 • Allen Woody • USA
CRIMES AT THE DARK HOUSE • 1940 • King George • UKN
CRIMES DE L'AMOUR, LES • 1951 • Astruc Alexandre, Barry Maurice, Clavel Maurice • FRN • MINA DE VANGHEL
CRIME'S END (UKN) see **MY SON IS GUILTY** • 1940
CRIME'S HIGHWAY (UKN) see **DESERT JUSTICE** • 1936
CRIMES IN THE WAX MUSEUM see **NIGHTMARE IN WAX** • 1969
CRIMES OF DR. MABUSE (UKN) see **TESTAMENT DES DR. MABUSE, DAS** • 1932
CRIMES OF PASSION • 1984 • Russell Ken • USA
CRIMES OF STEPHEN HAWKE, THE • 1936 • King George • UKN • STRANGLER'S MORGUE
CRIMES OF THE BLACK CAT (UKN) see **SETTE SCIALLI DI SETA GIALLA** • 1972
CRIMES OF THE BODY SNATCHERS see **GREED OF WILLIAM HART, THE** • 1948
CRIMES OF THE FUTURE • 1970 • Cronenberg David • CND
CRIMES OF THE HEART • 1986 • Beresford Bruce • USA
CRIME'S TRIANGLE • 1915 • Baggot King • USA
CRIMEWAVE • 1986 • Raimi Sam • USA • XYZ MURDERS, THE ◦ BROKEN HEARTS AND NOSES
CRIMEWAVE • 1987 • Paizs John • USA
CRIMINAL, THE • 1915 • Brooke Van Dyke • USA
CRIMINAL, THE • 1916 • Barker Reginald • USA
CRIMINAL, THE • 1960 • Losey Joseph • UKN • CONCRETE JUNGLE, THE (USA)
CRIMINAL, THE • 1978 • Abu Saif Salah • EGY
CRIMINAL, THE see **VOYOU, LE** • 1970
CRIMINAL ABORTION see **ABORTO CRIMINAL** • 1973
CRIMINAL ACT see **TUNNELS** • 1988
CRIMINAL AND THE LADY, THE see **ZBRODNIARZ I PANNA** • 1963
CRIMINAL AT LARGE see **FUGITIVE AT LARGE** • 1939
CRIMINAL AT LARGE (USA) see **FRIGHTENED LADY, THE** • 1932
CRIMINAL CARGO see **OUTSIDE THE THREE MILE LIMIT** • 1940
CRIMINAL CODE, THE • 1914 • Taylor William D. • USA
CRIMINAL CODE, THE • 1931 • Hawks Howard • USA
CRIMINAL CONVERSATION • Hickey Kieran • IRL
CRIMINAL CONVERSATIONS • 1974 • Kent Larry • MTV • CND
CRIMINAL COURT • 1946 • Wise Robert • USA
CRIMINAL COURT JUDGE, THE see **BROTTMALSDOMAREN** • 1917
CRIMINAL CRIED, THE • 1907 • Morland John • UKN
CRIMINAL FACE see **HO!** • 1968
CRIMINAL HYPNOTIST, THE • 1909 • Griffith D. W. • USA
CRIMINAL INVESTIGATOR • 1942 • Yarbrough Jean • USA
CRIMINAL IS BORN, A • 1938 • Fenton Leslie • SHT • USA
CRIMINAL JOURNEY OF A YOUNG BOSS see **WAKAOYABUN KYOJOTABI** • 1967
CRIMINAL KING, THE see **SUPERARGO EL GIGANTE** • 1967
CRIMINAL LAW • 1988 • Campbell Martin • USA
CRIMINAL LAWYER • 1937 • Cabanne W. Christy • USA
CRIMINAL LAWYER • 1951 • Friedman Seymour • USA
CRIMINAL LIFE OF ARCHIBALDO DE LA CRUZ, THE (USA) see **ENSAYO DE UN CRIMEN** • 1955
CRIMINAL OFFENCE see **PRESTOP** • 1981
CRIMINAL ON PROBATION, A see **MOGREM TAHT EL EKHTEBAR** • 1968
CRIMINAL PATH, THE • 1914 • Davis Will S. • USA
CRIMINAL RECORDS see **ZAPIS ZBRODNI** • 1975
CRIMINAL SHALL NOT ESCAPE, THE • 1966 • Tumanov Semyon • USS
CRIMINAL STORY (ITL) see **LIGNE DE DEMARCATION, LA** • 1966
CRIMINAL SYMPHONY see **SETTE UOMINI E UN CERVELLO** • 1968
CRIMINAL WHO STOLE THE CRIME, THE see **ZBRODNIARZ, KTORY UKRADL ZBRODNIC** • 1969
CRIMINALE, IL • 1963 • Baldi Marcello • ITL • NIGHT TRAIN TO MILAN ◦ TRAIN TO MILAN
CRIMINALI DELLA GALASSIA, I • 1966 • Margheriti Antonio • ITL • WILD, WILD PLANET, THE (USA) ◦ GALAXY CRIMINALS, THE
CRIMINALS • 1913 • Dwan Allan • *Rex* • USA
CRIMINALS • 1933 • Room Abram • USS
CRIMINALS see **JANAYAT** • 1981
CRIMINALS, THE • 1913 • *Mecca* • USA
CRIMINALS ALWAYS BLUNDER • 1938 • Delamar Mickey, Kavanagh Denis • UKN
CRIMINALS OF THE AIR • 1937 • Coleman C. C. Jr. • USA
CRIMINALS' ROAD see **JADEH TABAH KARAN** • 1968
CRIMINAL'S THUMB, THE • 1916 • Middleton Edwin • SHT • USA
CRIMINALS WITHIN • 1941 • Lewis Joseph H. • USA
CRIMINE A DUE • 1965 • Ferrara Romano • ITL • CASA SULLA FUNGAIA, LA
CRIMINEL • 1932 • Forrester Jack • FRN • CODE CRIMINEL, LE ◦ CRIMINELS
CRIMINEL A PEUR DES GOSSES, LE see **GOSSES MENENT L'ENQUETE, LES** • 1946
CRIMINELS see **CRIMINEL** • 1932
CRIMINOLOGIST, THE • 1912 • *Nestor* • USA
CRIMINOLOGY AND REFORM • 1914 • *Hennessy George* • USA
CRIMSON • 1985 • Fortuny Juan • SPN
CRIMSON AFFAIR, THE • 1917 • *Darkfeather Mona* • SHT • USA
CRIMSON AFFAIR, THE see **CURSE OF THE CRIMSON ALTAR** • 1968
CRIMSON ALTAR, THE see **CURSE OF THE CRIMSON ALTAR** • 1968
CRIMSON BLADE, THE • 1917 • Howard George Bronson • SHT • USA
CRIMSON BLADE, THE (USA) see **SCARLET BLADE, THE** • 1963
CRIMSON CANARY, THE • 1945 • Hoffman John • USA • HEAR THAT TRUMPET TALK
CRIMSON CANDLE, THE • 1934 • Mainwaring Bernerd • UKN
CRIMSON CANYON, THE • 1928 • Taylor Ray • USA
CRIMSON CHALLENGE, THE • 1922 • Powell Paul • USA
CRIMSON CIRCLE, THE • 1915 • *Santa Barbara* • USA
CRIMSON CIRCLE, THE • 1922 • Ridgwell George • UKN
CRIMSON CIRCLE, THE • 1936 • Denham Reginald • UKN
CRIMSON CIRCLE, THE see **ROTE KREIS, DER** • 1959
CRIMSON CIRCLE, THE (USA) see **ROTE KREIS, DER** • 1928
CRIMSON CITY, THE • 1928 • Mayo Archie • USA
CRIMSON CLUE • 1922 • *Richardson Jack* • USA
CRIMSON COFFIN see **KERANDA JINGGA** • 1970
CRIMSON COURAGE • 1930 • Levigard Josef • SHT • USA
CRIMSON CROSS, THE • 1913 • *Eclair* • USA
CRIMSON CROSS, THE • 1920 • Everett George • USA
CRIMSON CULT, THE (USA) see **CURSE OF THE CRIMSON ALTAR** • 1968
CRIMSON CURTAIN, THE see **RIDEAU CRAMOISI, LE** • 1952
CRIMSON DOVE, THE • 1917 • Fielding Romaine • USA
CRIMSON DYNASTY, THE see **KOENIGSMARK** • 1935
CRIMSON EXECUTIONER, THE see **BOIA SCARLATTO, IL** • 1965
CRIMSON FLASH, THE • 1927 • Heath Arch B. • SRL • USA
CRIMSON FLOWER, THE • 1953 • Atamanov A. L. • ANM • USS
CRIMSON GARDENIA, THE • 1919 • Barker Reginald • USA
CRIMSON GHOST, THE • 1946 • Witney William, Brannon Fred C. • SRL • USA
CRIMSON GOD, THE • 1917 • *Romayne Superfilm* • USA
CRIMSON GOLD • 1923 • Elfelt Clifford S. • USA
CRIMSON KEY, THE • 1947 • Forde Eugene J. • USA
CRIMSON KIMONO, THE • 1959 • Fuller Samuel • USA
CRIMSON MOTH, THE • 1915 • Vale Travers • USA
CRIMSON PIRATE, THE • 1952 • Siodmak Robert • USA
CRIMSON RAIN see **HONG YU** • 1975
CRIMSON ROMANCE • 1934 • Howard David • USA
CRIMSON RUNNER, THE • 1925 • Forman Tom • USA
CRIMSON SABRE, THE • 1915 • *Illian Isolde* • USA
CRIMSON SAILS see **ALYE PARUSA** • 1961
CRIMSON SCARS, THE • 1911 • Melies Gaston • USA
CRIMSON SHOALS • 1919 • Ford Francis • USA
CRIMSON SKULL, THE • 1921 • *Bush Anita* • USA
CRIMSON STAIN, THE • 1913 • Edwards Walter? • USA
CRIMSON STAIN MYSTERY, THE • 1916 • Hunter T. Hayes • SRL • USA
CRIMSON SUNSET see **BLODRAUTT SOLARLAG** • 1978
CRIMSON TRAIL, THE • 1916 • Kelley J. Winthrop • SHT • USA
CRIMSON TRAIL, THE • 1935 • Raboch Alfred • USA
CRIMSON TRIANGLE, THE • 1915 • Aylott Dave • UKN
CRIMSON WING, THE • 1915 • Calvert E. H. • USA
CRIMSON WINGS see **KURENAI NO TSUBASA** • 1958
CRIMSON YOKE, THE • 1916 • Madison Cleo, Mong William V. • SHT • USA
CRIN BLANC • 1953 • Lamorisse Albert • FRN • WHITE MANE (USA) ◦ WILD STALLION ◦ CHEVAL SAUVAGE
CRINGER, THE • 1912 • *Lubin* • USA

CRINOLINE, LA • 1906 • Blache Alice • FRN
CRINOLINE AND ROMANCE • 1923 • Beaumont Harry • USA
CRIOLLA, EL • 1944 • Mendez Fernando • MXC
CRIPPLE, THE • 1914 • *Gane Nolan* • USA
CRIPPLE CREEK • 1952 • Nazarro Ray • USA
CRIPPLE CREEK BAR-ROOM SCENE • 1899 • USA
CRIPPLE CREEK CINDERELLA, A • 1916 • Davis Ulysses • SHT • USA
CRIPPLE GIRL, THE see **KAERLIGHEDSLAENGEL** • 1915
CRIPPLE IN LOVE see **RAKASTUNUT RAMPA** • 1974
CRIPPLE OF YPRES, THE • 1915 • Tudor F. C. S. • UKN
CRIPPLED HAND, THE • 1916 • Leonard Robert Z., Kirkland David • USA
CRIPPLED TEDDY BEAR, THE • 1910 • *Imp* • USA
CRIPTA, LA • 1981 • del Real Cayetano • SPN, MXC • CRYPT, THE
CRIPTA E L'INCUBO, LA • 1964 • Mastrocinque Camillo • ITL, SPN • MALDICION DE LOS KARNSTEIN, LA (SPN) ○ TERROR IN THE CRYPT (USA) ○ CRYPT OF HORROR (UKN) ○ CURSE OF THE KARNSTEIN, THE ○ CRYPT AND THE NIGHTMARE, THE
CRIS SANS ECHO • 1954 • Masson Jean • SHT • FRN
CRISANTEMI PER UN BRANCO DI CAROGNE • 1968 • Pastore Sergio • ITL • CHRYSANTHEMUMS FOR A BUNCH OF SWINE
CRISE DU LOGEMENT, LA • 1955 • Dewever Jean • FRN
CRISE EST FINIE, LA • 1934 • Siodmak Robert • FRN • FINIE LA CRISE ○ SLUMP IS OVER, THE
CRISE MONDIALE • 1934 • Perojo Benito • SPN • WORLD CRISIS (USA)
CRISI • 1921 • Genina Augusto • ITL
CRISIS • 1950 • Brooks Richard • USA
CRISIS • 1963 • Pennebaker D. A., Leacock Richard, Lipscombe Jim, Dryden Hope • DOC • USA
CRISIS • 1968 • Revenga Luis • SPN • SOMBRE DE UN GIRASOL, LA
CRISIS • 1970 • Wendkos Paul • TVM • USA
CRISIS • 1972 • Hughes Bill • MTV • ASL
CRISIS see **ABWEGE** • 1928
CRISIS see **CRISIS: A FILM OF "THE NAZI WAY"** • 1938
CRISIS see **KRIS** • 1946
CRISIS, A • 1954 • Xie Jin • CHN
CRISIS, THE • 1911 • *Powers* • USA
CRISIS, THE • 1912 • Ince Thomas H. • USA
CRISIS, THE • 1913 • Lincoln W. J. • ASL
CRISIS, THE • 1915 • Campbell Colin • USA
CRISIS: A FILM OF "THE NAZI WAY" • 1938 • Kline Herbert • DOC • USA • CRISIS
CRISIS AT CENTRAL HIGH • 1981 • Johnson Lamont • TVM • USA
CRISIS AT SUN VALLEY • 1978 • Stanley Paul • TVM • USA • CRISIS IN SUN VALLEY
CRISIS EN EL CARIBE • 1962 • Alvarez Santiago • DOC • CUB
CRISIS IN MID-AIR • 1979 • Grauman Walter • TVM • USA
CRISIS IN SUN VALLEY see **CRISIS AT SUN VALLEY** • 1978
CRISOL • 1965 • Mariscal Alberto • MXC
CRISPINO E LA COMARE • 1938 • Sorelli Vincenzo • ITL
CRISS CROSS • 1949 • Siodmak Robert • USA
CRISS CROSS see **P.J.** • 1967
CRISSCROSS see **HITCHHIKE!** • 1974
CRISTAUX • 1928 • Gance Abel • SHT • FRN
CRISTEROS, LOS • 1946 • de Anda Raul • MXC
CRISTIANA MOACA INDEMONIATA • 1972 • Bergonzelli Sergio • ITL • VOCAZIONE, LA
CRISTINA • 1959 • Argemi Jose Maria • SPN
CRISTINA GUZMAN • 1942 • Delgras Gonzalo • SPN
CRISTINA GUZMAN • 1968 • Amadori Luis Cesar • SPN
CRISTO • 1953 • Aleixandre Margarita, Torrecilla Rafael • SPN
CRISTO DE LAMA • 1968 • Silva Wilson • BRZ • MUD CHRIST
CRISTO DE MI CABECERA, EL • 1950 • Cortazar Ernesto • MXC
CRISTO DE ORO, EL • 1927 • Ojeda Manuel R. • MXC
CRISTO DEL OCEANO, EL • 1970 • Fernandez Ramon • SPN, ITL • CHRIST OF THE OCEAN, THE
CRISTO E PASSATO SULL'AIA • 1953 • Palella Oreste • ITL
CRISTO IN INDIA • 1965 • Dal Fabbro Rinaldo • ITL
CRISTO NEGRO • 1962 • Torrado Ramon • SPN
CRISTO PROIBITO • 1951 • Malaparte Curzio • ITL • STRANGE DECEPTION ○ FORBIDDEN CHRIST
CRISTO SI E FERMATO A EBOLI • 1979 • Rosi Francesco • ITL • CHRIST STOPPED AT EBOLI
CRISTOBAL COLON • 1943 • Diaz Morales Jose • MXC • GRANDEZA DE AMERICA, LA
CRISTOFORO COLOMBO • 1984 • Lattuada Alberto • MTV • ITL, USA • CHRISTOPHER COLUMBUS
CRISTUS • 1915 • Guazzoni Enrico (c/d) • ITL
CRITIC • 1906 • *Bitzer Billy (Ph)* • USA
CRITIC, THE • 1963 • Pintoff Ernest, Brooks Mel • ANS • USA
CRITICAL AGE, THE (USA) see **GLENGARRY SCHOOLDAYS** • 1922
CRITICAL CONDITION • 1987 • Apted Michael • USA
CRITICAL LIST, THE • 1978 • Antonio Lou • TVM • USA
CRITICO, IL • 1912 • Mari Febo • ITL
CRITIC'S CHOICE • 1963 • Weis Don • USA
CRITICUS • 1961 • Jutrisa Vladimir, Marks Aleksandar • YGS
CRITIQUE EST AISEE, LA • 1960 • Laliberte Roger • DCS • CND
CRITTERS • 1986 • Hereck Stephen • USA
CRITTERS 2: THE MAIN COURSE • 1988 • Garris Mick • USA
CRNE PTICE • 1967 • Galic Eduard • YGS • BLACK BIRDS ○ UP THE RIVER
CRNI BISERI • 1958 • Janic Tomo • YGS • BLACK PEARLS
CRNO SEME • 1972 • Cenevski Kiril • YGS • BLACK SEED, THE ○ UPHO SEME
CROAZIERA • 1981 • Daneliuc Mircea • RMN • CRUISE, THE
CROC-BLANC (FRN) see **ZANNA BIANCA** • 1973
CROCE DI SANGUE, LA • 1916 • Lolli Alberto Carlo • ITL
CROCE SENZA NOME, UNA • 1952 • Covaz Tullio • ITL
CROCE SICILIANA, LA see **ESECUTORI, GLI** • 1976
CROCIFISSO DI OTTONE, IL • 1909 • Novelli Enrico • ITL
CROCKETT-DOODLE-DO • 1960 • McKimson Robert • ANS • USA
CROCODILE • 1981 • Sands Sampote, Cohen Herman • THL, HKG
CROCODILE DUNDEE • 1986 • Faiman Peter • ASL
CROCODILE DUNDEE II • 1988 • Cornell John • USA
CROCODILE HUNTERS • 1949 • Robinson Lee • DOC • ASL
CROCODILE MAJUSCULE, LE • 1964 • Ryssack Eddy, Rosy Maurice, Delire Jean • ANS • BLG
CROCODILE SAFARI • 1967 • Fancey Malcolm J. • DOC • UKN
CROCODILES IN AMSTERDAM see **KROKODILLEN IN AMSTERDAM** • 1990
CROFTERS • 1944 • Keene Ralph • DOC • UKN
CROGMERE RUBY, THE • 1915 • *Thanhouser* • USA
CROISADE, LA • 1923 • Le Somptier Rene • FRN
CROISEE DES CHEMINS, LA • 1942 • Berthomieu Andre • FRN
CROISEE DES CHEMINS, LA • 1975 • Brisseau Jean-Claude • FRN
CROISEMENTS ET PROFITS see **CROSSBREEDING FOR PROFIT** • 1961
CROISIERE DE L'ATALANTE, LA • 1926 • Gremillon Jean • FRN
CROISIERE JAUNE, LA • 1928 • Poirier Leon • FRN • EAST MEETS WEST
CROISIERE JAUNE, LA • 1933 • Poirier Leon, Sauvage Andre (U/c) • DOC • FRN • YELLOW CRUISE, THE
CROISIERE NOIRE, LA • 1927 • Poirier Leon • DOC • FRN • BLACK JOURNEY
CROISIERE PORU L'INCONNU • 1947 • Montazel Pierre • FRN
CROISIERE POUR COUPLES EN CHALEUR • 1980 • Bernard-Aubert Claude • FRN
CROISIERES SIDERALES • 1941 • Zwobada Andre • FRN • SIDEREAL CRUISES
CROISSANCE DE PARIS • 1954 • Gibaud Marcel • SHT • FRN
CROISSEUR EN FOLIE, LE see **CAPITAINE CRADDOCK, LE** • 1931
CROIX DE BOIS, LES • 1931 • Bernard Raymond • FRN • WOODEN CROSSES (USA)
CROIX DE LA BANNIERE, LA • 1960 • Ducrest Philippe • FRN
CROIX DES CIMES, LA • 1934 • Greville Edmond T. • FRN
CROIX DES VIVANTS, LA • 1962 • Govar Yvan • FRN • CROSS OF THE LIVING (USA)
CROIX DU MONT-ROYAL, LA see **CROIX SUR LA COLLINE, LA** • 1971
CROIX DU SUD, LA • 1931 • Hugon Andre • FRN
CROIX SUR LA COLLINE, LA • 1971 • Danis Aime • CND • CROIX DU MONT-ROYAL, LA
CROLLO DI ROMA, IL • 1962 • Margheriti Antonio • ITL • FALL OF ROME, THE (USA)
CROMWELL • 1912 • Desfontaines Henri • FRN
CROMWELL • 1970 • Hughes Ken • UKN
CROMWELL M.D. • 1975 • Rubie Howard • MTV • ASL
CRONACA DI ANNA MAGDALENA BACH (ITL) see **CHRONIK DER ANNA MAGDALENA BACH** • 1967
CRONACA DI DUE SECOLI see **PIAZZA S. SEPOLCRO** • 1943
CRONACA DI UN AMORE • 1950 • Antonioni Michelangelo • ITL • STORY OF A LOVE AFFAIR (USA) ○ CHRONICLE OF A LOVE
CRONACA DI UN DELITTO • 1953 • Sequi Mario • ITL
CRONACA DI UN GRUPPO • 1968 • Lorenzini Ennio • ITL
CRONACA DI UNA MORTE ANNUNCIATA • 1987 • Rosi Francesco • ITL, FRN • CHRONICLE OF A DEATH FORETOLD (UKN)
CRONACA EROTICA DI UNA COPPIA • 1973 • Coggio Roger • ITL
CRONACA FAMILIARE • 1962 • Zurlini Valerio • ITL • FAMILY HISTORY ○ FAMILY DIARY
CRONACA NERA • 1947 • Bianchi Giorgio • ITL
CRONACA (UNO SPARA NEL SOLE) • 1969 • Santini Gian Paolo • ITL
CRONACHE DEL '22 • 1962 • Cinieri Francesco, Guidi Guidarino, Rossi Moraldo, Ubezio Stefano, Orlandini Giuseppe • ITL
CRONACHE DI POVERI AMANTI • 1954 • Lizzani Carlo • ITL • TRUE STORIES OF POOR LOVERS ○ CHRONICLE OF POOR LOVERS ○ STORIES OF POOR LOVERS
CRONACHE DI UN CONVENTO (ITL) see **RELUCTANT SAINT, THE** • 1962
CRONICA ANEDOTICA see **LISBOA, CRONICA ANEDOTICA** • 1930
CRONICA DA CIDADE AMADA • 1965 • Christensen Carlos Hugo • ARG
CRONICA DE FAMILIA • 1985 • Lopez Diego • MXC • FAMILY CHRONICLE, A
CRONICA DE NUEVE MESES • 1967 • Ozores Mariano • SPN
CRONICA DE UM INDUSTRIAL • 1980 • Filho Luis Rosemberg • BRZ • CHRONICLE OF AN INDUSTRIAL
CRONICA DE UN AMOR • 1972 • *Cima* • MXC
CRONICA DE UN ATRACO • 1968 • Balcazar Jaime Jesus • SPN, ITL • DIARY OF A HOLD-UP
CRONICA DE UN INSTANTE • 1980 • Pangua Jose Antonio • SPN • STORY OF A MOMENT
CRONICA DE UN SUBVERSIVO LATINOAMERICANO • 1974 • Walerstein Mauricio • VNZ • CHRONICLE OF A LATIN-AMERICAN SUBVERTER
CRONICA DE UNA SENORA • 1972 • de la Torre Raul • ARG • CHRONICLE OF A LADY
CRONICA DEL ALBA • 1983 • Sender Ramon • SPN • CHRONICLE OF DAWN
CRONICA DO ESFORCO PERDIDO • 1966 • de Macedo Antonio • SHT • PRT
CRONICA DOS BONS MALANDROS • 1984 • Lopes Fernando • PRT
CRONICA INTIMA • 1978 • Isaac Claudio • MXC • INTIMATE CHRONICLE
CRONICA ROJA • 1977 • Vallejo Fernando • MXC
CRONICAS LEVANTINAS • 1968 • Briz Jose • SHT • SPN
CRONICON, EL • 1969 • Gimenez-Rico Antonio • SPN
CRONIN, AMERICAN CLUB MANIPULATOR • 1896 • *Paul R. W.* • UKN
CRONIN WITH THREE CLUBS • 1896 • *Paul R. W.* • UKN
CROOK, THE (USA) see **VOYOU, LE** • 1970
CROOK AND THE GIRL, THE • 1913 • O'Sullivan Tony • USA
CROOK BUSTER • 1925 • Wyler William • SHT • USA
CROOK OF DREAMS • 1919 • Apfel Oscar • USA
CROOK THAT CRIED WOLF, THE • 1963 • Hanna William, Barbera Joseph • ANS • USA
CROOKED ALLEY • 1923 • Hill Robert F. • USA • DAUGHTER OF CROOKED ALLEY, THE
CROOKED BANKERS, THE • 1913 • *Patheplay* • USA
CROOKED BILLET, THE • 1929 • Brunel Adrian • UKN
CROOKED BUT DUMB (UKN) see **AMATEUR CROOK** • 1937
CROOKED CHIMNEY, THE • 1970 • Prochazka Pavel • ANM • CZC
CROOKED CIRCLE • 1932 • Humberstone H. Bruce • USA
CROOKED CIRCLE, THE • 1957 • Kane Joseph • USA
CROOKED COIN, THE • 1919 • *Universal* • SHT • USA
CROOKED FROM THE START • 1916 • *Selby Gertrude* • SHT • USA
CROOKED HEARTS, THE • 1972 • Sandrich Jay • TVM • USA
CROOKED LADY, THE • 1932 • Hiscott Leslie • UKN
CROOKED MAN, THE • 1923 • Ridgwell George • UKN
CROOKED MIRROR see **KRIVE ZRCADLO** • 1956
CROOKED MIX-UP, A • 1916 • Beaudine William • SHT • USA
CROOKED PATH • 1909 • *Selig* • USA
CROOKED PATH, THE • 1912 • *Hawley Ormi* • USA
CROOKED PATH, THE • 1915 • Vignola Robert G. • USA
CROOKED RING (UKN) see **DOUBLE JEOPARDY** • 1955
CROOKED RIVER • 1951 • Carr Thomas • USA • LAST BULLET, THE
CROOKED ROAD see **LIKU-LIKONG LANDAS** • 1968
CROOKED ROAD, THE • 1911 • Powell Frank?, Griffith D. W.? • USA
CROOKED ROAD, THE • 1916 • Huntley Fred W. • SHT • USA
CROOKED ROAD, THE • 1940 • Rosen Phil • USA
CROOKED ROAD, THE • 1965 • Chaffey Don • UKN, YGS • KRIVI PUT (YGS)
CROOKED ROMANCE, A • 1917 • Parke William • USA
CROOKED SKY, THE • 1957 • Cass Henry • UKN
CROOKED STRAIGHT • 1919 • Storm Jerome • USA
CROOKED STREETS • 1920 • Powell Paul • USA
CROOKED TO THE END • 1915 • Frazee Edwin, Reed Walter C. • USA
CROOKED TRAIL, THE • 1910 • *Nestor* • USA
CROOKED TRAIL, THE • 1936 • Luby S. Roy • USA • LEAD LAW (UKN)
CROOKED TRAILS • 1916 • Mix Tom • SHT • USA
CROOKED TRAILS • 1930 • Levigard Josef • SHT • USA
CROOKED WAY, THE • 1949 • Florey Robert • USA
CROOKED WAY, THE (UKN) see **GANG BULLETS** • 1938
CROOKED WEB, THE • 1954 • Juran Nathan • USA
CROOKS, THE • 1914 • Fielding Romaine • USA
CROOKS AND CORONETS • 1969 • O'Connolly Jim • UKN • SOPHIE'S PLACE (USA)
CROOKS AND CREDULOUS • 1913 • *Coxen Ed* • USA
CROOKS AND CROCODILES • 1917 • *Voss Fatty* • SHT • USA
CROOKS ANONYMOUS • 1962 • Annakin Ken • UKN
CROOKS CAN'T WIN • 1928 • Arthur George M. • USA
CROOKS IN CLOISTERS • 1963 • Summers Jeremy • UKN
CROOKS IN CLOVER (UKN) see **PENTHOUSE** • 1933
CROOKS IN CLOVER (UKN) see **TONTONS FLINGEURS, LES** • 1963
CROOK'S ROMANCE, A • 1921 • *Mcgowan J. P.* • USA
CROOK'S SWEETHEART, A • 1914 • *Kb* • USA
CROOK'S TOUR • 1933 • McGowan Robert • SHT • USA
CROOK'S TOUR • 1940 • Baxter John • UKN
CROOKY • 1915 • Williams C. Jay • USA
CROON CRAZY • 1933 • Muffati Steve • ANS • USA
CROONER • 1932 • Bacon Lloyd • USA
CROP CHASERS • 1939 • Iwerks Ub • ANS • USA
CROQUE LA VIE • 1981 • Tacchella Jean-Charles • FRN
CROQUEMITAINE ET ROSALIE • 1916 • Cohl Emile • ANS • FRN
CROQUEMITOUFLE • 1958 • Barma Claude • FRN
CROQUET QUACKS • 1962 • *Vanderbeek Stan (P)* • USA
CROQUETTE • 1927 • Mercanton Louis • FRN • MONKEYNUTS
CROQUEZ.. ET VOUS TROUVEREZ • 1973 • Lamothe Arthur • DCS • CND
CROQUIS BRESILIENS • 1966 • Kast Pierre • SHT • FRN
CROREPATI • 1936 • *Sircar B. N. (P)* • IND
CROSBY CASE, THE • 1934 • Marin Edwin L. • USA • CROSBY MURDER CASE, THE (UKN)
CROSBY – COLUMBO – VALLEE • 1931-32 • Ising Rudolf • ANS • USA
CROSBY MURDER CASE, THE (UKN) see **CROSBY CASE, THE** • 1934
CROSBY'S REST CURE • 1916 • Drew Sidney • SHT • USA
CROSS, THE • 1911 • *Thanhouser* • USA
CROSS, THE • 1984 • SAF
CROSS AND AXE see **KRZYZ I TOPOR** • 1972
CROSS AND MAUSER • 1925 • Gardin Vladimir • USS
CROSS AND PASSION • 1981 • Longinotto Kim, Pollack Claire • UKN
CROSS AND THE SWITCHBLADE, THE • 1970 • Murray Don • USA
CROSS AND THE SWORD, THE see **CRUZ Y LA ESPADA, LA** • 1934
CROSS AT THE BROOK, THE see **KRIZ U POTOKA** • 1921
CROSS BAR see **TVARBALK** • 1967
CROSS-BEARER, THE see **CROSS BEARERS, THE** • 1918
CROSS BEARERS, THE • 1918 • Archainbaud George • USA • CROSS-BEARER, THE
CROSS BREED • 1927 • Smith Noel • USA
CROSS CHANNEL • 1955 • Springsteen R. G. • UKN
CROSS COUNTRY • 1969 • Djordjevic Purisa • YGS
CROSS COUNTRY • 1983 • Lynch Paul • CND
CROSS COUNTRY CRUISE • 1934 • Buzzell Edward • USA
CROSS COUNTRY DETOURS • 1940 • Avery Tex • ANS • USA
CROSS-COUNTRY ROMANCE • 1940 • Woodruff Frank • USA • CROSS COUNTRY ROMANCE
CROSS COUNTRY ROMANCE see **CROSS-COUNTRY ROMANCE** • 1940
CROSS CREEK • 1983 • Ritt Martin • USA
CROSS CURRENTS • 1916 • Grandon Francis J. • USA
CROSS CURRENTS • 1935 • Brunel Adrian • UKN
CROSS EXAMINATION • 1932 • Thorpe Richard • USA
CROSS-EYED SUBMARINE, THE • 1917 • Beaudine William • SHT • USA

CROSS-EYED TERROR, THE see **TERRORE CON GLI OCCHI STORTI, IL** • 1972
CROSS IN THE CACTI, THE • 1914 • *Eclair* • USA
CROSS IN THE DESERT, THE • 1914 • *Broncho* • USA
CROSS MY HEART • 1937 • Mainwaring Bernerd • UKN • LOADED DICE
CROSS MY HEART • 1946 • Berry John • USA
CROSS MY HEART see **AMERICAN DATE** • 1987
CROSS OF CRIME, THE • 1914 • *Shumway L. C.* • USA
CROSS OF FIRE, THE • 1915 • *Edwards Walter* • USA
CROSS OF IRON • 1977 • Peckinpah Sam • UKN, FRG • STEINER –DAS EISERNE KREUZ
CROSS OF IRON II see **BREAKTHROUGH** • 1978
CROSS OF LORRAINE, THE • 1943 • Garnett Tay • USA
CROSS OF PEARLS, THE • 1911 • Melies Gaston • USA
CROSS OF THE LIVING (USA) see **CROIX DES VIVANTS, LA** • 1962
CROSS OF VALOUR, THE see **KRZYZ WALECZNYCH** • 1959
CROSS-PATCH, THE see **KRIBBEBIJTER, DE** • 1936
CROSS PURPOSES • 1913 • Reid Wallace, Robards Willis • USA
CROSS PURPOSES • 1916 • Worthington William • SHT • USA
CROSS RED NURSE, THE • 1918 • *Dressler Marie* • SHT • USA
CROSS ROADS • 1914 • *Frontier* • USA
CROSS ROADS • 1922 • Ford Francis? • USA • LARIAT THROWER, THE (?)
CROSS ROADS • 1930 • Fogwell Reginald • UKN
CROSS ROADS, THE • 1908 • *Lubin* • USA
CROSS-ROADS, THE • 1912 • *Victor* • USA
CROSS ROADS, THE • 1912 • Thompson Frederick A. • USA
CROSS SHOT (USA) see **LEGGE VIOLENTA DELLA SQUADRA ANTICRIMINE, LA** • 1976
CROSS STREETS • 1934 • Strayer Frank • USA
'CROSS THE MEXICAN LINE • 1914 • Reid Wallace • USA
CROSS UP (USA) see **TIGER BY THE TAIL** • 1955
CROSS YOUR FINGERS • 1942 • Lilley Edward • USA
CROSS YOUR HEART • 1912 • *Eline Marie* • USA
CROSSBAR • 1979 • Trent John • CND
CROSSBEAM see **TVARBALK** • 1967
CROSSBOW, THE see **KUSZA** • 1963
CROSSBREEDING FOR PROFIT • 1961 • Patry Pierre • DCS • CND • CROISEMENTS ET PROFITS
CROSSCURRENT • 1971 • Thorpe Jerry • TVM • USA • CABLE CAR MURDER, THE
CROSSED CLUES • 1915 • *Courtot Marguerite* • USA
CROSSED FLAGS, THE • 1914 • *B & C* • UKN
CROSSED LOVE AND SWORDS • 1915 • Jones F. Richard • USA
CROSSED SIGNALS • 1926 • McGowan J. P. • USA
CROSSED SWORDS (USA) see **MAESTRO DI DON GIOVANNI, IL** • 1952
CROSSED SWORDS (USA) see **PRINCE AND THE PAUPER, THE** • 1978
CROSSED TRAILS • 1917 • *Knickerbocker Star* • SHT • USA
CROSSED TRAILS • 1924 • McGowan J. P. • USA
CROSSED TRAILS • 1948 • Hillyer Lambert • USA
CROSSED WIRES • 1915 • *Empress* • USA
CROSSED WIRES • 1923 • Baggot King • USA
CROSSED WIRES see **DAUGHTERS OF THE NIGHT** • 1924
CROSSED WIRES, THE • 1915 • *Thanhouser* • USA
CROSSEYED BULL, THE • 1944 • Newman Robert • USA
CROSSFIRE • 1933 • Brower Otto • USA
CROSSFIRE • 1947 • Dmytryk Edward • USA
CROSSFIRE • 1975 • Hale William • TVM • USA
CROSSFIRE • 1986 • Conrad Robert, Zacarias Alfredo • USA
CROSSFIRE see **JUJI HOKA** • 1939
CROSSING see **PRZEPRAWA** • 1988
CROSSING, THE • 1976 • Shields Frank • SHT • ASL
CROSSING, THE • 1989 • Ogilvie George • ASL
CROSSING, THE see **CRUCE, EL**
CROSSING, THE see **PARANMA, TO** • 1989
CROSSING BORDERS see **HERZLICH WILLKOMMEN** • 1990
CROSSING DELANCEY • 1988 • Silver Joan Micklin • USA
CROSSING OF THE RHINE, THE see **PASSAGE DU RHIN, LE** • 1960
CROSSING OVER • 1989 • Laird, Bampoe-Addo • T&T, GHN
CROSSING POLICEMAN, THE • 1913 • *Dayton Frank* • USA
CROSSING THE DELAWARE • 1961 • Bartsch Art • ANS • USA
CROSSING THE GREAT SAGRADA • 1924 • Brunel Adrian • UKN
CROSSING THE LINE • 1989 • Graver Gary • USA
CROSSING THE MOB see **MAN AGAINST THE MOB** • 1988
CROSSING THE RIVER • 1988 • Frieberg Camelia • DCS • CND
CROSSING THE ROAD • 1947 • Wildman Shaw • UKN
CROSSING TRAILS • 1921 • Smith Cliff • USA
CROSSING WATCHMAN OF THE MOUNTAINS, THE • 1923 • Shimazu Yasujiro • JPN
CROSSOVER see **MR. PATMAN** • 1980
CROSSOVER DREAMS • 1985 • Ichaso Leon • USA
CROSSPLOT • 1969 • Rakoff Alvin • UKN
CROSSROAD see **PEREKRESTOK** • 1963
CROSSROAD see **SHIH-TZU-LU K'OU** • 1977
CROSSROAD, THE see **GRIHAYADHYA** • 1982
CROSSROAD DRILL • 1947 • Cathles Ralph • UKN
CROSSROAD GALLOWS, THE • 1958 • Tully Montgomery • UKN
CROSSROADS • 1942 • Conway Jack • USA
CROSSROADS • 1955 • Fitchen John • UKN
CROSSROADS • 1957 • Haldane Don • SHT • CND
CROSSROADS • 1976 • Conner Bruce • USA
CROSSROADS • 1986 • Hill Walter • USA
CROSSROADS see **JUJIRO** • 1928
CROSSROADS see **SHIZI JIETOU** • 1937
CROSSROADS see **GYOCHARO** • 1955
CROSSROADS see **CHOWRINGHEE** • 1968
CROSSROADS FOR A NUN see **ENCRUCIJADA PARA UNA MONJA** • 1967
CROSSROADS OF LIFE see **AU CARREFOUR DE LA VIE** • 1949
CROSSROADS OF LIFE, THE see **I LIVETS BRANDING** • 1915
CROSSROADS OF NEW YORK, THE • 1922 • Jones F. Richard • USA • FOR LOVE OR MONEY ○ HEARTBALM
CROSSROADS: SOUTH AFRICA • 1980 • Wacks Jonathan • DOC • SAF
CROSSROADS TO CRIME • 1960 • Anderson Gerry • UKN
CROSSROADS (USA) see **CARREFOUR** • 1938
CROSSTALK • 1982 • Egerton Mark • ASL • WALL TO WALL
CROSSTRAP • 1962 • Hartford-Davis Robert • UKN
CROSSWAYS see **JUJIRO** • 1928
CROSSWIND • 1951 • Foster Lewis R. • USA • JUNGLE ATTACK
CROSSWINDS • 1951 • Pine William H. • USA
CROSSWINDS see **OUT OF CONTROL** • 1985
CROUCHING BEAST, THE • 1935 • Hanbury Victor • UKN
CROULANTS SE PORTENT BIEN, LES • 1961 • Boyer Jean • FRN
CROW, THE • 1919 • Eason B. Reeves • SHT • USA
CROW, THE see **CORBEAU, LE** • 1943
CROW, THE see **KALAAGH** • 1977
CROW AND THE CANARY, THE • 1988 • Lipsey Arnie • ANS • CND
CROW CRAZY • 1945 • Lundy Dick • ANS • USA
CROW HOLLOW • 1952 • McCarthy Michael • UKN
CROW KILLER, THE see **JEREMIAH JOHNSON** • 1972
CROW ON THE TOWER (USA) see **VARJU A TORONYORAN** • 1939
CROWD, THE • 1927 • Vidor King • USA • MOB, THE
CROWD, THE • 1984 • Thomas Ralph L. • MTV • CND
CROWD FOR LISETTE, A see **LISETTE** • 1961
CROWD INSIDE, THE • 1971 • Waxman Albert • CND
CROWD ROARS, THE • 1932 • Hawks Howard • USA
CROWD ROARS, THE • 1938 • Thorpe Richard • USA
CROWD SNORES, THE • 1932 • Lantz Walter, Nolan William • ANS • USA
CROWDED COFFIN, THE see **TRAFRACKEN** • 1966
CROWDED DAY, THE • 1954 • Guillermin John • UKN • SHOP SPOILED (USA) ○ SHOP SOILED ○ TOMORROW IS SUNDAY
CROWDED HOUR, THE • 1925 • Hopper E. Mason • USA
CROWDED PARADISE • 1955 • Pressburger Fred • USA
CROWDED SKY, THE • 1960 • Pevney Joseph • USA
CROWDED STREETCAR, THE see **MANIN DENSHA** • 1957
CROWDED TRAIN, THE see **MANIN DENSHA** • 1957
CROWHAVEN FARM • 1970 • Grauman Walter • TVM • USA
CROWIN' PAINS • 1962 • Smith Paul J. • ANS • USA
CROWING PAINS • 1947 • McKimson Robert • ANS • USA
CROWN CAPER, THE see **THOMAS CROWN AFFAIR, THE** • 1968
CROWN JEWELS • 1918 • Clements Roy • USA
CROWN OF LIES, THE • 1926 • Buchowetzki Dimitri • USA
CROWN OF TEARS see **CORONA DE LAGRIMAS** • 1968
CROWN OF THE RUSSIAN EMPIRE, THE see **KORONA RUSSKOI IMPERII** • 1971
CROWN OF THORNS see **I.N.R.I.** • 1923
CROWN OUTSIDE: OR, WAITING FOR YOU, THE • 1913 • Stow Percy • UKN
CROWN PRINCE, THE see **KRONPRINSEN** • 1979
CROWN PRINCE'S DOUBLE, THE • 1916 • Brooke Van Dyke • USA
CROWN TRAIL • 1938 • Ruffin John • UKN
CROWN V STEVENS • 1936 • Powell Michael • UKN • THIRD TIME UNLUCKY
CROWNING EXPERIENCE, THE • 1960 • Anderson Marion Clayton • USA
CROWNING GIFT, THE • 1967 • Walker Norman • UKN
CROWNING GLORY, THE • 1914 • *Lubin* • USA
CROWNING TOUCH, THE • 1959 • Eady David • UKN
CROWN'S CAVALIERS, THE see **KRONANS KAVALJERER** • 1930
CROWS • 1988 • Menachemi Ayeleth • ISR
CROWS, THE see **CORBEAUX, LES**
CROWS, THE see **VRANE** • 1969
CROWS AND SPARROWS see **WUYA YU MAQUE** • 1949
CROW'S DEFEAT • 1911 • *Bison* • USA
CROW'S FEAT • 1962 • Freleng Friz • ANS • USA
CROW'S FETE • 1963 • Hanna William, Barbera Joseph • ANS • USA
CROW'S NEST, THE • 1922 • Hurst Paul C. • USA
CROXLEY MASTER, THE • 1921 • Nash Percy • UKN
CROYANCES • Colson-Malleville Marie • DOC • FRN • BELIEFS
CRUCE, EL • Arzuaga Jose Maria • CLM • CROSSING, THE
CRUCERO 33 see **SANGRE EN EL BARRIO** • 1951
CRUCERO DE VERANO • 1964 • Lucia Luis • SPN
CRUCES SOBRE EL YERMO • 1965 • Mariscal Alberto • MXC
CRUCIAL MOMENT, THE (USA) see **DONTO PILLANAT** • 1938
CRUCIAL TEST, A • 1912 • *Darkfeather Mona* • USA
CRUCIAL TEST, THE • 1911 • *Prior Herbert* • USA
CRUCIAL TEST, THE • 1916 • *Lily* • USA
CRUCIAL TEST, THE • 1916 • Thornby Robert T., Ince John • *Paragon* • USA
CRUCIAL YEARS see **KRISTOVE ROKY** • 1967
CRUCIBLE, THE • 1914 • Johnston Lorimer • *American* • USA
CRUCIBLE, THE • 1914 • Porter Edwin S., Ford Hugh • *Famous Players* • USA
CRUCIBLE, THE • 1919 • *Lincoln E. K.* • USA
CRUCIBLE, THE • 1959 • Hart Harvey • MTV • CND
CRUCIBLE, THE (USA) see **SORCIERES DE SALEM, LES** • 1957
CRUCIBLE OF FATE, THE • 1914 • Lambart Harry • USA
CRUCIBLE OF HORROR • 1971 • Ritelis Viktors • UKN • VELVET HOUSE CORPSE, THE ○ VELVET HOUSE ○ CORPSE, THE
CRUCIBLE OF LIFE, THE • 1918 • Lambart Harry • USA
CRUCIBLE OF LOVE, THE • 1913 • *Pilot* • USA
CRUCIBLE OF TERROR • 1971 • Hooker Ted • UKN
CRUCIFICTION OF AL BRADY, THE • 1915 • *Greenwood Winnifred* • USA
CRUCIFIED GIRL, THE see **UKRIZOVANA** • 1921
CRUCIFIED LOVERS, THE see **CHIKAMATSU MONOGATARI** • 1954
CRUCIFIED WOMAN, A see **UWASA NO ONNA** • 1954
CRUCIFIJO DE PIEDRA, EL • 1954 • Toussaint Carlos • MXC
CRUCIFIX, THE • 1934 • Samuelson G. B. • UKN
CRUCIFIX OF DESTINY, THE • 1920 • Armstrong R. Dale • USA
CRUCIFIXION, THE • 1963 • Burstall Tim • SHT • ASL
CRUDE AWAKENING • 1984 • Pyke Roger • MTV • CND
CRUDE MISS PRUDE, THE • 1911 • *Comet* • USA
CRUDE OIL • 1967 • Mesaros Titus • DOC • RMN
CRUDELE MENZOGNA see **HO PIANTO PER TE** • 1954
CRUDELI, I • 1966 • Corbucci Sergio • ITL, SPN • DESPIADADOS, LOS (SPN) ○ HELLBENDERS, THE (USA)
CRUE, LA • 1976 • Benoit Denyse • CND
CRUEL ALSO LOVE, THE see **ZALIMLER DE SEVER** • 1967
CRUEL AND INNOCENT • 1989 • Yossifova Iskra • BUL
CRUEL AND UNUSUAL • 1916 • Myll Louis • SHT • USA
CRUEL, CRUEL LOVE • 1914 • Nicholls George • USA
CRUEL, CRUEL WORLD • 1914 • *Joker* • USA
CRUEL DESTINO • 1943 • Orol Juan • MXC
CRUEL DRAGON see **POHADKA O DRAKOVI** • 1953
CRUEL EMBRACE, THE • 1987 • Hansel Marion • BLG
CRUEL FATHER see **PAI TIRANO, O** • 1941
CRUEL GHOST LEGEND see **KAIDAN ZANKOKU MONOGATARI** • 1968
CRUEL HEART see **HATI BATU** • 1971
CRUEL HISTORY OF AFFAIRS see **JYOJI ZANKOKUSHI** • 1968
CRUEL HORIZON • 1989 • Thys Guy Lee • BLG
CRUEL LESSON, A • 1914 • *Gaumont* • USA
CRUEL LOVE see **LOVE FEROZ, EL** • 1972
CRUEL MAP OF WOMEN'S BODIES see **JOTAI ZANGYAKUZO** • 1967
CRUEL NEED, THE • 1968 • Skalenakis Giorgos • GRC
CRUEL PASSION • 1977 • Boger Chris • UKN • MARQUIS DE SADE'S JUSTINE ○ JUSTINE
CRUEL REVENGE, A • 1914 • Ince John • USA
CRUEL SEA, THE • 1953 • Frend Charles • UKN
CRUEL SEA, THE see **IKARI NO UMI** • 1944
CRUEL SEA, THE see **BAS YA BAHR** • 1971
CRUEL STEPMOTHER, THE • 1912 • *Imp* • USA
CRUEL STORY OF THE SAMURAI'S WAY see **BUSHIDO ZANKOKU MONOGATARI** • 1963
CRUEL STORY OF YOUTH see **SEISHUN ZANKOKU MONOGATARI** • 1960
CRUEL STORY OFF SEX FILM ACTORS, A see **SEX JOYU ZANKOKUSHI** • 1968
CRUEL SUMMER OF PARACELSUS • 1985 • Baker Douglas • UKN
CRUEL SUSPICION, A • 1913 • *Cummings Irving* • USA
CRUEL SWAMP see **SWAMP WOMEN** • 1955
CRUEL TALES OF BUSHIDO see **BUSHIDO ZANKOKU MONOGATARI** • 1963
CRUEL TALES OF YOUTH see **SEISHUN ZANKOKU MONOGATARI** • 1960
CRUEL TOWER, THE • 1956 • Landers Lew • USA
CRUEL TRUTH, THE • 1927 • Rosen Phil • USA
CRUEL WIND see **AANDHIYAN** • 1952
CRUEL WOMEN, THE see **CRUELES, LAS** • 1969
CRUELDADE MORTAL • 1980 • dos Santos Luiz Paulino • BRZ • MORTAL CRUELTY
CRUELES, LAS • 1969 • Aranda Vicente • SPN • CADAVER EXQUISITO, EL ○ EXQUISITE CADAVER ○ CRUEL WOMEN, THE
CRUELLE MEPRISE • 1962 • Rankovitch Jean-Michel • FRN • MEPRISE, LA
CRUELTY see **ZHESTOKOST** • 1959
CRUELTY see **ZANNIN** • 1967
CRUELTY TO A HORSE • 1904 • *Gaumont* • UKN • CRUELTY TO HORSES (USA)
CRUELTY TO HORSES (USA) see **CRUELTY TO A HORSE** • 1904
CRUISE, THE • 1967 • Hubley John, Hubley Faith • ANS • CND
CRUISE, THE see **REJS** • 1970
CRUISE, THE see **CROAZIERA** • 1981
CRUISE CAT • 1952 • Hanna William, Barbera Joseph • ANS • USA
CRUISE IN THE ALBERTINA, A (USA) see **KRYSS MED ALBERTINA, PAA** • 1940
CRUISE INTO TERROR • 1978 • Kessler Bruce • TVM • USA • VOYAGE INTO EVIL
CRUISE MISSILE see **MISSILE X** • 1978
CRUISE OF FATE, THE • 1916 • Warde Ernest C. • SHT • USA
CRUISE OF THE AIDEN BESSE, THE see **MUTINY** • 1917
CRUISE OF THE HELL SHIP, THE • 1914 • *Balboa* • USA
CRUISE OF THE HELLION, THE • 1927 • Worne Duke • USA
CRUISE OF THE JASPER B, THE • 1926 • Horne James W. • USA
CRUISE OF THE MAKE-BELIEVES, THE • 1918 • Melford George • USA
CRUISE OF THE MOLLY ANNE, THE • 1914 • *Broncho* • USA
CRUISER EMDEN see **KREUZER EMDEN** • 1932
CRUISER POTEMKIN see **BRONENOSETS POTYOMKIN** • 1925
CRUISIN' • 1973 • Lofven Chris • SHT • UKN
CRUISIN' • 1977 • Clark Curtis, Van Rellim Tim • UKN
CRUISIN' DOWN THE RIVER • 1953 • Quine Richard • USA
CRUISIN' HIGH • 1975 • Bushelman John • USA
CRUISING • 1980 • Friedkin William • USA
CRUISING BAR • 1990 • Menard Robert • CND • MEET MARKET
CRUISING CASANOVAS (UKN) see **GOBS AND GALS** • 1952
CRUISKEEN LAWN • 1922 • MacDonagh John • IRL
CRUMBLING CITADEL, THE see **CITADELA SFARIMATA** • 1957
CRUMBS OF THE WORLD, THE see **PSIHOULA TOU KOSMOU, TA** • 1967
CRUMLEY COGWELL • 1962 • Kneitel Seymour • ANS • USA
CRUMPLED LETTER, THE • 1915 • Montgomery Frank E. • USA
CRUNCH • 1980 • Warren Mark • CND • KINKY COACHES AND THE POM-POM PUSSYCATS, THE
CRUNCH see **BENGELCHEN LIEBT KREUZ UND QUER** • 1968
CRUNCH BIRD, THE • 1971 • Petok Ted • ANS • USA
CRUNCH CRUNCH • *Guest Group* • ANS • CND
CRUSADE • 1929 • Antonovsky B. • ANM • USS
CRUSADE AGAINST RACKETS • 1937 • Clifton Elmer • USA
CRUSADE FOR JAZZ see **BOUND TO BE HEARD** • 1972
CRUSADE FOR LIFE see **LOIS GIBBS AND THE LOVE CANAL** • 1982
CRUSADE OF THE INNOCENT • 1922 • *Popular Film Co.* • USA
CRUSADER, THE • 1911 • *Sawyer Laura* • USA
CRUSADER, THE • 1922 • Mitchell Howard M., Howard William K. • USA

CRUSADER, THE • 1932 • Strayer Frank • USA
CRUSADERS see **IF..** • 1968
CRUSADERS OF THE WEST • 1930 • *Lyons Cliff* • USA
CRUSADES, THE • 1935 • De Mille Cecil B. • USA
CRUSH PROOF • 1971 • De Menil Francois • USA
CRUSHED TO DEATH • 1967 • Ogawa Shinsuke • JPN
CRUSHED TRAGEDIAN, THE • 1908 • *Lubin* • USA
CRUSHING THE DRUG TRAFFIC • 1922 • Parkinson H. B. • UKN
CRUSOE • 1989 • Deschanel Caleb • USA
CRUST • 1987 • Hughes John E. • ANM • ASL
CRUZ DE FERRO, A • 1967 • do Canto Jorge Brum • PRT • IRON CROSS, THE
CRUZ DE MAYO, LA • 1954 • Rey Florian • SPN
CRUZ DEL DIABLO, LA • 1974 • Gilling John • SPN • DEVIL'S CROSS, THE
CRUZ DIABLO • 1934 • de Fuentes Fernando • MXC
CRUZ DIEZ, EL ILUSIONISTA DEL COLOR • 1979 • de Pedro Manuel • DCS • VNZ
CRUZ EN EL INFIERNO, UNA • 1954 • Elorrieta Jose Maria • SPN
CRUZ NA PRACA, A • 1959 • Rocha Glauber • SHT • BRZ
CRUZ Y LA ESPADA, LA • 1934 • Strayer Frank • USA • CROSS AND THE SWORD, THE
CRUZA • 1942 • Barth-Moglia Luis • ARG
CRUZADA ABC • 1966 • dos Santos Nelson Pereira • BRZ
CRUZADA EN EL MAR • 1967 • Ferry Isidoro Martinez • SPN
CRUZADO DE ORIENTE, EL • 1951 • Alfonso Raul • SPN
CRUZEIRO DO SUL • 1966 • Lopes Fernando • SHT • PRT
CRVENA ZEMLJA • 1976 • Jankovic Branimir Tori • YGS • RED EARTH, THE
CRVENI BUGI • 1983 • Godina Karpo • YGS • RDECI BOOGIE ALI KAJ TI JE DEKLICA ○ RED BOOGIE ○ CVRENI BOOGIE ILI STO TI JE DJEVOJKO ○ RED BOOGIE, OR WHAT'S UP, GIRL?
CRVENI CVET • 1950 • Gavrin Gustav • YGS
CRVENI I CRNI • 1985 • Mikuljan Miroslav • YGS • RED AND BLACK
CRVENI KONJ see **CRVENIOT KONJ** • 1981
CRVENI SAL see **PARTIZANSKE PRICE** • 1960
CRVENI UDAR • 1975 • Golubovic Predrag • YGS • MINERS' DETACHMENT, THE
CRVENIOT KONJ • 1981 • Popov Stole • YGS • RED HORSE, THE ○ CRVENI KONJ
CRVENO KLASJE • 1971 • Pavlovic Zivojin • YGS • RED WHEAT, THE ○ RDECE KLASJE
CRY, THE (UKN) see **GRIDO, IL** • 1957
CRY, THE (UKN) see **KRIK** • 1963
CRY AND CRY AGAIN see **KIALTAS ES KIALTAS** • 1988
CRY BABY • 1989 • Waters John* • USA
CRY BABY KILLER, THE • 1958 • Addiss Jus • USA
CRY BLOOD, APACHE • 1970 • Starrett Jack • USA
CRY DANGER • 1951 • Parrish Robert • USA
CRY DEMON see **EVIL, THE** • 1978
CRY DR. CHICAGO • 1971 • Manupelli George • USA
CRY DOUBLE CROSS (UKN) see **BUMERANG** • 1960
CRY FOR CINDY • 1975 • Locke Wendy • USA
CRY FOR HAPPY • 1961 • Marshall George • USA
CRY FOR HELP, A • 1912 • Griffith D. W. • USA
CRY FOR HELP, A • 1975 • Duke Daryl • TVM • USA • END OF THE LINE
CRY FOR HELP, A • 1986 • Roudarov Nikola • BUL
CRY FOR HELP, THE • 1964 • Stoney George C. • USA
CRY FOR JUSTICE, A • 1978 • Kelljan Bob • TVM • USA
CRY FOR JUSTICE, A see **SONG FOR EUROPE, A** • 1985
CRY FOR JUSTICE, THE • 1919 • Frenguelli Albert G. • UKN
CRY FOR LOVE, A • 1980 • Wendkos Paul • TVM • USA • ADDICTION: A CRY FOR LOVE
CRY FOR LUST see **SCHREI NACH LUST** • 1968
CRY FOR ME, BILLY • 1972 • Graham William A. • USA • FACE TO THE WIND ○ COUNT YOUR BULLETS ○ APACHE MASSACRE ○ LONG TOMORROW, THE ○ NAKED REVENGE
CRY FOR STRANGERS see **CRY FOR THE STRANGERS** • 1982
CRY FOR THE STRANGERS • 1982 • Medak Peter • TVM • USA • CRY FOR STRANGERS
CRY FREEDOM • 1959 • Avellana Lamberto V. • PHL
CRY FREEDOM • 1987 • Attenborough Richard • UKN • ASKING FOR TROUBLE
CRY FROM THE DUMB, A • 1913 • *Gail Jane* • USA
CRY FROM THE HEART, A • 1987 • Gerretsen Peter • CND
CRY FROM THE MOUNTAIN • 1985 • Collier James F. • USA
CRY FROM THE MUEZZIN, THE see **CRI DU MUEZZIN, LE** • 1973
CRY FROM THE STREETS, A • 1958 • Gilbert Lewis* • UKN
CRY FROM THE WILDERNESS, A • 1909 • Porter Edwin S. • USA
CRY HARD, CRY FAST • 1967 • Ritchie Michael • TVM • USA
CRY HAVOC • 1943 • Thorpe Richard • USA
CRY IN THE DARK, A • 1988 • Schepisi Fred • USA, ASL • EVIL ANGELS (ASL) ○ GUILTY BY SUSPICION
CRY IN THE NIGHT • 1956 • Tuttle Frank • USA
CRY IN THE NIGHT, A • 1915 • Batley Ernest G. • UKN
CRY IN THE WILDERNESS, A • 1974 • Hessler Gordon • TVM • USA
CRY IN THE WIND • 1966 • Schach Leonard, Heller Anthony • UKN, GRC
CRY ME A TEARDROP • 1974 • Van Der Watt Keith • SAF
CRY MURDER • 1950 • Glenn Jack • USA
CRY NO MORE see **BADHU BIDESHINI** • 1980
CRY OF BATTLE • 1963 • Lerner Irving • USA, PHL • TO BE A MAN
CRY OF CONSCIENCE, THE • 1916 • Elfelt Clifford S. • SHT • USA
CRY OF DEATH see **GRITO DE LA MUERTE, EL** • 1958
CRY OF ERIN, THE • 1916 • Ford Francis • SHT • USA
CRY OF INNOCENCE see **PRIME SUSPECT** • 1982
CRY OF JAZZ • 1959 • Bland Edward • USA
CRY OF JOY see **ONNA NO URESHINAKI** • 1968
CRY OF THE BANSHEE • 1970 • Hessler Gordon • UKN, USA
CRY OF THE BEWITCHED see **YAMBAO** • 1956
CRY OF THE BLACK WOLVES see **SCHREI DER SCHWARZEN WOLFE, DER** • 1972
CRY OF THE BLOOD, THE • 1913 • Terwilliger George W. • USA
CRY OF THE CAPTIVE, THE • 1914 • Wilson Frank • UKN
CRY OF THE CHILDREN, THE • 1912 • *Cruze James* • USA
CRY OF THE CITY • 1948 • Siodmak Robert • USA • MARTIN ROME
CRY OF THE FIRSTBORN, THE • 1915 • MacDonald Norman • USA
CRY OF THE HUNTED • 1953 • Lewis Joseph H. • USA
CRY OF THE INNOCENT • 1980 • O'Herlihy Michael • TVM • USA
CRY OF THE MOUNTAIN (USA) see **KITAHODAKA ZESSHO** • 1968
CRY OF THE NIGHTHAWK, THE • 1923 • Coleby A. E. • UKN
CRY OF THE PENGUINS (USA) see **MR. FORBUSH AND THE PENGUINS** • 1972
CRY OF THE PEOPLE, THE (UKN) see **AL GRITO DE ESTE PUEBLO** • 1972
CRY OF THE SWAMP see **LURE OF THE WILDERNESS** • 1952
CRY OF THE VAMPIRE, THE see **URLO DEL VAMPIRO, L'**
CRY OF THE WEAK, THE • 1919 • Fitzmaurice George • USA
CRY OF THE WEREWOLF • 1944 • Levin Henry • USA • DAUGHTER OF THE WEREWOLF
CRY OF THE WILD • 1972 • Mason William • DOC • CND • CHANT DE LA FORET, LE
CRY OF THE WORLD • 1932 • *De Rochemont Louis (Ed)* • DOC • USA
CRY OF THE WOUNDED see **AAKROSH** • 1978
CRY ONION (UKN) see **CIPOLLA COLT** • 1975
CRY PANIC • 1974 • Goldstone James • USA
CRY RAPE • 1972 • Allen Corey • TVM • USA
CRY SILENCE see **SILENCE** • 1974
CRY TERROR • 1958 • Stone Andrew L. • USA
CRY, THE BELOVED COUNTRY • 1952 • Korda Zoltan • UKN, SAF • AFRICAN FURY (USA)
CRY TO THE WIND • 1979 • Davison Robert W. • USA
CRY TOUGH • 1959 • Stanley Paul • USA
CRY UNCLE • 1971 • Avildsen John G. • USA • SUPER DICK (UKN) ○ AMERICAN ODDBALLS
CRY VENGEANCE • 1954 • Stevens Mark • USA
CRY WOLF • 1947 • Godfrey Peter • USA
CRY WOLF • 1968 • Davis John • UKN
CRY WOLF • 1981 • Ravn Jens • DNM
CRY WOLF see **ULVETID** • 1981
CRYBABY APPRENTICE see **NAKIMUSHI KOZO** • 1938
CRYING AND LAUGHING (USA) see **GENS QUI PLEURENT ET GENS QUI RIENT** • 1900
CRYING BLUE SKY see **EYES OF FIRE** • 1985
CRYING FOR THE SUN see **HINODE NO SAKEBI** • 1967
CRYING OUT LOUD see **COTTON QUEEN** • 1937
CRYING TO THE BLUE SKY see **AOZURA NI NAKU** • 1931
CRYING WOLF • 1947 • Rasinski Connie • ANS • USA
CRYING WOMAN, THE see **LLORONA, LA** • 1933
CRYING WOMAN, THE see **FEMME QUI PLEURE, LA** • 1979
CRYPT, THE see **HEARTS OF HUMANITY** • 1936
CRYPT, THE see **CRIPTA, LA** • 1981
CRYPT AND THE NIGHTMARE, THE see **CRIPTA E L'INCUBO, LA** • 1964
CRYPT OF DARK SECRETS • 1976 • *Ridley Maureen* • USA
CRYPT OF DARK SECRETS see **MARDI GRAS MASSACRE** • 1982
CRYPT OF HORROR (UKN) see **CRIPTA E L'INCUBO, LA** • 1964
CRYPT OF THE BLIND DEATH see **NOCHE DEL TERROR CIEGO, LA** • 1972
CRYPT OF THE DEAD see **CRYPT OF THE LIVING DEAD** • 1973
CRYPT OF THE LIVING DEAD • 1973 • Danton Ray • USA, SPN • TUMBA DE LA ISLA MALDITA, LA (SPN) ○ HANNAH, QUEEN OF THE VAMPIRES ○ VAMPIRE WOMAN (UKN) ○ CRYPT OF THE DEAD ○ YOUNG HANNAH, QUEEN OF THE VAMPIRES
CRYPTOGRAMME ROUGE, LE • 1915 • Feuillade Louis • FRN
CRYPTONYM "OKTAN" see **KRYPTONIM "OKTAN"** • 1959
CRYSTAL BALL see **SZKLANA KULA** • 1972
CRYSTAL BALL, THE • 1909 • *Centaur* • USA
CRYSTAL BALL, THE • 1914 • *Warner Features* • USA
CRYSTAL BALL, THE • 1943 • Nugent Elliott • USA
CRYSTAL BALLET • 1937 • Sparling Gordon • DCS • CND
CRYSTAL BRAWL, THE • 1957 • Kneitel Seymour • ANS • USA
CRYSTAL CAGES • 1983 • Patel Ishu • ANS • CND
CRYSTAL CASKET, THE see **GLASS COFFIN** • 1912
CRYSTAL CASKET, THE (USA) see **PHENIX OU LE COFFRET DE CRISTAL, LE** • 1905
CRYSTAL CUP, THE • 1927 • Dillon John Francis • USA
CRYSTAL EYE, THE • 1988 • Tornatore Joe • USA
CRYSTAL FIST see **JADE CLAW** • 1979
CRYSTAL GARDEN • 1980 • Casson Barry • DOC • CND
CRYSTAL GAZEBO, THE • 1932 • *Mintz Charles (P)* • ANS • USA
CRYSTAL GAZER, THE • 1912 • *Cosmopolitan* • UKN
CRYSTAL GAZER, THE • 1917 • Melford George • USA
CRYSTAL GAZER, THE • 1930 • Buzzell Edward • SHT • USA
CRYSTAL GAZER, THE • 1941 • *Mintz Charles (P)* • ANS • USA
CRYSTAL GAZING • 1982 • Mulvey Laura, Wollen Peter • UKN
CRYSTAL GLOBE, THE • 1915 • MacDonald Donald • USA
CRYSTAL HEART • 1987 • Bettman Gil • USA
CRYSTAL PRINCESS, THE • 1925 • Lamac Carl • CZC
CRYSTAL VOYAGER • 1973 • Falzon Franz, Greenough George • ASL
CRYSTALBRAIN L'UOMO DAL CERVELLO DI CRISTALLO • 1970 • Logar Juan • ITL, SPN • SEGRETO DEL DR. CHALMERS, IL (SPN) ○ UOMO CHE VISSE DUE VOLTE, L' ○ TRASPLANTE DE UN CEREBRO ○ SECRET OF DR. CHALMERS, THE ○ MAN WHO LIVED TWICE, THE ○ BRAIN TRANSPLANT
CRYSTALMAN see **SHUI-CHING JEN** • 1981
CRYSTALS • 1959 • Leacock Richard • DOC • USA
CRYSTALS see **KRISTALLEN** • 1930
CRYSTAL'S STRUCTURE see **STRUKTURA KRYSZTALU** • 1970
CRYSTAL'S WARNING, THE • 1916 • Hill Robert F. • SHT • USA
CRYSTALSTONE • 1987 • Pelaez Antonio • USA
CS BLUES see **COCKSUCKER BLUES** • 1976
CSAK EGY EJSZAKARA • 1936 • Sekely Steve • HNG
CSALADI TUZFESZEK • 1979 • Tarr Bela • HNG • FAMILY NEST
CSARDAS DES HERZENS • 1951 • Slatina Alexander V. • FRG
CSARDAS, IHRE TOLLSTE NACHT • 1937 • Kolm Walter
CSARDASKIRALYNO • 1971 • Szinetar Miklos • HNG • CZARDAS PRINCESS
CSASZAR PARANCSARA, A • 1956 • Ban Frigyes • HNG • EXTINGUISHED FLAMES
CSEMPESZEK • 1958 • Mariassy Felix • HNG • SMUGGLERS
CSEND ES KIALTAS • 1968 • Jancso Miklos • HNG • SILENCE AND CRY (USA)
CSENDES OTTHON • 1957 • Ban Frigyes • HNG • QUIET HOME, A
CSEPLO GYURI • 1978 • Schiffer Pal • HNG • GYURI
CSEREPEK • 1981 • Gaal Istvan • HNG • BUFFER ZONE ○ POTTERIES ○ SHARDS
CSIBSI DER FRATZ • 1934 • Neufeld Max • AUS
CSILLAG A MAGLYAN • 1979 • Adam Otto • HNG • BRIGHT STAR AT THE STAKE, A
CSILLAGOSOK, KATONAK • 1967 • Jancso Miklos • HNG, USS • ZVYOZDY I SOLDATY (USS) ○ RED AND THE WHITE, THE (USA)
CSODA VEGE, A • 1984 • Veszi Janos • HNG • END OF THE MIRACLE, THE
CSODALATOS MANDARIN, A • 1965 • *Fulop Zoltan* • HNG • MIRACULOUS MANDARIN, THE
CSOK, ANYU • 1986 • Rozsa Janos • HNG • LOVE, MOTHER ○ CSOKANYU ○ LOVEMUM
CSOKANYU see **CSOK, ANYU** • 1986
CSOKOLJ MEG EDES • 1932 • Gaal Bela • HNG
CSONTVARY • 1980 • Huszarik Zoltan • HNG
CSUNYA FIJU, A • 1918 • Curtiz Michael • HNG • UGLY BOY, THE
CSUNYA LANY, A • 1935 • Gaal Bela • HNG
C'T'AMOUR DE COUTURIER see **COUTURIER DE MON COEUR** • 1935
CTV'S NATIONAL CRIME TEST • 1980 • Pearson Peter • CND • NATIONAL CRIME TEST
CTYRI V KRUHU • 1967 • Makovec Milos • CZC • FOUR IN THE CIRCLE ○ CIRCLE OF FOUR, A
CTYRI VRAZDY STACI, DRAHOUSKU • 1971 • Lipsky Oldrich • CZC • FOUR MURDERS ARE ENOUGH, DARLING
CTYRICET DEDECKU • 1962 • Bedrich Vaclav • ANS • CZC • FORTY GRANDFATHERS
CTYRIKRAT O BULHARSKU • 1958 • Kachyna Karel • CZC • FOUR TIMES ABOUT BULGARIA
CU MIINILE CURATE • 1972 • Nicolaescu Sergiu • RMN • WITH CLEAN HANDS
CUADRILATERO • 1969 • de la Iglesia Eloy • SPN
CUALQUIER COSA • 1980 • Sanchez Douglas • MXC • ANYTHING
CUANDO ACABA LA NOCHE • 1950 • Gomez Muriel Emilio • MXC
CUANDO ACABA LA NOCHE • 1964 • Soler Julian • MXC, PRC
CUANDO BAJA LA MAREA • 1948 • Patino Gomez Alfonso • MXC
CUANDO CALIENTA EL SOL.. VAMOS ALLA PLAIA • 1984 • Guerrini Mino • ITL
CUANDO CANTA EL CORAZON • 1941 • Harlan Richard • ARG
CUANDO CONCHITA SE ESCAPA HAY TOCATA • 1976 • Delgado Luis Maria • SPN
CUANDO EL ALBA LLEGUE • 1949 • Ortega Juan J. • MXC
CUANDO EL AMOR RIE • 1933 • Howard David • USA • WHEN LOVE LAUGHS
CUANDO EL CUERNO SUENA • 1974 • Delgado Luis Maria • SPN
CUANDO EL DIABLO SOPLA • 1965 • Salvador Jaime • MXC
CUANDO EL VALLE SE CUBRA DE NIEVE • 1965 • Perez De Rozas Jose Luis • SPN
CUANDO ESCUCHES ESTE VALS • 1944 • Bueno Jose Luis • MXC
CUANDO ESTALLO LA PAZ see **QUE NO FUIMOS A LA GUERRA, LOS** • 1961
CUANDO HABLA EL CORAZON • 1943 • Segura Juan Jose • MXC
CUANDO LA PATRIA LO MANDE • 1920 • Canals De Home Juan • MXC
CUANDO LA PRIMAVERA SE EQUIVOCA • 1944 • Soffici Mario • ARG • WHEN SPRING MAKES A MISTAKE
CUANDO LA SAL PIERDE SU SABOR • 1975 • Franco Manuel • SHT • CLM • WHEN SALT LOSES ITS TASTE
CUANDO LA TIERRA TEMBLO • 1940 • Helu Antonio • MXC
CUANDO LEVANTA LA NIEBLA • 1952 • Fernandez Emilio • MXC
CUANDO LLEGUE LA NOCHE • 1946 • Mihura Jeronimo • SPN
CUANDO LLORAN LOS VALIENTES • 1945 • Rodriguez Ismael • MXC
CUANDO LOS ANGELES DUERMEN • 1947 • Gascon Jose • SPN
CUANDO LOS HIJOS CRECEN • 1971 • *Cima* • MXC
CUANDO LOS HIJOS PECAN • 1952 • Rodriguez Joselito • MXC
CUANDO LOS HIJOS SE PIERDEN • 1962 • de la Serna Mauricio • MXC
CUANDO LOS HIJOS SE VAN • 1941 • Bustillo Oro Juan • MXC • WHEN THE CHILDREN LEAVE
CUANDO LOS HOMBRES HABLAN DE MUJERES • 1967 • Ayala Fernando • ARG • WHEN MEN DISCUSS WOMEN
CUANDO LOS MARIDOS IBAN A LA GUERRA • 1975 • Fernandez Ramon • SPN
CUANDO LOS NINOS VIENEN DE MARSELLA • 1974 • Saenz De Heredia Jose Luis • SPN
CUANDO LOS PADRES SE QUEDAN SOLOS • 1948 • Bustillo Oro Juan • MXC
CUANDO ME VAYA • 1953 • Davison Tito • MXC
CUANDO MEXICO CANTA • 1956 • Soler Julian • MXC
CUANDO PIZARRO, CORTEZ Y ORELLANA ERAN AMIGOS • 1979 • Macedo Gilberto • MXC • WHEN PIZARRO, CORTEZ AND ORELLANA WERE FRIENDS
CUANDO QUIERE UN MEXICANO • 1944 • Bustillo Oro Juan • MXC

CUANDO QUIERO LLORAR NO LLORO • 1972 • Walerstein Mauricio • VNZ, MXC • WHEN I WANT TO CRY, I DON'T DO IT ○ I WANT TO CRY I WON'T CRY ○ WHEN I WANT TO CRY, I CAN'T
CUANDO REGRESE MAMA • 1959 • Baledon Rafael • MXC
CUANDO SE DESPIERTA EL PUEBLO • 1973 • DOC • CHL • WHEN THE PEOPLE AWAKE (UKN)
CUANDO SE QUIERE SE QUIERE • 1958 • Urueta Chano • MXC
CUANDO TE SUICIDAS? • 1928 • Romero Manuel • SPN
CUANDO TEJEN LAS ARANAS • 1977 • Gavaldon Roberto • MXC
CUANDO TU ME QUIERAS • 1950 • Cortazar Ernesto • MXC
CUANDO TU NO ESTAS • 1966 • Camus Mario • SPN
CUANDO VIAJAN LAS ESTRELLAS • 1942 • Gout Alberto • MXC
CUANDO, VIVA VILLA! ES LA MUERTE • 1958 • Rodriguez Ismael • MXC
CUANDO VUELVAS A MI • 1953 • Baviera Jose • MXC, GTM
CUANTO VALE TU HIJO • 1961 • de la Serna Mauricio • MXC
CUARENTA ANOS SIN SEXO • 1974 • Bosch Juan • DOC • SPN • FORTY YEARS WITHOUT SEX
CUARENTA GRADOS A LA SOMBRA • 1967 • Ozores Mariano • SPN, ARG • FORTY DEGREES IN THE SHADE
CUARENTA SIGLOS OS CONTEMPLAN • 1967 • Alonso-Pesquera Jose • SPN
CUARENTA Y OCHO HORAS • 1942 • Castellvi Jose Maria • SPN • FORTY-EIGHT HOURS
CUARTA CARABELA, LA • 1961 • Martin Miguel • SPN
CUARTA DIMENSION, LA • 1970 • Marcos Julian • SHT • SPN • FOURTH DIMENSION, THE
CUARTA VENTANA, LA • 1961 • Coll Julio • SPN
CUARTELAZO • 1976 • Isaac Alberto • MXC • COUP D'ETAT
CUARTELES DE INVIERNO • 1984 • Murua Lautaro • ARG • WINTER QUARTERS
CUARTO CERRADO, EL • 1952 • Urueta Chano • MXC
CUARTO CHINO, EL (MXC) see **CHINESE ROOM, THE** • 1966
CUARTO MANDAMIENTO, EL • 1948 • Aguilar Rolando • MXC
CUATREROS, LOS • 1964 • Torrado Ramon • SPN
CUATRO BALAZOS • 1963 • Navarro Agustin • SPN
CUATRO BODAS DE MARISOL, LAS • 1967 • Lucia Luis • SPN • MARISOL'S FOUR WEDDINGS
CUATRO BODAS Y PICO • 1962 • Catalan Feliciano • SPN
CUATRO CABALGARON (SPN) see **FOUR RODE OUT** • 1969
CUATRO CONTRA EL CRIMEN • 1968 • Vejar Sergio • MXC • FOUR AGAINST CRIME
CUATRO CONTRA EL IMPERIO • 1955 • Salvador Jaime • MXC
CUATRO CONTRA EL MUNDO • 1949 • Galindo Alejandro • MXC
CUATRO COPAS • 1957 • Demicheli Tulio • MXC
CUATRO CORAZONES • 1939 • Discepolo Enrique Santos (c/d) • ARG
CUATRO CURVAS PELIGROSAS see **MUCHACHAS QUE TRABAJAN** • 1961
CUATRO DE HOJALATA, EL • 1979 • Montagudo Alberto • VNZ • TIN-PLATE CUATRO, THE
CUATRO DE HOTEL • 1952 • Fernandez Bustamente Adolfo • MXC
CUATRO DESERTORES • 1969 • Cervera Pascual • SPN
CUATRO DOLARES DE VENGANZA • 1965 • Balcazar Alfonso • SPN, ITL • QUATTRO DOLLARI DI VENDETTA (ITL)
CUATRO EN LA FRONTERA • 1957 • Santillan Antonio • SPN
CUATRO HOMBRES MARCADOS • 1968 • Salvador Jaime • MXC • FOUR MARKED MEN
CUATRO HORAS ANTES DE MORIR • 1952 • Gomez Muriel Emilio • MXC
CUATRO JUANES, LOS • 1964 • Zacarias Miguel • MXC
CUATRO MILPAS, LAS • 1937 • Pereda Ramon • MXC • FOUR CORN PATCHES, THE (USA)
CUATRO MILPAS, LAS • 1958 • Pereda Ramon • MXC
CUATRO MUJERES • 1947 • del Amo Antonio • SPN
CUATRO MUSICOS DE BREMEN, LAS • 1988 • Delgado Cruz • ANM • SPN • BREMER MUSICIANS, THE
CUATRO NOCHES CONTIGO • 1951 • de Anda Raul • MXC
CUATRO NOCHES DE BODA • 1969 • Ozores Mariano • SPN
CUATRO NOCHES DE LA LUNA LLENA, LAS • 1964 • Martin Sobey • SPN • FOUR NIGHTS OF THE FULL MOON, THE
CUATRO NOVIAS DE AUGUSTO PEREZ, LAS see **NIEBLA** • 1975
CUATRO PUENTES, LOS • 1974 • Alvarez Santiago • DOC • CUB
CUATRO ROBINSONES, LOS • 1939 • Maroto Eduardo G. • SPN
CUATRO VERDADES, LAS see **QUATRE VERITES** • 1962
CUATRO VIDAS • 1949 • Giaccardi Jose • MXC
CUAUHTEMOC • 1918 • de la Bandera Manuel • MXC
CUB, THE • 1913 • Shaw Harold • USA
CUB, THE • 1915 • Tourneur Maurice • USA
CUB AND THE DAISY CHAIN, THE • 1915 • Drew Sidney • USA
CUB REPORTER, THE • 1909 • *Lubin* • USA
CUB REPORTER, THE • 1912 • *Edison* • USA
CUB REPORTER, THE • 1922 • Dillon John Francis • USA • NEW REPORTER, THE
CUB REPORTER'S ASSIGNMENT, THE • 1914 • *Ellis Robert* • USA
CUB REPORTER'S BIG SCOOP, THE • 1912 • *Lockwood Harold* • USA
CUB REPORTER'S TEMPTATION, THE • 1913 • *Foxe Earle* • USA
CUBA • 1979 • Lester Richard • USA
CUBA 58 • 1962 • Garcia Ascot Jose Miguel, Fraga Jorge • CUB
CUBA A MONTMARTRE • 1947-51 • Verneuil Henri • SHT • FRN
CUBA AND CASTRO TODAY • 1965 • Rasky Harry • MTV • USA
CUBA BAILA • 1959 • Espinosa Julio Garcia • CUB, MXC • CUBA DANCES
CUBA: BATTLE OF THE 10,000,000 (USA) see **BATAILLE DES DIX MILLIONS, LA** • 1969
CUBA CABANA • 1952 • Buch Fritz Peter • FRG
CUBA CROSSING • 1980 • Workman Chuck • USA • ASSIGNMENT: KILL CASTRO ○ SWEET DIRTY TONY ○ KILL CASTRO ○ MERCENARIES: SWEET VIOLENT TONY, THE
CUBA DANCES see **CUBA BAILA** • 1959
CUBA DOS DE ENERO • 1965 • Alvarez Santiago • DOC • CUB • CUBA, JANUARY 2
CUBA, ISLAND OF FLAMES see **CUBA SEGODNYA** • 1960
CUBA, JANUARY 2 see **CUBA DOS DE ENERO** • 1965
CUBA: LA BATAILLE DES DIX MILLIONS see **BATAILLE DES DIX MILLIONS, LA** • 1969
CUBA NO KOIBITO • 1970 • Kuroki Kazuo • JPN • MAS CERCA DE TI
CUBA, PUEBLO ARMADO see **PUEBLOS EN ARMAS** • 1961
CUBA SEGODNYA • 1960 • Karmen Roman • USS • CUBA, ISLAND OF FLAMES ○ ISLAND OF FLAME, THE ○ CUBA TODAY
CUBA SI! • 1961 • Marker Chris • DOC • FRN
CUBA SI • 1964 • Rachedi Ahmed • SHT • ALG
CUBA TODAY see **CUBA SEGODNYA** • 1960
CUBA, UN NOUVEAU MONDE • 1977 • Floquet Francois • DOC • CND
CUBA VA! • 1971 • Greene Felix • DOC • CUB
CUBAINA • 1944 • Poitevin Jean-Marie • DCS • CND
CUBAN, THE see **CUBAN LOVE SONG** • 1931
CUBAN FIGHT AGAINST THE DEMONS, A see **PELEA CUBANA CONTRA LOS DEMONIOS, UNA** • 1971
CUBAN FIREBALL • 1951 • Beaudine William • USA
CUBAN LOVE SONG • 1931 • Van Dyke W. S. • USA • CUBAN, THE
CUBAN MADNESS • 1945 • Collins Lewis D. • SHT • USA
CUBAN MELODY • 1961 • Henryson Robert • SHT • UKN
CUBAN PETE • 1946 • Yarbrough Jean • USA • DOWN CUBA WAY (UKN)
CUBAN REBEL GIRLS • 1959 • Mahon Barry • USA • ASSAULT OF THE REBEL GIRLS
CUBAN RHYTHM • 1941 • Jason Will • USA
CUBAN RHYTHM • 1961 • Henryson Robert • SHT • UKN
CUBAN STRUGGLE AGAINST THE DEMONS, A see **PELEA CUBANA CONTRA LOS DEMONIOS, UNA** • 1971
CUBA'S TEN YEARS see **TIZ EVES KUBA** • 1969
CUBBY'S PICNIC • 1933 • Muffati Steve, Donnelly Eddie • ANS • USA
CUBBY'S STRATOSPHERE FLIGHT • 1934 • Stallings George • ANS • USA
CUBBY'S WORLD FLIGHT • 1933 • Harman Hugh, Ising Rudolf • ANS • USA
CUBE, THE • 1968 • *Nbc* • USA
CUBES OLE • 1970 • Thomas Richard* • ANM • USA
CUBISTE PAR AMOUR • 1913 • Fescourt Henri • FRN
CUBISTES • 1953 • Hessens Robert • FRN
CUBOK • 1990 • Nikolic Dragan • YGS • LITTLE SOMETHING EXTRA, A
CUCARACHA, LA • 1934 • Corrigan Lloyd • SHT • USA
CUCARACHA, LA • 1959 • Rodriguez Ismael • MXC • BANDIT, THE
CUCCAGNA, LA • 1962 • Salce Luciano • ITL • LAND OF PLENTY, THE ○ STROKE OF LUCK, A
CUCHILLO • 1977 • de Anda Rodolfo • MXC
CUCHILLOS DE FUEGO • 1990 • Chalbaud Roman • VNZ, SPN • FLAMING KNIVES
CUCINA AL BURRO (ITL) see **CUISINE AU BUERRE, LA** • 1963
CUCKOO • 1984 • Kazakov Varna Velislav • ANM • BUL
CUCKOO see **HOTOTOGISU** • 1932
CUCKOO, THE • 1948 • Felstead Bert • UKN
CUCKOO AND THE STARLING, THE • 1951 • *Sovexportfilm* • ANS • USS
CUCKOO BIRD, THE • 1939 • Davis Mannie • ANS • USA
CUCKOO CAVALIERS • 1940 • White Jules • SHT • USA
CUCKOO CLOCK, THE • 1912 • *Sullivan T. T.* • USA
CUCKOO CLOCK, THE • 1950 • Avery Tex • ANS • USA
CUCKOO CLOCK THAT WOULDN'T CUCKOO, THE • 1958 • *Coronet* • SHT • USA
CUCKOO I.Q., THE • 1941 • Marcus Sid • ANS • USA
CUCKOO IN A CHOO CHOO • 1952 • White Jules • SHT • USA
CUCKOO IN A DARK WOOD, A see **KUKACKA V TEMNEM LESE** • 1985
CUCKOO IN THE NEST, A • 1933 • Walls Tom • UKN
CUCKOO LOVE • 1925 • Roach Hal • SHT • USA
CUCKOO MURDER CASE, THE • 1931 • *Iwerks Ub (P)* • ANS • USA
CUCKOO PATROL • 1965 • Wood Duncan • UKN
CUCKOO (USA) see **JIHI SHINCHO** • 1927
CUCKOO WALTZ • 1953 • van Morkerken Emile • SHT • NTH
CUCKOOS, THE • 1930 • Sloane Paul • USA • RADIO REVELS
CUCKOOVILLE GOES SKATING • 1914 • *Frontier* • USA
CUCURICHITO Y PINOCHO • 1944 • Vejar Carlos Jr. • MXC
CUCURRUCUCU PALOMA • 1964 • Delgado Miguel M. • MXC
CUD NAD WISLA • 1920 • Boleslawski Richard • PLN • MIRACLE OF THE VISTULA, THE
CUDESNI SAN DZIGE VERTOVA • 1990 • Petrovic Miroslav • YGS • AMAZING DREAMING OF DZIGA VERTOV, THE
CUDNA PTICA • 1969 • Dovnikovic Borivoj • ANS • YGS • STRANGE BIRD
CUDOTVORNI MAC • 1949 • Nanovic Vojislav • YGS • MAGIC SWORD, THE (USA) ○ LUDOT-VORNIMAC ○ MIRACULOUS SWORD, THE
CUDOVITI PRAH see **DIVOTA PRASINE** • 1976
CUDZA ZONA I MAZ POD LOZKIEM • 1962 • Wajda Andrzej • PLN • ANOTHER'S WIFE AND HUSBAND ○ UNDER THE BED
CUE AND MISCUE • 1913 • *Eclair* • USA
CUEBALL CAT • 1950 • Hanna William, Barbera Joseph • ANS • USA
CUEILLETTE DES ORANGES, LA • 1967 • Mazif Sid-Ali • SHT • ALG
CUEILLETTE DU TABAC, LA • 1977 • Bonin Laurier • MTV • CND
CUENCA • 1958 • Saura Carlos • SPN
CUENCA CRIME, THE see **CRIMEN DE CUENCA, EL** • 1979
CUENCA'S CRIME see **CRIMEN DE CUENCA, EL** • 1979
CUENTAN DE UNA MUJER • 1958 • Ortega Juan J. • MXC
CUENTO DE HADAS • 1951 • Neville Edgar • SPN • FAIRY TALE
CUENTOS DE ABELARDO • 1989 • Molina Luis • PRC • ABELARDO'S STORIES ○ ABELARDO'S SHORT STORIES
CUENTOS DE LA ALHAMBRA • 1950 • Rey Florian • SPN
CUENTOS DE LA MISTERIOSA BUENOS AIRES • 1981 • Fischermann Alberto, Wulicher Ricardo, Finn Oscar Barney • ARG • TALES FROM MYSTERIOUS BUENOS AIRES
CUENTOS DE LAS SABANAS BLANCAS • 1977 • Ozores Mariano • SPN
CUENTOS DE PANCHO VILLA • 1957 • Rodriguez Ismael • MXC
CUENTOS DEL ALHAMNARA: GUANCANAYABO • 1963 • Gomez Manuel Octavio • CUB
CUENTOS EROTICOS • 1979 • *Berlanga Luis Garcia* • SPN • EROTIC TALES
CUENTOS PARA MAYORES • 1963 • Chalbaud Roman • VNZ • STORIES FOR ADULTS
CUERDA DE PRESOS • 1955 • Lazaga Pedro • SPN
CUERNAVACA EN PRIMAVERA • 1965 • Bracho Julio • MXC • TRES COMEDIAS DE AMOR
CUERPO DE MUJER, UN • 1949 • Davison Tito • MXC
CUERPOS PERDIDOS • 1988 • de Gregorio Eduardo • ARG, FRN • CORPS PERDUS (FRN)
CUERTO REPARTIDO Y EL MUNDO AL REVES • 1975 • Ruiz Raul • CHL • SCATTERED BODY AND THE WORLD UPSIDE DOWN, THE ○ UTOPIA
CUERVOS ESTAN DE LUTO, LOS • 1965 • del Villar Francisco • MXC
CUERVOS, LOS • 1961 • Coll Julio • SPN
CUESTA ABAJO • 1934 • Gasnier Louis J. • SPN
CUEVA DE ALI BABA, LA • 1954 • Lugones Mario C. • ARG • CAVE OF ALI BABA, THE
CUEVA DE LOS TIBURONES, LA see **FOSSA MALEDETTA, LA** • 1978
CUEVAS, CAVERNAS Y UN PARQUE • 1988 • Casanova Luis Molina • DOC • PRC • CAVES, CAVERNS AND A PARK
CUGINA, LA • 1974 • Lado Aldo • ITL
CUGINE MIE • 1978 • Avallone Marcello • ITL
CUGINETTA AMORE MIO • 1977 • Mattei Bruno • ITL
CUGINI CARNALI • 1974 • Martino Sergio • ITL • LOVING COUSINS (USA) ○ VISITOR, THE (UKN)
CUGINO AMERICANO, IL • 1986 • Battiato Giacomo • ITL • BLOOD TIES ○ AMERICAN COUSIN, THE
CUIBUL DE VIESPI • Popescu Horea • RMN • WASPS' NEST
CUIDADO CON EL AMOR • 1954 • Zacarias Miguel • MXC
CUIDADO CON LAS MUJERES • 1952 • Cahen Enrique • ARG
CUIDADO CON LAS SENORAS • 1968 • Buchs Julio • SPN • BE CAREFUL WITH THE LADIES
CUIDADO CON LOS LADRONES! • 1920 • Buchs Jose • SPN
CUIDE A SU MARIDE • 1949 • Soler Fernando • MXC
CUIR DANS LA PEAU, LE • 1950 • Tavano Fred • SHT • FRN
CUIRASSE POTEMKIN, LE see **EVENEMENTS D'ODESSA, LES** • 1905
CUISINE AU BUERRE, LA • 1963 • Grangier Gilles • FRN, ITL • MY WIFE'S HUSBAND (USA) ○ CUCINA AL BURRO (ITL)
CUISINE DE L'OGRE, LA • 1908 • Melies Georges • FRN • IN THE BOGIE MAN'S CAVE (USA)
CUISINE EXPRESS • 1912 • Cohl Emile • ANS • FRN
CUISINE MAGNETIQUE • 1908 • de Chomon Segundo • FRN, SPN • COCINA MAGNETICA, LA (SPN) ○ MAGNETIC KITCHEN (USA) ○ ELECTRIC KITCHEN
CUISINE ROUGE, LA • 1980 • Baillargeon Paul, Collin Frederique • CND
CUISSARDES • Blanc Michel • FRN
CUISSES EN CHALEUR, LES • 1975 • Roy Jean-Claude • FRN
CUISSES ENTR'OUVERTES • Blanc Michel • FRN
CUISSES OUVERTES • 1980 • Roy Jean-Claude • FRN
CUIVRES A LA VOIX D'OR, LES • 1958 • Leduc • SHT • FRN
CUJO • 1984 • Teague Lewis • USA
CUKROVA BOUDA • 1980 • Kachyna Karel • CZC • LITTLE SUGAR HOUSE, THE ○ SUGAR COTTAGE ○ SUGAR SHACK
CUL-DE-JATTE EMBALLE, LE • 1908 • Feuillade Louis • FRN
CUL-DE-SAC • 1966 • Polanski Roman • UKN
CULASTRISCE NOBILE VENEZIANO • 1976 • Mogherini Flavio • ITL
CULINARY CARVING • 1939 • Feist Felix E. • SHT • USA
CULINARY SORCERY see **SORCELLERIE CULINAIRE, LA** • 1904
CULLODEN see **BATTLE OF CULLODEN, THE** • 1964
CULOTTES ROUGES, LES • 1963 • Joffe Alex • FRN • RED CULOTTES, THE (USA)
CULPA, A • 1972 • Oliveira Domingos • BRZ
CULPA, A • 1981 • de Almeida Antonio Vitorino • PRT • GUILT, THE
CULPA DE LOS HOMBRES, LA • 1954 • Rodriguez Roberto • MXC
CULPA DEL OTRO, LA • 1942 • Iquino Ignacio F. • SPN
CULPA LA TUVO EL OTRO • 1950 • Demare Lucas • ARG
CULPABLE! • 1945 • Iquino Ignacio F. • SPN
CULPABLE • 1960 • del Carril Hugo • ARG
CULPABLE, LA • 1944 • Diaz Morales Jose • MXC
CULPABLES • 1958 • Ruiz-Castillo Arturo • SPN
CULPABLES, LOS • 1962 • Forn Josep Maria • SPN
CULPABLES PARA UN DELITO • 1966 • Duce Jose Antonio • SPN
CULPEPPER CATTLE COMPANY, THE • 1972 • Richards Dick • USA
CULPRIT, THE see **APARADHI** • 1931
CULPRITS, THE see **MUZNIBUN, AL** • 1976
CULT OF THE COBRA, THE • 1955 • Lyon Francis D. • USA
CULT OF THE DAMNED see **ANGEL, ANGEL, DOWN WE GO** • 1969
CULT OF THE DEAD see **SNAKE PEOPLE** • 1968
CULT OF VIOLENCE, THE see **BERLINO, APPUNTAMENTO PER LE SPIE** • 1965
CULTA DAMA, LA • 1956 • Gonzalez Rogelio A. • MXC
CULTE DE LA BEAUTE, LE see **ARTHUR** • 1930
CULTE DU VAMPIRE, LE • 1971 • Rollin Jean • FRN • VAMPIRE CULT, THE
CULTIVATION OF LIVING TISSUE, THE • 1933 • Canti R. G. • DOC • UKN

CULTIVO DEL TABACO BALIZADO • 1967 • Villafuerte Santiago • DOC • CUB
CULTURA DA LARANJA NA REGIAO DE VALENCIA, A • 1931 • Coelho Jose Adolfo • SHT • PRT
CULTURA DE BANANAS NA MADEIRA, A • 1931 • Coelho Jose Adolfo • SHT • PRT
CULTURA DO CACAU EM S. TOME • 1909 • de Albuquerque Ernesto • SHT • PRT
CULTURA DO MELAO NO RIBATEJO, A • 1939 • Coelho Jose Adolfo • SHT • PRT
CULTURA DO MILHO EM PORTUGAL, A • 1929 • Coelho Jose Adolfo • SHT • PRT
CULTURAL LISBON see **LISBOA CULTURAL** • 1983
CULTURAL REVIEW NO.2/53 see **PRZEGLAD KULTURALNY 2/53** • 1952
CULTURE DE LA BETTERAVE A SUCRE, LA • 1949 • Proulx Maurice • DCS • CND
CULTURE DES TISSUS, LA • 1937 • Painleve Jean • SHT • FRN
CULTURE DU MIL, LA see **GENS DU MIL, LES** • 1951
CULTURE INTENSIVE • 1904 • Blache Alice • FRN • VIEUX MARI, LE
CULTURE MARAICHERE EN EVOLUTION, LA • 1961 • Proulx Maurice • DCS • CND
CULTURE VIVANTE DU CINEMA • 1967 • Dansereau Jean • DOC • CND
CULTURED APE, THE • 1960 • Halas John, Batchelor Joy • ANS • UKN
CUM-QUIBUS see **RINGO A CAMINHO DO INFERNO** • 1972
CUMALI, THE THIN ONE see **INCE CUMALI** • 1967
CUMARTESI CUMARTESI • Okan Tunc • SWT, TRK
CUMBERLAND ROMANCE, A • 1920 • Maigne Charles • USA
CUMBERLAND STORY, THE • 1947 • Jennings Humphrey • DOC • UKN
CUMBERNAULD HIT, THE • 1976 • McConnell Edward • UKN
CUMBERNAULD -TOWN FOR TOMORROW • 1970 • Crichton Robin • DOC • UKN
CUMBITE • 1964 • Alea Tomas Gutierrez • CUB
CUMBRE QUE NOS UNE, LA • 1979 • Alvarez Santiago • DOC • CUB
CUMBRES BORRASCOSAS • 1953 • Bunuel Luis • MXC • WUTHERING HEIGHTS (USA) ◦ ABISMO DE PASION ◦ ABYSS OF PASSION
CUMBRES LUMINOSAS • 1957 • Fogues Juan Jose • SPN
CUMMINGTON STORY, THE • 1945 • Grayson Helen, Madison Larry • USA
CUMMUNICANTS, THE (USA) see **NATTVARDSGASTERNA** • 1963
CUMPARSITA, LA • 1947 • Momplet Antonio • ARG
CUMPLEANOS DEL PERRO, EL • 1974 • *Conacine* • MXC
CUMPLIMOS • 1962 • Alvarez Santiago • DOC • CUB • WE ACCOMPLISHED
CUNA VACIA, LA • 1937 • Zacarias Miguel • MXC • EMPTY CRADLE, THE (USA)
CUNNING CANAL-BOAT CUPID, A • 1915 • *Cooper Claude* • USA
CUNNING CANINE, A • 1913 • Stow Percy • UKN • LITTLE DOGGEREL, A
CUNNING FOX, THE see **KOIYA KOI NASUNA KOI** • 1962
CUNNING LITTLE VIXEN, THE see **LISKA BYSTROUSKA** • 1954
CUNNINGHAMES ECONOMISE, THE • 1922 • Cooper George A. • UKN
CUODIAN YUANYANG • 1985 • Lu Jianming • HKG • LOVE WITH THE PROPER STRANGER
CUOR DI VAGABONDO (ITL) see **COEUR DE GUEUX** • 1936
CUORE • 1948 • Coletti Duilio • ITL • HEART AND SOUL (USA)
CUORE • 1975 • Scavolini Romano • ITL
CUORE • 1984 • Comencini Luigi • ITL
CUORE DEL TIRRANO, IL (ITL) see **ZSARNOK SZIVE AVAGY BOCCACCIO MAGYARORSZAGON, A** • 1981
CUORE DI CANE • 1975 • Lattuada Alberto • ITL • DOG'S HEART
CUORE DI MAMMA • 1955 • Capuano Luigi • ITL
CUORE DI MAMMA • 1968 • Samperi Salvatore • ITL • MOTHER'S HEART, A
CUORE DI SPIA • 1954 • Borracetti Renato • ITL
CUORE FORESTIERO • 1953 • Fizzarotti Armando • ITL
CUORE MATTO see **RIDERA** • 1967
CUORE MATTO.. MATTO DA LEGARE • 1967 • Amendola Mario • ITL • MAD, MAD HEART..
CUORE NAPOLETANO • 1940 • Palermi Amleto • ITL • NEAPOLITAN HEART (USA)
CUORE NEL MONDO, UN • 1920 • Palermi Amleto • ITL
CUORE RIVELATORE • 1948 • Risi Dino • SHT • ITL
CUORE SEMPLICE, UN • 1977 • Ferrara Giorgio • ITL
CUORI INFRANTI, I • 1963 • Caprioli Vittorio, Puccini Gianni • ITL
CUORI NELLA TORMENTA • 1941 • Campogalliani Carlo • ITL
CUORI NELLA TORMENTA • 1984 • Oldoini Enrico • ITL • HEARTS IN THE STORM
CUORI SENZA FRONTIERE • 1950 • Zampa Luigi • ITL • HEART KNOWS NO FRONTIERS, THE ◦ WHITE LINE, THE
CUORI SOLITARI • 1970 • Giraldi Franco • ITL
CUORI SUL MARE • 1950 • Bianchi Giorgio • ITL
CUOWEI • 1987 • Huang Jianxin • CHN • STAND-IN, THE ◦ DISLOCATION
CUP, THE see **KA'S, AL** • 1986
CUP FEVER • 1965 • Bracknell David • UKN
CUP FINAL MYSTERY, THE • 1914 • Elvey Maurice • UKN
CUP GLORY • 1971 • Maylam Tony • DOC • UKN
CUP OF CHANCE, THE • 1915 • Levering Joseph • USA
CUP OF COLD WATER, A • 1911 • *Selig* • USA
CUP OF FURY, THE • 1920 • Hunter T. Hayes • USA
CUP OF KINDNESS, A • 1934 • Walls Tom • UKN
CUP OF LIFE, THE • 1915 • West Raymond B. • USA
CUP OF LIFE, THE • 1921 • Lee Rowland V. • USA
CUP OF SAN SEBASTIAN, THE • 1967 • *Hunter Tab*
CUP OF TEA AND SHE, A • 1909 • Porter Edwin S. • USA
CUP-TIE HONEYMOON • 1948 • Blakeley John E. • UKN
CUP WINNER, THE • 1911 • Rolfe Alfred • ASL
CUPBOARD LOVE • 1931 • Mainwaring Bernerd • UKN
CUPBOARD WAS BARE, THE (USA) see **ARMOIRE VOLANTE, L'** • 1948
CUPID • 1907 • Gilbert Arthur • UKN
CUPID see **CUPIDO** • 1961
CUPID see **PANCHASHAR** • 1968
CUPID A VICTOR • 1914 • *Bright Mildred* • USA
CUPID AND A DRESS COAT • 1914 • *Fischer Marguerite* • USA
CUPID AND COHEN'S • 1916 • MacMackin Archer • SHT • USA
CUPID AND PSYCHE • 1897 • *Biograph* • USA
CUPID AND THE BRICK • 1917 • *Kerrigan J. Warren* • USA
CUPID AND THE BUTTON • 1917 • *American* • USA
CUPID AND THE COMETS • 1911 • *Solax* • USA
CUPID AND THE COOK • 1913 • Henderson Dell • USA
CUPID AND THE COP • 1918 • *Keystone* • SHT • USA
CUPID AND THE MOTOR BOAT • 1909 • *Vitagraph* • USA
CUPID AND THE PEST • 1915 • *Tincher Fay* • USA
CUPID AND THE RANCHMAN • 1912 • *Nestor* • USA
CUPID AND THE SCRUB LADY • 1915 • *L-Ko* • USA
CUPID AND THE WIDOW • 1906 • Fitzhamon Lewin • UKN
CUPID AND THREE • 1913 • *Essanay* • USA
CUPID ANGLING • 1918 • *Roland Ruth* • USA
CUPID AT THE CIRCUS • 1910 • *Thanhouser* • USA
CUPID AT THE POLO GAME • 1916 • *Griffith Ray* • SHT • USA
CUPID AT THE WASHTUB • 1897 • *Paul R. W.* • UKN
CUPID BACKS A WINNER • 1914 • *Roland Ruth* • USA
CUPID BACKS THE WINNERS • 1914 • *Kalem* • USA
CUPID BEATS FATHER • 1915 • Douglass James • USA
CUPID BY PROXY • 1918 • Bertram William • USA
CUPID CAMOUFLAGED • 1918 • Rolfe Alfred • ASL
CUPID ENTANGLED • 1915 • Coyle Walter • USA
CUPID FINDS A WAY • 1913 • *Nestor* • USA
CUPID FORECLOSES • 1919 • Smith David • USA
CUPID GETS HIS MAN • 1936 • Palmer Tom • ANS • USA
CUPID IN A DENTAL PARLOR • 1913 • Lehrman Henry, Sennett Mack (Spv) • USA • CUPID IN THE DENTAL PARLOR
CUPID IN A HOSPITAL • 1915 • *Ritchie Billie* • USA
CUPID IN CHAPS • 1911 • Dwan Allan • USA
CUPID IN CLOVER • 1929 • Miller Frank • UKN
CUPID IN QUARANTINE • 1918 • *Field Elinor* • USA
CUPID IN THE COW CAMP • 1913 • Duncan William • USA
CUPID IN THE DENTAL PARLOR see **CUPID IN A DENTAL PARLOR** • 1913
CUPID IN THE OLDEN TIME • 1915 • *Thanhouser* • USA
CUPID IN THE ROUGH (UKN) see **AGGIE APPLEBY, MAKER OF MEN** • 1933
CUPID IN UNIFORM • 1913 • *Imp* • USA
CUPID INCOGNITO • 1914 • Reid Wallace • USA
CUPID KICKS A GOAL • 1914 • Smallwood Ray C. • USA
CUPID MAKES A BULL'S EYE • 1913 • *Selig* • USA
CUPID NEVER AGES • 1913 • Dwan Allan • USA
CUPID ON THE JOB • 1912 • *Majestic* • USA
CUPID PULLS A TOOTH • 1914 • *Lyons Eddie* • USA
CUPID PUTS ONE OVER ON THE SHATCHEN • 1915 • Van Wally • USA
CUPID RIDES THE RANCH • 1939 • Brock Lou • SHT • USA
CUPID TAKES A TAXI • 1915 • MacMackin Archer • USA
CUPID THE CONQUEROR • 1911 • *Thanhouser* • USA
CUPID THE COWPUNCHER • 1920 • Badger Clarence • USA
CUPID THROUGH PADLOCKS • 1912 • Dwan Allan • USA
CUPID THROUGH THE KEYHOLE • 1913 • Brooke Van Dyke • USA
CUPID THROWS A BRICK • 1913 • Dwan Allan • USA
CUPID TRIMS HIS LORDSHIP • 1916 • Christie Al • SHT • USA
CUPID TURNS THE TABLES • 1914 • MacGregor Norval • USA
CUPID VERSUS MONEY • 1914 • Brooke Van Dyke • USA
CUPID VERSUS WOMEN'S RIGHTS • 1913 • Costello Maurice • USA
CUPID VS. ART • 1918 • Moore Vin • SHT • USA
CUPID VS. CIGARETTES • 1912 • *Majestic* • USA
CUPIDITY OF CUPID, THE • 1913 • *Gaumont* • USA
CUPIDO • 1961 • Kostelac Nikola • ANS • YGS • CUPID
CUPIDO CONTRABANDISTA • 1961 • Madruga Esteban • SPN
CUPIDO PIERDE A PAQUITA • 1954 • Rodriguez Ismael • MXC
CUPIDON AU PENSIONNAT see **PETITE SAUVAGE, LA** • 1935
CUPIDON AUX MANOEUVRES • 1912 • Perret Leonce • FRN
CUPID'S ARROW • 1935 • Starevitch Ladislas • ANM • FRN
CUPID'S ASSISTANTS • 1913 • *Nestor* • USA
CUPID'S BAD AIM • 1913 • *Nestor* • USA
CUPID'S BATH • 1915 • *Stockdale Carl* • USA
CUPID'S BIG SISTER • 1911 • *Powers* • USA
CUPIDS, BLACK AND WHITE see **AMOUR NOIR ET AMOUR BLANC** • 1927
CUPID'S BOOTS • 1925 • Kennedy Edgar • SHT • USA
CUPID'S BOW see **LUK EROSA** • 1988
CUPID'S BRAND • 1921 • Lee Rowland V. • USA
CUPID'S CADDIES • 1917 • *Hamilton Lloyd V.* • SHT • USA
CUPID'S CAMOUFLAGE • 1917 • *Compson Betty* • SHT • USA
CUPID'S CAPRICE • 1914 • *Selig* • USA
CUPID'S CARNIVAL • 1920 • Kellino W. P. • UKN
CUPID'S CHAUFFEUR • 1911 • *Neason Hazel* • USA
CUPID'S CLOSE SHAVE • 1914 • *Nestor* • USA
CUPID'S COLUMN • 1915 • Beggs Lee • USA
CUPID'S COMEDY • 1910 • *Bison* • USA
CUPID'S CONQUEST • 1911 • *Gaumont* • FRN
CUPID'S DAY OFF • 1919 • Cline Eddie • SHT • USA
CUPID'S FIREMAN • 1923 • Wellman William A. • USA
CUPID'S FOUR DARTS • 1909 • *Pathe* • FRN
CUPID'S HIRED MAN • 1913 • North Wilfred • USA
CUPID'S HOLDUP • 1919 • *Vernon Bobby* • USA
CUPID'S JOKE • 1911 • Sennett Mack • USA
CUPID'S KNOCKOUT • 1926 • Mitchell Bruce • USA
CUPID'S LARIAT • 1913 • *Kalem* • USA
CUPID'S LEAP YEAR PRANKS • 1912 • *Missimer Howard* • USA
CUPID'S LIEUTENANT • 1913 • *Princess* • USA
CUPID'S LOAF • 1909 • Fitzhamon Lewin • UKN
CUPID'S MESSAGE GOES ASTRAY • 1910 • Wilson Frank? • UKN
CUPID'S MONKEY WRENCH • 1911 • *Powers* • USA
CUPID'S POCKET BOOK • 1911 • *American* • USA
CUPID'S PRANKS • 1908 • Porter Edwin S. • USA
CUPID'S PRANKS • 1914 • *Eclectic* • USA
CUPID'S QUARTETTE • 1912 • *Mason William* • USA
CUPID'S REALM • 1908 • Blackton J. Stuart • USA • GAME OF HEARTS, A
CUPID'S RIVAL • 1917 • Gillstrom Arvid E. • SHT • USA
CUPID'S ROUND-UP • 1918 • Le Saint Edward J. • USA
CUPID'S RUSTLER • 1924 • Ford Francis • USA
CUPID'S STOLEN ARROW • 1912 • *Pathe* • USA
CUPID'S STOLEN ARROWS • 1912 • *Pathe* • FRN
CUPID'S TARGET • 1915 • Hevener Jerold T. • USA
CUPID'S THUMB-PRINT • 1917 • Thayer Otis B. • SHT • USA
CUPID'S TOUCHDOWN • 1917 • Beal Frank • SHT • USA
CUPID'S UPPERCUT • 1916 • Davey Horace • SHT • USA
CUPID'S VICTORY • 1911 • *Solax* • USA
CUPID'S VICTORY • 1912 • *Nestor* • USA
CUPID'S VICTORY • 1925 • Lamont Charles • SHT • USA
CUPID'S WINDOW • 1914 • *Melies* • USA
CUPOLA, WHERE THE FURNACES GLOW see **KYUPORA NO ARU MACHI** • 1962
CURA DE ALDEA, EL • 1926 • Rey Florian • SPN
CURA GAUCHO, EL • 1941 • *Lolito Salvador* • ARG
CURABLE DISEASE, A • 1912 • *Edison* • USA
CURARE • 1972 • Brandis Barbara • DOC • VNZ
CURARE ODER DER INDISCHE DOLCH • 1915 • Schmidthassler Walter • FRG • SCHLEIER DER FAVORITIN, DER
CURATE, THE see **NIPPER AND THE CURATE** • 1916
CURATE AT THE RACES, THE • 1909 • Fitzhamon Lewin • UKN
CURATE'S ADVENTURE, THE • 1903 • *Warwick Trading Co.* • UKN
CURATE'S BRIDE, THE • 1913 • Plumb Hay? • UKN
CURATE'S COURTSHIP, THE • 1908 • Fitzhamon Lewin • UKN
CURATE'S DILEMMA, THE • 1906 • Martin J. H.? • UKN
CURATE'S DOUBLE, THE • 1907 • Booth W. R. • UKN
CURATE'S HONEYMOON, THE • 1908 • Cooper Arthur • UKN
CURATE'S LOVE STORY, A • 1912 • Fitzhamon Lewin • UKN
CURATE'S NEW YEAR GIFTS, THE • 1910 • Stow Percy • UKN
CURATE'S OUTING, THE • 1913 • Matthews H. C. • USA
CURD JURGENS • 1977 • Wicki Bernhard • FRG
CURE, THE • 1913 • Finley Ned, Castle James W. • *Vitagraph* • USA
CURE, THE • 1913 • Henderson Dell • *Ab* • USA
CURE, THE • 1914 • *Broncho* • USA
CURE, THE • 1914 • *Joker* • USA
CURE, THE • 1917 • Chaplin Charles • SHT • USA
CURE, THE • 1924 • Fleischer Dave • ANS • USA
CURE, THE • 1928 • Montagu Ivor • SHT • UKN
CURE, THE • 1950 • Massingham Richard, Law Michael • UKN
CURE DE CUCUGNAN, LE • 1967 • Pagnol Marcel • FRN
CURE DE SAINT-AMOUR, LE • 1952 • Couzinet Emile • FRN
CURE DE VILLAGE, LE • 1949 • Gury Paul • CND
CURE DU NEURASTHENIQUE, LA • 1908 • Jasset Victorin • FRN
CURE FOR BASHFULNESS • 1909 • *Vitagraph* • USA
CURE FOR CARELESSNESS • 1913 • *Selig* • USA
CURE FOR CRIME, A • 1911 • Porter Edwin S. • USA
CURE FOR DYSPEPSIA, A • 1911 • *Edison* • USA
CURE FOR GOUT, A • 1909 • *Essanay* • USA
CURE FOR INSOMNIA, THE • 1987 • Timmis Iv John Henry • USA
CURE FOR JEALOUSY, A • 1912 • *Johnson Arthur* • USA
CURE FOR LAZINESS, A • 1911 • *American* • USA
CURE FOR LOVE, THE • 1950 • Donat Robert • UKN
CURE FOR LUMBAGO, A • 1906 • Fitzhamon Lewin • UKN
CURE FOR MICROBES, A • 1909 • *Cines* • ITL
CURE FOR POKERITIS, A • 1912 • *Bunny John* • USA
CURE FOR STAGE FEVER • 1912 • *Republic* • USA
CURE FOR SUFFRAGETTES, A • 1913 • Kirkwood James? • USA
CURE OF COWARDICE, THE • 1909 • *Linder Max* • FRN
CURE OF JOHN DOUGLAS, THE • 1911 • *Halliday John* • USA
CURE OF LOVE, A see **LEKARSTWO NA MILOSC** • 1965
CURE OF THE MOUNTAINS, THE • 1915 • Lloyd Frank • USA • NATURE'S TRIUMPH
CURE SENTIMENTALE, LA • 1932 • Weill Pierre, Dianville Max • FRN
CURE TERMALI A LACCO AMENO • 1957 • Heusch Paolo • DOC • ITL
CURE THAT FAILED, THE • 1912 • *Imp* • USA
CURE THAT FAILED, THE • 1913 • Nicholls George, Sennett Mack (Spv) • USA
CURED • 1911 • Sennett Mack • USA
CURED • 1912 • *Essanay* • USA
CURED • 1916 • Metcalfe Earl • SHT • USA
CURED DUCK • 1945 • King Jack • ANS • USA
CURED IN THE EXCITEMENT • 1927 • *Sennett Mack (P)* • SHT • USA
CURED OF HER LOVE • 1913 • France Charles H. • USA
CUREE, LA • 1916 • Negroni Baldassare • ITL
CUREE, LA • 1966 • Vadim Roger • FRN, ITL • CALDA PREDA, LA (ITL) ◦ GAME IS OVER, THE (USA)
CURFEW see **TOQUE DE QUEDA** • 1978
CURFEW AT SIMPTON CENTER • 1916 • Wolbert William • SHT • USA
CURFEW BELL, THE • 1909 • *Edison* • USA
CURFEW MUST NOT RING TONIGHT • 1912 • Plumb Hay • UKN
CURFEW MUST NOT RING TONIGHT • 1923 • Collins Edwin J. • UKN
CURFEW SHALL NOR RING TONIGHT • 1912 • Reid Hal • USA
CURFEW SHALL NOT RING TONIGHT • 1906 • Collins Alf • UKN
CURFEW SHALL NOT RING TONIGHT • 1907 • Gilbert Arthur • UKN
CURFEW SHALL NOT RING TONIGHT • 1913 • *La Badie Florence* • USA
CURFEW SHALL NOT RING TONIGHT • 1926 • Tilley Frank • UKN
CURIEUSE EVASION, UNE see **BENVENUTO CELLINI OU UNE CURIEUSE EVASION** • 1904
CURIEUSE HISTOIRE see **FLORENCE EST FOLLE** • 1944
CURIEUX CAS D'AMNESIE, UN • 1947-51 • Verneuil Henri • SHT • FRN
CURING A GROUCH • 1910 • *Atlas* • USA

CURING A HUSBAND • 1914 • *Beery Wallace* • USA
CURING A JEALOUS HUSBAND • 1909 • *Lubin* • USA
CURING A JEALOUS WIFE • 1907 • Smith Jack • UKN
CURING A MASHER • 1910 • *Essanay* • USA
CURING BILL • 1915 • *Stinger Bill* • USA
CURING CISSY • 1915 • Middleton Edwin • USA
CURING FATHER • 1915 • Dillon John Francis • USA
CURING HER EXTRAVAGANCE • 1913 • *Kalem* • USA
CURING HUBBY • 1912 • *Imp* • USA
CURING MR. GOODHEART • 1914 • Middleton Mr. • USA • CHEERING MR. GOODHEART
CURING OF MYRA MAY, THE • 1914 • Brooke Van Dyke? • USA
CURING THE BLIND • 1907 • Stow Percy • UKN
CURING THE COOK • 1915 • *Edison* • USA
CURING THE DOCTOR • 1913 • *Frontier* • USA
CURING THE OFFICE BOY • 1912 • *Boss Yale* • USA
CURING UNCLE • 1915 • *Wright Bertie* • USA
CURIO HUNTERS, THE • 1912 • Ince Ralph • USA
CURIO LAKE see **JEZIORO OSOBLIWOSCI** • 1973
CURIO MASTER, THE see **CHINPINDO** • 1960
CURIO SHOP • 1933 • *Mintz Charles (P)* • ANS • USA
CURIOSA, LA • 1972 • Escriva Vicente • SPN
CURIOSITE PUNIEE, LA • 1908 • Melies Georges • FRN • CRIME DE LA RUE DU CHERCHE-MIDI A 14 HEURES, LE ○ CURIOSITY PUNISHED
CURIOSITY • 1911 • Lehrman Henry, Sennett Mack (Spv) • USA
CURIOSITY • 1912 • *Essanay* • USA
CURIOSITY • 1915 • *Turpin Ben* • USA
CURIOSITY • 1966 • Ratz Gunter • ANM • GDR
CURIOSITY see **ZNATIZELJA** • 1966
CURIOSITY see **KIVANCSISAG** • 1970
CURIOSITY PUNISHED see **CURIOSITE PUNIEE, LA** • 1908
CURIOUS ADVENTURES OF MR. WONDERBIRD (USA) see **BERGERE ET LE RAMONEUR, LA** • 1953
CURIOUS CASE OF MEREDITH STANHOPE, THE • 1915 • *Millarde Harry* • USA
CURIOUS CASE OF THE CAMPUS CORPSE, THE see **HAZING, THE** • 1978
CURIOUS CONDUCT OF JUDGE LEGARDE, THE • 1915 • Davis Will S. • USA
CURIOUS CONTESTS • 1950 • *Smith Pete* • SHT • USA
CURIOUS DR. HUMPP, THE (USA) see **VENGANZA DEL SEXO, LA** • 1967
CURIOUS DREAM, A • 1907 • Blackton J. Stuart • USA
CURIOUS EVASION, A see **BENVENUTO CELLINI OU UNE CURIEUSE EVASION** • 1904
CURIOUS FAMILY, THE • 1912 • *Selig* • USA
CURIOUS FEMALE, THE • 1969 • Rapp Paul • USA • CURIOUS FEMALES
CURIOUS FEMALES see **CURIOUS FEMALE, THE** • 1969
CURIOUS HISTORY OF MONEY, THE • 1969 • Stevens Beryl • UKN
CURIOUS INVENTION, A • 1910 • *Pathe* • FRN
CURIOUS JOURNEY • 1979 • Jones Gareth Wyn • UKN
CURIOUS MR. CURIO • 1908 • Porter Edwin S. • USA
CURIOUS PETS OF OUR ANCESTORS • 1917 • O'Brien Willis • USA
CURIOUS PUPPY, THE • 1939 • Jones Charles M. • ANS • USA
CURIOUS TEENAGER • 1972 • Conte Lou • USA
CURIOUS WAY TO LOVE, A (UKN) see **MORTE HA FATTO L'UOVO, LA** • 1968
CURIOUS YELLOW BIRD see **YELLOW BIRD** • 1969
CURITA CANON, UN • 1974 • Delgado Luis Maria • SPN
CURLEW CORLISS • 1916 • Bertram William • SHT • USA
CURLEY • 1947 • Carr Bernard • USA • ADVENTURES OF CURLEY AND HIS GANG, THE ○ CURLY
CURLEY AND HIS GANG see **WHO KILLED DOC ROBBIN?** • 1948
CURLEY AND HIS GANG IN THE HAUNTED MANSION see **WHO KILLED DOC ROBBIN?** • 1948
CURLY • 1915 • MacDonald Donald • USA
CURLY • 1958 • Romero George A. • SHT • USA
CURLY see **ONCE UPON A TIME** • 1944
CURLY see **CURLEY** • 1947
CURLY TOP • 1935 • Cummings Irving • USA
CURLY'S HOLIDAY • 1917 • Carr J. F. • UKN
CURLYTOP • 1924 • Elvey Maurice • USA
CURRA VELETA • 1955 • Torrado Ramon • SPN
CURRENT, THE • 1913 • *Howard Lois* • USA
CURRENT (UKN) see **SODRASBAN** • 1964
CURRENTS OF YOUTH see **SEISHUN NO KIRYU** • 1942
CURRICULUM VITAE • 1986 • Koutsky Pavel • ANM • CZC
CURRITO DE LA CRUZ • 1936 • Delgado Fernando • SPN
CURRITO DE LA CRUZ • 1948 • Lucia Luis • SPN
CURRITO DE LA CRUZ • 1965 • Gil Rafael • SPN
CURRO VARGAS • 1923 • Buchs Jose • SPN
CURSA • 1975 • Daneliuc Mircea • RMN • LONG DRIVE ○ RACE, THE
CURSE, THE • 1913 • *Powers* • USA
CURSE, THE • 1913 • *Domino* • USA
CURSE, THE • 1915 • *Premier* • USA
CURSE, THE • 1971 • Shamshiev Bolotbek • USS
CURSE, THE see **XALA** • 1974
CURSE, THE see **FARM, THE** • 1987
CURSE AND THE COFFIN, THE (UKN) see **CHAMBRE ARDENTE, LA** • 1961
CURSE OF A FLIRTING HEART, THE • 1917 • Hutchinson Craig • SHT • USA
CURSE OF A NAME, THE • 1915 • *Gribbon Harry* • USA
CURSE OF ALPHA STONE • 1985 • Malleon Stewart • USA
CURSE OF BELPHEGOR, THE see **MALEDICTION DE BELPHEGOR, LA** • 1967
CURSE OF BIGFOOT, THE • 1972 • Fields Don • USA
CURSE OF CASTE, THE see **TRAGEDY OF THE ORIENT, A** • 1914
CURSE OF COCAINE, THE • 1909 • *Essanay* • USA
CURSE OF DARK SHADOWS see **NIGHT OF DARK SHADOWS** • 1971
CURSE OF DRACULA • Brzezinski Tony • SHT • USA
CURSE OF DRACULA see **RETURN OF DRACULA, THE** • 1958
CURSE OF DRINK, THE • 1912 • *Republic* • USA
CURSE OF DRINK, THE • 1922 • Hoyt Harry O. • USA
CURSE OF EVE, THE • 1917 • Beal Frank • USA
CURSE OF EVE, THE see **MOTHER, I NEED YOU** • 1918
CURSE OF FRANKENSTEIN, THE • 1957 • Fisher Terence • UKN • BIRTH OF FRANKENSTEIN
CURSE OF FRED ASTAIRE, THE • 1982 • Berger Mark • USA
CURSE OF GAMBLING, THE • 1910 • *Bison* • USA
CURSE OF GOLD, THE • 1909 • *Lubin* • USA
CURSE OF GOLD, THE see **MALDICION DEL ORO, LA** • 1964
CURSE OF GREED, THE see **TWIN PAWNS, THE** • 1919
CURSE OF HER FLESH, THE • 1968 • Findlay Michael • USA • CURSE OF THE CURIOUS, THE ○ CURSE OF THE FLESH, THE
CURSE OF HUMANITY, THE • 1914 • Sidney Scott • USA
CURSE OF IKU, THE • 1918 • Borzage Frank • USA
CURSE OF INAGAMI, THE see **INUGAMIKE NO TATARI** • 1977
CURSE OF KING TUTANKHAMEN'S TOMB, THE • 1980 • Leacock Philip • TVM • UKN, USA • CURSE OF KING TUT'S TOMB, THE (USA)
CURSE OF KING TUT'S TOMB, THE (USA) see **CURSE OF KING TUTANKHAMEN'S TOMB, THE** • 1980
CURSE OF LARADJONGRAN, THE • 1972 • Tammer Peter • DOC • ASL
CURSE OF MELISSA, THE • 1971 • Henderson Don • USA • TOUCH OF MELISSA, THE ○ TOUCH OF SATAN, A ○ NIGHT OF THE DEMON
CURSE OF MONEY, THE • 1909 • Bouwmeester Theo? • UKN
CURSE OF MY RACE, THE see **MALDICION DE MI RAZA, LA** • 1964
CURSE OF NOSTRADAMUS, THE (USA) see **MALDICION DE NOSTRADAMUS, LA** • 1959
CURSE OF QUON QWON, THE • 1917 • *Mandarine* • USA
CURSE OF RAVENSCROFT, THE • 1926 • Coleby A. E. • UKN
CURSE OF SIMBA (UKN) see **CURSE OF THE VOODOO** • 1965
CURSE OF SNAKE VALLEY, THE • 1988 • Piestrak Marek • PLN
CURSE OF THE ALLENBYS, THE (UKN) see **SHE-WOLF OF LONDON** • 1946
CURSE OF THE AZTEC MUMMY, THE (USA) see **MALDICION DE LA MOMIA AZTECA, LA** • 1957
CURSE OF THE BLACK PEARL • 1915 • Golden Joseph A.? • USA
CURSE OF THE BLACK WIDOW • 1977 • Curtis Dan • TVM • USA • LOVE TRAP
CURSE OF THE BLOOD see **KAIDAN ZANKOKU MONOGATARI** • 1968
CURSE OF THE BLOOD-GHOULS (USA) see **STRAGE DEI VAMPIRI, LA** • 1962
CURSE OF THE CAT PEOPLE, THE • 1944 • Wise Robert, Fritsch Gunther V. • USA
CURSE OF THE CRIMSON ALTAR • 1968 • Sewell Vernon • UKN • CRIMSON CULT, THE (USA) ○ REINCARNATION, THE ○ CRIMSON AFFAIR, THE ○ CRIMSON ALTAR, THE
CURSE OF THE CRYING WOMAN, THE (USA) see **MALDICION DE LA LLORONA, LA** • 1961
CURSE OF THE CURIOUS, THE see **CURSE OF HER FLESH, THE** • 1968
CURSE OF THE DEAD (UKN) see **OPERAZIONE PAURA** • 1966
CURSE OF THE DEMON (USA) see **NIGHT OF THE DEMON** • 1957
CURSE OF THE DESERT, THE • 1915 • *Bison* • USA
CURSE OF THE DEVIL see **RETORNO DE WALPURGIS, EL** • 1973
CURSE OF THE DOLL PEOPLE, THE (USA) see **MUNECOS INFERNALES** • 1960
CURSE OF THE FACELESS MAN • 1958 • Cahn Edward L. • USA
CURSE OF THE FLESH, THE see **CURSE OF HER FLESH, THE** • 1968
CURSE OF THE FLY, THE • 1965 • Sharp Don • UKN
CURSE OF THE FOREST, THE • 1916 • Earle William P. S. • SHT • USA
CURSE OF THE GHOULS see **STRAGE DEI VAMPIRI, LA** • 1962
CURSE OF THE GOLEM see **IT!** • 1966
CURSE OF THE GREAT SOUTHWEST, THE • 1913 • *Gazzolo Don* • USA
CURSE OF THE GREEN EYES, THE see **FLUCH DER GRUNEN AUGEN, DER** • 1964
CURSE OF THE HAUNTED FOREST see **DIAVOLI DI SPARTIVENTO, I** • 1963
CURSE OF THE HEADLESS HORSEMAN • 1971 • Kirkland John • USA • VALLEY OF THE HEADLESS HORSEMAN
CURSE OF THE HIDDEN VAULT, THE (USA) see **GRUFT MIT DEM RATSELSCHLOSS, DIE** • 1964
CURSE OF THE HINDOO PEARL, THE • 1912 • *Vitagraph* • USA
CURSE OF THE KARNSTEIN, THE see **CRIPTA E L'INCUBO, LA** • 1964
CURSE OF THE LAKE, THE • 1912 • *Vitagraph* • USA
CURSE OF THE LIVING CORPSE, THE • 1964 • Tenney Del • USA
CURSE OF THE LIVING DEAD see **OPERAZIONE PAURA** • 1966
CURSE OF THE MAYAN TEMPLE • 1977 • Burrud Bill • USA
CURSE OF THE MOON CHILD, THE • 1972 • *West Adam* • USA
CURSE OF THE MUMMY see **BLOOD FROM THE MUMMY'S TOMB** • 1972
CURSE OF THE MUMMY'S TOMB, THE • 1964 • Carreras Michael • UKN
CURSE OF THE NIGHT, THE see **YOTSUYA KAIDAN -OIWA NO BOREI** • 1969
CURSE OF THE OILY MAN see **SUMPAH ORANG MINYAK** • 1958
CURSE OF THE ONE-EYED CORPSE see **KAIDAN KATAME OTOKO** • 1965
CURSE OF THE PHARAOH see **PHARAOH'S CURSE** • 1957
CURSE OF THE PINK PANTHER • 1983 • Edwards Blake • USA
CURSE OF THE RED MAN, THE • 1911 • Boggs Frank • USA
CURSE OF THE SCARABEE RUBY, THE • 1914 • *Gaumont* • USA
CURSE OF THE SCREAMING DEAD • USA
CURSE OF THE STONE HAND • 1965 • Warren Jerry, Schleipper Carl • USA, MXC
CURSE OF THE SWAMP CREATURE • 1966 • Buchanan Larry • USA
CURSE OF THE SWASTIKA, THE • 1940 • Watts Fred • UKN
CURSE OF THE UNDEAD • 1959 • Dein Edward • USA • AFFAIRS OF A VAMPIRE ○ MARK OF THE WEST
CURSE OF THE VAMPIRE see **ULTIMA PREDA DEL VAMPIRO, L'** • 1960
CURSE OF THE VAMPIRES • 1970 • De Leon Gerardo • USA, PHL • CREATURES OF EVIL (UKN)
CURSE OF THE VOODOO • 1965 • Shonteff Lindsay • USA, UKN • CURSE OF SIMBA (UKN) ○ LION MAN
CURSE OF THE WEREWOLF, THE • 1961 • Fisher Terence • UKN
CURSE OF THE WITCH, THE see **FLUCH DER HEXE, DER** • 1920
CURSE OF THE WRAYDONS, THE • 1946 • Gover Victor M. • UKN • TERROR OF LONDON, THE
CURSE OF THE YELLOW SNAKE (USA) see **FLUCH DER GELBEN SCHLANGE, DER** • 1963
CURSE OF VERERBUNG, THE see **FLUCH DER VERERBUNG, DER** • 1927
CURSE OF WESTACOTT, THE • 1921 • Paul Fred, Raymond Jack • UKN
CURSE OF WORK, THE • 1915 • *Ritchie Billy* • USA
CURSED BE WAR see **MAUDITE SOIT LA GUERRE** • 1913
CURSED BY HIS BEAUTY • 1914 • Henderson Dell • USA
CURSED BY HIS CLEVERNESS • 1920 • *Gayety Comedies* • SHT • USA
CURSED CAGE, THE • 1909 • *Aquila* • SPN
CURSED JEWEL, THE • 1920 • de Barros Luis • BRZ
CURSED LOVE see **KATARAMENI AGAPI** • 1968
CURSED MILLIONS see **PROKLIATIYE MILLIONI** • 1917
CURSED OF THE TIME • 1979 • el Sabawi Ahmed • EGY
CURSED POND, THE see **KAIBYO NOROI NO NUMA** • 1968
CURSED TANGLE, A see **MALEDETTO IMBROGLIO, UN** • 1959
CURSED VALLEY OF CHAMBAL see **ABHISHAPTA CHAMBAL** • 1967
CURSES! JACK DALTON • 1915 • *Lubin* • USA
CURSES OF THE KNIFE see **TAO WEN** • 1989
"CURSES" SAID THE VILLAIN • 1913 • *Lyons Eddie* • USA
CURSES! THEY REMARKED • 1914 • Henderson Dell • USA
CURTAIN • 1920 • Young James • USA
CURTAIN, THE • 1914 • Buckland Warwick? • UKN
CURTAIN AT EIGHT • 1934 • Hopper E. Mason • USA
CURTAIN CALL • 1940 • Woodruff Frank • USA
CURTAIN CALL AT CACTUS CREEK • 1950 • Lamont Charles • USA • TAKE THE STAGE (UKN)
CURTAIN FALLS, THE • 1934 • Lamont Charles • USA
CURTAIN LECTURE, A • 1929 • Aylott Dave, Symmons E. F. • SHT • UKN
CURTAIN POLE, THE • 1909 • Griffith D. W. • USA
CURTAIN RAZOR • 1949 • Freleng Friz • ANS • USA
CURTAIN RISES, THE (USA) see **ENTREE DES ARTISTES** • 1938
CURTAIN TIME IN OTTAWA • 1953-54 • Devlin Bernard • DCS • CND
CURTAIN UP • 1952 • Smart Ralph • UKN • ON MONDAY NEXT
CURTAINS • 1983 • Ciupka Richard • CND
CURTAIN'S SECRET, THE see **BEHIND THE CURTAIN** • 1915
CURTATONE E MONTANARA • 1955-59 • Taviani Paolo, Taviani Vittorio • DCS • ITL
CURTIS AMY - PAUL BRYANT QUINTET • 1962 • Binder Steve • SHT • USA
CURTIS AMY SEXTET • 1962 • Markas Gary • SHT • USA
CURTISS'S SCHOOL OF AVIATION • 1912 • Dwan Allan • USA
CURUCU, BEAST OF THE AMAZON • 1956 • Siodmak Curt • USA
CURVAS PELIGROSAS • 1950 • Davison Tito • MXC
CUSTARD BOYS, THE • 1980 • Finbow Colin • UKN
CUSTARD CUP, THE • 1923 • Brenon Herbert • USA
CUSTER MASSACRE, THE see **GREAT SIOUX MASSACRE, THE** • 1965
CUSTER OF THE WEST • 1968 • Siodmak Robert • USA, SPN • GOOD DAY FOR FIGHTING, A
CUSTER'S LAST FIGHT • 1968 • Foster Norman (c/d) • TVM • USA
CUSTER'S LAST FIGHT see **LIEUTENANT'S LAST FIGHT** • 1912
CUSTER'S LAST RAID • 1912 • Ford Francis, Ince Thomas H. (Spv) • USA
CUSTER'S LAST SCOUT • 1915 • McRae Henry • USA
CUSTER'S LAST STAND • 1910 • *Chicago Film* • USA
CUSTER'S LAST STAND • 1921 • Elias Francisco • SHT • USA
CUSTER'S LAST STAND • 1936 • Clifton Elmer • SRL • USA
CUSTER'S LAST STAND see **BOB HAMPTON OF PLACER** • 1921
CUSTOMARY TWO WEEKS, THE • 1917 • Harrison Saul • USA
CUSTOMARY WIFE, THE • 1915 • *Broncho* • USA
CUSTOMER AND YOU NO.4: DEALING WITH OBJECTIONS, THE • 1968 • Inman Jeff • UKN
CUSTOMER AND YOU NO.6: THE INTERVIEW, THE • 1968 • Inman Jeff • UKN
CUSTOMERS WANTED • 1939 • Fleischer Dave • ANS • USA
CUSTOMS AGENT • 1950 • Friedman Seymour • USA
CUSTOMS FRONTIER see **VAMHATAR** • 1977
CUT AND RUN see **INFERNO IN DIRETTA** • 1985
CUT IT OUT • 1925 • Brunel Adrian • UKN
CUT NYAK DIEN • 1988 • Djarot Eros • INN
CUT THE CARDS • 1920 • Roach Hal • SHT • USA
CUT-THROATS NINE • 1973 • *Hundar Robert* • SPN
CUT-UPS, THE • 1967 • Balch Anthony • UKN
CUTE RECRUIT, THE • 1941 • *Mintz Charles (P)* • ANS • USA
CUTEY AND THE CHORUS GIRLS • 1913 • Young James • USA
CUTEY AND THE TWINS • 1913 • Young James • USA
CUTEY BECOMES A LANDLORD • 1915 • Van Wally • USA
CUTEY, FORTUNE HUNTING • 1915 • Van Wally • USA
CUTEY PLAYS DETECTIVE • 1913 • Trimble Larry • USA
CUTEY TRIES REPORTING • 1913 • Angeles Bert • USA
CUTEY'S AWAKENING • 1915 • Van Wally • USA
CUTEY'S SISTER • 1915 • Van Wally • USA
CUTEY'S VACATION • 1914 • Lambart Harry • USA
CUTEY'S WATERLOO • 1913 • Lackaye James • USA
CUTEY'S WIFE • 1914 • *Van Wally* • USA

CUTIE • 1928 • Taurog Norman • SHT • USA
CUTIE ON DUTY • 1943 • Holmes Ben • SHT • USA
CUTTER • 1972 • Irving Richard • TVM • USA
CUTTER AND BONE • 1981 • Passer Ivan • USA • CUTTER'S WAY
CUTTER TO HOUSTON • 1983 • Stern Sandor • MTV • CND
CUTTER'S TRAIL • 1969 • McEveety Vincent • TVM • USA
CUTTER'S WAY see **CUTTER AND BONE** • 1981
CUTTING CLASS • 1989 • Pallenberg Rospo • USA
CUTTING DOWN EXPENSES • 1915 • McKim Edwin • USA
CUTTING EDGE OF FEAR, THE see **FILO DEL MIEDO, EL** • 1967
CUTTING HEADS see **CABEZAS CORTADAS** • 1970
CUTTING IT SHORT (UKN) see **POSTRIZINY** • 1980
CUTTING LOOSE see **ALLNIGHTER, THE** • 1987
CUTTING LOOSE AT THE WOLFGANGSEE see **AUSSER RAND UND BAND AM WOLFGANGSEE** • 1972
CUTTING OUT HIS VACATION • 1920 • Davey Horace • SHT • USA
CUTTING OUT PICTURES • 1922 • Dudley Bernard • UKN
CUVAR PLAZE U ZIMSKOM PERIODU • 1977 • Paskaljevic Goran • YGS • BEACH KEEPER IN WINTERTIME ◦ BEACH GUARD IN WINTER
CVIJECE U JESEN • 1974 • Klopcic Matjaz • YGS • BLOSSOMS IN AUTUMN
CVOR • 1971 • Mimica Vatroslav • ANS • YGS
CVOR see **JAZOL** • 1985
CVRENI BOOGIE ILI STO TI JE DJEVOJKO see **CRVENI BUGI** • 1983
CY PERKINS IN THE CITY OF DELUSION • 1915 • McCray Roy • USA
CY WHITTAKER'S WARD • 1917 • Turbett Ben • USA
CYANKALI • 1930 • Tintner Hans • FRG
CYBELE see **DIMANCHES DE VILLE D'AVRAY, LES** • 1962
CYBERNETIC 5.3 see **CIBERNETIC 5.3** • 1969
CYBERNETIC AMATEUR, THE see **CYBERNETYK** • 1962
CYBERNETIC GRANDMA see **KYBERNETICKA BABICKA** • 1962
CYBERNETIC GRANDMOTHER, THE see **KYBERNETICKA BABICKA** • 1962
CYBERNETIC GRANNY see **KYBERNETICKA BABICKA** • 1962
CYBERNETICS • 1964 • Somlo Tamas • SHT • HNG
CYBERNETYK • 1962 • Szwakopf St. • ANS • PLN • CYBERNETIC AMATEUR, THE
CYBORG see **SIX MILLION DOLLAR MAN, THE** • 1973
CYBORG see **CYBORG -ATTACK FROM THE FUTURE** • 1988
CYBORG 009 see **SAIBOGU 009** • 1966
CYBORG 009 -KAIJU SENSO see **SAIBOGU 009 -KAIJU SENSO** • 1967
CYBORG 009 -UNDERGROUND DUEL see **SAIBOGU 009 -KAIJU SENSO** • 1967
CYBORG 2087 • 1966 • Adreon Franklin • USA • MAN FROM TOMORROW (UKN)
CYBORG -ATTACK FROM THE FUTURE • 1988 • Pyun Albert • USA • CYBORG
CYCLAMEN see **CIKLAMEN** • 1916
CYCLE • Albers Rudy • SHT • USA
CYCLE • 1971 • Gervais Suzanne • ANS • CND
CYCLE, THE see **DAYEREH MINA** • 1974
CYCLE OF ADVERSITY, THE • 1914 • *Leonard Robert* • USA
CYCLE OF FATE, THE • 1916 • Neilan Marshall • USA
CYCLE OF HATRED, THE • 1915 • *La Badie Florence* • USA
CYCLE SAVAGES, THE • 1969 • Brame Bill • USA
CYCLE TEACHER'S EXPERIENCES, A • 1904 • Mottershaw Frank • UKN
CYCLES • 1971 • Jassim Linda • SHT • USA
CYCLES SOUTH • 1971 • Marshall Don • USA
CYCLEWALI • 1938 • *Mohan* • IND
CYCLING HONEYMOON, A • 1909 • *Urban Trading Co.* • UKN
CYCLING TO THE MOON see **FIETSEN NAAR DE MAAN** • 1962
CYCLIST, THE • 1923 • Summerville Slim • USA
CYCLIST, THE • 1970 • Djordjevic Purisa • YGS
CYCLIST, THE see **BICYCLE RUN** • 1988
CYCLIST SCOUTS IN ACTION • 1901 • Williamson James • UKN
CYCLISTS ABROAD • 1957 • Thompson Tony • UKN
CYCLISTS AND PONY-TRAPS • 1900 • Paul Robert William • UKN
CYCLISTS ARE COMING, THE see **VIN CICLISTII** • 1968
CYCLISTS IN LOVE see **SZERELMES BICIK LISTAK** • 1965
CYCLIST'S MISHAP: OR, THE OLD MAID'S REVENGE, THE • 1902 • *Warwick Trading Co.* • UKN
CYCLONE • 1987 • Ray Fred Olen • USA
CYCLONE see **CICLON** • 1963
CYCLONE see **CICLON** • 1977
CYCLONE, THE • 1920 • Smith Cliff • USA
CYCLONE BLISS • 1921 • Ford Francis • USA
CYCLONE BOB • 1926 • McGowan J. P. • USA
CYCLONE BUDDY • 1924 • Neitz Alvin J. • USA
CYCLONE CAVALIER • 1925 • Rogell Albert S. • USA
CYCLONE COWBOY, THE • 1927 • Thorpe Richard • USA
CYCLONE FURY • 1951 • Nazarro Ray • USA
CYCLONE HIGGINS D.D. • 1918 • Cabanne W. Christy • USA • CYCLONE OF HIGGINS D.D.
CYCLONE JONES • 1923 • Seeling Charles R. • USA
CYCLONE KID, THE • 1931 • McGowan J. P. • USA
CYCLONE KID, THE • 1942 • Sherman George • USA
CYCLONE OF HIGGINS D.D. see **CYCLONE HIGGINS D.D.** • 1918
CYCLONE OF THE RANGE • 1927 • De Lacy Robert • USA
CYCLONE OF THE SADDLE • 1935 • Clifton Elmer • USA
CYCLONE ON HORSEBACK • 1941 • Killy Edward • USA
CYCLONE PETE IN MATRIMONY see **CYCLONE PETE'S MATRIMONY** • 1910
CYCLONE PETE'S MATRIMONY • 1910 • Melies Gaston • USA • CYCLONE PETE IN MATRIMONY
CYCLONE PRAIRIE RANGERS • 1944 • Kline Benjamin • USA
CYCLONE RANGER, THE • 1935 • Hill Robert F. • USA
CYCLONE RIDER, THE • 1924 • Buckingham Thomas • USA
CYCLONE SMITH • 1919 • SER • USA
CYCLONE SMITH PLAYS TRUMPS • 1919 • Jaccard Jacques • SHT • USA
CYCLONE SMITH'S COMEBACK • 1919 • Jaccard Jacques • SHT • USA
CYCLONE SMITH'S PARTNER • 1919 • Jaccard Jacques • SHT • USA
CYCLONE TRACY • 1975 • Noonan Chris • DCS • ASL
CYCLOPS • 1957 • Gordon Bert I. • USA
CYCLOPS, THE see **ZIKLOPAT** • 1976
CYCLOPS, THE see **KIKLOP** • 1983
CYCLOTRODE "X" • 1946 • Witney William, Brannon Fred C. • USA
CYKLEDRENGENE: TORVEGRAVEN • 1940 • Henning-Jensen Bjarne • SHT • DNM
CYKLISTEN • 1957 • Carlsen Henning • SHT • DNM
CYLINDER'S SECRET, THE • 1912 • *Vitagraph* • USA
CYMBELINE • 1913 • Marston Theodore • USA
CYNARA • 1932 • Vidor King • USA
CYNIC, THE • 1914 • Delmore Ralph • USA
CYNIC EFFECT, A see **COUNTRY FLAPPER, THE** • 1922
CYNIC, THE RAT AND THE FIST, THE see **CINICO, L'INFAME, IL VIOLENTO, IL** • 1977
CYNTHIA • 1947 • Leonard Robert Z. • USA • RICH FULL LIFE, THE (UKN)
CYNTHIA IN THE WILDERNESS • 1916 • Weston Harold • UKN
CYNTHIA-OF-THE-MINUTE • 1920 • Vekroff Perry N. • USA
CYNTHIANA • 1918 • Sargent George L. • SHT • USA
CYNTHIA'S SECRET • 1912 • Dawley J. Searle • USA
CYNTHIA'S SECRET (UKN) see **DARK DELUSION** • 1947
CYNTHY • 1913 • *Eclair* • USA
CYPRESS BOARDS see **HINOKI BUTAI** • 1946
CYPRUS see **KYPROS** • 1976
CYPRUS IS AN ISLAND • 1946 • Keene Ralph • DOC • UKN
CYRANO DE BERGERAC • 1910 • Durand Jean • FRN
CYRANO DE BERGERAC • 1923 • Genina Augusto, Gallone Carmine • ITL • CIRANO DE BERGERAC
CYRANO DE BERGERAC • 1945 • Rivers Fernand • FRN
CYRANO DE BERGERAC • 1950 • Gordon Michael • USA
CYRANO DE BERGERAC • 1989 • Rappeneau Jean-Paul • FRN
CYRANO E D'ARTAGNAN (ITL) see **CYRANO ET D'ARTAGNAN** • 1963
CYRANO ET D'ARTAGNAN • 1963 • Gance Abel • FRN, ITL, SPN • CYRANO E D'ARTAGNAN (ITL)
CYRANO ET D'ASSOUCY • 1911 • Capellani Albert • FRN
CYRIAS OUELLET • 1960 • Benoit Real • DOC • CND
CYRIL STAPLETON AND THE SHOW BAND • 1955 • Carreras Michael • SHT • UKN
CYRIUS OUELLET, HOMME DE SCIENCE • 1959 • Patry Pierre • DCS • CND
CYRK • 1954 • Haupe Wlodzimierz • PLN • CIRCUS, THE
CYRK • 1962 • Gordon Konstanty • PLN • CIRCUS UNDER THE STARS
CYROGRAF DOJRZALOSCI • 1967 • Lomnicki Jan • MTV • PLN • AFFIDAVIT OF MATURITY ◦ COMPACT OF MATURITY
CYROMORPHOSIS see **GYROMORPHOSIS** • 1958
CY'S TRIUMPH • 1915 • *Punchinello* • USA
CYTAT Z RAPORTU U THANTA • 1972 • Szczygiel Andrzej • PLN • QUOTATION FROM U TANT'S REPORT, A
CYTHEREA • 1924 • Fitzmaurice George • USA • FORBIDDEN WAY, THE
CZAR AND HIS CORTEGE GOING TO VERSAILLES, THE see **CORTEGE DU TZAR ALLANT A VERSAILLES** • 1896
CZAR AND POET see **TSAR I POET** • 1927
CZAR DURANDAI, THE see **SKAZKA O CARE DURANDAE** • 1934
CZAR I GENERAL see **TSAR I GENERAL** • 1966
CZAR KOLEK • 1967 • Urbanski Kazimierz • PLN • MAGIC OF WHEELS, THE ◦ MOTOR-STRUCK ◦ AUTOMANIA
CZAR OF BROADWAY, THE • 1930 • Craft William James • USA
CZAR OF THE SLOT MACHINES see **KING OF GAMBLERS** • 1937
CZARCI ZLEB • 1949 • Vergano Aldo, Kanski Tadeusz • PLN • DEVIL'S POWER, THE ◦ DEVIL'S PASS, THE
CZARDAS FURSTIN, DIE • 1951 • Marischka Hubert • FRG
CZARDAS-KONIG, DER • 1958 • Philipp Harald • FRG
CZARDAS PRINCESS see **CSARDASKIRALYNO** • 1971
CZARDASFURSTIN, DIE • 1927 • Schwarz Hanns • FRG
CZARDASFURSTIN, DIE • 1934 • Jacoby Georg • FRG
CZARDASFURSTIN, DIE • 1951 • Jacoby Georg • FRG
CZARINA (UKN) see **ROYAL SCANDAL, A** • 1945
CZARINA'S SECRET, THE • 1928 • Neill R. William • SHT • USA
CZARNA ONCA • 1971 • Passendorfer Jerzy • PLN • BLACK SHIP
CZARNA SUKNIA • 1967 • Majewski Janusz • SHT • PLN • BLACK DRESS, THE
CZARNE SKRZYDLA • 1963 • Petelska Ewa, Petelski Czeslaw • PLN • BLACK WINGS
CZARNE ZIELONE • 1971 • Gebski Jozef, Halor Antoni • PLN • BLACK GREEN
CZARNOKSIEZNIK • 1964 • Nehrebecki Wladyslaw • ANS • PLN • MAGICIAN, THE
CZARODZIEJ • 1962 • Makarczynski Tadeusz • PLN • MAGICIAN, THE
CZAR'S CORTEGE IN THE BOIS DE BOULOGNE, THE see **CORTEGE DU TZAR AU BOIS DE BOULOGNE** • 1896
CZAR'S FAVORITE, THE • 1920 • Hertz Aleksander • PLN
CZAS PRZEMIANY • 1968 • Piekutowski Andrzej • DOC • PLN • TIME OF CHANGE
CZAS PRZESZLY • 1961 • Buczkowski Leonard • PLN • TIME PAST (USA) ◦ PAST, THE
CZECH CONNECTION, THE • 1975 • Nemec Jan • DOC • FRG
CZECH GOTHIC PAINTING see **MISTR TREBONSKY** • 1950
CZECH HEAVEN see **CESKE NEBE** • 1918
CZECH MATE • 1984 • Hough John • UKN
CZECH YEAR, THE see **SPALICEK** • 1947
CZECHOSLOVAK GOTHIC see **MISTR TREBONSKY** • 1950
CZECHOSLOVAK PHILHARMONIC ORCHESTRA see **ETUDA O ZKOUSCE** • 1976
CZECHOSLOVAKIA • 1946 • Atasheva Pera
CZECHOSLOVAKIA • 1948 • Field Mary • DOC • UKN
CZECHOSLOVAKIA 1918-1968 • 1968 • Sanders Denis • SHT • USA
CZECHOSLOVAKIA 1918-1968 • 1969 • Nemec Jan • DOC • CZC
CZECHOSLOVAKIA ON PARADE • 1938 • Fitzpatrick James • SHT • USA
CZERWONE CIERNIE • 1976 • Dziedzina Julian • PLN
CZERWONE I CZARNE • 1963 • Giersz Witold • ANS • PLN • RED AND BLACK (USA) ◦ RED AND THE BLACK, THE
CZERWONE I ZLOTE • 1971 • Lenartowicz Stanislaw • PLN • RED AND GOLD
CZESC KAPITANIE • 1968 • Petelska Ewa, Petelski Czeslaw • MTV • PLN • GOODDAY CAPTAIN
CZEVERE • 1971 • Chalbaud Roman • SHT • VNZ
CZEVERE AND THE VICTORY OF WELLINGTON • 1971 • Chalbaud Roman • SHT • VNZ
CZLOWIEK I ANIOL • 1966 • Sturlis Edward • ANM • PLN • ANGEL AND MAN
CZLOWIEK NA TORZE • 1956 • Munk Andrzej • PLN • MAN ON THE TRACK ◦ HOMME SUR LA VOIE, UN ◦ MANN AUF DEN SCHIENEN, DER
CZLOWIEK O DWU NAZWISKACH • 1971 • Wionczek Roman • DOC • PLN • MAN WITH TWO NAMES, THE
CZLOWIEK Z M-3 • 1968 • Jeannot Leon • PLN • LOOKING FOR A WIFE
CZLOWIEK Z MARMARU • 1978 • Wajda Andrzej • PLN • MAN OF MARBLE
CZLOWIEK Z ZELAZA • 1980 • Wajda Andrzej • PLN • MAN OF IRON
CZTEREJ PANCERNI I PIES (I) • 1968 • Nalecki Konrad • PLN • FOUR ARTILLERYMEN AND A DOG
CZTEREJ PANCERNI I PIES (II) • 1968 • Nalecki Konrad • PLN • FOUR ARTILLERYMEN AND A DOG (II)
CZTEREJ PANCERNI I PIES (III) • 1968 • Nalecki Konrad • PLN • FOUR ARTILLERYMEN AND A DOG (III)
CZTEREJ PANCERNI I PIES (IV) • 1968 • Nalecki Konrad • PLN • FOUR ARTILLERYMEN AND A DOG (IV)
CZULE MIEJSCZ • 1981 • Szulkin Piotr • PLN • TENDER SPOTS
CZWARTKI UBOGICH • 1981 • Szyszko Sylwester • PLN • THURSDAYS FOR THE POOR
CZY JESTES WSROD NICH? • 1954 • Hoffman Jerzy, Skorzewski Edward • DOC • PLN • ARE YOU AMONGST THEM? ◦ ARE YOU AMONG THEM?

D

D.A.: CONSPIRACY TO KILL • 1970 • Webb Jack • TVM • USA
D.A. DRAWS A CIRCLE, THE see **THEY CALL IT MURDER** • 1971
D.A.: MURDER ONE • 1969 • Sagal Boris • TVM • USA • MURDER ONE
D.A.R.Y.L. • 1985 • Wincer Simon • USA • DARYL
D.C. CAB • 1983 • Schumacher Joel • USA • STREET FLEET
D-DAY ON MARS • 1945 • Bennet Spencer Gordon, Brannon Fred C. • USA
D-DAY THE SIXTH OF JUNE • 1956 • Koster Henry • USA
D. DEVANT, CONJUROR see **PRESTIDIGITATEUR D. DEVANT, LE** • 1897
D. DEVANT, PRESTIDIGITATEUR see **PRESTIDIGITATEUR D. DEVANT, LE** • 1897
D.F. • 1978 • Gonzalez • MXC
D' FIGHTING ONES • 1961 • Freleng Friz • ANS • USA
D.I., THE • 1957 • Webb Jack • USA
D III 88 • 1939 • Maisch Herbert • FRG • D III 88, DIE NEUE DEUTSCHE LUFTWAFFE GREIFT AN ◦ D III 88, THE NEW GERMAN AIR FORCE ATTACKS
D III 88, DIE NEUE DEUTSCHE LUFTWAFFE GREIFT AN see **D III 88** • 1939
D III 88, THE NEW GERMAN AIR FORCE ATTACKS see **D III 88** • 1939
D.O.A. • 1949 • Mate Rudolph • USA
D.O.A. • 1981 • Kowalski Lech • USA
D.O.A. • 1988 • Morton Rocky, Jankel Annabel • USA • DEAD ON ARRIVAL
D.O.A. see **MONSTER AND THE GIRL** • 1941
D.T'S: OR, THE EFFECT OF DRINK • 1905 • Haggar William • UKN
D.T'S : OR, THE HORRORS OF DRINK • 1899 • *Wolff Philipp* • UKN
D. W. GRIFFITH'S "THAT ROYLE GIRL" see **"THAT ROYLE GIRL"** • 1925
D-ZUG 13 HAT VERSPATUNG • 1931 • Zeisler Alfred • FRG
DA • 1988 • Clark Matt • USA
DA 077 CRIMINALI A HONG KONG (ITL) see **WEISSE FRACHT FUR HONGKONG** • 1964
DA 077: INTRIGO A LISBONA see **MISION LISBOA** • 1965
DA BERLINO L'APOCALISSE • 1967 • Maffei Mario • ITL, FRN, FRG • HEISSES PFLASTER FUR SPIONE (FRG) ◦ TIGRE SORT SANS SA MERE, LE ◦ SPY PIT, THE
DA BEST IN DA WEST • 1967 • Villaflor Romy • PHL • BEST IN THE WEST, THE
DA CAPO • 1985 • Honkasalo Pirjo, Lehto Pekka • FNL
DA CAPO • 1989 • Kornai Peter, Godros Frigyes • HNG
DA CORLEONE A BROOKLYN • 1979 • Lenzi Umberto • ITL • FROM CORLEONE TO BROOKLYN
DA DI DU • 1980 • Sattar Aziz • MLY
DA DUNKERQUE ALLA VITTORIA see **DE L'ENFER A LA VICTOIRE** • 1979
DA GONG HUANGDI • 1985 • Xu Ke • HKG • WORKING CLASS
DA GRANDE • 1988 • Amurri Franco • ITL • WHEN I GROW UP
DA HALT DIE WELT DEN ATEM AN • 1927 • Basch Felix • FRG
DA ICARO A DE PINEDO • 1927 • Rosa Silvio Laurenti • ITL
DA LACHT TIROL • 1967 • Brandler Lothar • FRG • TIROL LAUGHS AT THAT, THE
DA LANKARNA SMIDDES • 1939 • Natorp Arthur • SWD
DA LI ZNATE DOLLY BELL? • 1981 • Kusturica Emir • YGS • DO YOU KNOW DOLLY BELL?

DA NEW YORK: MAFIA UCCIDE! (ITL) see **JE VOUS SALUE, MAFIA** • 1965
DA NO TIEN GU • 1961 • Wan Lai-Ming • ANM • CHN • TROUBLES IN THE KINGDOM OF THE SKY ○ UPROAR IN HEAVEN ○ MONKEYKING, THE
DA PARTE DEGLI AMICI FIRMATO MAFIA (ITL) see **SAUT DE L'ANGE, LE** • 1971
DA QUI ALL'EREDITA • 1956 • Freda Riccardo • ITL
DA SCARAMOUCHE OR SE VUOI L'ASSOLUZIONE BACIAR DEVI'STO.. CORDONE! • 1973 • Baldanello Gianfranco • ITL
DA SERRA AO MAR • 1959 • Ribeiro Antonio Lopes • SHT • PRT
DA SHUI • 1989 • Tian Zhuangzhuang • CHN • GREAT WATERS
...DA SKA DU FA EN GUNGSTOL AV MIG –EN BLA see **SOMMARAVENTYR, ETT** • 1965
DA STERBEN, WENN SIE LIEBEN, DIE • 1921 • *Treumann Wanda* • FRG
DA STIMMT WAS NICHT • 1934 • Zerlett Hans H. • FRG
DA STIMMT WAS NICHT see **FALSCHE BRAUT, DIE** • 1944
DA SVANTE FORSVANDT • 1975 • Carlsen Henning • DNM • WHEN SVANTE DISAPPEARED
DA UNTEN, DIE • 1926 • Janson Victor • FRG
DA UOMO A UOMO • 1967 • Petroni Giulio • ITL • DEATH RIDES A HORSE
DA VINCI'S DREAM • 1978 • Langan Declan • SHT • IRL
DA YUEBING • 1985 • Chen Kaige • CHN • BIG PARADE, THE ○ TROOP REVIEW
DAAN EN DOORS OPPIE DIEGGINS • 1975 • SAF
DAAR DOER IN DIE BOSVELD • 1951 • SAF
DAAR DOER IN DIE STAD • 1954 • SAF
DAAR KOM TANT ALIE • 1975 • SAF
DAARSKAB • 1923 • Lauritzen Lau • DNM
DABBLING IN ART • 1920 • Kenton Erle C. • SHT • USA
DABBLING IN SOCIETY • 1919 • Morris Reggie • SHT • USA
DABLOVA PAST • 1961 • Vlacil Frantisek • CZC • DEVIL'S TRAP, THE
D'ABORD MENAGERES • 1978 • Guilbeault Luce • CND
DACHA • 1973 • Voinov Konstantin • USS
DACHNIKI • 1967 • Babochkin Boris • USS • SUMMER RESIDENTS IN THE COUNTRYSIDE ○ SUMMER RESIDENTS
DACHSHUND, THE see **ARTIST'S DREAM, THE** • 1910
DACHSHUND AND THE SAUSAGE, THE • 1910 • Bray John R. • ANS • USA
DACIANS, THE see **DACII** • 1966
DACII • 1966 • Nicolaescu Sergiu • RMN, FRN • DACIANS, THE
DACTYLO • 1931 • Thiele Wilhelm • FRN
DACTYLO SE MARIE • 1934 • Pujol Rene, May Joe • FRN
DAD • 1915 • *Mcquarrie Murdock* • USA
DAD • 1982 • Grgic Zlatko (c/d) • ANS • YGS
DAD • 1989 • Goldberg David • USA
DAD ALWAYS PAYS • 1949 • Yates Hal • SHT • USA
DAD AND DAVE COME TO TOWN • 1938 • Hall Ken G. • ASL • RUDD FAMILY GOES TO TOWN, THE
DAD AND THE GIRLS • 1914 • *Beauty* • USA
DAD BECOMES A GRANDAD • 1919 • *Austral Photoplay* • ASL
DAD, CAN I BORROW THE CAR? • 1970 • Kimball Ward • USA
DAD CAUGHT NAPPING • 1913 • Stow Percy • UKN
DAD FOR A DAY • 1939 • Cahn Edward L. • SHT • USA
DAD KNOWS BEST • 1930 • Roberts Stephen • SHT • USA
DAD RUDD, M.P. • 1940 • Hall Ken G. • ASL
DADA • Deses Greta • BLG
DADA DADA • 1929 • Aylott Dave, Symmons E. F. • SHT • UKN
DADAH IS DEATH see **LONG WAY FROM HOME: DADAH IS DEATH, A** • 1988
DADASCOPE I&II • 1956-57 • Richter Hans • SWT
DADAYAMA • 1984 • Obeyesekara Vasantha • SLN
DADDIES • 1924 • Seiter William A. • USA
DADDY • 1917 • Bentley Thomas • UKN
DADDY • 1923 • Hopper E. Mason • USA
DADDY • 1972 • Whitehead Peter, de Saint Phalle Niki • UKN, SWT
DADDY • 1987 • Herzfeld John • TVM • USA
DADDY • 1989 • Bhatt Mahesh • IND
DADDY O • 1959 • Place Lou • USA • OUT ON PROBATION ○ DOWNBEAT
DADDY AMBROSE • 1919 • *Swain Mack* • SHT • USA
DADDY AS OF OLD • 1908 • Smith Jack ? • UKN
DADDY BOY • 1927 • Edwards Harry J. • SHT • USA
DADDY COOL: EAGLE ROCK • 1973 • Lofven Chris • SHT • UKN
DADDY, DARLING • 1970 • Sarno Joe • USA, DNM
DADDY DUCK • 1948 • Hannah Jack • ANS • USA
DADDY GOES A GRUNTING • 1925 • Roach Hal • SHT • USA
DADDY, I DON'T LIKE IT LIKE THIS • 1978 • Aldrich Adell • TVM • USA
DADDY KNOWS BEST • 1933 • *Sennett Mack (P)* • SHT • USA
DADDY LONG LEGS • 1919 • Neilan Marshall • USA
DADDY LONG LEGS • 1931 • Santell Alfred • USA
DADDY LONG LEGS • 1955 • Negulesco Jean • USA
DADDY NOSTALGIE • 1990 • Tavernier Bertrand • FRN
DADDY NUMBER TWO • 1919 • *Osborne Marie* • SHT • USA
DADDY OF THEM ALL, THE • 1914 • *Lubin* • USA
DADDY PUTS ONE OVER • 1916 • *Gayety* • USA
DADDY SAID THE WORLD WAS LOVELY see **SALVARE LA FACCIA** • 1969
DADDY WANTS IT THAT WAY see **BABA AYEZ KEDA** • 1968
DADDY, WHY ARE YOU ANGRY –YOU DID IT YOURSELF IN YOUR YOUTH see **PAPPA, VARFOR AR DU ARG –DU GJORDE LIKADANT SJALV NAR DU VAR UNG** • 1968
DADDY'S BOY AND MAMMY • 1911 • *Casey Kenneth* • USA
DADDY'S BOYS • 1987 • Minion Joe • USA
DADDY'S DARLINGS • 1913 • Fitzhamon Lewin • UKN
DADDY'S DEADLY DARLING • 1972 • Lawrence Toni • USA • STRANGE EXORCISM OF LYNN HART, THE ○ LOVE EXORCIST ○ PIGS ○ KILLER, THE ○ DADDY'S GIRL
DADDY'S DELECTABLE DOZEN see **TURKISCHEN GURKEN, DIE** • 1963
DADDY'S DIDUMS AND THE BOX TRICK • 1913 • Noy Wilfred • UKN
DADDY'S DIDUMS AND THE TALE OF THE TAILOR • 1911 • Noy Wilfred • UKN
DADDY'S DIDUMS AND THE UMBRELLA • 1911 • Noy Wilfred • UKN
DADDY'S DOUBLE • 1910 • *Thanhouser* • USA
DADDY'S DYING, WHO'S GOT THE WILL • 1990 • Fisk Jack • USA
DADDY'S GIRL • 1918 • Bertram William • USA
DADDY'S GIRL see **DADDY'S DEADLY DARLING** • 1972
DADDY'S GONE A-HUNTING • 1969 • Robson Mark • USA
DADDY'S GONE A'HUNTING • 1925 • Borzage Frank • USA • MAN'S WORLD, A
DADDY'S GOT TO GO TO THE REFORM SCHOOL see **JAK DOSTAT TATINKA DO POLEPSOVNY** • 1979
DADDY'S HOME • 1989 • Heckerling Amy • USA
DADDY'S LITTLE DARLING • 1957 • Rasinski Connie • ANS • USA
DADDY'S LITTLE DIDUMS AND THE NEW BABY • 1911 • Noy Wilfred • UKN
DADDY'S LITTLE DIDUMS DID IT • 1910 • Noy Wilfred • UKN
DADDY'S LITTLE GIRL see **SHE'S OUT OF CONTROL** • 1989
DADDY'S LOVE • 1922 • *Klumb R. H.* • USA
DADDY'S LULLABY see **ZOKU ROKYOKU KOMORIUTA** • 1967
DADDY'S SOLDIER BOY • 1913 • Thornby Robert T. • USA
DADDYTHINGS • 1974 • Blagg Linda • SHT • ASL
DAD'S ALLOWANCE • 1914 • *Frontier* • USA
DADS AND KIDS • 1987 • Bruyere Christian • DCS • CND
DAD'S ARMY • 1971 • Cohen Norman • UKN
DAD'S AWFUL CRIME • 1915 • Curtis Allen • USA • DAD'S AWFUL DEED
DAD'S AWFUL DEED see **DAD'S AWFUL CRIME** • 1915
DAD'S COLLEGE WIDOW • 1916 • Walsh Phil • SHT • USA
DAD'S DARLING DAUGHTERS • 1916 • *Chamberlin Riley* • SHT • USA
DAD'S DAY • 1929 • McCarey Leo • SHT • USA
DAD'S DOLLARS AND DIRTY DOINGS • 1916 • *Howell Alice* • SHT • USA
DAD'S DOWNFALL • 1917 • *Sutherland Eddie* • USA
DAD'S GIRL • 1911 • *Reliance* • USA
DAD'S GIRL • 1919 • Fischer David G. • USA
DAD'S GIRLS • 1911 • *Selig* • USA
DAD'S INSANITY • 1913 • *Boulder Robert* • USA
DAD'S KNOCKOUT • 1918 • *Parsons William* • SHT • USA
DAD'S LITTLE GIRL • 1913 • Parker Lem B. • USA
DAD'S MASTERPIECE • 1916 • *Compson Betty* • USA
DAD'S MISTAKE • 1912 • *Nestor* • USA
DAD'S ORDERS • 1913 • *Fraunholz Fraunie* • USA
DAD'S OUTLAWS • 1914 • *Reliance* • USA
DAD'S SMASH-UP • 1911 • *Pathe* • USA
DAD'S STENOGRAPHER • 1913 • *Nestor* • USA
DAD'S SURPRISE • 1913 • *Nestor* • USA
DAD'S TERRIBLE MATCH • 1914 • *Mace Fred* • USA
DAD'S WAR see **GUERRA DE PAPA, LA** • 1977
DAD'S WATCH • 1912 • *Essanay* • USA
DAEMON • 1985 • Finbow Colin • UKN
DAEMON DER BERGE, DER • 1934 • Marton Andrew • SWT • DEMON OF THE HIMALAYAS, THE (USA) ○ BEAST OF THE HIMALAYAS (UKN)
DAERAT EL INTIQAM • 1976 • Sayf Samir • EGY • VENGEANCE TRIBUNAL
DAESH RADIO! • 1924 • Yutkevich Sergei, Grunberg S. • USS • GIVE US RADIO! ○ RADIO NOW!
DAESH VOZKUKH see **DAYESH VOZDUKH** • 1924
DAFFODIL KILLER see **GEHEIMNIS DER GELBEN NARZISSEN, DAS** • 1961
DAFFY see **WILD SEED, THE** • 1965
DAFFY DILLY • 1948 • Jones Charles M. • ANS • USA
DAFFY DOC, THE • 1938 • Clampett Robert • ANS • USA
DAFFY DOODLES • 1946 • McKimson Robert • ANS • USA
DAFFY DUCK AND EGGHEAD • 1938 • Avery Tex • ANS • USA
DAFFY DUCK AND THE DINOSAUR • 1939 • Jones Charles M. • ANS • USA
DAFFY DUCK HUNT • 1949 • McKimson Robert • ANS • USA
DAFFY DUCK IN HOLLYWOOD • 1938 • Avery Tex • ANS • USA
DAFFY DUCK SLEPT HERE • 1948 • McKimson Robert • ANS • USA
DAFFY DUCKAROO, THE • 1942 • McCabe Norman • ANS • USA
DAFFY DUCK'S MOVIE: FANTASTIC ISLAND • 1983 • Freleng Friz • ANM • USA
DAFFY RENTS • 1966 • McKimson Robert • ANS • USA
DAFFY THE COMMANDO • 1943 • Freleng Friz • ANS • USA
DAFFYDILLY DADDY • 1945 • Kneitel Seymour • ANS • USA
DAFFY'S DINER • 1967 • McKimson Robert • ANS • USA
DAFFY'S INN TROUBLE • 1961 • McKimson Robert • ANS • USA
DAFFY'S SOUTHERN EXERCISE • 1942 • McCabe Norman • ANS • USA
DAFGIN • 1926 • May Joe • FRG
DAFNIS KAI CHLOI • 1930 • Laskos Orestis • GRC • DAPHNIS ET CHLOE ○ DAPHNIS AND CHLOE
DAFTIE, THE • 1978 • Alexander Mike • UKN
DAG DOKTER • 1978 • de Jong Ate • NTH • INHERITANCE, THE
DAG I IVAN DENISOVIWICH'S LIV, EN (NRW) see **ONE DAY IN THE LIFE OF IVAN DENISOVICH** • 1971
DAG I STADEN, EN • 1956 • Hutten Pontus, Nordenstrom Hans • SWD • DAY IN THE CITY, A
DAG SKALL GRY, EN • 1944 • Ekman Hasse • SWD • DAY SHALL DAWN, A
DAG ZUIDERZEE, EEN • 1968 • Wiegel Jan • SHT • NTH
DAGE I MIN FARS HUS • 1968 • Nagata David • DNM • DAYS IN MY FATHER'S HOUSE ○ WHISTLE, THE
DAGEN MIJNER JAREN • 1960 • de Haas Max • NTH • DAYS OF MY YEARS
DAGENS DONNA • 1989 • Henszelman Stefan • DNM • MODERN WOMAN, A ○ DONNA OF THE DAY
DAGER FRA 1000 AR • 1969 • Breien Anja, Kolsto Egil, Thorstenson Espen • NRW • DAYS FROM 1000 YEARS
DAGG DAY AFTERNOON • 1977 • Murphy Geoff • NZL
DAGGER see **KORTIK** • 1954
DAGGER, THE see **DOLKEN** • 1915
DAGGERS • Cheung Sum, Tong Wilson • HKG
DAGGERS DRAWN (USA) see **A COUTEAUX TIRES** • 1963
DAGGERS OF BLOOD see **COL FERRO E COL FUOCO** • 1962
DAGJE NAAR HET STRAND, EEN • 1984 • van Gogh Theo • NTH • DAY AT THE BEACH, A
DAGLAR ASLANI • 1967 • Kan Kemal • TRK • LION OF THE MOUNTAINS, THE
DAGLARI BEKLEYEN KIZ • 1968 • Duru Sureyya • TRK • GIRL WHO WATCHES THE MOUNTAIN, THE
DAGLARIN KURDU KOCERO • 1964 • Utku Umit • TRK • KOCERO, MOUNTAIN WOLF
DAGLARIN OGLU • 1965 • Atadeniz Yilmaz • TRK
DAGLI APPENNINI ALLE ANDE • 1943 • Calzavara Flavio • ITL
DAGLI APPENNINI ALLE ANDE • 1959 • Quilici Folco • DOC • ITL, ARG
DAGLI ARCHIVI DELLA POLIZIA CRIMINALE • 1975 • Lombardo Paolo • ITL
DAGLI ZAR ALLA BANDIERA ROSSA • 1963 • Mangini Gino, Ghione Piero • DOC • ITL
DAGNY • 1976 • Sandoy Hakon • NRW, PLN
DAGOBERT • 1984 • Risi Dino • ITL, FRN • BON ROI DAGOBERT, LE (FRN)
DAGOBERT THE JESTER • 1913 • Noy Wilfred • UKN
DAGORA see **UCHU DAIKAIJU DOGORA** • 1964
DAGORA THE SPACE MONSTER (USA) see **UCHU DAIKAIJU DOGORA** • 1964
DAGUEMALUAHK, LE • 1968 • Robiolles Jacques • FRN
DAGUERRE OU LA NAISSANCE DE LA PHOTO see **NAISSANCE DE LA PHOTO** • 1965
DAGUERREOTYPES • 1975 • Varda Agnes • FRN
DAH NA BADEMI see **DAKH NA BADEMI, S** • 1967
DAHAN • 1985 • Ali Shaikh Neamat • BNG
DAHANA-ARANJA • 1976 • Ray Satyajit • IND • MASSES' MUSIC, THE (USA) ○ MIDDLEMAN, THE (UKN) ○ JANA ARANYA ○ MIDDLE MAN, THE
DAHASAK SITHUVILI • 1968 • Perera G. D. L. • SLN • THOUSAND THOUGHTS, A
DAHE BENLIU • 1978 • Xie Tieli, Chen Huai-Ai • CHN • GREAT RIVER FLOWS ON, THE
DAHEJ • 1950 • Shantaram Victor • IND • DOWRY, THE
DAHIL SA ISANG BULAKLAK • 1967 • Nepomuceno Luis • PHL • BECAUSE OF A FLOWER
DAHINTEN IN DER HEIDE • 1936 • Boese Carl • FRG • BACK IN THE COUNTRY (USA)
DAI CHUSHINGUSA • 1957 • Osone Tatsuo • JPN • MATTER OF VALOUR, A
DAI JONES • 1941 • Birt Daniel • DOC • UKN
DAI KANBU • 1968 • Masuda Toshio • JPN • GANGSTER V.I.P., THE (USA) ○ DAIKANBU
DAI KANBU BURAI • 1968 • Ozawa Keiichi • JPN • OUTLAW SWORD, THE ○ DAIKANBU-BURAI
DAI KANBU BURAI HIJO • 1968 • Ezaki Mio • JPN • GANGSTER V.I.P. –VILLAINOUS CRUELTY
DAI KOESU YONGKARI • 1967 • Kiduck Kim • SKR, JPN • YONGARY, MONSTER FROM THE DEEP (USA) ○ GREAT MONSTER YONGARY ○ MONSTER YONGARY
DAI KUSEN • 1966 • Moritani Shiro • JPN • ZERO FIGHTER
...DAI NEMICI MI GUARDO IO! • 1968 • Amendola Mario • ITL • ...I PROTECT MYSELF AGAINST MY ENEMIES!
DAI SANJI SEKAI TAISEN-YONJI-ICHI JIKAN NO KYOFU • 1960 • Hidaka Shigeaki • JPN • FINAL WAR, THE (USA) ○ WORLD WAR III BREAKS OUT ○ 41 JIKAN NO KYOFU ○ JIKAN NO KYOFU
DAI-SHINRIN • 1930 • Gosho Heinosuke • JPN • BIG FOREST, THE
DAI TATSUMAKI • 1964 • Inagaki Hiroshi • JPN • WHIRLWIND
DAI TENGU SHUTSUGEN • 1960 • Mori Masaki • JPN
DAI-TOKYO NO IKKAKU • 1930 • Gosho Heinosuke • JPN • CORNER OF GREAT TOKYO, A
DAIAKUTO • 1968 • Masumura Yasuzo • JPN • EVIL TRIO
DAIBOKEN • 1966 • Furusawa Kengo • JPN • DON'T CALL ME A CON MAN (USA) ○ CRAZY ADVENTURE
DAIBOSATSU PASS see **DAIBOSATSU TOGE** • 1935
DAIBOSATSU TOGE • 1935 • Inagaki Hiroshi • JPN • GREAT BODHISATTVA PASS, THE ○ DAIBOSATSU PASS
DAIBOSATSU TOGE • 1957 • Uchida Tomu • JPN • GREAT BODHISATTVA PASS, THE ○ MOONLIT SWORDS
DAIBOSATSU TOGE • 1960 • Misumi Kenji • JPN • SATAN'S SWORD
DAIBOSATSU TOGE • 1966 • Okamoto Kihachi • JPN
DAIBUTSU KAIGEN • 1952 • Kinugasa Teinosuke • JPN • DEDICATION OF THE GREAT BUDDHA ○ SAGA OF THE GREAT BUDDHA
DAICHI NI TATSU • 1932 • Uchida Tomu • JPN • MOTHER EARTH RISES
DAICHI NO KOMORI-UTA • 1975 • Masumura Yasuzo • JPN • CRADLESONG FROM THE EARTH, A
DAICHI WA HOHOEMU • 1925 • Mizoguchi Kenji • JPN • SMILING EARTH, THE (USA) ○ SMILE OF OUR EARTH, THE ○ EARTH SMILES, THE
DAIDOKORO TAIHEIKI • 1963 • Toyoda Shiro • JPN • KITCHEN PEACE
DAIGAKU NO NIJU-HACHININ SHU • 1959 • Aoyagi Nobuo • JPN • COLLEGE RUGGERS
DAIGAKU NO ONEICHAN • 1959 • Sugie Toshio • JPN • THREE DOLLS IN COLLEGE ○ YOUNG GIRL AT THE UNIVERSITY
DAIGAKU NO SAMURAI-TACHI • 1957 • Aoyagi Nobuo • JPN • SCHOOLDAYS
DAIGAKU NO WAKADAISHO • 1962 • Sugie Toshio • JPN • BULL OF THE CAMPUS
DAIGAKU WA DETA KEREDA • 1929 • Ozu Yasujiro • JPN • I GRADUATED BUT.. ○ I PASSED BUT..
DAIGAKU YOITOKO • 1936 • Ozu Yasujiro • JPN • COLLEGE IS SUCH A NICE PLACE ○ COLLEGE IS A NICE PLACE
DAIGAN JOJU • 1959 • Ikoma Chisato • JPN • FINE FELLOW
DAIGASHI • 1968 • Saeki Kiyoshi • JPN • THREE CHIVALROUS MEN
DAIGO FUKURYU MARU • 1959 • Shindo Kaneto • JPN • LUCKY DRAGON NO.5, THE
DAIHAO MEIZHOUBAO • 1988 • Zhang Yimou, Yang Fengliang • CHN • PUMA ACTION, THE ○ CODE NAME COUGAR
DAIKAIJU BARAN • 1958 • Honda Inoshiro • JPN • VARAN THE UNBELIEVABLE ○ MONSTER BARAN, THE

DAIKAIJU GAMERA • 1965 • Yuasa Noriaki • JPN • GAMMERA THE INVINCIBLE (USA) ○ GAMMERA ○ GAMERA

DAIKAIJU KUCHUSEN: GAMERA TAI GAOS see **GAMERA TAI GYAOS** • 1967

DAIKANBU see **DAI KANBU** • 1968

DAIKANBU-BURAI see **DAI KANBU BURAI** • 1968

DAIKON TO NINJIN • 1964 • Shibuya Minoru • JPN • TWILIGHT PATH (USA) ○ MR. RADISH AND MR. CARROT ○ RADISHES AND CARROTS

DAIKU TAIHEIKI • 1965 • Toyoda Shiro • JPN • TALE OF A CARPENTER

DAIKYAJU GAPPA • 1967 • Noguchi Haruyasu • JPN • MONSTER FROM A PREHISTORIC PLANET (USA) ○ GAPPA, TRIPHIBIAN MONSTER ○ GAPPA ○ GAPPA THE TRIFIBIAN MONSTER

DAILY BATTLE, THE • 1944 • Shimazu Yasujiro • JPN

DAILY DOUBLE, THE see **6-9 THE DAILY DOUBLE** • 1970

DAILY JESTERS • 1927 • Newman Widgey R. • SER • UKN

DAILY MIRROR COMPETITION FILMS, THE • 1926 • Tilley Frank • SER • UKN

DAILY NEWS see **NOVOSTI DNYA** • 1947-54

DAILY PASSION AT THE TURKISH BATHS see **TORUKOBORO YOGOTO NO JOHNETSU** • 1968

DAILY ROUND • 1937 • Massingham Richard, Urbahn Karl • UKN

DAIMAJIN • 1966 • Yasuda Kimiyoshi, Kuroda Yoshiyuki • JPN • MAJIN, THE MONSTER OF TERROR ○ VENGEANCE OF A MONSTER, THE ○ MAJIN (USA) ○ MAJIN, THE HIDEOUS IDOL ○ DEVIL GOT ANGRY, THE

DAIMAJIN GUAKUSHU • 1966 • Mori Issei, Kuroda Yoshiyuki • JPN • MAJIN STRIKES AGAIN (USA)

DAIMAJIN IKARU • 1966 • Misumi Kenji, Kuroda Yoshiyuki • JPN • RETURN OF GIANT MAJIN, THE (USA) ○ RETURN OF MAJIN, THE

DAIMAN EL QALBI see **DAIMAN FI KALBI** • 1947

DAIMAN FI KALBI • 1947 • Abu Saif Salah • EGY • ALWAYS IN MY HEART ○ DAIMAN EL QALBI

DA'IMAN MA'AK • 1953 • Barakat Henry • EGY • AVEC TOI POUR TOUJOURS

DAIN CURSE, THE • 1978 • Swackhamer E. W. • TVM • USA • PRIVATE EYE

DAINAH LA METISSE • 1931 • Gremillon Jean • SHT • FRN

DAINAI NO JINSEI • 1948 • Sekigawa Hideo • JPN • SECOND LIFE, A

DAINAI NO SEPPUN • 1954 • Shimizu Hiroshi • JPN

DAINAID'S BARREL, THE (USA) see **TONNEAU DES DANAIDES, LE** • 1900

DAINAMAITO NI HI O TSUKERO • 1959 • Kurahara Koreyoshi • JPN • DYNAMITE

DAINIPPON TEIKOKU • 1983 • Masuda Toshio • JPN • IMPERIAL JAPANESE EMPIRE, THE ○ EMPIRE OF JAPAN

DAINTY DAMSELS AND BOGUS COUNTS • 1919 • Stevens Walter • SHT • USA

DAINTY POLITICIAN, A • 1910 • *Thanhouser* • USA

DA'IRAT AL-INTIQAM • 1975 • Sayf Samir • EGY • MOI ET LA JUSTICE

DAIROKU NO YOGISHA • 1960 • Inoue Umeji • JPN • SIX SUSPECTS (USA)

DAIRY OF A CHAMBERMAID (USA) see **JOURNAL D'UNE FEMME DE CHAMBRE, LE** • 1963

DAISAN NO AKUMYO • 1963 • Tanaka Tokuzo • JPN • TOUGH GUY III ○ THIRD BAD NAME, THE

DAISAN NO SHIKAKU • 1959 • Kurahara Koreyoshi • JPN • THIRD ASSASSIN, THE

DAISAN NON ONNA • 1959 • Murayama Shinji • JPN • THIRD WOMAN, THE

DAISHOGEKI • 1968 • Ichimura Hirokazu • JPN • HOTSPRING'S HOTSHOP

DAISIES • 1910 • *Vitagraph* • USA

DAISIES • 1914 • *Julian Rupert* • USA

DAISIES see **SEDMIKRASKY** • 1966

DAISY • 1923 • Zelnik Friedrich • FRG

DAISY, THE see **MARGARITKA** • 1965

DAISY BELL • 1925 • Fleischer Dave • ANS • USA

DAISY BELL • 1929 • Fleischer Dave • ANS • USA

DAISY CHAIN, THE • 1969 • Davis Don • USA • CHAIN, THE

DAISY COWBOYS, THE • 1911 • *Fuller Mary* • USA

DAISY DOODAD'S DIAL • 1914 • Trimble Larry • UKN

DAISY GOES HOLLYWOOD see **HOLLYWOOD AND VINE** • 1945

DAISY KENYON • 1947 • Preminger Otto • USA

DAISY MILLER • 1974 • Bogdanovich Peter • USA

DAISY, THE DEMONSTRATOR • 1916 • *Close Ivy* • SHT • USA

DAISY (THE DOG) GOES HOLLYWOOD (UKN) see **HOLLYWOOD AND VINE** • 1945

DAISY: THE STORY OF A FACELIFT • 1983 • Rubbo Michael • CND

DAISY'S ADVENTURES IN THE LAND OF THE CHRYSANTHEMUMS • 1904 • *Mutoscope & Biograph* • UKN

DAITOA SENSO • 1968 • Oshima Nagisa • JPN • PACIFIC WAR, THE (UKN)

DAITOKAI RODOHEN • 1930 • Ushihara Kiyohiko • JPN • GREAT METROPOLIS: CHAPTER ON LABOUR, THE ○ GREAT CITY, THE

DAITOWA SENSO TO KOKUSAI SAIBAN • 1959 • Komori Kiyoshi • JPN • GREAT ASIA WAR AND THE INTERNATIONAL TRIBUNAL, THE ○ PACIFIC WAR AND THE INTERNATIONAL MILITARY TRIBUNE, THE

DAITOZOKU • 1963 • Taniguchi Senkichi • JPN • SAMURAI PIRATE (USA) ○ LOST WORLD OF SINBAD, THE

DAIYAT GAN • 1990 • Leung Raymond • HKG • FIRST TIME IS THE LAST TIME, THE

DAJ STO DAS • 1981 • Zizic Bogdan • YGS • WHATEVER YOU CAN SPARE

DAJAJ, AD- • 1976 • Amiralai Omar • DOC • SYR • HENS, THE ○ DAJAL, AL

DAJAL, AL see **DAJAJ, AD-** • 1976

DAK BANGLA • Ranjan Girish • IND

DAKARETA HANAYOME • 1957 • Nomura Hotaro • JPN • EMBRACED BRIDE

DAKARETE HANAYOME • 1962 • Bansho Yoshiaki • JPN

DAKH NA BADEMI, S • 1967 • Sharlandgiev Ljobomir • BUL • TASTE OF ALMONDS, A ○ SCENT OF ALMONDS ○ ALMOND-SCENTED ○ DAH NA BADEMI

DAKHAL • 1982 • Ghose Goutam • IND • OCCUPATION, THE

DAKHIL, EL • 1967 • el Demerdash Nour • EGY • INTRUDER, THE

DAKILANG TANGA • 1968 • Carlos Luciano B. • PHL • GREAT FOOL, THE

DAKKET QALB • 1976 • Aziz Mohamed Abdel • EGY • HEARTBEAT

DAKOO MANSOOR • 1934 • *Sircar B. N. (P)* • IND

DAKOTA • 1945 • Kane Joseph • USA

DAKOTA • 1974 • Verstappen Wim • NTH

DAKOTA 308 • 1950 • Daniel-Norman Jacques • FRN

DAKOTA DAN • 1917 • *W.h. Production* • USA

DAKOTA INCIDENT • 1956 • Foster Lewis R. • USA

DAKOTA KID, THE • 1951 • Ford Philip • USA

DAKOTA LIL • 1950 • Selander Lesley • USA

DAKSHA YAGNA • 1934 • Banerjee Jyotish • IND • SOUTHERN WAR FESTIVAL ○ SATI

DAKSHYA YAGNA • 1923 • *Radha* • IND • SATI

DAKTAR • 1940 • *Sircar B. N. (P)* • IND

DAKU MANSOOR • 1934 • *Roy Bimal (Ph)* • IND

DAL NOSTRO INVIATO A COPENHAGEN • 1970 • Cavallone Alberto • ITL

DAL REFERENDUM ALLA COSTITUZIONE • 1971 • De Sica Vittorio • MTV • ITL • DUE GIUGNO, IL

DAL SABATO AL LUNEDI • 1963 • Guerrasio Guido • ITL

DALAGANG BUKID • 1919 • Nepomuceno Jose • PHL

DALAHU • 1967 • Yasami Siyamak • IRN

DALAL L'EGYPTIENNE see **DALAL MISRIYA**

DALAL MISRIYA • Al Imam Hassan • EGY • DALAL L'EGYPTIENNE

DALAWANG MUKHA NG ANGHEL • 1968 • Torres Mar S. • PHL • TWO FACES OF AN ANGEL

DALAWANG MUKHA NG PAG-IBIG • 1967 • Garces Armando • PHL • TWO FACES OF LOVE

DALAWANG PUGAD, DALAWANG IBON • 1977 • Bernal Ishmael • PHL • TWO NESTS, TWO BIRDS

DALBICH MERRODI • 1985 • I Hwang-Lim • SKR • MOONLIGHT MELODY

DALE DURO CAYETANO • 1976 • Castro Alberto Giraldo • DOC • CLM

DALEKA CESTA • 1949 • Radok Alfred • CZC • LONG JOURNEY, THE ○ DISTANT JOURNEY ○ GHETTO TEREZIN

DALEKA JEST DROGA • 1963 • Poreba Bohdan • PLN • WAY IS LONG, THE ○ HIS LAST WILL

DALEKO JE SUNCE • 1953 • Novakovic Rados • YGS • SUN IS FAR AWAY, THE

DALEKO NA ZAPADE • 1969 • Fainzimmer Alexander • USS • FAR AWAY IN THE WEST

DALEKO NEBO • 1983 • Cikes Stjepan • YGS • DISTANT SKY, THE

DALEKO OT MOSKVY • 1950 • Stolper Alexander • USS • FAR FROM MOSCOW

DALEKS' INVASION OF EARTH 2150 A.D. • 1966 • Flemyng Gordon • UKN • DR. WHO: INVASION EARTH 2150 A.D. ○ INVASION EARTH 2150 A.D.

DALI MUSEUM see **MUSEE DALI** • 1981

DALIAS • 1972 • Bosch Juan • SPN

DALIAS IDOK • 1983 • Gemes Jozsef • HNG • HEROIC TIMES

DALIBOR • 1956 • Krska Vaclav • CZC

DALLAS • 1950 • Heisler Stuart • USA

DALLAS COWBOYS CHEERLEADERS, THE • 1979 • Bilson Bruce • TVM • USA

DALLAS COWBOYS CHEERLEADERS II, THE • 1980 • O'Herlihy Michael • TVM • USA

DALLAS: THE EARLY YEARS • 1986 • Elikann Larry • TVM • USA

DALLE ARDENNE ALL'INFERNO • 1968 • De Martino Alberto • ITL, FRN, FRG • ...UND MORGEN FAHRT IHR ZUR HOLLE (FRG) ○ GLOIRE DES CANAILLES, LA (FRN) ○ DIRTY HEROES (USA) ○ FROM THE ARDENNES TO HELL

DALLE CINQUE GIORNATE DI MILANO ALLA BRECCIA DI PORTE PIA • 1923 • Rosa Silvio Laurenti • ITL

DALLEGRET • 1967 • Sheppard Gordon H. • CND

DALMAS • 1973 • Deling Bert • ASL

DALMATIAN CHRONICLE, THE see **DALMATINSKA KRONIKA** • 1973

DALMATINISCHE HOCHZEIT • 1953 • von Bolvary Geza • FRG • EINMAL KEHR' ICH WIEDER

DALMATINSKA KRONIKA • 1973 • Zafranovic Lordan • YGS • DALMATIAN CHRONICLE, THE

DALOKAN • 1982 • Dosso Moussa • IVC • PAROLE DONNEE, LA

DALOLVA SZEP AZ ELET • 1950 • Keleti Marton • HNG • SINGING MAKES LIFE BEAUTIFUL

DALTON BOYS, THE • 1914 • SHT • USA

DALTON: CODE OF VENGEANCE II • 1986 • Smithee Alan • TVM • USA

DALTON GANG, THE • 1949 • Beebe Ford • USA • OUTLAW GANG, THE

DALTON GIRLS, THE • 1957 • Le Borg Reginald • USA

DALTON THAT GOT AWAY • 1960 • Salvador Jimmy • USA

DALTONS EN CAVALE, LES see **LUCKY LUKE, LES DALTONS EN CAVALE** • 1983

DALTONS RIDE AGAIN, THE • 1945 • Taylor Ray • USA

DALTONS' WOMEN, THE • 1951 • Carr Thomas • USA

DALYOKAYA NEVESTA • 1948 • Ivanov-Barkov Yevgeni • USS • FAR-AWAY BRIDE, THE

DAM • 1967 • Szemes Mihaly • HNG

DAM, THE • 1984 • Tsanev Emil • BUL

DAM, THE see **PRIEHRADA** • 1950

DAM, THE see **BARAJ** • 1978

DAM BUILDER, THE • 1912 • *Ogle Charlie* • USA

DAM BUSTERS, THE • 1955 • Anderson Michael • UKN

DAM OF ONE'S MIND, THE see **MANKO BANDH**

DAM ON THE YELLOW RIVER see **APOCALISSE SUL FIUME GIALLO** • 1960

DAM THE DELTA see **NEDERLAND -DELTALAND** • 1961

DAMA BIANCA, LA • 1938 • Mattoli Mario • ITL • LADY IN WHITE, THE (USA)

DAMA DE BEIRUT, LA • 1965 • Delgado Luis Maria, Vajda Ladislao (U/c) • SPN

DAMA DE COMPANIA • 1940 • de Zavalia Alberto • ARG

DAMA DE LA MUERTE, LA • 1946 • Christensen Carlos Hugo • CHL • LADY AND DEATH, THE

DAMA DE LAS CAMELIAS, LA • 1919 • Stahl Carlos • MXC

DAMA DE LAS CAMELIAS, LA • 1943 • Soria Gabriel • MXC

DAMA DEL ALBA, LA • 1949 • Gomez Muriel Emilio • MXC

DAMA DEL ALBA, LA • 1965 • Rovira Beleta Francisco • SPN

DAMA DEL ARMINO, LA • 1947 • Ardavin Eusebio F. • SPN

DAMA DEL MILLON, LA • 1956 • Cahen Enrique • ARG

DAMA DEL VELO, LA • 1948 • Crevenna Alfredo B. • MXC

DAMA DI PICCHE, LA • 1913 • *Gys Leda* • ITL • QUEEN OF SPADES, THE

DAMA DO CINE SHANGHAII, A • 1987 • Prado Guilherme De Almeida • BRZ • LADY FROM THE SHANGHAI CINEMA, THE (UKN) ○ LADY FROM THE MOVIE, THE

DAMA DUENDE, LA • 1945 • Saslavsky Luis • ARG

DAMA NA KOLEJICH • 1965 • Rychman Ladislav • CZC • LADY ON THE TRACKS, THE (USA) ○ LADY OF THE LINES, THE ○ LADY OF THE TRAM LINES

DAMA ROSSA UCCIDE SETTE VOLTE, LA • 1972 • Miraglia Emilio Paolo • ITL, FRG • CORPSE WHICH DIDN'T WANT TO DIE, THE (USA)

DAMA S MALOU NOZKOU • 1919 • Kolar J. S. • CZC • LADY WITH THE SMALL FOOT, THE ○ LADY WITH SHORT LEGS, THE

DAMA S SOBACHKOI • 1960 • Heifitz Josif • USS • LADY WITH THE DOG, THE (USA) ○ LADY WITH THE LITTLE DOG, THE ○ LADY WITH A LITTLE DOG

DAMA SPATHI • 1966 • Skalenakis Giorgos • GRC • LOVE CYCLES (USA) ○ QUEEN OF CLUBS

DAMA TORERA, LA • 1949 • Morayta Miguel • MXC

DAMAGED GOOD • 1918 • *Lyons Eddie* • USA

DAMAGED GOODNESS • 1917 • Hartigan P. C. • SHT • USA

DAMAGED GOODS • 1915 • Ricketts Thomas • USA

DAMAGED GOODS • 1917 • *Bennett Richard* • USA

DAMAGED GOODS • 1919 • Butler Alexander • UKN

DAMAGED GOODS see **MARRIAGE FORBIDDEN** • 1936

DAMAGED GOODS see **V.D.** • 1961

DAMAGED HEARTS • 1924 • Hunter T. Hayes • USA

DAMAGED LIVES • 1933 • Ulmer Edgar G. • USA

DAMAGED LOVE • 1930 • Willat Irvin V. • USA

DAMAGED -NO GOODS • 1917 • White Jack, Howe J. A. • SHT • USA

DAMAGES • 1972 • Dolan Marianne • SHT • USA

DAMAGES FOR BREACH • 1919 • Bocchi Arrigo • UKN

DAMAGES IN FULL • 1913 • *Imp* • USA

DAMALS • 1943 • Hansen Rolf • FRG

DAMALS IN PARIS • 1956 • Balhaus Carl • GDR

DAMASCAN SKY, THE • 1932 • SYR

DAMBANA NG KAGITINGAN • 1968 • Gallardo Cesar Chat • PHL • ALTAR OF THE BRAVE

DAME A LA LONGUE-VUE, LA • 1962 • Korber Serge • SHT • FRN

DAME AU RUBAN DE VELOURS, LA • 1923 • Guarino Joseph • FRN

DAME AUS BERLIN, DIE • 1925 • von Kabdebo Lorand • FRG

DAME AUS LISSABON, DIE see **GROSSE UNBEKANNTE 2, DIE** • 1923

DAME AUX CAMELIAS, LA • 1908 • Mercanton Louis • FRN

DAME AUX CAMELIAS, LA • 1910 • Calmettes Andre • FRN • CAMILLE

DAME AUX CAMELIAS, LA • 1912 • Pouctal Henri • FRN

DAME AUX CAMELIAS, LA • 1915 • De Liguoro Giuseppe • ITL

DAME AUX CAMELIAS, LA • 1934 • Rivers Fernand, Gance Abel • FRN

DAME AUX CAMELIAS, LA • 1953 • Bernard Raymond • FRN, ITL • SIGNORA DALLE CAMELIE, LA (ITL)

DAME AUX CAMELIAS, LA • 1981 • Bolognini Mauro • FRN, ITL, FRG • VERA STORIA DELLA SIGNORE DALLE CAMELIE, LA (ITL) ○ LADY OF THE CAMELIAS, THE ○ TRUE STORY OF CAMILLE, THE ○ SIGNORA DALLE CAMILIE, LA ○ KAMELIEN DAME, DIE

DAME AUX CAMELIAS, LA VRAIE, LA • 1942 • Gelinas Gratien • SHT • CND

DAME BLONDE, LA • 1917 • Roussell Henry • FRN

DAME CARE • 1928 • Land Robert • FRG

DAME CHANCE • 1926 • Bracken Bertram • USA

DAME DANS L'AUTO AVEC DES LUNETTES ET UN FUSIL, LA • 1970 • Litvak Anatole • FRN, UKN • LADY IN THE CAR WITH GLASSES AND A GUN, THE (UKN)

DAME DE CHEZ MAXIM, LA see **DAME DE CHEZ MAXIM'S, LA** • 1932

DAME DE CHEZ MAXIM'S, LA • 1912 • Chautard Emile • FRN

DAME DE CHEZ MAXIM'S, LA • 1923 • Palermi Amleto • ITL

DAME DE CHEZ MAXIM'S, LA • 1932 • Korda Alexander • FRN • DAME DE CHEZ MAXIM, LA

DAME DE CHEZ MAXIM'S, LA • 1950 • Aboulker Marcel • FRN

DAME DE COEUR, LA see **ENTRAINEUSE, L'** • 1938

DAME DE HAUT-LE-BOIS, LA • 1946 • Daroy Jacques • FRN

DAME DE MALACCA, LA • 1937 • Allegret Marc • FRN

DAME DE MONTE CARLO, LA see **INCONNUE DE MONTE CARLO, L'** • 1938

DAME DE MONTSOREAU, LA • 1912 • Chautard Emile • FRN

DAME DE MONTSOREAU, LA • 1913 • Tourneur Maurice • FRN

DAME DE MONTSOREAU, LA • 1923 • Le Somptier Rene • FRN

DAME DE PIQUE, LA • 1965 • Keigel Leonard • FRN • QUEEN OF SPADES, THE

DAME DE PIQUE, LA • 1986 • Plattner Patricia • SHT • SWT

DAME DE PIQUE, LA see **PIQUE DAME** • 1937

DAME DE VITTEL, LA • 1936 • Goupillieres Roger • FRN

DAME D'EMBARA, LA • 1974 • Rouch Jean • FRN

DAME, DER TEUFEL UND DIE PROBIERMAMSELL, DIE • 1918 • Biebrach Rudolf • FRG • LADY, THE DEVIL AND THE FASHION MODEL, THE

DAME D'ONZE HEURES, LA • 1947 • Devaivre Jean • FRN

DAME DU CHATEAU, LA see **SAIYIDAT AL-QASR** • 1958

DAME E I CAVALIERI, LE see **MAZURKA DI PAPA, LA** • 1938

DAME EN BLANC, LA • 1969 • Ledoux Patrick • BLG

DAME EN COLEURS, LA • 1984 • Jutra Claude • CND • WOMAN OF COLOURS, A ○ OUR LADY OF THE PAINTS

DAME FANTOME, LA • 1904 • Melies Georges • FRN • SHADOW LADY, THE (USA) ○ PHANTOM LADY, THE
DAME IM GLASHAUS, DIE • 1915 • Zangenberg Einar • FRG
DAME IM GLASHAUS, DIE • 1922 • Janson Victor • FRG
DAME IN GRAU, DIE • 1922 • Stein Josef • FRG
DAME IN SCHWARZ, DIE • 1920 • Janson Victor • FRG
DAME IN SCHWARZ, DIE • 1928 • Osten Franz • FRG
DAME IN SCHWARZ, DIE • 1951 • *Hartmann Paul* • FRG
DAME MASQUEE, LA • 1924 • Tourjansky Victor • FRN
DAME MIT DEM DIADEM, DIE • 1918 • Schubert Georg • FRG
DAME MIT DEM SCHWARZEN HANDSCHUH, DIE • 1919 • Curtiz Michael • AUS • LADY WITH THE BLACK GLOVE, THE
DAME MIT DEM TIGERFELL, DIE • 1927 • Wolff Willi • FRG
DAME MIT DEN SMARAGDEN, DIE • 1919 • Zelnik Friedrich • FRG
DAME MIT DEN SONNENBLUMEN, DIE • 1920 • Curtiz Michael • FRG
DAME MIT DER MASKE, DIE • 1928 • Thiele Wilhelm • FRG • LADY WITH THE MASK, THE
DAME NATURE • Lavoie Hermenegilde • DCS • CND
DAME OF SARK, THE • 1976 • Rakoff Alvin • MTV • UKN
DAME UN POCO DE AMOOOOR...! • 1968 • Forque Jose Maria • SPN • GIVE ME A BIT OF LOOOVE!
DAME UND DER LANDSTREICHER, DIE • 1921 • Halm Alfred • FRG
DAME UND IHR CHAUFFEUR, DIE • 1928 • Noa Manfred • FRG • LADY AND THE CHAUFFEUR, THE
DAME UND IHR FRISEUR, DIE • 1922 • Ullstein Heinz • FRG
DAME VRAIMENT BIEN, UNE • 1908 • Feuillade Louis • FRN • TRULY GOOD LADY, A
DAMEN I SVART • 1958 • Mattsson Arne • SWD • LADY IN BLACK, THE
DAMEN MED DE LYSER HANDSKER • 1942 • Christensen Benjamin • DNM • LADY WITH THE LIGHT GLOVES, THE (USA) ○ LADY WITH THE COLOURED GLOVES, THE
DAMEN MED KAMELIORNA • 1925 • Molander Olof • SWD • LADY OF THE CAMELIAS, THE
DAMENWAHL • 1953 • Emo E. W. • FRG
DAMERNES BLAD • 1911 • Blom August • DNM • LADIES' JOURNAL, THE
DAMERNES VEN • 1969 • Meineche Annelise • DNM
DAMES • 1934 • Enright Ray • USA
DAMES AHOY! • 1930 • Craft William James • USA • PARADISE AHOY
DAMES AND DENTISTS • 1920 • Smith Noel • SHT • USA
DAMES AND DYNAMITE see **FLIRTING WITH DANGER** • 1934
DAMES DU BOIS DE BOULOGNE, LES • 1945 • Bresson Robert • FRN • LADIES OF THE BOIS DE BOULOGNE, THE ○ LADIES OF THE PARK (USA)
DAMES GALANTES, LES • 1990 • Tacchella Jean-Charles • FRN
DAMGA • 1947 • Akat Lutfu • TRK
DAMI, WA DUMUI WA-BTISAMATI • 1973 • Kamal Hussein • EGY • MON SANG, MES LARMES ET MON SOURIRE
DAMIANA Y LOS HOMBRES • 1966 • Bracho Julio • MXC
DAMIEN • 1977 • Murray Don • USA
DAMIEN -OMEN II • 1978 • Taylor Don • USA • OMEN II
DAMIEN: THE LEPER PRIEST see **FATHER DAMIEN: THE LEPER PRIEST** • 1980
DAMIGELLA DI BARD, LA • 1936 • Mattoli Mario • ITL
D'AMI'UM, AD- • 1972 • Jamil Mohammed Shoukry • EGY • ASSOIFFES, LES
DAMM, DER • 1964 • Kristl Vlado • FRG
DAMMERNDE NACHTE • 1920 • Walther-Fein Rudolf • FRG
DAMN CITIZEN! • 1958 • Gordon Robert • USA
DAMN REAL see **HOT-REAL** • 1988
DAMN THE DEFIANT! (USA) see **H.M.S. DEFIANT** • 1962
DAMN YANKEES • 1958 • Abbott George, Donen Stanley • USA • WHAT LOLA WANTS (UKN)
DAMNATION • 1970 • Benvenuti Lamberto • ITL
DAMNATION • 1988 • Tarr Bela • HNG
DAMNATION! see **JAHANAM** • 1971
DAMNATION ALLEY • 1977 • Smight Jack • USA • SURVIVAL RUN
DAMNATION DE FAUST • 1898 • Melies Georges • FRN • DAMNATION OF FAUST (USA)
DAMNATION DE FAUST, LA see **FAUST AUX ENFERS** • 1903
DAMNATION DU DOCTEUR FAUST • 1904 • Melies Georges • FRN • FAUST AND MARGUERITE (USA) ○ FAUST ET MARGUERITE ○ FAUST
DAMNATION OF FAUST, THE (USA) see **FAUST AUX ENFERS** • 1903
DAMNATION OF FAUST (USA) see **DAMNATION DE FAUST** • 1898
DAMNED, THE • 1962 • Losey Joseph • UKN • THESE ARE THE DAMNED (USA) ○ ON THE BRINK
DAMNED, THE • 1979 • Yassin Ahmed • EGY
DAMNED, THE see **TWILIGHT FOR THE GODS** • 1958
DAMNED, THE see **KE I PENTE ISAN KOLASMENES** • 1968
DAMNED, THE (UKN) see **CADUTA DEGLI DEI, LA** • 1968
DAMNED, THE (USA) see **MAUDITS, LES** • 1946
DAMNED DON'T CRY, THE • 1950 • Sherman Vincent • USA • VICTIM, THE
DAMNED FINN see **SAATANAN SUOMALAINEN** • 1973
DAMNED HOLIDAY see **PROKLETI PRAZNIK** • 1958
DAMNED IN VENICE see **NERO VENEZIANO** • 1978
DAMNED LOVERS see **AMANTS MAUDITS, LES** • 1951
DAMNED MILLIONS see **PROKLIATIYE MILLIONI** • 1917
DAMNED RADICALS see **SAAT EL TAHRIR DAKKAT BARRA YA ISTI'MAR** • 1974
DAMNED RIVER • 1989 • Schroeder Michael • USA
DAMNED ROADS see **BAZA LUDZI UMARLYCH** • 1958
DAMNED SOIL see **PRZEKLETA ZIEMIA** • 1983
DAMNED SOULS see **OSSUDENI DUSHI** • 1975
DAMNING, THE see **DEATH MASK** • 1987
DAMO FANG • 1989 • Wu Ziniu • CHN • BIG MILL, THE
DAMON • Sturlis Edward • ANM • PLN
DAMON AND PYTHIAS • 1908 • Turner Otis • USA
DAMON AND PYTHIAS • 1914 • Turner Otis • USA
DAMON AND PYTHIAS (USA) see **TIRANNO DI SIRACUSA, IL** • 1962
DAMON BLUT • 1920 • Sauer Fred • FRG
DAMON DER FRAUEN, DER see **RASPUTIN, DAMON DER FRAUEN** • 1930
DAMON DER WELT 1 • 1919 • Del Zopp Rudolf • FRG • SCHICKSAL DES EDGAR MORTON
DAMON DER WELT 2 • 1919 • Dessauer Siegfried • FRG • WIRBEL DES VERDERBENS
DAMON DER WELT 3 • 1919 • Del Zopp Rudolf • FRG • GOLDENE GIFT, DAS
DAMON DES "GRAND HOTEL MAJESTIC", DER • 1920 • Forest Karl • AUS • SCHACH DEM LEBEN
DAMON DES HIMALAYA, DER • 1935 • Dyrenfurth Oskar • FRG, SWT
DAMON DES MEERES • 1931 • Curtiz Michael, Bacon Lloyd, Dieterle William • FRG, USA • MOBY DICK
DAMON GELD see **ERSTE STAND, DER GROSSKAPITALIST, DER** • 1925
DAMON IM FRACK • 1923 • *Kuhnast Film* • FRG
DAMON THE MOWER • 1973 • Dunning George • ANS • UKN
DAMON UND MENSCH • 1915 • Oswald Richard • FRG • DEMON AND MAN
DAMON VON KOLNO, DER • 1920 • Henning Hanna • FRG
DAMON ZIRKUS • 1923 • Justitz Emil • FRG • TODESSEIL DER BLANDIN-TRUPPE, DAS
DAMONE E PITIAS see **TIRANNO DI SIRACUSA, IL** • 1962
DAMONEN DER TIEFE • 1912 • Piel Harry • FRG
DAMONISCHE LIEBE • 1951 • Meisel Kurt • FRG
DAMONISCHE TREUE • 1921 • Del Zopp Rudolf • FRG
DAMONISCHE TREUE • 1925 • Del Zopp Rudolf • FRG
D'AMORE SI MUORE • 1972 • Carunchio Carlo • ITL
D'AMOUR ET D'EAU FRAICHE • 1933 • Gandera Felix • FRN • FACON DE SE DONNER, LA ○ PASSAGE CLOUTE
D'AMOUR ET D'EAU FRAICHE • 1975 • Blanc Jean-Pierre • FRN
DAMP DEED, A • 1913 • Plumb Hay • UKN • LOOK BEFORE YOU LEAP
DAMS AND WATERWAYS • 1911 • Dwan Allan • USA
DAMSEL IN DISTRESS, A • 1919 • Archainbaud George • USA
DAMSEL IN DISTRESS, A • 1937 • Stevens George • USA
DAMSELS AND DANDIES • 1919 • Pratt Gilbert • SHT • USA
DAMSELS BE DAMNED • 1987 • Thompson Wendy • SHT • ASL
DAMY • 1954 • Kulidjanov Lev, Segel Yakov • USS • LADIES
DAN • 1914 • *Dockstader Lew* • USA
DAN, AUNT AND LITTLE MISS SODERLUND see **DAN, TANT OCH LILLA FROKEN SODERLUND** • 1924
DAN BACKS A WINNER • 1913 • Kinder Stuart? • UKN
DAN BLAKE'S RIVAL • 1909 • *Centaur* • USA
DAN CANDY'S LAW see **ALIEN THUNDER** • 1973
DAN CETRNAESTI • 1960 • Velimirovic Zdravko • YGS • FOURTEENTH DAY, THE
DAN CUPID, ASSAYER • 1914 • *Valdez Reina* • USA
DAN CUPID, FIXER • 1915 • Davey Horace • USA
DAN CUPID, M.D. • 1918 • *Depp Harry* • USA
DAN DUZI OD GODINE • 1973 • Jankovic Branimir Tori • YGS • DAY LONGER THAN A YEAR, A
DAN FUNG STREET • 1956 • Li Han-Hsiang • HKG
DAN GREEGAN'S GHOST • 1913 • *Ab* • USA
DAN LENO AND HERBERT CAMPBELL EDIT "THE SUN" • 1902 • *Mutoscope & Biograph* • UKN
DAN LENO, MUSICAL DIRECTOR • 1901 • *Warwick Trading Co.* • UKN
DAN LENO'S ATTEMPT TO MASTER THE CYCLE • 1900 • *Warwick Trading Co.* • UKN
DAN LENO'S CRICKET MATCH • 1900 • *Acres Birt* • UKN
DAN LENO'S DAY OUT • 1901 • *Warwick Trading Co.* • UKN
DAN LES GRIFFES DU MANIAQUE (FRN) see **MISS MUERTE** • 1966
DAN MORGAN -NOTORIOUS AUSTRALIAN OUTLAW • 1911 • Rolfe Alfred • ASL
DAN MORGAN'S WAY • 1914 • *Kelsey Fred* • USA
DAN NOLAN'S CROSS • 1912 • Rains Fred • UKN
DAN ODMORA • 1957 • Gluscevic Obrad • YGS • DAY OF PEACE
DAN, TANT OCH LILLA FROKEN SODERLUND • 1924 • Wallen Sigurd • SWD • DAN, AUNT AND LITTLE MISS SODERLUND
DAN, THE ARIZONA SCOUT • 1910 • *Bison* • USA
DAN, THE DANDY • 1911 • Griffith D. W. • USA
DAN, THE LIGHTHOUSE KEEPER • 1911 • *Kalem* • USA
DAN ZA TETOVIRANJE • 1990 • Popov Stole • YGS • DAY FOR TATTOOING, A
DANA • 1968 • Gonzalez Victor M. • VNZ
DANA PRATAP • 1925 • *London Art Photo Co.* • BRM
DANARO DI GIUDA, IL • 1911 • Maggi Luigi • ITL
DANCA DOS BONECOS, A • 1986 • Raton Helvecio • BRZ • DANCE OF THE PUPPETS
DANCA DOS PAROXISMOS, A • 1929 • do Canto Jorge Brum • PRT
DANCAS POPULARES • 1935 • Contreiras Anibal • SHT • PRT
DANCE, THE • 1970 • Rimmer David • CND
DANCE ACADEMY • 1988 • Mather Ted • USA, ITL • SCUOLA DI BALLO (ITL) ○ BODY BEAT
DANCE AT ALECK FONTAINE'S, THE • 1915 • *Travers Richard* • USA
DANCE AT EAGLE PASS, THE • 1913 • *Essanay* • USA
DANCE AT SILVER GULCH, THE • 1912 • *Anderson Broncho Billy* • USA
DANCE AT THE RACES • 1899 • *Warwick Trading Co.* • UKN
DANCE BAND • 1935 • Varnel Marcel • UKN
DANCE BY THE DAISY QUARTETTE • 1898 • *Levi, Jones & Co.* • UKN
DANCE CHARLIE DANCE • 1937 • McDonald Frank • USA
DANCE CHROMATIC • 1959 • Emshwiller Ed • SHT • USA
DANCE CONTEST, THE • 1934 • Fleischer Dave • ANS • USA
DANCE CONTEST IN ESIRA see **DANSTAVLING I ESIRA** • 1937
DANCE CRAZE • 1980 • Massot Joe • DOC • UKN
DANCE DEMONS • 1957 • Cowan Will • SHT • USA
DANCE FEVER • 1984 • Sesani Riccardo • ITL
DANCE FEVER see **TANZER MEINER FRAU, DER** • 1925
DANCE, FOOLS, DANCE • 1930 • Beaumont Harry • USA
DANCE FOR MODERN TIMES • 1988 • Mossanen Moze • DOC • CND
DANCE GIRL DANCE • 1933 • Strayer Frank • USA
DANCE, GIRL, DANCE • 1940 • Arzner Dorothy • USA • HAVE IT YOUR OWN WAY
DANCE GOES ON, THE see **TANZ GEHT WEITER, DER** • 1930
DANCE HALL • 1929 • Brown Melville • USA
DANCE HALL • 1941 • Pichel Irving • USA
DANCE HALL • 1950 • Crichton Charles • UKN
DANCE HALL see **DANSSALONGEN** • 1955
DANCE HALL HOSTESS • 1933 • Eason B. Reeves • USA
DANCE HALL MARGE • 1931 • Sennett Mack • USA
DANCE HALL RACKET • 1953 • Tucker Phil • USA
DANCE IN RAIN see **PLES NA KISI** • 1961
DANCE IN THE RAIN see **PLES NA KISI** • 1961
DANCE IN THE SUN • 1953 • Clarke Shirley • SHT • USA
DANCE LEADER see **WODZIREJ** • 1978
DANCE LITTLE LADY • 1954 • Guest Val • UKN
DANCE MADNESS • 1925 • Leonard Robert Z. • USA
DANCE MAGIC • 1927 • Halperin Victor Hugo • USA
DANCE, MEPHISTO see **OBLONG BOX, THE** • 1969
DANCE MOVIE • 1963 • Warhol Andy • USA • ROLLER SKATE
DANCE MUSIC • 1984 • De Sisti Vittorio • ITL
DANCE MY DOLL see **DANSA MIN DOCKA** • 1953
DANCE MY LOVE see **DANSE MON AMOUR** • 1978
DANCE OF COBRA TO PLAYING OF VEENA see **NACHE NAGIN BAJE BEEN** • 1960
DANCE OF DEATH see **TOTENTANZ** • 1919
DANCE OF DEATH see **PAARUNGEN** • 1967
DANCE OF DEATH see **HOUSE OF EVIL, THE** • 1968
DANCE OF DEATH, THE • 1914 • Vignola Robert G. • USA
DANCE OF DEATH, THE • 1928 • Banfield George J., Eveleigh Leslie • SHT • UKN
DANCE OF DEATH, THE • 1938 • Blake Gerald • UKN • VENGEANCE OF KALI, THE
DANCE OF DEATH, THE • 1969 • Giles David • UKN
DANCE OF DEATH, THE see **DANSE DE MORT, LA** • 1946
DANCE OF DEATH, THE (USA) see **SAINT MENE LA DANSE, LE** • 1960
DANCE OF FIRE see **DANZA DEL FUEGO** • 1949
DANCE OF FIRE, THE • 1909 • *Pathe* • FRN
DANCE OF FIRE, THE see **DANSE DU FEU, LA** • 1899
DANCE OF HOPE • 1989 • Shaffer Beverly • DOC • USA
DANCE OF LIFE, THE • 1929 • Cromwell John, Sutherland A. Edward • USA • BURLESQUE
DANCE OF LIFE, THE • 1951 • Strate Walter • USA
DANCE OF LOVE • Weiner David • SHT • USA
DANCE OF LOVE, THE • 1916 • Weber Lois, Smalley Phillips • SHT • USA
DANCE OF LOVE (UKN) see **REIGEN** • 1974
DANCE OF THE ANGELS • 1962 • Burstall Tim • SHT • ASL
DANCE OF THE BEAR • 1981 • Tritsibidas Yiannis • GRC
DANCE OF THE COLORS (USA) see **TANZ DER FARBEN** • 1938
DANCE OF THE DAMNED • 1988 • Ruben Katt Shea • USA • HALF LIFE
DANCE OF THE DEAD, THE (USA) see **TOTENTANZ, DER** • 1912
DANCE OF THE DWARFS see **JUNGLE HEAT** • 1984
DANCE OF THE GOATS, THE • 1971 • Voulgaris Pantelis • GRC
DANCE OF THE HANDS • 1968 • *Monarch* • SHT • UKN
DANCE OF THE HERON (UKN) see **DANS VAN DE REIGER, DE** • 1966
DANCE OF THE LOONEY SPOONS • 1965 • Vanderbeek Stan • ANS • USA
DANCE OF THE MOTH, THE • 1972 • Dunkers O. • USS
DANCE OF THE PUPPETS see **DANCA DOS BONECOS, A** • 1986
DANCE OF THE SEVEN VEILS • 1970 • Russell Ken • MTV • UKN
DANCE OF THE VAMPIRE • 1914 • Protazanov Yakov • USS
DANCE OF THE VAMPIRES • 1967 • Polanski Roman • UKN • FEARLESS VAMPIRE KILLERS, THE (USA) ○ PARDON ME, YOUR TEETH ARE IN MY NECK
DANCE OF THE WEED • 1941 • Ising Rudolf • ANS • USA
DANCE OF THE WITCHES see **DANCE OF WITCHES** • 1933
DANCE OF WITCHES • 1933 • Milton Robert • UKN • DANCE OF THE WITCHES
DANCE ON THE VOLCANO, THE see **TANZ AUF DEM VULKAN 1, DER** • 1920
DANCE OR DIE • 1923 • Kenton Erle C. • SHT • USA
DANCE OR DIE • 1988 • Munchkin Richard W. • USA
DANCE OVER THE GRAVES see **TANSSI YLI HAUTOJEN** • 1950
DANCE PARTY • 1987 • Rosenthal Mark • USA • IN CROWD, THE
DANCE PRETTY LADY • 1932 • Asquith Anthony • UKN • CARNIVAL
DANCE PROGRAMME, THE see **CARNET DE BAL, UN** • 1937
DANCE SQUARED • 1961 • Jodoin Rene • ANS • CND
DANCE SQUARED see **SQUARE DANCE** • 1944
DANCE TEACHER, THE • 1970 • Sremec Rudolf • DOC • YGS
DANCE TEAM • 1932 • Lanfield Sidney • USA
DANCE TRAINING see **KYOREN NO BUTO** • 1924
DANCE WITH A STRANGER • 1985 • Newell Mike • UKN
DANCE WITH ME, HENRY • 1956 • Barton Charles T. • USA
DANCE WITH THE DEVIL see **JOHNNY APOLLO** • 1940
DANCER, THE • 1913 • Miller Ashley • USA
DANCER, THE • 1914 • *Thanhouser* • USA
DANCER, THE • 1914 • Vignola Robert G. • *Kalem* • USA
DANCER, THE • 1915 • Giblyn Charles • USA
DANCER, THE • 1916 • Le Viness Carl M. • SHT • USA
DANCER, THE see **MAIHIME** • 1951
DANCER AND THE KING, THE • 1908 • Blackton J. Stuart • USA
DANCER AND THE KING, THE • 1914 • Artaud E. • USA
DANCER FROM SONBAT see **GHAZIA MEN SONBAT** • 1967
DANCER IN DARKNESS, THE • 1914 • *Solograph* • UKN
DANCER OF BARCELONA, THE see **BERUHMTE FRAU, DIE** • 1927
DANCER OF IZU see **IZU NO ODORIKO** • 1933
DANCER OF PARIS, THE • 1926 • Santell Alfred • USA
DANCER OF THE NILE, THE • 1923 • Earle William P. S. • USA
DANCERS • 1987 • Ross Herbert • USA • GISELLE
DANCERS, THE • 1925 • Flynn Emmett J. • USA
DANCERS, THE • 1930 • Sprague Chandler • USA
DANCER'S DREAM, THE • 1905 • Martin J. H.? • UKN

DANCER'S DREAM, THE • 1912 • Kinder Stuart • UKN
DANCERS IN SCHOOL • 1971 • Pennebaker D. A., Taylor Kate • DOC • USA
DANCERS IN THE DARK • 1932 • Burton David • USA
DANCERS OF ARAN • 1934 • Davidson J. N. G. • UKN
DANCERS OF TOMORROW see **ASHITA NO ODORIKO** • 1939
DANCER'S PERIL, THE • 1917 • Vale Travers • USA
DANCER'S REDEMPTION, THE • 1913 • Campbell Colin • USA
DANCER'S REVENGE, THE see **DANSERINDENS HAEVN** • 1915
DANCER'S RUSE, THE • 1915 • O'Sullivan Tony • USA
DANCER'S STRANGE DREAM, A see **DANSERINDENS KAERLIGHEDSDROM** • 1915
DANCER'S TOUCH, THE • 1988 • Fraker William A. • TVM • USA • B.L. STRYKER: THE DANCER'S TOUCH
DANCERS WERE ONLY ALLOWED TO DANCE • 1980 • Burton Geoff (c/d) • DOC • ASL
DANCES • 1908 • *Hepworth* • UKN
DANCES AT MY WEDDINGS • 1989 • Malmuth Bruce • USA
DANCES IN JAPAN see **NIHON NO BUYO** • 1959
DANCES IN THE SAND see **DANSEN I SANDET** • 1984
DANCES OF THE AGES • 1913 • Dawley J. Searle • USA
DANCES WITH WOLVES • 1990 • Costner Kevin • USA
DANCIN' FOOL, THE • 1920 • Wood Sam • USA
DANCIN' THROUGH THE DARK • 1989 • Ockrent Mike • UKN
DANCING • 1951 • Morayta Miguel • MXC • SALON DE BAILE
DANCING • 1975 • Mancini Claudio • ITL
DANCING, EL • 1933 • Barth-Moglia Luis • ARG
DANCING AROUND THE TABLE • 1988 • Bulbulian Maurice • DOC • CND
DANCING BEAR, THE • 1937 • *Terry Paul (P)* • ANS • USA
DANCING BEATLE, THE • 1915 • *Carle Richard* • USA • DANCING BEETLE, THE
DANCING BEETLE, THE see **DANCING BEATLE, THE** • 1915
DANCING BOURNONVILLE see **AT DANSE BOURNONVILLE** • 1979
DANCING BULL see **MOU NGAU** • 1989
DANCING CHEAT, THE • 1924 • Cummings Irving • USA
DANCING CLASS • 1964 • Cowan Tom • DOC • ASL
DANCING CO-ED • 1939 • Simon S. Sylvan • USA • EVERY OTHER INCH A LADY (UKN)
DANCING CRAZE • 1914 • Smalley Phillips • USA
DANCING DADDIES • 1932 • Lord Del • SHT • USA
DANCING DADDY • 1926 • Beaudine Harold • USA
DANCING DAUGHTERS see **OUR DANCING DAUGHTERS** • 1928
DANCING DAYS • 1926 • Kelley Albert • USA
DANCING DOLL, THE • 1915 • *Wessell Vivian* • USA
DANCING DOLL, THE • 1922 • Fleischer Dave • ANS • USA • DRESDEN DOLL
DANCING DYNAMITE • 1931 • Smith Noel • USA
DANCING FEET • 1936 • Santley Joseph • USA
DANCING FEET (UKN) see **BROADWAY HOOFER, THE** • 1929
DANCING FIEND, THE • 1908 • *Lubin* • USA
DANCING FLEECE, THE • 1951 • Wilson Frederick • UKN
DANCING FOOL, THE • 1932 • Fleischer Dave • ANS • USA
DANCING FOOL, THE (UKN) see **HAROLD TEEN** • 1934
DANCING GIRL see **MAIHIME** • 1951
DANCING GIRL see **ODORIKO** • 1957
DANCING GIRL, THE • 1908 • Collins Alf? • UKN
DANCING GIRL, THE • 1912 • Collins Edwin J. • UKN
DANCING GIRL, THE • 1914 • *Captain Kettle* • UKN
DANCING GIRL, THE • 1915 • Dwan Allan • USA
DANCING GIRL, THE see **OUR DANCING DAUGHTERS** • 1928
DANCING GIRL OF BUTTE, THE • 1910 • Griffith D. W. • USA
DANCING GIRLS • 1896 • *Paul R. W.* • UKN
DANCING GIRLS • 1967 • de Waal Allan • DNM
DANCING GIRLS (JARDIN DE PARIS) see **DANSEUSES AU JARDIN DE PARIS** • 1897
DANCING GIRLS OF IZU see **IZU NO ODORIKO** • 1933
DANCING GIRLS OF IZU see **IZU NO ODORIKO** • 1954
DANCING GIRLS OF IZU see **IZU NO ODORIKO** • 1960
DANCING GIRLS OF IZU see **IZU NO ODORIKO** • 1963
DANCING GOSHAWK see **TANCZACY JASTRZAB** • 1977
DANCING HANDS see **TANZENDE HANDE** • 1959
DANCING HAWK see **TANCZACY JASTRZAB** • 1977
DANCING HEART, THE (USA) see **TANZENDE HERZ, DAS** • 1953
DANCING IN A HAREM see **DANSE AU SERAIL** • 1897
DANCING IN HITLER'S HEADQUARTERS • 1968 • Batory Jan • PLN
DANCING IN MANHATTAN • 1945 • Levin Henry • USA • TONIGHT WE DANCE
DANCING IN THE DARK • 1949 • Reis Irving • USA
DANCING IN THE DARK • 1986 • Marr Leon G. • CND
DANCING IN THE FOREST • 1988 • Roper Mark • USA
DANCING IN THE RAIN see **PLES NA KISI** • 1961
DANCING LADIES (UKN) see **TEN CENTS A DANCE** • 1945
DANCING LADY • 1933 • Leonard Robert Z. • USA
DANCING LESSON, THE • 1929 • Aylott Dave, Symmons E. F. • SHT • UKN
DANCING MACHINE • 1990 • Behat Gilles • FRN
DANCING MAD (UKN) see **TANZER MEINER FRAU, DER** • 1925
DANCING MAN • 1934 • Ray Albert • USA
DANCING MASTERS, THE • 1943 • St. Clair Malcolm • USA
DANCING MICE see **CLUB SANDWICH** • 1931
DANCING MIDGET, THE (USA) see **DANSEUSE MICROSCOPIQUE, LA** • 1902
DANCING MISTRESS see **KAIDAN IRO-ZANGE-KYOREN ONNA SHISHO** • 1957
DANCING MOTHERS • 1926 • Brenon Herbert • USA
DANCING NIGGERS • 1899 • Norton C. Goodwin • UKN
DANCING ON A DIME • 1941 • Santley Joseph • USA
DANCING ON ROSES see **DANS PA ROSOR** • 1954
DANCING ON THE MOON • 1935 • Fleischer Dave • ANS • USA
DANCING ON THE STARS • 1943 • Dreifuss Arthur • SHT • USA
DANCING PARADISE • 1982 • Avati Pupi • ITL
DANCING PARTNER, THE (UKN) see **JUST A GIGOLO** • 1931
DANCING PIRATE • 1936 • Corrigan Lloyd • USA
DANCING POWDER, THE • 1911 • *Pathe* • FRN
DANCING PRINCESS see **MAIHIME** • 1951
DANCING PRINCESSES, THE • 1978 • Scolfield Jon • MTV • UKN
DANCING PRINCESSES, THE • 1984 • Medak Peter • MTV • USA
DANCING ROMEO • 1944 • Endfield Cy • SHT • USA
DANCING SHOES • 1949 • Davis Mannie • ANS • USA
DANCING SONGS see **BECARAC** • 1966
DANCING SWEETIES • 1930 • Enright Ray • USA • THREE FLIGHTS UP
DANCING TABLOIDS • 1909 • Coleby A. E. • UKN
DANCING THE SIRTAKI (UKN) see **DIPLOPENIES** • 1967
DANCING THRU • 1946 • Gover Victor M. • UKN
DANCING VIENNA see **TANZENDE WIEN, DAS** • 1927
DANCING WITH CRIME • 1947 • Carstairs John Paddy • UKN
DANCING WITH FOLLY • 1916 • Calvert E. H. • SHT • USA
DANCING YEARS, THE • 1950 • French Harold • UKN
DANCING YEARS, THE • 1979 • Bramall Richard • USA
DANDELION see **TAMPOPO** • 1985
DANDIN • 1988 • Planchon Roger • FRN
DANDIN GYORGY • 1955 • Varkonyi Zoltan • HNG • GEORGES DANDIN
DANDY • 1970 • Wilson R. Charleton • USA
DANDY, THE • 1955 • Gavioli Roberto, Gavioli Gino • ANS • ITL
DANDY DICK • 1935 • Beaudine William • UKN
DANDY DICK OF BISHOPSGATE • 1911 • Bouwmeester Theo • UKN
DANDY DONOVAN, THE GENTLEMAN CRACKSMAN • 1914 • Waller Wallett • UKN
DANDY IN ASPIC, A • 1968 • Mann Anthony, Harvey Laurence • UKN, USA
DANDY LION, THE • 1940 • Fleischer Dave • ANS • USA
DANDY OR MR. DAWSON TURNS THE TABLES, THE • 1912 • Humphrey William • USA
DANDY, THE ALL-AMERICAN GIRL • 1977 • Schatzberg Jerry • USA • SWEET REVENGE
DANFOSS-JORDEN RUNDT DOGNET RUNDT • 1959 • Carlsen Henning • SHT • DNM
DANG KOU-TAN • 1969 • Ng See Yuen • HKG • BLOODY FISTS, THE ◦ BLOODY FIST, THE
DANG LENGGANG • 1971 • Kadarisman S. • MLY • WOMAN PATRIOT
DANGAN TAISHO • 1960 • Ieki Miyoji • JPN • BRASS PICKERS, THE
DANGER • 1923 • Elfelt Clifford S. • USA
DANGER see **ORENI SAWARUTO ABUNAINE**
DANGER see **NIEBEZPIECZENSTWO** • 1963
DANGER AHEAD • 1917 • *Bison* • SHT • USA
DANGER AHEAD • 1918 • *Gibson Helen* • SHT • USA
DANGER AHEAD • 1921 • Sturgeon Rollin S. • USA
DANGER AHEAD • 1923 • Howard William K. • USA
DANGER AHEAD • 1935 • Herman Al • USA
DANGER AHEAD • 1940 • Staub Ralph • USA
DANGER AREA • 1943 • Cass Henry • DCS • UKN
DANGER BY MY SIDE • 1962 • Saunders Charles • UKN • DANGER ON MY SIDE (USA)
DANGER CLAIM, THE • 1930 • Nelson Jack • SHT • USA
DANGER DE MORT • 1947 • Grangier Gilles • FRN
DANGER DE MORT see **CLANDESTINS, LES** • 1945
DANGER DE MORT see **MYSTERIEUX MONSIEUR SYLVAIN, LE** • 1946
DANGER: DIABOLIK see **DIABOLIK** • 1967
DANGER DOWN UNDER • 1988 • Mayberry Russ • TVM • USA, ASL • HARRIS DOWN UNDER
DANGER DU MORT • 1958-59 • Breer Robert, Fano Michel • USA
DANGER FLIGHT • 1939 • Bretherton Howard • USA • SCOUTS OF THE AIR
DANGER FORWARD see **OPERATION SECRET** • 1952
DANGER GAME, THE • 1918 • Pollard Harry • USA
DANGER GIRL, THE • 1916 • Badger Clarence • SHT • USA • LOVE ON SKATES (UKN)
DANGER GIRL, THE • 1926 • Dillon Eddie • USA
DANGER, GO SLOW • 1918 • Leonard Robert Z. • USA
DANGER GROWS WILD see **POPPY IS ALSO A FLOWER, THE** • 1966
DANGER IN PARIS (USA) see **CAFE COLETTE** • 1937
DANGER IN THE MIDDLE EAST (USA) see **BAL DES ESPIONS, LE** • 1960
DANGER IN THE PACIFIC • 1942 • Collins Lewis D. • USA
DANGER IN THE SKIES see **PILOT, THE** • 1979
DANGER IS A WOMAN see **QUAI DE GRENELLE** • 1950
DANGER ISLAND • 1931 • Taylor Ray • SRL • USA
DANGER ISLAND see **MR. MOTO IN DANGER ISLAND** • 1939
DANGER LIGHTS • 1930 • Seitz George B. • USA • RECORD RUN, THE
DANGER LINE, THE • 1910 • *Essanay* • USA
DANGER LINE, THE • 1914 • McRae Henry • USA
DANGER LINE, THE • 1915 • Myers Harry • USA
DANGER LINE, THE • 1916 • Ashley Charles E. • SHT • USA
DANGER LINE, THE • 1924 • Violet Edouard-Emile • USA • BATTLE, THE
DANGER LIST • 1957 • Arliss Leslie • UKN
DANGER -LOVE AT WORK • 1937 • Preminger Otto • USA
DANGER MAN, THE • 1930 • Pollard Bud • USA
DANGER MARK, THE • 1918 • Ford Hugh • USA
DANGER MEN • 1983 • Caulfield Michael • DOC • ASL
DANGER OF BEING LONESOME, THE • 1915 • *Washburn Bryant* • USA
DANGER ON MY SIDE (USA) see **DANGER BY MY SIDE** • 1962
DANGER ON OUR DOORSTEP see **CASTRO, CUBA AND COMMUNISM** • 1962
DANGER ON THE AIR • 1938 • Garrett Otis • USA
DANGER ON THE DANUBE (UKN) see **NEGYEN AZ ARBAN** • 1961
DANGER ON THE RIVER see **MISSISSIPPI GAMBLER** • 1942
DANGER ON WHEELS • 1940 • Cabanne W. Christy • USA
DANGER PATH, THE see **NARROW PATH, THE** • 1916
DANGER PATROL • 1919 • *Lowell John* • SHT • USA
DANGER PATROL • 1928 • Worne Duke • USA
DANGER PATROL • 1937 • Landers Lew • USA • HIGHWAY TO HELL
DANGER PAYS see **YABAIKITO NARA ZENI NI NARU** • 1962
DANGER POINT, THE • 1922 • Ingraham Lloyd • USA
DANGER POUR LA SOCIETE • 1969 • Martimbeau Jean • CND
DANGER QUEST • 1926 • Brown Harry J. • USA
DANGER RIDER, THE • 1925 • McRae Henry • USA
DANGER RIDES THE RANGE (UKN) see **THREE TEXAS STEERS** • 1939
DANGER ROUTE • 1967 • Holt Seth • UKN • ELIMINATOR, THE
DANGER SIGNAL • 1945 • Florey Robert • USA
DANGER SIGNAL, THE • 1915 • *Hoops Arthur* • USA
DANGER SIGNAL, THE • 1925 • Kenton Erle C. • USA
DANGER SIGNALS • 1917 • *Pioneer Films* • USA
DANGER STALKS NEAR see **FUZEN NO TOMOSHIBI** • 1957
DANGER STREET • 1928 • Ince Ralph • USA
DANGER STREET • 1947 • Landers Lew • USA
DANGER TOMORROW • 1960 • Bishop Terry • UKN
DANGER TRAIL • 1928 • Smith Noel • USA
DANGER TRAIL, THE • 1917 • Thompson Frederick A. • USA
DANGER TRAILS • 1935 • Hill Robert F. • USA
DANGER VALLEY • 1921 • *Hart Neal* • USA
DANGER VALLEY • 1937 • Bradbury Robert North • USA
DANGER VIENT DE L'ESPACE, LE see **MORTE VIENE DALLO SPAZIO, LA** • 1958
DANGER WITHIN • 1918 • Berger Rea • USA
DANGER WITHIN • 1959 • Chaffey Don • UKN • BREAKOUT (USA)
DANGER WOMAN • 1946 • Collins Lewis D. • USA • CLAUDE'S WIFE
DANGER! WOMEN AT WORK • 1943 • Newfield Sam • USA
DANGER ZONE • 1925 • Bradbury Robert North • USA
DANGER ZONE • 1951 • Berke William • USA
DANGER ZONE 2: REAPER'S REVENGE • 1988 • Bowers Geoffrey G. • USA
DANGER ZONE, THE • 1918 • Beal Frank • USA
DANGER ZONE, THE • 1986 • Vernon Henry • USA
DANGER ZONE, THE (UKN) see **FAIR PLAY** • 1925
DANGEROUS • 1935 • Green Alfred E. • USA • HARD LUCK DAME
DANGEROUS ACQUAINTANCE • 1941 • Shepherd Horace • UKN
DANGEROUS ADVENTURE see **GAME OF DEATH, A** • 1946
DANGEROUS ADVENTURE, A • 1922 • Warner Sam, Warner Jack L. • SRL • USA
DANGEROUS ADVENTURE, A • 1922 • Warner Sam, Warner Jack L. • USA
DANGEROUS ADVENTURE, A • 1937 • Lederman D. Ross • USA
DANGEROUS ADVENTURE, THE (USA) see **AVENTURA PELIGROSA, UNA** • 1940
DANGEROUS AFFAIR, A • 1919 • Miller Charles • USA
DANGEROUS AFFAIR, A • 1931 • Sedgwick Edward • USA
DANGEROUS AFFECTION • 1987 • Elikann Larry • TVM • USA
DANGEROUS AFTERNOON • 1961 • Saunders Charles • UKN
DANGEROUS AGE see **ZOKU JUDAI NO SEITEN** • 1953
DANGEROUS AGE, A • 1957 • Furie Sidney J. • CND
DANGEROUS AGE, A (UKN) see **BELOVED BRAT, THE** • 1938
DANGEROUS AGE, THE • 1922 • Stahl John M. • USA
DANGEROUS AGE (UKN) see **WILD BOYS OF THE ROAD** • 1933
DANGEROUS AGENT (USA) see **CET HOMME EST DANGEREUX** • 1953
DANGEROUS ASSIGNMENT • 1950 • Hart Ben R. • UKN • LONDON ASSIGNMENT
DANGEROUS BLONDE, THE • 1924 • Hill Robert F. • USA
DANGEROUS BLONDES • 1943 • Jason Leigh • USA
DANGEROUS BRUNETTE see **MAN WANTED** • 1932
DANGEROUS BUSINESS • 1920 • Neill R. William • USA
DANGEROUS BUSINESS • 1946 • Lederman D. Ross • USA
DANGEROUS BUSINESS see **PARTY GIRL** • 1930
DANGEROUS BUT PASSABLE see **MOON OVER HER SHOULDER** • 1941
DANGEROUS CARGO • 1954 • Harlow John • UKN
DANGEROUS CARGO • 1975 • Sagal Boris • USA
DANGEROUS CARGO (UKN) see **FORBIDDEN CARGO** • 1925
DANGEROUS CARGO (UKN) see **HELL'S CARGO** • 1939
DANGEROUS CASE, A • 1914 • *Lubin* • USA
DANGEROUS CHARTER • 1962 • Gottschalk Robert • USA
DANGEROUS COMMENT • 1940 • Carstairs John Paddy • UKN
DANGEROUS COMPANIONS • 1934 • Macklin A. N. C. • UKN
DANGEROUS COMPANY • 1982 • Johnson Lamont • TVM • USA
DANGEROUS CORNER • 1934 • Rosen Phil • USA
DANGEROUS COWARD • 1924 • Rogell Albert S. • USA • SPORTING BLOOD, THE
DANGEROUS CROSSING • 1953 • Newman Joseph M. • USA
DANGEROUS CROSSROADS • 1933 • Hillyer Lambert • USA
DANGEROUS CURB • 1983 • Nicolaescu Sergiu • RMN
DANGEROUS CURRENTS see **WHY WOMEN LOVE** • 1925
DANGEROUS CURVE AHEAD • 1921 • Hopper E. Mason • USA • MR. AND MISERABLE JONES
DANGEROUS CURVES • 1929 • Mendes Lothar • USA
DANGEROUS CURVES • 1988 • Lewis David* • USA
DANGEROUS CURVES • 1988 • Sugerman Andrew • USA • TAN LINES
DANGEROUS CURVES see **FARLIG KURVA** • 1952
DANGEROUS CURVES BEHIND • 1925 • Cline Eddie • SHT • USA
DANGEROUS DAN MCFOO • 1939 • Avery Tex • ANS • USA
DANGEROUS DAVIES -THE LAST DETECTIVE • 1979 • Guest Val • TVM • UKN
DANGEROUS DAYS • 1920 • Barker Reginald • USA
DANGEROUS DAYS see **WILD BOYS OF THE ROAD** • 1933
DANGEROUS DAYS OF KIOWA JONES, THE • 1966 • March Alex • MTV • USA
DANGEROUS DAZE • 1931 • Nye William • SHT • USA
DANGEROUS DOUBLE, A • 1917 • Hill Robert F. • SHT • USA
DANGEROUS DUB, THE • 1926 • Thorpe Richard • USA
DANGEROUS DUDE, THE • 1926 • Brown Harry J. • USA
DANGEROUS ENCOUNTERS OF THE FIRST KIND see **DIYI LEI YING WEIXIAN** • 1980
DANGEROUS ENEMY (UKN) see **FIGHTING ROOKIE, THE** • 1934
DANGEROUS EXILE • 1957 • Hurst Brian Desmond • UKN
DANGEROUS EXPERIMENT, A • 1913 • Byrne Jack • USA
DANGEROUS EXPERIMENT, A • 1914 • *Wells William* • USA
DANGEROUS EYES • 1920 • Blystone John G. • SHT • USA
DANGEROUS FEMALE see **MALTESE FALCON, THE** • 1931

DANGEROUS FEMALES • 1929 • Watson William • USA
DANGEROUS FINGERS • 1937 • Lee Norman • UKN • WANTED BY SCOTLAND YARD (USA)
DANGEROUS FISTS • 1925 • *Perrin Jack* • USA
DANGEROUS FLIRT, THE • 1924 • Browning Tod • USA • DANGEROUS FLIRTATION, A (UKN) ○ PRUDE, THE
DANGEROUS FLIRTATION, A (UKN) see **DANGEROUS FLIRT, THE** • 1924
DANGEROUS FOE, A • 1913 • Henderson Dell • USA
DANGEROUS FREEDOM see **FARLIG FRIHET** • 1955
DANGEROUS FRIEND, A see **TODD KILLINGS, THE** • 1971
DANGEROUS FRIENDS • 1926 • Fox Finis • USA
DANGEROUS GAME • 1988 • Hopkins Steve • ASL
DANGEROUS GAME • 1990 • Osterfelt Preben • DNM
DANGEROUS GAME see **FARLIGA LEKEN, DEN** • 1930
DANGEROUS GAME, A • 1922 • Baggot King • USA
DANGEROUS GAME, A • 1941 • Rawlins John • USA • WHO KILLED DOC ROBIN?
DANGEROUS GAMES see **EPIKINDIN PECHNIDIA** • 1981
DANGEROUS GAMES (USA) see **JEUX DANGEREUX** • 1958
DANGEROUS GOLFERS • 1905 • Stow Percy • UKN
DANGEROUS GROUND • 1934 • Walker Norman • UKN
DANGEROUS GROUND (UKN) see **ESCAPADE** • 1932
DANGEROUS HOLIDAY • 1937 • Barrows Nicholas • USA
DANGEROUS HOUR • 1923 • Hughes William • USA
DANGEROUS HOURS • 1920 • Niblo Fred • USA
DANGEROUS HOUSES • 1952 • Harrington Curtis • SHT • USA
DANGEROUS INHERITANCE (UKN) see **GIRLS' SCHOOL** • 1950
DANGEROUS INNOCENCE • 1925 • Seiter William A. • USA
DANGEROUS INTRIGUE • 1936 • Selman David • USA
DANGEROUS INTRUDER • 1945 • Keays Vernon • USA
DANGEROUS ISLAND see **ISLAND OF THE LOST** • 1967
DANGEROUS JOURNEY • 1944 • McCarey Ray • USA
DANGEROUS JOURNEY, THE • 1944 • Roosevelt Leila, Denis Armand • DOC • USA
DANGEROUS KISS, THE • 1960 • Kawashima Yuzo • JPN
DANGEROUS KISSES see **FARLIGE KYS** • 1972
DANGEROUS LADY • 1941 • Ray Bernard B. • USA
DANGEROUS LESSON, A • 1912 • *Mccoy Gertrude* • USA
DANGEROUS LIAISONS • 1988 • Frears Stephen • UKN, USA • LIAISONS DANGEREUSES, LES
DANGEROUS LIES • 1921 • Powell Paul • USA, UKN
DANGEROUS LIFE OF A FISHERMAN, THE • 1907 • *Lund Alma* • NRW
DANGEROUS LITTLE DEMON, THE • 1922 • Badger Clarence • USA
DANGEROUS LITTLE DEVIL, THE • 1919 • *Guinan Texas* • SHT • USA
DANGEROUS LOVE • 1989 • Ollstein Marty • USA • SINGLES
DANGEROUS LOVE, A see **BLACK MARKET BABY** • 1977
DANGEROUS LOVE AFFAIRS see **LIAISONS DANGEREUSES, LES** • 1959
DANGEROUS LUNATIC, THE (USA) see **FOU ASSASSIN, LE** • 1900
DANGEROUS MAID, THE • 1923 • Heerman Victor • USA
DANGEROUS MAN, A (USA) see **HOMBRE PELIGROSO, UN** • 1935
DANGEROUS MEDICINE • 1938 • Woods Arthur • UKN
DANGEROUS MILLIONS • 1946 • Tinling James • USA • HOUSE OF TAO LING, THE (UKN)
DANGEROUS MISSION • 1954 • King Louis • USA
DANGEROUS MISSION (UKN) see **TRIGGER TOM** • 1935
DANGEROUS MISTS (UKN) see **U-BOAT PRISONER** • 1944
DANGEROUS MODEL, A • 1912 • *Majestic* • USA
DANGEROUS MOMENT, THE • 1921 • De Sano Marcel • USA • DANGEROUS MOMENTS
DANGEROUS MOMENTS see **DANGEROUS MOMENT, THE** • 1921
DANGEROUS MONEY • 1924 • Tuttle Frank • USA
DANGEROUS MONEY • 1946 • Morse Terry O. • USA
DANGEROUS MOONLIGHT • 1941 • Hurst Brian Desmond • UKN • SUICIDE SQUADRON (USA)
DANGEROUS MOVES (USA) see **DIAGONALE DU FOU, LA** • 1984
DANGEROUS NAN MCGREW • 1919 • Sidney Scott • USA
DANGEROUS NAN MCGREW • 1930 • St. Clair Malcolm • USA
DANGEROUS NUMBER • 1936 • Thorpe Richard • USA
DANGEROUS ODDS • 1925 • *Cody Bill* • USA
DANGEROUS ORPHANS • 1985 • Laing John • NZL
DANGEROUS PAIR, A • 1909 • *Edison* • USA
DANGEROUS PARADISE • 1930 • Wellman William A. • USA • FLESH OF EVE
DANGEROUS PARADISE, THE • 1920 • Earle William P. S. • USA
DANGEROUS PARTNERS • 1945 • Cahn Edward L. • USA
DANGEROUS PASS (MONT BLANC), A see **PASSAGE DANGEREUX AU MONT-BLANC** • 1897
DANGEROUS PASSAGE • 1944 • Berke William • USA
DANGEROUS PASTIME • 1922 • Horne James W. • USA
DANGEROUS PATHS • 1921 • Worne Duke • USA
DANGEROUS PLEASURE • 1925 • Revier Harry • USA
DANGEROUS PROFESSION, A • 1949 • Tetzlaff Ted • USA • BAIL BOND STORY, THE
DANGEROUS PROMISE see **FARLIGT LOFTE** • 1955
DANGEROUS ROADS see **FARLIGA VAGAR** • 1942
DANGEROUS SEAS • 1931 • Dryhurst Edward • UKN
DANGEROUS SPRING see **FARLIG VAR** • 1948
DANGEROUS SUMMER • 1980 • Trenchard-Smith Brian • DOC • ASL • BUSHFIRE
DANGEROUS SUMMER • 1982 • Masters Quentin • ASL • BURNING MAN, THE
DANGEROUS SUMMER see **FARLIG SOMMER** • 1969
DANGEROUS SYMPATHY • 1913 • *Ramo* • USA
DANGEROUS TALENT, THE • 1920 • Cox George L. • USA
DANGEROUS TO KNOW • 1938 • Florey Robert • USA
DANGEROUS TO MEN • 1920 • Dowlan William C. • USA • ELIZA COMES TO STAY
DANGEROUS TOYS • 1921 • Bradley Samuel R. • USA • DON'T LEAVE YOUR HUSBAND
DANGEROUS TRAFFIC • 1926 • Cohn Bennett • USA
DANGEROUS TRAFFIC • 1979 • McDougall Don • USA • TOKE
DANGEROUS TRAILS • 1923 • Neitz Alvin J. • USA • DRAGON'S PREY, THE
DANGEROUS VENTURE • 1947 • Archainbaud George • USA
DANGEROUS VOYAGE • 1954 • Sewell Vernon • UKN • TERROR SHIP (USA)
DANGEROUS VOYAGE see **KIKEN RYOKO** • 1959
DANGEROUS WAGER, A • 1913 • *Kalem* • USA
DANGEROUS WATERS • 1919 • Franz Joseph J. • USA
DANGEROUS WATERS • 1936 • Hillyer Lambert • USA
DANGEROUS WHEN WET • 1953 • Walters Charles • USA
DANGEROUS WHITENESS • 1974 • Breigutu Bjorn • SHT • NRW
DANGEROUS WOMAN see **BUFERE** • 1953
DANGEROUS WOMAN, A • 1929 • Lee Rowland V. • USA • WOMAN WHO NEEDED KILLING, THE
DANGEROUS YEARS • 1948 • Pierson Arthur • USA
DANGEROUS YOUTH • 1953 • Lauritzen Lau Jr. • DNM
DANGEROUS YOUTH, THE • 1930 • Heath Arch B. • USA
DANGEROUS YOUTH (USA) see **THESE DANGEROUS YEARS** • 1957
DANGEROUSLY BEAUTIFUL see **ZIBAYE KHATARNAK** • 1967
DANGEROUSLY CLOSE • 1986 • Pyun Albert • USA • CHOICE KILL
DANGEROUSLY THEY LIVE • 1942 • Florey Robert • USA • REMEMBER TOMORROW
DANGEROUSLY THEY LIVE see **STEEL AGAINST THE SKY** • 1942
DANGEROUSLY YOURS • 1933 • Tuttle Frank • USA
DANGEROUSLY YOURS • 1937 • St. Clair Malcolm • USA
DANGERS DE L'ALCOOLISME, LES • 1899 • Blache Alice • FRN • DANGERS OF ALCOHOLISM, THE
DANGERS OF A BIG CITY see **STORSTADSFAROR** • 1918
DANGERS OF A BRIDE • 1917 • Kerr Robert, Hartman Ferris • SHT • USA
DANGERS OF ALCOHOLISM, THE see **DANGERS DE L'ALCOOLISME, LES** • 1899
DANGERS OF DORIS, THE • 1916-17 • SER • USA
DANGERS OF HYPNOSIS, THE see **VERLORENE ICH, DAS** • 1923
DANGERS OF THE ARCTIC • 1932 • USA
DANGERS OF THE CANADIAN MOUNTED • 1948 • Brannon Fred C., Canutt Yakima • SRL • USA
DANGERS OF THE VELDT • 1914 • Turner Otis • USA
DANGLING NOOSE, THE • 1913 • Le Saint Edward J. • USA
DANGLING PARTICIPLE • 1971 • Lawder Standish D. • USA
DANI • 1957 • Szemes Mihaly • HNG
DANI • 1963 • Petrovic Aleksandar • YGS • DAYS, THE
DANI • 1965 • Sekigawa Hideo • JPN • FANCY MAN
DANI, MICHI, RENATO UND MAX • 1986 • Dindo Richard • DOC • SWT
DANI OD SNOVA • 1981 • Gilic Vlatko • YGS • DREAM DAYS
DANI SAMRAT see **VAMAN AVATAR** • 1934
DANIE BOSMAN • 1969 • SAF
DANIEL • 1913 • Thompson Frederick A. • USA
DANIEL • 1983 • Lumet Sidney • USA
DANIEL AND NEBUCHADNEZZAR • 1979 • Davis Charles • MTV • USA
DANIEL AND THE DEVIL see **DEVIL AND DANIEL WEBSTER, THE** • 1941
DANIEL AND THE LION'S DEN • 1979 • *Vaughan Robert* • MTV • USA
DANIEL BOONE • 1907 • Porter Edwin S. • USA
DANIEL BOONE • 1936 • Howard David • USA • ADVENTURES OF DANIEL BOONE
DANIEL BOONE see **IN THE DAYS OF DANIEL BOONE** • 1923
DANIEL BOONE, FRONTIER TRAIL RIDER • 1967 • Sherman George • MTV • USA
DANIEL BOONE, JR. • 1960 • Tendlar Dave • ANS • USA
DANIEL BOONE THRU THE WILDERNESS • 1926 • Mattison Frank S.?, Bradbury Robert North? • USA
DANIEL BOONE, TRAIL BLAZER • 1956 • Gannaway Albert C., Rodriguez Ismael • USA
DANIEL BOONE'S BRAVERY • 1911 • *Kalem* • USA
DANIEL DERONDA • 1921 • Rowden W. C. • UKN
DANIEL IN THE LION'S DEN • 1905 • *Pathe* • FRN
DANIEL JAZZ, THE • 1971 • Cominos N. H. • SHT • USA
DANIEL TAKES A TRAIN see **SZERENCSES DANIEL** • 1983
DANIEL UND DER WELTMEISTER • 1963 • Meyer Ingrid • GDR
DANIELE CORTIS • 1947 • Soldati Mario • ITL
DANIELE E MARIA • 1973 • De Concini Ennio • ITL
DANIELLA BY NIGHT (USA) see **ZARTE HAUT IN SCHWARZER SEIDE** • 1961
DANIMARCA INCREDIBILE REALTA see **PRIMO PREMIO SI CHIAMA IRENE, IL** • 1969
DANISH BED AND BOARD (UKN) see **REKTOR PA SENGEKANTEN** • 1972
DANISH & BLUE • 1970 • Crilly Spence • USA
DANISH BLUE (UKN) see **KAERE LEGETOJ, DET** • 1968
DANISH BRIGADE IN SWEDEN see **BRIGADEN I SVERIGE** • 1945
DANISH DENTIST ON THE JOB (UKN) see **TANDLAEGE PA SENGEKANTEN** • 1971
DANISH DESIGN • 1960 • Roos Jorgen • DOC • DNM
DANISH ESCORT GIRLS see **HOPLA PA SENGEKANTEN** • 1976
DANISH ISLAND see **DANSKE SYDHAVSOER, DE** • 1944
DANISH MOTORBOAT STORY • 1953 • Carlsen Henning • SHT • DNM
DANISH PILLOW TALK (USA) see **ROMANTIK PA SENGEKANTEN** • 1973
DANISH VILLAGE CHURCH, THE see **DANSKE LANDSBYKIRKE, DEN** • 1947
DANITES, THE • 1912 • Boggs Frank • USA
DANIYA • 1988 • Mira Carlos • SPN • DANIYA, GARDEN OF THE HAREM
DANIYA, GARDEN OF THE HAREM see **DANIYA** • 1988
DANJO KILL (IF YOU LIVE SHOOT) see **SE SEI VIVO SPARA** • 1967
DANJURO SANDAI • 1944 • Mizoguchi Kenji • JPN • THREE GENERATIONS OF DANJURO (USA) ○ THREE DANJUROS ○ THREE GENERATIONS OF THE DANJURO FAMILY
DANKE ES GEHT MIR GUT see **REIZENDE FAMILIE, EINE** • 1945
DANKO PISTA • 1941 • Kalmar Laszlo • HNG
DANKON • 1969 • Moritani Shiro • JPN • BULLET WOUND
DANMARK DIT OG MIT • 1981 • Vestergaard Jorgen • DOC • DNM • DENMARK YOURS AND MINE
DANMARK ER LUKKET • 1981 • Tschernia Dan • DNM • DENMARK IS CLOSED
DANMARKSFILMEN • 1935 • Henningsen Poul • DOC • DNM
DANMARKSFILMEN see **DER ER ET YNDIGT LAND** • 1940
DANN SCHON LIEBER LEBERTRAN • 1930 • Ophuls Max • FRG
DANNATI DELLA TERRA, I • 1969 • Orsini Valentino • ITL
DANNI • 1983 • Gies Martin • FRG
D'ANNUNZIO • 1987 • Nasca Sergio • ITL
DANNY • 1977 • Feldman Gene • USA
DANNY AND NICKY • 1970 • Jackson Douglas • CND
DANNY AND RAEWYN • 1987 • Nicholas Gregor • SHT • NZL
DANNY ASKS WHY • 1919 • *Imel John F.* • USA
DANNY BOY • 1934 • Mitchell Oswald, Sanderson Challis • UKN
DANNY BOY • 1941 • Mitchell Oswald • UKN
DANNY BOY • 1946 • Morse Terry O. • USA
DANNY BOY (USA) see **ANGEL** • 1983
DANNY, CHAMPION OF THE WORLD • 1989 • Millar Gavin • UKN • DANNY THE CHAMPION OF THE WORLD
DANNY JONES • 1972 • Bricken Jules • UKN • FIRES OF YOUTH
DANNY THE CHAMPION OF THE WORLD see **DANNY, CHAMPION OF THE WORLD** • 1989
DANNY THE DRAGON • 1967 • Pennington-Richards C. M. • SRL • UKN
DANNY THE SUPER SNOOPER see **SUPER FUZZ** • 1981
DANNY TRAVIS • 1981 • Boulting Roy • USA
DANRYU • 1939 • Yoshimura Kozaburo • JPN • WARM CURRENT, A
DANRYU • 1957 • Masumura Yasuzo • JPN • WARM CURRENT, A
DANS ARLES OU SONT LES ALYSCAMPS • 1966 • Clergue Lucien • FRN
DANS LA BOUCHE DE SOPHIE • 1980 • Baudricourt Michel • FRN
DANS LA BROUSSE • 1912 • Feuillade Louis • FRN
DANS LA CHALEUR DES NUITS D'ETE • 1979 • Gotz Siggi • FRN, FRG
DANS LA FOURNAISE • 1913 • Jasset Victorin • FRN
DANS LA GUEULE DU LOUP • 1961 • Dudrumet Jean-Charles • USA
DANS LA POUSSIERE DU SOLEIL • 1971 • Balducci Richard • FRN, ITL, SPN • LUST IN THE SUN (UKN)
DANS LA RAFALE • 1914 • Pouctal Henri • FRN
DANS LA TOURMENTE • 1910 • Bourgeois Gerard • FRN
DANS LA VALLEE D'OSSAU • 1912 • Cohl Emile • ANS • FRN
DANS LA VIE • 1911 • Feuillade Louis • FRN
DANS LA VIE TOUT S'ARRANE • 1949 • Cravenne Marcel • FRN • IDYLLE AU CHATEAU
DANS LA VILLE BLANCHE • 1983 • Tanner Alain • SWT, PRT • IN THE WHITE CITY
DANS LE BOIS I & 2 • 1925-30 • Tessier Albert • DCS • CND
DANS LE VENT • 1963 • Rozier Jacques • SHT • FRN
DANS LE VENTRE DRAGON • 1988 • Simoneau Yves • CND • IN THE BELLY OF THE DRAGON (UKN)
DANS L'EAU QUI FAIT DES BULLES • 1961 • Delbez Maurice • FRN
DANS LES COULISSES • 1897 • Melies Georges • FRN • BEHIND THE SCENES
DANS LES COULISSES • 1900 • Blache Alice • FRN
DANS LES GRIFFES DE L'ARAIGNEE • 1920 • Starevitch Ladislas • ANS • FRN • IN THE SPIDER'S GRIP (USA) ○ CLAWS OF THE SPIDER, THE ○ IN THE CLUTCH OF THE SPIDER
DANS LES RUES D'ALEXANDRIE • 1912 • de Lagarne M. • EGY
DANS LES RUINES DE CARTHAGE • 1910 • Jasset Victorin • FRN
DANS LES TENEBRES • 1923 • Bergerat Theo • FRN
DANS L'OMBRE DU HAREM • 1928 • Mathot Leon • FRN
DANS L'OURAGAN DE LA VIE see **VENUS VICTRIX** • 1917
DANS NOS FORETS • 1971 • Bulbulian Maurice • DOC • CND
DANS PA ROSOR • 1954 • Bauman Schamyl • SWD • DANCING ON ROSES
DANS UN OCEAN DE MIEL see **WA SAQAT'AT FI BAHRIN MIN AL-ASAL** • 1976
DANS UNE ILE PERDUE • 1930 • Cavalcanti Alberto • FRN
DANS UNE NOUVELLE USINE • 1968 • Dansereau Fernand • DCS • CND
DANS VAN DE REIGER, DE • 1966 • Rademakers Fons • NTH, FRG • DANCE OF THE HERON (UKN)
DANS VAN DIE VLAMMINK • 1974 • SAF
DANSA MIN DOCKA • 1953 • Soderhjelm Martin • SWD • DANCE MY DOLL
DANSAN GWAITSUK • 1989 • Chan Norman • HKG • NOBLES, THE
DANSE, LA • 1972 • Floquet Francois • DCS • CND
DANSE AU SERAIL • 1897 • Melies Georges • FRN • DANCING IN A HAREM
DANSE AVEC L'AVEUGLE, LA • 1978 • D'Aix Alain (c/d) • DOC • CND
DANSE BASQUE • 1901 • Blache Alice • FRN
DANSE DE L'IVRESSE • 1900 • Blache Alice • FRN
DANSE DE MORT, LA • 1946 • Cravenne Marcel, von Stroheim Erich (U/c) • FRN, ITL • DANCE OF DEATH, THE
DANSE DES EPEES, LA • 1914 • Protazanov Yakov • USS
DANSE DES SABRES, LA • Lemaire Yvan • SHT • BLG • SABER DANCE, THE
DANSE DES SAISONS, LA • 1900 • Blache Alice • SER • FRN
DANSE DU FEU, LA • 1899 • Melies Georges • FRN • HAGGARD'S SHE -THE PILLAR OF FIRE (USA) ○ COLONNE DE FEU, LA ○ COLUMN OF FIRE, THE ○ DANCE OF FIRE, THE
DANSE DU PAPILLON • 1900 • Blache Alice • FRN
DANSE DU PAS DES FOULARDS PAR DES ALMEES • 1900 • Blache Alice • FRN
DANSE DU VENTRE, LA • 1900-01 • Blache Alice • FRN
DANSE FLEUR DE LOTUS • 1897 • Blache Alice • FRN
DANSE MACABRE • Bevis Donald L. • SHT • USA
DANSE MACABRE • 1922 • *Bolm Adolph (P)* • SHT • USA
DANSE MACABRE • 1932 • Newman Widgey R. • UKN
DANSE MACABRE see **TETTES ISMERETLEN, A** • 1957
DANSE MACABRE see **PAARUNGEN** • 1967
DANSE MACABRE, LA (FRN) see **DANZA MACABRA** • 1964

DANSE MAURESQUE • 1902 • Blache Alice • FRN
DANSE MON AMOUR • 1978 • Beni Alphonse • FRN • DANCE MY LOVE
DANSE SERPENTINE • 1896 • Melies Georges • FRN • SERPENTINE DANCE, A
DANSE SERPENTINE • 1900 • Blache Alice • FRN
DANSE SERPENTINE, THE
DANSE SERPENTINE PAR MME BOB WALTER • 1899-00 • Blache Alice • FRN
DANSEI NO.1 • 1955 • Yamamoto Kajiro • JPN • MAN AMONG MEN, A
DANSEI SHIIKU-HO • 1959 • Toyoda Shiro • JPN • BRINGING UP HUSBANDS
DANSEN I SANDET • 1984 • Bovin Mette • DOC • DNM • DANCES IN THE SAND
DANSEN MED REGITZE • 1989 • Rostrup Kaspar • DNM • WALTZING REGITZE
DANSERINDEN see **BALLETTENS DATTER** • 1913
DANSERINDENS HAEVN • 1915 • Holger-Madsen • DNM • DANCER'S REVENGE, THE ○ CIRCUS ARRIVES
DANSERINDENS KAERLIGHEDSDROM • 1915 • Holger-Madsen • DNM • DANCER'S STRANGE DREAM, A ○ DODSDOMTE, DEN ○ CONDEMNED, THE
DANSES • 1900 • Blache Alice • SER • FRN
DANSES DE TAMI, LES • 1956 • Ichac Marcel • DCS • FRN
DANSES ESPAGNOLES • 1900 • Lumiere Louis • FRN
DANSEUR, LE • 1979 • Tana Paul • CND
DANSEUR: RUDOLPH NUREYEV, UN • 1972 • Jourdan Pierre • FRN, UKN • I AM A DANCER (UKN)
DANSEURS DE LA MER, LES see **DANSEURS DE MER, LES** • 1960
DANSEURS DE MER, LES • 1960 • Painleve Jean • SHT • FRN • DANSEURS DE LA MER, LES
DANSEUSE DE MARRAKECH, LA • 1949 • Mathot Leon • FRN
DANSEUSE MICROSCOPIQUE, LA • 1902 • Melies Georges • FRN • DANCING MIDGET, THE (USA) ○ MARVELLOUS EGG PRODUCING WITH SURPRISING DEVELOPMENTS
DANSEUSE NUE, LA • 1952 • Pierre-Louis • FRN
DANSEUSE ORCHIDEE, LA • 1928 • Perret Leonce • FRN • ORCHID DANCER, THE
DANSEUSE ROUGE, LA • 1937 • Paulin Jean-Paul • FRN • CHEVRE AUX PIEDS D'OR, LA
DANSEUSES AU JARDIN DE PARIS • 1897 • Melies Georges • FRN • DANCING GIRLS (JARDIN DE PARIS)
DANSHUN • 1966 • Nakamura Noboru • JPN • SPRINGTIME
DANSK POLITI I SVERIGE • 1945 • Henning-Jensen Astrid • DOC • DNM
DANSK SEXUALITET see **SEXUAL FREEDOM IN DENMARK** • 1970
DANSKE LANDSBYKIRKE, DEN • 1947 • Dreyer Carl T. • DCS • DNM • DANISH VILLAGE CHURCH, THE ○ LANDSBYKIRKEN
DANSKE SYDHAVSOER, DE • 1944 • Henning-Jensen Bjarne • DNM • DANISH ISLAND
DANSSALONGEN • 1955 • Larsson Borje • SWD • DANCE HALL
DANSTAVLING I ESIRA • 1937 • Fejos Paul • DCS • SWD, DNM • DANCE CONTEST IN ESIRA
DANTE • 1921 • Caramba Luigi • ITL
DANTE DREAMER • 1958 • Sparber I. • ANS • USA
DANTE E BEATRICE • 1912 • Caserini Mario • ITL
DANTE IS NOT ONLY SEVERE see **DANTE NO ES UNICAMENTE SEVERO** • 1967
DANTE NO ES UNICAMENTE SEVERO • 1967 • Esteva Jacinto, Jorda Joaquin • SPN • DANTE IS NOT ONLY SEVERE
DANTE'S INFERNO • 1924 • Otto Henry • USA
DANTE'S INFERNO • 1935 • Lachman Harry • USA
DANTE'S INFERNO • 1967 • Russell Ken • MTV • UKN
DANTE'S INFERNO • 1982 • Marshak Philip • CND
DANTE'S INFERNO (USA) see **INFERNO, L'** • 1909
DANTE'S INFERNO (USA) see **INFERNO, L'** • 1910
DANTES MYSTERIER • 1931 • Merzbach Paul • SWD • DANTE'S MYSTERIES
DANTE'S MYSTERIES see **DANTES MYSTERIER** • 1931
DANTE'S PROGRESS AND EXPERIENCES THROUGH PARADISE • 1912 • *National* • USA
DANTE'S PURGATORIO • 1913 • *Cinema Prod.*
DANTON • 1920 • Buchowetzki Dimitri, Dreier Hans • FRG • ALL FOR A WOMAN (USA) ○ LOVES OF THE MIGHTY
DANTON • 1930 • Behrendt Hans • FRG
DANTON • 1932 • Roubaud Andre • FRN
DANTON • 1982 • Wajda Andrzej • FRN, PLN • AFFAIRE DANTON, L'
DANUBE, THE • 1961 • *Disney Walt (P)* • DOC • USA
DANUBE, THE see **DONAU -VOM SCHWARZWALD BIS ZUM SCHWARZEN MEER, DIE** • 1929
DANUBE BLEU, LE • 1939 • Reinert Emile Edwin, Rode Alfred • FRN
DANUBE – FISHES – BIRDS, THE see **DUNA – HALAK – MADARAK** • 1971
DANUBE PILOT, THE see **DUNAI HAJOS** • 1975
DANUBE WAVES, THE see **VALURILE DUNARII** • 1963
DANULON GYARTAS • 1961 • Meszaros Marta • DCS • HNG • DANULON PRODUCTION
DANULON PRODUCTION see **DANULON GYARTAS** • 1961
DANUN • 1924 • Yamamoto Kajiro • JPN
DANY, BITTE SCHREIBEN SIE! • 1956 • von Borsody Eduard • FRG
DANY LA RAVAGEUSE • 1972 • Rozier Willy • FRN • DANY THE RAVAGER (UKN)
DANY THE RAVAGER (UKN) see **DANY LA RAVAGEUSE** • 1972
DANZA D'AMORE SOTTO GLI OLMI see **PRIMA VOLTA SULL'ERBA, LA** • 1975
DANZA DE LA FORTUNA, LA • 1944 • Torres-Rios Leopoldo • ARG
DANZA DE LA FORTUNA, LA • 1960 • Klimovsky Leon • SPN
DANZA DE LOS DESEOS, LA • 1954 • Rey Florian • SPN
DANZA DEI MILIONI, LA • 1940 • Mastrocinque Camillo • ITL • QUADRANTE DELLA FORTUNA, IL
DANZA DEL CORAZON, LA • 1951 • Alfonso Raul, Iquino Ignacio F. • SPN
DANZA DEL FUEGO • 1949 • Tinayre Daniel • ARG • DANCE OF FIRE
DANZA DEL FUOCO, LA • 1943 • Simonelli Giorgio C. • ITL • DANZA PROIBITO, LA
DANZA DELLE LANCETTE, LA • 1936 • Baffico Mario • ITL
DANZA DELLE ORE, LA • 1920 • Maggi Luigi • ITL
DANZA MACABRA • 1964 • Margheriti Antonio, Corbucci Sergio • ITL, FRN • EDGAR ALLAN POE'S CASTLE OF BLOOD ○ LUNGA NOTTE DEL TERRORE, LA ○ COFFIN OF TERROR ○ DANSE MACABRE, LA (FRN) ○ TOMBS OF TERROR ○ CASTLE OF BLOOD (USA) ○ TERRORE
DANZA PROIBITO, LA see **DANZA DEL FUOCO, LA** • 1943
DAO MA DAN • 1987 • Xu Ke • HKG • PEKING OPERA BLUES
DAOMAZEI • 1985 • Tian Zhuangzhuang • CHN • HORSE THIEF
DAPHNE • 1909 • Perret Leonce • FRN
DAPHNE • 1936 • Rossellini Roberto • SHT • ITL
DAPHNE see **JINCHOGE** • 1966
DAPHNE AND THE DEAN • 1913 • Rains Fred • UKN
DAPHNE AND THE PIRATE • 1916 • Cabanne W. Christy • USA
DAPHNE POLLARD, THE ENGLISH COMEDIENNE IN WANTED A MAN • 1928 • USA
DAPHNE UND DER DIPLOMAT • 1937 • Stemmle R. A. • FRG
DAPHNIA • 1914 • Ricketts Thomas • USA
DAPHNIE, LA • 1929 • Painleve Jean • SHT • FRN
DAPHNIS AND CHLOE see **DAFNIS KAI CHLOI** • 1930
DAPHNIS AND CHLOE 66 see **DHAFNIS KE HLOI 66** • 1967
DAPHNIS ET CHLOE see **DAFNIS KAI CHLOI** • 1930
DAR EMTEDADE SHAB • 1975 • Daryoush Hagir • IRN • NIGHT NEVER ENDS, THE
DAR FYREN BLINKAR • 1924 • Kage Ivar • SWD • WHERE THE LIGHTHOUSE FLASHES
DAR GHORBAT • 1975 • Saless Sohrab Shahid • IRN • FAR FROM HOME
DAR JOSTOJOYE TABAHCARAN • 1967 • Safaei Reza • IRN • SEARCHING FOR CRIMINALS
DAR LA CARA • 1962 • Suarez Jose Martinez • ARG • RESPONSIBILITY
DAR MOLLARNA GA • 1956 • Jarrel Bengt • SWD • WHERE WINDMILLS RUN
DAR VIDA E DAR SANGUE • 1955 • Mendes Joao • SHT • PRT
DARAH PENGLIMA • 1971 • Kadarisman S. • MLY • BLOOD OF A WARRIOR
DARAKU SURU ONNA • 1967 • Yoshimura Kozaburo • JPN • CORRUPTED WOMAN, A ○ FALLEN WOMAN, A
DARB AL-MAHABIL • 1955 • Saleh Tewfik • EGY • RUELLE DES FOU ○ RUELLE DES IDIOTS
DARBET CHAMS • 1978 • Khan Mohamed • EGY • CHAM'S BLOW
DARBOS ON PARADE • 1978 • Bauman Peter • TVM • USA
DARBUJAN A PANDRHOLA • 1960 • Fric Martin • CZC • COMPACT WITH DEATH, A
DARBY AND JOAN • 1912 • *Buckley May* • USA
DARBY AND JOAN • 1919 • Nash Percy • UKN
DARBY AND JOAN • 1937 • Courtenay Syd • UKN
DARBY O'GILL AND THE LITTLE PEOPLE • 1959 • Stevenson Robert • USA
DARBY'S RANGERS • 1958 • Wellman William A. • USA • YOUNG INVADERS, THE (UKN)
DARCLEE • 1961 • Iacob Mihai • RMN
D'ARCY OF THE NORTHWEST MOUNTED • 1916 • Worthington William • SHT • USA
D'ARDENELLE see **HAREM** • 1985
DARE-DEVIL, THE • 1923 • *Sennett Mack (P)* • SHT • USA
DARE DEVIL BILL • 1916 • Metcalfe Earl • SHT • USA
DARE DEVIL DICK WINS A WIFE • 1912 • *Bison* • USA
DARE-DEVIL MOUNTAINEER, THE • 1913 • *Imp* • USA
DARE DEVIL RANCH GIRL, THE • 1916 • *Rancho* • USA
DARE-DEVILS AND DANGER • 1916 • MacMackin Archer • SHT • USA
DARE-DEVILS OF WAR, THE • 1916 • *Imp* • SHT • USA
DARE-DEVILS' TIME see **HAJDUCKA VREMENA** • 1977
DARE-DEVILTRY • 1936 • Miller David • SHT • USA
DARE NO ISU? • 1968 • Morinaga Kenjiro • JPN • CHAIR FOR SOMEBODY, A
DARE NO TAME NI AISURUKA • 1971 • Deme Masanobu • JPN • FOR WHOM DO WE LOVE?
DARE THE DEVIL • 1969 • Emery Robert J. • USA
DARE TO SAY NO see **UMYEI SKAZAT -NYET** • 1976
DAREDEVIL • 1968 • Feleo Ben • PHL
DAREDEVIL, THE • 1918 • Grandon Francis J. • USA
DAREDEVIL, THE • 1919 • Le Saint Edward J. • USA
DAREDEVIL, THE • 1920 • Mix Tom • USA
DAREDEVIL, THE • 1972 • Stringer Robert W. • USA
DAREDEVIL, THE (UKN) see **SKYWAYMAN, THE** • 1920
DAREDEVIL COMMANDOS • 1985 • Rapi R. • ITL
DAREDEVIL DAN • 1917 • Stonehouse Ruth • SHT • USA
DAREDEVIL DICK (UKN) see **YANKEE DON** • 1931
DAREDEVIL DRIVERS • 1938 • Eason B. Reeves • USA
DAREDEVIL DRIVERS • 1978 • Wilson Stanley, Miho Keitaro • JPN • MACH 78
DAREDEVIL DROOPY • 1951 • Avery Tex • ANS • USA
DAREDEVIL HARRY • 1915 • *Mina* • USA
DAREDEVIL IN THE CASTLE (USA) see **OSAKA-JO MONOGATARI** • 1961
DAREDEVIL JACK • 1920 • Van Dyke W. S. • SRL • USA
DAREDEVIL KATE • 1916 • Buel Kenean • USA
DAREDEVILS, THE see **SZALENCY** • 1928
DAREDEVILS, THE see **TSA-CHI WANG-MING TUI** • 1979
DAREDEVILS OF THE CLOUDS • 1948 • Blair George • USA
DAREDEVILS OF THE RED CIRCLE • 1939 • Witney William, English John • SRL • USA
DAREDEVILS OF THE WEST • 1943 • English John • SRL • USA
DAREDEVIL'S REWARD • 1928 • Forde Eugene J. • USA • $5000 REWARD
DAREDREAMER • 1990 • Callier Barry • USA
DAREK • 1947 • Trnka Jiri • ANM • CZC • GIFT, THE
DARIKO • 1937 • Dolidze Siko • USS
DARING AND DYNAMITE • 1918 • Hall Walter • SHT • USA
DARING CABALLERO, THE • 1949 • Fox Wallace • USA
DARING CHANCE, THE • 1917 • Mong William V. • SHT • USA
DARING CHANCES • 1924 • Smith Cliff • USA • HIS TRUST
DARING CIRCUS YOUTH (USA) see **CIRCUS DAREDEVILS** • 1953
DARING DANGER • 1922 • Smith Cliff • USA
DARING DANGER • 1932 • Lederman D. Ross • USA
DARING DAUGHTERS • 1933 • Cabanne W. Christy • USA • BEHIND THE COUNTER (UKN)
DARING DAYLIGHT BURGLARY, A • 1903 • Mottershaw Frank • UKN
DARING DAYS • 1925 • O'Brien John B. • USA
DARING DEED, A • 1911 • *Champion* • USA
DARING DEEDS • 1927 • Worne Duke • USA
DARING DOBERMANS, THE • 1973 • Chudnow Byron • USA
DARING GAME • 1968 • Benedek Laslo • USA
DARING GETAWAY, A • 1914 • O'Sullivan Tony • USA
DARING HEARTS • 1919 • Houry Henri • USA
DARING LIONS AND DIZZY LOVERS • 1919 • Watson William • SHT • USA
DARING LOVE • 1924 • Edwards Roland G. • USA
DARING NUN, THE see **AMAKUZURE** • 1968
DARING OF DIANA, THE • 1916 • Drew Sidney • USA
DARING YEARS, THE • 1923 • Webb Kenneth • USA
DARING YOUNG MAN • 1942 • Strayer Frank • USA
DARING YOUNG MAN, THE • 1935 • Seiter William A. • USA • MAN PROPOSES
DARING YOUNG MAN ON THE FLYING TRAPEZE, THE • 1944 • Munro Grant • ANS • CND
DARING YOUNG PERSON, THE • 1914 • *Stonehouse Ruth* • USA
DARING YOUTH • 1924 • Beaudine William • USA
DARK, THE • 1979 • Cardos John Bud • USA
DARK, THE see **HAUNTED HOUSE OF HORROR, THE** • 1969
DARK AGE • 1986 • Nicholson Arch • ASL
DARK ALIBI • 1946 • Karlson Phil • USA • FATAL FINGERPRINTS
DARK ALLEYS • 1968 • Grigoriou Grigoris, Kontellis Panos • GRC
DARK AND CLOUDY • 1919 • *Gayety Comedies* • USA
DARK ANGEL • 1989 • Baxley Craig R. • USA
DARK ANGEL, THE • 1925 • Fitzmaurice George • USA
DARK ANGEL, THE • 1935 • Franklin Sidney A. • USA
DARK AT THE TOP OF THE STAIRS, THE • 1960 • Mann Delbert • USA
DARK AUGUST • 1976 • Goldman Martin • USA
DARK AVENGER, THE • 1955 • Levin Henry • UKN • WARRIORS, THE (USA)
DARK BEFORE DAWN • 1989 • Totten Robert • USA
DARK BLUE see **INDUNILA** • 1968
DARK BUTTERFLIES see **MARIPOSAS NEGRAS** • 1953
DARK CIRCLE see **ALIAS NICK BEAL** • 1948
DARK CITY • 1950 • Dieterle William • USA
DARK CLAW see **KARA PENCE** • 1968
DARK COMMAND • 1940 • Walsh Raoul • USA
DARK CORNER, THE • 1946 • Hathaway Henry • USA
DARK CORNERS • 1916 • *Rex* • SHT • USA
DARK CRYSTAL, THE • 1982 • Henson Jim, Oz Frank • ANM • UKN, USA
DARK DAYS OF A MOTHER, THE see **ROUZHAYE TARIKE YEK MATHAR** • 1967
DARK DECEPTION, A • 1912 • *Lubin* • USA
DARK DEED, A • 1917 • Chaudet Louis W. • SHT • USA
DARK DELUSION • 1947 • Goldbeck Willis • USA • CYNTHIA'S SECRET (UKN)
DARK DREAMS • 1971 • Guermontes Roger • USA
DARK DREAMS OF AUGUST see **OSCUROS SUENOS DE AGOSTO** • 1967
DARK END OF THE STREET, THE • 1981 • Egleson Jan • USA
DARK ENEMY • 1984 • Finbow Colin • UKN
DARK-EYED WOMAN, THE see **MUHUR GOZLU KADIN** • 1967
DARK EYES • 1980 • Polakoff James • USA • FURY OF THE SUCCUBUS ○ SATAN'S MISTRESS ○ DEMON RAGE
DARK EYES see **OCI CIORNIE** • 1988
DARK EYES OF LONDON, THE • 1939 • Summers Walter • UKN • HUMAN MONSTER, THE (USA)
DARK EYES OF LONDON, THE see **TOTEN AUGEN VON LONDON, DIE** • 1960
DARK EYES (USA) see **YEUX NOIRS, LES** • 1935
DARK FORCES (USA) see **HARLEQUIN** • 1979
DARK GODS • 1958 • Kelly Ron • CND
DARK HABITS see **ENTRE TINIEBLAS** • 1983
DARK HAZARD • 1934 • Green Alfred E. • USA
DARK HISTORY OF JAPAN: STRUGGLE OF BLOOD see **NIHON ANKOKUSHI: CHI NO KOSO** • 1967
DARK HORSE • 1984 • Collins Robert • MTV • USA
DARK HORSE, THE • 1914 • *Imp* • USA
DARK HORSE, THE • 1915 • *Fuehrer Bobby* • USA
DARK HORSE, THE • 1932 • Green Alfred E., Leroy Mervyn (U/c) • USA
DARK HORSE, THE • 1946 • Jason Will • USA • KELLY IS MY NAME
DARK HOUR, THE • 1936 • Lamont Charles • USA
DARK ILLNESS, THE see **MALE OSCURO, IL** • 1990
DARK INTERLUDE • 1955 • Wendkos Paul • DCS • USA
DARK INTERVAL • 1950 • Saunders Charles • UKN
DARK INTRUDER, THE • 1965 • Hart Harvey • MTV • USA • SOMETHING WITH CLAWS ○ BLACK CLOAK, THE
DARK JOURNEY • 1937 • Saville Victor • UKN • ANXIOUS YEARS, THE
DARK LANTERN, A • 1920 • Robertson John S. • USA
DARK LIGHT, THE • 1951 • Sewell Vernon • UKN
DARK LOVE see **KARA SEVDA** • 1968
DARK LOVER'S PLAY, A • 1915 • Frazee Edwin, Cogley Nick • USA
DARK LULLABIES • 1986 • Angelico Irene Lilienheim • DOC • CND
DARK MAGIC • 1939 • Rowland Roy • USA
DARK MAKING OF AN HELIOGRAPHY, THE see **SKOTINI KATASKEVI MIAS ILIOGRAFIAS** • 1976
DARK MAN, THE • 1951 • Dell Jeffrey • UKN • MAN DETAINED
DARK MANSIONS • 1986 • London Jerry • TVM • USA
DARK MIRROR • 1984 • Lang Richard • TVM • USA
DARK MIRROR, THE • 1920 • Giblyn Charles • USA
DARK MIRROR, THE • 1946 • Siodmak Robert • USA
DARK MOON HOLLOW • 1971 • Hill Colin • SHT • IRL
DARK MOUNTAIN • 1944 • Berke William • USA
DARK MOVES • 1974 • Austin-Hunt Peter • SHT • UKN

DARK NIGHT • 1986 • Tan Han-Chang • TWN
DARK NIGHT, THE see **NOCHE OSCURA, LA** • 1989
DARK NIGHT OF THE SCARECROW • 1981 • De Felitta Frank • TVM • USA • NIGHT OF THE SCARECROW
DARK NIGHTS see **KARUTHA RATRIKAL** • 1967
DARK ODYSSEY • 1961 • Kyriakys William, Metzger Radley H. • USA • PASSIONATE SUNDAY
DARK OF THE NIGHT (USA) see **MR. WRONG** • 1986
DARK OF THE SUN (USA) see **MERCENARIES, THE** • 1967
DARK PAGE, THE (UKN) see **SCANDAL SHEET** • 1952
DARK PASSAGE • 1947 • Daves Delmer • USA
DARK PAST, THE • 1948 • Mate Rudolph • USA
DARK PLACES • 1974 • Sharp Don • UKN
DARK POWER, THE • 1985 • Smoot Phil • USA • DARK POWERS
DARK POWERS see **DARK POWER, THE** • 1985
DARK POWERS -GRIGORI RASPUTIN AND HIS ASSOCIATES see **TEMNIYE SILT -GRIGORII RASPUTIN I YEVO SPODVIZHNIKI** • 1917
DARK PURPOSE (USA) see **INTRIGO, L'** • 1964
DARK RAIN • 1990 • Hool Lance • USA
DARK RAPTURE • 1938 • Denis Armand • DOC • USA
DARK RED ROSES • 1929 • Hill Sinclair • UKN
DARK RIDE, THE • 1982 • Hoenak Jeremy • USA
DARK RIVER see **WHISPERS** • 1941
DARK RIVER, THE see **CIEMNA RZEKA** • 1974
DARK RIVER (USA) see **AGUAS BAJAN TURBIAS, LAS** • 1951
DARK ROAD, THE • 1917 • Miller Charles • USA • ROAD TO HONOUR, THE
DARK ROAD, THE • 1948 • Goulding Alf • UKN
DARK ROMANCE OF A TOBACCO CAN, THE • 1911 • *Essanay* • USA
DARK ROMANCES • 1987 • Shephard Mark • USA
DARK ROOM see **ANSHITSU** • 1984
DARK ROOM, THE • 1982 • Harmon Paul • ASL • DARKROOM, THE
DARK ROOM SECRET, A • 1917 • *Dewitt Elizabeth* • SHT • USA
DARK SANDS (USA) see **JERICHO** • 1937
DARK SANITY • 1980 • Greene Martin, McWhorter Tim, Sudderth Martha • USA • STRAIGHT JACKET
DARK SECRET • 1949 • Rogers Maclean • UKN
DARK SECRET OF HARVEST HOME • 1978 • Penn Leo • USA
DARK SECRETS • 1923 • Fleming Victor • USA
DARK SHADOWS • 1944 • Burnford Paul • USA
DARK SHADOWS • 1970 • Curtis Dan • USA • HOUSE OF DARK SHADOWS
DARK SHORE, THE see **FLOOD TIDE** • 1958
DARK SIDE, THE see **REINCARNATE, THE** • 1971
DARK SIDE OF INNOCENCE, THE • 1976 • Thorpe Jerry • TVM • USA
DARK SIDE OF MIDNIGHT, THE • 1986 • Olsen Wes • USA • CREEPER, THE
DARK SIDE OF THE MOON • 1984 • Tatarsky Aleksandr • ANS • USS
DARK SIDE OF THE MOON, THE see **MANDEN I MANEN** • 1986
DARK SIDE OF TOMORROW, THE • 1970 • Peeters Barbara, Deerson Jacques • USA
DARK SILENCE, THE • 1916 • Capellani Albert • USA
DARK SKIES • 1929 • Webb Harry S. • USA • DARKENED SKIES
DARK STAIRWAY, THE • 1938 • Woods Arthur • UKN
DARK STAIRWAY, THE • 1954 • Hughes Ken • UKN
DARK STAIRWAYS • 1924 • Hill Robert F. • USA
DARK STAR • 1972 • Carpenter John • USA
DARK STAR see **MIN AND BILL** • 1930
DARK STAR, THE • 1919 • Dwan Allan • USA
DARK STREETS • 1929 • Lloyd Frank • USA
DARK STREETS see **KARANLIK YOLLAR** • 1968
DARK STREETS OF CAIRO • 1940 • Kardos Leslie • USA
DARK SUN see **KARA GUNES** • 1968
DARK SUNDAY • 1978 • Huston Jimmy • USA
DARK SUNLIGHT see **SOLEIL NOIR** • 1966
DARK SUSPICION, A • 1916 • Curtis Allen • SHT • USA
DARK SWAN, THE • 1924 • Webb Millard • USA • BLACK SWAN, THE
DARK SWAN, THE see **WEDDING RINGS** • 1929
DARK THE MOUNTAIN SNOW (USA) see **ROKUJO YUKIYAMA TSUMUGI** • 1965
DARK TOWER • 1987 • Francis Freddie • UKN, USA
DARK TOWER see **MAN WITH TWO FACES, THE** • 1934
DARK TOWER, THE • 1943 • Harlow John • UKN
DARK TOWER, THE see **NIGHT MOVES** • 1975
DARK TOWN BELLE, THE • 1913 • Lehrman Henry • USA
DARK TUNNEL, THE • 1965 • Leibowitz Lawrence • USA
DARK-VEILED BRIDE, THE see **KARA CARSAFLI GELIN** • 1976
DARK VENTURE • 1956 • *Carradine John* • USA
DARK VICTORY • 1939 • Goulding Edmund • USA
DARK VICTORY • 1976 • Butler Robert • TVM • USA
DARK WARRIOR • 1984 • Clouse Robert • USA
DARK WATER • 1980 • Bogle Andrew • USA
DARK WATERS • 1944 • De Toth Andre • USA
DARK WEB, THE see **WEB, THE** • 1947
DARK WOODS (UKN) see **BOIS NOIRS, LES** • 1989
DARK WORLD • 1935 • Vorhaus Bernard • UKN
DARKENED ROOMS • 1929 • Gasnier Louis J. • USA
DARKENED SKIES see **DARK SKIES** • 1929
DARKENING TRAIL, THE • 1915 • Hart William S., Smith Cliff • USA
DARKER SIDE OF TERROR, THE • 1979 • Trikonis Gus • TVM • USA
DARKER THAN AMBER • 1970 • Clouse Robert • USA
DARKER THAN NIGHT -A LOVE STORY see **SVARTERE ENN NATTEN -EN KJAERLIGHETHISTORIE** • 1979
DARKEST AFRICA • 1913 • *United Film Co.* • USA
DARKEST AFRICA • 1936 • Eason B. Reeves, Kane Joseph • USA • HIDDEN CITY (UKN) ○ KING OF THE JUNGLELAND
DARKEST HOUR, THE • 1920 • Scardon Paul • USA
DARKEST HOUR, THE • 1923 • Roach Hal • SHT • USA
DARKEST HOUR, THE see **HELL ON FRISCO BAY** • 1955
DARKEST LONDON: OR, THE DANCER'S ROMANCE • 1915 • Haldane Bert? • UKN
DARKEST RUSSIA • 1917 • Vale Travers • USA
DARKFEATHER THE SQUAW • 1911 • *Bison* • USA
DARKFEATHER'S SACRIFICE • 1913 • *Darkfeather Mona* • USA
DARKFEATHER'S STRATEGY • 1912 • *Darkfeather Mona* • USA
DARKMAN • 1990 • Raimi Sam • USA
DARKNESS • 1923 • Cooper George A. • UKN
DARKNESS see **YAMI** • 1927
DARKNESS see **TEMNO** • 1950
DARKNESS see **TENEBRAE** • 1982
DARKNESS AND DAYLIGHT • 1923 • Plummer Albert • USA
DARKNESS AT NOON see **MAHIRU NO ANKOKU** • 1956
DARKNESS BEFORE DAWN, THE • 1915 • *Clayton Ethel* • USA
DARKNESS BY DAYLIGHT see **NAPPALI SOTETSEG** • 1963
DARKNESS IN DAYTIME see **NAPPALI SOTETSEG** • 1963
DARKNESS IN THE BRAIN, THE see **OSCURIDAD EN EL CEREBRO, LA** • 1971
DARKROOM • 1981 • Lynch Paul • TVM • USA
DARKROOM, THE see **DARK ROOM, THE** • 1982
DARKSIDE, THE • 1987 • Magnatta Constantino • USA
DARKTOWN BELLE, THE • 1913 • Sennett Mack • USA
DARKTOWN DUEL • 1912 • *Vitagraph* • USA
DARKTOWN REVIEW • 1931 • Micheaux Oscar • USA
DARKTOWN STRUTTERS see **GET DOWN AND BOOGIE** • 1975
DARKTOWN WOOING, A • 1914 • *Kalem* • USA
DARLIN' (UKN) see **COME ON OVER** • 1922
DARLING.. • 1965 • Schlesinger John • UKN
DARLING see **COME ON OVER** • 1922
DARLING see **MAZLICEK** • 1934
DARLING see **RAKAS** • 1961
DARLING see **DRAGAM** • 1969
DARLING, ARE WE A GOOD MATCH..? see **HODIME SE K SOBE, MILACKU?** • 1975
DARLING, ARE YOU BORED WITH MEN? • 1968 • Meyer John • USA • ARE YOU BORED WITH MEN? ○ DO I BORE YOU DARLING?
DARLING AT SEA see **ALSKLING PA VAGEN** • 1955
DARLING CONFUSION, A • 1910 • *Essanay* • USA
DARLING DANDY • 1915 • *Stonehouse Ruth* • USA
DARLING, DO YOU LOVE ME? • 1969 • Whittaker Bob, Sharp Martin • SHT • UKN
DARLING DOLLY GRAY • 1926 • Fleischer Dave • ANS • USA
DARLING, HOW COULD YOU? • 1951 • Leisen Mitchell • USA • RENDEZVOUS (UKN)
DARLING I SURRENDER see **ALSKLING, JAG GER MIG** • 1943
DARLING IN BUCKSKIN, A • 1917 • Mong William V. • SHT • USA
DARLING LILI • 1970 • Edwards Blake • USA
DARLING MINE • 1920 • Trimble Larry • USA
DARLING OF C.S.A., THE • 1912 • Olcott Sidney • USA
DARLING OF NEW YORK, THE • 1923 • Baggot King • USA • WANTED, A HOME
DARLING OF PARIS, THE • 1917 • Edwards J. Gordon • USA
DARLING OF PARIS, THE see **BELLE OF BROADWAY, THE** • 1926
DARLING OF THE GODS (USA) see **LIEBLING DER GOTTER** • 1930
DARLING OF THE MOUNTED, THE • 1912 • *Horton Clara* • USA
DARLING OF THE REGIMENT, THE • 1913 • *Bison* • USA
DARLING OF THE RICH, THE • 1922 • Adolfi John G. • USA
DARLING OF THE STOCKHOLM LADIES see **STOCKHOLMSDAMERNAS ALSKLING** • 1911
DARLING PUGGY • 1905 • Collins Alf? • UKN
DARLINGS see **SCHATJES** • 1983
DARLINGS OF FORTUNE see **LYCKANS GULLGOSSAR** • 1932
DARLINGS OF THE GODS • 1989 • Millar Catherine • TVM • ASL
DARLINGS OF THE GODS (UKN) see **SIRENS OF THE SEA** • 1917
DARMA KESUMA • 1971 • Kadarisman S. • MLY • PATRIOT, THE
DARN BARN • 1965 • Rasinski Connie • ANS • USA
DARN THAT STOCKING! • 1920 • Laver Jack • SHT • USA
DARNA AND THE PLANETMAN see **DARNA AT ANG PLANETMAN** • 1967
DARNA AT ANG BABAING TUOD • 1965 • PHL
DARNA AT ANG PLANETMAN • 1967 • Navarro Marcelino D. • PHL • DARNA AND THE PLANETMAN
DARO UN MILIONE • 1935 • Camerini Mario • ITL • I'LL GIVE A MILLION
DARSELA A GAMBE (ITL) see **POUDRE D'ESCAMPETTE, LA** • 1971
DARSKAB, DYD OD DRIVERT • 1923 • Holger-Madsen • DNM
DARSKAPENS HUS • 1951 • Ekman Hasse • SWD • HOUSE OF FOLLY
D'ARTAGNAN • 1916 • Swickard Charles • USA
D'ARTAGNAN CONTRO I TRE MOSCHETTIERI • 1963 • Tului Fulvio • ITL • REVENGE OF THE MUSKETEERS (USA)
D'ARTAGNAN L'INTREPIDE (FRN) see **GLORIOUS MUSKETEERS, THE** • 1974
DARTMOUTH DAYS • 1934 • Rapf Maurice • USA
DARTS ARE TRUMPS • 1938 • Rogers Maclean • UKN
DARU DUKA • 1967 • Jayawardena Dommie • SLN • PARENT'S LOVE, A
DARVAZE TAGHDEER • 1967 • Mojtahedi Hamid • IRN • GATE OF DESTINY, THE
DARWIN • 1919 • Bernhardt Fritz • FRG • MENSCH ODER AFFE ○ WELTRATSEL MENSCH, DAS
DARWIN ADVENTURE, THE • 1972 • Couffer Jack • UKN, USA
DARWIN -GATEWAY TO AUSTRALIA • 1946 • Robinson Lee • DOC • ASL
DARWIN WAS RIGHT • 1924 • Seiler Lewis • USA
DARY MAGOW • 1972 • Maruszewska Walentyna • PLN • GIFTS OF THE MAGI, THE
DARYL see **D.A.R.Y.L.** • 1985
DAS GAB'S NUR EINMAL • 1958 • von Bolvary Geza • FRG
DAS HAB' ICH IN PARIS GELERNT • 1960 • Engel Thomas • FRG
DAS HAB' ICH VON PAPA GELERNT • 1964 • von Ambesser Axel • FRG, AUS
DAS HABEN DIE MADCHEN GERN see **LUSTIGEN VAGABUNDEN, DIE** • 1963
DAS HAUT EINEN SEEMANN DOCH NICHT UM • 1958 • Rabenalt Arthur M. • FRG, DNM
DAS IST MEIN WIEN • 1965 • Hollmann Hans • AUS • ... EWIGES WIENERLIED
DAS KANN JEDEM PASSIEREN • 1952 • Verhoeven Paul • FRG
DAS KAPITAL • 1971 • Zilnik Zelimir • YGS
DAS LICHT SCHEUEN..!, DIE • 1920 • Jutzi Phil • FRG
DAS TRIPAS CORACAO • 1982 • Soares Ana Carolina Texeira, Nabuco Caroline? • BRZ • HEARTS AND GUTS
DAS WAR BUFFALO BILL (FRG) see **BUFFALO BILL, L'EROE DEL FAR WEST** • 1965
DAS WAR IN HEIDELBERG IN BLAUER SOMMERNACHT • 1926 • Hanus Emerich • FRG
DAS WAR MEIN LEBEN • 1944 • Martin Paul • FRG • THAT WAS MY LIFE
DAS WAR MEIN LEBEN see **SAUERBRUCH** • 1954
DASA AVATHAR • 1928 • *Guarany* • IND • DASA, INCARNATION OF GOD
DASA, INCARNATION OF GOD see **DASA AVATHAR** • 1928
DASAVATAR • 1936 • Murti • IND • TENTH INCARNATION
DASAVATHAR • 1935 • *Jayawani Films* • IND
DASENKU • 1975 • Pojar Bretislav • ANM • CZC • DASHENKA
DASH AHMAD • 1967 • Sadeghpoor Manouchehr • IRN
DASH AVTAR • 1951 • Desai Jayant • IND • TENTH INCARNATION
DASH FOR HELP, A • 1909 • Cooper Arthur • UKN
DASH FOR LIBERTY, A • 1908 • Aylott Dave • UKN
DASH FOR LIBERTY, A • 1913 • Fielding Romaine • USA
DASH FOR LIBERTY, A see **HOJT SPIL** • 1913
DASH FOR LIBERTY: OR, THE CONVICT'S ESCAPE AND CAPTURE, A • 1903 • Haggar William • UKN
DASH, LOVE AND SPLASH • 1914 • Henderson Dell • USA
DASH OF COURAGE, A • 1916 • Parrott Charles • SHT • USA
DASH THROUGH THE CLOUDS, A • 1912 • Sennett Mack • USA
DASH TO DEATH, A • 1909 • *Edison* • USA
DASH TO THE CANOE RALLY see **ZRYW NA SPLYW** • 1956
DASH WITH THE DISPATCHES, A • 1904 • Mottershaw Frank • UKN
DASHAKOL • 1972 • Kimiyaei Massoud • IRN
DASHENKA see **DASENKU** • 1975
DASHING DRUGGIST'S DILEMMA, THE • 1916 • *Keyes Francis* • USA
DASHING GIRLS see **SZIKRAZO LANYOK** • 1973
DASHING HUSSAR, THE • 1913 • *Barker* • UKN
DASHING THRU • 1925 • *Merrill Frank* • USA
DASHTE SORKH • 1968 • Aghanikyan Hekmat • IRN • RED PLAIN
DASSAN -AN ADVENTURE IN SEARCH OF LAUGHTER AND FEATURING NATURE'S GREATEST LITTLE COMEDIANS • 1930 • Kearton Cherry, Kearton Ada • UKN
DASSEHRA • 1956 • *Roy Nirupa* • IND
DASSO • 1963 • *Mikuni Rentaro* • JPN • ESCAPE
DASTAAN • 1950 • *Kapoor Raj* • IND
DASTAK • 1971 • Bedi Rajendra Singh • IND
DATA, THE • 1964 • Petrovic Aleksandar • SHT • YGS
DATAI LI LIANYING • 1990 • Tian Zhuangzhuang • CHN
DATE AT MIDNIGHT • 1960 • Grayson Godfrey • UKN
DATE BAIT • 1960 • Ireland O'Dale • USA
DATE-BAYARI • 1931 • Inagaki Hiroshi • JPN
DATE FOR DINNER, A • 1947 • Donnelly Eddie • ANS • USA
DATE FOR MARRIAGE see **TOTSUGU HI** • 1956
DATE OF BIRTH • 1950 • Fraser Donald • DOC • CND
DATE OF EXPECTATION • 1987 • Hashemi Asghar • IRN
DATE TO SKATE, A • 1938 • Fleischer Dave • ANS • USA
DATE WITH A DREAM, A • 1948 • Leeman Dicky • UKN
DATE WITH A LONELY GIRL, A see **T. R. BASKIN** • 1971
DATE WITH AN ANGEL • 1987 • McLoughlin Tom • USA
DATE WITH AN ANGEL, A (UKN) see **IT COMES UP LOVE** • 1943
DATE WITH DEATH, A • 1959 • Daniels Harold • USA
DATE WITH DESTINY, A (UKN) see **MAD DOCTOR, THE** • 1941
DATE WITH DESTINY, A (UKN) see **RETURN OF OCTOBER, THE** • 1948
DATE WITH DISASTER • 1957 • Saunders Charles • UKN
DATE WITH DIZZY • 1956 • Hubley John • SHT • USA
DATE WITH DUKE, A • 1946 • Pal George • ANS • USA
DATE WITH JUDY, A • 1948 • Thorpe Richard • USA
DATE WITH MARILIN see **CITA CON MARILIN** • 1968
DATE WITH THE FALCON, A • 1941 • Reis Irving • USA
DATELINE DIAMONDS • 1965 • Summers Jeremy • UKN
DATENIGHT see **ONE MORE SATURDAY NIGHT** • 1986
DATES • 1915 • *Casino* • USA
DATING DELILAH • 1987 • Cunningham Sean S. • USA
DATSUGOKO-SHU • 1957 • Suzuki Hideo • JPN • DECOY
DATSUGOKU • 1950 • Yamamoto Kajiro • JPN • ESCAPE FROM PRISON
DATSUGOKUSHA • 1967 • Ikehiro Kazuo • JPN • BREAKOUT, THE
DAUGHTER see **MUSUME** • 1926
DAUGHTER, THE • Reiniger Lotte • ANM • UKN
DAUGHTER, THE • 1972 • Guldbrandsen Peer • DNM, SWD
DAUGHTER ANGELE • 1918 • Dowlan William C. • USA
DAUGHTER: I, A WOMAN PART III, THE (USA) see **TRE SLAGS KAERLIGHED** • 1970
DAUGHTER-IN-LAW see **SNAHA** • 1954
DAUGHTER-IN-LAW see **BHALE KODALU** • 1968
DAUGHTER-IN-LAW, THE see **NEVESTKA** • 1972
DAUGHTER IN REVOLT, A • 1927 • Hughes Harry • UKN
DAUGHTER OF A CROOK, THE • 1914 • *Victor* • USA
DAUGHTER OF A WEREWOLF see **LUPA MANNARA, LA** • 1976
DAUGHTER OF AUSTRALIA • 1912 • Mervale Gaston • ASL
DAUGHTER OF AUSTRALIA, A • 1922 • Harris Lawson • ASL
DAUGHTER OF BELGIUM, A • 1914 • Thornton F. Martin? • UKN
DAUGHTER OF BRAHMA, A see **MAHARAJAENS YNDLINGSHUSTRU II** • 1918
DAUGHTER OF CLEOPATRA see **SEPOLCRO DEI RE, IL** • 1961
DAUGHTER OF CROOKED ALLEY, THE see **CROOKED ALLEY** • 1923
DAUGHTER OF DARING, A • 1917 • SER • USA
DAUGHTER OF DARKNESS • 1948 • Comfort Lance • UKN
DAUGHTER OF DAWN, A • 1920 • Myles Norbert • USA
DAUGHTER OF DAWN, THE • 1924 • *Chief Buffalo Bear* • USA

DAUGHTER OF DECEIT (USA) see **HIJA DEL ENGANO, LA** • 1951
DAUGHTER OF DESTINY • 1917 • Irving George • USA
DAUGHTER OF DESTINY, A see **ALRAUNE** • 1927
DAUGHTER OF DEVIL DAN • 1921 • *Harrison Irma* • USA
DAUGHTER OF DIXIE, A • 1910 • *Kalem* • USA
DAUGHTER OF DIXIE, A • 1911 • *Champion* • USA
DAUGHTER OF DIXIE, A • 1916 • *Big U* • SHT • USA
DAUGHTER OF DR. JEKYLL • 1957 • Ulmer Edgar G. • USA
DAUGHTER OF DON Q • 1946 • Bennet Spencer Gordon, Brannon Fred C. • SRL • USA
DAUGHTER OF EARTH, A • 1915 • MacDonald J. Farrell • USA
DAUGHTER OF EMMANUELLE • 1978 • Luret Jean • FRN, BLG
DAUGHTER OF ENGLAND, A • 1915 • Bantock Leedham • UKN
DAUGHTER OF ERIN ,A • 1908 • *Selig* • USA
DAUGHTER OF EVE, A • 1914 • O'Neil Barry • USA
DAUGHTER OF EVE, A • 1919 • West Walter • UKN
DAUGHTER OF EVIL see **ALRAUNE** • 1930
DAUGHTER OF FRANCE, A • 1914 • *Crusade* • UKN
DAUGHTER OF FRANCE, A • 1918 • Lawrence Edmund • USA
DAUGHTER OF FRANKENSTEIN, THE see **FIGLIA DI FRANKENSTEIN, LA** • 1971
DAUGHTER OF FRANKENSTEIN, THE see **SANTO CONTRA LA HIJA DE FRANKENSTEIN** • 1971
DAUGHTER OF GARCIA, BRIGAND, THE • 1914 • Aylott Dave • UKN
DAUGHTER OF GAS-HOUSE DAN, THE • 1917 • Thayer Otis B. • SHT • USA
DAUGHTER OF GIMBO see **GIMBO KI BETI** • 1960
DAUGHTER OF HORROR see **DEMENTIA** • 1953
DAUGHTER OF ISRAEL, A • 1915 • Brooke Van Dyke • USA
DAUGHTER OF ISRAEL (USA) see **PUITS DE JACOB, LES** • 1926
DAUGHTER OF ITALY, A • 1911 • *Walthall William* • USA
DAUGHTER OF JOAN, A • 1917 • Ingraham Lloyd • USA
DAUGHTER OF KINGS • 1915 • *Snow Marguerite* • USA
DAUGHTER OF LIBERTY, A • 1911 • Dwan Allan • USA
DAUGHTER OF LIGHTNING see **ANAK NG KIDLAT** • 1959
DAUGHTER OF LOVE see **BINT EL HAWA** • 1953
DAUGHTER OF LOVE, A • 1925 • West Walter • UKN
DAUGHTER OF LUXURY, A • 1922 • Powell Paul • USA
DAUGHTER OF LUXURY (UKN) see **FIVE AND TEN** • 1931
DAUGHTER OF MACGREGOR, A • 1916 • Olcott Sidney • USA
DAUGHTER OF MADAME X, THE • 1917 • Hertz Aleksander • PLN
DAUGHTER OF MARYLAND, A • 1917 • O'Brien John B. • USA
DAUGHTER OF MATA-HARI see **FIGLIA DI MATA HARI, LA** • 1955
DAUGHTER OF MINE • 1919 • Badger Clarence • USA
DAUGHTER OF PAN, A • 1913 • Gaskill Charles L. • USA
DAUGHTER OF PENANCE, A • 1916 • Otto Henry • SHT • USA
DAUGHTER OF ROMANY, A • 1913 • Brabin Charles J. • UKN
DAUGHTER OF ROSIE O'GRADY, THE • 1942 • Negulesco Jean • SHT • USA
DAUGHTER OF ROSIE O'GRADY, THE • 1950 • Butler David • USA
DAUGHTER OF SATAN • 1970 • *Janus Ii Productions* • USA • DAUGHTER OF THE DEVIL
DAUGHTER OF SATAN, A • 1914 • Collins Edwin J. • UKN
DAUGHTER OF SHANGHAI • 1937 • Florey Robert • USA • DAUGHTER OF THE ORIENT (UKN)
DAUGHTER OF THE CITY, A • 1915 • Calvert E. H. • USA
DAUGHTER OF THE CONFEDERACY, A • 1913 • Kirkland Hardee • *Selig* • USA
DAUGHTER OF THE CONFEDERACY, A • 1913 • Olcott Sidney, Melford George • *Gene Gauntier Feature Players* • USA
DAUGHTER OF THE CONGO • 1930 • Micheaux Oscar • USA
DAUGHTER OF THE DEVIL see **DAUGHTER OF SATAN** • 1970
DAUGHTER OF THE DON, THE • 1917 • Kabierske Henry • USA
DAUGHTER OF THE DON, THE • 1918 • *Hamilton Shorty* • USA
DAUGHTER OF THE DON, THE • 1921 • *Cooley Hal* • USA
DAUGHTER OF THE DRAGON • 1931 • Corrigan Lloyd • USA
DAUGHTER OF THE EAST • 1924 • Darling Roy • ASL
DAUGHTER OF THE FORTUNE TELLER, THE see **BLAA NATVIOL, DEN** • 1911
DAUGHTER OF THE GODS, A • 1916 • Brenon Herbert • USA
DAUGHTER OF THE GODS, A • 1917 • Edwards J. Gordon • USA
DAUGHTER OF THE HIGH MOUNTAIN see **HOGFJALLETS DOTTER** • 1914
DAUGHTER OF THE HILLS, A • 1913 • Dawley J. Searle • USA
DAUGHTER OF THE HILLS, A • 1916 • *Hiawatha* • USA
DAUGHTER OF THE JUNGLE • 1949 • Blair George • USA
DAUGHTER OF THE JUNGLES, A • 1915 • McRae Henry • USA
DAUGHTER OF THE LAW, A • 1920 • *Cunard Grace* • SHT • USA
DAUGHTER OF THE LAW, A • 1921 • Conway Jack • USA
DAUGHTER OF THE LIGHTHOUSE KEEPER, THE see **FYRVAKTARENS DOTTER** • 1918
DAUGHTER OF THE MIND • 1969 • Grauman Walter • TVM • USA
DAUGHTER OF THE MINE, A • 1910 • *Nestor* • USA
DAUGHTER OF THE MINES, A • 1910 • *Edison* • USA
DAUGHTER OF THE MOUNTAIN see **HOGFJALLETS DOTTER** • 1914
DAUGHTER OF THE NAVAJOS, A • 1911 • Blache Alice • USA
DAUGHTER OF THE NIGHT, A see **WHICH WAY?** • 1916
DAUGHTER OF THE NIGHT, THE • *Sannom Emilie* • DNM
DAUGHTER OF THE NIGHT -PSALM 69, A • 1927 • Barnett Charles • UKN
DAUGHTER OF THE NILE see **BINT EL NIL** • 1929
DAUGHTER OF THE NILE see **NI-LO-HO NU-ERH** • 1988
DAUGHTER OF THE NILE, A • 1915 • Henderson Lucius • USA
DAUGHTER OF THE OLD SOUTH, A • 1918 • Chautard Emile • USA
DAUGHTER OF THE ORIENT (UKN) see **DAUGHTER OF SHANGHAI** • 1937
DAUGHTER OF THE PEOPLE, A • 1915 • Dawley J. Searle • USA
DAUGHTER OF THE PLAINS, A • 1914 • *Nestor* • USA
DAUGHTER OF THE POOR, A • 1917 • Dillon Eddie • USA
DAUGHTER OF THE RAILWAY, THE see **JERNBANENS DATTER** • 1911
DAUGHTER OF THE REDSKINS, A • 1912 • *Bison* • USA
DAUGHTER OF THE REGIMENT • 1927 • Parkinson H. B. • UKN
DAUGHTER OF THE REVOLUTION, A • 1911 • Porter Edwin S. • USA
DAUGHTER OF THE SAMURAI, A see **ATARASHIKI TSUCHI** • 1937
DAUGHTER OF THE SANDS see **NOCES DE SABLE** • 1948
DAUGHTER OF THE SEA, A • 1915 • Seay Charles M. • USA
DAUGHTER OF THE SHEEP RANCHER, THE • 1913 • *Frontier* • USA
DAUGHTER OF THE SHERIFF, THE • 1912 • *Kalem* • USA
DAUGHTER OF THE SHERIFF, THE • 1913 • *Essanay* • USA
DAUGHTER OF THE SIOUX, A • 1909 • *Selig* • USA
DAUGHTER OF THE SIOUX, A • 1925 • Wilson Ben • USA
DAUGHTER OF THE SOUTHLAND, A • 1917 • Eagle Oscar • SHT • USA
DAUGHTER OF THE STORM • 1954 • Lindtberg Leopold • SWT
DAUGHTER OF THE SUN see **SURJOKANNYA** • 1977
DAUGHTER OF THE SUN, A • 1909 • Porter Edwin S. • USA
DAUGHTER OF THE SUN GOD • 1967 • Herts Kenneth • USA
DAUGHTER OF THE TONG • 1939 • Johnston Raymond K. • USA
DAUGHTER OF THE UNDERWORLD, A • 1913 • *Rhodes Billie* • USA
DAUGHTER OF THE WEREWOLF see **CRY OF THE WEREWOLF** • 1944
DAUGHTER OF THE WEST • 1949 • Daniels Harold • USA
DAUGHTER OF THE WEST, A • 1918 • Bertram William • USA
DAUGHTER OF THE WILDERNESS, A • 1913 • *Phillips Augustus* • USA
DAUGHTER OF THE WILDS • 1917 • Wilson Frank • UKN
DAUGHTER OF THE WOLF, A • 1919 • Willat Irvin V. • USA
DAUGHTER OF THE WOODS, A • 1916 • *Saunders Jackie* • SHT • USA
DAUGHTER OF TWO WORLDS, A • 1920 • Young James • USA
DAUGHTER OF UNCLE SAM, A • 1918 • Morton James • SRL • USA
DAUGHTER OF VIRGINIA, A • 1910 • *Powers* • USA
DAUGHTER OF VIRGINIA, A • 1913 • *Champion* • USA
DAUGHTER OF WAR, A • 1917 • *Mutual* • USA
DAUGHTER PAYS, THE • 1920 • Ellis Robert • USA
DAUGHTER WORTH WHILE, A • 1913 • *Cruze James* • USA
DAUGHTER'S CHOICE, THE • 1910 • *Lubin* • USA
DAUGHTERS COURAGEOUS • 1939 • Curtiz Michael • USA • AMERICAN FAMILY ○ FAMILY REUNION
DAUGHTERS! DAUGHTERS! see **ANOUL BANAT** • 1973
DAUGHTER'S DEVOTION, A • 1910 • *Nestor* • USA
DAUGHTERS OF CHINA see **ZHONGHUA NUER** • 1949
DAUGHTERS OF DARKNESS (USA) see **ROUGE AUX LEVRES, LE** • 1970
DAUGHTERS OF DESIRE • 1929 • King Burton L. • USA • RECKLESS YOUTH (UKN)
DAUGHTERS OF DESTINY (USA) see **DESTINEES** • 1953
DAUGHTERS OF DRACULA see **VAMPYRES** • 1974
DAUGHTERS OF FIRE see **FILHAS DO FOGO, AS** • 1979
DAUGHTERS OF JOSHUA CABE, THE • 1972 • Leacock Philip • TVM • USA
DAUGHTERS OF JOSHUA CABE RETURN, THE • 1975 • Rich David Lowell • TVM • USA
DAUGHTERS OF LESBOS see **DOMINIQUE** • 1968
DAUGHTERS OF MEN • 1914 • Terwilliger George W. • USA
DAUGHTERS OF PLEASURE • 1924 • Beaudine William • USA
DAUGHTERS OF SATAN • 1972 • Morse Hollingsworth • USA, PHL
DAUGHTERS OF SENOR LOPEZ, THE • 1912 • Dwan Allan • USA
DAUGHTERS OF THE DESERT see **ORIENT** • 1924
DAUGHTERS OF THE NIGHT • 1924 • Clifton Elmer • USA • CROSSED WIRES
DAUGHTERS OF THE NILE • 1981 • Molenaar Hillie, van Wijk Joop • DOC • NTH
DAUGHTERS OF THE RICH • 1923 • Gasnier Louis J. • USA
DAUGHTERS OF THE SUN • 1962 • Lewis Herschell G. • USA
DAUGHTERS OF THE WEST • 1911 • Dwan Allan • USA
DAUGHTERS OF TODAY • 1924 • Sturgeon Rollin S. • USA • WHAT'S YOUR DAUGHTER DOING?
DAUGHTERS OF TODAY • 1933 • Kraemer F. W. • UKN
DAUGHTERS OF YOSHIWARA see **TAKEKURABE** • 1955
DAUGHTER'S SACRIFICE, A • 1912 • *Joyce Alice* • USA
DAUGHTER'S STRANGE INHERITANCE, A • 1915 • Brooke Van Dyke • USA
DAUGHTERS WHO PAY • 1925 • Terwilliger George W. • USA
DAUGHTERS, WIVES AND A MOTHER see **MUSUME TSUMA HAHA** • 1960
DAUMIER • 1959 • Leenhardt Roger • DCS • FRN
DAUMIER, EYE WITNESS OF AN EPOCH see **DAUMIER - REPORTER OF HIS TIME** • 1972
DAUMIER -REPORTER OF HIS TIME • 1972 • Crama Nico • SHT • NTH • DAUMIER, EYE WITNESS OF AN EPOCH
DAUNTAUN HIROZU • 1988 • Yamada Yoji • JPN • HOPE AND PAIN
DAUPHIN SUR LA PLAGE, LE see **BANCO DE PRINCE** • 1950
DAUPHINE JAVA, LA • 1960 • Alexeieff Alexandre • SHT • FRN
DAUPHINS ET CETACES • 1949 • Cousteau Jacques • FRN
DAURIA see **DAURIYA** • 1972
DAURIYA • 1972 • Tregubovich Viktor • USS • DAURIA
D'AUTRES HISTOIRES • 1975 • Bokor Pierre • MTV • RMN
DAVANTI A LUI TREMAVA TUTTA ROMA • 1946 • Gallone Carmine • ITL • BEFORE HIM ALL ROME TREMBLED ○ AVANTI A LUI ○ TOSCA ○ INNANZI A LUI TREMAVA TUTTA ROMA
DAVE BRUBECK • 1970 • Leduc Francois • FRN
DAVE CLARK FIVE RUNS WILD, THE see **CATCH US IF YOU CAN** • 1965
DAVE PERRY • 1968 • Thoms Albie • ASL
DAVE'S LOVE AFFAIR • 1911 • Sennett Mack, Henderson Dell • USA
DAVEY CRICKET • 1965 • Smith Paul J. • ANS • USA
DAVEY JONES' LOCKER • 1903 • *Biograph* • USA
DAVEY JONES' LOCKER • 1966 • Goode Frederic • UKN
DAVID • 1924 • Southwell Harry • FRN
DAVID • 1951 • Dickson Paul • UKN
DAVID • 1962 • Leacock Richard, Pennebaker D. A. • DOC • USA
DAVID • 1967 • Barnet Enrique Pineda • CUB
DAVID • 1977 • Driessen Paul • ANM • CND
DAVID • 1979 • Lilienthal Peter • FRG
DAVID AND BATHSHEBA • 1951 • King Henry • USA
DAVID AND CATRIONA see **KIDNAPPED** • 1971
DAVID AND GOLIATH • 1908 • Olcott Sidney • USA
DAVID AND GOLIATH • 1979 • *Cassidy Ted* • MTV • USA
DAVID AND GOLIATH see **DAVID ET GOLIATH** • 1910
DAVID AND GOLIATH see **EDGAR'S SUNDAY COURTSHIP** • 1920
DAVID AND GOLIATH (USA) see **DAVID E GOLIA** • 1960
DAVID AND GOLIGHTLY • 1961 • Hill James • SHT • UKN
DAVID AND HAZEL • 1963 • Howe John • CND
DAVID AND JONATHAN • 1920 • Butler Alexander • UKN
DAVID AND LISA • 1963 • Perry Frank • USA
DAVID AND SANDY see **DAWID I SANDY** • 1988
DAVID AND THE ICE AGE see **WINTERMARCHEN** • 1971
DAVID-BEK • 1944 • Bek-Nazarov Amo • USS
DAVID BOWIE • 1975 • Pennebaker D. A. • DOC • USA
DAVID, CAROL, DON, WILL: A PORTRAIT • 1966 • Mottram Ron • USA • PORTRAIT
DAVID CHAPTER II • 1967 • Hart Harvey • MTV • CND
DAVID CHAPTER III • 1968 • Hart Harvey • MTV • CND
DAVID COPPERFIELD • 1911 • Marston Theodore • USA
DAVID COPPERFIELD • 1913 • Bentley Thomas • UKN
DAVID COPPERFIELD • 1922 • Sandberg Anders W. • DNM
DAVID COPPERFIELD • 1969 • Mann Delbert • MTV • UKN
DAVID COPPERFIELD • 1984 • Nicholas Alex, MacKenzie Ian • ANM • USA
DAVID COPPERFIELD see **PERSONAL HISTORY, ADVENTURES, EXPERIENCE AND OBSERVATION OF DAVID COPPERFIELD THE YOUNGER, THE** • 1935
DAVID CRAGGS, DETECTIVE • 1910 • Fitzhamon Lewin • UKN
DAVID CRAIG'S LUCK • 1917 • *Moore Matt* • SHT • USA
DAVID DEVANT, CONJUROR • 1903 • *Mutoscope & Biograph* • UKN
DAVID DEVANT'S LAUGHABLE HAND SHADOWS • 1903 • *Mutoscope & Biograph* • UKN
DAVID E GOLIA • 1960 • Pottier Richard, Baldi Ferdinando • ITL • DAVID AND GOLIATH (USA)
DAVID ET GOLIATH • 1910 • *Bovy Berthe* • FRN • DAVID AND GOLIATH
DAVID GARRICK • 1908 • *Dixey Henry E.* • USA
DAVID GARRICK • 1912 • Nash Percy • UKN
DAVID GARRICK • 1913 • Bantock Leedham • *Zenith* • UKN
DAVID GARRICK • 1913 • Plumb Hay • *Hepworth* • UKN
DAVID GARRICK • 1914 • Young James • USA
DAVID GARRICK • 1916 • Lloyd Frank • USA
DAVID GARRICK • 1922 • *Parkinson H. B. (P)* • SHT • UKN
DAVID GARRICK • 1928 • Banfield George J., Eveleigh Leslie • SHT • UKN
DAVID GOLDER • 1930 • Duvivier Julien • USA
DAVID GOLIATH see **PROUD VALLEY, THE** • 1940
DAVID GORELICK • 1931 • Roshal Grigori • USS • JEW AT WAR, A
DAVID GRAY'S ESTATE • 1914 • *Ayres Sydney* • USA
DAVID GURAMISHVILI • 1946 • Tumanishvili I., Sanishvili Nikolai • USS
DAVID HARDING, COUNTERSPY • 1950 • Nazarro Ray • USA
DAVID HARUM • 1915 • Dwan Allan • USA
DAVID HARUM • 1934 • Cruze James • USA
DAVID HOLZMAN'S DIARY • 1968 • McBride Jim • USA
DAVID LEAN • 1959 • Wilkinson Hazel • DOC • UKN • DIRECTOR AND THE FILM -DAVID LEAN, THE
DAVID LEAN: A SELF PORTRAIT • Craven Thomas • UKN
DAVID LIVINGSTONE • 1936 • Fitzpatrick James A. • UKN
DAVID LLOYD GEORGE see **SECRET LIVES OF THE BRITISH PRIME MINISTERS: LLOYD GEORGE** • 1983
DAVID LYNN'S SCULPTURE see **SCULPTURE OF DAVID LYNN, THE** • 1961
DAVID: OFF AND ON • Coolidge Martha • DOC • USA
DAVID OR GOLIATH • 1988 • Wivel Anne • DOC • DNM
DAVID SECTER • 1966 • Shebib Donald • CND
DAVID THE OUTLAW see **STORY OF DAVID, A** • 1960
DAVID THOMPSON, CARTOGRAPHE see **DAVID THOMPSON, THE GREAT MAP-MAKER** • 1964
DAVID THOMPSON, THE GREAT MAP-MAKER • 1964 • Devlin Bernard • SHT • CND • DAVID THOMPSON, CARTOGRAPHE
DAVID'S DAY • 1966 • Ohlsson Terry • SHT • UKN
DAVID'S IDOL DREAM • 1917 • Morton Walter • SHT • USA
DAVIS CUP, THE • 1923 • ASL
DAVOLJA POSLA • 1966 • Grgic Zlatko • ANS • YGS • WORK OF THE DEVIL, THE ○ DEVIL'S WORK, THE
DAVOLJI RAJ • 1989 • Grlic Rajko • YGS, UKN • THAT SUMMER OF WHITE ROSES
DAVON TRAUMEN ALLE MADCHEN • 1961 • Engel Thomas • FRG
DAVUDO • 1965 • Kazankaya Hasan • TRK
DAVY • 1957 • Relph Michael • UKN
DAVY CROCKETT • 1910 • Boggs Frank • USA
DAVY CROCKETT • 1916 • Taylor William D. • USA
DAVY CROCKETT AND THE RIVER PIRATES • 1956 • Foster Norman • MTV • USA
DAVY CROCKETT AT THE FALL OF THE ALAMO • 1926 • Bradbury Robert North • USA • WITH DAVY CROCKETT AT THE FALL OF THE ALAMO
DAVY CROCKETT -IN HEARTS UNITED • 1909 • Balshofer Fred J. • USA
DAVY CROCKETT, INDIAN SCOUT • 1950 • Landers Lew • USA • INDIAN SCOUT (UKN)
DAVY CROCKETT, KING OF THE WILD FRONTIER • 1956 • Foster Norman • MTV • USA
DAVY CROCKETT UP-TO-DATE • 1915 • *Bainbridge Rolinda* • USA
DAVY JONES AND CAPTAIN BRAGG • 1910 • Baker George D. • USA

DAVY JONES' DOMESTIC TROUBLES • 1910 • *Vitagraph* • USA

DAVY JONES IN THE SOUTH SEAS • 1911 • *Vitagraph* • USA

DAVY JONES' LANDLADIES • 1910 • *Vitagraph* • USA

DAVY JONES' LOCKER • 1934 • *Iwerks Ub (P)* • ANS • USA

DAVY JONES OR HIS WIFE'S HUSBAND • 1911 • *Vitagraph* • USA

DAVY JONES' PARROT • 1910 • *Vitagraph* • USA

DAWG GAWN • 1958 • Kneitel Seymour • ANS • USA

DAWGONE • 1920 • *Gibson Hoot* • SHT • USA

DAWID I SANDY • 1988 • Lutczyna Edward • ANM • PLN • DAVID AND SANDY

DAWN • 1914 • Le Saint Edward J. • USA

DAWN • 1917 • Lucoque H. Lisle • UKN

DAWN • 1919 • Blackton J. Stuart • USA

DAWN • 1928 • Wilcox Herbert • UKN

DAWN! • 1979 • Hannam Ken • ASL

DAWN • 1986 • Jancso Miklos • HNG

DAWN see **MORGENROT** • 1933

DAWN see **GRYNING** • 1944

DAWN see **FAJR, AL** • 1967

DAWN see **HAJNAL** • 1971

DAWN see **PRATVUSHA** • 1979

DAWN, THE • 1936 • Cooper Thomas G. • UKN • DAWN OVER IRELAND

DAWN, THE see **SVITANI** • 1933

DAWN, THE see **NAD NAMI SVITA** • 1952

DAWN, THE see **RAAT BHORE** • 1956

DAWN, THE see **SERANGAN FAJAR** • 1981

DAWN ABOVE US see **NAD NAMI SVITA** • 1952

DAWN ALL NIGHT see **SVITALO CELOU NOC** • 1979

DAWN AND TWILIGHT • 1914 • *Essanay* • USA

DAWN AT SOCORRO • 1954 • Sherman George • USA

DAWN COMES LATE see **GUERRILLA GIRL** • 1953

DAWN FIFTEENTH OF AUGUST see **REIMEI HACHIGATSU JUGO-NICHI** • 1952

DAWN FRASER STORY • 1964 • Robinson Lee, Cavill Joy • DOC • ASL

DAWN GUARD • 1941 • Boulting Roy • UKN

DAWN IN MANCHURIA see **MAMMO KENKOKU NO REIMEI** • 1932

DAWN IN PARIS see **ZORI PARISCHA** • 1937

DAWN IN THE BOULEVARD see **ASA NO NAMIKI-MICHI** • 1936

DAWN KILLER, THE • 1959 • Taylor Donald • SRL • UKN

DAWN MAKER, THE • 1916 • Hart William S. • USA

DAWN OF A NEW DAY see **FAJR YOM JADID** • 1964

DAWN OF A TOMORROW, THE • 1915 • Kirkwood James • USA

DAWN OF A TOMORROW, THE • 1924 • Melford George • USA

DAWN OF AN INDUSTRY • 1966 • Bryant Gerard, Stewart Derek • DOC • UKN

DAWN OF COURAGE, THE • 1915 • Morgan George • USA

DAWN OF DECENCY, THE • 1917 • *Big U* • SHT • USA

DAWN OF FREEDOM • 1910 • *Selig* • USA

DAWN OF FREEDOM, THE • 1916 • Scardon Paul, Marston Theodore • USA

DAWN OF HOPE, THE see **UMUTLU SAFAKLLAR** • 1985

DAWN OF INDIA see **UTRO INDIA** • 1959

DAWN OF IRAN • 1938 • Taylor John • UKN

DAWN OF ISLAM, THE see **FAJR AL-ISLAM** • 1970

DAWN OF JUSTICE • 1928 • CLM

DAWN OF LIFE, THE (UKN) see **LIFE BEGINS** • 1932

DAWN OF LOVE, THE • 1916 • Carewe Edwin • USA • LIGHT OF LOVE, THE

DAWN OF MANCHUKUO AND MONGOLIA, THE see **MAMMO KENKOKU NO REIMEI** • 1932

DAWN OF MONGOLIA, THE (USA) see **MAMMO KENKOKU NO REIMEI** • 1932

DAWN OF MOTORING • 1973 • Mason Bill • DOC • UKN

DAWN OF NETTA, THE • 1912 • *Nestor* • USA

DAWN OF OCTOBER, THE see **SWIT PAZDZIERNIKA** • 1958

DAWN OF PASSION, THE • 1912 • Dwan Allan • USA

DAWN OF REVENGE • 1922 • Sievel Bernard • USA

DAWN OF ROMANCE • 1914 • Tucker George Loane • USA

DAWN OF THE DAMNED see **AUBE DES DAMNES, L'** • 1964

DAWN OF THE DEAD see **ZOMBIES** • 1978

DAWN OF THE EAST • 1921 • Griffith Edward H. • USA

DAWN OF THE FOUNDATION OF MANCHUKUO AND MONGOLIA see **MAMMO KENKOKU NO REIMEI** • 1932

DAWN OF THE MUMMY • 1981 • Agrama Frank, Weston Armand • USA, ITL, EGY

DAWN OF THE NEW DAY, THE • 1914 • *Grandin Ethel* • USA

DAWN OF TRUTH, THE • 1920 • MacBean L. C. • UKN

DAWN OF UNDERSTANDING, THE • 1915 • Brooke Van Dyke • USA

DAWN OF UNDERSTANDING, THE • 1918 • Smith David • USA

DAWN OF WISDOM, THE • 1917 • *Mayo Frank* • SHT • USA

DAWN ON THE GREAT DIVIDE • 1943 • Bretherton Howard • USA

DAWN OVER FRANCE (USA) see **GASPARD DE BESSE** • 1935

DAWN OVER IRELAND see **DAWN, THE** • 1936

DAWN OVER THE DANUBE • 1956 • Grigorov Roumen • DOC • BUL

DAWN OVER THE DRAVA • 1974 • Heskiya Zako • BUL

DAWN OVER THE HOMELAND see **UTRO NAD RODINATA** • 1951

DAWN OVER THIRA • Sfikas Kostas • SHT • GRC

DAWN PATROL • 1930 • Hawks Howard • USA • FLIGHT COMMANDER

DAWN PATROL • 1938 • Goulding Edmund • USA

DAWN: PORTRAIT OF A TEENAGE RUNAWAY • 1976 • Kleiser Randall • TVM • USA

DAWN RENDEZVOUS • 1963 • Spencer Ronald • UKN

DAWN RIDER, THE • 1935 • Bradbury Robert North • USA

DAWN ROAD, THE • 1915 • Franz Joseph J. • USA

DAWN TO DAWN • 1933 • Berne Josef • USA

DAWN TO DUSK • 1968 • Wolf Mark • SHT • USA

DAWN TRAIL, THE • 1930 • Cabanne W. Christy • USA

DAWN VISITOR, THE • 1975 • Shoukry Mamdouh • EGY

DAWNBREAKERS • 1975 • Boulting Laurence • UKN

DAWNING, THE • 1912 • *Baird Leah* • USA

DAWNING, THE • 1988 • Knights Robert • UKN

DAWNING NATION see **YOAKE NO KUNI** • 1967

DAWNS ARE QUIET HERE, THE see **A ZORI ZYDES TIKHIYE..** • 1973

DAWNS HERE ARE QUIET, THE (USA) see **A ZORI ZYDES TIKHIYE..** • 1973

DAWSON J. • 1980 • Mason Don, Malleson Nicky • UKN

DAWSON PATROL, THE see **DAWSON PATROL: DEATH IN ALASKA, THE**

DAWSON PATROL: DEATH IN ALASKA, THE • Kelly Peter • CND • DEATH IN ALASKA ○ DAWSON PATROL, THE

DAY, THE • 1914 • Rolfe Alfred • ASL

DAY, THE • 1961 • Finch Peter, Turner Yolande • UKN • ANTONITO

DAY AFTER, THE • 1909 • Powell Frank, Griffith D. W. • USA

DAY AFTER, THE • 1983 • Meyer Nicholas • TVM • USA

DAY AFTER, THE see **UP FROM THE BEACH** • 1965

DAY AFTER DAY • 1943 • Slutsky Mikhail • USS

DAY AFTER DAY • 1971 • Ioseliani Otar • USS

DAY AFTER DAY see **JOUR APRES JOUR** • 1962

DAY AFTER HALLOWEEN, THE see **SNAPSHOT** • 1979

DAY AFTER THE DIVORCE, THE (USA) see **TAG NACH DER SCHEIDUNG, DER** • 1938

DAY AFTER TOMORROW, THE (UKN) see **STRANGE HOLIDAY** • 1945

DAY AFTER TRINITY: J. ROBERT OPPENHEIMER AND THE ATOMIC BOMB • 1981 • Else John • DOC • USA

DAY AHEAD, A • 1969 • Lyubimov Pavel • USS

DAY AND A NIGHT, A • 1911 • *Kalem* • USA

DAY AND A NIGHT, A • 1917 • Richmond J. A. • SHT • USA

DAY AND NIGHT • 1949 • UKN

DAY AND NIGHT see **RAAT AUR DIN** • 1968

DAY AND THE HOUR, THE (USA) see **JOUR ET L'HEURE, LE** • 1963

DAY AT BRIGHTON, A • 1904 • Collins Alf • UKN

DAY AT MIDLAND BEACH, A • 1915 • Perez Marcel • USA

DAY AT SCHOOL, A • 1916 • *Plump & Runt* • SHT • USA

DAY AT THE BEACH, A • 1938 • Freleng Friz • ANS • USA

DAY AT THE BEACH, A • 1970 • Hesera Simon • UKN

DAY AT THE BEACH, A see **DAGJE NAAR HET STRAND, EEN** • 1984

DAY AT THE CIRCUS, A • 1901 • Porter Edwin S. • USA

DAY AT THE RACES, A • 1937 • Wood Sam • USA

DAY AT THE SAN DIEGO FAIR, A • 1915 • Curtis Allen • USA

DAY AT THE ZOO, A • 1939 • Avery Tex • ANS • USA

DAY AT THE ZUYDERZEE, A • DOC • NTH

DAY AT UNIVERSAL CITY, A • 1915 • *Moran Lee* • USA

DAY BEFORE, THE see **VISPERA, LA** • 1982

DAY BEFORE, THE see **GIORNO PRIMA, IL** • 1987

DAY BEFORE YESTERDAY, THE see **TEGNAPELOTT** • 1981

DAY BY DAY • 1913 • *Watson Minor* • USA

DAY BY DAY see **ROZ GARAN** • 1968

DAY BY DAY see **DIA TRAS DIA** • 1979

DAY CHRIST DIED, THE • 1980 • Jones James Cellan • TVM • UKN

DAY COMES, THE see **IDU DANI** • 1968

DAY-DREAM (USA) see **HAKUJITSUMU** • 1964

DAY-DREAMERS, THE see **FANTASTERNE** • 1967

DAY DREAMS • 1919 • Badger Clarence • USA

DAY DREAMS • 1922 • Cline Eddie, Keaton Buster • SHT • USA

DAY DREAMS • 1933 • *Premier* • SHT • UKN

DAY DUTY • 1907 • Coleby A. E.? • UKN

DAY FOR LION-HEARTS, A see **GIORNO DA LEONI, UN** • 1961

DAY FOR MY LOVE, A see **DEN PRO MOU LASKU** • 1976

DAY FOR NIGHT (UKN) see **NUIT AMERICAINE, LA** • 1973

DAY FOR TATTOOING, A see **DAN ZA TETOVIRANJE** • 1990

DAY FOR THANKS ON WALTON MOUNTAIN, A • 1982 • Harris Harry • TVM • USA

DAY HAS GONE, THE see **ELTAVOZOTT NAP** • 1968

DAY I STOPPED SMOKING, THE • 1982 • Dragic Nedeljko • ANM • YGS

DAY I VANISHED, THE • 1959 • Glut Don • SHT • USA

DAY IN A FACTORY, A • 1940 • Anstey Edgar • DOC • UKN

DAY IN A NEW WORLD see **DEN NOVOGO MIRA** • 1940

DAY IN CAMP WITH THE VOLUNTEERS, A • 1902 • Williamson James • UKN

DAY IN COURT, A (USA) see **GIORNO IN PRETURA, UN** • 1954

DAY IN JERUSALEM, A • 1912 • Olcott Sidney • DOC • USA

DAY IN JUNE, A • 1944 • Donnelly Eddie • ANS • USA

DAY IN LONDON, A • 1912 • Fitzhamon Lewin? • UKN

DAY IN MOSCOW, A • 1957 • Poselsky I. • USS

DAY IN RIJEKA, A • 1955 • Babaja Ante • YGS

DAY IN SANTA FE, A • 1932 • Riggs Lynn • USA

DAY IN THE CITY, A see **DAG I STADEN, EN** • 1956

DAY IN THE COUNTRY, A • 1912 • Fitzhamon Lewin • UKN

DAY IN THE COUNTRY, A see **PARTIE DE CAMPAGNE, UNE** • 1936

DAY IN THE DEATH OF JOE EGG, A • 1972 • Medak Peter • UKN • JOE EGG

DAY IN THE LIFE OF A COAL MINER, A • 1910 • UKN

DAY IN THE LIFE OF A THAMES FIREMAN, A • 1904 • *Cricks & Sharp* • UKN

DAY IN THE LIFE OF A WARSAW BUSDRIVER, A see **WARSZAWSKI KIEROWCA JERZY WINNICKI** • 1973

DAY IN THE LIFE OF A WREN, A • 1949 • UKN

DAY IN THE LIFE OF DR. KALINNIKOVA, A • 1974 • Titov Victor • USS

DAY IN THE LIFE OF GESTAPO MAN SCHMIDT, A see **POWSZEDNI DZIEN GESTAPOWCA SCHMIDTA** • 1963

DAY IN THE LIFE OF JONATHON MOLE, A • 1959 • Brittain Don • CND

DAY IN THE NEW WORLD, A see **DEN NOVOGO MIRA** • 1940

DAY IT CAME TO EARTH, THE • 1979 • Thomason Harry • USA

DAY IT RAINED, THE (USA) see **AM TAG ALS DER REGEN KAM** • 1959

DAY LAPU, DRUG! • 1967 • Gurin Ilya • USS • GIVE ME YOUR PAW, FRIEND! ○ YOUR PAW, FRIEND!

DAY LIKE ANY OTHER DAY, A see **JOUR COMME UN AUTRE, UN** • 1974

DAY LONGER THAN A YEAR, A see **DAN DUZI OD GODINE** • 1973

DAY LONGER THAN NIGHT, THE see **DEN' DINNEIE NOCHI** • 1983

DAY MARS INVADED EARTH, THE • 1962 • Dexter Maury • USA • SPACERAID '63

DAY MUCH LIKE THE OTHERS, A • 1978 • Gunnarsson Sturla • CND

DAY MY GRANDFATHER DIED, THE • 1976 • Bonniere Rene • CND

DAY NEW YORK WAS INVADED, THE see **MOUSE THAT ROARED, THE** • 1959

DAY NURSE • 1932 • Lantz Walter, Nolan William • ANS • USA

DAY NURSING see **CHILDREN'S CORNER** • 1956

DAY OF A STRIPPER • 1964 • *St. Thomas Warren (P)* • USA

DAY OF ANGER (UKN) see **GIORNI DELL'IRA, I** • 1967

DAY OF DAYS, THE • 1914 • *Scott Cyril* • USA

DAY OF FAITH, THE • 1923 • Browning Tod • USA

DAY OF FEAR • 1957 • *Rojo Ruben* • SPN

DAY OF FREEDOM: OUR ARMY see **TAG DER FREIHEIT: UNSERE WEHRMACHT** • 1935

DAY OF FURY, A • 1956 • Jones Harmon • USA

DAY OF GRACE • 1957 • Searle Francis • DOC • UKN

DAY OF HAPPINESS, A see **DEN SCHASTYA** • 1963

DAY OF HAVOC, A • 1915 • Kaufman Joseph • USA

DAY OF JOY see **GLAEDENS DAG** • 1918

DAY OF JUDGEMENT • 1974 • Ovadia George • ISR

DAY OF JUDGEMENT, A • 1981 • Reynolds C. D. H. • USA • STORMBRINGER

DAY OF LIFE, A see **GIORNO NELLA VITA, UN** • 1946

DAY OF MARRIAGE see **TOTSUGU HI** • 1956

DAY OF PEACE see **DAN ODMORA** • 1957

DAY OF PLEASURE, A • 1910 • *Powers* • USA

DAY OF PURIFICATION see **DZIEN OCZYSZCZENIA** • 1969

DAY OF RECKONING • 1933 • Brabin Charles J. • USA • FOREVER FAITHFUL

DAY OF RECKONING see **GUNS OF DIABLO** • 1964

DAY OF RECKONING, THE • 1914 • *United States Film* • USA

DAY OF RECKONING, THE • 1915 • Eason B. Reeves • USA

DAY OF RECKONING, THE see **DEN ODPLATY** • 1960

DAY OF REMISSION see **DZIEN OCZYSZCZENIA** • 1969

DAY OF REST • 1970 • Clark Jim • SHT • UKN

DAY OF REST, A • 1915 • Cooper Toby? • UKN

DAY OF REST, THE • 1939 • Wrangell Basil • USA

DAY OF RESURRECTION, THE see **FUKKATSU NO HI** • 1979

DAY OF SIN, A see **GIORNATA BALORDA, LA** • 1960

DAY OF SUN AND RAIN, A see **DYEN SOLNTSA I DOZHDYA** • 1968

DAY OF THE ANIMALS • 1977 • Girdler William • USA • SOMETHING IS OUT THERE

DAY OF THE APOCALYPSE see **SENGOKU JIEITAI** • 1979

DAY OF THE ARROW • 1965 • Furie Sidney J. • USA

DAY OF THE ASSASSIN • 1981 • Trenchard-Smith Brian, Vasallo Carlos • MXC

DAY OF THE BAD MAN • 1958 • Keller Harry • USA

DAY OF THE COBRA see **COBRA** • 1980

DAY OF THE DEAD • 1957 • Eames Charles, Eames Ray • USA

DAY OF THE DEAD • 1985 • Romero George A. • USA

DAY OF THE DOG, THE • 1914 • *Selig* • USA

DAY OF THE DOLPHIN, THE • 1973 • Nichols Mike • USA

DAY OF THE ECLIPSE, THE see **GUNESIN TUTULDUGU GUN** • 1985

DAY OF THE EVIL GUN • 1968 • Thorpe Jerry • USA

DAY OF THE FIGHT • 1950 • Kubrick Stanley • DCS • USA

DAY OF THE HAWKER see **JOUR DU FORAIN, LE** • 1987

DAY OF THE HUNTER • 1989 • Gessner Nicolas

DAY OF THE IGUANA, THE • 1988 • Hellman Monte • USA

DAY OF THE JACKAL, THE • 1973 • Zinnemann Fred • UKN, USA, FRN

DAY OF THE LAND GRABBER see **LAND RAIDERS** • 1970

DAY OF THE LOCUST, THE • 1975 • Schlesinger John • USA

DAY OF THE NIGHTMARE • 1965 • Bushelman John • USA • DON'T SCREAM, DORIS MAYS

DAY OF THE OUTLAW • 1959 • De Toth Andre • USA

DAY OF THE OWL, THE see **GIORNO DELLA CIVETTA, IL** • 1967

DAY OF THE PANTHER, THE • 1987 • Trenchard-Smith Brian • ASL

DAY OF THE RULERS, THE • 1984 • Ikonomov Vladislav • BUL

DAY OF THE TRIFFIDS • 1962 • Sekely Steve, Francis Freddie (U/c) • UKN

DAY OF THE TRUMPET, THE • 1957 • Romero Eddie • PHL

DAY OF THE VICTORIOUS COUNTRY, THE • 1947 • Kopalin Ilya • DOC • USS

DAY OF THE WOLVES • 1973 • Grofe Ferde Jr. • TVM • USA

DAY OF THE WOMAN see **I SPIT ON YOUR GRAVE** • 1981

DAY OF TRIUMPH • 1954 • Pichel Irving, Coyle John T. • USA • GREAT BETRAYAL, THE

DAY OF VIOLENCE • *Norman Daria* • ITL

DAY OF WAR see **DEN VOINI** • 1942

DAY OF WRATH see **VREDENS DAG** • 1943

DAY OF WRATH see **GIORNI DELL'IRA, I** • 1967

DAY OF YOUTH see **SEINEN NO KI** • 1960

DAY OF YOUTH (USA) see **JEUGDDAG** • 1929

DAY OFF see **REPO** • 1981

DAY OFF, A • 1912 • *Selig* • USA

DAY OFF, A • 1917 • *Pokes & Jabbs* • SHT • USA

DAY OFF, THE • 1980 • Goldsmith Sidney • ANM • CND

DAY ON HIS OWN, A • 1906 • Williamson James • UKN

DAY ON ROLLERS, A • 1913 • Fitzhamon Lewin • UKN

DAY ON THE FORCE, A • 1915 • Hotaling Arthur D. • USA

DAY ON THE RIVER, A • 1955 • Babaja Ante • SHT • YGS

DAY OR NIGHT see **YO VAI PAIVA** • 1962

DAY OUR LIVES SHINE, THE see **WAGA SHOGAI NO KAGAYAKERU HI** • 1948

DAY OUT OF JAIL, A • 1917 • Hamilton Lloyd • SHT • USA

DAY RESURGENT, THE • 1920 • Totten Joseph Byron • SHT • USA

DAY SHALL DAWN see **JAGO HUA SAVERA** • 1958

DAY SHALL DAWN, A see **DAG SKALL GRY, EN** • 1944

DAY SHE PAID, THE • 1919 • Ingram Rex • USA

DAY STARS see **STARS BY DAY** • 1966

DAY THAT IS DEAD, A • 1913 • France Charles H. • USA

DAY THAT IS GONE, A • 1915 • *Clary Charles* • USA

DAY THAT SHOOK THE WORLD, THE see **SARAJEVSKI ATENTAT** • 1975

DAY THAT YOU LOVE ME, THE see **DIA QUE ME QUIERAS, EL** • 1935

DAY THE BOOKIES WEPT, THE • 1939 • Goodwins Leslie • USA
DAY THE BUBBLE BURST, THE • 1982 • Hardy Joseph • TVM • USA
DAY THE CLOWN CRIED, THE see **JOUR OU LE CLOWN PLEURA, LE** • 1974
DAY THE EARTH CAUGHT FIRE, THE • 1961 • Guest Val • UKN
DAY THE EARTH FROZE, THE (USA) see **SAMPO** • 1959
DAY THE EARTH GOT STONED, THE • 1978 • Patterson Richard • USA
DAY THE EARTH MOVED, THE • 1974 • Lewis Robert Michael • TVM • USA
DAY THE EARTH STOOD STILL, THE • 1950 • Wise Robert • USA
DAY THE EIFFEL TOWER RAN AWAY, THE • ANM • FRN
DAY THE FISH CAME OUT, THE • 1967 • Cacoyannis Michael • UKN, GRC, USA
DAY THE HOT LINE GOT HOT, THE (USA) see **ROUBLE A DEUX FACES, LE** • 1969
DAY THE LORD GOT BUSTED, THE • 1976 • Topper Burt • USA • MIRACLE MAN, THE
DAY THE LOVING STOPPED, THE • 1981 • Mann Daniel • TVM • USA
DAY THE MUSIC DIED, THE • 1977 • Tenzer Bert • DOC • USA
DAY THE RAINS CAME, THE see **AM TAG ALS DER REGEN KAM** • 1959
DAY THE SCREAMING STOPPED, THE see **COMEBACK, THE** • 1978
DAY THE SKY EXPLODED, THE(USA) see **MORTE VIENE DALLO SPAZIO, LA** • 1958
DAY THE SKY FELL IN, THE • 1961 • Shawzin Barry • UKN
DAY THE SUN ROSE, THE (USA) see **GION MATSURI** • 1968
DAY THE TREES WILL BLOOM, THE see **KDE REKY MAJI SLUNCE** • 1961
DAY THE WAR ENDED, THE (USA) see **PERVYI DEN MIRA** • 1959
DAY THE WOMEN GOT EVEN, THE • 1980 • Brinckerhoff Burt • TVM • USA
DAY THE WORLD CHANGED HANDS, THE see **FORBIN PROJECT, THE** • 1969
DAY THE WORLD ENDED, THE • 1956 • Corman Roger • USA
DAY THE WORLD ENDED, THE see **WHEN TIME RAN OUT..** • 1980
DAY THEY GAVE BABIES AWAY, THE (UKN) see **ALL MINE TO GIVE** • 1956
DAY THEY KILLED THE SNOWMAN, THE • 1970 • Carter Peter • CND
DAY THEY ROBBED THE BANK OF ENGLAND, THE • 1960 • Guillermin John • UKN
DAY THEY TOOK THE BABIES AWAY, THE • 1974 • Moxey John Llewellyn • TVM • USA
DAY TIME ENDED, THE • 1978 • Cardos John Bud • USA • TIME WARP ○ VORTEX
DAY-TIME WIFE • 1939 • Ratoff Gregory • USA
DAY TO LIVE, A • 1931 • *Terry Paul/ Moser Frank (P)* • ANS • USA
DAY TO REMEMBER, A • 1953 • Thomas Ralph • UKN
DAY TO WED, THE see **TOTSUGU HI** • 1956
DAY WHEN LOVE RETURNS, THE see **AI NI YOMIGAERU HI** • 1922
DAY WILL DAWN, THE • 1942 • French Harold • UKN • AVENGERS, THE (USA)
DAY WITH GOVERNOR WHITMAN, A • 1916 • Griffith D. W. • DOC • USA
DAY WITH MARY PICKFORD, A • 1916 • Griffith D. W. • DOC • USA
DAY WITH POACHERS, A • 1912 • *Urban Trading Co.* • UKN
DAY WITH THE BOYS, A • 1969 • Gulager Clu • SHT • USA
DAY WITH THE DEVIL, A see **DIA CON EL DIABLO, UN** • 1945
DAY WITH THE FRESH AIR FIEND, A • 1905 • Collins Alf? • UKN
DAY WITH THE HOP PICKERS, A • 1903 • Hepworth Cecil M. • UKN
DAY WITH THE RUSSIANS, A • 1961 • Karmen Roman, Boykov V. • ANT • USS • ONE DAY WITH THE RUSSIANS
DAY WITHOUT END see **BEWARE MY LOVELY** • 1952
DAY WITHOUT LAND • 1968 • Kovachev Hristo • DOC • BUL
DAY WITHOUT SUN see **DZIEN BEZ SLONCA** • 1959
DAY YOU LOVE ME, THE see **DIA QUE ME QUIERAS, EL** • 1935
DAY YOU LOVE ME, THE see **DIA QUE ME QUIERAS, EL** • 1988
DAYBREAK • 1914 • *Vale Louise* • USA
DAYBREAK • 1918 • Capellani Albert • USA
DAYBREAK • 1931 • Feyder Jacques • USA
DAYBREAK • 1946 • Bennett Compton • UKN
DAYBREAK • 1957 • Brakhage Stan • USA
DAYBREAK see **OUTSIDER, THE** • 1926
DAYBREAK AND WHITEYE • 1957 • Brakhage Stan • SHT • USA
DAYBREAK EXPRESS • 1953 • Pennebaker D. A. • SHT • USA
DAYBREAK IN UDI • 1949 • Bishop Terry • DOC • UKN
DAYBREAK (USA) see **JOUR SE LEVE, LE** • 1939
DAYBREAKERS, THE see **SACKETTS, THE** • 1979
DAYDREAM see **HAKUJITSU-MU** • 1980
DAYDREAMER • 1967 • Martin Michael • SHT • ASL
DAYDREAMER, THE • 1966 • Bass Jules • ANM • USA
DAYDREAMER, THE (USA) see **DISTRAIT, LE** • 1970
DAYDREAMS • 1913 • Collins Edwin J.? • UKN
DAYDREAMS • 1928 • Montagu Ivor • UKN
DAYDREAMS • 1965 • Buesst Nigel • SHT • ASL
DAYEREH MINA • 1974 • Mehrjui Dariush • IRN • MINA CYCLE ○ CYCLE, THE
DAYESH VOZDUKH • 1924 • Vertov Dziga • USS • LONG LIVE THE AIR ○ DAESH VOZKUKH ○ GIVE US AIR
DAYLIGHT • 1914 • *American* • USA
DAYLIGHT • 1974 • Nikolov Margarit • BUL
DAYLIGHT BURGLAR, THE • 1912 • Cabanne W. Christy • USA
DAYLIGHT BURGLAR, THE • 1913 • O'Sullivan Tony • USA
DAYLIGHT ROBBERY • 1913 • Calvert Charles? • UKN
DAYLIGHT ROBBERY • 1964 • Truman Michael • UKN
DAYLIGHT SAVING BILL, THE • 1916 • Batley Ethyle • UKN
DAYS • Stoyanov Yuli • DOC • BUL
DAYS, THE see **DANI** • 1963
DAY'S ADVENTURE, A • 1915 • O'Sullivan Tony • USA
DAYS AND NIGHTS • 1944 • Stolper Alexander • USS
DAYS AND NIGHTS IN LENINGRAD see **LENINGRAD V BORBYE** • 1942
DAYS AND NIGHTS IN THE FOREST see **ARANYE DINRATRI** • 1969
DAYS ARE NUMBERED, THE see **GIORNI CONTATI, I** • 1962
DAYS ARE PASSING see **IDU DANI** • 1971
DAYS ARE PASSING, THE see **ZEMALJSKI DANI TEKU** • 1980
DAYS BEFORE CHRISTMAS, THE • 1958 • Koenig Wolf, Jackson Stanley R., Macartney-Filgate Terence, Dufaux Georges • DCS • CND • BIENTOT NOEL
DAYS BEFORE LENT see **HOLIDAY FOR SINNERS** • 1952
DAYS BEFORE TOMORROW, THE see **BEFORE TOMORROW** • 1968
DAY'S BEGINNING, THE • 1975 • Petrov Dimitar • BUL
DAYS, DAYS see **ALAYAM, ALAYAM** • 1977
DAY'S DIET, A see **EDGAR'S FEAST DAY** • 1921
DAYS ELAPSE, THE see **IDU DANI** • 1968
DAY'S ENCOUNTERS, A see **INCONTRI DI UN GIORNO** • 1947
DAYS FROM 1000 YEARS see **DAGER FRA 1000 AR** • 1969
DAY'S HOLIDAY, A • 1908 • Williamson James? • UKN
DAYS IN LONDON • 1978 • Gousini Samir • SYR
DAYS IN MY FATHER'S HOUSE see **DAGE I MIN FARS HUS** • 1968
DAYS IN THE TREES see **DES JOURNEES ENTIERES DANS LES ARBRES** • 1976
DAYS LIKE OLD TIMES see **DIAS DE VIEJO COLOR** • 1968
DAYS, MONTHS, YEARS see **DNI, MIESIACE, LATA** • 1966
DAYS OF '36 (USA) see **IMERES TOU '36** • 1972
DAYS OF '49 • 1910 • *Nestor* • USA
DAYS OF '49 • 1912 • *Blackwell Carlyle* • USA
DAYS OF '49 • 1913 • Ince Thomas H. • USA
DAYS OF '49 • 1924 • Jaccard Jacques, Wilson Ben • SRL • USA
DAYS OF ANGER see **AYAM EL GHADAB** • 1988
DAYS OF ASHES see **DIAS DE CENIZA** • 1970
DAYS OF ASHES see **DIAS DE CENIZA** • 1978
DAYS OF BETRAYAL, THE see **DNY ZRADY** • 1973
DAYS OF BUFFALO BILL • 1946 • Carr Thomas • USA
DAYS OF BUFFALO BILL, THE see **IN THE DAYS OF BUFFALO BILL** • 1922
DAYS OF DANIEL BOONE, THE • 1923 • Messinger Frank • USA
DAYS OF DESIRE (UKN) see **ILS SONT NUS** • 1966
DAYS OF DESTRUCTION • 1973 • Steingrimsson Pall • DOC • ICL
DAYS OF DYLAN THOMAS, THE • 1965 • Ferguson Graeme • USA
DAYS OF ECLIPSE • 1989 • Sokurov Alexander • USS
DAYS OF EVIL WOMEN see **AKUJO NO KISETSU** • 1958
DAYS OF GLORY • 1944 • Tourneur Jacques • USA
DAYS OF HATE (USA) see **DIAS DE ODIO** • 1954
DAYS OF HATRED see **DIAS DE ODIO** • 1954
DAYS OF HEAVEN • 1978 • Malick Terence • USA
DAYS OF HELL • 1985 • Ricci Tonino • ITL
DAYS OF HOPE • 1976 • Loach Kenneth • MTV • UKN
DAYS OF HOPE see **ESPOIR** • 1939
DAYS OF INSPECTOR AMBROSIO, THE see **GIORNI DEL COMMISSARIO AMBROSIO, I** • 1988
DAYS OF JESSE JAMES • 1939 • Kane Joseph • USA
DAYS OF LOVE see **GIORNI D'AMORE** • 1955
DAYS OF LOVE see **AYYAM EL HOB** • 1968
DAYS OF LOVE see **DIAS DEL AMOR, LOS** • 1971
DAYS OF MAKE BELIEVE • 1946 • Williamson Cecil H. • UKN
DAYS OF MATTHEW, THE see **ZYWOT MATEUSZA** • 1968
DAYS OF MY YEARS see **DAGEN MIJNER JAREN** • 1960
DAYS OF MY YOUTH, THE see **WAGA SEISHUN NO TOKI** • 1974
DAYS OF NO RETURN see **KAEREZARU HIBI** • 1978
DAYS OF OCTOBER, THE see **OCTIABR' DNI** • 1958
DAYS OF OLD • 1922 • Parrott Charles • USA
DAYS OF OLD CHEYENNE • 1943 • Clifton Elmer • USA
DAYS OF OUR LIFE see **DNI NACHEI GIZNI** • 1914
DAYS OF OUR YEARS (USA) see **CE SIECLE A CINQUANTE ANS** • 1949
DAYS OF PEACE AND MUSIC see **MULATSAG** • 1989
DAYS OF SHAME AND NIGHTS OF EXCESS see **MELLEM VENNER** • 1963
DAYS OF SIN AND NIGHTS OF MADNESS see **MELLEM VENNER** • 1963
DAYS OF SIN AND NIGHTS OF NYMPHOMANIA (USA) see **MELLEM VENNER** • 1963
DAYS OF SIN, NIGHTS OF NYMPH.. see **MELLEM VENNER** • 1963
DAYS OF SMOKE see **DIAS DE HUMO** • 1989
DAYS OF SMOKE see **KE ARTEKO EGUNAK** • 1989
DAYS OF TEMPTATION, THE • 1966 • Gapo Branko • YGS
DAYS OF TERROR • 1912 • *Kent Charles* • USA
DAYS OF THE EARLY WEST • 1910 • *Champion* • USA
DAYS OF THE PAST see **DIAS DEL PASADA, LOS** • 1977
DAYS OF THE PONY EXPRESS • 1913 • *Stockdale Carl* • USA
DAYS OF THRILLS AND LAUGHTER • 1961 • Youngson Robert • CMP • USA
DAYS OF THUNDER • 1990 • Scott Anthony • USA
DAYS OF TORMENT see **JOURS DE TOURMENTES** • 1983
DAYS OF TREASON, THE see **DNY ZRADY** • 1973
DAYS OF VIOLENCE see **GIORNI DELLA VIOLENZA, I** • 1967
DAYS OF VOLOCHAYEV, THE see **VOLOCHAYEVSKIYE DNI** • 1938
DAYS OF WATER, THE see **DIAS DEL AGUA, LOS** • 1970
DAYS OF WHISKY GAP • 1961 • Low Colin • DOC • CND
DAYS OF WINE AND ROSES • 1958 • Frankenheimer John • MTV • USA
DAYS OF WINE AND ROSES • 1962 • Edwards Blake • USA
DAYS OF WRATH see **GIORNI DELL'IRA, I** • 1967
DAYS OF YOUTH see **JEUGDDAG** • 1929
DAYS OF YOUTH see **WAKAKIHI** • 1929
DAY'S OUTING, A • 1912 • *Lucas Wilfred* • USA
DAY'S OUTING, A • 1914 • *Lux* • USA
DAY'S OUTING AT MANLEY, A • 1912 • ASL
DAY'S PLEASURE, A • 1919 • Chaplin Charles • SHT • USA
DAY'S SPORT, A • 1912 • Melford Mark • UKN
DAY'S WORK, THE • 1916 • Humphrey Orral • USA
DAYS YOU GAVE ME, THE see **DIAS QUE ME DISTE, LOS** • 1975
DAYTIME WIVES • 1923 • Chautard Emile • USA
DAYTONA BEACH WEEKEND • 1965 • Welby Robert • USA
DAYTON'S DEVILS • 1968 • Shea Jack • USA
DAYUHAN, ANG • 1968 • Reyes Efren • PHL • STRANGER, THE
DAZE OF THE WEST • 1927 • Wyler William • SHT • USA
DAZZLE'S BLACK EYE • 1914 • *Crystal* • USA
DAZZLING AFFAIRS see **KYORETSU NO JYOJI** • 1968
DAZZLING MISS DAVISON, THE • 1917 • Powell Frank • USA • ON HER HONOR
DCERY EVINY • 1928 • Lamac Carl • CZC
DDAENG BYEOT • 1985 • Ha Myeong-Sung • SKR • BLAZING SUN, THE
DDANACH • 1970 • Cohen Robert* • SWT • AFTERMATH
DDQ10 • 1978 • Dobson Kevin • DOC • ASL
DE AMERICA SOY HIJO.. Y A ELLA ME DEBO • 1972 • Alvarez Santiago • DOC • CUB • I AM A SON OF AMERICA.. AND I'M INDEBTED TO IT
DE-AS FI HARAP ALB • 1965 • Popescu-Gopo Ion • RMN • WHITE MOOR ○ HARAP ALB
DE BABORD A TRIBORD • 1926 • Matras Christian • SHT • FRN
DE BARRO Y ORO • 1966 • Bollo Joaquin • SPN
DE BOUCHE A OREILLE • 1957 • Leduc • SHT • FRN
DE BRECKER • 1988 • Bodson Menn, Olinger Marc • LXM • TRAITOR, THE
DE BRUIT ET DE FUREUR • 1988 • Brisseau Jean-Claude • FRN • OF SOUND AND FURY
DE CAIN, LAS • 1957 • Momplet Antonio • SPN
DE CARA AL CIELO • 1979 • Dawi Enrique • ARG • FACING THE SKY
DE CARNE SOMOS • 1954 • Gavaldon Roberto • MXC
...DE CHICAGO • 1981 • Payer Roch Christophe (c/d) • CND
DE CIERTA MANERA • 1977 • Gomez Sara • CUB • ONE WAY OR ANOTHER ○ IN A CERTAIN WAY ○ IN A WAY
DE COEUR DE COEUR see **MINA AL-QALB LI AL-QALB** • 1951
DE COLOR MORENO • 1963 • Martinez Solares Gilberto • MXC, SPN
DE COLORES • 1968 • Garces Armando • PHL
DE COMO HERODES FUE DEGOLLADO POR LOS HIPPIES • 1972 • Plasencia Arturo • VNZ • HOW HERODES WAS BEHEADED BY THE HIPPIES
DE CUERPO PRESENTE • 1967 • Eceiza Antonio • SPN • PHYSICALLY PRESENT
DE DRAGUL TAU ANCA • 1984 • Nicolae Cristiana • RMN • FOR YOUR SAKE, ANCA
DE ESPALDAS A LA PUERTA • 1959 • Forque Jose Maria • SPN
DE FACTO • 1973 • Donev Donyo • ANS • BUL
DE FRESA, LIMON Y MENTA • 1977 • Diez Miguel Angel • SPN • OF STRAWBERRY, LEMON AND MINT
DE GAULLE LE VERBE ET L'IMAGE • Boutang Pierre-Andre • DOC • FRN
DE GLADA AREN see **EVIGA LANKAR** • 1947
DE GRACE ET D'EMBARRAS • 1979 • Carriere Marcel • CND
DE GRANDS EVENEMENTS ET DES GENS ORDINAIRES • 1979 • Ruiz Raul • FRN • OF GREAT EVENTS AND ORDINARY PEOPLE ○ GREAT EVENTS AND ORDINARY PEOPLE
DE GRAY -LE BANC DE DESOLATION • 1973 • Chabrol Claude • MTV • FRN • BANC DE LA DESOLATION, LE ○ BENCH OF DESOLATION, THE
DE HOMBRE A HOMBRE • 1949 • Fregonese Hugo • ARG
DE HOMBRE A HOMBRE • 1960 • Alazraki Benito • MXC
DE JOUR ET DE NUIT • 1964 • Cloche Maurice • FRN
DE LA CHAIR POUR FRANKENSTEIN (FRN) see **ANDY WARHOL'S FRANKENSTEIN** • 1974
DE LA CROUPE AUX LEVRES • Antony Michel • FRN
DE LA JUNGLE A L'ECRAN • 1929 • Machin Alfred • FRN
DE LA PART DES COPAINS (FRN) see **COLD SWEAT** • 1971
DE LA PIEL DEL DIABLO • 1961 • Perla Alejandro • SPN
DE LA TERRE ET DES HOMMES • 1962 • Ben Halima Hamouda • SHT • TNS
DE LA TOURBE ET DU RESTANT • 1979 • Belanger Fernand • CND
DE LA VEINE A REVENDRE see **ZEZOWATE SZCZESCIE** • 1960
DE L'ACADIE A SILLERY • 1961 • Lavoie Hermenegilde • DCS • CND
DE L'AGE DE PIERRE A L'AGE ATOMIQUE see **STONE AGE TO ATOM AGE** • 1961
DE L'AMOUR • 1964 • Aurel Jean • FRN, ITL • CALDA PELLE, LA (ITL) ○ ALL ABOUT LOVING (UKN) ○ CONCERNING LOVE
DE L'AUTRE COTE DE L'EAU • 1951 • Darene Robert • SHT • FRN
DE L'AUTRE COTE DU CHEMIN DE FER • 1967 • Patris Gerard, Ferrari L. • SHT • FRN
DE L'EAU POUR TOUS • 1969 • Merbah Lamine • DCS • ALG
DE L'ENFER A LA VICTOIRE • 1979 • Lenzi Umberto • FRN, ITL, SPN • FROM HELL TO VICTORY ○ DA DUNKERQUE ALLA VITTORIA ○ FORTRESS EUROPE
DE LENINE A HITLER • 1940 • Rony Georges • CMP • FRN
DE L'ESPRIT ET DU CORPS • 1976 • Kamba Sebastien • DOC • CNG
DE L'HOMME SINGE • 1908 • *Deed Andre* • FRN
DE LUXE ANNIE • 1918 • West Roland • USA
DE MADRID AL CIELO • 1952 • Gil Rafael • SPN
DE MAYERLING A SARAJEVO • 1940 • Ophuls Max • FRN • MAYERLING TO SARAJEVO (USA) ○ SARAJEVO (UKN)
DE MERE EN FILLE • 1968 • Poirier Anne-Claire • DOC • CND • MOTHER-TO-BE
DE MEXICO LLEGO EL AMOR • 1940 • Harlan Richard • ARG
DE MONTREAL A MANICOUAGAN • 1963 • Lamothe Arthur • DCS • CND
DE MUJER A MUJER • 1950 • Lucia Luis • SPN
DE MUJER A MUJER • 1987 • Walerstein Mauricio • VNZ • WOMAN TO WOMAN
DE NOTRE TEMPS • 1962 • Rossif Frederic • SHT • FRN
DE NUEVA YORK A HUIPANGUILLO • 1943 • Ojeda Manuel R. • MXC
DE PADRE DESCONOCIDO • 1949 • de Zavalia Alberto • ARG
DE PECADO EN PECADO • 1947 • Urueta Chano • MXC

DE PERE EN FILS • 1951 • Blais Roger • DCS • CND
DE PICOS PARDOS A LA CIUDAD • 1968 • Iquino Ignacio F. • SPN
DE PISIS • 1957 • Dona • SHT • ITL
DE PORTE EN PORTE see **PLOUM PLOUM TRA LA LA** • 1946
DE PROFESION: POLIGAMO • 1975 • Fons Angelino • SPN
DE PROFESION, SUS LABORES • 1970 • Aguirre Javier • SPN
DE PROFUNDIS • 1919 • Jacoby Georg • FRG
DE QUE COLOR ES EL VIENTO • 1972 • *Churubusco Azteca* • MXC
DE QUELQUES EVENEMENTS SANS SIGNIFICATION • 1975 • Derkaoui Mustafa • MRC
DE QUOI TU TE MELES, DANIELA! (FRN) see **ZARTE HAUT IN SCHWARZER SEIDE** • 1961
DE RANCHERO A EMPRESARIO • 1953 • Cardona Rene • MXC
DE RAZA AZTECA • 1922 • Contreras Torres Miguel, Calles Guillermo • MXC • OF AZTEC RACE
DE RENOIR A PICASSO • 1949 • Haesaerts Paul • BLG
DE ROVUMA AU MAPUTO • 1976 • Popovic Dragutin
DE SABLE ET DE FEU • 1958 • Haesaerts Luc • DOC • BLG
DE SADE • 1969 • Endfield Cy, Corman Roger (U/c), Hessler Gordon (U/c) • USA, FRG • AUSSCHWEIFENDE LEBEN DES MARQUIS DE SADE, DAS ○ MARQUIS DE SADE, DER (FRG)
DE SADE 70 • 1969 • Franco Jesus • SPN, FRN • INASSOUVIES, LES (FRN) ○ DEADLY SANCTUARY (USA)
DE SANGRE CHICANA • 1973 • Romay Pepito • MXC • OF CHICANO BLOOD
DE SFASURAREA • 1954 • Calinescu Paul • RMN • IN A VILLAGE
DE SOL A SOL • 1975 • Billon Yves • DOC • FRN
DE TAL PALO TAL ASTILLA • 1959 • Delgado Miguel M. • MXC
DE TAL PEDRO TAL ASTILLA • 1985 • Bernaza Luis Felipe • CUB • LIKE FATHER LIKE DAUGHTER
DE TEQUILA, SU MEZCAL • 1949 • Toussaint Carlos • MXC
DE TODOS MODOS JUAN TE LLAMAS • 1976 • Violante Marcela Fernandez • MXC • GENERAL'S DAUGHTER, THE
DE TOUT POUR FAIRE UN MONDE • 1962 • Cayrol Jean • FRN
DE TREI ORI BUCHAREST • 1967 • Popescu Horea, Iacob Mihai, Popescu-Gopo Ion • RMN • THREE TIMES BUCHAREST
DE WETS SPOOR • 1975 • SAF
DEA BIANCA, LA see **SENZA CIELO** • 1940
DEACON BILLINGTON'S DOWNFALL • 1914 • France Charles H. • USA
DEACON DEBS • 1911 • *Thanhouser* • USA
DEACON OUTWITTED, THE • 1913 • Lehrman Henry, Sennett Mack (Spv) • USA
DEACON STOPS THE SHOW, THE • 1916 • Curtis Allen • SHT • USA
DEACON'S CARD, THE • 1916 • Humphrey Orral • USA
DEACON'S DAUGHTER, THE • 1910 • Olcott Sidney • USA
DEACON'S DILEMMA, THE • 1913 • *Carney Augustus* • USA
DEACON'S LOVE LETTER, THE • 1909 • Brooke Van Dyke • USA
DEACON'S REWARD, THE • 1911 • *Missimer Howard* • USA
DEACON'S SHOES, THE • 1912 • *Majestic* • USA
DEACON'S SON, THE • 1914 • *Hart Lew* • USA
DEACON'S TROUBLES, THE • 1912 • Nicholls George • USA
DEACON'S WATERLOO, THE • 1916 • Christie Al • SHT • USA
DEACON'S WHISKERS, THE • 1915 • Dillon Eddie • USA
DEACON'S WIDOW, THE • 1916 • *Cub* • USA
DEAD, THE • 1960 • Brakhage Stan • SHT • USA
DEAD, THE • 1988 • Huston John • USA, UKN, FRG
DEAD ALIVE, THE • 1916 • Vernot Henry J. • USA
DEAD AMONG THE LIVING see **MRTVY MEZI ZIVYMI** • 1947
DEAD AND BURIED • 1981 • Sherman Gary • USA
DEAD AND MARRIED see **SHE'S BACK** • 1989
DEAD AND THE DEADLY, THE see **JEN HSIA JEN** • 1984
DEAD ARE ALIVE, THE see **MRTVI ZIJI** • 1922
DEAD ARE ALIVE, THE (USA) see **ETRUSCO UCCIDE ANCORA, L'** • 1972
DEAD ARE COUNTLESS, THE see **MORTI NON SI CONTANI, I** • 1968
DEAD AREA see **HOLT VIDEK** • 1971
DEAD AS A DOORMAN see **DOORMAN** • 1985
DEAD-BANG • 1989 • Frankenheimer John • USA • DEAD BANG
DEAD BANG see **DEAD-BANG** • 1989
DEAD BEAT AND BLOOD • 1978 • Rosso Franco • UKN
DEAD BIRDS • 1965 • Gardner Robert • USA, NTH
DEAD BIRD'S FLIGHT see **LET MRTVE PTICE** • 1974
DEAD BODY WITH THE SEVERED HEAD, THE • 1919 • Barsky • USS
DEAD BROKE • 1914 • *Prescott Vivian* • USA
DEAD BUT NOT BURIED • 1964 • Eceiza Antonio • SPN
DEAD CALM • 1988 • Noyce Phil • ASL
DEAD CANARY, THE • 1911 • *Comet* • USA
DEAD CAN'T LIE, THE • 1988 • Fonvielle Lloyd • USA • GOTHAM
DEAD CAT, THE • 1902 • Collins Alf? • UKN
DEAD CERT • 1974 • Richardson Tony • UKN
DEAD CERT, A • 1919 • Whiting Rowland • UKN
DEAD CERTAINTY, A • 1920 • Dewhurst George • UKN
DEAD CLASS, THE • 1978 • Wajda Andrzej • MTV • PLN
DEAD COME BACK, THE see **HOLTAK VISSZAJARNAK, A** • 1968
DEAD COUNTRY, THE see **HOLT VIDEK** • 1971
DEAD DIMENSION see **DEATH DIMENSION** • 1978
DEAD DON'T DIE, THE • 1974 • Harrington Curtis • TVM • USA
DEAD DON'T DREAM, THE • 1948 • Archainbaud George • USA
DEAD DON'T FORGIVE, THE see **MUERTOS NO PERDONAN, LOS** • 1963
DEAD DRIFTER, A see **HYORYU SHITAI** • 1959
DEAD EASY • 1927 • Christie Al • USA
DEAD EASY • 1970 • Buesst Nigel • ASL
DEAD EASY • 1982 • Deling Bert • ASL
DEAD END • 1937 • Wyler William • USA
DEAD END • 1972 • Papadopoulos John • SHT • ASL
DEAD END • 1987 • Dick Nigel • USA
DEAD END see **TEN TO SEN** • 1958
DEAD END see **BONBAST** • 1975
DEAD END see **HOLTPONT** • 1983
DEAD END CITY • 1988 • Yuval Peter • USA
DEAD END CREEK • 1964 • Jackson Pat • SRL • UKN
DEAD-END DRIVE-IN • 1986 • Trenchard-Smith Brian • ASL • DEAD END DRIVE IN
DEAD END DRIVE IN see **DEAD-END DRIVE-IN** • 1986
DEAD END KIDS see **DEAD END KIDS: A STORY OF NUCLEAR POWER** • 1986
DEAD END KIDS: A STORY OF NUCLEAR POWER • 1986 • Akalaitis Joanne • USA • DEAD END KIDS
DEAD END KIDS ON DRESS PARADE, THE see **DRESS PARADE** • 1939
DEAD END STREET see **KVISH LELO MOTZA** • 1983
DEAD END (USA) see **STRADA SENZA USCITA** • 1970
DEAD EVEN see **DEAD-TIME STORIES: VOLUME 3** • 1987
DEAD EYES OF LONDON (USA) see **TOTEN AUGEN VON LONDON, DIE** • 1960
DEAD FISHES, THE see **TOTEN FISCHE, DIE** • 1988
DEAD FLIGHT • 1979 • Rich David Lowell • USA
DEAD GAME • 1923 • Sedgwick Edward • USA • KATY DIDD
DEAD GAME see **SHOOTING STRAIGHT** • 1930
DEAD HEART, THE • 1914 • Plumb Hay • UKN
DEAD HEAT • 1926 • Barnett Charles • UKN
DEAD HEAT • 1987 • Ferrari Stefano • USA
DEAD HEAT • 1988 • Goldblatt Mark • USA
DEAD HEAT • 1988 • Sohmer Steve • USA
DEAD HEAT ON A MERRY-GO-ROUND • 1966 • Girard Bernard • USA
DEAD HOUSE see **CASA MUERTE** • 1974
DEAD I DICK • 1970 • *Stacey Dist.* • USA
DEAD IMAGE (UKN) see **DEAD RINGER** • 1964
DEAD KIDS • 1981 • Laughlin Michael • NZL • STRANGE BEHAVIOR (USA) ○ SMALL TOWN MASSACRE
DEAD LANDSCAPE see **HOLT VIDEK** • 1971
DEAD LETTER, THE • 1910 • *Lubin* • USA
DEAD LETTER, THE • 1915 • Louis Will • USA
DEAD LINE, THE • 1914 • *Nestor* • USA
DEAD LINE, THE • 1914 • *Princess* • USA
DEAD LINE, THE • 1917 • Middleton George E. • USA
DEAD LINE, THE • 1918 • *Hart Neal* • SHT • USA
DEAD LINE, THE • 1920 • Henderson Dell • USA
DEAD LINE, THE • 1926 • Nelson Jack • USA
DEAD LINE, THE see **GRAFT** • 1931
DEAD LUCKY • 1960 • Tully Montgomery • UKN
DEAD MAN, THE (USA) see **MYORTVETZ** • 1915
DEAD MAN DIED, THE (USA) see **MUERTO MURIO, EL** • 1939
DEAD MAN ON THE RUN • 1975 • Bilson Bruce • TVM • USA
DEAD MAN SEEKS HIS MURDERER, A see **VENGEANCE** • 1962
DEAD MAN WALKING • 1987 • Brown Gregory • USA
DEAD MAN WALKING • 1988 • Pearce Richard • CND
DEAD MAN WHO KILLED, THE (USA) see **MORT QUI TUE, LA** • 1914
DEAD MAN'S CHEST • 1965 • Dromgoole Patrick • UKN
DEAD MAN'S CLAIM, THE • 1912 • *Anderson Broncho Billy* • USA
DEAD MAN'S CURVE • 1928 • Rosson Richard • USA
DEAD MAN'S EVIDENCE • 1962 • Searle Francis • UKN
DEAD MAN'S EYES • 1944 • Le Borg Reginald • USA
DEAD MAN'S FLOAT • 1980 • Sharp Peter • ASL
DEAD MAN'S FOLLY see **AGATHA CHRISTIE'S DEAD MAN'S FOLLY** • 1986
DEAD MAN'S GOLD • 1948 • Taylor Ray • USA
DEAD MAN'S GULCH • 1943 • English John • USA
DEAD MAN'S HONOR, A • 1911 • *Vitagraph* • USA
DEAD MAN'S ISLE see **ISLAND OF DOOMED MEN** • 1940
DEAD MAN'S KEYS, THE • 1915 • *Delaney Bert* • USA
DEAD MAN'S PAPERS • 1914 • *Gaumont* • USA
DEAD MAN'S SHOES • 1913 • Reid Wallace • USA
DEAD MAN'S SHOES • 1939 • Bentley Thomas • UKN
DEAD MAN'S TRAIL • 1952 • Collins Lewis D. • USA
DEAD MELODY (USA) see **VERKLUNGENE MELODIE** • 1938
DEAD MEN ARE DANGEROUS • 1939 • French Harold • UKN
DEAD MEN DON'T WEAR PLAID • 1982 • Reiner Carl • USA
DEAD MEN RIDE (UKN) see **SOLE SOTTO TERRA, IL** • 1971
DEAD MEN TELL • 1941 • Lachman Harry • USA
DEAD MEN TELL NO TALES • 1914 • Thornton F. Martin? • UKN
DEAD MEN TELL NO TALES • 1920 • Terriss Tom • USA
DEAD MEN TELL NO TALES • 1938 • MacDonald David • UKN
DEAD MEN TELL NO TALES • 1971 • Grauman Walter • TVM • USA • TO SAVE HIS LIFE
DEAD MEN WALK • 1943 • Newfield Sam • USA • CREATURE OF THE DEVIL
DEAD MEN'S TALES • 1914 • *Hearne Fred* • USA
DEAD MOUNTAINEER HOTEL, THE see **OTEL 'U POGIBSHCHEGO ALPINISTA** • 1979
DEAD NIGHT see **DEATHDREAM** • 1972
DEAD OF LAUGHTER see **MUERTOS DE RISA** • 1957
DEAD OF NIGHT • 1945 • Dearden Basil, Hamer Robert, Crichton Charles, Cavalcanti Alberto • UKN
DEAD OF NIGHT • 1977 • Curtis Dan • TVM • USA
DEAD OF NIGHT see **DEATHDREAM** • 1972
DEAD OF NIGHT, THE • 1987 • Warren Deryn • USA
DEAD OF SUMMER (USA) see **ONDATA DI CALORE** • 1970
DEAD OF WINTER • 1987 • Penn Arthur • USA
DEAD ON ARRIVAL • 1979 • Martin Charles • USA
DEAD ON ARRIVAL see **GIRL IN 419, THE** • 1933
DEAD ON ARRIVAL see **D.O.A.** • 1988
DEAD ON COURSE (USA) see **WINGS OF DANGER** • 1952
DEAD ON TIME • 1955 • Chaffey Don • UKN
DEAD ONE, THE • 1961 • Mahon Barry • USA
DEAD ONE, THE see **MUERTO, EL** • 1975
DEAD ONES see **MORTACCI** • 1988
DEAD ONES, THE • 1948 • Markopoulos Gregory J. • USA
DEAD ONLY PERISH, THE see **OLUME YALNIZ GIDILAR** • 1963
DEAD OR ALIVE • 1921 • Henderson Dell • USA
DEAD OR ALIVE • 1944 • Clifton Elmer • USA
DEAD OR ALIVE • 1988 • Guillermin John • USA
DEAD OR ALIVE see **MINUTO PER PREGARE, UN ISTANTE PER MORIRE, UN** • 1967
DEAD OR ALIVE see **ELVE, VAGY HALVA!** • 1980
DEAD PAST RECALLED, THE • 1914 • Thornton F. Martin? • UKN
DEAD PAYS, THE • 1912 • West Raymond B. • USA
DEAD PEOPLE see **MESSIAH OF EVIL** • 1975
DEAD PERSON'S SHADOW see **UMARLI RZUCAJA CIEN** • 1978
DEAD PIGEON ON BEETHOVEN STREET see **KRESSIN UND DIE TOTE TAUBE IN DER BEETHOVENSTRASSE** • 1972
DEAD PIGEON ON BEETHOVENSTRASSE see **KRESSIN UND DIE TOTE TAUBE IN DER BEETHOVENSTRASSE** • 1972
DEAD PIT see **POZO MUERTO** • 1967
DEAD PIT, THE • 1988 • Leonard Brett • USA
DEAD POETS SOCIETY • 1989 • Weir Peter • USA
DEAD POOL, THE • 1988 • Van Horn Buddy • USA
DEAD QUEEN, THE see **INES DE CASTRO** • 1944
DEAD RECKONING • 1947 • Cromwell John • USA
DEAD REMAIN YOUNG, THE see **TOTEN BLEIBEN JUNG, DIE** • 1968
DEAD REVENGE THEMSELVES, THE see **TOTEN RACHEN SICH, DIE** • 1918
DEAD RINGER • 1964 • Henreid Paul • USA • DEAD IMAGE (UKN)
DEAD RINGER • 1982 • Castravelli Claude • CND
DEAD RINGER • 1982 • Nichols Allan • USA
DEAD RINGERS see **TWINS** • 1988
DEAD RUN (USA) see **GEHEIMNISSE IN GOLDENEN NYLONS** • 1966
DEAD SEASON see **MIERTVY SEZON** • 1969
DEAD SECRET, THE • 1913 • Taylor Stanner E. V. • USA
DEAD SEXY see **ICH SCHLAFE MIT MEINEM MORDER** • 1971
DEAD SHOT, THE • 1918 • Harvey Harry • SHT • USA
DEAD-SHOT BAKER • 1917 • Duncan William • USA
DEAD SLEEP • 1990 • Mills Alec • ASL
DEAD SOUL, THE • 1915 • *Routh George* • USA
DEAD SOULS see **MERTVIYE DUSHI** • 1960
DEAD SPEAK, THE (USA) see **MUERTOS HABLAN, LOS** • 1935
DEAD STAY YOUNG, THE see **TOTEN BLEIBEN JUNG, DIE** • 1968
DEAD THAT WALK, THE (UKN) see **ZOMBIES OF MORA-TAU** • 1957
DEAD TIME STORIES see **DEAD-TIME STORIES: VOLUME 1** • 1985
DEAD-TIME STORIES: VOLUME 1 • 1985 • Noyce Phil, Schenkel Carl • CND • DEAD TIME STORIES
DEAD-TIME STORIES: VOLUME 2 • 1987 • Nagy Ivan, Rothstein Richard • CND • SCREAM SHOW
DEAD-TIME STORIES: VOLUME 3 • 1987 • Wickes David, Verhoeven Paul* • CND • DEAD EVEN
DEAD TIMES, THE see **TEMPS MORTS, LES** • 1964
DEAD TO THE WORLD • 1960 • Webster Nicholas • USA
DEAD TO THE WORLD • 1990 • Gibson Ross • ASL
DEAD WATER see **DOOD WATER** • 1934
DEAD WITNESSES see **TESTIGOS MUERTOS** • 1972
DEAD WOMAN, THE • Hirszman Leon • BRZ
DEAD WOMAN FROM BEVERLY HILLS see **TOTE VON BEVERLY HILLS, DIE** • 1964
DEAD WOMAN IN THE THAMES, THE see **TOTE AUS DER THEMSE, DIE** • 1971
DEAD WOMAN'S KISS, A (USA) see **BACIO DI UNA MORTA, IL** • 1949
DEAD WRONG see **COLUMBIA CONNECTION, THE** • 1982
DEAD YESTERDAY, A • 1916 • Giblyn Charles • SHT • USA
DEAD ZONE, THE • 1983 • Cronenberg David • USA
DEADEND CATS • 1947 • Donnelly Eddie • ANS • USA
DEADFALL • 1967 • Forbes Bryan • UKN, USA
DEADGROUND • 1973 • Tombleson Richard • UKN
DEADHEAD MILES • 1972 • Zimmerman Vernon • USA
DEADLIER SEX, THE • 1920 • Thornby Robert T. • USA
DEADLIER THAN THE MALE • 1966 • Thomas Ralph • UKN
DEADLIER THAT THE MALE (USA) see **VOICI LE TEMPS DES ASSASSINS** • 1956
DEADLIEST SEASON, THE • 1977 • Markowitz Robert • TVM • USA
DEADLIEST SIN, THE (USA) see **CONFESSION** • 1955
DEADLINE • 1948 • Drake Oliver • USA
DEADLINE • 1970 • Olsson Stellan • SWD, DNM
DEADLINE • 1981 • Nicholson Arch • MTV • ASL
DEADLINE see **ANATOMY OF A HORROR** • 1980
DEADLINE see **WAR ZONE** • 1987
DEADLINE, THE • 1931 • Hillyer Lambert • USA
DEADLINE, THE see **SHADOWS OF THE NIGHT** • 1928
DEADLINE AT DAWN • 1946 • Clurman Harold • USA
DEADLINE AT DAWN see **NIGHT RIDE** • 1930
DEADLINE AT ELEVEN • 1920 • Fawcett George • USA
DEADLINE AUTO THEFT • 1983 • Halicki H. B. • USA
DEADLINE FOR MURDER • 1946 • Tinling James • USA
DEADLINE: MADRID • 1987 • Patterson John • TVM • USA
DEADLINE MIDNIGHT (UKN) see **-30-** • 1959
DEADLINE, U.S.A. • 1952 • Brooks Richard • USA • DEADLINE (UKN)
DEADLINE (UKN) see **DEADLINE, U.S.A.** • 1952
DEADLOCK • 1931 • King George • UKN
DEADLOCK • 1943 • Haines Ronald • UKN
DEADLOCK • 1957 • Weis Don • MTV • USA
DEADLOCK • 1966 • *Halas John (P)* • ANS • UKN
DEADLOCK • 1969 • Johnson Lamont • TVM • USA
DEADLOCK • 1970 • Klick Roland • FRG, ISR
DEADLOCK • 1988 • Dodson James • USA
DEADLOCK see **MAN-TRAP** • 1961
DEADLOCK see **SIKATOR** • 1966
DEADLY AFFAIR, THE • 1966 • Lumet Sidney • UKN
DEADLY AND THE BEAUTIFUL • 1973 • *Kwan Nancy* • USA
DEADLY ANGELS, THE • 1979 • *Kraft Evelyne* • HKG
DEADLY AUGUST • 1966 • *Carey Macdonald* • USA
DEADLY AVENGER see **LOVELY BUT DEADLY** • 1983
DEADLY BATTLE AT HICKSVILLE, THE • 1914 • *Roland Ruth* • USA
DEADLY BEES, THE • 1967 • Francis Freddie • UKN
DEADLY BLESSING • 1981 • Craven Wes • USA
DEADLY BREAKING SWORD, THE see **FENG-LIU TUAN-CHIEN HSIAO-HSIAO TAO** • 1979
DEADLY BROTHERS • 1967 • Garces Armando • PHL
DEADLY BUSINESS • 1986 • Korty John • TVM • USA
DEADLY CARE • 1987 • Anspaugh David • TVM • USA
DEADLY CHASE see **COMMISSARIO VERRAZZANO, IL** • 1979

DEADLY CHEROOT, THE • 1914 • *Ab* • USA
DEADLY CHINA DOLL • 1973 • Huang Feng • HKG • OPIUM TRAIL, THE
DEADLY COMPANIONS, THE • 1961 • Peckinpah Sam • USA • TRIGGER HAPPY
DEADLY DANCER • 1989 • Prior David A. • USA
DEADLY DAPHNE'S REVENGE • 1988 • Gardner Richard • USA
DEADLY DECEPTION • 1987 • Moxey John Llewellyn • TVM • USA • DEADLY DECEPTIONS
DEADLY DECEPTIONS see **DEADLY DECEPTION** • 1987
DEADLY DECISION (USA) see **CANARIS** • 1954
DEADLY DECOY, THE (USA) see **GORILLE A MORDU L'ARCHEVEQUE, LE** • 1962
DEADLY DIAPHANOIDS, THE see **DIAFANOIDI PORTANO LA MORTE, I** • 1965
DEADLY DISPATCH, THE • 1914 • *Ab* • USA
DEADLY DOUGHNUT, THE • 1917 • Santell Alfred • USA
DEADLY DREAM • 1971 • Kjellin Alf • USA
DEADLY DREAMS • 1989 • Peterson Kristine • USA
DEADLY DREAMS see **LIEBESTRAUM** • 1951
DEADLY DUO • 1962 • Le Borg Reginald • USA
DEADLY DUST • 1978 • *Hammond Nicholas* • MTV • USA
DEADLY EMBRACE • 1988 • Cabot Ellen, Decoteau David? • USA
DEADLY ENCOUNTER • 1979 • Hugh R. John • USA
DEADLY ENCOUNTER • 1982 • Graham William A. • TVM • USA
DEADLY ENEMY see **SMERTELNI VRAG** • 1971
DEADLY EYES • 1982 • Clouse Robert • USA • RATS, THE ○ NIGHT EYES
DEADLY FEMALES, THE • 1975 • Winter Donovan • UKN
DEADLY FOCUS, THE • 1915 • *Wells Raymond* • USA
DEADLY FORCE • 1983 • Aaron Paul • USA
DEADLY FRIEND • 1987 • Craven Wes • USA
DEADLY GAME • 1986 • Brickman Marshall • USA • MANHATTAN PROJECT: THE DEADLY GAME, THE ○ MANHATTAN PROJECT, THE
DEADLY GAME, THE • 1941 • Rosen Phil • USA
DEADLY GAME, THE • 1977 • Slate Lane • TVM • USA
DEADLY GAME, THE • 1989 • Forbes Bryan • TVM • UKN, ITL
DEADLY GAME, THE see **THIRD PARTY RISK** • 1955
DEADLY GAME, THE see **SERPICO: THE DEADLY GAME** • 1976
DEADLY GAME, THE see **STUNTS** • 1977
DEADLY GAMES • 1982 • Mansfield Scott • USA • ELIMINATOR, THE
DEADLY GASES, THE see **GAZ MORTELS, LES** • 1916
DEADLY HARVEST • 1972 • O'Herlihy Michael • TVM • USA
DEADLY HARVEST • 1978 • Bond Timothy • CND
DEADLY HATE, A • 1915 • Ridgely Richard • USA
DEADLY HERO • 1976 • Nagy Ivan • USA
DEADLY HONEYMOON see **NIGHTMARE HONEYMOON** • 1972
DEADLY HUNT, THE • 1971 • Newland John • TVM • USA
DEADLY ILLUSION • 1987 • Tannen William, Cohen Larry • USA • LOVE YOU TO DEATH
DEADLY ILLUSION see **TURNAROUND** • 1985
DEADLY IMPACT • 1983 • De Angelis Fabrizio • ITL, USA
DEADLY INNOCENTS • 1989 • Patterson John • USA
DEADLY INTENT • 1988 • Dick Nigel • USA
DEADLY INTENTIONS • 1985 • Black Noel • TVM • USA
DEADLY INTRUDER • 1985 • McCauley John • USA
DEADLY INVENTION, THE see **VYNALEZ ZKAZY** • 1958
DEADLY IS THE FEMALE • 1949 • Lewis Joseph H. • USA • GUN CRAZY
DEADLY JACKS • 1968 • Diaz Leody M. • PHL
DEADLY LESSON see **DEADLY LESSONS** • 1983
DEADLY LESSONS • 1983 • Wiard William • TVM • USA • DEADLY LESSON
DEADLY MANTIS, THE • 1957 • Juran Nathan • USA • INCREDIBLE PRAYING MANTIS, THE
DEADLY MESSAGES • 1985 • Bender Jack • TVM • USA
DEADLY MODEL • 1915 • Martinek H. O. • UKN
DEADLY NIGHTMARES • 1988 • Schenkel Carl, Leitch Christopher, Vadim Roger • CND
DEADLY NIGHTSHADE • 1953 • Gilling John • UKN
DEADLY OBSESSION • 1988 • Hodi Jeno • USA
DEADLY ODOUR, THE see **SMRTICI VUNE** • 1970
DEADLY ORGAN, THE (USA) see **PLACER SANGRIENTO** • 1967
DEADLY PASSION • 1985 • SAF
DEADLY PASSION • 1985 • Larson Larry • USA
DEADLY PERFUME see **SMRTICI VUNE** • 1970
DEADLY PREY • 1987 • Prior David A. • USA
DEADLY PRICE OF PARADISE, THE • 1978 • Frawley James • TVM • USA • NIGHTMARE AT PENDRAGON'S CASTLE (UKN)
DEADLY PURSUIT (UKN) see **SHOOT TO KILL** • 1988
DEADLY RAY FROM MARS • 1938 • Beebe Ford, Hill Robert F. • USA
DEADLY RAY FROM MARS, THE see **MARS ATTACKS THE WORLD** • 1938
DEADLY REACTOR see **REACTOR, THE** • 1989
DEADLY RECORD • 1959 • Huntington Lawrence • UKN
DEADLY REEF • 1978 • Randall John • USA
DEADLY RIVALS see **RIVALS** • 1972
DEADLY ROULETTE (UKN) see **HOW I SPENT MY SUMMER VACATION** • 1967
DEADLY RUN (UKN) see **MORTELLE RANDONNEE** • 1983
DEADLY SANCTUARY (USA) see **DE SADE 70** • 1969
DEADLY SEVEN • 1967 • Diaz Leody M. • PHL
DEADLY SHOTS IN BROADWAY see **TODESSCHUSSE AM BROADWAY** • 1968
DEADLY SILENCE, THE see **TARZAN'S DEADLY SILENCE** • 1970
DEADLY SIN, A see **DOODZONDE** • 1979
DEADLY SNAIL VERSUS KUNG FU KILLERS see **DEADLY SNAKE VERSUS KUNG FU KILLERS**
DEADLY SNAKE VERSUS KUNG FU KILLERS • *Wong Tony* • HKG • DEADLY SNAIL VERSUS KUNG FU KILLERS
DEADLY SPARK, THE • 1915 • *Kb* • USA
DEADLY SPAWN, THE • 1983 • McKeown Douglas • USA • RETURN OF THE ALIEN'S DEADLY SPAWN
DEADLY STING see **EVIL SPAWN** • 1987
DEADLY STRANGER • 1988 • Kleven Max • USA • MIXTEC
DEADLY STRANGERS • 1974 • Hayers Sidney • UKN
DEADLY STRIKE, THE • 1979 • Huang Lung • HKG
DEADLY SWEET (USA) see **COL CUORE IN GOLA** • 1967
DEADLY THIEF, THE see **RIVALS** • 1972
DEADLY TOWER, THE • 1975 • Jameson Jerry • TVM • USA
DEADLY TRACKERS, THE • 1973 • Shear Barry • USA, SPN • RIATA
DEADLY TRAP, THE (UKN) see **MAISON SOUS LES ARBRES, LA** • 1971
DEADLY TREASURE OF THE PIRANHA see **KILLER FISH** • 1979
DEADLY TRIANGLE, THE • 1977 • Dubin Charles S. • TVM • USA
DEADLY TRIO • 1968 • Gaudite Solano • PHL
DEADLY VENGEANCE • 1985 • Qamar A. C. • USA
DEADLY VISITOR • 1973 • *Verdon Gwen* • TVM • USA
DEADLY VOWS • 1988 • Freedman Jerrold • TVM • USA
DEADLY WARRIORS see **NINE DEATHS OF THE NINJA** • 1985
DEADLY WEAPONS • 1988 • Miner Michael • USA
DEADLY WEAPONS see **INCREDIBLE CHESTY (72-32-36) MORGAN AND HER DEADLY WEAPONS, THE** • 1974
DEADLY WHEN AROUSED see **GARCES, LES** • 1973
DEADMAN'S CURVE • 1978 • Compton Richard • TVM • USA
DEADRINGER • 1985 • Page Teddy • USA
DEADSHOT CASEY • 1928 • *Hoxie Al* • USA
DEADTIME STORIES • 1986 • Delman Jeffrey • USA
DEADWOOD '76 • 1965 • Landis James • USA
DEADWOOD COACH, THE • 1924 • Reynolds Lynn • USA
DEADWOOD DICK • 1940 • Horne James W. • SRL • USA
DEADWOOD DICK AND THE MORMONS • 1915 • Paul Fred, MacBean L. C. • SHT • UKN
DEADWOOD DICK SPOILS BRIGHAM YOUNG • 1915 • Paul Fred, MacBean L. C. • SHT • UKN
DEADWOOD DICK'S DETECTIVE PARD • 1915 • Paul Fred, MacBean L. C. • SHT • UKN
DEADWOOD DICK'S RED ALLY • 1915 • Paul Fred, MacBean L. C. • SHT • UKN
DEADWOOD DICK'S VENGEANCE • 1915 • Paul Fred, MacBean L. C. • SHT • UKN
DEADWOOD PASS • 1933 • McGowan J. P. • USA
DEADWOOD SLEEPER • 1905 • *Bitzer Billy (Ph)* • USA
DEAF AND MUTE HEROINE, THE see **LONGJA JIAN** • 1970
DEAF BURGLAR, A • 1913 • Lehrman Henry, Sennett Mack (Spv) • USA
DEAF, DUMB AND DAFFY • 1924 • Roach Hal • SHT • USA
DEAF-MUTES BALL • 1907 • *Bitzer Billy (Ph)* • USA
DEAF SMITH AND JOHNNY EARS (UKN) see **AMIGOS, LOS** • 1973
DEAF TO THE CITY see **SOURD DANS LA VILLE, LE** • 1986
DEAFULA • 1975 • Wechsberg Peter • USA
DEAL • 1977 • Schott John, Vaughn E. J. • USA
DEAL IN BONDS, A • 1917 • Ellis Robert • USA
DEAL IN BROKEN CHINA, A • 1910 • Martinek H. O. • UKN
DEAL IN CROCKERY, A • 1912 • Martinek H. O. • UKN
DEAL IN DIAMONDS, A • 1915 • Cooley Frank • USA
DEAL IN FURNITURE, A • 1917 • *Vim* • USA
DEAL IN INDIANS, A • 1910 • *Nestor* • USA
DEAL IN INDIANS, A • 1915 • *Ovey George* • USA
DEAL IN OIL, A • 1913 • *Myers Harry* • USA
DEAL IN REAL ESTATE, A • 1914 • *Jones Edgar* • USA
DEAL IN STATUARY, A • 1914 • Seay Charles M. • USA
DEAL ME IN • 1951 • Yates Hal • SHT • USA
DEAL OF THE CENTURY • 1983 • Friedkin William • USA
DEAL WITH THE DEVIL • 1916 • Wilson Frank • UKN
DEAL WITH THE DEVIL see **ZMLUVA S DIABLOM** • 1967
DEAL WITH THE DEVIL, A see **MYSTIKE FREMMEDE, DEN** • 1914
DEALER, THE • 1985 • SAF
DEALER PLAN, THE • 1951 • Heyer John • DOC • ASL
DEALERS • 1989 • Bucksey Colin • UKN
DEALERS IN DEATH, THE see **PROFANADORES DE TUMBAS** • 1966
DEALING: OR THE BERKELEY-TO-BOSTON FORTY-BRICK LOST-BAG BLUES • 1972 • Williams Paul • USA
DEAN CASE, THE • 1982 • Dobson Kevin • MTV • ASL
DEAN'S DAUGHTERS, THE • 1913 • Edwin Walter • USA
DEAN'S WIFE, THE • 1970 • Onivas Benjamin • USA • TALE OF THE DEAN'S WIFE, THE
DEAR AMERICA • 1987 • Couturie Bill • TVM • USA
DEAR BOYS see **LIEVE JONGENS** • 1979
DEAR BOYS HOME FOR THE HOLIDAYS, THE • 1903 • Williamson James • UKN • BOYS WILL BE BOYS
DEAR BRAT • 1951 • Seiter William A. • USA
DEAR BRIGITTE • 1965 • Koster Henry • USA • ERASMUS WITH FRECKLES
DEAR BROTHER CESAR see **DEAR KUYA CESAR** • 1968
DEAR CARDHOLDER • 1987 • Bennett Bill • ASL
DEAR CAROLINE (USA) see **CAROLINE CHERIE** • 1950
DEAR CHARLES see **LIEBER KARL** • 1985
DEAR COMRADES.. see **QUERIDOS COMPANEROS..** • 1979
DEAR DEAD DELILAH • 1972 • Farris John • USA
DEAR! DEER! • 1942 • Holmes Ben • SHT • USA
DEAR DEPARTED, THE • 1920 • Roach Hal • SHT • USA
DEAR DETECTIVE • 1979 • Hargrove Dean • TVM • USA
DEAR DETECTIVE (USA) see **TENDRE POULET** • 1978
DEAR EMPEROR see **HAIKEI TENNOHEIKA-SAMA** • 1963
DEAR EVA see **ARME EVA** • 1914
DEAR FAMILY see **KARA FAMILJEN, DEN** • 1962
DEAR FATHER see **CARO PAPA** • 1979
DEAR FOOL, A • 1921 • Shaw Harold • UKN
DEAR FRIENDS see **QUERIDAS AMIGAS** • 1980
DEAR GORBACHOV see **CARLO GORBACIOV** • 1988
DEAR HEART • 1964 • Mann Delbert • USA
"DEAR" HUNTER, THE • 1914 • *Glaum Louise* • USA
DEAR INSPECTOR see **TENDRE POULET** • 1978
DEAR IRENE see **DRAGA IRENA** • 1970
DEAR IRENE (UKN) see **KAERE IRENE** • 1971
DEAR JOHN • 1988 • Ord Catherine • CND
DEAR JOHN see **KARE JOHN** • 1964
DEAR KIND HUBBY • 1911 • *Selig* • USA
DEAR KUYA CESAR • 1968 • Pacheco Lauro • PHL • DEAR BROTHER CESAR
DEAR LIAR, A • 1925 • Granville Fred Leroy • UKN
DEAR LITTLE OLD TIME GIRL • 1915 • Dowlan William C. • USA
DEAR LITTLE TEACHER, THE • 1912 • Buckland Warwick? • UKN
DEAR MAESTRO • 1983 • Odorisio Luciano • ITL
DEAR MARJORIE BOOBS • 1977 • Godfrey Bob • ANS • UKN
DEAR MICHAEL see **CARO MICHELE** • 1976
DEAR MR. PROHACK • 1949 • Freeland Thornton • UKN • MR. PROHACK
DEAR MR. WONDERFUL • 1982 • Lilienthal Peter • FRG
DEAR MOTHER, I'M DOING WELL see **LIEBE MUTTER, MIR GEHT ES GUT** • 1971
DEAR MURDERER • 1947 • Crabtree Arthur • UKN
DEAR OCTOPUS • 1943 • French Harold • UKN • RANDOLPH FAMILY, THE (USA)
DEAR OLD DOG, THE • 1909 • Stow Percy • UKN
DEAR OLD GIRL • 1913 • Wharton Theodore • USA
DEAR OLD HYPOCRITE • 1915 • *Mcquarrie Murdock* • USA
DEAR OLD LONDON • 1934 • Flemming Claude • DOC • ASL
DEAR OLD PAL • 1924-26 • Fleischer Dave • ANS • USA
DEAR OLD SWITZERLAND • 1944 • Donnelly Eddie • ANS • USA
DEAR PAPA see **CARO PAPA** • 1979
DEAR PARIS see **PARIGI O CARA** • 1962
DEAR PERCY • 1916 • Dickson Charles • USA
DEAR RELATIVES see **KARA SLAKTEN** • 1933
DEAR ROSIE • 1990 • Cattano Peter • UKN
DEAR RUTH • 1947 • Russell William D. • USA
DEAR SUMMER SISTER (USA) see **NATSU NO IMOTO** • 1972
DEAR VIVIAN • 1929 • Kane Raymond • USA
DEAR WIFE • 1949 • Haydn Richard • USA
DEAREST EXECUTIONERS see **QUERIDISIMOS VERDUGOS** • 1974
DEAREST LOVE (UKN) see **SOUFFLE AU COEUR, LE** • 1971
DEARIE • 1927 • Mayo Archie • USA
DEARLY LOVED FACE, A see **NATSUKASHI NO KAO** • 1941
DEARLY PURCHASED FRIENDSHIP see **DYREKOBT VENSKAB** • 1912
DEARTH OF A SALESMAN • 1957 • Arliss Leslie • UKN
DEATH • 1911 • *Biorama*
DEATH see **GEVATTER TOD** • 1921
DEATH, A • 1979 • Norman Ron • USA
DEATH AMONG FRIENDS • 1975 • Wendkos Paul • TVM • USA • MRS. R.: DEATH AMONG FRIENDS
DEATH AND DEVIL • 1973 • Dwoskin Stephen • FRG
DEATH AND MOURNING • 1969 • Watson Patricia • CND
DEATH AND THE GREEN SLIME see **GAMMA SANGO UCHU DAISAKUSEN** • 1968
DEATH AND THE MAIDEN see **HAWKINS ON MURDER** • 1973
DEATH AND THE RIVER see **RIO Y LA MUERTE, EL** • 1954
DEATH AND THE SKY ABOVE • 1959 • *Williams Peter* • UKN
DEATH AND TRANSFIGURATIONS • 1965 • Davis James* • SHT • USA
DEATH AT BROADCASTING HOUSE • 1934 • Denham Reginald • UKN
DEATH AT DAWN see **MUERTE AL AMANECER** • 1979
DEATH AT DAWN (USA) see **AKATSUKI NO SHI** • 1924
DEATH AT DAYBREAK see **MUERTE AL AMANECER** • 1979
DEATH AT LOVE HOUSE • 1976 • Swackhamer E. W. • TVM • USA
DEATH AT ORWELL ROCK see **MORTE NON CONTA I DOLLARI, LA** • 1967
DEATH AT OSLO C see **DODEN PA OSLO S** • 1990
DEATH AVENGER see **MUERTO HACE LAS MALETAS, EL** • 1971
DEATH BAY see **BUKHTA SMERTI** • 1926
DEATH BE NOT PROUD • 1975 • Wrye Donald • TVM • USA
DEATH BEFORE DISHONOR • 1987 • Leonard Terry J. • USA
DEATH BELL, THE see **HALALSENGO, A** • 1917
DEATH BITE see **SPASMS** • 1982
DEATH BLOW • 1983 • Spring Tim • SAF
DEATH BLOW, THE see **TOUCH OF LEATHER** • 1968
DEATH BY DESIGN • 1943 • Faithfull Geoffrey • UKN
DEATH BY DIALOGUE • 1988 • Dewier Tom • USA
DEATH BY HANGING (UKN) see **KOSHIKEI** • 1968
DEATH BY INVITATION • 1971 • Friedman Ken • USA
DEATH BY WITCHCRAFT see **BYAKUYA NO YOJO** • 1958
DEATH CALLS ITSELF ENGELCHEN see **SMRT SI RIKA ENGELCHEN** • 1963
DEATH CAR see **DEATH CAR ON THE FREEWAY** • 1979
DEATH CAR ON THE FREEWAY • 1979 • Needham Hal • TVM • USA • DEATH ON THE FREEWAY ○ WHEELS OF DEATH ○ DEATH CAR ○ DEATH CARS
DEATH CARS see **DEATH CAR ON THE FREEWAY** • 1979
DEATH CHASE • *Smith William* • USA
DEATH CHASE • 1987 • Prior David A. • USA
DEATH CHEAT, THE see **BRENNENDE KUGEL, DIE** • 1923
DEATH CHERISHES MIDNIGHT see **MORTE ACCAREZZA A MEZZANOTTE, LA** • 1972
DEATH CLIFF see **SHI NO DANGAI** • 1951
DEATH CODE: NINJA • *Wilford John* • USA
DEATH COLLECTOR • 1977 • De Vito Ralph • USA • FAMILY ENFORCER ○ ENFORCER 2
DEATH COMES FROM OUTER SPACE see **MORTE VIENE DALLO SPAZIO, LA** • 1958
DEATH COMES FROM THE DARK see **COLECCIONISTA DE CADAVERES, EL** • 1967
DEATH COMMAND OF THE TOWER see **BORO NO KESSHITAI** • 1943
DEATH CORPS • 1970 • Wiederhorn Ken • USA • ALMOST HUMAN (UKN) ○ SHOCK WAVES ○ DEATH WAVES
DEATH CROONS THE BLUES • 1937 • MacDonald David • UKN
DEATH CROSSED THE RIO BRAVO see **MUERTE CRUZO EL RIO BRACO, LA** • 1985
DEATH CRUISE • 1974 • Senensky Ralph • TVM • USA
DEATH CURSE OF TARTU • 1968 • Grefe William • USA
DEATH DANCE, THE • 1918 • Dawley J. Searle • USA
DEATH DANCE AT MADELIA see **INTRUDERS, THE** • 1967
DEATH DAY see **QUE VIVA MEXICO!** • 1931
DEATH DEALER, THE see **PSYCHIC KILLER** • 1975
DEATH DEALERS (UKN) see **NAPOLI VIOLENTA** • 1976
DEATH DEVILS IN A PAPUAN PARADISE • 1924 • Ward J. E. • DOC • ASL
DEATH DICE, THE • 1915 • Walsh Raoul? • USA • DEATH DIES, THE

DEATH DIES, THE see **DEATH DICE, THE** • 1915
DEATH DIMENSION • 1978 • Adamson Al • USA • DEAD DIMENSION ○ BLACK ELIMINATOR, THE ○ DEATH DIMENSIONS ○ KILL FACTOR, THE ○ FREEZE BOMB
DEATH DIMENSIONS see **DEATH DIMENSION** • 1978
DEATH DIPLOMA see **DIPLOMA ZA SMRT** • 1989
DEATH DISC, THE • 1909 • Griffith D. W. • USA
DEATH DIVE see **FER-DE-LANCE** • 1974
DEATH DOES NOT COUNT THE DOLLARS see **MORTE NON CONTA I DOLLARI, LA** • 1967
DEATH DOLL • 1989 • Mims William • USA
DEATH DORM see **PRANKS** • 1981
DEATH DRIVE see **AUTOSTOP** • 1977
DEATH DRIVER • 1979 • Huston Jimmy • USA • HELL RACERS ○ HELL RACER
DEATH DRIVES THROUGH • 1935 • Cahn Edward L. • UKN
DEATH DRUG • 1978 • Williams Oscar • USA
DEATH DRUMS ALONG THE RIVER • 1963 • Huntington Lawrence • UKN
DEATH DUEL see **SAN SHAO-YEH-TE CHIEN** • 1978
DEATH FLASH see **DEATHFLASH** • 1987
DEATH FLIES EAST • 1935 • Rosen Phil • USA
DEATH FLIGHT see **SST -DEATH FLIGHT** • 1977
DEATH FORCE • 1978 • Santiago Cirio H. • PHL, USA • FORCE OF DEATH
DEATH FROM A DISTANCE • 1935 • Strayer Frank • USA
DEATH FROM OUTER SPACE see **MORTE VIENE DALLO SPAZIO, LA** • 1958
DEATH GAME • 1977 • Traynor Peter S. • USA • SEDUCERS, THE ○ MRS. MANNING'S WEEKEND
DEATH GAME see **DEATHGAME**
DEATH GAMES see **SOFIA CONSPIRACY, THE** • 1988
DEATH GOES NORTH • 1939 • McDonald Frank • USA
DEATH GOES TO SCHOOL • 1953 • Clarkson Stephen • UKN
DEATH HAS BLUE EYES see **PARAPSYCHICS** • 1974
DEATH HAS LAID AN EGG see **MORTE HA FATTO L'UOVO, LA** • 1968
DEATH HAS NO SEX see **MORTE NON HA SESSO, LA** • 1968
DEATH-HEAD VIRGIN, THE • 1974 • *Gaynor Jack* • USA
DEATH HOUSE • 1988 • Saxon John • USA
DEATH HOUSE see **SILENT NIGHT, BLOODY NIGHT** • 1972
DEATH HUNT • 1981 • Hunt Peter • USA
DEATH IN A FRENCH GARDEN (UKN) see **PERIL EN LA DEMEURE** • 1984
DEATH IN ALASKA see **DAWSON PATROL: DEATH IN ALASKA, THE**
DEATH IN BRUNSWICK • 1990 • Ruane John • ASL
DEATH IN CALIFORNIA • 1986 • Mann Delbert • TVM • USA
DEATH IN CANAAN, A • 1978 • Richardson Tony • TVM • USA
DEATH IN DALLAS • Gemma Giuliano • ITL
DEATH IN FULL VIEW see **DEATH WATCH** • 1979
DEATH IN HIGH HEELS • 1947 • Tomlinson Lionel • UKN
DEATH IN LOVE see **MUERTE ENAMORADA, LA** • 1950
DEATH IN PARADISE CANYON see **FAIR WARNING** • 1937
DEATH IN PERSEPOLIS see **AND THEN THERE WERE NONE** • 1974
DEATH IN ROME see **RAPPRESAGLIA** • 1973
DEATH IN SMALL DOSES • 1957 • Newman Joseph M. • USA
DEATH IN SPACE • 1974 • Dubin Charles S. • TVM • USA
DEATH IN THE AIR • 1936 • Clifton Elmer • USA • MURDER IN THE AIR (UKN)
DEATH IN THE ARENA (USA) see **MACISTE IL GLADIATORE PIU FORTE DEL MONDO** • 1962
DEATH IN THE DAWN see **AKATSUKI NO SHI** • 1924
DEATH IN THE DOLL'S HOUSE see **SHADOW ON THE WALL** • 1949
DEATH IN THE FAMILY, A • 1987 • Wells Peter, Main Stewart • NZL
DEATH IN THE FORENOON • Hill Jerome • SHT • USA • WHO'S AFRAID OF ERNEST HEMINGWAY?
DEATH IN THE GARDEN see **MORT EN CE JARDIN, LA** • 1956
DEATH IN THE HAND • 1948 • Barr-Smith A. • UKN
DEATH IN THE MIDDLE ROOM see **SMIERC W SRODKOWYM POKOJU** • 1965
DEATH IN THE RED JAGUAR see **TOD IM ROTEN JAGUAR, DER** • 1968
DEATH IN THE SADDLE • 1958 • Polak Jindrich • CZC
DEATH IN THE SNOW see **ECHIGO TSUTSUISHI OYASHIRAZU** • 1964
DEATH IN THE STREETS see **DODEN IGATERNE** • 1970
DEATH IN THE SUN see **WHISPERING DEATH** • 1975
DEATH IN THE VATICAN see **MORTE IN VATICANO** • 1982
DEATH IN VENICE (UKN) see **MORTE A VENEZIA** • 1971
DEATH IS A NUMBER • 1951 • Shepherd Horace • UKN
DEATH IS A WOMAN • 1966 • Goode Frederic • UKN • LOVE IS A WOMAN (USA) ○ SEX IS A WOMAN
DEATH IS CALLED ENGELCHEN see **SMRT SI RIKA ENGELCHEN** • 1963
DEATH IS CHILD'S PLAY see **QUIEN PUEDE MATAR A UN NINO?** • 1975
DEATH IS MY TRADE see **AUS EINEM DEUTSCHEN LEBEN** • 1978
DEATH IS NOT THE END • 1976 • Michaels Richard • USA
DEATH JOURNEY • 1976 • Williamson Fred • USA, SPN • JORNADA DE MUERTE (SPN)
DEATH KICK • 1974 • Ho Meng-Hua • HKG • MASTER OF KUNG FU, THE
DEATH KISS, THE • 1933 • Marin Edwin L. • USA
DEATH KISS, THE (USA) see **DODSKYSSEN** • 1917
DEATH LEGACY see **GIRLS' SCHOOL SCREAMERS** • 1986
DEATH LINE • 1972 • Sherman Gary • UKN • RAW MEAT (USA)
DEATH LISTENS see **MUERTE ESCUCHA, LE** • 1970
DEATH MACHINES • 1976 • Kyriazi Paul • USA • NINJA MURDERS
DEATH MARCH, THE • 1937 • Pollard Bud • USA
DEATH MASK • 1987 • Mundhra Jag • USA • DAMNING, THE ○ HACK O'LANTERN ○ DEATHMASK
DEATH MASK, THE • 1914 • *Aoki Tsuru* • USA
DEATH MAY BE YOUR SANTA CLAUS • 1969 • Dymon Frankie Jr. • UKN
DEATH MERCHANTS, THE see **TOD EINES FREMDEN, DER** • 1972
DEATH MOON • 1978 • Kessler Bruce • TVM • USA
DEATH NOOSE, THE see **TODESSCHLEIFE, DIE** • 1928
DEATH NURSE • 1987 • Phillips Nick • USA
DEATH OCCURRED LAST NIGHT (UKN) see **MORTE RISALE A IERI SERA, LA** • 1970
DEATH OF A BUREAUCRAT (UKN) see **MUERTE DE UN BUROCRATA, LA** • 1966
DEATH OF A CAMERAMAN see **MORTE DI UN OPERATORE** • 1979
DEATH OF A CENTERFOLD see **DEATH OF A CENTERFOLD: THE DOROTHY STRATTON STORY** • 1981
DEATH OF A CENTERFOLD: THE DOROTHY STRATTON STORY • 1981 • Beaumont Gabrielle • TVM • USA • DEATH OF A CENTERFOLD ○ DOROTHY STRATTEN STORY, THE ○ DOROTHY STRATTEN: UNTOLD STORY
DEATH OF A CHAMPION • 1939 • Florey Robert • USA
DEATH OF A COMMISSAR • 1966 • Karmen Roman • DOC • USS
DEATH OF A CYCLIST see **MUERTE DE UN CICLISTA** • 1955
DEATH OF A DOCTOR see **EK DOCTOR KI MAUT** • 1990
DEATH OF A DOUBLE, THE see **TOD EINES DOPPELGANGERS, DER** • 1967
DEATH OF A DREAM • 1950 • Reynolds Quentin • USA
DEATH OF A DREAM, THE see **MIRAGE, THE** • 1912
DEATH OF A FRIEND see **MORTE DI UN AMICO** • 1959
DEATH OF A GUNFIGHTER • 1969 • Smithee Alan • USA
DEATH OF A HOOKER see **WHO KILLED MARY WHAT'S'ERNAME?** • 1971
DEATH OF A JEW (USA) see **SABRA** • 1970
DEATH OF A KIDMAKER see **SMIERC DZIECIOROBA** • 1990
DEATH OF A LEGEND • 1971 • Mason William • DCS • CND
DEATH OF A LUMBERJACK see **MORT D'UN BUCHERON, LA** • 1973
DEATH OF A MAIDEN see **SHOJO NO SHI** • 1927
DEATH OF A NOBODY • 1970 • Gillespie Gordon • SHT • CND
DEATH OF A NUN see **DOOD VAN EEN NON, DE** • 1972
DEATH OF A NYMPHETTE • 1967 • Furri Malcolm • USA
DEATH OF A PHILATELIST • 1971 • Kalatozishvili Georgi • USS
DEATH OF A PRESIDENT, THE see **SMIERC PREZYDENTA** • 1977
DEATH OF A PROVINCIAL see **SMIERC PROWINCJALA** • 1966
DEATH OF A SALESMAN • 1951 • Benedek Laslo • USA
DEATH OF A SALESMAN • 1985 • Schlondorff Volker • TVM • USA
DEATH OF A SALESMAN see **MOST PEREYTI NELIEYA** • 1960
DEATH OF A SANDWICHMAN see **DOOD VAN EEN SANDWICHMAN, DE** • 1972
DEATH OF A SCHOOLBOY see **TOD EINES SCHULERS** • 1990
DEATH OF A SCOUNDREL • 1956 • Martin Charles • USA • LOVES AND DEATH OF A SCOUNDREL, THE
DEATH OF A SILENCE see **LYS CASSE, LE** • 1988
DEATH OF A SNOWMAN • 1976 • Rowley Christopher • SAF • BLACK TRASH
DEATH OF A SNOWQUEEN see **SUMMER WISHES, WINTER DREAMS** • 1973
DEATH OF A SOLDIER • 1986 • Mora Philippe • ASL • LEONSKI
DEATH OF A STRANGER • 1971 • Hengge Paul • ISR
DEATH OF A STRANGER (USA) see **TOD EINES FREMDEN, DER** • 1972
DEATH OF A SWAN, THE see **MORT DU CYNGE, LA** • 1937
DEATH OF A TALENTED COBBLER, THE see **SMRT TALENTOVANEHO SEVCE** • 1982
DEATH OF A TAXI-DRIVER see **OSTATNI KURS** • 1963
DEATH OF A USURER see **SMYERT ROSTOVSHCHIKA** • 1967
DEATH OF A VIRGIN see **SHOJO NO SHI** • 1927
DEATH OF ADOLF HITLER • 1973 • Firkin Rex • UKN
DEATH OF AGNES, THE • 1925 • Butler Alexander • UKN
DEATH OF ALEXANDER, THE see **THANATOS TOU ALEXANDROU, O** • 1967
DEATH OF AN ANGEL • 1952 • Saunders Charles • UKN
DEATH OF AN ANGEL • 1985 • Popescu Petru • USA
DEATH OF ANGELS see **WHERE THE BULLETS FLY** • 1966
DEATH OF BRUCE LEE • 1977 • Lu Chun • HKG
DEATH OF GANDJI see **MORT DE GANDJI, LA** • 1965
DEATH OF HEMINGWAY, THE • 1965 • Markopoulos Gregory J. • SHT • USA
DEATH OF HER INNOCENCE, THE see **OUR TIME** • 1974
DEATH OF HEROES, THE • 1979 • Owles Ian, Leatherbarrow Joy • UKN
DEATH OF INNOCENCE, A • 1971 • Wendkos Paul • TVM • USA
DEATH OF IVAN THE TERRIBLE • 1909 • Goncharov Vasili M. • USS
DEATH OF IVAN THE TERRIBLE, THE • 1909 • Protazanov Yakov • USS
DEATH OF JOE THE INDIAN, THE see **MOARTEA LUI JOE INDIANUL** • 1968
DEATH OF JULIUS CAESAR, THE see **REVE DE SHAKESPEARE, LE** • 1907
DEATH OF KING EDWARD III, THE • 1911 • Blackton J. Stuart • USA
DEATH OF MANOLETE, THE • 1957 • Frankenheimer John • MTV • USA
DEATH OF MARIA MALIBRAN, THE see **TOD DER MARIA MALIBRAN, DER** • 1971
DEATH OF MARIO RICCI, THE see **MORT DE MARIO RICCI, LA** • 1983
DEATH OF ME YET, THE • 1971 • Moxey John Llewellyn • TVM • USA
DEATH OF MICHAEL GRADY, THE • 1910 • *Vitagraph* • USA
DEATH OF MIKEL see **MUERTE DE MIKEL, LA** • 1984
DEATH OF MINNEHAHA, THE • 1910 • *Imp* • USA
DEATH OF MR. BALTISBERGER, THE see **SMRT PANA BALTISBERGA** • 1965
DEATH OF MR. FOERSTER, THE • 1963 • Menzel Jiri • CZC
DEATH OF MR. GOLUZA, THE see **SMRT GOSPODINA GOLUZE** • 1983
DEATH OF MY SISTER, THE see **IMOTO NO SHI** • 1921
DEATH OF NATHAN HALE, THE • 1911 • *Shaw Harold M.* • USA
DEATH OF NELSON, THE • 1897 • *Wolff Philip* • UKN
DEATH OF NELSON, THE • 1905 • Fitzhamon Lewin • UKN
DEATH OF OCEAN VIEW PARK, THE • 1979 • Swackhamer E. W. • TVM • USA
DEATH OF PAZUKHIN, THE • 1959 • Nikulin G. • USS
DEATH OF POOR JOE, THE • 1900 • *Warwick Trading Co.* • UKN
DEATH OF PRINCES, A • 1958 • Brahm John • MTV • USA
DEATH OF P'TOWN, THE • 1961 • Jacobs Ken • SHT • USA
DEATH OF RICHIE, THE • 1977 • Wendkos Paul • TVM • USA • RICHIE
DEATH OF SAUL, THE see **MORT DU SAUL, LA** • 1912
DEATH OF SIEGFRIED see **NIBELUNGEN 1, DIE** • 1924
DEATH OF SIMON LA GREE, THE • 1915 • *L-Ko* • USA
DEATH OF TARZAN, THE (USA) see **TARZANOVA SMRT** • 1963
DEATH OF THE APE MAN see **TARZANOVA SMRT** • 1963
DEATH OF THE FLEA CIRCUS DIRECTOR, THE see **MORT DU DIRECTEUR DE CIRQUE DE PUCES, LA** • 1974
DEATH OF THE FLY, THE see **SMRT MOUCHY** • 1975
DEATH OF THE GORILLA, THE • Mays Peter • SHT • USA
DEATH OF THE IRON HORSE, THE • 1905 • Cooper Arthur • UKN
DEATH OF THE LEOPARD • 1989 • Saleh Fariborz • IRN
DEATH OF THE PEASANT DJURICA, THE • 1971 • Golubovic Predrag • SHT • YGS
DEATH OF THE PRESIDENT see **SMIERC PREZYDENTA** • 1977
DEATH OF THE SUN, THE see **MORT DU SOLEIL, LA** • 1921
DEATH ON A SIDE STREET see **ONE-WAY STREET** • 1950
DEATH ON SAFARI • 1989 • Birkinshaw Alan • USA
DEATH ON SUGAR ISLAND • 1961 • Sequens Jiri • CZC
DEATH ON THE DIAMOND • 1934 • Sedgwick Edward • USA
DEATH ON THE FOUR-POSTER (USA) see **DELITTO ALLO SPECCHIO** • 1964
DEATH ON THE FREEWAY see **DEATH CAR ON THE FREEWAY** • 1979
DEATH ON THE MOUNTAIN see **ARU SONAN** • 1961
DEATH ON THE NILE • 1978 • Guillermin John • USA
DEATH ON THE ROAD • 1935 • Rotha Paul • DOC • UKN
DEATH ON THE RUN see **BERSAGLIO MOBILE** • 1967
DEATH ON THE SET • 1935 • Hiscott Leslie • UKN • MURDER ON THE SET
DEATH OR FREEDOM see **TOD ODER FREIHEIT** • 1977
DEATH OVER MY SHOULDER • 1958 • Crabtree Arthur • UKN
DEATH PACKS UP see **MUERTO HACE LAS MALETAS, EL** • 1971
DEATH PACT see **AKORD SMRTI** • 1919
DEATH PATROL see **PATROUILLE DE CHOC** • 1956
DEATH PENALTY • 1980 • Hussein Waris • TVM • USA
DEATH PENALTY see **PENA DE MUERTE** • 1973
DEATH PEOPLE'S MANSION see **SHIBIJIN YASHIKI** • 1954
DEATH PLAY • 1976 • *Leslie Karen* • USA
DEATH PREDICTER, THE see **MONDE TREMBLERA, LE** • 1939
DEATH PROMISE • 1978 • Warmflash Robert • USA • PAY-OFF TIME
DEATH RACE • 1973 • Rich David Lowell • TVM • USA • STATE OF DIVISION
DEATH RACE 2000 • 1975 • Bartel Paul • USA
DEATH RAGE see **CON LA RABBIA AGLI OCCHI** • 1976
DEATH RAIDERS • Ramos Segundo
DEATH RAILWAY • 1980 • Bilcock David Jr. • DOC • ASL
DEATH RATHER THAN A CHANCE LIKE THAT see **ANTES A MORTE QUE TAL SORTE** • 1976
DEATH RAY • 1977 • Baldanello Gianfranco • ITL
DEATH RAY 2000 • 1981 • Katzin Lee H. • TVM • USA
DEATH RAY, THE • 1924 • Grindell-Matthews H. • SHT • USA
DEATH RAY, THE • 1924 • Quiribet Gaston • UKN
DEATH RAY, THE see **LUCH SMERTI** • 1925
DEATH RAY, THE (UKN) see **MURDER AT DAWN** • 1932
DEATH RAYS OF DR. MABUSE, THE see **TODESSTRAHLEN DES DR. MABUSE, DIE** • 1964
DEATH REPAID, THE • 1910 • *Melies* • USA
DEATH RIDE see **CRASH!** • 1977
DEATH-RIDE UNDER THE BIG TOP, THE see **DODSRITTEN UNDER CIRKUSKUPOLEN** • 1912
DEATH RIDERS • 1976 • Wilson James L. • USA
DEATH RIDES A CAROUSEL see **CARNIVAL OF BLOOD** • 1971
DEATH RIDES A HORSE see **DA UOMO A UOMO** • 1967
DEATH RIDES THE PLAINS • 1943 • Newfield Sam • USA
DEATH RIDES THE RANGE • 1940 • Newfield Sam • USA
DEATH RIDES THIS TRAIL see **WILD HERITAGE** • 1958
DEATH RIDES TO OSAKA see **GIRLS OF THE WHITE ORCHID** • 1983
DEATH SCOUTS see **MAN FROM ATLANTIS: THE DEATH SCOUTS, THE** • 1977
DEATH SCREAM • 1975 • Heffron Richard T. • TVM • USA • WOMAN WHO CRIED MURDER, THE ○ HOMICIDE
DEATH SCREAM see **MAISON SOUS LES ARBRES, LA** • 1971
DEATH SCREAMS • 1982 • Nelson David • USA
DEATH SENTENCE • 1975 • Swackhamer E. W. • TVM • USA
DEATH SENTENCE (UKN) see **SENTENZA DI MORTE** • 1967
DEATH SHIP • 1980 • Rakoff Alvin • CND
DEATH SIGN OF HIGH NOON, THE • 1914 • *Sais Marin* • USA
DEATH SMILES ON A MURDERER (USA) see **MORTE SORRIDE ALL'ASSASSINO, LA** • 1973
DEATH SPAR • 1988 • Fischa Michael • USA • WITCH BITCH
DEATH SQUAD see **ESCUADRON DE LA MORTE** • 1985
DEATH SQUAD, THE • 1973 • Falk Harry • USA
DEATH STALK • 1975 • Day Robert • TVM • USA
DEATH STALKER see **CAZADOR DE LA MUERTE, EL** • 1982
DEATH STONE OF INDIA, THE • 1913 • *Bison* • USA
DEATH TAKES A HOLIDAY • 1934 • Leisen Mitchell • USA • STRANGE HOLIDAY
DEATH TAKES A HOLIDAY • 1971 • Butler Robert • TVM • USA
DEATH TAKES A HOLIDAY • 1990 • Brest Martin • USA
DEATH: THE ULTIMATE MYSTERY • 1975 • Emenegger Robert • USA
DEATH THREAT see **HOLLYWOOD MAN** • 1976
DEATH THROES see **AGONIYA** • 1976
DEATH TO THE INVADER see **MUERTE AL INVASOR** • 1961
DEATH TO THE PEE-WEE SQUAD • 1988 • Adams Neal • USA
DEATH TO THE WHORE see **VURUN KAHPEYE** • 1974
DEATH TRAIL, THE • 1913 • *Champion* • USA
DEATH TRAP • 1962 • Moxey John Llewellyn • UKN
DEATH TRAP • 1967 • Marquez Artemio • PHL
DEATH TRAP, THE • 1913 • *Lubin* • USA

DEATH TRAP, THE • 1920 • Bradbury Robert North • USA
DEATH TRAP, THE • 1920 • Jaccard Jacques • SHT • USA
DEATH TRAP (UKN) see **EATEN ALIVE** • 1976
DEATH TRAVELS TOO MUCH see **UMORISMO NERO** • 1965
DEATH TROUBLES see **MORT TROUBLE, LA** • 1968
DEATH VALLEY • 1927 • Powell Paul • USA
DEATH VALLEY • 1946 • Landers Lew • USA
DEATH VALLEY • 1982 • Richards Dick • USA
DEATH VALLEY GUNFIGHTER • 1949 • Springsteen R. G. • USA
DEATH VALLEY MANHUNT • 1943 • English John • USA
DEATH VALLEY OUTLAWS • 1941 • Sherman George • USA
DEATH VALLEY RANGERS • 1943 • Tansey Robert • USA
DEATH VALLEY SCOTTY'S MINE • 1912 • *Scott Walter* • USA
DEATH VENGEANCE see **FIGHTING BACK** • 1982
DEATH WALKS ALONE see **SOUL OF A MONSTER, THE** • 1944
DEATH WALKS BY NIGHT • 1955 • MacDonald David • UKN
DEATH WARD see **ANBAR EL MAWI** • 1988
DEATH WARMED UP • 1984 • Blyth David • NZL • BRAIN DAMAGE ○ DOCTOR DEATH
DEATH WARRANT, THE • 1914 • *Lubin* • USA
DEATH WAS A PASSENGER • 1958 • Zichy Theodore • UKN
DEATH WATCH • 1979 • Tavernier Bertrand • UKN, FRN, FRG • MORT EN DIRECT, LA (FRN) ○ DEATHWATCH ○ DEATH IN FULL VIEW
DEATH WATCH, THE see **BEFORE DAWN** • 1933
DEATH WAVE • 1986 • Shields Frank • ASL
DEATH WAVES see **DEATH CORPS** • 1970
DEATH WEB, THE • 1915 • Kent Leon D. • USA
DEATH WEEKEND • 1976 • Fruet William • CND • HOUSE BY THE LAKE, THE (USA)
DEATH WEIGHT, THE • 1913 • *Bailey William* • USA
DEATH WHEELERS, THE see **PSYCHOMANIA** • 1972
DEATH, WHERE IS THY STING? • 1920 • *Prizma* • USA
DEATH WISH • 1974 • Winner Michael • USA
DEATH WISH 3 • 1985 • Winner Michael • UKN
DEATH WISH 4: THE CRACKDOWN • 1987 • Thompson J. Lee • USA
DEATH WISH II • 1982 • Winner Michael • USA
DEATH WOMAN, THE (UKN) see **SENORA MUERTE, LA** • 1968
DEATH ZONE • 1985 • Woodland James • DOC • CND
DEATH ZONE see **ULTIMO DIA DE LA GUERRA, EL** • 1969
DEATHBED • 1973 • Foster Norman • USA
DEATHBLOW • 1988 • Nussbaum Raphael • USA
DEATHCHEATERS • 1976 • Trenchard-Smith Brian • ASL
DEATHDREAM • 1972 • Clark Bob • CND • DEAD OF NIGHT ○ DEAD NIGHT ○ KILL ○ NIGHT ANDY CAME HOME, THE ○ NIGHT WALK ○ VETERAN, THE
DEATHFLASH • 1987 • Zarindast Tony • USA • DEATH FLASH
DEATHGAME • Jameson Jerry • USA • DEATH GAME
DEATHHOUSE • 1981 • Gershuny Theodore • USA
DEATHLINE see **SNO-LINE** • 1984
DEATHLOCK, THE • 1915 • *Butler Fred J.* • USA
DEATHMASK • 1984 • Friedman Richard • USA
DEATHMASK see **DEATH MASK** • 1987
DEATHMASTER, THE • 1972 • Danton Ray • USA • KHORDA
DEATHROW GAMESHOW • 1988 • Pirro Mark • USA
DEATH'S ECSTACY see **BETE, LA** • 1975
DEATH'S MARATHON • 1913 • Griffith D. W. • USA
DEATH'S SHORT CUT • 1913 • Siegmann George • USA
DEATH'S WITNESS • 1914 • O'Sullivan Tony • USA
DEATHSHEAD VAMPIRE see **BLOOD BEAST TERROR, THE** • 1968
DEATHSPORT • 1978 • Suso Henry, Arkush Allan • USA
DEATHSTALKER II • 1987 • Wynorski Jim • USA • DEATHSTALKER II: DUEL OF THE TITANS ○ DUEL OF THE TITANS
DEATHSTALKER II: DUEL OF THE TITANS see **DEATHSTALKER II** • 1987
DEATHSTALKER III • 1988 • Corona Alfonso • USA • DEATHSTALKER III: THE WARRIORS FROM HELL
DEATHSTALKER III: THE WARRIORS FROM HELL see **DEATHSTALKER III** • 1988
DEATHSTALKER (USA) see **CAZADOR DE LA MUERTE, EL** • 1982
DEATHTRAP • 1982 • Lumet Sidney • USA
DEATHWATCH • 1965 • Morrow Vic • USA
DEATHWATCH see **DEATH WATCH** • 1979
DEBAIN FAMILY • 1969 • Bonniere Rene • DCS • CND
DEBAJO DEL MUNDO • 1986 • Feijoo Beda Ocampo, Stagnaro Juan Bautista • ARG, CZC • UNDER THE WORLD ○ UNDER EARTH
DEBARQUE-MOUE AU LAC DES VENTS • 1974 • Gauthier Michel • DOC • CND
DEBARQUEMENT • 1895 • Lumiere Louis • FRN • ARRIVEE DES CONGRESSISTES A NEUVILLE-SUR-SAONE
DEBARQUEMENT A QUIBERON • 1899 • Melies Georges • FRN
DEBARQUEMENT DE VOYAGEURS PORT DE GRANVILLE • 1899 • Melies Georges • FRN • PASSENGERS LANDING AT HARBOUR OF GRANVILLE
DEBARQUEMENT DU CONGRES DE PHOTOGRAPHIE • 1895 • Lumiere Louis • FRN • CONGRES DES SOCIETES PHOTOGRAPHIQUES DE FRANCE
DEBATIK • Hakani Hysen • ALB • DISCUSSION, THE
DEBAUCHEE, LA • 1970 • Davy Jean-Francois • FRN • WIFE SWAPPING -FRENCH STYLE (UKN)
DEBAUCHERS, THE • 1970 • Knight Sidney • USA
DEBAUCHERY see **RYOSHOKU** • 1967
DEBAUCHERY IS WRONG see **DORAKU GOSHINAN** • 1928
DEBBIE • 1965 • SAF
DEBBIE GOES DALLAS • 1978 • Clark Jim* • USA
DEBDAS see **DEVDAS** • 1935
DEBELI I MRSAVI • 1985 • Prelic Svetislav Bata • YGS • FAT AND THIN
DEBIERON AHORCARLOS ANTES • 1973 • *Filmadora Chapultepec* • MXC
DEBILES LEGERS, LES • 1974 • Moreau Michel • CND
DEBITIRTHA-KAMRUP • 1967 • Sen Manu • IND • HOLY PILGRIMAGE -KAMRUP, THE
DEBITO CONIUGALE, IL • 1970 • Prosperi Franco • ITL
DEBITO D'ODIO • 1920 • Genina Augusto • ITL
DEBLA, LA VIRGEN GITANA • 1950 • Torrado Ramon • SPN
DEBORAH • 1914 • *Fealy Maude* • USA
DEBORAH • 1968 • Navarro Marcelino D. • PHL
DEBORAH (USA) see **FIOCCO NERO PER DEBORAH, UN** • 1974
DEBOUT, LA-DEDANS! • 1935 • Wulschleger Henry • FRN
DEBOUT LES CRABES, LA MER MONTE! • 1983 • Grand-Jouan Jean-Jacques • FRN
DEBOUT LES MORTS • 1917 • Heuze Andre • FRN
DEBOUT SUR LEUR TERRE • 1982 • Bulbulian Maurice • DOC • CND
DEBROUILLE-TOI • 1917 • Feuillade Louis • FRN
DEBROUSSAILLAGE CHIMIQUE, LE • 1955 • Tadie, Lacoste • SHT • FRN
DEBT • 1910 • Salter Harry • USA
DEBT, THE • 1912 • *Rex* • USA
DEBT, THE • 1914 • *Lubin* • USA
DEBT, THE • 1917 • Powell Frank • USA
DEBT, THE see **HIS DEBT** • 1919
DEBT OF BLOOD, THE see **HANGYAKU** • 1967
DEBT OF GAMBLING • 1913 • Haldane Bert? • UKN
DEBT OF HONOR • 1914 • *Lewis Pennant Features* • USA
DEBT OF HONOR, A • 1916 • Nigh William • USA • HER DEBT OF HONOR
DEBT OF HONOR, THE • 1918 • Lund O. A. C. • USA
DEBT OF HONOUR • 1936 • Walker Norman • UKN • MAN WHO COULD NOT FORGET, THE
DEBT OF HONOUR see **NAMUS BORCU** • 1967
DEBT OF HONOUR, A • 1922 • Elvey Maurice • UKN
DEBT REPAID, THE • 1910-12 • Melies Gaston • USA
DEBTOR TO THE LAW, A • 1924 • *Starr Henry* • USA
DEBURAU • 1950 • Guitry Sacha • FRN
DEBUSSY FILM, THE • 1965 • Russell Ken • MTV • UKN
DEBUT, THE see **NACHALO** • 1971
DEBUT, THE see **DEBUUT, HET** • 1976
DEBUT DE SIECLE • 1968 • Allegret Marc • FRN
DEBUT IN THE SECRET SERVICE, A • 1914 • *Cruze James* • USA
DEBUTANT, LE • 1969 • Daert Daniel • FRN
DEBUTS D'UN CANOTIER, LES • 1908 • *Deed Andre* • FRN
DEBUTS D'UN CHAUFFEUR, LES • 1907 • Heuze Andre • FRN
DEBUTS D'UN PATINEUR, LES • 1906 • Linder Max • FRN • MAX'S ICE SCREAM
DEBUTS D'UN YACHTMAN, LES • 1913 • Linder Max • FRN
DEBUUT, HET • 1976 • van Brakel Nouchka • NTH • DEBUT, THE
DECA VOJVODE SMITA • 1967 • Pavlovic Vladimir • YGS • CHILDREN OF COMMANDER SCHMIDT, THE
DECADE PRODIGIEUSE, LA • 1971 • Chabrol Claude • FRN, ITL • DIECI INCREDIBILI GIORNI (ITL) ○ TEN DAY'S WONDER (UKN)
DECADENCE ET GRANDEUR • 1923 • Bernard Raymond • FRN • GRANDEUR ET DECADENCE
DECADENT INFLUENCE, THE see **FILLE ET DES FUSILS, UNE** • 1965
DECADENZA • 1977 • Magro A. M. • ITL
DECAIT • 1989 • Qaiser Jehangir • PKS
DECAK I VIOLINA • 1976 • Rancic Jovan • YGS • BOY AND THE VIOLIN, THE
DECAK JE VIKAO UBISTVO (YGS) see **BOY CRIED MURDER, THE** • 1966
DECAK MITA • 1951 • Novakovic Rados • YGS
DECAMERON 3 (UKN) see **DECAMERON N.3 -LE PIU BELLE DONNE DEL BOCCACCIO** • 1972
DECAMERON '69 • 1969 • Clarens Bernard, Herman Jean, Grospierre Louis, Desaillers Jean, Korber Serge • FRN
DECAMERON '300 • 1972 • Stefani Mauro • ITL
DECAMERON, THE (USA) see **DECAMERONE, IL** • 1971
DECAMERON II (UKN) see **DECAMERON N.2** • 1972
DECAMERON N.2 • 1972 • Guerrini Mino • ITL • DECAMERON N.2 -LE ALTRE NOVELLE DEL BOCCACCIO ○ DECAMERON II (UKN)
DECAMERON N.2 -LE ALTRE NOVELLE DEL BOCCACCIO see **DECAMERON N.2** • 1972
DECAMERON N.3 see **ULTIMO DECAMERONE, L'** • 1972
DECAMERON N.3 -LE PIU BELLE DONNE DEL BOCCACCIO • 1972 • Margheriti Antonio • ITL • NOVELLE GALEOTTE D'AMORE DEL DECAMERONE ○ DECAMERON 3 (UKN)
DECAMERON N.3 LE PIU BELLE DONNE DEL BOCCACCIO see **ULTIMO DECAMERONE, L'** • 1972
DECAMERON N.4 • 1972 • Bianchini Paolo • ITL • PIU BELLE NOVELLE DEL BOCCACCIO, LE
DECAMERON NIGHTS • 1924 • Wilcox Herbert • UKN, FRG • DEKAMERON-NACHTE (FRG)
DECAMERON NIGHTS • 1953 • Fregonese Hugo • USA, UKN
DECAMERON PROIBITISSIMO • 1972 • Girolami Marino • ITL • BOCCACCIO MIO STATTE ZITTO ○ SEXY SINNERS (UKN)
DECAMERONE, IL • 1971 • Pasolini Pier Paolo • ITL, FRN, FRG • DECAMERON, THE (USA)
DECAMERONE NERO, IL • 1972 • Vivarelli Piero • ITL • BLACK DECAMERON (UKN)
DECAMERONE PROIBITO • 1972 • Infascelli Carlo • ITL • FORBIDDEN DECAMERON (UKN)
DECAMERON'S JOLLY KITTENS(UKN) see **ULTIMO DECAMERONE, L'** • 1972
DECAMEROTICUS • 1972 • Ferretti Piergiorgio • ITL
DECAP I LOPTA • 1960 • *Zagreb* • ANS • YGS • CHILD AND THE BALL, THE
DECATHLON CHAMPION • 1937 • Feist Felix E. • SHT • USA • DECATHLON CHAMPION -THE STORY OF GLENN MORRIS
DECATHLON CHAMPION -THE STORY OF GLENN MORRIS see **DECATHLON CHAMPION** • 1937
DECEIT • 1923 • Micheaux Oscar • USA
DECEIT see **FAREB** • 1968
DECEIT see **NO WAY OUT** • 1987
DECEIT (UKN) see **UNHOLY LOVE** • 1932
DECEITFUL GOSHO • 1963 • Buchvarova Radka • ANS • BUL
DECEITFUL SHEPHERD, THE • 1970 • Donev Donyo • ANS • BUL
DECEITFUL YEARS see **YALAN YILLAR** • 1968
DECEIVED FOX, THE • 1952 • Calinescu Bob • ANM • RMN
DECEIVED ONES, THE see **MAKHDU UN, AL-** • 1972
DECEIVED SLUMMING PARTY • 1908 • McCutcheon Wallace • USA
DECEIVER, THE • 1909 • *Centaur* • USA
DECEIVER, THE • 1914 • Dillon Eddie • USA
DECEIVER, THE • 1920 • Hersholt Jean, Moomaw Lewis H. • USA
DECEIVER, THE • 1931 • King Louis • USA
DECEIVERS, THE • 1910 • *Powers* • USA
DECEIVERS, THE • 1912 • *Hawley Ormi* • USA
DECEIVERS, THE • 1913 • Sturgeon Rollin S. • USA
DECEIVERS, THE • 1915 • Drew Sidney • *Vitagraph* • USA
DECEIVERS, THE • 1915 • Giblyn Charles • *Gold Seal* • USA
DECEIVERS, THE • 1988 • Meyer Nicholas • UKN, USA
DECEIVERS, THE see **WHY ANNOUNCE YOUR MARRIAGE?** • 1922
DECEIVERS, THE see **INTIMACY** • 1966
DECEIVERS BOTH • 1913 • Plumb Hay? • UKN
DECEIVING COSTUME see **ITSUWARERU SEISO** • 1951
DECEIVING DAD • 1913 • *Komic* • USA
DECEIVING DAD • 1916 • *Unicorn* • USA
DECEIVING UNCLE • 1913 • Batley Ethyle • UKN
DECEIVING UNCLE ASA • 1913 • *Kalem* • USA
DECEMBARSKI DEZ • 1990 • Sprajc Bozo • YGS • DECEMBER RAIN, THE
DECEMBER see **JOULUKUU** • 1969
DECEMBER 7TH • 1943 • Ford John, Toland Gregg • DOC • USA
DECEMBER 32ND see **32 DICEMBRE** • 1988
DECEMBER BRIDE, THE • 1989 • O'Sullivan Thaddeus • IRL, UKN
DECEMBER, CHILDREN'S MONTH see **DECEMBRE, MOIS DES ENFANTS** • 1956
DECEMBER RAIN, THE see **DECEMBARSKI DEZ** • 1990
DECEMBRE • 1972 • Hamina Mohamed Lakhdar • ALG, FRN
DECEMBRE, MOIS DES ENFANTS • 1956 • Storck Henri • DOC • BLG • DECEMBER, CHILDREN'S MONTH
DECEMBRISTS • 1927 • Ivanovsky Alexander • USS
DECENT LIFE, A see **ANSTANDIGT LIV, ETT** • 1979
DECENTE, LA • 1970 • Saenz De Heredia Jose Luis • SPN
DECEPTION • 1913 • Bowman William J. • USA
DECEPTION • 1918 • Hunter A. C. • UKN
DECEPTION • 1933 • Seiler Lewis • USA
DECEPTION • 1946 • Rapper Irving • USA
DECEPTION • 1973 • *Dullea Keir* • MTV • USA
DECEPTION see **DU BARRY, WOMAN OF PASSION** • 1930
DECEPTION see **RICHTER UND SEIN HENKER, DER** • 1976
DECEPTION see **STRIPPED TO KILL** • 1987
DECEPTION, THE • 1909 • Griffith D. W. • USA
DECEPTION, THE • 1912 • *Reliance* • USA
DECEPTION, THE • 1912 • Haldane Bert? • UKN
DECEPTION, THE • 1915 • Kaufman Joseph • *Lubin* • USA
DECEPTION, THE • 1915 • Otto Henry • *American* • USA
DECEPTION (USA) see **ANNA BOLEYN** • 1921
DECEPTIONS • 1985 • Chenault Robert, Shavelson Melville • TVM • USA
DECEPTIONS see **INGANNI** • 1985
DECHAINEES, LES see **QUAND LES FILLES SE DECHAINENT** • 1973
DECHAINES, LES • 1950 • Keigel Leonard • SHT • FRN • SURBOUM
DECHAINES, LES • 1972 • Combret Georges • FRN
DECHARGE, LA • 1970 • Baratier Jacques • FRN, FRG
DECHARGE VICTORIEUSE, LA • 1981 • Baudricourt Michel • FRN
DECHARGEMENT DE BATEAUX AU HAVRE • 1896 • Melies Georges • FRN • UNLOADING THE BOAT (HAVRE)
DECHEANCE see **ODETTE** • 1934
DECHIRURE, LA • Apprederis Franck • FRN
DECHIRURE, LA • 1974 • Dansereau Fernand, Rossignol Yolande • SHT • CND
DECIDING KISS, THE • 1918 • Browning Tod • USA
DECIDING VOTE, THE • 1910 • *Imp* • USA
DECIDUOUS TREE, A see **RAKUYO-JU** • 1987
DECIMA VITTIMA, LA • 1965 • Petri Elio • ITL, FRN • DIXIEME VICTIME, LA (FRN) ○ 10TH VICTIM, THE (USA)
DECIMALS OF LOVE, THE see **KARLEKENS DECIMALER** • 1960
DECISION • 1981 • Dalen Zale R. • CND
DECISION, LA • 1964 • Massip Jose • CUB
DECISION, THE • 1915 • Otto Henry • USA
DECISION, THE • 1918 • *Duncan William* • SHT • USA
DECISION, THE see **LITTLE BLOND LADY, THE** • 1914
DECISION AGAINST TIME (USA) see **MAN IN THE SKY** • 1957
DECISION AT MIDNIGHT • 1963 • Allen Lewis • USA
DECISION AT SUNDOWN • 1957 • Boetticher Budd • USA
DECISION BEFORE DAWN • 1951 • Litvak Anatole • USA
DECISION CAPITALE, UNE see **MATTER OF SURVIVAL, A** • 1969
DECISION OF CHRISTOPHER BLAKE, THE • 1948 • Godfrey Peter • USA • CHRISTOPHER BLAKE
DECISION OF JIM O'FARRELL, THE • 1914 • Martin E. A. • USA
DECISION OF THE COURT, THE • 1915 • *Whitman Velma* • USA
DECISION TO DIE • 1978 • SAF
DECISIVE BATTLE see **KESSEN** • 1944
DECISIVE STEP, THE • 1966 • USS
DECK PASSAGE see **KANSIPAIKKA** • 1968
DECKNAME SCHLIER • 1985 • Kiener Wilma, Matzka Dieter • AUS • ASSUMED NAME: SCHLIER
DECKO KOJI OBECAVA • 1982 • Radivojevic Misa • YGS • PROMISING LAD, A
DECKS RAN RED, THE • 1958 • Stone Andrew L. • USA • INFAMY AT SEA
DECLARATION OF INDEPENDENCE, THE • 1911 • Dawley J. Searle • *Edison* • USA
DECLARATION OF INDEPENDENCE, THE • 1911 • Marston Theodore • *Thanhouser* • USA
DECLARATION OF LOVE see **ZAYAVLYENIYE O LYUBVI** • 1979
DECLASSEE • 1925 • Vignola Robert G. • USA • SOCIAL EXILE, THE
DECLIC ET DES CLAQUES • 1964 • Clair Philippe • FRN, ITL • DES CLICS ET DES CLACS ○ ESBROUFFE, L'
DECLIN • 1980 • Coderre Laurent • ANM • CND • RUSTING WORLD
DECLIN DE L'EMPIRE AMERICAIN, LE • 1986 • Arcand Denys • CND • DECLINE OF THE AMERICAN EMPIRE, THE
DECLINE AND FALL see **DECLINE AND FALL.. OF A BIRDWATCHER!** • 1968

DECLINE AND FALL.. OF A BIRDWATCHER! • 1968 • Krish John • UKN • DECLINE AND FALL

DECLINE OF A SHARPSHOOTER see **OCASO DE UN PISTOLERO** • 1968

DECLINE OF THE AMERICAN EMPIRE, THE see **DECLIN DE L'EMPIRE AMERICAIN, LE** • 1986

DECLINE OF THE WIZARDS • 1965 • Jaworski Tadeusz • DOC • PLN

DECLINE.. OF WESTERN CIVILISATION, THE • 1980 • Spheeris Penelope • DOC • USA

DECLINE OF WESTERN CIVILIZATION PART II: THE METAL YEARS • 1988 • Spheeris Penelope • DOC • USA

DECLIVE • 1951 • Aguirre Javier • SHT • SPN

DECOBERTA DE NOVAS TERRAS DE CULTURA, A • 1947 • Coelho Jose Adolfo • SHT • PRT

DECOLLETE DANS LE DOS, LE (FRN) see **RUCKENDEKOLLETE, DAS** • 1975

DECORATOR, THE • 1920 • Robbins Jess • SHT • USA

DECOY • Bocan Hynek • CZC

DECOY • 1946 • Bernhard Jack • USA

DECOY see **DATSUGOKO-SHU** • 1957

DECOY, THE • 1914 • *Princess* • USA

DECOY, THE • 1915 • *Lubin* • USA

DECOY, THE • 1915 • *Reliance* • USA

DECOY, THE • 1916 • Garwood William • *Imp* • SHT • USA

DECOY, THE • 1916 • Lederer George W. • *Mutual* • USA

DECOY, THE see **LOCKFAGELN** • 1972

DECOY, THE (UKN) see **STOOL PIGEON** • 1928

DECOY DUCK, THE • 1974 • Vazov Yanoush • BUL

DECOY FOR TERROR see **PLAYGIRL KILLER** • 1965

DECOY (UKN) see **ROUGH RIDIN' JUSTICE** • 1945

DECOY (USA) see **MYSTERY SUBMARINE** • 1963

DECREE OF DESTINY • 1915 • *Warner'S Features* • USA

DECREE OF DESTINY, A • 1911 • Griffith D. W. • USA

DECREE OF JUSTICE, A • 1914 • *Coxen Ed* • USA

DECYZJA • 1960 • Dziedzina Julian • PLN

DEDACEK • 1968 • Jires Jaromil • CZC • GRANPA

DEDAIN DE DIONISIO, LE • 1914 • Protazanov Yakov • USS

DEDANS LE SUD DE LA LOUISIANE • 1974 • Bruneau Jean-Pierre • DOC • FRN

DEDE • 1934 • Guissart Rene • FRN

DEDE • 1990 • Benoit Jean-Louis • FRN

DEDE DE MONTMARTRE see **DEDE LA MUSIQUE** • 1939

DEDE LA MUSIQUE • 1939 • Berthomieu Andre • FRN • DEDE DE MONTMARTRE

DEDE, SON PERE ET L'AMOUR see **SON AUTRE AMOUR** • 1933

DEDECEK AUTOMOBIL • 1956 • Radok Alfred • CZC • GRANDFATHER AUTOMOBILE ○ OLD MAN MOTOR-CAR

DEDECKEM PROTI SVE VULI • 1939 • Slavinsky Vladimir • CZC • GRANDPA INVOLUNTARILY

DEDEE D'ANVERS • 1947 • Allegret Yves • FRN • DEDEE (USA) ○ WOMAN OF ANTWERP

DEDEE (USA) see **DEDEE D'ANVERS** • 1947

DEDICACAO • 1954 • Rosa Americo Leite • SHT • PRT

DEDICATED GUNMAN, THE see **GOROTSUKI INO** • 1964

DEDICATED TO THE AEGEAN SEA see **EGE KAI NI SASAGU** • 1978

DEDICATION see **DEDICATORIA** • 1980

DEDICATION OF THE GREAT BUDDHA see **DAIBUTSU KAIGEN** • 1952

DEDICATO A PINELLI see **DOCUMENTI SU GIUSEPPE PINELLI** • 1970

DEDICATO A UN MEDICO • 1974 • Serra Gianni • MTV • ITL

DEDICATO A UNA STELLA • 1977 • Cozzi Luigi • ITL

DEDICATORIA • 1980 • Chavarri Jaime • SPN • DEDICATION

DEDISCINA • 1985 • Klopcic Matjaz • YGS • HERITAGE ○ NASLEDJE

DEDO DEL DESTINO, EL (SPN) see **FICKLE FINGER OF FATE, THE** • 1967

DEDO EN EL GATILLO, EL (SPN) see **FINGER ON THE TRIGGER** • 1965

DEDOUBLEMENT CABALISTIQUE • 1898 • Melies Georges • SHT • FRN • TRIPLE LADY, THE (USA)

DEDUCE YOU SAY • 1956 • Jones Charles M. • ANS • USA

DEEDAR • 1958 • Bose Nitin • IND

DEEDEE • 1974 • Shebib Donald • CND

DEEDEE'S BLIND MASTER • 1913 • *Pathe* • USA

DEEDS MEN DO, THE see **BATTLE OF THE CORONEL AND FALKLAND ISLANDS, THE** • 1927

DEEDS OF DARING • 1924 • Seeling Charles R. • USA

DEEDS THAT WON GALLIPOLI see **WITHIN OUR GATES** • 1915

DEELA • 1970 • Alassane Moustapha • DOC • NGR

DEEMSTER, THE • 1917 • Hansel Howell • USA

DEEP see **PROFUNDO** • 1988

DEEP, THE • 1969 • Welles Orson

DEEP, THE • 1977 • Yates Peter • USA

DEEP ADVENTURE • 1957 • *Allen Ross* • USA

DEEP BLUE NIGHT see **GIPGO PULD BAM** • 1985

DEEP BLUE SEA, THE • 1955 • Litvak Anatole • UKN

DEEP BOO SEA • 1952 • Kneitel Seymour • ANS • USA

DEEP DARK SECRETS • 1987 • Lewis Robert • TVM • USA

DEEP DESIRE OF GODS see **KAMIGAMI NO FUKAKI YOKUBO** • 1968

DEEP DOWN UNDER • 1956 • Monkman Noel • DOC • ASL

DEEP DYED DUBS • 1915 • *Heinie & Louie* • USA

DEEP DYED VILLAINY • 1917 • *Heinie & Louie* • SHT • USA

DEEP END • 1970 • Skolimowski Jerzy • UKN, FRG • STARTING OUT

DEEP END, THE see **ONE-WAY STREET** • 1950

DEEP FEELINGS • 1982 • *Jeremy Ron* • USA

DEEP-FREEZE SQUEEZE • 1964 • *Lantz Walter (P)* • ANS • USA

DEEP HOLLAND see **DIEP NEDERLAND** • 1956

DEEP ILLUSION see **FONTE DA SAUDADE, A** • 1986

DEEP IN LOVE see **SKIN DEEP IN LOVE** • 1967

DEEP IN MY HEART • 1954 • Donen Stanley • USA

DEEP IN THE HEART see **HANDGUN** • 1983

DEEP IN THE HEART OF TEXAS • 1942 • Clifton Elmer • USA

DEEP IN THE HEART OF TEXAS see **MEN OF TEXAS** • 1942

DEEP INSIDE • 1968 • Sarno Joe • USA

DEEP JAWS • 1975 • Dell Perry • USA

DEEP OF DELIVERANCE, THE • 1983 • van Brakel Nouchka • NTH

DEEP PURPLE • 1920 • Walsh Raoul • USA

DEEP PURPLE • 1949 • Cowan Will • SHT • USA • GENE KRUPA AND HIS ORCHESTRA

DEEP PURPLE, THE • 1916 • Young James • USA

DEEP RED: HATCHET MURDERS see **PROFONDO ROSSO** • 1975

DEEP RED (USA) see **PROFONDO ROSSO** • 1975

DEEP RIVER SAVAGES see **PAESE DEL SESSO SELVAGGIO, IL** • 1972

DEEP RUB • Gucci Leon • USA

DEEP SEA BOODLE • 1960 • Tendlar Dave • ANS • USA

DEEP SEA LIAR, THE • 1913 • *Thanhouser* • USA

DEEP SEA LIAR, THE • 1916 • Dillon John Francis • USA

DEEP SEA PANIC, A • 1924 • Del Ruth Roy • SHT • USA

DEEP SEAS AND DESPERATE DEEDS • 1917 • Moore Vin • SHT • USA

DEEP SIX, THE • 1958 • Mate Rudolph • USA

DEEP SLEEP • 1972 • Sole Alfred • USA

DEEP SOUTH • 1936 • Goodwins Leslie • SHT • USA

DEEP SOUTH see **THEY WON'T FORGET** • 1937

DEEP SPACE • 1987 • Ray Fred Olen • USA

DEEP STAR SIX • 1988 • Cunningham Sean S. • USA • DEEPSTAR SIX

DEEP STUFF • 1917 • *Vim* • USA

DEEP THOUGHTS see **PENSIERI MORBOSI** • 1981

DEEP THREAT see **MER MERE** • 1975

DEEP THROAT • 1972 • Damiano Gerard • USA

DEEP THROAT -PART II • 1974 • *Lovelace Linda* • USA

DEEP THRUST -THE HAND OF DEATH • 1973 • *Mao Angela* • HKG

DEEP VALLEY • 1947 • Negulesco Jean • USA

DEEP VALLEY OF DESIRE see **FUKIA YOKUBO NO TANIMA** • 1967

DEEP WATER • 1983 • Wirth Franz Peter • MTV • FRG

DEEP WATERS • 1920 • Tourneur Maurice • USA • CALEB WEST, MASTER DIVER

DEEP WATERS • 1948 • King Henry • USA

DEEP WATERS • 1979 • Eady David • UKN

DEEP WEST • 1975 • *Hilton George* • ITL

DEEPSTAR SIX see **DEEP STAR SIX** • 1988

DEER HUNT see **MRIGAYAA** • 1976

DEER HUNT, THE see **LOV NA JELENE** • 1972

DEER HUNTER, THE • 1978 • Cimino Michael • USA

DEER KING, THE • 1970 • Arsenov Pavel • USS • KING-DEER

DEER SLAYER'S RETRIBUTION, THE • 1912 • *Pathe* • USA

DEER STALKING WITH CAMERA • 1905 • *Bitzer Billy (Ph)* • USA

DEERS, THE see **GAVAZNHA** • 1974

DEERSLAYER, THE • 1913 • Reid Hal, Trimble Larry • USA

DEERSLAYER, THE • 1923 • *Mingo Pictures* • USA

DEERSLAYER, THE • 1943 • Landers Lew • USA

DEERSLAYER, THE • 1957 • Neumann Kurt • USA

DEERSLAYER, THE • 1978 • Friedenberg Richard • TVM • USA

DEESSE, LA • 1966 • Cayrol Jean • FRN

DEEWANJEE • 1976 • *Burman S. D. (M)* • IND

DEF BY TEMPTATION • 1990 • Bond James Iii • USA

DEF-CON 4 • 1985 • Donovan Paul, O'Connell Maura? • CND • GROUND ZERO ○ DEFENSE CONDITION FOUR

DEFA 70 • 1967 • Bergmann Werner • GDR

DEFAITE DE SATAN, LE • 1909 • *Pathe* • FRN • DEFEAT OF SATAN, THE (USA)

DEFAITE DU GENERAL PRINGLE, LA • 1952 • Bail Rene • CND

DEFAULTER, THE • 1914 • *Domino* • USA

DEFEAT see **DERROTA** • 1972

DEFEAT, THE see **DERROTA, A** • 1967

DEFEAT, THE see **DERROTA, LA** • 1981

DEFEAT DIPHTHERIA • 1941 • Peake Bladon • DOC • UKN

DEFEAT OF FATHER • 1914 • *Joker* • USA

DEFEAT OF HANNIBAL, THE see **SCIPIONE L'AFRICANO** • 1937

DEFEAT OF JAPAN, THE • 1946 • Heifitz Josif, Zarkhi Alexander • DOC • USS

DEFEAT OF SATAN, THE (USA) see **DEFAITE DE SATAN, LE** • 1909

DEFEAT OF THE BARBARIANS, THE • 1962 • *Clark Ken* • ITL

DEFEAT OF THE BREWERY GANG, THE • 1912 • *Kalem* • USA

DEFEAT OF THE CITY, THE • 1917 • Mills Thomas R. • USA

DEFEAT OF THE GERMAN ARMIES NEAR MOSCOW, THE see **RAZGROM NEMETZKIKHY VOISK POD MOSKVOI** • 1942

DEFEAT TUBERCULOSIS • 1943 • Nieter Hans M. • DOC • UKN

DEFEATED PEOPLE, A • 1946 • Jennings Humphrey • DOC • UKN

DEFEATING DELINQUENCY • 1951 • Garceau Raymond • DCS • CND • GUERRE A LA DELINQUANCE ○ FEMME POLICES

DEFECTION OF SIMAS KUDIRKA, THE • 1978 • Rich David Lowell • TVM • USA

DEFECTIVE DETECTIVE, THE • 1913 • Plumb Hay? • UKN

DEFECTIVE DETECTIVE, THE • 1916 • *Armstrong Billy* • USA

DEFECTIVE DETECTIVE, THE see **JEWELS AND JIMJAMS** • 1915

DEFECTIVE DETECTIVES • 1917 • Howe J. A. • SHT • USA

DEFECTIVE DETECTIVES • 1944 • Edwards Harry J. • SHT • USA

DEFECTOR, THE (USA) see **ESPION, L'** • 1966

DEFENCE COUNSEL SEDOV • 1988 • Tsymbal • USS

DEFENCE OF LENINGRAD, THE see **LENINGRAD V BORBYE** • 1942

DEFENCE OF MADRID, THE • 1936 • Montagu Ivor • DOC • UKN • IN DEFENCE OF MADRID

DEFENCE OF MINNIE DEAN, THE see **HANLON: IN DEFENCE OF MINNIE DEAN** • 1984

DEFENCE OF SEBASTOPOL, THE see **OKORANA SEVASTOPOLVA** • 1911

DEFENCE OF THE REALM • 1985 • Drury David • UKN

DEFENCE OF TSARITSIN, THE see **OBORONA TSARITSINA** • 1942

DEFENCE OF WESTERN EUROPE see **NISHI YOROPPA NO MAMORI** • 1968

DEFEND MY LOVE (USA) see **DIFENDO IL MIO AMORE** • 1956

DEFEND YOURSELF • 1925 • Henderson Dell • USA • RETRIBUTION

DEFENDAMOS O PAO NOSSO • 1947 • Coelho Jose Adolfo • SHT • PRT

DEFENDANT, THE see **OBZALOVANY** • 1964

DEFENDED BY BIRDS • 1954 • Dolin Boris • DOC • USS

DEFENDER OF THE NAME, THE • 1912 • *Leonard Marion* • USA

DEFENDERS OF THE EARTH: BATTLEGROUND • 1986 • ANM • USA

DEFENDERS OF THE EARTH: THE MOVIE • 1986 • ANM • USA

DEFENDERS OF THE EARTH: THE STORY BEGINS • 1986 • ANM • USA

DEFENDERS OF THE LAW • 1931 • Levering Joseph • USA

DEFENDERS OF THE SEA • 1981 • Stoneman John • MTV • CND

DEFENDING A REDOUBT • 1900 • *Paul R. W.* • UKN

DEFENDING THE FORT AT MANILA see **COMBAT NAVAL DEVANT MANILLE** • 1898

DEFENDING YOUR LIFE • 1990 • Brooks Albert • USA

DEFENSE CONDITION FOUR see **DEF-CON 4** • 1985

DEFENSE D'AFFICHER • 1896 • Melies Georges • FRN • POST NO BILLS

DEFENSE D'AFFICHER • 1958 • Hirsch Hy • SHT • FRN

DEFENSE D'AIMER • 1942 • Pottier Richard • FRN • COEUR SUR LA MAIN, LE ○ TOTTE ET SA CHANCE

DEFENSE DE CZESTOCHOWA, LA • 1923 • Puchalski Eduard • PLN

DEFENSE DE FUMER • 1961 • Rhein • SHT • FRN

DEFENSE DE JOUER • 1971 • Grand-Jouan Jean-Jacques • FRN

DEFENSE DE SAVOIR • 1973 • Trintignant Nadine • FRN, ITL • UOMO IN BASSO A DESTRA NELLA FOTO, L' (ITL)

DEFENSE DE TSARITSYNE, LE see **OBORONA TSARITSINA** • 1942

DEFENSE D'EN PARLER • Betremieux Bertrand • DOC • FRN

DEFENSE OF VOLOTCHAYEVSK, THE see **VOLOCHAYEVSKIYE DNI** • 1938

DEFENSE OR TRIBUTE? • 1916 • *Radio Film* • USA

DEFENSE PLAY • 1988 • Markham Monte • USA

DEFENSE RESTS, THE • 1934 • Hillyer Lambert • USA

DEFENSELESS • 1989 • Campbell Martin • USA

DEFENSEUR, LE • 1930 • Ryder Alexandre • FRN

DEFENSEUR DE CZESTOCHOWA • 1934 • Puchalski Eduard • PLN

DEFENSIVE PLAY • 1931 • Kelley Albert • SHT • USA

DEFI • 1975-77 • Bertolino Daniel, Floquet Francois • DSS • CND

DEFI, LE • 1976 • Dansereau Fernand, Rossignol Yolande • DCS • CND

DEFI A GIBRALTAR (FRN) see **FINCHE DURA LA TEMPESTA** • 1962

DEFI KILOWATTS • 1964 • Regnier Michel • DOC • CND

DEFIANCE • 1917 • *Fischer Marguerite* • SHT • USA

DEFIANCE • 1979 • Flynn John • USA

DEFIANCE see **TROTS** • 1952

DEFIANCE (UKN) see **TEXAS BAD MAN, THE** • 1932

DEFIANT DAUGHTERS see **SCHATTEN WERDEN LANGER, DIE** • 1962

DEFIANT DELTA, THE see **PRKOSNA DELTA** • 1981

DEFIANT GIANT, THE • 1966 • Post Howard • ANS • USA

DEFIANT ONES, THE • 1958 • Kramer Stanley • USA

DEFICIT, THE • 1915 • Kent Leon D. • USA

DEFILE DE POMPIERS • 1897 • Melies Georges • FRN • FIREMEN ON PARADE

DEFILERS, THE • 1965 • Frost R. L. • USA

DEFINITE OBJECT, THE • 1920 • Camiller Edgar J. • UKN

DEFINITIVE AFSLAG PA ANMODNINGEN OM ET KYS, DET • 1949 • Roos Jorgen (c/d) • DOC • DNM

DEFIZIT DAS • 1917 • Neuss Alwin • FRG

DEFRICHEMENT MOTORISE • 1946 • Proulx Maurice • DCS • CND

DEFROQUE, LE • 1953 • Joannon Leo • FRN • RENEGADE PRIEST, THE

DEFY TO THE LAST PARADISE see **MANGIATI VIVI DAI CANNIBALI** • 1980

DEFYING DESTINY • 1923 • Chaudet Louis W. • USA

DEFYING THE CHIEF • 1914 • *Darkfeather Mona* • USA

DEFYING THE LAW • 1922 • Horner Robert J. • USA

DEFYING THE LAW • 1924 • Bracken Bertram • USA

DEFYING THE LAW • 1935 • Horner Robert J. • USA

DEGENERATE, A see **HENSHITSUSHA** • 1967

DEGENERATES, THE • 1967 • Milligan Andy • USA

DEGENHARDTS, DIE • 1944 • Klinger Werner • FRG

DEGIRMEN see **SEY SARSILIYOR** • 1986

DEGOURDIS DE LA 11e, LES • 1937 • Christian-Jaque • FRN

DEGRADATION, LA • 1898 • Melies Georges • FRN

DEGREE OF MURDER, A see **MORD UND TOTSCHLAG** • 1967

DEGREE OF RISK see **STEPIEN RISKA** • 1969

DEGREES OF CHANGE • 1981 • Tingwell Charles • MTV • ASL

DEGUEJO • 1966 • Vari Giuseppe • ITL

DEHADAKA DUKA • 1968 • Tampoe Robin • SLN • SORROW OF TWO HEARTS, THE

DEHORS, DEDANS • 1975 • Fleischer Alain • FRN

DEHORS ET LE DEDANS, LE • 1978 • Guerin Gerard • FRN

DEIN BEGEHREN IST SUNDE • 1925 • Seitz Franz • FRG

DEIN HERZ IST MEINE HEIMAT • 1953 • Haussler Richard • FRG, AUS

DEIN IST MEIN HERZ • 1920 • Eriksen Erich • FRG

DEIN LEBEN GEHORT MIR • 1939 • Meyer Johannes • FRG

DEIN MANN, DAS UNBEKANNTE WESEN see **OSWALT KOLLE: DEIN MANN, DAS UNBEKANNTE WESEN** • 1970

DEIN MUND VERSPRICHT MIR LIEBE • 1954 • Neufeld Max • FRG

DEIN SCHICKSAL • 1928 • Fischinger Oskar • ANS • FRG • YOUR DESTINY

DEIN UNBEKANNTER BRUDER • 1984 • Weiss Ulrich • GDR

DEINE FRAU, DAS UNBEKANNTE WESEN see **OSWALT KOLLE: DEINE FRAU, DAS UNBEKANNTE WESEN** • 1969

DEINE ZARTLICHKEITEN • 1969 • Schamoni Peter • FRG

DEINES BRUDERS WEIB • 1921 • Eckstein Franz • FRG

DEIVA BALAM • 1959 • Reddy P. Vasanthakumar • IND • STRENGTH OF GOD, THE

DEIVA JANILE KUNI • 1967 • Patil Krishna • IND
DEJA S'ENVOLE LA FLEUR MAIGRE • 1960 • Meyer Paul • BLG • FRAIL FLOWERS ARE DISAPPEARING, THE ○ ENFANTS DU BORINAGE, LES ○ LANK FLOWER HAS ALREADY FLOWN, THE
DEJA VU • 1984 • Richmond Anthony* • UKN • ALWAYS
DEJECTED LOVER, THE • 1911 • Kinder Stuart? • UKN
DEJEUNER CHEZ LE MARECHAL DE LA NOBLESSE • 1953 • Rybakov Anatoly • USS
DEJEUNER DE BEBE, LE • 1895 • Lumiere Louis • FRN • REPAS DE BEBE, LE ○ BABY'S BREAKFAST
DEJEUNER DE SOLEIL, UN • 1937 • Cravenne Marcel • FRN
DEJEUNER DES ENFANTS, LES • 1899-00 • Blache Alice • FRN
DEJEUNER DU CHAT, LE • 1895 • Lumiere Louis • FRN
DEJEUNER IMPOSSIBLE, LE • 1898 • Melies Georges • FRN
DEJEUNER SUR L'HERBE, LE • 1959 • Renoir Jean • FRN • PICNIC ON THE GRASS (USA) ○ LUNCH ON THE GRASS (UKN)
DEJEUNER SUR L'HERBE, LE • 1975 • Le Grice Malcolm • UKN
DEKAMERON-NACHTE (FRG) see **DECAMERON NIGHTS** • 1924
DEKIGOKORO • 1933 • Ozu Yasujiro • JPN • PASSING FANCY
DEKKAI TAIYO • 1967 • Matsumori Takashi • JPN • GOAL FOR THE YOUNG
DEKUJEME, PANOVE • 1976 • Bedrich Vaclav • CZC • THANK YOU, SIRS
DEL AMOR Y DE LA MUERTE • 1977 • Gimenez-Rico Antonio • SPN
DEL AMOR Y OTRAS SOLEDADES • 1969 • Patino Basilio Martin • SPN • OF LOVE AND OTHER LONELY THINGS
DEL BRAZO Y POR LA CALLE • 1955 • Bustillo Oro Juan • MXC
DEL CAN CAN AL MAMBO • 1951 • Urueta Chano • MXC
DEL COURTNEY AND HIS ORCHESTRA • 1949 • Cowan Will • SHT • USA
DEL ESCAMBRAY.. EL CAMPESINO • 1971 • Paris Rogelio • DOC • CUB
DEL-KINA TAJAIN • 1957 • Jancso Miklos • SHT • HNG • LANDSCAPES OF SOUTHERN CHINA, THE ○ IN THE SOUTH CHINA COUNTRYSIDE
DEL MERO CORAZON • 1979 • Blank Les • USA • STRAIGHT FROM THE HEART -LOVE SONGS OF THE SOUTH WEST
DEL MISMO BARRO • 1930 • Howard David • USA
DEL ODIO NACIO EL AMOR • 1949 • Fernandez Emilio • MXC, USA • TORCH, THE (USA) ○ BANDIT GENERAL, THE (UKN) ○ BELOVED
DEL PINGO AL VOLANTE • 1928 • Kouri Roberto • URG
DEL RANCHO A LA CAPITAL • 1926 • Urriola Eduardo • MXC
DEL RANCHO A LA CAPITAL • 1941 • de Anda Raul • MXC
DEL RANCHO A LA TELEVISION • 1952 • Rodriguez Ismael • MXC
DEL RASTRO A LA CASTELLANA see **RELOJ DEL ANTICUARIO, EL** • 1925
DEL ROSA AL AMARILLO • 1963 • Summers Manuel • SPN
DEL SUELO NO PASO • 1958 • Urueta Chano • MXC
DEL TRES AL ONCE • 1968 • Artero Antonio • SHT • SPN
DELA I LYUDI see **DELA Y LYUDI** • 1932
DELA Y LYUDI • 1932 • Macheret Alexander • USS • MEN AND JOBS ○ JOBS AND MEN ○ DELA I LYUDI
DELACROIX, PAINTER OF ISLAM see **DELACROIX, PEINTRE D EL'ISLAM**
DELACROIX, PEINTRE D EL'ISLAM • Colson-Malleville Marie • DOC • FRN • DELACROIX, PAINTER OF ISLAM
DELAISSES, LES see **ADOLESCENCIA MARGINAL** • 1979
DELANCEY STREET: THE CRISIS WITHIN • 1975 • Frawley James • TVM • USA • SINNER, THE
DELATORA, LA • 1955 • Land Kurt • ARG
DELAVINE AFFAIR, THE • 1954 • Pierce Douglas • UKN • MURDER IS NEWS
DELAWARE WHIPPING POST, THE • 1914 • *Feature Photoplay* • USA
DELAYED ACTION • 1954 • Harlow John • UKN
DELAYED FLIGHT • 1964 • Wakefield John, Young Tony, Luckwell Michael • UKN
DELAYED IN TRANSIT • 1917 • Martin E. A. • SHT • USA
DELAYED LETTER, THE • 1913 • Ince Ralph • USA
DELAYED PROPOSAL, THE • 1911 • Sennett Mack • USA
DELAYED PROPOSALS • 1913 • Young James • USA
DELAYED REFORMATION, A • 1915 • Smiley Joseph • USA
DELAYED SPECIAL, THE • 1914 • *Kalem* • USA
DELAYED TELEGRAM, THE • 1909 • *Phoenix* • USA
DELE COLOR AL DIFUNTO • 1969 • Delgado Luis Maria • SPN
DELECTABLE TIME OF KALIMAGDORA, THE see **SUSSE ZEIT MIT KALIMAGDORA, DIE** • 1968
DELERIUM • 1984 • Zervos Nikos • GRC • BITTER MOVIE
DELFINI, I • 1960 • Maselli Francesco • ITL • DOLPHINS, THE
DELFTSBLAUW • 1966 • Geesink Joop • SHT • NTH
DELHI • 1937-40 • *Cardiff Jack (Ph)* • DCS • UKN
DELHI WAY, THE • 1964 • Ivory James • IND
DELI FISEK • 1967 • Gulyuz Aram • TRK • CRAZY ONE, THE
DELI KAN • 1982 • Yilmaz Atif • TRK • HOT BLOOD
DELI YUSUF • 1976 • Yilmaz Atif • TRK • CRAZY YUSUF
DELIBABOK ORSZAGA • 1984 • Meszaros Marta • HNG • LAND OF MIRAGES, THE
DELIBERATE STRANGER, THE • 1985 • Chomsky Marvin • TVM • USA
DELICATE BALANCE, A • 1973 • Richardson Tony • USA
DELICATE DELINQUENT, THE • 1957 • McGuire Don • USA
DELICATE SEX, THE • 1977 • Aziz Mohamed Abdel • EGY
DELICATESSEN MYSTERY, THE • 1917 • *Myers Harry* • SHT • USA
DELICATESSEN SHOP, THE • 1915 • *World* • USA
DELICESINE • 1976 • Seden Osman • TRK • MADLY
DELICIAS DE LOS VERDES ANOS, LAS • 1976 • Mercero Antonio • SPN
DELICIOSAMENTE TONTOS • 1943 • de Orduna Juan • SPN
DELICIOUS • 1931 • Butler David • USA
DELICIOUS LITTLE DEVIL, THE • 1919 • Leonard Robert Z. • USA
DELIGHTFUL DILEMMA • 1970 • Evans Richard Z. • USA
DELIGHTFUL DOLLY • 1910 • *Thanhouser* • USA
DELIGHTFUL ROGUE, THE • 1929 • Shores Lynn, Pearce A. Leslie • USA
DELIGHTFULLY DANGEROUS • 1945 • Lubin Arthur • USA
DELIGHTS OF AUTOMOBILING, THE (USA) see **EXPLOSION OF A MOTOR CAR, THE** • 1900
DELIJE • 1968 • Popovic Mica • YGS • TOUGH ONES, THE
DELIKANIS • 1963 • Skouloudis Manolis • GRC
DELIKATESSEN • 1930 • von Bolvary Geza • FRG
DELILAH • 1921 • Paul Fred • UKN
DELILAH • 1969 • *Distripix* • USA
DELILAH • 1972 • King Allan • CND
DELINCUENTES • 1956 • Fortuny Juan • SPN
DELINEATION • 1970 • Barge Roy • SHT • USA
DELINQUANT, LE see **SHARID, ASH-** • 1941
DELINQUENT, THE • 1973 • Chang Ch'Eh, Kuei Chih-Hung • HKG
DELINQUENT, THE (UKN) see **TATOWIERUNG** • 1967
DELINQUENT BRIDEGROOMS • 1916 • Dillon John Francis • SHT • USA
DELINQUENT DAUGHTERS • 1944 • Herman Al • USA • ACCENT ON CRIME (UKN)
DELINQUENT GIRL see **FURYO SHOJO** • 1949
DELINQUENTS • 1950 • *Marlen Gloria* • USA
DELINQUENTS • 1984 • Corarito Greg • USA
DELINQUENTS, THE • 1955 • Altman Robert • USA
DELINQUENTS, THE • 1989 • Thomson Chris • ASL
DELINQUENTS, THE see **MARGINAIS, OS** • 1968
DELINQUENTS OF PURE HEART see **GURENTAI JUNJOHA** • 1963
DELIRE A L'ATELIER see **ALI BARBOUYOU ET ALI BOUF A L'HUILE** • 1907
DELIRES PORNO • 1976 • Philippe-Gerard Didier • FRN
DELIRES SEUELS • Love John • FRN
DELIRIA • 1988 • Soavi Michele • ITL
DELIRIO CALDO • 1972 • Polselli Renato • ITL • DELIRIUM (USA)
DELIRIO (ITL) see **ORAGE** • 1952
DELIRIO TROPICAL • 1951 • Morayta Miguel • MXC
DELIRIOUS • 1990 • Mankiewicz Tom • USA
DELIRIUM • 1979 • Maris Peter • USA
DELIRIUM • 1988 • Bava Lamberto • ITL
DELIRIUM see **CRAVING, THE** • 1918
DELIRIUM see **MYTEN** • 1965
DELIRIUM IN A STUDIO (USA) see **ALI BARBOUYOU ET ALI BOUF A L'HUILE** • 1907
DELIRIUM TREMENS, LE • 1907 • Melies Georges • FRN • FIN D'UN ALCOOLIQUE, LA ○ DRINK! A GOOD TEMPERANCE STORY
DELIRIUM (USA) see **DELIRIO CALDO** • 1972
DELISTAVRO KAI GIOS • 1958 • Sakellarios Alekos • GRC • TROUBLE FOR FATHERS (USA)
DELIT DE FUITE • 1958 • Borderie Bernard • FRN, ITL, YGS
DELITTO A OXFORD • 1970 • Liberatore Ugo • ITL • MAY MORNING IN OXFORD ○ ALBA PAGANA
DELITTO A PORTA ROMANA • 1980 • Corbucci Bruno • ITL • CRIME AT PORTA ROMANA
DELITTO A POSILLIPO • 1967 • Parravicini Renato • ITL • LONDRA CHIAMA NAPOLI ○ CRIME AT POSILLIPO ○ LONDON CALLING NAPLES
DELITTO AL CIRCOLO DEL TENNIS • 1969 • Rossetti Franco • ITL, YGS • RAGE WITHIN, THE (UKN)
DELITTO AL LUNA PARK • 1952 • Polselli Renato • ITL
DELITTO ALLO SPECCHIO • 1964 • Molteni Ambrogio, Josipovici Jean • ITL, FRN • DEATH ON THE FOUR-POSTER (USA) ○ SEXY PARTY (UKN) ○ CRIME IN THE MIRROR
DELITTO D'AMORE • 1966 • de Orduna Juan • ITL
DELITTO D'AMORE • 1974 • Comencini Luigi • ITL • SOMEWHERE BEYOND LOVE
DELITTO D'AUTORE • 1974 • Sabatini Mario • ITL
DELITTO DEL DIAVOLO, IL • 1970 • Cervi Tonino • ITL, FRN • SORCIERES DU BORD DU LAC, LES (FRN) ○ QUEENS OF EVIL ○ REGINE, LE ○ SORCIERES, LES ○ WITCHES, THE
DELITTO DI ANNA SANDOVAL, IL • 1966 • Nieves Conde Jose Antonio • ITL
DELITTO DI CRETINETTI, IL • 1909 • *Deed Andre* • ITL
DELITTO DI GIOVANNI EPISCOPO, IL • 1947 • Lattuada Alberto • ITL • FLESH WILL SURRENDER (USA) ○ GIOVANNI EPISCOPO
DELITTO DU PRE, IL (ITL) see **BONNES CAUSES, LES** • 1963
DELITTO GRATUITO, UN • 1976 • Lizzani Carlo • ITL
DELITTO IN FORMULA UNO • 1984 • Corbucci Bruno • ITL • FORMULA ONE MURDER
DELITTO MATTEOTTI, IL • 1973 • Vancini Florestano • ITL
DELITTO NON PAGA, IL (ITL) see **CRIME NE PAIE PAS, LE** • 1962
DELITTO QUASI PERFETTO • 1966 • Camerini Mario • ITL, FRN • IMPERFECT MURDER (UKN)
DELIVER THE GOODS • 1915 • Batley Ethyle • UKN
DELIVER US FROM EVIL • 1973 • Sagal Boris • TVM • USA
DELIVER US FROM EVIL • 1975 • McCahon Robert • USA
DELIVER US FROM EVIL see **SZABADITS MEG A GONOSZTOL** • 1978
DELIVERANCE • 1919 • Platt George Foster • USA
DELIVERANCE • 1928 • Blake Ben K. • USA
DELIVERANCE • 1972 • Boorman John • USA
DELIVERANCE see **SADGATI** • 1981
DELIVERY BOY, THE • 1931 • Gillett Burt • ANS • USA
DELIVERY BOY, THE • 1987 • Mandell Howie • USA
DELIVERY BOYS • 1984 • Handler Ken • USA
DELIVERY PACKAGE, A • 1913 • *Ashton Sylvia* • USA
DELIVREZ-NOUS DU MAL • 1965 • Lord Jean-Claude • CND
DELL OF THE VIRGINS, THE see **RINCON DE LAS VIRGENES, EL** • 1972
DELLA • 1964 • Stevens Leslie • USA
DELLA NUBE ALLA RESISTENZA • 1979 • Straub Jean-Marie, Huillet Daniele • ITL, FRG, FRN • FROM THE CLOUD TO THE RESISTANCE (UKN)
DELNAMAK • 1989 • Ghavidel Amir • IRN
DELO ARTAMANOVICH • 1941 • Roshal Grigori • USS • ARTAMANOV AFFAIR, THE
DELO BYLO V PENKOVE • 1957 • Rostotsky Stanislav • USS • IT HAPPENED IN PENKOVO
DELO RUMYANTSEVA • 1955 • Heifitz Josif • USS • RUMIANTSEV CASE, THE
DELOS ADVENTURE, THE • 1987 • Purcell Joseph • USA • DELOS FILE, THE
DELOS FILE, THE see **DELOS ADVENTURE, THE** • 1987
DELOVAK ATHARA • 1966 • Peries Lester James • SLN • BETWEEN TWO WORLDS
DELOVYE LYUDI • 1963 • Gaidai Leonid • USS • BUSINESSMAN, THE
DELPHI BUREAU, THE • 1972 • Wendkos Paul • TVM • USA
DELPHICA • 1962 • Korber Serge • SHT • FRN
DELPHINE • 1931 • Capellani Roger, de Marguenat Jean • FRN
DELPHINE • 1968 • Le Hung Eric • FRN
DELTA 8-3 • 1960 • Baim Harold • UKN
DELTA, EL • 1939 • Fregonese Hugo • SHT • ARG
DELTA COUNTY, U.S.A. • 1977 • Jordan Glenn • TVM • USA
DELTA DATA • 1968 • Ferno John • SHT • NTH
DELTA FACTOR, THE • 1970 • Garnett Tay • USA
DELTA FEVER • 1987 • Webb William • USA
DELTA FORCE, THE • 1986 • Golan Menahem • USA
DELTA FORCE COMMANDO • 1987 • Valenti Frank • USA
DELTA FORCE II: AMERICA'S RED ARMY • 1989 • Norris Aaron • USA
DELTA FOX • 1977 • Sebastian Beverly, Sebastian Ferdinand • USA
DELTA PHASE 1 • 1962 • Haanstra Bert • DCS • NTH
DELTA PI see **MUGSY'S GIRLS** • 1985
DELTOL HAJNALIG • 1964 • Renyi Tamas • HNG • FROM NOON TO DAWN
DELUDED WIFE, A • 1916 • *Norden Virginia* • SHT • USA
DELUDING THE DADS • 1911 • *Urban Trading Co.* • UKN
DELUGE, LE • 1912 • Puchalski Eduard • PLN
DELUGE, THE • 1911 • *Vitagraph* • USA
DELUGE, THE • 1933 • Feist Felix E. • USA
DELUGE, THE • 1979 • Conway James L. • MTV • USA • NOAH
DELUGE, THE • 1985 • el Deek Bashir • EGY
DELUGE, THE (USA) see **POTOP** • 1974
DELUSION • 1981 • Beattie Alan • USA • HOUSE WHERE DEATH LIVES, THE ○ HOUSE WHERE DEATH LIVED, THE
DELUSION, A • 1902 • *Biograph* • SHT • USA
DELUSION, THE • 1934 • Samuelson G. B. • UKN
DELUSIONS OF GRANDEUR (USA) see **FOLIE DES GRANDEURS, LA** • 1971
DELUTAN KOPPANYMONOSTORBAN, EGY • 1955 • Jancso Miklos • SHT • HNG • ONE AFTERNOON IN KOPPANYMONOSTOR ○ AFTERNOON IN THE VILLAGE, AN
DEM GLUCK ENTGEGEN • 1919 • von Woringen Paul • FRG
DEM LICHT ENTGEGEN • 1918 • *Oswalda Ossie* • FRG
DEM TATER AUF DER SPUR: BLINDER HASS • 1973 • Roland Jurgen • FRG • ON THE TRAIL OF THE CULPRIT: BLIND HATRED
DEM TEUFEL VERSCHRIEBEN • 1919 • Molter Ernst • FRG
DEM WELKENGRAB ENTRONNEN see **STAATSANWALT BRIANDS ABENTEUER 2** • 1920
DEMAIN A NANGUILA • 1960 • Ivens Joris • MLI • NANGUILA TOMORROW
DEMAIN LA CHINE • 1965 • Otzenberger Claude • DOC • FRN
DEMAIN LA FIN DU MONDE • 1970 • Polac Michel • FRN
DEMAIN LES MOMES • 1975 • Pourtale Jean • FRN
DEMAIN, NOUS DIVORCONS • 1950 • Cuny Louis • FRN
DEMAIN PARIS • 1957 • Boschet Michel • ANM • FRN
DEMAIN PARIS • 1964 • Leenhardt Roger • DCS • FRN
DEMAIN UN JOUR NOUVEAU • 1978 • Dong Jean-Marie • GBN
DEMAND, THE see **PETICION, LA** • 1976
DEMAND FOR JUSTICE, A • 1913 • *Williams C. G.* • USA
DEMAND OF DUGAN, THE • 1919 • *World* • USA
DEMANDE EN MARIAGE MAL ENGAGEE, UNE • 1901 • Zecca Ferdinand • FRN
DEMANTY NOCI • 1964 • Nemec Jan • CZC • DIAMONDS OF THE NIGHT (USA)
DEMARCHEUSES EN CHALEUR • 1979 • Pradley Boris • FRN
DEMARIES, LES • 1980 • Pillault Jean-Daniel • SHT • FRN
DEMASIADA GENTE PARA UN FIN DE SEMANA • 1973 • Rodriguez Javier • SPN
DEMASIADAS MUERTES PARA TEX • 1972 • Martinez Celeiro Francisco • SPN
DEMASIADO PARA GALVEZ • 1981 • Gonzalo Juan Antonio • SPN • TOO MUCH FOR GALVEZ
DEMASKIERUNG see **NACHT DER VERWANDLUNG** • 1935
DEMENAGEMENT A LA CLOCHE DE BOIS • 1897-98 • Blache Alice • FRN
DEMENAGEMENT A LA CLOCHE DE BOIS • 1907 • Blache Alice • FRN
DEMENT DU LAC JEAN JEUNE, LE • 1947 • Jutra Claude • SHT • CND
DEMENTED • 1980 • Jeffreys Arthur • USA
DEMENTED, THE see **SZALENCY** • 1928
DEMENTED DEATH FARM MASSACRE • 1988 • Ray Fred Olen, Davison Donn • USA
DEMENTI, DAS see **VERLOBTE LEUTE** • 1945
DEMENTIA • 1953 • Parker John • USA • DAUGHTER OF HORROR
DEMENTIA 13 • 1963 • Coppola Francis Ford • USA • HAUNTED AND THE HUNTED, THE (UKN)
DEMENTIAE CALIGULAE IMPERATORIS • 1916 • Falena Ugo • ITL
DEMERDARDS, LES • 1974 • Balducci Richard • FRN
DEMETRIUS AND THE GLADIATORS • 1954 • Daves Delmer • USA • GLADIATORS, THE
DEMI-BRIDE, THE • 1926 • Leonard Robert Z. • USA
DEMI-HEURE DE MARIAGE, UNE see **NUCFU SA'A JAWAZ** • 1969
DEMI-PARADISE, THE • 1943 • Asquith Anthony • UKN • ADVENTURE FOR TWO (USA)
DEMI-TASSE • 1934 • Doane Warren • SHT • USA
DEMI-VIERGES see **MODERNE TOCHTER** • 1919
DEMI-VIERGES, LES • 1924 • du Plessis Armand • FRN
DEMI-VIERGES, LES • 1936 • Caron Pierre • FRN
DEMIMONDE-HEIRAT, EINE • 1920 • Zickel Martin • FRG
DEMIR KAPI • 1967 • Ucak Fikret • TRK • STEEL DOOR, THE
DEMIR YUMRUKLU UCLER • 1967 • Hancer Nisan • TRK • STEEL-FISTED TRIO, THE
DEMIREL'E SOYLERIM • 1967 • Saner Hulki • TRK • I'LL TELL DEMIREL

DEMIRYOLU • 1980 • Ozkan Yavuz • TRK • RAILROAD, THE
DEMISE OF FATHER MOURET, THE (USA) see **FAUTE DE L'ABBE MOURET, LA** • 1970
DEMISE OF HERMAN DURER, THE see **VERWORDING VAN HERMAN DURER, DE** • 1979
DEMOBBED • 1944 • Blakeley John E. • UKN
DEMOCRACY • 1918 • Morgan Sidney • UKN
DEMOCRACY • 1920 • Nigh William • USA • DEMOCRACY –THE VISION RESTORED
DEMOCRACY • 1976 • Safran Henri • SHT • ASL
DEMOCRACY –THE VISION RESTORED see **DEMOCRACY** • 1920
DEMOCRATS IN '66, THE • 1966 • Leiterman Douglas • DOC • USA
DEMOISELLE DES FOLIES, LA see **ATOMIQUE MONSIEUR PLACIDO, L'** • 1949
DEMOISELLE DU NOTAIRE, LA • 1912 • Feuillade Louis • FRN
DEMOISELLE DU TABAC, LA see **MIQUETTE** • 1940
DEMOISELLE ET LE VIOLONCELLISTE, LA • 1964 • Laguionie Jean-Francois • ANS • FRN • YOUNG LADY AND THE CELLIST, THE ○ GIRL AND THE CELLIST, THE
DEMOISELLE ET SON REVENANT, LA • 1951 • Allegret Marc • FRN
DEMOISELLE SAUVAGE, LA • 1989 • Pool Lea • CND, SWT
DEMOISELLES A PEAGE • Balducci Richard • FRN
DEMOISELLES DE ROCHEFORT, LES • 1966 • Demy Jacques • FRN • YOUNG GIRLS OF ROCHEFORT, THE
DEMOISELLES DE WILKO, LES (FRN) see **PANNY Z WILKO** • 1979
DEMOISELLES PERROTIN, LES • 1914 • Poirier Leon • FRN
DEMOLITION • 1978 • Dobson Kevin • MTV • ASL
DEMOLITION D'UN MUR • 1895 • Lumiere Louis • FRN • MUR, LE ○ PULLING DOWN A WALL
DEMOLITION SQUAD see **DIVERZANTI** • 1967
DEMON • 1911 • Vitrotti Giovanni • USS
DEMON • 1976 • Cohen Larry • USA • GOD TOLD ME TO
DEMON • 1977 • Emigholz Heinz • FRG
DEMON see **ONI** • 1972
DEMON, THE • 1911 • *Navatzi M.* • ITL
DEMON, THE • 1918 • Baker George D. • USA
DEMON, THE • 1926 • Smith Cliff • USA
DEMON, THE • 1967 • Dembinski Lucjan • ANM • PLN
DEMON, THE • 1979 • Rubens Percival • SAF, NTH • NIGHT CALLER
DEMON, THE see **DEMONIO, IL** • 1964
DEMON, THE see **ONIBABA** • 1964
DEMON AND MAN see **DAMON UND MENSCH** • 1915
DEMON AND THE MUMMY • 1975 • Weis Don, McDougall Don • MTV • USA
DEMON BALLAD see **ONI NO UTA** • 1975
DEMON BARBER OF FLEET STREET, THE (USA) see **SWEENEY TODD, THE DEMON BARBER OF FLEET STREET** • 1936
DEMON DANS LA CHAIR, LE (FRN) see **DEMONIO, IL** • 1964
DEMON DANS L'ILE, LE • 1982 • Leroi Francis • FRN
DEMON DE LA HAINE, LE • 1921 • Perret Leonce • FRN
DEMON DE MIDI • 1979 • Paureilhe Christian • FRN, BLG, SPN • DEMONS DE MIDI
DEMON DE ONZE HEURES, LE see **PIERROT LE FOU** • 1965
DEMON, DEMON • 1975 • Dunlop Richard • TVM • UKN
DEMON DOCTOR, THE (UKN) see **GRITOS EN LA NOCHE** • 1962
DEMON DOG, THE • 1911 • Fitzhamon Lewin? • UKN
DEMON FOR TROUBLE, A • 1934 • Hill Robert F. • USA
DEMON FROM DEVIL'S LAKE, THE • 1964 • Marker Russ • USA
DEMON HUNTERS • 1989 • Layton David • USA
DEMON IN ART, THE (USA) see **DEMONIACO' NELL'ARTE, IL** • 1950
DEMON IN THE BLOOD, THE see **DEMONIO EN LA SANGRE, EL**
DEMON IN THE CITY, THE • 1978 • Sayf Samir • EGY
DEMON LAND • 1948 • Meiyappan A. V. • IND
DEMON LOVER, THE • 1976 • Jackson Donald G., Younkins Jerry • USA
DEMON LOVER DIARY • 1980 • Demott Joel • USA
DEMON MOTORIST, THE • 1905 • Mottershaw Frank • UKN
DEMON MURDER CASE, THE • 1983 • Hale William • TVM • USA • RHODE ISLAND MURDERS, THE
DEMON OF DUNKIRQUE, THE • 1910 • *Ambrosio* • ITL
DEMON OF FEAR, THE • 1916 • Borzage Frank • SHT • USA
DEMON OF GOLD see **KONJIKI YASHA** • 1954
DEMON OF PARADISE • 1987 • Santiago Cirio H. • USA
DEMON OF THE HIMALAYAS, THE (USA) see **DAEMON DER BERGE, DER** • 1934
DEMON OF THE RAILS, THE • 1914 • McGowan J. P. • USA
DEMON OF THE STEPPES • 1930 • Scheffer Leo
DEMON PLANET, THE see **TERRORE NELLO SPAZIO** • 1965
DEMON POND (USA) see **YASHA-GA-IKE** • 1979
DEMON PRINCES: GENESIS OF THE VAMPIRE • 1987 • Wisco Victor • USA
DEMON RAGE see **DARK EYES** • 1980
DEMON RIDER, THE • 1925 • Hurst Paul C. • USA
DEMON SEED • 1977 • Cammell Donald • USA
DEMON WITCH CHILD (USA) see **ENDEMONIADA, LA** • 1975
DEMONE DELL'INCESTO, IL see **BYLETH** • 1971
DEMONER • 1986 • Brandt Carsten • SWD • DEMONS
DEMONI • 1985 • Bava Lamberto • ITL • DEMONS ○ DEMONS 1
DEMONI 2 • 1987 • Bava Lamberto • ITL • DEMONS 2 –THE NIGHTMARE IS BACK (USA) ○ DEMONS 2: THE NIGHTMARE BEGINS ○ DEMONS 2: THE NIGHTMARE CONTINUES ○ DEMONS 2
DEMONI 3 • 1988 • Bava Lamberto • ITL • DEMONS 3: THE OGRE ○ OGRE, THE
DEMONIAC see **LOUVES, LES** • 1957
DEMONIACO' NELL'ARTE, IL • 1950 • Gattinara Carlo Castelli • SHT • ITL • DEMON IN ART, THE (USA)
DEMONIAQUE see **LOUVES, LES** • 1957
DEMONIAQUE, LE • 1968 • Gainville Rene • FRN
DEMONIAQUES, LES • 1973 • Rollin Jean • FRN, BLG • DEUX VIERGES POUR SATAN ○ DIABLESSES, LES
DEMONIO, IL • 1964 • Rondi Brunello • ITL, FRN • DEMON DANS LA CHAIR, LE (FRN) ○ DEMON, THE
DEMONIO AZUL, EL • 1964 • Urueta Chano • MXC • BLUE DEMON, THE
DEMONIO CON ANGEL, UN • 1962 • Lluch Miguel • SPN
DEMONIO EN LA SANGRE, EL • Mujica Rene • ARG • DEMON IN THE BLOOD, THE
DEMONIO ES UN ANGEL, EL • 1949 • Christensen Carlos Hugo • ARG
DEMONIO NEL CERVELLO, IL • 1977 • Masi Marco • ITL
DEMONIO Y CARNE see **SUSANA** • 1950
DEMONIOS DE ALCACER-QUIBIR, OS • 1976 • Costa Jose Fonseca • PRT • DEMONS OF ALCACER-QUIBIR, THE
DEMONIOS EN EL JARDIN • 1982 • Gutierrez Aragon Manuel • SPN • DEVILS IN THE GARDEN ○ DEMONS IN THE GARDEN
DEMONIOS, LOS see **DEMONS, LES** • 1973
DEMONIOS, OS (PRT) see **DEMONS, LES** • 1973
DEMONIOS SOBRE RUEDAS • 1966 • Curiel Federico • MXC
DEMONOID see **DEMONOID, MESSENGER OF DEATH** • 1981
DEMONOID, MESSENGER OF DEATH • 1981 • Zacarias Alfredo • USA • DEMONOID ○ MACABRA
DEMONS see **DEMONI** • 1985
DEMONS see **DEMONER** • 1986
DEMONS 1 see **DEMONI** • 1985
DEMONS 2 see **DEMONI 2** • 1987
DEMONS 2: THE NIGHTMARE BEGINS see **DEMONI 2** • 1987
DEMONS 2: THE NIGHTMARE CONTINUES see **DEMONI 2** • 1987
DEMONS 2 –THE NIGHTMARE IS BACK (USA) see **DEMONI 2** • 1987
DEMONS 3: THE OGRE see **DEMONI 3** • 1988
DEMONS, LES • 1973 • de Nesle Robert • FRN, PRT, SPN • DEMONIOS, OS (PRT) ○ DEMONS DU SEXE, LES ○ DEMONS, THE ○ SEX DEMONS, THE ○ DEMONIOS, LOS
DEMONS, THE see **DEMONS, LES** • 1973
DEMONS AT MIDNIGHT see **DEMONS DE MINUIT, LES** • 1961
DEMONS DE L'AUBE, LES • 1945 • Allegret Yves • FRN • AMES QUI VIVENT
DEMONS DE MIDI see **DEMON DE MIDI** • 1979
DEMONS DE MINUIT, LES • 1961 • Allegret Marc, Gerard Charles • FRN • DEMONS AT MIDNIGHT
DEMONS DU SEXE, LES see **DEMONS, LES** • 1973
DEMONS ET MERVEILLES DE BALI • 1954 • Bourguignon Serge • FRN
DEMONS IN SPRING see **HARU KURU ONI** • 1989
DEMONS IN THE GARDEN see **DEMONIOS EN EL JARDIN** • 1982
DEMON'S MASK, THE see **MASCHERA DEL DEMONIO, LA** • 1960
DEMONS OF ALCACER-QUIBIR, THE see **DEMONIOS DE ALCACER-QUIBIR, OS** • 1976
DEMONS OF LUDLOW, THE • 1983 • Rebane Bill • USA
DEMONS OF THE DEAD • 1974 • Martino Sergio • ITL
DEMONS OF THE MIND • 1971 • Sykes Peter • UKN • BLOOD WILL HAVE BLOOD ○ NIGHTMARE OF TERROR ○ BLOOD EVIL
DEMONS OF THE SWAMP (UKN) see **ATTACK OF THE GIANT LEECHES** • 1958
DEMON'S TALE, THE • Kabrt Josef • ANS • CZC
DEMONS (USA) see **SHURA** • 1970
DEMON'S VICTIM, THE • 1916 • *Sunset* • SHT • USA
DEMONSTRATIE VAN PROLETARISCHE SOLIDARITEIT • 1930 • Ivens Joris • SHT • NTH • DEMONSTRATION OF PROLETARIAN SOLIDARITY
DEMONSTRATION OF PROLETARIAN SOLIDARITY see **DEMONSTRATIE VAN PROLETARISCHE SOLIDARITEIT** • 1930
DEMONSTRATIONS RELIGEUSES TRIFLUVIENNES 1933-1936 • 1936 • Tessier Albert • DCS • CND
DEMONSTRATOR • 1971 • Freeman Warwick • ASL
DEMONWARP • 1988 • Alston Emmett • USA
DEMONYTE • 1913 • *Cosmopolitan* • USA
DEMOS • 1921 • Clift Denison • UKN • WHY MEN FORGET (USA)
DEMPSEY • 1983 • Trikonis Gus • TVM • USA
DEMPSEY AND MAKEPEACE: THE MOVIE • 1985 • Wharmby Tony • TVM • UKN
DEMUTIGE UND DIE SANGERIN, DER • 1925 • Dupont E. A. • FRG • HUMBLE MAN AND THE SINGER, THE ○ MEURTRIERE, LA
DEN, THE see **MADRIGUERA, LA** • 1969
DEN, DER SEJRER see **SYNDENS DATTER** • 1915
DEN' DINNEIE NOCHI • 1983 • Gogoberidze Lana • USS • DAY LONGER THAN NIGHT, THE
DEN-EN NI SHISU • 1974 • Terayama Shuji • JPN • PASTORAL HIDE AND SEEK
DEN HAAG HOLLAND • 1968 • Willers Casper • DOC • NTH • HAAG HOLLAND, DEN
DEN, KTORY NEUMRIE • 1973 • Tapak Martin • CZC
DEN MUSSO • 1975 • Cisse Souleymane • MLI • FILLE, LA ○ GIRL, THE
DEN NAS KAZDODENNY • 1969 • Krivanek Otto • CZC • OUR DAILY DAY
DEN NASHEY ZHIZNI • 1960 • Karmen Roman • USS • SEPTEMBER 16
DEN NOVOGO MIRA • 1940 • Karmen Roman, Slutsky Mikhail • USS • ONE DAY IN THE NEW WORLD ○ DAY IN THE NEW WORLD, A ○ DAY IN A NEW WORLD ○ ONE DAY IN SOVIET RUSSIA
DEN ODPLATY • 1960 • Tyrlova Hermina, Pinkava Josef • ANS • CZC • DAY OF RECKONING, THE
DEN OF BEASTS see **KEDAMONO NO YADO** • 1951
DEN OF DOOM see **GLASS CAGE, THE** • 1964
DEN OF SPIRITS see **ANTRE DES ESPRITS, L'** • 1901
DEN OF THIEVES, A • 1904 • Fitzhamon Lewin • UKN
DEN OF THIEVES, A • 1914 • Reid Wallace • USA
DEN PERVYI see **PERVI DEN** • 1955
DEN POSLEDNII, DEN PERVYI • 1960 • Dolidze Siko • USS • LAST DAY AND THE FIRST DAY, THE ○ LAST AND FIRST DAY, THE ○ LAST DAY, FIRST DAY
DEN PRO MOU LASKU • 1976 • Herz Juraj • CZC • DAY FOR MY LOVE, A
DEN SCHASTYA • 1963 • Heifitz Josif • USS • DAY OF HAPPINESS, A ○ DEN STCHASTIA
DEN SEDMY, OSMA NOC • 1969 • Schorm Evald • CZC • SEVENTH DAY, THE EIGHTH NIGHT, THE ○ SEVENTH DAY, EIGHTH NIGHT ○ SEDMY DEN, OSMA NOC
DEN SOMMEREN JEG FYLTE 15 • 1974 • Andersen Knut • NRW • I WAS FIFTEEN
DEN STCHASTIA see **DEN SCHASTYA** • 1963
DEN STROMLINJEDE GRIS • 1952 • Roos Jorgen • DOC • DNM
DEN VOINI • 1942 • Slutsky Mikhail • USS • DAY OF WAR ○ ONE DAY OF WAR
DENA POONA • 1931 • *Sircar B. N. (P)* • IND
DENARA E D'AMORE • 1936 • Brignone Guido • ITL • MONEY AND LOVE
DENDAM PONTIANAK • 1957 • Rao B. N. • MLY • REVENGE OF THE VAMPIRE
DENDANG PERANTHU • 1977 • Sulong Jamil • MLY • WAYFARER
DENDRO POU PLIGONAME, TO • 1987 • Avdeliodis Dimos • GRC • TREE WE DAMAGED, THE
DENEIGEMENT • 1956 • Blais Roger • DCS • CND
DENEN KOKYOGAKU • 1938 • Yamamoto Satsuo • JPN • SYMPHONIE PASTORALE, LA
DENEVER MIELOTT BEFEJEZI ROPT see **MIELOTT BEFEJEZI ROPTET A DENEVER** • 1988
DENGUE DEL AMOR, EL • 1965 • Rodriguez Roberto • MXC
DENIAL, THE • 1925 • Henley Hobart • USA • SQUARE PEG, THE
DENICHEURS D'OISEAUX, LES • 1904 • Velle Gaston • FRN
DENIS LOW • 1975 • Dodd Thomas • MTV • UKN
DENIZ KIZI • 1987 • Cetinkaya Yavuzer • TRK • MERMAID
DENKI KURAGE • 1970 • Masumura Yasuzo • JPN • PLAY IT COOL (USA)
DENKWURDIGE WALLFAHRT DES KAISERS KANGA MUSSA VON MALI NACH MEKKA • 1977 • Hagmuller Gotz, Graf Dietmar • AUS • MEMORABLE PILGRIMAGE OF THE EMPEROR KANGA MUSSA FROM MALI TO MECCA
DENMARK BETWEEN DANES see **KORT FRA DANMARK** • 1972
DENMARK GROWS UP • 1947 • Henning-Jensen Astrid, Hasselbalch Hagen, Melson Soren • DOC • DNM
DENMARK IS CLOSED see **DANMARK ER LUKKET** • 1981
DENMARK YOURS AND MINE see **DANMARK DIT OG MIT** • 1981
DENN DAS WEIB IST SCHWACH • 1961 • Gluck Wolfgang • FRG
DENN DIE MUSIK UND DIE LIEBE IN TIROL • 1963 • Jacobs Werner • FRG
DENNIS THE MENACE • 1987 • Rogers Doug • TVM • USA
DENNIS THE MENACE MOVIE EXCLUSIVES: MEMORY MAYHEM see **DENNIS: THE MOVIE – MEMORY MAYHEM** • 1987
DENNIS: THE MOVIE – MEMORY MAYHEM • 1987 • ANM • USA • DENNIS THE MENACE MOVIE EXCLUSIVES: MEMORY MAYHEM
DENNY FROM IRELAND • 1918 • Clifford William H., Gray Bob • USA
DENNY OF THE RAILROAD (UKN) see **DYNAMITE DENNY** • 1932
DENOMME SQUARCIO, UN see **GRANDE STRADA AZZURRA, LA** • 1957
DENONCIATION, LA • 1962 • Doniol-Valcroze Jacques • FRN • IMMORAL MOMENT, THE (USA)
DENOUEMENT, THE • 1915 • *Ab* • USA
DENSO NINGEN • 1960 • Fukuda Jun • JPN • SECRET OF THE TELEGIAN (USA) ○ TELEGIAN, THE
DENT RECALCITRANTE, LA • 1902 • Blache Alice • FRN
DENTAL DISASTER, A • 1911 • *American* • USA
DENTE PER DENTE • 1943 • Elter Marco • ITL
DENTELLES • 1918 • Blom August • DNM
DENTELLES DE METAL • 1959 • Regnier Michel • DCS • CND
DENTELLIERE, LA • 1912 • Perret Leonce • FRN
DENTELLIERE, LA • 1918-19 • du Plessis Armand • BLG
DENTELLIERE, LA • 1977 • Goretta Claude • SWT, FRN, FRG • LACEMAKER, THE (USA)
DENTIST, THE • 1917 • Drew Sidney, Drew Sidney Mrs. • SHT • USA
DENTIST, THE • 1919 • Jones F. Richard • SHT • USA
DENTIST, THE • 1932 • Pearce A. Leslie • SHT • USA
DENTIST, THE see **LAUGHING GAS** • 1914
DENTIST IN THE CHAIR • 1960 • Chaffey Don • UKN
DENTIST ON THE JOB • 1961 • Pennington-Richards C. M. • UKN • CARRY ON TV (USA) ○ GET ON WITH IT!
DENTIST ON THE JOB see **TANDLAEGE PA SENGEKANTEN** • 1971
DENTISTE DIABOLIQUE, LA see **CHICOT, DENTISTE AMERICAIN** • 1896
DENTISTS • 1938 • *Coronel Films* • SHT • UKN
DENTIST'S DAUGHTER, THE • 1909 • Fitzhamon Lewin • UKN
DENTIST'S DILEMMA, THE • 1912 • *Comet* • USA
DENTIST'S JANITOR, THE • 1914 • *Ab* • USA
DENTIST'S REVENGE, THE • 1906 • Hough Harold • UKN
DENTS DU DIABLE, LES (FRN) see **SAVAGE INNOCENTS, THE** • 1959
DENTS DU SINGE, LES • 1960 • Laloux Rene • ANS • FRN • MONKEY'S TEETH, THE
DENTS DU SINGE, LES • 1980 • Laloux Rene • ANM • FRN
DENTS LONGUES, LES • 1953 • Gelin Daniel • FRN
DENTURE ADVENTURE, A • 1960 • *Halas John (P)* • ANS • UKN
DENVER AND RIO GRANDE, THE • 1952 • Haskin Byron • USA
DENVER DUDE, THE • 1927 • Eason B. Reeves • USA
DENVER KID, THE • 1948 • Ford Philip • USA
DENVER ROMANCE, A • 1914 • *Thanhouser* • USA
DENWA WA YUGATA NI NARU • 1959 • Yoshimura Kozaburo • JPN • TELEPHONE RINGS IN THE EVENING, THE ○ TELEPHONE RING IN THE EVENING, A
DENYSE BENOIT, COMEDIENNE • 1975 • Guilbeault Luce • CND
DEO GRATIS see **DROLE DE PAROISSIEN, UN** • 1963
DEONZO BROTHERS, THE • 1901 • *Paul R. W.* • UKN
DEPART, LE • 1968 • Skolimowski Jerzy • BLG • START, THE
DEPART A ZERO • 1941 • Cloche Maurice • FRN
DEPART DANS LA NUIT, LE • 1913 • Fescourt Henri • FRN
DEPART DES AUTOMOBILES • 1896 • Melies Georges • FRN • AUTOMOBILES STARTING A RACE
DEPART DES OFFICIERS • 1896 • Melies Georges • FRN • OFFICERS OF FRENCH ARMY LEAVING SERVICE
DEPART EN VOITURE • 1895 • Lumiere Louis • FRN
DEPART POUR LES VACANCES • 1904 • Blache Alice • FRN

DEPART SANS ADIEUX see **NOBODY WAVED GOODBYE** • 1964
DEPART TRAGIQUE see **INNI RAHILA** • 1955
DEPARTED FOR EVER see **BORTREIST PA UBESTEMT TID** • 1973
DEPARTEMENTET • 1981 • Svenstedt Carl-Henrik, Svenstedt Stefania Lopez • SWD • MINISTRY, THE
DEPARTMENT 5 • 1960 • Polak Jindrich • CZC
DEPARTMENT 66 • 1963 • Laporte Claude • DCS • FRN
DEPARTMENT OF THE NAVY • 1958 • Cannon Robert • ANS • USA
DEPARTMENT STORE see **UNIVERMAG** • 1922
DEPARTMENT STORE see **BARGAIN BASEMENT** • 1935
DEPARTMENT STORE, THE • 1911 • *Edison* • USA
DEPARTMENT STORE, THE • 1920 • Goodwins Fred • UKN
DEPARTMENTAL CASE, A • 1917 • Justice Martin • SHT • USA
DEPARTS see **HEUREUSE AVENTURE, L'** • 1935
DEPARTS NECESSAIRES, LES • 1965 • Dufaux Georges • DCS • CND
DEPARTS POUR L'ALLEMAGNE • 1946 • Leenhardt Roger • DCS • FRN
DEPARTURE • 1986 • Kavanagh Brian • ASL
DEPARTURE OF A GRAND OLD MAN, THE see **UKHOD VELIKOVO STARTZA** • 1912
DEPARTURE OF A STEAMER • 1901 • Hepworth Cecil M. • UKN
DEPARTURE OF FIRST EXPEDITIONARY FORCE, SOUTH AUSTRALIA • 1914 • ASL
DEPARTURE OF MR. HABETIN, THE see **PAN HABETIN OCHAZI** • 1949
DEPARTURE OF TRAIN FROM STATION • 1905 • *Bitzer Billy (Ph)* • USA
DEPENDANCE see **OVER-DEPENDANCY** • 1949
DEPILATORY POWDER, THE • 1908 • *Pathe* • FRN
DEPORTATE DELLA SEZIONE SPECIALE SS, LE • 1976 • Di Silvestro Rino • ITL
DEPORTED • 1950 • Siodmak Robert • USA
DEPORTIERT • 1922 • Mendes Lothar • FRG
DEPOSITED AFTER BANKING HOURS • 1911 • *Yankee* • USA
DEPOSITION • 1973 • Paliyannopoulos Christos • SHT • GRC
DEPOT • 1978 • Mann Ron • DOC • CND
DEPOT PLAYGROUND, THE see **REMISELEGEPLADSEN** • 1972
DEPOT ROMEO, A • 1917 • Hotaling Arthur D. • SHT • USA
DEPRAVEDI • 1967 • Milligan Andy • USA
DEPRAVED, THE • 1957 • Dickson Paul • UKN
DEPRAVED, THE (USA) see **ADELAIDE** • 1968
DEPRAVES DU PLAISIR, LES • 1974 • Launois Bernard • FRN
DEPREM • 1977 • Goren Serif • TRK • EARTHQUAKE
DEPRESSED AREA • 1963 • Van Dyke Willard • DOC • USA
DEPRESSION see **FEELINGS OF DEPRESSION** • 1950
DEPRESSION see **FUKEIKI JIDAI** • 1930
DEPRISA, DEPRISA • 1980 • Saura Carlos • SPN • HURRY, HURRY ○ FAST, FAST
DEPS • 1975 • Vrdoljak Antun • YGS
DEPTH CHARGE • 1960 • Summers Jeremy • UKN
DEPTH CHARGES • 1945-52 • Napier-Bell J. B. • DOC • UKN
DEPTH OF FEELING • 1989 • Nicholson Arch • ASL
DEPTHS, THE see **KAIDAN KASANE-GA-FUCHI** • 1957
DEPTHS BELOW, THE see **DEVIL'S PLAYGROUND** • 1937
DEPTHS OF HATE, THE • 1913 • *Sindelar Pearl* • USA
DEPTHS OF THE SEA see **DIEPTE** • 1932
DEPUCELAGES • 1978 • Roy Jean-Claude • FRN
DEPUTAT BALTIKI • 1937 • Heifitz Josif, Zarkhi Alexander • USS • BALTIC DEPUTY (USA)
DEPUTE 73 • 1973 • Savignac Jean-Paul • DOC • FRN
DEPUTE, LE • 1915 • Protazanov Yakov • USS
DEPUTIES, THE • 1976 • Vogel Virgil W. • TVM • USA
DEPUTY, THE • 1974 • Povolotskaya I. • USS
DEPUTY, THE see **DIPUTADO, EL** • 1978
DEPUTY AND THE GIRL, THE • 1912 • *Anderson Broncho Billy* • USA
DEPUTY DROOPY • 1955 • Avery Tex, Lah Michael • ANS • USA
DEPUTY DRUMMER, THE • 1935 • George Henry W. • UKN
DEPUTY MARSHAL • 1949 • Berke William • USA
DEPUTY SHERIFF'S STAR • 1914 • Mackley Arthur • USA
DEPUTY'S BEAUTY, THE • 1912 • *Comet* • USA
DEPUTY'S CHANCE THAT WON, THE • 1915 • Mackley Arthur • USA
DEPUTY'S DUTY, THE • 1915 • Physioc Wray • USA
DEPUTY'S HONOR, THE • 1911 • *Bison* • USA
DEPUTY'S LOVE, THE • 1910 • *Anderson Broncho Billy* • USA
DEPUTY'S LOVE AFFAIR, THE • 1912 • *Anderson Broncho Billy* • USA
DEPUTY'S PERIL, THE • 1912 • Fielding Romaine • USA
DEPUTY'S REWARD, THE • 1915 • *Premier* • USA
DEPUTY'S SWEETHEART, THE • 1912 • *Bison* • USA
DEPUTY'S SWEETHEART, THE • 1913 • *Duncan William* • USA
DER ER ET YNDIGT LAND • 1940 • Frank Preben • DNM • DANMARKSFILMEN
DER ER ET YNDIGT LAND • 1982 • Arnfred Morten • DNM • WHAT A CHARMING COUNTRY
DER FUEHRER'S FACE • 1943 • Kinney Jack • ANS • USA
DER KAPTAIN DISCOVERS THE NORTH POLE • 1917 • La Cava Gregory • ANS • USA
DER KAPTAIN IS EXAMINED FOR INSURANCE • 1917 • La Cava Gregory • ANS • USA
DER KAPTAIN'S VALET • 1917 • La Cava Gregory • ANS • USA
DER KOM EN SOLDAT • 1969 • Guldbrandsen Peer • DNM • TINDERBOX OR, THE STORY OF A LIGHTER, THE ○ SCANDAL IN DENMARK (USA)
DER MA VAERE EN SENGEKANT • 1974 • Hilbard John • DNM
DER VAR ENGANG • 1922 • Dreyer Carl T. • DNM • ONCE UPON A TIME
DER VAR ENGANG • 1922 • Schneevoigt George • SWD, NRW
DER VAR ENGANG EN KRIG • 1966 • Kjaerulff-Schmidt Palle • DNM • ONCE THERE WAS A WAR ○ ONCE UPON A WAR
DERACINEMENTS • 1957 • Rossetti Georges • FRN
DERACINES, LES see **BENI-HENDEL** • 1976
DERANGED • 1974 • Gillen Jeff, Ormsby Alan • USA
DERANGED • 1987 • Vincent Chuck • USA
DERANGED see **WELCOME TO ARROW BEACH** • 1973
DERANGED see **IDAHO TRANSFER** • 1975
DERAS OGON SER OSS see **VAGEN GENOM SKA** • 1957
DERBORENCE • 1985 • Reusser Francis • SWT
DERBY • 1926 • Reichmann Max • FRG
DERBY • 1949 • von Norman Roger • FRG
DERBY • 1971 • Kaylor Robert • DOC • USA • ROLLER DERBY (UKN)
DERBY 1895, THE • 1895 • Acres Birt • UKN
DERBY, DAS • 1919 • Dupont E. A. • FRG
DERBY, THE • 1896 • Paul Robert William • UKN
DERBY, THE • 1905 • Hepworth Cecil M. • UKN
DERBY DAY • 1923 • Roach Hal • SHT • USA
DERBY DAY • 1952 • Wilcox Herbert • UKN • FOUR AGAINST FATE (USA)
DERBY-KA-SHIKAR • 1935 • IND
DERBY WINNER, THE • 1915 • Shaw Harold • UKN
DEREBEYI • 1968 • Figenli Yavuz • TRK • FEUDAL LORD, THE
DERECHO A LA FELICIDAD, EL • 1968 • Rinaldi Carlos • ARG • RIGHT TO HAPPINESS, THE
DERECHO A LA VIDA, EL • 1958 • de la Serna Mauricio • MXC
DERECHO A LA VIDA, EL • 1973 • Balcazar Alfonso • SPN
DERECHO DE NACER, EL • 1951 • Gomez Urquiza Zacarias • MXC, CUB • RIGHT TO BE BORN, THE
DERECHO DE NACER, EL • 1966 • Davison Tito • MXC
DERECHO Y EL DEBER, EL • 1937 • Orol Juan • MXC
DERECHOS DE LA MUJER, LOS • 1963 • Saenz De Heredia Jose Luis • SPN
DERECHOS DE LOS HIJOS, LOS • 1962 • Morayta Miguel • MXC
DERELICT • 1930 • Lee Rowland V. • USA • TYPHOON BILL
DERELICT, THE • 1911 • Porter Edwin S. • USA
DERELICT, THE • 1912 • *Champion* • USA
DERELICT, THE • 1914 • Melford George • USA
DERELICT, THE • 1915 • Otto Henry • USA
DERELICT, THE • 1916 • *Lily* • USA
DERELICT, THE • 1917 • Harbaugh Carl • USA
DERELICT, THE • 1937 • Simpson Harold • UKN
DERELICT AND THE MAN, THE • 1914 • *Wallace Irene* • USA
DERELICT REPORTER, THE • 1911 • *Ince Ralph* • USA
DERELICTS • 1917 • Morgan Sidney • UKN
DERELICTS, THE • 1914 • Vale Travers • USA
DERELICT'S RETURN, THE • 1912 • *Buckley May* • USA
DERELITTA, LA • 1981 • Igoux Jean-Pierre • FRN
DERIVATIF, LE see **FOLLE NUIT, LA** • 1932
DERIVE, LA see **FILLE A LA DERIVE, UNE** • 1962
DERIVE DES CONTINENTS, LES see **CONTINENTAL DRIFT** • 1968
DERJI VORA • 1930 • Medvedkin Alexander • USS
DERKOVITZ GYULA 1894-1934 • 1958 • Jancso Miklos • SHT • HNG
DERMAN • 1985 • Goren Serif • TRK • REMEDY
DERMIS PROBE, THE • 1966 • Williams Richard • ANS • USA
DERNIER AMANT ROMANTIQUE, LE • 1978 • Jaeckin Just • FRN, SPN • LAST ROMANTIC LOVER, THE
DERNIER AMOUR • 1949 • Stelli Jean • FRN
DERNIER AMOUR, LE • 1915 • Perret Leonce • FRN
DERNIER ATOUT • 1942 • Becker Jacques • FRN
DERNIER BAISER, LE • 1977 • Grassian Dolores • FRN, BLG
DERNIER CHOC, LE • 1932 • de Baroncelli Jacques • FRN • BRUMES
DERNIER COMBAT, LE • 1982 • Besson Luc • FRN • LAST COMBAT, THE (UKN) ○ LAST BATTLE, THE
DERNIER CREPUSCULE, LE • 1969 • Hamina Mohamed Lakhdar • ALG
DERNIER DES COUREURS DES BOIS, LE • 1979 • Labrecque Jean-Claude • CND
DERNIER DES ROBIN DES BOIS, LE • 1952 • Berthomieu Andre • FRN
DERNIER DES SIX, LE • 1941 • Lacombe Georges • FRN
DERNIER DES VIKINGS, LE (FRN) see **ULTIMO DEI VICHINGHI, L'** • 1961
DERNIER DOMICILE CONNU • 1970 • Giovanni Jose • FRN, ITL • ULTIMO DOMICILIO CONOSCIUTO (ITL)
DERNIER ENVOL • 1977 • Desbiens Francine • ANS • CND
DERNIER GLACIER, LE • 1984 • Leduc Jacques (c/d) • CND
DERNIER HAVRE, LE • 1987 • Benoit Denyse • CND
DERNIER HOMME, LE • 1969 • Bitsch Charles L. • FRN • LAST MAN, THE
DERNIER MELODRAME, LE • 1978 • Franju Georges • MTV • FRN • LAST MELODRAMA, THE
DERNIER METRO • 1945 • de Canonge Maurice • FRN
DERNIER METRO, LE • 1980 • Truffaut Francois • FRN • LAST METRO, THE (USA)
DERNIER MILLIARDAIRE, LE • 1934 • Clair Rene • FRN • LAST MILLIONAIRE, THE
DERNIER MOMENT, LE see **LAST MOMENT, THE** • 1928
DERNIER PARDON, LE • 1913 • Tourneur Maurice • FRN
DERNIER PRINTEMPS, LE • 1977 • Brandt Henry • DOC • SWT
DERNIER QUART D'HEURE, LE • 1961 • Saltel Roger • FRN
DERNIER REFUGE • 1946 • Maurette Marc • FRN
DERNIER REFUGE • 1971 • Camus Marcel • FRN
DERNIER REFUGE, LE • 1965 • Puzenat Jean-Loup • SHT • FRN
DERNIER SAUT, LE • 1969 • Luntz Edouard • FRN, ITL • INDAGINE SU UN PARA ACCUSATO DI OMICIDA (ITL)
DERNIER SOU, LE • 1943 • Cayatte Andre • FRN
DERNIER TANGO A PARIS, LE (FRN) see **ULTIMO TANGO A PARIGI, L'** • 1972
DERNIER TIERCE, LE • 1964 • Pottier Richard • FRN
DERNIER TOURNANT, LE • 1939 • Chenal Pierre • FRN • POSTMAN ALWAYS RINGS TWICE, THE ○ LAST BEND, THE
DERNIER VOYAGE, LE see **RIHLA AL-AKHIRA, AR-** • 1966
DERNIER VOYAGE DE GULLIVER, LE • 1961 • Borowczyk Walerian • FRN
DERNIERE ATTAQUE, LA (FRN) see **GUERRA CONTINUA, LA** • 1962
DERNIERE AVENTURE • 1941 • Peguy Robert • FRN
DERNIERE BERCEUSE, LA • 1930 • Cassagne Jean, Righelli Gennaro • FRN • CHANSON DE L'AMOUR, LA ○ SILENCE
DERNIERE BOURREE A PARIS, LA • 1973 • Andre Raoul • FRN, ITL
DERNIERE CHEVAUCHEE, LA • 1946 • Mathot Leon • FRN • CAID, LE
DERNIERE ETE • 1980 • Guediguian Robert, Le Wita Frank • FRN
DERNIERE FEMME, LA (FRN) see **ULTIMA DONNA, L'** • 1976
DERNIERE HEURE • 1934 • Bernard-Derosne Jean • FRN
DERNIERE HEURE, EDITION SPECIALE • 1949 • de Canonge Maurice • FRN
DERNIERE INCARNATION DE LARSAN, LA see **ROULETABILLE 2** • 1912
DERNIERE JEUNESSE • 1939 • Musso Jeff • FRN, ITL • ULTIMA GIOVINEZZA (ITL) ○ FIN D'UNE VIE, LA
DERNIERE NEIGE, LA • 1973 • Theberge Andre • CND
DERNIERE NUIT, LA • 1933 • de Casembroot Jacques • FRN
DERNIERE NUIT, LA see **LEILA EL AKHIRA, EL** • 1963
DERNIERE SORTIE AVANT ROISSY • 1976 • Paul Bernard • FRN • LAST EXIT BEFORE ROISSY (USA)
DERNIERE VALSE, LA • 1935 • Mittler Leo • FRN
DERNIERES CARTOUCHES, LES • 1897 • Melies Georges • FRN • LAST CARTRIDGES, THE
DERNIERES FIANCAILLES, LES • 1973 • Lefebvre Jean-Pierre • CND • LAST BETROTHAL, THE
DERNIERES ROSES, LES see **MARTHA** • 1935
DERNIERES VACANCES, LES • 1947 • Leenhardt Roger • FRN • LAST VACATION, THE (USA)
DERNIERS HIVERS, LES • 1971 • Tacchella Jean-Charles • SHT • FRN
DERNIERS JOURS DE POMPEI, LES • 1948 • L'Herbier Marcel • FRN, ITL • ULTIMI GIORNI DI POMPEI, GLI (ITL) ○ LAST DAYS OF POMPEII, THE(USA) ○ SINS OF POMPEI
DERNIERS JOURS D'HERCULANUM, LES (FRN) see **ANNO 79, LA DISTRUZIONE DI ERCOLANO** • 1963
DEROBADE, LA • 1979 • Duval Daniel • FRN • MEMOIRS OF A FRENCH WHORE (USA) ○ GETAWAY LIFE, THE ○ LIFE, THE (UKN) ○ CONFESSIONS OF A STREETWALKER ○ EVASION, THE
DEROUTE, LA • 1957 • Kyrou Ado • SHT • FRN
DERRAPAGEM • 1974 • Esteves Constantino • PRT
DERRIERE CES MURS see **JERICHO** • 1945
DERRIERE LA FACADE • 1939 • Lacombe Georges, Mirande Yves • FRN • 32, RUE DE MONTMARTRE
DERRIERE LA GRANDE MURAILLE • 1956 • Menegoz Robert • DOC • FRN
DERRIERE LE MIROIR SANS TAIN • Roy Jean-Claude • FRN
DERRIERE L'IMAGE • 1978 • Godbout Jacques • CND
DERRIERE L'OMNIBUS see **PAULUS CHANTANT: DERRIERE L'OMNIBUS** • 1897
DERROTA • 1972 • Morantes Carlos Gonzalez • MXC • DEFEAT
DERROTA, A • 1967 • Fiorani Mario • BRZ • DEFEAT, THE
DERROTA, LA • 1981 • Vallejo Fernando • MXC • DEFEAT, THE
DERSU UZALA see **DERZU UZALA** • 1975
DERTLI GONLUM • 1968 • Olgac Bilge • TRK • MY SORROWFUL HEART
DERTLI PINAR • 1968 • Ergun Nuri • TRK • SORROWFUL SPRING, THE
DERVIS I SMRT • 1974 • Velimirovic Zdravko • YGS • DERVISH AND DEATH, THE
DERVISH AND DEATH, THE see **DERVIS I SMRT** • 1974
DERVISH'S REVENGE, THE • 1907 • *Gaumont* • FRN
DERYNE • 1951 • Kalmar Laszlo • HNG • MRS. DERY
DERYNE, HOL VAN? • 1975 • Maar Gyula • HNG • WHERE ARE YOU, MRS. DERY? ○ MRS. DERY, WHERE ARE YOU? ○ IN THE WINGS
DERZU UZALA • 1975 • Kurosawa Akira • JPN, USS • DERSU UZALA
DES AMANTS SUR L'HERBE • Jauniaux M. • FRN
DES ANGES ET DES DEMONS • 1976 • Rabinowicz Maurice, Michelems Yvette • MTV • BLG
DES ARMES ET LES HOMMES • 1973 • Melancon Andre • SHT • CND
DES ASTRES ET DESASTRES • 1978 • Sauve Alain • MTV • CND
DES CANONS, DES MUNITIONS • 1916 • Bernard-Deschamps • FRN
DES CHRISTS PAR MILLIERS • 1969 • Arthuys Philippe • FRN
DES CLICS ET DES CLACS see **DECLIC ET DES CLAQUES** • 1964
DES ENFANTS GATES • 1976 • Tavernier Bertrand • FRN • SPOILED CHILDREN (USA) ○ ENFANTS GATES, LES
DES FEMMES DANS MA VIE see **NISSA'UN FI HAYATI** • 1957
DES FEMMES DISPARAISSENT • 1959 • Molinaro Edouard • FRN • ROAD TO SHAME, THE (USA) ○ GIRLS DISAPPEAR
DES FEMMES ET DES FLEURS • 1963 • Leenhardt Roger • DCS • FRN
DES FILLES POUR L'ARMEE (FRN) see **SOLDATESSE, LE** • 1965
DES FRISSONS PARTOUT • 1963 • Andre Raoul • FRN, ITL
DES FUSILS POUR BANTA • 1970 • Maldoror Sarah • ANG
DES GARCONS ET DES FILLES • 1968 • Perier Etienne • BLG, FRN • GIRLS AND BOYS
DES GENS SANS IMPORTANCE • 1955 • Verneuil Henri • FRN • BE BEAUTIFUL BUT SHUT UP
DES GOLDES FLUCH • 1917 • Oswald Richard • FRG
DES GOLEMS LETZTE ABENTEUER see **DORFSGOLEM, DER** • 1921
DES GOUTS ET DES COULEURS • 1960 • Gerard • SHT • FRN
DES GUTEN ZUVIEL • 1915 • Del Zopp Rudolf • FRG
DES HAARES UND DER LIEBE WELLEN • 1929 • Ruttmann Walter • FRG
DES HISTOIRES DE NOTRE CARTIER • 1974 • Bokor Pierre • MTV • RMN
DES HOMMES DANS LE CIEL • 1959 • Languepin Jean-Jacques • DOC • FRN
DES HOMMES ET DES MONTAGNES • 1953 • Languepin Jean-Jacques, Rebuffat Gaston • SHT • FRN
DES HOMMES QU'ON APPELLE SAUVAGE • 1948 • Fichter Jean, Saenz Luis, Gaisseau Pierre-Dominique, Gheerbrandt Alain • DOC • FRN
DES HOMMES SOUS LE SOLEIL see **RIJALUN TAHTA ASH-SHAMS** • 1970

DES HOMMES.. UNE DOCTRINE • 1960 • Catenys • SHT • FRN
DES IMAGES QUI TRAVAILLENT I & II • 1972 • Chabot Jean • DCS • CND
DES JEUNES FILLES DANS LA NUIT • 1942 • Le Henaff Rene • FRN
DES JOURNEES ENTIERES DANS LES ARBRES • 1976 • Duras Marguerite • FRN • ENTIRE DAYS AMONG THE TREES (UKN) ○ DAYS IN THE TREES
DES JUNGEN DESSAUERS GROSSE LIEBE • 1933 • Robison Arthur • FRG
DES KAISERS ALTE KLEIDER • 1923 • Seitz Franz • FRG
DES KONIGS BEFEHL • 1926 • FRG
DES LEBENS RUTSCHBAHN • 1918 • Gunsburg Arthur • FRG
DES LEBENS UEBERFLUSS • 1950 • Liebeneiner Wolfgang • FRG
DES LEBENS UND DER LEIBE WELLEN • 1921 • Batz Lorenz • FRG
DES LEBENS UNGEMISCHTE FREUDE.. • 1917 • *Andra Fern* • FRG
DES LOGIS ET DES HOMMES • 1958 • Dewever Jean • FRN
DES MAINS COMME DES OISEAUX • 1964 • Rachedi Ahmed • ALG
DES MAISONS DES HOMMES • 1953 • Jallaud Sylvia • SHT • FRN
DES MORTS • 1979 • Ferbus Jean-Paul, Garny Dominique, Zeno Thierry • DOC • BLG, FRN
DES NACHSTEN WEIB • 1922 • Berger Josef? • *Union-Film* • FRG
DES NACHSTEN WEIB • 1923 • *Lu Synd-Film* • FRG
DES PARDES • 1978 • Anand Dev • IND • HOME AND ABROAD
DES PAS DANS L'UNIVERS • 1967 • Chabot Jean • SHT • CND
DES PIEDS ET DES MAINS • 1916 • Feyder Jacques, Ravel Gaston • FRN
DES PISSENLITS PAR LA RACINE • 1963 • Lautner Georges • FRN, ITL
DES PROKURATORS TOCHTER • 1917 • Wauer William • FRG
DES QUINTUPLES AU PENSIONNAT • 1952 • Jayet Rene • FRN
DES RAILS SOUS LES PALMIERS • 1951 • Colson-Malleville Marie, Colpi Henri • DOC • FRN • RAILS BENEATH THE PALM TREES
DES RHEINES UND DER LIEBE WELLEN. RHEINZAUBER • 1925 • *Filmverleih Max Banisch* • FRG • RHEINZAUBER
DES RUINES ET DES HOMMES • 1958 • Kast Pierre • SHT • FRN
DES SINGES DANS LE GRENIER see **MONKEYS IN THE ATTIC: A FILM OF EXPLODING DREAMS** • 1974
DES SONT SUR LE TAPIS, LES • 1960 • Collomb Jean • FRN • DIE IS CAST, THE
DES SOURIS ET DES HOMMES • 1958 • Menegoz Robert • SHT • FRN
DES TEUFELS ADVOKAT • 1920 • Eriksen Erich • FRG
DES TEUFELS ADVOKAT see **AVVOCATO DEL DIAVOLO, L'** • 1977
DES TEUFELS GENERAL • 1955 • Kautner Helmut • FRG • DEVIL'S GENERAL, THE
DES TEUFELS PARADIES • 1987 • Glowna Vadim • FRG • DEVIL'S PARADISE, THE
DES TEUFELS PUPPE • 1919 • Brenken Kurt • FRG
DES TROIS-RIVIERES A LA RIVIERE-AU-RAT • 1944 • Tessier Albert • DCS • CND
DES VACANCES EN OR • 1969 • Rigaud Francis • FRN, SPN • VIVA LA AVENTURA! (SPN) ○ HURRAH FOR ADVENTURE!
DES VATERS LETZTER WILLE • 1917 • May Joe • FRG
DES VATERS SCHULD • 1918 • Ziener Bruno • FRG
DESA NISA • 1972 • Peries Lester James • SLN • EYES, THE ○ DESE NISE
DESAFIO, EL • 1970 • Alvarez Santiago, Perez Manuel, Fraga Jorge, Egea Jose Luis, Guerin Claudio, Erice Victor • CUB
DESAFIO, EL • 1979 • Alvarez Santiago • DOC • CUB
DESAFIO A AVENTURA • 1972 • Fernandes Ary • BRZ
DESAFIO DE PANCHO VILLA, EL (SPN) see **PANCHO VILLA** • 1972
DESAFIO EN RIO BRAVO see **SFIDA A RIO BRAVO** • 1965
DESALMADO, EL • 1950 • Urueta Chano • MXC
DESAMPARADOS, LOS • 1960 • Santillan Antonio • SPN
DESANT NA DRVAR • 1963 • Hadzic Fadil • YGS • DESCENT ON DRVAR
DESARRAIGADAS, LAS • 1975 • Lara Polop Francisco • SPN
DESARRAIGADOS, LOS • 1958 • Gazcon Gilberto • MXC
DESARROI • 1946 • Dagan Robert-Paul • FRN • ODETTE
DESARROIS DE L'ELEVE TORLESS, LES (FRN) see **JUNGE TORLESS, DER** • 1966
DESASTER • 1973 • Hauff Reinhard • FRG
DESASTRE DE ANNUAL, EL • 1970 • Franco Ricardo • SPN
DESASTRES DE LA GUERRE, LES • 1951 • Kast Pierre • SHT • FRN
DESAXEES, LES • 1972 • Lemoine Michel • FRN • I AM AVAILABLE (UKN)
DESCARRIADA, LA • 1972 • Ozores Mariano • SPN
DESCARTE, O • 1974 • Duarte Anselmo • BRZ
DESCARTES • 1974 • Rossellini Roberto • MTV • ITL
DESCENDANTS OF TARO URASHIMA, THE see **URASHIMA TARO NO KOEI** • 1946
DESCENDEZ, ON VOUS DEMANDE • 1951 • Laviron Jean • FRN
DESCENSO AL PAIS DE LA NOCHE • 1974 • Gurrola Alfredo • MXC • DESCENT TO THE LAND OF NIGHT
DESCENT • 1975 • Walker Giles • CND
DESCENT OF THE NINE see **KATHODOS TON ENNEA** • 1984
DESCENT ON DRVAR see **DESANT NA DRVAR** • 1963
DESCENT TO HELL see **ZEJSCIE DO PIEKLA** • 1966
DESCENT TO THE LAND OF NIGHT see **DESCENSO AL PAIS DE LA NOCHE** • 1974
DESCENTES ET VIRAGES see **SKI SKILL** • 1946
DESCOBRIMENTO DO BRASIL, O • 1937 • Mauro-Humberto • BRZ
DESCOMEDIDOS Y CHASCONES • 1973 • *Cine Experimental* • DOC • CHL
DESCONHECIDO, O • 1980 • Santos Ruy • BRZ • UNKNOWN, THE
DESCONOCIDA, LA • 1954 • Urueta Chano • MXC
DESCONOCIDO, EL • 1973 • *Cinema Jalisco* • MXC
DESCRIPTION DE L'EGYPTE • 1972 • Tilmissani Abdel-Qadir At- • SHT • EGY
DESCRIPTION D'UN COMBAT • 1960 • Marker Chris • DOC • FRN, ISR
DESCRIPTION OF AN ISLAND see **BESCHREIBUNG EINER INSEL** • 1979
DESCUARTIZADOR DE BINBROOK, EL • 1971 • Skaife Michael • SPN • NECROPHAGUS (USA) ○ GRAVEYARD OF HORROR ○ DISMEMBERER OF BINBROOK, THE
DESDE EL ABISMO • 1980 • Ayala Fernando • ARG • FROM THE DEPTHS
DESDEMONA • 1908 • *Messter Oskar (P)* • FRG
DESDEMONA • 1911 • Blom August • DNM
DESE NISE see **DESA NISA** • 1972
DESEADA • 1950 • Gavaldon Roberto • MXC
DESEBAGATO • 1987 • Sanon Emmanuel K. • BRK, CUB • LAST SALARY, THE
DESEMBARCOS • 1989 • Meerapfel Jeanine, Chiesa • ARG, FRG • WHEN MEMORY SPEAKS (UKN)
DESEMPREGADOS, OS • 1972 • Thome Antonio B. • BRZ • IRMAOS SEM CORAGEM, OS
DESENCANTO, EL • 1976 • Chavarri Jaime • SPN • DISENCHANTMENT, THE
DESENCHANTEE, LA • 1989 • Jacquot Benoit • FRN
DESENE PE ASFALT • 1989 • Bostan Elisabeta • RMN • DRAWINGS ON ASPHALT
DESENFRENADOS, LOS • 1959 • Delgado Agustin P. • MXC
DESEO • 1975 • Balcazar Alfonso • SPN
DESEO, EL • 1945 • Urueta Chano • MXC
DESEOS • 1977 • Corkidi Rafael • MXC
DESEOS CONCEBIDOS, LOS • 1982 • Sanchez Christian • CHL • DESIRES CONCEIVED
DESERT • 1976 • Brakhage Stan • SHT • USA
DESERT see **PUSTYNYA** • 1967
DESERT, LE see **SERGENT X, LE** • 1931
DESERT, THE • 1912 • *Bison* • USA
DESERT ADVENTURES see **PRZYGODY NA PUSTYNI** • 1966
DESERT ARCHIPELAGO, THE see **MUJIN RETTO** • 1970
DESERT ASSAULT see **BATTAGLIA DEL DESERTO, LA** • 1969
DESERT ATTACK (USA) see **ICE COLD IN ALEX** • 1958
DESERT BANDIT • 1941 • Sherman George • USA
DESERT BATTLE (UKN) see **BATTAGLIA DEL DESERTO, LA** • 1969
DESERT BLOOM • 1986 • Corr Eugene • USA
DESERT BLOOMS • 1921 • Rosson Arthur • USA
DESERT BREED, THE • 1915 • De Grasse Joseph • USA
DESERT BRIDE, THE • 1928 • Lang Walter • USA
DESERT BRIDEGROOM, THE • 1922 • Clements Roy • USA
DESERT CALLS ITS OWN, THE • 1916 • Mix Tom • SHT • USA
DESERT CLAIM, THE • 1911 • *Essanay* • USA
DESERT COMMAND see **ATTENTATO AI TRE GRANDI** • 1967
DESERT DE PIGALLE, LE • 1957 • Joannon Leo • FRN, ITL • INFERNO DI PIGALLE, L' (ITL) ○ PRIEST IN PIGALLE, A
DESERT DEATH • 1935 • Seitz George B. • USA
DESERT DEMON, THE • 1925 • Thorpe Richard • USA
DESERT DES TARTARES, LE • 1970 • Schoendoerffer Pierre • FRN
DESERT DES TARTARES, LE • 1973 • Bertucelli Jean-Louis • FRN
DESERT DES TARTARES, LE (FRN) see **DESERTO EI TARTARI, IL** • 1976
DESERT DESPERADOES (USA) see **PECCATRICE DEL DESERTO, LA** • 1959
DESERT DRIVEN • 1923 • Paul Val • USA
DESERT DUST • 1917 • *Artcraft* • USA
DESERT DUST • 1937 • Wyler William • USA
DESERT FIGHTERS (USA) see **PATROUILLE DES SABLES, LA** • 1954
DESERT FLOWER, THE • 1925 • Cummings Irving • USA
DESERT FOX, THE • 1951 • Hathaway Henry • USA • ROMMEL -DESERT FOX (UKN)
DESERT FURY • 1947 • Allen Lewis • USA
DESERT GENERATION, THE see **GENERATION DU DESERT, LA** • 1957
DESERT GHOST, THE • 1917 • Marshall George • SHT • USA
DESERT GOLD • 1914 • Sidney Scott • USA • AFTER THE STORM
DESERT GOLD • 1919 • Hunter T. Hayes • USA
DESERT GOLD • 1919 • Smith Beaumont • ASL
DESERT GOLD • 1926 • Seitz George B. • USA
DESERT GOLD • 1936 • Hogan James P. • USA
DESERT GREED • 1926 • Jaccard Jacques • USA • GREED OF GOLD
DESERT GUNS • 1936 • Hutchison Charles • USA
DESERT HARMONIES • 1935 • Schwarzwald Milton • SHT • USA
DESERT HAWK, THE • 1924 • De La Mothe Leon • USA
DESERT HAWK, THE • 1944 • Eason B. Reeves • SRL • USA
DESERT HAWK, THE • 1950 • De Cordova Frederick • USA
DESERT HEALER, THE see **OLD LOVES AND NEW** • 1926
DESERT HEARTS • 1986 • Deitch Donna • USA
DESERT HELL • 1958 • Warren Charles Marquis • USA
DESERT HERO • 1919 • Arbuckle Roscoe • SHT • USA
DESERT HONEYMOON, A • 1915 • Fielding Romaine • USA
DESERT HORSEMAN, THE • 1946 • Nazarro Ray • USA • CHECKMATE (UKN)
DESERT INN • 1959 • SAF
DESERT ISLAND, THE • 1914 • *Captain Kettle* • UKN
DESERT JUSTICE • 1936 • Berke William • USA • CRIME'S HIGHWAY (UKN)
DESERT LAUGHS, THE see **YABAN GULU** • 1961
DESERT LAW • 1953 • Conway Jack • USA
DESERT LEGION • 1953 • Pevney Joseph • USA
DESERT LOVE • 1920 • Jaccard Jacques • USA
DESERT LOVERS • 1985 • Leblanc Michel • FRN
DESERT MADNESS • 1925 • Webb Harry S. • USA
DESERT MAN, THE • 1917 • Hart William S. • USA
DESERT MAN, THE • 1920 • *Dalton Emmett* • SHT • USA
DESERT MAN, THE • 1934 • Tansey Robert • USA
DESERT MESA • 1935 • James Alan • USA
DESERT MICE • 1959 • Relph Michael • UKN
DESERT MYSTERY, THE • 1920 • *Coburn Wallace* • SHT • USA
DESERT NIGHTS • 1929 • Nigh William • USA • THIRST
DESERT ODYSSEY see **HAREM BUNCH, OR WAR AND PIECE, THE** • 1969
DESERT OF DESIRE see **JOEN NO SABAKU** • 1967
DESERT OF GANGA, THE see **GANGAVATAREN** • 1937
DESERT OF LOST MEN • 1951 • Keller Harry • USA
DESERT OF THE LOST, THE • 1927 • Thorpe Richard • USA
DESERT OF WHEAT, THE see **RIDERS OF THE DAWN** • 1920
DESERT OUTLAW, THE • 1924 • Mortimer Edmund • USA
DESERT OUTPOST • 1954 • Newfield Sam, Cravenne Marcel • USA, FRN
DESERT PASSAGE • 1953 • Selander Lesley • USA
DESERT PATROL • 1938 • Newfield Sam • USA
DESERT PATROL (UKN) see **EL ALAMEIN** • 1953
DESERT PATROL (USA) see **SEA OF SAND** • 1958
DESERT PEOPLE • 1965 • Dunlop Ian • DOC • ASL
DESERT PHANTOM, THE • 1936 • Luby S. Roy • USA
DESERT PIRATE, THE • 1927 • Dugan James • USA
DESERT PRINCE, THE see **LIGHTNING** • 1927
DESERT PURSUIT • 1952 • Blair George • USA
DESERT RAIDERS (USA) see **DOMINATORE DEL DESERTO, IL** • 1964
DESERT RAT, THE • 1916 • Fielding Romaine • SHT • USA
DESERT RATS • 1988 • Wharmby Tony • TVM • USA
DESERT RATS, THE • 1953 • Wise Robert • USA
DESERT RAVEN, THE • 1965 • Lee Alan S. • USA
DESERT REGATTA • 1932 • White Jules • SHT • USA
DESERT RETOUR see **CHATELAINE DU LIBAN, LA** • 1956
DESERT RIDER • 1923 • Bradbury Robert North • USA
DESERT RIDER, THE • 1929 • Grinde Nick • USA
DESERT ROUGE, LE (FRN) see **DESERTO ROSSO, IL** • 1964
DESERT RUBY, THE • 1919 • *Steiner William* • USA
DESERT SANDS • 1954 • Selander Lesley • USA
DESERT SCORPION, THE • 1920 • Thayer Otis B. • USA
DESERT SECRET, THE • 1924 • Reel Frederick Jr. • USA
DESERT SHEIK, THE • 1924 • Terriss Tom • USA
DESERT SONG, THE • 1929 • Del Ruth Roy • USA
DESERT SONG, THE • 1943 • Florey Robert • USA
DESERT SONG, THE • 1953 • Humberstone H. Bruce • USA
DESERT SONG (USA) see **LIED DER WUSTE, DAS** • 1939
DESERT SUNK • 1930 • *Mintz Charles (P)* • ANS • USA
DESERT SWEETHEARTS, THE • 1912 • *Anderson Broncho Billy* • USA
DESERT TANKS (UKN) see **BATTAGLIA DI EL ALAMEIN, LA** • 1969
DESERT THIEVES • 1914 • Barker Reginald? • USA
DESERT TIGERS see **TIGROS DEL DESIERTO, LOS**
DESERT TRAIL, THE • 1912 • *Roland Ruth* • USA
DESERT TRAIL, THE • 1935 • Collins Lewis D. • USA
DESERT TRIBESMAN, THE • 1914 • *Cruze James* • USA
DESERT VALLEY • 1926 • Dunlap Scott R. • USA
DESERT VENGEANCE • 1931 • King Louis • USA
DESERT VICTORY • 1943 • Boulting Roy, MacDonald David • DOC • UKN
DESERT VIGILANTE • 1949 • Sears Fred F. • USA
DESERT VULTURE • 1920 • *Guinan Texas* • SHT • USA
DESERT VULTURES • 1930 • Adamson Victor • USA
DESERT WAR (USA) see **QUATTRO NOTTI CON ALBA** • 1962
DESERT WARRIOR • 1987 • Hool Lance • USA
DESERT WARRIOR • 1988 • Goldman Jim • USA
DESERT WARRIOR see **AMANTES DEL DESIERTO, LOS** • 1958
DESERT WARRIOR see **TUAREG IL GUERRIERO DEL DESERTO** • 1984
DESERT WARRIOR see **WHEELS OF FIRE** • 1984
DESERT WEDDING see **NOCES DE SABLE** • 1948
DESERT WELL, THE • 1911 • *Kalem* • USA
DESERT WOOING, A • 1918 • Storm Jerome • USA
DESERTED AT THE ALTAR • 1922 • Howard William K., Kelley Albert • USA
DESERTED AT THE AUTO • 1915 • Dillon John Francis • USA
DESERTED ENGINE, THE • 1917 • Davis James • USA
DESERTED SHAFT, THE • 1912 • *Imp* • USA
DESERTER • 1898 • Paul Robert William • UKN
DESERTER • 1988 • Korras Giorgos, Voupouras Christos • GRC
DESERTER see **DEZERTIR** • 1933
DESERTER, THE • 1903 • Williamson James • UKN
DESERTER, THE • 1908 • Fitzhamon Lewin • UKN
DESERTER, THE • 1912 • Ince Thomas H. • USA
DESERTER, THE • 1916 • Edwards Walter • USA
DESERTER, THE • 1956 • Biggs Julian • CND
DESERTER, THE see **DEZERTER** • 1958
DESERTER, THE see **DESERTOREN** • 1971
DESERTER, THE (UKN) see **DEZERTER** • 1966
DESERTER, THE (USA) see **SPINA DORSALE DEL DIAVOLO, LA** • 1970
DESERTER AND THE NOMADS, THE (USA) see **ZBEHOVIA A PUTNICI** • 1968
DESERTER U.S.A. • 1969 • Lambert Lars, Sjogren Olle • SWD
DESERTERS • 1983 • Darcus Jack • CND
DESERTERS AND PILGRIMS see **ZBEHOVIA A PUTNICI** • 1968
DESERTER'S COURAGE, A • 1916 • *Buffalo* • SHT • USA
DESERTEUR, LE • 1906 • Nonguet Lucien, Heuze Andre • FRN
DESERTEUR, LE • 1939 • Moguy Leonide • FRN • JE T'ATTENDRAI
DESERTEURS • 1969 • Sanchez-Ariza Jose • SWD
DESERTEUSE • 1917 • Feuillade Louis • FRN
DESERTION see **FANEFLUCKT** • 1974
DESERTION AND NON-SUPPORT • 1917 • Calvert E. H. • SHT • USA
DESERTO BIANCO see **RAGAZZO DAGLI OCCHI CHIARI, IL** • 1970
DESERTO DI FUOCO • 1971 • Merusi Renzo • ITL
DESERTO DI GLORIA see **EL ALAMEIN** • 1958
DESERTO EI TARTARI, IL • 1976 • Zurlini Valerio • ITL, FRN • DESERT DES TARTARES, LE (FRN)
DESERTO ROSSO, IL • 1964 • Antonioni Michelangelo • ITL, FRN • DESERT ROUGE, LE (FRN) ○ RED DESERT, THE (USA)
DESERTOREN • 1971 • Kragh Thomas, Brydesen Lars, Fredholm Gert, Kalo Sten • DNM • DESERTER, THE
DESERT'S CRUCIBLE, THE • 1922 • Clements Roy • USA
DESERT'S LURE, THE • 1911 • *Bison* • USA

DESERT'S PRICE, THE • 1925 • Van Dyke W. S. • USA
DESERT'S STING, THE • 1914 • Lucas Wilfred • USA
DESERT'S TOLL, THE • 1926 • Smith Cliff • USA • DEVIL'S TOLL, THE
DESESPERADO, LE see **LOI DU SURVIVANT, LA** • 1966
DESESPERADO, EL (SPN) see **DESPERADO, EL** • 1967
DESESPERADOS, LOS (SPN) see **QUEI DISPERATI CHE PUZZANO DI SUDORE E DI MORTE** • 1970
DESETI BRAT • 1983 • Duletic Vojko • YGS • TENTH BROTHER, THE
DESFORRA, A • 1967 • Palmisano Gino • BRZ • REDRESS, THE
DESHABILLAGE IMPOSSIBLE, LE • 1900 • Melies Georges • FRN • GOING TO BED UNDER DIFFICULTIES (USA) ○ INCREASING WARDROBE, AN
DESHEREDADOS, LOS • 1935 • Baqueriza Guillermo • MXC
DESHEREDADOS, LOS • 1963 • Curiel Federico • MXC, SPN, PRC
DESHERMATI • 1938 • *Sircar B. N. (P)* • IND
DESHIMA -INSEL DER FREMDEN • 1987 • Kuert Beat • SWT
DESIDERANDO GIULIA • 1987 • Barzini Andrea • ITL • DESIRING GIULIA
DESIDERI D'ESTATE • 1964 • Amadio Silvio • ITL
DESIDERI NEL SOLE • 1965 • Rozier Jacques • FRN, ITL
DESIDERIA, LA VITA INTERIORE • 1980 • Barcelloni • ITL • DESIRE, THE INTERIOR LIFE
DESIDERIO • 1946 • Pagliero Marcello, Rossellini Roberto • ITL
DESIDERIO • 1984 • Tato Anna Maria • ITL • DESIRE
DESIDERIO 'E SOLE • 1954 • Pastina Giorgio • ITL
DESIDERIUS ORBAN • 1981 • Pringle Ian • DOC • ASL
DESIGN FOR DEATH • 1947 • Fleischer Richard • USA
DESIGN FOR DYING, A see **ONNA NO KUNSHO** • 1961
DESIGN FOR LEAVING • 1954 • McKimson Robert • ANS • USA
DESIGN FOR LIVING • 1933 • Lubitsch Ernst • USA
DESIGN FOR LOVE see **CONFESSIONS OF A SEX MANIAC** • 1975
DESIGN FOR LOVING • 1962 • Grayson Godfrey • UKN • FASHION FOR LOVING
DESIGN FOR LUST see **CONFESSIONS OF A SEX MANIAC** • 1975
DESIGN FOR MURDER (USA) see **TRUNK CRIME** • 1939
DESIGN FOR SCANDAL • 1941 • Taurog Norman • USA
DESIGN FOR SWIMMING • 1949 • Sparling Gordon • DCS • CND
DESIGN IN MOTION / STUDY ONE • Kosower Herbert • ANS • USA
DESIGN OF A HUMAN BEING see **NINGEN MOYO** • 1949
DESIGNED BY FANNY HURST • 1942 • *O'Brien Joseph/ Mead Thomas (P)* • SHT • USA
DESIGNED FOR LIVING • 1956 • Palardy Jean • DCS • CND • FORMES VIVANTES ○ FORMES UTILES
DESIGNED TO COVER • 1971 • Clisby Ted • SHT • UKN
DESIGNING WOMAN • 1957 • Minnelli Vincente • USA
DESIGNING WOMAN, A • 1916 • *Shay William* • SHT • USA
DESIGNING WOMEN • 1934 • Campbell Ivar • UKN • HOUSE OF CARDS
DESIGNS ON JERRY • 1955 • Hanna William, Barbera Joseph • ANS • USA
DESINHERITED SON'S LOYALTY, A • 1909 • *Bison* • USA
DESIR 22 see **JEUNE FILLE ET UN MILLION,UNE** • 1932
DESIR ET LA VOLUPTE, LE • 1972 • Saint-Clair Julien • FRN
DESIR ET L'AMOUR, LE • 1951 • Decoin Henri • FRN, SPN
DESIR MENE LES HOMMES, LE see **AMOUR MENE LES HOMMES, L'** • 1957
DESIRABLE • 1934 • Mayo Archie • USA
DESIRABLE ET LE SUBLIME, LE • 1970 • Benazeraf Jose • FRN
DESIRABLE WOMAN see **WOMAN ON THE BEACH, THE** • 1946
DESIRADE, LA • 1968 • Cuniot Alain • FRN
DESIRE • 1920 • Hall George Edwardes • UKN • MAGIC SKIN, THE
DESIRE • 1923 • Lee Rowland V. • USA
DESIRE • 1936 • Borzage Frank • USA
DESIRE • 1937 • Guitry Sacha • FRN
DESIRE • 1983 • Romero Eddie • PHL
DESIRE see **ABWEGE** • 1928
DESIRE see **BEGAR** • 1946
DESIRE see **YOKUBO** • 1952
DESIRE see **TOUHA** • 1958
DESIRE see **YOKU** • 1958
DESIRE see **MIDARERU** • 1964
DESIRE see **VAASNA** • 1968
DESIRE see **SHAWQ** • 1976
DESIRE see **DESIDERIO** • 1984
DESIRE IN A PUBLIC DUMP • 1958 • *Pike Robert (P)* • SHT • USA
DESIRE IN THE DUST • 1960 • Claxton William F. • USA
DESIRE ME • 1947 • Cukor George (U/c), Leroy Mervyn (U/c), Conway Jack (U/c) • USA • WOMAN OF MY OWN, A
DESIRE OF NIGHT see **AIYOKU NO YORU** • 1930
DESIRE OF THE MOTH, THE • 1917 • Julian Rupert • USA
DESIRE TAKES THE MEN see **AMOUR MENE LES HOMMES, L'** • 1957
DESIRE, THE INTERIOR LIFE see **DESIDERIA, LA VITA INTERIORE** • 1980
DESIRE UNDER THE ELMS • 1958 • Mann Delbert • USA
DESIRE UNDER THE PALMS • 1969 • Sarno Joe • USA
DESIRED see **FOIRE AUX FEMMES, LA** • 1955
DESIRED WOMAN, THE • 1918 • Scardon Paul • USA
DESIRED WOMAN, THE • 1927 • Curtiz Michael • USA • OUTPOST, THE
DESIREE • 1954 • Koster Henry • USA
DESIRELLA • 1970 • Dague Jean-Claude • FRN • SEXTROVERT, THE (UKN)
DESIRES see **YOKUBO** • 1952
DESIRES CONCEIVED see **DESEOS CONCEBIDOS, LOS** • 1982
DESIRES OF A NAUGHTY NYMPHO see **JACK 'N' JILL 2** • 1981
DESIRES (USA) see **LETZTE REZEPT, DAS** • 1952
DESIRES WITHIN YOUNG GIRLS • 1977 • Karson Ramsay • USA
DESIRING GIULIA see **DESIDERANDO GIULIA** • 1987
DESIRS ET PERVERSIONS • 1976 • Rollin Jean • FRN
DESISTFILM • 1954 • Brakhage Stan • SHT • USA

DESK SET, THE • 1957 • Lang Walter • USA • HIS OTHER WOMAN (UKN)
DESNA, THE see **ZACHAROVANNAYA DESNA** • 1965
DESNUDA INQUIETUD • 1977 • Iglesias Miguel • SPN
DESNUDARSE O MORIR • 1966 • Morayta Miguel • MXC
DESNUDATE LUCRECIA • 1957 • Demicheli Tulio • MXC
DESNUDOS ARTISTICOS see **AMOR DE ADOLESCENTE** • 1963
DESOBEISSANCE, LA • 1981 • Lado Aldo • FRN, ITL
DESOEUVRES, LES • 1959 • Bail Rene • CND
DESOLATION ANGELS • 1983 • Fitchett Christopher • ASL
DESORDRE • 1927 • Derain Lucy • SHT • FRN
DESORDRE • 1949 • Baratier Jacques • FRN • DISORDER
DESORDRE • 1987 • Assayas Olivier • FRN
DESORDRE A VINGT ANS, LE • 1967 • Baratier Jacques • DOC • FRN • DISORDER IS TWENTY YEARS OLD ○ EDEN MISERIA
DESORDRE ET GENIE see **KEAN** • 1923
DESORDRE ET LA NUIT, LE • 1958 • Grangier Gilles • FRN • NIGHT AFFAIR (USA)
DESORDRE, LE (FRN) see **DISORDINE, IL** • 1962
DESPAIR • 1915 • Haydon J. Charles • USA
DESPAIR see **EINE REISE IN LICHTS** • 1978
DESPEDIDA DE CASADA • 1966 • de Orduna Juan • MXC, SPN
DESPEDIDA DE CASADOS • 1975 • Delgado Luis Maria • SPN
DESPEDIDA DE SOLTERA • 1965 • Soler Julian • MXC
DESPEDIDA DE SOLTERO • 1958 • Martin Eugenio • SPN
DESPEGUE A LAS 18.00 • 1969 • Alvarez Santiago • DOC • CUB • START AT THE 18.00
DESPENSA VIVA, UMA • 1942 • Coelho Jose Adolfo • SHT • PRT
DESPERACJA • 1989 • Kuzminski Zbigniew • PLN • IN DESPERATION
DESPERADO • 1987 • Vogel Virgil W. • TVM • USA
DESPERADO, EL • 1967 • Rossetti Franco • SPN, ITL • DIRTY OUTLAWS, THE (USA) ○ DESESPERADO, EL (SPN)
DESPERADO, LE • 1909 • Durand Jean • FRN
DESPERADO, THE • 1910 • *Anderson Broncho Billy* • USA
DESPERADO, THE • 1912 • *Pathe* • USA
DESPERADO, THE • 1914 • *Broncho* • USA
DESPERADO, THE • 1916 • Julian Rupert • SHT • USA
DESPERADO, THE • 1954 • Carr Thomas • USA
DESPERADO CITY • 1981 • Glowna Vadim • FRG
DESPERADO OUTPOST see **DOKURITSU GURENTAI NISHI-E** • 1960
DESPERADO TRAIL, THE (UKN) see **WINNETOU III** • 1965
DESPERADOES, THE • 1943 • Vidor Charles • USA
DESPERADOES ARE IN TOWN, THE see **DESPERADOS ARE IN TOWN, THE** • 1956
DESPERADOES OF DODGE CITY • 1948 • Ford Philip • USA
DESPERADOES OF THE WEST • 1950 • Brannon Fred C. • SRL • USA
DESPERADOES OUTPOST • 1952 • Ford Philip • USA
DESPERADOS, THE • 1969 • Levin Henry • USA
DESPERADOS ARE IN TOWN, THE • 1956 • Neumann Kurt • USA • DESPERADOES ARE IN TOWN, THE
DESPERADO'S TRAIL • 1966 • *Barker Lex* • FRG
DESPERATE • 1947 • Mann Anthony • USA
DESPERATE • 1987 • Markle Peter • TVM • USA
DESPERATE ADVENTURE, A • 1924 • McGowan J. P. • USA
DESPERATE ADVENTURE, A • 1938 • Auer John H. • USA • IT HAPPENED IN PARIS (UKN)
DESPERATE CARGO • 1941 • Beaudine William • USA
DESPERATE CHANCE • 1926 • McGowan J. P. • USA
DESPERATE CHANCE, A • 1908 • *World* • USA
DESPERATE CHANCE, A • 1913 • *Hollister Alice* • USA
DESPERATE CHANCE, A • 1914 • *Huff Justina* • USA
DESPERATE CHANCE, A (UKN) see **DESPERATE CHANCE FOR ELLERY QUEEN** • 1942
DESPERATE CHANCE, THE • 1916 • Fahrney Milton • USA
DESPERATE CHANCE FOR ELLERY QUEEN • 1942 • Hogan James P. • USA • DESPERATE CHANCE, A (UKN)
DESPERATE CHARACTER, A • 1908 • *Cresent Film* • USA
DESPERATE CHARACTERS • 1971 • Gilroy Frank D. • USA • DESPERATE ENCOUNTERS
DESPERATE CHASE, THE • 1974 • Kao Pao Shu • HKG • BLOOD OF THE DRAGON
DESPERATE CONDITION OF MR. BOGGS, THE • 1913 • Edwin Walter • USA
DESPERATE COURAGE • 1928 • Thorpe Richard • USA
DESPERATE CRIME, A see **INCENDIARES, LES** • 1906
DESPERATE DECISION (USA) see **JEUNE FOLLE, LA** • 1952
DESPERATE DESMOND ABDUCTS ROSAMUND • 1911 • *Keller Betsy* • USA
DESPERATE DESMOND ALMOSTS SUCCEEDS • 1911 • Ricketts Thomas • USA
DESPERATE DESMOND AT THE CANNON'S MOUTH • 1912 • *Keller Betsy* • USA
DESPERATE DESMOND FAILS • 1912 • *Nestor* • USA
DESPERATE DESMOND FOILED BY CLAUDE ECLAIRE • 1911 • *Keller Betsy* • USA
DESPERATE DESMOND ON THE TRAIL AGAIN • 1912 • *Nestor* • USA
DESPERATE DESMOND PURSUED BY CLAUDE ECLAIRE • 1911 • *Keller Betsy* • USA
DESPERATE DUD, THE PLUMBER • 1915 • *Kalem* • USA
DESPERATE DUEL, A • 1916 • *Hamilton Lloyd V.* • SHT • USA
DESPERATE ENCOUNTERS see **DESPERATE CHARACTERS** • 1971
DESPERATE FOOTPADS • 1907 • Haggar William • UKN
DESPERATE GAME, THE • 1926 • Franz Joseph J. • USA
DESPERATE HERO, A • 1914 • *Ab* • USA
DESPERATE HERO, THE • 1920 • Ruggles Wesley • USA
DESPERATE HOODLUM see **YOKOGAMI-YABURINO ZENKAMONO** • 1968
DESPERATE HOURS, THE • 1955 • Wyler William • USA
DESPERATE HOURS, THE • 1990 • Cimino Michael • USA
DESPERATE INTRUDER • 1983 • Havinga Nick • TVM • USA
DESPERATE JOURNEY • 1942 • Walsh Raoul • USA
DESPERATE LEAP, A • 1915 • McGowan J. P. • USA
DESPERATE LIVES • 1982 • Lewis Robert • TVM • USA
DESPERATE LIVING • 1977 • Waters John* • USA
DESPERATE LOVER, A • 1912 • Nicholls George, Sennett Mack (Spv) • USA

DESPERATE MAN, THE • 1959 • Maxwell Peter • UKN
DESPERATE MEN, THE see **CAT AND MOUSE** • 1958
DESPERATE MEN (UKN) see **EL DORADO PASS** • 1948
DESPERATE MILES, THE • 1975 • Haller Daniel • TVM • USA
DESPERATE MISSION • 1971 • Bellamy Earl • TVM • USA • MURIETTA
DESPERATE MISSION see **AGENTE Z55, MISSIONE DISPERATA** • 1965
DESPERATE MOMENT • 1953 • Bennett Compton • UKN
DESPERATE MOMENT, A • 1926 • Dawn Jack • USA
DESPERATE ODDS • 1925 • Carpenter Horace B. • USA
DESPERATE ONES, THE (USA) see **MAS ALLA DE LAS MONTANAS** • 1967
DESPERATE POACHING AFFRAY • 1903 • Haggar William • UKN
DESPERATE REMEDY, A • 1910 • *Nestor* • USA
DESPERATE REMEDY, A • 1916 • Bartlett Charles • SHT • USA
DESPERATE ROAD, THE see **AMANSIZ OUL** • 1985
DESPERATE SEARCH • 1952 • Lewis Joseph H. • USA
DESPERATE SIEGE see **RAWHIDE** • 1951
DESPERATE STRATAGEM, A • 1914 • Martinek H. O. • UKN
DESPERATE TRAILS • 1921 • Ford John • USA • CHRISTMAS EVE AT PILOT BUTTE
DESPERATE TRAILS • 1939 • Ray Albert • USA
DESPERATE VOYAGE • 1980 • O'Herlihy Michael • TVM • USA
DESPERATE WOMAN, A see **LADIES AT PLAY** • 1926
DESPERATE YOUTH • 1921 • Harris Harry B. • USA
DESPERATELY SEEKING SUSAN • 1985 • Seidelman Susan • USA
DESPERATION see **YABURE KABURE** • 1961
DESPERATION see **ZUIHOUDE FENGKUANG** • 1987
DESPERATION (USA) see **DRIVEN** • 1916
DESPERTAR DA REDENTORA, O • 1942 • Mauro-Humberto • SHT • BRZ
DESPERTO SU CORAZON • 1949 • Mihura Jeronimo • SPN
DESPIADADOS, LOS (SPN) see **CRUDELI, I** • 1966
DESPICABLE ONES, THE see **CANALLAS, LOS** • 1968
DESPIERTA, CHICA • 1971 • Pena Raul • SPN
DESPISED AND REJECTED • 1914 • Wilson Frank? • UKN
DESPITE EVERYTHING see **TROTZ ALLEDEM** • 1972
DESPITE EVERYTHING see **HERSEYE RAGMEN** • 1987
DESPOILER, THE • 1916 • *Washburn Bryant* • SHT • USA
DESPOT, THE see **SATRAPIS, O** • 1968
DESPOTIC FIANCE, THE see **TYRANNISKE FASTMANNEN, DEN** • 1912
DESPUES DE.. • 1981 • Bartolome Cecilia, Bartolome Jose Juan • DOC • SPN • AFTER
DESPUES DE LA TORMENTA • 1955 • Gavaldon Roberto • MXC
DESPUES DE LA TORMENTA • 1988 • Bauer Tristan • ARG • AFTER THE STORM
DESPUES DE LOS NUEVE MESES • 1970 • Ozores Mariano • SPN
DESPUES DEL DILUVIO • 1968 • Esteva Jacinto • SPN • AFTER THE FLOOD ○ AFTER THE DELUGE
DESPUES DEL GRAN ROBO • 1964 • Iglesias Miguel • SPN
DESPUES DEL SILENCIO • 1956 • Demare Lucas • ARG
DESQUITE, EL • 1945 • Ratti Roberto • MXC
DESQUITE, EL • 1982 • Desanzo Juan Carlos • ARG • RETALIATION, THE
DESSA FANTASTISKA SMALANNINGAR MED SINA FINURLIGA MASKINER • 1966 • *Frisk Ragnar (Edt)* • SWD
DESSINATEUR CHAMBERLAIN • 1896 • Melies Georges • FRN • LIGHTNING SKETCH: CHAMBERLAIN, A
DESSINATEUR EXPRESS • 1896 • Melies Georges • FRN • DESSINATEUR EXPRESS (M. THIERS) ○ LIGHTNING SKETCH (MR. THIERS)
DESSINATEUR EXPRESS (M. THIERS) see **DESSINATEUR EXPRESS** • 1896
DESSINATEUR (REINE VICTORIA) • 1896 • Melies Georges • FRN • LIGHTNING SKETCH (H.M. QUEEN VICTORIA)
DESSINATEUR VON BISMARCK • 1896 • Melies Georges • FRN • LIGHTNING SKETCH (VON BISMARCK), A
DESSINS ET MERVEILLES • 1961 • Kaplan Nelly • SHT • FRN • DRAWINGS AND WONDERS
DESSINS S'ANIMENT • 1952 • Boucquey Omer • FRN
DESSOUS DE PARIS, LES • 1906 • Nonguet Lucien, Heuze Andre • FRN
DESSOUS DE RAMATUELLE, LES see **BRANCHES A SAINT-TROPEZ, LES** • 1983
DESSOUS DES CARTES, LE • 1947 • Cayatte Andre • FRN • ASSASSIN, L'
DESTERRADO, O • 1949 • Guimaraes Manuel • SHT • PRT
DESTIN see **MOGHO DAKAN** • 1976
DESTIN DE JULIETTE, LE • 1982 • Issermann Aline • FRN
DESTIN DES MERES, LE • 1911 • Feuillade Louis • FRN
DESTIN EXECRABLE DE GUILLEMETTE BABIN, LE • 1948 • Radot Guillaume • FRN • EXECRABLE DESTINY OF GUILLEMETTE BABIN, THE
DESTIN FABULEUX DE DESIREÉ CLARY, LE • 1941 • Guitry Sacha, Le Henaff Rene • FRN • MLLE. DESIREE
DESTIN MIRACULEUX DU TIMBRE-POSTE, LE • 1950 • Tavano Fred • SHT • FRN
DESTIN S'AMUSE, LE • 1946 • Reinert Emile Edwin • FRN • COUP DE MAITRE
DESTIN TRAGIQUE • 1913 • Jasset Victorin • FRN
DESTINATION 60,000 • 1957 • Waggner George • USA
DESTINATION AMERICA • 1987 • Allen Corey • TVM • USA
DESTINATION BIG HOUSE • 1950 • Blair George • USA
DESTINATION DANGER (UKN) see **EYES OF THE JUNGLE** • 1953
DESTINATION DEATH • 1956 • Tully Montgomery • UKN
DESTINATION DEATH see **TRANSPORT, DER** • 1961
DESTINATION FURY (USA) see **MANI IN ALTO** • 1961
DESTINATION GOBI • 1953 • Wise Robert • USA • GOBI OUTPOST ○ SIXTY SADDLES FOR GOBI
DESTINATION HOSPITALITE • 1975 • Cardinal Roger • DCS • CND
DESTINATION INNER SPACE • 1966 • Lyon Francis D. • USA • TERROR OF THE DEEP
DESTINATION MAGOO • 1954 • Burness Pete • ANS • USA
DESTINATION MARS see **MISSION MARS** • 1968

DESTINATION MEATBALLS • 1951 • Lantz Walter • ANS • USA
DESTINATION MIAMI • 1966 • *Gora Claudio* • ITL
DESTINATION MILAN • 1954 • Gilling John (c/d)
DESTINATION MOON • 1950 • Pichel Irving • USA
DESTINATION MOON see **OBJECTIVE MOON** • 1962
DESTINATION MOONBASE ALPHA • 1975 • Anderson Gerry • MTV • UKN
DESTINATION MOONBASE ALPHA • 1979 • Clegg Tom • MTV • UKN • SPACE 1999: DESTINATION MOONBASE ALPHA
DESTINATION MURDER • 1950 • Cahn Edward L. • USA
DESTINATION NIGHTMARE • 1958 • Landres Paul • MTV • USA
DESTINATION OOTI see **OOTIVARAI URAVU** • 1967
DESTINATION PARADISE • 1971 • Lemke Klaus • FRG
DESTINATION: PARADISE see **PAKKETUR TIL PARADIS** • 1981
DESTINATION RIO see **VI FLYGER PA RIO** • 1949
DESTINATION RIVIERE LA GRANDE • 1982 • Labrecque Jean-Claude • CND
DESTINATION SATURN • 1939 • Beebe Ford, Goodkind Saul • USA
DESTINATION SPRING see **BAHARON KI MANZIL** • 1968
DESTINATION TOKYO • 1943 • Daves Delmer • USA
DESTINATION UNKNOWN • 1933 • Garnett Tay • USA
DESTINATION UNKNOWN • 1942 • Taylor Ray • USA
DESTINATION VIETNAM • 1968 • Avellana Lamberto V. • PHL
DESTINATIONS see **YEH WOH MANZIL TO NAHIN** • 1987
DESTINATIONS: UNKNOWN • 1982 • Murray Russell • UKN
DESTINAZIONE MARCIAPIEDE (ITL) see **VOYAGE DU PERE, LE** • 1966
DESTINAZIONE PIOVAROLO • 1955 • Paolella Domenico • ITL
DESTINAZIONE ROMA • 1977 • Williamson Fred • ITL, USA • MR. MEAN (USA) ○ TRACER, THE
DESTINAZIONE SANREMO • 1959 • Paolella Domenico • ITL
DESTINEE • 1920 • Linke Edmund • FRG
DESTINEE • 1923 • du Plessis Armand • FRN
DESTINEE • 1926 • Roussell Henry • FRN
DESTINEES • 1953 • Pagliero Marcello, Delannoy Jean, Christian-Jaque • FRN, ITL • DESTINI DI DONNE (ITL) ○ DAUGHTERS OF DESTINY (USA) ○ LOVE, SOLDIERS AND WOMEN
DESTINI DI DONNE (ITL) see **DESTINEES** • 1953
DESTINIES FULFILLED • 1914 • Johnston Lorimer • USA
DESTINIES OF THE GOOD SOLDIER SCHWEIK, THE • 1987 • Latal Stanislav • ANM • CZC
DESTINIES OF WOMEN see **NAISKOHTALOITA** • 1947
DESTINO • 1916 • Serena Gustavo • ITL
DESTINO • 1951 • Di Gianni Enzo • ITL
DESTINO, IL • 1938 • Mattoli Mario • ITL
DESTINO: BARAJAS • 1963 • Blasco Ricardo • SPN
DESTINO D'AMORE • 1943 • Emmer Luciano, Gras Enrico • ITL
DESTINO DE TRES VIDAS see **BAJO EL MANTO DE LA NOCHE** • 1962
DESTINO DI DONNA • 1937 • Brignone Guido • ITL
DESTINO E IL TIMONIERE, IL • 1919 • Gallone Carmine • ITL
DESTINO EM APUROS, O • 1953 • Remani Ernesto • BRZ • DESTINY IN TROUBLE (USA)
DESTINO: ESTAMBUL 68 • 1967 • Iglesias Miguel • SPN
DESTINO IN TASCA, IL • 1938 • Righelli Gennaro • ITL • FORTUNA IN TASCA, LA
DESTINO: LA MUERTE • 1972 • *Filmadora Chapultepec* • MXC
DESTINO MARCA A HORA, O • 1970 • Campos Henrique • PRT
DESTINO PARA DOS • 1968 • Dubois Albert • ARG • DESTINY FOR TWO
DESTINO SE DISCULPA, EL • 1944 • Saenz De Heredia Jose Luis • SPN
DESTINS • 1946 • Pottier Richard • FRN
DESTINS see **SYLVIE DESTIN** • 1927
DESTINY • 1909 • *Imp* • USA
DESTINY • 1915 • Carewe Edwin • USA • SOUL OF A WOMAN, THE
DESTINY • 1916 • Beaumont Harry? • USA
DESTINY • 1919 • Sturgeon Rollin S. • USA
DESTINY • 1944 • Le Borg Reginald, Duvivier Julien • USA • FUGITIVE, THE
DESTINY • 1983 • Korabov Nicolai • BUL
DESTINY see **WOMAN OF PARIS, A** • 1923
DESTINY see **WOLF MAN, THE** • 1941
DESTINY see **SON OF DRACULA** • 1943
DESTINY see **HOUSE OF FRANKENSTEIN** • 1945
DESTINY see **CHARKH-E-BAZIGAR** • 1968
DESTINY see **SUDBA** • 1978
DESTINY see **SUDBINE** • 1979
DESTINY DECIDES • 1915 • *Rea Isabel* • USA
DESTINY FOR TWO see **DESTINO PARA DOS** • 1968
DESTINY IN TROUBLE (USA) see **DESTINO EM APUROS, O** • 1953
DESTINY IS CHANGELESS • 1911 • *Vitagraph* • USA
DESTINY OF A CREDENTIAL AGENT see **ONMITSU SHICHISOKI** • 1958
DESTINY OF A MAN see **SUDBA CHELOVEKA** • 1959
DESTINY OF A SPY • 1969 • Sagal Boris • TVM • USA • GAUNT WOMAN, THE
DESTINY OF RUSSIA • 1927 • Rymowicz K. S. • USS
DESTINY OF THE SEA • 1913 • *Selig* • USA
DESTINY TO ORDER • 1988 • Purdy Jim • CND
DESTINY (USA) see **MUDE TOD, DER** • 1921
DESTINY'S BOOMERANG • 1916 • *Montague Frederick* • SHT • USA
DESTINY'S ISLE • 1922 • Earle William P. S. • USA
DESTINY'S NIGHT • 1914 • *Broncho* • USA
DESTINY'S SKEIN • 1915 • Terwilliger George W. • USA
DESTINY'S SON see **KIRU** • 1962
DESTINY'S TOY • 1916 • O'Brien John B. • USA
DESTINY'S TRUMP CARD • 1915 • Garwood William • USA
DESTROY ALL MONSTERS (USA) see **KAIJU SOSHINGEKI** • 1968
DESTROY ALL PLANETS (USA) see **GAMERA TAI UCHI KAIJU BAIRUSU** • 1968
DESTROY, SHE SAID see **DETRUIRE, DIT-ELLE** • 1969
DESTROYED CITY, THE see **CITE FOUDROYEE, LA** • 1923
DESTROYER • 1943 • Seiter William A., Enright Ray (U/c) • USA
DESTROYER • 1988 • Kirk Robert • USA • SHADOW OF DEATH ○ EDISON EFFECT
DESTROYER see **DESTROYERS, THE** • 1985
DESTROYER, THE • 1915 • *Imp* • USA
DESTROYER, THE • 1915 • Vignola Robert G. • *Kalem* • USA
DESTROYER, THE • 1915 • Windom Lawrence C. • *Essanay* • USA
DESTROYER YUKIKAZE see **KUCHIKUKAN YUKIKAZE** • 1964
DESTROYERS, THE • 1916 • Ince Ralph • USA
DESTROYERS, THE • 1985 • Santiago Cirio H. • USA • DEVASTATOR, THE ○ DESTROYER
DESTROYING ANGEL, THE • 1915 • Ridgely Richard • USA
DESTROYING ANGEL, THE • 1923 • Van Dyke W. S. • USA
DESTRUCTION • 1915 • Davis Will S. • USA
DESTRUCTION FORCE see **DIRTY GANG**
DESTRUCTION INC. • 1942 • Sparber I. • ANS • USA
DESTRUCTION OF HERCULANEUM, THE see **ANNO 79, LA DISTRUZIONE DI ERCOLANO** • 1963
DESTRUCTION OF ST. PATRICK'S COLLEGE 1971 • 1971 • Buesst Nigel • DOC • ASL
DESTRUCTION OF THE H.M.A.S. AUSTRALIA • 1924 • ASL
DESTRUCTION OF THE SPACE FLEET, THE see **UCHUTEI TO JINKO EISEN NO GEKITOTSU** • 1958
DESTRUCTORS, THE • 1968 • Lyon Francis D. • USA
DESTRUCTORS, THE (USA) see **MARSEILLE CONTRACT, THE** • 1974
DESTRY • 1954 • Marshall George • USA
DESTRY OF DEATH VALLEY see **RIDER OF DEATH VALLEY, THE** • 1932
DESTRY RIDES AGAIN • 1932 • Stoloff Ben, James Alan • USA
DESTRY RIDES AGAIN • 1939 • Marshall George • USA
DESYATY SHAG • 1967 • Ivchenko Viktor • USS • TENTH STEP, THE
DESZCZOWY LUPIEC • 1958 • Buczkowski Leonard • PLN • RAINY JULY, A (USA)
DET AR ALDRIG FOR SENT • 1956 • Boman Barbro • SWD • IT'S NEVER TOO LATE
DET AR HOS MIG HAN HAR VARIT • 1963 • Mattsson Arne • SWD • YES, HE HAS BEEN WITH ME
DET AR MIN MODELL • 1946 • Molander Gustaf • SWD • IT'S MY MODEL
DET AR MIN MUSIK • 1942 • Larsson Borje • SWD • IT IS MY MUSIC
DET BRINNER EN ELD • 1943 • Molander Gustaf • SWD • THERE BURNED A FLAME
DET ENDER MED BRYLLUP • 1943 • Lauritzen Lau Jr. • DNM
DET ER IKKE APPELSINER -DET ER HESTE • 1967 • Langberg Ebbe • DNM • IT IS NOT ORANGES -BUT HORSES
DET ER NAT MED FRU KNUDSEN • 1971 • Ornbak Henning • DNM • IT'S ALL UP WITH AUNTIE
DET ER SA SYND FOR FARMAND • 1968 • Langberg Ebbe • DNM • WHAT A PITY ABOUT DADDY
DET FINNS INGA GUDAR PA JORDEN • 1917 • Klercker Georg • SWD • THERE ARE NO GODS ON EARTH
DET GAELDER OS ALLE! • 1949 • O'Fredericks Alice • DNM • IT CONCERNS US ALL
DET HANDER I NATT see **ALDRIG I LIVET** • 1957
DET KOM EN GAST • 1947 • Mattsson Arne • SWD • GUEST CAME, A ○ UNEXPECTED VISITOR, THE
DET REGNAR PA VAR KARLEK • 1946 • Bergman Ingmar • SWD • MAN WITH AN UMBRELLA (UKN) ○ IT RAINS ON OUR LOVE (USA)
DET SVANGER PA SLOTTET • 1959 • Kjellin Alf • SWD • SWINGING AT THE CASTLE
DET VAR EN GANG.. • 1945 • Bornebusch Arne • SWD • ONCE UPON A TIME
DET VAR EN GANG EN SJOMAN • 1951 • Frisk Ragnar • SWD • ONCE UPON A TIME A SAILOR
DET VAR EN LORDAG AFTEN • 1968 • Balling Erik • DNM • ONCE UPON A SATURDAY NIGHT ○ ONE SATURDAY EVENING..
DET VAR I MAJ • 1915 • Sjostrom Victor • SWD • IT WAS IN MAY
DETACHABLE MAN, THE • 1910 • *Pathe* • USA
DETAILS OF A DUEL see **TECNICAS DE DUELO** • 1988
DETECKTERS • 1916 • *Cooper Claude* • USA
DETECTIVE • 1930 • Lantz Walter, Nolan William • ANS • USA
DETECTIVE • 1985 • Godard Jean-Luc • FRN
DETECTIVE, A see **DETECTIVE, UN** • 1969
DETECTIVE, THE • 1917 • *Sparkle* • SHT • USA
DETECTIVE, THE • 1919 • Kenton Erle C. • SHT • USA
DETECTIVE, THE • 1968 • Douglas Gordon • USA
DETECTIVE, THE (USA) see **FATHER BROWN** • 1954
DETECTIVE, UN • 1969 • Guerrieri Romolo • ITL • DETECTIVE BELLI (USA) ○ DETECTIVE, A ○ RING OF DEATH
DETECTIVE AND MATCHMAKER • 1914 • Davis Ulysses • USA
DETECTIVE AND THE JEWEL TRICK, THE • 1911 • Fitzhamon Lewin • UKN
DETECTIVE BELLI (USA) see **DETECTIVE, UN** • 1969
DETECTIVE BLINN • 1915 • Otto Henry • USA
"DETECTIVE CLIVE", BART. (UKN) see **SCOTLAND YARD** • 1930
DETECTIVE CON FALDAS • 1961 • Nunez Ricardo • SPN
DETECTIVE CRAIG'S COUP • 1914 • Mackenzie Donald • USA
DETECTIVE DAN CUPID • 1914 • *Nestor* • USA
DETECTIVE DARING AND THE THAMES COINERS • 1914 • Northcote Sidney • UKN
DETECTIVE DERVIEUX, LE • 1912-13 • Feuillade Louis • SER • FRN
DETECTIVE DOROTHY • 1912 • *Osman Sadie* • USA
DETECTIVE DOT • 1913 • Hotaling Arthur D. • USA
DETECTIVE FERRIS • 1912 • Southwell Gilbert • UKN
DETECTIVE FINN AND THE FOREIGN SPIES • 1914 • Finn Arthur • UKN • FOREIGN SPIES, THE (USA)
DETECTIVE FINN, OR, IN THE HEART OF LONDON • 1914 • Weston Charles • UKN • SOCIETY DETECTIVE
DETECTIVE FOR A DAY, A • 1912 • Wilson Frank? • UKN
DETECTIVE GERONIMO see **POLICE CONNECTION, THE** • 1976
DETECTIVE IN PERIL, A • 1910 • Fitzhamon Lewin • UKN
DETECTIVE KITTY O'DAY • 1944 • Beaudine William • USA
DETECTIVE LLOYD • 1932 • Taylor Ray • SRL • USA • GREEN SPOT MYSTERY, THE
DETECTIVE LLOYD (USA) see **LLOYD OF THE C.I.D.** • 1931
DETECTIVE MORGAN AND A MAN OF MYSTERY see **MORGAN KEIBU TO NAZO NO OTOKO** • 1961
DETECTIVE SCHOOL DROPOUTS see **PRIVATE DETECTIVE** • 1986
DETECTIVE SHARP AND THE STOLEN MINIATURES • 1912 • Calvert Charles? • UKN
DETECTIVE SHORT • 1914 • *Lubin* • USA
DETECTIVE STORY • 1951 • Wyler William • USA
DETECTIVE STORY see **KEIJI MONOGATARI** • 1982
DETECTIVE SWIFT • 1914 • Gasnier Louis J., Mackenzie Donald • USA
DETECTIVE TOM HOWARD OF THE SUICIDE SQUAD • 1933 • Cline Eddie • SHT • USA
DETECTIVES • 1928 • Franklin Chester M. • USA
DETECTIVE'S CONSCIENCE, THE • 1912 • *Fielding Romaine* • USA
DETECTIVE'S DANGER • 1917 • Davis James • USA
DETECTIVE'S DESPERATE CHANCE, THE • 1912 • *Pathe* • USA
DETECTIVE'S DOG, THE • 1910 • Fitzhamon Lewin? • UKN
DETECTIVE'S DOG, THE • 1912 • *Karr Darwin* • USA
DETECTIVE'S DREAM • 1910 • *Pathe* • FRN
DETECTIVES DU DIMANCHE, LES • 1952 • Orval Claude • FRN
DETECTIVES O LADRONES • 1966 • Morayta Miguel • MXC • DOS AGENTES INOCENTES
DETECTIVES OF THE ITALIAN BUREAU, THE • 1909 • *Kalem* • USA
DETECTIVE'S RUSE, THE • 1908 • Fitzhamon Lewin • UKN
DETECTIVE'S SANTA CLAUS, THE • 1913 • *Eclair* • USA
DETECTIVE'S SISTER, THE • 1914 • Melford George • USA
DETECTIVE'S STRATAGEM, THE • 1913 • Cabanne W. Christy • USA
DETECTIVE'S STRATEGY, A • 1912 • *Clary Charles* • USA
DETECTIVE'S TRAP, THE • 1913 • *Kalem* • USA
DETECTIVES WANTED • 1929 • Taurog Norman • SHT • USA
DETEKTIV DES KAISERS, DER • 1930 • Boese Carl • FRG
DETEKTIV-DUELL, EIN • 1917 • Alexander Georg • FRG
DETEKTIVDUELL, DAS • 1920 • Arnheim Valy • FRG • HARRY HILL CONTRA SHERLOCK HOLMES
DETEKTIVENS BARNEPIGE • 1914 • Davidsen Hjalmar • DNM
DETENTION GIRLS • 1969 • *Sam Lake Production* • USA
DETENUTO IN ATTESA DI GIUDIZIO • 1971 • Loy Nanni • ITL • WHY?
DETERMINATION • 1920 • Stoll Frederick F. • USA
DETERMINATION • 1922 • Levering Joseph • USA
DETERMINATION see **AZIMA, EL** • 1939
DETERMINATION (UKN) see **FINAL EDITION, THE** • 1932
DETERMINATIONS • 1988 • Hockenhull Oliver • DOC • CND
DETERMINES A VAINCRE • 1969 • Ivens Joris • FRN
DETI BURI • 1926 • Ermler Friedrich, Johanson Eduard • USS • CHILDREN OF THE STORM
DETI DON QUIXOTE • 1966 • Karelov Yevgyeni • USS • CHILDREN OF DON QUIXOTE, THE
DETI KAPITANA GRANTA • 1936 • Vainshtok Vladimir • USS • CAPTAIN GRANT'S CHILDREN
DETIK 12 MALAM • 1978 • Sudarmadji S. • MLY
DETOUR • 1945 • Ulmer Edgar G. • USA
DETOUR see **OBJIZDKA** • 1968
DETOUR see **JOURNEY** • 1972
DETOUR, THE • 1979 • Holland Rodney • UKN
DETOURING AMERICA • 1939 • Avery Tex • ANS • USA
DETOURING THRU MAINE • 1950 • Kneitel Seymour • ANS • USA
DETOURNEMENT DE MINEURES • 1959 • Kapps Walter • FRN • PRICE OF FLESH, THE (USA) ○ GIRLS LED ASTRAY
DETRAS DE UN LARGO MURO • 1957 • Demare Lucas • ARG
DETRESSE ET CHARITE see **ANGE DE NOEL, L'** • 1904
DETROIT 9000 • 1973 • Marx Arthur • USA • CALL DETROIT 9000 (UKN) ○ MOTOWN 9000 ○ POLICE CALL 9000
DETRUIRE, DIT-ELLE • 1969 • Duras Marguerite • FRN • DESTROY, SHE SAID
DETRUISEZ-VOUS • 1968 • Bard Serge • FRN
DETSTVO GORKOVO • 1938 • Donskoi Mark • USS • CHILDHOOD OF MAXIM GORKI, THE ○ GORKY'S CHILDHOOD ○ CHILDHOOD OF GORKY
DETSTVO IVANA see **IVANOVO DETSTVO** • 1962
DETTE, LA • 1914 • Burguet Charles • FRN
DETTE, LA • 1922 • Roudes Gaston • FRN
DETTE DE HAINE • 1915 • Pouctal Henri • FRN
DETTE D'HONNEUR, LA • 1912 • Perret Leonce • FRN
DETTE DU SANG, LA • 1923 • Bourgeois Gerard • FRN
DETYRE E POSACINE • Dhamo Kristaq • ALB • SPECIAL DUTY
DEU A LOUCA NO CANGACO • 1969 • Mendes Nelson Teixeira • BRZ • IT'S A MAD CANGACO
DEUCE AND TWO PAIR, THE • 1914 • *Powers* • USA
DEUCE CLASS AWAKES, THE see **HABABAM SINIFI UYANIYOR** • 1977
DEUCE DUNCAN • 1918 • Heffron Thomas N. • USA
DEUCE HIGH • 1926 • Thorpe Richard • USA
DEUCE OF A GIRL, A • 1916 • Collins Edwin J.? • UKN
DEUCE OF SPADES, THE • 1922 • Ray Charles • USA
DEUDA INTERNA, LA • 1987 • Pereira Miguel • ARG, UKN
DEUS E O DIABO NA TERRA DO SOL • 1964 • Rocha Glauber • BRZ • BLACK GOD AND THE WHITE DEVIL, THE ○ BLACK GOD, WHITE DEVIL (UKN) ○ BLACK GOD AND THE BLOND DEVIL, THE
DEUS EX • 1970 • Brakhage Stan • USA
DEUS EX MACHINA • 1971 • Mich Ludo • BLG
DEUS EX MACHINA • 1974 • Eastman Allan • MTV • CND, UKN
DEUS LO VOLT • 1978 • Monheim Luc • BLG • DIEU LE VENT
DEUS OS FEZ • 1950 • Garcia Fernando • SHT • PRT
DEUS, PATRIA, AUTORIDADE • 1976 • Simoes Rui • PRT • GOD, FATHERLAND AND AUTHORITY ○ GOD, HOME, AUTHORITY
DEUSA NEGRA, A • 1980 • Balogun Ola • BRZ • BLACK GODDESS
DEUSES E OS MORTOS, OS • 1970 • Guerra Ruy • BRZ • OF GODS AND THE UNDEAD (USA) ○ GODS AND THE DEAD, THE
DEUTSCHE FRAUEN -DEUTSCHE TREUE • 1928 • Neff Wolfgang • FRG
DEUTSCHE HELDEN IN SCHWERER ZEIT • 1924 • Blachnitzky Curt, Porten Franz • FRG

DEUTSCHE HERZEN AM DEUTSCHEN RHEIN • 1926 • Sauer Fred • FRG
DEUTSCHE LIED, DAS • 1928 • Pindl Karl • FRG
DEUTSCHE MUTTERHERZ, DAS • 1926 • von Bolvary Geza • FRG
DEUTSCHE PANZER • 1940 • Ruttmann Walter • FRG
DEUTSCHE WAFFENSCHMIEDE, DIE • 1940 • Ruttmann Walter • FRG • WAFFENKAMMERN DEUTSCHLAND
DEUTSCHER RUNDFUNK • 1928 • Ruttmann Walter • FRG
DEUTSCHLAND, BLEICHE MUTTER • 1980 • Sanders Helma • FRG • GERMANY, PALE MOTHER
DEUTSCHLAND, DEINE STERNCHEN see **IHRE HAUT ZU MARKTE TRAGEN, DIE** • 1962
DEUTSCHLAND ERWACHE! • 1966 • Leiser Erwin • SWT
DEUTSCHLAND IM HERBST • 1978 • Schlondorff Volker, Brustellin Alf, Fassbinder R. W., Kluge Alexander, Mainka Maximilliane, Reitz Edgar, Rupe Katya, Cloos Hans Peter, Sinkel Bernard • FRG • GERMANY IN AUTUMN
DEUTSCHMEISTER, DIE • 1955 • Marischka Ernst • AUS
DEUX • 1989 • Zidi Claude • FRN
DEUX AFFREUX SUR LE SABLE • 1979 • Gessner Nicolas • FRN, CND • IT RAINED ALL DAY THE NIGHT I LEFT ○ DEUX REQUINS SUR LE SABLE
DEUX AMIS • 1946 • Kirsanoff Dimitri • SHT • FRN
DEUX AMOURS • 1948 • Pottier Richard • FRN
DEUX AMOURS, LES • 1918 • Burguet Charles • FRN
DEUX ANGLAISES, LES see **DEUX ANGLAISES ET LE CONTINENT, LES** • 1971
DEUX ANGLAISES ET LE CONTINENT, LES • 1971 • Truffaut Francois • FRN • TWO ENGLISH GIRLS (USA) ○ DEUX ANGLAISES, LES ○ ANNE AND MURIEL
DEUX ANS ET PLUS • 1970 • Dufaux Georges, Theriens G. • DCS • CND
DEUX AVEUGLES, LES • 1900 • Melies Georges • FRN • TWO BLIND MEN, THE (USA)
DEUX BAISERS, LES • 1920 • Bergerat Theo • FRN
DEUX BALLES AU COEUR • 1934 • Heymann Claude (c/d) • FRN
DEUX BILLETS POUR MEXICO (FRN) see **GEHEIMNISSE IN GOLDENEN NYLONS** • 1966
DEUX CANARDS, LES • 1933 • Schmidt Erich • FRN
DEUX CENT MILLE LIEUES SOUS LES MERS: OU, LE CAUCHEMAR D'UN PECHEUR • 1907 • Melies Georges • FRN • 200,000 LEAGUES UNDER THE SEA (USA) ○ UNDER THE SEAS
DEUX CLOCHES A LA NEIGE • 1976 • Guillermou Jean-Louis • FRN
DEUX COMBINARDS, LES • 1937 • Houssin Jacques • FRN
DEUX COTES DE LA MEDAILLE 1er PARTIE: RACE DE BRONZE • 1973 • Cote Guy-L. • DOC • CND
DEUX COTES DE LA MEDAILLE 2e PARTIE: RISQUER SA PEAU • 1973 • Cote-Guy L. • DOC • CND
DEUX COUVERTS, LES • 1934 • Perret Leonce • FRN
DEUX DANS UNE VOITURE see **PARIS-MEDITERRANEE** • 1931
DEUX DE LA RESERVE • 1938 • Pujol Rene • FRN
DEUX DE L'ESCADRILLE • 1952 • Labro Maurice • FRN
DEUX EPISODES DANS LA VIE D'HUBERT AQUIN • 1979 • Godbout Jacques • CND
DEUX ET DEUX FONT QUATRE • 1975 • Chabrol Claude • MTV • FRN
DEUX FAVORIS, LES • 1936 • Hornez Andre, Jacoby Georg • FRN • MARIKA
DEUX FEMMES • 1965 • Fournier Claude • DCS • CND
DEUX FEMMES EN OR • 1970 • Fournier Claude • CND • FEMMES DE BANLIEU ○ TWO WOMEN OF GOLD ○ TWO WOMEN IN GOLD
DEUX FESTIVALS A GRENOBLE • 1974 • Abnudi Atiat Al- • SHT • FRN
DEUX FOIS • 1971 • Raynal Jackie • FRN • TWICE
DEUX FOIS DEUX YEUX • 1964 • de Hert Robbe • BLG
DEUX FOIS VINGT ANS • 1930 • Tavano Charles-Felix • FRN
DEUX FONT LA PAIRE, LES • 1954 • Berthomieu Andre • FRN • MORT EN FUITE, LE
DEUX FRANCAISES • 1915 • Feuillade Louis • FRN
DEUX GAGNANTS, LES see **OISEAU RARE, UN** • 1935
DEUX GAMINES, LES • 1920 • Feuillade Louis • SRL • FRN • TWO LITTLE URCHINS, THE
DEUX GAMINES, LES • 1936 • Hervil Rene, Champreux Maurice • FRN
DEUX GAMINES, LES • 1950 • de Canonge Maurice • FRN
DEUX GAMINES, LES • 1980 • Pierson Claude • FRN
DEUX GOSSES, LES • 1906 • Feuillade Louis • FRN
DEUX GOSSES, LES • 1924 • Mercanton Louis • FRN
DEUX GOSSES, LES • 1928 • Mercanton Louis • FRN • TWO LITTLE VAGABONDS ○ TWO ORPHANS, THE
DEUX GOSSES, LES • 1936 • Rivers Fernand • FRN
DEUX GOUINES, LES • 1975 • Benazeraf Jose • FRN
DEUX GRANDES FILLES DANS UN PYJAMA • 1974 • Girault Jean • FRN
DEUX GRANDES GUEULES (FRN) see **BESTIONE, IL** • 1974
DEUX HEURES A TUER • 1965 • Govar Yvan • FRN, BLG
DEUX HEURES DE COLLE POUR UN BAISER • 1977 • Farwagi Andre • FRN
DEUX HEURES MOINS LE QUART AVANT JESUS-CHRIST • 1983 • Yanne Jean • FRN, TNS
DEUX HOMMES DANS LA VILLE • 1973 • Giovanni Jose • FRN, ITL • DUE CONTRO LA CITTA (ITL) ○ TWO AGAINST THE LAW (USA)
DEUX HOMMES DANS MANHATTAN • 1959 • Melville Jean-Pierre • FRN • TWO MEN IN MANHATTAN
DEUX IMBECILES HEUREUX • 1975 • Fress Edmond • FRN • JE REVE D'ETRE UN IMBECILE HEUREUX
DEUX LIONS AU SOLEIL • 1980 • Faraldo Claude • FRN • TWO LIONS IN THE SUN
DEUX MAMANS, LES • 1926 • Guarino Joseph • FRN
DEUX MARSEILLAISES, LES • 1968 • Comolli Jean-Louis, Labarthe Andre S. • DOC • FRN
DEUX MEMOIRES, LES • 1973 • Semprun Jorge • FRN, SPN
DEUX MERES, LES • 1913 • Pouctal Henri • FRN
DEUX MONDES, LES • 1930 • Dupont E. A. • FRN
DEUX "MONSIEUR" DE MADAME, LES • 1933 • Jacquin Abel, Pallu Georges • FRN
DEUX "MONSIEUR" DE MADAME, LES • 1951 • Bibal Robert • FRN
DEUX ORPHELINES, LES • 1910 • Capellani Albert • FRN • TWO ORPHANS, THE
DEUX ORPHELINES, LES • 1910 • Monca Georges • FRN
DEUX ORPHELINES, LES • 1932 • Tourneur Maurice • FRN • TWO ORPHANS, THE
DEUX OU TROIS CHOSES QUE JE SAIS D'ELLE • 1967 • Godard Jean-Luc • FRN • TWO OR THREE THINGS I KNOW ABOUT HER (UKN)
DEUX PIEDS DANS LA MEME BOTTINE, LES • 1974 • Rose Pierre • CND • KLUTZ, THE
DEUX PIGEONS, LES • 1922 • Hugon Andre • FRN
DEUX PLUMES, LES • 1958 • Lacam Henri • ANS • FRN • TWO FEATHERS, THE
DEUX POUCES EN HAUT DE LA CARTE • 1976 • Lesaunier Daniel, Augustin Jacques • DOC • CND
DEUX REQUINS SUR LE SABLE see **DEUX AFFREUX SUR LE SABLE** • 1979
DEUX RIVALES, LES (FRN) see **INDIFFERENTI, GLI** • 1964
DEUX RIVAUX, LES • 1903-04 • Blache Alice • FRN
DEUX SAISONS DE LA VIE, LES • 1973 • Pavel Samy • BLG
DEUX SERMENTS, LES • 1918 • Burguet Charles • FRN
DEUX SOEURS VICIEUSES • 1978 • Franco Jesus • FRN
DEUX SOLDATS, LES • 1923 • Herve Jean • FRN
DEUX SOLITUDES • 1978 • Chetwynd Lionel • CND • TWO SOLITUDES
DEUX SOUS DE VIOLETTES • 1951 • Anouilh Jean • FRN
DEUX TIMIDES, LES • 1928 • Clair Rene • FRN • TWO TIMID ONES, THE
DEUX TIMIDES, LES see **JEUNES TIMIDES** • 1941
DEUX TUEURS • 1966 • Grospierre Louis • FRN, ITL • DUE KILLERS IN FUGA (ITL) ○ DU MOU DANS LA GACHETTE
DEUX URANIUMS, LES • 1965 • Leroux Jacques, Otero Manuel • SHT • FRN
DEUX VIERGES POUR SATAN see **DEMONIAQUES, LES** • 1973
DEUX VIEUX GARCONS • 1911 • Carre Michel • FRN
DEUX VISAGES DU SAHARA, LES • 1953 • Leherissey Jean • SHT • FRN
DEUX VOIX • 1966 • Stevenson Rosalind A. • USA • TWO VOICES
DEUXIEME BUREAU • 1935 • Billon Pierre • FRN
DEUXIEME BUREAU CONTRE INCONNU • 1957 • Stelli Jean • FRN
DEUXIEME BUREAU CONTRE KOMMANDANTUR • 1939 • Jayet Rene, Bibal Robert • FRN • TERRE D'ANGOISSE
DEUXIEME BUREAU CONTRE TERRORISTES • 1959 • Stelli Jean • FRN
DEUXIEME PROCES D'ARTHUR LONDON, LE • 1969 • Marker Chris • FRN
DEUXIEME SOUFFLE, LE • 1966 • Melville Jean-Pierre • FRN • SECOND BREATH (UKN) ○ SECOND WIND
DEV ADAM • 1968 • Engin Ilhan • TRK • GIANT, THE
DEV BALA • 1938 • Apte Baburao • IND • GOD BALA
DEV GIRI JATRA • 1932 • IND • TOWARDS THE ABODE OF GODS (USA)
DEVA KANYA • 1968 • Rao Hemambaradara • IND • ANGELS
DEVA TUZI SONYACHI JEJURI • 1967 • Bargir Raja • IND
DEVAKI • 1934 • Sarpotdar • IND
DEVALISEURS NOCTURNES, LES • 1904 • Velle Gaston • FRN
DEVANT'S EXHIBITION OF PAPER FOLDING • 1896 • *Paul R. W.* • UKN
DEVANT'S HAND SHADOWS • 1896 • *Paul R. W.* • UKN
DEVASSOS, OS • 1972 • Barros Carlos Alberto De Souza • BRZ
DEVASTATOR, THE see **DESTROYERS, THE** • 1985
DEVATE SRDCE • 1978 • Herz Juraj • CZC • NINTH HEART, THE
DEVCATA, NEDEJTE SE! • 1937 • Haas Hugo, Holman J. Alfred • CZC
DEVCATKO, NERIKEJ NE! • 1932 • Medeotti-Bahac • CZC • LITTLE GIRL, DON'T SAY NO!
DEVCE Z HOR • 1924 • Kubasek Vaclav • CZC • GIRL FROM THE MOUNTAINS
DEVCE Z PODSKALI • 1922 • Binovec Vaclav • CZC • GIRL FROM PODSKALI, THE
DEVCICA Z BEZKYD • 1944 • Cap Frantisek • CZC • MAIDEN OF BEZKYDY, THE
DEVDAS • 1935 • Barua Pramathesh Chandra • IND • DEBDAS
DEVDAS • 1956 • Roy Bimal • IND
DEVDASI • 1947 • Bose Chandra Sekhar • IND
DEVELOPING A FOOTBALL TEAM • 1931 • Kelley Albert • SHT • USA
DEVELOPMENT AREAS • 1947 • DOC • UKN • THIS MODERN AGE NO.9
DEVELOPMENT HISTORY OF THE SOUTHERN SEA: TRIBES OF THE OCEAN see **MAMPOU HATTENSHI: UMI NO GOZUKU** • 1942
DEVELOPMENT OF THE ENGLISH RAILWAYS • 1936 • Jones Andrew Miller • DOC • UKN
DEVELOPMENT OF THE STALK AND THE ROOT, THE see **SZAR ES A GYOKER FEJLODESE, A** • 1961
DEVELOPMENT OF WESTERN AUSTRALIAN AGRICULTURE • 1924 • ASL
DEVELOPPEMENT PSYCHOMOTEUR • 1973 • Chabot Jean • DOC • CND
DEVENI GAMANA • 1983 • Premaratna H. D. • SLN
DEVERAS ME ATRAPASTE • 1983 • Pardo Gerardo • MXC • YOU'VE REALLY GOT ME
DEVETI KRUG • 1960 • Stiglic France • YGS • NINTH CIRCLE, THE
DEVETNAEST DEVOJAKA I MORNA • 1971 • Kosovac Milutin • YGS • NINETEEN GIRLS AND A SAILOR
DEVETO CUDO NA ISTOKU • 1973 • Filipovic Vlatko • YGS • NINTH WONDER OF THE EAST, THE
DEVI • 1961 • Ray Satyajit • IND • GODDESS, THE
DEVI FULLARA • 1938 • Chakrabarti Tinkari • IND
DEVI TODI • 1922 • *Kohinoor* • IND
DEVIATION see **MAFU CAGE, THE** • 1978
DEVIATOE YANVARIA • 1926 • Viskovski Vyacheslav • USS • NINTH OF JANUARY
DEVICES AND DESIRES • 1990 • Davies John • UKN
DEVICHYA VESNA • 1960 • Dorman Veniamin, Oganisyan Genrikh • USS • SPRINGTIME ON THE VOLGA (USA) ○ SPRING OF THE VIRGIN
DEVIGA URAVU • 1968 • Satyam • IND • GODLY RELATIONS
DEVIL, THE • 1908 • Griffith D. W. • *Ab* • USA
DEVIL, THE • 1908 • Porter Edwin S. • *Edison* • USA
DEVIL, THE • 1910 • *Powers* • USA
DEVIL, THE • 1914 • Protazanov Yakov • USS
DEVIL, THE • 1915 • Ince Thomas H. • USA
DEVIL, THE • 1921 • Young James • USA
DEVIL, THE see **ORDOG, AZ** • 1918
DEVIL, THE see **DIAVOLO, IL** • 1963
DEVIL, THE see **DIABEL** • 1972
DEVIL AND ANGEL • 1974 • Lo Lieh • HKG
DEVIL AND DANIEL WEBSTER, THE • 1941 • Dieterle William • USA • ALL THAT MONEY CAN BUY (UKN) ○ DANIEL AND THE DEVIL ○ HERE IS A MAN
DEVIL AND FLESH see **SUSANA** • 1950
DEVIL AND IDLE HANDS, THE • 1915 • Dowlan William C. • USA
DEVIL AND KACHA, THE see **CHERT A KACHA** • 1955
DEVIL AND LEROY BASSETT, THE • 1973 • Pearson Robert E. • USA
DEVIL AND MAX DEVLIN, THE • 1981 • Stern Steven Hilliard • USA
DEVIL AND MISS JONES, THE • 1941 • Wood Sam • USA • MILLIONS IN STORE
DEVIL AND MISS SARAH, THE • 1971 • Caffey Michael • TVM • USA
DEVIL AND MRS. WALKER, THE • 1914 • *Brennan John E.* • USA
DEVIL AND THE ANGEL, THE (USA) see **FOIRE AUX CHIMERES, LA** • 1946
DEVIL AND THE CORNET, THE • 1908 • Fitzhamon Lewin • UKN
DEVIL AND THE DEEP • 1932 • Gering Marion • USA
DEVIL AND THE FLESH, THE (USA) see **SUSANA** • 1950
DEVIL AND THE GAMBLER, THE • 1908 • Blackton J. Stuart • USA
DEVIL AND THE LADY, THE see **DIABLO Y LA DAMA, EL** • 1983
DEVIL AND THE MADONNA, THE see **TEUFEL UND DIE MADONNA, DER** • 1919
DEVIL AND THE MAN FROM SMALAND, THE see **HIN OCH SMALANNINGEN** • 1927
DEVIL AND THE NUN, THE (UKN) see **MATKA JOANNA OD ANIOLOW** • 1961
DEVIL AND THE STATUE, THE (USA) see **DIABLE GEANT OU LE MIRACLE DE LA MADONNE, LE** • 1902
DEVIL AND THE TEN COMMANDMENTS, THE (USA) see **DIABLE ET LES DIX COMMANDEMENTS, LE** • 1962
DEVIL AND TOM WALKER, THE • 1913 • Kirkland Hardee • USA
DEVIL AS LAWYER, THE • 1911 • *Messter* • UKN
DEVIL AT 4 O'CLOCK, THE • 1961 • LeRoy Mervyn • USA
DEVIL AT HIS ELBOW, THE • 1916 • King Burton L. • USA
DEVIL AT MY HEELS (USA) see **BALLE AU COEUR, UNE** • 1965
DEVIL AT YOUR HEELS, THE • 1982 • Fortier Bob • CND
DEVIL BAT • 1941 • Yarbrough Jean • USA • KILLER BAT
DEVIL BAT'S DAUGHTER • 1946 • Wisbar Frank • USA
DEVIL BEAR see **CLAWS** • 1977
DEVIL BEAR, THE • 1929 • Chaudet Louis W. • CND
DEVIL BIRD see **HIMAKATHARA** • 1982
DEVIL BLADE (FRN) see **PASSI DI DANZA SU UNA LAMA SI RASOIO** • 1973
DEVIL BY THE TAIL, THE (USA) see **DIABLE PAR LA QUEUE, LE** • 1969
DEVIL CAME AT NIGHT, THE see **NACHTS, WENN DER TEUFEL KAM** • 1957
DEVIL CAME TO DRINK, THE • 1958 • Smith Jack* • SHT • UKN
DEVIL CAT • 1978 • *Pleasance Donald* • USA
DEVIL COMES AND THE WHISTLE BLOWS, THE see **AKUMA GA KITARITE FUE WO FUKU** • 1978
DEVIL COMMANDS, THE • 1941 • Dmytryk Edward • USA • WHEN THE DEVIL COMMANDS
DEVIL CRAG see **SEYTAN KAYALIKLARI** • 1970
DEVIL DANCER, THE • 1927 • Niblo Fred • USA
DEVIL DIAMOND, THE • 1937 • *Darro Frankie* • USA
DEVIL DODGER, THE • 1917 • Smith Cliff • USA
DEVIL DOG DAWSON • 1921 • *Hoxie Jack* • USA
DEVIL DOG: THE HOUND OF HELL • 1978 • Harrington Curtis • TVM • USA
DEVIL DOGS • 1928 • Windermere Fred • USA
DEVIL DOGS OF THE AIR • 1935 • Bacon Lloyd • USA
DEVIL DOLL, THE • 1936 • Browning Tod • USA • WITCH OF TIMBUKTU
DEVIL DOLL, THE • 1963 • Shonteff Lindsay • UKN, USA
DEVIL FISH see **MONSTER SHARK** • 1984
DEVIL FOX OF THE NORTH, THE • 1914 • Lund O. A. C. • USA
DEVIL GIRL FROM MARS • 1954 • MacDonald David • UKN
DEVIL GODDESS • 1955 • Bennet Spencer Gordon • USA
DEVIL GOT ANGRY, THE see **DAIMAJIN** • 1966
DEVIL HAS SEVEN FACES, THE see **DIAVOLO A SETTE FACCE, IL** • 1971
DEVIL HORSE, THE • 1926 • Jackman Fred • USA
DEVIL HORSE, THE • 1932 • Brower Otto • SRL • USA
DEVIL HUNTER • Conti Pier Luigi • ITL • TREASURE OF THE WHITE GODDESS
DEVIL IN A BOTTLE, THE see **LIEBE, TOD UND TEUFEL** • 1934
DEVIL IN A CONVENT, THE (USA) see **DIABLE AU CONVENT, LE** • 1899
DEVIL IN AMSTERDAM, THE see **DUIVEL IN AMSTERDAM, DE** • 1919
DEVIL-IN-CHIEF, THE • 1916 • Campbell Colin • SHT • USA
DEVIL IN CHURCH see **DIAVOLAT V TCHERKVATA** • 1969
DEVIL IN EVENING DRESS, THE • 1973 • Miller George • DOC • ASL
DEVIL IN HER, THE • 1974 • Chang Sen • HKG
DEVIL IN LOVE, THE (USA) see **ARCIDIAVOLO, L'** • 1966
DEVIL IN MISS JONES, THE • 1973 • Damiano Gerard • USA
DEVIL IN MISS JONES II, THE • 1982 • Pachard Henri • USA • DEVIL IN MISS JONES PART 2
DEVIL IN MISS JONES PART 2 see **DEVIL IN MISS JONES II, THE** • 1982
DEVIL IN MY FLESH see **SHIN IREZUMI MUZAN TEKKA NO JINGI** • 1968
DEVIL IN SILK (USA) see **TEUFEL IN SEIDE** • 1956

DEVIL IN THE BLOOD see **DIABO MORA NO SANGUE, O** • 1968
DEVIL IN THE BOX, THE see **DIABLE DANS LA BOITE, LE** • 1977
DEVIL IN THE BRAIN, THE see **DIAVOLO NEL CERVELLO, IL** • 1972
DEVIL IN THE CASTLE see **OSAKA-JO MONOGATARI** • 1961
DEVIL IN THE CITY, THE see **DIABLE DANS LA VILLE, LE** • 1924
DEVIL IN THE FLESH • 1986 • Murray Scott • ASL
DEVIL IN THE FLESH see **DIABLE AU CORPS, LE** • 1946
DEVIL IN THE FLESH see **SHIN IREZUMI MUZAN TEKKA NO JINGI** • 1968
DEVIL IN THE FLESH, THE see **DIAVOLO IN CORPO, IL** • 1985
DEVIL IN THE HEART, THE (USA) see **DIABLE AU COEUR, LE** • 1977
DEVIL IN THE HOUSE OF EXORCISM, THE see **CASA DELL'EXORCISMO, LA** • 1975
DEVIL IN THE STUDIO, THE • 1901 • Booth W. R.? • UKN
DEVIL IN THE TIN CUP, THE • 1911 • *Solax* • USA
DEVIL IN THE TOWN, THE see **DIABLE DANS LA VILLE, LE** • 1924
DEVIL IN VELVET • 1968 • Crane Larry • USA
DEVIL INCARNATE, THE see **AKUMA NO KESHIIN** • 1959
DEVIL INSIDE, THE see **OFFBEAT** • 1961
DEVIL INSIDE HER, THE • 1978 • De Leon Leon • USA
DEVIL IS A SISSY, THE • 1936 • Van Dyke W. S. • USA • DEVIL TAKES THE COUNT, THE (UKN)
DEVIL IS A WOMAN, THE • 1935 • von Sternberg Josef • USA • CAPRICE ESPAGNOL
DEVIL IS A WOMAN, THE see **LUPA, LA** • 1953
DEVIL IS A WOMAN, THE see **VELVET VAMPIRE, THE** • 1971
DEVIL IS A WOMAN, THE (UKN) see **DONA DIABLA** • 1949
DEVIL IS A WOMAN, THE (USA) see **SORRISO DEL GRANDE TENTATORE, IL** • 1974
DEVIL IS AN EMPRESS, THE see **JOUEUR D'ECHECS, LE** • 1938
DEVIL IS DEAD, THE • 1964 • Linder Carl • SHT • USA
DEVIL IS DRIVING, THE • 1932 • Stoloff Ben • USA
DEVIL IS DRIVING, THE • 1937 • Lachman Harry • USA
DEVIL LIVES BY BLOOD, THE see **DIABO MORA NO SANGUE, O** • 1968
DEVIL MADE A WOMAN, THE (USA) see **CARMEN, LA DE RONDA** • 1959
DEVIL MAKES THREE, THE • 1952 • Marton Andrew • USA
DEVIL MAY CARE • 1929 • Franklin Sidney A. • USA • BATTLE OF THE LADIES ○ DEVIL-MAY-CARE
DEVIL-MAY-CARE see **DEVIL MAY CARE** • 1929
DEVIL MAY HARE • 1954 • McKimson Robert • ANS • USA
DEVIL MAY WELL LAUGH, THE see **TEUFEL HAT GUT LACHEN, DER** • 1960
DEVIL MCCARE • 1919 • Johnston Lorimer • USA
DEVIL MEN FROM SPACE, THE see **DIAVOLI DELLO SPAZIO, I** • 1965
DEVIL MONSTER • 1935 • *Excelsior* • USA • SEA FIEND, THE (UKN)
DEVIL NEVER SLEEPS, THE see **SATAN NEVER SLEEPS** • 1962
DEVIL OBSESSION, THE see **OSSESSA, L'** • 1974
DEVIL OF A FELLOW, A (USA) see **TEUFELSKERL, EIN** • 1935
DEVIL OF A HONEYMOON, A • 1915 • Booth W. R. • UKN
DEVIL OF A TIME, THE • 1912 • *Punch* • USA
DEVIL OF A WOMAN, A see **WEIBSTEUFEL, DER** • 1966
DEVIL OF EDO see **OEDO NO ONI** • 1947
DEVIL OF THE DEEP • 1938 • Foster John • ANS • USA
DEVIL OF THE DEEP AND THE SEA URCHINS, THE • 1902 • *Warwick Trading Co.* • UKN
DEVIL OF THE DESERT, THE see **SHAITAN EL SAHARA** • 1954
DEVIL OF THE DESERT AGAINST THE SON OF HERCULES (USA) see **ANTHAR L'INVINCIBILE** • 1965
DEVIL ON DECK • 1932 • Fox Wallace • USA
DEVIL ON HORSEBACK • 1936 • Wilbur Crane • USA
DEVIL ON HORSEBACK • 1954 • Frankel Cyril • UKN
DEVIL ON SPRINGS, THE see **PERAK A SS** • 1946
DEVIL ON VACATION, THE see **DIABLO EN VACACIONES, EL** • 1963
DEVIL ON WHEELS, THE • 1947 • Wilbur Crane • USA
DEVIL ON WHEELS (UKN) see **BURN 'EM UP BARNES** • 1934
DEVIL ON WHEELS (UKN) see **INDIANAPOLIS SPEEDWAY** • 1939
DEVIL PAYS OFF • 1941 • Auer John H. • USA
DEVIL PLAYS, THE • 1931 • Thorpe Richard • USA • MURDOCK AFFAIR, THE (UKN)
DEVIL, PROBABLY, THE (USA) see **DIABLE, PROBABLEMENT, LE** • 1977
DEVIL RANCH see **RANCHO DIABLO** • 1968
DEVIL RESUSCITATION • 1980 • Fukasaku Kinji • JPN
DEVIL RIDER • 1971 • *Kananza Ross* • USA
DEVIL RIDERS • 1943 • Newfield Sam • USA
DEVIL RIDES OUT, THE • 1968 • Fisher Terence • UKN • DEVIL'S BRIDE, THE (USA)
DEVIL SHIP • 1947 • Landers Lew • USA
DEVIL-SHIP PIRATES, THE • 1964 • Sharp Don • UKN
DEVIL SLEEP see **FLYGANDE DRAKEN, DEN** • 1980
DEVIL STONE, THE • 1917 • De Mille Cecil B. • USA • DEVIL-STONE, THE
DEVIL-STONE, THE see **DEVIL STONE, THE** • 1917
DEVIL STRIKES AT NIGHT, THE (USA) see **NACHTS, WENN DER TEUFEL KAM** • 1957
DEVIL TAKE THE HINDMOST, THE see **POSLEDNI PROPADNE PEKLU** • 1982
DEVIL TAKES THE COUNT, THE (UKN) see **DEVIL IS A SISSY, THE** • 1936
DEVIL, THE SERVANT AND THE MAN, THE • 1910 • *Selig* • USA
DEVIL, THE SERVANT AND THE MAN, THE • 1912 • *Williams Kathlyn* • USA
DEVIL, THE SERVANT AND THE MAN, THE • 1916 • Beal Frank • USA
DEVIL THUMBS A RIDE, THE • 1947 • Feist Felix E. • USA
DEVIL TIGER, THE • 1934 • Elliott Clyde E. • USA
DEVIL TIMES FIVE see **PEOPLETOYS** • 1974
DEVIL TO PAY, THE • 1912 • Saunders, Bowden • UKN
DEVIL TO PAY, THE • 1915 • Collins Edwin J.? • UKN
DEVIL TO PAY, THE • 1920 • Warde Ernest C. • USA
DEVIL TO PAY, THE • 1931 • Fitzmaurice George • USA
DEVIL TO PAY, THE • 1962 • Beresford Bruce • SHT
DEVIL TO PAY, THE see **SAMMENSVERGELSEN** • 1984
DEVIL UNDER THE PILLOW, A see **DIABLO BAJA LA ALMOHADA, UN** • 1968
DEVIL WAS AN ANGEL, THE see **COLT IN PUGNA AL DIAVOLO, UNA** • 1967
DEVIL WAS COMING FROM AKASAWA, THE see **TEUFEL KAM AUS AKASAWA, DER** • 1971
DEVIL WITCH, THE see **BABA YAGA** • 1973
DEVIL WITH A BRIEFCASE, THE see **CHYORT S PORTFYELEM** • 1968
DEVIL WITH HITLER, THE • 1942 • Douglas Gordon • USA
DEVIL WITH LOVE, THE see **AL DIABLO CON AMOR** • 1972
DEVIL WITH SEVEN FACES, THE see **DIAVOLO A SETTE FACCE, IL** • 1971
DEVIL WITH THE WIMMIN, THE • 1917 • Hutchinson Craig • SHT • USA
DEVIL WITH WOMEN, A • 1930 • Cummings Irving • USA • ON THE MAKE
DEVIL WITHIN, THE • 1914 • *Ramo* • USA
DEVIL WITHIN, THE • 1921 • Durning Bernard J. • USA
DEVIL WITHIN HER, THE (UKN) see **CHI SEI?** • 1974
DEVIL WITHIN HER, THE (USA) see **I DON'T WANT TO BE BORN** • 1975
DEVIL WOLF OF SHADOW MOUNTAIN • 1964 • Kent Gary • USA
DEVIL WOMAN • 1970 • Sibal Jose Flores • PHL
DEVIL WOMAN see **WEIBSTEUFEL, DER** • 1951
DEVIL WOMAN see **ONIBABA** • 1964
DEVIL WORSHIPPERS, THE (USA) see **TEUFELSANBETER, DIE** • 1920
DEVILED HAMS • 1937 • Schwarzwald Milton • SHT • USA
DEVILISH BUSINESS • 1916 • Miller Rube • USA
DEVILISH DOCTOR, A • 1913 • *Mace Fred* • USA
DEVILISH DREAM, A • 1915 • Mitchell Bruce • USA
DEVILISH HONEYMOON, A • 1970 • Podskalsky Zdenek • CZC
DEVILISH MAGIC see **MAGIE DIABOLIQUE** • 1898
DEVILISH PLANK, THE (USA) see **PLANCHE DU DIABLE, LA** • 1904
DEVILLED CRABS • 1917 • *Pokes & Jabbs* • SHT • USA
DEVILMAN STORY • 1967 • Bianchini Paolo • ITL • DEVIL'S MAN, THE (UKN)
DEVILS see **GENII** • 1969
DEVIL'S 8, THE • 1969 • Topper Burt • USA
DEVILS, THE • 1971 • Russell Ken • UKN
DEVILS, THE see **DIABLY** • 1964
DEVIL'S ADVOCATE, THE see **AVVOCATO DEL DIAVOLO, L'** • 1977
DEVIL'S ADVOCATE, THE see **SORCERESS** • 1982
DEVIL'S AGENT, THE (UKN) see **IM NAMEN DES TEUFELS** • 1962
DEVIL'S ANGEL, THE • 1920 • A'Hiller Lejaren • USA
DEVIL'S ANGELS • 1967 • Haller Daniel • USA
DEVIL'S APPLE TREE, THE • 1929 • Clifton Elmer • USA
DEVILS ARE NOT TO BE TRIFLED WITH see **S CERTY NEJSOU ZERTY** • 1985
DEVIL'S ASSISTANT, THE • 1913 • *Neilson Asta* • SHT • FRN
DEVIL'S ASSISTANT, THE • 1917 • Pollard Harry • USA
DEVIL'S BAIT • 1959 • Scott Peter Graham • USA
DEVIL'S BAIT, THE • 1917 • Harvey Harry • USA
DEVIL'S BANKNOTES see **AKUMA NO SATSUTABA** • 1960
DEVIL'S BARGAIN, THE • 1908 • Coleby A. E. • UKN
DEVIL'S BED, THE see **WOLFIN VOM TEUFELSMOOR, DIE** • 1978
DEVIL'S BEDROOM, THE • 1964 • Jones L. Q. • USA
DEVIL'S BILLIARD TABLE, THE • 1910 • *Eclair* • FRN
DEVIL'S BISHOP, THE • 1988 • Pontecorvo Gillo • ITL
DEVIL'S BOND WOMAN, THE • 1916 • Carleton Lloyd B. • USA
DEVIL'S BONDMAN, THE • 1915 • Nash Percy • UKN • SCORPION'S STING, THE (USA)
DEVIL'S BOOK STORE, THE • 1969 • *Lust Bernard* • CMP • USA
DEVIL'S BOUNCING-BALL SONG, THE see **AKUMA NO TEMARI-UTA** • 1977
DEVIL'S BOWL, THE • 1923 • Hart Neal • USA • IN THE DEVIL'S BOWL
DEVIL'S BRIDE, THE (USA) see **DEVIL RIDES OUT, THE** • 1968
DEVIL'S BRIGADE, THE • 1968 • McLaglen Andrew V. • USA
DEVIL'S BROOD, THE see **HOUSE OF FRANKENSTEIN** • 1945
DEVIL'S BROTHER, THE • 1933 • Roach Hal, Rogers Charles • USA • FRA DIAVOLO (UKN) ○ VIRTUOUS TRAMPS, THE ○ BOGUS BANDITS
DEVIL'S CABARET, THE • 1931 • Grinde Nick • SHT • USA
DEVIL'S CAGE, THE • 1928 • Noy Wilfred • USA • GIRL IN THE RAIN, THE (UKN)
DEVIL'S CAGE, THE see **SEYTAN KAFESI** • 1968
DEVIL'S CAMERA see **SCUM OF THE EARTH!** • 1963
DEVIL'S CANYON • 1935 • Smith Cliff • USA
DEVIL'S CANYON • 1953 • Werker Alfred L. • USA • ARIZONA OUTPOST
DEVIL'S CARGO see **IN SPITE OF DANGER** • 1935
DEVIL'S CARGO, THE • 1925 • Fleming Victor • USA
DEVIL'S CARGO, THE • 1948 • Link John F. • USA
DEVIL'S CASTLE, THE see **MANOIR DU DIABLE, LE** • 1896
DEVIL'S CASTLE, THE see **CASTELLO DEL DIAVOLO, IL** • 1913
DEVIL'S CASTLE, THE (USA) see **CHATEAU HANTE, LE** • 1897
DEVIL'S CAVALIERS, THE (USA) see **CAVALIERI DEL DIAVOLO, I** • 1959
DEVIL'S CHAIR, THE see **SEDIA DEL DIAVOLO, LA** • 1912
DEVIL'S CHAPLAIN • 1929 • Worne Duke • USA
DEVIL'S CHARIOT, THE see **ARABAT AL SHAITAN** • 1962
DEVIL'S CHILDREN, THE • 1962 • Sheldon James • USA
DEVIL'S CIRCUS, THE • 1925 • Christensen Benjamin • USA • LIGHT ETERNAL, THE
DEVIL'S CLAIM, THE • 1920 • Swickard Charles • USA
DEVIL'S COMMANDMENT, THE (USA) see **VAMPIRI, I** • 1956
DEVIL'S CONFESSION, THE • 1921 • Lopez John S. • USA
DEVIL'S CROSS, THE see **CRUZ DEL DIABLO, LA** • 1974
DEVIL'S DAFFODIL, THE (UKN) see **GEHEIMNIS DER GELBEN NARZISSEN, DAS** • 1961
DEVIL'S DANSANT, THE • 1914 • Vignola Robert G. • USA
DEVIL'S DARLING, THE • 1915 • Haddock William F. • USA
DEVIL'S DAUGHTER, THE • 1915 • Powell Frank • USA
DEVIL'S DAUGHTER, THE • 1972 • Szwarc Jeannot • TVM • USA
DEVIL'S DAUGHTER, THE see **POCOMANIA** • 1939
DEVIL'S DAUGHTER (USA) see **FILLE DU DIABLE** • 1945
DEVIL'S DEFEAT see **AKUMA NO KANPAI** • 1947
DEVIL'S DICE • 1926 • Forman Tom • USA
DEVIL'S DICE, THE see **PURPLE LILY, THE** • 1918
DEVIL'S DIRTY WORK, THE • 1962 • D'Bomba Jorg • ANS • GDR
DEVIL'S DISCIPLE, THE • 1926 • Micheaux Oscar • USA
DEVIL'S DISCIPLE, THE • 1959 • Hamilton Guy • UKN
DEVIL'S DOLL see **NAKED GODDESS, THE** • 1959
DEVIL'S DOLL, THE see **SINTHIA, THE DEVIL'S DOLL** • 1970
DEVIL'S DOORWAY • 1950 • Mann Anthony • USA
DEVIL'S DOORYARD, THE • 1923 • King Louis • USA
DEVIL'S DOUBLE, THE • 1916 • Hart William S. • USA
DEVIL'S ELIXIRS see **ELIXIERE DES TEUFELS, DIE** • 1922
DEVIL'S ENVOYS, THE (USA) see **VISITEURS DU SOIR, LES** • 1942
DEVIL'S EXPRESS • 1975 • Rosen Barry • USA
DEVIL'S EYE, THE see **DJAVULENS OGA** • 1960
DEVIL'S FEUD CAKE • 1963 • Freleng Friz • ANS • USA
DEVIL'S FIDDLER, THE • 1914 • *Biograph* • DNM
DEVIL'S FOOT, THE • 1921 • Elvey Maurice • UKN
DEVILS FROM SPACE, THE see **DIAVOLI DELLO SPAZIO, I** • 1965
DEVILS FROM THE PLANETS see **KOTETSU NO KYOJIN - KAISEIJIN NO MAJYO** • 1957
DEVIL'S GARDEN see **COPLAN SAUVE SA PEAU** • 1967
DEVIL'S GARDEN, THE • 1920 • Webb Kenneth • USA
DEVIL'S GENERAL, THE see **DES TEUFELS GENERAL** • 1955
DEVIL'S GHOST, THE • 1922 • *Western Pictures Exploitation Co.* • USA
DEVIL'S GIFT, THE • 1984 • Barton Kenneth J. • USA
DEVIL'S GODMOTHER, THE (USA) see **MADRINA DEL DIABLO, LA** • 1937
DEVIL'S GROTTO, THE • 1912 • *Pathe* • FRN
DEVIL'S GULCH, THE • 1926 • Nelson Jack • USA
DEVIL'S HAIRPIN, THE • 1957 • Wilde Cornel • USA
DEVIL'S HAND, THE see **MAIN DU DIABLE, LA** • 1922
DEVIL'S HAND, THE see **NAKED GODDESS, THE** • 1959
DEVIL'S HAND, THE (USA) see **MAIN DU DIABLE, LA** • 1942
DEVIL'S HARBOR (USA) see **DEVIL'S POINT** • 1954
DEVIL'S HENCHMAN, THE • 1949 • Friedman Seymour • USA
DEVIL'S HOLIDAY, THE • 1930 • Goulding Edmund • USA
DEVIL'S HONEY, THE see **MIELE DEL DIAVOLO, IL** • 1987
DEVIL'S IMAGE, THE • 1916 • Otto Henry • SHT • USA
DEVIL'S IMPOSTER, THE see **POPE JOAN** • 1972
DEVILS-IN-LAW see **HARURANMAN** • 1968
DEVIL'S IN LOVE, THE • 1933 • Dieterle William • USA
DEVILS IN THE GARDEN see **DEMONIOS EN EL JARDIN** • 1982
DEVIL'S INSTRUMENT, THE see **DJAVULENS INSTRUMENT** • 1967
DEVIL'S ISLAND • 1926 • O'Connor Frank • USA
DEVIL'S ISLAND • 1940 • Clemens William • USA
DEVIL'S ISLAND see **AKURYO-TO** • 1982
DEVIL'S ISLAND, THE (USA) see **GOKUMON-TO** • 1977
DEVIL'S JEST, THE • 1954 • Goulding Alf • UKN
DEVIL'S LEFT HAND, THE see **AKUMA NO HIDARITE** • 1966
DEVIL'S LIEUTENANT, THE • 1984 • Goldschmidt John • MTV • UKN
DEVIL'S LOCKSMITH, THE see **TEUFELS-SCHLOSSER, DER** • 1919
DEVIL'S LONGEST NIGHT, THE see **PLUS LONGUE NUIT DU DIABLE, LA** • 1971
DEVIL'S LOTTERY • 1932 • Taylor Sam • USA
DEVIL'S LOVER, THE (USA) see **AMANTE DEL DEMONIO, L'** • 1972
DEVIL'S LOVERS, THE (USA) see **AMANTES DEL DIABLO, LES** • 1971
DEVIL'S MAN, THE (UKN) see **DEVILMAN STORY** • 1967
DEVIL'S MANOR, THE see **MANOIR DU DIABLE, LE** • 1896
DEVIL'S MARRIAGE, THE • 1931 • Elliot Grace • SHT • USA
DEVIL'S MASK, THE • 1946 • Levin Henry • USA
DEVIL'S MASTERPIECE, THE • 1927 • McCarthy John P. • USA
DEVIL'S MATCH, THE • 1923 • *Strasser Jan* • USA
DEVIL'S MATE • 1933 • Rosen Phil • USA • HE KNEW TOO MUCH (UKN)
DEVIL'S MATE, THE • 1966 • Zorfa T. G. • USA • SATAN'S MISTRESS ○ SATAN'S WOMAN
DEVIL'S MAZE, THE • 1929 • Gundrey V. Gareth • UKN
DEVIL'S MEN, THE see **LAND OF THE MINOTAUR** • 1976
DEVIL'S MESSENGER, THE • 1962 • Strock Herbert L., Siodmak Curt • USA, SWD
DEVIL'S MILL, THE (USA) see **CERTUV MLYN** • 1951
DEVIL'S MIRROR, THE • Sun Chung • HKG
DEVIL'S MISTRESS, THE • 1966 • Wanzer Orville • USA
DEVIL'S MONEY, THE see **DINERO DEL DIABLO, EL**
DEVIL'S MONEYBAGS, THE see **TRESORS DE SATAN, LES** • 1902
DEVIL'S MOTHER-IN-LAW, THE • 1910 • *Pathe* • USA
DEVIL'S NEEDLE, THE • 1916 • Withey Chet • USA
DEVIL'S NIGHTMARE (UKN) see **PLUS LONGUE NUIT DU DIABLE, LA** • 1971
DEVIL'S ODDS • 1987 • Bridges Beau • USA
DEVIL'S ODDS, THE • 1989 • Schroeder Michael • USA
DEVILS OF DARKNESS • 1964 • Comfort Lance • UKN
DEVILS OF MONZA • 1986 • Odorisio Luciano • ITL
DEVILS OF SPARTIVENTO, THE see **DIAVOLI DI SPARTIVENTO, I** • 1963
DEVIL'S OWN, THE • 1916 • Marshall George • SHT • USA
DEVIL'S OWN, THE (USA) see **WITCHES, THE** • 1966
DEVIL'S OWN ENVOY, THE see **VISITEURS DU SOIR, LES** • 1942
DEVIL'S PARADE, THE • 1930 • Hale George • SHT • USA
DEVIL'S PARADISE, THE see **DES TEUFELS PARADIES** • 1987
DEVIL'S PARTNER, THE • 1923 • Fleming Caryl S. • USA
DEVIL'S PARTNER, THE • 1958 • Rondeau Charles R. • USA
DEVIL'S PARTY, THE • 1938 • McCarey Ray • USA • HELL'S KITCHEN ○ RIOT PATROL
DEVIL'S PASS, THE • 1957 • Conyers Darcy • UKN
DEVIL'S PASS, THE see **CZARCI ZLEB** • 1949
DEVIL'S PASSION, THE • 1927 • Trystan Leon • PLN
DEVIL'S PASSKEY, THE • 1920 • von Stroheim Erich • USA

DEVIL'S PAWN, THE • 1922 • USA
DEVIL'S PAY DAY, THE • 1917 • Worthington William • USA
DEVIL'S PEOPLE, THE see **LAND OF THE MINOTAUR** • 1976
DEVIL'S PIPELINE, THE • 1940 • Cabanne W. Christy • USA
DEVIL'S PIT, THE • 1930 • Collins Lewis D. • DOC • USA • UNDER THE SOUTHERN CROSS (UKN)
DEVIL'S PLAYGROUND • 1937 • Kenton Erle C. • USA • DEPTHS BELOW, THE
DEVIL'S PLAYGROUND see **LADY WHO DARED, THE** • 1931
DEVIL'S PLAYGROUND, THE • 1918 • Webster Harry Mcrae • USA
DEVIL'S PLAYGROUND, THE • 1929 • *Bindley Victor (P)* • ASL
DEVIL'S PLAYGROUND, THE • 1946 • Archainbaud George • USA
DEVIL'S PLAYGROUND, THE • 1976 • Schepisi Fred • ASL
DEVIL'S PLAYTHING, THE • 1973 • Sarno Joe • USA
DEVIL'S PLAYTHING, THE see **BABI RIAZANSKIE** • 1927
DEVIL'S PLOT, THE see **COUNTERBLAST** • 1948
DEVIL'S POINT • 1954 • Tully Montgomery • UKN • DEVIL'S HARBOR (USA)
DEVIL'S POSSESSED, THE • Klimovsky Leon • SPN
DEVIL'S POWER, THE see **CZARCI ZLEB** • 1949
DEVIL'S PRAYER-BOOK, THE • 1916 • *Hoops Arthur* • USA
DEVIL'S PRICE, THE (UKN) see **LONE STAR VIGILANTES, THE** • 1942
DEVIL'S PRIZE, THE • 1916 • Bertsch Marguerite • USA
DEVIL'S PROFESSION, THE • 1915 • Tudor F. C. S. • UKN
DEVIL'S PROTEGE, THE see **HVIDE DJOEVEL, DEN** • 1916
DEVIL'S RAIN, THE • 1975 • Fuest Robert • USA, MXC
DEVIL'S RAVINE, THE see **RIPA DRACULUI** • 1957
DEVIL'S RIDDLE, THE • 1920 • Beal Frank • USA
DEVIL'S ROCK • 1938 • Burger Germain • UKN
DEVIL'S SADDLE, THE • 1927 • Rogell Albert S. • USA
DEVIL'S SADDLE LEGION, THE • 1937 • Connolly Bobby • USA
DEVIL'S SAINT, THE see **FLOR DE SANTIDAD** • 1972
DEVIL'S SIGNATURE, THE • 1914 • *Essanay* • USA
DEVIL'S SISTERS, THE • 1966 • Grefe William • USA
DEVIL'S SKIN, THE • 1970 • *Hu Ingrid* • SNG
DEVIL'S SKIPPER, THE • 1928 • Adolfi John G. • USA
DEVIL'S SON, THE see **HIJO DEL DIABLO, EL** • 1965
DEVIL'S SON, THE see **SEYTANIN OGLU** • 1967
DEVIL'S SON MAKES A NIGHT OF IT IN PARIS, THE see **MEPHISTO'S SON** • 1906
DEVIL'S SONATA, THE • 1911 • *Skandinavia* • SWD
DEVIL'S SONG, THE see **AKUMA NO TEMARI-UTA** • 1977
DEVIL'S SONG OF BALL, THE see **AKUMA NO TEMARI-UTA** • 1977
DEVIL'S SPAWN, THE see **LAST GUNFIGHTER, THE** • 1959
DEVIL'S SQUADRON • 1936 • Kenton Erle C. • USA
DEVIL'S STAIRCASE, THE see **POTOMOK DJAVOLA** • 1917
DEVIL'S SUMMER see **MASHO NO NATSU** • 1981
DEVIL'S SWORD • 1984 • Timoer Ratno • INN
DEVIL'S TEMPLE, THE see **ONI NO SUMA YAKATA** • 1969
DEVIL'S THREE see **MEAN BUSINESS**
DEVIL'S THREE SINS, THE • 1908 • *Pathe* • FRN
DEVIL'S TOAST see **AKUMA NO KANPAI** • 1947
DEVIL'S TOLL, THE see **DESERT'S TOLL, THE** • 1926
DEVIL'S TOUCH, THE see **SATAN'S SKIN** • 1970
DEVIL'S TOWER • 1928 • McGowan J. P. • USA
DEVIL'S TOY, THE • 1916 • Knoles Harley • USA
DEVIL'S TOY, THE see **ROULI-ROULANT** • 1966
DEVIL'S TRADEMARK, THE • 1928 • Meehan James Leo • USA
DEVIL'S TRAIL, THE • 1919 • Paton Stuart • USA
DEVIL'S TRAIL, THE • 1942 • Hillyer Lambert • USA • ROGUES' GALLERY (UKN)
DEVIL'S TRAP, THE see **DABLOVA PAST** • 1961
DEVIL'S TRIANGLE, THE • 1974 • Winer Richard • USA
DEVIL'S TRICKS, THE see **RUSES DU DIABLE, LES** • 1965
DEVIL'S TWIN, THE • 1927 • Maloney Leo • USA
DEVIL'S UNDEAD, THE (USA) see **NOTHING BUT THE NIGHT** • 1972
DEVIL'S VALLEY, THE • 1959 • Georgi Katja • ANM • GDR
DEVIL'S VISITATIONS, THE see **VISITACIONES DEL DIABLO, LAS** • 1968
DEVIL'S WANTON, THE see **FANGELSE** • 1949
DEVIL'S WEB • 1974 • O'Riordan Shaun • TVM • UKN • NURSE WILL MAKE IT BETTER
DEVIL'S WEDDING NIGHT, THE (USA) see **PLENILUNIO DELLE VERGINI, IL** • 1973
DEVIL'S WEED, THE (UKN) see **WILD WEED** • 1949
DEVIL'S WHEEL, THE • 1918 • Le Saint Edward J. • USA
DEVIL'S WHEEL, THE see **CHYORTOVO KOLESO** • 1926
DEVIL'S WIDOW, THE (USA) see **TAMLIN** • 1972
DEVIL'S WOMAN, THE see **TAMLIN** • 1972
DEVIL'S WORK, THE see **DAVOLJA POSLA** • 1966
DEVINE QUI VIENT PINER CE SOIR? • Antony Michel • FRN
DEVJANI • 1939 • Burma Phani • IND
DEVLERIN INTIKAMI • 1967 • Tuna Feyzi • TRK • VENGEANCE OF THE GIANTS, THE ○ REVENGE OF THE GIANTS, THE
DEVLIN • 1971 • Jeffrey Tom • MTV • ASL
DEVOCHKA I EKHO • 1964 • Zhebrunas Arunas • USS • GIRL AND THE ECHO, THE
DEVOIR, LE see **WAGIB, AL-** • 1947
DEVOIR ET L'HONNEUR, LE • 1911 • Andreani Henri • FRN
DEVOIRS DE VACANCES • 1952 • Paviot Paul • SHT • FRN
DEVOJACKI MOST • 1976 • Stamenkovic Miomir • YGS • MAIDEN'S BRIDGE, THE
DEVOJKA • 1965 • Djordjevic Purisa • YGS • GIRL, THE
DEVOJKA SA KOSMAJA • 1972 • Jovanovic Dragovan • YGS • NINA THE GIRL FROM KOSMAJ ○ GIRL FROM THE MOUNTAINS
DEVONSVILLE TERROR, THE • 1983 • Lommel Ulli • USA
DEVORADORA, LA • 1946 • de Fuentes Fernando • MXC
DEVOTED APE, THE • 1910 • Aylott Dave • UKN
DEVOTED SON • 1915 • *Johnson Emory* • USA
DEVOTEE see **NETSUAISHA** • 1960
DEVOTEE, THE see **PURAN BHAGAT** • 1933
DEVOTEE PRAHLAD see **BHAKT PRAHLAD** • 1934
DEVOTEE TO ISHWAR see **ISHWAR BHAKTI** • 1951
DEVOTEE TO THE GOD see **BHAKTA-KE-BHAGWAN** • 1934
DEVOTEE TO THE GOD see **HARI-HAR BHAKTI** • 1955
DEVOTION • 1913 • *Domino* • USA
DEVOTION • 1921 • George Burton • USA
DEVOTION • 1931 • Milton Robert • USA
DEVOTION • 1946 • Bernhardt Curtis • USA
DEVOTION • 1955 • Pyryev K.
DEVOTION see **HERR GENERALDIREKTOR, DER** • 1925
DEVOTION see **EDERA, L'** • 1950
DEVOTION NOW VANISHED see **SHUSHIN IMADA KIEZU** • 1949
DEVOTION OF THE RAILWAY, THE see **OINARU BAKUSHIN** • 1960
DEVOTION OF WOMEN, THE • 1910 • *Imp* • USA
DEVOURING ROCK, THE see **BATU BELAH BATU BERTANGKUP** • 1959
DEVOURING WAVES see **MONSTER SHARK** • 1984
DEVTA • 1956 • Pattanna • IND
DEVTCHATA • 1962 • Chulyukin Yuri • USS • GIRLS, THE
DEVUSHKA BEZ ADRESA • 1957 • Ryazanov Eldar • USS • GIRL WITHOUT AN ADDRESS, THE
DEVUSHKA S DALEKOI REKI • 1928 • Chervyakov Yevgeni • USS • GIRL FROM THE DISTANT RIVER, THE
DEVUSHKA S KOROBKOI • 1927 • Barnet Boris • USS • GIRL WITH THE HAT BOX, THE ○ WHEN MOSCOW LAUGHS
DEVYAT DNEI ODNOGO GODA • 1961 • Romm Mikhail • USS • NINE DAYS OF ONE YEAR ○ NINE DAYS IN ONE YEAR
DEW DROP INN • 1919 • Semon Larry • USA
DEW DROPS see **PINI BINDU** • 1968
DEWADASI, DIE • 1915 • Heiland Heinz Karl • FRG
DEWDROP BRAVES THE FLOODS OF MAIDENHEAD • 1915 • Batley Ernest G. • UKN
DEWEY • 1911 • *Champion* • USA
DEWI • 1974 • Prijono Ami • INN
DEXTER GORDON • 1971 • *Flip Film* • SHT • DNM
DEXTERITY • 1937 • Miller David • SHT • USA
DEZERTER • 1958 • Lesiewicz Witold • PLN • DESERTER, THE
DEZERTER • 1966 • Brdecka Jiri • ANS • CZC • DESERTER, THE (UKN)
DEZERTIR • 1933 • Pudovkin V. I. • USS • DESERTER
DEZINFEKCIJA • 1975 • Zaninovic Ante • YGS • DISINFECTION
D'GAJAO MATA PARA VINGAR • 1972 • Marins Jose Mojica • BRZ
DHADRAM KARAM • 1975 • *Kapoor Raj (P)* • IND
DHAFNIS KE HLOI 66 • 1967 • Zaharopoulou Mika • GRC • DAPHNIS AND CHLOE 66
DHAKAM • 1972 • Nanthencode Babu • IND • THIRST
DHAKRIA ORGIS • 1967 • Pitsios Kostas • GRC • TEARS OF RAGE
DHAKRISMENA MATIA • 1967 • Tegopoulos Apostolos • GRC • TEARS OF GRIEF ○ TEARFUL EYES
DHANWAN • 1937 • Atorthy P. • IND
DHARAM KI DEVI • 1935 • *Biswas Anil (M)* • IND
DHARATI-MATA • 1938 • Bose Nitin • IND • MOTHERLAND, THE
DHARMA KANYA • 1968 • Shinde Madhav • IND
DHARMAPATNI • 1968 • Ghanchkar G. B. • IND
DHARMATMA • 1935 • Shantaram Victor • IND
DHARMATMA • 1974 • Khan Feroz • IND • GODFATHER
DHARTI KE LAL • 1946 • Abbas Khwaya Ahmad • IND • CHILDREN OF THE EARTH
DHAW AL-KHAFIT, ADH- • 1961 • Wahab Fatin Abdel • EGY • LUMIERE DOUCE
DHEKATOS TRITOS, O • 1967 • Dadiras Dimis • GRC • THIRTEENTH MAN, THE
DHEN EHO DHROMO NA DHIAVO • 1968 • Lois Giorgos • GRC • NO WAY OUT
DHEN POULAO TIN KARDIA MOU • 1967 • Katsimitsoulias Andreas • GRC • I DON'T SELL MY HEART
DHEN THA XEHASO POTE TIN MORFI TOU • 1968 • Stratzalis Kostas • GRC • I'LL NEVER FORGET HIS FACE
DHIO FENGARIA TON AVGOUSTO • 1979 • Ferris Kostas • GRC • TWO MOONS IN AUGUST
DHIREY BAHE MEGHNA • 1973 • Kabir Alamgir • BNG • MEGHNA, MEGHNA
DHOKTOR ZI-VENGOS • 1968 • Vengos Thanasis • GRC • DOCTOR ZI-VENGOS
DHOLLARIATIS ASPASIAS, TA • 1967 • Fileris Xenophon • GRC • ASPASIA'S DOLLARS
D'HOMME A HOMME • 1956-57 • Devlin Bernard • SHT • CND
D'HOMME A HOMMES • 1948 • Christian-Jaque • FRN • MAN TO MEN (USA) ○ MAN IN WHITE, THE
DHOOMA KETHU • 1968 • Jayagopal R. N. • IND • METEOR
DHOON • 1953 • *Kapoor Raj* • IND
DHRUBA • 1953 • Bose Chandra Sekhar • IND
DHRUPAD • 1983 • Kaul Mani • IND • INDIAN CLASSICAL SCHOOL OF MUSIC, AN
DHRUV, DEVOTEE TO THE GOD see **BHAKTA DHRUV** • 1947
DHRUVA • 1934 • *Madan* • IND
DHRUVA • 1936 • *East India Film* • IND
DHRUVA • 1937 • Kale D. K. • IND
DHRUVA CHARITRA • 1921 • *Madan J. F. (P)* • IND • HISTORY OF DHRUVA
DHRUVA KUMAR • 1938 • Bhave K. P. • IND
DHUAAN • 1953 • Malhotra Roshanlal • IND
DHUL MALAK • 1975 • Sri Wijawa Dharma • SLN
DHUWAN-DHAR • 1935 • *Chitnis Lela* • IND
DI CHE SEGNO SEI? • 1975 • Corbucci Sergio • ITL
DI CHE SESSO SEI? • 1977 • Guerrieri Romolo • ITL
DI MAMA NON CE N'E UNA SOLA • 1974 • Giannetti Alfredo • ITL
DI PADRE IN FIGLIO • 1983 • Gassman Vittorio, Gassman Alessandro • ITL • FROM FATHER TO SON
DI QUA DI LA DEL PIAVE • 1959 • Leoni Guido • ITL
DI QUE ME QUIERES • 1939 • Snoddy Robert • SAY THAT YOU LOVE ME
DI TRESSETTE CE N'E UNO, TUTTI GLI ALTRI SON NESSUNO • 1974 • Carnimeo Giuliano • ITL
DIA COMENZO AYER, EL • 1965 • Cisneros Icaro • MXC • OPUS 65
DIA CON EL DIABLO, UN • 1945 • Delgado Miguel M. • MXC • DAY WITH THE DEVIL, A
DIA CON SERGIO, UN • 1975 • Romero-Marchent Rafael • SPN
DIA DE DICIEMBRE, UN • 1961 • Cortes Fernando • MXC
DIA DE LA BODA, EL • 1968 • Cardona Rene Jr. • MXC • WEDDING DAY, THE
DIA DE LLUVIA, UN see **ANGELICA** • 1951
DIA DE LOS ENAMORADOS, EL • 1960 • Palacios Fernando • SPN
DIA DE MANANA, EL • 1965 • Navarro Agustin • SPN
DIA DE NOVIEMBRE, UN • 1972 • Solas Humberto • CUB
DIA DE VIDA, UN • 1950 • Fernandez Emilio • MXC
DIA DE VIDA, UM • 1962 • Fraga Augusto • PRT
DIA DESPUES DE AGOSTO, UN • 1968 • Lorente German • SPN • ONE DAY AFTER AUGUST
DIA ES UN DIA, UN • 1968 • Prosper Francisco • SPN
DIA IBUKU • 1980 • Salleh Yassin • MLY
DIA PERDIDO, UN • 1954 • Forque Jose Maria • SPN
DIA QUE ME QUIERAS, EL • 1935 • Reinhardt John • USA • DAY YOU LOVE ME, THE ○ DAY THAT YOU LOVE ME, THE
DIA QUE ME QUIERAS, EL • 1988 • Dow Sergio • CLM, VNZ • DAY YOU LOVE ME, THE
DIA QUE ME QUITAS, EL • 1935 • *Lusiardo Tito* • ARG
DIA QUE ME QUITAS, EL • 1969 • *Lusiardo Tito* • ARG
DIA SANTO DE TIATIRA, EL • 1970 • Guedez Jesus Enrique • VNZ • SAINT DAY OF TIATIRA
DIA TRAS DIA • 1951 • del Amo Antonio • SPN
DIA TRAS DIA • 1979 • Rojas Guillermo Orlando • CUB • DAY BY DAY
DIA.. UN RIO, UN • 1979 • Garayucochea Oscar • DOC • VNZ • ONE DAY.. A RIVER
DIA YO PREGUNTE..., UN • 1970 • de Alvarez Julia • CLM • ONE DAY I ASKED..
DIABEL • 1972 • Zulawski Andrzej • PLN • DEVIL, THE
DIABLE AU COEUR, LE • 1927 • L'Herbier Marcel • FRN • LITTLE DEVIL-MAY-CARE
DIABLE AU COEUR, LE • 1977 • Queysanne Bernard • FRN • DEVIL IN THE HEART, THE (USA) ○ NUIT TRANSFIGUREE, LA ○ PUDEUR SINGULIERE, UNE
DIABLE AU CONVENT, LE • 1899 • Melies Georges • FRN • DEVIL IN A CONVENT, THE (USA) ○ SIGN OF THE CROSS, THE
DIABLE AU CORPS, LE • 1946 • Autant-Lara Claude • FRN • DEVIL IN THE FLESH
DIABLE AU CORPS, LE (FRN) see **DIAVOLO IN CORPO, IL** • 1985
DIABLE BOITEUX, LE • 1948 • Guitry Sacha • FRN
DIABLE DANS LA BOITE, LE • 1977 • Lary Pierre • FRN • DEVIL IN THE BOX, THE
DIABLE DANS LA VILLE, LE • 1924 • Dulac Germaine • FRN • DEVIL IN THE CITY, THE ○ DEVIL IN THE TOWN, THE
DIABLE DE SIBERIE, LE see **TRAGEDIE IMPERIALE, LA** • 1937
DIABLE EN BOUTEILLE, LE • 1935 • Hilpert Heinz, Steinbicker Reinhart • FRN
DIABLE EST PARMI NOUS, LE • 1972 • Beaudin Jean • CND • SENSUAL SORCERESS
DIABLE ET LA DAME, OU L'ITINERAIRE DE LA HAINE, LE (FRN) see **DIABLO Y LA DAMA, EL** • 1983
DIABLE ET LES DIX COMMANDEMENTS, LE • 1962 • Duvivier Julien • FRN, ITL • DEVIL AND THE TEN COMMANDMENTS, THE (USA) ○ TENTAZIONE QUOTIDIANE, LE(ITL) ○ DIAVOLO E I DIECI COMANDAMENTI, IL
DIABLE GEANT OU LE MIRACLE DE LA MADONNE, LE • 1902 • Melies Georges • FRN • DEVIL AND THE STATUE, THE (USA) ○ GIGANTIC DEVIL, THE
DIABLE NOIR, LE • 1905 • Melies Georges • FRN • BLACK IMP, THE (USA)
DIABLE PAR LA QUEUE, LE • 1969 • de Broca Philippe • FRN, ITL • NON TIRATE IL DIAVOLO PER LA CODA (ITL) ○ DEVIL BY THE TAIL, THE (USA)
DIABLE, PROBABLEMENT, LE • 1977 • Bresson Robert • FRN • DEVIL, PROBABLY, THE (USA)
DIABLE SOUFFLE, LE • 1947 • Greville Edmond T. • FRN
DIABLERIES D'UN SOURCIER, LES • 1966 • Garceau Raymond • SHT • CND
DIABLES BLEUS, LES see **SIDI-BRAHIM** • 1939
DIABLESSE, LA see **IFRITA HANIM** • 1948
DIABLESSES, LES • 1972 • Margheriti Antonio • FRN, ITL, FRG • CORRINGA
DIABLESSES, LES see **DEMONIAQUES, LES** • 1973
DIABLILLOS DE ARRABAL • 1938 • Sequeyro Adela • MXC
DIABLO A CABALLO, EL • 1954 • Aguilar Rolando • MXC
DIABLO BAJA LA ALMOHADA, UN • 1968 • Forque Jose Maria • SPN, ITL, FRN • DEVIL UNDER THE PILLOW, A
DIABLO COJUELO, EL • 1970 • Fernandez Ramon • SPN • LAME DEVIL, THE
DIABLO DESAPARECE, EL • 1954 • Aguilar Rolando • MXC
DIABLO EN VACACIONES, EL • 1963 • Elorrieta Jose Maria • SPN • DEVIL ON VACATION, THE
DIABLO NO ES TAN DIABLO, EL • 1949 • Soler Julian • MXC
DIABLO TAMBIEN LLORA, EL • 1963 • Nieves Conde Jose Antonio • SPN
DIABLO TOCA LA FLAUTA, EL • 1953 • Forque Jose Maria • SPN
DIABLO VENIA DE AKASAWA, EL (SPN) see **TEUFEL KAM AUS AKASAWA, DER** • 1971
DIABLO Y LA DAMA, EL • 1983 • Zuniga Ariel • MXC, FRN • DIABLE ET LA DAME, OU L'ITINERAIRE DE LA HAINE, LE (FRN) ○ DEVIL AND THE LADY, THE ○ DIABLO Y LA DAMA, O EL ITINERARIO DEL ODIO, EL
DIABLO Y LA DAMA, O EL ITINERARIO DEL ODIO, EL see **DIABLO Y LA DAMA, EL** • 1983
DIABLOS DEL TERROR, LOS • 1958 • Mendez Fernando • MXC
DIABLOS EN EL CIELO • 1964 • Baledon Rafael • MXC
DIABLOS ROJOS, LOS • 1966 • Viloria Jose Luis • SPN
DIABLY • 1964 • Urbanski Kazimierz • DOC • PLN • DEVILS, THE
DIABO DESCEU A VILA, O • 1979 • de Fonseca Teixeira • PRT • SATAN GOES TO TOWN
DIABO ERA OUTRO, O • 1969 • Esteves Constantino • PRT
DIABO MORA NO SANGUE, O • 1968 • Thire Cecil • BRZ • DEVIL LIVES BY BLOOD, THE ○ EVIL LIVES IN THE BLOOD ○ DEVIL IN THE BLOOD
DIABOLIC DUCHESS, THE see **DUQUESA DIABOLICA, LA** • 1963

DIABOLIC GAME see **JUEGO DIABOLICO** • 1958
DIABOLIC INVENTION, THE see **VYNALEZ ZKAZY** • 1958
DIABOLIC PACT see **PACTO DIABOLICO** • 1968
DIABOLIC QUEEN, THE see **DIABOLICAL QUEEN, THE** • 1962
DIABOLIC TENANT, THE see **LOCATAIRE DIABOLIQUE, LE** • 1909
DIABOLIC WEDDING • 1972 • Nash Gene • USA
DIABOLICAL AXE, THE see **HACHA DIABOLICA, EL** • 1964
DIABOLICAL BOX, THE • 1912 • *Urbanora*
DIABOLICAL DR. Z, THE (USA) see **MISS MUERTE** • 1966
DIABOLICAL HATCHET, THE see **HACHA DIABOLICA, EL** • 1964
DIABOLICAL MAGIC see **MAGIE DIABOLIQUE** • 1898
DIABOLICAL MEETINGS see **AMANTES DEL DIABLO, LES** • 1971
DIABOLICAL POT, THE see **MARMITE DIABOLIQUE, LA** • 1903
DIABOLICAL QUEEN, THE • 1962 • Li Han-Hsiang • CHN • DIABOLIC QUEEN, THE
DIABOLICAL SHUDDER see **ESCALOFRIO DIABOLICO** • 1971
DIABOLICALLY YOURS see **DIABOLIQUEMENT VOTRE** • 1967
DIABOLICAMENTE.. LETIZIA • 1975 • Bugnatelli Salvatore • ITL
DIABOLICAMENTE TUA (ITL) see **DIABOLIQUEMENT VOTRE** • 1967
DIABOLICI CONVEGNI see **AMANTES DEL DIABLO, LES** • 1971
DIABOLICI, I • 1920 • Genina Augusto • ITL
DIABOLICO, EL • 1976 • Korporaal Giovanni • MXC
DIABOLICO DR. MABUSE, IL (ITL) see **TAUSEND AUGEN DES DR. MABUSE, DIE** • 1960
DIABOLICO TRIANGULO DE LA BERMUDAS, EL • 1977 • Cardona Rene Jr. • MXC • TRIANGLE (THE BERMUDA MYSTERY) ○ BERMUDA TRIANGLE, THE
DIABOLIK • 1967 • Bava Mario • ITL, FRN • DANGER: DIABOLIK
DIABOLIQUE DOCTEUR MABUSE, LE (FRN) see **TAUSEND AUGEN DES DR. MABUSE, DIE** • 1960
DIABOLIQUE (USA) see **DIABOLIQUES, LES** • 1954
DIABOLIQUEMENT VOTRE • 1967 • Duvivier Julien • FRN, ITL, FRG • MIT TEUFLISCHEN GRUSSEN (FRG) ○ DIABOLICAMENTE TUA (ITL) ○ DIABOLICALLY YOURS
DIABOLIQUES, LES • 1954 • Clouzot Henri-Georges • FRN • FIENDS, THE (UKN) ○ DIABOLIQUE (USA)
DIABOLO MAD • 1908 • Coleby A. E. • UKN
DIABOLO MENTHE • 1977 • Kurys Diane • FRN • PEPPERMINT SODA
DIABOLO NIGHTMARE • 1907 • Booth W. R. • UKN
DIABOLO SE LLEVA A LOS MUERTOS see **CASA DELL'EXORCISMO, LA** • 1975
DIABOLO VIENA DE AKASAWA, EL • 1970 • Franco Jesus • SPN
DIADALMAS ELET • 1923 • *Lukas Paul* • HNG
DIADEM DER ZARIN, DAS • 1922 • Lowenbein Richard • FRG
DIADIA VANYA see **DYADYA VANYA** • 1971
DIADIKASIA, I • 1975 • Theos Dimosthenis • GRC • PROCEDURE, THE
DIAFANOIDI PORTANO LA MORTE, I • 1965 • Margheriti Antonio • ITL • WAR OF THE PLANETS (USA) ○ DEADLY DIAPHANOIDS, THE ○ DIAFANOIDI VENGONO DA MORTE ○ DIAPHANOIDS BRING DEATH, THE
DIAFANOIDI VENGONO DA MORTE see **DIAFANOIDI PORTANO LA MORTE, I** • 1965
DIAGNOSI see **ULTIMO ADDIO, L'** • 1942
DIAGNOSIS MURDER • 1974 • Hayers Sidney • UKN
DIAGNOSIS OF DEATH • 1979 • Schulhoff Petr • CZC
DIAGNOSIS OF SEXUAL DESIRE see **SHIKIJO SHINDAN** • 1968
DIAGNOSTIC C.I.V. • 1960 • Fabiani Henri • SHT • FRN
DIAGNOZA X • 1933 • Marten Leo • CZC • X-DIAGNOSIS, THE
DIAGONAL SINFONIE see **SYMPHONIE DIAGONALE** • 1920
DIAGONAL SYMPHONY see **SYMPHONIE DIAGONALE** • 1920
DIAGONALE DU FOU, LA • 1984 • Dembo Richard • FRN, SWT • DANGEROUS MOVES (USA)
DIAGRAM see **WYKRES** • 1966
DIAL 17 • 1952 • Anderson Michael • SHT • FRN
DIAL 999 • 1938 • Huntington Lawrence • UKN
DIAL 999 • 1955 • Tully Montgomery • UKN • WAY OUT, THE (USA)
DIAL 1119 • 1950 • Mayer Gerald • USA • VIOLENT HOUR, THE (UKN)
DIAL DOUBLE TWO DOUBLE FOUR • 1968 • Krishnasamy R. M. • IND
DIAL HELP • 1988 • Deodato Ruggero • ITL
DIAL HOT LINE • 1969 • Thorpe Jerry • TVM • USA
DIAL M FOR MURDER • 1954 • Hitchcock Alfred • USA
DIAL M FOR MURDER • 1967 • Moxey John Llewellyn • TVM • USA
DIAL M FOR MURDER • 1981 • Sagal Boris • TVM • USA
DIAL P FOR PINK • 1965 • Freleng Friz • ANS • USA
DIAL RAT see **DIAL RAT FOR TERROR** • 1972
DIAL RAT FOR TERROR • 1972 • Cohen Larry • USA • BEVERLY HILLS NIGHTMARE ○ FUNNY BONE ○ BONE ○ DIAL RAT ○ MAN WHO CAME TO KILL A RAT, THE
DIAL RED O • 1955 • Ullman Daniel B. • USA
DIALECTIQUE • 1966 • Guillemot Claude • SHT • FRN
DIALOG 20-40-60 • 1968 • Skolimowski Jerzy, Solan Peter, Brynych Zbynek • CZC • DIALOGUE 20-40-60
DIALOGHI DELLE CARMELITANE, I • 1960 • Bruckberger Raymond-Leopold, Agostini Philippe • ITL, FRN
DIALOGHI DI PLATONE, I see **PROCESSO E MORTE DI SOCRATE** • 1940
DIALOGO CON CHE • 1969 • Soltero Jose • USA • DIALOGUE WITH CHE ○ CHE IS ALIVE
DIALOGO DE EXILIADOS • 1975 • Ruiz Raul • FRN • DIALOGUES D'EXILES ○ DIALOGUE OF EXILES
DIALOGOS DE LA PAZ • 1965 • Feliu Jordi, Font Espina Jose Maria • SPN
DIALOGUE • 1968 • Lugo Alfredo • SHT • VNZ
DIALOGUE • 1974 • Majka Chris • UKN
DIALOGUE see **PARBESZED** • 1963
DIALOGUE see **HIWAR** • 1972
DIALOGUE 20-40-60 see **DIALOG 20-40-60** • 1968
DIALOGUE AVEC LA TERRE • 1962 • Lavoie Richard • DCS • CND
DIALOGUE DE ROME • 1982 • Duras Marguerite • FRN
DIALOGUE DES CARMELITES, LE • 1959 • Agostini Philippe, Bruckberger R. L. • FRN, ITL • CARMELITES, THE (UKN)
DIALOGUE DES SOLDATSMORTS, LE • 1961 • Martin Marcel • SHT • FRN
DIALOGUE D'UNE BRUME ANTIQUE see **DIALOGUE OF AN ANCIENT FOG** • 1978
DIALOGUE OF AN ANCIENT FOG • 1978 • Siegel Lois • CND • DIALOGUE D'UNE BRUME ANTIQUE
DIALOGUE OF EXILES see **DIALOGO DE EXILIADOS** • 1975
DIALOGUE OUVERT see **OPEN DIALOOG** • 1973
DIALOGUE WITH A WOMAN DEPARTED • 1980 • Hurwitz Leo T. • USA
DIALOGUE WITH CHE see **DIALOGO CON CHE** • 1969
DIALOGUES see **ROZHOVORY** • 1969
DIALOGUES D'EXILES see **DIALOGO DE EXILIADOS** • 1975
DIAMANT, LE • 1970 • Grimault Paul • ANS • FRN
DIAMANT BLEU, LE • 1956 • Laliberte Roger • CND
DIAMANT DE CENT SOUS, LE • 1947 • Daniel-Norman Jacques • FRN
DIAMANT DES TODES, DER • 1919 • AUS • DIAMOND OF THE DEAD, THE
DIAMANT DES ZARENS, DER • 1932 • Neufeld Max • FRG • ORLOW, DER
DIAMANT DU SENECHAL, LE • 1914 • Feuillade Louis • FRN
DIAMANT EN DIE DIEF • 1978 • SAF
DIAMANT NOIR • 1922 • Hugon Andre • FRN
DIAMANT NOIR • 1940 • Delannoy Jean • FRN
DIAMANT NOIR, LE • 1913 • Machin Alfred • NTH
DIAMANT VERT, LE • 1923 • Marodon Pierre • FRN
DIAMANTE, EL • 1967 • Valdes Oscar • DOC • CUB
DIAMANTE DEL MAHARAJA, EL • 1947 • de Ribon Roberto • CHL
DIAMANTE IS TROEWE • 1961 • SAF
DIAMANTE LOBO • 1977 • Parolini Gianfranco • ITL
DIAMANTEN-BILLARD (FRG) see **MILLIARD DANS UN BILLIARD, UN** • 1965
DIAMANTEN DES ZARENS, DIE • 1918 • Larsen Viggo • FRG
DIAMANTENHOLLE AM MEKONG, DIE (FRG) see **SFIDA VIENE DA BANGKOK, LA** • 1965
DIAMANTENKONKURRENZ, DIE • 1921 • Santen Trude • FRG
DIAMANTENPRINZ, DIE • 1969 • FRG
DIAMANTENSTIFTUNG, DIE • 1917 • Guter Johannes • FRG
DIAMANTES • 1971 • *Cinema Marte* • MXC
DIAMANTES A GO-GO (SPN) see **AD OGNI COSTO** • 1967
DIAMANTI • 1939 • D'Errico Corrado • ITL
DIAMANTI CHE NESSUNO VOLEVA RUBARE • 1967 • Mangini Gino • ITL
DIAMANTI SPORCHI DI SANGUE • 1978 • Di Leo Fernando • ITL
DIAMANTS D'ANVERS • 1969 • Thiele Rolf • BLG, FRG
DIAMANTS DU CANADA • 1958-60 • Bonniere Rene • DCS • CND
DIAMOND 33 see **ALMAS-E-33** • 1968
DIAMOND, THE • 1954 • Tully Montgomery, O'Keefe Dennis • UKN • DIAMOND WIZARD, THE (USA) ○ MILLION DOLLAR DIAMOND
DIAMOND ARM see **BRILLIANTOVAYA RUKA** • 1968
DIAMOND BANDIT, THE • 1924 • Ford Francis • USA
DIAMOND BROKER, THE • 1915 • *Ridgely Cleo* • USA
DIAMOND BROOCH, THE • 1912 • *Gordon Julia Swayne* • USA
DIAMOND CARLISLE • 1922 • Morante Milburn • USA • SOLACE OF THE WOODS
DIAMOND CATCH • 1985 • SAF
DIAMOND CITY • 1949 • MacDonald David • UKN
DIAMOND COUNTRY see **RUN LIKE A THIEF** • 1967
DIAMOND CROSS • 1910 • Percival Lacey? • ASL
DIAMOND CROWN, THE • 1913 • *Sawyer Laura* • USA
DIAMOND CUT DIAMOND • 1912 • *Bunny John* • USA
DIAMOND CUT DIAMOND • 1913 • Carleton Lloyd B. • USA
DIAMOND CUT DIAMOND • 1914 • Buckland Warwick? • UKN
DIAMOND CUT DIAMOND • 1915 • Aylott Dave? • UKN
DIAMOND CUT DIAMOND • 1916 • Evans Fred, Evans Joe • UKN
DIAMOND CUT DIAMOND • 1932 • Elvey Maurice, Niblo Fred • UKN • BLAME THE WOMAN (USA)
DIAMOND CUT DIAMOND see **BLACK MASKS, THE** • 1913
DIAMOND CUT DIAMOND see **MAN HUNT** • 1933
DIAMOND DEMON • 1947 • Barclay David • SHT • USA
DIAMOND DOLL, THE see **BONEKA PERMATA** • 1974
DIAMOND EARRINGS, THE see **MADAME DE..** • 1953
DIAMOND EXPERT, THE • 1955 • MacDonald David • UKN
DIAMOND FROM THE PIE, A • 1916 • *Juvenile Film* • USA
DIAMOND FROM THE SKY, THE • 1915 • Jaccard Jacques, Taylor William D. • SRL • USA
DIAMOND FRONTIER • 1940 • Schuster Harold • USA • MODERN MONTE CRISTO, A
DIAMOND GANG, THE • 1911 • *Essanay* • USA
DIAMOND HAND, THE see **BRILLIANTOVAYA RUKA** • 1968
DIAMOND HANDCUFFS • 1928 • McCarthy John P. • USA
DIAMOND HEAD • 1962 • Green Guy • USA
DIAMOND HORSESHOE • 1945 • Seaton George • USA • BILLY ROSE'S DIAMOND HORSESHOE
DIAMOND HUNTERS see **RUN LIKE A THIEF** • 1967
DIAMOND HUNTERS, THE • 1975 • De Villiers Dirk • SAF
DIAMOND IN THE ROUGH, A • 1911 • *Selig* • USA
DIAMOND IN THE ROUGH, A • 1914 • *Kalem* • USA
DIAMOND IN THE ROUGH, A • 1914 • Adolfi John G. • *Majestic* • USA
DIAMOND JIM • 1935 • Sutherland A. Edward • USA
DIAMOND JIM'S PARDNER • 1916 • *Mustang* • SHT • USA
DIAMOND LOCKET, THE • 1911 • *Comet* • USA
DIAMOND LURE, THE • 1916 • McDermott John • SHT • USA
DIAMOND MACHINE, THE (USA) see **VOUS PIGEZ?** • 1955
DIAMOND MAKER • 1914 • *Cines* • ITL
DIAMOND MAKER, THE • 1909 • Blackton J. Stuart • USA • FORTUNE AND MISFORTUNE ○ MAKER OF DIAMONDS, THE ○ FORTUNE OR MISFORTUNE
DIAMOND MAKER, THE • 1914 • *Eclair* • USA
DIAMOND MAKERS, THE • 1913 • *Leonard Robert Z.* • USA
DIAMOND MAN, THE • 1924 • Rooke Arthur • UKN
DIAMOND MASTER, THE • 1914 • *Eclair* • FRN
DIAMOND MASTER, THE • 1929 • Nelson Jack • SRL • USA
DIAMOND MERCENARIES, THE • 1975 • Guest Val • SWT, IRL, SAF • KILLER FORCE ○ SOELDNER, DIE ○ MERCENAIRES, LES
DIAMOND MYSTERY, THE • 1913 • *Baird Leah* • USA
DIAMOND NECKLACE, THE • 1909 • *Centaur* • USA
DIAMOND NECKLACE, THE • 1921 • Clift Denison • UKN
DIAMOND NINJA FORCE • 1986 • Ho Godfrey • HKG
DIAMOND NIPPERS, THE • 1914 • *Asher Max* • USA
DIAMOND OF DISASTER, THE • 1914 • Fleming Carroll • USA
DIAMOND OF THE ANDES see **SEKIDOO KAKERU OTOKO** • 1968
DIAMOND OF THE DEAD, THE see **DIAMANT DES TODES, DER** • 1919
DIAMOND OF THE LITTLE COCKEREL, THE see **KISKAKAS GYEMANT FELKRAJCARJA, A** • 1950
DIAMOND PATH, THE • 1912 • *Rex* • USA
DIAMOND QUEEN, THE • 1921 • Kull Edward • SRL • USA
DIAMOND QUEEN, THE • 1953 • Brahm John • USA
DIAMOND RUNNERS, THE • 1916 • McGowan J. P. • USA
DIAMOND RUSH (UKN) see **PARIA, LE** • 1968
DIAMOND S RANCH, THE • 1912 • *Selig* • USA
DIAMOND SAFARI • 1958 • Mayer Gerald • USA
DIAMOND SHIP, THE see **SPINNEN PART 2, DIE** • 1920
DIAMOND SKULLS • 1989 • Broomfield Nicholas • UKN
DIAMOND SMUGGLERS, THE • 1911 • Dwan Allan • USA • SMUGGLER AND THE GIRL, THE
DIAMOND SMUGGLERS, THE • 1914 • Whitman Frank • USA
DIAMOND SQUARE see **PLACA DEL DIAMANT, LA** • 1982
DIAMOND STAR, THE • 1911 • Griffith D. W. • USA
DIAMOND STAR, THE • 1913 • Collins Edwin J. • UKN
DIAMOND STUD • 1970 • Corarito Greg • USA
DIAMOND THIEVES • 1917 • *Fischer Marguerita* • SHT • USA
DIAMOND THIEVES, THE • 1908 • Raymond Charles? • UKN
DIAMOND THIEVES, THE • 1916 • Melville Wilbert • USA
DIAMOND TRAIL, THE • 1932 • Fraser Harry L. • USA
DIAMOND WALKERS, THE see **JAGD AUF BLAUE DIAMANTEN** • 1966
DIAMOND WIZARD, THE (USA) see **DIAMOND, THE** • 1954
DIAMONDS • 1947 • Pravov Ivan, Olenin A. • USS
DIAMONDS • 1975 • Golan Menahem • USA, ISR
DIAMONDS ADRIFT • 1921 • Bennett Chester • USA
DIAMONDS AND CRIME see **HI DIDDLE DIDDLE** • 1943
DIAMONDS AND DIMPLES • 1918 • Rains Fred • UKN
DIAMONDS AND GOLD see **PETCH SEAN TONG** • 1986
DIAMONDS AND PEARLS • 1918 • Archainbaud George • USA • HOUR GLASS, THE
DIAMONDS ARE BRITTLE (UKN) see **MILLIARD DANS UN BILLIARD, UN** • 1965
DIAMONDS ARE DANGEROUS • 1961 • SAF
DIAMONDS ARE DANGEROUS see **ADVENTURE IN DIAMONDS** • 1940
DIAMONDS ARE FOREVER • 1971 • Hamilton Guy • UKN
DIAMONDS ARE TRUMPS • 1916 • Daly William Robert • SHT • USA
DIAMONDS FOR BREAKFAST • 1968 • Morahan Christopher • UKN
DIAMONDS FOR DINNER • 1985 • SAF
DIAMONDS FOR THE DICTATORSHIP OF THE PROLETARIAT • 1975 • Kromanov Grigori • USS
DIAMONDS IN THE ROUGH see **FRAMED** • 1927
DIAMONDS OF DESTINY • 1917 • Ryder Maxwell • SHT • USA
DIAMONDS OF FATE • 1915 • Ayres Sydney • USA
DIAMONDS OF THE NIGHT (USA) see **DEMANTY NOCI** • 1964
DIAMONDS ON WHEELS • 1972 • Courtland Jerome • UKN
DIANA • 1916 • Allen Charles W. • SHT • USA
DIANA see **DIANA CAZADORA, LA** • 1956
DIANA AND DESTINY • 1916 • Thornton F. Martin • UKN
DIANA ARDWAY see **SATAN JUNIOR** • 1919
DIANA CAZADORA, LA • 1956 • Davison Tito • MXC • CALL ME BAD (USA) ○ BAD DIANE ○ DIANA
DIANA L'AFFASCINATRICE • 1915 • Serena Gustavo • ITL
DIANA OF DOBSON'S • 1917 • *Loftus Cecilia* • UKN
DIANA OF EAGLE MOUNTAIN • 1915 • *Bison* • USA
DIANA OF THE CROSSWAYS • 1922 • Clift Denison • UKN
DIANA OF THE FARM • 1915 • *Teare Ethel* • USA
DIANA OF THE FOLLIES • 1916 • Cabanne W. Christy • USA • DIANE OF THE FOLLIES
DIANA OF THE HUNTRESS • 1916 • *Braham Lionel* • USA
DIANA OF THE ISLANDS see **MUTINY** • 1924
DIANA SOREL • 1920 • Serena Gustavo • ITL
DIANA'S DRESS REFORM • 1914 • Ince Ralph • USA
DIANA'S LEGACY • 1912 • *Vitagraph* • USA
DIANE • 1929 • Waschneck Erich • FRG
DIANE • 1955 • Miller David • USA
DIANE LINKLETTER STORY, THE • 1970 • Waters John* • USA
DIANE OF STAR HOLLOW • 1921 • Sellers Oliver L. • USA
DIANE OF THE FOLLIES see **DIANA OF THE FOLLIES** • 1916
DIANE OF THE GREEN VAN • 1919 • Worsley Wallace • USA
DIANE, THE ZEBRA WOMAN • 1962 • Rochlin Sheldon, Rochlin Diane • SHT • USA
DIANKHA-BI • 1968 • Traore Mahama Johnson • SNL • YOUNG GIRL, THE
DIAPHANOIDS BRING DEATH, THE see **DIAFANOIDI PORTANO LA MORTE, I** • 1965
DIARIES, NOTES AND SKETCHES • 1969 • Mekas Jonas • USA • WALDEN: REELS ONE TO FOUR
DIARIES OF KAMIKAZE, THE see **AA DOKI NO SAKURA** • 1967
DIARIES OF THE PEASANTS see **PAMIETNIKI CHLOPOW** • 1952
DIARIO DE INVIERNO • 1988 • Regueiro Francisco • SPN • WINTER DIARY (UKN)
DIARIO DE LA GUERRA DEL CERDO see **GUERRA DEL CERDO, LA** • 1975
DIARIO DE MI MADRE, EL • 1956 • Rodriguez Roberto • MXC
DIARIO DE PROVINCIA • 1980 • Palmari Roberto • BRZ • DIARY OF A COUNTY
DIARIO DE UN FISCAL DE TRANSITO • 1972 • Carrera Guillermo • SHT • VNZ • DIARY OF A TRAFFIC COP
DIARIO DE UNA MUJER • 1944 • Benavides Jose Jr. • MXC
DIARIO DI UN ITALIANO • 1973 • Capogna Sergio • ITL
DIARIO DI UN MAESTRO • 1973 • De Seta Vittorio • MTV • ITL • DIARY OF A SCHOOLTEACHER ○ DIARY OF A TEACHER

DIARIO DI UNA CAMERIERA, IL (ITL) see **JOURNAL D'UNE FEMME DE CHAMBRE, LE** • 1963
DIARIO DI UNA DONNA AMATA, IL • 1936 • Koster Henry • ITL
DIARIO DI UNA SCHIZOFRENICA • 1968 • Risi Nelo • ITL • DIARY OF A SCHIZOPHRENIC GIRL (USA) ○ DIARY OF A SCHIZOPHRENIC ○ WHY ANNA?
DIARIO DI UNA STELLA, IL • 1939 • Pinoli Mattia, Valinotti Domenico • ITL • ALESSANDROWNA
DIARIO PROIBITO DI FANNY, IL • 1969 • Pastore Sergio • ITL
DIARIO SEGRETO DI UN CARCERE FEMMINILE • 1973 • Di Silvestro Rino • ITL, USA • SECRET DIARY FROM A WOMEN'S PRISON (UKN) ○ LOVE IN A WOMEN'S PRISON ○ HELL PRISON ○ WOMEN IN CELL BLOCK 7
DIARIO SEGRETO DI UNA MINORENNE, IL • 1968 • Brazzi Oscar • ITL • SECRET DIARY OF A MINOR, THE ○ E NATA UNA DONNA
DIARY • 1967 • Kovasznai Gyorgy • ANS • HNG
DIARY • 1972 • van der Keuken Johan • NTH
DIARY • 1988 • Perlov David • ISR
DIARY see **DVEVNIK** • 1974
DIARY see **TAGEBUCH** • 1975
DIARY, THE • 1981 • Vinton Will • ANS • USA
DIARY FOR IN SARAGOSSA, A see **REKOPIS ZNALEZIONY W SARAGOSSIE** • 1965
DIARY FOR MY CHILDREN see **NAPLO GYERMEKEIMNEK** • 1984
DIARY FOR MY FATHER AND MOTHER see **NAPLO APAMNAK, ANYAMNAK** • 1989
DIARY FOR MY LOVES see **NAPLO SZERELMEIMNEK** • 1987
DIARY FOR TIMOTHY, A • 1946 • Jennings Humphrey • DOC • UKN
DIARY OF A BACHELOR • 1964 • Howard Sandy • USA
DIARY OF A BAD GIRL (USA) see **LONG DES TROTTOIRS, LE** • 1956
DIARY OF A BED see **BETWEEN THE SHEETS** • 1984
DIARY OF A BRIDE (UKN) see **I, JANE DOE** • 1948
DIARY OF A CHAMBERMAID • 1946 • Renoir Jean • USA • JOURNAL D'UNE FEMME DE CHAMBRE, LE (FRN)
DIARY OF A CLOISTERED NUN (USA) see **STORIA DI UNA MONACA DI CLAUSURA** • 1973
DIARY OF A COUNTRY PRIEST (USA) see **JOURNAL D'UN CURE DE CAMPAGNE, LE** • 1950
DIARY OF A COUNTY see **DIARIO DE PROVINCIA** • 1980
DIARY OF A DOG see **KRONIKA POD PSEM** • 1959
DIARY OF A DRUNKARD, THE see **SHUCHU NIKKI** • 1924
DIARY OF A HALF VIRGIN • 1971 • Wickman Torgny • SWD
DIARY OF A HIGH SCHOOL BRIDE • 1959 • Topper Burt • USA
DIARY OF A HITCH-HIKER see **DIARY OF A TEENAGE HITCHHIKER** • 1979
DIARY OF A HOLD-UP see **CRONICA DE UN ATRACO** • 1968
DIARY OF A LOST GIRL (UKN) see **TAGEBUCH EINER VERLORENEN** • 1929
DIARY OF A LOST ONE see **TAGEBUCH EINER VERLORENEN** • 1929
DIARY OF A LOVER see **TAGEBUCH EINES LIEBENDEN** • 1977
DIARY OF A MAD HOUSEWIFE • 1970 • Perry Frank • USA
DIARY OF A MAD OLD MAN • 1987 • Rademakers Lili • NTH, UKN
DIARY OF A MAD OLD MAN see **FUTEN ROJIN NIKKI** • 1962
DIARY OF A MADMAN • 1963 • Le Borg Reginald • USA
DIARY OF A MADMAN • 1965 • Williams Richard • ANS • UKN
DIARY OF A MARRIED WOMAN see **TAGEBUCH EINER VERLIEBTEN** • 1953
DIARY OF A MODEL see **INTIMATE DIARY OF ARTISTS' MODELS** • 1964
DIARY OF A NAZI • 1943 • Savchenko Igor • USS
DIARY OF A NOBODY • 1964 • Russell Ken • MTV • UKN
DIARY OF A NUDIST see **NATURE CAMP CONFIDENTIAL** • 1961
DIARY OF A NYMPH see **AGGIE -THE DIARY OF A NYMPH** • 1969
DIARY OF A NYMPHOMANIAC (UKN) see **JOURNAL INTIME D'UNE NYMPHOMANE, LE** • 1972
DIARY OF A PERFECT MURDER • 1986 • Day Robert • TVM • USA
DIARY OF A PUPPY, THE • 1917 • Blackton J. Stuart • SHT • USA
DIARY OF A QUEBECER • 1965 • Lavoie Richard, Zolou J. • DCS • CND
DIARY OF A REVOLUTIONIST • 1932 • Urinof J. I.
DIARY OF A SCHIZOPHRENIC see **DIARIO DI UNA SCHIZOFRENICA** • 1968
DIARY OF A SCHIZOPHRENIC GIRL (USA) see **DIARIO DI UNA SCHIZOFRENICA** • 1968
DIARY OF A SCHOOLTEACHER see **DIARIO DI UN MAESTRO** • 1973
DIARY OF A SERGEANT • 1945 • Newman Joseph M. • DOC • USA
DIARY OF A SEX COUNSELLOR, THE see **ARU SEX DOCTOR NO KIROKU** • 1968
DIARY OF A SEXY ACTRESS see **ZOKU NIKUTAI JOYU NIKKI** • 1968
DIARY OF A SHINJUKU BURGLAR (USA) see **SHINJUKU DOROBO NIKKI** • 1969
DIARY OF A SHINJUKU THIEF(UKN) see **SHINJUKU DOROBO NIKKI** • 1969
DIARY OF A SINNER • 1973 • Hunt Ed • CND
DIARY OF A SPACE VIRGIN see **SEXPLORER, THE** • 1975
DIARY OF A SWINGER • 1967 • Amero John, Amero Lem • USA
DIARY OF A TEACHER see **DIARIO DI UN MAESTRO** • 1973
DIARY OF A TEENAGE HITCHHIKER • 1979 • Post Ted • TVM • USA • DIARY OF A HITCH-HIKER
DIARY OF A TEENAGER see **STINE OG DRENGENE** • 1969
DIARY OF A TENEMENT GENTLEMAN see **NAGAYA SHINSHI-ROKU** • 1948
DIARY OF A TIRED MAN see **NIHON NO SEISHUN** • 1968
DIARY OF A TRAFFIC COP see **DIARIO DE UN FISCAL DE TRANSITO** • 1972
DIARY OF A VIOLATED VIRGIN -FEMALE see **BOKO SHOJO NIKK-MESU** • 1968
DIARY OF A VOYAGE IN THE SOUTH PACIFIC see **ODISSEA NUDA** • 1961
DIARY OF A WORKER see **TYOMIEHEN PAIVAKIRJA** • 1967
DIARY OF AN UNKNOWN SOLDIER • 1959 • Watkins Peter • UKN
DIARY OF ANNE FRANK, THE • 1959 • Stevens George • USA
DIARY OF ANNE FRANK, THE • 1980 • Sagal Boris • TVM • USA
DIARY OF ARTISTS AND MODELS see **INTIMATE DIARY OF ARTISTS' MODELS** • 1964
DIARY OF CHUJI'S TRAVELS, A see **CHUJI TABINIKKI** • 1927
DIARY OF FALLEN LEAVES see **OCHIBA NIKKI** • 1954
DIARY OF FANNY HILL, THE • 1964 • USA
DIARY OF FORBIDDEN DREAMS see **CHE?** • 1972
DIARY OF KAY MCALLISTER see **DIARY OF KNOCKERS MCCALLA** • 1968
DIARY OF KNOCKERS MCCALLA • 1968 • *Mahon Barry (P)* • USA • DIARY OF KAY MCALLISTER ○ DIARY OF LOVE MCCALLA
DIARY OF LOVE MCCALLA see **DIARY OF KNOCKERS MCCALLA** • 1968
DIARY OF MAJOR THOMPSON, THE (UKN) see **CARNETS DU MAJOR THOMPSON, LES** • 1955
DIARY OF ONE WHO DISAPPEARED, THE see **ZAPISNIK ZMIZELEHO** • 1978
DIARY OF SUEKO see **NIANCHAN** • 1959
DIARY OF THE DEAD • 1976 • Brown Arvin • USA
DIARY OF THE PIG WAR see **GUERRA DEL CERDO, LA** • 1975
DIARY OF UMAGORO'S TRAVELLING THEATRE see **UKIGUSA NIKKI** • 1955
DIARY OF YUNBOGI, THE see **YUNBOGI NO NIKKI** • 1965
DIAS DE CABIRIO, LOS • 1971 • Merino Fernando • SPN
DIAS DE CENIZA • 1970 • Rojas Abigail, Lejter Herman • VNZ • DAYS OF ASHES
DIAS DE CENIZA • 1978 • Cordido Enver • VNZ • TODOS LOS DIAS SON SABADOS ○ EVERY DAY IS SATURDAY ○ DAYS OF ASHES
DIAS DE COMBATE • 1979 • Gurrola Alfredo • MXC
DIAS DE FERIA • 1959 • Salvia Rafael J. • SPN
DIAS DE HUMO • 1989 • Ezeiza Antonio • SPN • DAYS OF SMOKE ○ KE ARTEKO EGUNAK
DIAS DE ODIO • 1954 • Torre-Nilsson Leopoldo • ARG • DAYS OF HATE (USA) ○ DAYS OF HATRED
DIAS DE OTONO • 1962 • Gavaldon Roberto • MXC
DIAS DE VIEJO COLOR • 1968 • Olea Pedro • SPN • DAYS LIKE OLD TIMES
DIAS DEL AGUA, LOS • 1970 • Gomez Manuel Octavio • CUB • DAYS OF WATER, THE
DIAS DEL AMOR, LOS • 1971 • Isaac Alberto • MXC • DAYS OF LOVE
DIAS DEL ORO NEGRO, LOS • 1971 • Oropeza Daniel • VNZ • BLACK GOLD-DAYS
DIAS DEL PASADA, LOS • 1977 • Camus Mario • SPN • DAYS OF THE PAST
DIAS DIFICILES • 1987 • Pelayo Alejandro • MXC • HARD DAYS
DIAS DUROS, LOS • 1970 • Marmol Julio Cesar • VNZ • THOSE HARD DAYS
DIAS MELHORES VIRAO • 1989 • Diegues Carlos • BRZ • BETTER DAYS WILL COME
DIAS QUE ME DISTE, LOS • 1975 • Siro Fernando • ARG • DAYS YOU GAVE ME, THE
DIAS SE LO PAGUE • 1947 • Amadori Luis Cesar • ARG
DI'ASIMANDON AFORMIN • 1974 • Psarras Tasos • GRC • REASON WHY, THE ○ FOR TRIVIAL REASONS
DIAVOLAT V TCHERKVATA • 1969 • Vesselinov Ivan • ANS • BUL • DEVIL IN CHURCH
DIAVOLEZZA • 1958 • Ritter Otto • UKN, SWT
DIAVOLI DELLA GUERRA, I • 1969 • Albertini Bitto • ITL
DIAVOLI DELLO SPAZIO, I • 1965 • Margheriti Antonio • ITL • SNOW DEVILS (USA) ○ DEVIL MEN FROM SPACE, THE ○ SPACE DEVILS ○ SNOW DEMONS ○ DEVILS FROM SPACE, THE
DIAVOLI DI SPARTIVENTO, I • 1963 • Savona Leopoldo • ITL, FRN • WEAPONS OF VENGEANCE (USA) ○ FIGHTING LEGIONS, THE ○ CURSE OF THE HAUNTED FOREST ○ DEVILS OF SPARTIVENTO, THE
DIAVOLO, IL • 1963 • Polidoro Gian Luigi • ITL • TO BED.. OR NOT TO BED (USA) ○ AMORE IN STOCKHOLM ○ DEVIL, THE
DIAVOLO A QUATTRO, IL • 1977 • Tucci Alfredo M. • ITL
DIAVOLO A SETTE FACCE, IL • 1971 • Civirani Osvaldo • ITL • DEVIL WITH SEVEN FACES, THE ○ DEVIL HAS SEVEN FACES, THE
DIAVOLO BIANCO, IL • 1948 • Malasomma Nunzio • ITL
DIAVOLO CONTRO JUSTEX see **COUPLE IDEAL, LE** • 1945
DIAVOLO E I DIECI COMANDAMENTI, IL see **DIABLE ET LES DIX COMMANDEMENTS, LE** • 1962
DIAVOLO IN CONVENTO, IL • 1951 • Malasomma Nunzio • ITL
DIAVOLO IN CORPO, IL • 1985 • Bellocchio Marco • ITL, FRN • DIABLE AU CORPS, LE (FRN) ○ DEVIL IN THE FLESH, THE
DIAVOLO INNAMORATO, IL see **ARCIDIAVOLO, L'** • 1966
DIAVOLO NEL CERVELLO, IL • 1972 • Sollima Sergio • ITL, FRN • DEVIL IN THE BRAIN, THE
DIAVOLO NERO, IL • 1957 • Grieco Sergio • ITL
DIAVOLO VA IN COLLEGIO, IL • 1944 • Boyer Jean • ITL • SANTARELLINA
DIAVOLO'S DILEMMA • 1903 • *Paul R. W.* • UKN
DIBALIK KELAMBU • 1983 • Karya Teguh • INN • BEHIND THE MOSQUITO NET
DIBELAKANG TABIR • 1970 • Shamsuddin Jins • MLY • BEHIND THE CURTAIN
DICE, THE see **KOCKA** • 1972
DICE OF DESTINY • 1920 • King Henry • USA
DICE PLAYER'S LAST THROW, THE • 1903 • Booth W. R. • UKN
DICE WOMAN, THE • 1927 • Dillon Eddie • USA
DICEN QUE SOY COMUNISTA • 1951 • Galindo Alejandro • MXC
DICEN QUE SOY HOMBRE MALO • 1958 • Delgado Miguel M. • MXC
DICEN QUE SOY MUJERIEGO • 1948 • Rodriguez Roberto • MXC
DICH HAB' ICH GELIEBT • 1929 • Walther-Fein Rudolf • FRG
DICIOTTENNI, LE • 1956 • Mattoli Mario • ITL
DICIOTTENNI AL SOLE • 1962 • Mastrocinque Camillo • ITL • EIGHTEEN IN THE SUN (USA) ○ BEACH PARTY ITALIAN STYLE
DICK AND DAISY • 1912 • *Majestic* • USA
DICK BARTON AT BAY • 1950 • Grayson Godfrey • UKN
DICK BARTON -SPECIAL AGENT • 1948 • Goulding Alf • UKN
DICK BARTON STRIKES BACK • 1949 • Grayson Godfrey • UKN
DICK CARSON WINS THROUGH see **FAILURE, THE** • 1917
DICK CARTER • 1916 • *Dorsch Kathe* • FRG
DICK DEADEYE • 1975 • Melendez Bill • ANM • UKN, USA • DICK DEADEYE, OR DUTY DONE
DICK DEADEYE, OR DUTY DONE see **DICK DEADEYE** • 1975
DICK DOWN UNDER see **TRUE STORY OF ESKIMO NELL, THE** • 1975
DICK FARRELL'S PRIZE • 1911 • *Bison* • USA
DICK HENDERSON • 1926 • *Deforest Phonofilm* • SHT • UKN
DICK HENDERSON • 1930 • *Balcon Michael (P)* • SHT • UKN
DICK POTTER'S WIFE • 1914 • Miller Ashley • USA
DICK SMART 2007 • 1967 • Prosperi Franco • ITL
DICK, THE DEAD SHOT • 1913 • *Shea William* • USA
DICK THE KISSER • 1908 • Aylott Dave? • UKN
DICK TRACY • 1937 • Taylor Ray, James Alan • SRL • USA
DICK TRACY • 1990 • Beatty Warren • USA
DICK TRACY see **DICK TRACY, DETECTIVE** • 1945
DICK TRACY, DETECTIVE • 1945 • Berke William • USA • SPLITFACE (UKN) ○ DICK TRACY
DICK TRACY MEETS GRUESOME • 1947 • Rawlins John • USA • DICK TRACY'S AMAZING ADVENTURE (UKN)
DICK TRACY RETURNS • 1938 • Witney William, English John • SRL • USA
DICK TRACY VERSUS CUEBALL • 1946 • Douglas Gordon • USA
DICK TRACY VS. CRIME INC. • 1941 • English John, Witney William • SRL • USA • DICK TRACY VS. THE PHANTOM EMPIRE
DICK TRACY VS. THE PHANTOM EMPIRE see **DICK TRACY VS. CRIME INC.** • 1941
DICK TRACY'S AMAZING ADVENTURE (UKN) see **DICK TRACY MEETS GRUESOME** • 1947
DICK TRACY'S DILEMMA • 1947 • Rawlins John • USA • MARK OF THE CLAW (UKN)
DICK TRACY'S G-MEN • 1939 • Witney William, English John • SRL • USA
DICK TURPIN • 1925 • Blystone John G. • USA
DICK TURPIN • 1929 • *Banfield George J. (P)* • SER • UKN
DICK TURPIN • 1933 • Stafford John, Hanbury Victor • UKN
DICK TURPIN • 1974 • Merino Fernando • SPN
DICK TURPIN • 1980 • Poulson Gerry • TVM • UKN
DICK TURPIN -HIGHWAYMAN • 1956 • Paltenghi David • UKN
DICK TURPIN'S LAST RIDE TO YORK • 1906 • Raymond Charles? • UKN
DICK TURPIN'S RIDE TO YORK • 1906 • Fitzhamon Lewin • UKN
DICK TURPIN'S RIDE TO YORK • 1913 • Raymond Charles • UKN
DICK TURPIN'S RIDE TO YORK • 1922 • Elvey Maurice • UKN
DICK TURPIN'S RIDE (UKN) see **LADY AND THE BANDIT, THE** • 1951
DICK WHITTINGTON • 1899 • Smith G. A. • UKN
DICK WHITTINGTON AND HIS CAT • 1913 • Blache Alice • USA
DICK WHITTINGTON'S CAT • 1936 • *Iwerks Ub (P)* • ANS • USA
DICKE TURPIN'S RIDE TO YORKE • 1913 • Evans Fred, Evans Joe • UKN
DICKE UND ICH, DER • Lotz • GDR • FATTY AND ME, THE
DICKENS UP-TO-DATE • 1923 • Phillips Bertram • UKN
DICKENSIAN FANTASY, A • 1933 • Ginever Aveling • UKN
DICK'S AUNT • 1908 • *Lubin* • USA
DICK'S FAIRY • 1921 • Wynne Bert • UKN
DICK'S PREDICAMENT • 1912 • *Imp* • USA
DICK'S TURNING • 1913 • McGill Lawrence • USA
DICK'S WIFE • 1912 • *Tennant Barbara* • USA
DICKSON'S DIAMOND • 1914 • West Langdon • USA
DICKY see **TRAPPOLA D'AMORE** • 1940
DICKY DEE'S CARTOON • 1915 • Dyer Anson • ANM • UKN
DICKY MONTEITH • 1922 • Foss Kenelm • UKN
DICKY'S DEMON DACHSHUND • 1915 • *Parker Burnett* • USA
DICTATOR, THE • 1915 • Eagle Oscar • *Famous Players* • USA
DICTATOR, THE • 1915 • Porter Edwin S. • USA
DICTATOR, THE • 1922 • Cruze James • USA
DICTATOR, THE • 1935 • Saville Victor, Santell Alfred • UKN • LOVES OF A DICTATOR, THE (USA) ○ FOR LOVE OF A QUEEN ○ LOVE AFFAIR OF A DICTATOR, THE ○ FOR THE LOVE OF A QUEEN
DICTATOR KALI THANASSI • 1973 • Glykofridis Panos • GRC • THANASSIS AND THE DICTATOR
DICTATOR'S GUNS, THE (USA) see **ARME A GAUCHE, L'** • 1965
DICTEE DU BORDEREAU, LA • 1899 • Melies Georges • FRN
DICTIONARY OF LOVE see **DICTIONARY OF SEX** • 1964
DICTIONARY OF SEX • 1964 • Metzger Radley H. • CMP • USA • DICTIONARY OF LOVE
DICTIONARY OF SUCCESS, THE • 1920 • Physioc Wray • SHT • USA
DICTIONNAIRE DE JOACHIM, LE • 1965 • Borowczyk Walerian • ANS • FRN • JOACHIM'S DICTIONARY (UKN)
DICTIONNAIRE DES PIN-UP GIRLS, LE • 1951 • Gibaud Marcel • SHT • FRN
DID HE OR DID HE NOT? • 1916 • Currier Frank • SHT • USA
DID HE SAVE HER? • 1914 • Griffin Frank C. • USA
DID HE? THE BRUTE! • 1915 • Nash Percy? • UKN
DID I BETRAY? • 1936 • Martin Paul • UKN • BLACK ROSES
DID IT EVER HAPPEN TO YOU? • 1917 • Jackson Harry • SHT • USA
DID 'JA KNOW • 1950 • Barclay David • SHT • USA
DID MOTHER GET HER WISH? • 1912 • Sennett Mack • USA
DID SHE CURE HIM? • 1914 • MacGregor Norval • USA
DID SHE DO WRONG? • 1918 • Morris Reggie • SHT • USA
DID SHE RUN? • 1914 • *Royal* • USA

DID SOMEBODY LAUGH? see **HOR, VAR DER IKKE EN, SOM LO?** • 1978
DID YOU HEAR THE ONE ABOUT THE TRAVELING SALESLADY? • 1968 • Weis Don • USA
DID YOU KNOW THAT? • 1934 • Sparling Gordon • DCS • CND
DID YOU KNOW THAT? FIFTH EDITION • 1940 • Sparling Gordon • DCS • CND
DID YOU KNOW THAT? FOURTH EDITION • 1939 • Sparling Gordon • DCS • CND
DID YOU KNOW THAT? SECOND EDITION • 1936 • Sparling Gordon • DCS • CND
DID YOU KNOW THAT? SEVENTH EDITION • 1943 • Sparling Gordon • DCS • CND
DID YOU KNOW THAT? SIXTH EDITION • 1941 • Sparling Gordon • DCS • CND
DID YOU KNOW THAT? THIRD EDITION • 1937 • Sparling Gordon • DCS • CND
DIDA IBSENS GESCHICHTE see **TAGEBUCH EINER VERLORENEN 2, DAS** • 1918
DIDDLEDI • 1912 • Calvert Charles? • UKN
DIDI • 1937 • *Sircar B. N. (P)* • IND
DIDI IN FORM AGAIN see **DIDI WIEDER VOLL IN FORM** • 1989
DIDI WIEDER VOLL IN FORM • 1989 • Hallervorden Didi • FRG • DIDI IN FORM AGAIN
DIDN'T YOU KILL MY BROTHER? see **COMIC STRIP PRESENTS: DIDN'T YOU KILL MY BROTHER?** • 1987
DIDUMS AND A POLICEMAN • 1912 • Noy Wilfred • UKN
DIDUMS AND THE BATHING MACHINE • 1911 • Noy Wilfred • UKN
DIDUMS AND THE CHRISTMAS PUDDING • 1911 • Noy Wilfred • UKN
DIDUMS AND THE HADDOCK • 1911 • Noy Wilfred • UKN
DIDUMS AND THE MONKEY • 1912 • Noy Wilfred • UKN
DIDUMS AS AN ARTIST • 1912 • Noy Wilfred • UKN
DIDUMS AT SCHOOL • 1912 • Stow Percy • UKN
DIDUMS ON HIS HOLIDAYS • 1912 • Noy Wilfred • UKN
DIE • 1966 • Schofill John • SHT • USA
DIE, DARLING, DIE • 1973 • Wendkos Paul • TVM • USA
DIE! DIE! MY DARLING (USA) see **FANATIC** • 1965
DIE HARD • 1988 • McTiernan John • USA
DIE HARD 2 see **DIE HARD 2 –DIE HARDER** • 1990
DIE HARD 2 –DIE HARDER • 1990 • Harlin Renny • USA • DIE HARD 2
DIE-HARD SHOEMAKERS, THE see **SKALNI SEVCI** • 1931
DIE IS CAST, THE see **DES SONT SUR LE TAPIS, LES** • 1960
DIE IS CAST, THE see **TARNINGEN AR KASTAD** • 1960
DIE IS CAST, THE (UKN) see **JEUX SONT FAIT, LES** • 1947
DIE LAUGHING • 1980 • Werner Jeff • USA
DIE, MONSTER, DIE (USA) see **MONSTER OF TERROR** • 1965
DIE–ODER KEINE • 1932 • Froelich Carl • FRG
DIE SCREAMING, MARIANNE • 1970 • Walker Pete • UKN
...DIE SICH VERKAUFTEN • 1924 • Greiner Fritz • FRG
DIE SISTER DIE • 1974 • Hood Randall • USA
DIE, SISTER, DIE • 1980 • Foreman Ronald Kent • USA
DIE SLOWLY, YOU'LL ENJOY IT MORE see **MISTER DYNAMIT – MORGEN KUSST EUCH DER TOD** • 1967
DIE TO BE BORN • 1979 • Rivera Homera • SHT • NTH
DIE VOM ANDEREN UFER • 1926 • Bergen Arthur • FRG
DIE VOM NIEDERRHEIN • 1925 • Walther-Fein Rudolf • FRG
DIE VOM NIEDERRHEIN • 1933 • Obal Max • FRG
DIE VOM RUMMELPLATZ • 1930 • Lamac Carl • FRG
DIE VOM SCHICKSAL VERFOLGTEN • 1927 • Kleinmann Henk • FRG
DIE VON DER SCHOLLE SIND • 1928 • Lang Alexander • FRG
DIE VON DER WATERKANT • 1926 • Lisson Heinz • FRG
DIE WELT IST MEIN! see **UNSICHTBARER GEHT DURCH DIE STADT, EIN** • 1933
DIEB IM SCHLAFCOUPE, DER • 1929 • Lowenbein Richard • AUS • PRINZESSIN AUF URLAUB
DIEB SIENES EIGENTUMS, DER see **FLIEGENDEN BRIGANTEN 1, DIE** • 1921
DIEB UND WEIB • 1920 • Berger Martin? • FRG
DIEB VON SAN MARENGO, DER • 1963 • Reisch Gunter • GDR • THIEF OF SAN MARENGO, THE
DIEBARE DIPLOMAT • 1975 • SAF
DIEBE • 1928 • Heuberger Edmund, Gambino Domenico M. • FRG
DIEBE UND LIEBE • 1917 • Mack Max • FRG
DIEBESFALLE, DIE • 1920 • de Siqueira Waldemar • FRG
DIEBIN VON BAGDAD, DIE • 1952 • Lamac Carl • FRG
DIECI ANNI DELLA CECCOSLOVACCHIA, I • 1929 • Anton Karl • ITL
DIECI ANNI DELLA NOSTRA VITA • 1953 • Marcellini Romolo • DOC • ITL
DIECI BIANCHI UCCISI DA UN PICCOLO INDIANO • 1976 • Baldanello Gianfranco • ITL
DIECI CANZONI D'AMORE DA SALVARE • 1953 • Calzavara Flavio • ITL
DIECI COMANDAMENTI, I • 1945 • Chili Giorgio W. • ITL
DIECI GLADIATORI, I • 1964 • Parolini Gianfranco • ITL • TEN GLADIATORS, THE (USA) ○ TEN DESPERATE MEN
DIECI INCREDIBILI GIORNI (ITL) see **DECADE PRODIGIEUSE, LA** • 1971
DIECI ITALIANI PER UN TEDESCO • 1962 • Ratti Filippo M. • ITL • VIA RASELLA
DIECI MERAVIGLIE DELL'AMORE, LE • 1969 • Bergonzelli Sergio • ITL
DIECI MINUTI DI VITA • 1943 • Longanesi Leo • ITL • VIVERE ANCORA
DIECIMILA DOLLARI PER UN MASSACRO • 1967 • Guerrieri Romolo • ITL • TEN THOUSAND DOLLARS FOR A MASSACRE ○ 10,000 DOLLARS BLOOD MONEY
DIED ON DUTY see **UBIT PRI ISPOLNYENII** • 1978
DIEF • 1981 • Canning William • CND
DIEGO AND ALICIA see **DIEGO Y ALICIA** • 1972
DIEGO CORRIENTES • 1924 • Buchs Jose • SPN
DIEGO CORRIENTES • 1936 • Iquino Ignacio F. • SPN
DIEGO CORRIENTES • 1959 • Isasi Antonio • SPN
DIEGO, THE RAT see **DIEGONG DAGA** • 1968
DIEGO Y ALICIA • 1972 • Suarez Gonzalo • SPN • DIEGO AND ALICIA
DIEGONG DAGA • 1968 • Buenaventura Augusto • PHL • DIEGO, THE RAT
DIEGUE–BI • 1970 • Traore Mahama Johnson • SNL • WOMAN, THE
DIENER IHRES FREUNDES, DER • Mack Max • FRG
DIENER LASSEN BITTEN • 1936 • Zerlett Hans H. • FRG
DIENST IST DIENST • 1931 • Boese Carl • FRG
DIEP NEDERLAND • 1956 • van der Linden Charles Huguenot • DOC • NTH • DEEP HOLLAND
DIEPPE 1942 • 1979 • Macartney-Filgate Terence • CND
DIEPTE • 1932 • Baert Germain, Buysse Cyriel • BLG • PROFONDEURS DE LA MER, LES ○ DEPTHS OF THE SEA
DIES IRAE see **VREDENS DAG** • 1943
DIES IRAE see **VARIATIONS ON THE SAME THEME** • 1978
DIES RIGOROSE LEBEN • 1983 • Glowna Vadim • FRG
DIESE NACHT VERGESS' ICH NIE • 1949 • Meyer Johannes • FRG
DIESEL • 1942 • Lamprecht Gerhard • FRG
DIESEL • 1986 • Kramer Robert • FRN
DIESEL STORY, THE • 1951 • Cole Lionel • DOC • UKN
DIESER MANN GEHORT MIR • 1950 • Verhoeven Paul • FRG
DIESES LIED BLIEBT BEI DIR • 1954 • Forst Willi • FRG • CABARET (USA)
DIESMAL MUSS ES KAVIAR SEIN • 1961 • von Radvanyi Geza • FRG, FRN
DIETER, DER MENSCH UNTER STEINEN • 1924 • Berger Josef • FRG • WEIB IN NOT
DIETRO LA FACCIATA (ITL) see **DU MOURON POUR LES PETITS OISEAUX** • 1962
DIETRO LA MASCHERA • 1921 • Korda Alexander • ITL
DIEU A BESOIN DES HOMMES • 1950 • Delannoy Jean • FRN • ISLE OF SINNERS (UKN) ○ GOD NEEDS MAN (USA)
DIEU A CHOISI PARIS • 1969 • Arthuys Philippe, Prouteau Gilbert • CMP • FRN
DIEU DU HASARD, LE • 1919 • Pouctal Henri • FRN • GOD OF LUCK, THE
DIEU LE VENT see **DEUS LO VOLT** • 1978
DIEUX, LES • 1961 • Dufaux Georges, Godbout Jacques • DCS • CND
DIEUX DU DIMANCHE, LES • 1948 • Lucot Rene • FRN
DIEUX DU FEU, LES • 1961 • Storck Henri • DOC • BLG
DIEUX DU PASSE, LES • 1958 • Martin Marcel • SHT • FRN
DIEUX ONT SOIF, LES • 1926 • Marodon Pierre • FRN
DIEUX S'AMUSENT, LES • 1935 • Valentin Albert, Schunzel Reinhold • FRN • AMPHITRYON II
DIEXUE HEIGU • 1985 • Wu Ziniu, Li Jingmin • CHN • SECRET DECREE
DIEZ DIAS MILLONARIA • 1934 • Buchs Jose • SPN
DIEZ MIL DOLARES PARA LASSITER • 1965 • Romero-Marchent Rafael • SPN, ITL • 100,000 DOLLARI PER LASSITER (ITL)
DIEZ NEGRITOS see **AND THEN THERE WERE NONE** • 1974
DIFENDO IL MIO AMORE • 1956 • Macchi Giulio, Sherman Vincent • ITL • DEFEND MY LOVE (USA) ○ I'LL DEFEND YOU MY LOVE
DIFENDO IL MIO AMORE • 1956 • Matarazzo Raffaello • ITL • SCANDALO A MILANO
DIFERENTE • 1961 • Delgado Luis Maria, Grinan Jorge • SPN
DIFFERENCE 1965–66, A see **ROZNICA 1965–66** • 1966
DIFFERENCE, THE • 1986 • Lasry Pierre • MTV • CND
DIFFERENCE, THE see **HITCH–HIKER, THE** • 1953
DIFFERENCE N'A PAS D'IMPORTANCE, LA • 1984 • Goulet Stella (c/d) • MTV • CND
DIFFERENCE OF OPINION, A • 1915 • Physioc Wray • USA
DIFFERENCES • 1981 • Shapiro Nesya • CND
DIFFERENT AFFAIR, A • 1987 • Nosseck Noel • TVM • USA
DIFFERENT DRUMMER: ELVIN JONES • 1979 • Gray Edward • SHT • USA
DIFFERENT ENDING, A see **STARTLING CLIMAX, THE** • 1917
DIFFERENT FROM THE OTHERS see **ANDERS ALS DIE ANDERN** • 1919
DIFFERENT INCARNATIONS OF DURGA see **UMA CHANDI GOWRI SANKARULA KATHA** • 1968
DIFFERENT MAN, THE • 1914 • *Billington Francelia* • USA
DIFFERENT RULERS OF THE WORLD • 1909 • *Pathe* • FRN
DIFFERENT SONS • 1971 • Ofield Jack • USA
DIFFERENT SONS see **FUTARI NO MUSUKO** • 1962
DIFFERENT STORY, A • 1978 • Aaron Paul • USA
DIFFERENT SUNRISE, A see **DISTINTO AMANACER** • 1943
DIFFICILE MORIRE • 1977 • Silva Umberto • ITL
DIFFICULT COURTSHIP, A • 1910 • Fitzhamon Lewin? • UKN
DIFFICULT DAYS see **ROZHAI DUSHWAR** • 1974
DIFFICULT GUEST, THE see **KLOPOTLIWY GOSC** • 1971
DIFFICULT HAPPINESS, THE see **TRUDNOE SCHASTE** • 1958
DIFFICULT LIFE, A see **VITA DIFFICILE, UNA** • 1961
DIFFICULT LIFE OF AN ADVENTURER, THE see **TEZKY ZIVOT DOBRODRUHA** • 1941
DIFFICULT LOVE see **TRUDNA MILOSC** • 1953
DIFFICULT LOVE see **AMORES DIFICILES, LOS** • 1967
DIFFICULT LOVE, A see **OSTRE SLEDOVANE VLAKY** • 1966
DIFFICULT LOVE, A see **TROUDNA LYUBOV** • 1974
DIFFICULT PASS, THE • 1965 • Erzikian Yu. • USS
DIFFICULT PEOPLE see **NEHEZ EMBEREK** • 1964
DIFFICULT SHAVE, A • 1905 • Green Tom? • UKN
DIFFICULT TO GET ENGAGED see **...SCHWIERIG SICH ZU VERLOBEN** • 1983
DIFFICULT TRUTH, THE see **VERITA DIFFICILE, LA** • 1968
DIFFICULT WAY, THE • 1914 • Tucker George Loane • UKN
DIFFICULT WOMAN, A • 1988 • Lewin Ben?, Millar Catherine? • ASL
DIFFICULT YEARS (USA) see **ANNI DIFFICILI** • 1948
DIFFICULTE D'ETRE INFIDELE, LA • 1963 • Toublanc-Michel Bernard • FRN, ITL • PIACERI CONIUGALI, I (ITL)
DIFFICULTY • Andonov Ivan • ANS • BUL
DIFUNTO ES UN VIVO, EL • 1955 • Llado Juan • SPN
DIG • 1972 • Hubley John, Hubley Faith • ANS • USA
DIG A MILLION: MAKE A MILLION • 1969 • Haydon Tom • DOC • ASL
DIG FOR VICTORY • 1941 • Hankinson Michael • UKN
DIG THAT DOG • 1954 • Patterson Ray • ANS • USA
DIG THAT GOLD • 1948 • Yates Hal • SHT • USA
DIG THAT JULIET see **ROMANOFF AND JULIET** • 1961
DIG THAT URANIUM • 1956 • Bernds Edward • USA
DIG UP • 1922 • Roach Hal • SHT • USA
DIGA DEL GHIACCIAIO, LA • 1954 • Olmi Ermanno • DCS • ITL
DIGA DI MAGHMOD, LA • 1929 • Alessandrini Goffredo • DOC • ITL
DIGA SUL PACIFICO, LA (ITL) see **BARRAGE CONTRE LE PACIFIQUE** • 1958
DIGAN LO QUE DIGAN • 1968 • Camus Mario • SPN, ARG • SAY WHAT THEY MAY
DIGBY –THE BIGGEST DOG IN THE WORLD • 1973 • McGrath Joseph • UKN
DIGGER EARL, THE • 1924 • Smith Beaumont • ASL
DIGGERS • 1931 • Thring F. W. • ASL
DIGGERS IN BLIGHTY • 1933 • Hanna Pat • ASL
DIGGING DEEP see **MAN I WANT, THE** • 1934
DIGGING FOR GOLD • 1936 • Hopwood R. A. • UKN
DIGGING FOR VICTORY • 1942 • Halas John, Batchelor Joy • ANS • UKN
DIGITAL DREAMS • 1983 • Dornhelm Robert • AUS, UKN
DIGITAL KNIGHTS see **DUNGEONMASTER, THE** • 1985
DIGMAAN SA KARATE • 1967 • Gaudite Solano • PHL • KARATE WAR
DIGNIFIED FAMILY, A • 1915 • *Stonehouse Ruth* • USA
DIGNITY • 1971 • Boyadgieva Lada • BUL
DIGNITY see **JOM** • 1982
DIGTERKONGEN see **GUDERNES YNDLING** • 1919
DIGUE, LA • 1911 • Gance Abel • FRN • DIGUE, OU: POUR SAUVER LA HOLLANDE, LA
DIGUE, OU: POUR SAUVER LA HOLLANDE, LA see **DIGUE, LA** • 1911
DIH/DAH • 1984 • Sprajc Bozo • YGS • BREATH OF AIR, A
DIJK IS DICHT, DE • 1959 • Koolhaas Anton • NTH • DIKE IS SEALED, THE
DIJKBOUW • 1952 • Haanstra Bert • NTH • DIKE BUILDERS
DIKAIA OKHOTA KOROLIA STAKHA • 1979 • Roubinchik Valeri • USS
DIKAYA SOBAKA DINGO see **DINKAYA SOBAKA DINGO** • 1963
DIKE BUILDERS see **DIJKBOUW** • 1952
DIKE IS SEALED, THE see **DIJK IS DICHT, DE** • 1959
DIKI MYOD • 1967 • Chebotaryov Vladimir • USS • WILD HONEY
DIKI TIS CHOUNDAS, I • 1981 • Thedossopoulos Theodossis • GRC • TRIAL OF THE JUNTA, THE
DIKI TON DIKASTON, I • 1973 • Glykofridis Panos • GRC • TRIAL OF THE JUDGES, THE
DIKIE MOE • 1962 • Deitch Gene • ANS • USA
DIKSHUL WAPAS • 1943 • *Sircar B. N. (P)* • IND
DIKTATOREN, DIE • 1961 • Pomaniczky Felix • FRG
DIKTATUR DER LIEBE 1, DIE • 1921 • Zeyn Willy • FRG • BOSE LUST, DIE
DIKTATUR DER LIEBE 2, DIE • 1921 • Sauer Fred • FRG • WELT OHNE LIEBE (DIE FRAU OHNE HERZ), EINE ○ WELT OHNE LIEBE, DIE
DIL HI TO HAI • 1963 • *Kapoor Raj* • IND
DIL KI RAANI • 1947 • *Kapoor Raj* • IND
DIL NE PUKARA • 1967 • Mohan • IND • CALL OF THE HEART, THE
DILAN • 1987 • Kiral Erden • TRK, FRG
DILE QUE LA QUIERO • 1963 • Martinez Solares Gilberto • MXC
DILEMMA • 1962 • Carlsen Henning • DNM, SAF • WORLD OF STRANGERS, A
DILEMMA • 1989 • Coppens Freddy • BLG
DILEMMA see **DUVIDHA** • 1973
DILEMMA see **CHOICES** • 1981
DILEMMA, THE • 1912 • Cabanne W. Christy • USA
DILEMMA, THE • 1914 • Vale Travers • USA
DILES QUE NO ME MATEN • 1986 • Siso Freddy • VNZ • TELL THEM NOT TO KILL ME
DILIGENCIA DE LA MUERTE, LA • 1959 • Gonzalez Rogelio A. • MXC
DILIGENCIA DE LOS CONDENADOS, LA • 1970 • Bosch Juan • SPN
DILIZANSA SNOVA • 1960 • Jovanovic Soja • YGS • COACH OF DREAMS, THE
DILL JONES AND HIS ALL STARS • 1960 • Henryson Robert • SHT • UKN
DILLINGER • 1945 • Nosseck Max • USA
DILLINGER • 1973 • Milius John • USA
DILLINGER 70 see **TEMPS DES LOUPS –TEMPO DI VIOLENZA, LE** • 1970
DILLINGER E MORTO • 1969 • Ferreri Marco • ITL • DILLINGER IS DEAD (UKN)
DILLINGER IS DEAD (UKN) see **DILLINGER E MORTO** • 1969
DILLY AND DALLY • 1927 • Newman Widgey R. • UKN
DILOROM • 1969 • Khamraev Ali • USS
DIM • 1967 • Kosovalic Slobodan • YGS • SMOKE
DIM LITTLE ISLAND • 1949 • Jennings Humphrey • DOC • UKN
DIM SUM • 1985 • Wang Wayne • USA • DIM SUM: A LITTLE BIT OF HEART
DIM SUM: A LITTLE BIT OF HEART see **DIM SUM** • 1985
DIMA GORINA • 1961 • Dovlatyan Frunze, Mirsky Lev • USS • CAREER OF DIMA
DIMANA GAJAH BERDIRI TEGAK see **RUMAH PUAKA** • 1957
DIMANCHE, UN • 1948 • Vilardebo Carlos • SHT • FRN
DIMANCHE A LA COMPAGNE, UN • 1984 • Tavernier Bertrand • FRN • SUNDAY IN THE COUNTRY (UKN)
DIMANCHE A PEKIN • 1955 • Marker Chris • FRN
DIMANCHE D'AMERIQUE • 1961 • Carle Gilles • DCS • CND
DIMANCHE DE FLICS, UN • 1982 • Vianey Michel • FRN
DIMANCHE DE LA VIE, LE • 1967 • Herman Jean • FRN, FRG, ITL • SUNDAY OF LIFE, THE (USA)
DIMANCHE DE MAI, UN • 1963 • Goretta Claude • MTV • SWT
DIMANCHE D'ETE, UN (FRN) see **DOMENICA D'ESTATE, UNA** • 1962
DIMANCHE EN ALSACE • 1948 • Tedesco Jean • SHT • FRN
DIMANCHE–GRANIT • 1978 • Leduc Jacques • DCS • CND
DIMANCHES DE VILLE D'AVRAY, LES • 1962 • Bourguignon Serge • FRN • SUNDAYS AND CYBELE (USA) ○ CYBELE
DIMANCHES POUR L'ALGERIE • 1963 • Rachedi Ahmed • SHT • ALG
DIMBOOLA • 1979 • Duigan John • ASL
DIME BOX • 1971 • *Schwartz Marvin* • MXC
DIME NOVEL DETECTIVE, THE • 1909 • *Lubin* • USA
DIME NOVEL HERO, THE • 1915 • *Superba* • USA
DIME STORE • 1949 • Anderson Dorsey • SHT • USA

DIME TO RETIRE • 1955 • McKimson Robert • ANS • USA
DIME WITH A HALO • 1963 • Sagal Boris • USA
DIMENSION 5 • 1966 • Adreon Franklin • USA • DIMENSION FOUR (UKN)
DIMENSION FOUR (UKN) see **DIMENSION 5** • 1966
DIMENSION LUMINEUSE • 1962 • Regnier Michel • DCS • CND
DIMENSIONS • Munteanu Stefan • ANS • RMN
DIMENSIONS • 1966 • Longpre Bernard • ANS • CND
DIMENSIONS DE LA CLASSE • 1970 • Moreau Michel • DCS • CND
DIMENSIONS OF DIALOGUE see **MOZNOSTI DIALOGU** • 1982
DIMENTICA IL MIO PASSATO (ITL) see **RIO GUADALQUIVIR** • 1956
DIMENTICARE PALERMO • 1990 • Rosi Francesco • ITL, FRN • TO FORGET PALERMO
DIMENTICARE VENEZIA • 1979 • Brusati Franco • ITL • TO FORGET VENICE ○ FORGET VENICE
DIMENTICATI • 1959 • De Seta Vittorio • ITL
DIME'S WORTH, A • 1969 • Applebee Robert • SHT • CND
DIMINETILE UNUI BAIAT CUMINTE • 1966 • Blaier Andrei • RMN • MORNINGS OF A SENSIBLE YOUTH, THE
DIMITRI DONSKOI • 1944 • Yutkevich Sergei • DOC • USS
DIMITRI MOU, DIMITRI MOU • 1967 • Karayannis Kostas • GRC • MY DIMITRI, MY DIMITRI ○ DIMITRI, MY DARLING
DIMITRI, MY DARLING see **DIMITRI MOU, DIMITRI MOU** • 1967
DIMITRI SHOSTAKOVICH: VIOLA SONATA • Aranovich S., Sokurov Alexander • DOC • USS
DIMITRIE CANTEMIR • 1973 • Vitandis Gheorghe • RMN
DIMITROVGRADTSI • 1956 • Korabov Nicolai, Mundrov Dutcho • BUL • PEOPLE OF DIMITROVGRAD ○ MEN OF DIMITROVGRAD
DIMITRY ARAKISHVILI • 1952 • Abuladze Tengiz, Chkheidze Revaz • DOC • USS
DIMKA (USA) see **YA KAPIL PAPU** • 1963
DIMKY see **DYMKY** • 1966
DIMMI CHE FAI TUTTO PER ME • 1976 • Festa Campanile Pasquale • ITL
DIMPLES • 1916 • Jones Edgar • USA
DIMPLES • 1936 • Seiter William A. • USA
DIMPLES AND DANGERS • 1918 • *Gribbon Harry* • SHT • USA
DIMPLES AND TEARS • 1929 • Harrison Jack • SHT • UKN • CAMERA COCKTALES NO.3
DIMPLES AND THE RING • 1915 • North Wilfred • USA
DIMPLE'S BABY • 1917 • North Wilfred • SHT • USA
DIMPLES, THE AUTO SALESMAN • 1915 • North Wilfred • USA
DIMPLES, THE DIPLOMAT • 1917 • North Wilfred • SHT • USA
DIN NABOS SON • 1981 • Petersen Jorgen Flindt, Stephensen Erik • DNM • YOUR NEIGHBOUR'S SON
DIN STUND PA JORDEN • 1972 • Sjostrand • MTV • SWD • YOUR TIME ON EARTH
DIN TILLVAROS LAND • 1940 • Sucksdorff Arne • DCS • SWD • YOUR OWN LAND ○ THIS LAND IS FULL OF LIFE
DINA AND DJANGO see **DINA E DJANGO** • 1982
DINA CHEZ LES ROIS • 1966 • Delouche Dominique • SHT • FRN
DINA DZA-DZU • 1925 • Shengelaya Nikolai, Zhelyabuzhsky Yuri • USS
DINA E DJANGO • 1982 • Nordlund Solveig • PRT • DINA AND DJANGO
DINAH • 1933 • Fleischer Dave • ANS • USA
DINAH EAST • 1970 • Nash Gene • USA • STORY OF DINAH EAST, THE ○ HOLLYWOOD SUPERSTAR
DINAMITA ESTA SERVIDA, LA • 1968 • Merino Fernando • SPN • DYNAMITE IS READY, THE
DINAMITA JIM • 1966 • Balcazar Alfonso • SPN, ITL • DINAMITE JIM (ITL)
DINAMITA KID • 1960 • Curiel Federico • MXC
DINAMITE JIM (ITL) see **DINAMITA JIM** • 1966
DINAMITE JOE see **JOE L'IMPLACABILE** • 1967
DINAMITEROS, LOS • 1962 • Atienza Juan G. • SPN
DINAMO DELL'EROISMO, LA see **O LA BORSA O LA VITA** • 1933
DINANZI A NOI IL CIELO • 1958 • Savarese Roberto • ITL
DINASTIA DE DRACULA, LA • 1978 • Crevenna Alfredo B. • MXC
DINASTIA DE LA MUERTE, LA • 1975 • *Reynosa* • MXC
DINCOLO DE NISIPURI • 1973 • Gabrea Radu • RMN • BEYOND THE SANDS
DINCOLO DE POD • 1974 • Veroiu Mircea • RMN • OTHER SIDE OF THE BRIDGE, THE ○ BEYOND THE BRIDGE
DINDON, LE • 1913 • Pouctal Henri • FRN
DINDON, LE • 1951 • Barma Claude • FRN
DINE BORN FRA AMERIKA • 1969 • Reenberg Annelise • DNM • YOUR KIDS FROM THE STATES
DINER • 1982 • Levinson Barry • USA
DINER IMPOSSIBLE, LE • 1904 • Melies Georges • FRN • IMPOSSIBLE DINNER, THE (USA)
DINER TRES SPECIAL, UN • 1977 • Benazeraf Jose • FRN
DINERO DEL DIABLO, EL • *Clasa-Mohme* • MXC • DEVIL'S MONEY, THE
DINERO MALDITO • 1949 • Rivero Fernando A. • MXC
DINERO NO ES LA VIDA, EL • 1951 • Diaz Morales Jose • MXC
DINERO TIENE MIEDO, EL • 1970 • Lazaga Pedro • SPN
DINEROS DEL DIABLO, LOS • 1952 • Galindo Alejandro • MXC
DING-DONG • 1972 • Grgic Zlatko • ANS • YGS
DING DONG BELL • 1912 • *Champion* • USA
DING DONG DADDY • 1942 • Freleng Friz • ANS • USA
DING DONG DOGGIE • 1937 • Fleischer Dave • ANS • USA
DING DONG WILLIAMS • 1945 • Berke William • USA • MELODY MAKER (UKN)
DINGAKA • 1965 • Uys Jamie • SAF
DINGBAT LAND • 1949 • *Terry Paul (P)* • ANS • USA
DINGE GIBT'S DIE GIBT'S GAR NICHT • 1966 • Sacher Otto • ANS • GDR • THINGS EXIST THAT DO NOT EXIST AT ALL ○ THERE ARE MORE THINGS IN HEAVEN AND EARTH
DINGE ZWISCHEN HIMMEL UND ERDE see **GEHEIMBUNDSKLAVEN 1** • 1922
DINGERTJIE EN IDI • 1978 • De Villiers Dirk • SAF • LITTLE THING AND IDI, THE
DINGERTJIE IS DYNAMITE • 1975 • SAF
DINGLES, THE • 1990 • Drew Les • ANS • CND
DINGO • 1990 • De Heer Rolf • ASL
DINGO, THE • 1923 • Brampton Kenneth • ASL
DINGUE, LE • 1972 • Daert Daniel • FRN
DINHEIRO DOS POBRES, O • 1953 • Semedo Artur • PRT
DINKAYA SOBAKA DINGO • 1963 • Karasik Yuli • USS • WILD DOG DINGO ○ DIKAYA SOBAKA DINGO
DINKEY DOODLE • 1929 • Bray John R. • USA
DINKLESPIEL'S BABY • 1914 • Seay Charles M. • USA
DINKUM BLOKE, THE • 1923 • Longford Raymond • ASL
DINKUM OIL • 1921 • *Murphy Fred E. (Ph)* • ASL • ON THE TRACK OF OIL
DINKY • 1935 • Lederman D. Ross, Bretherton Howard • USA
DINKY DOODLE • 1924-26 • Lantz Walter • ASS • USA
DINKY DOODLE AND THE LITTLE ORPHAN • 1926 • Lantz Walter • ANS • USA
DINKY DOODLE IN EGYPT • 1926 • Lantz Walter • ANS • USA
DINKY DOODLE IN LOST AND FOUND • 1926 • Lantz Walter • ANS • USA
DINKY DOODLE IN THE ARCTIC • 1926 • Lantz Walter • ANS • USA
DINKY DOODLE IN THE ARMY • 1926 • Lantz Walter • ANS • USA
DINKY DOODLE IN THE CIRCUS • 1925 • Lantz Walter • ANS • USA
DINKY DOODLE IN THE WILD WEST • 1926 • Lantz Walter • ANS • USA
DINKY DOODLE IN UNCLE TOM'S CABIN • 1926 • Lantz Walter • ANS • USA
DINKY DOODLE'S BEDTIME STORY • 1926 • Lantz Walter • ANS • USA
DINKY FINDS A HOME • 1946 • Donnelly Eddie • ANS • USA
DINNER AT EIGHT • 1933 • Cukor George • USA
DINNER AT THE RITZ • 1937 • Schuster Harold • UKN
DINNER BELL ROMANCE, A • 1913 • *Nestor* • USA
DINNER DATE see **CLAUDIA** • 1985
DINNER DATE, THE • 1960 • *Halas John (P)* • ANS • UKN
DINNER FOR ADELE (USA) see **ADELA JESTE NEVECERELA** • 1977
DINNER HOUR • 1906 • Collins Alf? • UKN
DINNER HOUR, THE • 1920 • Roach Hal • SHT • USA
DINNER JEST, A • 1926 • *Sennett Mack (P)* • SHT • USA
DINNER TIME • 1928 • Terry Paul • ANS • USA
DINNER TIME • 1962 • Ermler Friedrich • USS
DINNER UNDER DIFFICULTIES, A (USA) see **SALLE A MANGER FANTASTIQUE** • 1898
DINO • 1957 • Carr Thomas • USA • KILLER DINO (UKN)
DINOSAUR • 1975 • Bicat Tony • UKN
DINOSAUR • 1980 • Vinton Will • ANS • USA
DINOSAUR AND THE MISSING LINK, THE • 1914 • O'Brien Willis • ANS • USA
DINOSAUR DESTROYER • 1959 • Glut Don • SHT • USA
DINOSAUR ISLAND see **ISLA DE LOS DINOSAUROS, LA** • 1966
DINOSAURA see **DINOZAURY** • 1962
DINOSAURS see **DINOZAURY** • 1962
DINOSAURS.. THE TERRIBLE LIZARDS • 1970 • Chang Wah • ANS • USA
DINOSAURUSI • 1960 • Yeaworth Irvin S. Jr. • USA
DINOZAURY • 1962 • Giersz Witold • ANS • PLN • DINOSAURA ○ DINOSAURS
DINSDAGAVOND • 1966 • van der Lecq Bas • NTH
DINTY • 1920 • Neilan Marshall, McDermott John • USA
DINTY'S DARING DASH • 1916 • *Russell Dan* • SHT • USA • WHERE IS MY HUSBAND?
DIO CHIAMATO DORIAN, IL • 1970 • Dallamano Massimo • ITL, FRG, LCH • BILDNIS DES DORIAN GRAY, DAS (FRG) ○ SECRET OF DORIAN GRAY, THE ○ DORIAN GRAY (USA) ○ GOD CALLS DORIAN ○ EVILS OF DORIAN GRAY, THE
DIO COME TI AMO! (ITL) see **COMO TE AMO!** • 1966
DIO E CON NOI see **GOTT MIT UNS** • 1964
DIO E CON NOI see **GOTT MIT UNS** • 1970
DIO IN CIELO.. ARIZONA IN TERRA • 1972 • Iquino Ignacio F. • ITL
DIO LI CREA, IO LI AMMAZZO • 1968 • Bianchini Paolo • ITL • GOD CREATED THEM, I KILL THEM
DIO LI FA POI LI ACCOPPIA • 1983 • Steno • ITL • GOD CREATES THEM AND THEN PUTS THEM TOGETHER
DIO NON C'ERA see **QUEL GIORNO DIO NON C'ERA** • 1970
DIO NON PAGA IL SABATO • 1967 • Boccia Tanio • ITL, SPN
DIO PERDONA.. IO NO! • 1967 • Colizzi Giuseppe • ITL, SPN • GOD FORGIVES -I DON'T (USA) ○ TU PERDONAS.. YO NO (SPN) ○ MAY GOD FORGIVE YOU.. I CAN'T ○ BLOOD RIVER
DIO PERDONI LA MIA PISTOLA • 1969 • Gariazzo Mario, Savona Leopoldo • ITL
DIO, SEI PROPRIA UN PADRETERNO see **SUO NOME FACEVA TREMARE.. INTERPOL IN ALLARME, IL** • 1973
DIO SERPENTE, IL (ITL) see **DIOS SERPIENTE, EL** • 1970
DIO SOTTO LA PELLE, IL • 1974 • Quilici Folco, Pinelli C. A. • ITL
DIOGENE see **OTE-TOI DE MON SOLEIL** • 1982
DIOGENES PERHAPS see **MOZDA DIOGEN** • 1968
DIOGENES WEEKLY NO.13 • 1914 • Henderson Dell • USA
DIOGENES WEEKLY NO.23 • 1915 • Henderson Dell • USA
DION BROTHERS, THE see **GRAVY TRAIN, THE** • 1974
DIONNE QUINTUPLETS, THE • 1978 • Brittain Don • DOC • CND
DIONYSOS • 1984 • Rouch Jean • FRN
DIONYSOS NOIR • 1973 • Garaudy Roger • FRN
DIONYSUS • 1963 • Boultenhouse Charles • SHT • USA
DIONYSUS IN '69 • 1970 • De Palma Brian, Fiore Robert, Rubin Bruce • USA
DIOS BENDIGA CADA RINCON DE ESTA CASA • 1977 • Chumez Chumy • SPN
DIOS ELIJIO SUS VIAJEROS see **HORA INCOGNITA, LA** • 1964
DIOS LOS CRIA... • 1953 • Martinez Solares Gilberto • MXC
DIOS LOS CRIA • 1975 • *Cima* • MXC
DIOS NO LO QUIERA • 1956 • Demicheli Tulio • MXC
DIOS NOS MANDA VIVIR • 1954 • Pardave Joaquin • MXC
DIOS SABRA JUZGARNOS • 1960 • Cortes Fernando • MXC
DIOS SERPIENTE, EL • 1970 • Vivarelli Piero • VNZ, ITL • DIO SERPENTE, IL (ITL) ○ SERPENT-GOD, THE ○ GOD SNAKE, THE
DIOS Y YO • 1973 • Melendez Ramiro • CLM • GOD AND I
DIOSA ARRODILLADA, LA • 1947 • Gavaldon Roberto • MXC
DIOSA DE TAHITI, LA • 1952 • Orol Juan • MXC • CHACALES DE LA ISLA VERDE, LOS
DIOSA IMPURA, LA • 1963 • Bo Armando • ARG, MXC
DIOSA SALVAJE, LA • 1974 • Iglesias Miguel • SPN
DIP 'EM AND DO 'EM LTD. • 1914 • Kellino W. P. • UKN
DIP IN THE BRINEY, A • 1913 • *Selig* • USA
DIP IN THE WATER, A • 1915 • Curtis Allen • USA
DIP INTO SOCIETY, A • 1913 • *White Pearl* • USA
DIPHUT YINGHUNG • 1989 • Woo John • HKG • KILLER, THE
DIPINGI DI GIALLO IL TUO POLIZIOTTO • 1970 • Pingitore Pier Francesco • ITL
DIPLODOCUS AT LARGE • 1953 • Glut Don • SHT • USA
DIPLOMA ZA SMRT • 1989 • Tomic Zivorad • YGS • DEATH DIPLOMA
DIPLOMACY • 1916 • *Powers* • SHT • USA
DIPLOMACY • 1916 • Olcott Sidney • *Famous Players* • USA
DIPLOMACY • 1926 • Neilan Marshall • USA
DIPLOMANIACS • 1933 • Seiter William A. • USA
DIPLOMAT INTERRUPTED, A • 1912 • *Selig* • USA
DIPLOMATEN • 1918 • Piel Harry • FRG
DIPLOMATENSAUGLING, DER • 1919 • Schonfelder Erich • FRG
DIPLOMATIC AMBROSE • *Swain Mack* • SHT • USA
DIPLOMATIC CORPSE, THE • 1958 • Tully Montgomery • UKN
DIPLOMATIC COURIER • 1952 • Hathaway Henry • USA
DIPLOMATIC ERROR • 1955 • MacDonald David • UKN
DIPLOMATIC FLO • 1914 • Salter Harry • USA
DIPLOMATIC HENRY • 1915 • Drew Sidney • USA
DIPLOMATIC LOVER, THE see **HOW'S CHANCES** • 1934
DIPLOMATIC MISSION, A • 1918 • Conway Jack • USA
DIPLOMATIC PASSPORT • 1954 • Martel Gene • UKN
DIPLOMATIC POUCH, THE see **SUMKA DIPKURIERA** • 1927
DIPLOMATS, THE • 1929 • Taurog Norman • SHT • USA
DIPLOMATS, THE • 1968 • Lisakovitch Viktor • DOC • USS
DIPLOMAT'S MANSION, THE see **TOKYO YAWA** • 1961
DIPLOMES DU DERNIER RANG, LES • 1982 • Gion Christian • FRN
DIPLOPENIES • 1967 • Skalenakis Giorgos • GRC • DANCING THE SIRTAKI (UKN)
DIPLOTERATOLOGY OR BARDO FOLLY • 1967 • Landow George • USA
DIPPY ADVERTISES FOR A PUP • 1911 • *Nestor* • USA
DIPPY DAN'S DOINGS • 1917 • Blystone John G. • SHT • USA
DIPPY DAUGHTER, THE • 1918 • Roach Hal • SHT • USA
DIPPY DENTIST, THE • 1920 • Roach Hal • SHT • USA
DIPPY DIPLOMAT, THE • 1945 • Culhane James • ANS • USA
DIPPY'S DREAM • 1914 • *Kalem* • USA
DIPPY'S PLIGHT (USA) see **MEPHISTO'S PLIGHT** • 1911
DIPSY GIPSY • 1941 • Pal George • ANS • USA
DIPTYCH see **DIPTYQUE** • 1967
DIPTYQUE • 1967 • Borowczyk Walerian • SHT • FRN • DIPTYCH
DIPUTADO, EL • 1978 • de la Iglesia Eloy • SPN • DEPUTY, THE
DIR GEHORT MEIN HERZ • 1938 • Gallone Carmine • FRG • MY HEART BELONGS TO THEE
DIR ZULIEBE • 1944 • Fric Martin • FRG
DIRECT AU COEUR • 1932 • Lion Roger, Arnaudy • FRN
DIRECT HEIRESS • Soloviev Sergei • USS
DIRECTED BY JOHN FORD • 1971 • Bogdanovich Peter • DOC • USA
DIRECTED BY WILLIAM WYLER • 1986 • Slesin Aviva • DOC • USA
DIRECTEUR ARTISTIQUE, LE see **MUDIRU AL-FANNI, AL-** • 1964
DIRECTION BERLIN see **KIERUNEK BERLIN** • 1968
DIRECTION D'ACTEUR PAR JEAN RENOIR, LA • 1968 • Braunberger Gisele • DCS • FRN
DIRECTION: NOWA HUTA see **KIERUNEK NOWA HUTA** • 1951
DIRECTION OF MAIN STRIKE, THE • 1970 • Ozerov Yury • USS
DIRECTION SOCIALISM see **KIERUNEK SOCJALIZM** • 1959
DIRECTION VENEZUELA see **KIERUNEK WENEZUELA** • 1958
DIRECTIONS OF HARRY HOOTON, THE • Preston Richard • USA
DIRECTISSIMO • 1980 • *Kristel Sylvia*
DIRECTIVITY • 1960 • Jodoin Rene • ANS • CND
DIRECTOIRE GOWN, THE • 1908 • *Essanay* • USA
DIRECTOR, THE • 1970 • Crain William • USA
DIRECTOR, THE see **DIREKTOR** • 1969
DIRECTOR AND THE FILM -DAVID LEAN, THE see **DAVID LEAN** • 1959
DIRECTOR Z.K.'S BIRTHDAY see **NAROZENINY REZISERA Z.K.** • 1987
DIRECTORS, THE see **FIRST NUDIE MUSICAL, THE** • 1976
DIRECTOR'S WIFE, THE see **SENORA DE INTENDENTE, LA** • 1967
DIREKTAN PRENOS • 1983 • Bajic Darko • YGS • LIVE BROADCAST
DIREKTOR • 1969 • Saltykov Alexei • USS • DIRECTOR, THE
DIREKTORENS DATTER • 1912 • Blom August • DNM • CAUGHT IN HIS OWN TRAP
DIRIGEABLE FANTASTIQUE OU LE CAUCHEMAR D'UN INVENTEUR, LE • 1906 • Melies Georges • FRN • INVENTOR CRAZYBRAINS AND HIS WONDERFUL AIRSHIP (USA) ○ FANTASTICAL AIRSHIP, THE
DIRIGIBLE • 1931 • Capra Frank • USA
DIRITTO D'AMARE, IL (ITL) see **DROIT D'AIMER, LE** • 1972
DIRK see **KORTIK** • 1954
DIRK BOUTS • 1976 • Delvaux Andre • BLG • AVEC DIRK BOUTS
DIRKIE • 1969 • Uys Jamie • SAF • LOST IN THE DESERT
DIRNENMORDER VON LONDON, DER • 1976 • Franco Jesus • SWT
DIRNENTRAGODIE • 1927 • Rahn Bruno • FRG • WOMEN WITHOUT MEN (USA) ○ TRAGEDY OF THE STREET
DIRNENTRAGODIE see **ZWISCHEN NACHT UND MORGEN** • 1931
DIRT • Heliczer Piero • USA
DIRT • 1979 • Karson Eric, Naylor Cal • USA
DIRT BIKE KID, THE • 1986 • Caston Hoite C. • USA
DIRT GANG, THE • 1972 • Jameson Jerry • USA
DIRTY ANGEL (UKN) see **SCHMUTZIGER ENGEL** • 1958

DIRTY ANGELS (UKN) see **VERGOGNA, SCHIFOSI!** • 1968
DIRTY BUSINESS, THE see **PRLJAVI FILM** • 1989
DIRTY DANCING • 1987 • Ardolino Emile • USA
DIRTY DAN'S DEMISE • 1915 • Mitchell Bruce • USA
DIRTY DIAMONDS • 1989 • *Reynolds Burt* • TVM • USA
DIRTY DINGUS MCGEE • 1970 • Kennedy Burt • USA
DIRTY DISHES (USA) see **JUMENT VAPEUR, LA** • 1978
DIRTY DR. JEKYLL (?) see **NAUGHTY DR. JEKYLL**
DIRTY DOZEN, THE • 1967 • Aldrich Robert • UKN, USA
DIRTY DOZEN, THE see **EIGHT IRON MEN** • 1953
DIRTY DOZEN: THE DEADLY MISSION, THE • 1987 • Katzin Lee H. • USA
DIRTY DOZEN: THE FATAL MISSION, THE • 1988 • Katzin Lee H. • TVM • USA
DIRTY DOZEN: THE NEXT MISSION, THE • 1985 • McLaglen Andrew V. • TVM • USA
DIRTY DREAMER see **SALE REVEUR** • 1978
DIRTY FACE DAN • 1915 • Franklin Sidney A., Franklin Chester M. • USA
DIRTY-FACE MAX • 1968 • Castillo Tony Ad. Jr. • PHL
DIRTY FILTHY SLIME, THE • 1988 • Decoteau David • USA
DIRTY FINGERS (USA) see **SMUTSIGA FINGRAR** • 1972
DIRTY FIVE, THE see **FILTHY FIVE, THE** • 1968
DIRTY GAME, THE (UKN) see **GUERRE SECRETE** • 1965
DIRTY GANG • *Merenda Luc* • ITL • DESTRUCTION FORCE
DIRTY GERTIE FROM HARLEM USA • 1946 • Williams Spencer • USA
DIRTY GIRLS, THE • 1965 • Metzger Radley H. • USA
DIRTY GIRLS, THE see **BUTA TO GUNKAN** • 1961
DIRTY HALF DOZEN see **HUSTLER SQUAD** • 1976
DIRTY HALF DOZEN, THE • 1983 • Makinen Visa • FNL
DIRTY HANDS (USA) see **MAINS SALES, LES** • 1951
DIRTY HANDS (USA) see **INNOCENTS AUX MAINS SALES, LES** • 1975
DIRTY HARRIET • 1985 • Shore Sig • USA
DIRTY HARRY • 1971 • Siegel Don • USA
DIRTY HAWK, THE see **MASTER BEATER, THE** • 1969
DIRTY HEROES (USA) see **DALLE ARDENNE ALL'INFERNO** • 1968
DIRTY-HO • 1981 • *Liu Gordon* • HKG
DIRTY JOBS see **TERRIFYING CONFESSIONS OF CAPTIVE WOMEN** • 1977
DIRTY JOKE • 1975 • USA
DIRTY KNIGHT'S WORK (USA) see **TRIAL BY COMBAT** • 1976
DIRTY LAUNDRY • 1987 • Webb William • USA
DIRTY LILLY • 1978 • Vincent Chuck • USA
DIRTY LITTLE BILLY • 1972 • Dragoti Stan • USA
DIRTY LITTLE BOY, THE see **BRUDASEK** • 1951
DIRTY LOOKS • 1982 • Vincent Chuck • USA
DIRTY LOOKS see **ALMOST SUMMER** • 1977
DIRTY LOVE • D'Amato Joe • ITL
DIRTY MARY, CRAZY LARRY • 1974 • Hough John • USA
DIRTY MARY (UKN) see **FIANCEE DU PIRATE, LA** • 1969
DIRTY MIND OF YOUNG SALLY, THE • 1972 • Novak Harry • USA • INNOCENT SALLY
DIRTY MOB, THE (UKN) see **AJUSTE DE CUENTAS** • 1973
DIRTY MONEY see **HRIMA ITAN VROMIKO, TO** • 1967
DIRTY MONEY see **MONEY, THE** • 1977
DIRTY MONEY see **GREAT RIVIERA BANK ROBBERY, THE** • 1979
DIRTY MONEY (UKN) see **FLIC, UN** • 1972
DIRTY NIGHT see **BLUE NOTTE** • 1989
DIRTY O'NEIL • 1974 • Freen Howard, Teague Lewis • USA • DIRTY O'NEIL -THE LOVE LIFE OF A COP
DIRTY O'NEIL -THE LOVE LIFE OF A COP see **DIRTY O'NEIL** • 1974
DIRTY OUTLAWS, THE (USA) see **DESPERADO, EL** • 1967
DIRTY PICTURE • 1981 • de la Parra Pim • NTH
DIRTY POOL • 1970 • *Distripix* • USA
DIRTY ROTTEN SCOUNDRELS • 1988 • Oz Frank • USA
DIRTY SEVEN, THE see **SHICHININ NO YAJU** • 1967
DIRTY STORY see **SMUTSIG HISTORIA, EN** • 1984
DIRTY STORY, A see **SALE HISTOIRE, UNE** • 1977
DIRTY TRICKS • 1980 • Rakoff Alvin • CND, USA • ACCROCHE-TOI.. J'ARRIVE
DIRTY TWO, THE see **DITO NELLA PIAGA, IL** • 1969
DIRTY WAR see **GUERRA SUCIA** • 1984
DIRTY WEEKEND see **MORDI E FUGGI** • 1973
DIRTY WESTERN, A • 1975 • Fleetwood David • USA
DIRTY WORK • 1933 • French Lloyd • SHT • USA
DIRTY WORK • 1934 • Walls Tom • UKN
DIRTY WORK IN A BEANERY • 1916 • *Morris Reggie* • SHT • USA
DIRTY WORK IN A LAUNDRY • 1915 • Parrott Charles • USA
DIRTYMOUTH • 1970 • Altman Herbert S. • USA • STORY OF LENNIE BRUCE -DIRTYMOUTH ○ TOUGH GIG, A
DIS BONJOUR A LA DAME • 1977 • Gerard Michel • FRN
DIS LEKKER OM TE LEWE • 1957 • SAF
DIS-MOI QUE TU M'AIMES • 1974 • Boisrond Michel • FRN
DIS-MOI QUI TUER? • 1965 • Perier Etienne • FRN
DISABLED MOTOR, THE • 1900 • Williamson James • UKN
DISAPPEARANCE, THE • 1977 • Cooper Stuart • CND
DISAPPEARANCE OF AIMEE, THE • 1976 • Harvey Anthony • TVM • USA
DISAPPEARANCE OF AZARIA CHAMBERLAIN, THE • 1983 • Rymer Judy • TVM • ASL
DISAPPEARANCE OF FLIGHT 412, THE • 1973 • Taylor Jud • TVM • USA
DISAPPEARANCE OF HARRY, THE • 1982 • Despins Joseph • UKN
DISAPPEARANCE OF HARRY WARRINGTON, THE • 1915 • *Roland Ruth* • USA
DISAPPEARANCE OF HELEN MINTERN, THE • 1916 • Horne James W. • SHT • USA
DISAPPEARANCE OF JOHNNY BRADY, THE • 1916 • *Lily* • SHT • USA
DISAPPEARANCE OF LADY FRANCES CARFAX, THE • 1923 • Ridgwell George • UKN
DISAPPEARANCE OF THE JUDGE, THE • 1919 • Butler Alexander • UKN
DISAPPEARANCES, THE see **MAN FROM ATLANTIS: THE DISAPPEARANCES, THE** • 1977
DISAPPEARED, THE see **PRESOS DESAPARECIDOS** • 1979
DISAPPEARED PRISONERS see **PRESOS DESAPARECIDOS** • 1979
DISAPPEARING GROOM, THE • 1916 • Davey Horace • SHT • USA
DISAPPEARING NECKLACE, THE • 1915 • Horne James W. • USA
DISAPPEARING TRAINS • 1966 • Sremec Rudolf • DOC • YGS • TRAIN THAT DISAPPEARED, THE
DISAPPEARING WATCH, THE • 1908 • *Urban-Eclipse* • USA
DISAPPEARING WORLD see **MIZEJICI SVET** • 1932
DISAPPOINTED LONDON • 1901 • Hepworth Cecil M. • UKN
DISAPPOINTED LOVE • 1917 • *Stull Walter* • USA
DISAPPOINTED MAMA, A • 1912 • Henderson Dell • USA
DISAPPOINTED SUITOR, A • 1915 • Mitchell Bruce • USA
DISAPPOINTED SUITOR'S STRATEGY AND REWARD, THE • 1905 • Green Tom? • UKN
DISAPPOINTED TOFFS, THE • 1904 • *Warwick Trading Co.* • UKN
DISAPPOINTED TOFFS, THE • 1905 • *Warwick Trading Co.* • UKN
DISARMAMENT CONFERENCE • 1931 • *Mintz Charles (P)* • ANS • USA
DISASTER • 1948 • Pine William H. • USA
DISASTER, THE see **UNHEIL, DAS** • 1972
DISASTER AT SILO 7 • 1988 • Elikann Larry • TVM • USA
DISASTER ON THE COASTLINER • 1979 • Sarafian Richard C. • TVM • USA
DISASTROUS BET, A • 1913 • *Lubin* • USA
DISASTROUS IMITATION, A • 1912 • *Cosmopolitan* • UKN
DISBARRED • 1939 • Florey Robert • USA
DISC, THE • 1987 • Perisic Zoran • YGS
DISC JOCKEY • 1951 • Jason Will • USA
DISC JOCKEY JAMBOREE (UKN) see **JAMBOREE** • 1957
DISCARD, THE • 1916 • Windom Lawrence C. • USA
DISCARDED LOVERS • 1932 • Newmeyer Fred • USA
DISCARDED WOMAN, THE • 1920 • King Burton L. • USA
DISCCOTECA, LA • 1984 • Laurenti Mariano • ITL • DISCOTHEQUE, THE
DISCHARGING THE COOK • 1911 • *Selig* • USA
DISCIPLE, THE • 1915 • Hart William S., Smith Cliff, Barker Reginald • *Kb* • USA
DISCIPLE OF DARWIN, A • 1912 • Wilson Frank? • UKN
DISCIPLE OF DEATH • 1972 • Parkinson Tom • UKN
DISCIPLE OF DRACULA see **DRACULA -PRINCE OF DARKNESS** • 1965
DISCIPLE OF NIETZSCHE, A • 1915 • *Welch Marshall* • USA
DISCIPLE OF PLATO, A • 1915 • Beggs Lee • USA
DISCIPLE OF SATAN see **KAMPON NI SATANAS** • 1970
DISCIPLES, THE see **TANITVANYOK, A** • 1985
DISCIPLES OF DEATH see **ENTER THE DEVIL** • 1975
DISCIPLES OF SHAOLIN see **HUNG CHU'A HSIAO TZU** • 1975
DISCIPLES' OFFERINGS TO THE PRIEST see **GURU DAKSHINA** • 1986
DISCIPLINE • 1935 • Riddell James, Imeson A. B. • UKN
DISCIPLING BABY • 1913 • North Wilfred • USA
DISCO • 1977 • Noyce Phil • DCS • ASL
DISCO DELIRIO • 1979 • Righini Oscar • ITL • DISCO MUSIC FEVER
DISCO DYNAMITE • *Boney M.* • USA
DISCO FEVER • 1978 • Card Lamar • USA
DISCO FIEBER • 1978 • Uberall Klaus, Frank Hubert • FRG
DISCO MUSIC FEVER see **DISCO DELIRIO** • 1979
DISCO ROJO • 1972 • Romero-Marchent Rafael • SPN
DISCO-STORY see **DISCOPRIBEH** • 1987
DISCO VOLANTE, IL • 1964 • Brass Tinto • ITL • FLYING SAUCER, THE (USA) ○ MARTIANS, THE ○ FLYING DISC, THE
DISCOLORED ROMANCE, A • 1914 • *Melies* • USA
DISCONNECTED • 1984 • Bechard Gorman • USA
DISCONTENT • 1916 • Weber Lois, Smalley Phillips • SHT • USA
DISCONTENT see **SHE GOT WHAT SHE WANTED** • 1930
DISCONTENTED CANARY, THE • 1934 • Ising Rudolf • ANS • USA
DISCONTENTED COWBOYS • 1930 • Ray Albert • SHT • USA
DISCONTENTED HUSBANDS • 1924 • Le Saint Edward J. • USA
DISCONTENTED MAN, THE • 1915 • *Gray Robert* • USA
DISCONTENTED WIVES • 1921 • McGowan J. P. • USA
DISCONTENTED WOMAN, A • 1910 • *Imp* • USA
DISCOPRIBEH • 1987 • Soukup Jaroslav • CZC • DISCO-STORY
DISCORD • 1928 • Molander Gustaf • SWD
DISCORD • 1933 • Edwards Henry • UKN
DISCORD see **SZAKADEK** • 1955
DISCORD AND HARMONY • 1914 • Dwan Allan • USA
DISCORD IN A FLAT, A • 1918 • *Triangle* • USA
DISCORD IN THREE FLATS • 1915 • Collins Edwin J.? • UKN
DISCORDANT NOTE, A • 1917 • *Triangle* • USA
DISCORDE, LA • 1978 • Franju Georges • MTV • FRN
DISCORDS IN A FLAT • 1917 • De La Parelle M. • SHT • USA
DISCOTECA DEL AMOR, LA • 1980 • Aristarain Adolfo • ARG • LOVE DISCO
DISCOTHEQUE see **LET'S HANG ON** • 1967
DISCOTHEQUE, THE see **DISCCOTECA, LA** • 1984
DISCOUNTERS OF MONEY • 1917 • Justice Martin • SHT • USA
DISCOURSE DE BIENVENUE DE NORMAN MCLAREN see **MESDAMES, MESSIEURS** • 1960
DISCOVER JAPAN WITH FIVE GENTS see **SHACHO SEN-ICHIYA** • 1967
DISCOVERER, THE • 1965 • Kolar Boris • ANS • YGS
DISCOVERERS, THE • 1908 • Blackton J. Stuart • USA
DISCOVERIES • 1939 • Davis Redd • UKN
DISCOVERING JAZZ • 1969 • *Wilets Bernard (P)* • SHT • USA
DISCOVERY • 1949 • Byrd Admiral • USA
DISCOVERY, THE • 1913 • *Bushman Francis X.* • USA
DISCOVERY OF AMERICA, THE • 1969 • Barrios Jaime • USA
DISCOVERY OF SERGEI RADONEZHSKY'S REMAINS see **VSKRYTIE MOSHCHEI SERGIYA RADONEZHSKOVO** • 1920
DISCOVERY OF THE BODY, THE • 1968 • Heinz John • SHT • USA
DISCOVERY OF ZERO, THE see **ZERO NO HAKKEN** • 1963
DISCOVERY ON THE SHAGGY MOUNTAIN see **OBJEV NA STRAPATE HURCE** • 1962
DISCREET CHARM OF THE BOURGEOISIE, THE (UKN) see **CHARME DISCRET DE LA BOURGEOISIE, LE** • 1972
DISCRETION WITH HONOR (USA) see **DISKRETION-EHRENSACHE** • 1938
DISCUSSION • 1895 • Lumiere Louis • FRN
DISCUSSION, THE see **DEBATIK**
DISCUSSION DE M. JANSSEN ET DE M. LAGRANGE • 1895 • Lumiere Louis • FRN
DISCUSSION POLITIQUE • 1901 • Zecca Ferdinand • FRN
DISEMBODIED, THE • 1957 • Grauman Walter • USA
DISENCHANTMENT, A • 1914 • Salter Harry • USA
DISENCHANTMENT, THE see **DESENCANTO, EL** • 1976
DISERTORE, IL see **SPINA DORSALE DEL DIAVOLO, LA** • 1970
DISERTORE E I NOMADI, IL (ITL) see **ZBEHOVIA A PUTNICI** • 1968
DISGRACED! • 1933 • Kenton Erle C. • USA
DISGRACED (CORRUPTION AND ARISTOCRACY), THE see **DROPIASMENI (SAPILA KE ARISTOKRATIA)** • 1967
DISGUISE, THE • 1913 • *Reliance* • USA
DISGUISE THE LIMIT • 1960 • Kneitel Seymour • ANS • USA
DISGUISED BUT DISCOVERED • 1915 • *Smith Dick* • USA
DISGUISERS • 1916 • *Cooper Claude* • SHT • USA
DISGUSTED BINCHESTER • 1973 • Spargo Nicholas • UKN
DISH RAN AWAY WITH THE SPOON, THE • 1933 • Ising Rudolf • ANS • USA
DISHA • 1990 • Paranjpye Sai • IND • UPROOTED, THE
DISHEVELLED HAIR see **MIDARE-GAMI** • 1961
DISHEVELLED HAIR see **MIDAREGAMI** • 1967
DISHING DICK'S DISHWASHER • 1914 • *Patheplay* • USA
DISHONEST BARBER, THE • 1908 • Fitzhamon Lewin? • UKN
DISHONEST BURGLAR, A • 1917 • *Dillon Jack* • USA
DISHONORABLE DISCHARGE (USA) see **CES DAMES PREFERENT LE MAMBO** • 1957
DISHONORED • 1931 • von Sternberg Josef • USA
DISHONORED LADY • 1947 • Stevenson Robert • USA
DISHONORED MEDAL, A • 1914 • Cabanne W. Christy • USA
DISHONOUR BRIGHT • 1936 • Walls Tom • UKN
DISHWASH DICK'S COUNTERFEIT • 1913 • Duncan William • USA
DISI KILLING • 1967 • Gulyuz Aram • TRK • SHE-KILLING, THE
DISILLUSION see **I BELIEVED IN YOU** • 1934
DISILLUSIONED • 1912 • *Bosworth Hobart* • USA
DISILLUSIONED • 1913 • *Kinemacolor* • USA
DISILLUSIONED • 1914 • *Kerrigan J. Warren* • USA
DISILLUSIONED BLUEBIRD • 1944 • Swift Howard • ANS • USA
DISILLUSIONMENT OF JANE, THE • 1915 • *Broncho* • USA
DISINFECTION see **DEZINFEKCIJA** • 1975
DISINHERITED NEPHEW, THE • 1912 • Haldane Bert? • UKN
DISINHERITED SON'S LOYALTY • 1909 • Balshofer Fred J. • USA
DISINTEGRATING RAY OR THE ADVENTURES OF QUIQUE AND ARTHUR THE ROBOT, THE see **RAYO DESINTEGRADOR O AVENTURAS DE QUIQUE Y ARTURO EL ROBOT, EL** • 1965
DISK-O-TEK HOLIDAY (USA) see **JUST FOR YOU** • 1964
DISKRET OPHOLD • 1947 • Palsbo Ole • DNM
DISKRETION-EHRENSACHE • 1938 • Meyer Johannes • FRG • DISCRETION WITH HONOR (USA)
DISLOCATION see **CUOWEI** • 1987
DISLOCATION EXTRAORDINARY see **DISLOCATION MYSTERIEUSE** • 1901
DISLOCATION MYSTERIEUSE • 1901 • Melies Georges • FRN • EXTRAORDINARY DISLOCATION, AN (USA) ○ DISLOCATIONS MYSTERIEUSES ○ EXTRAORDINARY ILLUSIONS ○ DISLOCATION EXTRAORDINARY
DISLOCATIONS MYSTERIEUSES see **DISLOCATION MYSTERIEUSE** • 1901
DISMANTLED BEAUTY, A • 1915 • *Gribbon Harry* • USA
DISMEMBERED CORPSE see **KAO NO NAI ONNA** • 1959
DISMEMBERED GHOST see **KAIDAN BARABARA YUREI** • 1968
DISMEMBERER OF BINBROOK, THE see **DESCUARTIZADOR DE BINBROOK, EL** • 1971
DISMISSAL see **PAYDOS** • 1968
DISMISSAL OF SILVER PHIL • 1918 • Watt Allen • SHT • USA
DISMISSED FROM SCHOOL see **MAGDAT KICSAPJAK** • 1935
DISNEYLAND AFTER DARK • 1962 • Luske Hamilton, Beaudine William • USA
DISOBEDIENCE see **OYAFUKO DORI** • 1958
DISOBEDIENT see **INTIMATE RELATIONS** • 1953
DISOBEDIENT MOUSE • 1938 • Kline Lester • ANS • USA
DISOBEDIENT ROBOT, THE see **NESTASNI ROBOT** • 1956
DISONORATA SENZA COLPA • 1954 • Chili Giorgio W. • ITL
DISORDER see **DESORDRE** • 1949
DISORDER see **DISORDINE, IL** • 1962
DISORDER AND EARLY SORROW see **UNORDNUNG UND FRUHES LEID** • 1975
DISORDER IN THE COURT • 1936 • Black Preston • SHT • USA
DISORDER IS TWENTY YEARS OLD see **DESORDRE A VINGT ANS, LE** • 1967
DISORDER OF THE BATH, THE • 1915 • *Tree Dolly* • UKN
DISORDER OF THE KURODA CLAN see **KURODA SODO** • 1956
DISORDERED MIND, THE • 1960 • Anderson Robert • SER • CND
DISORDERLIES • 1987 • Schultz Michael • USA
DISORDERLY CONDUCT • 1932 • Considine John W. Jr. • USA
DISORDERLY ORDERLY, THE • 1927 • Newfield Sam • SHT • USA
DISORDERLY ORDERLY, THE • 1964 • Tashlin Frank • USA
DISORDINE, IL • 1962 • Brusati Franco • ITL, FRN • DESORDRE, LE (FRN) ○ DISORDER
DISORGANISED CRIME • 1989 • Kouf Jim • USA • WAITING FOR SALAZAR ○ BANK JOB
DISPARATE NACIONAL • 1989 • SPN
DISPARU DE L'ASCENSEUR, LE • 1931 • Del Torre Giulio • FRN
DISPARUS, LES • 1960 • Vicas Victor • FRN
DISPARUS DE SAINT-AGIL, LES • 1938 • Christian-Jaque • FRN • BOYS' SCHOOL (USA)
DISPATCH BEARER, THE • 1900 • *Mitchell & Kenyon* • UKN

DISPATCH FROM REUTERS, A • 1940 • Dieterle William • USA • THIS MAN REUTER (UKN)
DISPENSATION, A • 1910 • *Reliance* • USA
DISPERATAMENTE L'ESTATE SCORSA • 1970 • Amadio Silvio • ITL
DISPERATI DELLA GLORIA, I (ITL) see **PARIAS DE LA GLOIRE** • 1963
DISPERATI DI CUBA, I • 1970 • Topart Robert • ITL
DISPERATO ADDIO • 1956 • De Felice Lionello • ITL
DISPERSING CLOUD see **WAKARE-GUMO** • 1951
DISPERSING CLOUDS see **WAKARE-GUMO** • 1951
DISPLACED PERSON, A see **RAZSELJENA OSEBA** • 1982
DISPOSABLE MAN, THE • 1971 • Bonniere Rene • CND
DISPOSTA A TUTTO • 1977 • Stegani Giorgio • ITL
DISPREZZO, IL (ITL) see **MEPRIS, LE** • 1963
DISPUTA, LA • 1972 • *P.r. Re-Al* • MXC
DISPUTED CLAIM, A • 1912 • *Prior Herbert* • USA
DISPUTED MARRIAGE see **GALATTA KALYANAM** • 1968
DISPUTED PASSAGE • 1939 • Borzage Frank • USA
DISQUE 413, LE • 1936 • Pottier Richard • FRN • SYMPHONIE D'AMOUR
DISQUE 927 • 1929 • Dulac Germaine • SHT • FRN
DISQUES D'HIER ET D'AUJOURD'HUI • 1951 • Gerard • SHT • FRN
DISRAELI • 1916 • Nash Percy, Calvert Charles • UKN
DISRAELI • 1921 • Kolker Henry • USA
DISRAELI • 1929 • Green Alfred E. • USA
DISRAELI see **SECRET LIVES OF THE BRITISH PRIME MINISTERS: DISRAELI, THE** • 1981
DISREPUTABLE MR. RAEGAN, THE • 1911 • *Edison* • USA
DISREPUTABLE UNCLE, THE see **ZIO INDEGNO, LO** • 1990
DISSENT ILLUSION • 1963 • Goldscholl Mildred • USA
DISSOLVED GOVERNMENT, THE • 1910 • Smith F. Percy • UKN
DISSOLVING THE GOVERNMENT • 1909 • Smith F. Percy • UKN
DISTACCO, IL see **PELLE A SCACCHI, LA** • 1969
DISTANCE • 1975 • Lover Anthony • USA
DISTANCE, LA • 1918 • Boudrioz Robert • FRN
DISTANCE, LA • 1974 • Dansereau Fernand, Rossignol Yolande • SHT • CND
DISTANCE, THE • 1981 • van der Velde Jean, Seegers Rene, de Winter Leon • NTH
DISTANT AUGUST TRAIN, THE • 1972 • Lysenko Vadim • USS
DISTANT CLOUDS see **TOI KUMO** • 1955
DISTANT COUSINS • 1935 • Sparling Gordon • DCS • CND
DISTANT CRY FROM SPRING, A • 1979 • Yamada Yoji • JPN
DISTANT DRUMS • 1951 • Walsh Raoul • USA
DISTANT EARLY WARNING • 1975 • Kenney Wes • TVM • USA
DISTANT FIELDS see **MARRIED AND IN LOVE** • 1940
DISTANT HARMONY • 1987 • Sage Dewitt • DOC • USA
DISTANT JAMAICA see **FERNES JAMAICA** • 1969
DISTANT JOURNEY see **DALEKA CESTA** • 1949
DISTANT LAND, THE see **WEITE LAND, DAS** • 1987
DISTANT NEIGHBOURS • 1956 • Durst John • UKN
DISTANT RELATIVE, A • 1912 • Dwan Allan • USA
DISTANT SCREAM, A • 1985 • Hough John • UKN
DISTANT SKY, THE see **DALEKO NEBO** • 1983
DISTANT THAMES see **ROYAL RIVER** • 1951
DISTANT THUNDER • 1988 • Rosenthal Rick • USA
DISTANT THUNDER see **EN-RAI** • 1982
DISTANT THUNDER (USA) see **ASHANI SANKET** • 1973
DISTANT TRUMPET • 1952 • Fisher Terence • UKN
DISTANT TRUMPET, A • 1964 • Walsh Raoul • USA
DISTANT VOICES, STILL LIVES • 1987 • Davies Terence • UKN
DISTILLATION • 1940 • Baylis Peter • UKN
DISTILLATION OF OIL • 1954 • Cons David • DOC • UKN
DISTILLED SPIRITS • 1915 • Fahrney Milton • USA
DISTINTO AMANACER • 1943 • Bracho Julio • MXC • DIFFERENT SUNRISE, A
DISTORTED DESIRE see **HIZUNDA JOYOKU** • 1967
DISTORTED SEX see **YUGANDA SEX** • 1968
DISTORTIONS • 1981 • Godbout Jacques • CND
DISTORTIONS • 1987 • Mastroianni Armand • USA
DISTRACTED BATHER, THE • 1899 • *Norton C. Goodwin* • UKN
DISTRACTIONS, LES • 1960 • Dupont Jacques • FRN, ITL • DISTRAZIONI, LE (ITL) ○ TRAPPED BY FEAR (USA)
DISTRAIT, LE • 1970 • Richard Pierre • FRN • DAYDREAMER, THE (USA)
DISTRAZIONI, LE (ITL) see **DISTRACTIONS, LES** • 1960
DISTRESS CALL • 1938 • Watt Harry • DOC • UKN
DISTRESSED see **NANIWA NO KOI NO MONOGATARI** • 1959
DISTRIBUTION DE MACHINES AGRICOLES AUX PAYSANS • 1970 • Al-Rawi Abdel-Hadi • SHT • IRQ
DISTRICT ATTORNEY, THE • 1910 • *Lubin* • USA
DISTRICT ATTORNEY, THE • 1911 • *Powers* • USA
DISTRICT ATTORNEY, THE • 1915 • O'Neil Barry • USA
DISTRICT ATTORNEY'S BEAUTY, THE • 1914 • *Kalem* • USA
DISTRICT ATTORNEY'S BROTHER, THE • 1914 • *Gold Seal* • USA
DISTRICT ATTORNEY'S BURGLAR, THE • 1914 • Vale Travers • USA
DISTRICT ATTORNEY'S CONSCIENCE, THE • 1912 • Kirkwood James • USA
DISTRICT ATTORNEY'S CONSCIENCE, THE • 1913 • Johnson Arthur • USA
DISTRICT ATTORNEY'S TRIUMPH, THE • 1910 • *Lubin* • USA
DISTRICT NURSE • 1952 • Hill James • UKN
DISTRICT NURSE, THE • 1942 • Page John • UKN
DISTRITO QUINTO • 1957 • Coll Julio • SPN
DISTURBING HIS REST • 1907 • Stow Percy • UKN
DISZMAGYAR • 1948 • Gertler Viktor • HNG • GALA SUIT
DIT IS NOORD-BRABANT • 1966 • van Neijenhoff Otto • NTH
DIT VINDARNA BAR • 1948 • Ohberg Ake • SWD, NRW • JORUND SMED (NRW) ○ WHERE THE WINDS LEAD
DIT WAS AAND EN DIT WAS MORE • 1978 • Marx Franz • SAF • IT WAS EVENING AND IT WAS MORNING
DITA SAXOVA • 1967 • Moskalyk Antonin • CZC
DITES 33 (FRN) see **TOTO, VITTORIO E LA DOTTORESSA** • 1957
DITES-LE AVEC DES FLEURS • 1974 • Grimblat Pierre • FRN
DITES-LUI QUE JE L'AIME • 1977 • Miller Claude • FRN • THIS SWEET SICKNESS (UKN)
DITIRAMBO • 1967 • Suarez Gonzalo • SPN
DITO NELLA PIAGA, IL • 1969 • Ricci Tonino • ITL • AD OGNI CESTO OGNANO PER SE ○ DIRTY TWO, THE ○ BADGE OF COURAGE
DITTE: CHILD OF MAN see **DITTE MENNESKEBARN** • 1946
DITTE MENNESKEBARN • 1946 • Henning-Jensen Bjarne • DNM • DITTE: CHILD OF MAN
DITTO • 1937 • Lamont Charles • SHT • USA
DITYA BOLSHOVA GORODA • 1914 • Bauer Yevgeni • USS • CHILD OF THE BIG CITY
DIVA • 1981 • Beineix Jean-Jacques • FRN
DIVANKATZEN • 1922 • Neff Wolfgang • FRG
DIVE, THE see **DYKKET** • 1989
DIVE BOMBER • 1941 • Curtiz Michael • USA
DIVE IN • 1932 • McCarey Ray • SHT • USA
DIVER, THE • 1913 • Lambart Harry • USA
DIVER-SIONS • 1909 • Aylott Dave • UKN • DIVER'S DIVERSIONS
DIVERGENT VIEWS: NOS. 41 AND 42 JOHN STREET • 1914 • Cooper Toby? • UKN
DIVERGING PATHS • 1913 • Parker Lem B. • USA
DIVERS AT WORK ON A WRECK UNDER SEA see **VISITE SOUS-MARINE DU MAINE** • 1898
DIVERS AT WORK ON THE WRECK OF THE MAINE see **VISITE SOUS-MARINE DU MAINE** • 1898
DIVER'S DIVERSIONS see **DIVER-SIONS** • 1909
DIVER'S LAST KISS, THE • 1918 • *Sunshine* • SHT • USA
DIVER'S REMORSE, THE • 1909 • *Vitagraph* • USA
DIVER'S STORY, THE • 1902 • Moss Hugh • UKN
DIVER'S WIFE, THE • 1910 • *London Cinematograph Co.* • UKN
DIVERSIA • 1989 • Kuliev Eldar • USS • SUBVERSIVE ACTION
DIVERSION • 1913 • O'Sullivan Tony • USA
DIVERSION • 1987 • Lyne Adrian • USA
DIVERTISSEMENT • 1960 • Alexeieff Alexandre • SHT • FRN
DIVERTISSEMENT, LE • 1952 • Rivette Jacques • SHT • FRN
DIVERTISSEMENT ROCOCCO • 1952 • Hirsch Hy • SHT • FRN
DIVERZANTI • 1967 • Krvavac Hajrudin • YGS • DEMOLITION SQUAD
DIVETTA DEL REGIMENTO, LA • 1916 • Caserini Mario • ITL
DIVIDE AND CONQUER • 1943 • Litvak Anatole, Capra Frank • DOC • USA • WHY WE FIGHT (PART 3): DIVIDE AND CONQUER
DIVIDED FAMILY, A • 1912 • Davis Ulysses • USA
DIVIDED HEART, THE • 1954 • Crichton Charles • UKN
DIVIDED HEAVEN see **GETEILTE HIMMEL, DER** • 1964
DIVIDED HOUSE, A • 1912 • *Comet* • USA
DIVIDED HOUSE, THE • 1913 • *Essanay* • USA
DIVIDED INTERESTS • 1911 • *Lubin* • USA
DIVIDED LOCKET, THE • 1915 • Reehm George E. • USA
DIVIDED LOVE • 1916 • *Buffalo* • USA
DIVIDED LOYALTIES • 1985 • Hart Harvey • USA
DIVIDED RING, THE • 1911 • *Solax* • USA
DIVIDED SKY see **GETEILTE HIMMEL, DER** • 1964
DIVIDED TRAIL, THE • 1980 • Aronson Jerry, Goldman Mical • DOC • USA
DIVIDED WORLD, A see **KLUVEN VARLD, EN** • 1948
DIVIDEND, THE • 1916 • Edwards Walter • USA
DIVIDING LINE, THE • 1912 • Brenon Herbert • USA
DIVIDING LINE, THE • 1913 • Physioc Wray • USA
DIVIDING LINE, THE • 1916 • *Hiawatha* • USA
DIVIDING LINE, THE (UKN) see **LAWLESS, THE** • 1949
DIVIDING WALL, THE • 1951 • Chu Shih-Ling • HKG
DIVIETO DI SOSTA • 1943 • Albani Marcello • ITL
DIVINA, LA • O'Connor John • USA
DIVINA CREATURA • 1975 • Patroni Griffi Giuseppe • ITL • DIVINE NYMPH, THE
DIVINA GARZA, LA • 1962 • Gomez Landero Humberto • MXC
DIVINAS PALABRAS • 1977 • Ibanez Juan • MXC
DIVINAS PALABRAS • 1987 • Garcia Sanchez Jose Luis • SPN • DIVINE WORDS
DIVINATIONS • 1965 • De Hirsch Storm • SHT • USA
DIVINE • 1935 • Ophuls Max • FRN
DIVINE • 1975 • Delouche Dominique • FRN
DIVINE CASTE, THE see **CASTA DIVINA, LA** • 1976
DIVINE COUNCIL see **SHINSAI KAIGI** • 1949
DIVINE COUNCILS see **RAT DER GOTTER, DER** • 1950
DIVINE CROISIERE, LA • 1928 • Duvivier Julien • FRN
DIVINE DAMNATION, THE • 1967 • Markopoulos Gregory J. • USA
DIVINE DECREE, THE • 1915 • Otto Henry • USA
DIVINE EMMA, THE (USA) see **BOZSKA EMA** • 1983
DIVINE GIFT, THE • 1918 • Bentley Thomas • UKN
DIVINE JETTA, THE (USA) see **GOTTLICHE JETTE, DIE** • 1937
DIVINE LADY, THE • 1929 • Lloyd Frank • USA
DIVINE LOVE (UKN) see **NO GREATER LOVE** • 1932
DIVINE MADNESS • 1980 • Ritchie Michael • USA
DIVINE MR. J., THE see **THORN, THE** • 1980
DIVINE NYMPH, THE see **DIVINA CREATURA** • 1975
DIVINE OBSESSION, THE • 1976 • Kaufman Lloyd • USA
DIVINE ONE, THE see **MALAKOOT** • 1975
DIVINE PLAN, THE see **CHHATRABHANG** • 1976
DIVINE PUNISHMENT, THE • 1925 • IND
DIVINE SACRIFICE, THE • 1918 • Archainbaud George • USA
DIVINE SARAH • 1984 • Suissa Daniele J. • MTV • CND
DIVINE SINNER • 1928 • Pembroke Scott • USA
DIVINE SOLITUDE • 1987 • Lariviere Jean Marc • DCS • CND
DIVINE SOLUTION, THE • 1912 • *Lubin* • USA
DIVINE SPARK, THE • 1935 • Gallone Carmine • UKN
DIVINE WOMAN, THE • 1927 • Sjostrom Victor • USA
DIVINE WORDS see **DIVINAS PALABRAS** • 1987
DIVINERS, THE • 1983 • Altman Robert • USA
DIVING FOOL, A • 1924 • Lamont Charles • SHT • USA
DIVING FOR TREASURE • 1900 • Booth W. R. • UKN
DIVING GIRL, THE • 1911 • Sennett Mack • USA
DIVING GIRLS' ISLAND, THE see **VIOLATED PARADISE** • 1963
DIVING GIRLS OF JAPAN see **VIOLATED PARADISE** • 1963
DIVING LUCY • 1903 • *Mitchell & Kenyon* • UKN
DIVINO BOEMO, IL • 1975 • Jires Jaromil • DOC • CZC
DIVINO MISTERO, IL • 1950 • De Ruffo D. • ITL • EUCARESTIA
DIVISION BRANDENBURG • 1960 • Philipp Harald • FRG
DIVISION HEADQUARTERS see **FIREBALL FORWARD** • 1972
DIVISION HOMICIDIOS • 1978 • Doria Alejandro • ARG • HOMICIDE SECTION: COUNTERSTROKE
DIVISION NARCOTICOS • 1963 • Mariscal Alberto • MXC
DIVISIONE FOLGORE • 1955 • Coletti Duilio • ITL
DIVISIONS DE LA NATURE ,LES • 1977 • Ruiz Raul • SHT • FRN • DIVISIONS OF NATURE, THE
DIVISIONS OF NATURE, THE see **DIVISIONS DE LA NATURE , LES** • 1977
DIVKA NA KOSTETI • 1971 • Vorlicek Vaclav • CZC • GIRL ON THE BROOMSTICK, THE (USA) ○ GIRL ON A BROOM
DIVKA S MUSLI • 1979 • Svoboda Jiri • CZC • GIRL WITH A SHELL, THE
DIVKA SE TREMI VELBLOUDY • 1967 • Krska Vaclav • CZC • GIRL WITH THE THREE CAMELS, THE ○ GIRL WITH THREE CAMELS, A
DIVKA V MODREM • 1939 • Vavra Otakar • CZC • GIRL IN BLUE, THE
DIVLJE SENKE • 1968 • Rakonjac Kokan • YGS • WILD SHADOWS
DIVLJI ANDELI • 1970 • Hadzic Fadil • YGS • WILD ANGELS
DIVOKA HOLKA • 1966 • Tucek Petr • CZC
DIVORCE • 1911 • *Reliance* • USA
DIVORCE • 1911 • *Thanhouser* • USA
DIVORCE • 1914 • West Raymond B. • USA
DIVORCE • 1923 • Bennett Chester • USA
DIVORCE • 1945 • Nigh William • USA • HILLSBORO STORY, THE
DIVORCE A LA CARTE • 1931 • Lamont Charles • SHT • USA
DIVORCE A LA MODE • 1932 • *Sennett Mack (P)* • SHT • USA
DIVORCE, AMERICAN STYLE • 1967 • Yorkin Bud • USA
DIVORCE AMONG FRIENDS • 1931 • Del Ruth Roy • USA
DIVORCE AND THE DAUGHTER • 1916 • Sullivan Frederick • USA
DIVORCE COUPONS • 1922 • Campbell Webster • USA
DIVORCE COURTSHIP, A • 1933 • Stevens George • SHT • USA
DIVORCE CURE, THE • 1912 • *Francis Evelyn* • USA
DIVORCE DODGER, THE • 1926 • *Sennett Mack (P)* • SHT • USA
DIVORCE GAME, THE • 1917 • Vale Travers • USA
DIVORCE HEUREUX, UN (FRN) see **LYKKELIG SKILSMISSE, EN** • 1974
DIVORCE HIS -DIVORCE HERS • 1973 • Hussein Waris • TVM • USA
DIVORCE IN BUDAPEST • 1964 • Szemes Marianne • DOC • HNG
DIVORCE IN THE FAMILY • 1932 • Reisner Charles F. • USA • FATHER AND SONS
DIVORCE IS FASHIONABLE see **DIVORCIO ESTA DE MODA, LA** • 1978
DIVORCE, ITALIAN STYLE (USA) see **DIVORZIO ALL'ITALIANA** • 1961
DIVORCE LAS VEGAS STYLE • 1970 • White William • USA
DIVORCE MADE EASY • 1929 • Burns Neal • SIL • USA
DIVORCE MADE EASY • 1929 • Graham Walter • SND • USA
DIVORCE OF CONVENIENCE, A • 1921 • Ellis Robert • USA
DIVORCE OF LADY X, THE • 1938 • Whelan Tim • UKN
DIVORCE SCANDAL, A • 1913 • *Coxen Ed* • USA
DIVORCE TRAP, THE • 1919 • Beal Frank • USA
DIVORCE (UKN) see **SAN FRANCISCO NIGHTS** • 1928
DIVORCE WARS: A LOVE STORY • 1982 • Wrye Donald • TVM • USA
DIVORCED • 1915 • Golden Joseph A. • USA
DIVORCED see **FRANSKILD** • 1951
DIVORCED, THE • 1975 • el Kadi Ismail • EGY
DIVORCED AT HOME see **SEPARATI IN CASA** • 1985
DIVORCED SWEETHEARTS • 1930 • Sennett Mack • USA
DIVORCEE, THE • 1912 • Henderson Dell • USA
DIVORCEE, THE • 1914 • *Powers* • USA
DIVORCEE, THE • 1917 • Wolbert William • USA
DIVORCEE, THE • 1919 • Blache Herbert • USA • LADY FREDERICK
DIVORCEE, THE • 1930 • Leonard Robert Z. • USA
DIVORCEE, THE • 1969 • Stephen A. C. • USA • CONFESSIONS OF A DIVORCEE
DIVORCEMENT, LE • 1979 • Barouh Pierre • FRN
DIVORCES, DIVORCES • 1988 • Vulchanov Rangel • ANT • BUL
DIVORCIADAS • 1943 • Galindo Alejandro • MXC
DIVORCIO, UN • 1952 • Gomez Muriel Emilio • MXC
DIVORCIO A LA ANDALUZA • 1967 • Zabalza Jose Maria • SPN
DIVORCIO EN MONTEVIDEO • 1940 • Romero Manuel
DIVORCIO ESTA DE MODA, LA • 1978 • Siro Fernando • ITL • DIVORCE IS FASHIONABLE
DIVORCONS • 1912 • *Eclair* • USA
DIVORCONS • 1915 • Henderson Dell • USA
DIVORZIATA, LA (ITL) see **FEUX DE LA CHANDELEUR, LES** • 1972
DIVORZIO, IL • 1970 • Guerrieri Romolo • ITL
DIVORZIO ALLA SICILIANA • 1963 • Di Gianni Enzo • ITL
DIVORZIO ALL'ITALIANA • 1961 • Germi Pietro • ITL • DIVORCE, ITALIAN STYLE (USA)
DIVOT DIGGERS • 1936 • McGowan Robert • SHT • USA
DIVOTA PRASINE • 1976 • Ljubic Milan • YGS • CUDOVITI PRAH ○ GLORIOUS DUST, THE
DIVOTVORNY KLOBOUK • 1952 • Radok Alfred • CZC • MAGICAL HAT, THE
DIWAN • 1973 • Nekes Werner • FRG
DIWANA • 1968 • Kaul Mahesh • IND • LOVER
DIX CHAPEAUX EN 60 SECONDES • 1896 • Melies Georges • FRN • CONJURER MAKING TEN HATS IN SIXTY SECONDS (USA)
DIX DE HOLLYWOOD • 1951 • Berry John • DOC • FRN
DIX FEMMES POUR UN MARI • 1905 • Nonguet Lucien, Heuze Andre • FRN
DIX FEMMES POUR UN MARI • 1905 • Zecca Ferdinand • FRN
DIX GRAMMES D'ARC-EN-CIEL • 1962 • Menegoz Robert • SHT • FRN
DIX-HUIT HEURES D'ESCALE • 1954 • Jolivet Rene • FRN
DIX PETITS INDIENS, LES see **AND THEN THERE WERE NONE** • 1945

DIX PETITS NEGRES • Misonne Claude • ANS • BLG • TEN LITTLE NIGGER BOYS
DIX SIECLES D'ELEGANCE • 1910 • Cohl Emile • ANS • FRN
DIX SOLEILS D'AUDERGHERN, LES • 1969 • Lagrange Yvan • FRN
DIXIA QING • 1987 • Guan Jinpeng • HKG • LOVE UNTO WASTE
DIXIANA • 1930 • Reed Luther • USA
DIXIE • 1910 • *Imp* • USA
DIXIE • 1925 • Fleischer Dave • ANS • USA
DIXIE • 1929 • Fleischer Dave • ANS • USA
DIXIE • 1943 • Sutherland A. Edward • USA
DIXIE: CHANGING HABITS • 1982 • Englund George • TVM • USA
DIXIE DAYS • 1930 • Foster John, Davis Mannie • ANS • USA
DIXIE DUGAN • 1943 • Brower Otto • USA
DIXIE DYNAMITE • 1980 • Frost Lee • USA
DIXIE FLYER, THE • 1926 • Hunt Charles J. • USA
DIXIE FRYER, THE • 1960 • McKimson Robert • ANS • USA
DIXIE HANDICAP, THE • 1924 • Barker Reginald • USA
DIXIE JAMBOREE • 1945 • Cabanne W. Christy • USA
DIXIE LANES • 1988 • Cato Don • USA • INDIAN SUMMER ○ RELATIVE SECRETS
DIXIE MERCHANT, THE • 1926 • Borzage Frank • USA
DIXIE MOTHER, A • 1910 • Brooke Van Dyke • USA
DIXIE MOTHER, A • 1913 • Edwards Walter? • USA
DIXIE RAY: HOLLYWOOD STAR see **IT'S CALLED MURDER BABY** • 1982
DIXIE WINNER, THE • 1916 • *Maupain Ernest* • SHT • USA
DIXIELAND • 1913 • Kirkland Hardee • USA
DIXIELAND DROOPY • 1954 • Avery Tex • ANS • USA
DIXIEME SYMPHONIE, LA • 1918 • Gance Abel • FRN • TENTH SYMPHONY, THE
DIXIEME VICTIME, LA (FRN) see **DECIMA VITTIMA, LA** • 1965
DIXIE'S DAY OFF • 1915 • MacMackin Archer • USA
DIXON'S RETURN • 1924 • Haynes Manning • UKN
DIYAMANTHI • 1976 • Obeysekara Vasantha • SLN
DIYET • 1975 • Akat Lutfu • TRK
DIYI LEI YING WEIXIAN • 1980 • Xu Ke • HKG • DANGEROUS ENCOUNTERS OF THE FIRST KIND ○ DON'T PLAY WITH FIRE
DIYOSA • 1957 • Conde Conrado • PHL
DIZENGOFF 99 • 1979 • Nesher Avi • ISR
DIZZY see **SECRET LIVES OF THE BRITISH PRIME MINISTERS: DISRAELI, THE** • 1981
DIZZY ACROBAT, THE • 1943 • Lovy Alex • ANS • USA
DIZZY DADDIES • 1926 • Roach Hal • SHT • USA
DIZZY DAMES • 1935 • Nigh William • USA
DIZZY DATES • 1930 • Foster Lewis R. • SHT • USA
DIZZY DAY, A • 1933 • Bailey Harry • ANS • USA
DIZZY DETECTIVES • 1943 • White Jules • SHT • USA
DIZZY DINOSAURS • 1952 • Kneitel Seymour • ANS • USA
DIZZY DISHES • 1930 • Fleischer Dave • ANS • USA
DIZZY DISHES • 1955 • Sparber I. • ANS • USA
DIZZY DIVERS • 1935 • Fleischer Dave • ANS • USA
DIZZY DOCTORS • 1937 • Lord Del • SHT • USA
DIZZY DOINGS • 1941 • Le Borg Reginald • SHT • USA
DIZZY DUCKS • 1936 • *Mintz Charles (P)* • ANS • USA
DIZZY DWARF, THE • 1934 • Nolan William • ANS • USA
DIZZY GILLESPIE • 1965 • Blank Les • SHT • USA
DIZZY GILLESPIE QUINTET • 1964 • *Gleason Ralph J./ Christian Richard (P)* • SHT • USA
DIZZY HEIGHTS AND DARING HEARTS • 1916 • Wright Walter • SHT • USA
DIZZY JOE'S CAREER • 1914 • *Komic* • USA
DIZZY KITTY • 1941 • Lantz Walter • ANS • USA
DIZZY LIMIT, THE • 1930 • Dryhurst Edward • UKN • KIDNAPPED
DIZZY NEWSREEL • 1943 • Geiss Alec • ANS • USA
DIZZY PILOTS • 1943 • White Jules • SHT • USA
DIZZY RED RIDING HOOD • 1931 • Fleischer Dave • ANS • USA
DJALAMBU • 1961 • Holmes Cecil • DOC • ASL
DJAMILA see **JAMILA EL GAZAIRIA** • 1958
DJANGER "LOVE RITE OF BALI" see **VIRGINS OF BALI** • 1932
DJANGO • 1966 • Corbucci Sergio • ITL, SPN • MERCENARIO, IL (SPN) ○ PROFESSIONAL GUN, A ○ MERCENARY, THE
DJANGO 2 –IL GRANDE RITORNO • 1988 • Rossati Nello • ITL • DJANGO 2 –THE BIG COMEBACK
DJANGO 2 –THE BIG COMEBACK see **DJANGO 2 –IL GRANDE RITORNO** • 1988
DJANGO –DIE GEIER STEHEN SCHLANGE • 1969 • Cardone Alberto • FRG, ITL
DJANGO –DIE TOTENGRABER WARTEN SCHON • 1968 • Castellari Enzo G. • FRG, ITL
DJANGO E SARTANA • Fidani Demofilo • ITL
DJANGO –EIN SARG VOLL BLUT • 1968 • Carnimeo Giuliano • FRG, ITL
DJANGO IL BASTARDO • 1969 • Garrone Sergio • ITL • STRANGER'S GUNDOWN, THE (USA) ○ DJANGO THE BASTARD
DJANGO KILL (UKN) see **SE SEI VIVO SPARA** • 1967
DJANGO, KILLER PER ONORE (ITL) see **PROSCRITO DEL RIO COLORADO, EL** • 1965
DJANGO REINHARDT • 1958 • Paviot Paul • DCS • FRN
DJANGO, RIDER OF DEATH see **CANGO OLUM SUVARISI** • 1967
DJANGO SFIDA SARTANA • 1970 • Squitieri Pasquale • ITL
DJANGO SHOOTS FIRST see **DJANGO SPARA PER PRIMO** • 1966
DJANGO SPARA PER PRIMO • 1966 • De Martino Alberto • ITL, SPN • HE WHO SHOOTS FIRST (UKN) ○ DJANGO SHOOTS FIRST
DJANGO STORY see **GIU LE MANI.. CAROGNA** • 1971
DJANGO STRIKES AGAIN see **GRANDE RITORNO DI DJANGO, IL** • 1987
DJANGO THE BASTARD see **DJANGO IL BASTARDO** • 1969
DJANGO'S CUT PRICE CORPSES • *Cameron Jeff* • ITL
DJAVOLJA KICMA see **SPINA DORSALE DEL DIAVOLO, LA** • 1970
DJAVULENS INSTRUMENT • 1967 • Fischer Gunnar • SHT • SWD • DEVIL'S INSTRUMENT, THE
DJAVULENS OGA • 1960 • Bergman Ingmar • SWD • DEVIL'S EYE, THE

DJECAK I LOPTA • 1960 • Kolar Boris • ANS • YGS • BOY AND THE BALL ○ BOY AND A BALL, A
DJECAK JE ISAO ZA SUNCEM • 1983 • Bastac Branislav • YGS • BOY WHO FOLLOWED THE SUN, THE
DJELI • 1981 • Kramo-Lancine Fadika • IVC
DJEMILE see **CEMILE** • 1968
DJERBA • 1947 • Lamorisse Albert • SHT • FRN
DJEVA U SAOBRACAJU • 1968 • Vunak Dragutin • ANM • YGS • CHILDREN IN TRAFFIC
DJEVOJCICA I HRAST • 1954 • Golik Kreso • YGS • GIRL AND THE OAK, THE ○ DJEVOJKA I HRAST ○ LITTLE GIRL AND THE OAK, THE
DJEVOJKA I HRAST see **DJEVOJCICA I HRAST** • 1954
DJEVOJKE I MUSKARCI • 1957 • *Vich Vaclav (Ph)* • CZC
DJEZAIR AR-RAIS, AL- • 1975 • Laradji Rabah • SHT • ALG • ALGER DES CORSAIRES
DJIM CHUANTE see **SOL SVANETII** • 1930
DJINN • Hirsch Hy • USA
DJOEVELENS PROTEGE see **HVIDE DJOEVEL, DEN** • 1916
DJOOU • 1933 • Litvinof • DOC • USS
DJUNGELAVENTYRET CAMPA, CAMPA • 1976 • Anderberg Torgny • SWD • JUNGLE ADVENTURE CAMPA, CAMPA
DJUNGELDANSEN • 1937 • Fejos Paul • DCS • DNM, SWD • JUNGLE DANCE
DJUNGELDROTTNINGENS SMYCKE • 1917 • Magnussen Fritz • SWD • JUNGLE QUEEN'S JEWELS, THE
DJUNGELSAGA, EN • 1957 • Sucksdorff Arne • DOC • SWD • FLUTE AND THE ARROW, THE
DJURA • 1964 • Bergunkev Adolf • USS
DJURADO • 1966 • Narzisi Gianni • ITL
DJURGARDSKVALLAR • 1947 • Husberg Rolf • SWD • EVENINGS AT DJURGARDEN
DJURGARDSNATTER • 1933 • Rodin Gosta • SWD • NIGHTS IN THE DJURGARD
D'KLASSEZAMMEKUNFT • 1988 • Deuber Walter, Stierlin Peter • SWT • KLASSEZAMMEKUNFT
DLUGOSZEWSKI CONCERT • 1965 • Emshwiller Ed • USA
DM-KILLER • 1964 • Thiele Rolf • AUS
DNES NAPOSLED • 1958 • Fric Martin • CZC • TODAY FOR THE LAST TIME
DNES VECER VSECHNO SKONCI • 1954 • Kachyna Karel, Jasny Vojtech • CZC • EVERYTHING ENDS TONIGHT ○ IT WILL ALL BE OVER TONIGHT
DNESKA PRISEL NOVY KLUK • 1981 • Drha Vladimir • CZC • NEW BOY STARTED TODAY, A
DNEVNYE ZVEZDI • 1968 • Talankin Igor • USS
DNI, MIESIACE, LATA • 1966 • Slesicki Wladyslaw • DOC • PLN • DAYS, MONTHS, YEARS
DNI NACHEI GIZNI • 1914 • Gardin Vladimir • USS • DAYS OF OUR LIFE
DNI OSWIATY • 1958 • Borowczyk Walerian, Lenica Jan • ANS • PLN • EDUCATION DAYS
DNY ZRADY • 1973 • Vavra Otakar • CZC • DAYS OF TREASON, THE ○ DAYS OF BETRAYAL, THE
DO A GOOD DEED • 1935 • *Lantz Walter (P)* • ANS • USA
DO AND DARE • 1922 • Sedgwick Edward • USA • KISS IN THE DARK, A
DO ANKHEN BARAH HAATH • 1958 • Shantaram Victor • IND • TWO EYES, TWELVE HANDS
DO BHAI • 1947 • *Burman S. D. (M)* • IND
DO BIGHA ZAMIN • 1953 • Roy Bimal • IND • CALCUTTA CRUEL CITY ○ TWO ACRES OF LAND
DO BOOND PARI • 1972 • Abbas Khwaya Ahmad • IND
DO BRASIL PARA O MUNDO • 1967 • Manzon Jean • DOC • BRZ
DO CHILDREN COUNT? • 1917 • SER • USA
DO DETECTIVES THINK • 1927 • Guiol Fred • USA
DO DILON KI DASTAN • 1967 • Kumar Pradeep • IND • MEETING OF TWO HEARTS
DO DO • 1964 • Halas John • ASS • UKN
DO DOONI CHAR • 1968 • *Roy Bhimal (P)* • IND
DO DREAMS COME TRUE? • 1912 • *Essanay* • USA
DO DUSHMAN • 1968 • Hussain Mohammed • IND • TWO ENEMIES
DO GENTLEMEN SNORE? • 1928 • Heath Arch B. • SHT • USA
DO-GOOD WOLF, THE • 1960 • Hanna William, Barbera Joseph • ANS • USA
DO HUSBANDS DECEIVE? • 1918 • Roach Hal • SHT • USA
DO I BORE YOU DARLING? see **DARLING, ARE YOU BORED WITH MEN?** • 1968
DO I HAVE TO KILL MY CHILD? • 1976 • Crombie Donald • MTV • ASL
DO I KILL THEM? see **MATO ELES?** • 1982
DO I LOVE YOU? see **LIUBLIU LITEBIA?** • 1934
DO I REALLY WANT TO DIE? see **WIL IK WEL DOOD?** • 1974
DO IT AGAIN see **THREE-RING MARRIAGE** • 1928
DO IT NOW • 1913 • *Powers* • USA
DO IT NOW • 1924 • Worne Duke • USA
DO IT UP see **CRACK IN THE MIRROR** • 1988
DO-IT-YOURSELF CARTOON KIT, THE • 1961 • Godfrey Bob • ANS • UKN
DO-IT-YOURSELF DEMOCRACY, THE • 1963 • Zetterling Mai • DCS • UKN
DO-IT-YOURSELF HAPPENING KIT see **YEAR THE UNIVERSE LOST THE PENNANT, THE** • 1961
DO JASSOS • 1975 • *Kapoor Raj* • IND
DO KALIYAN • 1968 • Panju Krishnan • IND • TWO BUDS
DO KONCA IN NAPREJ • 1990 • Pervanje Jure • YGS • TILL THE END AND ONWARD
DO KRWI OSTATNIEJ • 1978 • Hoffman Jerzy • PLN • STEFAN STARZYNSKI, MAYOR OF WARSAW ○ TO THE LAST DROP OF BLOOD
DO LESICKA NA CEKANOU • 1966 • Brdecka Jiri • CZC • IN THE FOREST, IN THE SITES ○ LET'S GO HUNTING IN THE WOODS ○ FORESTER'S SONG ○ ON THE WATCH IN THE FOREST
DO ME A FAVOR • 1922 • Roach Hal • SHT • USA
DO ME A FAVOUR see **INGEN ROSER, TAKK** • 1979
DO ME! DO ME! DO ME! • 1969 • Ransom Wes • USA
DO MEN LOVE WOMEN? • 1912 • Rolfe Alfred • ASL
DO NOT ANNOY THE LION • 1960 • Wilkosz Tadeusz • ANS • PLN • NEVER TEASE A LION

DO NOT COME ALONG THE SAME ROAD see **PO ISTI POTI SE NE VRACAJ** • 1966
DO NOT COME BACK ALONG THE SAME ROAD see **PO ISTI POTI SE NE VRACAJ** • 1966
DO NOT DISTURB • 1965 • Levy Ralph • USA
DO NOT FOLD, SPINDLE OR MUTILATE • 1971 • Post Ted • TVM • USA
DO NOT FOLD, STAPLE, SPINDLE OR MUTILATE • 1967 • Howe John • CND
DO NOT FORSAKE MY LOVE see **ZISE VIA TIN AGAPI MAS** • 1968
DO NOT JUDGE see **DOMEN ICKE** • 1914
DO NOT LEAN OUT OF THE WINDOW see **KIHAJOLNI VESZELYES** • 1978
DO NOT MENTION THE CAUSE OF DEATH see **UZROK SMRTI NE POMINJATI** • 1968
DO NOT MUDDY THE WATER see **LET'S NOT MUDDLE THE WATER** • 1989
DO OR DIE • 1921 • McGowan J. P. • USA
DO OR DIET • 1947 • Yates Hal • SHT • USA
DO OR DIET • 1953 • Sparber I. • ANS • USA
DO PANSKEHO STAVU • 1925 • Anton Karl • CZC • BECOMING MIDDLE-CLASS ○ TO THE LORD'S ESTATE
DO PIVNICE • 1982 • Svankmajer Jan • ANM • CZC • DOWN TO THE CELLAR
DO RAHA • 1952 • *Biswas Anil (M)* • IND
DO-RE-ME-BOOM! see **DO-RE-ME-FA!** • 1915
DO-RE-ME-FA! • 1915 • Parrott Charles • USA • DO-RE-ME-BOOM!
DO-RE-MI • 1966 • Gedris Marionas Vintzo • SHT • USS
DO SITARE • 1951 • *Biswas Anil (M)* • IND
DO SKLEPA • Svankmajer Jan • ANM • CZC • CELLAR, THE
DO SOMEONE A FAVOR • 1954 • Barclay David • SHT • USA
DO SVIDANIJA, GULSAI • 1967 • Urusevsky Sergei • USS • FAREWELL, GYULSARY
DO SVIDANIYA, MALCHIKI • 1965 • Kalik Moisei • USS • GOODBYE, BOYS
DO THE DEAD RETURN see **DRAME AU CHATEAU D'ACRE, UN** • 1915
DO THE DEAD TALK? • 1920 • MacDonald Jack, MacCullough Jack • USA
DO THE RIGHT THING • 1989 • Lee Spike • USA
DO THEY EVER CRY IN AMERICA? see **PACIFIC INFERNO** • 1978
DO UNTO OTHERS • 1915 • *Badgley Helen* • USA
DO UNTO OTHERS • 1915 • Haldane Bert? • UKN
DO UNTO OTHERS • 1925 • Butler Alexander • UKN
DO USTAD • 1959 • *Kapoor Raj* • IND
DO VIDENIA V PEKLE, PRIATELIA • 1970 • Jakubisko Juraj • CZC • SEE YOU IN HELL, FELLOWS! ○ SEE YOU IN HELL, FRIENDS
DO WIDZENIA DO JUTRA • 1960 • Morgenstern Janusz • PLN • SEE YOU TOMORROW (UKN)
DO YOU BELIEVE IN SWEDISH SIN see **SOM HON BADDAR FAR HAN LIGGA** • 1970
DO YOU BELIVE IN ANGELS? (UKN) see **ANGLAR, FINNS DOM?** • 1961
DO YOU GET IT? • 1975 • van Gasteren Louis A. • SER • NTH
DO YOU GET IT NOW, WHY I'M CRYING? see **BEGRIJPT U NU WAAROM IK HUIL?** • 1970
DO YOU HEAR THE DOGS BARKING? see **NO OYES LADRAR A LOS PERROS?** • 1974
DO YOU KEEP A LION AT HOME? see **MATE DOMA IVA?** • 1964
DO YOU KNOW DOLLY BELL? see **DA LI ZNATE DOLLY BELL?** • 1981
DO YOU KNOW "SUNDAY-MONDAY"? see **ISMERI A SZANDI-MANDIT?** • 1969
DO YOU KNOW THIS VOICE? • 1964 • *Duryea Dan* • UKN
DO YOU KNOW THIS WOMAN? • 1911 • *American* • USA
DO YOU KNOW WHAT STALIN DID TO WOMEN? see **SAI COSA FACEVA STALIN ALLE DONNE?** • 1969
DO YOU KNOW WHO I AM? see **NAAN YAAR THERIYUMA?** • 1967
DO YOU LIKE WOMEN? see **AIMEZ-VOUS LES FEMMES?** • 1964
DO YOU LOVE ME? • 1946 • Ratoff Gregory • USA • KITTEN ON THE KEYS
DO YOU LOVE YOUR WIFE? • 1919 • Roach Hal • SHT • USA
DO YOU REMEMBER? • 1922 • Quiribet Gaston • UKN
DO YOU REMEMBER DOLLY BELL? see **SJECAS LI SE DOLLY BELL?** • 1981
DO YOU REMEMBER LOVE? • 1985 • Bleckner Jeff • TVM • USA
DO YOU TAKE THIS STRANGER? • 1970 • Heffron Richard T. • TVM • USA • KNOCK AT THE WRONG DOOR, A ○ STRANGERS AND LOVERS
DO YOU WANT TO REMAIN A VIRGIN FOREVER? (UKN) see **WILLST DU EWIG JUNGFRAU BLEIBEN?** • 1968
DO YOUR DUTY • 1926 • Roach Hal • SHT • USA
DO YOUR DUTY • 1928 • Beaudine William • USA
DO YOUR EXAMS FIRST see **PASSE TON BAC D'ABORD** • 1979
DO YOUR STUFF • 1923 • Roach Hal • SHT • USA
DO YOUR THING • 1973 • Low Colin, Henaut Dorothy • DOC • CND
DOA EL-KARAWAN • 1959 • UAR • CALL OF THE NIGHTINGALE
DOBAR DECKO • 1981 • Radivojevic Milos • YGS • GOOD BOY
DOBBELTE MAND, DEN • 1975 • Ernst Franz • DNM • DOUBLE MAN, THE
DOBBS FORGOT THE COAL • 1913 • *Komic* • USA
DOBBS THE DAUBER • 1911 • *Lubin* • USA
DOBERMAN GANG, THE • 1972 • Chudnow Byron • USA
DOBERMAN PATROL • 1973 • De Felitta Frank • TVM • USA • TRAPPED
DOBLE HISTORIA DEL DR. VALMY, LA • 1978 • Klimovsky Leon • SPN
DOBOL WEDDING • 1968 • de Villa Jose • PHL • DOUBLE WEDDING
DOBRE BYDLENI • 1960 • Pojar Bretislav • ANS • CZC
DOBRE PLACENA PROCHAZKA • 1965 • Forman Milos • CZC • WELL PAID STROLL, A

DOBRE SVETIO • 1985 • Kachyna Karel • CZC • AMATEUR PHOTOGRAPHER

DOBRO MORJE • 1958 • Grobler Mirko • YGS • GOOD SEA

DOBRO POZHALOVAT • 1964 • Klimov Elem • USS • NO HOLIDAY FOR INOCHKIN (UKN) ○ WELCOME KOSTYA! (USA) ○ DOBRO POZHALOVAT ILI POSTORONNIM VKHOD VOSPRESHCHEN

DOBRO POZHALOVAT ILI POSTORONNIM VKHOD VOSPRESHCHEN see **DOBRO POZHALOVAT** • 1964

DOBRODRUZSTVI NA ZLATE ZATOCE • 1955 • Pojar Bretislav • CZC • GOLD BAY ADVENTURE, THE ○ BIG FISH, THE ○ BAY OF GOLD

DOBRODRUZSTVI PANA PROKOUKA • 1947-58 • Zeman Karel • ASS • CZC • ADVENTURES OF MR. PROKOUK (USA)

DOBRODRUZSTVI ROBINSONA CRUSOE, NAMORNIKA Z YORKU • 1982 • Latal Stanislav • ANM • CZC, FRG • ADVENTURES OF ROBINSON CRUSOE, THE SAILOR OF YORK ○ LIFE AND INCREDIBLE ADVENTURES OF ROBINSON CRUSOE, THE SAILOR FROM YORK, THE

DOBROVOLTSY • 1958 • Yegorov Yuri • USS • VOLUNTEERS

DOBRY VOJAK SVEIK • 1929 • Antonovsky B. • ANM • USS • GOOD SOLDIER SCHWEIK, THE (USA)

DOBRY VOJAK SVEJK • 1926 • Lamac Carl • CZC • GOOD SOLDIER SCHWEIK

DOBRY VOJAK SVEJK • 1931 • Fric Martin • CZC • GOOD SOLDIER SCHWEIK

DOBRY VOJAK SVEJK • 1957 • Stekly Karel • CZC • GOOD SOLDIER SCHWEIK PARTS I & 2, THE

DOBRY VOJAK SVEJK see **OSUDY DOBREHO VOYAKA SVEJKA** • 1954

DOBRZYNSKIEGO WITRAZE • 1958 • Lomnicki Jan • DOC • PLN • DOBRZYNSKI'S STAINED GLASS WINDOWS

DOBRZYNSKI'S STAINED GLASS WINDOWS see **DOBRZYNSKIEGO WITRAZE** • 1958

DOBS AT THE SHORE • 1914 • *Hardy Babe* • USA

DOBU • 1954 • Shindo Kaneto • JPN • GUTTER

DOBUNEZUMI SAKUSEN • 1962 • Okamoto Kihachi • JPN • OPERATION X

DOBUROKU NO TATSU • 1949 • Tasaka Tomotaka • JPN • TATSU THE DRUNKARD

DOBUROKU NO TATSU • 1962 • Inagaki Hiroshi • JPN • TATSU

DOBUTSU TAKARAJIMA • 1971 • Ikeda Hiroshi • JPN • TREASURE ISLAND

DOBUTSUEN NIKKI • 1957 • Hani Susumu • JPN • ZOO DIARY ○ ZOO STORY

DOC • 1914 • *Seaword Sydney* • USA

DOC • 1971 • Perry Frank • USA, SPN

DOC see **CALLALOO** • 1937

DOC HOOKER'S BUNCH • 1978 • Belcher Zach • USA

DOC, MANOS DE PLATA • 1966 • Balcazar Alfonso • SPN

DOC SAVAGE, THE MAN OF BRONZE • 1975 • Anderson Michael • USA

DOCE ESPORTE DO SEXO, O • 1972 • Viano Zelito • BRZ

DOCE HOMBRES Y UNA MUJER • 1934 • Delgado Fernando • SPN

DOCE HORAS DE VIDAS • 1948 • Rovira Beleta Francisco • SPN

DOCE LUNAS DE MIEL • 1943 • Vajda Ladislao • SPN

DOCE MALDITOS, LOS • 1972 • *Estudios America* • MXC

DOCE MUJERES • 1939 • Barth-Moglia Luis • ARG • TWELVE WOMEN (USA)

DOCE MULHER AMADA, A • 1968 • Santos Ruy • BRZ • SWEET AND BELOVED WOMAN, THE

DOCE SILLAS, LOS • 1962 • Alea Tomas Gutierrez • CUB • TWELVE CHAIRS, THE

DOCENT HAMLER • 1964 • Majewski Janusz • PLN • PROFESSOR HAMLER

DOCH DIE LIEBE FAND DEN WEG • 1915 • Moest Hubert • FRG

DOCH DIE LIEBE FAND DEN WEG • 1917 • Moest Hubert • FRG

DOCH MIT DES SCHICKSALS MACHTEN • 1923 • *Admiral-Film* • FRG

DOCHKI MATERI • 1975 • Gerasimov Sergei • USS • MOTHERS AND DAUGHTERS

DOCHU SUGOROKU BUNE • 1927 • Kinugasa Teinosuke • JPN

DOCHU SUGOROKU KAGO • 1927 • Kinugasa Teinosuke • JPN • PALANQUIN, THE

DOCI I OSTATI • 1965 • Bauer Branko • YGS • TO COME AND STAY

DOCK • 1955 • Degelin Emile • BLG

DOCK BRIEF, THE • 1962 • Hill James • UKN • TRIAL AND ERROR (USA) ○ CASE FOR THE JURY, A

DOCK SUD • 1953 • Demicheli Tulio • ARG

DOCKER, THE • 1974 • Rogov Yu. • USS

DOCKHEM, ETT • 1955 • Henrikson Anders • SWD

DOCKPOJKEN • 1990 • Hellwig Hilda • SWD • BOY-DOLL

DOCKS AT MARSEILLES, THE see **QUAIS A MARSEILLES, LES** • 1896

DOCKS OF HAMBURG • Waschneck Erich • FRG

DOCKS OF NEW ORLEANS • 1948 • Abrahams Derwin • USA

DOCKS OF NEW YORK • 1948 • Fox Wallace • USA

DOCKS OF NEW YORK, THE • 1928 • von Sternberg Josef • USA

DOCKS OF SAN FRANCISCO • 1932 • Seitz George B. • USA

DOC'S KINGDOM • 1989 • Kramer Robert • USA

DOC'S LAST STAND • 1961 • Hannah Jack • ANS • USA

DOCTEUR CARNAVAL • 1909 • Cohl Emile • ANS • FRN

DOCTEUR FRANCOISE GAILLAND • 1975 • Bertucelli Jean-Louis • FRN • NO TIME FOR BREAKFAST (USA) ○ DR. FRANCOISE ○ CRI, UN ○ JUST A WOMAN

DOCTEUR JEKYLL ET LES FEMMES • 1981 • Borowczyk Walerian • FRN • STRANGE CASE OF DR. JEKYLL AND MISS OSBOURNE, THE ○ DR. JEKYLL AND THE WOMEN ○ BLOODBATH OF DR. JEKYLL ○ BLOOD OF DR. JEKYLL, THE ○ DOCTOR JEKYLL AND MISS OSBOURNE

DOCTEUR LAENNEC • 1948 • Cloche Maurice • FRN

DOCTEUR LOUISE see **ON NE TRICHE PAS AVEC LA VIE** • 1949

DOCTEUR NO HA MUERTO, EL • 1972 • Franco Jesus • SPN

DOCTEUR PETIOT • 1990 • de Chalonge Christian • FRN

DOCTEUR PHANTOM • 1909 • Jasset Victorin • FRN

DOCTEUR POPAUL • 1972 • Chabrol Claude • FRN, ITL • TRAPPOLA PER UN LUPO (ITL) ○ SCOUNDREL IN WHITE (UKN) ○ HIGH HEELS (USA) ○ PIEGE A LOUP, LE ○ TRAPPOLI PER LUPI

DOCTEUR TEYRAN • 1980 • Chapot Jean • MTV • FRN

DR. • 1962 • Jovanovic Soja • YGS

DR. • 1990 • Babic Vuk • YGS • DOCTOR

DOCTOR see **DR.** • 1990

DOCTOR, THE • 1911 • Dawley J. Searle • USA

DOCTOR, THE • 1912 • *Blanchard Eleanor* • USA

DOCTOR, THE see **DOKTOR UR** • 1916

DOCTOR, THE see **ONE MAN'S JOURNEY** • 1933

DR. ALIEN • 1988 • Decoteau David • USA

DOCTOR AND THE DEBUTANTE, THE (UKN) see **DOCTOR KILDARE'S VICTORY** • 1941

DOCTOR AND THE DEVILS, THE • 1965 • Ray Nicholas • USA

DOCTOR AND THE DEVILS, THE • 1985 • Francis Freddie • UKN

DOCTOR AND THE GIRL, THE • 1949 • Bernhardt Curtis • USA

DOCTOR AND THE MONKEY, THE (USA) see **SAVANT ET LE CHIMPANZE, LE** • 1900

DOCTOR AND THE NURSE see **AIZEN KATSURA** • 1954

DOCTOR AND THE PLAYGIRL, THE • 1963 • Martin William • USA • DR. WARD STORY, THE

DOCTOR AND THE QUACK see **MEDICO E LO STREGONE, IL** • 1957

DOCTOR AND THE WIZARD, THE see **MEDICO E LO STREGONE, IL** • 1957

DOCTOR AND THE WOMAN, THE • 1918 • Weber Lois, Smalley Phillips • USA

DOCTOR AND THE WOMAN DOCTOR, THE • Lee Doo-Yong • SKR

DOCTOR AT LARGE • 1957 • Thomas Ralph • UKN

DOCTOR AT SEA • 1955 • Thomas Ralph • UKN

DR. BESSELS VERWANDLUNG • 1927 • Oswald Richard • FRG

DOCTOR BETHUNE see **BAIQUEN DAIFU** • 1964

DOCTOR BEWARE (USA) see **TERESA VENERDI** • 1941

DOCTOR BILL'S PATIENT • 1911 • *Essanay* • USA

DR. BLACK AND MR. HYDE see **DR. BLACK, MR. HYDE** • 1976

DR. BLACK, MR. HYDE • 1976 • Crain William • USA • DR. BLACK AND MR. HYDE ○ WATTS MONSTER, THE

DOCTOR BLOOD'S COFFIN • 1961 • Furie Sidney J. • UKN

DOCTOR BLUEBIRD • 1936 • *Mintz Charles (P)* • ANS • USA

DR. BREEDLOVE see **KISS ME QUICK!** • 1964

DR. BREEDLOVE OR HOW I LEARNED TO STOP WORRYING AND LOVE see **KISS ME QUICK!** • 1964

DR. BRIAN PELLIE AND THE BANK ROBBERY • 1911 • Noy Wilfred • UKN

DR. BRIAN PELLIE AND THE BARONET'S BRIDE • 1911 • Noy Wilfred • UKN

DR. BRIAN PELLIE AND THE SECRET DESPATCH • 1912 • Stow Percy • UKN

DR. BRIAN PELLIE AND THE SPANISH GRANDEES • 1912 • Noy Wilfred • UKN

DR. BRIAN PELLIE AND THE WEDDING GIFTS • 1913 • Stow Percy • UKN

DR. BRIAN PELLIE ESCAPES FROM PRISON • 1912 • Noy Wilfred • UKN

DR. BRIAN PELLIE, THIEF AND COINER • 1910 • Noy Wilfred • UKN

DR. BRIDGET • 1912 • Thompson Frederick A. • USA

DOCTOR BROADWAY • 1942 • Mann Anthony • USA

DR. BROMPTON-WATTS ADJUSTER • 1912 • *Sturgeon John* • USA • DR. BROMPTON-WATTS AGE ADJUSTER (UKN)

DR. BROMPTON-WATTS AGE ADJUSTER (UKN) see **DR. BROMPTON-WATTS ADJUSTER** • 1912

DOCTOR BULL • 1933 • Ford John • USA • LIFE'S WORTH LIVING

DR. BUTCHER M.D. (MEDICAL DEVIATE) see **REGINA DEI CANNIBALI, LA** • 1979

DR. BYRD see **RAGINA'S SECRETS** • 1969

DR. BYRD UNLOCKS RAGINA'S SECRETS see **RAGINA'S SECRETS** • 1969

DR. CADMAN'S SECRET see **BLACK SLEEP, THE** • 1956

DR. CHARLIE IS A GREAT SURGEON • 1911 • *Eclair* • FRN

DR. CHRISTIAN MEETS THE WOMEN • 1940 • McGann William • USA

DR. COOK'S GARDEN • 1970 • Post Ted • TVM • USA

DR. COPPELIUS (USA) see **FANTASTICO MUNDO DEL DR. COPPELIUS, EL** • 1966

DR. CRATHERN'S EXPERIMENT • 1913 • Brooke Van Dyke • USA

DOCTOR CRIMEN see **MONSTRUO RESUCITADO, EL** • 1953

DR. CRIPPEN • 1962 • Lynn Robert • UKN

DR. CRIPPEN AN BORD • 1942 • Engels Erich • FRG

DR. CRIPPEN LEBT • 1958 • Engels Erich • FRG • DR. CRIPPEN LIVES

DR. CRIPPEN LIVES see **DR. CRIPPEN LEBT** • 1958

DOCTOR CUPID • 1911 • *Vitagraph* • USA

DOCTOR CUPID • 1915 • *Baxter Marie* • USA

DR. CUREM'S PATIENTS • 1908 • *Lubin* • USA

DR. CURETO'S CLINIC see **CLINICA DEL DOCTOR CURETA, LA** • 1987

DR. CUT'EMUP • 1904 • Collins Alf? • UKN

DR. CYCLOPS • 1940 • Schoedsack Ernest B. • USA

DR. DEATH see **DR. DEATH, SEEKER OF SOULS** • 1972

DOCTOR DEATH see **DEATH WARMED UP** • 1984

DR. DEATH, SEEKER OF SOULS • 1972 • Saeta Eddie • USA • DR. DEATH

DOCTOR DETROIT • 1983 • Pressman Michael • USA

DR. DEVIL AND MR. HARE • 1964 • McKimson Robert • ANS • USA

DR. DILDOE'S SECRET • 1970 • *Stacey Dist.* • USA

DR. DIPPY'S SANITARIUM • 1906 • *Bitzer Billy (Ph)* • USA

DOCTOR DOLITTLE • 1967 • Fleischer Richard • USA

DR. DOLITTLE IN THE LION'S DEN • 1928 • Reiniger Lotte • ANS • FRG

DR. DOLITTLE'S TRIP TO AFRICA see **REISE NACH AFRIKA, DIE** • 1928

DOCTOR DON'TLITTLE see **DOKTOR ZA ZIVOTINJE** • 1972

DR. DOSEM'S DEPUTY • 1914 • Kellino W. P. • UKN

DR. DRACULA • 1977 • Aratow Paul, Adamson Al • USA

DR. EDUARD WIRTHS, STANDORTARZT AUSCHWITZ • 1975 • Orthel Rolf • DOC • NTH

DR. EHRLICH'S MAGIC BULLET • 1940 • Dieterle William • USA • STORY OF DR. EHRLICH'S MAGIC BULLET, THE (UKN) ○ MAGIC BULLET, THE

DR. ENGEL, CHILD SPECIALIST (USA) see **KINDERARZT DR. ENGEL** • 1936

DR. EPAMEINONDAS • 1938 • Mizrahi Togo • EGY

DR. EVANS' SILENCE see **MOLCHANIYE DOKTORA IVENSA** • 1973

DR. FABIAN -LACHEN IST DIE BESTE MEDIZIN • 1969 • Reinl Harald • FRG • DR. MED. FABIAN

DOCTOR FAUSTUS • 1967 • Coghill Nevill, Burton Richard • UKN, ITL

DR. FAUSTUS see **PAN TVARDOVSKI** • 1937

DOCTOR, FEEL MY PULSE • 1944 • *Vague Vera* • SHT • USA

DR. FENTON'S ORDEAL • 1914 • Wilson Frank? • UKN

DR. FISCHER OF GENEVA • 1983 • Lindsay-Hogg Michael • UKN

DOCTOR FOR AN HOUR, A • 1912 • *Wadsworth William* • USA

DOCTOR FOR ANIMALS see **DOKTOR ZA ZIVOTINJE** • 1972

DR. FRANCOISE see **DOCTEUR FRANCOISE GAILLAND** • 1975

DOCTOR FRANKEN • 1980 • Chomsky Marvin • TVM • USA

DOCTOR FRANKENSTEIN see **FRANKENSTEIN: THE TRUE STORY** • 1973

DR. FRANKENSTEIN ON CAMPUS (USA) see **FLICK** • 1970

DR. FRANKENSTEIN'S CASTLE OF FREAKS see **CASTELLO DELLE DONNE MALEDETTE, IL** • 1973

DOCTOR FRANKENSTEIN'S CASTLE OF FREAKS see **CASTELLO DELLE DONNE MALEDETTE, IL** • 1973

DOCTOR FROM HALBERSTADT, A see **ARZT AUS HALBERSTADT, EIN** • 1969

DOCTOR FROM SEVEN DIALS, THE see **CORRIDORS OF BLOOD** • 1958

DR. G AND THE BIKINI MACHINE (UKN) see **DR. GOLDFOOT AND THE BIKINI MACHINE** • 1966

DR. G. AND THE LOVE BOMBS see **SPIE VENGONO DAL SEMIFREDDO, LE** • 1966

DR. GILLESPIE'S CRIMINAL CASE • 1943 • Goldbeck Willis • USA • CRAZY TO KILL (UKN)

DR. GILLESPIE'S NEW ASSISTANT • 1942 • Goldbeck Willis • USA

DOCTOR GLAS see **DOKTOR GLAS** • 1968

DR. GOLDFOOT AND THE BIKINI MACHINE • 1966 • Taurog Norman • USA • DR. G AND THE BIKINI MACHINE (UKN)

DR. GOLDFOOT AND THE GIRL BOMBS (USA) see **SPIE VENGONO DAL SEMIFREDDO, LE** • 1966

DR. GORE • 1975 • Patterson Pat • USA

DR. GOUDRON'S SYSTEM see **SYSTEME DU DOCTEUR GOUDRON ET DU PROFESSEUR PLUME, LE** • 1909

DR. GYLLENBORGS DOPPELTES GESICHT • 1921 • Ralph Louis • FRG

DR. HA HA HA • 1966 • Bakshi Ralph • ANS • USA

DR. HACKENSTEIN • 1989 • Clark Richard • USA

DR. HALLERS see **ANDERE, DER** • 1930

DR. HALLIN • 1921 • Lampel Alfred • AUS

DR. HECKYL AND MR. HYPE • 1980 • Griffith Charles B. • USA

DR. HEGL'S PATIENT see **PACIENTKA DR. HEGLA** • 1940

DR. HEIDEGGER'S EXPERIMENT • 1954 • *Woolley Monty* • SHT • USA

DR. HOFFMANN • 1971 • Schottle Valeska • SHT • FRG

DOCTOR HOMER'S BROTHER see **BRAT DOKTORA HOMERA** • 1968

DOCTOR, I'M COMING • 1970 • Killy Rod • USA

DOCTOR IN CLOVER • 1966 • Thomas Ralph • UKN • CARNABY M.D. (USA)

DOCTOR IN DISTRESS • 1963 • Thomas Ralph • UKN

DOCTOR IN LOVE • 1960 • Thomas Ralph • UKN

DOCTOR IN THE HOUSE • 1954 • Thomas Ralph • UKN

DOCTOR IN THE NUDE (UKN) see **TRAITEMENT DE CHOC** • 1972

DOCTOR IN THE VILLAGE see **DORP AAN DE RIVEIR** • 1958

DOCTOR IN TROUBLE • 1970 • Thomas Ralph • UKN

DOCTOR JACK • 1922 • Newmeyer Fred • USA • DOCTOR'S ORDERS

DOCTOR JEKYLL see **DOTTOR JEKYLL** • 1964

DOCTOR JEKYLL AND MISS OSBOURNE see **DOCTEUR JEKYLL ET LES FEMMES** • 1981

DR. JEKYLL AND MR. BLOOD see **MAN WITH TWO HEADS, THE** • 1971

DR. JEKYLL AND MR. HYDE • 1908 • *Selig William N.* • USA • MODERN DR. JEKYLL, THE

DR. JEKYLL AND MR. HYDE • 1908 • Olcott Sidney • USA

DR. JEKYLL AND MR. HYDE • 1912 • Henderson Lucius • SHT • USA

DR. JEKYLL AND MR. HYDE • 1913 • *Kinemacolour* • UKN

DR. JEKYLL AND MR. HYDE • 1913 • Brenon Herbert • USA

DR. JEKYLL AND MR. HYDE • 1914 • *Starlight* • USA

DR. JEKYLL AND MR. HYDE • 1920 • *Arrow Film Corp.* • USA

DR. JEKYLL AND MR. HYDE • 1920 • Hall George Edwardes • *Louis B. Mayer Prod.* • USA

DR. JEKYLL AND MR. HYDE • 1920 • Robertson John S. • *Paramount* • USA

DR. JEKYLL AND MR. HYDE • 1925 • *Standard* • USA

DR. JEKYLL AND MR. HYDE • 1932 • Mamoulian Rouben • USA

DR. JEKYLL AND MR. HYDE • 1932 • Vance William • SHT • USA

DR. JEKYLL AND MR. HYDE • 1939 • *Pixilated Pictures* • USA

DR. JEKYLL AND MR. HYDE • 1941 • Fleming Victor • USA

DR. JEKYLL AND MR. HYDE • 1973 • Winters David • TVM • UKN

DR. JEKYLL AND MR. HYDE • 1981 • Reid Alastair • MTV • UKN

DR. JEKYLL AND MR. HYDE see **SKAEBNESVANGRE OPFINDELSE, DEN** • 1910

DR. JEKYLL AND MR. HYDE see **SELTSAMER FALL, EIN** • 1914

DR. JEKYLL AND MR. HYDE see **STRANGE CASE OF DR. JEKYLL AND MR. HYDE, THE** • 1967

DR. JEKYLL AND MR. HYDE -A JOURNEY INTO FEAR • 1988 • Kikoine Gerard • UKN • EDGE OF SANITY

DR. JEKYLL AND MR. HYDE DONE TO A FRAZZLE • 1914 • *Warner Features* • USA

DR. JEKYLL AND MR. HYDE (UKN) see **JANUSKOPF, DER** • 1920

DR. JEKYLL AND MR. HYDE (USA) see **SHADA KALO** • 1953

DR. JEKYLL AND MR. MOUSE • 1947 • Hanna William, Barbera Joseph • ANS • USA
DR. JEKYLL AND SISTER HYDE • 1972 • Baker Roy Ward • UKN
DR. JEKYLL AND THE WEREWOLF see **DR. JEKYLL Y EL HOMBRE LOBO, EL** • 1972
DR. JEKYLL AND THE WOLFMAN (USA) see **DR. JEKYLL Y EL HOMBRE LOBO, EL** • 1972
DR. JEKYLL AND THE WOMEN see **DOCTEUR JEKYLL ET LES FEMMES** • 1981
DR. JEKYLL Y EL HOMBRE LOBO, EL • 1972 • Klimovsky Leon • SPN • DR. JEKYLL AND THE WOLFMAN (USA) ○ DR. JEKYLL AND THE WEREWOLF
DOCTOR JEKYLL Y MR. HYDE • 1969 • Franco Jesus • SPN
DR. JEKYLL'S DUNGEON OF DARKNESS see **DR. JEKYLL'S DUNGEON OF DEATH** • 1979
DR. JEKYLL'S DUNGEON OF DEATH • 1979 • Wood James • USA • DR. JEKYLL'S DUNGEON OF DARKNESS ○ JEKYLL EXPERIMENT, THE
DR. JEKYLL'S HIDE • 1932 • De Mond Albert • SHT • USA
DOCTOR JERKYLE'S HIDE • 1954 • Freleng Friz • ANS • USA
DOCTOR JERRY • 1915 • *Ovey George* • USA
DOCTOR JIM • 1915 • *Burns Fred* • USA
DR. JIM • 1921 • Worthington William • USA
DR. JOSSER K.C. • 1931 • Lee Norman • UKN • HOUSE FULL
DOCTOR JUDYM see **DOKTOR JUDYM** • 1975
DR. JUSTICE • 1975 • Christian-Jaque • FRN, SPN
DR. K. see **GOD KNOWS WHY BUT IT WORKS** • 1976
DOCTOR KALIE • 1968 • Hall Ivan • SAF
DR. KILDARE GOES HOME • 1940 • Bucquet Harold S. • USA
DR. KILDARE'S CRISIS • 1940 • Bucquet Harold S. • USA • SHOULD DR. KILDARE TELL?
DR. KILDARE'S STRANGE CASE • 1940 • Bucquet Harold S. • USA
DOCTOR KILDARE'S VICTORY • 1941 • Van Dyke W. S. • USA • DOCTOR AND THE DEBUTANTE, THE (UKN)
DR. KILDARE'S WEDDING DAY • 1941 • Bucquet Harold S. • USA • MARY NAMES THE DAY (UKN)
DR. KILLEM'S DOPE • 1914 • *Premier* • USA
DR. KNOCK (USA) see **KNOCK** • 1950
DOCTOR KNOWS-ALL • 1911 • *Itala* • ITL
DR. KURCZAK • 1989 • Wajda Andrzej • PLN, FRG • KORCZAK
DR. LAFLUER'S THEORY • 1912 • *Costello Maurice* • USA
DR. LOVE see **TEENIE TULIP** • 1970
DOCTOR LUKE • 1982 • SAF
DR. M. • 1989 • Chabrol Claude • FRG, FRN
DR. M. SCHLAGT ZU • 1972 • Franco Jesus • FRG
DR. MABUSE see **DR. MABUSE, DER SPIELER** • 1922
DR. MABUSE, EL • 1971 • Franco Jesus • SPN, FRG • DOKTOR MABUSE, DER (FRG)
DR. MABUSE, DER SPIELER • 1922 • Lang Fritz • FRG • FATAL PASSION OF DR. MABUSE ○ DR. MABUSE THE GAMBLER ○ DR. MABUSE ○ FATAL PASSIONS, THE
DR. MABUSE, DER SPIELER 1 • 1922 • Lang Fritz • FRG • GROSSE SPIELER -EIN BILD DER ZEIT, DER ○ SPIELER AUS LEIDENSCHAFT ○ GREAT GAMBLER -AN IMAGE OF OUR TIME, THE
DR. MABUSE, DER SPIELER 2 • 1922 • Lang Fritz • FRG • INFERNO -EIN SPIEL VON MENSCHEN UNSERER ZEIT ○ INFERNO -MENSCHEN DER ZEIT ○ INFERNO -MEN OF OUR TIME ○ INFERNO DES VERBRECHENS
DR. MABUSE THE GAMBLER see **DR. MABUSE, DER SPIELER** • 1922
DR. MABUSE VS. SCOTLAND YARD (USA) see **SCOTLAND YARD JAGT DOKTOR MABUSE** • 1963
DR. MACDONALDS SANATORIUM see **HUND VON BASKERVILLE 5, DER** • 1920
DR. MANIAC see **MAN WHO CHANGED HIS MIND, THE** • 1936
DOCTOR MANIAC see **HOUSE OF THE LIVING DEAD, THE** • 1973
DR. MARION HILLIARD • 1981 • Dalen Zale R. • CND
DR. MARIUS HUGO • 1978 • SAF
DR. MASHER • 1969 • Duffy Kevin • USA
DR. MASON'S TEMPTATION • 1915 • Lloyd Frank • USA
DR. MAWSON IN THE ANTARCTIC • 1913 • Hurley Frank • ASL • LIFE IN THE ANTARCTIC ○ HOME OF THE BLIZZARD
DR. MAX • 1974 • Goldstone James • TVM • USA
DOCTOR MAXWELL'S EXPERIMENT • 1913 • Johnson Arthur • USA
DOCTOR, ME GUSTAN LAS MUJERES, ES GRAVE? • 1973 • Fernandez Ramon • SPN
DR. MED. FABIAN see **DR. FABIAN -LACHEN IST DIE BESTE MEDIZIN** • 1969
DR. MED HIOB PRATORIUS • 1965 • Hoffmann Kurt • FRG
DR. MESNER'S FATAL PRESCRIPTION • 1910 • *Warwick* • UKN
DR. MINX • 1975 • Avedis Howard • USA
DOCTOR MLADEN see **DOKTOR MLADEN** • 1974
DR. MONICA • 1934 • Keighley William, Dieterle William (U/c) • USA
DR. MONNIER UND DIE FRAUEN • 1928 • Molander Gustaf • FRG • DOCTOR'S WOMEN, THE ○ PARISERINNEN ○ PARISER EHEN
DR. MORELLE see **DR. MORELLE -THE CASE OF THE MISSING HEIRESS** • 1949
DR. MORELLE -THE CASE OF THE MISSING HEIRESS • 1949 • Grayson Godfrey • UKN • DR. MORELLE
DR. MORS • 1917 • Heymann Robert • FRG
DR. NEIGHBOR • 1916 • Carleton Lloyd B. • USA
DR. NICOLA • 1909 • *Blom August* • DNM • HVORLEDES DR. NICOLA ERHVERVEDE DEN KINESISKE STOK ○ HOW DR. NICOLA PROCURED THE CHINESE CANE
DR. NICOLA I • 1909 • *Blom August* • DNM • SKJULTE SKAT, DEN
DR. NICOLA III • 1909 • *Blom August* • DNM • MYSTERY OF THE LAMA CONVENT, THE ○ DR. NICOLA IN TIBET
DR. NICOLA IN TIBET see **DR. NICOLA III** • 1909
DR. NIKOLA see **DOKTOR NIKOLA** • 1909
DR. NO • 1962 • Young Terence • UKN
DOCTOR NO • 1970 • *Stacey Dist.* • USA
DOCTOR NYE see **IDLE TONGUES** • 1924
DR. O'DOWD • 1940 • Mason Herbert • UKN
DOCTOR OF DOOM (USA) see **LUCHADORAS CONTRA EL MEDICO ASESINO, LAS** • 1962
DOCTOR OF GAFIRE, THE see **MEDECIN DE GAFIRE, LE**
DOCTOR OF ST. PAULI, THE see **ARZT VON ST. PAULI, DER** • 1968
DOCTOR OF THE AFTERNOON ARM, THE • 1916 • Hill Robert F. • SHT • USA
DR. ORLOFF'S MONSTER (USA) see **SECRETO DEL DR. ORLOFF, EL** • 1964
DR. ORLOFF'S SECRET see **SECRETO DEL DR. ORLOFF, EL** • 1964
DOCTOR OSWALD • 1935 • *Lantz Walter (P)* • ANS • USA
DR. OTTO AND THE RIDDLE OF THE GLOOM BEAM • 1986 • Cherry John • USA
DR. PAUL JOSEPH GOEBBELS see **ENEMY OF WOMEN** • 1944
DR. PAXTON'S LAST CRIME • 1914 • Morgan Sidney • UKN
DR. PHIBES see **ABOMINABLE DR. PHIBES, THE** • 1971
DR. PHIBES RISES AGAIN • 1972 • Fuest Robert • UKN
DR. PHIL. DODERLEIN • 1945 • Klinger Werner • FRG
DR. PIEN • 1968 • Bedel Jean-Pierre • CND
DR. POENARU • 1978 • Tanase Dinu • RMN
DOCTOR POLLY • 1914 • North Wilfred, Van Wally • USA
DOCTOR PRAETORIUS see **PEOPLE WILL TALK** • 1951
DOCTOR PULDER SOWS POPPIES see **DOKTER PULDER ZAAIT PAPAVERS** • 1975
DR. PYCKLE AND MR. PRIDE • 1925 • *Laurel Stan* • SHT • USA
DR. RAMEAU • 1915 • Davis Will S. • USA • INFIDELITY
DOCTOR RED ADAMS see **BETWEEN TWO WOMEN** • 1944
DR. RENAULT'S SECRET • 1942 • Lachman Harry • USA • BURIED ALIVE
DR. RHINESTONE'S THEORY • 1967 • Bakshi Ralph • ANS • USA
DR. RHYTHM • 1938 • Tuttle Frank • USA
DR. ROCK AND MR. ROLL • 1967 • *Rathbone Basil* • USA
DR. RUSHDI • 1970 • Ramlee P. • MLY
DR. RUSSELL'S LIE • 1912 • Coleby A. E. • UKN
DR. SACROBOSCO, DER GROSSE UNHEIMLICHE • 1923 • Firmans Josef • FRG
DR. SATAN see **DR. SHAITAN** • 1959
DR. SATAN see **DR. SHAITAN** • 1960
DR. SATAN, EL • 1966 • Morayta Miguel • MXC • DR. SATAN AND THE BLACK MAGIC
DOCTOR SATAN AND BLACK MAGIC see **DR. SATAN Y LA MAGIA NEGRA, EL** • 1967
DR. SATAN AND THE BLACK MAGIC see **DR. SATAN, EL** • 1966
DR. SATAN Y LA MAGIA NEGRA, EL • 1967 • Gonzalez Rogelio A. • MXC • DOCTOR SATAN AND BLACK MAGIC ○ VUELVE EL DR. SATAN ○ RETURN OF DR. SATAN
DOCTOR SATAN'S ROBOT • 1940 • Witney William, English John • USA
DOCTOR SAYS, THE (USA) see **ARZT STELLT FEST... DER** • 1966
DR. SCHOTTE • 1918 • Wauer William • FRG
DR. SCORPION • 1978 • Lang Richard • TVM • USA
DR. SEMMELWEISS see **SEMMELWEISS -REITER DER MUTTER** • 1950
DR. SENERATH PARANAVITANE • Hettiarachi P. • DOC • SLN
DR. SEX • 1964 • *Romike Films* • USA
DR. SEXUAL AND MR. HYDE • 1971 • Brzezinski Tony • USA
DR. SHAITAN • 1959 • Aziz S. A. • PKS • DR. SATAN
DR. SHAITAN • 1960 • Shreeram • IND • DR. SATAN
DR. SHRINK • 1970 • *Cosmos Films* • USA
DR. SIN FANG • 1937 • Frenguelli Tony • UKN
DR. SIN FANG DRAMAS • 1928 • Paul Fred • SER • UKN
DR. SKINNEM'S WONDERFUL INVENTION • 1912 • *Kalem* • USA
DR. SKINUM • 1907 • *Biograph* • USA
DR. SMITH'S AUTOMATON • 1910 • *Pathe* • FRN
DOCTOR SMITH'S BABY • 1914 • Costello Maurice, Gaillord Robert • USA
DR. SOCRATES • 1935 • Dieterle William • USA
DOCTOR SPEAKS OUT, THE see **ARZT STELLT FEST... DER** • 1966
DR. STEFFANS SELTSAMSTER FALL • 1921 • Attenberger Toni • FRG
DR. STRANGE • 1978 • Deguere Philip • TVM • USA
DR. STRANGELOVE see **DR. STRANGLOVE: OR, HOW I LEARNED TO STOP WORRYING AND LOVE THE BOMB** • 1963
DR. STRANGLOVE: OR, HOW I LEARNED TO STOP WORRYING AND LOVE THE BOMB • 1963 • Kubrick Stanley • UKN • DR. STRANGELOVE
DOCTOR STUDLEY • 1969 • Evans Richard Z. • USA
DR. SUN YAT-SEN • 1986 • Ding Yinnan • CHN
DR. SUNSHINE (UKN) see **POTASH AND PERLMUTTER** • 1923
DR. SYN • 1937 • Neill R. William • UKN
DR. SYN see **CAPTAIN CLEGG** • 1962
DR. SYN -ALIAS THE SCARECROW • 1963 • Neilson James • UKN • SCARECROW OF ROMNEY MARSH, THE
DOCTOR TAKES A WIFE, THE • 1940 • Hall Alexander • USA
DR. TARR'S TORTURE DUNGEON (USA) see **SYSTEM OF DR. TARR AND PROFESSOR FEATHER** • 1972
DR. TERROR'S GALLERY OF HORRORS see **RETURN FROM THE PAST** • 1967
DR. TERROR'S HOUSE OF HORRORS • 1943 • *National Roadshow* • CMP • USA
DR. TERROR'S HOUSE OF HORRORS • 1964 • Francis Freddie • UKN
DR. TRIMBALL'S VERDICT • 1913 • Wilson Frank? • UKN
DR. TURNER TURNS THE TABLES • 1913 • *Patheplay* • USA
DR. VAN DER VELDE -DIE VOLLKOMMENE EHE 1 • 1968 • Gottlieb Franz J. • FRG
DOCTOR VERA see **DOKTOR VYERA** • 1968
DR. VIDYA • 1962 • *Burman S. D. (M)* • IND
DR. VIOLET DARING • 1915 • Birch Cecil • UKN
DOCTOR VLIMMEN • 1976 • Pieters Guido • NTH, BLG
DR. WAKE'S PATIENT • 1916 • Paul Fred • UKN
DR. WARD STORY, THE see **DOCTOR AND THE PLAYGIRL, THE** • 1963
DR. WHO AND THE DALEKS • 1965 • Flemyng Gordon • UKN
DR. WHO AND THE REVENGE FO THE CYBERMEN • 1975 • Briant Michael E. • MTV • UKN • DR. WHO: REVENGE OF THE CYBERMEN
DR. WHO: DEATH TO THE DALEKS • 1974 • Briant Michael E. • MTV • UKN
DR. WHO: INVASION EARTH 2150 A.D. see **DALEKS' INVASION OF EARTH 2150 A.D.** • 1966
DR. WHO: REVENGE OF THE CYBERMEN see **DR. WHO AND THE REVENGE FO THE CYBERMEN** • 1975
DR. WHO: SPEARHEAD FROM SPACE • 1970 • Martinus Derek • MTV • UKN
DR. WHO: TERROR OF THE ZIGONS • 1975 • Camfield Douglas • MTV • UKN
DR. WHO: THE BRAIN OF MORBIUS • 1976 • Barry Christopher • MTV • UKN
DR. WHO: THE DAY OF THE DALEKS • 1972 • Bernard Paul • MTV • UKN
DR. WHO: THE FIVE DOCTORS • 1983 • Moffatt Peter • MTV • UKN
DR. WHO: THE PYRAMID OF MARS • 1975 • Russell Paddy • MTV • UKN • PYRAMID OF MARS, THE
DR. WHO: THE ROBOTS OF DEATH • 1977 • Briant Michael E. • MTV • UKN
DR. WHO: THE SEEDS OF DEATH • 1969 • Ferguson Michael • MTV • UKN
DR. WHO: THE TALONS OF WENG-CHIANG • 1977 • Maloney David • MTV • UKN
DR. WISLIZENUS • 1924 • Kobe Hanns • FRG
DOCTOR WITHOUT SCRUPLES (USA) see **ARZT OHNE GEWISSEN** • 1959
DR. WRIGHT'S INVENTION • 1909 • *Pathe* • FRN
DOCTOR X • 1932 • Curtiz Michael • USA
DOCTOR, YOU'VE GOT TO BE KIDDING • 1967 • Tewkesbury Peter • USA • THREE FOR A WEDDING ○ THIS WAY OUT, PLEASE
DOCTOR Z • 1960 • *Shakila* • IND
DOCTOR ZHIVAGO • 1965 • Lean David • USA
DOCTOR ZI-VENGOS see **DHOKTOR ZI-VENGOS** • 1968
DOCTORA CASTANUELAS, LA • 1950 • Barth-Moglia Luis • ARG
DOCTORED AFFAIR, A • 1913 • Lehrman Henry, Sennett Mack (Spv) • USA
DOCTORED BEER, THE • 1906 • Martin J. H.? • UKN
DOCTORING A LEAK • 1916 • Miller Rube • SHT • USA
DOCTORS, THE see **MEDICOS, LOS** • 1978
DOCTORS, THE (USA) see **HOMMES EN BLANC, L'** • 1955
DOCTOR'S ALIBI, THE (UKN) see **MEDICO OF PAINTED SPRINGS, THE** • 1941
DOCTORS AND NURSES • 1982 • Murphy Maurice • ASL
DOCTORS AT WAR • 1943 • Shumlin Herman • SHT • USA
DOCTOR'S BLIND CHILD • 1912 • *Pathe* • USA
DOCTOR'S BRIDE, THE • 1909 • *Lubin* • USA
DOCTOR'S CARRIAGE, THE • 1910 • *Thanhouser* • USA
DOCTOR'S CLOSE CALL, THE • 1911 • *Champion* • USA
DOCTORS CONDEMNED see **HAITOKU NO MESU** • 1960
DOCTOR'S COURAGE, THE (UKN) see **CRIME DOCTOR'S COURAGE** • 1945
DOCTOR'S CRIME, THE • 1914 • *Weston Charles* • UKN
DOCTOR'S DAY OFF, THE see **HONJITSU KYUSHIN** • 1952
DOCTOR'S DEBT, THE • 1912 • *Clayton Ethel* • USA
DOCTOR'S DECEIT, A • 1914 • *Imp* • USA
DOCTOR'S DECEPTION, THE • 1917 • *Baird Leah* • SHT • USA
DOCTOR'S DIARY, A • 1937 • Vidor Charles • USA
DOCTOR'S DILEMMA, THE • 1911 • *Reliance* • USA
DOCTOR'S DILEMMA, THE • 1911 • Stow Percy • UKN • WHAT COULD THE DOCTOR DO?
DOCTOR'S DILEMMA, THE • 1913 • *Reliance* • USA
DOCTOR'S DILEMMA, THE • 1959 • Asquith Anthony • UKN
DOCTOR'S DINNER PAIL, THE • 1909 • Porter Edwin S. • USA
DOCTOR'S DODGE, THE • 1908 • Fitzhamon Lewin • UKN
DOCTORS DON'T TELL • 1941 • Tourneur Jacques • USA
DOCTOR'S DOUBLE, THE • 1912 • Balshofer Fred J. • USA
DOCTOR'S DUTY, THE • 1912 • *Eclair* • USA
DOCTOR'S DUTY, THE • 1913 • *Essanay* • USA
DOCTOR'S DUTY, THE • 1913 • Lessey George A. • *Edison* • USA
DOCTOR'S EXPERIMENT, THE • 1908 • *Gaumont* • FRN • REVERSING DARWIN'S THEORY
DOCTOR'S FORGIVENESS, THE • 1908 • *Urban-Eclipse* • USA
DOCTORS FROM OH! COPENHAGEN • 1970 • *Century Cinema Corp.*
DOCTOR'S GAMBLE, THE (UKN) see **CRIME DOCTOR'S GAMBLE** • 1947
DOCTOR'S HORRIBLE EXPERIMENT, THE (USA) see **TESTAMENT DU DR. CORDELIER, LE** • 1959
DOCTORS IN LOVE see **YOUNG DOCTOR IN LOVE** • 1982
DOCTOR'S LEGACY, THE see **ENSOM KVINDE, EN** • 1914
DOCTOR'S LOVE STORY, THE • 1910 • *Powers* • USA
DOCTOR'S MISTAKE, THE • 1914 • Eagle Oscar • USA
DOCTOR'S ORDERS • 1930 • Heath Arch B. • SHT • USA
DOCTOR'S ORDERS • 1932 • Breslow Lou • SHT • USA
DOCTOR'S ORDERS • 1934 • Lee Norman • UKN • MEDICINE MAN, THE
DOCTOR'S ORDERS see **DOCTOR JACK** • 1922
DOCTOR'S ORDERS, THE • 1913 • *Powers* • USA
DOCTOR'S PERFIDY, A • 1910 • Salter Harry • USA
DOCTOR'S PHOTOGRAPH, THE • 1913 • Edwin Walter • USA
DOCTORS' PRIVATE LIVES • 1978 • Stern Steven Hilliard • TVM • USA
DOCTOR'S ROMANCE, THE • 1913 • *Myers Harry* • USA
DOCTOR'S ROUND see **POZOR, VIZITA** • 1981
DOCTOR'S RUSE, THE • 1913 • *Mace Fred* • USA
DOCTOR'S SACRIFICE, THE • 1913 • *Gaumont* • USA
DOCTOR'S SACRIFICE, THE (UKN) see **KLONDIKE** • 1932
DOCTOR'S SECRET, THE • 1913 • Brooke Van Dyke • USA
DOCTOR'S SECRET, THE • 1915 • *Nordisk* • DNM
DOCTOR'S SECRET, THE • 1930 • De Mille William C. • USA • HALF AN HOUR
DOCTOR'S SECRET, THE (USA) see **HYDROTHERAPIE FANTASTIQUE** • 1909
DOCTOR'S STORY, A • 1984 • Levin Peter • TVM • USA
DOCTOR'S STORY, THE • 1913 • *Powers* • USA
DOCTOR'S STRATEGY, THE • 1915 • Cooley Frank • USA
DOCTOR'S TALE, THE see **DOKTORKA POHADKA** • 1963
DOCTOR'S TESTIMONY, THE • 1914 • Salter Harry • USA
DOCTOR'S TRUST, THE • 1914 • O'Sullivan Tony • USA

DOCTOR'S WARNING, THE (UKN) see **CRIME DOCTOR'S WARNING** • 1945
DOCTORS WEAR SCARLET see **INCENSE FOR THE DAMNED** • 1970
DOCTORS' WIVES • 1931 • Borzage Frank • USA
DOCTORS' WIVES • 1971 • Schaefer George • USA
DOCTOR'S WOMEN, THE see **DR. MONNIER UND DIE FRAUEN** • 1928
DOCTRESS' CONSULTING OFFICE see **FUJINKAI NO HIMITSU** • 1959
DOCUMENT IN CIPHER see **SHIFROVANNY DOKUMENT** • 1928
DOCUMENT SECRET, LE • 1913 • Navarre Rene • FRN
DOCUMENTAL A PROPOSITO DEL TRANSITO, UN • 1971 • Gomez Sara • DOC • CUB
DOCUMENTATOR, THE see **DOKUMENTATOR, A** • 1988
DOCUMENTEUR • 1981 • Varda Agnes • FRN • DOCUMENTEUR: AN EMOTION PICTURE
DOCUMENTEUR: AN EMOTION PICTURE see **DOCUMENTEUR** • 1981
DOCUMENTI SU GIUSEPPE PINELLI • 1970 • Risi Nelo, Petri Elio • ITL • DEDICATO A PINELLI
DOCUMENTO, IL • 1939 • Camerini Mario • ITL
DOCUMENTO UMANO, IL • 1919 • Deed Andre • ITL
DOCUMENTO Z3 • 1942 • Guarini Alfredo • ITL
DOCUMENTS OF FIGHT see **DOKUMENTY WALKI** • 1967
DOCUMENTS SECRETS • 1940 • Joannon Leo • FRN • MER EN FLAMMES, LA ○ MISSIONS SECRETES
DODDET HALSBAND, DEN • 1910 • Blom August • DNM • NECKLACE OF THE DEAD, THE
DODDINGTON DIAMONDS, THE • 1922 • Denton Jack • UKN
DODEDANSEN see **TOTENTANZ, DER** • 1912
DODEK NA FRONCIE • 1936 • Waszynski Michael • PLN
DODEN IGATERNE • 1970 • Berg Arnljot • NRW • DEATH IN THE STREETS
DODEN PA OSLO S • 1990 • Isaksen Eva • NRW • DEATH AT OSLO C
DODEN TAR STUDENTEN see **FARLIG VAR** • 1948
DODENS BRUD • 1911 • Blom August • DNM • BRIDE OF DEATH, A
DODENS GAADE (DNM) see **ZUM TODE GEHETZT** • 1912
DODENS KONTRAKT see **HENDES MODERS LOFTE** • 1916
DODES "O", DE • 1913 • Gluckstadt Wilhelm • DNM • ISLE OF THE DEAD (USA) ○ ISLAND OF THE DEAD
DODES ROST, DEN see **TESTAMENTETS HEMMELIGHED** • 1916
DODES SJAEL, DEN see **KUNSTNERS GENNEMBRUD, EN** • 1915
DODESKA DEN • 1970 • Kurosawa Akira • JPN • SOUNDS OF STREET CARS ○ DODESUKADEN
DODESUKADEN see **DODESKA DEN** • 1970
DODGE CITY • 1939 • Curtiz Michael • USA
DODGE CITY TRAIL • 1936 • Coleman C. C. Jr. • USA
DODGE YOUR DEBTS • 1921 • Roach Hal • SHT • USA
DODGERS, THE • 1918 • Lyons Eddie, Moran Lee • SHT • USA
DODGERS DODGED, THE • 1907 • Mottershaw Frank • UKN
DODGING A MILLION • 1918 • Tucker George Loane • USA
DODGING HIS DOOM • 1917 • Williams Harry, Campbell William • SHT • USA
DODGING HIS DOOM • 1920 • *Hallmark* • USA
DODGING THE BEER TAX • 1915 • *Excel Films* • UKN
DODGING THE DOLE • 1936 • Blakeley John E. • UKN
DODGING THE LANDLORD • 1913 • Lepard Ernest • UKN
DODGING THE SHERIFF • 1912 • Melies Gaston • USA
DODGING TROUBLE • 1926 • Beaudine Harold • SHT • USA
DODICI DICEMBRE • 1972 • Bonfanti Giovanni, Ponzi Maurizio, Pasolini Pier Paolo (U/c) • ITL
DODICI DONNE D'ORO (ITL) see **KOMMISSAR X: JAGD AUF UNBEKANNT** • 1965
DODOMPA SUIKODEN • 1961 • Tanaka Tokuzo • JPN
DODSDOMTE, DEN see **DANSERINDENS KAERLIGHEDSDROM** • 1915
DODSDROMMEN • 1911 • Blom August • DNM • DREAM OF DEATH, A
DODSHOPPET FRAN CIRKUSKUPOLEN see **DODSRITTEN UNDER CIRKUSKUPOLEN** • 1912
DODSKYSSEN • 1917 • Sjostrom Victor • SWD • DEATH KISS, THE (USA) ○ KISS OF DEATH, THE
DODSRITTEN UNDER CIRKUSKUPOLEN • 1912 • Klercker Georg • SWD • DEATH-RIDE UNDER THE BIG TOP, THE ○ DODSHOPPET FRAN CIRKUSKUPOLEN
DODSSEJLEREN • 1911 • *Holger-Madsen* • DNM • DYNAMITATTENTATET PA FYRTAARNET
DODSSPRINGET TIL HEST FRA CIRKUSKUPLEN • 1912 • Schnedler-Sorensen • DNM • STORE ATTRAKTION, DEN
DODSWORTH • 1936 • Wyler William • USA
DOEA TANDA MATA • 1985 • Karya Teguh • INN • MEMENTOS
DOES, THE see **BICHES, LES** • 1968
DOES ADVERTISING PAY? • 1913 • Trimble Larry • USA
DOES ADVERTISING PAY? • 1915 • *Waters Tom* • USA
DOES ANYBODY HERE KNOW DENNY? • 1969 • Carter Peter • CND
DOES DRACULA REALLY SUCK? • 1969 • USA • DRACULA AND THE BOYS
DOES FLIRTING PAY? • 1915 • *Gribbon Harry* • USA
DOES IT END RIGHT? • 1914 • Ayres Sydney • USA
DOES IT END RIGHT? • 1915 • Stanton Richard • USA
DOES IT PAY? • 1912 • *Powers* • USA
DOES IT PAY? • 1923 • Horan Charles • USA
DOES MOTHER KNOW BEST see **MOTHER KNOWS BEST** • 1928
DOES SHE DO-DO-DO • 1929 • Aylott Dave, Symmons E. F. • SHT • UKN
DOES SHE LOVE ME? • 1910 • *Vinter M.* • FRN
DOES THE JAZZ LEAD TO DESTRUCTION? • 1919 • Ward Fred • ASL
DOES THE WOMAN FORGET? • 1915 • *Stonehouse Ruth* • USA
DOES YOUR SWEETHEART FLIRT? • 1918 • *Vernon Bobby* • USA
DOES YOUR WIFE LOVE YOU? • 1912 • *Majestic* • USA
DOG, THE • 1977 • Bardem Juan Antonio
DOG, A MOUSE AND A SPUTNIK, A (USA) see **A PIED, A CHEVAL ET EN SPOUTNIK** • 1958
DOG AND CAT • 1938 • Atamanov A. L. • ANS • USS
DOG AND CAT • 1977 • Kelljan Bob • TVM • USA
DOG AND CAT see **CANE E GATTO** • 1983
DOG AND CAT II • 1955 • Atamanov A. L. • ANS • USS
DOG AND THE BONE, THE • 1909 • Fitzhamon Lewin • UKN
DOG AND THE BONE, THE • 1937 • Gordon George • ANS • USA
DOG AND THE DIAMONDS, THE • 1953 • Thomas Ralph • UKN
DOG BARBOSS AND THE UNUSUAL CROSS, THE see **BARBOS, THE DOG AND A CROSS-COUNTRY RUN** • 1961
DOG BLIGHT • 1936 • Yarbrough Jean • SHT • USA
DOG CAME BACK, THE • 1909 • Fitzhamon Lewin • UKN
DOG, CAT AND CANARY • 1945 • Swift Howard • ANS • USA
DOG CATCHER, THE • 1917 • Cline Eddie • SHT • USA • DOG CATCHER'S LOVE, THE
DOG CATCHER'S BRIDE, THE • 1915 • *Chamberlin Riley* • USA
DOG CATCHER'S LOVE, THE see **DOG CATCHER, THE** • 1917
DOG CHAPERONE, THE • 1910 • Fitzhamon Lewin • UKN
DOG COLLARED • 1950 • McKimson Robert • ANS • USA
DOG DAY AFTERNOON • 1975 • Lumet Sidney • USA
DOG DAY (USA) see **CANICULE** • 1983
DOG DAYS • 1919 • Reisner Charles F. • SHT • USA
DOG DAYS • 1925 • Roach Hal • SHT • USA
DOG DAYS see **HUNDSTAGE** • 1958
DOG DAYS see **ROTMANAD** • 1970
DOG DAZE • 1925 • Lamont Charles • SHT • USA
DOG DAZE • 1937 • Freleng Friz • ANS • USA
DOG DAZE • 1939 • Sidney George • SHT • USA
DOG DETECTIVE, THE • 1906 • Hough Harold • UKN
DOG DOCTOR, THE • 1931 • Whitman Phil • SHT • USA
DOG EAT DOG (USA) see **EINER FRISST DEN ANDEREN** • 1964
DOG FACTORY • 1904 • Porter Edwin S. • USA • EDISON'S DOG FACTORY
DOG-GONE BARON, A • 1913 • *Holmes Stuart* • USA
DOG-GONE CLEVER • 1919 • Reisner Charles F. • SHT • USA
DOG GONE CLEVER • 1920 • *Century* • SHT • USA
DOG GONE DOG CATCHER • 1955 • *Halas John (P)* • ANS • UKN
DOG GONE IT • 1927 • Lantz Walter • ANS • USA
DOG-GONE LUCK • 1915 • *Levering James* • USA
DOG GONE MODERN • 1939 • Jones Charles M. • ANS • USA
DOG-GONE QUESTION, THE • 1912 • *Solax* • USA
DOG GONE ROMANCE, A • 1916 • *Unicorn* • USA
DOG GONE SHAME, A • 1919 • Lyons Eddie, Moran Lee • SHT • USA
DOG-GONE SHAME, A • 1920 • Williamson Robin E. • SHT • USA
DOG GONE SOUTH • 1950 • Jones Charles M. • ANS • USA
DOG HEAVEN • 1929 • Mack Anthony • SHT • USA
DOG HOUSE • 1943 • Wilmot Robert • SHT • USA
DOG HOUSE, THE • 1952 • Hanna William, Barbera Joseph • ANS • USA
DOG HOUSE BUILDERS, THE • 1913 • Young James • USA
DOG IN A MANSION, A • 1940 • Donnelly Eddie • ANS • USA
DOG IN ORBIT, A see **PERRO EN ORBITA** • 1966
DOG IN THE BAGGAGE CAR, A • 1913 • *Thanhouser* • USA
DOG IN THE MANGER, A • 1917 • Richmond J. A. • SHT • USA
DOG IN THE ORCHARD, A • 1940 • Negulesco Jean • SHT • USA
DOG JUSTICE • 1928 • Storm Jerome • USA
DOG LAW • 1928 • Storm Jerome • USA
DOG MEETS DOG • 1942 • Tashlin Frank • ANS • USA
DOG NAPPER, THE • 1934 • Hand David • ANS • USA
DOG OF FLANDERS, A • 1935 • Sloman Edward • USA
DOG OF FLANDERS, A • 1959 • Clark James B. • USA
DOG OF FLANDERS, THE • 1914 • *Snow Marguerite* • USA
DOG OF THE REGIMENT, A • 1927 • Lederman D. Ross • USA
DOG OF WAR, THE see **UNDER THE BLACK EAGLE** • 1928
DOG ON BUSINESS, A • 1910 • *Essanay* • USA
DOG OUTWITS THE KIDNAPPERS, THE • 1908 • Fitzhamon Lewin • USA
DOG POUND, THE • 1960 • *Halas John (P)* • ANS • UKN
DOG POUNDED • 1954 • Freleng Friz • ANS • USA
DOG RAFFLES, THE • 1914 • *Sterling* • USA
DOG SHOW, THE • 1934 • *Terry Paul/ Moser Frank (P)* • ANS • USA
DOG SHOW, THE • 1950 • Donnelly Eddie • ANS • USA
DOG SHOW-OFF, THE • 1948 • Kneitel Seymour • ANS • USA
DOG SHY • 1926 • McCarey Leo • SHT • USA
DOG SNATCHER, THE • 1952 • Burness Pete • ANS • USA
DOG SNATCHERS, THE • 1931 • *Mintz Charles (P)* • ANS • USA
DOG SOLDIERS (UKN) see **WHO'LL STOP THE RAIN** • 1978
DOG SQUAD • 1973 • SAF
DOG STAR MAN • 1965 • Brakhage Stan • USA
DOG TAGS • 1986 • Jones Dalu • USA
DOG TAGS • 1986 • Scavolini Romano • ITL
DOG TALES • 1958 • McKimson Robert • ANS • USA
DOG TAX DODGERS • 1948 • Lundy Dick • ANS • USA
DOG THAT CRIED WOLF, THE • 1953 • Smith Paul J. • ANS • USA
DOG THAT STOPPED THE WAR, THE see **GUERRE DES TUQUES, LA** • 1985
DOG THIEF, THE • 1908 • Fitzhamon Lewin • UKN
DOG TIRED • 1942 • Jones Charles M. • ANS • USA
DOG TROUBLES • 1942 • Hanna William, Barbera Joseph • ANS • USA
DOG VS. DOG • 1918 • *Boy City Films* • SHT • USA
DOG WATCH • 1945 • Nichols Charles • ANS • USA
DOG WHO LIKED TRAINS, THE see **PAS KOJI JE VOLEO VOZOVE** • 1978
DOG WHO LOVED TRAINS, THE see **PAS KOJI JE VOLEO VOZOVE** • 1978
DOG WHO STOPPED THE WAR, THE see **GUERRE DES TUQUES, LA** • 1985
DOGADJAJ • 1969 • Mimica Vatroslav • YGS • EVENT, AN
DOGE DI VENEZIA • 1909 • De Liguoro Giuseppe • ITL
DOGFIGHT • 1988 • Dinner Michael • USA
DOGFIGHT • 1990 • Savoca Nancy • USA
DOGFLUTE see **INUBUE** • 1977
DOGGIE BAG • 1969 • Walsh C. • USA
DOGGIE MARCH see **WANWAN CHUSHINGURA** • 1965
DOGGIE MARCH, THE • 1964 • Okawa Hiroshi • ANM • JPN
DOGGIE'S DEBUT • 1912 • *Thanhouser* • USA
DOGGONE CATS • 1947 • Davis Arthur • ANS • USA
DOGGONE IT • 1915 • *Royal* • USA
DOGGONE MIXUP, A • 1938 • Lamont Charles • SHT • USA
DOGGONE PEOPLE • 1960 • McKimson Robert • ANS • USA
DOGGONE TIRED • 1949 • Avery Tex • ANS • USA
DOGGY AND THE FOUR see **PUNT'A A CTYRLISTEK** • 1954
DOGHEADS see **PSOHLAVCI** • 1954
DOGKESELYU • 1983 • Andras Ferenc • ANM • HNG • VULTURE, THE
DOGODILO SE NA DANASNJI DAN • 1987 • Lekic Miroslav • YGS • IT HAPPENED ON THIS DAY
DOGORA see **UCHU DAIKAIJU DOGORA** • 1964
DOGPOUND SHUFFLE • 1975 • Bloom Jeffrey • CND, UKN • SPOT
DOGS • 1912 • Miles David • USA
DOGS • 1977 • Brinckerhoff Burt • USA • SLAUGHTER
DOGS, THE (USA) see **CHIENS, LES** • 1979
DOGS AND PEOPLE see **PSI A LIDE** • 1970
DOGS AND THE DESPERADO, THE • 1913 • Wilson Frank • UKN
DOGS AT WORK • 1953 • Sparling Gordon • DCS • CND
DOG'S BEST FRIEND, A • 1959 • Cahn Edward L. • USA
DOG'S DEVOTION, THE • 1908 • Aylott Dave? • UKN
DOG'S DEVOTION, THE • 1911 • Fitzhamon Lewin • UKN
DOGS, DO YOU WANT TO LIVE FOREVER see **HUNDE! WOLLT IHR EWIG LEBEN?** • 1959
DOG'S DREAM, THE • 1941 • Donnelly Eddie • ANS • USA
DOG'S EYES see **OJOS DE PERRO** • 1982
DOGS FOR SHOW • 1945 • *Universal* • SHT • USA
DOG'S GOOD DEED, A • 1914 • *Jones Morgan* • USA
DOG'S HEADS see **PSOHLAVCI** • 1954
DOG'S HEART see **CUORE DI CANE** • 1975
DOG'S HEAVEN • 1967 • Tyrlova Hermina • ANM • CZC
DOG'S HOLIDAY see **PRAZDNINY PRO PSA** • 1981
DOGS IN SPACE • 1986 • Lowenstein Richard • ASL
DOGS IS DOGS • 1931 • McGowan Robert • SHT • USA
DOG'S LIFE, A • 1918 • Chaplin Charles • SHT • USA
DOG'S LIFE, A • 1977 • Cheyaroon Permpol • THL
DOG'S LIFE, A see **ZIVOT JE PES** • 1933
DOG'S LIFE, A see **MONDO CANE** • 1962
DOG'S LIFE, A see **PASJI ZIVOT** • 1966
DOG'S LIFE, A see **VIDA PERRA** • 1983
DOG'S LOVE, A • 1914 • *Thanhouser Kidlet* • USA
DOGS 'N DUCKS • 1953 • *Smith Pete* • SHT • USA
DOG'S NEWSREEL, THE see **KRONIKA POD PSEM** • 1959
DOG'S NIGHT SONG, THE see **KUTYA EJI DALA** • 1983
DOGS OF HELL • 1982 • Keeter Worth • USA • ROTTWEILER: THE DOGS OF HELL ○ ROTTWEILER
DOGS OF WAR • 1923 • Roach Hal • SHT • USA
DOGS OF WAR, THE • 1980 • Irvin John • UKN
DOG'S OWN TALE, A • 1917 • *Binns George H.* • SHT • USA
DOG'S TALE, A • 1983 • Hickey Aidan • IRL
DOG'S TALE, A see **PSI POHADKA** • 1959
DOGS TO THE RESCUE • 1972 • Fritz-Nemeth Paul • CND, RMN
DOGSDAY see **CANICULE** • 1983
DOGVILLE COMEDIES • 1930-31 • White Jules, Myers Zion • SHS • USA
DOGWAY MELODY • 1930 • Myers Zion, White Jules • SHT • USA
DOHATSU • 1926 • Ito Daisuke • JPN • FIRST SHRINE
DOHAYA, EL • 1933 • *Hafez Bahija* • EGY • VICTIMS, THE
DOHYO MONOGATARI KAH CHAN WA HANNINJA NOI • 1958 • Murayama Mitsuo • JPN
DOHYOSAI • 1944 • Marune Santaro • JPN • WRESTLING-RING FESTIVAL ○ DOHYOU MATSURI ○ SUMO FESTIVAL
DOHYOU MATSURI see **DOHYOSAI** • 1944
DOI IEPURASI • 1952 • Popescu-Gopo Ion • ANS • RMN • TWO LITTLE RABBITS ○ TWO RABBITS
DOI VECINI • 1958 • Saizescu Geo • RMN • TWO NEIGHBOURS
DOIDA DEMAIS • 1988 • Rezende Sergio • BRZ • TOO CRAZY
DOIGT DANS L'ENGRENAGE, LE • 1973 • Rachedi Ahmed • ALG
DOIGTS CROISES, LES (FRN) see **CATCH ME A SPY** • 1971
DOIGTS DANS LA TETE, LES • 1975 • Doillon Jacques • FRN
DOIGTS DE LUMIERE, LES • 1947 • Colson-Malleville Marie • DOC • FRN • FINGERS OF LIGHT
DOIGTS QUI ENTRANGLENT, LES • 1913 • Durand Jean • FRN
DOIGTS QUI VOIENT, LES • 1911 • Feuillade Louis • FRN
DOIN' THE TOWN • 1935 • Schwarzwald Milton • SHT • USA
DOIN' THE TOWN • 1941 • Ceballos Larry • SHT • USA
DOIN' THEIR BIT • 1942 • Glazer Herbert • SHT • USA
DOIN' TIME • 1984 • Mendeluk George • USA • BIG HOUSE, THE
DOIN' TIME ON PLANET EARTH • 1987 • Matthau Charles • USA
DOING HER BIT • 1916 • Payne John M. • UKN
DOING HER BIT • 1917 • *Gilbert John* • USA
DOING HIS BEST see **MAKING A LIVING** • 1914
DOING HIS BIT • 1917 • *Powers* • SHT • USA
DOING HIS BIT • 1917 • Collins Edwin J. • UKN
DOING HIS DUTY • 1929 • Croise Hugh • UKN
DOING IMPOSSIBLE STUNTS • 1940 • Fleischer Dave • ANS • USA
DOING IT • 1984 • Gordon Bert I. • USA • LET'S DO IT
DOING LIFE • 1986 • Reynolds Gene • TVM • USA
DOING LIKE DAISY • 1913 • *Lubin* • USA
DOING OUR BIT see **DOING THEIR BIT** • 1918
DOING THE DEMONSTRATOR • 1916 • *Close Ivy* • USA
DOING THE ROUND-UP • 1913 • Griffith D. W.? • USA
DOING THEIR BIT • 1918 • Buel Kenean • USA • DOING OUR BIT
DOING THEIR BIT • 1942 • *Terry Paul (P)* • ANS • USA
DOING TIME • 1920 • Goulding Alf, Roach Hal • SHT • USA
DOING TIME (USA) see **PORRIDGE** • 1979
DOING WHAT'S FRIGHT • 1959 • Kneitel Seymour • ANS • USA
DOINGS AT THE RANCH • 1910 • *Champion* • USA
DOINGS IN DOLLY LAND • 1905 • *Urban Trading Co.* • UKN

DOIS DIAS NO PARAISO • 1957 • Duarte Arthur • PRT

DOIS PISOS • 1970 • Tropa Alfredo • SHT • PRT

DOIS TIROS NO SOL • 1977 • Esteves Constantino • PRT • TWO SHOTS IN THE SUN

DOITY DEED, A • 1920 • Nolan William • SHT • USA

DOJO YABURI • 1964 • Uchikawa Seiichiro • JPN • SAMURAI FROM NOWHERE (USA) ○ KEMPO SAMURAI

DOJOJI • 1976 • Kawamoto Kihachiro • ANS • JPN • DOJOJI TEMPLE

DOJOJI TEMPLE see **KYOKANOKO MUSUME DOJOJI** • 1956

DOJOJI TEMPLE see **DOJOJI** • 1976

DOK JITAUN NULGURI • 1969 • Ha Won Choi • KOR • OLD CRAFTSMAN OF THE JARS, THE

DOKA O • 1926 • Mizoguchi Kenji • JPN • COPPER KING, THE ○ COPPER COIN KING, THE ○ KING OF A PENNY ○ DOKA-WO

DOKA-WO see **DOKA O** • 1926

DOKAD IDZIECIE • 1961 • Karabasz Kazimierz • DCS • PLN • WHERE ARE YOU GOING? ○ WHERE DO YOU GO?

DOKHTA LOR • 1934 • Sepenta Abdol Hoseyn • IRN

DOKHTAR TALA • 1968 • Sadeghpoor Manouchehr • IRN • GOLDEN GIRL

DOKHTARE ESHVEGAR • 1968 • Jourak Fereydoun • IRN • COQUETTE, THE

DOKKOI IKITEIRU • 1951 • Imai Tadashi • JPN • AND YET WE LIVE ○ STILL WE LIVE

DOKOKU • 1952 • Saburi Shin • JPN • WAIL

DOKONJO MONOGATARI -ZENI NO ODORI • 1964 • Ichikawa Kon • JPN • ZENI NO ODORI ○ MONEY TALKS ○ MONEY DANCE, THE

DOKOSVANIA • 1989 • Garcia Raul • SHT • BUL

DOKTER PULDER ZAAIT PAPAVERS • 1975 • Haanstra Bert • NTH • DOCTOR PULDER SOWS POPPIES ○ WHEN THE POPPIES BLOOM AGAIN

DOKTOR DOLITTLE UND SEINEN TIEREN • 1928 • Reiniger Lotte • ANS • FRG • ADVENTURES OF DR. DOLITTLE, THE ○ ABENTEUER DES DR. DOLITTLE, DAS

DOKTOR FAUST • 1958 • Radok Alfred • ANS • CZC • FAUST

DOKTOR FAUSTUS • 1981 • Seitz Franz* • FRG

DOKTOR GLAS • 1942 • Carlsten Rune • SWD

DOKTOR GLAS • 1968 • Zetterling Mai • SWD • DOCTOR GLAS

DOKTOR HOLL • 1951 • Hansen Rolf • FRG • ANGELIKA (USA) ○ AFFAIRS OF DR. HOLL

DOKTOR HOLM • 1915 • Schmidthassler Walter • FRG

DOKTOR JUDYM • 1975 • Haupe Wlodzimierz • PLN • DOCTOR JUDYM

DOKTOR KLAUS • 1920 • Bolten-Baeckers Heinrich • FRG

DOKTOR MABUSE, DER (FRG) see **DR. MABUSE, EL** • 1971

DOKTOR MLADEN • 1974 • Mutapcic Midhat • YGS • DOCTOR MLADEN

DOKTOR MURKES SAMLADE TYSTNAD • 1968 • Berglund Per • SWD

DOKTOR NIKOLA • 1909 • Larsen Viggo • DNM • HIDDEN TREASURE, THE ○ DR. NIKOLA

DOKTOR RUHLAND • 1920 • *Haid Liane* • AUS

DOKTOR SATANSOHN • 1916 • Edel Edmund • FRG

DOKTOR UR • 1916 • Curtiz Michael • HNG • DOCTOR, THE

DOKTOR VOLUNTAS • 1915 • Dinesen Robert • DNM

DOKTOR VYERA • 1968 • Vyatich-Berezhnykh Damir • USS • DOCTOR VERA

DOKTOR ZA ZIVOTINJE • 1972 • Grgic Zlatko • ANS • YGS • DOCTOR FOR ANIMALS ○ DOCTOR DON'TLITTLE

DOKTORKA POHADKA • 1963 • Hofman Eduard • ANS • PLN • DOCTOR'S TALE, THE

DOKTORNS HEMLIGHET • 1930 • Brunius John W. • FRG

DOKUD MAS MAMINKU • 1934 • Svitak • CZC • UNTIL YOU HAVE MAMMA

DOKUGA • 1967 • Yamashita Osamu • JPN • POISONOUS TUSKS

DOKUGA OKOKU • 1959 • Akasaka Chogi • JPN • SUPER GIANT 9 (USA) ○ KINGDOM OF THE POISON MOTH

DOKUGANRYU MASAMUNE • 1942 • Inagaki Hiroshi • JPN • ONE-EYED DRAGON

DOKUGANRYU MASAMUNE • 1959 • Kono Juichi • JPN • HAWK OF THE NORTH

DOKUMENTATOR, A • 1988 • Darday Istvan, Szalai Gyorgyi • HNG • DOCUMENTATOR, THE

DOKUMENTY WALKI • 1967 • Bossak Jerzy • PLN • DOCUMENTS OF FIGHT

DOKURITSU GURENTAI NISHI-E • 1960 • Okamoto Kihachi • JPN • WESTWARD DESPERADO (USA) ○ DESPERADO OUTPOST

DOKURITSU KIKANJUTAI IMADA SHAGEKICHU • 1963 • Taniguchi Senkichi • JPN • OUTPOST OF HELL (USA)

DOKURO KYOJO • 1957 • Fukuda Seiichi • JPN • MASKED TERROR

DOKURO NO MAI • 1923 • Tanaka Eizo • JPN

DOKUSHIN-SHA GOYOJIN • 1930 • Gosho Heinosuke • JPN • BACHELORS BEWARE

DOKUYAKU NO NIOU ONNA • 1967 • Tomimoto Sokichi • JPN • SMELL OF POISON, THE

DOKUZUNCU HARICIYE KOGUSU • 1967 • Saydam Nejat • TRK • NINTH EXTERNAL WARD

DOLANDIRICILAR SAHI • 1961 • Yilmaz Atif • TRK • KING OF THIEVES, THE

DOLAPBEYGIRI • 1982 • Yilmaz Atif • TRK • WORKHORSE

DOLAR DE FUEGO, UN • 1965 • Iquino Ignacio F. • SPN, ITL • DOLLARE DI FUOCO, UN (ITL)

DOLAR DE RECOMPENSA, UN • 1971 • Romero-Marchent Rafael • SPN

DOLAR PARA SARTANA, UN • 1971 • Klimovsky Leon • SPN

DOLAR Y UNA TUMBA, UN • 1970 • Klimovsky Leon • SPN

DOLCE CORPO DI DEBORAH, IL • 1968 • Guerrieri Romolo • ITL, FRN • ADORABLE CORPS DE DEBORAH, L' (FRN) ○ SOFT BODY OF DEBORAH, THE ○ SWEET BODY OF DEBORAH, THE (USA) ○ SWEET BODY, THE

DOLCE FEBBRE AZZURRA, LA • 1970 • Castellani Massimo • ITL

DOLCE MATTATOIO see **SPELL** • 1977

DOLCE PELLE DI DONNA • 1974 • Santini Alessandro • ITL

DOLCE VITA, LA • 1959 • Fellini Federico • ITL, FRN • DOUCEUR DE VIVRE, LA (FRN) ○ SWEET LIFE, THE

DOLCEZZE DEL PECCATO, LE (ITL) see **TURM DER VERBOTENEN LIEBE, DER** • 1968

DOLCH DES MALAYEN, DER • 1919 • Lasko Leo • FRG

DOLCI INGANNI, I • 1960 • Lattuada Alberto • ITL, FRN • ADOLESCENTES, LES (FRN) ○ SWEET DECEPTIONS (USA)

DOLCI NOTTI, LE • 1962 • Marinucci Vinicio • DOC • ITL

DOLCI SIGNORE, LE • 1967 • Zampa Luigi • ITL • ANYONE CAN PLAY ○ SWEET LADIES, THE ○ LADIES AND LADIES

DOLCI VIZI DELLA CASTA SUSANNA, I see **SUSANNE -DIE WIRTIN VON DER LAHN** • 1967

DOLDERTAL 7 • 1971 • Markopoulos Gregory J. • USA

DOLE OF DESTINY, THE • 1914 • O'Sullivan Tony • USA

DOLE PLOTOVI • 1962 • Makavejev Dusan • SHT • YGS • DOWN WITH THE FENCES

DOLEMITE • 1975 • Martin D'Urville • USA • HUMAN TORNADO

DOLGAYA SCHASTLIVAYA ZHIZN • 1967 • Shpalikov Gennadi • USS • LONG AND HAPPY LIFE, A

DOLGII PUT • 1956 • Gaidai Leonid, Nevzorov V. • USS • LONG PATH, THE ○ LONG WAY, THE

DOLI TEY HATHKARI • 1987 • PKS

DOLINA ISSY • 1983 • Konwicki Tadeusz • PLN • ISSA VALLEY, THE

DOLINA MIRU • 1956 • Stiglic France • YGS • SERGEANT JIM (USA) ○ VALLEY OF PEACE, THE ○ MR. JIM -AMERICAN, SOLDIER AND GENTLEMAN ○ PEACE VALLEY

DOLKEN • 1915 • Stiller Mauritz • SWD • DAGGER, THE

DOLL, A • 1961 • Vukotic Dusan • ANS • YGS

DOLL, A see **LUTKICA** • 1961

DOLL, THE • 1911 • *Pathe* • USA

DOLL, THE • 1911 • Blache Alice • USA • CHILD'S SACRIFICE, A

DOLL, THE • 1963 • Rybkowski Jan • PLN

DOLL, THE see **POUPEE, LA** • 1899

DOLL, THE see **PUPPE, DIE** • 1919

DOLL, THE see **POUPEE, LA** • 1958

DOLL, THE see **VAXDOCKAN** • 1962

DOLL, THE see **PUPA, LA** • 1963

DOLL, THE see **LALKA** • 1968

DOLL, THE see **DOLLS** • 1987

DOLL AND THE DEVIL, THE • 1913 • *Pilot* • USA

DOLL DOCTOR, THE • 1916 • Harvey John • SHT • USA

DOLL FACE • 1945 • Seiler Lewis • USA • COME BACK TO ME (UKN)

DOLL FOR THE BABY, A • 1913 • Bowman William J. • USA

DOLL HOSPITAL • 1952 • Peterson Sidney • USA

DOLL HOUSE, THE see **BRICK DOLLHOUSE, THE** • 1967

DOLL HOUSE MYSTERY, THE • 1915 • Franklin Sidney A., Franklin Chester M. • USA

DOLL MAKER, THE • 1983 • Petrie Daniel • TVM • USA • DOLLMAKER, THE

DOLL MAKER'S DAUGHTER, THE • 1906 • Fitzhamon Lewin • UKN

DOLL MAKER'S DAUGHTER, THE • 1908 • *Centaur* • USA

DOLL MERCHANT AND THE BEAUTIFUL LILITH, THE see **NUKKEKAUPPIAS JA KAUNIS LILITH** • 1955

DOLL OF THE HEIR TUTTI, THE • 1966 • Batalov Alexei • USS

DOLL SHOP • 1918 • Dillon Eddie • USA

DOLL SHOP, THE • 1929 • Lee Sammy • SHT • USA

DOLL SQUAD, THE • 1973 • Mikels Ted V. • USA • HUSTLER SQUAD

DOLL THAT TOOK THE TOWN, THE (USA) see **DONNA DEL GIORNO, LA** • 1957

DOLL WITH MILLIONS, THE see **KUKLA S MILLIONAMI** • 1928

DOLLAR • 1938 • Molander Gustaf • SWD

DOLLAR A DAY, A see **SPACE RAGE** • 1985

DOLLAR A TESTA, UN see **NAVAJO JOE** • 1966

DOLLAR-A-YEAR MAN, THE • 1921 • Cruze James • USA

DOLLAR AND THE LAW, THE • 1916 • North Wilfred • USA

DOLLAR BILL • 1913 • *Kinemacolor* • USA

DOLLAR BILLS AT A CENT APIECE • 1913 • *Gaumont* • USA

DOLLAR BOTTOM, THE • 1981 • Christian Roger • UKN

DOLLAR DANCE • 1943 • McLaren Norman • ANS • CND

DOLLAR DAWN, A • 1916 • *Pokes & Jabbs* • USA

DOLLAR DEVILS • 1923 • Schertzinger Victor • USA

DOLLAR DID IT, A • 1913 • Lehrman Henry, Sennett Mack (Spv) • USA

DOLLAR DIZZY • 1930 • Horne James W. • SHT • USA

DOLLAR DOWN • 1925 • Browning Tod • USA

DOLLAR DOWN, A • 1917 • *Essanay* • SHT • USA

DOLLAR DOWN, DOLLAR A WEEK • 1913 • Campbell Colin • USA

DOLLAR FOR DOLLAR • 1920 • Keenan Frank • USA

DOLLAR MARK, THE • 1914 • Lund O. A. C. • USA

DOLLAR OF FIRE, A see **DOLLARO DI FUOCO, UN** • 1968

DOLLAR - POUNDS - CENTS • 1913 • *Essanay* • USA

DOLLAR SAVED IS A DOLLAR EARNED, A • 1912 • *Phillips Augustus* • USA

DOLLAR TRAP, THE see **DOLLARFALLE, DIE** • 1988

DOLLAR TROUE, LE (FRN) see **DOLLARO BUCATO, UN** • 1965

DOLLARD DES ORMEAUX see **BATTLE OF THE LONG SAULT, THE** • 1913

DOLLARE DI FUOCO, UN (ITL) see **DOLAR DE FUEGO, UN** • 1965

DOLLARFALLE, DIE • 1988 • Koerfer Thomas • SWT • DOLLAR TRAP, THE

DOLLARI E FRAKS • 1919 • Ghione Emilio • SRL • ITL

DOLLARMILJONEN • 1926 • Wallen Sigurd • SWD • MILLION DOLLARS, A

DOLLARO BUCATO, UN • 1965 • Ferroni Giorgio • ITL, FRN • ONE SILVER DOLLAR (USA) ○ DOLLAR TROUE, LE (FRN) ○ BLOOD FOR A SILVER DOLLAR

DOLLARO DI FIFA, UN • 1960 • Simonelli Giorgio C. • ITL

DOLLARO DI FUOCO, UN • 1968 • Iquino Ignacio F. • ITL, SPN • DOLLAR OF FIRE, A

DOLLARO FRA I DENTI, UN • 1967 • Vanzi Luigi • ITL, USA • FOR A DOLLAR IN THE TEETH (UKN) ○ STRANGER IN TOWN, A (USA)

DOLLARO PER 7 VIGLIACCHI, UN see **MILLIPILLERI** • 1966

DOLLARPRINZESSIN UND IHRE SECHS FREIER, DIE • 1927 • Basch Felix • FRG

$ DOLLARS • 1971 • Brooks Richard • USA • HEIST, THE (UKN)

DOLLARS AND SENSE • 1916 • Wright Walter, Anderson Andy • SHT • USA • TWINS, THE

DOLLARS AND SENSE • 1920 • Beaumont Harry • USA • TWO CENTS WORTH OF HUMAN KINDNESS

DOLLARS AND THE WOMAN • 1916 • Kaufman Joseph • USA

DOLLARS AND THE WOMAN • 1920 • Terwilliger George W. • USA

DOLLARS FOR A FAST GUN • *Hundar Robert*

DOLLARS FOR SALE • 1955 • Kavanagh Denis, Hartford-Davis Robert (U/c) • UKN

DOLLARS IN SURREY • 1921 • Dewhurst George, Dyer Anson • UKN

DOLLARS OF DROSS • 1916 • Borzage Frank • USA

DOLLMAKER, THE see **DOLL MAKER, THE** • 1983

DOLLS • 1912 • *Horton Clara* • USA

DOLLS • 1968 • Zwartjes Frans • SHT • NTH

DOLLS • 1987 • Gordon Stuart • USA • DOLL, THE

DOLLS, THE see **BAMBOLE, LE** • 1964

DOLLS AND BALLS see **BRUDAR OCH BOLLAR** • 1955

DOLLS FOR HIRE • 1967 • Rowe George • PHL

DOLL'S HOUSE, A • 1911 • *Thanhouser* • USA

DOLL'S HOUSE, A • 1917 • De Grasse Joseph • USA

DOLL'S HOUSE, A • 1918 • Tourneur Maurice • USA

DOLL'S HOUSE, A • 1922 • Bryant Charles • USA

DOLL'S HOUSE, A • 1973 • Garland Patrick • UKN

DOLL'S HOUSE, A see **NORA** • 1944

DOLL'S HOUSE, A (UKN) see **MAISON DE POUPEE** • 1972

DOLLS IN DREAMLAND • 1907 • *Biograph* • USA

DOLLS OF INTRIGUE, THE • 1915 • *Pathe Exchange* • USA

DOLLS OF VICE see **GEFAHRDETE MADCHEN** • 1958

DOLL'S REVENGE, THE • 1907 • Fitzhamon Lewin • UKN

DOLL'S REVENGE, THE • 1911 • Stow Percy • UKN

DOLL'S SECRET, THE • 1910 • *Walturdaw* • UKN

DOLLS' THIEF • 1989 • Honarmand Mohammad-Reza • IRN

DOLLY • 1928 • Colombier Piere • FRN

DOLLY AND HER LOVER see **RAPSY JA DOLLY** • 1989

DOLLY AND THE BURGLAR • 1913 • *Powers* • USA

DOLLY AT THE HELM • 1914 • Edwin Walter • USA

DOLLY DOES HER BIT • 1918 • Bertram William • USA

DOLLY DOINGS • 1917 • Moss Howard S. • ANM • USA

DOLLY GETS AHEAD see **DOLLY MACHT KARRIERE** • 1930

DOLLY IL SESSO BIONDO • 1979 • Russo Luigi • ITL

DOLLY MACHT KARRIERE • 1930 • Litvak Anatole • FRG • DOLLY'S WAY TO STARDOM (USA) ○ DOLLY GETS AHEAD ○ DOLLY'S CAREER

DOLLY PLAYS DETECTIVE • 1914 • Edwin Walter • USA

DOLLY PUT THE KETTLE ON • 1947 • Halas John, Batchelor Joy • ANS • UKN

DOLLY SAVES HER GRANDMOTHER • 1913 • *Gaumont* • USA

DOLLY SISTERS, THE • 1945 • Cummings Irving • USA

DOLLY TAKES HER CHANCE see **DOLLY TAR CHANSEN** • 1944

DOLLY TAR CHANSEN • 1944 • Edgren Gustaf • SWD • DOLLY TAKES HER CHANCE

DOLLY, THE CIRCUS QUEEN • 1908 • *Imp* • USA

DOLLY, THE TOMBOY • 1912 • *Imp* • USA

DOLLY VARDEN • 1906 • Collins Alf? • UKN

DOLLY VARDEN • 1913 • Brabin Charles J. • USA

DOLLY WHO SHED REAL TEARS, THE see **O PANENCE, KTERA PLAKALA** • 1954

DOLLY'S BIRTHDAY PRESENT • 1911 • Stow Percy • UKN

DOLLY'S CAREER see **DOLLY MACHT KARRIERE** • 1930

DOLLY'S DELIVERANCE • 1914 • *Frontier* • USA

DOLLY'S PAPA • 1907 • *Selig William (P)* • USA

DOLLY'S PAPA • 1907 • *Walturdaw* • UKN

DOLLY'S SCOOP • 1916 • De Grasse Joseph • SHT • USA

DOLLY'S STRATAGEM • 1913 • *Gaumont* • USA

DOLLY'S TOYS • 1901 • Cooper Arthur? • UKN

DOLLY'S VACATION • 1918 • Bertram William • USA

DOLLY'S WAY TO STARDOM (USA) see **DOLLY MACHT KARRIERE** • 1930

DOLLYWOOD PUPPETS, THE • Geesink Joop • NTH

DOLMEN TRAGIQUE, LE • 1947 • Mathot Leon • FRN • TROIS MORTS DANS UN DOLMEN

DOLMETSCH STORY, THE • 1971 • Annraghain Ciaran, Moore Keiron • UKN

DOLOR DE LOS HIJOS, EL • 1948 • Zacarias Miguel • MXC

DOLOR DE PAGAR LA RENTA, EL • 1959 • Delgado Agustin P. • MXC

DOLORES • 1980 • Garcia Sanchez Jose Luis • SPN

DOLORES see **LIGHT WOMAN, A** • 1928

DOLORES, LA • 1939 • Rey Florian • SPN

DOLORES D'ARADA, LADY OF SORROW • 1914 • *Madison Cleo* • USA

DOLORES DECISION • 1913 • Nicholls George • USA

DOLORES THE BEAUTIFUL (UKN) see **TEX TAKES A HOLIDAY** • 1932

DOLORETES • 1923 • Buchs Jose • SPN

DOLOROSA, LA • 1934 • Gremillon Jean • SPN

DOLOVAI NABOB LEANYA, A • 1916 • Korda Alexander, Janovics Jeno • HNG

DOLPHIN • 1979 • Jones Hardy, Wiese Michael • DOC • USA

DOLPHINS, THE see **DELFINI, I** • 1960

DOLUNAY • 1988 • Kaygun Sahin • TRK • FULL MOON

DOLWYN see **LAST DAYS OF DOLWYN, THE** • 1949

DOM • 1958 • Borowczyk Walerian, Lenica Jan • ANS • PLN • HOUSE ○ HOME

DOM BEZ OKIEN • 1962 • Jedryka Stanislaw • PLN • HOUSE WITHOUT WINDOWS ○ PROVINCIAL CIRCUS

DOM I KHOZYAIN • 1967 • Metalnikov Budimir • USS • HOUSE AND MASTER

DOM JOZEF MATUSA • 1978 • Jakubisko Juraj • CZC • HOUSE OF JOZEF MATUS, THE

DOM KALLAR OSS MODS • 1967 • Lindqvist Jan, Jarl Stefan • SWD • THEY CALL US MISFITS (USA)

DOM MATYSIAKOW • 1966 • Ziarnik Jerzy • DOC • PLN • MATYSIAK'S HOUSE, THE

DOM NA PUSTKOWIU • 1949 • Rybkowski Jan • PLN • HOUSE ON THE WASTELANDS ○ HOUSE IN THE WILDERNESS

DOM NA TRUBNOI • 1928 • Barnet Boris • USS • HOUSE ON TRUBNAYA SQUARE, THE ○ DOMA NA TRUBNOI ○ HOUSE ON CHIMNEY SQUARE

DOM ROBERTO • 1962 • de Sousa Ernesto • PRT

DOM S MEZONINOM • 1961 • Bazelyan Yakov • USS • HOUSE WITH AN ATTIC (USA)
DOM STARYCH KOBIET • 1956 • Lomnicki Jan • DOC • PLN • HOUSE OF OLD WOMEN, THE
DOM, V KOTOROM YA ZHIVU • 1957 • Kulidjanov Lev, Segel Yakov • USS • HOUSE WHERE I LIVE, THE ○ HOUSE I LIVE IN, THE
DOM V SUGROBAKH • 1928 • Ermler Friedrich • USS • HOUSE IN THE SNOW DRIFTS, THE
DOM ZA VESANJE • 1987 • Kusturica Emir • YGS, USA • HOME FROM HANGING, A ○ GYPSY CARAVAN ○ TIME OF GIPSIES, THE
DOM ZHDANOSTI • 1934 • Ivanovsky Alexander • USS
DOMA NA TRUBNOI see **DOM NA TRUBNOI** • 1928
DOMADOR, THE • 1978 • Cortes Joaquin • VNZ • HORSEBREAKER, THE
DOMAIN OF THE MOMENT, THE • 1977 • Brakhage Stan • SHT • USA
DOMANDA DI GRAZIA (ITL) see **OBSESSION** • 1954
DOMANI • 1974 • Rafele Mimmo • ITL • TOMORROW
DOMANI ACCADRA • 1988 • Luchetti Daniele • ITL • IT WILL HAPPEN TOMORROW
DOMANI E TROPPO TARDI • 1950 • Moguy Leonide • ITL • TOMORROW IS TOO LATE (UKN)
DOMANI E UN ALTRO GIORNO • 1951 • Moguy Leonide • ITL
DOMANI NON SIAMO PIU QUI • 1967 • Rondi Brunello • ITL
DOMANI PASSERO A SALUTARE LA TUA VEDOVA.. PAROLA DI EPIDEMIA • 1972 • Iquino Ignacio F. • ITL
DOMANI SI BALLA • 1982 • Nichetti Maurizio • ITL • TOMORROW WE'LL DANCE
DOMAREN • 1960 • Sjoberg Alf • SWD • JUDGE, THE
DOMBEY AND SON • 1917 • Elvey Maurice • UKN
DOMEN ICKE • 1914 • Sjostrom Victor • SWD • DO NOT JUDGE
DOMENICA • 1951 • Cloche Maurice • FRN
DOMENICA D'AGOSTO • 1950 • Emmer Luciano • ITL • SUNDAY IN AUGUST
DOMENICA DELLA BUONA GENTE, LA • 1954 • Majano Anton Giulio • ITL
DOMENICA D'ESTATE, UNA • 1962 • Petroni Giulio • ITL, FRN • DIMANCHE D'ETE, UN (FRN) ○ ALWAYS ON SUNDAY (USA)
DOMENICA E SEMPRE DOMENICA • 1958 • Mastrocinque Camillo • ITL
DOMENICA SI', UNA • 1987 • Bastelli Cesare • ITL • YES SUNDAY, A
DOMESTIC COSINESS see **HJEMLIG HUGGE** • 1983
DOMESTIC ECONOMY • 1914 • *Favourite Films* • UKN
DOMESTIC GAME HUNT, THE • 1914 • Kellino W. P. • UKN
DOMESTIC HOT WATER • 1951 • Gould-Marks L. • DOC • UKN
DOMESTIC HOUND, A • 1917 • Mann Hank • SHT • USA
DOMESTIC MEDDLERS • 1928 • Flood James • USA
DOMESTIC RELATIONS • 1922 • Withey Chet • USA
DOMESTIC REVOLUTION, A • 1915 • *Punch* • USA
DOMESTIC RIVALS • 1909 • McDowell J. B.? • UKN
DOMESTIC TROUBLES • 1928 • Enright Ray • USA
DOMESTICO, IL • 1974 • D'Amico Luigi Filippo • ITL
DOMICILE CONJUGALE • 1970 • Truffaut Francois • FRN, ITL • NON DRAMMATIZZIAMO: E SOLO QUESTIONE DI CORNA (ITL) ○ BED AND BOARD (USA)
DOMINANT SEX, THE • 1937 • Brenon Herbert • UKN
DOMINANT WILL, THE see **FORCES OF EVIL** • 1914
DOMINATORE DEI SETTE MARI, IL • 1962 • Mate Rudolph, Zeglio Primo, Freda Riccardo (U/c) • ITL • SEVEN SEAS TO CALAIS (USA) ○ SIR FRANCIS DRAKE ○ SIR FRANCIS DRAKE ,IL RE DEI SETTE MARI ○ RE DEI SETTE MARI, IL
DOMINATORE DEL DESERTO, IL • 1964 • Boccia Tanio • ITL • DESERT RAIDERS (USA)
DOMINATORE DEL FERRO, IL see **GUERRA DEL FERRO, LA** • 1983
DOMINEERING MALE, THE • 1940 • Hines Johnny • USA
DOMINGA • 1979 • Cote Guy-L. • CND
DOMINGO • 1961 • Diegues Carlos • SHT • BRZ
DOMINGO A TARDE • 1965 • de Macedo Antonio • PRT • SUNDAY IN THE AFTERNOON ○ SUNDAY AFTERNOON
DOMINGO DE CARNAVAL • 1945 • Neville Edgar • SPN
DOMINGO DE GLORIA • 1981 • Bustamente Juan Carlos, Bustamente Patricio • CHL • GLORIOUS SUNDAY
DOMINGO EN LA TARDE, UN • 1938 • Portas Rafael E. • MXC • ON A SUNDAY AFTERNOON (USA)
DOMINGO FELIZ, UN • 1988 • Barrera Olegario • VNZ, SPN • HAPPY SUNDAY, A
DOMINGO SALVAJE • 1966 • del Villar Francisco • MXC
DOMINICK AND EUGENE • 1988 • Young Robert Malcolm • USA • NICKY AND GINO (UKN)
DOMINIKA'S NAME-DAY see **KDYZ MA SVATEK DOMINIKA** • 1967
DOMINIK'S FLITTING see **PRZEPROWADZKA DOMINIKA** • 1968
DOMINION • 1974 • Brakhage Stan • USA
DOMINION OF FERNANDEZ, THE • 1917 • Horne James W. • SHT • USA
DOMINIQUE • 1950 • Noe Yvan • FRN
DOMINIQUE • 1968 • *Chancellor Films* • USA • DOMINIQUE IN DAUGHTERS OF LESBOS ○ DAUGHTERS OF LESBOS
DOMINIQUE • 1978 • Anderson Michael • UKN • DOMINIQUE IS DEAD (USA)
DOMINIQUE IN DAUGHTERS OF LESBOS see **DOMINIQUE** • 1968
DOMINIQUE IS DEAD (USA) see **DOMINIQUE** • 1978
DOMINO • 1943 • Richebe Roger • FRN
DOMINO • 1988 • Brasch Thomas • FRG
DOMINO see **DOMINO KID, THE** • 1957
DOMINO KID, THE • 1957 • Nazarro Ray • USA • DOMINO
DOMINO KILLINGS, THE (UKN) see **DOMINO PRINCIPLE, THE** • 1977
DOMINO PRINCIPE, EL (MXC) see **DOMINO PRINCIPLE, THE** • 1977
DOMINO PRINCIPLE, THE • 1977 • Kramer Stanley • USA, UKN, MXC • DOMINO KILLINGS, THE (UKN) ○ DOMINO PRINCIPE, EL (MXC)
DOMINO VERT, LE • 1935 • Decoin Henri, Selpin Herbert • FRN
DOMITILA DE CHUNGARA: THE WOMAN AND THE ORGANIZATION • 1980 • Dagron Alfonso Gumucio • BLV
DOMNISOARA AURICA • Marinescu Serban • RMN • OLD MAID, THE
DOMPTEUR, LE • 1938 • Colombier Piere • FRN
DON BOSCO • 1935 • Alessandrini Goffredo • ITL
DON BOSCO • Tessier Albert • DOC • CND
DON BOSCO • 1988 • Castellani Leandro • ITL
DON BOSCO TENORIO • 1921 • de Banos Ricardo • SPN
DON BUFFALO BILL see **SOBRINO DE DON BUFFALO BILL, EL** • 1944
DON BUONAPARTE • 1941 • Calzavara Flavio • ITL
DON CAESAR DE BAZAN • 1912 • *Cummings Irving* • USA
DON CAESAR DE BAZAN • 1915 • Vignola Robert G. • USA
DON CAMILLO • 1983 • Hill Terence • ITL
DON CAMILLO see **PETIT MONDE DE DON CAMILLO, LE** • 1951
DON CAMILLO E I GIOVANI D'OGGI • 1972 • Camerini Mario • ITL
DON CAMILLO E L'ONOREVOLE PEPPONE • 1955 • Gallone Carmine • ITL, FRN • GRANDE BAGARRE DE DON CAMILLO, LA (FRN) ○ DON CAMILLO'S LAST ROUND
DON CAMILLO EN RUSSIE (FRN) see **COMPAGNO DON CAMILLO, IL** • 1965
DON CAMILLO ET LES CONTESTAIRES • 1970 • Christian-Jaque • FRN
DON CAMILLO, MONSEIGNEUR (FRN) see **DON CAMILLO MONSIGNORE.. MA NON TROPPO** • 1961
DON CAMILLO MONSIGNORE.. MA NON TROPPO • 1961 • Gallone Carmine • ITL, FRN • DON CAMILLO, MONSEIGNEUR (FRN)
DON CAMILLO'S LAST ROUND see **DON CAMILLO E L'ONOREVOLE PEPPONE** • 1955
DON CARLOS • 1910 • Calmettes Andre • FRN
DON CARLOS • 1950 • Stoger Alfred • AUS
DON CARLOS • 1977 • Bugajski Ryszard • MTV • PLN
DON CARLOS AND ELIZABETH see **CARLOS UND ELISABETH** • 1924
DON CESAR DE BAZAN • 1957 • Shapiro Mikhail • USS
DON CESARE DI BAZAN • 1942 • Freda Riccardo • ITL • LAMADEL GIUSTIZIERE, LA
DON CHERRY • 1973 • Delamarre Jean-Noel • DCS • FRN
DON CHICAGO • 1945 • Rogers Maclean • UKN
DON CHISCIOTTE E SANCHO PANZA • 1968 • Grimaldi Gianni • ITL • DON QUIXOTE AND SANCHO PANZA
DON COO-COO • 1925 • Ruggles Wesley • SHT • USA
DON CORNELL SINGS • 1952 • *Univ-International* • SHT • USA
DON COSSACK ORCHESTRA, THE • 1942 • Negulesco Jean • SHT • USA
DON D'ADELE, LE • 1950 • Couzinet Emile • FRN
DON DAREDEVIL • 1925 • Smith Cliff • USA
DON DAREDEVIL RIDES AGAIN • 1951 • Brannon Fred C. • SRL • USA
DON DESPERADO • 1927 • Maloney Leo • USA
DON DIEGO AND PELAGEIA see **DONDIEGO I PELAGUYA** • 1928
DON DONALD • 1937 • Sharpsteen Ben • ANS • USA
DON DOUGIO FAIRABANCA • 1930 • *Ottorino Gorno'S Marionettes* • ANS • UKN
DON ERRE QUE ERRE • 1970 • Saenz De Heredia Jose Luis • SPN
DON FLORIPONDIO • 1939 • Ardavin Eusebio F. • SPN
DON FRANCO E DON CICCIO NELL'ANNO DELLA CONTESTAZIONE • 1970 • Girolami Marino • ITL • NELL'ANNO DELLA CONTESTAZIONE
DON FULGENCIO • 1950 • Cahen Enrique • ARG
DON GABRIEL • 1966 • Petelska Ewa, Petelski Czeslaw • PLN
DON GIL DE ALCALA see **CAPITAN AVENTURERO, EL** • 1938
DON GIOVANNI • 1942 • Falconi Dino • ITL • DON JUAN
DON GIOVANNI • 1955 • Czinner Paul, Travers Alfred • UKN • DON JUAN
DON GIOVANNI • 1970 • Bene Carmelo • ITL • DON JUAN
DON GIOVANNI • 1979 • Losey Joseph • ITL, FRN, FRG
DON GIOVANNI IN SICILIA • 1967 • Lattuada Alberto • ITL • DON GIOVANNI IN SICILY
DON GIOVANNI IN SICILY see **DON GIOVANNI IN SICILIA** • 1967
DON IS DEAD, THE • 1973 • Fleischer Richard • USA • BEAUTIFUL BUT DEADLY
DON JOSE, PEPE Y PEPITO • 1959 • Pamplona Clemente • SPN
DON JUAN • 1907 • Capellani Albert • FRN
DON JUAN • 1922 • Collins Edwin J. • UKN
DON JUAN • 1922 • Heine Albert • FRG
DON JUAN • 1924 • Bonanova Fortunio • SPN
DON JUAN • 1926 • Crosland Alan • USA
DON JUAN • 1950 • Saenz De Heredia Jose Luis • SPN
DON JUAN • 1956 • Berry John • FRN, ITL, SPN • GRAND SEDUTTORE, IL (ITL) ○ AMOR DE DON JUAN, EL (SPN) ○ PANTALOONS (USA) ○ GREAT LOVER, THE
DON JUAN • 1956 • Kolm-Veltee H. Walter • AUS • DON JUAN'S FAREWELL
DON JUAN • 1963 • Zitzman Jerzy • ANS • PLN
DON JUAN see **DON GIOVANNI** • 1942
DON JUAN see **DON GIOVANNI** • 1955
DON JUAN see **DON GIOVANNI** • 1970
DON JUAN see **DON SAJN** • 1970
DON JUAN 67 • 1966 • Velo Carlos • MXC
DON JUAN 68 • 1968 • Jires Jaromil • CZC
DON JUAN 73 see **DON JUAN 1973, OU SI DON JUAN ETAIT UNE FEMME** • 1973
DON JUAN 1973, OU SI DON JUAN ETAIT UNE FEMME • 1973 • Vadim Roger • FRN, ITL • DON JUAN, OR IF DON JUAN WERE A WOMAN (UKN) ○ SI DON JUAN ETAIT UNE FEMME ○ DON JUAN 73 ○ MS. DON JUAN
DON JUAN DE SERRALLONGA • 1913 • de Banos Ricardo • SPN
DON JUAN DE SERRALLONGA • 1948 • Gascon Jose • SPN
DON JUAN ET FAUST • 1922 • L'Herbier Marcel • FRN
DON JUAN HEIRATET • 1909 • Porten Franz (c/d) • FRG
DON JUAN IN DER MADCHENSCHULE • 1928 • Schunzel Reinhold • FRG
DON JUAN MANUEL • 1920 • Castilla Enrique, Cortes Ladislao • MXC
DON JUAN OF THE WEST • 1928 • *Cheyenne Bill* • USA
DON JUAN, OR IF DON JUAN WERE A WOMAN (UKN) see **DON JUAN 1973, OU SI DON JUAN ETAIT UNE FEMME** • 1973
DON JUAN QUILLIGAN • 1945 • Tuttle Frank • USA • TWO-FACED QUILLIGAN
DON JUAN TENORIO • 1898 • Barragan Salvador Toscano • MXC
DON JUAN TENORIO • 1910 • de Banos Ricardo • SPN
DON JUAN TENORIO • 1937 • Cardona Rene • MXC
DON JUAN TENORIO • 1949 • Amadori Luis Cesar • ARG
DON JUAN TENORIO • 1952 • Perla Alejandro • SPN
DON JUAN UND DIE DREI MARIEN • 1922 • Schunzel Reinhold • FRG • DREI MARIEN UND DER HERR VON MARANA, DIE
DON JUAN UTOLSO KAIANDJA • 1958 • Keleti Marton • HNG • DON JUAN'S LAST ADVENTURE
DON JUAN'S COMPACT • 1913 • *Milano* • ITL
DON JUAN'S FAREWELL see **DON JUAN** • 1956
DON JUAN'S LAST ADVENTURE see **DON JUAN UTOLSO KAIANDJA** • 1958
DON JUAN'S NIGHT OF LOVE see **AVVENTURE DI MANDRIN, LE** • 1952
DON JUAN'S THREE NIGHTS • 1926 • Dillon John Francis • USA
DON KEY, SON OF BURRO • 1926 • Roach Hal • SHT • USA
DON KIHOT • 1961 • Kristl Vlado • ANS • YGS • DON QUIXOTE (USA)
DON KIKHOT • 1957 • Kozintsev Grigori • USS • DON QUIXOTE (USA)
DON LORENZO • 1952 • Bragaglia Carlo Ludovico • ITL
DON LUCIO Y EL HERMANO PIO • 1960 • Nieves Conde Jose Antonio • SPN
DON MANUEL, DER BANDIT • 1929 • Mengon Romano • FRG • FARMER OF CORDOBA, THE ○ JUAN CARIZZA
DON MESSER: HIS LAND AND HIS MUSIC • 1971 • Defalco Martin • DOC • CND
DON MIKE • 1927 • Ingraham Lloyd • USA
DON MILANI • 1976 • Angeli Ivan • ITL
DON MUANG INCIDENT • 1984 • Sani Asrul • INN
DON PABLO IL BANDITO see **LUCI SOMMERSE** • 1934
DON PASQUALE • 1940 • Mastrocinque Camillo • ITL
DON PIETRO CARUSO • 1914 • Ghione Emilio • ITL
DON Q AND THE ARTIST • 1912 • Martinek H. O. • UKN
DON Q -HOW HE OUTWITTED DON LUIS • 1912 • Martinek H. O. • UKN
DON Q -HOW HE TREATED THE PAROLE OF GEVIL HAY • 1912 • Martinek H. O. • UKN
DON Q, SON OF ZORRO • 1925 • Crisp Donald • USA
DON QUICHOTTE • 1903 • Nonguet Lucien, Zecca Ferdinand • FRN
DON QUICHOTTE • 1909 • Cohl Emile • ANS • FRN • DON QUIXOTE (USA)
DON QUICHOTTE • 1913 • de Morlhon Camille • FRN
DON QUICHOTTE • 1932 • Pabst G. W. • FRN • ADVENTURES OF DON QUIXOTE ○ DON QUIXOTE
DON QUICHOTTE • 1964-69 • Rohmer Eric • MTV • FRN
DON QUICHOTTE see **AVENTURES DE DON QUICHOTTE** • 1908
DON QUICKSHOT OF THE RIO GRANDE • 1923 • Marshall George • USA
DON QUIJOTE • 1961 • Ruutsalo Eino • FNL
DON QUIJOTE AYER Y HOY • 1964 • Ardavin Cesar • SHT • SPN
DON QUIJOTE CABALGA DE NUEVA see **DON QUIXOTE CABALGA DE NUEVA** • 1972
DON QUIJOTE DE LA MANCHA see **DON QUIXOTE DE LA MANCHA** • 1947
DON QUINTIN EL AMARGAO • 1935 • Marquina Luis, Bunuel Luis (U/c) • SPN
DON QUINTIN, EL AMARGAO see **HIJA DEL ENGANO, LA** • 1951
DON QUIXOTE • 1916 • Dillon Eddie • USA
DON QUIXOTE • 1923 • Elvey Maurice • UKN
DON QUIXOTE • 1926 • Lauritzen Lau • DNM
DON QUIXOTE • 1932 • Farrow John, Pabst G. W. • UKN
DON QUIXOTE • 1934 • Iwerks Ub • ANS • USA
DON QUIXOTE • 1959 • Welles Orson • USA
DON QUIXOTE • 1971 • Bokor Pierre • MTV • RMN
DON QUIXOTE • 1972 • Rakoff Alvin • MTV • UKN
DON QUIXOTE • 1973 • Helpmann Robert, Nureyev Rudolph • ASL
DON QUIXOTE see **DON QUICHOTTE** • 1932
DON QUIXOTE see **DON QUIXOTE DE LA MANCHA** • 1947
DON QUIXOTE AND SANCHO PANZA see **DON CHISCIOTTE E SANCHO PANZA** • 1968
DON QUIXOTE CABALGA DE NUEVA • 1972 • Gavaldon Roberto • MXC • DON QUIJOTE CABALGA DE NUEVA ○ DON QUIXOTE RIDES AGAIN
DON QUIXOTE DE LA MANCHA • 1947 • Gil Rafael • SPN • DON QUIJOTE DE LA MANCHA ○ DON QUIXOTE
DON QUIXOTE RIDES AGAIN see **DON QUIXOTE CABALGA DE NUEVA** • 1972
DON QUIXOTE (USA) see **DON QUICHOTTE** • 1909
DON QUIXOTE (USA) see **DON KIKHOT** • 1957
DON QUIXOTE (USA) see **DON KIHOT** • 1961
DON QUIXOTE'S DREAM • 1908 • Fitzhamon Lewin? • UKN
DON RAMON'S DAUGHTER • 1911 • *Kalem* • USA
DON REDMAN AND HIS ORCHESTRA • 1934 • Henabery Joseph • SHT • USA
DON RENEGADE see **MARK OF THE RENEGADE** • 1951
DON RUY see **A FIL DI SPADA** • 1953
DON SAJN • 1970 • Svankmajer Jan • ANM • CZC • DON JUAN
DON SEGUNDO SOMBRA • 1969 • Antin Manuel • ARG
DON SIMON DE LIRA • 1946 • Bracho Julio • MXC
DON STORY, THE • 1964 • Fetin Vladimir • USS • TALE OF THE DON, A
DON VESUVIO see **BACIO DEL SOLE, IL** • 1961
DON WINSLOW OF THE COAST GUARD • 1943 • Beebe Ford, Taylor Ray • SRL • USA
DON WINSLOW OF THE NAVY • 1942 • Beebe Ford, Taylor Ray • SRL • USA
DON X • 1925 • Sheldon Forrest • USA
DONA BARBARA • 1943 • de Fuentes Fernando • MXC

DONA BARBARA • 1972 • de Fuentes Fernando Jr. • VNZ, MXC

DONA CLARINES • 1950 • Ugarte Eduardo • MXC

DONA DIABLA • 1949 • Davison Tito • MXC • DEVIL IS A WOMAN, THE (UKN)

DONA FLOR AND HER TWO HUSBANDS (USA) see **DONA FLOR E SEUS DOIS MARIDOS** • 1978

DONA FLOR E SEUS DOIS MARIDOS • 1978 • Barreto Bruno • BRZ • DONA FLOR AND HER TWO HUSBANDS (USA)

DONA FRANCISQUITA • 1935 • Behrendt Hans • FRG

DONA FRANCISQUITA • 1952 • Vajda Ladislao • SPN

DONA HERLINDA AND HER SON see **DONA HERLINDA Y SU HIJO** • 1986

DONA HERLINDA Y SU HIJO • 1986 • Hermosillo Jaime Humberto • MXC • DONA HERLINDA AND HER SON

DONA JUANA • 1928 • Czinner Paul • FRG

DONA MACABRA • 1971 • *Churubusco Azteca* • MXC

DONA MALINCHE • 1934 • Paullada Hilario • MXC

DONA MARIA LA BRAVA • 1947 • Marquina Luis • SPN

DONA MARIQUITA DE MI CORAZON • 1952 • Pardave Joaquin • MXC

DONA MENTIRAS • 1930 • Millar Adelqui • SPN

DONA MESALINA • 1977 • Grau Jorge • SPN

DONA PERFECTA • 1915 • Wilson Elsie Jane • USA

DONA PERFECTA • 1950 • Galindo Alejandro • MXC

DONA PERFECTA • 1977 • Ardavin Cesar • SPN

DONALD AND PLUTO • 1936 • Sharpsteen Ben • ANS • USA

DONALD APPLECORE • 1952 • Hannah Jack • ANS • USA

DONALD AT THE WHEEL • 1961 • Luske Hamilton • ANS • USA

DONALD DUCK • 1934-61 • *Disney Walt (P)* • ASS • USA

DONALD DUCK AND THE GORILLA • 1944 • King Jack • ANS • USA

DONALD GETS DRAFTED • 1942 • King Jack • ANS • USA

DONALD IN MATHMAGIC LAND • 1959 • Luske Hamilton • ANS • USA

DONALD'S BETTER SELF • 1938 • King Jack • ANS • USA

DONALD'S BIRTHDAY GIFT • 1914 • *Captain Kettle Films* • UKN

DONALD'S CAMERA • 1941 • Lundy Dick • ANS • USA

DONALD'S COUSIN GUS • 1939 • King Jack • ANS • USA

DONALD'S CRIME • 1945 • King Jack • ANS • USA

DONALD'S DAY OFF • 1944 • Hannah Jack • ANS • USA

DONALD'S DIARY • 1954 • Kinney Jack • ANS • USA

DONALD'S DILEMMA • 1947 • King Jack • ANS • USA

DONALD'S DOG LAUNDRY • 1940 • King Jack • ANS • USA

DONALD'S DOUBLE TROUBLE • 1946 • Hannah Jack • ANS • USA

DONALD'S DREAM VOICE • 1948 • King Jack • ANS • USA

DONALD'S GARDEN • 1942 • Lundy Dick • ANS • USA

DONALD'S GOLD MINE • 1942 • Lundy Dick • ANS • USA

DONALD'S GOLF GAME • 1938 • King Jack • ANS • USA

DONALD'S HAPPY BIRTHDAY • 1949 • Hannah Jack • ANS • USA

DONALD'S LUCKY DAY • 1939 • King Jack • ANS • USA

DONALD'S NEPHEWS • 1938 • King Jack • ANS • USA

DONALD'S OSTRICH • 1937 • King Jack • ANS • USA

DONALD'S PENGUIN • 1939 • King Jack • ANS • USA

DONALD'S SNOW FIGHT • 1942 • King Jack • ANS • USA

DONALD'S TIRE TROUBLE • 1943 • Lundy Dick • ANS • USA

DONALD'S VACATION • 1940 • King Jack • ANS • USA

DONATA • 1968 • Cayado Tony • PHL

DONATELLA • 1956 • Monicelli Mario • ITL

DONATOR • 1989 • Bulajic Velko • YGS • DONATOR, THE

DONATOR, THE see **DONATOR** • 1989

DONAU -VOM SCHWARZWALD BIS ZUM SCHWARZEN MEER, DIE • 1929 • Curlis Hans • FRG • DANUBE, THE

DONAUMELODIEN • 1936 • Reiber Willy • FRG

DONAUSCHIFFER • 1940 • Stemmle R. A. • FRG

DONAUWALZER • 1930 • Janson Victor • FRG

DONCEL DE LA REINA, EL • 1944 • Ardavin Eusebio F. • SPN

DONCELLA DE LA DUQUESA, LA • 1941 • Delgras Gonzalo • SPN

DONCELLA DE PIEDRA, LA • 1955 • Delgado Miguel M. • MXC

DONDE EL CIRCULO TERMINA • 1955 • Crevenna Alfredo B. • MXC

DONDE ESTAS, CORAZON? • 1960 • Gonzalez Rogelio A. • MXC

DONDE HAY PATRON.. • 1978 • Ozores Mariano • SPN

DONDE LAS DAN LAS TOMAN • 1957 • Bustillo Oro Juan • MXC

DONDE MUEREN LAS PALABRAS • 1946 • Fregonese Hugo • ARG • WHERE WORDS FAIL

DONDE PONGO A ESTE MUERTO? • 1961 • Ramirez Pedro L. • SPN

DONDE TU ESTES • 1963 • Lorente German • SPN

DONDE VAS, ALFONSO XII • 1959 • Amadori Luis Cesar • ARG

DONDE VAS, TRISTE DE TI? • 1960 • Balcazar Alfonso • SPN

DONDI • 1961 • Zugsmith Albert • USA

DONDIEGO I PELAGUYA • 1928 • Protazanov Yakov • USS • DON DIEGO AND PELAGEIA

DONE IN OIL • 1917 • *Anderson Claire* • USA

DONE IN OIL • 1934 • Meins Gus • SHT • USA

DONE IN WAX • 1915 • *Beery Wallace* • USA

DONEGALS, THE • 1978 • Alexander Mike • UKN

DONETS MINERS see **DONETSKY SHAKTERY** • 1950

DONETSKY SHAKTERY • 1950 • Lukov Leonid • USS • MINERS OF THE DON ○ MINERS OF DONETSK, THE ○ DONETS MINERS

DONG OF ARCHIDONA, THE see **CIPOTE DE ARCHIDONA, EL** • 1979

DONGDONG DE JIAQUI • 1984 • Hou Hsiao-Hsien • TWN • SUMMER AT GRANDPA'S, A

DONGIOVANNI DELLA COSTA AZZURRA, I • 1963 • Sala Vittorio • ITL • BEACH CASANOVA (USA)

DONGURI TONBEI • 1935 • Yamamoto Kajiro • JPN

DONIZETTI see **CAVALIERE DEL SOGNO, IL** • 1946

DONKER AFRIKA • 1957 • SAF

DONKER SPORE • 1944 • SAF

DONKEY, THE see **ASINUS** • 1964

DONKEY AND CLOWN • 1919 • *Chance Frank S.* • SHT • USA

DONKEY AND THE SERPENTINE, THE • 1902 • Smith G. A. • UKN

DONKEY BASEBALL • 1935 • Waters John • SHT • USA

DONKEY DID IT, THE • 1918 • Moore Vin • SHT • USA

DONKEY IN A BRAHMIN VILLAGE see **AGRAHARATHIL KAZHUTHAI** • 1977

DONKEY PARTY • 1901 • Porter Edwin S. • USA

DONKEY PRINCE, THE • Wasilewski Zenon • ANM • PLN

DONKEY SKIN see **PEAU D'ANE** • 1908

DONKEY SKIN, THE see **SZAMARBOR** • 1918

DONKEY SKIN (USA) see **PEAU D'ANE** • 1970

DONKEY, THE HERRING AND THE BROOM, THE see **OSLIC, SELEDKA I MEDLA** • 1969

DONKEY'S HOUR see **HORA DEL BURRO, LA** • 1978

DONKEYS' YEARS • 1979 • Ives Kenneth • UKN

DONKOSAKENLIED, DAS • 1929 • Asagaroff Georg • FRG

DONKOSAKENLIED, DAS • 1956 • von Bolvary Geza • FRG

DONNA '70 • 1972 • Salvatore Anna • ITL

DONNA ABANDONATA, LA • 1917 • Negroni Baldassare • ITL

DONNA AD UNA DIMENSIONE • 1969 • Baratti Bruno • ITL • MARCUSIANA, LA

DONNA ALLA FINESTRA, UNA see **FEMME A SA FENETRE, UNE** • 1976

DONNA AND LISA • 1969 • Winters Larry • USA

DONNA CHE INVENTO L'AMORE, LA • 1952 • Cerio Ferruccio • ITL

DONNA CHE NON EBBE CUORE, LA • 1917 • Falena Ugo • ITL

DONNA CHIAMATA APACHE, UNA • 1976 • Mariuzzo Giorgio • ITL

DONNA.. COSA SI FA PER TE • 1976 • Biagetti Giuliano • ITL

DONNA DEI FARAOINI, LA • 1960 • Rivalta Giorgio, Tourjansky Victor • ITL • PHARAOHS' WOMAN, THE (USA)

DONNA DEL FIUME, LA • 1955 • Soldati Mario • ITL • WOMAN OF THE RIVER (USA) ○ RIVER GIRL, THE

DONNA DEL GIORNO, LA • 1957 • Maselli Francesco • ITL • DOLL THAT TOOK THE TOWN, THE (USA)

DONNA DEL LAGO, LA • 1965 • Bazzoni Luigi, Rossellini Franco • ITL • POSSESSED, THE (UKN) ○ LADY OF THE LAKE, THE

DONNA DEL PECCATO, LA • 1942 • Hasso Harry • ITL

DONNA DELLA DOMENICA, LA • 1976 • Comencini Luigi • ITL • SUNDAY WOMAN, THE (USA)

DONNA DELLA LUNA, LA • 1988 • Zagarrio Vito • ITL • WOMAN OF THE MOON, THE ○ NIGHT OF THE FULL MOON

DONNA DELLA MONTAGNA, LA • 1943 • Castellani Renato • ITL • WOMAN FROM THE MOUNTAIN, THE ○ OMBRA DELLA MONTAGNA, L'

DONNA DELL'ALTRO, LA (ITL) see **JONS UND ERDME** • 1959

DONNA DELLE MERAVIGLIE, LA • 1985 • Bevilacqua Alberto • ITL • WOMAN OF WONDERS

DONNA DI GHIACCIO, LA • 1961 • Racioppi Antonio • ITL

DONNA DI NOTTE, LA • 1962 • Loy Mino • ITL

DONNA DI NOTTE, UNA • 1979 • Rossati Nello • ITL

DONNA DI SECONDA MANO, UNA • 1977 • Tosini Pino • ITL

DONNA DI UNA NOTTE, LA • 1930 • Palermi Amleto • ITL

DONNA DI VITA see **LOLA** • 1961

DONNA DONNA!! • 1987 • van Beek Hans, van Beek Luc • NTH

DONNA E BELLO • 1964 • Bazzini Sergio • ITL

DONNA E DONNA, LA (ITL) see **FEMME EST UNE FEMME, UNE** • 1961

DONNA E IL CADAVERE, LA • 1919 • Genina Augusto • ITL

DONNA E MOBILE, LA • 1942 • Mattoli Mario • ITL • LADY IS FICKLE, THE (USA)

DONNA E UNA CANAGLIA, UNA (ITL) see **BONNE ANNEE, LA** • 1973

DONNA E UNA COSA MERAVIGLIOSA, LA • 1964 • Bolognini Mauro, Zac Pino • ITL

DONNA FRA DUE MONDI, UNA • 1937 • Alessandrini Goffredo • MXC

DONNA HA UCCISO, UNA • 1952 • Cottafavi Vittorio • ITL

DONNA, IL SESSO E IL SUPERUOMO, LA • 1968 • Spina Sergio • ITL • FANTABULOUS INC. (USA) ○ FANTABULOUS

DONNA INVISIBILE, LA • 1969 • Spinola Paolo • ITL

DONNA LIBERA, UNA • 1956 • Cottafavi Vittorio • ITL, FRN • FEMMES LIBRES (FRN)

DONNA NEL MONDO, LA • 1963 • Jacopetti Gualtiero, Cavara Paolo, Prosperi Franco* • DOC • ITL • WOMEN OF THE WORLD (USA) ○ EVA SCONOSCIUTA

DONNA NUDA, LA • 1914 • Gallone Carmine • ITL

DONNA NUDA, LA • 1918 • Roberti Roberto Leone • ITL

DONNA OF THE DAY see **DAGENS DONNA** • 1989

DONNA PER RINGO, UN • 1966 • Romero-Marchent Rafael • ITL

DONNA PER SETTE BASTARDI, UNA • 1974 • Grottoli Pier Fabio • ITL

DONNA PERDUTA, LA • 1941 • Gambino Domenico M. • ITL

DONNA PIU BELLA DEL MONDO, LA • 1955 • Leonard Robert Z. • ITL • BEAUTIFUL BUT DANGEROUS (USA) ○ BELLA DES BELLES, LA (FRN)

DONNA PREGA, UNA • 1954 • Majano Anton Giulio • ITL

DONNA SCARLATTA, LA (ITL) see **FEMME ECARLATE, LA** • 1969

DONNA SCIMMIA, LA • 1964 • Ferreri Marco • ITL, FRN • MARI DE LA FEMME A BARBE, LE (FRN) ○ APE WOMAN, THE (USA) ○ MOST UNUSUAL WOMAN, A ○ MONKEY WOMAN ○ BEARDED LADY, THE

DONNA SENZA NOME, UNA see **TURBINE** • 1941

DONNA SOLA, UNA see **LACRIME DE SANGUE** • 1944

DONNA TRA DUE MONDI, UNA (ITL) see **LIEBE DES MAHARADSCHA, DIE** • 1936

DONNACCIA, LA • 1963 • Siano Silvio • ITL

DONNE ALLA FRONTIERA (ITL) see **SIETE MAGNIFICAS, LAS** • 1966

DONNE, AMORE E MATRIMONI • 1958 • Montero Roberto Bianchi • ITL

DONNE.. BOTTE E BERSAGLIERI • 1968 • Deodato Ruggero • ITL • UOMO PIANGE SOLO PER AMORE, UN ○ MAN ONLY CRIES FOR LOVE ○ WOMEN.. BOTTLES AND SHARPSHOOTERS

DONNE CHE VENNE DAL MARE, LA • 1957 • De Robertis Francesco • ITL, SPN

DONNE CI TENGONO ASSAI, LE • 1959 • Amendola Toni • ITL

DONNE DI SPAGNA see **PECCATO DI ROGELIA SANCHEZ, IL** • 1939

DONNE E BRIGANTI • 1951 • Soldati Mario • ITL • OF LOVE AND BANDITS (USA)

DONNE E DIAVOLI see **GUERRA DEI TOPLESS, LA** • 1965

DONNE E MAGIA CON SATANASSO IN COMPAGNIA • 1974 • Montero Roberto Bianchi • ITL

DONNE E SOLDATI • 1955 • Malerba Luigi, Marchi Antonio • ITL

DONNE FACILI, LE (ITL) see **BONNES FEMMES, LES** • 1960

DONNE, MITRA E DIAMANTI (ITL) see **GENTLEMAN DE COCODY, LE** • 1965

DONNE-MOI LA MAIN • 1958 • Blanc • SHT • FRN

DONNE-MOI TES YEUX • 1943 • Guitry Sacha • FRN • GIVE ME YOUR EYES ○ NUIT BLANCHE, LA

DONNE PROIBITE • 1953 • Amato Giuseppe • ITL • ANGELS OF DARKNESS (USA) ○ FORBIDDEN WOMEN

DONNE SENZA NOME • 1950 • von Radvanyi Geza • ITL • WOMEN WITHOUT NAMES (USA) ○ INDESIDERABILI, LE ○ UNWANTED WOMEN

DONNE SENZA PARADISO (ITL) see **AXEL MUNTHE, DER ARZT VON SAN MICHELE** • 1962

DONNE SOLE • 1956 • Sala Vittorio • ITL

DONNE SONO DEBOLI, LE (ITL) see **FAIBLES FEMMES** • 1959

DONNE SOPRA FEMMINE SOTTO • 1972 • Draskovic Boro • ITL

DONNER, LITZ UND SONNENSCHEIN • 1936 • Engels Erich • FRG

DONNER PASS: THE ROAD TO SURVIVAL • 1978 • Conway James L. • TVM • USA

DONNERWETTER, DONNERWETTER, BONIFATIUS KEISEWETTER • 1968 • Weiss Helmut • FRG

DONNEUSE, LA • 1975 • Pallardy Jean-Marie • BLG

DONNEZ-MOI DIX HOMMES DESESPERES • 1961 • Zimmer Pierre • FRN, ISR • GIVE ME TEN DESPERATE MEN

DONNEZ-MOI UNE CHANCE • 1957 • Moguy Leonide • FRN

DONNEZ-NOUS NOTRE AMOUR QUOTIDIEN • 1973 • Pierson Claude • FRN, ITL, CND • AMORE QUOTIDIANO (ITL)

DONO DEL MATTINO, IL • 1932 • Guazzoni Enrico • ITL

DONOGOO • 1936 • Chomette Henri, Schunzel Reinhold • FRN

DONOGOO TONKA • 1936 • Schunzel Reinhold • FRG

DONOVAN AFFAIR, THE • 1929 • Capra Frank • USA

DONOVAN'S BRAIN • 1953 • Feist Felix E. • USA

DONOVAN'S KID • 1978 • McEveety Bernard • USA

DONOVAN'S KID (UKN) see **YOUNG DONOVAN'S KID** • 1931

DONOVAN'S REEF • 1963 • Ford John • USA

DON'S FOUNTAIN OF YOUTH • 1953 • Hannah Jack • ANS • USA

DON'S PARTY • 1976 • Beresford Bruce • ASL

DON'T • 1925 • Goulding Alf • USA • REBELLIOUS GIRL, THE

DON'T ANSWER THE PHONE! • 1980 • Hammer Robert • USA • HOLLYWOOD STRANGLER, THE

DON'T AXE ME • 1958 • McKimson Robert • ANS • USA

DON'T BE A BABY, BABY • 1946 • Crouch William Forest • SHT • USA

DON'T BE A DUMMY • 1932 • Richardson Frank • UKN

DON'T BE AFRAID OF THE DARK • 1973 • Newland John • TVM • USA

DON'T BE BLUE see **TOUT PEUT ARRIVER** • 1969

DON'T BE GREEDY • 1904 • *Warwick Trading Co.* • UKN

DON'T BE LIKE THAT • 1936 • Yarbrough Jean • SHT • USA

DON'T BE TOO POLITE • 1975 • Ansara Martha • DOC • ASL

DON'T BELIEVE EVERYTHING • 1918 • *Mason Billy* • USA

DON'T BELIEVE IN MONUMENTS see **SPOMENICIMA NE TREBA VEROVATI** • 1958

DON'T BELIEVE IT • 1930 • Watson William • USA

DON'T BET ON BLONDES • 1935 • Florey Robert • USA

DON'T BET ON LOVE • 1933 • Roth Murray • USA

DON'T BET ON LOVE see **LOVE ON A BET** • 1936

DON'T BET ON WOMEN • 1931 • Howard William K. • USA • MORE THAN A KISS (UKN)

DON'T BITE YOUR DENTIST • 1930 • Cline Eddie • SHT • USA

DON'T BLAME THE STORK • 1920 • *Gribbon Harry* • SHT • USA

DON'T BLAME THE STORK • 1954 • von Rathony Akos • UKN

DON'T BLOW THEM UP • Doicheva Zdenka • BUL

DON'T BOTHER TO KNOCK • 1952 • Baker Roy Ward • UKN

DON'T BOTHER TO KNOCK • 1961 • Frankel Cyril • UKN • WHY BOTHER TO KNOCK? (USA)

DON'T CALL IT LOVE • 1924 • De Mille William C. • USA

DON'T CALL ME A CON MAN (USA) see **DAIBOKEN** • 1966

DON'T CALL ME A LITTLE GIRL • 1921 • Henabery Joseph • USA

DON'T CALL ME MOTHER see **LET'S MAKE IT LEGAL** • 1951

DON'T CALL ME VASICK see **NERIKEJ MI VA SIKU** • 1972

DON'T CHANGE YOUR HUSBAND • 1919 • De Mille Cecil B. • USA

DON'T CRY • 1972 • Krolikiewicz Grzegorz • DOC • PLN

DON'T CRY FOR ME LITTLE MOTHER see **LITTLE MOTHER** • 1972

DON'T CRY, IT'S ONLY THUNDER • 1981 • Werner Peter • USA

DON'T CRY, MY LOVE • 1979 • Yehia Ahmed • EGY

DON'T CRY, PETER see **NE JOCI, PETRE** • 1965

DON'T CRY, PRETTY GIRLS see **SZEP LANYOK, NE SIRJATOK** • 1970

DON'T CRY WITH YOUR MOUTH FULL see **PLEURE PAS LA BOUCHE PLEINE** • 1974

DON'T CRY WOLF see **CRAWLING HAND, THE** • 1963

DON'T DECEIVE YOURSELF, MY HEART see **NO TE ENGANES CORAZON** • 1936

DON'T DELIVER US FROM EVIL see **MAIS NE NOUS DELIVREZ PAS DU MAL** • 1970

DON'T DISTURB! see **SZEDULES** • 1989

DON'T DIVORCE HIM • 1931 • Watson William • USA

DON'T DOUBT YOUR HUSBAND • 1924 • Beaumont Harry • USA

DON'T DOUBT YOUR WIFE • 1922 • Horne James W. • USA

DON'T DRINK THE WATER • 1969 • Morris Howard • USA

DON'T EVER ASK ME IF I LOVE • 1979 • Noble Barbara • ISR

DON'T EVER LEAVE ME • 1949 • Crabtree Arthur • UKN

DON'T EVER MARRY • 1920 • *Independent Film Assoc.* • SHT • USA

DON'T EVER MARRY • 1920 • Neilan Marshall, Heerman Victor • *Marshall Neilan Productions* • USA

DON'T FAIL • 1924 • Bacon Lloyd • SHT • USA
DON'T FENCE ME IN • 1945 • English John • USA
DON'T FLIRT • 1918 • *Moore Marcia* • SHT • USA
DON'T FLIRT • 1923 • Roach Hal • SHT • USA
DON'T FLIRT NEAR A POND • 1905 • *Urban Trading Co.* • UKN
DON'T FOOL THYSELF –HEART see **NO TE ENGANES CORAZON** • 1936
DON'T FOOL YOUR WIFE • 1948 • Roberts Charles E. • SHT • USA
DON'T FORGET • 1924 • Roach Hal • SHT • USA
DON'T FORGET • 1979 • Spry Robin • MTV • CND • DON'T FORGET "JE ME SOUVIENS" ○ JE ME SOUVIENS
DON'T FORGET "JE ME SOUVIENS" see **DON'T FORGET** • 1979
DON'T FORGET MY TRAUDEL see **VERGESST MIR MEINE TRAUDEL NICHT** • 1957
DON'T FORGET.. THE LUGOVAYA STATION see **NYE ZABUD.. STANTSIYA LUGOVAYA** • 1967
DON'T FORGET TO KISS YOUR WIFE see **VERGISS NICHT DEINE FRAU ZU KUSSEN** • 1967
DON'T FORGET TO REMEMBER see **THERE GOES THE GROOM** • 1937
DON'T GAMBLE WITH LOVE • 1936 • Murphy Dudley • USA
DON'T GAMBLE WITH STRANGERS • 1946 • Beaudine William • USA
DON'T GET BLUE, MY DARK-EYED ONE see **KARA GOZLUM EFKARLANMA** • 1968
DON'T GET CAUGHT see **SISTA BUDET** • 1980
DON'T GET EXCITED see **GOOD-BY GIRLS!** • 1923
DON'T GET GAY WITH YOUR MANICURE • 1903 • *Bitzer Billy (Ph)* • USA
DON'T GET INVOLVED (UKN) see **NO TE METAS** • 1989
DON'T GET JEALOUS • 1929 • *Sennett Mack (P)* • SHT • USA
DON'T GET ME WRONG • 1937 • Woods Arthur, Purdell Reginald • UKN
DON'T GET PERSONAL • 1922 • Badger Clarence • USA
DON'T GET PERSONAL • 1936 • Nigh William • USA
DON'T GET PERSONAL • 1936 • Thiele Wilhelm • USA
DON'T GET PERSONAL • 1942 • Lamont Charles • USA
DON'T GET YOUR KNICKERS IN A TWIST (UKN) see **JOSEFINE MUTZENBACHER 2 TEIL: MEINE 365 LIEBHABER** • 1971
DON'T GIVE A DAMN • 1987 • Imberman Samuel • ISR • I DON'T GIVE A DAMN
DON'T GIVE UP see **TAPPA INTE SUGEN** • 1947
DON'T GIVE UP see **KID, HUWAG KANG SUSUKO** • 1988
DON'T GIVE UP THE SHEEP • 1952 • Jones Charles M. • ANS • USA
DON'T GIVE UP THE SHIP • 1959 • Taurog Norman • USA
DON'T GO AWAY • 1976 • Kirkov Lyudmil • BUL
DON'T GO IN THE BEDROOM see **SCREAM.. AND DIE!** • 1973
DON'T GO IN THE HOUSE • 1980 • Ellison Joseph • USA • BURNING, THE
DON'T GO IN THE WOODS see **DON'T GO IN THE WOODS.. ALONE** • 1980
DON'T GO IN THE WOODS.. ALONE • 1980 • Bryan James • USA • DON'T GO INTO THE WOODS ○ DON'T GO IN THE WOODS
DON'T GO INTO THE BEDROOM see **SCREAM.. AND DIE!** • 1973
DON'T GO INTO THE WOODS see **DON'T GO IN THE WOODS.. ALONE** • 1980
DON'T GO NEAR THE PARK • 1981 • Foldes Lawrence D. • USA • NIGHTSTALKER
DON'T GO NEAR THE WATER • 1957 • Walters Charles • USA
DON'T GO TO SLEEP • 1982 • Lang Richard • TVM • USA
DON'T GO TO THE LAW • 1907 • Coleby A. E.? • UKN
DON'T GRIEVE! see **NE GORIUY!** • 1970
DON'T HAVE ANY MORE, MRS. MOORE • 1929 • Aylott Dave, Symmons E. F. • SHT • UKN
DON'T INTERFERE WITH A COALHEAVER • 1904 • Fitzhamon Lewin • UKN
DON'T IRRITATE THE MOUSE • 1967 • Nepp Jozsef • ANM • HNG
DON'T JUMP TO CONCLUSIONS • 1915 • Birch Cecil • UKN
DON'T JUST LAY THERE • 1970 • Pine Phillip • USA
DON'T JUST LIE THERE, SAY SOMETHING! • 1973 • Kellett Bob • UKN
DON'T JUST STAND THERE! • 1968 • Winston Ron • USA
DON'T KID YOUR WIFE • 1919 • *Lyons Eddie* • USA
DON'T KILL YOURSELF see **ONGYILKOS** • 1970
DON'T KNOCK THE OX • 1970 • Ianzelo Tony • DOC • CND
DON'T KNOCK THE ROCK • 1956 • Sears Fred F. • USA
DON'T KNOCK THE TWIST • 1962 • Rudolph Oscar • USA
DON'T LABEL ME • 1962 • Leiterman Douglas • CND
DON'T LEAN OUT see **NE NAGINJI SE VAN** • 1978
DON'T LEAN OUT OF THE WINDOW see **KIHAJOLNI VESZELYES** • 1978
DON'T LEAN OUT THE WINDOW see **NE NAGINJI SE VAN** • 1978
DON'T LEAVE HOME • 1930 • Watson William • USA
DON'T LEAVE ME see **JANGAN TINGGAL DAKU** • 1971
DON'T LEAVE ME ALONE • 1975 • el Imam Hassan • EGY
DON'T LEAVE THE DOOR OPEN see **NO DEJES LA PUERTA ABIERTA** • 1933
DON'T LEAVE YOUR HUSBAND see **DANGEROUS TOYS** • 1921
DON'T LEAVE YOUR LOVED ONES see **SLYUBIMYMI NE RASSTAVAITES** • 1980
DON'T LET GO • 1987 • Brock Deborah • USA
DON'T LET IT GET YOU • 1967 • O'Shea John • ASL, NZL
DON'T LET IT KILL YOU see **IL NE FAUT PAS MOURIR** • 1968
DON'T LET ME DIE see **JANGAN AMBIL NYAWAKU** • 1981
DON'T LET MOTHER KNOW • 1913 • *Winterhoff Carl* • USA
DON'T LET THE ANGELS FALL • 1968 • Kaczender George • CND • SEULS LES ENFANTS ETAIENT PRESENTS
DON'T LET THEM SHOOT THE KITE see **UCURTRAYI VURMASINLAR** • 1988
DON'T LIE • 1942 • Cahn Edward L. • SHT • USA
DON'T LIE TO YOUR HUSBAND • 1913 • *Blanchard Eleanor* • USA
DON'T LOOK BACK • 1967 • Pennebaker D. A. • DOC • USA
DON'T LOOK BACK see **DON'T LOOK BACK: THE STORY OF LEROY "SATCHEL" PAGE** • 1981
DON'T LOOK BACK, SON see **NE OKRECI SE, SINE** • 1956
DON'T LOOK BACK: THE STORY OF LEROY "SATCHEL" PAGE • 1981 • Colla Richard A. • TVM • USA • DON'T LOOK BACK
DON'T LOOK IN THE BASEMENT • 1973 • Brownrigg S. F. • USA
DON'T LOOK NOW • 1936 • Avery Tex • ANS • USA
DON'T LOOK NOW • 1973 • Roeg Nicolas • UKN, ITL • A VENEZIA UN DICEMBRE ROSSO SHOCKING (ITL)
DON'T LOOK NOW (USA) see **GRANDE VADROUILLE, LA** • 1966
DON'T LOOK NOW.. WE'RE BEING SHOT AT! (UKN) see **GRANDE VADROUILLE, LA** • 1966
DON'T LOSE YOUR COAT • 1917 • Rastrelli Amedee • SHT • USA
DON'T LOSE YOUR HEAD • 1966 • Thomas Gerald • UKN • CARRY ON DON'T LOSE YOUR HEAD
DON'T LOSE YOUR TEMPER, NAPOLEON see **PSIHREMIA NAPOLEON** • 1968
DON'T MAKE LOVE ON SUNDAY • 1962 • Georgiadis Vassilis • GRC
DON'T MAKE ME LAUGH • 1970 • *Anvil* • CMP • UKN
DON'T MAKE WAR, MAKE LOVE see **NON FACCIO LA GUERRA, FACCIO L'AMORE** • 1966
DON'T MAKE WAVES • 1967 • Mackendrick Alexander • USA
DON'T MARRY • 1928 • Tinling James • USA
DON'T MARRY FOR MONEY • 1923 • Brown Clarence • USA
DON'T MENTION THE CAUSE OF DEATH see **UZROK SMRTI NE POMINJATI** • 1968
DON'T MESS WITH MY SISTER • 1985 • Zarchi Meir • USA
DON'T MESS WITH THE MARTIANS see **NE JOUEZ PAS AVEC LES MARTIANS** • 1967
DON'T MONKEY WITH THE BUZZ-SAW • 1914 • *Roland Ruth* • USA
DON'T MOVE (USA) see **NE BOURGEONS PLUS** • 1900
DON'T NEGLECT YOUR WIFE • 1921 • Worsley Wallace • USA • NOBLESSE OBLIGE
DON'T OPEN THE DOOR • 1979 • Brownrigg S. F. • USA
DON'T OPEN THE WINDOW (USA) see **FIN DE SEMANA PARA LOS MUERTOS** • 1974
DON'T OPEN TILL CHRISTMAS • 1984 • Purdom Edmund • UKN
DON'T PANIC • 1987 • Galindo Ruben Jr. • USA
DON'T PANIC CHAPS! • 1959 • Pollock George • UKN
DON'T PARK HERE • 1919 • *Banks Monty* • USA
DON'T PARK THERE • 1924 • Guiol Fred • SHT • USA
DON'T PINCH MY PUP • 1919 • *Thanhouser* • USA
DON'T PLAY BRIDGE WITH YOUR WIFE • 1933 • *Sennett Mack (P)* • SHT • USA
DON'T PLAY HOOKEY • 1923 • Mayo Archie • SHT • USA
DON'T PLAY WITH FIRE see **DIYI LEI YING WEIXIAN** • 1980
DON'T PLAY WITH LOVE see **MAN SPIELT NICHT MIT DER LIEBE!** • 1926
DON'T PLAY WITH MARTIANS see **NE JOUEZ PAS AVEC LES MARTIANS** • 1967
DON'T PULL MY BEARD! see **ERESZD EL A SZAKALLAMAT!** • 1975
DON'T PULL MY LEG • 1908 • *Essanay* • USA
DON'T PULL YOUR PUNCHES (UKN) see **KID COMES BACK, THE** • 1938
DON'T PUSH, I'LL CHARGE WHEN I'M READY • 1969 • Lande Nathaniel • TVM • USA
DON'T PUSH ME • 1970 • *Reynolds Brian* • USA
DON'T RAISE THE BRIDGE, LOWER THE RIVER • 1968 • Paris Jerry • USA
DON'T ROCK THE BOAT • 1920 • Roach Hal • SHT • USA
DON'T RUSH ME • 1936 • Lee Norman • UKN
DON'T SAY • 1973 • Le Grice Malcolm • UKN
DON'T SAY DIE • 1923 • Roach Hal • SHT • USA
DON'T SAY DIE see **NEVER SAY DIE** • 1950
DON'T SAY IT! see **KUNG-FU-MASTER** • 1988
DON'T SCREAM, DORIS MAYS see **DAY OF THE NIGHTMARE** • 1965
DON'T SEARCH FOR THREE FEET.. see **NO LE BUSQUES TRES PIES..** • 1968
DON'T SHOOT • 1918 • Lyons Eddie, Moran Lee • SHT • USA
DON'T SHOOT • 1922 • Conway Jack • USA
DON'T SHOOT • 1926 • Wyler William • SHT • USA
DON'T SHOOT NO. 26 see **V 26-VO NYE STRELYAT** • 1967
DON'T SHOOT THE COMPOSER • 1966 • Russell Ken • MTV • UKN
DON'T SHOVE • 1919 • Roach Hal • SHT • USA
DON'T SLEEP • 1919 • Barsky • SHT • USS
DON'T SPILL THE BEANS • 1965 • Bakshi Ralph • ANS • USA
DON'T STEAL MY BABY see **BLACK MARKET BABY** • 1977
DON'T STING THE MOSQUITO (USA) see **NON STUZZICATE LA ZANZARA** • 1967
DON'T TAKE IT TO HEART • 1944 • Dell Jeffrey • UKN
DON'T TAKE SHELTER FROM THE RAIN see **NESCHOVAVAJTE SE KDYZ PRSI** • 1962
DON'T TAKE SHELTER WHEN IT RAINS see **NESCHOVAVAJTE SE KDYZ PRSI** • 1962
DON'T TALK • 1942 • Newman Joseph M. • SHT • USA
DON'T TALK TO STRANGE MEN • 1962 • Jackson Pat • UKN
DON'T TEASE THE MOSQUITO see **NON STUZZICATE LA ZANZARA** • 1967
DON'T TELL DAD • 1925 • *Sennett Mack (P)* • SHT • USA
DON'T TELL EVERYTHING • 1921 • Wood Sam • USA
DON'T TELL EVERYTHING • 1927 • Roach Hal • SHT • USA
DON'T TELL HER IT'S ME • 1990 • Mowbray Malcolm • USA
DON'T TELL MY DAUGHTER see **KIZIM DUYMASIN** • 1967
DON'T TELL THE WIFE • 1927 • Stein Paul L. • USA
DON'T TELL THE WIFE • 1937 • Cabanne W. Christy • USA • ONCE OVER LIGHTLY
DON'T TELL THEM I FELL see **NO LES DIGAS QUE CAI** • 1988
DON'T TEMPT THE DEVIL (USA) see **BONNES CAUSES, LES** • 1963
DON'T THROW THE KNIFE • 1951 • White Jules • SHT • USA
DON'T TICKLE • 1920 • Blystone John G. • SHT • USA
DON'T TORTURE THE DUCKLING (USA) see **NON SI SEVIZIA UN PAPERINO** • 1972
DON'T TOUCH IT! • 1912 • Stow Percy • UKN
DON'T TOUCH MY HALO • 1960 • Barfod Bent • ANS • DNM
DON'T TOUCH MY SISTER see **GLASS CAGE, THE** • 1964
DON'T TOUCH THE LITTLE GIRL see **NO TOQUEN A LA NEVA** • 1976
DON'T TOUCH THE LOOT see **TOUCHEZ PAS AU GRISBI** • 1953
DON'T TOUCH YOUNG GIRLS see **WAKKAI ONNA NI TE O DASUNA** • 1967
DON'T TRUST YOUR HUSBAND see **INNOCENT AFFAIR, AN** • 1948
DON'T TRY IT WITH ME see **FORSOK INTE MED MEJ** • 1946
DON'T TURN BACK see **NE SE OBRUSHTAI NAZAD** • 1971
DON'T TURN 'EM LOOSE • 1936 • Stoloff Ben • USA
DON'T WEAKEN • 1918 • Lyons Eddie, Moran Lee • SHT • USA
DON'T WEAKEN • 1920 • Roach Hal • *Rolin* • USA
DON'T WEAKEN • 1920 • St. Clair Malcolm • *Sennett* • SHT • USA
DON'T WORRY • 1913 • Williams C. Jay • USA
DON'T WORRY TOO MUCH • 1975 • Verstappen Wim? • NTH
DON'T WORRY, WE'LL THINK OF A TITLE • 1966 • Jones Harmon • USA
DON'T WRITE LETTERS • 1922 • Baker George D. • USA
DON'T YOU BELIEVE IT • 1943 • Cahn Edward L. • SHT • USA
DON'T YOU CRY see **MY LOVER, MY SON** • 1970
DON'T YOU CRY see **JANGAN KAU TANGISI** • 1972
DON'T YOU HEAR THE DOGS BARK? see **NO OYES LADRAR A LOS PERROS?** • 1974
DONTO OKOZE • 1959 • Nomura • JPN
DONTO PILLANAT • 1938 • Vajda Ladislao • HNG • CRUCIAL MOMENT, THE (USA)
DONUS • 1973 • Soray Turkan • TRK • COMEBACK, THE ○ GOING BACK
DONYAYE GHAHREMANAN • 1967 • Saeid Esmaeil Poor • IRN • HERO'S WORLD, THE
DONZELO, O • 1971 • Wohl Stefan • BRZ
DONZOKO • 1957 • Kurosawa Akira • JPN • LOWER DEPTHS, THE
DOOD VAN EEN NON, DE • 1972 • Collet Paul, Drouot Pierre • BLG • DEATH OF A NUN
DOOD VAN EEN SANDWICHMAN, DE • 1972 • de Hert Robbe, Henderickx Guido • BLG • DEATH OF A SANDWICHMAN
DOOD WATER • 1934 • Rutten Gerard • NTH • DEAD WATER
DOODKRY IS MIN • 1961 • SAF
DOODLE FILM • 1970 • Winkler Donald • CND
DOODZONDE • 1979 • van Nie Rene • NTH • DEADLY SIN, A
DOOIE DUIKERS DEEL NIE • 1974 • SAF
DOOLEY AND HIS DOG • 1913 • *Solax* • USA
DOOLEY REFEREES THE BIG FIGHT • 1910 • *Bison* • USA
DOOLEY'S HOLIDAY • 1910 • *Bison* • USA
DOOLEY'S REWARD • 1912 • *Essanay* • USA
DOOLEY'S SCHEME • 1911 • Sennett Mack • USA
DOOLEY'S THANKSGIVING TURKEY • 1909 • *Bison* • USA
DOOLINS OF OKLAHOMA, THE • 1949 • Douglas Gordon • USA • GREAT MANHUNT, THE (UKN)
DOOM, THE see **OSINDA** • 1976
DOOM ASYLUM • 1988 • Friedman Richard • USA
DOOM OF DRACULA see **HOUSE OF FRANKENSTEIN** • 1945
DOOM OF DUTY, THE • 1914 • Forman Tom • USA
DOOM OF THE CRINOLINE, THE • 1905 • *Urban Trading Co.* • UKN
DOOM OF THE SQUADRON, THE • 1966 • Dovgan Vladimir • USS
DOOMED • 1909 • *Pathe* • FRN
DOOMED • 1917 • *Ambrosio* • ITL
DOOMED • 1917 • Cochrane George • SHT • USA
DOOMED see **IKIRU** • 1952
DOOMED AT SUNDOWN • 1937 • Newfield Sam • USA
DOOMED BATTALION see **BERG IN FLAMMEN** • 1931
DOOMED BATTALION, THE • 1932 • Gardner Cyril • USA • MOUNTAINS IN FLAME
DOOMED CARAVAN • 1941 • Selander Lesley • USA
DOOMED CARGO see **SEVEN SINNERS** • 1940
DOOMED CARGO (USA) see **SEVEN SINNERS** • 1936
DOOMED GROOM, THE • 1915 • *Winninger Charles* • USA
DOOMED HERO, A • 1915 • *Ritchie Billie* • USA
DOOMED LOVE see **AMOR DE PERDICAO** • 1977
DOOMED SHIP, THE • 1911 • Porter Edwin S. • USA
DOOMED SOULS see **OSSUDENI DUSHI** • 1975
DOOMED TO DIE • 1940 • Nigh William • USA • MYSTERY OF THE WENTWORTH CASTLE, THE (UKN)
DOOMED TO DIE see **MANGIATI VIVI DAI CANNIBALI** • 1980
DOOMED TO DIE (UKN) see **SMOKING GUNS** • 1934
DOOMI NGACC • 1979 • Mbaye Ousmane William • SNL • CHILD FROM NGATCH, THE
DOOMOORER PHOOL • 1978 • Dutta Subhash • BNG • UNSEEN FLOWER ○ PARADOX
DOOMSDAY • 1928 • Lee Rowland V. • USA
DOOMSDAY • 1938 • Rasinski Connie • ANS • USA
DOOMSDAY AT ELEVEN • 1963 • Zichy Theodore • UKN
DOOMSDAY CHRONICLES • 1979 • Thornton James • USA
DOOMSDAY FLIGHT, THE • 1966 • Graham William A. • TVM • USA
DOOMSDAY MACHINE • 1967 • Sholem Lee • USA
DOOMSDAY VOYAGE • 1972 • Vidette John, Adamson Al? • USA
DOOMSHOW • Wisniewski Ray • SHT • USA
DOOMWATCH • 1972 • Sasdy Peter • UKN
DOON PO SA AMIN • 1968 • de Villa Jose • PHL • HOMETOWN
DOOR, THE • 1968 • Mundie Ken • ANS • USA
DOOR, THE • 1970 • Dragic Nedeljko • ANM • YGS
DOOR, THE • 1970 • Eckert John M. • CND
DOOR, THE see **STRANGE DOOR, THE** • 1951
DOOR, THE see **PORTE, LA** • 1964
DOOR, THE see **PUERTA, LA** • 1968
DOOR, THE see **VRATA** • 1972
DOOR BETWEEN, THE • 1917 • Julian Rupert • USA
DOOR BETWEEN, THE • 1919 • *Strand* • SHT • USA
DOOR IN A WALL see **DRZWI W MURZE** • 1973
DOOR IN THE MOUNTAIN, THE • 1917 • Horne James W. • USA
DOOR IN THE WALL, THE • 1956 • Alvey Glenn H. Jr. • UKN
DOOR IS LEFT OPEN, THE see **VRATA OSTAJU OTVORENA** • 1959

DOOR KNOCKER, THE • 1932 • Cline Eddie • SHT • USA
DOOR STAYS OPEN, THE see **VRATA OSTAJU OTVORENA** • 1959
DOOR THAT HAS NO KEY, THE • 1921 • Crane Frank H. • UKN
DOOR TO DOOR • 1984 • Bailey Patrick • USA
DOOR TO-DOOR MANIAC see **FIVE MINUTES TO LIVE** • 1961
DOOR TO THE OPEN SEA see **PORTE DU LARGE, LA** • 1936
DOOR WILL OPEN, A • 1940 • Sidney George • SHT • USA
DOOR WITH BARS, THE see **KANGELOPORTA, I** • 1979
DOOR WITH SEVEN LOCKS, THE • 1940 • Lee Norman • UKN • CHAMBER OF HORROR (USA)
DOOR WITH SEVEN LOCKS, THE (USA) see **TUR MIT DEN SIEBEN SCHLOSSERN, DIE** • 1962
DOOR-WOMAN, THE see **THIRORINA, I** • 1968
DOORMAN • 1985 • Youngman Gary • USA • DEAD AS A DOORMAN
DOORMAN see **TOO SCARED TO SCREAM** • 1982
DOORS • 1969 • Storm Esben • SHT • ASL
DOORS, THE • 1963 • Gassan Arnold • SHT • USA
DOORS, THE • 1990 • Stone Oliver • USA
DOORSTEPS • 1916 • Edwards Henry • UKN
DOORWAY OF DESTRUCTION, THE • 1915 • Ford Francis • USA
DOORWAY TO HELL, THE • 1930 • Mayo Archie • USA • HANDFUL OF CLOUDS, A (UKN)
DOORWAY TO SUSPICION • 1957 • Bower Dallas • UKN
DOOSRA BADSHAH URF CHOUTHA SULEMAN • 1988 • Daylani H. R. • IND
DOP BEY KUAN WAN • 1972 • Wang Yu • HKG • ONE ARMED BOXER (UKN) ○ ONE-ARMED BOXER
DOP DOCTOR, THE • 1915 • Paul Fred, MacBean L. C. • UKN • TERRIER AND THE CHILD, THE ○ LOVE TRAIL, THE
DOPE • 1924 • Webb Dunstan • ASL
DOPE • 1968 • Rochlin Diane, Rochlin Sheldon • USA • BOOTS AT MIDNIGHT ○ HEAD
DOPE ADDICT see **BURNING QUESTION, THE** • 1940
DOPE HEAD CLANCY • 1909 • *Phoenix* • USA
DOPE MANIA • 1987 • Legend Johnny, Vilencia Jeff • DOC • USA
DOPED YOUTH see **BURNING QUESTION, THE** • 1940
DOPEY DICK AND THE PINK WHALE • 1957 • Smith Paul J. • ANS • USA
DOPEY DICKS • 1950 • Bernds Edward • SHT • USA
DOPEY NUMBSKULL USELESS-BROOK see **UUNO TURHAPURO** • 1974
DOPING • 1971 • Marton Thomas • DOC • SWT
...DOPO DI CHE UCCIDE IL MASCHIO E LO DIVORA • 1971 • Nieves Conde Jose Antonio • ITL
DOPO DIVORZIEREMO • 1940 • Malasomma Nunzio • ITL
DOPO IL VEGLIONE • 1914 • Genina Augusto • ITL
DOPO LA MORTE • 1913 • *Hesperia* • ITL • AFTER DEATH (USA)
DOPO L'ADOLESCENZA see **LEZIONI DI VIOLONCELLO CON TOCCATA E FUGA** • 1976
DOPO L'ALTRA, UNA (ITL) see **FILLE LIBRE, UNE** • 1970
DOPO UNA NOTTE D'AMORE • 1935 • Brignone Guido • ITL • AFTER A NIGHT OF LOVE (USA)
DOPPELBRAUTIGAM, DER • 1934 • Fric Martin • FRG, CZC • DOUBLE FIANCEE, THE
DOPPELGANGER • 1969 • Parrish Robert • UKN • JOURNEY TO THE FAR SIDE OF THE SUN ○ FAR SIDE OF THE SUN, THE (USA)
DOPPELGANGER, DER • 1934 • Emo E. W. • FRG
DOPPELGANGER DES HERRN SCHNEPFE, DER see **HOCHSTAPLER WIDER WILLEN** • 1924
DOPPELKONZERT • 1963 • Spieker Franz-Josef • FRG
DOPPELMORD VON SERAJEWO, DER • 1920 • Randolf Rolf • FRG
DOPPELNATUR, DIE • 1914 • FRG
DOPPELSELBSTMORD, DER • 1918 • Fleck Jacob, Fleck Luise • AUS
DOPPELTE EHEMAN, DER • 1955 • Dorfler Ferdinand • FRG
DOPPELTE LOTTCHEN, DAS • 1950 • von Baky Josef • FRG • LISA AND LOTTIE
DOPPIA COPPIA CON REGINA • 1974 • Buchs Julio • ITL
DOPPIA FERITA, LA • 1915 • Genina Augusto • ITL
DOPPIA MORTE AL GOVERNO VECCHIO see **DOPPIO DELITTO** • 1977
DOPPIA TAGLIA PER MINNESOTA STINKY • 1971 • Fidani Demofilo • ITL
DOPPIO A META, UN see **ULTIME ORE DI UNA VERGINE, LE** • 1972
DOPPIO DELITTO • 1977 • Steno • ITL • DOPPIA MORTE AL GOVERNO VECCHIO ○ DOUBLE MURDER
DOPPIO SOGNO DEL SIGNOR X, IL • 1979 • Tato Anna Maria • ITL
DORA • 1909 • Olcott Sidney • USA
DORA • 1910 • Haldane Bert? • UKN
DORA • 1912 • *Barker Florence* • USA
DORA • 1912 • Martinek H. O.? • UKN
DORA • 1913 • *Loveridge Marguerite* • USA
DORA • 1915 • Vale Travers • USA
DORA • 1927 • Newman Widgey R. • UKN
DORA • 1933 • Clowes St. John L. • UKN
DORA BRANDES • 1916 • Stifter Magnus • FRG
DORA ET LA LANTERNE MAGIQUE • 1977 • Kane Pascal • FRN
DORA JELENTI • 1978 • Ban Robert • HNG • CODE NAME: DORA
DORA, LA ESPIA • 1943 • Matarazzo Raffaello • ITL
DORA NELSON • 1935 • Guissart Rene • FRN
DORA NELSON • 1939 • Soldati Mario • ITL
DORA O LE SPIE • 1917 • Roberti Roberto Leone • ITL
DORA THORNE • 1910 • *Selig* • USA
DORA THORNE • 1915 • Marston Lawrence • USA
DORADO DE PANCHO VILLA, UN • 1966 • Fernandez Emilio • MXC • LOYAL SOLDIER OF PANCHO VILLA, A
DORAKU GOSHINAN • 1928 • Gosho Heinosuke • JPN • DEBAUCHERY IS WRONG ○ GUIDANCE TO THE INDULGENT
DORAMUNDO • 1979 • de Andrade Joao Batista • BRZ
DORAN • 1979 • Moritani Shiro • JPN • UPHEAVAL
DORAN NO BETONAMU • 1965 • Akasa Masaharu • DOC • JPN • VIETNAM IN TURMOIL (USA)
DORA'S DUNKIN' DONUTS • 1933 • Edwards Harry J. • SHT • USA
DORCE SOK AKRAB • 1990 • INN
DORDU DE SEVIYORDU • 1967 • Erakalin Ulku • TRK • FOUR IN LOVE
DOREI KOJO • 1968 • Yamamoto Satsuo, Takeda Atsushi • JPN • SLAVE FACTORY, THE
DOREI MIBOJIN • 1967 • Watanabe Yuzuru • JPN • SLAVE WIDOW
DORELLIK ARRIVES see **ARRIVA DORELLIK** • 1967
DORELLIK (USA) see **ARRIVA DORELLIK** • 1967
DORF AND THE FIRST GAMES OF MOUNT OLYMPUS • 1988 • Elliott Lang • SHT • USA
DORF IM ROTEN STURM see **FRIESENNOT** • 1935
DORF UND STADT • 1915 • Schonfeld Carl • FRG
DORF UNTERM HIMMEL • 1953 • Haussler Richard • FRG
DORFHEXE, DIE • 1920 • Bauer Leopold • FRG
DORFMONARCH, DER see **SIN SIND DIE FRAUEN** • 1950
DORFPRINZESSIN, DIE • 1916 • Albes Emil • FRG
DORFSGOLEM, DER • 1921 • Szomogyi Julius • AUS • DES GOLEMS LETZTE ABENTEUER ○ GOLEM'S LAST ADVENTURE, THE
DORIAN GRAY IM SPIEGEL DER BOULEVARD-PRESSE • 1984 • Ottinger Ulrike • FRG
DORIAN GRAY (USA) see **DIO CHIAMATO DORIAN, IL** • 1970
DORIAN'S DIVORCE • 1916 • Lund O. A. C. • USA
DORIS MCCARTHY: HEART OF A PAINTER • 1983 • Leiterman Richard • DOC • CND
DORM THAT DRIPPED BLOOD, THE see **PRANKS** • 1981
DORMANT POWER, THE • 1917 • Vale Travers • USA
DORMEUR, LE • Aubier Pascal • SHT • FRN
DORMEUSE, LA • 1909 • Carre Michel • FRN
DORMEUSE, LA • 1962 • Pons • SHT • FRN
DORMEZ-VOUS • 1965 • Chabot Jean • SHT • CND
DORMIR Y LIGAR, TODO ES EMPEZAR • 1974 • Ozores Mariano • SPN
DORMITORIO PARA SENORITAS • 1959 • Cortes Fernando • MXC
DORNENWEG EINER FURSTIN • 1928 • Larin Nikolai • FRG
DORNROSCHEN • 1917 • Leni Paul • FRG • SLEEPING BEAUTY
DORNROSCHEN • 1922 • Reiniger Lotte • ANS • FRG • SLEEPING BEAUTY
DORNROSCHEN • 1929 • Rudolph Karl Heinz • FRG • SLEEPING BEAUTY
DORNROSCHEN • 1955 • Genschow Fritz • FRG • SLEEPING BEAUTY (USA)
DORNROSCHEN • Beck Walter • GDR • SLEEPING BEAUTY
DORNWITTCHEN UND SCHNEEROSCHEN • 1970 • Klein Erwin • FRG • SLEEPING BEAUTY AND SNOW WHITE
DORO NO KAWA • 1981 • Oguri Kohei • JPN • MUDDY RIVER ○ MUD RIVER
DORODARAKE NO JUNJO • 1963 • Nakahira Ko • JPN • WHEN THE SNOWS FELL
DORODARAKE NO SEIFUKU • 1967 • Shindo Takae • JPN • MUDDY UNIFORM
DORODARAKE NO SEISHUN • 1954 • *Mikuni Rentaro* • JPN • YOUTH COVERED WITH MUD
DOROGA • 1955 • Stolper Alexander • USS • ROAD, THE
DOROGA BEZ SNA • 1946 • Yarmatov Kamil • USS • ROAD WITHOUT SLEEP
DOROGA GORYASHCHEVO FURGONA • 1967 • Atakhanov Mered • USS • ROAD OF THE BURNING VAN
DOROGA K ZVEZDAM • 1957 • Klushantsev Pavel • USS • BLAZING A TRAIL TO THE STARS ○ RUSSIAN ROCKET TO THE MOON ○ ROAD TO THE STARS
DOROGA U MIR • 1929 • Ships Boris • USS • LIFE ROADS
DOROGA V TYSYACHU VYERST • 1968 • Karpov Alexander • USS • THOUSAND-MILE ROAD, A
DOROGOI MOI CHELOVEK • 1958 • Heifitz Josif • USS • MY BELOVED ○ MY DEAR MAN
DOROGOI TSENOI • 1957 • Donskoi Mark • USS • HORSE THAT CRIED, THE ○ AT A HIGH COST ○ AT A HIGH PRICE ○ AT GREAT COST
DORONKO TENGOKU • 1958 • Hozumi Toshimasa • JPN
DOROTEJ • 1981 • Velimirovic Zdravko • YGS
DOROTHEA AND THE CHIEF RAZAMATAZ • 1913 • *Frontier* • USA
DOROTHEA ANGERMANN • 1959 • Siodmak Robert • FRG
DOROTHEA TANNING, OU LE REGARD EBLOUI • 1960 • Desvilles • SHT • FRN
DOROTHEAS RACHE • 1973 • Fleischmann Peter • FRG
DOROTHEE CHERCHE L'AMOUR • 1945 • Greville Edmond T. • FRN
DOROTHY • 1915 • Brooke Van Dyke • USA
DOROTHY AND SCARECROW IN OZ • 1910 • *Selig* • USA • DOROTHY AND THE SCARECROW IN OZ
DOROTHY AND THE SCARECROW IN OZ see **DOROTHY AND SCARECROW IN OZ** • 1910
DOROTHY DALTON IN A LIBERTY LOAN APPEAL • 1918 • *Paramount* • SHT • USA
DOROTHY DANESBRIDGE, MILITANT • 1914 • Marston Theodore • USA
DOROTHY DARES • 1917 • Stonehouse Ruth • SHT • USA
DOROTHY STRATTEN STORY, THE see **DEATH OF A CENTERFOLD: THE DOROTHY STRATTON STORY** • 1981
DOROTHY STRATTEN: UNTOLD STORY see **DEATH OF A CENTERFOLD: THE DOROTHY STRATTON STORY** • 1981
DOROTHY VERNON OF HADDON HALL • 1924 • Neilan Marshall • USA
DOROTHY'S ADOPTION • 1913 • *Selig* • USA
DOROTHYS BEKENNTNIS see **FRAU DOROTHY'S BEKENNTNIS** • 1921
DOROTHY'S DREAM • 1903 • Smith G. A. • UKN
DOROTHY'S FAMILY • 1911 • *Imp* • USA
DOROTHY'S MOTOR CAR • 1910 • Rosenthal Joe • UKN
DORP AAN DE RIVEIR • 1958 • Rademakers Fons • NTH • DOCTOR IN THE VILLAGE ○ VILLAGE ON THE RIVER
DORRIT BEKOMMT 'NE LEBENSSTELLUNG • 1916 • Heidemann Paul • FRG
DORRITCHENS VERGNUGUNGSREISE • 1916 • Heidemann Paul • FRG
DORRITS CHAUFFEUR • 1915 • Otto Paul • FRG
DORRITS EHEGLUCK • 1916 • Otto Paul • FRG
DORSEY BROTHERS ENCORE, THE • 1953 • Cowan Will • SHT • USA
DORT IN DER WACHAU • 1957 • Carl Rudolf • AUS
DORTOIR DES GRANDES • 1953 • Decoin Henri • FRN • INSIDE A GIRLS' DORMITORY (USA) ○ GIRLS' DORMITORY
DORTOIR DES GRANDES • 1984 • Unia Pierre • FRN
DORUCAK SA DAVOLOM • 1972 • Antic Miroslav • YGS • BREAKFAST WITH THE DEVIL
DOS • 1980 • del Amo Alvaro • SPN • TWO
DOS AGENTES INOCENTES see **DETECTIVES O LADRONES** • 1966
DOS ALAS • 1967 • Cervera Pascual • SPN • TWO WINGS
DOS ALEGRES GAVILANES • 1963 • Crevenna Alfredo B. • MXC
DOS ALMAS EN EL MUNDO • 1948 • Urueta Chano • MXC
DOS ANGELES Y UN PECADOR • 1945 • Amadori Luis Cesar • ARG
DOS ANOS DE VACACIONES • 1962 • Gomez Muriel Emilio • SPN • SHIPWRECK ISLAND (USA)
DOS APOSTOLES, LOS • 1964 • Salvador Jaime • MXC
DOS AU MUR • 1958 • Molinaro Edouard • FRN • EVIDENCE IN CONCRETE ○ BACK TO THE WALL
DOS AU MUR, LE • 1981 • Thorn Jean-Pierre • DOC • FRN
DOS BASURAS • 1958 • Land Kurt • ARG
DOS CABALLEROS DE ESPADA • 1963 • Martinez Arturo • MXC
DOS CADETES • 1938 • Cardona Rene • MXC
DOS CAMINOS • 1953 • Ruiz-Castillo Arturo • SPN
DOS CARAS TIENE EL DESTINO • 1951 • Delgado Agustin P. • MXC
DOS CHICAS DE REVISTA • 1972 • Ozores Mariano • SPN
DOS CHICOS LOCAS, LOCAS • 1964 • Lazaga Pedro • SPN
DOS CORAZONES Y UN TANGO • 1942 • del Rio Mario • MXC
DOS COSMONAUTAS A LA FUERZA (SPN) see **002 OPERAZIONE LUNA** • 1965
DOS CRIADOS MALCRIADOS • 1959 • Delgado Agustin P. • MXC
DOS CRUCES EN DANGER PASS • 1967 • Romero-Marchent Rafael • SPN, ITL • DUE CROCI A DANGER PASS (ITL) ○ TWO CROSSES IN DANGER PASS
DOS CUATREROS, LOS • 1964 • Mariscal Alberto • MXC
DOS CUENTOS PARA DOS • 1947 • Lucia Luis • SPN
DOS DE LA VIDA AIRADA • 1947 • Bustillo Oro Juan • MXC
DOS DE MAYO, EL • 1927 • Buchs Jose • SPN
DOS DESTINOS • 1936 • Etchebchere Juan • URG
DOS DIABLILLOS EN APUROS • 1955 • Rodriguez Roberto • MXC
DOS EN EL MUNDO • 1965 • Solly • ARG, ITL
DOS FANTASMAS Y UNA MUCHACHA • 1958 • Gonzalez Rogelio A. • MXC • TWO GHOSTS AND A GIRL
DOS GALLERAS, LAS • 1963 • Curiel Federico • MXC
DOS GALLOS DE PELEA • 1949 • de Anda Raul • MXC
DOS GALLOS EN PALENQUE • 1959 • Baledon Rafael • MXC
DOS GALLOS Y DOS GALLINAS • 1962 • Gomez Muriel Emilio • MXC
DOS GOLFILLOS, LOS • 1960 • del Amo Antonio • SPN
DOS HERMANOS, LOS • 1970 • *Magna* • MXC
DOS HIJOS DESOBEDIENTES • 1958 • Salvador Jaime • MXC
DOS HOMBRES VAN A MORIR • 1968 • Romero-Marchent Rafael • SPN
DOS HOMBRES Y EN MEDIO DOS MUJERES • 1977 • Gil Rafael • SPN
DOS HUERFANAS, LAS • 1944 • Benavides Jose Jr. • MXC
DOS HUERFANITAS, LAS • 1950 • Rodriguez Roberto • MXC
DOS INOCENTES MUJERIEGOS • 1963 • Crevenna Alfredo B. • MXC
DOS LOCOS EN ESCENA • 1959 • Delgado Agustin P. • MXC
DOS MARIDOS BARATOS • 1959 • Salvador Jaime • MXC
DOS MAS UNO DOS • 1934 • Reinhardt John • USA • TWO AND ONE TWO
DOS MESEROS MAJADEROS • 1965 • Martinez Solares Gilberto • MXC
DOS MEXICANAS EN MEXICO see **MEXICO DE MI CORAZON** • 1963
DOS MEXICANOS EN SEVILLA • 1941 • Orellana Carlos • MXC
DOS MIL DOLARES POR COYOTE • 1967 • Klimovsky Leon • SPN • TWO THOUSAND DOLLARS FOR COYOTE
DOS MONJES • 1934 • Bustillo Oro Juan • MXC • TWO MONKS
DOS MUJERES EN LA NIEBLA • 1947 • Viladomat Domingo • SPN
DOS MUJERES Y UN DON JUAN • 1933 • Buchs Jose • SPN
DOS MUNDOS DE ANGELITA, LOS • 1982 • Morrison Jeanne • USA • TWO WORLDS OF ANGELITA, THE
DOS MUNDOS Y UN AMOR • 1954 • Crevenna Alfredo B. • MXC
DOS NOCHES • 1933 • Borcosque Carlos • ARG
DOS NOVIAS PARA UN TORERO • 1956 • Roman Antonio • SPN
DOS PESOS DEJADA • 1949 • Pardave Joaquin • MXC
DOS PILLETES, LOS • 1942 • Patino Gomez Alfonso • MXC
DOS PINTORES PINTOESCOS • 1966 • Cardona Rene Jr. • MXC
DOS PISTOLAS GEMELAS • 1965 • Romero-Marchent Rafael • SPN
DOS POR DOS • 1968 • Garces Armando • PHL • TWO BY TWO
DOS PUERTOS Y UN CERRO • 1977 • Handler Mario • DOC • VNZ • TWO PORTS AND A MOUNTAIN ○ TWO PORTS AND A MINE
DOS PUTAS, O HISTORIA DE AMOR QUE TERMINA EN BODA • 1974 • Almodovar Pedro • SPN • TWO WHORES: OR A LOVE STORY WHICH ENDS IN MARRIAGE
DOS RIVALES, LOS • 1965 • Zacarias Miguel • MXC
DOS RIVALES, LOS (SPN) see **MERAVIGLIOSA** • 1958
DOS TENORIOS DE BARRIO • 1948 • Vejar Carlos • MXC
DOS TIPOS DE CUIDADO • 1952 • Rodriguez Ismael • MXC
DOS TONTOS Y UN LOCO • 1960 • Morayta Miguel • MXC
DOS VIAJEROS DEL ESPACIO see **ASTRONAUTAS, LOS** • 1960

DOS VIDAS • 1951 • Povedo Emilio • SPN

DOS Y MEDIA Y VENENO, LAS • 1959 • Ozores Mariano • SPN

DOSHABURI • 1957 • Nakamura Noboru • JPN • CLOUDBURST ○ HARD RAIN

DOSLO DOBA DA SE LJUBAV PROBA • 1981 • Calic Zoran • YGS • TIME FOR LOVE

DOSS HOUSE • 1933 • Baxter John • UKN

DOSSIER 51, LE • 1978 • Deville Michel • FRN, FRG

DOSSIER 212 –DESTINAZIONE MORTE (ITL) see **PEAU DE TORPEDO, LA** • 1970

DOSSIER 1413 • 1959 • Rode Alfred • FRN • SECRET FILE 1413 (USA)

DOSSIER DE CREDIT, LE • 1973 • Lavoie Richard • SHT • CND

DOSSIER NELLIGAN, LE • 1968 • Fournier Claude • CND

DOSSIER NOIR, LE • 1955 • Cayatte Andre • FRN, ITL • FASCICOLO NERO (ITL)

DOSSIER PROSTITUTION • 1969 • Roy Jean-Claude • FRN • SECRET FRENCH PROSTITUTION REPORT (UKN) ○ GIRLS FOR PLEASURE

DOST DOBRI CHLAPI • 1972 • Rezucha Jozef • CZC • QUITE GOOD CHAPS

DOSTAVENICKO VE MLYNICI • 1898 • Krizenecky Jan • CZC • RENDEZ-VOUS AT THE GRINDING ROOM ○ APPOINTMENT AT THE MILL

DOSTE TA HERIA • 1970 • Andreou Errikos • GRC • HOLD HANDS

DOSTIGAEV AND OTHERS • 1959 • Muzykant Yu., Rashevskaya Natalya • USS

DOSTIH • 1981 • Soukup Jaroslav • CZC • RACE, THE

DOT, LA • 1913 • Ravel Gaston • FRN

DOT AND CARRIE • 1927 • Newman Widgey R. • UKN

DOT AND SANTA CLAUS • 1982 • Gross Yoram • ANM • ASL • AROUND THE WORLD WITH DOT ○ DOT AROUND THE WORLD

DOT AND THE BUNNY • 1983 • Gross Yoram • ANM • ASL

DOT AND THE KANGAROO • 1977 • Gross Yoram • ANM • ASL

DOT AND THE KOALA • 1986 • Gross Yoram • ANM • ASL

DOT AND THE LINE, THE • 1965 • Jones Charles M. • ANS • USA

DOT AROUND THE WORLD see **DOT AND SANTA CLAUS** • 1982

DOT, DOT, COMMA, DASH see **PUNKTUR, PUNKTUR, COMMA, STRIK** • 1980

DOT DOT DOT see **. . .** • 1971

DOT ON THE DAY LINE BOAT • 1915 • *Anderson Mignon* • USA

DOTANBA • 1957 • Uchida Tomu • JPN • THEY ARE BURIED ALIVE ○ ELEVENTH HOUR, THE

DOTEI SHACHO TO ONNA-HISHO • 1959 • Matsubayashi Shue • JPN • JOURNEY OF A PRESIDENT AND HIS SECRETARY

DOTHEBOYS HALL: OR, NICHOLAS NICKLEBY • 1903 • Collins Alf • UKN

DOTKNIECIE NOCY • 1960 • Bareja Stanislaw • PLN • TOUCH OF THE NIGHT, THE

DOTO ICHIMAN-KAIRI • 1966 • Fukuda Jun • JPN • MAD ATLANTIC

DOTS • 1940 • McLaren Norman • ANS • USA • POINTS

DOTS AND DASHES • 1910 • *Thanhouser* • USA

DOT'S CHAPERONE • 1914 • *Asher Max* • USA

DOT'S ELOPEMENT • 1914 • *Sterling* • USA

DOTTED LINE, THE see **LET WOMEN ALONE** • 1925

DOTTER FODD, EN • 1944 • Cederlund Gosta • SWD • BORN: A DAUGHTER

DOTTIE'S NEW DOLL • 1912 • *Snow Marguerite* • USA

DOTTOR ANTONIO, IL • 1937 • Guazzoni Enrico • ITL

DOTTOR JEKYLL • 1964 • Guardamagna? • ITL • DOCTOR JEKYLL

DOTTOR JEKYLL E GENTILE SIGNORA • 1979 • Steno • ITL

DOTTOR YEKYLL see **EXTRANO CASO DEL HOMBRE Y LA BESTIA, EL** • 1951

DOTTORESSA DEL DISTRETTO MILITARE, LA • 1976 • Cicero Nando • ITL

DOTTORESSA SOTTO IL LENZVOLO, LA • 1976 • Martucci Gianni Antonio • ITL

DOTTY, THE DANCER • 1912 • *Chamberlain Riley* • USA

DOTTY WORLD OF JAMES LLOYD, THE • 1964 • Russell Ken • MTV • UKN

D'OU VIENS-TU, JOHNNY? • 1963 • Howard Noel • FRN

D'OU VIENT MARIE-MARTINE? see **MARIE-MARTINE** • 1942

DOUANCE, LA • 1986 • Beaudry Michel • MTV • CND

DOUANIERS ET CONTREBANDIERS • 1905 • Blache Alice • FRN • GUERITE, LA

DOUAUMONT • 1930 • Joannon Leo • FRN

DOUAUMONT • 1931 • Paul Heinz • FRG

DOUBLE, THE • 1910 • *Imp* • USA

DOUBLE, THE • 1963 • Harris Lionel • UKN

DOUBLE ACTION DANIELS • 1925 • Thorpe Richard • USA

DOUBLE ADVENTURE • 1921 • Van Dyke W. S. • SRL • USA

DOUBLE AFFAIR, THE see **SPY WITH MY FACE, THE** • 1965

DOUBLE AGENT • 1987 • Vejar Mike • TVM • USA

DOUBLE AGENT 73 • 1975 • Wishman Doris • USA

DOUBLE AGENTS, THE see **NUIT DES ESPIONS, LA** • 1959

DOUBLE ALIBI • 1937 • MacDonald David • UKN

DOUBLE ALIBI • 1940 • Rosen Phil • USA

DOUBLE ALIBI, THE see **LAW AND ORDER** • 1942

DOUBLE AMOUR, LE • 1925 • Epstein Jean • FRN

DOUBLE AND QUITS • 1915 • Cooper Toby • UKN

DOUBLE-BARREL MIRACLE, THE • 1954 • *Bowman Lee* • USA

DOUBLE-BARRELED COURTSHIP, A • 1916 • Ellis Robert • USA

DOUBLE-BARRELLED JUSTICE • 1925 • *Farnum Franklin* • USA

DOUBLE-BARRELLED DETECTIVE STORY, THE • 1965 • Mekas Adolfas • USA

DOUBLE BED, THE see **LIT A DEUX PLACES, LE** • 1965

DOUBLE-BEDDED ROOM, THE • 1903 • Collins Alf? • UKN

DOUBLE BLUFF • 1933 • Jeffrey R. E. • UKN

DOUBLE BUNK • 1961 • Pennington-Richards C. M. • UKN

DOUBLE CHASE, THE • 1913 • *Mann Frankie* • USA

DOUBLE CHASER • 1942 • Freleng Friz • ANS • USA

DOUBLE CINCHED • 1923 • Beebe Ford, Maloney Leo • USA

DOUBLE CON, THE see **TRICK BABY** • 1973

DOUBLE CONFESSION • 1950 • Annakin Ken • UKN • ALL ON A SUMMER'S DAY

DOUBLE COURTSHIP, A • 1912 • *Lubin* • USA

DOUBLE CRIME SUR LA LIGNE MAGINOT • 1937 • Gandera Felix • FRN • CRIME IN THE MAGINOT LINE (USA)

DOUBLE CROSS • 1918 • *Sparkle* • SHT • USA

DOUBLE CROSS • 1938 • Bhavnani Mohan Dayaram • IND

DOUBLE CROSS • 1941 • Kelley Albert • USA

DOUBLE CROSS see **FIGLIA DEL CAPITANO, LA** • 1947

DOUBLE CROSS, THE • 1912 • *Imp* • USA

DOUBLE CROSS, THE • 1912 • *Selig* • USA

DOUBLE CROSS, THE • 1912 • *Eclair* • USA

DOUBLE CROSS, THE • 1913 • *Frontier* • USA

DOUBLE CROSS, THE • 1915 • Fahrney Milton • USA

DOUBLE CROSS, THE • 1916 • *Burbridge Elizabeth* • SHT • USA

DOUBLE CROSS COUNTRY RACE • 1951 • Kneitel Seymour • ANS • USA

DOUBLE CROSS ROADS • 1930 • Werker Alfred L. • USA

DOUBLE CROSSBONES • 1950 • Barton Charles T. • USA

DOUBLE CROSSED • 1914 • Nicholls George • USA

DOUBLE CROSSED • 1916 • Bertram William • SHT • USA

DOUBLE CROSSED • 1917 • *W. H. Productions* • USA

DOUBLE CROSSED • 1917 • Chautard Emile • USA

DOUBLE CROSSED • 1917 • Vignola Robert G. • *Paramount* • USA

DOUBLE CROSSED • 1935 • Goulding Alf • SHT • USA

DOUBLE CROSSED see **CASH PARRISH'S PAL** • 1915

DOUBLE-CROSSING MARMADUKE • 1915 • Miller Rube • USA

DOUBLE-CROSSING OF SLIM, THE • 1915 • Beranger George A. • USA

DOUBLE-CROSSING THE DEAN • 1916 • Christie Al • SHT • USA

DOUBLE DANGER • 1920 • Russell Albert • SHT • USA

DOUBLE DANGER • 1938 • Landers Lew • USA • PERFECT ALIBI, THE

DOUBLE DANGER, A • 1912 • *Vitagraph* • USA

DOUBLE DARING • 1926 • Thorpe Richard • USA

DOUBLE DARING (UKN) see **FIXER DUGAN** • 1939

DOUBLE DATE • 1941 • Tryon Glenn • USA

DOUBLE DATE • 1967 • Torres Mar S. • PHL

DOUBLE DEADLY see **SILENT PARTNER, THE** • 1978

DOUBLE DEAL • 1938 • Dreifuss Arthur • USA

DOUBLE DEAL • 1950 • Berlin Abby • USA

DOUBLE DEAL • 1982 • Kavanagh Brian • ASL

DOUBLE DEAL • 1984 • SAF

DOUBLE DEAL IN PORK, A • 1915 • Lloyd Frank • USA

DOUBLE DEALING • 1923 • Lehrman Henry • USA • POOR WORM, THE ○ KNOCKER, THE

DOUBLE DEALING • 1928 • Malins Geoffrey H. • UKN

DOUBLE DEALING • 1932 • Hiscott Leslie • UKN

DOUBLE DECEPTION, A • 1911 • Fitzhamon Lewin? • UKN

DOUBLE DECEPTION, A • 1913 • *Imp* • USA

DOUBLE DECEPTION, A • 1915 • *Empress* • USA

DOUBLE DECEPTION, A • 1917 • *Boardman True* • SHT • USA

DOUBLE DECEPTION, THE • 1915 • *Majestic* • USA

DOUBLE DECEPTION (USA) see **MAGICIENNES, LES** • 1960

DOUBLE DESTIN (FRN) see **ZWEITE LEBEN, DAS** • 1954

DOUBLE DESTINY see **ZWEITE LEBEN, DAS** • 1954

DOUBLE DIVING • 1939 • Feist Felix E. • SHT • USA

DOUBLE DOOR • 1933 • Vidor Charles • USA

DOUBLE DOUBLE CROSS, A • 1916 • *L-Ko* • USA

DOUBLE DOUBLE CROSS, THE • 1916 • Currier Frank • *Vitagraph* • USA

DOUBLE DRAGON IN LAST DUEL • 1985 • Key Nam Nam • HKG

DOUBLE DRIBBLE • 1946 • Hannah Jack • ANS • USA

DOUBLE DUKES • 1917 • Smith Dick, Mayo Archie • SHT • USA

DOUBLE-DYED DECEIVER, THE • 1920 • Green Alfred E. • USA

DOUBLE DYNAMITE • 1951 • Cummings Irving Jr. • USA • IT'S ONLY MONEY

DOUBLE-EDGED CRIME see **CRIMEN DE DOBLE FILO** • 1964

DOUBLE-EDGED MURDER see **CRIMEN DE DOBLE FILO** • 1964

DOUBLE ELOPEMENT, A • 1910 • *Vitagraph* • USA

DOUBLE ELOPEMENT, A • 1911 • *Lubin* • USA

DOUBLE ELOPEMENT, A • 1914 • Seay Charles M. • USA

DOUBLE ELOPEMENT, A • 1916 • Ellis Robert • SHT • USA

DOUBLE ELOPEMENT, THE • 1911 • *Solax* • USA

DOUBLE ELOPEMENT, THE • 1911 • Fitzhamon Lewin? • UKN

DOUBLE ERROR see **PRICE OF FOLLY, THE** • 1937

DOUBLE ERROR, A • 1914 • Marston Theodore • USA

DOUBLE EVENT, THE • 1911 • Lincoln W. J. • ASL

DOUBLE EVENT, THE • 1914 • Buckland Warwick? • UKN

DOUBLE EVENT, THE • 1921 • Foss Kenelm • UKN

DOUBLE EVENT, THE • 1934 • Gordon Leslie H. • UKN

DOUBLE EXISTENCE DE LORD SAMSEY, LA • 1924 • Monca Georges, Keroul Maurice • FRN

DOUBLE EXPOSURE • 1944 • Berke William • USA

DOUBLE EXPOSURE • 1954 • Gilling John • UKN

DOUBLE EXPOSURE • 1976 • Webb William • UKN

DOUBLE EXPOSURE • 1982 • Hillman William Byron • USA

DOUBLE EXPOSURE see **TERMINAL EXPOSURE** • 1987

DOUBLE EXPOSURE, A • 1914 • Collins Edwin J.? • UKN

DOUBLE EXPOSURE, A • 1915 • *Burke Peggy* • USA

DOUBLE EXPOSURE (UKN) see **CORRUPTION** • 1933

DOUBLE EXPOSURES • 1937 • Carstairs John Paddy • UKN • ALIBI BREAKER

DOUBLE FACE see **A DOPPIA FACCIA** • 1969

DOUBLE FEATURE see **SESION CONTINUA** • 1984

DOUBLE FIANCEE, THE see **DOPPELBRAUTIGAM, DER** • 1934

DOUBLE FIRE DECEPTION, A • 1916 • Moore Matt • SHT • USA

DOUBLE FISTED • 1925 • Webb Harry S. • USA

DOUBLE FURLOUGH see **I'LL BE SEEING YOU** • 1944

DOUBLE GAMES • 1989 • Tozum Irfan • TRK

DOUBLE HARNESS • 1933 • Cromwell John • USA

DOUBLE-HEADED ARROW, THE see **‡—×(BACK AND FORTH)** • 1969

DOUBLE HEADED EAGLE • 1973 • Becker Lutz • DOC • UKN

DOUBLE-HEADED EAGLE, THE • 1972 • Mora Philippe, Becker Lutz • DOC • UKN

DOUBLE-HEARTED MAN, A see **KETSZIVU FERFI, A** • 1916

DOUBLE HIT see **NEXT MAN, THE** • 1976

DOUBLE HOLD-UP, THE • 1919 • Rosen Phil • SHT • USA

DOUBLE HONEYMOON • 1945 • Yates Hal • SHT • USA

DOUBLE IDENTITY see **RIVER'S END** • 1940

DOUBLE IDENTITY see **HURRICANE SMITH** • 1941

DOUBLE IDENTITY, A • 1915 • Horne James W. • USA

DOUBLE INDEMNITY • 1944 • Wilder Billy • USA

DOUBLE INDEMNITY • 1973 • Smight Jack • TVM • USA

DOUBLE INITIATION • 1970 • Tobalina Carlos • USA

DOUBLE INSOMNIE, LA • 1966 • Lethem Roland • BLG

DOUBLE JAM • 1958 • Hirsch Hy • SHT • USA

DOUBLE JEOPARDY • 1955 • Springsteen R. G. • USA • CROOKED RING (UKN)

DOUBLE JEOPARDY see **TASTE OF SIN, A** • 1983

DOUBLE JEU, LE • 1916 • Burguet Charles • FRN

DOUBLE JEU, LE • 1916 • Feuillade Louis • FRN

DOUBLE KNOCKING • 1967 • Kishi Shintaro, Fijita Junya • JPN

DOUBLE KNOT, THE • 1914 • Walsh Raoul • USA

DOUBLE LIFE, A • 1906 • Stow Percy • UKN

DOUBLE LIFE, A • 1912 • Buckland Warwick? • UKN

DOUBLE LIFE, A • 1913 • Haldane Bert? • UKN

DOUBLE LIFE, A • 1948 • Cukor George • USA • DOUBLE TROUBLE ○ IMAGINATION

DOUBLE LIFE, A see **CONVICTED BY HYPNOTISM** • 1912

DOUBLE LIFE, A (USA) see **ZWEITE LEBEN, DAS** • 1954

DOUBLE LIFE, THE • 1914 • Myers Harry • USA

DOUBLE LIFE OF A DRAGONFLY see **PODWOJNE ZYCIE WAZKI** • 1958

DOUBLE LIFE OF MR. ALFRED BURTON, THE • 1919 • Rooke Arthur • UKN

DOUBLE LIVES (UKN) see **TRAIL OF THE HORSE THIEVES, THE** • 1929

DOUBLE MAN, THE • 1967 • Schaffner Franklin J. • UKN

DOUBLE MAN, THE see **DOBBELTE MAND, DEN** • 1975

DOUBLE MARRIAGE see **KEKKON NIJUSO** • 1927

DOUBLE MCGUFFIN, THE • 1979 • Camp Joe • USA

DOUBLE MESSIEURS • 1985 • Stevenin Jean-Francois • FRN

DOUBLE MISUNDERSTANDING, A • 1912 • *Tennant Barbara* • USA

DOUBLE MURDER see **DOPPIO DELITTO** • 1977

DOUBLE MURDERS • 1977 • *Andress Ursula*

DOUBLE NEGATIVE • 1980 • Bloomfield George • CND

DOUBLE NICKELS • 1977 • Vacek Jack • USA

DOUBLE O, THE • 1921 • Clements Roy • USA

DOUBLE OR MUTTON • 1955 • Jones Charles M. • ANS • USA

DOUBLE OR NOTHING • 1937 • Reed Theodore • USA

DOUBLE OR QUITS • 1938 • Neill R. William • UKN

DOUBLE PENALTY, A • 1916 • *Buffalo* • SHT • USA

DOUBLE PENETRATION • 1976 • Baudricourt Michel • FRN

DOUBLE PLAY see **LILY IN LOVE** • 1985

DOUBLE PLEASURE see **DOUBLE YOUR PLEASURE** • 1969

DOUBLE PORTRAIT see **ATVALTOZASOK** • 1964

DOUBLE POSSESSION see **GANJA AND HESS** • 1973

DOUBLE POSSESSION: THE DOCTOR CANNOT DIE see **GANJA AND HESS** • 1973

DOUBLE PROFILE see **SECOND FACE** • 1954

DOUBLE PUNCH, THE (UKN) see **DOWN RIO GRANDE WAY** • 1942

DOUBLE PURSUIT see **MY BROTHER'S KEEPER** • 1948

DOUBLE RANSOM see **OBSESSION** • 1976

DOUBLE REVENGE • 1917 • *Kerrigan J. Warren* • USA

DOUBLE REVENGE • 1988 • Mastroianni Armand • USA

DOUBLE REWARD • 1915 • *Navajo* • USA

DOUBLE REWARD, A • 1912 • Ince Thomas H. • USA

DOUBLE REWARD, A • 1914 • *Warner'S Features* • USA

DOUBLE REWARD, A • 1916 • *Rancho* • USA

DOUBLE ROLE, A • 1915 • *Lubin* • USA

DOUBLE-ROOM MYSTERY, THE • 1917 • Henley Hobart • USA

DOUBLE SACRIFICE, A • 1913 • *Nestor* • USA

DOUBLE SHADOW, THE • 1914 • *Phillips Augustus* • USA

DOUBLE SHOJO • 1967 • Kishi Shintaro, Miki Hideki • JPN • DOUBLE VIRGINITY

DOUBLE SKULLS • 1986 • Gilmour Ian • TVM • ASL

DOUBLE SPEED • 1920 • Wood Sam • USA

DOUBLE STANDARD, THE • 1915 • Dowlan William C. • USA

DOUBLE STANDARD, THE • 1917 • Smalley Phillips • USA

DOUBLE-STOP • 1968 • Sindell Gerald Seth • USA • DOUBLE STOP

DOUBLE STOP see **DOUBLE-STOP** • 1968

DOUBLE SUICIDE see **SHINJU TEN NO AMIJIMA** • 1969

DOUBLE SUICIDE AT AMIJIMA see **SHINJU TEN NO AMIJIMA** • 1969

DOUBLE SUICIDE AT SONEZAKI see **SONEZAKI SHINJUH** • 1981

DOUBLE SUSPICION • 1917 • Marshall George • SHT • USA

DOUBLE SWITCH • 1987 • Greenwalt David • TVM • USA

DOUBLE TALK GIRL • 1942 • *O'Brien Joseph/ Mead Thomas (P)* • SHT • USA

DOUBLE TARGET • 1987 • Mattei Bruno • USA

DOUBLE-TOPPED TRUNK, THE • 1917 • Holubar Allen • SHT • USA

DOUBLE TRAIL, THE • 1912 • *Forde Victoria* • USA

DOUBLE TROUBLE • 1915 • Cabanne W. Christy • USA

DOUBLE TROUBLE • 1951 • Robinson Lee • DOC • ASL

DOUBLE TROUBLE • 1964 • *Eto Yumi* • JPN

DOUBLE TROUBLE • 1967 • Taurog Norman • USA

DOUBLE TROUBLE see **DOUBLE LIFE, A** • 1948

DOUBLE TROUBLE see **INAFFERRABILE 12, L'** • 1950

DOUBLE TROUBLE see **SWINGIN' ALONG** • 1962

DOUBLE TROUBLE see **IZVRNUTA PRICA** • 1972

DOUBLE TROUBLE see **BROTHERS O'TOOLE, THE** • 1973

DOUBLE TROUBLE see **IO, TU, LORO E GLI ALTRI** • 1984

DOUBLE UP • 1943 • Holmes Ben • SHT • USA

DOUBLE VERDICT see **EN VOTRE AME ET CONSCIENCE** • 1960

DOUBLE VIRGINITY see **DOUBLE SHOJO** • 1967

DOUBLE WEDDING • 1933 • Richardson Frank • UKN

DOUBLE WEDDING • 1937 • Thorpe Richard • USA

DOUBLE WEDDING see **DOBOL WEDDING** • 1968

DOUBLE WEDDING, A • 1913 • Sennett Mack • USA

DOUBLE WHOOPEE • 1929 • Foster Lewis R. • SHT • USA

DOUBLE WINNING, A • 1915 • *Ab* • USA
DOUBLE X • 1986 • Cunningham Julie • SHT • ASL
DOUBLE YOUR PLEASURE • 1969 • *Dragon Films* • USA • TWILIGHT AFFAIR ○ DOUBLE PLEASURE
DOUBLECROSS • 1956 • Squire Anthony • UKN
DOUBLECROSSERS, THE • 1975 • Cheng Chang-Wa • HKG, INN
DOUBLES • 1981 • Wilson Bruce • USA
DOUBLES, THE • 1922 • Dewhurst George • UKN
DOUBLES AND TROUBLES • 1917 • Santell Alfred • USA
DOUBLES BRING TROUBLES • 1914 • *Eclectic* • USA
DOUBLE'S FATE, THE • 1909 • *Urban-Eclipse* • USA
DOUBLE'S TROUBLES, THE • 1916 • *Howell Alice* • SHT • USA
DOUBLETAKE • 1985 • Taylor Jud • TVM • USA
DOUBLING FOR ROMEO • 1922 • Badger Clarence • USA • BASHFUL ROMEO, THE
DOUBLING IN THE QUICKIES • 1932 • *Sennett Mack (P)* • SHT • USA
DOUBLING WITH DANGER • 1926 • Dunlap Scott R. • USA
DOUBLY DESIRED ORPHAN, A • 1911 • *De Garde Adele* • USA
DOUBTFUL DEAL IN DOGS, A • 1914 • Plumb Hay? • UKN
DOUBTING THOMAS • 1935 • Butler David • USA
DOUCE • 1943 • Autant-Lara Claude • FRN • LOVE STORY
DOUCE ENQUETE SUR LA VIOLENCE • 1981 • Guerin Gerard • FRN
DOUCE MOMENTS DU PASSE (FRN) see **DULCES HORAS** • 1981
DOUCE VIOLENCE • 1962 • Pecas Max • FRN • SWEET ECSTASY (USA) ○ SWEET VIOLENCE ○ VIOLENT ECSTASY
DOUCEMENT LES BASSES! • 1971 • Deray Jacques • FRN, ITL • UOMO DI SAINT-MICHEL, L' (ITL) ○ EASY DOWN THERE! (USA)
DOUCEUR D'AIMER, LA • 1930 • Hervil Rene • FRN • MON COUSIN ALBERT
DOUCEUR DE VIVRE, LA (FRN) see **DOLCE VITA, LA** • 1959
DOUCEUR DU PECHE, LA • 1911 • Puchalski Eduard • PLN
DOUCEUR DU VILLAGE, LA • 1965 • Reichenbach Francois • DOC • FRN
DOUCHE APRES LE BAIN • 1896-97 • Lumiere Louis • FRN
DOUCHE DE COLONEL, LA • 1901 • Melies Georges • FRN • PAINTER'S MISHAP IN THE BARRACKS, THE ○ COLONEL'S SHOWER BATH, THE
DOUCHE D'EAU BOUILLANTE, LA • 1907 • Melies Georges • FRN • ROGUES' TRICKS (USA)
DOUCHE EST LA REVANCHE • 1972 • Simenon Marc • FRN
DOUGAL AND THE BLUE CAT (UKN) see **POLLUX ET LE CHAT BLEU** • 1970
DOUGH AND DYNAMITE • 1914 • Chaplin Charles • USA • DOUGHNUT DESIGNER, THE ○ COOK, THE
DOUGH BOYS, THE • 1930 • Sedgwick Edward • USA • FORWARD MARCH (UKN) ○ DOUGHBOYS ○ BIG SHOT, THE
DOUGH FOR THE DO-DO • 1949 • Freleng Friz • ANS • USA
DOUGH NUTS • 1915 • *Heinie & Louie* • USA
DOUGH-NUTS • 1917 • Gillstrom Arvid E. • SHT • USA
DOUGH RAY ME-OW • 1948 • Davis Arthur • ANS • USA
DOUGHBOYS see **DOUGH BOYS, THE** • 1930
DOUGHBOYS IN IRELAND • 1943 • Landers Lew • USA
DOUGHGIRLS, THE • 1944 • Kern James V. • USA
DOUGHNUT DESIGNER, THE see **DOUGH AND DYNAMITE** • 1914
DOUGHNUT VENDOR, THE • 1915 • King Burton L. • USA
DOUGHNUTS • 1916 • *Chamberlin Riley* • USA
DOUGHNUTS • 1933 • Sherman Frank, Rufle George • ANS • USA
DOUGHNUTS AND SOCIETY • 1936 • Collins Lewis D. • USA • STEPPING INTO SOCIETY (UKN) ○ STEPPING IN SOCIETY
DOUGLAS • 1970 • Bang-Hansen Pal • NRW
DOUGLAS FAIRBANKS IN ROBIN HOOD see **ROBIN HOOD** • 1922
DOUKHOBORS, THE • 1958 • Leiterman Douglas • CND
DOULEUR, LA • 1925 • Roudes Gaston • FRN
DOULOS, LE • 1962 • Melville Jean-Pierre • FRN, ITL • DOULOS -THE FINGER MAN (USA) ○ SPIONE, LO (ITL) ○ FINGERMAN, THE
DOULOS -THE FINGER MAN (USA) see **DOULOS, LE** • 1962
DOULOUREUSE, LA • 1920 • Genina Augusto • ITL
DOULOUREUSE COMEDIE, LA • 1922 • Bergerat Theo • FRN
DOUREN, TY DOUREN • 1931 • Medvedkin Alexander • USS
DOURO, FAINA FLUVIAL • 1931 • de Oliveira Manoel • SHT • PRT • HARD LABOR ON THE RIVER DOURO
DOUWE VAN DEN BERG, ONGEWENST • 1972 • Crama Nico • SHT • NTH • DOUWE VAN DEN BERG, UNDESIRABLE
DOUWE VAN DEN BERG, UNDESIRABLE see **DOUWE VAN DEN BERG, ONGEWENST** • 1972
DOUX AVEUX, LES • 1982 • Dansereau Fernand • CND • SWEET LIES AND TENDER OATHS
DOUX VOYAGE DE MONSIEUR MICHALON, LE see **PAS DE PROBLEME!** • 1975
DOUZAINE D'OEUFS FRAIS, UNE • 1908 • *Deed Andre* • FRN
DOUZE HEURES DE BONHEUR • 1952 • Grangier Gilles • FRN
DOUZE HEURES D'HORLOGE • 1958 • von Radvanyi Geza • FRN, FRG
DOUZE MOIS EN FRANCE • 1970 • Leenhardt Roger (c/d) • DCS • FRN
DOUZE TRAVAUX D'ASTERIX, LES • 1976 • Goscinny Rene, Uderzo Albert • ANM • FRN • ASTERIX THE GAUL 2: THE TWELVE TASKS OF ASTERIX ○ TWELVE TASKS OF ASTERIX, THE
DOUZE TRAVAUX D'HERCULE, LES • 1910 • Cohl Emile • ANS • FRN • DOZEN LABORS OF HERCULES, THE ○ HERCULES AND THE BIG STICK
DOUZIEME HEURE, LA • 1966 • Martimbeau Jean • CND
DOVE see **HOLUBICE** • 1960
DOVE, THE • 1927 • West Roland • USA
DOVE, THE • 1968 • Coe George, Lover Anthony • SHT • USA
DOVE, THE • 1974 • Jarrott Charles • USA, UKN
DOVE, THE see **GIRL AND THE GAMBLER, THE** • 1939
DOVE, THE (UKN) see **GIRL OF THE RIO, THE** • 1932
DOVE AND THE SERPENT, THE • 1912 • *Fischer Margarita* • USA
DOVE ANDIAMO, SIGNORA? • 1943 • Cominetti Gian M. • ITL
DOVE EYE'S GRATITUDE • 1909 • *Bison* • USA
DOV'E FINITA LA 7a COMPAGNIA? (ITL) see **MAIS OU EST DONC PASSE LA 7e COMPAGNIE?** • 1973
DOVE IN THE EAGLE'S NEST, THE • 1913 • *Snow Marguerite* • USA
DOV'E LA LIBERTA? • 1954 • Rossellini Roberto • ITL
DOVE NON E PECCATO • 1970 • Colantuoni Antonio • ITL
DOVE SI SPARA DI PIU • 1967 • Puccini Gianni • ITL, SPN
DOVE STA ZAZA? • 1948 • Simonelli Giorgio C. • ITL
DOVE VAI IN VACANZA? • 1978 • Bolognini Mauro, Salce Luciano, Sordi Alberto • ITL
DOVE VAI SE IL VIZIETTO NON CE L'HAI? • 1979 • Girolami Marino • ITL
DOVE VAI TUTTA NUDA? • 1969 • Festa Campanile Pasquale • ITL • WHERE ARE YOU GOING ALL NAKED? (UKN)
DOVE VOLANO I CORVI D'ARGENTO • 1977 • Livi Piero • ITL
DOVE WITH CLIPPED WINGS, A • 1975 • Muller John • MTV • CND
DOVER BOYS, THE • 1942 • Jones Charles M. • ANS • USA
DOVER -FRONT LINE • 1940 • Watt Harry • DCS • UKN • FRONT LINE, THE
DOVER REVISITED • 1942 • Watt Harry • DOC • UKN
DOVER ROAD, THE see **LITTLE ADVENTURESS, THE** • 1927
DOVER ROAD, THE (UKN) see **WHERE SINNERS MEET** • 1934
DOVER ROAD MYSTERY, THE • 1960 • Bryant Gerard • UKN
DOVES, THE see **COLOMBES, LES** • 1972
DOVE'S FLIGHT, THE see **VUELO DE LA PALOMA, EL** • 1988
DOVETREE see **GEZI SHU** • 1985
DOVIDJENJA U SLIJEDECEM RATU see **NASVIDENJE V NASLEDNJI VOJNI** • 1981
DOVOLENA S ANDELEM • 1952 • Zeman • CZC • HOLIDAYS WITH AN ANGEL
DOWELL'S DUELS • 1915 • Collins Edwin J.? • UKN
DOWN A LONG WAY • 1954 • Privett Bob • ANS • UKN
DOWN AMONG THE SHELTERING PALMS • 1953 • Goulding Edmund • USA
DOWN AMONG THE SUGAR CANE • 1932 • Fleischer Dave • ANS • USA
DOWN AMONG THE Z MEN • 1952 • Rogers Maclean • UKN • STAND EASY (USA) ○ SOME KIND OF NUT ○ GOON SHOW MOVIE, THE
DOWN AND DIRTY • 1969 • Everett Edward • USA
DOWN AND DIRTY see **BRUTTI, SPORCHI E CATTIVI** • 1976
DOWN AND OUT • 1912 • *Majestic* • USA
DOWN AND OUT • 1922 • Roach Hal • ANS • USA
DOWN AND OUT see **LAUGHING GAS** • 1914
DOWN AND OUT IN BEVERLY HILLS • 1986 • Mazursky Paul • USA
DOWN AND OUTING • 1961 • Deitch Gene • ANS • USA
DOWN ARGENTINE WAY • 1940 • Cummings Irving • USA
DOWN BOY! • 1964 • Cohen Norman • UKN
DOWN BUT NOT OUT • 1919 • Jaccard Jacques • SHT • USA
DOWN BY LAW • 1986 • Jarmusch Jim • USA
DOWN BY THE OLD BULL AND BUSH • 1906 • Green Tom? • UKN
DOWN BY THE OLD BULL AND BUSH • 1907 • Morland John • UKN
DOWN BY THE OLD MILL STREAM • 1933 • Fleischer Dave • ANS • USA
DOWN BY THE RIO GRANDE • 1924 • Neitz Alvin J. • USA
DOWN BY THE SEA • 1914 • Ricketts Thomas • USA
DOWN BY THE SEA • 1917 • Christie Al • SHT • USA
DOWN BY THE SOUNDING SEA • 1912 • *Gem* • USA
DOWN BY THE SOUNDING SEA • 1914 • Cabanne W. Christy • USA
DOWN BY THE STATION • 1977 • Dunkley-Smith John • ASL
DOWN CHANNEL • 1929 • Barringer Michael • UKN
DOWN CUBA WAY (UKN) see **CUBAN PETE** • 1946
DOWN DAKOTA WAY • 1949 • Witney William • USA
DOWN FOR DOUBLE • 1970 • *Stacey Dist.* • USA
DOWN FRIDAY STREET • 1966 • Hooper Tobe • SHT • USA
DOWN GRADE • 1927 • Hutchison Charles • USA
DOWN HOME • 1920 • Willat Irvin V. • USA
DOWN HOME • 1987 • Berry Thomas • USA
DOWN HOME IN TENNESSEE • 1916 • *Tress Henry* • SHT • UKN
DOWN IN ARKANSAS • 1938 • Grinde Nick • USA
DOWN IN DIXIE • 1932 • Foster John, Bailey Harry • ANS • USA
DOWN IN MEXICO • 1910 • *Actophone* • USA
DOWN IN SAN DIEGO • 1941 • Sinclair Robert B. • USA • YOUNG AMERICANS
DOWN JAYVILLE WAY • 1912 • *Steppling John* • USA
DOWN LAREDO WAY • 1953 • Witney William • USA
DOWN LIBERTY ROAD • 1956 • Schuster Harold • USA
DOWN LONE GAP WAY • 1914 • *Patheplay* • USA
DOWN MELODY LANE • 1943 • *Schofield Johnnie* • UKN
DOWN MEMORY LANE • 1932 • Brice Monte • SHT • USA
DOWN MEMORY LANE • 1949 • Karlson Phil • USA
DOWN MEXICO WAY • 1941 • Santley Joseph • USA
DOWN MISSOURI WAY • 1969 • Berne Josef • USA
DOWN NORTH • 1920 • Scott J. Booth • CND
DOWN ON THE BARN • 1938 • Schwarzwald Milton • SHT • USA
DOWN ON THE FARM • 1905 • Porter Edwin S. • USA
DOWN ON THE FARM • 1914 • Madden Mr. • USA
DOWN ON THE FARM • 1915 • Christie Al • USA
DOWN ON THE FARM • 1920 • Kenton Erle C., Grey Ray • USA
DOWN ON THE FARM • 1920 • Sandground Maurice • UKN
DOWN ON THE FARM • 1922 • Smith Eric L'Epine • UKN
DOWN ON THE FARM • 1935 • Hill Lee, Pitt Stuart • NZL
DOWN ON THE FARM • 1938 • St. Clair Malcolm • USA
DOWN ON THE LEVEE • 1933 • *Terry Paul/ Moser Frank (P)* • ANS • USA
DOWN ON THE RIO GRANDE • 1913 • *Carewe Edwin* • USA
DOWN ON US • 1984 • Buchanan Larry • USA
DOWN OUR STREET • 1932 • Lachman Harry • UKN
DOWN OUR STREET • 1942 • Bishop Terry • DOC • UKN
DOWN RIO GRANDE WAY • 1942 • Berke William • USA • DOUBLE PUNCH, THE (UKN)
DOWN RIVER • 1931 • Godfrey Peter • UKN
DOWN SWING • 1933 • Marshall George • SHT • USA
DOWN TEXAS WAY • 1942 • Bretherton Howard • USA
DOWN THE ANCIENT STAIRCASE see **PER LE ANTICHE SCALE** • 1975
DOWN THE ANCIENT STAIRS (USA) see **PER LE ANTICHE SCALE** • 1975
DOWN THE CORNER • 1978 • Comerford Joe • IRL, UKN
DOWN THE HILL TO CREDITVILLE • 1914 • Crisp Donald • USA
DOWN THE LONG HILLS • 1987 • Kennedy Burt • TVM • USA • LOUIS L'AMOUR'S DOWN THE LONG HILLS
DOWN THE MAJESTIC ST. LAWRENCE • Lavoie Hermenegilde • DCS • CND
DOWN THE RIBBER • 1936 • Boasberg Al • SHT • USA
DOWN THE RIVER • 1918 • Chapin Benjamin • SHT • USA
DOWN THE RIVER • 1951 • Cowan Will • SHT • USA
DOWN THE SHORE see **BEACH HOUSE** • 1982
DOWN THE STRETCH • 1927 • Baggot King • USA
DOWN THE STRETCH • 1936 • Clemens William • USA
DOWN THE WIND • 1975 • McKenzie Kim, Hicks Scott • ASL
DOWN THE WYOMING TRAIL • 1939 • Herman Al • USA
DOWN THREE DARK STREETS • 1954 • Laven Arnold • USA
DOWN THROUGH THE AGES • 1912 • Olcott Sidney • USA
DOWN TO EARTH • 1917 • Emerson John • USA
DOWN TO EARTH • 1932 • Butler David • USA
DOWN TO EARTH • 1947 • Hall Alexander • USA
DOWN TO EARTH see **SPRAVCA SKANZENU** • 1988
DOWN TO MIRTH • 1959 • Kneitel Seymour • ANS • USA
DOWN TO THE CELLAR see **DO PIVNICE** • 1982
DOWN TO THE SEA • 1972 • Walker Giles • MTV • CND, USA
DOWN TO THE SEA IN SHIPS • 1922 • Clifton Elmer • USA
DOWN TO THE SEA IN SHIPS • 1949 • Hathaway Henry • USA
DOWN TO THE SEA IN SHIPS see **LAST ADVENTURERS, THE** • 1937
DOWN TO THE SEA IN SHOES • 1923 • *Sennett Mack (P)* • SHT • USA
DOWN TO THEIR LAST YACHT • 1934 • Sloane Paul • USA • HAWAIIAN NIGHTS (UKN)
DOWN TOWN see **MIXED BLOOD** • 1984
DOWN TRIP see **NEDTUR** • 1979
DOWN TWISTED • 1987 • Pyun Albert • USA • TREASURE OF SAN LUCAS, THE ○ DOWNTWISTED
DOWN UNDER • 1926 • Southwell Harry • ASL
DOWN UNDER • 1939 • Smith Percy • UKN
DOWN UNDER see **SQUATTER'S DAUGHTER, THE** • 1933
DOWN UNDER DONOVAN • 1922 • Lambart Harry • UKN
DOWN UNDER THE SEA • 1936 • Collins Lewis D. • USA
DOWN UPON THE SUWANEE RIVER • 1925 • Kennedy Lem F. • USA
DOWN WENT MCGINTY (UKN) see **GREAT MCGINTY, THE** • 1940
DOWN WENT THE KEY • 1917 • Chaudet Louis W. • SHT • USA
DOWN WITH CATS • 1943 • Rasinski Connie • ANS • USA
DOWN WITH HUSBANDS! • 1930 • Watson William • USA
DOWN WITH THE FENCES see **DOLE PLOTOVI** • 1962
DOWN WITH THE MEN • 1912 • *Lubin* • USA
DOWN WITH WEAPONS (USA) see **NED MED VAABNENE** • 1914
DOWNBEAT see **DADDY O** • 1959
DOWNBEAT BEAR • 1956 • Hanna William, Barbera Joseph • ANS • USA
DOWNFALL • 1964 • Moxey John Llewellyn • UKN
DOWNFALL see **ABSTURZ, DER** • 1922
DOWNFALL, THE • 1969 • Chebotaryov Vladimir • USS • FALL-DOWN, THE
DOWNFALL, THE (UKN) see **ORIZURU OSEN** • 1934
DOWNFALL OF OSEN, THE (USA) see **ORIZURU OSEN** • 1934
DOWNFALL OF POTTS, THE • 1915 • Christie Al • USA
DOWNFALL OF THE BURGLAR'S TRUST, THE • 1908 • Stow Percy • UKN
DOWNFALL OF URIAH SNOOP, THE • 1913 • *Albert Elsie* • USA
DOWNHEARTED DUCKLING • 1954 • Hanna William, Barbera Joseph • ANS • USA
DOWNHILL • 1927 • Hitchcock Alfred • UKN • WHEN BOYS LEAVE HOME (USA)
DOWNHILL • 1973 • Spry Robin • CND
DOWNHILL RACER • 1969 • Ritchie Michael • USA • DOWNHILL RACERS, THE
DOWNHILL RACERS, THE see **DOWNHILL RACER** • 1969
DOWNING AN UPRISING • 1920 • Lyons Eddie, Moran Lee • SHT • USA
DOWNPAYMENT ON MURDER • 1987 • Hussein Waris • TVM • USA
DOWNPOUR see **LIVEN** • 1929
DOWNPOUR see **RAGBAR** • 1972
DOWNSTAIRS • 1932 • Bell Monta • USA
DOWNSTAIRS AT RAMSEY'S • 1969 • LeRoy Mervyn • USA
DOWNSTREAM • 1929 • Guarino Joseph • UKN
DOWNSTREAM FROM THE SUN see **NIZVODNO OD SUNCA** • 1969
DOWNSTREAM THE SUN see **NIZVODNO OD SUNCA** • 1969
DOWNTOWN • Kassner Joe • SHT • USA
DOWNTOWN • 1989 • Benjamin Richard • USA
DOWNTOWN see **SHITAMACHI** • 1957
DOWNTOWN FLAT • 1977 • Fadel Mohamed • EGY
DOWNTWISTED see **DOWN TWISTED** • 1987
DOWNWARD PATH, THE • 1914 • Melville Wilbert • USA
DOWNWARD SPIRAL see **SYOKSYKIERRE** • 1982
DOWNY GIRL see **DUNUNGEN** • 1941
DOWNY GIRL, THE (USA) see **DUNUNGEN** • 1919
DOWRY, THE • 1969 • Pearson Peter • CND
DOWRY, THE see **DAHEJ** • 1950
DOWRY, THE see **WIANO** • 1963
DOWRY FOR ROBAB • 1988 • Shayeghi Siamak • IRN
DOWRY OF LADY RALU, THE • 1969 • Cocea Dinu • RMN
DOX, CACCIA ALL'UOMO see **CACCIA ALL'UOMO** • 1961
DOXOBUS • 1988 • Lambrinos Fotos • GRC
DOYOBI NO TENSHI • 1954 • Yamamoto Kajiro • JPN • ANGEL OF SATURDAY, AN ○ SATURDAY ANGEL
DOZDE-SIYAHPOUSH • 1968 • Shervan Amir • IRN • THIEF IN A BLACK DRESS
DOZEN DADDIES, A see **TUCET MYCH TATINKU** • 1960
DOZEN LABORS OF HERCULES, THE see **DOUZE TRAVAUX D'HERCULE, LES** • 1910

DOZEN SOCKS, A • 1927 • *Sennett Mack (P)* • SHT • USA
DOZENS, THE • 1981 • Dall Christine, Conrad Randall • USA
DOZHIVEM DO PONEDELNIKA see **DOZHIVYOM DO PONEDYELNIKA** • 1968
DOZHIVYOM DO PONEDYELNIKA • 1968 • Rostotsky Stanislav • USS • WE'LL GET BY TILL MONDAY ○ DOZHIVEM DO PONEDELNIKA ○ LET'S WAIT TILL MONDAY ○ UNTIL MONDAY ○ LET'S LIVE UNTIL MONDAY
DOZNANIYE PILOTA PIKRSA see **TEST PILOTA PIRXA** • 1978
D'R HERR MAIRE see **MONSIEUR LE MAIRE** • 1939
DRAB SISTER, THE • 1915 • Vale Travers • USA
DRACHENFUTTER • 1987 • Schutte Jan • FRG, SWT • DRAGON FEED ○ DRAGON'S FOOD ○ SPICY RICE
DRACOS • 1956 • Koundouros Nikos • GRC • OGRE OF ATHENS, THE ○ OGRE IN ATHENS, THE
DRACULA • 1931 • Browning Tod • USA
DRACULA • 1931 • Melford George • USA
DRACULA • 1958 • Fisher Terence • UKN • HORROR OF DRACULA (USA)
DRACULA • 1964 • Warhol Andy • USA
DRACULA • 1973 • Curtis Dan • UKN
DRACULA • 1979 • Badham John • USA, UKN
DRACULA • 1984 • ANM • JPN
DRACULA see **NOSFERATU –EINE SYMPHONIE DES GRAUENS** • 1921
DRACULA see **ANDY WARHOL'S DRACULA** • 1974
DRACULA A.D.1972 • 1972 • Gibson Alan • UKN • DRACULA CHELSEA '72 ○ DRACULA TODAY
DRACULA AND HIS VAMPIRE BRIDE see **SATANIC RITES OF DRACULA, THE** • 1973
DRACULA AND SON see **DRACULA PERE ET FILS** • 1976
DRACULA AND THE BOYS see **DOES DRACULA REALLY SUCK?** • 1969
DRACULA AND THE SEVEN GOLDEN VAMPIRES see **LEGEND OF 7 GOLDEN VAMPIRES, THE** • 1974
DRACULA BLOWS HIS COOL • 1979 • Ombra Carlo • FRG
DRACULA CERCA SANGUE DI VERGINE E.. MORI DI SETE! see **ANDY WARHOL'S DRACULA** • 1974
DRACULA CHELSEA '72 see **DRACULA A.D.1972** • 1972
DRACULA CONTRA EL DR. FRANKENSTEIN • 1971 • Franco Jesus • SPN, FRN • DRACULA PRISONNIER DU DOCTEUR FRANKENSTEIN (FRN) ○ DRACULA VS. DR. FRANKENSTEIN ○ SCREAMING DEAD, THE
DRACULA EXOTICA see **LOVE AT FIRST GULP** • 1980
DRACULA HAS RISEN FROM THE GRAVE • 1968 • Francis Freddie • UKN
DRACULA HUNTS FRANKENSTEIN see **HOMBRE QUE VINO DEL UMMO, EL** • 1970
DRACULA IM SCHLOSS DES SCHRECKENS (FRG) see **NELLA STRETTA MORSA DEL RAGNO** • 1971
DRACULA IN ISTANBUL see **DRAKULA ISTANBULDA** • 1953
DRACULA IS DEAD AND WELL AND LIVING IN LONDON see **SATANIC RITES OF DRACULA, THE** • 1973
DRACULA JAGD FRANKENSTEIN (FRG) see **HOMBRE QUE VINO DEL UMMO, EL** • 1970
DRACULA MEETS THE OUTER SPACE CHICKS • 1968 • USA
DRACULA PERE ET FILS • 1976 • Molinaro Edouard • FRN • DRACULA AND SON
DRACULA –PRINCE OF DARKNESS • 1965 • Fisher Terence • UKN • BLOODY SCREAM OF DRACULA, THE ○ REVENGE OF DRACULA ○ DISCIPLE OF DRACULA
DRACULA PRISONNIER DU DOCTEUR FRANKENSTEIN (FRN) see **DRACULA CONTRA EL DR. FRANKENSTEIN** • 1971
DRACULA SAGA, THE see **SAGA DE LOS DRACULA, LA** • 1972
DRACULA SUCKS • 1978 • Marshak Philip • USA • LUST AT FIRST BITE ○ DRACULA'S BRIDE
DRACULA: THE BLOODLINE CONTINUES see **SAGA DE LOS DRACULA, LA** • 1972
DRACULA (THE DIRTY OLD MAN) • 1969 • Edwards William • USA
DRACULA, THE GREAT UNDEAD • 1985 • DOC • USA
DRACULA THE TERROR OF THE LIVING DEAD see **ORGIA DE LOS MUERTOS, LA** • 1972
DRACULA TODAY see **DRACULA A.D.1972** • 1972
DRACULA VS. DR. FRANKENSTEIN see **DRACULA CONTRA EL DR. FRANKENSTEIN** • 1971
DRACULA VS. FRANKENSTEIN • 1971 • Adamson Al • USA • BLOOD OF FRANKENSTEIN ○ BLOOD SEEKERS, THE ○ REVENGE OF DRACULA
DRACULA VS. FRANKENSTEIN (UKN) see **HOMBRE QUE VINO DEL UMMO, EL** • 1970
DRACULA VUOLE VIVERE: CERCA SANGUE DI VERGINE (ITL) see **ANDY WARHOL'S DRACULA** • 1974
DRACULA'S BRIDE see **DRACULA SUCKS** • 1978
DRACULA'S CASTLE see **BLOOD OF DRACULA'S CASTLE** • 1969
DRACULA'S DAUGHTER • 1936 • Hillyer Lambert • USA
DRACULA'S DISCIPLE • 1984 • Schaaf Allen • USA
DRACULA'S DOG • 1978 • Band Albert • USA • ZOLTAN.. HOUND OF DRACULA ○ ZOLTAN, HOUND OF HELL ○ ZOLTAN
DRACULA'S GREAT LOVE (USA) see **GRAN AMOR DEL CONDE DRACULA, EL** • 1972
DRACULA'S LAST RITES see **LAST RITES** • 1980
DRACULA'S LUST FOR BLOOD see **CHIOSU ME** • 1971
DRACULAS LUSTERNE VAMPIRE • 1970 • D'Alcala Mario • SWT • DRACULA'S VAMPIRE LUST
DRACULA'S SAGA see **SAGA DE LOS DRACULA, LA** • 1972
DRACULA'S VAMPIRE LUST see **DRACULAS LUSTERNE VAMPIRE** • 1970
DRACULA'S VIRGIN LOVERS see **GRAN AMOR DEL CONDE DRACULA, EL** • 1972
DRACULA'S WEDDING DAY • 1967 • Jacobson Mike • SHT • USA
DRACULA'S WIDOW • 1987 • Coppola Christopher • USA
DRAEGERMAN COURAGE • 1937 • King Louis • USA • CAVE-IN, THE (UKN)
DRAFT 258 • 1917 • Cabanne W. Christy • USA
DRAFT HORSE, THE • 1942 • Jones Charles M. • ANS • USA
DRAFTED IN THE DEPOT • 1940 • French Lloyd • SHT • USA
DRAFTEE DAFFY • 1945 • Clampett Robert • ANS • USA
DRAG • 1929 • Lloyd Frank • USA • PARASITES (UKN)
DRAG, THE • 1966 • Koenig Wolf • ANS • CND
DRAG-ALONG DROOPY • 1954 • Avery Tex • ANS • USA
DRAG HARLAN • 1920 • Edwards J. Gordon • USA
DRAGA IRENA • 1970 • Stojanovic Nikola • YGS • DEAR IRENE
DRAGA, THE GYPSY • 1913 • *Rex* • USA
DRAGAM • 1969 • Kenyeres Gabor • HNG • DARLING
DRAGAO DA MALDADE CONTRA O SANTO GUERREIRO, O see **ANTONIO DAS MORTES** • 1969
DRAGEE HAUTE, LA • 1959 • Kerchner Jean • FRN
DRAGEES AU POIVRE • 1963 • Baratier Jacques • FRN, ITL • CONFETTI AL PEPE (ITL) ○ SWEET AND SOUR (USA)
DRAGEN • 1984 • Rostotsky Stanislav • USS, NRW • DRAGON, THE
DRAGENS FANGE • 1984 • Andersen Knut, Rostotsky Stanislav • NRW, USS • CAPTURE OF THE DRAGON, THE
DRAGNET • 1928 • von Sternberg Josef • USA
DRAGNET • 1947 • Goodwins Leslie • USA
DRAGNET • 1954 • Webb Jack • USA
DRAGNET • 1969 • Webb Jack • TVM • USA
DRAGNET • 1987 • Mankiewicz Tom • USA
DRAGNET, THE • 1916 • Beal Frank • SHT • USA
DRAGNET, THE • 1936 • Moore Vin • USA
DRAGNET GIRL see **HIJOSEN NO ONNA** • 1933
DRAGNET PATROL • 1931 • Strayer Frank • USA • LOVE REDEEMED (UKN)
DRAGOMAN, THE • 1916 • Sloman Edward • SHT • USA
DRAGON, THE • 1916 • Pollard Harry • USA
DRAGON, THE • 1974 • Dinov Todor • BUL
DRAGON, THE see **BAJKA O SMOKU** • 1962
DRAGON, THE see **DRAGEN** • 1984
DRAGON AROUND • 1954 • Hannah Jack • ANS • USA
DRAGON BEARD DITCH see **LONGXU GOU** • 1952
DRAGON BRUCE LEE • *Le Bruce* • HKG • CHALLENGE OF THE TIGER
DRAGON BRUCE LEE: PART 2 • *Le Bruce* • HKG
DRAGON CITY see **LUNG-CH'ANG SHIH-JIH** • 1969
DRAGON DE KOMODO, LE • 1958 • Bourdelon • SHT • FRN
DRAGON DIES HARD, THE see **CHIN-SE TAI YANG** • 1976
DRAGON DOWN THE LANE see **ZA HUMNY JE DRAK** • 1982
DRAGON EXPEDITION, THE see **SMOK-XPEDITION** • 1969
DRAGON FEED see **DRACHENFUTTER** • 1987
DRAGON FIST • 1985 • Lo Wei • HKG
DRAGON FLIES, THE see **CHIH TAO HUANG LUNG** • 1975
DRAGON FLY, THE (USA) see **LIBELLULE, LA** • 1901
DRAGON FORCE • 1982 • Key Nam Nam • HKG
DRAGON GATE INN (USA) see **LUNG-MEN K'E-CHEN** • 1966
DRAGON HORSE, THE see **SILK BOUQUET, THE** • 1926
DRAGON INN see **LUNG-MEN K'E-CHEN** • 1966
DRAGON LADY • 1975 • Reed Joel M. • USA
DRAGON LADY see **G.I. EXECUTIONER** • 1971
DRAGON LIVES, THE see **YUNG-CH'UN TA-HSIUNG** • 1978
DRAGON LIVES AGAIN, THE • 1979 • *Leong Bruce* • HKG
DRAGON, LIZARD, BOXER see **DRAGON, THE LIZARD AND THE BOXER, THE**
DRAGON LORD see **LUNG SHAO-YEH** • 1981
DRAGON MASTER see **CANNON FOR CORDOBA** • 1970
DRAGON MURDER CASE, THE • 1934 • Humberstone H. Bruce • USA
DRAGON OF CRACOW, THE see **PRINCESS AND THE DRAGON, THE** • 1948
DRAGON OF KOMODO, THE see **DRAKEN PA KOMODO** • 1938
DRAGON OF PENDRAGON CASTLE, THE • 1950 • Baxter John • UKN
DRAGON ON FIRE • Chiang Hung, Ho Chih-Chiang • HKG
DRAGON PAINTER, THE • 1919 • Worthington William • USA
DRAGON PRINCE, THE • 1930 • Teschner Richard • ANM • AUS
DRAGON RAPIDE • 1985 • Camino Jaime • SPN
DRAGON RETURNS, THE see **DRAK SA VRACIA** • 1967
DRAGON SEED • 1944 • Conway Jack, Bucquet Harold S., Van Dyke W. S. (U/c) • USA
DRAGON SKY (USA) see **OISEAU DE PARADIS, L'** • 1962
DRAGON SQUADS • 1976 • Wang Juan • HKG
DRAGON STORY • 1956 • Tyrlova Hermina • CZC
DRAGON STORY, A see **BRUCE LEE STORY, THE** • 1974
DRAGON SWAMP • 1971 • Lo Wei • HKG
DRAGON TATTOO, THE see **BAKUCHIUCHI IPPIKIRYU** • 1967
DRAGON TATTOO: FULL OF BLOOD see **SHOWA ZANKYODEN: CHIZOME NO KARAJISHI** • 1967
DRAGON THAT WASN'T.. OR WAS HE?, THE • 1983 • ANM • NTH
DRAGON, THE HERO, THE • 1981 • Ho Godfrey • HKG
DRAGON, THE LIZARD AND THE BOXER, THE • Lo Ke • HKG • DRAGON, THE LIZARD, THE BOXER, THE ○ DRAGON, LIZARD, BOXER
DRAGON, THE LIZARD, THE BOXER, THE see **DRAGON, THE LIZARD AND THE BOXER, THE**
DRAGON, THE YOUNG MASTER, THE • Ho Godfrey • HKG
DRAGON ZOMBIES RETURN • 1983 • Hau Ching • HKG
DRAGONARD • 1987 • Kikoine Gerard • MASTER OF DRAGONARD HILL
DRAGONEN • 1925 • Blom August • DNM
DRAGONERLIEBCHEN • 1928 • Walther-Fein Rudolf • FRG
DRAGONES DE HA-LONG, LOS • 1976 • Alvarez Santiago • DOC • CUB
DRAGONFLY • 1976 • Cates Gilbert • USA • ONE SUMMER LOVE
DRAGONFLY, THE see **INEVITABLE, THE** • 1917
DRAGONFLY SQUADRON • 1954 • Selander Lesley • USA
DRAGONNADES SOUS LOUIS XIV, LES • 1909 • Jasset Victorin • SRL • FRN
DRAGONS • 1971 • Aristopoulos Konstantinos • SHT • GRC
DRAGONS see **LITTLE DRAGONS, THE** • 1980
DRAGON'S BLOOD see **SIGFRIDO** • 1959
DRAGON'S BREATH, THE • 1913 • *Weber Lois* • USA
DRAGON'S CLAW see **DRAGON'S CLAWS** • 1974
DRAGON'S CLAW, THE • Cavanaugh John • SHT • USA
DRAGON'S CLAW, THE • 1915 • Taylor Stanner E. V. • USA
DRAGON'S CLAW, THE • 1922 • May Joe
DRAGON'S CLAWS • 1974 • Kong Joseph • HKG • DRAGON'S CLAW
DRAGONS DE VILLARS, LES • 1906 • Blache Alice • FRN
DRAGON'S FANGS, THE • 1967 • JPN
DRAGON'S FOOD see **DRACHENFUTTER** • 1987
DRAGONS FOREVER • 1988 • Hong Jinbao • HKG
DRAGON'S GOLD • 1953 • Wisberg Aubrey, Pollexfen Jack • USA
DRAGON'S GREATEST REVENGE see **BRUCE LEE'S GREATEST REVENGE** • 1978
DRAGON'S LORD, THE see **LUNG SHAO-YEH** • 1981
DRAGON'S NET, THE • 1920 • McRae Henry • SRL • USA
DRAGONS OF DEATH • 1975 • Pascual Jimmy Lo • HKG
DRAGON'S PASS see **TANGE EJDEHA** • 1968
DRAGON'S PREY, THE see **DANGEROUS TRAILS** • 1923
DRAGON'S RETURN, THE see **DRAK SA VRACIA** • 1967
DRAGON'S TEETH, THE see **SHAOLIN TZU-TI** • 1975
DRAGONSLAYER • 1981 • Robbins Matthew • USA, UKN
DRAGONWYCK • 1946 • Mankiewicz Joseph L. • USA
DRAGOON WELLS MASSACRE • 1957 • Schuster Harold • USA
DRAGOSTE LA 0 • 1964 • Saizescu Geo • RMN • LOVE AT FREEZING POINT
DRAGOTZENNYE ZERNA • 1948 • Heifitz Josif, Zarkhi Alexander • USS • PRECIOUS SEEDS, THE ○ PRECIOUS GRAIN
DRAGSTRIP DRACULA • 1962 • Glut Don • USA
DRAGSTRIP GIRL • 1957 • Cahn Edward L. • USA
DRAGSTRIP RIOT • 1958 • Bradley David • USA • RECKLESS AGE, THE (UKN)
DRAGUEURS, LES • 1959 • Mocky Jean-Pierre • FRN • CHASERS, THE (USA) ○ YOUNG HAVE NO MORALS, THE
DRAHOUSEK KLEMENTYNA • 1959 • Brdecka Jiri • ANM • CZC • MY DARLING CLEMENTINE
DRAINS IN THE CITY see **MACHI TO GESUI** • 1953
DRAK SA VRACIA • 1967 • Grecner Eduard • CZC • DRAGON'S RETURN, THE ○ DRAGON RETURNS, THE
DRAKE • 1958 • Topaldgikov Stefan • BUL
DRAKE CASE, THE • 1929 • Laemmle Edward • USA
DRAKE OF ENGLAND • 1935 • Woods Arthur • UKN • DRAKE THE PIRATE (USA) ○ ELIZABETH OF ENGLAND
DRAKE THE PIRATE (USA) see **DRAKE OF ENGLAND** • 1935
DRAKEN PA KOMODO • 1938 • Fejos Paul • DCS • SWD • DRAGON OF KOMODO, THE
DRAKE'S LOVE STORY • 1913 • Plumb Hay • UKN • LOVE ROMANCE OF ADMIRAL SIR FRANCIS DRAKE, THE (USA)
DRAKULA • 1921 • Lajtham Karoly • HNG
DRAKULA ISTANBULDA • 1953 • Muhtar Mehmet • TRK • DRACULA IN ISTANBUL
DRAKUT IL VENDICATORE • 1962 • Capuano Luigi • ITL • REVENGE OF THE CONQUERED (USA)
DRAMA AMONG THE PUPPETS (USA) see **DRAME CHEZ LES FANTOCHES, UNE** • 1908
DRAMA AT THE BOTTOM OF THE SEA, A see **DRAME AU FOND DE LA MER, UN** • 1901
DRAMA DE LA ARISTOCRACIA, UN • 1925 • Saenz De Sicilia Gustavo • MXC
DRAMA DE LUXE • 1927 • Taurog Norman • SHT • USA
DRAMA FROM OLDEN TIMES see **DRAMA IZ STARINNOI ZHIZNI** • 1971
DRAMA IN HEYVILLE, THE • 1914 • Miller Ashley • USA
DRAMA IN THE AIR, A • 1913 • *Pathe* • USA
DRAMA IN THE FUTURIST'S CABARET NO.13 • 1914 • Kasyanov Vladimir • USS
DRAMA IN THE SKY, A see **DRAME DANS LES AIRS, UN** • 1904
DRAMA IZ STARINNOI ZHIZNI • 1971 • Averbach Ilya • USS • DRAMA OF FORMER TIMES, A ○ DRAMA FROM OLDEN TIMES
DRAMA NUEVO, UN • 1946 • de Orduna Juan • SPN
DRAMA OF FORMER TIMES, A see **DRAMA IZ STARINNOI ZHIZNI** • 1971
DRAMA OF GOD see **INDRA LEELA** • 1954
DRAMA OF JEALOUSY (AND OTHER THINGS), A see **DRAMMA DELLA GELOSIA –TUTTI I PARTICOLARI IN CRONACA** • 1970
DRAMA OF JEALOUSY (USA) see **DRAMMA DELLA GELOSIA –TUTTI I PARTICOLARI IN CRONACA** • 1970
DRAMA OF KRISHNA see **KRISHNA LEELA** • 1935
DRAMA OF KRISHNA see **KRISHNA LEELA** • 1945
DRAMA OF THE CASTLE, A see **DRAME AU CHATEAU D'ACRE, UN** • 1915
DRAMA OF THE PRESENT, A • 1910 • *Kalem* • USA
DRAMA OF THE RICH see **FATTI DI GENTE PER BENE** • 1974
DRAMA OF THE SEA see **DRAME EN MER** • 1905
DRAMA ON THE THRESHING FLOOR • Jacoby Georg • FRG
DRAMA PA SLOTTET • 1943 • Ipsen Bodil • DNM
DRAMA VON GLOSSOW, DAS • 1920 • Eckstein Franz • FRG
DRAMA VON MAYERLING, DAS see **TRAGODIE IM HAUSE HABSBURG** • 1924
DRAMA'S DREADFUL DEED • 1917 • *Lampton Skinny* • USA
DRAMATIC DEMISE • 1945 • Anger Kenneth • SHT • USA • DRASTIC DEMISE
DRAMATIC LIFE OF ABRAHAM LINCOLN, THE see **ABRAHAM LINCOLN** • 1924
DRAMATIC MISTAKE, A • 1914 • *Sterling* • USA
DRAMATIC SCHOOL • 1938 • Sinclair Robert B. • USA
DRAMATIC STORY OF THE VOTE, THE • 1913 • Stow Percy • UKN
DRAMATIST'S DREAM, THE • 1909 • *Vitagraph* • USA
DRAME A LA MINE, UN • 1907 • Zecca Ferdinand • FRN
DRAME A LA NANDA DEVI • 1951 • Languepin Jean-Jacques • FRN • ASSAUT DE HIMALAYA, L' ○ ASCENT DE HIMALAYA, L' ○ HIMALAYAN EPIC
DRAME A VENISE, UN • 1907 • Zecca Ferdinand • FRN
DRAME AU CHATEAU D'ACRE, UN • 1915 • Gance Abel • FRN • MORTS REVIENNENT-ILS?, LES ○ DO THE DEAD RETURN ○ DRAMA OF THE CASTLE, A
DRAME AU COLLEGE see **GOSSES MENENT L'ENQUETE, LES** • 1946
DRAME AU FOND DE LA MER, UN • 1901 • Zecca Ferdinand • FRN • DRAMA AT THE BOTTOM OF THE SEA, A
DRAME AU PAYS BASQUE, UN • 1913 • Feuillade Louis • FRN
DRAME AU TELEPHONE, UN • 1914 • Protazanov Yakov • USS
DRAME AU VEL' D'HIV, UN • 1949 • Cam Maurice • FRN
DRAME BEDOUIN • 1965 • Khalifa Omar • SHT • TNS
DRAME CHEZ LES FANTOCHES, UNE • 1908 • Cohl Emile • ANS • FRN • DRAMA AMONG THE PUPPETS (USA) ○ LOVE AFFAIR IN TOYLAND, A ○ MYSTICAL LOVE-MAKING
DRAME DANS LA TEMPETE, UN • 1929 • Diamant-Berger Henri • FRN

DRAME DANS LES AIRS, UN • 1904 • Velle Gaston • FRN • DRAMA IN THE SKY, A

DRAME DE L'HONNEUR, UN • 1914 • Burguet Charles • FRN

DRAME DE LOURDES, LE see **VIERGE DU ROCHER, LA** • 1933

DRAME DE SHANGHAI, LE • 1938 • Pabst G. W. • FRN • SHANGHAI DRAMA, THE

DRAME DU CHATEAU DE SAINT-PRIVAT, LE • 1917 • de Baroncelli Jacques • FRN

DRAME EN MER • 1905 • Velle Gaston • FRN • DRAMA OF THE SEA

DRAME PASSIONEL • 1906 • Zecca Ferdinand • FRN

DRAME SOUS RICHELIEU, UN • 1908 • Bourgeois Gerard • FRN

DRAME SUR LA PLANCHE A CHAUSSURES, UN • 1915 • Cohl Emile • ANS • FRN

DRAME SUR UNE LOCOMOTIVE • 1907 • Durand Jean • FRN

DRAMES DU BOIS DE BOULOGNE, LES • 1947 • Loew Jacques • SHT • FRN

DRAMMA AL CIRCO, UN see **MANEGE** • 1937

DRAMMA AL LUNA PARK see **GIUDICATEMI** • 1948

DRAMMA BORGHESE, UN • 1979 • Vancini Florestano • ITL

DRAMMA DELLA CORONA, IL • 1916 • Genina Augusto • ITL

DRAMMA DELLA GELOSIA -TUTTI I PARTICOLARI IN CRONACA • 1970 • Scola Ettore • ITL, SPN • JEALOUSY, ITALIAN STYLE (USA) ○ PIZZA TRIANGLE, THE (UKN) ○ DRAMA OF JEALOUSY (AND OTHER THINGS), A ○ DRAMA OF JEALOUSY (USA)

DRAMMA DI CRISTO, IL • 1948 • Emmer Luciano, Gras Enrico • ITL

DRAMMA DI UNA NOTTE, IL • 1917 • Caserini Mario • ITL

DRAMMA IGNORATA, UN • 1916 • Ghione Emilio • ITL

DRAMMA NEL PORTO • 1956 • Montero Roberto Bianchi • ITL • ULTIMO ADDIO

DRAMMA NELLA KASBAH (ITL) see **MAN FROM CAIRO, THE** • 1953

DRAMMA SUL TEVERE • 1952 • Boccia Tanio • ITL

DRANEM • 1900-07 • Blache Alice • SER • FRN

DRANGO • 1957 • Bartlett Hall, Bricken Jules • USA

DRANKERSKEN • 1914 • Davidsen Hjalmar • DNM

DRAPEAU BLANC D'OXALA, LE • 1969 • Kast Pierre • FRN • CANDOMBLE ET MACUMBA ○ MACUMBA

DRAPEAU NOIR FLOTTE SUR LA MARMITE, LE • 1971 • Audiard Michel • FRN

DRAPIEZCY • 1990 • Szulkin Piotr • PLN • BEASTS OF PREY

DRASTIC DEMISE see **DRAMATIC DEMISE** • 1945

DRASTIC MEASURES see **ISAAC LITTLE-FEATHERS** • 1985

DRASTIC REMEDY, A • 1914 • *Melies* • USA

DRAT THAT BOY! • 1904 • *Paul R. W.* • UKN

DRAUFGANGER, DER • 1931 • Eichberg Richard • FRG

DRAUGHTSMAN'S CONTRACT, THE • 1982 • Greenaway Peter • UKN

DRAUGHTSMAN'S REVENGE, THE • 1912 • Haldane Bert? • UKN

DRAUPADI • 1939 • Chaudhury Ahindra • IND

DRAUPADI MANASAMRAKSHANAM • 1936 • *Bai Kamala* • IND

DRAVCI • 1948 • Weiss Jiri • CZC • WILD BEASTS ○ BEASTS OF PREY

DRAVE, LA • 1957 • Garceau Raymond • DCS • CND • LOG DRIVE, THE

DRAW! • 1984 • Stern Steven Hilliard • TVM • CND, USA

DRAW-BACK, THE • 1927 • Taurog Norman • SHT • USA

DRAWING, THE • 1912 • *Vitagraph* • USA

DRAWING FOR CATS see **MALOVANI PRO KOCKU** • 1960

DRAWING LESSON, THE (USA) see **STATUE ANIMEE, LA** • 1903

DRAWING THE COLOR LINE • 1909 • *Edison* • USA

DRAWING THE LINE • 1912 • *Rex* • USA

DRAWING THE LINE • 1915 • Eason B. Reeves • USA

DRAWINGS AND WONDERS see **DESSINS ET MERVEILLES** • 1961

DRAWINGS FROM LIFE: CHARLES WHITE • 1980 • *Moss Carlton* • USA

DRAWINGS ON ASPHALT see **DESENE PE ASFALT** • 1989

DRAWN BLIND, THE • 1910 • Batley Ernest G. • UKN

DRAWN BLIND, THE • 1914 • Batley Ethyle? • UKN

DRAWS see **AMERICAN TICKLER OR THE WINNER OF 10 ACADEMY AWARDS** • 1976

DRAYTON CASE, THE • 1953 • Hughes Ken • UKN

DREAD INHERITANCE, THE • 1913 • *Victor* • USA

DREAD PERSUASION, THE see **NARCOTIC STORY, THE** • 1958

DREADED MAFIA, THE see **SALVATORE GIULIANO** • 1962

DREADED TUBE, THE • 1917 • Howard George Bronson • SHT • USA

DREADNOUGHT TO THE RESCUE • 1909 • Rosenthal Joe • UKN

DREAM • 1966 • Cantrill Arthur • SHT • ASL

DREAM see **MECHTA** • 1943

DREAM, A see **HIS PREHISTORIC PAST** • 1914

DREAM, THE • 1911 • *Solax* • USA

DREAM, THE • 1911 • Ince Thomas H., Tucker George Loane • *Imp* • USA

DREAM, THE • 1912 • *Republic* • USA

DREAM, THE • 1913 • *Rex* • USA

DREAM, THE • 1920 • Totten Joseph Byron • SHT • USA

DREAM, THE • *Sibley Antoinette* • UKN

DREAM, THE • 1985 • Verhoeff Pierre • NTH

DREAM, THE see **SAN** • 1966

DREAM A LITTLE DREAM • 1989 • Rocco Marc • USA

DREAM A40 • 1965 • Reckford Lloyd • SHT • UKN

DREAM ABOUT A HOUSE see **ALOM A HAZROL** • 1971

DREAM BABY • 1989 • Pope Angela • TVM • UKN

DREAM BAD, LUCK DITTO • 1915 • Collins Edwin J.? • UKN

DREAM BALLERINA (USA) see **BALLERINA** • 1949

DREAM BOY see **YUMEMI-DOJI** • 1958

DREAM BOY see **DROMPOJKEN** • 1964

DREAM BREAKERS • 1989 • Millar Stuart • TVM • USA

DREAM BRIDGE • 1986 • Than Htut • BRM

DREAM-BRIGADE see **ALOMBRIGAD** • 1983

DREAM CASTLE see **SOME CALL IT LOVING** • 1973

DREAM CASTLES see **SOME CALL IT LOVING** • 1973

DREAM CHASERS • 1984 • Jackson David E., Dubbs Arthur • USA

DREAM CHEATER, THE • 1920 • Warde Ernest C. • USA

DREAM CHILD see **DREAMCHILD** • 1986

DREAM CHILD, THE • 1914 • *Greenwood Winnifred* • USA

DREAM CIRCUS • 1939 • Reiniger Lotte • ANM • UKN

DREAM CITY • 1976 • *Oscarsson Per* • FRG, CZC

DREAM CLOUD • 1971 • Hitchins Hitch • UKN

DREAM COME TRUE, A see **MESHTE NASTRESHU** • 1963

DREAM DANCE, THE • 1915 • Kent Leon D. • USA

DREAM DAYS see **DANI OD SNOVA** • 1981

DREAM DEMON, THE • 1988 • Cokliss Harley • UKN

DREAM DOCTOR, THE • 1936 • Lotinga R. W. • UKN

DREAM DOLL • 1979 • Grgic Zlatko, Godfrey Bob • ANS • UKN • LUTKA SNOVA

DREAM DOLL, THE • 1917 • Moss Howard S. • USA

DREAM DUST • 1949 • *Universal* • SHT • USA

DREAM ENCOUNTER • 1957 • Kostelac Nikola • ANS • YGS • MEETING IN A DREAM

DREAM FACES • 1926 • Croise Hugh • UKN

DREAM FACTORY, THE • 1979 • Finegan Peter • SHT • IRL

DREAM FAIRY, THE • 1913 • Miller Ashley • USA

DREAM FLIGHT see **POLIOTY VO SNE I NAIAVOU** • 1983

DREAM FLIGHTS see **POLIOTY VO SNE I NAIAVOU** • 1983

DREAM FOR CHRISTMAS, A • 1973 • Senensky Ralph • TVM • USA

DREAM GIRL • 1948 • Leisen Mitchell • USA

DREAM GIRL see **FEMME DES REVES, LA** • 1964

DREAM GIRL, THE • 1914 • Santschi Thomas • USA

DREAM GIRL, THE • 1916 • De Mille Cecil B. • USA

DREAM HOLIDAY see **DROMSEMESTER** • 1952

DREAM HOME see **VILLA MON REVE** • 1961

DREAM HOME, THE • 1913 • McGill Lawrence • USA

DREAM HOUSE • 1981 • Hardy Joseph • TVM • USA

DREAM HOUSE, THE • 1932 • *Sennett Mack (P)* • SHT • USA

DREAM IS ALIVE, THE • 1984 • Ferguson Graeme • CND • EN DIRECT DE L'ESPACE

DREAM KIDS, THE • 1944 • Wickersham Bob • ANS • USA

DREAM KNIGHT, THE see **RYTSAR MECHTY** • 1964

DREAM LADY, THE • 1918 • Wilson Elsie Jane • USA

DREAM LIFE see **VIE REVEE, LA** • 1972

DREAM LOVER • 1986 • Pakula Alan J. • USA

DREAM LOVERS see **MENGZHONG REN** • 1985

DREAM MACHINE • 1987 • Kazanjian Howard • USA

DREAM MACHINE, THE see **ESCAPEMENT** • 1957

DREAM MAKER, THE see **IT'S ALL HAPPENING** • 1963

DREAM MAKER, THE see **MAGO DE LOS SUENOS, EL** • 1966

DREAM MAKERS, THE • 1975 • Sagal Boris • TVM • USA

DREAM MATES • 1983 • Allen Tom C. • DOC • CND

DREAM MELODY, THE • 1929 • King Burton L. • USA

DREAM MERCHANT • 1964 • Jordan Larry • SHT • USA

DREAM MERCHANTS, THE • 1980 • Sherman Vincent • TVM • USA

DREAM MOTHER (UKN) see **MIDNIGHT LADY** • 1932

DREAM-NAPPING • 1966 • Bakshi Ralph • ANS • USA

DREAM NEVER DIES, THE • 1981 • Johnson William • DOC • CND

DREAM NO MORE • 1950 • Krumgold Joseph • ISR

DREAM, NYC, THE RETURN, THE FLOWER, THE • 1976 • Brakhage Stan • SHT • USA

DREAM OF A COSSACK see **KAVALER ZOLOTOI ZVEZDY** • 1950

DREAM OF A FATHER see **FADERN** • 1969

DREAM OF A HINDU BEGGAR, THE (USA) see **REVE DU PARIA, LE** • 1902

DREAM OF A LOBSTER FIEND • 1912 • *Hevener Jerold T.* • USA

DREAM OF A MOTION PICTURE DIRECTOR • 1912 • *Lubin* • USA

DREAM OF A NIGHT see **HILM LAYLA** • 1949

DREAM OF A PAINTING, THE • 1914 • *Fazenda Louise* • USA

DREAM OF A RAREBIT FIEND • 1906 • Porter Edwin S. • USA

DREAM OF A WORLD • 1970 • Gosling Nicholas • UKN

DREAM OF AN ARTIST see **MOUNA, OU LE REVE D'UN ARTISTE** • 1969

DREAM OF AN OPIUM FIEND, THE (USA) see **REVE D'UN FUMEUR D'OPIUM, LE** • 1908

DREAM OF BUTTERFLY, THE see **SOGNO DI BUTTERFLY, IL** • 1939

DREAM OF CHRISTMAS see **VANOCNI SEN** • 1945

DREAM OF DAN MCGUIRE, THE • 1913 • Huntley Fred W. • USA

DREAM OF DEATH, A see **DODSDROMMEN** • 1911

DREAM OF EGYPT, A • 1917 • Stedman Marshall • SHT • USA

DREAM OF EUGENE ARAM, THE • 1916 • Campbell Colin • SHT • USA

DREAM OF EUGENE ARAM, THE • 1923 • Greenwood Edwin • UKN

DREAM OF EVIL • 1974 • Hayes John • USA

DREAM OF FAIR WOMEN, A • 1920 • *Getwell Anetha* • SHT • USA

DREAM OF FREEDOM, A see **STRAFF** • 1969

DREAM OF GENERAL SANDINO, THE see **TRAUM DES SANDINO, DER** • 1981

DREAM OF GLORY, A • 1913 • Coleby A. E.? • UKN

DREAM OF HAPPINESS see **LYCKODROMMEN** • 1963

DREAM OF HELL • Bonomi Nardo • ITL

DREAM OF KINGS, A • 1969 • Mann Daniel • USA

DREAM OF LOCO JUAN, THE • 1914 • *Balboa* • USA

DREAM OF LOVE • 1928 • Niblo Fred • USA • ANDRIENNE LECOUVREUR

DREAM OF LOVE • 1967 • Haymeen Benjamin • USA

DREAM OF LOVE • 1970 • *Sakai Wakako* • JPN

DREAM OF LOVE, A • 1938 • Fitzpatrick James A. • UKN

DREAM OF LOVERS, A see **TRAUM DE LIEBENDEN, EIN** • 1964

DREAM OF MY PEOPLE, THE • 1934 • Bloome A. J.

DREAM OF OLD SCROOGE, THE • 1910 • *Cines* • ITL

DREAM OF OLWEN see **WHILE I LIVE** • 1947

DREAM OF PARADISE, A • 1910 • *Wrench Films* • UKN

DREAM OF PASSION, A • 1978 • Dassin Jules • GRC

DREAM OF ROSES, A • 1904 • *Biograph* • USA

DREAM OF SHAKESPEARE, THE see **REVE DE SHAKESPEARE, LE** • 1907

DREAM OF THE BALLET MASTER, THE (UKN) see **REVE DU MAITRE DE BALLET, LE** • 1903

DREAM OF THE CIRCUS, A • 1914 • *Lubin* • USA

DREAM OF THE MOON see **REVE A LA LUNE** • 1905

DREAM OF THE RACETRACK FIEND • 1905 • *Bitzer Billy (Ph)* • USA

DREAM OF THE RED CHAMBER • Li Han-Hsiang • HKG

DREAM OF THE RED CHAMBER '77 see **HUNG LOU MENGHSING** • 1977

DREAM OF THE RED CHAMBER, THE (USA) see **HUNG LOU MENG** • 1966

DREAM OF THE SPHINX • Gore James • ANS • USA

DREAM OF THE STARS • 1953 • Dollens Morris Scott • SHT • USA

DREAM OF THE WILD, A • 1913 • *Darkfeather Mona* • USA

DREAM OF TOMORROW, A see **WAKE UP! OR, A DREAM OF TOMORROW** • 1914

DREAM OF WEALTH, A • 1908 • *Vitagraph* • USA

DREAM OF WINGS, A • Jankovics Marcell • ANS • HNG

DREAM ONE • 1983 • Selignac Arnaud • UKN, FRN

DREAM OR TWO AGO, A • 1916 • Kirkwood James • USA

DREAM PAINTINGS • 1912 • Neame Elwin • UKN

DREAM PATH OF YOUTH, THE (USA) see **SEISHUN NO YUMEJI** • 1922

DREAM PILL, THE • 1910 • *Lubin* • USA

DREAM SEEKERS, THE • 1915 • Horne James W. • USA

DREAM SHIP, THE • 1914 • Pollard Harry • USA

DREAM SLAYER see **DREAMSLAYER** • 1974

DREAM SOUND • 1958 • Heyer John • SHT • ASL

DREAM SPECTRES • 1909 • *Gaumont* • FRN

DREAM STREET • 1921 • Griffith D. W. • USA

DREAM STUFF • 1934 • Beaudine William • SHT • USA

DREAM TEAM, THE • 1989 • Zieff Howard • USA

DREAM THAT CAME TRUE, THE • 1919 • Miller Frank • SHT • UKN

DREAM TO BELIEVE • 1985 • Lynch Paul • CND

DREAM VALLEY see **DROMDA DALEN, DEN** • 1947

DREAM WALK see **DROMMARES VANDRING, EN** • 1957

DREAM WALKING • 1950 • Rasinski Connie • ANS • USA

DREAM WALKING, A • 1934 • Fleischer Dave • ANS • USA

DREAM WALTZ, THE see **SAG DET I TONER** • 1929

DREAM WIFE • 1953 • Sheldon Sidney • USA

DREAM WITHOUT AN END see **DROOM ZONDER EINDE** • 1964

DREAM WITHOUT END see **DROOM ZONDER EINDE** • 1964

DREAM WOMAN, THE • 1914 • Blache Alice • USA

DREAM WORLD OF HARRISON MARKS, THE see **NAKED WORLD OF HARRISON MARKS, THE** • 1967

DREAM YOUNG MAN'S DREAM see **OTOKO NARA YUME O MIRO** • 1959

DREAMANIAC • 1986 • Decoteau David • USA

DREAMBOAT • 1952 • Binyon Claude • USA

DREAMBOATS • 1985 • Wynne Cordell • MTV • CND

DREAMCHILD • 1986 • Millar Gavin • UKN • DREAM CHILD

DREAMER • 1979 • Nosseck Noel • USA

DREAMER, THE • 1915 • Fielding Romaine • USA

DREAMER, THE • 1916 • Hollingsworth Alfred • SHT • USA

DREAMER, THE • 1920 • *West Billy* • SHT • USA

DREAMER, THE • 1976 • Paisz John • CND

DREAMER, THE see **SONADORA, LA** • 1917

DREAMER, THE see **SANJAR** • 1961

DREAMER, THE see **HA'TIMHONI** • 1970

DREAMER, THE (USA) see **MORBIDONE, IL** • 1965

DREAMERS • Andonov Ivan • BUL

DREAMERS see **SVAERMERE** • 1974

DREAMERS, THE • 1912 • *Tennant Barbara* • USA

DREAMERS, THE • 1933 • Cadman Frank • UKN

DREAMERS, THE • 1988 • Barbash Uri • ISR • ONCE WE WERE DREAMERS ○ UNSETTLED LAND

DREAMERS, THE see **FANTASTERNE** • 1967

DREAMER'S WALK, A see **DROMMARES VANDRING, EN** • 1957

DREAMING • 1944 • Baxter John • UKN

DREAMING • 1980 • Vanderbeek Stan • USA

DREAMING see **TRAUMEREI** • 1944

DREAMING, THE • 1988 • Andreacchio Mario • ASL

DREAMING IN THE PARK • 1965 • Carruana Jorge, Rodriguez Luis • ANS • CUB

DREAMING LIPS • 1935 • Garmes Lee, Czinner Paul • UKN

DREAMING LIPS (USA) see **TRAUMENDE MUND, DER** • 1953

DREAMING MOUTH see **TRAUMENDE MUND, DER** • 1932

DREAMING MOUTH see **TRAUMENDE MUND, DER** • 1953

DREAMING OF ROBINSON CRUSOE • 1915 • *Fay Films* • UKN

DREAMING OUT LOUD • 1940 • Young Harold • USA

DREAMING YOUTH see **ALMODO IFJUSAG** • 1974

DREAMLAND • 1937 • Bhatt Vijay • IND

DREAMLAND • 1938 • *Shalini* • ANS • IND

DREAMLAND • 1982 • Saks Mady • NTH

DREAMLAND • 1983 • Scott Oz, Baker Nancy, Schulman Joel • USA

DREAMLAND see **DREAMLAND: A HISTORY OF EARLY CANADIAN MOVIES 1895-1939** • 1974

DREAMLAND: A HISTORY OF EARLY CANADIAN MOVIES 1895-1939 • 1974 • Brittain Don • DOC • CND • DREAMLAND

DREAMLAND ADVENTURES • 1907 • Booth W. R. • UKN

DREAMLAND CAPERS • 1958 • *Wald Harry* • USA • GIRL FROM OUT OF THIS WORLD, THE

DREAMLAND FROLIC, A • 1919 • *Lane Lupino* • SHT • UKN

DREAMLAND IN THE SKY • 1966 • Pojar Bretislav • ANS • CZC

DREAMLAND OF DESIRE see **TRAUMLAND DER SEHNSUCHT** • 1960

DREAMLAND OF GANJADRAO, THE • 1913 • Phalke Dada • SHT • IND

DREAMLAND TRAGEDY, A • 1912 • *Barker Florence* • USA

DREAMS • 1920 • *Claypole Comedies* • USA

DREAMS • 1940 • Feist Felix E. • SHT • USA

DREAMS • 1970 • Fischer Max • NTH

DREAMS • 1973 • Siegel Lois, Passet Jean-Pol • CND

DREAMS • 1990 • Kurosawa Akira • JPN

DREAMS AND NIGHTMARES • 1975 • Osheroff Abe, Klingman Larry • DOC • USA

DREAMS BEYOND MEMORY • 1988 • Markiewicz Andrzej • CND

DREAMS COME TRUE • 1936 • Denham Reginald • UKN

DREAMS COME TRUE • 1960 • Vinyarsky M. • USS

DREAMS COME TRUE • 1985 • Kalmanowicz Max • USA

DREAMS COME TRUE AT NIGHT see **YUME NO YORU HIRAKU** • 1967

DREAMS DIE FIRST • 1979 • USA
DREAMS DON'T DIE • 1982 • Young Roger • TVM • USA
DREAMS DON'T MAKE A NOISE WHEN THEY DIE see **DROEMME STOEJER IKKE, NAAR DE DOER** • 1979
DREAMS GONE WITH THE WIND see **PIRE O ANEMOS TA ONIRA MOU** • 1968
DREAMS IN A PICTURE GALLERY see **MUSEUM SPOOKS** • 1910
DREAMS IN THE DRAWER see **SOGNI NEL CASSETTO, I** • 1957
DREAMS IN THE STREET see **TOSA ONIRA STOUS DROMOUS** • 1968
DREAMS, LIFE AND DEATH OF FILIP FILIPOVIC see **SNOVI, ZIVOT, SMRT FILIPA FILIPOVICA** • 1981
DREAMS LOST, DREAMS FOUND • 1987 • Patterson Willi • TVM • USA
DREAMS MAKE NO NOISE WHEN THEY DIE see **DROEMME STOEJER IKKE, NAAR DE DOER** • 1979
DREAMS OF A POLICEMAN • 1908 • Blackton J. Stuart • USA
DREAMS OF AN OPIUM SMOKER see **REVES D'UN FUMEUR D'OPIUM** • 1906
DREAMS OF DEATH (USA) see **LIEBESTRAUM** • 1951
DREAMS OF G • Bode Boris • USA
DREAMS OF GLASS • 1970 • Clouse Robert • USA
DREAMS OF GLORY see **SUENOS DE GLORIA** • 1952
DREAMS OF GOLD • 1985 • Weston Eric, Garcia Agraz Jose Luis • MXC, USA
DREAMS OF GOLD: THE MEL FISHER STORY • 1986 • Goldstone James • TVM • USA
DREAMS OF HIND AND CAMILIA see **ALHAN HIND WA CAMILIA** • 1987
DREAMS OF LOVE (USA) see **REVES D'AMOUR** • 1946
DREAMS OF MONTE CARLO see **MONTE CARLO** • 1926
DREAMS OF SPRING see **BAHARON KE SAPNE** • 1967
DREAMS OF THE CITY see **AHLAM AL MADINA** • 1984
DREAMS OF THE RAREBIT FIEND • 1921 • McCay Winsor • ASS • USA • ADVENTURES OF A RAREBIT EATER
DREAMS OF THIRTEEN • 1974 • Ray Nicholas (c/d) • USA
DREAMS OF TOYLAND • 1908 • Cooper Arthur • ANM • UKN
DREAMS OF YOU • 1969 • Henriksen R. Lasse • NRW
DREAMS OF YOUTH see **SEISHUN NO YUMEJI** • 1922
DREAMS OF YOUTH see **WAKADO NO YUME** • 1928
DREAMS OF YOUTH see **AHLAM EL CHABAB** • 1943
DREAMS ON ICE • 1939 • Marcus Sid • ANS • USA
DREAMS ON SUNDAY see **SNY NA NEDELI** • 1959
DREAMS REALIZED • 1915 • Cooley Frank • USA
DREAMS THAT MONEY CAN BUY • 1947 • Richter Hans • USA
DREAMS THAT NEVER CAME TRUE see **ONIRO APATILO** • 1968
DREAMS (USA) see **KVINNODROM** • 1955
DREAMS WITHOUT END • 1965 • Lisakovitch Viktor • DOC • USS
DREAMSCAPE • 1984 • Ruben Joseph • USA
DREAMSLAYER • 1974 • Levi Alan J. • USA • HUNTERS, THE ○ DREAM SLAYER
DREAMSPEAKER • 1977 • Jutra Claude • CND
DREAMTOWN see **TRAUMSTADT** • 1973
DREAMWEAVER • 1968 • Rosso Franco, Thomson David • UKN
DREAMWOOD • 1972 • Broughton James • USA
DREAMWORLD see **COVERGIRL** • 1982
DREAMY CHINATOWN • 1920 • *Reelcraft* • SHT • USA
DREAMY DUD • 1916 • *Bray John R. (P)* • SHS • USA
DREAMY DUD HAS A LAUGH ON THE BOSS • 1916 • *Essanay* • SHT • USA
DREAMY DUD IN THE AFRICAN WAR ZONE • 1916 • *Essanay* • SHT • USA
DREAMY DUD JOYRIDING WITH PRINCESS ZLIM • 1916 • *Essanay* • SHT • USA
DREAMY DUD LOST AT SEA • 1916 • *Essanay* • SHT • USA
DREAMY EYES • 1905 • Gilbert Arthur? • UKN
DREAMY JIMMY DREAMS AGAIN • 1914 • Aylott Dave • UKN
DREAMY KNIGHTS • 1916 • *Plump & Runt* • SHT • USA
DREAMY LOVE BED see **CANDY BABY** • 1969
DREARY HOUSE • 1928 • Stone Andrew L. • USA
DRECHT TUNNEL, THE • 1977 • van Eijk Kees, Linschoten Bob • SHT • NTH
DREGS • 1913 • Smiley Joseph • USA
DREGS see **BUNDFALD** • 1957
DREI, DIE see **SEILERGASSE 8** • 1960
DREI AMERIKANISCHE LPS • 1969 • Wenders Wim • SHT • FRG • THREE AMERICANS LP'S
DREI BIRKEN AUF DER HEIDE • 1956 • Erfurth Ulrich • FRG
DREI BLAUE JUNGS -EIN BLONDES MADEL • 1933 • Boese Carl • FRG
DREI DOLCHE IM STEIN • 1920 • Dessauer Siegfried • FRG
DREI DORFHEILIGEN, DIE • 1949 • Dorfler Ferdinand • FRG
DREI FRAUEN see **SEINE DREI FRAUEN** • 1920
DREI FRAUEN VON URBAN HELL, DIE • 1928 • Speyer Jaap • FRG • HELL IN FRAUENSEE
DREI HASELNUSSE FUR ASCHENBRODEL see **TRI ORISKY PRO POPELKU** • 1973
DREI KAISERJAGER • 1933 • Land Robert, Hofer Franz • FRG
DREI KAPITEL GLUCK • 1961 • Beck Walter • GDR • THREE CHAPTERS OF LUCK
DREI KAVALIERE • 1951 • Stockel Joe • FRG
DREI KUCKUCKSUHREN, DIE • 1926 • Mendes Lothar • FRG
DREI LIEBESBRIEFE AUS TIROL • 1962 • Jacobs Werner • AUS
DREI LORRIS, DIE see **GESCHWISTER LORRIS** • 1915
DREI MADCHEN IHR GLUCK see **TEURE HEIMAT** • 1929
DREI MADCHEN VON FINSTERVIERECK, DIE • 1923 • Fiala Hans • FRG
DREI MADELS UND IHRE FREIER see **GLUCK IM WINKEL** • 1927
DREI MADELS VOM RHEIN • 1955 • Jacoby Georg • FRG
DREI MADERL UM SCHUBERT • 1936 • Emo E. W. • FRG • DREIMADERLHAUS
DREI MANN AUF EINEM PFERD • 1957 • Meisel Kurt • FRG
DREI MANN IN EINEN BOOT • 1961 • Weiss Helmut • FRG, AUS
DREI MANNEQUINS, DIE • 1926 • Speyer Jaap • FRG
DREI MANNER IM SCHNEE • 1955 • Hoffmann Kurt • FRG
DREI MARIEN UND DER HERR VON MARANA, DIE see **DON JUAN UND DIE DREI MARIEN** • 1922
DREI MINUTEN VOR ZEHN see **TAT DES ANDREAS HARMER, DIE** • 1930
DREI NACHTE • 1920 • Boese Carl • FRG
DREI NIEMANDSKINDER, DIE • 1927 • Freisler Fritz • FRG
DREI PORTIERMADEL, DIE • 1925 • Boese Carl • FRG
DREI SCHWEDINNEN AUF DER REEPERBAHN • 1980 • Boos Walter • FRG • THREE SWEDISH GIRLS ON THE REEPERBAHN ○ THREE SWEDISH GIRLS IN HAMBURG ○ NYMPHO GIRLS
DREI SCHWEDINNEN IM OBERBAYERN • 1977 • Gotz Siggi • FRG
DREI SEELEN -EIN GEDANKE • 1927 • Sauer Fred • FRG
DREI SUPERMANNER RAUMEN AUF, DIE • 1967 • Parolini Gianfranco • FRG, FRN, ITL • THREE SUPERMEN CLEAN UP, THE
DREI TAGE ANGST • 1952 • Waschneck Erich • FRG
DREI TAGE AUF LEBEN UND TOD • 1929 • Paul Heinz • FRG
DREI TAGE LIEBE • 1931 • Hilpert Heinz • FRG • THREE DAYS OF LOVE (USA)
DREI TAGE MITTELARREST • 1915 • Bernhardt Fritz • FRG
DREI TAGE MITTELARREST • 1930 • Boese Carl • FRG • THREE DAYS IN THE GUARDHOUSE
DREI TAGE MITTELARREST • 1955 • Jacoby Georg • FRG • THREE DAYS IN THE GUARDHOUSE
DREI TANZE DER MARY WILFORD, DIE • 1920 • Wiene Robert • FRG
DREI TOLLE KERLE • 1968 • Albertini Bitto • FRG, ITL • TRE SUPERMEN A TOKIO (ITL) ○ THREE CRAZY FELLOWS
DREI TOLLE MADELS (FRG) see **TRE RAGAZZE VIENNESI** • 1942
DREI TOLLE TAGE • 1936 • Deppe Hans • FRG
DREI UM CHRISTINE, DIE • 1936 • Deppe Hans • FRG
DREI UM EDITH, DIE • 1929 • Waschneck Erich • FRG
DREI UNTEROFFIZIERE • 1939 • Hochbaum Werner • FRG • THREE NON-COMS (USA)
DREI VAN HELLS, DIE • 1918 • Brenken Arthur • FRG
DREI VATER UM ANNA • 1939 • Boese Carl • FRG • THREE FATHERS FOR ANNA (USA)
DREI VATERUNSER FUR VIER HALUNKEN (FRG) see **GRANDE DUELLO, IL** • 1973
DREI VOM VARIETE • 1954 • Neumann Kurt • FRG
DREI VON DENEN MAN SPRICHT see **GLUCK MUSS MAN HABEN** • 1953
DREI VON DER STEMPELSTELLE • 1932 • Thiele Eugen • FRG
DREI VON DER STRASSE, DIE • 1922 • Bock-Stieber Gernot • FRG
DREI VON DER TANKSTELLE, DIE • 1930 • Thiele Wilhelm • FRG • THREE FROM THE GAS STATION, THE ○ THREE MEN AND LILLIAN (UKN) ○ THREE OF THE FILLING STATION, THE
DREI VON DER TANKSTELLE, DIE • 1955 • Wolff Hans, Forst Willi • FRG
DREI WEISSE BIRKEN • 1961 • Albin Hans • FRG
DREI WUNDERSCHONE TAGE • 1939 • Kirchhoff Fritz • FRG
DREI ZIRKUSKONIGE, DIE see **EIN MADEL UND DREI CLOWNS** • 1928
DREIFACH HOCH DEM SANITATSGEFREITEN NEUMANN • 1969 • FRG
DREIGROSCHENOPER, DIE • 1930 • Pabst G. W. • FRG • THREEPENNY OPERA, THE ○ BEGGAR'S OPERA, THE
DREIGROSCHENOPER, DIE • 1962 • Staudte Wolfgang • FRG, FRN • THREEPENNY OPERA, THE
DREIKLANG • 1938 • Hinrich Hans • FRG
DREIKLANG DER NACHT • 1924 • Gerhardt Karl • FRG
DREIMADERLHAUS see **DREI MADERL UM SCHUBERT** • 1936
DREIMADERLHAUS, DAS • 1918 • Oswald Richard • FRG
DREIMADERLHAUS, DAS • 1958 • Marischka Ernst • FRG • HOUSE OF THE THREE GIRLS, THE (USA)
DREIMAL HOCHZEIT • 1941 • von Bolvary Geza • FRG
DREIMAL KLINGELN see **INTIMITATEN** • 1944
DREIMAL KOMODIE • 1945 • Tourjansky Victor • FRG • LIEBESWIRBEL
DREIN VON DER KAVALLARIE • 1932 • Boese Carl • FRG
DREISSIG JAHRE • 1989 • Schaub Christoph • SWT • THIRTY YEARS
DREIZEHN, DIE • 1918 • Halm Alfred • FRG
DREIZEHN AUS STAHL, DIE • 1920 • Guter Johannes • FRG
DREIZEHN MANN UND EINE KANONE • 1938 • Meyer Johannes • FRG
DREIZEHNTE KREUZ, DAS • 1918 • Moest Hubert • FRG
DRENCHED LOVER, THE • 1900 • *Paul R. W.* • UKN
DRENCHED PASSION see **NURETA YOKUJO** • 1972
DRENGE • 1976 • Malmros Nils • DNM • BOYS IN THE DARK ○ BOYS
DRENGEN DER FORSVANT • 1984 • Nyvold Ebbe • DNM • BOY WHO DISAPPEARED, THE
DRENGENE I TORVEMOSSEN • 1943 • Henning-Jensen Bjarne • DNM
DRESDEN DOLL see **DANCING DOLL, THE** • 1922
DRESS, THE • 1902 • Manuel Eugene • FRN
DRESS, THE • 1967 • Ne'Eman Yehuda • SHT • ISR
DRESS, THE • 1969 • Ne'Eman Yehuda • ISR
DRESS, THE • 1984 • Sereny Eva • SHT • UKN
DRESS, THE (UKN) see **KLANNINGEN** • 1964
DRESS GRAY • 1986 • Jordan Glenn • TVM • USA
DRESS OF LOLITA, THE • 1913 • *Hunt Irene* • USA
DRESS PARADE • 1927 • Crisp Donald • USA
DRESS PARADE • 1939 • Clemens William • USA • DEAD END KIDS ON DRESS PARADE, THE ○ ON DRESS PARADE
DRESS REFORM • 1913 • *White Pearl* • USA
DRESS REHEARSAL, THE • 1949 • Gilkison Anthony • UKN
DRESS REVERSAL • 1965 • Bakshi Ralph • ANS • USA
DRESS SUITS IN PAWN • 1912 • *Edison* • USA
DRESSED AS A BRIDE see **VESTIDA DE NOVIA** • 1966
DRESSED IN BLUE see **VESTIDA DE AZUL** • 1984
DRESSED TO KILL • 1928 • Cummings Irving • USA
DRESSED TO KILL • 1941 • Forde Eugene J. • USA
DRESSED TO KILL • 1946 • Neill R. William • USA • SHERLOCK HOLMES AND THE SECRET CODE (UKN)
DRESSED TO KILL • 1980 • De Palma Brian • USA
DRESSED TO THRILL • 1935 • Lachman Harry • USA • DRESSMAKER, THE
DRESSEL FAMILY, THE see **FAMILIA DRESSEL, LA** • 1935
DRESSER, THE • 1983 • Yates Peter • UKN
DRESSIERTE FRAU, DIE • 1972 • Hofbauer Ernst • FRG
DRESSMAKER, THE • 1988 • O'Brien Jim • UKN
DRESSMAKER, THE see **DRESSED TO THRILL** • 1935
DRESSMAKER FROM PARIS, THE • 1925 • Bern Paul • USA
DRESZCZE • 1981 • Marczewski Wojciech • PLN • SHIVERS (USA) ○ CREEPS
DREVO ZHELANYA • 1976 • Abuladze Tengiz • USS • WISHING TREE, THE ○ NATVRIS KHE
DREWNIANY ROZANIEC • 1965 • Petelska Ewa, Petelski Czeslaw • PLN • WOODEN ROSARY, THE
DREYFUS • 1930 • Oswald Richard • FRG
DREYFUS • 1931 • Kraemer F. W., Rosmer Milton • UKN • DREYFUS CASE, THE (USA)
DREYFUS AFFAIR, THE see **AFFAIRE DREYFUS, L'** • 1899
DREYFUS ALLANT DU LYCEE DE RENNES A LA PRISON • 1899 • Melies Georges • FRN
DREYFUS CASE, THE (USA) see **DREYFUS** • 1931
DREYFUS COURT MARTIAL see **AFFAIRE DREYFUS, L'** • 1899
DREYFUS, L'INTOLERABLE VERITE • 1973 • Cherasse Jean-A. • DOC • FRN
DRIBBLE • De Gaetano Michael A. • USA
DRIBBLE DRABBLE • 1968 • Bartsch Art • ANS • USA
DRIE VAN DER MERWES, DIE • 1970 • SAF
DRIE WENSCHEN see **TRE DESIDERI, I** • 1937
DRIE WENSEN, DE (NTH) see **TRE DESIDERI, I** • 1937
DRIFT, A • 1911 • *Young Lucille* • USA
DRIFT, THE • 1914 • *Marion Leonard Players* • USA
DRIFT FENCE • 1936 • Lovering Otho • USA • TEXAS DESPERADOES
DRIFTER • 1975 • Rocco Pat • USA
DRIFTER, THE • 1916 • Garrick Richard • USA
DRIFTER, THE • 1917 • Kelsey Fred A. • SHT • USA
DRIFTER, THE • 1922 • Maloney Leo, Beebe Ford • USA
DRIFTER, THE • 1929 • De Lacy Robert • USA • TWO BIG VAGABONDS (UKN)
DRIFTER, THE • 1932 • O'Connor William A. • USA
DRIFTER, THE • 1944 • Newfield Sam • USA
DRIFTER, THE • 1967 • Matter Alex • USA
DRIFTER, THE • 1988 • Brand Larry • USA
DRIFTER, THE see **GALLOPING ACE, THE** • 1924
DRIFTERS • 1929 • Grierson John • DOC • UKN
DRIFTERS, THE • 1919 • Hampton Jesse D. • USA
DRIFTERS, THE see **VITELLONI, I** • 1953
DRIFTERS DESUYO see **TOTTE TOTTE TORIMAKURE** • 1968
DRIFTIN' KID, THE • 1941 • Tansey Robert • USA
DRIFTIN' RIVER • 1946 • Tansey Robert • USA
DRIFTIN' SANDS • 1928 • Fox Wallace • USA
DRIFTIN' THRU • 1926 • Dunlap Scott R. • USA
DRIFTING • 1911 • *Lubin* • USA
DRIFTING • 1915 • *Alhambra* • USA
DRIFTING • 1915 • Bartlett Charles • *American* • USA
DRIFTING • 1923 • Browning Tod • USA
DRIFTING • 1976 • Ricketson James • SHT • ASL
DRIFTING • Guttman Amos • ISR
DRIFTING see **FORBIDDEN** • 1953
DRIFTING ALONG • 1946 • Abrahams Derwin • USA
DRIFTING AVENGER, THE see **KOYA NO TOSEININ** • 1968
DRIFTING BOYS see **SHONEN HYORYUKI** • 1960
DRIFTING CLOUDS see **WAKARE-GUMO** • 1951
DRIFTING HEARTS • 1914 • *Fischer Marguerite* • USA
DRIFTING KID, THE • 1928 • *Maynard Tex* • USA
DRIFTING ON • 1927 • *Bay Tom* • USA
DRIFTING SOULS • 1932 • King Louis • USA
DRIFTING UPSTREAM see **ENTRE LA MER ET L'EAU DOUCE** • 1967
DRIFTING WEEDS see **UKIGUSA** • 1959
DRIFTING WESTWARDS • 1939 • Hill Robert F. • USA
DRIFTWOOD • 1912 • *Selig* • USA
DRIFTWOOD • 1912 • Dwan Allan • *American* • USA
DRIFTWOOD • 1916 • Farnum Marshall • USA
DRIFTWOOD • 1924 • *Ferguson Al* • USA
DRIFTWOOD • 1928 • Cabanne W. Christy • USA
DRIFTWOOD • 1948 • Dwan Allan • USA • HEAVEN FOR JENNY
DRIFTWOOD OF THE CITY see **TREIBGUT DER GROSSTADT** • 1967
DRILLER KILLER • 1979 • Ferrara Abel • USA
DRILLINGE AN BORD • 1959 • Muller Hans • FRG
DRILLS AND THRILLS see **ONE PUNCH O'DAY** • 1926
DRINGUE • 1954 • Barth-Moglia Luis • ARG
DRINGUE, CASTRITO Y LA LAMPARA DE ALADINO • 1954 • Barth-Moglia Luis • ARG
DRINK • 1907 • Fitzhamon Lewin • UKN
DRINK • 1917 • Morgan Sidney • UKN
DRINK see **FACE ON THE BARROOM FLOOR, THE** • 1923
DRINK! A GOOD TEMPERANCE STORY see **DELIRIUM TREMENS, LE** • 1907
DRINK AND REPENTANCE • 1905 • Green Tom? • UKN
DRINK CURE, A • 1907 • Coleby A. E.? • UKN
DRINK HEARTY • 1920 • Roach Hal • SHT • USA
DRINK HEARTY • 1946 • Crouch William Forest • SHT • USA
DRINK NO LONGER WATER • 1979 • Fraser Chris • DOC • ASL
DRINK THE MOON • 1981 • Foster Mark • ASL
DRINKER'S DREAM, THE see **REVE D'UN BUVEUR, LE** • 1898
DRINKING see **PIJANSTWO** • 1958
DRINKING MAN'S WAR, THE see **SVERIGE AT SVENSKARNA** • 1980
DRINK'S LURE • 1913 • *Mcdowell Claire* • USA
DRINK'S LURE, THE • 1912 • Cabanne W. Christy • USA
DRINKS ON THE MOUSE • 1953 • Tendlar Dave • ANS • USA
DRIP-ALONG DAFFY • 1951 • Jones Charles M. • ANS • USA
DRIP DIPPY DONALD • 1948 • King Jack • ANS • USA
DRIPPING DEEP RED see **PROFONDO ROSSO** • 1975
DRIPPING WATER • 1969 • Snow Michael, Wieland Joyce • USA
DRIPPY MISSISSIPPI • 1951 • Kneitel Seymour • ANS • USA
DRIPS AND STRIPS • 1961-65 • Menken Marie • SHT • USA
DRISHTI • 1990 • Nihalani Govind • IND • VISION

DRITTE, DER • 1972 • Gunther Egon • GDR • THIRD ONE, THE ○ THIRD, THE
DRITTE, LE • 1958 • Amendola Mario • ITL
DRITTE ESKADRON, DIE • 1926 • Wilhelm Carl • FRG
DRITTE GENERATION, DER • 1979 • Fassbinder R. W. • FRG • THIRD GENERATION, THE (USA)
DRITTE GESCHLECHT, DAS see **ANDERS ALS DU UND ICH** • 1957
DRITTE GRAD, DER • 1975 • Fleischmann Peter • FRG
DRITTE VON RECHTS, DER • 1950 • von Cziffra Geza • FRG
DRITTI, I • 1957 • Amendola Mario • ITL
DRIVE A CROOKED ROAD • 1954 • Quine Richard • USA
DRIVE FOR A LIFE, THE • 1909 • Griffith D. W. • USA
DRIVE HARD, DRIVE FAST • 1969 • Heyes Douglas • TVM • USA
DRIVE, HE SAID • 1972 • Nicholson Jack • USA
DRIVE-IN • 1976 • Amateau Rod • USA
DRIVE-IN MASSACRE • 1976 • Segall Stuart • USA
DRIVE ON NUDNIK • 1965 • Deitch Gene • ANS • USA
DRIVE TO WIN, THE see **SHA OU** • 1981
DRIVEN • 1916 • Elvey Maurice • UKN • DESPERATION (USA)
DRIVEN • 1923 • Brabin Charles J. • USA
DRIVEN BY FATE • 1915 • Adolfi John G. • USA
DRIVEN BY HUNGER • 1915 • Evans Fred • UKN
DRIVEN FROM HOME • 1904 • *Mitchell & Kenyon* • UKN
DRIVEN FROM HOME • 1909 • *Lubin* • USA
DRIVEN FROM HOME • 1925 • Butler Alexander • UKN
DRIVEN FROM HOME • 1927 • Young James • USA
DRIVEN FROM HOME see **AUSTREIBUNG, DIE** • 1923
DRIVEN FROM THE RANCH • 1912 • *Gaumont* • USA
DRIVEN OUT OF PARADISE see **IZGONEN OT RAYA** • 1967
DRIVEN OUT OF PARADISE see **KHOUROUG MIN EL GUANA, EL** • 1967
DRIVEN TO EXTRACTION • 1963 • Bartsch Art • ANS • USA
DRIVER, THE • 1978 • Hill Walter • USA
DRIVER DAGG FALLER REGN • 1946 • Edgren Gustaf • SWD • IF DEW FALLS RAIN FOLLOWS ○ SUNSHINE FOLLOWS RAIN
DRIVER OF THE DEADWOOD COACH • 1912 • *West William H.* • USA
DRIVER OF THE RISK CATEGORY see **JEZDEC FORMULE RISK** • 1973
DRIVERS IN CHAINS see **OKOVANI SOFERI** • 1976
DRIVER'S SEAT, THE (USA) see **IDENTIKIT** • 1974
DRIVERS TO HELL see **WILD ONES ON WHEELS** • 1967
DRIVIN' FOOL, THE • 1923 • Thornby Robert T. • USA
DRIVING ACADEMY • 1988 • Scott Oz • USA
DRIVING CATTLE TO PASTURE • 1904 • Porter Edwin S. • USA
DRIVING HOME THE COWS • 1911 • Olcott Sidney • USA
DRIVING IN THE NIGHT see **TUR I NATTEN** • 1968
DRIVING MISS DAISY • 1989 • Beresford Bruce • USA
DRIVING SCHOOL • 1987 • Stephan Bernhard • GDR
DRIVING SCHOOL • 1990 • Hafsham Othman • MLY
DRIVING TEST • 1958 • Godfrey Bob • SHT • UKN
DRIVING TO A SYSTEM • 1968 • Baker David • DOC • ASL
DRIZZLE see **LLOVIZNA** • 1977
DROEMME STOEJER IKKE, NAAR DE DOER • 1979 • Thomsen Christian Braad • DNM • DREAMS DON'T MAKE A NOISE WHEN THEY DIE ○ DREAMS MAKE NO NOISE WHEN THEY DIE
DROGA • 1971 • Kijowicz Miroslaw • ANS • PLN • ROAD, THE
DROGA DO JEDNOSCI • 1948 • Bossak Jerzy • DOC • PLN • ROAD TO UNITY, THE
DROGA DO NIEBA • 1958 • Ronisz Wincenty, Zanussi Krzysztof • PLN • STREETCAR TO HEAVEN ○ WAY TO THE SKIES, THE
DROGA MALDITA, LA see **OPIO** • 1949
DROGA MLODYCH • 1935 • Ford Aleksander • PLN • STREET OF THE YOUNG ○ CHILDREN MUST LAUGH ○ ROAD FOR YOUTH, THE
DROGA NA FRONT • 1975 • Konic Andrzej • PLN • WAY TO THE FRONT, THE
DROGA NA ZACHOD • 1961 • Poreba Bohdan • PLN • ROAD WEST, THE ○ WESTWARD
DROGUE DU VICE, LA • 1963 • Benazeraf Jose • FRN • NIGHT OF LUST (USA) ○ CONCERTO DE LA PEUR, LA ○ NOTTE EROTIQUE ○ NIGHT OF LOVE
DROHENDE FAUST, DIE • 1921 • Eichgrun Bruno • FRG
DROHENDE WOLKEN AM FIRMAMENT • 1918 • *Andra Fern* • FRG
DROIT A LA VIE, LE • 1916 • Gance Abel • FRN
DROIT D'AIMER, LE • 1972 • Le Hung Eric • FRN, ITL • DIRITTO D'AMARE, IL (ITL) ○ RIGHT TO LOVE, THE ○ BRAINWASHED
DROIT DE CUISSAGE • 1979 • Bernard-Aubert Claude • FRN
DROIT DE L'ENFANT, LE • 1914 • Pouctal Henri • FRN
DROIT DE L'ENFANT, LE • 1948 • Daroy Jacques • FRN
DROIT DE TUER, LE • 1920 • Maudru Charles • FRN
DROIT DE VISITE • 1966 • Garrel Philippe • SHT • FRN
DROLE DE BALLADE, UNE • 1977 • Lavoie Richard • CND
DROLE DE BOURRIQUE, UNE • 1969 • Canolle Jean • FRN
DROLE DE CAID, UN see **SOURIS CHEZ LES HOMMES, UNE** • 1964
DROLE DE COLONEL, UN • 1968 • Girault Jean • FRN
DROLE DE DIAM'S see **LAISSE-MOI REVER** • 1978
DROLE DE DIMANCHE, UN • 1958 • Allegret Marc • FRN • SUNDAY ENCOUNTER (USA)
DROLE DE DRAME • 1937 • Carne Marcel • FRN • BIZARRE BIZARRE (USA) ○ AFFAIRE MOLYNEUX, L'
DROLE DE JEU • 1968 • Kast Pierre • FRN • MOST DANGEROUS GAME, THE
DROLE DE NOCE • 1952 • Joannon Leo • FRN
DROLE DE PAROISSIEN, UN • 1963 • Mocky Jean-Pierre • FRN • THANK HEAVEN FOR SMALL FAVORS (USA) ○ FUNNY PARISHIONER, THE ○ HEAVEN SENT (UKN) ○ DEO GRATIS
DROLE D'ENDROIT POUR UNE RENCONTRE • 1988 • Dupeyron Francoise • FRN • STRANGE PLACE TO MEET, A (UKN)
DROLES DE BOBINES • 1957 • Pialat Maurice • SHT • FRN
DROLES DE PHENOMENES • 1958 • Vernay Robert • FRN • CES CHERS PETITS
DROLES DE ZEBRES • 1977 • Lux Guy • FRN
DROLESSE, LA • 1979 • Doillon Jacques • FRN • HUSSY, THE (USA)
DROLL STORIES see **COSE DA PAZZI** • 1954
DROM OM FRIHET, EN see **STRAFF** • 1969
DROMDA DALEN, DEN • 1947 • Sucksdorff Arne • DCS • SWD • DREAM VALLEY ○ TALE OF THE FJORDS ○ SORIA-MORIA
DROMI TIS AGAPIS INE NICHTERIN, I • 1981 • Liappa Frieda • GRC • LOVE WANDERS IN THE NIGHT ○ NIGHT ROADS OF LOVE, THE
DROMMARES VANDRING, EN • 1957 • Lindgren Lars-Magnus • SWD • ENDONMARES VANDRING ○ DREAMER'S WALK, A ○ DREAM WALK
DROMMEN OM AMERIKA • 1976 • Abrahamsen Christer • SWD • AMERICAN DREAM, THE
DROMMESLOTTET • 1984 • Wam Svend, Vennerod Petter • NRW • CASTLE IN THE AIR
DROMPOJKEN • 1964 • Falck Karin • SWD • ANTE I DROMPOJKEN ○ DREAM BOY
DROMSEMESTER • 1952 • Bernhard Gosta • SWD • DREAM HOLIDAY
DROOLER'S DELIGHT • 1949 • Lundy Dick • ANS • USA
DROOM ZONDER EINDE • 1964 • de Haas Max • NTH • DREAM WITHOUT AN END ○ DREAM WITHOUT END
DROOPY • 1943-57 • ASS • USA
DROOPY LEPRECHAUN • 1958 • Lah Michael • ANS • USA
DROOPY'S DOUBLE TROUBLE • 1951 • Avery Tex • ANS • USA
DROOPY'S GOOD DEED • 1951 • Avery Tex • ANS • USA
DROP, THE • Sorescu Maria • ANS • RMN
DROP A BOMB ON THE PALESTINIANS • 1982 • Sluizer George • DOC • NTH
DROP DEAD, DARLING • 1966 • Hughes Ken • UKN • ARRIVEDERCI, BABY (USA) ○ MY LAST DUCHESS
DROP DEAD DEAREST see **I MISS YOU, HUGS AND KISSES** • 1978
DROP DEAD, MY LOVE see **MARITO E MIO E L'AMMAZZO QUANDO MI PARE, IL** • 1967
DROP KICK, THE • 1927 • Webb Millard • USA • GLITTER
DROP OF BLOOD, A • 1913 • *Solax* • USA
DROP OF BLOOD, THE • 1913 • Thompson Frederick A. • *Vitagraph* • USA
DROP OF POISON, A • 1965 • Makhnach Leonid • DOC • USS
DROP OF WATER, A (USA) see **VANDRABEN** • 1969
DROP OUT • 1970 • Verstappen Wim • NTH
DROP-OUT FATHER • 1982 • Taylor Don • TVM • USA
DROP-OUT MOTHER • 1988 • Dubin Charles S. • TVM • USA
DROP OUTS, THE • 1969 • USA
DROP THAT TURNED INTO A PEARL, THE see **BOOND JO BAN GAYE MOTI** • 1968
DROP THEM OR I'LL SHOOT (UKN) see **SPECIALISTI, GLI** • 1969
DROP TO MUCH, A see **PICK-POCKET ET POLICEMAN** • 1899
DROP TOO MUCH, A (USA) see **OSKLENICKU VIC** • 1954
DROPIASMENI (SAPILA KE ARISTOKRATIA) • 1967 • Karayannis Kostas • GRC • DISGRACED (CORRUPTION AND ARISTOCRACY), THE
DROPOUT • 1971 • Brass Tinto • ITL
DROPPED FROM THE CLOUDS • 1909 • *Gaumont* • FRN
DROPPED FROM THE CLOUDS • 1917 • McRae Henry • SHT • USA
DROPPED INTO SCANDAL • 1919 • Hutchinson Craig • USA
DROPPINGTON'S DEVILISH DREAM • 1915 • Henderson Dell • USA
DROPPINGTON'S FAMILY TREE • 1915 • Henderson Dell • USA
DROPS OF BLOOD (UKN) see **MULINO DELLE DONNE DI PIETRA, IL** • 1960
DROSKE 519 • 1909 • Larsen Viggo • DNM • CAB NO.519 ○ SHERLOCK HOLMES FIVE
DROSO I ARHONTOPOULA • 1968 • Katsimitsoulias Andreas • GRC • DROSO, THE RICH MAN'S DAUGHTER ○ BACK TO MY VILLAGE
DROSO, THE RICH MAN'S DAUGHTER see **DROSO I ARHONTOPOULA** • 1968
DROSS AND DIAMONDS • 1916 • *Wehlen Emmy* • SHT • USA
DROTTNINGEN AV PELLAGONIEN • 1927 • Wallen Sigurd • SWD • QUEEN OF PELLAGONIA, THE
DROTTNINGHOLM PALACE THEATRE, THE see **DROTTNINGHOLMS SLOTTSTEATER** • 1965
DROTTNINGHOLMS SLOTTSTEATER • 1965 • Fischer Gunnar • SHT • SWD • DROTTNINGHOLM PALACE THEATRE, THE
DROUGHT see **VIDAS SECAS** • 1963
DROUGHT see **SUSZA** • 1969
DROUGHT see **BARRA** • 1979
DROUPADI VASTRAPAHARAN • 1935 • IND
DROVER'S SWEETHEART, THE • 1911 • Gavin John F. • ASL
DROVER'S WIFE, THE • 1968 • Gow Keith • SHT • ASL
DROWNED • 1956 • Zalakevicius Vitautus • SHT • USS • DROWNED MAN, A
DROWNED MAN, A see **DROWNED** • 1956
DROWNING BY NUMBERS • 1988 • Greenaway Peter • UKN, NTH
DROWNING IN THE SHALLOW END • 1989 • Gregg Colin • UKN
DROWNING POOL, THE • 1975 • Rosenberg Stuart • USA
DROWSY DICK DREAMS HE'S A BURGLAR • 1910 • Martinek H. O. • UKN
DROWSY DICK'S DREAM • 1909 • Martinek H. O. • UKN
DRRA PA -EN KUL GREJ HANDE PA VAG TILL GOTET • 1967 • Wallman Hasse • SWD • FUNNY THING HAPPENED ON THE WAY TO GOTHENBURG, A
DRSNA PLANINA • 1980 • Soukup Jaroslav • CZC • ROUGH PLATEAU
DRUDGE, THE • 1914 • Johnson Tefft • USA
DRUDGE, THE • 1917 • Mong William V. • SHT • USA
DRUG ADDICT • 1948 • Anderson Robert • DCS • CND
DRUG ADDICT see **PENAGIH DADAH** • 1977
DRUG CLERK, THE • 1915 • *Essanay* • USA
DRUG MOI, KOLKA • 1961 • Mitta Alexander, Saltykov Alexei • USS • MY FRIEND, KOLKA! ○ KOLKA
DRUG MONSTER, THE • 1923 • *Warning Films* • USA
DRUG PREDSEDNIK CENTARFOR • 1960 • Skrigin Zorz • YGS • DRUG PREDSEDNIK CENTRE FORWARD
DRUG PREDSEDNIK CENTRE FORWARD see **DRUG PREDSEDNIK CENTARFOR** • 1960
DRUG QUEEN, THE see **TA TU HOU** • 1976
DRUG STORE COWBOY • 1925 • Frame Park • USA
DRUG TERROR, THE • 1914 • *Lubin* • USA
DRUG TRAFFIC • 1923 • Cummings Irving • USA
DRUG TRAFFIC, THE • 1914 • *Walpole Stanley* • USA
DRUGA GENERACIJA • 1983 • Zilnik Zelimir • YGS • SECOND GENERATION, THE
DRUGA STRANA MEDALJE • 1965 • Hadzic Fadil • YGS • OTHER SIDE OF THE MEDAL, THE
DRUGARCINE • 1980 • Milosevic Mica • YGS • PALS, THE
DRUGE • 1973 • Tadic Zoran • SHT • YGS • FRIENDS
DRUGGED WATERS • 1916 • Dowlan William C. • USA
DRUGGIST'S DILEMMA, THE • 1933 • Sandrich Mark • SHT • USA
DRUGI BRZEG • 1962 • Kuzminski Zbigniew • PLN • OTHER BANK, THE ○ ANOTHER SHORE
DRUGI COVEK • 1989 • Zivkovic Milan • YGS • OTHER MAN, THE
DRUGI CZLOWIEK • 1961 • Nalecki Konrad • PLN • OTHER MAN, THE ○ NEW MAN, THE
DRUGOI I STALIN • 1989 • Lopatin V. • USS • OTHERS AND STALIN
DRUGOTO SHTASTIE • 1960 • Marinovich Anton • BUL • OTHER HAPPINESS, THE
DRUGSTORE COWBOY • 1989 • Van Sant Gus • USA
DRUHA SMENA • 1940 • Fric Martin • CZC • SECOND TOUR (USA) ○ SECOND SHIFT, THE ○ SECOND LAWYER ○ SECOND PART
DRUHA TAH PESCEM • 1985 • Olmer Vit • CZC • SECOND MOVE WITH A PAWN, THE
DRUIDES, LES • 1906 • Blache Alice • FRN
DRUM • 1976 • Carver Steve • USA
DRUM, THE • Dinov Todor • ANS • BUL
DRUM, THE • 1924 • Hill Sinclair • UKN
DRUM, THE • 1937 • Korda Zoltan • UKN • DRUMS (USA)
DRUM, THE • 1952 • Brummer Richard S. • SHT • USA
DRUM BEAT • 1954 • Daves Delmer • USA
DRUM CRAZY (UKN) see **GENE KRUPA STORY, THE** • 1960
DRUM OF TABU, THE (USA) see **TABU (FUGITIVOS DE LAS ISLAS DEL SUR)** • 1966
DRUM ROLL • 1961 • Tendlar Dave • ANS • USA
DRUM-STICKED • 1962 • Hanna William, Barbera Joseph • ANS • USA
DRUM TAPS • 1933 • McGowan J. P. • USA
DRUM UP A TENANT • 1963 • Kneitel Seymour • ANS • USA
DRUMBEATS see **BEI BARABAN** • 1962
DRUMBEATS OF BATTLE see **RANABHERI** • 1968
DRUMMER, THE • 1912 • *Hale Allen* • USA
DRUMMER, THE • 1956 • Eisimont Viktor • USS
DRUMMER, THE see **TROMMLER, DER** • 1969
DRUMMER BOY OF SHILOH, THE • 1911 • *Yankee* • USA
DRUMMER GIRL OF VICKSBURG, THE • 1912 • *Cooper Marian* • USA
DRUMMER MAN • 1947 • Cowan Will • SHT • USA
DRUMMER OF THE EIGHTH, THE • 1913 • Ince Thomas H. • USA
DRUMMER OF VENGEANCE see **GIORNO DEL GIUDIZIO, IL** • 1971
DRUMMER'S HONEYMOON, THE • 1913 • *Coxen Ed* • USA
DRUMMER'S NARROW ESCAPE, THE • 1913 • *Lubin* • USA
DRUMMER'S NOTE BOOK, THE • 1913 • Smalley Phillips • USA
DRUMMER'S TRUNK, THE • 1915 • Douglass James • USA
DRUMMER'S UMBRELLA, THE • 1913 • *Essanay* • USA
DRUMMER'S VACATION, THE • 1912 • Sennett Mack • USA
DRUMS • 1958 • Barfod Bent • ANS • DNM
DRUMS • 1961 • Casparius Hans G. • UKN
DRUMS • 1964 • Novak Ivo • CZC
DRUMS see **TAMBOURS** • 1968
DRUMS ACROSS THE RIVER • 1954 • Juran Nathan • USA
DRUMS ALONG THE AMAZON (UKN) see **ANGEL ON THE AMAZON** • 1948
DRUMS ALONG THE MOHAWK • 1939 • Ford John • USA
DRUMS IN THE DEEP SOUTH • 1951 • Menzies William Cameron • USA
DRUMS O' VOODOO • 1934 • Hoerl Arthur • USA
DRUMS OF AFRICA • 1963 • Clark James B. • USA
DRUMS OF ARABY see **ARABIA** • 1922
DRUMS OF DESTINY • 1937 • Taylor Ray • USA
DRUMS OF DESTINY • 1961 • Michael George • SAF
DRUMS OF DESTINY see **DRUMS OF FATE** • 1923
DRUMS OF FATE • 1923 • Maigne Charles • USA • DRUMS OF DESTINY
DRUMS OF FU MANCHU • 1940 • Witney William, English John • SRL • USA
DRUMS OF JEOPARDY • 1931 • Seitz George B. • USA • MARK OF TERROR
DRUMS OF JEOPARDY, THE • 1923 • Dillon Eddie • USA
DRUMS OF LOVE • 1928 • Griffith D. W. • USA
DRUMS OF TAHITI • 1954 • Castle William • USA
DRUMS OF THE CONGO • 1942 • Cabanne W. Christy • USA
DRUMS OF THE DESERT • 1927 • Waters John • USA
DRUMS OF THE DESERT • 1940 • Waggner George • USA
DRUMS OF THE JUNGLE • 1935 • Terwilliger George W. • USA • OUANGA (UKN) ○ CRIME OF VOODOO
DRUMS (USA) see **DRUM, THE** • 1937
DRUMSTICKS • 1910 • Trimble Larry • USA
DRUNK • 1965 • Warhol Andy • USA
DRUNK DRIVING • 1939 • Miller David • SHT • USA
DRUNK MONKEY IN THE TIGER'S EYES see **TSUI CH'UAN** • 1979
DRUNK OF THE PORT, THE see **METHISTAKAS TOU LIMANIOU, O** • 1967
DRUNK THAT CAME BACK, THE see **KAETTE KITA YOPPARAI** • 1968
DRUNKARD, THE • 1935 • Herman Al • USA
DRUNKARD, THE see **METHYSTAKAS, O** • 1950
DRUNKARD, THE see **KONYAKCI** • 1965
DRUNKARD, THE see **AKSAMCI** • 1967

DRUNKARD AND INVENTOR (USA) see **POCHARD ET L'INVENTEUR, LE** • 1902
DRUNKARDS, THE see **IVROGNES, LES** • 1896
DRUNKARD'S CHILD, THE • 1909 • *Lubin* • USA
DRUNKARD'S CONVERSION, THE • 1901 • Booth W. R. • UKN • HORRORS OF DRINK, THE
DRUNKARD'S DREAM, A • 1908 • *Pathe* • FRN
DRUNKARD'S DREAM, A (USA) see **VISION D'IVROGNE** • 1897
DRUNKARD'S DREAM, THE • 1908 • Collins Alf? • UKN
DRUNKARD'S FAITH, THE • 1909 • *Selig* • USA
DRUNKARD'S HOME, THE • 1904 • *Cricks & Sharp* • UKN
DRUNKARD'S REFORMATION, A • 1909 • Griffith D. W. • USA
DRUNKARD'S SON, A • 1909 • Fitzhamon Lewin • UKN
DRUNKEN ANGEL see **YOIDORE TENSHI** • 1948
DRUNKEN MASTER • Yu'An Ho-P'Ing • HKG
DRUNKEN MOTORCYCLIST, THE • 1907 • Collins Alf? • UKN
DRUNKEN SWORDSMAN, THE • Chang Jen-Tsei • HKG
DRUNTER UND DRUBER • 1932 • Neufeld Max • AUS
DRUNTER UND DRUBER • 1939 • Marischka Hubert • FRG
DRUNTER UND DRUBER? see **HASENKLEIN KANN NICHTS DAFUR** • 1932
DRUNTER UND DRUBER see **MAL DRUNTER, MAL DRUBER** • 1960
DRUSILLA WITH A MILLION • 1925 • Weight F. Harmon • USA
DRUSTVENA IGRA • 1973 • Karanovic Srdjan • YGS • SOCIAL GAME
DRUVA-VIJAYM • 1936 • Pillayya C. • IND • DRUVA'S VICTORY
DRUVA'S VICTORY see **DRUVA-VIJAYM** • 1936
DRUZBA PERE KVRZICE • 1971 • Tadej Vladimir • YGS • LITTLE PETER'S DIARY
DRUZHOK • 1957 • Eisimont Viktor • USS • LITTLE FRIEND
DRUZINA CERNEHO PERA • 1973 • Koval Ota • CZC • COMPANY OF THE BLACK FEATHER, THE
DRY AND THIRSTY • 1920 • *Bletcher Billy* • USA
DRY BIKINI, THE see **HER BIKINI NEVER GOT WET** • 1962
DRY CLEANED • 1920 • *Franey William* • SHT • USA
DRY DOCK • 1936 • Hawes Stanley • UKN
DRY DOCK, A see **SUCHY DOK** • 1964
DRY EARTH see **CHI WA KAWAITEIRU** • 1960
DRY EARTH see **TIERRA SECA** • 1962
DRY GOODS AND DAMP DEEDS • 1917 • Moore Vin • SHT • USA
DRY LAKE see **KAWAITA MIZUUMI** • 1960
DRY LIVES see **VIDAS SECAS** • 1963
DRY MARTINI • 1928 • D'Arrast Harry D'Abbadie • USA
DRY ROT • 1956 • Elvey Maurice • UKN
DRY SUMMER (USA) see **SUSUZ YAZ** • 1963
DRY TOWN, A • 1912 • *Eclair* • USA
DRY VALLEY JOHNSON • 1917 • *Broadway Star* • USA
DRY WHITE SEASON, A • 1988 • Palcy Euzhan • USA
DRY WOOD AND HOT PEPPER • 1973 • Blank Les • DOC • USA
DRYING UP THE STREETS • 1979 • Spry Robin • CND
DRYLANDERS • 1963 • Haldane Don • CND • AUTRE PAYS, UN
DRZANJE ZA VAZDUH • 1985 • Sotra Zdravko • YGS • HANGING ON TO THIN AIR
DRZWI W MURZE • 1973 • Rozewicz Stanislaw • PLN • DOOR IN A WALL
DSCHIHAD • 1916 • Weidemann Fritz • FRG
DSCHINGIS KHAN see **GENGHIS KHAN** • 1965
DSCHUNGEL RUFT, DER • 1936 • Piel Harry • FRG
DSCHUNGELMADCHEN FUR ZWEI HALUNKEN • 1973 • Hofbauer Ernst • FRG, CLM, ITL
D'SOUND BEATS -SOUL DISCOTHEQUE A-GO-GO • 1967 • Marquez Artemio • PHL
DU AR MITT AVENTYR • 1958 • Olin Stig • SWD • YOU ARE MY ADVENTURE
DU BARRY • 1918 • Edwards J. Gordon • USA • MADAME DUBARRY
DU BARRY, LA see **MADAME DU BARRY** • 1954
DU BARRY (UKN) see **DU BARRY, WOMAN OF PASSION** • 1930
DU BARRY WAS A LADY • 1943 • Del Ruth Roy • USA
DU BARRY, WOMAN OF PASSION • 1930 • Taylor Sam • USA • DU BARRY (UKN) ○ DECEPTION ○ FLAME OF THE FLESH
DU-BEAT-E-O • 1984 • Sacks Alan • USA
DU BETON ET DES HOMMES • 1965 • Rivard Fernand • DCS • CND
DU BIST DAS LEBEN • 1921 • Eckstein Franz • FRG
DU BIST DIE RICHTIGE • 1955 • Engel Erich • FRG, AUS
DU BIST DIE ROSE VOM WORTHERSEE • 1952 • Marischka Hubert • FRG
DU BIST DIE SCHONSTE FUR MICH! see **ZWEI IN EINEM AUTO** • 1951
DU BIST DIE WELT FUR MICH • 1953 • Marischka Ernst • AUS • YOU ARE THE WORLD FOR ME (USA) ○ RICHARD TAUBER STORY, THE
DU BIST ENTZUCKEND, ROSEMARIE • 1933 • von Wolzogen Hans • FRG • ROSL VOM TRAUNSEE, DIE
DU BIST MEIN, EIN DEUTSCHES TAGEBUCH • 1969 • Thorndike Andrew, Thorndike Annelie • GDR • GERMAN DIARY, A
DU BIST MEIN GLUCK • 1936 • Martin Karl Heinz • FRG • THOU ART MY JOY (USA)
DU BIST MUSIK • 1956 • Martin Paul • FRG
DU BIST NICHT ALLEIN • 1949 • Verhoeven Paul • FRG
DU BIST WUNDERBAR • 1959 • Martin Paul • FRG
DU BLE EN LIASSES • 1969 • Brunet Alain • FRN
DU BLUES DANS LA TETE • 1981 • Palud Herve • FRN
DU BOUT DES LEVRES • 1976 • Degesves Jean-Marie • BLG • AT THE TIP OF THE TONGUE ○ TIP OF THE TONGUE
DU BUERRE AUX ALLEMANDS see **BLUE JEANS** • 1977
DU BUERRE DANS LES TARTINES • 1981 • Bonmariage Manu • BLG
DU CHARBON ET DES HOMMES • 1952 • Leenhardt Roger • DCS • FRN
DU CHOC DES IDEES • 1956 • Portugais Louis • DCS • CND
DU CIEL PLEIN LE COEUR • 1971 • Maloumian Serge • DOC • FRN
DU COEUR A L'OUVRAGE see **WORKING CHANCE, A** • 1976
DU COQ A L'ANE • 1973 • Hebert Pierre, Desbiens Francine, Gervais Suzanne • ANS • CND
DU COTE DE LA COTE • 1958 • Varda Agnes • SHT • FRN • RIVIERA, TODAY'S EDEN, THE
DU COTE DE LA TASSAOUT • 1968 • Lahalolo Latif • SHT • MRC
DU COTE DE ROBINSON • 1964 • Eustache Jean • FRN • ROBINSON'S PLACE
DU COTE DE SAINTE-ADELE see **FLYING SKIS** • 1951
DU COTE DES TENNIS • 1976 • Hartmann-Clausset Madeleine • FRN
DU COTE D'OROUET • 1969 • Rozier Jacques • FRN
DU CREPUSCULE A L'AUBE see **SOIXANTE-DIX-SEPT RUE CHALGRIN** • 1931
DU DARFST NICHT LANGER SCHWEIGEN • 1955 • Stemmle R. A. • FRG
DU ER IKKE ALENE • 1978 • Nielsen Lasse, Johansen Ernst • DNM • YOU'RE NOT ALONE ○ YOU ARE NOT ALONE
DU FIL A L'AIGULLE • 1924 • Gremillon Jean • SHT • FRN
DU GAMLA, DU FRIA • 1938 • Olsson Gunnar • SWD • THOU OLD, THOU FREE (USA) ○ YOU FREE OLD COUNTRY
DU GAMLA, DU FRIA • 1970 • Fahlstrom Oyvind • SWD • YOU OLD, YOU FREE ○ PROVOCATION
DU GEHORST MIR • 1959 • Ten Haaf Wilm • FRG • YOUR BODY BELONGS TO ME (USA)
DU GEHORST ZU MIR • 1943 • Lamprecht Gerhard • FRG
DU GENERAL AU PARTICULIER • 1967 • Fournier Claude • DCS • CND
DU GRABUGE CHEZ LES VEUVES • 1963 • Poitrenaud Jacques • FRN, ITL • STRANA VOGLIA DI UNA VEDOVA (ITL)
DU GUESCLIN • 1948 • de Latour Bernard • FRN
DU HAUT EN BAS • 1933 • Pabst G. W. • FRN • HIGH AND LOW
DU KANNST NICHT TREU SEIN • 1936 • Seitz Franz • FRG
DU MANUAL AU ROBOT • Colson-Malleville Marie • FRN • FROM MANUAL LABOR TO THE MACHINE
DU MEIN STILLES TAL • 1955 • Steckel Leonard • FRG
DU MEINE HIMMELSKONIGIN • 1919 • Wilhelm Carl • FRG
DU MICH AUCH • 1986 • Levy Dani, Franke Anja, Berger Helmut • SWT
DU MOU DANS LA GACHETTE see **DEUX TUEURS** • 1966
DU MOURON POUR LES PETITS OISEAUX • 1962 • Carne Marcel • FRN, ITL • DIETRO LA FACCIATA (ITL)
DU PLAISIR A LA JOIE • 1978 • Leenhardt Roger • DCS • FRN
DU POINT DE VUE D'ANTON • 1954 • Colson-Malleville Marie • SHT • FRN
DU RIFIFI A PANAMA • 1966 • de La Patelliere Denys • FRN, ITL, FRG • RIFIFI INTERNACIONALE (ITL) ○ RIFIFI IN PARIS (UKN) ○ UPPER HAND, THE (USA)
DU RIFIFI A TOKYO • 1963 • Deray Jacques • FRN, ITL • RIFIFI IN TOKYO (USA)
DU RIFIFI CHEZ LES FEMMES • 1959 • Joffe Alex • FRN, ITL • RIFIFI FRA LE DONNE (ITL) ○ RIFF RAFF GIRLS (USA) ○ RIFIFI FOR GIRLS
DU RIFIFI CHEZ LES HOMMES • 1955 • Dassin Jules • FRN • RIFIFI (USA)
DU SANG DANS LA SCIURE see **CHICAGO DIGEST** • 1951
DU SANG DANS LE SOLEIL see **PROIBITO** • 1955
DU SANG DE LA VOLUPTE ET DE LA MORT • 1948 • Markopoulos Gregory J. • USA
DU SANG SOUS LE CHAPITEAU • 1956 • Peclet Georges • FRN
DU SEL, DU CALCAIRE ET DU COKE • 1955 • Venard Jean • SHT • FRN
DU SKAL AERE DIN HUSTRU • 1918 • Magnussen Fritz • SWD
DU SKAL AERE DIN HUSTRU • 1925 • Dreyer Carl T. • DNM • MASTER OF THE HOUSE ○ THOU SHALT HONOR THY WIFE
DU SKAL ELSKE DIN NAESTE • 1915 • Blom August • DNM • SAMARITAN, THE ○ FOR DE ANDRE
DU SOLEIL PLEIN LES YEUX • 1969 • Boisrond Michel • FRN
DU SOLLST DER KAISER MEINER SEELE SEIN • 1928 • Arnheim Valy • FRG
DU SOLLST DICH NIE VOR EINEM LEBENDEN MENSCHEN BUCKEN • 1978 • Richter Wolfgang, Karnick Hannes • DOC • FRG • NEVER BE HUMBLE BEFORE ANY LIVING PERSON ○ NEVER BOW DOWN BEFORE A LIVING PERSON!
DU SOLLST KEINE ANDEREN GOTTER HABEN • 1917 • Gartner Adolf • FRG
DU SOLLST NICHT BEGEHREN • 1933 • Schneider-Edenkoben Richard • FRG
DU SOLLST NICHT EHEBRECHEN! (FRG) see **THERESE RAQUIN** • 1928
DU SOLLST NICHT RICHTEN • 1916 • von Woringen Paul • FRG
DU SOLLST NICHT STEHLEN • 1928 • Janson Victor • FRG • LOVE COMMANDMENT, THE (USA)
DU SOLLST NICHT TOTEN • 1923 • *Wiking-Film* • FRG
DU TAM-TAM AU JAZZ • 1969 • Brunet Philippe • FRN
DU THE POUR MONSIEUR JOSE see **INVITE DU MARDI, L'** • 1949
DU UND ICH • 1938 • Liebeneiner Wolfgang • FRG
DU UND MANCHER KAMARAD.. • 1956 • Thorndike Andrew, Thorndike Annelie • GDR • YOU AND OTHER COMRADES ○ GERMAN STORY, THE ○ KRIEG ODER FRIEDEN
DU ZAIRE AU CONGO • 1981 • Mesnil Christian • DOC • BLG
DUA MOSKETYRI see **BLAZNOVA KRONIKA** • 1964
DU'A'AL-KARAWAN • 1959 • Barakat Henry • EGY • APPEL DU COURLIS, L'
DUAL ALIBI • 1947 • Travers Alfred • UKN
DUAL CONTROL • 1932 • Summers Walter • UKN
DUAL LIFE, A • 1908 • *Selig* • USA
DUAL PERSONALITY, A • 1912 • *Republic* • USA
DUALITY OF MAN, THE • 1910 • *Wrench Films* • UKN
½-DUAN QING • 1985 • Ho Kangqiao • HKG • INFATUATION
DUANG DUANG MYEE TAI ATHAI • 1982 • Nyunt Win • BRM • HEART THAT GOES DING DING, THE
DUAS CAUSAS • 1952 • Campos Henrique • PRT
DUAS FACES DA MOEDA, AS • 1970 • Oliveira Domingos • BRZ
DUB, THE • 1919 • Cruze James • USA
DUBARRY • 1915 • Kleine George • USA
DUBARRY, DIE • 1951 • Wildhagen Georg • FRG
DUBARRY, THE see **I GIVE MY HEART** • 1935
DUBARRY VON HEUTE, EINE • 1926 • Korda Alexander • FRG • MODERN DUBARRY, A
DUBIOUS PATRIOTS see **SECRET INVASION, THE** • 1964
DUBIOUS PATRIOTS, THE see **YOU CAN'T WIN 'EM ALL** • 1970
DUBLIN • 1970 • Marcus Louis • DOC • IRL
DUBLIN DAN • 1912 • Warren Edward • USA
DUBLIN NIGHTMARE • 1958 • Pomeroy John • UKN
DUBOIS ET FILS • 1961 • Devlin Bernard, Leboursier Raymond • CND
DUBRAVKA • 1968 • Vasilevski Radomir • USS
DUBROVACKI PASTELLI • 1957 • Vajda Marijan • YGS • DUBROVNIK PASTELS, THE
DUBROVNIK PASTELS, THE see **DUBROVACKI PASTELLI** • 1957
DUBROVSKY • 1936 • Ivanovsky Alexander • USS
DUBROWSKY see **VENDICATORE, IL** • 1959
DUBS • 1978 • Emshwiller Ed • USA
DUBS AND DRYGOODS • 1917 • Semon Larry • SHT • USA
DUCA E FORSE UNA DUCHESSA, UN see **IDILLIO A BUDAPEST** • 1941
DUCA NERO, IL • 1963 • Mercanti Pino • ITL, SPN • DUQUE NEGRO, EL (SPN) ○ BLACK DUKE, THE (USA)
DUCH Z CANTERVILLE • 1967 • Petelska Ewa, Petelski Czeslaw • MTV • PLN • CANTERVILLE GHOST, THE
DUCH ZAMCZYSKA SACRAMENTO • 1962 • Pulchny Leonard • ANS • PLN • GHOST OF SACRAMENTO, THE
DUCHESS, THE • 1915 • McCulley W. T. • USA
DUCHESS AND THE DIRTWATER FOX, THE • 1976 • Frank Melvin • USA
DUCHESS OF BROADWAY see **TALK ABOUT A LADY** • 1946
DUCHESS OF BUFFALO, THE • 1926 • Franklin Sidney A. • USA • SYBIL
DUCHESS OF DOUBT, THE • 1917 • Baker George D. • USA
DUCHESS OF IDAHO • 1950 • Leonard Robert Z. • USA
DUCHESS OF LANGEAIS, THE see **ETERNAL FLAME, THE** • 1922
DUCHESS OF SEVEN DIALS, THE • 1920 • Paul Fred • UKN
DUCHESS OF THE FOLIES BERGERES, THE see **KONIGIN VOM MOULIN-ROUGE, DIE** • 1926
DUCHESSA DI SANTA LUCIA, LA • 1959 • Montero Roberto Bianchi • ITL
DUCHESSE DE BERRY, LA • 1910 • Leprince Rene • FRN
DUCHESSE DE LANGEAIS, LA • 1942 • de Baroncelli Jacques • FRN • WICKED DUCHESS, THE (USA)
DUCHESSE DE TILSITT, LA see **SANS LENDEMAIN** • 1939
DUCHESSE OF NEW ORLEANS, THE see **FLAME OF NEW ORLEANS, THE** • 1941
DUCHIN STORY, THE see **EDDY DUCHIN STORY, THE** • 1956
DUCHY OF CORNWALL, THE • 1938 • Pollard William • DOC • UKN
DUCK AMUCK • 1953 • Jones Charles M. • ANS • USA
DUCK-AND-DRAKE ADVENTURE, A see **SZEGENY DZSONI ES ARNIKA** • 1984
DUCK AND SWAN see **HANGSA - MITHUN** • 1968
DUCK DOCTOR • 1952 • Hanna William, Barbera Joseph • ANS • USA
DUCK DODGERS OF THE 24½TH CENTURY • 1953 • Jones Charles M. • ANS • USA
DUCK FEVER • 1955 • Rasinski Connie • ANS • USA
DUCK HUNT • 1937 • *Lantz Walter (P)* • ANS • USA
DUCK HUNT, THE • 1932 • Gillett Burt • ANS • USA
DUCK HUNTER, THE • 1922 • Del Ruth Roy • SHT • USA
DUCK IN ORANGE SAUCE (USA) see **ANITRA AL'ARANCIA, L'** • 1975
DUCK INN • 1920 • Pratt Gilbert • USA
DUCK JOURNEY DIARY see **OSHIDORI TABI NIKKI** • 1929
DUCK OUT OF WATER, A • 1918 • Lyons Eddie, Moran Lee • SHT • USA
DUCK PIMPLES • 1945 • Kinney Jack • ANS • USA
DUCK, RABBIT, DUCK • 1953 • Jones Charles M. • ANS • USA
DUCK RINGS AT SEVEN-THIRTY, THE see **ENTE KLINGELT UM ½ ACHT, DIE** • 1968
DUCK SOUP • 1927 • Guiol Fred • USA
DUCK SOUP • 1933 • McCarey Leo • USA
DUCK SOUP • 1942 • Holmes Ben • SHT • USA
DUCK SOUP TO NUTS • 1944 • Freleng Friz • ANS • USA
DUCK TALES -THE MOVIE: THE TREASURE OF THE LOST LAMP • 1990 • Hatchcock Bob • ANM • USA
DUCK, YOU SUCKER (USA) see **GIU LA TESTA** • 1971
DUCKING A DISCORD • 1916 • Miller Rube • SHT • USA
DUCKING STOOL, THE • 1905 • Cooper Arthur • UKN
DUCKING THE DEVIL • 1957 • McKimson Robert • ANS • USA
DUCKS AND DRAKES • 1921 • Campbell Maurice • USA
DUCKS IS DUCKS • 1916 • *Rolma Film* • SHT • USA
DUCKS ON SALE OR RETURN • 1904 • Cooper Arthur • UKN
DUCKSTERS, THE • 1950 • Jones Charles M. • ANS • USA
DUCKTATOR, THE • 1942 • McCabe Norman • ANS • USA
DUCKWEED • 1981 • Yang Te-Ch'Ang • MTV • TWN
DUCKWEED STORY see **UKIGUSA NIKKI** • 1955
DUD CHEQUE CHICANERY • 1926 • Engholm F. W. • UKN
DUDA • 1951 • Salvador Julio • SPN
DUDA, LA • 1953 • Galindo Alejandro • MXC
DUDA, LA • 1972 • Gil Rafael • SPN
DUDAS see **JUDAS** • 1918
DUDE AND THE BURGLAR • 1903 • *Bitzer Billy (Ph)* • USA
DUDE BANDIT, THE • 1933 • Melford George • USA
DUDE COWBOY • 1941 • Howard David • USA
DUDE COWBOY, THE • 1911 • *Kalem* • USA
DUDE COWBOY, THE • 1911 • *Bison* • USA
DUDE COWBOY, THE • 1926 • Nelson Jack • USA
DUDE DUCK • 1951 • Hannah Jack • ANS • USA
DUDE GOES WEST, THE • 1948 • Neumann Kurt • USA
DUDE OPERATOR, THE • Harrison Saul? • SHT • USA
DUDE RAFFLES • 1915 • *Sterling* • USA
DUDE RANCH • 1931 • Tuttle Frank • USA
DUDE RANCH, THE • 1931 • Ray Albert • USA
DUDE RANCH, THE • 1934 • Cline Eddie • USA
DUDE RANCH HARMONY • 1949 • *Groom Dewey* • SHT • USA
DUDE RANGER, THE • 1934 • Cline Eddie • USA
DUDE WRANGLER, THE • 1930 • Thorpe Richard • USA • FEMININE TOUCH (UKN)
DUDES • 1987 • Spheeris Penelope • USA

DUDES ARE PRETTY PEOPLE • 1942 • Roach Hal Jr. • USA
DUDES FOR A DAY • 1916 • *Hamilton Lloyd V.* • SHT • USA
DUDOSA VIRILIDAD DE CRISTOBAL, LA • 1975 • Bosch Juan • SPN
DUDS • 1920 • Mills Thomas R. • USA
DUDU, EIN MENSCHENSCHICKSAL • 1924 • Meinert Rudolf • FRG • GESCHICHTE EINES CLOWNS, DIE ○ MENSCHEN
DUE ASSI DEL GUANTONE, I • 1971 • Laurenti Mariano • ITL
DUE BARBIERI, I • 1937 • Coletti Duilio • ITL
DUE BIANCHI NELL'AFRICA NERA • 1970 • Corbucci Bruno • ITL
DUE CAMPANILI E.. TANTE SPERANZE • 1961 • Romero-Marchent Joaquin Luis • ITL, SPN
DUE CARABINIERI, I • 1984 • Verdone Carlo • ITL • TWO CARABINEERS, THE
DUE CASTELLI, I • 1963 • Bozzetto Bruno, Manuli Guido • ANS • ITL • TWO CASTLES, THE
DUE + CINQUE MISSIONE HYDRA see **2 + 5 MISSIONE HYDRA** • 1966
DUE COLONNELLI, I • 1962 • Steno • ITL • TWO COLONELS, THE
DUE COMPARI, I • 1955 • Borghesio Carlo • ITL
DUE CONTRO LA CITTA (ITL) see **DEUX HOMMES DANS LA VILLE** • 1973
DUE CONTRO TUTTI • 1962 • Momplet Antonio • ITL, SPN
DUE CROCI A DANGER PASS (ITL) see **DOS CRUCES EN DANGER PASS** • 1967
DUE CROCIATA, I • 1968 • Orlandini Giuseppe • ITL • TWO CRUSADERS, THE
DUE CROCIFISSI, I • 1918 • Genina Augusto • ITL
DUE CUORI • 1943 • Borghesio Carlo • ITL • CASA SUL FIUME, LA
DUE CUORI FELICI • 1932 • Negroni Baldassare • ITL
DUE CUORI FRA LE BELVE • 1943 • Simonelli Giorgio C. • ITL
DUE CUORI SOTTO SEQUESTRO • 1941 • Bragaglia Carlo Ludovico • ITL
DUE CUORI UNA CAPELLA • 1975 • Lucidi Maurizio • ITL
DUE DELLA FORMULA 1 ALLA CORSA PIU PAZZA, PAZZA DEL MONDO • 1971 • Civirani Osvaldo • ITL
DUE DELLA LEGIONE, IL • 1962 • Fulci Lucio • ITL
DUE DEPUTATI, I • 1968 • Grimaldi Gianni • ITL
DUE DERELITTI, I • 1952 • Calzavara Flavio • ITL
DUE DOZZINE DI ROSE SCARLATTE see **ROSE SCARLATTE** • 1940
DUE ESISTENZE, LE • 1920 • Falena Ugo • ITL
DUE EVASI DI SING SING, I • 1964 • Fulci Lucio • ITL
DUE FACCE DEL DOLLARO, LE • 1967 • Montero Roberto Bianchi • ITL, FRN • TWO SIDES OF THE DOLLAR, THE
DUE FIGLI DI RINGO, I • 1966 • Simonelli Giorgio C. • ITL
DUE FIGLI DI TRINITA, I • 1972 • Civirani Osvaldo • ITL
DUE FOSCARI, I • 1942 • Fulchignoni Enrico • ITL
DUE GATTONI A NOVE CODE.. E MEZZA AD AMSTERDAM • 1972 • Civirani Osvaldo • ITL
DUE GIUGNO, IL see **DAL REFERENDUM ALLA COSTITUZIONE** • 1971
DUE GLADIATORI, I • 1964 • Caiano Mario • ITL • TWO GLADIATORS (USA)
DUE GONDOLIERI, I see **VENEZIA, LA LUNA E TU** • 1958
DUE KENNEDY, I • 1969 • Bisiach Gianni • ITL • TWO KENNEDYS.. A VIEW FROM EUROPE, THE ○ TWO KENNEDYS, THE (USA)
DUE KILLERS IN FUGA (ITL) see **DEUX TUEURS** • 1966
DUE LACRIME • 1955 • Vari Giuseppe • ITL
DUE LEGGI, LE • 1963 • Mulargia Edoardo • ITL
DUE LETTERE ANONIME • 1945 • Camerini Mario • ITL • TWO ANONYMOUS LETTERS
DUE MADONNE, LE • 1950 • Simonelli Giorgio C., Di Gianni Enzo • ITL
DUE MADRI, I • 1938 • Palermi Amleto • ITL • TWO MOTHERS, THE (USA)
DUE MAFIOSI CONTRO AL CAPONE • 1966 • Simonelli Giorgio C. • ITL
DUE MAFIOSI CONTRO GOLDGINGER • 1965 • Simonelli Giorgio C. • ITL, SPN • AMAZING DR. G., THE (USA) ○ TWO MAFIOSI VS. GOLDGINGER
DUE MAFIOSI DELL'F.B.I., I see **SPIE VENGONO DAL SEMIFREDDO, LE** • 1966
DUE MAFIOSI, I • 1964 • Simonelli Giorgio C. • ITL, SPN
DUE MAFIOSI NEL FAR WEST • 1964 • Simonelli Giorgio C. • ITL, SPN
DUE MAGGIOLINI PIU MATTI DEL MONDO, I • 1970 • Orlandini Giuseppe • ITL
DUE MAGHI DEL PALLONE, I • 1970 • Laurenti Mariano • ITL
DUE MAGNIFICI FRESCONI, I • 1969 • Girolami Marino • ITL
DUE MAGNUM 38 PER UN CITTA DI CAROGNE • 1975 • Pinzauti Mario • ITL
DUE MARESCIALLI, I • 1961 • Corbucci Sergio • ITL
DUE MARIE, LE • 1917 • Falena Ugo • ITL
DUE MARINES E UN GENERALE • 1966 • Scattini Luigi • ITL • WAR ITALIAN STYLE (USA) ○ TWO MARINES AND A GENERAL
DUE MASCHI PER ALEXIA • 1972 • Logar Juan • ITL
DUE MATTACCHIONI AL MOULIN ROUGE • 1964 • Infascelli Carlo • ITL
DUE MILIONI PER UN SORRISO • 1939 • Borghesio Carlo, Soldati Mario • ITL
DUE MISANTROPI, I • 1937 • Palermi Amleto • ITL
DUE MOGLI SONO TROPPE • 1951 • Camerini Mario • ITL
DUE NEMICI, I • 1962 • Hamilton Guy • ITL, UKN • BEST OF ENEMIES, THE (UKN)
DUE NOTTI CON CLEOPATRA • 1953 • Mattoli Mario • ITL • TWO NIGHTS WITH CLEOPATRA
DUE OCCHI DIABOLICI • 1990 • Romero George A., Argento Dario • ITL, USA • TWO EVIL EYES
DUE OCCHI PER NON VEDERE • 1939 • Righelli Gennaro • ITL
DUE OCCHI PER UCCIDERE • 1968 • Borraccetti Renato • ITL
DUE ONCE DI PIOMBO • 1966 • Lucidi Maurizio • ITL • MIO NOME E PECOS, IL ○ MY NAME IS PECOS
DUE ORFANELLE, LE • 1942 • Gallone Carmine • ITL • TWO ORPHANS, THE
DUE ORFANELLE, LE • 1955 • Gentilomo Giacomo • ITL, FRN
DUE ORFANELLE, LE • 1966 • Freda Riccardo • ITL • TWO ORPHANS, THE (USA)
DUE ORFANELLE, LE • 1978 • Savona Leopoldo • ITL
DUE ORFANELLI, I • 1947 • Mattoli Mario • ITL
DUE PARA, I • 1966 • Fulci Lucio • ITL
DUE PERICOLI PUBBLICI, I • 1965 • Fulci Lucio • ITL • TWO PUBLIC ENEMIES ○ TWO DANGEROUS AGENTS
DUE PEZZI DA GO • 1971 • Civirani Osvaldo • ITL
DUE PEZZI DI PANE • 1979 • Citti Sergio • ITL
DUE PISTOLE E UN VIGLIACCO • 1968 • Ferroni Giorgio • ITL • TWO PISTOLS AND A COWARD
DUE POMPIERI, I • 1968 • Corbucci Sergio • ITL • TWO FIREMEN, THE
DUE RAGAZZI DA MARCIAPIEDE • 1971 • Fernandez Ramon • ITL
DUE RRRINGOS NEL TEXAS • 1967 • Girolami Marino • ITL • TWO RRRINGOS OF TEXAS
DUE SAMURAI PER 100 GEISHE • 1963 • Simonelli Giorgio C. • ITL
DUE SANCULOTTI, I • 1966 • Simonelli Giorgio C. • ITL
DUE SELVAGGI A CORTE • 1959 • Baldi Ferdinando • ITL
DUE SERGENTI DEL GENERALE CUSTER, I • 1965 • Simonelli Giorgio C. • ITL, SPN
DUE SERGENTI, I • 1908 • Pasquali Ernesto Maria • ITL
DUE SERGENTI, I • 1936 • Guazzoni Enrico • ITL
DUE SERGENTI, I • 1952 • Chiesa Carlo Alberto • ITL
DUE SOGNI A OCCHI APERTI, I • 1920 • D'Ambra Lucio • ITL
DUE SOLDI DI FELICITA • 1955 • Amoroso Roberto • ITL
DUE SOLDI DI SPERANZA • 1951 • Castellani Renato • ITL • TWO CENTS WORTH OF HOPE (USA) ○ TWO PENNYWORTH OF HOPE ○ TWO PENNIES OF HOPE
DUE SORELLE, LE • 1950 • Volpe Mario • ITL
DUE SORELLE AMANO • 1951 • Comin Jacopo • ITL
DUE SOSIA IN ALLEGRIA • 1958 • Ferronetti Ignazio • ITL
DUE SPORCHE CAROGNE (ITL) see **ADIEU L'AMI** • 1968
DUE SUL PIANEROTTOLO • 1976 • Amendola Mario • ITL
DUE SUPERPIEDI QUASI PIATTI, I • 1977 • Clucher E. B. • ITL • CRIME BUSTERS (USA) ○ TWO SUPERCOPS
DUE TIGRI, LE • 1941 • Simonelli Giorgio C. • ITL
DUE TO AN ACT OF GOD see **IM ZEICHEN DES KREUZES** • 1983
DUE TORERI, I • 1964 • Simonelli Giorgio C. • ITL, SPN
DUE VERITA, LE • 1952 • Leonviola Antonio • ITL
DUE VIGILI, I • 1967 • Orlandini Giuseppe • ITL • TWO POLICEMEN, THE
DUE VIOLENTI, I • 1965 • Zeglio Primo • ITL, SPN
DUE VOLTE GUIDA • 1968 • Cicero Nando • ITL, SPN • TWO TIMES GUIDE
DUE VOLTI DELLA PAURA, I • 1972 • Demicheli Tulio • ITL • TWO FACES OF FEAR, THE (UKN)
DUEL • 1927 • de Baroncelli Jacques • FRN
DUEL • 1960 • Heyer John • SHT • ASL
DUEL • 1961 • Berezantseva Tatyana, Rudnik Lev • USS
DUEL • 1962 • Thomsen Knud Leif • DNM
DUEL • 1971 • Spielberg Steven • TVM • USA
DUEL see **POYEDINOK** • 1945
DUEL see **PARBAJ** • 1959
DUEL, LE • 1939 • Fresnay Pierre • FRN
DUEL, THE • 1905 • Fitzhamon Lewin • UKN
DUEL, THE • 1912 • *Reliance* • USA
DUEL, THE • 1912 • Sennett Mack • *Keystone* • USA
DUEL, THE • 1922 • Gardin Vladimir • USS
DUEL, THE • 1962 • Shebib Donald • CND
DUEL, THE • Bijlsma Ronald • ANS • NTH
DUEL, THE see **POEDINOK** • 1957
DUEL, THE see **POJEDYNEK** • 1964
DUEL, THE see **PLOKHOY KHOROSHYI CHELOVEK** • 1974
DUEL A DAKAR • 1952 • Combret Georges, Orval Claude • FRN
DUEL A LA DYNAMITE • Cloche Maurice • FRN
DUEL A L'AMERICAINE • 1913 • Durand Jean • FRN
DUEL A MORT, UN • 1950 • *Keaton Buster* • SHT • FRN
DUEL A RIO BRAVO (FRN) see **SFIDA A RIO BRAVO** • 1965
DUEL ABRACADABRANT • 1902 • Zecca Ferdinand • FRN • AMAZING DUEL
DUEL AMERICAIN, UN • 1922 • Madzelewski Eugenjusz • PLN
DUEL AT APACHE WELLS • 1957 • Kane Joseph • USA
DUEL AT DAWN, A • 1915 • Curtis Allen • USA
DUEL AT DIABLO • 1966 • Nelson Ralph • USA
DUEL AT EZO (USA) see **EZO YAKATA NO KETTO** • 1970
DUEL AT GANRYU ISLAND see **KETTO GANRYU JIMA** • 1955
DUEL AT HANNYA-ZAKA see **KETTO HANNYA-ZAKA** • 1943
DUEL AT ICHIJOJI TEMPLE see **ICHIJOJI NO KETTO** • 1941
DUEL AT ICHIJOJI TEMPLE see **ICHIJOJI NO KETTO** • 1955
DUEL AT ICHIJOJI TEMPLE, THE see **MIYAMOTO MUSASHI IV** • 1964
DUEL AT KAGIYA CORNER, THE see **KETTO KAGIYA NO TSUJI** • 1951
DUEL AT RED VALLEY see **AKAI TANIMA KETTO** • 1965
DUEL AT RIO BRAVO see **SFIDA A RIO BRAVO** • 1965
DUEL AT SILVER CREEK • 1952 • Siegel Don • USA
DUEL AT THE KEYMAKER'S CORNER see **KETTO KAGIYA NO TSUJI** • 1951
DUEL AT THE QUARRY see **KANTO ONNA YAKUZA** • 1968
DUEL AT THE RIO GRANDE (USA) see **SEGNO DI ZORRO, IL** • 1963
DUEL DANS LE MONDE • 1967 • Combret Maurice • FRN, ITL
DUEL DE MAX, LE • 1913 • Linder Max • FRN
DUEL I HESHTUR • 1967 • Anagosti Dhimiter • ALB • SILENT DUEL
DUEL IN DURANGO see **GUN DUEL IN DURANGO** • 1957
DUEL IN MID-AIR, A • 1909 • *Edison* • USA
DUEL IN SPACE • 1954 • *Reed Roland (P)* • MTV • USA
DUEL IN THE DARK, THE • 1915 • *Foster Morris* • USA
DUEL IN THE FOREST (USA) see **SCHINDERHANNES, DER** • 1958
DUEL IN THE JUNGLE • 1954 • Marshall George • UKN
DUEL IN THE MOUNTAINS see **POYEDINOK V GORAKH** • 1968
DUEL IN THE STORM, THE see **ARASHI NO HATASHIJO** • 1968
DUEL IN THE SUN • 1946 • Vidor King, von Sternberg Josef (U/c) • USA
DUEL OF A SNOWY NIGHT, THE see **YUKI NO YO NO KETTO** • 1954
DUEL OF CANDLES, A • 1911 • Dwan Allan • USA • DUEL OF THE CANDLES
DUEL OF CHAMPIONS (USA) see **ORAZI E CURIAZI** • 1961
DUEL OF FIRE (USA) see **DUELLO NELLA SILA** • 1962
DUEL OF FISTS, THE • 1973 • Chang Ch'Eh • HKG
DUEL OF HEARTS, THE • 1915 • *Ramona* • USA
DUEL OF THE BRAVE ONES • *Chang Wu Lang* • HKG
DUEL OF THE CANDLES see **DUEL OF CANDLES, A** • 1911
DUEL OF THE CHAMPIONS see **ORAZI E CURIAZI** • 1961
DUEL OF THE GARGANTUAS see **FURANKENSHUTAIN NO KAIJU -SANDA TAI GAILAH** • 1966
DUEL OF THE IRON FIST • 1971 • Chang Ch'Eh • HKG
DUEL OF THE MASTERS • Tang Wei Cheng • HKG
DUEL OF THE SEVEN TIGERS see **SHADOW OF THE TIGER**
DUEL OF THE SPACE MONSTERS (UKN) see **FRANKENSTEIN MEETS THE SPACE MONSTER** • 1965
DUEL OF THE TITANS see **DEATHSTALKER II** • 1987
DUEL OF THE TITANS (USA) see **ROMOLO E REMO** • 1961
DUEL OF THE TOUGH • 1982 • Ho Chih-Chiang • HKG
DUEL ON THE CLIFFS • 1986 • Traore Falaba Issa • MLI
DUEL ON THE MISSISSIPPI • 1955 • Castle William • USA
DUEL ON THE SILVER PEAK see **HAKUGIN-JO** • 1960
DUEL PERSONALITIES • 1939 • Sidney George • SHT • USA
DUEL PERSONALITY • 1966 • Jones Charles M. • ANS • USA
DUEL POLITIQUE • 1899 • Melies Georges • FRN • POLITICAL DUEL, A
DUEL SCENE FROM "THE TWO ORPHANS" • 1902 • Haggar William • UKN
DUEL SUR LE NIL see **SIRAUN FI AN-NIL** • 1959
DUEL TRAGIQUE • 1904 • Blache Alice • FRN
DUEL WITH DEATH (USA) see **UND EWIG SINGEN DIE WALDER** • 1959
DUEL WITHOUT END see **MIYAMOTO MUSASHI II** • 1962
DUEL WITHOUT HONOR (USA) see **DUELLO SENZA ONORE** • 1950
DUELL IN DEN BERGEN • 1949 • Trenker Luis • FRG
DUELL MIT DEM TOD • 1949 • May Paul • AUS • AM RANDE DES LEBENS
DUELL VOR SONNENUNTERGANG • 1965 • Lahola Leopold • FRG, YGS, ITL
DUELLE • 1976 • Rivette Jacques • FRN • WOMEN DUELLING (USA) ○ FILLES DE FEU, LES ○ TWILIGHT
DUELLISTE MARSEILLAIS see **PAULUS CHANTANT: DUELLISTE MARSEILLAIS** • 1897
DUELLISTS, THE • 1913 • *Moore Owen* • USA
DUELLISTS, THE • 1977 • Scott Ridley • UKN
DUELLO NEL MONDO • 1966 • Scattini Luigi • ITL
DUELLO NEL TEXAS see **GRINGO** • 1964
DUELLO NELLA SILA • 1962 • Lenzi Umberto • ITL • DUEL OF FIRE (USA)
DUELLO NELL'OMBRA • 1949 • Amata Gaetano • ITL
DUELLO SENZA ONORE • 1950 • Mastrocinque Camillo • ITL • DUEL WITHOUT HONOR (USA)
DUELO AL ATARDECER • 1971 • *Cine Vision* • MXC
DUELO DE PASIONES • 1954 • Seto Javier • SPN
DUELO DE PISTOLEROS • 1965 • Delgado Miguel M. • MXC
DUELO DE VALIENTES • 1962 • Delgado Miguel M. • MXC • CAZADORES DE ASESINOS
DUELO EN EL AMAZONAS • 1964 • Martin Eugenio • SPN
DUELO EN LA CANADA • 1959 • Mur Oti • SPN
DUELO EN LA DESIERTO • 1963 • Martinez Arturo? • MXC
DUELO EN LAS MONTANAS • 1949 • Fernandez Emilio • MXC
DUELO INDIO • 1957 • Aguilar Rolando • MXC
DUELS see **COUPS DE FEU** • 1939
DUENA Y SENORA • 1948 • Davison Tito • MXC
DUENDE • 1989 • Junod Jean-Blaise • SWT, FRN
DUENDE DE JEREZ, EL • 1953 • Mangrane Daniel • SPN
DUENDE Y EL REY, EL • 1948 • Perla Alejandro • SPN
DUENDE Y MISTERIO DEL FLAMENCO • 1952 • Neville Edgar • SPN • FLAMENCO (USA)
DUENDE Y YO, EL • 1960 • Martinez Solares Gilberto • MXC
DUENDES DE ANDALUCIA, LOS • 1968 • Mariscal Ana • SPN • ELVES OF ANDALUCIA, THE
DUERME, DUERME, MI AMOR • 1974 • Regueiro Francisco • SPN • SLEEP, SLEEP, MY LOVE
DUES AND THE UNION • 1953 • Bairstow David • DOC • CND
DUET • 1961 • Donev Donyo • ANS • BUL
DUET • 1964 • Szczechura Daniel • ANM • PLN
DUET • 1968 • Lehky Vladimir • ANM • CZC
DUET FOR CANNIBALS (USA) see **DUETT FOR KANNIBALER** • 1969
DUET FOR FOUR • 1982 • Burstall Tim • ASL
DUET FOR ONE • 1986 • Konchalovsky Andrei • USA
DUETT FOR KANNIBALER • 1969 • Sontag Susan • SWD • DUET FOR CANNIBALS (USA)
DUETT ZU DRITT • 1977 • Janda Gerhard • AUS • A DUO-TRIO
DUETTO VAGABONDO • 1939 • Giannini Guglielmo • ITL
DUFFER • 1971 • Despins Joseph, Dumaresq William • UKN
DUFFY • 1968 • Parrish Robert • UKN, USA • AVEC-AVEC
DUFFY OF SAN QUENTIN • 1954 • Doniger Walter • USA • MEN BEHIND BARS (UKN)
DUFFY'S TAVERN • 1945 • Walker Hal • USA
DUGAN OF THE BADLANDS • 1931 • Bradbury Robert North • USA
DUGAN OF THE DUGOUTS • 1928 • Ray Robert • USA
DUGAY NA SA MAYNILA • 1968 • San Juan Luis • PHL • OLD-TIMER IN MANILA
DUGI BRODOVI (YGS) see **LONG SHIPS, THE** • 1964
DUGO SA BUHANGIN • 1967 • Herrera Armando A. • PHL • BLOOD ON SAND
DUGUN • 1974 • Akat Lutfu • TRK • MARRIAGE, THE
DUHALLOW HOME • 1973 • Hill Colin • SHT • IRL
DUHOVITA PRICA • 1978 • Grgic Zlatko • ANS • YGS • SAD LITTLE GHOST, THE
DUHUL AURULUI • 1974 • Veroiu Mircea, Pita Dan • RMN • LUST FOR GOLD ○ GOLD FEVER
DUI PURUSH • 1945 • *Sircar B. N. (P)* • IND
DUIOS ANASTASIA TRECEA • 1979 • Tatos Alexandru • RMN • GENTLY PASSED ANASTASIA ○ ANASTASIA PASSING GENTLY ○ ANASTASIA PASSED BY ○ GENTLY WAS ANASTASIA PASSING
DUIVEL IN AMSTERDAM, DE • 1919 • Frenkel Theo Sr. • NTH • DEVIL IN AMSTERDAM, THE
DUKE, THE see **UP AGAINST THE ODDS** • 1979
DUKE AND THE ACTOR, THE • 1913 • *Champion* • USA
DUKE COMES BACK, THE • 1937 • Pichel Irving • USA • CALL OF THE RING, THE (UKN)

DUKE DE RIBBON COUNTER • 1911 • Salter Harry • USA

DUKE ELLINGTON AND HIS ORCHESTRA • 1943 • Bonafield Jay • SHT • USA

DUKE ELLINGTON AND HIS ORCHESTRA • 1962 • *Bryan Mike (P)* • USA

DUKE ELLINGTON AT THE COTE D'AZUR WITH ELLA FITZGERALD • 1966 • *Granz Norman (P)* • MTV • USA

DUKE ELLINGTON AT THE WHITE HOUSE • 1969 • *Stiber Sidney J. (P)* • MTV • USA

DUKE ELLINGTON -LOVE YOU MADLY • 1966 • Moore Richard • DOC • USA

DUKE ELLINGTON SWINGS THROUGH JAPAN • 1964 • Poor Peter • SHT • USA

DUKE FOR A DAY • 1915 • Curtis Allen • USA

DUKE FOR A DAY, A • 1917 • Turbett Ben • SHT • USA

DUKE FOR A DAY, A • 1934 • Parrott James • SHT • USA

DUKE IS TOPS, THE • 1938 • *Horne Lena* • USA • BRONZE VENUS

DUKE OF CHICAGO • 1949 • Blair George • USA

DUKE OF CHIMNEY BUTTE, THE • 1921 • Borzage Frank • USA

DUKE OF THE NAVY • 1942 • Beaudine William • USA

DUKE OF WELLINGTON, THE see **SECRET LIVES OF THE BRITISH PRIME MINISTERS: THE IRON DUKE, THE** • 1983

DUKE OF WEST POINT, THE • 1938 • Green Alfred E. • USA

DUKE OF YORK'S SPEECH AT CANBERRA • 1927 • *De Forest Phonofilm* • ASL

DUKE OF YORK'S SPEECH AT SYDNEY • 1927 • *Sully Wally (Ph)* • ASL

DUKE STEPS OUT, THE • 1929 • Cruze James • USA

DUKE WORE JEANS, THE • 1958 • Thomas Gerald • UKN

DUKES AND DOLLARS • 1918 • Hall Walter • SHT • USA

DUKE'S DILEMMA, THE • 1913 • Edwin Walter • USA

DUKE'S GOOD JOKE, THE • 1908 • Melies Georges • FRN

DUKE'S JESTER, OR A FOOL'S REVENGE, THE • 1909 • Blackton J. Stuart (Spv) • USA

DUKE'S MOTTO, THE • 1908 • *Selig* • USA

DUKE'S PLAN, THE • 1910 • Griffith D. W. • USA

DUKE'S SON • 1920 • Dyall Franklyn • UKN • SQUANDERED LIVES (USA)

DUKHIYARI • 1937 • *Biswas Anil (M)* • IND

DUKKESTUEN • 1950 • Carlsen Henning • SHT • DNM

DULCE ENEMIGA, LA • 1956 • Davison Tito • MXC

DULCE MADRE MIA • 1942 • Patino Gomez Alfonso • MXC

DULCE NOMBRE • 1951 • Gomez Bascuas Enrique • SPN

DULCEMENTE MORIRAS POR AMOR • 1976 • Demicheli Tulio • SPN

DULCES HORAS • 1981 • Saura Carlos • SPN, FRN • DOUCE MOMENTS DU PASSE (FRN) ○ TENDER HOURS (UKN) ○ SWEET HOURS

DULCIE'S ADVENTURE • 1916 • Kirkwood James • USA

DULCIMA • 1970 • Dorn Rudi • CND

DULCIMA • 1971 • Nesbitt Frank • UKN

DULCIMER STREET (USA) see **LONDON BELONGS TO ME** • 1948

DULCINEA • 1962 • Escriva Vicente • SPN • GIRL FROM LA MANCHA

DULCY • 1923 • Franklin Sidney A. • USA

DULCY • 1940 • Simon S. Sylvan • USA

DULCY see **NOT SO DUMB** • 1930

DULHA DULHAN • 1964 • *Kapoor Raj* • IND

DULHAN EK RAAT KI • 1967 • Kashyap Dharm Dev • IND • BRIDE FOR A SINGLE NIGHT

DULL CARE • 1919 • Semon Larry • SHT • USA

DULL CLANG, A see **HARD KLANG** • 1952

DULL RAZOR • 1900 • Porter Edwin S. • USA

DULL RAZOR, THE • 1900 • Smith G. A. • UKN

DULL RAZOR, THE • 1910 • *Selig* • USA

DULSCY • 1976 • Rybkowski Jan • PLN

DUM-BOM • 1953 • Poppe Nils • SWD • STUPID BOM

DUM NA PREDMESTI • 1933 • Cikan Miroslav • CZC • HOUSE IN THE SUBURBS, A ○ SUBURBAN HOUSE, THE

DUM PATROL, THE • 1930 • Harman Hugh, Ising Rudolf • ANS • USA

DUM PRO DVA • 1988 • Zabransky Milos • CZC • HOUSE FOR TWO, A

DUM ZTRACENYCH DUSI • 1967 • Hanibal Jiri • CZC • HOUSE OF LOST SOULS, THE

DUMA EL SILENCIO • 1968 • Berriatua Luciano • SHT • SPN

DUMB, THE see **STUMME, DER** • 1976

DUMB BANDIT, THE • 1916 • Ford Francis • SHT • USA

DUMB BELL, THE • 1922 • Parrott Charles • USA

DUMB-BELL, THE • 1922 • Roach Hal • SHT • USA

DUMB-BELLS IN ERMINE • 1930 • Adolfi John G. • USA • DUMBELLES IN ERMINE

DUMB BUT DISCIPLINED see **BETE MAIS DISCIPLINE** • 1978

DUMB CLUCK, THE • 1937 • *Lantz Walter (P)* • ANS • USA

DUMB COMRADES • 1910 • Fitzhamon Lewin • UKN

DUMB CONSCIOUS MIND, THE • 1942 • Sommer Paul, Hubley John • ANS • USA

DUMB DADDIES • 1928 • Yates Hal • SHT • USA

DUMB DICKS see **PRIVATE DETECTIVE** • 1986

DUMB DORA DISCOVERS TOBACCO • 1945 • Hawtrey Charles • UKN • FAG END

DUMB DRAGONS GO TO SEA see **SHA LUNG CH'UN-HAI** • 1989

DUMB GIRL OF PORTICI, THE • 1916 • Weber Lois, Smalley Phillips • USA

DUMB HALF BREED'S DEFENCE, THE • 1910 • *Anderson Broncho Billy* • USA

DUMB HEIRESS, THE • 1916 • Ellis Robert • USA

DUMB HERO, A • 1908 • Porter Edwin S. • USA

DUMB HOUNDED • 1943 • Avery Tex • ANS • USA

DUMB LIKE A FOX • 1941 • *Mintz Charles (P)* • ANS • USA

DUMB LIKE A FOX • 1964 • Marcus Sid • ANS • USA

DUMB MAN OF MANCHESTER, THE • 1908 • Haggar William • UKN

DUMB MAN'S EVIDENCE, THE • 1915 • Batley Ernest G. • UKN

DUMB MATCHMAKER, THE • 1912 • Haldane Bert? • UKN

DUMB MESSENGER, THE • 1911 • *Imp* • USA

DUMB MESSENGER, THE • 1913 • *Kalem* • USA

DUMB PATROL • 1964 • Chiniquy Gerry • ANS • USA

DUMB SAGACITY • 1907 • Fitzhamon Lewin • UKN

DUMB WAITER, A • 1928 • Edwards Harry J. • SHT • USA

DUMB WAITER, THE • 1989 • Altman Robert • USA

DUMB WITNESS, THE • 1908 • Brooke Van Dyke • USA

DUMB WOOING, THE • 1912 • Louis Will • USA

DUMBO • 1941 • Sharpsteen Ben • ANM • USA

DUMBBELL OF THE YUKON • 1946 • King Jack • ANS • USA

DUMBBELLS IN DERBIES • 1931 • Foster Lewis R. • SHT • USA

DUMBELLES IN ERMINE see **DUMB-BELLS IN ERMINE** • 1930

DUMBELLS, THE • 1965 • Barclay Robert • MTV • CND

DUMB'S THE WORD • 1937 • Goodwins Leslie • SHT • USA

DUMELA SAM • 1981 • SAF

DUMINICA LA ORA 6 • 1965 • Pintile Lucian • RMN • SUNDAY AT 6 O'CLOCK

DUMKA • 1964 • Paradjanov Sergei • USS • BALLAD, THE

DUMME AUGUST DES ZIRKUS ROMANELLI, DER • 1926 • Jacoby Georg • FRG

DUMMERJONS OCH SVINAHERDEN • 1952 • *Kinch Olle (Edt)* • SWD, USA

DUMMIES AND DECEPTIONS • 1917 • Kernan Henry • SHT • USA

DUMMKOPF, DER • 1920 • Pick Lupu • FRG • IDIOT, THE

DUMMY • 1979 • Perry Frank • USA • SILENCE OF DONALD LANG, THE

DUMMY, THE • 1916 • Kellino W. P. • UKN

DUMMY, THE • 1917 • Grandon Francis J. • USA

DUMMY, THE • 1929 • Milton Robert • USA

DUMMY ACHE • 1936 • Goodwins Leslie • SHT • USA

DUMMY DIRECTOR, THE • 1912 • *Champion* • USA

DUMMY OF DEATH see **NUR TOTE ZEUGEN SCHWEIGEN** • 1963

DUMMY OWNER • 1938 • Yarbrough Jean • SHT • USA

DUMMY PARTNER see **BLIND MAKKER** • 1976

DUMMY TALKS, THE • 1943 • Mitchell Oswald • UKN

DUNA BULL, THE • 1971 • Henson Laurence • UKN

DUNA – HALAK – MADARAK • 1971 • Szabo Istvan • DCS • HNG • DANUBE – FISHES – BIRDS, THE

DUNAI HAJOS • 1975 • Markos Miklos • HNG • DANUBE PILOT, THE

DUNANAL, A • 1988 • Magyar Balint, Schiffer Pal • DOC • HNG

DUNAPARTI RANDEVU • 1937 • Sekely Steve • HNG • RIVER RENDEZVOUS

DUNCAN HINES • 1964 • Goldman Peter Emanuel • USA

DUNCAN'S WIFE • 1907 • *Walturdaw* • UKN

DUNCES AND DANGERS • 1918 • Semon Larry • SHT • USA

DUNDEE-CRIQUI BOXING EXHIBITION • 1923 • *Brittain Leon D. (P)* • USA

DUNDEN SONRA, YARINDAN ONCE • 1988 • Yonder Nisan • TRK • AFTER YESTERDAY, BEFORE TOMORROW

DUNDERKLUMPEN • 1975 • Ahlin Per • ANM • SWD • THUNDERING FATTY

DUNE • 1975 • Jodorowsky Alejandro • FRN

DUNE • 1984 • Lynch David • USA

DUNE ROLLER, THE see **CREMATORS, THE** • 1972

DUNERA BOYS, THE • 1986 • Lewin Ben • MTV • ASL

DUNFERMLINE • 1974 • Alexander Mike • DCS • UKN

DUNG-AW • 1981 • Brocka Lino • PHL • LAMENTATIONS

DUNGEON, THE • 1922 • Micheaux Oscar • USA

DUNGEON, THE see **SCARF, THE** • 1951

DUNGEON MASTER • 1968 • USA

DUNGEON OF DEATH, THE • 1915 • Weston Charles • UKN

DUNGEON OF HORROR see **DUNGEONS OF HORROR** • 1964

DUNGEONMASTER, THE • 1985 • Turko Rosemarie, Buechler John, Band Charles, Ford Steve, Allen David*, Nicolaou Ted, Manoogian Peter • USA • DIGITAL KNIGHTS ○ RAGEWAR

DUNGEONS OF HARROW see **DUNGEONS OF HORROR** • 1964

DUNGEONS OF HORROR • 1964 • Boyette Pat • USA • DUNGEONS OF HARROW ○ DUNGEON OF HORROR

DUNHUANG YE TAN • 1990 • Li Han-Hsiang • CHN, HKG

DUNIA AL-BANAT • 1962 • Arafa Saad • EGY • UNIVERS DES FILLES, L'

DUNIYA NA MANE • 1937 • Shantaram Rajaram • IND • UNEXPECTED, THE

DUNIYA NACHEGI • 1967 • Parvez K. • IND • WORLD WILL DANCE, THE

DUNJA • 1955 • von Baky Josef • AUS

DUNKED IN THE DEEP • 1949 • White Jules • SHT • USA

DUNKEL BEI TAGESLICHT see **NAPPALI SOTETSEG** • 1963

DUNKI-SCHOTT • 1986 • Wyss Tobias • SWT

DUNKIRK • 1958 • Norman Leslie • UKN

DUNKLE GASSEN • 1923 • *Duval Charlotte* • FRG

DUNKLE PUNKT, DER • 1940 • Zoch Georg • FRG

DUNKLE SCHLOSS, DAS • 1915 • Zeyn Willy • FRG

DUNKLE STERN, DER • 1955 • Kugelstadt Hermann • FRG

DUNKLE TAG, DER • 1943 • von Bolvary Geza • FRG

DUNKLING OF THE CIRCUS • 1917 • Moss Howard S. • ANM • USA

DUNOYER DE SEGONZAC • 1965 • Reichenbach Francois • SHT • FRN

DUNUNGEN • 1919 • Hedqvist Ivan, Jaenzon Julius • SWD • DOWNY GIRL, THE (USA) ○ QUEST OF HAPPINESS, THE

DUNUNGEN • 1941 • Hildebrand Weyler • SWD • DOWNY GIRL

DUNWICH HORROR, THE • 1970 • Haller Daniel • USA

DUNYANIN EN GUZEL KADINI • 1968 • Saydam Nejat • TRK • MOST BEAUTIFUL GIRL IN THE WORLD, THE

DUO • 1969 • USA

DUO see **PAS DE DEUX** • 1968

DUO CONCERTANTES • 1964 • Jordan Larry • ANS • USA

DUO.. TRIO.. CUARTETO • 1971 • *Filman International* • MXC

DUOMO DI MILANO, IL • 1946 • Blasetti Alessandro • DOC • ITL

DUOS SUR CANAPE • 1980 • Camoletti Marc • FRN

DUPAAMIAZA OBISNUITA • 1968 • Pita Dan • SHT • RMN • COMMON AFTERNOON

DUPE, THE • 1914 • *Frazer Robert* • USA

DUPE, THE • 1916 • *Knickerbocker Star* • SHT • USA

DUPE, THE • 1916 • Reicher Frank • *Lasky* • USA

DUPE, THE • 1916 • Worthington William • *Gold Seal* • SHT • USA

DUPE, THE see **KAMO** • 1965

DUPED • 1925 • McGowan J. P. • USA

DUPED BY DETERMINATION • 1912 • Rains Fred • UKN

DUPED JOURNALIST, THE see **BECSAPOTT UJSAPIRO, A** • 1914

DUPED OTHELLO, THE • 1909 • Smith Jack • UKN • THEATRICAL CHIMNEY SWEEP, THE

DUPED TILL DOOMSDAY see **BETROGEN BIS ZUM JUNGSTEN TAG** • 1957

DUPES, LES see **MAKHDU UN, AL-** • 1972

DUPKATA • 1967 • Doicheva Zdenka • BUL • HOLE, THE

DUPLICATA see **COPIE CONFORME** • 1946

DUPLICITY • 1916 • Drew Sidney • SHT • USA

DUPLICITY • 1978 • Brakhage Stan • SHT • USA

DUPLICITY II • 1978 • Brakhage Stan • SHT • USA

DUPLICITY III • 1980 • Brakhage Stan • SHT • USA

DUPLICITY OF HARGRAVES, THE • 1917 • Mills Thomas R. • USA

DUPLIZITAT DER EREIGNISSE, DER • 1919 • Gartner Adolf • FRG

DUPONT-BARBES • 1951 • Lepage Henri • FRN • MALOU DE MONTMARTRE

DUPONT LA JOIE • 1975 • Boisset Yves • FRN • RAPE OF INNOCENCE (USA)

DUQUE NEGRO, EL (SPN) see **DUCA NERO, IL** • 1963

DUQUESA DE BENAMEJI, LA • 1949 • Lucia Luis • SPN

DUQUESA DEL TEPETATE, LA • 1951 • Segura Juan Jose • MXC • PRETENDIENTE ARDIENTE, EL

DUQUESA DIABOLICA, LA • 1963 • Martinez Arturo • MXC • DIABOLIC DUCHESS, THE

DUR DESIR DE DIRE, LE • 1981 • D'Aix Alain • DOC • CND

DUR, DUR • 1981 • Korber Serge • FRN

DUR METIER DE FRERE, LE • 1980 • Moreau Michel (c/d) • MTV • CND

DURA LEX see **PO ZAKONU** • 1926

DURA MINGA see **MAZURKA DI PAPA, LA** • 1938

DURAND BIJOUTIER • 1938 • Stelli Jean • FRN

DURAND CONTRE DURAND • 1931 • Joannon Leo, Thiele Eugen • FRN

DURAND OF THE BAD LANDS • 1917 • Stanton Richard • USA

DURAND OF THE BAD LANDS • 1925 • Reynolds Lynn • USA

DURANGO • 1967 • Diaz Leody M. • PHL

DURANGO KID, THE • 1940 • Hillyer Lambert • USA • MASKED STRANGER, THE (UKN)

DURANGO VALLEY RAIDERS • 1938 • Newfield Sam • USA

DURANT AFFAIR, THE • 1962 • Grayson Godfrey • UKN

DURANTE L'ESTATE • 1971 • Olmi Ermanno • ITL • DURING THE SUMMER (USA) ○ IN THE SUMMERTIME

DURATION see **WHITCHURCH DOWN** • 1972

DURATION OF THE WAR, THE see **LONGITUD DE GUERRA** • 1975

DURATON, LES • 1955 • Berthomieu Andre • FRN

DURBARGATI PADMA • 1971 • *Ghatak Ritwik* • IND

"DURCH" • 1915 • *Lunafilm* • FRG

DURCH ALLE HOLLEN • 1920 • Attenberger Toni • FRG

DURCH DICK UND DUNN • 1915 • Del Zopp Rudolf • FRG

DURCH DICK UND DUNN • 1951 • Lingen Theo • FRG

DURCH DIE QUARTIERE DES ELENDS UND VERBRECHENS • 1920 • Land Robert • AUS

DURCH DIE WALDER, DURCH DIE AUEN • 1956 • Pabst G. W. • FRG

DURCH FLAMMEN ZUM GLUCK • 1925 • *Problem-Film* • FRG

DURCH LIEBE ERLOST • 1921 • Eckstein Franz • FRG

DURCH NACHT ZUM LICHT • 1915 • Schonfeld Carl • FRG

DURCH SELIGKEIT UND SUNDEN • 1920 • *Andersen Iven* • FRG

DURCH WAHRHEIT ZUM NARREN • 1920 • Fleck Jacob, Fleck Luise • AUS

DURCH WIE WUSTE • 1936 • Hubler-Kahla J. A. • FRG

DURCHBRUCH LOK 234 • 1963 • Wisbar Frank • FRG • BREAKTHROUGH, THE

DURCHGANGERIN, DIE • 1928 • Schwarz Hanns • FRG • LOVE'S SACRIFICE

DURCHLAUCHT AMUSIERST SICH • 1932 • Wiene Conrad • FRG

DURCHLAUCHT DER REISENDE • 1915 • Karfiol William • FRG

DURCHLAUCHT HYPOCHONDER • 1917 • Dupont E. A. • FRG

DURCHLAUCHT RADIESCHEN • 1927 • Eichberg Richard • FRG

DURCHLAUT, DIE WASCHERIN see **PURPUR UND WASCHBLAU** • 1931

DURCHS BRANDENBURGER TOR • 1929 • Knaake Max • FRG

DURCHS WILDE KURDISTAN • 1965 • Gottlieb Franz J. • FRG, SPN • WILD KURDISTAN (UKN)

DURFEN SIE WIEDERKOMMEN? • 1971 • Nestler Peter • FRG

DURFEN WIR SCHWEIGEN? • 1926 • Oswald Richard • FRG

DURGA AS THE GODDESS OF DESTRUCTION see **ADYASAKTI MAHAMAYA** • 1968

DURI A MORIRE • 1979 • D'Amato Joe • ITL

DURING CHERRY TIME • 1911 • Salter Harry • USA

DURING ONE NIGHT • 1961 • Furie Sidney J. • UKN • NIGHT OF PASSION

DURING THE DAY -AT NIGHT see **TAGSUBER -ABENDS** • 1973

DURING THE PLAGUE see **MENS PESTEN RASER** • 1913

DURING THE ROUND-UP • 1913 • Cabanne W. Christy • USA

DURING THE SUMMER (USA) see **DURANTE L'ESTATE** • 1971

DURJANA • 1970 • Rojik Omar • MLY • WICKED

DURS A CUIRE, LES • 1964 • Pinoteau Jack • FRN

DUS-INTORS • Daneliuc Mircea • SHT • RMN • ALLER-RETOUR

DUS LAKH • 1967 • Goel Devendra • IND • TEN LAKHS

DUSHMAN • 1938 • *Sircar B. N. (P)* • IND

DUSHMAN • 1943 • Guha Dulal • IND

DUSHMANOON KEY DUSHMAN • 1988 • Fazil Javed • PKS • ENEMY

DUSHTU PARJAPATI • 1967 • Chakravarty Shyam • IND • MISCHEVIOUS BUTTERFLY

DUSK TO DAWN • 1922 • Vidor King • USA

DUSKS AND DAWNS see **ALKONYOK ES HAJNALOK** • 1961

DUSKY MELODIES • 1930 • Oumansky Alexander • UKN

DUSMAN • 1980 • Okten Zeki • TRK • ENEMY, THE

DUSMAN ASIKLAR • 1967 • Gorec Ertem • TRK • HOSTILE LOVERS

DUSSELDORF, EQUILIBRE URBAIN • 1974 • Regnier Michel • DOC • CND

DUSSELDORF -MODISCH, HEITER, IM WIND VERSPIELT • 1961 • Vesely Herbert • FRG

DUST • 1916 • Sloman Edward • USA
DUST • Winzentsen Franz, Winzentsen Ursula • ANS • FRG
DUST • 1985 • Hansel Marion • BLG, FRN
DUST AND GOLD • 1955 • Guillermin John • UKN
DUST BE MY DESTINY • 1939 • Seiler Lewis • USA
DUST FEVER • 1962 • Watkins Peter • UKN
DUST FLOWER, THE • 1922 • Lee Rowland V. • USA
DUST IN FRONT OF THE SUN see **STAUB VOR DER SONNE** • 1990
DUST IN THE SUN • 1958 • Robinson Lee • ASL
DUST OF DESIRE • 1919 • Vekroff Perry N. • USA
DUST OF DESIRE see **SONG OF LOVE, THE** • 1923
DUST OF EGYPT, THE • 1915 • Baker George D. • USA
DUST, VICTOR OVER THE SUN see **POLVO VENCEDOR DEL SOL** • 1979
DUSTBIN PARADE • 1942 • Halas John, Batchelor Joy • ANS • UKN
DUSTCAP DOORMAT • 1958 • Kouzel Al • ANS • USA
DUSTERE SCHATTEN, STRAHLENDES GLUCK • 1924 • Ehrhardt Max • FRG
DUSTMAN'S HOLIDAY, THE • 1913 • Kellino W. P. • UKN
DUSTMAN'S NIGHTMARE, THE • 1915 • Kellino W. P. • UKN
DUSTMAN'S OUTING, THE • 1916 • Kellino W. P. • UKN
DUSTMAN'S WEDDING, THE • 1916 • Kellino W. P. • UKN
DUSTS OF THE EARTH see **MGA ALABOK SA LUPA** • 1967
DUSTY • 1982 • Richardson John • ASL
DUSTY AND SWEETS MCGEE • 1971 • Mutrux Floyd • DOC • USA
DUSTY BATES • 1947 • Catling Darrell • SRL • UKN
DUSTY BROWN see **ADVENTURES OF BUSTY BROWN, THE** • 1964
DUSTY DICK'S AWAKENING • 1911 • Coleby A. E. • UKN • DUSTY GETS A SHOCK (USA)
DUSTY ERMINE • 1936 • Vorhaus Bernard • UKN • HIDEOUT IN THE ALPS (USA)
DUSTY GETS A SHOCK (USA) see **DUSTY DICK'S AWAKENING** • 1911
DUSTY PLACE see **JINKYO** • 1924
DUSTY RHODES TAKES A FLIGHT • 1911 • *Pathe* • FRN
DUSTY WORLD see **JINKYO** • 1924
DUSTY'S FINISH • 1915 • *Banner* • USA
DUTCH COURAGE • 1922 • Dunstall George • UKN
DUTCH ELM DISEASE • 1948 • Garceau Raymond • DCS • CND • ORME EN PERIL, L'
DUTCH GIRLS • 1985 • Foster Giles • MTV • UKN
DUTCH GOLD MINE, THE • 1911 • Sennett Mack • USA
DUTCH IN SEVEN LESSONS • 1948 • van der Linden Charles Huguenot • NTH, UKN
DUTCH SCULPTURE see **NEDERLANDSE BEELDHOUWKUNST TIJDENS DE LATE MIDDELEEUWEN** • 1951
DUTCH T.T., THE • 1954 • Mason Bill • DOC • UKN
DUTCH TREAT • 1930 • *Terry Paul/ Moser Frank (P)* • ANS • USA
DUTCH TREAT • 1956 • Sparber I. • ANS • USA
DUTCH TREAT • 1987 • *Dots Dolly* • NTH
DUTCH TREAT • 1987 • Davidson Boaz • USA
DUTCH WIVES OF THE WILD, THE see **KOYA NO DUTCHWIVES** • 1967
DUTCHMAN • 1967 • Harvey Anthony • UKN
DUTIFUL BUT DUMB • 1941 • Lord Del • SHT • USA
DUTIFUL DUB, THE • 1919 • Roach Hal • SHT • USA
DUTTURU DUNYA • 1988 • Okten Zeki • TRK • QUEEN WORLD, THE
DUTY • 1911 • *Imp* • USA
DUTY • 1914 • *Francis Alec B.* • USA
DUTY • 1914 • Shaw Harold • UKN
DUTY see **FARZ** • 1967
DUTY see **ROMIOS EHI FILOTIMO, O** • 1968
DUTY AND LOVE see **RING, THE** • 1927
DUTY AND THE BEAST • 1943 • Geiss Alec • ANS • USA
DUTY AND THE MAN • 1913 • Apfel Oscar • USA
DUTY FIRST • 1922 • Perez Marcel • USA
DUTY-FREE MARRIAGE see **VAMMENTES HAZASSAG** • 1981
DUTY OF BROTHERHOOD: A DAREDEVIL OF KANTO see **KYODAI JINGI: KANTO INOCHISHIRAZU** • 1967
DUTY OF BROTHERHOOD: KANTO AFFAIR see **KYODAI JINGI: KANTO ANIKIBUN** • 1967
DUTY OF BROTHERHOOD: THREE BROTHERS OF KANTO see **KYODAI JINGI: ZOKU KANTO SANKYODAI** • 1967
DUTY VERSUS REVENGE • 1908 • Brooke Van Dyke • USA
DUTY'S REWARD • 1927 • Bracken Bertram • USA
DUVAD • 1959 • Fabri Zoltan • HNG • BRUTE, THE ○ SCHEUSAL, DAS
DUVAR see **MUR, LE** • 1983
DUVIDHA • 1973 • Kaul Mani • IND • DILEMMA
DVA BILYETA NA DNEVNOY SEANS • 1967 • Rappaport Herbert • USS • TWO TICKETS FOR THE MATINEE ○ TWO TICKETS FOR A DAY SHOW
DVA BOITSA • 1943 • Lukov Leonid • USS • TWO SOLDIERS
DVA, BOULDEJ, DVA • 1930 • Kuleshov Lev, Agadzhanova-Shutko Nina • USS • TWO, BULDI, TWO ○ GREAT BULDIS, THE ○ 2-BOULDY-2 ○ 2-BULDI-2
DVA DNYA • 1927 • Stabovoi Grigori • USS • SHADOW OF ANOTHER TIME ○ FATHER AND SON ○ TWO DAYS
DVA DRUGA • 1955 • Eisimont Viktor • USS • TWO FRIENDS ○ CHUMS
DVA FEDORA • 1958 • Khutsiev Marlen • USS • TWO FYODORS ○ TWO FEDORS
DVA GODA NAD PROPASTYU • 1967 • Levchuk Timofey • USS • TWO YEARS ON THE EDGE OF A PRECIPICE
DVA KAPITANA • 1956 • Vengerov Vladimir • USS • TWO CAPTAINS
DVA KVINNOR: DEN VITA VAGGEN see **VITA VAGGEN, DEN** • 1975
DVA MRAZICI • 1954 • Trnka Jiri • ANM • CZC • TWO FROSTS, THE ○ TWO LITTLE FROSTS
DVA OHNE • 1949 • Kubasek Vaclav (c/d) • CZC
DVA PUZA • 1960 • Ranitovic Branko • ANS • YGS • TWO SNAILS (USA)
DVA ROKY PRAZDNIN see **UKRADENA VZDUCHOLOD** • 1966
DVA VOSKRESENYA • 1963 • Shredel Vladimir • USS • TWO SUNDAYS
DVA Z ONOHO SVETA • 1962 • Makovec Milos • CZC
DVA ZRNA GROZDJA • 1955 • Djordjevic Purisa • YGS • TWO GRAPES
DVADTSAT DNEI BEZ VOINI • 1976 • Gherman Alexei • USS • TWENTY DAY RESPITE FROM WAR, A ○ TWENTY DAYS WITHOUT WAR
DVADTSAT SHESJ KOMISSAROV • 1936 • Shengelaya Nikolai • USS • TWENTY-SIX BAKU COMMISSARS ○ 26 COMMISSARS
DVADZATDVA NESHCHASTIA • 1930 • Gerasimov Sergei, Bartenev D. • USS • TWENTY-TWO MISHAPS ○ 22 MISFORTUNES
DVAERGEN • 1974 • Raski Vidal • DNM, USA
DVAKRAT KAUCEK • 1939-40 • *Hammid Alexander* • CZC • RUBBER TWICE
DVAMA POD NEBETO • 1962 • Shariliev Borislav • BUL • TWO UNDER THE SKY
DVE POBEDI • 1956 • Shariliev Borislav • USS • TWO VICTORIES
DVE ZHIZNI • 1961 • Voinov Konstantin • USS • TWO LIVES
DVENADTSATAYA NOCH • 1955 • Frid Ya. • USS • TWELFTH NIGHT
DVENADTSTAT STULYEV see **DVINATSAT STULYEV** • 1971
DVEVNIK • 1974 • Dragic Nedeljko • ANM • YGS • DIARY
DVIJE POLOVINE SRCA • 1983 • Hadzismajlovic Vefik • YGS • TWO HALVES OF THE HEART, THE
DVINATSAT STULYEV • 1971 • Gaidai Leonid • USS • TWELVE CHAIRS, THE ○ DVENADTSTAT STULYEV
DVOBOJ ZA JUZNU PRUGU • 1979 • Velimirovic Zdravko • YGS • FIGHT FOR THE SOUTH RAILWAY, A
DVOE see **DVOYE** • 1965
DVOJE • 1961 • Petrovic Aleksandar • YGS • WHERE LOVE HAS GONE ○ WHEN LOVE HAS GONE ○ TWO
DVOJI SVET V HOTELU PACIFIK • 1975 • Majewski Janusz • PLN • HOTEL PACIFIC ○ ZAKLETE REWIRY
DVOJI ZIVOT • 1924 • Kubasek Vaclav • CZC • TWO LIVES
DVORETS I KREPOST • 1925 • Ivanovsky Alexander • USS • PALACE AND FORTRESS
DVORIANSKOE GNEZDO • 1969 • Konchalovsky Andrei • USS • NEST OF GENTLEFOLK, A (UKN) ○ NEST OF THE GENTRY, A
DVORYANSKOYE GNEZDO • 1915 • Gardin Vladimir • USS
DVOYE • 1965 • Bogin Mikhail • USS • BALLAD OF LOVE, A (USA) ○ TWO IN LOVE ○ TWO, THE ○ DVOE
DVOYE I ODNA • 1989 • Gavrilov Eduard • USS • TWO GROWNUPS AND A CHILD
DWA I POL KILOGRAMA SILY • 1966 • Trzos-Rastawiecki Andrzej • DOC • PLN • TWO AND A HALF KILOGRAMMES OF STRENGTH ○ TWO AND A HALF KILOGRAMMES OF POWER
DWA OBLICZA BOGA • 1960 • Hoffman Jerzy, Skorzewski Edward • DCS • PLN • TWO FACES OF GOD
DWA SMYCZKI • 1970 • Nehrebecki Wladyslaw • ANS • PLN • TWO BOW STRINGS, THE
DWA ZEBRA ADAMA • 1964 • Morgenstern Janusz • PLN • ADAM'S TWO RIBS
DWAALLICHT, HET • 1973 • Buyens Frans • BLG
DWADZIESCIA CZTERY GODZINY JADWIGI L. • 1967 • Gryczelowska Krystyna • DOC • PLN • JADWIGA L'S 24 HOURS
DWAJ LUDZIE Z SZAFA • 1958 • Polanski Roman • PLN • TWO MEN AND A WARDROBE
DWAJ PANOWIE N. • 1962 • Chmielewski Tadeusz • PLN • TWO MYSTERIOUS MEN
DWAJ RYCERZE • 1964 • Nehrebecki Wladyslaw • ANS • PLN • TWO KNIGHTS ○ KNIGHTS, THE
DWAJ ZOLNIERZE • 1970 • Gradowski Bohdan • DOC • PLN • TWO SOLDIERS
DWARF AND THE CATERPILLAR, THE see **KOBITO TO AOMUSHI** • 1950
DWARF AND THE GIANT, THE (USA) see **NAIN ET GEANT** • 1902
DWARF NOSE see **ZWERG NASE** • 1921
DWARFS ARE COMING, THE • 1987 • Arafa Sherif • EGY
DWARF'S CAKE WALK, THE • 1905 • *Pathe* • FRN
DWARF'S SPRING ADVENTURES, A see **WIOSENNE PRZYGODY KRASNALA** • 1959
DWATZAT SCHEST DNEJ IS SHISNI DOSTOJEWSKOGO • 1981 • Zarkhi Alexander • USS • TWENTY SIX DAYS IN THE LIFE OF DOSTOEVSKY
DWEEP • 1976 • Kariat Ramu • IND
DWELLER IN THE DESERT, THE see **BURNING SANDS** • 1922
DWELLERS IN GLASS HOUSES • 1915 • Vale Travers • USA
DWELLING PLACE OF LIGHT, THE • 1920 • Conway Jack • USA
DWIE BRYGADY • 1950 • Nasfeter Janusz (c/d) • PLN • TWO BRIGADES
DWIE LEWE RECE • 1968 • Piwowski Marek • DOC • PLN • TWO LEFT HANDS
DWIE NAPRAWY • 1964 • Halladin Danuta • DOC • PLN • TWO REPAIRS
DWIE WARSZAWY • 1962 • Wionczek Roman • DOC • PLN • TWO WARSAWS
DWIGHTANIA • 1959 • Menken Marie • ANS • USA
DWOJE Z WIELKIEJ RZEKI • Nalecki Konrad • PLN • TWO FROM THE GREAT RIVER
DWUDZIESTA PIERWSZA • 1964 • Slesicki Wladyslaw • DOC • PLN • TWENTY FIRST, THE
DYADYA VANYA • 1971 • Konchalovsky Andrei • USS • UNCLE VANYA ○ DIADIA VANYA
DYADYUSHKIN SON • 1967 • Voinov Konstantin • USS • UNCLE'S DREAM, AN
DYBBUK • 1937 • Waszynski Michael • PLN • DYBBUK, THE
DYBBUK, THE • 1960 • Hart Harvey • MTV • CND
DYBBUK, THE see **DYBBUK** • 1937
DYBBUK, THE see **HADYBBUK** • 1968
DYCKERPOTTS ERBEN • 1928 • Behrendt Hans • FRG
DYD OG DRIVERTER • 1923 • Lauritzen Lau • DNM
D'YE KEN JOHN PEEL • 1908 • Gilbert Arthur • UKN
D'YE KEN JOHN PEEL? • 1935 • Edwards Henry • UKN • CAPTAIN MOONLIGHT (USA)
DYED, BUT NOT DEAD • 1913 • Dillon Eddie • USA
DYEN ROZHDYENIYA • 1978 • Odzhagov Rasim • USS • BIRTHDAY
DYEN SOLNTSA I DOZHDYA • 1968 • Sokolov Viktor • USS • DAY OF SUN AND RAIN, A
DYESELBEL • 1954 • PHL
DYESTUFFS • 1968 • Iliesu Mirel • DOC • RMN
DYETI VANYUSHINA • 1974 • Tashkov Yevgyeni • USS • VANYUSHIN'S CHILDREN
DYEVOCHKA IZ BERYOZOVSKA • 1975 • Titov Victor • USS • GIRL FROM BERYOZOVSK, THE
DYEVOCHKA NA SHARYE • 1967 • Shenghelia Levan, Komarovski Gleb • USS • GIRL ON A BALL, A
DYEVUSHKA V CHYORNOM • 1968 • Kasper Veljo • USS • GIRL IN BLACK, THE
DYING, A PART OF LIVING • 1989 • Bonfils Dola • DOC • DNM
DYING DETECTIVE, THE • 1921 • Elvey Maurice • UKN
DYING FOR A SMOKE • 1966 • Batchelor Joy • ANS • UKN
DYING FOR LOVE see **MASQUERADE** • 1987
DYING HARD • 1978 • Haldane Don • MTV • CND
DYING IN THE GULF see **MORIR EN EL GOLFO** • 1990
DYING OF THIRST • 1907 • Fitzhamon Lewin • UKN
DYING ROOM ONLY • 1973 • Leacock Philip • TVM • USA
DYING TO BE PERFECT • 1988 • Hoeter Eileen • DCS • CND
DYKKERKLOKKENS HEMMELIGHED • 1916 • Schneevoigt George • DNM
DYKKET • 1989 • Cole Tristan De Vere • NRW • DIVE, THE
DYM BRAMBOROVE NATE • 1976 • Vlacil Frantisek • CZC • FIRE ON THE POTATO FIELD ○ SMOKE OF POTATO HAULM
DYMKY • 1966 • Jasny Vojtech • CZC, AUS • PFEIFEN, BETTEN, TURTELTAUBEN (AUS) ○ PIPES ○ DIMKY ○ PFEIFEN
DYNAMIT • 1916 • Neuss Alwin • FRG
DYNAMIT • 1947 • Ohberg Ake • SWD • DYNAMITE
DYNAMIT IN GRUNER SEIDE • 1968 • Reinl Harald • FRG, ITL • DYNAMITE IN GREEN SILK
DYNAMITATTENTATET PA FYRTAARNET see **DODSSEJLEREN** • 1911
DYNAMITE • 1919 • Kull Edward • SHT • USA
DYNAMITE • 1920 • Pratt Gilbert • SHT • USA
DYNAMITE • 1929 • De Mille Cecil B. • USA
DYNAMITE • 1938 • *Biswas Anil (M)* • IND
DYNAMITE • 1949 • Pine William H. • USA
DYNAMITE • 1972 • Mills Michael • ANS • CND
DYNAMITE see **MANPOWER** • 1927
DYNAMITE see **DYNAMIT** • 1947
DYNAMITE see **DAINAMAITO NI HI O TSUKERO** • 1959
DYNAMITE ALLEN • 1921 • Henderson Dell • USA
DYNAMITE ANCHORAGE see **MURDER IS MY BEAT** • 1954
DYNAMITE BROTHERS, THE see **STUD BROWN** • 1975
DYNAMITE BROTHERS, THE (USA) see **FRATELLI DINAMITE, I** • 1950
DYNAMITE CANYON • 1941 • Tansey Robert • USA
DYNAMITE CHICKEN • 1971 • Pintoff Ernest • USA
DYNAMITE DAN • 1924 • Mitchell Bruce • USA
DYNAMITE DELANEY • 1938 • Rothman Joseph • USA • FIGHTING CHUMP, THE
DYNAMITE DENNY • 1932 • Strayer Frank • USA • DENNY OF THE RAILROAD (UKN)
DYNAMITE DOCTOR see **YOIDORE HAKASE** • 1966
DYNAMITE DON DON • 1978 • Okamoto Kihachi • JPN
DYNAMITE-EXPERT SAFER'S RIGHT-TO-HOUSING see **STANARSKO PRAVO LAGUMASA SAFERA** • 1974
DYNAMITE GIRLS see **GREAT TEXAS DYNAMITE CHASE, THE** • 1976
DYNAMITE IN GREEN SILK see **DYNAMIT IN GRUNER SEIDE** • 1968
DYNAMITE IS READY, THE see **DINAMITA ESTA SERVIDA, LA** • 1968
DYNAMITE JACK • 1961 • Bastia Jean • FRN, ITL
DYNAMITE JACKSON see **TNT JACKSON** • 1975
DYNAMITE JOHNSON • 1978 • Suarez Bobby A. • PHL, USA, HKG • NEW ADVENTURES OF THE BIONIC BOY, THE ○ 12 MILLION DOLLAR BOY, THE ○ RETURN OF THE BIONIC BOY, THE
DYNAMITE JONES • 1973 • Starrett Jack • USA
DYNAMITE MAN • 1908 • *Kalem* • USA
DYNAMITE MAN • 1975 • Gries Tom • USA
DYNAMITE MAN FROM GLORY JAIL (UKN) see **FOOL'S PARADE** • 1971
DYNAMITE PASS • 1950 • Landers Lew • USA
DYNAMITE RANCH • 1932 • Sheldon Forrest • USA
DYNAMITE SHAOLIN HEROES • Ho Godfrey • HKG
DYNAMITE SMITH • 1924 • Ince Ralph • USA
DYNAMITE SPECIAL, THE • 1917 • Davis James • SHT • USA
DYNAMITE TRIO see **CH'I-SOU SHIN ERH TAO** • 1982
DYNAMITE WOMEN see **GREAT TEXAS DYNAMITE CHASE, THE** • 1976
DYNAMITED DOG, THE • 1913 • *Solax* • USA
DYNAMITED LOVE • 1912 • *Pathe* • USA
DYNAMITERS, THE • 1911 • *Imp* • USA
DYNAMITERS, THE • 1912 • Duncan William • USA
DYNAMITERS, THE (USA) see **GELIGNITE GANG, THE** • 1956
DYNAMO • 1972 • Dwoskin Stephen • UKN
DYNAMO • 1981 • Hwa I Hung • HKG
DYNASTY • 1976 • Chang Mei-Chun • HKG
DYNASTY OF FEAR see **FEAR IN THE NIGHT** • 1972
DYPLOMATYCZNA ZONA • Krawicz Mecislas • PLN
DYPLOMATYCZNA ZONA • 1938 • Boese Carl • FRG
DYRA • 1932 • Medvedkin Alexander • USS
DYREKOBT GLIMMER see **HULDA RASMUSSEN** • 1911
DYREKOBT VENSKAB • 1912 • Blom August • DNM • DEARLY PURCHASED FRIENDSHIP
DYRLAEGENS PLEJEBORN • 1968 • Ottosen Carl • DNM • VETERINARY SURGEON'S FOSTER-CHILD, THE
DYRYGENT • 1980 • Wajda Andrzej • PLN • CONDUCTOR, THE (UKN) ○ ORCHESTRA CONDUCTOR, THE
DYSPEPTIC, THE • 1916 • Bertram William • SHT • USA
DYSPEPTIC AND HIS DOUBLE, THE • 1909 • *Kalem* • USA
DZHOI AND HIS FRIENDS • 1928 • Petrov Vladimir (c/d) • USS
DZIADEK DO ORZECHOW • 1967 • Bielinska Halina • PLN • NUTCRACKER, THE
DZIECI OSKARZAJA • 1956 • Hoffman Jerzy, Skorzewski Edward • DOC • PLN • CHILDREN ACCUSE

DZIECI Z RAMPY • 1963 • Hornicka Lidia • PLN • CHILDREN IN THE LIMELIGHT
DZIECIOL • 1970 • Gruza Jerzy • PLN • WOODPECKER, THE
DZIECIOM • 1968 • Lomnicki Jan • DOC • PLN • TO CHILDREN
DZIEJE GRZECHU • 1911 • Bednarczyk Antoni • PLN
DZIEJE GRZECHU • 1975 • Borowczyk Walerian • PLN • STORY OF A SIN, THE (USA) ○ STORY OF SIN, THE
DZIEN BEZ SLONCA • 1959 • Karabasz Kazimierz, Slesicki Wladyslaw • DCS • PLN • DAY WITHOUT SUN
DZIEN OCZYSZCZENIA • 1969 • Rybkowski Jan?, Passendorfer Jerzy? • PLN • DAY OF PURIFICATION ○ DAY OF REMISSION
DZIEN UPRAGNIONY • 1939 • Szaro Henryk • PLN • ANTICIPATED DAY, THE (USA)
DZIESIEC DNI PIERWSZYCH • 1973 • Brzozowski Andrzej • PLN • FIRST TEN DAYS, THE
DZIESIEC KOLOBRZESKICH DNI • 1971 • Wionczek Roman • DOC • PLN • TEN KOLOBRZEG DAYS
DZIESIECIU Z PAWIAKA • 1932 • Ordynski Ryszard • PLN
DZIEWCZETA Z BUKARESZTU • 1964 • Wionczek Roman • MTV • PLN • GIRL FROM BUCHAREST
DZIEWCZETA Z NOWOLIPEK • 1938 • Lejtes Joseph • PLN • GIRLS OF NOWOLIPEK
DZIEWCZYNA, PRZYGODA I.. • 1961 • Hoffman Jerzy, Skorzewski Edward • DCS • PLN • GIRL, AN ADVENTURE AND..
DZIEWCZYNA Z DOBREGO DOMU • 1962 • Bohdziewicz Antoni • PLN • GIRL FROM A GOOD FAMILY
DZINGIS-KAN see **GENGHIS KHAN** • 1965
DZIS W NOCY UMRZE MIASTO • 1961 • Rybkowski Jan • PLN • TOWN WILL DIE TONIGHT, A ○ TONIGHT A TOWN DIES
DZIURA W ZIEMI • 1970 • Kondratiuk Andrzej • PLN • HOLE IN THE GROUND, A ○ HOLE IN THE EARTH
DZIWNY SEN PROFESORA FILUTEKA • 1956 • Nehrebecki Wladyslaw • ANS • PLN • STRANGE DREAM OF PROFESSOR FILUTEK, THE ○ PROFESSOR FILUTEK'S DREAM
DZUNGLE VELKOMESTA see **JUNGLE D'UNE GRAND VILLE** • 1929

E

E ALLA FINE LO CHIAMARONO JERUSALEMME L'IMPLACABILE • 1972 • Secchi Toni • ITL • PADELLA CALIBRO 38
E ANCHTLANG FUURLAND • 1982 • Klopfenstein Clemens, Legnazzi Remo • SWT • TIERRA DEL FUEGO, A WHOLE NIGHT LONG
E ARRIVATA LA PARIGINA • 1958 • Mastrocinque Camillo • ITL, FRN
E ARRIVATO IL CAVALIERE • 1950 • Steno, Monicelli Mario • ITL
E ARRIVATO L'ACCORDATORE • 1952 • Coletti Duilio • ITL • ZERO IN AMORE
E' ARRIVATO MIO FRATELLO • 1985 • Castellano, Pipolo • ITL • MY BROTHER HAS COME
E.B. WHITE'S CHARLOTTE'S WEB see **CHARLOTTE'S WEB** • 1973
E CADUTA UNA DONNA • 1941 • Guarini Alfredo • ITL
E COMINCIO IL VIAGGIO DELLA VERTIGINE • 1974 • De Gregorio Toni • ITL
...E CONTINUAVANO A CHIAMARLO FIGLIO DI... • 1972 • Romero-Marchent Rafael • ITL
...E CONTINUAVANO A FREGARSI IL MILIONE DI DOLLARI • 1971 • Martin Eugenio • ITL, SPN, FRN • HOMBRE DEL RIO MALO, EL (SPN) ○ BAD MAN'S RIVER (USA)
...E COSI DIVENNERO I TRE SUPERMEN DEL WEST • 1973 • Martinengo Italo • ITL
E, DER SCHARLACHROTE BUCHSTABE • 1918 • Hanus Emerich • FRG • SCHARLACHROTE BUCHSTABE, DER
...E DI SHAUL E DEI SICARI SULLA VIA DI DAMASCO • 1974 • Toti Gianni • ITL
E DIO DISSE A CAINO • 1969 • Margheriti Antonio • ITL, FRG, MNC
...E DIVENNE IL PIU SPIETATO BANDITO DEL SUD • 1967 • Buchs Julio • ITL, SPN • HOMBRE QUE MATO A BILLY EL NINO, EL (SPN) ○ FEW BULLETS MORE, A (USA) ○ MAN WHO KILLED BILLY THE KID, THE
E.F.P.E.U.M. • 1970 • Odreman Mauricio • VNZ • EFPEUM
E-FLAT see **KOMAL GANDHAR** • 1961
E FLAT MAN, THE • 1935 • Lamont Charles • SHT • USA
...E INTORNO A LUI FU MORTE • 1967 • Klimovsky Leon • ITL, SPN • ...AND AROUND HIM WAS DEATH
E LA NAVE VA • 1983 • Fellini Federico • ITL • AND THE SHIP SAILS ON (USA) ○ SHIP SAILS ON, THE
E L'AMOR CHE MI ROVINA • 1951 • Soldati Mario • ITL • LOVE IS MY UNDOING
...E LO CHIAMARONO SPIRITO SANTO! • 1971 • Mauri Roberto, Martin Eugenio? • ITL
'E LOLLIPOP • 1975 • Lazarus Ashley • SAF • FOREVER YOUNG, FOREVER FREE (USA)
E LUCEAN LE STELLE • 1935 • Gallone Carmine • ITL
E MEZZANOTTE, BUTTA GIU ILL CADAVERE • 1966 • Zurli Guido • ITL
E, NAO E? • 1977 • Peyroteo Herlander • PRT
...E NAPOLI CANTA • 1953 • Grottini Armando • ITL
E NATA UNA DONNA see **DIARIO SEGRETO DI UNA MINORENNE, IL** • 1968
E NON DIRSI ADDIO • 1948 • Rosa Silvio Laurenti • ITL
...E PER TETTO UN CIELO DI STELLE • 1968 • Petroni Giulio • ITL • ...AND FOR A ROOF A SKY FULL OF STARS
E PERIGOSO DEBRUCAR-SE • 1946 • Duarte Arthur • PRT, SPN • ES PELIGROSO ASOMARSE AL EXTERIOR (SPN)
E PERMESSO MARESCIALLO? • 1958 • Bragaglia Carlo Ludovico • ITL • TUPPE, TUPPE, MARESCIA
E PIU FACILE CHE UN CAMMELLO • 1950 • Zampa Luigi • ITL, FRN • POUR L'AMOUR DU CIEL (FRN) ○ HIS LAST TWELVE HOURS (USA) ○ TWELVE HOURS TO LIVE ○ SUE ULTIME 12 ORE, LE
E PLURIBUS UNUM • 1969 • Jacobson Alan • SHT • USA • ONE OUT OF MANY
...E POI LO CHIAMARONO IL MAGNIFICO • 1972 • Clucher E. B. • ITL, FRN • MAN OF THE EAST (UKN) ○ MAN FROM THE EAST, A
...E POI NON RIMASE NESSUNO (ITL) see **SELLOUT, THE** • 1975
E PRIMAVERA • 1949 • Castellani Renato • ITL • IT'S FOREVER SPRINGTIME (USA) ○ SPRINGTIME IN ITALY ○ SPRINGTIME
E-ROCK • 1984 • Simoneau Guy • MTV • CND
E-SAITE, DIE • 1921 • Popper Georg • FRG
E SBARCATO UN MARINAIO • 1940 • Ballerini Piero • ITL
E SE PER CASO UNA MATTINA • 1972 • Sindoni Vittorio • ITL
E SIMPATICO MA GLI ROMPEREI IL MUSO (ITL) see **CESAR ET ROSALIE** • 1972
E SPECIALISTE DEL 44 • 1977 • *Saxon John* • ITL, AUS • SPECIALIST, THE
E STATO BELLO AMARTI • 1968 • Sala Adimaro • ITL
E STATO COSI • 1977 • Sherman Tomaso • ITL
E.T. THE EXTRA-TERRESTRIAL • 1982 • Spielberg Steven • USA
E.T.:THE EXTRA-TERRESTRIAL NASTIE see **NIGHT FRIGHT** • 1968
...E TANTA PAURA • 1977 • Cavara Paolo • ITL
E TORNATO CARNEVALE • 1937 • Matarazzo Raffaello • ITL
E TORNATO SABATA.. HAI CHIUSO UN'ALTRA VOLTE • 1971 • Parolini Gianfranco • ITL, FRN, FRG • RETURN OF SABATA (UKN) ○ RITORNO DI SABATA, IL
E TU VIVRAI NEL TERRORE! L'ALDILA see **ALDILA, L'** • 1981
E TUDO A AGUA LEVOU • 1952 • Coelho Jose Adolfo • SHT • PRT
E UNA RUOTA CHE GIRA • 1979 • Rossetti Claudio • ITL
E VENNE IL GIORNO DEI LIMONI NERI • 1970 • Bazzoni Camillo • ITL
...E VENNE IL TEMPO DI UCCIDERE • 1968 • Dell'Acquila Enzo • ITL
E VENNE L'ALBA.. MA TINTA DIROSSO see **NELLA STRETTA MORSA DEL RAGNO** • 1971
E VENNE UN UOMO • 1964 • Olmi Ermanno • ITL • MAN NAMED JOHN, A (UKN) ○ AND THERE CAME A MAN
E VENNERO IN QUATTRO PER UCCIDERE SARTANA • 1969 • Fidani Demofilo • ITL
EA-BANI • 1979 • Carmeno Alex • ITL
EACH ACCORDING TO HIS FAITH • 1955 • Beaudine William • USA
EACH DAWN I DIE • 1939 • Keighley William • USA
EACH DAWN I CROW • 1949 • Freleng Friz • ANS • USA
EACH DAY I CRY see **HIKO SHOJO** • 1963
EACH DAY LIFE BEGINS ANEW see **HAYAT HERGUN YENIDEN BASLAR** • 1978
EACH DOG HAS HIS DAY see **ATTE GONDUKALA SOSE GONDUKALA** • 1968
EACH GOES HIS OWN WAY see **VAR SIN VAG** • 1948
EACH HEART HAS ITS STORY see **VART HJARTA HAR SIN SAGA** • 1948
EACH MAN FOR HIMSELF see **GOLD VON SAM COOPER, DAS** • 1968
EACH MAN'S SON • 1953 • Blais Roger • DCS • CND • MAINS BRISEES, LES
EACH ONE FOR HIMSELF see **GOLD VON SAM COOPER, DAS** • 1968
EACH OTHER see **MOMENTS DE LA VIE D'UNE FEMME** • 1979
EACH PEARL A TEAR • 1916 • Melford George • USA
EACH TO HIS KIND • 1917 • Le Saint Edward J. • USA • RAJAH'S AMULET, THE
EACH WITHIN HIS SHELL see **JIBUN NO ANA NO NAKADE** • 1955
EADIE WAS A LADY • 1945 • Dreifuss Arthur • USA
EADWEARD MUYBRIDGE -ZOOPRAXOGRAPHER • 1975 • Andersen Thom • USA
EAGER BEAVER • 1945 • Crouch William Forest • SHT • USA
EAGER BEAVER, THE • 1946 • Jones Charles M. • ANS • USA
EAGER BEAVERS see **SWINGING BARMAIDS, THE** • 1975
EAGER FINGERS, EAGER LIPS see **SLIP UP** • 1974
EAGER LIPS • 1927 • Noy Wilfred • USA
EAGER TO LIVE see **FEBBRE DI VIVERE** • 1953
EAGER TO WORK see **RARIN' TO GO** • 1924
EAGLE, THE • 1915 • Kent Leon D. • USA
EAGLE, THE • 1918 • Clifton Elmer • USA
EAGLE, THE • 1925 • Brown Clarence • USA • LONE EAGLE, THE
EAGLE, THE • 1986 • Hulette Donald • USA
EAGLE, THE see **AQUILA** • 1981
EAGLE, THE see **ORAO** • 1990
EAGLE AND THE HAWK, THE • 1933 • Walker Stuart, Leisen Mitchell (U/c) • USA
EAGLE AND THE HAWK, THE • 1950 • Foster Lewis R. • USA • SPREAD EAGLE
EAGLE AND THE HAWK, THE see **WASHI TO TAKA** • 1957
EAGLE AND THE LAMB, THE see **SHADOW OF THE EAGLE** • 1950
EAGLE AND THE SPARROW, THE • 1915 • King Burton L. • USA
EAGLE AND THE WOLF, THE see **TAKA TO OKAMI** • 1968
EAGLE BOY see **BOY AGUILA** • 1967
EAGLE CLAWS CHAMPION • *Han Conan* • HKG
EAGLE COMMANDOS • 1968 • Cruz Jose Miranda • PHL
EAGLE FEATHER, THE • 1916 • *Hiawatha* • USA
EAGLE FIST, THE • Cheng Kay Ying • HKG
EAGLE HAS LANDED, THE • 1976 • Sturges John • UKN
EAGLE HAS TWO HEADS, THE (UKN) see **AIGLE A DEUX TETES, L'** • 1948
EAGLE IN A CAGE • 1971 • Cook Fielder • USA, UKN, YGS
EAGLE ISLAND • 1987 • Olsson Mats Helge • SWD
EAGLE OF CAUCASUS, THE see **KAFKAS KARTALI** • 1968
EAGLE OF THE CAUCASUS, THE • 1932 • Mikhin B. A.
EAGLE OF THE NIGHT, THE • 1928 • Fulton Jimmie • SRL • USA
EAGLE OF THE PACIFIC see **TAIHEIYO NO WASHI** • 1953
EAGLE OF THE PLAIN, THE see **YAYLA KARTALI** • 1968
EAGLE OF THE SEA, THE • 1926 • Lloyd Frank • USA • SEA EAGLE, THE
EAGLE-OWLS AND OWLETS see **VOM UHU UND ANDEREN GESICHTERN DER NACHT** • 1936
EAGLE ROCK • 1964 • Geddes Henry • UKN
EAGLE SHADOW FIST • Hdeng Tsu • HKG
EAGLE SQUADRON • 1942 • Lubin Arthur • USA
EAGLE VERSUS DRAGON • 1943 • *O'Brien Joseph/ Mead Thomas (P)* • SHT • USA
EAGLE VERSUS SILVER FOX • Ho Godfrey • HKG
EAGLE WITH TWO HEADS, THE (USA) see **AIGLE A DEUX TETES, L'** • 1948
EAGLES ATTACK AT DAWN • 1970 • Golan Menahem • ISR
EAGLE'S BROOD, THE • 1935 • Bretherton Howard • USA
EAGLE'S CEMETERY, THE (USA) see **CEMETARIO DE LAS AGUILAS, EL** • 1938
EAGLE'S CLAW, THE • 1924 • Seeling Charles R. • USA
EAGLE'S DANCE, THE • 1976 • Zhivolub Viktor • USS
EAGLE'S EYE, THE • 1918 • Lessey George A., Playter Wellington • SRL • USA
EAGLE'S FEATHER, THE • 1923 • Sloman Edward • USA
EAGLE'S FEATHERS see **ORLIE PIERKO** • 1972
EAGLES FLY EARLY, THE see **ORLOVI RANO LETE** • 1966
EAGLE'S MATE, THE • 1914 • Kirkwood James • USA
EAGLE'S NEST, THE • 1915 • Fielding Romaine • USA
EAGLES OF THE FLEET • 1950 • Frankel Cyril • DCS • UKN
EAGLES OF THE FLEET (UKN) see **FLAT TOP** • 1952
EAGLES ON PATROL see **AGUIAS EM PATRULLA** • 1969
EAGLES OUT ON THE HILLS • NKR
EAGLES OVER BRITAIN see **BATTAGLIA D'INGHILTERRA, LA** • 1969
EAGLES OVER LONDON see **BATTAGLIA D'INGHILTERRA, LA** • 1969
EAGLE'S PREY • 1909 • *Powhatan* • USA
EAGLE'S SHADOW, THE see **SHE-HSING TIAO SHOU** • 1978
EAGLE'S TALONS, THE • 1923 • Worne Duke • USA
EAGLE'S WING • 1979 • Harvey Anthony • USA, UKN
EAGLE'S WINGS, THE • 1916 • Leonard Robert Z. • USA
EAR, THE see **UCHO** • 1970
EAR IS NOT A CRYSTAL, THE see **HATI BUKAN KRISTAL** • 1989
EAR-RING, THE • 1915 • Batley Ethyle • UKN
EARGOGH • Lederberg Dov • USA
EARL CARROLL SKETCHBOOK • 1946 • Rogell Albert S. • USA • HATS OFF TO RHYTHM ○ STAND UP AND SING
EARL CARROLL VANITIES • 1945 • Santley Joseph • USA
EARL "FATHA" HINES • 1964 • Moore Richard • USA
EARL OF CAMELOT, THE • 1914 • Wilson Henry • UKN
EARL OF CHICAGO, THE • 1939 • Thorpe Richard • USA
EARL OF PAWTUCKET, THE • 1915 • Myers Harry • USA
EARL OF PUDDLESTONE • 1940 • Meins Gus • USA • JOLLY OLD HIGGINS (UKN)
EARLE BIRNEY: PORTRAIT OF A POET • 1981 • Winkler Donald • MTV • CND
EARLE WILLIAMS IN A LIBERTY LOAN APPEAL • 1918 • *Vitagraph* • SHT • USA
EARL'S ADVENTURE, THE • 1915 • *Hall Thurston* • USA
EARLY ABSTRACTIONS • 1946 • Smith Harry • SHT • USA
EARLY AUTUMN see **KOHAYAGAWA-KE NO AKI** • 1961
EARLY BIRD, THE • 1913 • *Santschi Thomas* • USA
EARLY BIRD, THE • 1925 • Hines Charles • USA
EARLY BIRD, THE • 1936 • Pedelty Donovan • UKN
EARLY BIRD, THE • 1938 • *Mintz Charles (P)* • ANS • USA
EARLY BIRD, THE • 1965 • Asher Robert • UKN
EARLY BIRD AND THE WORM, THE • 1936 • Ising Rudolf • ANS • USA
EARLY BIRD DOOD IT, THE • 1942 • Avery Tex • ANS • USA
EARLY BIRDS • 1906 • Jeapes Harold? • UKN
EARLY BIRDS • 1923 • Brouett Albert • UKN
EARLY CLUE TO A NEW DIRECTION, AN • 1966 • Meyer Andrew • DCS • USA
EARLY CRANES see **RANNIE ZHURAVLI** • 1979
EARLY DAYS IN COMMUNICATION • 1958 • Halas John • ANS • UKN
EARLY DAYS IN THE WEST • 1909 • *Powhatan* • USA
EARLY DAYS IN THE WEST • 1912 • *Bison* • USA
EARLY DAYS OUT WEST • 1912 • Turner • USA
EARLY FASHIONS ON BRIGHTON PIER • 1898 • Smith G. A. • UKN • SCENE ON BRIGHTON PIER
EARLY FROST see **SOMETHING WICKED** • 1982
EARLY FROST, AN • 1985 • Erman John • TVM • USA
EARLY HANDLING OF SPINAL INJURIES • 1954 • Mulholland Donald • SHT • CND
EARLY IN THE MORNING • 1912 • *Cumpson Johnny* • USA
EARLY IN THE MORNING see **RANO UTROM** • 1965
EARLY MORNING see **MORGONVAKT** • 1945
EARLY MORNING see **RANO UTROM** • 1965
EARLY MORNINGS see **PETITS MATINS, LES** • 1961
EARLY OKLAHOMA • 1913 • *Reliance* • USA
EARLY ROUND WITH THE MILKMAN, THE • 1906 • *Urban* • UKN
EARLY SETTLERS, THE • 1910 • *Selig* • USA
EARLY SPORTS QUIZ • 1947 • Barclay David • SHT • USA
EARLY SPRING • 1962 • Bahna Vladimir • CZC
EARLY SPRING see **SOSHUN** • 1956
EARLY SPRING see **BEFORE SPRING** • 1958
EARLY SPRING see **ZAOCHUN ERYUE** • 1963
EARLY SPRING see **BARNDOMMENS GADE** • 1987
EARLY SUMMER see **BAKUSHU** • 1951
EARLY TO BED • 1928 • Flynn Emmett J. • SHT • USA
EARLY TO BED • 1932 • Berger Ludwig • UKN
EARLY TO BED • 1936 • McLeod Norman Z. • USA
EARLY TO BED • 1941 • King Jack • ANS • USA
EARLY TO BED • 1970 • *Stacey Dist.* • USA
EARLY TO BED see **OUT ALL NIGHT** • 1933
EARLY TO BET • 1951 • McKimson Robert • ANS • USA
EARLY TO WED • 1926 • Borzage Frank • USA
EARLY WORKS (USA) see **RANI RADOVI** • 1969
EARLY WORM, THE • 1911 • Fitzhamon Lewin • UKN
EARLY WORM GETS THE BIRD, THE • 1940 • Avery Tex • ANS • USA
EARLY YEARS, THE see **MLADA LETA** • 1952
EARLY'S AWAKENING • 1912 • *Powers* • USA

EARNEST MAN, THE • 1962 • Kristl Vlado • ANM • YGS
EARNING HIS SALT • 1916 • *Teare Ethel* • SHT • USA
EARRINGS OF MADAME DE.., THE (USA) see **MADAME DE..** • 1953
EARS OF EXPERIENCE • 1938 • Goodwins Leslie • SHT • USA
EARTH • 1963 • Sremec Rudolf • DCS • YGS • SOIL, THE
EARTH see **ZEMLYA** • 1930
EARTH see **ZEMYA** • 1957
EARTH see **JORD** • 1986
EARTH, THE see **TSUCHI** • 1939
EARTH, THE see **ARD, EL** • 1969
EARTH, THE see **KHAK** • 1973
EARTH AND BLOOD see **HOMA KE EMA** • 1967
EARTH AND COAL see **ZIEMIA I WEGIEL** • 1961
EARTH AND MANKIND, THE • 1961 • Fraser Donald • SER • CND
EARTH AND THE SKY, THE see **TIERRA Y EL CIELO, LA** • 1977
EARTH BEFORE MAN, THE • 1957 • Glut Don • SHT • USA
EARTH CRIES OUT, THE (USA) see **GRIDO DELLA TERRA, IL** • 1948
EARTH DAYS PASS BY see **ZEMALJSKI DANI TEKU** • 1980
EARTH DEFENCE FORCE see **CHIKYU BOEIGUN** • 1957
EARTH DEFENSE FORCES see **CHIKYU BOEIGUN** • 1957
EARTH DIES SCREAMING, THE • 1964 • Fisher Terence • UKN
EARTH ENTRANCED (USA) see **TERRA EM TRANSE** • 1967
EARTH FALL • 1984 • Donovan Paul • CND
EARTH GIRLS ARE EASY • 1989 • Temple Julien • USA
EARTH II • 1971 • Gries Tom • TVM • USA • EARTH TWO
EARTH IN CHAINS see **ZEMLYA V PLENU** • 1928
EARTH IN DANGER, THE see **ATOMIC RULERS OF THE WORLD** • 1964
EARTH IN LABOUR • 1950 • Halas John • ANS • UKN
EARTH IN REVOLT see **TERRA EM TRANSE** • 1967
EARTH IS A SINFUL SONG, THE (USA) see **MAA ON SYNTINEN LAULAU** • 1973
EARTH IS FLAT, THE see **JORDEN ER FLAD** • 1976
EARTH IS MAN'S HOME • 1967 • Chaparos Nick, Chaparos Ann • SHT • CND
EARTH IS OUR MOTHER, THE see **JORDEN ER VORES MOR** • 1987
EARTH IS OUR SINFUL SONG see **MAA ON SYNTINEN LAULAU** • 1973
EARTH IS SINGING, THE see **ZEM SPIEVA** • 1933
EARTH MESSAGE • 1970 • Cantrill Arthur, Cantrill Corinne • ASL
EARTH PATROL • 1978 • Schultz Carl • SHT • ASL
EARTH SINGS, THE see **ZEM SPIEVA** • 1933
EARTH SMILES, THE see **DAICHI WA HOHOEMU** • 1925
EARTH SPIRIT see **ERDGEIST** • 1923
EARTH STAR VOYAGER see **EARTH*STAR VOYAGER** • 1988
EARTH THIRSTS, THE see **ZEMLYA ZHAZHDYOT** • 1930
EARTH TREMBLES, THE see **TERRA TREMA, LA** • 1950
EARTH TWO see **EARTH II** • 1971
EARTH VS. THE FLYING SAUCERS • 1956 • Sears Fred F. • USA • INVASION OF THE FLYING SAUCERS
EARTH VS. THE GIANT SPIDER see **EARTH VS. THE SPIDER, THE** • 1958
EARTH VS. THE SPIDER, THE • 1958 • Gordon Bert I. • USA • EARTH VS. THE GIANT SPIDER ○ SPIDER, THE
EARTH WAITS, THE see **ZIEMIA CZEKA** • 1954
EARTH WOMAN, THE • 1926 • Lang Walter • USA
EARTH YEAR 2069 • 1970 • *Able Film Co.* • USA
EARTHBOTTOM • 1956 • Romero George A. • DCS • USA
EARTHBOUND • 1920 • Hunter T. Hayes • USA
EARTHBOUND • 1940 • Pichel Irving • USA
EARTHBOUND • 1981 • Conway James L. • USA
EARTHENWARE POTS • 1986 • Volev Nikolai • DOC • BUL
EARTHKEEPING • 1973 • Goldscholl Morton • USA
EARTHLING, THE • 1981 • Collinson Peter • ASL
EARTHLY LOVE • 1976 • Matveyev Yevgeni • USS
EARTHLY PARADISE (USA) see **PARADISO TERRESTRE, IL** • 1940
EARTHLY RITUALS see **KANKON SOSAI** • 1959
EARTHQUAKE • 1974 • Robson Mark • USA
EARTHQUAKE see **DEPREM** • 1977
EARTHQUAKE 7.9 see **JISHIN RETTO** • 1980
EARTHQUAKE ALARM, THE • 1909 • *Schultze* • FRG
EARTHQUAKE IN CHILE see **ERDBEBEN IN CHILE** • 1975
EARTHRIGHT see **RETURN, THE** • 1980
EARTH'S REVENGE, THE see **OMSTRIDTE JORD, DEN** • 1915
EARTH*STAR VOYAGER • 1988 • Goldstone James • TVM • USA • EARTH STAR VOYAGER
EARTHWORM TRACTORS • 1936 • Enright Ray • USA • NATURAL BORN SALESMAN, A (UKN)
EASIEST PROFESSION, THE (USA) see **CHOMEUR DE CLOCHEMERLE, LE** • 1957
EASIEST WAY, THE • 1917 • Capellani Albert • USA
EASIEST WAY, THE • 1931 • Conway Jack • USA
EAST AFRICAN COLLEGE • 1950 • Davies Robert Kingston • DOC • UKN
EAST AFRICAN SAFARI • 1965 • Reichenbach Francois • SHT • FRN
EAST AND ITS HOPES, THE see **ORIENTE Y SU ESPERANZA** • 1970
EAST AND THE WEST, THE • 1911 • *Thanhouser* • USA
EAST AND WEST • 1913 • *Kinemacolor* • USA
EAST CHINA SEA, THE see **HIGASHI SHINAKI** • 1968
EAST END CHANT see **LIMEHOUSE BLUES** • 1934
EAST END HUSTLE • 1976 • Vitale Frank • CND • EAST SIDE HUSTLE
EAST IS EAST • 1916 • Edwards Henry • UKN
EAST IS RED, THE • 1966 • *August First Film Studio* • CHN
EAST IS WEST • 1922 • Franklin Sidney A. • USA
EAST IS WEST • 1930 • Bell Monta • USA
EAST LYNNE • 1902 • Winslow Dicky • UKN
EAST LYNNE • 1908 • *Selig* • USA
EAST LYNNE • 1910 • *Precision Films* • UKN
EAST LYNNE • 1912 • Nicholls George, Marston Theodore • USA
EAST LYNNE • 1913 • Charrington Arthur • *Brightonia* • UKN
EAST LYNNE • 1913 • Haldane Bert • *Barker* • UKN
EAST LYNNE • 1915 • Vale Travers • USA
EAST LYNNE • 1916 • Bracken Bertram • USA
EAST LYNNE • 1921 • Ballin Hugo • USA
EAST LYNNE • 1922 • *Hardy Charles (P)* • ASL
EAST LYNNE • 1922 • *Parkinson H. B.* • SHT • UKN
EAST LYNNE • 1925 • Flynn Emmett J. • USA
EAST LYNNE • 1931 • Lloyd Frank • USA
EAST LYNNE IN BUGVILLE • 1914 • Smalley Phillips • USA
EAST LYNNE ON THE WESTERN FRONT • 1931 • Pearson George • UKN
EAST LYNNE WITH VARIATIONS • 1919 • Cline Eddie • SHT • USA
EAST MEETS WEST • 1936 • Mason Herbert • UKN
EAST MEETS WEST see **CROISIERE JAUNE, LA** • 1928
EAST OF BORNEO • 1931 • Melford George • USA
EAST OF BROADWAY • 1924 • Howard William K. • USA
EAST OF EDEN • 1955 • Kazan Elia • USA
EAST OF EDEN • 1982 • Hart Harvey • TVM • USA • JOHN STEINBECK'S EAST OF EDEN
EAST OF ELEPHANT ROCK • 1976 • Boyd Don • UKN
EAST OF FIFTH AVENUE • 1933 • Rogell Albert S. • USA • TWO IN A MILLION (UKN)
EAST OF FIFTH AVENUE (UKN) see **OBEY THE LAW** • 1933
EAST OF JAVA • 1935 • Melford George • USA • JAVA SEAS (UKN)
EAST OF JAVA (UKN) see **SOUTH SEA SINNER** • 1949
EAST OF KILIMANJARO (USA) see **GRANDE CACCIA, LA** • 1957
EAST OF LUDGATE HILL • 1937 • Haynes Manning • UKN
EAST OF MARACAIBO see **AL ESTE DE MARACAIBO** • 1972
EAST OF PICCADILLY • 1939 • Huth Harold • UKN • STRANGLER, THE (USA)
EAST OF SHANGHAI see **RICH AND STRANGE** • 1931
EAST OF SUDAN • 1964 • Juran Nathan • UKN
EAST OF SUEZ • 1925 • Johnson Martin E. • DOC • USA
EAST OF SUEZ • 1925 • Walsh Raoul • USA
EAST OF SUMATRA • 1953 • Boetticher Budd • USA
EAST OF THE RISING SUN (UKN) see **MALAYA** • 1949
EAST OF THE RIVER • 1940 • Green Alfred E. • USA
EAST OF THE WATER PLUG • 1924 • *Sennett Mack (P)* • SHT • USA
EAST SIDE HUSTLE see **EAST END HUSTLE** • 1976
EAST SIDE KIDS • 1940 • Hill Robert F. • USA
EAST SIDE KIDS MEET BELA LUGOSI, THE see **GHOSTS ON THE LOOSE** • 1943
EAST SIDE OF HEAVEN • 1939 • Butler David • USA
EAST SIDE SADIE • 1929 • Goldin Sidney M. • USA
EAST SIDE -WEST SIDE • 1923 • Cummings Irving • USA
EAST SIDE, WEST SIDE • 1927 • Dwan Allan • USA
EAST SIDE, WEST SIDE • 1927 • Fleischer Dave • ANS • USA
EAST SIDE, WEST SIDE • 1949 • LeRoy Mervyn • USA
EAST SIDE, WEST SIDE • 1972 • Miller Arnold Louis • DOC • UKN
EAST, WEST, HOME IS BEST • Kluge Josef • ANS • CZC
EAST WIND see **VENT D'EST, LE** • 1969
EASTER BABIES • 1911 • *Vitagraph* • USA
EASTER BONNET, THE • 1912 • *Eclair* • USA
EASTER CELEBRATION AT JERUSALEM • 1912 • Olcott Sidney • DOC • USA
EASTER DINNER, THE see **PIGEON THAT TOOK ROME, THE** • 1962
EASTER EGGS • 1907 • *Walturdaw* • UKN • EGGS!
EASTER IN SICILY see **PASQUA IN SICILIA** • 1955
EASTER ISLAND see **ILE DE PAQUES** • 1935
EASTER LILY, AN • 1914 • Johnson Tefft • USA
EASTER PARADE • 1948 • Walters Charles • USA
EASTER SUNDAY see **BEING, THE** • 1983
EASTER YEGGS • 1947 • McKimson Robert • ANS • USA
EASTERN CORRIDOR see **VOSTOCHNY KORIDOR** • 1968
EASTERN COWBOY, THE • 1911 • Dwan Allan • USA
EASTERN CYCLONE AT BLUFF RANCH, AN • 1913 • *Frontier* • USA
EASTERN FLOWER, AN • 1913 • Dwan Allan • USA
EASTERN GIRL, THE • 1912 • Dwan Allan • USA • HER MOUNTAIN HOME
EASTERN NIGERIAN NEWSREEL NO.30 • 1965 • Beresford Bruce • SHT • NGR
EASTERN PERIPHERY • 1980 • Vafeas Vassilis • GRC
EASTERN STAR, THE see **SARK YILDIZI** • 1967
EASTERN WESTERNER, AN • 1920 • Roach Hal • SHT • USA
EASTERN WIND see **KHAMSIN** • 1982
EASTERNER'S PERIL, AN • 1911 • *Bison* • USA
EASTERNER'S SACRIFICE, THE • 1911 • *Standing Jack* • USA
EASTSIDE SUMMER • 1957 • Burckhardt Rudy • SHT • USA
EASTWARD HO! • 1919 • Flynn Emmett J. • USA
EASY • 1978 • Spinelli Anthony • USA
EASY ALLEY see **NONKI YOKOCHO** • 1939
EASY-BREEZY SEEKS THE EASY WAY • 1961 • Topouzanov Christo • ANM • BUL
EASY COME EASY GO • 1914 • *Melies* • USA
EASY COME, EASY GO • 1928 • Tuttle Frank • USA
EASY COME, EASY GO • 1947 • Farrow John • USA
EASY COME, EASY GO • 1967 • Rich John • USA
EASY CURVES • 1927 • Watson William • USA
EASY DOES IT see **MEILTAHAN TAMA KAY** • 1974
EASY DOWN THERE! (USA) see **DOUCEMENT LES BASSES!** • 1971
EASY ED • 1916 • Windom Lawrence C. • SHT • USA
EASY GO see **FREE AND EASY** • 1930
EASY GOING • 1926 • Thorpe Richard • USA
EASY GOING see **WAY OUT WEST** • 1930
EASY GOING see **ON AGAIN, OFF AGAIN** • 1937
EASY GOING GORDON • 1925 • Worne Duke • USA • NO MORE TROUBLES
EASY IN MIND (UKN) see **AIR DE RIEN, L'** • 1989
EASY LIFE • 1944 • Hart Walter • SHT • USA
EASY LIFE, THE see **SORPASSO, IL** • 1962
EASY LIVING • 1937 • Leisen Mitchell • USA
EASY LIVING • 1949 • Tourneur Jacques • USA • INTERFERENCE
EASY MAN, THE see **UOMO FACILE, UN** • 1959
EASY MARK, AN • 1912 • *Thanhouser* • USA
EASY MARKS • 1912 • *Pathe* • USA
EASY MILLIONS • 1933 • Newmeyer Fred • USA
EASY MILLIONS see **EVERYBODY'S DOING IT** • 1938
EASY MONEY • 1913 • *Patheplay* • USA
EASY MONEY • 1914 • *Kalem* • USA
EASY MONEY • 1914 • Smalley Phillips • *Crystal* • USA
EASY MONEY • 1915 • *Pearce Peggy* • USA
EASY MONEY • 1917 • Vale Travers • USA
EASY MONEY • 1922 • *Morton Edna* • USA
EASY MONEY • 1925 • Rogell Albert S. • USA
EASY MONEY • 1934 • Davis Redd • UKN
EASY MONEY • 1936 • Rosen Phil • USA
EASY MONEY • 1948 • Knowles Bernard • UKN
EASY MONEY • 1983 • Signorelli James • USA
EASY MONEY see **STAGE MONEY** • 1915
EASY MONEY see **PLATA DULCE** • 1982
EASY MONEY see **BONY A KLID** • 1987
EASY MONEY (UKN) see **BIG MONEY** • 1930
EASY ON THE EYE • 1933 • Marshall George • SHT • USA
EASY PAYMENTS • 1913 • *Stonehouse Ruth* • USA
EASY PAYMENTS • 1919 • *Strand* • SHT • USA
EASY PECKIN'S • 1953 • McKimson Robert • ANS • USA
EASY PICKINGS • 1927 • Archainbaud George • USA
EASY PREY • 1986 • Stern Sandor • USA
EASY RICHES • 1938 • Rogers Maclean • UKN
EASY RIDER • 1969 • Hopper Dennis • USA
EASY ROAD see **ASYMVIVASTOS** • 1979
EASY ROAD, THE • 1921 • Forman Tom • USA
EASY STREET • 1917 • Chaplin Charles • SHT • USA
EASY STREET • 1930 • Micheaux Oscar • USA
EASY TO GET • 1920 • Edwards Walter • USA
EASY TO LOOK AT • 1945 • Beebe Ford • USA
EASY TO LOVE • 1934 • Keighley William • USA
EASY TO LOVE • 1953 • Walters Charles • USA
EASY TO LOVE • 1960 • Boyer Jean
EASY TO MAKE MONEY • 1919 • Carewe Edwin • USA
EASY TO TAKE • 1936 • Tryon Glenn • USA
EASY TO WED • 1946 • Buzzell Edward • USA
EASY VIRTUE • 1927 • Hitchcock Alfred • UKN
EASY WAY, THE see **ROOM FOR ONE MORE** • 1952
EASY WHEELS • 1989 • O'Malley David • USA • WOMEN ON WHEELS
EASY YEARS see **ANNI FACILI** • 1953
EAT • 1964 • Warhol Andy • USA
EAT A BOWL OF TEA • 1989 • Wang Wayne • USA
EAT AND GROW HUNGRY • 1916 • *Dunham Phil* • SHT • USA
EAT AND RUN • 1986 • Hart Christopher • USA • MANGIA ○ MANIA
EAT IT • 1968 • Casaretti Francesco • ITL
EAT ME KITTY, EIGHT TO THE BAR • 1942 • Davis Mannie • ANS • USA
EAT MY DUST! • 1976 • Griffith Charles B. • USA
EAT OR BE EATEN • 1986 • Austin Phil • USA
EAT THE DOCUMENT • 1972 • Dylan Bob, Alk Howard • USA
EAT THE PEACH • 1987 • Ormrod Peter • IRL, UKN
EAT THE RICH • 1987 • Richardson Peter • UKN
EAT YOUR MAKE UP • 1967 • Waters John* • USA
EATEN ALIVE • 1976 • Hooper Tobe • USA • DEATH TRAP (UKN) ○ STARLIGHT SLAUGHTER ○ SLAUGHTER HOTEL ○ LEGEND OF THE BAYOU
EATEN ALIVE see **MANGIATI VIVI DAI CANNIBALI** • 1980
EATEN ALIVE BY THE CANNIBALS see **MANGIATI VIVI DAI CANNIBALI** • 1980
EATEN-UP SHOP, THE see **U SNEDENEHO KRAMU** • 1933
EATER, AN • 1963 • Fujino Kazutomo • JPN
EATIN' ON THE CUFF • 1942 • Clampett Robert • ANS • USA
EATING • 1969 • Zwartjes Frans • SHT • NTH
EATING • 1990 • Jaglom Henry • USA
EATING OUT WITH TOMMY • 1941 • Dickinson Desmond • UKN
EATING RAOUL • 1982 • Bartel Paul • USA
EATING TOO FAST • 1966 • Warhol Andy • USA
EATS • 1914 • Beggs Lee • USA
EAU, L' • 1966 • Alexeieff Alexandre • FRN
EAU, L' • 1968 • Bedel Jean-Pierre • CND
EAU A LA BOUCHE, L' • 1959 • Doniol-Valcroze Jacques • FRN • GAME FOR SIX LOVERS, A (USA) ○ GAMES FOR SIX LOVERS ○ GAME OF LOVE, THE
EAU CHAUDE, L'EAU FRETTE, L' • 1976 • Forcier Andre • CND • HOT WATER, COLD WATER
EAU D'EVIAN • 1938 • Alexeieff Alexandre • SHT • FRN
EAU DU NIL, L' • 1928 • Vandal Marcel • FRN
EAU ET LA PIERRE, L' • 1959 • Vilardebo Carlos • SHT • FRN
EAU NOIRE, L' • 1986 • Sauriol Brigitte • CND, FRN
EAU QUI COULE SOUS LES PONTS, L' • 1929 • Guyot Albert • FRN • WATER WHICH FLOWS UNDER THE BRIDGES, THE
EAU VIVE • 1938 • Epstein Jean • FRN
EAU VIVE • 1941 • Decae Henri (c/d) • SHT • FRN
EAU VIVE, L' • 1956 • Villiers Francois • FRN • GIRL AND THE RIVER, THE
EAUX D'ARTIFICE • 1953 • Anger Kenneth • SHT • FRN
EAUX PROFONDES • 1981 • Deville Michel • FRN
EAUX SOUTERRAINES, LES • 1956 • Tazieff Haroun • SHT • FRN
EAUX TROUBLES, LES • 1948 • Calef Henri • FRN
EAUX VIVES, LES • 1952 • Mitry Jean • SHT • FRN • FLEUVE: LE TARN, LA
EAVESDROPPER, THE • 1909 • Griffith D. W. • USA
EAVESDROPPER, THE • 1912 • Young James • USA
EAVESDROPPER, THE • 1914 • Henderson Dell • USA
EAVESDROPPER, THE (UKN) see **OJO DE LA CERRAUDURA, EL** • 1964
EB URA FAKO • 1940 • Martonffy Emil • HNG
EBACHE D'UN FILM: LA MAURICIE • 1952 • Tessier Albert • DOC • CND
EBB TIDE • 1915 • Campbell Colin • USA
EBB TIDE • 1922 • Melford George • USA
EBB TIDE • 1932 • Rosson Arthur • UKN
EBB TIDE • 1937 • Hogan James P. • USA
EBB TIDE see **OSEKA** • 1968
EBBE UND FLUT • 1921 • Hartwig Martin • FRG
EBBERODS BANK • 1926 • Wallen Sigurd • SWD
EBBERODS BANK • 1935 • Wallen Sigurd • SWD
EBBERODS BANK • 1947 • Jahr Adolf • SWD
EBBING TIDE, THE • 1915 • Physioc Wray • USA
EBBREZZA DEL CIELO, L' • 1940 • Ferroni Giorgio • ITL

EBENE KITSO • 1968 • Papakostas Giorgos • GRC • ALL THE DOORS FLEW OPEN FOR KITSOS
EBENEZER EXPLAINS • 1915 • *Chamberlin Riley* • USA
EBIRAH, HORROR OF THE DEEP (UKN) see **NANKAI NO DAI KETTO** • 1966
EBIRAH, TERROR OF THE DEEP see **NANKAI NO DAI KETTO** • 1966
EBN AL DAAL, EL • 1976 • Shahin Youssef • EGY • PRODIGAL SON
EBN EL HETTA • 1968 • el Saifi Hassan • EGY • BOY OF THE DISTRICT, THE
EBONY CASKET, THE • 1915 • Davis Ulysses • USA
EBONY, IVORY AND JADE • 1977 • Santiago Cirio H. • USA
EBONY, IVORY AND JADE • 1979 • Moxey John Llewellyn • TVM • USA
EBONY PARADE • 1947 • *Calloway Cab* • USA
EBONY TOWER, THE • 1987 • Knights Robert • TVM • UKN
EBRANLEES, LES • 1972 • de Nesle Robert • FRN
EBREO ERRANTE, L' • 1913 • *Roma* • ITL • WANDERING JEW, THE (USA)
EBREO ERRANTE, L' • 1947 • Alessandrini Goffredo • ITL • WANDERING JEW, THE
ECCE BOMBO • 1978 • Moretti Nanni • ITL
ECCE HOMO • 1915 • Gance Abel • FRN
ECCE HOMO • 1969 • Gaburro Bruno Alberto • ITL • SOPRAVVISSUTI, I
ECCE HOMO • 1972 • Marks Aleksandar, Jutrisa Vladimir, Garnier Max Massimino • YGS
ECCE HOMO • 1978 • Popescu-Gopo Ion • ANM • RMN
ECCE HOMO see **GOLGOTHA** • 1935
ECCE HOMO HOMOLKA • 1969 • Papousek Jaroslav • CZC
ECCENTRIC BARBER, THE • 1908 • *Tyler Walter* • UKN
ECCENTRIC BURGLARY, AN • 1905 • Mottershaw Frank • UKN
ECCENTRIC COMIQUES • 1914 • *Joker* • USA
ECCENTRIC DANCER, THE • 1900 • Hepworth Cecil M. • UKN
ECCENTRIC LODGER, AN see **ORIGINAL LOCATAIRE, UN**
ECCENTRIC SPORTSMAN, THE • 1912 • Booth W. R. • UKN
ECCENTRIC THIEF, THE • 1906 • Mottershaw Frank • UKN
ECCENTRIC UNCLE'S WILL, THE • 1912 • Haldane Bert? • UKN
ECCENTRICITIES OF TRAVEL, THE • 1905 • *Warwick Trading Co.* • UKN
ECCENTRICITIES OF WOMEN see **NOI DOLGOK** • 1963
ECCENTRICS, THE see **CHUDAKI** • 1974
ECCEZZZIUNALE.. VERAMENTE • 1982 • Vanzina Carlo • ITL • REALLY EXCEPTIONAL
ECCITANTI GUERRE DI ADELEINE, LE (ITL) see **A LA GUERRE COMME A LA GUERRE** • 1971
ECCO.. IL FINIMONDO • 1964 • Nuzzi Paolo • DOC • ITL
ECCO LA FELICITA • 1940 • L'Herbier Marcel • ITL • COMMEDIA DELLA FELICITA, LA
ECCO LA FELICITA! (ITL) see **COMEDIE DU BONHEUR, LA** • 1940
ECCO LA RADIO! • 1940 • Gentilomo Giacomo • ITL
ECCO LINGUA D'ARGENTO • 1976 • Ivaldi Mauro O. • ITL • EMMANUELLE'S SILVER TONGUE ○ LINGUA D'ARGENTO
ECCO NOI PER ESEMPIO • 1977 • Corbucci Sergio • ITL
ECCO (USA) see **MONDO DI NOTTE N.3** • 1963
ECELIN GELDI YAVRUM • 1967 • Okcugil Nejat • TRK • YOUR TERM HAS COME, BABY
ECHAFAUD PEUT ATTENDRE, L' • 1948 • Valentin Albert • FRN
ECHAME A MI LA CULPA! • 1958 • Cortes Fernando • SPN, MXC
ECHANGES DE PARTENAIRES • 1976 • Mulot Claude • FRN
ECHAPPATOIRE, L' • 1976 • Patin Claude • FRN
ECHAPPEMENT LIBRE • 1964 • Becker Jean • FRN, ITL, SPN • SCAPPAMENTO APERTO (ITL) ○ ESCAPE LIBRE (SPN) ○ BACKFIRE (USA)
ECHAPPES DE CHARENTON see **OMNIBUS DES TOQUES BLANCS ET NOIRS, L'** • 1901
ECHEBKA see **RAYHA WINE** • 1976
ECHEC AU PORTEUR • 1957 • Grangier Gilles • FRN
ECHEC AU ROI • 1931 • d'Usseau Leon, de La Falaise Henri • FRN • MARI DE LA REINE, LA ○ ROI S'ENNUIE, LE
ECHEC AU ROY • 1943 • Paulin Jean-Paul • FRN
ECHEC D'UN ASSASSIN, L' see **PORTRAIT ROBOT** • 1960
ECHEC ET MAT • 1931 • Goupillieres Roger • FRN • AMOURS TRAGIQUES
ECHELLE BLANCHE, L' see **PROMESSE, LA** • 1969
ECHELON OF DR. M., THE see **ESALON DOKTORA M.** • 1955
ECHENME AL GATO • 1957 • Galindo Alejandro • MXC
ECHENME AL VAMPIRO • 1961 • Crevenna Alfredo B. • MXC • BRING ME THE VAMPIRE (USA) ○ THROW ME TO THE VAMPIRE
ECHIGO TSUTSUISHI OYASHIRAZU • 1964 • Imai Tadashi • JPN • OYASHIRAZU IN THE ECHIGO REGIME ○ STORY FROM ECHIGO, A ○ STORY OF ECHIGO, A ○ STORY FOR ECHIGO, A ○ DEATH IN THE SNOW
ECHIQUER DE DIEU, L' see **FABULEUSE AVENTURE DE MARCO POLO, LA** • 1965
ECHIZEN TAKENINGYO • 1963 • Yoshimura Kozaburo • JPN • BAMBOO DOLL, THE ○ BAMBOO DOLL OF ECHIZEN
ECHO, L' see **SADA', AS-** • 1973
ECHO, THE • 1915 • Ricketts Thomas • USA
ECHO, THE • 1964 • Rozewicz Stanislaw • PLN
ECHO, THE see **YAMA NO OTO** • 1954
ECHO AND NARCISSUS • 1924 • Fleischer Dave • ANS • USA
ECHO MURDERS, THE • 1945 • Harlow John • UKN
ECHO OF A SHOT • 1970 • Nielsen Erik Frohn • DNM
ECHO OF A SONG, THE • 1913 • Dwan Allan • USA
ECHO OF AN ERA • 1957 • Freeman Henry • SHT • USA
ECHO OF APPLAUSE • 1946 • Anderson James M. • UKN
ECHO OF BARBARA • 1961 • Hayers Sidney • UKN
ECHO OF DIANA • 1963 • Morris Ernest • UKN
ECHO OF DISTANT SNOW, THE • 1969 • Golovnya L. • USS
ECHO OF LOVE see **YAMA TO TANI TO KUMO** • 1959
ECHO OF TERROR see **PSYCHO A GO-GO!** • 1965
ECHO OF THE 45 • 1931 • Hogan James P. • USA
ECHO OF THE BADLANDS • 1976 • Eady David, King Tim • UKN
ECHO OF THE FAR MOUNTAIN see **HARUKANARU YAMA NO YOBIGOE** • 1979
ECHO OF YOUTH, THE • 1919 • Abramson Ivan • USA
ECHO PARK • 1985 • Dornhelm Robert • USA, AUS
ECHO RANCH • 1948 • Crouch William Forest • SHT • USA
ECHO SCHOOL see **YAMABIKO GAKKO** • 1952
ECHOES • 1982 • Holender Jacques • SHT • CND
ECHOES • 1983 • Seidelman Arthur Allan • USA • LIVING NIGHTMARE
ECHOES • 1988 • Rennie Barbara • UKN
ECHOES FROM THE PAST • 1971 • Melik-Avekyan G. • USS
ECHOES IN THE DARKNESS • 1987 • Jordan Glenn • TVM • USA
ECHOES OF A SUMMER • 1975 • Taylor Don • CND, USA • LAST CASTLE, THE
ECHOES OF PARADISE • 1989 • Noyce Phil • ASL
ECHOES OF SILENCE • 1965 • Goldman Peter Emanuel • USA
ECHOES OF THE JUNGLE see **COOL WORLD, THE** • 1964
ECHOES OF THE ROAD (UKN) see **PICKUP ON 101** • 1972
ECHOES OF THE WILDERNESS see **KAIKUJA ERAMAASSA** • 1986
ECHOES OF WOLVES see **WILCZE ECHA** • 1968
ECHOES ON THE SHORE see **OSHETIME NE BREGDET**
ECHOES –PINK FLOYD • 1972 • Maben D'Adriann • DOC • FRG, FRN
ECHOES WITHOUT SAYING • 1983 • Mann Ron • CND
ECHOUERIES, LES • 1965-66 • Garceau Raymond • DCS • CND
ECHT DEUTSCHER SIEG, EIN • 1915 • Halm Alfred • FRG
ECHTZEIT • 1983 • Costard Hellmuth, Ebert Jurgen • FRG • REAL TIME
ECI, PEC, PEC • 1961 • Makavejev Dusan • SHT • YGS • ONE POTATO, TWO POTATO
ECLAIR AU CHOCOLAT • 1979 • Lord Jean-Claude • CND
ECLAIR JOURNAL SERIES • 1915 • Cohl Emile • ASS • FRN
ECLAIR JOURNAL SERIES • 1916 • Cohl Emile • ASS • FRN
ECLAIREURS SKIEURS, LES • 1950 • Bonniere Rene • DCS • FRN
ECLAT DE GLOIRE see **MI TI LAMPSI STA MATIA** • 1966
ECLIPSE • 1911 • Blache Alice • USA
ECLIPSE • 1977 • Perry Simon • UKN
ECLIPSE, THE see **GRAHANA** • 1979
ECLIPSE, THE (UKN) see **ECLISSE, L'** • 1962
ECLIPSE, THE (USA) see **ECLIPSE DE SOLEIL EN PLEINE LUNE, L'** • 1907
ECLIPSE AT GRAND'MERE • 1963 • Jackson Douglas • CND
ECLIPSE DE SOLEIL EN PLEINE LUNE, L' • 1907 • Melies Georges • FRN • ECLIPSE, THE (USA)
ECLIPSE DEL SOL • 1943 • Saslavsky Luis • ARG
ECLIPSE OF THE MOON, AN • 1905 • Williamson James • UKN
ECLIPSE OF THE SUN see **ZACMIENIE SLONCA** • 1955
ECLIPSE OF THE SUN VIRGIN • 1967 • Kuchar George • USA
ECLIPSE SUR UN ANCIEN CHEMIN VERS COMPOSTELLE • 1978 • Ferie Bernard • FRN • BRAVADE LEGENDAIRE, LA
ECLISSE, L' • 1962 • Antonioni Michelangelo • ITL, FRN • ECLIPSE, THE (UKN)
ECO DELLA GLORIA, L' (ITL) see **BEAUX JOURS DU ROI MURAT, LES** • 1946
ECOLE #8, L' • 1946 • Petel Pierre • DCS • CND
ECOLE, L' • 1962 • Tanner Alain • SWT
ECOLE, L' see **SZKOLA** • 1958
ECOLE BUISSONIERE, L' • 1948 • Le Chanois Jean-Paul • FRN • I HAVE A NEW MASTER (UKN) ○ PASSION FOR LIFE
ECOLE DE LA LIBERTE • 1959 • Haesaerts Paul (c/d) • BLG
ECOLE DES AUTRES, L' • 1968 • Regnier Michel • DOC • CND
ECOLE DES COCOTTES, L' • 1935 • Colombier Piere • FRN
ECOLE DES COCOTTES, L' • 1957 • Audry Jacqueline • FRN • SCHOOL FOR STRUMPETS
ECOLE DES CONTRIBUABLES, L' • 1934 • Guissart Rene • FRN
ECOLE DES DETECTIVES, L' • 1934 • Delannoy Jean • SHT • FRN
ECOLE DES FACTEURS, L' • 1947 • Tati Jacques • SHT • FRN
ECOLE DES FEMMES, L' • 1940 • Ophuls Max • FRN
ECOLE DES GENDRES, L' • 1897 • Melies Georges • FRN • SCHOOL FOR SONS–IN–LAW, THE
ECOLE DES JOURNALISTES, L' • 1936 • Christian-Jaque • FRN
ECOLE DES VIERGES, L' • 1935 • Weill Pierre • FRN
ECOLE DU MALHEUR, L' • 1908 • Zecca Ferdinand • FRN
ECOLE DU SOLDAT, L' • 1909 • Cohl Emile • ANS • FRN • ARMEE D'AGENOR, L'
ECOLE EST FINIE, L' • 1979 • Nolin Olivier • FRN
ECOLE INFERNALE, L' • 1901 • Melies Georges • FRN • TRIALS OF A SCHOOLMASTER, THE (USA)
ECOLE MILITAIRE, L' • 1969 • Nasser George • SHT • LBN
ECOLE SAUVAGE, L' • 1971 • Natsis Costa, Pianko Adam • DOC • FRN
ECOLES, LES • 1963 • Borowczyk Walerian • ANS • FRN
ECOLES DE BONHEUR • 1954 • Tessier Albert • DCS • CND
ECOLES DE PILOTAGE • 1956 • Mitry Jean • SHT • FRN
ECOLES D'INFIRMIERES • 1957 • Masson Jean • SHT • FRN
ECOLES ET ECOLIERS • Tessier Albert • DCS • CND
ECOLES MENAGERES REGIONALES • 1941 • Tessier Albert • DCS • CND
ECOLES MENAGERES REGIONALES II see **FEMMES DEPAREILLEES** • 1941
ECOLIERES TRES POLISSONNES • Lean Bruce J. • FRN
ECOLOGIA DEL DELITTO see **REAZIONE A CATENA** • 1971
ECOLOGY OF A CRIME see **REAZIONE A CATENA** • 1971
ECOLOGY OF A VIRGIN see **SHOJO SEITAI** • 1967
ECONOMIA DO DINHEIRA • 1954 • Mendes Joao • SHT • PRT
ECONOMICAL BROWN • 1912 • *Simpson Fanny* • USA
ECONOMICAL PETER • 1912 • Collins Edwin J.? • UKN
ECONOMICAMENTE DEBILES, OS • 1960 • Lazaga Pedro • SPN
ECONOMICS OF SEPARATION, THE • 1978 • Bittman Roman • DOC • CND
ECONOMIE DES METAUX, L' • 1943 • Rouquier Georges • SHT • FRN
ECONOMISTS, THE • 1916 • Payne John M. • UKN
ECONOMY • 1912 • *Essanay* • USA
ECONOMY • 1917 • Kellino W. P. • UKN
ECOUTE VOIR.. • 1978 • Santiago Hugo • FRN • SEE HEAR MY LOVE ○ SEE HERE MY LOVE
ECOUTEZ BIZEAU • 1981 • Baissat Bernard • DOC • FRN
ECOUTEZ MAY PICQUERAY • 1984 • Baissat Bernard • DOC • FRN
ECRAN D'EPINGLES, L' • 1973 • McLaren Norman • DCS • CND
ECRIN DU RADJAH, L' • 1913 • Feuillade Louis • FRN
ECRIN DU RAJAH, L' • 1906 • Velle Gaston • FRN • RAJAH'S CASKET, THE
ECRIT SUR LE SABLE • 1966 • Clement Rene • FRN
ECRITURE, L' • 1963 • Borowczyk Walerian • ANS • FRN
ECRITURE DE LA DANSE • 1948 • Painleve Jean • SHT • FRN
ECRIVISSE MATHEMATIQUE, L' • 1969 • Lemaitre Maurice • FRN
ECSTASIES OF WOMEN, THE • 1969 • Hansen Mark • USA
ECSTASY • Thornberg Billy • USA
ECSTASY see **EXTASE** • 1932
ECSTASY see **LOVE SCENES** • 1984
ECSTASY FROM 7 TO 10 see **EXTAZIS 7–TOL 10–IG** • 1969
ECSTASY GIRLS see **SMALL TOWN GIRLS** • 1979
ECSTASY GIRLS, THE • 1979 • McCallum Robert • USA
ECSTASY INC. see **SWEDISH SEX CLINIC** • 1981
ECSTASY OF LOVERS see **HONEYMOON OF TERROR** • 1961
ECSTASY OF YOUNG LIFE (USA) see **REKA** • 1933
ECSTASY ON LOVERS ISLAND see **HONEYMOON OF TERROR** • 1961
ECUELLES, LES • 1983 • Ouedraogo Idrissa • SHT • BRK • WOODEN BOWLS, THE
ECUME, L' see **JEU ETERNEL, LE** • 1971
ECUME DES JOURS, L' • 1967 • Belmont Charles • FRN • FROTH OF TIME, THE
ECURIE, L' • 1956 • Bail Rene • CND
ECUYERE, L' • 1922 • Perret Leonce • FRN
ED ORA RACCOMANDA L'ANIMA A DIO • 1968 • Fidani Demofilo • ITL
ED SULLIVAN'S HEADLINERS • 1934 • Schwarzwald Milton • SHT • USA
EDAD DE LA INOCENCIA, LA • 1962 • Davison Tito • MXC
EDAD DE LA PIEDRA, LA • 1965 • Blanco Gabriel • ANS • SPN • STONE AGE, THE
EDAD DE LA TENTACION, LA • 1958 • Galindo Alejandro • MXC
EDAD DE LA VIOLENCIA, LA • 1963 • Soler Julian • MXC
EDAD DE PIEDRA, LA • 1962 • Cardona Rene • MXC
EDAD PELIGROSA, LA • 1950 • Diaz Morales Jose • MXC
EDDIE • 1958 • Smight Jack • MTV • USA
EDDIE see **EDDIE SACHS AT INDIANAPOLIS** • 1961
EDDIE AND SUZANNE see **EDDIE OG SUZANNE** • 1976
EDDIE AND THE CRUISERS • 1984 • Davidson Martin • USA
EDDIE CANTOR • 1929 • Florey Robert • SHT • USA
EDDIE CANTOR STORY, THE • 1953 • Green Alfred E. • USA
EDDIE CARROLL AND HIS BOYS • 1939 • Shepherd Horace • UKN
EDDIE CONDON • 1961 • Rubin Bernard • SHT • USA
EDDIE CONDON'S • 1951 • *Columbia* • SHT • USA
EDDIE CUTS IN see **TIP–OFF, THE** • 1931
EDDIE, GET THE MOP • 1918 • Beaudine William • USA
EDDIE MACON'S RUN • 1983 • Kanew Jeff • USA
EDDIE MURPHY –DELIRIOUS • 1983 • Gowers Bruce • USA
EDDIE MURPHY RAW • 1987 • Townsend Robert • USA
EDDIE OG SUZANNE • 1976 • Kristo Arild • NRW • EDDIE AND SUZANNE
EDDIE PEABODY AND SONNY BURKE'S ORCHESTRA • 1951 • Cowan Will • SHT • USA
EDDIE PEABODY IN BANJOMANIA • 1927 • Foy Bryan • SHT • USA
EDDIE SACHS AT INDIANAPOLIS • 1961 • Leacock Richard • USA • ON THE POLE ○ EDDIE
EDDIE'S AWFUL PREDICAMENT • 1915 • *Lyons Eddie* • USA
EDDIE'S EXPLOIT • 1912 • *Edison* • USA
EDDIE'S LITTLE LOVE AFFAIR • 1915 • Christie Al • USA
EDDIE'S LITTLE NIGHTMARE • 1915 • Lyons Eddie • USA
EDDIE'S NIGHT OUT • 1916 • Christie Al • SHT • USA
EDDINI AKHLAK • 1953 • Kamel Morsi Ahmad • EGY • IT IS UNBELIEVABLE
EDDY • 1969 • *Astro-Jemco* • USA
EDDY DUCHIN STORY, THE • 1956 • Sidney George • USA • DUCHIN STORY, THE
EDDY MERCKX see **COURSE EN TETE, LA** • 1974
EDDY POLO IM WESPENNEST • 1928 • Lasko Leo • FRG
EDDY POLO MIT PFERD UND LASSO • 1918 • Polo Eddie • FRG
EDELSTEINE • 1917 • Biebrach Rudolf • FRG
EDELSTEINSAMMLUNG, DIE • 1918 • Larsen Viggo • FRG
EDELWEISS • 1919 • Zelnik Friedrich • FRG
EDELWEISS • 1923 • *Imperial-Film* • FRG • JENSEITS DER GRENZE
EDELWEISSKONIG, DER • 1919 • Ostermayr Peter • FRG
EDELWEISSKONIG, DER • 1938 • May Paul • FRG
EDELWEISSKONIG, DER • 1957 • Ucicky Gustav • FRG
EDELWILD • 1918 • Schmidthassler Walter • FRG
EDEN AND AFTER (USA) see **EDEN ET APRES, L'** • 1970
EDEN AND RETURN • 1921 • Seiter William A. • USA
EDEN BOYS • 1967 • Navarro Rod • PHL
EDEN CRIED • 1967 • Johnson Fred • USA • IN THE FALL OF '55 EDEN CRIED
EDEN ET APRES, L' • 1970 • Robbe-Grillet Alain • FRN, CZC • EDEN AND AFTER (USA)
EDEN MISERIA see **DESORDRE A VINGT ANS, LE** • 1967
EDEN NO UMI • 1950 • Nakamura Noboru • JPN
EDEN PALACE • Compain Frederic • FRN
EDERA, L' • 1950 • Genina Augusto • ITL • DEVOTION
EDES A BOSSZU • 1938 • Vaszary Janos • SWEET REVENGE (USA)
EDES ANNA • 1958 • Fabri Zoltan • HNG • ANNA ○ SCHULDIG?
EDES ES KESERU • 1966 • Szemes Mihaly • HNG • SWEET AND BITTER
EDES MOSTOHA • 1935 • Balazs Bela • HNG
EDGAR ALLAN POE • 1909 • Griffith D. W. • USA
EDGAR ALLAN POE'S BURIED ALIVE • 1989 • Kikoine Gerard

EDGAR ALLAN POE'S CASTLE OF BLOOD see **DANZA MACABRA** • 1964
EDGAR ALLAN POE'S CONQUEROR WORM see **WITCHFINDER GENERAL** • 1968
EDGAR ALLAN POE'S THE OBLONG BOX see **OBLONG BOX, THE** • 1969
EDGAR AND GOLIATH • 1937 • Goodwins Leslie • SHT • USA
EDGAR AND KRISTINA see **EDGAR I KRISTINA** • 1967
EDGAR AND THE TEACHER'S PET • 1920 • Hopper E. Mason • SHT • USA
EDGAR CAMPS OUT • 1920 • Hopper E. Mason • SHT • USA
EDGAR HAMLET • 1935 • Ripley Arthur • SHT • USA
EDGAR I KRISTINA • 1967 • Leimanis Leonidis • USS • EDGAR AND KRISTINA ○ EDGARS AND KRISTINE
EDGAR POE • 1964-69 • Rohmer Eric • MTV • FRN
EDGAR RUNS IN • 1940 • Davis Mannie • ANS • USA
EDGAR TAKES THE CAKE • 1920 • Litson Mason N. • SHT • USA
EDGAR THE DETECTIVE • 1921 • *Jones Johnny* • SHT • USA
EDGAR THE EXPLORER • 1921 • *Jones Johnny* • SHT • USA
EDGARS AND KRISTINE see **EDGAR I KRISTINA** • 1967
EDGAR'S COUNTRY COUSIN • 1921 • Litson Mason N. • SHT • USA
EDGAR'S FEAST DAY • 1921 • Litson Mason N. • SHT • USA • DAY'S DIET, A
EDGAR'S HAMLET • 1920 • Hopper E. Mason • SHT • USA
EDGAR'S JONAH DAY • 1920 • Hopper E. Mason • SHT • USA
EDGAR'S LITTLE SAW • 1920 • Litson Mason N. • SHT • USA • LITTLE SAW, THE
EDGAR'S SUNDAY COURTSHIP • 1920 • Hopper E. Mason • SHT • USA • DAVID AND GOLIATH
EDGE, THE • 1968 • Kramer Robert • USA
EDGE O'BEYOND • 1919 • Durrant Fred W. • UKN
EDGE OF DARKNESS • 1943 • Milestone Lewis • USA
EDGE OF DARKNESS • 1985 • Campbell Martin • MTV • USA
EDGE OF DARKNESS see **TRUE BLOOD** • 1989
EDGE OF DIVORCE (USA) see **BACKGROUND** • 1953
EDGE OF DOOM • 1950 • Robson Mark • USA • STRONGER THAN FEAR (UKN)
EDGE OF ETERNITY • 1959 • Siegel Don • USA
EDGE OF FEAR • 1964 • Klimovsky Leon • SPN • NIGHT OF FEAR
EDGE OF FURY • 1958 • Lerner Irving, Gurney Robert Jr. • USA
EDGE OF FURY • 1978 • Lee Tso Nam • HKG
EDGE OF FURY • 1981 • Ho George • HKG
EDGE OF HELL • 1956 • Haas Hugo • USA • TENDER HEARTS
EDGE OF HELL • 1986 • Fasano John • USA • ROCK 'N' ROLL NIGHTMARE
EDGE OF POWER • 1988 • Safran Henri • ASL
EDGE OF SANITY see **DR. JEKYLL AND MR. HYDE -A JOURNEY INTO FEAR** • 1988
EDGE OF TERROR, THE see **WIND, THE** • 1987
EDGE OF THE ABYSS, THE • 1915 • West Raymond B.? • USA
EDGE OF THE AXE • 1987 • Braunstein Joseph • USA
EDGE OF THE CITY • 1956 • Ritt Martin • USA • MAN IS TEN FEET TALL, A (UKN)
EDGE OF THE CITY see **CITY'S EDGE, THE** • 1983
EDGE OF THE LAW, THE • 1917 • Chaudet Louis W. • USA
EDGE OF THE WORLD, THE • 1937 • Powell Michael • UKN
EDGE OF THINGS, THE • 1913 • *Essanay* • USA
EDGE OF THINGS, THE • 1915 • *Mayo Edna* • USA
EDGE OF YOUTH, THE • 1920 • Calvert Charles • UKN
EDHIR NEECHAL • 1968 • Balachandar K. • IND • AGAINST ALL OBSTACLES
EDICION EXTRA • 1949 • Barth-Moglia Luis • ARG
EDICT see **ZERO POPULATION GROWTH** • 1972
EDIE • 1989 • Byrum John • USA • GIRL OF THE YEAR, THE ○ WAR AT HOME, THE
EDIFICATION DU BONHEUR, L' • Lavoie Hermenegilde • DCS • CND
EDINBURGH • 1952 • Eady David • DOC • UKN
EDINBURGH ON PARADE • 1970 • Littlewood Mark • DCS • UKN
EDINSTVENNAIA see **YEDINSTVENNAYA** • 1976
EDIPEON • 1970 • Artale Lorenzo • ITL
EDIPO RE • 1967 • Pasolini Pier Paolo • ITL, MRC • OEDIPUS THE KING ○ OEDIPUS REX
EDISON BUGG'S INVENTION • 1916 • Hevener Jerold T. • SHT • USA
EDISON EFFECT see **DESTROYER** • 1988
EDISON MAES DAGBOG see **NATTEVANDREREN** • 1917
EDISON, MARCONI & CO. • 1928 • Mack Anthony • SHT • USA
EDISON THE MAN • 1940 • Brown Clarence • USA
EDISON TWINS, THE • 1983 • Dalen Zale R., Bonniere Rene, Shapiro Paul • SER • CND
EDISON'S DOG FACTORY see **DOG FACTORY** • 1904
EDIT, THE • 1986 • Todd Michael • SHT • CND
EDITH • 1970 • Hustaix Lucien • FRN
EDITH AND MARCEL (USA) see **EDITH ET MARCEL** • 1983
EDITH CAVELL • 1916 • Lincoln W. J. • ASL
EDITH ET MARCEL • 1983 • Lelouch Claude • FRN • EDITH AND MARCEL (USA)
EDITH PIAF • Derrien Denis • DOC • FRN
EDITH SITWELL • 1927 • Newman Widgey R. • UKN
EDITH STEIN • 1962 • Delouche Dominique • SHT • FRN
EDITH'S VICTORY FOR DEMOCRACY • 1918 • *Storey Edith* • SHT • USA
EDITIE SPECIALA • 1978 • Daneliuc Mircea • RMN • SPECIAL ISSUE
EDITIONS DE LUXE • 1915 • *Sears A. D.* • USA
EDITOR, THE • 1912 • *Champion* • USA
EDITOR AND THE MILLIONAIRE, THE • 1912 • Fitzhamon Lewin? • UKN
EDLE BLUT, DAS • 1927 • Boese Carl • FRG
EDMUND KEAN, PRINCE AMONG PLAYERS • 1927 • St. Louis Albert
EDMUNDO ROS HALF HOUR • 1957 • Carreras Michael • SHT • UKN
EDNA, THE INEBRIATE WOMAN • 1971 • Kotcheff Ted • MTV • UKN
EDNA'S IMPRISONMENT • 1911 • *Edison* • USA
EDO MIYAGE KOMORI UTA • 1936 • Ito Daisuke • JPN
EDO NO AKUTARO • 1959 • Makino Masahiro • JPN
EDO NO SAIGO NO HI see **EDO SAIGO NO HI** • 1941
EDO NO YUBAE • 1954 • Nakamura Noboru • JPN • EDO SUNSET
EDO PORN • Shindo Kaneto • JPN
EDO SAIGO NO HI • 1941 • Inagaki Hiroshi • JPN • LAST DAYS OF EDO, THE ○ EDO NO SAIGO NO HI
EDO SUNSET see **EDO NO YUBAE** • 1954
EDOICKO HANJOKI • 1961 • Makino Masahiro • JPN
EDOKKO MATSURI • 1958 • Shima Koji • JPN • SHOGUN'S HOLIDAY
EDOUARD ET CAROLINE • 1950 • Becker Jacques • FRN • EDWARD AND CAROLINE
EDOUARD SARRAZIN • 1968 • Dansereau Fernand • DCS • CND
EDRAB AL SHAHATIN • 1967 • el Imam Hassan • EGY • BEGGARS' STRIKE, THE
EDU CORACAO DE OURO • 1968 • de Oliveira Domingos • BRZ • EDU HEART OF GOLD
EDU HEART OF GOLD see **EDU CORACAO DE OURO** • 1968
EDUCANDA, L' • 1976 • Lo Cascio Franco • ITL
EDUCANDE AL TABARIN • 1961 • Regamey Maurice • FRN, ITL
EDUCANDE DI SAINT-CYR, LE • 1941 • Righelli Gennaro • ITL
EDUCANDO A PAPA • 1954 • Soler Fernando • MXC, SPN
EDUCANDO A UNA IDIOTA • 1968 • Torrado Ramon • SPN
EDUCATED ABROAD • 1909 • *Essanay* • USA
EDUCATED EVANS • 1936 • Beaudine William • UKN
EDUCATED FISH • 1937 • Fleischer Dave • ANS • USA
EDUCATING BUSTER • 1925 • Lamont Charles • SHT • USA
EDUCATING FATHER • 1936 • Tinling James • USA
EDUCATING HIS DAUGHTERS • 1914 • *Davies Howard* • USA
EDUCATING JULIE • 1985 • Hardman Gale • UKN
EDUCATING NINA • 1984 • Anderson Juliet • USA
EDUCATING PAPA • 1934 • Lamont Charles • SHT • USA
EDUCATING RITA • 1983 • Gilbert Lewis* • UKN
EDUCATING THE GENERALS see **MI GENERAL** • 1987
EDUCATION • 1915 • *Beery Wallace* • USA
EDUCATION • 1975 • Noonan Chris • DOC • ASL
EDUCATION see **PAIDEIA** • 1977
EDUCATION AMOUREUSE DE VALENTIN, L' • 1974 • L'Hote Jean • FRN, FRG, SPN
EDUCATION ANGLAISE • 1982 • Roy Jean-Claude • FRN
EDUCATION DAYS see **DNI OSWIATY** • 1958
EDUCATION DE BOUT DE ZAN, L' • 1913 • Feuillade Louis • FRN
EDUCATION DE PRINCE • 1926 • Diamant-Berger Henri • FRN
EDUCATION DE PRINCE • 1938 • Esway Alexander • FRN • BARGE-KEEPER'S DAUGHTER, THE
EDUCATION FOR DEATH • 1943 • Geronimi Clyde • ANS • USA
EDUCATION FOR LIVING • 1947 • Lazarus Felix • USA
EDUCATION OF ALLISON TATE, THE • 1987 • Leder Paul • USA
EDUCATION OF AUNT GEORGIANNA, THE • 1913 • Costello Maurice, Gaillord Robert • USA
EDUCATION OF ELIZABETH, THE • 1910 • *Kalem* • USA
EDUCATION OF ELIZABETH, THE • 1921 • Dillon Eddie • USA
EDUCATION OF FATHER, THE • 1915 • *United Film Service* • USA
EDUCATION OF MARY JANE, THE • 1910 • *Defender* • USA
EDUCATION OF MR. PIPP, THE • 1914 • Thomas Augustus • USA
EDUCATION OF NICKY, THE • 1921 • Rooke Arthur • UKN
EDUCATION OF PHYLLISTINE, THE • 1963 • Keatley Philip • CND
EDUCATION OF SONNY CARSON, THE • 1974 • Campus Michael • USA
EDUCATION OF STANLEY EVANS, THE see **SUNSTRUCK** • 1972
EDUCATION OF THE DEAF • 1946 • Ellitt Jack • DOC • UKN
EDUCATION OF VERA, THE see **ANGI VERA** • 1979
EDUCATION PROFESSIONNELLE DES CONDUCTORS DE TRAMWAY • 1925 • Gremillon Jean • SHS • FRN
EDUCATION SENTIMENTALE, L' • 1961 • Astruc Alexandre • FRN, ITL • LESSONS IN LOVE (UKN)
EDUCATIONAL AIM: CLASS-FIGHTER see **ERZIEHUNGSZIEL KLASSENKAMPFER** • 1967
EDUCATIONAL FAIRY TALE see **PEDAGOSKA BAJKA** • 1961
EDUCATORE AUTORIZZATO • 1979 • Odorisio Luciano • ITL
EDUCATRICE, L' • Gregory Gerard • FRN
EDUCATRICE, L' see **C'EST JEUNE ET CA SAIT TOUT!** • 1974
EDUCAZZIONE CIVICA • 1974 • Comencini Luigi • SHT • ITL
EDUT ME ONESS • 1984 • Rebibo Raphael • ISR • FORCED WITNESS
EDVARD MUNCH • 1976 • Watkins Peter • SWD, NRW
EDWARD AND CAROLINE see **EDOUARD ET CAROLINE** • 1950
EDWARD AND MRS. SIMPSON • 1979 • Hussein Waris • MTV • UKN
EDWARD BURRA • 1973 • Smith Peter K. • UKN
EDWARD MY SON • 1948 • Cukor George • UKN, USA
EDWARD SCISSORHANDS • 1990 • Burton Tim • USA
EDWIN MASQUERADES • 1913 • Henderson Dell • USA
EDWIN'S BADGE OF HONOR • 1913 • Henderson Dell • USA
EE BABA LEBA • 1947 • *Gillespie Dizzy* • SHT • USA
EE BY GUM • 1929 • Aylott Dave, Symmons E. F. • SHT • UKN
EE PUT • 1929 • Strizhak Alexander, Poznanski Dimitri • USS • HER WAY OF LOVE
EEGAH! • 1962 • Hall Arch Sr. • USA
EEL, THE • 1916 • Millarde Harry • SHT • USA
EEL STRIKES AGAIN see **PALOS STRIKES AGAIN** • 1968
EEN BLANDT MANGE • 1961 • Henning-Jensen Astrid • DNM • ONE AMONG MANY
EEN MAAND LATER • 1987 • van Brakel Nouchka • NTH • ONE MONTH LATER
EEN PAK SLAAG • 1979 • Haanstra Bert • NTH • MR. SLOTTER'S JUBILEE (UKN)
EENA DEENA DINAH DO • 1919 • Miller Frank • SHT • UKN
EENAM MARANNA KATTU • 1987 • Easaw Thomas J. • IND
EENDAG OP 'N REENDAG • 1975 • SAF
EENDAG VIR ALTYD • 1985 • SAF
EENY, MEENY, MINEY, MOE see **PIC ET PIC ET COLEGRAM** • 1970
EENY MEENY MINY MOE see **OLE DOLE DOFF** • 1968
EERIE MIDNIGHT HORROR SHOW, THE see **OSSESSA, L'** • 1974
EESTGAH-E-TRAIN • 1967 • Alkhas Mardouk • IRN • RAILWAY STATION
EFELERIN OCU • 1968 • Okcugil Cevat • TRK • REVENGE OF THE MASTERS, THE
EFENIN INTIKAMI • 1967 • Yalinkilic Yavuz • TRK • REVENGE OF THE MASTER, THE
EFFECT OF A SHAVE, THE • 1908 • *Essanay* • USA
EFFECT OF GAMMA RAYS ON MAN-IN-THE-MOON MARIGOLDS, THE • 1972 • Newman Paul • USA
EFFECTING A CURE • 1910 • Sennett Mack, Griffith D. W.? • USA
EFFECTIVE HAIR GROWER, THE • 1908 • *Lux* • FRN
EFFECTS • 1969 • Gati John • ANS • USA
EFFECTS OF A ROCKET, THE • 1911 • *Itala* • ITL
EFFECTS OF TOO MUCH SCOTCH, THE • 1903 • Collins Alf? • UKN
EFFEMINATE ONE, THE see **MAZLICEK** • 1934
EFFET DE MER SUR LES ROCHERS • 1896 • Melies Georges • FRN • SEA BREAKING ON THE ROCKS
EFFETS D'UNE VALSE LENTE, LES • 1907 • Zecca Ferdinand • FRN
EFFETTO NOTTE (ITL) see **NUIT AMERICAINE, LA** • 1973
EFFI BRIEST see **ROSEN IM HERBST** • 1955
EFFI BRIEST (USA) see **FONTANE EFFI BRIEST** • 1974
EFFICACY OF A PRAYER, THE • 1913 • *Glaum Louise* • USA
EFFICIENCY • 1918 • *Christie* • USA
EFFICIENCY EDGAR'S COURTSHIP • 1917 • Windom Lawrence C. • USA
EFFICIENCY EXPERTS? • 1917 • Santell Alfred • SHT • USA
EFFICIENCY SQUAD, THE • 1915 • *Ab* • USA
EFFIE BRIEST see **SCHRITT VOM WEGE, DER** • 1939
EFFLUVES FUNESTES • 1916 • de Morlhon Camille • FRN
EFFORT see **KOSHISH** • 1972
EFFRACTION • 1983 • Duval Daniel • FRN
EFFROI, L' • 1913 • Feuillade Louis • FRN
EFFRONTEE, L' • 1985 • Miller Claude • FRN • IMPUDENT GIRL, AN (UKN)
EFKARLI SOSYETEDE • 1968 • Inanoglu Turker • TRK • BLUE-ONE IN HIGH SOCIETY, THE
EFPEUM see **E.F.P.E.U.M.** • 1970
EFTERLYST • 1939 • Bauman Schamyl • SWD • WANTED
EFTERMIDDAGSGOESTEN • 1963 • Refn Peter • SHT • DNM • STOLEN FEAST, THE
EGAREMENTS, LES see **VACANCES PORTUGAISES, LES** • 1963
EGE KAI NI SASAGU • 1978 • Ikeda Masuo • JPN • DEDICATED TO THE AEGEAN SEA
EGEN INGANG • 1956 • Ekman Hasse • SWD • PRIVATE ENTRANCE
EGER ES OROSZLAN • 1957 • Macskassy Gyula • ANS • HNG • MOUSE AND THE LION, THE
EGESZSEGES EROTIKA • 1985 • Timar Peter • HNG • SOUND EROTICISM
EGG see **EI** • 1987
EGG, THE • Steinbach Heinz • ANM • GDR
EGG, THE • 1916 • Ashley Charles E. • SHT • USA
EGG, THE • 1922 • Pratt Gilbert • SHT • USA • WEAK-END PARTY, THE
EGG, THE • 1989 • Bergman Daniel • SHT • SWD
EGG, THE see **JAJE** • 1973
EGG, THE (USA) see **JAJE** • 1960
EGG AND I, THE • 1947 • Erskine Chester • USA
EGG AND JERRY, THE • 1956 • Hanna William, Barbera Joseph • DCS • USA
EGG AND SPOON RACE FOR LADY CYCLISTS • 1898 • Hepworth Cecil M. • UKN
EGG-CITED ROOSTER, THE • 1952 • McKimson Robert • ANS • USA
EGG COLLECTOR, THE • 1940 • Jones Charles M. • ANS • USA
EGG CRACKER SUITE • 1943 • Hardaway Ben, Schaffer Milt • ANS • USA
EGG CRATE WALLOP, THE • 1919 • Storm Jerome • USA • EGG-CRATE WALLOP, THE ○ KNOCK-OUT BLOW, THE
EGG-CRATE WALLOP, THE see **EGG CRATE WALLOP, THE** • 1919
EGG! EGG? A HARDBOILED STORY see **AGGET AR LOST! EN HARDKOKT SAGA** • 1975
EGG HUNT, THE • 1940 • Iwerks Ub • ANS • USA
EGG IN BLACK ART, THE see **OEUF DU SORCIER OU L'OEUF MAGIQUE PROLIFIQUE, L'** • 1902
EGG-LAYING MAN, THE • 1896 • *Paul R. W.* • UKN
EGG-LAYING MAN, THE • 1900 • Hepworth Cecil M. • UKN
EGG SCAMBLE, AN • 1950 • McKimson Robert • ANS • USA
EGG SONG, THE • 1929 • Aylott Dave, Symmons E. F. • SHT • UKN
EGG-THIEVES see **EIERDIEBE** • 1977
EGG TRUST, THE • 1910 • *Essanay* • USA
EGG YEGG, THE • 1944 • Wickersham Bob • ANS • USA
EGGED ON • 1917 • Jackson Harry • SHT • USA
EGGHEAD ON HILL 656, THE see **RELUCTANT HEROES, THE** • 1971
EGGHEAD RIDES AGAIN • 1937 • Avery Tex • ANS • USA
EGGHEAD'S ROBOT • 1970 • Lewis Milo • UKN
EGGNAPPER • 1961 • Hannah Jack • ANS • USA
EGGS • 1915 • Kellino W. P. • UKN
EGGS • 1970 • Hubley John, Hubley Faith • ANS • USA
EGGS! see **EASTER EGGS** • 1907
EGGS, THE (USA) see **SADO-NO TAMAGO** • 1966
EGGS AND EGGS-SPERIMENTS • 1913 • *Kinemacolor* • USA
EGGS AND MARROW BONE • *Hart Ralph/ Roe Carol (P)* • ANS • USA
EGGS DON'T BOUNCE • 1943 • Sparber I. • ANS • USA
EGGS IS EGGS • 1914 • Somers Dalton • UKN
EGGS-TRAORDINARY AFFAIR, AN • 1913 • Plumb Hay? • UKN
EGGS-TRAORDINARY COMPLAINT, AN • 1914 • Aylott Dave • UKN
EGGSHELLS • 1972 • Hooper Tobe • USA
EGI BARANY • 1970 • Jancso Miklos • HNG • AGNUS DEI (UKN)

EGLANTINE • 1971 • Brialy Jean-Claude • FRN
EGLISE TRADITIONNELLE, L' • 1976 • Dansereau Fernand, Rossignol Yolande • DCS • CND
EGO • Cobar Nell • ANS • RMN
EGO • 1969 • Bozzetto Bruno • ANS • ITL
EGO TRIP • 1970 • *Cosmos Films* • USA
EGOIST, THE see **SAMOLUB** • 1966
EGOISTEN • 1924 • Linke Edmund • FRG
EGOISTI, GLI (ITL) see **MUERTE DE UN CICLISTA** • 1955
EGON, DER FRAUENHELD • 1957 • Albin Hans • FRG
EGON SCHIELE • 1982 • Goldschmidt John • MTV • UKN
EGON SCHIELE: EXCESSES see **EGON SCHIELE: EXZESSE** • 1980
EGON SCHIELE: EXZESSE • 1980 • Vesely Herbert • FRG, AUS, FRN • EGON SCHIELE: EXCESSES
EGOR BULYCHOV • 1953 • Solntseva Yulia • USS • IGOR BULICHOV
EGOUTS DU PARADIS, LES • 1978 • Giovanni Jose • FRN • SEWERS OF PARIS, THE
EGRET HUNT, THE see **EGRET HUNTER, THE** • 1910
EGRET HUNTER, THE • 1910 • Olcott Sidney • *Kalem* • USA • AIGRETTE HUNTER, THE ○ EGRET HUNT, THE
EGRI CSILLAGOK • 1923 • Fejos Paul • HNG • STARS OF EGER, THE
EGRI CSILLAGOK • 1968 • Varkonyi Zoltan • HNG • STARS OF EGER
EGUNGUN • 1982 • Brajsblat Carlos • BRZ
EGY BAGATELL • 1975 • Body Gabor • SHT • HNG • ONE BAGATELLE
EGY FIUNAK A FELE • 1924 • *Lukas Paul* • HNG
EGY HUSZASOS LANY, AZ • 1923 • *Lukas Paul* • HNG
EGYMASRA NEZVE • 1983 • Makk Karoly • HNG • ANOTHER WAY
EGYMILLIO FONTOS BANKO, AS • 1916 • Korda Alexander • HNG • MILLION POUND NOTE, THE ○ ONE MILLION POUND NOTE, THE
EGYPT • 1912 • Olcott Sidney • DOC • USA
EGYPT THE MYSTERIOUS • 1912 • Olcott Sidney • DOC • USA
EGYPTE DE 1952 A 1965, L' • 1965 • Tilmissani Abdel-Qadir At- • SHT • EGY
EGYPTE ETERNELLE, L' • 1953 • de Gastyne Marco • SHT • FRN
EGYPTIAN, THE • 1954 • Curtiz Michael • USA
EGYPTIAN MELODIES • 1931 • Jackson Wilfred • ANS • USA
EGYPTIAN MUMMY, THE • 1913 • *Kalem* • USA
EGYPTIAN MUMMY, THE • 1914 • Beggs Lee • USA
EGYPTIAN MYSTERY, THE • 1909 • Dawley J. Searle • USA
EGYPTIAN PRINCESS, AN • 1914 • Bellows Walter Clark • USA
EGYPTIAN SPORTS • 1912 • Olcott Sidney • DOC • USA
EGYPTIAN STORY, AN see **HADDUTA MISRIYA** • 1982
EGYSZEREGY • 1978 • Kardos Ferenc • HNG • PETER AND PAUL ○ ONCE ONE
EGYUTT KAROLYI MIHALLYAL –BESZELGETES KAROLYI MIHALYNEVAL • 1973 • Kovacs Andras • HNG • MY LIFE WITH MIHALY KAROLYI
EGYUTTELES • 1983 • Boszormenyi Geza • HNG • COEXISTENCE
EGZAMIN • 1969 • Trzos-Rastawiecki Andrzej • DOC • PLN • EXAMINATION, THE ○ EXAM, THE
EHE, DIE • 1929 • Frowein Eberhard • FRG
EHE AUS HAUS, DIE • 1919 • Ziener Bruno • FRG
EHE DER CHARLOTTE VON BRAKEL, DIE • 1918 • von Woringen Paul • FRG
EHE DER FRAU MARY, DIE • 1919 • Coenen Josef? • FRG
EHE DER FURSTIN DEMIDOFF, DIE • 1921 • Zelnik Friedrich • FRG
EHE DER GRAFIN WETTERBERG, DIE • 1923 • *Heros-Film* • FRG
EHE DER HEDDA OLSEN ODER DIE BRENNENDE AKROBATIN, DIE • 1921 • Eichberg Richard • FRG • BRENNENDE AKROBATIN, DIE
EHE DER LUISE ROHRBACH • 1916 • Biebrach Rudolf • FRG
EHE DER MARIA BRAUN, DIE • 1979 • Fassbinder R. W. • FRG • MARRIAGE OF MARIA BRAUN, THE (UKN)
EHE DES DR. MED. DANWITZ, DIE • 1956 • Rabenalt Arthur M. • FRG
EHE DES HERRN MISSISSIPPI, DIE • 1961 • Hoffmann Kurt • FRG, SWT
EHE, EIN • 1968 • Strobel Hans Rolf, Tichawsky Heinz • FRG
EHE EINER ACHTZEHNJAHRIGEN, DIE • 1919 • *Dominici Lili* • FRG
EHE FUR EINE NACHT • 1953 • Tourjansky Victor • FRG
EHE IM SCHATTEN • 1947 • Maetzig Kurt • FRG • MATRIMONY IN THE SHADOWS ○ MARRIAGE IN THE SHADOW
EHE IN DOSEN • 1939 • Meyer Johannes • FRG
EHE IN NOT • 1929 • Oswald Richard • FRG • EHEN ZU DRITT
EHE M.B.H. • 1931 • Wenzler Franz • FRG
EHE MAN EHEMAN WIRD • 1941 • Elling Alwin • FRG
EHEFERIEN • 1927 • Janson Victor • FRG • MATRIMONIAL HOLIDAYS
EHEGATTIN, DIE • 1971 • Schlondorff Volker • FRG
EHEGEHEIMNISSE see **WIE BLEIBE ICH JUNG UND SCHON** • 1926
EHEINSTITUT AURORA • 1962 • Schleif Wolfgang • FRG
EHEKONFLIKTE • 1927 • Rahn Bruno • FRG
EHEKRACH see **KLEINER GOLDENER BERG, EIN** • 1936
EHEMANNER REPORT • 1970 • Philipp Harald • FRG • FREEDOM FOR LOVE (UKN)
EHEMANNS URLAUB • 1916 • Larsen Viggo • FRG
EHEN ZU DRITT see **EHE IN NOT** • 1929
EHERNE GESETZ, DAS • 1920 • Speyer Jaap? • FRG
EHES INGOVANY • 1989 • Acs Miklos • HNG • HUNGRY SWAMP
EHESACHE LORENZ • 1959 • Kunert Joachim • GDR • LORENZ V. LORENZ
EHESANATORIUM • 1955 • Antel Franz • FRG
EHESANATORIUM, DAS • 1938 • Huppertz Toni • FRG
EHESCHULE, DIE • 1917 • Karfiol William • FRG
EHESKANDAL IM HAUSE FROMONT JUN. UND RISLER SEN. • 1927 • Sandberg Anders W. • FRG
EHESTIFTER, DER • 1918 • Schmidthassler Walter • FRG
EHESTREIK • 1930 • Boese Carl • FRG
EHESTREIK • 1935 • Jacoby Georg • FRG
EHESTREIK, DER • 1953 • Stockel Joe • FRG
EHI AMICO.. C'E SABATA, HAI CHIUSO • 1969 • Parolini Gianfranco • ITL • SABATA
EHI, AMICO, SEI MORTO • 1970 • Bianchini Paolo • ITL
EHMALOTI TOU MISOUS • 1971 • Foskolos Nikos • GRC • PRISONERS OF HATE
EHON MUSHASHUGYO • 1929 • Inagaki Hiroshi • JPN • SWORDSMAN'S PICTURE BOOK, A
EHRE DEINE MUTTER • 1928 • Stein Paul L. • FRG • SEINE MUTTER
EHRE GERETTET, DIE • 1915 • *Seldeneck Herman* • FRG
EHRENMANNER • 1966 • Heynowski Walter, Scheumann Gerhard • GDR
EHRENREICHS, DIE • 1920 • Del Zopp Rudolf • FRG
EHRENSCHULD • 1921 • Stein Paul L. • FRG
EHRLICHE NAME, DER see **SIE KANNTEN SICH ALLE** • 1958
EHTHROS TOU LAOU, O • 1972 • Dalianidis Ioannis • GRC • ENEMY OF THE PEOPLE, THE
EI • 1987 • Danniel Danniel • NTH • EGG
EI OM ZEEP • 1977 • Driessen Paul • NTH • KILLING OF AN EGG, THE
EIB, EL • 1967 • el Sharkawy Galal • EGY • BAD, THE
EICHMANN see **HOUSE ON GARIBALDI STREET, THE** • 1979
EICHMANN AND THE THIRD REICH see **EICHMANN UND DAS DRITTE REICH** • 1961
EICHMANN UND DAS DRITTE REICH • 1961 • Leiser Erwin • SWT • EICHMANN AND THE THIRD REICH ○ MURDER BY SIGNATURE
EID DES FURSTEN ULRICH see **SPITZEN** • 1926
EID DES STEPHAN HULLER 1, DER • 1919 • Bruck Reinhard • FRG
EID DES STEPHAN HULLER 2, DER • 1921 • Bruck Reinhard • FRG
EID DES STEPHAN HULLER, DER • 1913 • Larsen Viggo • FRG
EIDECHSE, DIE • 1920 • Dessauer Siegfried • FRG
EIEN NO HITO • 1961 • Kinoshita Keisuke • JPN • IMMORTAL LOVE ○ BITTER SPIRIT ○ ETERNAL LOVE
EIERDIEBE • 1977 • Fengler Michael • FRG • EGG–THIEVES
EIERHELD, DER • 1924 • *Schaffer Sylvester* • FRG
EIFERSUCHT • 1925 • Grune Karl • FRG • JEALOUSY
EIGA JOYUH • 1987 • Ichikawa Kon • JPN • FILM ACTRESS, A
EIGEN POORT NAAR EUROPA • 1966 • Wassenaar J. • SHT • NTH
EIGER SANCTION, THE • 1975 • Eastwood Clint • USA
EIGHT AND A HALF see **OTTO E MEZZO** • 1963
EIGHT BALL ANDY • 1948 • Bernds Edward • SHT • USA
EIGHT BELLS • 1916 • Byrne John F. • USA
EIGHT BELLS • 1935 • Neill R. William • USA
EIGHT BRAVE BROTHERS see **SATOMI HAKKEN–DEN** • 1959
EIGHT BRIDES see **HACHININ NO HANAYOME** • 1958
EIGHT CYLINDER BULL • 1926 • Lanfield Sidney (c/d) • SHT • USA
EIGHT CYLINDER LOVE • 1934 • Saunders Peter • UKN
EIGHT CYLINDER ROMANCE, AN • 1917 • Heffron Thomas N. • SHT • USA
EIGHT DEADLY SHOTS see **KAHDEKSAN SURMANLUOTIA** • 1972
EIGHT DIAGRAM POLE FIGHTER, THE see **INVINCIBLE POLE FIGHTER, THE**
EIGHT FATAL BULLETS see **KAHDEKSAN SURMANLUOTIA** • 1972
EIGHT GIRLS IN A BARREL see **TONNEAU DES DANAIDES, LE** • 1900
EIGHT GIRLS IN A BOAT • 1934 • Wallace Richard • USA
EIGHT GIRLS IN A BOAT see **ACHT MADELS IM BOOT** • 1959
EIGHT IMMORTALS • 1971 • Chen Hung-Ming • HKG
EIGHT IRON MEN • 1953 • Dmytryk Edward • USA • DIRTY DOZEN, THE
EIGHT IS ENOUGH: A FAMILY REUNION • 1987 • Harris Harry • TVM • USA
EIGHT KILOS OF HAPPINESS see **OSAM KILA GRECE** • 1981
EIGHT MASTERS, THE • 1974 • Kuo Joseph • HKG
EIGHT MEN OUT • 1989 • Sayles John • USA
EIGHT MINUTES TO MIDNIGHT: A PORTRAIT OF DR. HELEN CALDICOTT • 1981 • Benjamin Mary, Estus Boyd • DOC • USA
EIGHT O'CLOCK WALK • 1954 • Comfort Lance • UKN
EIGHT ON THE LAM • 1966 • Marshall George • USA • EIGHT ON THE RUN (UKN)
EIGHT ON THE RUN (UKN) see **EIGHT ON THE LAM** • 1966
EIGHT PER CENT OF LOVE • 1988 • Kraev Vladimir • BUL
EIGHT TAELS OF GOLD see **BAT LEUNG KAM** • 1989
EIGHT–THIRTEEN see **"813"** • 1920
EIGHT TO FOUR • 1981 • Lewis Louie • USA • 8 TO 4
EIGHTEEN AGAIN! see **18 AGAIN!** • 1988
EIGHTEEN AND ANXIOUS • 1957 • Parker Joe • USA
EIGHTEEN BRONZE GIRLS OF SHAOLIN, THE • 1983 • Chien Lai Yen • HKG • 18 BRONZE GIRLS OF SHAOLIN, THE ○ BRONZE GIRLS OF SHAOLIN
EIGHTEEN IN THE SUN (USA) see **DICIOTTENNI AL SOLE** • 1962
EIGHTEEN MINUTES • 1935 • Banks Monty • UKN
EIGHTEEN PENNY LUNCH, THE • 1905 • *Walturdaw* • UKN
EIGHTEEN ROUGHS see **ARASHI O YOBU JUHACHI–NIN** • 1963
EIGHTEEN–YEAR OLD GIRL see **OSMNACTILETA** • 1939
EIGHTEEN YEARS' IMPRISONMENT see **CHOEKI JUHACHINEN** • 1967
EIGHTEEN YEARS' IMPRISONMENT: PAROLE see **CHOEKI JUHACHINEN: KARI SHUTSUGOKU** • 1967
EIGHTH, THE • 1969 • Heskiya Zako • BUL
EIGHTH BROTHER, THE see **KAHDEKSAS VELJES** • 1971
EIGHTH DAY, THE • 1967 • Gagnon Charles • SHT • CND
EIGHTH DAY, THE see **ATTONDE DAGEN, DET** • 1979
EIGHTH DAY, THE see **ACHTE TAG, DER** • 1989
EIGHTH DAY OF THE WEEK, THE see **HASHTOMIN ROOZE HAFTEH** • 1973
EIGHTH DAY OF THE WEEK, THE (USA) see **OSMY DZIEN TYGODNIA** • 1958
EIGHTH DOOR, THE see **OSMA VRATA** • 1959
EIGHTH FREE MAY DAY, THE see **NYOCADIK SZABAD MAJUS 1, A** • 1952
EIGHTH INCARNATION, THE see **KRISHNA SAMBHAV** • 1926
EIGHTH NOTCH, THE • 1913 • *Kalem* • USA
EIGHTH PLAGUE, THE • 1945 • Lee Jack • DOC • UKN
EIGHTH WONDER, THE see **8e MERVEILLE, LA** • 1964
EIGHTH WONDER, THE see **ATAWENI PUDUMAYA** • 1968
EIGHTH WONDER OF THE WORLD, THE see **KING KONG** • 1933
EIGHTY DAYS, THE • 1945 • Jennings Humphrey • DCS • UKN
EIGHTY HUSSARS see **NYOLCVAN HUSZAR** • 1978
EIGHTY PERCENT OF THE VILLAGE see **MURA HACHIBU** • 1953
EIGHTY STEPS TO JONAH • 1969 • Oswald Gerd • USA
EIJANAIKA see **EJA NAIKA** • 1981
EIKA KATAPPA • 1970 • Schroeter Werner • FRG
EIKO EN MICHI • 1950 • Nakamura Noboru • JPN • ROAD TO RISE AND FALL
EIKO ENO CHOSEN • 1966 • Masuda Toshio • JPN • CHALLENGE FOR GLORY
EIKO ENO GOSEN–KIRO • 1969 • Kurahara Koreyoshi • JPN • EIKO'S 5,000 KILOGRAMS
EIKO ENO KUROHYO • 1969 • Ichimura Hirokazu • JPN • FIGHT FOR THE GLORY (USA)
EIKON • 1969 • Cantrill Arthur, Cantrill Corinne • ASL
EIKO'S 5,000 KILOGRAMS see **EIKO ENO GOSEN–KIRO** • 1969
EILAND • 1966 • Terpstra Erik • SHT • NTH
EILEEN ALLANAH • 1909 • *Warwick Trading Co.* • UKN
EILEEN ALLANAH • 1921 • Rowden W. C. • SHT • UKN
EILEEN OF ERIN • 1913 • Sidney Scott • USA
EILEEN OF THE TREES • 1928 • Cutts Graham • UKN • GLORIOUS YOUTH
EIMAN • 1967 • Reis-Firouz Mehdi • IRN • FAITH, THE
EIN MADEL UND DREI CLOWNS • 1928 • Steinhoff Hans • FRG • DREI ZIRKUSKONIGE, DIE
EIN SOMMERTAG MACHT KEINE LIEBE • 1960 • Klein Gerhard • GDR • ONE SUMMER DAY DOES NOT MEAN LOVE
EIN SPIEL UMS LEBEN • 1924 • Curtiz Michael • AUS
EIN WENIG STERBEN • 1981 • Madavi Mansur • AUS • TO DIE A LITTLE
EINAR SCHANKES GLEDEHUS • 1975 • Schanke Einar • NRW
EINAUGIGE, DER • 1920 • Coenen Josef • FRG
EINBRECHER • 1930 • Schwarz Hanns • FRG • MURDER FOR SALE (USA) ○ BURGLARS
EINBRECHER WIDER WILLEN, DER • 1918 • Larsen Viggo • FRG
EINBRUCH • 1927 • Osten Franz • FRG
EINBRUCH IM BANKHAUS REICHENBACH • 1930 • Fleck Jacob, Fleck Luise • FRG
EINBRUCH IN DIE VILLA HOWARTH • 1927 • Tamara Eric • FRG
EINDE VAN DE REIS, HET • 1981 • Simons Peter • BLG
EINDRINGLING, DER • 1911 • Stark Kurt • FRG
EINE ALTE LIEBE • 1959 • Beyer Frank • GDR • OLD LOVE
EINE MINUTE VOR ZWOLF • 1925 • Malasomma Nunzio • FRG • ONE MINUTE TO TWELVE
EINE REISE IN LICHTS • 1978 • Fassbinder R. W. • FRG • DESPAIR
EINE WEISSE UNTER KANNIBALEN • 1921 • Schomburgk Hans • FRG
EINEN JUX WILL ER SICH MACHEN see **EINMAL KEINE SORGEN HABEN** • 1953
EINER FRAU MUSS MAN ALLES VERZEIH'N • 1931 • Thiele Eugen • FRG
EINER FRISST DEN ANDEREN • 1964 • Nazarro Ray, Zugsmith Albert • FRG, ITL, USA • MORTE VESTITA DI DOLLARI, LA (ITL) ○ DOG EAT DOG (USA) ○ WHEN STRANGERS MEET
EINER GEGEN ALLE • 1927 • Malasomma Nunzio • FRG
EINER SPIELT FALSCH (FRG) see **MIVTZA KAHIR** • 1966
EINER TRAGE DES ANDEREN LAST • 1987 • Warneke Lothar • GDR • BEAR YE ONE ANOTHER'S BURDENS
EINER UNTER MILLIONEN see **5 JUNI, DER** • 1942
EINER VON UNS • 1960 • Spiess Helmut • GDR
EINER VON UNS BEIDEN • 1973 • Petersen Wolfgang • FRG
EINER ZUVIEL AN BORD • 1935 • Lamprecht Gerhard • FRG
EINES PRINZEN JUNGE LIEBE • 1933 • Robison Arthur • FRG
EINFACHE MADCHEN, DAS • 1957 • Jacobs Werner • FRG
EINGEBILDETE KRANKE, DER • 1952 • Konig Hans H. • FRG
EINHORN, DAS • 1978 • Patzak Peter • FRG • UNICORN, THE
EINLADUNG ZUM NACHTESSEN • 1928 • Szekely Hans • FRG
EINLEITUNG ZU ARNOLD SCHOENBERG BEGLEIT MUSIK EINER LICHTSPIELSCENE • 1969 • Straub Jean-Marie, Huillet Daniele • MTV • FRG • INTRODUCTION TO ARNOLD SCHOENBERG'S ACCOMPANIMENT FOR A CINEMATOGRAPHIC SCENE
EINMAL AM RHEIN • 1952 • Weiss Helmut • FRG
EINMAL DER LIEBE HERRGOTT SEIN • 1942 • Zerlett Hans H. • FRG
EINMAL EINE GROSSE DAME SEIN • 1933 • Lamprecht Gerhard • FRG
EINMAL EINE GROSSE DAME SEIN • 1957 • Ode Erik • FRG
EINMAL IST KEINMAL • 1955 • Wolf Konrad • GDR • ONE IS LESS THAN ONE ○ ONCE IS NONCE
EINMAL KEHR' ICH WIEDER see **DALMATINISCHE HOCHZEIT** • 1953
EINMAL KEINE SORGEN HABEN • 1953 • Marischka Georg • FRG, AUS • EINEN JUX WILL ER SICH MACHEN
EINMAL KU' DAMM UND ZURUCK • 1983 • Ballmann Herbert • FRG • GIRL IN A BOOT
EINMAL MOCHT' ICH KEINE SORGEN HABEN • 1932 • Nosseck Max • FRG
EINMAL MOCHT ICH NOCH SO JUNG SEIN see **GROSSE CHANCE, DIE** • 1934
EINMAL UM MITTERNACHT • 1929 • Krause Karl Otto • FRG
EINMAL WERD' ICH DIR GEFALLEN • 1937 • Riemann Johannes • FRG
EINMALEINS DER LIEBE, DAS • 1935 • Hoffmann Carl • FRG
EINOD SPFARRE, DIE • 1915 • Delmont Joseph • FRG
EINS • 1971 • Schamoni Ulrich • FRG
EINS BERLIN–HARLEM • 1974 • Fassbinder R. W. • FRG
EINS OG SKEPNAN DEYR • 1986 • Oddsson Hilmar • ICL • AS THE BEAST DIETH ○ BEAST, THE
EINS PLUS EINS GLEICH DREI • 1927 • Basch Felix • FRG

EINS – ZWEI – DREI CORONA • 1948 • Muller Hans • GDR
EINSAM GRAB, EIN • 1916 • May Joe • FRG
EINSAME, DIE • 1916 • Sauer Fred • FRG
EINSAME FRAU, DIE • 1915 • Del Zopp Rudolf • FRG
EINSAME FRAU, DIE • 1919 • von Woringen Paul • FRG
EINSAME INSEL, DIE • 1920 • Mierendorff Hans • FRG
EINSAME INSEL, DIE see **HYANEN DER WELT 2** • 1921
EINSAME WRACK, DAS • 1919 • Heiland Heinz Karl • FRG
EINSIEDLER VON ST. GEORG, DER • 1916 • Hanus Emerich • FRG
EINSPANNER NO.13 see **FIAKER NR.13** • 1926
EINSTEIN THEORY OF RELATIVITY, THE • 1923 • Fleischer Max • DOC • USA • EINSTEIN'S THEORY OF RELATIVITY
EINSTEIN VS. BABINSKY • 1964 • Podskalsky Zdenek • CZC
EINSTEIN'S THEORY OF RELATIVITY see **EINSTEIN THEORY OF RELATIVITY, THE** • 1923
EINSTWEILEN WIRD ES MITTAG • 1988 • Brandauer Karin • AUS • IN THE MEANTIME IT'S MIDDAY
EINTANZER, DER • 1978 • Horn Rebecca • FRG • GIGOLO, THE
EIREI-TACHI NO OENKA • 1979 • Okamoto Kihachi • JPN • CHEERS ON THE UNKNOWN SOLDIERS
EIS AM STIEL, 6 TEIL see **HAREEMU OHGEN LEMON POPSICLE 6** • 1984
EISENBAHN • 1966 • Mommartz Lutz • FRG
EISENBAHNKONIG 1, DER • 1921 • Illes Eugen • FRG • MENSCH UND MAMMON
EISENBAHNKONIG 2, DER • 1921 • Illes Eugen • FRG • LAUERNDER TOD
EISENBAHNMARDER, DER • 1918 • Guter Johannes • FRG
EISENBAHNRAUBER, DIE • 1920 • Stranz Fred • FRG
EISENHANS • 1983 • Dorst Tankred • FRG
EISENKONIG, DER • 1923 • Neufeld Max • AUS
EISENSTEIN IN MEXICO see **QUE VIVA MEXICO!** • 1931
EISERNE ACHT, DIE • 1921 • Justitz Emil • FRG
EISERNE BRAUT, DIE • 1925 • Boese Carl • FRG
EISERNE FAUST, DIE • 1921 • Delmont Joseph • FRG
EISERNE GUSTAV, DER • 1958 • Hurdalek Georg • FRG
EISERNE KAFIG, DER • 1918 • Dessauer Siegfried • FRG
EISERNE KREUZ, DER • 1914 • Oswald Richard • FRG • IRON CROSS, THE
EISERNE RING, DER • 1915 • von Woringen Paul • FRG
EISERNE UND DAS ROTE KREUZ, DAS • 1915 • Larsen Viggo • FRG
EISERNE WILLE, DER • 1917 • Gartner Adolf • FRG
EISMEER RUFT, DAS • Foth • GDR • ARCTIC SEA IS CALLING, THE
EISZEIT • 1975 • Zadek Peter • FRG, NRW • ICE AGE ○ ISTID
EJA NAIKA • 1981 • Imamura Shohei • JPN • IT'S NICE ISN'T IT? ○ EIJANAIKA ○ WHY NOT?
EJECTION see **AMERICAN TICKLER OR THE WINNER OF 10 ACADEMY AWARDS** • 1976
EJERCICIO GENERAL DE BOMBEROS, UN • 1902 • CHL
EJERCITO BLANCO • 1959 • Moro Francesco De Borja • SPN
EJERCITO EN VILLA ANTA, EL • 1980 • Dagron Alfonso Gumucio • BLV • ARMY IN VILLA ANTA, THE
EJSZAKA RABJA, AZ • 1914 • Curtiz Michael • HNG • SLAVES OF THE NIGHT
EK see **ONE GLORIOUS DAY** • 1922
EK AADMI • 1987 • Abbas Khwaya Ahmad • IND • ONE MAN
EK ADHURI KAHANI • 1972 • Sen Mrinal • IND • UNFINISHED STORY, AN
EK BAAR PHIR • 1980 • Pande Vinod • IND • ONCE AGAIN (USA)
EK DIL SOU AFSANE • 1963 • *Kapoor Raj* • IND
EK DIN PRATIDIN • 1979 • Sen Mrinal • IND • AND STILL BREAKS THE DAWN ○ AND QUIET ROLLS THE DAWN ○ QUIET ROLLS THE DAY
EK DOCTOR KI MAUT • 1990 • Sinha Tapan • IND • DEATH OF A DOCTOR
EK GAON BARA BHANGADI • 1968 • Mane Anant • IND
EK HI RAASTA • 1939 • *Biswas Anil (M)* • IND
EK KE BAAD EK • 1960 • *Burman S. D. (M)* • IND
EK MATI ANEK NATI • 1968 • Patil Krishna • IND
EK NAUJAWAN • 1951 • *Burman S. D. (M)* • IND
EK PAL • 1985 • Lajmi Kalpana • IND
EK PHOOL, EK BHOOL • 1968 • Kapoor Kedar • IND • FLOWER, A MISTAKE, A
EK SAAL PABLE • 1965 • Kumar Dharam • IND
EK SAL OPSTAAN • 1958 • SAF
EKATERINA VORONINA • 1957 • Annensky Isider • USS • YEKATERINA VORONINA
EKDIN ACHANAK • 1989 • Sen Mrinal • IND • SUDDENLY ONE DAY.. (UKN) ○ AND SUDDENLY ONE DAY..
EKDROMI, I • 1967 • Kanellopoulos Takis • GRC • EXCURSION, THE
EKEL, DAS • 1931 • Schufftan Eugen, Wenzler Franz • FRG
EKEL, DAS • 1939 • Deppe Hans • FRG
EKEZET • 1977 • Kardos Ferenc • HNG • ACCENT, THE
EKHANEY AAMAR SWARGA • 1989 • Gowda Chandrashekhar • IND
EKHI ROSTA • 1941 • Khan Mehboob • IND • ONLY LIFE, THE
EKHONEE • 1971 • Sinha Tapan • IND
EKHTIAR, AL • 1970 • Shahin Youssef • EGY • IKHTIAR, AL- ○ CHOIX, LE ○ CHOICE, THE
EKI • 1982 • Furuhata Yasuo • JPN • STATION
EKIMAE HYAKUNEN • 1967 • Toyoda Shiro • JPN • TOKYO CENTURY PLAZA
EKIMAE KAIUN • 1968 • Toyoda Shiro • JPN • LUCK OF STATION FRONT PLAZA, THE
EKIMAE MANGAN • 1967 • Saeki Kozo • JPN • MAHJONG MADNESS
EKIMAE RYUKAN • 1958 • Toyoda Shiro • JPN • HOTELMAN'S HOLIDAY
EKINI POU XEROUN N'AGAPOUN • 1968 • Koliatis Dimitris • GRC • THOSE WHO KNOW HOW TO LOVE
EKINO TO KALOKERI • 1971 • Georgiadis Vassilis • GRC • THAT SUMMER
EKINOS KI EKINI • 1967 • Andreou Errikos • GRC • HE AND SHE
EKLABYA • 1938 • Banerjee Jyotish • IND
EKPOMBI, I • 1968 • Angelopoulos Theo • GRC • BROADCAST ○ EMISSION, L'
EKSPEDITRICEN • 1911 • Blom August • DNM • IN THE PRIME OF LIFE ○ UNGDOM OG LETSIND
EKSPLOATACIJA • 1971 • Dragic Nedeljko • ANM • YGS • EXPLOITATION
EKSTASE • 1932 • Machaty Gustav • FRG • SYMPHONIE DER LIEBE
EKTEE • 1968 • Thakur Raja • IND
EKTI JIBAN • 1988 • Mitra Raja • IND • PORTRAIT OF LIFE
EL • 1952 • Bunuel Luis • MXC • THIS STRANGE PASSION ○ HE
EL ALAMEIN • 1953 • Sears Fred F. • USA • DESERT PATROL (UKN)
EL ALAMEIN • 1958 • Malatesta Guido • ITL • DESERTO DI GLORIA
EL CAPITAN AND THE LAND GRABBERS • 1912 • *Inslee Charles* • USA
EL CID • 1961 • Mann Anthony • USA
EL CISCO • 1966 • Bergonzelli Sergio • ITL
EL CONDOR • 1970 • Guillermin John • USA
EL CORDOBES • 1966 • Reichenbach Francois • SHT • FRN
EL DIABLO • 1916 • MacQuarrie Murdock • SHT • USA
EL DIABLO • 1984 • Carpenter John • USA
EL DIABLO RIDES • 1939 • Webb Ira • USA
EL DJEZAIR • 1947 • Leherissey Jean • SHT • FRN
EL DORADO • 1951 • Alderson John • UKN
EL DORADO • 1963 • Golan Menahem • ISR
EL DORADO • 1967 • Hawks Howard • USA
EL DORADO • 1988 • Saura Carlos • SPN
EL DORADO PASS • 1948 • Nazarro Ray • USA • DESPERATE MEN (UKN)
EL ES DIOS • 1965 • Anteo Victor, Bonfil Guillermo, Warman Arturo, Munoz Alfonso • MXC
EL GASSI • 1960 • Heinrich • SHT • FRN
EL-GJORT ER VELGJORT • 1953 • Carlsen Henning • SHT • DNM
EL GRECO • 1966 • Salce Luciano • ITL, FRN • LE GRECO
EL GUELMOUNA, MARCHAND DE SABLE see **MARCHAND DE SABLE, LE** • 1931
EL HAKIM • 1957 • Thiele Rolf • FRG
EL MACHO see **MACHO, EL** • 1977
EL OUED, CITY OF A THOUSAND DOMES see **EL OUED ,LA VILLE AUX MILLE COUPOLES** • 1947
EL OUED ,LA VILLE AUX MILLE COUPOLES • 1947 • Colson-Malleville Marie • DOC • FRN • EL OUED, CITY OF A THOUSAND DOMES
EL PASO • 1949 • Foster Lewis R. • USA
EL PASO KID, THE • 1946 • Carr Thomas • USA
EL PASO STAMPEDE • 1953 • Keller Harry • USA
EL QUE MURIO DE AMOR • 1945 • Morayta Miguel • MXC
EL ROJO • 1966 • Savona Leopoldo • ITL
EL SALVADOR: ANOTHER VIETNAM • 1981 • Silber Glenn, Vasconcellos Tete • DOC • USA
EL SALVADOR: POTRAIT OF A LIBERATED ZONE • 1982 • Chanan Michael, Chappell Peter • DOC • UKN
EL SALVEJO see **MACHISMO -40 GRAVES FOR 40 GUNS** • 1970
EL SAVADOR, REVOLUTION OR DEATH • 1980 • Diamand Frank • NTH
EL SUPER • 1979 • Ichaso Leon, Jiminez-Leal Orlando • USA
EL TERRIBLE TOREADOR • 1928 • Disney Walt, Iwerks Ub • ANS • USA
EL TOPO • 1971 • Jodorowsky Alejandro • MXC
EL ZORRO • 1968 • Zurli Guido • ITL
ELADAS MUVESZETE, AZ • 1960 • Jancso Miklos, Meszaros Marta • DCS • HNG • ART OF SALESMANSHIP, THE ○ ART OF REVIVAL, THE ○ SALESMANSHIP
ELAINE • Stanton Richard • USA
ELAMAN KOREUS see **RUNOILIJA JA MUUSA** • 1978
ELAS • 1970 • Noronha Jose Roberto • BRZ
ELASTIC AFFAIR, AN • 1930 • Hitchcock Alfred • UKN
ELASTIC BATTALION, THE (USA) see **BATAILLON ELASTIQUE, LE** • 1902
ELASTIC TRANSFORMATION • 1909 • *Pathe* • FRN
ELBOW see **ELBOW AS SUCH, AN** • 1961
ELBOW AS SUCH, AN • 1961 • Babaja Ante • SHT • YGS • ELBOW
ELBOW PLAY (UKN) see **ELLENBOGENSPIELE** • 1969
ELBOWING • 1980 • Driessen Paul • ANS • NTH
ELCKERLYC • 1975 • Stelling Jos • NTH • EVERYMAN
ELD OMBORD • 1922 • Sjostrom Victor • SWD • FIRE ON BOARD ○ HELL SHIP, THE ○ TRAGIC SHIP, THE
ELDA OF THE MOUNTAINS • 1911 • *Nestor* • USA
ELDDONET • 1951 • Hagerman Helge • SWD
ELDER ALDEN'S INDIAN WARD • 1910 • *Kalem* • USA
ELDER BROTHER, THE • 1913 • Merwin Bannister • USA
ELDER BROTHER, THE • 1914 • *Bushman Francis X.* • USA
ELDER BROTHER, THE • 1937 • Hayward Frederick • UKN
ELDER BROTHER'S WIFE see **BOUDI** • 1968
ELDER CITIZEN • 1956 • Haldane Don • SHT • CND
ELDER MISS BLOSSOM, THE • 1918 • Nash Percy • UKN • WANTED A WIFE (USA)
ELDER SISTER see **OPPOL** • 1980
ELDER SISTER, THE see **STARSHAYA SESTRA** • 1967
ELDER VASILI GRYAZNOV see **STARETS VASILI GRYAZNOV** • 1924
ELDEST SISTER see **PEDDA AKKAYYA** • 1967
ELDEST SON RULES, THE • 1912 • *Eclair* • USA • IRON HAND, THE
ELDFAGELN • 1952 • Ekman Hasse • SWD, ITL • UCCELLO DI FUOCO, L' (ITL) ○ FIRE BIRD, THE
ELDORA • 1952 • Markopoulos Gregory J. • SHT • USA
ELDORA, THE FRUIT GIRL • 1911 • *Edison* • USA
ELDORADO • 1921 • L'Herbier Marcel • FRN
ELDORADO • 1988 • Beremenyi Geza • HNG • MIDAS TOUCH, THE
ELDORADO LODE, THE • 1913 • *Gordon James* • USA
ELDRED'S GREAT EQUESTRIAN ACT • 1902 • *Warwick Trading Co.* • UKN
ELDRIDGE CLEAVER see **ELDRIDGE CLEAVER, BLACK PANTHER** • 1969
ELDRIDGE CLEAVER, BLACK PANTHER • 1969 • Klein William • FRN, ALG • ELDRIDGE CLEAVER ○ BLACK PANTHER
ELDSMIDURINN • 1981 • Fridriksson Fridrik Thor • DCS • ICL • BLACKSMITH, THE
ELDUR I HEIMAEY • 1975 • Knudsen Vilhjalmur, Knudsen Osvaldur • ICL • FIRE ON HEIMAEY
ELE, O BOTO • 1988 • Lima Walter Jr. • BRZ • HE, THE DOLPHIN
ELEAGABAL KUPERUS see **NACHTGESTALTEN** • 1920
ELEANA • 1969 • Doules Seemore • USA
ELEANOR AND FRANKLIN • 1976 • Petrie Daniel • TVM • USA
ELEANOR AND FRANKLIN: THE WHITE HOUSE YEARS • 1977 • Petrie Daniel • TVM • USA
ELEANOR, FIRST LADY IN THE WORLD • 1982 • Erman John • TVM • USA
ELEANOR ROOSEVELT: AN UNCOMMON WOMAN • 1980 • Clark Barry • MTV • USA
ELEANOR ROOSEVELT: FIRST LADY OF THE WORLD • 1963 • Rasky Harry • MTV • USA
ELEANOR ROOSEVELT STORY, THE • 1965 • Kaplan Richard • USA
ELEANORA DUSE • 1950 • Ratti Filippo M. • ITL
ELEANORE CUYLER • 1911 • *Nesbitt Miriam* • USA
ELEANOR'S CATCH • 1916 • Madison Cleo • SHT • USA
ELECCIONES MUNICIPALES • 1970 • Guzman Patricio • DOC • CHL • MUNICIPAL ELECTIONS
ELECT, THE see **IZBRANNYE** • 1983
ELECTED, THE see **ELEGIDOS, LOS** • 1963
ELECTION see **ILEKSEN** • 1978
ELECTION BET, THE • 1912 • *Imp* • USA
ELECTION BET, THE • 1916 • Metcalfe Earl • SHT • USA
ELECTION DAY IN CALIFORNIA • 1912 • *Kalem* • USA
ELECTION DAZE • 1943 • Glazer Herbert • SHT • USA
ELECTIVE AFFINITIES see **WAHLVERWANDTSCHAFTEN, DIE** • 1975
ELECTOFRENIA • 1979 • Nery Julio • DOC • VNZ
ELECTRA • 1907 • USA
ELECTRA see **LEKTRO** • 1927
ELECTRA see **ELEKTRA** • 1962
ELECTRA GLIDE IN BLUE • 1973 • Guercio James William • USA • LEGEND OF BIG JOHN, THE ○ BIG JOHN
ELECTRA, MY LOVE see **SZERELMEM ELEKTRA** • 1974
ELECTRIC ALARM, THE • 1915 • Browning Tod • USA
ELECTRIC BATH TUB, THE • 1910 • *Pantograph* • USA
ELECTRIC BATTERY, THE see **PILE ELECTRIQUE, LA** • 1906
ELECTRIC BELT, THE • 1907 • *Gaumont* • FRN
ELECTRIC BELT, THE • 1912 • *Cosmopolitan* • UKN
ELECTRIC BELT, THE see **CEINTURE ELECTRIQUE, LA** • 1912
ELECTRIC BLUE -THE MOVIE • 1982 • Cole Adam • UKN
ELECTRIC BOOTS • 1911 • *Pathe* • FRN
ELECTRIC BULB FACTORY see **FABRYKA ZAROWEK** • 1946
ELECTRIC CURRENT • 1906 • *Pathe* • FRN
ELECTRIC DOLL, THE • 1914 • Collins Edwin J. • UKN
ELECTRIC DREAMS see **ELECTRIC DREAMS: THE MOVIE** • 1984
ELECTRIC DREAMS: THE MOVIE • 1984 • Barron Steve • UKN, USA • ELECTRIC DREAMS
ELECTRIC EARTHQUAKE • 1942 • Fleischer Dave • ANS • USA
ELECTRIC ESKIMO, THE • 1979 • Godwin Frank • UKN
ELECTRIC FIRE GIRL, THE • 1907 • *Walturdaw* • UKN
ELECTRIC GIRL, THE • 1914 • *Eclair* • USA
ELECTRIC GOOSE, THE • 1905 • Collins Alf? • UKN
ELECTRIC HORSEMAN, THE • 1979 • Pollack Sydney • USA
ELECTRIC HOTEL, THE • 1908 • Blackton J. Stuart • USA
ELECTRIC HOTEL, THE (USA) see **HOTEL ELECTRICO, EL** • 1906
ELECTRIC HOUSE, THE • 1922 • Cline Eddie, Keaton Buster • SHT • USA
ELECTRIC INSOLES • 1910 • *Essanay* • USA
ELECTRIC KITCHEN see **CUISINE MAGNETIQUE** • 1908
ELECTRIC LAUNDRY • 1912 • *C.g.p.c.* • FRN
ELECTRIC LEG, THE • 1912 • Stow Percy • UKN
ELECTRIC MAN, THE (UKN) see **MAN MADE MONSTER** • 1941
ELECTRIC MOON • 1990 • Krishen Pradip • IND, UKN
ELECTRIC MULE, THE • 1905 • Porter Edwin S. • USA
ELECTRIC POLICEMAN, THE • 1909 • *Gaumont* • FRN
ELECTRIC SERVANT, THE • 1909 • Booth W. R. • UKN
ELECTRIC SHOCK see **ARAMUTES** • 1978
ELECTRIC SHOCK, THE • 1904 • Collins Alf? • UKN
ELECTRIC SNUFF, THE • 1913 • Calvert Charles? • UKN
ELECTRIC TORCH, THE • 1908 • Fitzhamon Lewin? • UKN
ELECTRIC TRANSFORMATION • 1909 • Stow Percy • UKN
ELECTRIC VILLA, THE • 1911 • *Pathe* • FRN
ELECTRIC VITALISER, THE • 1910 • Booth W. R. • UKN
ELECTRICAL HOUSE BUILDING • 1912 • Stow Percy • UKN
ELECTRICAL VITALIZER, THE • 1910 • Bouwmeester Theo? • UKN
ELECTRICIAN'S HAZARD, THE • 1913 • *Kalem* • USA
ELECTRICIDAD DE CARACAS • 1972 • Blanco Javier • DOC • VNZ • ELECTRICITY OF CARACAS
ELECTRICITY AND LIGHT • 1951 • Durst John • DOC • UKN
ELECTRICITY CURE, THE • 1900 • Hepworth Cecil M. • UKN
ELECTRICITY FOR NERVOUSNESS • 1909 • *Gaumont* • FRN
ELECTRICITY -GENERATION AND DISTRIBUTION • 1952 • DOC • UKN
ELECTRICITY OF CARACAS see **ELECTRICIDAD DE CARACAS** • 1972
ELECTRICITY SUPPLY -EARLY WARNING see **SITE BETTER, A** • 1970
ELECTRIFICATION DE LA LIGNE BRUXELLES-ANVERS • 1935 • Storck Henri • DOC • BLG
ELECTRIFICATION DE LA LIGNE PARIS-VIERZON, L' • 1925 • Gremillon Jean • SHT • FRN
ELECTRIFIED HUMP, THE • 1914 • *Alpha* • FRN
ELECTRIFIED PIG, THE • 1911 • *Cosmopolitan* • USA
ELECTRO-SEX • 1970 • USA
ELECTROCORD FILMS • 1929 • Aylott Dave, Symmons E. F. • SHS • UKN
ELECTROCUTE, L' • 1911 • Morlhon • FRN
ELECTROCUTED • 1907 • *Pathe* • FRN
ELECTROCUTEE • 1904 • Blache Alice • FRN
ELECTROCUTION OF THE WORD • 1968 • Markson Morley • SHT • USA
ELECTRONIC FISH FINDERS • 1969 • Goldsmith Sidney • CND
ELECTRONIC MONSTER, THE (USA) see **ESCAPEMENT** • 1957

ELECTRONIC MOUSE TRAP, THE • 1946 • Davis Mannie • ANS • USA
ELECTRONICA • 1960 • Kneitel Seymour • ANS • USA
ELECTRONICUS • Munteanu Stefan • ANM • RMN
ELECTRONIQUE ET MACHINES-OUTILS • 1955 • Tavano Fred • SHT • FRN
ELECTRON'S TALE, THE • 1970 • Godfrey Bob, Green Peter • ANS • UKN
ELECTROPHORESE DU NITRATE D'ARGENT • 1932 • Painleve Jean • SHT • FRN
ELECTRORYTMES • 1967 • Foldes Peter • ANM • FRN
ELECTROSHOW • 1966 • Guzman Patricio • SHT • CHL
ELEF NESHIKOTH KETANOTH • 1981 • Recanati Mira • ISR • THOUSAND LITTLE KISSES, A
ELEFANT IM PORZELLANLADEN, DER • 1958 • Paul Heinz • FRG
ELEFANTENJAGER • 1914-18 • Zelnik Friedrich • FRG
ELEFTHERIOS VENIZELOS • 1980 • Voulgaris Pantelis • GRC
ELEGANCE OF LIFE, THE see **RUNOILIJA JA MUUSA** • 1978
ELEGANT BEAST see **SHITOYAKANA KEDAMONO** • 1963
ELEGANTES PACK • 1925 • Speyer Jaap • FRG
ELEGIA • 1966 • Huszarik Zoltan • SHT • HNG • ELEGY
ELEGIDO, EL • 1975 • Gonzalez Servando • MXC
ELEGIDOS, LOS • 1963 • Demicheli Tulio • SPN • ELECTED, THE
ELEGIJA • 1965 • Dragic Nedeljko • ANM • YGS • ELEGY
ELEGY • 1983 • Zahariev Edward • BUL
ELEGY see **HIKA** • 1951
ELEGY see **ELEGIJA** • 1965
ELEGY see **ELEGIA** • 1966
ELEGY see **AGIT** • 1971
ELEGY see **BANKA** • 1975
ELEGY, AN see **BANKA** • 1957
ELEGY, THE • 1927 • Stone Andrew L. • SHT • USA
ELEGY FOR A QUARREL see **KENKA SEREJII** • 1966
ELEGY FOR OUR TIME see **SHOWA KARESUSUKI** • 1974
ELEGY OF HELL II-III see **ZOKU BANKA JIGOKU** • 1929
ELEGY OF THE NORTH see **BANKA** • 1957
ELEKSIR BODROSTI • 1941 • Yutkevich Sergei • USS • ELIXIR OF COURAGE
ELEKTRA • 1910 • Blackton J. Stuart • USA
ELEKTRA • 1962 • Cacoyannis Michael • GRC • ELECTRA
ELEKTRA • 1962 • Zarpas Ted • GRC
ELEKTRA • 1970 • *Liebermann Rolf (P)* • MTV • FRG
ELEKTRA see **SZERELMEM ELEKTRA** • 1974
ELEKTREIA see **SZERELMEM ELEKTRA** • 1974
ELEMENT 3 • 1965 • Giraldeau Jacques • DOC • CND
ELEMENT OF CRIME, THE see **FORBRYDELSENS ELEMENT** • 1984
ELEMENT OF MIGHT, THE • 1919 • *Hart Neal* • SHT • USA
ELEMENTS, THE • 1968 • Arnold Steven, Wiese Michael • SHT • USA
ELEMENTS POUR UNE ETUDE DE RHYTHME see **TAMBOUR DE PIERRE** • 1964
ELENA • 1954 • Pascual Jesus • SPN
ELENA ET LES HOMMES • 1956 • Renoir Jean • FRN, ITL • NIGHT DOES STRANGE THINGS, THE (UKN) ○ ELIANA E GLI UOMINI (ITL) ○ PARIS DOES STRANGE THINGS (USA)
ELENA FONTANA • 1914 • Gad Urban • FRG
ELENA SI, MA.. DI TROIA • 1973 • Brescia Alfonso • ITL
ELENA Y RAQUEL • 1970 • *Cima* • MXC
ELENDEN DER STRASSE, DIE • 1926 • Kramer Albert • FRG
ELENI • 1985 • Yates Peter • USA • ELENI -A SON'S REVENGE
ELENI -A SON'S REVENGE see **ELENI** • 1985
ELEPHANT, AN see **ZO** • 1957
ELEPHANT AND THE SKIPPING ROPE, THE see **SLON I VEREVOCHKA** • 1945
ELEPHANT AT THE PICNIC, THE • 1905 • *Cricks & Sharp* • UKN
ELEPHANT BOY • 1937 • Flaherty Robert, Korda Zoltan • USA, UKN
ELEPHANT BOY • 1975 • Safran Henri • ASL
ELEPHANT CA TROMPE ENORMEMENT, UN • 1977 • Robert Yves • FRN • PARDON MON AFFAIRE (USA)
ELEPHANT CALLED SLOWLY, AN • 1970 • Hill James • UKN
ELEPHANT FURY • 1955 • *Piel Harry* • FRG
ELEPHANT GOD, THE see **JAI BABA FELUNATH** • 1977
ELEPHANT GUN (USA) see **NOR THE MOON BY NIGHT** • 1958
ELEPHANT KEEPER, THE • 1990 • Yukol Prince Chatri • THL
ELEPHANT MAN, THE • 1980 • Lynch David • UKN
ELEPHANT MAN, THE • 1981 • Hofsiss Jack • TVM • USA
ELEPHANT MOUSE, THE • 1951 • Davis Mannie • ANS • USA
ELEPHANT NEVER FORGETS, AN • 1935 • Fleischer Dave • ANS • USA
ELEPHANT ON HIS HANDS, AN • 1913 • Christie Al • USA
ELEPHANT ON THEIR HANDS, AN • 1912 • Thompson Frederick A. • USA
ELEPHANT PARTS • 1981 • Dear William • USA
ELEPHANT STAMPEDE • 1951 • Beebe Ford • USA • BOMBA AND THE ELEPHANT STAMPEDE (UKN)
ELEPHANT WALK • 1954 • Dieterle William • USA
ELEPHANT WALK see **BARNFORBJUDET** • 1979
ELEPHANTASTIC • 1964 • Hanna William, Barbera Joseph • ANS • USA
ELEPHANTRIO • 1985 • Weldon John (c/d) • ANM • CND
ELEPHANT'S DINNER, THE • 1916 • *Vitagraph* • SHT • USA
ELEPHANT'S GRATITUDE, AN • 1916 • Santschi Thomas • USA
ELEPHANTS HAVE RIGHT OF WAY • 1962 • Joseph Stanley • DCS • UKN
ELEPHANTS NEVER FORGET (UKN) see **ZENOBIA** • 1939
ELEPHANT'S NIGHTMARE, AN • 1920 • Moore Vin • SHT • USA
ELES NAO USAM BLACK TIE • 1981 • Hirszman Leon • BRZ • THEY DON'T WEAR BLACK TIE
ELET KIRALYA: DORIAN GRAY, AZ • Desy Alfred • HNG • PICTURE OF DORIAN GRAY, THE (USA)
ELET MEGY TOVABB, AZ • 1959 • Meszaros Marta • DCS • HNG • LIFE GOES ON
ELET VIZE, AZ • 1970 • Jankovics Marcell • ANM • HNG • WATER OF LIFE, THE
ELETBE TANCOLTATOTT LANY • 1964 • Banovich Tamas • HNG • GIRL DANCED INTO LIFE, THE ○ ETERNAL DANCE
ELETJEL • 1954 • Fabri Zoltan • HNG • FOURTEEN LIVES IN DANGER ○ FOURTEEN LIVES SAVED ○ VIERZEHN MENSCHENLEBEN ○ LIFE SIGNS
ELETMU • 1972 • Vajda Bela • HNG
ELEVATING FATHER • 1916 • *Orth Louise* • SHT • USA
ELEVATION A see **V RAIONYE VYSOTY A** • 1941
ELEVATOR • 1971 • Breer Robert • USA
ELEVATOR, THE • 1974 • Jameson Jerry • TVM • USA
ELEVATOR MAN, THE • 1914 • *Chamberlin Riley* • USA
ELEVATOR ROMANCE, AN • 1911 • *Thanhouser* • USA
ELEVATOR TO THE GALLOWS see **ASCENSEUR POUR L'ECHAFAUD, L'** • 1957
ELEVEN DAYS ELEVEN NIGHTS see **UNDICI GIORNI, UNDICI NOTTI** • 1987
ELEVEN DAYS, ELEVEN NIGHTS: PART 2 • 1988 • D'Amato Joe • ITL • TOP MODEL
ELEVEN DAYS ELEVEN NIGHTS: PART 3 • 1988 • D'Amato Joe • ITL • 11 DAYS 11 NIGHTS: PART 3 -THE FINAL CHAPTER
ELEVEN HOPES • 1975 • Sadovsky Viktor • USS
ELEVEN MEN see **KET FELIDO A POKOLBAN** • 1961
ELEVEN SAMURAI see **JUICHININ NO SAMURAI** • 1967
ELEVEN-THIRTY P.M. • 1915 • Walsh Raoul • USA
ELEVEN TO ONE • 1915 • Lloyd Frank • USA
ELEVEN WHO WERE LOYAL • Meinert Rudolf • FRG
ELEVEN YEARS OLD • 1966 • Junge Winifried • DOC • GDR
ELEVENTH, THE see **ODINNADTSATI** • 1928
ELEVENTH COMMANDMENT, THE • 1913 • *Cooper Gladys* • UKN
ELEVENTH COMMANDMENT, THE • 1916 • *Veritas Photoplay* • USA
ELEVENTH COMMANDMENT, THE • 1918 • Ince Ralph • USA
ELEVENTH COMMANDMENT, THE • 1924 • Cooper George A. • UKN
ELEVENTH COMMANDMENT, THE • 1933 • Melford George, Cabanne W. Christy? • USA
ELEVENTH COMMANDMENT, THE see **JEDENACTE PRIKAZANI** • 1925
ELEVENTH COMMANDMENT, THE see **JEDENACTE PRIKAZANI** • 1935
ELEVENTH COMMANDMENT, THE see **JEDANAESTA ZAPOVEST** • 1970
ELEVENTH COMMANDMENT, THE see **SWORD OF GIDEON, THE** • 1986
ELEVENTH DIMENSION, THE • 1915 • Easton Clem • USA
ELEVENTH HOUR • 1942 • Gordon Dan • ANS • USA
ELEVENTH HOUR, THE • 1912 • *Stirling Sydney* • ASL
ELEVENTH HOUR, THE • 1914 • *Bison* • USA
ELEVENTH HOUR, THE • 1916 • Batley Ernest G. • UKN
ELEVENTH HOUR, THE • 1918 • O'Donovan Fred • IRL
ELEVENTH HOUR, THE • 1922 • Ridgwell George • UKN • PURPLE PHIAL, THE
ELEVENTH HOUR, THE • 1923 • Durning Bernard J. • USA
ELEVENTH HOUR, THE see **ODINNADTSATI** • 1928
ELEVENTH HOUR, THE see **DOTANBA** • 1957
ELEVENTH HOUR REFORMATION, AN • 1914 • Edwards Walter • USA
ELEVENTH VICTIM, THE • 1979 • Kaplan Jonathan • TVM • USA
ELEVENTH YEAR, THE see **ODINNADTSATI** • 1928
ELF JAHRE UND EIN TAG • 1963 • Reinhardt Gottfried • FRG
ELF KING, THE • 1908 • Blackton J. Stuart • USA
ELF SCHILLERSCHEN OFFIZIERE, DIE • 1926 • Meinert Rudolf • FRG
ELF SCHILLERSCHEN OFFIZIERE, DIE • 1932 • Meinert Rudolf • FRG
ELF TEUFEL, DIE • 1927 • Korda Zoltan • FRG
ELFEGO BACA: SIX GUN LAW • 1962 • Nyby Christian • MTV • USA • SIX GUN LAW
ELFENSZENE AUS DEM SOMMERNACHTSTRAUM • 1917 • *Harmonie-Film* • SHT • FRG • MIDSUMMER NIGHT'S DREAM, A (USA)
ELGAR • 1962 • Russell Ken • MTV • UKN
ELGE, QUEEN OF SNAKES • 1965 • Grivikas V. • USS
ELGHORBA see **GHORBA, EL** • 1971
ELI SJURSDOTTER • 1938 • Bornebusch Arne, Sinding Leif • SWD, NRW • SISTE KAROLEN, DEN
ELIA KAZAN, OUTSIDER • 1982 • Tresgot Annie, Ciment Michel • DOC • FRN
ELIANA E GLI UOMINI (ITL) see **ELENA ET LES HOMMES** • 1956
ELIETTE OU INSTANTS DE LA VIE D'UNE FEMME • 1971 • Reichenbach Francois • SHT • FRN
ELIF LAILA WA LAILA • 1964 • el Imam Hassan • EGY • THOUSAND AND ONE NIGHTS, A
ELIMINATOR, THE see **DANGER ROUTE** • 1967
ELIMINATOR, THE see **TEHERAN '43** • 1979
ELIMINATOR, THE see **DEADLY GAMES** • 1982
ELIMINATORS • 1986 • Manoogian Peter • USA
ELINE 0 - 16 MANEDER • 1974 • Roos Lise • DCS • DNM • ELINE 0 - 16 MONTHS
ELINE 0 - 16 MONTHS see **ELINE 0 - 16 MANEDER** • 1974
ELINOR NORTON • 1935 • MacFadden Hamilton • USA • STATE VERSUS ELINOR NORTON, THE
ELIPATHAYAM see **ELIPPATHAYAM** • 1981
ELIPPATHAYAM • 1981 • Gopalakrishnan Adoor • IND • MOUSE TRAP ○ ELIPATHAYAM ○ RAT-TRAP ○ ELLIPATHAYAM
ELISA see **FILLE ELISA, LA** • 1956
ELISA, MY LIFE see **ELISA, VIDA MIA** • 1977
ELISA, MY LOVE (USA) see **ELISA, VIDA MIA** • 1977
ELISA, VIDA MIA • 1977 • Saura Carlos • SPN • ELISA, MY LOVE (USA) ○ ELISA, MY LIFE
ELISABETH • 1968 • Gelabert Alejandro Marti • SPN
ELISABETH, DIE WEISSE SCHWESTER VON ST. VEITH see **ELISABETH UND IHR NARR** • 1933
ELISABETH REINE D'ANGLETERRE see **AMOURS DE LA REINE ELISABETH, LES** • 1912
ELISABETH UND IHR NARR • 1933 • von Harbou Thea • FRG • ELISABETH, DIE WEISSE SCHWESTER VON ST. VEITH ○ WEISSE SCHWESTER
ELISABETH VON OESTERREICH • 1931 • Trotz Adolf • FRG
ELISE ET LA MER • 1986 • Goulet Stella • MTV • CND
ELISE OU LA VRAIE VIE • 1970 • Drach Michel • FRN, ALG
ELISE, THE FORESTER'S DAUGHTER • 1913 • *Fuller Mary* • USA
ELISIR D'AMORE • 1947 • Costa Mario • ITL • THIS WINE OF LOVE (USA)
ELISIR D'AMORE, L' • 1939 • Reiniger Lotte • ANM • UKN
ELISIR D'AMORE, L' • 1941 • Palermi Amleto • ITL • ELIXIR OF LOVE, THE
ELISO • 1928 • Shengelaya Nikolai • USS • CAUCASIAN LOVE ○ ELISSO
ELISSO see **ELISO** • 1928
ELITE BALL, THE • 1913 • Sennett Mack • USA
ELITE KILLER, THE see **STALKING MOON, THE** • 1969
ELIXIERE DES TEUFELS, DIE • 1922 • Abter Adolf • FRG • DEVIL'S ELIXIRS
ELIXIERE DES TEUFELS, DIE • 1973 • Kirsten Ralf • GDR, CZC
ELIXIR OF BRAVERY, THE • 1911 • *Eclair* • FRN
ELIXIR OF COURAGE see **ELEKSIR BODROSTI** • 1941
ELIXIR OF DREAMS, THE • 1909 • *Pathe* • FRN
ELIXIR OF LIFE, THE • 1901 • Williamson James • UKN
ELIXIR OF LIFE, THE • 1907 • *Pathe* • FRN • ELIXIR OF STRENGTH, THE (UKN)
ELIXIR OF LIFE, THE • 1916 • Curtis Allen • SHT • USA
ELIXIR OF LIFE, THE see **VERS L'IMMORTALITE** • 1911
ELIXIR OF LONG LIFE, THE • 1912 • *Cines* • ITL
ELIXIR OF LOVE, THE • 1914 • *Imp* • USA
ELIXIR OF LOVE, THE see **ELISIR D'AMORE, L'** • 1941
ELIXIR OF STRENGTH, THE (UKN) see **ELIXIR OF LIFE, THE** • 1907
ELIXIR OF YOUTH • 1910 • *Pathe* • FRN
ELIXIR OF YOUTH, THE • 1913 • *Powers* • USA
ELIZA • 1969 • Sheppard Gordon H. • CND
ELIZA COMES TO STAY • 1936 • Edwards Henry • UKN
ELIZA COMES TO STAY see **DANGEROUS TO MEN** • 1920
ELIZA FRASER see **ROLLICKING ADVENTURES OF ELIZA FRASER, THE** • 1976
ELIZA ON THE ICE • 1944 • Rasinski Connie • ANS • USA
ELIZA RUNS AGAIN • 1938 • Rasinski Connie • ANS • USA
ELIZABETH • 1968 • Cayado Tony • PHL
ELIZABETH AND ESSEX see **PRIVATE LIVES OF ELIZABETH AND ESSEX, THE** • 1939
ELIZABETH AND MARY • 1965 • Pennebaker D. A. • USA
ELIZABETH IS QUEEN • 1953 • Ashwood Terry • UKN
ELIZABETH OF ENGLAND see **DRAKE OF ENGLAND** • 1935
ELIZABETH OF LADYMEAD • 1949 • Wilcox Herbert • UKN • GIRL HE LEFT BEHIND, THE
ELIZABETH THE QUEEN see **PRIVATE LIVES OF ELIZABETH AND ESSEX, THE** • 1939
ELIZABETHAN ROMANCE, AN • 1911 • Bouwmeester Theo • UKN
ELIZABETH'S PRAYER • 1914 • Huntley Fred W. • USA
ELIZA'S FAIRY PRINCE • 1915 • Frank Alexander F. • USA
ELIZA'S HOROSCOPE • 1974 • Sheppard Gordon H. • CND
ELIZA'S ROMEO • 1922 • Haldane Bert • UKN
ELIZAVETA UVAROVA • 1974 • Panfilov Gleb • USS
ELJEGYZES • 1959 • Zolnay Pal • HNG • ENGAGEMENT
ELJEN SVERVAC! • 1987 • Foky Otto • ANM • HNG • LONG LIVE SERVATIUS!
ELLA • 1946 • Peon Ramon • MXC
ELLA • 1964 • Casson Philip • UKN
ELLA • 1972 • Demicheli Tulio • SPN
ELLA CINDERS • 1926 • Green Alfred E. • USA
ELLA, EL Y SUS MILLONES • 1944 • de Orduna Juan • SPN
ELLA LOLA, A LA TRILBY • 1898 • *Edison* • USA
ELLA, LUCIFER Y YO • 1952 • Morayta Miguel • MXC • SHE, LUCIFER AND I
ELLA WANTS TO ELOPE • 1916 • Douglass James • SHT • USA
ELLA Y EL MIEDO • 1968 • Klimovsky Leon • SPN • SHE AND FEAR
ELLA Y LOS VETERANOS • 1961 • Torrado Ramon • SPN
ELLA Y YO • 1951 • Delgado Miguel M. • MXC
ELLAS LOS PREFIEREN LOCAS • 1977 • Ozores Mariano • SPN
ELLAS TAMBIEN SON REBELDES • 1959 • Galindo Alejandro • MXC
ELLE AIME CA AUSSI PAR DERRIERE • Antony Michel • FRN
ELLE BOIT PAS, ELLE FUME PAS, ELLE DRAGUE PAS, MAIS.. ELLE CAUSE! • 1969 • Audiard Michel • FRN
ELLE CAUSE PLUS.. ELLE FLINGUE • 1972 • Audiard Michel • FRN, ITL • ROSAMUNDA NON PARLA.. SPARA (ITL)
ELLE COURT, ELLE COURT, LA BANLIEUE • 1973 • Pires Gerard • FRN, ITL
ELLE EN VEUT • 1975 • Sala Henri • FRN
ELLE EST BICIMIDINE • 1927 • Brunius John. W., Greville Edmond T. • SHT • FRN • SHE IS BICIMIDINE
ELLE EST MOI • 1952 • Lefranc Guy • FRN
ELLE ET LUI • 1959 • Jabely Jean • ANM • FRN
ELLE ETAIT UNE FOIS see **ELLE ETAIT UNE FOIS.. UNE AUTRE FOIS** • 1971
ELLE ETAIT UNE FOIS.. UNE AUTRE FOIS • 1971 • Noel Jean-Guy • SHT • CND • ELLE ETAIT UNE FOIS
ELLE LUI DIRAIT DANS L'ILE • 1972 • Le Hung Eric • FRN, ITL
ELLE-VIS • 1990 • Holmes Mary • SHT • CND
ELLE VOIT DES NAINS PARTOUT • 1982 • Sussfeld Jean-Claude • FRN
ELLEHAMMER • 1957 • Roos Jorgen • DNM • FLYING DANE, THE
ELLEN IN WINDOW LAND • 1956-57 • Vickrey Robert • SHT • USA
ELLEN (UKN) see **SECOND WOMAN, THE** • 1949
ELLENBOGENSPIELE • 1969 • Becker Wolfgang • FRG • ELBOW PLAY (UKN)
ELLER SANGEN OM DEN ELDRODA HUMMERN see **OJ OJ OJ..** • 1966
ELLERY QUEEN • 1975 • Greene David • TVM • USA • TOO MANY SUSPECTS
ELLERY QUEEN AND THE MURDER RING • 1941 • Hogan James P. • USA • MURDER RING, THE (UKN)

ELLERY QUEEN AND THE PERFECT CRIME • 1941 • Hogan James P. • USA • PERFECT CRIME, THE (UKN)
ELLERY QUEEN: DON'T LOOK BEHIND YOU • 1971 • Shear Barry • TVM • USA
ELLERY QUEEN, MASTER DETECTIVE • 1940 • Neumann Kurt • USA
ELLERY QUEEN'S PENTHOUSE MYSTERY • 1941 • Hogan James P. • USA
ELLES • 1966 • Lallem Ahmed • ALG • WOMEN ○ SHE
ELLES EN VEULENT • 1980 • Turbay Max • FRN
ELLES ETAIENT DOUZE FEMMES • 1940 • Lacombe Georges • FRN
ELLES FONT TOUT • 1978 • Franco Jesus • FRN
ELLES S'ECLATENT AU SOLEIL • Pary Jack • FRN
ELLIE • 1984 • Wittman Peter • USA
ELLIPATHAYAM see **ELIPPATHAYAM** • 1981
ELLIPSIS see **. . .** • 1971
ELLIS ISLAND • 1936 • Rosen Phil • USA
ELLIS ISLAND • 1984 • London Jerry • MTV • USA
ELLIS LARKINS • 1975 • Leiser Erwin • SHT • SWT
ELLOPTAKA VITAMINAT • 1967 • Perc Otto • ANM • HNG • VITAMIN THIEF
ELM-CHANTED FOREST, THE • 1986 • Blazekovic Milan • ANM • YGS
ELMER • 1976 • Cain Christopher • USA
ELMER AND ELSIE • 1934 • Pratt Gilbert • USA • LADIES FIRST
ELMER ELEPHANT • 1936 • Jackson Wilfred • ANS • USA
ELMER GANTRY • 1960 • Brooks Richard • USA
ELMER THE GREAT • 1933 • LeRoy Mervyn • USA
ELMER THE GREAT DANE • 1935 • Avery Tex • ANS • USA
ELMER'S CANDID CAMERA • 1940 • Jones Charles M. • ANS • USA
ELMER'S PET RABBIT • 1941 • Jones Charles M. • ANS • USA
ELMETTO PIENO DI.. FIFA (ITL) see **MUR DE L'ATLANTIQUE, LE** • 1970
ELMO THE FEARLESS • 1920 • McGowan J. P. • SRL • USA
ELMO THE MIGHTY • 1919 • McRae Henry • SRL • USA
ELMOLO, GLI • 1979 • Maraini Dacia • ITL
ELNOEK KISASSZONY • 1935 • Marton Andrew
ELOGE DU CHIAC • 1968 • Brault Michel • DCS • CND
ELOIGNEMENT, L' • 1969 • Lamothe Arthur • DCS • CND
ELOISA ESTA DEBAJO DE UN ALMENDRO • 1943 • Gil Rafael • SPN
ELOISE • 1956 • Frankenheimer John • MTV • USA
ELOKUU • 1956 • Kassila Matti • FNL • AUGUST ○ HARVEST MONTH
ELOPE IF YOU MUST • 1922 • Wallace C. R. • USA
ELOPEMENT • 1907 • *Bitzer Billy (Ph)* • USA
ELOPEMENT • 1923 • Ramster P. J. • SHT • ASL • CATTIVA EVASIONE
ELOPEMENT • 1951 • Koster Henry • USA
ELOPEMENT, THE • 1911 • Powell Paul • UKN
ELOPEMENT, THE • 1912 • *Crystal* • USA
ELOPEMENT, THE • 1916 • *Mutual* • USA
ELOPEMENT, THE see **BUMPS AND WILLIE** • 1913
ELOPEMENT, THE see **KAWIN LARI** • 1975
ELOPEMENT AT HOME, AN • 1913 • Brooke Van Dyke • USA
ELOPEMENT IN ROME, AN • 1914 • Neilan Marshall • USA
ELOPEMENT OF ELIZA • 1914 • *Melies* • USA
ELOPEMENTS ON DOUBLE L RANCH, THE • 1911 • Dwan Allan • USA
ELOPING WITH AUNTIE • 1909 • Griffith D. W. • USA
ELOQUENTS, LES • 1956 • Guillon Jacques, Ford Charles • DOC • FRN
ELPIDHES POU NAVAYISAN • 1968 • Doukas Kostas • GRC • HOPES GONE WITH THE WIND
ELPIDIO VALDES • 1979 • Padron Juan • ANM • CUB
ELSA • 1966 • Varda Agnes • SHT • FRN
ELSA, FRAULEIN SS • 1977 • Stern Mark • FRN
ELSA MAXWELL'S HOTEL FOR WOMEN see **HOTEL FOR WOMEN** • 1939
ELSA SE GEHEIM • 1979 • SAF
ELSA'S BROTHER • 1915 • Brooke Van Dyke • USA
ELSE DIE RAUBERBRAUT • *Kampers Fritz* • FRG
ELSE VOM ERLENHOF • 1919 • Kortner Fritz • AUS
ELSEWHERE see **KAHIN AURCHAL** • 1968
ELSIE PERCIVAL AND RAY RAYMOND • 1930 • *Balcon Michael (P)* • SHT • UKN
ELSIE THE GAMEKEEPER'S DAUGHTER • 1911 • Haldane Bert? • UKN
ELSIE VENNER • 1914 • *Maude Arthur* • USA
ELSIE'S AMBITION • 1915 • *Federal* • USA
ELSIE'S AUNT • 1913 • *Powers* • USA
ELSIE'S NIGHTMARE see **NIGHTMARE OF THE GLAD-EYE TWINS, THE** • 1913
ELSIE'S UNCLE • 1914 • *Victor* • USA
ELSIETETT HAZASSAG • 1968 • Keleti Marton • HNG • HASTY MARRIAGE
ELSK.. DIN NAESTE • 1967 • Kolsto Egil • DNM • LOVE.. THY NEIGHBOUR
ELSKER HVERANDRE see **GEZEICHNETEN, DIE** • 1921
ELSKOVMAGT • 1913 • Holger-Madsen • DNM
ELSKOVS MAGT • 1912 • Blom August • DNM • MAN'S GREAT ADVERSARY ○ GOGLEREN
ELSKOVS OPFINFSOMHED • 1913 • Wolder • DNM • INVENTIVE LOVE
ELSKOVSLEG • 1913 • Holger-Madsen, Blom August • DNM • LIEBELEI ○ LOVE'S DEVOTEE
ELSO KETSZAZ EVEM • 1985 • Maar Gyula • HNG • MY FIRST TWO HUNDRED YEARS
ELSTREE CALLING • 1930 • Hitchcock Alfred, Hulbert Jack, Murray Paul, Charlot Andre, Brunel Adrian • UKN
ELSTREE STORY • 1952 • Gunn Gilbert • UKN
ELTAVOZOTT NAP • 1968 • Meszaros Marta • HNG • DAY HAS GONE, THE ○ GIRL, THE ○ CATI -THE GIRL
ELTERN, DIE • 1973 • Geissendorfer Hans W. • FRG • PARENTS, THE
ELTERNLOS • 1927 • Hofer Franz • FRG
ELTETO TISZA-VIZ • 1954 • Jancso Miklos • SHT • HNG • HEALTH-GIVING WATERS OF TISZA, THE ○ LIFE-BRINGING WATER
ELUS DE LA MER, LES • 1921 • Roudes Gaston, Dumont • FRN
ELUSIVE AVENGERS, THE see **NEULOVIMYYE MSTITELI** • 1967
ELUSIVE CORPORAL, THE (USA) see **CAPORAL EPINGLE, LE** • 1961
ELUSIVE DIAMOND, THE • 1914 • *Anderson Mignon* • USA
ELUSIVE ENEMY, THE • 1916 • Ford Francis • SHT • USA
ELUSIVE ISABEL • 1916 • Paton Stuart • USA
ELUSIVE JAN, THE • 1942 • Petrov Vladimir, Annensky I. • USS
ELUSIVE KISS, THE • 1913 • Wharton Leopold • USA
ELUSIVE MISS PINKHURST, THE • 1912 • *Warwick Trading Co.* • UKN
ELUSIVE PIMPERNEL, THE • 1919 • Elvey Maurice • UKN
ELUSIVE PIMPERNEL, THE • 1950 • Powell Michael, Pressburger Emeric • UKN • FIGHTING PIMPERNEL, THE (USA) ○ SCARLET PIMPERNEL, THE
ELUSIVE TURKEY, THE • 1913 • *Patheplay* • USA
ELVE, VAGY HALVA! • 1980 • Renyi Tamas • HNG • DEAD OR ALIVE
ELVEDA • 1967 • Basaran Tunc • TRK • FAREWELL
ELVES OF ANDALUCIA, THE see **DUENDES DE ANDALUCIA, LOS** • 1968
ELVESZETT ILLUZIOK • 1983 • Gazdag Gyula • HNG • LOST ILLUSIONS
ELVESZETT PARADICSOM, AZ • 1962 • Makk Karoly • HNG • LOST PARADISE, THE ○ PARADISE LOST
ELVIRA • Waxman Daniel • SHT • ISR
ELVIRA MADIGAN • 1943 • Ohberg Ake • SWD
ELVIRA MADIGAN • 1967 • Widerberg Bo • SWD
ELVIRA, MISTRESS OF THE DARK • 1988 • Signorelli James • USA
ELVIS! • 1979 • Carpenter John • TVM • USA
ELVIS AND ME • 1988 • Peerce Larry • TVM • USA
ELVIS AND THE BEAUTY QUEEN • 1981 • Trikonis Gus • TVM • USA
ELVIS! ELVIS! • 1977 • Pollak Kay • SWD
ELVIS GRATTON LE KING DES KINGS • 1986 • Falardeau Pierre, Poulin Julien • CND
ELVIS ON TOUR • 1972 • Adidge Pierre • USA
ELVIS -THAT'S THE WAY IT IS • 1970 • Sanders Denis • USA
EM BUSCA DO TESOURO • 1967 • Barros Carlos Alberto De Souza • BRZ • IN SEARCH OF TREASURE
EM FAMILIA • 1971 • Porto Paulo • BRZ • GAME OF LIFE, THE
EM PORTUGAL JA SE FAZEM AUTOMOVEIS • 1938 • de Oliveira Manoel • SHT • PRT • JA SE FAZEM AUTOMOVEIS EM PORTUGAL
EMA TON AGALMATON, TO • 1981 • Lycouressis Tony • GRC • MUSEUM PIECES
EMAK BAKIA • 1926 • Ray Man • SHT • FRN • GIVE US A REST ○ LEAVE ME ALONE
EMANCIPATED WOMEN • 1913 • *Brennan John E.* • USA
EMANCIPATION CENTENNIAL, THE see **CEM ANOS DE ABOLICAO** • 1989
EMANON • 1986 • Paul Stuart • USA
EMANUELLE AND FRANCOISE see **EMANUELLE E FRANCOISE LE SORELLINE** • 1976
EMANUELLE AND THE LAST CANNIBALS see **EMANUELLE E GLI ULTIMI CANNIBALI** • 1977
EMANUELLE BIANCA E NERA • 1976 • Pinzauti Mario • ITL
EMANUELLE E FRANCOISE see **EMANUELLE E FRANCOISE LE SORELLINE** • 1976
EMANUELLE E FRANCOISE LE SORELLINE • 1976 • D'Amato Joe • ITL • EMANUELLE E FRANCOISE ○ EMANUELLE AND FRANCOISE
EMANUELLE E GLI ULTIMI CANNIBALI • 1977 • D'Amato Joe • ITL • EMANUELLE AND THE LAST CANNIBALS
EMANUELLE E LE PORNO NOTTI • 1978 • Mattei Bruno • ITL
EMANUELLE GIALLA • 1971 • Albertini Bitto • ITL, HKG • YELLOW EMMANUELLE ○ KINGDOM OF EROTICISM, THE
EMANUELLE IN AMERICA • 1977 • D'Amato Joe • ITL
EMANUELLE NERA • 1975 • Albertini Bitto • ITL • BLACK EMMANUELLE
EMANUELLE NERA N.2 • 1975 • Albertini Bitto • ITL • BLACK EMMANUELLE 2 ○ NEW BLACK EMMANUELLE, THE
EMANUELLE NERA ORIENT REPORTAGE • 1976 • D'Amato Joe • ITL • BLACK EMMANUELLE IN BANGKOK ○ BLACK EMMANUELLE GOES EAST
EMANUELLE PERCHE VIOLENZA ALLA DONNE? • 1977 • D'Amato Joe • ITL • CONFESSIONS OF EMMANUELLE ○ SHE'S SEVENTEEN AND ANXIOUS
EMANUELLE REPORTAGE DA UN CARCERE FEMMINILE • 1982 • Mattei Bruno • ITL, FRN • EMMANUELLE REPORTS FROM A WOMEN'S PRISON ○ CAGED WOMEN
EMBAJADOR, EL • 1949 • Davison Tito • MXC
EMBAJADOR DE LA INDIA, EL • 1989 • Ribero Mario • CLM • AMBASSADOR FROM INDIA, THE
EMBAJADORES EN EL INFIERNO • 1956 • Forque Jose Maria • SPN
EMBALAGEM DO VIDRO, A • 1966 • de Almeida Manuel Faria • SHT • PRT
EMBALMED see **MORTUARY** • 1984
EMBALMER, THE (USA) see **MOSTRO DI VENEZIA, IL** • 1965
EMBARQUEMENT POUR LE PROMENADE • 1896-97 • Lumiere Louis • FRN
EMBARRASSED BRIDEGROOM, AN • 1913 • Duncan William • USA
EMBARRASSING MOMENTS • 1930 • Craft William James • USA
EMBARRASSING MOMENTS • 1934 • Laemmle Edward • USA
EMBARRASSING PREDICAMENT, AN • 1914 • MacGregor Norval • USA
EMBARRASSING PRESENT, AN • 1909 • *Urban-Eclipse* • USA
EMBARRASSMENT see **ZATRUDNENIE** • 1967
EMBARRASSMENT OF RICHES, THE • 1913 • Seay Charles M. • USA
EMBARRASSMENT OF RICHES, THE • 1918 • Dillon Eddie • USA
EMBASSY • 1957 • Haldane Don • CND
EMBASSY • 1972 • Hessler Gordon • UKN
EMBASSY • 1985 • Lewis Robert • TVM • USA
EMBASSY AMERICAN PARADES see **PARADES** • 1976
EMBASSY GIRL (UKN) see **HAT CHECK GIRL** • 1932
EMBER A HID ALLATT • 1934 • Vajda Ladislao • HNG • MAN UNDER THE BRIDGE, THE
EMBER NEHA TEVED, AZ • 1938 • Gaal Bela • HNG • MAN SOMETIMES ERRS
EMBEREK A HAVASON • 1942 • Szots Istvan • HNG • MEN IN THE MOUNTAINS ○ PEOPLE ON THE MOUNTAIN ○ MEN ON THE MOUNTAIN
EMBEREK! NE ENGEDJETEK! • 1954 • Jancso Miklos (c/d) • SHT • HNG • COMRADES! DON'T PUT UP WITH IT, DON'T ALLOW IT!
EMBERS • 1916 • Maude Arthur • USA
EMBERS see **SHOLAY** • 1975
EMBEZZLED HEAVEN (USA) see **VERUNTREUTE HIMMEL, DER** • 1958
EMBEZZLER, THE • 1914 • Dwan Allan • *Gold Seal* • USA
EMBEZZLER, THE • 1914 • Osborne George • *Kb* • USA
EMBEZZLER, THE • 1954 • Gilling John • UKN
EMBLEMS OF LOVE • 1924 • *Drumier Jack* • USA
EMBODIED THOUGHT, THE • 1916 • Sloman Edward • SHT • USA
EMBODIMENT OF FORBIDDEN PLEASURE, THE see **CHINA GIRL** • 1976
EMBORAKOS, O • 1967 • Plita Maria • GRC • SMALL SALESMAN, THE
EMBOSCADA MORTAL, LA • 1960 • Munoz Manuel • MXC
EMBOSCADOS DE CUPIDO, LAS • 1924 • Palau Francisco • DMN
EMBOUCHURE, L' • 1972 • Chouikh Mohamed • ALG
EMBRACE, THE see **ZAGRLJAJ** • 1989
EMBRACEABLE YOU • 1948 • Jacoves Felix • USA
EMBRACED BRIDE see **DAKARETA HANAYOME** • 1957
EMBRACERS, THE • 1963 • Graver Gary • USA • GREAT DREAM, THE ○ BABY GIRL ○ NOW
EMBRACES AND OTHER THINGS see **UMARMUNGEN UND ANDERE SACHEN** • 1976
EMBRASSEZ-MOI • 1928 • Peguy Robert, de Rieux Max • FRN
EMBRASSEZ-MOI • 1932 • Mathot Leon • FRN
EMBRAYE BIDASSE, CA FUME • 1978 • Pecas Max • FRN
EMBRIOK • 1985 • Zolnay Pal • HNG • EMBRYOS
EMBROIDERED DREAMS see **VEZANI METCHTI** • 1956
EMBROIDERY EXTRAORDINARY • 1910 • Hepworth Cecil M.? • UKN
EMBRUJO • 1941 • ARG • BEWITCHED
EMBRUJO • 1947 • Serrano De Osma Carlos • SPN
EMBRUJO ANTILLANO • 1945 • Polaty Geza P., Orol Juan • MXC
EMBRUJO DE SEVILLA, EL • 1930 • Perojo Benito • SPN
EMBRUJO EN CERROS BLANCOS • 1955 • Rossi Julio • ARG • BEWITCHED IN THE WHITE MOUNTAINS
EMBRYO • 1976 • Nelson Ralph • USA • CREATED TO KILL
EMBRYO, THE • 1966 • Wakamatsu Koji • JPN
EMBRYOS see **EMBRIOK** • 1985
EMBUN • 1954 • Effendy Basuki • INN
EMBUN • 1956 • Ismai Osman • INN
EMBUSCADE, L' • 1939 • Rivers Fernand • FRN
EMDEN, THE see **KREUZER EMDEN** • 1932
EMERALD see **CODE NAME: EMERALD** • 1985
EMERALD BROOCH, THE • 1915 • Ingraham Lloyd • USA
EMERALD CITY • 1988 • Jenkins Michael • ASL
EMERALD CITY OF OZ, THE • 1987 • *Kidder Margot (Nar)* • ANM • USA
EMERALD FOREST, THE • 1985 • Boorman John • UKN, USA
EMERALD GOD, THE • 1915 • Melville Wilbert • USA
EMERALD HUNTER, THE see **CACADOR DE ESMERALDAS, O** • 1980
EMERALD ISLE, THE • 1949 • Kneitel Seymour • ANS • USA
EMERALD OF ARTATAMA, THE (UKN) see **MUCHACHA DEL NILO, LA** • 1967
EMERALD OF DEATH (USA) see **KNABE IN BLAU, DER** • 1919
EMERALD OF THE EAST • 1928 • De Kuharski Jean • UKN • HERZ DES MAHARADSCHA, DAS
EMERALD PIN, THE • 1916 • George Burton • SHT • USA
EMERAUDE, L' • 1916 • Burguet Charles • FRN
EMERGENCY • 1962 • Searle Francis • UKN
EMERGENCY • 1971 • Nyby Christian • TVM • USA
EMERGENCY • 1979 • Fenady George • TVM • USA
EMERGENCY CALL • 1933 • Cahn Edward L. • USA
EMERGENCY CALL • 1952 • Gilbert Lewis* • UKN • HUNDRED HOUR HUNT, THE (USA)
EMERGENCY ESCAPE, AN see **WYJSCIE AWARYJNE** • 1983
EMERGENCY HOSPITAL • 1956 • Sholem Lee • USA
EMERGENCY IN MOROCCO • 1960 • Macartney-Filgate Terence • DOC • CND
EMERGENCY LANDING • 1941 • Beaudine William • USA
EMERGENCY RESCUE • 1956 • Macartney-Filgate Terence • DOC • CND
EMERGENCY ROOM • 1983 • Katzin Lee H. • TVM • USA
EMERGENCY SQUAD • 1940 • Dmytryk Edward • USA
EMERGENCY WARD see **SALA DE GUARDIA** • 1952
EMERGENCY WARD see **CAREY TREATMENT, THE** • 1972
EMERGENCY WARD 10 see **LIFE IN EMERGENCY WARD 10** • 1959
EMERGENCY WEDDING • 1950 • Buzzell Edward • USA • JEALOUSY (UKN) ○ THAT BEDSIDE MANNER
EMERSON, LAKE & PALMER IN CONCERT • 1981 • Kantor Ron • USA
EMGODINI • 1985 • SAF
EMIGRADO, EL • 1946 • Torrado Ramon • SPN
EMIGRANT, THE • 1910 • *Selig* • USA
EMIGRANT, THE • 1910 • Gobbett T. J.? • UKN
EMIGRANT, THE • 1965 • Jakubisko Juraj • CZC
EMIGRANTE, EL • 1959 • Almeida Sebastian • SPN
EMIGRANTE, L' • 1939 • Joannon Leo, Allegret Yves • FRN
EMIGRANTE, L' • 1973 • Festa Campanile Pasquale • ITL
EMIGRANTE, O • 1955 • Mendes Joao • SHT • PRT
EMIGRANTES • 1949 • Fabrizi Aldo • ITL • EMIGRANTI, GLI
EMIGRANTI, GLI see **EMIGRANTES** • 1949
EMIGRANTS, THE see **LANDSFLYKTIGE, DE** • 1921
EMIGRANTS, THE (UKN) see **UTVANDRARNA** • 1970
EMIGRANT'S PERIL, THE • 1915 • *Brunette Fritzie* • USA
EMIGRATING BIRDS, THE • 1979 • Youssef Hassan • EGY
EMIL AND THE DETECTIVES • 1935 • Rosmer Milton • UKN • EMIL (USA)

EMIL AND THE DETECTIVES • 1964 • Tewkesbury Peter • USA, FRG
EMIL AND THE DETECTIVES see **EMIL UND DIE DETEKTIVE** • 1931
EMIL AND THE DETECTIVES see **EMIL UND DIE DETEKTIVE** • 1955
EMIL AND THE DETECTIVES see **EMILER GOENDA BAHINI** • 1978
EMIL I LONNEBERGA • 1971 • Hellbom Olle • SWD, FRG
EMIL OCH GRISEKNOEN • 1973 • Hellbom Olle • SWD
EMIL UND DIE DETEKTIVE • 1931 • Lamprecht Gerhard • FRG • EMIL AND THE DETECTIVES
EMIL UND DIE DETEKTIVE • 1955 • Stemmle R. A. • FRG • EMIL AND THE DETECTIVES
EMIL (USA) see **EMIL AND THE DETECTIVES** • 1935
EMILE ASSELIN, FORGERON • 1974 • Plamondon Leo • DCS • CND
EMILE COLEMAN AND HIS ORCHESTRA IN ON THE MELLOW SIDE • 1944 • Collins Lewis D. • SHT • USA
EMILE GRIMSHAW BANJO QUARTETTE • 1929 • *Bsfp* • SHT • UKN • MUSIC WITHOUT WORDS ○ MUSICAL MEDLEY NO.3
EMILE L'AFRICAIN • 1947 • Vernay Robert • FRN
EMILE VERHAEREN, POETE DE LA FLANDRE ET DU MONDE • 1954 • Haesaerts Paul • BLG
EMILE ZOLA • Arcady • SHT • FRN
EMILER GOENDA BAHINI • 1978 • Rahman Badal • BNG • EMIL AND THE DETECTIVES
EMILIA GALOTTI • 1958 • Hellberg Martin • GDR
EMILIA LA DONNA DELLE TENEBRE • 1977 • Dallamano Massimo • ITL
EMILIA, PARADA Y FONDA • 1976 • Fons Angelino • SPN • EMILY.. HALT AND INN
EMILIANO ZAPATA • 1970 • Cazals Felipe • MXC
EMILIE HOGQUIST • 1939 • Molander Gustaf • SWD
EMILIENNE • 1975 • Casaril Guy • FRN
EMILLE JONG • 1961 • Seungkie Hong • SKR • BELL OF EMILLE, THE
EMILY • 1976 • Herbert Henry • UKN • AWAKENING OF EMILY, THE
EMILY • 1979 • Le Grice Malcolm • UKN • THIRD PARTY SPECULATION
EMILY see **AMERICANIZATION OF EMILY, THE** • 1964
EMILY AND JOE • 1973 • Sargent Joseph • TVM • USA
EMILY.. HALT AND INN see **EMILIA, PARADA Y FONDA** • 1976
EMINE see **YATIK EMINE** • 1975
EMINENT DOMAIN • 1990 • Irvin John • USA
EMIR • 1918 • D'Ambra Lucio • ITL
EMIR ABDEL-KADER • 1966 • Cherif Hachemi • SHT • ALG
EMIR PREFERE LES BLONDES, L' • 1983 • Payet Alain • FRN
EMISSARY, THE • 1988 • Scholtz Jan • USA
EMISSARY WHO DID NOT RETURN, THE • 1984 • NKR
EMISSION, L' see **EKPOMBI, I** • 1968
EMITAI • 1972 • Sembene Ousmane • SNL • THUNDERGOD, THE
EMLEKEZZ, IFJUSAG! • 1955 • Jancso Miklos • SHT • HNG • YOUNG PEOPLE, REMEMBER
EMMA • 1931 • Brown Clarence • USA
EMMA • 1965 • Perry Anthony • UKN
EMMA • 1977 • Mahot Jean-Pierre • FRN
EMMA HAMILTON see **LADY HAMILTON ZWISCHEN SCHMACH UND LIEBE** • 1968
EMMA JANE MAKES GOOD • 1915 • Matthews H. C. • USA
EMMA MAE • 1977 • Fanaka Jamaa • USA • BLACK SISTER'S REVENGE
EMMA, PUERTAS OSCURAS • 1972 • Larraz Jose R. • SPN
EMMA, QUEEN OF THE SOUTH SEAS • 1988 • Banas John • TVM • USA
EMMA ZUNZ • Delpeut Peter • SHT • NTH
EMMAHU, DER SCHRECKEN AFRIKAS • 1918 • *Rieck Arnold* • FRG
EMMANUELLE • 1974 • Jaeckin Just • FRN
EMMANUELLE 2, L'ANTIVIERGE see **EMMANUELLE L'ANTIVIERGE** • 1975
EMMANUELLE 2 (UKN) see **EMMANUELLE L'ANTIVIERGE** • 1975
EMMANUELLE 3 • *Castell Silvia* • FRN
EMMANUELLE 4 • 1983 • Leroi Francis • FRN
EMMANUELLE 5 • 1986 • Borowczyk Walerian • FRN
EMMANUELLE AND THE WHITE SLAVE TRADE see **VIA DELLA PROSTITUZIONE, LA** • 1978
EMMANUELLE AND THE WHITE SLAVE TRADERS see **VIA DELLA PROSTITUZIONE, LA** • 1978
EMMANUELLE GOES TO CANNES • 1984 • Pallardy Jean-Marie • FRN
EMMANUELLE IN DENMARK see **I SKYTTENS TEGN** • 1978
EMMANUELLE IN EGYPT see **VELLUTO NERO** • 1976
EMMANUELLE IN SOHO • 1982 • Hughes David • UKN
EMMANUELLE IN THE COUNTRY see **CORNETTI A COLAZIONE** • 1978
EMMANUELLE IN TOKYO see **TOKYO EMMANUELLE FUJIN** • 1975
EMMANUELLE L'ANTIVIERGE • 1975 • Giacobetti Francis • FRN • EMMANUELLE, THE JOYS OF A WOMAN (USA) ○ EMMANUELLE 2 (UKN) ○ EMMANUELLE 2, L'ANTIVIERGE
EMMANUELLE QUEEN BITCH see **EMMANUELLE: QUEEN OF THE SADOS** • 1979
EMMANUELLE: QUEEN OF THE SADOS • 1979 • Milonakos Ilias • GRC, CYP • EMMANUELLE QUEEN BITCH ○ EMMANUELLE'S DAUGHTER
EMMANUELLE REPORTS FROM A WOMEN'S PRISON see **EMANUELLE REPORTAGE DA UN CARCERE FEMMINILE** • 1982
EMMANUELLE, THE JOYS OF A WOMAN (USA) see **EMMANUELLE L'ANTIVIERGE** • 1975
EMMANUELLE'S DAUGHTER see **EMMANUELLE: QUEEN OF THE SADOS** • 1979
EMMANUELLE'S SILVER TONGUE see **ECCO LINGUA D'ARGENTO** • 1976
EMMA'S SHADOW see **SKYGGEN AF EMMA** • 1987
EMMA'S WAR • 1987 • Jessop Clytie • USA
EMMENEZ-MOI AU RITZ • 1977 • Grimblat Pierre • MTV • FRN
EMMERDEUR, L' • 1973 • Molinaro Edouard • FRN, ITL • ROMPIBALLE, IL (ITL) ○ PAIN IN THE A.., A (USA) ○ ALLEZ VOUS PENDRE AILLEURS
EMMIGRANT, THE see **PAWEOGO** • 1983
EMMY • 1934 • Sekely Steve • HNG
EMMY OF STORK'S NEST see **STORK'S NEST, THE** • 1915
EMOTION DISSONANTE, L' • 1984 • Belanger Fernand • CND
EMOTIONAL EDUCATION, AN see **SELSKAYA UCHITELNITSA** • 1947
EMOTIONAL MISS VAUGHAN, THE • 1920 • Drew Sidney Mrs. • SHT • USA • EMOTIONAL MRS. VAUGHAN
EMOTIONAL MRS. VAUGHAN see **EMOTIONAL MISS VAUGHAN, THE** • 1920
EMOTIONS AT SUNSET • 1968 • Gati John • SHT • USA
EMOZIONE IN PIU, UN' • 1979 • Longo Francesco • ITL
EMPERADOR DE LOS NEVADOS, EL • 1979 • Perez Liko • VNZ, SPN
EMPEREUR DES PAUVRES, L' • 1921 • Leprince Rene • FRN
EMPEREUR DES VACHES, L' see **JEUNESSE D'ABORD** • 1935
EMPEREUR DU PEROU, L' • 1982 • Arrabal Fernando • FRN
EMPEROR, THE • 1968 • Lucas George • USA
EMPEROR, THE • 1989 • el Erian Tarek • EGY
EMPEROR, THE see **KEJSAREN** • 1978
EMPEROR AND A GENERAL, THE see **NIHON NO ICHIBAN NAGAI HI** • 1967
EMPEROR AND THE GOLEM, THE (USA) see **CISARUV PEKAR** • 1951
EMPEROR AND THE NIGHTINGALE, THE see **CISARUV SLAVIK** • 1948
EMPEROR CALIGULA: THE UNTOLD STORY see **CALIGULA: THE UNTOLD STORY**
EMPEROR CHIEN LUNG AND THE BEAUTY see **CH'IEN LUNG HUANG YU KU-NIANG** • 1980
EMPEROR CHIEN LUNG PART II see **CH'IEN LUNG HUANG-TI** • 1977
EMPEROR FRANZ JOSEF OPENING THE MILLENIAL EXHIBITION • 1896 • Sziklay Arnold • HNG
EMPEROR JONES, THE • 1933 • Murphy Dudley • USA
EMPEROR MEIJI AND THE RUSSO-JAPANESE WAR, THE see **MEIJI-TENNO TO MICHIRO-SENSO** • 1957
EMPEROR OF CALIFORNIA, THE see **KAISER VON KALIFORNIEN, DER** • 1936
EMPEROR OF MONKEYS see **OPICI CISAR** • 1955
EMPEROR OF PERU, THE • 1981 • Arrabal Fernando • CND, FRN • ODYSSEY OF THE PACIFIC
EMPEROR OF PORTUGAL, THE see **KEJSARN AV PORTUGALLIEN** • 1944
EMPEROR OF THE EUCALYPTS • 1953 • Monkman Noel • DOC • ASL
EMPEROR OF THE NORTH see **EMPEROR OF THE NORTH POLE, THE** • 1973
EMPEROR OF THE NORTH POLE, THE • 1973 • Aldrich Robert • USA • EMPEROR OF THE NORTH
EMPEROR PENGUINS, THE see **APTENODYTES FORSTERI** • 1953
EMPEROR TOMATO-KETCHUP see **TOMATO KETCHUP KOTEI** • 1972
EMPEROR WALTZ, THE • 1948 • Wilder Billy • USA
EMPEROR'S BAKER, THE see **CISARUV PEKAR** • 1951
EMPEROR'S CANDLESTICKS, THE • 1937 • Fitzmaurice George • USA
EMPEROR'S CANDLESTICKS, THE see **LEUCHTER DES KAISERS, DIE** • 1936
EMPEROR'S MESSENGER, THE • 1912 • Plumb Hay • UKN
EMPEROR'S NEW ARMOR, THE • 1970 • Blechman R. O. • ANS • USA
EMPEROR'S NEW CLOTHES, THE • 1919 • Zhelyabuzhsky Yuri • USS
EMPEROR'S NEW CLOTHES, THE • 1953 • Parmelee Ted • ANS • USA
EMPEROR'S NEW CLOTHES, THE • 1958 • Schulz Kurt Herbert • ANM • GDR
EMPEROR'S NEW CLOTHES, THE • 1965 • Clark Bob • CND
EMPEROR'S NEW CLOTHES, THE • 1984 • Medak Peter • MTV • USA
EMPEROR'S NEW CLOTHES, THE • 1987 • Irving David • USA • CANNON MOVIE TALES: THE EMPEROR'S NEW CLOTHES
EMPEROR'S NEW CLOTHES, THE see **CAREVO NOVO RUHO** • 1961
EMPEROR'S NIGHTINGALE, THE see **CISARUV SLAVIK** • 1948
EMPEROR'S SPY, THE • 1914 • *Foster Morris* • USA
EMPEZO EN BUDA • 1944 • Matarazzo Raffaello • ITL
EMPIRE • 1965 • Warhol Andy • USA
EMPIRE AU SERVICE DE LA FRANCE, L' see **VISION SAHARIENNE** • 1939
EMPIRE BLEND, THE • 1977 • Phelps Richard • UKN
EMPIRE BUILDERS • 1924 • *Baker Snowy* • USA
EMPIRE BUILDERS see **IT'S A GREAT LIFE** • 1920
EMPIRE BUILDERS, THE see **WHITE RENEGADE, THE** • 1931
EMPIRE D'ALEXANDRE, L' see **STAVISKY..** • 1973
EMPIRE DE LA NUIT, L' • 1962 • Grimblat Pierre • FRN
EMPIRE DE M., L' see **IMBRAT'URIYYAT MIN** • 1972
EMPIRE DES PASSIONS, L' (FRN) see **AI NO BOREI** • 1977
EMPIRE DES SENS, L' (FRN) see **AI NO CORRIDA** • 1976
EMPIRE DU DIAMANT, L' see **EMPIRE OF DIAMONDS, THE** • 1920
EMPIRE GLIDE, THE • 1913 • *Selsior Films* • UKN
EMPIRE IN THE SUN (USA) see **IMPERO DEL SOLE, L'** • 1956
EMPIRE, INC. see **TYCOON** • 1982
EMPIRE OF ASH • 1987 • Simandl Lloyd A., Mazo Michael • USA
EMPIRE OF DIAMONDS, THE • 1920 • Perret Leonce • USA • EMPIRE DU DIAMANT, L'
EMPIRE OF DRACULA (USA) see **IMPERIO DE DRACULA, EL** • 1966
EMPIRE OF DREAMS see **AHLAM** • 1987
EMPIRE OF FORTUNE, THE see **IMPERIO DE LA FORTUNAM, EL** • 1986
EMPIRE OF ILLUSION, THE • 1914 • *Kerrigan J. Warren* • USA
EMPIRE OF JAPAN see **DAINIPPON TEIKOKU** • 1983
EMPIRE OF PASSION (UKN) see **AI NO BOREI** • 1977
EMPIRE OF SATAN, THE see **BEDAYA, EL** • 1986
EMPIRE OF THE ANTS • 1977 • Gordon Bert I. • USA
EMPIRE OF THE LAZY, THE • 1961 • Sibianu Gheorghe • ANM • RMN
EMPIRE OF THE SENSES see **AI NO CORRIDA** • 1976
EMPIRE OF THE SUN • 1987 • Spielberg Steven • USA
EMPIRE SONRAI, L' see **SONGHAYS** • 1963
EMPIRE STATE • 1987 • Peck Ron • UKN
EMPIRE STRIKES BACK -STAR WARS II, THE • 1980 • Kershner Irvin • USA
EMPIRE WAS BUILT, AN see **PRIME MINISTER, THE** • 1941
EMPLOI CANADA • 1981 • Payer Roch Christophe • MTV • CND
EMPLOYEE, THE see **IMPIEGATO, L'** • 1959
EMPLOYEES' ENTRANCE, THE • 1933 • Del Ruth Roy • USA
EMPLOYER'S LIABILITY • 1912 • *Nestor* • USA
EMPLOYMENT WITH INVESTMENT AND THE MASKED FRAUD • 1926 • Engholm F. W. • UKN
EMPOR • 1973 • Jegersberg Otto • FRG
EMPREINTE DU DIEU, L' • 1940 • Moguy Leonide • FRN
EMPREINTE ROUGE, L' • 1936 • de Canonge Maurice • FRN
EMPRESA PERDONA UN MOMENTO DE LOCURA, LA • 1977 • Walerstein Mauricio • VNZ • FIRM FORGIVES A MOMENT OF MADNESS, THE ○ COMPANY PARDONS A FIT OF MADNESS, THE
EMPRESS, THE • 1917 • Blache Alice • USA
EMPRESS DOWAGER, THE see **CH'ING KUO CH'ING CH'ENG** • 1975
EMPRESS JOSEPHINE: OR, WIFE OF A DEMI-GOD, THE • 1923 • Greenwood Edwin • UKN
EMPRESS MESSALINA MEETS THE SON OF HERCULES see **ULTIMO GLADIATORE, L'** • 1965
EMPRESS WU (USA) see **WU-HOU** • 1964
EMPRESS YANG KWEI FEI, THE (UKN) see **YOKIHI** • 1955
EMPRESS'S LOVE LETTER, THE see **LIEBESBRIEF DER KONIGIN, DER** • 1916
EMPRISE, L' • 1923 • Diamant-Berger Henri • FRN
EMPTIED-OUT GROCER'S SHOP, THE see **U SNEDENEHO KRAMU** • 1933
EMPTY ARMS • 1920 • Reicher Frank • USA
EMPTY BEACH, THE • 1985 • Thomson Chris • ASL
EMPTY BOX, AN • 1913 • *Smalley Phillips* • USA
EMPTY CAB, THE • 1918 • Gerrard Douglas • USA
EMPTY CANVAS, THE (USA) see **NOIA, LA** • 1964
EMPTY CHAIR, THE see **CHAISE VIDE, LA** • 1975
EMPTY CRADLE, THE • 1923 • King Burton L. • USA
EMPTY CRADLE, THE (USA) see **CUNA VACIA, LA** • 1937
EMPTY CRIB, THE • 1911 • *Fearnley Jane* • USA
EMPTY CRIB, THE • 1916 • *Supreme* • USA
EMPTY EYES see **PUSTE OCSY** • 1969
EMPTY GRAVE, THE • 1912 • *Pathe* • USA
EMPTY GUN, THE • 1917 • De Grasse Joseph • SHT • USA
EMPTY HANDS • 1924 • Fleming Victor • USA
EMPTY HEARTS • 1924 • Santell Alfred • USA
EMPTY HOLSTERS • 1937 • Eason B. Reeves • USA
EMPTY HOUSE, THE • 1921 • Elvey Maurice • UKN
EMPTY HOUSE, THE see **LEGE HUIS, HET** • 1975
EMPTY PILLOW, THE see **WESSADA EL KHALIA, EL** • 1957
EMPTY POCKETS • 1918 • Brenon Herbert • USA
EMPTY RUN, AN • 1963 • Vengerov Vladimir • USS
EMPTY SADDLE, THE • 1911 • *Essanay* • USA
EMPTY SADDLE, THE • 1925 • Webb Harry S. • USA
EMPTY SADDLES • 1936 • Selander Lesley • USA
EMPTY SADDLES • 1973 • Blagg Linda • SHT • ASL
EMPTY SEA see **SVART HAV** • 1979
EMPTY SHELL, THE • 1911 • Ince Thomas H. • USA
EMPTY SLEEVE, THE • 1914 • Santschi Thomas • USA
EMPTY SLEEVE, OR MEMORIES OF BYGONE DAYS, THE • 1909 • Brooke Van Dyke • USA
EMPTY SOCKS • 1927 • Disney Walt • ANS • USA
EMPTY STAR, THE (USA) see **ESTRELLA VACIA, LA** • 1958
EMPTY STUDIO, THE • 1913 • Kirkland Hardee • USA
EMPTY TABLE, THE see **SHOKUTAKU NO NAI IE** • 1985
EMPTY TEPEE, THE • 1911 • *Bison* • USA
EMPTY WATER KEG, THE • 1912 • *Bison* • USA
EMRAA WA SHAITAN • 1961 • Shawkat Saifeddine • EGY • WOMAN AND THE DEVIL, THE
EMULE DE TARTARIN see **MAX EMULE DE TARTARIN** • 1912
EN AFRIQUE CENTRALE, FACHODA • 1910 • Machin Alfred • FRN
EN ANDALUCIA NACIO EL AMOR • 1966 • Eguiluz Enrique L. • SPN
EN AV DE MANGA • 1915 • Sjostrom Victor • SWD • ONE OUT OF MANY ○ ONE OF THE MANY
EN BALDIRI DE LA COSTA • 1967 • Font Espina Jose Maria • SPN
EN BATEAU • 1952 • *Mitry Jean (P)* • SHT • FRN • BY BOAT
EN BORDEE • 1931 • Wulschleger Henry, Francis Joe • FRN
EN BORDEE • 1957 • Chevalier Pierre • FRN
EN BUSCA DE UNA CANCION • 1937 • Ardavin Eusebio F. • SPN
EN CABINET PARTICULIER • 1897 • Melies Georges • FRN • PRIVATE DINNER, A
EN CADA FERIA UN AMOR • 1960 • Gonzalez Rogelio A. • MXC
EN CADA PUERTO UN AMOR • 1948 • Cortazar Ernesto • MXC
EN CARNE PROPIA • 1959 • Ortega Juan J. • MXC
EN CARNE VIVA • 1950 • Gout Alberto • MXC
EN CARNE VIVA • 1955 • Cahen Enrique • ARG
EN CAS DE GUERRE MONDIALE, JE FILE A L'ETRANGER.. • 1982 • Ardouin Jacques • FRN
EN CAS DE MALHEUR • 1958 • Autant-Lara Claude • FRN, ITL • RAGAZZA DEL PECCATO, LA (ITL) ○ LOVE IS MY PROFESSION (USA)
EN CE JOUR MEMORABLE • 1971 • Bulbulian Maurice • DCS • CND
EN CE TEMPS-LA • 1962 • Boigelot Jacques • BLG
EN CHERCHANT SON PERE • 1969 • Roudakoff Michel • FRN
EN CLASSE • 1897-98 • Blache Alice • FRN
EN COMPAGNIE DE MAX LINDER • 1964 • Linder Maud • CMP • FRN • LAUGH WITH MAX LINDER (UKN)
EN COURS DE ROUTE see **UTKOZBEN** • 1980
EN CRETE SANS LES DIEUX • 1934 • Leenhardt Roger (c/d) • FRN
EN DALIG FLICKA see **EN FASTMAN I TAGET** • 1952

EN DE ZEE WAS NIET MEER • 1956 • Haanstra Bert • NTH • AND THERE WAS NO MORE SEA
EN DEFENSA PROPIA • 1917 • Coss Joaquin • MXC • IN SELF DEFENSE
EN DERNIER RECOURS • 1988 • Godbout Jacques • DOC • CND
EN DERNIERES PAGES • 1983 • Tessier Jean • CND
EN DESCENDANT LA VOLGA • 1916 • Protazanov Yakov • USS
EN DIAS COMO ESTOS • 1960 • Fraga Jorge • CUB
EN DIE VONKE SPAT • 1961 • SAF
EN DIRECT DE L'ESPACE see **DREAM IS ALIVE, THE** • 1984
EN EFFEUILLANT LA MARGUERITE • 1956 • Allegret Marc • FRN • PLEASE MR. BALZAC (USA) ○ MAM'SELLE STRIPTEASE
EN EL BALCON VACIO • 1962 • Garcia Ascot Jose Miguel • MXC • ON AN EMPTY BALCONY ○ ON THE EMPTY BALCONY
EN EL NOMBRE DEL HIJO • 1987 • Polaco Jorge • ARG • IN THE NAME OF THE SON
EN EL RIO • 1961 • Borau Jose Luis • SPN • IN THE RIVER
EN EL ULTIMO PISO • 1942 • Catrani Catrano • ARG
EN EL VIEJO GUANAJUATO see **JINETES DE LA BRUJA, LOS** • 1965
EN EL VIEJO TAMPICO see **GRAN CASINO** • 1946
EN ENDA NATT • 1938 • Molander Gustaf • SWD • ONE SINGLE NIGHT ○ ENDA NATT, EN
EN ES A NAGYAPAM • 1954 • Gertler Viktor • HNG • ME AND MY GRANDFATHER
EN ESTE PUEBLO NO HAY LADRONES • 1965 • Isaac Alberto • MXC • IN THIS TOWN THERE ARE NO THIEVES
EN ETES-VOUS BIEN SUR? • 1946 • Houssin Jacques • FRN, BLG
EN FACTION • 1902 • Blache Alice • FRN
EN FANGE HAR RYMT • 1943 • Ahrle Elof • SWD
EN FASTMAN I TAGET • 1952 • Bauman Schamyl • SWD • ONE FIANCE AT A TIME ○ EN DALIG FLICKA
EN FEVRIER see **FEVRIER** • 1967
EN FLUGA GOR INGEN SOMMAR • 1947 • Ekman Hasse • SWD • ONE SWALLOW DOESN'T MAKE A SUMMER
EN GHENTAR SE MUERE FACIL (SPN) see **A GHENTAR SI MUORE FACILE** • 1967
EN GRANDES POMPES • Teisseire Andre • FRN
EN GREVE.. • 1911 • Feuillade Louis • FRN
EN HAUT DES MARCHES • 1983 • Vecchiali Paul • FRN
EN HERRE I KJOLE OG HVIDT • 1942 • Ipsen Bodil • DNM
EN LA CORTE DE NAPOLEON see **MADAME SANS-GENE** • 1945
EN LA CRESTA DE LA OLA • 1974 • Lazaga Pedro • SPN
EN LA FRONTERA DE LA MUERTE • 1954 • Catalan Feliciano • SPN
EN LA HACIENDA • 1920 • Vollrath Ernesto • MXC
EN LA HACIENDA DE LA FLOR • 1948 • Cortazar Ernesto • MXC
EN LA LUGAR DE LA MANGA • 1970 • Ozores Mariano • SPN
EN LA LUZ DE UNA ESTRELLA • 1941 • Discepolo Enrique Santos • ARG
EN LA MITAD DEL MUNDO • 1963 • Pereda Ramon • MXC, ECD
EN LA OTRA ISLA • 1968 • Gomez Sara • DOC • CUB
EN LA PALMA DE TU MANO • 1950 • Gavaldon Roberto • MXC • KILL HIM FOR ME
EN LA RED DE MI CORAZON • 1971 • Ozores Mariano • SPN
EN LA SELVA NO HAY ESTRELLAS • 1968 • Godoy Armando Robles • ARG, PRU • THERE ARE NO STARS IN THE JUNGLE ○ NO STARS IN THE JUNGLE
EN LA SOMBRA • 1917 • Coss Joaquin • MXC
EN LA TORMENTA • 1980 • Vallejo Fernando • MXC • IN THE STORM
EN LA TRAMPA • 1978 • Araiza Raul • MXC • IN THE TRAP
EN LA VIEJA CALIFORNIA • 1962 • Marin Jesus • MXC
EN LANYON NEM OLYAN, AZ • 1936 • Vajda Ladislao • HNG • MY DAUGHTER IS DIFFERENT
EN L'AUTRE BORD • 1978 • Kanapa Jerome • FRN
EN LEGIOM, AZ • 1989 • Ledniczky Marton • HNG, FRN • MY LEGION
EN LEGITIME DEFENSE • 1958 • Berthomieu Andre • FRN, ITL
EN LIBERTE SUR LES ROUTES D'U.R.S.S. • 1956 • Lapierre Dominique, Pedrazzini Jean-Pierre • DOC • FRN
EN LISANT LE JOURNAL • 1932 • Cavalcanti Alberto • FRN
EN LOS ACTOS DE JALISCO • 1948 • Urueta Chano • MXC
EN MAN FOR MYCKET • 1941 • Stevens Gosta • SWD • ONE MAN TOO MANY
EN MARCHANT see **WALKING** • 1968
EN MET ETT LEJON • 1940 • Molander Gustaf • SWD • ONE BUT A LION
EN MI CASA MANDO YO • 1968 • Ayala Fernando • ARG • IN MY HOUSE I'M BOSS
EN-NAR, LA CIUDAD DE FUEGO • 1951 • Gonzalez Jose • SPN
EN NATT • 1931 • Molander Gustaf • SWD • ONE NIGHT ○ SERMENTS ○ NATT, EN
EN NOLLA FOR MYCKET • 1962 • Nyberg Borje • SWD • ONE ZERO TOO MANY
EN NORSK LASSE MAJA • 1940 • Ibsen Tancred • SWD
EN NY MANNISKA • 1966 • Stromblad Curt • SWD
EN OCH EN • 1978 • Josephson Erland, Nykvist Sven, Thulin Ingrid • SWD • ONE AND ONE (UKN)
EN OPSTANDELSE • 1914 • Holger-Madsen • DNM • GENOPSTANDELSEN ○ RESURRECTION, A
EN PASSANT • 1943 • Alexeieff Alexandre • CND • IN PASSING
EN PASSANT PAR LA LORRAINE • 1950 • Franju Georges • DOC • FRN
EN PASSANT PAR MASCOUCHE • 1981 • Moreau Michel, Labonte Francois • DOC • CND
EN PAYS NEUFS • 1937 • Proulx Maurice • DOC • CND
EN PAYS PITTORESQUES • 1939 • Proulx Maurice • DOC • CND
EN PELIGRO DE MUERTE! • 1962 • Cardona Rene • MXC
EN PLEIN CIRAGE • 1961 • Lautner Georges • FRN, ITL • OPERATION GOLD INGOT (USA)
EN PLEIN MIDI • 1958 • Leenhardt Roger • DCS • FRN
EN PLEINE BAGARRE (FRN) see **MANI IN ALTO** • 1961
EN PODER DE BARBA AZUL • 1940 • Buchs Jose • SPN
EN PREMIER, L' • 1976-77 • Brault Michel, Gladu Andre • DCS • CND
EN RADE • 1927 • Cavalcanti Alberto • FRN • SEA FEVER (USA)
EN-RAI • 1982 • Arai Kichitaro • JPN • DISTANT THUNDER
EN REKRUT FRA '64 • 1912 • Lind Alfred • DNM
EN REMONTANT LE MISSISSIPPI • 1971 • Manthoulis Robert • FRN, FRG • OUT OF THE BLACKS, INTO THE BLUES
EN RESIDENCE SURVEILLEE • 1981 • Vieyra Paulin • SNL • UNDER HOUSE ARREST
EN RETIRADA • 1984 • Desanzo Juan Carlos • ARG • IN RETREAT
EN REVENANT DE SAINT-HILARION • 1958-60 • Bonniere Rene • DCS • CND
EN REVENNAT D'LA REVUE see **PAULUS CHANTANT: EN REVENANT D'LA REVUE** • 1897
EN ROULANT MA BOULE • 1944 • MacKay Jim • ANS • CND
EN ROULANT MA BOULE see **GOIN' DOWN THE ROAD** • 1970
EN ROUTE • 1910 • Cohl Emile • ANS • FRN
EN ROUTE • 1961 • Andjaparidze Marija • USS
EN ROUTE TO BRASILIA see **RUMBO A BRASILIA** • 1960
EN ROUTE VERS LA TERRE PROMISE • 1971 • Tanner Alain • SWT
EN SAN STRALANDE DAG • 1967 • Gimtell Kage G. • SWD • WHAT A BEAUTIFUL DAY
EN SCENE • 1982 • Letourneau Diane • CND
EN SEPTIEMBRE • 1981 • de Arminan Jaime • SPN • IN SEPTEMBER
EN SIX HEURES • 1973 • Shawqi Khalil • SHT • EGY
EN SONS KAERLIGHED • 1915 • Davidsen Hjalmar • DNM
EN STAERKERE MAGT • 1914 • Davidsen Hjalmar • DNM
EN TERRITORIO EXTRANJERO • 1990 • Penzo Jacobo • VNZ • ON FOREIGN SHORES
EN TIEMPOS DE DON PORFIRIO • 1939 • Bustillo Oro Juan • MXC • MELODIAS DE ANTANO ○ IN THE TIMES OF DON PORFIRIO
EN TIEMPOS DE LA INQUISICION • 1946 • Bustillo Oro Juan • MXC
EN TO IU ONNA • 1971 • Imai Tadashi • JPN • GIRL NAMED EN, A ○ WOMAN NAMED EN, A
EN TOUT INNOCENCE • 1988 • Jessua Alain • FRN
EN UN BURRO TRES BATURROS • 1939 • Benavides Jose Jr. • MXC
EN UN FIN DE CURSO • 1970 • Cortazar Octavio • DOC • CUB
EN UN MUNDO NUEVO • 1971 • Garcia de la Vega Fernando, Torrado Ramon • SPN • IN THE NEW WORLD
EN UN RINCON DE ESPANA • 1948 • Mihura Jeronimo • SPN
EN VACKER DAG • 1963 • Gentele Goran • SWD • ONE FINE DAY
EN VAROSOM, AZ • 1959 • Monich Laszlo • HNG • MY TOWN
EN VOTRE AME ET CONSCIENCE • 1960 • Saltel Roger • FRN • DOUBLE VERDICT ○ JUGEZ-LES BIEN
EN VOYAGE AVEC JEAN MOHR • 1989 • Herman Villi • DOC • SWT
EN XX. SZAZADOM, A • 1988 • Enyedi Ildiko • HNG • MY 20TH CENTURY (UKN)
ENA KORITSI ALLIOTIKO APO T'ALLA • 1968 • Varveris Nikos • GRC • GIRL DIFFERENT FROM THE OTHERS, A ○ GIRL LIKE ME, A
ENA REISS • 1930 • *Balcon Michael (P)* • SHT • UKN
ENAMORADA • 1946 • Fernandez Emilio • MXC • IN LOVE
ENAMORADO, EL • 1951 • Zacarias Miguel • MXC • VUELVE MARTIN CORONA
ENARMADE BANDITEN, DEN • 1974 • Kruse Peter • SWD • ONE ARMED BANDIT
ENAS APENTAROS LEFTAS • 1967 • Kiriakopoulos Hristos • GRC • RICH MAN WITHOUT A PENNY, A
ENAS IPPOTIS ME TSAROUHIA • 1968 • Papakostas Giorgos • GRC • KNIGHT RUNNING WILD, A ○ KNIGHT IN SANDALS, A
ENAS IPPOTIS YIA TI VASOULA • 1968 • Dalianidis Ioannis • GRC • KNIGHT AND THE GIRL, THE ○ KNIGHT FOR VASOULA, A
ENAS ISICHOS THANATOS • 1987 • Liappa Frieda • GRC • QUIET DEATH, A
ENAS NOMOTAGIS POLITIS • 1973 • Thalassinos Errikos • GRC • LAW-ABIDING CITIZEN, A
ENAS VENGOD GIA OLES TIS DOULIES • 1969 • Katsouridis Dinos • GRC • JACK OF ALL TRADES
ENCADENADA, LA • 1972 • Mur Oti • SPN
ENCALHE, O see **SETE DIAS DE AGONIA** • 1982
ENCAPUCHADOS DEL INFIERNO, LOS • 1961 • Curiel Federico • MXC
ENCERCLES, LES • 1968 • Gion Christian • FRN
ENCHAINEMENT, L' see **ANGELA DAVIS ET L'ENCHAINEMENT** • 1978
ENCHANTED see **ENCHANTMENT** • 1916
ENCHANTED APRIL • 1934 • Beaumont Harry • USA
ENCHANTED BARN • 1919 • Smith David • USA
ENCHANTED BASKET, THE (USA) see **CORBEILLE ENCHANTEE, LA** • 1903
ENCHANTED BEAN, THE see **FEVE ENCHANTEE, LA**
ENCHANTED BOOTS, THE • 1908 • *Gaumont* • FRN
ENCHANTED CASTLE, THE • 1910 • *Kalem* • USA
ENCHANTED CASTLE IN DUDINCI, THE see **ZACARANI DVORAC U DUDINCINA** • 1951
ENCHANTED CITY, THE • 1921 • *Newcombe Warren A. (P)* • SHT • USA • LAND OF LOVE'S DREAMS, THE
ENCHANTED COTTAGE, THE • 1924 • Robertson John S. • USA
ENCHANTED COTTAGE, THE • 1945 • Cromwell John • USA
ENCHANTED CUP, THE • 1902 • Booth W. R. • UKN
ENCHANTED DESNA, THE see **ZACHAROVANNAYA DESNA** • 1965
ENCHANTED DRAWING, THE • 1900 • Blackton J. Stuart • USA
ENCHANTED DRAWING, THE • 1900 • Porter Edwin S. • USA
ENCHANTED FIFER, THE • 1912 • *C.g.p.c.* • FRN
ENCHANTED FOREST, THE • 1930 • Justice Martin • SHT • USA
ENCHANTED FOREST, THE • 1945 • Landers Lew • USA
ENCHANTED FOREST, THE (USA) see **VERZAUBERTE WALD, DER** • 1928
ENCHANTED GLASSES, THE • 1906 • *Pathe* • FRN
ENCHANTED GUITAR, THE • 1908 • *Gaumont* • FRN
ENCHANTED HAND, THE • 1967 • Brdecka Jiri • ANS • CZC • BEWITCHED HAND, THE
ENCHANTED HERITAGE see **CAROVNE DEDICTVI** • 1985
ENCHANTED HILL, THE • 1926 • Willat Irvin V. • USA
ENCHANTED HOUSE, THE see **KOUZELNY DUM** • 1939
ENCHANTED ISLAND • 1958 • Dwan Allan • USA
ENCHANTED ISLAND see **MADOL DUWA** • 1975
ENCHANTED ISLAND, THE • 1927 • Crosby William G. • USA
ENCHANTED KISS, THE • 1917 • Smith David • USA
ENCHANTED LAKE, THE see **FEE LIBELLULE, LA** • 1908
ENCHANTED LEG, THE • 1913 • *Kinemacolor* • USA
ENCHANTED MATCHES, THE • 1916 • *Jockey* • USA
ENCHANTED MATTRESS, THE • 1907 • *Lubin* • USA
ENCHANTED MIRROR, THE (USA) see **VOLSHEVNOYE ZERKALO** • 1958
ENCHANTED PILLS, THE • *Patankar Friends* • IND
ENCHANTED POND • 1907 • *Pathe* • FRN
ENCHANTED PRINCESS, THE see **HATSUHARA TANUKI GOTEN** • 1959
ENCHANTED PROFILE, THE • 1918 • Justice Martin • SHT • USA
ENCHANTED ROCK, THE • Karpas Jan • ANS • CZC
ENCHANTED SEDAN-CHAIR, THE (USA) see **CHAISE A PORTEURS ENCHANTEE, LA** • 1905
ENCHANTED SQUARE, THE • 1947 • Kneitel Seymour • ANS • USA
ENCHANTED SWORD, THE • 1960 • *Fox* • ANM • SPN
ENCHANTED TOYMAKER, THE • 1904 • Cooper Arthur • UKN • OLD TOYMAKER'S DREAM, THE
ENCHANTED VALLEY, THE • 1948 • Tansey Robert • USA
ENCHANTED VOICE, AN • 1914 • *Eclair* • USA
ENCHANTED VOYAGE see **WAKE UP AND DREAM** • 1946
ENCHANTED WALK see **FORTROLLAD VANDRING** • 1954
ENCHANTED WAMPUM, THE • 1965 • Hornicka Lidia • ANM • PLN
ENCHANTED WELL, THE (USA) see **PUITS FANTASTIQUE, LE** • 1903
ENCHANTED WREATH, THE • 1910 • *Warwick* • UKN
ENCHANTER, THE see **ENCHANTEUR ALCOFRISBAS, L'** • 1903
ENCHANTEUR ALCOFRISBAS, L' • 1903 • Melies Georges • FRN • ALCOFRISBAS, THE MASTER MAGICIAN ○ MASTER MAGICIAN ALCOFRISBAS ○ ENCHANTER, THE
ENCHANTING ADVENTURE, AN see **KOUZELNE DOBRODRUZSTVI** • 1983
ENCHANTING EYES, THE see **EYOUN SAHERA** • 1934
ENCHANTING HOUSE, THE see **KOUZELNY DUM** • 1939
ENCHANTING PRAGUE OF RUDOLF II, THE see **KOUZELNA PRAHA RUDOLFA II** • 1982
ENCHANTING SHADOW see **CH'IEN-NU YU-HUN** • 1959
ENCHANTMENT • 1916 • Le Viness Carl M. • *American* • SHT • USA • ENCHANTED
ENCHANTMENT • 1920 • Bruun Einar J. • UKN
ENCHANTMENT • 1921 • Vignola Robert G. • USA
ENCHANTMENT • 1948 • Reis Irving • USA
ENCHANTRESS see **JADUGARIN** • 1937
ENCHANTRESS see **MESU INU** • 1951
ENCHANTRESS, THE see **BYAKUYA NO YOJO** • 1958
ENCHANTRESS, THE see **SKIACHTRA, I** • 1985
ENCHANTRESS, THE (USA) see **JALIM JADUGARIN** • 1929
ENCIKLOPEDIJA KRVNIKA • 1974 • Majdak Nikola • YGS • ENCYCLOPAEDIA OF THE EXECUTIONER
ENCLOS, L' • 1961 • Gatti Armand • BLG, FRN, YGS
ENCLOSURE, THE see **IN KLUIS** • 1978
ENCOBERTO, O • 1975 • Lopes Fernando • SHT • PRT
ENCONTRO COM A MORTE • 1964 • Duarte Arthur • BRZ
ENCONTRO COM A VIDA • 1960 • Duarte Arthur • PRT
ENCORE • 1951 • French Harold, Jackson Pat, Pelissier Anthony • UKN
ENCOSTALADOS, LOS • 1974 • Samper Gabriela • SHT • CLM
ENCOUNTER see **IMBARCO A MEZZANOTTE** • 1952
ENCOUNTER see **TALAKOZAS**
ENCOUNTER, THE • 1977 • Shafik Sobhi • EGY
ENCOUNTER AT KWACHA HOUSE • 1967 • Klein Bonnie • DOC • CND
ENCOUNTER AT THE HARBOUR see **ENCUENTRO EN LA PUERTO** • 1978
ENCOUNTER IN JULY, AN see **SETKANI V CERVENI** • 1977
ENCOUNTER IN THE MOUNTAINS see **VSTRYECHA V GORAKH** • 1967
ENCOUNTER OF CLOUDS AND THE DRAGON • 1983 • Le Lam • VTN
ENCOUNTER ON URBAN ENVIRONMENT • 1971 • Hart Roger • DOC • CND
ENCOUNTER WITH FRANCE see **VSTRETCHA S FRANTZIEI** • 1960
ENCOUNTER WITH SAUL ALINSKY • 1967 • Klein Bonnie • DOC • CND
ENCOUNTER WITH THE BASILISK see **BAZYLISZEK** • 1961
ENCOUNTER WITH THE UNKNOWN • 1973 • Thomason Harry • USA
ENCOUNTERS AT DUSK see **MOTEN I SKYMNINGEN** • 1957
ENCOUNTERS IN THE DARK see **SPOTKANIA W MROKU** • 1960
ENCOUNTERS IN THE DEEP • 1985 • *Andre Carol* • USA
ENCOUNTERS IN THE DEEP see **ENCUENTRO EN EL ABISMO** • 1978
ENCOUNTERS IN THE NIGHT see **INTIMATE ENCOUNTERS** • 1986
ENCOUNTERS IN THE SHADOWS see **SPOTKANIA W MROKU** • 1960
ENCOUNTERS OF THE FIRST KIND see **TI-YI-LEI-HSING WEI-HSIEN** • 1981
ENCOUNTERS WITH NATURE see **SPOTKANIE Z PRZYRODA** • 1971
ENCRUCIJADA • 1948 • Lazaga Pedro • SPN
ENCRUCIJADA • 1955 • Sevilla Raphael J. • MXC
ENCRUCIJADA, LA • 1959 • Balcazar Alfonso • SPN
ENCRUCIJADA PARA UNA MONJA • 1967 • Buchs Julio • SPN, ITL • VIOLENZA PER UN MONACA (ITL) ○ NUN AT THE CROSSROADS, A (USA) ○ CROSSROADS FOR A NUN ○ AMBUSH FOR A NUN
ENCRUDIJADA, LA • 1951 • Torres-Rios Leopoldo • ARG

ENCUENTRO, EL • 1952 • Royan Eladio • SPN
ENCUENTRO, EL • 1972 • Olhovich Sergio • MXC • MEETING, THE
ENCUENTRO, EL • 1977 • Forque Jose Maria • SPN
ENCUENTRO CON FREDDY REYNA • 1979 • Guevara De Suarez Rosa • MEETING WITH FREDDY REYNA, A
ENCUENTRO DE UN HOMBRE SOLO • 1973 • *Olhovich Sergio* • MXC
ENCUENTRO EN EL ABISMO • 1978 • Ricci Tonino • ITL, SPN • ENCOUNTERS IN THE DEEP
ENCUENTRO EN LA CIUDAD • 1952 • Elorrieta Jose Maria • SPN
ENCUENTRO EN LA PUERTO • 1978 • Odreman Mauricio • VNZ • ENCOUNTER AT THE HARBOUR
ENCUENTRO: LA SALACION, EL • 1965 • Gomez Manuel Octavio • CUB • SALACION, LA
ENCYCLOPAEDIA OF THE EXECUTIONER see **ENCIKLOPEDIJA KRVNIKA** • 1974
ENCYCLOPEDIE DE GRAND'MAMAN EN 13 VOLUMES, L' • 1963 • Borowczyk Walerian • ANM • FRN • GRANDMOTHER'S ENCYCLOPAEDIA
END, THE • 1953 • MacLaine Christopher • USA
END, THE • 1968 • Beresford Bruce • SHT • UKN
END, THE • 1970 • Blazekovic Milan • ANM • YGS
END, THE • 1978 • Reynolds Burt • USA
END, THE • 1985 • Talebi Ali • IRN
END, THE see **SLUT** • 1966
END AS A MAN (UKN) see **STRANGE ONE, THE** • 1957
END GAME IN PARIS • 1982 • Soul Veronika • ANS • CND
END OF A GREAT ERA, THE see **KONEC VELKE EPOCHY** • 1966
END OF A PERFECT DAY, THE • 1917 • *Mann Hank* • SHT • USA
END OF A PRIEST see **FARARUV KONEC** • 1968
END OF A PROLONGED JOURNEY see **HANA NO NAGADOSU** • 1954
END OF A SONG, THE see **KRASSIMIRA POPOVA** • 1971
END OF A SUMMER DAY • 1969 • Fortier Bob • MTV • CND
END OF ADVENTURE see **GIRL FROM SCOTLAND YARD, THE** • 1948
END OF AGENT W4C THROUGH MR. FOUSTKA'S DOG, THE see **KONEC AGENTA W4C PROSTREDNICTVIM PSA PANA FOUSTKY** • 1967
END OF ALL THINGS, THE see **MAKING SAUSAGES** • 1897
END OF AN ERA see **YUGANTHAYO** • 1983
END OF ARTHUR'S MARRIAGE, THE • 1965 • Loach Kenneth • MTV • UKN
END OF AUGUST, THE • 1981 • Graham Bob • USA
END OF AUGUST AT THE HOTEL OZONE, THE (USA) see **KONEC SRPNA V HOTELU OZON** • 1966
END OF AUGUST IN HOTEL OZONE see **KONEC SRPNA V HOTELU OZON** • 1966
END OF AUTUMN, THE see **MAN CHU** • 1983
END OF BATTLE FIRE, THE see **SENKA NO HATE** • 1950
END OF BELLE, THE see **MORT DE BELLE, LA** • 1961
END OF BLACK BART, THE • 1913 • *Coxen Ed* • USA
END OF DAWN, THE • 1964 • Warhol Andy • SHT • USA
END OF DESIRE (USA) see **VIE, UNE** • 1958
END OF ENGAGEMENT see **SHIMAI NO YAKUSOKU** • 1940
END OF INNOCENCE see **CASA DEL ANGEL, LA** • 1957
END OF INNOCENCE, THE see **FINE DELL'INNOCENZA, LA** • 1976
END OF LOVEMAKING see **KONEC MILOVANI** • 1913
END OF MILTON LEVY, THE • 1979 • Dayan Nissim • ISR
END OF NANCY J., THE • 1970 • Devlin Bernard • SHT • CND • NANCY J. NE PECHERA PAS, LE
END OF NIGHT see **KONIEC NOCY** • 1957
END OF NIGHT, THE see **SFIRSITUL NOPTI** • 1982
END OF OLD TIMES, THE (UKN) see **KANEC STARYCH CASU** • 1989
END OF ONE, THE • 1973 • Kocela Paul • SHT • USA
END OF OUR WORLD, THE see **KONIEC NASZEGO SWIATA** • 1964
END OF ST. PETERSBURG, THE see **KONYETS SANKT-PETERBURGA** • 1927
END OF "SATURN", THE see **KONYETS "SATURNA"** • 1968
END OF SUMMER see **KRAYAT NA LYATOTO** • 1967
END OF SUMMER, THE see **KOHAYAGAWA-KE NO AKI** • 1961
END OF SUMMER, THE see **TEMPS PERDU, LE** • 1964
END OF THE ACT, THE • 1934 • Samuelson G. B. • UKN
END OF THE AFFAIR, THE • 1955 • Dmytryk Edward • UKN
END OF THE BRAVE see **HANGGANAN NG MATATAPANG** • 1967
END OF THE BRIDGE, THE • 1914 • *Balboa* • USA
END OF THE CHIEFTAIN, THE • 1970 • *Konchalovsky Andrei (Sc)* • USS
END OF THE CIRCLE, THE • 1912 • Porter Edwin S. • USA
END OF THE CIRCLE, THE • 1913 • *Blevins Eleanor* • USA
END OF THE CUBE, THE see **KONEC KRYCHLE** • 1979
END OF THE DAY, THE (USA) see **FIN DU JOUR, LA** • 1938
END OF THE DIALOGUE (UKN) see **PHELA-NDABA** • 1970
END OF THE EARTH, THE see **NA KRAY SYVETA..** • 1976
END OF THE FEUD, THE • 1912 • *Lubin* • USA
END OF THE FEUD, THE • 1912 • *Essanay* • USA
END OF THE FEUD, THE • 1912 • Dwan Allan • *Rex* • USA
END OF THE FEUD, THE • 1914 • Dwan Allan • USA
END OF THE GALLEY, THE • 1914 • *Broncho* • USA
END OF THE GAME, THE • 1919 • Hampton Jesse D. • USA
END OF THE GAME, THE see **FIN DEL JUEGO, EL**
END OF THE GAME, THE see **ENDEN PA LEGEN** • 1960
END OF THE GAME (USA) see **RICHTER UND SEIN HENKER, DER** • 1976
END OF THE LINE • 1959 • Macartney-Filgate Terence • DOC • CND
END OF THE LINE • 1987 • Russell Jay • USA
END OF THE LINE see **CRY FOR HELP, A** • 1975
END OF THE LINE, THE • 1957 • Saunders Charles • UKN
END OF THE LONELY FARM BERHOF • 1984 • Svoboda Jiri • CZC
END OF THE LYUBAVINS, THE • 1972 • Golovnya L. • USS
END OF THE MIRACLE, THE see **CSODA VEGE, A** • 1984
END OF THE NIGHT, THE see **KONIEC NOCY** • 1957
END OF THE NIGHT, THE see **SFIRSITUL NOPTI** • 1982
END OF THE PLAY, THE • 1915 • *Perley Charles* • USA
END OF THE QUEST, THE • 1913 • *August Edwin* • USA
END OF THE RAINBOW, THE • 1916 • Reynolds Lynn • USA
END OF THE RAINBOW, THE see **ENDE DES REGEN BOGENS, DAS** • 1980
END OF THE RAINBOW (UKN) see **NORTHWEST OUTPOST** • 1947
END OF THE RIVER, THE • 1947 • Twist Derek • UKN
END OF THE ROAD • 1944 • Blair George • USA
END OF THE ROAD • 1970 • Avakian Aram • USA
END OF THE ROAD, THE • 1913 • *Victor* • USA
END OF THE ROAD, THE • 1913 • Daly William Robert • *Gem* • USA
END OF THE ROAD, THE • 1915 • Ricketts Thomas • USA
END OF THE ROAD, THE • 1919 • Griffith Edward H. • USA
END OF THE ROAD, THE • 1923 • *Berstein Saul (P)* • USA
END OF THE ROAD, THE • 1936 • Bryce Alex • UKN • SONG OF THE ROAD (USA)
END OF THE ROAD, THE • 1954 • Rilla Wolf • UKN
END OF THE ROAD, THE • 1958 • Lomnicki Jan • DOC • PLN
END OF THE ROAD, THE see **LOVEBOUND** • 1923
END OF THE ROMANCE, THE • 1912 • *Besserer Eugenie* • USA
END OF THE ROPE • 1923 • Seeling Charles R. • USA
END OF THE RUN, THE • 1913 • *Kalem* • USA
END OF THE RUN, THE • 1917 • Davis James • SHT • USA
END OF THE SUMMER, THE see **KRAYAT NA LYATOTO** • 1967
END OF THE SUN see **HI NO HATE** • 1954
END OF THE TOUR, THE • 1917 • Baker George D. • USA
END OF THE TRAIL • 1932 • Lederman D. Ross • USA
END OF THE TRAIL • 1936 • Kenton Erle C. • USA • REVENGE! (UKN)
END OF THE TRAIL, THE • 1911 • *Nestor* • USA
END OF THE TRAIL, THE • 1913 • *Powers* • USA
END OF THE TRAIL, THE • 1916 • Apfel Oscar • USA
END OF THE TROUBLE, THE • 1906 • Jeapes Harold? • UKN
END OF THE UMBRELLA, THE • 1914 • Edwin Walter • USA
END OF THE WAR, THE see **KRAJ RATA** • 1985
END OF THE WORLD • 1977 • Hayes John • USA
END OF THE WORLD see **WORLD, THE FLESH AND THE DEVIL, THE** • 1959
END OF THE WORLD, THE • 1913 • Dillon Eddie • USA
END OF THE WORLD, THE • 1925 • *Terry Paul (P)* • SHT • USA
END OF THE WORLD, THE • 1925 • Matherson Harvey G. • USA
END OF THE WORLD, THE • 1929 • Barker Bradley • SHT • USA
END OF THE WORLD, THE (?) see **WAKING UP THE TOWN** • 1925
END OF THE WORLD, THE see **PANIC IN YEAR ZERO** • 1962
END OF THE WORLD, THE see **NA KRAY SYVETA..** • 1976
END OF THE WORLD, THE (USA) see **VERDENS UNDERGANG** • 1916
END OF THE WORLD, THE (USA) see **FIN DU MONDE, LA** • 1930
END OF THE WORLD IN OUR USUAL BED IN A NIGHT FULL OF RAIN, THE (USA) see **FINE DEL MONDO NEL NOSTRO SOLITO LETTO IN UNA NOTTEPIENA DI PIOGGIA, LA** • 1978
END OF THE WORLD MAN, THE • 1986 • Miskelly Bill • IRL
END OF TWO FAMOUS BANDITS • 1909 • *Powhatan* • USA
END OF WAR DISASTERS see **SENKA NO HATE** • 1950
END PLAY • 1975 • Burstall Tim • ASL
END WITHOUT END see **ANAADI ANANT** • 1986
ENDA NATT, EN see **EN ENDA NATT** • 1938
ENDAMA NOVHEA • 1967 • Wahab Fatin Abdel • EGY • WHEN IN LOVE ○ INDAMA NUHIBB
ENDAMA TEHOBEL MERAA • 1933 • *Assis* • EGY • WHEN A WOMAN LOVES
ENDANGERED • 1989 • Hammer Barbara • SHT • USA
ENDANGERED, THE • 1989 • Engels Mark • SAF
ENDANGERED SPECIES • 1983 • Rudolph Alan • USA
ENDE DES ABENTEURERS PAOLO DE CASPADO • 1920 • Seitz Franz • FRG • PAOLO DE CASPADO
ENDE DES HOMUNCULUS, DAS see **HOMUNCULUS 6** • 1917
ENDE DES REGEN BOGENS, DAS • 1980 • Friessner Uwe • FRG • END OF THE RAINBOW, THE
ENDE VOM LIEDE, DAS • 1915 • Biebrach Rudolf • FRG
ENDE VOM LIEDE, DAS • 1919 • Grunwald Willy • FRG • LUGE, DIE ○ GELOBNIS, DAS
ENDEAVOUR see **NASTOJANJE** • 1983
ENDELIG ALENE • 1914 • Holger-Madsen • DNM • ALONE AT LAST
ENDEMONIADA, LA • 1975 • de Ossorio Amando • SPN • DEMON WITCH CHILD (USA) ○ POSSESSED, THE
ENDEMONIADOS DEL RING, LOS • 1964 • Crevenna Alfredo B. • MXC
ENDEN PA LEGEN • 1960 • Christensen Theodor • DNM • END OF THE GAME, THE
ENDGAME • 1985 • Benson Steven • ITL • ENDGAMES
ENDGAMES see **ENDGAME** • 1985
ENDISE • 1975 • Goren Serif • TRK • ANXIETY ○ TROUBLE
ENDLESS DAY, THE • 1962 • Rudzitis Maris • USS
ENDLESS DESIRE, THE see **HATESHINAKI YOKUBO** • 1958
ENDLESS DEVILRY, AN see **ZRAK** • 1978
ENDLESS DREAM see **SONHO SEM FIM** • 1986
ENDLESS DUEL, THE see **KETTO** • 1967
ENDLESS HORIZONS see **HORIZONS SAN FIN** • 1952
ENDLESS LAND OF ALEXIS DROEVEN, THE see **GRAND PAYSAGE D'ALEXIS DROEVEN, LE** • 1981
ENDLESS LOVE • 1981 • Zeffirelli Franco • USA
ENDLESS NIGHT • 1913 • *Johnson Arthur* • USA
ENDLESS NIGHT • 1971 • Gilliat Sidney • UKN • AGATHA CHRISTIE'S ENDLESS NIGHT
ENDLESS PASSION, THE see **HATESHINAKI JONETSU** • 1949
ENDLESS PRETENSIONS • 1975 • Krolikiewicz Grzegorz • PLN
ENDLESS SHORE, THE see **TARMUL N-ARE SFIRSIT** • 1962
ENDLESS SUMMER, THE • 1966 • Brown Bruce • DOC • USA
ENDLESS TRAIL see **GOLAPI EKHON TRENE** • 1977
ENDLESS WAY, THE see **UNENDLICHE WEG, DER** • 1943
ENDLOSE NACHT, DIE • 1963 • Tremper Will • FRG
ENDONMARES VANDRING see **DROMMARES VANDRING, EN** • 1957
ENDS OF THE EARTH, THE • 1911 • *Vitagraph* • USA
ENDSTATION • 1935 • Emo E. W. • FRG
ENDSTATION DREIZEHN SAHARA • 1962 • Holt Seth • FRG • STATION SIX SAHARA (UKN)
ENDSTATION FREIHEIT • 1981 • Hauff Reinhard • FRG • SLOW ATTACK
ENDSTATION LIEBE • 1957 • Tressler Georg • FRG • TWO WORLDS (USA) ○ TERMINUS LOVE
ENDSTATION "ROTE LATERNE" • 1960 • Jugert Rudolf • FRG
ENDURANCE see **IN THE GRIP OF POLAR ICE** • 1917
ENDURANCE see **SOUTHWARD ON THE 'QUEST'** • 1923
ENDURANCE CONTEST PARIS-NEW YORK BY AUTOMOBILE, THE see **RAID PARIS NEW YORK EN AUTOMOBILE, LE** • 1908
ENDURING FLAME, THE see **STEEL PREFERRED** • 1926
ENEK A BUZAMEZOKROL • 1947 • Szots Istvan • HNG • SONG OF THE CORNFIELDS
ENEMIES, THE • 1915 • Davenport Harry • USA
ENEMIES, THE • 1938 • Ivanovsky Alexander • USS
ENEMIES, THE see **VIJANDEN, DE** • 1968
ENEMIES, THE see **ENEMIGOS, LOS** • 1982
ENEMIES, A LOVE STORY • 1989 • Mazursky Paul • USA
ENEMIES OF CHILDREN • 1923 • Ducey Lillian, Voshell John M. • USA • YOUTH TRIUMPHANT
ENEMIES OF FREEDOM, THE see **ENNEMIS DE LA LIBERTE, LES** • 1967
ENEMIES OF PROGRESS • 1934 • Beresnyef Nikolai
ENEMIES OF SOCIETY see **MOULDERS OF MEN** • 1927
ENEMIES OF SOCIETY (UKN) see **BIG BRAIN, THE** • 1933
ENEMIES OF THE LAW • 1931 • Windom Lawrence C. • USA
ENEMIES OF THE PUBLIC (UKN) see **PUBLIC ENEMY, THE** • 1931
ENEMIES OF WOMEN, THE • 1923 • Crosland Alan • USA
ENEMIES OF YOUTH • 1925 • Berthelet Arthur • USA
ENEMIGO PRINCIPAL, EL • 1973 • Sanjines Jorge • BLV • MAIN ENEMY, THE ○ PRINCIPAL ENEMY, THE
ENEMIGOS • 1933 • Urueta Chano • MXC
ENEMIGOS • 1943 • Santillan Antonio • SPN
ENEMIGOS • 1955 • de Anda Raul • MXC • VALIENTES DE JALISCO, LOS
ENEMIGOS, LOS • 1982 • Calcagno Eduardo • ARG • ENEMIES, THE
ENEMY • 1974 • Bagley Anthony • UKN
ENEMY • 1990 • Hussnain • PKS
ENEMY see **DUSHMANOON KEY DUSHMAN** • 1988
ENEMY, THE • 1916 • Scardon Paul • USA
ENEMY, THE • 1927 • Niblo Fred • USA
ENEMY, THE • 1930-40 • Bose Nitin • IND
ENEMY, THE see **TALK ABOUT A STRANGER** • 1952
ENEMY, THE see **SOVRAZNIK** • 1965
ENEMY, THE see **HELL IN THE PACIFIC** • 1968
ENEMY, THE see **DUSMAN** • 1980
ENEMY AGENT • 1940 • Landers Lew • USA • SECRET ARMY (UKN)
ENEMY AGENT (UKN) see **BRITISH INTELLIGENCE** • 1940
ENEMY AGENTS MEET ELLERY QUEEN • 1942 • Hogan James P. • USA • LIDO MYSTERY, THE (UKN)
ENEMY AIR ATTACK see **TEKKI KUSHU** • 1943
ENEMY ALIEN • 1975 • Lerman Jeanette • CND
ENEMY AMONGST US, THE • 1916 • Batley Ernest G. • UKN
ENEMY BELOW, THE • 1957 • Powell Dick • USA
ENEMY FROM SPACE (USA) see **QUATERMASS II** • 1956
ENEMY GENERAL, THE • 1960 • Sherman George • USA
ENEMY IN OUR MIDST • 1914 • Stow Percy • UKN
ENEMY IN THE BOTTLE, THE • 1966 • Janik Stefan • ANS • PLN
ENEMY IN THE CAMP, AN • 1908 • Fitzhamon Lewin? • UKN
ENEMY MINE • 1985 • Petersen Wolfgang • FRG
ENEMY OF MAN see **STORY OF LOUIS PASTEUR, THE** • 1936
ENEMY OF MEN • 1930 • Strayer Frank • USA
ENEMY OF MEN, AN • 1925 • Strayer Frank • USA
ENEMY OF SOAP, AN • 1918 • Roach Hal • SHT • USA
ENEMY OF THE KING, AN • 1916 • Blackton J. Stuart • USA
ENEMY OF THE LAW • 1945 • Fraser Harry L. • USA
ENEMY OF THE PEOPLE • 1960 • Hart Harvey • MTV • CND
ENEMY OF THE PEOPLE, AN • 1978 • Schaefer George • USA
ENEMY OF THE PEOPLE, AN see **MINSHU NO TEKI** • 1946
ENEMY OF THE PEOPLE, AN (UKN) see **GANASHATRU** • 1989
ENEMY OF THE PEOPLE, THE see **EHTHROS TOU LAOU, O** • 1972
ENEMY OF THE POLICE • 1933 • King George • UKN
ENEMY OF WOMEN • 1944 • Zeisler Alfred • USA • LIFE AND LOVES OF DR. PAUL JOSEPH GOEBBELS, THE ○ DR. PAUL JOSEPH GOEBBELS ○ MAD LOVER ○ PRIVATE LIFE OF DR. PAUL JOSEPH GOEBBELS, THE
ENEMY SEX, THE • 1924 • Cruze James • USA
ENEMY SISTERS see **SOEURS ENNEMIES, LES** • 1915
ENEMY TERRITORY • 1987 • Manoogian Peter • USA
ENEMY TERRITORY see **WOMAN AGAINST WOMAN** • 1938
ENEMY, THE SEA, THE see **TAIHEIYO HITORIBOTCHI** • 1963
ENEMY TO SOCIETY, AN • 1915 • Jones Edgar • USA
ENEMY TO THE KING, AN • 1916 • Thompson Frederick A. • USA
ENEMY WITHIN, THE • 1918 • Stavely Roland • ASL
ENEMY WITHIN, THE see **TO SAVE THE KING** • 1914
ENEMY WITHIN, THE (UKN) see **RED MENACE, THE** • 1949
ENEMY'S AID, AN • 1913 • *Jones Edgar* • USA
ENEMY'S BABY, THE • 1913 • Griffith D. W.? • USA
ENERGETIC EVA • 1916 • *Tanguay Eva* • USA
ENERGETIC MEMBER OF THE S.P.C.A., AN • 1912 • *Powers* • USA
ENERGETIC STREET-CLEANER, THE • 1909 • *Essanay* • USA
ENERGIA • 1967 • Slesicki Wladyslaw • DOC • PLN • ENERGY
ENERGIA, LA UNIVERSIDAD Y LOS ANDES, LA • 1967 • San Andres Miguel • DOC • VNZ • ENERGY, THE UNIVERSITY AND LOS ANDES
ENERGIC DANCE OU UN CERTAIN ART DE VIVRE, L' • Jaeckin Just • FRN
ENERGIE ELECTRIQUE • 1939 • Clement Rene • SHT • FRN
ENERGIE ET VOUS, L' • 1961 • Storck Henri • DOC • BLG
ENERGIES • 1957 • Davis James* • SHT • USA
ENERGIZER • 1908 • McCutcheon Wallace • USA
ENERGY • Catling Darrell • DCS • UKN
ENERGY • 1976 • Bonniere Rene • DOC • CND

ENERGY see **ENERGIA** • 1967
ENERGY AND MATTER • 1966 • Verrall Robert A. • ANM • CND
ENERGY B.C. • 1979 • Dodd Thomas • SHS • CND
ENERGY CAROL • 1975 • Drew Les • CND
ENERGY FIRST • 1955 • Anderson Lindsay • DCS • UKN
ENERGY FROM THE PEACE • 1980 • Dodd Thomas • DOC • CND
ENERGY PICTURE, THE • 1958 • Potterton Gerald, Halas John • UKN
ENERGY –SEARCH FOR AN ANSWER • 1984 • Pyke Roger • DOC • CND
ENERGY, THE UNIVERSITY AND LOS ANDES see **ENERGIA, LA UNIVERSIDAD Y LOS ANDES, LA** • 1967
ENERI • 1953 • Hirsch Hy • SHT • FRN
ENES DOED.., DEN • 1980 • Olsson Stellan • SWD
ENEZ EUSSA • 1961 • Page, Gestin • SHT • FRN • ILE D'OUESSANT, L'
ENFALDIGE MORDAREN, DEN • 1982 • Alfredson Hans • SWD • SIMPLE-MINDED MURDERER, THE
ENFANCE DE L'ART, L' • 1910 • Cohl Emile • ANS • FRN
ENFANCE DE L'ART, L' • 1988 • Girod Francis • FRN
ENFANCE DU CIEL, L' • 1984 • Rodde Michel • SWT
ENFANCE NUE, L' • 1968 • Pialat Maurice • FRN • ME (USA) ○ NAKED CHILDHOOD
ENFANT AIME, L' • 1971 • Akerman Chantal • BLG
ENFANT AU CORAIL, L' • 1952 • Leherissey Jean • SHT • FRN
ENFANT AU FENNEC, L' • 1954 • Dupont Jacques • SHT • FRN
ENFANT COMME LES AUTRES, UN • 1972 • Heroux Denis • CND
ENFANT DANS LA FOULE, UN • 1976 • Blain Gerard • FRN
ENFANT DANS LA TOURMENTE, L' see **RETOUR A BONHEUR** • 1940
ENFANT DANS LA TOURMENTE, UNE • 1951 • Gourguet Jean • FRN
ENFANT DE LA BARRICADE, L' see **SUR LA BARRICADE** • 1907
ENFANT DE LA ROULOTTE, L' • 1914 • Feuillade Louis • FRN
ENFANT DE L'AMOUR, L' • 1930 • L'Herbier Marcel • FRN
ENFANT DE L'AMOUR, L' • 1944 • Stelli Jean • FRN
ENFANT DE L'HIVER, L' • 1988 • Assayas Olivier • FRN
ENFANT DE MA SOEUR, L' • 1932 • Wulschleger Henry • FRN
ENFANT DE MINUIT, L' • 1930 • Revol Claude, Caire Reda • FRN • MIDNIGHT CHILD, THE
ENFANT DE NUIT, L' • 1978 • Gobbi Sergio • FRN • ENFANTASME
ENFANT DE PARIS, L' • 1913 • Perret Leonce • FRN
ENFANT DE TROUPE, L' see **CEUX DE DEMAIN** • 1938
ENFANT DES HALLES, L' • 1924 • Leprince Rene • FRN
ENFANT DES NEIGES, L' • 1950 • Guyot Albert • FRN
ENFANT DU CARNAVAL, L' • 1921 • Volkov Alexander, Mosjoukine Ivan • FRN
ENFANT DU CARNAVAL, L' • 1934 • Volkov Alexander • FRN
ENFANT DU DANUBE, L' • 1935 • Le Derle Charles, Alexandre Andre • FRN
ENFANT DU MIRACLE, L' • 1932 • Maurice D. B. • FRN
ENFANT ET CHIEN • 1896-97 • Lumiere Louis • FRN
ENFANT ET LE CHIEN, L' • 1913-18 • Durand Jean • FRN
ENFANT ET LES MATHEMATIQUES, L' • 1971 • Melancon Andre • SHT • CND
ENFANT FRAGILE, L' • 1980 • Vamos Thomas, Hazanavicius Claude • CND
ENFANT INVISIBLE, L' • 1978 • Lindon Andre • ANM • FRN
ENFANT PRODIGE, L' see **FEU DE PAILLE, LE** • 1939
ENFANT PRODIGUE, L' • 1902 • Zecca Ferdinand • FRN
ENFANT PRODIGUE, L' • 1907 • Carre Michel • FRN
ENFANT ROI, L' • 1924 • Kemm Jean • FRN
ENFANT ROI, L' • 1979 • Feret Rene • FRN
ENFANT SAUVAGE, L' • 1970 • Truffaut Francois • FRN • WILD CHILD, THE (USA) ○ WILD BOY, THE (UKN)
ENFANT SECRET, L' • 1982 • Garrel Philippe • FRN
ENFANT TERRIBLE, L' see **KAUHUKAKARA** • 1971
ENFANT.. UN PAYS, UN • 1967 • Moretti Pierre • CND
ENFANTASME see **ENFANT DE NUIT, L'** • 1978
ENFANTS, LES • 1975 • Brault Francois • DCS • FRN
ENFANTS AU BORD DE LA MER • 1896-97 • Lumiere Louis • FRN
ENFANTS AUX JOUETS • 1895 • Lumiere Louis • FRN
ENFANTS DANS LA FORET, LES • 1971-74 • Bertolino Daniel • DOC • CND
ENFANTS DE CHOEUR, LES (FRN) see **EROI, GLI** • 1973
ENFANTS DE FRANCE ET LA GUERRE, LES • 1916 • Desfontaines Henri • FRN
ENFANTS DE GAYAN, LES see **MONSIEUR ALBERT** • 1975
ENFANTS DE LA COUR, LA LONGUE MARCHE EN INSTITUTION, LES • 1977 • Favreau Robert • DCS • CND
ENFANTS DE LA COUR, UNE CHANCE SUR MILLE, LES • 1977 • Favreau Robert • DCS • CND
ENFANTS DE LA PEUR, LES see **FILHOS DO MEDO, OS** • 1978
ENFANTS DE L'AMOUR, LES • 1953 • Moguy Leonide • FRN • CHILDREN OF LOVE
ENFANTS DE L'EMOTION, LES • 1975-77 • Moreau Michel, Fournier Eric • DCS • CND
ENFANTS DE L'OUBLI, LES • 1979 • Correa Joao • BLG
ENFANTS DE NOVEMBRE, LES • 1975 • Haddad Moussa • ALG
ENFANTS DE PARIS • 1936 • Roudes Gaston • FRN • JEUNE FILLES DEVANT L'AMOUR
ENFANTS D'EDOUARD, LES • 1909 • Bourgeois Gerard • FRN
ENFANTS D'EDOUARD, LES • 1914 • Andreani Henri • FRN
ENFANTS DES COURANTS D'AIR, LES • 1959 • Luntz Edouard • FRN • CHILDREN ADRIFT
ENFANTS DES NORMES, LES • 1978 • Dufaux Georges • SER • CND
ENFANTS DES NORMES POST SCRIPTUM, LES • 1983 • Dufaux Georges • DOC • CND
ENFANTS DESACCORDES, LES • 1967 • Garrel Philippe • SHT • FRN
ENFANTS DORMENT LA NUIT, LES • 1948 • Bonniere Rene • SHT • FRN
ENFANTS DU BORINAGE, LES see **DEJA S'ENVOLE LA FLEUR MAIGRE** • 1960
ENFANTS DU DESORDRE, LES • 1989 • Bellon Yannick • FRN • CHILDREN OF CHAOS (UKN)
ENFANTS DU MIRACLE, LES • 1903-04 • Blache Alice • FRN
ENFANTS DU NEANT, LES • 1968 • Brault Michel • DOC • FRN
ENFANTS DU PARADIS, LES • 1944 • Carne Marcel • FRN • CHILDREN IN PARADISE (USA)
ENFANTS DU PEUPLE • 1967 • Laradji Rabah • SHT • ALG
ENFANTS DU PLACARD, LES • 1977 • Jacquot Benoit • FRN • CLOSET CHILDREN, THE (UKN)
ENFANTS DU QUEBEC, LES • 1979 • Moreau Michel • DOC • CND
ENFANTS DU SILENCE, LES • 1964 • Jutra Claude, Brault Michel • DCS • CND
ENFANTS DU SOLEIL, LES • 1961 • Dayan David • FRN, MRC
ENFANTS DU SOLEIL, LES • 1968 • Bertolino Daniel, Floquet Francois • DCS • CND
ENFANTS GATES, LES see **DES ENFANTS GATES** • 1976
ENFANTS, HEUREUX ENFANTS • 1955 • Haesaerts Luc • DOC • BLG
ENFANTS JOUANT SUR LA PLAGE • 1896 • Melies Georges • FRN • CHILDREN PLAYING ON THE BEACH
ENFANTS TERRIBLES, LES • 1949 • Melville Jean-Pierre • FRN • STRANGE ONES, THE (UKN)
ENFER, L' • 1964 • Clouzot Henri-Georges • FRN
ENFER, L' see **HOLLE, DIE** • 1971
ENFER A DIX ANS, L' • 1968 • Bouguermouh Abderrahmane, Mazif Sid-Ali, Bendeddouche Ghaouti, Laskri Amar, Akika Youcef • ALG • HELL AT THE AGE OF TEN
ENFER BLANC, L' • 1972 • Lavoie Richard • DCS • CND
ENFER DANS LA PEAU, L' • 1965 • Benazeraf Jose • FRN • SEXUS (USA) ○ NUIT LA PLUS LONGUE, LA
ENFER DANS LA VILLE, L' (FRN) see **NELLA CITTA L'INFERNO** • 1958
ENFER DE LA PROSTITION, L' • Davy Jean-Francois • FRN
ENFER DE RODIN, L' • 1959 • Alekan Henri • SHT • FRN
ENFER DES ANGES, L' • 1939 • Christian-Jaque • FRN • PLUS GRAND CRIME, LE ○ A L'OMBRE DES HOMMES
ENFER DES FARDS, L' • 1949 • Perdrix Jean • FRN
ENFER DU JEU, L' see **MACAO, L'ENFER DU JEU** • 1939
ENFER SUR LA PLAGE, L' • 1966 • Benazeraf Jose • FRN
ENFILEES, LES • 1979 • Roy Jean-Claude • FRN
ENFIM SOS.. COM O OUTRO • 1968 • Silva Wilson • BRZ • AT LAST ALONE.. WITH SOMEONE ELSE
ENFONCEUSES EXPERTES, LES • 1979 • Love John • FRN
ENFORCER 2 see **DEATH COLLECTOR** • 1977
ENFORCER, THE • 1951 • Windust Bretaigne, Walsh Raoul (U/c) • USA • MURDER INC. (UKN)
ENFORCER, THE • 1976 • Fargo James • USA
ENFORCER FROM DEATH ROW • 1978 • Pinon Efren C., Bordon Marshall M. • PHL
ENGAGED IN PLEASURE see **SURUGA YUKYODEN** • 1964
ENGAGEMENT see **ELJEGYZES** • 1959
ENGAGEMENT, THE • 1970 • Joyce Paul • UKN
ENGAGEMENT, THE see **PETICION, LA** • 1976
ENGAGEMENT, THE (UKN) see **FIDANZATI, I** • 1963
ENGAGEMENT ITALIANO (USA) see **RAGAZZA IN PRESTITO, LA** • 1965
ENGAGEMENT OF ANNA see **PROXENIO TIS ANNAS, TO** • 1971
ENGAGEMENT OF CONVENIENCE, AN • 1914 • Plumb Hay? • UKN
ENGAGEMENT RING see **KONYAKU YUBIWA** • 1950
ENGAGEMENT RING, THE • 1909 • *Selig* • USA
ENGAGEMENT RING, THE • 1912 • Sennett Mack • USA
ENGAGING KID, THE • 1913 • *Hotely Mae* • USA
ENGALUCKUM KALAM VARUM • 1967 • Vincent A. • IND • EVERY DOG HAS HIS DAY
ENGANADAS, LAS • 1954 • Bustillo Oro Juan • MXC
ENGANO, O • 1968 • Fiorani Mario • BRZ • MISTAKE, THE
ENGEIJI RINGU see **KONYAKU YUBIWA** • 1950
ENGEL AUF ERDEN, EIN • 1959 • von Radvanyi Geza • FRG, FRN • MADEMOISELLE ANGE (FRN) ○ ANGEL ON EARTH (USA) ○ ANGEL ON WHEELS, AN
ENGEL AUS EISEN • 1981 • Brasch Thomas • FRG • IRON ANGEL
ENGEL DER LUST see **VERWUNDBAREN, DIE** • 1967
ENGEL, DER SEINE HARFE VERSETZTE, DER • 1959 • Hoffmann Kurt • FRG
ENGEL DER SUNDE • 1968 • Arive Jean-Christophe • FRG
ENGEL, DIE IHRE FLUGEL VERBRENNEN • 1970 • Brynych Zbynek • FRG
ENGEL IM ABENDKLEID • 1951 • von Rathony Akos • FRG
ENGEL IM FEGEFEUER • 1964 • *Hoffmann Jutta Ann* • GDR • ANGELS IN PURGATORY
ENGEL IM SEPAREE –MADCHEN IN GEFAHR • 1929 • Mayer Erno • FRG • MADCHEN IN GEFAHR
ENGEL MIT DEM FLAMMENSCHWERT, DER • 1954 • Lamprecht Gerhard • FRG
ENGEL MIT DEM SAITENSPIEL • 1944 • Ruhmann Heinz • FRG
ENGEL MIT DER POSAUNE, DER • 1948 • Hartl Karl, Bushell Anthony • AUS, UKN • ANGEL WITH THE TRUMPET, THE (UKN)
ENGEL MIT KLEINEN FEHLERN • 1936 • Boese Carl • FRG
ENGEL VON ST. PAULI, DIE • 1969 • Roland Jurgen • FRG • ANGELS OF THE STREET (UKN)
ENGELCHEN MACHT WEITER, HOPPE HOPPE REITER • 1968 • Verhoeven Michael • FRG
ENGELCHEN –ODER DIE JUNGFRAU VON BAMBERG • 1968 • Gosov Marran • FRG • LITTLE ANGEL –OR THE VIRGIN OF BAMBERG ○ ANGEL BABY (USA)
ENGELEIN • 1912 • Gad Urban • FRG, DNM • LILLE ENGELS, DEN (DNM)
ENGELEINS HOCKZEIT • 1913 • Gad Urban • FRG, DNM • LILLE ENGELS BRYLLUP, DEN (DNM)
ENGENHOS E USINAS • 1945-56 • Mauro-Humberto • SHT • BRZ
ENGINE, THE • 1956 • Mason Bill • UKN
ENGINEER, THE • 1908 • *Lubin* • USA
ENGINEER GARIN'S DEATH RAY see **GIPERBOLOID INGENERA GARINA** • 1965
ENGINEER PRITE'S PROJECT see **PROYEKT INZHENERA PRAITA** • 1918
ENGINEER'S DAUGHTER, THE • 1909 • *Selig* • USA
ENGINEER'S DAUGHTER, THE • 1911 • *Kalem* • USA
ENGINEER'S DAUGHTER, THE • 1913 • *Pathe* • USA
ENGINEER'S REVENGE, THE • 1914 • *Smiley John* • USA
ENGINEER'S ROMANCE, THE • 1910 • Porter Edwin S. • USA
ENGINEER'S SWEETHEART, AN • 1910 • *Bison* • USA
ENGINEER'S THUMB, THE • 1923 • Ridgwell George • UKN
ENGINEMEN • 1959 • Grigsby Michael • UKN
ENGLAND AWAKE • 1932 • Woolfe H. Bruce, Buchan John • UKN
ENGLAND EXPECTS • 1914 • Tucker George Loane • UKN
ENGLAND INVADED • 1909 • Stormont Leo • UKN
ENGLAND MADE ME • 1972 • Duffell Peter • UKN, USA, YGS • RAPE OF THE THIRD REICH, THE
ENGLAND OF ELIZABETH, THE • 1957 • Taylor John • UKN
ENGLAND'S CALL • 1914 • Aylott Dave • UKN
ENGLAND'S FUTURE SAFEGUARD • 1916 • Batley Ethyle • UKN
ENGLAND'S HISTORIC CHURCHES • 1972 • Scott James • DOC • UKN
ENGLAND'S MENACE • 1914 • Shaw Harold • UKN
ENGLAND'S WARRIOR KING • 1915 • Williams Eric • UKN
ENGLENE • 1973 • *Topsy* • DNM
ENGLER I SNEEN • 1982 • Sandoy Hakon • NRW • ANGELS IN THE SNOW
ENGLIMA STO KAVOURI • 1973 • Karayannis Kostas • GRC • HE MURDERED HIS WIFE ○ WIFE KILLER, THE
ENGLISCHE HEIRAT, DIE • 1934 • Schunzel Reinhold • FRG
ENGLISH ABROAD, THE • 1979 • Shillingford Peter • UKN
ENGLISH BY RADIO • 1949 • Dobson Quentin • UKN
ENGLISH CRIMINAL JUSTICE • 1946 • Annakin Ken • DCS • UKN
ENGLISH JIG see **MISS DE VERE (GIGUE ANGLAISE)** • 1896
ENGLISH NELL • 1900 • *Tempest Marie* • UKN
ENGLISH OIL WELLS • 1939 • Searle Francis • DCS • UKN
ENGLISH POTTER, THE • 1933 • Flaherty Robert • DCS • UKN
ENGLISH ROSE, THE • 1920 • Paul Fred • UKN
ENGLISH SILK –THE CRAFT OF HAND BLOCK MAKING • 1985 • Shaw-Smith David • DOC • IRL
ENGLISH VILLAGE • Catling Darrell • DCS • UKN
ENGLISH WALNUT INDUSTRY, THE • 1913 • Hutchinson Samuel • USA
ENGLISH WITHOUT TEARS • 1944 • French Harold • UKN • HER MAN GILBEY (USA)
ENGLISHMAN ABROAD, AN • 1985 • Schlesinger John • TVM • UKN
ENGLISHMAN AND THE GIRL, THE • 1910 • Griffith D. W. • USA
ENGLISHMAN'S HOME, AN • 1914 • Batley Ernest G. • UKN
ENGLISHMAN'S HOME, AN • 1939 • De Courville Albert • UKN • MADMEN OF EUROPE (USA) ○ MAD MEN OF EUROPE
ENGLISHMAN'S HONOR, AN • 1911 • *Selig* • USA
ENGLISHMAN'S HONOUR, AN • 1915 • *English Films* • UKN
ENGLISHMAN'S TRIP TO PARIS FROM LONDON, AN (USA) see **TRIP TO PARIS, A** • 1904
ENGRAVER, THE • 1913 • Grandon Francis J. • USA
ENGRENAGE • 1980 • Vidal Ghislain • FRN
ENGRENAGE, L' • 1919 • Feuillade Louis • FRN
ENGRENAGE, L' • 1960 • Kalifa Max • FRN
ENHORNINGEN • 1955 • Molander Gustaf • SWD • UNICORN, THE
ENID BENNETT IN A LIBERTY LOAN SPECIAL • 1918 • *Paramount* • SHT • USA
ENID IS SLEEPING • 1990 • Phillips Maurice • USA
ENID'S IDYLL • Jordan Larry • SHT • USA
ENIGMA • 1982 • Szwarc Jeannot • UKN, FRN
ENIGMA see **FRAU, NACH DER MAN SICH SEHNT, DIE** • 1929
ENIGMA, THE • 1981 • Furie Sidney J. • USA
ENIGMA DE MUJER • 1956 • Cahen Enrique • ARG
ENIGMA OF KASPER HAUSER, THE (UKN) see **JEDER FUR SICH UND GOTT GEGEN ALLE** • 1974
ENIGMA PARA DEMONIOS • 1974 • Christensen Carlos Hugo • ARG
ENIGMA ROSSO • 1978 • Negrin Alberto • ITL, SPN, FRG • RED RINGS OF FEAR
ENIGMA VARIATIONS, THE • 1970 • Archibald James • UKN
ENIGMATIC INDIAN, THE • 1966 • Todorovsky Podor • USS • MYSTERIOUS HINDU, A
ENIGMATIC MONSIEUR PARKES, L' • 1930 • Gasnier Louis J. • FRN
ENIGMATIQUE GENTLEMAN, L' see **SECRET DR L'EMERALDE, LE** • 1936
ENIGMATIQUE MADAME UNTEL, L' see **ETRANGE MADAME X, L'** • 1950
ENIGME, L' • 1919 • Feuillade Louis • FRN • MOT DE L'ENIGME
ENIGME, L' • 1921 • Kemm Jean • FRN
ENIGME AUX FOLIES BERGERE • 1959 • Mitry Jean • FRN
ENIGME DE DIX HEURES, L' • 1916 • Gance Abel • FRN
ENIGME DE LA RIVIERE, L' • 1915 • Perret Leonce • FRN
ENIGME DU MONT AGEL, L' • 1923 • Wulschleger Henry, Machin Alfred • FRN
ENJO • 1958 • Ichikawa Kon • JPN • CONFLAGRATION (USA) ○ FLAME OF TORMENT (UKN)
ENJOLEUSE, L' see **FRAUDEUR, LE** • 1937
ENJOYMENT see **OTANOSHIMI** • 1968
ENKEL MELODI, EN • 1974 • Grede Kjell • SWD • SIMPLE MELODY, A
ENLEVEMENT D'ANTOINE BIGUT, L' • 1964 • Doniol-Valcroze Jacques • FRN
ENLEVEMENT DE DEJANIRE GOLDEBOIS, L' • 1917 • Cohl Emile • ANS • FRN
ENLEVEMENT DE PERSEPHONE see **ARPAYI TIS PERSEFONIS, I** • 1956
ENLEVEMENT DES SABINES, L' (FRN) see **RATTO DELLE SABINE, IL** • 1962
ENLEVEMENT EN AUTOMOBILE ET MARIAGE PRECIPITE • 1903 • Blache Alice • FRN
ENLEVEMENT PAR HYDRO-AEROPLANE • 1912 • Linder Max • FRN
ENLEVEZ-MOI • 1932 • Perret Leonce • FRN
ENLIGHTEN THY DAUGHTER • 1917 • Abramson Ivan • USA

ENLIGT LAG • 1957 • Weiss Peter, Nordenstrom Hans • SWD • ACCORDING TO THE LAW ○ LIGT LAG, EN ○ ACCORDING TO LAW

ENLISTED MAN'S HONOR, AN • 1911 • Blache Alice • USA

ENMASCARADO DE ORO CONTRA EL ASESINO INVISIBLE, EL see **ASESINO INVISIBLE, EL** • 1964

ENMASCARADOS DE MAZATLAN, LOS • 1920 • Abitia Jesus B. • MXC

ENMASCARADOS DE PLATA, EL • 1952 • Cardona Rene • MXC

ENMEI-IN NO SEMUSHIOTOKO • 1924 • *Tsuburaya Eijo (Ph)* • JPN • HUNCHBACK OF ENMEI-IN, THE ○ ENMEIIN NO SEMUSHI

ENMEIIN NO SEMUSHI see **ENMEI-IN NO SEMUSHIOTOKO** • 1924

ENMESHED BY FATE • 1914 • Warren Edward • USA

ENN THAMBI • 1968 • Thirulokachander A. C. • IND • MY YOUNGER BROTHER

ENNEMI DANS L'OMBRE, L' • 1960 • Gerard Charles • FRN

ENNEMI PUBLIC, L' see **SAHHAR, AS-** • 1969

ENNEMI PUBLIC, UN • 1937 • Storck Henri • DOC • BLG

ENNEMI PUBLIC NO.1 • 1953 • Verneuil Henri • FRN, ITL • NEMICO PUBBLICO N.1, IL (ITL) ○ MOST WANTED MAN, THE (USA) ○ MOST WANTED MAN IN THE WORLD, THE ○ PUBLIC ENEMY NO.1

ENNEMI SANS VISAGE, L' • 1946 • Cammage Maurice, Dagan Robert-Paul • FRN

ENNEMIE, L' see **TENDRE ENNEMIE, LA** • 1935

ENNEMIS, LES • 1961 • Molinaro Edouard • FRN • TOUCH OF TREASON, A (USA)

ENNEMIS DE LA LIBERTE, LES • 1967 • Marzouk Said • SHT • EGY • ENEMIES OF FREEDOM, THE

ENNEMIS DE LA POMME DE TERRE, LES • 1949 • Proulx Maurice • DOC • CND

ENNUI, L' see **BOREDOM** • 1970

ENNUI ET SA DIVERSION, L'EROTISME, L' (FRN) see **NOIA, LA** • 1964

ENO • 1973 • Sinniger Alfons • DCS • USA

ENO UTAGASSEN • 1939 • Makino Masahiro • JPN

ENOCH AND EZRA'S FIRST SMOKE • 1913 • France Charles H. • USA

ENOCH ARDEN • 1914 • Nash Percy • UKN

ENOCH ARDEN • 1915 • Cabanne W. Christy • USA • AS FATE ORDAINED (UKN) ○ FATAL MARRIAGE, THE

ENOCH ARDEN PARTS I & II • 1911 • Griffith D. W. • USA

ENOKEN HAS HIS HAIR CROPPED see **ENOKEN NO ZANGIRI KINTA** • 1940

ENOKEN IS SURPRISED AT LIFE see **ENOKEN NO BIKKURI JINSEI** • 1938

ENOKEN NO BIKKURI JINSEI • 1938 • Yamamoto Kajiro • JPN • ENOKEN IS SURPRISED AT LIFE

ENOKEN NO CHAKKIRI KINTA • 1937 • Yamamoto Kajiro • JPN • ENOKEN'S PICKPOCKET

ENOKEN NO GAKKURI JIDAI • 1939 • Yamamoto Kajiro • JPN

ENOKEN NO HOKAIBO • 1938 • Saito Torajiro • JPN • ENOKEN THE PRIEST

ENOKEN NO KONDO ISAMU • 1935 • Yamamoto Kajiro • JPN

ENOKEN NO SEISHUN SUIKODEN • 1934 • Yamamoto Kajiro • JPN

ENOKEN NO SENMAN CHOJA • 1936 • Yamamoto Kajiro • JPN • ENOKEN'S MILLIONAIRE

ENOKEN NO ZANGIRI KINTA • 1940 • Yamamoto Kajiro • JPN • ENOKEN HAS HIS HAIR CROPPED

ENOKEN -ROPPA NO SHIN BAKA JIDAI • 1947 • Yamamoto Kajiro • JPN

ENOKEN THE PRIEST see **ENOKEN NO HOKAIBO** • 1938

ENOKEN'S MILLIONAIRE see **ENOKEN NO SENMAN CHOJA** • 1936

ENOKEN'S PICKPOCKET see **ENOKEN NO CHAKKIRI KINTA** • 1937

ENOLA GAY see **ENOLA GAY: THE MEN, THE MISSION, THE ATOMIC BOMB** • 1980

ENOLA GAY: THE MEN, THE MISSION, THE ATOMIC BOMB • 1980 • Rich David Lowell • TVM • USA • ENOLA GAY

ENORMOUS CHANGES AT THE LAST MINUTE • 1983 • Bank Mirra, Hovde Ellen • USA

ENORMOUS EGG, THE • Reig June • USA

ENORMOUS MIDNIGHT, THE • 1967 • Rotsler William • USA

ENOUGH, MY HEART • 1977 • Youssef Hassan • EGY

ENOUGH OF IT see **HUSKORS, ET** • 1914

ENOUGH PRAYING see **YA NO BASTA CON REZAR** • 1971

ENOUGH ROPE (USA) see **MEURTRIER, LE** • 1962

ENOUGH TO EAT? • 1936 • Anstey Edgar • UKN

ENQUETE ABOUTIT, L' • 1954 • Delbez Maurice • SHT • FRN

ENQUETE DE MARIE • 1952 • Gibaud Marcel • SHT • FRN

ENQUETE SUR LE 58, L' • 1944 • Tedesco Jean • SHT • FRN

ENQUETE SUR UN CORPS • 1959 • Lapoujade Robert • ANS • FRN

ENQUIQUINEURS, LES • 1965 • Quignon Roland-Jean • FRN

ENQUIRY, THE see **INCHIESTA, L'** • 1987

ENQUIRY INTO GENERAL PRACTICE • 1957 • Dickson Paul • DOC • UKN

ENRACINEMENT, L' • 1978 • Lesaunier Daniel • MTV • CND

ENRACINES, LES • 1981 • Harris Andre, de Sedouy Alain • FRN

ENRAGED SEX, THE see **SEXE ENRAGE, LE** • 1970

ENRAGED SHEEP, THE see **MOUTON ENRAGE, LE** • 1974

ENRAPTURED see **ONNAMAI** • 1961

ENREDO Y VERAS • 1948 • Orellana Carlos • MXC

ENREDO DE FAMILIA, UN • 1943 • Iquino Ignacio F. • MXC

ENREDOS DE PAPA, LOS • 1938 • Zacarias Miguel • MXC

ENREDOS DE UNA GALLEGA, LOS • 1951 • Soler Fernando • MXC

ENRICO see **ENRICO CUISINIER** • 1955

ENRICO CARUSO • 1951 • Gentilomo Giacomo • ITL • YOUNG CARUSO, THE (USA) ○ LEGGENDA DI UNA VOCE

ENRICO CUISINIER • 1955 • Grimault Paul • SHT • FRN • ENRICO

ENRICO IV • 1926 • Palermi Amleto • ITL

ENRICO IV • 1944 • Pastina Giorgio • ITL

ENRICO IV • 1984 • Bellocchio Marco • ITL • HENRY IV

ENRIQUE DE LAGARDERE see **JOROBADO, EL** • 1943

ENSAYO DE UN CRIMEN • 1955 • Bunuel Luis • MXC • CRIMINAL LIFE OF ARCHIBALDO DE LA CRUZ, THE (USA) ○ REHEARSAL FOR A CRIME ○ ARCHIBALDO ○ VIDA CRIMINAL DE ARCHIBALDO DE LA CRUZ, LA ○ PRACTICE OF A CRIME

ENSAYO DE UNA NOCHE DE BODAS • 1968 • Fernandez Unsain Jose Maria • MXC • WEDDING NIGHT ESSAY, A

ENSAYO FINAL • 1955 • Lugones Mario C. • ARG

ENSAYO GENERAL PARA LA MUERTE • 1962 • Coll Julio • SPN

ENSEMBLE EN ROUTE • 1946 • van Neyenhoff • NTH

ENSENAME A BESAR • 1951 • Davison Tito • MXC

ENSENANZA DE LA LECTURA Y LA ESCRITURA • 1971 • Delgado Cruz • SHS • SPN

ENSENAR A UN SINVERGUENZA • 1970 • Navarro Agustin • SPN

ENSETSU MEIJI JAKYODEN • 1968 • Doi Michiyoshi • JPN • WORSHIP OF THE FLESH, THE

ENSHO MORI NO ISHIMATSU • 1958 • Makino Masahiro • JPN

ENSIGN NUN, THE see **MONJA ALFEREZ, LA** • 1944

ENSIGN PULVER • 1964 • Logan Joshua • USA

ENSLIGENS HUSTRU • 1916 • Magnussen Fritz • SWD • HERMIT'S WIFE

ENSLINGEN I BLASVADER • 1959 • Bernhard Gosta • SWD • HERMIT IN STORMY WEATHER

ENSLINGEN JOHANNES • 1957 • Bernhard Gosta • SWD • HERMIT JOHANNES

ENSOM KVINDE, EN • 1914 • Blom August • DNM • HVEM ER HAN? ○ DOCTOR'S LEGACY, THE

ENSORCELLEMENT DE SEVILLE, L' • 1931 • Perojo Benito • FRN

ENTANGLED • 1988 • Hooper Tobe • USA

ENTANGLEMENT, THE see **KARAMI-AI** • 1962

ENTANGLEMENT OF LUST see **JOSHOKU NO MOTSURE** • 1968

ENTBLATTERTE BLUTEN • 1920 • Speyer Jaap • FRG

ENTDECKUNG DES JULIAN BOLL, DIE • 1962 • Knittel Johannes • GDR

ENTDECKUNGSFAHRTEN INS UNBEWUSSTE • 1964 • Schamoni Peter • SHT • FRG

ENTE KLINGELT UM ½ ACHT, DIE • 1968 • Thiele Rolf • FRG, ITL • DUCK RINGS AT SEVEN-THIRTY, THE

ENTEBBE: OPERATION THUNDERBOLT see **OPERATION THUNDERBOLT** • 1977

ENTENAS DE MADRID, LA • 1923 • Perojo Benito • SPN

ENTENDS-TU LES CHIENS BOYER? see **NO OYES LADRAR A LOS PERROS?** • 1974

ENTENTE CORDIALE • 1939 • L'Herbier Marcel • FRN

ENTENTE CORDIALE see **MAX ET L'ENTENTE CORDIALE** • 1912

ENTER ARSENE LUPIN • 1944 • Beebe Ford • USA

ENTER HAMLET • 1967 • Mogubgub Fred • ANS • USA

ENTER HOROWITZ • 1973 • Moxey John Llewellyn • TVM • USA

ENTER INSPECTOR DUVAL • 1961 • Varnel Max • UKN

ENTER INSPECTOR MAIGRET (USA) see **MAIGRET UND SEIN GROSSTER FALL** • 1966

ENTER LAUGHING • 1967 • Reiner Carl • USA

ENTER MADAME • 1922 • Worsley Wallace • USA

ENTER MADAME • 1935 • Nugent Elliott • USA

ENTER MY HOUSE see **VOYDI V MOY DOM** • 1968

ENTER THE DEVIL • 1975 • Dobbs Frank Q., Cass David • USA • DISCIPLES OF DEATH

ENTER THE DEVIL see **OSSESSA, L'** • 1974

ENTER THE DRAGON (USA) see **LUNG-CHENG-HU TOU** • 1973

ENTER THE INVINCIBLE HERO • *Lee Dragon* • HKG

ENTER THE NINJA • 1982 • Golan Menahem • USA

ENTER THE QUEEN • 1930 • Varney-Serrao Arthur • UKN

ENTER THE SEVEN VIRGINS • 1975 • Kuei Chih-Hung, Hofbauer Ernst • HKG, FRG

ENTER THE STREETFIGHTER see **GEKITOTSU SATSUJINKEN** • 1973

ENTER THREE DRAGONS • 1981 • Kong Joseph, Ho Godfrey • HKG

ENTERPRISE • 1950 • Sachs Peter • UKN

ENTERPRISING FLORIST, AN • 1908 • *Essanay* • USA

ENTERRADO VIVO • 1957 • Aguilar Rolando • MXC

ENTERRADOR DE CUENTOS, EL • 1978 • Cuchi Victor • VNZ • GRAVEDIGGER OF STORIES, THE

ENTERREMENT DE KENNEDY • 1963 • Reichenbach Francois • SHT • FRN

ENTERRO DA CAFETINA, O • 1970 • Pieralisi Alberto • BRZ

ENTERTAINER, THE • 1960 • Richardson Tony • UKN

ENTERTAINER, THE • 1976 • Wrye Donald • TVM • USA

ENTERTAINING MR. SLOANE • 1970 • Hickox Douglas • UKN, AUS

ENTERTAINING THE BOSS • 1922 • St. Clair Malcolm • SHT • USA

ENTERTAINING UNCLE • 1913 • *Brennan John* • USA

ENTERTAINING UNCLE • 1914 • Plumb Hay? • UKN

ENTERVUE AVEC MONIQUE LEONARD, UNE • 1968 • Dansereau Fernand • DCS • CND

ENTFESSELTE MENSCHHEIT, DIE • 1920 • Delmont Joseph • FRG

ENTFESSELTE WIEN, DAS see **SEINE HOHEIT, DER EINTANZER** • 1927

ENTFUHRUNG, DIE • 1936 • von Bolvary Geza • FRG

ENTGLEIST • 1921 • Karfiol William • FRG

ENTHUSIASM see **ENTUZIAZM** • 1931

ENTHUSIASTIC INVENTOR, AN see **ORIGINAL LOCATAIRE, UN**

ENTHUSIASTIC PHOTOGRAPHER, AN • 1911 • Wilson Frank? • UKN

ENTICEMENT • 1925 • Archainbaud George • USA

ENTICEMENT (UKN) see **SENSUALITA** • 1952

ENTIERRO DE UN FUNCIONARIO EN PRIMAVERA • 1957 • Zabalza Jose Maria • SPN

ENTIRE DAYS AMONG THE TREES (UKN) see **DES JOURNEES ENTIERES DANS LES ARBRES** • 1976

ENTIRE LIFE, THE see **VIDA ENTERA, LA** • 1987

ENTITY, THE • 1982 • Furie Sidney J. • USA

ENTITY FORCE, THE see **REST IN PEACE** • 1982

ENTLARVUNG, DIE • 1921 • *Mabeck Ria* • FRG

ENTLASSEN AUF BEWAHRUNG • 1965 • Groschopp Richard • GDR

ENTLASSUNG, DIE • 1942 • Liebeneiner Wolfgang • FRG • BISMARCK'S DISMISSAL (UKN)

ENTOMBED ALIVE • 1909 • *Vitagraph* • USA

ENTOMBED WARRIORS, THE see **QIN YONG** • 1989

ENTOTSU NO MIERU BASHO • 1953 • Gosho Heinosuke • JPN • FOUR CHIMNEYS (UKN) ○ FROM WHERE CHIMNEYS ARE SEEN ○ WHERE CHIMNEYS ARE SEEN ○ THREE CHIMNEYS

ENTOURLOUPE, L' • 1979 • Pires Gerard • FRN

ENTR'ACTE • 1924 • Clair Rene • SHT • FRN • CINEMA ○ INTERVAL BETWEEN ACTS

ENTRACTE • 1966 • Sanchez-Ariza Jose • PLN

ENTRAINEUSE, L' • 1938 • Valentin Albert • FRN • DAME DE COEUR, LA ○ TABARIN

ENTRANCE EXAMINATION see **MATURA** • 1965

ENTRAPMENT see **COLUMBIA CONNECTION, THE** • 1982

ENTRE ABOGADOS TE VEAS • 1950 • Fernandez Bustamente Adolfo • MXC

ENTRE AMIS see **BETWEEN FRIENDS** • 1973

ENTRE AUSSI PAR DERRIERE • Baudricourt Michel • FRN

ENTRE BALA Y BALA • 1962 • Ortega Juan J. • MXC

ENTRE CALAIS ET DOUVRES • 1897 • Melies Georges • FRN • BETWEEN CALAIS AND DOVER

ENTRE CHIEN ET LOUP • 1978 • Hebert Pierre • CND

ENTRE CIEL ET NIEGE see **FLIGHT IN WHITE** • 1969

ENTRE CIEL ET TERRE • 1960 • Rebuffat Gaston • DOC • FRN

ENTRE CIEL ET TERRE • 1977 • Reichenbach Francois • MTV • FRN

ENTRE DANS LA DANSE • 1948 • Leenhardt Roger • DCS • FRN

ENTRE DEUX FORCES see **COMPLICE, LA** • 1932

ENTRE DEUX TRAINS • 1947-51 • Verneuil Henri • SHT • FRN

ENTRE DEUX VAGUES • 1985 • Groulx Sylvie (c/d) • CND

ENTRE DOS AMORES • 1973 • Lucia Luis • SPN

ENTRE DOS ROSAS • 1953 • Baron Carlos Barrios • SHT • ARG • BETWEEN TWO ROSES

ENTRE DUNES ET VALLEES • 1952 • Tavano Fred • SHT • FRN

ENTRE GOLPES Y BOLEROS • 1988 • Dickenson John • VNZ • BETWEEN BLOWS AND BOLEROS ○ AMONG BLOWS AND BOLEROS

ENTRE HERMANOS • 1944 • Peon Ramon • MXC

ENTRE HOY Y LA ETERNIDAD (SPN) see **ZWISCHEN ZEIT UND EWIGKEIT** • 1956

ENTRE KAMPUCHEA Y VIETNAM • 1978 • Alvarez Santiago • DOC • CUB

ENTRE LA MER ET L'EAU DOUCE • 1967 • Brault Michel • CND • DRIFTING UPSTREAM ○ GENEVIEVE

ENTRE LA TERRE ET LE CIEL • 1957 • Vilardebo Carlos • SHT • FRN

ENTRE L'ARBRE ET L'ENCORCE • 1983 • Beaudry Michel • MTV • CND

ENTRE LAS REDES (SPN) see **MORESQUE OBIETTIVO ALLUCINANTE** • 1967

ENTRE LES DEUX PALAIS see **BAYN AL-QASRAYN**

ENTRE LES RUINES see **BIN AL-ATLAL** • 1948

ENTRE MONJAS ANDA EL DIABLO • 1972 • *Cima* • MXC

ENTRE NOUS (USA) see **COUP DE FOUDRE** • 1983

ENTRE ONZE HEURES ET MINUIT • 1948 • Decoin Henri • FRN • BETWEEN ELEVEN AND MIDNIGHT (USA) ○ ODEON 36.72

ENTRE SEINE ET MER • 1960 • Leenhardt Roger • DCS • FRN

ENTRE TINIEBLAS • 1983 • Almodovar Pedro • SPN • IN THE DARK ○ DARK HABITS

ENTRE TU AMOR Y EL CIELO • 1950 • Gomez Muriel Emilio • MXC

ENTRE TU ET VOUS • 1969 • Groulx Gilles • CND

ENTREATY, THE see **MOLBA** • 1969

ENTRECHATTES • 1978 • Kikoine Gerard • FRN

ENTRECUISSES • 1977 • Reinhard Pierre B. • FRN

ENTREE DES ARTISTES • 1938 • Allegret Marc • FRN • CURTAIN RISES, THE (USA)

ENTREE D'UN PAQUEBOT PORT DE JERSEY • 1899 • Melies Georges • FRN • STEAMER ENTERING THE HARBOUR OF JERSEY

ENTREGA, LA • 1954 • Soler Julian • MXC

ENTREGA DE CHUCHO EL ROJO, LA • 1959 • Munoz Manuel • MXC

ENTREGA IMMEDIATA • 1963 • Delgado Miguel M. • MXC

ENTREMEZ FAMOSO SOBRE A PESCA NO RIO MINHO • 1974 • Teles Luis Galvao • PRT

ENTREPRISE DE TOUTE UNE VIE, L' • 1973 • Gagne Jacques, Labrecque Jean-Claude • DCS • CND

ENTREPRISE ET SES COMPES, L' • 1956 • Tavano Fred • SHT • FRN

ENTRESANGEN UR DOLLARPRINSESSAN • 1910 • Magnusson Charles • SWD • ENTRY SONG FROM THE DOLLAR PRINCESS

ENTRETIEN AVEC HENRI LEFEBVRE • 1972 • Regnier Michel • DCS • CND

ENTRETIEN DE DREYFUS ET DE SA FEMME A RENNES • 1899 • Melies Georges • FRN

ENTRETIEN SUR LA MECANOLOGIE I, UN • 1970 • Parent Jacques • DOC • CND

ENTRETIEN SUR LA MECANOLOGIE II, UN • 1970 • Parent Jacques • DOC • CND

ENTREVISTA SOBRE PLANAS • 1973 • Rodriguez Martha, Silva Jorge • SHT • CLM • INTERVIEWS ON PLANAS

ENTREVUE AVEC GUY MONETTE, UNE • 1968 • Dansereau Fernand • DCS • CND

ENTREVUE AVEC M. EDWIN-B. MARTIN, UNE • 1968 • Dansereau Fernand • DCS • CND

ENTREVUE AVEC M. FERNAND COUPAL, UNE • 1968 • Dansereau Fernand • DCS • CND

ENTREVUE AVEC M. GUY BROSSARD, UNE • 1968 • Dansereau Fernand • DCS • CND

ENTREVUE AVEC M. HUBERT MURRAY, UNE • 1968 • Dansereau Fernand • DCS • CND

ENTREVUE AVEC M. JEAN-PAUL CORBEIL, UNE • 1968 • Dansereau Fernand • DCS • CND

ENTREVUE AVEC M. LUCIEN ROLLAND, UNE • 1968 • Dansereau Fernand • DCS • CND

ENTREVUE AVEC MME. F. ROLLAND BEAUDRY, UNE • 1968 • Dansereau Fernand • DCS • CND
ENTREVUE AVEC MME. LOUISE BOUVRETTE, UNE • 1968 • Dansereau Fernand • DCS • CND
ENTREVUE DE SELECTION, L' • 1984 • Kinsey Nicholas • DOC • CND
ENTRY, THE see **VSTUPLENIE** • 1962
ENTRY SONG FROM THE DOLLAR PRINCESS see **ENTRESANGEN UR DOLLARPRINSESSAN** • 1910
ENTSAGUNGEN • 1913 • May Joe • FRG
ENTSCHEIDUNG DES DR. AHRENDT, DIE • 1960 • Vogel Frank • GDR
ENTSCHLEIERTE MAJA, DIE • 1917 • Beck Ludwig • FRG
ENTSIEGELTE LIPPEN • 1925 • *Vampyr-Film* • FRG
ENTUZIAZM • 1931 • Vertov Dziga • USS • SYMPHONY OF THE DON BASIN ○ SYMPHONY OF THE DONBAS ○ ENTHUSIASM ○ SIMFONIYA DONBASA
ENVAR SIN EGEN LYCKAS SMED • 1917 • Eide Egil • SWD • ARCHITECT OF ONE'S OWN FUTURE
ENVASES VENEZOLANOS • 1978 • Blanco Javier • DCS • VNZ
ENVELOPE JIVE • 1962 • Goldscholl Morton, Goldscholl Mildred • ANS • USA
ENVEROUNEN • 1973 • Mallin Simon, Diver William • UKN
ENVERS DU PARADIS, L' • 1953 • Greville Edmond T. • FRN
ENVIRONMENT • 1914 • Cabanne W. Christy • USA
ENVIRONMENT • 1915 • *Mica* • USA
ENVIRONMENT • 1917 • Kirkwood James • USA
ENVIRONMENT • 1922 • Cummings Irving • USA • CHICAGO SAL
ENVIRONMENT • 1927 • Hayle Gerald M.?, Marshall Vaughan C.? • ASL
ENVIRONMENTAL HEALTH OFFICER, THE • 1982 • von Puttkamer Peter • DOC • CND
ENVOI DE FLEURS • 1949 • Stelli Jean • FRN
ENVOLEE, L' • 1919 • Ravel Gaston • FRN
ENVOY EXTRAORDINARY, THE • 1914 • Johnston Lorimer • USA
ENVOYEZ DE L'AVANT NOS GENS • 1976-77 • Brault Michel, Gladu Andre • DCS • CND
ENVOYONS D'L'AVANT NOS GENS • 1944-46 • Ladouceur Jean-Paul • ANS • CND
ENVY • 1917 • Ridgely Richard • USA
ENVY • 1980 • Pilliod Philippe • MTV • SWT
ENVY, HATRED AND MALICE • 1911 • Fitzhamon Lewin • UKN
ENZOVOORT • 1972 • Keesom Peter • SHT • NTH
EO KAKU KODOMOTACHI • 1956 • Hani Susumu • DOC • JPN • CHILDREN WHO DRAW PICTURES
EO U-DONG • 1985 • I Jang-Ho • SKR • ER WOO-DONG, THE ENTERTAINER
EOLOMEA • 1972 • Zschoche Hermann • GDR
EOMI • 1985 • Bak Cheol-Su • SKR • MOTHER, THE
EPAIS MANTEAU DE SANG, UN • 1968 • Benazeraf Jose • FRN • SUBJECT IS SEX, THE (UKN)
EPANASTATIS POPOLAROS • 1971 • Dalianidis Ioannis • GRC • REVOLUTIONARY, THE
EPATOZOIDES • 1968 • Foldes Peter • ANM • FRN
EPAVE, L' • 1920 • Hervil Rene • FRN
EPAVE, L' • 1949 • Rozier Willy • FRN
EPAVES • 1945 • Cousteau Jacques • FRN
EPAVES DE L'AMOUR, LES • 1915 • Capellani Albert • FRN
EPAVES DE L'AMOUR, LES • 1918 • Le Somptier Rene • FRN
EPERON D'OR • 1930 • Matras Christian • SHT • FRN
EPERVIER, L' • 1924 • Boudrioz Robert • FRN
EPERVIER, L' • 1933 • L'Herbier Marcel • FRN • AMOUREUX, LES ○ BIRD OF PREY
EPHEMETRES, LES • 1963-64 • Portugais Louis • DCS • CND
EPH'S DREAM • 1913 • *Powers* • USA
EPI ESKHATI PRODHOSIA • 1968 • Papageorgiou Thanasis • GRC • HIGH TREASON
EPIC • 1984 • Gross Yoram • ANM • ASL
EPIC HERO AND THE BEAST, THE (UKN) see **ILYA MUROMETS** • 1956
EPIC OF EVEREST • 1924 • Noel J. B. L. • UKN
EPIC THAT NEVER WAS, THE • 1965 • Duncalf Bill • UKN
EPIDEMIC • 1987 • von Trier Lars • DNM
EPIDEMIC see **JARVANY** • 1975
EPIDEMIC, THE • 1914 • *Beery Wallace* • USA
EPIDEMIC, THE see **ZAVAZA** • 1972
EPIDEMIC IN PARADISE GULCH, THE • 1912 • *Harte Betty* • USA
EPIHIRISIS APOLLON • 1968 • Skalenakis Giorgos • GRC, SWD • APOLLO GOES ON HOLIDAY ○ OPERATION APOLLO
EPIKINDIN PECHNIDIA • 1981 • Caripidis Giorgos • GRC • DANGEROUS GAMES
EPILEPSY • 1976 • Benegal Shyam • DCS • IND
EPILOG • 1950 • Kautner Helmut • FRG
EPILOGO • 1983 • Suarez Gonzalo • SPN • EPILOGUE
EPILOGUE see **EPILOGO** • 1983
EPILOGUE (USA) see **HVAD MED OS?** • 1963
EPINE AU PIED, UNE • 1954 • Rozier Jacques • SHT • FRN
EPINGLES, LES • 1913 • Perret Leonce • FRN
EPISODE • 1935 • Reisch Walter • AUS
EPISODE • 1968 • Carriere Marcel • DOC • CND
EPISODE see **MY LOVE CAME BACK** • 1940
EPISODE, AN • 1914 • *Smalley Phillips* • USA
EPISODE AT CLOUDY CANYON, THE • 1913 • *Essanay* • USA
EPISODE DE 1812 • 1912 • de Morlhon Camille • FRN
EPISODE DE GUERRE (GRECO-TURQUE) • 1897 • Melies Georges • FRN • WAR EPISODE
EPISODE DE WATERLOO, UN • 1913 • Machin Alfred • FRN
EPISODE IN THE LIFE OF A LODGER, AN • 1902 • Smith G. A. • UKN
EPISODE OF EARLY MORMON DAYS, AN • 1911 • *Pathe* • USA
EPISODE OF LIFE IN GREATER LONDON, AN • 1921 • Storrie Kelly • UKN
EPISODE OF THE CUBAN WAR • 1909 • *Powhatan* • USA
EPISODE OF THE DERBY, AN • 1906 • Fitzhamon Lewin • UKN
EPISODIO DEL MARE see **TERRA TREMA, LA** • 1950
EPISODIO PASTORIL • 1954 • Garcia Fernando • SHT • PRT
EPISTEMOLOGY OF JEAN PIAGET, THE see **JEAN PIAGET** • 1977
EPISTROFI TIS MIDIAS, I • 1968 • Hristian Yan • GRC • MEDEA'S RETURN
EPITAPH • 1986 • Merhi Joseph • USA
EPITAPH FOR A SPY see **BERLINO, APPUNTAMENTO PER LE SPIE** • 1965
EPITAPH TO MY LOVE see **WAGA KOI NO TABIJI** • 1961
EPITOME see **SHUKUZU** • 1953
EPOCH OF LOYALTY see **KINNO JIDAI** • 1927
EPOCH OF MURDER MADNESS see **SATSUJINKYOJIDAI** • 1967
EPOPEA DEI NIBELUNGHI, L' • 1913 • *Ambrosio* • ITL • NIBELUNGEN SAGA, THE
EPOPEE DU RAMAYANA, L' • 1979 • Oger Jacques, Salvini Milena • DOC • FRN
EPOPEYA • 1922 • Elias Francisco • SHT • SPN
EPOPEYA DE SIMON BOLIVAR, LA see **SIMON BOLIVAR** • 1968
EPOPEYA DEL CAMINO, LA • 1941 • Elias Francisco • MXC
EPOPEYAS DE LA REVOLUCION • 1963 • Cabello Nosser R. • DOC • MXC
EPOUSE DE BARISS, UNE see **ZAWGATUN MIN BARISS** • 1966
EPOUSE POUR CINQUE HOMMES, UNE see **ZAWGA LI KHAMSA RIGAL** • 1970
EPOUSEZ MA FEMME see **EPOUX SCANDALEUX, LES** • 1935
EPOUVANTAIL, L' • 1921 • Starevitch Ladislas • ANM • FRN • SCARECROW, THE (USA)
EPOUVANTAIL, L' • 1943 • Grimault Paul • ANS • FRN • SCARECROW, THE (USA)
EPOUVANTE, L' • 1910 • Carre Michel • FRN
EPOUX CELEBATAIRES, LES • 1935 • Boyer Jean, Robison Arthur • FRN • VEUVE CELIBATAIRE, LA
EPOUX SCANDALEUX, LES • 1935 • Lacombe Georges • FRN • JEAN ET LOULOU ○ EPOUSEZ MA FEMME
EPPISURES DE SABLES • 1981 • Ferrand Carlos • MTV • CND
EPREUVE, L' • 1914 • Feuillade Louis • FRN
EPREUVE TRAGIQUE, L' • 1914 • Burguet Charles • FRN
EPROPIACION • 1977 • Robles Mario • VNZ, PRU • EXPROPRIATION
EPURATION DES EAUX, L' • 1963 • Regnier Michel • DCS • CND
EQUAL CHANCE, AN • 1913 • *Selig* • USA
EQUAL OPPORTUNITY, AN • 1982 • Leaf Caroline • CND
EQUAL TO THE EMERGENCY • 1910 • *Edison* • USA
EQUALISER 2000 • 1986 • Santiago Cirio H. • USA
EQUALISER: BLOOD AND WINE, THE • 1987 • Metzger Alan • TVM • USA • BLOOD AND WINE
EQUALISER: THE MYSTERY OF MANON, THE • 1988 • May Bradford • TVM • USA • MYSTERY OF MANON, THE
EQUALITY • 1983 • Jannes Martti • ANS • FNL
EQUALS, THE • 1982 • Frankenheimer John • USA
EQUATEUR • 1983 • Gainsbourg Serge • FRN, GBN
EQUATEUR AUX CENT VISAGES, L' • 1948 • Cauvin Andre • BLG • BLACK SHADOWS
EQUATION • 1973 • O'Shea John • DCS • NZL
EQUATION A DEUX INCONNUS • 1979 • de Velsa Dietrich • FRN
EQUATION X + X + A SIN NIT, THE • 1937 • Salt Brian • UKN
EQUATOR TRAMP, THE see **WENN DU EINMAL DEIN HERZ VERSCHENKST** • 1929
EQUATORE • 1939 • Valori Gino • ITL
EQUATORIAL AFRICA: ROOSEVELT'S HUNTING GROUNDS • 1924 • *Klein A. J. (Ph)* • DOC • USA
EQUESTRIAN ACROBATICS • 1937 • Miller David • DOC • USA
EQUESTRIAN QUIZ • 1946 • *O'Brien Dave* • SHT • USA
EQUILIBRE IMPOSSIBLE, L' • 1902 • Melies Georges • FRN • IMPOSSIBLE BALANCING FEAT, AN (USA)
EQUILIBRISTE, L' • 1902 • Blache Alice • FRN
EQUINE HERO, AN • 1910 • *Edison* • USA
EQUINE HERO, AN • 1912 • *Selig* • USA
EQUINE HERO, AN • 1913 • *Pathe* • USA
EQUINE SPY, THE • 1912 • Warren Edward • USA
EQUINOX • 1967 • McGee Mark • USA
EQUINOX • 1970 • Woods Jack • USA • BEAST, THE
EQUINOX see **NEVJERA** • 1953
EQUINOX see **EQUINOZIO** • 1971
EQUINOX FLOWER see **HIGANBANA** • 1958
EQUINOXE • 1987 • Lamothe Arthur • CND
EQUINOZIO • 1971 • Ponzi Maurizio • ITL • EQUINOX
EQUIPAGE, L' • 1927 • Tourneur Maurice • FRN • LAST FLIGHT, THE (USA) ○ CREW, THE (UKN)
EQUIPAGE, L' • 1935 • Litvak Anatole • FRN
EQUIPE 13, L' see **AMOUR EN VITESSE, L'** • 1932
EQUITY MUSICAL REVUE • 1935 • *Smith Herbert (P)* • SHS • UKN
EQUUS • 1977 • Lumet Sidney • USA, UKN
ER DU GRONLAENDER see **KALALIUVIT** • 1970
ER ET YNDIGT LAND, DER • 1983 • Arnfred Morten • DNM • LAND OF PLENTY
ER GEHT RECHTS -SIE GEHT LINKS • 1928 • Sauer Fred • FRG
ER I BANGE? • 1971 • Carlsen Henning • DNM • ARE YOU AFRAID? ○ HVAD ER I BANGE FOR?
ER IST DEIN BRUDER • 1923 • Stahl Walter Richard • FRG • MUTTER HERZBLUT, EINER
ER KANN'S NICHT LASSEN • 1962 • von Ambesser Axel • FRG
ER MUSS SIE HABEN • May Joe • AUS
ER ODER ICH • 1930 • Piel Harry • FRG
ER ODER ICH see **SEIN GROSSTER BLUFF** • 1927
ER PIU -STORIA D'AMORE E DI COLTELLO • 1971 • Corbucci Sergio • ITL
ER RECHTS, SIE LINKS • 1915 • Wiene Robert • FRG
ER SELBST -SEIN GOTT see **SKLAVEN DER SEELEN** • 1919
ER SOLL DEIN HERR SEIN • *Mack Max* • FRG
ER SOLL DEIN HERR SEIN ODER IN DER EIGENEN SCHLINGE GEFANGEN • 1915 • Del Zopp Rudolf • FRG
ER TILLADT AT VAERE ANDSSVAG, DET • 1969 • Roos Jorgen • DOC • DNM
ER UND SEIN DIENER • 1931 • Sekely Steve • FRG, HNG
ER UND SEIN SCHWESTER • 1931 • Lamac Carl • FRG, SWT
ER UND SEIN TIPPFRAULEIN see **WENN DEM ESEL ZU WOHL IST** • 1932
ER WOO-DONG, THE ENTERTAINER see **EO U-DONG** • 1985
ERA DI VENERDI 17 • 1956 • Soldati Mario • ITL, FRN • SOUS LE CIEL DE PROVENCE (FRN) ○ VIRTUOUS BIGAMIST, THE
ERA E LISI • 1981 • Sahatciu Besim • YGS • WIND AND THE OAK, THE ○ VJETAR I HRAST
ERA LEI CHE LO VOLEVA! • 1953 • Girolami Marino, Simonelli Giorgio C. • ITL
ERA LUI, SI, SI.. • 1951 • Metz Vittorio, Marchesi Marcello, Girolami Marino • ITL
ERA NOTTE A ROMA • 1960 • Rossellini Roberto • ITL, FRN • EVADES DE LA NUIT, LES (FRN) ○ ESCAPE BY NIGHT (USA) ○ WAIT FOR THE DAWN ○ IT WAS NIGHT IN ROME
ERA O VENTO E ERA O MAR • 1966 • Costa Jose Fonseca • SHT • PRT
ERA SAM WALLASH.. LO CHIAMAVANO COSI SIA • 1971 • Fidani Demofilo • ITL
ERA UMA VEZ AMANHA • 1971 • Lopes Fernando • SHT • PRT
ERADICATING AUNTY • 1909 • Griffith D. W. • USA
ERAKU NARE • 1932 • Naruse Mikio • JPN • ERRONEOUS PRACTICE ○ BE GREAT!
ERAM 200 IRMAOS • 1952 • Esteves Constantino, Garcia Fernando • PRT
ERAMOS SIETE A LA MESA • 1942 • Rey Florian • SPN
ERAN TRECE • 1932 • Howard David • USA
ERAN TRECENTO • 1952 • Callegari Gian Paolo • ITL • SPIGOLATRICE DI SAPRI, LA
ERASE UN NINO, UN GUERRILLERO, UN COBALLO.. • 1967 • Soto Helvio • CHL • ONCE THERE WAS A BOY, A PARTISAN, A HORSE..
ERASE UNA VEZ UN PILLO • 1972 • *Churubusco Azteca* • MXC
ERASERHEAD • 1977 • Lynch David • USA
ERASMOS UNA VEZ • 1979 • de la Barra Leonardo • DCS • BLG • ONCE WE WERE
ERASMUS • 1963 • Kumel Harry • BLG
ERASMUS, DE STEMM VAN DE REDE • 1961 • Hulsker Jan • DOC • NTH • ERASMUS: THE VOICE OF REASON
ERASMUS: THE VOICE OF REASON see **ERASMUS, DE STEMM VAN DE REDE** • 1961
ERASMUS WITH FRECKLES see **DEAR BRIGITTE** • 1965
ERASTE TOU MESEOU TIHOU, I • 1968 • Jackson Stelios, Ikonomou Nikos • GRC • LOVERS BEHIND TWO WALLS
ERASTIS ERCHETE, O • 1956 • Tzavellas Georges • GRC • LOVERS ARRIVE, THE
ERATHA PEY • 1968 • Muban • IND • BLOODY GHOST
ERAVAMO SETTE SORELLE • 1938 • Malasomma Nunzio • ITL • WE WERE SEVEN SISTERS
ERAVAMO SETTE VEDOVE • 1939 • Mattoli Mario • ITL • WE WERE SEVEN WIDOWS (USA)
ERBE, DAS • 1923 • Wiene Conrad • FRG
ERBE DER VAN DIEMEN, DER • 1921 • Ziener Bruno • FRG
ERBE VOM PRUGGERHOF, DAS • 1956 • Konig Hans H. • AUS
ERBE VON BJORNDAL, DAS • 1960 • Ucicky Gustav • AUS • HERITAGE OF BJORNDAL, THE
ERBE VON HET-STEEN, DER • 1917 • *Kaiser-Titz Erich* • FRG
ERBE VON PRETORIA • 1934 • Meyer Johannes • FRG
ERBE VON SKIALDINGSHOLM, DER • 1919 • Burg Eugen • FRG
ERBE VON WALKERAU, DER • 1915 • Larsen Viggo • FRG
ERBE WIRD GESUCHT, EIN • 1915 • Delmont Joseph • FRG
ERBEFORSTER, DER • 1944 • Lippl Alois J. • FRG
ERBEN, DIE • 1982 • Bannert Walter • AUS • INHERITORS, THE (USA) ○ HEIRS, THE
ERBEN DES GEIZHALSES, DIE • 1915 • *Zilzer Max* • FRG
ERBFOLGESTREIT, EIN see **SCHWEIGEN IM WALDE 1** • 1918
ERBFORSTER, DER • 1915 • Oberlander Hans • FRG
ERBIN, DIE • 1919 • Moest Hubert • FRG
ERBIN DES GRAFEN VON MONTE CRISTO, DIE • 1919 • Zelnik Friedrich • FRG
ERBIN VOM BERGHOF, DIE • 1954 • Haussler Richard • FRG
ERBIN VOM ROSENHOF, DIE • 1942 • Seitz Franz • FRG
ERBIN VON ST. ALBAN, DIE • 1925 • *Hermann Li-Lo* • FRG
ERBIN VON TORDIS, DIE • 1921 • Dinesen Robert • FRG
ERBLICH BELASTET • 1917 • Alexander Georg • FRG
ERBORGTES GLUCK • 1918 • *Moissi Alexander* • FRG
ERBSCHAFT, DER • 1936 • Geis Jacob • FRG
ERBSCHAFT DER INGE STANHOPE, DER • 1920 • Bach Rudi • FRG
ERBSCHAFT MIT HINDERNISSEN, EINE see **TESTAMENT DES CORNELIUS GULDEN, DAS** • 1932
ERBSCHAFT VON NEW YORK, DIE • 1919 • *Fichtner Erwin* • FRG
ERBSCHLEICHER, DER • 1925 • *M. Stambulki & Co.* • FRG
ERCOLE • 1917 • Mari Febo • ITL
ERCOLE AL CENTRO DELLA TERRA • 1961 • Bava Mario • ITL • HERCULES AT THE CENTRE OF THE EARTH (UKN) ○ HERCULES AND THE HAUNTED WORLD ○ HERCULES IN THE HAUNTED WORLD (USA) ○ HERCULES IN THE CENTRE OF THE EARTH
ERCOLE ALLA CONQUISTA DI ATLANTIDE • 1961 • Cottafavi Vittorio, Cristallini Giorgio • ITL, FRN • HERCULES AND THE CONQUEST OF ATLANTIS ○ HERCULES CONQUERS ATLANTIS ○ HERCULE A LA CONQUETE DE L'ATLANTIDE ○ HERCULES AND THE HAUNTED WOMEN ○ HERCULES AND THE CAPTIVE WOMEN
ERCOLE CONTRO I FIGLI DEL SOLE • 1964 • Civirani Osvaldo • ITL, SPN • HERCULES AGAINST THE SONS OF THE SUN (USA) ○ HERCULES CONTRA LOS HIJOS DEL SOL (SPN)
ERCOLE CONTRO I TIRANNI DI BABILONIA • 1964 • Paolella Domenico • ITL • HERCULES AND THE TYRANTS OF BABYLON (USA)
ERCOLE CONTRO MOLOCH • 1964 • Ferroni Giorgio • ITL, FRN • CONQUEST OF MYCENE (USA) ○ HERCULE CONTRE MOLOCH ○ HERCULES ATTACKS ○ HERCULES CHALLENGE ○ HERCULES AGAINST MOLOCH ○ HERCULES VS. MOLOCH
ERCOLE CONTRO ROMA • 1964 • Pierotti Piero • ITL, FRN • HERCULE CONTRE ROME (FRN) ○ HERCULES AGAINST ROME (USA)

ERCOLE E LA REGINA DI LIDIA • 1959 • Francisci Pietro • ITL, FRN • HERCULES AND THE QUEEN OF SHEBA (USA) ○ HERCULES UNCHAINED (UKN) ○ HERCULE ET LA REINE DE LYDIE (FRN) ○ HERCULES AND THE QUEEN OF LIDIA
ERCOLE L'INVINCIBILE • 1963 • Mancori Alvaro • ITL • HERCULES THE INVINCIBLE (USA)
ERCOLE, SANSONE, MACISTE E URSUS: GLI INVINCIBILE • 1965 • Capitani Giorgio • ITL, FRN, SPN • SAMSON AND THE MIGHTY CHALLENGE (USA) ○ SAMSON AND THE SEVEN CHALLENGES ○ HERCULES, MACISTE, SAMSON AND URSUS VS. THE UNIVERSE
ERCOLE SFIDA SANSONE • 1964 • Francisci Pietro • ITL • HERCULES, SAMSON AND ULYSSES (USA) ○ HERCULES CHALLENGES SAMSON
ERDBEBEN IN CHILE • 1975 • Sanders Helma • FRG • EARTHQUAKE IN CHILE
ERDE • 1947 • Hainisch Leopold • AUS • TROTZIGE HERZEN
ERDEI SPORTVERSENY • 1951 • Macskassy Gyula • ANS • HNG • SPORTS COMPETITION IN THE FOREST ○ RACES IN THE FOREST
ERDGEIST • 1923 • Jessner Leopold • FRG • EARTH SPIRIT
ERDGIFT • 1919 • Otto Paul • FRG
ERDSTROMMOTOR, DER • 1917 • Wolff Carl Heinz • FRG
ERE D'ACIER, UNE • 1968 • Danis Aime • DCS • CND
ERE ERERA BALEIBU ICIK SUBUA ARUAREN • 1976 • Sistiaga Jose Antonio • SPN
ERECTIONS • 1975 • Desvilles Jean • FRN
EREDE, L' (ITL) see **HERITIER, L'** • 1973
EREDITA CONTESA, L' see **ASTUTO BARONE, L'** • 1948
EREDITA DELLO ZIO BUONANIMA, L' • 1934 • Palermi Amleto • ITL
EREDITA DELLO ZIO BUONANIMA, L' • 1975 • Brescia Alfonso • ITL
EREDITA FERRAMONTI, L' • 1975 • Bolognini Mauro • ITL • INHERITANCE, THE (USA) ○ INHERITORS, THE
EREDITA IN CORSA, L' • 1939 • Biancoli Oreste • ITL
EREDITIERA, L' • 1914 • Negroni Baldassare • ITL
EREKI NO WAKADAISHO • 1966 • Iwauchi Katsumi • JPN • CAMPUS A GO-GO (USA)
EREMIT, DER • 1915 • Hofer Franz • FRG
EREMITKRAFTEN • 1965 • Hellbom Olle • SWD • HERMIT CRAB, THE
EREMITTEN see **SYNDIG KAERLIGHED** • 1915
ERENDIRA • 1971 • Benacerraf Margot • VNZ
ERENDIRA • 1982 • Guerra Ruy • MXC, FRN, FRG
ERESZD EL A SZAKALLAMAT! • 1975 • Bacso Peter • HNG • DON'T PULL MY BEARD! ○ LET GO OF MY BEARD
ERETICO, L' • 1958 • Moro Francesco De Borja • ITL, SPN • HEREJE, EL (SPN)
ERFARINGER • 1976 • Billing Kjell • SHT • NRW
ERFGENAAM, DIE • 1971 • SAF
ERFGOED IS STERFGOED • 1976 • SAF
ERFINDER, DER • 1981 • Gloor Kurt • SWT • INVENTOR, THE
ERFOLG • 1990 • Seitz Franz* • FRG • SUCCESS
ERGASTOLO • 1953 • Capuano Luigi • ITL
ERGENS IN NEDERLAND • 1940 • Berger Ludwig • NTH • SOMEWHERE IN HOLLAND
ERGOSTASIO, TO • 1981 • Psarras Tasos • GRC • FACTORY, THE
ERH-TZU-TE TA WAN-OU • 1983 • Hou Hsiao-Hsien, Wan Jen, Tseng Chuang-Hsiang • TWN • SANDWICH MAN, THE
ERIC • 1975 • Goldstone James • TVM • USA
ERIC CLAPTON AND HIS ROLLING HOTEL • 1980 • Pyke Rex • DOC • UKN
ERIC DELANEY AND HIS NEW BAND • 1960 • Henryson Robert • SHT • UKN
ERIC SOYA'S "17" (USA) see **SYTTEN** • 1965
ERIC TABARLY ET LES AUTRES • 1976 • Hussenot Yves • DOC • FRN
ERIC THE GREAT see **LAST PERFORMANCE, THE** • 1927
ERIC THE GREAT ILLUSIONIST see **LAST PERFORMANCE, THE** • 1927
ERIC THE RED'S WOOING • 1914 • *Domino* • USA
ERIC WINSTONE BAND SHOW, THE • 1955 • Carreras Michael • SHT • UKN
ERIC WINSTONE'S STAGECOACH • 1956 • Carreras Michael • SHT • UKN
ERICA MINOR • 1974 • Van Effenterre Bertrand • SWT, FRN
ERIK • 1990 • Kennedy Michael • CND • ONE MAN OUT
ERIK A BUZAKALASZ • 1939 • Gaal Bela • HNG • WHEAT RIPENS, THE
ERIK EL VIKINGO (SPN) see **ERIK, IL VICHINGO** • 1965
ERIK, IL VICHINGO • 1965 • Caiano Mario • ITL, SPN • VENGEANCE OF THE VIKINGS (UKN) ○ ERIK EL VIKINGO (SPN)
ERIK THE CONQUEROR (USA) see **INVASORI, GLI** • 1961
ERIK THE VIKING • 1989 • Jones Terry • UKN
ERIK XIV see **KARIN MANSDOTTER** • 1954
ERIKA • 1970 • Capetanis Leon • FRG
ERIKA • 1971 • Ratti Filippo M. • ITL
ERIKA/ONE • 1969 • Denby Jerry • USA
ERIKA'S HOT SUMMER • 1970 • Graver Gary • USA
ERIKLER CICEK ACTI • 1968 • Ergun Nuri • TRK • PLUMP BLOSSOMS
ERIKO TO TOMONI • 1951 • Toyoda Shiro • JPN
ERIKSSON • 1969 • Edwall Allan • SWD
ERIN EREINTEE • 1970 • Aubert Jean-Paul • SHT • FRN
ERINNERUNG AN EINEN SOMMER IN BERLIN • 1972 • Hadrich Rolf • FRG • MEMORIES OF A SUMMER IN BERLIN
ERINNERUNGEN • 1986 • Quendlinger Albert • DOC • AUS • REMEMBRANCES OF O.K.
ERINNERUNGEN AUS DER ZUKUNFT • 1969 • Reinl Harald • FRG • CHARIOTS OF THE GODS (UKN) ○ BACK TO THE STARS (USA) ○ MEMORIES OF THE FUTURE
ERINNERUNGEN EINER NONNE • 1927 • Bergen Arthur • FRG
ERISKAY • 1935 • Kissling Werner • UKN
ERKEK ADAM SOZUNDE DURUR • 1967 • Aslan Mehmet • TRK • MAN'S WORD, A
ERKEL • 1952 • Keleti Marton • HNG
ERKENNTNIS, DIE • 1915 • *Vallis Lo* • FRG
ERKOLCSOS EJSZAKA, EGY • 1978 • Makk Karoly • HNG • VERY MORAL NIGHT, A
ERL KING, THE see **ROI DES AULNES, LE** • 1930
ERLEBNIS EINER NACHT, DAS • 1929 • Brignone Guido • FRG
ERLEBNIS GEHT WEITER, DAS • 1940 • Gallone Carmine • FRG • ANOTHER EXPERIENCE
ERLEBNISSE DER BERUHMTEN TANZERIN FANNY ELSSLER, DIE • 1920 • Zelnik Friedrich • FRG
ERLEBNISSE DER PUPPE • 1966 • Winzenstein Franz • FRG
ERLEBNISSE EINER KAMMERZOFF, DIE • 1921 • Lamprecht Gerhard • FRG
ERLEBNISSE EINER SEKRETARIN • 1922 • *Burg Rita* • FRG
ERLEBNISSE ZWEIER NAHMADCHEN, DIE see **PRATER** • 1924
ERLENKONIGS TOCHTER • 1914 • Rye Stellan • FRG
ERLKONIG, DER • 1931 • Brauer Peter P., Iribe Marie-Louise • FRG
ERLOSCHENE AUGEN • 1917 • Stein Josef • FRG
ERMA BIFRONTE, L' • 1920 • Lolli Alberto Carlo • ITL
ERMINE AND RHINESTONES • 1925 • King Burton L. • USA
ERNEST GOES TO CAMP • 1987 • Cherry John • USA
ERNEST HEMINGWAY'S THE KILLERS see **KILLERS, THE** • 1964
ERNEST LE REBELLE • 1938 • Christian-Jaque • FRN
ERNEST MALTRAVERS • 1914 • Vale Travers • USA
ERNEST MALTRAVERS • 1920 • Denton Jack • UKN
ERNEST MEETS THE VOODOO QUEEN • 1989 • Cherry John • USA
ERNEST SAVES CHRISTMAS • 1988 • Cherry John • USA
ERNESTO • 1979 • Samperi Salvatore • ITL, SPN, FRG
ERNIE • 1977 • Tranter Barbara • SHT • CND
ERNIE see **ERNIE GAME, THE** • 1967
ERNIE AND ROSE • 1982 • Huckert John W. • USA
ERNIE GAME, THE • 1967 • Owen Don • CND • ERNIE
ERNIE KOVACS: BETWEEN THE LAUGHTER • 1984 • Johnson Lamont • TVM • USA
ERNIE KOVACS: TELEVISION'S ORIGINAL GENIUS • 1982 • Burns Keith • TVM • USA
ERNIEDRIGTE UND BELEIDIGTE • 1922 • Zelnik Friedrich • FRG
ERNST BUSCH • 1967 • Gass Karl • DOC • GDR
ERNST FUCHS • 1976 • Jasny Vojtech • SHT • UKN
ERNST IST DAS LEBEN.. • 1916 • Andra Fern • FRG
ERNST THALMAN PT.1 see **ERNST THALMANN -SOHN SEINER KLASSE** • 1954
ERNST THALMAN PT.2 see **ERNST THALMANN -FUHRER SEINER KLASSE** • 1955
ERNST THALMANN -FUHRER SEINER KLASSE • 1955 • Maetzig Kurt • GDR • ERNST THALMAN PT.2
ERNST THALMANN -SOHN SEINER KLASSE • 1954 • Maetzig Kurt • GDR • ERNST THALMAN PT.1
ERNTE see **JULIKA, DIE** • 1936
EROBERUNG DER ZITADELLE, DIE • 1976 • Wicki Bernhard • FRG • CONQUEST OF THE CITADEL, THE
EROD, AZ • 1979 • Szinetar Miklos • HNG • FORTRESS, THE
ERODE IL GRANDE • 1958 • Genoino Arnaldo, Tourjansky Victor • ITL, FRN • HEROD THE GREAT (USA)
EROE DEI NOSTRI TEMPI, UN • 1955 • Monicelli Mario • ITL
EROE DEL NOSTRO TEMPO, UN • 1960 • Capogna Sergio • ITL • CAMICIA NERA
EROE DELLA STRADA, L' • 1948 • Borghesio Carlo • ITL
EROE DELLA VANDEA, L' (ITL) see **REVOLTES DE LOMANACH, LES** • 1953
EROE DI BABILONIA, L' • 1963 • Marcellini Siro • ITL, FRN • BEAST OF BABYLON AGAINST THE SON OF HERCULES, THE (USA) ○ HERO OF BABYLON, THE
EROE SONO IO, L' • 1951 • Bragaglia Carlo Ludovico • ITL • I'M THE HERO
EROE VAGABONDO • 1966 • Santesso Walter • ITL
EROGAMI NO ONRYO • 1930 • Ozu Yasujiro • JPN • REVENGEFUL SPIRIT OF EROS, THE
EROGENA ZONA • 1981 • Karaklajic Dejan • YGS • EROGENOUS ZONE
EROGENOUS ZONE see **EROGENA ZONA** • 1981
EROGENY • 1976 • Broughton James • USA
EROI, GLI • 1973 • Tessari Duccio • ITL, FRN, SPN • ENFANTS DE CHOEUR, LES (FRN)
EROI ALL'INFERNO • 1974 • Wotruba Michael • ITL • HEROES IN HELL
EROI DEL DOPPIO GIOCO, GLI • 1962 • Mastrocinque Camillo • ITL
EROI DEL WEST, GLI • 1963 • Steno • ITL, SPN
EROI DELLA DOMENICA, GLI • 1952 • Camerini Mario • ITL
EROI DELL'ARTIDE, GLI • 1954 • Emmer Luciano • DOC • ITL
EROI DI FORT WORTH, GLI • 1964 • De Martino Alberto • ITL
EROI DI IERI, OGGI, DOMANI, GLI • 1965 • Tau Sergio, Dell'Acquila Enzo, Di Leo Fernando, Wedsz Franz • ITL
EROICA • 1949 • Kolm-Veltee H. Walter • AUS
EROICA • 1958 • Munk Andrzej • PLN • HEROISM ○ EROICA -POLEN 44
EROICA • 1960 • Cacoyannis Michael • GRC • OUR LAST SPRING
EROICA, L' • 1919 • Mari Febo • ITL
EROICA -POLEN 44 see **EROICA** • 1958
EROICA (THE BEETHOVEN STORY) • 1951 • Hartl Karl • FRG
EROS + GYAKUSATSU • 1970 • Yoshida Yoshishige • JPN • EROS + MASSACRE
EROS IN KETTEN • 1930 • Wiene Conrad • AUS • SEXUALNOT
EROS + MASSACRE see **EROS + GYAKUSATSU** • 1970
EROS, O BASILEUS • 1967 • Markopoulos Gregory J. • USA
EROS STERNA see **HIJIRI KANNON DAIBOSATSU** • 1976
EROS.. THE BIZARRE see **NOITE VAZIA** • 1965
EROS (USA) see **NOITE VAZIA** • 1965
EROSTRATUS • 1958 • Marzano Joseph • SHT • USA
EROTES STI LESVO • 1967 • Sequens Jiri • GRC • ROMANCE IN LESVOS
EROTIC ADVENTURES OF CANDY, THE • 1978 • Palmer Gail • USA
EROTIC ADVENTURES OF PINOCCHIO see **PINOCCHIO** • 1971
EROTIC ADVENTURES OF ROBINSON CRUSOE • 1975 • Dixon Ken • USA
EROTIC ADVENTURES OF SIEGFRIED, THE (UKN) see **SIEGFRIED UND DAS SAGENHAFTE LIEBESLEBEN DER NIBELUNGEN** • 1971
EROTIC ADVENTURES OF SNOW WHITE, THE see **GRIMMS MARCHEN VON LUSTERNEN PARCHEN** • 1969
EROTIC ADVENTURES OF ZORRO, THE • 1972 • Freeman Robert • USA, FRN, FRG
EROTIC BLUE (UKN) see **PERCHE QUELLE STRANE GOCCE DI SANGUE SUL CORPO DI JENNIFER?** • 1972
EROTIC CIRCUS, THE • 1969 • Sullivan Ron • USA
EROTIC CONFESSIONS see **COMING ATTRACTIONS** • 1976
EROTIC DEVIL see **KOSHOKUMA** • 1968
EROTIC DIARY see **JOURNAL EROTIQUE D'UN BUCHERON, LE** • 1973
EROTIC ENCOUNTERS see **AMOUR CHEZ LES POIDS LOURDS, L'** • 1978
EROTIC EVA see **EVA NERA** • 1976
EROTIC FANTASIES • 1972 • Leigh Malcolm • UKN
EROTIC FANTASIES • 1978 • Ford Derek, Selway Paul • ITL
EROTIC FUUDOKI -KAEDOKO • 1968 • Seki Koji • JPN • EROTIC TOPOGRAPHY -BED EXCHANGE
EROTIC INFERNO • 1975 • Wrenn Trevor • UKN • ADAM AND NICOLE ○ NAKED AND WILLING
EROTIC LOVE GAMES (UKN) see **FILLE LIBRE, UNE** • 1970
EROTIC MR. ROSE, THE • 1964 • Millard Nicholas • USA • CONQUESTS OF MR. ROSE, THE
EROTIC ODYSSEY • 1976 • Milas Nick • GRC • ROXANA
EROTIC PARADE • 1968 • Roy Jean-Claude • FRN
EROTIC PLEASURES see **PLAISIRS SOLITAIRES, LES** • 1976
EROTIC PLEASURES: THE BODIES DESIRE see **PLAISIRS SOLITAIRES, LES** • 1976
EROTIC PROFESSOR, THE see **PROFESOR EROTICO, EL** • 1976
EROTIC RADIO WSEX • 1984 • Augustus Bob • USA • EROTIC RADIO WSSX
EROTIC RADIO WSSX see **EROTIC RADIO WSEX** • 1984
EROTIC REVENGE see **CARNALITA** • 1974
EROTIC STORIES see **CONTOS EROTICOS** • 1980
EROTIC TALES see **CUENTOS EROTICOS** • 1979
EROTIC TALES see **CONTES PERVERS** • 1980
EROTIC THREE, THE (UKN) see **SCRATCH HARRY** • 1970
EROTIC TOPOGRAPHY -BED EXCHANGE see **EROTIC FUUDOKI -KAEDOKO** • 1968
EROTIC TOUCH, THE see **BAIE DU DESIR, LA** • 1964
EROTIC TOUCH OF HOT SKIN, THE (USA) see **BAIE DU DESIR, LA** • 1964
EROTIC URGE (UKN) see **TROIS FILLES VERS LE SOLEIL** • 1967
EROTIC WITCHCRAFT (UKN) see **GOULVE, LA** • 1971
EROTIC WOMAN, THE see **FIEBRE** • 1972
EROTIC WORLD OF ANGEL CASH • 1982 • Howard Howard A. • USA
EROTICA • 1961 • Meyer Russ • USA • EROTICON
EROTICA • 1980 • Smedley-Aston Brian • UKN • PAUL RAYMOND'S EROTICA
EROTICA see **AMORE DIFFICILE, L'** • 1962
EROTICAS VACACIONES DE STELA, LAS • 1978 • Urbiola Zacarias • SPN, FRN • INTIMATE CONFESSIONS OF STELLA ○ INGENUE LIBERTINE, UNE
EROTICISM ON THE SCHOOL BENCH see **EROTIK AUF DER SCHULBANK** • 1968
EROTICIST, THE see **ALL'ONOREVOLE PIACCIONO LE DONNE** • 1972
EROTICON • 1974 • Balcazar Alfonso • SPN
EROTICON see **EROTICA** • 1961
EROTIK AUF DER SCHULBANK • 1968 • Dahlberg Hans, Fritz Roger, Schmidt Eckhardt • FRG • EROTICISM ON THE SCHOOL BENCH
EROTIK IM BERUF • 1971 • Hofbauer Ernst • FRG • SEX IN THE OFFICE (UKN)
EROTIKILL • 1975 • Johnson J. P. • SPN
EROTIKON • 1920 • Stiller Mauritz • SWD • BONDS THAT CHAFE (UKN) ○ RIDDAREN AV IGAR
EROTIKON • 1929 • Machaty Gustav • CZC • SEDUCTION
EROTIKON -KARUSSELL DER LEIDENSCHAFTEN • 1963 • Hladnik Bostjan • FRG
EROTIKOS see **HOW TO PICK UP A GIRL** • 1967
EROTIQUE, L' see **EROTYK** • 1960
EROTIQUE (USA) see **TRAQUENARDS** • 1969
EROTIQUES PASSIONS • Thierry Alain • FRN
EROTISME A L'ETUDE, L' • 1972 • Pallardy Jean-Marie • FRN
EROTISMO Y LA INFORMATICA, EL • 1975 • Merino Fernando • SPN
EROTISSIMO • 1969 • Pires Gerard • ITL, FRN
EROTOMANE, L' • 1974 • Vicario Marco • ITL
EROTOMANIAC, AN see **IROKURUI** • 1968
EROTYK • 1960 • Skolimowski Jerzy • SHT • PLN • EROTIQUE, L'
ERPRESSER • 1929 • Decroix Henry • FRG
ERPRESSERTRICK, EIN • 1921 • Schonfelder Erich • FRG
ERRAND see **RECARDO**
ERRAND BOY, THE • 1962 • Lewis Jerry • USA
ERRAND BOY FOR RHYTHM • 1946 • Crouch William Forest • SHT • USA
ERRAND OF MERCY, AN • 1913 • *Thanhouser* • USA
ERRANT HUSBAND HYPNOTISED, AN • 1910 • *Pathe Freres* • FRN
ERRATIC POWER • 1910 • Aylott Dave • UKN
ERREUR DE JEUNESSE • 1989 • Tadic Radovan • FRN
ERREUR DE POIVROT • 1904 • Blache Alice • FRN
ERREUR DE PORTE • 1902 • Zecca Ferdinand • FRN
ERREUR D'UN PERE, L' see **GHALT'AT ABB** • 1952
ERREUR JUDICIAIRE • 1899-00 • Blache Alice • FRN
ERREUR JUDICIAIRE • 1947 • de Canonge Maurice • FRN
ERREUR TRAGIQUE • 1913 • Feuillade Louis • FRN
ERRIGAL • 1969 • Carey Patrick • DOC • IRL
ERRING, THE • 1914 • Ince John • USA
ERRING BROTHER, THE • 1913 • *Patheplay* • USA
ERRING SON'S AWAKENING, THE • 1911 • *Yankee* • USA
ERRONEOUS PRACTICE see **ERAKU NARE** • 1932
ERROR IN KIDNAPPING, AN • 1913 • Thompson Frederick A. • USA
ERROR OF OMISSION, THE • 1912 • *Essanay* • USA
ERRORS OF YOUTH (UKN) see **OSHIBKI YUNISTI** • 1989
ERSATZ see **SUROGAT** • 1961
ERSCHEINEN PFLICHT • 1984 • Dziuba Helmut • GDR • ATTENDANCE COMPULSORY
ERSCHIESSUNG DES LANDESVERRATERS ERNST S., DIE • 1976 • Meienberg Niklaus, Dindo Richard • DOC • SWT • EXECUTION OF TRAITOR ERNST S., THE ○ SHOOTING OF TRAITOR ERNST S., THE

ERSKINE • 1974 • Marzaroli Oscar • DOC • UKN
ERSKINE NEW TOWN • 1975 • Marzaroli Oscar • DOC • UKN
ERSTE FRUHLINGSTAG, DER • 1956 • Weiss Helmut • FRG
ERSTE KUSS, DER • 1928 • Lamac Carl • FRG
ERSTE KUSS, DER • 1954 • Ode Erik • FRG, AUS
ERSTE LIEBE • 1919 • Gunsburg Arthur • FRG
ERSTE LIEBE • 1970 • Schell Maximilian • FRG, SWT, UKN • FIRST LOVE
ERSTE LIEBE see **SEXTANERIN, DIE**
ERSTE PATIENT, DER • 1916 • Lubitsch Ernst • FRG
ERSTE POLKA • 1978 • Emmerich Klaus • FRG • FIRST POLKA, THE
ERSTE RECHT DES KINDES, DAS • 1932 • Wendhausen Fritz • FRG • AUS DEM TAGEBUCH EINER FRAUENARZTIN
ERSTE SCHNEE, DER • 1979 • Weber Walter • SWT
ERSTE STAND, DER GROSSKAPITALIST, DER • 1925 • *Klopfer Eugen* • FRG • DAMON GELD
ERSTE WALZER, DER • 1978 • Dorrie Doris • FRG • FIRST WALTZ, THE
ERSTEN TAGE, DIE • 1971 • Holba Herbert • AUS • FIRST DAYS, THE
ERSTWHILE SUSAN • 1919 • Robertson John S. • USA
ERTRAUMTES • 1918 • Gartner Adolf • FRG
ERUPTIA • 1959 • Ciulei Liviu • RMN • ERUPTION
ERUPTION • 1978 • Kurlan Stanley • USA
ERUPTION • 1978 • Stojanovic Nikola • YGS
ERUPTION see **ERUPTIA** • 1959
ERUPTION DE L'ETNA, L' • 1951-55 • Tazieff Haroun • SHT • FRN
ERUPTION DU MONT PELE, L' see **ERUPTION VOLCANIQUE A LA MARTINIQUE** • 1902
ERUPTION OF ETNA, THE see **TRAGEDIA DELL'ETNA, LA** • 1951
ERUPTION OF MOUNT PELEE, THE see **ERUPTION VOLCANIQUE A LA MARTINIQUE** • 1902
ERUPTION VOLCANIQUE A LA MARTINIQUE • 1902 • Melies Georges • FRN • ERUPTION OF MOUNT PELEE, THE ○ ERUPTION DU MONT PELE, L' ○ TERRIBLE ERUPTION OF MOUNT PELEE AND DESTRUCTION OF ST. PIERRE, MARTINIQUE, THE
ERVINKA • 1967 • Kishon Ephraim • ISR
ERWACHEN DES WEIBES, DAS • 1927 • Sauer Fred • FRG • GIRL DOWNSTAIRS
ERWACHSEN SEIN.. • 1956 • Hart Wolf • FRG
ERWTEN EN WORTELTJES • 1972 • Schelfthout D. • BLG
ERZAHLUNGEN AUS DER NEUEN WELT • 1968 • Hellwig Joachim, Cohn-Vossen Richard, Mida Massimo • GDR • TALES FROM THE NEW WORLD
ERZEBETH see **ROUGE AUX LEVRES, LE** • 1970
ERZEKENY BUCSU A FEJEDELEMTOL • 1986 • Vitezy Laszlo • HNG • FAREWELL TO THE PRINCE
ERZGAUNER • 1921 • Eichgrun Bruno • FRG
ERZHERZOG JOHANN • 1930 • Neufeld Max • AUS
ERZHERZOG JOHANNS GROSSE LIEBE • 1950 • Schott-Schobinger Hans • AUS
ERZIEHER MEINER TOCHTER, DER • 1929 • von Bolvary Geza • FRG
ERZIEHERIN GESUCHT • 1945 • Erfurth Ulrich • FRG
ERZIEHUNGSZIEL KLASSENKAMPFER • 1967 • Jakob Ernst Otto • GDR • EDUCATIONAL AIM: CLASS-FIGHTER
ERZKOKETTE, DIE • 1917 • Portegg R. • FRG
ES • 1965 • Schamoni Ulrich • FRG • IT
ES BEGANN UM MITTERNACHT • 1951 • Bauer Peter P. • FRG
ES BLASEN DIE TROMPETEN • 1926 • Boese Carl • FRG
ES BLEIBT IN DER FAMILIE • 1922 • Bolten-Baeckers Heinrich • FRG
ES FIEL EIN REIF IN DER FRUHLINGSNACHT • 1915 • Matull Kurt • FRG
ES FING SO HARMLOS AN • 1944 • Lingen Theo • FRG
ES FLUSTERT DIE LIEBE • 1935 • von Bolvary Geza • AUS
ES FLUSTERT DIE NACHT.. • 1929 • Janson Victor • FRG
ES GEHOREN ZWEI DAZU see **TOD EINES DOPPELGANGERS, DER** • 1967
ES GEHT NICHT OHNE GISELA • 1951 • Deppe Hans • FRG
ES GEHT UM ALLES • 1932 • Nosseck Max • FRG
ES GEHT UM MEIN LEBEN • 1936 • Eichberg Richard • FRG
ES GESCHAH AM 20 JULI • 1955 • Pabst G. W. • FRG • JACKBOOT MUTINY
ES GESCHAH AM HELLICHTEN TAG • 1958 • Vajda Ladislao • FRG, SWT • IT HAPPENED IN BROAD DAYLIGHT (USA) ○ ASSAULT IN BROAD DAYLIGHT
ES GESCHEHEN NOCH WUNDER • 1951 • Forst Willi • FRG • MIRACLES STILL HAPPEN
ES GIBT EINE FRAU, DIE DICH NIEMALS VERGISST • 1930 • Mittler Leo • FRG
ES GIBT NUR EINE LIEBE • 1933 • Meyer Johannes • FRG
ES GIBT NUR EINE MELODIE see **LIED VOM GLUCK, DAS** • 1933
ES HAT NICHT SOLLEN SEIN • 1915 • Del Zopp Rudolf • FRG
ES HERRSCHT RUHE IM LAND • 1976 • Lilienthal Peter • FRG • COUNTRY IS CALM, THE
ES HILFT NICHT, WO GEWALT HERRSCHT see **NICHT VERSOHNT ODER "ES HILFT NUR GEWALT, WO GEWALT HERRSCHT"** • 1965
ES IST EINE ALTE GESCHICHTE • 1972 • Warneke Lothar • GDR
ES KOMMT ALLE TAGE VOR.. • 1930 • Natge Hans • FRG
ES KOMMT DER TAG • 1922 • Krause Karl Otto • FRG
ES KOMMT DRAUF AN, SIE ZU VARANDERN • 1973 • Alemann Claudia • DOC • FRG • POINT IS TO CHANGE IT, THE (UKN)
ES KOMMT EIN TAG • 1950 • Jugert Rudolf • FRG
ES LEBE DAS LEBEN • 1949 • Emo E. W. • AUS
ES LEBE DIE LIEBE • 1944 • Engel Erich • FRG
ES LEUCHTEN DIE STERNE • 1938 • Zerlett Hans H. • FRG • STARS SHINE, THE (USA)
ES LEUCHTET MEINE LIEBE • 1922 • Stein Paul L. • FRG
ES LIEGT WAS IN DER LUFT • 1950 • Emo E. W. • FRG, SWT
ES MI HOMBRE • 1928 • Fernandez Cuenca Carlos • SPN
ES MI HOMBRE • 1935 • Perojo Benito • SPN
ES MI HOMBRE • 1966 • Gil Rafael • SPN
ES MUSS NICHT IMMER KAVIAR SEIN • 1961 • von Radvanyi Geza • FRG
ES NALUNK LEHTETLEN • 1965 • Macskassy Gyula, Varnai Gyorgy • ANS • HNG • IT CAN'T HAPPEN HERE
ES PECADO.. PERO ME GUSTA • 1977 • Bosch Juan • SPN
ES PECADO PERO ME GUSTA • 1979 • de la Rosa Antonio • VNZ • IT IS SIN.. BUT I LIKE IT
ES PELIGROSO ASOMARSE AL EXTERIOR (SPN) see **E PERIGOSO DEBRUCAR-SE** • 1946
ES QUAN DORMO QUE HI VEIG CLAR • 1988 • *Septimania Films* • SPN • IN MY SLEEP I SEE CLEARLY
ES SCHLAGT DREIZEHN see **JETZT SCHLAGTS 13** • 1950
ES STEHT EIN WIRTSHAUS AN DER LAHN • 1927 • Neff Wolfgang • FRG
ES TUT SICH WAS UM MITTERNACHT • 1934 • Stemmle R. A. • FRG • MADEL MIT TEMPO, EIN
ES USTED MI PADRE? • 1970 • Gimenez-Rico Antonio • SPN
ES WAR DIE ERSTE LIEBE • 1958 • Stapenhorst Fritz • FRG
ES WAR EIN MENSCH • 1950 • Oertel Curt • FRG
ES WAR EIN TRAUM • 1915 • *Morena Erna* • FRG
ES WAR EINE RAUSCHENDE BALLNACHT • 1939 • Froelich Carl • FRG • ONE ENCHANTED EVENING ○ THAT NIGHT AT THE BALL ○ IT WAS A GAY BALL NIGHT
ES WAR EINMAL EIN MUSIKUS • 1933 • Zelnik Friedrich • FRG
ES WAR EINMAL EIN TREUER HUSAR • 1929 • Wolff Carl Heinz • FRG
ES WAR EINMAL EIN WALZER • 1932 • Janson Victor • FRG
ES WAR EINST EIN PRINZESSCHEN • 1916 • Matull Kurt • FRG
ES WAR MIR EIN VERGNUGEN • 1963 • Moszkowicz Imo • FRG
ES WAR NICHT DIE NACHTIGALL • 1974 • Rothemund Sigi • FRG • JULIA (USA) ○ LIEBERSCHULER, DER
ES WARD LICHT see **FIAT LUX** • 1923
ES WAREN ZWEI JUNGGESELLEN • 1935 • Seitz Franz • FRG
ES WAREN ZWEI KONIGSKINDER.. • 1921 • Gunsburg Arthur • FRG
ES WERDE LICHT! 1 • 1918 • Oswald Richard • FRG • LET THERE BE LIGHT
ES WERDE LICHT! 2 • 1917 • Oswald Richard • FRG
ES WERDE LICHT! 3 • 1918 • Oswald Richard • FRG
ES WIRD ALLES WIEDER GUT • 1957 • von Bolvary Geza • FRG
ES WIRD SCHON WIEDER BESSER • 1932 • Gerron Kurt • FRG • THINGS WILL BE BETTER AGAIN
ES ZOGEN DREI BURSCHEN • 1927 • Wilhelm Carl • FRG
ESA MUJER • 1968 • Camus Mario • SPN
ESA PAREJA FELIZ • 1951 • Bardem Juan Antonio, Berlanga Luis Garcia • SPN • THAT HAPPY PAIR (USA) ○ THAT HAPPY COUPLE
ESA PICARA PELIRROJA • 1961 • Elorrieta Jose Maria • SPN
ESA VOZ ES UNA MINA • 1955 • Lucia Luis • SPN
ESALON DR. M. see **ESALON DOKTORA M.** • 1955
ESALON DOKTORA M. • 1955 • Mitrovic Zika • YGS • ECHELON OF DR. M., THE ○ ESALON DR. M.
ESBOZO DE DANIEL • 1986 • Marin Mariano • NCR • SKETCH OF DANIEL
ESBROUFFE, L' see **DECLIC ET DES CLAQUES** • 1964
ESBROUFFEUR, L' see **VOUS SEREZ MA FEMME** • 1932
ESCA-LATORS • 1971 • Cox Peter • SHT • ASL
ESCADRADRILEI ALBE see **SQUADRIGLIA BIANCA** • 1942
ESCADRILLE see **WOMAN I LOVE, THE** • 1937
ESCADRILLE DE LA CHANCE, L' • 1937 • de Vaucorbeil Max • FRN
ESCADRON BLANC, L' • 1948 • Chanas Rene • FRN
ESCADRON DE LA MUERTE, EL • 1966 • SPN • MUTINY AT FORT SHARP (USA)
ESCADRON DE LA MUERTE, EL (SPN) see **PER UN DOLLARO DI GLORIA** • 1966
ESCADRON VOLAPUK, L' • 1971 • Gilson Rene • FRN
ESCALA EN HI-FI • 1963 • Ferry Isidoro Martinez • SPN • SCALE IN HI-FI
ESCALA EN LA CIUDAD • 1935 • de Zavalia Alberto • ARG
ESCALA EN LA CIUDAD • 1936 • Saslavsky Luis • ARG
ESCALA EN TENERIFE • 1964 • Klimovsky Leon • SPN
ESCALADA DE LA MUERTE, LA • 1965 • Torres Manuel • SPN
ESCALADA DEL CHANTAJE, LA • 1965 • Alvarez Santiago • DOC • CUB
ESCALATION • 1967 • Faenza Roberto • ITL
ESCALATION • 1968 • Kimball Ward • ANS • USA
ESCALE • 1935 • Valray Louis • FRN • THIRTEEN DAYS OF LOVE (USA)
ESCALE • 1959 • Bourguignon Serge • FRN
ESCALE A ORAN • Colson-Malleville Marie • DOC • FRN • PORT-OF-CALL AT ORAN
ESCALE A ORLY • 1955 • Dreville Jean • FRN, FRG • ZWISCHENLANDUNG IN PARIS (FRG) ○ FASTEN YOUR SEAT BELTS
ESCALE A PARIS • 1951 • Lukine • SHT • FRN
ESCALE AU SOLEIL • 1947 • Verneuil Henri • SHT • FRN
ESCALE DE VERDURE see **MY ISLAND HOME** • 1961
ESCALE DES OIES SAUVAGES • 1964 • Dansereau Fernand • DCS • CND
ESCALIER C • 1984 • Tacchella Jean-Charles • FRN • STAIRCASE C
ESCALIER DE SERVICE • 1955 • Carlo-Rim • FRN
ESCALIER DE SERVICE, L' see **SULLAM AL-KHALFI, AS-** • 1970
ESCALIER SANS FIN, L' • 1943 • Lacombe Georges • FRN
ESCALOFRIO • 1978 • Puerto Carlos • SPN
ESCALOFRIO DIABOLICO • 1971 • Martinez Celeiro Francisco • SPN • DIABOLICAL SHUDDER
ESCAMBRAY • 1961 • Alvarez Santiago • DOC • CUB
ESCAMOTAGE D'UNE DAME CHEZ ROBERT-HOUDIN • 1896 • Melies Georges • FRN • CONJURING A LADY AT ROBERT-HOUDIN'S ○ VANISHING LADY, THE
ESCANDALO, EL • 1920 • Cuellar Alfredo B. • MXC
ESCANDALO, EL • 1934 • Urueta Chano • MXC
ESCANDALO, EL • 1943 • Saenz De Heredia Jose Luis • SPN
ESCANDALO, EL • 1963 • Seto Javier • SPN
ESCANDALO, EL • 1986 • Oteyza Carlos • VNZ • SCANDAL, THE
ESCANDALO DE ESTRELLAS • 1944 • Rodriguez Ismael • MXC
ESCANDALO EN LA FAMILIA • 1968 • Porter Julio • SPN, ARG • SCANDAL IN THE FAMILY
ESCANDALO EN LA RESIDENCIA • 1976 • Martin Eugenio • SPN
ESCAPADE • 1932 • Thorpe Richard • USA • DANGEROUS GROUND (UKN)
ESCAPADE • 1935 • Leonard Robert Z. • USA • MASQUERADE
ESCAPADE • 1955 • Leacock Philip • UKN
ESCAPADE • 1957 • Habib Ralph • FRN
ESCAPADE see **PARADIS DES VOLEURS, LE** • 1939
ESCAPADE see **ATOLL K** • 1952
ESCAPADE see **CAR NAPPING** • 1980
ESCAPADE, L' • 1974 • Soutter Michel • SWT
ESCAPADE, THE • 1983 • Diaconu Cornel • RMN
ESCAPADE DE FILOCHE, L' • 1915 • Feuillade Louis • FRN
ESCAPADE IN FLORENCE • 1962 • Previn Steven • USA
ESCAPADE IN JAPAN • 1957 • Lubin Arthur • USA
ESCAPADES OF EVA, THE see **EVA TROPI HLOUPOSTI** • 1939
ESCAPADES OF TEDDY BEAR, THE • 1909 • Smith Jack ? • UKN
ESCAPATE CONMIGO • 1989 • MXC
ESCAPE • 1930 • Dean Basil • UKN
ESCAPE • 1940 • Bute Mary Ellen, Nemeth Ted J. • ANS • USA
ESCAPE • 1940 • LeRoy Mervyn • USA • WHEN THE DOOR OPENED
ESCAPE • 1948 • Mankiewicz Joseph L. • UKN
ESCAPE • 1965 • Dembinski Lucjan • ANM • PLN
ESCAPE • 1970 • Moxey John Llewellyn • TVM • USA
ESCAPE • 1980 • Lewis Robert Michael • TVM • USA
ESCAPE • 1988 • Styles Richard • USA
ESCAPE • 1989 • Flynn John • USA
ESCAPE see **DASSO** • 1963
ESCAPE see **UTEK** • 1967
ESCAPE see **WOMAN HUNT, THE** • 1972
ESCAPE 2000 (USA) see **TURKEY SHOOT** • 1982
ESCAPE, THE • 1913 • *Pathe* • USA
ESCAPE, THE • 1913 • *Kalem* • USA
ESCAPE, THE • 1913 • *Powers* • USA
ESCAPE, THE • 1914 • Griffith D. W. • USA
ESCAPE, THE • 1926 • Greenwood Edwin • UKN
ESCAPE, THE • 1926 • Morante Milburn • USA
ESCAPE, THE • 1928 • Rosson Richard • USA
ESCAPE, THE • 1939 • Cortez Ricardo • USA
ESCAPE, THE see **FUGA, LA** • 1943
ESCAPE, THE see **FUGA, LA** • 1965
ESCAPE, THE see **FIRAR** • 1985
ESCAPE ARTIST, THE • 1982 • Deschanel Caleb • USA
ESCAPE AT DAWN see **AKATSUKI NO DASSO** • 1950
ESCAPE BY NIGHT • 1937 • MacFadden Hamilton • USA • FOOLS IN PARADISE
ESCAPE BY NIGHT • 1954 • Gilling John • UKN
ESCAPE BY NIGHT (USA) see **ERA NOTTE A ROMA** • 1960
ESCAPE BY NIGHT (USA) see **CLASH BY NIGHT** • 1963
ESCAPE DANGEROUS • 1947 • Smith Digby • UKN
ESCAPE DE LA ISLA DEL DIABLO (MXC) see **I ESCAPED FROM DEVIL'S ISLAND** • 1973
ESCAPE EPISODE • 1946 • Anger Kenneth • SHT • USA
ESCAPE EPISODE (SOUND VERS.) • 1946 • Anger Kenneth • USA
ESCAPE FROM ALCATRAZ • 1979 • Siegel Don • USA
ESCAPE FROM ANDERSONVILLE, THE • 1909 • Olcott Sidney • USA
ESCAPE FROM ANGOLA • 1976 • Martinson Leslie H. • USA, SAF • RETURN TO AFRICA
ESCAPE FROM APARTHEID see **GITANOS: ESCAPE FROM APARTHEID** • 1976
ESCAPE FROM BAD GIRLS' DORMITORY • 1985 • Kincaid Tim • USA
ESCAPE FROM BATAAN see **LONGEST HUNDRED MILES, THE** • 1967
ESCAPE FROM BOGEN COUNTY • 1977 • Stern Steven Hilliard • TVM • USA
ESCAPE FROM BROADMOOR • 1948 • Gilling John • UKN
ESCAPE FROM BROADMOOR (USA) see **BROKEN CHISEL, THE** • 1913
ESCAPE FROM CELL BLOCK 3 • 1978 • Osborne Kent • USA
ESCAPE FROM COLDITZ • 1977 • Slater W., Gregreen P. • TVM • UKN
ESCAPE FROM CRIME • 1942 • Lederman D. Ross • USA
ESCAPE FROM CRIME see **BIG SHOT, THE** • 1942
ESCAPE FROM DEVIL'S ISLAND • 1935 • Rogell Albert S. • USA • SONG OF THE DAMNED
ESCAPE FROM DS-3 • 1981 • Sandler Allan, Emenegger Robert • USA
ESCAPE FROM EAST BERLIN • 1962 • Siodmak Robert • USA, FRG • TUNNEL 28
ESCAPE FROM EL DIABLO • 1983 • Hessler Gordon • USA
ESCAPE FROM FORT BRAVO • 1953 • Sturges John • USA
ESCAPE FROM GALAXY 3 • 1986 • Norman Ben • ITL
ESCAPE FROM HELL see **LISSU WA AL-KILAB, AL-** • 1962
ESCAPE FROM HELL see **MUSHUKU NINBETSUCHU** • 1963
ESCAPE FROM HELL see **SAVAGE ISLAND** • 1985
ESCAPE FROM HELL ISLAND see **MAN IN THE WATER, THE** • 1963
ESCAPE FROM HONG KONG • 1942 • Nigh William • USA
ESCAPE FROM IRAN • 1982 • Johnson Lamont • TVM • CND • ESCAPE FROM IRAN: THE CANADIAN CAPER ○ CANADIAN CAPER, THE
ESCAPE FROM IRAN: THE CANADIAN CAPER see **ESCAPE FROM IRAN** • 1982
ESCAPE FROM JAPAN see **NIPPON DASSHUTSU** • 1964
ESCAPE FROM LIMBO • 1953 • Callagher Charles E. • USA
ESCAPE FROM NEW YORK • 1981 • Carpenter John • USA
ESCAPE FROM PRISON see **DATSUGOKU** • 1950
ESCAPE FROM RED ROCK • 1958 • Bernds Edward • USA
ESCAPE FROM SAFEHAVEN • 1988 • Jones Brian Thomas • USA
ESCAPE FROM SAHARA (USA) see **MADELEINE UND DER LEGIONAR** • 1958
ESCAPE FROM SAIGON (USA) see **CAPTIF, LE** • 1957
ESCAPE FROM SAN QUENTIN • 1957 • Sears Fred F. • USA
ESCAPE FROM SINGAPORE • 1974 • Power John • DOC • ASL

ESCAPE FROM SOBIBOR • 1987 • Gold Jack • TVM • UKN, USA, YGS
ESCAPE FROM TERROR • 1960 • Coogan Jackie, Coogan George • USA
ESCAPE FROM THE BRONX (USA) see **FUGA DAL BRONX** • 1984
ESCAPE FROM THE DARK • 1976 • Jarrott Charles • UKN, USA • LITTLEST HORSE THIEVES, THE (USA)
ESCAPE FROM THE DEAD STREET see **SHI NO MACHI O NOGARATE** • 1952
ESCAPE FROM THE PLANET OF THE APES • 1971 • Taylor Don • USA
ESCAPE FROM THE SEA • 1968 • Seabourne Peter • UKN
ESCAPE FROM THE SHADOWS see **UTEK ZE STINU** • 1958
ESCAPE FROM YESTERDAY (UKN) see **BANDERA, LA** • 1935
ESCAPE FROM YESTERDAY (UKN) see **RIDE A CROOKED MILE** • 1938
ESCAPE FROM ZAHRAIN • 1962 • Neame Ronald • USA
ESCAPE IF YOU CAN (UKN) see **ST. BENNY THE DIP** • 1951
ESCAPE IN THE DESERT • 1945 • Blatt Edward A., Florey Robert (U/c) • USA • STRANGERS IN OUR MIDST
ESCAPE IN THE FOG • 1945 • Boetticher Budd • USA
ESCAPE IN THE SUN • 1956 • Breakston George • USA
ESCAPE IN THE WIND • 1965 • Taborsky Vaclav • CZC
ESCAPE INTO DREAMS (USA) see **NATALE AL CAMPO 119** • 1948
ESCAPE INTO TERROR see **TAIYO E NO DASSHUTSU** • 1963
ESCAPE LIBRE (SPN) see **ECHAPPEMENT LIBRE** • 1964
ESCAPE ME NEVER • 1935 • Czinner Paul • UKN
ESCAPE ME NEVER • 1947 • Godfrey Peter • USA
ESCAPE OF BRONCHO BILLY, THE • 1915 • *Anderson Broncho Billy* • USA
ESCAPE OF JIM DOLAN, THE • 1913 • Duncan William • USA
ESCAPE OF MEGAGODZILLA, THE see **MEKAGOJIRA NO GYAKUSHU** • 1975
ESCAPE OF THE AMETHYST see **YANGTSE INCIDENT** • 1957
ESCAPE OF THE APE, THE • 1908 • *Essanay* • USA
ESCAPE OF THE BIRDMEN see **BIRDMEN, THE** • 1971
ESCAPE OF THE RED, THE see **FUGA DEL ROJO, LA** • 1983
ESCAPE ROUTE • 1952 • Scott Peter Graham, Friedman Seymour • UKN • I'LL GET YOU (USA)
ESCAPE ROUTE CAPE TOWN • 1967 • Webb Robert D. • SAF • CAPE TOWN AFFAIR, THE
ESCAPE ROUTE TO MARSEILLES see **FLUCHTWEG NOCH MARSEILLE** • 1977
ESCAPE THE CITY • 1955 • Dimond Peter • DOC • ASL
ESCAPE TO ATHENA • 1979 • Cosmatos George Pan • UKN • GOLDEN RAIDERS
ESCAPE TO BERLIN (USA) see **FLUCHT NACH BERLIN** • 1961
ESCAPE TO BURMA • 1955 • Dwan Allan • USA
ESCAPE TO DANGER • 1943 • Comfort Lance, Greenbaum Mutz • UKN • MURDER IN A CONVOY
ESCAPE TO ECSTASY see **ESCAPE TO EXSTASY** • 1970
ESCAPE TO ENTEBBE • 1977 • Grant David • UKN
ESCAPE TO EXSTASY • 1970 • *Stacey Dist.* • USA • ESCAPE TO ECSTASY
ESCAPE TO GLORY • 1940 • Brahm John • USA • SUBMARINE ZONE ○ PASSAGE WEST
ESCAPE TO HAPPINESS (UKN) see **INTERMEZZO** • 1939
ESCAPE TO JUSTICE • 1942 • Knight C. Pattinson • UKN
ESCAPE TO LOVE • 1982 • Stein Herb • USA
ESCAPE TO MINDINAO • 1968 • McDougall Don • TVM • USA
ESCAPE TO NOWHERE • 1960 • Spielberg Steven • USA
ESCAPE TO NOWHERE see **SILENCIEUX, LE** • 1972
ESCAPE TO PARADISE • 1939 • Kenton Erle C. • USA
ESCAPE TO THE SUN • 1972 • Golan Menahem • ISR, FRN, FRG • HABRICHA EL HASHEMESH
ESCAPE TO VICTORY • 1980 • Huston John • UKN, USA • VICTORY (USA)
ESCAPE TO WITCH MOUNTAIN • 1975 • Hough John • USA
ESCAPED CONVICT • 1919 • *Capital* • SHT • USA
ESCAPED FROM DARTMOOR (USA) see **COTTAGE ON DARTMOOR, A** • 1929
ESCAPED FROM HELL (USA) see **FLUCHT AUS DER HOLLE** • 1928
ESCAPED FROM SIBIRIA • 1914 • Goldin Sidney M. • USA
ESCAPED FROM THE ASYLUM • 1913 • *Imp* • USA
ESCAPED LUNATIC, THE • 1911 • *Cumpson John R.* • USA
ESCAPED THE LAW, BUT.. see **STORSTE KAERLIGHED, DEN** • 1914
ESCAPEMENT • 1957 • Tully Montgomery • UKN • ELECTRONIC MONSTER, THE (USA) ○ DREAM MACHINE, THE ○ ZEX, THE ELECTRONIC FIEND ○ ZEX
ESCAPES • 1985 • Steensland David • USA
ESCAPES see **BEKSTVA** • 1968
ESCAPES HOME see **UTEKY DOMU** • 1980
ESCAPING FROM PRISON see **STICI PRE SVITANJA BEGSTVO SA ROBIJE** • 1979
ESCAPING FROM THE EARTHQUAKE see **HUYENDO DEL SISMO** • 1970
ESCAPING FROM TRUTH see **FARAR AZ HAGHIGHAT** • 1967
ESCAPULARIO, EL • 1966 • Gonzalez Servando • MXC
ESCARAVELHO DA BATATEIRA, O • 1943 • Coelho Jose Adolfo • SHT • PRT
ESCARGOT DANS LA TETE, UN • 1980 • Siry Jean-Etienne • FRN
ESCARGOTS, LES • 1965 • Laloux Rene • ANS • FRN • SNAILS, THE (UKN)
ESCARLATA • 1969 • Crisostomo Fely • PHL
ESCARPINS DE MAX, LES • 1913 • Linder Max • FRN
ESCARPOLETTE FANTASTIQUE, L' see **CAUCHEMAR DU PECHEUR, LE** • 1905
ESCARPOLETTE TRAGIQUE, L' • 1913 • de Morlhon Camille • FRN
ESCENAS CALLEJERAS • 1902 • Cardini Eugenio • ARG
ESCENAS DE LOS MUELLES • 1968 • Valdes Oscar • DOC • CUB
ESCENAS MARAVILLOSAS DE MEXICO • 1918 • *Alvarez Arrondo Y Cia* • MXC
ESCLAVA DEL DESEO • 1968 • Gomez Muriel Emilio • MXC • SLAVE OF DESIRE
ESCLAVA DEL PARAISO, LA • 1968 • Elorrieta Jose Maria • SPN, ITL • SLAVE OF PARADISE, THE
ESCLAVA TE DOY • 1975 • Martin Eugenio • SPN
ESCLAVAS DE LA MODA • 1930 • Howard David • USA
ESCLAVE • 1923 • Monca Georges • FRN
ESCLAVE, L' • 1953 • Ciampi Yves • FRN, ITL • SCHIAVITU (ITL) ○ SLAVE, THE (USA)
ESCLAVE BLANC, L' • 1936 • Paulin Jean-Paul • FRN, ITL • JUNGLA NERA (ITL) ○ MUDUNDU
ESCLAVE BLANCHE, L' • 1927 • *Vanel Charles* • FRN • WHITE SLAVE, THE (USA)
ESCLAVE BLANCHE, L' • 1939 • Sorkin Marc • FRN • PASHA'S WIVES, THE (USA)
ESCLAVE DE PHIDIAS, L' • 1914 • Perret Leonce • FRN
ESCLAVES DE L'ARGENT, LES see **ABID AL-MAL** • 1953
ESCLAVES EXISTENT TOUJOURS, LES (FRN) see **SCHIAVE ESISTONO ANCORA, LE** • 1964
ESCOLAS PRIMARIAS • 1962 • de Barros Jose Leitao • PRT
ESCOMBRERAS • 1967 • Aguirre Javier • SHT • SPN
ESCONDIDA, LA • 1955 • Gavaldon Roberto • MXC • HIDDEN WOMAN, THE
ESCONDIDO see **MINUTO PER PREGARE, UN ISTANTE PER MORIRE, UN** • 1967
ESCONDITES, LOS • 1969 • Yague Jesus • SPN
ESCOPETA NACIONAL, LA • 1978 • Berlanga Luis Garcia • SPN • NATIONAL SHOTGUN, THE ○ NATIONAL RIFLE, THE ○ SPANISH SHOTGUN, THE
ESCORPIAO ESCARLATE, O • 1989 • Cardoso Ivan • BRZ • SCARLET SCORPION, THE
ESCORT • 1915 • *Royal* • USA
ESCORT FOR HIRE • 1960 • Grayson Godfrey • UKN
ESCORT GIRLS • 1974 • Winter Donovan • UKN
ESCORT GIRLS see **HOPLA PA SENGEKANTEN** • 1976
ESCORT WEST • 1958 • Lyon Francis D. • USA
ESCROCS, LES see **QUAND PASSENT LES FAISANS** • 1965
ESCUADRILLA • 1941 • Roman Antonio • SPN
ESCUADRILLA DE VUELO • 1962 • Comeron Luis Jose • SPN
ESCUADRON 201 • 1945 • Salvador Jaime • MXC
ESCUADRON DE LA MORTE • 1985 • Gurrola Alfredo • MXC • DEATH SQUAD
ESCUADRON DEL PANICO, EL • 1966 • Mur Oti • SPN
ESCUCHA MI CANCION • 1959 • del Amo Antonio • SPN
ESCUDO DEL CONDOR, EL • 1988 • Palomares Luis • ANM • ARG • SHIELD OF THE CONDOR
ESCUELA DE ENFERMERAS • 1964 • de Ossorio Amando • SPN
ESCUELA DE MUSICA • 1955 • Zacarias Miguel • MXC
ESCUELA DE PERIODISMO • 1955 • Pascual Jesus • SPN
ESCUELA DE RATEROS • 1956 • Gonzalez Rogelio A. • MXC
ESCUELA DE SEDUCTORAS • 1962 • Klimovsky Leon • SPN
ESCUELA DE SORDOMUDOS • 1967 • Guzman Patricio • SPN • SCHOOL FOR DEAFMUTES
ESCUELA DE VAGABUNDOS • 1954 • Gonzalez Rogelio A. • MXC
ESCUELA DE VALIENTES • 1961 • Soler Julian • MXC • TIGRE, EL
ESCUELA DE VERANO • 1958 • Martinez Solares Gilberto • MXC
ESCUELA EN EL CAMPO, UNA • 1961 • Gomez Manuel Octavio • DOC • CUB
ESCUELA PARA CASADAS • 1949 • Zacarias Miguel • MXC
ESCUELA PARA SOLTERAS • 1964 • Zacarias Miguel • MXC • AGUILA CON LAS HERMANAS
ESCUELA PARA SUEGRAS • 1956 • Martinez Solares Gilberto • MXC
ESCUELA RURAL • 1960 • Almendros Nestor • DCS • CUB
ESCUELITA DEL RELAJO, LA • 1958 • Porter Julio • MXC
ESCULTERAL REVOLUTION see **BEIJO DE VIDA, O** • 1976
ESE LOCO AMOR LOCO • 1978 • Landeck Eva • ARG • THAT CRAZY, CRAZY LOVE
ESECUTORE OLTRE LA LEGGE (ITL) see **SEINS DE GLACE, LES** • 1974
ESECUTORI, GLI • 1976 • Lucidi Maurizio • ITL • SICILIAN CROSS, THE (UKN) ○ STREET PEOPLE (USA) ○ CROCE SICILIANA, LA ○ EXECUTORS, THE
ESEK A FIATALOK • 1967 • Banovich Tamas • HNG • OH, THESE POOR PEOPLE ○ THESE YOUNGSTERS
ESERCITO DI 5 UOMINI, UN • 1969 • Zingarelli Italo, Taylor Don • ITL • FIVE-MAN ARMY, THE (USA)
ESERCITO DI SCIPIONE, L' • 1978 • Berlinguer Giuliana • ITL
ESFINGE DE CRISTAL, LA (SPN) see **SFINGE D'ORO, LA** • 1967
ESFINGE MARAGATA, LA • 1948 • Obregon Antonio • SPN
ESFINGE SUMERGIDA, LA • 1968 • Alonso-Pesquera Jose • SPN
ESHATI PRODOSIA • 1970 • Glykofridis Panos • GRC • HIGH TREASON
ESHGHE GHAROON • 1968 • Bagheri Ebrahim • IRN • LOVE OF GHAROON, THE
ESILIATI DEL VOLGA, GLI • 1927 • Righelli Gennaro • ITL
ESKADRILYA N5 • 1939 • Room Abram • USS • SQUADRON NO.5 ○ FIVE SQUADRON
ESKAPADE • 1936 • Waschneck Erich • FRG • SEINE OFFIZIELLE FRAU
ESKIMAE DANCHI • 1961 • Hisamatsu Seiji • JPN • URBAN AFFAIR, AN
ESKIMO • 1930 • Schneevoigt George • DNM
ESKIMO • 1933 • Van Dyke W. S. • USA • MALA THE MAGNIFICENT (UKN)
ESKIMO, THE • 1919 • Kenton Erle C. • SHT • USA
ESKIMO, THE • 1922 • Summerville Slim • SHT • USA
ESKIMO, THE see **JUSTICE OF THE FAR NORTH** • 1925
ESKIMO LIMON • 1978 • Davidson Boaz • ISR • LEMON POPSICLE (USA)
ESKIMO LIMON 6 see **HAREEMU OHGEN LEMON POPSICLE 6** • 1984
ESKIMO NELL • 1974 • Campbell Martin • UKN
ESKIMO VILLAGE • 1933 • Anstey Edgar • DOC • UKN
ESKIMO WOMAN FEELS COLD see **ESZKIMO ASSZONY FAZIK** • 1984
ESKIMOBABY, DAS • 1916 • Schmidthassler Walter • FRG
ESKINITA 29 • 1968 • Osorio Consuelo P. • PHL • INTERIOR 29
ESKIYA CELLADI • 1967 • Conturk Remzi • TRK • OUTLAW'S HANGMAN
ESKIYA HALIL • 1968 • Heper Alp Zeki • TRK • HALIL THE BRIGAND ○ HAYDUT
ESKIYA KANI • 1968 • Figenli Yavuz • TRK • BRIGAND'S BLOOD ○ HAKIMO
ESMERALDA • 1915 • Kirkwood James • USA
ESMERALDA • 1917 • Falena Ugo • ITL
ESMERALDA • 1922 • Collins Edwin J. • UKN
ESMERALDA, LA • 1905 • Blache Alice • FRN
ESMERALDA, LA • 1905 • Jasset Victorin • FRN
ESODACSATAR, A • 1956 • Keleti Marton • HNG • FOOTBALL STAR, THE
ESOK MASIH ADA • 1979 • Shamsuddin Jins • MLY • HOPES FOR TOMORROW
ESOK UNTUK SIAPA • 1982 • Shamsuddin Jins • MLY
ESORCICCIO, L' • 1975 • Ingrassia Ciccio • ITL • EXORCIST – ITALIAN STYLE, THE (USA)
ESORCISTA N.2, L' see **URLO DALLE TENEBRE, UN** • 1975
ESOS DE PENJAMO • 1952 • Bustillo Oro Juan • MXC
ESOS HOMBRES! • 1936 • Aguilar Rolando • MXC • MALDITOS SEAN LOS HOMBRES
ESOS VASARNAP • 1962 • Keleti Marton • HNG • RAINY SUNDAY, A
ESOTIKA, EROTIKA, PSICOTIKA FAB • 1975 • Metzger Radley H. • USA
ESPACE D'UN CRI, L' • 1984 • Charles Freddy • BLG
ESPACE D'UN ETE, L' • 1980 • Melancon Andre • CND
ESPACE D'UN MATIN, L' • 1960 • Gobbi Sergio • FRN
ESPACE D'UN VIE, L' • 1949 • Dekeukeleire Charles • BLG
ESPACIO DE PLAYA • 1967 • Aguirre Javier • SHT • SPN
ESPACIO DOS • 1961 • Aguirre Javier • SHT • SPN
ESPADA DEL CID, LA see **SPADA DEL CID, LA** • 1962
ESPADA NEGRA, LA • 1976 • Rovira Beleta Francisco • SPN
ESPADA NORMANDA, LA (SPN) see **SPADA NORMANNA, LA** • 1971
ESPADACHIN, EL • 1963 • Martinez Arturo • MXC
ESPADACHINES DE LA REINA, LOS • 1960 • Rodriguez Roberto • MXC • QUEEN'S SWORDSMEN, THE (USA)
ESPADIN, EL • 1969 • Floralvalle • SHT • SPN • RAPIER, THE
ESPALDAS MOJADAS • 1953 • Galindo Alejandro • MXC • WETBACKS
ESPANA DEBE SABER • 1976 • Manzanos Eduardo • DOC • SPN • SPAIN OUGHT TO KNOW
ESPANA INSOLITA • 1964 • Aguirre Javier • SPN
ESPANA LEAL EN ARMAS • 1937 • Bunuel Luis (U/c) • SPN • MADRID 36
ESPANA OTRA VEZ • 1968 • Camino Jaime • SPN • SPAIN AGAIN (USA)
ESPANJANKAVIJAT • 1980 • Wahlforss Mikael • FNL • WAR WE LEFT BEHIND, THE
ESPANOLAS EN PARIS • 1970 • Bodegas Roberto • SPN • SPANISH GIRLS IN PARIS
ESPANOLEAR • 1969 • Balcazar Jaime Jesus • SPN
ESPANTO SURGE DE LA TUMBA, EL • 1972 • Aured Carlos • SPN • HORROR RISES FROM THE TOMB (USA)
ESPECIALISTA EN CHAMACAS • 1965 • Urueta Chano • MXC
ESPECIALISTA EN SENORAS • 1951 • Cahen Enrique • ARG
ESPECIALISTA EN SENORAS • 1951 • Morayta Miguel • MXC
ESPECTRO DE LA GUERRA • 1988 • Deshon Lacayo • NCR, CUB, MXC
ESPECTRO DE LA NOVIA, EL • 1943 • Cardona Rene • MXC
ESPECTRO DE TELEVICENTRO, EL see **VARIEDADES DE MEDIANOCHE** • 1959
ESPECTRO DEL ESTRANGULADOR, EL • 1963 • Cardona Rene • MXC • SANTO CONTRA EL ESPECTRO ○ GHOST OF THE STRANGLER, THE
ESPECTRO DEL TERROR ,EL • 1972 • Elorrieta Jose Maria • SPN
ESPECTROS DE TOLNIA, LOS • 1972 • Klimovsky Leon • SPN
ESPEJISMO • 1973 • Godoy Armando Robles • PRU • MIRAGE
ESPEJISMO DE LA CIUDAD • 1975 • *Conacine* • MXC
ESPEJO DE LA BRUJA, EL • 1960 • Urueta Chano • MXC • WITCH'S MIRROR, THE (USA) ○ MIRROR OF THE WITCH, THE
ESPEJOS DEL SILENCIO, LOS • 1989 • Fritz Sonia • DCS • PRC • MIRRORS OF SILENCE, THE
ESPELHO DE CARNE, O • 1984 • Fontoura Antonio Carlos • BRZ • MIRROR OF FLESH, THE
ESPERA, LA • 1956 • Lluch Vicente • SPN
ESPERADO AMOR DESESPERADO, EL • 1975 • Pastor Julian • MXC • EXPECTED AND UNEXPECTED LOVE, AN
ESPERAME • 1933 • Gasnier Louis J., Rey Florian • FRN, SPN
ESPERAME EN EL CIELO • 1988 • Mercero Antonio • SPN • WAIT FOR ME IN HEAVEN
ESPERAME MUCHO • 1982 • Jusid Juan Jose • ARG • KEEP WAITING FOR ME
ESPERANCE • 1969 • Ben Ammar Abdul Latif • SHT • TNS
ESPERANCE STORY, THE • 1969 • Thornhill Michael • DOC • ASL
ESPERANZA • 1967 • Andonov Ivan • ANS • BUL
ESPERANZA • 1972 • Alcoriza Luis • MXC
ESPERANZA • 1989 • Olhovich Sergio • MXC, USS • EXPECTATIONS
ESPERANZA LLAMADA BOLIVIA, UNA • Ruiz Jorge • DCS • BLV • HOPE NAMED BOLIVIA, A
ESPEREN LA LLEGADA DE HALLEWYN • 1972 • Bejo Miguel • ARG • WAIT FOR THE ARRIVAL OF HALLEWYN
ESPERIENZA DEL CURISMO, L' • 1949 • Pellegrini Glauco • SHT • ITL
ESPERIMENTO • 1978 • Torricella Edoardo • ITL
ESPIA QUE ENTROU EM FRIA, A • 1967 • Cherques Sanin • BRZ • FEMALE SPY WHO WENT INTO THE COLD, THE
ESPIANDO • 1966 • Ariza Francisco • SPN
ESPIAS MANTAN EL SILENCIO, LOS • 1966 • Caiano Mario • SPN, ITL, FRN • SPIE UCCIDONO IN SILENZIO, LE (ITL) ○ SPY STRIKES SILENTLY, THE ○ SPIES KILL SILENTLY
ESPINAS DE UNA FLOR • 1945 • Peon Ramon • MXC
ESPION, L' • 1966 • Levy Raoul J. • FRN, FRG • LAUTLOSE WAFFEN (FRG) ○ DEFECTOR, THE (USA)
ESPION LEVE-TOI • 1981 • Boisset Yves • FRN
ESPIONAGE • 1937 • Neumann Kurt • USA
ESPIONAGE • 1988 • Thomas Ramzi (Smithee Alan) • USA
ESPIONAGE AGENT • 1939 • Bacon Lloyd • USA
ESPIONAGE IN LISBON see **MISION LISBOA** • 1965
ESPIONAGE IN TANGIERS (USA) see **S 077 SPIONAGGIO A TANGERI** • 1965
ESPIONAGE INC. • 1967 • Wenceslao Jose Pepe • PHL

ESPIONAJE EN EL GOLFO • 1942 • Aguilar Rolando • MXC
ESPIONNAGE OU LA GUERRE SANS ARMES • 1928 • Choux Jean • FRN
ESPIONNE, L' • 1923 • Desfontaines Henri • FRN
ESPIONNE, L' • 1925 • Roudes Gaston • FRN
ESPIONNE AUX YEUX NOIRS, L' • 1925 • Desfontaines Henri • FRN
ESPIONNE SERA A NOUMEA, L' • 1960 • Peclet Georges • FRN
ESPIONS, LES • 1957 • Clouzot Henri-Georges • FRN, ITL
ESPIONS A L'AFFUT • 1966 • Pecas Max • FRN • HEAT OF MIDNIGHT ○ CHALEUR DE MINUIT, LA ○ HEAT AT MIDNIGHT
ESPIONS MEURENT A BEYROUTH, LES (FRN) see **SPIE UCCIDONO A BEIRUT, LE** • 1965
ESPIRITISMO • 1961 • Alazraki Benito • MXC • SPIRITISM (USA)
ESPIRITU DE LA COLMENA, EL • 1973 • Erice Victor • SPN • SPIRIT OF THE BEEHIVE, THE (USA)
ESPLORATI A CAVALLO • 1960 • Zane Angio • ITL
ESPLOSIONE DEL FORTINO B.12, L' • 1915 • Rosa Silvio Laurenti • ITL
ESPOIR • 1939 • Malraux Andre • FRN, SPN • SIERRA DE TERUEL (SPN) ○ MAN'S HOPE (UKN) ○ DAYS OF HOPE
ESPOIRS • 1940 • Rozier Willy • FRN • CHAMP MAUDIT, LE
ESPOLIO • 1970 • Goldsmith Sidney • ANM • CND
ESPONTANEO, EL • 1964 • Grau Jorge • SPN
ESPOSA DE DIA, AMANTE DE NOCHE • 1977 • Aguirre Javier • SPN
ESPOSA O AMANTE • 1959 • Blake Alfonso Corona • MXC, ARG
ESPOSA TE DOY • 1956 • Galindo Alejandro • MXC
ESPOSA Y AMANTE • 1977 • Fons Angelino • SPN
ESPOSAS INFIELES • 1955 • Diaz Morales Jose • MXC
ESPRIT DE FAMILLE, L' • 1978 • Blanc Jean-Pierre • FRN
ESPRIT DE FAMILLE, L' see **BONHEUR EN LOCATION** • 1948
ESPRIT DU MAL, L' • 1953 • Bigras Jean-Yves • CND
ESPRIT DU TEMPS, L' • 1981 • Mongredien Jean-Michel • FRN
ESPUELA, LA • 1976 • Fandino Roberto • SPN
ESPUELAS DE ORO • 1947 • Delgado Agustin P. • MXC
ESQUELETO DE LA SENORA MORALES, EL • 1959 • Gonzalez Rogelio A. • MXC • SKELETON OF MRS. MORALES, THE
ESQUILACHE • 1988 • Molina Josefina • SPN
ESQUIMAUX • 1972 • Blais Gilles • CND
ESQUINA BAJAN! • 1948 • Galindo Alejandro • MXC • CORNER, GETTING OFF!
ESQUINA DE MI BARRIO, LA • 1957 • Mendez Fernando • MXC
ESREFPASALI • 1966 • Tokatli Erdogan • TRK
ESSAI A LA MILLE • 1970 • Labrecque Jean-Claude • DCS • CND
ESSAI FILMIQUE SUR MUSIQUE JAPONAISE • 1974 • Gagnon Claude • JPN
ESSAI SUR L'AGRESSION • 1974 • Rivette Jacques • SHT • FRN
ESSAI SUR UN BARRAGE DANS LA VALLEE DE L'EUPHRATE see **NUHAWWALU SUDD AL-FURAT** • 1970
ESSANAY-CHAPLIN REVUE OF 1916, THE • 1916 • CMP • USA
ESSAY IN FILM • 1960 • Chapman Christopher • DOC • CND
ESSAY ON PORNOGRAPHY, AN • 1973 • Carey Chris • ASL
ESSAY ON REHEARSING, AN see **ETUDA O ZKOUSCE** • 1976
ESSAY ON SCIENCE, AN • 1962 • Cote Guy-L. • DCS • CND • CITE SAVANTE
ESSENCE, THE see **SUSMAN** • 1985
ESSENE • 1972 • Wiseman Frederick • DOC • USA
ESSENTIAL JOBS • 1942 • Rotha Paul • DOC • UKN
ESSERE DONNE • 1964 • Mangini Cecilia • SHT • ITL • TO BE WOMEN
ESSINGTON • 1976 • Pringle Julian • MTV • ASL
ESSO • 1954 • Alexeieff Alexandre • SHT • FRN
ESSOR, L' • 1920 • Burguet Charles • FRN
EST-CE BIEN RAISSONNABLE? • 1981 • Lautner Georges • FRN
EST-CE QU'ON A LE DROIT DE FAIRE UN SOLEIL? • 1968 • Dansereau Jean • SHT • CND
EST COUPABLE • 1917 • Volkov Alexander • USS
ESTA NOCHE NO • 1965 • Baledon Rafael • MXC
ESTA NOITE ENCARNAREI NO TEU CADAVER • 1967 • Marins Jose Mojica • BRZ • THIS NIGHT WILL MAKE YOUR CORPSE INCARNATE
ESTA NOITE ENCARNAREI SEU CADAVER • 1966 • Marins Jose Mojica • BRZ • TONIGHT I WILL PAINT IN FLESH-COLOR ○ TONIGHT I WILL ENTER YOUR CORPSE
ESTA QUE LO ES • 1975 • Fernandez Ramon • SPN
ESTA TIERRA ES MIA • 1960 • del Carril Hugo • ARG
ESTA TIERRA NUESTRA • 1959 • Alea Tomas Gutierrez • DOC • CUB • THIS LAND OF OURS
ESTACION CENTRAL • 1988 • Salgot Jose Antonio • SPN • CENTRAL STATION
ESTADO DE SITIO • 1971 • Chavarri Jaime • SHT • SPN
ESTAFA DE AMOR • 1954 • Delgado Miguel M. • MXC
ESTAMBUL 65 (SPN) see **COLPO GROSSO A GALATA BRIDGE** • 1965
ESTAMPAS ANTIGAS DE PORTUGAL • 1947 • Ribeiro Antonio Lopes • SHT • PRT
ESTAMPIDA • 1958 • de Anda Raul • MXC
ESTAMPIDA, LA • 1971 • Alvarez Santiago • DOC • CUB
ESTANCIA DEL GAUCHO CRUZ, LA • 1938 • Torres-Rios Leopoldo • ARG
ESTATE, L' • 1966 • Spinola Paolo • ITL
ESTATE CON SENTIMENTO, UN' • 1970 • Scarsella Roberto B. • ITL • WITHIN AND WITHOUT (UKN)
ESTATE IN QUATTRO, UN' see **VIOLENZA AL SOLE** • 1969
ESTATE OF INSANITY see **BLACK TORMENT, THE** • 1964
ESTATE STA FINENDO, L' • 1987 • Cortini Bruno • ITL • SUMMER IS NEARLY OVER
ESTATE VIOLENTA • 1959 • Zurlini Valerio • ITL, FRN • VIOLENT SUMMER (USA) ○ WIDOW IS WILLING, THE (USA) ○ ETE VIOLENT (FRN)
ESTATUA, LA • 1957 • Gamboa Jose Luis • SPN
ESTATUA DE CARNE, LA • 1951 • Urueta Chano • MXC
ESTATUAS DE LISBOA • 1932 • de Oliveira Manoel • PRT • STATUES OF LISBON, THE
ESTE AMOR SI ES AMOR • 1962 • Toussaint Carlos • MXC
ESTER OCH ALBERT see **UNG MAN SOKER SALLSKAP** • 1954
ESTERBROOK CASE, THE • 1915 • Johnston Lorimer • USA
ESTERINA • 1959 • Lizzani Carlo • ITL
ESTHAPPAN • 1979 • Aravindan G. • IND
ESTHER • 1910 • Feuillade Louis • FRN
ESTHER • 1913 • Andreani Henri • FRN
ESTHER • 1916 • Elvey Maurice • UKN
ESTHER AND THE KING (USA) see **ESTHER E IL RE** • 1961
ESTHER AND THE MEN see **MI LESZ VELED ESZTERKE?** • 1968
ESTHER E IL RE • 1961 • Walsh Raoul, Bava Mario • ITL • ESTHER AND THE KING (USA)
ESTHER REDEEMED • 1915 • Morgan Sidney • UKN
ESTHER, RUTH & JENNIFER see **NORTH SEA HIJACK** • 1980
ESTHER WATERS • 1948 • Dalrymple Ian, Proud Peter • UKN • SIN OF ESTHER WATERS, THE
ESTIMADO SENOR JUEZ • 1978 • Lazaga Pedro • SPN
ESTO ES ALEGRIA! • 1967 • Carreras Enrique • ARG • THIS IS FUN!
ESTORETA VELLETA, UNA • 1971 • Aznar Tomas • SHT • SPN
ESTOS ANOS VIOLENTOS • 1959 • Diaz Morales Jose • MXC
ESTOS Y AQUELLOS • 1970 • Villafuerte Santiago • DOC • CUB
ESTOUFFADE A LA CARAIBE • 1966 • Besnard Jacques • FRN, ITL • PAGATI PER MORIRE (ITL) ○ LOOTERS, THE (UKN) ○ GOLD ROBBERS
ESTOY CASADO JA..! JA..! • 1961 • Delgado Miguel M. • MXC
ESTOY EN CRISIS • 1983 • Colomo Fernando • SPN • I HAVE A CRISIS
ESTOY HECHO UN CHAVAL • 1975 • Lazaga Pedro • SPN
ESTOY TAAAN ENAMORADA • 1954 • Salvador Jaime • MXC
ESTRABURGO DE CHILE • 1980 • Avril Philippe • DOC • FRN
ESTRADA 62 • 1962 • Perski Ludwik • DOC • PLN • CONCERT HALL 62
ESTRADA DA VIDA • 1968 • Campos Henrique • PRT • A ESTRADA DA VIDA ○ ROAD OF LIFE
ESTRADA DA VIDA, A • 1943 • Duarte Arthur • SHT • PRT
ESTRANGEIRA, A • 1983 • Grilo Joao Mario • PRT
ESTRANGEMENT • 1914 • Eagle Oscar • USA
ESTRANGER -OH! DE LA CALLE CRUZ DEL SUR, EL • 1985 • Grau Jorge • SPN • STRANGER FROM CRUZ DEL SUR STREET
ESTRANGULADORES, OS • 1906 • Leal Antonio?, Sandenberg Isaac? • BRZ
ESTRANHA HISTORIA DE AMOR, UMA • 1980 • Doo John • BRZ • STRANGE LOVE STORY, A
ESTRANHO ENCONTRO • 1958 • Khouri Walter Hugo • BRZ
ESTRANHO MUNDO DE ZE DO CAIXAO, O • 1969 • Marins Jose Mojica • BRZ • STRANGE WORLD OF ZE DO CAIXAO, THE
ESTRATEGIA DEL CARACOL • 1989 • Cabrera Sergio • CLM • SNAIL'S STRATEGY
ESTRATEGIA MATRIMONIO • 1966 • Gout Alberto • MXC • COMO CASARSE CON UN MILLONARIO
ESTRATTO DAGLI ARCHIVI SEGRETI DELLA POLIZIA DI UNA CAPITALE EUROPEA • 1972 • Freda Riccardo • ITL
ESTRELA NULA, A • 1984 • Martins Icaro, Garcia Jose Antonio • BRZ • NAKED STAR, THE
ESTRELA SOBE, A • 1974 • Barreto Bruno • BRZ
ESTRELLA • 1913 • Stafl Otakar, Urban Max • CZC
ESTRELLA DE SIERRA MORENA, LA • 1952 • Torrado Ramon • SPN
ESTRELLA SIN LUZ • 1952 • Cortazar Ernesto • MXC
ESTRELLA VACIA, LA • 1958 • Gomez Muriel Emilio • MXC • EMPTY STAR, THE (USA)
ESTRELLA Y DOS ESTRALLADOS, UNA • 1959 • Martinez Solares Gilberto • MXC
ESTRELLADOS • 1930 • Sedgwick Edward • USA
ESTRELLAS DE BUENOS AIRES • 1956 • Land Kurt • ARG
ESTRELLAS ESTAN VERDE, LAS • 1973 • Lazaga Pedro • SPN
ESTRELLAS, LAS • 1961 • Lluch Miguel • SPN
ESTRELLITA • 1910 • Maggi Luigi • ITL
ESTRELLITA • 1938 • Cardona Rene • MXC
ESTUARY, THE see **KAKO** • 1961
ESTUDIO AMUEBLADO 2-P • 1969 • Forque Jose Maria • SPN
ESTUDIOS PARA UN RETRATO • 1978 • Castanedo R., Goded A., Leduc Paul • SHT • MXC
ESZKIMO ASSZONY FAZIK • 1984 • Xantus Janos • HNG • ESKIMO WOMAN FEELS COLD
ESZMELES • 1985 • Grunwalsky Ferenc • HNG • REALISATION
ESZTERHAZA MUZSIKUSA, HAYDN • 1960 • Takacs Gabor • HNG • PRINCE'S COURT MUSICIAN, HAYDN, THE ○ JOSEPH HAYDN ○ HAYDN
ESZTERKE see **MI LESZ VELED ESZTERKE?** • 1968
ESZTERKONYV • 1989 • Deak Krisztina • HNG • BOOK OF ESTHER, THE
ET AVEC CA, MADAME see **SCANDALE AUX GALERIES, UN** • 1937
ET BUDSKA TIL NAPOLEON PA ELBA • 1909 • Larsen Viggo • DNM • NAPOLEON ON THE ISLAND OF ELBA
ET CETERA see **ETCETERA** • 1966
ET DE NOVEAU LE MATIN • 1961 • Kazansky Gennadi • USS
ET DEMAIN.. see **WA GHADAN..** • 1972
ET DIEU CREA LA FEMME • 1956 • Vadim Roger • FRN • AND GOD CREATED WOMAN (USA) ○ AND WOMAN.. WAS CREATED (UKN)
ET DIEU CREA LES HOMMES • Estienne Jean • FRN
...ET DIEU CREA L'ETE! • 1974 • Fournier Claude, Raymond Marie-Josee • DCS • CND
ET DIX DE DER • 1947 • Hennion Robert • FRN
ET DOGN MED ILSE • 1971 • Hovmand Annelise • DNM • PRIVATE PARTY
ET DU FILS • 1971 • Garceau Raymond • CND
ET IL VOULUT ETRE UN FEMME • Ricaud Michel • DOC • FRN
ET LA FEMME CREA L'AMOUR • 1964 • Collin Fabien • FRN
ET LA LUMIERE FUT • 1989 • Ioseliani Otar • FRN, FRG, ITL • AND THEN THERE WAS LIGHT (UKN)
ET LA NEIGE N'ETAIT PLUS • 1965 • Samb Ababacar • SNL • AND THE SNOW WAS NO MORE
ET LA TENDRESSE? ...BORDEL! • 1978 • Schulmann Patrick • FRN
ET LA TERREUR COMMENCE see **NEW YORK NE REPOND PAS** • 1977
ET L'ON REVIENT TOUJOURS • 1917 • Rivers Fernand • FRN
ET MOI J'TE DIS QU'ELLE T'A FAIT D' L'OEIL • 1950 • Gleize Maurice • FRN
ET MOI J'TE DIS QU'ELLE T'A FAIT DE L'OEIL • 1935 • Forrester Jack • FRN • J'TE DIS QU'ELLE T'A FAIT DE L'OEIL
ET MOURIR DE DESIR • 1973 • Bastia Jean • FRN
ET MOURIR DE PLAISIR • 1960 • Vadim Roger • FRN, ITL • SANGUE E LA ROSA, IL (ITL) ○ BLOOD AND ROSES (USA) ○ AND DIE OF PLEASURE ○ SANG ET LA ROSE, LE
ET PAR ICI LA SORTIE • 1957 • Rozier Willy • FRN
ET POURQUOI PAS? • 1969 • Beaudin Jean • DCS • CND
ET POURTANT, ELLE TOURNE • 1980 • Raoul-Duval Francois • FRN
ET PUIS APRES • 1974 • Dansereau Fernand, Rossignol Yolande • SHT • CND
ET QU'CA SAUTE! • 1970 • Lefranc Guy • FRN
ET RAAT • 1968 • Nath Raj • IND • ONE NIGHT
ET REVOLUTIONS BRYLLUP • 1909 • Larsen Viggo • DNM
ET ROULE LE MONDE • 1954 • Masson Jean • SHT • FRN
ET SATAN CONDUIT LE BAL • 1962 • Dabat Grisha M. • FRN • SATAN LEADS THE DANCE
ET SI NOUS BUVIONS UN COUP see **SI NOUS BUVIONS UN COUP** • 1909
ET SI ON FAISANT L'AMOUR (FRN) see **SCUSI, FACCIAMO L'AMORE?** • 1968
ET SPOKELSE FORELSKER SEG • 1947 • Ibsen Tancred • NRW • GHOST IN LOVE, A (USA) ○ AMOROUS GHOST, AN
ET TA SOEUR.. • 1951 • Lepage Henri • FRN
ET TA SOEUR • 1958 • Delbez Maurice • FRN
ET TU OTTO • 1962 • Kneitel Seymour • ANS • USA
ET VIVE LA LIBERTE • 1977 • Korber Serge • FRN
ET ZEUS SE GRATTA LA CUISSE • 1964 • Dumoulin Georges • FRN
ETA BYLO V DONBASE • 1945 • Lukov Leonid • USS • IT HAPPENED IN DONBAS
ETA CRITICA, L' • 1921 • Palermi Amleto • ITL
ETA DEL FERRO, L' • 1964 • Rossellini Renzo Jr. • DOC • ITL • IRON AGE, THE (USA)
ETA DEL MALESSERE, L' • 1968 • Biagetti Giuliano • ITL • LOVE PROBLEMS (USA) ○ AGE OF UNEASINESS, THE
ETA DELLA PACE, L' • 1974 • Carpi Fabio • ITL • AGE OF PEACE, THE
ETA DELL'AMORE, L' • 1953 • De Felice Lionello • ITL, FRN • TOO YOUNG FOR LOVE (USA) ○ AGE DE L'AMOUR, L' (FRN) ○ AGE OF INDISCRETION, THE
ETA DI COSIMO DE' MEDICI, L' • 1972 • Rossellini Roberto • MTV • ITL • AGE OF THE MEDICI (USA)
ETALON, L' • 1970 • Mocky Jean-Pierre • FRN
ETANG, L' • 1978 • Cayeux Jean-Paul • FRN
ETANG, L' see **WORLD IN A MARSH** • 1955
ETANG TRAGIQUE, L'(FRN) see **SWAMP WATER** • 1941
ETAPES DE LA SCULPTURE EN EGYPTE, LES • 1960 • Shawqi Khalil • SHT • EGY
ETAPES ET RENCONTRES INTERNATIONALES • 1953 • Tessier Albert • DOC • CND
ETAPPENHASE, DER • 1937 • Stockel Joe • FRG
ETAT DE BONHEUR.. PERMANENT!, L' • 1981 • Koleva Maria • FRN
ETAT DE SIEGE • 1972 • Costa-Gavras • FRN, ITL, FRG • STATE OF SIEGE (UKN) ○ AMERIKANO, L' (ITL)
ETAT SAUVAGE, L' • 1978 • Girod Francis • FRN
ETATS D'AME • 1985 • Fansten Jacques • FRN
ETATS GENERAUX DU CINEMA, LES • 1969 • Derkaoui Mustafa • DCS • FRN
ETAU, L' • 1918 • Negroni Baldassare • ITL
ETC. • 1975 • Breer Robert • USA
ETCETCETC.. • 1972 • UKN
ETCETERA • 1966 • Svankmajer Jan • ANS • CZC • ET CETERA
ETE, L' • 1968 • Bex Ludo • SHT • BLG
ETE, L' • 1968 • Hanoun Marcel • FRN
ETE A SAINT-TROPEZ, UN • 1981 • Hamilton David • FRN • SUMMER IN SAINT TROPEZ, A
ETE AMERICAIN, UN • 1969 • Chapier Henri • DOC • FRN
ETE AND ALI • Kahane Peter • GDR
ETE DE NOS QUINZE ANS, L' • 1982 • Jullian Marcel • FRN
ETE D'ENFER, UN • 1984 • Schock Michael • FRN
ETE EN PENTE DOUCE, L' • 1986 • Krawczyk Gerard • FRN
ETE INDIEN, L' • 1957 • Reichenbach Francois • SHT • FRN
ETE INDIEN, L' • 1977 • Delannoy Jean • MTV • FRN
ETE MEURTRIER, UN • 1983 • Becker Jean • FRN • ONE DEADLY SUMMER (USA)
ETE PAS COMME LES AUTRES, UN see **JULIE ETAIT BELLE** • 1976
ETE PROCHAIN, L' • 1985 • Trintignant Nadine • FRN • NEXT SUMMER (USA)
ETE SAUVAGE, UN • 1970 • Camus Marcel • FRN
ETE TORRIDE, UN • 1965 • Borowczyk Walerian • ANS • FRN
ETE VIOLENT (FRN) see **ESTATE VIOLENTA** • 1959
ETERNA AGONIA • 1949 • Soler Julian • MXC
ETERNA CATENA, L' • 1956 • Majano Anton Giulio • ITL • ETERNAL CHAINS (USA) ○ ETERNAL CHAIN, THE
ETERNA FEMMINA see **AMANTE DI PARIDE, L'** • 1955
ETERNA MARTIR • 1937 • Orol Juan • MXC
ETERNA SONRISA DE NEW JERSEY • 1988 • Sorin Carlos • ARG, UKN • EVERSMILE NEW JERSEY (UKN) ○ ETERNAL NEW JERSEY SMILE
ETERNAL AMOUR, L' • 1921 • Colombani Gaston • FRN
ETERNAL BONDS (USA) see **EVIGA LANKAR** • 1947
ETERNAL CAUSE see **KAIGUN TOKUBETSU SHONEN HEI** • 1972
ETERNAL CHAIN, THE see **ETERNA CATENA, L'** • 1956
ETERNAL CHAINS (USA) see **ETERNA CATENA, L'** • 1956
ETERNAL CHALLENGE, THE • 1916 • *Aubrey Helen* • SHT • USA
ETERNAL CHILDREN • 1959 • Haldane Don • CND
ETERNAL CITY, THE • 1915 • Porter Edwin S., Ford Hugh • USA

ETERNAL CITY, THE • 1923 • Fitzmaurice George • USA

ETERNAL CONFLICT, THE • 1912 • *Rex* • USA

ETERNAL DANCE see **ELETBE TANCOLTATOTT LANY** • 1964

ETERNAL DUEL, THE • 1914 • Bracken Bertram • USA

ETERNAL ECSTASY see **MAIN CHAUDE, LA** • 1959

ETERNAL EVIL see **BLUE MAN, THE** • 1986

ETERNAL FEMININE, THE • 1915 • Nicholls George • SHT • USA

ETERNAL FEMININE, THE • 1931 • Varney-Serrao Arthur • UKN

ETERNAL FIRE, THE • 1937-40 • *Cardiff Jack (Ph)* • DCS • UKN

ETERNAL FLAME, THE • 1922 • Lloyd Frank • USA • DUCHESS OF LANGEAIS, THE

ETERNAL FOOLS • 1930 • Goldin Sidney M. • USA • EWIGE NARANIM

ETERNAL GENERATION, THE see **ONNA NO SONO** • 1954

ETERNAL GRIND, THE • 1916 • O'Brien John B. • USA

ETERNAL HAT, THE • 1968 • Rotmil Charles • SHT • USA

ETERNAL HEART, THE see **CHIBUSA YO EIEN NARE** • 1955

ETERNAL HUSBAND, THE (USA) see **HOMME AU CHAPEAU ROND, L'** • 1946

ETERNAL LIFE see **YABUREZARU MONO** • 1964

ETERNAL LIGHT see **AMAR JYOTI** • 1936

ETERNAL LIGHT, THE • 1919 • *Catholic Art Association* • USA

ETERNAL LINKS see **EVIGA LANKAR** • 1947

ETERNAL LOVE • 1917 • Gerrard Douglas • USA

ETERNAL LOVE • 1929 • Lubitsch Ernst • USA • KING OF THE MOUNTAINS

ETERNAL LOVE see **EIEN NO HITO** • 1961

ETERNAL LOVE see **LIANG SHAN-PO YU CHU YING-T'AI** • 1963

ETERNAL LOVE see **ZANSETSU** • 1968

ETERNAL LOVE see **MYITTAR ATHIN-CHE** • 1982

ETERNAL MAGDALENE, THE • 1919 • Hopkins Arthur • USA

ETERNAL MASCULINE, THE • 1912 • *Prior Herbert* • USA

ETERNAL MASK, THE (USA) see **EWIGE MASKE, DIE** • 1935

ETERNAL MELODIES see **MELODIE ETERNE** • 1940

ETERNAL MOTHER, THE • 1912 • Griffith D. W. • USA

ETERNAL MOTHER, THE • 1917 • Reicher Frank • USA

ETERNAL MOTHER, THE • 1921 • Davis Will S. • USA

ETERNAL MUSIC • 1937 • Bose Hiren • IND

ETERNAL NEW JERSEY SMILE see **ETERNA SONRISA DE NEW JERSEY** • 1988

ETERNAL PEACE • 1922 • *Harte Betty* • USA

ETERNAL PEACE see **PAX AETERNA** • 1916

ETERNAL PRAGUE • 1941 • Weiss Jiri • DOC • UKN

ETERNAL QUESTION, THE • 1916 • King Burton L. • USA

ETERNAL RAINBOW, THE see **KONO TEN NO NIJI** • 1958

ETERNAL RENAISSANCE • 1966 • Kollanyi Agoston • HNG

ETERNAL RETURN, THE (USA) see **ETERNEL RETOUR, L'** • 1943

ETERNAL ROAD, THE see **ROUTE ETERNELLE, LA**

ETERNAL SACRIFICE, THE • 1913 • *Reliance* • USA

ETERNAL SAPHO, THE • 1916 • Bracken Bertram • USA • ETERNAL SAPPHO, THE ○ BOHEMIA

ETERNAL SAPPHO, THE see **ETERNAL SAPHO, THE** • 1916

ETERNAL SEA, THE • 1955 • Auer John H. • USA

ETERNAL SIN, THE • 1917 • Brenon Herbert • USA • LUCRETIA BORGIA

ETERNAL STRUGGLE, THE • 1923 • Barker Reginald • USA • MAN THOU GAVEST ME, THE ○ MASTER OF WOMAN, THE

ETERNAL SUMMER • 1961 • Hearn J. Van • USA

ETERNAL TEMPTRESS, THE • 1917 • Chautard Emile • USA

ETERNAL THREE, THE • 1923 • Neilan Marshall, Urson Frank • USA

ETERNAL TIDAL RACE see **PULSSCHLAG DES MEERES** • 1938

ETERNAL TIMES • 1975 • Shopov Assen • BUL

ETERNAL TREE see **OLMEZ AGACI** • 1985

ETERNAL TRIANGLE, THE • 1910 • Salter Harry • USA

ETERNAL TRIANGLE, THE • 1917 • Wilson Frank • UKN

ETERNAL TRIANGLE, THE • 1919 • Dawn Norman • SHT • USA

ETERNAL TRIANGLE, THE • 1922 • *Terry Paul* • ANS • USA

ETERNAL TRIANGLE, THE • 1925 • Butler Alexander • UKN

ETERNAL TRUTH, THE • 1916 • *Supreme* • USA

ETERNAL WALTZ, THE (USA) see **EWIGER WALZER** • 1954

ETERNAL WAY, THE • 1916 • Elfelt Clifford S. • SHT • USA

ETERNAL WOMAN, THE • 1929 • McCarthy John P. • USA

ETERNAL YOUTH see **WEST POINT** • 1927

ETERNAL YOUTH see **WEST POINT** • 1928

ETERNALLY PAGU see **ETERNAMENTE PAGU** • 1988

ETERNALLY YOURS • 1939 • Garnett Tay • USA

ETERNAMENTE PAGU • 1988 • Bengell Norma • BRZ • ETERNALLY PAGU

ETERNEL CONFLIT • 1947 • Lampin Georges • FRN • LILI

ETERNEL ESPOIR • 1951 • Joly Max • FRN

ETERNEL RETOUR, L' • 1943 • Delannoy Jean • FRN • ETERNAL RETURN, THE (USA) ○ LOVE ETERNAL (UKN)

ETERNITE POUR NOUS, L' see **CRI DE LA CHAIR, LE** • 1963

ETERNITY FOR US see **CRI DE LA CHAIR, LE** • 1963

ETERNITY OF LOVE see **WAKARATE IKIRU TOKI MO** • 1961

ETES-VOUS FIANCEE A UN MARIN GREC OU A UN PILOTE DE LIGNE? • 1970 • Aurel Jean • FRN

ETES-VOUS JALOUSE? • 1937 • Chomette Henri • FRN

ETHEL GAINS CONSENT • 1915 • *Tincher Fay* • USA

ETHEL GETS THE EVIDENCE • 1915 • *Tincher Fay* • USA

ETHEL HAS A STEADY • 1914 • *Tincher Fay* • USA

ETHEL HOOK • 1926 • *Deforest Phonofilms* • SHT • UKN

ETHEL SMITH AND THE HENRY KING ORCHESTRA • 1950 • *Universal* • SHT • USA

ETHEL'S BURGLAR • 1915 • MacQuarrie Murdock • USA

ETHEL'S DANGER • 1912 • Haldane Bert? • UKN

ETHEL'S DEADLY ALARM CLOCK • 1915 • *Booth Elmer* • USA

ETHEL'S DISGUISE • 1915 • *Tincher Fay* • USA

ETHEL'S DOGGONE LUCK • 1915 • Dillon Eddie • USA

ETHEL'S FIRST CASE • 1915 • *Komic* • USA

ETHEL'S LUNCHEON • 1909 • *Browning Ethel* • USA

ETHEL'S NEW DRESS • 1915 • *Tincher Fay* • USA

ETHEL'S ROMANCE • 1915 • *Komic* • USA

ETHEL'S ROMEOS • 1915 • Middleton Edwin • USA

ETHEL'S ROOF PARTY • 1914 • *Komic* • USA

ETHEL'S SACRIFICE • 1912 • *Charles John* • USA

ETHEL'S TEACHER • 1914 • *Komic* • USA

ETHER SHIP see **SHIP OF THE ETHER** • 1935

ETHICS OF THE PROFESSION, THE • 1914 • Vale Travers • USA

ETHIOPIA, DIARY OF A VICTORY see **ETIOPIA, CRONICA DE UNA VICTORIA** • 1979

ETHIRIGAL JAGGIRITHAI • 1967 • Sundaram R. • IND • BEWARE OF THE ENEMY

ETHNIC BROADCASTING • 1978 • Blagg Linda • DOC • ASL

ETHNOCIDE see **ETNOCIDIO** • 1976

ETHNOGRAPHICAL MUSEUM see **SKANSEN** • 1978

ETIENNE • 1933 • Tarride Jean • FRN

ETIENNE BRULE GIBIER DE POTENCE • 1952 • Turner Melburn E. • CND

ETIENNE ET SARA • 1984 • Hebert Pierre • CND

ETIENNE OF THE GLAD HEART • 1914 • Campbell Colin • USA

ETINCELLE, L' • 1983 • Lang Michel • FRN, UKN

ETIOPIA, CRONICA DE UNA VICTORIA • 1979 • Fleitas Miguel • DOC • CUB • ETHIOPIA, DIARY OF A VICTORY

ETIQUETTE • 1924 • Seiler Lewis, Stoloff Ben • SHT • USA

ETIRAGE DES AMPOULES ELECTRIQUES, L' • 1924 • Gremillon Jean • SHT • FRN

ETIUDA SPORTOWA • 1965 • Trzos-Rastawiecki Andrzej • DOC • PLN • SPORT ETUDE

ETNA, L' • 1976 • Tazieff Haroun • DOC • FRN

ETNOCIDIO • 1976 • Leduc Paul • DOC • CND, MXC • ETNOCIDIO: NOTAS SOBRE EL MEZQUITAL ○ ETHNOCIDE

ETNOCIDIO: NOTAS SOBRE EL MEZQUITAL see **ETNOCIDIO** • 1976

ETO LOSHADI • 1965 • Okeyev Tolomush • USS • THESE ARE HORSES ○ HORSES

ETO NACHINADOS TAK.. • 1956 • Kulidjanov Lev, Segel Yakov • USS • THIS IS HOW IT BEGAN.. ○ IT STARTED LIKE THIS

ETO SLADKOE SLOVO-SVOBODA • 1973 • Zalakevicius Vitautus • USS • THIS SWEET WORD -FREEDOM ○ THAT SWEET WORD "FREEDOM"

ETOCK • 1974 • Valcour Pierre, Hebert Y. • DOC • CND

ETOILE • 1988 • Del Monte Peter • ITL

ETOILE AU SOLEIL, UNE • 1942 • Zwobada Andre • FRN

ETOILE AUX DENTS, L' • 1971 • Berkani Deri • FRN • POULOU LE MAGNIFIQUE

ETOILE DE MER, L' • 1928 • Ray Man • SHT • FRN

ETOILE DE MER, L' • 1959 • Bourguignon Serge • FRN

ETOILE DE VALENCIA, L' • 1933 • de Poligny Serge • FRN

ETOILE DISPARAIT, UNE • 1932 • Villers Robert • FRN • STAR DISAPPEARS, A (USA) ○ ETOILE EST MORTE, UNE ○ ETOILE S'ETAIENT, UNE

ETOILE DU NORD, L' • Sarde Alain • FRN

ETOILE DU NORD, L' • 1982 • Granier-Deferre Pierre • FRN • NORTHERN STAR, THE (USA)

ETOILE DU SUD, L' (FRN) see **SOUTHERN STAR, THE** • 1969

ETOILE EST MORTE, UNE see **ETOILE DISPARAIT, UNE** • 1932

ETOILE NOIRE, L' • 1973 • Djingareye Maiga • NGR

ETOILE SANS LUMIERE • 1945 • Blistene Marcel • FRN • STAR WITHOUT LIGHT (USA)

ETOILE S'ETAIENT, UNE see **ETOILE DISPARAIT, UNE** • 1932

ETOILES DE MIDI, LES • 1958 • Ertaud Jacques, Ichac Marcel • DOC • FRN

ETOILES EN CROISETTE • 1955 • Guillon Jacques • DCS • FRN

ETOILES ET TEMPETES • 1955 • Rebuffat Gaston • DOC • FRN

ETOILES NE MEURENT JAMAIS, LES • 1957 • de Vaucorbeil Max • FRN

ETOILES NUCLEAIRES • 1961 • Pessis Georges • DCS • FRN

ETRANGE AFFAIRE, UNE • 1981 • Granier-Deferre Pierre • FRN

ETRANGE AMAZONE, L' • 1975 • Vallee Jean • FRN

ETRANGE AVENTURE, L' • 1922 • Hamman Joe • FRN

ETRANGE AVENTURE DE ISABELLA, L' • Marischka Franz • ITL, FRG

ETRANGE AVENTURE DU DOCTEUR WORK, L' • 1921 • Saidreau Robert • FRN

ETRANGE AVENTURE DU DOCTEUR WORK, L' • 1924 • Herve Jean • FRN

ETRANGE DESIR DE M. BARD, L' • 1953 • von Radvanyi Geza • FRN • STRANGE DESIRE OF MONSIEUR BARD, THE

ETRANGE DESTIN • 1945 • Cuny Louis • FRN

ETRANGE ENIGME DES ORANG KUBUS, L' • 1971-74 • Floquet Francois • DOC • CND

ETRANGE FIANCEE, L' • 1930 • Pallu Georges • FRN

ETRANGE HISTOIRE DE GILLES DE RAIS, L' see **IMAGES A PROPOS DE "ENLUMINURES AUTOUR DES MINUTES DU PROCES DE GILLES DE RAIS"** • 1975

ETRANGE M. VICTOR, L' • 1937 • Gremillon Jean • FRN • STRANGE MR. VICTOR, THE (UKN)

ETRANGE MADAME CLAPAIN, L' see **SECRET DE MADAME CLAPAIN, LE** • 1943

ETRANGE MADAME X, L' • 1950 • Gremillon Jean • FRN • ENIGMATIQUE MADAME UNTEL, L'

ETRANGE MONSIEUR STEVE, L' • 1957 • Bailly Raymond • FRN • MR. STEVE (USA) ○ PLUS MORT QUE VIF

ETRANGE MORT DE MONSIEUR CRAUQUAL, L' see **GOSSES MENENT L'ENQUETE, LES** • 1946

ETRANGE NUIT DE NOEL, L' • 1939 • Noe Yvan • FRN

ETRANGE SUZY, L' • 1941 • Ducis Pierre-Jean • FRN

ETRANGE VOYAGE, UN • 1981 • Cavalier Alain • FRN

ETRANGER, L' see **GHARIB, EL** • 1955

ETRANGER, L' (FRN) see **STRANIERO, LO** • 1967

ETRANGERE, L' • 1930 • Ravel Gaston • FRN

ETRANGERE, L' • 1968 • Gobbi Sergio • FRN • SEX WITH A STRANGER

ETRANGERS see **GHURUBA'** • 1973

ETRANGERS, LES • 1968 • Desagnat Jean-Pierre • FRN, ITL, FRG • QUELLI CHE SANNO UCCIDERE (ITL) ○ GEIER KONNEN WARTEN (FRG)

ETRANGLEUR, L' • 1970 • Vecchiali Paul • FRN

ETRE ANALPHABETE A 20 ANS see **JEUNE SAIT PAS LIRE** • 1985

ETRE LIBRE • 1968 • Bertault Paul, Jauvert Claude, Bourlat Jean-Claude, Lefebvre Catherine, Dianoux Robert, Glasbert Jimmy • FRN • ETRE LIBRE -AVIGNON 68

ETRE LIBRE -AVIGNON 68 see **ETRE LIBRE** • 1968

ETRE OU NE PAS ETRE • 1922 • Leprince Rene • FRN

ETREINTE, L' • 1969 • Drouot Pierre, Collet Paul • BLG • GISELE (UKN)

ETREINTE DE LA STATUE, L' • 1908 • Jasset Victorin • FRN

ETREINTE DU PASSE, L' • 1918 • Perret Leonce • FRN

ETRENNES A TRAVERS LES AGES, LES • 1925 • Colombier Piere • FRN

ETRENNES DE BOUT DE ZAN, LES • 1913 • Feuillade Louis • FRN

ETRUSCANS KILL AGAIN, THE see **ETRUSCO UCCIDE ANCORA, L'** • 1972

ETRUSCO UCCIDE ANCORA, L' • 1972 • Crispino Armando • ITL, FRG, YGS • DEAD ARE ALIVE, THE (USA) ○ ETRUSCANS KILL AGAIN, THE

ETSI GENNITHIKE MIA MEGALI AGAPI • 1968 • Rabenalt Arthur M. • GRC • THUS GREW A GREAT LOVE ○ GREAT LOVE, A

ETSURAKU • 1965 • Oshima Nagisa • JPN • PLEASURES OF THE FLESH, THE

ETTA OF THE FOOTLIGHTS • 1914 • Costello Maurice, Gaillord Robert • USA

ETTARO DI CIELO, UN • 1959 • Casadio Aglauco • ITL

ETTEHAM, EL • 1937 • *Hafez Bahija* • EGY • ACCUSATION, THE

ETTER RUBICON • 1987 • Risan Leidulv • NRW • RUBICON

ETTERKRIGSTID • 1982 • Skagen Solve, Wadman Malte • NRW

ETTORE FIERAMOSCA • 1909 • Pasquali Ernesto Maria • ITL

ETTORE FIERAMOSCA • 1938 • Blasetti Alessandro • ITL

ETTORE LO FUSTO • 1972 • Castellari Enzo G. • ITL, FRN, SPN • RAPTO DE ELENA, LA DELENTE ITALIANA, EL ○ HECTOR LE FORTICHE ○ HECTOR THE MIGHTY ○ PROXENETES, LES

ETUDA • 1962 • Hofman Eduard • ANS • PLN

ETUDA O ZKOUSCE • 1976 • Schorm Evald • CZC • CZECHOSLOVAK PHILHARMONIC ORCHESTRA ○ ESSAY ON REHEARSING, AN

ETUDE • 1959 • Gaal Istvan • SHT • ITL

ETUDE • 1961 • Kamler Piotr • ANS • FRN

ETUDE • 1970 • Greenwald Barry • CND

ETUDE 021 • 1956 • Puttemans Pierre • BLG

ETUDE ABOUT A WORKING DAY see **STUDY OF A WORKING DAY** • 1961

ETUDE ANATOMIQUE DU PHOTOGRAPHE • 1961 • Hirsch Hy • FRN

ETUDE CINEMATOGRAPHIQUE SUR UNE ARABESQUE • 1928 • Dulac Germaine • FRN • ARABESQUE

ETUDE EN 21 POINTS • 1968 • Bobet Jacques • CND

ETUDE VOOR LOUIZA SEULE • 1969 • Collet Paul, Drouot Pierre • BLG

ETUDES • 1963 • Grospierre Louis • SHT • FRN

ETUDES DE MOUVEMENTS • 1928 • Ivens Joris • SHT • FRN • STUDIES IN MOVEMENT (USA)

ETUDES DE RHYTHME RAPIDE • 1924 • Bull Lucien • FRN

ETUDIANT, L' • 1960 • Dansereau Jean • SHT • CND

ETUDIANTE D'AUJOURD'HUI • 1967 • Rohmer Eric • SHT • FRN

ETUDIANTS, LES • 1960 • Grospierre Louis • SHT • FRN

ETWAS ANDERES • 1986 • Graf Urs • DOC • SWT

ETWAS VERSPRICHT see **KOCICI SIOVO** • 1960

EU + EU + EU • 1969 • Popescu-Gopo Ion • RMN • ME + ME + ME

EU FUI AO JARDIM DA CELESTE • 1952 • Vitorino Orlando • SHT • PRT

EU MATEI LUCIO FLAVIO • 1980 • Calmon Antonio • BRZ • I KILLED LUCIO FLAVIO

EU SEI QUE VOU TE AMAR • 1986 • Jabor Arnaldo • BRZ • I KNOW I'M GOING TO LOVE YOU

EU TE AMO • 1981 • Jabor Arnaldo • BRZ • I LOVE YOU

EUCALYPTUS • 1973 • Tropa Alfredo • SHT • PRT

EUCARESTIA see **DIVINO MISTERO, IL** • 1950

EUCH WERD' ICH'S ZEIGEN • 1972 • Losansky Rolf • GDR

EUCHARIST CONGRESS IN MONTREAL, THE • 1910 • Ouimet Leo • CND

EUCHRED • 1912 • *Eyton Bessie* • USA

EUCLIDEAN ILLUSIONS • 1978 • Vanderbeek Stan • USA

EUGEN • 1968 • Lyssy Rolf • SWT

EUGEN HEISST WOHLGEBOREN • 1968 • Lyssy Rolf • SWT • EUGEN MEANS WELL-BORN

EUGEN MEANS WELL-BORN see **EUGEN HEISST WOHLGEBOREN** • 1968

EUGEN ONEGIN • 1918 • Halm Alfred • FRG

EUGENE AMOUREUX • 1912 • Perret Leonce • FRN

EUGENE ARAM • 1914 • Collins Edwin J. • UKN

EUGENE ARAM • 1915 • Ridgely Richard • USA

EUGENE ARAM • 1929 • Rooke Arthur • UKN

EUGENE DIONNE, FERBLANTIER • 1975 • Plamondon Leo • DCS • CND

EUGENE ONEGIN see **IEVGENY ONYEGIN** • 1958

EUGENE PINI AND HIS ORCHESTRA • 1948 • Shepherd Horace • SHT • UKN

EUGENE PINI AND HIS TANGO ORCHESTRA • 1936 • Shepherd Horace • SHT • UKN

EUGENE WRAYBURN • 1911 • *Karr Darwin* • USA

EUGENIA GRANDET • 1947 • Soldati Mario • ITL

EUGENIA GRANDET • 1952 • Gomez Muriel Emilio • MXC

EUGENIC BOY, THE • 1914 • *Chester Lila* • USA

EUGENIC GIRL, THE • 1914 • Santschi Thomas • USA

EUGENICS AT BAR U RANCH • 1914 • Farnum Marshall • USA

EUGENICS VERSUS LOVE • 1914 • Pollard Harry • USA

EUGENIE see **EUGENIE.. THE STORY OF HER JOURNEY INTO PERVERSION** • 1970

EUGENIE.. THE STORY OF HER JOURNEY INTO PERVERSION • 1970 • Franco Jesus • UKN, SPN, FRG • EUGENIE

EULALLIE QUITTE LES CHAMPS • 1974 • Savary Jerome • FRN

EULE 1, DIE • 1927 • Polo Eddie • FRG • TOLLEN LAUNEN EINES MILLIONARS, DIE

EULE 2, DIE • 1927 • Polo Eddie • FRG • UNBEKANNTE, DIE

EULENHAUS, DAS • 1917 • Mendel Georg Victor • FRG

EUNICE • 1984 • Korman Harvey, Beatty Roger • TVM • USA

EUNUCH see **NAESI** • 1986

EUR WEG FUHRT DURCH DIE HOLLE • 1984 • von Theumer Ernst Ritter • FRG, MXC • JUNGLE WARRIORS ○ JUNGLE FEVER
EUREKA • 1913 • *Gardner Helen* • USA
EUREKA • 1974 • Gehr Ernie • USA
EUREKA • 1982 • Roeg Nicolas • USA, UKN
EUREKA STOCKADE • 1907 • *Australatian Cinematograph* • ASL
EUREKA STOCKADE • 1948 • Watt Harry • ASL, UKN • MASSACRE HILL (USA)
EUREKA STOCKADE • 1984 • Hardy Rod • MTV • ASL
EUREKA STOCKADE see **LOYAL REBEL, THE** • 1915
EURIDICE BA-2037 see **EVRIDIKI BA-2037** • 1975
EUROPA '51 • 1952 • Rossellini Roberto • ITL • GREATEST LOVE, THE (USA) ○ NO GREATER LOVE (UKN) ○ EUROPE 51
EUROPA CANTA • 1966 • Merino Jose Luis • SPN
EUROPA DALL'ALTO • 1960 • Casara Severino • DOC • ITL • MERAVIGLIA DELLE ALPI, LA
EUROPA DI NOTTE • 1959 • Blasetti Alessandro • DOC • ITL • EUROPEAN NIGHTS (USA)
EUROPA IL MIO PAESE • 1962 • Loy Mino • ITL
EUROPA -LEUCHTFEUER DER WELT • 1971 • Stummer Alfons • DOC • AUS
EUROPA NEUE MUSIKPARADE • 1957 • Martin Paul • FRG
EUROPA: OPERAZIONE STRIP-TEASE • 1964 • Russo Renzo • DOC • ITL
EUROPA POSTLAGERND • 1918 • Dupont E. A. • FRG • POST OFFICE EUROPE
EUROPA RADIO • 1931 • Richter Hans • NTH
EUROPAS NEUE MUSIKPARADE see **WENN FRAUEN SCHWINDELN** • 1957
EUROPE • 1964 • Leenhardt Roger • DCS • FRN
EUROPE 51 see **EUROPA '51** • 1952
EUROPE AFTER THE RAIN • 1978 • Gold Mick • UKN
EUROPE CONTINENTALE AVANT 1900 • 1969 • Allegret Marc • SHT • FRN
EUROPE IN THE RAW • 1963 • Meyer Russ • USA
EUROPE MERIDIONALE AU TEMPS DES ROI • 1969 • Allegret Marc • SHT • FRN
EUROPEAN CHAMPIONS • 1966 • Csoke Jozsef • DOC • HNG
EUROPEAN DIARIES • 1966 • Mead Taylor • USA
EUROPEAN GRASS SKI • 1975 • Howard John • DOC • UKN
EUROPEAN MUSIC REVOLUTION see **AMOUGIES** • 1970
EUROPEAN NIGHTS (USA) see **EUROPA DI NOTTE** • 1959
EUROPEAN REST CURE • 1904 • Porter Edwin S. • USA
EUROPEAN VACATION see **NATIONAL LAMPOON'S EUROPEAN VACATION** • 1985
EUROPEANS, THE • 1979 • Ivory James • UKN
EURYNOME • 1970 • Straiton John S. • ANS • CND
EUSEBE, DEPUTE • 1938 • Berthomieu Andre • FRN • MON DEPUTE
EUSEBE ET MELANIE • 1975 • Delimal Henri-Paul • CND
EUSKADI HORS D'ETAT • 1984 • Maccaig Arthur • DOC • FRN
EUSTAKI • 1936 • Le Henaff Rene • SHT • FRN
EUTANASIA DI UN AMORE • 1978 • Salerno Enrico Maria • ITL
EVA • 1912 • Stark Kurt • FRG
EVA • 1935 • Riemann Johannes • AUS • EVA, DAS FABRIKSMADEL
EVA • 1948 • Molander Gustaf • SWD
EVA • 1953 • Plytas Maria
EVA • 1962 • Losey Joseph • FRN, ITL • EVA (THE DEVIL'S WOMAN) ○ EVE
EVA • 1968 • Ballmann Herbert • FRG • EVA -THE WAY TO LOVE
EVA • 1983 • Slak Franci • YGS
EVA see **FACE OF EVE, THE** • 1968
EVA 63 • 1963 • Lazaga Pedro • SPN
EVA A 5116 • 1963 • Nadasy Laszlo • HNG • EVA IS CLEVER
EVA AND THE GRASSHOPPER • 1928 • Diehle Bros • ANM • FRG
EVA AND THE GRASSHOPPER (USA) see **JUGENDRAUSCH** • 1927
EVA BRAUN AND HITLER STORY see **IT MUST NOT HAPPEN AGAIN** • 1948
EVA, DAS FABRIKSMADEL see **EVA** • 1935
EVA -DEN UTSTOTTA • 1969 • Wickman Torgny • SWD • EVA.. WAS EVERYTHING BUT LEGAL (USA) ○ SWEDISH AND UNDERAGE
EVA, DIE SUNDE • 1920 • Fleck Jacob, Fleck Luise • AUS
EVA EN LA SELVA see **FACE OF EVE, THE** • 1968
EVA ERBT DAS PARADIES • 1951 • Antel Franz • AUS
EVA ET L'AMOUR • Regis Jack • FRN
"EVA" EXPERIMENT, THE see **EXPERIMENT "EVA"** • 1985
EVA GAR OMBORD • 1934 • Marmstedt Lorens • SWD • EVA GOES ON BOARD
EVA GOES ON BOARD see **EVA GAR OMBORD** • 1934
EVA: GUERRILLERA • 1988 • Levitin Jacqueline • CND
EVA IM FRACK • 1951 • Verhoeven Paul • FRG
EVA IN SEIDE • 1928 • Boese Carl • FRG
EVA IS CLEVER see **EVA A 5116** • 1963
EVA IS FOOLING see **EVA TROPI HLOUPOSTI** • 1939
EVA KUSST NUR DIKTATOREN • 1958 • Jugert Rudolf • AUS
EVA, LA VENERE SELVAGGIA • 1968 • Mauri Roberto • ITL • EVE, THE SAVAGE VENUS ○ EVE, THE WILD WOMAN
EVA LIMPIA COMO LOS CHORROS DEL ORO • 1976 • Truchado Jose • SPN
EVA LOVED A TURK see **BIR TURK'E GONUL VERDIM** • 1969
EVA NERA • 1954 • Tomei Giuliano • ITL
EVA NERA • 1976 • D'Amato Joe • ITL • BLACK COBRA ○ EROTIC EVA
EVA PLAYS THE FOOL see **EVA TROPI HLOUPOSTI** • 1939
EVA, QUE HACE ESE HOMBRE EN TU CAMA? • 1975 • Demicheli Tulio • SPN
EVA SCANDAL, THE see **SKANDAL UM EVA** • 1930
EVA SCONOSCIUTA see **DONNA NEL MONDO, LA** • 1963
EVA, SUR PAYSAGE ORDINAIRE • 1984 • Ciepka Emmanuel • FRN
EVA THE CIGARETTE GIRL • 1914 • *Ab* • USA
EVA (THE DEVIL'S WOMAN) see **EVA** • 1962
EVA THE FIFTH see **GIRL IN THE SHOW, THE** • 1930
EVA -THE WAY TO LOVE see **EVA** • 1968
EVA TROPI HLOUPOSTI • 1939 • Fric Martin • CZC • EVA PLAYS THE FOOL ○ EVA IS FOOLING ○ ESCAPADES OF EVA, THE
EVA UND DER FRAUENARZT • 1951 • Kobler Erich • FRG
EVA.. WAS EVERYTHING BUT LEGAL (USA) see **EVA -DEN UTSTOTTA** • 1969
EVA Y ADAN, EL PRIMER PECADO see **PECADO DE ANAN Y EVA, EL** • 1967
EVA Y DARIO • 1972 • *Churubusco Azteca* • MXC
EVACUATED see **EVAKKO** • 1956
EVACUEES, THE • 1974 • Parker Alan • MTV • UKN
EVADE, L' • 1971 • Danis Aime • CND
EVADE DE L'ENFER see **LISSU WA AL-KILAB, AL-** • 1962
EVADE DE L'ENFER, L' see **FEU DE DIEU, LE** • 1966
EVADE DE TUILERIES, L' • 1910 • Capellani Albert • FRN
EVADEE, L' • 1922 • Burel Leonce-Henry (c/d) • FRN
EVADES, LES • 1955 • Le Chanois Jean-Paul • FRN
EVADES DE LA NUIT, LES (FRN) see **ERA NOTTE A ROMA** • 1960
EVADES DE LA TERRE, LES • 1970 • Brault Francois, Daviault L. • DCS • CND
EVADIDOS, LOS • 1964 • Carreras Enrique • ARG
EVAKKO • 1956 • Salminen Ville • FNL • EVACUATED
EVANGELIEMANDENS LIV • 1914 • Holger-Madsen • DNM • LIFE OF THE LAY PREACHER, THE ○ EVANGELIST PREACHER, THE ○ CANDLE AND THE MOTH, THE
EVANGELIMANN, DER • 1923 • Holger-Madsen • FRG
EVANGELINA • 1959 • Land Kurt • ARG
EVANGELINE • 1911 • *Selig* • USA
EVANGELINE • 1913 • Sullivan E. P., Cavanaugh William H. • CND
EVANGELINE • 1919 • Walsh Raoul • USA
EVANGELINE • 1929 • Carewe Edwin • USA
EVANGELINE DEUSSE • 1984 • Suissa Daniele J. • MTV • CND
EVANGELINE ET LE TONNERRE see **TONNERRE, LE** • 1921
EVANGELIO A SOLENTINAME • 1979 • Mallet Marilu • DCS • CND • GOSPEL OF SOLENTINAME, THE
EVANGELIST, THE • 1916 • O'Neil Barry • USA
EVANGELIST PREACHER, THE see **EVANGELIEMANDENS LIV** • 1914
EVANGILE SELON SAINT-MATHIEU, L' (FRN) see **VANGELO SECONDO MATTEO, IL** • 1964
EVAN'S LUCKY DAY • 1915 • Cooley Verdinal • USA
EVARISTE GALOIS • 1964 • Astruc Alexandre • FRN
EVA'S FAITHFUL FURNITURE • 1911 • *C.g.p.c.* • USA
EVAS SEELENGROSSE • 1915 • Del Zopp Rudolf • FRG
EVA'S SIN see **EVIN HRICH** • 1919
EVAS TOCHTER • 1928 • Lamac Carl • FRG
EVASANA DANA • 1967 • Jayasinghe H. E. • SLN • PATIENT MASSES, THE
EVASE, LE • 1978 • Brusadori Giovanni • ITL
EVASION • 1947 • *Lamas Fernando* • ARG
EVASION • 1963 • Lacko Jan • CZC
EVASION see **MANEATER** • 1973
EVASION, THE see **DEROBADE, LA** • 1979
EVASION DES CARROUSELS, L' • 1968 • Longpre Bernard • ANS • CND • CARROUSEL
EVASION DU MORT, L' • 1916 • Feuillade Louis • FRN
EVASIONS DE BOB WALTER, LES • 1916 • Cohl Emile • ANS • FRN
EVASIVE PEACE see **CAST A GIANT SHADOW** • 1966
EVASO, L' (ITL) see **VEUVE COUDERC, LE** • 1971
EVDOKIA • 1971 • Damianos Alexis • GRC
EVE see **EVA** • 1962
EVE ADOPTS A LONELY SOLDIER • 1918 • Leigh J. L. V. • SHT • UKN
EVE AND THE HANDYMAN • 1961 • Meyer Russ • USA
EVE AND THE INTERNMENT QUESTION • 1918 • Leigh J. L. V. • SHT • UKN
EVE AND THE MERMAN • 1965 • Royton Chev • USA
EVE AND THE MONKEY see **HAWAA WAL KERD** • 1968
EVE AND THE NERVOUS CURATE • 1918 • Leigh J. L. V. • SHT • UKN
EVE AS MRS. ADAM • 1918 • Leigh J. L. V. • SHT • UKN
EVE ASSISTS THE CENSOR • 1918 • Leigh J. L. V. • SHT • UKN
EVE AT THE CROSSROADS see **HAWAA ALAL TARIK** • 1968
EVE CHERCHE UN PERE • 1933 • Bonnard Mario • FRN
EVE ET LE SERPENT • 1949 • Tavano Charles-Felix • FRN
EVE ET LES BONNES POMMES • 1964 • Walter Claude • FRN
EVE + EVE see **EWA + EWA** • 1971
EVE GOES TO THE EAST COAST • 1918 • Leigh J. L. V. • SHT • UKN
EVE IN EXILE • 1919 • George Burton • USA
EVE IN THE COUNTRY • 1918 • Leigh J. L. V. • SHT • UKN
EVE KNEW HER APPLES • 1945 • Jason Will • USA
EVE OF A HOLIDAY see **PRZEDSWIATECZNY WIECZOR** • 1966
EVE OF DESTRUCTION • 1990 • Gibbins Duncan • USA
EVE OF ST. MARK, THE • 1944 • Stahl John M. • USA
EVE OF THE WILD WOMAN see **KING OF KONG ISLAND** • 1978
EVE ON THE THIRD FLOOR • 1986 • Grubcheva Ivanka • BUL
EVE OUTWITS ARTFUL ADAM • 1918 • Leigh J. L. V. • SHT • UKN
EVE RESOLVES TO DO WAR WORK • 1918 • Leigh J. L. V. • SHT • UKN
EVE, THE SAVAGE VENUS see **EVA, LA VENERE SELVAGGIA** • 1968
EVE, THE WILD WOMAN see **EVA, LA VENERE SELVAGGIA** • 1968
EVE (USA) see **FACE OF EVE, THE** • 1968
EVE WANTS TO SLEEP see **EWA CHCE SPAC** • 1958
EVEIL • 1967 • Foldes Peter • SHT • USA
EVEIL, L' • 1925 • Roudes Gaston • FRN
EVEIL DE L'AMOUR, L' • 1955 • Jaffe Georges, Roy Jean-Claude • FRN
EVEIL D'UN MONDE, L' • 1951 • Dupont Jacques • SHT • FRN
EVEILLES DU PONT DE L'ALMA, L' • 1986 • Ruiz Raul • FRN
EVEL KNIEVEL • 1972 • Chomsky Marvin • USA
EVELESS EDEN, THE see **EVELESS EDEN CLUB, THE** • 1916
EVELESS EDEN CLUB, THE • 1916 • Beaudine William • SHT • USA • EVELESS EDEN, THE
EVELINA AND HER CHILDREN see **EVELINA E I SUOI FIGLI** • 1990
EVELINA E I SUOI FIGLI • 1990 • Giampalmo Livia • ITL • EVELINA AND HER CHILDREN
EVELYN PRENTICE • 1934 • Howard William K. • USA
EVELYN THE BEAUTIFUL see **SKONNE EVELYN, DEN** • 1916
EVELYN'S STRATEGY • 1913 • *De Lespine Edgena* • USA
EVEN ANGELS EAT BEANS see **ANCHE GLI ANGELI MANGIANO FAGIOLI** • 1973
EVEN AS A WORM WILL TURN • 1907 • Coleby A. E.? • UKN
EVEN AS EVE • 1920 • Rolfe B. A., De Vonde Chester M. • USA
EVEN AS HIM AND HER • 1917 • Dunham Phil • SHT • USA
EVEN AS I.O.U. • 1942 • Lord Del • SHT • USA
EVEN AS YOU AND I • 1917 • Weber Lois • USA
EVEN AS YOU AND I • 1937 • Hirsch Hy, Barlow Roger, Hay Harry, Robbins Leroy • SHT • USA
EVEN BREAK, AN • 1912 • *Mersereau Violet* • USA
EVEN BREAK, AN • 1917 • Hillyer Lambert • USA
EVEN DWARFS STARTED SMALL (UKN) see **AUCH ZWERGE HABEN KLEIN ANGEFANGEN** • 1970
EVEN EXCHANGE, AN • 1913 • *American* • USA
EVEN IN THE WEST THERE WAS GOD ONCE UPON A TIME see **ANCHE NEL WEST, C'ERA UNA VOLTA DIO** • 1968
EVEN MONEY • 1919 • *Morrison Pete* • SHT • USA
EVEN STILTE • 1966 • van der Keuken Johan • SHT • NTH
EVEN SUCH A GLANCE SUFFICES • 1989 • *Poe Fernando* • PHL
EVEN THE WIND IS AFRAID see **HASTA EL VIENTO TIENE MIEDO** • 1968
EVEN UNTO DEATH • 1914 • Hamilton G. P. • USA
EVEN WALLFLOWERS WANT TO BLOOM see **AUCH MIMOSEN WOLLENBLUHEN** • 1976
EVENEMENT LE PLUS IMPORTANT DEPUIS QUE L'HOMME A MARCHE SUR LA LUNE, L' • 1973 • Demy Jacques • FRN, ITL • NIENTE DI GRAVE, SUO MARITO E INCINTO (ITL) ○ SLIGHTLY PREGNANT MAN, THE ○ MOST IMPORTANT EVENT SINCE MAN EVER SET FOOT ON THE MOON, THE
EVENEMENTS DE RESTIGOUCHE, LES see **INCIDENT AT RESTIGOUCHE** • 1984
EVENEMENTS D'OCTOBRE 1970, LES see **ACTION: THE OCTOBER CRISIS OF 1970** • 1974
EVENEMENTS D'ODESSA, LES • 1905 • Nonguet Lucien • FRN • CUIRASSE POTEMKIN, LE ○ BATTLESHIP POTEMKIN, THE ○ REVOLUTION IN RUSSIA ○ REVOLTE DU CUIRASSE POTEMKINE, LA
EVENING see **SERATA** • 1971
EVENING ALONE, AN • 1938 • Rowland Roy • USA
EVENING AT "SZPAKS", AN see **WIECZOR W "SZPAKU"** • 1960
EVENING AT THE CLUB "FESZEK" • Horvath Adam • HNG
EVENING BELL see **WAN ZHONG** • 1988
EVENING CALM see **YUNAGI** • 1957
EVENING CLOTHES • 1927 • Reed Luther • USA
EVENING DRESS see **TENUE DE SOIREE** • 1986
EVENING GLORY OF HEAVEN see **AMA NO YUHGAO** • 1948
EVENING IN BYZANTIUM • 1978 • London Jerry • TVM • USA
EVENING IN PARIS • 1967 • Samanta Shakti • IND
EVENING LAND see **AFTENLANDET** • 1976
EVENING.. NIGHT.. MORNING see **ABEND - NACHT - MORGEN** • 1920
EVENING OF THE FAIR see **MARKNADSAFTON** • 1948
EVENING SONG see **SANDHYA RAG** • 1977
EVENING STAR • 1937 • Nemeth Ted J. • SHT • USA
EVENING STREAM see **YORU NO NAGARE** • 1960
EVENING SUN IS CRYING, THE see **YUHI GA NAITEIRU** • 1967
EVENING WITH BATMAN AND ROBIN, AN • 1966 • Hillyer Lambert • USA
EVENING WITH ROBIN WILLIAMS, AN • 1983 • Mischer Don • USA
EVENING WITH THE ROYAL BALLET, AN • 1963 • Asquith Anthony, Havelock-Allan Anthony • UKN
EVENING WITH WILDER SPENCER, AN • 1913 • *Ab* • USA
EVENINGS see **AVONDEN, DE** • 1989
EVENINGS AT DJURGARDEN see **DJURGARDSKVALLAR** • 1947
EVENINGS FOR SALE • 1932 • Walker Stuart • USA
EVENINGS WITH JINDRICH PLACHTA see **VECERY S JINDRICHEM PLACHTOU** • 1954
EVENSONG • 1934 • Saville Victor • UKN
EVENT, AN see **DOGADJAJ** • 1969
EVENT IN THE STADIUM see **SLUCHAI NA STADIONE** • 1929
EVENT NO ONE NOTICED, AN see **PROISHYESTVIYE, KOTOROVO NIKTO NYE ZAMYETIL** • 1968
EVENTAIL, L' • 1947 • Reinert Emile Edwin • FRN • ILE AUX NUAGES, L'
EVENTAIL ANIME, L' • 1909 • Cohl Emile • ANS • FRN • ANIMATED FAN, THE ○ HISTORICAL FAN ○ MAGIC FAN
EVENTAIL MAGIQUE, L' see **MERVEILLEUX EVENTAIL VIVANT, LE** • 1904
EVENTFUL BARGAIN DAY, AN • 1912 • *Horner Violet* • USA
EVENTFUL ELOPEMENT, AN • 1912 • Ranous William V. • USA
EVENTFUL EVENING, AN • 1911 • *Edison* • USA
EVENTFUL EVENING, AN • 1916 • Mix Tom • SHT • USA
EVENTFUL JOURNEY (UKN) see **HITCH HIKE LADY** • 1936
EVENTFUL TRIP, AN • 1909 • *Pathe* • FRN
EVENTS • 1969 • Llewellyn John • UKN
EVENTS • 1970 • Baker Fred • USA
EVENTS HIT THANASSIS SMACK ON THE NOSE see **THANASSIS STI HORA TIS SFALIARAS, O** • 1975
EVENTS OF THE COMING YEAR see **WAQA'II AL AAM AL MUQBIL** • 1986
EVENTUALLY BUT NOT NOW • 1931 • Foster Lewis R. • SHT • USA
EVENTYR PAA FODREJSEN • 1911 • Blom August • DNM • UDBRUDTE SLAVE, DEN ○ 2 CONVICTS, THE
EVENTYRET OM CARL GUSTAV, GJENGEN OG PARKERINGSBANDITTENE • 1982 • Solum Ola • NRW
EVER AFTER ALL see **GOLDEN APPLES OF THE SUN** • 1972
EVER BEEN HAD? • 1915 • Birch Cecil • UKN
EVER BEEN HAD? • 1917 • Buxton Dudley • ANM • UKN
EVER BEEN ON A TRIP? • 1970 • *Stacey Dist.* • USA
EVER BRAVEST HEART • 1929 • Aylott Dave, Symmons E. F. • SHT • UKN
EVER-CHANGING MOTOR CAR, THE • 1962 • Dunning George, Ball Alan • ANS • UKN

EVER-GALLANT MARQUISE, THE • 1914 • Miller Ashley • USA
EVER IN MY HEART • 1933 • Mayo Archie • USA
EVER-LIVING ISLES, THE • 1915 • Powers Francis • USA
EVER ON THEE • 1909 • *Warwick Trading Co.* • UKN
EVER-OPEN DOOR, THE • 1920 • Goodwins Fred • UKN
EVER-READY WOMEN see **UVEK SPREMNE ZENE** • 1987
EVER SINCE EVE • 1921 • Mitchell Howard M. • USA
EVER SINCE EVE • 1934 • Marshall George • USA • HEIR TO THE HOORAH
EVER SINCE EVE • 1937 • Bacon Lloyd • USA
EVER SINCE VENUS • 1944 • Dreifuss Arthur • USA
EVER-SO-SAD PRINCESS, THE see **SILENE SMUTNA PRINCEZNA** • 1968
EVER THE ACCUSER • 1911 • *Davenport Helen* • USA
EVERDALE PLACE • 1967 • Shebib Donald • CND
EVERGLADE KILLINGS, THE see **HOOKED GENERATION, THE** • 1969
EVERGLADE RAID, THE • 1958 • Smith Paul J. • ANS • USA
EVERGREEN • 1934 • Saville Victor • UKN
EVERGREEN • 1984 • Cook Fielder • MTV • USA
EVERHARDTS CLEVER HOOP MANIPULATION, THE • 1902 • *Warwick Trading Co.* • UKN
EVERLASTING CHIVALRY • *Meng Fei* • HKG
EVERLASTING JUDY, THE • 1912 • Fahrney Milton • USA
EVERLASTING SECRET FAMILY, THE • 1987 • Thornhill Michael • ASL
EVERLASTING TRIANGLE, THE • 1914 • Collins John H., Seay Charles M. • USA
EVERLASTING WHISPER, THE • 1925 • Blystone John G. • USA
EVERSMILE NEW JERSEY (UKN) see **ETERNA SONRISA DE NEW JERSEY** • 1988
EVERY BASTARD A KING (USA) see **KOL MAMZER MELECH** • 1968
EVERY BEGINNING IS HARD see **MINDEN KEZDET NEHEZ** • 1966
EVERY CHILD • 1979 • Fedorenko Eugene • ANM • CND
EVERY DAY AS ONE DAY see **TODOS LOS DIAS UN DIA** • 1977
EVERY DAY CHALLENGE • 1981 • Ricketson James • DOC • ASL
EVERY DAY EVERY NIGHT • 1984 • Mueller Kathy • SHT • ASL
EVERY DAY EXCEPT CHRISTMAS • 1957 • Anderson Lindsay • UKN
EVERY DAY IS A HOLIDAY • 1966 • Ferrer Mel • USA, SPN • CABRIOLA
EVERY DAY IS SATURDAY see **DIAS DE CENIZA** • 1978
EVERY DAY'S A HOLIDAY • 1937 • Sutherland A. Edward • USA
EVERY DAY'S A HOLIDAY • 1964 • Hill James • UKN • SEASIDE SWINGERS (USA)
EVERY DAY'S A HOLIDAY see **ORO DI NAPOLI, L'** • 1954
EVERY DOG HAS HIS DAY see **LIEBE AUF KRUMMEN BEINEN** • 1959
EVERY DOG HAS HIS DAY see **ENGALUCKUM KALAM VARUM** • 1967
EVERY DOG'S GUIDE TO COMPLETE HOME SAFETY • 1987 • Drew Les • ANS • CND
EVERY DOUBLE CAUSES TROUBLE • 1913 • *Patheplay* • USA
EVERY FIVE MINUTES • 1950 • Anderson Max • SHT • UKN
EVERY GIRL SHOULD BE MARRIED • 1948 • Hartman Don • USA
EVERY GIRL SHOULD HAVE ONE • 1975 • Hyatt Robert • USA
EVERY GIRL'S DREAM • 1917 • Millarde Harry • USA
EVERY HOME SHOULD HAVE ONE • 1970 • Clark Jim • UKN • THINK DIRTY (USA)
EVERY INCH A HERO • 1913 • *Quirk Billy* • USA
EVERY INCH A HERO • 1915 • *L-Ko* • USA
EVERY INCH A KING • 1914 • *Bushman Francis X.* • USA
EVERY INCH A MAN • 1912 • Humphrey William • USA
EVERY LASSIE HAS A LOVER • 1916 • *Dovoy Alice* • USA
EVERY LITTLE BIT HELPS • 1907 • Gilbert Arthur • UKN
EVERY LITTLE CROOK AND NANNY • 1972 • Howard Cy • USA
EVERY MAN A KING see **KOL MAMZER MELECH** • 1968
EVERY MAN FOR HIMSELF • 1924 • Roach Hal • SHT • USA
EVERY MAN FOR HIMSELF AND GOD AGAINST ALL see **JEDER FUR SICH UND GOTT GEGEN ALLE** • 1974
EVERY MAN FOR HIMSELF (USA) see **SAUVE QUI PEUT** • 1980
EVERY MAN HAS HIS PRICE • 1914 • Mackley Arthur • USA
EVERY MAN HIS OWN CIGAR LIGHTER (USA) see **PEU DE FEU, S.V.P., UN** • 1904
EVERY MAN IS MY ENEMY (USA) see **QUALCUNO HA TRADITO** • 1967
EVERY MAN NEEDS ONE • 1972 • Paris Jerry • TVM • USA
EVERY MAN'S MONEY • 1915 • Reynolds Lynn • USA
EVERY MAN'S WIFE • 1925 • Elvey Maurice • USA
EVERY MAN'S WOMAN (UKN) see **ROSA PER TUTTI, UNA** • 1967
EVERY MINUTE COUNTS see **ASSASSINS DU DIMANCHE, LES** • 1956
EVERY MINUTE COUNTS (UKN) see **COUNT THE HOURS** • 1952
EVERY MOTHER'S SON • 1919 • Walsh Raoul • USA
EVERY MOTHER'S SON • 1926 • Cullen Robert J. • UKN
EVERY MOVE SHE MAKES • 1984 • Millar Catherine • TVM • ASL
EVERY NIGHT AT EIGHT • 1935 • Walsh Raoul • USA
EVERY NIGHT OF THE WEEK (UKN) see **PUPA, LA** • 1963
EVERY NIGHT OF THE WEEK (UKN) see **VAN DER VELDE: DAS LEBEN ZU ZWEIT, DIE SEXUALITAT IN DER EHE** • 1972
EVERY OTHER INCH A LADY (UKN) see **DANCING CO-ED** • 1939
EVERY PENNY COUNTS see **KAZDA KORUNA DOBRA** • 1961
EVERY PERSON IS GUILTY • 1979 • Almond Paul • MTV • CND
EVERY PICTURE TELLS A STORY • 1984 • Scott James • MTV • UKN
EVERY REVOLUTION IS A THROW OF THE DICE see **TOUTE REVOLUTION EST UN COUP DE DES** • 1977
EVERY ROSE HAS A STEM • 1912 • *Mccoy Gertrude* • USA
EVERY SATURDAY NIGHT • 1936 • Tinling James • USA
EVERY SECOND CAR • 1964 • Watson Patricia, Tasker Rex • CND
EVERY SECOND COUNTS (USA) see **ASSASSINS DU DIMANCHE, LES** • 1956
EVERY SPARROW MUST FALL • 1964 • Budsan Ronald R. • USA
EVERY SUNDAY • 1936 • Feist Felix E. • SHT • USA
EVERY SUNDAY see **W KAZDA NIEDZIELE** • 1965
EVERY SUNDAY MORNING see **TUTTE LE DOMENICHE MATTINA** • 1972
EVERY THIEF LEAVES A CLUE • 1913 • *Essanay* • USA
EVERY TIME THAT.. see **CADA VEZ QUE..** • 1968
EVERY TIME WE SAY GOODBYE • 1986 • Mizrahi Moshe • USA
EVERY WEDNESDAY see **MINDEN SZERDAN** • 1980
EVERY WHICH WAY BUT LOOSE • 1978 • Fargo James • USA
EVERY WOMAN'S MAN (UKN) see **PRIZEFIGHTER AND THE LADY, THE** • 1933
EVERY WOMAN'S PROBLEM • 1921 • Robards Willis • USA
EVERY WRONG SHALL BE RIGHTED • 1910 • Raymond Charles • UKN
EVERY YEAR AGAIN see **ALLE JAHRE WIEDER** • 1967
EVERY YOUNG MAN see **KAZDY MLADY MUZ** • 1965
EVERYBODY AND A CHICKEN • Gardner Frank • SHT • USA
EVERYBODY AND NOBODY • 1978 • Azarian Krikor • BUL
EVERYBODY AT HIS STATION see **ALLE MAN PA POST** • 1940
EVERYBODY CALLS ME GATO see **TODOS ME LLAMAN GATO** • 1981
EVERYBODY DANCE • 1936 • Reisner Charles F. • UKN
EVERYBODY DOES IT • 1949 • Goulding Edmund • USA
EVERYBODY GO HOME! (USA) see **TUTTI A CASA** • 1960
EVERYBODY GOES APE • 1970 • *Able Film Co.* • USA
EVERYBODY HELPS TEDDY • Anderson Monika • ANM • GDR
EVERYBODY IN LOVE see **TUTTI INNAMORATI** • 1959
EVERYBODY IS GOOD see **TO EL MUNDO ES GUENO** • 1981
EVERYBODY, LET'S GO! see **NANIWANAKUTOMO ZEN-IN SHUGO!!** • 1967
EVERYBODY LIKES MOUNTAIN WOMEN see **UNDRESSED WEST, THE** • 1964
EVERYBODY LIKES MUSIC • 1934 • Jason Leigh • SHT • USA
EVERYBODY LOVES A FAT MAN • 1916 • Williams C. Jay • SHT • USA
EVERYBODY LOVES IT • 1964 • *Paramore Edward E. (P)* • USA
EVERYBODY RIDES THE CAROUSEL • 1975 • Hubley John • ANM • USA
EVERYBODY SAVES FATHER • 1911 • *Thanhauser* • USA
EVERYBODY SING • 1937 • *Lantz Walter (P)* • ANS • USA
EVERYBODY SING • 1937 • Marin Edwin L. • USA
EVERYBODY WAS SATISFIED • 1917 • MacGregor Norval • SHT • USA
EVERYBODY WAS VERY NICE see **LOVE, HONOR AND BEHAVE** • 1938
EVERYBODY WINS • 1989 • Reisz Karel • USA
EVERYBODY WORKS BUT FATHER • 1905 • Porter Edwin S. • USA
EVERYBODYS • 1977 • Pecas Max • FRN
EVERYBODY'S ACTING • 1926 • Neilan Marshall • USA
EVERYBODY'S ALL-AMERICAN • 1988 • Hackford Taylor • USA
EVERYBODY'S AT IT (UKN) see **FEMALE RESPONSE, THE** • 1972
EVERYBODY'S BABY • 1939 • St. Clair Malcolm • USA
EVERYBODY'S BUSINESS • 1917 • Dewsbury Ralph • UKN
EVERYBODY'S BUSINESS • 1919 • Dawley J. Searle • USA
EVERYBODY'S CELEBRATION see **FIESTA DE TODOS, LA** • 1979
EVERYBODY'S CHEERING (UKN) see **TAKE ME OUT TO THE BALL GAME** • 1948
EVERYBODY'S DOING IT • 1913 • *Turner Florence* • USA
EVERYBODY'S DOING IT • 1913 • Kellino W. P. • UKN
EVERYBODY'S DOING IT • 1914 • *Melies* • USA
EVERYBODY'S DOING IT • 1916 • Browning Tod • USA
EVERYBODY'S DOING IT • 1919 • Malins Geoffrey H. • UKN
EVERYBODY'S DOING IT • 1938 • Cabanne W. Christy • USA • EASY MILLIONS
EVERYBODY'S GIRL • 1918 • Terriss Tom • USA
EVERYBODY'S HOBBY • 1939 • McGann William • USA • HOBBY FAMILY, THE
EVERYBODY'S OLD MAN • 1936 • Flood James • USA
EVERYBODY'S PREJUDICED • 1961 • Brittain Don • CND
EVERYBODY'S SWEETHEART • 1920 • Trimble Larry • USA
EVERYBODY'S TROUBLES • 1911 • *Essanay* • USA
EVERYBODY'S WEARING THEM • 1913 • *Powers* • USA
EVERYBODY'S WOMAN see **JEDERMANNS FRAU** • 1924
EVERYDAY • 1929 • Richter Hans • FRG
EVERYDAY • 1949 • Makarczynski Tadeusz • DOC • PLN
EVERYDAY see **ICH DZIEN POWSZEDNI** • 1963
EVERYDAY CHRONICLE (USA) see **MALA KRONIKA** • 1962
EVERYDAY COURAGE see **KAZDY DEN ODVAHU** • 1964
EVERYDAY FRAUDS • 1926 • Engholm F. W. • SER • UKN
EVERYDAY LIFE IN A SYRIAN VILLAGE see **HAYAT AL-YAWMIYYA FI QARIA SURIYYA, AL-** • 1974
EVERYDAY STORIES see **MINDENNAPI TORTENETEK** • 1955
EVERYDAY -SUNDAY see **PIROSBETOS HETKOZNAPOK** • 1962
EVERYGIRL • 1915 • *Victor* • USA
EVERYGIRL • 1915 • *Knickerbocker Star* • USA
EVERYHEART • 1915 • MacMackin Archer • USA
EVERYMAN • 1913 • *Kinemacolor* • USA
EVERYMAN • 1914 • *Crawley Constance* • USA
EVERYMAN • *Dobie Alan* • UKN
EVERYMAN • 1962 • Baillie Bruce • SHT • USA
EVERYMAN • 1971 • Mathers James • USA
EVERYMAN see **ELCKERLYC** • 1975
EVERYMAN CAMEOS • 1916 • Gilbert Lewis, Frenguelli Alfonse • SER • UKN
EVERYMAN (USA) see **JEDERMANN** • 1961
EVERYMAN'S LAW • 1936 • Ray Albert • USA
EVERYMAN'S PRICE • 1921 • King Burton L. • USA
EVERYMAN'S WOMAN see **ROSA PER TUTTI, UNA** • 1967
EVERYNIGHT DREAMS see **YOGOTO NO YUME** • 1933
EVERYONE • 1915 • *Warner Features* • USA
EVERYONE A GOOD FELLOW-COUNTRYMAN see **VSICHNI DOBRI RODACI** • 1968
EVERYONE FOR HIMSELF see **GOLD VON SAM COOPER, DAS** • 1968
EVERYONE'S BUSINESS • 1982 • Armstrong Mary • MTV • CND
EVERYONE'S GREAT see **TO EL MUNDO ES GUENO** • 1981
EVERYTHING AGAINST HIM • 1914 • Davis Ulysses • USA
EVERYTHING AT A LOW PRICE see **PARE KOSME** • 1967
EVERYTHING BEGINS WITH A JOURNEY see **VSE NACHINAETSYA S DOROGI** • 1959
EVERYTHING BUT THE TRUTH • 1920 • Lyons Eddie, Moran Lee • USA
EVERYTHING BUT THE TRUTH • 1956 • Hopper Jerry • USA
EVERYTHING COMES TO HIM WHO WAITS • 1912 • *Edison* • USA
EVERYTHING ENDS TONIGHT see **DNES VECER VSECHNO SKONCI** • 1954
EVERYTHING FLOWS see **PANTA RHEI** • 1951
EVERYTHING FOR EVERYBODY • 1969 • Amero John? • USA
EVERYTHING FOR SALE • 1921 • O'Connor Frank • USA
EVERYTHING FOR SALE see **WSZYSTKO NA SPRZEDAZ** • 1969
EVERYTHING GOES • 1976 • Desvilles Jean • FRN
EVERYTHING HAPPENS AT NIGHT • 1939 • Cummings Irving • USA
EVERYTHING HAPPENS TO ANNE see **HALF A SINNER** • 1940
EVERYTHING HAPPENS TO ME • 1938 • Neill R. William • UKN
EVERYTHING HAPPENS TO US (UKN) see **HI'YA, CHUM** • 1943
EVERYTHING HERE IS FINE see **NOS POR CA TODOS BEM** • 1977
EVERYTHING I HAVE IS YOURS • 1952 • Leonard Robert Z. • USA
EVERYTHING IN LIFE • 1936 • Wills J. Elder • UKN • BECAUSE OF LOVE
EVERYTHING IS A NUMBER see **WSZYSTKO JEST LICZBA** • 1967
EVERYTHING IS IN ORDER, BUT ON THE OTHER HAND.. see **NAI MEN ALLA..** • 1972
EVERYTHING IS RHYTHM • 1936 • Goulding Alf • UKN
EVERYTHING IS THUNDER • 1936 • Rosmer Milton • UKN
EVERYTHING OKAY see **ON TOP OF THE WORLD** • 1936
EVERYTHING STARTS ON THE ROAD see **VSE NACHINAETSYA S DOROGI** • 1959
EVERYTHING THAT LIVES see **IKITOSHI IKERUMONO** • 1934
EVERYTHING THAT LIVES see **IKITOSHI IKERUMONO** • 1955
EVERYTHING TURNS, EVERYTHING REVOLVES see **ALLES DREHT SICH, ALLES BEWEGT SICH!** • 1929
EVERYTHING YOU ALWAYS WANTED TO KNOW ABOUT SEX (BUT WERE AFRAID TO ASK) • 1972 • Allen Woody • USA
EVERYTHING'S ALL RIGHT see **OKKOMA HARI** • 1967
EVERYTHING'S DUCKY • 1934 • Holmes Ben • SHT • USA
EVERYTHING'S DUCKY • 1961 • Taylor Don • USA
EVERYTHING'S IN ORDER BUT NOTHING WORKS see **TUTTO A POSTO E NIENTE IN ORDINE** • 1974
EVERYTHING'S ON ICE • 1939 • Kenton Erle C. • USA
EVERYTHING'S READY NOTHING WORKS see **TUTTO A POSTO E NIENTE IN ORDINE** • 1974
EVERYTHING'S ROSIE • 1931 • Bruckman Clyde • USA
EVERYWOMAN • 1919 • Melford George • USA
EVERYWOMAN'S HUSBAND • 1918 • Hamilton G. P. • USA
EVE'S BURGLAR • 1918 • Leigh J. L. V. • SHT • UKN
EVE'S DAUGHTER • 1914 • North Wilfred • USA
EVE'S DAUGHTER • 1916 • MacBean L. C. • UKN • LOVE
EVE'S DAUGHTER • 1918 • Kirkwood James • USA
EVE'S FALL • 1930 • Banks Monty • UKN
EVES FUTURES • 1964 • Baratier Jacques • SHT • FRN
EVE'S LEAVES • 1926 • Sloane Paul • USA
EVE'S LOVE LETTERS • 1927 • Roach Hal • SHT • USA
EVE'S LOVER • 1925 • Del Ruth Roy • USA
EVES ON SKIS • 1963 • Keatering Michael • UKN
EVE'S SECRET • 1925 • Badger Clarence • USA
EVICTED • 1911 • Fitzhamon Lewin • UKN
EVICTION • 1986 • Chbib Bachar • CND
EVICTION, THE • 1904 • Collins Alf • UKN
EVICTIONS • 1979 • Lowenstein Richard • DOC • ASL
EVICTORS, THE • 1979 • Pierce Charles B. • USA
EVIDENCE • 1915 • August Edwin • USA
EVIDENCE • 1918 • Edwards Walter • USA • ARGUMENT, THE
EVIDENCE • 1922 • Archainbaud George • USA
EVIDENCE • 1929 • Adolfi John G. • USA
EVIDENCE • 1965 • Kidawa Janusz • DOC • PLN
EVIDENCE see **SVEDECTVI** • 1961
EVIDENCE, THE • 1912 • *Nestor* • USA
EVIDENCE, THE • 1916 • Leonard Robert Z. • SHT • USA
EVIDENCE IN CAMERA (UKN) see **HEADLINE SHOOTERS** • 1933
EVIDENCE IN CONCRETE • 1960 • Hales Gordon • UKN
EVIDENCE IN CONCRETE see **DOS AU MUR** • 1958
EVIDENCE OF POWER • 1979 • Piehl Vern • USA
EVIDENCE OF THE FILM, THE • 1913 • *Thanhouser* • USA
EVIDENCE: PART 1: BETRAYAL • 1961 • Toman Ivo, Hasa Pavel • DOC • CZC
EVIDENCE: PART 2: VICTORY • 1961 • Toman Ivo, Hasa Pavel • DOC • CZC
EVIGA LANKAR • 1947 • Carlsten Rune • SWD • ETERNAL BONDS (USA) ○ ETERNAL LINKS ○ DE GLADA AREN
EVIGE HAD, DET • 1915 • Davidsen Hjalmar • DNM
EVIGE NAT, DEN (DNM) see **EWIGE NACHT, DIE** • 1914
EVIL, THE • 1978 • Trikonis Gus • USA • FORCE BEYOND, THE ○ HOUSE OF EVIL ○ CRY DEMON
EVIL ALTAR • 1987 • Winburn Jim • USA
EVIL ANGELS (ASL) see **CRY IN THE DARK, A** • 1988
EVIL BE TO HIM WHO EVIL THINKS • 1912 • *Republic* • USA
EVIL BELOW, THE • 1989 • Crawford Wayne • USA
EVIL BOY, THE see **ZLY CHLOPIEC** • 1950
EVIL BRAIN FROM OUTER SPACE • 1959 • JPN
EVIL COME, EVIL GO see **YELLOW CANARY, THE** • 1963
EVIL DEAD, THE • 1983 • Raimi Sam • USA
EVIL DEAD II • 1987 • Raimi Sam • USA • EVIL DEAD II: DEAD BY DAWN
EVIL DEAD II: DEAD BY DAWN see **EVIL DEAD II** • 1987

EVIL-DOER'S SAD END, THE • 1903 • Williamson James • UKN
EVIL EDEN see **MORT EN CE JARDIN, LA** • 1956
EVIL EYE see **KATARAMENI ORA** • 1968
EVIL EYE, THE • 1909 • *Gaumont* • USA
EVIL EYE, THE • 1913 • Fielding Romaine • USA
EVIL EYE, THE • 1914 • *Apex* • USA
EVIL EYE, THE • 1917 • Melford George • USA
EVIL EYE, THE • 1920 • Cooper J. Gordon • SRL • USA
EVIL EYE, THE • 1975 • *Conte Richard* • ITL
EVIL EYE, THE (USA) see **RAGAZZA CHE SAPEVA TROPPO, LA** • 1962
EVIL EYES see **ONDA OGON** • 1947
EVIL FINGERS (UKN) see **GIORNATA NERA PER L'ARIETE** • 1971
EVIL FORCE, THE (UKN) see **4D MAN, THE** • 1959
EVIL FOREST, THE see **PARSIFAL** • 1951
EVIL GENIUS, THE • 1913 • Wilson Frank • UKN • AT THE PROMPTING OF THE DEVIL
EVIL GENIUS, THE see **TRUET LYKKE** • 1915
EVIL HALF, THE see **WOLVES OF THE NORTH** • 1921
EVIL HANDS • 1917 • McDermott John • USA
EVIL IN CLEAR RIVER • 1988 • Arthur Karen • TVM • USA
EVIL IN THE DEEP • 1976 • Stone Virginia Lively • USA • TREASURE OF JAMAICA REEF, THE
EVIL INHERITANCE, THE • 1912 • Dwan Allan • USA
EVIL LAUGH • 1988 • Brascia Dominic • USA
EVIL LIVES IN THE BLOOD see **DIABO MORA NO SANGUE, O** • 1968
EVIL LOVE see **AMOR BRUJO, EL** • 1967
EVIL MAGICIAN, THE • Ericsson Alvar • ANM • SWD
EVIL MEN DO, THE • 1915 • Costello Maurice, Gaillord Robert • USA
EVIL MIND, THE see **CLAIRVOYANT, THE** • 1935
EVIL OF DIVORCE, THE • 1914 • *Russell Martha* • USA
EVIL OF DRACULA see **CHIO SU BARA** • 1975
EVIL OF EDEN see **MORT EN CE JARDIN, LA** • 1956
EVIL OF FRANKENSTEIN, THE • 1964 • Francis Freddie • UKN
EVIL OF SUSPICION, THE • 1915 • Julian Rupert • USA
EVIL OF THE SLUMS, AN • 1913 • *Powers* • USA
EVIL ONE, THE • 1913 • Grandon Francis J. • USA
EVIL PHILTER, THE • 1909 • *Pathe* • FRN
EVIL PLEASURE, THE • 1966 • Delvos Jamie • USA • PORNOGRAFI –THE EVIL PLEASURE ○ PORNOGRAFI
EVIL POWER, AN • 1911 • *Selig* • USA
EVIL POWER, THE • 1913 • Turner Otis • USA
EVIL PRIEST, THE see **GOKUAKU BOZU** • 1968
EVIL ROY SLADE • 1971 • Paris Jerry • USA
EVIL SAG, THE • 1917 • Thayer Otis B. • SHT • USA
EVIL SENSES • 1987 • Lavia Gabriele • ITL
EVIL SHE DID, THE • 1914 • Martin E. A. • USA
EVIL SPAWN • 1987 • Hall Kenneth J. • USA • METAMORPHOSIS ○ ALIVE BY NIGHT ○ DEADLY STING
EVIL SPELL see **MALEFICES** • 1962
EVIL SPIRIT see **IKIRYO** • 1927
EVIL SPIRITS see **MALEFICES** • 1962
EVIL SPIRITS OF THE EUPHRATES, THE see **FIRATIN CINLERI** • 1979
EVIL STREET see **GERMANIA, ANNO ZERO** • 1947
EVIL THAT IS EVE, THE see **MANCHE ET LA BELLE, UNE** • 1957
EVIL THAT MEN DO, THE • 1909 • Brooke Van Dyke • USA
EVIL THAT MEN DO, THE • 1983 • Thompson J. Lee • USA, MXC
EVIL THAT MEN DO, THE see **LITTLE DOOR INTO THE WORLD, THE** • 1923
EVIL THEREOF, THE • 1913 • *Milford Bliss* • USA
EVIL THEREOF, THE • 1916 • Vignola Robert G. • USA
EVIL THOUGHTS see **CATTIVI PENSIERI** • 1976
EVIL TIMES see **ZEIT IST BOSE, DIE** • 1982
EVIL TOWN • 1977 • Traynor Peter S., Spiegel Larry, Collins Edward • USA
EVIL TRIO see **DAIAKUTO** • 1968
EVIL UNDER THE SUN • 1982 • Hamilton Guy • UKN
EVIL VILLAGE see **FALU ROSSZA, A** • 1938
EVIL WE DO, THE • 1914 • *Selig* • USA
EVIL WOMEN DO, THE • 1916 • Julian Rupert • USA • CLIQUE OF GOLD, THE
EVIL/HATE/KILLER see **PSYCHO FROM TEXAS** • 1982
EVILS OF CHINATOWN (UKN) see **CONFESSIONS OF AN OPIUM EATER** • 1962
EVILS OF DORIAN GRAY, THE see **DIO CHIAMATO DORIAN, IL** • 1970
EVILS OF THE NIGHT • 1983 • Rustam Mardi • USA
EVILSPEAK • 1982 • Weston Eric • USA
EVIN HRICH • 1919 • Binovec Vaclav • CZC • EVA'S SIN
EVINTRUDE, DIE GESCHICHTE EINES ABENTEURERS • 1914 • Gliese Rochus, Rye Stellan, Wegener Paul • FRG
EVITA –IF SOMEBODY WANTS TO LISTEN, LET HIM LISTEN see **EVITA –WUIEN QUIERE OIR QUE OIGA** • 1984
EVITA PERON • 1981 • Chomsky Marvin • TVM • USA • EVITA, THE FIRST LADY
EVITA, THE FIRST LADY see **EVITA PERON** • 1981
EVITA –WUIEN QUIERE OIR QUE OIGA • 1984 • Mignogna Eduardo • ARG • EVITA –IF SOMEBODY WANTS TO LISTEN, LET HIM LISTEN
EVITEZ LE DESORDRE • 1949 • Decae Henri • SHT • FRN
EVLAT UGRUNA • 1967 • Inanoglu Turker • TRK • FOR MY SON
EVOCATION • 1938 • Ciampi Yves • FRN
EVOCATION SPIRITE • 1899 • Melies Georges • FRN • SUMMONING THE SPIRITS (USA)
EVOIA–MANTOUDI 76 • 1977 • Antonopoulos Giorgos • DOC • GRC
EVOLUON • 1969 • de Wit Ted, Erends Ronny • SHT • NTH
EVOLUTION • 1923 • Fleischer Max • DOC • USA
EVOLUTION • 1932 • Carrick Allyn B. • USA
EVOLUTION • 1971 • Mills Michael • ANS • CND
EVOLUTION • 1980 • Graber Sheila • UKN
EVOLUTION DE L'OEUF • 1925 • Painleve Jean • SHT • FRN
EVOLUTION OF CUTEY, THE • 1915 • Van Wally • USA
EVOLUTION OF LIFE • 1964 • *Halas John (P)* • ANS • UKN
EVOLUTION OF MAN, THE • 1920 • *Aywon Film Co.* • USA • JACK THE MAN–APE
EVOLUTION OF PERCIVAL, THE • 1914 • Beggs Lee • USA
EVOLUTION OF THE MOTION PICTURE, THE • 1921 • Griffith D. W. • USA
EVOLUTIONS • 1955 • Davis James* • SHT • USA
EVRIDIKI BA–2037 • 1975 • Nikolaidis Nikos • GRC • EURIDICE BA–2037
EWA CHCE SPAC • 1958 • Chmielewski Tadeusz • PLN • EVE WANTS TO SLEEP
EWA + EWA • 1971 • Fiwek Wojciech • DOC • PLN • EVE + EVE
EWIGE FLUCH, DER • 1921 • Wendhausen Fritz • FRG
EWIGE KAMPF, DER • 1921 • Stein Paul L. • FRG
EWIGE KLANG, DER • 1943 • Rittau Gunther • FRG • GEIGER, DER
EWIGE LEBEN, DAS see **THEOPHRASTUS PARACELSUS** • 1916
EWIGE MASKE, DIE • 1935 • Hochbaum Werner • AUS, SWT • ETERNAL MASK, THE (USA)
EWIGE MONCH IM BANNE DER MUSIK, DER • 1920 • *Fery-Film* • FRG
EWIGE NACHT, DIE • 1914 • Gad Urban • FRG, DNM • EVIGE NAT, DEN (DNM)
EWIGE NARANIM see **ETERNAL FOOLS** • 1930
EWIGE QUELL, DER • 1939 • Kirchhoff Fritz • FRG
EWIGE RATSEL, DAS • 1919 • Coenen Josef • FRG
EWIGE SCHONHEIT • 1919 • Walther-Fein Rudolf • FRG
EWIGE SPIEL, DAS • 1951 • Cap Frantisek • FRG
EWIGE TRAUM, DER • 1934 • Fanck Arnold • FRG • KONIG DES MONT-BLANC, DER
EWIGE VERRAT, DER see **JUDAS VON TIROL, DER** • 1933
EWIGE ZWEIFEL, DER • 1917 • Dupont E. A. • FRG
EWIGER STROM • 1919 • Guter Johannes • FRG
EWIGER WALD • 1936 • Springer Hans, von Sonjevski-Jamrowski Rolf • FRG
EWIGER WALZER • 1954 • Verhoeven Paul • FRG • ETERNAL WALTZ, THE (USA)
...EWIGES WIENERLIED see **DAS IST MEIN WIEN** • 1965
EWIGKEIT VON GESTERN see **BRUTALITAT IN STEIN** • 1960
EWIGKEIT VON GESTERN, DIE • 1963 • Schamoni Peter • SHT • FRG
EWOK ADVENTURE, AN see **CARAVAN OF COURAGE: AN EWOK ADVENTURE** • 1984
EWOKS: THE BATTLE FOR ENDOR • 1985 • Wheat Jim, Wheat Ken • TVM • USA
EX–BAD BOY • 1931 • Moore Vin • USA • HIS TEMPORARY AFFAIR (UKN) ○ WHOLE TOWN'S TALKING, THE
EX–CHAMP • 1936 • Rosen Phil • USA • GOLDEN GLOVES (UKN)
EX–CONVICT • 1904 • Porter Edwin S. • USA
EX–CONVICT • 1967 • Reyes Efren • PHL
EX–CONVICT 4287 • 1915 • Mackley Arthur • USA
EX–CONVICT, THE • 1913 • Eagle Oscar • USA
EX–CONVICT, THE • 1914 • *Coombs Guy* • USA
EX–CONVICT NO.900 • 1908 • Porter Edwin S. • USA
EX–CONVICT'S ORDEAL, AN • 1912 • *Republic* • USA
EX–CONVICT'S PLUNGE, THE • 1913 • Kirkland Hardee • USA
EX–FLAME • 1930 • Halperin Victor Hugo • USA • MIXED DOUBLES
EX–LADY • 1933 • Florey Robert • USA
EX–MISTRESS see **MY PAST** • 1931
EX–MRS. BRADFORD, THE • 1936 • Roberts Stephen • USA • ONE TO TWO
EX–PLUMBER • 1931 • Arbuckle Roscoe • USA
EX–ROOSTER • 1932 • Sandrich Mark • SHT • USA
EX–SWEETIES • 1931 • Neilan Marshall • SHT • USA
EX VOTO • 1986 • Langjahr Erich • SWT
EX–VOTO, L' • 1919 • L'Herbier Marcel • FRN
EXALTED FLAPPER, THE • 1929 • Tinling James • USA
EXAM see **IZPIT** • 1971
EXAM, THE see **ZALICZENIE** • 1968
EXAM, THE see **EGZAMIN** • 1969
EXAMINATION, AN see **ZALICZENIE** • 1968
EXAMINATION, THE • 1952 • Thorndike Andrew, Thorndike Annelie • DOC • GDR
EXAMINATION, THE see **EGZAMIN** • 1969
EXAMINATION DAY AT SCHOOL • 1910 • Griffith D. W. • USA
EXAMPLE, AN • 1915 • *Macquarrie Murdock* • USA
EXAMPLE, THE see **IBRET** • 1971
EXAMS AT AN IN APPROPRIATE TIME see **IZPITI PO NIKOYE VREME** • 1974
EXAMS AT ANY OLD TIME see **IZPITI PO NIKOYE VREME** • 1974
EXCALIBUR • 1981 • Boorman John • UKN • MERLIN AND THE KNIGHTS OF KING ARTHUR ○ KNIGHTS
EXCEEDING HIS DUTY • 1911 • Fitzhamon Lewin? • UKN
EXCEEDING HIS LEGAL SPEED • 1904 • *Warwick Trading Co.* • UKN
EXCEEDING THE LIMIT • 1919 • Rooke Arthur • UKN
EXCELLENSEN • 1944 • Ekman Hasse • SWD • HIS EXCELLENCY
EXCELSIOR! • 1901 • Melies Georges • FRN • PRINCE OF MAGICIANS, THE (UKN)
EXCELSIOR • 1906 • Gilbert Arthur • UKN
EXCELSIOR • 1909 • *Powers* • USA
EXCELSIOR • 1909 • *Warwick Trading Co.* • UKN
EXCELSIOR • Pinschewer Julius • ANM • FRG
EXCELSIOR • 1914 • Comerio Luca • ITL
EXCELSIOR • 1931 • UKN
EXCENTRIQUE, L' see **MON AMANT L'ASSASSIN** • 1931
...EXCEPT PEOPLE GET KILLED see **MISSION BATANGAS** • 1967
EXCEPTION TO THE RULE, AN • 1911 • Porter Edwin S. • USA
EXCEPTIONAL SITUATION, AN see **VYJIMECNA SITUACE** • 1985
EXCERPT FROM A NEWSPAPER • 1987 • Tsankov Pancho • DOC • BUL
EXCES PORNOGRAPHIQUES • 1978 • Bernard-Aubert Claude • FRN
EXCESS BAGGAGE • 1920 • Edwards Harry J. • SHT • USA
EXCESS BAGGAGE • 1926 • Lamont Charles • SHT • USA
EXCESS BAGGAGE • 1928 • Cruze James • USA
EXCESS BAGGAGE • 1933 • Davis Redd • UKN
EXCESS BAGGAGE, THE • 1911 • *Essanay* • USA
EXCHANGE, THE • 1911 • *Champion* • USA
EXCHANGE AND DIVIDE • 1980 • Dickinson Margaret • UKN
EXCHANGE IS NO ROBBERY • 1898 • Hepworth Cecil M. • UKN
EXCHANGE IS NO ROBBERY • 1902 • *Warwick Trading Co* • UKN • UNFAIR EXCHANGE IS ROBBERY
EXCHANGE OF LABELS, THE • 1912 • *Pollard Harry* • USA
EXCHANGE OF WIVES, AN • 1925 • Henley Hobart • USA
EXCHANGE STUDENT • 1970 • *Distripix* • USA
EXCITATION • 1975 • Emerson Les • FRN
EXCITATION see **CALDE LABBRA** • 1976
EXCITE ME (UKN) see **TUO VIZIO E UNA STANZA CHIUSA E SOLO IO NE HO LE CHIAVI, IL** • 1972
EXCITED • 1969 • Telmig Akdov • USA
EXCITEMENT • 1924 • Hill Robert F. • USA • THRILL GIRL, THE
EXCITEMENT see **KOFUN** • 1968
EXCITEMENT OF A YOUNG DAY see **WAKAKI HI NO KANGEKI** • 1931
EXCITERS, THE • 1923 • Campbell Maurice • USA
EXCITING ADVENTURE, AN see **KOUZELNE DOBRODRUZSTVI** • 1983
EXCITING COURTSHIP, AN • 1914 • *Komic* • USA
EXCITING HONEYMOON, AN • 1913 • *Pates Gwendolyne* • USA
EXCITING OUTING, AN • 1912 • *Cumpson John* • USA
EXCITING WIVES see **CASE OF THE STRIPPING WIVES, THE** • 1966
EXCLAMATION POINT see **WYKRZKNIK**
EXCLUDED, THE see **AUSGESPERRTEN, DIE** • 1982
EXCLUSIVE • 1937 • Hall Alexander • USA
EXCLUSIVE MODEL, THE • 1922 • Dunstall George • UKN
EXCLUSIVE PATTERN, THE • 1913 • *Lubin* • USA
EXCLUSIVE RIGHTS • 1926 • O'Connor Frank • USA
EXCLUSIVE STORY • 1935 • Seitz George B. • USA
EXCURSION, THE see **EKDROMI, I** • 1967
EXCURSION A VUELTABAJO • 1965 • Gomez Sara • DOC • CUB
EXCURSION HOUSE • 1954 • Van Dyke Willard • DOC • USA
EXCURSION INTO THE COSMOS see **WYCIECZKA W KOSMOS** • 1961
EXCURSION INTO THE UNKNOWN see **WYCIECZKA W NIEZNANE** • 1968
EXCURSION TO AUSCHWITZ–BIRKENAU see **WYCIECZKA W NIEZNANE** • 1968
EXCURSION TO THE MOON • 1907 • *Pathe* • FRN
EXCURSIONS DANS LA VILLE see **SI TU VEUX** • 1932
EXCUSE ME • 1916 • Savage Henry W. • USA
EXCUSE ME • 1924 • Goulding Alf • USA
EXCUSE ME • 1925 • Grinde Nick • USA
EXCUSE ME, ARE YOU FAMILIAR WITH SEX? see **SCUSI, LEI CONOSCE IL SESSO?** • 1968
EXCUSE ME, ARE YOU WATCHING FOOTBALL? see **VERZEIHUNG, SEHEN SIE FUSSBALL** • 1983
EXCUSE ME, BUT THERE'S A COMPUTER ASKING FOR YOU • 1983 • Howe John • CND
EXCUSE ME, DO THEY BEAT HERE? see **PRZEPRASZAM, CZY TU BIJA?** • 1977
EXCUSE ME, DO YOU LIKE SEX? (UKN) see **SCUSI, LEI CONOSCE IL SESSO?** • 1968
EXCUSE ME, IS IT HERE THEY BEAT UP PEOPLE? see **PRZEPRASZAM, CZY TU BIJA?** • 1977
EXCUSE ME, SHALL WE MAKE LOVE? see **SCUSI, FACCIAMO L'AMORE?** • 1968
EXCUSE MY DUST • 1920 • Wood Sam • USA • BEAR TRAP, THE
EXCUSE MY DUST • 1951 • Rowland Roy • USA
EXCUSE MY GLOVE • 1925 • Roach Hal • SHT • USA
EXCUSE MY GLOVE • 1936 • Davis Redd • UKN
EXECRABLE DESTINY OF GUILLEMETTE BABIN, THE see **DESTIN EXECRABLE DE GUILLEMETTE BABIN, LE** • 1948
EXECUTED AT DAWN • 1964 • Andrikanis Yevgeni • USS
EXECUTION • 1968 • Paolella Domenico • ITL
EXECUTION, L' • Gobbi Sergio • FRN
EXECUTION, THE • 1913 • *Monogram Exhibition Co.* • USA
EXECUTION, THE • 1985 • Wendkos Paul • TVM • USA
EXECUTION, THE see **FUSILACION** • 1962
EXECUTION, THE see **TIRBARAN** • 1974
EXECUTION, THE see **MARTIN** • 1980
EXECUTION, THE (UKN) see **TOD EINES FREMDEN, DER** • 1972
EXECUTION D'UN ESPION • 1897 • Melies Georges • FRN • EXECUTION OF A SPY
EXECUTION IN AUTUMN see **CH'IU CHUEH** • 1971
EXECUTION NIGHT • 1957 • *Lowe Edmund* • MTV • USA
EXECUTION OF A SPY see **EXECUTION D'UN ESPION** • 1897
EXECUTION OF MARY, QUEEN OF SCOTS, THE • 1895 • Heiss William?, Clark Alfred? • USA
EXECUTION OF PRIVATE SLOVIK, THE • 1974 • Johnson Lamont • TVM • USA
EXECUTION OF RAYMOND GRAHAM, THE • 1985 • Petrie Daniel • TVM • USA
EXECUTION OF TRAITOR ERNST S., THE see **ERSCHIESSUNG DES LANDESVERRATERS ERNST S., DIE** • 1976
EXECUTION SQUAD (USA) see **POLIZIA RINGRAZIA, LA** • 1972
EXECUTIONER 2 see **EXECUTIONER, PART II, THE** • 1984
EXECUTIONER, THE • 1970 • Wanamaker Sam • UKN
EXECUTIONER, THE • 1978 • Mitchell Duke • USA
EXECUTIONER, THE see **MASTERMAN** • 1920
EXECUTIONER, THE see **BOIA DI VENEZIA, IL** • 1964
EXECUTIONER, THE see **VERDUGO, EL** • 1964
EXECUTIONER, THE see **MAJSTER KAT** • 1965
EXECUTIONER, THE see **AZRAIL BENIM** • 1968
EXECUTIONER, THE see **SKARPRETTEREN** • 1972
EXECUTIONER, THE see **EXECUTIONER, PART II, THE** • 1984
EXECUTIONER OF VENICE, THE see **BOIA DI VENEZIA, IL** • 1964
EXECUTIONER ON THE HIGH SEAS, THE see **GIUSTIZIERE DEI MARE, IL** • 1962
EXECUTIONER ON THE SEAS, THE see **GIUSTIZIERE DEI MARE, IL** • 1962
EXECUTIONER, PART II, THE • 1984 • Bryan James • USA • EXECUTIONER 2 ○ EXECUTIONER, THE

EXECUTIONERS, THE see **NURNBERGER PROZESS, DER** • 1958
EXECUTIONERS FROM SHAOLIN see **HUNG HSI-KUAN** • 1977
EXECUTIONER'S SONG, THE see **EXECUTIONER'S SONG -THE GARY GILMORE STORY, THE** • 1982
EXECUTIONER'S SONG -THE GARY GILMORE STORY, THE • 1982 • Schiller Lawrence • TVM • USA • EXECUTIONER'S SONG, THE
EXECUTIONS CAPITALES, LES • 1906 • Zecca Ferdinand • FRN • PEINE DE MORT A TRAVERS LES AGES, LA
EXECUTIVE ACTION • 1973 • Miller David • USA
EXECUTIVE CLEMENCY • 1911 • *Baggot King* • USA
EXECUTIVE HOUSEWIVES see **JEUX POUR COUPLES INFIDELES** • 1972
EXECUTIVE SUITE • 1954 • Wise Robert • USA
EXECUTORS, THE see **ESECUTORI, GLI** • 1976
EXEMPLE ETRETAT • 1962 • Lepeuve Monique • SHT • FRN
EXERCICE DU POUVOIR, L' • 1976 • Galland Philippe • FRN
EXERCISE GREEN • 1982 • Ohlsson Terry (c/d) • DOC • ASL • OPERATION CELLULOID
EXERCISE RUNNING JUMP II • 1972 • Kroitor Roman • CND
EXHIBITION • 1975 • Davy Jean-Francois • FRN
EXHIBITION 79 • 1979 • Davy Jean-Francois • FRN
EXHIBITION II • 1978 • Davy Jean-Francois • FRN
EXHIBITION OF PAINTINGS see **CHITRA MELA** • 1967
EXHIBITION SAUSAGE VENDOR, THE see **VYSTAVNI PARKAR A LEPIC PLAKATU** • 1898
EXHIBITIONS DANOISES • 1977 • Ayranu Lino • FRN
EXHUMATION OF THE REMAINS OF SERGEI RADONEZHKOVO, THE see **VSKRYTIE MOSHCHEI SERGIYA RADONEZHSKOVO** • 1920
EXIGENCE, L' • 1974 • Dansereau Fernand, Rossignol Yolande • SHT • CND
EXIGENCE DES TEMPS, L' see **HUKM AZ-ZAMAN** • 1952
EXIL, L' • 1971 • Vamos Thomas • CND
EXILE • 1917 • Tourneur Maurice • USA
EXILE • 1965 • Irvin John • UKN
EXILE see **EXILIO** • 1979
EXILE, L' • 1980 • Ganda Oumarou • NGR • EXILE, THE
EXILE, THE • 1913 • *Lamon Isabelle* • USA
EXILE, THE • 1931 • Micheaux Oscar • USA
EXILE, THE • 1947 • Ophuls Max • USA
EXILE, THE • 1985 • Pinsent Gordon • MTV • CND
EXILE, THE see **EXILE, L'** • 1980
EXILE AND HOPE see **EXILIO Y ESPERANZA**
EXILE EXPRESS • 1939 • Garrett Otis • USA
EXILE FROM EDEN • *Living Book* • SHT • USA
EXILE OF BAR-K RANCH, THE • 1915 • Eason B. Reeves • USA
EXILED see **AEVENTYRERSKEN** • 1914
EXILED see **JILT, THE** • 1922
EXILED see **HEIMWEH** • 1927
EXILED CHIEF, THE • 1910 • *Kalem* • USA
EXILED ON MAIN STREET • 1980 • Zervos Nikos • GRC
EXILED TO SHANGHAI • 1937 • Grinde Nick • USA
EXILES, THE • 1923 • Mortimer Edmund • USA
EXILES, THE • 1961 • MacKenzie Kent • USA
EXILES, THE (UKN) see **LANDSFLYKTIGE, DE** • 1921
EXILE'S LOVE, AN • 1910 • *Lubin* • USA
EXILIO • 1979 • de la Barra Leonardo • DCS • BLG • EXILE
EXILIO Y ESPERANZA • Lubbert Jorge, Poelmans Christian • BLG • EXILE AND HOPE
EXIPNAKIAS, O • 1967 • Karayannis Kostas • GRC • QUICK-WIT, THE
EXISTENCE see **14, THE** • 1973
EXISTING LOVE see **JEEVITHA BANDHAM** • 1968
EXISTIO OTRA HUMANIDAD • 1976 • Marcos Julian • SPN
EXIT • 1970 • Lokkeberg Pal • NRW, DNM
EXIT • 1987 • Menard Robert • CND
EXIT 7 • 1980 • Degelin Emile • BLG
EXIT 10 • 1978 • Gyllenhaal Stephen • SHT • USA
EXIT 19 see **IZLAZ 19** • 1989
EXIT.. BUT DON'T PANIC! see **EXIT -NUR KEINE PANIK!** • 1980
EXIT-EXIL • 1986 • Monheim Luc • BLG, FRN
EXIT GENUA • 1989 • Koerfer Thomas • SWT, FRG, FRN • GENOA EXIT, THE
EXIT LAUGHING see **ARE YOU THERE?** • 1930
EXIT -NO PANIC! see **EXIT -NUR KEINE PANIK!** • 1980
EXIT -NUR KEINE PANIK! • 1980 • Novotny Franz • AUS, FRG • EXIT -NO PANIC! ○ EXIT.. BUT DON'T PANIC!
EXIT QUIETLY • 1921 • Christie Al • USA
EXIT SMILING • 1926 • Taylor Sam • USA
EXIT THE DRAGON, ENTER THE TIGER • 1976 • Lee Tso Nam • HKG
EXIT THE VAMP • 1921 • Urson Frank • USA
EXITUS • 1988 • Kroumov Krassimir • BUL
EXO-MAN • 1977 • Irving Richard • TVM • USA
EXO PTOCHIA • 1932 • Gaziadis Dimitrios • GRC • BE HAPPY
EXODE, L' • 1910 • Feuillade Louis • FRN
EXODOS • 1976 • Lintzeris Yannis • GRC • EXODUS
EXODUS • 1960 • Preminger Otto • USA
EXODUS see **KHOUROUJ 67, AL-** • 1968
EXODUS see **EXODOS** • 1976
EXONERATION • 1913 • *Buckham Hazel* • USA
EXORCISM • 1986 • UKN
EXORCISM see **EXORCISMO** • 1974
EXORCISM AT MIDNIGHT see **NAKED EVIL** • 1966
EXORCISMO • 1974 • Bosch Juan • SPN • EXORCISM
EXORCISM'S DAUGHTER • 1974 • Moreno Alba Rafael • SPN • HOUSE OF INSANE WOMEN
EXORCIST 3: CRIES AND SHADOWS, THE see **URLO DALLE TENEBRE, UN** • 1975
EXORCIST, THE • 1973 • Friedkin William • USA
EXORCIST II: THE HERETIC • 1977 • Boorman John • USA • HERETIC, THE
EXORCIST III: THE LEGION • 1990 • Blatty William Peter • USA
EXORCIST -ITALIAN STYLE, THE (USA) see **ESORCICCIO, L'** • 1975
EXOSMOSIS • 1976 • Aguirre Javier • SHT • SPN
EXOTIC DREAMS OF CASANOVA, THE • 1971 • *Rocco Johnny* • USA • YOUNG SWINGERS, THE
EXOTIC ONES, THE • 1968 • Ormond Ron • USA
EXPANSION OF GERMANY 1870-1914, THE • 1936 • Jones Andrew Miller • DOC • UKN
EXPATRIADOS, LOS • 1963 • Cortes Fernando • MXC, PRC • EXPATRIATES, THE
EXPATRIATES, THE see **EXPATRIADOS, LOS** • 1963
EXPECTANTS see **VARAKOSOK** • 1975
EXPECTATION • 1972 • Shariliev Borislav • BUL
EXPECTATION, THE • 1970 • Creanga Serban • RMN
EXPECTATIONS • Beller Arvid • USA
EXPECTATIONS see **OCZEKIWANIE** • 1962
EXPECTATIONS see **VARAKOSOK** • 1975
EXPECTATIONS see **ESPERANZA** • 1989
EXPECTED AND UNEXPECTED LOVE, AN see **ESPERADO AMOR DESESPERADO, EL** • 1975
EXPECTED SINS, THE see **LICZE NA WASZE GRZECHY** • 1963
EXPEDIENTE LEONARDO • 1977 • Cosmi Carlo • VNZ • LEONARDO PROCEEDINGS, THE
EXPEDITION • 1962 • Stitt Alexander • DCS • ASL
EXPEDITION see **POHOD** • 1968
EXPEDITION, THE (UKN) see **ABHIJAN** • 1962
EXPEDITION MOON see **ROCKET SHIP X-M** • 1950
EXPEDITION RODA HAVET • 1957 • *Borjeson Bengt (Edt)* • SWD • AVENTYR I HAJARNAS HAV
EXPEDITION TO THE BLACK ISLAND, AN see **WYPRAWA NA CZARNA WYSPE** • 1955
EXPEDITION TO THE RED PLANET • 1968 • Villard Raymond • SHT • USA
EXPELLED FROM PARADISE see **IZGONEN OT RAYA** • 1967
EXPENDABLES, THE • 1988 • Moos A. I. • USA
EXPENSIVE DRINK, AN • 1913 • *Crystal* • USA
EXPENSIVE ECONOMY • 1915 • *Wadsworth William* • USA
EXPENSIVE HUSBANDS • 1938 • Connolly Bobby • USA
EXPENSIVE KISSES • 1930 • Christie Al • USA
EXPENSIVE KISSES • 1931 • Watson William • USA
EXPENSIVE SHINE, AN • 1912 • *Finch Flora* • USA
EXPENSIVE TASTE • 1979 • *Wells Elaine* • USA
EXPENSIVE VISIT, AN • 1915 • Louis Will • USA
EXPENSIVE WOMEN • 1931 • Henley Hobart • USA
EXPERIENCE • 1921 • Fitzmaurice George • USA
EXPERIENCE • 1969 • Neal Peter • DOC • UKN
EXPERIENCE • 1983 • Brocka Lino • PHL
EXPERIENCE, THE see **TAJROBE** • 1975
EXPERIENCE DE GUYENNE, L' • 1965-66 • Garceau Raymond • DCS • CND
EXPERIENCE, MY BOY! see **ANUBAVI RAJA ANUBAVI** • 1967
EXPERIENCE PREFERRED -BUT NOT ESSENTIAL • 1983 • Duffell Peter • UKN
EXPERIENCER, THE • 1977 • Kohler Michael • UKN
EXPERIENCIA PREMATRIMONIAL • 1972 • Maso Pedro • SPN
EXPERIMENT • 1943 • Fric Martin • CZC
EXPERIMENT • Hirsch Hy • SHT • USA
EXPERIMENT • 1977 • Al-Tohamy Foa'Ad • IRQ
EXPERIMENT, THE • 1915 • West Langdon • USA
EXPERIMENT, THE • 1922 • Hill Sinclair • UKN
EXPERIMENT ALCATRAZ • 1950 • Cahn Edward L. • USA
EXPERIMENT DES PROF. MITHRANY, DAS • 1920 • Buchowetzki Dimitri • FRG
EXPERIMENT "EVA" • 1985 • Balik Jaroslav • CZC • "EVA" EXPERIMENT, THE
EXPERIMENT IN EVIL (UKN) see **TESTAMENT DU DR. CORDELIER, LE** • 1959
EXPERIMENT IN MURDER see **KRONVITTNET** • 1989
EXPERIMENT IN TEACHING • 1968 • Crabb Lawrence • UKN
EXPERIMENT IN TERROR • 1962 • Edwards Blake • USA • GRIP OF FEAR, THE (UKN)
EXPERIMENT NO.1 • 1915-20 • *Bray John R. (P)* • ANS • USA
EXPERIMENT NO.2 • 1915-20 • *Bray John R. (P)* • ANS • USA
EXPERIMENT NO.3 • 1915-20 • *Bray John R. (P)* • ANS • USA
EXPERIMENT PERILOUS • 1944 • Tourneur Jacques • USA
EXPERIMENT WITH TIME, AN • Dunne J. W. • USA
EXPERIMENTAL ANIMATION • 1933 • Lye Len • SHT • UKN • PEANUT VENDOR
EXPERIMENTAL MARRIAGE • 1919 • Vignola Robert G. • USA
EXPERIMENTS IN MOTION GRAPHICS • 1968 • Whitney John • SHT • USA
EXPERIMENTS OF YALON, THE • 1966 • *Unbehaan Klaus (P)* • FRG
EXPERIMENTS ON THE HUMAN BODY see **ZANKI: SEITAIJIKKEN** • 1967
EXPERT, THE • 1932 • Mayo Archie • USA • OLD MAN MINICK
EXPERT ELOPER, THE • 1919 • Lyons Eddie, Moran Lee • SHT • USA
EXPERTS, THE • 1967 • Cortez Abelardo • PHL
EXPERTS, THE • 1988 • Thomas Dave • USA
EXPERTS, THE see **SACHVERSTANDIGEN, DIE** • 1974
EXPERT'S OPINION • 1935 • Campbell Ivar • UKN
EXPERT'S REPORT, THE • 1911 • *Thanhouser* • USA
EXPIACION • 1920 • Buchs Jose • SPN
EXPIACION, LA • 1910 • de Chomon Segundo • SPN
EXPIATED GUILT see **SONAD SKULD** • 1915
EXPIATION • 1916 • Terwilliger George W. • SHT • USA
EXPIATION • 1918 • de Morlhon Camille • FRN
EXPIATION • 1922 • Hill Sinclair • UKN
EXPIATION see **PO ZAKONU** • 1926
EXPIATION, L' • 1915 • Feuillade Louis • FRN
EXPIATION, THE • 1909 • Griffith D. W. • USA
EXPLANATION OF LOVE, AN see **LIEBESERKLARUNG** • 1988
EXPLODING PLASTIC INEVITABLES, THE see **VELVET UNDERGROUND AND NICO, THE** • 1966
EXPLODING THE MYTH • 1980 • Schulz Bob (c/d) • MTV • CND
EXPLOIT ON THE ICE see **PODVIG VO IDACH** • 1928
EXPLOITATION see **EKSPLOATACIJA** • 1971
EXPLOITEERS, THE see **ACOSADA** • 1963
EXPLOITERS, THE see **SEXPLOITERS, THE** • 1965
EXPLOITS D'APACHES A MONTMARTRE see **PARIS LA NUIT** • 1904
EXPLOITS DE FARFADET, LES • 1916 • Cohl Emile • ANS • FRN
EXPLOITS DE FEU-FOLLET, LES • 1912 • Cohl Emile • ANS • FRN
EXPLOITS EROTIQUES DE MACISTE DANS L'ATLANTIDE • 1973 • de Nesle Robert • FRN
EXPLOITS OF AN INTELLIGENCE AGENT see **PODVIG RAZVEDCHIKA** • 1947
EXPLOITS OF ELAINE, THE • 1915 • Gasnier Louis J., Seitz George B. • SRL • USA
EXPLOITS OF JANNE VANGMAN see **JANNE VANGMANS BRAVADER** • 1948
EXPLOITS OF PARKER, THE • 1918 • *Austin Charles* • UKN
EXPLOITS OF PRIVATE 91 KARLSSON see **91:AN KARLSSONS BRAVADER** • 1951
EXPLOITS OF THE EMDEN, THE • 1928 • *Hall Ken G. (Ed)* • ASL
EXPLOITS OF THREE-FINGERED KATE, THE • 1909 • Martinek H. O. • UKN
EXPLOITS OF TUBBY, THE • 1916 • Wilson Frank • SER • UKN
EXPLORACION • 1972 • Camacho Carlos Antonio • DCS • VNZ • EXPLORATION
EXPLORATION • 1967 • Crabtree Grant • SHT • CND
EXPLORATION • 1967 • Markson Morley • CND
EXPLORATION see **EXPLORACION** • 1972
EXPLORATION DU LAC DE LAVE DU NIRAGONGO, L' • 1959 • Tazieff Haroun • FRN
EXPLORATION IN FRONT OF THE STATION see **KIGEKI EKIMAE TANKEN** • 1967
EXPLORE -EXPO 67 • 1967 • Vaitiekunas Vince • CND
EXPLORER, THE • 1912 • *Powers* • USA
EXPLORER, THE • 1915 • Melford George • USA
EXPLORER, THE • 1931 • *Terry Paul/ Moser Frank (P)* • ANS • USA
EXPLORER, THE • 1963 • Burstall Tim • SHT • ASL
EXPLORERS • 1985 • Dante Joe • USA
EXPLORERS OF THE DEPTHS • 1950 • Frankel Cyril • SHT • UKN
EXPLORERS OF THE WORLD • 1931 • Noice Harold • USA
EXPLORING CHEMISTRY • 1966 • Parker Robert • DOC • UKN
EXPLORING EPHRAIM'S EXPLOIT • 1915 • *Bray John R. (P)* • ANS • USA
EXPLORING THE MARCHES OF BRANDENBERG • 1982 • Graf Roland • GDR
EXPLORING THE UNKNOWN • 1977 • *Lancaster Burt (Nar)* • DOC • USA
EXPLOSION • 1970 • Bricken Jules • CND
EXPLOSION see **PURSUIT** • 1972
EXPLOSION, L' • 1970 • Simenon Marc • FRN, ITL, CND
EXPLOSION, THE see **INFIJAR, EL** • 1986
EXPLOSION CAME see **OTOKO GA BAKUHATSU SURU** • 1959
EXPLOSION COURSE see **INDI RACE: BAKUSO** • 1967
EXPLOSION DEMOGRAPHIQUE • 1967 • Hebert Pierre • ANS • CND • POPULATION EXPLOSION
EXPLOSION OF A MOTOR CAR, THE • 1900 • Hepworth Cecil M. • UKN • DELIGHTS OF AUTOMOBILING, THE (USA)
EXPLOSIVE "D" • 1914 • *Kalem* • USA
EXPLOSIVE GENERATION, THE • 1961 • Kulik Buzz • USA
EXPLOSIVE MR. MAGOO, THE • 1958 • Burness Pete • ANS • USA
EXPLOSIVES -THE TWO METRE LIFELINE • 1972 • Crombie Donald • DOC • ASL
EXPLOSIVO 008 • 1940 • Bauer James • ARG
EXPO 1900 • 1966 • Allegret Marc • SHT • FRN
EXPONERAD • 1971 • Wiklund Gustav • SWD • EXPOSED
EXPORT IN BLOND • 1956 • York Eugen • FRG
EXPORTACAO DE CEREJAS • 1931 • Coelho Jose Adolfo • SHT • PRT
EXPORTACAO DE MELOES • 1938 • Coelho Jose Adolfo • SHT • PRT
EXPORTACAO DE UVAS • 1931 • Coelho Jose Adolfo • SHT • PRT
EXPOSE • 1975 • Clarke James Kenelm • UKN • HOUSE ON STRAW HILL, THE ○ TRAUMA
EXPOSE ME LOVELY • 1976 • Weston Armand • USA
EXPOSE ME NOW • 1982 • Sherman Joe • USA
EXPOSED • 1932 • Herman Al • USA • STRANGE ROADS (UKN)
EXPOSED • 1938 • Schuster Harold • USA
EXPOSED • 1947 • Blair George • USA
EXPOSED • 1980 • Fairbanks Jeffrey • USA
EXPOSED • 1983 • Toback James • USA
EXPOSED see **EXPONERAD** • 1971
EXPOSED BY THE CRIME DOCTOR see **JUST BEFORE DAWN** • 1946
EXPOSED BY THE DICTOGRAPH • 1912 • *Stedman Myrtle* • USA
EXPOSICAO COLONIAL NO PORTO • 1934 • Contreiras Anibal • SHT • PRT
EXPOSICAO DE MARQUINAS AGRICOLAS NA AJUDA • 1953 • Semedo Artur • SHT • PRT
EXPOSICAO DE TAPECARIA • 1968 • Vasconcelos Antonio-Pedro • SHT • PRT
EXPOSICAO DO MUNDO PORTUGUES • 1941 • Ribeiro Antonio Lopes • SHT • PRT
EXPOSICAO HISTORICA DA OCUPACAO NO SECULO XIX • 1938 • Ribeiro Antonio Lopes • SHT • PRT
EXPOSICAO PECUARIA DA GOLEGA, A • 1939 • Coelho Jose Adolfo • SHT • PRT
EXPOSING THE HANDCUFF KINGS • 1914 • *Powers* • USA
EXPOSITION D'ARTISANAT A L'ILE SAINTE-HELENE • Tessier Albert • DCS • CND
EXPOSITION DE 1900, L' see **EXPOSITION DE PARIS, L'** • 1900
EXPOSITION DE CARICATURES see **UNFORSEEN METAMORPHOSIS** • 1912-14
EXPOSITION DE PARIS, L' • 1900 • Melies Georges • FRN • PARIS EXPOSITION 1900 ○ EXPOSITION DE 1900, L'
EXPOSITION FRANCAISE A MOSCOU • 1962 • Pagliero Marcello • SHT • FRN
EXPOSITION PROVINCIALE DE QUEBEC, L' • 1962 • Lavoie Richard • DCS • CND
EXPOSTULATIONS • 1962 • Romero George A. • USA
EXPOSURE! • 1967 • *Lima Productions* • USA
EXPOSURE • 1978 • Hickey Kieran • IRL
EXPOSURE see **RAZOBLATCHENIE** • 1970
EXPOSURE, THE • 1914 • Kelsey Fred A. • USA
EXPOSURE OF THE LAND SWINDLERS • 1913 • Buel Kenean • USA
EXPRESO DE ANDALUCIA • 1956 • Rovira Beleta Francisco • SPN

EXPRESS C.O.D. • 1913 • *Thanhouser* • USA
EXPRESS CAR MYSTERY, THE • 1913 • *Kalem* • USA
EXPRESS DELIVERY • 1913 • Collins Edwin J.? • UKN
EXPRESS ENVELOPE, THE • 1911 • *Kalem* • USA
EXPRESS LOVE • 1929 • Geneen Sasha • UKN
EXPRESS MESSENGER, THE • 1914 • *Holmes Helen* • USA
EXPRESS MESSENGER, THE • 1915 • *Crawford Florence* • USA
EXPRESS SEDAN see **SUTTOBI KAGO** • 1952
EXPRESS TO HORROR see **SUPERTRAIN** • 1979
EXPRESS TRAIN see **KIGEKI KYUKO RESSHA** • 1967
EXPRESS TRAIN A RAILWAY CUTTING • 1898 • Hepworth Cecil M. • UKN
EXPRESS TRAIN OF LOVE see **BLITZZUG DER LIEBE** • 1925
EXPRESSENS MYSTERIUM • 1913 • Davidsen Hjalmar • DNM
EXPRESSIONS • 1899 • Norton C. Goodwin • UKN
EXPRESSIVE I, THE see **IZRAZI JA** • 1969
EXPRESSO BONGO • 1959 • Guest Val • UKN
EXPROPRIACION, LA • 1972 • Ruiz Raul • CHL • EXPROPRIATION, THE
EXPROPRIATION • 1976 • Mankiewicz Francis • CND
EXPROPRIATION see **EPROPIACION** • 1977
EXPROPRIATION, THE see **EXPROPRIACION, LA** • 1972
EXPULSION see **AUSTREIBUNG, DIE** • 1923
EXPULSION FROM PARADISE see **VERTREIBUNG AUS DEM PARADIES, DIE** • 1977
EXPULSION OF TEARS see **OTOKO NAMIDA NON HAMONJO** • 1967
EXQUISITE CADAVER see **CRUELES, LAS** • 1969
EXQUISITE CORPSES • 1989 • Lopez Temistocles • USA
EXQUISITE SINNER, THE • 1926 • von Sternberg Josef, Rosen Phil • USA
EXQUISITE THIEF, THE • 1919 • Browning Tod • USA
EXTASE • 1932 • Machaty Gustav • CZC • ECSTASY ○ MY LIFE
EXTASE • 1932 • Machaty Gustav • FRN
EXTASE see **REGARD, LE** • 1976
EXTASE, L' see **VERS L'EXTASE** • 1960
EXTAZIS 7-TOL 10-IG • 1969 • Kovacs Andras • DOC • HNG • ECSTASY FROM 7 TO 10
EXTENTION TABLE, THE • 1912 • *Delaney Leo* • USA
EXTENUATING CIRCUMSTANCES (USA) see **CIRCONSTANCES ATTENUANTES** • 1946
EXTERIEUR NUIT • 1979 • Bral Jacques, Leca J.-P., Levi Lucien • FRN
EXTERMINATING ANGEL, THE (USA) see **ANGEL EXTERMINADOR, EL** • 1962
EXTERMINATOR 2, THE • 1984 • Buntzman Mark • USA
EXTERMINATOR, THE • 1945 • Donnelly Eddie • ANS • USA
EXTERMINATOR, THE • 1980 • Glickenhaus James • USA
EXTERMINATORS, THE (USA) see **COPLAN FX18 CASSE TOUT** • 1965
EXTERMINATORS OF THE YEAR 3000 • 1984 • Harrison Jules • SPN, ITL
EXTINCTION OF A SOUL • 1956 • Kosower Herbert • SHT • USA
EXTINGUISHED CINDERS see **BRAZA DORMIDA** • 1928
EXTINGUISHED FLAMES see **CSASZAR PARANCSARA, A** • 1956
EXTORTION • 1938 • Hillyer Lambert • USA
EXTRA, EL • 1962 • Delgado Miguel M. • MXC
EXTRA BABY, THE • 1913 • *Hodges Runa* • USA
EXTRA BRIDEGROOM, THE • 1918 • Lyons Eddie, Moran Lee • SHT • USA
EXTRA CONIUGALE • 1965 • Franciosa Massimo, Guerrini Mino, Montaldo Giuliano • ITL
EXTRA DAY, THE • 1956 • Fairchild William • UKN • 12 DESPERATE HOURS ○ ONE EXTRA DAY
EXTRA DOLLARS • 1954 • Quine Richard • SHT • USA
EXTRA! EXTRA! • 1922 • Howard William K. • USA
EXTRA! EXTRA! • 1932 • Sweet Harry • USA
EXTRA GIRL, THE • 1923 • Jones F. Richard • USA
EXTRA KNOT, THE • 1922 • Wynn George • UKN
EXTRA MAN AND THE MILK-FED LION, THE • 1916 • Bertram William • SHT • USA
EXTRA-TERRESTRIAL NASTIE see **NIGHT FRIGHT** • 1968
EXTRA TERRESTRIAL VISITORS see **NUEVOS EXTRA TERRESTRES, LOS** • 1983
EXTRA TURN, AN • 1902 • Williamson James • UKN • EXTREY TURN, THE
EXTRACTING A CHEQUE FROM UNCLE • 1910 • Fitzhamon Lewin? • UKN
EXTRADITION, THE see **AUSLIEFERUNG, DIE** • 1974
EXTRAMUROS • 1985 • Picazo Miguel • SPN • OUTSIDE THE CITY
EXTRANA AVENTURA DE LUIS CANDELAS • 1926 • Buchs Jose • SPN
EXTRANA AVENTURA DE UN HOMBRE, LA see **AMOR A LA VIDA, EL** • 1950
EXTRANA CITA • 1947 • Martinez Solares Gilberto • MXC
EXTRANA OBSESION • 1946 • Diaz Morales Jose • MXC
EXTRANA PASAJERA, LA • 1952 • Rivero Fernando A. • MXC
EXTRANJERA, LA • 1958 • Xiol Juan • SPN
EXTRANO AMANECER • 1947 • Gomez Bascuas Enrique • SPN
EXTRANO AMOR DE LOS VAMPIROS, EL • 1975 • Klimovsky Leon • SPN
EXTRANO CASO DE LA MUJER ASESINADA, EL • 1949 • Hardy Boris H. • ARG
EXTRANO CASO DE MORGAN, EL • 1973 • *Filmadora Chapultepec* • MXC
EXTRANO CASO DEL DR. FAUSTO, EL • 1969 • Suarez Gonzalo • SPN • MEFISTOFELES! ○ STRANGE CASE OF DR. FAUST, THE
EXTRANO CASO DEL HOMBRE Y LA BESTIA, EL • 1951 • Soffici Mario • ARG • STRANGE CASE OF THE MAN AND THE BEAST, THE ○ HOMBRE Y LA BESTIA, EL ○ DOTTOR YEKYLL ○ MAN AND THE BEAST, THE ○ SENSACIONAL Y EXTRANO CASO DEL HOMBRE Y LA BESTIA, EL
EXTRANO EN LA CASA, UN • 1966 • Zacarias Miguel • MXC, VNZ
EXTRANO EN LA ESCALERA, UN • 1954 • Demicheli Tulio • MXC, CUB
EXTRANO HOMBRE DE BERLIN, EL • 1969 • Madrid Jose Luis • SPN
EXTRANO MUJER, UNA • 1946 • Delgado Miguel M. • MXC
EXTRANO VIAJE, EL • 1964 • Fernan-Gomez Fernando • SPN • STRANGE JOURNEY, THE
EXTRAORDINAIRES EXERCICES DE LA FAMILLE COEUR-DE-BUIS, LES • 1912 • Cohl Emile • ANS • FRN • AVENTURES DE LA FAMILLE COEUR DE BOIS, LES
EXTRAORDINARY ADVENTURES OF JULES VERNE, THE see **AVENTURES EXTRAORDINAIRES DE JULES VERNE** • 1952
EXTRAORDINARY ADVENTURES OF MR. WEST IN THE LAND OF THE BOLSHEVIKS see **NEOBYCHAINIYE PRIKLUCHENIYA MISTERA VESTA V STRANYE BOLSHEVIKOV** • 1924
EXTRAORDINARY ADVENTURES OF THE MOUSE AND HIS CHILD, THE • 1977 • Wolf Fred, Swenson Charles • ANM • USA, JPN • MOUSE AND HIS CHILD, THE
EXTRAORDINARY CAB ACCIDENT, AN • 1903 • Booth W. R.? • UKN
EXTRAORDINARY CHILD, THE • 1954 • Brakhage Stan • SHT • USA
EXTRAORDINARY DISLOCATION, AN (USA) see **DISLOCATION MYSTERIEUSE** • 1901
EXTRAORDINARY EVENT, AN • 1959 • Ivchenko Viktor • USS
EXTRAORDINARY EXHIBITION, AN see **NEOBYKNOVENNAIA VYSTAVKA** • 1968
EXTRAORDINARY EXPERIENCE OF SEX see **SEI NO ISHOKU TAIKEN** • 1968
EXTRAORDINARY ILLUSIONS see **DISLOCATION MYSTERIEUSE** • 1901
EXTRAORDINARY ILLUSIONS (USA) see **ILLUSIONS FUNAMBULESQUES** • 1903
EXTRAORDINARY SEAMAN, THE • 1968 • Frankenheimer John • USA
EXTRAORDINARY VOYAGES OF JULES VERNE, THE see **VOYAGES EXTRAORDINAIRES DE JULES VERNE** • 1952
EXTRAORDINARY WAITER, THE • 1902 • Booth W. R. • UKN • MYSTERIOUS HEADS, THE
EXTRAORDINARY WRESTLING MATCH, AN (USA) see **LUTTES EXTRAVAGANTES** • 1899
EXTRAORDINARY YEARS see **NEOBYCEJNA LETA** • 1952
EXTRAVAGANCE • 1912 • *La Badie Florence* • USA
EXTRAVAGANCE • 1915 • Giblyn Charles • USA
EXTRAVAGANCE • 1916 • King Burton L. • USA
EXTRAVAGANCE • 1919 • Schertzinger Victor • USA
EXTRAVAGANCE • 1921 • Rosen Phil • USA
EXTRAVAGANCE • 1930 • Rosen Phil • USA
EXTRAVAGANT BRIDE, THE • 1917 • Calvert E. H. • SHT • USA
EXTRAVAGANT MOLLY • 1915 • Kellino W. P. • UKN
EXTRAVAGANTE MISSION, L' • 1945 • Calef Henri • FRN • MILLIARDAIRE!
EXTRAVAGANTE THEODORA, L' • 1949 • Lepage Henri • FRN
EXTRAVAGANZA • 1968 • Beresford Bruce • SHT • UKN
EXTRAVAGANZA OF GOLGOTHA SMUTS, THE • Holmes Andrew • SHT • UKN
EXTREMADURA • 1967 • Enciso Luis S. • SHT • SPN
EXTREME CLOSE-UP • 1973 • Szwarc Jeannot • USA • SEX THROUGH A WINDOW
EXTREME CLOSE-UP • 1981 • De Sante Charles • USA
EXTREME CLOSE-UP • 1981 • Siegel Lois • CND • PROFOND REGARD, UN
EXTREME PREJUDICE • 1987 • Hill Walter • USA
EXTREME SADNESS see **AYA NI KANASHIKI** • 1956
EXTREME UNCTION • 1967 • Hayeem Benjamin • SHT • USA
EXTREMENOS SE TOCAN, LOS • 1970 • Paso Alfonso • SPN
EXTREMES • 1971 • Klinger Tony, Lytton Mike • DOC • UKN
EXTREMITIES • 1913 • Costello Maurice • USA
EXTREMITIES • 1986 • Young Robert Malcolm • USA
EXTREY TURN, THE see **EXTRA TURN, AN** • 1902
EXTROVERT, THE see **FIGOURATZIS, O** • 1968
EXURBIA • 1988 • Blyth David • NZL
EXZELLENZ UNTERROCK • 1920 • Klitsch Edgar • FRG
EYE see **NAZAR** • 1990
EYE, THE see **SE** • 1948
EYE ABOVE THE WELL, THE • 1988 • van der Keuken Johan • DOC • NTH
EYE CREATURES, THE • 1965 • Buchanan Larry • USA
EYE FOR AN EYE see **OEIL POUR OEIL** • 1918
EYE FOR AN EYE, AN • 1910 • *Vitagraph* • USA
EYE FOR AN EYE, AN • 1913 • *O'Brien Jack* • USA
EYE FOR AN EYE, AN • 1915 • Taylor William D. • USA
EYE FOR AN EYE, AN • 1917 • *Boardman True* • SHT • USA
EYE FOR AN EYE, AN • 1966 • Lewis Herschell G. • USA
EYE FOR AN EYE, AN • 1966 • Moore Michael • USA
EYE FOR AN EYE, AN • 1981 • Carver Steve • USA
EYE FOR AN EYE, AN (USA) see **OEIL POUR OEIL** • 1957
EYE FOR AN EYE, A TOOTH FOR A TOOTH, AN see **OCCHIO PER OCCHIO, DENTE PER DENTE** • 1967
EYE FOR EYE • 1918 • Capellani Albert • USA
EYE HEARS AND THE EAR SEES, THE • 1970 • McLaren Norman • ANS • CND
EYE MUSIC IN RED MAJOR • 1961 • Menken Marie • SHT • USA
EYE MYTH • 1972 • Brakhage Stan • USA
EYE MYTH • 1981 • Brakhage Stan • USA
EYE OF A GOD, THE • 1913 • Golden Joseph A. • USA
EYE OF CONSCIENCE, THE • 1911 • *Selig* • USA
EYE OF COUNT FLICKENSTEIN, THE • 1966 • Conrad Tony • SHT • USA
EYE OF ENVY, THE • 1917 • Ingraham Harrish • USA
EYE OF EVIL see **TAUSEND AUGEN DES DR. MABUSE, DIE** • 1960
EYE OF GOD, THE • 1916 • Weber Lois, Smalley Phillips • USA
EYE OF KRISHLA, THE • 1913 • *Benham Harry* • USA
EYE OF STONE • 1990 • Vachani Nilita • DOC • IND
EYE OF THE BEHOLDER • 1980 • Till Eric • CND
EYE OF THE CAT • 1969 • Rich David Lowell • USA • WYLIE
EYE OF THE DEVIL • 1966 • Thompson J. Lee • USA, UKN • 13
EYE OF THE EAGLE • 1987 • Santiago Cirio H. • USA
EYE OF THE EAGLE 2: INSIDE THE ENEMY see **EYE OF THE EAGLE II** • 1989
EYE OF THE EAGLE II • 1989 • Franklin Carl • USA • EYE OF THE EAGLE 2: INSIDE THE ENEMY ○ K.I.A. KILLED IN ACTION ○ KIA
EYE OF THE EVIL DEAD, THE see **OCCHIO DEL MALE, L'** • 1982
EYE OF THE GOVERNMENT, THE • 1914 • Olcott Sidney • USA
EYE OF THE IDOL, THE • 1912 • Noy Wilfred • UKN
EYE OF THE LABYRINTH, THE see **OCCHIO NEL LABIRINTO, L'** • 1972
EYE OF THE MONOCLE, THE (USA) see **OEIL DU MONOCLE, L'** • 1962
EYE OF THE NEEDLE • 1981 • Marquand Richard • UKN
EYE OF THE NEEDLE, THE (USA) see **SMANIA ADDOSSO, LA** • 1963
EYE OF THE NIGHT, THE • 1916 • Edwards Walter • USA
EYE OF THE SOUL, THE • 1915 • Vale Travers • USA
EYE OF THE SPIDER • 1987 • Hirsch John • USA
EYE OF THE SPIDER see **OCCHIO DEL RAGNO, L'** • 1971
EYE OF THE TIGER • 1986 • Sarafian Richard C. • USA
EYE ON THE SPARROW • 1987 • Korty John • TVM • USA
EYE PUPILS OF TOKYO see **TOKYO NO HITOMI** • 1958
EYE THAT NEVER SLEEPS, THE • 1912 • *Essanay* • USA
EYE TOO MANY, AN • 1915 • *Williams Margot* • USA
EYE UPON THE WIND see **PUPILA AL VIENTO** • 1949
EYE WITNESS • 1939 • Llewellyn Richard • UKN
EYE WITNESS (USA) see **YOUR WITNESS** • 1950
EYEBALL • 1978 • Lenzi Umberto • ITL
EYES • Gour Rajendra • SHT • USA
EYES • 1968 • Singh Hardev • PLN
EYES • 1970 • Brakhage Stan • USA
EYES see **ANKHEN** • 1968
EYES, THE see **DESA NISA** • 1972
EYES AND EARS • 1972 • Polak Dick • SHT • NTH
EYES BEHIND THE STARS (USA) see **OCCHI DALLE STELLE** • 1978
EYES BEYOND THE STARS see **OCCHI DALLE STELLE** • 1978
EYES CLOSED, THE see **YEUX FERMES, LES** • 1972
EYES DO NOT WANT TO CLOSE AT ALL TIMES OR PERHAPS ONE DAY ROME WILL PERMIT HERSELF TO CHOOSE IN H... see **YEUX NE PEUVENT PAS EN TOUT TEMPS SE FERMER OU PEUT-ETRE QU'UN JOUR ROME SE PERMETTRA DE CHOISIR A..** • 1970
EYES DOWN • 1976 • Dunkley R. • UKN
EYES FROM ANOTHER COUNTRY see **AUGEN AUS EINEM ANDEREN LAND** • 1975
EYES HAVE IT • 1932 • Edwards Harry J. • SHT • USA
EYES HAVE IT, THE • 1914 • *Lubin* • USA
EYES HAVE IT, THE • 1945 • Hannah Jack • ANS • USA
EYES IN OUTER SPACE • 1959 • Kimball Ward • SHT • USA
EYES IN THE DARK, THE • 1917 • Crane Frank H. • SHT • USA
EYES IN THE NIGHT • 1942 • Zinnemann Fred • USA
EYES LIKE DADDY see **OJOS COME PAPA, LOS** • 1979
EYES OF A STRANGER • 1981 • Wiederhorn Ken • USA
EYES OF ANNIE JONES, THE • 1963 • Le Borg Reginald • UKN, USA
EYES OF BIRDS, THE see **YEUX DES OISEAUX, LES** • 1982
EYES OF CHARLES SAND, THE • 1972 • Badiyi Reza • TVM • USA
EYES OF FATE • 1933 • Campbell Ivar • UKN
EYES OF FEAR, THE • 1916 • Julian Rupert • SHT • USA
EYES OF FIRE • 1985 • Crouse Avery • USA • CRYING BLUE SKY
EYES OF HELL, THE (UKN) see **MASK, THE** • 1961
EYES OF HOLLYWOOD • 1925 • *Wing Ward* • USA
EYES OF JULIA DEEP, THE • 1918 • Ingraham Lloyd • USA
EYES OF LAURA MARS, THE • 1978 • Kershner Irvin • USA
EYES OF LOVE, THE • 1916 • Kelsey Fred A. • SHT • USA
EYES OF LOVE, THE see **KARLEKENS OGON** • 1922
EYES OF MY CITY, THE see **OCHII DRASULUI MEU** • 1963
EYES OF MYSTERY, THE • 1918 • Browning Tod • USA
EYES OF SATAN, THE • 1913 • *Solax* • USA
EYES OF TEXAS • 1948 • Witney William • USA
EYES OF THE AMARYLLIS, THE • 1982 • Keller Frederick King • USA
EYES OF THE ARMY: WITH R.F.C. AT THE FRONT, THE • 1916 • UKN
EYES OF THE DESERT • 1926 • Reel Frederick Jr. • USA
EYES OF THE DRAGON • 1981 • Vieira George • USA
EYES OF THE DRAGON, THE (USA) see **YEUX DU DRAGON, LES** • 1925
EYES OF THE FOREST • 1923 • Hillyer Lambert • USA
EYES OF THE GOD OF FRIENDSHIP, THE • 1913 • *Frontier* • USA
EYES OF THE HEART • 1920 • Powell Paul • USA
EYES OF THE JUNGLE • 1953 • Landres Paul • USA • DESTINATION DANGER (UKN)
EYES OF THE MUMMY, THE (UKN) see **AUGEN DER MUMIE MA, DIE** • 1918
EYES OF THE MUMMY MA (USA) see **AUGEN DER MUMIE MA, DIE** • 1918
EYES OF THE SAHARA see **OEIL POUR OEIL** • 1957
EYES OF THE SEA • 1963 • Grigorov Roumen • DOC • BUL
EYES OF THE SKIES (UKN) see **MISSION OVER KOREA** • 1953
EYES OF THE SOUL • 1919 • Chautard Emile • USA
EYES OF THE TOTEM • 1927 • Van Dyke W. S. • USA • TOTEM POLE BEGGAR, THE ○ EYES OF TOTEM, THE
EYES OF THE UNDERWORLD • 1929 • Jason Leigh, Taylor Ray • USA
EYES OF THE UNDERWORLD • 1942 • Neill R. William • USA
EYES OF THE WORLD, THE • 1917 • Crisp Donald • USA
EYES OF THE WORLD, THE • 1930 • King Henry • USA
EYES OF TOTEM, THE see **EYES OF THE TOTEM** • 1927
EYES OF YOUTH • 1919 • Parker Albert • USA
EYES ON THE PRIZE: AMERICA'S CIVIL RIGHTS 1954-1965 • 1986 • *Hampton Henry (P)* • DOC • USA
EYES ONLY • 1981 • Ferrand Carlos • MTV • CND
EYES RIGHT • 1905 • Collins Alf? • UKN
EYES RIGHT! • 1926 • Chaudet Louis W. • USA
EYES THAT CANNOT SEE • 1915 • *Balboa* • USA
EYES THAT COULD NOT CLOSE, THE • 1913 • Blache Alice • USA
EYES THAT KILL • 1947 • Grey Richard M. • UKN

EYES THAT KILL, THE see **YEUX QUI MEURENT, LES** • 1912
EYES THAT SEE NOT • 1911 • *Powers* • USA
EYES THAT SEE NOT • 1912 • Porter Edwin S. • USA
EYES THAT SEE NOT • 1915 • Roach Joseph A. • USA
EYES, THE MOUTH, THE (USA) see **OCCHI, LA BOCCA, GLI** • 1983
EYES THE SEA AND A BALL, THE see **NATSUKASHIKI FUE YA TAIKO** • 1967
EYES WITHOUT A FACE (UKN) see **YEUX SANS VISAGE, LES** • 1959
EYEWASH • 1959 • Breer Robert • SHT • USA
EYEWITNESS • 1956 • Box Muriel • UKN
EYEWITNESS • 1970 • Hough John • UKN • SUDDEN TERROR
EYEWITNESS • 1981 • Yates Peter • USA • JANITOR, THE (UKN)
EYOUN SAHERA • 1934 • *Assis* • EGY • ENCHANTING EYES, THE
EZEKIEL • Heinz John • SHT • USA
EZERKILENCSZAZOTVENKETTO see **NYOCADIK SZABAD MAJUS 1, A** • 1952
EZEROV TRIAL, THE see **PROZESS ESEROV** • 1922
EZO GELIN • 1968 • Elmas Orhan • TRK • EZO THE BRIDE
EZO THE BRIDE see **EZO GELIN** • 1968
EZO YAKATA NO KETTO • 1970 • Furusawa Kengo • JPN • DUEL AT EZO (USA)
EZOP • 1969 • Vulchanov Rangel • BUL, CZC • AESOP
EZRA AND THE FORTUNE TELLER • 1911 • *Eclipse* • FRN
EZRA POUND, 80 • 1966 • Bienek Horst • FRG
EZREDES, AZ • 1917 • Curtiz Michael • HNG • COLONEL, THE
EZUST KECSKE, AZ • 1916 • Curtiz Michael • HNG • SILVER GOAT, THE

F

F • Bergeret John • BLG
F-100 • 1956 • Leacock Richard • DOC • USA • HOW THE F-100 GOT ITS TAIL
F-104, BAIL OUT see **JET F-104 DASSYUTSU SEYO** • 1968
F.B.I., THE • 1965 • Graham William A. • TVM • USA
F.B.I. CHIAMA ISTANBUL • 1964 • Salvi Emimmo • ITL • NONE BUT THE LONELY SPY (USA)
F.B.I. CODE 98 • 1964 • Martinson Leslie H. • USA
F.B.I. CONTRO DR. MABUSE see **IM STAHLNETZ DES DR. MABUSE** • 1961
F.B.I. GIRL • 1951 • Berke William • USA
F.B.I. OPERAZIONE BAALBECK • 1964 • Giannini Marcello • ITL, FRN, LBN
F.B.I. OPERAZIONE PAKISTAN see **KOMMISSAR X: JAGT DIE ROTEN TIGER** • 1971
F.B.I. OPERAZIONE VIPERA GIALLA • 1966 • Medori Alfredo • ITL, FRG
F.B.I. STORY, THE • 1959 • LeRoy Mervyn • USA
F.B.I. STORY -THE F.B.I. VERSUS ALVIN KARPIS PUBLIC ENEMY NUMBER ONE, THE • 1974 • Chomsky Marvin • TVM • USA
F COMME FAIRBANKS • 1976 • Dugowson Maurice • FRN
F.D.R., THE LAST YEAR • 1980 • Page Anthony • TVM • USA
F.E.N. • 1980 • Hernandez Antonio • SPN • FORMATION OF THE NATIONAL SPIRIT
F- FIVE, THE see **FILTHY FIVE, THE** • 1968
F FOR FAKE • 1977 • Welles Orson • FRN, FRG, IRN • VERITES ET MENSONGES (FRN) ○ QUESTION MARK ○ FAKE! ○ ?
F.I.S.T. • 1978 • Jewison Norman • USA • FIST
F.J. HOLDEN, THE see **FJ HOLDEN, THE** • 1977
F-MAN • 1936 • Cline Eddie • USA
F.P.1 • 1932 • Hartl Karl • UKN • SECRETS OF F.P.1
F.P.1 ANTWORTET NICHT • 1932 • Hartl Karl • FRG • F.P.1. DOES NOT ANSWER ○ NO ANSWER FROM F.P.1
F.P.1. DOES NOT ANSWER see **F.P.1 ANTWORTET NICHT** • 1932
F- PATTERN OF EVIL see **FORNICON -PATTERN OF EVIL** • 1970
F.R.O. 7 • 1989 • Acevski Jon • ANM • UKN
F.R. SCOTT: RHYME AND REASON • 1982 • Winkler Donald • MTV • CND
F. SCOTT FITZGERALD AND "THE LAST OF THE BELLES" • 1974 • Schaefer George • TVM • USA
F. SCOTT FITZGERALD IN HOLLYWOOD • 1976 • Page Anthony • TVM • USA
"F" STREET see **GIRLS ON F- STREET, THE** • 1966
F.T.A. • 1972 • Parker Francine • DOC • USA • FOXTROT TANGO ALPHA ○ FREE THE ARMY ○ FTA ○ FUCK THE ARMY
F.V.V.A. see **FEMME - VILLA - VOITURE - ARGENT** • 1972
F - W - L see **FINGER - WATER - LIGHT**
FA CH'IEN HAN • 1978 • Wu Yusen • HKG • MONEY CHASERS
FA'A SAMOA -THE SAMOAN WAY • 1972 • Siers James • DOC • NZL
FABBRICA DEI SOLDI, LA • 1965 • Pazzaglia Riccardo • ITL
FABBRICA DEL DUOMO, LA • 1948 • Risi Dino • SHT • ITL
FABBRICA DELL'IMPREVISTO, LA • 1943 • Comin Jacopo • ITL • QUELLO CHE NON T'ASPETTI
FABBRO DEL CONVENTO, IL • 1949 • Calandri Max • ITL • RIVOLTA DEI COSACCHI, LA
FABEL • 1979 • Lochen Erik • NRW • FABLE
FABIAN • 1980 • Gremm Wolfgang • FRG
FABIAN BALINT TALALKOZASA ISTENNEL • 1981 • Fabri Zoltan • HNG • BALINT FABIAN MEETS GOD
FABIAN OCH FLICKAN see **HON KOM SOM EN VIND** • 1952
FABIEN BECOMES AN ARCHITECT see **COMMENT FABIEN DEVIENT ARCHITECTE** • 1901
FABIENNE • 1920 • de Morlhon Camille • FRN
FABIENNE SANS SON JULES • 1964 • Godbout Jacques • SHT • CND
FABIOLA • 1918 • Guazzoni Enrico • ITL
FABIOLA • 1948 • Blasetti Alessandro • ITL
FABLE • 1964 • Buchvarova Radka • ANS • BUL
FABLE see **FABEL** • 1979
FABLE, A • 1971 • Freeman Al Jr. • USA
FABLE, A see **BASNA** • 1979
FABLE OF ...., THE • 1922-23 • *Terry Paul (P)* • ASS • USA
FABLE OF A DREAMER, THE (USA) see **YUMEMI-DOJI** • 1958
FABLE OF A NIGHT GIVEN OVER TO REVELRY, THE • 1915 • *Stine Charles* • USA
FABLE OF AGGIE AND THE AGGRAVATED ATTACKS, THE • 1914 • *Essanay* • USA
FABLE OF ALL THAT TRIANGLE STUFF AS SIZED UP BY THE MEAL TICKET, THE • 1917 • Baker Richard Foster • SHT • USA
FABLE OF BOOKS MADE TO BALANCE, THE • 1916 • Baker Richard Foster • SHT • USA
FABLE OF ELVIRA AND FARINA AND THE MEAL TICKET, THE • 1915 • Baker Richard Foster • USA
FABLE OF FLORA AND ADOLPH AND A HOME GONE WRONG, THE • 1916 • *Essanay* • SHT • USA
FABLE OF HANDSOME JETHRO, WHO WAS SIMPLY CUT OUT TO BE A MERCHANT, THE • 1915 • Baker Richard Foster • USA
FABLE OF HAZEL'S TWO HUSBANDS AND WHAT BECAME OF THEM, THE • 1915 • Baker Richard Foster • USA
FABLE OF HIGH FALUTING TILLIE AND HER PLAIN PARENTS, THE • 1915 • *Essanay* • USA
FABLE OF HIGHER EDUCATION THAT WAS TOO HIGH FOR THE OLD MAN, THE • 1914 • *Beery Wallace* • USA
FABLE OF HOW UNCLE BREWSTER WAS TOO SHIFTY FOR THE TEMPTER, THE • 1914 • *Owens Frank* • USA
FABLE OF HOW WISENSTEIN DID NOT LOSE OUT TO BUTTINSKY, THE • 1916 • Baker Richard Foster • SHT • USA
FABLE OF LUTIE, THE FALSE ALARM, THE • 1914 • *Stonehouse Ruth* • USA
FABLE OF MAY see **POHADKA MAJE** • 1926
FABLE OF MAY see **POHADKA MAJE** • 1940
FABLE OF NAPOLEON AND THE BUMPS, THE • 1914 • Ade George • USA
FABLE OF ONE SAMARITAN WHO GOT PARALYSIS OF THE HELPING HAND, THE • 1914 • *Essanay* • USA
FABLE OF PRINCE FORTUNATUS, WHO MOVED AWAY FROM EASY STREET, AND SILAS, THE SAVER, WHO MOVED IN, THE • 1917 • Wright Fred E. • SHT • USA
FABLE OF SISTER MAE, WHO DID AS WELL AS COULD BE EXPECTED, THE • 1915 • *Scott Betty* • USA
FABLE OF THE ADULT GIRL WHO GOT BUSY, THE • 1914 • *Essanay* • USA
FABLE OF THE AUTHOR AND THE DEAR PUBLIC AND THE PLATE OF MUSH, THE • 1914 • *Cuneo Lester* • USA
FABLE OF THE BACHELOR AND THE BACK-PEDAL, THE • 1915 • *Ainsworth Sidney* • USA
FABLE OF THE BACK-TRACKERS FROM THE HOT SIDEWALKS, THE • 1917 • Metford Lee • SHT • USA
FABLE OF THE BRASH DRUMMER AND THE NECTARINE, THE • 1914 • Ade George • USA
FABLE OF THE BUSH LEAGUE LOVER WHO FAILED TO QUALIFY, THE • 1914 • Ade George • USA
FABLE OF THE BUSY BUSINESS BOY AND THE DROPPERS-IN, THE • 1914 • *Beery Wallace* • USA
FABLE OF THE BUSY MAN AND THE IDLE WOMAN, THE • 1915 • *Essanay* • USA
FABLE OF THE CITY GRAFTER AND THE UNPROTECTED RUBES, THE • 1915 • *Essanay* • USA
FABLE OF THE CLUB GIRLS AND THE FOUR TIMES VETERANS, THE • 1914 • *Essanay* • USA
FABLE OF THE COLD GRAY DAWN OF THE MORNING AFTER, THE • 1915 • *Holmes Rapley* • USA
FABLE OF THE COMING CHAMPION WHO WAS DELAYED, THE • 1914 • Ade George • USA
FABLE OF THE DEMAND THAT MUST BE SUPPLIED, THE • 1915 • *Holmes Gerda* • USA
FABLE OF THE DIFFERENCE BETWEEN LEARNING AND LEARNING HOW, THE • 1914 • *Essanay* • USA
FABLE OF THE DIVINE SPARK THAT HAD A SHORT CIRCUIT, THE • 1915 • *Stonehouse Ruth* • USA
FABLE OF THE ESCAPE OF ARTHUR AND THE SALVATION OF HERBERT, THE • 1915 • Baker Richard Foster • USA
FABLE OF THE FABRICS • 1942 • Mackendrick Alexander • UKN
FABLE OF THE FAMILY THAT DID TOO MUCH FOR NELLIE, THE • 1914 • *Holmes Gerda* • USA
FABLE OF THE FEARSOME FEUD BETWEEN THE FIRST FAMILIES, THE • 1916 • Baker Richard Foster • SHT • USA
FABLE OF THE FELLOW WHO HAD A FRIEND WHO KNEW A GIRL WHO HAD A FRIEND, THE • 1915 • *White Leo* • USA
FABLE OF THE FILM FED FAMILY, THE • 1917 • Baker Richard Foster • SHT • USA
FABLE OF THE FISHERMAN AND THE FISH, THE see **SKAZKA O RYBAKE I RYBKE** • 1913
FABLE OF THE GALLOPING PILGRIM WHO KEPT ON GALLOPING, THE • 1915 • *Maupain Ernest* • USA
FABLE OF THE GALUMPTIOUS GIRL, THE • 1915 • *Stonehouse Ruth* • USA
FABLE OF THE GIRL WHO TOOK NOTES AND GOT WISE AND THEN FELL DOWN, THE • 1917 • Baker Richard Foster • SHT • USA
FABLE OF THE "GOOD FAIRY", THE • 1914 • *Eaton Mabel* • USA
FABLE OF THE GOOD FAIRY WITH THE LORGNETTE AND WHY SHE GOT IT GOOD, THE • 1916 • *Essanay* • SHT • USA
FABLE OF THE GOOD PEOPLE WHO RALLIED TO THE SUPPORT OF THE CHURCH, THE • 1915 • *Essanay* • USA
FABLE OF THE GRASS WIDOW AND THE MESMEREE AND THE SIX DOLLARS, THE • 1916 • *Essanay* • SHT • USA
FABLE OF THE HEIR AND THE HEIRESS, THE • 1915 • *Stine Charles J.* • USA
FABLE OF THE HIGHROLLER AND THE BUZZING BLONDINE, THE • 1915 • *Washburn Bryant* • USA
FABLE OF THE HOME TREATMENT AND THE SURE CURE, THE • 1915 • *Stine Charles J.* • USA
FABLE OF THE HONEYMOON THAT TRIED TO COME BACK, THE • 1914 • Baker Richard Foster • USA
FABLE OF THE HUSBAND WHO SHOWED UP AND DID HIS DUTY, THE • 1914 • *Travers Richard C.* • USA
FABLE OF THE INTERMITTENT FUSSER, THE • 1915 • *Essanay* • USA
FABLE OF THE KID WHO SHIFTED HIS IDEALS TO GOLF AND FINALLY BECAME A BASEBALL FAN AND TOOK....., THE • 1916 • Baker Richard Foster • SHT • USA
FABLE OF THE KITTENISH SUPER-ANNS AND THE WORLD-WEARY SNIPES, THE • 1916 • Baker Richard Foster • SHT • USA
FABLE OF THE LONG RANGE LOVER AND THE LALLYPALOOZE, THE • 1914 • *Dunkinson Harry* • USA
FABLE OF THE LOW DOWN EXPERT ON THE SUBJECT OF BABIES, THE • 1915 • *Maupain Ernest* • USA
FABLE OF THE MANOEUVRES OF JOEL AND FATHER'S SECOND TIME ON EARTH, THE • 1914 • *Essanay* • USA
FABLE OF THE MEN AT THE WOMEN'S CLUB, THE • 1915 • *Essanay* • USA
FABLE OF THE PEOPLE'S CHOICE WHO ANSWERED THE CALL OF DUTY AND TOOK SELTZER, THE • 1914 • *Essanay* • USA
FABLE OF THE PREACHER WHO FLEW HIS KITE BUT NOT BECAUSE HE WISHED TO DO SO, THE • 1916 • *Essanay* • SHT • USA
FABLE OF THE REGULAR BEANERY AND THE PEACHY NEWCOMER, THE • 1914 • Baker Richard Foster • USA
FABLE OF THE ROISTERING BLADES, THE • 1915 • Baker Richard Foster • USA
FABLE OF THE SCOFFER WHO FELL HARD, THE • 1915 • *Dunkinson Harry* • USA
FABLE OF THE SEARCH FOR CLIMATE, THE • 1915 • *Essanay* • USA
FABLE OF THE SLIM GIRL WHO TRIED TO KEEP A DATE THAT WAS NEVER MADE, THE • 1916 • Baker Richard Foster • SHT • USA
FABLE OF THE SMALL TOWN FAVORITE WHO WAS RUINED BY TOO MUCH COMPETITION, THE • 1916 • *Essanay* • SHT • USA
FABLE OF THE SORROWS OF THE UNEMPLOYED AND THE DANGER OF CHANGING FROM BILL TO HAROLD, THE • 1915 • Baker Richard Foster • USA
FABLE OF THE SPEEDY SPRITE, THE • 1917 • Baker Richard Foster • SHT • USA
FABLE OF THE STATESMAN WHO DIDN'T MAKE GOOD, THE • 1915 • Baker Richard Foster • USA
FABLE OF THE STRUGGLE BETWEEN PERSONAL LIBERTY AND THE WAVE OF REFORM, THE • 1915 • *Essanay* • USA
FABLE OF THE SYNDICATE LOVER, THE • 1915 • *Essanay* • USA
FABLE OF THE THROBBING GENIUS OF A TANK TOWN WHO WAS ENCOURAGED BY HER FOLKS WHO WERE PROMINENT, THE • 1916 • Baker Richard Foster • SHT • USA
FABLE OF THE THROUGH TRAIN, THE • 1915 • Baker Richard Foster • USA
FABLE OF THE TIP AND THE TREASURE, THE • 1915 • Baker Richard Foster • USA
FABLE OF THE TOILSOME ASCENT AND THE SHINING TABLE LAMP, THE • 1917 • McGuirk Charles J. • SHT • USA
FABLE OF THE TWELVE-CYLINDER SPEED OF THE LEISURE CLASS, THE • 1917 • Baker Richard Foster • SHT • USA
FABLE OF THE TWO MANDOLIN PLAYERS AND THE WILLING PERFORMER, THE • 1915 • *Essanay* • USA
FABLE OF THE TWO PHILANTHROPIC SONS, THE • 1916 • *Essanay* • SHT • USA
FABLE OF THE TWO SENSATIONAL FAILURES, THE • 1915 • *Holton Lloyd* • USA
FABLE OF THE TWO UNFETTERED BIRDS, THE • 1915 • *Douglas Royal* • USA
FABLE OF THE UNDECIDED BRUNETTE, THE • 1916 • *Essanay* • SHT • USA
FABLE OF THE UPLIFTER AND HIS DANDY LITTLE OPUS, THE • 1917 • Baker Richard Foster • SHT • USA
FABLE OF THE WANDERING BOY AND THE WAYWARD PARENTS, THE • 1917 • Baker Richard Foster • SHT • USA
FABLE OF THE WILLING COLLEGIAN WHO WANTED TO GET A FOOTHOLD, THE • 1916 • *Essanay* • SHT • USA
FABLE OF WHAT THE BEST PEOPLE ARE NOT DOING, THE • 1917 • Baker Richard Foster • SHT • USA
FABLE OF WHAT TRANSPIRES AFTER THE WIND-UP, THE • 1917 • Baker Richard Foster • SHT • USA
FABLE ON LITTLE FISHES, A • 1989 • Pirhasan Baris • TRK
FABLE PROVING THAT SPONGERS ARE FOUND IN A DRUGSTORE, THE • 1914 • *Essanay* • USA
FABLES ABOUT POWER see **SATUJA VALLASTA** • 1970-72
FABLES DE LA FONTAINE, LES • 1925 • O'Galop Marius • ANM • FRN
FABLES FROM HANS CHRISTIAN ANDERSEN see **ANDERSEN MONOGATARI** • 1968
FABLES OF THE GREEN FOREST • ANM • USA
FABRICA DE BOLACHAS TRIUNFU • 1953 • Garcia Fernando • SHT • PRT
FABRICACAO DE CARRUAGENS • 1954 • Mendes Joao • SHT • PRT
FABRICANT DE DIAMANTS, LE • 1908 • Melies Georges • FRN • HABIT NE FAIT PAS LE MOINE, L' ○ FAKE-DIAMOND SWINDLER, A
FABRICANTE DE SUICIDIOS, EL • 1928 • Elias Francisco • SPN
FABRICATION DU CIMENT ARTIFICIEL, LA • 1924 • Gremillon Jean • SHT • FRN
FABRICATION DU FIL, LA • 1924 • Gremillon Jean • SHT • FRN
FABRICATION D'UN ASCENSEUR • Lavoie Hermenegilde • DOC • CND
FABRICATION INDUSTRIELLE DES COMPRIMES ET DRAGEES • 1952 • Gerard • SHT • FRN

FABRICATION INDUSTRIELLE DES SOLUTES INJECTABLES • 1951 • Gerard • SHT • FRN

FABRICS OF THE FUTURE • 1947 • DOC • UKN • THIS MODERN AGE NO.4

FABRIK DER OFFIZIERE • 1960 • Wisbar Frank • FRG

FABRIQUE D'ARGENT • 1908 • de Chomon Segundo • FRN

FABRYKA ZAROWEK • 1946 • Bossak Jerzy • DOC • PLN • ELECTRIC BULB FACTORY

FABULA DA LEITURA • 1952 • Vitorino Orlando • SHT • PRT

FABULEUSE AVENTURE DE MARCO POLO, LA • 1965 • de La Patelliere Denys, Christian-Jaque, Howard Noel • FRN, ITL, YGS • MERAVIGLIOSE AVVENTURE DI MARCO POLO, LE (ITL) ○ MARKO POLO (YGS) ○ ECHIQUER DE DIEU, L' ○ FABULOUS ADVENTURES OF MARCO POLO, THE ○ MARCO THE MAGNIFICENT (USA)

FABULEUSES AVENTURES DU BARON DE MUNCHAUSEN, LES see **FABULEUSES AVENTURES DU LEGENDAIRE BARON DE MUNCHHAUSEN, LES** • 1965

FABULEUSES AVENTURES DU LEGENDAIRE BARON DE MUNCHHAUSEN, LES • 1965 • Image Jean • ANM • FRN, HNG • FABULOUS ADVENTURES OF BARON VON MUNCHAUSEN, THE ○ FABULEUSES AVENTURES DU BARON DE MUNCHAUSEN, LES

FABULOSOS DE TRINIDAD, LA • 1972 • Iquino Ignacio F. • SPN

FABULOSOS VEINTES, LOS see **AMORES DE MARIETA, LOS** • 1963

FABULOUS ADVENTURES OF BARON VON MUNCHAUSEN, THE see **FABULEUSES AVENTURES DU LEGENDAIRE BARON DE MUNCHHAUSEN, LES** • 1965

FABULOUS ADVENTURES OF MARCO POLO, THE see **FABULEUSE AVENTURE DE MARCO POLO, LA** • 1965

FABULOUS BAKER BOYS, THE • 1989 • Kloves Steve • USA

FABULOUS BARON MUNCHAUSEN, THE (USA) see **BARON PRASIL** • 1962

FABULOUS BASTARD FROM CHICAGO, THE • 1969 • Corarito Greg • USA • FABULOUS KID FROM CHICAGO, THE ○ CHICAGO KID, THE ○ BASTARD WENCH FROM CHICAGO, THE

FABULOUS DORSEYS, THE • 1947 • Green Alfred E. • USA

FABULOUS FIFTIES • 1981 • McLennan Don • DOC • ASL

FABULOUS FIREWORK FAMILY, THE • 1959 • Kouzel Al • ANS • USA

FABULOUS FORTUNE FUMBLERS • 1918 • Binney Josh • SHT • USA

FABULOUS FRAUD, THE • 1948 • Cahn Edward L. • SHT • USA

FABULOUS HOLLYWOOD • 1956 • Staub Ralph • SHT • USA

FABULOUS IRISHMAN, THE • 1957 • Frankenheimer John • MTV • USA

FABULOUS JOE, THE • 1947 • Carr Bernard, Foster Harve • USA

FABULOUS JOURNEY TO THE CENTRE OF THE EARTH see **VIAJE AL CENTRO DE LA TIERRA** • 1977

FABULOUS KID FROM CHICAGO, THE see **FABULOUS BASTARD FROM CHICAGO, THE** • 1969

FABULOUS SENORITA, THE • 1952 • Springsteen R. G. • USA

FABULOUS SPAIN • 1963 • De La Varre Andre Jr. • DOC • USA

FABULOUS SUZANNE, THE • 1946 • Sekely Steve • USA

FABULOUS TEXAN, THE • 1947 • Ludwig Edward • USA

FABULOUS WORLD OF JULES VERNE, THE (USA) see **VYNALEZ ZKAZY** • 1958

FAC EN DELIRE, LA • 1980 • Antel Franz • FRN, FRG, ITL

FACA DE DOIS GUMES • 1988 • Salles Murilo • BRZ • TWO-EDGED KNIFE

FACA SEGUNDO A ARTE • 1965 • de Almeida Manuel Faria • SHT • PRT

FACADE • 1966 • Wiertsema Jan • SHT • NTH

FACADE • 1968 • Kent Larry • CND

FACADE SUR L'OCEAN • 1960 • Leherissey Jean • SHT • FRN

FACCE DELL'ASIA CHE CAMBIA (L'ORBITA DELLA CINA) • 1972 • Lizzani Carlo • MTV • ITL

FACCIA A FACCIA • 1967 • Sollima Sergio • ITL, SPN • FACE TO FACE (UKN)

FACCIA A FACCIA CON EL DIABLO see **LOLA COLT** • 1967

FACCIA DA LADRO • 1977 • Zurli Guido • ITL

FACCIA DA MASCALZONE • 1955 • Andreassi Raffaele, Comfort Lance • ITL

FACCIA DA SCHIAFFI • 1969 • Crispino Armando • ITL

FACCIA D'ANGELO see **LUNGHI GIORNI DELLA VENDETTA, I** • 1967

FACCIA DI SPIA • 1975 • Ferrara Giuseppe • ITL

FACE • 1966 • Warhol Andy • USA • FACES

FACE • 1968 • Zwartjes Frans • SHT • NTH

FACE • 1975 • Spry Robin • CND

FACE • 1980 • Stevenson Erika • UKN

FACE see **MUKRA** • 1988

FACE, THE • 1967 • Kosower Herbert • ANS • USA

FACE, THE see **KAO** • 1960

FACE, THE see **KAO** • 1965

FACE, THE see **ARC** • 1970

FACE, THE see **TVAR** • 1973

FACE, THE (UKN) see **ANSIKTET** • 1958

FACE A FACE see **PROSSOPO ME PROSSOPO** • 1966

FACE A L'OCEAN • 1920 • Leprince Rene • FRN

FACE AT MIDNIGHT see **MAYONAKA NO KAO** • 1958

FACE AT THE CURTAIN, THE • 1915 • *Anderson Broncho Billy* • USA

FACE AT THE TELEPHONE, THE • 1915 • Paul Fred, MacBean L. C. • UKN

FACE AT THE WINDOW see **TVAR V OKNE** • 1963

FACE AT THE WINDOW, THE • 1910 • Griffith D. W. • USA

FACE AT THE WINDOW, THE • 1912 • *Republic* • USA

FACE AT THE WINDOW, THE • 1912 • Blache Alice • *Solax* • USA

FACE AT THE WINDOW, THE • 1913 • *Boyle Irene* • USA

FACE AT THE WINDOW, THE • 1914 • *Princess* • USA

FACE AT THE WINDOW, THE • 1915 • Grandon Francis J. • USA

FACE AT THE WINDOW, THE • 1919 • Villiers Charles • ASL

FACE AT THE WINDOW, THE • 1920 • *Lowell John* • SHT • USA

FACE AT THE WINDOW, THE • 1920 • Noy Wilfred • UKN

FACE AT THE WINDOW, THE • 1932 • Hiscott Leslie • UKN

FACE AT THE WINDOW, THE • 1939 • King George • UKN

FACE AT YOUR WINDOW, THE • 1920 • Stanton Richard • USA

FACE AU DESTIN • 1939 • Fescourt Henri • FRN

FACE AUX LOUPS • 1926 • Durand Jean • FRN

FACE BEHIND THE MASK, THE • 1938 • Tourneur Jacques • SHT • USA

FACE BEHIND THE MASK, THE • 1941 • Florey Robert • USA

FACE BEHIND THE SCAR, THE (USA) see **RETURN OF A STRANGER** • 1937

FACE BETWEEN, THE • 1922 • Veiller Bayard • USA • PHANTOM BRIDE, THE

FACE CACHEE D'HITLER, LA • 1976 • Balducci Richard • FRN

FACE DOWNSTAIRS, THE • 1917 • Weber Lois • SHT • USA

FACE FROM THE PAST, A • 1913 • Edwin Walter • USA

FACE FROM THE PAST, A see **NATSUKASHI NO KAO** • 1941

FACE IN THE CROWD, A • 1957 • Kazan Elia • USA

FACE IN THE CROWD, THE • 1914 • Powell Paul • USA

FACE IN THE DARK, THE • 1918 • Henley Hobart • USA

FACE IN THE FOG, A • 1936 • Hill Robert F. • USA

FACE IN THE FOG, THE • 1922 • Crosland Alan • USA

FACE IN THE MIRROR, THE • 1915 • *Johnstone Lamar* • USA

FACE IN THE MIRROR, THE • 1916 • Ashley Charles E. • SHT • USA

FACE IN THE MOONLIGHT, THE • 1915 • Capellani Albert • USA

FACE IN THE NIGHT • 1957 • Comfort Lance • UKN • MENACE IN THE NIGHT (USA)

FACE IN THE RAIN, A • 1963 • Kershner Irvin • USA

FACE IN THE SALAD, THE • 1970 • Silver Mitchell L. • SHT • USA

FACE IN THE SKY • 1933 • Lachman Harry • USA

FACE IN THE WATCH, THE • 1919 • Kull Edward • SHT • USA

FACE IN THE WINDOW, THE • 1908 • *Lubin* • USA

FACE MOST FAIR, THE • 1915 • *Beauty* • USA

FACE OF A FLOWER see **HANA NO SUGAO** • 1949

FACE OF A FUGITIVE • 1959 • Wendkos Paul • USA

FACE OF A HERO • 1959 • Frankenheimer John • MTV • USA

FACE OF A MURDERER, THE see **SATSUJINSHA NO KAO** • 1950

FACE OF A STRANGER • 1964 • Moxey John Llewellyn • UKN

FACE OF A STRANGER see **PROMISE, THE** • 1979

FACE OF ANOTHER, THE see **TANIN NO KAO** • 1966

FACE OF BRITAIN, THE • 1935 • Rotha Paul • UKN

FACE OF DARKNESS, THE • 1976 • Lloyd Ian F. H. • UKN

FACE OF DEATH, THE see **ROSTRO DE LA MUERTE, EL** • 1963

FACE OF EVE, THE • 1968 • Summers Jeremy • UKN, USA, SPN • EVA EN LA SELVA ○ EVE (USA) ○ EVA

FACE OF FEAR see **PEEPING TOM** • 1960

FACE OF FEAR see **CARA DEL TERROR, LA** • 1962

FACE OF FEAR, THE • 1913 • Bowman William J. • USA

FACE OF FEAR, THE • 1971 • McCowan George • TVM • USA

FACE OF FIRE (USA) see **MANNEN UTAN ANSIKTE** • 1959

FACE OF FU MANCHU, THE • 1965 • Sharp Don • UKN • MASK OF FU MANCHU, THE

FACE OF MARBLE • 1946 • Beaudine William • USA

FACE OF MEDUSA, THE see **PROSOPO TES MEDOUSAS, TO** • 1967

FACE OF RAGE, THE • 1982 • Wrye Donald • TVM • USA

FACE OF SCOTLAND, THE • 1938 • Wright Basil • DOC • UKN

FACE OF SIN, THE see **GIRL WITH HUNGRY EYES, THE** • 1967

FACE OF TERROR, THE see **SADIST, THE** • 1963

FACE OF TERROR (USA) see **CARA DEL TERROR, LA** • 1962

FACE OF THE CAT, THE see **CHATTE, LA** • 1958

FACE OF THE EARTH • 1975 • Mason William • DOC • CND

FACE OF THE ENEMY, THE see **FASCHISM BUDET RASBYT** • 1941

FACE OF THE FLOWER, THE • 1988 • Rygard Elisabeth • SHT • DNM

FACE OF THE FROG (USA) see **FROSCH MIT DER MASKE, DER** • 1959

FACE OF THE MADONNA, THE • 1915 • Buel Kenean • USA

FACE OF THE MEDUSA see **PROSOPO TES MEDOUSAS, TO** • 1967

FACE OF THE MURDERER, THE see **ROSTRO DEL ASESINO, EL** • 1965

FACE OF THE SCREAMING WEREWOLF (USA) see **CASA DEL TERROR, LA** • 1959

FACE OF THE WORLD • 1921 • Willat Irvin V. • USA

FACE OF WAR, A • 1968 • Jones Eugene S. • DOC • USA

FACE OF WAR, THE (USA) see **KRIGETS VANVETT** • 1963

FACE OFF • 1972 • McCowan George • CND

FACE OFF • 1977 • Emshwiller Ed • USA

FACE OFF see **VON METZ INCIDENT, THE** • 1988

FACE ON THE ACE, THE • 1911 • *Tress Henry (P)* • UKN

FACE ON THE BARROOM FLOOR, THE • 1908 • Porter Edwin S. • USA

FACE ON THE BARROOM FLOOR, THE • 1914 • Chaplin Charles • USA • HAM ARTIST, THE

FACE ON THE BARROOM FLOOR, THE • 1923 • Ford John • USA • LOVE IMAGE, THE (UKN) ○ DRINK

FACE ON THE BARROOM FLOOR, THE • 1932 • Bracken Bertram • USA

FACE ON THE CEILING, THE • 1915 • *Edwards Walter* • USA

FACE ON THE SCREEN, THE • 1917 • Salter Harry • SHT • USA

FACE OR THE VOICE, THE • 1912 • *Vitagraph* • USA

FACE POWDER see **USUGESHO** • 1985

FACE THAT I RECOGNISE, THE see **ANDRU KANDA MUGAM** • 1968

FACE THAT LAUNCHED A THOUSAND SHIPS, THE (UKN) see **AMANTE DI PARIDE, L'** • 1955

FACE THE CAMERA • 1922 • Roach Hal • SHT • USA

FACE THE MUSIC • 1954 • Fisher Terence • UKN • BLACK GLOVE, THE (USA)

FACE TO FACE • 1913 • Noy Wilfred • UKN

FACE TO FACE • 1916 • Wilson Frank • UKN

FACE TO FACE • 1920 • Grossman Harry • USA

FACE TO FACE • 1952 • Brahm John, Windust Bretaigne • USA

FACE TO FACE • 1972 • Mathoulis Robert • GRC

FACE TO FACE • 1982 • Shandel Thomas (c/d) • MTV • CND

FACE TO FACE see **LICEM U LICE** • 1963

FACE TO FACE see **PROSSOPO ME PROSSOPO** • 1966

FACE TO FACE see **TWARZA W TWARZ** • 1967

FACE TO FACE see **CARA A CARA** • 1968

FACE TO FACE see **SZEMTOL-SZEMBE** • 1970

FACE TO FACE see **WAGHAN LI WAGH** • 1976

FACE TO FACE see **MUKHAMUKHAM** • 1984

FACE TO FACE see **ANSIGT TIL ANSIGT** • 1987

FACE TO FACE (UKN) see **FACCIA A FACCIA** • 1967

FACE TO FACE (USA) see **ANSIKTE MOT ANSIKTE** • 1976

FACE TO THE WIND see **PLUS DE VACANCES POUR LE BON DIEU** • 1949

FACE TO THE WIND see **CRY FOR ME, BILLY** • 1972

FACE UNDER THE MASK see **TVAR POD MASKOU** • 1970

FACE VALUE • 1914 • Lessey George A. • USA

FACE VALUE • 1918 • Leonard Robert Z. • USA

FACE VALUE • 1927 • Florey Robert • USA

FACE WORK see **CONVICTED** • 1938

FACELESS MAN, THE • 1966 • Rosenberg Stuart • TVM • USA

FACELESS MEN, THE see **INCIDENT AT PHANTOM HILL** • 1966

FACELESS MONSTER, THE (UKN) see **AMANTI D'OLTRETOMBA** • 1965

FACES • 1934 • Morgan Sidney • UKN

FACES • 1968 • Cassavetes John • USA

FACES • 1976 • Siegel Lois • ANS • CND

FACES see **FACE** • 1966

FACES AFTER THE STORM • 1983 • Jha Prakesh • IND

FACES IN THE DARK • 1960 • Eady David • UKN

FACES IN THE FOG • 1944 • English John • USA

FACES IN THE NIGHT • 1915 • *Ogle Charles* • USA

FACES IN THE SHADOWS see **ANSIKTEN I SKUGGA** • 1956

FACES IN THE SUN • 1961 • Holmes Cecil • DOC • ASL

FACES OF AMERICA • 1965 • Emshwiller Ed • USA

FACES OF BRONZE see **VISAGES DE BRONZE** • 1957

FACES OF CHILDREN (USA) see **VISAGES D'ENFANTS** • 1923

FACES OF DEATH I • 1983 • Scott Rosilyn T. • USA

FACES OF DEATH II • 1983 • Scott Rosilyn T. • USA

FACES OF DEPRESSION, THE • 1959 • Anderson Robert • DOC • CND

FACES OF FEAR see **TASTE OF SIN, A** • 1983

FACES OF HARLOW • 1964 • Knight Derrick • UKN

FACES OF LOVE, THE • 1978 • Soutter Michel • SWT

FACES OF NEW ENGLAND • 1932 • Rodakiewicz Henwar • USA

FACES OF ONTARIO • 1972-73 • Owen Don • SER • CND • ONTARIO TOWNS AND VILLAGES

FACESCAPES • 1965 • Vanderbeek Stan • SHT • USA

FACETS OF LOVE • 1973 • Li Han-Hsiang • HKG

FACHEUX MODERNES, LES see **CASSE-PIEDS, LES** • 1948

FACIAL EXPRESSION • 1902 • Porter Edwin S. • USA

FACIAL EXPRESSIONS • 1902 • *Paul R. W.* • UKN

FACING THE AUDIENCE • 1954 • Stiopul Savel • RMN

FACING THE CLOUDS see **KUMO NI MUKATTE TATSU** • 1962

FACING THE ENEMY • 1914 • Weston Charles • UKN

FACING THE MUSIC • 1933 • Hughes Harry • UKN • JEWEL SONG, THE

FACING THE MUSIC • 1941 • Rogers Maclean • UKN

FACING THE SKY see **DE CARA AL CIELO** • 1979

FACING THE TRUTH see **PRAWDZIE W OCZY** • 1970

FACING THE WIND see **VETER V LITSO** • 1929

FACKELTRAGER, DER • 1918 • Holger-Madsen • FRG, DNM

FACKELTRAGER, DER • 1957 • Knittel Johannes • GDR

FACON DE SE DONNER, LA see **D'AMOUR ET D'EAU FRAICHE** • 1933

FACT AND FICTION • 1980 • Noyce Phil • DOC • ASL

FACTEUR, LE • 1974 • Dussault Louis • CND

FACTEUR DU TOUR DE FRANCE, LE see **HARDI LES GARS!** • 1931

FACTEUR S'EN VA-T-EN GUERRE, LE • 1966 • Bernard-Aubert Claude • FRN • POSTMAN GOES TO WAR, THE (USA)

FACTEUR TROP FERRE, UN • 1908 • Feuillade Louis • FRN

FACTORIES • 1973 • Ondaatje Kim • DCS • CND

FACTORY • 1970 • Kieslowski Krzysztof • MTV • PLN

FACTORY, THE see **ERGOSTASIO, TO** • 1981

FACTORY FRONT see **CAUSE COMMUNE, LA** • 1940

FACTORY GIRL, THE • 1912 • Olcott Sidney • USA

FACTORY GIRL'S HONOUR, A • 1912 • Brett B. Harold • UKN

FACTORY IN GERMANY • 1954 • Gass Karl • DOC • GDR

FACTORY INSPECTOR • Reeve Leonard • DOC • UKN

FACTORY MAGDALEN, A • 1914 • Bostwick Elwood • USA

FACTORY TOWN, A see **RABOUCHI POSSELOK** • 1965

FACTORY WORKERS IN REVOLT see **MYATYEZHNAYA ZASTAVA** • 1967

FACTS AND FANCIES • 1950 • Law Michael • UKN

FACTS AND FIGURES • 1935 • Sewell Vernon • DCS • UKN

FACTS AND FOLLIES • 1919-20 • SER • USA

FACTS OF LIFE, THE • 1960 • Frank Melvin • USA

FACTS OF LIFE, THE see **29 ACACIA AVENUE** • 1945

FACTS OF LIFE DOWN UNDER, THE • 1987 • Margolin Stuart • TVM • USA

FACTS OF LIFE GO TO PARIS, THE • 1982 • Kelada Asaad • TVM • USA

FACTS OF LOVE, THE (USA) see **29 ACACIA AVENUE** • 1945

FACTS OF MURDER, THE see **MALEDETTO IMBROGLIO, UN** • 1959

FACULTAD DE LETRAS • 1950 • Ballesteros Pio • SPN

FAD JAL • 1979 • Faye Safi • SNL • GRANDFATHER ○ WORK NEWCOMER

FADA, LA • 1923 • Burel Leonce-Henry • FRN

FADDIJA • 1950 • Montero Roberto Bianchi • ITL • LEGGE DELLA VENDETTA, LA ○ LAW OF VENGEANCE, THE

FADDISTS, THE • 1914 • *Ab* • USA

FADE-IN • 1968 • Smithee Alan • USA • FADE IN

FADE IN see **FADE-IN** • 1968

FADE TO BLACK • 1980 • Zimmerman Vernon • USA

FADEAWAY, THE • 1926 • Fleischer Dave • ANS • USA

FADED FLOWER, THE • 1916 • Abramson Ivan • USA

FADED LILIES, THE • 1909 • Griffith D. W. • USA

FADED ROSES • 1911 • *Yankee* • USA

FADED WRITING, THE see **SETRELE PISMO** • 1920

FADER OG SON • 1911 • Blom August • DNM • ONKEL OG NEVO ○ POISONOUS LOVE, A

FADEREN • 1909 • *Blom August* • DNM • FATHER'S GRIEF, A

FADERN • 1969 • Sjoberg Alf • SWD • FATHER, THE (UKN) ○ DREAM OF A FATHER

FADERULLAN UR GOTEBORGSSYSTEMET I GRONKOPING • 1910 • Magnusson Charles • SWD
FADNI ODPOLENE • 1965 • Passer Ivan • SHT • CZC • BORING AFTERNOON, A
FADO • 1947 • Queiroga Perdigao • PRT
FADO CORRIDO • 1964 • do Canto Jorge Brum • PRT
FADO -LISBOA 68 • 1968 • de Macedo Antonio • SHT • PRT
FADREN • 1912 • Hoffman-Uddgren Anna • SWD
FADS AND FANCIES • 1934 • Schwarzwald Milton • SHT • USA
FAEDRENES SYND • 1914 • Blom August • DNM • NEMESIS
FAEDRENES SYND see **SUNDEN DER VATER, DIE** • 1913
FAEDRENES SYNDER • 1915 • Schneevoigt George • DNM
FAENGSLENDE FERIEDAGE • 1978 • Henriksen Finn • DNM
FAETRENE PA TORNDAL • 1973 • Mossin Ib • DNM
FAFALARIFLA • 1911 • Velle Gaston • FRN
FAG END see **DUMB DORA DISCOVERS TOBACCO** • 1945
FAGASA • 1928 • Wells Raymond • USA
FAGIN • 1922 • Parkinson H. B. • UKN
FAGIN'S FRESHMEN • 1939 • Hardaway Ben, Dalton Cal • ANS • USA
FAGR • 1955 • Salem Atef • EGY • AUBE
FAGR YAWN GADID see **FAJR YOM JADID** • 1964
FAGYONGYOK • 1979 • Ember Judit • HNG • MISTLETOES
FAGYOSSZENTEK • 1962 • Revesz Gyorgy • HNG • HAIL DAYS
FAHD, AL- • 1972 • Maleh Nabil • SYR • LEOPARD, LE ○ PANTHER, THE
FAHHAM, AL- • 1972 • Bouamari Mohamed • ALG • CHARBONNIER, LE
FAHLSTROM • 1980 • Ruiz Raul • SHT • FRN
FAHNE VON KRIWOJ ROG, DIE • 1967 • Maetzig Kurt • GDR • FLAG OF KRIVOY ROG, THE
FAHNENTRAGER VON SEDAN, DER • 1927 • Brandt Johannes • FRG
FAHNLEIN DER VERSPRENGTEN, DAS see **ALTE KAMERADEN** • 1934
FAHRENDES VOLK • 1921 • Gartner Adolf • FRG
FAHRENDES VOLK • 1925 • *Nosskess-Film* • FRG
FAHRENDES VOLK • 1938 • Feyder Jacques • FRG
FAHRENHEIT 451 • 1966 • Truffaut Francois • UKN
FAHRMANN MARIA • 1936 • Wisbar Frank • FRG • FERRYMAN MARIA (USA) ○ FERRYBOAT WOMAN MARIA ○ FERRYWOMAN MARIA
FAHRT IN ABENTEUER, DIE • 1926 • Mack Max • FRG
FAHRT IN DIE JUGEND, DIE • 1935 • Boese Carl • AUS
FAHRT INS ABENTEUER • 1943 • von Alten Jurgen • FRG
FAHRT INS BLAUE, DIE • 1919 • Biebrach Rudolf • FRG
FAHRT INS BLAUE, DIE see **SEEFAHRT, DIE IST LUSTIG, EINE** • 1935
FAHRT INS GLUCK • 1945 • Engel Erich • FRG
FAHRT INS GLUCK, DIE • 1923 • Bolten-Baeckers Heinrich • FRG • BOB UND MARY
FAHRT INS GLUCK, DIE • 1926 • Lisson Heinrich • FRG
FAHRT INS GRUNE, DIE • 1933 • Obal Max • FRG
FAHRT INS LEBEN • 1940 • Hoffmann Bernd • FRG
FAHRT INS VERDERBEN, DIE • 1924 • Bauer James • FRG • HOFFNUNG AUF SEGEN
FAI IN FRETTA AD UCCIDERMI.. HO FREDDO • 1967 • Maselli Francesco • ITL • KILL ME QUICK, I'M COLD
FAIBLE FEMME, UNE • 1932 • de Vaucorbeil Max • FRN
FAIBLES FEMMES • 1959 • Boisrond Michel • FRN • DONNE SONO DEBOLI, LE (ITL) ○ THREE MURDERESSES (USA) ○ WOMEN ARE WEAK (UKN)
FAIL-SAFE • 1964 • Lumet Sidney • USA
FAILING OF RAYMOND, THE • 1971 • Sagal Boris • TVM • USA
FAILLE, LA • 1975 • Fleischmann Peter • FRN, FRG, ITL • WEAK SPOT, THE
FAILURE • 1925 • Keefe Daniel • USA
FAILURE, THE • 1911 • Griffith D. W. • USA
FAILURE, THE • 1915 • *Domino* • USA
FAILURE, THE • 1915 • Cabanne W. Christy • *Reliance* • USA
FAILURE, THE • 1917 • Edwards Henry • UKN • DICK CARSON WINS THROUGH
FAILURE, THE see **MISLUKKING, DE** • 1987
FAILURE AT FIFTY, A • 1916 • Baker Richard Foster • SHT • USA
FAILURE OF IDOLATERS, THE see **GHOROUBE BOTPARASTAN** • 1968
FAILURE OF SUCCESS, THE • 1913 • *Elder Charles* • USA
FAILURE'S SONG IS SAD (USA) see **HAIZAN NO UTA WA KANASHI** • 1922
FAIM, LA • 1973 • Foldes Peter • ANS • CND • HUNGER
FAIM DES CAVES, LA • 1973 • Favreau Robert • DCS • CND
FAIM DU MONDE, LA • 1958 • Grimault Paul • ANS • FRN • HUNGER OF THE WORLD, THE ○ MONDE EN RACCOURCI, LE
FAIM DU MONDE, LA • 1978 • Hondo Abib Med, Robichet Theo • DOC • FRN, ALG
FAIM.. L'OCCASION.. L'HERBE TENDRE, LA • 1904 • Blache Alice • FRN
FAINAS DO RIO E DO MAR • 1959 • Ribeiro Antonio Lopes • SHT • PRT
FAINT HEART • 1922 • La Cava Gregory • SHT • USA
FAINT HEART AND FAIR LADY • 1917 • De Vonde Chester M. • USA
FAINT HEART NE'ER WON FAIR LADY • 1914 • Seay Charles M. • USA
FAINT PERFUME • 1925 • Gasnier Louis J. • USA
FAINTING LOVER • 1931 • Sennett Mack • SHT • USA
FAIR see **FERIA** • 1962
FAIR AND COLD • 1933 • Sparling Gordon • DCS • CND
FAIR AND MUDDY • 1928 • Oelze Charles • SHT • USA
FAIR AND WARMER • 1919 • Otto Henry • USA
FAIR AND WORMER • 1946 • Jones Charles M. • ANS • USA
FAIR ANGEL, THE see **FOIRE AUX CHIMERES, LA** • 1946
FAIR BARBARIAN, THE • 1917 • Thornby Robert T. • USA
FAIR BUT FALSE • 1920 • *Vernon Bobby* • SHT • USA
FAIR BUT FOOLISH • 1926 • Christie Al • USA
FAIR CHEAT, THE • 1923 • King Burton L. • USA
FAIR CO-ED, THE • 1927 • Wood Sam • USA • VARSITY GIRL, THE
FAIR DENTIST, THE • 1911 • *Pickford Mary* • USA
FAIR ENOUGH • 1919 • Sloman Edward • USA
FAIR EXCHANGE • 1936 • Ince Ralph • UKN
FAIR EXCHANGE, A • 1909 • Griffith D. W. • USA
FAIR EXCHANGE, A • 1910 • *Essanay* • USA
FAIR EXCHANGE, A • 1911 • *Selig* • USA
FAIR EXCHANGE, A • 1913 • *Kirkwood James* • USA
FAIR EXCHANGE, A • 1916 • *Stull Walter* • USA
FAIR EXCHANGE, A see **GETTING ACQUAINTED** • 1914
FAIR FARE, THE • 1916 • Hiller Frederick W. • SHT • USA
FAIR, FAT AND SAUCY • 1915 • Williams C. Jay • USA
FAIR GAME • 1914 • Wilson Frank • UKN
FAIR GAME • 1988 • Orfini Mario • ITL
FAIR GAME see **SHE WAS FAIR GAME** • 1985
FAIR GOD OF SUN ISLAND, THE • 1915 • Worthington William • USA
FAIR-HEADED HARE • 1951 • Freleng Friz • ANS • USA
FAIR IMPOSTER, A • 1916 • Butler Alexander • UKN
FAIR IS FAIR see **LEGEND OF BILLIE JEAN, THE** • 1985
FAIR IS HERE, THE see **PRIJELA K NAM POUT** • 1973
FAIR LADY • 1922 • Webb Kenneth • USA
FAIR MAID OF PERTH, THE • 1923 • Greenwood Edwin • UKN
FAIR MAID OF PERTH, THE • 1926 • Mander Miles • UKN
FAIR ORIANA • 1961 • Mason Bill • UKN
FAIR PLAY • 1925 • Crane Frank H. • USA • DANGER ZONE, THE (UKN)
FAIR PLAY • 1970 • Zeman Bronislaw • PLN
FAIR PLAY see **REGLE DU JEU, LA** • 1939
FAIR PRETENDER, THE • 1918 • Miller Charles • USA
FAIR REBEL, A • 1914 • Kirkwood James • USA
FAIR RODRIGUEZ, THE see **GUERA RODRIGUEZ, LA** • 1976
FAIR SAMPLE, A • 1919 • *Strand* • SHT • USA
FAIR SUSSEX • 1912 • Pearson George • DCS • UKN
FAIR TODAY • 1941 • Lantz Walter • USA
FAIR TRADE • 1988 • Davis B. J. • USA • FLIGHT TO HELL
FAIR WARNING • 1925 • Roberts Stephen • SHT • USA
FAIR WARNING • 1931 • Werker Alfred L. • USA
FAIR WARNING • 1937 • Foster Norman • USA • DEATH IN PARADISE CANYON
FAIR WEATHER FIENDS see **FAIR WEATHER FRIENDS** • 1946
FAIR WEATHER FRIENDS • 1946 • Culhane James • ANS • USA • FAIR WEATHER FIENDS
FAIR WEEK • 1922 • Roach Hal • SHT • USA
FAIR WEEK • 1924 • Wagner Robert • USA
FAIR WIND TO JAVA • 1953 • Kane Joseph • USA
FAIRE LA COUR • 1974 • Dansereau Fernand, Rossignol Yolande • SHT • CND
FAIRE LA DEMENAGEUSE • 1971 • Varela Jose • FRN
FAIRE L'AMOUR: DE LA PILULE A L'ORDINATEUR* • 1968 • Fantl Thomas, Albicocco Jean-Gabriel, Hoglund Gunnar • FRN, FRG, SWD • AMOUR AU FEMININ, L'
FAIRE MARIE PLEINE DE GRACE • 1971 • Varela Jose • FRN
FAIRFAX AVENUE • 1949 • Lewis Jerry • SHT • USA
FAIRIES, THE see **FATE, LE** • 1966
FAIRIES' BANQUET, THE • 1911 • *Clarke Edwin* • USA
FAIRIES' HALLOWE'EN, THE • 1910 • *Thanhouser* • USA
FAIRIES' REVENGE, THE • 1913 • Plumb Hay? • UKN
FAIRS • 1964 • Petrovic Aleksandar • SHT • YGS
FAIRUZ HANIN • 1951 • Kamel Abbas • EGY • MADAME FAIRUZ
FAIRY, THE • 1898 • *Paul R. W.* • UKN
FAIRY AND THE WAIF, THE • 1915 • Frohman Mary Hubert, Irving George • USA
FAIRY BOOKSELLER, THE (USA) see **MARCHAND D'IMAGES, LE** • 1910
FAIRY BOTTLE, THE • 1913 • Aylott Dave? • UKN
FAIRY DANCE, THE • 1976 • Andonov Ivan • BUL
FAIRY DOLL, THE • 1912 • Laird Laurence • UKN
FAIRY DRAGONFLY, THE see **FEE LIBELLULE, LA** • 1908
FAIRY FERN SEED • 1915 • Harvey John • USA
FAIRY FOX AND GHOST, THE • Chin Sheng-En • HKG
FAIRY GODFATHER, THE • 1917 • Blackton J. Stuart • SHT • USA
FAIRY GODMOTHER, THE • 1906 • Cooper Arthur • UKN
FAIRY HANDS see **MANI DI FATA** • 1984
FAIRY JEWEL, THE • 1910 • *Milano* • ITL
FAIRY OF BAGHDAD • 1932 • Vakil Nanubhai • IND
FAIRY OF CEYLON (USA) see **LANKAKI LADI** • 1925
FAIRY OF SINHALDWIP • 1937 • Desai Kikubhai • IND
FAIRY OF SOLBAKKEN (USA) see **SYNNOVE SOLBAKKEN** • 1919
FAIRY OF THE FLUTE (USA) see **BANSARIBALA** • 1935
FAIRY OF THE SPRING, THE • 1906 • *Pathe* • FRN
FAIRY RING, THE • 1966 • Wilkosz Tadeusz • ANM • PLN
FAIRY SPECTACLES, THE see **LUNETTES FEERIQUES, LES** • 1909
FAIRY STORY • Mocanu Virgil • ANS • RMN
FAIRY STORY • 1968 • Cattaneo Tony • UKN
FAIRY STORY, THE see **BAJKA** • 1970
FAIRY TALE see **CUENTO DE HADAS** • 1951
FAIRY TALE see **MESE** • 1963
FAIRY TALE CASTLE see **MARCHENSCHLOSS, DAS** • 1961
FAIRY TALE FOR ADULTS: OR, THE HALF-FAST LOVER, THE • 1970 • *Shane Forman* • USA • FAIRY TALES FOR ADULTS ○ MIXED FRUIT
FAIRY TALE MURDER (UKN) see **RIVER GANG** • 1945
FAIRY TALE OF BLOOD see **KRVAVA BAJKA** • 1971
FAIRY TALE OF MALICEK, THE see **POHADKA O MALICKOVI** • 1985
FAIRY TALE OF MAY see **POHADKA MAJE** • 1940
FAIRY TALE OF PATTERNS, A • Belov Vyacheslav • ANM • USS
FAIRY-TALE OF PILGRIMAGE, THE see **POHADKA O PUTOVANI** • 1982
FAIRY TALES • 1978 • Hurwitz Harry • USA • ADULT FAIRY TALES (UKN)
FAIRY TALES FOR ADULTS see **FAIRY TALE FOR ADULTS: OR, THE HALF-FAST LOVER, THE** • 1970
FAIRYLAND • 1916 • Lucoque H. Lisle • UKN
FAIRYLAND, THE (USA) see **ROYAUME DES FEES, LE** • 1903
FAIRYLAND BRIDE, A • 1912 • *Reliance* • USA
FAIRYLAND FOLLIES • 1931 • Foster John, Bailey Harry • ANS • USA
FAIRY'S PRESENTS, THE • 1909 • *Pathe* • FRN
FAIRY'S SWORD, THE • 1908 • Fitzhamon Lewin • UKN
FAIRYTALE • 1973 • Djurkovic Dejan • YGS
FAIS GAFFE A LA GAFFE! • 1981 • Boujenah Paul • FRN
FAIS GAFFE A LA MARCHE see **HOROSCOPE, L'** • 1978
FAIS M'EN PLUS • 1979 • Love John • FRN
FAIS-MOI TOUT • Warren Ken • FRN
FAIS MOI TRES MAL, MAIS COUVRE-MOI DE BAISERS (FRN) see **STRAZIAMI MA DI BACI SAZIAMI** • 1968
FAISEUR, LE • 1936 • Hugon Andre • FRN
FAISEUR DE FOUS, LE • 1914 • Chautard Emile • FRN
FAISEURS DE PLUIE, LES see **HOMMES QUI FONT LA PLUIE, LES** • 1951
FAISEURS DE SUISSES, LES see **SCHWEIZERMACHER, DIE** • 1979
FAISONS UN REVE • 1936 • Guitry Sacha • FRN
FAIT ACCOMPLI, UN • 1974 • Theberge Andre • SHT • CND
FAIT DIVERS • 1923 • Autant-Lara Claude • SHT • FRN
FAIT DIVERS • 1956 • Degelin Emile • BLG
FAIT DIVERS D'UNE ADOLESCENTE • 1980 • Berard Herve • FRN
FAITES DONC PLAISIR AUX AMIS • 1968 • Rigaud Francis • FRN
FAITES LE SAUT AVEC S.L.M. • 1981 • Kinsey Nicholas • DOC • CND
FAITES-MOI CONFIANCE • 1953 • Grangier Gilles • FRN
FAITES-MOI JOUIR • 1977 • Baudricourt Michel • FRN
FAITES SAUTER LA BANQUE • 1963 • Girault Jean • FRN, ITL
FAITES SOIGNER VOS EGRATIGNURES • 1949 • Decae Henri • SHT • FRN
FAITES VOS JEUX, MESDAMES see **FEU A VOLONTE** • 1965
FAITH • 1911 • Porter Edwin S. • USA
FAITH • 1916 • Kirkwood James • USA
FAITH • 1919 • Swickard Charles • USA
FAITH • 1919 • Wilson Rex • UKN • IN BONDAGE
FAITH • 1920 • Mitchell Howard M. • USA
FAITH, THE see **EIMAN** • 1967
FAITH AND ENDURIN' • 1918 • Smith Cliff • USA • FAITH ENDURIN', A
FAITH AND FORTUNE • 1915 • McGlynn Frank • USA
FAITH ENDURIN', A see **FAITH AND ENDURIN'** • 1918
FAITH FOR GOLD • 1930 • *Mission Film Society* • USA
FAITH HEALER, THE • 1911 • Haldane Bert? • UKN
FAITH HEALER, THE • 1912 • *Cummings Irving* • USA
FAITH HEALER, THE • 1913 • *Johnston J. W.* • USA
FAITH HEALER, THE • 1921 • Melford George • USA • GOODHEART
FAITH, HOPE, AND CHARITY see **FE, ESPERANZA Y CARIDAD** • 1972
FAITH, HOPE AND WITCHCRAFT see **TRO, HAB OG TROLDDOM** • 1960
FAITH IN DESTINY see **FE ENSU DESTINO** • 1978
FAITH LOST AND WON • 1910 • *Lubin* • USA
FAITH OF A CHILD, THE • 1915 • Thornton F. Martin • UKN
FAITH OF A GIRL • 1913 • *Clayton Ethel* • USA
FAITH OF A ROBOT • 1935 • Pal George • ANS • NTH
FAITH OF HER FATHER, THE • 1914 • Lewis Edgar • USA
FAITH OF HER FATHERS, THE • 1915 • Giblyn Charles • USA
FAITH OF MILLIONS • 1927 • *Chester Productions* • DOC • USA
FAITH OF SONNY JIM, THE • 1915 • Johnson Tefft • USA
FAITH OF THE STRONG, THE • 1919 • Bradbury Robert North • USA
FAITH OF TWO, THE • 1914 • *August Edwin* • USA
FAITHFUL • 1910 • Griffith D. W. • USA
FAITHFUL • 1936 • Stein Paul L. • UKN
FAITHFUL see **NOTORIOUS AFFAIR, A** • 1930
FAITHFUL 47, THE see **CHUSHINGURA** • 1962
FAITHFUL BUTLER, THE • 1914 • *Kineto* • UKN
FAITHFUL CITY • 1952 • Leytes Joseph • ISR
FAITHFUL CLOCK, THE • 1909 • Fitzhamon Lewin • UKN
FAITHFUL DEPARTED • 1969 • Hickey Kieran • DOC • IRL
FAITHFUL FRIENDS see **VERNYE DRUZYA** • 1954
FAITHFUL HEART, THE • 1922 • Samuelson G. B. • UKN
FAITHFUL HEART, THE • 1932 • Saville Victor • UKN • FAITHFUL HEARTS (USA)
FAITHFUL HEART, THE • 1958 • Dolin Boris • DOC • USS
FAITHFUL HEART, THE see **COEUR FIDELE** • 1923
FAITHFUL HEARTS (USA) see **FAITHFUL HEART, THE** • 1932
FAITHFUL IN MY FASHION • 1946 • Salkow Sidney • USA
FAITHFUL IN MY FASHION • 1969 • Maley Jean • FRN
FAITHFUL INDIAN, THE • 1911 • *Anderson Bronco Billy* • USA
FAITHFUL MAX • 1910 • *Imp* • USA
FAITHFUL NARRATIVE OF THE CAPTURE, SUFFERINGS AND MIRACULOUS ESCAPE OF ELIZA FRASER, A see **ROLLICKING ADVENTURES OF ELIZA FRASER, THE** • 1976
FAITHFUL PUP, THE • 1929 • Terry Paul • ANS • USA
FAITHFUL RIVER see **WIERNA RZEKA** • 1936
FAITHFUL RIVER see **WIERNA RZEKA** • 1988
FAITHFUL SERVANT, A • 1913 • Costello Maurice • USA
FAITHFUL SERVANTS, THE see **FIELES SIRVIENTES, LOS** • 1980
FAITHFUL SERVITOR, THE • 1913 • *Gebhardt George* • USA
FAITHFUL SHEP • 1913 • *Reliance* • USA
FAITHFUL TAXICAB, THE • 1913 • Sennett Mack • USA
FAITHFUL TO THE FINISH • 1915 • Dillon Eddie • USA
FAITHFUL TO THE RESCUE • 1956 • Negus Olive • UKN
FAITHFUL UNTO DEATH • 1910 • FRN
FAITHFUL UNTO DEATH • 1912 • *Vitagraph* • USA
FAITHFUL UNTO DEATH • 1919 • *Capital* • SHT • USA
FAITHFUL UNTO DEATH see **HJERTETS GULD** • 1912
FAITHFUL WIFE • 1909 • *Bison* • USA
FAITHFUL WIVES • 1926 • Myles Norbert • USA
FAITHFULNESS see **VERNOST** • 1965
FAITHHEALER, THE • 1967 • Vrijman Jan • NTH
FAITHLESS • 1932 • Beaumont Harry • USA • TINFOIL
FAITHLESS FRIEND, A • 1908 • Fitzhamon Lewin • UKN
FAITHLESS FRIEND, THE • 1908 • *Williams, Brown & Earle* • USA
FAITHLESS FRIEND, THE • 1913 • *Patheplay* • USA
FAITHLESS LOVER, THE • 1928 • Windom Lawrence C. • USA • PASTEBOARD LOVER, THE
FAITHLESS MAN, A • 1911 • *Imp* • USA
FAITHLESS SEX, THE • 1922 • Napier Henry J. • USA

FAITH'S REWARD • 1916 • Horkheimer H. M., Horkheimer E. D. • SHT • USA

FAITS D'HIVER • 1951 • Decae Henri • SHT • FRN

FAITS DIVERS • 1983 • Depardon Raymond • DOC • FRN

FAITS DIVERS A PARIS • 1949 • Kirsanoff Dimitri • FRN

FAIZA, AL- • 1975 • Lallem Ahmed • ALG • ZONE INTERDITE

FAIZE HUCUM • 1985 • Okten Zeki • TRK • RAID ON THE INTERESTS

FAJA LOBBI • 1960 • van der Horst Herman • NTH • SYMPHONY OF THE TROPICS ○ FIERY LOVE

FAJA PETROLIFERA DE ORINOCO • 1974 • Camacho Carlos Antonio • DOC • VNZ

FAJR, AL • 1967 • Khalifa Omar • TNS • AUBE, L' ○ DAWN

FAJR AL-HAD'ARA: AL-FANN AS-SUMARY • 1976 • Saleh Tewfik • IRQ • AUBE DE LA CIVILISATION: L'ART DE SUMER, L'

FAJR AL-ISLAM • 1970 • Abu Saif Salah • EGY • DAWN OF ISLAM, THE ○ FAJR EL ISLAM

FAJR EL ISLAM see **FAJR AL-ISLAM** • 1970

FAJR YOM JADID • 1964 • Shahin Youssef • EGY • DAWN OF A NEW DAY ○ FAGR YAWN GADID

FAKE! see **F FOR FAKE** • 1977

FAKE, THE • 1927 • Jacoby Georg • UKN

FAKE, THE • 1953 • Grayson Godfrey • UKN

FAKE BLIND MAN, THE • 1906 • Raymond Charles? • UKN

FAKE BLONDES, THE see **FINTE BIONDE, LE** • 1988

FAKE DIAMOND SWINDLER, A • 1908 • *Melies* • USA

FAKE-DIAMOND SWINDLER, A see **FABRICANT DE DIAMANTS, LE** • 1908

FAKE GAME, THE see **IKASAMA BAKUCHI** • 1968

FAKE GAS MAN, THE • 1913 • *Crystal* • USA

FAKE GIRL see **KARAKURI MUSUME** • 1927

FAKE ISABELLA, THE see **HAMIS IZABELLA, A** • 1968

FAKE OUT • 1983 • Cimber Matt • USA

FAKE RUSSIAN PROPHET, THE (USA) see **JOYEUX FAUX PROPHETE RUSSE, LE** • 1904

FAKE SOLDIERS, THE • 1913 • Stull Walter • USA

FAKE SPIRITUALISM EXPOSED see **SPIRITUALISM EXPOSED** • 1926

FAKER, THE • 1929 • Rosen Phil • USA

FAKERS, THE • 1920 • Harbaugh Carl • SHT • USA

FAKERS, THE see **HELL'S BLOODY DEVILS** • 1967

FAKE'S PROGRESS • 1950 • Fairbairn Kenneth • UKN

FAKING FAKERS • 1917 • Howe J. A. • SHT • USA

FAKING WITH SOCIETY see **CAUGHT IN A CABARET** • 1914

FAKIR, DER • 1918 • Dessauer Siegfried • FRG

FAKIR, LE see **FAKIR, MYSTERE INDIEN, LE** • 1896

FAKIR, THE • 1915 • *Edwards Walter* • USA

FAKIR (A HINDOO MYSTERY), THE see **FAKIR, MYSTERE INDIEN, LE** • 1896

FAKIR AND THE FOOTPADS, THE • 1906 • Martin J. H.? • UKN

FAKIR DE SINGAPOUR, LE • 1908 • Melies Georges • FRN • INDIAN SORCERER, THE (USA)

FAKIR DU GRAND HOTEL, LE • 1933 • Billon Pierre • FRN

FAKIR IM FRACK, DER • 1916 • Mack Max • FRG

FAKIR, MYSTERE INDIEN, LE • 1896 • Melies Georges • FRN • FAKIR (A HINDOO MYSTERY), THE ○ FAKIR, LE

FAKIR'S DREAM, THE • 1908 • *Pathe* • FRN

FAKIR'S FAN, THE • 1911 • Booth W. R. • UKN • MAGIC FAN, THE

FAKIR'S FLUTE, THE • 1910 • Fitzhamon Lewin • UKN

FAKIRS, FUMISTES ET COMPAGNIE • 1927 • Machin Alfred • FRN

FAKIR'S NEW SERVANT, THE • 1911 • DNM

FAKIR'S SPELL, THE • 1914 • Newman Frank • UKN

FAKKELGANG • 1932 • de Haas Max • NTH • TORCHLIGHT PROCESSION

FAKLEN see **HVO SOM ELSKER SIN FADER** • 1915

FALA • 1943 • Fritsch Gunther V. • SHT • USA

FALA • 1986 • Lazarkiewicz Piotr • DOC • PLN • WAVE, THE

FALA AT HYDE PARK • 1946 • Fritsch Gunther V. • SHT • USA

FALA, BRASILIA • 1965 • dos Santos Nelson Pereira • BRZ

FALAK • 1968 • Kovacs Andras • HNG • LOST GENERATION ○ WALLS

FALAMOS DE RIO DE ONOR • 1974 • Campos Antonio • PRT

FALASHA -AGONY OF THE BLACK JEWS • 1982 • Raymont Peter • DOC • CND

FALASHA: EXILE OF THE BLACK JEWS • 1983 • Boyd Jamie, Jacobovici Simcha • DOC • CND

FALASTINI AL SAER, AL • 1970 • Mattar Ghassan, Myassar Reda • LBN • PALESTINIAN REVOLT

FALATO • 1988 • Kouyate Djibril • MLI • ORPHAN, THE

FALBALAS • 1945 • Becker Jacques • FRN • PARIS FRILLS (USA)

FALCO D'ORO, IL • 1956 • Bragaglia Carlo Ludovico • ITL

FALCO ROSSO, IL • 1950 • Bragaglia Carlo Ludovico • ITL

FALCON, THE see **SAKR, EL** • 1950

FALCON, THE see **SAQR, AS-** • 1965

FALCON, THE see **SOKO** • 1981

FALCON, THE see **SHAHEEN** • 1985

FALCON AND THE CO-EDS, THE • 1943 • Clemens William • USA

FALCON AND THE SNOWMAN, THE • 1984 • Schlesinger John • USA

FALCON FIGHTERS, THE (USA) see **AA RIKUGUN HAYABUSA SENTOTAI** • 1969

FALCON IN DANGER, THE • 1943 • Clemens William • USA

FALCON IN HOLLYWOOD, THE • 1944 • Douglas Gordon • USA

FALCON IN MEXICO, THE • 1944 • Berke William • USA

FALCON IN SAN FRANCISCO, THE • 1945 • Lewis Joseph H. • USA

FALCON OUT WEST, THE • 1944 • Clemens William • USA

FALCON STRIKES BACK, THE • 1943 • Dmytryk Edward • USA

FALCON TAKES OVER, THE • 1942 • Reis Irving • USA

FALCONS, THE see **MAGASISKOLA** • 1970

FALCON'S ADVENTURE, THE • 1946 • Berke William • USA

FALCON'S ALIBI, THE • 1946 • McCarey Ray • USA

FALCON'S BROTHER, THE • 1942 • Logan Stanley • USA

FALCON'S GOLD • 1985 • Schulz Bob • TVM • CND • ROBBERS OF THE SACRED MOUNTAIN ○ ROBBERS OF SACRED MOUNTAIN

FALCON'S MALTESER, THE see **JUST ASK FOR DIAMOND** • 1988

FALENA, LA • 1916 • Gallone Carmine • ITL

FALFURO • 1985 • Szomjas Gyorgy • HNG • WALL DRILLER, THE

FALKE, DER • 1983 • Mimica Vatroslav • FRG

FALL • Dewitt Tom • SHT • USA

FALL 7 A 9, DER see **FALSCHMUNZER AM WERK** • 1951

FALL, THE • 1969 • Whitehead Peter • UKN

FALL, THE see **CAIDA, LA** • 1959

FALL, THE see **QUEDA, A** • 1978

FALL, THE see **STURZ, DER** • 1979

FALL, THE see **ZUHANAS KOZBEN** • 1987

FALL AND RISE OF REGINALD PERRIN, THE • 1980 • Davies John Howard • MTV • UKN

FALL AND RISE OF THE ROMAN EMPIRE, THE see **CALIGULA E MESSALINA** • 1982

FALL BENKEN, DER • 1934 • Lamac Carl • FRG • UBERFALL IM HOTEL

FALL BERND K., DER • 1967 • Heynowski Walter, Scheumann Gerhard • GDR

FALL CLIFFORD, DER • 1917 • Kahn William • FRG • GETUPFTE KRAWATTE, DIE

FALL DERUGA, DER • 1938 • Buch Fritz Peter • FRG

FALL DES GENERALSTABS-OBERST REDL, DER • 1931 • Anton Karl • FRG

FALL DES STAATSANWALTS M...., DER • 1928 • Meinert Rudolf • FRG • STRANGE CASE OF DISTRICT ATTORNEY M., THE ○ WERA MIRZEWA

FALL DR. WAGNER, DER • 1954 • Mannl Harald • GDR

FALL DOMBRONOSKA-CLEMENCEAU, DER see **FALL DOMBRONOWSKA...!, DER** • 1917

FALL DOMBRONOWSKA...!, DER • 1917 • Kahn William • FRG • FALL DOMBRONOSKA-CLEMENCEAU, DER

FALL-DOWN, THE see **DOWNFALL, THE** • 1969

FALL DUIF, DER see **SCHATTEN DER NACHT** • 1918

FALL FARE • 1973 • Dalen Zale R. • CND

FALL GIRL see **LISETTE** • 1961

FALL GLEIWITZ, DER • 1961 • Klein Gerhard • GDR • GLEIWITZ CASE, THE

FALL GREHN...!, DER • 1916 • Kahn William • FRG

FALL GUY • 1945 • Burnford Paul • SHT • USA

FALL GUY • 1947 • Le Borg Reginald • USA

FALL GUY • 1955 • *O'Brien Dave* • SHT • USA

FALL GUY, THE • 1921 • Taurog Norman, Semon Larry • SHT • USA

FALL GUY, THE • 1930 • Pearce A. Leslie • USA • TRUST YOUR WIFE (UKN)

FALL GUY, THE • 1982 • Fukasaku Kinji • JPN

FALL GUY, THE see **FALLGUY** • 1962

FALL HARRER, DER • 1986 • Lepeniotis Antonis • AUS • HARRER CASE, THE

FALL HIRN, DER • 1917 • Mack Max • FRG

FALL HOOP, DER • 1916 • Kahn William • FRG

FALL IN • 1942 • Neumann Kurt • USA

FALL IN! see **NASTUP** • 1952

FALL INTO LUCK, A • 1913 • *American* • USA

FALL JAGERSTATTER, DER • 1972 • Corti Axel • AUS • JAGERSTATTER CASE, THE ○ VERWEIGERUNG, DIE ○ REFUSAL, THE

FALL KLERK, DER • 1916 • Kahn William • FRG

FALL MANOEUVRES (USA) see **HERBSTMANOVER** • 1935

FALL MOLANDER, DER • 1945 • Pabst G. W. • FRG

FALL OF A KNIGHT, THE • 1911 • Porter Edwin S. • USA

FALL OF A NATION, THE • 1916 • Cushing Bartley • USA

FALL OF A SAINT, THE • 1920 • Kellino W. P. • UKN

FALL OF AKO-JO, THE see **AKOJO DANZETSU** • 1978

FALL OF ALEXANDER THE GREAT, THE see **GIBELTA NA ALEKASANDAR VILIKI** • 1968

FALL OF BABYLON, THE • 1919 • Griffith D. W. • USA

FALL OF BERLIN, THE • 1965 • Rossif Frederic • DOC • FRN

FALL OF BERLIN, THE see **BERLIN** • 1945

FALL OF BERLIN, THE see **ZAGLADA BERLIN** • 1945

FALL OF BERLIN, THE (USA) see **PADENIYE BERLINA** • 1949

FALL OF BLACK HAWK, THE • 1912 • Sullivan Joseph, Lee William • USA

FALL OF BLACK WATER see **KALU DIYA DHARA** • 1974

FALL OF DEACON STILLWATERS, THE • 1916 • Curtis Allen • USA

FALL OF EVE, THE • 1929 • Strayer Frank • USA

FALL OF ITALY, THE see **PAD ITALIJA** • 1982

FALL OF LOLA MONTES, THE (UKN) see **LOLA MONTES** • 1955

FALL OF MONTEZUMA, THE • 1912 • Webster Harry Mcrae • USA

FALL OF MUSCLE-BOUND HICKS, THE • 1914 • Henderson Dell • USA

FALL OF ROME, THE see **SOLO CONTRO ROMA** • 1962

FALL OF ROME, THE (USA) see **CROLLO DI ROMA, IL** • 1962

FALL OF THE ALAMO, THE • 1914 • *Myers Ray* • USA

FALL OF THE CONDOR, THE see **CAIDA DEL CONDOR, LA** • 1982

FALL OF THE GODS, THE see **CADUTA DEGLI DEI, LA** • 1968

FALL OF THE HOUSE OF USHER, THE • 1928 • Webber Melville, Watson James Sibley • SHT • USA

FALL OF THE HOUSE OF USHER, THE • 1941 • SHT • UKN

FALL OF THE HOUSE OF USHER, THE • 1942 • Harrington Curtis • SHT • USA

FALL OF THE HOUSE OF USHER, THE • 1950 • Barnett Ivan • UKN

FALL OF THE HOUSE OF USHER, THE • 1955 • Pizzo Sal • USA

FALL OF THE HOUSE OF USHER, THE • 1958 • *Tryon Tom* • USA

FALL OF THE HOUSE OF USHER, THE • 1960 • Corman Roger • USA • HOUSE OF USHER, THE

FALL OF THE HOUSE OF USHER, THE • 1979 • Conway James L. • USA

FALL OF THE HOUSE OF USHER, THE see **CHUTE DE LA MAISON USHER, LA** • 1928

FALL OF THE HOUSE OF USHER, THE see **ZANIK DOMU USHERU** • 1981

FALL OF THE ROMAN EMPIRE, THE • 1964 • Mann Anthony • USA

FALL OF THE ROMANOFFS, THE • 1917 • Brenon Herbert • USA

FALL OF THE ROMANOV DYNASTY, THE see **PADENIYE DINASTI ROMANOVIKH** • 1927

FALL OF THE ROMANOVS, THE see **PADENIYE DINASTI ROMANOVIKH** • 1927

FALL OF TROY, THE see **CADUTA DI TROIA, LA** • 1910

FALL OUT -FALL IN • 1943 • King Jack • ANS • USA

FALL POPINOFF, DER • 1919 • *Forster Rudolf* • AUS

FALL RABANSER, DER • 1950 • Hoffmann Kurt • FRG

FALL RAINIER, DER • 1942 • Verhoeven Paul • FRG • ICH WARTE AUF DICH

FALL ROBERTS, DER see **NACHT IM FORSTHAUS, DIE** • 1933

FALL ROSENTOPF, DER • 1918 • Lubitsch Ernst • FRG • ROSENTOPF CASE, THE

FALL ROUTT...!, DER • 1916 • Kahn William • FRG

FALL TO ARMS, A • 1930 • Foster Lewis R. • SHT • USA

FALL TOKERAMO, DER see **POLIZEIAKTE 909** • 1934

FALL X701, DER • 1964 • Knowles Bernard • FRG, UKN • FROZEN ALIVE (UKN)

FALLADA -THE LAST CHAPTER • 1988 • Graf Roland • GDR

FALLAGA see **FELLAGHAS** • 1970

FALLAH AL-FACIH, AL- • 1970 • Abdes-Salam Shadi • EGY • PAYSAN ELOQUENT, LE ○ FELLAH AL FASSIEH, AL

FALLAVENTYRET • 1927 • Sinding Leif • NRW

FALLE, DIE • Mack Max • FRG

FALLE, DIE see **SALON DORA GREEN** • 1933

FALLEN • 1975 • Watkins Peter • SWD • TRAP, THE

FALLEN ANGEL • 1914 • Vale Travers • USA

FALLEN ANGEL • 1945 • Preminger Otto • USA

FALLEN ANGEL • 1981 • Lewis Robert • TVM • USA

FALLEN ANGEL see **SCHMUTZIGER ENGEL** • 1958

FALLEN ANGEL, THE • 1913 • *Smalley Phillips* • USA

FALLEN ANGEL, THE • 1918 • Thornby Robert T. • USA

FALLEN ANGEL, THE see **CAMILLE OF THE BARBARY COAST** • 1925

FALLEN ANGELS see **MAN, WOMAN AND WIFE** • 1929

FALLEN APPLE see **APFEL IST AB, DER** • 1948

FALLEN ARCHES • 1933 • Meins Gus • SHT • USA

FALLEN BY THE WAY • 1922 • Sanderson Challis • UKN

FALLEN HERO, A • 1913 • Dillon Eddie • USA

FALLEN IDOL, THE • 1910 • *Imp* • USA

FALLEN IDOL, THE • 1913 • Elvey Maurice • UKN

FALLEN IDOL, THE • 1919 • Buel Kenean • USA

FALLEN IDOL, THE • 1948 • Reed Carol • UKN • LOST ILLUSION, THE

FALLEN IN HELL, THE see **CAIDOS EN EL INFIERNO** • 1954

FALLEN LEAVES • 1919 • SAF

FALLEN LEAVES • 1922 • Cooper George A. • UKN

FALLEN LEAVES FROM THE TREES see **OPADLY LISCIE Z DRZEW** • 1975

FALLEN ROSEBUD see **BARAIRO NO FUTARI** • 1967

FALLEN SPARROW, THE • 1943 • Wallace Richard • USA

FALLEN STANDARD, THE • 1915 • *Balboa* • USA

FALLEN STAR, A • 1916 • Hepworth Cecil M. • UKN

FALLEN STAR, A • 1917 • *Mccoy Harry* • USA

FALLEN WOMAN, A see **DARAKU SURU ONNA** • 1967

FALLENDE STERN, DER • 1950 • Braun Harald • FRG • FALLING STAR, THE (USA)

FALLET INGEGERD BREMSSEN • 1942 • Henrikson Anders • SWD • INGEGERD BREMSSEN CASE, THE

FALLGROPEN • 1989 • Sjoman Vilgot • SWD • PITFALL, THE

FALLGUY • 1962 • Harling Donn • USA • FALL GUY, THE

FALLIBLE FABLE, A • 1962 • Hanna William, Barbera Joseph • ANS • USA

FALLIN' OUT, THE • 1911 • *Imp* • USA

FALLING, THE see **ALIEN PREDATORS** • 1987

FALLING AMONG THIEVES see **NAMI Z LODEJI** • 1964

FALLING ANGELS • 1975 • Conrad Derek • UKN

FALLING BLOSSOMS see **HANA NO UTAGE** • 1967

FALLING FOR YOU • 1933 • Hulbert Jack, Stevenson Robert • UKN

FALLING FROM LADDERS • 1969 • Ransen Mort • CND

FALLING HARE • 1943 • Clampett Robert • ANS • USA

FALLING IN LOVE • 1934 • Banks Monty • UKN • TROUBLE AHEAD

FALLING IN LOVE • 1985 • Grosbard Ulu • USA

FALLING IN LOVE AGAIN • 1980 • Paul Steven • USA

FALLING IN LOVE WITH INEZ • 1913 • Williams C. Jay • USA

FALLING LEAVES • 1912 • Blache Alice • USA

FALLING LEAVES see **LISTOPAD** • 1968

FALLING LEAVES, THE see **YAPREK DOKUMU** • 1967

FALLING MAN, THE • 1971 • Michaels Billy • USA

FALLING STAR, THE (USA) see **FALLENDE STERN, DER** • 1950

FALLING STARS see **HOLLYWOOD CAVALCADE** • 1939

FALLING STONES (UKN) see **OVERLAND TO DEADWOOD** • 1942

FALLING UNCONSCIOUS see **IJO NA HANNO: MONZETSU** • 1967

FALLOW LAND see **MAGYAR UGARAON, A** • 1973

FALLS • 1946 • Mulholland Donald • SHT • CND • CHUTES, LES

FALLS, THE • 1980 • Greenaway Peter • UKN

FALLS THE SHADOW • 1958 • McConnell Edward, Henson Laurence • SHT • UKN

FALLSTRICKE DER LEIDENSCHAFT • 1924 • *Revera-Film* • FRG

FALN • 1965 • Kramer Robert • USA

FALOSNY PRINC • 1985 • Rapos Dusan • CZC, FRG • FALSE PRINCE, A

FALPALA see **NINI FALPALA** • 1933

FALSA AMANTE, LA • 1920 • D'Ambra Lucio • ITL

FALSARI, I • 1952 • Rossi Franco • ITL

FALSCHE ADAM, DER • 1955 • von Cziffra Geza • FRG

FALSCHE ARZT, DER see **NAMENLOS** • 1923

FALSCHE BARONET, DER • 1920 • Eichgrun Bruno • FRG

FALSCHE BEWEGUNG • 1975 • Wenders Wim • FRG • WRONG MOVEMENT (UKN) ○ WRONG MOVE

FALSCHE BRAUT, DIE • 1944 • Stockel Joe • FRG • DA STIMMT WAS NICHT

FALSCHE DEMETRIUS, DER • 1918 • Grunwald Willy • FRG

FALSCHE DIMITRY, DER • 1922 • Steinhoff Hans • FRG

FALSCHE EHEMANN, DER • 1931 • Guter Johannes • FRG

FALSCHE EMIR, DER see **MENSCHEN UND MASKEN 1** • 1923

FALSCHE FELDMARSCHALL, DER • 1930 • Lamac Carl • FRG • K. UND K. FELDMARSCHALL, DER ○ FIELD MARSHALL, THE
FALSCHE GEWICHT, DAS • 1971 • Wicki Bernhard • FRG • WANTING WEIGHT, THE
FALSCHE KATZE, DIE see **HEIRATEN -ABER WEN?** • 1938
FALSCHE PRINZ, DER • 1922 • Prager Wilhelm? • FRG
FALSCHE PRINZ, DER • 1927 • Paul Heinz • FRG
FALSCHE SCHAM • 1926 • Biebrach Rudolf • FRG
FALSCHE SCHEIN, DER • 1915 • Zeyn Willy • FRG
FALSCHE SCHEIN, DER • 1919 • Justitz Emil • FRG
FALSCHE WITTWE, DIE see **HURRAH! ICH LIEBE!** • 1928
FALSCHEN HOND, DE • 1990 • Bodson Menn, Rollinger Gast, Olinger Marc • LXM • TRAITOR, THE
FALSCHER FUFFZIGER, EIN • 1935 • Boese Carl • FRG
FALSCHER START • 1920 • *Alexander Georg* • FRG
FALSCHER VON LONDON, DER • 1961 • Reinl Harald • FRG • FORGER OF LONDON, THE (USA)
FALSCHES GELD • 1918 • Dessauer Siegfried?, Matull Kurt? • FRG
FALSCHMUNZER • 1940 • Pfeiffer Hermann • FRG
FALSCHMUNZER AM WERK • 1951 • Agotay Louis • FRG • FALL 7 A 9, DER
FALSCHSPIELER • 1920 • Justitz Emil • FRG
FALSCHUNG, DIE • 1981 • Schlondorff Volker • FRG, FRN • CIRCLE OF DECEIT (UKN) ○ FAUSSAIRE, LE (FRN) ○ FALSE WITNESS ○ FORGERY, THE
FALSE ACCUSATION, A • 1909 • Brooke Van Dyke • USA
FALSE ACCUSATION, A • 1913 • *Patheplay* • USA
FALSE ALARM • 1922 • Kenton Erle C. • SHT • USA
FALSE ALARM • 1923 • Fleischer Dave • ANS • USA
FALSE ALARM, A • 1917 • *Triangle* • USA
FALSE ALARM, THE • Hempel Johannes • ANM • GDR
FALSE ALARM, THE • 1913 • *Crystal* • USA
FALSE ALARM, THE • 1926 • O'Connor Frank • USA
FALSE ALARM, THE • 1933 • *Mintz Charles (P)* • ANS • USA
FALSE ALARM; OR, THE MASHER'S DUCKING, A • 1905 • Collins Alf? • UKN
FALSE ALARMS • 1936 • Lord Del • SHT • USA
FALSE AMBITION • 1918 • Hamilton G. P. • USA
FALSE AND THE TRUE, THE • 1914 • Marston Theodore • USA
FALSE AS WATER • 1985 • Alfredson Hans • SWD
FALSE BEAUTY, A • 1914 • Sterling Ford • USA
FALSE BRANDS • 1922 • Craft William James • USA
FALSE BRIDE, THE • 1914 • Salter Harry • USA • TEST, THE
FALSE CLUE, THE • 1913 • Coleby A. E.? • UKN
FALSE CLUE, THE • 1915 • *Horseshoe* • UKN
FALSE CLUE, THE • 1915 • *Boardman True* • USA
FALSE CLUE, THE • 1916 • *Davenport Dorothy* • SHT • USA
FALSE CLUES (UKN) see **NORTH OF THE ROCKIES** • 1942
FALSE CODE, THE • 1919 • Warde Ernest C. • USA
FALSE COIN, THE see **KALPIKI LIRA, I** • 1955
FALSE COLORS • 1914 • Weber Lois, Smalley Phillips • USA
FALSE COLORS • 1943 • Archainbaud George • USA
FALSE COLORS see **REPUTATION** • 1921
FALSE COLORS see **TRUE HEAVEN** • 1929
FALSE COLOURS • 1927 • Mander Miles • UKN
FALSE CUE, THE • 1915 • *Horseshoe* • SHT • UKN
FALSE DOOR, THE see **POR LA PUERTA FALSA** • 1950
FALSE DREAM see **ONIRO APATILO** • 1968
FALSE EVIDENCE • 1919 • Carewe Edwin • USA • MADELON OF THE REDWOODS
FALSE EVIDENCE • 1922 • Shaw Harold • UKN
FALSE EVIDENCE • 1937 • Pedelty Donovan • UKN
FALSE EVIDENCE see **FOR SIN FADERS SKYLD** • 1916
FALSE EVIDENCE (UKN) see **RETURN OF WILD BILL, THE** • 1940
FALSE FACE see **SCALPEL** • 1976
FALSE FACES • 1932 • Sherman Lowell • USA • WHAT PRICE BEAUTY (UKN)
FALSE FACES • 1943 • Sherman George • USA • ATTORNEY'S DILEMMA, THE (UKN)
FALSE FACES see **FAUX VISAGES, LES** • 1962
FALSE FACES, THE • 1919 • Willat Irvin V. • USA
FALSE FACES (UKN) see **LET 'EM HAVE IT** • 1935
FALSE FATHERS • 1929 • Carpenter Horace B. • USA
FALSE FRIEND, A • 1911 • Noy Wilfred • UKN
FALSE FRIEND, A • 1913 • Melville Wilbert • USA
FALSE FRIEND, THE • 1913 • Le Saint Edward J. • USA
FALSE FRIEND, THE • 1917 • Davenport Harry • USA
FALSE FRIENDS • 1926 • Ford Francis • USA
FALSE FRIENDS AND FIRE ALARMS • 1916 • *Ritchie Billie* • SHT • USA
FALSE FRONTS • 1922 • Bradley Samuel R. • USA
FALSE GEMS, THE • 1916 • Julian Rupert • SHT • USA
FALSE GODS • 1914 • Ricketts Thomas • USA
FALSE GODS • 1919 • Van Wally • USA
FALSE GRETA see **FALSKA GRETA** • 1934
FALSE GUARDIAN, THE • 1914 • Vignola Robert G. • USA
FALSE HAIR, THE • 1915 • *Powell Russ* • USA
FALSE HARE • 1964 • McKimson Robert • ANS • USA
FALSE HERO (UKN) see **ROARING RANGERS** • 1946
FALSE IDOL, THE (UKN) see **FALSE MADONNA, THE** • 1932
FALSE IMPRESSIONS • 1932 • *Sennett Mack (P)* • SHT • USA
FALSE KISSES • 1921 • Scardon Paul • USA • ROPES
FALSE LOVE see **AMOUR MENSONGE, L'** • 1979
FALSE LOVE AND TRUE • 1910 • *Lubin* • USA
FALSE LOVE AND TRUE • 1913 • *Crystal* • USA
FALSE MADONNA, THE • 1932 • Walker Stuart • USA • FALSE IDOL, THE (UKN)
FALSE MAGISTRATE, THE see **FAUX MAGISTRAT, LE** • 1914
FALSE MILLIONAIRE see **FALSKA MILLIONAREN** • 1931
FALSE MONEY • 1905 • Fitzhamon Lewin • UKN
FALSE MORALS • 1927 • *Glass Gaston* • USA
FALSE MOVE, A • 1914 • Thornby Robert T. • USA
FALSE NEWS • 1913 • *Gaumont* • USA
FALSE NEWS (UKN) see **BARBED WIRE** • 1952
FALSE NOTE, THE see **VALSE NOOT, DE**
FALSE ORDER, THE • 1913 • Eagle Oscar • USA
FALSE PARADISE • 1948 • Archainbaud George • USA
FALSE PART, THE • 1916 • Worthington William • SHT • USA
FALSE PASSPORT, THE see **VIZA NO ZLOTO** • 1958
FALSE PLAY • 1923 • Marchant Jay • USA
FALSE PLAY see **LONE HAND, THE** • 1922
FALSE POUND STERLING, THE see **KALPIKI LIRA, I** • 1955
FALSE PRETENCES • 1935 • Lamont Charles • USA
FALSE PRIDE • 1914 • *Majestic* • USA
FALSE PRIDE • 1926 • Dierker Hugh • USA
FALSE PRIDE HAS A FALL • 1914 • *Farley Dot* • USA
FALSE PRINCE, A see **FALOSNY PRINC** • 1985
FALSE PROPHET, THE • 1917 • Horne James W. • SHT • USA
FALSE ROAD, THE • 1920 • Niblo Fred • USA
FALSE ROOMERS • 1931 • Sandrich Mark • SHT • USA
FALSE ROOMERS • 1938 • Goodwins Leslie • SHT • USA
FALSE SHADOW, THE • 1914 • *Ince John* • USA
FALSE SHAME (USA) see **WORUBER MAN NICHT SPRICHT** • 1958
FALSE STEP, THE (USA) see **SCHRITT VOM WEGE, DER** • 1939
FALSE STUDENT, THE see **NISE DAIGAKUSEI** • 1960
FALSE SUSPICION, A • 1911 • *Moore Mabel* • USA
FALSE SVENSSON see **KONSTGJORDA SVENSSON** • 1929
FALSE TO BOTH • 1912 • *Imp* • USA
FALSE TO THE FINISH • 1917 • Morris Reggie • SHT • USA
FALSE TRAILS • 1924 • *Morrison Pete* • USA
FALSE UNIFORMS • 1932 • Lopashinsky Faust
FALSE WIRELESS, THE • 1914 • Martinek H. O. • UKN
FALSE WITNESS • 1988 • Seidelman Arthur Allan • USA
FALSE WITNESS see **FALSCHUNG, DIE** • 1981
FALSE WITNESS (UKN) see **TRANSIENT LADY** • 1936
FALSE WITNESS (UKN) see **ARKANSAS JUDGE** • 1941
FALSE WITNESS (UKN) see **ZIGZAG** • 1970
FALSE WOMEN • 1921 • Armstrong R. Dale • USA
FALSELY ACCUSED • 1905 • Fitzhamon Lewin • UKN
FALSELY ACCUSED • 1907 • *Gaumont* • UKN
FALSELY ACCUSED • 1907 • *Bitzer Billy (Ph)* • USA
FALSELY ACCUSED • 1912 • *Bison* • USA
FALSELY ACCUSED • 1913 • *Solax* • USA
FALSELY ACCUSED • 1915 • Batley Ethyle • UKN
FALSELY ACCUSED • 1915 • Golden Joseph A.? • USA
FALSELY ACCUSED • 1916 • *Hiawatha* • USA
FALSH • 1987 • Dardenne Luc, Dardenne Jean-Pierre • BLG
FALSIFICADORES ASESINOS • 1964 • Gomez Urquiza Zacarias • MXC
FALSKA GRETA • 1934 • Brunius John W. • SWD • FALSE GRETA
FALSKA MILLIONAREN • 1931 • Merzbach Paul • SWD • FALSE MILLIONAIRE
FALSOS HEROES, LOS • 1961 • Toussaint Carlos • MXC
FALSTAFF • 1911 • Desfontaines Henri • FRN
FALSTAFF IN WIEN • 1940 • Hainisch Leopold • FRG
FALSTAFF THE TAVERN KNIGHT • 1923 • Greenwood Edwin • UKN
FALSTAFF (UKN) see **CAMPANADAS A MEDIANOCHE** • 1966
FALU ROSSZA, A • 1938 • Pasztor Bela • HNG • VILLAGE ROGUE, A (USA) ○ EVIL VILLAGE
FALUDY GYORGY KOLTO • 1988 • Boszormenyi Geza, Gyarmathy Livia • DOC • HNG • POET GYORGY FALUDY, THE
FAMA • 1921 • Roberti Roberto Leone • ITL
FAMALICAO • 1941 • de Oliveira Manoel • SHT • PRT
FAME • 1936 • Hiscott Leslie • UKN
FAME • 1980 • Parker Alan • USA
FAME see **RECAPTURED LOVE** • 1930
FAME see **SLAVA** • 1959
FAME AND FORTUNE • 1918 • Reynolds Lynn • USA • MR. LOGAN
FAME AND THE DEVIL (USA) see **AL DIAVOLO LA CELEBRITA** • 1949
FAME AT LAST • 1916 • Beery Wallace • SHT • USA
FAME IS THE NAME OF THE GAME • 1966 • Rosenberg Stuart • TVM • USA
FAME IS THE SPUR • 1947 • Boulting Roy • UKN
FAME OF LORD KRISHNA see **THIRUMAL PERUMAI** • 1968
FAME STREET • 1932 • King Louis • USA
FAMIGLIA, LA • 1987 • Scola Ettore • ITL, FRN • FAMILY, THE
FAMIGLIA BRAMILLA IN VACANZA, LA • 1942 • Boese Carl • ITL
FAMIGLIA IMPOSSIBILE, UNA • 1940 • Bragaglia Carlo Ludovico • ITL
FAMIGLIA PASSAGUAI, LA • 1951 • Fabrizi Aldo • ITL
FAMIGLIA PASSAGUAI FA FORTUNA, LA • 1952 • Fabrizi Aldo • ITL
FAMILIA DE TANTAS, UNA • 1948 • Galindo Alejandro • MXC • ORDINARY FAMILY, AN
FAMILIA DECENTE, UNA • 1977 • Comeron Luis Jose • SPN
FAMILIA DRESSEL, LA • 1935 • de Fuentes Fernando • MXC • DRESSEL FAMILY, THE
FAMILIA OROZCO, LA • 1982 • Reyes Jorge • PRU
FAMILIA PEREZ, LA • 1948 • Martinez Solares Gilberto • MXC
FAMILIA PICHILIN, LA • 1978 • Getino Octavio • ARG
FAMILIA PROVISIONAL • 1955 • Rovira Beleta Francisco • SPN
FAMILIA VILA, LA • 1949 • Iquino Ignacio F. • SPN
FAMILIA Y UNO MAS, LA • 1965 • Palacios Fernando • SPN
FAMILIAR, EL • 1973 • Getino Octavio • ARG
FAMILIAR FACES AND MIXED FEELINGS • 1981 • de Jong Ate • NTH
FAMILIARI DELLE VITTIME NON SARANNO AVVERTITI, I • 1972 • De Martino Alberto • ITL • CRIME BOSS (USA) ○ NEW MAFIA BOSS, THE
FAMILIARIDADES • 1969 • Cazals Felipe • MXC • FAMILIARITIES
FAMILIARITIES see **FAMILIARIDADES** • 1969
FAMILIE BENTHIN • 1950 • Maetzig Kurt, Dudow Slatan • GDR
FAMILIE BUCHHOLZ • 1944 • Froelich Carl • FRG • NEIGUNGSEHE
FAMILIE OHNE MORAL • 1927 • Neufeld Max • AUS
FAMILIE SCHIMEK • 1925 • Halm Alfred • FRG • WIENER HERZEN
FAMILIE SCHIMEK • 1935 • Emo E. W. • FRG
FAMILIE SCHIMEK • 1956 • Jacoby Georg • AUS
FAMILIEBILLEDER • 1964 • Carlsen Henning • DNM • FAMILY PORTRAITS
FAMILIEN GYLDENKAL • 1975 • Axel Gabriel • DNM
FAMILIEN GYLDENKAL SPRAENGER BANKEN • 1976 • Axel Gabriel • DNM
FAMILIEN GYLDENKAL VINDER VALGET • 1977 • Christensen Bent • DNM
FAMILIEN MED DE 100 BORN • 1972 • Methling Sven • DNM
FAMILIEN SWEDENHJELM • 1947 • Lauritzen Lau Jr. • DNM
FAMILIENANSCHLUSS • 1941 • Boese Carl • FRG
FAMILIENGLUCK • 1975 • Ludcke Marianne, Kratisch Ingo • FRG • HAPPY FAMILY LIFE
FAMILIENPARADE • 1936 • Wendhausen Fritz • FRG
FAMILIENTAG IM HAUSE PRELLSTEIN • 1927 • Steinhoff Hans • FRG
FAMILIES • 1986 • Dueck David B. • CND
FAMILIES IN CRISIS • 1982 • Noonan Chris • DOC • ASL
FAMILJEN ANDERSSON • 1937 • Wallen Sigurd • SWD • ANDERSSON FAMILY, THE
FAMILJEN BJORCK • 1940 • Henrikson Anders • SWD • VILLE, ALLA TIDERS KILLE ○ BJORCK FAMILY, THE
FAMILJEN SOM VAR EN KARUSELL • 1936 • Bauman Schamyl • SWD • FAMILY THAT WAS A MERRY-GO-ROUND, THE
FAMILJENS HEMLIGHET • 1936 • Molander Gustaf • SWD • FAMILY SECRET, THE
FAMILJENS TRADITIONER • 1920 • Carlsten Rune • SWD • FAMILY TRADITIONS
FAMILLE 1949, DOUVILLE 1949 • 1949 • Tessier Albert • DCS • CND
FAMILLE, LA • 1970 • Lagrange Yvan • FRN
FAMILLE, LA see **ABUSAN** • 1973
FAMILLE CARDINAL, LA see **PETITES CARDINALES, LES** • 1950
FAMILLE CUCUROUX, LA • 1953 • Couzinet Emile • FRN
FAMILLE DE CHOIX, UNE see **IN SEARCH OF HOME** • 1953
FAMILLE DE CONIQUES see **FOUR-LINE CONICS** • 1962
FAMILLE DE ZIZI, LA see **A'ILAT ZIZI** • 1962
FAMILLE DURATON, LA • 1939 • Stengel Christian • FRN
FAMILLE ET VARIATIONS • 1977 • Dansereau Fernand • DOC • CND
FAMILLE FENOUILLARD, LA • 1960 • Robert Yves • FRN
FAMILLE HERNANDEZ, LA • 1964 • Bailac Genevieve • FRN
FAMILLE HEUREUSE, LA • 1958 • Shawqi Khalil • SHT • EGY
FAMILLE KLEPKENS, LA • 1930 • Schoukens Gaston, Flon Paul • BLG
FAMILLE MARTIN, LA • 1948 • Mander Kay • UKN
FAMILLE NOMBREUSE • 1934 • Hugon Andre • FRN
FAMILLE PONT-BIQUET, LA • 1935 • Christian-Jaque • FRN
FAMILLE SCHMIDT, LA • 1951 • Palsbo Ole • DNM
FAMILLES DE DROITES ET DE PARABOLES • Cantagrel Marc • DOC • FRN
FAMILY • 1971 • Graef Roger • UKN
FAMILY see **CHIA** • 1953
FAMILY see **JIA** • 1957
FAMILY see **KUDUMBAM** • 1967
FAMILY see **PARIVAR** • 1968
FAMILY, A see **KAZOKU** • 1942
FAMILY, A see **KAZOKU** • 1971
FAMILY, A see **RODZINA** • 1975
FAMILY, THE • 1969 • Alexander Mike • UKN
FAMILY, THE • 1974 • de Boer Lodewijk • NTH
FAMILY, THE see **CITTA VIOLENTA** • 1970
FAMILY, THE see **RODZINA** • 1971
FAMILY, THE see **ABUSAN** • 1973
FAMILY, THE see **KAREINARU ICHIZOKU** • 1973
FAMILY, THE see **PYHA PERHE** • 1976
FAMILY, THE see **FAMIGLIA, LA** • 1987
FAMILY AFFAIR, A • 1913 • *Kinemacolor* • USA
FAMILY AFFAIR, A • 1916 • Badger Clarence • SHT • USA
FAMILY AFFAIR, A • 1937 • Seitz George B. • USA
FAMILY AFFAIR, A • 1942 • Diamant-Berger Henri
FAMILY AFFAIR, A • 1955 • Jacoby Irving • SHT • USA
FAMILY AFFAIR (USA) see **LIFE WITH THE LYONS** • 1954
FAMILY ALBUM see **BLAKES SLEPT HERE, THE** • 1954
FAMILY ALBUM see **SEMEINYE FOTOGRAFI** • 1989
FAMILY AND HONOR • 1985 • Zarchi Meir • USA
FAMILY BIBLE, THE • 1915 • *Prior Herbert* • USA
FAMILY BUSINESS • 1982 • Stix John • TVM • USA
FAMILY BUSINESS • 1986 • Costa-Gavras • FRN
FAMILY BUSINESS • 1989 • Lumet Sidney • USA
FAMILY CENTERED MATERNITY CARE • 1961 • Hammid Alexander • DOC • USA
FAMILY CHRONICLE, A see **CRONICA DE FAMILIA** • 1985
FAMILY CIRCLE • 1949 • Parker Morten • DOC • CND
FAMILY CIRCUS, THE • 1951 • Babbitt Art • ANS • USA
FAMILY CLOSET, THE • 1921 • O'Brien John B. • USA
FAMILY CONFERENCE see **KAZOKU KAIGI** • 1954
FAMILY CUPBOARD, THE • 1915 • Crane Frank H. • USA
FAMILY DIARY see **KATEI NIKKI** • 1938
FAMILY DIARY see **CRONACA FAMILIARE** • 1962
FAMILY DIVIDED, THE • 1915 • Haydon J. Charles? • USA
FAMILY DOCTOR • 1958 • Twist Derek • UKN • RX MURDER (USA)
FAMILY DOCTOR, THE • 1915 • *Blue G. M.* • USA
FAMILY ENFORCER see **DEATH COLLECTOR** • 1977
FAMILY ENTRANCE, THE • 1925 • McCarey Leo • SHT • USA
FAMILY FACE, A • 1967 • Thompson Peter • DOC • ASL
FAMILY FEUD, A • 1910 • *Vitagraph* • USA
FAMILY FEUD, A • 1914 • *Lux* • USA
FAMILY FEUD, A • 1943 • *Errol Leon* • SHT • USA
FAMILY FLIGHT • 1972 • Chomsky Marvin • TVM • USA
FAMILY FLIVVER, A • 1917 • Baker Graham • SHT • USA
FAMILY FOCUS • 1975 • Emshwiller Ed • USA
FAMILY GAME see **KAZUKO GEEMU** • 1983
FAMILY GROUP, THE • 1928 • Guiol Fred • SHT • USA
FAMILY HISTORY see **CRONACA FAMILIARE** • 1962
FAMILY HOME see **HIS TRYSTING PLACE** • 1914
FAMILY HONEYMOON • 1948 • Binyon Claude • USA
FAMILY HONOR, THE • 1917 • Chautard Emile • USA
FAMILY HONOR, THE • 1920 • Vidor King • USA
FAMILY HOUSE, THE see **HIS TRYSTING PLACE** • 1914
FAMILY IN LOVE see **AINO FAMILY** • 1978
FAMILY IN THOUSANDS, A see **WAN HU CH'IEN CHIA** • 1976
FAMILY INTERMINGLE, A • 1914 • *Columbus* • USA
FAMILY JAR, THE • 1913 • *Pathe* • USA
FAMILY JARS • 1899 • *Warwick Trading Co.* • UKN
FAMILY JEWELS see **BIJOUX DE FAMILLE, LES** • 1974
FAMILY JEWELS, THE • 1965 • Lewis Jerry • USA
FAMILY JEWELS, THE see **BIJUTERII DE FAMILIE** • 1958

FAMILY KOVACK, THE • 1974 • Senensky Ralph • TVM • USA
FAMILY LIFE • 1971 • Loach Kenneth • UKN • WEDNESDAY'S CHILD (USA)
FAMILY LIFE see **ZYCIE RODZINNE** • 1971
FAMILY LIFE OF THE GOLDEN EAGLE, THE • 1935 • Gordon Seton • UKN
FAMILY LIGHT AFFAIR see **CH'ENG-SHIH-CHIH KUANG** • 1984
FAMILY MAN see **HIS GREATEST GAMBLE** • 1934
FAMILY MAN, THE • 1979 • Jordan Glenn • TVM • USA
FAMILY MIX-UP, A • 1912 • Sennett Mack • USA
FAMILY MIX-UP, A • 1915 • *Thistle* • USA
FAMILY-NESS, THE • 1984 • ANM • UKN
FAMILY NEST see **CSALADI TUZFESZEK** • 1979
FAMILY NEXT DOOR, THE • 1912 • *Fielding Romaine* • USA
FAMILY NEXT DOOR, THE • 1939 • Santley Joseph • USA
FAMILY NISKAVUORI, THE see **NISKAVUORI** • 1984
FAMILY NOBODY WANTED, THE • 1956 • Frankenheimer John • MTV • USA
FAMILY NOBODY WANTED, THE • 1975 • Senensky Ralph • TVM • USA
FAMILY OF MAN, THE see **RODZINA CZLOWIECZA** • 1966
FAMILY OF THE RECKLESS see **KAN NG HARAGAN, ANG** • 1967
FAMILY OF VEGETARIANS, A • 1911 • *Edison* • USA
FAMILY OUTING, THE • 1914 • *Melies* • USA
FAMILY PICNIC, A • 1915 • Stratton Edmund F. • USA
FAMILY PLOT • 1976 • Hitchcock Alfred • USA
FAMILY PORTRAIT • 1950 • Jennings Humphrey • DOC • UKN
FAMILY PORTRAIT see **RETRATO DE FAMILIA** • 1976
FAMILY PORTRAIT, A see **IKOGENIA HORAFA** • 1968
FAMILY PORTRAITS see **FAMILIEBILLEDER** • 1964
FAMILY RECORD, THE • 1914 • MacGregor Norval • USA
FAMILY RELATIONS see **RODNIA** • 1983
FAMILY REUNION • 1981 • Cook Fielder • TVM • USA
FAMILY REUNION • 1988 • Hawes Michael • USA
FAMILY REUNION see **DAUGHTERS COURAGEOUS** • 1939
FAMILY REUNION see **SAKHA PRASAKHA** • 1990
FAMILY RICO, THE • 1972 • Wendkos Paul • TVM • USA
FAMILY ROBINSON ON THE FARM see **SEX FAMILY ROBINSON ON THE FARM** • 1969
FAMILY ROCK • 1982 • Pinheiro Jose • FRN
FAMILY SECRET, THE • 1916 • Worthington William • SHT • USA
FAMILY SECRET, THE • 1924 • Seiter William A. • USA
FAMILY SECRET, THE • 1951 • Levin Henry • USA
FAMILY SECRET, THE see **FAMILJENS HEMLIGHET** • 1936
FAMILY SECRETS • 1984 • Hofsiss Jack • TVM • USA
FAMILY SHOE, THE • 1931 • Foster John, Davis Mannie • ANS • USA
FAMILY SINS • 1987 • Freedman Jerrold • TVM • USA
FAMILY SKELETON, THE • 1914 • *Brennan John E.* • USA
FAMILY SKELETON, THE • 1918 • Schertzinger Victor • USA
FAMILY SOLICITOR, THE • 1914 • Noy Wilfred • UKN
FAMILY STAIN, THE • 1915 • Davis Will S. • USA
FAMILY STORY, A (UKN) see **MOM AND DAD** • 1944
FAMILY THAT DWELT APART, THE • 1973 • Mallette Yvon • CND
FAMILY THAT WAS A MERRY-GO-ROUND, THE see **FAMILJEN SOM VAR EN KARUSELL** • 1936
FAMILY TIES VACATION • 1985 • Mackenzie Will • TVM • USA
FAMILY TRADITIONS see **FAMILJENS TRADITIONER** • 1920
FAMILY TREE • 1950 • Lambart Evelyn, Dunning George • ANS • CND
FAMILY TREE, THE see **FOOLS AND THEIR MONEY** • 1919
FAMILY TROUBLES • 1914 • *Powers* • USA
FAMILY TROUBLES • 1916 • *Hippo* • USA
FAMILY TROUBLES • 1932 • Stevens George • SHT • USA
FAMILY TROUBLES • 1943 • Glazer Herbert • SHT • USA
FAMILY TYRANT, THE • 1912 • *Kalem* • USA
FAMILY UPSIDE DOWN, A • 1978 • Rich David Lowell • TVM • USA
FAMILY UPSTAIRS, THE • 1926 • Blystone John G. • USA
FAMILY VICES see **VIZIO DI FAMIGLIA, IL** • 1975
FAMILY VIEWING • 1986 • Egoyan Atom • CND
FAMILY WAY, THE • 1966 • Boulting Roy • UKN • ALL IN GOOD TIME
FAMILY WITHOUT A DINNER TABLE see **SHOKUTAKU NO NAI IE** • 1985
FAMILY'S HONOR, THE • 1913 • Ridgely Richard • USA
FAMINE • 1915 • Barker Reginald • USA
FAMINE • 1934 • *Prabhat* • ANS • IND
FAMINE, THE see **BARA** • 1979
FAMINE IN THE FOREST OR THE TRAPPER'S GRATITUDE • 1909 • *Kalem* • USA
FAMORO LE TYRAN see **PAYSANS NOIRS** • 1947
FAMOUS 702, THE see **CEREBRUL 702** • 1962
FAMOUS ALL OVER TOWN • 1988 • Demme Jonathan • USA
FAMOUS BONERS • 1942 • Foster Douglas • SHT • USA
FAMOUS BOX TRICK, THE (USA) see **ILLUSIONS FANTASMAGORIQUES** • 1898
FAMOUS CONJURING TRICKS • 1904 • *Urban Trading Co.* • UKN
FAMOUS DUEL, A • 1911 • Porter Edwin S. • USA
FAMOUS ESCAPE • 1908 • *Bitzer Billy (Ph)* • USA
FAMOUS FERGUSON CASE, THE • 1932 • Bacon Lloyd • USA
FAMOUS ILLUSION OF DE KOLTA, THE • 1901 • Booth W. R. • UKN
FAMOUS MORGAN PEARLS, THE see **WATERFRONT WOLVES** • 1924
FAMOUS MRS. FAIR, THE • 1923 • Niblo Fred • USA
FAMOUS MUSIC MELODIES • 1925 • Fitzpatrick James A. • SER • UKN
FAMOUS PLAYS • 1931 • Kelley Albert • SHT • USA
FAMOUS POEMS BY GEORGE R. SIMS • 1922 • SER • UKN
FAMOUS RIDE, THE • 1960 • Rasinski Connie • ANS • USA
FAMOUS SCOUT TO THE RESCUE, THE • 1912 • *Pathe* • USA
FAMOUS SONG SCENAS • 1926 • Croise Hugh • SER • UKN
FAMOUS SOVIET HEROES see **SLAVA SOVETSKIM GEROINYAM** • 1938
FAMOUS SWORD BIJOMARU, THE (USA) see **MEITO BIJOMARU** • 1945
FAMOUS WILLE BROTHERS, THE • 1901 • *Warwick Trading Co.* • UKN
FAN, A • 1968 • Zwartjes Frans • SHT • NTH
FAN, THE • 1909 • *Pathe* • FRN
FAN, THE • 1949 • Preminger Otto • USA • LADY WINDERMERE'S FAN (UKN)
FAN, THE • 1981 • Bianchi Edward • USA
FAN, THE see **KIPAS AKAR WANGI** • 1981
FAN FAN • 1918 • Franklin Chester M., Franklin Sidney A. • USA • MIKADO, THE
FAN-FAN LA TULIPE • 1907 • Blache Alice • FRN
FAN-MU AN-K'AO • 1990 • Tang Jiming • TNS
FANAKALO • 1984 • SAF
FANATIC • 1965 • Narizzano Silvio • UKN • DIE! DIE! MY DARLING (USA)
FANATIC see **LAST HORROR FILM, THE** • 1982
FANATICS • 1917 • Wells Raymond • USA
FANATICS, THE • 1963 • *Stevens Craig* • MTV • UKN
FANATICS, THE see **MEGSZALLOTTAK** • 1961
FANATICS, THE (UKN) see **FANATIQUES, LES** • 1957
FANATIKER DES LEBENS • 1917 • Heymann Robert • FRG
FANATIQUES, LES • 1957 • Joffe Alex • FRN • BOMB FOR THE DICTATOR, A (USA) ○ FANATICS, THE (UKN)
FANATISME • 1934 • Ravel Gaston, Lekain Tony • FRN • SAVELLI, LA
FANCHON, THE CRICKET • 1912 • *Imp* • USA
FANCHON THE CRICKET • 1915 • Kirkwood James • USA
FANCIULLA, LA • 1920 • Gallone Carmine • ITL
FANCIULLA DELL'ALTRA RIVA, LA • 1942 • Ballerini Piero • ITL
FANCIULLA DELL'ALTRO MONDO, LA • 1934 • Righelli Gennaro • ITL
FANCIULLA DI POMPEI, LA see **PAPA, TI RICORDO!** • 1954
FANCIULLA DI PORTICI, LA • 1940 • Bonnard Mario • ITL
FANCIULLE DI LUSSO • 1953 • Mussetta Piero, Vorhaus Bernard • ITL • FINISHING SCHOOL (UKN) ○ LUXURY GIRLS (USA)
FANCIULLO DEL WEST, IL • 1943 • Ferroni Giorgio • ITL
FANCY ANSWERS • 1941 • Wrangell Basil • SHT • USA
FANCY BAGGAGE • 1929 • Adolfi John G. • USA
FANCY CURVES • 1932 • Breslow Lou • SHT • USA
FANCY DRESS • 1919 • Foss Kenelm • UKN
FANCY DRESS BALL, THE • 1909 • Fitzhamon Lewin • UKN
FANCY FOOLING FATHER • 1919 • *Strand* • SHT • USA
FANCY MAN see **DANI** • 1965
FANCY MAN AND A FANCY WOMAN, A see **JOFU TO JOFU** • 1967
FANCY PANTS • 1950 • Marshall George • USA
FANCY PLANTS • 1967 • Bakshi Ralph • ANS • USA
FANCY STEP JIG • 1899 • *Warwick Trading Co.* • UKN
FANDANGO • 1948 • Reinert Emile Edwin • FRN
FANDANGO • 1970 • Hayes John • USA
FANDANGO • 1984 • Reynolds Kevin • USA
FANDANGO see **SONG OF SCHEHERAZADE** • 1947
FANDO AND LIS (USA) see **FANDO Y LIS** • 1968
FANDO Y LIS • 1968 • Jodorowsky Alejandro • MXC • FANDO AND LIS (USA) ○ TAR BABIES (UKN) ○ FANDO Y LYS
FANDO Y LYS see **FANDO Y LIS** • 1968
FANDY see **FANDY O FANDY** • 1983
FANDY O FANDY • 1983 • Kachyna Karel • CZC • FANDY
FANEFLUCKT • 1974 • Einarson Eldar • NRW • DESERTION
FANFAN LA TULIPE • 1926 • Leprince Rene • FRN
FANFAN LA TULIPE • 1952 • Christian-Jaque • FRN, ITL • FANFAN THE TULIP (USA) ○ SOLDIER OF LOVE
FANFAN THE TULIP (USA) see **FANFAN LA TULIPE** • 1952
FANFARE • 1958 • Haanstra Bert • NTH
FANFARE D'AMOUR • 1935 • Pottier Richard • FRN
FANFARE FOR A DEATH SCENE • 1967 • Stevens Leslie • TVM • USA
FANFARE FOR FIGLEAVES see **IT STARTED IN PARADISE** • 1952
FANFAREN DER EHE • 1953 • Grimm Hans • FRG
FANFAREN DER LIEBE • 1951 • Hoffmann Kurt • FRG
FANFARON see **FANFARON, MALI KLAUN** • 1968
FANFARON, MALI KLAUN • 1968 • Pojar Bretislav • ANM • CZC • FANFARON, THE LITTLE CLOWN ○ FANFARON
FANFARON, THE LITTLE CLOWN see **FANFARON, MALI KLAUN** • 1968
FANFARRON, EL see **AQUI LLEGO EL VALENTON** • 1938
FANFARRONES, LOS • 1960 • Gonzalez Rogelio A. • MXC
FANFULLA DA LODI • 1940 • Duse Carlo • ITL
FANG AND CLAW • 1935 • Buck Frank, Taylor Ray • DOC • USA
FANG DER DETEKTIVIN, DER • 1915 • Del Zopp Rudolf • FRG
FANG SHIH-YU HU HU-CH'IEN • 1976 • Chang Ch'Eh • HKG • SHAOLIN AVENGERS
FANGAD AV EN ROST • 1943 • Johansson Ivar • SWD • CAPTIVATED BY A VOICE
FANGAN 53 see **COTTAGE ON DARTMOOR, A** • 1929
FANGE NR.1 • 1935 • Fejos Paul • DNM • PRISONER NO.1
FANGE NR.113 • 1917 • Holger-Madsen • DNM • PRISONER NO.113 ○ CONVICT NO.113
FANGELSE • 1949 • Bergman Ingmar • SWD • DEVIL'S WANTON, THE ○ PRISON
FANGEN PA KARLSTENS FASTNING • 1916 • Klercker Georg • SWD • PRISONER AT KARLSTEN FORT, THE
FANGENS SON • 1913 • Davidsen Hjalmar • DNM
FANGERFAMILIE I THULEDISTRIKTET • 1967 • Roos Jorgen • DOC • DNM
FANGO • 1976 • Balbuena Silvio F. • SPN
FANGO BOLLENTE • 1975 • Salerno Vittorio • ITL
FANGORIA'S WEEKEND OF HORRORS • 1986 • DOC • USA
FANG'S FATE AND FORTUNE • 1918 • *Fang Charlie* • SHT • USA
FANGS OF A FEMALE see **ONNA MEKURA HANA TO KIBA** • 1968
FANGS OF DEATH see **FEAR** • 1927
FANGS OF DESTINY • 1927 • Paton Stuart • USA
FANGS OF FATE • 1925 • Carpenter Horace B. • USA
FANGS OF FATE • 1928 • Smith Noel • USA
FANGS OF HATE, THE • 1913 • *Ramo* • USA
FANGS OF JUSTICE • 1926 • Smith Noel • USA
FANGS OF THE ARCTIC • 1953 • Bailey Rex • USA
FANGS OF THE LIVING DEAD (USA) see **MALENKA, LA SOBRINA DEL VAMPIRO** • 1968
FANGS OF THE NIGHT see **YORU NO KIBA** • 1958
FANGS OF THE TATLER, THE • 1916 • Horne James W. • SHT • USA
FANGS OF THE WILD • 1928 • Storm Jerome • USA
FANGS OF THE WILD • 1954 • Claxton William F. • USA
FANGS OF THE WOLF • 1920 • *Lowell John* • SHT • USA
FANGS OF THE WOLF • 1924 • Hoyt Harry O.?, Golden Joseph A.? • USA
FANGS OF WOLFHEART • 1925 • *Williams Big Boy* • USA
FANGSCHUSS, DER • 1976 • Schlondorff Volker • FRG, FRN • COUP DE GRACE
FANNY • 1932 • Allegret Marc • FRN
FANNY • 1933 • Almirante Mario • ITL
FANNY • 1948 • Allegret Marc • FRN
FANNY • 1961 • Logan Joshua • USA
FANNY AND ALEXANDER see **FANNY OCH ALEXANDER** • 1983
FANNY, BALLERINA DELLA SCALA see **BALLERINE** • 1936
FANNY BY GASLIGHT • 1944 • Asquith Anthony • UKN • MAN OF EVIL (USA)
FANNY EISSLER • 1937 • Martin Paul • FRG
FANNY FOLEY HERSELF • 1931 • Brown Melville • USA • TOP OF THE BILL (UKN)
FANNY HAWTHORNE (USA) see **HINDLE WAKES** • 1927
FANNY HILL • 1964 • Meyer Russ • FRG, USA • FANNY HILL: MEMOIRS OF A WOMAN OF PLEASURE (USA) ○ ROMP OF FANNY HILL
FANNY HILL • 1968 • Ahlberg Mac • SWD • SWEDISH FANNY HILL, THE
FANNY HILL • 1983 • O'Hara Gerry • UKN
FANNY HILL MEETS DR. EROTICO • 1967 • Mahon Barry • USA
FANNY HILL MEETS LADY CHATTERLEY • 1967 • Mahon Barry, Matsui George • USA
FANNY HILL MEETS THE RED BARON • 1968 • Mahon Barry • USA
FANNY HILL: MEMOIRS OF A WOMAN OF PLEASURE (USA) see **FANNY HILL** • 1964
FANNY HURST AND HER PETS • 1943 • *O'Brien Joseph/ Mead Thomas (P)* • SHT • USA
FANNY IN THE LION'S DEN • 1933 • *Terry Paul/ Moser Frank (P)* • ANS • USA
FANNY OCH ALEXANDER • 1983 • Bergman Ingmar • SWD • FANNY AND ALEXANDER
FANNY PELOPAJA • 1984 • Aranda Vicente • SPN, FRN • A COUP DE CROSSE (FRN) ○ FANNY STRAWHAIR ○ STRAWHAIRED FANNY
FANNY STRAWHAIR see **FANNY PELOPAJA** • 1984
FANNY THE MULE • 1930 • Lantz Walter, Nolan William • ANS • USA
FANNY'S CONSPIRACY • 1913 • Brooke Van Dyke • USA
FANNY'S MELODRAMA • 1914 • North Wilfred, Van Wally • USA
FANNY'S WEDDING DAY • 1933 • *Terry Paul/ Moser Frank (P)* • ANS • USA
FANOUS EL SEHRI, EL • 1959 • Wahab Fatin Abdel • EGY • MAGIC LAMP, THE ○ FANUSS AS-SIHRI, AL-
FANRIK STALS SAGNER • 1909 • Engdahl Carl • SWD
FANRIK STALS SAGNER • 1926 • Brunius John W. • SWD • TALES OF ENSIGN STEEL, THE
FANS see **GET-RICH-QUICK EDGAR** • 1920
FAN'S NOTES, A • 1972 • Till Eric • CND
FANT • 1937 • Ibsen Tancred, Maurstad Alfred • NRW, SWD
FANTABULOUS see **DONNA, IL SESSO E IL SUPERUOMO, LA** • 1968
FANTABULOUS INC. (USA) see **DONNA, IL SESSO E IL SUPERUOMO, LA** • 1968
FANTAISIE DE MILLIARDAIRE • 1912 • Fescourt Henri • FRN
FANTAISIE D'UN JOUR • 1954 • Cardinal Pierre • FRN
FANTAISIE EGYPTIENNE • 1903 • Melies Georges • FRN
FANTAISIES D'AGENOR MALTRACE, LES • 1911 • Cohl Emile • ANS • FRN
FANTAISIES POUR CLARINETTE • 1947-51 • Verneuil Henri • SHT • FRN
FANTAISIES TRUQUEES • 1915 • Cohl Emile • ANS • FRN
FANTASCA, THE GYPSY • 1912 • *Joyce Alice* • USA
FANTASIA • 1940 • Sharpsteen Ben, Armstrong Samuel, Algar James, Roberts Bill, Satterfield Paul, Luske Hamilton, Handley Jim, Beebe Ford, Hee T., Ferguson Norman, Jackson Wilfred • ANM • USA
FANTASIA...3 • 1966 • de la Iglesia Eloy • SPN • FANTASY...3
FANTASIA CHEZ LES PLOUCS • 1970 • Pires Gerard • FRN, ITL
FANTASIA ESPANOLA • 1953 • Seto Javier • SPN
FANTASIA OF STAMPS see **KITTE-NO GENSO** • 1959
FANTASIA ON A ROMANTIC THEME • 1978 • Tracz Vitek • ISR
FANTASIA PARA UM RALLY • 1973 • Silva Jaime • SHT • PRT
FANTASIA RANCHERA • 1943 • Segura Juan Jose • MXC
FANTASIA SOTTOMARINA • 1939 • Rossellini Roberto • SHT • ITL
FANTASIA TRAGICA • 1950 • Fite Enrique • SPN
FANTASIE AU VIEUX-COLOMBIER • 1953 • Allain Yves • SHT • FRN
FANTASIE: DRESDEN CHINA • 1913 • Booth W. R.? • UKN
FANTASIES • 1967 • Calinescu Bob • ANS • RMN
FANTASIES • 1980 • Wiard William • TVM • USA
FANTASIES • 1981 • Derek John • USA • AND ONCE UPON A LOVE
FANTASIES POUR COUPLES • 1979 • FRN
FANTASIST, THE • 1986 • Hardy Robin • UKN
FANTASM • 1976 • Franklin Richard • ASL
FANTASM COMES AGAIN • 1977 • Ram Eric • ASL
FANTASMA • 1914 • Seay Charles M. • USA
FANTASMA, IL • 1909 • *Cines* • ITL • PHANTOM, THE
FANTASMA D'AMORE • 1980 • Risi Dino • ITL, FRN, FRG • FANTOME D'AMOUR (FRN) ○ GHOST OF LOVE
FANTASMA DE LA CASA ROJA, EL • 1954 • Delgado Miguel M. • MXC • PHANTOM OF THE RED HOUSE, THE (USA)
FANTASMA DE LA OPERETA, EL • 1955 • Carreras Enrique • ARG • PHANTOM OF THE OPERETTA, THE
FANTASMA DE LA OPERETA, EL • 1959 • Cortes Fernando • MXC • PHANTOM OF THE OPERETTA, THE
FANTASMA DE LAS NIEVES, EL see **MONSTRUO DE LOS VOLCANES, EL** • 1962

FANTASMA DE MEDIANOCHE, EL • 1939 • Sevilla Raphael J. • MXC

FANTASMA DE MINA PRIETA, EL • 1973 • *Cinetelmex* • MXC

FANTASMA DEL CASTILLO, EL • 1919 • Buchs Jose, Roesset Julio • SPN

FANTASMA DEL CONVENTO, EL • 1934 • de Fuentes Fernando • MXC • FANTASY IN A MONASTERY ○ PHANTOM OF THE CONVENT, THE

FANTASMA DEL LAGO, EL • 1978 • Alazraki Benito • MXC

FANTASMA DELLA LIBERTA, IL (ITL) see **FANTOME DE LA LIBERTE, LE** • 1974

FANTASMA DELLA MEZZANOTTE • 1911 • *Ambrosia* • ITL • MIDNIGHT PHANTOM

FANTASMA DELLE MORTE, IL • 1950 • Ferronetti Ignazio • ITL

FANTASMA LLAMADO AMOR, UN • 1956 • Torrado Ramon • SPN

FANTASMA SE ENAMORA, EL • 1952 • Portillo Rafael • MXC

FANTASMA Y DONA JUANITA, EL • 1944 • Gil Rafael • SPN • GHOST AND DONA JUANITA, THE

FANTASMAGORIA • 1946 • Crockwell Douglas • SHT • USA

FANTASMAGORICAL ILLUSIONS see **ILLUSIONS FANTASMAGORIQUES** • 1898

FANTASMAGORIE • 1908 • Cohl Emile • ANS • FRN • FANTASY, A ○ METAMORPHOSIS ○ BLACK AND WHITE

FANTASMAGORIE • Molinard Patrice • FRN

FANTASMAS ASUSTADOS • 1951 • Rinaldi Carlos • ARG • FRIGHTENED GHOSTS

FANTASMAS BURLONES, LOS • 1964 • Baledon Rafael • MXC • GHOST JESTERS, THE

FANTASMAS DEL TALLER, LOS • 1967 • Ardavin Cesar • SHT • SPN • PHANTOMS OF THE WORKSHOP, THE

FANTASMAS EN BUENOS AIRES • 1942 • Discepolo Enrique Santos, Amadori Luis Cesar? • ARG • GHOSTS IN BUENOS AIRES

FANTASMAS EN LA CASA • 1958 • Ramirez Pedro L. • SPN • GHOSTS IN THE HOUSE

FANTASMATIC • 1968 • Ansorge Ernest, Ansorge Giselle • ANS • SWT

FANTASMI A ROMA • 1961 • Pietrangeli Antonio • ITL • GHOSTS IN ROME (USA) ○ PHANTOM LOVERS (UKN) ○ GHOSTS OF ROME

FANTASMI DEL MARE • 1948 • De Robertis Francesco • ITL

FANTASMI E LADRI • 1959 • Simonelli Giorgio C. • ITL • GHOSTS AND THIEVES

FANTASMITAS CON QUESO • 1970 • Carretero Amaro • ANS • SPN • GHOSTS WITH CHEESE

FANTASSIN GUIGNARD, LA • 1905 • Blache Alice • FRN

FANTASTERNE • 1967 • Stenbaek Kirsten • DNM • DAY-DREAMERS, THE ○ DREAMERS, THE

FANTASTIC ANIMATION FESTIVAL • 1977 • ANM • USA

FANTASTIC ARGOMAN see **COME RUBARE LA CORONA D'INGHILTERRA** • 1967

FANTASTIC BALLAD, A see **FANTASTICNA BALADA** • 1954

FANTASTIC BUTTERFLIES, THE see **PAPILLON FANTASTIQUE, LE** • 1910

FANTASTIC CASTLE, THE • 1944 • *O'Brien Joseph/ Mead Thomas (P)* • SHT • USA

FANTASTIC COMEDY, A see **COMEDIA FANTASTICA** • 1975

FANTASTIC DISAPPEARING MAN, THE (UKN) see **RETURN OF DRACULA, THE** • 1958

FANTASTIC DIVER, THE see **PLONGEUR FANTASTIQUE, LE** • 1906

FANTASTIC FURNITURE • 1910 • *Eclair* • FRN

FANTASTIC HEADS • 1909 • Zecca Ferdinand • FRN

FANTASTIC INVASION OF PLANET EARTH see **BUBBLE, THE** • 1967

FANTASTIC JOURNEY • 1977 • McLaglen Andrew V. • USA

FANTASTIC MAGIC BABY, THE see **HUNG HAI-ARH** • 1975

FANTASTIC NIGHT (USA) see **NUIT FANTASTIQUE, LA** • 1941

FANTASTIC PLANET (USA) see **PLANETE SAUVAGE, LA** • 1973

FANTASTIC PLASTIC MACHINE, THE • 1969 • Blum Eric, Blum Lowell • DOC • USA

FANTASTIC PUPPET PEOPLE, THE see **ATTACK OF THE PUPPET PEOPLE** • 1958

FANTASTIC SEVEN see **STUNT SEVEN** • 1979

FANTASTIC TALE OF NARUTO, A see **NARUTO HICHO** • 1957

FANTASTIC THREE, THE (UKN) see **FANTASTICI 3 SUPERMEN, I** • 1967

FANTASTIC VOYAGE • 1966 • Fleischer Richard • USA • MICROSCOPIA

FANTASTIC WORLD OF D.C. COLLINS, THE • 1984 • Martinson Leslie H. • TVM • USA

FANTASTIC WORLD OF DR. COPPELIUS, THE see **FANTASTICO MUNDO DEL DR. COPPELIUS, EL** • 1966

FANTASTIC WORLD OF MARIA MONTIEL, THE see **FANTASTICO MUNDO DE LA MARIA MONTIEL, EL** • 1977

FANTASTICA • 1980 • Carle Gilles • CND, FRN

FANTASTICAL AIRSHIP, THE see **DIRIGEABLE FANTASTIQUE OU LE CAUCHEMAR D'UN INVENTEUR, LE** • 1906

FANTASTICAL ILLUSIONS (USA) see **CREATIONS SPONTANEES** • 1898

FANTASTICAL MEAL, A (USA) see **REPAS FANTASTIQUE, LE** • 1900

FANTASTICI 3 SUPERMEN, I • 1967 • Parolini Gianfranco • ITL, FRN, FRG • TRE FANTASTICI SUPERMEN, I ○ FANTASTIC THREE, THE (UKN) ○ THREE FANTASTIC SUPERMEN, THE

FANTASTICNA BALADA • 1954 • Hladnik Bostjan • YGS • FANTASTIC BALLAD, A

FANTASTICO see **NUREGAMI BOTAN** • 1961

FANTASTICO MUNDO DE LA MARIA MONTIEL, EL • 1977 • Juri Jorge Zuhair • ARG • FANTASTIC WORLD OF MARIA MONTIEL, THE

FANTASTICO MUNDO DEL DR. COPPELIUS, EL • 1966 • Kneeland Ted • SPN, USA • DR. COPPELIUS (USA) ○ MYSTERIOUS HOUSE OF DR. C, THE ○ COPPELIA ○ FANTASTIC WORLD OF DR. COPPELIUS, THE

FANTASTIQUE • 1962 • Rivard Fernand • ANS • CND

FANTASTIQUE HISTOIRE VRAIE D'EDDIE CHAPMAN, LA (FRN) see **TRIPLE CROSS** • 1966

FANTASTIQUE ILE DE PAQUES • 1973-74 • Valcour Pierre • DOC • CND

FANTASY • Giorgio Bob • SHT • USA

FANTASY • 1927 • Stone Andrew L. • SHT • USA • APPLEJOY'S GHOST (UKN)

FANTASY see **FASCINATION** • 1978

FANTASY...3 see **FANTASIA...3** • 1966

FANTASY, A see **FANTASMAGORIE** • 1908

FANTASY BAZAAR see **MAYA BAZAR** • 1939

FANTASY BAZAAR see **MAYA BAZAR** • 1949

FANTASY BAZAAR see **MAYA BAZAR** • 1959

FANTASY CITY • Shimamura Tatsuo • ANS • JPN

FANTASY FILM WORLD OF GEORGE PAL, THE • 1986 • Leibovit Arnold • DOC • USA

FANTASY FOR FOUR STRINGS • SHT • FRN

FANTASY FOR LEFT HAND AND THE HUMAN CONSCIENCE see **FANTAZIE PRO LEVOU RUKU A LIDSKE SVENDOMI** • 1961

FANTASY FOR PIANO • 1972 • Kuri Yoji • ANS • JPN

FANTASY GIRL see **FANTASY GIRLS** • 1976

FANTASY GIRLS • 1976 • De Renzy Alex • USA • FANTASY GIRL

FANTASY IN A MONASTERY see **FANTASMA DEL CONVENTO, EL** • 1934

FANTASY IN COLOR AND SOUND • 1968 • Dexter Steve • SHT • USA

FANTASY IN G MINOR -JOHANN SEBASTIAN BACH see **JOHANN SEBASTIAN BACH: FANTASIA G-MOLL** • 1965

FANTASY IN LIGHT • 1957 • Scheyer Betty • USA

FANTASY ISLAND • 1976 • Lang Richard • TVM • USA

FANTASY MISSION FORCE • 1984 • Chu Yen Ping • HKG

FANTASY OF LONDON LIFE, A • 1950 • Stringer G. Henry • UKN • LONDON FANTASY

FANTASY SEQUENCE • 1975 • Hartman Rivka • SHT • ASL

FANTASY WORLD • 1979 • Chinn Robert C., Fairbanks Jeffrey • USA

FANTAZIE PRO LEVOU RUKU A LIDSKE SVENDOMI • 1961 • Hobl Pavel • CZC • FANTASY FOR LEFT HAND AND THE HUMAN CONSCIENCE

FANTEE • 1920 • Willoughby Lewis • UKN

FANTEGUTTEN • 1932 • Sinding Leif • NRW, SWD

FANTINE • 1909 • Brooke Van Dyke • USA

FANTOCHE • 1976 • de la Rosa Jorge • MXC

FANTOCHE CHERCHE UN LOGEMENT see **MAISON DU FANTOCHE, LA** • 1916

FANTOCHE'S NIGHTMARE see **CAUCHEMAR DU FANTOCHE, LE** • 1908

FANTOMA -APPOINTMENT IN ISTANBUL see **FANTOMA ISTANBULDA BULUSALIM** • 1967

FANTOMA ISTANBULDA BULUSALIM • 1967 • Baytan Natuk • TRK • FANTOMA -APPOINTMENT IN ISTANBUL

FANTOMAS • 1913 • Feuillade Louis • SRL • FRN • FANTOMAS UNDER THE SHADOW OF THE GUILLOTINE

FANTOMAS • 1920-21 • Sedgwick Edward • SRL • USA

FANTOMAS • 1932 • Fejos Paul • FRN

FANTOMAS • 1946 • Sacha Jean • FRN

FANTOMAS • 1964 • Hunebelle Andre • FRN

FANTOMAS CONTRE FANTOMAS • 1914 • Feuillade Louis • SRL • FRN • FANTOMAS, THE CROOK DETECTIVE ○ FANTOMAS IV

FANTOMAS CONTRE FANTOMAS • 1948 • Vernay Robert • FRN

FANTOMAS CONTRE SCOTLAND YARD • 1967 • Hunebelle Andre • FRN, ITL • FANTOMAS CONTRO SCOTLAND YARD (ITL) ○ FANTOMAS VS. SCOTLAND YARD

FANTOMAS CONTRO SCOTLAND YARD (ITL) see **FANTOMAS CONTRE SCOTLAND YARD** • 1967

FANTOMAS II see **JUVE CONTRE FANTOMAS** • 1914

FANTOMAS III see **MORT QUI TUE, LA** • 1914

FANTOMAS IV see **FANTOMAS CONTRE FANTOMAS** • 1914

FANTOMAS MINACCIA IL MONDO (ITL) see **FANTOMAS SE DECHAINE** • 1965

FANTOMAS REVIENT • 1965 • Hunebelle Andre • FRN • VENGEANCE OF FANTOMAS (USA)

FANTOMAS SE DECHAINE • 1965 • Hunebelle Andre • FRN, ITL • FANTOMAS MINACCIA IL MONDO (ITL) ○ PHANTOM, THE ○ FANTOMAS STRIKES BACK

FANTOMAS STRIKES BACK see **FANTOMAS SE DECHAINE** • 1965

FANTOMAS, THE CROOK DETECTIVE see **FANTOMAS CONTRE FANTOMAS** • 1914

FANTOMAS UNDER THE SHADOW OF THE GUILLOTINE see **FANTOMAS** • 1913

FANTOMAS V see **FAUX MAGISTRAT, LE** • 1914

FANTOMAS VS. SCOTLAND YARD see **FANTOMAS CONTRE SCOTLAND YARD** • 1967

FANTOME, LE • 1936 • Schwab Pierre • FRN • GHOST, THE

FANTOME A VENDRE, LE (FRN) see **GHOST GOES WEST, THE** • 1935

FANTOME D'ALGER, LE • 1906 • Melies Georges • FRN • SPIRITUALISTIC MEETING, A (USA)

FANTOME D'AMOUR (FRN) see **FANTASMA D'AMORE** • 1980

FANTOME DE LA LIBERTE, LE • 1974 • Bunuel Luis • FRN, ITL • FANTASMA DELLA LIBERTA, IL (ITL) ○ PHANTOM OF LIBERTY, THE (UKN)

FANTOME DU MOULIN ROUGE, LE • 1925 • Clair Rene • FRN • PHANTOM OF THE MOULIN ROUGE, THE ○ PHANTOM OF MOULIN ROUGE, THE

FANTOMES DE HURLEVENT, LES see **NELLA STRETTA MORSA DEL RAGNO** • 1971

FANTOMES DU CHAPELIER, LES • 1981 • Chabrol Claude • FRN • HATTER'S GHOSTS, THE ○ HATMAKER, THE

FANTOM'S HOTEL • 1932 • Colline Paul • FRN • PHANTOM'S HOTEL, THE

FANTORRO, LE DERNIER JUSTICIER • 1973 • Lenica Jan • ANS • FRN • FANTORRO, THE LAST JUST MAN

FANTORRO, THE LAST JUST MAN see **FANTORRO, LE DERNIER JUSTICIER** • 1973

FANTOZZI • 1975 • Salce Luciano • ITL

FANTOZZI CONTRA TUTTI • 1980 • Villaggio Paolo, Parenti Neri • ITL

FANTOZZI RETIRES see **FANTOZZI VA IN PENSIONE** • 1988

FANTOZZI SUBISCE ANCORA • 1984 • Parenti Neri • ITL • FANTOZZI SUFFERS AGAIN

FANTOZZI SUFFERS AGAIN see **FANTOZZI SUBISCE ANCORA** • 1984

FANTOZZI VA IN PENSIONE • 1988 • Parenti Neri • ITL • FANTOZZI RETIRES

FANUSS AS-SIHRI, AL- see **FANOUS EL SEHRI, EL** • 1959

FANY O EL ROBO DE LOS VEINTE MILLONES • 1925 • Valtierra Manuel Sanchez • MXC

FAPADOS SZERELEM • 1959 • Mariassy Felix • HNG • THIRD CLASS LOVE ○ SIMPLE LOVE, A

FAR AWAY AND LONG AGO see **ALLA LEJOS Y HACE TIEMPO** • 1978

FAR-AWAY BRIDE, THE see **DALYOKAYA NEVESTA** • 1948

FAR AWAY I SAW MIST AND MUD see **I VIDEL SEM DALJINE MEGLENE I KALNE** • 1964

FAR AWAY IN THE WEST see **DALEKO NA ZAPADE** • 1969

FAR BEYOND THE WAVES see **ANO NAMI NO HATEMADE I** • 1961

FAR CALL, THE • 1929 • Dwan Allan • USA

FAR COUNTRY, THE • 1916 • Beal Frank • SHT • USA

FAR COUNTRY, THE • 1955 • Mann Anthony • USA

FAR CRY, THE • 1926 • Balboni Silvano • USA

FAR CRY FROM HOME, A • 1981 • Pinsent Gordon • MTV • CND

FAR EAST • 1982 • Duigan John • ASL

FAR EAST see **VOLOCHAYEVSKIYE DNI** • 1938

FAR EAST MARTIAL COURT, THE see **TOKYO SAIBAN** • 1983

FAR FREEDOM • 1945 • Bielik Palo • CZC

FAR FROM DALLAS • 1971 • Toledano Philippe • FRN

FAR FROM ERIN'S ISLE • 1912 • Olcott Sidney • USA

FAR FROM HOME see **DAR GHORBAT** • 1975

FAR FROM HOME see **IN DER FREMDE** • 1975

FAR FROM MOSCOW see **DALEKO OT MOSKVY** • 1950

FAR FROM THE BEATEN TRACK • 1912 • *Baggot King* • USA

FAR FROM THE MADD'ING CROWD • 1909 • *Edison* • USA

FAR FROM THE MADDING CROWD • 1915 • Trimble Larry • UKN

FAR FROM THE MADDING CROWD • 1967 • Schlesinger John • UKN

FAR FROM THE SOIL see **WATAN SE DOOR** • 1968

FAR FROM VIETNAM see **LOIN DU VIETNAM** • 1967

FAR FROM WAR see **YUANLIZHANZHENGDE NIANDAI** • 1988

FAR FRONTIER, THE • 1948 • Witney William • USA

FAR HORIZONS • Gurney Philip • DOC • UKN

FAR HORIZONS, THE • 1955 • Mate Rudolph • USA • UNTAMED WEST

FAR JAG LANA DIN FRU? • 1959 • Mattsson Arne • SWD • MAY I BORROW YOUR WIFE?

FAR JAG LOV, MAGISTERN! • 1947 • Larsson Borje • SWD • MAY I SIR?

FAR LAVER SOVSEN • 1967 • Henriksen Finn • DNM • LIFE WITH DADDY

FAR NORTH • 1988 • Shepard Sam • USA

FAR OCH FLYG • 1955 • Bernhard Gosta • SWD • BEAT IT

FAR OCH SON see **AN EN GANG GOSTA EKMAN** • 1940

FAR OUT MAN • 1989 • Chong Thomas • USA

FAR OUT WEST, THE • 1968 • *Sheridan Ann* • TVM • USA

FAR PARADISE, THE • 1928 • McDonagh Paulette • ASL

FAR PAVILIONS, THE • 1983 • Duffell Peter • MTV • UKN

FAR ROAD, THE see **TOI IPPONNO MICHI** • 1977

FAR SHORE, THE • 1976 • Wieland Joyce • CND • AUTRE RIVE, L'

FAR SIDE OF PARADISE, THE see **FOXTROT** • 1976

FAR SIDE OF THE SUN, THE (USA) see **DOPPELGANGER** • 1969

FAR TIL FIRE I HOJT HUMOR • 1971 • Mossin Ib • DNM

FAR TILL SOL OCH VAR • 1958 • Kjellgren Lars-Eric • SWD • TRAVEL TO SUN AND SPRING

FAR-WEST, LE • 1973 • Brel Jacques • FRN, BLG • FAR WEST, LE

FAR WEST, LE see **FAR-WEST, LE** • 1973

FAR WESTERN TRAILS • 1929 • Horner Robert J. • USA

FARANDOLE • 1944 • Zwobada Andre • FRN

FARANDULA, LA • 1936 • Momplet Antonio • SPN

FARAON • 1965 • Kawalerowicz Jerzy • PLN • PHARAOH, THE

FARAONA, LA • 1955 • Cardona Rene • MXC, SPN

FARAON'S COURT see **CORTE DE FARAON, LA** • 1985

FARAR • 1955 • *Biswas Anil (M)* • IND

FARAR AZ HAGHIGHAT • 1967 • Malak-Motiei Nasser • IRN • ESCAPING FROM TRUTH

FARARI • 1967 • Kassaei Abas • IRN • FUGITIVE, THE

FARARUV KONEC • 1968 • Schorm Evald • CZC • END OF A PRIEST ○ PARSON'S END, THE ○ PASTOR'S END ○ PRIEST'S END, THE

FARAWAY FIELDS • 1912 • *Weber Lois* • USA

FARBENPRACHT AUF DEM MEERESGRUND • 1938 • FRG

FARBENSPIEL • 1934 • Fischinger Oskar • ANM • FRG • SPIEL IN FARBEN, EIN ○ PLAY IN COLORS, A

FARBROR BLAS NYA BAT • 1969 • Schmidt Mille • SWD • UNCLE BLUE'S NEW BOAT

FARBROR FRANS • 1926 • Wallen Sigurd • SWD • UNCLE FRANS

FARBROR JOHANNES ANKOMST TILL STOCKHOLM • 1912 • Jaenzon Julius • SWD • UNCLE JOHN'S ARRIVAL IN STOCKHOLM

FARCE DE MARMITON • 1900 • Melies Georges • FRN • SCULLION'S JOKE ON THE CHEF (USA)

FARCE DE MODELES • 1898 • Melies Georges • FRN

FARCES DE CUISINIERE • 1902 • Blache Alice • FRN

FARCES DE JOCKO, LES • 1897-98 • Blache Alice • FRN

FARCEUR, LE • 1960 • de Broca Philippe • FRN • JOKER, THE (USA)

FARDAYE BA SHOKOH • 1968 • Sabahi Samad • IRN • MAGNIFICENT TOMORROW

FARE, LADY • 1916 • *Chamberlin Riley* • USA

FARE-PLAY • 1932 • *Mintz Charles (P)* • ANS • USA

FARE, PLEASE • 1918 • *Rolin* • SHT • USA

FARE THEE WELL, MOLLY DARLING • 1916 • *Tress Henry* • SHT • UKN

FAREB • 1968 • Kishore Jugal • IND • DECEIT

FARENDJ • 1990 • Prenczina Sabine • FRN

FARES AND FAIR ONES • 1919 • Rock Joseph • SHT • USA

FARES, PLEASE! • 1915 • MacMackin Archer • USA

FARES PLEASE • 1925 • Roberts Stephen (c/d) • SHT • USA

FAREWELL see **ABSCHIED** • 1930

FAREWELL see **STASTNOU CESTU** • 1943

FAREWELL see **ELVEDA** • 1967

FAREWELL see **PROSHCHAY** • 1967
FAREWELL see **ABSCHIED** • 1968
FAREWELL see **PROSCANIE** • 1983
FAREWELL, THE see **AFSCHEID, HET** • 1967
FAREWELL, THE see **AVSKEDET** • 1980
FAREWELL AGAIN • 1937 • Whelan Tim • UKN • TROOPSHIP (USA)
FAREWELL AUTUMN see **POZEGNANIE JESIENI** • 1990
FAREWELL CHINA see **NAU YEUK HAK** • 1990
FAREWELL CONCERT OF CREAM, THE • 1969 • Palmer Tony • USA • CREAM'S FAREWELL CONCERT
FAREWELL DINNER, A • 1915 • *West Billie* • USA
FAREWELL, DOVES! (USA) see **PROSHCHAYTE, GOLUBI!** • 1961
FAREWELL FRIEND (USA) see **ADIEU L'AMI** • 1968
FAREWELL, FRIENDS! see **SBOGOM, PRIYATELI!** • 1970
FAREWELL, GYULSARY see **DO SVIDANIJA, GULSAI** • 1967
FAREWELL IN THE NEXT WAR see **NASVIDENJE V NASLEDNJI VOJNI** • 1981
FAREWELL, MY BELOVED (USA) see **WAKARE** • 1969
FAREWELL MY LOVELY • 1975 • Richards Dick • USA
FAREWELL MY LOVELY (UKN) see **MURDER MY SWEET** • 1945
FAREWELL, OAK STREET • 1953 • McLean Grant • DCS • CND
FAREWELL PARTY (UKN) see **MORALS FOR WOMEN** • 1931
FAREWELL PERFORMANCE • 1963 • Tronson Robert • UKN
FAREWELL, RIVERSIDE PILLBOX see **ZBOGOM OSTAJ, BUNKERU NA RECI** • 1972
FAREWELL SCARLET • 1976 • Vincent Chuck • USA
FAREWELL TO A SPY see **SPOTKANIE ZE SZPIEGEM** • 1964
FAREWELL TO ARMS, A • 1932 • Borzage Frank • USA
FAREWELL TO ARMS, A • 1957 • Vidor Charles • USA
FAREWELL TO CHILDHOOD • 1950 • Peries Lester James • SHT • SLN
FAREWELL TO CINDERELLA • 1937 • Rogers Maclean • UKN
FAREWELL TO FALSE PARADISE • 1989 • Baser Tecfik • FRG
FAREWELL TO FAME (UKN) see **LET'S GO COLLEGIATE** • 1941
FAREWELL TO INNOCENCE see **TSUKI NI TOBU KARI** • 1955
FAREWELL TO LOVE (USA) see **CITY OF SONG, THE** • 1930
FAREWELL TO MANZANAR • 1976 • Korty John • TVM • USA
FAREWELL TO MATJORA see **PROSCANIE** • 1983
FAREWELL TO MUMBO • 1978 • Jolly Sara • UKN
FAREWELL TO MY SWEETHEART see **SARABA ITOSHIKI HITOYO** • 1988
FAREWELL TO SUMMER LIGHT see **SARABA NATSU NO HIKARI** • 1968
FAREWELL TO THE ARK see **SARABA HAKOBUNE** • 1984
FAREWELL TO THE CHANNEL, A see **HSI-PIEH HAI-AN** • 1987
FAREWELL TO THE DEVIL see **POZEGNANIE Z DIABLEM** • 1956
FAREWELL TO THE DUMAN RIVER • Lim Kwon-Taek • SKR
FAREWELL TO THE KING • 1988 • Milius John • USA
FAREWELL TO THE LAND, A • 1982 • Yanagimachi Mitsuo • JPN
FAREWELL TO THE PLANET OF THE APES • 1974 • McDougall Don, Lucas J. M. • MTV • USA
FAREWELL TO THE PRESIDENT see **JAAHYVAISET PRESIDENTILLE** • 1987
FAREWELL TO THE PRINCE see **ERZEKENY BUCSU A FEJEDELEMTOL** • 1986
FAREWELL TO THEE • 1915 • *Reliance* • USA
FAREWELL TO YESTERDAY • 1950 • *Reek Edmund (P)* • DOC • USA
FAREWELL TO YOUR LOVE see **WADAAT HUBAK** • 1956
FAREWELL UNCLE TOM (USA) see **ZIO TOM** • 1971
FAREWELLS see **POZEGNANIA** • 1958
FAREWELLS see **AFSCHEID, HET** • 1967
FARFALLA CON LE ALI INSANGUINATE, UNA • 1971 • Tessari Duccio • ITL
FARFALLON • 1974 • Pazzaglia Riccardo • ITL
FARGO • 1952 • Collins Lewis D. • USA
FARGO see **WILD SEED, THE** • 1965
FARGO EXPRESS • 1932 • James Alan • USA
FARGO KID, THE • 1940 • Killy Edward • USA
FARGO PHANTOM, THE • 1949 • Cowan Will • SHT • USA
FARHAD'S ACHIEVEMENT see **PODVIG FARKHADA** • 1968
FARI NELLA NEBBIA • 1942 • Franciolini Gianni • ITL • LIGHTHOUSE IN THE FOG ○ GELOSIA ○ NEBBIA ○ HEADLIGHTS IN THE FOG
FARIAHO • 1983 • Graf Roland • GDR
FARIB • 1953 • *Biswas Anil (M)* • IND
FARINET, ODER DAS FALSCHE GELD see **OR DANS LA MONTAGNE, L'** • 1938
FARINET, OU LA FAUSSE MONNAIE see **OR DANS LA MONTAGNE, L'** • 1938
FARKAS, A • 1916 • Curtiz Michael • HNG • WOLF, THE
FARKHAD'S FEAT see **PODVIG FARKHADA** • 1968
FARLEY MOWAT • 1970 • Bonniere Rene • DCS • CND
FARLIG FORBRYDER, EN • 1913 • Blom August • DNM • MODERN JACK THE RIPPER, A ○ KNIVSTIKKEREN
FARLIG FRIHET • 1955 • Ragneborn Arne • SWD • DANGEROUS FREEDOM
FARLIG KURVA • 1952 • Holmsen Egil • SWD • DANGEROUS CURVES
FARLIG SOMMER • 1969 • Bro Christopher • DNM • DANGEROUS SUMMER
FARLIG VAR • 1948 • Mattsson Arne • SWD • DANGEROUS SPRING ○ DODEN TAR STUDENTEN
FARLIGA LEKEN, DEN • 1930 • Bergman Gustaf • SWD • DANGEROUS GAME
FARLIGA LEKEN, DEN • 1933 • Hildebrand Weyler • SWD
FARLIGA VAGAR • 1942 • Henrikson Anders • SWD • DANGEROUS ROADS ○ FLYKTINGAR
FARLIGE ALDER, DEN • 1911 • Blom August • DNM • PRICE OF BEAUTY, THE
FARLIGE KYS • 1972 • Stangerup Henrik • DNM • DANGEROUS KISSES
FARLIGT LOFTE • 1955 • Bergstrom Hakan • SWD • DANGEROUS PROMISE
FARM, THE • 1987 • Keith David • USA • CURSE, THE
FARM, THE see **BONDESGARDEN** • 1949
FARM AND THE FLAT, THE • 1912 • *Thanhouser* • USA
FARM BULLY, THE • 1912 • *Nilsson Anna Q.* • USA
FARM CALENDAR • 1955 • Kroitor Roman • CND
FARM DIARY • 1970 • Ball Gordon • DOC • USA
FARM FACTORY, THE • 1935 • Field Mary • DOC • UKN
FARM FOOLERY • 1930 • Foster John • ANS • USA
FARM FOOLERY • 1949 • Kneitel Seymour • ANS • USA
FARM FROLICS • 1941 • Clampett Robert • ANS • USA
FARM GIRL see **FARMER'S OTHER DAUGHTER, THE** • 1965
FARM HANDS • 1943 • Glazer Herbert • SHT • USA
FARM HOMES BEAUTIFUL • 1947 • Garceau Raymond • DCS • CND • MON DOMAINE
FARM IN THE FENS, A • 1945 • Annakin Ken • DCS • UKN • FENLANDS
FARM MUSEUM • 1953-54 • Devlin Bernard • DCS • CND
FARM OF THE YEAR see **MILES FROM HOME** • 1988
FARM OF TOMORROW • 1954 • Avery Tex • ANS • USA
FARM ON THE FRONTIER, THE • 1973 • Ostrovski Grisha • BUL
FARM RELIEF • 1929 • *Mintz Charles (P)* • ANS • USA
FARM SCENES • 1934 • Cones James, Cones Nancy Ford • ANM • USA
FARM YARD, A see **COUR DE FERME** • 1897
FARM YARD FOLLIES • 1920 • Del Ruth Roy • SHT • USA • FARMYARD FOLLIES
FARMACIA DE GUARDIA • 1958 • Pamplona Clemente • SPN
FARMAN-E-KHAN • 1967 • Ghasemivand • IRN • KHAN'S COMMAND
FARMER see **VIVASAAYEE** • 1967
FARMER see **BONDI** • 1978
FARMER, THE • 1931 • Lantz Walter, Nolan William • ANS • USA
FARMER, THE • 1977 • Berlatsky David • USA
FARMER AL FALFA • 1916-17 • Terry Paul • ASS • USA
FARMER AL FALFA • 1919-36 • *Terry Paul (P)* • ASS • USA
FARMER ALFALFA'S APE GIRL • 1932 • *Terry Paul/ Moser Frank (P)* • ANS • USA
FARMER ALFALFA'S BEDTIME STORY • 1932 • *Terry Paul/ Moser Frank (P)* • ANS • USA
FARMER ALFALFA'S BIRTHDAY PARTY • 1932 • *Terry Paul/ Moser Frank (P)* • ANS • USA
FARMER ALFALFA'S PRIZE PACKAGE • 1936 • *Terry Paul (P)* • ANS • USA
FARMER ALFALFA'S TWENTIETH ANNIVERSARY • 1936 • Davis Mannie, Gordon George • ANS • USA
FARMER ALLEN'S DAUGHTER • 1912 • *Prior Herbert* • USA
FARMER AND THE BAD BOYS, THE • 1901 • Porter Edwin S. • USA
FARMER AND THE BELLE • 1950 • Kneitel Seymour • ANS • USA
FARMER AUS TEXAS, DER • 1925 • May Joe • FRG
FARMER BORCHARDT • 1918 • Boese Carl • FRG
FARMER CHARLEY • 1949 • Halas John, Batchelor Joy • ANS • UKN
FARMER -FEAST OR FAMINE, THE • 1965 • Van Dyke Willard, Barlow Roger • DOC • USA
FARMER FOR A DAY • 1943 • White Jules • SHT • USA
FARMER GENE SARAZEN • 1943 • *O'Brien Joseph/ Mead Thomas (P)* • SHT • USA
FARMER GILES AND HIS PORTRAIT • 1900 • Cooper Arthur • UKN
FARMER GILES IN LONDON • 1909 • Bouwmeester Theo? • UKN
FARMER HAD A WIFE, THE • 1987 • Laine Edvin • FNL
FARMER IN THE DELL, THE • 1936 • Holmes Ben • USA
FARMER JENKINS' VISIT TO WHITE CITY • 1910 • *Walturdaw* • UKN
FARMER OF CORDOBA, THE see **DON MANUEL, DER BANDIT** • 1929
FARMER RODNEY'S DAUGHTER • 1914 • Ridgely Richard • USA
FARMER SPUDD AND HIS MISSUS TAKE A TRIP TO TOWN • 1915 • Leigh J. L. V. • UKN
FARMER TAKES A WIFE, THE • 1935 • Fleming Victor • USA
FARMER TAKES A WIFE, THE • 1953 • Levin Henry • USA
FARMER TOM THUMB • 1940 • *Mintz Charles (P)* • ANS • USA
FARMERETTE • 1932 • *Van Beuren* • ANS • USA
FARMER'S DAUGHTER, THE • 1910 • Fitzhamon Lewin? • UKN
FARMER'S DAUGHTER, THE • 1910 • Porter Edwin S. • USA
FARMER'S DAUGHTER, THE • 1912 • Collins Edwin J.? • UKN
FARMER'S DAUGHTER, THE • 1913 • *Bushman Francis X.* • USA
FARMER'S DAUGHTER, THE • 1928 • Taurog Norman?, Rosson Arthur? • USA
FARMER'S DAUGHTER, THE • 1940 • Hogan James P. • USA
FARMER'S DAUGHTER, THE • 1947 • Potter H. C. • USA
FARMER'S DAUGHTERS, THE • 1913 • *Thanhouser* • USA
FARMERS OF FERMATHE, THE • 1960 • Polidoro Gian Luigi • SHT • UNN
FARMER'S OTHER DAUGHTER, THE • 1965 • Hayes John • USA • FARM GIRL
FARMER'S SON, A • 1912 • *Lubin* • USA
FARMERS THREE • 1969 • Cobham David • UKN
FARMER'S TWO SONS, THE • 1910 • Haldane Bert • UKN
FARMER'S WIFE, THE • 1928 • Hitchcock Alfred • UKN
FARMER'S WIFE, THE • 1941 • Lee Norman, Arliss Leslie • UKN
FARMERSVILLE • 1969 • Low Colin • DSS • CND
FARMING • 1985 • Bocking Robert • DOC • CND
FARMING FOOLS • 1936 • *Lantz Walter (P)* • ANS • USA
FARMING FOR BOYS • 1930 • UKN
FARMING FOR THE FUTURE • 1949 • Benson Shan • DOC • ASL • LOOK TO THE LAND
FARMING IN EAST ANGLIA • 1934 • Field Mary • DOC • UKN
FARMING TO STAY • 1947 • Clifford William T. • USA
FARMORS REVOLUTION • 1933 • Branner Per-Axel • SWD • GRANDMOTHER'S REVOLUTION
FARMS AND FUMBLES • 1918 • Pratt Gilbert • SHT • USA
FARMYARD FOLLIES see **FARM YARD FOLLIES** • 1920
FARMYARD FOLLIES (UKN) see **HOOSIER HOLIDAY** • 1943
FARMYARD SYMPHONY • 1938 • Cutting Jack • ANS • USA
FARO 1979 see **FARO-DOKUMENT 1979** • 1979
FARO ABBANDONATO, IL see **MISTERI DI VENEZIA, I** • 1951
FARO DA PADRE, LE • 1974 • Lattuada Alberto • ITL • BAMBINA
FARO DOCUMENT, THE see **FARO-DOKUMENT** • 1969
FARO-DOKUMENT • 1969 • Bergman Ingmar • MTV • SWD • FARO DOCUMENT, THE
FARO-DOKUMENT 1979 • 1979 • Bergman Ingmar • SWD • FARO 1979
FARO JACK (UKN) see **OUTLAWS OF THE PANHANDLE** • 1941
FARO NELL, LOOKOUT • 1918 • Sargent George L. • SHT • USA
FAROL DE LA VENTANA, EL • 1955 • Orol Juan • MXC, SPN
FARORNAS PARADIS • 1930 • Carlsten Rune • SWD
FARREBIQUE: OU LES QUATRE SAISONS • 1947 • Rouquier Georges • DOC • FRN • FARREBIQUE (USA) ○ FOUR SEASONS, THE
FARREBIQUE (USA) see **FARREBIQUE: OU LES QUATRE SAISONS** • 1947
FARRELL FOR THE PEOPLE • 1982 • Wendkos Paul • TVM • USA
FARS SORG see **SMIL** • 1916
FARSA, LA • 1969 • Xiol Juan • SPN
FARSANTES DEL AMOR, LOS • 1972 • Xiol Juan • SPN
FARSANTES, LOS • 1963 • Camus Mario • SPN
FARTFEBER • 1953 • Holmsen Egil • SWD • POSSESSED BY SPEED
FARVAL TILL 40-TALET see **SODRANS REVY** • 1951
FARY L'ANESSE • 1987 • Wade Mansour Sora • SNL
FARZ • 1967 • Naghaich Ravi • IND • DUTY
FASCHING • 1920 • Zelnik Friedrich • FRG
FASCHING • 1939 • Schweikart Hans • FRG
FASCHING DER SINNE see **IM FASCHING DER SINNE** • 1920
FASCHING IN WIEN • 1939 • Marischka Hubert • FRG
FASCHINGSFEE, DIE • 1931 • Steinhoff Hans • FRG
FASCHINGSKONIG, DER • 1928 • Jacoby Georg • FRG
FASCHINGSLIEBE • 1923 • Somlay • FRG
FASCHINGSPRINZ, DER • 1928 • Walther-Fein Rudolf • FRG
FASCHINGSZAUBER • 1927 • Walther-Fein Rudolf • FRG
FASCHISM BUDET RASBYT • 1941 • Shub Esther • USS • FACE OF THE ENEMY, THE ○ FASCISM WILL BE DESTROYED
FASCICOLO NERO (ITL) see **DOSSIER NOIR, LE** • 1955
FASCINANTE AMAZONIE • 1965 • Lambert Paul • DOC • FRN • FRATERNELLE AMAZONIE
FASCINATIE • 1969 • Balasa Sabin • ANS • RMN • FASCINATION
FASCINATING BACHELOR, A • 1911 • Salter Harry • USA
FASCINATING EYE, THE • 1914 • *Joker* • USA
FASCINATING FLUFFY DIMPLES • 1908 • *Lubin* • USA
FASCINATING GAME, A • 1908 • Fitzhamon Lewin • UKN
FASCINATING MODEL, THE • 1916 • Clements Roy • SHT • USA
FASCINATING MRS. FRANCIS, THE • 1909 • Griffith D. W. • USA
FASCINATING NUISANCE, THE see **LIKELY STORY, A** • 1947
FASCINATING VAMP, A • 1928 • Freund Karl • UKN
FASCINATING WIDOW, A • 1911 • *Solax* • USA
FASCINATING YOUTH • 1926 • Wood Sam • USA • GLORIOUS YOUTH
FASCINATION • 1922 • Leonard Robert Z. • USA
FASCINATION • 1931 • Mander Miles • UKN
FASCINATION • 1978 • Damiano Gerard • USA • THAT PRICKLY FEELING ○ FANTASY
FASCINATION • 1979 • Rollin Jean • FRN
FASCINATION see **LOVE IN THE AFTERNOON** • 1957
FASCINATION see **FASCINATIE** • 1969
FASCINATION, THE • 1987 • Bourguignon Serge • FRN
FASCINATION OF THE FLEUR DE LIS, THE • 1915 • De Grasse Joseph • USA
FASCINO • 1939 • Solito Giacinto • ITL
FASCINO DISCRETO DELLA BORGHESIA, IL (ITL) see **CHARME DISCRET DE LA BOURGEOISIE, LE** • 1972
FASCISM WILL BE DESTROYED see **FASCHISM BUDET RASBYT** • 1941
FASCIST, THE (USA) see **FEDERALE, IL** • 1961
FASCISTA • 1974 • Naldini Nico • ITL
FASHION see **FASSHON** • 1960
FASHION 99 • 1986 • Firus Karen • CND
FASHION AND FURY • 1916 • Beaudine William • USA
FASHION AND THE SIMPLE LIFE • 1915 • *Thanhouser* • USA
FASHION FANTASY • 1946 • Grey Richard M. • DOC • UKN
FASHION FOLLIES OF 1934 see **FASHIONS OF 1934** • 1934
FASHION FOR LOVING see **DESIGN FOR LOVING** • 1962
FASHION FOR MEN see **FINE CLOTHES** • 1925
FASHION HOUSE OF DEATH see **SEI DONNE PER L'ASSASSINO** • 1964
FASHION MADNESS • 1928 • Gasnier Louis J. • USA
FASHION MODEL • 1945 • Beaudine William • USA
FASHION MODEL, THE see **MANNEKANGEN** • 1913
FASHION ROW • 1923 • Leonard Robert Z. • USA
FASHION SHOP, THE • 1915 • *Ab* • USA
FASHION SHOP, THE • 1915 • *Kleine George (P)* • USA
FASHIONABLE FAKERS • 1923 • Worthington William • USA • WORM, THE
FASHIONABLE MAN, THE see **HOMBRA DE MODA, EL** • 1980
FASHIONS see **FASHIONS OF 1934** • 1934
FASHIONS FOR WOMEN • 1927 • Arzner Dorothy • USA
FASHIONS IN LOVE • 1929 • Schertzinger Victor • USA
FASHIONS OF 1934 • 1934 • Dieterle William • USA • FASHION FOLLIES OF 1934 ○ FASHIONS
FASHION'S TOYS • 1913 • *Hawley Ormi* • USA
FASSADENGESPENST • 1927 • Bock-Stieber Gernot • FRG
FASSHON • 1960 • Kuri Yoji • ANS • JPN • FASHION
FAST AND FEARLESS • 1924 • Thorpe Richard • USA
FAST AND FURIOUS • 1915 • *Miller Rube* • USA
FAST AND FURIOUS • 1924 • Taurog Norman • SHT • USA
FAST AND FURIOUS • 1927 • Brown Melville • USA
FAST AND FURIOUS • 1931 • Lamont Charles • SHT • USA
FAST AND FURIOUS • 1939 • Berkeley Busby • USA
FAST AND FURRY-OUS • 1949 • Jones Charles M. • ANS • USA
FAST AND LOOSE • 1930 • Newmeyer Fred • USA • BEST PEOPLE, THE
FAST AND LOOSE • 1939 • Marin Edwin L. • USA
FAST AND LOOSE • 1954 • Parry Gordon • UKN
FAST AND SEXY (USA) see **ANNA DI BROOKLYN** • 1958
FAST AND THE FURIOUS, THE • 1954 • Sampson Edwards, Ireland John • USA

FAST ANSTANDGES MADCHEN, EIN • 1963 • Vajda Ladislao • FRG, SPN
FAST BLACK • 1924 • Roach Hal • SHT • USA
FAST BREAK see **FASTBREAK** • 1979
FAST BUCK DUCK • 1963 • McKimson Robert, Bonnicksen Ted • ANS • USA
FAST BULLETS • 1936 • Webb Harry S. • USA • LAW AND ORDER (UKN)
FAST, BUT CAREFUL see **BRZINA, ALI OPREZ** • 1968
FAST CARS see **FAST CARS, FAST WOMEN** • 1979
FAST CARS, FAST WOMEN • 1979 • McHaley Scott • USA • FAST CARS
FAST CHARLIE AND THE MOONBEAM see **FAST CHARLIE.. THE MOONBEAM RIDER** • 1979
FAST CHARLIE.. THE MOONBEAM RIDER • 1979 • Carver Steve • USA • FAST CHARLIE AND THE MOONBEAM
FAST COMPANIONS • 1932 • Neumann Kurt • USA • INFORMATION KID
FAST COMPANY • 1918 • Reynolds Lynn • USA
FAST COMPANY • 1924 • Roach Hal • SHT • USA
FAST COMPANY • 1929 • Sutherland A. Edward • USA
FAST COMPANY • 1938 • Buzzell Edward • USA • RARE BOOK MURDER, THE
FAST COMPANY • 1953 • Sturges John • USA
FAST COMPANY • 1978 • Cronenberg David • CND
FAST EIN HELD see **KOMMANDANT VON MOLINETTE, DER** • 1967
FAST EINE WEIHNACHTSGESCHICHTE • 1984 • Zeindler Werner • SWT
FAST EXPRESS, THE • 1924 • Duncan William • SRL • USA
FAST, FAST see **DEPRISA, DEPRISA** • 1980
FAST FIGHTIN' • 1925 • Thorpe Richard • SHT • USA
FAST FOOD • 1989 • Simpson Michael A. • USA
FAST FORWARD • 1985 • Poitier Sidney • USA
FAST FREIGHT 3205 • 1914 • *Kalem* • USA
FAST FREIGHT, THE • 1921 • Cruze James • USA • VIA FAST FREIGHT ○ FREIGHT PREPAID
FAST FRIENDS • 1979 • Stern Steven Hilliard • USA
FAST GUN, THE see **QUICK GUN, THE** • 1964
FAST KILL, THE • 1972 • Shonteff Lindsay • UKN
FAST LADY, THE • 1962 • Annakin Ken • UKN
FAST LANE FEVER (USA) see **RUNNIN' ON EMPTY** • 1982
FAST LIFE • 1929 • Dillon John Francis • USA
FAST LIFE • 1932 • Pollard Harry • USA • LET'S GO
FAST LIVER, THE see **GOKUDO** • 1968
FAST & LOOSE see **KONNYUVER** • 1989
FAST MAIL, THE • 1918 • Marshall George • SHT • USA
FAST MAIL, THE • 1922 • Durning Bernard J. • USA
FAST MALE, THE • 1925 • Ruggles Wesley • SHT • USA
FAST MONEY • 1962 • Holloway Douglas • USA
FAST ON THE DRAW • 1950 • Carr Thomas • USA • SUDDEN DEATH
FAST ONE, THE see **SIBAD** • 1967
FAST ONE AND THE HAWK, THE see **ANG LIMBAS AT ANG LAWIN** • 1967
FAST ONES, THE see **IVY LEAGUE KILLERS** • 1962
FAST PLAY (UKN) see **CAMPUS CONFESSIONS** • 1938
FAST SET, THE • 1924 • De Mille William C. • USA
FAST TALKING • 1983 • Cameron Ken • ASL
FAST TIMES AT RIDGEMONT HIGH • 1982 • Heckerling Amy • USA
FAST-WALKING • 1981 • Harris James B. • USA
FAST WORK • 1930 • Horne James W. • SHT • USA
FAST WORKER, THE • 1924 • Seiter William A. • USA • LIGHTNING LOVER, THE
FAST WORKERS • 1924 • USA • RIVETS (UKN)
FAST WORKERS • 1933 • Browning Tod • USA
FASTBREAK • 1979 • Smight Jack • USA • FAST BREAK
FASTEN YOUR SEAT BELTS see **ESCALE A ORLY** • 1955
FASTEN YOUR SEATBELTS: A REPORT ON AIRLINE SAFETY • 1968 • Leiterman Douglas • DOC • CND
FASTER see **PLUS VITE** • 1966
FASTER AND FASTER • 1956 • Jones Charles M. • ANS • USA
FASTER, PUSSYCAT! KILL! KILL! • 1965 • Meyer Russ • USA • LEATHER GIRLS, THE ○ MANKILLERS, THE ○ PUSSYCAT
FASTER THAN SOUND • 1949 • Pine Diana • UKN
FASTERS, THE • 1916 • Wolbert William • SHT • USA
FASTERS MILLIONER • 1934 • Molander Gustaf • SWD • MY AUNT'S MILLIONS
FASTEST GUITAR ALIVE, THE • 1967 • Moore Michael • USA
FASTEST GUN ALIVE, THE • 1956 • Rouse Russell • USA
FASTEST WITH THE MOSTEST • 1960 • Jones Charles M. • ANS • USA
FASTMO UTHYRES • 1951 • Molander Gustaf • SWD • FIANCEE FOR HIRE
FASTNACHTSBEICHTE, DIE • 1960 • Dieterle William • FRG • ASH WEDNESDAY CONFESSION
FAT ALBERT VS. BILL COSBY IN THE GREAT GO CART RACE • 1972 • Sutherland Hal • USA
FAT AND FATE • 1913 • *Kalem* • USA
FAT AND FICKLE • 1917 • *Hardy Babe* • USA
FAT AND FOOLISH • 1917 • *Three C* • USA
FAT AND FOOLISH • 1917 • Clements Roy • *Victor* • SHT • USA
FAT AND FURIOUS • 1917 • Moore Vin • SHT • USA
FAT AND LEAN WRESTLING MATCH (USA) see **NOUVELLES LUTTES EXTRAVAGANTES** • 1900
FAT AND THE LEAN, THE (UKN) see **GROS ET LE MAIGRE, LE** • 1961
FAT AND THIN see **DEBELI I MRSAVI** • 1985
FAT AND THIN OF IT, THE • 1914 • *Crystal* • USA
FAT ANGELS (USA) see **ANGELES GORDOS** • 1980
FAT BILL'S WOOING • 1912 • *Brennan John E.* • USA
FAT BLACK PUSSYCAT, THE • 1964 • Lea Harold • USA
FAT CHANCE see **PEEPER** • 1975
FAT CITY • 1972 • Huston John • USA
FAT FEET • 1966 • Grooms Red • SHT • USA
FAT GIRL'S ROMANCE, THE • 1914 • *De Forrest Charles* • USA
FAT GUY GOES NUTZOID • 1986 • Golden John • USA • ZEISTERS
FAT IN THE SADDLE • 1968 • Smith Paul J. • ANS • USA
FAT MAN • 1970 • Weintraub William • CND
FAT MAN, THE • 1951 • Castle William • USA
FAT MAN'S BURDEN, THE • 1914 • *Pathe* • USA
FAT MAN/THIN MAN • 1990 • Rogers Derek • SHT • CND
FAT PEOPLE, SKINNY PEOPLE • 1968 • Savage Lee • SHT • USA
FAT SPY, THE • 1966 • Cates Joseph • USA
FAT WIVES FOR THIN • 1930 • Sennett Mack • SHT • USA
FATA MORGANA • 1920 • Boese Carl • FRG
FATA MORGANA • 1966 • Aranda Vicente • SPN • LEFT-HANDED FATE (USA)
FATA MORGANA • 1970 • Herzog Werner • FRG
FATA MORGANA • 1982 • Pavlinic Zlatko, Jutrisa Vladimir • ANM • YGS
FATAL 30, THE • 1921 • Hayes John J. • USA
FATAL APPETISER, THE • 1909 • Fitzhamon Lewin? • UKN
FATAL ARMS see **TONE NO CHISHIBUKI** • 1959
FATAL ATTRACTION • 1987 • Lyne Adrian • USA
FATAL ATTRACTION (USA) see **HEAD ON** • 1980
FATAL BALL, THE • 1909 • Melies Gaston • USA
FATAL BEAN, THE • 1916 • McKim Edwin • SHT • USA
FATAL BEAUTY • 1987 • Holland Tom • USA
FATAL BLACK BEAN, THE • 1915 • Walsh Raoul • USA
FATAL CARD, A • 1914 • *Lubin* • USA
FATAL CARD, THE • 1914 • *Frontier* • USA
FATAL CARD, THE • 1915 • Kirkwood James • USA
FATAL CARD, THE • 1930 • Taurog Norman • SHT • USA
FATAL CHARM • 1989 • Medak Peter • USA
FATAL CHOCOLATE, THE • 1912 • Sennett Mack • USA
FATAL CLAWS AND DEADLY KICKS • *Hsian Kuang-Li* • HKG
FATAL CLUES, THE • 1914 • *Blackwell Carlyle* • USA
FATAL CONFESSION: A FATHER DOWLING MYSTERY • 1987 • Hibler Christopher • TVM • USA
FATAL DESIRE see **CAVALLERIA RUSTICANA** • 1953
FATAL DRESS SUIT, THE • 1914 • *Komic* • USA
FATAL EXIT see **PROFESSIONE: REPORTER** • 1975
FATAL FINGER PRINTS, THE • 1915 • Dillon Eddie • USA
FATAL FINGERPRINTS see **DARK ALIBI** • 1946
FATAL FINGERS • 1916 • Bramble A. V., Stannard Eliot • UKN
FATAL FLIRTATION • 1914 • Sennett Mack • USA
FATAL FLOWER, THE • 1918 • Seiter William A. • USA
FATAL FLOWER, THE • 1930 • Harcourt Harold A. • CND
FATAL FLYING GUILLOTINE, THE • *Cheng Sang* • HKG
FATAL FORMULA, THE • 1915 • Stather Frank • UKN
FATAL FORTUNE, THE • 1919 • Mackenzie Donald • SRL • USA
FATAL GAMES • 1984 • Elliott Michael • USA • KILLING TOUCH, THE
FATAL GLASS, THE • 1912 • *Champion* • USA
FATAL GLASS OF BEER, THE • 1916 • Browning Tod • USA
FATAL GLASS OF BEER, THE • 1933 • Bruckman Clyde • SHT • USA
FATAL GOLD, THE • 1910 • *Bison* • USA
FATAL HAND, THE • 1907 • Martin J. H.? • UKN
FATAL HANSOM, THE • 1914 • *Wolbert William* • USA
FATAL HIGH C • 1914 • Henderson Dell • USA
FATAL HOUR, THE • 1908 • Griffith D. W. • USA
FATAL HOUR, THE • 1915 • *West Charles* • USA
FATAL HOUR, THE • 1920 • Terwilliger George W. • USA
FATAL HOUR, THE • 1937 • Pearson George • UKN
FATAL HOUR, THE • 1940 • Nigh William • USA • MR. WONG AT HEADQUARTERS (UKN)
FATAL INTRODUCTION, THE • 1916 • MacQuarrie Murdock • SHT • USA
FATAL JOURNEY • 1954 • Gherzo Paul • UKN
FATAL KISS, THE • 1915 • Curtis Allen • USA
FATAL KISS, THE see **FATAL MISTAKE, THE** • 1924
FATAL KISS, THE (USA) see **BESO MORTAL, EL** • 1938
FATAL LADY • 1936 • Ludwig Edward • USA • BRAZEN
FATAL LEAP, THE • 1906 • Fitzhamon Lewin • UKN
FATAL LEGACY, THE • 1913 • *Vincent James* • USA
FATAL LETTER, THE • 1898 • *Mutoscope & Biograph Co.* • UKN
FATAL LETTER, THE • 1914 • *Asher Max* • USA
FATAL LIE, A see **FRU POTIFAR** • 1911
FATAL LIKENESS, A • 1908 • *Lubin* • USA
FATAL MALLET, THE • 1914 • Chaplin Charles, Sennett Mack • USA • PILE DRIVER, THE ○ RIVAL SUITORS ○ HIT HIM AGAIN
FATAL MARRIAGE, THE • 1914 • *L-Ko* • USA
FATAL MARRIAGE, THE • 1918 • Campbell William • SHT • USA
FATAL MARRIAGE, THE see **ENOCH ARDEN** • 1915
FATAL MIRROR, THE • 1912 • Dwan Allan • USA
FATAL MISTAKE, THE • 1924 • Dunlap Scott R. • USA • FATAL KISS, THE
FATAL NECKLACE, THE • 1905 • Martin J. H.? • UKN
FATAL NIGHT, THE • 1915 • *Crawley Constance* • USA
FATAL NIGHT, THE • 1948 • Zampi Mario • UKN
FATAL NOTE, THE • 1914 • Martin E. A. • USA
FATAL NOTE, THE • 1915 • Edwards Harry J. • USA
FATAL NOTE, THE • 1933 • *Van Beuren* • ANS • USA
FATAL OPAL, THE • 1914 • Melford George • USA
FATAL ORCHIDS, THE (UKN) see **BLACK ORCHIDS** • 1916
FATAL ORGULLO • 1916 • *Mexico Lux* • MXC
FATAL PACT, THE • 1912 • *Pathe* • USA
FATAL PASSION OF DR. MABUSE see **DR. MABUSE, DER SPIELER** • 1922
FATAL PASSIONS, THE see **DR. MABUSE, DER SPIELER** • 1922
FATAL PLUNGE, THE • 1924 • Hoyt Harry O. • USA
FATAL PORTRAIT, THE • 1914 • *Boyle Irene* • USA
FATAL POSING, THE • 1911 • *Pathe* • USA
FATAL QUART OF PERFUME, THE • 1918 • *Luke Mcluke Producing Co.* • USA
FATAL RECKONING, THE • 1913 • *Ammex* • USA
FATAL RING, THE • 1917 • Seitz George B. • SRL • USA
FATAL SCAR, THE • 1913 • Fielding Romaine • USA
FATAL SHOT, THE • 1913 • *Kalem* • USA
FATAL SHOT, THE see **FEJLOVES** • 1968
FATAL SIGN, THE • 1920 • Paton Stuart • SRL • USA
FATAL SKIES • 1989 • Yuval Peter • USA
FATAL SKY • 1989 • Shields Frank • ASL • NO CAUSE FOR ALARM
FATAL SNEEZE, THE • 1908 • Fitzhamon Lewin • UKN
FATAL STEP, THE • 1914 • *Imp* • USA
FATAL SWEET TOOTH, THE • 1914 • Wright Walter • USA
FATAL TAXICAB, THE • 1913 • Sennett Mack • USA
FATAL TELEPHONE, THE see **USODNI TELEFON** • 1987
FATAL VERDICT • 1913 • Smith Frank L. • USA
FATAL VIOLIN, THE • 1916 • *Duncan Bud* • USA
FATAL VISION • 1984 • Greene David • TVM • USA
FATAL WAGER, THE see **V POLNOCH NA KLADBISCHE** • 1909
FATAL WALLOP, THE • 1920 • *Ovey George* • USA
FATAL WARNING, THE • 1929 • Thorpe Richard • SRL • USA
FATAL WEDDING, THE • 1911 • Longford Raymond • ASL
FATAL WEDDING, THE • 1913 • Cabanne W. Christy • USA
FATAL WEDDING, THE • 1914 • Marston Lawrence • USA
FATAL WEDDING, THE see **HIS WEDDING DAY** • 1914
FATAL WIG, THE • 1904 • Collins Alf? • UKN
FATAL WITNESS, THE • 1945 • Selander Lesley • USA
FATALE • 1987 • Marx Gerard
FATALE MEPRISE • 1900 • Melies Georges • FRN • RAILROAD PICKPOCKET, THE (USA) ○ RAILWAY PICKPOCKET, THE
FATALI-CHAN • 1948 • Dzigan Yefim • USS
FATALIDAD, LA • 1910 • de Chomon Segundo • SPN
FATALITA • 1947 • Bianchi Giorgio • ITL
FATALLY INJURED BY LOVE OF LIFE see **SA MORI RANIT DIN DRAGOSTE DE VIATA** • 1983
FATAWA, EL • 1956 • Abu Saif Salah • EGY • FETEWA, EL ○ FUTUWWA, AL- ○ TOUGH, THE
FATE • 1911 • Bouwmeester Theo • UKN
FATE • 1911 • Porter Edwin S. • USA
FATE • 1913 • Griffith D. W., Powell Frank • USA
FATE • 1921 • *Ince John* • USA
FATE see **TAQDEER** • 1967
FATE, LE • 1966 • Salce Luciano, Monicelli Mario, Bolognini Mauro, Pietrangeli Antonio • ITL, FRN • OGRESSES, LES (FRN) ○ FAIRIES, THE ○ QUEENS, THE ○ SEX QUARTET
FATE AND FORTUNE • 1918 • De Barge C. R. • SHT • USA
FATE AND FUGITIVE • 1914 • Powell Paul • USA
FATE AND THE CHILD • 1917 • Sloman Edward • USA
FATE AND THE WOMAN • 1911 • Coleby A. E. • UKN
FATE AND THE WOMAN • 1916 • Durrant Fred W. • UKN
FATE AND THREE • 1913 • *August Edwin* • USA
FATE FASHIONS A LETTER • 1913 • Huntley Fred W. • USA
FATE GAVE ME TWENTY CENTS see **GOD GAVE ME TWENTY CENTS** • 1926
FATE IS THE HUNTER • 1964 • Nelson Ralph • USA
FATE LARGO AI MOSCHETTIERI! (ITL) see **TROIS MOUSQUETAIRES, LES** • 1953
FATE NAMED KAMILA • 1974 • Schulhoff Petr • CZC
FATE OF A FLIRT, THE • 1925 • Strayer Frank • USA • GAY NIGHTS
FATE OF A KING, THE • 1913 • Coleby A. E. • UKN
FATE OF A MAN (USA) see **SUDBA CHELOVEKA** • 1959
FATE OF A SELF-DEFENCE CORPS MEMBER • NKR
FATE OF A SQUAW, THE • 1914 • *Darkfeather Mona* • USA
FATE OF AMERICA, THE • 1916 • Ellis Robert • USA
FATE OF AN EMPIRE • 1948 • DOC • UKN • THIS MODERN AGE NO.20
FATE OF ELIZABETH, THE • 1913 • Kirkland Hardee • USA
FATE OF GUM HUI AND UN HUI • NKR
FATE OF JOE DORR • 1911 • *Bison* • USA
FATE OF JUAN GARCIA, THE • 1917 • *Sais Marin* • SHT • USA
FATE OF LEE KHAN, THE see **YING CH'UN KO CHIH FENG-PO** • 1973
FATE OF MARINA, THE • 1954 • Ivchenko Viktor • USS
FATE OF PERSISTENT PETE, THE • 1915 • *Powers* • USA
FATE OF THE CASTLE, THE FATE OF THE COUNTRY.., THE see **LOSY ZAMKU, LOSY KRAJU..** • 1971
FATE OF THE DOLPHIN, THE • 1916 • Ricketts Thomas • SHT • USA
FATE OF THE EMDEN, THE • 1915 • ASL • HOW WE FOUGHT THE EMDEN
FATE OF THE HUNTER see **CAPTIVE HEARTS** • 1987
FATE TAKES A HAND • 1915 • Grandon Francis J. • USA
FATE TAKES A HAND • 1962 • Varnel Max • UKN
FATE (UKN) see **TAQDEER** • 1943
FATE WILLED IT SO see **KADER BOYLE ISTEDI** • 1968
FATEFUL BELL see **ODESDIGRA KLOCKAN, DEN** • 1966
FATEFUL DIAMOND, THE • 1912 • *Eclair* • USA
FATEFUL GIFT, A • 1910 • *Solax* • USA
FATEFUL MISTAKE see **ROKOVAYA OSHIBKA** • 1989
FATE'S ALIBI • 1915 • Lloyd Frank • USA
FATES AND FLORA FOURFLUSH, THE • 1914 • Van Wally • SRL • USA • TEN BILLION DOLLAR VITAGRAPH MYSTERY SERIAL, THE
FATES AND RYAN, THE • 1914 • Le Saint Edward J. • USA
FATE'S AWFUL JEST • 1912 • *Casey Kenneth* • USA
FATE'S BOOMERANG • 1916 • Crane Frank H. • USA
FATE'S CHESSBOARD • 1920 • *Lowell John* • SHT • USA
FATE'S DAUGHTER • 1915 • *Wallace Inez* • USA
FATE'S DECISION • 1916 • Swickard Charles • SHT • USA
FATE'S DECREE • 1912 • *Pathe* • USA
FATE'S DECREE • 1914 • *West Billie* • USA
FATE'S DECREE • 1916 • *Utah* • USA
FATE'S DOUBLE CROSS • 1920 • Van Dyke W. S. • SHT • USA
FATE'S FATHEAD • 1934 • Parrott Charles • SHT • USA
FATE'S FINGER • 1914 • *Bright Mildred* • USA
FATE'S FRAME-UP • 1920 • Van Dyke W. S. • SHT • USA
FATE'S FUNNY FROLIC • 1911 • Baker R. E. • USA
FATE'S HEALING HAND • 1915 • Morgan George • USA
FATE'S INTERCEPTION • 1912 • Griffith D. W. • USA
FATE'S MIDNIGHT HOUR • 1914 • Buel Kenean • USA
FATE'S MOCKERY • 1920 • *Jennings Al* • SHT • USA
FATES OF WOMEN see **FRAUENSCHICKSALE** • 1952
FATE'S PLAYTHING • 1920 • Doxat-Pratt B. E. • UKN
FATE'S PROTECTING ARM see **FATE'S PROTECTIVE ARM** • 1915
FATE'S PROTECTIVE ARM • 1915 • Reehm George E. • USA • FATE'S PROTECTING ARM
FATE'S ROUND-UP • 1913 • *American* • USA
FATE'S TURNING • 1911 • Griffith D. W. • USA
FATE'S VENGEANCE • 1913 • *Powers* • USA
FATE'S VENGEANCE • 1915 • MacDonald Donald • USA

FATE'S WARNING • 1912 • *Rex* • USA
FATE'S WAY • 1912 • *Powers* • USA
FATEVI VIVI: LA POLIZIA NON INTERVERRA • 1974 • Fago Giovanni • ITL
FATHER • 1912 • *Reliance* • USA
FATHER • 1966 • Sara Sandor • SHT • HNG
FATHER • 1987 • Benchev Detelin • BUL
FATHER • 1989 • Power John • ASL
FATHER see **CHICHI** • 1924
FATHER see **CHICHI** • 1988
FATHER, THE • 1912 • *Edison* • USA
FATHER, THE • 1915 • Powers Francis • USA
FATHER, THE • 1974 • Steinhardt Alfred • ISR
FATHER, THE see **OJCIEC** • 1967
FATHER, THE see **BABA** • 1971
FATHER, THE see **OTAC** • 1973
FATHER, THE (UKN) see **FADERN** • 1969
FATHER -A MEMBER OF THE PURITY LEAGUE • 1914 • *Premier* • USA
FATHER AMINE see **BABA AMINE** • 1950
FATHER AND HIS CHILD see **OYAJI TO SONO KO** • 1929
FATHER AND HIS SON see **OYAJI TO SONO KO** • 1929
FATHER AND SON • 1910 • Noy Wilfred • UKN
FATHER AND SON • 1912 • *Williams Earle* • USA
FATHER AND SON • 1915 • *Trump* • USA
FATHER AND SON • 1915 • Grandon Francis J. • *Mutual* • USA
FATHER AND SON • 1916 • *Dixey Henry E.* • USA
FATHER AND SON • 1917 • Thayer Otis B. • SHT • USA
FATHER AND SON • 1929 • Kenton Erle C. • USA
FATHER AND SON • 1934 • Banks Monty • UKN
FATHER AND SON see **DVA DNYA** • 1927
FATHER AND SON see **FU-TZU CH'ING** • 1981
FATHER AND SON see **CHICHI TO KO** • 1983
FATHER AND SON OR THE CURSE OF THE GOLDEN LAND • 1913 • *Foote Courtenay* • USA
FATHER AND SON (USA) see **MARKURELLS I WADKOPING** • 1930
FATHER AND SONS see **DIVORCE IN THE FAMILY** • 1932
FATHER AND THE BOOKMAKER see **FATHER'S DERBY TRIP** • 1906
FATHER AND THE BOYS • 1912 • *Quirk Billy* • USA
FATHER AND THE BOYS • 1915 • De Grasse Joseph • USA
FATHER AND THE GIRLS • 1911 • *Lubin* • USA
FATHER AT 21, A see **NIJU-ISSAI NO CHICHI** • 1964
FATHER BEAUCLAIRE • 1912 • Reid Hal • USA
FATHER BROWN • 1954 • Hamer Robert • UKN • DETECTIVE, THE (USA)
FATHER BROWN see **SANCTUARY OF FEAR** • 1979
FATHER BROWN, DETECTIVE • 1935 • Sedgwick Edward • USA
FATHER BROWN, DETECTIVE see **SANCTUARY OF FEAR** • 1979
FATHER BUYS A BALE • 1914 • *Victor* • USA
FATHER BUYS A CHEAP GOOSE • 1909 • *Anglo-American Films* • UKN
FATHER BUYS A LAWN ROLLER • 1907 • Collins Alf? • UKN
FATHER BUYS A PICTURE • 1908 • Coleby A. E. • UKN
FATHER BUYS A SCREEN • 1910 • Fitzhamon Lewin? • UKN
FATHER BUYS AN ARMCHAIR • 1909 • Rosenthal Joe • UKN
FATHER BUYS SOME LINOLEUM see **ADVENTURES OF A ROLL OF LINO, THE** • 1907
FATHER BUYS THE FIREWORKS • 1909 • Gobbett T. J. • UKN
FATHER BY FORCE see **SILOM OTAC** • 1970
FATHER CAME TOO • 1963 • Scott Peter Graham • UKN
FATHER CHRISTMAS HAS BLUE EYES see **PERE NOEL A LES YEUX BLEUS, LE** • 1966
FATHER CLEMENTS STORY, THE • 1987 • Sherin Edwin • TVM • USA
FATHER DAMIEN see **GREAT HEART, THE** • 1938
FATHER DAMIEN: THE LEPER PRIEST • 1980 • Gethers Steve • TVM • USA • DAMIEN: THE LEPER PRIEST
FATHER DEAR FATHER • 1972 • Stewart William G. • UKN
FATHER FIGURE • 1980 • London Jerry • USA
FATHER FORGOT • 1915 • Fahrney Milton • USA
FATHER FROST see **MOROZKO** • 1924
FATHER GETS IN THE GAME • 1908 • Griffith D. W. • USA
FATHER GETS IT WRONG • 1916 • Curtis Allen • SHT • USA
FATHER GOES A-SAILING • 1911 • *Walturdaw* • UKN
FATHER GOOSE • 1964 • Nelson Ralph • USA
FATHER, HOLD MY WOOL • 1909 • Coleby A. E. • UKN
FATHER IN THE KITCHEN • 1905 • Collins Alf? • UKN
FATHER IS A BACHELOR • 1950 • Foster Norman, Berlin Abby • USA • MOTHER FOR MAY, A
FATHER IS A PRINCE • 1940 • Smith Noel • USA
FATHER JIM • 1989 • Green Terry • UKN
FATHER KNISH'S GANG • 1924 • Rasumny Alexander • USS
FATHER KNOWS BEST • 1935 • Horne James W. • SHT • USA
FATHER KNOWS BEST REUNION • 1977 • Daniels Marc • TVM • USA
FATHER KNOWS BEST (USA) see **JO AS A HAZNAL** • 1935
FATHER KONDELIK AND BRIDEGROOM VEJVARA see **OTEC KONDELIK A ZENICH VEJVARA** • 1926
FATHER KONDELIK AND BRIDEGROOM VEJVARA see **OTEC KONDELIK A ZENICH VEJVARA** • 1937
FATHER LOVE • 1911 • *Lubin* • USA
FATHER LOVE • 1915 • Dillon Eddie • USA
FATHER MAKES GOOD • 1951 • Yarbrough Jean • USA
FATHER MAKES HIMSELF USEFUL • 1911 • *Lubin* • USA
FATHER MAKES LOVE TO THE PUMP • 1905 • Collins Alf? • UKN
FATHER MALACHY'S MIRACLE (USA) see **WUNDER DES MALACHIAS, DAS** • 1961
FATHER MANOLO see **PADRE MANOLO, EL** • 1967
FATHER MASTER (USA) see **PADRE PADRONE** • 1977
FATHER MINDS THE BABY • 1910 • Collins Alf? • UKN
FATHER, MOTHER WANTS YOU • 1906 • *Urban Trading Co.* • UKN
FATHER MURPHY • 1981 • Landon Michael • TVM • USA
FATHER NILE • 1931 • Bray John R. • USA
FATHER NOAH'S ARK • 1933 • Jackson Wilfred • ANS • USA
FATHER O' NINE • 1938 • Kellino Roy • UKN
FATHER OF A DEAD SOLDIER (USA) see **OTETS SOLDATA** • 1965
FATHER OF HELL TOWN • 1985 • Medford Don • TVM • USA
FATHER OF HER CHILD, THE • 1916 • *Calvert Ethel* • SHT • USA
FATHER OF MORE THAN FOUR (USA) see **PADRE DE MAS DE CUATRO** • 1938
FATHER OF THE BRIDE • 1950 • Minnelli Vincente • USA
FATHER OF THE EGG, THE see **BASHTATA NA YAITSETO** • 1990
FATHER OF THE GIRL, THE see **PERE DE MADEMOISELLE, LE** • 1953
FATHER O'FLYNN • 1909 • *Warwick Trading Co.* • UKN
FATHER O'FLYNN • 1919 • Watts Tom • UKN
FATHER O'FLYNN • 1935 • Noy Wilfred, Tennyson Walter • UKN
FATHER SAID HE'D FIX IT • 1915 • Louis Will • USA
FATHER SERGI see **OTYETS SERGII** • 1979
FATHER SERGIUS see **OTETS SERGEI** • 1918
FATHER SERGIUS see **OTYETS SERGII** • 1979
FATHER SORROW see **SMIL** • 1916
FATHER STEPS OUT • 1937 • Rogers Maclean • UKN
FATHER STEPS OUT • 1941 • Yarbrough Jean • USA • CITY LIMITS
FATHER TAKES A WIFE • 1941 • Hively Jack • USA
FATHER TAKES THE AIR • 1951 • McDonald Frank • USA
FATHER TAKES THE BABY OUT • 1913 • Wilson Frank? • UKN
FATHER TAMED • 1913 • *Punch* • USA
FATHER THAMES' TEMPERANCE CURE • 1902 • Booth W. R. • UKN
FATHER TO BE see **JAG AR MED BARN** • 1979
FATHER TOM • 1921 • O'Brien John B. • USA
FATHER (UKN) see **APA** • 1966
FATHER VOJTECH see **PATER VOJTECH** • 1928
FATHER VOJTECH see **PATER VOJTECH** • 1937
FATHER WANTED, A see **PAPPA SOKES** • 1947
FATHER WAS A FULLBACK • 1949 • Stahl John M. • USA
FATHER WAS A LOAFER • 1915 • *Ritchie Billie* • USA
FATHER WAS NEUTRAL • 1915 • Edwards Harry J. • USA
FATHER WAS RIGHT • 1917 • *Alden Hazel* • USA
FATHER WINS A TURKEY see **CHRISTMAS RAFFLE, A** • 1908
FATHERHOOD • 1915 • Bosworth Hobart • USA
FATHERHOOD OF BUCK MCGEE, THE • 1912 • *Vitagraph* • USA
FATHERLAND • 1987 • Loach Kenneth • UKN, FRN, FRG
FATHERLAND, THE • 1939 • Shengelaya Nikolai • USS
FATHERLAND, ROBBERY AND FAMILY • Zervos Nikos • GRC
FATHERS see **OTSY** • 1989
FATHERS AND CHILDREN see **OJCOWIE I DZIECI** • 1969
FATHERS AND SONS • Rashevskaya Natalya • USS
FATHERS AND SONS • 1912 • *Champion* • USA
FATHERS AND SONS • 1945 • Lukov Leonid • USS
FATHERS AND SONS • 1960 • Bergunkev Adolf • USS
FATHERS ARE PEOPLE • 1951 • Kinney Jack • ANS • USA
FATHER'S BABY BOY • 1909 • Stow Percy • UKN
FATHER'S BEARD • 1914 • Ransom Charles • USA
FATHER'S BIRTHDAY CHEESE • 1905 • Stow Percy • UKN
FATHER'S BIRTHDAY PARTY • 1904 • Collins Alf? • UKN
FATHER'S BIRTHDAY RING • 1911 • *Myers Harry* • USA
FATHER'S BLUFF • 1912 • *Wadsworth William* • USA
FATHER'S BRIDE • 1914 • *Meredyth Bess* • USA
FATHER'S BRIGHT IDEA • 1917 • Christie Al • USA
FATHER'S BRILLIANT IDEA • 1915 • *Pathe Exchange* • USA
FATHER'S BUST • 1912 • *Majestic* • USA
FATHER'S CHICKEN DINNER • 1913 • *Morris David* • USA
FATHER'S CHILD • 1915 • Myers Harry • USA
FATHER'S CHOICE • 1913 • Hotaling Arthur D. • *Lubin* • USA
FATHER'S CHOICE • 1913 • Nicholls George, Sennett Mack (Spv) • *Keystone* • USA
FATHER'S CLOSE SHAVE • 1920 • Morris Reggie • SHT • USA
FATHER'S DAY • 1913 • *Stowell William* • USA
FATHER'S DAY see **RICHEST MAN IN THE WORLD, THE** • 1930
FATHER'S DAY OFF • 1953 • Kinney Jack • ANS • USA
FATHER'S DERBY TRIP • 1906 • Green Tom • UKN • FATHER AND THE BOOKMAKER
FATHER'S DEVOTION, A • 1914 • Smalley Phillips • USA
FATHER'S DILEMMA (USA) see **PRIMA COMMUNIONE** • 1950
FATHER'S DOING FINE • 1952 • Cass Henry • UKN
FATHER'S DRESS SUIT • 1911 • Merwin Bannister • USA
FATHER'S ESTATE see **ODAL FEDRANNA** • 1980
FATHER'S FAVORITE • 1912 • Dwan Allan • USA • FAVORED SON, THE
FATHER'S FIGHTING FEVER • 1914 • Aylott Dave • UKN
FATHER'S FINISH • 1913 • *American* • USA
FATHER'S FIRST BABY • 1908 • Mottershaw Frank • UKN
FATHER'S FIRST HALF HOLIDAY • 1909 • Porter Edwin S. • USA
FATHER'S FIRST MURDER • 1915 • *Pearce Peggy* • USA
FATHER'S FLIRTATION • 1914 • Baker George D. • USA
FATHER'S FLIRTATION • 1916 • *Hippo* • USA
FATHER'S GOT THE SACK FROM THE WATERWORKS • 1916 • *Tress Henry* • SHT • UKN
FATHER'S GRIEF, A see **FADEREN** • 1909
FATHER'S HAT; OR GUY FAWKES'DAY • 1904 • Stow Percy • UKN
FATHER'S HATBAND • 1913 • Brooke Van Dyke • USA
FATHER'S HEART, A • 1914 • *Larkin Dolly* • USA
FATHER'S HELPING HAND • 1908 • Davey Horace • USA
FATHER'S HOLIDAY • 1908 • *Wrench* • UKN
FATHER'S HOT TODDY • 1912 • *Vitagraph* • USA
FATHER'S LEGACY -A GOAT • 1910 • Rosenthal Joe • UKN
FATHER'S LESSON • 1908 • Fitzhamon Lewin • UKN
FATHER'S LESSON, A • 1913 • Henderson Dell • USA
FATHER'S LION • 1952 • Kinney Jack • ANS • USA
FATHER'S LITTLE DIVIDEND • 1950 • Minnelli Vincente • USA
FATHER'S LITTLE FLUTTER • 1913 • Wilson Frank? • UKN
FATHER'S LOVE, A • 1909 • Wormald S.? • UKN
FATHER'S LOVE, A • 1910 • *Powers* • USA
FATHER'S LOVE, A • 1913 • *Lubin* • USA
FATHER'S LOVE, A see **BLOODBROTHERS** • 1978
FATHER'S LUCKY ESCAPE • 1915 • Davey Horace • USA
FATHER'S MISTAKE • 1909 • Bouwmeester Theo? • UKN
FATHER'S MONEY • 1915 • *Victor* • USA
FATHER'S NAME see **IMIE OJCA** • 1969
FATHER'S NEW MAID • 1915 • *Beery Wallace* • USA
FATHER'S NIGHT OFF • 1916 • Greene Clay M. • USA
FATHERS OF MEN • 1916 • Humphrey William • USA
FATHER'S PICNIC ON THE SANDS • 1905 • *Cricks & Sharp* • UKN
FATHER'S REVENGE, A • 1988 • Herzfeld John • TVM • USA • FATHER'S REVENGER: THE TERRORISTS ○ TERRORISTS, THE
FATHER'S REVENGER: THE TERRORISTS see **FATHER'S REVENGE, A** • 1988
FATHER'S SACRIFICE, A • 1912 • Raymond Charles? • UKN
FATHER'S SATURDAY AFTERNOON • 1911 • Coleby A. E.? • UKN
FATHER'S SCAPEGOAT, THE • 1914 • Vale Travers • USA
FATHER'S SON • 1931 • Beaudine William • USA
FATHER'S SON • 1941 • Lederman D. Ross • USA
FATHERS, SONS AND CHORUS GIRLS • 1918 • Davis James • SHT • USA
FATHER'S STRATEGY • 1915 • *Moore Matt* • USA
FATHER'S TEMPER • 1914 • *Lubin* • USA
FATHERS THREE • 1915 • *Myers Harry* • USA
FATHER'S TIMEPIECE • 1914 • Beggs Lee • USA
FATHER'S VENGEANCE, A • 1902 • *New Century Pictures* • UKN
FATHER'S VENGEANCE, A • 1907 • Fitzhamon Lewin • UKN
FATHER'S WAR see **GUERRA DE PAPA, LA** • 1977
FATHER'S WASHING DAY • 1906 • *Walturdaw* • UKN
FATHER'S WEEKEND • 1953 • Kinney Jack • ANS • USA
FATHER'S WILD GAME • 1950 • Leeds Herbert I. • USA
FATHOM • 1967 • Martinson Leslie H. • UKN
FATIA NEGRA see **SZEGENY GAZDAGOK** • 1959
FATICHE DI ERCOLE, LE • 1957 • Francisci Pietro • ITL • HERCULES (UKN)
FATIK AND THE JUGGLER see **FATIKCHAND** • 1982
FATIKCHAND • 1982 • Ray Sandip • IND • FATIK AND THE JUGGLER
FATIMA • 1959 • Dolidze Siko • USS
FATIMA see **BUDAK NAFSU** • 1984
FATIMA, ESPERANCA DO MUNDO • 1963 • Ribeiro Antonio Lopes, Spiguel Miguel • SHT • PRT
FATIMA STORY • 1975 • de Macedo Antonio • MTV • PRT
FATIMA, TERRA DE FE • 1943 • do Canto Jorge Brum • PRT
FATINA WAL SOOLUK, AL • 1976 • Emara Hussein • EGY • WOMAN AND PUPPET
FATINAT AL-JAMAHIR • 1964 • Salman Mohammed • LBN • IDOLE DES FOULES, L'
FATMA BACI • 1973 • Refig Halit • TRK
FATMAN AND LITTLE BOY • 1989 • Joffe Roland • USA
FATRICIDE, LE • 1967 • Belmont Charles • SHT • FRN
FATS AND THINS see **GORDOS E MAGROS** • 1980
FATSO • 1980 • Bancroft Anne • USA
FATTACCIO, ER • 1954 • Moschino Riccardo • ITL
FATTENED FOR THE MARKET • 1901 • *Bitzer Billy (Ph)* • USA
FATTI DI BRONTE, I see **BRONTE: CRONACA DI UN MASSACRO CHE I LIBRI DI STORIA NON HANNO RACCONTATO** • 1972
FATTI DI GENTE PER BENE • 1974 • Bolognini Mauro • FRN, ITL • GRANDE BOURGEOISE, LA (FRN) ○ MURRI AFFAIR, THE (USA) ○ DRAMA OF THE RICH
FATTIG MILJONAR, EN • 1941 • Wallen Sigurd • SWD • POOR MILLIONAIRE, A
FATTIGA RIDDARE • 1944 • Holmberg Tage • SWD
FATTO DI SANGUE FRA DUE UOMINI PER CAUSA DI UNA VEDOVA (SI SOSPETTANO MOVENTI POLITICI) • 1978 • Wertmuller Lina • ITL • BLOOD FEUD (USA) ○ REVENGE
FATTY AGAIN • 1914 • Arbuckle Roscoe • USA
FATTY AND MABEL ADRIFT • 1916 • Arbuckle Roscoe • SHT • USA
FATTY AND MABEL AT THE SAN DIEGO EXPOSITION • 1915 • Dillon Eddie • USA
FATTY AND MABEL VIEWING THE WORLD'S FAIR AT SAN FRANCISCO • 1915 • Arbuckle Roscoe, Normand Mabel • USA
FATTY AND MABEL'S SIMPLE LIFE see **MABEL'S AND FATTY'S SIMPLE LIFE** • 1915
FATTY AND ME, THE see **DICKE UND ICH, DER**
FATTY AND MINNIE HE-HAW • 1915 • Arbuckle Roscoe, Dillon Eddie • USA
FATTY AND THE BANDITS • 1913 • *Nestor* • USA
FATTY AND THE BROADWAY STARS • 1915 • Arbuckle Roscoe • USA
FATTY AND THE HEIRESS • 1914 • Arbuckle Roscoe, Dillon Eddie • USA
FATTY AND THE SCHYSTER LAWYER • 1914 • *Brennan John E.* • USA
FATTY ARBUCKLE IN A LIBERTY LOAN APPEAL see **SCRAPS OF PAPER** • 1918
FATTY AT CONEY ISLAND • 1917 • Arbuckle Roscoe • SHT • USA • CONEY ISLAND
FATTY AT E Z RANCH • 1912 • *Nestor* • USA
FATTY AT SAN DIEGO • 1913 • Lehrman Henry • USA
FATTY FINN • 1981 • Murphy Maurice • ASL
FATTY JOINS THE FORCE • 1913 • Lehrman Henry • USA
FATTY ON THE JOB • 1914 • Ince Ralph • USA
FATTY'S AFFAIR OF HONOR • 1913 • Ince Ralph • USA
FATTY'S BIG MIX-UP • 1912 • *Nestor* • USA
FATTY'S BUSY DAY • 1913 • *Kalem* • USA
FATTY'S CHANCE ACQUAINTANCE • 1915 • Dillon Eddie • USA
FATTY'S DAY OFF • 1913 • Lehrman Henry • USA
FATTY'S DEBUT • 1914 • Arbuckle Roscoe, Dillon Eddie • USA
FATTY'S DECEPTION • 1913 • *Roland Ruth* • USA
FATTY'S ECHO • 1915 • *Kalem* • USA
FATTY'S FAITHFUL FIDO • 1915 • Arbuckle Roscoe • USA
FATTY'S FATAL FUN • 1915 • *Hardy Oliver* • USA
FATTY'S FEATURE FILLUM • 1917 • Voss Fatty • SHT • USA
FATTY'S FINISH • 1914 • Arbuckle Roscoe, Dillon Eddie • USA
FATTY'S FLIRTATION • 1913 • Nicholls George • USA
FATTY'S GIFT • 1914 • Arbuckle Roscoe, Dillon Eddie • USA
FATTY'S INFATUATION • 1915 • *Gardner Willard* • USA
FATTY'S JONAH DAY • 1914 • Arbuckle Roscoe, Dillon Eddie • USA

FATTY'S LOYAL FRIEND • 1916 • *Arbuckle Roscoe* • USA

FATTY'S MAGIC PANTS • 1914 • Arbuckle Roscoe, Dillon Eddie • USA

FATTY'S NEW ROLE • 1915 • Arbuckle Roscoe, Dillon Eddie • USA

FATTY'S OVERTIME • 1922 • Roberts Edward D. • UKN

FATTY'S PLUCKY PUP see **FOILED BY FIDO** • 1915

FATTY'S RECKLESS FLING • 1915 • Dillon Eddie • USA

FATTY'S SWEETHEART • 1914 • Ince Ralph • USA

FATTY'S TIN TYPE TANGLE see **FIDO'S TIN TYPE TANGLE** • 1915

FATTY'S WINE PARTY • 1914 • Arbuckle Roscoe, Dillon Eddie • USA

FAUBOURG-MONTMARTRE • 1923 • Burguet Charles • FRN

FAUBOURG-MONTMARTRE • 1931 • Bernard Raymond • FRN

FAUBOURG SAINT-MARTIN • 1986 • Guiguet Jean-Claude • FRN

FAUBOURGS DE MOSCOU, LES • 1915 • Protazanov Yakov • USS

FAUCET • 1960 • Menken Marie • USA

FAUCET, THE • 1916 • Wing William E. • USA

FAUCON, LE • 1983 • Boujenah Paul • FRN

FAUCON, LE see **SAQR, AS-** • 1965

FAULTS see **GUNAH** • 1981

FAULTS OF YOUTH see **WAKAKIHI NO AYAMACHI** • 1952

FAULTY PRONOUN REFERENCE, COMPARISON AND PUNCTUATION OF THE PARTICIPLE PHRASE • Landow George • USA

FAUN, THE • 1908 • *Pathe* • FRN

FAUN, THE • 1917 • Korda Alexander • HNG

FAUN, THE see **MARRIAGE MAKER, THE** • 1923

FAUN, THE (UKN) see **BOUGHT AND PAID FOR** • 1916

FAUNO, IL • 1916 • Mari Febo • ITL

FAUNO DAS MONTANHAS • 1926 • Vieira Manuel Luis • PRT

FAUNOVO VELMI POZDNI ODPOLEDNE • 1984 • Chytilova Vera • CZC • LATE AFTERNOON OF A FAUN, THE

FAUSSAIRE, LE (FRN) see **FALSCHUNG, DIE** • 1981

FAUSSE ALERTE • 1940 • de Baroncelli Jacques • FRN • FRENCH WAY, THE (USA) ○ SOIR D'ALERTE, UN ○ A PARIS UN SOIR ○ ABRI 39

FAUSSE IDENTITE • 1946 • Chotin Andre • FRN

FAUSSE MAITRESSE, LA • 1942 • Cayatte Andre • FRN

FAUSSES CONFIDENCES, LES • 1984 • Moosmann Daniel • FRN

FAUSSES INGENUES (FRN) see **LABBRA ROSSE** • 1960

FAUSSES NOUVELLES see **BREAK THE NEWS** • 1938

FAUST • 1897 • *Lumiere* • FRN

FAUST • 1898 • Smith G. A. • UKN

FAUST • 1906 • Blache Alice • FRN

FAUST • 1907 • *Pathe* • FRN

FAUST • 1907 • Gilbert Arthur • UKN

FAUST • 1909 • Fagot Georges, Andreani M. • FRN

FAUST • 1909 • Porter Edwin S., Dawley J. Searle • USA

FAUST • 1910 • *Negri-Pouget Fernanda* • ITL

FAUST • 1910 • Andreani Henri • FRN

FAUST • 1910 • Barnett David • UKN

FAUST • 1911 • Hepworth Cecil M. • UKN

FAUST • 1912 • Hlavsa Stanislav • CZC

FAUST • 1915 • *Commercial Biophone* • USA

FAUST • 1915 • Sloman Edward • UKN

FAUST • 1918 • UKN

FAUST • 1921 • *Todd Frederick A.* • USA

FAUST • 1922 • Bourgeois Gerard • ITL

FAUST • 1922 • Sanderson Challis • UKN

FAUST • 1923 • Phillips Bertram • UKN

FAUST • 1926 • Murnau F. W. • FRG • FAUST –EINE DEUTSCHE VOLKSSAGE

FAUST • 1927 • Parkinson H. B. • UKN

FAUST • 1936 • Hopkins Albert • UKN

FAUST • 1960 • Gorski Peter • FRG

FAUST • 1964 • Susman Michael • USA

FAUST • 1970 • Syberberg Hans-Jurgen • SHT • FRG

FAUST • 1980 • Rumbelow Steven • UKN

FAUST see **DAMNATION DU DOCTEUR FAUST** • 1904

FAUST see **DOKTOR FAUST** • 1958

FAUST see **JOHANES DOKTOR FAUST** • 1958

FAUST see **SFIDA AL DIAVOLO** • 1965

FAUST AND MARGUERITE • 1900 • Porter Edwin S. • USA

FAUST AND MARGUERITE • 1911 • Durand Jean • FRN

FAUST AND MARGUERITE (USA) see **FAUST ET MARGUERITE** • 1897

FAUST AND MARGUERITE (USA) see **DAMNATION DU DOCTEUR FAUST** • 1904

FAUST AND MEPHISTOPHELES • 1898 • Smith G. A. • UKN

FAUST AND MEPHISTOPHELES see **FAUST ET MEPHISTO** • 1902

FAUST AND THE DEVIL see **LEGGENDA DI FAUST, LA** • 1949

FAUST AND THE LILY • 1913 • *Biograph* • USA

FAUST AND THE LILY • 1913 • Henderson Dell • *Ab* • USA

FAUST AUX ENFERS • 1903 • Melies Georges • FRN • DAMNATION OF FAUST, THE (USA) ○ DAMNATION DE FAUST, LA ○ CONDEMNATION OF FAUST, THE

FAUST DES RIESEN, DIE • 1917 • Biebrach Rudolf • FRG

FAUST DES SCHICKSALS, DIE • 1917 • Neuss Alwin • FRG

FAUST DES SCHICKSALS, DIE • 1921 • Schirokauer Alfred • FRG

FAUST –EINE DEUTSCHE VOLKSSAGE see **FAUST** • 1926

FAUST ET MARGUERITE • 1897 • Melies Georges • FRN • FAUST AND MARGUERITE (USA)

FAUST ET MARGUERITE see **DAMNATION DU DOCTEUR FAUST** • 1904

FAUST ET MEPHISTO • 1902 • Blache Alice • FRN • FAUST AND MEPHISTOPHELES

FAUST FANTASY • 1935 • *Booth Webster* • UKN

FAUST IM DUNKEL, DIE • 1919 • Tollen Otz • FRG

FAUST XX • 1966 • Popescu-Gopo Ion • RMN • FAUSTUS XX

FAUSTAU • 1971 • Coutinho Eduardo • BRZ

FAUSTINA • 1956 • Saenz De Heredia Jose Luis • SPN

FAUSTINA • 1968 • Magni Luigi • ITL

FAUSTINE AND THE BEAUTIFUL SUMMER see **FAUSTINE ET LE BEL ETE** • 1971

FAUSTINE ET LE BEL ETE • 1971 • Companeez Nina • FRN • FAUSTINE AND THE BEAUTIFUL SUMMER ○ FAUSTINE (UKN)

FAUSTINE (UKN) see **FAUSTINE ET LE BEL ETE** • 1971

FAUSTO • 1924 • Martinez, Gunche • ARG

FAUSTO CRIOLLO, EL • 1980 • Saslavsky Luis • ARG • NATIVE FAUST, A

FAUSTRECHT • 1922 • Ehmann Karl • FRG

FAUSTRECHT • 1922 • Neufeld Max • AUS

FAUSTRECHT DER FREIHEIT • 1975 • Fassbinder R. W. • FRG • FOX AND HIS FRIENDS (UKN) ○ FIST-RIGHT OF FREEDOM ○ CLUB-LAW OF FREEDOM ○ FOX

FAUSTUS XX see **FAUST XX** • 1966

FAUT ALLER PARMI L'MONDE POUR LE SAVOIR • 1971 • Dansereau Fernand • DOC • CND

FAUT CE QU'IL FAUT • 1940 • Pujol Rene • FRN • MONSIEUR BIBI

FAUT-IL SE COUPER L'OREILLE? • 1970 • Giraldeau Jacques • DCS • CND

FAUT-IL SE MARIER? • 1929 • Noa Manfred • FRN

FAUT-ILS LES MARIER? • 1932 • Billon Pierre, Lamac Carl • FRN

FAUT PAS L'DIRE • 1976-77 • Brault Michel, Gladu Andre • DCS • CND

FAUT PAS PRENDRE LES ENFANTS DU BON DIEU POUR DES CANARDS SAUVAGES • 1968 • Audiard Michel • FRN • OPERATION LEONTINE (USA) ○ LEONTINE (UKN)

FAUT REPARER SOPHIE • 1933 • Ryder Alexandre • FRN

FAUT S'LES FAIRE! ..CES LEGIONNAIRES • 1981 • Nauroy Alain C. • FRN

FAUTE DE L'ABBE MOURET, LA • 1970 • Franju Georges • FRN, ITL • AMANTE DEL PRETE, L' (ITL) ○ SIN OF FATHER MOURET, THE ○ DEMISE OF FATHER MOURET, THE (USA) ○ C'EST LA FAUTE DE L'ABBE MOURET

FAUTE DE MONIQUE, LA • 1929 • Gleize Maurice • FRN

FAUTE DE PIERRE DAISY, LA • 1916 • de Baroncelli Jacques • FRN

FAUTE DES AUTRES, LA • 1953 • Guez Robert • SHT • FRN

FAUTE D'ODETTE MARECHAL, LA • 1919 • Roussell Henry • FRN

FAUTE D'ORTHOGRAPHE, LA • 1919 • Feyder Jacques • FRN

FAUTE PATERNELLE, LA see **H'AD'A MA GANARU ABY** • 1945

FAUTEUIL 47, LE • 1926 • Ravel Gaston, Lekain Tony • FRN

FAUTEUIL 47, LE • 1937 • Rivers Fernand • FRN

FAUVE EST LACHE, LE • 1958 • Labro Maurice • FRN

FAUVES, LES • 1984 • Daniel Jean-Louis • FRN

FAUVES ET BANDITS • 1913-18 • Durand Jean • FRN

FAUX-CUL, LE • 1975 • Hanin Roger • FRN, FRG • FAUX CUL, LE ○ PHONEY, THE

FAUX CUL, LE see **FAUX-CUL, LE** • 1975

FAUX ET USAGE DE FAUX • 1990 • Heynemann Laurent • FRN

FAUX-FUYANTS • 1982 • Bergala Alain, Limosin Jean-Pierre • FRN • FAUX FUYANTS

FAUX-FUYANTS • 1986 • Favreau Robert • CND

FAUX FUYANTS see **FAUX-FUYANTS** • 1982

FAUX MAGISTRAT, LE • 1914 • Feuillade Louis • FRN • FALSE MAGISTRATE, THE ○ FANTOMAS V

FAUX MONNAYEURS see **OR DANS LA MONTAGNE, L'** • 1938

FAUX MUTANT, LE • 1967 • Lemaire Yvan • BLG

FAUX PAS, LE • 1964 • d'Ormesson Antoine • FRN

FAUX VISAGES, LES • 1962 • Bonniere Rene • DOC • CND • FALSE FACES

FAVELA DO MEUS AMORES • 1934 • Mauro-Humberto (c/d) • BRZ • FAVELA OF MY LOVES

FAVELA OF MY LOVES see **FAVELA DO MEUS AMORES** • 1934

FAVOLOSE NOTTI D'ORIENTE, LE • 1973 • Guerrini Mino • ITL

FAVOR, THE see **VERY SPECIAL FAVOR, A** • 1965

FAVOR CORRESSE ATRAS • 1976 • Naranjo Lisandro Duque • DOC • CLM

FAVOR TO A FRIEND, A • 1919 • Ince John • USA

FAVORED SON, THE see **FATHER'S FAVORITE** • 1912

FAVORIS DE LA LUNE, LES • 1984 • Ioseliani Otar • FRN • FAVOURITES OF THE MOON

FAVORIT DER KAISERIN, DER • 1936 • Hochbaum Werner • FRG • TSARINA'S FAVOURITE, THE

FAVORIT DER KONIGIN, DER • 1922 • Seitz Franz • FRG

FAVORITA, LA • 1953 • Barlacchi Cesare • ITL

FAVORITE FOOL, A • 1915 • Henderson Dell, Frazee Edwin • USA

FAVORITE MELODIES • 1929 • *Etting Ruth* • SHT • USA

FAVORITE NURSERY SCENE, A • 1898 • *Paul R. W.* • UKN

FAVORITE OF THE REGIMENT, THE see **MILACEK PLUKU** • 1931

FAVORITE SON, THE • 1913 • Ford Francis • USA

FAVOURABLE OUTCOME • 1990 • Zhivkov Vassil • BUL

FAVOURITE, THE • 1988 • Smight Jack • USA

FAVOURITE, THE • 1989 • Guillermin John • USA

FAVOURITE AIRS • 1929 • *Paikin Luella* • SHT • UKN

FAVOURITE FOR THE JAMAICA CUP, THE • 1913 • Raymond Charles • UKN

FAVOURITE NO.13 see **LYUBIMETZ 13** • 1958

FAVOURITE OF THE GODS see **LIEBLING DER GOTTER** • 1960

FAVOURITE WIFE OF THE MAHARAJA II, THE see **MAHARAJAENS YNDLINGSHUSTRU II** • 1918

FAVOURITES OF THE MOON see **FAVORIS DE LA LUNE, LES** • 1984

FAZIL • 1928 • Hawks Howard • USA

FAZILET • 1989 • Tozum Irfan • TRK

FBI 99 • 1945 • Bennet Spencer Gordon, Grissell Wallace A., Canutt Yakima • USA

FBI MISSION BALBECK see **OPERAZIONE BAALBECK** • 1965

FBI MURDERS, THE • 1988 • Lowry Dick • USA

FE, LA • 1947 • Gil Rafael • SPN

FE EN DOS, LA • 1949 • de Anda Raul • MXC

FE ENSU DESTINO • 1978 • Ordosgoitti Napoleon • VNZ • FAITH IN DESTINY

FE, ESPERANZA Y CARIDAD • 1972 • Bojorquez Alberto, Alcoriza Luis, Fons Jorge • MXC • FAITH, HOPE, AND CHARITY

FE-MAIL SPECIAL DELIVERY • 1965 • *Ron Lawrence Productions* • USA • FEMALE SPECIAL DELIVERY

FEAR • 1916 • Mitchell Howard M. • SHT • USA

FEAR • 1927 • Greenwood Edwin • UKN • FANGS OF DEATH

FEAR • 1943 • Schwartz Zac • ANS • USA

FEAR • 1945 • Cannon Robert • ANS • USA

FEAR • 1946 • Zeisler Alfred • USA

FEAR • 1963 • Schulhoff Petr • CZC

FEAR • 1965 • *Ghatak Ritwik* • DOC • IND

FEAR • 1981 • Freda Riccardo • ITL

FEAR • 1988 • Ferretti Robert A. • USA • HONOR BETRAYED ○ FLASHBACK

FEAR see **WOMAN IN THE HOUSE, THE** • 1942

FEAR see **PAURA, LA** • 1954

FEAR see **STRACH** • 1975

FEAR see **STRAH** • 1975

FEAR see **PAURA, LA** • 1980

FEAR see **ANGST** • 1983

FEAR, THE • 1912 • Dwan Allan • USA

FEAR, THE • 1913 • *Essanay* • USA

FEAR, THE • 1913 • *Powers* • USA

FEAR, THE see **FOVOS, HO** • 1966

FEAR AND DESIRE • 1954 • Kubrick Stanley • USA

FEAR AND LOVE see **PEUR ET L'AMOUR, LA** • 1967

FEAR AND PETER BROWN • 1940 • Massingham Richard • UKN

FEAR, ANXIETY AND DEPRESSION • 1989 • Solandz Todd • USA

FEAR-BOUND • 1925 • Nigh William • USA

FEAR CHAMBER, THE • 1968 • Hill Jack, Ibanez Juan • USA, MXC • CHAMBER OF FEAR ○ CAMERA DEL TERROR, LA ○ TORTURE ZONE, THE

FEAR CITY • 1985 • Ferrara Abel • USA

FEAR EATS THE SOUL (UKN) see **ANGST ESSEN SEELE AUF** • 1973

FEAR FIGHTER, THE • 1925 • Rogell Albert S. • USA

FEAR HAS A THOUSAND EYES see **SKRACKEN HAR TUSEN OGON** • 1971

FEAR IN A HANDFUL OF DUST see **FLESHBURN** • 1983

FEAR IN THE CITY see **PAURA IN CITTA** • 1976

FEAR IN THE NIGHT • 1947 • Shane Maxwell • USA

FEAR IN THE NIGHT • 1972 • Sangster Jimmy • UKN • DYNASTY OF FEAR

FEAR IS THE KEY • 1972 • Tuchner Michael • UKN

FEAR MARKET, THE • 1920 • Webb Kenneth • USA

FEAR NO EVIL • 1949 • Scotese Giuseppe Maria • ITL

FEAR NO EVIL • 1969 • Wendkos Paul • TVM • USA

FEAR NO EVIL • 1981 • La Loggia Frank • USA

FEAR NO MORE • 1961 • Wiesen Bernard • USA

FEAR NOT • 1917 • Holubar Allen • USA

FEAR O' GOD (USA) see **MOUNTAIN EAGLE, THE** • 1926

FEAR OF FEAR see **ANGST VOR DER ANGST** • 1975

FEAR OF LITTLE MEN, THE see **LUCK OF THE IRISH, THE** • 1948

FEAR OF LOVE • 1970 • Portici Emilio • USA

FEAR OF POVERTY, THE • 1916 • Sullivan Frederick • USA

FEAR OF THE HANGMAN • 1914 • *Solograph* • UKN

FEAR OF THE SNAKE WOMAN see **KAIDAN HEBIONNA** • 1968

FEAR ON THE CITY see **PEUR SUR LA VILLE** • 1975

FEAR ON TRIAL • 1975 • Johnson Lamont • TVM • USA

FEAR OVER THE CITY see **PEUR SUR LA VILLE** • 1975

FEAR SHIP, THE • 1933 • Edwards J. Steven • UKN

FEAR STRIKES OUT • 1957 • Mulligan Robert • USA • JIM PIERSALL STORY, THE

FEAR WITHIN, THE • 1915 • Giblyn Charles • USA

FEAR WOMAN, THE • 1919 • Barry J. A. • USA

FEARFUL DECISION see **RANSOM** • 1955

FEARLESS see **POLIZIOTTO SENZA PAURA** • 1978

FEARLESS DEPUTY, THE (UKN) see **LARIATS AND SIX SHOOTERS** • 1931

FEARLESS DICK • 1922 • *Hatton Dick* • USA

FEARLESS DRAGONS • *Ko Philip* • HKG

FEARLESS FAGAN • 1952 • Donen Stanley • USA

FEARLESS FOSDICK • 1952 • SHS • USA

FEARLESS FOSDICK IN BATULA see **BATULA** • 1952

FEARLESS FOSDICK IN FRANK N. STEIN see **FRANK N. STEIN** • 1952

FEARLESS FRANK • 1969 • Kaufman Philip • USA • FRANK'S GREATEST ADVENTURE

FEARLESS FUZZ see **POLIZIOTTO SENZA PAURA** • 1978

FEARLESS HYENA 2 • 1985 • Chan Jackie • HKG

FEARLESS HYENA, THE see **HSIAO CH'UAN YI CHAO** • 1979

FEARLESS JINX, THE (UKN) see **GALLOPING JINX** • 1925

FEARLESS LOVER, THE • 1925 • McRae Henry • USA

FEARLESS OPPOSITION see **FUTEKINARU HANKO** • 1958

FEARLESS RIDER, THE • 1928 • Lewis Edgar • USA

FEARLESS STRANGER, THE see **KORKUSUZ YABANCI** • 1968

FEARLESS VAMPIRE KILLERS, THE (USA) see **DANCE OF THE VAMPIRES** • 1967

FEARLESS YOUNG BOXER, THE see **AVENGING BOXER**

FEARMAKERS, THE • 1958 • Tourneur Jacques • USA

FEARS see **MIEDOS, LOS** • 1980

FEARSOME BEAST, THE • Zarubin Leonid • ANM • USS

FEAST see **UTAGE** • 1967

FEAST, THE see **PRAZNIK** • 1967

FEAST AND FAMINE • 1914 • Ayres Sydney • USA

FEAST AND FURIOUS • 1952 • Sparber I. • ANS • USA

FEAST AT SEA see **MEREN JUHLAT** • 1963

FEAST AT ZHIRMUNKA see **PIR V ZHIRMUNKE** • 1941

FEAST BY THE SEA see **MEREN JUHLAT** • 1963

FEAST OF FLESH see **BLOOD FEAST** • 1963

FEAST OF FLESH see **PLACER SANGRIENTO** • 1967

FEAST OF FRIENDS • 1970 • *Doors The* • DOC • USA

FEAST OF FRIENDSHIP • 1967 • Bottcher Jurgen • DOC • GDR

FEAST OF HARMONY, A • 1930 • Jeffrey R. E. • UKN

FEAST OF LIFE, THE • 1916 • Capellani Albert • USA

FEAST OF ST. JORGEN, THE see **PRAZDNIK SVYATOVO IORGENE** • 1930

FEAST OF SATAN, THE see **FESTIN DE SATANAS, EL**

FEAST OUT AT SEA, THE see **MEREN JUHLAT** • 1963

FEASTS OF SINCELEJO see **CORRALEJAS DE SINCELEJO** • 1975

FEAT OF LENINGRAD, THE see **PODVIG LENINGRADA** • 1973

FEATHER, THE • 1929 • Hiscott Leslie • UKN

FEATHER AND FATHER • 1977 • Kulik Buzz • TVM • USA • FEATHER AND FATHER GANG, THE

FEATHER AND FATHER GANG, THE see **FEATHER AND FATHER** • 1977

FEATHER BLUSTER • 1958 • McKimson Robert • ANS • USA

FEATHER DUSTER • 1955 • McKimson Robert • ANS • USA

FEATHER FINGER • 1966 • McKimson Robert • ANS • USA
FEATHER IN HER HAT, A • 1935 • Santell Alfred • USA
FEATHER IN HIS CAP, A • 1907 • Fitzhamon Lewin • UKN
FEATHER IN HIS HARE, A • 1948 • Jones Charles M. • ANS • USA
FEATHER TOP • 1912 • *Eclair* • USA
FEATHER YOUR NEST • 1937 • Beaudine William • UKN
FEATHER YOUR NEST • 1944 • Yates Hal • SHT • USA
FEATHERED FOLLIES • 1932 • *Van Beuren* • ANS • USA
FEATHERED NEST, THE • 1916 • Griffin Frank C., Chandler Edward • SHT • USA
FEATHERED PESTS • 1939 • Roberts Charles E. • SHT • USA
FEATHERED SERPENT, THE • 1934 • Rogers Maclean • UKN
FEATHERED SERPENT, THE • 1948 • Beaudine William • USA
FEATHERED SHADOWS, THE see **OPERENE STINY** • 1930
FEATHERS • 1987 • Ruane John • SHT • ASL
FEATHERTOP • 1912 • *Eclair* • FRN
FEATHERTOP • 1913 • *Kinemacolor* • USA
FEATHERTOP • 1916 • Vernot Henry J. • USA
FEATHERWEIGHT CHAMP • 1953 • Donnelly Eddie • ANS • USA
FEBBRE see **ACCADDE A DAMASCO E FEBBRE** • 1943
FEBBRE DA CAVALLO • 1976 • Steno • ITL
FEBBRE DEL CINEMA, LA see **MOVIE RUSH** • 1976
FEBBRE DI VIVERE • 1953 • Gora Claudio • ITL • EAGER TO LIVE
FEBRERO 28 DE 1970 • 1970 • Alvarez Carlos • SHT • CLM • COLOMBIA '70
FEBRUARY 29 see **LEAP YEAR COMEDY, A** • 1912
FECHTER VON RAVENNA, DER • 1923 • *Golaor Alfredo* • FRG
FEDAI KOMANDOLAR KIBRISTA • 1968 • Okcugil Nejat • TRK • VOLUNTEER COMMANDOS IN CYPRUS, THE
FEDE • 1916 • Gallone Carmine • ITL
FEDERAL, THE see **FEDERALE, IL** • 1961
FEDERAL AGENT • 1936 • Newfield Sam • USA
FEDERAL AGENT AT LARGE • 1950 • Blair George • USA
FEDERAL AGENTS VS. UNDERWORLD, INC. • 1949 • Brannon Fred C. • SRL • USA
FEDERAL BULLETS • 1937 • Brown Karl • USA
FEDERAL FUGITIVES • 1941 • Beaudine William • USA
FEDERAL MAN • 1950 • Tansey Robert • USA
FEDERAL MAN-HUNT • 1939 • Grinde Nick • USA • FLIGHT FROM JUSTICE (UKN)
FEDERAL OFFENSE see **UNDERCOVER DOCTOR** • 1939
FEDERAL OPERATOR 99 • 1945 • Bennet Spencer Gordon, Grissell Wallace A. • SRL • USA
FEDERALE, IL • 1961 • Salce Luciano • ITL • FASCIST, THE (USA) ○ FEDERAL, THE
FEDERICO BARBAROSSA • 1910 • Caserini Mario • ITL
FEDERICO FELLINI'S INTERVISTA (USA) see **INTERVISTA** • 1987
FEDORA • 1916 • De Liguoro Giuseppe • ITL
FEDORA • 1916 • Serena Gustavo • ITL
FEDORA • 1918 • Chautard Emile • USA
FEDORA • 1918 • Jose Edward • *Paramount* • USA
FEDORA • 1926 • Manoussi Jean • FRG
FEDORA • 1928 • Manoussi Jean • FRN
FEDORA • 1934 • Gasnier Louis J. • FRN
FEDORA • 1942 • Mastrocinque Camillo • ITL
FEDORA • 1978 • Wilder Billy • FRG, FRN
FEDORA see **PRINCESS ROMANOFF** • 1915
FEDORA see **FEHER EJSZAKAK** • 1916
FEDRA • 1956 • Mur Oti • SPN • FEDRA, THE DEVIL'S DAUGHTER (USA) ○ STEPMOTHER, THE
FEDRA, THE DEVIL'S DAUGHTER (USA) see **FEDRA** • 1956
FEDRA WEST • 1968 • Romero-Marchent Joaquin Luis • SPN, ITL • PHAEDRA WEST
FEDS • 1988 • Goldberg Dan • USA
FEE AUX CHOUX, LA • 1896 • Blache Alice • FRN • CABBAGE FAIRY, THE
FEE CARABOSSE: OU, LE POIGNARD FATAL, LA • 1906 • Melies Georges • FRN • WITCH, THE (USA) ○ POIGNARD FATAL, LE ○ PRINCESSE FATALE, LA
FEE DES FLEURS, LA • 1904 • Velle Gaston • FRN • FLOWER FAIRY, THE (USA)
FEE FIE FOES • 1961 • Hanna William, Barbera Joseph • ANS • USA
FEE LIBELLULE, LA • 1908 • Melies Georges • FRN • LAC ENCHANTE, LE ○ FAIRY DRAGONFLY, THE ○ ENCHANTED LAKE, THE
FEE PAS COMME LES AUTRES, UNE • 1956 • Tourane Jean • ANM • FRN, ITL • SECRET OF MAGIC ISLAND, THE (USA) ○ PAESE DI PAPERINO, IL ○ SECRET OF OUTER SPACE ISLAND ○ ONCE UPON A TIME
FEE PRINTEMPS, LA • 1902 • Zecca Ferdinand • FRN • SPRING FAIRY, THE (USA)
FEE PRINTEMPS, LA • 1906 • Blache Alice • FRN • SPRING FAIRY, THE (USA)
FEE SANGUINAIRE, LA • 1968 • Lethem Roland • SHT • BLG • BLOODTHIRSTY FAIRY, THE ○ BLOODY FAIRY, THE
FEE VON SAINT MENARD, DIE • 1919 • Lund Erik • FRG
FEED 'EM AND WEEP • 1929 • Guiol Fred • SHT • USA
FEED 'EM AND WEEP • 1938 • Douglas Gordon • SHT • USA
FEED THE KITTY • 1938 • Lovy Alex • ANS • USA
FEED THE KITTY • 1952 • Jones Charles M. • ANS • USA
FEEDBACK • 1965 • Vanderbeek Stan • USA
FEEDBACK • 1978 • Doukas Bill • USA
FEEDER see **PALANDAI** • 1967
FEEDIN' THE KIDDIE • 1957 • Hanna William, Barbera Joseph • ANS • USA
FEEDING THE "KITTY" • 1914 • *Nestor* • USA
FEEDING TIME • 1913 • Sennett Mack • USA
FEEL MY MUSCLE • 1915 • *Lubin* • USA
FEEL MY PULSE • 1928 • La Cava Gregory • USA
FEEL THE HEAT see **CATCH THE HEAT** • 1987
FEELIN' GOOD • 1966 • Pike James A. • USA
FEELING see **ANUBHAV** • 1972
FEELING ALL RIGHT • 1944 • Lassee Fred • USA
FEELING OF HOSTILITY, THE • 1948 • Anderson Robert • DCS • CND • HOSTILITE
FEELING OF REJECTION, THE • 1947 • Anderson Robert • DCS • CND • BANNIS IMAGINAIRES, LES
FEELING ROSY • 1933 • Edwards Harry J. • USA
FEELINGS • 1976 • Britten Laurence • UKN
FEELINGS see **CHUVSTVA** • 1971
FEELINGS -MIRTA FROM LINIERS TO ISTANBUL see **SENTIMIENTOS -MIRTA DE LINIERS A ESTAMBUL** • 1987
FEELINGS OF DEPRESSION • 1950 • Jackson Stanley R. • DCS • CND • DEPRESSION
FEELS SO GOOD • 1980 • Mann Ron • CND
FEENEY'S SOCIAL EXPERIMENT • 1913 • *Reliance* • USA
FEENHANDE • 1912 • Stark Kurt • FRG
FEENHANDE • 1916 • Biebrach Rudolf • FRG
FEEST, HET • 1963 • Verhoeven Paul* • SHT • NTH • LET'S HAVE A PARTY ○ PARTY
FEET see **NOGE** • 1967
FEET AND DEFEAT • 1918 • De Barge C. R. • SHT • USA
FEET FIRST • 1930 • Bruckman Clyde • USA
FEET IS FEET • 1916 • *International Film Service* • SHT • USA
FEET OF CLAY • 1917 • Harvey Harry • USA
FEET OF CLAY • 1924 • De Mille Cecil B. • USA
FEET OF CLAY • 1960 • Marshall Frank • UKN
FEET OF MUD • 1924 • Edwards Harry J. • SHT • USA
FEGEFEUER DER LIEBE • 1951 • Reinl Harald • AUS • WEISSE HOLLE MONTBLANC ○ NACHT AM MONTBLANC
FEGYVER • 1971 • Macskassy Gyula, Varnai Gyorgy • ANS • HNG • WEAPONS
FEHER EJSZAKAK • 1916 • Korda Alexander • HNG • WHITE NIGHTS ○ WHITE NIGHT ○ FEDORA
FEHER ROZSA • 1920 • Korda Alexander • HNG • WHITE ROSE
FEHERLOFIA • 1982 • Jankovics Marcell • ANM • HNG • SON OF THE WHITE MARE ○ WHITE MARE'S SON, THE
FEHERVARI HUSZAROK • 1939 • Keleti Marton • HNG • HUSSARS OF FEHERVARI (USA)
FEI-HU-WAI CHUAN • 1981 • Chang Ch'Eh • HKG • LEGEND OF THE FOX
FEI TAO, YU CHIEN FEI TAO • 1981 • Liu Chia-Liang • HKG • RETURN OF THE DEADLY BLADE
FEIFA SHENGMING • 1990 • Tian Zhuangzhuang • CHN
FEIFA YIMIN • 1985 • Zhang Wanting • HKG • ILLEGAL IMMIGRANT, THE
FEIND IM BLUT • 1931 • Ruttmann Walter • DOC • FRG, SWT
FEINDE • 1940 • Tourjansky Victor • FRG
FEINDLICHE GATTEN see **KAMPF UM DIE EHE 2, DER** • 1919
FEINDLICHES BLUT • 1920 • Achsel Willy • FRG
FEINE GESELLSCHAFT BESCHRANKTE HAFTUNG • 1982 • Runze Ottokar • FRG • HIGH SOCIETY LIMITED
FEIRA, A • 1970 • de Almeida Manuel Faria • SHT • PRT
FEIRA POPULAR DE LISBOA • 1944 • Mendes Joao, Acursio Oscar, Mendes Santos • SHT • PRT
FEIRAS E MERCADOS • 1941 • Coelho Jose Adolfo • SHT • PRT
FEITICO DO IMPERIO • 1940 • Ribeiro Antonio Lopes • PRT
FEIYIT WONGFAN • 1988 • Cheung Chi-Leung • HKG • BEYOND THE SUNSET
FEJLOVES • 1968 • Bacso Peter • HNG • HEAD WOUND, THE ○ SHOT IN THE HEAD ○ FATAL SHOT, THE
FEKETE GYEMANTOK • 1937 • Vajda Ladislao • HNG
FEKETE GYEMANTOK • 1977 • Varkonyi Zoltan • HNG • BLACK DIAMOND
FEKETE KAPITANY • 1920 • Fejos Paul • HNG • BLACK CAPTAIN, THE
FEKETE SZEM EJSZAKAJA • 1958 • Keleti Marton • HNG • LADY AND THE GYPSY, THE
FEKETE SZIVARVANY, A • 1916 • Curtiz Michael • HNG • BLACK RAINBOW, THE
FELD MARECHAL see **MONSIEUR LE MARECHAL** • 1931
FELDARZT, DER see **TAGEBUCH DES DR. HART, DAS** • 1916
FELDGRAUE GROSCHEN, DER • 1916 • Jacoby Georg • FRG
FELDHERRENHUGEL, DER • 1926 • Schonfelder Erich, Lowenstein Hans Otto • FRG, ITL
FELDHERRENHUGEL, DER • 1932 • Thiele Eugen • FRG
FELDHERRENHUGEL, DER • 1953 • Marischka Ernst • AUS
FELDMANN CASE, THE see **FELDMANN-SAKEN** • 1986
FELDMANN-SAKEN • 1986 • Erichsen Bente • NRW • FELDMANN CASE, THE ○ OVER GRENSEN
FELDMARESCIALLA, LA • 1967 • Steno • ITL, FRN • RITA FLEES.. LUI CORRE.. EGLI SCAPPA ○ GIRL FIELD-MARSHAL, THE ○ RITA FLEES.. HE RUNS.. THEY ESCAPE
FELDMARSCHALL, DER • 1927 • Mengon Romano • FRG
FELDOBOTT KO • 1969 • Sara Sandor • HNG • THROWN UP STONE, THE ○ UPTHROWN STONE, THE
FELHOLJATEK! • 1984 • Maar Gyula • HNG • PASSING FANCY
FELICES PASCUAS • 1954 • Bardem Juan Antonio • SPN
FELICES SESENTA, LOS • 1963 • Camino Jaime • SPN
FELICIA • 1969 • Shiffen Arlo • USA
FELICIA IS HAPPY • 1968 • Robertson George C. • CND
FELICIDAD • 1956 • Blake Alfonso Corona • MXC
FELICIE NANTEUIL • 1942 • Allegret Marc • FRN • PLUS GRAND AMOUR, LE ○ HISTOIRE COMIQUE
FELICITA COLOMBO • 1937 • Mattoli Mario • ITL
FELICITA IN PERICOLO see **C'E SEMPRE UN MA!** • 1943
FELICITA PERDUTA • 1947 • Ratti Filippo M. • ITL
FELICITA SOTTO LA PIOGGIA see **FINALMENTE SI** • 1943
FELICITAS GROLANDIN • 1922 • Biebrach Rudolf • FRG
FELICITE • 1979 • Pascal Christine • FRN
FELICITY • 1979 • Lamond John • ASL
FELICITY ARRIVES AT 9 see **SRECA DOLACI U 9** • 1961
FELIKS DZIERZYNSKI • 1978 • Bobrovsky Anatoli • PLN
FELINE FOLLIES see **FELIX THE CAT** • 1919-21
FELINE FRAME-UP • 1954 • Jones Charles M. • ANS • USA
FELINEOUS ASSAULT • 1959 • Kneitel Seymour • ANS • USA
FELINES, LES • 1973 • Daert Daniel • FRN • CATS, THE (UKN)
FELINS, LES • 1964 • Clement Rene • FRN • LOVE CAGE, THE (UKN) ○ JOY HOUSE, THE (USA)
FELIPE FUE DESGRACIADO • 1947 • Cardona Rene • MXC
FELIX • 1983 • Clausen Erik • DNM
FELIX • 1988 • Sanders Helma, Sander Helke, von Trotta Margarethe, Buschmann Christel • FRG
FELIX AND OTILIA see **FELIX SI OTILIA** • 1972
FELIX AT THE BALL • 1912 • *Lubin* • USA
FELIX DZERJINSKY • 1957 • Kalatozov Mikhail • USS
FELIX FOLLOWS SWALLOWS • 1924 • Sullivan Pat • ANS • USA
FELIX GETS IN WRONG • 1916 • Ormston Frank • SHT • USA
FELIX HOLT • 1915 • Vale Travers? • USA
FELIX IN ARABIANTICS • 1928 • Sullivan Pat • ANS • USA
FELIX IN COLD RUSH • 1925 • Sullivan Pat • ANS • USA
FELIX IN GERMANIA • 1927 • Sullivan Pat • ANS • USA
FELIX IN HOLLYWOOD • 1923 • Sullivan Pat • ANS • USA
FELIX IN OCEANTICS • 1930 • Sullivan Pat • ANS • USA
FELIX IN THE BONE AGE • 1922 • Sullivan Pat • ANS • USA
FELIX KNIGHT ERRANT • 1923 • Sullivan Pat • ANS • USA
FELIX LECLERC -TROUBADOUR • 1959 • Jutra Claude • DCS • CND
FELIX MINDS THE BABY • 1923 • Sullivan Pat • ANS • USA
FELIX O'DAY • 1920 • Thornby Robert T. • USA
FELIX ON THE JOB • 1916 • De Grasse Joseph • SHT • USA
FELIX REVOLTS • 1922 • Sullivan Pat • ANS • USA
FELIX SI OTILIA • 1972 • Mihu Iulian • RMN • FELIX AND OTILIA
FELIX THE CAT • 1919-21 • *Sullivan Pat (P)* • ASS • USA • FELINE FOLLIES
FELIX THE CAT • 1922-25 • *Sullivan Pat (P)* • ASS • USA
FELIX THE CAT • 1925-32 • *Sullivan Pat (P)* • ASS • USA
FELIX THE CAT AND THE GOOSE THAT LAID THE GOLDEN EGGS • 1936 • Gillett Burt, Palmer Tom • ANS • USA
FELIX THE CAT AT THE RAINBOW'S END • 1925 • *Sullivan Pat (P)* • ANS • USA
FELIX THE CAT IN ASTRONOMEOWS • 1928 • *Sullivan Pat (P)* • ANS • USA
FELIX THE CAT IN DRAGGIN TH' DRAGON • 1928 • *Sullivan Pat (P)* • ANS • USA
FELIX THE CAT SWITCHES WITCHES • 1927 • *Sullivan Pat (P)* • ANS • USA
FELIX THE CAT TRIFLES WITH TIME • 1925 • *Sullivan Pat (P)* • ANS • USA
FELIX THE CAT TRIPS THROUGH TOYLAND • 1925 • *Sullivan Pat (P)* • ANS • USA
FELIX THE FOX • 1948 • Davis Mannie • ANS • USA
FELIX WINS AND LOSES • 1925 • Sullivan Pat • SHT • USA
FELIZ AND VELHO • 1988 • Gervitz Roberto • BRZ • HAPPY OLD YEAR
FELIZ ANO, AMOR MIO • 1955 • Demicheli Tulio • MXC
FELIZES PARA SEMPRE • 1984 • Barreto Bruno • BRZ • HAPPILY EVER AFTER
FELL LOCOMOTIVE, THE • 1952 • Harris Roy, De Normanville Peter • UKN
FELLA WITH THE FIDDLE, THE • 1937 • Freleng Friz • ANS • USA
FELLAGHAS • 1970 • Khalifa Omar • TNS • REBELS ○ FALLAGA
FELLAH • 1921 • Vorins Henri • FRN
FELLAH AL FASSIEH, AL see **FALLAH AL-FACIH, AL-** • 1970
FELLERS • 1930 • Higgins Arthur, Fay Austin • ASL
FELLINI -A DIRECTOR'S NOTEBOOK • 1968 • Fellini Federico • DOC • USA • BLOCK-NOTES DI UN REGISTA
FELLINI-ROMA (FRN) see **ROMA** • 1972
FELLINI-SATYRICON • 1969 • Fellini Federico • ITL, FRN • SATYRICON
FELLINI'S AMARCORD see **AMARCORD** • 1973
FELLINI'S CASANOVA see **CASANOVA** • 1976
FELLINI'S ROMA (USA) see **ROMA** • 1972
FELLOW AMERICANS • 1942 • Kanin Garson • DOC • USA
FELLOW CADETS see **KADETTKAMRATER** • 1939
FELLOW CITIZENS • 1920 • Goulding Alf, Roach Hal • SHT • USA
FELLOW CLERKS • 1909 • Bouwmeester Theo • UKN
FELLOW FROM OUR TOWN, A see **PAREN IZ NASHEGO GORODA** • 1942
FELLOW ON A FURLOUGH • 1944 • Keays Vernon • SHT • USA
FELLOW ROMANS • 1921 • Roach Hal • SHT • USA
FELLOW STUDENTS • 1930 • Newfield Sam • SHT • USA
FELLOW TRAVELLER • 1989 • Saville Philip • UKN
FELLOW TRAVELLERS • 1983 • Nee'Man Yehuda • MTV • ISR
FELLOW VILLAGERS • 1975 • Vinogradov Valentin • USS
FELLOW VOYAGERS • 1913 • Costello Maurice • USA
FELLOWS WHO ATE THE ELEPHANT, THE see **ZO O KUTTA RENCHU** • 1947
FELLOWSHIP OF THE FROG see **FROSCH MIT DER MASKE, DER** • 1959
FELONS, THE see **HUDODELCI** • 1987
FELSZABADULT FOLD • 1950 • Ban Frigyes • HNG • LIBERATED LAND
FELURE, THE • 1973 • Climent Antonio • SPN
FEM DOGN I AUGUST • 1973 • Wam Svend • NRW • FIVE DAYS IN AUGUST
FEM KOPIER • 1913 • Blom August • DNM • 5 COPIES
FEM OG SPIONERNE, DE • 1969 • Hedman Trine • DNM • FIVE GO ADVENTURING
FEMALE • 1933 • Curtiz Michael, Dieterle William (U/c) • USA
FEMALE see **VIOLENT YEARS, THE** • 1956
FEMALE, THE • 1924 • Wood Sam • USA
FEMALE, THE see **FEMME ET LE PANTIN, LA** • 1958
FEMALE, THE see **SETENTA VECES SIETE** • 1962
FEMALE AND THE FLESH see **LUMIERE D'EN FACE, LA** • 1955
FEMALE ANIMAL, THE • 1958 • Keller Harry • USA
FEMALE ANIMAL, THE (USA) see **GEHEIMNIS DER VENUS, DAS** • 1955
FEMALE ANIMAL (USA) see **MUJER DEL GATO, LA** • 1970
FEMALE ARTILLERY • 1973 • Chomsky Marvin • TVM • USA
FEMALE BANDIT, THE • 1910 • *Bison* • USA
FEMALE BLUEBEARD, THE • 1908 • *Kalem* • USA
FEMALE BOOK AGENT, THE • 1914 • *Hotely Mae* • USA
FEMALE BUNCH, THE • 1971 • Adamson Al • USA
FEMALE BUTCHER see **CEREMONIA SANGRIETA** • 1972
FEMALE CHAUVINISTS • 1977 • Jackson Jay • USA
FEMALE COBRA see **NAGIN** • 1959
FEMALE COP, THE • 1914 • Hevener Jerold T. • USA
FEMALE CORRESPONDENT (UKN) see **ADVENTURE IN WASHINGTON** • 1941
FEMALE DEMON see **CHOKON YASHA** • 1928
FEMALE DETECTIVE, THE • 1913 • *Hotely Mae* • USA
FEMALE FAGIN, A • 1913 • *Kalem* • USA
FEMALE FANTASIES • *Spelvin Georgina* • USA
FEMALE FRIENDS (USA) see **STRANGE AWAKENING** • 1958

FEMALE FUGITIVE • 1938 • Nigh William • USA • FUGITIVE LADY (UKN)
FEMALE HIGHWAYMAN, THE • 1906 • *Selig William (P)* • USA
FEMALE IMPERSONATOR, THE see **MASQUERADER, THE** • 1914
FEMALE INSTINCT see **SNOOP SISTERS, THE** • 1972
FEMALE JUNGLE • 1956 • Ve Sota Bruno • USA
FEMALE OF THE SPECIES see **FEMININE TOUCH, THE** • 1941
FEMALE OF THE SPECIES, THE • 1912 • Griffith D. W. • USA
FEMALE OF THE SPECIES, THE • 1913 • Weber Lois • USA
FEMALE OF THE SPECIES, THE • 1916 • West Raymond B. • USA
FEMALE ON THE BEACH • 1955 • Pevney Joseph • USA
FEMALE POLITICIAN, THE • 1908 • *Vitagraph* • USA
FEMALE PRINCE, THE • 1966 • Chou See-Loke • HKG
FEMALE PRISONER, THE see **PRISONNIERE, LA** • 1968
FEMALE REBELLION see **YEOJAEUI BANRAN** • 1985
FEMALE REPORTER, A • 1909 • *Essanay* • USA
FEMALE RESPONSE, THE • 1972 • Kincaid Tim • USA • EVERYBODY'S AT IT (UKN)
FEMALE: SEVENTY TIMES SEVEN (USA) see **SETENTA VECES SIETE** • 1962
FEMALE SEXUALITY see **OSWALT KOLLE: DEINE FRAU, DAS UNBEKANNTE WESEN** • 1969
FEMALE SPECIAL DELIVERY see **FE-MAIL SPECIAL DELIVERY** • 1965
FEMALE SPY 503 see **KVINNLIG SPION 503** • 1959
FEMALE SPY WHO WENT INTO THE COLD, THE see **ESPIA QUE ENTROU EM FRIA, A** • 1967
FEMALE SWINDLER, THE • 1916 • Ward Albert • UKN
FEMALE THREE TIMES see **FEMMINE TRE VOLTE** • 1957
FEMALE TRAP see **NAME OF THE GAME IS KILL, THE** • 1968
FEMALE TROUBLE • 1974 • Waters John* • USA
FEMALE WOLF see **MESU OOKAMI** • 1967
FEMALES, THE see **WEIBCHEN, DIE** • 1970
FEMALES IS FICKLE • 1940 • Fleischer Dave • ANS • USA
FEME • 1927 • Oswald Richard • FRG
FEMEILE ZILELOR NOASTRE • 1958 • Meszaros Marta • DCS • RMN
FEMINA RIDENS • 1969 • Schivazappa Piero • ITL • LAUGHING WOMAN, THE (USA)
FEMININ-FEMININ • 1973 • Calef Henri, Correa Joao Manso • BLG, FRN
FEMININ FLEUR, LA • 1965 • Lenica Jan • ANS • FRN • WOMAN IS A FLOWER (UKN) ○ FLOWER WOMAN, THE ○ FEMME-FLEUR, LA
FEMININE FAMILY see **JOSEI KAZOKU** • 1963
FEMININE TOUCH, THE • 1941 • Van Dyke W. S. • USA • FEMALE OF THE SPECIES
FEMININE TOUCH, THE • 1956 • Jackson Pat • UKN • GENTLE TOUCH, THE (USA)
FEMININE TOUCH (UKN) see **DUDE WRANGLER, THE** • 1930
FEMININE WIT • 1915 • *Ivans Elaine* • USA
FEMINIST AND THE FUZZ, THE • 1970 • Paris Jerry • TVM • USA
FEMME, LA • 1975 • Brault Francois • DCS • CND
FEMME A L'ORCHIDEE, LA • 1951 • Leboursier Raymond • FRN
FEMME A MENTI, UNE • 1930 • de Rochefort Charles • FRN
FEMME A SA FENETRE, UNE • 1976 • Granier-Deferre Pierre • FRN, ITL, FRG • WOMAN AT HER WINDOW, A (USA) ○ DONNA ALLA FINESTRA, UNA
FEMME AU CORBEAU, LA see **RIVER, THE** • 1928
FEMME AU COUTEAU, LA • 1968 • Bassori Timite • IVC • WOMAN WITH THE KNIFE, THE
FEMME AU VOLANT, UNE • 1933 • Gerron Kurt, Billon Pierre • FRN
FEMME AUX ABOIS, UNE • 1967 • Pecas Max • FRN • PRISONNIERE DU DESIR, LA ○ SLAVE, THE (USA)
FEMME AUX BOTTES ROUGES, LA • 1974 • Bunuel Juan • FRN, ITL, SPN • RAGAZZA CON GLI STIVALI ROSSI, LA (ITL) ○ WOMAN WITH RED BOOTS, THE(USA)
FEMME AUX DEUX VISAGES, LA • 1920 • Marodon Pierre • FRN
FEMME AUX LOUPS, LA • 1943 • Pottier Richard • FRN
FEMME CHERCHE JEUNE HOMME SEUL • 1971 • Marchal Jean • FRN, SPN, BLG
FEMME CHIPEE, UNE • 1934 • Colombier Piere • FRN • FEMME RAVIE, UNE
FEMME COCHERE, LA • 1911 • Desfontaines Henri • FRN
FEMME COQUETTE, UNE • 1955 • Godard Jean-Luc • SHT • FRN
FEMME COUPEE EN MORCEAUX, UNE • 1945 • Noe Yvan • FRN • NOUS CHERCHONS UNE FEMME
FEMME CREA L'AMANT, LA see **CHALEURS** • 1970
FEMME D'A COTE, LA • 1981 • Truffaut Francois • FRN • WOMAN NEXT DOOR, THE (USA)
FEMME D'AFFAIRES TRES SPECIALE, UNE • Bernard Jean Laurent • FRN
FEMME DANGEREUSE, UNE see **JUDITH TERPEAUVE** • 1979
FEMME DANS LA NUIT, UNE • 1941 • Gance Abel, Greville Edmond T. • FRN
FEMME DE CHAMBRE JENNI, LA • 1918 • Protazanov Yakov • USS
FEMME DE JEAN, LA • 1961 • Bellon Yannick • FRN
FEMME DE JEAN, LA • 1974 • Bellon Yannick • FRN • JOHN'S WIFE (USA)
FEMME DE L'AVIATEUR, LA • 1980 • Rohmer Eric • FRN • ON NE SAURAIT PENSER A RIEN ○ AVIATOR'S WIFE, THE (UKN) ○ FEMME DE L'AVIATEUR OU: ON NE SAURAIT PENSER A RIEN, LA
FEMME DE L'AVIATEUR OU: ON NE SAURAIT PENSER A RIEN, LA see **FEMME DE L'AVIATEUR, LA** • 1980
FEMME DE L'HOTEL, LA • 1985 • Pool Lea • CND • WOMAN IN TRANSIT
FEMME DE MAUVAISE REPUTATION, UNE see **IMRA'ATUN SAIYI'ATA AS-SUMA** • 1972
FEMME DE MENAGE, LA • 1954 • Forest Leonard • SHT • CND • CHARWOMAN, THE
FEMME DE MES REVES, LA • 1931 • Bertin Jean • FRN
FEMME DE MON POTE, LA • 1983 • Blier Bertrand • FRN • MY BEST FRIEND'S GIRL (USA)
FEMME DE NULLE PART, LA • 1922 • Delluc Louis • FRN • WOMAN FROM NOWHERE, THE
FEMME DE ROSE HILL, LA • 1989 • Tanner Alain • FRN, SWT • WOMAN FROM ROSE HILL, THE (UKN)
FEMME DE SADE • 1978 • *Obel* • USA
FEMME DES AUTRES, LA • 1920 • Marodon Pierre • FRN
FEMME DES REVES, LA • 1964 • Sheppard Gordon H. • CND • DREAM GIRL
FEMME DISPARAIT, UNE • 1942 • Feyder Jacques • SWT • PORTRAIT OF A WOMAN ○ WOMAN DISAPPEARED, A
FEMME DOUCE, UNE • 1969 • Bresson Robert • FRN • GENTLE CREATURE, A (UKN)
FEMME DU BOULANGER, LA • 1938 • Pagnol Marcel • FRN • BAKER'S WIFE, THE (USA)
FEMME DU BOUT DU MONDE, LA • 1937 • Epstein Jean • FRN
FEMME DU GANGE, LA • 1973 • Duras Marguerite • FRN, ITL • RAGAZZA DI PASSAGGIO, LA (ITL) ○ WOMAN OF THE GANGES
FEMME DU PRETRE, LA (FRN) see **MOGLIE DEL PRETE, LA** • 1970
FEMME DU VOISIN, LA • 1929 • de Baroncelli Jacques • FRN
FEMME D'UNE NUIT, LA • 1930 • L'Herbier Marcel • FRN
FEMME ECARLATE, LA • 1969 • Valere Jean • FRN, ITL • DONNA SCARLATTA, LA (ITL) ○ SCARLET WOMAN, THE
FEMME EN BLANC SE REVOLTE, UNE see **NOUVEAU JOURNAL D'UNE FEMME EN BLANC, LE** • 1966
FEMME EN BLEU, LA • 1973 • Deville Michel • FRN, ITL
FEMME EN HOMME, LA • 1932 • Genina Augusto • FRN
FEMME EN ROUGE, LA • 1946 • Cuny Louis • FRN
FEMME ENFANT, LA • 1980 • Billetdoux Raphaele • FRN
FEMME ENTRE CHIEN ET LOUP, UNE (FRN) see **VROUW TUSSEN HOND EN WOLF, EEN** • 1979
FEMME EST UNE FEMME, UNE • 1961 • Godard Jean-Luc • FRN, ITL • WOMAN IS A WOMAN, A (USA) ○ DONNA E DONNA, LA (ITL)
FEMME ET LE DIAMANT, LA see **COUP DE FEU A L'AUBE** • 1932
FEMME ET LE PANTIN, LA • 1929 • de Baroncelli Jacques • FRN
FEMME ET LE PANTIN, LA • 1958 • Duvivier Julien • FRN, ITL • WOMAN LIKE SATAN, A (USA) ○ FEMALE, THE
FEMME ET LE ROSSIGNOL, LA • 1930 • Hugon Andre • FRN
FEMME FARDEE, LA • 1990 • Pinheiro Jose • FRN
FEMME FATALE • 1912 • *Roch Madeleine* • FRN
FEMME FATALE, LA • 1917 • Feuillade Louis • FRN
FEMME FATALE, LA • 1945 • Boyer Jean • FRN
FEMME FATALE, UNE • 1976 • Doniol-Valcroze Jacques • FRN, FRG
FEMME FIDELE, UNE • 1976 • Vadim Roger • FRN • WHEN A WOMAN IN LOVE.. (UKN) ○ WHEN A WOMAN IS IN LOVE
FEMME-FLEUR, LA see **FEMININ FLEUR, LA** • 1965
FEMME FLIC, LA • 1979 • Boisset Yves • FRN • FEMME-FLIC, LA
FEMME-FLIC, LA see **FEMME FLIC, LA** • 1979
FEMME FORTE • 1938 • Tessier Albert • DCS • CND
FEMME IDEALE, LA • 1933 • Berthomieu Andre • FRN • IDEAL WOMAN, THE (USA)
FEMME IMAGE, LA • 1960 • Borremans Guy • SHT • CND
FEMME INCONNUE, LA • 1914 • Ravel Gaston • FRN
FEMME INCONNUE, LA • 1916 • Gance Abel • FRN
FEMME INCONNUE, LA • 1923 • de Baroncelli Jacques • FRN
FEMME INFIDELE, LA • 1968 • Chabrol Claude • FRN, ITL • STEPHANE, UNA MOGLIE INFEDELE (ITL) ○ UNFAITHFUL WIFE ○ UNFAITHFUL WIVES
FEMME INTEGRALE, LA • 1979 • Guilmain Claudine • FRN
FEMME INVISIBLE, LA • 1933 • Lacombe Georges • FRN • INVISIBLE WOMAN, THE
FEMME IVOIRE, LA • 1984 • Cheminal Dominique • FRN
FEMME LIBRE, UNE see **FILS DE L'AUTRE, LE** • 1931
FEMME LIBRE, UNE see **FILLE LIBRE, UNE** • 1970
FEMME, L'OISELEUR ET LA MAISON, LA • 1960 • Borremans Guy • CND
FEMME MARIEE, LA see **FEMME MARIEE, UNE** • 1964
FEMME MARIEE, UNE • 1964 • Godard Jean-Luc • FRN • FEMME MARIEE, LA ○ MARRIED WOMAN, A ○ MARRIED WOMAN, THE
FEMME METAMORPHOSEE EN CHATTE, LA • 1912 • Carre Michel • FRN
FEMME NUE, LA • 1926 • Perret Leonce • FRN • MODEL FROM MONTMARTRE, THE (USA) ○ BOHEMIAN LOVE
FEMME NUE, LA • 1932 • Paulin Jean-Paul • FRN
FEMME NUE, LA • 1949 • Berthomieu Andre • FRN • NAKED WOMAN, THE (USA)
FEMME OBJET, LA • 1980 • Mulot Claude • FRN
FEMME OU DEUX, UNE • 1985 • Vigne Daniel • FRN • ONE WOMAN OR TWO (USA) ○ WOMAN OR TWO, A
FEMME PAR JOUR, UNE • 1948 • Boyer Jean • FRN
FEMME PERDUE, LA • 1942 • Choux Jean • FRN
FEMME POLICES see **DEFEATING DELINQUENCY** • 1951
FEMME POUR LES AUTRES, UNE • 1964 • Patry Pierre • CND
FEMME PUBLIQUE, LA • 1984 • Zulawski Andrzej • FRN
FEMME QUE J'AI ASSASSINE, LA • 1948 • Daniel-Norman Jacques • FRN
FEMME QUE J'AI LE PLUS AIMEE, LA • 1942 • Vernay Robert • FRN
FEMME QUI PLEURE, LA • 1979 • Doillon Jacques • FRN • CRYING WOMAN, THE
FEMME QUI SE PARTAGE, UNE • 1936 • Cammage Maurice • FRN
FEMME RAVIE, UNE see **FEMME CHIPEE, UNE** • 1934
FEMME REVEE, LA • 1929 • Durand Jean • FRN
FEMME SANS IMPORTANCE, UNE • 1937 • Choux Jean • FRN • SECRET D'UNE VIE, LE
FEMME SANS PASSE • 1948 • Grangier Gilles • FRN
FEMME SPECTACLE, LA • 1964 • Lelouch Claude • DOC • FRN • NIGHT WOMEN (USA) ○ PARIS IN THE RAW
FEMME-STATUE, LA • 1969 • Behi Ridha • SHT • TNS
FEMME SUR LA PLAGE, LA (FRN) see **WOMAN ON THE BEACH, THE** • 1946
FEMME SUR LA ROUTE, UNE see **IMRA'A FI AT-TARIQ** • 1958
FEMME, UN JOUR, UNE • 1977 • Keigel Leonard • FRN • WOMAN, ONE DAY, A
FEMME – VILLA – VOITURE – ARGENT • 1972 • Alassane Moustapha • NGR • WOMAN – VILLA – CAR – MONEY ○ F.V.V.A. ○ FVVA
FEMME VOLANTE, LA • 1902 • Melies Georges • FRN • MARVELOUS SUSPENSION AND EVOLUTION (USA)
FEMMES • 1936 • Bernard-Roland • FRN
FEMMES • 1983 • Kaleya Tana • FRN, SPN
FEMMES, LES • 1969 • Aurel Jean • FRN, ITL • WOMEN
FEMMES, LES see **BAL DES VOYOUS, LE** • 1968
FEMMES AU SOLEIL • 1974 • Dreyfus Liliane • FRN
FEMMES COLLANTES, LES • 1920 • Monca Georges • FRN
FEMMES COLLANTES, LES • 1938 • Caron Pierre • FRN
FEMMES COMPLICES • Pierson Claude • FRN
FEMMES D'ABORD, LES • 1962 • Andre Raoul • FRN • LADIES FIRST (USA)
FEMMES DANS LA MELEE, LES see **WOMEN ARE WARRIORS** • 1942
FEMMES DE BANLIEU see **DEUX FEMMES EN OR** • 1970
FEMMES DE BONNE VOLANTE see **APPEL DU BLED, L'** • 1942
FEMMES DE DEMAIN see **GRAND-PERE** • 1938
FEMMES DE PARIS • 1951 • Boyer Jean • FRN • WOMEN OF PARIS
FEMMES DE PARIS see **AHI LES BELLES BACCHANTES** • 1954
FEMMES DE PERSONNE • 1984 • Frank Christopher • FRN • NOBODY'S WOMEN
FEMMES DEPAREILLEES • 1941 • Tessier Albert • DCS • CND • ECOLES MENAGERES REGIONALES II
FEMMES DEPAREILLEES • 1948 • Tessier Albert • DCS • CND
FEMMES DEVANT L'AMOUR, LES see **CHANT DE L'AMOUR, LE** • 1935
FEMMES DU LOUVRES, LES • 1951 • Kast Pierre • FRN
FEMMES D'UN ETE (FRN) see **RACCONTI D'ESTATE** • 1958
FEMMES ENTRE HOMMES • 1981 • Ayranu Lino • FRN
FEMMES FATALES see **CALMOS** • 1976
FEMMES, FEMMES • 1974 • Vecchiali Paul • FRN
FEMMES FLAMBOYANTES, LES see **SVENSKA FLICKOR I PARIS** • 1960
FEMMES IMPUDIQUES • 1975 • Pierson Claude • FRN
FEMMES LIBRES (FRN) see **DONNA LIBERA, UNA** • 1956
FEMMES MENENT LE JEU, LES (FRN) see **SCAMPOLO '53** • 1954
FEMMES NOIRES, FEMMES NUES see **A NOUS DEUX, LA FRANCE!** • 1970
FEMMES PARMI NOUS, LES • 1961 • Bobet Jacques • CND
FEMMES POUR NOUMEA see **ROUTE DU BAGNE, LA** • 1945
FEMMES PREFERENT LES GROSSES!!! • Ray John* • FRN
FEMMES SAVANTES, LES • 1965 • Meyer Jean • FRN
FEMMES S'EN BALANCENT, LES • 1953 • Borderie Bernard • FRN
FEMMES SONT DES ANGES, LES • 1952 • Aboulker Marcel • FRN
FEMMES SONT FOLLES, LES • 1950 • Grangier Gilles • FRN
FEMMES SONT MARRANTES, LES • 1958 • Hunebelle Andre • FRN • WOMEN ARE TALKATIVE (USA)
FEMMES VICIEUSES • 1974 • Cachoux Georges • FRN • MA FEMME VOUS PLAIT, J'ADORE LA VOTRE
FEMMINA • 1917 • Genina Augusto • ITL
FEMMINA see **AMANTE DI PARIDE, L'** • 1955
FEMMINA INCATENATA • 1949 • Martin G. D. • ITL
FEMMINA (ITL) see **GRANDE SAUTERELLE, LA** • 1967
FEMMINA SENZA CUORE • 1953 • Borraccetti Renato • ITL
FEMMINE DI LUSSO • 1960 • Bianchi Giorgio • ITL • LOVE, THE ITALIAN WAY (USA) ○ LOVE ITALIAN STYLE
FEMMINE INSAZIABILI see **INSAZIABILI, GLI** • 1969
FEMMINE TRE VOLTE • 1957 • Steno • ITL, SPN • THREE TIMES A LADY ○ FEMALE THREE TIMES
FENCE, THE see **GARDUL** • 1969
FENCE OF WOMEN, A see **ONNA NO SAKA** • 1960
FENCE ON BAR Z RANCH, THE • 1910 • *Essanay* • USA
FENCE RIDERS • 1950 • Fox Wallace • USA
FENCING AT THE JOINVILLE SCHOOL see **ASSAUT D'ESCRIME (ECOLE DE JOINVILLE)** • 1898
FENCING CONTEST FROM "THE THREE MUSKETEERS" • 1898 • *Mutoscope & Biograph Co.* • UKN
FENCING MASTER • 1907 • *Bitzer Billy (Ph)* • USA
FENCING MASTER see **TATESHI DAMPEI** • 1950
FENCING MASTER, THE • 1915 • Walsh Raoul • USA
FENESTA CA LUCIVE see **AMANTI DI RAVELLO, GLI** • 1951
FENETRE OUVERTE, LA see **OPEN WINDOW, THE** • 1952
FENETRE SUR CA • 1986 • Ferrand Carlos • CND
FENG CHIEH • 1980 • Hsu An-Hua • HKG • SECRET, THE
FENG HUA HSUEH YUEH • 1977 • Li Han-Hsiang • HKG • MOODS OF LOVE
FENG-KUEI-LAI-TE JEN • 1983 • Hou Hsiao-Hsien • TWN • BOYS FROM FENGKUEI, THE ○ ALL THE YOUTHFUL DAYS
FENG-LIU TUAN-CHIEN HSIAO-HSIAO TAO • 1979 • Sun Chung • HKG • DEADLY BREAKING SWORD, THE
FENGBAO • 1959 • Jin Shan • CHN • STORM
FENGKUANGDE DAIJIA • 1988 • Zhou Xiaowen • CHN • OBSESSION
FENGRIFFEN see **AND NOW THE SCREAMING STARTS!** • 1973
FENGSLENDE DAGER FOR CHRISTINA BERG • 1988 • Kolsto Egil • NRW
FENLANDS see **FARM IN THE FENS, A** • 1945
FENOMENA • 1990 • Osman Aziz M. • MLY • PHENOMENON
FENOMENAL AND THE TREASURE OF TUT-ANKH-AMEN see **FENOMENAL E IL TESORO DI TUTANKAMEN** • 1968
FENOMENAL E IL TESORO DI TUTANKAMEN • 1968 • Deodato Ruggero • ITL • FENOMENAL AND THE TREASURE OF TUT-ANKH-AMEN ○ PHENOMENAL AND THE TREASURE OF TUTANKAMEN
FENOMENO, EL • 1956 • Elorrieta Jose Maria • SPN
FENOMENOS DEL FUTBOL, LOS • 1962 • Munoz Manuel • MXC
FENSAME ULUG • 1979 • SAF
FENTON see **GELDTEUFEL, DER** • 1923
FENTON OF THE 42D • 1909 • *Edison* • USA
FENYES SZELEK • 1968 • Jancso Miklos • HNG • CONFRONTATION, THE (UKN) ○ SPARKLING WINDS
FER A CHEVAL, LE • 1915 • Feuillade Louis • FRN
FER-DE-LANCE • 1974 • Mayberry Russ • TVM • USA • DEATH DIVE
FER ET L'ACIER, LE • 1958 • Shawqi Khalil • SHT • EGY
FERAT VAMPIRE see **UPIR Z FERATU** • 1982
FERDA THE ANT • 1944 • Tyrlova Hermina • ANS • CZC
FERDIE, BE BRAVE! • 1912 • *Imp* • USA

FERDIE'S FAMILY FEUD • 1912 • *Cumpson John* • USA
FERDIE'S VACATION • 1910 • *Lubin* • USA
FERDINAND AND THE CENTIPEDE see **FERDINAND Y EL CIEMPIES** • 1970
FERDINAND LASSALLE • 1918 • Meinert Rudolf • FRG
FERDINAND LE NOCEUR • 1935 • Sti Rene • FRN
FERDINAND THE BULL • 1938 • Rickard Dick • ANS • USA
FERDINAND Y EL CIEMPIES • 1970 • Pey Marti • ANS • SPN • FERDINAND AND THE CENTIPEDE
FERDINANDO I RE DI NAPOLI • 1959 • Franciolini Gianni • ITL
FERDY FINK'S FLIRTATION • 1915 • *Chamberlain Riley* • USA
FERDYDURKE • 1990 • Skolimowski Jerzy • PLN
FERESTADEH see **MISSION, THE** • 1984
FERFIARCKEP • 1964 • Gyongyossy Imre • SHT • HNG • PORTRAIT OF A MAN
FERGANA CANAL, THE • 1939 • Eisenstein Sergei • DCS • USS
FERIA • 1962 • Luna Ricardo • ARG • FAIR
FERIA DE JALISCO, LA • 1947 • Urueta Chano • MXC
FERIA DE LA CANCION, LA see **SU PRIMER AMOR** • 1959
FERIA DE LAS FLORES, LA • 1942 • Benavides Jose Jr. • MXC
FERIA DE SAN MARCOS, LA • 1957 • Martinez Solares Gilberto • MXC
FERIA DE SAN SEBASTIAN • 1974 • de Pedro Manuel • DCS • VNZ
FERIA DE SEVILLA • 1960 • Mariscal Ana, Carreras Enrique • SPN
FERIAS A BEIRA-MAR • 1942 • Duarte Arthur • SHT • PRT
FERIAS DE MEXICO • 1958 • Portillo Rafael • MXC
FERIAS EM LOURENCO MARQUES • 1961 • Spiguel Miguel • SHT • PRT
FERIAS NO SUL • 1967 • de Barros Reynaldo Paes • BRZ • HOLIDAYS IN THE SOUTH
FERIEBORN • 1952 • Roos Jorgen • DOC • DNM
FERIEN • 1961 • Houwer Rob • FRG
FERIEN AUF IMMENHOF • 1957 • Leitner Hermann • FRG
FERIEN IN TIROL see **ZARTLICHES GEHEIMNIS** • 1956
FERIEN MIT PIROSCHKA • 1965 • Gottlieb Franz J. • FRG, AUS, HNG
FERIEN MIT SYLVESTER • 1990 • Neuberger Bernd • AUS • VACATION WITH SYLVESTER
FERIEN VOM ICH • 1934 • Deppe Hans • FRG
FERIEN VOM ICH • 1952 • Deppe Hans • FRG
FERIEN VOM ICH • 1963 • Grimm Hans • FRG
FERIENBETT MIT 100PS, EIN • 1965 • Becker Wolfgang • FRG
FERIENKIND, DAS • 1943 • Leiter Karl • FRG
FERITA, LA • 1921 • Roberti Roberto Leone • ITL
FERKO THE POUCH • 1968 • Tyrlova Hermina • ANM • CZC
FERMATE IL MONDO, VOGLIO SCENDERE • 1970 • Cobelli Giancarlo • ITL
FERMATI COPLAN see **COPLAN FX18 CASSE TOUT** • 1965
FERME DES SEPT PECHES, LA • 1948 • Devaivre Jean • FRN
FERME DU CHOQUART, LA • 1921 • Kemm Jean • FRN
FERME DU MAUDIT, LA see **FERME DU PENDU, LA** • 1945
FERME DU PENDU, LA • 1945 • Dreville Jean • FRN • FERME DU MAUDIT, LA ○ HANGED MAN'S FARM
FERMI TUTTI ARRIVO IO! • 1953 • Grieco Sergio • ITL
FERMI TUTTI: E UNA RAPINA • 1976 • Battaglia Enzo • ITL
FERMIERE A MONTFAUCON • 1968 • Rohmer Eric • SHT • FRN
FERMO CON LE MANI! • 1937 • Zambuto Gero • ITL
FERMONT P.Q. • 1980 • Fortier Monique, Perron Clement • DOC • CND
FERN, THE RED DEER • 1976 • Darnley-Smith Jan • UKN
FERNAND • 1980 • Feret Rene • FRN
FERNAND CLOCHARD • 1957 • Chevalier Pierre • FRN
FERNAND COW-BOY • 1956 • Lefranc Guy • FRN
FERNAND JOLICOEUR • 1968 • Dansereau Fernand • DCS • CND
FERNANDA • 1917 • Serena Gustavo • ITL
FERNANDEL JOINS THE ARMY see **UNIFORMES ET GRANDES MANOEUVRES** • 1950
FERNANDEL, THE DRESSMAKER (USA) see **COUTURIER DE CES DAMES, LE** • 1956
FERNANDEZ DE PERALVILLO, LOS • 1953 • Galindo Alejandro • MXC • FERNANDEZES OF PERALVILLO, THE
FERNANDEZES OF PERALVILLO, THE see **FERNANDEZ DE PERALVILLO, LOS** • 1953
FERNANDO ARMENDARIZ • 1979 • Cameron Ken • DOC • ASL
FERNANDO NAMORA • 1969 • Guimaraes Manuel • SHT • PRT
FERNES JAMAICA • 1969 • Moland • FRG • DISTANT JAMAICA
FEROCE SALADINO, IL • 1937 • Bonnard Mario • ITL
FEROCIOUS see **FEROZ** • 1983
FEROCIOUS ONE, THE see **LYUTY** • 1974
FEROCIOUS PAL, THE • 1934 • Bennet Spencer Gordon • USA • HIS FEROCIOUS PAL (UKN)
FEROZ • 1983 • Gutierrez Aragon Manuel • SPN • FEROCIOUS ○ WILD
FERRAGOSTO IN BIKINI • 1961 • Girolami Marino • ITL
FERRAGUS • 1923 • Ravel Gaston • FRN
FERRARESE, LA • 1977 • Mauri Roberto • ITL
FERRENTE • 1973 • *Kennedy Arthur* • ITL • KISS MY HAND
FERREOL • 1920 • Hofer Franz • FRG
FERRET, THE • 1915 • Julian Rupert? • USA
FERRETS, THE • 1913 • Eagle Oscar • USA
FERRETS DE LA REINE, LES • 1932 • Diamant-Berger Henri • FRN
FERRIS BUELLER'S DAY OFF • 1986 • Hughes John • USA
FERROVIERE, IL • 1956 • Germi Pietro • ITL • RAILROAD MAN, THE (USA) ○ MAN OF IRON (UKN)
FERRUM • Hoglund Gunnar • DCS • SWD
FERRY see **KHEYA** • 1967
FERRY, THE see **PROM** • 1970
FERRY CROSS THE MERSEY • 1964 • Summers Jeremy • UKN
FERRY PILOT • 1941 • Jackson Pat • DCS • UKN
FERRY TO HONG KONG • 1959 • Gilbert Lewis* • UKN
FERRYBOAT WOMAN MARIA see **FAHRMANN MARIA** • 1936
FERRYMAN FROM ACCRA, THE • 1960 • Jaworski Tadeusz • DOC • PLN
FERRYMAN MARIA (USA) see **FAHRMANN MARIA** • 1936
FERRYMAN'S SWEETHEART, THE • 1909 • *Gaumont* • USA
FERRYWOMAN MARIA see **FAHRMANN MARIA** • 1936
FERTILE LAND see **SARU BIMA** • 1967
FERTILITY GOD, THE see **RISHYA SHRUNGA** • 1976
FERTILITY RITES FOR THE 21ST CENTURY • 1977 • Bonniere Rene • DOC • CND
FERTILIZZANTI COMPLESSI • 1956 • Olmi Ermanno (Spv) • DOC • ITL
FERTILIZZANTI PRODUTTI DALLA SOCIETA DEL GRUPPA EDISON • 1959 • Olmi Ermanno (Spv) • DOC • ITL
FESCHE ERZHERZOG, DER • 1926 • Land Robert • FRG • RIGHT TO LOVE, THE
FESCHE HUSAR, DER • 1928 • von Bolvary Geza • FRG
FESCHE RUDI, DER • 1915 • Schmelter Franz • FRG
FESCHE TIROLER, DER • 1910 • *Krahly Hanns* • FRG
FESSEE, LA • 1937 • Caron Pierre • FRN
FESSEE, LA • Bernard-Aubert Claude • FRN
FESSELN • 1918 • Moest Hubert • FRG
FESSES EN FEU • 1978 • Davy Jean-Sebastien • FRN
FEST AUF HADERSLEVHUUS • 1922 • Weigert August • FRG
FEST DER ROSELLA, DAS • 1919 • Zelnik Friedrich? • FRG
FEST DER SCHONHEIT • 1938 • Riefenstahl Leni • FRG • OLYMPIA-FILM II
FEST DER VOLKER • 1938 • Riefenstahl Leni • FRG • OLYMPIA-FILM I
FEST DES SCHWARZEN TULPE, DAS • 1920 • Droop Marie Luise • FRG
FESTA • 1988 • Giorgetti Ugo • BRZ • PARTY
FESTA, A • 1975 • Campos Antonio • PRT
FESTA DA FLOR • 1915 • de Albuquerque Ernesto • SHT • PRT
FESTA DI ISIDORA see **GOYA** • 1950
FESTA DI LAUREA • 1985 • Avati Pupi • ITL • GRADUATION PARTY
FESTA DI MAGGIO (ITL) see **PREMIER MAI** • 1958
FESTA VINDIMARIA • 1938 • Coelho Jose Adolfo • SHT • PRT
FESTAS DA CURIA • 1926 • de Barros Jose Leitao, Fonseca Joao De Sousa • SHT • PRT
FESTIN DE BALTHAZAR, LE • 1910 • Feuillade Louis • FRN
FESTIN DE BUITRES • 1946 • Peon Ramon • MXC
FESTIN DE LA LOBA, EL • 1972 • *Del Villar* • MXC
FESTIN DE SATANAS, EL • Papier Ralph • ARG • FEAST OF SATAN, THE
FESTIN DES MORTS, LE • 1964 • Dansereau Fernand • CND
FESTIVAL • 1952 • York Derek • SHT • UKN
FESTIVAL • 1960 • Ardavin Cesar • SPN
FESTIVAL • 1967 • Lerner Murray • USA • NEWPORT FESTIVAL
FESTIVAL • 1970 • Chapman Christopher • DOC • CND
FESTIVAL ACROSS THE SEA see **UMI O WATARU SAIREI** • 1941
FESTIVAL AT ST. JURGEN see **PRAZDNIK SVYATOVO IORGENE** • 1930
FESTIVAL COURTELINE • 1933 • Hugon Andre • FRN
FESTIVAL DANS LE DESERT • 1969 • Reichenbach Francois • SHT • FRN
FESTIVAL DE BALLET see **BALLET FESTIVAL** • 1949
FESTIVAL DEL NINO • 1973 • de Pedro Manuel • DOC • VNZ • CHILDREN'S FESTIVAL
FESTIVAL DU BLE D'INDE • 1978 • Dussault Louis • CND
FESTIVAL EN BENIDORM • 1960 • Salvia Rafael J. • SPN
FESTIVAL EN EL PASO • 1921 • Elias Francisco • SHT • SPN
FESTIVAL GAME, THE • 1969 • Klinger Tony, Lytton Mike • DOC • UKN
FESTIVAL GIRLS, THE • 1962 • Jason Leigh • USA
FESTIVAL IN ADELAIDE • 1962 • Otton Malcolm, Mason Richard, Townsend Loch, Dunlop Ian • ASL
FESTIVAL IN BRITAIN • 1951 • Leacock Philip • DOC • UKN
FESTIVAL IN MOSCOW • 1958 • Slutsky Mikhail • USS
FESTIVAL IN PUERTO RICO • 1961 • Koenig Wolf, Kroitor Roman • CND
FESTIVAL OF FIRE, THE see **HOLI** • 1984
FESTIVAL OF FOOLS • 1973 • McMillan Ian, Seeger Peggy • UKN
FESTIVAL OF JAZZ • 1961 • Gomelsky Giorgio • SHT • UKN
FESTIVAL OF LOVE • 1970 • Verstappen Wim • NTH
FESTIVAL OF NYAN-NYAN-MYAN see **NYAN-NYAN-MYAN-HOI** • 1940
FESTIVAL OF RUSSIAN SONG AND DANCES see **PESNI RODNOY STORONY** • 1953
FESTIVAL PAN AFRICAN D'ALGER • 1970 • Klein William • DOC • FRN, ALG • FESTIVAL PANAFRICAN ○ PAN-AFRICAN FESTIVAL
FESTIVAL PANAFRICAN see **FESTIVAL PAN AFRICAN D'ALGER** • 1970
FESTIVAL UNITA 72 • 1972 • Scola Ettore • ITL
FESTIVALS see **UTSAV** • 1983
FESTIVALS OF THE SEA see **MEREN JUHLAT** • 1963
FESTIVE DAY IN SARAJEVO, A see **PRAZNIK U SARAJEVU** • 1990
FESTIVITETSSALONGEN • 1965 • Ericson Stig Ossian • SWD • BALLROOM, THE
FESTOK VAROSA -SZENTENDRE, A • 1964 • Meszaros Marta • SHT • HNG • SZENTENDRE -TOWN OF PAINTERS ○ TOWN OF PAINTERS, THE
FETARD, LE • Cohl Emile • ANS • FRN • REVELLER, THE
FETE A HENRIETTE, LA • 1953 • Duvivier Julien • FRN • HOLIDAY FOR HENRIETTA (USA) ○ HENRIETTE'S HOLIDAY ○ HENRIETTE
FETE A JULES, LA see **HOME SWEET HOME** • 1973
FETE AU PERE MATHIEU, LA • 1904 • Melies Georges • FRN • UNCLE RUBE'S BIRTHDAY (USA)
FETE AUJOURD'HUI, LA FETE DEMAIN, LA • 1972 • Koleva Maria • DOC • FRN
FETE CHEZ LES HAMBA • 1955 • de Heusch Luc • BLG
FETE DES MORTS, LA • 1970 • Reichenbach Francois • SHT • FRN
FETE DES NEIGES see **SNOW FIESTA** • 1950
FETE DES PERES, LA • 1990 • *Lhermitte Thierry* • FRN
FETE DES PERES, LA see **MORDS PAS -ON T'AIME** • 1976
FETE DU MAYROUN, LA see **ID AL-MAIRUN** • 1967
FETE DU SONNEUR, LA see **GENIE DES CLOCHES, LES** • 1908
FETE ESPAGNOL, LA • 1919 • Dulac Germaine • FRN
FETE ESPAGNOLE, LA • 1961 • Vierne Jean-Jacques • FRN • NO TIME FOR ECSTASY (USA)
FETE IN THE BOTANICAL GARDENS, THE see **SLAVNOST V BOTANICKEJ ZAHRADE** • 1969
FETE SAUVAGE, LA • 1975 • Rossif Frederic • DOC • FRN
FETES DE BELGIQUES • 1969-72 • Storck Henri • DOC • BLG
FETES DE FRANCE • 1940 • Leenhardt Roger, Zuber Rene • DCS • FRN
FETES DE LA JEUNESSE, LES see **AFRAH' ASH-SHABAB** • 1964
FETES DU CENTENAIRE, LES • 1930 • Storck Henri • DOC • BLG
FETES DU LAC-SAINT-JEAN, LES • 1947 • Imbault Thomas-Louis, Larouche Leonidas • DOC • CND
FETES GALANTES, LES • 1965 • Clair Rene, Vitandis Gheorghe • FRN, RMN • SERBARILOR GALANTE (RMN)
FETEWA, EL see **FATAWA, EL** • 1956
FETICHE • 1933 • Starevitch Ladislas • SHT • FRN • CHARM, THE
FETISHES OF MONIQUE • Davian Joe • USA
FETITA MINCINOASA • 1953 • Popescu-Gopo Ion • RMN • LITTLE LIAR
FETTERED • 1919 • Bocchi Arrigo • UKN
FETTERED WOMAN, THE • 1917 • Terriss Tom • USA
FETTERS • 1987 • Beshara Khairy • EGY • COLLAR AND THE BRACELET, THE
FETTERS see **POUTA** • 1961
FETTERS OF FEAR • 1915 • Seldon-Truss Leslie • UKN
FEU! • 1927 • de Baroncelli Jacques • FRN
FEU! • 1937 • de Baroncelli Jacques • FRN • FEU! MARINE D'ABORD!
FEU • 1970 • Jaeger Claude • SHT • FRN
FEU A VOLONTE • 1965 • Ophuls Marcel • FRN, ITL • FAITES VOS JEUX, MESDAMES ○ FIRE AT WILL
FEU AU SEXE, LE • 1977 • Desvilles Jean • FRN
FEU AU VENTRE, LE • 1975 • Nauroy Alain C. • FRN
FEU AUX LEVRES, LE • 1972 • Kalfon Pierre • FRN
FEU AUX POUDRES, LE • 1956 • Decoin Henri • FRN, ITL • X 3 OPERAZIONE DINAMITE (ITL)
FEU DANS LA PEAU, LE • 1953 • Blistene Marcel • FRN, ITL • FIRE UNDER HER SKIN (USA) ○ FIRE IN THE SKIN
FEU D'ARTIFICE IMPROVISE, UN • 1905 • Melies Georges • FRN • UNEXPECTED FIREWORKS (USA)
FEU D'ARTIFICE INATTENDU • 1905 • Melies Georges • FRN
FEU DE DIEU, LE • 1966 • Combret Georges • FRN, ITL • FIRE OF LOVE (UKN) ○ EVADE DE L'ENFER, L'
FEU DE PAILLE, LE • 1939 • Benoit-Levy Jean • FRN • FIRE IN THE STRAW (USA) ○ ENFANT PRODIGE, L'
FEU DES PASSIONS, LE • 1955 • Sassy Jean-Paul • SHT • FRN
FEU FOLLET, LE • 1963 • Malle Louis • FRN, ITL • TIME TO LIVE AND A TIME TO DIE, A (UKN) ○ FIRE WITHIN, THE (USA) ○ FOX FIRE ○ WILL O' THE WISP
FEU L'OBJECTIVITE • 1979 • Godbout Jacques • CND
FEU! MARINE D'ABORD! see **FEU!** • 1937
FEU MATTHIAS PASCAL • 1925 • L'Herbier Marcel • FRN • LATE MATTHEW PASCAL, THE ○ LIVING DEAD MAN, THE (USA)
FEU NICOLAS • 1943 • Houssin Jacques • FRN
FEU? PAS POUR LES HOMMES, LE see **HOT STUFF** • 1971
FEU SACRE • 1941 • Cloche Maurice • FRN
FEU SACRE, LE • 1934 • Forgency Vladimir • FRN
FEU SUR LE CANDIDAT • 1990 • Delarive Agnes • FRN, ITL
FEU TOUPINEL • 1933 • Capellani Roger • FRN
FEUD, THE • 1910 • *Bison* • USA
FEUD, THE • 1910 • Olcott Sidney • *Kalem* • USA
FEUD, THE • 1911 • *Lubin* • USA
FEUD, THE • 1914 • *Madison Cleo* • USA
FEUD, THE • 1915 • Butler Fred J. • USA
FEUD, THE • 1919 • Le Saint Edward J. • USA
FEUD, THE • 1936 • *Terry Paul/ Moser Frank (P)* • ANS • USA
FEUD, THE • 1990 • D'Elia Bill • USA
FEUD AND THE TURKEY, THE • 1908 • Griffith D. W. • USA
FEUD AT BEAVER CREEK, THE • 1914 • *Kb* • USA
FEUD GIRL, THE • 1916 • Thompson Frederick A. • USA
FEUD IN THE KENTUCKY HILLS, A • 1912 • Griffith D. W. • USA
FEUD MAKER, THE • 1938 • Newfield Sam • USA
FEUD OF THE RANGE • 1939 • Webb Harry S. • USA
FEUD OF THE TRAIL, THE • 1937 • Hill Robert F. • USA
FEUD OF THE WEST • 1936 • Fraser Harry L. • USA • VENGEANCE OF GREGORY WALTERS, THE (UKN)
FEUD THERE WAS, A • 1938 • Avery Tex • ANS • USA
FEUD WITH A DUDE, A • 1968 • Lovy Alex • ANS • USA
FEUD WOMAN, THE • 1926 • Williamson Robin E. • USA
FEUDAL DEBT, THE • 1912 • Ricketts Thomas • USA
FEUDAL LORD, THE see **DEREBEYI** • 1968
FEUDIN' FIGHTIN' 'N' FUSSIN' • 1968 • Smith Paul J. • ANS • USA
FEUDIN' FOOLS • 1952 • Beaudine William • USA
FEUDIN' FUSSIN' AND A-FIGHTIN' • 1948 • Sherman George • USA
FEUDIN' RHYTHM • 1949 • Bernds Edward • USA • ACE LUCKY (UKN)
FEUDING HILLBILLIES, THE • 1948 • Rasinski Connie • ANS • USA
FEUDISTS, THE • 1913 • North Wilfred • USA
FEUER, DAS • 1914 • Gad Urban • FRG • FIRE, THE
FEUER, EIS UND DYNAMIT • 1990 • Bogner Willy • FRG • FIRE, ICE AND DYNAMITE
FEUER FREI AUF FRANKIE • 1967 • de la Loma Jose Antonio • FRG, SPN, ITL • OPEN FIRE ON FRANKIE
FEUERLOSCHER E.A. WINTERSTEIN • 1968 • Kluge Alexander • SHT • FRG • FIREMAN E.A. WINTERSTEIN
FEUERROTE BARONESSE, DIE • 1959 • Jugert Rudolf • FRG • SCARLET BARONESS, THE (USA)
FEUERSCHIFF, DAS • 1922 • Lowenbein Richard • FRG
FEUERSCHIFF, DAS • 1963 • Vajda Ladislao • FRG • LIGHTSHIP, THE
FEUERTANZERIN, DIE • 1925 • Dinesen Robert • FRG
FEUERTAUFE • 1940 • Pabst G. W. • DOC • FRG
FEUERTEUFEL, DER • 1940 • Trenker Luis • FRG • FIREDEVIL, THE
FEUERWERK • 1959 • Hoffmann Kurt • FRG • OH! MY PAPA
FEUERZANGENBOWLE, DIE • 1944 • Weiss Helmut • FRG
FEUERZANGENBOWLE, DIE • 1970 • Kautner Helmut • FRG

FEUERZEICHEN see **LEBENSZEICHEN** • 1967
FEUERZEUG, DAS • 1959 • Hartmann Siegfried • GDR • TINDER BOX, THE (USA)
FEUILLE QUI BRISE LES REINS, LA see **BACK-BREAKING LEAF, THE** • 1959
FEUX DE JOIE • 1938 • Houssin Jacques • FRN
FEUX DE LA CHANDELEUR, LES • 1972 • Korber Serge • FRN, ITL • DIVORZIATA, LA (ITL)
FEUX DE LA MER, LES • 1948 • Epstein Jean • FRN
FEUX ET COULEURS • 1959 • Regnier Michel • DCS • CND • CERAMIQUE
FEUX QUI MEURENT, LES • 1943 • Tedesco Jean • SHT • FRN
FEVE ENCHANTEE, LA • Blache Alice • FRN • ENCHANTED BEAN, THE
FEVER • 1988 • Lahiff Craig • ASL
FEVER see **LAZ** • 1957
FEVER see **HORECKA** • 1958
FEVER see **FIEBRE** • 1977
FEVER see **GORACZKA** • 1980
FEVER, THE see **FEVER PITCH** • 1985
FEVER HEAT • 1968 • Doughton Russell S. Jr. • USA
FEVER HEAT (USA) see **BOB LE FLAMBEUR** • 1955
FEVER IN THE BLOOD, A • 1961 • Sherman Vincent • USA
FEVER MOUNTS AT EL PAO, THE see **FIEVRE MONTE A EL PAO, LA** • 1959
FEVER ON THE ROADS see **PIRETOS STIN ASFALTO** • 1967
FEVER PITCH • 1985 • Brooks Richard • USA • FEVER, THE
FEVERHOUSE, THE • 1984 • Walmsley Howard • UKN
FEVERISH YEARS, THE see **TOPLE GODINE** • 1966
FEVRIER • 1967 • Longpre Bernard • DCS • CND • EN FEVRIER
FEW BULLETS MORE, A (USA) see **...E DIVENNE IL PIU SPIETATO BANDITO DEL SUD** • 1967
FEW DAYS AT WEASEL CREEK, A • 1981 • Lowry Dick • TVM • USA
FEW DAYS IN THE LIFE OF I.I. OBLOMOV, A see **NESKOLKO DNEI IZ ZHIZNI I.I. OBLOMOV** • 1980
FEW DOLLARS FOR DJANGO, A (UKN) see **POCHI DOLLARI PER DJANGO** • 1966
FEW DOLLARS FOR GYPSY • 1967 • *Steffan Anthony* • ITL
FEW MORE DAYS, A see **A QUELQUES JOURS PRES** • 1968
FEW OUNCES A DAY, A • 1941 • Rotha Paul • DOC • UKN
FEW STEPS TO THE FRONTIER, A see **PAR LEPES A HATAR** • 1959
FEW WORDS OF INTRODUCTION, A see **UVODNI SLOVO PRONESE** • 1964
FFOLKES (USA) see **NORTH SEA HIJACK** • 1980
FI BAYTINA RAGOL see **FI BAYTINA RAJUL** • 1960
FI BAYTINA RAJUL • 1960 • Barakat Henry • EGY • IL Y A UN HOMME CHEZ NOUS ○ FI BAYTINA RAGOL ○ YOU HAVE A MAN IN THE HOUSE
FIA JANNSON FRAN SODER • 1944 • Falck Ragnar • SWD
FIACA, LA • 1969 • Ayala Fernando • ARG
FIACRE 13 • 1947 • Andre Raoul, Hugon Andre • FRN
FIACRE N.13 • 1916 • Capozzi Alberto (c/d) • ITL
FIACRE N.13, IL • 1947 • Mattoli Mario • ITL
FIAKER NR.13 • 1926 • Curtiz Michael • FRG • EINSPANNER NO.13
FIAKERLIED • 1936 • Emo E. W. • FRG
FIAKERMILLI, DIE • 1953 • Rabenalt Arthur M. • AUS
FIAMMA CHE NON SI SPEGNE, LA • 1949 • Cottafavi Vittorio • ITL
FIAMMATA, LA • 1924 • Gallone Carmine • ITL
FIAMMATA, LA • 1952 • Blasetti Alessandro • ITL • PRIDE, LOVE AND SUSPICION
FIAMME IN ORIENTE see **ODESSA IN FIAMME** • 1942
FIAMME SU ODESSA see **ODESSA IN FIAMME** • 1942
FIAMME SUL MARE • 1948 • Waszynski Michael • ITL
FIAMME SULLA LAGUNA • 1951 • Scotese Giuseppe Maria • ITL • VENEZIA, RIO DELL'ANGELO
FIANCAILLES D'AGENOR, LES • 1916 • Feuillade Louis • FRN
FIANCAILLES DE FLAMBEAU, LES • 1916 • Cohl Emile (c/d) • ANS • FRN
FIANCE DE MA MERE, LE see **KHATIB MAMA** • 1971
FIANCE IN SIGHT see **NOVIO A LA VISTA** • 1953
FIANCEE, THE • Klimov Elem • USS • SUITOR, THE
FIANCEE, THE see **VERLOBTE, DIE** • 1979
FIANCEE AND THE FAIRY, THE • 1913 • Carleton Lloyd B. • USA
FIANCEE DE L'AVIATEUR, LA • 1914 • Burguet Charles • FRN
FIANCEE DES TENEBRES, LA • 1944 • de Poligny Serge • FRN • FIANCEE OF THE NIGHT
FIANCEE DU DIABLE, LA • 1916 • Perret Leonce • FRN
FIANCEE DU GLADIATEUR, LA • 1908 • Jasset Victorin • FRN
FIANCEE DU NIL, LA see **AROUSS EL NIL** • 1963
FIANCEE DU PIRATE, LA • 1969 • Kaplan Nelly • FRN • VERY CURIOUS GIRL, A (USA) ○ DIRTY MARY (UKN) ○ PIRATE'S FIANCEE
FIANCEE DU TOREADOR, LA • 1913 • Durand Jean • FRN
FIANCEE ENSORCELEE, LA • 1903 • Blache Alice • FRN • BEWITCHED FIANCEE, THE
FIANCEE FOR HIRE see **FASTMO UTHYRES** • 1951
FIANCEE FROM THE OTHER WORLD see **ZHENIKH S TOGO SVETA** • 1958
FIANCEE OF THE NIGHT see **FIANCEE DES TENEBRES, LA** • 1944
FIANCEE QUI VENAIT DU FROID, LA • 1983 • Nemes Charles • FRN
FIANCEES EN LOCATION see **JEUX DE FEMMES** • 1945
FIANCES, THE (USA) see **FIDANZATI, I** • 1963
FIANCES DE 1914, LES • 1914 • Feuillade Louis • FRN
FIANCES DE SEVILLE, LES • 1914 • Feuillade Louis • FRN
FIASCO IN MILAN see **AUDACE COLPI DEI SOLITI IGNOTI** • 1959
FIAT LUX • 1923 • Thiele Wilhelm • AUS, FRG • ES WARD LICHT
"FIAT VOLUNTAS DEI" • 1935 • Palermi Amleto • ITL
FIBBER AND THE GIRL, THE • 1915 • *Imp* • USA
FIBBERS, THE • 1917 • Wright Fred E. • USA
FIBRA DEL DOLORE, LA • 1919 • Negroni Baldassare • ITL
FIBRE E CIVILTA • 1957 • Olmi Ermanno (Spv) • DOC • ITL
FIBRES DE PIERRE see **MAGIC MINERAL** • 1959
FICHERAS, LAS • 1976 • *Cinema Calderon* • MXC • B GIRLS, THE
FICHU METIER, UN • 1938 • Ducis Pierre-Jean • FRN
FICKLE ALL ROUND • 1916 • *Miller Rube* • SHT • USA
FICKLE BLACKSMITH, THE • 1918 • *Sedgwick Eileen* • SHT • USA
FICKLE BRIDGET • 1911 • *Beggs Lee* • USA
FICKLE ELSIE • 1914 • *Mcleod Elsie* • USA
FICKLE FANCY • 1920 • Kenton Erle C. • SHT • USA
FICKLE FATTY'S FALL • 1915 • Arbuckle Roscoe • USA
FICKLE FIDDLER'S FINISH, THE • 1916 • Ellis Robert • SHT • USA
FICKLE FINGER OF FATE, THE • 1967 • Rush Richard • USA, SPN • DEDO DEL DESTINO, EL (SPN)
FICKLE FLO'S FLIRTATION • 1915 • Collins Edwin J.? • UKN
FICKLE FORTUNE'S FAVOR • 1913 • *Gore Rose* • USA
FICKLE FREAK, THE • 1913 • *Roland Ruth* • USA
FICKLE GIRL, A • 1910 • Fitzhamon Lewin • UKN
FICKLE HUSBAND AND THE BOY, THE • 1908 • Fitzhamon Lewin • UKN
FICKLE MADGE • 1916 • *Vogue* • USA
FICKLE MARY JANE • 1914 • *Royal* • USA
FICKLE SOLDIER, THE • 1912 • *Pathe* • USA
FICKLE SPANIARD, THE • 1912 • Sennett Mack, Henderson Dell • USA
FICKLE TRAMP, THE • 1913 • *Majestic* • USA
FICKLE WOMAN • 1920 • Butler Fred J. • USA
FICKLENESS GETS ON THE TRAIN see **UWAKI WA KISHA NI NOTTE** • 1931
FICKLENESS OF SWEEDIE, THE • 1914 • *Beery Wallace* • USA
FICO D'INDIA • 1980 • Steno • ITL • PRICKLY PEARS
FICTION • 1977 • Rentzis Thanasis
FICTION D'AMOUR • 1986 • Dussault Louis • CND
FICTION-MAKERS, THE • 1967 • Baker Roy Ward • UKN
FICTION NUCLEAIRE, LA • 1978 • Chabot Jean • CND
FIDALGOS DA CASA MOURISCA, OS • 1938 • Duarte Arthur • PRT
FIDANZAMENTO, IL • 1975 • Grimaldi Gianni • ITL
FIDANZATI DELLA MORTE, I • 1957 • Marcellini Romolo • ITL
FIDANZATI, I • 1963 • Olmi Ermanno • ITL • ENGAGEMENT, THE (UKN) ○ FIANCES, THE (USA)
FIDANZATO DI MIA MOGLIE, IL • 1943 • Bragaglia Carlo Ludovico • ITL
FIDARSI E BENE, SPARARE E MEGLIO • 1968 • Civirani Osvaldo • ITL • TRUSTING IS GOOD, SHOOTING IS BETTER
FIDAYINES, LES • 1969 • Bedjaoui Ahmed • ALG
FIDAYUN, AL- • 1970 • Haddad Moussa • ALG
FIDDLE DE DEE • 1947 • McLaren Norman • ANS • CND
FIDDLE FADDLE • 1960 • Kneitel Seymour • ANS • USA
FIDDLE-FADDLE see **TRZY PO TRZY** • 1965
FIDDLE FANATICS, THE • 1931 • *First National* • SHT • UKN
FIDDLER ON THE ROOF • 1971 • Jewison Norman • USA
FIDDLER PETE • 1913 • *Rex* • USA
FIDDLERS, THE • 1909 • *Pathe* • FRN
FIDDLERS, THE • 1915 • *Novelty* • USA
FIDDLERS GROVE • Hodgson Dana • USA
FIDDLERS OF JAMES BAY • 1979 • Rodgers Bob • MTV • CND
FIDDLERS THREE • 1944 • Watt Harry • UKN
FIDDLERS THREE • 1948 • White Jules • SHT • USA
FIDDLE'S REQUIEM, THE • 1911 • Olcott Sidney • USA
FIDDLESTICKS • 1927 • Edwards Harry J. • SHT • USA
FIDDLESTICKS • 1931 • *Iwerks Ub (P)* • ANS • USA
FIDDLIN' AROUND • 1962 • Kneitel Seymour • ANS • USA
FIDDLIN' AROUND see **JUST MICKEY** • 1930
FIDDLIN' BUCKAROO, THE • 1933 • Maynard Ken • USA
FIDDLIN' FUN • 1934 • Stallings George • ANS • USA
FIDDLING AROUND • 1938 • Lamont Charles • SHT • USA
FIDDLING FOOL, THE • 1923 • La Cava Gregory • SHT • USA
FIDEL • 1970 • Landau Saul • DOC • USA
FIDELE BAUER, DER • 1927 • Seitz Franz • FRG
FIDELE BAUER, DER • 1951 • Marischka Georg • AUS
FIDELE HERRENPARTIE, DIE • 1929 • Walther-Fein Rudolf • FRG
FIDELE TANKSTELLE, DIE • 1950 • Dorfler Ferdinand • FRG
FIDELEN DETEKTIVE, DIE • 1957 • Kugelstadt Hermann • FRG
FIDELES GEFANGNIS, EIN • 1917 • Lubitsch Ernst • FRG
FIDELIA • 1970 • O'Hara Gerry • UKN
FIDELIO • 1919 • Halm Alfred?, Sauer Fred? • FRG
FIDELIO • 1956 • Felsenstein Walter • AUS
FIDELIO • 1968 • Hess Joachim • MTV • FRG
FIDELIO see **BEETHOVEN FIDELIO** • 1977
FIDELITE ROMAINE • 1911 • Feuillade Louis • FRN
FIDELITY • 1912 • Dwan Allan • USA
FIDELITY see **VERNOST** • 1965
FIDGETT'S SUPERSTITIONS • 1914 • Kellino W. P. • UKN
FIDGETY FLY, THE • 1907 • Martin J. H.? • UKN
FIDLOVACKA • 1931 • Innemann Svatopluk • CZC • VILLAGE FESTIVAL, THE
FIDO BETA KAAPA • 1954 • Sparber I. • ANS • USA
FIDO'S DRAMATIC CAREER • 1914 • *L-Ko* • USA
FIDO'S FATE • 1916 • Griffin Frank C. • SHT • USA
FIDO'S TIN TYPE TANGLE • 1915 • Arbuckle Roscoe • USA • FATTY'S TIN TYPE TANGLE
FIEBERSONATE, DIE • 1916 • Hanus Emerich • FRG
FIEBERZEIT • 1986 • Schertenleib Christof • SWT
FIEBRE • 1972 • Bo Armando • ARG • EROTIC WOMAN, THE
FIEBRE • 1977 • Santana Juan, Anzola Alfredo J. • VNZ • FEVER
FIEBRE AMARILLA • 1981 • Torre Javier • ARG • YELLOW FEVER
FIEBRE DE JUVENTUD • 1965 • Blake Alfonso Corona • MXC, ECD
FIEBRE DEL DESEO, LA • 1964 • Mistral Jorge • MXC, PRC
FIEL INFANTERIA, LA • 1959 • Lazaga Pedro • SPN
FIELD • 1970 • Gehr Ernie • USA
FIELD, THE • 1990 • Sheridan Jim • IRL
FIELD, THE see **PRATO, IL** • 1979
FIELD AND SCREAM • 1955 • Avery Tex • ANS • USA
FIELD DAY, THE • 1963 • King Allan • CND
FIELD DAY, THE • 1972 • Weir Peter • SHT • ASL
FIELD-FLOWERS SMELL see **MIRIS POLJSKOG CVECA** • 1977
FIELD FOREMAN, THE • 1913 • *Kerrigan J. Warren* • USA
FIELD MARSHALL, THE see **FALSCHE FELDMARSCHALL, DER** • 1930
FIELD MOUSE, THE • 1941 • Harman Hugh • ANS • USA
FIELD OF DREAMS • 1989 • Robinson Phil Alden • USA • SHOELESS JOE
FIELD OF HONOR see **FIELDS OF HONOR** • 1918
FIELD OF HONOR see **FIELD OF HONOUR** • 1985
FIELD OF HONOR, THE • 1911 • *American* • USA
FIELD OF HONOR, THE • 1917 • Holubar Allen • USA
FIELD OF HONOUR • 1985 • Scheepmaker Hans • NTH • FIELD OF HONOR
FIELD OF HONOUR, THE • 1922 • Moran Percy • UKN
FIELD OF RED, THE • 1958 • Watkins Peter • UKN
FIELD OF SPACE • 1969 • Goldsmith Sidney • SHT • CND
FIELD POPPY, THE (UKN) see **GUBIJINSO** • 1935
FIELDS OF ENDLESS DAY • 1978 • Macartney-Filgate Terence • CND
FIELDS OF HONOR • 1918 • Ince Ralph • USA • FIELD OF HONOR
FIELDS OF HONOR see **SHENANDOAH** • 1965
FIELDS OF SACRIFICE • 1963 • Brittain Don • CND • CHAMPS D'HONNEUR
FIELES SIRVIENTES, LOS • 1980 • Betriu Francisco • SPN • FAITHFUL SERVANTS, THE
FIEND • 1981 • Dohler Don • USA
FIEND, THE • 1971 • Hartford-Davis Robert • UKN • BEWARE OF THE BRETHREN ○ BEWARE MY BRETHREN (USA)
FIEND OF DOPE ISLAND • 1961 • Watt Nate • USA
FIEND WHO WALKED THE WEST, THE • 1958 • Douglas Gordon • USA • HELL BENT KID, THE
FIEND WITH THE ATOMIC BRAIN, THE see **BLOOD OF GHASTLY HORROR** • 1972
FIEND WITH THE ELECTRONIC BRAIN, THE see **PSYCHO A GO-GO!** • 1965
FIEND WITH THE ELECTRONIC BRAIN, THE see **BLOOD OF GHASTLY HORROR** • 1972
FIEND WITHOUT A FACE • 1958 • Crabtree Arthur • UKN
FIENDISH GHOULS, THE see **FLESH AND THE FIENDS, THE** • 1960
FIENDISH PLOT OF DR. FU MANCHU, THE • 1980 • Haggard Piers • UKN
FIENDISH TENANT, THE • 1910 • *Gaumont* • USA
FIENDS, THE (UKN) see **DIABOLIQUES, LES** • 1954
FIENDS OF HELL, THE see **GUARDING BRITAIN'S SECRETS** • 1914
FIERA, LA • 1954 • Peon Ramon • MXC
FIERAS SIN JAULA • 1971 • Logar Juan • SPN
FIERCE CHARGER AND THE KNIGHT, THE (UKN) see **CHEVALIER DEMONTABLE ET LE GENERAL BOUM, LE** • 1901
FIERCE ONE, THE see **LYUTY** • 1974
FIERCEST HEART, THE • 1961 • Sherman George • USA
FIERECILLA • 1950 • Mendez Fernando • MXC
FIERECILLA DEL PUERTO, LA • 1962 • Crevenna Alfredo B. • MXC
FIERECILLA DOMADA, LA • 1955 • Roman Antonio • SPN
FIERRO OU L'ETE DES SECRETS • 1988 • Malancon Andre • CND, ARG • SUMMER OF THE COLT
FIERY DEEDS OF THE TERRIBLE TWO, THE • 1914 • Evans Joe • UKN
FIERY HAND, THE • 1923 • Coleby A. E. • UKN
FIERY INTRODUCTION, A • 1915 • Giblyn Charles • USA
FIERY LOVE see **FAJA LOBBI** • 1960
FIERY MILES, THE see **OGNENNYE VERSTY** • 1957
FIERY SPUR see **HOT SPUR** • 1968
FIERY SUMMER see **OHNIVE LETO** • 1939
FIERY TEARS see **NAGBABAGANG LUHA** • 1988
FIERY TRANSPORT, THE see **TRANSPORT OF FIRE** • 1929
FIESCO • 1913 • *Dieterle Wilhelm* • FRG
FIESCO see **VERSCHWORUNG ZU GENUA, DIE** • 1920
FIESTA • 1941 • Prinz Leroy • USA
FIESTA • 1947 • Thorpe Richard • USA
FIESTA BRAVA (ITL) see **TORO BRAVO** • 1956
FIESTA DE SANTA BARBARA, LA • 1935 • Lewyn Louis • SHT • USA
FIESTA DE TODOS, LA • 1979 • Renan Sergio • ARG • EVERYBODY'S CELEBRATION
FIESTA DEL DIABLO, LA • 1930 • Millar Adelqui • SPN
FIESTA EN EL CARIBE (SPN) see **BALDORIA NEI CARAIBI** • 1956
FIESTA EN EL CORAZON • 1957 • Salvador Jaime • MXC
FIESTA EN SATURNO • 1969 • Gijon Salvador • ANS • SPN • FIESTA ON SATURN
FIESTA FIASCO • 1967 • Lovy Alex • ANS • USA
FIESTA ON SATURN see **FIESTA EN SATURNO** • 1969
FIESTA SIGUE, LA • 1948 • Gomez Bascuas Enrique • SPN
FIESTA TIME • 1945 • Wickersham Bob • ANS • USA
FIESTA TIME • 1950 • Kneitel Seymour • ANS • USA
FIETSEN NAAR DE MAAN • 1962 • van der Heyden Jef • NTH • CYCLING TO THE MOON
FIEVRE • 1921 • Delluc Louis • FRN
FIEVRE DE L'OR, LA • 1911 • Leprince Rene • FRN
FIEVRE DU ZLOTY, LA • 1926 • Bieganski Victor • PLN
FIEVRE MONTE A EL PAO, LA • 1959 • Bunuel Luis • FRN, MXC • AMBICIOSOS, LOS (MXC) ○ REPUBLIC OF SIN ○ FEVER MOUNTS AT EL PAO, THE
FIEVRES • 1941 • Delannoy Jean • FRN
FIEVRES D'ETE • Reinhard Pierre B. • FRN
FIFA E ARENA • 1948 • Mattoli Mario • ITL
FIFI • 1911 • *Urban Trading Co.* • UKN
FIFI BLOWS HER TOP • 1958 • White Jules • SHT • USA
FIFI LA PLUME • 1964 • Lamorisse Albert • FRN • FIFI THE FEATHER
FIFI TAMBOUR • 1915 • Feuillade Louis • FRN
FIFI THE FEATHER see **FIFI LA PLUME** • 1964
FIFRES ET TAMBOURS D'ENTRE-SAMBRE-ET-MEUSE • 1974-75 • Storck Henri • DOC • BLG
FIFTEEN MINUTES • 1921 • Roach Hal • SHT • USA
FIFTEEN SCAFFOLDS FOR A MURDERER see **QUINDICI FORCHE PER UN ASSASSINO** • 1968
FIFTEEN SONG TRAITS see **XV SONG TRAITS** • 1965
FIFTEEN STREETS, THE • 1989 • Wheatley David • TVM • UKN
FIFTEEN STRINGS OF CASH see **SHIWU GUAN** • 1956

FIFTEEN WIVES • 1934 • Strayer Frank • USA • MAN WITH THE ELECTRIC VOICE, THE (UKN)
FIFTEEN YEARS LATER • 1914 • *Melies* • USA
FIFTH, THE see **PETI** • 1964
FIFTH ACE, THE • 1916 • Parke William • SHT • USA
FIFTH AMBUSH, THE • 1969 • Kosmac France • YGS
FIFTH AVENUE • 1916 • Fitzmaurice George • USA
FIFTH AVENUE • 1926 • Vignola Robert G. • USA • OCTOPUS, THE
FIFTH AVENUE GIRL • 1939 • La Cava Gregory • USA
FIFTH AVENUE MODELS • 1925 • Gade Svend • USA
FIFTH CHAIR, THE (UKN) see **IT'S IN THE BAG** • 1945
FIFTH CLASS WAS ALSO CALLED, THE see **PROZVAN JE I VB** • 1962
FIFTH COLUMN HORSE • 1943 • Freleng Friz • ANS • USA
FIFTH COMMANDMENT, THE • 1915 • *Steger Julius* • USA
FIFTH COMMANDMENT, THE • 1927 • *Kaufman Film Co.* • USA
FIFTH DAY OF PEACE, THE (USA) see **GOTT MIT UNS** • 1970
FIFTH FACADE, THE • 1973 • Crombie Donald • SHT • ASL
FIFTH FILM • 1944 • Whitney John, Whitney James • SHT • USA
FIFTH FLOOR, THE • 1980 • Avedis Howard • USA
FIFTH FORM AT ST. DOMINIC'S, THE • 1921 • Coleby A. E. • UKN
FIFTH HORSEMAN, THE • 1924 • *Merkel Una* • USA
FIFTH HORSEMAN IS FEAR, THE (USA) see **...A PATY JEZDEC JE STRACH** • 1964
FIFTH MAN, THE • 1914 • Grandon Francis J. • SHT • USA
FIFTH MISSILE, THE • 1986 • Peerce Larry • USA, ITL
FIFTH MONKEY, THE • 1990 • Rochat Eric • USA
FIFTH MUSKETEER, THE • 1977 • Annakin Ken • USA, AUS
FIFTH OF JULY, THE • 1983 • Mason Marshall W. • TVM • USA
FIFTH OF JUNE FLIGHT • 1989 • Samiazar Alireza • IRN
FIFTH OF NOVEMBER, THE • 1907 • *Walturdaw* • UKN
FIFTH OF NOVEMBER, THE see **HENNESSY** • 1975
FIFTH OFFENSIVE, THE see **SUTJESKA** • 1974
FIFTH ONE, THE see **PETI** • 1964
FIFTH RIDER IS FEAR, THE (UKN) see **...A PATY JEZDEC JE STRACH** • 1964
FIFTH ROUND, THE (UKN) see **TOUGH KID** • 1939
FIFTH SEAL, THE see **OTODIK PECSET, AZ** • 1977
FIFTH SEASON • 1978 • Vorster Gordon • SAF, UKN • VYFDE SEISOEN
FIFTH STRING, THE • 1913 • *Carrigan Thomas* • USA
FIFTH WHEEL, THE • 1918 • Smith David • SHT • USA
FIFTH YEAR, THE • 1923 • *Friends Of Russia* • DOC • USA
FIFTIES TRIP -A SIXTIES TRIP, A • 1970 • Rowe Peter • CND
FIFTY BUCKS A WEEK • 1967 • Sheppard Gordon H. • CND
FIFTY CANDLES • 1921 • Willat Irvin V. • USA
FIFTY FATHOMS DEEP • 1931 • Neill R. William • USA
FIFTY-FIFTY • 1915 • *Imp* • USA
FIFTY-FIFTY • 1915 • Easton Clem • *Essanay* • USA
FIFTY-FIFTY • 1916 • Dwan Allan • USA
FIFTY-FIFTY • 1925 • Diamant-Berger Henri • USA
FIFTY-FIFTY • 1980 • Vidal Pascal • FRN • FIFTY FIFTY
FIFTY FIFTY • 1984 • Falk Harry • TVM • USA
FIFTY-FIFTY see **IT NEARLY HAPPENED** • 1916
FIFTY-FIFTY see **HALBE-HALBE** • 1978
FIFTY FIFTY see **FIFTY-FIFTY** • 1980
FIFTY-FIFTY GIRL, THE • 1928 • Badger Clarence • USA
FIFTY FIRST DRAGON, THE • 1953 • Bosustow Steve • ANS • USA
FIFTY-FIVE BROTHERS see **CINCUENTICINCO HERMANOS** • 1979
FIFTY MILE AUTO CONTEST • 1912 • Dwan Allan • USA • AUTO RACE -LAKESIDE
FIFTY MILES FROM TOMBSTONE • 1913 • *Kinemacolor* • USA
FIFTY MILLION FRENCHMEN • 1931 • Bacon Lloyd • USA
FIFTY MILLION HUSBANDS • 1930 • Kennedy Edgar, Horne James W. • SHT • USA
FIFTY ROADS TO TOWN • 1937 • Taurog Norman • USA
FIFTY-SHILLING BOXER • 1937 • Rogers Maclean • UKN
FIFTY-TWO PICK-UP see **52 PICK-UP** • 1987
FIFTY-VYFTIG • 1953 • SAF
FIFTY YEARS AFTER • 1912 • Evans Fred • UKN
FIFTY YEARS AFTER APPOMATTOX • 1915 • *Huling Lorraine* • USA
FIFTY YEARS AGO • 1911 • *Powers* • USA
FIFTY YEARS BEFORE YOUR EYES • 1950 • Youngson Robert • USA
FIFTY YEARS BEHIND • 1915 • Ayres Sydney • USA
FIFTY YEARS OF COUNTRY MUSIC • 1978 • Miller Walter C. • MTV • USA
FIG-LEAF see **FUGEFALEVEL** • 1966
FIG LEAVES • 1926 • Hawks Howard • USA
FIGARO • Steinbach Heinz • ANM • GDR
FIGARO • 1928 • Ravel Gaston
FIGARO AND CLEO • 1943 • Kinney Jack • ANS • USA
FIGARO AND FRANKIE • 1947 • Nichols Charles • ANS • USA
FIGARO, BARBIERE DI SIVIGLIA • 1955 • Mastrocinque Camillo • ITL
FIGARO E LA SUO GRAN GIORNATA • 1931 • Camerini Mario • ITL
FIGARO ET L'AUVERGNAT • 1897 • Melies Georges • FRN • BARBER AND THE FARMER, THE
FIGARO QUA, FIGARO LA • 1950 • Bragaglia Carlo Ludovico • ITL
FIGAROS HOCHZEIT • 1920 • Mack Max • FRG • MARRIAGE OF FIGARO, THE
FIGAROS HOCHZEIT • 1949 • Wildhagen Georg • GDR • MARRIAGE OF FIGARO, THE
FIGAROS HOCHZEIT see **HOCHZEIT DES FIGARO, DIE** • 1968
FIGHT, THE • 1915 • Lederer George W. • USA
FIGHT, THE • 1924 • Marshall George • SHT • USA
FIGHT, THE see **KUZDOK** • 1977
FIGHT AGAINST EVIL, A • 1913 • *Fischer Marguerite* • USA
FIGHT AND WIN • 1924 • Kenton Erle C. • SHS • USA
FIGHT AT GRIZZLY GULCH, THE • 1913 • *Wolfe Jane* • USA
FIGHT AT THE MILL, THE • 1912 • *American* • USA
FIGHT BETWEEN A MILLER AND A SWEEP • 1899 • Cooper Arthur • UKN
FIGHT BETWEEN YAKUZA FAMILIES see **JINGI NAKI TATAKAI, CHOJO SAKUSEN** • 1973

FIGHT FOR A MILLION, A • 1914 • *Warner'S Features* • USA
FIGHT FOR FREEDOM see **AUTOBIOGRAPHY OF MISS JANE PITTMAN, THE** • 1974
FIGHT FOR FREEDOM see **IJA OMINIRA** • 1979
FIGHT FOR FREEDOM, THE • 1908 • McCutcheon Wallace • USA
FIGHT FOR FREEDOM, OR EXILED TO SIBERIA, A • 1914 • Blache Herbert • USA
FIGHT FOR FRIENDSHIP, A • 1912 • *Nestor* • USA
FIGHT FOR GLORY • Hu Sin Yue • HKG
FIGHT FOR HAPPINESS see **KAMPF UMS GLUCK** • 1988
FIGHT FOR HIS HEART, THE see **KAMPEN OM HANS HJARTA** • 1916
FIGHT FOR HONOR, A • 1924 • McRae Henry • USA
FIGHT FOR HONOUR, A • 1908 • Coleby A. E. • UKN
FIGHT FOR JENNY, A • 1986 • Moses Gilbert • TVM • USA
FIGHT FOR LIFE • 1987 • Silverstein Elliot • TVM • USA
FIGHT FOR LIFE see **GYONGYVIRAGTOL LOMBHULLASIG** • 1954
FIGHT FOR LIFE, A • 1912 • Haldane Bert? • UKN
FIGHT FOR LIFE, A • 1915 • Kellino W. P. • UKN
FIGHT FOR LIFE, THE • 1940 • Lorentz Pare • DOC • USA
FIGHT FOR LOVE, A • 1914 • *Pyramid* • USA
FIGHT FOR LOVE, A • 1916 • Jaccard Jacques • SHT • USA
FIGHT FOR LOVE, A • 1919 • Ford John • USA
FIGHT FOR MILLIONS, A • 1910 • *Yankee* • USA
FIGHT FOR MILLIONS, A • 1918 • Duncan William • SRL • USA
FIGHT FOR MILLIONS, THE • 1913 • Blache Herbert • USA
FIGHT FOR OUR SOVIET UKRAINE, THE see **BITVA ZA NASHA SOVIETSKAYA UKRAINU** • 1943
FIGHT FOR PARADISE VALLEY, THE • 1916 • Horne James W. • SHT • USA
FIGHT FOR RIGHT, THE • 1912 • *Nestor* • USA
FIGHT FOR RIGHT, THE • 1913 • Apfel Oscar • USA
FIGHT FOR THE GLORY (USA) see **EIKO ENO KUROHYO** • 1969
FIGHT FOR THE GUN, THE • 1901 • *Mitchell & Kenyon* • UKN
FIGHT FOR THE REMBRANDT PAINTING, THE see **KAMPEN OM EN REMBRANDT** • 1915
FIGHT FOR THE SOUTH RAILWAY, A see **DVOBOJ ZA JUZNU PRUGU** • 1979
FIGHT FOR US • 1989 • Brocka Lino • PHL • INSOUMIS, LES
FIGHT FOR YOUR LADY • 1937 • Stoloff Ben • USA
FIGHT FOR YOUR LIFE • 1977 • Endelson Robert A. • USA
FIGHT GAME, THE • 1969 • Renwick David W. • SHT • USA
FIGHT GOES ON, THE see **STRIDEN GAR VIDARE** • 1941
FIGHT GOES ON, THE see **LUTA CONTINUA, LA** • 1971
FIGHT IN A THIEVES' KITCHEN • 1921 • Gordon Edward R. • UKN
FIGHT IN LONELY GULCH, THE • 1914 • *Frontier* • USA
FIGHT IN THE DARK, THE • 1912 • *Solax* • USA
FIGHT IS OUT • 1920 • Russell Albert • SHT • USA
FIGHT IS RIGHT • 1936 • Yarbrough Jean • SHT • USA
FIGHT NEVER ENDS, THE • 1947 • Lerner Joseph • USA
FIGHT NIGHT • 1926 • Pratt Gilbert, Moffitt Jefferson • SHT • USA • FIGHT NITE
FIGHT NITE see **FIGHT NIGHT** • 1926
FIGHT OF DEADWOOD TRAIL, THE • 1914 • *Darkfeather Mona* • USA
FIGHT OF THE WILD STALLION • 1947 • *Mead Thomas (P)* • DOC • USA
FIGHT ON, MARINES see **MARINES COME THROUGH, THE** • 1943
FIGHT ON THE DAM, THE • 1916 • *Kerrigan J. Warren* • USA
FIGHT PEST, THE • 1928 • Guiol Fred • SHT • USA
FIGHT THE GHOST • 1952 • Beaudine William? • USA
FIGHT TO A FINISH, A • 1913 • *Holmes Helen* • USA
FIGHT TO A FINISH, A • 1915 • McGowan J. P. • USA
FIGHT TO THE FINISH, A • 1920 • *Ridgeway Fritzi* • SHT • USA
FIGHT TO THE FINISH, A • 1925 • Eason B. Reeves • USA
FIGHT TO THE FINISH, A • 1937 • Coleman C. C. Jr. • USA
FIGHT TO THE FINISH, A • 1947 • Rasinski Connie • ANS • USA
FIGHT WITH FIRE, A • 1911 • Fitzhamon Lewin? • UKN
FIGHT WITH SLEDGEHAMMERS • 1902 • Winslow Dicky • UKN
FIGHT WITH THE DRAGON (USA) see **KAMPF MIT DEM DRACHEN, DER** • 1935
FIGHT WITH THE PANTHER, THE see **LUCHA CON LA PANTERA, LA** • 1974
FIGHTEN • 1962 • *Stivell Arne (Ed)* • DOC • SWD
FIGHTER, THE • 1921 • Kolker Henry • USA
FIGHTER, THE • 1952 • Kline Herbert • USA
FIGHTER, THE • 1982 • Rich David Lowell • TVM • USA
FIGHTER, THE see **BADEK LANG BVANA** • 1979
FIGHTER ATTACK • 1953 • Selander Lesley • USA
FIGHTER PILOT • 1943 • Weiss Jiri • DOC • UKN
FIGHTER PILOT • 1974 • Marx Franz • SAF
FIGHTER PLANES, THE • 1939 • Pentzlin E. • USS
FIGHTER SQUADRON • 1948 • Walsh Raoul • USA
FIGHTERS see **AGONISTES** • 1970
FIGHTERS, THE • 1974 • Greaves William • DOC • USA
FIGHTERS GO TO PARADISE see **BOKSERI IDU U RAJ** • 1967
FIGHTERS IN THE SADDLE see **FIGHTERS OF THE SADDLE** • 1929
FIGHTERS OF THE PLAINS • 1913 • *Bison* • USA
FIGHTERS OF THE SADDLE • 1929 • *Acord Art* • USA • FIGHTERS IN THE SADDLE
FIGHTERS ON FIRE see **NIPPON GERIRA JIDAI** • 1968
FIGHTER'S PARADISE • 1924 • Neitz Alvin J. • USA
FIGHTIN' COMEBACK, THE • 1927 • Wright Tenny • USA
FIGHTIN' DEVIL • 1922 • McKenzie Robert • USA
FIGHTIN' FISH • 1935 • *Mgm* • SHT • USA
FIGHTIN' FOOLS • 1941 • Cahn Edward L. • USA
FIGHTIN' MAD • 1921 • Franz Joseph J. • USA
FIGHTIN' ODDS • 1925 • Cohn Bennett • USA
FIGHTIN' PALS • 1940 • Fleischer Dave • ANS • USA
FIGHTIN' REDHEAD, THE • 1928 • King Louis • USA
FIGHTIN' TERROR, THE • 1920 • Gibson Ed Hoot • SHT • USA
FIGHTIN' THRU • 1924 • Hughes Roy M. • USA
FIGHTING 69TH, THE • 1940 • Keighley William • USA
FIGHTING 69½TH, THE • 1941 • Freleng Friz • ANS • USA

FIGHTING ACE, THE see **FLYING ACE, THE** • 1928
FIGHTING ADVENTURER, THE see **FIGHTING AMERICAN, THE** • 1924
FIGHTING AMERICAN, THE • 1924 • Forman Tom • USA • FIGHTING ADVENTURER, THE
FIGHTING BACK • 1917 • Wells Raymond • USA
FIGHTING BACK • 1948 • St. Clair Malcolm • USA
FIGHTING BACK • 1949 • Holmes Cecil • DOC • NZL
FIGHTING BACK • 1980 • Lieberman Robert • TVM • USA
FIGHTING BACK • 1982 • Caulfield Michael • ASL
FIGHTING BACK • 1982 • Teague Lewis • USA • DEATH VENGEANCE
FIGHTING BILL CARSON • 1945 • Newfield Sam • USA
FIGHTING BILL FARGO • 1942 • Taylor Ray • USA • VIGILANTES, THE
FIGHTING BILLY • 1915 • Kellino W. P. • UKN
FIGHTING BLADE, THE • 1923 • Robertson John S. • USA
FIGHTING BLOOD • 1911 • Griffith D. W. • USA
FIGHTING BLOOD • 1914 • *Fielding Romaine* • USA
FIGHTING BLOOD • 1916 • Apfel Oscar • USA
FIGHTING BLOOD • 1923 • St. Clair Malcolm, Lehrman Henry • SRL • USA
FIGHTING BOB • 1909 • *Selig* • USA
FIGHTING BOB • 1915 • Noble John W. • USA
FIGHTING BOOB, THE • 1926 • Nelson Jack • USA
FIGHTING BREED, THE • 1921 • Lucas Wilfred • USA
FIGHTING BROTHERS, THE • 1919 • Ford John • SHT • USA
FIGHTING BUCKAROO, THE • 1926 • Neill R. William • USA
FIGHTING BUCKAROO, THE • 1943 • Berke William • USA
FIGHTING CABALLERO • 1935 • Clifton Elmer • USA
FIGHTING CARAVANS • 1930 • Burton David, Brower Otto • USA • BLAZING ARROWS
FIGHTING CHAMP, THE • 1933 • McCarthy John P. • USA
FIGHTING CHANCE, A • 1909 • *Selig* • USA
FIGHTING CHANCE, A • 1913 • Ince Ralph • USA
FIGHTING CHANCE, THE • 1912 • *Conway Jack* • USA
FIGHTING CHANCE, THE • 1920 • Maigne Charles • USA
FIGHTING CHANCE, THE • 1955 • Witney William • USA
FIGHTING CHAPLAIN, THE • 1913 • Melford George • USA
FIGHTING CHEAT, THE • 1926 • Thorpe Richard • USA
FIGHTING CHOICE • 1985 • Fairfax Ferdinand • USA
FIGHTING CHUMP, THE see **DYNAMITE DELANEY** • 1938
FIGHTING COASTGUARD • 1951 • Kane Joseph • USA
FIGHTING COBBLER, THE see **COBBLER, THE** • 1915
FIGHTING CODE, THE • 1933 • Hillyer Lambert • USA
FIGHTING COLLEEN, A • 1919 • Smith David • USA • LOVE AT FIRST FIGHT
FIGHTING CORSAIR, THE see **SURCOUF, L'EROE DEI SETTE MARI** • 1966
FIGHTING COURAGE • 1925 • Elfelt Clifford S. • USA
FIGHTING COWARD, THE • 1924 • Cruze James • USA
FIGHTING COWBOY • 1930 • *Hoxie Al* • USA
FIGHTING COWBOY, THE • 1932 • Adamson Victor • USA
FIGHTING COWBOY, THE • 1933 • Dixon Denver • USA
FIGHTING CRESSY • 1919 • Thornby Robert T. • USA
FIGHTING CUB, THE • 1925 • Hurst Paul C. • USA • SON O' MINE
FIGHTING CURATE, THE • 1908 • Mottershaw Frank • UKN • LITTLE FLOWER GIRL, THE
"FIGHTING DAN" MCCOOL • 1912 • *Nilsson Anna Q.* • USA
FIGHTING DEACON, THE • 1926 • *Miller Walk (P)* • USA • LIFE OF TIGER FLOWERS, THE
FIGHTING DEATH • 1914 • Blache Herbert • USA
FIGHTING DEMON, THE • 1925 • Rosson Arthur • USA
FIGHTING DEPUTY, THE • 1937 • Newfield Sam • USA
FIGHTING DERVISHES OF THE DESERT, THE • 1912 • Olcott Sidney • USA
FIGHTING DESTINY • 1919 • Scardon Paul • USA
FIGHTING DEVIL DOGS • 1938 • Witney William, English John, Beche Robert • SRL • USA
FIGHTING DOCTOR, THE • 1926 • Bradbury Robert North • USA
FIGHTING DRAGON, THE • 1980 • Peng Chien • HKG
FIGHTING DUDE, THE • 1925 • Arbuckle Roscoe • USA
FIGHTING EAGLE, THE • 1927 • Crisp Donald • USA • BRIGADIER GERARD
FIGHTING EDGE, THE • 1926 • Lehrman Henry • USA
FIGHTING ENGINEERS, THE • 1943 • Eason B. Reeves • SHT • USA
FIGHTING FAILURE, THE • 1926 • Boyle E. G. • USA
FIGHTING FANNY • 1928 • Kerr Robert • USA
FIGHTING FATE • 1920 • Duncan William • SRL • USA
FIGHTING FATE • 1925 • Rogell Albert S. • USA
FIGHTING FATHER DUNNE • 1948 • Tetzlaff Ted • USA
FIGHTING FATHERS • 1927 • Guiol Fred • SHT • USA
FIGHTING FIGHTERS, THE • 1927 • Jaccard Jacques • SRL • USA
FIGHTING FILM ALBUM NO.1 see **BOYEVOYE KINOSBORNIK N.1** • 1941
FIGHTING FILM ALBUM NO.9 see **BOEVOI KINOSBORNIK 9** • 1942
FIGHTING FISH see **TOGYO** • 1941
FIGHTING FISTS OF SHANGHAI JOE, THE see **MIO NOME E SHANGHAI JOE, IL** • 1973
FIGHTING FLUID • 1925 • McCarey Leo • SHT • USA
FIGHTING FOOL, THE • 1929 • Harrison Jack • UKN
FIGHTING FOOL, THE • 1932 • Hillyer Lambert • USA
FIGHTING FOOLS • 1949 • Le Borg Reginald • USA
FIGHTING FOR FAME • 1926 • Worne Duke • SRL • USA
FIGHTING FOR GOLD • 1919 • Le Saint Edward J. • USA
FIGHTING FOR JUSTICE • 1924 • De Courcy Walter • USA
FIGHTING FOR JUSTICE • 1932 • Brower Otto • USA
FIGHTING FOR LOVE • 1917 • Wells Raymond • USA
FIGHTING FOR OUR LIVES • 1974 • Pearcy Glen • DOC • USA
FIGHTING FOUR, THE • 1915 • *Ovey George* • USA
FIGHTING FRIENDS, JAPANESE STYLE see **WASEI KENKA TOMODACHI** • 1929
FIGHTING FRONTIER • 1943 • Hillyer Lambert • USA
FIGHTING FRONTIERSMAN, THE • 1946 • Abrahams Derwin • USA • GOLDEN LADY (UKN)
FIGHTING FURY • 1924 • Smith Cliff • USA
FIGHTING FURY see **OUTLAWS' HIGHWAY** • 1934
FIGHTING GENTLEMAN, THE • 1932 • Newmeyer Fred • USA

FIGHTING GENTLEMAN, THE see **MY FIGHTING GENTLEMAN** • 1917
FIGHTING GLADIATOR, THE • 1926 • Malins Geoffrey H., Parkinson H. B. • UKN
FIGHTING GOB, THE • 1926 • Fraser Harry L. • USA
FIGHTING GRIN, THE • 1918 • De Grasse Joseph • USA • CATAMOUNT, THE
FIGHTING GRINGO, THE • 1917 • Kelsey Fred A. • USA • RED SAUNDERS PLAYS CUPID
FIGHTING GRINGO, THE • 1939 • Howard David • USA
FIGHTING GUARDSMAN, THE • 1945 • Levin Henry • USA
FIGHTING GUIDE, THE • 1922 • Duncan William, Clark Don • USA
FIGHTING HEART, A • 1924 • Nelson Jack • USA
FIGHTING HEART, THE • 1919 • Eason B. Reeves • USA
FIGHTING HEART, THE • 1925 • Ford John • USA • ONCE TO EVERY MAN (UKN)
FIGHTING HEARTS • 1922 • *Fairbanks William* • USA
FIGHTING HEARTS see **VERGODO SZIVEK** • 1916
FIGHTING HEIRESS, THE • 1916 • Horne James W. • SHT • USA
FIGHTING HERO • 1934 • Webb Harry S. • USA
FIGHTING HIS BATTLES OVER AGAIN • 1902 • Williamson James • UKN
FIGHTING HOMBRE, THE • 1927 • Nelson Jack • USA
FIGHTING HOPE, THE • 1915 • Melford George • USA
FIGHTING IN THE STREETS IN INDIA see **COMBAT DANS UNE RUE AUX INDES** • 1897
FIGHTING INSTINCT see **MANDEN, DER SEJREDE** • 1917
FIGHTING INSTINCT, THE • 1912 • Duncan William • USA
FIGHTING IS NO BUSINESS • 1914 • Goetz Ben • USA
FIGHTING JACK • 1926 • Chaudet Louis W. • USA
FIGHTING JACK see **CORINTHIAN JACK** • 1921
FIGHTING JIM GRANT • 1923 • Adcook W. • USA
FIGHTING JOE • 1916 • Mong William V. • SHT • USA
FIGHTING KENTUCKIAN, THE • 1949 • Waggner George • USA
FIGHTING KENTUCKIANS, THE • 1920 • Edwards J. Harrison • USA
FIGHTING KID, THE • 1915 • *Ovey George* • USA
FIGHTING KID, THE • 1922 • *Horner Robert J. (P)* • USA
FIGHTING LADY, THE • 1943 • Wyler William • DOC • USA
FIGHTING LADY, THE • 1944 • Radford Arthur W. • USA
FIGHTING LADY, THE • 1944 • Steichen Edward J. • USA
FIGHTING LAWMAN, THE • 1953 • Carr Thomas • USA
FIGHTING LEGION, THE • 1930 • Brown Harry J. • USA
FIGHTING LEGIONS, THE see **DIAVOLI DI SPARTIVENTO, I** • 1963
FIGHTING LIEUTENANT, THE • 1913 • Martin E. A. • USA
FIGHTING LINE, THE • 1919 • Eason B. Reeves • SHT • USA
FIGHTING LOVE • 1927 • Chrisander Nils • USA • IF THE GODS LAUGH
FIGHTING LOVER, THE • 1921 • Granville Fred Leroy • USA
FIGHTING LUCK • 1926 • McGowan J. P. • USA
FIGHTING MAD • 1917 • Le Saint Edward J. • USA
FIGHTING MAD • 1919 • Terwilliger George W. • SHT • USA
FIGHTING MAD • 1939 • Newfield Sam • USA • RENFREW OF THE ROYAL MOUNTED IN FIGHTING MAD
FIGHTING MAD • 1948 • Le Borg Reginald • USA • JOE PALOOKA IN FIGHTING MAD
FIGHTING MAD • 1957 • Kavanagh Denis • UKN
FIGHTING MAD • 1976 • Demme Jonathan • USA
FIGHTING MAD • 1977 • Santiago Cirio H. • USA, PHL
FIGHTING MAN OF THE PLAINS • 1949 • Marin Edwin L. • USA
FIGHTING MARINE, THE • 1926 • Bennet Spencer Gordon • USA
FIGHTING MARINE, THE (UKN) see **UNITED STATES SMITH** • 1928
FIGHTING MARINES • 1935 • Eason B. Reeves, Kane Joseph • SRL • USA
FIGHTING MARSHAL, THE • 1932 • Lederman D. Ross • USA
FIGHTING MARSHAL, THE (UKN) see **CHEROKEE STRIP** • 1940
FIGHTING MEN, THE • 1977 • Shebib Donald • TVM • CND
FIGHTING MINISTER, THE • 1915 • *Santa Barbara* • USA
FIGHTING MUSTANG • 1948 • Drake Oliver • USA
FIGHTING NAVY, THE see **OUR FIGHTING NAVY** • 1937
FIGHTING NEAR TSARITSIN see **BOI POD TSARITSYNOM** • 1919
FIGHTING ODDS • 1917 • Dwan Allan • USA
FIGHTING OF SHAOLIN MONKS, THE • *Chen Hsing* • HKG
FIGHTING O'FLYNN, THE (UKN) see **O'FLYNN, THE** • 1948
FIGHTING PALS • 1920 • Feeney Edward • SHT • USA
FIGHTING PARSON, THE • 1908 • *Selig* • USA
FIGHTING PARSON, THE • 1910 • *Nestor* • USA
FIGHTING PARSON, THE • 1912 • Haldane Bert, Gray George • UKN
FIGHTING PARSON, THE • 1930 • Rogers Charles, Guiol Fred • USA
FIGHTING PARSON, THE • 1933 • Fraser Harry L. • USA
FIGHTING PEACEMAKER, THE • 1926 • Smith Cliff • USA
FIGHTING PHANTOM see **MYSTERIOUS RIDER, THE** • 1933
FIGHTING PILOT • 1935 • Smith Noel • USA
FIGHTING PIMPERNEL, THE (USA) see **PIMPERNEL SMITH** • 1941
FIGHTING PIMPERNEL, THE (USA) see **ELUSIVE PIMPERNEL, THE** • 1950
FIGHTING PIONEERS • 1935 • Fraser Harry L. • USA
FIGHTING PRESIDENT, THE • 1933 • *Universal* • DOC • USA
FIGHTING PRINCE OF DONEGAL, THE • 1966 • O'Herlihy Michael • UKN, USA
FIGHTING RANGER • 1926 • Hurst Paul C. • USA
FIGHTING RANGER, THE • 1922 • *Miller Bill* • USA
FIGHTING RANGER, THE • 1925 • Marchant Jay • USA
FIGHTING RANGER, THE • 1934 • Seitz George B. • USA • FIGHTING RANGERS, THE
FIGHTING RANGER, THE • 1948 • Hillyer Lambert • USA
FIGHTING RANGERS, THE see **FIGHTING RANGER, THE** • 1934
FIGHTING RATS OF TOBRUK (USA) see **RATS OF TOBRUK, THE** • 1944
FIGHTING REDHEAD, THE • 1949 • Collins Lewis D. • USA
FIGHTING RENEGADE, THE • 1939 • Newfield Sam • USA
FIGHTING REV. CALDWELL, THE • 1911 • Davis Ulysses • USA
FIGHTING ROMANCE • 1931 • Adamson Victor • USA
FIGHTING ROMEO, THE • 1925 • Ferguson Al • USA
FIGHTING ROOKIE, THE • 1934 • Bennet Spencer Gordon • USA • DANGEROUS ENEMY (UKN)
FIGHTING ROOSEVELTS, THE • 1919 • Nigh William • USA • OUR TEDDY
FIGHTING SAP, THE • 1924 • Rogell Albert S. • USA
FIGHTING SCHOOLMASTER, THE • 1911 • *Storey Edith* • USA
FIGHTING SCHOOLMASTER, THE (UKN) see **JUCKLINS, THE** • 1920
FIGHTING SEABEES, THE • 1944 • Ludwig Edward • USA
FIGHTING SELINA • 1915 • Aylott Dave • UKN
FIGHTING SEVENTH, THE (UKN) see **LITTLE BIG HORN** • 1951
FIGHTING SHADOWS • 1935 • Selman David • USA
FIGHTING SHEPHERDESS, THE • 1920 • Jose Edward • USA
FIGHTING SHERIFF, THE • 1919 • Kull Edward • SHT • USA
FIGHTING SHERIFF, THE • 1925 • McGowan J. P. • USA
FIGHTING SHERIFF, THE • 1931 • King Louis • USA
FIGHTING SKIPPER, THE • 1923 • Ford Francis • SRL • USA
FIGHTING SMILE, THE • 1925 • Marchant Jay • USA
FIGHTING SNUB REILLY • 1924 • Wilson Andrew P. • UKN
FIGHTING SPIRIT, THE see **OBANTO KOBANTO** • 1967
FIGHTING SPIRIT (UKN) see **SPIRIT OF STANFORD, THE** • 1942
FIGHTING STALLION, THE • 1926 • Wilson Ben • USA
FIGHTING STALLION, THE • 1950 • Tansey Robert • USA
FIGHTING STOCK • 1935 • Walls Tom • UKN
FIGHTING STRAIN, THE • 1923 • Hart Neal • USA • BILL BARLOW'S CLAIM
FIGHTING STRAIN OF OLD ENGLAND, THE • 1914 • Aylott Dave • UKN
FIGHTING STRANGER, THE • 1921 • Cullison Webster • USA
FIGHTING STREAK, THE • 1922 • Rosson Arthur • USA
FIGHTING SULLIVANS, THE see **SULLIVANS, THE** • 1944
FIGHTING TERROR, THE • 1929 • McGowan J. P. • USA
FIGHTING TEST, THE (UKN) see **CHEYENNE KID, THE** • 1930
FIGHTING TEXAN, THE • 1937 • Abbott Charles • USA
FIGHTING TEXANS, THE • 1933 • Schaefer Armand • USA • RANDY STRIKES OIL (UKN)
FIGHTING THE FIRE • 1905 • USA
FIGHTING THE FLAMES • 1925 • Eason B. Reeves • USA
FIGHTING THE IRIQUOIS IN CANADA • 1910 • *Kalem* • USA
FIGHTING THOROBREDS • 1926 • Brown Harry J. • USA
FIGHTING THOROUGHBREDS • 1939 • Salkow Sidney • USA
FIGHTING THREE, THE • 1927 • Rogell Albert S. • USA
FIGHTING THROUGH • 1919 • Cabanne W. Christy • USA • AMERICAN SPIRIT, THE
FIGHTING THROUGH • 1934 • Fraser Harry L. • USA
FIGHTING THRU: OR, CALIFORNIA IN 1878 • 1930 • Nigh William • USA • CALIFORNIA IN 1878
FIGHTING TO LIVE • 1934 • Cline Eddie • USA
FIGHTING TRAIL, THE • 1917 • Duncan William • SRL • USA
FIGHTING TROOPER, THE • 1934 • Taylor Ray • USA • TROOPER, THE (UKN)
FIGHTING TROUBLE • 1956 • Blair George • USA
FIGHTING VALLEY • 1943 • Drake Oliver • USA
FIGHTING VIGILANTES, THE • 1947 • Taylor Ray • USA
FIGHTING WASHERWOMEN • 1904 • Stow Percy • UKN
FIGHTING WESTERNER see **ROCKY MOUNTAIN MYSTERY** • 1935
FIGHTING WILDCATS (USA) see **WEST OF SUEZ** • 1957
FIGHTING WITH BUFFALO BILL • 1926 • Taylor Ray • SRL • USA
FIGHTING WITH KIT CARSON • 1933 • Schaefer Armand, Clark Colbert • SRL • USA
FIGHTING YOUTH • 1925 • Eason B. Reeves • USA
FIGHTING YOUTH • 1935 • MacFadden Hamilton • USA
FIGHTS OF NATIONS • 1907 • *Bitzer Billy (Ph)* • USA
FIGHTS THROUGH THE AGES • 1924 • SER • UKN
FIGLI CHIEDONO PERCHE, I • 1972 • Zanchin Nino • ITL
FIGLI CRESCONO, I • 1977 • Vani Bruno • ITL
FIGLI DEL LEOPARDO, I • 1965 • Corbucci Sergio • ITL
FIGLI DEL MARCHESE LUCERA, I • 1938 • Palermi Amleto • ITL
FIGLI DELLA LAGUNA, I • 1945 • De Robertis Francesco • ITL
FIGLI DELLA NOTTE, I • 1939 • Perojo Benito • ITL
FIGLI DELL'ETNA, I see **VENDETTA DI FUOCO** • 1955
FIGLI DI NESSUNO, I • 1951 • Matarazzo Raffaello • ITL
FIGLI DI NESSUNO, I • 1974 • Gaburro Bruno Alberto • ITL
FIGLI DI ZANNA BIANCA, I • 1974 • Pradeaux Maurizio • ITL
FIGLI NON SI TOCCANO!, I • 1978 • Rossati Nello • ITL
FIGLI NON SI VENDONO, I • 1952 • Bonnard Mario • ITL
FIGLIA DEL CAPITANO, LA • 1947 • Camerini Mario • USA • CAPTAIN'S DAUGHTER, THE (USA) ○ DOUBLE CROSS
FIGLIA DEL CORSARO VERDE, LA • 1941 • Guazzoni Enrico • ITL
FIGLIA DEL DIAVOLO, LA • 1953 • Zeglio Primo • ITL
FIGLIA DEL FORZATO, LA • 1955 • Amata Gaetano • ITL • MORTE CIVILE, LA
FIGLIA DEL MENDICANTE, LA • 1950 • Campogalliani Carlo • ITL
FIGLIA DEL PECCATO, LA • 1949 • Ingegnero Armando • ITL • VOCE 'E NOTTE
FIGLIA DEL REGGIMENTO, LA (ITL) see **TOCHTER DER KOMPANIE, DIE** • 1951
FIGLIA DEL TEMPESTA, LA • 1920 • Gallone Carmine • ITL
FIGLIA DELLA MADONNA, LA • 1949 • Montero Roberto Bianchi • ITL
FIGLIA DELLA TEMPESTA, LA • 1922 • Gallone Carmine • ITL
FIGLIA DELLO SCEICCO, LA see **AMANTES DEL DESIERTO, LOS** • 1958
FIGLIA DI FRANKENSTEIN, LA • 1971 • von Theumer Ernst Ritter • ITL • LADY FRANKENSTEIN (USA) ○ MADAME FRANKENSTEIN ○ DAUGHTER OF FRANKENSTEIN, THE
FIGLIA DI MATA HARI, LA • 1955 • Merusi Renzo, Gallone Carmine • ITL, FRN • MATA HARI'S DAUGHTER (USA) ○ FILLE DE MATA-HARI, LA (FRN) ○ DAUGHTER OF MATA-HARI
FIGLIASTRA (STORIA DI CORNA E PASSIONE) • 1977 • Mulargia Edoardo • ITL
FIGLIE DEL MARE, LA • 1919 • Gallone Carmine • ITL
FIGLIO DEL CAPITANO BLOOD, IL (ITL) see **HIJO DEL CAPITAN BLOOD, EL** • 1962
FIGLIO DEL CIRCO, IL • 1963 • Grieco Sergio • ITL
FIGLIO DEL CORSARO ROSSO, IL • 1942 • Elter Marco • ITL
FIGLIO DEL CORSARO ROSSO, IL • 1960 • Zeglio Primo • ITL • SON OF THE RED CORSAIR (USA) ○ SON OF THE RED PIRATE
FIGLIO DELLA GUERRA, IL • 1915 • Falena Ugo • ITL
FIGLIO DELLA SEPOLTA VIVA, IL • 1974 • Ercoli Luciano • ITL
FIGLIO DELLE SELVE, IL • 1909 • Maggi Luigi • ITL
FIGLIO DELLE STELLE, IL • 1979 • Vanzina Carlo • ITL • TU SEI L'UNICA DONNA PER ME ○ MAKING IT
FIGLIO DELLO SCEICCO, IL • 1962 • Costa Mario • ITL, FRN • FILS DU CHEIKH, LE (FRN)
FIGLIO DELLO SCEICCO, IL • 1978 • Corbucci Sergio • ITL
FIGLIO DELL'UOMO, IL • 1955 • Sabel Virgilio • ITL • SHADOW ON THE HILL, THE (UKN) ○ SON OF MAN, THE
FIGLIO DI AQUILA NERA, IL • 1968 • Malatesta Guido • ITL • SON OF BLACK EAGLE, THE
FIGLIO DI CLEOPATRA, IL • 1965 • Baldi Ferdinando • ITL, EGY
FIGLIO DI D'ARTAGNAN, IL • 1949 • Freda Riccardo • ITL • SON OF D'ARTAGNAN (USA) ○ GAY SWORDSMAN, THE
FIGLIO DI DJANGO, IL • 1967 • Civirani Osvaldo • ITL • SON OF DJANGO
FIGLIO DI LAGARDERE, IL • 1952 • Cerchio Fernando • ITL
FIGLIO DI MADAME SANS-GENE, IL • 1922 • Negroni Baldassare • ITL • LITTLE CORPORAL, THE
FIGLIO DI SPARTACUS, IL • 1962 • Corbucci Sergio • ITL • SLAVE, THE (USA) ○ SON OF SPARTACUS, THE
FIGLIO DI UN ALTRO, IL see **CENTO PICCOLE MAMME** • 1952
FIGLIO DI ZORRO, IL • 1973 • Baldanello Gianfranco • ITL
FIGLIO D'OGGI, UN • 1961 • Graziano Domenico, Girolami Marino • ITL
FIGLIO MIO INFINITAMENTE CARO • 1985 • Orsini Valentino • ITL • MY VERY BELOVED SON
FIGLIO MIO, SONO INNOCENTE! • 1977 • Caiano Carlo • ITL
FIGLIOCCIO DEL PADRINO, IL • 1973 • Laurenti Mariano • ITL
FIGOURATZIS, O • 1968 • Melissinos Vangelis • GRC • GIVE AWAY THE SHOW ○ EXTROVERT, THE
FIGUEIRA DA FOZ • 1974 • Tropa Alfredo • SHT • PRT
FIGUI BIREN • 1987 • Gao Zhizen • HKG • IT'S A MAD, MAD WORLD
FIGURANTE, LA • 1922 • D'Ambra Lucio • ITL
FIGURANTS DU NOUVEAU MONDE, LES see **CAPRICES DE MARIE, LES** • 1969
FIGURE DE PROUE • 1947 • Stengel Christian • FRN
FIGURE IN BLACK, THE • 1915 • *Sais Marin* • USA
FIGURE TO SUPPORT, A see **POSTAVA K PODPIRANI** • 1963
FIGUREHEAD • 1953 • Halas John, Batchelor Joy • ANS • UKN
FIGUREHEAD, THE • 1920 • Ellis Robert • USA
FIGURES • Prochazka Pavel • ANM • CZC
FIGURES DE CIRE • 1912 • Tourneur Maurice • FRN • HOMME AUX FIGURES DE CIRE, L' ○ MAN WITH WAX FACES, THE
FIGURES DE CIRE ET TETES DE BOIS • 1916 • Cohl Emile • ANS • FRN
FIGURES DON'T LIE • 1927 • Sutherland A. Edward • USA
FIGURES IN A LANDSCAPE • 1954 • Ashton Dudley Shaw • UKN
FIGURES IN A LANDSCAPE • 1970 • Losey Joseph • UKN • HUNTED, THE
FIGURETTA • 1920 • Maggi Luigi • ITL
FIJATE QUE SUAVE • 1947 • Bustillo Oro Juan • MXC
FIKRIMIN INCE GULU see **SARI MERSEDES** • 1987
FIL A LA PATTE, LE • 1954 • Lefranc Guy • FRN
FIL A LA PATTE, UN • 1914 • Pouctal Henri • FRN
FIL A LA PATTE, UN • 1924 • Saidreau Robert • FRN
FIL A LA PATTE, UN • 1933 • Anton Karl • FRN
FIL FIN, LE see **KHAIT' AR-RAFI, AL-** • 1971
FIL, FOND, FOSFOR • 1980 • Nahoun Philippe • FRN
FILASSE (FRN) see **WITTE VAN SICHEM, DE** • 1980
FILE 222 see **222 NO. LU DOSYA** • 1967
FILE 1365 -THE CONNORS CASE • 1947 • Mulholland Donald • CND
FILE, THE see **KARTOTEKA** • 1966
FILE NO.113 • 1915 • *Ritchie Franklin* • USA
FILE NO.113 • 1932 • Franklin Chester M. • USA
FILE OF THE GOLDEN GOOSE, THE • 1968 • Wanamaker Sam • UKN
FILE ON JILL HATCH, THE • 1983 • Reid Alastair • TVM • USA, UKN
FILE ON THELMA JORDON, THE (UKN) see **THELMA JORDON** • 1949
FILE X FOR SEX • 1967 • *Lake Sam* • USA • STORY OF THE PERVERTED, THE
FILES FROM SCOTLAND YARD • 1951 • Squire Anthony • UKN
FILES OF DETECTIVE X see **SECRET FILES OF DETECTIVE "X", THE** • 1968
FILET AMERICAIN, LE • 1977 • de Hert Robbe • BLG
FILET DE SOIE, LE • 1966 • Levy Jacques • FRN
FILET MEOW • 1966 • Levitow Abe • ANS • USA
FILEZ, FILEZ, O MON NAVIRE • 1944 • MacKay Jim • ANS • CND
FILHAS DO FOGO, AS • 1979 • Khouri Walter Hugo • BRZ • DAUGHTERS OF FIRE
FILHO PRODIGO, O • 1980 • Pontes Ipojuca • BRZ • PRODIGAL SON, THE
FILHOS DO MEDO, OS • 1978 • Diegues Carlos • DOC • BRZ • ENFANTS DE LA PEUR, LES
FILIAL LOVE • 1912 • *Horton Clara* • USA
FILIBUSTERISMO, EL • 1962 • De Leon Gerardo • PHL
FILIBUSTERS, THE • 1912 • *Kalem* • USA
FILIBUSTER'S SHIP, THE • 1912 • *Pathe* • USA
FILIGRANA • 1949 • Marquina Luis • SPN
FILIP CEL BUN • 1975 • Pita Dan • RMN • FILIP THE KIND
FILIP THE KIND see **FILIP CEL BUN** • 1975
FILLE, LA see **DEN MUSSO** • 1975
FILLE A CROQUER, UNE • 1950 • Andre Raoul • FRN • PETIT CHAPERON ROUGE, LE
FILLE A LA DERIVE, UNE • 1962 • Delsol Paula • FRN • DERIVE, LA
FILLE A LA VALISE, LA (FRN) see **RAGAZZA CON LA VALIGIA, LA** • 1961
FILLE A L'ENVERS, LA • 1973 • Roullet Serge • FRN
FILLE A PAPA, UNE • 1935 • Guissart Rene • FRN
FILLE AU FOUET, LA • 1951 • Dreville Jean, Le Henaff Rene (U/c) • FRN, SWT

FILLE AU VIOLONCELLE, LA • 1973 • Butler Yvan • FRN, SWT
FILLE AUX YEUX CLAIRS, LA see **FILLE AUX YEUX GRIS, LA** • 1945
FILLE AUX YEUX D'OR, LA • 1961 • Albicocco Jean-Gabriel • FRN • GIRL WITH THE GOLDEN EYES, THE (USA)
FILLE AUX YEUX GRIS, LA • 1945 • Faurez Jean • FRN • FILLE AUX YEUX CLAIRS, LA
FILLE BIEN GARDEE, LA • 1924 • Feuillade Louis • FRN
FILLE COUSUE DE FIL BLANC, LA • 1976 • Lang Michel • FRN • STRAIT-LACED GIRL, A
FILLE D'AMERIQUE, LA • 1974 • Newman David • FRN • CRAZY AMERICAN GIRL (USA)
FILLE DANGEREUSE see **BUFERE** • 1953
FILLE DANS LA MONTAGNE, UNE • 1964 • Leenhardt Roger • MTV • FRN
FILLE DANS LA VITRINE, LA (FRN) see **RAGAZZA IN VETRINA, LA** • 1960
FILLE DANS LE SOLEIL, LA • 1952 • Cam Maurice • FRN
FILLE D'AUBERGE • 1913 • Pouctal Henri • FRN
FILLE DE 15 ANS, LA • 1988 • Doillon Jacques • FRN
FILLE DE CHIFFONNIERS, LA • 1922 • Desfontaines Henri • FRN
FILLE DE DELFT, LA • 1912 • Machin Alfred • NTH
FILLE DE FEU, LA • 1958 • Rode Alfred • FRN • FIRE IN THE FLESH (USA)
FILLE DE HAMBOURG, LA • 1958 • Allegret Yves • FRN • PORT OF DESIRE (USA) ○ GIRL FROM HAMBURG, THE
FILLE DE JEPHTE, LA • 1910 • Feuillade Louis • FRN
FILLE DE JEPHTE, LA • 1913 • Andreani Henri • FRN
FILLE DE LA MADELON, LA • 1937 • Pallu Georges, Mugeli Jean • FRN
FILLE DE LA MER MORTE, LA • 1966 • Golan Menahem • FRN, ISR • SEDUCED IN SODOM (UKN) ○ GIRL FROM THE DEAD SEA, THE
FILLE DE LA RIZIERE, LA (FRN) see **RISAIA, LA** • 1956
FILLE DE LA ROUTE, LA • 1962 • Terme Louis • FRN • GIRL OF THE ROAD, THE
FILLE DE LA SORCIERE, LA • 1908 • Jasset Victorin • FRN
FILLE DE L'EAU, LA • 1924 • Renoir Jean • FRN • WHIRLPOOL OF FATE (UKN) ○ GIRL OF THE WATER, THE ○ WHIRLPOOL OF LIFE, THE
FILLE DE MADAME ANGOT, LA • 1935 • Bernard-Derosne Jean • FRN
FILLE DE MATA-HARI, LA (FRN) see **FIGLIA DI MATA HARI, LA** • 1955
FILLE DE PACHAS, LA • 1926 • Hamman Joe (c/d) • FRN
FILLE DE PRAGUE AVEC UN SAC TRES LOURD, LA • 1978 • Jaeggi Danielle • FRN, ISR
FILLE DE PRINCE • 1914 • Fescourt Henri • FRN
FILLE DE RIEN • 1921 • Hugon Andre • FRN
FILLE D'EN FACE, LA • 1968 • Simon Jean-Daniel • FRN • GIRL OPPOSITE, THE
FILLE DES COLLINES, LA • 1990 • Davis Robin • FRN
FILLE DU BOCHE, LA • 1915 • Pouctal Henri • FRN
FILLE DU BOUIF, LA • 1931 • Bussy Rene • FRN
FILLE DU DIABLE • 1945 • Decoin Henri • FRN • DEVIL'S DAUGHTER (USA) ○ VIE D'UN AUTRE, LA
FILLE DU GARDE-BARRIERE, LA • 1975 • Savary Jerome • FRN • GATEKEEPER'S DAUGHTER, THE (UKN)
FILLE DU GARDIEN, LA see **BINT AL-H'ARIS** • 1968
FILLE DU JUGE D'INSTRUCTION, LA • 1911 • Feuillade Louis • FRN
FILLE DU MARGRAVE, LA • 1912 • Feuillade Louis • FRN
FILLE DU PECHEUR, LA • 1912 • Peguy Robert • FRN
FILLE DU PEUPLE • 1920 • de Morlhon Camille • FRN
FILLE DU PUISATIER, LA • 1940 • Pagnol Marcel • FRN • WELL-DIGGER'S DAUGHTER, THE (USA)
FILLE DU REGIMENT, LA • 1933 • Billon Pierre, Lamac Carl • FRN
FILLE DU ROY, LA • 1971 • Heroux Denis • CND
FILLE DU TORRENT, LA • 1960 • Herwig Hans • FRN, ITL
FILLE ELISA, LA • 1956 • Richebe Roger • FRN • ELISA ○ THAT GIRL ELISA
FILLE EN NOIR, LA see **KORITSI META MAVRA, TO** • 1956
FILLE EPATANTE, UNE • 1955 • Andre Raoul • FRN
FILLE ET DES FUSILS, UNE • 1965 • Lelouch Claude • FRN • TO BE A CROOK (USA) ○ DECADENT INFLUENCE, THE
FILLE ET LA GARCON, LA • 1931 • Thiele Wilhelm, Le Bon Roger • FRN • GIRL AND THE BOY, THE
FILLE LIBRE, UNE • 1970 • Pierson Claude • FRN, ITL, CND • EROTIC LOVE GAMES (UKN) ○ DOPO L'ALTRA, UNA (ITL) ○ FEMME LIBRE, UNE
FILLE NOMMEE AMOUR, UNE • 1968 • Gobbi Sergio • FRN, ITL • RAGAZZA CHIAMATA AMORE, UNA (ITL) ○ GIRL CALLED LOVE, A
FILLE NOMMEE DESIR, UNE • 1973 • Laurent Germaine • FRN
FILLE PERDUE, LA • 1953 • Gourguet Jean • FRN
FILLE POUR L'ETE, UNE • 1960 • Molinaro Edouard • FRN, ITL • MISTRESS FOR THE SUMMER, A (USA) ○ RAGAZZA PER L'ESTATE, UNA(ITL) ○ GIRLS FOR THE SUMMER (UKN) ○ LOVER FOR THE SUMMER, A ○ GIRL FOR THE SUMMER, A
FILLE POUR SAINT-TROPEZ, UNE (FRN) see **RAGAZZINA PERVERSA, LA** • 1975
FILLE PRODIGUE, LA • 1980 • Doillon Jacques • FRN • PRODIGAL DAUGHTER, THE (USA)
FILLE SAGE, LA • 1964 • Borowczyk Walerian • ANS • FRN
FILLE SUR LA ROUTE, UNE • 1951 • Stelli Jean • FRN
FILLE UNIQUE, UNE • 1976 • Nahoun Philippe • FRN
FILLERES GYOERS • 1933 • Gaal Bela • HNG
FILLES C'EST PAS PAREIL, LES • 1974 • Girard Helene • CND
FILLES DE FERME, LES • Reinhard Pierre B. • FRN
FILLES DE FEU, LES see **DUELLE** • 1976
FILLES DE GRENOBLE, LES • 1980 • Le Moign' Joel • FRN
FILLES DE LA CONCIERGE, LES • 1934 • Tourneur Jacques • FRN • TROIS FILLES DE LA CONCIERGE, LES
FILLES DE LA ROCHELLE, LES • 1961 • Deflandre Bernard • FRN
FILLES DE L'EXIL see **ANGES DU PECHES, LES** • 1943
FILLES DE MALEMORT, LES • 1973 • Daert Daniel • FRN • CARNAVAL DE MALEMORT, LE
FILLES DE NEIGE, LES • Brandau Walter • LXM • SNOW GIRLS
FILLES DE NUIT • 1958 • Cloche Maurice • FRN, ITL • LEGGE DEL VIZIO, LA (ITL) ○ GIRLS OF THE NIGHT (USA)
FILLES D'EVE • 1916 • Burguet Charles • FRN
FILLES DOIVENT SE MARIER, LES see **BANAT LAZIM TITZAWWIG, AL-** • 1973
FILLES DU CANTONNIER, LES • 1909 • Feuillade Louis • FRN
FILLES DU DIABLE, LES • 1903 • Melies Georges • FRN • BEELZEBUB'S DAUGHTERS (USA) ○ WOMEN OF FIRE, THE
FILLES DU GOLDEN SALOON, LES see **ORGIES DU GOLDEN SALOON, LES** • 1973
FILLES DU REGIMENT, LES • 1978 • Bernard-Aubert Claude • FRN
FILLES DU RHONE, LES • 1937 • Paulin Jean-Paul • FRN
FILLES DU ROY, LES • 1974 • Poirier Anne-Claire • CND • THEY CALLED US "LES FILLES DU ROY"
FILLES DU SOLEIL, LES • 1949 • Baratier Jacques • FRN
FILLES ET L'ETE, LES see **BANAT WA AC-CAIF, AL-** • 1960
FILLES EXPERTES EN JEUX CLANDESTINS • 1975 • Maria Guy • FRN • MAID FOR PLEASURE
FILLES INSATIABLES • 1975 • Matalon Eddy • FRN
FILLES SEMENT LE VENT, LES • 1961 • Soulanes Louis • FRN, ITL • FRUIT IS RIPE, THE (USA)
FILLEULE D'AMERIQUE, UNE • 1920 • de Carbonnat Louis • FRN
FILLING HIS OWN SHOES • 1917 • Beaumont Harry • USA
FILLING THE GAP • 1941 • Halas John, Batchelor Joy • ANS • UKN
FILLMORE • 1972 • Heffron Richard T. • DOC • USA
FILLY, THE • 1913 • *Stanton Bob* • USA
FILM • 1979 • Clark David Rayner • UKN
FILM • 1979 • Pomar Vitor • NTH
FILM 2 TEIL 1 • 1966 • Herzog Ulrich • FRG
FILM 100% BRASILEIRO, UM • 1986 • Sette Jose • BRZ • 100% BRAZILIAN FILM, A
FILM 1941 see **1941** • 1941
FILM 1965 • 1965 • Schneider Alan • USA
FILM A • Siani Toni • SHT • USA
FILM -A WONDERFUL WORLD see **FILMENS VIDUNDERLIGE VERDEN** • 1978
FILM ABOUT A WOMAN WHO... • 1974 • Rainer Yvonne • USA
FILM ABOUT ELISE see **FILMEN OG ELISE** • 1984
FILM ABOUT LOVE, A see **SZERELMESFILM** • 1970
FILM ABOUT LOVE, A see **OM KARLEK** • 1987
FILM ABOUT THE BOOK see **FILM O KNJIZI A.B.C.** • 1962
FILM ABSTRACTIONS • Sutton Denver • SHT • UKN
FILM ACTRESS, A see **EIGA JOYUH** • 1987
FILM AND REALITY • 1942 • Cavalcanti Alberto • CMP • UKN
FILM ANTICS • 1954 • Barclay David • SHT • USA
FILM AUS DEM SUEDEN, EIN see **GRUNE MANUELA, DIE** • 1923
FILM, AUTOPORTRAIT, UN • 1982 • Hanoun Marcel • FRN
FILM BEZ RECI • 1973 • Radivojevic Misa • YGS • FILM WITHOUT WORDS
FILM BITTI • 1988 • Ozkan Yavuz • TRK • FILM IS OVER
FILM COMME LES AUTRES, UNE • 1968 • Godard Jean-Luc • FRN • FILM LIKE ALL OTHERS, A
FILM CONCERT FOR THE RED ARMY'S 25TH ANNIVERSARY see **KINOKONCERT K25 LETIJU KRASNOJ ARMII** • 1943
FILM D'AMORE E D'ANARCHIA: OVVERO STAMATTINA ALLE IO IN VIA DEI FIORI NELLA NOTA CASA DI TOLLERANZA • 1973 • Wertmuller Lina • ITL • LOVE AND ANARCHY (USA) ○ AMORE E ANARCHIA ○ STORY OF LOVE AND ANARCHY ○ FILM OF LOVE AND ANARCHY
FILM D'ARIANE OU PETITE HISTOIRE DE FEMMES 1925-80, LE • 1986 • Beaudet Josee • DOC • CND
FILM DE ESTACAO • 1984 • Silva Jaime • PRT
FILM DE JEAN, LE see **JEAN COTON** • 1953
FILM DU POILU, LE • 1928 • Desfontaines Henri • FRN
FILM ELATION OF SPEJBL, THE see **SPEJBLOVO OPOJENI** • 1931
FILM EST DEJA COMMENCE • 1951 • Lemaitre Maurice • FRN
FILM EXERCISES #1-5 • 1941-45 • Whitney John, Whitney James • SHT • USA
FILM EXPOSURE, A • 1917 • *Dwiggins Jay* • USA
FILM FAN, THE • 1939 • Clampett Robert • ANS • USA
FILM FAVORITE'S FINISH, THE • 1915 • *Chamberlin Riley* • USA
FILM FAVOURITES • 1914 • Trimble Larry • UKN • FLORENCE TURNER IMPERSONATES FILM FAVORITES (USA)
FILM FAVOURITES • 1924 • Hepworth Cecil M. • UKN
FILM, FILM, FILM • 1968 • Hitruck Fedor • USS
FILM FOR DISCUSSION • 1973 • Ansara Martha • DOC • ASL
FILM FOR GUITAR • 1965 • Beresford Bruce • SHT • UKN
FILM FOR LUCEBERT, A see **FILM VOOR LUCEBERT** • 1967
FILM FOR MARIA, A • 1962 • Smith Jack* • UKN
FILM FOR MAX, A • 1971 • May Derek • CND
FILM FORM NO.1 • 1970 • Vanderbeek Stan • USA
FILM FORM NO.2 • 1970 • Vanderbeek Stan • SHT • USA
FILM FROM THE CLYDE • 1977 • Cinema Action • UKN • CLASS STRUGGLE: FILM FROM THE CLYDE
FILM GEGEN DIE VOLKKRANKHEIT KREBS -JEDER ACHTE..., EIN • 1941 • Ruttmann Walter • FRG • VOLKSKRANKHEIT KREBS -JEDER ACHTE
FILM HI FILM • 1983 • Nag Hiren • IND
FILM IM FILM, DER • 1924 • Porges Friedrich • FRG
FILM IN RHYTHM see **RHYTHMUS** • 1921-27
FILM IN WHICH THERE APPEAR SPROCKET HOLES, EDGE LETTERING, DIRT PARTICLES, ETC. • 1966 • Landow George • SHT • USA
FILM IS OVER see **FILM BITTI** • 1988
FILM IST RHYTHMUS see **RHYTHMUS 21** • 1921
FILM JOHNNIE, A • 1914 • Nicholls George, Sennett Mack • USA • MOVIE NUT ○ CHARLIE AT THE STUDIO ○ MILLION DOLLAR JOB
FILM-KATHI, DIE • 1919 • Portegg R. • FRG
FILM LIKE ALL OTHERS, A see **FILM COMME LES AUTRES, UNE** • 1968
FILM MAGAZINE OF THE ARTS • 1963 • Mekas Jonas • SHT • USA
FILM NOTITIES UIT DE SOVJET-UNIE • 1930 • Ivens Joris • SHT • NTH • NEWS FROM THE SOVIET UNION
FILM NOVEL -THREE SISTERS see **FILMREGENY -HAROM NOVER** • 1978
FILM O KNJIZI A.B.C. • 1962 • Makavejev Dusan • SHT • YGS • FILM ABOUT THE BOOK
FILM OF LOVE AND ANARCHY see **FILM D'AMORE E D'ANARCHIA: OVVERO STAMATTINA ALLE IO IN VIA DEI FIORI NELLA NOTA CASA DI TOLLERANZA** • 1973
FILM OF THEIR SPRING TOUR COMMISSIONED BY THE CHRISTIAN WORLD LIBERATION FRONT OF BERKELEY CALIFORNI • 1974 • Landow George • USA
FILM OHNE NAMEN, DER • 1922 • Schonfelder Erich • FRG
FILM OHNE TITEL • 1949 • Jugert Rudolf • FRG • FILM WITHOUT A NAME (USA) ○ FILM WITHOUT TITLE
FILM PARADE, THE • 1933 • Blackton J. Stuart • USA • CAVALCADE OF THE MOVIES ○ MARCH OF THE MOVIES
FILM PIE • 1920 • Malins Geoffrey H., Bruce Neville • SER • UKN
FILM REGENY see **FILMREGENY -HAROM NOVER** • 1978
FILM REPORT ON THE WAR NO.4 • 1941 • Alexandrov Grigori • USS
FILM SONG ALBUM • 1921 • SHS • UKN
FILM SONG ALBUM • 1922 • SHS • UKN
FILM SPOILERS, THE • 1917 • Parrott Charles • SHT • USA
FILM STAR'S PERFECT DAY, THE • 1921 • Bruce Neville • UKN
FILM STUDY see **FILMSTUDIE** • 1926
FILM SUR QUELQU'UN, UN • 1972 • Weyergans Francois • FRN
FILM TEMPO • 1915 • Bertram William • USA
FILM TEST, THE see **ZDJECIA PROBNE** • 1978
FILM THAT NEVER WAS, THE • 1957 • Dickson Paul • UKN
FILM THAT RISES TO THE SURFACE OF CLARIFIED BUTTER, THE • 1968 • Landow George • USA
FILM THAT WAS LOST, THE • 1942 • Lee Sammy • SHT • USA
FILM TRUTH see **KINO PRAVDA** • 1922-25
FILM VOOR LUCEBERT • 1967 • van der Keuken Johan • DOC • NTH • FILM FOR LUCEBERT, A
FILM WITH THREE DANCERS • 1970 • Emshwiller Ed • USA
FILM WITHOUT A NAME see **ZA SADA BEZ DOBROG NASLOVA** • 1987
FILM WITHOUT A NAME (USA) see **FILM OHNE TITEL** • 1949
FILM WITHOUT TITLE see **FILM OHNE TITEL** • 1949
FILM WITHOUT WORDS see **FILM BEZ RECI** • 1973
FILMABENTEUER • May Joe • AUS
FILMAVIS • Tuhus Oddvar Bull • SHT • NRW
FILMBANDITEN • 1921 • Hartenstein Paul • FRG
FILME DER PRINZESSIN FANTOCHE, DIE • 1921 • Neufeld Max • AUS
FILMEN OG ELISE • 1984 • Ploug Claus • DNM • FILM ABOUT ELISE
FILMENS DATTER • 1915 • Davidsen Hjalmar • DNM
FILMENS VIDUNDERLIGE VERDEN • 1978 • Greve Bruno • NRW • FILM -A WONDERFUL WORLD
FILMGORE • 1983 • Dixon Ken • CMP • USA
FILMING OF OTHELLO, THE • 1977 • Welles Orson
FILMINUTO • Padron Juan • ANM • CUB
FILMORE BUS, THE • 1961 • Branaman Bob • USA
FILMPRIMADONNA, DIE • 1913 • Gad Urban • FRG, DNM • FILMPRIMADONNA, DEN (DNM)
FILMPRIMADONNA, DEN (DNM) see **FILMPRIMADONNA, DIE** • 1913
FILMREGENY -HAROM NOVER • 1978 • Darday Istvan, Szalai Gyorgyi • HNG • FILM NOVEL -THREE SISTERS ○ FILM REGENY ○ SISTERS
FILMS BY BOB BRANAMAN • Branaman Bob • SHT • USA
FILMS BY STAN BRAKHAGE: AN AVANT-GARDE HOME MOVIE • 1961 • Brakhage Stan • SHT • USA
FILMS OF HARRY SMITH, THE • 1965 • Smith Harry • ANT • USA
FILMS OF THE PARIS EXHIBITION • 1900 • Hepworth Cecil M. • UKN
FILMSTUDIE • 1926 • Richter Hans • FRG • FILM STUDY
FILMSTUDY -ZEEDIJK see **ZEEDIJK FILM STUDIE** • 1927
FILO DEL MIEDO, EL • 1967 • Balcazar Jaime Jesus • SPN • CUTTING EDGE OF FEAR, THE
FILO DELLA VITA, IL • 1918 • Caserini Mario • ITL
FILO D'ERBA, IL • 1952 • Vassarotti Vittorio • ITL • HA DA VENI'.. DON CALOGERO
FILO DI SPERANZA, UN (ITL) see **JUSQU'AU BOUT DU MONDE** • 1962
FILOPAT UND PATOFIL • Steinbach Heinz • GDR
FILOSOFSKA HISTORIE • 1937 • Vavra Otakar • CZC • PHILOSOPHICAL STORY, A ○ PHILOSOPHICAL HISTORY
FILOU • 1988 • Aldin Samir Jamal • SWT
FILS ET CIE • 1957 • Saytor Tony • FRN
FILS, LE • 1973 • Granier-Deferre Pierre • FRN, ITL • BATTITO D'ALI DOPO LA STRAGE, UN (ITL)
FILS A PAPA see **PAPA SANS LE SAVOIR** • 1931
FILS D'AMERIQUE, UN • 1925 • Fescourt Henri • FRN
FILS D'AMERIQUE, UN • 1932 • Gallone Carmine • FRN, HNG • AMERIKAI FLU, AZ (HNG)
FILS D'AMIDOU, LE see **IBN HAMIDU** • 1956
FILS D'AMR EST MORT, LE see **MENSONGE, LE** • 1974
FILS DE CAROLINE CHERIE, LE • 1954 • Devaivre Jean • FRN • SON OF DEAR CAROLINE, THE (USA)
FILS DE CHARLES QUINT, LE • 1912 • Andreani Henri • FRN
FILS DE FIERRO, LES • 1978 • Salinas Fernando E. • FRN, FRG
FILS DE FRANCE • 1945 • Blondy Pierre • FRN • COMBATS D'ALSACE
FILS DE LA LIBERTE, LES • 1981 • Boissol Claude • CND
FILS DE LA NUIT, LE • 1919 • Bourgeois Gerard • FRN
FILS DE LA SUNAMITE, LE • 1911 • Feuillade Louis • FRN
FILS DE L'AUTRE, LE • 1931 • de La Falaise Henri • FRN • FEMME LIBRE, UNE ○ MADAME JULIE
FILS DE L'EAU, LES • 1955 • Rouch Jean • DOC • FRN
FILS DE L'ELEPHANT, LES • 1952 • Philippe Anne • SHT • BLG
FILS DE L'INNOCENT, LE • 1914 • Burguet Charles • FRN
FILS DE LOCUSTE, LE • 1911 • Feuillade Louis • FRN
FILS DE TARASS-BULBA, LE • 1961 • Zaphiratos Henri-T. • FRN, ITL
FILS DU BOURREAU, LE • 1913 • Protazanov Yakov • USS

FILS DU CHARPENTIER, LE • 1908 • Perret Leonce • FRN
FILS DU CHEIKH, LE (FRN) see **FIGLIO DELLO SCEICCO, IL** • 1962
FILS DU DIABLE, LE • 1906 • Lepine Charles • FRN • SON OF THE DEVIL
FILS DU FLIBUSTIER, LE • 1922 • Feuillade Louis • FRN • SON OF A BUCCANEER, THE
FILS DU GARDE-CHASSE, LE • 1906 • Blache Alice • FRN
FILS DU RAJAH, LE • 1931 • Autant-Lara Claude • FRN
FILS DU SOLEIL, LE • 1925 • Le Somptier Rene • FRN
FILS DU VENT, LE • 1920 • de Carbonnat Louis • FRN
FILS IMPROVISE, LE • 1932 • Guissart Rene • FRN
FILS NATUREL • 1918 • de Baroncelli Jacques • FRN
FILS POUR L'ETE, UN see **TRIBUTE** • 1981
FILS PRODIGUE, LE • 1974 • Goretta Claude • SWT
FILS PUNI, LE • 1978 • Collin Philippe • FRN
FILS UNIQUE, LE see **FILS UNIQUE, UN** • 1967
FILS UNIQUE, UN • 1967 • Polac Michel • FRN • FILS UNIQUE, LE
FILTH SHOP, THE • 1969 • *Sex Susan* • USA
FILTHIEST SHOW IN TOWN, THE • 1973 • Engelson Bob, Engelson Rick • USA
FILTHY FIVE, THE • 1968 • Milligan Andy • USA • F- FIVE, THE ○ DIRTY FIVE, THE
FILTRATION DES EAUX, LA • 1963 • Regnier Michel • DCS • CND
FILUMENA MARTURANO • 1951 • De Filippo Eduardo • ITL
FIM DE FESTA • 1980 • Porto Paulo • BRZ • PARTY'S END
FIM DE SEMANA COM A MORTE • 1967 • Coll Julio • PRT • WEEK-END WITH DEATH
FIM DO ANO NA MADEIRA • 1957 • Garcia Fernando • SHT • PRT
FIMPEN • 1974 • Widerberg Bo • SWD • STUBBY
FIN DE CURSO • 1943 • Iquino Ignacio F. • SPN
FIN DE DON JUAN, LA • 1911 • Jasset Victorin • FRN
FIN DE FIESTA • 1960 • Torre-Nilsson Leopoldo • ARG • PARTY IS OVER, THE ○ BLOOD FEAST
FIN DE FIESTA • 1971 • Walerstein Mauricio • MXC
FIN DE JEU • 1971 • Ledoux Patrick • BLG
FIN DE LA INOCENCIA, EL • 1976 • Larraz Jose R. • SPN
FIN DE MES • 1953 • Cahen Enrique • ARG
FIN DE PAGANINI, LA • 1910 • *Gance Abel* • FRN
FIN DE SEMANA • 1962 • Lazaga Pedro • SPN
FIN DE SEMANA AL DESNUDO • 1976 • Ozores Mariano • VNZ, SPN • UNCOVERED WEEKEND
FIN DE SEMANA PARA LOS MUERTOS • 1974 • Grau Jorge • SPN, ITL • LIVING DEAD AT THE MANCHESTER MORGUE, THE ○ DON'T OPEN THE WINDOW (USA) ○ BREAKFAST AT MANCHESTER MORGUE ○ BREAKFAST AT THE MANCHESTER MORGUE ○ ITL ○ NO PROFANAR EL SUENO DE LOS MUERTOS
FIN DE SIECLE see **PATTES DE MOUCHE, LES** • 1936
FIN DE UN IMPERIO, EL • 1956 • Salvador Jaime • MXC
FIN DEL JUEGO, EL • Cornejo Luis • CHL • END OF THE GAME, THE
FIN DES ETES, LA • 1964 • Poirier Anne-Claire • SHT • CND
FIN DES PYRENEES, LA • 1970 • Lajournade Jean-Pierre • FRN
FIN DES ROMANOFF, LA see **TRAGEDIE IMPERIALE, LA** • 1937
FIN DU JOUR, LA • 1938 • Duvivier Julien • FRN • END OF THE DAY, THE (USA)
FIN DU MONDE, LA • 1930 • Gance Abel • FRN • END OF THE WORLD, THE (USA)
FIN D'UN ALCOOLIQUE, LA see **DELIRIUM TREMENS, LE** • 1907
FIN D'UN DESERT • 1958 • Menegoz Robert • SHT • FRN
FIN D'UNE REVOLUTION AMERICAINE, LA • 1912 • Feuillade Louis • FRN
FIN D'UNE VIE, LA see **DERNIERE JEUNESSE** • 1939
FIN ET LES MOYENS, LA • 1953 • Novik William • SHT • FRN
FIN' 'N CATTY • 1943 • Jones Charles M. • ANS • USA
FINAL ACCORD (UKN) see **SCHLUSSAKKORD** • 1936
FINAL ALLIANCE • 1989 • Dileo Mario • USA
FINAL APPOINTMENT • 1954 • Fisher Terence • UKN
FINAL ARRANGEMENT, THE see **TILINTEKO** • 1987
FINAL ASSIGNMENT • 1980 • Almond Paul • CND
FINAL BLOW, THE • 1970 • *Stacey Dist.* • USA
FINAL CHAPTER -WALKING TALL • 1977 • Starrett Jack • USA • WALKING TALL 3: THE FINAL CHAPTER
FINAL CLOSE-UP, THE • 1919 • Edwards Walter • USA
FINAL COLUMN • 1955 • MacDonald David • UKN
FINAL COMEDOWN, THE • 1972 • Williams Oscar • USA • BLAST
FINAL CONFLICT, THE • 1981 • Baker Graham* • USA • OMEN 3: THE FINAL CONFLICT ○ FINAL CONFLICT: OMEN 3, THE
FINAL CONFLICT: OMEN 3, THE see **FINAL CONFLICT, THE** • 1981
FINAL COUNTDOWN, THE • 1979 • Taylor Don • USA
FINAL CRASH, THE see **STEELYARD BLUES** • 1973
FINAL CURTAIN, THE • 1916 • *Hanlon Alma* • USA
FINAL CUT • 1980 • Dimsey Ross • ASL
FINAL CUT • 1987 • Brown Larry • USA
FINAL CUT • 1989 • Nel Frans • SAF
FINAL DE UNA LEYENDA, EL • 1950 • Gascon Jose • SPN
FINAL DECISION, THE see **ZOKU OTOSHIMAE** • 1968
FINAL DEFEAT, THE see **SETTE WINCHESTER PER UN MASSACRO** • 1967
FINAL EDITION, THE • 1932 • Higgin Howard • USA • DETERMINATION (UKN)
FINAL EDITION, THE • 1981 • Rowe Peter • MTV • CND
FINAL EXAM • 1981 • Huston Jimmy • USA
FINAL EXECUTIONER, THE • 1983 • Guerrieri Romolo • ITL • LAST WARRIOR, THE ○ FINAL EXECUTOR
FINAL EXECUTOR see **FINAL EXECUTIONER, THE** • 1983
FINAL EXTRA, THE • 1927 • Hogan James P. • USA
FINAL EYE, THE see **COMPUTERCIDE** • 1982
FINAL FRAUD, THE • 1916 • Haydon J. Charles • SHT • USA
FINAL HOUR, THE • 1936 • Lederman D. Ross • USA
FINAL HOUR, THE • 1963 • Douglas Robert • MTV • USA
FINAL IMPULSE, THE • 1914 • *American* • USA
FINAL JEOPARDY • 1985 • Pressman Michael • TVM • USA
FINAL JUDGEMENT, THE • 1913 • MacMackin Archer • USA
FINAL JUDGEMENT, THE • 1915 • Carewe Edwin • USA
FINAL JUSTICE • 1984 • Clark Greydon • USA, ITL • MALTESE CONNECTION, THE ○ MALTESE PROJECT, THE
FINAL JUSTICE, THE • 1913 • *Lytton L. Rogers* • USA
FINAL LAUGHTER see **SAIGO NI WARAU OTOKO** • 1949
FINAL LIE, THE see **TELEFTEO PSEMMA, TO** • 1957
FINAL MISSION • 1984 • Santiago Cirio H. • PHL, USA
FINAL OFFER see **FINAL OFFER: BOB WHITE AND THE UNITED AUTO WORKERS FIGHT FOR INDEPENDENCE** • 1986
FINAL OFFER: BOB WHITE AND THE UNITED AUTO WORKERS FIGHT FOR INDEPENDENCE • 1986 • Gunnarsson Sturla • CND • FINAL OFFER
FINAL OPTION, THE (USA) see **WHO DARES WINS** • 1982
FINAL PARDON, THE • 1912 • Porter Edwin S. • USA
FINAL PAYMENT, THE • 1916 • Kent Leon D., Melville Wilbert • SHT • USA
FINAL PAYMENT, THE • 1917 • Powell Frank • USA
FINAL PROBLEM, THE • 1923 • Ridgwell George • UKN
FINAL PROGRAMME, THE • 1973 • Fuest Robert • UKN • LAST DAYS OF MAN ON EARTH
FINAL RECKONING, THE • 1914 • Edwards Walter • USA • RECKONING, THE
FINAL RECKONING, THE • 1915 • *La Badie Florence* • USA
FINAL RECKONING, THE • 1932 • Argyle John F. • UKN
FINAL SANCTION • 1989 • Prior David A. • USA
FINAL SETTLEMENT, THE • 1910 • Griffith D. W. • USA
FINAL TACTIC see **FORCE FIVE** • 1975
FINAL TERROR, THE • 1981 • Davis Andrew • USA • CAMPSITE MASSACRE
FINAL TEST • Ben Art • USA
FINAL TEST, THE • 1914 • *Princess* • USA
FINAL TEST, THE • 1953 • Asquith Anthony • UKN
FINAL VERDICT, THE • 1914 • Walsh Raoul • USA • FINAL VOTE, THE
FINAL VOTE, THE see **FINAL VERDICT, THE** • 1914
FINAL WAR, THE see **SEKAI DAI SENSO** • 1961
FINAL WAR, THE (USA) see **DAI SANJI SEKAI TAISEN-YONJI-ICHI JIKAN NO KYOFU** • 1960
FINALE • 1948 • Erfurth Ulrich • FRG
FINALE • 1962 • Vas Robert, Darlow Michael • UKN
FINALE • 1970 • Wein George, Stiber Sidney J. • DOC • USA
FINALE see **UNRUHIGEN MADCHEN, DIE** • 1938
FINALE DER LIEBE • 1925 • Basch Felix • FRG
FINALEMENT.. • 1971 • Martin Richard • CND
FINALEMENT SOLI • 1942 • Gentilomo Giacomo • ITL • HO PERDUTO MIA MOGLIE
FINALLY SUNDAY see **VIVEMENT DIMANCHE** • 1983
FINALMENTE LE MILLE E UNA NOTTE • 1972 • Margheriti Antonio • ITL • BED OF A THOUSAND PLEASURES ○ 1001 NIGHTS
FINALMENTE LIBERO! • 1953 • Amendola Mario, Maccari Ruggero • ITL
FINALMENTE SI • 1943 • Kish Ladislao • ITL • FELICITA SOTTO LA PIOGGIA
FINANCE NOIRE • 1940 • Gandera Felix • FRN • GUET-APENS DANS LA FORET NOIRE
FINANCES OF THE GRAND DUKE, THE see **FINANZEN DES GROSSHERZOGS, DIE** • 1924
FINANCIAL FRENZY, A • 1917 • *Myers Harry* • USA
FINANCIAL JITTERS • 1934 • Horne James W. • SHT • USA
FINANCING THE FOURTH • 1918 • *Drew Sidney* • SHT • USA
FINANZEN DES GROSSHERZOGS, DIE • 1924 • Murnau F. W. • FRG • FINANCES OF THE GRAND DUKE, THE ○ GRAND DUKE'S FINANCES, THE
FINANZEN DES GROSSHERZOGS, DIE • 1934 • Grundgens Gustaf • FRG • GRAND DUKE'S FINANCES, THE
FINCHE C'E GUERRA C'E SPERANZA • 1974 • Sordi Alberto • ITL • WHILE THERE'S WAR THERE'S HOPE (USA)
FINCHE DURA LA TEMPESTA • 1962 • Frend Charles, Vailati Bruno • ITL, FRN • DEFI A GIBRALTAR (FRN) ○ TORPEDO BAY (USA) ○ BETA SOM
FINCHO • 1958 • Zebra Sam • NGR
FIND A PLACE TO DIE see **JOE, CERCATI UN POSTO PER MORIRE** • 1968
FIND A WAY, COMRADE see **SNADJI SE DRUZE** • 1982
FIND, FIX AND STRIKE • 1942 • Bennett Compton • DOC • UKN
FIND LIVINGSTONE • 1968 • SAF
FIND ME see **NAYDI MENYA** • 1968
FIND OUT TALK ABOUT • 1981 • McLennan Don • DOC • ASL
FIND THE BLACKMAILER • 1943 • Lederman D. Ross • USA
FIND THE GIRL • 1920 • Roach Hal • SHT • USA
FIND THE LADY • 1936 • Gillett Burt • UKN
FIND THE LADY • 1956 • Saunders Charles • UKN
FIND THE LADY • 1976 • Trent John • CND
FIND THE WITNESS • 1937 • Selman David • USA
FIND THE WOMAN • 1918 • Beranger George A. • USA
FIND THE WOMAN • 1918 • Terriss Tom • *Vitagraph* • USA
FIND THE WOMAN • 1922 • Terriss Tom • USA
FIND THE WOMAN • 1926 • Malins Geoffrey H., Parkinson H. B. • UKN
FIND YOUR MAN • 1924 • St. Clair Malcolm • USA
FINDEN SIE, DASS CONSTANZE SICH RICHTING VERHALT? • 1962 • Pevsner Tom • FRG • CONSTANT WIFE, THE
FINDERS KEEPERS • 1921 • Thayer Otis B. • USA
FINDERS KEEPERS • 1928 • Ruggles Wesley • USA
FINDERS KEEPERS • 1951 • De Cordova Frederick • USA
FINDERS KEEPERS • 1966 • Hayers Sidney • UKN
FINDERS KEEPERS • 1984 • Lester Richard • UKN
FINDERS KEEPERS, LOVERS WEEPERS • 1968 • Meyer Russ • USA
FINDING A NEW PATH • 1984 • von Puttkamer Peter • DOC • CND
FINDING FREDDY WORK • 1912 • *Cosmopolitan* • USA
FINDING HIS VOICE • 1929 • Goldman F. Lyle, Fleischer Max • ANS • USA
FINDING KATIE • 1983 • Sharp Peter • NZL • TRESPASSES ○ OMEN OF EVIL
FINDING MARY MARCH • 1988 • Pittman Ken • CND
FINDING MAUBEE see **MIGHTY QUINN, THE** • 1989
FINDING THE LAST CHANCE MINE • 1912 • Melies Gaston • USA
FINDLING, DER • 1968 • Moorse Georg • FRG
FINDS OF THE FORTNIGHT • 1960 • Jordan Larry • ANM • USA
FINE AND DANDY (UKN) see **WEST POINT STORY, THE** • 1950
FINE ARTS AT YORK • 1977 • Vaitiekunas Vince • CND
FINE ARTS OF JOCKO, THE see **BEAUX-ARTS DE JOCKO, LES** • 1909
FINE CLOTHES • 1925 • Stahl John M. • USA • FASHION FOR MEN
FINE DEL GIOCO, LA • 1971 • Amelio Gianni • MTV • ITL
FINE DEL MONDO NEL NOSTRO SOLITO LETTO IN UNA NOTTEPIENA DI PIOGGIA, LA • 1978 • Wertmuller Lina • ITL, USA • NIGHT FULL OF RAIN ○ END OF THE WORLD IN OUR USUAL BED IN A NIGHT FULL OF RAIN, THE (USA)
FINE DELL'INNOCENZA, LA • 1976 • Dallamano Massimo • ITL, UKN • BLUE BELLE (UKN) ○ END OF INNOCENCE, THE
FINE FEATHER • 1968 • Lambart Evelyn • ANS • CND
FINE-FEATHERED FIEND • 1960 • Kneitel Seymour • ANS • USA
FINE FEATHERED FRENZY • 1954 • Patterson Don • ANS • USA
FINE FEATHERED FRIEND • 1942 • Hanna William, Barbera Joseph • ANS • USA
FINE FEATHERS • 1912 • *Weber Lois* • USA
FINE FEATHERS • 1915 • *Beecher Janet* • USA
FINE FEATHERS • 1915 • Elvey Maurice • UKN
FINE FEATHERS • 1921 • Sittenham Fred • USA
FINE FEATHERS • 1933 • White Jules • SHT • USA
FINE FEATHERS • 1937 • Hiscott Leslie • UKN
FINE FEATHERS • 1941 • Buchanan Andrew • UKN
FINE FEATHERS MAKE FINE BIRDS • 1914 • *Melies* • USA
FINE FEATHERS MAKE FINE BIRDS • 1914 • Humphrey William • *Vitagraph* • USA
FINE FEATHERS (UKN) see **FOOTLOOSE WIDOWS** • 1926
FINE FELLOW see **DAIGAN JOJU** • 1959
FINE FELLOWS DURING THE MOBILISATION see **TOFFE JONGENS ONDER DE MOBILISATIE** • 1914
FINE FISHERMAN, THE • 1903 • *Paul R. W.* • UKN
FINE GOLD • 1988 • de la Loma Jose Antonio • SPN
FINE MADNESS, A • 1966 • Kershner Irvin • USA
FINE MANNERS • 1926 • Rosson Richard • USA
FINE MANNERS see **BELLES MANIERES, LES** • 1978
FINE MESS, A • 1986 • Edwards Blake • USA
FINE PAIR, A (USA) see **RUBA AL PROSSIMO TUO** • 1968
FINE POINTE, LA • 1979 • Payer Roch Christophe • CND
FINE POINTS • 1933 • Marshall George • SHT • USA
FINE SNOW see **SASAME YUKI** • 1983
FINE SON-IN-LAW, A see **YOI MUKODONO** • 1954
FINE TOLERANCE, A • 1979 • *Nihalani Govind (Ph)* • DOC • IND
FINE WHITE LINE, THE see **COCAINE WARS** • 1985
FINE WINDY DAYS • Lee Chang-Ho • SKR
FINER METAL, THE • 1916 • Schrock Raymond L. • SHT • USA
FINER THINGS, THE • 1913 • Dwan Allan • USA
FINEST GOLD, THE • 1915 • MacQuarrie Murdock • USA
FINEST HOURS, THE • 1964 • Baylis Peter • DOC • UKN
FINESTRA SUL LUNA PARK, LA • 1957 • Comencini Luigi • ITL
FINESTRE • 1950 • Maselli Francesco • DOC • ITL
FINGAL'S CAVE • 1946 • Vorkapich Slavko • SHT • USA
FINGER MAN • 1955 • Schuster Harold • USA • FINGERMAN
FINGER OF DESTINY, THE • 1914 • Raymond Charles • UKN
FINGER OF FATE, THE • 1911 • Noy Wilfred • UKN
FINGER OF FATE, THE • 1913 • *Woodruff Eleanor* • USA
FINGER OF GOD, THE see **PALEC BOZY** • 1972
FINGER OF GUILT see **INTIMATE STRANGER, THE** • 1956
FINGER OF JUSTICE, THE • 1918 • Chaudet William • USA
FINGER OF SCORN, THE • 1912 • *Thanhouser* • USA
FINGER OF SUSPICION, THE • 1912 • *Joyce Alice* • USA
FINGER OF SUSPICION, THE • 1916 • Batley Ethyle • UKN
FINGER ON THE TRIGGER • 1965 • Pink Sidney • USA, SPN • DEDO EN EL GATILLO, EL (SPN)
FINGER POINTS, THE • 1931 • Dillon John Francis • USA
FINGER PRESSING TREATMENT see **AI NO SANPUNKAN SHIATSU** • 1968
FINGER PRINT, THE • 1913 • Eagle Oscar • USA
FINGER PRINTS • 1914 • *Bushman Francis X.* • USA
FINGER PRINTS • 1920 • Sowders Edward • SHT • USA
FINGER PRINTS • 1923 • Levering Joseph • USA
FINGER PRINTS • 1923 • Roach Hal • SHT • USA
FINGER PRINTS • 1927 • Bacon Lloyd • USA
FINGER PRINTS • 1931 • Taylor Ray • SRL • USA
FINGER PRINTS, THE • 1912 • *Karr Darwin* • USA
FINGER PRINTS OF FATE • 1915 • *Thanhouser* • USA
FINGER - WATER - LIGHT • Beattie Paul • SHT • USA • F - W - L
FINGER WAVE • 1987 • Nagy Gyula • ANS • HNG
FINGERMAN see **LADY KILLER** • 1933
FINGERMAN see **FINGER MAN** • 1955
FINGERMAN, THE see **DOULOS, LE** • 1962
FINGERNAGEL, DER see **FUND IM NEUBAU 1, DER** • 1915
FINGERPRINT see **AMPRENTA** • 1967
FINGERPRINTS DON'T LIE • 1950 • Newfield Sam • USA
FINGERS • 1940 • Mason Herbert • UKN
FINGERS • 1978 • Toback James • USA
FINGERS see **FIVE FINGERS** • 1952
FINGERS AND POCKETS • 1920 • Goldaine Mark • SHT • USA
FINGERS AND THUMBS • 1938 • Cherry Evelyn Spice • UKN
FINGERS AT THE WINDOW • 1942 • Lederer Charles • USA
FINGERS OF LIGHT see **DOIGTS DE LUMIERE, LES** • 1947
FINIAN'S RAINBOW • 1968 • Coppola Francis Ford • USA
FINIE LA CRISE see **CRISE EST FINIE, LA** • 1934
FINIS TERRAE • 1929 • Epstein Jean • FRN
FINISCE SEMPRE COSI • 1939 • Susini Enrique T. • ITL
FINISH, THE • 1917 • Windom Lawrence C. • SHT • USA
FINISH LINE • 1988 • Nicolella John • USA
FINISH OF BRIDGET MCKEEN, THE • 1901 • Porter Edwin S. • USA
FINISHED • 1923 • Cooper George A. • UKN
FINISHED ACTOR, A • 1927 • Sennett Mack • SHT • USA
FINISHED PRODUCT ,A • 1917 • *Dwiggins Jay* • SHT • USA
FINISHING MARY • 1918 • *Rhodes Billie* • USA

FINISHING SCHOOL • 1934 • Tuchock Wanda, Nicholls George Jr. • USA
FINISHING SCHOOL • 1975 • Brummer Alois • FRG
FINISHING SCHOOL see **GEFAHRLICHER SEX FRUHREIFER MADCHEN** • 1971
FINISHING SCHOOL (UKN) see **FANCIULLE DI LUSSO** • 1953
FINISHING STROKE see **QUEMA DE JUDAS, LA** • 1974
FINISHING TOUCH see **YOUR TICKET IS NO LONGER VALID** • 1980
FINISHING TOUCH, THE • 1916 • Cochrane George • SHT • USA
FINISHING TOUCH, THE • 1928 • Bruckman Clyde • SHT • USA
FINISHING TOUCH, THE • 1932 • Stevens George • SHT • USA
FINLAND • 1951 • D'Avino Carmen • USA
FINLAND, MY SWEET HOME see **KOTIMAANI OMPI SUOMI**
FINLANDE • 1951 • Bonniere Rene • SHT • FRN
FINLAND'S LAST WOLF see **SUOMEN VIIMEINEN SUSI** • 1973
FINN AND HADDIE • 1915 • Winter Percy • USA
FINN AND HATTIE • 1931 • McLeod Norman Z., Taurog Norman • USA • FINN AND HATTIE ABROAD
FINN AND HATTIE ABROAD see **FINN AND HATTIE** • 1931
FINNEGAN • 1913 • *Essanay* • USA
FINNEGAN BEGIN AGAIN • 1985 • Silver Joan Micklin • TVM • USA
FINNEGAN'S BALL • 1927 • Hogan James P. • USA
FINNEGAN'S BOMB • 1914 • Nicholls George • USA
FINNEGANS CHIN • 1982 • Le Grice Malcolm • UKN
FINNEGAN'S FLEA • 1958 • Sparber I. • ANS • USA
FINNEGAN'S WAKE see **PASSAGES FROM "FINNEGAN'S WAKE"** • 1967
FINNEY • 1969 • Hare Bill • USA
FINNEY'S LUCK • 1913 • *Punch* • USA
FINNIGAN'S INITIATION • 1909 • *Lubin* • USA
FINNISH FABLE, A • 1965 • D'Avino Carmen • SHT • USA
FINNISH FABLES see **SUOMALAISIA ELAINTARINOITA** • 1973-75
FINNISH FRUSTRATIONS see **AMPUMARATA** • 1970
FINNSKOGENS FOLK • 1955 • Johansson Ivar • SWD • PEOPLE FROM THE DEPTHS OF THE FOREST
FINO A FARTI MALE (ITL) see **ADELAIDE** • 1968
FINSTERNIS UND IHR EIGENTUM, DIE • 1922 • Hartwig Martin • FRG
FINTE BIONDE, LE • 1988 • Vanzina Carlo • ITL • FAKE BLONDES, THE
FINYE • 1982 • Cisse Souleymane • MLI • VENT, LE ○ WIND, THE
FINZAN • 1988 • Sissoko Cheikh Oumar • MLI
FINZI DETECTIVE AGENCY, THE see **AGENZIA RICCARDO FINZI.. PRATICAMENTE DETECTIVE** • 1979
FIOCCO NERO PER DEBORAH, UN • 1974 • Andrei Marcello • ITL • BLACK RIBBON FOR DEBORAH, A ○ DEBORAH (USA) ○ TORMENT
FIOLE ENCHANTEE, LA • 1902 • Blache Alice • FRN
FIONA see **LET'S GET LAID** • 1977
FIONA ON FIRE • 1978 • Evans Warren • USA • WHITE FLESH IS WEAK
FIOR D'AMORE • 1920 • Caserini Mario • ITL
FIOR DEL MALE • 1914 • Oxilia Nino • ITL
FIOR DI MALE • 1915 • Gallone Carmine • ITL
FIORDALISI D'ORO • 1936 • Forzano Giovacchino • ITL
FIORE DAI PETALI D'ACCACIAIO, IL • 1973 • Piccioli Gianfranco • ITL
FIORE DELLE MILLE E UNA NOTTE, IL • 1974 • Pasolini Pier Paolo • ITL • THOUSAND AND ONE NIGHTS, A ○ ARABIAN NIGHTS
FIORE SELVAGGIO • 1920 • Serena Gustavo • ITL
FIORE SOTTO GLI OCCHI, IL • 1944 • Brignone Guido • ITL
FIORENZO, IL TERZO UOMO • 1951 • Canzio Stefano • DOC • ITL
FIORI D'ARANCIO see **ANIMALI PAZZI** • 1939
FIORINA LA VACCA • 1972 • De Sisti Vittorio • ITL
FIORITURE: OU, LA SOURCE DE BEAUTE see **FIORITURES OU SOURCES DE BEAUTE** • 1915
FIORITURES OU SOURCES DE BEAUTE • 1915 • Gance Abel • FRN • FIORITURE: OU, LA SOURCE DE BEAUTE
FIPS THE TROUBLEMAKER • Hempel Johannes • ANM • GDR
FIR TREE, THE • 1979 • Sullivan Kevin • MTV • CND
FIRAR • 1985 • Goren Serif • TRK • ESCAPE, THE
FIRATIN CINLERI • 1979 • Yurtsever Korhan • TRK • EVIL SPIRITS OF THE EUPHRATES, THE
FIRE! • 1901 • Williamson James • UKN
FIRE! • 1977 • Bellamy Earl • TVM • USA • IRWIN ALLEN'S PRODUCTION OF FIRE!
FIRE • 1989 • Keppy Martin • NTH
FIRE! see **FIRE BRIGADE, THE** • 1926
FIRE see **OGON** • 1930
FIRE see **AAG** • 1945
FIRE see **AAG** • 1968
FIRE! see **FUOCO!** • 1968
FIRE see **OGIEN** • 1971
FIRE see **AGNI** • 1977
FIRE see **YANGIN** • 1977
FIRE see **AAG HI AAG** • 1988
FIRE, THE see **FEUER, DAS** • 1914
FIRE, THE see **POZHARAT** • 1968
FIRE, THE see **BRANNEN** • 1973
FIRE, THE see **POZAR** • 1975
FIRE ALARM see **FLAMES** • 1932
FIRE ALARM, THE • 1936 • King Jack • ANS • USA
FIRE AND ICE • 1982 • Bakshi Ralph • ANM • USA
FIRE AND ICE • 1987 • Bogner Willy • FRG • SKI DANCE
FIRE AND ICE (USA) see **COMBAT DANS L'ILE, LE** • 1962
FIRE AND PASSION see **FOGO E PAIXAO** • 1988
FIRE AND STEEL • 1927 • Bracken Bertram • USA
FIRE AND STRAW • 1912 • *Hawley Ormi* • USA
FIRE AND SWORD • 1914 • Hunter T. Hayes • USA
FIRE AND SWORD see **COL FERRO E COL FUOCO** • 1962
FIRE AT SEA • 1908 • *Kalem* • USA
FIRE AT WILL see **FEU A VOLONTE** • 1965
FIRE AWAY • 1925 • Roberts Stephen • SHT • USA
FIRE-BABY, THE see **MOTOTO** • 1932
FIRE BARRIER, THE • 1926 • Wyler William • SHT • USA
FIRE BELOW! • 1962 • Busby Geoff • UKN
FIRE BIRD see **HINOTORI** • 1948
FIRE BIRD, THE see **ELDFAGELN** • 1952
FIRE BRAND, THE • 1970 • Bonniere Rene • CND
FIRE BRIDE, THE • 1913 • *Patheplay* • USA
FIRE BRIDE, THE • 1922 • Rosson Arthur • USA
FIRE BRIGADE, THE • 1926 • Nigh William • USA • FIRE!
FIRE BRIGADE, THE • 1928 • *Wilton Robb* • SHT • UKN
FIRE BRIGADE TURN-OUT IN THE COUNTRY • 1899 • Norton C. Goodwin • UKN • COUNTRY FIRE BRIGADE
FIRE BUGS • 1930 • Fleischer Dave • ANS • USA
FIRE CALL AND RESCUE BY FIRE ESCAPES • 1899 • *Warwick Trading Co.* • UKN
FIRE CAT, THE • 1921 • Dawn Norman • USA
FIRE CHEESE • 1941 • Fleischer Dave • ANS • USA
FIRE CHIEF • 1940 • King Jack • ANS • USA
FIRE CHIEF, THE see **LOVER'S MIGHT, A** • 1916
FIRE CHIEF, THE see **CHIEF, THE** • 1933
FIRE CHIEF'S BRIDE, THE • 1914 • Henderson Dell • USA
FIRE CHIEF'S DAUGHTER, THE • 1910 • Boggs Frank • USA
FIRE COP, THE • 1912 • *Selig* • USA
FIRE COWARD, THE • 1913 • *Foxe Earle* • USA
FIRE DETECTIVE, THE • 1929 • Bennet Spencer Gordon, Storey Thomas L. • SRL • USA
FIRE DIAEVLE, DE • 1911 • Dinesen Robert • DNM • FOUR DEVILS, THE
FIRE DJAEVLE, DE • 1920 • Sandberg Anders W. • DNM • FOUR DEVILS, THE
FIRE DOWN BELOW • 1957 • Parrish Robert • USA
FIRE EATER, THE • 1921 • Eason B. Reeves • USA
FIRE ESCAPE, THE • 1915 • Van Deusen Courtlandt • USA
FIRE ESCAPE FINISH, THE • 1917 • Edwards Harry J. • SHT • USA
FIRE FESTIVAL see **HIMATSURI** • 1985
FIRE FIGHTERS, THE • 1922 • Roach Hal • SHT • USA
FIRE FIGHTERS, THE • 1930 • Gillett Burt • ANS • USA
FIRE-FIGHTER'S LOVE, THE • 1912 • Eagle Oscar • USA
FIRE FIGHTERS (UKN) see **ARSON RACKET SQUAD** • 1938
FIRE-FIGHTING ZOUAVES, THE • 1913 • Melford George • USA
FIRE! FIRE! • 1914 • *Lubin* • USA
FIRE! FIRE! • 1919 • *Briggs* • SHT • USA
FIRE! FIRE! • 1932 • *Iwerks Ub (P)* • ANS • USA
FIRE! FIRE! see **HORI, MA PANENKO!** • 1967
FIRE, FIRE, SOMETHING IS HAPPENING AT LAST! see **POZAR, POZAR, COS NARESZCIE DZIEJE SIE!** • 1967
FIRE FLINGERS, THE • 1919 • Julian Rupert • USA
FIRE HAS BEEN ARRANGED, A • 1935 • Hiscott Leslie • UKN
FIRE, ICE AND DYNAMITE see **FEUER, EIS UND DYNAMIT** • 1990
FIRE IN EDEN • 1986 • Moore Tara • USA
FIRE IN THE BLOOD see **RAGE AU CORPS, LA** • 1953
FIRE IN THE FLESH (USA) see **FILLE DE FEU, LA** • 1958
FIRE IN THE NIGHT • 1985 • Soet John Steven • USA
FIRE IN THE OPERA HOUSE see **BRAND IN DER OPER** • 1930
FIRE IN THE SKIN see **FEU DANS LA PEAU, LE** • 1953
FIRE IN THE SKY, A • 1978 • Jameson Jerry • TVM • USA
FIRE IN THE STRAW (USA) see **FEU DE PAILLE, LE** • 1939
FIRE IN THE WATER • 1980 • Whitehead Peter • UKN
FIRE IN THE WIND • *Sander Stephen* • USA
FIRE IN THEIR HEARTS see **QUEST FOR LOVE** • 1987
FIRE IN TOWN • 1958 • Biggs Julian • CND
FIRE JUGGLERS, THE • 1914 • *Eyton Bessie* • USA
FIRE MAIDENS FROM OUTER SPACE • 1955 • Roth Cy • UKN • FIRE MAIDENS OF OUTER SPACE
FIRE MAIDENS OF OUTER SPACE see **FIRE MAIDENS FROM OUTER SPACE** • 1955
FIRE MONSTERS, THE • 1959 • Glut Don • SHT • USA
FIRE MONSTERS AGAINST THE SON OF HERCULES (USA) see **MACISTE CONTRO I MOSTRI** • 1962
FIRE OF A THOUSAND SUNS, THE see **BRULERE DE MILLE SOLEILS, LA** • 1964
FIRE OF LIFE, THE • 1912 • Sorensen Schnedler • DNM
FIRE OF LOVE (UKN) see **FEU DE DIEU, LE** • 1966
FIRE OF WATERS • 1965 • Brakhage Stan • SHT • USA
FIRE ON BOARD see **ELD OMBORD** • 1922
FIRE ON HEIMAEY see **ELDUR I HEIMAEY** • 1975
FIRE ON THE MOUNTAIN • 1981 • Wrye Donald • TVM • USA
FIRE ON THE POTATO FIELD see **DYM BRAMBOROVE NATE** • 1976
FIRE OVER AFRICA (USA) see **MALAGA** • 1954
FIRE OVER ENGLAND • 1937 • Howard William K. • UKN
FIRE OVER THE WOMEN'S CASTLE see **YOSHIWARA ENJOW** • 1987
FIRE PATROL see **MAN'S GAME, A** • 1934
FIRE PATROL, THE • 1924 • Stromberg Hunt • USA
FIRE PLUG, THE • 1937 • *Mintz Charles (P)* • ANS • USA
FIRE PROOF • 1929 • Lamont Charles • SHT • USA
FIRE RAISERS, THE • 1933 • Powell Michael • UKN
FIRE RESCUE SCENE • 1894 • *Edison* • USA
FIRE SALE • 1977 • Arkin Alan • USA
FIRE TEST see **AGNI PARIKSHA** • 1951
FIRE THE COOK • 1918 • Roach Hal • SHT • USA
FIRE THE FIREMAN • 1922 • Roach Hal • SHT • USA
FIRE THE FLAG! see **ANO HATA O UTE** • 1944
FIRE THE KAISER • 1918 • *Fairbanks Douglas* • SHT • USA
FIRE UNDER HER SKIN (USA) see **FEU DANS LA PEAU, LE** • 1953
FIRE UNDER THE ASHES see **POD PYEPLOM OGON** • 1968
FIRE WALKER, THE see **GIRL OF THE PORT** • 1930
FIRE, WATER AND BRASS TRUMPETS • 1967 • Rou Aleksandr • USS
FIRE WITH FIRE • 1986 • Gibbins Duncan • USA • CAPTIVE HEARTS
FIRE WITHIN, THE (USA) see **FEU FOLLET, LE** • 1963
FIRE WOMAN • Kim Key Yong • SKR
FIRE WOMAN VILLAGE see **HWA NYEO CHON** • 1985
FIREBACK • 1978 • Page Teddy • USA
FIREBALL see **SPIE UCCIDONO A BEIRUT, LE** • 1965
FIREBALL 500 • 1966 • Asher William • USA
FIREBALL, THE • 1950 • Garnett Tay • USA
FIREBALL FORWARD • 1972 • Chomsky Marvin • TVM • USA • DIVISION HEADQUARTERS
FIREBALL JUNGLE • 1968 • Prieto Joseph G. • USA • JUNGLE TERROR
FIREBIRD see **HI NO TORI** • 1979
FIREBIRD 2015 A.D. • 1981 • Robertson David M. • CND
FIREBIRD, THE • 1934 • Dieterle William • USA
FIREBRAND see **AFFAIRS OF CELLINI, THE** • 1934
FIREBRAND see **TULIPAA** • 1980
FIREBRAND, THE • 1918 • Lawrence Edmund • USA
FIREBRAND, THE • 1922 • Neitz Alvin J. • USA
FIREBRAND, THE • 1962 • Dexter Maury • USA
FIREBRAND JORDAN • 1930 • Neitz Alvin J. • USA
FIREBRAND TREVISION • 1920 • Heffron Thomas N. • USA
FIREBRANDS OF ARIZONA • 1944 • Selander Lesley • USA
FIREBUG • 1905 • *Bitzer Billy (Ph)* • USA
FIREBUGS, THE • 1913 • Sennett Mack • USA
FIRECHASERS, THE • 1970 • Hayers Sidney • TVM • UKN • CAUSE FOR ALARM
FIRECRACKER • 1981 • Santiago Cirio H. • USA, PHL • NAKED FIST
FIRECREEK • 1968 • McEveety Vincent • USA
FIRED • 1917 • *Dressler Marie* • SHT • USA
FIRED COOK, THE • 1913 • *Roland Ruth* • USA
FIRED MAN, THE • 1941 • Roberts Charles E. • SHT • USA
FIRED WIFE • 1943 • Lamont Charles • USA
FIREDEVIL, THE see **FEUERTEUFEL, DER** • 1940
FIREFALL, THE (USA) see **CASCADE DE FEU, LA** • 1904
FIREFIGHT • 1963 • Spielberg Steven • USA
FIREFIGHT • 1987 • Pfeiffer Scott • USA
FIREFIGHTERS, THE • 1974 • Ingrams Jonathan • UKN
FIREFIST OF INCREDIBLE DRAGON • 1980 • Tseng Jimmy • HKG
FIREFLIES see **HOTARUBI** • 1958
FIREFLIES OF THE NORTH • 1985 • Gosha Hideo • JPN
FIREFLY, THE • 1937 • Leonard Robert Z. • USA
FIREFLY LIGHT see **HOTARUBI** • 1958
FIREFLY OF FRANCE, THE • 1918 • Crisp Donald • USA
FIREFLY OF TOUGH LUCK • 1917 • Hopper E. Mason • USA
FIREFLY'S LIGHT see **HOTARUBI** • 1958
FIREFOX • 1982 • Eastwood Clint • USA
FIREGUARD • 1937-45 • Bell Geoffrey • DOC • UKN
FIREHOUSE • 1972 • March Alex • USA • NIGHT WATCH
FIREHOUSE • 1987 • Ingvordsen J. Christian • USA
FIREHOUSE FIVE PLUS TWO • 1962 • Binder Steve • SHT • USA
FIREHOUSE FIVE PLUS TWO, THE see **TERESA BREWER AND THE FIREHOUSE FIVE PLUS TWO** • 1951
FIREHOUSE HONEYMOON, A • 1932 • Marshall George • SHT • USA
FIRELADY • De Grasse Herbert Jean • SHT • USA
FIRELIGHT • 1914 • *Lund O. A. C.* • USA
FIRELIGHT • 1966 • Carpenter John • SHT • USA
FIREMAN see **BRANDSOLDATEN** • 1916
FIREMAN, THE • 1907 • Gilbert Arthur • UKN
FIREMAN, THE • 1916 • Chaplin Charles • USA
FIREMAN, THE • 1931 • Lantz Walter, Nolan William • ANS • USA
FIREMAN, THE see **MANN IM FEUER, DER** • 1926
FIREMAN, THE see **POMPIERI, I** • 1985
FIREMAN AND THE GIRL, THE • 1914 • *Esmond Elsie* • USA
FIREMAN E.A. WINTERSTEIN see **FEUERLOSCHER E.A. WINTERSTEIN** • 1968
FIREMAN, SAVE MY CHILD! • 1918 • Roach Hal • SHT • USA
FIREMAN, SAVE MY CHILD • 1927 • Sutherland A. Edward • USA
FIREMAN, SAVE MY CHILD • 1932 • Bacon Lloyd • USA
FIREMAN SAVE MY CHILD • 1935 • *Terry Paul/ Moser Frank (P)* • ANS • USA
FIREMAN SAVE MY CHILD • 1954 • Goodwins Leslie • USA
FIREMAN SAVE MY CHILD see **SANDY GETS HER MAN** • 1940
FIREMAN, SAVE MY CHOO CHOO • 1940 • Lord Del • SHT • USA
FIREMAN, SAVE MY GAL! • 1920 • *Ovey George* • USA
FIREMAN'S BALL, THE (UKN) see **HORI, MA PANENKO!** • 1967
FIREMAN'S BRAWL • 1953 • Sparber I. • ANS • USA
FIREMAN'S BRIDE, THE • 1917 • *Moore Matt* • SHT • USA
FIREMAN'S BRIDE, THE • 1931 • *Terry Paul/ Moser Frank (P)* • ANS • USA
FIREMAN'S DAUGHTER, THE • 1908 • Raymond Charles? • UKN
FIREMAN'S DAUGHTER, THE • 1911 • Fitzhamon Lewin • UKN
FIREMAN'S LIFE, A see **BUHAY BOMBERO** • 1968
FIREMAN'S PICNIC • 1937 • *Lantz Walter (P)* • ANS • USA
FIREMAN'S SNAPSHOT, THE • 1899 • Cooper Arthur • UKN
FIREMAN'S SONG, THE • 1906 • Gilbert Arthur • UKN
FIREMAN'S STORY, A • 1905 • Mottershaw Frank • UKN
FIREMAN'S WEDDING, THE • 1910 • Raymond Charles • UKN
FIREMAN'S WEDDING, THE • 1918 • *Williams Eric* • UKN
FIREMEN ON PARADE see **DEFILE DE POMPIERS** • 1897
FIREMEN TO THE RESCUE • 1903 • Hepworth Cecil M. • UKN
FIREMEN'S BALL, THE (USA) see **HORI, MA PANENKO!** • 1967
FIREMEN'S SOCIAL, THE • 1914 • *Ab* • USA
FIREPOWER • 1979 • Winner Michael • UKN, USA
FIRES AND BURNT OUT PLACES • Kachlik Antonin • CZC
FIRES OF AMBITION, THE • 1914 • *Domino* • USA
FIRES OF BAKU see **OGNI BAKU** • 1950
FIRES OF CONSCIENCE • 1914 • Reid Wallace • USA
FIRES OF CONSCIENCE • 1916 • Apfel Oscar • USA
FIRES OF CONSCIENCE, THE • 1912 • Apfel Oscar • USA
FIRES OF DRIFTWOOD • 1911 • *Vitagraph* • USA
FIRES OF ENVY • 1957 • Haldane Don • CND
FIRES OF FAITH • 1919 • Jose Edward • USA • FIRES OF FATE
FIRES OF FATE • 1911 • *Vitagraph* • USA
FIRES OF FATE • 1913 • Reid Wallace, Robards Willis • USA
FIRES OF FATE • 1914 • *Travers Richard C.* • USA
FIRES OF FATE • 1916 • *Sunset* • USA
FIRES OF FATE • 1923 • Terriss Tom • UKN
FIRES OF FATE • 1932 • Walker Norman • UKN
FIRES OF FATE see **FIRES OF FAITH** • 1919
FIRES OF HATE (UKN) see **SERPENT, THE** • 1916
FIRES OF INNOCENCE • 1922 • Morgan Sidney • UKN
FIRES OF LOVE see **LIEBESFEUER** • 1925
FIRES OF REBELLION • 1917 • Park Ida May • USA
FIRES OF YOUTH • 1917 • Chautard Emile • USA

FIRES OF YOUTH • 1918 • Julian Rupert • USA
FIRES OF YOUTH • 1924 • *Edwards Ted* • USA
FIRES OF YOUTH • 1931 • Bell Monta • USA
FIRES OF YOUTH see **MAN, WOMAN AND SIN** • 1927
FIRES OF YOUTH see **DANNY JONES** • 1972
FIRES ON THE PLAIN see **NOBI** • 1959
FIRES WERE STARTED • 1943 • Jennings Humphrey • DOC • UKN • I WAS A FIREMAN
FIRESIDE BREWER, A • 1920 • Smith Noel • ANS • USA • HOME BREW
FIRESIDE REALIZATION, A • 1915 • Wilson Ben • USA
FIRESIDE REMINISCENCES • 1908 • Porter Edwin S. • USA
FIRESIGN THEATER PRESENTS "HOT SHORTS" • 1983 • USA
FIRESTARTER • 1984 • Lester Mark L. • USA
FIRETRAP, THE • 1935 • Lynwood Burt • USA
FIREWALKER • 1987 • Thompson J. Lee • USA
FIREWORDS see **TERRIBLES VIVANTES, LES** • 1986
FIREWORKS • 1947 • Anger Kenneth • SHT • USA
FIREWORKS OVER THE SEA see **UMI NO HANABI** • 1951
FIRING FATHER • 1917 • *Rhodes Billie* • SHT • USA
FIRING LINE, THE • 1919 • Maigne Charles • USA
FIRING THE BUTLER OR THE BUTLER'S FIRE • 1916 • *Morris Reggie* • USA
FIRM FORGIVES A MOMENT OF MADNESS, THE see **EMPRESA PERDONA UN MOMENTO DE LOCURA, LA** • 1977
FIRM MAN, THE • 1975 • Duigan John • ASL
FIRM OF GIRDLESTONE, THE • 1915 • Shaw Harold • UKN
FIRMA HEIRATET, DIE • 1913 • Wilhelm Carl • FRG
FIRMA HEIRATET, DIE • 1931 • Wilhelm Carl • FRG
FIRMAFESTEN • 1973 • Halldoff Jan • SWD • OFFICE PARTY, THE
FIRMASKOVTUREN • 1978 • Hilbard John • DNM
FIRMIN, LE MUET DE SAINT-PATAGET • 1938 • Severac Jacques • FRN
FIRMLING, DER • 1934 • Valentin Karl • FRG • CONFIRMATION CANDIDATE, THE
FIRM'S SECRET, THE • 1935 • Shmidthoff V. • USS
FIRNENRAUSCH • 1922 • Karfiol William • FRG
FIRQAT AL-MARAH' • 1970 • Wahab Fatin Abdel • EGY • TROUPE DE LA BONNE HUMEUR, LA
FIRST 36 HOURS OF DR. DURANT, THE • 1975 • Singer Alexander • TVM • USA
FIRST 100 YEARS, THE • 1924 • Jones F. Richard • SHT • USA
FIRST A GIRL • 1935 • Saville Victor • UKN
FIRST AFFAIR • 1983 • Trikonis Gus • TVM • USA
FIRST AID • 1918 • Raymaker Herman C. • USA
FIRST AID • 1931 • Paton Stuart • USA • IN STRANGE COMPANY (UKN)
FIRST AID • 1943 • Jason Will • SHT • USA
FIRST AID FLIRTATION • 1911 • Stow Percy • UKN
FIRST AID IN ACTION • 1944 • Massingham Richard • UKN
FIRST AID ON THE SPOT • 1943 • Searle Francis • DCS • UKN
FIRST AIDERS • 1944 • Nichols Charles • ANS • USA
FIRST AMERICAN TEENAGER, THE see **JAMES DEAN, THE FIRST AMERICAN TEENAGER** • 1975
FIRST AND GOAL see **WILDCATS** • 1986
FIRST AND LAST • 1988 • Schlesinger John • UKN
FIRST AND THE LAST, THE • 1937 • Dean Basil • UKN • 21 DAYS TOGETHER (USA) ○ 21 DAYS
FIRST AND THE LAST, THE see **ILK VE SON** • 1968
FIRST ANIMATED STEP, THE • 1976 • Gross Yoram • ANS • ASL
FIRST AS A CHILD • 1949 • Glover Guy • USA
FIRST ASSAULT WITH MACHETES, THE see **PRIMERA CARGA AL MACHETE, LA** • 1968
FIRST AUTO, THE • 1927 • Del Ruth Roy • USA
FIRST BABY • 1904 • *Bitzer Billy (Ph)* • USA
FIRST BABY, THE • 1936 • Seiler Lewis • USA
FIRST BAD MAN, THE • 1955 • Avery Tex • ANS • USA
FIRST BLOOD • 1982 • Kotcheff Ted • USA
FIRST BLOOD, LAST RITES see **VIGIL** • 1984
FIRST-BORN, THE • 1910 • *Melies* • USA
FIRST BORN, THE • 1910-12 • Melies Gaston • USA
FIRST BORN, THE • 1921 • Campbell Colin • USA
FIRST BORN, THE • 1928 • Mander Miles • UKN
FIRST CANADIAN ASTRONAUT, THE • 1984 • Walker John • CND
FIRST CAR, THE • 1957 • Fetin Vladimir • SHT • USS
FIRST CASE -MAN, THE • 1965 • Skanata Krsto • DOC • YGS
FIRST CHARGE OF THE MACHETE, THE (UKN) see **PRIMERA CARGA AL MACHETE, LA** • 1968
FIRST CHRISTMAS, THE • 1913 • Miller Ashley • USA
FIRST CHRONICLES OF DON Q -THE DARK BROTHERS OF THE CIVIL GUARD • 1912 • Martinek H. O. • UKN
FIRST CIRCLE, THE see **FORSTE KREDS, DEN** • 1971
FIRST CIRCLE OF HELL, THE see **FORSTE KREDS, DEN** • 1971
FIRST CITIZEN IN A SMALL TOWN, THE see **PRVI GRADJANIN MALE VAROSI** • 1966
FIRST CLASS COOK, A • 1914 • Henderson Dell • USA
FIRST CLASS PILOT • 1972 • Vekhotko A., Troshchenko N. • USS
FIRST CLASS TEACHING see **ITTORYU SHINAN** • 1936
FIRST COMES COURAGE • 1943 • Arzner Dorothy • USA • ATTACK BY NIGHT
FIRST COMMANDMENT, THE • 1915 • Moore Tom • USA
FIRST COMMUNION see **PRIMA COMMUNIONE** • 1950
FIRST CONTACT • Connolly Bob, Anderson Robyn • DOC • ASL
FIRST CORNET STRESHNEV see **PERVYI KORNET STRECHNEV** • 1928
FIRST COURIER, THE see **PYERVY KURYER** • 1968
FIRST CRY, THE see **KRIK** • 1963
FIRST DATE see **TI-YI-TS'E YUEH-HUI** • 1988
FIRST DAY, THE see **PERVI DEN** • 1955
FIRST DAY AT WORK see **PIERWSZY DZIEN W PRACY** • 1969
FIRST DAY OF FREEDOM, THE see **PIERWSZY DZIEN WOLNOSCI** • 1964
FIRST DAY OF PEACE, THE see **PERVYI DEN MIRA** • 1959
FIRST DAY OF SCHOOL • 1978 • Paakspuu Kalli • DOC • CND
FIRST DAYS • 1949 • Zhandov Zahari • BUL
FIRST DAYS see **PIERWSZE DNI** • 1951
FIRST DAYS, THE • 1939 • Jackson Pat, Watt Harry, Jennings Humphrey • DCS • UKN • CITY PREPARES, A
FIRST DAYS, THE see **ERSTEN TAGE, DIE** • 1971
FIRST DEADLY SIN, THE • 1980 • Hutton Brian G. • USA
FIRST DEGREE, THE • 1923 • Sedgwick Edward • USA
FIRST DIVISION see **FORSTA DIVISIONEN** • 1941
FIRST ECHELON, THE see **PERVYI ESHELON** • 1956
FIRST EDITION OF MOTHER GOOSE RHYMES • 1911 • *Champion* • USA
FIRST EFFORT see **OPERA PRIMA** • 1980
FIRST ENDORSEMENT, THE • 1914 • Lambart Harry • USA
FIRST EXPEDITION, THE see **PIERWSZA WYPRAWA** • 1964
FIRST EXPERIENCE, THE see **ARU JOSHIKOKOI NO KIROKU HATSUTAIKEN** • 1968
FIRST FAMILY • 1980 • Henry Buck • USA
FIRST FAST MAIL, THE • 1961 • Tendlar Dave • ANS • USA
FIRST FEAR • 1952 • Brummer Richard S. • SHT • USA
FIRST FLEET, THE see **PRIMEROS METROS, LOS** • 1980
FIRST FLIGHT UP • 1962 • Tytla Bill • ANS • USA
FIRST FLYER, THE • 1918 • *Bray* • ANM • USA
FIRST FLYING FISH, THE • 1955 • Rasinski Connie • ANS • USA
FIRST FRONT, THE • 1949 • Petrov Vladimir • USS
FIRST GENERATION, THE see **PIERWSZE POKOLENIE** • 1963
FIRST GENTLEMAN, THE • 1948 • Cavalcanti Alberto • UKN • AFFAIRS OF A ROGUE (USA)
FIRST GIRL • 1969 • Yashin Boris • USS
FIRST GLASS, THE • 1912 • *Barker Florence* • USA
FIRST GRADE see **PIERWSZA KLASA** • 1959
FIRST GRADE, THE see **PERVOKLASSNIZA** • 1948
FIRST GREAT TRAIN ROBBERY, THE (UKN) see **GREAT TRAIN ROBBERY, THE** • 1979
FIRST HARVEST, THE • 1973 • Jubenvill Ken • MTV • CND
FIRST HARVEST, THE see **PIERWSZY PLON** • 1950
FIRST HELLO, THE see **HIGH COUNTRY, THE** • 1981
FIRST HUNDRED YEARS, THE • 1938 • Thorpe Richard • USA • WOODEN WEDDING
FIRST IN WAR • 1932 • Doane Warren • SHT • USA
FIRST INNOCENT, THE • 1975 • Farmanara Bahman • IRN
FIRST KISS, THE • 1928 • Lee Rowland V. • USA
FIRST KISS, THE see **PRVNI POLIBENI** • 1935
FIRST KISS, THE see **KUCHIZUKE III: ONNA DOSHI** • 1955
FIRST LAD, THE see **PERVYI PAREN** • 1958
FIRST LADY • 1937 • Logan Stanley • USA
FIRST, LAST AND ALWAYS see **CAPTAIN EDDIE** • 1944
FIRST LAW, THE • 1914 • Reehm George E. • USA
FIRST LAW, THE • 1918 • McGill Lawrence • USA
FIRST LAW OF NATURE, THE • 1914 • *Warner'S Features* • USA
FIRST LEFT PAST ADEN • 1961 • Bennett Compton • SHT • UKN
FIRST LEGION, THE • 1951 • Sirk Douglas • USA
FIRST LESSON see **PARVI UROK** • 1959
FIRST LINE OF DEFENCE • 1947 • Halas John, Batchelor Joy • ANS • UKN
FIRST LOVE • 1913 • *White Pearl* • USA
FIRST LOVE • 1921 • Campbell Maurice • USA • HEART OF YOUTH, THE ○ HER FIRST LOVE
FIRST LOVE • 1939 • Koster Henry • USA
FIRST LOVE • 1974 • Kieslowski Krzysztof • MTV • PLN
FIRST LOVE • 1977 • Darling Joan • USA
FIRST LOVE • 1983 • Ninh Nguyen Hai • VTN
FIRST LOVE see **HATSUKOI** • 1926
FIRST LOVE see **SEXTANERIN, DIE**
FIRST LOVE see **YOTTSU NO KOI NO MONOGATARI** • 1947
FIRST LOVE see **ERSTE LIEBE** • 1970
FIRST LOVE see **PRVA LJABAV** • 1971
FIRST LOVE see **CINTA PERTAMA** • 1973
FIRST LOVE IS BEST • 1910 • *Lubin* • USA
FIRST LOVE QUESTIONS AND ANSWERS see **HATSUKOI MONDO** • 1950
FIRST LOVE (USA) see **PRIMO AMORE** • 1959
FIRST MAN, THE • 1911 • *Essanay* • USA
FIRST MAN INTO SPACE • 1959 • Day Robert • UKN • SATELLITE OF BLOOD
FIRST MAN INTO TOKYO see **FIRST YANK INTO TOKYO** • 1945
FIRST MAN ON THE SUN • 1970 • Kaufman Nathan • ANS • USA
FIRST MAN TO THE MOON • 1920 • *Bray John R. (P)* • ANS • USA
FIRST MAN TO THE MOON, THE • 1921 • Fleischer Dave • ANS • USA
FIRST MARINES see **TRIPOLI** • 1950
FIRST MASS, THE see **PRIMEIRA MISSA, A** • 1961
FIRST MEN IN THE MOON • 1964 • Juran Nathan • UKN, USA
FIRST MEN IN THE MOON, THE • 1919 • Leigh J. L. V. • UKN
FIRST MILE UP, THE • 1963 • Bairstow David • DOC • CND
FIRST MISSION, THE • Hong Jinbao • HKG • HEART OF DRAGON
FIRST MONDAY IN OCTOBER • 1981 • Neame Ronald • USA
FIRST MRS. FRASER, THE • 1932 • Hill Sinclair • UKN
FIRST NAME: CARMEN see **PRENOM: CARMEN** • 1983
FIRST NIGHT • 1937 • Pedelty Donovan • UKN
FIRST NIGHT, THE • 1927 • Thorpe Richard • USA
FIRST NIGHT, THE see **PREMIERE NUIT, LA** • 1958
FIRST NIGHT OF PYGMALION, THE • 1975 • Till Eric • MTV • CND
FIRST NIGHT OF QUIET see **PRIMA NOTTE DI QUIETE, LA** • 1972
FIRST NINETY DAYS, THE • 1980 • Hicks Scott • SHT • ASL
FIRST NINETY-NINE, THE • 1958 • Batchelor Joy • ANS • UKN
FIRST NOTCH, THE see **NOTCH NUMBER ONE** • 1924
FIRST NOVEL • 1958 • Wilder Donald A. • CND
FIRST NUDIE MUSICAL, THE • 1976 • Haggard Mark, Kimmel Bruce • USA • DIRECTORS, THE ○ NYMPHO SUPERSTARS, THE
FIRST NUGGET, THE • 1914 • *Tennant Barbara* • USA
FIRST OF JANUARY, THE see **ZERO POPULATION GROWTH** • 1972
FIRST OF THE FEW, THE • 1942 • Howard Leslie • UKN • SPITFIRE (USA) ○ SPITFIRE: THE FIRST OF THE FEW
FIRST OFFENCE • 1936 • Mason Herbert • UKN • BAD BLOOD
FIRST OFFENDERS • 1939 • McDonald Frank • USA
FIRST OLYMPICS -ATHENS 1896, THE • 1984 • Rakoff Alvin • TVM • USA
FIRST ON THE ROAD • 1960 • Losey Joseph • UKN
FIRST PAVILION, THE see **PIERWSZY PAWILON** • 1964
FIRST PIANO IN CAMP, THE • 1915 • Physioc Wray • USA
FIRST POINT OF THE ORDER, THE see **TOTCHKA PARVA** • 1956
FIRST POLISH PEACE CONGRESS see **1 POLSKI KONGRES POKOJU** • 1950
FIRST POLKA, THE see **ERSTE POLKA** • 1978
FIRST POSITION • 1972 • Richert William • DOC • USA
FIRST PRIZE • 1927 • Sandrich Mark • SHT • USA
FIRST PRIZE see **HOGSTA VINSTEN** • 1915
FIRST PRIZE, THE • 1913 • Nicholls George • USA
FIRST PRIZE, THE see **HOGSTA VINSTEN** • 1916
FIRST PRIZE IRENE (UKN) see **PRIMO PREMIO SI CHIAMA IRENE, IL** • 1969
FIRST QUARREL, THE • 1916 • Douglass James • USA
FIRST REBEL, THE (UKN) see **ALLEGHENY UPRISING** • 1940
FIRST RENDEZVOUS • 1960 • Babich I. • USS
FIRST RESCUE PARTY, THE see **PRVNI PARTA** • 1959
FIRST RHAPSODY • 1946 • Villiers Kenneth • DOC • UKN
FIRST RIDER OF THE SAHARA see **TAKTAZANE SAHRA** • 1968
FIRST ROBIN, THE • 1939 • Rasinski Connie • ANS • USA
FIRST ROUND-UP • 1934 • Meins Gus • SHT • USA
FIRST RUSSIANS • 1967 • Ivanov Alexander • USS
FIRST SEASON, THE • 1990 • Thomas Ralph L. • CND
FIRST, SECOND, THIRD see **PIERWSZY, DRUGI, TRZECI** • 1964
FIRST SETTLER'S STORY, THE • 1912 • *Gordon James* • USA
FIRST SEVEN YEARS, THE • 1930 • McGowan Robert • SHT • USA
FIRST SHIFT, THE • 1962 • Kidawa Janusz • DOC • PLN
FIRST SHOCK BRIGADE, THE • Keko Endri • DOC • ALB
FIRST SHRINE see **DOHATSU** • 1926
FIRST SNOW • 1965 • Grigoriev Yuri, Shvyrev Yuri • USS
FIRST SNOW, THE • 1935 • *Terry Paul/ Moser Frank (P)* • ANS • USA
FIRST SNOW, THE • 1947 • Davis Mannie • ANS • USA
FIRST SON see **JANGAM** • 1985
FIRST SOUND FILM • 1943 • Whitney John, Whitney James • SHT • USA
FIRST SPACESHIP ON VENUS (USA) see **SCHWEIGENDE STERN, DER** • 1960
FIRST SPLIT DETACHMENT, THE see **PRVI SPLITSKI ODRED** • 1973
FIRST SPRING RACES AT TBILISI, THE • Digmelov Alexander • USS
FIRST START, THE see **PIERWSZY START** • 1951
FIRST STEEPLECHASE, THE • 1913 • Fitzhamon Lewin • UKN
FIRST STEP, THE see **PIERWSZY KROK** • 1962
FIRST STEP, THE see **PIRVELI MERTSKHALI** • 1976
FIRST STEP OF MARRIED LIFE see **WAKAOKUSAMA ICHIBAN SHOBU** • 1952
FIRST STEPS • Povh Dusan • SHT • YGS
FIRST STEPS • 1985 • Larry Sheldon • TVM • USA
FIRST STEPS, THE see **PIERWSZY KROK** • 1962
FIRST STEPS ASHORE • 1932 • Shimazu Yasujiro • JPN
FIRST STEPS TO THE MOON see **PASI SPRE LUNA** • 1963
FIRST STONE, THE • 1915 • Cooley Frank • USA
FIRST SURRENDER, THE see **PRIMERA ENTREGA DE UNA MUJER CASADA** • 1971
FIRST SWALLOW, THE • 1942 • Brewer Jerry • ANS • USA
FIRST SWALLOW, THE see **PIRVELI MERTSKHALI** • 1976
FIRST TASTE OF LOVE (USA) see **NYMPHETTES, LES** • 1961
FIRST TEACHER, THE see **PERVYI UCHITEL** • 1965
FIRST TEN DAYS, THE see **DZIESIEC DNI PIERWSZYCH** • 1973
FIRST TEXAN, THE • 1956 • Haskin Byron • USA
FIRST, THE SUMMER see **ANTES, O VERAO** • 1968
FIRST TIME, THE • 1952 • Tashlin Frank • USA • SMALL WONDER
FIRST TIME, THE • 1968 • Neilson James, Grasshoff Alex • USA • YOU DON'T NEED PYJAMAS AT ROSIE'S ○ BEGINNERS THREE, THE ○ THEY DON'T WEAR PAJAMAS AT ROSIE'S
FIRST TIME, THE • 1982 • Nosseck Noel • TVM • USA
FIRST TIME, THE • 1983 • Loventhal Charles • USA
FIRST TIME, THE (USA) see **PREMIERE FOIS, LA** • 1976
FIRST TIME HERE • 1964 • Myers Richard • SHT • USA
FIRST TIME IS THE LAST TIME, THE see **DAIYAT GAN** • 1990
FIRST TO FIGHT • 1931 • Edwards Harry J. • SHT • USA
FIRST TO FIGHT • 1967 • Nyby Christian • USA
FIRST TRAIN, THE see **PERVYI ESHELON** • 1956
FIRST TRAVELING SALESLADY, THE • 1956 • Lubin Arthur • USA
FIRST TRIP TO THE STARS see **PERVI REJS V ZVEZDAM** • 1961
FIRST TURN ONI, THE • 1984 • Herz Michael, Weil Samuel • USA
FIRST VIOLIN, THE • 1912 • Brooke Van Dyke • USA
FIRST VISITOR, THE • 1966 • Kvinikhidze Leonid • USS
FIRST WALTZ, THE see **ERSTE WALZER, DER** • 1978
FIRST WEAPONS (USA) see **PREMIERES ARMES** • 1949
FIRST WHITE AND RED, THE see **PIERWSZY BIALO-CAERWONY** • 1969
FIRST WIFE see **WIVES AND LOVERS** • 1963
FIRST WOMAN, THE • 1922 • Lyons Glen • USA
FIRST WOMAN IN THE FORESTS, THE see **SHANLINZHONGTOU YIGE NUREN** • 1988
FIRST WOMAN INTO SPACE see **SPACE MONSTER** • 1965
FIRST WOMAN JURY IN AMERICA • 1912 • *Bunny John* • USA
FIRST WORLD WAR, THE • 1934 • de Rochemont Louis (c/d) • CMP • USA
FIRST YANK INTO TOKYO • 1945 • Douglas Gordon • USA • MASK OF FURY (USA) ○ HIDDEN SECRET ○ FIRST MAN INTO TOKYO
FIRST YEAR • 1932 • Howard William K. • USA
FIRST YEAR, THE • 1926 • Borzage Frank • USA
FIRST YEAR, THE see **ROK PIERWSWY** • 1960
FIRST YEAR, THE see **PRIMER ANO, EL** • 1972
FIRST YEAR AT SCHOOL see **PERVOKLASSNIZA** • 1948
FIRST-YEAR LOVE see **SANA ULA HOB** • 1976

FIRST YEAR OF THE MEIJI ERA, THE see **MEIJI GANNEN** • 1932
FIRST YEARS, THE see **VITET E PARA**
FIRST YEARS, THE see **PIERWSZE LATA** • 1949
FIRST YOU CRY • 1978 • Schaefer George • TVM • USA
FIRSTBORN • 1984 • Apted Michael • USA • MOVING IN
FISCHER UND FANGER AM WATT • 1938 • FRG
FISCHER VOM HEILIGENSEE, DER • 1955 • Konig Hans H. • FRG
FISCHERIN VOM BODENSEE, DIE • 1956 • Reinl Harald • FRG
FISCHIA IL SESSO • 1974 • Polidoro Gian Luigi • ITL • INSTANT COFFEE
FISCHIO AL NASO, IL • 1967 • Tognazzi Ugo • ITL • SEVENTH FLOOR, THE (USA) ○ WHISTLING IN THE NOSE, THE ○ MAN WITH THE WHISTLING NOSE, THE
FISH • 1916 • *Williams Bert* • SHT • USA
FISH • 1936 • McGann William • USA
FISH, THE • 1922 • Fleischer Dave • ANS • USA
FISH, THE • 1989 • Partovi Kambuzia • IRN
FISH, THE see **RIBA** • 1976
FISH AND CHILLS • 1915 • Williams C. Jay • USA
FISH AND CHIPS • 1963 • Hannah Jack • ANS • USA
FISH AND MILLIGAN • 1966 • Mason Christopher • UKN
FISH AND SLIPS • 1962 • McKimson Robert • ANS • USA
FISH AND THE FISHERMAN see **FISHERMAN AND THE FISH, THE** • 1952
FISH AND THE RING, THE • 1913 • Thornton F. Martin, Callum R. H. • UKN
FISH BENEATH THE STONE, THE • 1978 • Jonsson Thorsteinn • SHT • ICL
FISH CALLED WANDA, A • 1988 • Crichton Charles • UKN
FISH FEATHERS • 1932 • Sweet Harry • SHT • USA
FISH FOLLIES • 1940 • *Mintz Charles (P)* • ANS • USA
FISH, FOOTBALL AND GIRLS see **HASHECHOUNA SHELANOU** • 1968
FISH FRY • 1944 • Culhane James • ANS • USA
FISH HAWK • 1980 • Shebib Donald • CND
FISH HOOKED • 1960 • Smith Paul J. • ANS • USA
FISH HOOKY • 1933 • McGowan Robert • SHT • USA
FISH MEN, THE see **ISOLA DEGLI UOMINI PESCE, L'** • 1979
FISH PIRATES, THE • 1909 • *Kalem* • USA
FISH PROFESSOR, THE see **POISSON PROF, THE**
FISH SPOILAGE CONTROL • 1956 • Potterton Gerald • CND
FISH STORY, A • 1909 • *Lubin* • USA
FISH STORY, A • 1912 • *Kalem* • USA
FISH STORY, A • 1972 • Smith Paul J. • ANS • USA
FISH TALES • 1936 • King Jack • ANS • USA
FISH TALES • 1954 • *Smith Pete* • SHT • USA
FISH THAT SAVED PITTSBURGH, THE • 1979 • Moses Gilbert • USA
FISH THAT SMOKES, THE see **PEX QUE FUMA, EL** • 1977
FISHE DA KRIN see **KLATSCHE, DIE** • 1939
FISHED FEELINGS see **GEFISCHTE GEFUUHLE** • 1979
FISHER FOLKS • 1911 • Griffith D. W. • USA
FISHER LADY, THE • 1913 • *Mecca* • USA
FISHER LASS, THE • 1915 • *Kriterion* • USA
FISHER-MAID, THE • 1911 • Ince Thomas H. • USA
FISHERBOY'S FAITH, THE • 1912 • Campbell Colin • USA
FISHERGIRL OF CORNWALL, THE • 1912 • Northcote Sidney • UKN
FISHERGIRL'S FOLLY, A • 1914 • Pearson George • UKN
FISHERGIRL'S LOVE, A • 1913 • Collins Edwin J.? • UKN
FISHERLESS CARTOON, A • 1918 • *Fisher* • USA
FISHERMAID OF BALLYDAVID, THE • 1911 • Olcott Sidney • USA
FISHERMAID'S LOVE STORY, THE • 1912 • *Pate Gwendolyn* • USA
FISHERMAID'S ROMANCE, A see **ROMANCE OF A FISHERMAID** • 1909
FISHERMAN, THE • 1909 • Brooke Van Dyke • USA
FISHERMAN, THE • 1931 • Lantz Walter, Nolan William • ANS • USA
FISHERMAN AND THE FISH, THE • 1952 • ANM • USS • FISH AND THE FISHERMAN
FISHERMAN FROM HANSTHOLM, A see **FISKER I HANSTHOLM, EN** • 1977
FISHERMAN KATE • 1914 • Lambart Harry • USA
FISHERMAN'S BRIDE, THE • 1909 • *Selig* • USA
FISHERMAN'S CHOICE, THE • 1916 • *Puritan* • USA
FISHERMAN'S DAUGHTER, THE • 1911 • Bouwmeester Theo • UKN
FISHERMAN'S FALL • 1968 • Nichol Robert L. • CND
FISHERMAN'S FORTUNE, THE • 1913 • *Reliance* • USA
FISHERMAN'S GRANDDAUGHTER, THE • 1910 • *Kalem* • USA
FISHERMAN'S INFATUATION, A • 1912 • Waller Wallett • UKN
FISHERMAN'S INFATUATION, A • 1915 • Waller Wallett • UKN
FISHERMAN'S LOVE STORY, A • 1912 • Fitzhamon Lewin • UKN
FISHERMAN'S LUCK • 1899 • *Warwick Trading Co.* • UKN
FISHERMAN'S LUCK • 1900 • Smith Jack • UKN
FISHERMAN'S LUCK • 1913 • *Solax* • USA
FISHERMAN'S LUCK • 1913 • Haldane Bert? • UKN
FISHERMAN'S LUCK • 1931 • Foster John, Bailey Harry • ANS • USA
FISHERMAN'S LUCK • 1945 • Donnelly Eddie • ANS • USA
FISHERMAN'S LUCK • 1970 • *Cosmos Films* • USA
FISHERMAN'S LUCK, A • 1906 • *Cricks & Sharp* • UKN
FISHERMAN'S LUCK, THE • 1912 • *Missimer Howard* • USA
FISHERMAN'S NIGHTMARE, THE • 1911 • *Pathe* • USA
FISHERMAN'S PARADISE • 1931 • *Smith Pete* • SHT • USA
FISHERMAN'S PERFECT DAY, THE • 1921 • Bruce Neville • UKN
FISHERMAN'S RIVAL, THE • 1908 • *Selig* • USA
FISHERMAN'S WHARF • 1939 • Vorhaus Bernard • USA
FISHERMEN • 1959 • Cote Guy-L. • DCS • CND • PECHEURS, LES
FISHERMEN see **PESCHERECCI** • 1957
FISHERMEN OF DUWA • 1980 • Burton Geoff (c/d) • DOC • ASL
FISHERMEN'S TOWN IN TOSA see **TOSA NO IPPONZURI** • 1981
FISHERMEN'S WALTZ FROM BOHUSLAN see **FISKARVALS FRAN BOHUSLAN** • 1909
FISHER'S GHOST • 1924 • Longford Raymond • ASL
FISHERWOMAN, THE • 1915 • *O'Brien Geraldine* • USA
FISHEYE see **RIBLJE OKO** • 1979
FISHIN' AROUND • 1931 • Gillett Burt • ANS • USA
FISHING • 1921 • Fleischer Dave • ANS • USA
FISHING BANKS OF SKYE, THE • 1934 • Grierson John • DOC • UKN • ON THE FISHING BANKS OF SKYE
FISHING BEAR, THE • 1940 • Ising Rudolf • ANS • USA
FISHING BOAT, THE see **RYURI NO KISHI** • 1956
FISHING BY THE SEA • 1947 • Rasinski Connie • ANS • USA
FISHING CATASTROPHE, A • 1898 • *Cinematograph Co.* • UKN
FISHING FEATS • 1951 • Trego Charles T. • SHT • USA
FISHING FOR FUN • 1949 • Ossi Lewis • SHT • USA
FISHING FOR TROUBLE • 1920 • Forde Walter • UKN
FISHING GROUNDS OF THE WORLD • 1947 • Gilbert Lewis* • DCS • UKN
FISHING IN THE GULF see **PESCA NEL GOLFO** • 1933
FISHING MADE EASY • 1941 • Donnelly Eddie • ANS • USA
FISHING STORY, A • 1913 • *Barker* • UKN
FISHING TACKLER • 1957 • Sparber I. • ANS • USA
FISHING TRIP, THE see **RIBOLOV** • 1972
FISHING TRIP, THE see **VEIDIFERDIN** • 1980
FISHING, U.S.A. • 1969 • *Gaddis Gadabout* • DOC • USA
FISHING VILLAGE, THE (USA) see **FISKEBYN** • 1920
FISHKE DER DRUME • 1939 • Ulmer Edgar G. • USA • FISHKE THE LAME ONE
FISHKE GOES TO WAR • 1970 • Obadiah George • ISR
FISHKE THE LAME ONE see **FISHKE DER DRUME** • 1939
FISHMONGER AND THE FISH see **SKAZKA O RYBAKE I RYBKE** • 1937
FISHMONGER'S APPRENTICE, THE • 1913 • Thornton F. Martin? • UKN
FISHY AFFAIR, A • 1913 • Sennett Mack • USA
FISHY STORY, A • 1913 • Collins Edwin J. • UKN
FISHY STORY, A • 1920 • Fishback Fred C. • SHT • USA
FISHY STORY, A see **BATTUTMATDIK YAN** • 1989
FISHY TALES • 1937 • Douglas Gordon • SHT • USA
FISKARVALS FRAN BOHUSLAN • 1909 • Magnusson Charles • SWD • FISHERMEN'S WALTZ FROM BOHUSLAN
FISKEBYN • 1920 • Stiller Mauritz • SWD • FISHING VILLAGE, THE (USA) ○ CHAINS (UKN) ○ VENGEANCE OF JACOB VINDAS, THE
FISKELIVETS FAVOR • 1908 • *Jaenzon Julius (Ph)* • SWD
FISKER I HANSTHOLM, EN • 1977 • Carlsen Jon Bang • DNM • FISHERMAN FROM HANSTHOLM, A
FIST see **BLACK FIST** • 1976
FIST see **F.I.S.T.** • 1978
FIST FIGHT • 1964 • Breer Robert • SHT • USA
FIST FIGHTER • 1985 • SAF
FIST IN HIS POCKET (USA) see **PUGNI IN TASCA, I** • 1965
FIST OF FEAR, TOUCH OF DEATH • 1980 • Mallinson Matthew • USA
FIST OF FURY see **CHING-WU MEN** • 1972
FIST OF FURY, PART 2 see **CHING-WU MEN SU-TSI** • 1976
FIST OF POWER see **KARATE WARRIOR** • 1988
FIST OF SHAOLIN see **FISTS OF SHAOLIN** • 1973
FIST OF VENGEANCE see **FISTS OF VENGEANCE** • 1974
FIST-RIGHT OF FREEDOM see **FAUSTRECHT DER FREIHEIT** • 1975
FIST TO FIST • 1972 • Chu Huan Jan • HKG
FISTFIGHTER • 1989 • Zuniga Frank • USA
FISTFUL OF CHOPSTICKS, A see **THEY CALL ME BRUCE?** • 1983
FISTFUL OF DEATH, A • *Tate Lincoln* • ITL
FISTFUL OF DOLLARS, A see **PER UN PUGNO DI DOLLARI** • 1964
FISTFUL OF DRAGONS, A • 1977 • Lahardi Iksan • HKG
FISTFUL OF DYNAMITE, A (UKN) see **GIU LA TESTA** • 1971
FISTFUL OF RAWHIDE • 1970 • Beggs W. G. • USA
FISTFUL OF TIME, A see **HANDFULL TID, EN** • 1988
FISTIC MYSTIC • 1969 • McKimson Robert • ANS • USA
FISTIC MYSTIC, A • 1946 • Kneitel Seymour • ANS • USA
FISTICUFFS • 1928 • George Henry W. • USA
FISTICUFFS • 1938 • Miller David • SHT • USA
FISTOL DEL DIABLO, EL • 1958 • Fernandez Fernando • MXC
FISTS AND FODDER • 1920 • Robbins Jess • SHT • USA
FISTS AND GUTS • *Lau Ka-Wing* • HKG
FISTS BEFORE THE CANNON see **PUNOS FRENTE AL CANON**
FISTS IN THE DARK see **PESTI VE TME** • 1987
FISTS IN THE POCKET see **PUGNI IN TASCA, I** • 1965
FISTS OF BLOOD see **STRIKE OF THE PANTHER, THE** • 1987
FISTS OF FURY 2 see **CHING-WU MEN SU-TSI** • 1976
FISTS OF FURY (USA) see **T'ANG-SHAN TA-HSIUNG** • 1971
FISTS OF SHAOLIN • 1973 • Li Hsun • HKG • FIST OF SHAOLIN
FISTS OF STEEL see **HANDS OF STEEL** • 1986
FISTS OF VENGEANCE • 1974 • Chan Hong Man • HKG • TWO FIST VERSUS SEVEN SAMURAI ○ FIST OF VENGEANCE
FIT FOR A KING • 1937 • Sedgwick Edward • USA
FIT FOR BURNING • 1916 • *Sisson Vera* • SHT • USA
FIT FOR NON-COMBATANT DUTY see **GODEN K NESTROYEVOY** • 1968
FIT TO BE A KING see **RAJAYOGAM** • 1968
FIT TO BE TIED • 1930 • Cozine Ray • USA
FIT TO BE TIED • 1952 • Hanna William, Barbera Joseph • ANS • USA
FIT TO BE TOYED • 1959 • Kneitel Seymour • ANS • USA
FIT TO BE UNTIED (USA) see **MATTI DA SLEGARE** • 1976
FIT TO FIGHT • 1919 • Griffith Edward H. • USA
FIT TO WIN • 1919 • Griffith Edward H. • USA
FITFUL MURDER • 1978 • Kinoshita Keisuke • JPN
FITILJ • 1971 • Grgic Zlatko • ANS • YGS • FUSE, THE
FITS • 1915 • *B & C* • UKN
FITS AND MISFITS • 1910 • Fitzhamon Lewin? • UKN
FITS IN A FIDDLE • 1933 • White Sam • USA
FITZ AND LILY see **LILY IN LOVE** • 1985
FITZCARRALDO • 1981 • Herzog Werner • FRG
FITZHUGH'S RIDE • 1914 • *Lubin* • USA
FITZNOODLE'S HUNT FOR WEALTH • 1914 • Calvert Charles? • UKN
FITZNOODLE'S WOOING • 1911 • Wilson Frank? • UKN
FITZROY COMING UP FOR AIR • 1979 • Dodds Peter • DOC • ASL
FITZWILLY • 1967 • Mann Delbert • USA • FITZWILLY STRIKES BACK (UKN)
FITZWILLY STRIKES BACK (UKN) see **FITZWILLY** • 1967
FIUK A TERROL • 1968 • Szasz Peter • HNG • BOYS FROM THE SQUARE ○ BOYS IN THE STREETS
FIUME DEI FARAONI, IL • 1955 • Ragona Ubaldo • DOC • ITL
FIUME DEL GRANDE CAIMANO, IL • 1979 • Martino Sergio • ITL
FIUME DI DOLLARI, UN • 1967 • Lizzani Carlo • ITL • HILLS RUN RED, THE (UKN) ○ RIVER OF DOLLARS, A
FIUME GIALLO, IL see **MURAGLIA CINESE, LA** • 1958
FIUNAK A FELE, EGY • 1922 • von Bolvary Geza • HNG
FIVE • 1951 • Oboler Arch • USA
FIVE, THE • 1969 • Batchelor Joy • ANS • UKN
FIVE ACCURSED GENTLEMEN, THE see **CINQ GENTLEMEN MAUDITS, LES** • 1920
FIVE ACRES see **AKKARA PAHA** • 1969
FIVE ACRES OF LAND see **AKKARA PAHA** • 1969
FIVE AGAINST CAPRICORN • 1972 • Perier Etienne
FIVE AGAINST THE HOUSE • 1955 • Karlson Phil • USA
FIVE AND A HALF OF PALE JOE see **PIEC I POL BLADEGO JOZKA** • 1970
FIVE AND DIME • 1933 • Lantz Walter, Nolan William • ANS • USA
FIVE AND SIX see **LUCKY NUMBER, THE** • 1933
FIVE AND TEN • 1931 • Leonard Robert Z., Conway Jack (U/c) • USA • DAUGHTER OF LUXURY (UKN)
FIVE AND TEN CENT ANNIE • 1928 • Del Ruth Roy • USA • AMBITIOUS ANNIE (UKN)
FIVE AND THE SKIN see **CINQ ET LA PEAU** • 1982
FIVE AND UNDER • 1941 • Alexander Donald • DOC • UKN
FIVE ANGLES ON MURDER (USA) see **WOMAN IN QUESTION, THE** • 1950
FIVE ASHORE IN SINGAPORE see **CINQ GARS POUR SINGAPOUR** • 1967
FIVE AT THE FUNERAL, THE see **HOUSE OF TERROR** • 1972
FIVE BAD MEN • 1935 • Smith Cliff • USA
FIVE BAR GATE • 1976 • Parsons David • UKN
FIVE BELLS • 1979 • Semler Dean • SHT • ASL
FIVE BLOODY DAYS TO TOMBSTONE see **GUN RIDERS** • 1970
FIVE BLOODY GRAVES see **GUN RIDERS** • 1970
FIVE BOLD MEN • 1911 • *Essanay* • USA
FIVE BOLD WOMEN • 1960 • Lopez-Portillo Jorge • USA
FIVE BOYS FROM BARSKA STREET see **PIATKA Z ULICY BARSKIEJ** • 1953
FIVE BOYS OF BARSKA STREET see **PIATKA Z ULICY BARSKIEJ** • 1953
FIVE BRANDED WOMEN (USA) see **JOVANKA E LE ALTRE** • 1960
FIVE BRIDGES, THE see **KOIBITO O SAGASO** • 1967
FIVE BROTHERS AND SISTERS see **GONIN NO KYODAI** • 1939
FIVE BULLETS see **FUNF PATRONENHULSEN** • 1960
FIVE CAME BACK • 1939 • Farrow John • USA
FIVE CANDLES • 1971 • Verwey Walt, Gage Leighton D. • SHT • NTH
FIVE CARD STUD • 1968 • Hathaway Henry • USA
FIVE CARTRIDGES see **FUNF PATRONENHULSEN** • 1960
FIVE CENTS A GLASS see **BEST OF ENEMIES, THE** • 1933
FIVE CHARGING SOLDIERS see **GONIN NO TOTSUGEKITAI** • 1961
FIVE CHOCOLATE AND ONE STRAWBERRY ICE CREAM see **CINCO DE CHOCOLATE Y UNO DE FRESA** • 1968
FIVE CLUES TO FORTUNE • 1957 • Mendoza Joe • SRL • UKN
FIVE CORNERS • 1988 • Bill Tony • USA
FIVE CRAZY BOYS, THE (UKN) see **BIDASSES EN FOLIE, LES** • 1971
FIVE DAY LOVER, THE (USA) see **AMANT DE CINQ JOURS, L'** • 1960
FIVE DAYS • 1954 • Tully Montgomery • UKN • PAID TO KILL (USA)
FIVE DAYS -FIVE NIGHTS see **PYAT DNEI -PYAT NOCHEI** • 1961
FIVE DAYS FROM HOME • 1978 • Peppard George • USA
FIVE DAYS HOME see **WELCOME HOME, SOLDIER BOYS** • 1972
FIVE DAYS IN AUGUST see **FEM DOGN I AUGUST** • 1973
FIVE DAYS IN FALKOPING • Ahrne Marianne • SWD
FIVE DAYS IN SUMMER • 1982 • Zinnemann Fred • USA
FIVE DAYS OF A LIFE see **CINQ JOURS D'UNE VIE** • 1971
FIVE DAYS TO LIVE • 1922 • Dawn Norman • USA • STREET OF THE FLYING DRAGON, THE
FIVE DESPERATE WOMEN • 1971 • Post Ted • TVM • USA
FIVE DOLLAR BABY, THE • 1922 • Beaumont Harry • USA
FIVE DOLLAR BILL, THE • 1917 • Windom Lawrence C. • SHT • USA
FIVE DOLLAR PLATE, THE • 1920 • Harbaugh Carl • SHT • USA
FIVE DOLLS FOR AN AUGUST MOON see **CINQUE BAMBOLE PER LA LUNA DI AGOSTO** • 1970
FIVE DOOMED GENTLEMEN see **CINQ GENTLEMEN MAUDITS, LES** • 1920
FIVE EASY PIECES • 1970 • Rafelson Bob • USA
FIVE ENDLESS HOURS see **BES UZUN SAAT** • 1967
FIVE EVENINGS • 1912 • *Solax* • USA
FIVE EVENINGS see **PYAT VECHEROV** • 1979
FIVE FACES see **FIVE FACES OF MALAYA** • 1938
FIVE FACES OF MALAYA • 1938 • Shaw Alexander • UKN • FIVE FACES
FIVE FAULTS OF FLO, THE • 1916 • Platt George Foster • USA
FIVE FINGER EXERCISE • 1962 • Mann Daniel • USA
FIVE FINGERS • 1952 • Mankiewicz Joseph L. • USA • FINGERS
FIVE FINGERS OF DEATH see **HAND OF DEATH** • 1962
FIVE FINGERS OF DEATH see **KING BOXER** • 1971
FIVE FIVE • 1979 • Imberman Samuel • ISR
FIVE-FOOT RULER, A • 1917 • De Haven Carter • SHT • USA
FIVE FOR CASABLANCA see **ATTENTATO AI TRE GRANDI** • 1967
FIVE FOR FOUR • 1942 • McLaren Norman • ANS • CND
FIVE FOR HELL • 1985 • Parolini Gianfranco • ITL
FIVE FOR HELL (UKN) see **CINQUE PER L'INFERNO** • 1969
FIVE FRANC PIECE, THE • 1916 • Grandon Francis J. • SHT • USA

FIVE GATES TO HELL • 1959 • Clavell James • USA
FIVE GENTS AND A CHINESE MERCHANT see ZOKU SHACHO HANJOKI • 1968
FIVE GENTS AND KARATE GRANDPA see SHACHO HANJOKI • 1968
FIVE GENTS AT SUNRISE see SHACHO GUOJOKI • 1966
FIVE GENTS ON THE SPOT see ZOKU SHACHO GYOJOKI • 1966
FIVE GENTS PREFER GEISHA see SHACHO SEN-ICHIYA • 1967
FIVE GENT'S TRICK BOOK see SHACHO NINPOCHI • 1965
FIVE GIANTS FROM TEXAS see CINQUE DELLA VENDETTA, I • 1966
FIVE GIRLS AROUND ONE'S NECK see PET HOLEK NA KRKU • 1967
FIVE GIRLS LIKE A MILLSTONE ROUND ONE'S NECK see PET HOLEK NA KRKU • 1967
FIVE GIRLS TO COPE WITH see PET HOLEK NA KRKU • 1967
FIVE GIRLS TO DEAL WITH see PET HOLEK NA KRKU • 1967
FIVE GO ADVENTURING see FEM OG SPIONERNE, DE • 1969
FIVE GO TO HELL • 1988 • Richardson Peter • UKN
FIVE GOLDEN DRAGONS • 1967 • Summers Jeremy • UKN
FIVE GOLDEN HOURS • 1961 • Zampi Mario • UKN, ITL • CINQUE ORE IN CONTANTI (ITL)
FIVE GRAVES FOR THE MEDIUM see CINQUE TOMBE PER UN MEDIUM • 1966
FIVE GRAVES TO CAIRO • 1943 • Wilder Billy • USA
FIVE GUINEAS A WEEK • 1956 • Monat Donald • UKN
FIVE GUNS TO TOMBSTONE • 1961 • Cahn Edward L. • USA
FIVE GUNS WEST • 1955 • Corman Roger • USA
FIVE HAVE A MYSTERY TO SOLVE • 1964 • Morris Ernest • SRL • UKN
FIVE HEARTBEATS, THE • 1990 • Townsend Robert • USA
FIVE HOT WOMEN see BES ATESLI KADIN • 1968
FIVE HOURS • 1911 • Porter Edwin S. • USA
FIVE HUNDRED DOLLAR KISS, THE • 1914 • Eagle Oscar • USA
FIVE HUNDRED OR BUST • 1919 • French George • USA
FIVE IN JAIL see CINCO EN LA CARCEL • 1968
FIVE IN THE SNOW, THE • 1958 • Strbac Milenko • YGS
FIVE-INCH BATHER, THE • 1942 • Massingham Richard • UKN
FIVE KISSES see AFFAIRS OF ANATOL, THE • 1921
FIVE LAST DAYS see FUNF LETZTE TAGE • 1983
FIVE-LEGGED HARE, THE see LEPURI ME PESE KEMBE • 1983
FIVE LITTLE PEPPERS see FIVE LITTLE PEPPERS AND HOW THEY GREW • 1939
FIVE LITTLE PEPPERS AND HOW THEY GREW • 1939 • Barton Charles T. • USA • FIVE LITTLE PEPPERS
FIVE LITTLE PEPPERS AT HOME • 1940 • Barton Charles T. • USA
FIVE LITTLE PEPPERS IN TROUBLE • 1940 • Barton Charles T. • USA
FIVE LITTLE WIDOWS • 1917 • Christie Al • SHT • USA
FIVE LITTLE WOLVES see CINCO LOBITAS • 1972
FIVE-MAN ARMY, THE (USA) see ESERCITO DI 5 UOMINI, UN • 1969
FIVE MASKED MEN see MASKELI BESLER • 1968
FIVE MEN, THE • 1964 • Komorowski Pawel • PLN
FIVE MEN IN THE CIRCUS see SAKASU GONINGUMI • 1935
FIVE MEN OF EDO see OEDO GONIN OTOKO • 1951
FIVE MILE CREEK • 1984 • Miller George* • MTV • ASL
FIVE MILES TO MIDNIGHT (USA) see COUTEAU DANS LA PLAIE, LE • 1962
FIVE MILLION YEARS TO EARTH (USA) see QUATERMASS AND THE PIT • 1967
FIVE MILLIONS SEEK AN HEIR (USA) see FUNF MILLIONEN SUCHEN EINEN ERBEN • 1938
FIVE-MINUTE FIVE-BILLION-YEAR MOVIE, THE • 1980 • Borenstein Joyce • CND
FIVE MINUTE KISS, THE • 1970 • Wilmer Otto • USA
FIVE MINUTE MURDER • 1966 • Nepp Jozsef • ANM • HNG
FIVE MINUTE THRILL • Nepp Jozsef • ANS • HNG
FIVE MINUTES OF PARADISE see PET MINUTA RAJA • 1959
FIVE MINUTES OF PURE CINEMA see CINQ MINUTES DE CINEMA PUR • 1926
FIVE MINUTES TO FREEDOM • 1973 • Nagy Ivan • USA
FIVE MINUTES TO LIVE • 1961 • Karn Bill • USA • DOOR TO-DOOR MANIAC
FIVE NIGHTS • 1915 • Haldane Bert? • UKN
FIVE O'CLOCK FINISH • 1954 • Irwin John • UKN
FIVE O'CLOCK GIRL, THE • 1929 • Green Alfred E. • USA
FIVE OF A KIND • 1938 • Leeds Herbert I. • USA
FIVE OF ME, THE • 1981 • Wendkos Paul • TVM • USA
FIVE ON A TREASURE ISLAND • 1957 • Landau Gerald • SRL • UKN
FIVE ON THE BLACK HAND SIDE • 1973 • Williams Oscar • USA
FIVE ON THE FOUR DAYS' RACE • van Nie Rene • NTH
FIVE OUT OF A MILLION see PET Z MILIONU • 1959
FIVE PATTERN DRAGON CLAWS • Ho Godfrey • HKG
FIVE PENNIES, THE • 1959 • Shavelson Melville • USA
FIVE PHILOSOPHICAL FABLES • Richie Donald • USA, JPN
FIVE PLUS ONE • 1977 • Vaptsarova Maya • BUL
FIVE-POUND NOTE, THE • 1915 • Baggot King • USA
FIVE POUNDS REWARD • 1913 • Kinder Stuart • UKN
FIVE POUNDS REWARD • 1920 • Brunel Adrian • SHT • UKN
FIVE PUPLETS • 1935 • Terry Paul/ Moser Frank (P) • ANS • USA
FIVE REBELLIOUS MEN see BES ASI ADAM • 1968
FIVE ROSE SISTERS, THE • 1911 • Thanhouser • USA
FIVE SAVAGE MEN see ANIMALS, THE • 1971
FIVE SCOUTS see GONIN NO SEKKOHEI • 1938
FIVE SEASONS • 1960 • Gass Karl • DOC • GDR
FIVE SENSES, THE • 1915 • Early Baby • USA
FIVE SENSES OF MAN, THE see PET SMYSLU CLOVECKA • 1912
FIVE SHAOLIN MASTERS see SHAOLIN WU TSU • 1975
FIVE SINISTER STORIES see FUNF UNHEIMLICHE GESCHICHTEN • 1919
FIVE SINISTER STORIES see FUNF UNHEIMLICHE GESCHICHTEN • 1933
FIVE SINNERS • 1964 • Balik Jaroslav • CZC
FIVE SISTERS see ONNA NO KOYOMI • 1954
FIVE SONS-OF-BITCHES see CINQUE FIGLI DI CANE • 1968
FIVE SQUADRON see ESKADRILYA N5 • 1939
FIVE STAR EGGO • Roman Joseph (P) • SHT • USA
FIVE STAR FINAL • 1931 • LeRoy Mervyn • USA • ONE FATAL HOUR
FIVE STEPS • 1968 • Mendoza Joe • DCS • UKN
FIVE STEPS TO DANGER • 1957 • Kesler Henry S. • USA
FIVE-STORIED PAGODA, THE see GOJU NO TU • 1944
FIVE SUMMER STORIES • 1973 • MacGillivray Greg, Freeman Jim • CMP • USA
FIVE SUPERFIGHTERS • 1979 • Lo Mar • HKG
FIVE TALES OF HORROR (USA) see FUNF UNHEIMLICHE GESCHICHTEN • 1919
FIVE THE HARD WAY • 1969 • Trikonis Gus • USA • SIDEHACKERS, THE
FIVE THOUSAND AN HOUR • 1918 • Ince Ralph • USA
FIVE THOUSAND DOLLAR DREAM, THE • 1916 • Griffith Beverly • SHT • USA
FIVE THOUSAND DOLLAR ELOPEMENT, A • 1916 • Mix Tom • SHT • USA
FIVE TO FIVE • 1918 • Christie Al • USA
FIVE TO ONE • 1963 • Flemyng Gordon • UKN
FIVE TOWNS • 1947 • Bishop Terry • DOC • UKN
FIVE WEEKS IN A BALLOON • 1962 • Allen Irwin • USA
FIVE WILD GIRLS (USA) see CINQ FILLES EN FURIE • 1964
FIVE WILD KIDS see CINQ FILLES EN FURIE • 1964
FIVE WISHES, THE • 1916 • Noy Wilfred? • UKN
FIVE WOMEN AROUND UTAMARO(UKN) see UTAMARO O MEGURU GONIN NO ONNA • 1946
FIVE WOMEN FOR ONE MAN see PENTE YINEKES YIA ENAN ANDHRA • 1967
FIVE YEAR PLAN, THE see PLAN VELIKH RABOT • 1930
FIVE YEARS IN THE LIFE OF THE LEVESQUE FAMILY • 1968 • Bonniere Rene • DCS • CND
FIVE YEARS IN THE LIFE OF THE WHYLLIE FAMILY • 1970 • Bonniere Rene • DCS • CND
FIVE YEARS OF STRUGGLE AND VICTORY see PYAT LET BOBBY I POBEDY • 1923
FIVER FOR A PENNY, A • 1913 • Gaumont • UKN
FIX, THE • 1984 • Zens Will • USA
FIX, THE see PICO, EL • 1984
FIX IT FOR ME • 1920 • Edwards Harry J. • SHT • USA
FIX THAT CLOCK • 1964 • Kneitel Seymour • ANS • USA
FIXATION see SHE MAN, THE • 1967
FIXED BAYONETS • 1951 • Fuller Samuel • USA • OLD SOLDIERS NEVER DIE
FIXED BY GEORGE • 1920 • Lyons Eddie, Moran Lee • USA
FIXER, THE • 1913 • Burns Robert • USA
FIXER, THE • 1915 • Morrisey Edward • USA
FIXER, THE • 1929 • Lamont Charles • SHT • USA
FIXER, THE • 1968 • Frankenheimer John • USA
FIXER, THE see HELLO BILLI • 1915
FIXER DUGAN • 1939 • Landers Lew • USA • DOUBLE DARING (UKN)
FIXER FIXED, A • 1912 • Solax • USA
FIXER-UPPERS, THE • 1935 • Rogers Charles • SHT • USA
FIXIN' FOOL • 1951 • Barclay David • SHT • USA
FIXIN' TRICKS • 1943 • Jason Will • SHT • USA
FIXING A FLIRT • 1912 • Lubin • USA
FIXING A STEW • 1934 • Boasberg Al • SHT • USA
FIXING AUNTIE UP • 1913 • Hotaling Arthur D. • USA
FIXING LIZZIE • 1920 • Franey William • SHT • USA
FIXING THE FAKER • 1918 • Ebony • SHT • USA
FIXING THE FAKIRS • 1913 • Imp • USA
FIXING THE FLIRTS • 1913 • Imp • USA
FIXING THE SWING • 1904 • Collins Alf? • UKN
FIXING THEIR DADS • 1914 • Baker George D. • USA
FIZESSEN NAGYSAG • 1937 • Rathonyi August
FIZZICLE FIZZLE • 1964 • Kneitel Seymour • ANS • USA
FJ HOLDEN, THE • 1977 • Thornhill Michael • ASL • F.J. HOLDEN, THE
FJARILEN OCH LJUSLAGAN • 1954 • Werner Gosta • SHT • SWD • BUTTERFLY AND THE FLAME, THE
FJELA'S CHILD • 1989 • Heyns Katinka • SAF
FJOLLS TIL FJELLS • 1957 • Kalmar Edith • NRW
F**K see BLUE MOVIE • 1969
FLACARI PE COMORI • 1988 • Margineanu Nicolae • RMN • WILL O'THE WISP
FLACHSACKER, DER see WENN DIE SONNE WIEDER SCHEINT • 1943
FLACHSMANN ALS ERZIEHER • 1920 • Achsel Willy • FRG
FLACHSMANN ALS ERZIEHER • 1930 • Wolff Carl Heinz • FRG
FLADENS FRISKE FYRE • 1965 • Henriksen Finn • DNM
FLAG, THE see SZTANDAR • 1965
FLAG, THE see PEI-KUO-CH'I-TE JEN • 1981
FLAG DELIT • 1930 • Treville Georges, Schwarz Hanns • FRN • CAMBRIOLEUR, LE
FLAG LIEUTENANT, THE • 1919 • Nash Percy • UKN
FLAG LIEUTENANT, THE • 1926 • Elvey Maurice • UKN
FLAG LIEUTENANT, THE • 1932 • Edwards Henry • UKN
FLAG NAZII • 1929 • Schmidgof • USS • FLAGS OF NATIONS
FLAG OF DISTRESS, THE • 1912 • Mack H. S. • USA
FLAG OF FORTUNE, THE • 1915 • MacQuarrie Murdock • USA
FLAG OF FREEDOM, THE • 1912 • Neason Hazel • USA
FLAG OF HIS COUNTRY, THE • 1910 • Thanhouser • USA
FLAG OF HUMANITY, THE • 1940 • Negulesco Jean • SHT • USA
FLAG OF IRON, THE see T'IEH-CH'I MEN • 1981
FLAG OF KRIVOY ROG, THE see FAHNE VON KRIWOJ ROG, DIE • 1967
FLAG OF MERCY • 1942 • Cahn Edward L. • SHT • USA
FLAG OF MOTHERS, THE see SERVICE STAR, THE • 1918
FLAG OF TWO WARS, A • 1913 • Huntley Fred W. • USA
FLAG SPEAKS, THE • 1940 • Miller David • SHT • USA
FLAGELADOS DO VENTO LESTE, OS • 1988 • Faria Antonio • CPV
FLAGELLO DI DIO, IL • 1917 • Mari Febo • ITL
FLAGPOLE • 1977 • Casson Barry • DOC • CND
FLAGPOLE JITTERS • 1956 • White Jules • SHT • USA
FLAGRANT DESIR • 1985 • Faraldo Claude • FRN • CERTAIN DESIRE, A
FLAGS see ZASTAVE • 1973
FLAGS OF NATIONS see FLAG NAZII • 1929
FLAK • 1977 • Mann Ron • DOC • CND
FLAKLYPA GRAND PRIX • 1972-75 • Caprino Ivo • NRW
FLAM • 1966 • Hubacek Miroslav • CZC • NIGHT ON THE TOWN, A
FLAMBEAU AU PAYS DES SURPRISES • 1916 • Cohl Emile (c/d) • ANS • FRN • FLAMBEAU AUX LIGNES
FLAMBEAU AUX LIGNES see FLAMBEAU AU PAYS DES SURPRISES • 1916
FLAMBEAU CHIEN PERDU • 1916 • Cohl Emile • ANS • FRN • FLAMBEAU THE LOST DOG (USA) ○ JOURNEE DE FLAMBEAU, LA
FLAMBEAU THE LOST DOG (USA) see FLAMBEAU CHIEN PERDU • 1916
FLAMBEE, LA • 1916 • Pouctal Henri • FRN
FLAMBEE, LA • 1934 • de Marguenat Jean • FRN
FLAMBEE DES REVES, LA • 1923 • de Baroncelli Jacques • FRN
FLAMBERERDE HJERTER • 1986 • Ryslinge Helle • DNM • COEURS FLAMBES ○ HENRY
FLAMBERGE AU VENT see CAPITAN, LE • 1945
FLAMBEUSE, LA • 1980 • Weinberg Rachel • FRN
FLAMBIERTE FRAU, DIE • 1983 • van Ackeren Robert • FRG • WOMAN IN FLAMES, A (USA)
FLAMBOYANT ARMS, THE • 1959 • Rasinski Connie • ANS • USA
FLAMBOYANT SEX, THE (USA) see SVENSKA FLICKOR I PARIS • 1960
FLAMBOYANTS, THE see SVENSKA FLICKOR I PARIS • 1960
FLAME • 1974 • Loncraine Richard • UKN
FLAME, THE • 1920 • Thornton F. Martin • UKN
FLAME, THE • 1947 • Auer John H. • USA
FLAME, THE see FLAMMAN • 1956
FLAME AND THE ARROW, THE • 1950 • Tourneur Jacques • USA
FLAME AND THE FIRE • 1965 • Gaisseau Pierre-Dominique • DOC • FRN
FLAME AND THE FLESH, THE • 1954 • Brooks Richard • USA
FLAME BARRIER, THE • 1958 • Landres Paul • USA • IT FELL FROM THE FLAME BARRIER
FLAME IN MY HEART, A (UKN) see FLAMME DANS MA COEUR, UNE • 1987
FLAME IN THE ASHES, THE • 1913 • Morty Frank • USA
FLAME IN THE HEATHER • 1935 • Pedelty Donovan • UKN
FLAME IN THE SKY see SATELLITE IN THE SKY • 1956
FLAME IN THE STREETS • 1961 • Baker Roy Ward • UKN
FLAME IS LOVE, THE • 1979 • O'Herlihy Michael • TVM • USA, UKN
FLAME OF AFRICA • 1954 • Bulpin T. V. • SAF
FLAME OF ANGER, THE see SHOLEHAYE KHASHM • 1968
FLAME OF ARABY • 1951 • Lamont Charles • USA
FLAME OF CALCUTTA • 1953 • Friedman Seymour • USA
FLAME OF DEVOTION, THE see SHUEN • 1964
FLAME OF HELLGATE, THE • 1920 • Middleton George E. • USA
FLAME OF LIFE, THE • 1923 • Henley Hobart • USA • THAT LASS O' LOWRIE'S
FLAME OF LIFE, THE see SANGEN OM DEN ELDRODA BLOMMAN • 1918
FLAME OF LOVE • 1930 • Summers Walter, Eichberg Richard • UKN
FLAME OF MY LOVE (USA) see WAGA KOI WA MOENU • 1949
FLAME OF NEW ORLEANS, THE • 1941 • Clair Rene • USA • DUCHESSE OF NEW ORLEANS, THE ○ BELLE ENSORCELEUSE ○ COUNTESS OF NEW ORLEANS, THE
FLAME OF PASSION, THE • 1915 • Terriss Tom • USA
FLAME OF SACRAMENTO see IN OLD SACRAMENTO • 1946
FLAME OF STAMBOUL • 1951 • Nazarro Ray • USA
FLAME OF THE ARGENTINE • 1926 • Dillon Eddie • USA
FLAME OF THE BARBARY COAST • 1945 • Kane Joseph • USA
FLAME OF THE DESERT • 1919 • Barker Reginald • USA
FLAME OF THE FLESH see DU BARRY, WOMAN OF PASSION • 1930
FLAME OF THE ISLANDS • 1955 • Ludwig Edward • USA
FLAME OF THE WEST • 1945 • Hillyer Lambert • USA
FLAME OF THE WEST, THE • 1918 • Madison Cleo • SHT • USA
FLAME OF THE YUKON, THE • 1917 • Miller Charles • USA
FLAME OF THE YUKON, THE • 1926 • Melford George • USA
FLAME OF TORMENT (UKN) see ENJO • 1958
FLAME OF TRIPOLI see SLAVE GIRL • 1947
FLAME OF YOUTH • 1920 • Mitchell Howard M. • USA
FLAME OF YOUTH • 1949 • Springsteen R. G. • USA
FLAME OF YOUTH, THE • 1917 • Clifton Elmer • USA
FLAME OF YOUTH, THE see MOERO SEISHUN • 1968
FLAME OVER INDIA (USA) see NORTH WEST FRONTIER • 1959
FLAME OVER VIETNAM • 1967 • Elorrieta Jose Maria • SPN, FRG
FLAME TO THE PHOENIX, A • 1985 • Geoffrey Paul • USA
FLAME-TOP see TULIPAA • 1980
FLAME TREES OF THIKA, THE • 1981 • Baker Roy Ward • MTV • UKN
FLAME WITHIN, THE • 1935 • Goulding Edmund • USA
FLAMENCA see SPANISH AFFAIR • 1958
FLAMENCA LA GITANE • 1928 • Andreani Henri • FRN
FLAMENCO • 1976 • Aguirre Javier • SHT • SPN
FLAMENCO see SAETA DEL RUISENOR • 1957
FLAMENCO AT 5.15 • 1983 • Scott Cynthia • DCS • CND
FLAMENCO (USA) see DUENDE Y MISTERIO DEL FLAMENCO • 1952
FLAMENCOS, LOS • 1968 • Yague Jesus • SPN • ANDALUSIAN GIPSIES, THE
FLAMES • 1917 • Elvey Maurice • UKN
FLAMES • 1926 • Moomaw Lewis H. • USA
FLAMES • 1932 • Brown Karl • USA • FIRE ALARM
FLAMES • 1975 • Chetverikov Vitali • USS
FLAMES see AAG AUR SHOLEY • 1987
FLAMES AND FORTUNE • 1911 • Thanhouser • USA
FLAMES IN THE DARK see LAGOR I DUNKLET • 1942
FLAMES OF BAKU see OGNI BAKU • 1950
FLAMES OF CHANCE • 1918 • Wells Raymond • USA
FLAMES OF DESIRE • 1924 • Clift Denison • USA
FLAMES OF DEVOTION • 1968 • Kurahosa • JPN
FLAMES OF FEAR • 1930 • Barnett Charles • UKN

FLAMES OF JOHANNIS, THE • 1916 • Lewis Edgar • USA
FLAMES OF LIFE, THE see **PLAMENY ZIVOTA** • 1920
FLAMES OF PASSION • 1922 • Cutts Graham • UKN • TIDES OF PASSION (USA) ○ WOMAN'S SECRET, A ○ CAUGHT IN THE MESH
FLAMES OF PASSION • 1923 • Moody H. G. • USA
FLAMES OF THE BORDER • 1958 • Lin Lung • CHN
FLAMES OF THE FLESH • 1920 • Le Saint Edward J. • USA
FLAMES OF TREACHERY • 1917 • MacDonald Donald • SHT • USA
FLAMES OF VENGEANCE • 1916 • Middleton Edwin • SHT • USA
FLAMES OF WRATH • 1923 • *Mankins Roxie* • USA
FLAMES ON THE VOLGA see **VOLGA EN FLAMMES** • 1933
FLAMES ON THE VOLGA see **VOLTINITSA** • 1956
FLAMES OVER THE CAFEZAL see **CHAMAS NO CAFEZAL** • 1954
FLAMES SPREADING ACROSS THE LAND • NKR
FLAMETTI • 1920 • Eichgrun Bruno • FRG
FLAMING ALTAR see **NAGAAPOY NA DAMBANA** • 1967
FLAMING ARROW, THE • 1913 • Carter Lincoln J.? • USA
FLAMING ARROW, THE (USA) see **BRANDENDE STRAAL, DE** • 1911
FLAMING ARROWS, THE • 1911 • Golden Joseph A. • USA
FLAMING BARRIERS • 1924 • Melford George • USA
FLAMING BORDERS see **HUDUD AL MULTAHIBA, AL** • 1986
FLAMING BULLETS • 1945 • Fraser Harry L. • USA
FLAMING CITY, THE • 1965 • Higgins Dick • USA
FLAMING CLUE, THE • 1920 • Hollywood Edwin L. • USA
FLAMING CREATURES • 1963 • Smith Jack** • USA
FLAMING CRISIS, THE • 1924 • *Nicholson Calvin* • USA
FLAMING DESIRE see **SMALL HOURS, THE** • 1962
FLAMING DIAGRAM, THE • 1914 • *Baggot King* • USA
FLAMING DISC, THE • 1921 • Hill Robert F. • SRL • USA • FLAMING DISK, THE
FLAMING DISK, THE see **FLAMING DISC, THE** • 1921
FLAMING FEATHER, THE • 1951 • Enright Ray • USA • FORT SAVAGE
FLAMING FEATHERS • 1927 • Roach Hal • SHT • USA
FLAMING FLAPPERS • 1925 • Roach Hal • SHT • USA
FLAMING FOREST, THE • 1926 • Barker Reginald • USA
FLAMING FORGE, THE • 1913 • Bartlett Lanier • USA
FLAMING FORTIES, THE • 1924 • Forman Tom • USA
FLAMING FRONTIER • 1958 • Newfield Sam • USA
FLAMING FRONTIER, THE • 1926 • Sedgwick Edward • USA
FLAMING FRONTIER (UKN) see **OLD SUREHAND I** • 1965
FLAMING FRONTIERS • 1938 • Taylor Ray, James Alan • SRL • USA
FLAMING FURY • 1926 • Hogan James P. • USA
FLAMING FURY • 1949 • Blair George • USA
FLAMING GOLD • 1934 • Ince Ralph • USA
FLAMING GUNS • 1932 • Rosson Arthur • USA • ROUGH RIDING ROMEO (UKN)
FLAMING HEARTS • 1913 • Baker George D. • USA
FLAMING HEARTS • 1922 • Elfelt Clifford S. • USA
FLAMING HOUR, THE • 1922 • Sedgwick Edward • USA • HOT-HEAD, THE
FLAMING JUSTICE (UKN) see **LITTLE WILD GIRL, THE** • 1928
FLAMING KNIVES see **CUCHILLOS DE FUEGO** • 1990
FLAMING LEAD • 1939 • Newfield Sam • USA
FLAMING LOVE • 1925 • McDonald J. K. • USA
FLAMING OMEN, THE • 1917 • Wolbert William • USA
FLAMING PASSION see **LUCRETIA LOMBARD** • 1923
FLAMING ROMANCE • 1926 • Roberts Stephen • SHT • USA
FLAMING SEA, THE • 1972 • Saakov Leon • USS
FLAMING SIGNAL • 1933 • Roberts Charles E., Jeske George • USA
FLAMING SKY see **MOERU OZORA** • 1940
FLAMING STAR • 1960 • Siegel Don • USA
FLAMING SWORD • 1915 • Middleton Edwin • USA
FLAMING SWORD, THE see **VERDENS UNDERGANG** • 1916
FLAMING TORCH, THE (UKN) see **BOB MATHIAS STORY, THE** • 1954
FLAMING WATERS • 1925 • Weight F. Harmon • USA
FLAMING WEST, THE (USA) see **HI-JACKING RUSTLERS** • 1926
FLAMING YEARS see **ALEVLI YILLAR** • 1968
FLAMING YEARS, THE see **POVEST PLAMENNYKH LET** • 1960
FLAMING YOUTH • 1923 • Dillon John Francis • USA
FLAMINGO • 1942 • Berne Josef • SHT • USA
FLAMINGO • 1947 • *Dandridge Dorothy* • USA
FLAMINGO AFFAIR, THE • 1948 • Shepherd Horace • UKN • BLONDE FOR DANGER (USA)
FLAMINGO KID, THE • 1984 • Marshall Garry • USA
FLAMINGO PARK • 1978 • Hoffman Sonia • SHT • ASL
FLAMINGO ROAD • 1949 • Curtiz Michael • USA
FLAMINGO ROAD • 1980 • Trikonis Gus • TVM • USA
FLAMMAN • 1956 • Ragneborn Arne • SWD • GIRLS WITHOUT ROOMS (USA) ○ FLAME, THE
FLAMME, DIE • 1922 • Lubitsch Ernst • FRG • MONTMARTRE
FLAMME, LA • 1923 • Leprieur Gaston • FRN
FLAMME, LA • 1925 • Hervil Rene • FRN
FLAMME, LA • 1936 • Berthomieu Andre • FRN
FLAMME BLANCHE • 1928 • Dekeukeleire Charles • BLG
FLAMME CACHEE, LA • 1919 • Musidora, Lasseyre Jacques • FRN • HIDDEN FLAME, THE
FLAMME DANS MA COEUR, UNE • 1987 • Tanner Alain • SWT • FLAME IN MY HEART, A (UKN)
FLAMME MERVEILLEUSE, LA • 1903 • Melies Georges • FRN • MYSTICAL FLAME, THE (USA)
FLAMMEN LUGEN, DIE • 1926 • Froelich Carl • FRG
FLAMMENDE BERG see **WILHELM TELL –BERGEN IN FLAMMEN** • 1960
FLAMMENDE KREIS, DER • 1917 • Dessauer Siegfried • FRG
FLAMMENDE VOLKER • 1922 • Reinert Robert • FRG
FLAMMENFAHRT DES PACIFIC–EXPRESS, DIE • 1921 • Paster-Saterp Fred • FRG
FLAMMENZEICHEN see **SONNE ASIENS, DIE** • 1920
FLAMMES • 1978 • Arrieta Adolfo • FRN
FLAMMES DE PIERRE • 1947 • Rebuffat Gaston (c/d) • SHT • FRN
FLAMMES SUR L'ADRIATIQUE • 1968 • Astruc Alexandre, Cikes Stjepan • FRN, YGS • PLAMEN NAD JADRANOM (YGS)
FLAMMESVAERDET see **VERDENS UNDERGANG** • 1916
FLANAGAN • 1975 • Ditvoorst Adriaan • NTH
FLANAGAN • 1985 • Goldstein Scott • USA • WALLS OF GLASS
FLANAGAN BOY, THE • 1953 • Le Borg Reginald • UKN • BAD BLONDE (USA)
FLANNELFOOT • 1953 • Rogers Maclean • UKN
FLAP • 1969 • Reed Carol • USA • LAST WARRIOR, THE (UKN) ○ NOBODY LOVES FLAPPING EAGLE ○ NOBODY LOVES A DRUNKEN INDIAN
FLAPJACKS • 1918 • Beaudine William • SHT • USA
FLAPPER, THE • 1920 • Crosland Alan • USA
FLAPPER AND THE CURATES, THE • 1912 • Fitzhamon Lewin • UKN
FLAPPER AND THE FAN, THE • 1914 • *Crusade* • UKN
FLAPPER GOES TO SCHOOL • 1916 • *Wheeler Nettie* • SHT • USA
FLAPPER WIVES • 1924 • Murfin Jane, McCloskey Justin H. • USA • PERILOUS LOVE
FLAPPERS AND FRISKIES • 1918 • Howe J. A. • SHT • USA
FLAPPERS AND THE COLONEL, THE • 1913 • Fitzhamon Lewin • UKN
FLAPPERS AND THE NUTS, THE • 1913 • Fitzhamon Lewin • UKN
FLAPPER'S ELOPEMENT, THE • 1912 • Fitzhamon Lewin • UKN
FLAPPERS IN KHAKI (UKN) see **RILEY OF THE RAINBOW DIVISION** • 1928
FLARE AND FLICKER see **TEKETORIA** • 1977
FLARE-UP • 1969 • Neilson James • USA
FLARE-UP SAL • 1918 • Neill R. William • USA
FLASH • 1962 • Zien Allen • FRN
FLASH, THE • 1915 • Turner Otis • USA
FLASH, THE • 1923 • Craft William James • USA
FLASH AND THE FIRECAT • 1975 • Sebastian Beverly, Sebastian Ferdinand • USA
FLASH BACKS • Brian J. • USA
FLASH FRAME • 1986 • Winning David • CND
FLASH GORDON • 1936 • Stephani Frederick • SRL • USA • SPACE SOLDIERS
FLASH GORDON • ANM • USA
FLASH GORDON • 1980 • Hodges Mike • USA
FLASH GORDON CONQUERS THE UNIVERSE • 1940 • Beebe Ford, Taylor Ray • SRL • USA • SPACE SOLDIERS CONQUER THE UNIVERSE
FLASH GORDON –THE GREATEST ADVENTURE OF ALL • 1979 • Wetzler Gwen • ANM • USA
FLASH GORDON: TO SAVE THE EARTH • 1989 • ANM • USA
FLASH GORDON'S BATTLE IN SPACE see **BAYTEKIN FEZADA CARPISANLAR** • 1967
FLASH GORDON'S TRIP TO MARS • 1938 • Beebe Ford, Hill Robert F. • SRL • USA
FLASH IN THE DARK, A • 1914 • Reid Wallace • USA
FLASH IN THE NIGHT, A • 1911 • *Kalem* • USA
FLASH LOVE • 1971 • Pontiac Jean-Marie • FRN • LOVE–MAKING HOT STYLE ○ NIGHT GAMES
FLASH O' LIGHTNING • 1925 • Maloney Leo • USA
FLASH OF AN EMERALD, THE • 1915 • Capellani Albert • USA
FLASH OF DEATH, THE • 1917 • *Big U* • SHT • USA
FLASH OF FATE, THE • 1914 • *Bison* • USA
FLASH OF FATE, THE • 1918 • Clifton Elmer • USA
FLASH OF GREEN, A • 1984 • Nunez Victor • USA
FLASH OF LIGHT, A • 1910 • Griffith D. W. • USA
FLASH OF LIGHTNING, A • 1913 • Raymond Charles • UKN
FLASH OF LIGHTNING, A see **INAZUMA** • 1967
FLASH OF THE FOREST • 1928 • *Braveheart* • USA
FLASH PANTS • 1984 • Milan Eve • USA
FLASH PIMPLE THE MASTER CROOK • 1915 • Evans Fred, Evans Joe • UKN
FLASH THE SHEEPDOG • 1967 • Henson Laurence • UKN
FLASHBACK • 1968 • Andreassi Raffaele • ITL
FLASHBACK • 1977 • Corneau Alain • FRN
FLASHBACK • 1989 • Amurri Franco • USA
FLASHBACK see **FEAR** • 1988
FLASHBACKS • 1938 • Jeffrey R. E. • UKN
FLASHDANCE • 1983 • Lyne Adrian • USA
FLASHDANCE FEVER • 1983 • Roberts Alan • USA
FLASHER, THE • 1975 • Kerr Barry • USA
FLASHES OF ACTION • 1925 • *U.s. Army Signal Corps* • USA
FLASHING BLADES • 1940 • Sparling Gordon • DCS • CND
FLASHING FANGS • 1926 • McCarty Henry • USA
FLASHING GUNS • 1947 • Hillyer Lambert • USA
FLASHING HOOFS • 1928 • *Lyons Cliff* • USA
FLASHING LIGHTS see **NEW YORK AFTER MIDNIGHT** • 1983
FLASHING SPIKES • 1962 • Ford John • MTV • USA
FLASHING SPURS • 1924 • Eason B. Reeves • USA • SPIDER'S WEB (UKN)
FLASHING STEEDS • 1925 • Carpenter Horace B. • USA
FLASHLIGHT, THE • 1915 • Carleton Lloyd B. • USA
FLASHLIGHT, THE • 1917 • Park Ida May • USA
FLASHLIGHT FLIVVER, A • 1915 • *Hamilton Lloyd V.* • USA
FLASHMAN • 1967 • Loy Mino • ITL, FRN • FLASHMAN CONTRE LES HOMMES INVISIBLES (FRN) ○ FLASHMAN VS. THE INVISIBLE MEN
FLASHMAN CONTRE LES HOMMES INVISIBLES (FRN) see **FLASHMAN** • 1967
FLASHMAN VS. THE INVISIBLE MEN see **FLASHMAN** • 1967
FLASHPOINT • 1972 • Hannant Brian • ASL
FLASHPOINT • 1984 • Tannen William • USA
FLASHPOINT AFRICA • 1978 • Megahy Francis • SAF, FRG • REBELLEN, DIE (FRG) ○ ONE TAKE TWO
FLASKEN • 1987 • Nielsen Per Tonnes • ANS • DNM • BOTTLE, THE
FLASKEPOST • 1988 • Straume Unni • NRW • MAIL BY BOTTLE ○ TIL EN UKJENT ○ TO AN UNKNOWN ○ TO A STRANGER
FLAT 15 • 1973 • Johnston S. • UKN
FLAT, THE • 1921 • Paul Fred • UKN
FLAT, THE • 1963 • Berkovic Zvonimir • DOC • YGS • MY FLAT
FLAT, THE see **BYT** • 1968
FLAT BROKE • 1920 • Roach Hal • SHT • USA
FLAT CHARLESTON, THE • 1926 • Ponting Dudley • UKN
FLAT FOOT FLEDGLING • 1952 • Davis Mannie • ANS • USA
FLAT FOOT ON THE NILE see **PIEDONE D'EGITTO** • 1980
FLAT FOOT STOOGES • 1938 • Parrott Charles • SHT • USA
FLAT FOR RENT • 1910 • *Essanay* • USA
FLAT HARMONY • 1917 • Curtis Allen • SHT • USA
FLAT HATTING • 1946 • Hubley John, Eastman Phil • ANS • USA
FLAT HUNTING • 1920 • *Celebrated Players* • USA
FLAT JUNGLE, THE • 1978 • van der Keuken Johan • DOC • NTH
FLAT NO.3 • 1934 • Hiscott Leslie • UKN
FLAT NO.9 • 1932 • Richardson Frank • UKN
FLAT ON YOUR FACE see **AL HAPANIM** • 1989
FLAT TOP • 1952 • Selander Lesley • USA • EAGLES OF THE FLEET (UKN)
FLAT TWO • 1962 • Cooke Alan • UKN
FLAT UPSTAIRS, THE • 1912 • *Prior Herbert* • USA
FLATBED ANNIE & SWEETIEPIE see **FLATBED ANNIE & SWEETIEPIE: LADY TRUCKERS** • 1979
FLATBED ANNIE & SWEETIEPIE: LADY TRUCKERS • 1979 • Greenwald Robert • TVM • USA • FLATBED ANNIE & SWEETIEPIE ○ LADY TRUCKERS
FLATFOOT see **PIEDONE LO SBIRRO** • 1973
FLATHEADS AND FLIVVERS • 1917 • Semon Larry • SHT • USA
FLATLAND • 1965 • Martin Eric • ANM • USA
FLATLINERS • 1990 • Schumacher Joel • USA
FLATS AND SHARPS • 1915 • *Starlight* • USA
FLATTERY • 1925 • Forman Tom • USA
FLAUTO IN PARADISO, UN • 1958 • Gamna Vincenzo • ITL
FLAUTO MAGICO, IL • 1978 • Luzzati Emmanuele • ANM • ITL
FLAVIA LA MONACA MUSULMANA • 1974 • Mingozzi Gianfranco • ITL, FRN • REBEL NUN, THE (UKN)
FLAVOUR OF GREEN TEA OVER RICE, THE see **OCHAZUKE NO AJI** • 1952
FLAW, THE • 1933 • Walker Norman • UKN
FLAW, THE • 1955 • Fisher Terence • UKN
FLAW IN THE ALIBI, THE • 1914 • *Holmes Helen* • USA
FLAW IN THE EVIDENCE, A • 1916 • *Thanhouser* • SHT • USA
FLAX • 1944 • Taylor Donald • UKN
FLAXY MARTIN • 1949 • Bare Richard L. • USA
FLAYED ROSE, THE see **ROSE ECORCHEE, LA** • 1970
FLEA CEOIL • Marcus Louis • DOC • IRL
FLEA CIRCUS, THE • 1954 • Avery Tex • ANS • USA
FLEA FOR TWO • 1955 • Patterson Ray • ANS • USA
FLEA IN HER EAR, A • 1968 • Charon Jacques • USA, FRN • PUCE A L'OREILLE, LA (FRN)
FLEA IN HER EAR, A see **PULGA EN LA OREJA, LA** • 1981
FLEA IN THE EAR see **VI SPILLOPPER** • 1979
FLEBUS • 1957 • Pintoff Ernest • ANS • USA
FLECHA ENVENENADA, LA • 1956 • Baledon Rafael • MXC
FLECHE D'ARGENT • 1938 • Clement Rene • DCS • FRN
FLEDERMAUS '55 see **OH ROSALINDA!** • 1955
FLEDERMAUS, DIE • 1923 • Mack Max • FRG
FLEDERMAUS, DIE • 1931 • Lamac Carl • FRG
FLEDERMAUS, DIE • 1937 • Verhoeven Paul • FRG
FLEDERMAUS, DIE • 1945 • von Bolvary Geza • FRG • BAT, THE (USA)
FLEDERMAUS, DIE • 1962 • von Cziffra Geza • AUS
FLEDERMAUS, DIE • 1966 • Meineche Annelise • DNM • FLEGERMUSEN
FLEDERMAUS SQUADRON, THE see **GESCHWADER FLEDERMAUS** • 1958
FLEDGED SHADOWS see **OPERENE STINY** • 1930
FLEDGLINGS • 1965 • Vane Norman Thaddeus • UKN
FLEE, YOU'RE DISCOVERED • 1914 • *Melies* • USA
FLEEING FROM THE FLEAS • 1914 • Neilan Marshall • USA
FLEET THAT CAME TO STAY, THE • 1946 • Boetticher Budd • USA
FLEET'S IN, THE • 1928 • St. Clair Malcolm • USA
FLEET'S IN, THE • 1942 • Schertzinger Victor • USA
FLEETS OF STRE'TH • 1942 • Fleischer Dave • ANS • USA
FLEETWING • 1928 • Hillyer Lambert • USA
FLEGERMUSEN see **FLEDERMAUS, DIE** • 1966
FLEISCH • 1980 • Erler Rainer • FRG • SPARE PARTS (USA)
FLEISCHER'S ALBUM see **ALBUM FLEISCHERA** • 1963
FLEISCHWOLF • 1990 • Allahyari Houchang • AUS • MEAT–GRINDER
FLEISSIGEN BIENEN VOM FROHLICHEN BOCK, DIE • 1970 • Billian Hans • FRG • SEX IS NOT FOR VIRGINS (UKN)
FLEMENCO VIVO • Mertens Reni, Marti Walter • DOC • SWT
FLEMING FALOON • 1964 • Landow George • SHT • USA • FLEMING FALOON SCREENING
FLEMING FALOON SCREENING see **FLEMING FALOON** • 1964
FLEMISH FARM, THE • 1943 • Dell Jeffrey • UKN
FLESH • 1932 • Ford John • USA
FLESH • 1968 • Morrissey Paul • USA
FLESH see **MIDNIGHT GUEST, THE** • 1923
FLESH see **CARNE** • 1968
FLESH, THE see **ZOKU NIKU** • 1968
FLESH AND BLOOD • 1912 • Blache Alice • USA
FLESH AND BLOOD • 1922 • Cummings Irving • USA
FLESH AND BLOOD • 1951 • Kimmins Anthony • UKN
FLESH AND BLOOD • 1979 • Taylor Jud • TVM • USA
FLESH AND BLOOD • 1985 • Verhoeven Paul* • USA, NTH
FLESH AND BLOOD SHOW, THE • 1972 • Walker Pete • UKN • ASYLUM OF THE INSANE
FLESH AND DESIRE (USA) see **CHAIR ET LE DIABLE, LA** • 1953
FLESH AND FANTASY • Desimone Tom • FRN
FLESH AND FANTASY • 1943 • Duvivier Julien • USA • OBSESSIONS ○ FOR ALL WE KNOW
FLESH AND FANTASY • 1967 • Benazeraf Jose • USA
FLESH AND FLAME see **NIGHT OF THE QUARTER MOON, THE** • 1959
FLESH AND FURY • 1952 • Pevney Joseph • USA • HEAR NO EVIL
FLESH AND LACE • 1965 • Sarno Joe • USA • FRESH & LACE ○ FRESH 'N' LACEY
FLESH AND LACE: PART 1 • 1983 • Tobalina Carlos • USA
FLESH AND SPIRIT • 1922 • Levering Joseph • USA
FLESH AND THE DEVIL • 1926 • Brown Clarence • USA
FLESH AND THE FIENDS, THE • 1960 • Gilling John • UKN • MANIA (USA) ○ PSYCHO KILLERS ○ FIENDISH GHOULS, THE

FLESH AND THE SPUR • 1957 • Cahn Edward L. • USA

FLESH AND THE WOMAN (USA) see **GRAND JEU, LE** • 1954

FLESH AND WOMAN see **GRAND JEU, LE** • 1954

FLESH CONTRACT, THE see **NIKUTAI NO KEIYAKUSHO** • 1968

FLESH CREATURES, THE see **HORROR OF THE BLOOD MONSTERS** • 1970

FLESH CREATURES OF THE RED PLANET see **HORROR OF THE BLOOD MONSTERS** • 1970

FLESH EATER • 1989 • Hinzman Bill • USA

FLESH EATERS, THE • 1964 • Curtis Jack • USA

FLESH FEAST • 1970 • Grinter Brad F. • USA

FLESH FOR FRANKENSTEIN (UKN) see **ANDY WARHOL'S FRANKENSTEIN** • 1974

FLESH GAME, THE • 1966 • Mitchell M. M. • USA • FRESH GAME, THE ○ FRESH GAMES

FLESH GORDON • 1972 • Light Mike • USA

FLESH GORDON • 1974 • Benveniste Michael, Ziehm Howard • USA

FLESH HUSTLER, THE • 1970 • Irving Limp • USA

FLESH IS HOT, THE (USA) see **BUTA TO GUNKAN** • 1961

FLESH IS WEAK, THE • 1957 • Chaffey Don • UKN

FLESH IS WEAK, THE see **BITOKU NO YOROMEKI** • 1957

FLESH MERCHANTS, THE • 1956 • Connell W. Merle • USA

FLESH OF EVE see **DANGEROUS PARADISE** • 1930

FLESH OF HIS FLESH • 1913 • Pollard Harry • USA

FLESH OF MORNING • 1956 • Brakhage Stan • SHT • USA

FLESH OF MY FLESH • 1969 • Macready Michael, Kelljan Bob • USA • LITTLE SISTER

FLESH ON FIRE • 1973 • Papakostas Giorgos • GRC

FLESH TORTURE see **NIKUZEME** • 1968

FLESH WILL SURRENDER (USA) see **DELITTO DI GIOVANNI EPISCOPO, IL** • 1947

FLESHBURN • 1983 • Gage George • USA • FEAR IN A HANDFUL OF DUST

FLESHDANCE • 1984 • Gibb Ken • USA

FLETCH • 1985 • Ritchie Michael • USA

FLETCH II see **FLETCH LIVES** • 1989

FLETCH LIVES • 1989 • Ritchie Michael • USA • FLETCH II

FLEUR, UNE see **WARDA** • 1971

FLEUR AUX DENTS, LA • 1975 • Vamos Thomas • CND

FLEUR BLEUE • 1970 • Kent Larry • CND • APPRENTICE, THE

FLEUR D'AMOUR • 1927 • Vandal Marcel • FRN

FLEUR DANS LES LES RONCES, UNE • 1921 • de Morlhon Camille • FRN

FLEUR DE FOUGERE • 1949 • Starevitch Ladislas, Bo Soniko • SHT • FRN • FLOWER OF THE FERN (USA)

FLEUR DE L'AGE, LA • 1947 • Carne Marcel • FRN

FLEUR DE L'AGE, LA (FRN) see **RAPTURE** • 1965

FLEUR DE L'AGE, OU LES ADOLESCENTES, LA see **ADOLESCENTI, LE** • 1964

FLEUR-DE-LIS RING, THE • 1914 • Physioc Wray • USA

FLEUR-DE-LYS • 1914 • Gaskill Charles L. • USA

FLEUR DE MAI • 1977 • Noel Jean-Guy • CND

FLEUR DE PAVE • 1909 • Carre Michel • FRN

FLEUR DES INDES, LA • 1921 • Bergerat Theo • FRN

FLEUR DES RUINES, LA • 1916 • Gance Abel • FRN

FLEUR D'ORANGER, LA • 1932 • Roussell Henry • FRN

FLEUR D'OSEILLE • 1967 • Lautner Georges • FRN • FRIC MET LES VOILES, LE

FLEUR DU GOLAN, LA • 1974 • Dehni Salah • DOC • SYR • ROSE OF THE GOLAN, THE

FLEUR EMPOISONNEE, LA • 1909 • Jasset Victorin • FRN

FLEUR ET LE FUSIL, LA • 1976 • Valet Gerard • BLG

FLEUR SANGLANTE, LA • 1912 • Machin Alfred • FRN

FLEURS, LES • 1963 • Dyja Andre • FRN

FLEURS, C'EST POUR ROSEMONT, LES • 1969 • Giraldeau Jacques • DOC • CND

FLEURS D'AMOUR see **WARDI AL-GHARAM** • 1951

FLEURS DE MACADAM, LES • 1969 • Coderre Laurent • ANS • CND • MACADAM FLOWERS, THE (USA) ○ ASPHALT FLOWERS, THE

FLEURS DE VIGNE • 1935 • Benoit-Levy Jean • FRN

FLEURS DU MIEL, LES • 1976 • Faraldo Claude • FRN

FLEURS DU SOLEIL, LES (FRN) see **GIRASOLI, I** • 1969

FLEURS ET FLEURS • Lavoie Hermenegilde • DCS • CND

FLEURS SAUVAGES see **ZUHURUN BARRIYYA** • 1972

FLEURS SAUVAGES, LES • 1982 • Lefebvre Jean-Pierre • CND • WILD FLOWERS

FLEUVE, LE see **NAHR, AL** • 1977

FLEUVE D'ARGENT, LE • 1956 • Chenal Pierre • FRN

FLEUVE INVISIBLE, LA • 1960 • Vilardebo Carlos • SHT • FRN

FLEUVE, LE (FRN) see **RIVER, THE** • 1951

FLEUVE: LE TARN, LA see **EAUX VIVES, LES** • 1952

FLEUVE SOUVERAIN, UN see **ROYAL RIVER** • 1958

FLIBUSTIER, DIE • 1922 • Stein Josef • FRG

FLIBUSTIERI DELLA MARTINICA, I (ITL) see **MARIE DES ISLES** • 1959

FLIC, UN • 1947 • de Canonge Maurice • FRN

FLIC, UN • 1972 • Melville Jean-Pierre • FRN, ITL • NOTTE SULLA CITTA (ITL) ○ DIRTY MONEY (UKN)

FLIC HORS LA LOI, UN (FRN) see **UOMO DELLA STRADA FA GIUSTIZIA, L'** • 1975

FLIC OU VOYOU? • 1979 • Lautner Georges • FRN

FLIC STORY • 1975 • Deray Jacques • FRN, ITL

FLIC STORY (UKN) see **IL ETAIT UNE FOIS UN FLIC** • 1972

FLICEK THE BALL • 1956 • Schaeffer Dusan • ANS • CZC • NAUGHTY BALL, THE ○ GAY BALL, THE

FLICK • 1970 • Taylor Gilbert W. • CND • DR. FRANKENSTEIN ON CAMPUS (USA) ○ FRANKENSTEIN ON CAMPUS (UKN)

FLICKA FOR MEJ, EN • 1943 • Larsson Borje • SWD • GIRL FOR ME, A

FLICKA FRAN BACKAFALL • 1953 • Bugler Bror • SWD • GIRL FROM BACKAFALL

FLICKA I KASERN • 1955 • Larsson Borje • SWD • GIRL IN THE BARRACKS

FLICKA KOMMER TILL STAN, EN • 1937 • Brooks Thor L., Keil-Moller Carlo • SWD • GIRL COMES TO TOWN, A

FLICKA MED MELODI • 1954 • Soderhjelm Martin • SWD • GIRL WITH A MELODY

FLICKA OCH HYACINTER • 1950 • Ekman Hasse • SWD • GIRL WITH HYACINTHS ○ SUICIDE

FLICKA UTAN NAMN • 1954 • Wickman Torgny • SWD • GIRL WITHOUT A NAME

FLICKAN AR ETT FYND • 1943 • Eklund Ernst • SWD • THAT GIRL IS A DISCOVERY

FLICKAN FRAN BYN • 1980 • Lohman Axel • SWD • GIRL FROM THE VILLAGE, THE

FLICKAN FRAN FJALLBYN • 1948 • Henrikson Anders • SWD • GIRL FROM THE MOUNTAIN VILLAGE, THE

FLICKAN FRAN PARADISET • 1924 • Berthels Theodor • SWD • GIRL FROM PARADISE

FLICKAN FRAN TREDJE RADEN • 1949 • Ekman Hasse • SWD • GIRL FROM THE GALLERY, THE

FLICKAN FRAN VARUHUSET • 1933 • Henrikson Anders, Lundqvist Torsten • SWD • GIRL FROM THE DEPARTMENT STORE, THE

FLICKAN I FONSTRET see **UNG MAN SOKER SALLSKAP** • 1954

FLICKAN I FONSTRET MITTEMOT • 1942 • Jerring Nils • SWD • GIRL IN THE WINDOW OPPOSITE

FLICKAN I FRACK • 1926 • Swanstrom Karin • SWD • GIRL IN A DRESS-COAT

FLICKAN I FRACK • 1956 • Mattsson Arne • SWD • GIRL IN A DRESS-COAT

FLICKAN I REGNET • 1955 • Kjellin Alf • SWD • GIRL IN THE RAIN, THE

FLICKAN OCH DJAVULEN • 1943 • Faustman Erik • SWD • GIRL AND THE DEVIL, THE

FLICKER, THE • 1966 • Conrad Tony • USA

FLICKER FEVER • 1935 • Sennett Mack • USA

FLICKER FLASHBACKS • 1943 • Fleischer Richard • SHS • USA

FLICKER MEMORIES • 1941 • Sidney George • SHT • USA

FLICKER OF THE SILVER THAW see **JUHYO NO YOROMEKI** • 1968

FLICKER UP • 1946 • *Eckstine Billy* • USA

FLICKERING LIGHT, THE • 1916 • Borzage Frank, Berger (Mr.) • SHT • USA

FLICKERING YOUTH • 1924 • *Sennett Mack (P)* • SHT • USA

FLICKERS • 1940 • Huntington Lawrence • DOC • UKN

FLICKOR I HAMN • 1945 • Ohberg Ake • SWD • GIRLS IN THE HARBOUR

FLICKOR PA FABRIK • 1935 • Cederstrand Solve • SWD • GIRLS IN A FACTORY

FLICKORNA • 1968 • Zetterling Mai • SWD • GIRLS, THE

FLICKORNA FRAN ARE • 1920 • Lauritzen Lau • SWD • GIRLS FROM ARE

FLICKORNA FRAN GAMLA STA'N • 1934 • Bauman Schamyl • SWD • GIRLS FROM THE OLD TOWN, THE

FLICKORNA GYURKOVICS • 1926 • Hytten-Cavallius Ragnar • SWD, FRG • SIEBEN TOCHTER DER FRAU GYURKOVICS, DIE (FRG) ○ SISTER OF SIX, A

FLICKORNA GYURKOVICS • 1926 • Merzbach Paul • SWD • GYURKOVICS GIRLS

FLICKORNA I SMALAND • 1945 • Bauman Schamyl • SWD • GIRLS OF SMALAND

FLICKORNA PA SOLVIK • 1926 • Klercker Georg • SWD • GIRLS OF SOLVIK, THE

FLICKORNA PA UPPAKRA • 1936 • Marmstedt Lorens, Eklund Alice • SWD • GIRLS OF UPPAKRA, THE

FLICKORNAS ALFRED • 1935 • Adolphson Edvin • SWD • ALFRED LOVED BY THE GIRLS

FLICKS • 1987 • Winograd Peter • USA • LOOSE JOINTS

FLICS DE CHOC • 1983 • Desagnat Jean-Pierre • FRN

FLIEGEN DE UNTERTASSEN • 1953 • *Filmaufbau Goettingen* • DOC • FRG • FLYING SAUCERS

FLIEGENDE AHNFRAU, DIE see **HERR SENATOR, DER** • 1934

FLIEGENDE AUTO, DAS • 1920 • Piel Harry • FRG

FLIEGENDE HOLLANDER, DER • 1918 • Neumann Hans • FRG

FLIEGENDE HOLLANDER, DER • 1965 • Herz Joachim • GDR • FLYING DUTCHMAN, THE (UKN)

FLIEGENDE KLASSENZIMMER, DAS • 1954 • Hoffmann Kurt • FRG • FLYING CLASSROOM, THE (USA)

FLIEGENDE KOFFER, DER • 1921 • Reiniger Lotte • ANM • FRG • FLYING COFFER, THE (UKN)

FLIEGENDE SCHATTEN • 1917 • *Landa Max* • FRG

FLIEGENDE TOD, DER • 1920 • Tostary Alfred • FRG

FLIEGENDEN ARZTE VON OSTAFRIKA, DIE • 1969 • Herzog Werner • FRG • FLYING DOCTORS OF EAST AFRICA, THE (UKN)

FLIEGENDEN BRIGANTEN 1, DIE • 1921 • Felmy Max • FRG • DIEB SIENES EIGENTUMS, DER

FLIEGENDEN BRIGANTEN 2, DIE • 1921 • Felmy Max • FRG • RACHE DES MONGOLEN, DIE

FLIEGENTUTEN -OTHELLO • 1918 • Boese Carl • FRG

FLIEGER, DER • 1987 • Keusch Erwin • FRG • AVIATOR, THE

FLIEGER.. FLIEGER.. KANONIERE! • 1936 • Rikli Martin • FRG • GERMAN AIR-FORCE, THE

FLIEGER VON GOERZ, DER • 1918 • Meinert Rudolf • FRG

FLIEHENDE SCHATTEN see **AUS DEN ERINNERUNGEN EINES FRAUENARZTES 1** • 1921

FLIES • 1923 • Fleischer Dave • ANS • USA

FLIES, THE see **THOSE FLIES** • 1908

FLIES AIN'T HUMAN • 1941 • Fleischer Dave • ANS • USA

FLIES' GROCERY, THE see **SINEKLI BAKKAL** • 1967

FLIES HUNTING see **POLOWANIE NA MUCHY** • 1969

FLIGHT • 1929 • Capra Frank • USA

FLIGHT • 1952 • Fancey E. J. • UKN

FLIGHT • 1958 • Belson Jordan • ANS • USA

FLIGHT • 1960 • Neyman Michael • USA

FLIGHT • 1974 • Brakhage Stan • USA

FLIGHT #90: DISASTER ON THE POTOMAC • 1984 • Lewis Robert Michael • TVM • USA

FLIGHT 54321 • 1971 • Vukotic Dusan • ANS • YGS

FLIGHT, THE see **FLUGTEN** • 1942

FLIGHT, THE see **OD RZEMYCZKA..** • 1961

FLIGHT, THE see **BEG** • 1971

FLIGHT ABOVE THE MARSHES • 1957 • Petrovic Aleksandar • YGS

FLIGHT ANGELS • 1940 • Seiler Lewis • USA • WOMEN ARE TOUGH ANGELS

FLIGHT AT MIDNIGHT • 1939 • Salkow Sidney • USA

FLIGHT BEYOND THE SUN see **SPACE MONSTER** • 1965

FLIGHT COMMAND • 1940 • Borzage Frank • USA

FLIGHT COMMANDER see **DAWN PATROL** • 1930

FLIGHT COMMANDER, THE • 1927 • Elvey Maurice • UKN

FLIGHT FOR A FORTUNE, A • 1914 • *Majestic* • USA

FLIGHT FOR FREEDOM • 1943 • Mendes Lothar • USA • STAND BY TO DIE

FLIGHT FROM ASHIYA • 1964 • Anderson Michael • USA, JPN • ASHIYA KARA NO HIKO (JPN)

FLIGHT FROM DESTINY • 1941 • Sherman Vincent • USA • INVITATION TO A MURDER ○ TRIAL AND ERROR

FLIGHT FROM FOLLY • 1945 • Mason Herbert • UKN

FLIGHT FROM GLORY • 1937 • Landers Lew • USA

FLIGHT FROM JUSTICE (UKN) see **FEDERAL MAN-HUNT** • 1939

FLIGHT FROM LIFE, THE see **HAR JEG RET TIL AT TAGE MIT EGET LIV** • 1917

FLIGHT FROM MEMORY • 1970 • *Universal* • MXC

FLIGHT FROM MILLIONS see **FLUGTEN FRA MILLIONERNE** • 1934

FLIGHT FROM SINGAPORE • 1962 • Birch Dudley • UKN

FLIGHT FROM TERROR see **SATAN NEVER SLEEPS** • 1962

FLIGHT FROM THE MILLIONS (UKN) see **FLUGTEN FRA MILLIONERNE** • 1934

FLIGHT FROM TREASON • 1960 • *Gregson John* • UKN

FLIGHT FROM VIENNA • 1956 • Kavanagh Denis • UKN

FLIGHT FROM WRONG • 1956 • Kneitel Seymour • ANS • USA

FLIGHT IN WHITE • 1969 • Canning William • CND • ENTRE CIEL ET NIEGE

FLIGHT INTO DANGER (UKN) see **SKY RACKET** • 1937

FLIGHT INTO FRANCE (UKN) see **FUGA IN FRANCIA** • 1948

FLIGHT INTO NOWHERE • 1938 • Collins Lewis D. • USA

FLIGHT LEVEL 450 see **FLYGNIVA 450** • 1980

FLIGHT LIEUTENANT • 1942 • Salkow Sidney • USA

FLIGHT NURSE • 1953 • Dwan Allan • USA

FLIGHT OF A NIGHT BIRD, THE • 1915 • Giblyn Charles • USA

FLIGHT OF DEATH, THE • 1914 • *Carew James* • UKN

FLIGHT OF FANCY see **THEY TRAVEL BY AIR (FLIGHT OF FANCY)** • 1947

FLIGHT OF LUDLOW'S AERODROME • 1905 • *Bitzer Billy (Ph)* • USA

FLIGHT OF MR. MACKINLEY, THE • 1975 • Schweitzer Mikhail • USS

FLIGHT OF MR. MCKINLEY, THE • 1965 • Roshal Grigori • USS

FLIGHT OF PARROTS see **RANA GIRAW** • 1967

FLIGHT OF POINCARE, THE see **BEGSTVO PUANKARE** • 1932

FLIGHT OF RAINBIRDS, A • 1981 • de Jong Ate • NTH

FLIGHT OF RED WING • 1910 • *Bison* • USA

FLIGHT OF THE ANGRY DRAGON • 1986 • Foong Wu Ma • HKG

FLIGHT OF THE BIRD see **A VOL D'OISEAU** • 1962

FLIGHT OF THE COUGAR • 1976 • Hively Jack • USA

FLIGHT OF THE CROW, THE • 1913 • Martin E. A. • USA

FLIGHT OF THE DOVE, THE see **VUELO DE LA PALOMA, EL** • 1988

FLIGHT OF THE DOVES • 1971 • Nelson Ralph • UKN

FLIGHT OF THE DRAGON, THE • 1982 • Rankin Arthur Jr., Bass Jules • ANM • USA

FLIGHT OF THE DUCHESS, THE • 1916 • Nowland Eugene • USA

FLIGHT OF THE EAGLE, THE see **INGENJOR ANDREES LUFTFARD** • 1983

FLIGHT OF THE GREY WOLF, THE • 1976 • Zuniga Frank • USA

FLIGHT OF THE INTRUDER • 1990 • Milius John • USA

FLIGHT OF THE "JUNE BUG" • 1908 • *Kalem* • USA

FLIGHT OF THE KING, THE • 1922 • Ridgwell George • UKN

FLIGHT OF THE LOST BALLOON • 1961 • Juran Nathan • USA

FLIGHT OF THE NAVIGATOR • 1986 • Kleiser Randall • USA

FLIGHT OF THE PHOENIX • 1965 • Aldrich Robert • USA

FLIGHT OF THE SANDPIPER, THE see **SANDPIPER, THE** • 1965

FLIGHT OF THE SOUTHERN CROSS: OR, THE FOUR HUMAN EAGLES, THE • 1929 • *Hancock G. Allan* • DOC • USA • FOUR HUMAN EAGLES, THE

FLIGHT OF THE SPRUCE GOOSE, THE • 1986 • Majewski Lech

FLIGHT OF THE WHITE HERON, THE • 1954 • Craig Gordon • UKN

FLIGHT OF THE WHITE STALLIONS, THE (UKN) see **MIRACLE OF THE WHITE STALLIONS, THE** • 1962

FLIGHT OF WEALTH, THE • 1913 • Kellino W. P. • UKN

FLIGHT PATROL see **INTERNATIONAL SQUADRON** • 1941

FLIGHT PLAN • 1949 • Hawes Stanley • ASL

FLIGHT THAT DISAPPEARED, THE • 1961 • Le Borg Reginald • USA • FLIGHT THAT VANISHED, THE

FLIGHT THAT FAILED, THE • 1917 • De La Parelle M. • SHT • USA

FLIGHT THAT VANISHED, THE see **FLIGHT THAT DISAPPEARED, THE** • 1961

FLIGHT TO BERLIN • 1983 • Petit Christopher • UKN

FLIGHT TO FAME • 1938 • Coleman C. C. Jr. • USA • WINGS OF DOOM

FLIGHT TO FURY • 1966 • Hellman Monte • USA, PHL • CORDILLERA

FLIGHT TO HELL see **FAIR TRADE** • 1988

FLIGHT TO HOLOCAUST • 1977 • Kowalski Bernard • TVM • USA

FLIGHT TO HONG KONG • 1956 • Newman Joseph M. • USA

FLIGHT TO MARS • 1951 • Selander Lesley • USA

FLIGHT TO NOWHERE • 1946 • Rowland William • USA

FLIGHT TO ROPOTAMO see **BYAGSTVO V ROPOTAMO** • 1973

FLIGHT TO TANGIER • 1953 • Warren Charles Marquis • USA

FLIGHT TO THE FINISH, A • 1962 • Tendlar Dave • ANS • USA

FLIGHT TO THE MOON • 1953 • Brumberg Valentina, Brumberg L. • ANS • USS

FLIGHT TO THE ROPOTAMO see **BYAGSTVO V ROPOTAMO** • 1973

FLIGHT ZONE see **TOBO CHITAI** • 1953

FLIGHTS • 1977 • Pringle Ian • SHT • ASL

FLIGHTS BETWEEN DREAM AND REALITY see **POLIOTY VO SNE I NAIAVOU** • 1983

FLIM-FLAM MAN, THE • 1967 • Kershner Irvin • USA • ONE BORN EVERY MINUTE (UKN)

FLIMMERPRINZ, DER • 1919 • Mack Max • FRG

FLIMMERSTERNE • 1919 • Neumann Hans • FRG

FLIN FLON STRIKE • 1971 • Rodgers Bob • MTV • CND

FLING IN THE RING • 1955 • White Jules • SHT • USA

FLINKEVLEUGEL • 1969 • van Hemert Ruud • SHT • NTH

FLINTS OF STEEL see **TWO-FISTED JEFFERSON** • 1922
FLINTSTONE CHRISTMAS, A see **FLINTSTONES: A FLINTSTONE CHRISTMAS** • 1977
FLINTSTONES: A FLINTSTONE CHRISTMAS • 1977 • Nichols Charles • ANM • USA • FLINTSTONE CHRISTMAS, A
FLINTSTONES: MEET ROCKULA AND FRANKENSTONE • 1977 • ANM • USA
FLINTSTONES: THE JETSONS MEET THE FLINTSTONES • 1987 • Lusk Don • ANM • USA • JETSONS MEET THE FLINTSTONES, THE
FLIP AND DOCTOR PILL • 1914 • McCay Winsor • ANS • USA
FLIP FLAP • 1948 • Sparber I. • ANS • USA
FLIP FLOPS • 1923 • Del Ruth Roy • SHT • USA
FLIP OF A COIN, THE • 1919 • Dillon John Francis • SHT • USA
FLIP THE FROG • 1929-33 • *Iwerks Ub (P)* • ASS • USA
FLIPOTTE • 1920 • de Baroncelli Jacques • FRN
FLIPPER • 1963 • Clark James B. • USA
FLIPPER AND THE PIRATES see **FLIPPER'S NEW ADVENTURE** • 1964
FLIPPER FROLICS • 1952 • Rasinski Connie • ANS • USA
FLIPPER'S FROLICS • 1936 • Schwarzwald Milton • SHT • USA
FLIPPER'S NEW ADVENTURE • 1964 • Benson Leon • USA • FLIPPER AND THE PIRATES
FLIPS AND FLOPS • 1919 • Pratt Gilbert • SHT • USA
FLIP'S LUNCHROOM • 1933 • *Iwerks Ub (P)* • ANS • USA
FLIPSIDE OF DOMINICK HIDE, THE • 1981 • Gibson Alan • MTV • UKN
FLIRT • 1984 • Russo Roberto • ITL
FLIRT, THE • 1909 • *Powhatan* • USA
FLIRT, THE • 1912 • *Rex* • USA
FLIRT, THE • 1913 • *Reliance* • USA
FLIRT, THE • 1913 • Humphrey William • *Vitagraph* • USA
FLIRT, THE • 1914 • *Sterling* • USA
FLIRT, THE • 1914 • Ransom Charles • *Edison* • USA
FLIRT, THE • 1916 • Quirk William • *Rolma* • SHT • USA
FLIRT, THE • 1916 • Weber Lois, Smalley Phillips • *Bluebird* • USA
FLIRT, THE • 1917 • *Rolin* • SHT • USA
FLIRT, THE • 1917 • Roach Hal • SHT • USA
FLIRT, THE • 1922 • Henley Hobart • USA
FLIRT, THE see **PIROPO, EL** • 1979
FLIRT AND THE BANDIT, THE • 1913 • *American* • USA
FLIRT OF FORLOVELSE • 1923 • Lauritzen Lau • DNM
FLIRT OR HEROINE • 1912 • Brooke Van Dyke • USA
FLIRT SE SLECNOU STRIBRNOU • 1969 • Gajer Vaclav • CZC • FLIRTING WITH MISS SILVER ○ FLIRT WITH MISS STRIBRNOU, A
FLIRT THERE WAS, A • 1919 • *Devore Dorothy* • USA
FLIRT WITH MISS STRIBRNOU, A see **FLIRT SE SLECNOU STRIBRNOU** • 1969
FLIRTATION A LA CARTE • 1916 • *Smith Dick* • SHT • USA
FLIRTATION AT SEA, A • 1913 • Raymond Charles • UKN
FLIRTATION COLLAR • 1909 • *Phoenix* • USA
FLIRTATION IN A BOAT • 1898 • *Cinematograph Co.* • UKN
FLIRTATION IN THE ARCHIPELAGO see **SKARGARDSFLIRT** • 1935
FLIRTATION WALK • 1934 • Borzage Frank • USA
FLIRTATIONS OF PHYLLIS, THE • 1921 • Paul Fred, Raymond Jack • UKN
FLIRTATIOUS LIZZIE • 1915 • *Kalem* • USA
FLIRTATIOUS WIFE see **UWAKIZUMA** • 1967
FLIRTING • 1990 • Duigan John • ASL
FLIRTING BRIDE, THE • 1916 • Horkheimer H. M., Horkheimer E. D. • SHT • USA
FLIRTING HUSBAND, THE • 1912 • Nicholls George, Sennett Mack (Spv) • USA
FLIRTING IN THE PARK • 1933 • Stevens George • SHT • USA
FLIRTING WIDOW, THE • 1930 • Seiter William A. • USA • GREEN STOCKINGS
FLIRTING WITH DANGER • 1917 • Miller Rube • SHT • USA
FLIRTING WITH DANGER • 1934 • Moore Vin • USA • DAMES AND DYNAMITE ○ RECKLESS ROMEOS
FLIRTING WITH DEATH • 1917 • Clifton Elmer • USA
FLIRTING WITH FATE • 1916 • Cabanne W. Christy • USA
FLIRTING WITH FATE • 1938 • McDonald Frank • USA
FLIRTING WITH LOVE • 1924 • Dillon John Francis • USA
FLIRTING WITH MISS SILVER see **FLIRT SE SLECNOU STRIBRNOU** • 1969
FLIRTO-MANIAC, THE • 1910 • *Lubin* • USA
FLIRTS • 1919 • Parrott Charles • USA
FLIRTS, THE see **BETWEEN SHOWERS** • 1914
FLIRTS AND FAKERS • 1918 • Howe J. A. • SHT • USA
FLIRT'S MISTAKE, A • 1914 • Lehrman Henry • USA
FLIRT'S REPENTANCE, A • 1914 • *Selig* • USA
FLIRTY APPLICATION, A • 1910 • *Essanay* • USA
FLIRTY BIRDY • 1945 • Hanna William, Barbera Joseph • ANS • USA
FLIRTY FLORENCE • 1913 • *Frontier* • USA
FLIRTY FOUR FLUSHERS • 1926 • Cline Eddie • SHT • USA
FLIRTY SLEEPWALKER, THE • 1932 • *Sennett Mack (P)* • SHT • USA
FLISACY • 1963 • Grabowski Stanislaw • DOC • PLN • BARGEMEN, THE
FLIT, IMBATTIBILE SUPREMO see **VOSTRO SUPER AGENTE FLIT, IL** • 1966
FLIT, SUPREMELY UNBEATABLE see **VOSTRO SUPER AGENTE FLIT, IL** • 1966
FLITTER-DORTJE • 1919 • Leffler Robert • FRG
FLITTERWOCHEN • 1928 • Emo E. W. • FRG
FLITTERWOCHEN • 1936 • Lamac Carl • FRG
FLITTERWOCHEN-CONTROLLEUR, DER • 1915 • *Davis Alvine* • FRG
FLITTERWOCHEN IN DER HOLLE • 1960 • Kai Johannes • FRG • ISLE OF SIN (USA)
FLIVVER, THE • 1922 • Roach Hal • SHT • USA
FLIVVER WEDDING, A • 1920 • Pratt Gilbert • SHT • USA
FLIVVERING • 1917 • Jackson Harry • SHT • USA
FLIVVER'S ART OF MYSTERY (USA) see **PIMPLE'S ART OF MYSTERY** • 1915
FLIVVER'S DILEMMA (USA) see **PIMPLE'S DILEMMA** • 1915
FLIVVER'S FAMOUS CHEESE HOUND (USA) see **PIMPLE'S MILLION DOLLAR MYSTERY** • 1915
FLIVVER'S GOOD TURN (USA) see **PIMPLE'S GOOD TURN** • 1915
FLIVVER'S STILL ALARM (USA) see **PIMPLE'S BURLESQUE OF THE STILL ALARM** • 1915
FLIVVER'S TERRIBLE PAST (USA) see **PIMPLE'S PAST** • 1915
FLIYVENDE CIRKUS, DEN • 1912 • Lind Alfred • DNM
FLO AND MARIANNA -A MATTER OF LANGUAGE • 1978 • Blagg Linda • DOC • ASL
FLO THE FLAPPER • 1912 • Fitzhamon Lewin • UKN
FLOAT LIKE A BUTTERFLY, STING LIKE A BEE • 1969 • Klein William • USA
FLOATING • 1975 • Edols Michael • DOC • ASL
FLOATING CALL, THE • 1914 • *Hunt Irene* • USA
FLOATING CLOUDS see **UKIGUMO** • 1955
FLOATING COLLEGE, THE • 1928 • Crone George J. • USA
FLOATING DEATH, THE • 1915 • Stanton Richard • USA
FLOATING DUTCHMAN, THE • 1953 • Sewell Vernon • UKN
FLOATING FREE see **UGY EREZTE, SZABADON EL** • 1988
FLOATING VESSEL see **UKIFUNE** • 1957
FLOATING WEEDS (USA) see **UKIGUSA** • 1959
FLOCH • 1971 • Wolman Dan • ISR
FLOCK OF ANGELS, THE see **REBANO DE LOS ANGELES, EL** • 1979
FLOCK OF SKELETONS, A • 1916 • Ellis Robert • USA
FLOCKING TOGETHER see **WILD FEMALES, THE** • 1968
FLOCONS D'OR see **GOLD FLOCKEN** • 1975
FLODDER • 1987 • Maas Dick • NTH
FLOFLOCHE • 1934 • Roudes Gaston • FRN
FLOH IM OHR • 1943 • Heidemann Paul • FRG
FLOOD • 1915 • Chardynin Pyotr • USS
FLOOD! • 1976 • Bellamy Earl • TVM • USA
FLOOD see **MABUL** • 1927
FLOOD, THE • 1931 • Tinling James • USA
FLOOD, THE • 1963 • Goode Frederic • UKN
FLOOD, THE see **LIVEN** • 1929
FLOOD, THE see **POWODZ** • 1947
FLOOD, THE see **POVODEN** • 1958
FLOOD, THE see **POTOP** • 1974
FLOOD, THE (UKN) see **JOHNSTOWN FLOOD, THE** • 1926
FLOOD SEASON, THE • 1989 • VTN
FLOOD TIDE • 1913 • *Thanhouser* • USA
FLOOD TIDE • 1913 • Brabin Charles J. • *Edison* • USA, UKN • FLOODTIDE, THE (UKN)
FLOOD TIDE • 1934 • Baxter John • UKN
FLOOD TIDE • 1958 • Biberman Abner • USA • ABOVE ALL THINGS (UKN) ○ DARK SHORE, THE
FLOOD WATERS • 1948 • Parker Benjamin R. • SHT • USA
FLOODED MINE, THE • 1912 • Noy Wilfred • UKN
FLOODED OUT see **INUNDADOS, LOS** • 1962
FLOODED WITH TROUBLE • 1916 • Miller Rube • USA
FLOODGATES • 1924 • Irving George • USA
FLOODS OF FEAR • 1958 • Crichton Charles • UKN
FLOODTIDE • 1949 • Wilson Frederick • UKN
FLOODTIDE, THE (UKN) see **FLOOD TIDE** • 1913
FLOOEY AND AXEL • 1915 • *Komic* • USA
FLOOR ABOVE, THE • 1914 • Kirkwood James • USA
FLOOR BELOW, THE • 1918 • Badger Clarence • USA
FLOOR BELOW, THE • 1920 • Roach Hal • SHT • USA
FLOOR FLUSHER • 1954 • Sparber I. • ANS • USA
FLOOR SHOW • 1978 • Myers Richard • USA
FLOORWALKER, THE • 1916 • Chaplin Charles • SHT • USA • STORE, THE
FLOORWALKER'S TRIUMPH, THE • 1913 • *Thanhouser* • USA
FLOP • 1990 • Mignogna Eduardo • ARG
FLOP GOES THE WEASEL • 1943 • Jones Charles M. • ANS • USA
FLOP HOUSE • 1932 • *Mintz Charles (P)* • ANS • USA
FLOP POPULAIRE • 1943 • Gelinas Gratien • SHT • CND
FLOP SEACRET • 1952 • Donnelly Eddie • ANS • USA
FLOPPING UPLIFTER, THE • 1917 • Hartigan P. C. • SHT • USA
FLOR DE CANA • 1948 • Orellana Carlos • MXC
FLOR DE CANELA • 1957 • Pereda Ramon • MXC
FLOR DE DURAZNO • 1945 • Zacarias Miguel • MXC
FLOR DE FANGO • 1941 • Ortega Juan J. • MXC
FLOR DE MAYO • 1957 • Gavaldon Roberto • MXC • BEYOND ALL LIMITS ○ SPOILERS OF THE SEA ○ FLOWERS OF MAY ○ MEXICAN AFFAIR, A
FLOR DE OTONO see **HOMBRE LLAMADO FLOR DE OTONO, UN** • 1978
FLOR DE SANGRE • 1950 • Gomez Urquiza Zacarias • MXC
FLOR DE SANTIDAD • 1972 • Marsillach Adolfo • SPN • DEVIL'S SAINT, THE
FLOR DE UN DIA • 1945 • Peon Ramon • MXC
FLOR DEL IRUPE, LA • 1964 • Dubois Albert • ARG • LOVE HUNGER (USA)
FLOR DO MAR • 1956 • Vitorino Orlando, Ehrardt Alfred • SHT • PRT
FLOR DO MAR, A • 1986 • Monteiro Joao Cesar • PRT
FLOR SILVESTRE • 1943 • Fernandez Emilio • MXC • WILD FLOWER
FLORA • 1948 • Lovy Alex • ANS • USA
FLORA • 1964 • Hayeem Benjamin • SHT • USA
FLORA LE BRETON • 1929 • *B.s.f.p.* • SHT • UKN
FLORA: SCENES FROM A LEADERSHIP CONVENTION • 1977 • Raymont Peter • DOC • CND
FLORA Y MARIANA • 1941 • Buchs Jose • SPN
FLORADAS NA SERRA • 1953 • Salce Luciano • BRZ
FLORADORA GIRL, THE • 1930 • Beaumont Harry • USA • GAY NINETIES, THE (UKN)
FLORAISON, LA • 1913 • Burel Leonce-Henry • SHT • FRN
FLORAL STUDIES see **CADRES FLEURIS** • 1910
FLORED ROBADAS EN LOS JARDINES DE QUILMMES • 1984 • Ottone Antonio • ARG • FLOWERS STOLEN FROM A SUBURBAN GARDEN
FLORENCE 13.30 • 1957 • Mach Josef • CZC • BUS TERMINAL
FLORENCE -DAYS OF DESTRUCTION • 1966 • Zeffirelli Franco • DOC • ITL
FLORENCE EST FOLLE • 1944 • Lacombe Georges • FRN • MONSIEUR BENOIT PERD LA TETE ○ CURIEUSE HISTOIRE
FLORENCE NIGHTINGALE • 1915 • Elvey Maurice • UKN
FLORENCE NIGHTINGALE • 1985 • Duke Daryl • TVM • USA
FLORENCE TURNER IMPERSONATES FILM FAVORITES (USA) see **FILM FAVOURITES** • 1914
FLORENTINE • 1937 • Lamac Carl • FRG • WIR FAHREN GEGEN DEN WIND
FLORENTINE DAGGER, THE • 1935 • Florey Robert • USA
FLORENTINE TRAGEDY, THE • 1913 • *Crawley Constance* • USA
FLORENTINER HUT, DER • 1939 • Liebeneiner Wolfgang • FRG • LEGHORN HAT, THE (USA)
FLORENTINISCHE NACHTE • 1920 • Wienskowitz Kathe, Wassung Hermann • FRG
FLORENTINISCHE NACHTE • 1929 • Wienskowitz Kathe, Wassung Hermann • FRG
FLORES DEL MIEDO, LAS • 1972 • Oliveira Jose Maria • SPN
FLORES DEL VALLE • 1941 • CLM
FLORES Y PERLAS • 1910 • de Chomon Segundo • SPN
FLORESCENCE OF A WOMAN'S BODY see **JYOTAI KAIKA** • 1968
FLORETTE E PATAPON • 1913 • Caserini Mario • ITL
FLORETTE E PATAPON • 1927 • Palermi Amleto • ITL
FLORIAN • 1938 • Buczkowski Leonard • PLN
FLORIAN • 1940 • Marin Edwin L. • USA
FLORIAN • 1973 • Emmerich Klaus • FRG
FLORIANS TANTE • 1916 • Otto Paul? • FRG
FLORIDA CONNECTION, THE see **HOOKED GENERATION, THE** • 1969
FLORIDA CRACKERS • 1908 • Olcott Sidney • USA • FLORIDA FEUD, A
FLORIDA ENCHANTMENT, A • 1914 • Drew Sidney • USA
FLORIDA FEUD, A see **FLORIDA CRACKERS** • 1908
FLORIDA ROMANCE, A • 1913 • Nicholls George • USA
FLORIDA SPECIAL • 1936 • Murphy Ralph • USA
FLORIDA STRAITS • 1986 • Hodges Mike • TVM • USA
FLORIDA: WEALTH OR WASTE? • 1947 • Seltzer Leo • USA
FLORINE • 1913 • Wilmeth T. Beauregard • USA
FLORIS • 1969 • Verhoeven Paul* • SER • NTH
FLORISTA DE LA REINA, LA • 1940 • Ardavin Eusebio F. • SPN
FLO'S DISCIPLINE • 1912 • Salter Harry • USA
FLOSS DER TOTEN, DAS • 1920 • Boese Carl • FRG
FLOSSIE • 1974 • Ahlberg Mac • SWD • SWEDISH SEX KITTEN
FLOSSIE VISITS BAR U RANCH • 1913 • *Frontier* • USA
FLOSSIE'S DARING LOYALTY • 1914 • Murphy J. A. • USA
FLOTENKONZERT VON SANSSOUCI, DAS • 1930 • Ucicky Gustav • FRG • FLUTE CONCERT AT SANS SOUCI, THE
FLOTILLA THE FLIRT • 1914 • Trimble Larry • UKN
FLOTSAM • 1913 • *Kb* • USA
FLOTSAM • 1921 • Blake Edmund • UKN
FLOTSAM see **SO ENDS OUR NIGHT** • 1941
FLOTTANS GLADA GOSSAR • 1954 • Husberg Rolf • SWD • MERRY BOYS OF THE NAVY
FLOTTANS KAVALJERER • 1949 • Edgren Gustaf • SWD • GENTLEMEN OF THE NAVY
FLOTTANS LILLA FASTMO • 1930 • Andersson Fredrik • SWD • MARIANNE -FLOTTANS LILLA FASTMO
FLOTTANS MUNTERGOKAR • 1955 • Frisk Ragnar • SWD • MERRY BOYS OF THE FLEET
FLOTTANS OVERMAN • 1958 • Olin Stig • SWD • OVERLORD OF THE NAVY
FLOTTARE MED FARG • 1953 • Frisk Ragnar • SWD
FLOURISH OF TUBES, A • 1961 • Hornby Clifford • UKN
FLOURISHING VILLAGE, THE • NKR
FLOW DIAGRAM • Whitaker Harold • ANS • UKN
FLOWER see **HANA** • 1941
FLOWER, THE see **HANA NO BOJO** • 1958
FLOWER, THE see **HANA** • 1967
FLOWER, A MISTAKE, A see **EK PHOOL, EK BHOOL** • 1968
FLOWER AND THORN see **HOOVU MULLU** • 1968
FLOWER ANGEL, THE see **ANGEL CLOUD** • 1975
FLOWER BLOOMS, A see **HANA HIRAKU** • 1948
FLOWER CHILD • 1967 • Meyer Andrew • SHT • USA
FLOWER DRUM SONG • 1961 • Koster Henry • USA
FLOWER FAIRY, THE (USA) see **FEE DES FLEURS, LA** • 1904
FLOWER FOR CONDUCT, A see **KAYTOS-KUKKA** • 1966
FLOWER GARDEN • 1930 • Brooks Marty • USA
FLOWER GIRL, A • NKR
FLOWER GIRL, THE • 1913 • *Rex* • USA
FLOWER GIRL AND THE COUNTERFEITER, THE • 1913 • *Imp* • USA
FLOWER GIRL OF LAS PALMAS, THE • 1911 • *Pathe* • USA
FLOWER GIRL OF PARIS, THE • 1908 • Brooke Van Dyke • USA
FLOWER GIRL'S LIFE STORY, A • 1908 • *Tyler Walter* • UKN
FLOWER GIRL'S ROMANCE, A • 1912 • *Wolff Jane* • USA
FLOWER IN A STORM see **AIZEN KATSURA** • 1962
FLOWER IN HIS MOUTH, THE (USA) see **GENTE DI RISPETTO** • 1975
FLOWER IN THE DESERT, A • 1915 • Miller Charles? • USA
FLOWER IN THE RAINY NIGHT, A see **K'AN-HAI-TE JIH-TZU** • 1983
FLOWER IN WINTER see **FUYU NO HANA** • 1977
FLOWER LAKE see **GUL SANOVAR** • 1934
FLOWER LOVERS, THE see **LJUBITELJI CVIJECA** • 1970
FLOWER OF AUTUMN see **HOMBRE LLAMADO FLOR DE OTONO, UN** • 1978
FLOWER OF DOOM, THE • 1917 • Ingram Rex • USA
FLOWER OF FAITH, THE • 1914 • Grandon Francis J. • USA
FLOWER OF FAITH, THE • 1916 • King Burton L. • USA
FLOWER OF GOLD • 1930 • Steuart Ronald • UKN
FLOWER OF GOLD see **BUNGA MAS** • 1972
FLOWER OF NIGHT • 1925 • Bern Paul • USA
FLOWER OF NO MAN'S LAND • 1916 • Collins John H. • USA
FLOWER OF THE DUSK • 1918 • Collins John H. • USA
FLOWER OF THE FERN (USA) see **FLEUR DE FOUGERE** • 1949
FLOWER OF THE FOREST see **FORSTERCHRISTL, DIE** • 1926
FLOWER OF THE FOREST, A • 1911 • *Yankee* • USA
FLOWER OF THE FOREST, THE • 1912 • Christie Al • USA
FLOWER OF THE HILLS, THE • 1915 • Humphrey William • USA
FLOWER OF THE NATION see **BUNGA BANGSA** • 1983
FLOWER OF THE NORTH • 1921 • Smith David • USA

FLOWER OF THE RANCH, THE • 1910 • *Anderson Broncho Billy* • USA
FLOWER OF THE RANGE • 1921 • Ford Francis • USA
FLOWER OF THE TISZA (USA) see **TISZAVIRAG** • 1938
FLOWER OF THE TRIBE, THE • 1911 • *Nestor* • USA
FLOWER OF YOUTH, THE • 1907 • *Pathe* • FRN
FLOWER ON THE STONE, THE see **TSVETOK NA KAMNE** • 1962
FLOWER ON THE TOKNO RIVER, A • Pak Hak • NKR
FLOWER PATH, THE see **POOVANAM** • 1968
FLOWER, STORM AND GANG see **HANA TO ARASHI TO GANG** • 1961
FLOWER THAT WITHERED IN SPRING, THE see **BAHARDA SOLAN CICEK** • 1968
FLOWER THIEF, THE • 1962 • Rice Ron • USA
FLOWER WOMAN, THE see **FEMININ FLEUR, LA** • 1965
FLOWERGIRL'S ROMANCE, A • 1910 • Haldane Bert • UKN
FLOWERING LOTUS see **PIPENA KUMUDU** • 1967
FLOWERING TIME see **BLOMSTERTID, DEN** • 1940
FLOWERPOT • 1969 • Hawkins John H. • SHT • USA
FLOWERS, THE • 1964 • Koundouros Nikos • GRC
FLOWERS, THE • 1965 • van der Linden Rupert • ANS • NTH
FLOWERS AND MOLES see **HANA TO MOGURA** • 1969
FLOWERS AND TREES • 1932 • Gillett Burt • ANS • USA
FLOWERS AND VERMILION see **POOVUM POTTUM** • 1968
FLOWERS FOR MADAME • 1936 • Freleng Friz • ANS • USA
FLOWERS FOR THE GODS see **BLOMMOR AT GUDARNA** • 1957
FLOWERS FOR THE MAN IN THE MOON see **BLUMEN FUR DEN MANN IM MOND** • 1975
FLOWERS FROM NICE see **BLUMEN AUS NIZZA** • 1936
FLOWERS IN THE ATTIC • 1987 • Bloom Jeffrey • USA
FLOWERS IN THE SAND • 1980 • Marr Leon G. • MTV • CND
FLOWERS OF ANSIS, THE • 1970 • ANM • USS
FLOWERS OF ASPHALT • 1951 • Markopoulos Gregory J. • SHT • USA
FLOWERS OF DARKNESS see **NIGHT ROSE, THE** • 1921
FLOWERS OF HELL see **JIGOKUBANA** • 1957
FLOWERS OF MAY see **FLOR DE MAYO** • 1957
FLOWERS OF ST. FRANCIS, THE see **FRANCESCO GUILLARE DI DIO** • 1950
FLOWERS OF SOFIA see **KWIATY SOFII** • 1967
FLOWERS OF THE VALLEY • 1939 • Garzon Pedro Moreno, Calvo Maximo • CLM
FLOWERS OF THE VALLEY see **ZIELARZE Z KAMIENNEJ DOLINY** • 1952
FLOWERS ON A ONE-WAY STREET • 1969 • Spry Robin • CND
FLOWERS STOLEN FROM A SUBURBAN GARDEN see **FLORED ROBADAS EN LOS JARDINES DE QUILMMES** • 1984
FLOWERS THAT BLOOM IN THE SPRING, THE • 1906 • Gilbert Arthur • UKN
FLOWERS THAT BLOOM IN THE SPRING, THE • 1907 • Morland John • UKN
FLOWING see **NAGARERU** • 1956
FLOWING GOLD • 1921 • De Grasse Joseph • USA
FLOWING GOLD • 1921 • Franchon Leonard • USA
FLOWING GOLD • 1940 • Green Alfred E. • USA
FLOWING NIGHT see **YORU NO NAGARE** • 1960
FLOWING SEA see **MAR CORRENTE** • 1967
'FLU THAT FLEW, THE • 1928 • *De Forest Phonofilm* • SHT • UKN
FLUCH, DER • 1925 • Land Robert • AUS • MEIN IST DER RACHE
FLUCH DER ALTEN MUHLE, DER • 1918 • Hanus Emerich • FRG
FLUCH DER BOSEN TAT, DER • 1925 • Obal Max • FRG • GEHEIMNIS AUF SCHLOSS ELMSHOH, DAS
FLUCH DER GELBEN SCHLANGE, DER • 1963 • Gottlieb Franz J. • FRG • CURSE OF THE YELLOW SNAKE (USA)
FLUCH DER GRUNEN AUGEN, DER • 1964 • von Rathony Akos • FRG, YGS • CAVE OF THE LIVING DEAD (UKN) ○ CURSE OF THE GREEN EYES, THE
FLUCH DER HEXE, DER • 1920 • AUS • CURSE OF THE WITCH, THE
FLUCH DER MENSCHHEIT 1, DER • 1920 • Eichberg Richard • FRG • TOCHTER DER ARBEIT, DIE
FLUCH DER MENSCHHEIT 2, DER • 1920 • Eichberg Richard • FRG • IM RAUSCHE DER MILLIARDEN
FLUCH DER PROTEKTION, DER • 1923 • *Arnold Und Richter* • FRG
FLUCH DER SCHONHEIT • 1915 • Rector D. I. • FRG
FLUCH DER SONNE, DER • 1916 • Reinert Robert • FRG
FLUCH DER VERERBUNG, DER • 1927 • Trotz Adolf • FRG • CURSE OF VERERBUNG, THE
FLUCH DER VERGANGENHEIT • 1919 • Burghardt Georg • FRG
FLUCH DES NURI, DER • 1918 • Boese Carl • FRG
FLUCH DES SCHWARZEN RUBINS, DER • 1965 • Kohler Manfred R. • FRG, FRN, ITL
FLUCH DES SCHWEIGENS, DER • 1921 • Basch Felix • FRG
FLUCH DES SPIELS, DER • 1918 • Meinert Rudolf • FRG
FLUCHBELADENE, DER • 1917 • Heymann Robert • FRG
FLUCHT, DIE • 1963 • Zbonek Edwin • FRG, YGS • BESTIE MENSCH
FLUCHT AUS DEM DER HEIMATLOSEN, DIE • 1920 • *Film-Haus Kruger* • FRG
FLUCHT AUS DEM GOLDENEN KERKER, DIE see **CHRISTIAN WAHNSCHAFFE 2** • 1921
FLUCHT AUS DEM LEBEN, DIE • 1923 • Bock-Stieber Gernot • FRG
FLUCHT AUS DEM LEBEN, DIE see **ABENTEUER EINES ERMORDETEN 1, DIE** • 1921
FLUCHT AUS DER HOLLE • 1928 • Asagaroff Georg • FRG • ESCAPED FROM HELL (USA) ○ HOLLE VON CAYENNE, DIE
FLUCHT DES ARNO JESSEN, DIE • 1917 • Eichberg Richard • FRG
FLUCHT DURCH FLAMMEN, DIE • 1920 • Romer Josef • FRG
FLUCHT IN DEN NORDEN • 1986 • Engstrom Ingemo • FRG
FLUCHT IN DEN ZIRKUS, DIE • 1926 • Bonnard Mario, Schamberg Guido • FRG • CIRCUS OF LIFE, THE
FLUCHT IN DIE DOLOMITEN • 1955 • Trenker Luis • FRG, ITL • PRIGIONIERO DELLA MONTAGNA, IL (ITL)
FLUCHT IN DIE EHE, DIE • 1922 • Retzbach-Erasimy Artur • FRG
FLUCHT IN DIE FREMDENLEGION • 1929 • Ralph Louis • FRG
FLUCHT IN DIE NACHT, DIE • 1926 • Palermi Amleto • FRG
FLUCHT IN DIE TROPENNACHT • 1957 • May Paul • FRG
FLUCHT INS DUNKEL • 1939 • Rabenalt Arthur M. • FRG
FLUCHT INS JENSEITS ODER; DIE DUNKLE GASSE VON NEW YORK, DIE • 1920 • Seitz Franz • FRG
FLUCHT INS PARADIES, DIE • 1924 • *Weser-Film* • FRG
FLUCHT NACH BERLIN • 1961 • Tremper Will • FRG, USA, SWT • ESCAPE TO BERLIN (USA) ○ CAPTIVES, THE
FLUCHT NACH NIZZA • 1932 • Bauer James • FRG • GANZ VERFLIXTER KERL
FLUCHT VOR BLOND • 1928 • Ralph Louis • FRG • BLOND! – GEFAHR!
FLUCHT VOR DEM TODE, DIE • 1915 • Schonfeld Carl • FRG
FLUCHT VOR DEM TODE, DIE see **HEILIGE HASS 2, DER** • 1921
FLUCHT VOR DER KRONE ODER DER SCHRECKEN VON SCHLOSS WOOD, DIE • 1919 • Hanus Emerich • FRG
FLUCHT VOR DER LIEBE, DIE • 1929 • Behrendt Hans • FRG
FLUCHTGEFAHR • 1975 • Imhoof Markus • SWT
FLUCHTIGE BEZIEHUNGEN • 1982 • Ludcke Marianne • FRG • CASUAL RELATIONS
FLUCHTLING AUS CHIKAGO, DER • 1934 • Meyer Johannes • FRG
FLUCHTLINGE • 1933 • Rohrig Walter, Ucicky Gustav • FRG • REFUGEES
FLUCHTVERSUCH • 1976 • Jasny Vojtech • AUS, FRG • ATTEMPT AT FLIGHT ○ ATTEMPTED ESCAPE ○ IVO
FLUCHTWEG NOCH MARSEILLE • 1977 • Engstrom Ingemo, Theuring Gerhard • FRG • ESCAPE ROUTE TO MARSEILLES
FLUCHTWEG ST. PAULI see **FLUCHTWEG ST. PAULI – GROSSALARM FUR DIE DAVIDSWACHE** • 1971
FLUCHTWEG ST. PAULI –GROSSALARM FUR DIE DAVIDSWACHE • 1971 • Staudte Wolfgang • FRG • HEISSE SPUR ST. PAULI ○ FLUCHTWEG ST. PAULI
FLUCTUATIONS • 1970 • Landwehr Joel • USA
FLUFFY • 1965 • Bellamy Earl • USA
FLUG IN DEN TOD, DER • 1921 • Ziener Bruno • FRG
FLUG UM DEN ERDBALL 2, DER • 1925 • Wolff Willi • FRG • INDIEN – EUROPA
FLUG UM DEN ERDBALL, DER • 1925 • Wolff Willi • FRG • PARIS BIS CEYLON
FLUG ZUR WESTGRENZE • *Hameister Willy (Ph)* • FRG
FLUGJAHR, DAS • 1982 • Fischer Markus • SWT, FRG • HARD TIME FAMILY
FLUGTEN • 1942 • Roos Jorgen, Mertz Albert • DOC • DNM • FLIGHT, THE
FLUGTEN • 1972 • Kristensen Hans • DNM
FLUGTEN FRA LIVET see **HAR JEG RET TIL AT TAGE MIT EGET LIV** • 1917
FLUGTEN FRA MILLIONERNE • 1934 • Fejos Paul • DNM • FLIGHT FROM THE MILLIONS (UKN) ○ MILLIONS IN FLIGHT (USA) ○ MILLIONS EN FUITE, LES ○ FLIGHT FROM MILLIONS
FLUGTEN GENNEM SKYERNE see **SANDE KAERLIGHED, DEN** • 1912
FLUKE IN THE 'FLUENCE, A • 1915 • Collins Edwin J.? • UKN
FLUKTEN FRA DAKAR • 1951 • Vibe-Muller Titus • NRW
FLUNKY, WORK HARD! see **KOSHIBEN GANBARE** • 1931
FLURINA • 1968 • Halas John • ANM • UKN
FLURRY IN ART, A • 1914 • *Komic* • USA
FLURRY IN DIAMONDS, A • 1913 • *Essanay* • USA
FLURRY IN FURNITURE, A • 1912 • *Essanay* • USA
FLURRY IN HATS, A • 1914 • Pollard Harry • USA
FLUSH • 1981 • Kuehn Andrew J. • USA
FLUSSPIRATEN VOM MISSISSIPPI, DIE • 1963 • Roland Jurgen • FRG, FRN, ITL • PIRATES OF THE MISSISSIPPI, THE (USA) ○ AGGUATO SUL GRANDE FIUME (ITL) ○ PIRATES DU MISSISSIPPI, LES (FRN)
FLUSTERNDE TOD, DER (FRG) see **WHISPERING DEATH** • 1975
FLUTE • 1964 • Ryssack Eddy • ANS • BLG
FLUTE A SIX SCHTROUMPFS, LA • 1975 • Dutillieu Jose, Rust John • ANM • BLG, FRN • SMURFS AND THE MAGIC FLUTE, THE ○ SIX-SMURF FLUTE, THE
FLUTE AND THE ARROW, THE see **DJUNGELSAGA, EN** • 1957
FLUTE CONCERT AT SANS SOUCI, THE see **FLOTENKONZERT VON SANSSOUCI, DAS** • 1930
FLUTE ENCHANTEES, LA • 1943 • Deslaw Eugene • FRN
FLUTE ET TROTTE • Daix Andre • ANM • FRN
FLUTE MAGIQUE, LA • 1906 • *Pathe* • FRN • MAGIC FLUTE, THE
FLUTE MAGIQUE, LA • 1946 • Grimault Paul • ANS • FRN • MAGIC FLUTE, THE
FLUTE MAGIQUE, LA see **MAGIC FLUTE, THE** • 1977
FLUTEMAN • 1982 • Maxwell Peter • ASL
FLUTTERING HEARTS • 1927 • Parrott James • SHT • USA
FLUTTERING OF A SPARROW, THE see **FRULLO DEL PASSERO, IL** • 1988
FLUX • 1971 • Tammer Peter • SHT • ASL
FLUXES • 1967 • Lipsett Arthur • CND
FLY • Reitano Robert • SHT • USA
FLY, THE • 1958 • Neumann Kurt • USA
FLY, THE • 1986 • Cronenberg David • USA
FLY, THE (USA) see **MUHA** • 1967
FLY A FLAG FOR POPLAR • 1975 • Collective • UKN
FLY ABOUT THE HOUSE • 1949 • Halas John, Batchelor Joy • ANS • UKN
FLY ANN • 1907 • Morland John • UKN
FLY-AWAY BABY • 1937 • McDonald Frank • USA • CRIME IN THE CLOUDS (UKN)
FLY AWAY HOME • 1981 • Krasny Paul • TVM • USA
FLY AWAY PETER • 1948 • Saunders Charles • UKN
FLY BALL, THE • 1918 • Seiter William A. • USA
FLY BY NIGHT • 1942 • Siodmak Robert • USA • SECRET OF G 32 (UKN)
FLY CATCHERS • 1904 • Mottershaw Frank • UKN
FLY COP, THE • 1917 • Gillstrom Arvid E. • SHT • USA
FLY COP, THE • 1920 • Semon Larry, Taurog Norman, Peebles Mort • SHT • USA
FLY FROLIC • 1932 • Foster John, Bailey Harry • ANS • USA
FLY GOD, THE • 1918 • Smith Cliff • USA
FLY GUY, THE • 1931 • Foster John, Bailey Harry • ANS • USA
FLY HI • 1931 • Foster John, Bailey Harry • ANS • USA
FLY HUNT, THE see **POLOWANIE NA MUCHY** • 1969
FLY II, THE • 1989 • Walas Chris • USA • FLY II: THE INSECT AWAKENS, THE
FLY II: THE INSECT AWAKENS, THE see **FLY II, THE** • 1989
FLY IN THE OINTMENT, A • 1920 • Goldaine Mark • SHT • USA
FLY IN THE OINTMENT, THE • 1943 • Sommer Paul • ANS • USA
FLY-KILLER, THE see **MUCHOTLUK** • 1967
FLY LEAF OF FATE, THE • 1913 • *Bailey Consuelo* • USA
FLY ME • 1973 • Santiago Cirio H. • PHL
FLY ME TO THE BANK • 1973 • Donner Clive • SHT • UKN
FLY MEJ EN GREVE • 1959 • Anderberg Torgny • SWD • HAND ME A COUNT
FLY MY KITE • 1931 • McGowan Robert • SHT • USA
FLY NOW, PAY LATER • 1969 • Dial B. H. • USA
FLY PAPER • 1908 • Porter Edwin S. • USA
FLY TIME, A • 1912 • *Lubin* • USA
FLY WITH MONEY, A see **O MUSCA CU BANI** • 1954
FLYER AND MAGIC SWORD • 1970 • *Chaibanca Mitre* • HKG
FLYER IN FLAPJACKS, A • 1917 • *Ham & Bud* • SHT • USA
FLYER IN FOLLY, A • 1918 • Kerr Robert • SHT • USA
FLYER IN SPRING WATER, A • 1915 • *Tincher Fay* • USA
FLYERS • 1985 • Moore Dennis Earl • USA
FLYERS see **LYOTCHIKI** • 1935
FLYERS IN THE GREAT SKY see **LETACI VELIKOG NEBA** • 1978
FLYERS OF THE OPEN SKY, THE see **LETACI VELIKOG NEBA** • 1978
FLYG-BOM • 1952 • Kjellgren Lars-Eric • SWD • FLYING-BOMB
FLYGANDE DRAKEN, DEN • 1980 • Floyd Calvin • SWD, IRL • INN OF THE FLYING DRAGON, THE ○ SLEEP OF DEATH, THE ○ ONDSKANS VARDSHUS ○ DEVIL SLEEP
FLYGANDE HOLLANDAREN • 1925 • Swanstrom Karin • SWD • FLYING DUTCHMAN
FLYGNIVA 450 • 1980 • Axelman Torbjorn • SWD • FLIGHT LEVEL 450
FLYGPLAN SAKNAS • 1965 • Gunwall Per • SWD • AIRCRAFT MISSING
FLYIN' COWBOY, THE • 1928 • Eason B. Reeves • USA
FLYIN' THRU • 1925 • Mitchell Bruce • USA
FLYING • 1986 • Lynch Paul • CND
FLYING ACE, THE • 1928 • *Corman Lawrence* • USA • FIGHTING ACE, THE
FLYING ANGEL, THE • 1961 • Wilder Donald A. • CND
FLYING BEAR, THE • 1941 • Ising Rudolf • ANS • USA
FLYING BLIND • 1941 • McDonald Frank • USA
FLYING-BOMB see **FLYG-BOM** • 1952
FLYING BONEHEADS see **LENTAVAT LUUPAAT** • 1984
FLYING BUCKAROO, THE • 1928 • Thorpe Richard • SHT • USA
FLYING CADETS • 1941 • Kenton Erle C. • USA
FLYING CARPET, THE • Bamberger Peter • FRG
FLYING CARPET, THE see **TAPIS VOLANT, LE** • 1960
FLYING CARPET, THE (USA) see **STARI KHOTTABYCH** • 1956
FLYING CAT • 1952 • Hanna William, Barbera Joseph • ANS • USA
FLYING CIRCUS • 1968 • Lovy Alex • ANS • USA
FLYING CIRCUS, THE (UKN) see **FLYING DEVILS** • 1933
FLYING CLASSROOM, THE (USA) see **FLIEGENDE KLASSENZIMMER, DAS** • 1954
FLYING CLIPPER –TRAUMREISE UNTER WEISSEN SEGELN • 1962 • Leitner Hermann, Nussgruber Rudolf • FRG • MEDITERRANEAN HOLIDAY (USA)
FLYING CLUE, THE • 1914 • *Savoia* • USA
FLYING COFFER, THE (UKN) see **FLIEGENDE KOFFER, DER** • 1921
FLYING COLORS • 1917 • Borzage Frank • USA
FLYING COURAGE (UKN) see **RECKLESS COURAGE** • 1925
FLYING CUPS AND SAUCERS • 1949 • Rasinski Connie • ANS • USA
FLYING DANE, THE see **ELLEHAMMER** • 1957
FLYING DESPATCH, THE • 1912 • Kinder Stuart • UKN
FLYING DEUCES, THE • 1939 • Sutherland A. Edward • USA
FLYING DEVILS • 1933 • Birdwell Russell J. • USA • FLYING CIRCUS, THE (UKN)
FLYING DEVILS, THE see **FLYVENDE DJAEVLE, DE** • 1985
FLYING DIMWITS see **LENTAVAT LUUPAAT** • 1984
FLYING DISC, THE see **DISCO VOLANTE, IL** • 1964
FLYING DISC MAN FROM MARS • 1951 • Brannon Fred C. • SRL • USA
FLYING DOCTOR, THE • 1936 • Mander Miles • UKN, ASL
FLYING DOCTORS OF EAST AFRICA, THE (UKN) see **FLIEGENDEN ARZTE VON OSTAFRIKA, DIE** • 1969
FLYING DOWN TO RIO • 1933 • Freeland Thornton • USA
FLYING DOWN TO ZERO • 1935 • Marcus Lee • USA
FLYING DRAGON HEROES • 1967 • *Shaws* • HKG
FLYING DRAGON MOUNTAIN • 1971 • Chen Hung-Ming • HKG
FLYING DUTCHMAN see **FLYGANDE HOLLANDAREN** • 1925
FLYING DUTCHMAN, THE • 1923 • Carleton Lloyd B. • USA
FLYING DUTCHMAN, THE see **ROTTERDAM –EUROPOORT** • 1966
FLYING DUTCHMAN, THE (UKN) see **FLIEGENDE HOLLANDER, DER** • 1965
FLYING ELEPHANTS • 1927 • Butler Fred J. • SHT • USA
FLYING ELEPHANTS see **SQUADRON 992** • 1940
FLYING EYE, THE • 1955 • Hammond William C. • UKN
FLYING FABIAN see **LETECI FABIJAN** • 1968
FLYING FEVER • 1941 • Davis Mannie • ANS • USA
FLYING FIFTY-FIVE • 1939 • Denham Reginald • UKN
FLYING FIFTY-FIVE, THE • 1924 • Coleby A. E. • UKN
FLYING FISTS • 1924 • Ginsberg Henry, Wilk Jacob • USA
FLYING FISTS • 1931 • Iwerks Ub • ANS • USA
FLYING FISTS • 1938 • Hill Robert F. • USA
FLYING FLEET, THE • 1928 • Hill George W. • USA • GOLD BRAID
FLYING FONTAINES, THE • 1959 • Sherman George • USA
FLYING FOOL • 1925 • Mattison Frank S. • USA
FLYING FOOL, A • 1925 • Seiler Lewis • SHT • USA
FLYING FOOL, THE • 1929 • Garnett Tay • USA

FLYING FOOL, THE • 1931 • Summers Walter • UKN
FLYING FORTRESS • 1942 • Forde Walter • UKN
FLYING FOX IN A FREEDOM TREE • 1989 • Sanderson Martyn • NZL
FLYING FROGS, THE • Velichko • ANM • USS
FLYING FROGS, THE (USA) see **CETYRE CORTA** • 1913
FLYING FROM JUSTICE • 1913 • Charrington Arthur • UKN
FLYING FROM JUSTICE • 1915 • Nash Percy • UKN
FLYING FURY see **WHEELS OF DESTINY** • 1934
FLYING FURY (UKN) see **STRAWBERRY ROAN, THE** • 1933
FLYING G-MEN • 1939 • Taylor Ray, Horne James W. • SRL • USA
FLYING GAUCHITO, THE • 1945 • Kinney Jack • ANS • USA
FLYING GUILLOTINE, THE see **HSUEH TI TZU** • 1975
FLYING HIGH • 1926 • Hutchison Charles • USA
FLYING HIGH • 1931 • Reisner Charles F. • USA • HAPPY LANDING (UKN)
FLYING HIGH • 1978 • Hunt Peter • TVM • USA
FLYING HOOFS • 1925 • Smith Cliff • USA • BEYOND THE LAW
FLYING HORSEMAN, THE • 1926 • Dull Orville O. • USA • WHITE EAGLE
FLYING HOSTESS • 1936 • Roth Murray • USA
FLYING HOUSE, THE • 1916 • McCay Winsor, McCay Robert • ANS • USA
FLYING HUNTERS • 1934 • Draper Lauron A. • SHT • USA
FLYING INSECTS see **AVIACIONNAJA NEDELJA NASEKOMYCH** • 1912
FLYING IRISHMAN, THE • 1939 • Jason Leigh • USA
FLYING JALOPY • 1943 • Lundy Dick • USA
FLYING KILLER, THE • 1970 • *Ting Ying* • HKG
FLYING LARIATS • 1931 • Neitz Alvin J. • USA
FLYING LEATHERNECKS • 1951 • Ray Nicholas • USA
FLYING LESSONS see **LEKCJA LATANIA** • 1978
FLYING LUCK • 1927 • Raymaker Herman C. • USA
FLYING MACHINE, THE see **A LA CONQUETE DE L'AIR** • 1901
FLYING MAIL, THE • 1926 • Smith Noel • USA
FLYING MAN, THE • 1962 • Dunning George • ANS • UKN
FLYING MAN, THE • 1972 • Gregg Colin • UKN
FLYING-MAN VS. KILLING see **UCAN ADAM KILLINGE KARSI** • 1967
FLYING MARINE, THE • 1929 • Rogell Albert S. • USA
FLYING MATCHMAKER, THE (USA) see **SHNEI KUNI LEMEL** • 1965
FLYING MISFITS • 1976 • Mayberry Russ • USA • BAA BAA BLACKSHEEP
FLYING MISSILE, THE • 1950 • Levin Henry • USA
FLYING MOUSE, THE • 1934 • Hand David • ANS • USA
FLYING NUT, THE see **HERO FOR A NIGHT, A** • 1927
FLYING OIL • 1935 • *Terry Paul/ Moser Frank (P)* • ANS • USA
FLYING PADRE • 1951 • Kubrick Stanley • DCS • USA
FLYING PAT • 1920 • Jones F. Richard • USA
FLYING PHANTOM SHIP see **SORATOBU YUREISEN** • 1969
FLYING QUEEN, THE see **FLYING RANEE** • 1959
FLYING RANEE • 1959 • Vakil Nanubhai • IND • FLYING QUEEN, THE
FLYING ROMEOS • 1928 • LeRoy Mervyn • USA
FLYING SAUCER see **KONTE PILLA** • 1967
FLYING SAUCER, THE • 1950 • Conrad Mikel • USA
FLYING SAUCER, THE (USA) see **DISCO VOLANTE, IL** • 1964
FLYING SAUCER DAFFY • 1958 • White Jules • SHT • USA
FLYING SAUCER MYSTERY, THE • 1950 • *Telenews* • SHT • USA
FLYING SAUCERS see **FLIEGEN DE UNTERTASSEN** • 1953
FLYING SAUCERS, THE see **PLATILLOS VOLADORES, LOS** • 1955
FLYING SAUCERS COMING! see **TALIRE NAD VELKYM MALIKOVEM** • 1977
FLYING SAUCERS OVER THE TOWN see **TALIRE NAD VELKYM MALIKOVEM** • 1977
FLYING SCHTROUMPF, THE see **SCHTROUMPF VOLANT, LE** • 1963
FLYING SCOT, THE • 1957 • Bennett Compton • UKN • MAIL BAG ROBBERY (USA)
FLYING SCOTS, THE • 1900 • *Warwick Trading Co.* • UKN
FLYING SCOTSMAN, THE • 1929 • Knight Castleton • UKN
FLYING SERPENT, THE • 1946 • Newfield Sam • USA
FLYING SEX see **SESSO PROFONDO** • 1980
FLYING SKIS • 1951 • Blais Roger • DCS • CND • DU COTE DE SAINTE-ADELE
FLYING SORCERER, THE • 1974 • Booth Harry • UKN
FLYING SORCERESS, THE • 1956 • Hanna William, Barbera Joseph • ANS • USA
FLYING SOUTH • 1937 • Davis Mannie, Gordon George • ANS • USA
FLYING SOUTH • 1947 • Davis Mannie • ANS • USA
FLYING SPIKES • 1932 • McCarey Ray • SHT • USA
FLYING SQUAD • 1971 • SAF
FLYING SQUAD, THE • 1929 • Maude Arthur • UKN
FLYING SQUAD, THE • 1932 • Kraemer F. W. • UKN
FLYING SQUAD, THE • 1940 • Brenon Herbert • UKN • FLYING SQUADRON, THE
FLYING SQUADRON, THE see **FLYING SQUAD, THE** • 1940
FLYING SQUIRREL, THE • 1954 • Hannah Jack • ANS • USA
FLYING SWITCH, THE • 1913 • *Holmes Helen* • USA
FLYING TARGET, THE • 1917 • Fahrney Milton • SHT • USA
FLYING THE FOAM AND SOME FANCY DIVING • 1906 • Williamson James • UKN
FLYING TIGERS • 1942 • Miller David • USA
FLYING TO FORTUNE • 1912 • *Cruze James* • USA
FLYING TORPEDO, THE • 1916 • O'Brien Jack, Cabanne W. Christy • USA
FLYING TOY • 1978 • Czurko Edward • MTV • CND
FLYING TRAPEZE, THE see **CITE DU MIDI** • 1952
FLYING TURTLE, THE • 1953 • Smith Paul J. • ANS • USA
FLYING TWINS, THE • 1915 • *Fairbanks Madeline* • USA
FLYING U RANCH, THE • 1927 • De Lacy Robert • USA
FLYING WILD • 1941 • West William • USA • AIR DEVILS
FLYING WITH MUSIC • 1942 • Archainbaud George • USA
FLYING WITHOUT WINGS see **VLIEGEN ZONDER VLEUGELS** • 1977
FLYKTINGAR see **FARLIGA VAGAR** • 1942
FLYKTINGER FINNER EN HAMN • 1945 • Henning-Jensen Bjarne • DOC • SWD • FUGITIVES FIND SHELTER
FLYNN • 1990 • Kavanagh Brian • ASL
FLYNN'S BIRTHDAY CELEBRATIONS • 1904 • Haggar William • UKN
FLYPAPER • 1906 • Collins Alf? • UKN
FLY'S BRIDE • 1929 • Foster John • ANS • USA
FLY'S LAST FLIGHT, THE • 1949 • Kneitel Seymour • ANS • USA
FLY'S REVENGE, THE • 1911 • Wilson Frank? • UKN
FLYVENDE DJAEVLE, DE • 1985 • Refn Anders • DNM • FLYING DEVILS, THE
FLYVEREN OG JOURNALISTE ENS HUSTRU • 1911 • Blom August • DNM • AVIATIKEREN OG JOURNALISTENS HUSTRU ○ LEKTION, EN ○ AVIATOR AND THE JOURNALIST'S WIFE, THE
FM • 1978 • Alonzo John A. • USA • CITIZEN'S BAND
FOAL, THE • 1959 • Fetin Vladimir • SHT • USS
FOCH THE MAN • 1918 • Dyer Anson • ANM • UKN
FOCOLARE SPENTO, IL • 1925 • Genina Augusto • ITL • PIU GRANDE AMORE, IL
FODDER AND SON • 1957 • Smith Paul J. • ANS • USA
FODELSEDAGSPRESENTEN • 1914 • Breidahl Axel • SWD • BIRTHDAY PRESENT
FODSELS FORLOB, EN • 1972 • Roos Lise • DOC • DNM • COURSE OF A BIRTH, THE
FODSELSDAGSGAVEN • 1912 • Blom August • DNM • BIRTHDAY GIFT, THE ○ GAVEN
FOE see **FOES** • 1977
FOES • 1977 • Coats John • USA • FOE
FOG • 1912 • Merwin Bannister • *Edison* • USA
FOG • 1912 • Miller Ashley • USA, UKN
FOG • 1934 • Rogell Albert S. • USA
FOG see **STUDY IN TERROR, A** • 1965
FOG see **NIEBLA** • 1978
FOG see **SIS** • 1989
FOG, THE • 1923 • Powell Paul • USA
FOG, THE • 1979 • Carpenter John • USA
FOG AND MUD see **I VIDEL SEM DALJINE MEGLENE I KALNE** • 1964
FOG AND RAIN see **KIRI NO AME** • 1924
FOG BOUND • 1923 • Willat Irvin V. • USA
FOG HORN see **MUTEKI** • 1952
FOG ISLAND • 1945 • Morse Terry O. • USA
FOG MURDERER, THE see **NEBELMORDER** • 1964
FOG OVER FRISCO • 1934 • Dieterle William • USA
FOG OVER THE RIVER BANKS • 1986 • Karasik Yuli • USS, BUL
FOG PUMAS • 1967 • Wiley Dorothy, Nelson Gunvor • SHT • USA
FOG UNDER THE SUN • 1980 • Lygouris Nikos • GRC
FOGADO AZ OROK VILAGOSSAGHOZ • 1981 • Ban Robert • HNG
FOGG'S MILLIONS • 1914 • Brooke Van Dyke • USA
FOGGY HARBOR (USA) see **KIRI NO MINATO** • 1923
FOGGY NIGHT BLUES see **YOGIRI NO BURUSU** • 1963
FOGGY NIGHT IN JAPAN, A see **NIHON NO YORU TO KIRI** • 1960
FOGHORN LEGHORN • 1948 • McKimson Robert • ANS • USA
FOGLIO DI VIA • 1955 • Campogalliani Carlo • ITL
FOGO! • 1949 • Duarte Arthur • PRT, SPN • FUEGO! (SPN)
FOGO E PAIXAO • 1988 • Weinfeld Isay, Kogan Marcio • BRZ • FIRE AND PASSION
FOGO ISLAND • 1968 • Low Colin • SER • CND
FOGO MORTO • 1976 • Farias Marcos • BRZ • LAST PLANTATION, THE
FOGS OF ANDROMEDA • USS
FOHN • 1920 • Werckmeister Hans • FRG
FOHN • 1950 • Hansen Rolf • FRG • WHITE HELL OF PITZ PALU, THE (USA)
FOILED • 1915 • *Teare Ethel* • SHT • USA
FOILED • 1916 • *Morris Dave* • SHT • USA
FOILED see **MIDNIGHT MESSAGE, THE** • 1926
FOILED AGAIN • 1914 • *Komic* • USA
FOILED AGAIN • 1932 • Lamont Charles • SHT • USA
FOILED AGAIN • 1935 • *Terry Paul/ Moser Frank (P)* • ANS • USA
FOILED BY A GIRL • 1912 • Stow Percy • UKN
FOILED BY A WOMAN; OR, FALSELY ACCUSED • 1906 • Green Tom? • UKN
FOILED BY FIDO • 1915 • Arbuckle Roscoe • USA • FATTY'S PLUCKY PUP
FOILING A FORTUNE HUNTER • 1912 • *Tennant Barbara* • USA
FOILING FATHER'S FOES • 1915 • *Campbell Colin* • USA
FOILING FICKLE FATHER • 1913 • Sennett Mack • USA
FOILING OF RED DUGAN, THE • 1911 • *Essanay* • USA
FOILING THE CAMORRA • 1911 • *Yankee* • USA
FOIRE AUX CANCRES, LA • 1963 • Daquin Louis • FRN
FOIRE AUX CHIMERES, LA • 1946 • Chenal Pierre • FRN • DEVIL AND THE ANGEL, THE (USA) ○ FAIR ANGEL, THE ○ ILLUSIONS
FOIRE AUX FEMMES, LA • 1955 • Stelli Jean • FRN • DESIRED
FOIRE INTERNATIONALE DE BRUXELLES, LA • 1940 • Storck Henri • DOC • BLG
FOIS DANS LA VIE, UNE • 1933 • de Vaucorbeil Max • FRN • SEULE FOIS DANS LA VIE, UNE ○ RONDE AUX MILLIONS, LA
FOIS DE PLUS, UNE • 1963 • Hamina Mohamed Lakhdar • DCS • ALG
FOK EL SUHAB • 1948 • Zulficar Mahmoud • EGY • ABOVE THE CLOUDS
FOKUSNIK • 1968 • Todorovsky Petr • USS • CONJURER
FOL ETE, LE see **SECRETS** • 1942
FOLD EMBRE, A • 1917 • Curtiz Michael • HNG • MAN OF THE SOIL, THE
FOLGEN EINER UNGLUCKLICHEN EHE, DIE • 1919 • Illes Eugen • FRG • GEFLUSTER DES TEUFELS
FOLIE DE JEUNESSE see **GUNUN ASH-SHABAB** • 1972
FOLIE DES GRANDEURS, LA • 1971 • Oury Gerard • FRN, ITL, FRG • MANIA DI GRANDEZZA (ITL) ○ DELUSIONS OF GRANDEUR (USA)
FOLIE DES VAILLANTS, LA • 1926 • Dulac Germaine • FRN • MADNESS OF THE VALIANT, THE
FOLIE DOUCE • 1950 • Paulin Jean-Paul • FRN
FOLIE DU DOCTEUR TUBE, LA • 1916 • Gance Abel • FRN • MADNESS OF DR. TUBE, THE ○ STORY OF A MADMAN
FOLIE DU DOUTE, LA • 1923 • Leprince Rene • FRN
FOLIES-BERGERE • 1935 • Del Ruth Roy • USA • MAN FROM THE FOLIES BERGERE, THE (UKN) ○ FOLIES BERGERE
FOLIES BERGERE • 1956 • Decoin Henri • FRN
FOLIES BERGERE see **FOLIES-BERGERE** • 1935
FOLIES BOURGEOISES • 1976 • Chabrol Claude • FRN, ITL, FRG • TWIST, THE
FOLIES D'ELODIE, LES • 1981 • Genoves Andre • FRN • SECRETS OF THE SATIN BLUES ○ NAUGHTY BLUE KNICKERS
FOLIES DOUCES • 1978 • Ronet Maurice • MTV • FRN
FOLIES MASQUEES • 1901 • Blache Alice • SER • FRN
FOLIES PARISIENNE • 1940 • Ceballos Larry • SHT • USA
FOLK CARNIVAL • Sara Sandor • SHT • HNG
FOLK DANCES OF THE U.S.S.R. • 1939 • Kaufman Mikhail • DOC • USS
FOLK-LORE see **CHANTE ET DANSE** • 1944
FOLK OG ROVERE I KARDEMOMME BY • 1988 • Erichsen Bente • NRW • PEOPLE AND ROBBERS OF CARDAMOM TOWN ○ CARDAMOM TOWN ○ KARDAMOM TOWN
FOLK SONG FANTASY • 1951 • Duncan Alma • ANS • CND
FOLK SONG "THE DISOBEDIENT SON", THE see **CORRIDO DE "EL HIJO DESOBEDIENTE", EL** • 1968
FOLK TALE, A see **BHAVNI BHAVAI** • 1980
FOLK TALES OF LU BAN see **LU BAN DE CHUANSHUO** • 1958
FOLKET I FALT • 1953 • Cederstrand Solve, Logardt Bengt • SWD • PEOPLE ON MANOEUVRES
FOLKET I SIMLANGSDALEN • 1924 • Berthels Theodor • SWD • PEOPLE OF SIMLANGEN VALLEY
FOLKET I SIMLANGSDALEN • 1948 • Ohberg Ake • SWD • PEOPLE OF SIMLANGEN VALLEY
FOLKET PA HOGBOGARDEN • 1939 • Weel Arne • SWD, DNM • PEOPLE OF HOGBO FARM
FOLKETINGSVALG 1945 • 1945 • Henning-Jensen Bjarne, Henning-Jensen Astrid • DNM
FOLKETS VEN • 1918 • Holger-Madsen • DNM • FRIEND OF THE PEOPLE, A
FOLKEVILJE • 1973 • Tuhus Oddvar Bull • SHT • NRW • PEOPLE'S WILL, THE
FOLKLORE A MONASTIR • 1963 • Ben Halima Hamouda • SHT • TNS
FOLKS see **GENTE, LA** • 1973
FOLKS AT RED WOLF INN, THE see **TERROR HOUSE** • 1972
FOLKS BACK HOME, THE • 1911 • *Yankee* • USA
FOLKS FROM WAY DOWN EAST • 1924 • *Horner Violet* • USA
FOLKS FROM WAY DOWN EAST, THE • 1914 • *Photo Drama Motion Picture Co.* • USA
FOLKS OF OLD VIRGINIA • 1911 • *Champion* • USA
FOLKS OF THE FAIR • 1916 • Batley Ethyle • UKN
FOLKSONG FANTASY • 1957 • Duncan Alma • ANM • CND
FOLKWANGSCHULE • 1960 • Vesely Herbert • FRG
FOLLA, LA • 1951 • Rosa Silvio Laurenti • ITL
FOLLE A TUER • 1975 • Boisset Yves • FRN, ITL
FOLLE AVENTURE, LA • 1930 • Antoine Andre-Paul, Froelich Carl • FRN
FOLLE D'AMOUR • 1918 • Perret Leonce • FRN
FOLLE DE TOUJANE, LA • 1975 • Vautier Rene, Le Garrec Nicole • FRN • COMMENT ON DEVIENT UN ENNEMI DE L'INTERIEUR
FOLLE ENVIE D'AIMER, UNE (FRN) see **ORGASMO** • 1968
FOLLE.. FOLLE.. FOLLEME TIM • 1978 • Almodovar Pedro • SPN • FUCK, FUCK, FUCK ME TIM
FOLLE NUIT, LA • 1932 • Bibal Robert • FRN • DERIVATIF, LE
FOLLET • 1943 • Henning-Jensen Bjarne • DNM
FOLLI AVVENTURE DI RABBI JACOB, LE (ITL) see **AVENTURES DE RABBI JACOB, LES** • 1973
FOLLIA DEL GIUDICE PASSMANN, LA see **TENTAZIONE** • 1942
FOLLIE DEL SECOLO • 1939 • Palermi Amleto • ITL
FOLLIE D'ESTATE • 1966 • Anton Edoardo • ITL
FOLLIE D'EUROPA • 1964 • Baldi Ferdinando • DOC • ITL
FOLLIE PER L'OPERA • 1948 • Costa Mario • ITL • MAD ABOUT OPERA (USA)
FOLLIES GIRL • 1943 • Rowland William • USA
FOLLIES GIRL, THE • 1919 • Dillon John Francis • USA
FOLLIES OF A DAY AND A NIGHT • 1913 • *Field Goerge* • USA
FOLLOW A STAR • 1959 • Asher Robert • UKN
FOLLOW ME • 1930 • Edwards Harry J. • SHT • USA
FOLLOW ME • 1969 • McCabe Gene • DOC • USA
FOLLOW ME • 1989 • Knilli Maria • FRG
FOLLOW ME, BOYS • 1966 • Tokar Norman • USA
FOLLOW ME IF YOU DARE • 1979 • Sherman Gary • TVM • USA • MYSTERIOUS TWO
FOLLOW ME QUIETLY • 1949 • Fleischer Richard • USA
FOLLOW ME.. THE FULL STORY OF THE SIX DAY WAR • 1968 • Ephrati Yigael • ISR
FOLLOW ME (UKN) see **PUBLIC EYE, THE** • 1972
FOLLOW TEACHER • 1928 • Lamont Charles • SHT • USA
FOLLOW THAT BIRD • 1985 • Kwapis Ken • USA • (SESAME STREET PRESENTS) FOLLOW THAT BIRD
FOLLOW THAT BLONDE • 1946 • Yates Hal • SHT • USA
FOLLOW THAT CAMEL • 1967 • Thomas Gerald • UKN • CARRY ON FOLLOW THAT CAMEL
FOLLOW THAT CAR • 1958 • Potterton Gerald • UKN
FOLLOW THAT CAR • 1964 • *Halas John (P)* • ANS • UKN
FOLLOW THAT CAR • 1981 • Haller Daniel • USA
FOLLOW THAT DREAM • 1962 • Douglas Gordon • USA
FOLLOW THAT GUY WITH THE ONE BLACK SHOE (UKN) see **GRAND BLOND AVEC UNE CHAUSSURE NOIRE, LE** • 1972
FOLLOW THAT HORSE! • 1960 • Bromly Alan • UKN
FOLLOW THAT MAN • 1961 • Epstein Jerome • UKN
FOLLOW THAT MUSIC • 1946 • Dreifuss Arthur • SHT • USA • FOLLOW THE MUSIC
FOLLOW THAT RAINBOW see **RUNAWAY MELODY** • 1979
FOLLOW THAT WOMAN • 1945 • Landers Lew • USA
FOLLOW THE ARROW • 1938 • Feist Felix E. • SHT • USA
FOLLOW THE BAND • 1943 • Yarbrough Jean • USA • TROMBONE FROM HEAVEN
FOLLOW THE BOYS • 1944 • Sutherland A. Edward • USA • THREE CHEERS FOR THE BOYS
FOLLOW THE BOYS • 1963 • Thorpe Richard • USA

FOLLOW THE CROWD • 1918 • Roach Hal • USA
FOLLOW THE FLEET • 1936 • Sandrich Mark • USA
FOLLOW THE GIRL • 1917 • Chaudet Louis W. • USA
FOLLOW THE LADY • 1923 • Brunel Adrian • UKN
FOLLOW THE LEADER • 1901 • Porter Edwin S. • USA
FOLLOW THE LEADER • 1930 • Taurog Norman • USA • MANHATTAN MARY
FOLLOW THE LEADER • 1944 • Beaudine William • USA
FOLLOW THE MUSIC see **FOLLOW THAT MUSIC** • 1946
FOLLOW THE NORTH STAR • 1972 • Till Eric • CND
FOLLOW THE STAR see **TA SHA-HSING YU HSAIO-MEI T'OU** • 1978
FOLLOW THE SUN • 1951 • Lanfield Sidney • USA
FOLLOW THE SWALLOW • 1927 • Fryer Bryant • ANS • CND
FOLLOW THE SWALLOW • 1930 • Goulding Alf • USA
FOLLOW THE TRACKS • 1917 • Chaudet Louis W. • SHT • USA
FOLLOW THRU • 1930 • Schwab Laurence, Corrigan Lloyd • USA
FOLLOW YOUR DREAMS see **INDEPENDENCE DAY** • 1983
FOLLOW YOUR HEART • 1936 • Scotto Aubrey • USA
FOLLOW YOUR LEADER • 1914 • Plumb Hay? • UKN
FOLLOW YOUR LEADER AND THE MASTER FOLLOWS LAST • 1908 • Stow Percy • UKN
FOLLOW YOUR STAR • 1938 • Hill Sinclair • UKN
FOLLOWING A CLUE • 1915 • *Roland Ruth* • USA
FOLLOWING COUSIN'S FOOTSTEPS • 1911 • *Solax* • USA
FOLLOWING FATHER'S FOOTSTEPS • 1915 • Christie Al • USA
FOLLOWING IN FATHER'S FOOTSTEPS • 1906 • Booth W. R.? • UKN
FOLLOWING IN FATHER'S FOOTSTEPS • 1908 • Gilbert Arthur • UKN
FOLLOWING IN MOTHER'S FOOTSTEPS • 1908 • Booth W. R. • UKN
FOLLOWING MOTHER'S FOOTSTEPS • 1909 • *Urban-Eclipse* • USA
FOLLOWING MOTHER'S FOOTSTEPS • 1911 • Bouwmeester Theo • UKN • IN MOTHER'S FOOTSTEPS
FOLLOWING THE FLAG • 1916 • *Selig* • SHT • USA
FOLLOWING THE SCENT • 1915 • Drew Sidney • USA
FOLLOWING THE STAR • 1912 • *Storey Edith* • USA
FOLLOWING THE SUN see **CHELOVEK IDYOT ZA SOLNTSEM** • 1962
FOLLOWING THE TRAIL • 1914 • Cooper Toby • UKN
FOLLY • 1916 • *Karr Darwin* • SHT • USA
FOLLY OF A LIFE OF CRIME, THE • 1915 • *Walker & Duke* • USA
FOLLY OF ANNE, THE • 1914 • O'Brien John B. • USA
FOLLY OF DESIRE, THE • 1916 • Tucker George Loane • USA • SHULAMITE, THE
FOLLY OF FANCHETTE, THE • 1917 • McDermott John • SHT • USA
FOLLY OF FEAR, THE • 1916 • *August Edwin* • SHT • USA
FOLLY OF IT ALL, THE • 1913 • *August Edwin* • USA
FOLLY OF REVENGE, THE • 1916 • *Lyle Warren E.* • USA
FOLLY OF SIN, THE • 1916 • *Peterson Joan* • DNM
FOLLY OF VANITY, THE • 1924 • Elvey Maurice, Otto Henry • USA
FOLLY OF YOUTH • 1925 • *Sable Productions* • USA
FOLLY TO BE WISE • 1952 • Launder Frank • UKN
FOLTERKAMMER DES DR. FU MAN CHU, DIE (FRG) see **CASTLE OF FU MANCHU, THE** • 1968
FOMA GORDEEV • 1959 • Donskoi Mark • USS • GORDEYEV FAMILY, THE (USA) ○ FOMA GORDEYEV
FOMA GORDEYEV see **FOMA GORDEEV** • 1959
FOME DE AMOR • 1968 • dos Santos Nelson Pereira • BRZ • HUNGRY FOR LOVE ○ HUNGER FOR LOVE ○ SOIF D'AMOUR
FOMOU FUNGWAN • 1988 • Cheung Tung-Tsou • HKG • BET ON FIRE
FOND DE L'AIR EST ROUGE, LE • 1977 • Marker Chris • DOC • FRN
FOND HEART SAVES THE DAY • 1913 • *Champion* • USA
FOND THINGS see **COSAS DEL QUERER, LAS** • 1989
FONDATEUR, LE • 1947 • Dekeukeleire Charles • BLG
FONDATION MAEGHT, LA • Carre Cesar • FRN
FONDERIES MARTIN, LES • 1938 • Alexeieff Alexandre • SHT • FRN
FONEY FABLES • 1942 • Freleng Friz • ANS • USA
FONIAS, O • 1984 • Christopoulos Takis • GRC • MURDERER, THE
FONISSA, I • 1974 • Ferris Kostas • GRC • MURDERESS, THE
FONT OF COURAGE, THE • 1917 • King Burton L. • USA
FONTAINE D'ARETHUSE, LA • 1936 • Kirsanoff Dimitri • SHT • FRN
FONTAINE DE VAUCLUSE, LA • 1955 • Malle Louis • DCS • FRN
FONTAINE MERVEILLEUSE, LA • 1908 • Melies Georges • FRN • MARVELOUS FOUNTAIN, THE
FONTAINE SACREE OU LA VENGEANCE DE BOUDHA, LA • 1901 • Melies Georges • FRN • SACRED FOUNTAIN, THE (USA) ○ VENGEANCE DU BOUDHA, LA
FONTAMARA • 1980 • Lizzani Carlo • ITL
FONTAN • 1989 • Mamin Yuri • USS • FOUNTAIN, THE (UKN)
FONTANA DI TREVI • 1960 • Campogalliani Carlo • ITL, SPN
FONTANE DI ROMA • 1938 • Costa Mario • DCS • ITL • FOUNTAINS OF ROME, THE
FONTANE EFFI BRIEST • 1974 • Fassbinder R. W. • FRG • EFFI BRIEST (USA)
FONTE DA SAUDADE, A • 1986 • Altberg Marcos • BRZ • DEEP ILLUSION
FOO FOO • 1960 • *Halas John (P)* • ASS • UKN
FOO FOO'S NEW HAT • 1960 • *Halas John (P)* • ANS • UKN
FOO FOO'S SLEEPLESS NIGHT • 1960 • *Halas John (P)* • ANS • UKN
FOOD CHOPPER WAR, THE • 1913 • Johnston Lorimer • USA
FOOD FOR FAMINE • 1962 • Legg Stuart, Varley M., Bailey A. • UKN
FOOD FOR FEUDIN' • 1950 • Nichols Charles • ANS • USA
FOOD FOR FREDDY • 1953 • Crawley Judith • DOC • CND
FOOD FOR KINGS AND RILEY • 1915 • Louis Will • USA
FOOD FOR SCANDAL • 1920 • Cruze James • USA
FOOD FOR THOUGHT • 1940 • Brunel Adrian • UKN
FOOD FOR THOUGHT • 1952 • *Hall Cameron* • SHT • UKN
FOOD GAMBLERS, THE • 1917 • Parker Albert • USA
FOOD INSPECTOR, THE • 1915 • *Superba* • USA
FOOD MACHINE, THE • 1950 • Holmes Cecil • DOC • ASL
FOOD OF LOVE, THE • 1916 • Kerrigan J. M. • IRL
FOOD OF THE GODS, THE • 1976 • Gordon Bert I. • USA
FOOD OF THE GODS II • 1988 • Lee Damian • CND • GNAW: FOOD OF THE GODS II ○ AFTER FOOD OF THE GODS
FOOD PRESERVATION • 1965 • Hudson Hugh • DCS • UKN
FOOFLE'S PICNIC • 1960 • Tendlar Dave • ANS • USA
FOOFLE'S TRAIN RIDE • 1959 • Tendlar Dave • ANS • USA
FOOL, THE • 1913 • Pearson George • UKN
FOOL, THE • 1916 • Wilson Ben • SHT • USA
FOOL, THE • 1925 • Millarde Harry • USA
FOOL ABOUT WOMEN, A • 1932 • Edwards Harry J. • SHT • USA
FOOL AND HIS FRIEND, A • 1916 • Wolbert William • SHT • USA
FOOL AND HIS MONEY, A • 1911 • Haldane Bert • UKN
FOOL AND HIS MONEY, A • 1912 • *Russell James* • USA
FOOL AND HIS MONEY, A • 1914 • Weber Lois • USA
FOOL AND HIS MONEY, A • 1920 • Ellis Robert • USA
FOOL AND HIS MONEY, A • 1925 • Kenton Erle C. • USA
FOOL AND THE PRINCESS, THE • 1948 • Hammond William C. • UKN
FOOL COVERAGE • 1938 • Goodwins Leslie • SHT • USA
FOOL COVERAGE • 1952 • McKimson Robert • ANS • USA
FOOL FOR BLONDES, A see **MAGNIFICENT BRUTE, THE** • 1936
FOOL FOR LOVE • 1986 • Altman Robert • USA
FOOL FOR LUCK • 1908 • Porter Edwin S. • USA
FOOL FOR LUCK, A • 1913 • *Nestor* • USA
FOOL KILLER, THE • 1963 • Gonzalez Servando • USA, MXC • LEGEND OF THE FOOL KILLER, THE ○ ASESINO DE TONTOS, EL (MXC) ○ VIOLENT JOURNEY, A
FOOL LUCK • 1913 • *Kalem* • USA
FOOL THERE WAS, A • 1914 • *Lubin* • USA
FOOL THERE WAS, A • 1915 • Powell Frank • USA
FOOL THERE WAS, A • 1922 • Flynn Emmett J. • USA
FOOL WHO MADE MIRACLES, THE see **TONTO QUE HACIA MILAGROS, EL** • 1983
FOOLERY see **NARROHUT** • 1982
FOOLIN' AROUND • 1980 • Heffron Richard T. • USA
FOOLING FANNY'S FATHER • 1914 • *Lubin* • USA
FOOLING FATHER • 1912 • *Lubin* • USA
FOOLING FATHER • 1915 • *Joker* • USA
FOOLING THE SPECIALIST • 1912 • *Reliance* • USA
FOOLING THEIR WIVES • 1913 • *Lubin* • USA
FOOLING UNCLE • 1914 • *Fischer Marguerita* • USA
FOOLING UNCLE • 1916 • *Don Dave* • SHT • USA
FOOLISH AGE, THE • 1919 • Jones F. Richard • SHT • USA
FOOLISH AGE, THE • 1921 • Seiter William A. • USA
FOOLISH AGREEMENT, A • 1914 • Miller Ashley • USA
FOOLISH BUNNY, THE • 1938 • Davis Arthur • ANS • USA
FOOLISH DAUGHTERS see **ALICE ADAMS** • 1923
FOOLISH DUCKLING • 1952 • Davis Mannie • ANS • USA
FOOLISH FAT FLORA • 1916 • *Cunningham Arthur* • USA
FOOLISH FOLLIES • 1930 • Foster John, Bailey Harry • ANS • USA
FOOLISH FORTIES, THE • 1931 • Watson William • USA
FOOLISH HUSBANDS • 1929 • *Sennett Mack (P)* • SHT • USA
FOOLISH HUSBANDS (USA) see **HISTOIRE DE RIRE** • 1941
FOOLISH LIVES • 1922 • *Chatman Frank* • USA
FOOLISH LOVE, A see **OI ATTEANTI** • 1981
FOOLISH LOVERS • 1914 • *Prescott Vivian* • USA
FOOLISH MATRONS, THE • 1921 • Tourneur Maurice, Brown Clarence • USA • IS MARRIAGE A FAILURE? (UKN)
FOOLISH MONTE CARLO • 1922 • Humphrey William • USA
FOOLISH MOTHERS • 1923 • *Coxen Edward* • USA
FOOLISH ROMANCE, A • 1916 • Schneider James • SHT • USA
FOOLISH TWINS, THE • 1923 • *Terry Twins* • USA
FOOLISH VIRGIN, THE • 1917 • Capellani Albert • USA
FOOLISH VIRGIN, THE • 1924 • Hill George W. • USA
FOOLISH WIVES • 1922 • von Stroheim Erich • USA
FOOLISH WORLD see **MONDO BALORDO** • 1964
FOOLISHNESS OF JEALOUSY, THE • 1911 • *Swayne Julia* • USA
FOOLISHNESS OF OLIVER, THE • 1912 • *Brunette Fritzie* • USA
FOOLPROOF • 1936 • Cahn Edward L. • SHT • USA
FOOLS • 1970 • Gries Tom • USA
FOOL'S ADVICE, A • 1932 • Ceder Ralph • USA
FOOLS AND DUELS • 1919 • Lehrman Henry • SHT • USA
FOOLS AND FIRES • 1918 • Hutchinson Craig • SHT • USA
FOOLS AND PAJAMAS • 1915 • *Joker* • USA
FOOLS AND RICHES • 1923 • Blache Herbert • USA • TWENTY DOLLARS
FOOLS AND THEIR MONEY • 1919 • Blache Herbert • USA • FAMILY TREE, THE
FOOLS AWAKE (UKN) see **STRAWBERRY ROAN, THE** • 1948
FOOL'S AWAKENING, A • 1924 • Shaw Harold • USA
FOOL'S FANCY (USA) see **SCROGGINS WINS THE FIDDLE-FADDLE PRIZE** • 1911
FOOLS FIRST • 1922 • Neilan Marshall • USA
FOOLS FOR LUCK • 1917 • Windom Lawrence C. • USA
FOOLS FOR LUCK • 1928 • Reisner Charles F. • USA
FOOLS FOR SCANDAL • 1938 • LeRoy Mervyn • USA
FOOL'S GAME, THE • 1916 • Broadwell Robert B. • SHT • USA
FOOL'S GOLD • 1915 • Physioc Wray • USA
FOOLS' GOLD • 1916 • *Essanay* • SHT • USA
FOOL'S GOLD • 1919 • Trimble Larry • USA
FOOL'S GOLD • 1947 • Archainbaud George • USA
FOOL'S GOLD see **KRAKGULDET** • 1969
FOOL'S GOLD see **1857** • 1981
FOOL'S GOLD, A • 1916 • Stanton Richard • *Laemmle* • SHT • USA • RICHES
FOOL'S GOLD (UKN) see **WHITE RENEGADE, THE** • 1931
FOOL'S HAIKUS, A • 1963 • Mekas Jonas • USA
FOOL'S HEART, THE • 1915 • *Myles Norbert* • USA
FOOLS' HIGHWAY • 1924 • Cummings Irving • USA
FOOLS IN PARADISE see **ESCAPE BY NIGHT** • 1937
FOOLS IN THE DARK • 1924 • Santell Alfred • USA
FOOL'S LOVE see **CHIJIN NO AI** • 1949
FOOL'S LUCK • 1926 • Arbuckle Roscoe • USA
FOOL'S MATE • 1989 • Carriere Mathieu • FRN, FRG
FOOL'S NIGHT see **KILLER PARTY** • 1986
FOOLS OF FASHION • 1926 • McKay James C. • USA
FOOLS OF FATE • 1909 • Griffith D. W. • USA
FOOLS OF FORTUNE • 1989 • O'Connor Pat • IRL, UKN
FOOL'S PARADE • 1971 • McLaglen Andrew V. • USA • DYNAMITE MAN FROM GLORY JAIL (UKN)
FOOL'S PARADISE • 1921 • De Mille Cecil B. • USA
FOOL'S PARADISE, A • 1916 • Abramson Ivan • USA
FOOL'S PROMISE, A • 1921 • *White Film Corp.* • USA
FOOL'S REVENGE, A • 1909 • Griffith D. W. • USA
FOOL'S REVENGE, THE • 1916 • Davis Will S. • USA
FOOLS RUSH IN • 1949 • Carstairs John Paddy • UKN
FOOLS RUSH IN see **BLONDE INSPIRATION** • 1940
FOOLS STEP IN • 1938 • Byass Nigel • UKN
FOOLS, WATER SPRITES, AND IMPOSTERS see **BLAZNI, VODNICI, A PODVODNICI** • 1980
FOORSTADSPRASTEN • 1917 • Klercker Georg • SWD • CLERGYMAN FROM THE SUBURBS, THE
FOOT AND MOUTH • 1955 • Anderson Lindsay • DCS • UKN
FOOT BRAWL • 1966 • Smith Paul J. • ANS • USA
FOOT FILM see **VOLLEYBALL** • 1968
FOOT OF ROMANCE, A • 1914 • *Beery Wallace* • USA
FOOT ROMANCE, A • 1911 • *Walton Fred* • USA
FOOTBALL • 1935 • *Terry Paul/ Moser Frank (P)* • ANS • USA
FOOTBALL • 1961 • Leacock Richard, Drew Robert L. • DOC • USA • MOONEY VS. FOWLE
FOOTBALL • 1962 • Languepin Jean-Jacques • SHT • FRN
FOOTBALL, THE • 1962 • Doicheva Zdenka • ANS • BUL
FOOTBALL ABSURDITY, A • 1912 • *Gaumont* • USA
FOOTBALL BUGS • 1936 • *Mintz Charles (P)* • ANS • USA
FOOTBALL COACH (UKN) see **COLLEGE COACH** • 1933
FOOTBALL CRAZY see **ARBITRO, L'** • 1974
FOOTBALL CRAZY (UKN) see **NEUE FIMMEL, DER** • 1960
FOOTBALL DAFT • 1921 • Rowe Victor W. • UKN
FOOTBALL FAVOURITE, A • 1922 • Wynn George • UKN
FOOTBALL FEVER • 1937 • Lantz Walter • ANS • USA
FOOTBALL FIEND, THE • 1908 • *Selig* • USA
FOOTBALL FINAL, THE • 1901 • Paul Robert William • UKN
FOOTBALL FOOL, THE see **GRIDIRON FLASH** • 1934
FOOTBALL FOOTWORK • 1932 • Feist Felix E. • SHT • USA
FOOTBALL FORTY YEARS AGO • 1931 • Kelley Albert • SHT • USA
FOOTBALL FREAKS • 1971 • Vester Paul • ANS • UKN
FOOTBALL, FRED AND TEETH • 1913 • *Apollo* • USA
FOOTBALL FUN • 1922 • Dudley Bernard • UKN
FOOTBALL HERO, A • 1911 • *Essanay* • USA
FOOTBALL (NOW AND THEN) • 1953 • Hannah Jack • ANS • USA
FOOTBALL OF THE GOOD OLD DAYS see **REGI IDOK FOCIJA** • 1974
FOOTBALL POOLS AND THE BOUZOUKI, THE see **PRO-PO KE TA BOUZOUKIA, TO** • 1968
FOOTBALL ROMEO • 1938 • Sidney George • SHT • USA
FOOTBALL STAR, THE see **ESODACSATAR, A** • 1956
FOOTBALL TEAMWORK • 1935 • Feist Felix E. • SHT • USA
FOOTBALL THRILLS #9 • 1946 • *Smith Pete* • SHT • USA
FOOTBALL THRILLS #10 • 1947 • *Smith Pete* • SHT • USA
FOOTBALL THRILLS #11 • 1948 • *Smith Pete* • SHT • USA
FOOTBALL THRILLS #12 • 1949 • *Smith Pete* • SHT • USA
FOOTBALL THRILLS #13 • 1950 • *Smith Pete* • SHT • USA
FOOTBALL THRILLS #14 • 1951 • *Smith Pete* • SHT • USA
FOOTBALL THRILLS #15 • 1952 • *Smith Pete* • SHT • USA
FOOTBALL THRILLS OF 1937 • 1938 • *Smith Pete* • SHT • USA
FOOTBALL THRILLS OF 1938 • 1939 • *Smith Pete* • SHT • USA
FOOTBALL THRILLS OF 1939 • 1940 • *Smith Pete* • SHT • USA
FOOTBALL THRILLS OF 1940 • 1941 • *Smith Pete* • SHT • USA
FOOTBALL THRILLS OF 1941 • 1942 • *Smith Pete* • SHT • USA
FOOTBALL THRILLS OF 1942 • 1943 • *Smith Pete* • SHT • USA
FOOTBALL THRILLS OF 1943 • 1944 • *Smith Pete* • SHT • USA
FOOTBALL THRILLS OF 1944 • 1945 • *Smith Pete* • SHT • USA
FOOTBALL TOUCHER DOWNER, THE • 1937 • Fleischer Dave • ANS • USA
FOOTBALL WARRIOR • 1908 • Porter Edwin S. • USA
FOOTBALLER'S HONOUR, A • 1914 • Fitzhamon Lewin? • UKN
FOOTBALLS AND FRAUDS • 1919 • Howe J. A. • SHT • USA
FOOTBRIDGE, THE see **LEVIATHAN** • 1966
FOOTFALLS • 1921 • Brabin Charles J. • USA
FOOTHILL PROBLEM, A • 1915 • Physioc Wray • USA
FOOTLIGHT FEVER • 1941 • Reis Irving • USA • SHOW BUSINESS
FOOTLIGHT FLAME, A • 1917 • Reed Walter C. • USA
FOOTLIGHT GLAMOUR • 1943 • Strayer Frank • USA
FOOTLIGHT GLAMOUR (UKN) see **UPSTREAM** • 1927
FOOTLIGHT LURE, THE see **BURLESQUE BLACKMAILERS, THE** • 1917
FOOTLIGHT MAIDS • 1919 • Blystone John G. • SHT • USA
FOOTLIGHT PARADE • 1933 • Bacon Lloyd • USA
FOOTLIGHT RANGER, THE • 1923 • Dunlap Scott R. • USA
FOOTLIGHT SERENADE • 1942 • Ratoff Gregory • USA • STRICTLY DYNAMITE
FOOTLIGHT VARIETIES • 1951 • Yates Hal • USA
FOOTLIGHTS • 1921 • Robertson John S. • USA
FOOTLIGHTS • 1937 • Hopwood R. A. • UKN
FOOTLIGHTS see **SUNNY SIDE UP** • 1926
FOOTLIGHTS see **LUCI DEL VARIETA** • 1950
FOOTLIGHTS AND FAKERS • 1917 • Semon Larry • SHT • USA
FOOTLIGHTS AND FOOLS • 1929 • Seiter William A. • USA
FOOTLIGHTS AND SHADOWS • 1920 • Noble John W. • USA
FOOTLIGHTS AND SHADOWS (UKN) see **HITCH HIKE TO HEAVEN** • 1935
FOOTLIGHTS OF FATE, THE • 1916 • Humphrey William • USA
FOOTLIGHTS OR THE FARM, THE • 1910 • *Edison* • USA

FOOTLOOSE • 1983 • Ross Herbert • USA
FOOTLOOSE see **BOMZH** • 1989
FOOTLOOSE HEIRESS • 1937 • Clemens William • USA
FOOTLOOSE WIDOWS • 1926 • Del Ruth Roy • USA • FINE FEATHERS (UKN)
FOOTMARK OF A SNOW FAIRY see **YUKIONNA NO ASHIATO** • 1959
FOOTNOTE, THE see **PRZYPIS** • 1970
FOOTNOTE TO FACE • 1932 • Jacobs Lewis • USA
FOOTPATH TO HAPPINESS, THE • 1913 • *Nestor* • USA
FOOTPRINT CLUE, THE • 1913 • *Wells Charles* • USA
FOOTPRINTS • 1914 • Le Saint Edward J. • USA
FOOTPRINTS • 1920 • Jones Grover • SHT • USA
FOOTPRINTS see **STOPY** • 1960
FOOTPRINTS see **SLADY** • 1974
FOOTPRINTS BLOW AWAY, THE see **VERWEHTE SPUREN** • 1938
FOOTPRINTS OF A WOMAN see **ONNA NI ASHIATO** • 1956
FOOTPRINTS OF MOZART • 1914 • *American* • USA
FOOTPRINTS ON THE MOON -APOLLO 11 • 1969 • Gibson Bill • DOC • USA
FOOTROT FLATS • 1986 • Ball Murray • ANS • NZL
FOOTSTEPS • 1972 • Wendkos Paul • TVM • USA • FOOTSTEPS: NICE GUYS FINISH LAST ○ NICE GUYS FINISH LAST
FOOTSTEPS • 1973 • Parker Alan • SHT • UKN
FOOTSTEPS • 1979 • Barrie Scott • SHT • CND
FOOTSTEPS IN THE DARK • 1941 • Bacon Lloyd • USA
FOOTSTEPS IN THE DARK see **SHAGI V NOCHI** • 1963
FOOTSTEPS IN THE FOG • 1955 • Lubin Arthur • UKN
FOOTSTEPS IN THE NIGHT • 1957 • Yarbrough Jean • USA
FOOTSTEPS IN THE NIGHT see **SHAGI V NOCHI** • 1963
FOOTSTEPS IN THE NIGHT (USA) see **HONEYMOON ADVENTURE, A** • 1931
FOOTSTEPS IN THE SNOW • 1966 • Green Martin • CND
FOOTSTEPS: NICE GUYS FINISH LAST see **FOOTSTEPS** • 1972
FOOTSTEPS OF CAPTAIN KIDD, THE • 1917 • *Grand Feature Films* • USA
FOOTSTEPS ON THE SAND • 1988 • Honarmand Mohammad-Reza • IRN
FOOZLE AT THE TEA PARTY, A • 1915 • Roach Hal • USA
FOOZLE TAKES UP GOLF • 1911 • Wilson Frank? • UKN
FOP, THE see **PIZHON** • 1929
FOR $200 • 1911 • *Melies* • USA
FOR £50,000 • 1913 • Butler Alexander? • UKN
FOR 50,000 DAMNED DOLLARS see **PER 50,000 MALEDETTI DOLLARI** • 1968
FOR 100,000 DOLLARS I'LL KILL YOU see **PER CENTOMILA DOLLARI TI AMMAZZO** • 1967
FOR A BABY'S SAKE • 1911 • Fitzhamon Lewin • UKN
FOR A CHILD CALLED MICHAEL • 1979 • Cox Paul • DOC • ASL
FOR A DOLLAR IN THE TEETH (UKN) see **DOLLARO FRA I DENTI, UN** • 1967
FOR A FEW BULLETS MORE (UKN) see **VADO.. L'AMMAZZO E TORNO** • 1967
FOR A FEW DOLLARS MORE (USA) see **PER QUALCHE DOLLARI IN PIU** • 1965
FOR A FISTFUL OF DOLLARS (USA) see **PER UN PUGNO DI DOLLARI** • 1964
FOR A JOYFUL LIFE see **ZA ZIVOT RADOSTNY** • 1951
FOR A NAMELESS STAR see **MONA, L'ETOILE SANS NOM** • 1966
FOR A NIGHT OF LOVE • 1988 • Makavejev Dusan
FOR A THOUSAND DOLLARS • 1915 • *Premier* • USA
FOR A THOUSAND DOLLARS A DAY see **PER MILLE DOLLARI AL GIORNI** • 1966
FOR A WESTERN GIRL • 1910 • *Bison* • USA
FOR A WIDOW'S LOVE • 1914 • Hotaling Arthur D. • USA
FOR A WIFE'S HONOR • 1908 • Griffith D. W. • USA
FOR A WOMAN • 1914 • *White Pearl* • USA
FOR A WOMAN'S EYES • 1926 • Malins Geoffrey H., Parkinson H. B. • UKN
FOR A WOMAN'S FAIR NAME • 1916 • Davenport Harry • USA
FOR A WOMAN'S HONOR • 1910 • Olcott Sidney • USA
FOR A WOMAN'S HONOR • 1919 • Frame Park • USA
FOR A YELLOW JERSEY (UKN) see **POUR UN MAILLOT JAUNE** • 1965
FOR ADULTS ONLY see **BARNFORBJUDET** • 1979
FOR ALIMONY ONLY • 1926 • De Mille William C. • USA
FOR ALL ETERNITY • 1917 • Coleby A. E., Rooke Arthur • UKN
FOR ALL ETERNITY • 1935 • Grierson Marion • UKN
FOR ALL WE KNOW see **FLESH AND FANTASY** • 1943
FOR AN OLD LOVE'S SAKE • 1908 • *Walturdaw* • UKN
FOR ANOTHER WOMAN • 1924 • Kirkland David • USA
FOR ANOTHER'S CRIME • 1913 • *Scardon Paul* • USA
FOR ANOTHER'S CRIME • 1915 • Humphrey William • USA
FOR ANOTHER'S SIN • 1913 • *Benham Harry* • USA
FOR ART AND LOVE • 1913 • *Joker* • USA
FOR ART'S SAKE • 1918 • *Rhodes Billie* • USA
FOR ART'S SAKE • 1923 • Roach Hal • SHT • USA
FOR ATT INTE TALA OM ALLA DESSA KVINNOR • 1964 • Bergman Ingmar • SWD • NOW ABOUT THESE WOMEN (UKN) ○ ALL THESE WOMEN (USA) ○ AS FOR ALL THESE WOMEN
FOR AULD LANG SYNE • 1914 • *Ab* • USA
FOR AUSTRALIA • 1915 • Luke Monty • ASL
FOR BABY'S SAKE • 1912 • Haldane Bert? • UKN
FOR BEAUTY'S SAKE • 1941 • Traube Shepard • USA
FOR BETTER -BUT WORSE • 1915 • Sennett Mack • USA
FOR BETTER, FOR WORSE • 1919 • De Mille Cecil B. • USA
FOR BETTER, FOR WORSE • 1954 • Thompson J. Lee • UKN • COCKTAILS IN THE KITCHEN (USA)
FOR BETTER FOR WORSE • 1959 • Halas John, Batchelor Joy • ANS • UKN
FOR BETTER, FOR WORSE see **ZANDY'S BRIDE** • 1974
FOR BETTER OR FOR WORSE • 1913 • *Francis Alec B.* • USA
FOR BETTER OR FOR WORSE • 1989 • Quintano Gene • USA
FOR BETTER OR NURSE • 1945 • Sparber I. • ANS • USA
FOR BETTER OR WORSE • 1911 • *Revier* • USA
FOR BETTER OR WORSE • 1911 • Haldane Bert • UKN
FOR BETTER OR WORSE • 1916 • *Stull Walter* • USA
FOR BETTER OR WORSER • 1935 • Fleischer Dave • ANS • USA
FOR BIG BROTHER'S SAKE • 1911 • *Solax* • USA
FOR BIG STAKES • 1922 • Reynolds Lynn • USA
FOR BOREDOM'S SAKE see **SKUKI RADI** • 1968
FOR CASH • 1915 • Chaney Lon • USA
FOR CLEMENCE see **POUR CLEMENCE** • 1977
FOR CRIMES NOT THEIRS (USA) see **ZA WINY NIEPOPELNIONE** • 1939
FOR CRIMIN' OUT LOUD • 1956 • White Jules • SHT • USA
FOR DAGENE ER ONDE • 1990 • Einarson Eldar • NRW • BECAUSE THESE ARE EVIL DAYS
FOR DE ANDRE see **DU SKAL ELSKE DIN NAESTE** • 1915
FOR DODEN OS SKILLER • 1970 • Karlsson Finn • DNM • TILL DEATH DO US PART
FOR EAST IS EAST • 1913 • Aylott Dave • UKN • IN THE PYTHON'S DEN
FOR ENGLAND'S SAKE • 1915 • *Urban* • UKN
FOR EVER AND FOR EVER • 1909 • *Warwick Trading Co.* • UKN
FOR EVERY CHILD • 1953 • Beaudine William • USA
FOR EXAMPLE • 1972 • Arakawa • USA
FOR EXAMPLE -SILBITZ IN COMPETITION • Nickel Gitta • DOC • GDR
FOR EYES ONLY see **STRENG GEHEIM** • 1963
FOR FADERNESLANDET • 1913 • Klercker Georg • SWD • FOR YOUR COUNTRY
FOR FIVE THOUSAND DOLLARS A YEAR • 1915 • *Huff Louise* • USA
FOR FOREIGN AND GERMAN WORKERS see **FUR AUSLANDISCHE UND DEUTSCHE ARBEITER** • 1973
FOR FOREST LONELINESS see **ZE SVETA LESNICH SAMOT** • 1933
FOR FRANCE • 1917 • Ruggles Wesley • USA
FOR FREEDOM • 1919 • Lloyd Frank • USA
FOR FREEDOM • 1940 • Elvey Maurice • UKN
FOR FRIENDSHIP see **FOR VANSKAPS SKULL** • 1965
FOR FRIHED OG RET • 1949 • Methling Sven • DNM
FOR FUN -FOR PLAY see **KALEIDOSKOP VALESKA GERT -NUR ZUM SPASS NUR ZUM SPIEL** • 1977
FOR GOESTERNE KOMMER • 1987 • Carlsen Jon Bang • SHT • DNM • BEFORE THE GUESTS ARRIVE
FOR GOODNESS SAKE • 1940 • *New Realm* • SHT • UKN
FOR GUESTS ONLY • 1923 • Roach Hal • SHT • USA
FOR HEAVEN'S SAKE • 1926 • Taylor Sam • USA
FOR HEAVEN'S SAKE • 1950 • Seaton George • USA
FOR HEM OCH HARD • 1917 • Klercker Georg • SWD • FOR HOME AND HEARTH
FOR HEMMET OCH FLICKAN • 1925 • Larsson William • SWD • FOR THE HOME AND THE GIRL
FOR HENNES SKULL • 1930 • Merzbach Paul • SWD, FRG • MACH MIR DIE WELT ZUM PARADIES (FRG) ○ FOR HER SAKE
FOR HER • 1912 • Merwin Bannister • USA
FOR HER BOY'S SAKE • 1913 • *Snow Marguerite* • USA
FOR HER BROTHER'S SAKE • 1911 • *Vitagraph* • USA
FOR HER BROTHER'S SAKE • 1911 • *Kalem* • USA
FOR HER BROTHER'S SAKE • 1911 • Ince Thomas H., Tucker George Loane • *Imp* • USA
FOR HER BROTHER'S SAKE • 1913 • *Lubin* • USA
FOR HER BROTHER'S SAKE • 1914 • Hunt Jay • USA
FOR HER BROTHER'S SAKE • 1915 • Evans Fred • UKN
FOR HER CHILD • 1914 • *Cummings Irving* • USA
FOR HER COUNTRY'S SAKE • 1909 • Blackton J. Stuart (Spv) • USA
FOR HER COUNTRY'S SAKE • 1910 • *Selig* • USA
FOR HER COUNTRY'S SAKE • Waschneck Erich • FRG
FOR HER FATHER'S HONOR • 1910 • *Bison* • USA
FOR HER FATHER'S SAKE • 1912 • Davis Ulysses • USA
FOR HER FATHER'S SAKE • 1921 • Butler Alexander • UKN
FOR HER FATHER'S SINS • 1914 • O'Brien John B. • USA
FOR HER FRIEND • 1915 • Reehm George E. • USA
FOR HER GOOD NAME • 1916 • Broadwell Robert B. • SHT • USA
FOR HER GOVERNMENT • 1913 • O'Sullivan Tony • USA
FOR HER HAPPINESS • 1915 • Reehm George E. • USA
FOR HER MOTHER'S SAKE • 1912 • Noy Wilfred • UKN
FOR HER MOTHER'S SAKE • 1913 • Collins Edwin J. • UKN • TYPIST'S LOVE AFFAIR, A
FOR HER MOTHER'S SAKE • 1916 • Elfelt Clifford S. • SHT • USA
FOR HER PEOPLE • 1914 • *Howley Irene* • USA
FOR HER PEOPLE • 1914 • Trimble Larry • UKN
FOR HER SAKE • 1909 • *Vitagraph* • USA
FOR HER SAKE • 1909 • Aylott Dave • UKN
FOR HER SAKE • 1911 • *Garwood William* • USA
FOR HER SAKE • 1913 • *Nestor* • USA
FOR HER SAKE see **FOR HENNES SKULL** • 1930
FOR HER SIN • 1911 • *Champion* • USA
FOR HER SISTER'S SAKE • 1910 • Porter Edwin S. • USA
FOR HER SISTER'S SAKE • 1913 • *Joyce Alice* • USA
FOR HER SISTER'S SAKE see **BRILLANTSTJERNEN** • 1912
FOR HER SON'S SAKE • 1910 • *Centaur* • USA
FOR HER SWEETHEART'S SAKE • 1909 • Brooke Van Dyke • USA
FOR HE'S A JOLLY GOOD FELLOW • 1911 • *Essanay* • USA
FOR HIGH ENDS see **HOGRE ANDAMAL** • 1921
FOR HIGH STAKES • 1915 • *Courtot Marguerite* • USA
FOR HIS BROTHER'S CRIME • 1914 • *Premier* • USA
FOR HIS BROTHER'S SAKE • 1916 • *Puritan* • USA
FOR HIS CHILD • 1912 • *Champion* • USA
FOR HIS CHILD'S SAKE • 1908 • Aylott Dave • UKN
FOR HIS CHILD'S SAKE • 1913 • *Lubin* • USA
FOR HIS CHILD'S SAKE • 1913 • *Eclair* • USA
FOR HIS COUNTRY'S HONOUR see **FOR SIT LANDS AERE** • 1915
FOR HIS FATHER'S LIFE • 1914 • *Ryan Joe* • USA
FOR HIS LOVED ONE • 1913 • *Johnstone Lamar* • USA
FOR HIS MASTER • 1914 • Cabanne W. Christy • USA
FOR HIS MOTHER • 1915 • Beaumont Harry • USA
FOR HIS MOTHER'S SAKE • 1912 • *Handworth Octavia* • USA
FOR HIS MOTHER'S SAKE • 1922 • *Johnson Jack* • USA
FOR HIS PAL • 1915 • *Sears A. D.* • USA
FOR HIS PAL'S SAKE • 1911 • *Selig* • USA
FOR HIS SAKE • 1911 • *Vitagraph* • USA
FOR HIS SAKE • 1911 • *Reliance* • USA
FOR HIS SAKE • 1912 • *Rex* • USA
FOR HIS SAKE • 1922 • Lawrence John S. • USA
FOR HIS SISTER'S HONOR • 1910 • *Bison* • USA
FOR HIS SISTER'S SAKE • 1908 • *Lubin* • USA
FOR HIS SON • 1912 • Griffith D. W. • USA
FOR HIS SUPERIOR'S HONOR • 1915 • Lloyd Frank • USA
FOR HIS WIFE'S SAKE • 1915 • *French Charles K.* • USA
FOR HOME AND COUNTRY see **FOR THE EMPIRE** • 1914
FOR HOME AND HEARTH see **FOR HEM OCH HARD** • 1917
FOR HOME AND HONOR • 1912 • *Champion* • USA
FOR HONOR'S SAKE • 1917 • *Big U* • SHT • USA
FOR HUSBANDS ONLY • 1918 • Weber Lois, Smalley Phillips • USA
FOR I HAVE TOILED • 1914 • *Macquarrie Murdock* • USA
FOR IRELAND'S SAKE • 1914 • Olcott Sidney • USA
FOR KATTEN • 1959 • Skoglund Gunnar • SWD
FOR KEEPS • 1988 • Avildsen John G. • USA • MAYBE BABY
FOR KING AND COUNTRY • 1914 • Finn Arthur • UKN
FOR KING OR KAISER • 1915 • *Apex* • USA
FOR LACK OF EVIDENCE • 1917 • Stevens Edwin • SHT • USA
FOR LADIES ONLY • 1927 • Pembroke Scott, Lehrman Henry • USA
FOR LADIES ONLY • 1981 • Damski Mel • TVM • USA
FOR LADIES ONLY • 1982 • Kramreither Anthony • CND
FOR LIBERTY • 1918 • Bracken Bertram • USA
FOR LIFE • 1919 • Jaccard Jacques • SHT • USA
FOR LIFE see **INOCHI ARUKAGHIRI** • 1946
FOR LIFE, AGAINST THE WAR • 1968 • CMP • USA
FOR LIFE AND LIBERTY • 1914 • *Imp* • USA
FOR LIZZIE'S SAKE • 1913 • Sennett Mack • USA
FOR LOVE ALONE • 1986 • Wallace Stephen • ASL
FOR LOVE AND GLORY • 1911 • *Vitagraph* • USA
FOR LOVE AND GOLD • 1916 • McRae Henry • SHT • USA
FOR LOVE AND HONOR • 1983 • Nelson Gary • TVM • USA
FOR LOVE AND LIFE • 1912 • Plumb Hay • UKN
FOR LOVE AND THE CROWN • 1914 • *Hallows Lillian* • UKN
FOR LOVE AND THE KING see **ROMANCE OF A ROYALIST MAID, THE** • 1912
FOR LOVE.. FOR MAGIC see **PER AMORE.. PER MAGIA** • 1967
FOR LOVE, LIFE AND RICHES • 1912 • *Bison* • USA
FOR LOVE & MONEY • 1967 • Davis Don • USA • FOR LOVE OF MONEY
FOR LOVE OF A LADY • 1924 • *Regent Films* • SHT • UKN
FOR LOVE OF A MAN • 1913 • *Walpole Stanley* • USA
FOR LOVE OF A QUEEN see **DICTATOR, THE** • 1935
FOR LOVE OF ANGELA • 1982 • Vejar Rudy • USA
FOR LOVE OF BENJI • 1977 • Camp Joe • USA • FOR THE LOVE OF BENJI
FOR LOVE OF BETTY • 1919 • *Strand* • SHT • USA
FOR LOVE OF COLUMBINE • 1913 • Apfel Oscar • USA
FOR LOVE OF COUNTRY • 1908 • *Kalem* • USA
FOR LOVE OF GOLD • 1908 • Griffith D. W. • USA
FOR LOVE OF HER • 1912 • *Robinson Gertrude* • USA
FOR LOVE OF HIM • 1913 • Buckland Warwick? • UKN
FOR LOVE OF HIM • 1914 • Martin E. A. • USA
FOR LOVE OF IVY • 1968 • Mann Daniel • USA
FOR LOVE OF MABEL • 1913 • Sennett Mack • USA
FOR LOVE OF MARY ELLEN • 1915 • *Stone George* • USA
FOR LOVE OF MONEY see **FOR LOVE & MONEY** • 1967
FOR LOVE OF SERVICE • 1922 • *Morante Milburn (P)* • USA
FOR LOVE OF THE FLAG • 1913 • *Kb* • USA
FOR LOVE OF YOU • 1933 • Gallone Carmine • UKN
FOR LOVE OR MONEY • 1914 • *Nestor* • USA
FOR LOVE OR MONEY • 1919 • *Christie* • USA
FOR LOVE OR MONEY • 1930 • Pearce A. Leslie • USA
FOR LOVE OR MONEY • 1939 • Rogell Albert S. • USA • TOMORROW AT MIDNIGHT (UKN)
FOR LOVE OR MONEY • 1963 • Gordon Michael • USA
FOR LOVE OR MONEY • 1984 • Hughes Terry • TVM • USA
FOR LOVE OR MONEY see **CROSSROADS OF NEW YORK, THE** • 1922
FOR LOVE OR MONEY see **THIS HAPPY FEELING** • 1958
FOR LOVE OR MONEY (USA) see **CASH** • 1933
FOR LOVERS ONLY • 1982 • Guzman Claudio • TVM • USA
FOR LOVE'S SAKE • 1909 • *Essanay* • USA
FOR LOVE'S SWEET SAKE • 1909 • *Lubin* • USA
FOR MARION'S SAKE • 1913 • Buckland Warwick? • UKN
FOR MASSA'S SAKE • 1911 • Golden Joseph A. • USA
FOR MAYOR -BESS SMITH • 1913 • *Patheplay* • USA
FOR ME AND MY GAL • 1942 • Berkeley Busby • USA • FOR ME AND MY GIRL (UKN)
FOR ME AND MY GIRL (UKN) see **FOR ME AND MY GAL** • 1942
FOR MEMORY'S SAKE • 1911 • *Essanay* • USA
FOR MEN ONLY see **TALL LIE, THE** • 1952
FOR MEN ONLY see **I LIKE BIRDS** • 1967
FOR MEN ONLY see **BEL AMI** • 1975
FOR MEN ONLY (USA) see **PER UOMINI SOLI** • 1939
FOR MIN HETA UNGDOMS SKULL • 1952 • Mattsson Arne • SWD • BECAUSE OF MY HOT YOUTH
FOR MONEY AND GLORY • 1984 • SAF
FOR MOTHER'S SAKE • 1913 • *Kb* • USA
FOR MOTHER'S SAKE • 1914 • Ray A. • UKN
FOR MY FELLOW see **PRO KAMARADA** • 1941
FOR MY LADY'S HAPPINESS • 1926 • Malins Geoffrey H. • UKN
FOR MY PAL • 1911 • *Powers* • USA
FOR MY SON see **EVLAT UGRUNA** • 1967
FOR NATIVE SOIL see **ZA RODNOU HROUDU** • 1930
FOR OLD LOVE'S SAKE • 1913 • *White Glen* • USA
FOR OLD TIME'S SAKE • 1913 • *Pilot* • USA
FOR OLD TIME'S SAKE • 1913 • Wharton Theodore • *Essanay* • USA
FOR OLD TIME'S SAKE • 1914 • *Nestor* • USA
FOR OLD TIME'S SAKE • 1948 • Barralet Paul • UKN
FOR ONE MOTH-EATEN DRACHMA see **YIA MIA TRIPIA DRAHMI** • 1968
FOR ONE SILVER DOLLAR • 1980 • Bologna Ugo • USA, ITL
FOR OUR VINES HAVE TENDER GRAPES see **OUR VINES HAVE TENDER GRAPES** • 1945
FOR PETE'S SAKE • 1934 • Meins Gus • SHT • USA
FOR PETE'S SAKE! • 1966 • Collier James F. • USA
FOR PETE'S SAKE • 1966 • Hornicka Lidia • ANM • PLN

FOR PETE'S SAKE • 1974 • Yates Peter • USA • JULY PORK BELLIES
FOR PROFESSIONAL REASONS • 1915 • King Burton L. • USA
FOR PROFESSIONAL SERVICES • 1912 • *Wadsworth William* • USA
FOR QUEEN AND COUNTRY • 1988 • Stellman Martin • UKN
FOR REMEMBRANCE • 1911 • *Reliance* • USA
FOR REPAIRS • 1914 • Powell Paul • USA
FOR REWARD OF SERVICE • 1917 • Green Alfred E. • SHT • USA
FOR SADIE'S SAKE • 1926 • Beaudine Harold • USA
FOR SAFE KEEPING • 1923 • Roach Hal • SHT • USA
FOR SALE • 1918 • Wright Fred E. • USA
FOR SALE • 1924 • Archainbaud George • USA
FOR SALE see **POULIMENOS, O** • 1967
FOR SALE, A BABY • 1909 • Melies Georges • FRN
FOR SALE A BUNGALOW • 1927 • *Sennett Mack (P)* • SHT • USA
FOR SALE -A DADDY • 1916 • *Juvenile Films* • SHT • USA
FOR SALE -A LIFE • 1912 • *Snow Marguerite* • USA
FOR SCENT-IMENTAL REASONS • 1949 • Jones Charles M. • ANS • USA
FOR SERVICES RENDERED • *Summers Cyndee* • USA
FOR SIN FADERS SKYLD • 1916 • Holger-Madsen • DNM • VEILED LADY, THE ○ FALSE EVIDENCE
FOR SIN KARLEKS SKULL • 1914 • Stiller Mauritz • SWD • BECAUSE OF HER LOVE ○ BECAUSE OF LOVE ○ STOCKBROKER, THE
FOR SINGLE SWINGERS ONLY • 1968 • Davis Don • USA • SINGLE SWINGERS ONLY
FOR SINGLES ONLY • 1968 • Dreifuss Arthur • USA
FOR SIT LANDS AERE • 1915 • Blom August • DNM • HENDES AERE ○ FOR HIS COUNTRY'S HONOUR
FOR SOVIET POWER • 1956 • Buneyev Boris • USS
FOR SUCH IS THE KINGDOM OF HEAVEN • 1913 • Buckland Warwick • UKN • CHRISTMAS STRIKE, THE
FOR SWEET CHARITY • 1916 • *Hamilton Lloyd V.* • USA
FOR SWEET CHARITY • 1917 • *Rhodes Billie* • USA
FOR TAPPERHET I TALT • 1965 • Stivell Arne • SWD
FOR TEN THOUSAND BUCKS • 1916 • Dillon John Francis?, Miller Rube? • SHT • USA
FOR THE ALLIES • 1915 • *B & C* • UKN
FOR THE CAUSE • 1912 • Cabanne W. Christy • USA
FOR THE CAUSE • 1914 • Vale Travers • USA
FOR THE CAUSE OF SUFFRAGE • 1909 • Melies Georges • FRN
FOR THE CAUSE OF THE SOUTH • 1912 • Merwin Bannister • USA
FOR THE CHILD'S SAKE • 1911 • *Revier* • USA
FOR THE CHILD'S SAKE see **KUZHANTHAIKKAGA** • 1968
FOR THE CHILD'S SAKE see **PAPAKOSAM** • 1968
FOR THE COMMON DEFENSE • 1942 • Kenward Allan • USA
FOR THE COMMONWEALTH • 1912 • *Fuller Mary* • USA
FOR THE COMMONWEALTH • 1915 • *Balboa* • USA
FOR THE CROWN • 1913 • Johnston Lorimer • USA
FOR THE DEFENCE • 1914 • *Phillips Ethel* • USA
FOR THE DEFENCE • 1916 • Reicher Frank • USA • FOR THE DEFENSE
FOR THE DEFENSE • 1922 • Powell Paul • USA
FOR THE DEFENSE • 1930 • Cromwell John • USA
FOR THE DEFENSE see **FOR THE DEFENCE** • 1916
FOR THE EMPIRE • 1914 • Shaw Harold • UKN • FOR HOME AND COUNTRY
FOR THE EMPIRE • 1916 • Pearson George • UKN
FOR THE FAMILY HONOR • 1914 • *Leonard Robert* • USA
FOR THE FIRST TIME see **POR PRIMERA VEZ** • 1967
FOR THE FIRST TIME (USA) see **SERENADE EINER GROSSEN LIEBE** • 1959
FOR THE FLAG • 1913 • Johnston Lorimer • USA
FOR THE FLAG OF FRANCE • 1911 • *Hartman Gretchen* • USA
FOR THE FLOURISH OF THE HOMELAND • 1955 • Stoyanov Yuli • DOC • BUL
FOR THE FREEDOM OF CUBA • 1914 • Turner Otis • USA
FOR THE FREEDOM OF IRELAND • 1920 • *Coleman Vincent* • USA
FOR THE FREEDOM OF THE EAST • 1918 • Lowry Ira M. • USA
FOR THE FREEDOM OF THE NATION see **ZA SVOBODU NARODA** • 1920
FOR THE FREEDOM OF THE WORLD • 1917 • Lowry Ira M., Carroll F. J. • USA
FOR THE FREEDOM OF THE WORLD • 1918 • Fielding Romaine • USA
FOR THE GIRL see **O DEVCICU** • 1918
FOR THE GIRL'S SAKE • 1910 • *Powers* • USA
FOR THE GOOD OF ALL • 1912 • *Powers* • USA
FOR THE GOOD OF HER MEN • 1912 • Dwan Allan • USA
FOR THE GOOD OF THE CAUSE • 1915 • *Nestor* • USA
FOR THE GOVERNOR'S CHAIR • 1916 • *Knickerbocker Star* • SHT • USA
FOR THE HAND OF A PRINCESS • 1904 • Fitzhamon Lewin • UKN
FOR THE HAND OF JANE • 1914 • *Shields Ernest* • USA
FOR THE HEART OF A PRINCESS • 1913 • Matthews H. C. • USA
FOR THE HEART OF THE BEAUTIFUL HELEN see **YIA TI KARDIA TIS OREAS ELENIS** • 1967
FOR THE HOME AND THE GIRL see **FOR HEMMET OCH FLICKAN** • 1925
FOR THE HONOR OF BAR X • 1915 • *Frith Vick* • USA
FOR THE HONOR OF BETTINA • 1915 • *Sampson Teddy* • USA
FOR THE HONOR OF THE 7TH • 1912 • Barker Reginald • USA
FOR THE HONOR OF THE CREW • 1915 • Earle William P. S. • USA
FOR THE HONOR OF THE FAMILY • 1912 • *Costello Maurice* • USA
FOR THE HONOR OF THE NAME • 1912 • Golden Joseph A. • USA
FOR THE HONOR OF THE TRIBE • 1912 • *Bison* • USA
FOR THE HONOUR OF BELGIUM • 1914 • Collins Edwin J.? • UKN
FOR THE HONOUR OF THE HOUSE • 1913 • Buckland Warwick? • UKN
FOR THE IMPROVEMENT OF THE INDIVIDUAL see **ZUR BESSERUNG DER PERSON** • 1982
FOR THE LAST EDITION • 1914 • Kelsey Fred A. • USA
FOR THE LITTLE LADY'S SAKE • 1908 • Fitzhamon Lewin • UKN
FOR THE LIVING see **VO IMYA ZHIZNI** • 1947
FOR THE LOVE O' LIL • 1930 • Tinling James • USA
FOR THE LOVE O' PETE • 1926 • Lantz Walter • ANS • USA
FOR THE LOVE OF A GIRL • 1912 • O'Neil Barry • USA
FOR THE LOVE OF A GIRL • 1916 • Carey Harry • SHT • USA
FOR THE LOVE OF A QUEEN see **DICTATOR, THE** • 1935
FOR THE LOVE OF A SHOWMAN • 1910 • *London Cinematograph Co.* • UKN
FOR THE LOVE OF ADA • 1972 • Baxter Ronnie • UKN
FOR THE LOVE OF AN ENEMY • 1911 • *Kalem* • USA
FOR THE LOVE OF ANNA see **LARGO RETORNO, UN** • 1974
FOR THE LOVE OF BALDY • 1914 • *Belmont Claude* • USA
FOR THE LOVE OF BENJI see **FOR LOVE OF BENJI** • 1977
FOR THE LOVE OF DANCE • 1981 • Scott Cynthia (c/d) • MTV • CND
FOR THE LOVE OF IT • 1980 • Kanter Hal • TVM • USA
FOR THE LOVE OF LUDWIG • 1932 • Harberger Emil • SHT • USA
FOR THE LOVE OF MAN see **LYUBIT CHELOVYEKA** • 1972
FOR THE LOVE OF MARY • 1948 • De Cordova Frederick • USA • MISS NUMBER PLEASE ○ WASHINGTON GIRL
FOR THE LOVE OF MIKE • 1911 • *Essanay* • USA
FOR THE LOVE OF MIKE • 1912 • *Rex* • USA
FOR THE LOVE OF MIKE • 1914 • *Kalem* • USA
FOR THE LOVE OF MIKE • 1927 • Capra Frank • USA
FOR THE LOVE OF MIKE • 1932 • Banks Monty • UKN
FOR THE LOVE OF MIKE • 1960 • Sherman George • USA • NONE BUT THE BRAVE
FOR THE LOVE OF MIKE AND ROSIE • 1916 • *Lehrman Henry* • SHT • USA
FOR THE LOVE OF PIZZA • 1972 • Smith Paul J. • ANS • USA
FOR THE LOVE OF PLEASURE • 1980 • Brown Edwin Scott • USA
FOR THE LOVE OF RED WING • 1910 • *Bison* • USA
FOR THE LOVE OF RUSTY • 1947 • Sturges John • USA
FOR THE LOVE OF TILLIE see **TILLIE'S PUNCTURED ROMANCE** • 1914
FOR THE MAN SHE LOVED • 1913 • *Thanhouser* • USA
FOR THE MAN SHE LOVED • 1913 • *Eclair* • USA
FOR THE MAN SHE LOVED • 1915 • *Trunelle Mabel* • USA
FOR THE MASTERY OF THE WORLD • 1914 • *Francis Alec B.* • USA
FOR THE MASTERY OF THE WORLD • 1914 • *Eclair* • FRN
FOR THE MIKADO • 1912 • *Takagi Taku* • USA
FOR THE PAPOOSE • 1912 • *Pathe* • USA
FOR THE PAPOOSE • 1916 • *Utah* • USA
FOR THE PEACE OF BEAR VALLEY • 1913 • *Nestor* • USA
FOR THE PEOPLE • 1914 • *Moore Matt* • USA
FOR THE QUEEN • 1911 • *Flugrath Leonie* • USA
FOR THE QUEEN'S HONOR • 1911 • *Pickford Mary* • USA
FOR THE RIGHT SOLUTION see **KUEI-MA CHIH-TO HSING** • 1981
FOR THE SAKE OF KATE • 1914 • *Reliance* • USA
FOR THE SAKE OF THE LITTLE ONES AT HOME • 1911 • Wilson Frank? • UKN
FOR THE SAKE OF THE PAPOOSE • 1912 • *Pathe* • USA
FOR THE SECRET SERVICE • 1914 • *Leonard Robert* • USA
FOR THE SERVICE • 1936 • Jones Buck • USA
FOR THE SINS OF ANOTHER • 1913 • Daly William Robert • USA
FOR THE SON OF THE HOUSE • 1913 • Henderson Dell • USA
FOR THE SOUL OF RAFAEL • 1920 • Garson Harry • USA
FOR THE SOVIET MOTHERLAND • 1937 • Muzykant R., Muzykant Yu. • USS
FOR THE SQUAW • 1911 • *Pathe* • USA
FOR THE SUNDAY EDITION • 1910 • *Imp* • USA
FOR THE TERM OF HIS NATURAL LIFE • 1908 • MacMahon Charles • ASL
FOR THE TERM OF HIS NATURAL LIFE • 1927 • Dawn Norman • ASL
FOR THE TRIBE • 1911 • *Powers* • USA
FOR THE WEARING OF THE GREEN • 1911 • *Yankee* • USA
FOR THE WEARING OF THE GREEN • 1914 • *Ray Charles* • USA
FOR THE YOUNGER SISTER see **CHELLELI KOSAM** • 1968
FOR THEM THAT TRESPASS • 1949 • Cavalcanti Alberto • UKN
FOR THIS WE FIGHT see **MACHI KARA MACHI E TSUMUJI-KAGE** • 1961
FOR THOSE I LOVED see **AU NOM DE TOUS LES MIENS** • 1983
FOR THOSE IN PERIL • 1944 • Crichton Charles • UKN
FOR THOSE UNBORN • 1914 • Cabanne W. Christy • USA
FOR THOSE WE LOVE • 1921 • Rosson Arthur • USA
FOR THOSE WHO ARE AT SEA see **SA TEKH KTO V MORE** • 1948
FOR THOSE WHO THINK YOUNG • 1964 • Martinson Leslie H. • USA
FOR TORS SKYLD see **KAMERATER** • 1982
FOR TRIVIAL REASONS see **DI'ASIMANDON AFORMIN** • 1974
FOR TWO PINS • 1914 • *Lubin* • USA
FOR UNCLE SAM'S NAVY • 1916 • *Stanley Edwin* • USA
FOR US see **ORA PRO NOBIS: OR, THE POOR ORPHAN'S LAST PRAYER** • 1901
FOR US THE LIVING • 1982 • Schultz Michael • TVM • USA • FOR US THE LIVING: THE MEDGAR EVERS STORY
FOR US THE LIVING: THE MEDGAR EVERS STORY see **FOR US THE LIVING** • 1982
FOR VALOR • 1972 • Trenchard-Smith Brian • DOC • ASL
FOR VALOUR • 1912 • Dawley J. Searle • USA
FOR VALOUR • 1917 • Parker Albert • USA
FOR VALOUR • 1928 • Samuelson G. B. • UKN
FOR VALOUR • 1937 • Walls Tom • UKN
FOR VALUE RECEIVED • 1916 • *Stull Walter* • USA
FOR VANSKAPS SKULL • 1965 • Abramson Hans • SWD • JUST LIKE FRIENDS ○ FOR FRIENDSHIP
FOR WASHINGTON • 1911 • *Thanhouser* • USA
FOR WHOM DO WE LOVE? see **DARE NO TAME NI AISURUKA** • 1971
FOR WHOM THE BELL TOLLS • 1943 • Wood Sam • USA
FOR WHOM THE BELL TOLLS • 1959 • Frankenheimer John • MTV • USA
FOR WHOM THE BIG BELL TOLLS see **YIA PION HTIPA I KOUDHOUNA** • 1968
FOR WHOM THE BULLS TOIL • 1953 • Kinney Jack • ANS • USA
FOR WHOM THE LARKS SING see **AKIKET A PACSIRTA ELKISER** • 1959
FOR WIVES ONLY • 1926 • Heerman Victor • USA
FOR WOMAN'S FAVOR • 1924 • Lund O. A. C. • USA
FOR YOU ALONE • 1945 • Faithfull Geoffrey • UKN
FOR YOU ALONE (UKN) see **WHEN YOU'RE IN LOVE** • 1937
FOR YOU I DIE • 1947 • Reinhardt John • USA
FOR YOU MR. BELL • 1972 • Canning William • CND • HOMAGE A M. BELL
FOR YOU MY BOY • 1923 • Roubert William L. • USA
FOR YOUR COUNTRY see **FOR FADERNESLANDET** • 1913
FOR YOUR EDIFICATION see **MIHEZTARTAS VEGETT** • 1971
FOR YOUR ENTERTAINMENT NOS.1-4 • 1952 • Bell Colin • SER • UKN
FOR YOUR EYES ONLY • 1981 • Glen John • UKN
FOR YOUR FREEDOM AND OURS see **ZA WASZA I NASZA WOLNOSC** • 1968
FOR YOUR LOVE ONLY • 1976 • Petersen Wolfgang • FRG
FOR YOUR PLEASURE see **SLUMRANDE TONER** • 1978
FOR YOUR SAKE, ANCA see **DE DRAGUL TAU ANCA** • 1984
FORA DAS GRADES • 1972 • Araujo Astolfo • BRZ
FORAGER, THE • 1910 • Olcott Sidney • USA
FORAGING • 1911 • *Costello Maurice* • USA
FORAGING ON THE ENEMY • 1912 • *Champion* • USA
FORAJIDOS, LOS • 1962 • Cortes Fernando • MXC
FORARSDAG I HELVEDE, EN • 1976 • Leth Jorgen • DNM • SUNDAY IN HELL, A
FORASTERA, LA • 1951 • Roman Antonio • SPN
FORASTERO VENGADOR, EL • 1966 • Fernandez Fernando • MXC
FORBID THEM NOT • 1962 • Kimble Robert L. • USA
FORBIDDEN • 1919 • Weber Lois, Smalley Phillips • USA • FORBIDDEN BOX, THE
FORBIDDEN • 1932 • Capra Frank • USA
FORBIDDEN • 1949 • King George • UKN • LADY WAS TO DIE, A ○ SCARLET HEAVEN
FORBIDDEN • 1953 • Mate Rudolph • USA • DRIFTING
FORBIDDEN • 1986 • Page Anthony • TVM • USA, FRG, UKN • VERSTECKT (FRG)
FORBIDDEN see **PROIBITO** • 1955
FORBIDDEN, THE • 1966 • Andrews Benjamin • FRN
FORBIDDEN ADVENTURE • 1934 • Cook J. C. • USA • INYAH, THE JUNGLE GODDESS
FORBIDDEN ADVENTURE, THE • 1915 • Swickard Charles • USA • CITY OF THE DEAD
FORBIDDEN ADVENTURE (UKN) see **NEWLY RICH** • 1931
FORBIDDEN AFFAIR see **KINDAN NO JOJI** • 1967
FORBIDDEN ALLIANCE see **BARRETTS OF WIMPOLE STREET, THE** • 1934
FORBIDDEN AREA • 1956 • Frankenheimer John • MTV • USA
FORBIDDEN BACCHANAL, THE • 1981 • Verstappen Wim • NTH
FORBIDDEN BOX, THE see **FORBIDDEN** • 1919
FORBIDDEN BREW • 1920 • Moore Vin • SHT • USA
FORBIDDEN CARGO • 1925 • Buckingham Thomas • USA • DANGEROUS CARGO (UKN)
FORBIDDEN CARGO • 1954 • French Harold • UKN
FORBIDDEN CARGO see **QUEEN WAS IN THE PARLOUR, THE** • 1927
FORBIDDEN CARGOES • 1925 • Granville Fred Leroy • UKN
FORBIDDEN CASTLE see **BINAN-JO** • 1959
FORBIDDEN CHRIST see **CRISTO PROIBITO** • 1951
FORBIDDEN CITY, THE • 1918 • Franklin Sidney A. • USA
FORBIDDEN COMPANY • 1932 • Thorpe Richard • USA
FORBIDDEN DECAMERON (UKN) see **DECAMERONE PROIBITO** • 1972
FORBIDDEN DREAMS see **SMRT KRASNYCH SRNCU** • 1987
FORBIDDEN FEMININITY see **SEXY PROIBITISSIMO** • 1963
FORBIDDEN FIRE • 1919 • Rosson Arthur • USA
FORBIDDEN FLESH: AS SEEN FROM A HAYLOFT IN THE HILLS • 1968 • *Mahon Barry* • USA
FORBIDDEN FLOWER GARDEN see **JOSHIDAISEI NO KINJIRARETA HANAZONO** • 1967
FORBIDDEN FRUIT • 1909 • *Pathe* • USA
FORBIDDEN FRUIT • 1916 • Abramson Ivan • USA
FORBIDDEN FRUIT • 1921 • De Mille Cecil B. • USA
FORBIDDEN FRUIT • 1988 • Shapiro Ken • USA
FORBIDDEN FRUIT see **FRUIT DEFENDU, LE** • 1952
FORBIDDEN FRUIT, THE see **KINDAN NO KAJITSU** • 1968
FORBIDDEN GAME, THE • 1917 • Millarde Harry • SHT • USA
FORBIDDEN GAMES (USA) see **JEUX INTERDITS** • 1948
FORBIDDEN GRASS • 1928 • Eldridge E. M. • USA
FORBIDDEN GROUND • 1969 • Gabor Pal • HNG
FORBIDDEN HEAVEN • 1936 • Barker Reginald • USA
FORBIDDEN HOURS • 1928 • Beaumont Harry • USA
FORBIDDEN IS IN FASHION, THE see **PROHIBIDO ESTA DE MODA, LO** • 1968
FORBIDDEN ISLAND • 1959 • Griffith Charles B. • USA
FORBIDDEN JOURNEY • 1949 • Jarvis Richard, Maiden Cecil • CND
FORBIDDEN JUNGLE • 1950 • Tansey Robert • USA
FORBIDDEN JUSTICE • Young Robert William • USA
FORBIDDEN LAND, THE see **JUNGLE JIM IN THE FORBIDDEN LAND** • 1952
FORBIDDEN LIPS see **KINJIRARETA KUCHIBIRU** • 1957
FORBIDDEN LOVE • 1921 • Van Loan Philip • USA • WOMEN WHO WAIT
FORBIDDEN LOVE • 1982 • Stern Steven Hilliard • TVM • USA
FORBIDDEN LOVE • 1989 • Fisher Jack • USA
FORBIDDEN LOVE see **QUEEN WAS IN THE PARLOUR, THE** • 1927
FORBIDDEN LOVE see **FREAKS** • 1932
FORBIDDEN LOVE see **MIZU DE KAKARETA MONOGATARI** • 1965
FORBIDDEN LOVE see **CAMBIO DE SEXO** • 1977
FORBIDDEN LOVE AFFAIR see **ASFALTO SELVAGEM** • 1964
FORBIDDEN LOVE (USA) see **HOMME DU NIGER, L'** • 1939

FORBIDDEN LOVER • 1923 • Deverich Nat C. • USA
FORBIDDEN LOVER, THE • 1898 • Williamson James • UKN
FORBIDDEN MELODY see **MELODIA PROHIBIDA** • 1934
FORBIDDEN MOON • 1953 • *Reed Roland (P)* • MTV • USA
FORBIDDEN MUSIC (USA) see **LAND WITHOUT MUSIC** • 1936
FORBIDDEN ON WEDDING-NIGHT see **MAMNU FI LEILET EL DOKHLA** • 1976
FORBIDDEN PARADISE • 1924 • Lubitsch Ernst • USA
FORBIDDEN PARADISE see **HURRICANE** • 1979
FORBIDDEN PASSAGE • 1941 • Zinnemann Fred • SHT • USA
FORBIDDEN PATH, THE • 1918 • Edwards J. Gordon • USA
FORBIDDEN PATHS • 1917 • Thornby Robert T. • USA
FORBIDDEN PLANET • 1956 • Wilcox Fred M. • USA
FORBIDDEN PLEASURE • 1969 • *Garva Productions* • USA
FORBIDDEN PLEASURES • 1986 • Leblanc Michel • SWT
FORBIDDEN RANGE, THE • 1923 • Hart Neal • USA
FORBIDDEN RELATIONS see **VISSZAESOK** • 1983
FORBIDDEN ROOM, THE • 1914 • Dwan Allan • USA
FORBIDDEN ROOM, THE • 1919 • Reynolds Lynn • USA
FORBIDDEN ROOM, THE see **STANZA DEL VESCOVO, LA** • 1977
FORBIDDEN SCOOP see **HIJI TOSHI** • 1960
FORBIDDEN SOIL • 1920 • *Coburn Wallace* • SHT • USA
FORBIDDEN SONGS (USA) see **ZAKAZANE PIOSENKI** • 1947
FORBIDDEN STEPS see **SEUILS INTERDITS** • 1972
FORBIDDEN STREET (USA) see **BRITANNIA MEWS** • 1948
FORBIDDEN SUBJECTS see **KINJITE** • 1989
FORBIDDEN SUN see **BULLDANCE** • 1989
FORBIDDEN TALES OF TOM THUMB see **HISTORIAS PROHIBIDAS DE PULGARCITO** • 1979
FORBIDDEN TERRITORY • 1934 • Rosen Phil • UKN
FORBIDDEN THING, THE • 1920 • Dwan Allan • USA
FORBIDDEN TRAIL, THE • 1923 • Bradbury Robert North • USA
FORBIDDEN TRAIL, THE • 1932 • Hillyer Lambert • USA
FORBIDDEN TRAILS • 1920 • Dunlap Scott R. • USA
FORBIDDEN TRAILS • 1928 • Horner Robert J. • USA
FORBIDDEN TRAILS • 1942 • Bradbury Robert North • USA
FORBIDDEN VALLEY • 1920 • Blackton J. Stuart • USA
FORBIDDEN VALLEY • 1938 • Gittens Wyndham • USA
FORBIDDEN WATERS • 1926 • Hale Alan • USA
FORBIDDEN WAY, THE • 1912 • *Walthall Henry B.* • USA
FORBIDDEN WAY, THE • 1913 • *Essanay* • USA
FORBIDDEN WAY, THE see **CYTHEREA** • 1924
FORBIDDEN WOMAN, THE • 1920 • Garson Harry • USA
FORBIDDEN WOMAN, THE • 1927 • Stein Paul L. • USA
FORBIDDEN WOMEN see **DONNE PROIBITE** • 1953
FORBIDDEN WORLD • 1982 • Holzman Allan • USA • MUTANT
FORBIDDEN WORLD see **GALAXY OF TERROR** • 1981
FORBIDDEN ZONE • 1980 • Elfman Richard • USA
FORBIN PROJECT, THE • 1969 • Sargent Joseph • USA • COLOSSUS THE FORBIN PROJECT ○ COLOSSUS 1980 ○ DAY THE WORLD CHANGED HANDS, THE
FORBODINGS see **PREDTUCHA** • 1947
FORBRYDELSENS ELEMENT • 1984 • von Trier Lars • DNM • ELEMENT OF CRIME, THE
FORBRYDERS LIV OG LEVNED, EN • 1916 • Christian • DNM • LIFE AND TIMES OF A CRIMINAL, THE ○ FORBRYDERS MEMOIRER, EN ○ MEMOIRS OF A CRIMINAL, THE
FORBRYDERS MEMOIRER, EN see **FORBRYDERS LIV OG LEVNED, EN** • 1916
FORCA AEREA, ESSA DESCONHECIDA • 1956 • Mendes Joao • SHT • PRT
FORCA AEREA NO ULTRAMAR • 1962 • Simoes Quirino • SHT • PRT
FORCA DE XANGO, A • 1980 • Cavalcanti Ibere • BRZ • FORCE OF XANGO, THE
FORCA PER DJANGO, UNA • 1972 • Pellegrini Giuseppe • ITL
FORCATS DER LA MER, LES see **MON AMI TIM** • 1932
FORCATS D'HONNEUR • 1946 • de Meyst E. G. • FRN
FORCE see **TAQAT KA TOOFAN** • 1988
FORCE 8 see **FORCE "8" OU LE PRIX DE LA CASSE** • 1972
FORCE "8" OU LE PRIX DE LA CASSE • 1972 • Sisser Pierre • FRN, SPN • FORCE 8
FORCE 10 FROM NAVARONE • 1978 • Hamilton Guy • USA, UKN
FORCE AND CONSCIENCE see **GEWALT UND GEWISSEN** • 1967
FORCE BEYOND, THE • 1978 • Sachs William • USA
FORCE BEYOND, THE see **EVIL, THE** • 1978
FORCE CENTRIFUGE, LA • Cantagrel Marc • DOC • FRN
FORCE DE LA VIE, LA • 1920 • Leprince Rene • FRN
FORCE DE L'ARGENT, LA • 1914 • Perret Leonce • FRN
FORCE DE L'ENFANT, LA • 1908 • Cohl Emile • ANS • FRN
FORCE DOIT RESTER A LA LOI • 1899 • Melies Georges • FRN • SLIPPERY BURGLAR, THE
FORCE ET LE DROIT, LA • 1970 • Carne Marcel • FRN
FORCE FIVE • 1975 • Grauman Walter • TVM • USA • FINAL TACTIC
FORCE: FIVE • 1981 • Clouse Robert • USA
FORCE FOUR • 1975 • Fink Michael • USA
FORCE MAJEURE • 1989 • Jolivet Pierre • FRN
FORCE OF ARMS • 1951 • Curtiz Michael • USA
FORCE OF DARKNESS • 1985 • Hauge Alan • USA
FORCE OF DEATH see **DEATH FORCE** • 1978
FORCE OF DESTINY, THE see **FORZA DEL DESTINO, LA** • 1950
FORCE OF DESTINY, THE see **MOC OSUDU** • 1969
FORCE OF EVIL • 1948 • Polonsky Abraham • USA
FORCE OF EXAMPLE, THE • 1915 • Wilson Ben • USA
FORCE OF IMPULSE • 1961 • Swimmer Saul • USA
FORCE OF ONE, A • 1979 • Aaron Paul • USA
FORCE OF XANGO, THE see **FORCA DE XANGO, A** • 1980
FORCE ON THUNDER MOUNTAIN, THE • 1978 • Good Peter B. • USA
FORCE SASQUATCH SERVICE • 1984 • Woodland James • CND
FORCED BRAVERY • 1913 • Nicholls George, Sennett Mack (Spv) • USA
FORCED CONFESSION, THE • 1912 • Noy Wilfred • UKN
FORCED ENTRY see **LAST VICTIM, THE** • 1975
FORCED IMPACT see **ROMA VIOLENTA** • 1975
FORCED INTO MATRIMONY • 1918 • *Jaxon* • USA
FORCED LABOUR see **KATORGA** • 1928
FORCED LANDING • 1935 • Brown Melville • USA
FORCED LANDING • 1941 • Wiles Gordon • USA
FORCED LANDING see **NODLANDING** • 1952
FORCED LANDING ON PLANET EGGATRON • 1968 • Yeatman Hoyt • ANS • USA
FORCED MARCH • 1989 • King Rick • USA
FORCED TO BE STYLISH • 1914 • *Princess* • USA
FORCED TO CONSENT see **THOUGHTLESS BEAUTY, A** • 1908
FORCED VENGEANCE • 1982 • Fargo James • USA
FORCED WITNESS see **EDUT ME ONESS** • 1984
FORCEFUL YEARS, THE see **ZESTOKE GODINE** • 1980
FORCES OCCULTES • 1943 • Mamy Jean • FRN
FORCES OF EVIL • 1914 • *Leading Players* • USA • DOMINANT WILL, THE
FORCES OF INDUCTION, THE • 1969 • Evans David • UKN
FORCES' SWEETHEART • 1953 • Rogers Maclean • UKN
FORCIER: "EN ATTENDANT.." • 1990 • Berthiaume Marc Andre • DOC • CND
FORCING DAD'S CONSENT • 1914 • Beggs Lee • USA
FORCING THE FORCE • 1914 • *Eclectic* • USA
FORCING THE ISSUE • 1913 • *Nestor* • USA
FORD see **FORD: THE MAN AND THE MACHINE** • 1987
FORD: HIS MISTRESS AND HIS MACHINE see **FORD: THE MAN AND THE MACHINE** • 1987
FORD: THE MAN AND THE MACHINE • 1987 • Eastman Allan • TVM • USA • FORD: HIS MISTRESS AND HIS MACHINE ○ FORD
FORD WORLD • 1960 • Stevens Frank • UKN
FORDINGTON TWINS, THE • 1920 • Kellino W. P. • UKN
FORDS ON WATER • 1983 • Bliss Barry • UKN
FORE see **LESSON IN GOLF, A** • 1932
FORE AND AFT • 1916 • Myll Louis • SHT • USA
FORECAST, THE • 1915 • Otto Henry • USA
FORECLOSURE, THE • 1912 • Dwan Allan • USA
FOREIGN AFFAIR, A • 1948 • Wilder Billy • USA
FOREIGN AFFAIRES • 1935 • Walls Tom • UKN
FOREIGN AFFAIRS: 25 YEARS OF AUSTRALIAN MUSIC • 1984 • Cox Peter • MTV • ASL
FOREIGN AGENT • 1942 • Beaudine William • USA
FOREIGN BODY • 1987 • Neame Ronald • UKN
FOREIGN CORRESPONDENT • 1940 • Hitchcock Alfred • USA
FOREIGN CURRENCY • 1989 • Bani-Etemad Rakhshan • IRN
FOREIGN DEVILS • 1927 • Van Dyke W. S. • USA
FOREIGN EXCHANGE • 1969 • Baker Roy Ward • TVM • UKN
FOREIGN GIFT see **SOGHAT-E-FARANG** • 1967
FOREIGN HARBOUR see **FRAMMANDE HAMN** • 1948
FOREIGN INTRIGUE • 1956 • Reynolds Sheldon • USA
FOREIGN INVASION, THE • 1912 • *Imp* • USA
FOREIGN LEGION, THE • 1928 • Sloman Edward • USA
FOREIGN NIGHTS • 1990 • Musallam Izidore K. • CND
FOREIGN SPIES, THE (USA) see **DETECTIVE FINN AND THE FOREIGN SPIES** • 1914
FOREIGN SPY, THE • 1911 • Haldane Bert • UKN
FOREIGN SPY, THE • 1912 • Ricketts Thomas • USA
FOREIGN SPY, THE • 1913 • Calvert Charles? • UKN
FOREIGN SPY, THE • 1913 • Reid Wallace • *American* • USA
FOREIGN STUDENTS see **LIU HSUEH-SHENG** • 1977
FOREIGN TONGUE • 1970 • Sharpe Mal • SHT • USA • FRENCH VOCABULARY REVIEW, A
FOREIGNER see **BIDESIYA** • 1968
FOREIGNER, THE • 1928 • Mayo Archie • SHT • USA
FOREIGNER, THE • 1978 • Poe Amos • USA
FOREIGNER, THE see **GOD'S CRUCIBLE** • 1920
FOREIGNERS • 1975 • Eastman Allan • MTV • CND, UKN
FOREIGNERS see **KOCKSGATAN 48** • 1972
FORELSKET I KOBENHAVN • 1960 • Henriksen Finn • DNM • IN LOVE WITH COPENHAGEN
FOREMAN, THE • 1910 • *Selig* • USA
FOREMAN HASSAN see **OSTA HASSEN, EL** • 1952
FOREMAN OF BAR Z RANCH, THE • 1924 • *Mix Tom* • USA
FOREMAN OF THE BAR Z RANCH, THE • 1915 • Mix Tom • USA
FOREMAN OF THE JURY, THE • 1913 • Sennett Mack • USA
FOREMAN WENT TO FRANCE, THE • 1942 • Frend Charles • UKN • SOMEWHERE IN FRANCE (USA)
FOREMAN'S BRIDE, THE • 1911 • *Bison* • USA
FOREMAN'S CHOICE, THE • 1915 • Mix Tom • USA
FOREMAN'S COURAGE, THE • 1911 • *Bison* • USA
FOREMAN'S COUSIN, THE • 1912 • *Anderson Broncho Billy* • USA
FOREMAN'S FIXUP, THE see **RANCH TENOR, THE** • 1911
FOREMAN'S MINE, THE • 1911 • *Bison* • USA
FOREMAN'S TREACHERY, THE • 1913 • Brabin Charles J. • USA, UKN
FOREPLAY • 1975 • Avildsen John G., McCarty Robert, Malmuth Bruce, Ross Vinnie • USA • PRESIDENT'S WOMEN, THE
FOREPLAY see **SON OF ALVIN** • 1984
FOREPLAY: THE PREQUEL see **ALVIN RIDES AGAIN** • 1974
FORERUNNER, THE • 1957 • Heyer John • DOC • ASL
FOREST, THE • 1965 • Spotton John • CND
FOREST, THE • 1983 • Jones Don • USA • TERROR IN THE FOREST
FOREST, THE see **WOODS, THE** • 1931
FOREST, THE see **LES** • 1953
FOREST, THE see **KAADU** • 1974
FOREST DRAGON • 1949 • Felstead Bert • UKN • GINGER NUTT'S FOREST DRAGON
FOREST FANTASY • 1952 • Kneitel Seymour • ANS • USA
FOREST FRUIT see **FRUCTE DE PADURE** • 1984
FOREST HAVOC • 1926 • Paton Stuart • USA
FOREST IS OUR INHERITANCE, THE see **SKOGEN AR VAR ARVIDEL** • 1944
FOREST KING, THE • 1922 • Hartman F. G. • USA
FOREST MAIDEN, THE see **PADUREANCA** • 1988
FOREST MURMURS • 1947 • Vorkapich Slavko • SHT • USA
FOREST NYMPH, THE • 1917 • Leonard Robert Z.? • SHT • USA
FOREST OF FEAR see **BLOODEATERS** • 1980
FOREST OF HANGED MEN see **PADUREA SPINZURATILOR** • 1965
FOREST OF HANGING FOXES • 1986 • Suikkari Jouko • FNL
FOREST OF KNIGHTS see **WU-LIN WAI SHIH** • 1978
FOREST OF NO ESCAPE see **KAJITSU NO NAI MORI** • 1964
FOREST OF THE FALCONS see **KEKVERCSEK ERDEJEBEN, A** • 1954
FOREST OF THE HANGED, THE see **PADUREA SPINZURATILOR** • 1965
FOREST ON THE HILL, THE • 1919 • Hepworth Cecil M. • UKN
FOREST PONY • 1946 • Leacock Philip • UKN
FOREST RANGER, THE • 1910 • *Anderson Broncho Billy* • USA
FOREST RANGER, THE • 1912 • Fielding Romaine • USA
FOREST RANGERS • 1965 • Haldane Don • SER • CND
FOREST RANGERS, THE • 1942 • Marshall George • USA
FOREST RANGER'S DAUGHTER, THE • 1909 • Salter Harry • USA
FOREST RENEWAL NOW see **POUR UNE FORET NOUVELLE** • 1985
FOREST RING, THE • 1930 • Markham Kyra, Gaither David
FOREST RIVALS • 1919 • Hoyt Harry O. • USA
FOREST ROMANCE, A • 1911 • *Reliance* • USA
FOREST ROMANCE, A • 1913 • Montgomery Frank E. • USA
FOREST ROSE, THE • 1912 • Marston Theodore • USA
FOREST RUNNERS, THE • 1920 • Jaccard Jacques • SHT • USA
FOREST STORY see **LYESNAYA BYL** • 1927
FOREST SYMPHONY • 1967 • Zguridi Alexander • DOC • USS
FOREST THIEVES, THE • 1914 • Mackley Arthur • USA
FOREST VAMPIRES, THE • 1914 • Hamilton G. P.? • USA
FOREST WATCHERS, THE • 1974 • Raymont Peter • DOC • CND
FORESTALLED (UKN) see **TWO-FISTED RANGERS** • 1940
FORESTER MADE KING, A (USA) see **BERNARD LE BUCHERON** • 1907
FORESTER'S PLEA, THE • 1911 • *Essanay* • USA
FORESTER'S REMEDY, THE • 1908 • *Melies* • USA
FORESTER'S REMEDY, THE (?) see **JUGEMENT DU GARDE CHAMPETRE** • 1908
FORESTER'S SONG see **DO LESICKA NA CEKANOU** • 1966
FORESTER'S SWEETHEART, THE • 1910 • *Bison* • USA
FORESTS OF QUEBEC, THE see **QUEBEC FORESTIER, LE** • 1984
FORET • 1970 • Rechiche Majid • SHT • MRC
FORET, LA • 1965-66 • Garceau Raymond • DCS • CND
FORET BIENFAISANTE, LA • 1942-43 • Tessier Albert • DCS • CND
FORET DE L'ADIEU, LA • 1952 • Habib Ralph • FRN
FORET DES HOMMES ROUGES, THE • 1959 • Leherissey Jean • SHT • FRN
FORET EST UN TRESOR, LA see **TREASURE OF THE FOREST** • 1958
FORET QUI ECOUTE, LA • 1913 • Desfontaines Henri • FRN
FORET QUI TUE, LA • Le Somptier Rene • BLG
FORET SACREE • 1954 • Gaisseau Pierre-Dominique • DOC • FRN
FORET SECRETE D'AFRIQUE • 1968 • Sielmann Heinz, Brandt Henry • DOC • BLG • SECRET AFRICAN FOREST
FOREVER • 1921 • Fitzmaurice George • USA • GREAT ROMANCE, THE ○ PETER IBBETSON
FOREVER • 1978 • Korty John • USA
FOREVER • 1988 • Khouri Walter Hugo • BRZ
FOREVER see **ILAL ABAD** • 1941
FOREVER see **MAGPAKAILAN MAN** • 1968
FOREVER AFTER • 1926 • Weight F. Harmon • USA
FOREVER AMBER • 1947 • Preminger Otto • USA
FOREVER AND A DAY • 1943 • Lloyd Frank, Stevenson Robert, Hardwicke Cedric, Wilcox Herbert, Goulding Edmund, Clair Rene, Saville Victor • USA, UKN
FOREVER AND BEYOND • 1982 • Flood Thomas • USA
FOREVER BE MINE see **KIMI SHINITAMAU KOTO NAKARE** • 1954
FOREVER DARLING • 1955 • Hall Alexander • USA
FOREVER ENGLAND see **BROWN ON RESOLUTION** • 1935
FOREVER EVIL • 1987 • Evans Roger • USA
FOREVER FAITHFUL see **DAY OF RECKONING** • 1933
FOREVER FEMALE • 1953 • Rapper Irving • USA
FOREVER FREE • 1983 • *Moss Carlton* • USA
FOREVER IN LOVE (UKN) see **PRIDE OF THE MARINES** • 1945
FOREVER, LULU • 1987 • Kollek Amos • USA
FOREVER MY LOVE see **SISSI** • 1956
FOREVER MY LOVE see **SISSI, DIE JUNGE KAISERIN** • 1956
FOREVER MY LOVE see **SISSI SCHICKSALJAHRE EINER KAISERIN** • 1957
FOREVER YOUNG • 1984 • Drury David • UKN
FOREVER YOUNG, FOREVER FREE (USA) see **'E LOLLIPOP** • 1975
FOREVER YOURS • 1944 • Nigh William • USA • RIGHT TO LIVE, THE (UKN) ○ THEY SHALL HAVE FAITH
FOREVER YOURS see **AMAZING MRS. HOLLIDAY, THE** • 1943
FOREVER YOURS see **HUB ILAL ABAD** • 1958
FOREVER YOURS, MONTGOMERY CLIFT • 1990 • Peck Ron • UKN
FOREVER YOURS (USA) see **FORGET-ME-NOT** • 1936
FORFAITURE • 1937 • L'Herbier Marcel • FRN • CHEAT, THE
FORFEIT, THE • 1919 • Powell Frank • USA
FORFEJLET SPRING, ET see **HOJT SPIL** • 1913
FORFOLGELSEN • 1981 • Breien Anja • NRW, SWD • WITCH HUNT, THE
FORGED BRIDE, THE • 1920 • Gerrard Douglas • USA
FORGED DISPATCH, THE • 1911 • *Imp* • USA
FORGED PASSPORT • 1939 • Auer John H. • USA
FORGED TESTAMENT, THE • 1915 • Nicholls George • USA
FORGED WILL, THE (UKN) see **BLAZING TRAIL, THE** • 1949
FORGER, THE • 1928 • Samuelson G. B. • UKN
FORGER, THE (UKN) see **PRAIRIE RAIDERS** • 1947
FORGER OF LONDON, THE (USA) see **FALSCHER VON LONDON, DER** • 1961
FORGERONS • 1895 • Lumiere Louis • FRN
FORGERONS, LES • 1896 • Melies Georges • FRN • BLACKSMITH IN HIS WORKSHOP
FORGERS OF PEACE see **FORJADORES DE LA PAZ** • 1962
FORGERY, THE see **FALSCHUNG, DIE** • 1981
FORGERY OF THE £1 NOTES, THE • 1916 • Batley Ethyle • UKN
FORGERY (UKN) see **SOUTHSIDE 1-1000** • 1950
FORGES • 1956 • Delvaux Andre, Brismee Jean, Bettendorf Andre • DOC • BLG
FORGET IF YOU CAN • 1987 • Bossilkov Nikolai • BUL

FORGET IT JACK • 1974 • Duckworth Martin • DOC • CND
FORGET-ME-NOT • 1920 • McGowan Robert • SHT • USA
FORGET-ME-NOT • 1922 • Van Dyke W. S. • USA
FORGET-ME-NOT • 1936 • Korda Zoltan, Irving Stanley • UKN • FOREVER YOURS (USA) ○ LULLABY
FORGET-ME-NOT • 1986 • Michel Franz • SWT
FORGET-ME-NOT see **FORGET-ME-NOTS** • 1917
FORGET-ME-NOT see **VERGISS MEIN NICHT** • 1935
FORGET-ME-NOTS • 1917 • Chautard Emile • USA • FORGET-ME-NOT
FORGET-ME-NUTS • 1967 • Culhane Shamus • ANS • USA
FORGET SNYDER! see **VERGISS SNEIDER!** • 1987
FORGET VENICE see **DIMENTICARE VENEZIA** • 1979
FORGETFUL FLOSSIE • 1913 • *White Pearl* • USA
FORGETTING • 1914 • *Grandin Ethel* • USA
FORGING AHEAD • 1933 • Walker Norman • UKN
FORGIVE AND FORGET • 1923 • Mitchell Howard M. • USA
FORGIVE ME see **AFFET BENI** • 1967
FORGIVE ME FOR YOUR PORTRAYAL see **PERDOA-ME POR ME TRAIRES** • 1986
FORGIVE ME, MY GOD see **AFFET BENI ALLAHIM** • 1968
FORGIVE ME, SON • 1937 • Peon Ramon • MXC
FORGIVE US OUR TRESPASSES • 1912 • *Melies* • USA
FORGIVE US OUR TRESPASSES • 1913 • *Thanhouser* • USA
FORGIVE US OUR TRESPASSES • 1919 • MacBean L. C. • UKN
FORGIVE US OUR TRESPASSES see **PARDONNEZ NOS OFFENCES** • 1956
FORGIVEN • 1910 • *Centaur* • USA
FORGIVEN • 1910 • *Selig* • USA
FORGIVEN • 1910 • *Defender* • USA
FORGIVEN IN DEATH • 1911 • *Essanay* • USA
FORGIVEN OR THE JACK O'DIAMONDS • 1914 • Daly William Robert • USA
FORGIVEN SINNER, THE (USA) see **LEON MORIN, PRETRE** • 1961
FORGIVING HEART, THE see **HARUBIYORI** • 1967
FORGOTTEN • 1909 • *Urban-Eclipse* • USA
FORGOTTEN • 1911 • Brooke Van Dyke • USA
FORGOTTEN • 1933 • Thorpe Richard • USA
FORGOTTEN see **RIP VAN WINKLE** • 1914
FORGOTTEN, THE • 1989 • Keach James • USA
FORGOTTEN BABIES • 1933 • McGowan Robert • SHT • USA
FORGOTTEN CHILDREN see **WASURERARETA KORA** • 1949
FORGOTTEN CINEMA • 1967 • Buckley Anthony • DOC • ASL
FORGOTTEN CITY OF THE PLANET OF THE APES • 1974 • *Mcdowall Roddy* • MTV • USA
FORGOTTEN COMMANDMENTS • 1932 • Gasnier Louis J., Schorr William • USA
FORGOTTEN COVE, THE see **CALETA OLVIDIDA, LA** • 1958
FORGOTTEN CREEK, THE see **CALETA OLVIDIDA, LA** • 1958
FORGOTTEN DOLL, THE • Hempel Johannes • ANM • GDR
FORGOTTEN FACES • 1928 • Schertzinger Victor • USA
FORGOTTEN FACES • 1936 • Dupont E. A. • USA • SOMETHING TO LIVE FOR
FORGOTTEN FACES see **LISMONIMENA PROSSOPA** • 1946
FORGOTTEN FACES, THE • 1961 • Watkins Peter • UKN
FORGOTTEN GIRLS • 1940 • Rosen Phil • USA
FORGOTTEN HEROES • 1989 • Marino Jack • USA
FORGOTTEN II, THE see **ZABORAVLJENI II** • 1989
FORGOTTEN LATCHKEY, THE • 1913 • Ince Ralph • USA
FORGOTTEN LAW, THE • 1922 • Horne James W. • USA
FORGOTTEN LETTER, THE • 1913 • *Nestor* • USA
FORGOTTEN LONELINESS • 1965 • Lofven Chris • SHT • ASL
FORGOTTEN MAN, THE • 1941 • Roush Leslie • SHT • USA
FORGOTTEN MAN, THE • 1971 • Grauman Walter • USA
FORGOTTEN MELODY, THE • 1913 • *Broncho* • USA
FORGOTTEN MELODY, THE see **FORLORADE MELODIEN, DEN** • 1957
FORGOTTEN MEN, THE • 1934 • Lee Norman • UKN
FORGOTTEN MOTHER • 1990 • Amato Adrienne • DCS • CND
FORGOTTEN ONES, THE see **OLVIDADOS, LOS** • 1950
FORGOTTEN PARALLEL, THE see **HOW SLEEP THE BRAVE** • 1981
FORGOTTEN POCKETBOOK, THE • 1912 • *Lubin* • USA
FORGOTTEN PRAYER, THE • 1916 • Borzage Frank • SHT • USA
FORGOTTEN STEP, THE • 1938 • Fenton Leslie • SHT • USA
FORGOTTEN SUMMER • 1970 • Rennie Howard • SAF
FORGOTTEN SWEETIES • 1927 • Roach Hal • SHT • USA
FORGOTTEN TREASURE • 1943 • Lee Sammy • SHT • USA
FORGOTTEN TUNE FOR THE FLUTE, A • 1987 • Ryazanov Eldar • USS
FORGOTTEN VICTORY • 1939 • Zinnemann Fred • SHT • USA • MARK CARLETON
FORGOTTEN VILLAGE, THE • 1941 • Kline Herbert • DOC • USA
FORGOTTEN VOWS (UKN) see **ROSE OF KILDARE, THE** • 1927
FORGOTTEN WAR, THE see **GUERRA OLVIDADA, LA** • 1967
FORGOTTEN WAR, THE see **GUERRE OUBLIEE, LA** • 1988
FORGOTTEN WARRIOR, THE • 1986 • Cacas Nick C., Ordonez Charles • PHL
FORGOTTEN WATCH, THE • 1909 • *Vitagraph* • USA
FORGOTTEN WOMAN • 1921 • Frame Park • USA
FORGOTTEN WOMAN • 1939 • Young Harold • USA
FORGOTTEN WOMEN • 1913 • *Kerrigan J. Warren* • USA
FORGOTTEN WOMEN • 1932 • Thorpe Richard • USA
FORGOTTEN WOMEN • 1949 • Beaudine William • USA
FORGOTTEN WOMEN (UKN) see **ISLE OF FORGOTTEN WOMEN** • 1927
FORGOTTEN WOMEN (UKN) see **MAD PARADE, THE** • 1931
FORHUS OG BAGHUS (DNM) see **VORDERHAUS UND HINTERHAUS** • 1914
FORJA DE ALMAS • 1943 • Ardavin Eusebio F. • SPN
FORJADORES DE LA PAZ • 1962 • Alvarez Santiago • DOC • CUB • FORGERS OF PEACE
FORK IN THE ROAD, THE • 1915 • Santschi Thomas • USA
FORK OVER • 1918 • *Triangle* • USA
FORKED TRAILS • 1915 • Mix Tom • USA
FORLORADE MELODIEN, DEN • 1957 • Werner Gosta • SHT • SWD • FORGOTTEN MELODY, THE
FORLORN HOPE, THE • 1913 • *Kb* • USA
FORLORN RIVER • 1927 • Waters John • USA • RIVER OF DESTINY
FORLORN RIVER • 1937 • Barton Charles T. • USA
FORM 9A see **MY Z DIVIATEJ A** • 1961
FORM IN MOTION • Pavone Jose • ANS • USA • FORMS IN MOTION
FORM PHASES I-IV • 1953-54 • Breer Robert • SHS • USA
FORMATION • 1952 • Godfrey Bob (c/d) • ANS • UKN
FORMATION OF THE NATIONAL SPIRIT see **F.E.N.** • 1980
FORMATORS: ATTACK OF THE XELANS • Terry Jim • ANM • JPN
FORMATORS: EARTH'S DEFENCE • Terry Jim • ANM • JPN
FORME DES CHOSES, LA • 1965 • Giraldeau Jacques • DCS • CND
FORMERLAERE, I • 1949 • Carlsen Henning • SHT • DNM
FORMERLY, YOU HAD A BIG TIME see **VROEGER KON JE LACHEN** • 1982
FORMES UTILES see **DESIGNED FOR LIVING** • 1956
FORMES VIVANTES see **DESIGNED FOR LIVING** • 1956
FORMICA PADANA, LA • 1978 • Sala Vittorio • MTV • ITL
FORMING OF METALS, THE • 1957 • De Normanville Peter • UKN
FORMS IN MOTION see **FORM IN MOTION**
FORMULA 1, 1956: AN IMPRESSION OF SEVEN INTERNATIONAL GRANDS PRIX • 1956 • Barden Michael • DOC • UKN
FORMULA 1 -NELL'INFERNO DEL GRAND PRIX • 1970 • Civirani Osvaldo • ITL
FORMULA, THE • 1916 • *Lily* • SHT • USA
FORMULA, THE • 1980 • Avildsen John G. • USA
FORMULA FOR LOVE see **KAERLIGHEDENS MELODI** • 1959
FORMULA OF THE RAINBOW, THE see **CALL ME ROBERT**
FORMULA ONE MURDER see **DELITTO IN FORMULA UNO** • 1984
FORMULA SECRETA, LA • 1965 • Gamez Ruben • MXC • SECRET FORMULA, THE (USA) ○ KOKA KOLA EN LA SANGRE ○ KOKA KOLA IN THE BLOOD
FORMULA UNO FEBBRE DELLA VELOCITA • 1978 • Morra Mario, Orefici Oscar • ITL • SPEED FEVER
FORMULA UNO NELL'INFERNO DEL GRAND PRIX • 1970 • Malatesta Guido • ITL
FORMULAS • 1949 • Hofman Eduard • ANS • CZC
FORMULE X24 • 1964 • Misonne Claude • ANS • BLG
FORMYDERNE • 1978 • Mace Nicole • NRW • GUARDIANS, THE ○ PROFESSOREN
FORNARETTO DI VENEZIA, IL • 1914 • Maggi Luigi • ITL
FORNARETTO DI VENEZIA, IL • 1939 • Coletti Duilio • ITL
FORNARETTO DI VENEZIA, IL • 1963 • Tessari Duccio • ITL, FRN • SCAPEGOAT, THE (USA)
FORNARINA, LA • 1944 • Guazzoni Enrico • ITL
FORNICON -PATTERN OF EVIL • 1970 • Marks George Harrison • USA • F- PATTERN OF EVIL ○ PATTERN OF EVIL
FOROYAR FAEROERNE • 1960 • Roos Jorgen • DOC • DNM • ISLES FEROE, LES
FORRAEDEREN • 1910 • *Blom August* • DNM • TRAITOR TO HIS COUNTRY, A
FORRAEDERNE • 1983 • Roos Ole • DNM • TRAITOR, THE ○ TRAITORS, THE
FORRIERE • 1971 • Alawiya Burhan • BLG
FORSAKEN see **HOROKI** • 1954
FORSAKEN, THE • 1913 • Buckland Warwick • UKN
FORSAKEN GARDEN, THE see **OF LOVE AND DESIRE** • 1963
FORSAKEN PEDALS see **BOKYAKU NO HANABIRA** • 1957
FORSAKING ALL OTHERS • 1922 • Chautard Emile • USA
FORSAKING ALL OTHERS • 1934 • Van Dyke W. S. • USA
FORSE ERI TU L'AMORE • 1940 • Righelli Gennaro • ITL
FORSE QUE SI FORSE QUE NO • 1918 • Ravel Gaston • FRN
FORSEGLADE LAPPAR • 1927 • Molander Gustaf • SWD • SEALED LIPS
FORSFARARENSBRUD • 1922 • Karu Erkki • FNL
FORSOK INTE MED MEJ • 1946 • Larsson Borje • SWD • DON'T TRY IT WITH ME
FORSTA DIVISIONEN • 1941 • Ekman Hasse • SWD • FIRST DIVISION
FORSTE HONORAR, DET • 1912 • Blom August • DNM • HANS FORSTE HONORAR ○ HIS FIRST PATIENT
FORSTE KAERLIGHED, DEN • 1912 • Blom August • DNM • HER FIRST LOVE AFFAIR
FORSTE KREDS, DEN • 1971 • Ford Aleksander • DNM, FRG, USA • FIRST CIRCLE OF HELL, THE ○ FIRST CIRCLE, THE
FORSTERBUBEN, DIE • 1955 • Stemmle R. A. • FRG
FORSTERCHRISTL, DIE • 1926 • Zelnik Friedrich • FRG • FLOWER OF THE FOREST
FORSTERCHRISTL, DIE • 1931 • Zelnik Friedrich • FRG
FORSTERCHRISTL, DIE • 1952 • Rabenalt Arthur M. • FRG
FORSTERCHRISTL, DIE • 1962 • Gottlieb Franz J. • FRG
FORSTHAUS IM TIROL, DAS • 1955 • Kugelstadt Hermann • FRG
FORSUMMAD AV SIN FRU • 1947 • Folke Gosta • SWD • NEGLECTED BY HIS WIFE
FORSVUNDNE FULDMAEGTIG, DEN • 1972 • Fredholm Gert • DNM • CASE OF THE MISSING CLERK, THE ○ MISSING PRINCIPAL, THE
FORT, THE (UKN) see **RENEGADES OF THE SAGE** • 1949
FORT ALGIERS • 1953 • Selander Lesley • USA
FORT APACHE • 1948 • Ford John • USA
FORT APACHE, THE BRONX • 1981 • Petrie Daniel • USA
FORT BOWIE • 1958 • Koch Howard W. • USA
FORT COURAGEOUS • 1965 • Selander Lesley • USA
FORT DE LA SOLITUDE • 1947 • Vernay Robert • FRN • POSTE SUD ○ RAS EL GUA
FORT DEFIANCE • 1951 • Rawlins John • USA
FORT DOBBS • 1958 • Douglas Gordon • USA
FORT DODGE STAMPEDE • 1951 • Keller Harry • USA
FORT-DOLORES • 1938 • Le Henaff Rene • FRN • A L'OMBRE D'UNE FEMME
FORT-DU-FOU • 1962 • Joannon Leo • FRN, ITL • OUTPOST IN INDO-CHINA (USA) ○ FORT DU FOU
FORT DU FOU see **FORT-DU-FOU** • 1962
FORT FRAYNE • 1926 • Wilson Ben • USA
FORT GRAVEYARD see **CHI TO SUNA** • 1965
FORT MASSACRE • 1958 • Newman Joseph M. • USA
FORT OF NASIMPUR see **GAR NASIMPUR** • 1968
FORT OSAGE • 1952 • Selander Lesley • USA
FORT SAGANNE • 1984 • Corneau Alain • FRN
FORT SAVAGE see **FLAMING FEATHER, THE** • 1951
FORT SAVAGE RAIDERS • 1951 • Nazarro Ray • USA
FORT TI • 1953 • Castle William • USA
FORT UTAH • 1968 • Selander Lesley • USA
FORT VENGEANCE • 1953 • Selander Lesley • USA
FORT WORTH • 1951 • Marin Edwin L. • USA
FORT WORTH ROBBERY • 1914 • Vidor King • SHT • USA
FORT YUMA • 1955 • Selander Lesley • USA
FORT YUMA GOLD (USA) see **PER POCHI DOLLARI ANCORA** • 1966
FORTE, O • 1974 • Sao Paulo Olney • BRZ
FORTE TETE • 1942 • Mathot Leon • FRN
FORTERESSE, LA • 1947 • Ozep Fedor • CND • WHISPERING CITY ○ CRIME CITY
FORTERESSE DE CHURCHILL, LA see **CHURCHILL'S ISLAND** • 1941
FORTEZZE VUOTE • 1975 • Serra Gianni, Benelli Gioia • ITL
FORTICHES, LES • 1937 • Kapps Walter • FRN
FORTICHES, LES • 1960 • Combret Georges • FRN
FORTIFICATION PLANS, THE • 1915 • *Clifton Elmer* • USA
FORTIN ALTO • 1941 • Barth-Moglia Luis • ARG
FORTINI see **CANI** • 1976
FORTJUSANDE FROKEN, EN • 1946 • Larsson Borje • SWD • LOVELY YOUNG LADY
FORTRESS • 1985 • Nicholson Arch • ASL
FORTRESS, THE see **EROD, AZ** • 1979
FORTRESS EUROPE see **DE L'ENFER A LA VICTOIRE** • 1979
FORTRESS OF PEACE • 1965 • Ferno John • SHT • NTH
FORTRESS OF THE DEAD • 1965 • *Hackett Joan* • PHL, USA
FORTRESS ON THE RHINE • 1962 • Toman Ivo • CZC
FORTRESS WARDEN, THE • 1974 • Nikolov Milen • BUL
FORTROLLAD VANDRING • 1954 • Mattsson Arne • SWD • ENCHANTED WALK
FORTSETZUNG FOLGT • 1938 • Martin Paul • FRG
FORTSYTE SAGA, THE • 1967 • Giles David, Jones James Cellan • MTV • UKN
FORTSYTE SAGA, THE (UKN) see **THAT FORTSYTE WOMAN** • 1949
FORTUNA • 1940 • Neufeld Max • ITL
FORTUNA • 1959 • Dhamo Kristaq • ALB • STORM
FORTUNA • 1959 • Ozerov Yury • USS • STORM
FORTUNA • 1968 • Golan Menahem • ISR
FORTUNA • 1973 • Amiradzibi Helena • MTV • PLN
FORTUNA DI ESSERE DONNA, LA • 1956 • Blasetti Alessandro • ITL, FRN • CHANCE D'ETRE FEMME, LA (FRN) ○ LUCKY TO BE A WOMAN (USA) ○ MATING MODERN STYLE ○ WHAT A WOMAN!
FORTUNA DI ZANZE, LA • 1933 • Palermi Amleto • ITL • ZANZE
FORTUNA IN TASCA, LA see **DESTINO IN TASCA, IL** • 1938
FORTUNA VIENE DAL CIELO, LA • 1942 • von Rathony Akos • ITL
FORTUNAT • 1960 • Joffe Alex • FRN, ITL
FORTUNATA AND JACINTA see **FORTUNATA Y JACINTA** • 1969
FORTUNATA Y JACINTA • 1969 • Fons Angelino • SPN • FORTUNATA AND JACINTA
FORTUNATE, THE see **THAIKKU THALAIMAGAN** • 1967
FORTUNATE, THE see **ADRUSHTA VANTHALU** • 1968
FORTUNATE FOOL, THE • 1933 • Walker Norman • UKN
FORTUNATE FUGITIVE, THE see **OLIVER TWIST, JR.** • 1921
FORTUNATE MAN, A • 1972 • Perks Jeff • UKN
FORTUNATE MISFORTUNE, A • 1910 • *Essanay* • USA
FORTUNATE PILGRIM, THE see **MARIO PUZO'S "THE FORTUNATE PILGRIM"** • 1988
FORTUNATE YOUTH, THE • 1916 • *Merkyl Wilmuth* • USA
FORTUNATO • 1942 • Delgado Fernando • SPN
FORTUNATO 1 • 1921 • Halden Karl • FRG • TANZENDE DAMON, DER
FORTUNATO 2 • 1921 • Halden Karl • FRG • TODESFAHRT IN DEN LUFTEN, DIE
FORTUNATO 3 • 1921 • Halden Karl • FRG • LETZTE ATEMZUG, DER
FORTUNE, LA • 1931 • Hemard Jean • FRN
FORTUNE, THE • 1913 • North Wilfred • USA
FORTUNE, THE • 1974 • Nichols Mike • USA
FORTUNE AND MEN'S EYES • 1971 • Hart Harvey • CND, USA • AUX YEUX DU SORT ET DES HUMAINS
FORTUNE AND MISFORTUNE see **DIAMOND MAKER, THE** • 1909
FORTUNE AT STAKE, A • 1918 • West Walter • UKN
FORTUNE CARREE • 1954 • Borderie Bernard • FRN, ITL • SHAITAN, IL DIAVOLO DEL DESERTO (ITL) ○ CONQUEROR OF THE DESERT (USA)
FORTUNE COMES ON SUNDAY • 1958 • Lacko Jan • CZC
FORTUNE COOKIE, THE • 1966 • Wilder Billy • USA • MEET WHIPLASH WILLIE (UKN)
FORTUNE DANE • 1986 • Sgarro Nicholas, Corell Charles • USA
FORTUNE DE MARSEILLE • 1951 • Lepage Henri, Mere Pierre • FRN
FORTUNE FAVORS THE BRAVE • 1909 • Melies Georges • FRN
FORTUNE HUNTER, A see **HUNTER OF FORTUNES, A** • 1915
FORTUNE HUNTER, A see **LYCKORIDDARE, EN** • 1921
FORTUNE HUNTER, THE • 1914 • O'Neil Barry • USA
FORTUNE HUNTER, THE • 1916 • *Puritan* • SHT • USA
FORTUNE HUNTER, THE • 1920 • Terriss Tom • USA
FORTUNE HUNTER, THE • 1927 • Reisner Charles F. • USA
FORTUNE HUNTER, THE (UKN) see **OUTCAST, THE** • 1954
FORTUNE HUNTER (UKN) see **SING ME A SONG OF TEXAS** • 1945
FORTUNE HUNTERS • 1946 • Rasinski Connie • ANS • USA
FORTUNE HUNTERS, THE • 1909 • *Lubin* • USA
FORTUNE HUNTERS, THE • 1911 • *Selig* • USA
FORTUNE HUNTERS, THE • 1914 • Blache Alice • USA
FORTUNE HUNTERS OF HICKSVILLE, THE • 1913 • Thornby Robert T. • USA
FORTUNE IN DIAMONDS (USA) see **ADVENTURERS, THE** • 1951
FORTUNE IN PANTS, A • 1914 • *Simon Louis* • USA
FORTUNE IN THE TEA-CUP, THE • 1912 • Hale Albert W. • USA

FORTUNE IS A WOMAN • 1957 • Gilliat Sidney • UKN • SHE PLAYED WITH FIRE (USA)
FORTUNE IS STANDING AROUND IN THE STREETS, A see **CAR NAPPING** • 1980
FORTUNE LANE • 1947 • Baxter John • UKN
FORTUNE OF CHRISTINA MCNAB • 1921 • Kellino W. P. • UKN • CHRISTINA MCNAB
FORTUNE OR MISFORTUNE see **DIAMOND MAKER, THE** • 1909
FORTUNE TELLER, THE • 1915 • *Starlight* • USA
FORTUNE TELLER, THE • 1920 • Capellani Albert • FRN
FORTUNE TELLER, THE • 1923 • Fleischer Dave • ANS • USA
FORTUNE-TELLER, THE see **HARTORRIHTRA, I** • 1967
FORTUNE TELLER, THE (USA) see **KAPHETZOU** • 1961
FORTUNELLA • 1958 • De Filippo Eduardo • ITL
FORTUNE'S CHILD • 1919 • Gleason Joseph • USA
FORTUNE'S FOOL • 1910 • *Edison* • USA
FORTUNE'S FOOL see **ALLES FUR GELD** • 1923
FORTUNE'S FOOLS see **SCOURGE, THE** • 1922
FORTUNE'S MASK • 1922 • Ensminger Robert • USA
FORTUNES OF A COMPOSER • 1912 • Kent Charles • USA
FORTUNES OF CAPTAIN BLOOD • 1950 • Douglas Gordon • USA
FORTUNES OF CORINNE • 1918 • *Joy Gloria* • SHT • USA
FORTUNES OF FIFI, THE • 1917 • Vignola Robert G. • USA
FORTUNES OF MARGARET, THE • 1914 • *Daintry Isabel* • USA
FORTUNES OF MARIANA, THE • 1915 • *Razetto Stella* • USA
FORTUNES OF PIERRE, THE • 1915 • Mackenzie Donald • USA
FORTUNES OF WAR • 1914 • Hunt Jay • USA
FORTUNES OF WAR, THE • 1911 • *Imp* • USA
FORTUNES OF WAR, THE • 1912 • *Lindsay Howard* • USA
FORTUNE'S PET • 1913 • *Tennant Barbara* • USA
FORTUNE'S TURN • 1913 • North Wilfred • USA
FORTUNE'S WHEEL • 1910 • *Imp* • USA
FORTY ACRE FEUD • 1965 • Ormond Ron • USA
FORTY AND ONE NIGHTS, THE • 1963 • Jordan Larry, Collins Jess • USA • JESS'S DIDACTIC NICKELODEON
FORTY CARATS • 1973 • Katselas Milton • USA
FORTY DAYS • 1979 • Marx Franz • SAF
FORTY DEGREES IN THE SHADE see **CUARENTA GRADOS A LA SOMBRA** • 1967
FORTY DEUCE • 1981 • Morrissey Paul • USA
FORTY-EIGHT HOUR MILE, THE • 1970 • Levitt Gene • TVM • USA
FORTY-EIGHT HOURS see **CUARENTA Y OCHO HORAS** • 1942
FORTY-EIGHT YEAR OLD REBEL see **YONJU HASSAI NO TEIKO** • 1956
FORTY-EIGHTH COMRADE, THE see **YONJUHAICHI-NIN-ME NO DOSHI** • 1936
FORTY-FIRST, THE see **SOROK PERVYI** • 1927
FORTY-FIRST, THE see **SOROK PERVYI** • 1956
FORTY-FIVE MINUTES FROM HOLLYWOOD • 1926 • Guiol Fred • SHT • USA
FORTY-FIVE MINUTES FROM NOWHERE • 1915 • *Mina* • USA
FORTY-FOUR see **STYRIDSATSTYRI** • 1957
FORTY-FOUR SOHO SQUARE see **SOHO INCIDENT** • 1956
FORTY GRANDFATHERS see **CTYRICET DEDECKU** • 1962
FORTY GRAVES FOR FORTY GUNS see **MACHISMO -40 GRAVES FOR 40 GUNS** • 1970
FORTY GUNS • 1957 • Fuller Samuel • USA
FORTY GUNS TO APACHE PASS • 1967 • Witney William • USA
FORTY HEARTS see **SOROK SERDETS** • 1931
FORTY LEAGUES FROM PARADISE • 1970 • Peries Lester James • SHT • SLN
FORTY LITTLE MOTHERS • 1940 • Berkeley Busby, Moguy Leonide • USA
FORTY MILLION BUCKS • 1978 • Levin Henry • USA • FORTY MILLION BUCKS ON A DEAD MAN'S CHEST ○ TREASURE SEEKERS, THE ○ CONTRABAND ○ GOLD ○ JAMAICAN GOLD ○ FORTY MILLION DOLLARS ○ TREASURE OF DEATH
FORTY MILLION BUCKS ON A DEAD MAN'S CHEST see **FORTY MILLION BUCKS** • 1978
FORTY MILLION DOLLARS see **FORTY MILLION BUCKS** • 1978
FORTY MILLION PEOPLE see **HEALTH OF A NATION** • 1939
FORTY NAUGHTY GIRLS • 1937 • Cline Eddie • USA
FORTY-NINE DAYS IN HELL • Lee Doo-Yong • SKR
FORTY-NINE DAYS (USA) see **49 DNEY** • 1962
FORTY-NINERS, THE • 1932 • McCarthy John P. • USA
FORTY-NINERS, THE • 1954 • Carr Thomas • USA
FORTY-NINTH PARALLEL, THE see **49TH PARALLEL** • 1941
FORTY POUNDS OF TROUBLE • 1962 • Jewison Norman • USA
FORTY-SECOND STREET see **42ND STREET** • 1933
FORTY SOUNDS OF ENGLISH, THE • 1962 • Starbecker Gene • USA
FORTY THIEVES • 1944 • Selander Lesley • USA
FORTY THIEVES, THE • 1932 • *Terry Paul/ Moser Frank (P)* • ANS • USA
FORTY THOUSAND HORSEMEN • 1940 • Chauvel Charles • ASL
FORTY WINKS • 1920 • Finn Arthur • UKN
FORTY WINKS • 1925 • Urson Frank, Iribe Paul • USA
FORTY YEARS see **VEERTIG JAREN** • 1938
FORTY YEARS OF EXPERIMENT IN FILM • 1961 • Richter Hans, Eggeling Viking, Ruttmann Walter, Duchamp Marcel • CMP • USA
FORTY YEARS WITHOUT SEX see **CUARENTA ANOS SIN SEXO** • 1974
FORUM • 1969 • Dansereau Mireille • DOC • UKN
FORUM, THE • 1962 • Sheppard Gordon H. • CND
FORVANDLINGEN • 1975 • Dvorak Ivo • SWD • METAMORPHOSIS (USA)
FORVISTE, DE • 1914 • Holger-Madsen • DNM • UDEN FAEDRELAND ○ WITHOUT A COUNTRY
FORWARD see **CALA NAPRZOD** • 1967
FORWARD see **NO PINCHA** • 1970
FORWARD A CENTURY • 1951 • Napier-Bell J. B. • SHT • UKN
FORWARD -ALWAYS FORWARD • 1919 • *Miller-Hodkinson* • SHT • USA
FORWARD, ARMY OF GOD see **YUKI YUKITE SHINGUN**
FORWARD CANADA! • 1931 • Sparling Gordon • CND
FORWARD COMMUNICATIONS • 1949 • Gandy Bern • ASL
FORWARD COOPERATION • 1935 • Ford Aleksander • DOC • PLN
FORWARD FIREBASE GLORIA • 1988 • Trenchard-Smith Brian • ASL • SIEGE AT FIREBASE GLORIA, THE ○ SIEGE OF FIREBASE GLORIA, THE
FORWARD FLAG OF INDEPENDENCE see **SUSUME DOKURITSUKI** • 1943
FORWARD INTO THE FUTURE • 1964 • Peries Lester James • SHT • SLN
FORWARD MARCH • 1923 • Smith John P. • USA
FORWARD MARCH HARE • 1953 • Jones Charles M. • ANS • USA
FORWARD MARCH (UKN) see **DOUGH BOYS, THE** • 1930
FORWARD PASS, THE • 1929 • Cline Eddie • USA
FORWARD THE PEOPLE see **PEUPLE EN MARCHE** • 1963
FORWARD, TIME! • 1966 • Schweitzer Mikhail, Milkina S. • USS
FORWARD TO THE STRUGGLE FOR FREEDOM AND SOCIALISM see **NAPRZOD DO WALKI O POKOJ I SOCJALIZM** • 1950
FORWARD YOUNG MINERS see **NAPRZOD MLODZIEZY GORNICZA** • 1950
FORZA BRUTA, LA • 1941 • Bragaglia Carlo Ludovico • ITL • SERATA DI GALA
FORZA DEL DESTINO, LA • 1950 • Gallone Carmine • ITL • FORCE OF DESTINY, THE
FORZA "G" • 1972 • Tessari Duccio • ITL • WINGED DEVILS (UKN)
FORZA ITALIA! • 1978 • Faenza Roberto • ITL
FORZADA • 1964 • Artero Antonio • SHT • SPN
FORZATO DELLA GUIANA, IL (ITL) see **CHERI-BIBI** • 1954
FOSA COMUN • Gordon Rafael • SHT • SPN • COMMON GRAVE
FOSSA DEGLI ANGELI, LA • 1937 • Bragaglia Carlo Ludovico • ITL • ANGEL'S PIT, THE
FOSSA MALEDETTA, LA • 1978 • Ricci Tonino • ITL, SPN • BERMUDE: LA FOSSA MALEDETTA ○ SHARK'S CAVE (UKN) ○ CAVE OF THE SHARKS ○ CUEVA DE LOS TIBURONES, LA
FOSSE, LE see **HUFRA, AL-** • 1969
FOSSILS see **KASEKI** • 1975
FOSTER AND LAURIE • 1975 • Moxey John Llewellyn • TVM • USA
FOSTER BROTHER, THE • 1915 • *Wayne Justina* • USA
FOSTER BROTHERS, THE • 1913 • Melies Gaston • USA
FOSTER CHILD, THE • 1912 • *Brooke Van Dyke* • USA
FOSTER CHILDREN • Sajko Mako • DCS • YGS
FOSTER GANG, THE • 1964 • SAF
FOSTERLING, THE see **HRANJENIK** • 1970
FOSTER'S CANARY COLLEGE • 1944 • *O'Brien Joseph/ Mead Thomas (P)* • SHT • USA
FOTEL • 1963 • Szczechura Daniel • ANS • PLN • ARMCHAIR, THE ○ SEAT, THE ○ CHAIR, THE
FOTO DI GIOIA, LE • 1987 • Bava Lamberto • ITL • GIOIA'S PHOTOS
FOTO HABER • 1963 • Varkonyi Zoltan • HNG • PHOTO HABER
FOTO PROIBITE DI UNA SIGNORA PER BENE, LE • 1970 • Ercoli Luciano • ITL
FOTO: SVEN NYKVIST • 1973 • Silleck Bayley • DOC • UKN
FOTODEATH • Kouzel Al • SHT • USA
FOTOGENICO, EL • 1957 • Lazaga Pedro • SPN
FOTOGRAFIA see **RETUSOR, A** • 1972
FOTOROMANZO • 1985 • Laurenti Mariano • ITL
FOTYGRAFT GALLERY • 1919 • *Carr Johnny* • SHT • USA
FOU • 1958 • Duvivier Eric • ANT • FRN
FOU, LE • 1970 • Goretta Claude • FRN, SWT • MADMAN, THE
FOU ASSASSIN, LE • 1900 • Melies Georges • FRN • DANGEROUS LUNATIC, THE (USA)
FOU D'AMOUR • 1942 • Mesnier Paul • FRN
FOU DE LA FALAISE, LE • 1916 • Gance Abel • FRN
FOU DE MAI, LE • 1979 • Defrance Philippe • FRN
FOU DU LABO 4, LE • 1967 • Besnard Jacques • FRN • MADMAN OF LAB 4, THE
FOU DU ROI, LE • 1984 • Chiffre Yvan • FRN
FOUAD, EL- • 1966 • Harzallah Ahmed, de Givozy Claude • SHT • TNS
FOUGERE ET LA ROUILLE, COLLAGE 2, LA • 1974 • Giraldeau Jacques • CND
FOUGERES BLEUES, LES • 1977 • Sagan Francoise • FRN
FOUINARD N'EST PAS SYNDICALISTE • 1911 • Machin Alfred • FRN
FOUL AND FEARFUL PLOT, A • 1913 • Dillon Eddie • USA
FOUL BALL PLAYER, THE • 1940 • Fleischer Dave • ANS • USA
FOUL HUNTING • 1947 • Hannah Jack • ANS • USA
FOUL PLAY • 1911 • *Brower Robert* • USA
FOUL PLAY • 1915 • Birch Cecil • UKN
FOUL PLAY • 1920 • *Kelly Renee* • USA
FOUL PLAY • 1976 • Bardem Juan Antonio
FOUL PLAY • 1978 • Higgins Colin • USA
FOUL PLAY • 1985 • SAF
FOUL PLAY see **PRZEPRASZAM, CZY TU BIJA?** • 1977
FOULARD MERVEILLEUX, LE • 1908 • *Deed Andre* • FRN
FOULE, LA • 1966 • Rihouet Pierre • FRN
FOULE HURLE, LA • 1932 • Daumery John, Hawks Howard • FRN
FOULES • 1959 • Lapoujade Robert • ANS • FRN
FOUND -A FLESH REDUCER • 1915 • Ransom Charles • USA
FOUND AGAIN see **WEERGEVONDEN** • 1914
FOUND ALIVE • 1934 • Hutchison Charles • USA
FOUND FILM NO.1 • 1968-70 • Vanderbeek Stan • USA
FOUND GUILTY • 1922 • *Santschi Tom* • USA
FOUND IN SPACE • 1969 • *Zenith* • USA
FOUND MONEY • 1983 • Persky Bill • TVM • USA
FOUND ON THE ROCKS • 1909 • *Urban-Eclipse* • USA
FOUND OUT • 1913 • *Carney Augustus* • USA
FOUNDATION OF THE ORDINATION, THE see **SEISHOKU NO ISHIZUE** • 1978
FOUNDATIONS OF FREEDOM, THE • 1918 • Branscombe Arthur • UKN
FOUNDATIONS OF PROGRESS • 1972 • Benegal Shyam • DCS • IND
FOUNDED ON SCIENCE • 1966 • Allen James • SHT • UKN
FOUNDLING, THE • 1909 • Brooke Van Dyke • USA
FOUNDLING, THE • 1912 • *Champion* • USA
FOUNDLING, THE • 1912 • Miller Ashley • *Edison* • USA, UKN
FOUNDLING, THE • 1913 • *All-British Films* • UKN
FOUNDLING, THE • 1915 • Dwan Allan • *Famous Players* • USA
FOUNDLING, THE • 1916 • O'Brien John B. • USA
FOUNDLING HOSPITAL SPORTS DAY • 1897 • Norton C. Goodwin • UKN • CHILDREN'S SPORTS
FOUNDLING OF FATE, THE see **HITTEBARNET** • 1916
FOUNDLINGS OF FATHER TIME, THE • 1914 • *Mackenzie Murdock* • USA
FOUNDRY TOWN, THE see **KYUPORA NO ARU MACHI** • 1962
FOUNTAIN, THE • 1934 • Cromwell John • USA • BREAKING THE NEWS
FOUNTAIN, THE see **IZUMI** • 1956
FOUNTAIN, THE (UKN) see **FONTAN** • 1989
FOUNTAIN OF BAKHCHISRAI, THE • 1909 • Protazanov Yakov • USS
FOUNTAIN OF LOVE see **MATA AU HIMADE: KOIBITO NO IZUMI** • 1967
FOUNTAIN OF LOVE, THE (USA) see **LIEBESQUELLE, DIE** • 1965
FOUNTAIN OF PRETTY GIRLS see **MOOIMEISIESFONTEIN** • 1978
FOUNTAIN OF TROUBLE, THE • 1917 • Beaudine William • SHT • USA
FOUNTAIN OF YOUTH • 1907 • Blackton J. Stuart • USA
FOUNTAIN OF YOUTH • 1909 • *Pathe* • FRN
FOUNTAIN OF YOUTH • 1911 • *Lubin* • USA
FOUNTAIN OF YOUTH • 1921 • Abramson Ivan • USA
FOUNTAIN OF YOUTH, THE • 1958 • Welles Orson • USA
FOUNTAIN OF YOUTH, THE (USA) see **WAKAGERI NO IZUMI** • 1956
FOUNTAINHEAD, THE • 1949 • Vidor King • USA
FOUNTAINHEAD, THE see **IZUMI** • 1956
FOUNTAINS OF ROME, THE see **FONTANE DI ROMA** • 1938
FOUNTAINS OF THE SUN • 1970 • Feeny John • DOC • CND, UAR • YANABIE EL SHAMS
FOUQUET • 1911 • de Morlhon Camille • FRN
FOUR $100 BILLS • 1913 • *Reliance* • USA
FOUR, THE see **CHETVERO** • 1957
FOUR A CHAUX, LE • 1910 • Carre Michel • FRN
FOUR ADVENTURES OF REINETTE AND MIRABELLE see **QUATRE AVENTURES DE REINETTE ET MIRABELLE** • 1987
FOUR AGAINST CRIME see **CUATRO CONTRA EL CRIMEN** • 1968
FOUR AGAINST FATE (USA) see **DERBY DAY** • 1952
FOUR AROUND A WOMAN see **KAMPFENDE HERZEN** • 1921
FOUR ARTILLERYMEN AND A DOG see **CZTEREJ PANCERNI I PIES (I)** • 1968
FOUR ARTILLERYMEN AND A DOG (II) see **CZTEREJ PANCERNI I PIES (II)** • 1968
FOUR ARTILLERYMEN AND A DOG (III) see **CZTEREJ PANCERNI I PIES (III)** • 1968
FOUR ARTILLERYMEN AND A DOG (IV) see **CZTEREJ PANCERNI I PIES (IV)** • 1968
FOUR BAGS FULL (USA) see **TRAVERSEE DE PARIS, LA** • 1956
FOUR BARRIERS • 1937 • Cavalcanti Alberto • DCS • UKN
FOUR BEARS BEFORE THE MAST • 1949 • *Universal* • SHT • USA
FOUR BILLION MOMENTS • 1980 • Pyhala Jaakko • FNL
FOUR BIT MAN, THE • 1919 • Eason B. Reeves • SHT • USA • FOUR-BIT MAN, THE
FOUR-BIT MAN, THE see **FOUR BIT MAN, THE** • 1919
FOUR BODIES WALLOWING IN DESIRE • 1970 • *Able Film Co.* • USA
FOUR BOYS AND A GUN • 1955 • Berke William • USA
FOUR BRIGHT GIRLS see **FOUR GIRLS IN TOWN** • 1956
FOUR CARDS • 1922 • Wheeler Leonard • USA
FOUR CENT COURTSHIP, A • 1917 • Windom Lawrence C. • SHT • USA
FOUR CENTS A WORD see **BLONDE INSPIRATION** • 1940
FOUR CHILDREN IN THE FLOOD see **NEGYEN AZ ARBAN** • 1961
FOUR CHIMNEYS (UKN) see **ENTOTSU NO MIERU BASHO** • 1953
FOUR CLOWNS • 1970 • Youngson Robert • CMP • USA
FOUR CORN PATCHES, THE (USA) see **CUATRO MILPAS, LAS** • 1937
FOUR CORNERED TRIANGLE see **SCREAM OF THE BUTTERFLY** • 1965
FOUR CORNERED TRIANGLE, A • 1918 • Baker Graham • SHT • USA
FOUR-CORNERED WEDDING, A • 1912 • *Mansfield Gus* • USA
FOUR CYLINDER FRAME-UP, A • 1920 • *Supreme Comedies* • USA
FOUR D MAN, THE see **4D MAN, THE** • 1959
FOUR DARK HOURS • 1937 • Menzies William Cameron, Howard William K. • UKN • GREEN COCKATOO, THE ○ RACE GANG
FOUR DAUGHTERS • 1938 • Curtiz Michael • USA • SISTER ACT
FOUR DAYS • 1913 • *Price Kate* • USA
FOUR DAYS • 1914 • *Larkin Dolly* • USA
FOUR DAYS • 1951 • Guillermin John • UKN
FOUR DAYS A WIDOW • 1912 • *Walker Lillian* • USA
FOUR DAYS ABOUT FREEDOM • 1968 • Tuhus Oddvar Bull • CZC
FOUR DAYS IN DALLAS see **RUBY AND OSWALD** • 1978
FOUR DAYS IN NOVEMBER • 1964 • Stuart Mel • DOC • USA
FOUR DAYS IN PARIS (USA) see **QUATRE JOURS A PARIS** • 1954
FOUR DAYS LEAVE • 1950 • Lindtberg Leopold • SWT, USA • SWISS TOUR
FOUR DAYS OF NAPLES, THE see **QUATTRO GIORNATE DI NAPOLI, LE** • 1962
FOUR DAYS OF SNOW AND BLOOD (2-2-6) • 1989 • Gosha Hideo • JPN

FOUR DAYS TILL DEATH see **CETIRI DANA DO SMRTI** • 1977
FOUR DAY'S WONDER • 1936 • Salkow Sidney • USA
FOUR DAY'S WONDER • 1971 • Bonniere Rene • CND
FOUR DESPERATE MEN (USA) see **SIEGE OF PINCHGUT, THE** • 1959
FOUR DEUCES, THE • 1975 • Bushnell William H. Jr. • USA
FOUR DEVILS • 1913 • Starevitch Ladislas • USS
FOUR DEVILS • 1929 • Murnau F. W. • USA
FOUR DEVILS, THE see **FIRE DIAEVLE, DE** • 1911
FOUR DEVILS, THE see **FIRE DJAEVLE, DE** • 1920
FOUR DIMENSIONS OF GRETA, THE • 1972 • Walker Pete • UKN
FOUR ELEMENTS, THE • 1966 • Harrington Curtis • SHT • USA
FOUR FACES OF INDIA (UKN) see **CHAR DIL CHAR RAHEN** • 1959
FOUR FACES WEST • 1948 • Green Alfred E. • USA • THEY PASSED THIS WAY (UKN) ○ NEW MEXICO ○ WANTED
FOUR FAST GUNS • 1959 • Hole William Jr. • USA
FOUR FEATHERS • 1915 • Dawley J. Searle • USA
FOUR FEATHERS, THE • 1921 • Plaissetty Rene • UKN
FOUR FEATHERS, THE • 1929 • Cooper Merian C., Schoedsack Ernest B., Mendes Lothar • USA
FOUR FEATHERS, THE • 1939 • Korda Zoltan • UKN
FOUR FEATHERS, THE • 1978 • Sharp Don • TVM • USA
FOUR FLIES ON GREY VELVET (UKN) see **QUATTRO MOSCHE DE VELLUTO GRIGIO** • 1971
FOUR FLIGHTS TO LOVE (USA) see **PARADIS PERDU** • 1939
FOUR FLUSH ACTOR, THE • 1912 • *Quirk Billy* • USA
FOUR FLUSHER, THE • 1919 • Franklin Harry L. • USA
FOUR FLUSHER, THE • 1923 • Taurog Norman • SHT • USA
FOUR FLUSHER, THE see **BLUFF** • 1924
FOUR FOOLS AND A MAID • 1913 • *Karr Darwin* • USA
FOUR-FOOTED DESPERADO, A • 1914 • Williams C. Jay • USA
FOUR-FOOTED HERO, A • 1912 • *Bison* • USA
FOUR-FOOTED PEST, A • 1910 • *Vitagraph* • USA
FOUR-FOOTED RANGER, THE • 1928 • Paton Stuart • USA
FOUR FOR TEXAS • 1963 • Aldrich Robert • USA
FOUR FOR THE MORGUE • 1962 • Sledge John • USA
FOUR FRIENDS • 1912 • *Solax* • USA
FOUR FRIENDS • 1981 • Penn Arthur • USA • GEORGIA'S FRIENDS (UKN) ○ GEORGIA
FOUR FRIENDS see **CHAR DOST** • 1956
FOUR FRIGHTENED PEOPLE • 1934 • De Mille Cecil B. • USA
FOUR FROM NOWHERE, THE • 1925 • Ford Francis • USA
FOUR FROM THE INFANTRY see **WESTFRONT 1918** • 1930
FOUR GIRLS • 1967 • Dewdney Alexander Keewatin • CND
FOUR GIRLS IN TOWN • 1956 • Sher Jack • USA • FOUR BRIGHT GIRLS
FOUR GIRLS IN WHITE • 1938 • Simon S. Sylvan • USA
FOUR GRAINS OF RICE • 1915 • Marston Theodore • USA
FOUR-GUN BANDIT, THE • 1919 • Holt George • SHT • USA
FOUR GUNS TO THE BORDER • 1954 • Carlson Richard • USA
FOUR HEARTS • 1945 • Yudin Konstantin • USS • HEARTS OF THE FOUR, THE
FOUR HITS AND A MISTER • 1962 • Hickox Douglas • SHT • UKN
FOUR HOOLIGANS, THE • 1906 • Collins Alf? • UKN
FOUR HOROSCOPES see **HATARA KENDARE** • 1967
FOUR HORSEMEN OF THE APOCALYPSE, THE • 1921 • Ingram Rex • USA
FOUR HORSEMEN OF THE APOCALYPSE, THE • 1961 • Minnelli Vincente • USA
FOUR HOURS TO KILL • 1935 • Leisen Mitchell • USA
FOUR HUMAN EAGLES, THE see **FLIGHT OF THE SOUTHERN CROSS: OR, THE FOUR HUMAN EAGLES, THE** • 1929
FOUR HUMBLE MEN see **CHAHAR DARVISH** • 1968
FOUR HUNDRED CUBIC CENTIMETRES • 1966 • Heynowski Walter, Scheumann Gerhard • GDR • 400 cm3
FOUR IN A JEEP (USA) see **VIER IM JEEP, DIE** • 1951
FOUR IN BED • 1970 • *Able Film Co.* • USA
FOUR IN LOVE see **DORDU DE SEVIYORDU** • 1967
FOUR-IN-ONE • 1970 • Sagal Boris • TVM • USA
FOUR IN ONE • 1970 • Spielberg Steven • TVM • USA
FOUR IN THE AFTERNOON • 1951 • Broughton James • SHT • USA
FOUR IN THE CIRCLE see **CTYRI V KRUHU** • 1967
FOUR IN THE MORNING • 1953 • Ivory James • SHT • USA
FOUR IN THE MORNING • 1965 • Simmons Anthony • UKN
FOUR INFERNOS TO CROSS • *Musung Kwak* • HKG
FOUR JACKS AND A JILL • 1941 • Hively Jack • USA • FOUR JACKS AND A QUEEN
FOUR JACKS AND A QUEEN see **FOUR JACKS AND A JILL** • 1941
FOUR JILLS IN A JEEP • 1944 • Seiter William A. • USA
FOUR JOLLY SAILOR BOYS FROM "THE PRINCESS OF KENSINGTON" • 1907 • Morland John • UKN
FOUR JOLLY SAILORMEN • 1909 • *Warwick Trading Co.* • UKN
FOUR JUST MEN, THE • 1921 • Ridgwell George • UKN
FOUR JUST MEN, THE • 1939 • Forde Walter • UKN • SECRET FOUR, THE
FOUR KEYS, THE see **VIER SCHLUSSEL** • 1965
FOUR KILOMETRES PER HOUR see **CETIRI KILOMETRA NA SAT** • 1958
FOUR KINDS OF LOVE • 1968 • Carse Shannon • USA
FOUR KINDS OF LOVE see **BAMBOLE, LE** • 1964
FOUR-LEGGED MAN, THE see **COVEK SA CETIRI NOGE** • 1984
FOUR-LINE CONICS • 1962 • Longpre Bernard, Fletcher Trevor • ANS • CND • FAMILLE DE CONIQUES
FOUR LITTLE TAILORS, THE see **QUATRE PETITS TAILLEURS, LES** • 1910
FOUR LOVE STORIES see **YOTTSU NO KOI NO MONOGATARI** • 1947
FOUR LOVES see **YOTTSU NO KOI NO MONOGATARI** • 1966
FOUR LOVES see **SEI TSINGAM** • 1989
FOUR MARKED MEN see **CUATRO HOMBRES MARCADOS** • 1968
FOUR MARYS, THE see **MAN-PROOF** • 1937
FOUR MASKED MEN • 1934 • Pearson George • UKN • BEHIND THE MASKS
FOUR MEN AND A PRAYER • 1938 • Ford John • USA
FOUR MEN IN A VAN • 1921 • Croise Hugh • UKN
FOUR MEN IN PRISON • 1950 • Anderson Max • DOC • UKN
FOUR MEN OF INDIA • 1967 • Doncaster Caryl • UKN
FOUR MINUTES LATE • 1914 • Grandon Francis J. • USA
FOUR MONKS, THE see **QUATTRO MONACI, I** • 1962
FOUR MONTHS • 1916 • Le Viness Carl M. • SHT • USA
FOUR MOODS (USA) see **HSI, NOU, AI, LUEH** • 1970
FOUR MOTHERS • 1941 • Keighley William • USA
FOUR MURDERS ARE ENOUGH, DARLING see **CTYRI VRAZDY STACI, DRAHOUSKU** • 1971
FOUR MUSICIANS OF BREMEN, THE • 1922 • Disney Walt • ANS • USA
FOUR MUSKETEERS, THE • 1975 • Lester Richard • UKN, SPN • FOUR MUSKETEERS: THE REVENGE OF MILADY ○ REVENGE OF MILADY, THE
FOUR MUSKETEERS, THE see **QUATTRO MOSCHETTIERI, I** • 1963
FOUR MUSKETEERS, THE (USA) see **VIER MUSKETIERE, DIE** • 1935
FOUR MUSKETEERS: THE REVENGE OF MILADY see **FOUR MUSKETEERS, THE** • 1975
FOUR NARRATIVES • 1916 • Powell Paul • SHT • USA
FOUR NEW APPLE DISHES • 1940 • Crawley Judith • DOC • CND
FOUR NIGHTS OF A DREAMER (USA) see **QUATRE NUITS D'UN REVEUR** • 1971
FOUR NIGHTS OF THE FULL MOON, THE see **CUATRO NOCHES DE LA LUNA LLENA, LAS** • 1964
FOUR OF A KIND • 1919 • *Christie* • USA
FOUR OF A KIND • 1920 • *Cohn Productions* • SHT • USA
FOUR OF THE AVE MARIA, THE see **QUATTRO DELL'AVE MARIA, I** • 1968
FOUR OF THEM see **QUATRE D'ENTRE ELLES** • 1968
FOUR OF US, THE • 1911 • *Powers* • USA
FOUR ON THE FLOOR • 1970 • Hansen Kenneth • USA
FOUR ORPHANS, THE • 1923 • La Cava Gregory • SHT • USA
FOUR PAGES FROM A YOUNG LIFE see **CHYETYRYE STRANITSY ODNOY MOLODY ZHIZNI** • 1968
FOUR PAGES OF A YOUNG LIFE see **CHYETYRYE STRANITSY ODNOY MOLODY ZHIZNI** • 1968
FOUR PARTS • 1934 • Parrott Charles, Dunn Eddie • SHT • USA
FOUR PEOPLE • 1962 • Brenton Guy • UKN
FOUR PORTRAITS • 1978 • Leiterman Richard, McCammon Jim • DOC • CND
FOUR QUEENS AND A JACK • 1913 • *Nestor* • USA
FOUR RIDERS see **HELL FIGHTERS OF THE EAST** • 1972
FOUR RODE OUT • 1969 • Peyser John • USA, SPN • CUATRO CABALGARON (SPN)
FOUR SEASONS • 1921 • Ditmars Raymond L. • USA
FOUR SEASONS • 1970 • Ivanov-Vano Ivan • ANS • USS • SEASONS, THE
FOUR SEASONS, THE • 1981 • Alda Alan • USA
FOUR SEASONS, THE see **FARREBIQUE: OU LES QUATRE SAISONS** • 1947
FOUR SEASONS, THE see **GODISNJA DOBA** • 1980
FOUR SEASONS OF CHILDREN see **KODOMO NO SHIKI** • 1939
FOUR SEASONS OF LOVE, THE see **SHIKI NO AIYOKU** • 1958
FOUR SEASONS OF TATESHINA see **TATESHINA NO SHIKI** • 1966
FOUR SEASONS OF WOMAN, THE see **ONNA NO SHIKI** • 1950
FOUR SHAOLIN CHALLENGERS, THE • *Wong Yuen* • HKG
FOUR SHOTS WERE HEARD see **SONARON CUATRO BALAZOS** • 1967
FOUR SIDED TRIANGLE • 1953 • Fisher Terence • UKN
FOUR-SIDED TRIANGLE see **TRIANGULO DE CUATRO** • 1975
FOUR SISTERS see **CHAHAR KHAHAR** • 1967
FOUR SKULLS OF JONATHAN DRAKE, THE • 1959 • Cahn Edward L. • USA
FOUR SOLDIERS see **AUF DEN BERGEN ROTER MOHN** • 1966
FOUR SOLDIERS FROM STALINGRAD see **SOLDATY** • 1956
FOUR SONS • 1928 • Ford John • USA
FOUR SONS • 1940 • Mayo Archie • USA
FOUR-STAR BOARDER, THE • 1935 • Parrott Charles • SHT • USA
****** (FOUR STARS)** • 1967 • Warhol Andy • USA • TWENTY-FOUR HOUR MOVIE, THE
FOUR STEPS IN THE CLOUDS see **QUATTRO PASSI FRA LE NUVOLE** • 1942
FOUR STEPS TO THE INFINITE see **LA PATRU PASI DE INFINIT** • 1964
FOUR THOUSAND STEPS TO THE SKY • 1963 • Mesaros Titus • DOC • RMN
FOUR TIGERS IN LIPSTICK • 1979 • *Andress Ursula*
FOUR TIMES ABOUT BULGARIA see **CTYRIKRAT O BULHARSKU** • 1958
FOUR TIMES FOILED • 1920 • *Chester* • SHT • USA
FOUR TIMES ONLY see **VAIN NELJA KERTAA** • 1968
FOUR TIMES THAT NIGHT (USA) see **QUANTE VOLTE.. QUELLA NOTTE** • 1972
FOUR TO FOUR • 1978 • Yalden-Tomson Peter • MTV • CND
FOUR TO ONE • 1899 • *Warwick Trading Co.* • UKN
FOUR TOMBOYS, THE • 1909 • Collins Alf? • UKN
FOUR TROUBLESOME HEADS, THE (USA) see **HOMME DE TETES, UN** • 1898
FOUR VISITS OF SAMUEL VULF, THE • 1934 • Stolper Alexander • USS
FOUR WALL DURATION • 1973 • Le Grice Malcolm • UKN
FOUR WALLS • 1928 • Nigh William • USA
FOUR WALLS • 1969 • Armstrong Gillian • SHT • ASL
FOUR WAYS OUT (USA) see **CITTA SI DIFENDE, LA** • 1951
FOUR WHEELS AND NO BRAKE • 1955 • Parmelee Ted • ANS • USA
FOUR WINDS ISLAND • 1961 • Villiers David • UKN
FOUR WISE GIRLS see **LADIES MUST LOVE** • 1933
FOUR WIVES • 1939 • Curtiz Michael • USA
FOUR WOMEN see **QUATRE D'ENTRE ELLES** • 1968
FOUR WOMEN FOR ONE HERO (UKN) see **HOMENAJE A LA HORA DE LA SIESTA** • 1964
FOUR YALE MEN • 1912 • *Powers* • USA
FOURBERIES DE PINGOUIN, LES • 1916 • Feuillade Louis • FRN
FOURBERIES DE SCAPIN, LES • 1980 • Coggio Roger • FRN
FOURCHAMBAULT, LES • 1929 • Monca Georges • FRN
FOURFLUSHER, THE • 1928 • Ruggles Wesley • USA • COLLEGIANS IN BUSINESS
FOURPOSTER, THE • 1952 • Reis Irving • USA
FOURRAGE • 1966 • Lahalolo Latif • MRC
FOUR'S A CROWD • 1938 • Curtiz Michael • USA
FOURS FAIMBIERS • 1959 • Novik William • SHT • FRN
FOURTEEN, THE see **14, THE** • 1973
FOURTEEN AMERICANS • 1981 • *Blackwood Michael/ Rosen Nancy (P)* • DOC • USA
FOURTEEN GOING ON THIRTY see **14 GOING ON 30** • 1988
FOURTEEN HOURS • 1951 • Hathaway Henry • USA
FOURTEEN LIVES IN DANGER see **ELETJEL** • 1954
FOURTEEN LIVES SAVED see **ELETJEL** • 1954
FOURTEEN MILLION LEAGUES FROM EARTH see **HIMMELSKIBET** • 1917
FOURTEENTH DAY, THE see **DAN CETRNAESTI** • 1960
FOURTEENTH LOVER, THE • 1922 • Beaumont Harry • USA
FOURTEENTH MAN, THE • 1917 • *Palmer Patricia* • USA
FOURTEENTH MAN, THE • 1920 • Henabery Joseph • USA • MAN FROM BLANKLEYS, THE
FOURTEENTH OF JULY, THE see **QUATORZE JUILLET** • 1932
FOURTEENTH WINTER, THE • NKR
FOURTH, THE • 1973 • Stolper Alexander • USS
FOURTH ALARM • 1926 • Roach Hal • SHT • USA
FOURTH ALARM, THE • 1930 • Whitman Phil • USA
FOURTH COMMANDMENT, THE • 1927 • Johnson Emory • USA
FOURTH DIMENSION, THE see **CUARTA DIMENSION, LA** • 1970
FOURTH DIMENSION, THE see **STVRTY ROZMER** • 1983
FOURTH ESTATE, THE • 1916 • Powell Frank • USA
FOURTH ESTATE, THE see **FOURTH ESTATE: A FILM OF A BRITISH NEWSPAPER, THE** • 1940
FOURTH ESTATE: A FILM OF A BRITISH NEWSPAPER, THE • 1940 • Rotha Paul • DOC • UKN • FOURTH ESTATE, THE
FOURTH FACE, THE • 1920 • *Climax Film* • USA
FOURTH FENCE ALONG THE WHARF • 1985 • Nicolae Cristiana • RMN • FOURTH FENCE ON THE WHARF, THE
FOURTH FENCE ON THE WHARF, THE see **FOURTH FENCE ALONG THE WHARF** • 1985
FOURTH FILM • 1944 • Whitney John, Whitney James • SHT • USA
FOURTH FOR MARRIAGE, A see **WHAT'S UP FRONT** • 1964
FOURTH HORSEMAN, THE • 1932 • MacFadden Hamilton • USA • PONY BOY
FOURTH IN SALVADOR, THE • 1918 • Smith David • SHT • USA
FOURTH MAN, THE (UKN) see **VIERDE MAN, DE** • 1983
FOURTH MARRIAGE OF DAME MARGARET, THE see **PRASTANKAN** • 1920
FOURTH MUSKETEER, THE • 1923 • Howard William K. • USA
FOURTH PARTY, THE see **CETVRTI SUPUTNIK** • 1967
FOURTH PROPOSAL, THE • 1914 • *Leonard Robert* • USA
FOURTH PROTOCOL, THE • 1987 • Mackenzie John • UKN
FOURTH ROOM, THE see **CHETVERTAYA KOMNATA** • 1974
FOURTH SEX, THE (USA) see **QUATRIEME SEXE, LE** • 1962
FOURTH SQUARE, THE • 1961 • Davis Allan • UKN
FOURTH TRAVELLING COMPANION, THE see **CETVRTI SUPUTNIK** • 1967
FOURTH WAR, THE • 1989 • Frankenheimer John • USA
FOURTH WAVE, THE • 1971 • Rodgers Bob • MTV • CND
FOURTH WISE MAN, THE • 1985 • Rhodes Michael Ray • TVM • USA
FOURTH WISH, THE • 1976 • Chaffey Don • ASL
FOURTH WITNESS, THE • 1917 • McDermott John • SHT • USA
FOURVIERE • 1948 • Maudru • SHT • FRN
FOUS DE BASSAN, LES • 1986 • Simoneau Yves • CND • IN THE SHADOW OF THE WIND
FOUS DU STADE, LES • 1972 • Zidi Claude • FRN
FOVOS, HO • 1966 • Manoussakis Kostas • GRC • FEAR, THE ○ PEUR, LA
FOWL AFFAIR, A • 1931 • Burns Neal, McGill Barney • SHT • USA
FOWL BALL, THE • 1930 • Lantz Walter, Nolan William • ANS • USA
FOWL BRAWL • 1947 • Swift Howard • ANS • USA
FOWL DEED, A • 1914 • Henderson Dell • USA
FOWL FEATHER • 1953 • Freleng Friz • ANS • USA
FOWL PLAY • 1937 • Fleischer Dave • ANS • USA
FOWL PLAY • 1973 • McKimson Robert • ANS • USA
FOWL PROCEEDING, A • 1925 • Hiscott Leslie • UKN
FOWLED-UP BIRTHDAY • 1962 • Hannah Jack • ANS • USA
FOWLED-UP FALCON • 1960 • Smith Paul J. • ANS • USA
FOWLED-UP PARTY • 1957 • Lovy Alex • ANS • USA
FOX see **FAUSTRECHT DER FREIHEIT** • 1975
FOX, THE • 1914 • *Leonard Robert* • USA
FOX, THE • 1921 • Thornby Robert T. • USA • PARTNERS
FOX, THE • 1968 • Rydell Mark • USA
FOX, THE see **KITSUNE** • 1939
FOX, THE see **LISKA BYSTROUSKA** • 1954
FOX, THE see **RAVEN** • 1987
FOX AND BEAR see **KETTU JA KARHU** • 1973
FOX AND HARE • 1973 • Norshtein Yuri • ANM • USS • VIXEN AND THE HARE, THE
FOX AND HEDGEHOG • Wiemer Hans Ulrich • ANM • GDR
FOX AND HIS FRIENDS (UKN) see **FAUSTRECHT DER FREIHEIT** • 1975
FOX AND THE CROW, THE • 1943-46 • Wickersham Bob • ASS • USA
FOX AND THE CROW, THE • 1948-49 • ASS • USA
FOX AND THE DUCK, THE • 1945 • Davis Mannie • ANS • USA
FOX AND THE GRAPES, THE • 1921 • *Terry Paul* • ANS • USA
FOX AND THE GRAPES, THE • 1941 • Tashlin Frank • ANS • USA
FOX AND THE HARE, THE • 1969 • Carretero Amaro • ASS • SPN
FOX AND THE HOUND, THE • 1981 • Stevens Art, Berman Ted, Rich Richard • ANM • USA
FOX AND THE JUG, THE (USA) see **LISKA A DZABAN** • 1947

FOX AND THE RABBIT, THE • 1935 • Lantz Walter • ANS • USA
FOX AND THE THRUSH • 1945 • Ivanov A. • ANS • USS
FOX AND THE WOLF, THE see **LISKA A VLK** • 1956
FOX CHASE • 1952 • Lye Len • SHT • USA
FOX CHASE, THE • 1928 • Disney Walt • ANS • USA
FOX FARM • 1922 • Newall Guy • UKN
FOX FIRE see **FEU FOLLET, LE** • 1963
FOX FIRE CHILD WATCH • 1971 • Brakhage Stan • USA
FOX FOLLIES OF 1929 see **FOX MOVIETONE FOLLIES OF 1929** • 1929
FOX HUNT • 1906 • *Bitzer Billy (Ph)* • USA
FOX HUNT • 1936 • Gross Anthony • ANS • UKN
FOX HUNT • 1950 • Rasinski Connie • ANS • USA
FOX HUNT, THE • 1925 • Roach Hal • SHT • USA
FOX HUNT, THE • 1931 • Jackson Wilfred • ANS • USA
FOX HUNT, THE • 1938 • Sharpsteen Ben • ANS • USA
FOX HUNTING • Abdrakhitov Vadim • USS
FOX HUNTING • 1982 • Daneliuc Mircea • RMN
FOX HUNTING THE ROMAN CAMPAGNA • 1937-40 • *Cardiff Jack (Ph)* • DCS • UKN
FOX IN A FIX, A • 1950 • McKimson Robert • ANS • USA
FOX IN THE CHICKEN COOP • 1978 • Kishon Ephraim • ISR
FOX MOVIETONE FOLLIES OF 1929 • 1929 • Butler David, Silver Marcel • USA • MOVIETONE FOLLIES OF 1929, THE (UKN) ○ FOX FOLLIES OF 1929 ○ WILLIAM FOX MOVIETONE FOLLIES OF 1929
FOX MOVIETONE FOLLIES OF 1930 • 1930 • Stoloff Ben • USA • MOVITONE FOLLIES OF 1930 (UKN) ○ NEW MOVIETONE FOLLIES OF 1930
FOX POP • 1942 • Jones Charles M. • ANS • USA
FOX STORY see **KITAKITSUNE MONGATARI** • 1978
FOX STYLE • 1986 • Houston Clyde • USA
FOX TALES • 1927 • Roberts Stephen • SHT • USA
FOX TERROR • 1957 • McKimson Robert • ANS • USA
FOX TROT CRAZE, THE • 1915 • *Sterling* • USA
FOX TROT FINESSE, THE • 1915 • Drew Sidney • USA
FOX WITH NINE TAILS, THE (USA) see **KYUBI NO KITSUNE TO TOBIMARU** • 1969
FOX WOMAN, THE • Yueh Griffi • HKG, SKR
FOX WOMAN, THE • 1915 • Ingraham Lloyd • USA
FOXBAT • 1977 • Liang Puzhi • HKG
FOXED BY A FOX • 1955 • Rasinski Connie • ANS • USA
FOXES • 1980 • Lyne Adrian • USA • TWENTIETH CENTURY FOXES
FOXES, THE • 1970 • Papic Krsto • YGS
FOXES OF HARROW, THE • 1947 • Stahl John M. • USA
FOXFIRE • 1955 • Pevney Joseph • USA
FOXHOLE IN CAIRO • 1960 • Moxey John Llewellyn • UKN
FOXHOLES see **VLCIE DIERY** • 1948
FOXHUNTER: CHAMPION JUMPER • 1953 • Wark Victor • DOC • UKN
FOXIEST GIRL IN PARIS, THE (USA) see **NATHALIE** • 1957
FOXTRAP • 1986 • Williamson Fred • USA
FOXTROT • 1976 • Ripstein Arturo • MXC, SWT, UKN • OTHER SIDE OF PARADISE, THE ○ FAR SIDE OF PARADISE, THE
FOXTROT • 1987 • Tryggvason Jon • ICL, NRW
FOXTROT TANGO ALPHA see **F.T.A.** • 1972
FOXY AMBROSE • Raymaker Herman C. • SHT • USA
FOXY BROWN • 1974 • Hill Jack • USA
FOXY BY PROXY • 1952 • Freleng Friz • ANS • USA
FOXY CUPID • 1916 • *Hippo* • USA
FOXY DUCKLING, THE • 1947 • Davis Arthur • ANS • USA
FOXY FLATFOOTS • 1946 • Wickersham Bob • ANS • USA
FOXY-FOX, THE • 1935 • *Terry Paul/ Moser Frank (P)* • ANS • USA
FOXY GRANDMA • 1911 • *Thanhouser* • USA
FOXY HUNTER, THE • 1937 • Fleischer Dave • ANS • USA
FOXY LADY • 1971 • Reitman Ivan • CND
FOXY PUP, THE • 1937 • *Mintz Charles (P)* • ANS • USA
FOXY TERROR, THE • 1935 • Gillett Burt • ANS • USA
FOXY TROTTERS, THE • 1916 • Smith David • SHT • USA
FOYER PERDU • 1952 • Loubignac Jean • FRN
FOYER PERDU, LE • 1913 • Jasset Victorin • FRN
FPA • 1966 • Beloufa Farouq • DOC • ALG
FRA DIAVOLO • 1906 • *Messter Oskar (P)* • FRG
FRA DIAVOLO • 1912 • Blache Alice • USA
FRA DIAVOLO • 1922 • Lange Bruno • FRG
FRA DIAVOLO • 1922 • Sanderson Challis • UKN
FRA DIAVOLO • 1925 • Roberti Roberto Leone (c/d) • ITL
FRA DIAVOLO • 1930 • Bonnard Mario • FRN
FRA DIAVOLO • 1930 • Bonnard Mario • FRG
FRA DIAVOLO • 1942 • Zampa Luigi • ITL
FRA DIAVOLO see **LEGGENDA DI FRA' DIAVOLO, LA** • 1962
FRA DIAVOLO (SPN) see **TROMBONI DI FRA'DIAVOLI, I** • 1962
FRA DIAVOLO (UKN) see **DEVIL'S BROTHER, THE** • 1933
FRA FYRSTE TIL KNEJPEVAERT • 1913 • Holger-Madsen • DNM • GAMBLER'S WIFE, THE
FRA GIACONE • 1913 • *Williams Eric* • UKN
FRA' MANISCO CERCA GUAI • 1964 • Tamburella Armando W. • ITL
FRA PIAZZA DEL POPOLO • 1925 • Sandberg Anders W. • DNM
FRA' TAZIO DA VELLETRI • 1974 • Gastaldi Romano • ITL
FRA VINCENTI • 1909 • Feuillade Louis • FRN
FRACASSA E L'ALTRO • 1919 • Mari Febo • ITL
FRACCHIA AGAINST DRACULA see **FRACCHIA CONTRO DRACULA** • 1985
FRACCHIA CONTRO DRACULA • 1985 • Parenti Neri • ITL • FRACCHIA AGAINST DRACULA
FRACHT VON BALTIMORE • 1938 • Hinrich Hans • FRG
FRACTURE • 1973 • Rimmer David • CND
FRACTURED FRIENDSHIP • 1965 • Marcus Sid • ANS • USA
FRACTURED LEGHORN, A • 1950 • McKimson Robert • ANS • USA
FRAGE SIEBEN • 1961 • Rosenberg Stuart, Wolff Lothar • FRG, USA • QUESTION SEVEN (USA)
FRAGILE BONHEUR • 1913 • Jasset Victorin • FRN
FRAGILE SEA, THE • 1979 • Stoneman John • MTV • CND
FRAGILE TREE, A • 1984 • Walker John • CND
FRAGILE TREE HAS ROOTS, THE • 1985 • Muller John • MTV • CND
FRAGILES ESPOIRS • 1975-77 • Moreau Michel • DCS • CND
FRAGILITE, TON NOM EST FEMME • 1956 • Varda Agnes • SHT • FRN • FRAGILITY, THY NAME IS WOMAN
FRAGILITE -TON NOM EST FEMME • 1965 • Trintignant Nadine • SHT • FRN
FRAGILITY, THY NAME IS WOMAN see **FRAGILITE, TON NOM EST FEMME** • 1956
FRAGMENT • 1966 • *Mantic* • SHT • UKN
FRAGMENT -DIVINA COMMEDIA • 1973 • Meschke Michael • SWD • FRAGMENT -THE DIVINE COMEDY
FRAGMENT OF AN EMPIRE see **OBLOMOK IMPERII** • 1929
FRAGMENT OF ASH, A • 1914 • West Langdon • USA
FRAGMENT OF FEAR • 1970 • Sarafian Richard C. • UKN
FRAGMENT OF SEEKING • 1946 • Harrington Curtis • SHT • USA • SYMBOL OF DECADENCE
FRAGMENT -THE DIVINE COMEDY see **FRAGMENT -DIVINA COMMEDIA** • 1973
FRAGMENTED LOVE • 1988 • Cherkelov Ivan • BUL
FRAGMENTOS DE VIDA • 1929 • Medina Jose • BRZ
FRAGMENTS • 1944 • Whitney John, Whitney James • SHT • USA
FRAGMENTS • 1976 • Voogd Juri • NTH
FRAGMENTS OF ISABELLA • 1989 • O'Leary Ronan • IRL
FRAGMENTS POUR UN DISCOURS THEATRAL-VITEZ-LE CONSERVATOIRE • 1976 • Koleva Maria • DOC • FRN
FRAGRANCE OF BREASTS see **CHIBUSA NO KAORI** • 1967
FRAGRANCE OF WILD FLOWERS, THE see **MIRIS POLJSKOG CVECA** • 1977
FRAGRANT YOUNG WIFE see **WAKAZUMA NO NIOI** • 1967
'FRAID CAT • 1914 • Johnson Tefft • USA
FRAIDY CAT • 1942 • Hanna William, Barbera Joseph • ANS • USA
FRAIDY CAT, THE • 1924 • Roach Hal • SHT • USA
FRAIL FLOWERS ARE DISAPPEARING, THE see **DEJA S'ENVOLE LA FLEUR MAIGRE** • 1960
FRAIL WOMEN • 1932 • Elvey Maurice • UKN
FRAILTY • 1921 • Thornton F. Martin • UKN
FRAILTY see **TEMPTATION HOURS** • 1916
FRAIRIE, LA • 1975 • Chauvaud Francis • FRN
FRAISES DE L'ILE D'ORLEANS • 1945 • Petel Pierre • DCS • CND
FRAM FOR FRAMGANG • 1938 • Skoglund Gunnar • SWD • LET'S HAVE SUCCESS
FRAM FOR LILLA MARTA • 1945 • Ekman Hasse • SWD • THREE CHEERS FOR LITTLE MARTHA
FRAME FOR MY LOVE • 1969 • Idrizovic Mirza • YGS
FRAME OF MIND, A see **SPOSOB BYCIA** • 1965
FRAME UP • 1967 • Diaz Leody M. • PHL
FRAME UP, A see **MODERN JEAN VAL JEAN: OR, A FRAME UP, A** • 1930
FRAME-UP, THE • 1912 • *Red Wing* • USA
FRAME-UP, THE • 1913 • *Broncho* • USA
FRAME-UP, THE • 1913 • *Majestic* • USA
FRAME-UP, THE • 1915 • *Kalem* • USA
FRAME-UP, THE • 1915 • MacDonald Donald • *Monty* • USA
FRAME-UP, THE • 1915 • Turner Otis • *Universal* • USA
FRAME-UP, THE • 1916 • *Lasky* • USA
FRAME-UP, THE • 1916 • *Vim* • USA
FRAME-UP, THE • 1917 • Sloman Edward • USA
FRAME UP, THE • 1923 • Moody Harry • USA
FRAME-UP, THE • 1937 • Lederman D. Ross • USA • FRAME UP, THE
FRAME-UP, THE • 1938 • Rasinski Connie • ANS • USA
FRAME UP, THE see **FRAME-UP, THE** • 1937
FRAME UP, THE see **INBREKER, DE** • 1972
FRAME-UP ON DAD, THE • 1915 • Davey Horace • USA
FRAMED • 1915 • Ayres Sydney • USA
FRAMED • 1926 • Roberts Stephen • SHT • USA
FRAMED • 1927 • Brabin Charles J. • USA • DIAMONDS IN THE ROUGH
FRAMED • 1930 • Archainbaud George • USA
FRAMED • 1940 • Schuster Harold • USA
FRAMED • 1947 • Wallace Richard • USA • PAULA (UKN)
FRAMED • 1975 • Karlson Phil • USA
FRAMED see **STRUL** • 1988
FRAMED CAT, THE • 1950 • Hanna William, Barbera Joseph • ANS • USA
FRAMED MINATURE, THE • 1917 • King Burton L. • SHT • USA
FRAMED (UKN) see **RIO GRANDE ROMANCE** • 1936
FRAMED UP • 1919 • Perez Marcel • USA
FRAMING FATHER • 1936 • Goodwins Leslie • SHT • USA
FRAMING FATHER • 1942 • Roberts Charles E. • SHT • USA
FRAMING FRAMERS • 1918 • Hurn Philip, Hartman Ferris • USA
FRAMING YOUTH • 1937 • Douglas Gordon • SHT • USA
FRAMLINGEN FRAN SKYN • 1956 • Husberg Rolf • SWD • STRANGER FROM THE SKY
FRAMMANDE HAMN • 1948 • Faustman Erik • SWD • FOREIGN HARBOUR
FRAMMENTI D'AMORE see **TEMA DI MARCO, IL** • 1972
FRAN • 1985 • Hambley Glenda • ASL
FRAN YTTERSTA SKAREN see **HAVETS MELODI** • 1934
FRANC-JEU • 1974 • Lavoie Richard • DOC • CND
FRANCAIS, LANGUE DE TRAVAIL • 1972 • Cardinal Roger • DCS • CND
FRANCAIS, SI VOUS SAVIEZ! • 1972 • Harris Andre, de Sedouy Alain • DOC • FRN
FRANCAIS, SORRY I DON'T • 1974 • Cardinal Roger • DCS • CND
FRANCAISE ET L'AMOUR, LA • 1960 • Le Chanois Jean-Paul, Decoin Henri, Clair Rene, Boisrond Michel, Christian-Jaque, Delannoy Jean, Verneuil Henri • FRN • LOVE AND THE FRENCHWOMAN (USA)
FRANCAISES, VEILLEZ! • 1915 • Perret Leonce • FRN
FRANCE • 1930 • *Holmes Burton* • DOC • USA
FRANCE BONNE HUMEUR • 1933 • Rigal Andre • ASS • FRN
FRANCE DE GISCARD, LA • 1977 • Kollatos Dimitris • FRN
FRANCE EST UN EMPIRE, LA • 1939 • Barrois Georges, Chelle Gaston, Missir Herve, Mejat Raymond, Percin Andre • DOC • FRN
FRANCE EST UN JARDIN, LA • 1953 • Leenhardt Roger • DCS • FRN
FRANCE ET ANGLETERRE FOREVER • 1915 • Perret Leonce • FRN
FRANCE INCONNUE • 1976 • Reichenbach Francois • SER • FRN
FRANCE INTERDITE, LA • 1983 • Imbrohoris Jean-Pierre, Garnier Jean-Pierre, Delannoy Gilles • FRN
FRANCE LIBERATED see **OSVOBOZHDENNAYA FRANTSYA** • 1946
FRANCE, MERE-PATRIE • 1976 • Barbero Guy • DOC • FRN
FRANCE, SOCIETE ANONYME • 1974 • Corneau Alain • FRN
FRANCE SUR MER • 1969 • Reichenbach Francois • SHT • FRN
FRANCE SUR UN CAILLOU, LA • 1960 • Fournier Claude, Groulx Gilles • DCS • CND
FRANCES • 1982 • Clifford Graeme • USA
FRANCESCA • 1987 • Rudolph Verena • FRG
FRANCESCA see **FRANCISCA** • 1981
FRANCESCA DA RIMINI • 1910 • *Vitagraph* • USA
FRANCESCA DA RIMINI • 1913 • Falena Ugo • ITL
FRANCESCA DA RIMINI see **PAOLO E FRANCESCA** • 1950
FRANCESCA DA RIMINI OR, THE TWO BROTHERS • 1907 • Ranous William V. • USA
FRANCESCO • 1988 • Cavani Liliana • ITL, FRG • SAN FRANCESCO
FRANCESCO D'ASSISI • 1966 • Cavani Liliana • MTV • ITL • FRANCESCO DI ASSISI ○ FRANCIS OF ASSISI
FRANCESCO DI ASSISI see **FRANCESCO D'ASSISI** • 1966
FRANCESCO GUILLARE DI DIO • 1950 • Rossellini Roberto • ITL • FLOWERS OF ST. FRANCIS, THE
FRANCHE-COMTE, LA • 1951 • Tavano Fred • SHT • FRN
FRANCHES LIPPEES • 1933 • Delannoy Jean • SHT • FRN
FRANCHESCA'S SEXUAL WHIRLPOOL • 1967 • *Century Cinema Corp.* • USA
FRANCHETTE: LES INTRIGUES • 1969 • Shiffen Arlo • USA
FRANCHISE, THE • 1916 • *Coxen Edward* • SHT • USA
FRANCHISE AFFAIR, THE • 1951 • Huntington Lawrence • UKN
FRANCINE • 1914 • Davis Ulysses • USA
FRANCINE DUGAL FLUTISTE • 1972-73 • Brault Francois • DCS • CND
FRANCIS • 1949 • Lubin Arthur • USA
FRANCIS COVERS THE BIG TOWN • 1953 • Lubin Arthur • USA
FRANCIS GARY POWERS:THE TRUE STORY OF THE U-2 SPY INCIDENT • 1976 • Mann Delbert • TVM • USA
FRANCIS GOES TO THE RACES • 1951 • Lubin Arthur • USA
FRANCIS GOES TO WEST POINT • 1952 • Lubin Arthur • USA
FRANCIS IN THE HAUNTED HOUSE • 1956 • Lamont Charles • USA
FRANCIS IN THE NAVY • 1955 • Lubin Arthur • USA
FRANCIS JOINS THE WACS • 1954 • Lubin Arthur • USA
FRANCIS MARION, THE SWAMP FOX • 1914 • *Coombs Guy* • USA
FRANCIS OF ASSISI • 1961 • Curtiz Michael • USA
FRANCIS OF ASSISI see **FRANCESCO D'ASSISI** • 1966
FRANCIS THE FIRST (USA) see **FRANCOIS 1er** • 1937
FRANCISCA • 1981 • de Oliveira Manoel • PRT • FRANCESCA
FRANCISCAIN DE BOURGES, LE • 1968 • Autant-Lara Claude • FRN
FRANCISCAINES MISSIONNAIRES DE MARIE • 1950 • Lavoie Hermenegilde • CND
FRANCISCAINES MISSIONNAIRES DE MARIE, LES • 1959 • Lavoie Hermenegilde, Lavoie Richard • DCS • CND
FRANCISCO FLOR Y ARCILLA • 1982 • Procopiuk Carlos • ARG • FRANCISCO, FLOWER AND CLAY
FRANCISCO, FLOWER AND CLAY see **FRANCISCO FLOR Y ARCILLA** • 1982
FRANCK AROMA • 1936 • Alexeieff Alexandre • SHT • FRG
FRANCO CICCIO AND THE MERRY WIDOWS see **FRANCO, CICCIO E LE VEDOVE ALLEGRE** • 1968
FRANCO, CICCIO E IL PIRATA BARBANERA • 1969 • Amendola Mario • ITL
FRANCO, CICCIO E LE VEDOVE ALLEGRE • 1968 • Girolami Marino • ITL • FRANCO CICCIO AND THE MERRY WIDOWS
FRANCO DE PORT • 1937 • Kirsanoff Dimitri • FRN • VIA BUENOS AIRES
FRANCO E CICCIO.. LADRO E GUARDIA • 1969 • Ciorciolini Marcello • ITL
FRANCO E CICCIO SUL SENTIERO DI GUERRA • 1970 • Grimaldi Aldo • ITL
FRANCO E CICCIO SUPERSTARS • 1974 • Agliani Giorgio Geo • ITL
FRANCO, ESE HOMBRE • 1964 • Saenz De Heredia Jose Luis • SPN
FRANCO-GERMAN INVASION, THE see **WAR OF WARS, THE** • 1914
FRANCO ZEFFIRELLI: A FLORENTINE ARTIST • 1973 • Mills Reginald • DOC • UKN
FRANCOIS 1er • 1937 • Christian-Jaque • FRN • AMOURS DE LA BELLE FERRONIERE, LES ○ FRANCIS THE FIRST (USA)
FRANCOIS 1er ET TRIBOULET • 1908 • Melies Georges • FRN • KING AND THE JESTER, THE (USA)
FRANCOIS IL CONTRABBANDIERE • 1954 • Parolini Gianfranco • ITL • BACIO DELL'AURORA, IL
FRANCOIS MAURIAC • 1954 • Leenhardt Roger • DCS • FRN
FRANCOIS S'EVADE • 1959 • Image Jean • ANS • FRN
FRANCOIS VILLON • 1945 • Zwobada Andre • FRN
FRANCOIS VILLON • 1988 • Nicolaescu Sergiu • RMN, FRN, FRG
FRANCOISE DUROCHER, WAITRESS • 1972 • Brassard Andre • SHT • CND
FRANCOISE ET LE VILLE • 1955 • Boigelot Jacques • BLG
FRANCOISE STEPS OUT (UKN) see **RUE DE L'ESTRAPADE** • 1953
FRANCOTIRADOR, EL • 1977 • Puerto Carlos • SPN
FRANCS-MACONS see **RIEN QUE DES MENSONGES** • 1932
FRANGINES, LES • 1959 • Gourguet Jean • FRN
FRANK AND EVA see **FRANK & EVA LIVING APART TOGETHER** • 1974
FRANK AND I see **LADY LIBERTINE** • 1983
FRANK COSTELLO FACCIA D'ANGELO (ITL) see **SAMOURAI, LE** • 1967
FRANK DUCK BRINGS 'EM BACK ALIVE • 1946 • Hannah Jack • ANS • USA

FRANK EN EVA see **FRANK & EVA LIVING APART TOGETHER** • 1974

FRANK & EVA LIVING APART TOGETHER • 1974 • de la Parra Pim • NTH • FRANK EN EVA ○ FRANK AND EVA

FRANK FILM • 1973 • Mouris Frank • USA

FRANK GARDINER -KING OF THE ROAD • 1911 • Gavin John F. • ASL

FRANK HANSENS GLUCK • 1917 • Larsen Viggo • FRG

FRANK JAMES RIDES AGAIN (UKN) see **GUNFIRE** • 1950

FRANK N. STEIN • 1952 • *Cowan Louis G.* • SHT • USA • FEARLESS FOSDICK IN FRANK N. STEIN

FRANK NORTON • 1920 • Bauer Leopold • FRG

FRANK ROSOLINO QUARTET • 1962 • Binder Steve • SHT • USA

FRANK W'S YEAR see **ROK FRANKA W.** • 1967

FRANKENCAR • 1988 • Bartel Paul • USA

FRANKENHEIMER • 1971 • Pittman Bruce • CND

FRANKENHOOKER • 1989 • Henenlotter Frank • USA

FRANKENSTEIN • 1910 • Dawley J. Searle • USA

FRANKENSTEIN • 1931 • Whale James • USA

FRANKENSTEIN • 1939 • *Pixilated Pictures* • USA

FRANKENSTEIN • 1968 • Smith Ryle • SHT • USA

FRANKENSTEIN • 1973 • Jordan Glenn • TVM • USA

FRANKENSTEIN • 1984 • ANM • JPN

FRANKENSTEIN • 1984 • Ormerod James • UKN

FRANKENSTEIN '80 • 1973 • Mancini Mario • ITL • FRANKENSTEIN 1980

FRANKENSTEIN '88 • 1984 • Lord Jean-Claude • CND • FRANKENSTEIN FACTOR, THE ○ VINDICATOR, THE

FRANKENSTEIN 90 • 1984 • Jessua Alain • FRN

FRANKENSTEIN -1970 • 1958 • Koch Howard W. • USA

FRANKENSTEIN 1980 see **FRANKENSTEIN '80** • 1973

FRANKENSTEIN ALL'ITALIANA • 1975 • Crispino Armando • ITL • FRANKENSTEIN ITALIAN STYLE

FRANKENSTEIN AND THE GIANT LIZARD see **FURANKENSHUTAIN TAI BARAGON** • 1964

FRANKENSTEIN AND THE MONSTER FROM HELL • 1973 • Fisher Terence • UKN

FRANKENSTEIN CONQUERS THE WORLD (UKN) see **FURANKENSHUTAIN TAI BARAGON** • 1964

FRANKENSTEIN CREATED WOMAN • 1967 • Fisher Terence • UKN

FRANKENSTEIN DE SADE see **HOLLOW-MY-WEANIE, DR. FRANKENSTEIN** • 1969

FRANKENSTEIN, EL VAMPIRO Y CIA • 1961 • Alazraki Benito • MXC • FRANKENSTEIN, THE VAMPIRE AND CO.

FRANKENSTEIN EXPERIMENT, THE see **ANDY WARHOL'S FRANKENSTEIN** • 1974

FRANKENSTEIN FACTOR, THE see **FRANKENSTEIN '88** • 1984

FRANKENSTEIN GENERAL HOSPITAL • 1988 • Roberts Deborah • USA

FRANKENSTEIN ISLAND • 1981 • Warren Jerry • USA • FRANKENSTEIN'S ISLAND

FRANKENSTEIN ITALIAN STYLE see **FRANKENSTEIN ALL'ITALIANA** • 1975

FRANKENSTEIN LIVES AGAIN see **BRIDE OF FRANKENSTEIN** • 1935

FRANKENSTEIN MEETS DRACULA • 1957 • Glut Don • SHT • USA

FRANKENSTEIN MEETS THE SPACE MONSTER • 1965 • Gaffney Robert • USA, PRC • DUEL OF THE SPACE MONSTERS (UKN) ○ MARTE INVADE A PUERTO RICO ○ FRANKENSTEIN MEETS THE SPACEMEN ○ MARS INVADES PUERTO RICO

FRANKENSTEIN MEETS THE SPACEMEN see **FRANKENSTEIN MEETS THE SPACE MONSTER** • 1965

FRANKENSTEIN MEETS THE WOLF MAN • 1943 • Neill R. William • USA

FRANKENSTEIN MUST BE DESTROYED • 1969 • Fisher Terence • UKN

FRANKENSTEIN ON CAMPUS (UKN) see **FLICK** • 1970

FRANKENSTEIN STORY, THE • 1958 • Glut Don • SHT • USA

FRANKENSTEIN: THE TRUE STORY • 1973 • Smight Jack • TVM • USA • DOCTOR FRANKENSTEIN

FRANKENSTEIN, THE VAMPIRE AND CO. see **FRANKENSTEIN, EL VAMPIRO Y CIA** • 1961

FRANKENSTEIN TRESTLE, WHITE MTS. • 1899 • *Bitzer Billy (Ph)* • USA

FRANKENSTEIN UNBOUND • 1990 • Corman Roger • USA

FRANKENSTEIN VS. THE GIANT DEVILFISH see **FURANKENSHUTAIN TAI BARAGON** • 1964

FRANKENSTEIN'S BABY • 1990 • Bierman Robert • TVM • UKN

FRANKENSTEIN'S BLOODY TERROR (USA) see **MARCA DEL HOMBRE LOBO, LA** • 1968

FRANKENSTEIN'S CAT • 1942 • Davis Mannie • ANS • USA

FRANKENSTEIN'S DAUGHTER • 1959 • Cunha Richard E. • USA • SHE MONSTER OF THE NIGHT

FRANKENSTEIN'S EXPERIMENT • 1963 • *Marks Aub* • SHT • UKN

FRANKENSTEIN'S GREAT AUNT TILLIE • 1985 • Gold Myron J. • MXC

FRANKENSTEIN'S ISLAND see **FRANKENSTEIN ISLAND** • 1981

FRANKENSTEIN'S SPUKSCHLOSS see **CRIME AND PASSION** • 1975

FRANKENSTYMIED • 1961 • Hannah Jack • ANS • USA

FRANKFURTER SALESMAN'S DREAM, THE • 1914 • *Shield Ernest* • USA

FRANKFURTERS AND QUAIL • 1912 • *Thanhouser* • USA

FRANKIE AND JOHNNIE • 1935 • Auer John H. • USA

FRANKIE AND JOHNNIE • 1985 • Campbell Martin • TVM • UKN

FRANKIE AND JOHNNY • Murphy Dudley • SHT • USA

FRANKIE AND JOHNNY • 1935 • Erskine Chester • USA

FRANKIE AND JOHNNY • 1966 • De Cordova Frederick • USA

FRANKISCHE LIED, DAS • 1922 • Moest Hubert, Weissenberg Friedrich • FRG

FRANKLIN ARRIVE see **GRAND RENDEZ-VOUS, LE** • 1949

FRANK'S GREATEST ADVENTURE see **FEARLESS FRANK** • 1969

FRANK'S NIGHTMARE • 1915 • *Alhambra* • USA

FRANS ZWARTJES -FILM-MAKER • 1972 • Coelho Rene • DOC • NTH

FRANSKILD • 1951 • Molander Gustaf • SWD • DIVORCED

FRANSSON DEN FORSKRACKLIGE • 1941 • Cederlund Gosta • SWD • FRANSSON THE TERRIBLE

FRANSSON THE TERRIBLE see **FRANSSON DEN FORSKRACKLIGE** • 1941

FRANTIC • 1988 • Polanski Roman • USA

FRANTIC see **MAGICIENNES, LES** • 1960

FRANTIC (USA) see **ASCENSEUR POUR L'ECHAFAUD, L'** • 1957

FRANTISEK • ANS • USS

FRANZ • 1971 • Brel Jacques • BLG, FRN

FRANZ HELLENS • 1969 • Deroisy Lucien • BLG

FRANZ LEHAR • 1923 • Thiele Wilhelm, Torre Hans • AUS

FRANZISKA • 1957 • Liebeneiner Wolfgang • FRG • AUF WIEDERSEHN, FRANZISKA

FRAPPE LOVE • 1913 • Henderson Dell • USA

FRASCONI • 1976 • Darino Eduardo • URG

FRASER, THE • 1964 • Kelly Ron • CND

FRASER'S RIVER • 1958 • Sparling Gordon • CND

FRASIER, THE SENSUOUS LION • 1973 • Shields Pat • USA

FRASQUITA • 1934 • Lamac Carl • AUS

FRAT HOUSE • 1979 • Conrad Sven • USA

FRATE FRANCESCO • 1926 • Antamoro Giulio • ITL • FRIAR FRANCESCO

FRATE SOLE • 1918 • Falena Ugo • ITL

FRATELLI CASTIGLIONI, I • 1937 • D'Errico Corrado • ITL

FRATELLI CORSI, I • 1961 • Majano Anton Giulio • ITL, FRN • CORSICAN BROTHERS, THE (USA) ○ FRERES CORSES, LES (FRN)

FRATELLI DINAMITE, I • 1950 • Pagot Nino, Pagot Tony • ANM • ITL • DYNAMITE BROTHERS, THE (USA) ○ BROTHERS DYNAMITE, THE

FRATELLI D'ITALIA • 1953 • Saraceni Fausto • ITL

FRATELLI D'ITALIA • 1990 • Parenti Neri • ITL • ITALIAN BROTHERS

FRATELLI KARAMAZOFF, I • 1948 • Gentilomo Giacomo • ITL

FRATELLI MIRACOLOSI, I • 1949 • Emmer Luciano • ITL • MIRACULOUS BROTHERS, THE

FRATELLO, IL • 1975 • Mida Massimo • ITL

FRATELLO CRUDELE • 1978 • De Rosa Mario • ITL

FRATELLO HOMO, SORELLA BONA • 1972 • Sequi Mario • ITL • GET THEE TO A NUNNERY (UKN) ○ ROMAN SCANDALS '73 ○ FRATELLO HOMO, SORELLA BONA – NEL BOCCACCIO SUPERPROIBITO

FRATELLO HOMO, SORELLA BONA -NEL BOCCACCIO SUPERPROIBITO see **FRATELLO HOMO, SORELLA BONA** • 1972

FRATELLO LADRO • 1972 • Tosini Pino • ITL

FRATELLO MARE • 1975 • Quilici Folco • ITL

FRATELLO SOLE, SORELLA LUNA • 1972 • Zeffirelli Franco • ITL, UKN • BROTHER SUN, SISTER MOON (UKN)

FRATERNALLY YOURS (UKN) see **SONS OF THE DESERT** • 1933

FRATERNELLE AMAZONIE see **FASCINANTE AMAZONIE** • 1965

FRATERNITY, THE • 1970 • USA

FRATERNITY HOUSE see **AGE OF CONSENT** • 1932

FRATERNITY PIN, THE • 1913 • *Billington Francelia* • USA

FRATERNITY ROW • 1977 • Tobin Thomas J. • USA

FRATERNITY VACATION • 1985 • Frawley James • USA • WENDELL

FRATII JDERI • 1973 • Dragan Mircea • RMN • CAPTAIN MARTENS BROTHERS, THE

FRATSE VAN DIE VLOOT • 1958 • SAF

FRAU AM DUNKLEN FENSTER, EINE • 1960 • Wirth Franz Peter • FRG

FRAU AM SCHEIDEWEGE, DIE • 1938 • von Baky Josef • FRG, HNG • SCHICKSAL EINER ARZTIN, DAS

FRAU AM SCHEIDEWEGE, DIE see **KREUZIGET SIE!** • 1919

FRAU AM STEUER • 1939 • Martin Paul • FRG

FRAU AM WEG, DIE • 1948 • von Borsody Eduard • AUS

FRAU ANNAS PILGERFAHRT • 1915 • Wilhelm Carl • FRG

FRAU AUF DER FOLTER, DIE • 1928 • Wiene Robert • FRG • SCANDAL IN PARIS, A ○ BUTTERFLY ON THE WHEEL, THE

FRAU AUF DER SCHILDKROTE, DIE • 1920 • Attenberger Toni • FRG

FRAU AUS DEM ORIENT, DIE • 1923 • *Orphid-Film* • FRG

FRAU BLACKBURN, BORN 5 JAN. 1872, IS FILMED see **FRAU BLACKBURN, GEB. 5 JAN. 1872, WIRD GEFILMT** • 1967

FRAU BLACKBURN, GEB. 5 JAN. 1872, WIRD GEFILMT • 1967 • Kluge Alexander • SHT • FRG • FRAU BLACKBURN, BORN 5 JAN. 1872, IS FILMED ○ FRAU BLACKBURN WIRD GEFILMT

FRAU BLACKBURN WIRD GEFILMT see **FRAU BLACKBURN, GEB. 5 JAN. 1872, WIRD GEFILMT** • 1967

FRAU CHENEY'S ENDE • 1961 • Wild Franz J. • FRG, SWT

FRAU DES ABGEORDNETEN, DIE • Mack Max • FRG

FRAU DES BOTSCHAFTERS, DIE • 1955 • Deppe Hans • FRG

FRAU, DIE JEDER LIEBT, BIST DU!, DIE • 1929 • Froelich Carl • FRG

FRAU -DIE NACHTIGALL, DIE • 1930 • Lasko Leo • FRG • PERLE DES SUDENS, DIE

FRAU, DIE NICHT "NEIN" SAGEN KANN, DIE • 1926 • Sauer Fred • FRG

FRAU, DIE WEISS, WAS SIE WILL, EINE • 1934 • Janson Victor • FRG

FRAU, DIE WEISS, WAS SIE WILL, EINE • 1958 • Rabenalt Arthur M. • FRG

FRAU DOROTHY'S BEKENNTNIS • 1921 • Curtiz Michael • FRG • DOROTHYS BEKENNTNIS

FRAU EVA see **ARME EVA** • 1914

FRAU FUR 3 TAGE, EINE • 1944 • Kirchhoff Fritz • FRG

FRAU FUR 24 STUNDEN, DIE • 1925 • Schunzel Reinhold • FRG

FRAU FUR ALFIE, EINE • 1989 • Kuert Beat • SWT • WIFE FOR ALFIE, A

FRAU FUR DREI, EINE see **MARGUERITE: 3** • 1939

FRAU FURS GANZE LEBEN, EINE • 1960 • Liebeneiner Wolfgang • FRG

FRAU GEGENUBER, DIE • 1978 • Noever Hans • FRG

FRAU GENUGT NICHT?, EINE • 1955 • Erfurth Ulrich • FRG

FRAU HEMPELS TOCHTER • 1919 • Dewald Julius? • FRG

FRAU HOLLE • 1985 • Jakubisko Juraj • FRG, AUS, CZC

FRAU IM BESTEN MANNESALTER • 1959 • von Ambesser Axel • FRG

FRAU IM DELPHIN ODER 30 TAGE AUF DEM MEERESGRUND, DIE • 1920 • Kiekebusch-Brenken Artur • FRG

FRAU IM DOKTORHUT, DIE • 1920 • Brenken Arthur • FRG

FRAU IM FEUER, DIE • 1924 • Boese Carl • FRG

FRAU IM HIMMEL, DIE • 1920 • Guter Johannes • FRG

FRAU IM KAFIG • 1919 • Guter Johannes • FRG

FRAU IM MOND, DIE • 1929 • Lang Fritz • FRG • BY ROCKET TO THE MOON (UKN) ○ WOMAN IN THE MOON ○ GIRL IN THE MOON

FRAU IM SCHRANK, DIE • 1927 • Biebrach Rudolf • FRG

FRAU IM SPIEGEL, DIE • 1916 • Heymann Robert • FRG

FRAU IM STROM • 1939 • Lamprecht Gerhard • FRG

FRAU IM TALAR, DIE • 1929 • Trotz Adolf • FRG

FRAU IM TUNNEL, DIE • 1921 • *Treumann Wanda* • FRG

FRAU IN DEN WOLKEN, DIE • 1920 • Philippi Siegfried • FRG

FRAU IN GOLD, DIE • 1926 • Marodon Pierre • FRG

FRAU IN VERSUCHUNG, DIE • 1924 • *Gura Sascha* • FRG

FRAU IN WEISS, DIE • 1921 • Neufeld Max • AUS

FRAU IRENE BESSER • 1960 • Olden John • FRG

FRAU IS EINE FRAU, EINE • 1972 • Weidenmann Alfred • FRG

FRAU KOMMT IN DIE TROPEN, EINE • 1938 • Paulsen Harald • FRG

FRAU LEHMANNS TOCHTER • 1932 • Wolff Carl Heinz • FRG

FRAU LENES SCHEIDUNG • 1917 • Grunwald Willy? • FRG

FRAU LUNA • 1941 • Lingen Theo • FRG

FRAU MARIAS ERLEBNIS • 1917 • Halm Alfred? • FRG

FRAU MEINER TRAUME, DIE • 1944 • Jacoby Georg • FRG

FRAU MIT DEM ETWAS, DIE • 1925 • Schonfelder Erich • FRG

FRAU MIT DEM SCHLECHTEN RUF, DIE • 1925 • Christensen Benjamin • FRG, DNM • WOMAN WHO DID, THE

FRAU MIT DEM WELTREKORD, DIE • 1927 • Waschneck Erich • FRG

FRAU MIT DEN KARFUNKELSTEINEN, DIE • 1917 • Mendel Georg Victor • FRG

FRAU MIT DEN MILLIARDEN, DIE see **HERRIN DER WELT 6, DIE** • 1919

FRAU MIT DEN MILLIONEN 1, DIE • 1923 • Wolff Willi • FRG • SCHUSS IN DER PARISER OPER, DER

FRAU MIT DEN MILLIONEN 2, DIE • 1923 • Wolff Willi • FRG • PRINZ OHNE LAND, DER

FRAU MIT DEN MILLIONEN 3, DIE • 1923 • Wolff Willi • FRG • KONSTANTINOPEL – PARIS

FRAU MIT DEN OPALAUGEN, DIE • 1918 • *Alldorf Ria* • FRG

FRAU MIT DEN ORCHIDEEN, DIE • 1919 • Rippert Otto • FRG • WOMAN WITH THE ORCHID, THE

FRAU MIT DEN ZEHN MASKEN 1, DIE • 1921 • Dessauer Siegfried • FRG • BEGEBENHEIT: DAS GRAB OHNE TOTEN

FRAU MIT DEN ZEHN MASKEN 2, DIE • 1921 • Dessauer Siegfried • FRG • BEGEBENHEIT: DAS SCHATTEN DES GEHENKTEN

FRAU MIT DEN ZEHN MASKEN 3, DIE • 1922 • Dessauer Siegfried • FRG • BEGEBENHEIT: TOTE, DIE LEBEN

FRAU MIT DEN ZEHN MASKEN 4, DIE see **HAUS DER VERRUFENEN, DAS** • 1922

FRAU MIT DEN ZWEI SEELEN, DIE • 1916 • Robison Arthur • FRG

FRAU MIT HERZ, EINE • 1951 • Jugert Rudolf • FRG

FRAU MIT VERANTWORTUNG, EINE • 1978 • Stockl Ula • FRG • WOMAN AND HER RESPONSIBILITIES, A

FRAU MIT VERGANGENHEIT, EINE • 1920 • Ziener Bruno • FRG

FRAU MIT VERGANGENHEIT, EINE see **FRAUENMORAL** • 1923

FRAU, NACH DER MAN SICH SEHNT, DIE • 1929 • Bernhardt Curtis • FRG • ENIGMA ○ THREE LOVES

FRAU NACH MASS • 1940 • Kautner Helmut • FRG

FRAU NAMENS HARRY, EIN • 1990 • Frankel Cyril • FRG • HARRY AND HARRIET

FRAU OHNE BETEUTUNG, EINE • 1936 • Steinhoff Hans • FRG • WOMAN OF NO IMPORTANCE, A (USA)

FRAU OHNE GELD, DIE • 1925 • Kaufmann Fritz • FRG

FRAU OHNE GEWISSEN, DIE • 1925 • *Bjornstad-Justitz Film* • FRG

FRAU OHNE HERZ, DIE • 1919 • Illes Eugen • FRG

FRAU OHNE HERZ, DIE • 1925 • *Dorry-Renu-Film* • FRG

FRAU OHNE NAMEN 1, DIE • 1927 • Jacoby Georg • FRG • UNDER EASTERN SKIES

FRAU OHNE NAMEN 2, DIE • 1927 • Jacoby Georg • FRG

FRAU OHNE NERVEN, DIE • 1929 • Wolff Willi • FRG

FRAU OHNE SEELE, DIE • 1920 • Lasko Leo • FRG

FRAU OHNE VERGANGENHEIT, DIE • 1939 • Malasomma Nunzio • FRG

FRAU SCHLANGE • 1923 • Holstein Eugen • FRG

FRAU SIXTRA • 1938 • Ucicky Gustav • FRG

FRAU SORGE • 1928 • Land Robert • FRG

FRAU SUCHT LIEBE, EINE • 1968 • Azderball Robert • FRG • WOMAN NEEDS LOVING, A (UKN)

FRAU SUNDE • 1922 • Sauer Fred • FRG

FRAU SYVELIN • 1938 • Maisch Herbert • FRG

FRAU UBER BORD • 1945 • Staudte Wolfgang • FRG • KABINE 27

FRAU UND DER FREMDE, DIE • 1985 • Simon Rainer • GDR

FRAU UND DER TOD, DIE see **ABENTEUER IN MAROKKO** • 1939

FRAU VAN VINKLE'S CRULLERS • 1913 • Mack H. S. • USA

FRAU VENUS AND HER DEVIL see **FRAU VENUS UND IHR TEUFEL** • 1967

FRAU VENUS UND IHR TEUFEL • 1967 • Kirsten Ralf • GDR • FRAU VENUS AND HER DEVIL ○ VENUS AND HER DEVIL

FRAU, VON DER MAN SPRICHT, DIE • 1931 • Janson Victor • FRG

FRAU VON FORMAT, EINE • 1928 • Wendhausen Fritz • FRG

FRAU VON GESTERN NACHT, DIE • 1950 • Rabenalt Arthur M. • FRG

FRAU VON HEUTE, DIE • 1954 • Verhoeven Paul • FRG

FRAU VON MORGEN, DIE • 1921 • Oberlander Hans • FRG

FRAU VON VIERZIG JAHREN, DIE • 1925 • Oswald Richard • FRG

FRAU WARRENS GEWERBE • 1960 • von Rathony Akos • FRG, SWT

FRAU WIE DU, EINE • 1933 • Boese Carl • FRG

FRAU WIE DU, EINE • 1939 • Tourjansky Victor • FRG

FRAU WIRTIN BLAST AUCH GERN TROMPETE • 1972 • Antel Franz • FRG, ITL, AUS • SEXY SUSAN KNOWS HOW

FRAU WIRTIN HAT AUCH EINE NICHTE • 1968 • Antel Franz • FRG, ITL, AUS • HOUSE OF PLEASURE (UKN)
FRAU WIRTIN HAT AUCH EINEN GRAFEN • 1968 • Antel Franz • FRG, ITL, AUS • HOSTESS ALSO HAS A COUNT, THE ◦ SEXY SUSAN SINS AGAIN
FRAU WIRTIN TREIBT ES JETZT NOCH TOLLER • 1971 • Antel Franz • FRG, AUS
FRAU WIRTIN'S DAREDEVIL DAUGHTERS see **FRAU WIRTINS TOLLE TOCHTERLEIN** • 1973
FRAU WIRTINS TOLLE TOCHTERLEIN • 1973 • Antel Franz • AUS, FRG, ITL • FRAU WIRTIN'S DAREDEVIL DAUGHTERS
FRAUD • 1973 • Monat Donald • SAF
FRAUD see **SHAKKAR** • 1988
FRAUD AT THE HOPE MINE, THE • 1912 • *Nilsson Anna Q.* • USA
FRAUD THAT FAILED, THE • 1912 • Dwan Allan • USA
FRAUDE MATRIMONIAL • 1976 • Iquino Ignacio F. • SPN
FRAUDES ANDERSEN, DIE • 1936 • Selpin Herbert • FRG
FRAUDEUR, LE • 1937 • Simons Leopold • FRN • CEUX DE LA DOUANE ◦ ENJOLEUSE, L'
FRAUDS • 1915 • *Mayo Edna* • USA
FRAUDS AND FREE LUNCH • 1917 • Kernan Henry • SHT • USA
FRAUDS AND FRENZIES • 1918 • Semon Larry • SHT • USA
FRAUDULENT BEGGAR, THE • 1898 • Williamson James • UKN
FRAUDULENT SOLICITOR, THE • 1907 • Fitzhamon Lewin • UKN
FRAUDULENT SPIRITUALISM EXPOSED see **SPIRITUALISM EXPOSED** • 1913
FRAUEN.. • 1920 • Kahn William • FRG
FRAUEN AM ABGRUND • 1929 • Jacoby Georg • FRG
FRAUEN AUS DER WIENER VORSTADT • 1925 • Hanus Heinz • AUS • 15 JAHRE SCHWEREN KERKER
FRAUEN DER LEIDENSCHAFT • 1926 • Randolf Rolf • FRG
FRAUEN DER NACHT see **TRAGODIE DER ENTEHRTEN, DIE** • 1924
FRAUEN DES HERRN S., DIE • 1951 • Martin Paul • FRG
FRAUEN DES JOSIAS GRASSENREUTH, DIE • 1918 • Rippert Otto • FRG
FRAUEN, DIE DEN WEG VERLOREN • 1926 • Rahn Bruno • FRG
FRAUEN, DIE DER ABGRUND VERSCHLINGT • 1918 • Wauer William • FRG
FRAUEN, DIE DURCH DIE HOLLE GEHEN (AUS) see **SIETE MAGNIFICAS, LAS** • 1966
FRAUEN, DIE EHE BRECHEN • 1922 • Walther-Fein Rudolf • FRG
FRAUEN, DIE MAN OFT NICHT GRUSST • 1925 • Zelnik Friedrich • FRG
FRAUEN, DIE NICHT HEIRATEN SOLLTEN • 1919 • Illes Eugen • FRG
FRAUEN, DIE NICHT LIEBEN DURFEN • 1925 • von Bolvary Geza • FRG • FRAUEN, DIE VOM WEG ABIRREN
FRAUEN, DIE SICH OPFERN • 1916 • Eichberg Richard • FRG
FRAUEN, DIE VOM WEG ABIRREN see **FRAUEN, DIE NICHT LIEBEN DURFEN** • 1925
FRAUEN FUR GOLDEN HILL • 1938 • Waschneck Erich • FRG
FRAUEN, HUTET EURE MUTTERSCHAFT! • 1925 • *Projektions-Ag Union* • FRG • KEIMENDES LEBEN ◦ MUSS DIE FRAU MUTTER WERDEN?
FRAUEN IM SUMPF • 1924 • *Makowska Helena* • FRG
FRAUEN IN MAROKKO • 1928 • Righelli Gennaro • FRG
FRAUEN IN NEW YORK • 1977 • Fassbinder R. W. • FRG • WOMEN IN NEW YORK
FRAUEN IN TEUFELS HAND • 1960 • Leitner Hermann • AUS
FRAUEN SIND DOCH BESSERE DIPLOMAT • 1941 • Jacoby Georg • FRG
FRAUEN SIND KEINE ENGEL • 1942 • Forst Willi • FRG
FRAUEN UM DEN SONNENKONIG see **LISELOTTE VON DER PFALZ** • 1935
FRAUEN UND BANKNOTEN • 1926 • Kaufmann Fritz • FRG
FRAUEN UND DIAMANTEN • 1919 • Boese Carl • FRG
FRAUEN UND FRAUEN • 1923 • *Clermont Rita* • FRG
FRAUEN VOM GNADENSTEIN, DIE • 1920 • Dinesen Robert • FRG
FRAUEN VOM TANNHOF, DIE • 1934 • Seitz Franz • FRG
FRAUEN VON FOLIES BERGERES, DIE • 1926 • Obal Max • FRG
FRAUEN ZWEIER JUNGGESELLEN, DIE • 1925 • Seitz Franz • FRG
FRAUENARZT DR. BERTRAM • 1957 • Klinger Werner • FRG
FRAUENARZT DR. PRATORIUS • 1950 • Goetz Curt, Gillmann Karl P. • FRG
FRAUENARZT DR. SCHAFER • 1928 • Fleck Jacob, Fleck Luise • FRG
FRAUENARZT DR. SIBELIUS • 1962 • Jugert Rudolf • FRG
FRAUENARZT KLAGT AN, EIN • 1964 • Harnack Falk • FRG
FRAUENBEICHTE 1 • 1921 • Lamprecht Gerhard • FRG • BEICHTE DER AUSGESTOSSENEN, DIE
FRAUENBEICHTE 2 • 1921 • Lamprecht Gerhard • FRG • BEICHTE DER MORDERIN, DIE
FRAUENBEICHTE 3 • 1921 • Lamprecht Gerhard • FRG • BEICHTE DER KRANKENSCHWESTER, DIE
FRAUENBRIEFE • 1920 • Walther-Fein Rudolf • FRG
FRAUENDIPLOMAT, DER • 1932 • Emo E. W. • FRG
FRAUENEHRE • 1918 • Kundert Georg • AUS
FRAUENGASSE VON ALGIER, DIE • 1927 • Hoffmann-Harnisch Wolfgang • FRG
FRAUENHAUS VON BRESCIA, DAS • 1920 • Moest Hubert • FRG
FRAUENHAUS VON RIO, DAS • 1927 • Steinhoff Hans • FRG • PLUSCH UND PLUMOWSKI
FRAUENKONIG, DER • 1923 • Speyer Jaap • FRG
FRAUENLIEBE • 1920 • Capello Carlo • FRG
FRAUENLIEBE -FRAUENLIED • 1937 • Genina Augusto • FRG
FRAUENMARDER, DER • 1925 • Wenter Adolf • FRG
FRAUENMORAL • 1923 • Frenkel-Bouwmeester Theo • FRG • FRAU MIT VERGANGENHEIT, EINE
FRAUENNOT -FRAUENGLUCK • 1930 • Tisse Eduard • DOC • SWT
FRAUENOPFER • 1922 • Grune Karl • FRG • SACRIFICE OF A WOMAN
FRAUENPARADIES, DAS • 1922 • Mack Max • FRG
FRAUENPARADIES, DAS • 1939 • Rabenalt Arthur M. • FRG • WOMAN'S PARADISE (USA)
FRAUENRAUB see **RAPT** • 1934
FRAUENRUHM • 1920 • Fiedler-Spies Ernst • FRG • UM RHUM UND FRAUENGLUCK
FRAUENSCHICKSAL • 1922 • von Parisch-Schamberg Guido • FRG
FRAUENSCHICKSAL • 1929 • Robison Arthur • FRG
FRAUENSCHICKSALE • 1952 • Dudow Slatan • GDR • FATES OF WOMEN ◦ WOMAN'S FATE ◦ WOMEN'S DESTINY
FRAUENSCHONHEIT UNTER DEM SEZIERMESSER, EINE • 1920 • Neff Wolfgang • FRG • IN DEN KRALLEN DES VAMPYRES
FRAUENSEE • 1958 • Jugert Rudolf • AUS
FRAULEIN • 1939 • Waschneck Erich • FRG
FRAULEIN • 1958 • Koster Henry • USA
FRAULEIN AUS ARGENTINIEN, DAS • 1928 • Philippi Siegfried • FRG • O JUGEND, WIE BIST DU SO SCHON!
FRAULEIN BARONIN • 1919 • Muller-Hagen Carl? • FRG
FRAULEIN BIMBI • 1951 • von Rathony Akos • AUS • UNMOGLICHE MADCHEN, DAS
FRAULEIN CASANOVA • 1953 • Emo E. W. • AUS
FRAULEIN CHAUFFEUR • 1928 • Speyer Jaap • FRG • MISS CHAUFFEUR
FRAULEIN DOKTOR • 1969 • Lattuada Alberto • ITL, YGS • GOSPODIJICA DOKTOR -SPIJUNKA BEZ IMENA (YGS) ◦ BETRAYAL, THE ◦ NAMELESS
FRAULEIN ELSE • 1929 • Czinner Paul • FRG
FRAULEIN FAHNRICH • 1929 • Sauer Fred • FRG
FRAULEIN -FALSCH VERBUNDEN • 1932 • Emo E. W. • FRG
FRAULEIN FELDWEBEL • 1915 • *Muller-Lincke Anna* • FRG
FRAULEIN FRAU • 1934 • Boese Carl • FRG
FRAULEIN HOCHMUT • 1915 • Hofer Franz • FRG
FRAULEIN HOFFMANNS ERZAHLUNGEN • 1933 • Lamac Carl • FRG
FRAULEIN JOSETTE, MEINE FRAU • 1926 • Ravel Gaston • FRG, FRN • MADEMOISELLE JOSETTE, MA FEMME ◦ MARRIAGE OF CONVENIENCE, THE
FRAULEIN JULIE • 1921 • Basch Felix • FRG • LADY JULIA
FRAULEIN KADETT • 1918 • *Hoffman Ernst* • FRG
FRAULEIN LAUSBUB • 1929 • Schonfelder Erich • FRG
FRAULEIN LISELOTT • 1934 • Guter Johannes • FRG
FRAULEIN MAMA • 1926 • von Bolvary Geza • FRG
FRAULEIN MUTTER • 1918 • *Haack Kate* • FRG
FRAULEIN PFIFFIKUS • 1918 • Hofer Franz • FRG
FRAULEIN PICCOLO • 1914 • Hofer Franz • FRG
FRAULEIN RAFFKE • 1923 • Eichberg Richard • FRG
FRAULEIN SEIFENSCHAUM • 1914 • Lubitsch Ernst • FRG
FRAULEIN UND DER VAGABUND, DAS • 1949 • Benitz Albert • FRG
FRAULEIN VOM AMT, DAS • 1925 • Schwarz Hanns • FRG • LIEBE UND TELEPHON
FRAULEIN VOM SPITTELMARKT, DAS • 1925 • Dammann Gerhard • FRG
FRAULEIN VON AMT • 1954 • Schroth Carl-Heinz • FRG
FRAULEIN VON BARNHELM, DAS • 1940 • Schweikart Hans • FRG
FRAULEIN VON KASSE 12, DAS • 1927 • Schonfelder Erich • FRG
FRAULEIN VON SCUDERI, DAS • 1955 • York Eugen • GDR, SWT
FRAULEIN ZAHNARZT • 1919 • May Joe • FRG
FRAULEINS IN UNIFORM (UKN) see **ARMEE GRETCHEN, EINE** • 1973
FRAUMONT JNR., REISLER SEN. see **ARME EVA** • 1914
FRAY DOLAR • 1970 • Pena Raul • SPN
FRAY ESCOBA • 1961 • Torrado Ramon • SPN
FRAY TORERO • 1966 • Saenz De Heredia Jose Luis • SPN
FRAYED FAGIN'S ADVENTURES • 1913 • *Brennan John E.* • USA
FRAYLE, EL • 1959 • Olmi Ermanno (Spv) • DOC • ITL
FRAZZLED FINANCE • 1913 • *Thanhouser* • USA
FREAK BARBER, THE • 1905 • Martin J. H.? • UKN
FREAK OF FERNDALE FOREST, THE • 1910 • *Warwick* • UKN
FREAK ORLANDO • 1980 • Ottinger Ulrike • FRG
FREAK TEMPERANCE WAVE, A • 1914 • *Asher Max* • USA
FREAKMAKER, THE see **MUTATIONS, THE** • 1973
FREAKS • 1915 • Curtis Allen • USA
FREAKS • 1932 • Browning Tod • USA • FORBIDDEN LOVE ◦ NATURE'S MISTAKES ◦ BARNUM ◦ MONSTER SHOW, THE
FREAKS! see **SHE FREAK** • 1967
FREAKS OF THE DEEP • 1932 • Sennett Mack • DOC • USA
FREAKSHOW • 1989 • Magnatta Constantino • USA
FREAKY FRIDAY • 1976 • Nelson Gary • USA
FRECCIA, LA see **FRECCIA NEL FIANCO, LA** • 1943
FRECCIA D'ORO • 1935 • D'Errico Corrado, Ballerini Piero • ITL
FRECCIA D'ORO, LA • 1962 • Margheriti Antonio • ITL • ARCIERE DELLE MILLE E UNA NOTTE, L' ◦ GOLDEN ARROW, THE (USA)
FRECCIA NEL CUORE, LA • 1924 • Palermi Amleto • ITL
FRECCIA NEL FIANCO, LA • 1943 • Lattuada Alberto • ITL • FRECCIA, LA ◦ ARROW, THE
FRECH UND VERLIEBT • 1944 • Schweikart Hans • FRG
FRECHDACHS, DER • 1932 • Boese Carl, Hille Heinz • FRG
FRECKLED FISH, THE • 1919 • Le Brandt Joseph • SHT • USA
FRECKLED RASCAL, THE • 1929 • King Louis • USA
FRECKLES • 1912 • Thompson Frederick A. • USA
FRECKLES • 1914 • Miller Charles? • USA
FRECKLES • 1917 • Neilan Marshall • USA
FRECKLES • 1928 • Meehan James Leo • USA
FRECKLES • 1935 • Hamilton William, Killy Edward • USA
FRECKLES • 1960 • McLaglen Andrew V. • USA
FRECKLES see **SOMMERSPROSSEN** • 1968
FRECKLES COME HOME • 1942 • Yarbrough Jean • USA
FRECKLES' FIGHT FOR HIS BRIDE • 1913 • *Powers* • USA
FRED BARNES • 1926 • *De Forest Phonofilms* • SHT • UKN
FRED BARRY see **FRED BARRY, COMEDIEN** • 1959
FRED BARRY, COMEDIEN • 1959 • Jutra Claude • DCS • CND • FRED BARRY
FRED GOES IN FOR HORSES • 1913 • *Apollo* • USA
FRED OTT'S SNEEZE OR RECORD OF A SNEEZE • 1894 • *Edison* • USA
FREDAINES DE PIERRETTE, LES • 1900 • Blache Alice • SER • FRN
FREDA'S PHOTO • 1913 • Noy Wilfred • UKN
FREDDA ALBA DEL COMMISSARIO JOSS, LA (ITL) see **PACHA, LE** • 1968
FREDDIE SLACK AND HIS ORCHESTRA • 1950 • *Universal* • SHT • USA
FREDDIE STEPS OUT • 1946 • Dreifuss Arthur • USA • SWEET SIXTEEN
FREDDIE THE FAKE FISHERMAN • 1915 • *Howell William Al* • USA
FREDDIE THE FRESHMAN • 1931-32 • Ising Rudolf • ANS • USA
FREDDIE THE GREAT see **HE'S A COCKEYED WONDER** • 1950
FREDDIE'S COURTSHIP • 1910 • *Powers* • USA
FREDDIE'S FRIGID FINISH • 1916 • *Keyes Francis* • USA
FREDDIE'S IN LOVE • 1971 • SAF
FREDDIE'S NIGHTMARES: A NIGHTMARE ON ELM STREET • 1988 • Hooper Tobe, McLoughlin Tom • TVM • USA
FREDDY • 1978 • Thomas Robert • FRN • JEANNOT LA FRIME
FREDDY AIDS MATRIMONY • 1916 • Currier Frank • SHT • USA
FREDDY CAN MANAGE IT see **FREDDY KLARAR BIFFEN** • 1968
FREDDY, DIE GITARRE UND DAS MEER • 1959 • Schleif Wolfgang • FRG
FREDDY FOILS THE FLOATERS • 1916 • Currier Frank • SHT • USA
FREDDY KLARAR BIFFEN • 1968 • Frisk Ragnar • SWD • FREDDY CAN MANAGE IT
FREDDY LOOSEBELT FROM AFRICA • 1913 • *Mace Fred* • USA
FREDDY MARTIN AND HIS ORCHESTRA • 1941 • Negulesco Jean • SHT • USA
FREDDY OF THE JUNGLE • 1981 • Konski Josi • SPN
FREDDY THE FIXER • 1916 • Currier Frank • SHT • USA
FREDDY, TIERE, SENSATIONEN • 1964 • Vibach Karl • FRG
FREDDY UND DAS LIED DER PRARIE • 1964 • Martin Sobey • FRG, YGS • SHERIFF WAS A LADY, THE (USA)
FREDDY UND DAS LIED DER SUDSEE • 1962 • Jacobs Werner • FRG
FREDDY UND DER MILLIONAR • 1961 • May Paul • FRG
FREDDY UND DIE MELODIE DER NACHT • 1960 • Schleif Wolfgang • FRG
FREDDY UNTER FREMDEN STERNEN • 1962 • Schleif Wolfgang • FRG
FREDDY VERSUS HAMLET • 1916 • Currier Frank • SHT • USA
FREDDY'S DUMB PLAYMATES • 1913 • Fitzhamon Lewin • UKN
FREDDY'S LAST BEAN • 1916 • Currier Frank • SHT • USA
FREDDY'S LITTLE LOVE AFFAIR • 1908 • Coleby A. E. • UKN
FREDDY'S NARROW ESCAPE • 1916 • Currier Frank • SHT • USA
FREDDY'S NIGHTMARE: OR, TOO MUCH MONEY • 1914 • Doff Mr. • UKN
FREDDY'S NIGHTMARES 2 • 1988 • Wiederhorn Ken • TVM • USA
FREDERIC CHOPIN • 1961 • Wrestler Philip • UKN
FREDERIC CHOPIN -VALSE MINUTE • 1967 • Marzynski Marian, Kaminski Andrzej • PLN
FREDERICA • 1942 • Boyer Jean • FRN
FREDERICK DOUGLAS: THE HOUSE ON CEDAR HILL • 1977 • *Moss Carlton* • USA
FREDERICK HOLMES' WARD • 1915 • Coyle Walter • USA
FREDERICK THE GREAT • 1914 • Edwin Walter • USA
FREDLOS • 1935 • Schneevoigt George • SWD, DNM • OUTLAWED ◦ OUTCAST
FRED'S FICTITIOUS FOUNDLING • 1918 • Binney Josh • SHT • USA
FRED'S FIGHTING FATHER • 1918 • *Filbert Fatty* • SHT • USA
FRED'S I.O.U. • 1913 • *Apollo* • USA
FRED'S LOUNGE • 1976-77 • Brault Michel, Gladu Andre • DCS • CND
FRED'S POLICE FORCE • 1912 • *Evans Fred* • UKN
FRED'S TRAINED NURSE • 1913 • *Mace Fred* • USA
FRED'S WATERLOO • 1913 • *Mace Fred* • USA
FREE • 1973 • Tenzer Bert • DOC • USA
FREE AIR • 1922 • Griffith Edward H. • USA
FREE AND EASY • 1930 • Sedgwick Edward • USA • EASY GO ◦ ON THE SET
FREE AND EASY • 1941 • Sidney George • USA
FREE AND EASY • 1960 • Henryson Robert • UKN
FREE, BLONDE AND TWENTYONE • 1940 • Cortez Ricardo • USA
FREE BREATHING see **SZABAD LELEGZET** • 1973
FREE CHRISTMAS DINNERS • 1909 • *Lubin* • USA
FREE CITY see **WOLNE MIASTO** • 1958
FREE EATS • 1932 • McCarey Ray • SHT • USA
FREE ENTERPRISE • 1948 • Davis Mannie • ANS • USA • RUNNING FROM THE GUNS (USA)
FREE ENTERPRISE • 1986 • Dixon John • ASL • RUNNING FROM THE GUNS
FREE FALL • 1964 • Lipsett Arthur • ANS • CND
FREE FALL • 1967 • Vanderbeek Stan • USA
FREE FOR ALL • 1949 • Barton Charles T. • USA
FREE FOR ALL see **PIEDRA LIBRE** • 1976
FREE FROM CARE • 1965 • Perry Margaret • DOC • CND
FREE GRASS • 1969 • Brame Bill • USA • SCREAM FREE
FREE HOUSE • 1942 • Cass Henry • DCS • UKN
FREE ISLAND, THE see **KIGEKI-OBUROSHIKI** • 1967
FREE KISSES • 1926 • Nye William • USA • WANTON KISSES
FREE LIPS • 1928 • MacDonald Wallace • USA
FREE LOVE • 1930 • Henley Hobart • USA • BLIND WIVES ◦ MODERN WIFE, THE
FREE LOVE see **SINNERS IN SILK** • 1924
FREE LOVE see **AMORE LIBRE** • 1974
FREE LOVE see **AMOR LIBRE, EL** • 1977
FREE LOVE CONFIDENTIAL • 1967 • Heller Gordon?, Hess Gordon? • USA
FREE MAN see **VOLNITSA** • 1956

FREE–MASON VILLE–KALLE see **VAPAA–DUUNARI VILLE–KALLE** • 1984
FREE PARDON, A • 1908 • Fitzhamon Lewin? • UKN
FREE PEASANTS • 1965 • Huisken Joop • DOC • GDR
FREE RADICALS • 1957 • Lye Len • SHT • USA
FREE RENT • 1936 • Lord Del • SHT • USA
FREE RIDE • 1986 • Trbovich Tom • USA
FREE RIDE, A • 1903 • Stow Percy • UKN
FREE–SHOOTER, THE see **FREISCHUTZ, DER** • 1968
FREE SONG see **CANTO LIBRE** • 1979
FREE SONG, THE see **CANTO LIVRE, O** • 1968
FREE SOUL, A • 1931 • Brown Clarence • USA
FREE SPEECH • 1916 • Drew Sidney • SHT • USA
FREE SPIRIT see **MAXIE** • 1985
FREE SPIRIT (USA) see **BELSTONE FOX, THE** • 1973
FREE THE ARMY see **F.T.A.** • 1972
FREE TO LIVE (UKN) see **HOLIDAY** • 1938
FREE TO LOVE • 1925 • O'Connor Frank • USA
FREE TRADE • 1910 • *Gaumont* • UKN
FREE TRADE BENCH, THE • 1903 • Smith G. A. • UKN
FREE WHEELING • 1932 • McGowan Robert • SHT • USA
FREE, WHITE AND 21 • 1963 • Buchanan Larry • USA
FREE WIND see **VOLNYI VETER** • 1961
FREE WOMAN, A (USA) see **STROHFEUER** • 1972
FREEBIE AND THE BEAN • 1974 • Rush Richard • USA
FREEBOOTERS • 1909 • *Selig* • USA
FREEBOOTERS, THE • 1908 • Coleby A. E. • UKN
FREED BIRD see **VOLNAYA PTITSA** • 1913
FREED BY FIDO • 1917 • Davis James • SHT • USA
FREED 'EM AND WEEP • 1929 • McCarey Leo • SHT • USA
FREED FROM SUSPICION • 1912 • *Kalem* • USA
FREED HANDS (USA) see **BEFREITE HANDE** • 1939
FREEDOM • 1981 • Sargent Joseph • TVM • USA
FREEDOM • 1982 • Hicks Scott • ASL
FREEDOM see **SAOIRSE?** • 1961
FREEDOM COMMITTEE see **FRIHEDSFONDEN** • 1945
FREEDOM FIGHTER • 1988 • Davis Desmond • TVM • USA
FREEDOM FIGHTERS • 1987 • Shelakh Riki • SAF • MERCENARY FIGHTERS
FREEDOM FOR LOVE (UKN) see **EHEMANNER REPORT** • 1970
FREEDOM FOR REBEL see **REVAK, LO SCHIAVO DI CARTAGINE** • 1960
FREEDOM FOR SALE see **PAROLE RACKET** • 1937
FREEDOM FOR US see **A NOUS LA LIBERTE** • 1931
FREEDOM FOR YOU AND FOR US • 1968 • Makhnach Leonid • DOC • USS
FREEDOM FORCE, THE • 1978 • ANM • USA
FREEDOM, FREEDOM ABOVE ALL • 1960 • Gass Karl • DOC • GDR
FREEDOM IS PARADISE • Bodrov Sergei • USS
FREEDOM MUST HAVE WINGS • 1941 • Bennett Compton • DCS • UKN
FREEDOM NOW see **FRIHETEN NA** • 1973
FREEDOM OF CHOICE • 1983 • White Helene B. • CND
FREEDOM OF THE CITY • 1974 • Till Eric • CND
FREEDOM OF THE PRESS • 1928 • Melford George • USA • POWER OF THE PRESS ○ MUZZLE, THE ○ GRAFT ○ UNCONQUERED
FREEDOM OF THE SEAS • 1934 • Varnel Marcel • UKN
FREEDOM OR STRIP see **SLOBODA ILI STRIP** • 1973
FREEDOM RADIO • 1941 • Asquith Anthony • UKN • VOICE IN THE NIGHT, THE (USA)
FREEDOM RIDERS, THE see **UNDERCOVER WITH THE KKK** • 1979
FREEDOM ROAD • 1979 • Kadar Jan • TVM • USA
FREEDOM SCHOOL see **JIYU GAKKU** • 1951
FREEDOM TO DIE • 1962 • Searle Francis • UKN
FREEDOM TO LOVE see **VITA E BELLA, LA** • 1980
FREEDOM TO LOVE (USA) see **FREIHEIT FUR DIE LIEBE** • 1969
FREEDOM TO MOVE, A • 1985 • Brault Michel • CND
FREELANCE • 1970 • Megahy Francis • UKN
FREELANCE SAMURAI see **MOMOTARO SAMURAI** • 1957
FREELOADING • 1982 • Sutherland Joseph, Terry Chris • CND
FREELOADING FELINE • 1960 • Hannah Jack • ANS • USA
FREEM • 1966 • Schmeink K. • SHT • NTH
FREEMEN • 1955 • Roshal Grigori • USS
FREEWAY • 1988 • Delia Francis • USA
FREEWAY F19 • 1976 • Patterson Garry • DOC • ASL
FREEWAY FRACAS • 1964 • Smith Paul J. • ANS • USA
FREEWAY KILLINGS, THE see **POLICE STORY: THE FREEWAY KILLINGS** • 1987
FREEWAY MANIAC, THE • 1987 • Winters Paul • USA • BREAKDOWN
FREEWAYPHOBIA NO.1 • 1965 • Clark Les • ANS • USA
FREEWAYPHOBIA NO.2 see **GOOFY'S FREEWAY TROUBLE** • 1965
FREEWHEELIN' • 1976 • Dittrich Scott • USA
FREEZE BOMB see **DEATH DIMENSION** • 1978
FREEZE FRAME AT TABLE see **STOP CADRU LA MASA** • 1980
FREEZE OUT, THE • 1921 • Ford John • USA
FREEZING AUNTIE • 1911 • *West William* • USA
FREEZING MIXTURE • 1910 • Bouwmeester Theo, Booth W. R. • UKN • POTTED PLAYS NO.3
FREEZING POINT see **HYOTEN** • 1966
FREGOLA • 1948 • Robbeling Harald • AUS
FREGOLI THE PROTEAN ARTISTE • 1898 • *Paul R. W.* • UKN
FREI LUIS DE SOUSA • 1949 • Ribeiro Antonio Lopes • PRT
FREI TANTEN, DIE • 1921 • Biebrach Rudolf • FRG
FREIE BAHN DEM TUCHTIGEN • 1921 • Bolten-Baeckers Heinrich • FRG
FREIE LIEBE • 1919 • Mack Max • FRG
FREIES LAND • 1946 • Harbich Milo • GDR
FREIES VOLK • 1925 • Berger Martin • FRG
FREIGHT 249 • 1918 • Craft William James • DOC • CND
FREIGHT CAR HONEYMOON, A • 1915 • *La Badie Florence* • USA
FREIGHT FRIGHT • 1965 • Rasinski Connie • ANS • USA
FREIGHT PREPAID see **FAST FREIGHT, THE** • 1921
FREIGHT STOP • 1954 • Downs Allen • SHT • USA
FREIGHT TRAIN DRAMA, A • 1912 • *Greenwood Winnifred* • USA
FREIGHTERS OF DESTINY • 1931 • Allen Fred • USA
FREIHEIT FUR DIE LIEBE • 1969 • Kronhausen Phyllis, Kronhausen Eberhard • FRG • FREEDOM TO LOVE (USA)
FREIHEIT, GLEICHHEIT, BRUDERLICHKEIT! • 1919 • Mendel Georg Victor • FRG
FREIHEIT IN FESSELN • 1929 • Wolff Carl Heinz • FRG • BEWAHRUNGSFRIST
FREISCHUTZ, DER • 1968 • Hess Joachim • MTV • FRG • FREE–SHOOTER, THE ○ MARKSMAN, THE
FREISPRUCH MANGELS BEWEISEN • 1962 • Groschopp Richard • GDR
FREITAG DER 13 • 1944 • Engels Erich • FRG • FRIDAY THE 13TH
FREITAG, DER 13 see **UNHEIMLICHE HAUS 2, DAS** • 1916
FREIWILD • 1928 • Holger-Madsen • FRG
FRELSENDE FILM, DEN • 1915 • Holger-Madsen • DNM • WOMAN TEMPTED ME, THE
FREM OG TILBAKE ER LIKE LANGT? • 1973 • Lochen Erik • NRW • THERE AND BACK FOR NOTHING?
FREMD BIN ICH EINGEZOGEN • 1978 • Leber Titus • AUS, FRG • I CAME A STRANGER
FREMD IM SUDETENLAND • 1938 • Wassermann H. • STRANGE TO THE SUDETEN COUNTRY (USA)
FREMDE, DER • 1961 • Arpe Johannes • GDR
FREMDE, DIE • 1917 • Rippert Otto • FRG
FREMDE, DIE • 1930 • Sauer Fred • FRG
FREMDE AUS DER ELSTERGASSE, DIE • 1921 • Tostary Alfred • FRG
FREMDE FRAU, DIE • 1939 • von Norman Roger • FRG
FREMDE FURST, DER • 1918 • Wegener Paul • FRG • STRANGE PRINCE, THE
FREMDE LEBEN, DAS • 1945 • Meyer Johannes • FRG
FREMDE MADCHEN, DAS • 1913 • *Von Hoffmansthal Hugo* • FRG • STRANGE GIRL, THE
FREMDE MIT DER TEUFELSFRATZE, DER • 1920 • Carstennsen Carlo • FRG
FREMDE STADT • 1972 • Thome Rudolf • FRG • STRANGE TOWN ○ STRANGE CITY
FREMDE VOGEL, DER • 1911 • Gad Urban • FRG • STRANGE BIRD, THE
FREMDE WELTEN • 1920 • Walther-Fein Rudolf • FRG
FREMDENFUHRER VON LISSABON, DER • 1956 • Deppe Hans • FRG
FREMDENHEIM FILODA • 1937 • Hinrich Hans • FRG
FREMDENLEGIONAR, DER see **WENN DIE SCHWALBEN HEIMWARTS ZIEHN** • 1927
FREMDENLEGIONAR NR.37 see **NACHT DER VERSUCHUNG, DIE** • 1932
FREMMED BANKER PA, EN • 1959 • Jacobsen Johan • DNM • STRANGER KNOCKS, A (USA)
FREMTID SOGES • 1983 • Bonfils Dola • DNM • FUTURE WANTED
FREMTIDENS BORN • 1984 • Nyholm Ove • DNM • CHILDREN OF THE FUTURE
FRENCH, THE • 1982 • Klein William • DOC • FRN
FRENCH BLUE see **BIJOUX DE FAMILLE, LES** • 1974
FRENCH CANCAN • 1954 • Renoir Jean • FRN • ONLY THE FRENCH CAN (USA)
FRENCH CONNECTION, THE • 1971 • Friedkin William • USA
FRENCH CONNECTION II • 1975 • Frankenheimer John • USA
FRENCH CONSPIRACY, THE (USA) see **ATTENTAT, L'** • 1972
FRENCH COPS LEARNING ENGLISH see **FRENCH INTERPRETER POLICEMAN** • 1908
FRENCH COUSINS, THE see **COUSINES, LES** • 1970
FRENCH CUISINE • 1953-54 • Devlin Bernard • DCS • CND
FRENCH DETECTIVE, THE (USA) see **ADIEU POULET** • 1975
FRENCH DOLL, THE • 1923 • Leonard Robert Z. • USA
FRENCH DOWNSTAIRS, THE • 1916 • Weber Lois • USA
FRENCH DRESSING • 1927 • Dwan Allan • USA • LESSONS FOR WIVES (UKN)
FRENCH DRESSING • 1964 • Russell Ken • UKN
FRENCH DUEL, THE • 1909 • Griffith D. W. • USA
FRENCH ERECTION • 1977 • Love John • FRN
FRENCH EROTIC FANTASIES see **GRANDES JOUISSEUSES, LES** • 1978
FRENCH FRIED • 1930 • *Terry Paul/ Moser Frank (P)* • ANS • USA
FRENCH GAME, THE (USA) see **COEUR BATTANT, LE** • 1960
FRENCH HEELS • 1922 • Hollywood Edwin L. • USA
FRENCH HONEYMOON, A • 1964 • Hakim Gaston
FRENCH INTERPRETER POLICEMAN • 1908 • Melies Georges • FRN • FRENCH COPS LEARNING ENGLISH
FRENCH KEY, THE • 1946 • Colmes Walter • USA
FRENCH KISS see **HOT TOUCH, THE** • 1981
FRENCH KISSES • 1930 • Roberts Stephen • SHT • USA
FRENCH LEAVE • 1930 • Newfield Sam • SHT • USA
FRENCH LEAVE • 1930 • Raymond Jack • UKN
FRENCH LEAVE • 1937 • Lee Norman • UKN
FRENCH LEAVE • 1948 • McDonald Frank • USA • KILROY ON DECK (UKN)
FRENCH LEAVE see **POUDRE D'ESCAMPETTE, LA** • 1971
FRENCH LEAVE see **VOYAGE EN DOUCE, LE** • 1980
FRENCH LEAVE (UKN) see **LEGIONNAIRES IN PARIS** • 1927
FRENCH LESSON see **FROG PRINCE, THE** • 1985
FRENCH LIEUTENANT'S WOMAN, THE • 1981 • Reisz Karel • UKN
FRENCH LINE, THE • 1953 • Bacon Lloyd • USA
FRENCH LOVE, THE • 1972 • Benazeraf Jose • FRN
FRENCH LOVE (UKN) see **AMOUR COMME LE NOTRE, UN** • 1975
FRENCH LOVERS, THE • 1979 • Pecas Max • FRN
FRENCH MILLINER, THE • 1916 • *Tincher Fay* • USA
FRENCH MISTRESS, A • 1960 • Boulting Roy • UKN
FRENCH MUSTARD see **MOUTARDE ME MONTE AU NEZ, LA** • 1974
FRENCH NYMPHO see **CANDICE CANDY** • 1975
FRENCH OFFICERS' MEETING see **REUNION D'OFFICIERS** • 1896
FRENCH PASTRY • 1925 • Baker Eddie • USA
FRENCH PASTRY • 1925 • Beaudine Harold • USA
FRENCH PEEP SHOW • 1952 • USA • FRENCH POSTCARDS ○ PEEP SHOWS OF PARIS
FRENCH POSTCARDS • 1979 • Huyck Willard • USA • AMERICAN FRENCH POSTCARDS
FRENCH POSTCARDS see **FRENCH PEEP SHOW** • 1952
FRENCH PROVINCIAL (USA) see **SOUVENIRS D'EN FRANCE** • 1975
FRENCH QUARTER • 1978 • Kane Dennis • USA
FRENCH QUARTER UNDERCOVER • 1985 • Catalanotto Joseph, Poole Patrick C. • USA
FRENCH RAREBIT • 1951 • McKimson Robert • ANS • USA
FRENCH REGIMENT GOING TO THE PARADE see **REGIMENT, LE** • 1896
FRENCH REVOLUTION, THE see **REVOLUTION FRANCAISE, LA** • 1989
FRENCH SHAMPOO • 1977 • Drexler Philip T. • USA
FRENCH SPY, THE • 1912 • Trimble Larry • USA
FRENCH THEY ARE A FUNNY RACE, THE see **CARNETS DU MAJOR THOMPSON, LES** • 1955
FRENCH TICKLER see **HISTOIRES DE Q** • 1974
FRENCH TOUCH, THE (USA) see **COIFFEUR POUR DAMES** • 1951
FRENCH TOWN, SEPTEMBER 1944 • 1945 • Shaw Alexander • UKN
FRENCH V ENGLISH • 1912 • Southwell Gilbert • UKN
FRENCH VOCABULARY REVIEW, A see **FOREIGN TONGUE** • 1970
FRENCH WAY, THE see **MOUTON ENRAGE, LE** • 1974
FRENCH WAY, THE (USA) see **FAUSSE ALERTE** • 1940
FRENCH WAY OF LOOKING AT IT, THE (UKN) see **VINGT MILLE ANS A LA FRANCAISE** • 1967
FRENCH WHITE CARGO see **CHEMIN DE RIO, LE** • 1936
FRENCH WITHOUT DRESSING • 1965 • Leversuch Ted • CND
FRENCH WITHOUT TEARS • 1939 • Asquith Anthony • UKN
FRENCH WOMAN, THE (USA) see **MADAME CLAUDE** • 1978
FRENCHIE • 1950 • King Louis • USA
FRENCHMAN'S CREEK • 1944 • Leisen Mitchell • USA
FRENCHMAN'S FARM • 1986 • Way Ron • ASL
FRENCHY • 1914 • *Pegg Vester* • USA
FRENESIA • 1939 • Bonnard Mario • ITL • FRENZY
FRENESIA DELL'ESTATE • 1964 • Zampa Luigi • ITL, FRN • SHIVERS IN SUMMER
FRENTE AL DESTINO • 1963 • Ortega Juan J. • MXC
FRENTE AL MAR • 1980 • Garcia Pelayo Gonzalo • SPN • ON THE SEA FRONT
FRENTE AL PECADO DE AYER • 1954 • Ortega Juan J. • MXC, CUB
FRENTE DE LOS SUSPIROS, EL • 1942 • de Orduna Juan • SPN
FRENTE DE MADRID • 1939 • Neville Edgar • SPN
FRENTE INFINITO, EL • 1956 • Lazaga Pedro • SPN
FRENZIED FILM • 1918 • *Lyons Eddie* • SHT • USA
FRENZIED FINANCE • 1912 • *Pathe* • USA
FRENZIED FINANCE • 1912 • *Selig* • USA
FRENZIED FINANCE • 1916 • Stull Walter, Burns Bobby • USA
FRENZIED FLAMES • 1926 • Paton Stuart • USA
FRENZY • 1929 • Stone Andrew L. • SHT • USA
FRENZY • 1970 • Feels C. W. • USA
FRENZY • 1972 • Hitchcock Alfred • UKN, USA
FRENZY see **FRENESIA** • 1939
FRENZY see **HETS** • 1944
FRENZY OF FIREWATER, THE • 1912 • *Kalem* • USA
FRENZY (USA) see **LATIN QUARTER** • 1945
FRERE AINE, LE see **AKH AL-KABIR, AL-** • 1958
FRERE ANDRE, LE • 1982 • Dansereau Mireille • CND
FRERE ANDRE, LE • 1988 • Labrecque Jean-Claude • CND • BROTHER ANDRE
FRERE DE LAIT, LE • 1916 • Feyder Jacques • FRN
FRERE JACQUES • 1944-45 • Jodoin Rene • ANS • CND
FRERES BOUQUINQUANT, LES • 1947 • Daquin Louis • FRN
FRERES BOUTDEBOIS, LES • 1908 • Cohl Emile • ANS • FRN • ACROBATIC TOYS ○ BROTHERS WOOD
FRERES CORSES • 1938 • Kelber Geo • FRN
FRERES CORSES, LES • 1917 • Antoine Andre • FRN • CORSICAN BROTHERS, THE (USA)
FRERES CORSES, LES (FRN) see **FRATELLI CORSI, I** • 1961
FRERES DAVENPORT, LES see **ARMOIRE DES FRERES DAVENPORT, L'** • 1902
FRERES ENNEMIS, LES • 1913 • Andreani Henri • FRN
FRERES ENNEMIS, LES • 1979 • Rached Tahani • MTV • CND
FRERES KARAMAZOFF, LES • 1931 • Ozep Fedor • FRN
FRESCOS IN DANISH CHURCHES see **KALKMALERIER** • 1954
FRESCOS ON THE WHITE • 1968 • Lotyanu Emil • USS
FRESH AGENT, THE • 1915 • *Bowers Billy* • USA
FRESH AIR • 1917 • *Mcevoy Tom* • SHT • USA
FRESH AIR • 1987 • Mansouri Touraj • IRN
FRESH AIR see **JINY VZDUCH** • 1939
FRESH AIR CURE, THE • 1914 • *Lubin* • USA
FRESH AIR FIEND, THE • 1910 • *Wrench Films* • UKN
FRESH AIR FILKINS • 1913 • *Horner Violet* • USA
FRESH AIR ROMANCE, A • 1912 • *West William* • USA
FRESH AIREDALE • 1945 • Jones Charles M. • ANS • USA
FRESH AS A FRESHMAN • *Columbia* • SHT • USA
FRESH EGGS • 1923 • Roach Hal • SHT • USA
FRESH EVERY HOUR see **HOW TO HANDLE WOMEN** • 1928
FRESH FISH • 1939 • Avery Tex • ANS • USA
FRESH FRESHMAN, THE • 1913 • *Mace Fred* • USA
FRESH FROM COLLEGE see **GIRL SAID NO, THE** • 1930
FRESH FROM PARIS see **PARIS FOLLIES OF 1956** • 1955
FRESH FROM THE CITY • 1920 • Wright Walter • SHT • USA
FRESH FROM THE FARM • 1915 • Roach Hal • USA
FRESH GAME, THE see **FLESH GAME, THE** • 1966
FRESH GAMES see **FLESH GAME, THE** • 1966
FRESH HAM • 1933 • *Van Beuren* • ANS • USA
FRESH HARE • 1942 • Freleng Friz • ANS • USA
FRESH HORSES • 1988 • Anspaugh David • USA
FRESH KILL • Merhi Joseph • USA
FRESH & LACE see **FLESH AND LACE** • 1965
FRESH LEAVES see **WAKAI HITO** • 1962
FRESH 'N' LACEY see **FLESH AND LACE** • 1965
FRESH PAINT • 1920 • Roach Hal • SHT • USA
FRESH PAINT see **PRENEZ GARDE A LA PEINTURE** • 1898
FRESH PAINT see **WET PAINT** • 1926
FRESH PAINTER • 1953 • Yates Hal • SHT • USA
FRESH START, A • 1910 • *Thanhouser* • USA
FRESH START, A • 1920 • White Jack • SHT • USA
FRESH VEGETABLE MYSTERY, THE • 1939 • Fleischer Dave • ANS • USA
FRESH VEGETABLES see **JUNGES GEMUSE** • 1956

FRESH YEGGS • 1950 • Kneitel Seymour • ANS • USA
FRESHET, THE • 1911 • *Tapley Rose* • USA
FRESHIE, THE • 1922 • Curran William Hughes • USA
FRESHMAN, THE • 1925 • Taylor Sam, Newmeyer Fred • USA • COLLEGE DAYS
FRESHMAN, THE • 1990 • Bergman Andrew • USA
FRESHMAN LOVE • 1936 • McGann William • USA • RHYTHM ON THE RIVER (UKN)
FRESHMAN YEAR • 1938 • McDonald Frank • USA
FRESHMAN'S FINISH, THE • 1931 • Christie Al • USA
FRESHMAN'S GOAT, THE • 1930 • Christie Al • USA
FRESHWATER WORLD • 1974 • Walker Giles • MTV • CND
FRESNO • 1986 • Bleckner Jeff • MTV • USA
FRESQUE INACHEVEE, LA • 1917 • Protazanov Yakov • USS
FRESTELSE • 1940 • Bornebusch Arne • SWD
FREUD • 1963 • Huston John • USA • FREUD -THE SECRET PASSION ○ SECRET PASSION, THE
FREUD STRIKES BACK • 1947 • Petroff Paul • USA
FREUD: THE HIDDEN NATURE OF MAN • 1968 • Kaczender George • DOC • CND
FREUD -THE SECRET PASSION see **FREUD** • 1963
FREUDE AM FLIEGEN • 1977 • Gottlieb Franz J. • FRG • SEX AT 7,000 FEET ○ JOY OF FLYING
FREUDENHAUS, DAS • 1971 • Weidenmann Alfred • FRG
FREUDLOSE GASSE, DIE • 1925 • Pabst G. W. • FRG • STREET OF SORROW, THE (USA) ○ JOYLESS STREET, THE (UKN) ○ CHEERLESS LANE
FREUDUS SEXUALIS • 1965 • Starkey William H. • USA • STORY OF A MAN AND HIS WOMAN, THE ○ MAN AND HIS WOMAN, A ○ STORY OF MAN AND HIS WOMAN, THE
FREUDY CAT • 1964 • McKimson Robert • ANS • USA
FREUHLING IM WIEN • Hubler-Kahla J. A. • FRG
FREUND DES FURSTEN, DER • 1916 • *Flink Hugo* • FRG
FREUND RIPP • 1923 • Halm Alfred • FRG
FREUNDE • 1944 • Emo E. W. • FRG
FREUNDE MEINER FRAU, DIE • 1949 • Deppe Hans • FRG
FREUNDIN DES GELBEN MANNES, DIE see **HERRIN DER WELT 1, DIE** • 1919
FREUNDIN EINES GROSSEN MANNES, DIE • 1934 • Wegener Paul • FRG
FREUNDIN MEINES MANNES, DIE • 1957 • von Ambesser Axel • FRG
FREUNDIN SO GOLDIG WIE DU, EINE • 1930 • Lamac Carl • FRG
FREUNDINNEN • 1915 • Del Zopp Rudolf • FRG
FREUNDSCHAFT SIEGT (GDR) see **MY ZA MIR** • 1951
FREUT EUCH DES LEBENS • 1920 • Fleck Jacob, Fleck Luise • AUS
FREUT EUCH DES LEBENS • 1934 • Steinhoff Hans • FRG
FRG see **VAMPYR** • 1931
FRG see **HOMBRE QUE VINO DEL UMMO, EL** • 1970
FRG see **PROCESO DE LAS BRUJAS, EL** • 1970
FRIAR FRANCESCO see **FRATE FRANCESCO** • 1926
FRIARANNONSEN • 1955 • Werner Gosta • SWD • MATRIMONIAL ANNOUNCEMENT
FRIAREN FRAN LANDSVAGEN • 1923 • Wallen Sigurd • SWD • SUITOR FROM THE ROADS, THE
FRIARS ROAD • 1986 • Tropia Marc C. • USA
FRIC, LE • 1959 • Cloche Maurice • FRN, ITL • GRANA, LA (ITL)
FRIC-FRAC • 1939 • Lehmann Maurice, Autant-Lara Claude • FRN
FRIC-FRAC EN DENTELLES • 1956 • Radot Guillaume • FRN
FRIC MET LES VOILES, LE see **FLEUR D'OSEILLE** • 1967
FRIDA see **FRIDA NATURALEZA VIVA** • 1985
FRIDA KAHLO see **FRIDA NATURALEZA VIVA** • 1985
FRIDA NATURALEZA VIVA • 1985 • Leduc Paul • MXC • FRIDA KAHLO ○ FRIDA
FRIDA'S SONGS see **FRIDAS VISOR** • 1930
FRIDAS VISOR • 1930 • Molander Gustaf • SWD • FRIDA'S SONGS
FRIDAY see **VRIJDAG** • 1981
FRIDAY EVENING see **LAILAT EL JUMAA** • 1945
FRIDAY FOSTER • 1975 • Marks Arthur • USA
FRIDAY NIGHT • 1986 • Kirkov Lyudmil • BUL
FRIDAY NIGHT ADVENTURE • 1976 • Vitale Frank • CND
FRIDAY ON MY MIND • 1970 • Schotten Wayne • USA
FRIDAY ROSE (USA) see **PENTEK REZI** • 1936
FRIDAY THE 13TH • 1911 • Loomis Charles Battell • USA
FRIDAY THE 13TH • 1916 • Chautard Emile • USA
FRIDAY THE 13TH • 1922 • Roach Hal • SHT • USA
FRIDAY THE 13TH • 1953 • Davis Mannie • ANS • USA
FRIDAY THE 13TH • 1980 • Cunningham Sean S. • USA
FRIDAY THE 13TH see **FREITAG DER 13** • 1944
FRIDAY THE 13TH PART 2 • 1981 • Miner Steve • USA
FRIDAY THE 13TH PART 3 • 1982 • Miner Steve • USA
FRIDAY THE 13TH PART V: A NEW BEGINNING • 1985 • Steinmann Danny • USA
FRIDAY THE 13TH PART VI: JASON LIVES • 1986 • McLoughlin Tom • USA
FRIDAY THE 13TH PART VII -THE NEW BLOOD • 1988 • Buechler John • USA
FRIDAY THE 13TH PART VIII: JASON TAKES MANHATTAN • 1989 • Heddon Rob • USA
FRIDAY THE 13TH -THE FINAL CHAPTER • 1984 • Zito Joseph • USA
FRIDAY THE 13TH: THE LEGACY -THE INHERITANCE/ CUPID'S QUIVER • 1987 • Fruet William • USA
FRIDAY THE RABBI SLEPT LATE see **LANIGAN'S RABBI** • 1976
FRIDAY THE THIRTEENTH • 1913 • *Princess* • USA
FRIDAY THE THIRTEENTH • 1933 • Saville Victor • UKN
FRIDAY THE THIRTEENTH see **V PIATOK TRINASTEHO** • 1953
FRIDAY THE THIRTEENTH.. THE ORPHAN • 1979 • Ballard John • USA • ORPHAN, THE
FRIDAY'S CURSE 4: QUILT OF HATHOR/ THE AWAKENING • 1987 • Bond Timothy, Mancuso Frank • MTV • USA • QUILT OF HATHOR
FRIDAY'S CURSE 5: THE EXECUTIONER/ FAITH HEALER • 1988 • Heddon Rob, Cronenberg David • MTV • USA
FRIDAY'S CURSE: DOCTOR JACK/ SHADOW BOXER • 1987 • Chubbock Lyndon, Fruet William • MTV • USA
FRIDAY'S CURSE: QUILT OF HATHOR/ THE AWAKENING • 1987 • Egoyan Atom • MTV • USA
FRIDAY'S CURSE: TALES OF THE UNDEAD/ SCARECROW • 1987 • Chubbock Lyndon, Fruet William • MTV • USA
FRIDAYS OF ETERNITY see **VIERNES DE LA ETERNIDAD, LOS** • 1981
FRIDEHENS PRIS • 1960 • Hovmand Annelise • DNM • PRICE OF LIBERTY, THE
FRIDERICUS • 1936 • Meyer Johannes • FRG
FRIDERICUS REX (EIN KONIGSSCHICKSAL) 1 • 1922 • von Cserepy Arzen • FRG • STURM UND DRANG
FRIDERICUS REX (EIN KONIGSSCHICKSAL) 2 • 1922 • von Cserepy Arzen • FRG • VATER UND SOHN
FRIDERICUS REX (EIN KONIGSSCHICKSAL) 3 • 1923 • von Cserepy Arzen • FRG • SANSSOUCI
FRIDERICUS REX (EIN KONIGSSCHICKSAL) 4 • 1923 • von Cserepy Arzen • FRG • SCHICKSALSWENDE
FRIDOLF I LEJONKULAN • 1933 • Hildebrand Weyler • SWD • RIDOLF IN THE LION'S CAGE
FRIDOLF IS REBELLIOUS see **FRIDOLF STICKER OPP!** • 1958
FRIDOLF STICKER OPP! • 1958 • Anderberg Torgny • SWD • FRIDOLF IS REBELLIOUS
FRIDOLF'S DANGEROUS AGE see **FRIDOLFS FARLIGA ALDER** • 1959
FRIDOLFS FARLIGA ALDER • 1959 • Anderberg Torgny • SWD • FRIDOLF'S DANGEROUS AGE
FRIDOLINONS • 1945 • Blais Roger • DCS • CND
FRIED CHICKEN • 1930 • *Terry Paul/ Moser Frank* • ANS • USA
FRIED EGG HERO, THE • 1917 • *Watson Harry Jr.* • USA
FRIEDA • 1947 • Dearden Basil • UKN
FRIEDE see **ALTE FRITZ 1, DER** • 1927
FRIEDEMANN BACH • 1941 • Muller Traugott • FRG
FRIEDENSFAHRT • 1952 • Ivens Joris • SHT • GDR, PLN • WYSCIG POKOJU WARSZAWA – BERLIN – PRAGA ○ PEACE TOUR (USA) ○ FRIENDSHIP TOUR 1952
FRIEDENSREITER, DER • 1918 • Werckmeister Hans • FRG
FRIEDERICKE • 1932 • Friedmann-Friedrich Fritz • FRG
FRIEDERICKE VON BARRING • 1956 • Thiele Rolf • FRG
FRIEDERIKE VON SESENHEIM see **JUGENDGELIEBTE, DIE** • 1930
FRIEDHOF DER LEBENDEN, DER • 1921 • Lamprecht Gerhard • FRG
FRIEDL VOM HOCHLAND, DER • 1918 • Beck Ludwig • FRG
FRIEDLICHE ZEITEN • 1966 • Rischert Christian • FRG
FRIEDRICH SCHILLER • 1923 • Goetz Curt • FRG
FRIEDRICH SCHILLER • 1940 • Maisch Herbert • FRG • TRIUMPH EINES GENIES, DER ○ TRIUMPH OF A GENIUS
FRIEDRICH SCHILLER • 1955 • Jaap Max • GDR
FRIEDRICH WERDERS SENDUNG • 1916 • Rippert Otto • FRG
FRIEND see **ARKADAS** • 1975
FRIEND, A see **PRZY JACIEL** • 1960
FRIEND, A see **AMICO, UN** • 1968
FRIEND, THE • 1914 • *Ray Charles* • USA
FRIEND, THE see **PRZYJACIEL** • 1963
FRIEND, THE see **HURRY UP OR I'LL BE 30** • 1973
FRIEND AMONG ENEMIES, ENEMY AMONG FRIENDS see **SVOI SREDI CHUZHIGH, CHUZHOI SREDI SVOIKH** • 1974
FRIEND, BUT A STAR BOARDER, A • 1916 • *Rogers Gene* • SHT • USA
FRIEND FLEEING • 1961 • Baillie Bruce • SHT • USA
FRIEND HEDGEHOG see **SUN BARATOM** • 1977
FRIEND HUSBAND • 1918 • Badger Clarence • *Goldwyn* • USA
FRIEND HUSBAND • 1918 • Wright Walter • *Sennett* • SHT • USA
FRIEND HUSBAND • 1924 • Roach Hal • SHT • USA
FRIEND IN BLUE, THE • 1914 • Martinek H. O. • UKN
FRIEND IN NEED, A • 1909 • Fitzhamon Lewin • UKN
FRIEND IN NEED, A • 1914 • *Eclair* • USA
FRIEND IN NEED, A • 1914 • *Selig* • USA
FRIEND IN NEED, A • 1914 • Wilson Frank • UKN
FRIEND IN NEED, A • 1915 • *Alhambra* • USA
FRIEND IN NEED, A • 1915 • Douglass James • *Beauty* • USA
FRIEND IN NEED, A see **KAMARAD DO DESTE** • 1988
FRIEND IN NEED IS A FRIEND INDEED, A • 1909 • *Vitagraph* • USA
FRIEND IN NEED IS FRIEND INDEED • 1906 • *Bitzer Billy (Ph)* • USA
FRIEND IN THE ENEMY'S CAMP, A • 1909 • Blackton J. Stuart (Spv) • USA
FRIEND IN TWEED, A • 1964 • Kneitel Seymour • ANS • USA
FRIEND INDEED • 1938 • Zinnemann Fred • SHT • USA
FRIEND INDEED, A • 1912 • *Nestor* • USA
FRIEND JOHN • 1913 • Johnson Arthur?, Smiley Joseph? • USA
FRIEND OF CUPID, A • 1924 • Hiscott Leslie • UKN
FRIEND OF THE DISTRICT ATTORNEY, A • 1914 • Vale Travers • USA
FRIEND OF THE FAMILY • 1949 • Hill James • SHT • UKN
FRIEND OF THE FAMILY, A • 1913 • *Shepard Iva* • USA
FRIEND OF THE FAMILY, THE • 1909 • Griffith D. W. • USA
FRIEND OF THE FAMILY (USA) see **PATATE** • 1964
FRIEND OF THE PEOPLE, A see **FOLKETS VEN** • 1918
FRIEND OF THE SONG, THE • 1961 • Fogelman Yu., Kasesalu R. • USS
FRIEND OR FOE • 1982 • Krish John • UKN
FRIEND OR PHONY • 1952 • Sparber I. • ANS • USA
FRIEND WILL COME TONIGHT, A (USA) see **AMI VIENDRA CE SOIR, UN** • 1945
FRIEND WILSON'S DAUGHTER • 1915 • West Langdon • USA
FRIENDLESS INDIAN, THE • 1913 • *Patheplay* • USA
FRIENDLY CALL, THE • 1920 • Mills Thomas R. • SHT • USA
FRIENDLY ENEMIES • 1925 • Melford George • USA
FRIENDLY ENEMIES • 1942 • Dwan Allan • USA
FRIENDLY ENEMIES see **TAIKETSU** • 1967
FRIENDLY FIRE • 1979 • Greene David • TVM • USA
FRIENDLY GHOST, THE • 1945 • Sparber I. • ANS • USA
FRIENDLY HUSBAND, A • 1923 • Blystone John G. • USA
FRIENDLY INTERCHANGE • 1961 • Duncan Alma • ANM • CND
FRIENDLY KILLER, THE (USA) see **NOBORIRYU TEKKAHADA** • 1969
FRIENDLY LAD, A • 1974 • Lyubimov L. • USS
FRIENDLY MARRIAGE, A • 1911 • *Vitagraph* • USA
FRIENDLY NEIGHBORS • 1913 • *Powers* • USA
FRIENDLY NEIGHBORS • 1941 • Grinde Nick • USA
FRIENDLY NEIGHBORS • 1970 • *Stacey Dist.* • USA
FRIENDLY NEIGHBORS see **VERY FRIENDLY NEIGHBORS, THE** • 1969
FRIENDLY PERSUASION • 1956 • Wyler William • USA • THEE I LOVE
FRIENDLY PERSUASION • 1975 • Sargent Joseph • TVM • USA
FRIENDS • 1910 • *Kalem* • USA
FRIENDS • 1912 • Griffith D. W. • USA
FRIENDS • 1971 • Gilbert Lewis* • UKN
FRIENDS • 1988 • Andersson Kjelle-Ake • SWD, JPN
FRIENDS see **PODRUGI** • 1936
FRIENDS see **DRUGE** • 1973
FRIENDS see **YAHALU YEHELI** • 1981
FRIENDS see **KAMERATER** • 1982
FRIENDS see **BEACHES** • 1988
FRIENDS, THE see **KOLEDZY** • 1956
FRIENDS, THE see **KAMARATKY** • 1978
FRIENDS AND ENEMIES • 1987 • Zubrycki Tom • DOC • ASL
FRIENDS AND HUSBANDS see **HELLER WAHN** • 1983
FRIENDS AND LOVERS • 1931 • Schertzinger Victor • USA • SPHINX HAS SPOKEN, THE
FRIENDS AND LOVERS see **VIXENS, THE** • 1969
FRIENDS AND NEIGHBORS (USA) see **FRIENDS AND NEIGHBOURS** • 1959
FRIENDS AND NEIGHBOURS • 1959 • Parry Gordon • UKN • FRIENDS AND NEIGHBORS (USA)
FRIENDS ARE BETTER THAN MONEY • 1959 • Kazansky Gennadi • USS
FRIENDS, COMRADES see **YSTAVAT, TOVERIT** • 1989
FRIENDS FOR LIFE see **AMICI PER LA PELLE** • 1955
FRIENDS FOREVER see **VENNER FOR ALTID** • 1986
FRIEND'S FORGIVENESS, A • 1914 • *Melies* • USA
FRIENDS IN SAN ROSARIO • 1912 • *Selig* • USA
FRIENDS IN SAN ROSARIO • 1917 • Mills Thomas R. • SHT • USA
FRIENDS OF EDDIE COYLE, THE • 1973 • Yates Peter • USA
FRIENDS OF GOSHO THE ELEPHANT, THE • 1967 • Donev Donyo • ANM • BUL
FRIENDS OF MR. SWEENEY • 1934 • Ludwig Edward • USA
FRIENDS OF THE FAMILY • 1954 • Thomson Margaret • SHT • UKN
FRIENDS OF THE SEA, THE • 1915 • *Salisbury Monroe* • USA
FRIENDS ON MATCHSTICKS see **PRATELE NA SIRKACH** • 1960
FRIENDS, ROMANS AND LEO • 1917 • Crosland Alan • SHT • USA
FRIENDS V. FOES • 1914 • Bocchi Arrigo • UKN
FRIENDSHIP see **YUJO** • 1975
FRIENDSHIP HOUSE • 1944 • Bolton Peter • DOC • UKN
FRIENDSHIP MARRIAGE see **YUAI KEKKON** • 1930
FRIENDSHIP OF BEAUPERE, THE • 1917 • Green Alfred E. • SHT • USA
FRIENDSHIP OF DAVID AND JONATHAN, THE see **CHOSEN PRINCE, THE** • 1917
FRIENDSHIP OF LAMOND, THE • 1915 • *Hawley Ormi* • USA
FRIENDSHIP TOUR 1952 see **FRIEDENSFAHRT** • 1952
FRIENDSHIP TRIUMPHS (USA) see **MY ZA MIR** • 1951
FRIENDSHIP (USA) see **AMICIZIA** • 1938
FRIENDSHIP'S DEATH • 1987 • Wollen Peter • UKN
FRIENDSHIPS, SECRETS AMD LIES • 1979 • Shanks Ann Zane, Laird Marlena • TVM • USA
FRIESENBLUT • 1925 • Sauer Fred • FRG
FRIESENNOT • 1935 • Hagen Peter, Kortwich Werner • FRG • DORF IM ROTEN STURM
FRIEZE -AN UNDERGROUND FILM • 1973 • *Miller George (Ed)* • SHT • ASL
FRIGHT • 1956 • Wilder W. Lee • USA • SPELL OF THE HYPNOTIST
FRIGHT • 1971 • Collinson Peter • UKN • GIRL IN THE DARK
FRIGHT see **VISITING HOURS** • 1982
FRIGHT NIGHT • 1947 • Bernds Edward • SHT • USA
FRIGHT NIGHT • 1985 • Holland Tom • USA
FRIGHT NIGHT II • 1988 • Wallace Tommy Lee • USA • FRIGHT NIGHT PART 2
FRIGHT NIGHT PART 2 see **FRIGHT NIGHT II** • 1988
FRIGHT TO THE FINISH • 1954 • Kneitel Seymour • ANS • USA
FRIGHTDAY THE 13TH • 1953 • Sparber I. • ANS • USA
FRIGHTENED BRIDE, THE see **TALL HEADLINES, THE** • 1952
FRIGHTENED CITY, THE • 1961 • Lemont John • UKN
FRIGHTENED CITY, THE (UKN) see **KILLER THAT STALKED NEW YORK, THE** • 1950
FRIGHTENED FLIRTS • 1917 • Williamson Robin E. • SHT • USA
FRIGHTENED FREDDY AND THE DESPERATE ALIEN • 1911 • Stow Percy • UKN
FRIGHTENED FREDDY AND THE MURDEROUS MARAUDER • 1911 • Stow Percy • UKN
FRIGHTENED FREDDY -HOW FREDDY WON A HUNDRED POUNDS • 1910 • Stow Percy • UKN
FRIGHTENED FREDDY THE FEARFUL POLICEMAN • 1910 • Stow Percy • UKN
FRIGHTENED GHOSTS see **FANTASMAS ASUSTADOS** • 1951
FRIGHTENED LADY, THE • 1932 • Hunter T. Hayes • UKN • CRIMINAL AT LARGE (USA)
FRIGHTENED LADY, THE (USA) see **CASE OF THE FRIGHTENED LADY, THE** • 1940
FRIGHTENED MAN, THE • 1952 • Gilling John • UKN
FRIGHTENED STIFF, A see **NIGHT TO REMEMBER, A** • 1943
FRIGHTENING CONFLICT, THE see **KORKUNC MUCADELE** • 1967
FRIGHTENING FIST, THE see **KORKUNC YUMRUK** • 1967
FRIGHTENING MOMENT, A see **UNHEIMLICHER MOMENT, EIN** • 1970
FRIGHTFUL BLUNDER, A • 1913 • O'Sullivan Tony • USA
FRIGHTMARE • 1974 • Walker Pete • UKN • FRIGHTMARE II ○ ONCE UPON A FRIGHTMARE
FRIGHTMARE see **HORROR STAR** • 1981
FRIGHTMARE II see **FRIGHTMARE** • 1974
FRIGHTY CAT • 1958 • Sparber I. • ANS • USA
FRIGID BIRD, THE • 1970 • *Stacey Dist.* • USA
FRIGID-HARE • 1950 • Jones Charles M. • ANS • USA
FRIGID SEA, THE see **FROZEN SEA, THE** • 1955
FRIGID WIFE • 1962 • Weinstein Julius • USA

FRIGID WIFE see **MODERN MARRIAGE, A** • 1950
FRIGOLIN • 1944 • Gelinas Gratien • ANT • CND
FRIGORELSE see **STUDIE IV** • 1954
FRIHED, LIGHED OG LOUISE • 1944 • Lauritzen Lau Jr. • DNM
FRIHEDSFONDEN • 1945 • Henning-Jensen Bjarne • DNM • FREEDOM COMMITTEE
FRIHETEN NA • 1973 • Kolsto Egil • NRW • FREEDOM NOW
FRIHETENS MURAR • 1978 • Ahrne Marianne • SWD • ROOTS OF GRIEF ○ WALLS OF FREEDOM, THE
FRILBY FRILLED • 1916 • McKim Edwin • SHT • USA
FRILLS • 1916 • Phillips Bertram • UKN
FRILUFT • 1959 • Roos Jorgen • DOC • DNM • PURE AIR ○ OPEN AIR
FRIM FRAM SAUCE • 1945 • Crouch William Forest • SHT • USA
FRINE CORTAGIANA D'ORIENTE • 1953 • Bonnard Mario • ITL
FRINGE BENEFIT • 1969 • Bonniere Rene • DOC • CND
FRINGE BENEFITS • 1973 • Gordon Al, Reese Ed • USA
FRINGE DWELLERS, THE • 1986 • Beresford Bruce • ASL
FRINGE OF SIN, THE • 1913 • *Imp* • USA
FRINGE OF SOCIETY, THE • 1918 • Ellis Robert • USA
FRINGE OF WAR, THE • 1914 • Tucker George Loane • UKN
FRINGE ON THE GLOVE, THE • 1914 • *Blackwell Carlyle* • USA
FRIOS OJOS DEL MIEDO, LOS (SPN) see **OCCHI FREDDI DELLA PAURA, GLI** • 1971
FRIOS SENDEROS DEL CRIMEN, LOS • 1972 • Aured Carlos • SPN
FRIPONS, VOLEURS ET CIE see **BOULOT AVIATEUR** • 1937
FRIPOUILLARD ET CIE (FRN) see **TARTASSATI, I** • 1959
FRIPOUILLES ET CIE see **MON COEUR ET SES MILLIONS** • 1931
FRIQUET, LE • 1912 • Tourneur Maurice • FRN
FRISCHER WIND AUS KANADA • 1935 • Kenter Heinz, Holder Erich • FRG
FRISCO JENNY • 1933 • Wellman William A. • USA • COMMON GROUND, THE (UKN)
FRISCO KID • 1935 • Bacon Lloyd • USA
FRISCO KID, THE • 1979 • Aldrich Robert • USA • NO KNIFE
FRISCO LADY see **CHINATOWN SQUAD** • 1935
FRISCO LIL • 1942 • Kenton Erle C. • USA
FRISCO SAL • 1945 • Waggner George • USA
FRISCO SALLY LEVY • 1927 • Beaudine William • USA
FRISCO TORNADO • 1950 • Springsteen R. G. • USA
FRISCO WATERFRONT • 1935 • Lubin Arthur • USA • WHEN WE LOOK BACK (UKN)
FRISCO WATERFRONT see **I COVER THE WATERFRONT** • 1933
FRISCOT DRINKS A BOTTLE OF HORSE EMBROCATION • 1910 • USA
FRISEE AUX LARDONS, LA • 1978 • Jaspard Alain • FRN
FRISKY LIONS AND WICKED HUSBANDS • 1919 • Moore Vin • SHT • USA
FRISKY MRS. JOHNSON, THE • 1920 • Dillon Eddie • USA
FRISKY (USA) see **PANE AMORE E GELOSIA** • 1954
FRISOU • 1973 • Bral Jacques • FRN
FRISSON DES VAMPIRES, LE • 1970 • Rollin Jean • FRN • SEX AND THE VAMPIRE (UKN) ○ VAMPIRE THRILLS
FRISSONS see **PARASITE MURDERS, THE** • 1975
FRISSONS AFRICAINS • 1976 • Soulanes Louis • FRN
FRITIDEN ER ALLEREDE BEGYNDT • 1962 • Roos Ole • DNM • LEISURE HAS COME TO STAY
FRITTATA ALL'ITALIANA • 1976 • Brescia Alfonso • ITL
FRITZ BAUER • 1930 • Petrov Vladimir • USS
FRITZ KORTNER RECITES FAUST see **FRITZ KORTNER SPRICHT FAUST** • 1966
FRITZ KORTNER RECITES MONOLOGUES FOR A RECORD see **FRITZ KORTNER SPRICHT MONOLOGE FUR EINE SCHALLPLATTE** • 1966
FRITZ KORTNER RECITES SHYLOCK see **FRITZ KORTNER SPRICHT SHYLOCK** • 1966
FRITZ KORTNER SPRICHT FAUST • 1966 • Syberberg Hans-Jurgen • SHT • FRG • FRITZ KORTNER RECITES FAUST
FRITZ KORTNER SPRICHT MONOLOGE FUR EINE SCHALLPLATTE • 1966 • Syberberg Hans-Jurgen • DOC • FRG • FRITZ KORTNER RECITES MONOLOGUES FOR A RECORD
FRITZ KORTNER SPRICHT SHYLOCK • 1966 • Syberberg Hans-Jurgen • SHT • FRG • FRITZ KORTNER RECITES SHYLOCK ○ KORTNER SPRICHT SHYLOCK
FRITZ THE CAT • 1972 • Bakshi Ralph • ANM • USA
FRITZ UND FRIEDERIKE • 1952 • von Bolvary Geza • FRG
FRITZ UND FRITZI see **SECHZEHN TOCHTER UND KEIN PAPA** • 1928
FRITZE BOLLMANN WOLLTE ANGELN • 1943 • von Collande Volker • FRG • WER ZULETZT LACHT
FRITZIGLI CHERCHE UN LOGEMENT • 1920-23 • Rastrelli Amedee • FRN
FRITZIGLI VEUT SE METTRE EN MENAGE.. • 1920-23 • Rastrelli Amedee • FRN
FRITZIS TOLLER EINFALL • 1916 • Mack Max • FRG
FRIVOLITE • 1901 • Blache Alice • FRN
FRIVOLOUS HEART, A • 1912 • *Eclair* • USA
FRIVOLOUS SAL • 1925 • Schertzinger Victor • USA
FRIVOLOUS WIVES • 1920 • Maxwell Joseph • USA
FRN see **MISTERO DEI TRE CONTINENTI, IL** • 1959
FRN see **TODESSTRAHLEN DES DR. MABUSE, DIE** • 1964
FRN see **ROUGE AUX LEVRES, LE** • 1970
FRN see **NELLA STRETTA MORSA DEL RAGNO** • 1971
FRO • 1965 • Esadze Rezo • SHT • USS
FROCKS AND FRILLS • 1916 • McKim Edwin • SHT • USA
FROG, THE • 1908 • *Pathe* • FRN
FROG, THE • 1929 • Smith Percy • UKN
FROG, THE • 1937 • Raymond Jack • UKN
FROG, THE see **SILKS AND SADDLES** • 1929
FROG, THE see **PSYCHOMANIA** • 1972
FROG AND THE PRINCESS, THE • 1944 • Donnelly Eddie • ANS • USA
FROG AND THE WHALE, THE see **TADPOLE AND THE WHALE** • 1988
FROG DREAMING • 1985 • Trenchard-Smith Brian • ASL • SPIRIT CHASER, THE ○ QUEST, THE ○ GO KIDS, THE
FROG POND, THE • 1938 • Iwerks Ub • ANS • USA
FROG PRINCE, THE • 1954 • Reiniger Lotte • ANS • UKN
FROG PRINCE, THE • 1961 • Reiniger Lotte • ANS • UKN
FROG PRINCE, THE • 1985 • Gilbert Brian • UKN • FRENCH LESSON
FROG-PRINCE, THE • 1987 • GDR
FROG PRINCE, THE • 1987 • Hunsicker Jackson • USA
FROG PRINCESS, THE • 1928 • *Peroff Paul (Anim)* • ANM • USA
FROG PRINCESS, THE • 1957 • *Coronet* • SHT • USA
FROG THAT WANTED TO BE A KING, THE • 1921 • *Terry Paul* • ANS • USA
FROGGO AND DROGGO see **KAIRYU DAIKESSEN** • 1966
FROGGY'S LITTLE BROTHER • 1921 • Coleby A. E. • UKN • CHILDREN OF COURAGE
FROGLAND see **GRENOUILLES QUI DEMANDENT UN ROI, LES** • 1922
FROGMAN-2 • 1975 • Khmelnitsky V. • USS
FROGMAN SPY (UKN) see **MIZAR** • 1953
FROGMEN, THE • 1951 • Bacon Lloyd • USA
FROGS • 1972 • McCowan George • USA
FROGS see **KURBAGALAR** • 1985
FROG'S LEGS • 1962 • Kneitel Seymour • ANS • USA
FROGS THAT WANTED A KING, THE • 1921 • *Terry Paul (Anim)* • ANM • USA
FROGS WHO WANTED A KING, THE (USA) see **GRENOUILLES QUI DEMANDENT UN ROI, LES** • 1922
FROGS WHO WANTED A KING, THE (USA) see **GRENOUILLES QUI DEMANDENT UN ROI, LES** • 1969
FROHLICHE DORF, DAS • 1955 • Schundler Rudolf • FRG • KRACH UM JOLANTHE
FROHLICHE WALLFAHRT, DIE • 1956 • Dorfler Ferdinand • FRG
FROHLICHE WANDERER, DER • 1955 • Quest Hans • FRG • HAPPY WANDERER, THE (USA)
FROHLICHE WEINBERG, DER • 1927 • Fleck Jacob, Fleck Luise • FRG • HAPPY VINEYARD, THE ○ GAY VINEYARD, THE
FROHLICHE WEINBERG, DER • 1952 • Engel Erich • FRG • GRAPES ARE RIPE, THE (USA) ○ HAPPY VINEYARD, THE ○ GAY VINEYARD, THE
FROHLICHE WISSENSCHAFT, DIE (FRG) see **GAI SAVOIR, LE** • 1967
FROHLICHES HAUS, EIN • 1944 • Guter Johannes • FRG
FROKEN APRIL • 1958 • Gentele Goran • SWD • MISS APRIL
FROKEN BLIR PIGA • 1936 • Johansson Ivar • SWD • LADY BECOMES A MAID
FROKEN CHIC • 1959 • Ekman Hasse • SWD • MISS CHIC
FROKEN JULIE • 1912 • Hoffman-Uddgren Anna • SWD • MISS JULIE
FROKEN JULIE • 1951 • Sjoberg Alf • SWD • MISS JULIE
FROKEN KYRKRATTA • 1941 • Bauman Schamyl • SWD • MISS CHURCH MOUSE
FROKEN PA BJORNEBORG • 1922 • Edgren Gustaf • SWD • YOUNG LADY OF BJORNEBORG, THE
FROKEN SOLKATT • 1948 • Werner Gosta • SWD • MISS SUNBEAM
FROKEN STATSADVOKAT • 1930 • Schneevoigt George • DNM
FROKEN VILDKATT • 1941 • Hildebrand Weyler • SWD • MISS WILDCAT
FROKENS FORSTA BARN • 1950 • Bauman Schamyl • SWD • TEACHER'S FIRST CHILD, THE
FROLEUSES, LES • Lemoine Michel • FRN
FROLICKING FISH • 1930 • Gillett Burt • ANS • USA
FROLICSOME POWDERS • 1908 • *Ambrosio* • ITL
FROM A CHINESE NOTEBOOK see **Z CINSKEO ZAPISNIKU** • 1954
FROM A FAR COUNTRY: POPE JOHN PAUL II • 1981 • Zanussi Krzysztof • TVM • UKN, ITL, PLN • MAN FROM A FAR COUNTRY, A
FROM A GERMAN LIFE see **AUS EINEM DEUTSCHEN LEBEN** • 1978
FROM A LIFE OF CRIME • 1915 • *Dumar Jean* • USA
FROM A ROMAN BALCONY (USA) see **GIORNATA BALORDA, LA** • 1960
FROM A TO Z-Z-Z-Z • 1954 • Jones Charles M. • ANS • USA
FROM A WHISPER TO A SCREAM • 1987 • Burr Jeff • USA • OFFSPRING, THE
FROM ACORN TO OAK • 1937 • Tully Montgomery • DCS • UKN
FROM AFAR I SEE MY COUNTRY see **AUS DER FERNE SEHE ICH DIESES LAND** • 1978
FROM ALTAR TO HALT'ER • 1916 • *Hamilton Lloyd V.* • USA
FROM BAD TO WORSE • 1916 • *Aubrey & Kendig* • USA
FROM BAD TO WORSE • 1917 • *Pokes & Jabbs* • SHT • USA
FROM BAD TO WORSE • 1937 • Lord Del • SHT • USA
FROM BANGKOK WITH ORDERS TO KILL • 1972 • James Shaw Fung • HKG • YELLOW KILLER, THE
FROM BEANERY TO BILLIONS • 1915 • *Howell Alice* • USA
FROM BEHIND THE FLAG • 1912 • Booth W. R. • UKN
FROM BEYOND • 1986 • Gordon Stuart • USA
FROM BEYOND THE GRAVE • 1973 • Connor Kevin • UKN, USA • TALES FROM BEYOND THE GRAVE ○ TALES FROM THE BEYOND ○ UNDEAD, THE ○ CREATURES FROM BEYOND THE GRAVE
FROM BLACKSTONE TO STONE • 1915 • *Mina* • USA
FROM BLOSSOM TIME TO AUTUMN FROST see **GYONGYVIRAGTOL LOMBHULLASIG** • 1954
FROM BLOSSOM TIME TO AUTUMN LEAVES see **GYONGYVIRAGTOL LOMBHULLASIG** • 1954
FROM BROADWAY TO A THRONE • 1916 • Bowman William J. • USA
FROM BROADWAY TO CHEYENNE • 1932 • Fraser Harry L. • USA • BROADWAY TO CHEYENNE (UKN)
FROM CABIN BOY TO KING • 1909 • *Vitagraph* • USA
FROM CACTUS TO KALE • 1917 • Smith Noel • SHT • USA
FROM CANTO TO TANGO • 1989 • Giritioglu Tomris • TRK
FROM CATERPILLAR TO BUTTERFLY • 1918 • Curtis Allen • SHT • USA
FROM CHAMPION TO TRAMP • 1915 • Fielding Romaine • USA
FROM CHINA WITH DEATH • 1974 • Wu Ma Chan • HKG
FROM CHINA WITH DEATH see **CHINESE HERCULES** • 1973
FROM COAL-MINE TO ROAD • 1931 • UKN
FROM CORLEONE TO BROOKLYN see **DA CORLEONE A BROOKLYN** • 1979
FROM COUNTRY TO TOWN • 1912 • Coleby A. E.? • UKN
FROM COWARDICE TO HONOUR • 1912 • Raymond Charles • UKN
FROM DADA TO REALISM • 1961 • Richter Hans • SWT
FROM DAWN TILL DARK • 1913 • *Ford Francis* • USA
FROM DEATH -LIFE • 1913 • *Gail Jane* • USA
FROM DEATH TO LIFE • 1911 • Porter Edwin S. • USA
FROM DEATH TO LIFE IN SOVIET RUSSIA • 1924 • *Broms Allan S.* • DOC • USA
FROM DEVASTATED UKRANIA TO THE STATUE OF LIBERTY • 1921 • *Gross Samuel M.* • DOC • USA
FROM DIME TO DIME • 1960 • Kneitel Seymour • ANS • USA
FROM DORIC TO GOTHIC • 1947 • Gillet • SHT • FRN
FROM EAR TO EAR (USA) see **COUSINES, LES** • 1970
FROM EGG TO CHICK • 1921 • Urban Charles • USA
FROM FACTORY GIRL TO PRIMA DONNA • 1910 • Bouwmeester Theo • UKN
FROM FATHER TO SON • 1914 • Leonard Robert Z. • USA
FROM FATHER TO SON see **DI PADRE IN FIGLIO** • 1983
FROM FATHER TO SON see **BLINDSIDE** • 1988
FROM FIREMAN TO ENGINEER • 1912 • *Lubin* • USA
FROM FLOWER GIRL TO RED CROSS NURSE • 1915 • Bantock Leedham • UKN
FROM GENERATION TO GENERATION • Stapp Philip • ANS • USA
FROM GIPSY HANDS • 1910 • Aylott Dave • UKN
FROM HAMBURG TO STRALSUND • 1949 • Thorndike Andrew, Thorndike Annelie • DOC • GDR
FROM HAND TO MOUSE • 1944 • Jones Charles M. • ANS • USA
FROM HAND TO MOUTH • 1919 • Goulding Alf, Roach Hal • SHT • USA
FROM HARE TO HEIR • 1960 • Freleng Friz • ANS • USA
FROM HEADQUARTERS • 1915 • Ince Ralph • USA
FROM HEADQUARTERS • 1919 • Ince Ralph • USA
FROM HEADQUARTERS • 1929 • Bretherton Howard • USA
FROM HEADQUARTERS • 1933 • Dieterle William • USA
FROM HEAVEN TO EARTH see **AHASIN POLA WATHA** • 1976
FROM HELL IT CAME • 1957 • Milner Dan • USA
FROM HELL TO BORNEO • 1964 • Montgomery George • USA
FROM HELL TO HEAVEN • 1933 • Kenton Erle C. • USA
FROM HELL TO TEXAS • 1958 • Hathaway Henry • USA • MANHUNT (UKN)
FROM HELL TO VICTORY see **DE L'ENFER A LA VICTOIRE** • 1979
FROM HEN TO HOSPITAL • 1916 • Croise Hugh • UKN
FROM HERE TO ETERNITY • 1953 • Zinnemann Fred • USA
FROM HERE TO ETERNITY • 1978 • Kulik Buzz • TVM • USA
FROM HERE TO THERE • 1964 • Bass Saul • SHT • USA
FROM HOUSE TO HOUSE • 1961 • Kokochashvili Merab, Abesadze Otar • SHT • USS
FROM IGNORANCE TO LIGHT • 1913 • *Carewe Edwin* • USA
FROM INNER SPACE • 1961 • Marzano Joseph • ANS • USA
FROM ISTANBUL -ORDERS TO KILL • 1965 • Butler Alex
FROM ITALY'S SHORES • 1915 • Turner Otis • USA
FROM JERUSALEM TO THE DEAD SEA • 1912 • Olcott Sidney • USA
FROM JERUSALEM WITH LOVE see **APO TA JEROSOLIMA ME AGAPI** • 1967
FROM LADY TO TRAMP see **AGONY OF LOVE, THE** • 1966
FROM LITTLE ACORNS see **IT'S A GREAT LIFE** • 1936
FROM MAD TO WORSE • 1957 • Kneitel Seymour • ANS • USA
FROM MAN TO MAN see **CHELOVIEKU CHELOVIEK** • 1958
FROM MANUAL LABOR TO THE MACHINE see **DU MANUAL AU ROBOT**
FROM MAO TO MOZART: ISAAC STERN IN CHINA • 1980 • Lerner Murray • DOC • USA
FROM MARS TO MUNICH • 1925 • *Fox* • SHT • USA
FROM MINUET TO FOXTROT • 1938 • Parsons Herbert R. • UKN
FROM MOCAMBO TO COPACABANA see **OD MOCAMBO SO COPACABANY** • 1959
FROM MORN TO MIDNIGHT see **VON MORGENS BIS MITTERNACHTS** • 1920
FROM MORNING TO NIGHT see **OT ZARI DO ZARI** • 1976
FROM MOUNTAIN TO SEASHORE see **MILLI FJALLS OG FJORU** • 1948
FROM MY LIFE see **Z MEHO ZIVOTA** • 1955
FROM MY LIFE see **Z MEHO ZIVOTA** • 1970
FROM NAGS TO WITCHES • 1966 • Post Howard • ANS • USA
FROM NASHVILLE WITH MUSIC • 1969 • Crandall Eddie, Patrick Robert • USA
FROM NEW YORK TO ISSANAIA POLIANA • 1963 • Ermler Friedrich • USS
FROM NEW YORK WITH LOVE • 1985 • Kollek Amos • ISR
FROM NIGERIA WITH LOVE • 1965 • Ritchie Michael • TVM • USA
FROM NINE TO NINE • 1935 • Ulmer Edgar G. • USA
FROM NOON TILL THREE • 1975 • Gilroy Frank D. • USA
FROM NOON TO DAWN see **DELTOL HAJNALIG** • 1964
FROM NOW ON • 1920 • Walsh Raoul • USA
FROM NUDNIK WITH LOVE • 1966 • Deitch Gene • ANS • USA
FROM NURSE TO WORSE • 1940 • White Jules • SHT • USA
FROM ONE FRIDAY TO THE NEXT see **OD PETKA DO PETKA** • 1985
FROM ONE TO EIGHT • 1966 • Kovachev Hristo • DOC • BUL
FROM ORBIT TO ORBIT • 1967 • Culhane Shamus • ANS • USA
FROM OUT OF THE BIG SNOWS • 1915 • Marston Theodore • USA
FROM OUT OF THE PAST • 1916 • *Rancho* • USA
FROM OUT OF THE PAST • 1916 • Humphrey William • *Broadway Star* • SHT • USA
FROM OUT THE DEPTHS • 1913 • *Peerless* • USA
FROM OUT THE DIARY • 1913 • *Essanay* • USA
FROM OUT THE FLOOD • 1913 • *Lubin* • USA
FROM OUT THE STORM • 1913 • *Broncho* • USA
FROM PASTURE TO TABLE • 1913 • *Krischock H. (Ph)* • ASL
FROM PATCHES TO PLENTY • 1915 • Wright Walter • USA
FROM PEN TO PICK • 1913 • *Pates Gwendoline I.* • USA
FROM PERIL TO PERIL • 1914 • *Holmes Helen* • USA
FROM PLAN INTO ACTION • 1951 • Alexander • SHT • UKN

FROM RAGS TO BRITCHES • 1925 • *Sennett Mack (P)* • SHT • USA

FROM RAGS TO RICHES • 1973 • SAF

FROM RAGS TO RICHES see **RAGS TO RICHES** • 1922

FROM RAIL SPLITTER TO PRESIDENT • 1913 • Ford Francis • USA

FROM ROGUES TO RICHES • 1951 • Goodwins Leslie • SHT • USA

FROM RUSSIA WITH LOVE • 1963 • Young Terence • UKN

FROM RUSSIA WITH ROCK see **SIRPPI JA KITARA** • 1988

FROM SATURDAY TO SUNDAY see **ZE SOBOTY NA NEDELI** • 1931

FROM SCOTLAND YARD • 1915 • Vernon Charles • UKN

FROM SERVANT GIRL TO DUCHESS • 1909 • Collins Alf? • UKN

FROM SHADOW TO SUNSHINE • 1910 • *Vitagraph* • USA

FROM SHOPGIRL TO DUCHESS • 1915 • Elvey Maurice • UKN

FROM SING SING TO LIBERTY • 1913 • *Atlas* • USA

FROM SKIN TO SKIN see **VON HAUT ZU HAUT** • 1969

FROM SNOW TO SNOW see **OT SNYEGA DO SNYEGA** • 1968

FROM SOUP TO NUTS • 1928 • Kennedy Edgar • SHT • USA

FROM STORM TO SUNSHINE • 1910 • Bouwmeester Theo? • UKN

FROM THE 400 TO THE HERD • 1912 • Dwan Allan • USA

FROM THE ARDENNES TO HELL see **DALLE ARDENNE ALL'INFERNO** • 1968

FROM THE BEYOND • 1913 • *Tennant Barbara* • USA

FROM THE BOTTOM OF THE SEA • 1911 • *Pickford Mary* • USA

FROM THE CIRCUS TO THE MOON • 1963 • Richter Hans • SWT

FROM THE CITY OF LODZ • 1969 • Kieslowski Krzysztof • MTV • PLN

FROM THE CLOUD TO THE RESISTANCE (UKN) see **DELLA NUBE ALLA RESISTENZA** • 1979

FROM THE CZECH MILLS see **Z CESKYCH MYLYNU** • 1929

FROM THE DEAD OF NIGHT • 1989 • Wendkos Paul • TVM • USA

FROM THE DEEP • 1916 • *Moore Joyce* • SHT • USA

FROM THE DEPTHS • 1913 • Collins Edwin J.? • UKN

FROM THE DEPTHS see **DESDE EL ABISMO** • 1980

FROM THE DEPTHS OF DESPAIR • 1915 • Watts Tom • UKN

FROM THE DRAIN • 1967 • Cronenberg David • SHT • CND

FROM THE DREGS • 1915 • Belmore Lionel • USA

FROM THE EARTH TO THE MOON • 1958 • Haskin Byron • USA

FROM THE EARTH TO THE MOON • 1979 • ANM

FROM THE FAMILY OF THE CROCODILE see **AUS DER FAMILIE DER PANZERECHSEN** • 1974

FROM THE FLAMES • 1914 • *Thanhouser* • USA

FROM THE FOUR CORNERS • 1941 • Havelock-Allan Anthony • DOC • UKN

FROM THE FOUR HUNDRED TO THE HERD • 1912 • Dwan Allan • USA

FROM THE FROZEN SOUTH • 1912 • *Spencer'S* • ASL

FROM THE GROUND UP • 1921 • Hopper E. Mason • USA

FROM THE HIGHWAY • 1971 • Chang Tseng-Tse • HKG

FROM THE HIP • 1969 • Lester Richard • USA

FROM THE HIP • 1987 • Clark Bob • USA

FROM THE KREMLIN TO THE COSMOS • 1963 • CMP • USS

FROM THE LAWYER'S WINDOW • 1912 • *Pathe* • USA

FROM THE LIFE OF THE MARIONETTES (USA) see **AUS DEM LEBEN DER MARIONETTEN** • 1980

FROM THE LION'S JAWS • 1914 • McRae Henry • USA

FROM THE MANGER TO THE CROSS • 1912 • Olcott Sidney • USA • JESUS OF NAZARETH

FROM THE MIXED-UP FILES OF MRS. BASIL E. FRANKWEILER • 1973 • Cook Fielder • USA • HIDEAWAYS, THE

FROM THE ORIENT WITH FURY (UKN) see **AGENTE 077, DALL'ORIENTE CON FURORE** • 1965

FROM THE OTHER SIDE see **OTRA ORILLA, LA** • 1966

FROM THE PATH DIRECT • 1912 • *Republic* • USA

FROM THE PORTALS OF DESPAIR • 1913 • *American* • USA

FROM THE RIVER BANK OF THE VISTULA • 1958 • Karabasz Kazimierz • DCS • PLN

FROM THE RIVER'S DEPTHS • 1915 • *Marshall Boyd* • USA

FROM THE ROGUES GALLERY • 1916 • Beery Wallace • SHT • USA

FROM THE SHADOW • 1915 • O'Sullivan Tony • USA

FROM THE SHADOWS • 1913 • Barker Reginald? • USA

FROM THE SHADOWS • 1914 • *Cummings Irving* • USA

FROM THE SHADOWS • 1915 • Lloyd Frank • USA

FROM THE SUBMERGED • 1912 • Wharton Theodore • USA

FROM THE TERRACE • 1960 • Robson Mark • USA

FROM THE TROPICS TO THE SNOW • 1964 • Lee Jack, Mason Richard • DOC • ASL

FROM THE UNKNOWN • Marinelli Lawrence A. • SHT • USA

FROM THE UTTERMOST ISLANDS see **HAVETS MELODI** • 1934

FROM THE VALLEY OF SHADOW • 1911 • *Reliance* • USA

FROM THE VALLEY OF THE MISSING • 1915 • Powell Frank • USA

FROM THE VILLAGE TO THE TOWN see **KOYDEN INDIM SEHIRE** • 1975

FROM THE WEST • 1920 • *American* • USA • TORCH BEARER, THE

FROM THE WILD • 1912 • *Rex* • USA

FROM THE WORLD OF WOOD COTTAGES see **ZE SVETA LESNICH SAMOT** • 1933

FROM THIS DAY FORWARD • 1946 • Berry John • USA

FROM TIME TO TIME see **VON ZEIT ZU ZEIT** • 1988

FROM TOMORROW ON • 1963 • Nepp Jozsef • ANM • HNG

FROM TWO TO SIX • 1918 • Parker Albert • USA

FROM TYRANNY TO LIBERTY • 1910 • Dawley J. Searle • USA

FROM VICTORY TO VICTORY • 1974 • CHN

FROM WALLACE TO GRANT • 1911 • *Champion* • USA

FROM WASH TO WASHINGTON • 1914 • *Snow Marguerite* • USA

FROM WHERE CHIMNEYS ARE SEEN see **ENTOTSU NO MIERU BASHO** • 1953

FROM WOMAN TO WOMAN TO WOMAN • 1968 • *Rowland William* • USA

FROM WORKING HOUSE TO MANSION • 1909 • Booth W. R.? • UKN

FROM WORRY TO WORRY see **APO LAHTARA SE LAHTARA** • 1967

FROMAGES AUTOMOBILES, LES • 1907 • Melies Georges • FRN • SKIPPING CHEESES, THE

FROMME HELENE, DIE • 1965 • von Ambesser Axel • FRG

FROMME LUGE, DIE • 1938 • Malasomma Nunzio • FRG

FROMONT JEUNE ET RISLER AINE • 1921 • Krauss Henry • FRN

FROMONT JEUNE ET RISLER AINE • 1941 • Mathot Leon • FRN

FRON MED MASKEN (DNM) see **FROSCH MIT DER MASKE, DER** • 1959

FRONA • 1954 • Krejcik Jiri • CZC • SISTERS, THE

FRONT • 1943 • Vasiliev Georgi, Vasiliev Sergei • USS • FRONT, THE

FRONT, THE • 1976 • Ritt Martin • USA

FRONT, THE see **FRONT** • 1943

FRONT AND CENTER see **WHEN WILLIE COMES MARCHING HOME** • 1950

FRONT LINE, THE • 1981 • Bradbury David • DOC • USA

FRONT LINE, THE see **DOVER –FRONT LINE** • 1940

FRONT LINE ARTISTS • 1945 • *Mead Thomas (P)* • SHT • USA

FRONT LINE KIDS • 1942 • Rogers Maclean • UKN

FRONT–LINE ROMANCE, A see **VOIENNO–POLEVOI ROMAN** • 1983

FRONT PAGE, THE • 1931 • Milestone Lewis • USA

FRONT PAGE, THE • 1974 • Wilder Billy • USA

FRONT PAGE STORY • 1954 • Parry Gordon • UKN • NEWSPAPER STORY

FRONT PAGE STORY, A • 1922 • Robbins Jess • USA

FRONT PAGE WOMAN • 1935 • Curtiz Michael • USA

FRONT ROW see **KABURITSUKI JINSEI** • 1968

FRONT WITHOUT FLANKS • 1975 • Gostev Igor • USS

FRONTEIRA DAS ALMAS • 1988 • Penna Hermano • BRZ • FRONTIER OF THE SOULS

FRONTEIRAS DO INFERNO • 1959 • Khouri Walter Hugo • BRZ • LONESOME WOMEN (USA)

FRONTERA AL SUR • 1966 • Merino Jose Luis • SPN

FRONTERA DE DIOS, LA • 1963 • Ardavin Cesar • SPN

FRONTERA DEL MIEDO, LA • 1957 • Lazaga Pedro • SPN

FRONTERA NORTE • 1953 • Orona Vicente • MXC

FRONTERA SIN LEY, LA • 1964 • Salvador Jaime • MXC

FRONTERA SUR • 1942 • *Lamas Fernando* • ARG

FRONTERAS DE LA LEY • 1941 • Navarro Isidoro • ARG

FRONTERAS DEL AMOR, LAS • 1934 • Strayer Frank • USA • LOVE'S FRONTIERS

FRONTERIZO, EL • 1952 • Delgado Miguel M. • MXC

FRONTGOCKEL, DER • 1955 • Dorfler Ferdinand • FRG

FRONTIER see **AEROGRAD** • 1935

FRONTIER, THE • 1935 • Dubson M. • USS • BORDER, THE

FRONTIER AGENT • 1948 • Hillyer Lambert • USA

FRONTIER ALASKA see **JONIKO AND THE KUSH TA KA** • 1969

FRONTIER BADMAN • 1943 • McGann William, Beebe Ford (U/c) • USA • FRONTIER BADMEN

FRONTIER BADMEN see **FRONTIER BADMAN** • 1943

FRONTIER CHILD, A • 1912 • *Bison* • USA

FRONTIER CRUSADER • 1940 • Newfield Sam • USA

FRONTIER DAY IN THE WEST • 1910 • *Nestor* • USA

FRONTIER DAYS • 1920 • *Hall'S Western Prod.* • USA

FRONTIER DAYS • 1934 • Hill Robert F. • USA

FRONTIER DAYS • 1945 • Scholl Jack • SHT • USA

FRONTIER DOCTOR, A • 1911 • *Fisher Edna* • USA

FRONTIER FEUD, A • 1945 • Hillyer Lambert • USA

FRONTIER FIGHTERS see **WESTERN CYCLONE** • 1943

FRONTIER FROLIC • 1946 • Collins Lewis D. • SHT • USA

FRONTIER FUGITIVES • 1945 • Fraser Harry L. • USA

FRONTIER FURY • 1943 • Berke William • USA

FRONTIER FURY (UKN) see **LONE RIDER IN FRONTIER FURY, THE** • 1941

FRONTIER GAL • 1945 • Lamont Charles • USA • BRIDE WASN'T WILLING, THE (UKN)

FRONTIER GAMBLER • 1956 • Newfield Sam • USA

FRONTIER GIRL'S COURAGE, A • 1911 • *Selig* • USA

FRONTIER GUN • 1958 • Landres Paul • USA

FRONTIER GUNLAW • 1946 • Abrahams Derwin • USA • MENACING SHADOWS (UKN)

FRONTIER HELLCAT (USA) see **UNTER GEIERN** • 1964

FRONTIER HERO, A • 1910 • *Edison* • USA

FRONTIER HORIZON see **NEW FRONTIER** • 1939

FRONTIER INTERLUDE • 1951 • Hughes Reg • UKN • NEW LIFE FOR GHAZI, A

FRONTIER JUSTICE • 1935 • McGowan Robert • USA

FRONTIER LAW • 1943 • Clifton Elmer • USA • GUNFIGHTER

FRONTIER MARSHAL • 1934 • Seiler Lewis • USA

FRONTIER MARSHAL • 1939 • Dwan Allan • USA • FRONTIER MARSHAL, THE SAGA OF TOMBSTONE, ARIZONA

FRONTIER MARSHAL • 1949 • Brannon Fred C. • USA

FRONTIER MARSHAL, THE SAGA OF TOMBSTONE, ARIZONA see **FRONTIER MARSHAL** • 1939

FRONTIER MOTHER, A • 1914 • *Domino* • USA

FRONTIER MYSTERY, A • 1913 • *Forde Victoria* • USA

FRONTIER OF THE SOULS see **FRONTEIRA DAS ALMAS** • 1988

FRONTIER OF THE STARS, THE • 1921 • Maigne Charles • USA

FRONTIER OUTLAWS • 1944 • Newfield Sam • USA

FRONTIER OUTPOST • 1950 • Nazarro Ray • USA

FRONTIER PEOPLE see **GRANSFOLKEN** • 1914

FRONTIER PHANTOM, THE • 1952 • Ormond Ron • USA

FRONTIER PONY EXPRESS • 1939 • Kane Joseph • USA

FRONTIER PROVIDENCE, A • 1913 • Turner Otis • USA

FRONTIER RANGERS • 1959 • Tourneur Jacques, Waggner George • MTV • USA

FRONTIER REVENGE • 1948 • Taylor Ray • USA

FRONTIER ROMANCE, A • 1914 • *Larkin Dolly* • USA

FRONTIER SCOUT • 1938 • Newfield Sam • USA

FRONTIER SCOUT (UKN) see **QUINCANNON, FRONTIER SCOUT** • 1956

FRONTIER STREET see **ULICA GRANICZNA** • 1948

FRONTIER TOWN • 1938 • Taylor Ray • USA

FRONTIER TRAIL, THE • 1926 • Dunlap Scott R. • USA

FRONTIER TWIN'S HEROISM, THE • 1913 • *Frontier* • USA

FRONTIER TWINS START SOMETHING, THE • 1913 • *Frontier* • USA

FRONTIER UPRISING • 1961 • Cahn Edward L. • USA

FRONTIER VENGEANCE • 1940 • Watt Nate, Sherman George • USA

FRONTIER WIFE, A • 1913 • Ford Francis • USA

FRONTIER WOLF • 1950 • *Lulli Piero* • ITL

FRONTIER WOMAN • 1956 • Ormond Ron • USA

FRONTIERE • 1934 • Meano Cesare, Carafoli Mario • ITL

FRONTIERE, LA • 1961 • Cayrol Jean • FRN

FRONTIERES DU COEUR, LES • 1914 • Bernard-Deschamps • FRN

FRONTIERES DU REVE OU JEAN–PIERRE, ANNE ET JULIETTE, LES • 1975 • Faber Jacques • BLG

FRONTIERS see **GRENS, DE** • 1984

FRONTIERS OF '49 • 1938 • Levering Joseph • USA

FRONTIERS OF NEWS • 1964 • Van Dyke Willard • DOC • USA

FRONTIERS OF POWER • 1967 • Fairbairn Kenneth • SHT • UKN

FRONTIERSMAN, THE • 1927 • Barker Reginald • USA

FRONTIERSMAN, THE • 1938 • Selander Lesley • USA

FRONTIERSMAN, THE see **BUCKSKIN** • 1968

FRONTIERSMAN'S BRIDE, THE • 1908 • *Kalem* • USA

FRONTLINE • 1975 • Vautier Rene • FRN

FRONTLINE CAMERAS 1935–1965 • 1965 • Van Dyke Willard • DOC • USA

FRONTOVYYE PODRUGI • 1942 • Eisimont Viktor • USS • GIRL FROM LENINGRAD, THE ○ GIRLFRIENDS AT THE FRONT ○ NATASHA

FRONTTHEATER • 1942 • Rabenalt Arthur M. • FRG

FROSCH MIT DER MASKE, DER • 1959 • Reinl Harald • FRG, DNM • FRON MED MASKEN (DNM) ○ FACE OF THE FROG (USA) ○ FELLOWSHIP OF THE FROG

FROSCHKONIG, DER • 1954 • Meyer Otto • FRG

FROSTY ROADS • 1985 • Jozani Massoud Jafari • IRN

FROTA MERCANTE PORTUGUESA, A • 1960 • Mendes Joao • SHT • PRT

FROTH OF TIME, THE see **ECUME DES JOURS, L'** • 1967

FROU FROU • 1914 • *Fealy Maude* • USA

FROU–FROU • 1922 • Rippert Otto • FRG

FROU–FROU • 1955 • Genina Augusto • ITL, FRN

FROU FROU DEL TABARIN • 1976 • Grimaldi Gianni • ITL

FROU FROU (UKN) see **TOY WIFE, THE** • 1938

FROUKTY–OVOCHTCHI • 1931 • Medvedkin Alexander • USS

FROZEN AFFAIR • 1937 • Dreifuss Arthur • SHT • USA

FROZEN AIR see **KALT, KALTER, AM KALTESTEN!** • 1938

FROZEN ALIVE (UKN) see **FALL X701, DER** • 1964

FROZEN APE, A • 1910 • Powers Mr. • USA

FROZEN ASSETS • 1933 • Edwards Harry J. • SHT • USA

FROZEN BRAIN, THE (USA) see **CERVEAU GELE** • 1969

FROZEN DEAD, THE • 1966 • Leder Herbert J. • UKN

FROZEN FACE • 1931 • Ceder Ralph • USA

FROZEN FATE • 1929 • Hart Ben R., Clowes St. John L. • UKN

FROZEN FEET • 1939 • Rasinski Connie • ANS • USA

FROZEN FLASHES see **GEFRORENEN BLITZE, DIE** • 1967

FROZEN FROLICS • 1930 • Foster John, Bailey Harry • ANS • USA

FROZEN GHOST, THE • 1945 • Young Harold • USA

FROZEN HEART, THE see **GEFRORENE HERZ, DAS** • 1979

FROZEN HEARTS • 1923 • Roach Hal • SHT • USA

FROZEN HOMES see **HIMGHAR** • 1987

FROZEN JUSTICE • 1929 • Dwan Allan • USA

FROZEN LEOPARD, THE see **FRUSNA LEOPARDEN, DEN** • 1986

FROZEN LIGHTNINGS see **GEFRORENEN BLITZE, DIE** • 1967

FROZEN LIMITS, THE • 1939 • Varnel Marcel • UKN

FROZEN LOGGER, THE see **ZMRZLY DREVAR** • 1962

FROZEN NORTH, THE • 1922 • Cline Eddie, Keaton Buster • SHT • USA

FROZEN NORTH, THE • 1941 • Rasinski Connie • ANS • USA

FROZEN NORTH, THE (UKN) see **KOMSOMOLSK** • 1938

FROZEN ON LOVE'S TRAIL • 1912 • *Solax* • USA

FROZEN PONDS • 1980 • Taylor Richard, McIntosh Roger • UKN

FROZEN RIVER • 1929 • Weight F. Harmon • USA

FROZEN SCREAM • 1980 • Roach Frank • USA

FROZEN SEA, THE • 1955 • Yegorov Yuri • USS • FRIGID SEA, THE

FROZEN SPARKLERS • 1967 • Bakshi Ralph • ANS • USA

FROZEN TERROR see **MACABRO** • 1980

FROZEN WARNING, THE • 1918 • Eagle Oscar • USA

FRPS • 1973 • Le Grice Malcolm • UKN

FRU BONNETS FELSTEG • 1917 • Eide Egil • SWD • MRS. B'S LAPSE

FRU INGER TOL OSTRAT • 1975 • Udnaes Sverre • NRW • LADY INGER OF OSTRAT

FRU POTIFAR • 1911 • Blom August • DNM • SKAEBNESVANGRE LOGN, DEN ○ MADAME PUTIPHAR ○ FATAL LIE, A

FRUCHT OHNE LIEBE • 1956 • Erfurth Ulrich • FRG

FRUCHTBARKEIT • 1929 • Frowein Eberhard • FRG

FRUCHTCHEN • 1934 • Eichberg Richard • FRG

FRUCHTE DER ARBEIT, DIE • 1976 • Seiler Alexander J. • SWT

FRUCTE DE PADURE • 1984 • Tatos Alexandru • RMN • FOREST FRUIT

FRUHERE VERHALTNISSE • 1927 • Bergen Arthur • FRG

FRUHJAHRSPARADE • 1935 • von Bolvary Geza • FRG, AUS

FRUHLING AUF IMMENHOF • 1974 • Schleif Wolfgang • FRG

FRUHLING IN BERLIN • 1957 • Rabenalt Arthur M. • FRG

FRUHLINGS ERWACHEN • 1929 • Oswald Richard • FRG • AWAKENING OF SPRING, THE

FRUHLINGS–SINFONIE • 1983 • Schamoni Peter • FRG, GDR • SPRING SYMPHONY

FRUHLINGSERWACHEN • 1923 • Fleck Jacob, Fleck Luise • FRG

FRUHLINGSFLUTEN • 1924 • Malikoff Nikolai • FRG

FRUHLINGSLIED • 1954 • Albin Hans • FRG

FRUHLINGSLIED, DAS • 1918 • Halm Alfred • FRG

FRUHLINGSLUFT • 1938 • Lamac Carl • FRG

FRUHLINGSMARCHEN • 1934 • Froelich Carl • FRG • VERLIEB' DICH NICHT IN SIZILIEN

FRUHLINGSMELODIE • 1945 • Bortfeldt Hans R. • FRG

FRUHLINGSRAUSCHEN • 1929 • Dieterle William • FRG • TRANEN DIE ICH DIR GEWEINT ○ REVES DE PRINTEMPS ○ NOSTALGIE
FRUHLINGSROMANZE see **SEHNSUCHT DES HERZENS** • 1951
FRUHLINGSSTIMMEN • 1952 • Thimig Hans • AUS
FRUHLINGSSTURME IM HERBSTE DES LEBENS • 1918 • Bluen Georg • FRG
FRUHLINGSTIMMEN • 1933 • Fejos Paul • AUS • VOIX DU PRINTEMPS, LES
FRUHLINGSTRAUM, EIN • 1919 • Muller-Hagen Carl • FRG
FRUHREIFEN, DIE • 1957 • von Baky Josef • FRG
FRUHREIFEN-REPORT • 1974 • Hofbauer Ernst • FRG
FRUHSTUCK IM DOPPELBETT • 1963 • von Ambesser Axel • FRG • BREAKFAST IN BED (USA)
FRUHSTUCK MIT DEM TOD • 1964 • Antel Franz • FRG, AUS
FRUIT DE PARADIS, LE (BLG) see **OVOCE STROMU RAJSKYCH JIME** • 1969
FRUIT DEFENDU, LE • 1952 • Verneuil Henri • FRN • FORBIDDEN FRUIT
FRUIT IS RIPE, THE see **GRIECHISCHE FEIGER** • 1976
FRUIT IS RIPE, THE (USA) see **FILLES SEMENT LE VENT, LES** • 1961
FRUIT MACHINE, THE • 1988 • Saville Philip • UKN • WONDERLAND (USA)
FRUIT MORDU, LE • 1943 • Remy Jacques • CHL
FRUIT OF DIVORCE, THE see **SAN FRANCISCO NIGHTS** • 1928
FRUIT OF EVIL, THE • 1914 • Reid Wallace • USA
FRUIT OF FOLLY, THE • 1915 • *Roland Ruth* • USA
FRUIT OF PARADISE, THE see **OVOCE STROMU RAJSKYCH JIME** • 1969
FRUIT OF THE TREES OF PARADISE, THE see **OVOCE STROMU RAJSKYCH JIME** • 1969
FRUIT SPRAYING • 1942 • Anstey Edgar • DOC • UKN
FRUITFUL EARTH, THE • 1951 • Sparling Gordon • DCS • CND
FRUITFUL VINE, THE • 1921 • Elvey Maurice • UKN
FRUITLANDS OF KENT • 1934 • Field Mary • DOC • UKN
FRUITLESS ERRAND, A • 1915 • *Horseshoe* • UKN
FRUITS AMERS • 1967 • Audry Jacqueline • FRN, ITL, YGS • FRUTTI AMARI (ITL) ○ BITTER FRUIT ○ SOLEDAD
FRUITS AND FLOWERS • 1914 • *Nestor* • USA
FRUITS AND THE FLOWERS • 1910 • *Imp* • USA
FRUITS COMMUNS • 1960 • Forestier • SHT • FRN
FRUITS DE LA PASSION, LES (FRN) see **SHINA NINGYO** • 1981
FRUITS DE L'ETE, LES • 1954 • Bernard Raymond • FRN, FRG • FRUITS OF SUMMER
FRUITS DE SAISON • 1902 • Blache Alice • FRN
FRUITS ET LEGUMES ANIMES • 1915 • Cohl Emile • ANS • FRN
FRUITS ET LEGUMES VIVANTS • 1912 • Cohl Emile • ANS • FRN
FRUITS OF DESIRE, THE • 1916 • Eagle Oscar • USA
FRUITS OF FAITH see **FRUITS OF THE FAITH** • 1922
FRUITS OF LOVE, THE see **YAGODKI LYUBVI** • 1926
FRUITS OF MATRIMONY, THE • 1904 • Collins Alf? • UKN
FRUITS OF PASSION • 1919 • Ridgwell George • USA
FRUITS OF PASSION, THE see **SHINA NINGYO** • 1981
FRUITS OF SUMMER see **FRUITS DE L'ETE, LES** • 1954
FRUITS OF THE FAITH • 1922 • Badger Clarence • SHT • USA • FRUITS OF FAITH
FRUITS OF VENGEANCE • 1910 • *Vitagraph* • USA
FRUITS OF VENGEANCE, THE • 1913 • Thompson Frederick A. • USA
FRUITS SAUVAGES, LES • 1953 • Bromberger Herve • FRN • WILD FRUIT (USA)
FRULLO DEL PASSERO, IL • 1988 • Mingozzi Gianfranco • ITL • FLUTTERING OF A SPARROW, THE
FRUMENTO, IL • 1958 • Olmi Ermanno (Spv) • DOC • ITL
FRUN TILLHANDA • 1939 • Olsson Gunnar • SWD • AT THE LADY'S SERVICE
FRUSNA LEOPARDEN, DEN • 1986 • Oskarsson Larus • SWD • FROZEN LEOPARD, THE
FRUSTA E IL CORPO, LA • 1963 • Bava Mario • ITL, FRN, UKN • NIGHT IS THE PHANTOM (UKN) ○ CORPS ET LE FOUET, LE (FRN) ○ WHAT! (USA) ○ WHIP AND THE BODY, THE ○ BODY AND THE WHIP, THE
FRUSTRATED • 1912 • Southwell Gilbert • UKN
FRUSTRATED CHERIE • 1969 • Dean Arthur • USA
FRUSTRATED ELOPEMENT, THE • 1902 • Stow Percy • USA
FRUSTRATED FUTURE see **BEHINDERTE ZUKUNFT** • 1971
FRUSTRATED HOLDUP • 1919 • Hurst Paul C. • USA
FRUSTRATED WOMEN (UKN) see **FRUSTRATION** • 1971
FRUSTRATION • 1971 • Benazeraf Jose • FRN • FRUSTRATED WOMEN (UKN) ○ FRUSTRATION OU LES DEREGLEMENTS D'UNE JEUNE PROVINCIALE
FRUSTRATION OU LES DEREGLEMENTS D'UNE JEUNE PROVINCIALE see **FRUSTRATION** • 1971
FRUSTRATION (USA) see **SKEPP TILL INDIALAND** • 1947
FRUSTRATIONS (USA) see **TRAITE DES BLANCHES, LA** • 1965
FRUTILLA • 1980 • Carreras Enrique • ARG • STRAWBERRY
FRUTO PROHIBIDO • 1952 • Crevenna Alfredo B. • MXC
FRUTTI AMARI (ITL) see **FRUITS AMERS** • 1967
FRUTTO ACERBO • 1934 • Bragaglia Carlo Ludovico • ITL
FTA see **F.T.A.** • 1972
FU MANCHU AND THE KISS OF DEATH see **TODESKUSS DES DR. FU MAN CHU, DER** • 1968
FU MANCHU Y EL BESO DE LA MUERTE (SPN) see **TODESKUSS DES DR. FU MAN CHU, DER** • 1968
FU MANCHU'S KISS OF DEATH see **TODESKUSS DES DR. FU MAN CHU, DER** • 1968
FU MATTIA PASCAL, IL • 1937 • D'Errico Corrado • ITL
FU-TZU CH'ING • 1981 • Fong Yuk-Ping • HKG • FATHER AND SON ○ FUZI QING
FUBUKITOGE • 1929 • *Hasegawa Kazuo* • JPN • BLIZZARD PASS
FUCHS DE PARIS, DER • 1957 • May Paul • FRG • MISSION DIABOLIQUE
FUCHS VON GLENARVON, DER • 1940 • Kimmich Max W. • FRG
FUCHSJAGD AUF SKIERN DURCHS ENGADIN, EINE see **WUNDER DES SCHNEESCHUHS 2, DAS** • 1922
FUCILLATO ALL'ALBA • 1943 • Gallone Carmine • ITL
FUCK see **BLUE MOVIE** • 1969
FUCK, FUCK, FUCK ME TIM see **FOLLE.. FOLLE.. FOLLEME TIM** • 1978
FUCK OFF! -IMAGES OF FINLAND (USA) see **PERKELE!** • 1971
FUCK THE ARMY see **F.T.A.** • 1972
FUDATSUKI SHOJO • 1967 • Sakao Masanao • JPN • NOTORIOUS VIRGINS
FUDDY DUDDY BUDDY • 1951 • Hubley John • ANS • USA
FUDGET'S BUDGET • 1954 • Cannon Robert • ANS • USA
FUEFUKI DORI • 1954 • *Nakamura Kinnosuke* • JPN • WHISTLING BOY
FUEFUKI-GAWA • 1960 • Kinoshita Keisuke • JPN • RIVER FUEFUKI, THE
FUEGO • 1964 • Coll Julio • SPN, USA • PYRO -THE THING WITHOUT A FACE ○ PHANTOM OF THE FERRIS WHEEL ○ WHEEL OF FIRE (UKN) ○ PYRO (USA) ○ PYRO -MAN WITHOUT A FACE ○ COLD WIND FROM HELL, A
FUEGO • 1969 • Bo Armando • ARG • PASSIONATE DESIRES
FUEGO EN LA SANGRE • 1953 • Iquino Ignacio F. • SPN
FUEGO EN LA SANGRE • 1964 • Cardona Rene Jr. • MXC, ARG, VNZ
FUEGO! (SPN) see **FOGO!** • 1949
FUEL FOR BATTLE • 1944 • Eldridge John • DOC • UKN
FUEL OF LIFE • 1917 • Edwards Walter • USA
FUELIN' AROUND • 1949 • Bernds Edward • SHT • USA
FUENTE ENTERRADA, LA • 1951 • Roman Antonio • SPN
FUENTE MAGICA, LA (SPN) see **MAGIC FOUNTAIN, THE** • 1962
FUENTEOVEJUNA • 1947 • Roman Antonio • SPN
FUENTEOVEJUNA • 1972 • Guerrero Zamora Juan • SPN
FUERA DE AQUI! • 1977 • Sanjines Jorge • BLV • GET OUT OF HERE!
FUERA DE LA LEY • 1940 • Romero Manuel • OUTSIDE THE LAW (USA)
FUERA DE LA LEY • 1962 • Klimovsky Leon • SPN • BILLY THE KID
FUERA DE LA REY • 1965 • de Anda Raul Jr. • MXC
FUERTE, AUDAZ Y VALIENTE • 1962 • Cardona Rene • MXC
FUERTE PERDIDO • 1965 • Elorrieta Jose Maria • SPN • MASSACRE AT FORT PERDITION (USA)
FUERZA CIEGA, LA • 1950 • Barth-Moglia Luis • ARG
FUERZA DE LA SANGRE, LA • 1946 • Magdaleno Mauricio • MXC
FUERZA DE LOS HUMILDES, LA • 1954 • Morayta Miguel • MXC, CUB • STRENGTH OF THE HUMBLE, THE
FUERZA DEL DESEO, LA • 1955 • Delgado Miguel M. • MXC
FUERZA DEL DESTINO, LA • 1910 • de Banos Ricardo • SPN
FUERZA DEL QUERER, LA • 1930 • Ince Ralph • USA
FUERZAS VIVAS, LAS • 1975 • Alcoriza Luis • MXC
FUFU • 1953 • Naruse Mikio • JPN • HUSBAND AND WIFE
FUFU GASSHO • 1959 • Tabata Tsuneo • JPN
FUFU KOKAN • 1968 • Umesawa Kaoru • JPN • MIXED COUPLE SEX
FUGA • 1960 • Diegues Carlos (c/d) • SHT • BRZ
FUGA, LA • 1937 • Saslavsky Luis • ARG
FUGA, LA • 1943 • Foster Norman • MXC • ESCAPE, THE
FUGA, LA • 1965 • Spinola Paolo • ITL • ESCAPE, THE
FUGA A DUE VOCI • 1943 • Bragaglia Carlo Ludovico • ITL
FUGA DAL BRONX • 1984 • Castellari Enzo G. • ITL • BRONX WARRIORS 2: THE BATTLE OF MANHATTAN ○ ESCAPE FROM THE BRONX (USA)
FUGA DEGLI AMANTI, LA • 1914 • Genina Augusto • ITL
FUGA DEL ROJO, LA • 1983 • Gurrola Alfredo • MXC • ESCAPE OF THE RED, THE
FUGA DESESPERADA • 1959 • de la Loma Jose Antonio, Vernay Robert • SPN
FUGA IN CITTA • 1950 • Risi Dino • SHT • ITL
FUGA IN FRANCIA • 1948 • Soldati Mario • ITL • FLIGHT INTO FRANCE (UKN)
FUGA NEL SOLE (ITL) see **GOUBBIAH MON AMOUR** • 1956
FUGA NELLA TEMPESTA • 1946 • Ferronetti Ignazio • ITL
FUGARD'S PEOPLE • 1981 • Nogueira Helena • DOC • SAF
FUGEFALEVEL • 1966 • Mariassy Felix • HNG • FIG-LEAF
FUGGITIVA, LA • 1941 • Ballerini Piero • ITL
FUGITIF, LE • 1946 • Bibal Robert • FRN • CAMP DES HOMMES PERDUS, LE
FUGITIF, LE see **HARIB, AL-** • 1973
FUGITIF DE LA VIE, LE see **HARIB MINA AL-HAYAT** • 1963
FUGITIFS, LES • 1960 • de Gastyne Marco • FRN
FUGITIFS, LES see **AU BOUT DU MONDE** • 1933
FUGITIVE see **BRIGANTE MUSOLINO, IL** • 1950
FUGITIVE, A see **BEGUNEC** • 1974
FUGITIVE, LA • 1918 • Hugon Andre • FRN
FUGITIVE, THE • 1910 • Griffith D. W. • USA
FUGITIVE, THE • 1912 • *Solax* • USA
FUGITIVE, THE • 1912 • *101 Bison* • USA
FUGITIVE, THE • 1912 • *Nestor* • USA
FUGITIVE, THE • 1913 • *Patheplay* • USA
FUGITIVE, THE • 1913 • Dwan Allan • *American* • USA
FUGITIVE, THE • 1913 • France Charles H. • *Selig* • USA
FUGITIVE, THE • 1914 • Barker Reginald • USA
FUGITIVE, THE • 1916 • Sullivan Frederick • USA
FUGITIVE, THE • 1917 • Kelsey Fred A. • SHT • USA
FUGITIVE, THE • 1925 • Wilson Ben • USA
FUGITIVE, THE • 1932 • Petrov Vladimir • USS
FUGITIVE, THE • 1933 • Fraser Harry L. • USA
FUGITIVE, THE • 1946 • Ford John, Fernandez Emilio • USA, MXC • FUGITIVO, EL (MXC)
FUGITIVE, THE • 1990 • Miner Steve • USA
FUGITIVE, THE see **TAKING OF LUKE MCVANE, THE** • 1915
FUGITIVE, THE see **DESTINY** • 1944
FUGITIVE, THE see **FARARI** • 1967
FUGITIVE, THE see **KACAK** • 1968
FUGITIVE, THE (USA) see **ON THE NIGHT OF THE FIRE** • 1939
FUGITIVE ALIEN • *Azuma Tatsuya* • JPN
FUGITIVE APPARITIONS, THE see **APPARITIONS FUGITIVES** • 1904
FUGITIVE AT LARGE • 1939 • Collins Lewis D. • USA • CRIMINAL AT LARGE
FUGITIVE FAMILY • 1980 • Krasny Paul • TVM • USA
FUGITIVE FROM A PRISON CAMP • 1940 • Collins Lewis D. • USA • PRISON CAMP
FUGITIVE FROM JUSTICE, A • 1912 • *King Burt* • USA
FUGITIVE FROM JUSTICE, A • 1914 • Kendall Preston • USA
FUGITIVE FROM JUSTICE, A • 1940 • Morse Terry O. • USA
FUGITIVE FROM MATRIMONY • 1919 • King Henry • USA
FUGITIVE FROM NOWHERE, A see **KIGA KAIGYO** • 1965
FUGITIVE FROM SONORA • 1943 • Bretherton Howard • USA
FUGITIVE FROM TERROR see **WOMAN IN HIDING** • 1949
FUGITIVE FROM THE PAST, A see **KIGA KAIGYO** • 1965
FUGITIVE FROM TIME (UKN) see **RIDING WEST** • 1944
FUGITIVE FUTURIST, THE • 1924 • Quiribet Gaston • UKN
FUGITIVE GIRLS • 1975 • Stephen A. C. • USA
FUGITIVE HERO see **MINAMOTO NO YOSHITSUNE** • 1955
FUGITIVE IN BELGRADE see **VELIKI I MALI** • 1956
FUGITIVE IN SAIGON (USA) see **MORT EN FRAUDE** • 1956
FUGITIVE IN THE SKY • 1937 • Grinde Nick • USA
FUGITIVE KILLER • 1975 • Harvard Emile • USA
FUGITIVE KIND, THE • 1959 • Lumet Sidney • USA
FUGITIVE LADY • 1951 • Salkow Sidney • USA
FUGITIVE LADY, THE • 1934 • Rogell Albert S. • USA
FUGITIVE LADY (UKN) see **FEMALE FUGITIVE** • 1938
FUGITIVE LADY (USA) see **STRADA BUIA, LA** • 1949
FUGITIVE LOVERS • 1933 • Boleslawski Richard • USA • TRANSCONTINENTAL BUS
FUGITIVE OF THE EMPIRE see **ARCHER AND THE SORCERESS, THE** • 1980
FUGITIVE OF THE PLAINS • 1943 • Newfield Sam • USA • RAIDERS OF RED ROCK
FUGITIVE PASSENGER, THE • 1917 • *Boardman True* • SHT • USA
FUGITIVE ROAD, THE • 1934 • Strayer Frank • USA
FUGITIVE SHERIFF, THE • 1936 • Bennet Spencer Gordon • USA • LAW AND ORDER (UKN)
FUGITIVE: THE JUDGEMENT, THE • 1966 • Medford Don • TVM • USA
FUGITIVE VALLEY • 1941 • Luby S. Roy • USA
FUGITIVES • 1929 • Beaudine William • USA • WISE BABY
FUGITIVES, LES see **TRIQUE, GAMIN DE PARIS** • 1960
FUGITIVES, THE • 1912 • Brenon Herbert • USA
FUGITIVES, THE see **SANDE KAERLIGHED, DEN** • 1912
FUGITIVES, THE see **KACAKLAR** • 1971
FUGITIVES FIND SHELTER see **FLYKTINGER FINNER EN HAMN** • 1945
FUGITIVES FOR A NIGHT • 1938 • Goodwins Leslie • USA • BIRTHDAY OF A STOOGE
FUGITIVE'S LIFE, THE • 1919 • Bergman H. W. • SHT • USA
FUGITIVES OF ALL KINDS • 1981 • Makela Visa • FNL
FUGITIVES OF RAIN see **YAGMUR KACAKLARI** • 1987
FUGITIVO, EL • 1964 • Gomez Muriel Emilio • MXC
FUGITIVO DE AMBERES, EL • 1954 • Iglesias Miguel, Le Henaff Rene • SPN
FUGITIVO, EL (MXC) see **FUGITIVE, THE** • 1946
FUGITIVOS • 1955 • Mendez Fernando • MXC • PUEBLO DE PROSCRITOS
FUGL FONIX • 1984 • Carlsen Jon Bang • DNM • PHOENIX BIRD
FUGS • 1965 • English Edward • DCS • USA
FUGUE DE BEBE, LA • 1911 • Feuillade Louis • FRN
FUGUE DE JIM BAXTER, LA see **SON ONCLE DE NORMANDIE** • 1938
FUGUE DE LILY, LA • 1917 • Feuillade Louis • FRN
FUGUE DE M. PERLE, LA • 1952 • Richebe Roger • FRN
FUGUE DE MAHMOOD, LA • 1950 • Leenhardt Roger • DCS • FRN
FUGUE DE SUZANNE, LA • 1974 • Buchet Jean-Marie • BLG
FUHRE UNS NICHT IN VERSUCHUNG • 1922 • Goldin Sidney M. • AUS • UND FUHRE UNS NICHT IN VERSUCHUNG
FUHRER EN FOLIE, LE • 1973 • Clair Philippe • FRN, ITL, FRG
FUHRMANN HENSCHEL • 1918 • Lubitsch Ernst • FRG
FUHRMANN HENSCHEL • 1922 • Mendes Lothar • FRG
FUHRMANN HENSCHEL • 1956 • von Baky Josef • AUS
FUIR • 1978 • Girard Helene • CND
FUITE, LA • 1985 • Cornellier Robert • SHT • CND
FUITE A L'ANGLAISE, LA see **AMOUR ET DISCIPLINE** • 1931
FUITE DE GAZ, LA • 1912 • Linder Max • FRN
FUITE EN AVANT, LA • 1980 • Zerbib Christian • FRN
FUJI • 1959 • Akasa Masaharu • JPN
FUJI • 1974 • Breer Robert • USA
FUJI NO SHIRAYUKI • 1935 • Inagaki Hiroshi • JPN • WHITE SNOW OF FUJI
FUJI SANCHO • 1948 • Saeki • JPN • SUMMIT OF MOUNT FUJI, THE
FUJI TAKESHI MONOGATARI: YAMATO DAMASHII • 1968 • Sekigawa Hideo • JPN
FUJICHO • 1947 • Kinoshita Keisuke • JPN • PHOENIX
FUJIMINA AITSU • 1967 • Saito Buichi • JPN • INVINCIBLE ONE, THE
FUJINKAI • 1959 • Yoshimura Ren • JPN • WOMAN'S SECRET, A
FUJINKAI NO HIMITSU • 1959 • Yoshimura Ren • JPN • LADY DOCTOR'S SURGERY ○ DOCTRESS' CONSULTING OFFICE
FUKEBA TOBUYONA OTOKODAGA • 1968 • Yamada Yoji • JPN • SHY DECEIVER, THE
FUKEIKI JIDAI • 1930 • Naruse Mikio • JPN • DEPRESSION PERIOD ○ HARD TIMES
FUKEYO HARUKAZE • 1930 • Tasaka Tomotaka • JPN • SPRING WIND
FUKEYO HARUKAZE • 1953 • *Mifune Toshiro* • JPN • MY WONDERFUL YELLOW CAR
FUKEYO KOIKAZE • 1935 • Gosho Heinosuke • JPN • BLOW, LOVE WIND ○ BREEZES OF LOVE
FUKIA YOKUBO NO TANIMA • 1967 • Sawa Kensuke • JPN • DEEP VALLEY OF DESIRE
FUKKATSU • 1950 • *Kyo Machiko* • JPN • RESURRECTION
FUKKATSU NO HI • 1979 • Fukasaku Kinji • JPN • DAY OF RESURRECTION, THE ○ VIRUS (USA) ○ RESURRECTION DAY
FUKUSHU NO UTA GA KIKOERU • 1968 • Sadanaga Yoshihisa, Yamane Shigeyuki • JPN • SONG OF VENGEANCE
FUKUSHU SURUWA WARE NI ARI • 1978 • Imamura Shohei • JPN • MY ROLE IS REVENGE ○ VENGEANCE IS MINE
FUKUSHUKI • 1968 • Wakamatsu Koji • JPN • REVENGER, THE
FUKUSUKE • 1957 • Yokoyama Ryuichi • ANS • JPN • TOP-HEAVY FROG, THE
FULANINHA • 1986 • Neves David • BRZ
FULANITA Y SUS MENGANOS • 1976 • Lazaga Pedro • SPN

FULANO Y MENGANO • 1955 • Romero-Marchent Joaquin Luis • SPN
FULFILLED DREAMS (USA) see **SPELNIONE MARZENIA** • 1939
FULFILLMENT, THE • 1914 • Webster Harry Mcrae • USA
FULFILLMENT, SOMETHING WORTH REMEMBERING • 1969 • Conner Charles M. • USA • SOMETHING WORTH REMEMBERING
FULFILMENT OF THE LAW, THE • 1914 • Batley Ethyle • UKN
FULGURACION DE LA RAZA • 1922 • Contreras Torres Miguel • MXC • RESPLENDENCE OF THE RACE
FULL AHEAD see **CALA NAPRZOD** • 1967
FULL CIRCLE • 1935 • King George • UKN
FULL CIRCLE • 1954 • Sachs Peter • UKN
FULL CIRCLE • 1971 • Wood Tim • UKN
FULL CIRCLE see **HAUNTING OF JULIA, THE** • 1976
FULL CONFESSION • 1939 • Farrow John • USA
FULL COVERAGE • 1934 • Horne James W. • SHT • USA
FULL DAY, A see **TELJES NAP, EGY** • 1988
FULL DAY'S WORK, A (USA) see **JOURNEE BIEN REMPLIE, UNE** • 1973
FULL DRESS FIZZLE, A • 1918 • *Triangle* • USA
FULL HEARTS AND EMPTY POCKETS (USA) see **VOLLES HERZ UND LEERE TASCHEN** • 1964
FULL HOUSE see **BOOT IST VOLL, DAS** • 1981
FULL HOUSE, A • 1919 • *Devore Dorothy* • USA
FULL HOUSE, A • 1920 • Cruze James • USA
FULL LIFE, A (USA) see **MITASARETA SEIKATSU** • 1962
FULL METAL JACKET • 1987 • Kubrick Stanley • USA
FULL MOON see **DOLUNAY** • 1988
FULL MOON see **LUNACHEIA** • 1988
FULL MOON HIGH • 1981 • Cohen Larry • USA
FULL MOON IN BLUE WATER • 1988 • Masterson Peter • USA
FULL MOON IN NEW YORK see **YAN TSOI NAU YEUK** • 1989
FULL MOON IN PARIS (UKN) see **NUITS DE LA PLEINE LUNE, LA** • 1984
FULL MOON SCIMITAR see **YUAN-YUEH WAN-TAO** • 1978
FULL O' PEP • 1922 • Roach Hal • SHT • USA
FULL O' SPIRITS • 1920 • *Swain Mack* • SHT • USA
FULL OF LIFE • 1956 • Quine Richard • USA • LADY IS WAITING, THE
FULL OF NOTIONS • 1931 • Seiter William A. • USA
FULL OF PEP • 1919 • Franklin Harry L. • USA
FULL SPEED • 1925 • Thorpe Richard • USA
FULL SPEED AHEAD • 1923 • St. John Al (c/d) • SHT • USA
FULL SPEED AHEAD • 1936 • Huntington Lawrence • UKN
FULL SPEED AHEAD • 1939 • Hunt John • UKN
FULL STEAM • 1936 • Hopwood R. A. • UKN
FULL STEAM AHEAD see **TELJES GOZZEL** • 1951
FULL STEAM AHEAD see **CALA NAPRZOD** • 1967
FULL STOP, FULL STOP, COMMA.. see **TOCHKA, TOCHKA, ZAPYATAYA..** • 1973
FULL TREATMENT, THE • 1961 • Guest Val • UKN • STOP ME BEFORE I KILL! (USA) ○ TREATMENT, THE
FULL UP • 1914 • West Walter • UKN
FULL VALUE, THE • 1912 • Dwan Allan • USA
FULLA BLUFF MAN, THE • 1940 • Fleischer Dave • ANS • USA
FULLER BRUSH GIRL, THE • 1950 • Bacon Lloyd • USA • AFFAIRS OF SALLY, THE
FULLER BRUSH MAN, THE • 1948 • Simon S. Sylvan • USA • THAT MAD MR. JONES (UKN)
FULLER REPORT see **RAPPORTO FULLER, BASE STOCCOLMA** • 1967
FULLER REPORT, BASE STOCKHOLM see **RAPPORTO FULLER, BASE STOCCOLMA** • 1967
FULLFILLMENT • Thornberg Billy • FRN
FULLY INSURED • 1923 • Roach Hal • SHT • USA
FULTAH FISHER'S BOARDING HOUSE • 1922 • Capra Frank • SHT • USA
FUMAVANO LE COLT.. LO CHIAMAVANO CAMPOSANTO • 1971 • Carnimeo Giuliano • ITL
FUMEE • 1963 • Borowczyk Walerian • ANM • FRN
FUMEE BLONDE • 1957 • Vernay Robert • FRN
FUMEE NOIRE • 1920 • Delluc Louis, Coiffart Rene • FRN
FUMEES • 1930 • Jaeger-Schmidt Andre, Benoit Georges • FRN
FUMEES • 1951 • Alexeieff Alexandre, Violet George • SHT • FRN
FUMERIO D'OPPIO, LA • 1947 • Matarazzo Raffaello • ITL • RITORNA ZA-LA MORT
FUMETSU NO NEKKYU • 1955 • Suzuki Hideo • JPN • IMMORTAL PITCHER
FUMEUR D'OPIUM • 1911 • Jasset Victorin • FRN
FUMIHAZUSHITA HARU • 1958 • Suzuki Seijun • JPN • BOY WHO CAME BACK, THE
FUMO-CHITAI • 1975 • Yamamoto Satsuo • JPN • MARGINAL LAND, THE
FUMO DI LONDRA • 1966 • Sordi Alberto • ITL
FUMO NO AIYOKU • 1967 • Yamashita Osamu • JPN • BARREN DESIRE
FUN see **TAWAMURE** • 1967
FUN AND FANCY FREE • 1947 • Boyle Charles P. • USA
FUN AND FANCY FREE • 1947 • Morgan William, Sharpsteen Ben, Kinney Jack, Roberts Bill, Luske Hamilton • ANM • USA
FUN AND GAMES • 1971 • Austin Ray • UKN
FUN AND GAMES • 1980 • Smithee Alan • TVM • USA
FUN AT A FINGLAS FAIR • 1916 • McCormick F. J. • IRL
FUN AT ST. FANNY'S • 1956 • Elvey Maurice • UKN
FUN AT THE BALL GAME • 1915 • *Mendel Jewel* • USA
FUN AT THE BARBER'S • 1903 • Stow Percy? • UKN
FUN AT THE EX • 1973 • Borris Clay, Phillips John • CND
FUN AT THE FAIR • 1926 • Parkinson H. B. • UKN
FUN AT THE FAIR • 1952 • Sparber I. • ANS • USA
FUN AT THE MOVIES • 1957 • Dickson Paul • UKN
FUN AT THE SEASIDE see **FUN ON THE SANDS AT BLACKPOOL** • 1914
FUN AT THE WAXWORKS • 1905 • Haggar William • UKN
FUN AT THE ZOO • 1950 • *Universal* • SHT • USA
FUN BEGINS AT HOME • 1937 • Schwarzwald Milton • SHT • USA
FUN FROM THE PRESS • 1923 • Fleischer Dave • ANS • USA
FUN HOUSE • 1936 • *Lantz Walter (P)* • ANS • USA
FUN HOUSE, THE see **LAST HOUSE ON DEAD END STREET** • 1981
FUN IN A BAKERY SHOP • 1902 • Porter Edwin S. • USA
FUN IN A BUTCHER'S SHOP • 1901 • Porter Edwin S. • USA
FUN IN A FIREHOUSE • 1936 • Schwarzwald Milton • SHT • USA
FUN IN A FLAT • 1919 • Lyons Eddie, Moran Lee • SHT • USA
FUN IN ACAPULCO • 1963 • Thorpe Richard • USA
FUN IN CAMP • 1904 • *Urban Trading Co.* • UKN
FUN IN COURT (USA) see **NOCE AU VILLAGE, UNE** • 1901
FUN IN THE STUDIO • 1907 • Coleby A. E.? • UKN
FUN LIFE OF AN AMSTERDAM STREETWALKER see **WAT ZIEN IK** • 1971
FUN LOVERS, THE see **SEX AND THE COLLEGE GIRL** • 1964
FUN LOVING see **QUACKSER FORTUNE HAS A COUSIN IN THE BRONX** • 1970
FUN ON A WEEKEND • 1947 • Stone Andrew L. • USA • PRETENDERS, THE ○ STRANGE BEDFELLOWS
FUN ON A WEEKEND • 1956 • Negus Olive • UKN
FUN ON FURLOUGH • 1959 • Kneitel Seymour • ANS • USA
FUN ON THE BEACH see **CHATEI EL MARAH** • 1967
FUN ON THE CLOTHESLINE • 1897 • *Paul R. W.* • UKN
FUN ON THE FARM • 1926 • *Burns Sammy* • USA
FUN ON THE FARM • 1952 • Burn Oscar • UKN
FUN ON THE ICE • 1931 • Foster John, Davis Mannie • ANS • USA
FUN ON THE JOY LINE • 1905 • *Bitzer Billy (Ph)* • USA
FUN ON THE SANDS AT BLACKPOOL • 1914 • *Hannaford E.* • UKN • FUN AT THE SEASIDE
FUN PARK see **BREAKING ALL THE RULES** • 1985
FUN WITH BOCCACCIO see **LATTJO MED BOCCACCIO** • 1949
FUN WITH DICK AND JANE • 1977 • Kotcheff Ted • USA
FUN WITH THE BRIDAL PARTY see **MARIAGE DE THOMAS POIVROT** • 1908
FUNAMBULE • 1973 • Poljinsky Serge • FRN
FUNCION DE NOCHE • 1982 • Molina Josefina • SPN • LATE PERFORMANCE
FUNCTION, THE see **MIEJSCE** • 1965
FUNCTIONAL ACTION • 1975 • Sinden Tony • UKN
FUNCTIONARY, THE • 1930 • Pyriev Ivan • USS
FUNCTIONS AND RELATIONS • 1968 • *Halas John (P)* • ANS • UKN
FUND IM NEUBAU 1, DER • 1915 • Oswald Richard • FRG • FINGERNAGEL, DER
FUND IM NEUBAU 2, DER • 1915 • Oswald Richard • FRG • BEKENNTNISSE
FUNDA • 1968 • Dinler Mehmet • TRK
FUNDA, THE SENSIBLE GIRL see **ICLI KIZ FUNDA** • 1967
FUNDACOMUN, UN CAMINO • 1972 • Blanco Javier • DOC • VNZ • ROAD OF PROGRESS
FUNDAMENTALS OF FISH SPOILAGE • 1962 • Goldsmith Sidney • DOC • CND
FUNDAMENTALS OF OFFENSE • 1931 • Kelley Albert • SHT • USA
FUNDAMENTY • 1972 • Jaraczewski Jerzy • PLN • BASIS, THE
FUNDERFUL SUBURBIA • 1962 • Kneitel Seymour • ANS • USA
FUNDOSHI ISHA • 1960 • Inagaki Hiroshi • JPN • LIFE OF THE COUNTRY DOCTOR ○ LIFE OF A COUNTRY DOCTOR ○ COUNTRY DOCTOR, THE
FUNDUQ AS-SAADA • 1971 • Wahab Fatin Abdel • LBN • HOTEL DU BONHEUR
FUNDVOGEL • 1930 • Hoffmann-Harnisch Wolfgang • FRG
FUNEBRAK • 1932 • Lamac Carl • CZC
FUNERAILLES, LES • 1934 • Gross Anthony • ANS • FRN
FUNERAILLES DE FELIX FAURE • 1899 • Melies Georges • FRN • FUNERAL OF FELIX FAURE
FUNERAILLES DE N'KRUMAH • 1971 • Diakite Moussa • SHT • GUN
FUNERAIS DE SALAZAR • 1970 • Ribeiro Antonio Lopes • SHT • PRT
FUNERAL • Gemes Jozsef • ANS • HNG
FUNERAL, THE see **OSOSHIKI** • 1984
FUNERAL CEREMONIES see **SMUTECNI SLAVNOST** • 1970
FUNERAL DO PATRAO, O • 1975 • Geada Eduardo • PRT
FUNERAL FEAST see **SEDMINA** • 1969
FUNERAL FEAST, THE • 1987 • Mansurov Bulat • USS
FUNERAL FOR AN ASSASSIN • 1974 • Hall Ivan • SAF
FUNERAL HOME see **CRIES IN THE NIGHT** • 1980
FUNERAL IN BERLIN • 1966 • Hamilton Guy • UKN • HARRY PALMER RETURNS
FUNERAL MARCH OF A MARIONETTE • 1932 • Newman Widgey R. • SHT • UKN
FUNERAL MARCH OF A MARIONETTE • 1937 • Newman Widgey R. • SHT • UKN
FUNERAL OF FELIX FAURE see **FUNERAILLES DE FELIX FAURE** • 1899
FUNERAL OF QUEEN VICTORIA • 1901 • Hepworth Cecil M. • UKN
FUNERAL OF ROSES see **BARA NO SORETSU** • 1970
FUNERAL OF THE CATHOLICS IN ECHMIADZIN, THE • Digmelov Alexander • USS
FUNERAL OF U TUN SHEIN, THE • 1920 • U Ohn Maung • BRM
FUNERAL PARADE OF ROSES see **BARA NO SORETSU** • 1970
FUNERAL RACKET, THE see **TOMURAISHI-TACHI** • 1968
FUNERAL RITES see **SMUTECNI SLAVNOST** • 1970
FUNERAL RITES see **SAMSKARA** • 1972
FUNERAL THAT FLASHED IN THE PAN, A • 1912 • *Edison* • USA
FUNERALE A LOS ANGELES (ITL) see **HOMME EST MORT, UN** • 1972
FUNF BANGE TAGE • 1928 • Righelli Gennaro • FRG
FUNF FRANKFURTER, DIE • 1922 • Schonfelder Erich • FRG
FUNF GEGEN CASABLANCA (FRG) see **ATTENTATO AI TRE GRANDI** • 1967
FUNF KAPITEL AUS EINEM ALTEN BUCH see **WEIB, EIN TIER, EIN DIAMANT, EIN** • 1923
FUNF KARNICKEL, DIE • 1953 • Steinwender Kurt • AUS • IM KRUG ZUM GRUNEN KRANZE
FUNF LETZTE TAGE •.1983 • Adlon Percy • FRG • FIVE LAST DAYS
FUNF MILLIONEN SUCHEN EINEN ERBEN • 1938 • Boese Carl • FRG • FIVE MILLIONS SEEK AN HEIR (USA)
FUNF-MINUTEN-VATER, DER • 1951 • Hubler-Kahla J. A. • AUS
FUNF MINUTEN ZU SPAT • 1918 • Krafft Uwe Jens • FRG
FUNF PATRONENHULSEN • 1960 • Beyer Frank • GDR • FIVE CARTRIDGES ○ FIVE BULLETS
FUNF TAGE -FUNF NACHTE (GDR) see **PYAT DNEI -PYAT NOCHEI** • 1961
FUNF UNHEIMLICHE GESCHICHTEN • 1919 • Oswald Richard • FRG • FIVE TALES OF HORROR (USA) ○ FIVE SINISTER STORIES
FUNF UNHEIMLICHE GESCHICHTEN • 1933 • Oswald Richard • FRG • LIVING DEAD, THE (USA) ○ HISTOIRES EXTRAORDINAIRES ○ FIVE SINISTER STORIES
FUNF UNTER VERDACHT • 1950 • Hoffmann Kurt • FRG • MORD IN BELGESUND ○ STADT IM NEBEL
FUNF VERFLUCHTEN GENTLEMEN, DIE • 1931 • Duvivier Julien • FRG
FUNF VOM TITAN, DIE see **VOR UNS LIEGT DAS LEBEN** • 1948
FUNF VON DER JAZZBAND • 1932 • Engel Erich • FRG
FUNF VOR ZWOLF IN CARACAS • 1966 • Baldi Marcello • FRG, ITL, FRN • INFERNO A CARACAS (ITL)
FUNFTE ELEMENT, DAS see **VIJFDE ELEMENT, HET** • 1966
FUNFTE STAND, DER see **VERRUFENEN, DIE** • 1925
FUNFTE STRASSE, DIE • 1923 • Hartwig Martin • FRG • SPIEL AUS DEM LEBEN DER ERSTEN VIERHUNDERT, EIN
FUNFTER AKT, SIEBTE SZENE. FRITZ KORTNER PROBT KABALE UND LIEBE • 1965 • Syberberg Hans-Jurgen • DOC • FRG • ACT FIVE, SCENE SEVEN. FRITZ KORTNER REHEARSES KABALE UND LIEBE
FUNFUHRTEE IN DER ACKERSTRASSE • 1926 • Stein Paul L. • FRG
FUNGI CELLARS, THE • 1923 • Coleby A. E. • UKN
FUNHOUSE, THE • 1981 • Hooper Tobe • USA • CARNIVAL OF TERROR
FUNIVIA DEL FALORIA, LA • 1950 • Antonioni Michelangelo • DCS • ITL
FUNKEN UNTER DER ASCHE • 1919 • Molter Ernst • FRG
FUNKENRUF DER RIOBAMBA, DER • 1920 • Gartner Adolf • FRG
FUNKSTREIFE GOTTES, DIE • 1968 • Frank Hubert • AUS, FRG • GOD'S RADIO PATROL
FUNKZAUBER • 1927 • Oswald Richard • FRG
FUNLAND • 1986 • Vanderkloot William • USA
FUNLAND • 1987 • Simpson Michael A. • USA
FUNNICUS' HUNTING EXPLOITS • 1912 • *Eclair* • USA
FUNNIEST GAME, THE see **JUEGO MAS DIVERTIDO, EL** • 1988
FUNNIEST MAN IN THE WORLD, THE • 1968 • Becker Vernon P. • DOC • USA
FUNNY ABOUT LOVE • 1990 • Nimoy Leonard • USA
FUNNY BIRDS see **PTACI KOHACI** • 1965
FUNNY BONE see **DIAL RAT FOR TERROR** • 1972
FUNNY BUNNY BUSINESS • 1942 • Donnelly Eddie • ANS • USA
FUNNY COW • 1980 • Sens Al • ANS • CND
FUNNY DIRTY LITTLE WAR, A see **NO HABRA MAS PENSAS NI OLVIDO** • 1985
FUNNY FACE • 1927 • Lamont Charles • SHT • USA
FUNNY FACE • 1933 • *Iwerks Ub (P)* • ANS • USA
FUNNY FACE • 1957 • Donen Stanley • USA
FUNNY FACE (UKN) see **BRIGHT LIGHTS** • 1935
FUNNY FACES • 1904 • Paul Robert William • UKN
FUNNY FARM • 1988 • Hill George Roy • USA
FUNNY FARM, THE • 1982 • Clark Ron • CND
FUNNY GIRL • 1968 • Wyler William • USA
FUNNY GIRL • 1969 • Vouyouklakis Takis • GRC
FUNNY LADY • 1975 • Ross Herbert • USA
FUNNY LITTLE BUNNIES • 1934 • Jackson Wilfred • ANS • USA
FUNNY MAHOMETAN, A see **MUSULMAN RIGOLO, LE** • 1897
FUNNY MAN, THE see **SMESNY PAN** • 1969
FUNNY MR. DINGLE • 1914 • *Victor* • USA
FUNNY MONEY • 1983 • Clarke James Kenelm • UKN
FUNNY NOTE • 1977 • Takeda Kazunari • JPN
FUNNY OLD MAN, THE see **SMESNY PAN** • 1969
FUNNY PARISHIONER, THE see **DROLE DE PAROISSIEN, UN** • 1963
FUNNY PEOPLE • 1976 • Uys Jamie • SAF
FUNNY PEOPLE II • 1984 • Uys Jamie • SAF
FUNNY SIDE OF JEALOUSY, THE • 1915 • Williams C. Jay • USA
FUNNY SIDE OF LIFE, THE see **HAROLD LLOYD'S FUNNY SIDE OF LIFE** • 1966
FUNNY STORY, A • 1900 • Smith Jack • UKN
FUNNY STORY, A • 1905 • Redfern Jasper • UKN
FUNNY STORY, A • 1910 • Wilson Frank? • UKN
FUNNY SUMMER, THE see **HULLA KESA** • 1980
FUNNY THING HAPPENED ON MY WAY TO GOLGOTHA, A • 1967 • de Hert Robbe • BLG
FUNNY THING HAPPENED ON THE WAY TO GOTHENBURG, A see **DRRA PA -EN KUL GREJ HANDE PA VAG TILL GOTET** • 1967
FUNNY THING HAPPENED ON THE WAY TO THE FORUM, A • 1966 • Lester Richard • USA
FUNNY THINGS HAPPEN DOWN UNDER • 1965 • McCormick Joe • NZL, ASL
FUNNY TOUR see **SPIDERS NO BARITO CHINDOCHU** • 1968
FUNNY YEARS, THE see **SJOVE AR, DE** • 1959
FUNNYMAN • 1967 • Korty John • USA • NATURALLY FUNNY MAN, A
FUNNYMOONERS • 1926 • *Sennett Mack (P)* • SHT • USA
FUNOSHA • 1967 • Kobayashi Satoru • JPN • IMPOTENT, THE
FUNSEEKERS, THE see **COMIC STRIP PRESENTS: THE FUNSEEKERS** • 1987
FUNSHINE STATE, THE • 1949 • Kneitel Seymour • ANS • USA
FUNTOOSH • 1956 • *Burman S. D. (M)* • IND
FUNTOWN • 1981 • Kardash Virlana • UKN
FUOCHI D'ARTIFICIO • 1938 • Righelli Gennaro • ITL
FUOCO! • 1968 • Baldi Gian Vittorio • ITL • FIRE!
FUOCO, IL • 1915 • Pastrone Giovanni • ITL
FUOCO NELLE VENE, IL (ITL) see **CHAIR ET LE DIABLE, LA** • 1953
FUOCO NERO • 1952 • Siano Silvio • ITL
FUOCO SACRO • 1909 • Lolli Alberto Carlo • ITL
FUORI CAMPO • 1969 • Del Monte Peter • ITL
FUORI IL MALLOPPO (ITL) see **POPSY POP** • 1970

FUORI UNO SOTTO UN ALTRO, ARRIVA IL PASSATORE! • 1973 • Carnimeo Giuliano • ITL
FUORILEGGE DEL MATRIMONIO, I • 1964 • Orsini Valentino, Taviani Paolo, Taviani Vittorio • ITL • OUTLAWS OF LOVE, THE
FUORILEGGE, I • 1950 • Vergano Aldo • ITL
FUR AND FEATHERS • 1912 • *Nestor* • USA
FUR AUSLANDISCHE UND DEUTSCHE ARBEITER • 1973 • Trautmann Christine, Rosenthal Kurt, Kohler Klaus • FRG • FOR FOREIGN AND GERMAN WORKERS
FUR COAT, THE • 1910 • *Imp* • USA
FUR COAT, THE • 1916 • Currier Frank • SHT • USA
FUR COATS see **SIDE STREETS** • 1934
FUR COLLAR, THE • 1962 • Huntington Lawrence • UKN
FUR DEN RUHM DES GELIEBTEN • 1916 • Reinert Robert • FRG
FUR DIE EHRE DES VATERS • 1917 • Eichberg Richard • FRG
FUR DIE KATZ • 1940 • Pfeiffer Hermann • FRG
FUR DIE LIEBE NOCH ZU MAGER? • 1975 • Stephan Bernhard • GDR
FUR EIN PAAR DOLLAR MEHR (FRG) see **PER QUALCHE DOLLARI IN PIU** • 1965
FUR EINE HANDVOLL DIAMANTEN • 1966 • Drach Michel • FRG, FRN • SAFARI DIAMANTS (FRN)
FUR EINE HANDVOLL DOLLARS (FRG) see **PER UN PUGNO DI DOLLARI** • 1964
FUR SMUGGLERS, THE • 1912 • *Robinson Gertrude* • USA
FUR TRAP, THE • 1978 • *Anderson Colleen* • USA • LUSTFUL DESIRES
FUR TRIMMED COAT, THE • 1916 • Julian Rupert • SHT • USA
FUR ZWEI GROSCHEN ZARTLICHKEIT • 1957 • Rabenalt Arthur M. • FRG, DNM • KAERLIGHED MOD BETALING (DNM)
FURAI MONOGATARI • 1959 • Watanabe Kunio • JPN • GAMBLER AS I AM
FURANKENSHUTAIN NO KAIJU -SANDA TAI GAILAH • 1966 • Honda Inoshiro • JPN • WAR OF THE GARGANTUAS, THE ○ DUEL OF THE GARGANTUAS ○ SANDA TAI GAILA ○ SANDA VS. GAILA
FURANKENSHUTAIN TAI BARAGON • 1964 • Honda Inoshiro • JPN • FRANKENSTEIN CONQUERS THE WORLD (UKN) ○ FRANKENSTEIN VS. THE GIANT DEVILFISH ○ FRANKENSTEIN AND THE GIANT LIZARD
FURCHT • 1918 • Wiene Robert • FRG
FURCHT VOR DEM WEIBE, DIE • 1921 • Henning Hanna • FRG
FURCHT VOR DER WAHRHEIT, DIE • 1917 • *Neumann Lotte* • FRG
FURCHTEN UND LIEBEN see **PAURA E AMORE** • 1987
FUREDI ANNA-BAL • 1973 • Szomjas Gyorgy • SHT • HNG • ANNA-BALL
FURENZOKU SATSUJIN JIKEN • 1976 • Sone Chusei • JPN • MURDER CASES
FURESSHUMAN WAKADAISHO • 1969 • Fukuda Jun • JPN • YOUNG GUY GRADUATES (USA)
FURET, LE • 1949 • Leboursier Raymond • FRN • CRIMES A VENDRE
FUREUR SUR LE BOSPHORE see **AGENTE 077, DALL'ORIENTE CON FURORE** • 1965
FURIA • 1946 • Alessandrini Goffredo • ITL
FURIA A BAHIA POUR OSS 117 • 1965 • Hunebelle Andre, Besnard Jacques • FRN, ITL • OSS 117 -MISSION FOR A KILLER (USA) ○ OSS 117 FURIA A BAHIA (ITL) ○ MISSION FOR A KILLER ○ TROUBLE IN BAHIA FOR OSS 117
FURIA A MARRAKESCH • 1966 • Loy Mino • ITL
FURIA DEGLI APACHE, LA see **HOMBRE DE LA DILIGENCIA ,EL** • 1963
FURIA DEGLI UOMINI, LA (ITL) see **GERMINAL** • 1963
FURIA DEI BARBARI, LA • 1960 • Malatesta Guido • ITL • FURY OF THE PAGANS (USA)
FURIA DEI KYBER, LA (ITL) see **TIGRE DE KYBER, EL** • 1970
FURIA DEL HOMBRE LOBO, LA • 1970 • Zabalza Jose Maria • SPN • FURY OF THE WOLF MAN, THE (USA)
FURIA DEL RING, LA • 1961 • Davison Tito • MXC • LUCHA LIBRE
FURIA DI ERCOLE, LA • 1962 • Parolini Gianfranco • ITL, FRN • FURY OF HERCULES, THE (USA) ○ FURY OF SAMSON, THE
FURIA EN EL EDEN • 1962 • de la Serna Mauricio • MXC
FURIA ESPANOLA • 1974 • Betriu Francisco • SPN • SPANISH FURY
FURIA NERA • 1975 • Fidani Demofilo • ITL
FURIA ROJA • 1950 • Sekely Steve • MXC, USA • STRONGHOLD
FURIAS DESATADAS • 1957 • Urueta Chano • MXC
FURIE see **LOULOUS, LES** • 1976
FURIES, THE • 1930 • Crosland Alan • USA
FURIES, THE • 1950 • Mann Anthony • USA
FURIES, THE see **PLAYING AROUND** • 1930
FURIES SEXUELLES • Payet Alain • FRN
FURIN • 1965 • Tanaka Shigeo • JPN • STRANGE TRIANGLE
FURIN KAZAN • 1969 • Inagaki Hiroshi • JPN • UNDER THE BANNER OF SAMURAI (USA) ○ SAMURAI BANNERS
FURIN NO TANOSHIMI • 1968 • Sasaki Moto • JPN • PLEASURES OF LIAISONS, THE
FURIOUS ENCOUNTER • 1962 • *Montesco Ofelia* • MXC
FURISODE MATOI • 1958 • Misumi Kenji • JPN
FURISODE-ZUKIYO • 1960 • Matsuda Sadatsugu • JPN
FURLOUGH ON WORD OF HONOR (USA) see **URLAUB AUF EHRENWORT** • 1937
FURNACE, THE • 1920 • Taylor William D. • USA
FURNACE MAN, THE • 1915 • *Clayton Ethel* • USA
FURNACE TROUBLE • 1929 • Parrott James • SHT • USA
FURNISHED ON EASY TERMS • 1904 • *Warwick Trading Co.* • UKN
FURNISHED ROOM, THE • 1917 • Mills Thomas R. • SHT • USA
FURNISHED ROOMS • 1916 • *Stull Walter* • SHT • USA
FURNISHED ROOMS TO LET • 1909 • *Edison* • USA
FURNISHING EXTRAORDINARY • 1913 • Aylott Dave? • UKN
FURNITURE MOVERS, THE • 1918 • Roach Hal • SHT • USA
FURONCLE, LE • 1915 • Feuillade Louis • FRN
FURONG GARRISON see **FURONG ZHEN** • 1985
FURONG ZHEN • 1985 • Xie Jin • CHN • SMALL TOWN CALLED HISBISCUS, A ○ FURONG GARRISON ○ HISBISCUS TOWN
FURORE DI VIVERE (ITL) see **CHEMIN DES ECOLIERS, LE** • 1959
FURORE NELLA SAVANA • 1979 • Montero Roberto Bianchi • ITL
FURS, THE • 1912 • Sennett Mack • USA
FURSAN ATH-THALATHA, AL- • 1961 • Wahab Fatin Abdel • EGY • TROIS CAVALIERS, LES
FURST DER BERGE, DER • 1921 • Piel Harry • FRG
FURST DER DIEBE UND SEINE LIEBE, DER • 1919 • Larsen Viggo • FRG
FURST DER LANDSTRSSE, DER • 1923 • Bock-Stieber Gernot • FRG
FURST DER NACHT, DER • 1919 • *Albers Hans* • FRG
FURST LAHORY, DER KONIG DER DIEBE see **MANOLESCUS MEMOIREN** • 1920
FURST ODER CLOWN • 1927 • Rasumny Alexander • FRG • PRINCE OR CLOWN (USA)
FURST SEPPL • 1915 • Froelich Carl • FRG
FURST SEPPL • 1932 • Osten Franz • FRG • SKANDAL IM GRANDHOTEL
FURST VON PAPPENHEIM ,DER • 1927 • Eichberg Richard • FRG
FURST VON PAPPENHEIM, DER • 1952 • Deppe Hans • FRG
FURST WORONZEFF • 1934 • Robison Arthur • FRG
FURSTENKIND, DAS • 1927 • Fleck Jacob, Fleck Luise • FRG
FURSTENLIEBE • 1919 • *Deutsche Bioscop* • FRG
FURSTIN DER OZEANWERFT, DIE • 1922 • Neff Wolfgang • FRG
FURSTIN DER RIVIERA, DIE • 1926 • von Bolvary Geza • FRG
FURSTIN UND IHR NARR, DIE • 1928 • *Pentagramm-Film* • FRG
FURSTIN VON BERANIEN, DIE • 1918 • Reicher Ernst • FRG
FURSTIN WORONZOFF ,DIE • 1920 • Gartner Adolf • FRG
FURSTLICHES BLUT • 1915 • Oberlander Hans • FRG
FURTHER ADVENTURES OF A GIRL SPY, THE • 1910 • Olcott Sidney • UKN
FURTHER ADVENTURES OF SAMMY ORPHEUS • 1915 • *Santschi Thomas* • USA
FURTHER ADVENTURES OF SHERLOCK HOLMES, THE • 1922 • Ridgwell George • SER • UKN
FURTHER ADVENTURES OF STINGAREE, THE • 1917 • SER • USA
FURTHER ADVENTURES OF TENNESSEE BUCK • 1987 • Keith David • USA • TENNESSEE BUCK ○ SACRIFICE
FURTHER ADVENTURES OF THE FLAG LIEUTENANT, THE • 1927 • Kellino W. P. • UKN
FURTHER ADVENTURES OF THE UGLY DUCKLING, THE see **HVORDAN DET VIDERE GIK DEN GRIMME AELLING** • 1981
FURTHER ADVENTURES OF THE WILDERNESS FAMILY, PART II • 1978 • Zuniga Frank • USA • ADVENTURES OF THE WILDERNESS FAMILY PART 2 ○ WILDERNESS FAMILY PART 2
FURTHER ADVENTURES OF UNCLE SAM, THE • 1970 • Mitchell Robert, Case Dale • ANS • USA
FURTHER EXPLOITS OF JUDEX, THE see **NOUVELLE MISSION DE JUDEX, LA** • 1917
FURTHER EXPLOITS OF SEXTON BLAKE -THE MYSTERY OF THE S.S. OLYMPIC, THE • 1919 • Lorraine Harry • UKN
FURTHER GLIMPSE OF JOEY, A • 1967 • Owen Don • CND
FURTHER MYSTERIES OF DR. FU MANCHU • 1924 • Paul Fred • SER • UKN
FURTHER PERILS OF LAUREL AND HARDY, THE • 1968 • Youngson Robert • USA
FURTHER PROPHECIES OF NOSTRADAMUS, THE • 1942 • Miller David • SHT • USA
FURTHER RIGHT THAN THE RIGHT see **MORE TO THE RIGHT THAN THE LEFT** • 1989
FURTHER TALES FROM THE CRYPT see **VAULT OF HORROR** • 1973
FURTHER UP THE CREEK • 1958 • Guest Val • UKN
FURTIVES see **FURTIVOS** • 1975
FURTIVOS • 1975 • Borau Jose Luis • SPN • FURTIVES ○ POACHERS
FURTO DI SERA BEL COLPO SI SPERA • 1973 • Laurenti Mariano • ITL
FURTO E L'ANIMA DEL COMMERCIO, IL • 1971 • Corbucci Bruno • ITL • IO NON GRATTO.. RUBO!
FURUERU SHITA • 1981 • Nomura Yoshitaro • JPN • TREMBLING TANG
FURUSATO • 1922 • Mizoguchi Kenji • JPN • HOMETOWN (USA)
FURUSATO • 1930 • Mizoguchi Kenji • JPN • HOMETOWN (USA) ○ HOME TOWN
FURUSATO • 1984 • Koyama Seijiro • JPN • HOMETOWN
FURUSATO see **KOKYO** • 1923
FURUSATO HARETE • 1934 • Yamamoto Kajiro • JPN • PUBLIC ACTIVITY
FURUSATO NO UTA • 1925 • Mizoguchi Kenji • JPN • SONG OF HOME, THE (USA) ○ SONG OF HOMETOWN, THE ○ SONG OF THE NATIVE COUNTRY, THE
FURY • 1923 • King Henry • USA
FURY • 1936 • Lang Fritz • USA • MOB RULE
FURY, THE • 1978 • De Palma Brian • USA
FURY AND THE WOMAN • 1937 • Collins Lewis D. • USA
FURY AT FURNACE CREEK • 1948 • Humberstone H. Bruce • USA • BALLAD OF FURNACE CREEK, THE
FURY AT GUNSIGHT PASS • 1956 • Sears Fred F. • USA
FURY AT RED GULCH • 1955 • Landers Lew • MTV • USA
FURY AT SHOWDOWN • 1957 • Oswald Gerd • USA
FURY AT SMUGGLER'S BAY • 1961 • Gilling John • UKN
FURY BELOW • 1938 • Fraser Harry L. • USA
FURY DISCO • Sarrazin Antoine • FRN
FURY FEMINA • 1973 • Bo Armando • ARG
FURY IN ISTANBUL see **AGENTE 077, DALL'ORIENTE CON FURORE** • 1965
FURY IN PARADISE • 1955 • Bruce George, Aguilar Rolando • USA, MXC • SENOR GRINGO
FURY IN PARADISE (UKN) see **ZAMBOANGA** • 1937
FURY IN SHAOLIN TEMPLE • Ho Godfrey • HKG
FURY IN THE PACIFIC • 1945 • Powell Bonney • USA
FURY IS A WOMAN (USA) see **SIBIRSKA LEDI MAGBET** • 1962
FURY OF ACHILLES (USA) see **IRA DI ACHILLE, L'** • 1962
FURY OF HERCULES, THE (USA) see **FURIA DI ERCOLE, LA** • 1962
FURY OF SAMSON, THE see **FURIA DI ERCOLE, LA** • 1962
FURY OF SHAOLIN FIST • 1977 • Li Chih Sho, Liu Yeh • HKG
FURY OF THE APACHES see **HOMBRE DE LA DILIGENCIA ,EL** • 1963
FURY OF THE CONGO • 1951 • Berke William • USA
FURY OF THE DRAGON • 1966 • Beaudine William • MTV • USA • GREEN HORNET, THE
FURY OF THE JUNGLE • 1934 • Neill R. William • USA • JURY OF THE JUNGLE (UKN)
FURY OF THE PAGANS (USA) see **FURIA DEI BARBARI, LA** • 1960
FURY OF THE SEMINOLES • Hugh R. John • USA
FURY OF THE SUCCUBUS see **DARK EYES** • 1980
FURY OF THE VIKINGS see **INVASORI, GLI** • 1961
FURY OF THE WILD • 1929 • d'Usseau Leon • USA • CHUMS (UKN)
FURY OF THE WOLF MAN, THE (USA) see **FURIA DEL HOMBRE LOBO, LA** • 1970
FURY ON WHEELS see **JUMP** • 1971
FURY RIVER • 1959 • Tourneur Jacques, Waggner George, Lang Otto, Crosland Alan Jr. • MTV • USA
FURY TO FREEDOM • 1985 • Jacobson Erik • USA
FURY (UKN) see **THUNDERHOOF** • 1948
FURY (UKN) see **GIORNO DEL FURORE, IL** • 1973
FURY UNLEASHED (UKN) see **HOT ROD GANG** • 1958
FURYO BANCHO • 1968 • Noda Yukio • JPN • WOLVES OF THE CITY
FURYO SHOJO • 1949 • Naruse Mikio • JPN • BAD DAUGHTER ○ BAD GIRL, THE ○ DELINQUENT GIRL
FURYO SHONEN • 1961 • Hani Susumu • JPN • BAD BOYS (USA)
FURYU FUKAGAWA • 1960 • Yamamura So • JPN • SONG OF FUKAGAWA
FUSE, THE see **FITILJ** • 1971
FUSE OF DEATH, THE • 1914 • Montgomery Frank E. • USA
FUSEE, LA • 1933 • Natanson Jacques • FRN • GRANDEUR ET DECADENCE
FUSEN • 1956 • Kawashima Yuzo • JPN • BALLOON, THE
FUSETSU NIJYUNEN • 1951 • Saburi Shin • JPN • TWENTY YEARS IN A STORM
FUSHIGINA ZUKIN • 1958 • *Toei* • JPN • MAGIC HOOD, THE (USA)
FUSHIN NO TOKI • 1968 • Imai Tadashi • JPN • TIME OF RECKONING, THE ○ TIME OF LOSING FAITH
FUSIL CHARGE • 1970 • Lombardini Carlo • FRN, ITL
FUSILACION • 1962 • Catrani Catrano • ARG • EXECUTION, THE
FUSILAMIENTO, EL • 1961 • Toussaint Carlos • MXC
FUSILAMIENTO DE DORREGO, EL • 1908 • Gallo Mario, Rosich Salvador • ARG • SHOOTING OF DORREGO, THE
FUSILAMIENTO DE RIZAL, EL • PHL
FUSILIER WIPF • 1938 • Lindtberg Leopold, Haller Hermann • SWT
FUSILLE A L'AUBE • 1950 • Haguet Andre • FRN • SECRET DOCUMENT -VIENNA (USA)
FUSILS, LES • 1961 • Herman Jean • FRN
FUSILS DE LA LIBERTE, LES see **BANADIQ AL-HURIA** • 1962
FUSILS POUR LA LIBERTE, LES see **BANADIQ AL-HURIA** • 1962
FUSION • 1967 • Emshwiller Ed, Nikolais Alwin • USA
FUSOKU YONJU METORU • 1958 • Kurahara Koreyoshi • JPN • MAN WHO RODE THE TYPHOON, THE
FUSS AND FEATHERS • 1909 • Porter Edwin S. • USA
FUSS AND FEATHERS • 1918 • Niblo Fred • USA
FUSS, HOGY UTOLERJENEK • 1972 • Keleti Marton • HNG • RUN TO BE CAUGHT
FUSS OVER FEATHERS (USA) see **CONFLICT OF WINGS** • 1954
FUSSGANGER, DER • 1974 • Schell Maximilian • FRG, SWT, USA • PEDESTRIAN, THE (USA)
FUSSPUR, DIE • 1917 • Meinert Rudolf • FRG
FUST • 1970 • Jancso Miklos • SHT • HNG • SMOKE
FUTARI • 1963 • Richie Donald • JPN
FUTARI DAKE NO HASHI • 1958 • Maruyama Seiji • JPN
FUTARI DAKE NO TORIDE • 1963 • Shibuya Minoru • JPN • RAT AMONG THE CATS
FUTARI DE ARUITA IKU-HARU-AKI • 1962 • Kinoshita Keisuke • JPN • SEASONS WE WALKED TOGETHER, THE
FUTARI DE ARUITA IKUSHUNJU • 1962 • Kinoshita Keisuke • JPN • BALLAD OF A WORKMAN
FUTARI NO GINZA • 1967 • Kaji Noboru • JPN • GINZA FOR TWO OF US
FUTARI NO IDA • 1976 • Matsuyama Zenzo • JPN • YUKO AND THE LIVING CHAIR
FUTARI NO MUSASHI • 1960 • Watanabe Kunio • JPN
FUTARI NO MUSUKO • 1962 • Chiba Yasuki • JPN • DIFFERENT SONS
FUTARI NO SEKAI • 1966 • Matsuo Akinori • JPN • COUPLE OF THE WORLD
FUTARI NO TAIYO • 1961 • Murayama Shinji • JPN
FUTARI SHIZUKA • 1922 • Obora G. • JPN • QUIET TWO, THE
FUTARIZUMA see **TSUMA YO BARA NO YONI** • 1935
FUTATSO-NO YAKIZAKANA • 1968 • Kuri Yoji • ANS • JPN • TWO GRILLED FISH (USA) ○ NI YAKI ZAKANA ○ NIHIKINO SAMNA
FUTATSU DORO • 1933 • Kinugasa Teinosuke • JPN • TWO STONE LANTERNS
FUTBOL, AMOR Y TOROS • 1929 • Rey Florian • SPN
FUTBOL ARGENTINO • 1990 • Dinenzon Victor • DOC • ARG • ARGENTINE SOCCER
FUTBOLISTA FENOMENA, EL • 1978 • Cortes Fernando • MXC
FUTEIZUMA • 1968 • Mukoi Hiroshi • JPN • UNFAITHFUL WIFE
FUTEKI NA OTOKO • 1958 • Masumura Yasuzo • JPN • LOWEST MAN, THE
FUTEKINARU HANKO • 1958 • Makino Masahiro • JPN • FEARLESS OPPOSITION
FUTEN ROJIN NIKKI • 1962 • Kimura Keigo • JPN • DIARY OF A MAD OLD MAN

FUTHER ADVENTURES OF THE GIRL SPY • 1910 • *Kalem* • USA
FUTILITY OF REVENGE, THE • 1914 • *Imp* • USA
FUTTOCKS END • 1970 • Kellett Bob • UKN
FUTUR AUX TROUSSES, LE • 1974 • Grassian Dolores • FRN
FUTUR INTERIEUR, LE • 1983 • Chabot Jean • CND
FUTURE • Vanderbeek Stan • SHT • USA
FUTURE BLOCK • 1988 • McCracken Kevin • ANS • CND
FUTURE COP see **TRANCERS** • 1985
FUTURE COPS • 1976 • Taylor Jud • TVM • USA
FUTURE FARMERS OF AMERICAN SILVER ANNIVERSARY • 1954 • Murphy Owen • USA
FUTURE FELICITIES see **ZUKUNFTIGEN GLUCKSELIGKEITEN, DIE** • 1989
FUTURE FORCE see **C.O.P.S.** • 1989
FUTURE FORCE II • 1989 • Prior David A. • USA
FUTURE HACKENSCHMIDTS • 1904 • Collins Alf? • UKN
FUTURE HUNTERS • 1985 • Santiago Cirio H. • USA
FUTURE IS WOMAN, THE see **FUTURO E' DONNA, IL** • 1984
FUTURE-KILL • 1984 • Moore Ronald W. • USA • FUTURE KILL ○ NIGHT OF THE ALIEN ○ SPLATTER
FUTURE KILL see **FUTURE-KILL** • 1984
FUTURE MAN, THE • 1916 • Quirk William • SHT • USA
FUTURE MERE, LA • 1975 • Brault Francois • DCS • CND
FUTURE OF EMILY, THE see **AVENIR D'EMILIE, L'** • 1984
FUTURE OF US ALL, THE • 1974 • Tyrrell Robert • UKN
FUTURE ONE • 1963 • Holt Niels • SHT • DNM
FUTURE PAST • Stewart Bob • USA
FUTURE PROSPECTS • 1981 • van Zuylen Erik • NTH
FUTURE SCHLOCK • 1984 • Peak Barry, Kiely Chris • ASL
FUTURE VISION, A see **PERSPECTIV, ETT** • 1973
FUTURE WANTED see **FREMTID SOGES** • 1983
FUTURE WOMEN • 1975 • Franco Jesus • SPN • RIO '80
FUTURE'S IN THE AIR, THE • 1936 • Shaw Alexander • DOC • UKN
FUTURES IN WATER • 1984 • Walton Lloyd A. • MTV • CND
FUTURES VEDETTES • 1955 • Allegret Marc • FRN • SCHOOL FOR LOVE (USA) ○ SWEET SIXTEEN (UKN) ○ JOY OF LIVING
FUTUREWORLD • 1976 • Heffron Richard T. • USA
FUTURISMO see **INHUMAINE, L'** • 1923
FUTURO E' DONNA, IL • 1984 • Ferreri Marco • ITL, FRN, FRG • FUTURE IS WOMAN, THE
FUTUWWA, AL- see **FATAWA, EL** • 1956
FUTZ • 1969 • O'Horgan Tom • USA
FUUN • 1934 • Inagaki Hiroshi • JPN • BAD LUCK
FUUN SENRYOBUNE • 1952 • Inagaki Hiroshi • JPN
FUUN SYOGIDANI • 1940 • Arai Ryohei • JPN
FUUNJI ODA NOBUNAGA • 1959 • Kono Juichi • JPN • YOUNG FURY
FUUNJO SHI • 1928 • *Tsuburaya Eijo (Ph)* • JPN
FUXI FUXI • 1989 • Zhang Yimou • CHN • INCESTUOUS, THE
FUXING GAOZHAO • 1985 • Hong Jinbao • HKG • MY LUCKY STARS
FUYARD, LE • 1914 • Volkov Alexander • USS
FUYU NO HANA • 1977 • Furuhata Yasuo • JPN • FLOWER IN WINTER
FUYU NO YADO • 1938 • Toyoda Shiro • JPN • WINTER INN
FUYUKI SHINJU • 1934 • Kinugasa Teinosuke • JPN
FUZ, THE • 1967 • Bakshi Ralph • ANS • USA
FUZEN NO TOMOSHIBI • 1957 • Kinoshita Keisuke • JPN • CANDLE IN THE WIND, A ○ DANGER STALKS NEAR
FUZI QING see **FU-TZU CH'ING** • 1981
FUZIS, OS • 1964 • Guerra Ruy • BRZ • RIFLES, THE ○ GUNS, THE
FUZZ • 1970 • *Stacey Dist.* • USA
FUZZ • 1972 • Colla Richard A. • USA
FUZZY PINK NIGHTGOWN, THE • 1957 • Taurog Norman • USA
FUZZY SETTLES DOWN • 1944 • Newfield Sam • USA
FVVA see **FEMME – VILLA – VOITURE – ARGENT** • 1972
F/X see **FX MURDER BY ILLUSION** • 1985
F/X 2 • 1990 • Franklin Richard • USA
FX-18 SECRET AGENT see **ORDEN: FX 18 DEBE MORIR** • 1965
FX-18 SUPERSPY see **COPLAN FX18 CASSE TOUT** • 1965
FX MURDER BY ILLUSION • 1985 • Mandel Robert • USA • F/X
FYRA GANGER FYRA • 1965 • Kjaerulff-Schmidt Palle, Kurkvaara Maunu, Clemens Rolf, Troell Jan • DNM, FNL, NRW • 4 X 4 ○ NORDISK KVADRILLE ○ UPPEHALLE I MYRLANDET ○ PIKE MED HVIT BALL
FYRE • 1979 • Grand Richard • USA
FYRSTINDENS SKAEBNE • 1915 • Schneevoigt George • DNM
FYRTOJET • 1946 • Johnsen Allan • ANM • DNM • MAGIC LIGHTER (USA)
FYRVAKTARENS DOTTER • 1918 • Klercker Georg • SWD • DAUGHTER OF THE LIGHTHOUSE KEEPER, THE

G

G-DOG see **ROOKIE COP, THE** • 1939
G.G. PASSION • 1966 • Bailey David • SHT • UKN
G.I. BLUES • 1960 • Taurog Norman • USA
G.I. EXECUTIONER • 1971 • Reed Joel M. • USA • WIT'S END ○ DRAGON LADY
G.I. HONEYMOON • 1945 • Karlson Phil • USA
G.I. JANE • 1951 • Le Borg Reginald • USA
G.I. JOE see **STORY OF G.I. JOE, THE** • 1945
G.I. JOE: THE MOVIE • 1987 • Jurwich Don • ANM • USA
G.I. WANNA GO HOME • 1946 • White Jules • SHT • USA
G.I. WAR BRIDES • 1946 • Blair George • USA
G.m.b.H. TENOR, DER • 1916 • Lubitsch Ernst • FRG • TENOR, INC.
G-MAN see **MELVIN PURVIS, G-MAN** • 1974
G-MAN JITTERS • 1939 • Donnelly Eddie • ANS • USA
G-MAN'S WIFE (UKN) see **PUBLIC ENEMY'S WIFE, THE** • 1936
G-MEN • 1935 • Keighley William • USA
G-MEN NEVER FORGET • 1948 • Brannon Fred C., Canutt Yakima • SRL • USA
G-MEN OF THE SEA see **UMI NO G-MEN: TAIHEIYO NO YOJINBO** • 1967
G-MEN VS. THE BLACK DRAGON • 1943 • Witney William • SRL • USA
G.P. AS BASIL THE BRAINLESS • 1915 • Huntley G. P. • UKN
G.P.U. • 1942 • Ritter Karl • FRG
G.R. STEIN • 1972 • Grigor Murray • DCS • UKN
G-STRING MURDERS, THE see **LADY OF BURLESQUE** • 1943
GA, GA -GLORY TO HEROES • Szulkin Piotr • PLN
GA PA VATTNET, OM DU KAN • 1979 • Bjorkman Stig • SWD • WALK ON WATER, IF YOU CAN
GAA MED MIG HJEM • 1941 • Christensen Benjamin • DNM • RETURN WITH ME ○ COME HOME WITH ME
GAANO KITA KAMAHAL • 1968 • Crisostomo Fely • PHL • HOW MUCH I LOVE YOU
GABAL, AL- • 1965 • Shawqi Khalil • EGY • MONTAGNE, LA
GABBIA, LA • 1977 • Tuzii Carlo • ITL
GABBIA, LA • 1985 • Patroni Griffi Giuseppe • ITL • CAGE, THE
GABBIA MALEDETTA, LA • 1909 • Lolli Alberto Carlo • ITL
GABBIANI VOLANO BASSO, I • 1978 • Cristallini Giorgio • ITL
GABBIANO, IL • 1977 • Bellocchio Marco • ITL • SEA GULL, THE (USA)
GABBY • 1941 • Fleischer Dave • ASS • USA
GABBY GOES FISHING • 1941 • Fleischer Dave • ANS • USA
GABBY'S DINER • 1961 • Hannah Jack • ANS • USA
GABINO BARRERA • 1964 • Cardona Rene • MXC • CAPORAL, EL
GABLE AND LOMBARD • 1976 • Furie Sidney J. • USA
GABLES MYSTERY, THE • 1938 • Hughes Harry • UKN
GABLES MYSTERY, THE (USA) see **MAN AT SIX, THE** • 1931
GABRIEL CHURCH KITTEN • 1944 • Kneitel Seymour • ANS • USA
GABRIEL GOES TO THE CITY • 1979 • Obomsawin Alanis • CND
GABRIEL GRUB THE SURLY SEXTON • 1904 • Williamson James • UKN
GABRIEL HEATTER REPORTING • 1945 • *Mead Thomas (P)* • SHT • USA
GABRIEL OVER THE WHITE HOUSE • 1933 • La Cava Gregory • USA
GABRIEL SCHILLINGS FLUCHT • 1962 • Dieterle William • MTV • FRG
GABRIELA • 1950 • von Cziffra Geza • FRG
GABRIELA • 1984 • Barreto Bruno • BRZ, ITL
GABRIELE • 1954 • Ekman Hasse • SWD
GABRIELE DAMBRONE • 1943 • Steinhoff Hans • FRG
GABRIELE, EINS, ZWEI, DREI • 1937 • Hansen Rolf • FRG
GABRIELLA • 1974 • Bing Mack • USA
GABRIELLE • 1970 • Shiffen Arlo • USA
GABRIELLE see **YESTERDAY** • 1980
GABY • 1956 • Bernhardt Curtis • USA
GABY • 1986 • Mandoki Luis • MXC, UKN, USA • GABY, A TRUE STORY
GABY see **PAID TO LOVE** • 1927
GABY, A TRUE STORY see **GABY** • 1986
GABY BEN YAKAR • Barbash Uri • MTV • ISR
GABY'S GASOLINE GLIDE • 1916 • *Selby Gertrude* • SHT • USA • GERTIE'S GASOLINE GLIDE
GACHO • 1942 • Torres-Rios Leopoldo • ARG
GADFLIES • 1976 • Brakhage Stan • SHT • USA
GADFLY, THE • 1928 • Mardzhanishvili Kote • USS
GADFLY, THE see **POPPYGUNYA** • 1955
GADFLY, THE see **OVOD** • 1957
GADIS MARATHON • 1981 • Umam Chaerul • INN • MARATHON GIRL
GADMOUSE THE APPRENTICE GOOD FAIRY • 1965 • Bakshi Ralph • ANS • USA
GADO BRAVO • 1934 • Ribeiro Antonio Lopes, Nosseck Max (Spv) • PRT
GAELLE, MALOU ET VIRGINE • 1977 • Renau-Pieri • FRN
GAEST FRA EN ANDEN VERDEN, EN see **TUGTHUSFANGE NO. 97** • 1914
GAESTEARBEJDERE • 1973 • Miladinovich Voja • DNM • GUEST WORKERS
GAETAN OU LE COMMIS AUDACIEUX • 1921 • Feuillade Louis • FRN
GAFAT AL-AMTAR • 1966 • Issa Sayyed • EGY • PLUIES ONT TARI, LES
GAFE, EL • 1958 • Ramirez Pedro L. • SPN
GAFFET EL AMTAR • 1967 • Essa Sayed • EGY • SOFT RAINS, THE
GAFFNEY'S GLADIATOR • 1913 • *Majestic* • USA
GAG AND BAGGAGE • 1952 • Sparber I. • ANS • USA
GAG BUSTER • 1957 • Rasinski Connie • ANS • USA
GAGAKU • 1957 • JPN
GAGAMBA AT SI SCORPIO • 1969 • Rowe George • PHL • SPIDER AND THE SCORPION
GAGE D'AMOUR • 1904 • Blache Alice • FRN
GAGLIARDI E PUPE • 1958 • Montero Roberto Bianchi • ITL
GAGNANT, LE • 1935 • Allegret Yves • SHT • FRN
GAGNANT, LE • 1979 • Gion Christian • FRN
GAGNANT, LE see **A NOUS DEUX, MADAME LA VIE** • 1936
GAGNE TA VIE • 1931 • Berthomieu Andre • FRN
GAI DIMANCHE • 1935 • Berr Jacques • SHT • FRN
GAI, GAI, DEMARIONS-NOUS see **SOYONS GAIS** • 1931
GAI SAVOIR, LE • 1967 • Godard Jean-Luc • FRN, FRG • FROHLICHE WISSENSCHAFT, DIE (FRG) ○ JOYFUL WISDOM, THE
GAIBI TALWAR • 1946 • Khan A. M. • IND
GAIETES DE LA FINANCE, LES • 1935 • Forrester Jack • FRN • HOMME QUI A VENDU SA TETE, L' ○ BENGALI VII
GAIETES DE L'ESCADRILLE, LES • 1958 • Peclet Georges • FRN
GAIETES DE L'ESCADRON, LES • 1912 • Chautard Emile • FRN
GAIETES DE L'ESCADRON, LES • 1913 • Tourneur Maurice • FRN
GAIETES DE L'ESCADRON, LES • 1932 • Tourneur Maurice • FRN
GAIETES DE L'EXPOSITION, LES • 1938 • Hajos Ernest • FRN
GAIETES DU PALACE, LES • 1936 • Kapps Walter • FRN
GAIETY COMEDIES • 1919 • Sandground Maurice • SER • UKN
GAIETY DUET, A • 1909 • Gilbert Arthur? • UKN
GAIETY GEORGE • 1945 • King George • UKN • SHOWTIME (USA)
GAIETY GIRL, THE • 1924 • Baggot King • USA • INHERITORS, THE
GAIETY GIRLS, THE (USA) see **PARADISE FOR TWO** • 1937
GAIJIN see **OJA NO KEN** • 1959
GAIJIN, A BRAZILIAN ODYSSEY see **GAIJIN -CAMINHOS DA LIBERDADE** • 1980
GAIJIN -CAMINHOS DA LIBERDADE • 1980 • Yamasaki Tizuka • BRZ • GAIJIN, A BRAZILIAN ODYSSEY ○ GAIJIN – ROADS TO FREEDOM
GAIJIN -ROADS TO FREEDOM see **GAIJIN -CAMINHOS DA LIBERDADE** • 1980
GAIJO NO SUKECHI • 1925 • Mizoguchi Kenji (c/d) • JPN • STREET SKETCHES (USA) ○ SKETCH ON THE ROAD, A ○ STREET SCENES
GAILY, GAILY • 1969 • Jewison Norman • USA • CHICAGO, CHICAGO (UKN)
GAINES ROUSSEL, LES • 1939 • Alexeieff Alexandre • SHT • FRN
GAINS OF FORTUNE see **KALISOCHINA ADHRUSHTAM** • 1968
GAINSBOROUGH BURLESQUES • 1925 • Brunel Adrian • SER • UKN
GAINSBOROUGH GEMS • 1929 • *Balcon Michael (P)* • SHS • UKN
GAINSBOROUGH PICTURE SHOW, THE • 1930 • Oumansky Alexander • UKN
GAIS LURONS, LES • 1936 • Natanson Jacques, Martin Paul • FRN
GAITES DE L'ESCADRON, LES see **ALLEGRO SQUADRONE, L'** • 1954
GAITO • 1957 • Nakahira Ko • JPN
GAITO NO KISHI • 1928 • Gosho Heinosuke • JPN • KNIGHT OF THE STREET
GAITUNGAP GONG • 1988 • Gao Zhizen • HKG • CHICKEN AND DUCK TALK
GAJ GOURI • 1958 • Thakur Raja • IND
GAJRE • 1948 • *Biswas Anil (M)* • IND
GAKI ZOSHI • 1972 • Takabayashi Yoichi • JPN • WATER IS SO CLEAR, THE
GAKUDA NO ONNATACHI • 1989 • Furuhata Yasuo • JPN • YAKUZA'S LADIES
GAKUSEI SHOFU • 1968 • Shinagawa Shoji • JPN • STUDENT PROSTITUTE
GAKUSEI YARO TO MUSUMETACHI • 1960 • Nakahira Ko • JPN • GIRLS AND THE STUDENTS, THE
GAKUSO O IDETE • 1925 • Mizoguchi Kenji • JPN • AFTER YEARS OF STUDY ○ OUT OF COLLEGE
GAL WHO TOOK THE WEST, THE • 1949 • De Cordova Frederick • USA • WESTERN STORY, THE
GAL YOUNG UN • 1979 • Nunez Victor • USA
GALA • 1961 • Pollet Jean-Daniel • SHT • FRN
GALA • 1982 • Scott Cynthia (c/d) • CND
GALA ARTISTIQUE • 1949 • Petel Pierre • DCS • CND
GALA DAY • 1963 • Irvin John • UKN
GALA DINNER see **UNNEPI VACSORA** • 1956
GALA SUIT see **DISZMAGYAR** • 1948
GALACTIC GIGOLO • 1988 • Bechard Gorman • USA • CLUB EARTH
GALACTICA 3: CONQUEST OF THE EARTH see **CONQUEST OF THE EARTH** • 1980
GALANTE KONIG, DER • 1920 • Halm Alfred • FRG • AUGUST DER STARKE
GALAPAGOS see **GALAPAGOS -LANDUNG IN EDEN** • 1961
GALAPAGOS ISLANDS • 1938 • Leacock Richard • DOC • USA
GALAPAGOS -LANDUNG IN EDEN • 1961 • Sielmann Heinz • FRG • GALAPAGOS
GALAS DE LA PARAMOUNT • 1930 • Venturini Edward D. • USA • GALAS PARAMOUNT
GALAS PARAMOUNT see **GALAS DE LA PARAMOUNT** • 1930
GALATALI MUSTAFA • 1967 • Gulyuz Aram • TRK • MUSTAFA FROM GALATA
GALATEE • 1910 • Melies Georges • SHT • FRN
GALATHEA • 1935 • Reiniger Lotte • ANS • FRG
GALATTA KALYANAM • 1968 • Rajendran C. V. • IND • DISPUTED MARRIAGE
GALAVORSTELLUNG DER FRATELLINIS, DIE see **SPIONE IM SAVOY-HOTEL** • 1932
GALAX • 1984 • Popescu-Gopo Ion • RMN
GALAXIA • 1960 • Kneitel Seymour • ANS • USA
GALAXIE • 1965 • Kamler Piotr • ANS • FRN
GALAXIE • 1966 • Markopoulos Gregory J. • USA
GALAXIE • 1971 • Meregny Mathias-R. • FRN
GALAXINA • 1980 • Sachs William • USA
GALAXIS • 1966 • SHT • FRG
GALAXY • 1964 • Cantrill Arthur, Cantrill Corinne • SHT • ASL
GALAXY CRIMINALS, THE see **CRIMINALI DELLA GALASSIA, I** • 1966
GALAXY EXPRESS • 1979 • Rin Taro • ANM • JPN
GALAXY INVADER • 1985 • Dohler Don • USA
GALAXY OF TERROR • 1981 • Clark Bruce • USA • MINDWARP: AN INFINITY OF TERROR ○ PLANET OF HORRORS ○ FORBIDDEN WORLD
GALE DANSKER, DEN • 1970 • Stenbaek Kirsten • DNM • MAD DANE, THE
GALE OF VERSE, A • 1917 • Curtis Allen • SHT • USA
GALE-WARNING see **STORMVARSEL** • 1968
GALEERENSTRAFLING, DER • 1919 • Gliese Rochus • FRG
GALEOTTO, DER GROSSE KUPPLER • 1919 • Moest Hubert • FRG
GALERIE DES MONSTRES, LA • 1924 • Catelain Jacques • FRN • GALLERY OF MONSTERS, THE
GALERIE SENS DESSUS-DESSOUS, LA • 1906 • Melies Georges • FRN
GALERIES DE MALGOVERT, LES • 1952 • Rouquier Georges • SHT • FRN
GALERIES LEVY ET CIE, LES • 1931 • Hugon Andre • FRN • GALERIES WASHINGTON, LES
GALERIES WASHINGTON, LES see **GALERIES LEVY ET CIE, LES** • 1931

GALETS D'ETRETAT, LES • 1971 • Gobbi Sergio • FRN, ITL • IMPROVVISAMENTE UNA SERA, UN AMORE (ITL)

GALETTES DE PONT-AVEN, LES • 1975 • Seria Joel • FRN

GALGA MENTEN • 1954 • Jancso Miklos • SHT • HNG • ALONG THE GALGU RIVER ○ AT THE RIVER GALGA

GALGENBRAUT, DIE • 1924 • Berger Josef, Nier Dr. • FRG • AUS DEUTSCHLANDS SCHWEREN TAGEN

GALGENSTEIGER, DER • 1979 • Koller Xavier • MTV • SWT • GALLOWS MAN

GALGMANNEN • 1945 • Molander Gustaf • SWD • MANDRAGORA

GALIA • 1966 • Lautner Georges • FRN, ITL • I, AND MY LOVERS ○ I AND MY LOVE

GALILAER, DER • 1921 • Buchowetzki Dimitri • FRG

GALILEO • 1968 • Cavani Liliana • ITL, BUL

GALILEO • 1975 • Losey Joseph • UKN, CND

GALL AND GOLF • 1917 • Semon Larry • SHT • USA

GALL OF THE NORTH, THE • 1932 • Buzzell Edward • SHT • USA

GALLAGHER'S TRAVELS • 1986 • Caulfield Michael • ASL

GALLANT BESS • 1946 • Marton Andrew • USA • STAR FROM HEAVEN

GALLANT BLADE, THE • 1948 • Levin Henry • USA

GALLANT DEFENDER • 1935 • Selman David • USA

GALLANT FOOL • 1933 • Bradbury Robert North • USA

GALLANT FOOL, THE • 1926 • Worne Duke • USA

GALLANT GHOST HOUNDS • 1918 • Hamilton Lloyd • USA

GALLANT GIRL, THE see **HSIA NU** • 1968

GALLANT GRINGO, THE (UKN) see **ADVENTURER, THE** • 1928

GALLANT HOURS, THE • 1960 • Montgomery Robert • USA

GALLANT JOURNEY • 1946 • Wellman William A. • USA

GALLANT LADY • 1933 • La Cava Gregory • USA

GALLANT LADY • 1942 • Beaudine William • USA

GALLANT LEGION, THE • 1948 • Kane Joseph • USA

GALLANT LITTLE TAILOR, THE • 1954 • Reiniger Lotte • ANS • UKN

GALLANT MAN see **THAT'S MY MAN** • 1947

GALLANT ONE, THE • 1961 • Stell Aaron • USA, PRU

GALLANT REBEL see **VANQUISHED, THE** • 1953

GALLANT RESCUE, A • 1900 • *Harrison* • UKN

GALLANT SCOUT, A • 1909 • *Manufacturer'S Film Agency* • UKN

GALLANT SONS • 1940 • Seitz George B. • USA

GALLANT THIEF, THE • 1958 • Lacko Jan • CZC

GALLANTRY OF JIMMY ROGERS, THE • 1915 • *Essanay* • USA

GALLEGA BAILA MAMBA, UNA • 1950 • Gomez Muriel Emilio • MXC

GALLEGA EN LA HABANA, UNA • 1955 • Cardona Rene • MXC, CUB

GALLEGA EN MEXICO, UNA • 1949 • Soler Julian • MXC

GALLEGHER • 1910 • Porter Edwin S. • USA

GALLEGHER • 1917 • Turbett Ben • SHT • USA

GALLEGHER (UKN) see **LET 'ER GO GALLEGHER** • 1928

GALLEGUITA • 1940 • Irigoyen Julio • ARG

GALLEGUITO DE LA CARA SUCIA, EL • 1966 • Cahen Enrique • ARG

GALLERO, EL • 1948 • Gomez Muriel Emilio • MXC

GALLEROS DE JALISCO, LOS • 1973 • *Filmicas Agrasanchez* • MXC

GALLERY • 1970 • Pavlinic Zlatko • ANS • YGS

GALLERY: A VIEW OF TIME, A • 1969 • Owen Don • DCS • CND

GALLERY MURDERS, THE (UKN) see **UCCELLO DALLE PIUME DE CRISTALLO, L'** • 1970

GALLERY OF HORRORS see **RETURN FROM THE PAST** • 1967

GALLERY OF MONSTERS, THE see **GALERIE DES MONSTRES, LA** • 1924

GALLEY SLAVE, THE • 1909 • Blackton J. Stuart (Spv) • USA

GALLEY SLAVE, THE • 1915 • Edwards J. Gordon • USA

GALLEY SLAVE'S ROMANCE, A • 1912 • *Rex* • USA

GALLI DEL MARE, I see **NON SCHERZARE CON LE DONNE** • 1957

GALLINA CLUECA, LA • 1941 • de Fuentes Fernando • MXC

GALLINA VOGELBIRDAE • 1963 • Brdecka Jiri • ANS • CZC • SPATNE NAMALOVANA SLEPICE ○ GROTESQUE CHICKEN, THE ○ VOGEL'S SPECIES ○ BADLY-DRAWN HEN

GALLIPOLI • 1982 • Weir Peter • ASL

GALLO COLORADO, EL • 1957 • Gomez Muriel Emilio • MXC

GALLO CON ESPOLONES, UN • 1964 • Gomez Urquiza Zacarias • MXC, PRU • OPERACION NONGOS

GALLO CORRIENTE GALLO VALIENTE • 1964 • Salvador Jaime • MXC

GALLO DE ORO, EL • 1964 • Gavaldon Roberto • MXC

GALLO EN CORRAL AJENO, UN • 1951 • Soler Julian • MXC

GALLO GIRO, EL • 1948 • Gout Alberto • MXC

GALLO GIRO EN ESPANA, EL see **MI NOCHE DE BODAS** • 1961

GALLOP OF DEATH, THE • 1913 • *Francis Alec B.* • USA

GALLOP PAST OF SYDNEY FIRE BRIGADE • 1898 • ASL

GALLOPER, THE • 1915 • Mackenzie Donald • USA

GALLOPIN' GALS • 1940 • Hanna William, Barbera Joseph • ANS • USA

GALLOPIN' GAUCHO • 1928 • Disney Walt, Iwerks Ub • ANS • USA

GALLOPIN' THROUGH see **GALLOPING THRU** • 1923

GALLOPING ACE, THE • 1924 • Bradbury Robert North • USA • CREED THAT WEAKENS, THE ○ DRIFTER, THE ○ HARD ROCK

GALLOPING BUNGALOWS • 1924 • Cline Eddie • SHT • USA

GALLOPING COWBOY, THE • 1926 • Craft William James • USA

GALLOPING DEVILS • 1920 • Watt Nate • USA

GALLOPING DYNAMITE • 1937 • Fraser Harry L. • USA

GALLOPING FANNY • 1933 • Muffati Steve, Donnelly Eddie • ANS • USA • GALLOPING HOOVES

GALLOPING FISH • 1924 • Ince Thomas H., Andrews Del • USA

GALLOPING FURY • 1927 • Eason B. Reeves • USA

GALLOPING GALLAGHER • 1924 • Rogell Albert S. • USA • SHERIFF OF GOPHER FLATS, THE ○ SHERIFF OF TOMBSTONE, THE

GALLOPING GHOST, THE • 1931 • Eason B. Reeves • SRL • USA

GALLOPING GHOSTS • 1926 • Ceder Ralph, Parrott James • SHT • USA

GALLOPING GOBS, THE • 1927 • Thorpe Richard • USA

GALLOPING HOOFS • 1924 • Seitz George B., Bennet Spencer Gordon • SRL • USA

GALLOPING HOOVES see **GALLOPING FANNY** • 1933

GALLOPING JINX • 1925 • Eddy Robert • USA • FEARLESS JINX, THE (UKN)

GALLOPING JUSTICE • 1927 • Wyler William • SHT • USA

GALLOPING KID, THE • 1922 • Ross Nat • USA • MISFIT BECOMES CHAPERON

GALLOPING KID, THE • 1932 • Tansey Robert • USA

GALLOPING LOVER, THE • 1929 • *Lyons Cliff* • USA

GALLOPING MAJOR, THE • 1909 • *Warwick Trading Co.* • UKN

GALLOPING MAJOR, THE • 1951 • Cornelius Henry • UKN

GALLOPING ON • 1925 • Thorpe Richard • USA

GALLOPING ROMEO • 1933 • Bradbury Robert North • USA

GALLOPING ROMEO, THE • 1913 • Duncan William • USA

GALLOPING THRU • 1923 • Bradbury Robert North • USA • GALLOPIN' THROUGH

GALLOPING THRU • 1932 • Nosler Lloyd • USA

GALLOPING THUNDER • 1927 • Pembroke Scott • USA

GALLOPING THUNDER • 1946 • Nazarro Ray • USA

GALLOPING VENGEANCE • 1925 • Craft William James • USA

GALLOS DE LA MADRUGADA, LOS • 1970 • Saenz De Heredia Jose Luis • SPN

GALLOS DE PELEA • 1970 • Moreno Alba Rafael • SPN

GALLOWS MAN see **GALGENSTEIGER, DER** • 1979

GALO GIMBAL • 1968 • Buenaventura Augusto • PHL

GALOPPERANDE OSTEN, DEN see **STJARNSMALL I FRUKOSTKLUBBEN** • 1950

GALOSE STASTIA • 1985 • Herz Juraj • CZC • OVERSHOES OF HAPPINESS

GALS AND GALLONS • 1939 • Schwarzwald Milton • SHT • USA

GALS, INC. • 1943 • Goodwins Leslie • USA

GALSKAPENS STILLHET • 1984 • Kolsto Egil • NRW • SILENCE OF MADNESS, THE

GALUCCI BROTHERS • 1988 • Magder Murray • USA • BROTHERS SPAGHETTI, THE

GALVANIC FLUID • 1908 • Blackton J. Stuart • USA • MORE FUN WITH LIQUID ELECTRICITY

GALVESTON HURRICANE SHOTS • 1900 • *Bitzer Billy (Ph)* • USA

GALYON • Tors Ivan • USA • GALYON: THE INDESTRUCTIBLE MAN ○ GAYLON

GALYON: THE INDESTRUCTIBLE MAN see **GALYON**

GAMAN • 1977 • Ali Muzaffar • IND • GOING

GAMBARA VERSUS BARUGON see **GAMERA TAI BARUGON** • 1966

GAMBARE! KENTA • 1957 • Harada Hasuo • JPN

GAMBE D'ORO • 1958 • Vasile Turi • ITL

GAMBERGE, LA • 1961 • Carbonnaux Norbert • FRN

GAMBERROS, LOS • 1954 • Llado Juan • SPN

GAMBIER'S ADVOCATE • 1915 • *Dawn Hazel* • USA • CLARISSA

GAMBIT • 1966 • Neame Ronald • USA

GAMBLE, THE • 1916 • Ricketts Thomas • SHT • USA

GAMBLE FOR LOVE, A • 1917 • Wilson Frank • UKN

GAMBLE IN LIVES, A • 1920 • Ridgwell George • UKN

GAMBLE IN SOULS, A • 1916 • Edwards Walter • USA

GAMBLE WITH DEATH, A • 1913 • O'Sullivan Tony • USA

GAMBLE WITH HEARTS, A • 1923 • Collins Edwin J. • UKN

GAMBLE WITH LOVE, A • 1911 • *Powers* • USA

GAMBLER • 1971 • *Burman S. D. (M)* • IND

GAMBLER see **JUARI** • 1968

GAMBLER see **SPIELER** • 1989

GAMBLER, THE • 1914 • *Imp* • USA

GAMBLER, THE • 1916 • Reynolds Lynn • SHT • USA

GAMBLER, THE • 1974 • Reisz Karel • USA

GAMBLER, THE see **MICHIGAN KID, THE** • 1928

GAMBLER, THE see **JOUEUR, LE** • 1958

GAMBLER, THE see **BAKUCHIUCHI** • 1967

GAMBLER, THE see **GHOMAR BAZ** • 1968

GAMBLER, THE see **IGROK** • 1972

GAMBLER, THE see **KENNY ROGERS AS THE GAMBLER** • 1980

GAMBLER, THE see **KATALA** • 1989

GAMBLER AND THE DEVIL, THE • 1908 • *Vitagraph* • USA

GAMBLER AND THE GIRL, THE • 1912 • *Bison* • USA

GAMBLER AND THE LADY, THE • 1952 • Jenkins Pat, Newfield Sam • UKN

GAMBLER AS I AM see **FURAI MONOGATARI** • 1959

GAMBLER BIOGRAPHY see **BAKUTO RETSUDEN** • 1968

GAMBLER FROM NATCHEZ, THE • 1954 • Levin Henry • USA

GAMBLER IN THE SEA see **UMI NO SHOBUSHI** • 1961

GAMBLER OF THE WEST, A • 1911 • *Anderson Broncho Billy* • USA

GAMBLER OF THE WEST, THE • 1915 • *Butler William J.* • USA

GAMBLER SERIES: THE GREAT CASINO see **BAKUCHIUCHI: SOCHO TOBAKU** • 1968

GAMBLER WORE A GUN, THE • 1961 • Cahn Edward L. • USA

GAMBLERS, THE • 1897 • *Paul R .w.* • UKN

GAMBLERS, THE • 1905 • Stow Percy • UKN

GAMBLERS, THE • 1912 • *Vitagraph* • USA

GAMBLERS, THE • 1914 • O'Neil Barry • USA

GAMBLERS, THE • 1919 • Scardon Paul • USA

GAMBLERS, THE • 1929 • Curtiz Michael • USA

GAMBLERS, THE • 1970 • Winston Ron • USA

GAMBLERS, THE (UKN) see **JUDGE, THE** • 1949

GAMBLERS ALL • 1919 • Aylott Dave • UKN

GAMBLER'S BLOOD see **TEKKABA YABURI** • 1964

GAMBLER'S CHANCE, THE • 1911 • *Lubin* • USA

GAMBLER'S CHARM, THE • 1910 • *Lubin* • USA

GAMBLER'S CHOICE • 1944 • McDonald Frank • USA

GAMBLER'S CODE • 1966 • *Takahashi Hideki* • JPN

GAMBLER'S DAUGHTER, THE • 1912 • *Robinson Ruth* • USA

GAMBLER'S DISPERSION see **BAKUTO KAISAN SHIKI** • 1968

GAMBLER'S FATE: OR, THE ROAD TO RUIN, THE • 1901 • Paul Robert William • UKN

GAMBLER'S GAMBOL, A • 1916 • *Voss Fatty* • SHT • USA

GAMBLER'S GOLD • 1911 • *Wilkins George (Ph)* • ASL

GAMBLER'S HEART, A • 1913 • *Melies* • USA

GAMBLER'S HEART, THE • 1912 • *Bison* • USA

GAMBLER'S HONOR, A • 1913 • O'Sullivan Tony • USA

GAMBLER'S I.O.U., THE • 1915 • *Furey Barney* • USA

GAMBLERS IN GREENBACKS • 1916 • MacMackin Archer • SHT • USA

GAMBLERS IN OKINAWA see **BAKUTO GAIJIN BUTAI** • 1971

GAMBLER'S INFLUENCE, THE • 1911 • *Lubin* • USA

GAMBLERS: INVINCIBLE GAME see **BAKUCHIUCHI: FUJIMI NO SHOBU** • 1967

GAMBLER'S LAST TRICK, A • 1913 • *Bison* • USA

GAMBLER'S LAW, THE see **KYOKAKUDO** • 1967

GAMBLER'S LOST LOVE, THE • 1916 • MacQuarrie Murdock • SHT • USA

GAMBLER'S NIGHTMARE, THE • 1906 • Raymond Charles? • UKN

GAMBLER'S OATH, THE • 1913 • *Bison* • USA

GAMBLERS OF TOKYO see **TOKYO BAKUTO** • 1967

GAMBLER'S PAL, THE • 1913 • Sidney Scott? • USA

GAMBLER'S REFORMATION, THE • 1912 • *Gebhardt George* • USA

GAMBLER'S REFORMATION, THE • 1914 • *Kalem* • USA

GAMBLER'S RUIN, THE • 1913 • *Gaumont* • USA

GAMBLER'S STORY OF SURUGA: BROKEN IRON FIRE see **SURUGA YUHKYOU-DEN: YABURE TAKKA** • 1964

GAMBLER'S VILLAINY, A • 1911 • Bouwmeester Theo • UKN

GAMBLER'S WAY, A • 1914 • *Essanay* • USA

GAMBLER'S WIFE, THE • 1899 • Smith G. A. • UKN

GAMBLER'S WIFE, THE • 1908 • *Graphic Cinematograph Co.* • UKN

GAMBLER'S WIFE, THE see **FRA FYRSTE TIL KNEJPEVAERT** • 1913

GAMBLERS' WORLD (TWO), THE see **ZOKU TOSEININ** • 1967

GAMBLIN' FOOL, A • 1920 • Maloney Leo • SHT • USA

GAMBLIN' MAN see **COCKFIGHTER** • 1974

GAMBLING • 1934 • Lee Rowland V. • USA

GAMBLING see **PANDHAYAM** • 1967

GAMBLING DAUGHTERS • 1941 • Nosseck Max • USA

GAMBLING FOOL, THE • 1925 • McGowan J. P. • USA

GAMBLING HELL (UKN) see **MACAO, L'ENFER DU JEU** • 1939

GAMBLING HOUSE • 1950 • Tetzlaff Ted • USA • ALIAS MIKE FURY

GAMBLING IN SOULS • 1919 • Millarde Harry • USA

GAMBLING LADY • 1934 • Mayo Archie • USA

GAMBLING ON THE GREEN • 1916 • *Rogers Gene* • SHT • USA

GAMBLING ON THE HIGH SEAS • 1940 • Amy George • USA

GAMBLING RUBE, A • 1914 • Henderson Dell • USA

GAMBLING SAMURAI see **KUNISADA CHUJI** • 1960

GAMBLING SEX, THE • 1932 • Newmeyer Fred • USA

GAMBLING SHIP • 1933 • Gasnier Louis J., Marcin Max • USA

GAMBLING SHIP • 1938 • Scotto Aubrey • USA

GAMBLING TERROR, THE • 1937 • Newfield Sam • USA

GAMBLING WITH DEATH • 1909 • *Vitagraph* • USA

GAMBLING WITH SOULS • 1936 • Clifton Elmer • USA

GAMBLING WITH THE GULF STREAM • 1922 • *Bray John R. (P)* • SHT • USA

GAMBLING WIVES • 1924 • Henderson Dell • USA

GAMBROS APO TO LONDHINO, O • 1967 • Dalianidis Ioannis • GRC • BRIDEGROOM FROM LONDON, THE

GAMBROS MOU O PRIKOTHIRAS, O • 1967 • Silinos Vangelis • GRC • MY SON-IN-LAW IS A DOWRY HUNTER

GAME, A • 1967 • Badzian Teresa • ANM • PLN

GAME, A see **ZABAWA** • 1961

GAME, THE • 1909 • *Essanay* • USA

GAME, THE • 1915 • *Foster Morris* • USA

GAME, THE • 1963 • Kaczender George • CND

GAME, THE • 1989 • McKay Cole • USA

GAME, THE • 1990 • Brown Curtis • USA

GAME, THE see **ZABAWA** • 1961

GAME, THE see **GRA** • 1968

GAME, THE (USA) see **IGRA** • 1962

GAME CALLED LOVE, A see **LADY TAKES A FLYER, THE** • 1958

GAME CALLED SCRUGGS, A • 1965 • Hart David • UKN • SCRUGGS

GAME CHICKEN, THE • 1922 • Franklin Chester M. • USA

GAME CHICKEN, THE • 1926 • Parkinson H. B. • UKN

GAME FIGHTER, A • 1924 • Gibson Tom • USA

GAME FOR LIFE, A • 1910 • *Defender* • USA

GAME FOR SIX LOVERS, A (USA) see **EAU A LA BOUCHE, L'** • 1959

GAME FOR THREE LOSERS • 1965 • O'Hara Gerry • UKN

GAME FOR TWO, A • 1910 • Salter Harry • USA

GAME FOR TWO, A • 1912 • *Trunnelle Mabel* • USA

GAME FOR TWO, A • 1921 • Paul Fred, Raymond Jack • UKN

GAME FOR VULTURES • 1980 • Fargo James • UKN, SWT, SAF

GAME GAMBLER, A • 1918 • *Triangle* • USA

GAME IS OVER, THE (USA) see **CUREE, LA** • 1966

GAME IS SET, THE see **GAME IS SEX, THE** • 1969

GAME IS SEX, THE • 1969 • Wuest Harry • USA • NAME OF THE GAME IS SEX, THE ○ GAME OF SEX, THE ○ GAME IS SET, THE

GAME IS THE GAME, THE • 1974 • Cardinal Roger • DCS • CND • PLUS CA CHANGE, PLUS C'EST PAREIL

GAME IS UP, THE • 1935 • Sparling Gordon • DCS • CND

GAME KEEPER'S DAUGHTER, THE • 1914 • *Domino* • USA

GAME OF BLUFF, A • 1912 • *Bassett Russell* • USA

GAME OF BLUFF, A • 1914 • Birch Cecil • UKN

GAME OF BRIDGE, A • 1911 • *Comet* • USA

GAME OF CARDS see **JEUX DE CARTES** • 1959

GAME OF CARDS see **JUEGO DE NAIPES** • 1969

GAME OF CARDS, A • 1913 • Finley Ned • USA

GAME OF CHANCE see **ONNENPELI** • 1965

GAME OF CHANCE see **GIOCARE D'AZZARDO** • 1983

GAME OF CHANCE, A • 1932 • Barnett Charles • UKN

GAME OF CHESS, A • 1912 • *Prior Herbert* • USA

GAME OF CHESS AND KISSES, A • 1899 • Smith G. A. • UKN

GAME OF DANGER see **BANG YOU'RE DEAD** • 1954

GAME OF DEATH see **SZU-WAN YU-HSI** • 1978

GAME OF DEATH 2 • 1981 • Ng See Yuen • HKG • NEW GAME OF DEATH, THE

GAME OF DEATH, A • 1946 • Wise Robert • USA • DANGEROUS ADVENTURE ○ MOST DANGEROUS GAME, THE
GAME OF DECEPTION, A • 1911 • Salter Harry • USA
GAME OF FREEZE-OUT, A • 1914 • Henderson Dell • USA
GAME OF HEARTS, A • 1910 • *Power* • USA
GAME OF HEARTS, A • 1910 • *Imp* • USA
GAME OF HEARTS, A see **CUPID'S REALM** • 1908
GAME OF IMAGINATION see **STUDIE V** • 1955
GAME OF LIBERTY, THE • 1916 • Tucker George Loane • UKN • UNDER SUSPICION (USA)
GAME OF LIFE, THE • 1914 • *Kb* • USA
GAME OF LIFE, THE • 1914 • *Selig* • USA
GAME OF LIFE, THE • 1915 • *Kalem* • USA
GAME OF LIFE, THE • 1915 • Davis Ulysses • USA
GAME OF LIFE, THE • 1922 • Samuelson G. B. • UKN
GAME OF LIFE, THE see **EM FAMILIA** • 1971
GAME OF LIVING WHIST, A • 1903 • *Urban Trading Co.* • UKN
GAME OF LOVE, A • 1915 • *Morris Reggie* • USA
GAME OF LOVE, THE • 1987 • Roth Bobby • USA
GAME OF LOVE, THE see **EAU A LA BOUCHE, L'** • 1959
GAME OF LOVE, THE (USA) see **BLE EN HERBE, LE** • 1953
GAME OF LUCK see **ONNENPELI** • 1965
GAME OF LUCK, THE see **BAZY-E-SHANCE** • 1968
GAME OF MEN see **JUEGO DE HOMBRES** • 1964
GAME OF POKER, A • 1913 • Sennett Mack • USA
GAME OF POLITICS, THE • 1914 • *Campbell William* • USA
GAME OF POOL, A • 1913 • Sennett Mack • USA
GAME OF SEX, THE see **GAME IS SEX, THE** • 1969
GAME OF SNOWBALLING, A • 1899 • *Norton C. Goodwin* • UKN
GAME OF SOLITAIRE, THE see **JEU DE SOLITAIRE, LE** • 1975
GAME OF SURVIVAL • 1988 • Gazarian Armand • USA
GAME OF THREE, THE • 1915 • *Gilmore Barney* • USA
GAME OF THRILLS, A • 1969 • Schuyler Helmud
GAME OF THRILLS, THE • 1915 • *Reliance* • USA
GAME OF TRUTH see **SALLSKAPSLEK** • 1963
GAME OF WITS, A • 1914 • *Holloway Carol* • USA
GAME OF WITS, A • 1917 • King Henry • USA
GAME OLD KNIGHT, A • 1915 • Jones F. Richard • USA
GAME PASS see **WILDWECHSEL** • 1972
GAME PEOPLE PLAY, THE • 1967 • Johnsen S. N. • USA • SEX IS THE GAME PEOPLE PLAY ○ SEX IS GAMES, PEOPLE PLAY
GAME RESERVE see **COTO DE CAZA** • 1984
GAME SHOW MODELS • 1977 • Gottlieb David Neil • USA
GAME THAT FAILED, THE • 1913 • *Crystal* • USA
GAME THAT FAILED, THE • 1916 • Wolbert William • SHT • USA
GAME THAT KILLS, THE • 1937 • Lederman D. Ross • USA
GAME THEY CALL SEX, THE see **HUANG-SE KU-SHIH** • 1988
GAME WARDEN, THE • 1913 • *Kalem* • USA
GAME WITH FAME, A • 1910 • *Kalem* • USA
GAME WITH FATE, A • 1918 • Scardon Paul • USA
GAME WITH STONES, A see **SPIEL MIT STEINEN** • 1965
GAME WITHOUT A DRAW see **IGRA BYEZ NICHYEY** • 1967
GAMEKEEPER see **WILDSCHUT** • 1986
GAMEKEEPER, THE • 1980 • Loach Kenneth • TVM • UKN
GAMEKEEPER'S DAUGHTER, THE • 1910 • Aylott Dave? • UKN
GAMEKEEPER'S DOG, THE • 1907 • Hough Harold • UKN
GAMEKEEPER'S REVENGE, THE • 1912 • Noy Wilfred • UKN
GAMERA see **DAIKAIJU GAMERA** • 1965
GAMERA TAI BARUGON • 1966 • Tanaka Shigeo • JPN • WAR OF THE MONSTERS (USA) ○ GAMERA VERSUS BARUGON ○ GAMBARA VERSUS BARUGON
GAMERA TAI DAIMAJU JAIGA • 1970 • Yuasa Noriaki • JPN • GAMERA VS. MONSTER X (USA) ○ MONSTERS INVADE EXPO '70 ○ GAMERA VERSUS JIGER
GAMERA TAI GURON • 1969 • Yuasa Noriaki • JPN • ATTACK OF THE MONSTERS ○ GAMERA VS. GUIRON
GAMERA TAI GYAOS • 1967 • Yuasa Noriaki • JPN • RETURN OF THE GIANT MONSTERS, THE (USA) ○ BOYICHI AND THE SUPERMONSTER ○ DAIKAIJU KUCHUSEN: GAMERA TAI GAOS ○ GAMERA VS. GAOS ○ GAMERA VS. GYAOS
GAMERA TAI SHINKAI KAIJU JIGURA • 1971 • Yuasa Noriaki • JPN • GAMERA VERSUS THE DEEP SEA MONSTER ZIGRA ○ GAMERA VS. ZIGRA
GAMERA TAI UCHI KAIJU BAIRUSU • 1968 • Yuasa Noriaki • JPN • DESTROY ALL PLANETS (USA) ○ GAMERA TAI UCHI KAIJU VIRAS ○ GAMERA TAI VIRAS ○ GAMERA VS. OUTER SPACE MONSTER VIRAS ○ GAMERA VS. VIRAS
GAMERA TAI UCHI KAIJU VIRAS see **GAMERA TAI UCHI KAIJU BAIRUSU** • 1968
GAMERA TAI VIRAS see **GAMERA TAI UCHI KAIJU BAIRUSU** • 1968
GAMERA VERSUS BARUGON see **GAMERA TAI BARUGON** • 1966
GAMERA VERSUS JIGER see **GAMERA TAI DAIMAJU JAIGA** • 1970
GAMERA VERSUS THE DEEP SEA MONSTER ZIGRA see **GAMERA TAI SHINKAI KAIJU JIGURA** • 1971
GAMERA VS. GAOS see **GAMERA TAI GYAOS** • 1967
GAMERA VS. GUIRON see **GAMERA TAI GURON** • 1969
GAMERA VS. GYAOS see **GAMERA TAI GYAOS** • 1967
GAMERA VS. MONSTER X (USA) see **GAMERA TAI DAIMAJU JAIGA** • 1970
GAMERA VS. OUTER SPACE MONSTER VIRAS see **GAMERA TAI UCHI KAIJU BAIRUSU** • 1968
GAMERA VS. VIRAS see **GAMERA TAI UCHI KAIJU BAIRUSU** • 1968
GAMERA VS. ZIGRA see **GAMERA TAI SHINKAI KAIJU JIGURA** • 1971
GAMES • 1967 • Harrington Curtis • USA
GAMES • 1974 • Kohanyi Julius • CND
GAMES see **GRY I ZABAWY** • 1966
GAMES see **PEHNIDHIARA, I** • 1967
GAMES see **JEUX** • 1979
GAMES, THE • 1969 • Winner Michael • UKN
GAMES AFFAIR, THE • 1974 • Clark Bruce • SRL • NZL
GAMES AND VARIATIONS see **SUGAR DADDY** • 1968
GAMES FOR CHILDREN OF SCHOOL AGE • 1986 • Laius Leida, Iho Arvo • USS
GAMES FOR GROWN-UPS • 1969 • Rudas I. • USS
GAMES FOR SIX LOVERS see **EAU A LA BOUCHE, L'** • 1959
GAMES GAMBLERS PLAY see **KUEI MAH SUENG SING** • 1975
GAMES GIRLS PLAY • 1974 • Arnold Jack • UKN • BUNNY CAPER, THE (USA) ○ SEX PLAY
GAMES MEN PLAY, THE (USA) see **CIGARRA NO ES UN BICHO, LA** • 1963
GAMES MOTHER NEVER TAUGHT YOU • 1982 • Philips Lee • TVM • USA
GAMES OF DESIRE (USA) see **LADY, DIE** • 1964
GAMES OF LOVE • 1916 • Sandberg Anders W. • DNM
GAMES OF LOVE AND LONELINESS see **ALLVARSAMMA LEKEN, DEN** • 1977
GAMES OF THE ANGELS, THE (USA) see **JEUX DES ANGES, LES** • 1964
GAMES THAT LOVERS PLAY • 1970 • Leigh Malcolm • UKN
GAMES THAT NURSES PLAY see **YOUNG NURSES, THE** • 1973
GAME'S UP, THE • 1919 • Wilson Elsie Jane • USA
GAMES WOMEN PLAY • 1982 • Vincent Chuck • USA
GAMESTERS, THE • 1920 • Cox George L. • USA
GAMETSUI YATSU • 1961 • Chiba Yasuki • JPN • THIS GREEDY OLD SKIN (USA)
GAMILA AL-GAZA'IRIYYA see **JAMILA EL GAZAIRIA** • 1958
GAMILA BOHRAID see **JAMILA EL GAZAIRIA** • 1958
GAMIN DE PARIS • 1953 • Jaffe Georges • FRN
GAMIN DE PARIS, LE • 1910 • Chautard Emile • FRN
GAMIN DE PARIS, LE • 1923 • Feuillade Louis • FRN
GAMIN DE PARIS, LE • 1932 • Roudes Gaston • FRN
GAMINE EN CHALEUR • Xavier Robert • FRN
GAMINES OUVERTES • 1980 • Roy Jean-Claude • FRN
GAMIN'S ATTITUDE, A • 1909 • Fitzhamon Lewin • UKN
GAMJA • 1988 • Bae Chang-Ho • SKR • POTATOES
GAMLA HERRGARDEN, DEN • 1925 • Persson Edvard • SWD • OLD MANOR, THE
GAMLA KVARNEN, DE • 1964 • Troell Jan • DOC • SWD • OLD MILL, THE
GAMLA STAN • 1931 • Almqvist Stig, Asklund Erik, Johnson Eyvind, Lundkvist Arthur • SWD • SYMPHONY OF THE STREETS ○ OLD CITY, THE
GAMLE, DE • 1947 • *Dreyer Carl T.* • DCS • DNM • SEVENTH AGE, THE
GAMLE, DE • 1961 • Carlsen Henning • SHT • DNM • OLD PEOPLE
GAMLE BAENK, DEN see **UNDER MINDERNES TRAE** • 1913
GAMLE CHATOL, DET see **CHATOLLETS HEMMELIGHED** • 1913
GAMLE KOBMANDSHUS, DET • 1911 • Blom August • DNM • MIDSUMMER-TIME ○ MIDSOMMER
GAMLET • 1964 • Kozintsev Grigori • USS • HAMLET
GAMMA 693 see **NIGHT OF THE ZOMBIES** • 1981
GAMMA PEOPLE, THE • 1956 • Gilling John • UKN
GAMMA SANGO UCHU DAISAKUSEN • 1968 • Fukasaku Kinji • JPN, USA • GREEN SLIME, THE (USA) ○ BATTLE BEYOND THE STARS ○ DEATH AND THE GREEN SLIME
GAMMELION • 1967 • Markopoulos Gregory J. • USA
GAMMELT ISFISKERI PA RINGKOBING FJORD • 1947 • Rasmussen Holger • DNM
GAMMERA see **DAIKAIJU GAMERA** • 1965
GAMMERA THE INVINCIBLE (USA) see **DAIKAIJU GAMERA** • 1965
GAMMICK, LA • 1974 • Godbout Jacques • CND
GAMOUDI • 1965 • Essid Hamadi, Harzallah Ahmed • SHT • TNS
GAMPEKI • 1953 • Nakamura Noboru • JPN • CLIFF, THE
GAMPERILAYA • 1964 • Peries Lester James • SLN • REVOLUTION IN THE VILLAGE ○ CHANGING COUNTRYSIDE, THE ○ CHANGES IN THE VILLAGE
GAN • 1953 • Toyoda Shiro • JPN • MISTRESS, THE (USA) ○ WILD GEESE
GAN NO TERA • 1962 • Kawashima Yuzo • JPN • TEMPLE OF THE WILD GEESE
GANASHATRU • 1989 • Ray Satyajit • IND • ENEMY OF THE PEOPLE, AN (UKN)
GANBARE SANTA • 1953 • *Hidari Sachiko* • JPN • TENACIOUS SANTA
GANCHEROS, LOS • 1957 • Berlanga Luis Garcia • SPN
GANCIA • 1964 • Borowczyk Walerian • ANS • FRN
GANDER AT MOTHER GOOSE, A • 1940 • Avery Tex • ANS • USA
GANDHI • 1982 • Attenborough Richard • UKN
GANDY GOOSE • 1938-54 • *Terry Paul (P)* • ASS • USA
GANDY GOOSE AND THE CHIPPER CHIPMUNK • 1948 • Davis Mannie • ANS • USA
GANDY GOOSE IN THE GHOST TOWN • 1944 • Davis Mannie • ANS • USA • GHOST TOWN, THE
GANDY THE GOOSE • 1938 • Foster John • ANS • USA
GANDYDANCE • 1973 • Dalen Zale R. • CND
GANDY'S DREAM GIRL • 1944 • Davis Mannie • ANS • USA
GANESH AVATAR • 1922 • *Hindustan* • IND
GANESH AVATAR • 1925 • *Hindustan* • IND
GANESH JANMA • 1930 • *Madan* • IND
GANESH MAHIMA • 1950 • Wadia Homi • IND • KRISHNA VIVAH ○ KRISHNA'S MARRIAGE ○ SUPERNATURAL GANESH
GANG see **WALK PROUD** • 1979
GANG, LE • 1977 • Deray Jacques • FRN, ITL
GANG, THE • 1914 • Finley Ned • USA • REFORMATION OF THE GANG, THE
GANG, THE • 1917 • Smith David • SHT • USA
GANG, THE see **BANDA** • 1965
GANG BANG • 1970 • USA
GANG BULLETS • 1938 • Hillyer Lambert • USA • CROOKED WAY, THE (UKN)
GANG BUSTER, THE • 1931 • Sutherland A. Edward • USA • ON THE SPOT
GANG BUSTERS • 1942 • Taylor Ray, Smith Noel • SRL • USA
GANG DES OTAGES, LE • 1972 • Molinaro Edouard • FRN, ITL • QUELLI DELLA BANDA BERETTA (ITL) ○ HOSTAGES, THE (USA)
GANG DES PIANOS A BRETELLES, LE • 1952 • de Turenne Gilles A. • FRN • HOLD-UP EN MUSIQUE
GANG DES TRACTIONS-ARRIERE, LE • 1950 • Loubignac Jean • FRN
GANG DOMES • 1963 • Fukasaku Kinji • JPN • LEAGUE OF GANGSTERS
GANG DURCH DIE HOLLE, DER • 1921 • Boese Carl • FRG
GANG FIGHTER, THE • 1912 • *Robinson Ruth* • USA
GANG IN DIE NACHT, DER • 1920 • Murnau F. W. • FRG • JOURNEY INTO THE NIGHT
GANG MADE GOOD, THE (UKN) see **TUXEDO JUNCTION** • 1941
GANG NO TEIO • 1967 • Furuhata Yasuo • JPN • SOVEREIGN OF ALL GANGSTERS, THE
GANG OF FOUR, THE (UKN) see **BANDE DES QUATRE, LA** • 1988
GANG SHOW, THE • 1937 • Goulding Alf • UKN
GANG SMASHERS see **GUN MOLL** • 1938
GANG TAI GANG • 1962 • Ishii Teruo • JPN • GANG VERSUS GANG
GANG THAT COULDN'T SHOOT STRAIGHT, THE • 1971 • Goldstone James • USA
GANG VERSUS GANG see **GANG TAI GANG** • 1962
GANG WAR • 1928 • Glennon Bert • USA • ALL SQUARE (UKN)
GANG WAR • 1958 • Fowler Gene Jr. • USA
GANG WAR • 1962 • Marshall Frank • UKN
GANG WAR see **ODD MAN OUT** • 1947
GANGA • 1960 • Tarafdar Rajen • IND • RIVER GANGES, THE
GANGA ADDARA • Peries Sumitra • SLN • RIVER BANK
GANGA AND GOURI see **GANGE GOWRI** • 1967
GANGA AVTARAN see **GANGAVATAREN** • 1937
GANGA BRUTA • 1932 • Mauro-Humberto • BRZ • ROUGH DIAMOND
GANGA, JAMUNA, SARASWATI • 1988 • *Bachchan Amitabh* • IND
GANGA MAIYA • 1953 • *Trivedi C. M. (P)* • IND • MYSTERY OF THE GANGES RIVER
GANGA MAYA • 1983 • Segarra Ludovic • FRN
GANGA SAGAR • 1979 • Chandragupta Bansi • DOC • IND
GANGA ZUMBA • 1963 • Diegues Carlos • BRZ
GANGAVATAREN • 1937 • Phalke Dada • IND • DESERT OF GANGA, THE ○ GANGA AVTARAN ○ ORIGIN OF THE GANGES RIVER
GANGBUSTERS • 1955 • Karn Bill • USA
GANGE GOWRI • 1967 • Panthalu B. R. • IND • GANGA AND GOURI
GANGLAND: THE VERNE MILLER STORY • 1987 • Hewitt Rod • USA • VERNE MILLER
GANGLEADER'S REFORM, THE • 1910 • *Yankee* • USA
GANGS see **TONG DANG** • 1988
GANG'S ALL HERE, THE • 1939 • Freeland Thornton • UKN • AMAZING MR. FORREST, THE (USA)
GANG'S ALL HERE, THE • 1941 • Yarbrough Jean • USA • IN THE NIGHT (UKN)
GANG'S ALL HERE, THE • 1943 • Berkeley Busby • USA • GIRLS HE LEFT BEHIND, THE (UKN) ○ BANANA SPLIT
GANGS INCORPORATED see **PAPER BULLETS** • 1941
GANG'S NEW MEMBER, THE • 1915 • *Mulhall Jack* • USA
GANGS OF CHICAGO • 1940 • Lubin Arthur • USA
GANGS OF NEW YORK • 1938 • Cruze James • USA
GANGS OF SONORA • 1941 • English John • USA
GANGS OF THE WATERFRONT • 1945 • Blair George • USA
GANGSTER '70 • 1968 • Guerrini Mino • ITL
GANGSTER, EL • 1964 • Alcoriza Luis • MXC
GANGSTER, THE • 1913 • *Lubin* • USA
GANGSTER, THE • 1947 • Wiles Gordon • USA
GANGSTER BOSS (USA) see **GRAND CHEF, LE** • 1959
GANGSTER MAIGRE LUI • 1935 • Hugon Andre • FRN
GANGSTER MOVIE, THE see **GANGSTERFILMEN EN FRAMLING STEG AV TAGET** • 1974
GANGSTER MOVIE A STRANGER CAME BY TRAIN, THE see **GANGSTERFILMEN EN FRAMLING STEG AV TAGET** • 1974
GANGSTER NIGHTMARE, A • 1935 • *Hill Charles* • SHT • UKN
GANGSTER PER UN MASSACRO • 1968 • Parolini Gianfranco • ITL
GANGSTER STORY • 1960 • Matthau Walter • USA
GANGSTER STORY see **SUO NOME FACEVA TREMARE.. INTERPOL IN ALLARME, IL** • 1973
GANGSTER V.I.P., THE (USA) see **DAI KANBU** • 1968
GANGSTER V.I.P. -VILLAINOUS CRUELTY see **DAI KANBU BURAI HIJO** • 1968
GANGSTER VENUTO DA BROOKLYN, UN • 1966 • Salvi Emimmo • ITL
GANGSTER WARS • 1981 • Sarafian Richard C. • MTV • USA
GANGSTER WARS 2 • 1981 • Sarafian Richard C. • MTV • USA
GANGSTER WE MADE, THE (UKN) see **VICIOUS YEARS, THE** • 1950
GANGSTERENS LAERLING • 1975 • Carlsen Esben Hoilund • DNM • GANGSTER'S APPRENTICE, THE
GANGSTERFILMEN EN FRAMLING STEG AV TAGET • 1974 • Thelestam Lars G. • SWD • GANGSTER MOVIE A STRANGER CAME BY TRAIN, THE ○ GANGSTER MOVIE, THE
GANGSTERJAGD IN LEDERHOSEN • 1959 • von Blucher Hubert • FRG
GANGSTERMEISJE, HET • 1967 • Weisz Frans • NTH • ILLUSION IS A GANGSTER GIRL ○ GANGSTER'S MOLL, THE
GANGSTERPREMIERE • 1951 • Jurgens Curd • AUS
GANGSTERS see **RITORNANO QUELLI DELLA CALIBRO 38** • 1977
GANGSTER'S DEN • 1945 • Newfield Sam • USA
GANGSTERS, THE • 1913 • Sennett Mack • USA
GANGSTERS, THE • 1914 • *Mutual* • USA
GANGSTERS, THE see **ANATOMIA MIAS LISTIAS** • 1973
GANGSTERS AND PHILANTHROPISTS see **GANGSTERZY I FILANTROPI** • 1962
GANGSTERS AND THE GIRL, THE • 1914 • Sidney Scott • USA
GANGSTER'S APPRENTICE, THE see **GANGSTERENS LAERLING** • 1975
GANGSTER'S BOY • 1938 • Nigh William • USA
GANGSTER'S BRIDE, THE (UKN) see **SECRET VALLEY** • 1937
GANGSTERS CONTRA CHARROS • 1947 • Orol Juan • MXC
GANGSTERS DALLA FACCIA PULITA, I • 1969 • Fornbacher Helmut • ITL

GANGSTERS DE L'EXPOSITION, LES • 1937 • de Meyst E. G. • FRN
GANGSTER'S DECOY, THE • 1916 • *Supreme* • USA
GANGSTER'S DOLL, THE see **PUPA DEL GANGSTER, LA** • 1975
GANGSTERS DU CHATEAU D'IF, LES • 1939 • Pujol Rene • FRN
GANGSTER'S ENEMY NO.1 (UKN) see **TRAIL OF TERROR** • 1935
GANGSTERS' LAW see **LEGGE DEI GANGSTERS, LA** • 1969
GANGSTER'S MOLL, THE see **GANGSTERMEISJE, HET** • 1967
GANGSTERS OF NEW YORK, THE • 1914 • Cabanne W. Christy • USA
GANGSTERS OF THE FRONTIER • 1944 • Clifton Elmer • USA
GANGSTERS OF THE HILLS • 1915 • *Garcia Al Ernest* • USA
GANGSTERS ON BROADWAY (UKN) see **BROADWAY AFTER MIDNIGHT** • 1927
GANGSTER'S REVENGE see **GET OUTTA TOWN** • 1959
GANGSTERZY I FILANTROPI • 1962 • Hoffman Jerzy, Skorzewski Edward • PLN • GANGSTERS AND PHILANTHROPISTS
GANGWAY • 1937 • Hale Sonnie • UKN
GANGWAY FOR TOMORROW • 1943 • Auer John H. • USA
GANITO KAMI NOON, PAANO KAYO NGAYON? • 1977 • Romero Eddie • PHL • WE WERE LIKE THIS YESTERDAY, HOW IS IT TODAY? ○ AS WE WERE
GANJ • 1973 • Golestan Ebrahim • IRN • TREASURE, THE
GANJ-VA-RANJ • 1967 • Sabahi Samad • IRN • SORROW AND TREASURE
GANJA AND HESS • 1973 • Gunn Bill • USA • DOUBLE POSSESSION: THE DOCTOR CANNOT DIE ○ BLOOD COUPLE ○ DOUBLE POSSESSION
GANJINEH SOLIMAN • 1967 • Rafiei Aziz • IRN • SULIMAN TREASURE
GANOVENEHRE • 1933 • Oswald Richard • FRG
GANOVENEHRE • 1966 • Staudte Wolfgang • FRG • HOODLUM'S HONOR
GANS VON SEDAN, DIE • 1959 • Kautner Helmut • FRG, FRN • SANS TAMBOUR NI TROMPETTE (FRN)
GANSE VON BUTZOW, DIE • 1986 • Vogel Frank • GDR • GEESE OF BUTZOW, THE
GANSELIESEL • 1918 • *Weise Lisa* • FRG
GANSEMAGD, DIE • 1958 • Genschow Fritz • FRG • GOOSE GIRL, THE (USA)
GANTELET VERT, LE see **GREEN GLOVE, THE** • 1952
GANTRY THE GREAT see **PRIDE OF THE BLUEGRASS** • 1939
GANTS BLANCS DE SAINT-CYR, LES • 1915 • Diamant-Berger Henri • FRN
GANTS BLANCS DU DIABLE, LES • 1972 • Szabo Laszlo • FRN
GANVIE, MON VILLAGE • 1966 • Abikanlou Pascal • BNN
GANZ FAIRE PROZESS DES MARCEL G., DER • 1978 • Meier Hans-Peter • FRG
GANZ GROSSE DING, DAS see **BABYSITTER, LA** • 1975
GANZ GROSSEN TORHEITEN, DIE • 1937 • Froelich Carl • FRG
GANZ GROSSES KIND, EIN • 1952 • Verhoeven Paul • FRG • LEIBHAFTIGE UNSCHULD, DIE
GANZ UND GAR VERWAHRLOSTES MADCHEN, EIN • 1977 • Bruckner Jutta • FRG • GONE TO SEED
GANZ VERFLIXTER KERL see **FLUCHT NACH NIZZA** • 1932
GANZE LEBEN, DAS • 1983 • Moll Bruno • SWT • WHOLE LIFE, THE
GANZE WELT DREHT SICH UM LIEBE, DIE • 1935 • Tourjansky Victor • FRG • WORLD'S IN LOVE, THE (USA) ○ LIEBESMELODIE
GANZE WELT IST HIMMELBLAU, DIE • 1964 • Antel Franz • AUS • ROTE LIPPEN SOLL MAN KUSSEN
GANZE WELT SINGT NUR AMORE, DIE • 1956 • Stemmle R. A. • FRG
GANZER KERL, EIN • 1935 • Boese Carl • FRG • KARL RAUMT AUF
GANZER KERL, EIN • 1939 • Buch Fritz Peter • FRG
GAOL BREAK • 1936 • Ince Ralph • UKN • BILL AND SON
GAOLBREAK • 1962 • Searle Francis • UKN • JAILBREAK (USA)
GAOSHANXIADE HUA HUAN • 1985 • Xie Jin • CHN • GARLANDS AT THE FOOT OF THE MOUNTAIN ○ REEDS AT THE FOOT OF THE MOUNTAIN
GAOU UTAGGASEN • 1939 • Makino Masahiro • JPN • GEESE AND DUCK'S SINGING CONTEST, THE
GAP, THE • 1937 • Carter Donald • UKN
GAP, THE see **JOE** • 1970
GAP OF DEATH, THE • 1914 • *Leading Players Film* • USA
GAPDUNG KEIHAP • 1989 • Fok Yiu-Leung • HKG • ICEMAN COMETH, THE
GAPPA see **DAIKYAJU GAPPA** • 1967
GAPPA THE TRIFIBIAN MONSTER see **DAIKYAJU GAPPA** • 1967
GAPPA, TRIPHIBIAN MONSTER see **DAIKYAJU GAPPA** • 1967
GAR NASIMPUR • 1968 • Lahiri Ajit • IND • FORT OF NASIMPUR
GARAGE, THE • 1920 • Arbuckle Roscoe • SHT • USA
GARAGE, THE see **GARAGET** • 1975
GARAGE GIRLS • 1980 • McCallum Robert • USA
GARAGET • 1975 • Sjoman Vilgot • SWD • GARAGE, THE
GARAKUTA • 1964 • Inagaki Hiroshi • JPN • RABBLE, THE
GARANTIERE ROLLAND, IL • 1910 • Maggi Luigi • ITL
GARASU NO USAGI • 1979 • Tachibana Yuten • JPN • GLASS RABBIT
GARATGARAN • 1981 • Shaban Abbas • AFG • THIEVES
GARBAGE • 1969 • Wilson Sandra • CND
GARBAGE MAN, THE • 1963 • Sayers Eric • USA • GARBAGE MAN COMETH, THE
GARBAGE MAN COMETH, THE see **GARBAGE MAN, THE** • 1963
GARBAGE MOVIE, THE • 1981 • Defalco Martin • DOC • CND
GARBAGE PAIL KIDS MOVIE, THE • 1987 • Amateau Rod • USA
GARBANCITO DE LA MANCHA • 1946 • Moreno Antonio, Blay Jose Maria • ANM • SPN • LITTLE KNIGHT, THE ○ LITTLE BEAN OF LA MANCHA
GARBANZA NEGRA QUE EN PAZ DESCANSE • 1971 • Delgado Luis Maria • SPN
GARBO • 1972 • Noonan Chris • SHT • ASL
GARBO TALKS • 1984 • Lumet Sidney • USA
GARCA E A SERPENTE, A • 1952 • Duarte Arthur • PRT
GARCE, LA • 1984 • Pascal Christine • FRN
GARCE EN CHALEUR, UNE • 1977 • Benazeraf Jose • FRN
GARCES, LES • 1973 • Matalon Eddy • FRN, ITL • LOVE-HUNGRY GIRLS (UKN) ○ DEADLY WHEN AROUSED ○ SEX HUNGRY GIRLS
GARCIAS RETURN, THE see **VUELVEN LOS GARCIA** • 1946
GARCON! • 1983 • Sautet Claude • FRN
GARCON DIVORCE, LE see **MARI GARCON, LE** • 1933
GARCON PLEIN D'AVENIR, UN • 1965 • Foldes Peter • ANS • FRN • BOY WITH A FUTURE, A
GARCON SAUVAGE, LE • 1951 • Delannoy Jean • FRN • SAVAGE TRIANGLE (USA) ○ WILD BOY
GARCON SAVOYARD, LE • 1967 • Diserens Jean-Claude • SWT, FRN, BLG • SAVOYAN BOY, THE ○ BOY FROM.., THE
GARCONNE, LA • 1924 • du Plessis Armand • FRN
GARCONNE, LA • 1936 • de Limur Jean • FRN
GARCONNE, LA • 1956 • Audry Jacqueline • FRN • BACHELOR GIRL
GARCONNIERE, LA • 1960 • De Santis Giuseppe • ITL
GARCONS DE PLAGE • Cadinot Jean-Daniel • SHT • FRN
GARCONS DE REVE • Cadinot Jean-Daniel • SHT • FRN
GARCONS, LES (FRN) see **NOTTE BRAVA, LA** • 1959
GARDAREM LOU LARZAC see **LARZAC** • 1973
GARDARNA RUNT SJON • 1957 • Spjuth Arthur • SWD • MANORS AROUND THE LAKE
GARDE A VUE • 1982 • Miller Claude • FRN • INQUISITOR, THE
GARDE CHAMPETRE, LE • Delbez Maurice • FRN
GARDE-CHASSE, LE • 1951 • Decae Henri • SHT • FRN
GARDE-DIVA, DIE • 1929 • Blachnitzky Curt • FRG
GARDE DU CORPS, LE • 1983 • Leterrier Francois • FRN
GARDE FANTOME, LA • 1904 • Velle Gaston • FRN • PHANTOM GUARD, THE
GARDE-MOTEUR, LE • 1953 • Devlin Bernard • DCS • CND
GARDEN, THE • 1990 • Jarman Derek • UKN
GARDEN, THE see **ZAHRADA** • 1968
GARDEN, THE see **ZAHRADU** • 1975
GARDEN, THE see **HAGAN** • 1977
GARDEN DWARFS, THE see **GARTENZWERGE, DIE** • 1962
GARDEN GAIETIES • 1935 • *Mintz Charles (P)* • ANS • USA
GARDEN GOPHER • 1950 • Avery Tex • ANS • USA
GARDEN MURDER CASE, THE • 1936 • Marin Edwin L. • USA
GARDEN OF ALLAH see **JARDIM DE ALAH** • 1988
GARDEN OF ALLAH, THE • 1916 • Campbell Colin • USA
GARDEN OF ALLAH, THE • 1927 • Ingram Rex • USA
GARDEN OF ALLAH, THE • 1936 • Boleslawski Richard • USA
GARDEN OF AUNT ELIZABETH, THE see **JARDIN DE TIA ISABEL, EL** • 1971
GARDEN OF DEATH see **GARDENER, THE** • 1974
GARDEN OF DELIGHTS, THE see **GIARDINO DELLE DELIZIE, IL** • 1968
GARDEN OF DELIGHTS, THE see **JARDIN DE LA DELICIAS, EL** • 1970
GARDEN OF DESIRE, THE • 1987 • Khamraev Ali • USS
GARDEN OF EARTHLY DELIGHTS, THE • 1981 • Brakhage Stan • USA
GARDEN OF EDEN • 1957 • Nosseck Max • USA
GARDEN OF EDEN, THE • 1928 • Milestone Lewis • USA
GARDEN OF EVIL • 1954 • Hathaway Henry • USA
GARDEN OF FATE, THE • 1910 • *Neason Hazel* • USA
GARDEN OF FOLLY, A see **PASTEBOARD CROWN, A** • 1922
GARDEN OF LIES, THE • 1915 • Thomas Augustus • USA
GARDEN OF RESURRECTION, THE • 1919 • Rooke Arthur • UKN
GARDEN OF SHADOWS, THE • 1916 • Henderson Lucius • SHT • USA
GARDEN OF STONES see **BAGHE SANGUI** • 1975
GARDEN OF THE DEAD • 1972 • Hayes John • USA • TOMB OF THE UNDEAD
GARDEN OF THE FINZI-CONTINIS, THE (UKN) see **GIARDINO DEI FINZI-CONTINI, IL** • 1970
GARDEN OF THE MOON • 1938 • Berkeley Busby • USA
GARDEN OF WEEDS, THE • 1924 • Cruze James • USA
GARDEN OF WOMEN, THE see **ONNA NO SONO** • 1954
GARDEN QUARRELS see **QUERELLES DE JARDINS** • 1982
GARDEN SUBURB see **KERTES HAZAK UTCAJA** • 1962
GARDEN TRAVELLERS see **PASAJEROS DEL JARDIN, LOS** • 1982
GARDENER, THE • 1960 • *Halas John (P)* • ANS • UKN
GARDENER, THE • 1972 • Alexander Mike • SHT • UKN
GARDENER, THE • 1974 • Kay James H. Iii • USA, PRC • SEEDS OF EVIL ○ GARDEN OF DEATH
GARDENER, THE see **ARROSEUR ARROSE, L'** • 1895
GARDENER, THE see **TRADGARDSMASTAREN** • 1912
GARDENER BURNING WEEDS see **JARDINIER BRULANT DES HERBES** • 1896
GARDENER OF EDEN, THE • 1981 • Broughton James • USA
GARDENER'S DAUGHTER, THE • 1913 • Noy Wilfred • UKN
GARDENER'S DAUGHTER, THE • 1914 • Noy Wilfred • UKN
GARDENER'S HOSE, THE • 1914 • Wilson Frank • UKN
GARDENER'S LADDER, THE • 1911 • *Edison* • USA
GARDENER'S LOT, A • 1938 • Alderson John • UKN
GARDENER'S NAP, THE • 1905 • Collins Alf? • UKN
GARDENIA • 1979 • Paolella Domenico • ITL • GIUSTIZIERE DELLA MALA, IL
GARDENS BY THE SEA • 1973 • McConnell Edward • DOC • UKN
GARDENS OF ATOS, THE see **ATOSKI VRTOVI** • 1989
GARDENS OF STONE • 1987 • Coppola Francis Ford • USA
GARDEOFFIZIER, DER • 1926 • Wiene Robert • AUS • GUARDSMAN, THE ○ LIEBGARDIST, DIE
GARDEZ LE SOURIRE • 1933 • Sti Rene, Fejos Paul • FRN • RAYON DE SOLEIL
GARDIAN, LE • 1920 • Hamman Joe • FRN
GARDIAN, LE • 1945 • de Marguenat Jean • FRN
GARDIAN DE LA NUIT • 1985 • Limosin Jean-Pierre • FRN
GARDIEN DU FEU, LE • 1924 • Ravel Gaston • FRN
GARDIEN MUET, LE • 1918 • Protazanov Yakov • USS
GARDIENNE DU FEU, LA • 1913 • Feuillade Louis • FRN
GARDIENS DU PHARE • 1928 • Gremillon Jean • FRN • GUARDIANS OF PHARE
GARDINENTRAUM, DER • 1969 • Georgi Katja, Preistragger Heinrich Greif • ANM • GDR
GARDUL • 1969 • Muresan Gelu • ANS • RMN • FENCE, THE
GARE CENTRALE see **BAB EL HADID** • 1957
GARE SAINT-LAZARE, LA • 1896 • Melies Georges • FRN • ST. LAZARE RAILROAD STATION
GAREEB • 1942 • *Biswas Anil (M)* • IND
GARGA M'BOSE • 1974 • Traore Mahama Johnson • SNL, SWD • CACTUS
GARGALHADA FINAL • 1980 • de Oliveira Xavier • BRZ • LAST LAUGH
GARGON TERROR, THE (UKN) see **TEEN-AGERS FROM OUTER SPACE** • 1959
GARGOULETTE, LA see **QULLA, AL-** • 1961
GARGOUSSE • 1938 • Wulschleger Henry • FRN • VACANCES JOYEUSES, LES
GARGOYLES • 1972 • Norton B. W. L. • TVM • USA
GARIBAH NO UCHU RYOKO • 1966 • Kuroda Yoshio • ANM • JPN • GULLIVER'S TRAVELS BEYOND THE MOON (UKN) ○ GULLIVER NO UCHU RYOKO
GARIBALDI • 1907 • Caserini Mario • ITL
GARIBALDI E I SUOI TEMPI • 1926 • Rosa Silvio Laurenti • ITL
GARIBALDI (USA) see **VIVA L'ITALIA** • 1961
GARIBALDINO AL CONVENTO, UN • 1942 • De Sica Vittorio • ITL
GARIBAN DERLER BIZE • 1967 • Olgac Bilge • TRK • THEY CALL US TRAMPS
GARIBEH VA MEH see **GHARIBEH VA MEH** • 1974
GARIMA FIL HAY EL HADY • 1967 • Mustafa Hassam Eddin • EGY • CRIME IN A PEACEFUL STREET, A
GARIMAT HUBB • 1959 • Salem Atef • EGY • CRIME PASSIONNEL
GARIPLER SOKAGI • 1967 • Palay Abdurrahman • TRK • STREET OF THE STRANGE ONES, THE
GARLAND OF FOLK-SONGS, A • 1955 • Tyrlova Hermina • ANM • CZC
GARLAND OF SONG, A • 1934 • *Piccaver Alfred* • SHT • UKN
GARLANDS AT THE FOOT OF THE MOUNTAIN see **GAOSHANXIADE HUA HUAN** • 1985
GARLIC IS AS GOOD AS TEN MOTHERS • 1979 • Blank Les • DOC • USA
GARM COAT • 1955 • Kumar Amar • IND • CLERK AND THE COAT, THE
GARM HAVA • 1973 • Sathyu M. S. • IND • HOT WIND ○ HOT WINDS ○ WARM WIND
GARMENT CENTER, THE see **GARMENT JUNGLE, THE** • 1957
GARMENT JUNGLE, THE • 1957 • Sherman Vincent, Aldrich Robert (U/c) • USA • GARMENT CENTER, THE
GARMENTS OF TRUTH • 1921 • Baker George D. • USA
GARMON • 1934 • Savchenko Igor • USS • ACCORDION
GARNET BRACELET, THE (USA) see **GRANATOVYY BRASLET** • 1965
GARNISON AMOUREUSE, LA • 1933 • de Vaucorbeil Max • FRN
GAROFANO ROSSO • 1976 • Faccini Luigi • ITL
GAROTA DE IPANEMA • 1967 • Hirszman Leon • BRZ • GIRL FROM IPANEMA
GAROU-GAROU LE PASSE-MURAILLE • 1950 • Boyer Jean • FRN • MR. PEEK-A-BOO (USA) ○ PASSE-MURAILLE, LE
GARRA DEL LEOPARDO, LA • 1962 • Salvador Jaime • MXC
GARRA NEGRA DE HIERRO, LA • 1978 • Cosmi Carlo • DOC • VNZ • BLACK CLAW OF IRON, THE
GARRAGAN • 1924 • Wolff Ludwig • FRG
GARRAS DE LORELEI, LAS • 1972 • de Ossorio Amando • SPN • LORELEI'S GRASP, THE (USA) ○ WHEN THE SCREAMING STOPS
GARRET IN BOHEMIA, A • 1915 • Shaw Harold • UKN
GARRINGO • 1969 • Romero-Marchent Rafael • SPN, ITL
GARRISON FOLLIES • 1940 • Rogers Maclean • UKN
GARRISON JOKE, A • 1912 • *Prior Herbert* • USA
GARRISON TRIANGLE, THE • 1912 • *101 Bison* • USA
GARRISON'S FINISH • 1914 • Grandon Francis J. • USA
GARRISON'S FINISH • 1923 • Rosson Arthur • USA
GARROTTING A MOTOR CAR • 1904 • Hough Harold? • UKN
GARRY OWEN • 1920 • Pearson George • UKN • GARRYOWEN
GARRY SHANDLING: ALONE IN VEGAS • 1984 • Dear William • USA
GARRYOWEN see **GARRY OWEN** • 1920
GARS D'ANVERS, LE see **Y'EN A MARRE** • 1959
GARS DE LAPALME, LES • 1972 • Lamothe Arthur, Dupuis Francois • DCS • CND
GARS DES VUES, LE • 1976 • Lefebvre Jean-Pierre • CND
GARS DU TABAC, LES • 1977 • Bulbulian Maurice • DCS • CND
GARTEN DER LUST, DER see **PLEASURE GARDEN, THE** • 1926
GARTEN EDEN, DER • 1977 • Mommartz Lutz • FRG
GARTENZWERGE, DIE • 1962 • Urchs Wolfgang • SHT • FRG • GARDEN DWARFS, THE ○ GNOMES
GARTER COLT see **GIARRETTIERA COLT** • 1967
GARTER GIRL, THE • 1920 • Griffith Edward H. • USA
GARTERS AND LACE • 1981 • Vincent Chuck • USA
GARTERS VERSUS BRACES: OR, ALGY IN A FIX • 1901 • *Paul R. W.* • UKN
GARU THE MAD MONK see **GURU THE MAD MONK** • 1970
GARY COOPER QUE ESTES EN LOS CIELOS • 1980 • Miro Pilar • SPN • GARY COOPER WHO ART IN HEAVEN
GARY COOPER WHO ART IN HEAVEN see **GARY COOPER QUE ESTES EN LOS CIELOS** • 1980
GARY'S STORY • 1981 • Michalak Richard • SHT • ASL
GAS • 1981 • Rose Les • CND
GAS AND AIR • 1923 • Roach Hal • SHT • USA
GAS HOUSE KIDS • 1946 • Newfield Sam • USA
GAS HOUSE KIDS GO WEST • 1947 • Beaudine William • USA
GAS HOUSE KIDS IN HOLLYWOOD • 1947 • Cahn Edward L. • USA
GAS IN THE VEINS see **BENSAA SUONISSA** • 1971
GAS LOGIC • 1918 • Drew Sidney, Drew Sidney Mrs. • SHT • USA
GAS -NATURAL ENERGY • 1978 • Robertson Michael • DOC • ASL

GAS NUNCA SE ACABA, EL • 1966 • Comeron Luis Jose • SHT • SPN
GAS-OIL • 1955 • Grangier Gilles • FRN • HI-JACK HIGHWAY (USA)
GAS, OIL AND WATER • 1922 • Ray Charles • USA
GAS, OR HOW IT BECAME NECESSARY TO DESTROY THE WORLD IN ORDER TO SAVE IT see **GAS-S-S-S!** • 1970
GAS PUMP GIRLS • 1979 • Bender Joel • USA
GAS-S-S-S! • 1970 • Corman Roger • USA • ARROWFEATHER ○ GAS, OR HOW IT BECAME NECESSARY TO DESTROY THE WORLD IN ORDER TO SAVE IT
GAS TURBINE, THE • 1954 • De Normanville Peter • UKN
GASBAGS • 1940 • Varnel Marcel • UKN
GASDUCTO CENTRAL DEL LAGO • 1974 • Camacho Carlos Antonio • DOC • VNZ
GASHIRAM KOTWAL • 1977 • IND
GASLIGHT • 1940 • Dickinson Thorold • UKN • ANGEL STREET (USA) ○ STRANGER CASE OF MURDER, A
GASLIGHT • 1944 • Cukor George • USA • MURDER IN THORTON SQUARE, THE (UKN)
GASLIGHT FOLLIES • 1955 • Levine Joseph E. • USA
GASMANN, DER • 1941 • Froelich Carl • FRG
GASOLINE ALLEY • 1951 • Bernds Edward • USA
GASOLINE BUCKAROO, THE • 1920 • *Cunard Grace* • SHT • USA
GASOLINE COWBOY • 1926 • Reel Frederick Jr. • USA
GASOLINE ENGAGEMENT, A • 1911 • *Pickford Mary* • USA
GASOLINE GUS • 1915 • *Booth Elmer* • USA
GASOLINE GUS • 1921 • Cruze James • USA
GASOLINE HABIT, THE • 1916 • Clements Roy • SHT • USA
GASOLINE: PART 2: CRACKING • 1948 • Segaller Denis • UKN • CRACKING
GASOLINE WEDDING, A • 1918 • Roach Hal • SHT • USA
GASOLOONS • 1936 • Ripley Arthur • SHT • USA
GASP see **KICMA** • 1976
GASPARD DE BESSE • 1935 • Hugon Andre • FRN • DAWN OVER FRANCE (USA)
GASPARD ET FILS • 1988 • Labonte Francois • CND
GASPARDS, LES • 1975 • Tchernia Pierre • FRN
GASPARONE • 1937 • Jacoby Georg • FRG
GASPARONE • 1956 • Paryla Karl • AUS
GASPESIE, LA • Lavoie Hermenegilde • DCS • CND
GASPESIE OUI, J'ECOUTE • 1972 • Danis Aime • DCS • CND
GASPESIE PITTORESQUE, LA • 1957 • Proulx Maurice • DCS • CND
GASSAN • 1979 • Murano Tetsutaro • JPN • MT. GASSAN
GASSE DER LEIBE UND SUNDE, DIE • 1923 • *Comedia-Film* • FRG
GASSENHAUER • 1931 • Pick Lupu • FRG
GASSENKONIGIN, DIE • 1921 • *De Lalsky Gertrude* • FRG
GAST I EGET HUS • 1957 • Olin Stig • SWD • GUEST IN ONE'S HOME, A
GASTHAUS AN DER THEMSE, DAS • 1962 • Vohrer Alfred • FRG • INN ON THE RIVER, THE (USA)
GASTHAUS VON CHICAGO, DAS • 1920 • Eichgrun Bruno • FRG
GASTHAUS ZUR EHE, DAS • 1926 • Jacoby Georg • FRG • MARRIAGE HOTEL, THE
GASTHAUS ZUR TREUEN LIEBE see **LUSTIGE KLEEBLATT, DAS** • 1933
GASTMAHL DES SATANS, DAS • 1920 • Bach Rudi • FRG
GASTON AND LEO IN HONGKONG • 1988 • *Gaston & Leo* • BLG
GASTON, GO HOME • 1958 • Rasinski Connie • ANS • USA
GASTON IS HERE • 1957 • Rasinski Connie • ANS • USA
GASTON ISABEL HAUTERIVE • 1981 • Lesaunier Daniel • MTV • CND
GASTON LE CRAYON • 1957-59 • ASS • USA
GASTON MIRON • 1971 • Frappier Roger • DOC • CND
GASTONE • 1960 • Bonnard Mario • ITL
GASTON'S BABY • 1958 • Rasinski Connie • ANS • USA
GASTON'S EASEL LIFE • 1958 • Tendlar Dave • ANS • USA
GASTON'S MAMA LISA • 1959 • Rasinski Connie • ANS • USA
GASTRONOMIE, LA • 1973 • Jackson Douglas • DOC • CND
GASTSPIEL IM PARADIES • 1938 • Hartl Karl • FRG
GASU NINGEN DAIICHIGO • 1960 • Honda Inoshiro • JPN • HUMAN VAPOUR, THE
GAT DE TIJD, EEN • 1974 • Severijn Jonne • DOC • NTH • PAUSE IN TIME, A
GATA, LA • 1955 • Aleixandre Margarita, Torrecilla Rafael • SPN
GATA CON BOTAS, LA • 1971 • *America* • MXC
GATAN • 1949 • Werner Gosta • SWD • STREET, THE
GATANS BARN • 1914 • Sjostrom Victor • SWD • CHILDREN OF THE STREET
GATAS TIENEN FRIO, LAS • 1967 • Serrano Carlos • SPN
GATE, THE • 1987 • Takacs Tibor • USA
GATE CRASHER, THE • 1928 • Craft William James • USA
GATE II, THE • 1989 • Takacs Tibor • USA
GATE OF DESTINY, THE see **DARVAZE TAGHDEER** • 1967
GATE OF FLESH (USA) see **NIKUTAI NO MON** • 1964
GATE OF HELL (USA) see **JIGOKUMON** • 1953
GATE OF LILACS see **PORTE DE LILAS** • 1957
GATE OF THE YOUTH, THE see **SEISHUN NO MON** • 1974
GATE OF YOUTH, THE see **SEISHUN NO MON** • 1974
GATE OF YOUTH II, THE see **SEISHUN NO MON, JIRITSU HEN** • 1982
GATE OF YOUTH: INDEPENDENCE, THE see **SEISHUN NO MON, JIRITSU HEN** • 1976
GATE OF YOUTH, PART 2, THE see **SEISHUN NO MON, JIRITSU HEN** • 1976
GATE SHE LEFT OPEN, THE • 1913 • *Pathe* • USA
GATE TO THE BLUE SKY see **SOKYU NO MON** • 1933
GATEGUTTER • 1949 • Skouen Arne, Greber • NRW • GODS OF THE STREETS ○ GUTTERSNIPES
GATEKEEPER'S DAUGHTER, THE (UKN) see **FILLE DU GARDE-BARRIERE, LA** • 1975
GATES OF ALCATRAZ, THE (UKN) see **THOSE HIGH GREY WALLS** • 1939
GATES OF BRASS • 1919 • Warde Ernest C. • USA
GATES OF DAWN, THE see **ADVENT** • 1956
GATES OF DIVORCE • 1916 • Middleton Edwin • SHT • USA
GATES OF DOOM, THE • 1917 • Swickard Charles • USA
GATES OF DOOM, THE • 1919 • Goldin Sidney M. • UKN
GATES OF DOOM, THE • 1920 • Ford Francis • SRL • USA
GATES OF DUTY see **TOWER OF STRENGTH** • 1919
GATES OF EDEN, THE • 1916 • Collins John H. • USA
GATES OF GLADNESS • 1918 • Knoles Harley • USA
GATES OF HEAVEN • 1978 • Morris Errol • DOC • USA
GATES OF HELL • 1972 • Kohanyi Julius • CND
GATES OF HELL, THE see **PAURA, LA** • 1980
GATES OF HOLLYWOOD see **MAKE ME A STAR!** • 1932
GATES OF JEALOUSY, THE • 1914 • *Eclectic* • USA
GATES OF NIGHT see **PORTES DE LA NUIT, LES** • 1946
GATES OF PARADISE see **VRATA RAJA** • 1967
GATES OF PARIS (USA) see **PORTE DE LILAS** • 1957
GATES OF THE LOUVRE, THE see **GUICHETS DU LOUVRE, LES** • 1974
GATES OF THE NIGHT (USA) see **PORTES DE LA NUIT, LES** • 1946
GATES TO PARADISE see **VRATA RAJA** • 1967
GATEWAY • 1938 • Werker Alfred L. • USA
GATEWAY OF REGRET, THE • 1914 • *Pates Gwendoline* • USA
GATEWAY OF THE MOON, THE • 1928 • Wray John Griffith • USA • UPSTREAM
GATEWAY TO AMERICA, THE • 1912 • *Champion* • USA
GATEWAY TO ASIA • 1945 • Daly Tom • DOC • CND
GATEWAY TO GLORY see **AA KAIGUN** • 1969
GATEWAY TO THE ANTARCTIC • 1955 • Carse Duncan • UKN
GATEWAY TO THE CATSKILLS • 1906 • *Bitzer Billy (Ph)* • USA
GATEWAY TO THE WEST • 1937 • Elder John C. • UKN
GATHER NO MOSS see **T.A.M.I. SHOW, THE** • 1964
GATHERING, THE • 1977 • Kleiser Randall • TVM • USA
GATHERING AT BATOUCHE • 1972 • Rodgers Bob • MTV • CND
GATHERING CLOUDS see **INTUNECARE**
GATHERING OF EAGLES, A • 1963 • Mann Delbert • USA
GATHERING OF EVIL • 1969 • Bertini Victor • USA
GATHERING OF OLD MEN, A • 1987 • Schlondorff Volker • TVM • USA
GATHERING PART II, THE • 1979 • Dubin Charles S. • TVM • USA
GATHERING STORM, THE • 1974 • Wise Herbert • UKN
GATILLO VELOZ • 1965 • Salvador Jaime • MXC
GATITA, LA • 1971 • *Cine Vision* • MXC
GATLING GUN see **QUEL CALDO MALEDETTO GIORNO DI FUOCO** • 1968
GATLING GUN, THE • 1972 • Gordon Robert • USA • SERGEANT BLUE ○ KING GUN
GATO, EL • 1930 • Melford George • USA
GATO, EL • 1959 • Delgado Miguel M. • MXC
GATO CON BOTAS, EL • 1961 • Rodriguez Roberto • MXC • PUSS 'N BOOTS (USA)
GATO CON BOTAS, EL • 1964 • Delgado Cruz • SHT • SPN
GATO SIN BOTAS, EL • 1956 • Cortes Fernando • MXC • CAT WITHOUT BOOTS, THE
GATOR • 1976 • Reynolds Burt • USA
GATOR BAIT • 1974 • Sebastian Beverly, Sebastian Ferdinand • USA • SWAMP BAIT
GATOR BAIT 2 • 1988 • Sebastian Beverly, Sebastian Ferdinand • USA
GATOS NEGROS, LOS • 1964 • Monter Jose Luis • SPN • BLACK CATS, THE
GATTA CI COVA • 1937 • Righelli Gennaro • ITL
GATTA DAGLI ARTIGLI D'ORO, LA (ITL) see **LOUVE SOLITAIRE, LA** • 1968
GATTA IN CALORE, LA • 1972 • Rossati Nello • ITL
GATTE, DER • 1989 • Rissi Mark M. • SWT • HUSBAND, THE
GATTESTELLVERTRETER, DER • 1919 • Gartner Adolf • FRG
GATTI ROSSI IN UN LABIRINTO DI VETRO • 1975 • Lenzi Umberto • ITL
GATTIN, DIE • 1943 • Jacoby Georg • FRG
GATTO, IL • 1978 • Comencini Luigi • USA • CAT, THE (USA)
GATTO A NOVE CODE, IL • 1971 • Argento Dario • ITL, FRN, FRG • CAT O' NINE TAILS, THE (UKN) ○ NEUNSCHWANZIGE KATZE, DIE
GATTO DAGLI OCCHI DI GIADA, IL • 1977 • Bido Antonio • ITL
GATTO DI BROOKLYN ASPIRANTE DETECTIVE, IL • 1973 • Brazzi Oscar • ITL
GATTO FILIPPO LICENZA DI UCCIDERE • 1966 • Zac Pino • ITL
GATTO MAMMONE, IL • 1975 • Cicero Nando • ITL
GATTO NERO, IL • 1981 • Fulci Lucio • ITL • BLACK CAT, THE
GATTO SELVAGGIO, IL • 1969 • Frezza Andrea • ITL
GATTOPARDO, IL • 1963 • Visconti Luchino • ITL, FRN • LEOPARD, THE (USA) ○ GUEPARD, LE (FRN)
GAUCHO, IL • 1964 • Risi Dino • ITL, ARG • GAUCHO, THE
GAUCHO, THE • 1928 • Jones F. Richard • USA
GAUCHO, THE see **GAUCHO, IL** • 1964
GAUCHO AND THE DEVIL, THE see **GAUCHO Y EL DIABLO, EL** • 1952
GAUCHO CHIVALRY (USA) see **NOBLEZA GAUCHA** • 1938
GAUCHO NOBILITY see **NOBLEZA GAUCHA** • 1915
GAUCHO SERENADE • 1940 • McDonald Frank • USA
GAUCHO WAR see **GUERRA DES GAUCHOS, LA** • 1942
GAUCHO Y EL DIABLO, EL • 1952 • Remani Ernesto • ARG • GAUCHO AND THE DEVIL, THE
GAUCHOS JUDIOS, LOS • 1975 • Jusid Juan Jose • ARG • JEWISH GAUCHOS, THE
GAUCHOS OF ELDORADO • 1941 • Orlebeck Lester • USA
GAUDEAMUS • 1912 • Starevitch Ladislas • ANM • USS • VESEL'YE SCENKI IZ ZIZNI ZIVOTNYCH ○ LET US REJOICE ○ HAPPY SCENES OF THE LIFE OF THE ANIMALS ○ HAPPY SCENES FROM ANIMAL LIFE
GAUDEAMUS • 1959 • Hoffman Jerzy, Skorzewski Edward • DOC • PLN
GAUDEAMUS IGITUR • 1964 • Vitandis Gheorghe • RMN
GAUDI • 1960 • Argemi Jose Maria • SPN
GAUDI • 1988 • Huerga Manuel • SPN
GAUGRAFIN FIFI • 1916 • *Orla Resel* • FRG
GAUGUIN • 1951 • Resnais Alain • SHT • FRN
GAUGUIN, LE LOUP DANS LE SOLEIL • 1985 • Carlsen Henning • FRN, DNM
GAUGUIN THE SAVAGE • 1980 • Cook Fielder • TVM • USA
GAUKLER DER STRASSE • 1922 • Stein Josef • FRG
GAUKLER (FRG) see **SALTIMBANQUES, LES** • 1930
GAUKLER VON PARIS, DER • 1922 • Gunsburg Arthur • FRG
GAULOISES BLEUES, LES • 1968 • Cournot Michel • FRN
GAUNER DER GESELLSCHAFT • 1920 • Boese Carl • FRG
GAUNER IM FRACK • 1927 • Noa Manfred • FRG
GAUNER IN UNIFORM • 1960 • von Cziffra Geza • FRG, AUS
GAUNER UND DER LIEBE GOTT, DER • 1960 • von Ambesser Axel • FRG
GAUNERLIEBCHEN • 1928 • Reichmann Max • FRG
GAUNERSERENADE • 1960 • Engel Thomas • FRG
GAUNT STRANGER, THE • 1938 • Forde Walter • UKN • PHANTOM STRIKES, THE (USA)
GAUNT WOMAN, THE see **SEALED CARGO** • 1951
GAUNT WOMAN, THE see **DESTINY OF A SPY** • 1969
GAUNTLET, THE • 1920 • Hollywood Edwin L. • USA
GAUNTLET, THE • 1977 • Eastwood Clint • USA
GAUNTLET, THE see **KUJANJUOKSU** • 1971
GAUNTLETS OF WASHINGTON, THE • 1913 • Edwin Walter, Dawley J. Searle • USA
GAUTAMA THE BUDDHA • 1955 • Roy Bimal (c/d) • DOC • IND
GAV • 1968 • Mehrjui Dariush • IRN • COW, THE (UKN)
GAVAZNHA • 1974 • Kimiyaei Massoud • IRN • DEERS, THE
GAVEA GIRLS see **BAIXO GAVEA** • 1986
GAVEN see **FODSELSDAGSGAVEN** • 1912
GAVILAN, EL • 1939 • Pereda Ramon • MXC • HAWK, THE (USA)
GAVILAN POLLERO, EL • 1950 • Gonzalez Rogelio A. • MXC
GAVILAN VENGADOR, EL • 1954 • Salvador Jaime • MXC
GAVILANES, LOS • 1954 • Orona Vicente • MXC
GAVILANES NEGROS, LOS • 1965 • Urueta Chano • MXC
GAVIOTA, LA • 1954 • de Anda Raul • MXC
GAVIOTA ROJA, LA see **MAR SANGRIENTO** • 1964
GAVOTTE • 1967 • Borowczyk Walerian • SHT • FRN
GAVOTTE, LA • 1902 • Blache Alice • FRN
GAVROCHE AND THE GHOSTS see **GAVROCHE ET LES ESPRITS** • 1912
GAVROCHE ET LES ESPRITS • 1912 • Bosetti Romeo • FRN • GAVROCHE AND THE GHOSTS
GAWAIN AND THE GREEN KNIGHT • 1973 • Weeks Stephen • UKN
GAWAZ ALAL HAWAA • 1976 • Sarwat Ahmed • EGY • MARRIAGE ON THE AIR
GAY ADVENTURE, THE • 1936 • Hill Sinclair • UKN
GAY ADVENTURE, THE • 1953 • Parry Gordon • UKN
GAY ADVENTURE, THE see **THREE MEN AND A GIRL** • 1949
GAY AMIGO, THE • 1949 • Fox Wallace • USA
GAY AND DEVILISH • 1922 • Seiter William A. • USA
GAY ANTIES, THE • 1947 • Freleng Friz • ANS • USA
GAY BACHELOR, A • 1911 • *Solax* • USA
GAY BACK ALLEY see **YOKI NO URAMACHI** • 1939
GAY BALL, THE see **FLICEK THE BALL** • 1956
GAY BLADES • 1946 • Blair George • USA • TOURNAMENT TEMPO
GAY BLADE'S LAST SCRAPE, A • 1916 • MacMackin Archer • USA
GAY BRAGGART, THE (USA) see **NIPPON ICHINO HORAFUKI OTOKO** • 1964
GAY BRIDE, THE • 1934 • Conway Jack • USA • REPEAL
GAY BUCKAROO, THE • 1931 • Rosen Phil • USA
GAY CABALLERO, THE • 1929 • Aylott Dave, Symmons E. F. • SHT • UKN
GAY CABALLERO, THE • 1932 • Werker Alfred L. • USA
GAY CABALLERO, THE • 1940 • Brower Otto • USA • GHOST OF THE CISCO KID
GAY CABALLERO, THE see **CAPTAIN THUNDER** • 1930
GAY CANARY, THE see **VESELAYA KANAREIKA** • 1929
GAY CAVALIER, THE • 1946 • Nigh William • USA
GAY CITY, THE (UKN) see **LAS VEGAS NIGHTS** • 1941
GAY CORINTHIAN, THE • 1924 • Rooke Arthur • UKN • THREE WAGERS, THE
GAY DECEIVER, A • 1912 • *Champion* • USA
GAY DECEIVER, A • 1916 • *Jockey* • USA
GAY DECEIVER, A • 1917 • *Rhodes Billie* • USA
GAY DECEIVER, THE • 1926 • Stahl John M. • USA • TOTO
GAY DECEIVER, THE see **CHICKEN A LA KING** • 1928
GAY DECEIVERS, THE • 1916 • Aylott Dave • UKN
GAY DECEIVERS, THE • 1969 • Kessler Bruce • USA
GAY DECEPTION, THE • 1935 • Wyler William • USA
GAY DEFENDER, THE • 1927 • La Cava Gregory • USA
GAY DESPERADO, THE • 1936 • Mamoulian Rouben • USA
GAY DIPLOMAT • 1931 • Boleslawski Richard • USA • KISSES BY COMMAND
GAY DIVORCE, THE (UKN) see **GAY DIVORCEE, THE** • 1934
GAY DIVORCEE, THE • 1934 • Sandrich Mark • USA • GAY DIVORCE, THE (UKN)
GAY DOG, THE • 1954 • Elvey Maurice • UKN
GAY DUELLIST, THE (USA) see **MEET ME AT DAWN** • 1947
GAY FALCON, THE • 1941 • Reis Irving • USA
GAY GAUCHO, THE • 1933 • Hamilton Rollin, McKimson Tom • ANS • USA
GAY HARRY see **HARRY MUNTER** • 1969
GAY HUSKIES, THE see **LYKKEHJULET** • 1926
GAY IMPOSTORS, THE (UKN) see **GOLDDIGGERS IN PARIS** • 1938
GAY INTRUDERS, THE • 1948 • McCarey Ray • USA
GAY INTRUDERS, THE (USA) see **MEDAL FOR THE GENERAL** • 1944
GAY LADY, THE see **BATTLE OF PARIS, THE** • 1929
GAY LADY, THE (UKN) see **LADY TUBBS** • 1935
GAY LADY, THE (USA) see **TROTTIE TRUE** • 1948
GAY LIFE, THE • 1968 • Foley John • USA
GAY LORD DUCIE, THE • 1911 • Fitzhamon Lewin? • UKN
GAY LORD QUEX, THE • 1917 • Elvey Maurice • UKN
GAY LORD QUEX, THE • 1920 • Beaumont Harry • USA
GAY LORD WARING, THE • 1916 • Turner Otis • USA
GAY LOVE • 1934 • Hiscott Leslie • UKN
GAY MASQUERADE see **BENTEN KOZO** • 1928
GAY MASQUERADE see **BENTEN KOZO** • 1958
GAY MRS. TREXEL, THE (UKN) see **SUSAN AND GOD** • 1940
GAY MUSICIANS see **MUNTRA MUSIKANTER** • 1932
GAY NIGHTS see **FATE OF A FLIRT, THE** • 1925
GAY NINETIES • 1942 • Ceballos Larry • SHT • USA
GAY NINETIES, THE • 1931 • Sandrich Mark • SHT • USA
GAY NINETIES, THE • 1942 • Le Borg Reginald • SHT • USA

GAY NINETIES, THE see **NAUGHTY NINETIES, THE** • 1945
GAY NINETIES, THE (UKN) see **FLORADORA GIRL, THE** • 1930
GAY OLD BIRD, THE • 1927 • Raymaker Herman C. • USA
GAY OLD DOG • 1935 • King George • UKN
GAY OLD DOG, THE • 1919 • Henley Hobart • USA
GAY PARADE see **GLADA PARADEN** • 1948
GAY PARISIAN, THE • 1942 • Negulesco Jean • SHT • USA
GAY PARTY, THE see **GLADA KALASET, DET** • 1946
GAY PURR-EE • 1963 • Levitow Abe • ANM • USA
GAY RANCHERO, THE • 1948 • Witney William • USA
GAY RASPLYEV DAYS see **VESYOLYYE RASPLYUYEVSKIYE DNI** • 1966
GAY RETREAT, THE • 1927 • Stoloff Ben, Marshall George (Spv) • USA
GAY REVENGERS see **OBOXU TENGO** • 1958
GAY SALOME • 1979 • Tarantini Michele Massimo • ITL
GAY SENORITA, THE • 1945 • Dreifuss Arthur • USA
GAY SHOE CLERK, THE • 1903 • Porter Edwin S. • USA
GAY SISTERS, THE • 1942 • Rapper Irving • USA
GAY SWORDSMAN, THE see **FIGLIO DI D'ARTAGNAN, IL** • 1949
GAY TAILOR, THE see **GLADE SKRADDAREN, DEN** • 1945
GAY TIME IN ATLANTIC CITY, A • 1911 • *Hopkins Jack* • USA
GAY TIME IN JACKSONVILLE, FLA., A • 1912 • *Reehm George E.* • USA
GAY TIME IN NEW YORK CITY, A • 1911 • *Hopkins Jack* • USA
GAY TIME IN QUEBEC, A • 1912 • *Lubin* • USA
GAY TIME IN WASHINGTON, A • 1911 • *Lubin* • USA
GAY VAGABOND, THE • 1941 • Morgan William • USA
GAY VINEYARD, THE see **FROHLICHE WEINBERG, DER** • 1927
GAY VINEYARD, THE see **FROHLICHE WEINBERG, DER** • 1952
GAYANE • 1979 • King Horace • USS
GAYARRE • 1958 • Viladomat Domingo • SPN
GAYE KNIGHTIES • 1941 • Pal George • ANS • USA
GAYEST OF THE GAY, THE see **HER REDEMPTION** • 1924
GAYLON see **GALYON**
GAZ, LE • 1939 • Alexeieff Alexandre • SHT • FRN
GAZ DE LACQ, LE • 1960 • Lanoe Henri • SHT • FRN
GAZ MORTELS, LES • 1916 • Gance Abel • FRN • GAZ MORTELS: OU, LE BROUILLARD SUR LA VILLE, LES ○ DEADLY GASES, THE
GAZ MORTELS: OU, LE BROUILLARD SUR LA VILLE, LES see **GAZ MORTELS, LES** • 1916
GAZEBO, THE • 1959 • Marshall George • USA
GAZEBO, THE see **JO** • 1971
GAZELL CLUB • 1950 • Dahlgren Sten • SHT • SWD
GAZIJA • 1981 • Dizdarevic Nenad • YGS
GAZING AT LOVE AND DEATH see **AI TO SHI O MITSUMETE** • 1964
GAZL EL BANAT -L'ADOLESCENTE SUCRE D'AMOUR • 1986 • Saab Jocelyne • CND
GAZOLAS • 1955 • Gertler Viktor • HNG • HIT AND RUN
GAZOROS SERRON • 1974 • Hatzopoulos Dimitris • GRC
GAZZA LADRA, LA • 1964 • Gianini Giulio, Luzzati Emmanuele • ANS • ITL • THIEVING MAGPIE, THE (USA)
GBH: GREVIOUS BODILY HARM see **GRIEVOUS BODILY HARM** • 1987
GDANSK -STARE MIASTO • 1968 • Riesser Jan • DOC • PLN • GDANSK -THE OLD TOWN
GDANSK -THE OLD TOWN see **GDANSK -STARE MIASTO** • 1968
GDANSK TRADE FAIR, THE see **TARGI GDANSKIE** • 1947
GDANSK WROUGHT IRON see **GDANSKA SZTUKA KUZNICZA** • 1968
GDANSKA SZTUKA KUZNICZA • 1968 • Zukowska Jadwiga • PLN • GDANSK WROUGHT IRON
GDY SPADAJA ANIOLY • 1959 • Polanski Roman • PLN • WHEN ANGELS FALL
GDYNIA RADIO • 1963 • Wionczek Roman • DOC • PLN
GDZIE DIABEL MOWI DOBRANOC • 1956 • Karabasz Kazimierz, Slesicki Wladyslaw • DCS • PLN • WHERE THE DEVIL SAYS GOODNIGHT
GDZIE JEST GENERAL? • 1964 • Chmielewski Tadeusz • PLN • WHERE IS THE GENERAL?
GDZIE JEST TRZECI KROL? • 1967 • Ber Ryszard • PLN • WHERE IS THE THIRD KING?
GDZIE JESTES LUIZO? • 1964 • Kubik Janusz • PLN • WHERE ARE YOU, LUIZO? ○ WHERE ARE YOU, LOUISA?
GDZIE SIE PODZIALY KOCHANE DINOZAURY • 1973 • Wiktorowski Janusz • PLN
GDZIE WODA CZYSTA I TRAWA ZIELONA • 1977 • Poreba Bohdan • PLN • WHERE THE WATER IS CLEAN AND THE GRASS IS GREEN
GDZIESKOLWIRK JEST, JESUS JEST • 1989 • Zanussi Krzysztof • PLN, FRG • WHEREVER YOU ARE..
GE-GE-GE NO KITARO • 1968 • Shitara Hiroshi • ANM • JPN • KITRO
GEACHTETEN, DIE • 1917 • Stein Josef • FRG
GEACHTETEN, DIE • 1919 • Delmont Joseph • FRG • RITUALMORD, DER
GEANT A LA COUR DE KUBLAI KHAN, LE (FRN) see **MACISTE ALLA CORTE DEL GRAN KHAN** • 1961
GEANT DE LA VALLEE DES ROIS, LE (FRN) see **MACISTE NELLA VALLE DEI RE** • 1960
GEANT DE THESALIE, LE (FRN) see **GIGANTI DELLA TESSAGLIA, I** • 1960
GEARED FOR PROFIT • 1970 • Gormley Charles • DCS • UKN
GEARED TO GO • 1924 • Rogell Albert S. • USA
GEBANNT UND ERLOST • 1919 • Bluen Georg • FRG
GEBIETERIN VON ST. TROPEZ, DIE • 1921 • Hofer Franz • FRG
GEBIETERISCHE RUF, DER • 1944 • Ucicky Gustav • FRG • VOICE OF CONSCIENCE, THE
GEBISSEN WIRD NUR NACHTS -HAPPENING DER VAMPIRE • 1971 • Francis Freddie • FRG • VAMPIRE HAPPENING, THE ○ HAPPENING DER VAMPIRE
GEBOORTE, DIE • 1968 • Verhavert Roland • SHT • BLG
GEBOORTEGROND • 1946 • SAF
GEBORGTE LEBEN, DAS • 1917 • *Deutsche-Bioscop* • FRG
GEBOT DER LIEBE, DAS • 1919 • Lund Erik • FRG
GEBROCHENE BLUTEN, MENSCHENSCHICKSALE UND GEDANKEN • 1925 • *Europa-Filmverleih* • FRG
GEBROKEN DIJKEN • 1945 • Ferno John • DOC • NTH • BROKEN DIKES
GEBROKEN SPIEGELS • 1984 • Gorris Marleen • NTH • BROKEN MIRRORS
GEBT EUCH NICHT DER TRAUER HIN • 1961 • Houwer Rob • FRG
GECE DANSI TUTSAKLARI • 1988 • Ergun Mahinur • TRK • CAPTIVES OF A NIGHT DANCE
GECE YOLCULUGU • 1988 • Kavur Omer • TRK • NIGHT VOYAGE
GECEKONDU PESINDE • 1967 • Tuna Feyzi • TRK • IN SEARCH OF A HOUSE
GECELERIN KRALI • 1967 • Ergun Nuri • TRK • KING OF THE KNIGHTS, THE
GEDANKENSUNDEN • 1924 • Linke Edmund • FRG
GEE! BUT IT'S GREAT TO BE STUNG • 1914 • *Crystal* • USA
GEE, IF MY MUDDER COULD SEE ME • 1905 • *Bitzer Billy (Ph)* • USA
GEE MY JOU HAND • 1963 • SAF
GEE! MY PANTS! • 1912 • *Wilbur Crane* • USA
GEE WHIZ • 1911 • *Essanay* • USA
GEE WHIZ • 1919 • Perez Marcel • USA
GEE WHIZ! • 1920 • Jones F. Richard • SHT • USA
GEE WHIZ GENEVIEVE! • 1924 • Howe J. A. • SHT • USA
GEE WHIZ-Z-Z-Z-Z-Z-Z! • 1956 • Jones Charles M. • ANS • USA
GEEK • 1987 • Crow Dean • USA • BACKWOODS
GEEK MAGGOT BINGO • 1983 • Zedd Nick • USA
GEEL • 1978 • Blanchet Vincent, Van In Andre • DOC • FRN, BLG
GEEL TRUI VIR 'N WENNER • 1983 • Marx Franz • SAF • YELLOW JERSEY FOR A WINNER
GEESE AND DUCK'S SINGING CONTEST, THE see **GAOU UTAGGASEN** • 1939
GEESE OF BUTZOW, THE see **GANSE VON BUTZOW, DIE** • 1986
GEET • 1969 • Sagar Ramanand • IND
GEET GOVIND • 1947 • Thakur Ramchandra • IND • MUSIC OF GOVIND
GEEZER OF BERLIN, THE • 1918 • Hotaling Arthur D. • SHT • USA
GEFAHRDETE MADCHEN • 1927 • Schall Heinz • FRG
GEFAHRDETE MADCHEN • 1958 • Gluck Wolfgang • FRG • DOLLS OF VICE
GEFAHREN DER BRAUTZEIT • 1929 • Sauer Fred • FRG
GEFAHREN DER BRAUTZEIT see **LIEBESNACHTE** • 1929
GEFAHREN DER GROSSTADT-STRASSE • 1924 • *Cabinet-Film* • FRG
GEFAHREN DER HYPNOSE see **VERLORENE ICH, DAS** • 1923
GEFAHREN DER LIEBE • 1931 • Thiele Eugen • FRG
GEFAHRLICHE ALTER, DAS • 1911 • Stark Kurt • FRG
GEFAHRLICHE ALTER, DAS • 1927 • Illes Eugen • FRG
GEFAHRLICHE FAHRT, EINE • 1920 • Kahn William? • FRG
GEFAHRLICHE FRACHT • 1954 • von Wangenheim Gustav • GDR
GEFAHRLICHE FREUNDSCHAFT • 1924 • Dammann Gerhard • FRG
GEFAHRLICHE GASTE • 1949 • von Cziffra Geza • FRG
GEFAHRLICHE SPIEL, EIN • 1919 • Wiene Robert • AUS
GEFAHRLICHER FRUHLING • 1943 • Deppe Hans • FRG
GEFAHRLICHER SEX FRUHREIFER MADCHEN • 1971 • Brummer Alois • FRG • FINISHING SCHOOL
GEFAHRLICHES ABENTEUER • 1953 • Reinert Emile Edwin • AUS • ABENTEUER IN WIEN
GEFAHRLICHES SPIEL • 1937 • Engel Erich • FRG
GEFAHRLICHES SPIEL, EIN see **MENSCHEN UND MASKEN 2** • 1923
GEFAHRTIN MEINES SOMMERS • 1943 • Buch Fritz Peter • FRG
GEFANGENE, DER • 1920 • Wolff Carl Heinz • FRG • SKLAVEN DES XX JAHRHUNDERTS ○ SKLAVEN DES 20 JAHRHUNDERTS
GEFANGENE DER BERNINA, DER see **SPUREN IM SCHNEE** • 1929
GEFANGENE DER LIEBE • 1954 • Jugert Rudolf • FRG
GEFANGENE DES KONIGS, DER • 1935 • Boese Carl • FRG
GEFANGENE DES MAHARADSCHA, DIE • 1954 • Harlan Veit • FRG
GEFANGENE SEELE • 1917 • Biebrach Rudolf • FRG
GEFANGENE SEELE • 1952 • Wolff Hans • FRG
GEFANGENE SEELEN • 1912 • Stark Kurt • FRG
GEFANGENE VON DAHOMEY, DER • 1918 • *Deutsche Kolonial* • FRG
GEFANGENE VON SHANGHAI, DIE • 1927 • von Bolvary Geza • FRG
GEFANGNIS AUF DEM MEERESGRUND, DAS • 1920 • Piel Harry • FRG
GEFESSELTE POLO, DER • 1928 • Lasko Leo • FRG
GEFISCHTE GEFUUHLE • 1979 • Kaufmann Manfred • AUS • FISHED FEELINGS
GEFLUSTER DES TEUFELS see **FOLGEN EINER UNGLUCKLICHEN EHE, DIE** • 1919
GEFOLTERTE HERZEN 1 • 1920 • Speyer Jaap • FRG • OHNE HEIMAT
GEFOLTERTE HERZEN 2 • 1920 • Speyer Jaap • FRG • GLUCK UND GLAS
GEFRORENE HERZ, DAS • 1979 • Koller Xavier • MTV • SWT • FROZEN HEART, THE
GEFRORENEN BLITZE, DIE • 1967 • Veiczi Janos • GDR • FROZEN LIGHTNINGS ○ FROZEN FLASHES
GEFUNDENE BRAUT, DIE • 1925 • Gliese Rochus • FRG
GEGE BELLAVITA • 1979 • Festa Campanile Pasquale • ITL
GEGEN DEN STROM • 1920 • *Andersen Iven* • FRG
GEGNER NACH MASS • 1963 • Bottge Bruno J. • ANS • GDR • RIVAL MADE TO MEASURE
GEH' MACH DEIN FENSTERL AUF • 1953 • Kutter Anton • AUS, DNM
GEHEIM VAN NANTES • 1969 • SAF
GEHEIM VAN ONDERPLAAS • 1962 • SAF
GEHEIMAGENT, DER • 1932 • Piel Harry • FRG • MANN FALLT VOM HIMMEL, EIN ○ SECRET AGENT (UKN)
GEHEIMAKTE WB1 • 1942 • Selpin Herbert • FRG
GEHEIMAKTEN SOLVAY • 1952 • Hellberg Martin • GDR • SOLVAY DOSSIER, THE ○ SECRET SOLVAY FILE, THE
GEHEIMAKTION SCHWARZE KAPELLE • 1960 • Habib Ralph • FRG, FRN, ITL • R.P.Z. APPELLE BERLIN (FRN) ○ SICARI DI HITLER, I (ITL) ○ BLACK CHAPEL, THE (USA) ○ SCHWARZE KAPELLE, DIE
GEHEIMARCHIV AN DER ELBE • 1963 • Jung-Alsen Kurt • GDR
GEHEIMBUND DER FALKEN • 1920 • Arnheim Valy • FRG
GEHEIMBUNDSKLAVEN 1 • 1922 • Linke Edmund • FRG • DINGE ZWISCHEN HIMMEL UND ERDE
GEHEIMBUNDSKLAVEN 2 • 1922 • Linke Edmund • FRG • MACHT DER VERSCHWORENEN
GEHEIME AGENT, DER • 1924 • Schonfelder Erich • FRG
GEHEIME KURIER, DER • 1928 • Righelli Gennaro • FRG • ROUGE ET NOIR ○ SECRET COURIER, THE
GEHEIME MACHT, DIE • 1927 • Waschneck Erich • FRG • SECRET POWER
GEHEIMIS EINER EHE, DAS • 1951 • Weiss Helmut • FRG
GEHEIMNIS AUF SCHLOSS CHANTILLY, DAS • 1925 • *Dorry-Renu-Film* • FRG
GEHEIMNIS AUF SCHLOSS ELMSHOH, DAS see **FLUCH DER BOSEN TAT, DER** • 1925
GEHEIMNIS DER 17 • 1963 • Losansky Rolf • GDR
GEHEIMNIS DER ALTEN MAMSELL, DAS • 1925 • Merzbach Paul • FRG
GEHEIMNIS DER ALTEN TRUHE, DAS • 1919 • *Smolowa Sibyl* • FRG • HERZBLUT 2
GEHEIMNIS DER AMERIKA-DOCKS, DAS • 1918 • Dupont E. A. • FRG • SECRET OF THE AMERICA DOCK, THE
GEHEIMNIS DER BETTLER, DAS • 1921 • Attenberger Toni • FRG
GEHEIMNIS DER BRIEFMARKE, DAS • 1917 • Alexander Georg • FRG
GEHEIMNIS DER BURGRUINE, DAS • 1924 • *Lohbauer Hans (P)* • FRG
GEHEIMNIS DER CHINESISCHEN NELKE, DAS • 1964 • Zehetgruber Rudolf • FRG, ITL, SPN • SECRET OF THE CHINESE CARNATION, THE (USA) ○ SEGRETO DEL GAROFANO CINESE, IL (ITL)
GEHEIMNIS DER CHRYSANTHEMEN, DAS • 1920 • Molter Ernst • FRG
GEHEIMNIS DER DIAMANDFELDER, DAS • 1916 • Dessauer Siegfried • FRG
GEHEIMNIS DER DREI DSCHUNKEN, DAS • 1965 • Hofbauer Ernst • FRG, ITL • A-009 MISSIONE HONG KONG (ITL) ○ RED DRAGON (USA) ○ MISSION TO HONG KONG ○ SECRET OF THE THREE JUNKS, THE
GEHEIMNIS DER GELBEN MONCHE, DAS • 1966 • Kohler Manfred R. • FRG, AUS, ITL • SEGRETO DEI FRATI GIALLI, IL (ITL) ○ TARGET FOR KILLING (USA) ○ WIE TOTET MAN EINE DAME? ○ TIRO A SEGNO PER UCCIDERE ○ COME SI UCCIDE UNA SIGNORA? ○ HOW TO KILL A LADY ○ AUS ○ SECRET OF THE YELLOW MONKS, THE
GEHEIMNIS DER GELBEN NARZISSEN, DAS • 1961 • von Rathony Akos • FRG • DEVIL'S DAFFODIL, THE (UKN) ○ DAFFODIL KILLER
GEHEIMNIS DER GLADIATORENWERKE 1, DAS • 1920 • Eichgrun Bruno • FRG • IM BANNE DER FRAU
GEHEIMNIS DER GLADIATORENWERKE 2, DAS • 1920 • Eichgrun Bruno • FRG • UNTER DER MASKE DES JUWELIERS
GEHEIMNIS DER GRUEN STECKNADELN, DAS (FRG) see **COSA AVETE FATTO A SOLANGE?** • 1972
GEHEIMNIS DER GRUNEN VILLA, DAS • 1921 • Mayring Philipp L. • FRG
GEHEIMNIS DER HERZOGIN, DAS • 1923 • *Landlicht-Ag* • FRG
GEHEIMNIS DER JUNGEN WITWE, DAS (FRG) see **MORTE NON HA SESSO, LA** • 1968
GEHEIMNIS DER KATAKOMBEN • 1921 • Piel Harry • FRG
GEHEIMNIS DER LATEN MAMSELL, DAS • 1917 • Mendel Georg Victor • FRG
GEHEIMNIS DER LEDERSCHLINGE, DAS (FRG) see **MISTERI DELLA GIUNGLA NERA, I** • 1964
GEHEIMNIS DER LEEREN WASSERFLASCHE, DAS • 1917 • May Joe • FRG
GEHEIMNIS DER LUFTE, DAS • 1913 • *Brandt Julius* • AUS, FRN
GEHEIMNIS DER M-STRAHLEN, DAS • 1923 • *Venus-Film* • FRG
GEHEIMNIS DER MARTHE LUDERS, DAS • 1930 • Wiene Conrad • FRG
GEHEIMNIS DER MITTERNACHSSTUNDE, DAS • 1920 • Neff Wolfgang • FRG
GEHEIMNIS DER MUMIE, DAS • 1921 • Janson Victor • FRG
GEHEIMNIS DER PAGODE, DER see **PAGODE, DIE** • 1917
GEHEIMNIS DER ROTEN KATZE, DAS • 1931 • Schonfelder Erich • FRG
GEHEIMNIS DER ROTEN KATZE, DAS • 1949 • Weiss Helmut • FRG • SECRET OF THE BLACK WIDOW
GEHEIMNIS DER SANTA MARGHERITA, DAS • 1921 • Randolf Rolf • FRG
GEHEIMNIS DER SANTA MARIA, DAS • 1921 • Mendes Lothar • FRG • SANTA MARIA. DAS GEHEIMNIS EINER BRIGG ○ SANTA MARIA
GEHEIMNIS DER SCHWARZEN HANDSCHUHE, DAS (FRG) see **UCCELLO DALLE PIUME DE CRISTALLO, L'** • 1970
GEHEIMNIS DER SCHWARZEN KOFFER, DAS • 1962 • Klinger Werner • FRG • SECRET OF THE BLACK TRUNK, THE (USA) ○ SCHLOSS DES SCHRECKENS, DAS ○ CASTLE OF THE TERRIFIED
GEHEIMNIS DER SCHWARZEN LUCY, DAS • 1924 • *Valy Arnheim-Film* • FRG
GEHEIMNIS DER SCHWARZEN WITWE, DAS • 1963 • Gottlieb Franz J. • FRG, SPN • SECRET OF THE BLACK WIDOW, THE (USA)
GEHEIMNIS DER SECHS SPIELKARTEN 1, DAS • 1920 • Kahn William • FRG • KARO 10
GEHEIMNIS DER SECHS SPIELKARTEN 2, DAS • 1921 • Kahn William • FRG • PIQUE BUBE
GEHEIMNIS DER SECHS SPIELKARTEN 3, DAS • 1921 • Kahn William • FRG • TREFF AS
GEHEIMNIS DER SECHS SPIELKARTEN 4, DAS • 1921 • Brunner Rolf • FRG • PIQUE SIEBEN

GEHEIMNIS DER SECHS SPIELKARTEN 5, DAS • 1921 • Kahn William • FRG • HERZ KONIG
GEHEIMNIS DER SECHS SPIELKARTEN 6, DAS • 1921 • Kahn William • FRG • HERZ DAME
GEHEIMNIS DER SPIELHOLLE VON SEBASTOPOL, DAS • 1920 • Klopfer Eugen • FRG
GEHEIMNIS DER TODESINSEL, DAS • 1967 • von Theumer Ernst Ritter • FRG, SPN, ITL • ISLAND OF THE DOOMED (USA) ○ ISLA DE LA MUERTE, LA (SPN) ○ BLOODSUCKERS, THE (UKN) ○ MAN EATER OF HYDRA ○ SECRET OF DEATH ISLAND ○ ISLAND OF THE DEAD
GEHEIMNIS DER TOTEN, DAS • 1910 • Porten Franz • FRG
GEHEIMNIS DER VENUS, DAS • 1955 • Rieger August • AUS, FRG • FEMALE ANIMAL, THE (USA)
GEHEIMNIS DER VILLA DOX, DAS • 1916 • Trautmann Ludwig • FRG
GEHEIMNIS DER WEISSEN NONNE, DAS • 1966 • Frankel Cyril • FRG, UKN
GEHEIMNIS DER WERA BORANSKA, DAS • 1919 • *Treumann Wanda* • FRG
GEHEIMNIS DER WETTERFAHNE, DAS • 1918 • Matull Kurt • FRG
GEHEIMNIS DES 15 SEPTEMBER, DAS • 1923 • *Filma-Film* • FRG
GEHEIMNIS DES ABBE X, DAS • 1927 • Dieterle William • FRG • MANN, DER NICHT LIEBEN DARF, DER ○ BEHIND THE ALTAR
GEHEIMNIS DES BLAUEN ZIMMERS • 1932 • Engels Erich • FRG
GEHEIMNIS DES BUDDHA, DAS • 1920 • Mayring Philipp L. • FRG
GEHEIMNIS DES CARLO CAVELLI, DAS see **HOHE SCHULE** • 1934
GEHEIMNIS DES FABRIKANTEN HENDERSON, DAS • 1920 • Neisser Karl • FRG
GEHEIMNIS DES FREMDENLEGIONARS, DAS see **SERGEANT X** • 1931
GEHEIMNIS DES HOHEN FALKEN, DAS • 1950 • Hallig Christian • FRG • STEINE GOTTIN, DIE
GEHEIMNIS DES KILOMETERSTEINS 13, DAS • 1916 • Zangenberg Einar • FRG
GEHEIMNIS DES KNOTENS, DAS • 1915 • *Luna-Film* • FRG
GEHEIMNIS DES RENNGRAFEN, DAS • 1923 • Bergson A. • FRG
GEHEIMNIS DES SCHAFOTTS, DAS • 1919 • *Marion Oscar* • FRG
GEHEIMNIS DES ZIRKUS BARRE, DAS • 1920 • Piel Harry • FRG
GEHEIMNIS EINER AERZTIN, DAS • 1955 • Rieger August, Stanzl Karl • AUS • LIEBE AM SCHEIDEWEG
GEHEIMNIS EINER NACHT ,DAS • 1915 • *Kaiser-Titz Erich* • FRG
GEHEIMNIS EINER NACHT, DAS • 1919 • *Kaiser-Titz Erich* • FRG
GEHEIMNIS EINER SCHULD • 1921 • Rippert Otto • FRG
GEHEIMNIS EINER SEELE • 1926 • Oertel Curt • FRG
GEHEIMNIS EINER STUNDE, DAS • 1925 • Obal Max • FRG
GEHEIMNIS EINES ALTEN HAUSES • 1936 • van der Noss Rudolf • FRG
GEHEIMNIS LORD PERCIVALS, DAS • 1921 • Neufeld Max • AUS
GEHEIMNIS TIBET • 1942 • Lettow Hans H., Schafer Ernst • FRG
GEHEIMNIS UM BETTY BONN, DAS • 1937 • Stemmle R. A. • FRG
GEHEIMNIS UM JOHANN ORT, DAS • 1932 • Wolff Willi • FRG • LIEBESROMAN IM HAUSE HABSBURG, EIN
GEHEIMNIS VOM KONIGSSEE, DAS see **MONCH VON ST. BARTHOLOMA, DER** • 1930
GEHEIMNIS VON BOMBAY, DAS • 1920 • Holz Artur • FRG • ABENTEUER EINER NACHT, DAS
GEHEIMNIS VON BRINKENHOF, DAS • 1923 • Gade Svend • FRG
GEHEIMNIS VON D14, DAS • 1915 • Piel Harry • FRG
GEHEIMNIS VON GENF, DAS • 1927 • Reiber Willy • FRG
GEHEIMNIS VON ST. PAULI, DAS • 1926 • Randolf Rolf • FRG
GEHEIMNIS VON SCHLOSS HOLLOWAY, DAS • 1919 • Zeyn Willy • FRG
GEHEIMNIS VON SCHLOSS TOTENSTEIN, DAS • 1920 • Bach Rudi • FRG
GEHEIMNIS VON ZERMATT, DAS see **SOHN DER WEISSEN BERG, DER** • 1930
GEHEIMNISSE DER SEELE see **VERFUHRTE, DIE** • 1913
GEHEIMNISSE DES BLUTES see **VERFUHRTE, DIE** • 1913
GEHEIMNISSE DES ORIENTS • 1928 • Volkov Alexander • FRG • SECRETS OF THE ORIENT (USA) ○ MYSTERIES OF THE ORIENT ○ SHEHERAZADE ○ SECRETS OF THE EAST
GEHEIMNISSE EINER SEELE • 1926 • Pabst G. W. • FRG • SECRETS OF A SOUL
GEHEIMNISSE IN GOLDENEN NYLONS • 1966 • Christian-Jaque • FRG, ITL, FRN • DEUX BILLETS POUR MEXICO (FRN) ○ QUI VEUT TUER CARLOS? ○ DEAD RUN (USA) ○ CHAUD LES SECRETS ○ SEGRETI CHE SCOTTANO (ITL) ○ WHO WANTS TO SHOOT CARLOS?
GEHEIMNISSE VON BERLIN 1, DIE • 1921 • Teuber Arthur • FRG • BERLIN N. DIE DUNKLE GROSSTADT
GEHEIMNISSE VON BERLIN 2, DIE • 1921 • *Eva Evi* • FRG • BERLIN W. DIE GROSSTADT IN GLANZ UND LICHT
GEHEIMNISSE VON BERLIN 3, DIE • 1921 • *Eva Evi* • FRG • BERLIN–MOABIT. HINTER GITTERFENSTERN
GEHEIMNISSE VON BERLIN 4, DIE • 1922 • *Eva Evi* • FRG • BERLIN FROBELSTRASSE. IM ASYL FUR OBDACHLOSE
GEHEIMNISSE VON BERLIN, DIE • 1921 • Mack Max • FRG
GEHEIMNISSE VON LONDON, DIE • 1920 • Oswald Richard • FRG, AUS • SIEBENTE GEBOT, DAS ○ TRAGODIE EINES KINDES, DIE ○ OLIVER TWIST
GEHEIMNISSE VON NEW YORK, DIE • 1920 • *Loos Theodor* • FRG
GEHEIMNISTRAGER, DER • 1975 • Gottlieb • FRG
GEHEIMNISVOLLE BUCH, DAS see **HOMUNCULUS 2** • 1916
GEHEIMNISVOLLE ENTFUHRUNG, EINE • 1925 • *Standard-Film* • FRG
GEHEIMNISVOLLE FREMDE, DER • 1919 • Bauer Leopold • FRG
GEHEIMNISVOLLE GEWALTEN • 1915 • *Andra Fern* • FRG
GEHEIMNISVOLLE MACHT, DIE see **REITER OHNE KOPF 2, DER** • 1921
GEHEIMNISVOLLE MISTER X, DER • 1936 • Hubler-Kahla J. A. • FRG • MYSTERIOUS MR. X, THE (USA)
GEHEIMNISVOLLE NACHT, DIE see **RATTEN DER GROSSTADT 1** • 1920
GEHEIMNISVOLLE SCHACHPARTIE, DIE • 1920 • *Liehr Charlotte* • FRG
GEHEIMNISVOLLE SPIEGEL, DER • 1928 • Hoffmann Carl, Teschner Prof. • FRG • MYSTIC MIRROR, THE (USA)
GEHEIMNISVOLLE TELEPHON, DAS • 1916 • Piel Harry • FRG
GEHEIMNISVOLLE TIEFEN • 1951 • Pabst G. W. • AUS
GEHEIMNISVOLLE VILLA, DIE • 1914 • May Joe • FRG
GEHEIMNISVOLLE WANDERER, DER • 1915 • Wauer William • FRG • UNHEIMLICHE FREMDE, DER
GEHEIMNISVOLLE WRACK, DAS • 1954 • Ballmann Herbert • GDR • MYSTERIOUS WRECK, THE
GEHEIMNISVOLLEN PIRATEN, DIE • 1922 • Gerhardt Karl • FRG
GEHEIMPOLIZISTEN • 1929 • Heuberger Edmund • FRG • KRIMINALPOLIZEI –ABTEILUNG MORD
GEHEIMSEKRETAR, DER • 1915 • May Joe • FRG
GEHEIMTRESOR, DER • 1927 • Polo Eddie • FRG
GEHEIMZEICHEN LB17 • 1938 • Tourjansky Victor • FRG
GEHENU LAMAI • 1977 • Peries Sumitra • SLN • GIRLS, THE
GEHETZTE FRAUEN • 1923 • Seitz Franz? • FRG
GEHETZTE FRAUEN • 1927 • Oswald Richard • FRG • LEBENDE WARE
GEHETZTE MADCHEN • 1930 • Schonfelder Erich • FRG
GEHETZTE MENSCHEN • 1924 • Schonfelder Erich • FRG
GEHETZTE MENSCHEN • 1932 • Feher Friedrich • FRG, UKN • ROBBER SYMPHONY, THE (UKN) ○ STECKBRIEF Z 48 ○ HUNTED PEOPLE ○ LOUP GARON, LE
GEHN SIE NICHT ALLEIN NACH HAUSE • 1961 • Marischka Franz • AUS
GEHORSAME REBELL, DER • 1952 • Oertel Curt • FRG
GEHULFE, DER • 1976 • Koerfer Thomas • SWT • ASSISTANT, THE
GEHVERSUCHE • 1982 • Zbonek Edwin • AUS • VINOPOLIS
GEH'ZIEH DEIN DIRNDL AUS • 1974 • Gotz Siggi • FRG
GEIDO ICHIDAI OTOKO • 1940 • Mizoguchi Kenji • JPN • LIFE OF AN ARTIST, THE (USA) ○ LIFE OF AN ACTOR, THE
GEIER KONNEN WARTEN (FRG) see **ETRANGERS, LES** • 1968
GEIER-WALLY, DIE • 1921 • Dupont E. A. • FRG • WOMAN WHO KILLED A VULTURE, THE ○ ROMAN AUS DEN BERGEN, EIN ○ GEIERWALLY
GEIERWALLY see **GEIER-WALLY, DIE** • 1921
GEIERWALLY, DIE • 1940 • Steinhoff Hans • FRG
GEIERWALLY, DIE • 1956 • Cap Frantisek • FRG
GEIGE DES THOMASO, DIE • 1918 • Hanus Emerich • FRG
GEIGENMACHER VON MITTENWALD, DER • 1950 • Schundler Rudolf • FRG
GEIGENSPIELER, DER • 1917 • von Woringen Paul • FRG
GEIGER, DER see **EWIGE KLANG, DER** • 1943
GEIGER VON FLORENZ, DER • 1926 • Czinner Paul • FRG • IMPETUOUS YOUTH (UKN) ○ VIOLINIST OF FLORENCE, THE
GEIGER VON MEISSEN, DER • 1920 • Robert Ferdinand • FRG
GEIGERKONIG, DER • 1923 • Krause Karl Otto • FRG
GEILE NICHTEN • 1978 • Saller Eddy • AUS • WANTON NIECES
GEININ • 1976 • Gagnon Claude • JPN
GEISHA • 1967 • Seki Koji • JPN
GEISHA, A (USA) see **GION BAYASHI** • 1953
GEISHA, THE • 1914 • Barker Reginald • USA
GEISHA BOY, THE • 1958 • Tashlin Frank • USA
GEISHA GIRL GINKO, A see **SHUKUZU** • 1953
GEISHA IN THE OLD CITY, A see **JOTAI WA KANASHIKU** • 1957
GEISHA KONATSU • 1954 • Sugie Toshio • JPN
GEISHA MASSEUSES see **ONSEN ANMA GEISHA** • 1968
GEISHA UND DER SAMURAI, DIE • 1919 • Boese Carl • FRG
GEISHA WHO SAVED JAPAN, THE • 1909 • Olcott Sidney • USA
GEISHA'S DIARY see **ONNA WA NIDO UMARERU** • 1961
GEISHA'S SUICIDE, A see **SHIROGANE SHINJU** • 1956
GEISSEL DES FLEISCHES • 1965 • Saller Eddy • AUS
GEIST UND EIN WENIG GLUCK • 1965 • Schamoni Ulrich • MTV • FRG
GEISTERJAGD, DIE • 1918 • Guter Johannes • FRG
GEISTERSEHER, DER • 1915 • Hecker Waldemar • FRG
GEISTERSEHER, DER • 1923 • Brandt Heinrich • FRG
GEISTERTANZ, DER • 1920 • Eichgrun Bruno • FRG
GEISTERZUG, DIE • 1927 • von Bolvary Geza • FRG
GEITERSTUNDE • 1967 • Heynowski Walter, Scheumann Gerhard • GDR
GEJAGT BIS ZUM MORGEN • 1957 • Hasler Joachim • FRG
GEKAUFTE GLUCK, DAS • 1989 • Odermatt Urs • SWT • HAPPINESS FOR SALE
GEKIJO NO CHIBUSA • 1967 • Kataoka Hitoshi • JPN • PASSIONATE BREASTS
GEKIRYU • 1944 • Hieki Mioji • JPN
GEKIRYU • 1952 • *Mifune Toshiro* • JPN
GEKIRYU • 1967 • Inoue Umeji • JPN • STREAM OF LIFE
GEKITO SANKAKU TOBI • 1958 • Namiki Kyotaro • JPN
GEKITOTSU • 1989 • Furuhata Yasuo • JPN • SHOGUN'S SHADOW
GEKITOTSU SATSUJINKEN • 1973 • Ozawa Shigehiro • JPN • STREETFIGHTER, THE (USA) ○ KARATE, THE ○ ENTER THE STREETFIGHTER
GEKKA NO KYOJIN • 1927 • Kinugasa Teinosuke • JPN • MOONLIGHT MADNESS
GEKKO KAMEN • 1958 • Kobayashi Tsuneo • JPN • MAN IN THE MOONLIGHT MASK, THE ○ MOONBEAM MAN, THE
GEKKO KAMEN • 1959 • Ainuda Satoru • JPN • MONSTER GORILLA, THE
GEKKO KAMEN • 1959 • Shimazu Shoichi • JPN • CHALLENGING GHOST, THE ○ LAST DEATH OF THE DEVIL, THE
GEKKO KAMEN –SATAN NO TSUME • 1959 • Wakabayashi Eijiro • JPN
GEKNECHTETE SEELEN • 1924 • *Spera-Film* • FRG
GELBE BESTIEN see **MANN OHNE NAMEN 3, DER** • 1920-21
GELBE DIPLOMAT, DER • 1920 • Sauer Fred • FRG
GELBE FLAGGE, DIE • 1937 • Lamprecht Gerhard • FRG
GELBE FRATZE, DIE • 1919 • Zickel Martin • FRG
GELBE GAUKLER, DER • 1919 • Osten Franz • FRG
GELBE HAUS, DAS see **PROSTITUTION, DIE** • 1919
GELBE HAUS AM PINNASBERG, DAS • 1970 • Vohrer Alfred • FRG
GELBE HAUS DES KING–FU, DAS • 1930 • Grune Karl • FRG
GELBE KOFFER, DER • 1970 • Marino Fernando • FRG
GELBE SCHATTEN, DER • 1919 • Speyer Jaap? • FRG
GELBE SCHEIN, DER • 1918 • Janson Victor, Illes Eugen • FRG
GELBE STERN, DER • 1981 • Hildebrandt Dieter • FRG • YELLOW STAR, THE
GELBE TOD 1, DER • 1919 • Wilhelm Carl • FRG
GELBE TOD 2, DER • 1919 • Wilhelm Carl • FRG
GELBE ULSTER, DER • 1916 • Meinert Rudolf • FRG
GELBE WAGEN, DER see **HUTET EURE TOCHTER** • 1962
GELBER WURGER, DER • 1921 • *Stranz Fred* • FRG
GELBSTERN • 1910 • Rippert Otto • FRG
GELBSTERN • 1921 • Neff Wolfgang • FRG
GELD AUF DER STRASSE • 1930 • Jacoby Georg • FRG, AUS
GELD AUF DER STRASSE, DAS • 1922 • Schunzel Reinhold • FRG • BETRUGER DES VOLKES
GELD AUS DER LUFT • 1954 • von Cziffra Geza • FRG
GELD FALLT VOM HIMMEL • 1938 • Helbig Heinz • FRG, SWD
GELD INS HAUS • 1945 • Stemmle R. A. • FRG • MILLIONAR, DER
GELD LIEGT AUF DER STRASSE, DAS • 1970 • Staudte Wolfgang • FRG
GELD MUSS MAN HABEN • 1945 • Lingen Theo • FRG • ARME JONATHAN, DER
GELD ODER LEBEN (FRG) see **BOURSE ET LA VIE, LA** • 1965
GELD REGIERT DIE WELT • 1934 • Neufeld Max • AUS
GELD SOOS BOSSIES • 1955 • SAF
GELDTEUFEL, DER • 1923 • Goldberg Heinz • FRG • FENTON
GELEGENHEIT MACHT DIEBE see **MEIDEKEN** • 1937
GELEGENHEITSARBEIT EINER SKLAVIN • 1974 • Kluge Alexander • FRG • OCCASIONAL WORK OF A FEMALE SLAVE (UKN) ○ PART–TIME WORK OF A DOMESTIC SLAVE (USA)
GELIEBTE, DIE • 1921 • Zelnik Friedrich • FRG • GELIEBTE DES GRAFEN VARENNE, DIE
GELIEBTE, DIE • 1927 • Wiene Robert • FRG • BELOVED, THE
GELIEBTE, DIE • 1939 • Lamprecht Gerhard • FRG
GELIEBTE BESTIE • 1959 • Rabenalt Arthur M. • AUS, FRG • HIPPODROME (USA) ○ MANNER MUSSEN SO SEIN ○ ARENA OF FEAR ○ MADCHEN IM TIGERFELL, DAS ○ MEINE HEIMAT IST TAGLICH WOANDERS
GELIEBTE CORINNA • 1956 • von Borsody Eduard • FRG
GELIEBTE DES GOUVERNEURS, DIE • 1927 • Feher Friedrich • FRG
GELIEBTE DES GRAFEN VARENNE, DIE see **GELIEBTE, DIE** • 1921
GELIEBTE DES KONIGS, DIE • 1922 • Zelnik Friedrich • FRG
GELIEBTE DES SCHAH, DIE see **ABENTEUERIN VON MONTE CARLO 1, DIE** • 1921
GELIEBTE FEINDIN • 1955 • Hansen Rolf • FRG
GELIEBTE HOCHSTAPLERIN • 1961 • von Rathony Akos • FRG
GELIEBTE MILENA • 1990 • Belmont Vera • FRG • BELOVED MILENA
GELIEBTE ROSWOLSKYS, DIE • 1921 • Basch Felix • FRG
GELIEBTE SEINER FRAU, DER • 1930 • Neufeld Max • FRG
GELIEBTE SEINER HOHEIT, DIE • 1928 • Fleck Jacob, Fleck Luise • FRG
GELIEBTE TOTE, DIE • 1919 • Baron Erwin • FRG
GELIEBTE WEISS MAUS • 1964 • Kolditz Gottfried • GDR
GELIEBTE WELT • 1942 • Burri Emil • FRG
GELIEBTER LUGNER • 1950 • Schweikart Hans • FRG
GELIEBTER SCHATZ • 1943 • Martin Paul • FRG
GELIEBTES FRAULEIN DOKTOR • 1954 • Konig Hans H. • FRG • LIEBESBRIEFE AUS MITTENWALD
GELIEBTES LEBEN • 1953 • Thiele Rolf • FRG
GELIGNITE GANG, THE • 1956 • Fisher Terence • UKN • DYNAMITERS, THE (USA)
GELIJKENIS • 1966 • Frenkel Micha • SHT • NTH
GELIN • 1973 • Akat Lutfu • TRK • BRIDE, THE
GELINCIK TARLASI • 1968 • Aslan Mehmet • TRK • POPPY FIELD, THE
GELOBNIS, DAS see **ENDE VOM LIEDE, DAS** • 1919
GELOBT SIE, WAS HART MACHT • 1972 • Thiele Rolf • FRG
GELOMBANG • 1980 • B. Rahman • MLY
GELORA • 1970 • Ramlee P. • MLY • TROUBLED
GELOSIA • 1915 • Genina Augusto • ITL
GELOSIA • 1943 • Poggioli Ferdinando M. • ITL
GELOSIA • 1953 • Germi Pietro • ITL • JEALOUSY
GELOSIA see **FARI NELLA NEBBIA** • 1942
GELOSTE KETTEN • 1916 • Biebrach Rudolf • FRG
GELUBDE, DAS • 1921 • Biebrach Rudolf • FRG
GELUBDE DER KEUSCHHEIT, DAS • 1919 • Chrisander Nils • FRG • VOW OF CHASTITY
GELUKSDAL • 1974 • SAF
GELURE, LA • 1967 • Audy Michel • CND
GEM AND GERMS • 1914 • *L-Ko* • USA
GEM FROM THE DEEP, THE see **PLOY TALAY** • 1986
GEM JAMS • 1943 • Hillyer Lambert • SHT • USA
GEM OF A JAM, A • 1943 • Lord Del • SHT • USA
GEMBAKO NO ZU • 1952 • Imai Tadashi • JPN • PICTURES OF THE ATOM BOMB
GEMEINDE VON ST. HELENE UND IHR KAPLAN VOLKSSCHAUSPIEL, DIE • 1920 • Seitz Franz • FRG
GEMEINDEPRASIDENT, DER • 1983 • Giger Bernhard • SWT
GEMELAS, LAS • 1963 • del Amo Antonio • SPN
GEMELLI DEL TEXAS, I • 1964 • Steno • ITL, SPN
GEMING JIATING • 1960 • Shui Hua • CHN • REVOLUTIONARY FAMILY, A
GEMINI • 1979 • Du Toit Chris • SAF
GEMINI AFFAIR • 1975 • Cimber Matt • USA
GEMINI MAN • 1976 • Levi Alan J. • TVM • USA • CODE NAME: MINUS ONE
GEMINI TWINS, THE see **TWINS OF EVIL** • 1972

GEMISCHTE FRAUENCHOR, DER • 1916 • Lubitsch Ernst • FRG
GEMMA • 1949 • Serna Rene • MXC • SECRETO DE MUERTE
GEMMA ORIENTALE DI PAPA, LA • 1946 • Blasetti Alessandro • DOC • ITL
GEMS FROM GEMINI • 1966 • Tendlar Dave • ANS • USA
GEMS OF LITERATURE • 1923 • *Godal Edward (P)* • SER • UKN
GEMS OF THE SCREEN (USA) see **Q-RIOSITIES BY "Q"** • 1922
GEMUTLICH BEIM KAFFEE • 1898 • Messter Oskar • FRG
GEN. MARION, THE SWAMP FOX • 1911 • *Champion* • USA
GEN. MEADE'S FIGHTING DAYS • 1911 • *Champion* • USA
GEN TO FUDO MYOO • 1962 • Inagaki Hiroshi • JPN • YOUTH AND HIS AMULET, THE (USA)
GENBAKU NO KO • 1952 • Shindo Kaneto • JPN • CHILDREN OF THE ATOM BOMB ○ CHILDREN OF HIROSHIMA ○ ATOM BOMBED CHILDREN
GENBOERNE • 1940 • *Henning-Jensen* • DNM
GENC ASLANLAR • 1967 • Ucak Fikret • TRK • YOUNG LIONS, THE
GENCLIK TURKUSU • 1967 • Saner Hulki • TRK • SONG OF YOUTH, A
GENDAI AI NO JITEN: SHIRITAI TOSHIGORO • 1967 • Yamamoto Shinya • JPN • CONTEMPORARY DICTIONARY OF LOVE: AGE OF CURIOSITY
GENDAI AKUTO JINGI • 1965 • Nakahira Ko • JPN • MORAL OF MODERN HOOLIGANS, THE
GENDAI INCHIKI MONOGATARI • 1964 • Masumura Yasuzo • JPN
GENDAI JOI IGAKU • 1967 • Ogawa Kinya • JPN • CONTEMPORARY MEDICAL SCIENCE ON WOMEN
GENDAI KUNOICHI NIKU JIGOKU • 1968 • Mukoi Hiroshi • JPN • INFERNO OF THE FLESH
GENDAI NO JOO • 1924 • Mizoguchi Kenji • JPN • QUEEN OF MODERN TIMES, THE (USA) ○ GENDAI NO JOWO
GENDAI NO JOWO see **GENDAI NO JOO** • 1924
GENDAI NO KYOGU • 1967 • Ito Fumihiro • JPN • CONTEMPORARY HORROR
GENDAI NO YOKUBO • 1956 • Maruyama Seiji • JPN • AMBITION
GENDAIJIN • 1952 • Shibuya Minoru • JPN • POSTWAR JAPANESE ○ MODERNS, THE
GENDARME A NEW YORK, LE • 1965 • Girault Jean • FRN, ITL • TRE GENDARMI A NEW YORK (ITL)
GENDARME DE CHAMPIGNOL, LE • 1959 • Bastia Jean • FRN
GENDARME DE LA ESQUINA, EL • 1950 • Pardave Joaquin • MXC
GENDARME DE SAINT-TROPEZ, LE • 1964 • Girault Jean • FRN, ITL • RAGGAZZA A SAINT TROPEZ, UNA (ITL) ○ GENDARME OF SAINT TROPEZ, THE
GENDARME DESCONOCIDO, EL • 1941 • Delgado Miguel M. • MXC • UNKNOWN POLICEMAN, THE
GENDARME EN BALLADE, LE • 1970 • Girault Jean • FRN, ITL • 6 GENDARMI IN FUGA (ITL) ○ BALLADE DU GENDARME, LA
GENDARME EST SAN PITIE, LE • 1932 • Autant-Lara Claude • FRN
GENDARME EST SANS CULOTTE, LE • 1914 • Feuillade Louis • FRN
GENDARME ET LES EXTRA-TERRESTRES, LE • 1978 • Girault Jean • FRN
GENDARME ET LES GENDARMETTES • 1982 • Girault Jean, Aboyantz Tony • FRN
GENDARME OF SAINT TROPEZ, THE see **GENDARME DE SAINT-TROPEZ, LE** • 1964
GENDARME SE MARIE, LE • 1968 • Girault Jean • FRN, ITL • CALMA RAGAZZO, OGGI MI SPOSO (ITL)
GENDARMES, LES • 1907 • Blache Alice • FRN
GENDRE DE MONSIEUR POIRIER, LE • 1933 • Pagnol Marcel • FRN
GENDRE INGENIEUX, L • 1911 • Desfontaines Henri • FRN
GENE • 1986 • Vassev Pavel • DOC • BUL
GENE AUTRY AND THE MOUNTIES • 1951 • English John • USA
GENE KRUPA, AMERICA'S ACE DRUMMER MAN AND HIS ORCHESTRA • 1941 • Roush Leslie • SHT • USA
GENE KRUPA AND HIS ORCHESTRA see **DEEP PURPLE** • 1949
GENE KRUPA STORY, THE • 1960 • Weis Don • USA • DRUM CRAZY (UKN)
GENE OF THE NORTHLAND • 1915 • Clark Jack J. • USA
GENE THE MATCHMAKER • 1910 • *Vitagraph* • USA
GENEALOGY • 1978 • Lim Kwon-Taek • SKR
GENERACION HALLEY, LA • 1986 • Urguelles Thaelman • VNZ • HALLEY GENERATION, THE
GENERAL see **GENERALEN** • 1930
GENERAL, LE see **REBELLE, LE** • 1930
GENERAL, THE • 1917 • Hotaling Arthur D. • USA
GENERAL, THE • 1927 • Keaton Buster, Bruckman Clyde • USA
GENERAL, THE • 1930 • Grinde Nick • SHT • USA
GENERAL, THE see **LAST COMMAND, THE** • 1928
GENERAL, THE see **VIRTUOUS SIN, THE** • 1930
GENERAL, THE see **KAKKA** • 1940
GENERAL, THE see **GENERALEN** • 1966
GENERAL A VOS ORDRES • 1931 • Diamant-Berger Henri • FRN
GENERAL AMIN (UKN) see **IDI AMIN DADA** • 1974
GENERAL AND A FLY, A • 1961 • Zitzman Jerzy • ANS • PLN
GENERAL AND DAISIES, THE • 1964 • Chiaureli Mikhail • USS
GENERAL ASSEMBLY see **ASAMBLEA GENERAL** • 1960
GENERAL BABKA • 1924 • Curtiz Michael • AUS
GENERAL BUNKO'S VICTORY • 1913 • *Brennan John E.* • USA
GENERAL CONFUSION (USA) see **ALLE STEHEN KOPF** • 1940
GENERAL CRACK • 1929 • Crosland Alan • USA
GENERAL CUSTER AT THE LITTLE BIG HORN • 1926 • Fraser Harry L. • USA • WITH GENERAL CUSTER AT LITTLE BIG HORN
GENERAL DAFT • 1912 • *Lubin* • USA
GENERAL DE L'ARMEE MORTE, LE (FRN) see **GENERALE DELL'ARMATA MORTA, IL** • 1983
GENERAL DELLA ROVERE, LE (FRN) see **GENERALE DELLA ROVERE, IL** • 1959
GENERAL DIED AT DAWN, THE • 1936 • Milestone Lewis • USA • CHINESE GOLD
GENERAL DORME IN PIEDI, IL • 1972 • Massaro Francesco • ITL
GENERAL FREDERICK • 1966 • Erler Rainer • FRG
GENERAL GABALDON IN THE TIME OF DICTATORS CASTRO AND GOMEZ see **TIEMPOS DE CASTRO Y GOMEZ APROXIMACION AL GENERAL GABALDON** • 1974
GENERAL GINSBURG • 1930 • Sandrich Mark • SHT • USA
GENERAL HOUSECLEANING (USA) see **GROSSREINEMACHEN** • 1935
GENERAL IDI AMIN DADA: AUTOPORTRAIT see **IDI AMIN DADA** • 1974
GENERAL IDI AMIN DADA (USA) see **IDI AMIN DADA** • 1974
GENERAL JOHN REGAN • 1921 • Shaw Harold • UKN
GENERAL JOHN REGAN • 1933 • Edwards Henry • UKN
GENERAL JOSE'S ODYSSEY see **ODISEA DEL GENERAL JOSE, LA** • 1968
GENERAL KATO'S FALCON FIGHTERS see **KATO HAYABUSA SENTOTAI** • 1944
GENERAL LINE, THE see **STAROIE I NOVOIE** • 1929
GENERAL MASSACRE • 1971 • Jerger Burr • BLG
GENERAL MIXUP • 1916 • *Jockey* • USA
GENERAL NOGI AND KUMA-SAN (USA) see **NOGI TAISHO TO KUMA-SAN** • 1926
GENERAL NOUS VOILA! • 1978 • Besnard Jacques • FRN
GENERAL NUISANCE • 1941 • *Keaton Buster* • SHT • USA
GENERAL OF THE DEAD ARMY, THE see **GENERALE DELL'ARMATA MORTA, IL** • 1983
GENERAL POST • 1920 • Bentley Thomas • UKN
GENERAL RAKHIMOV • 1968 • Sabitov Zakir • USS
GENERAL SCOTT'S PROTEGE • 1913 • *Pathe* • USA
GENERAL SPANKY • 1936 • Douglas Gordon, Newmeyer Fred • USA
GENERAL, STAFF OFFICER AND SOLDIERS see **SHOGUN TO SAMBO TO HEI** • 1942
GENERAL SUVOROV see **SUVOROV** • 1941
GENERAL VON DOBELN • 1942 • Molander Olof • SWD
GENERAL WALTER see **WALTER** • 1971
GENERAL YAMASHITA see **TOMOYUKI YAMASHITA** • 1953
GENERALE DELLA ROVERE, IL • 1959 • Rossellini Roberto • ITL, FRN • GENERAL DELLA ROVERE, LE (FRN)
GENERALE DELL'ARMATA MORTA, IL • 1983 • Tovoli Luciano • ITL, FRN • GENERAL DE L'ARMEE MORTE, LE (FRN) ○ GENERAL OF THE DEAD ARMY, THE
GENERALEN • 1930 • Bergman Gustaf • SWD • GENERAL
GENERALEN • 1966 • Hastrup Jannik • DNM • GENERAL, THE
GENERALENS BORN (DNM) see **KINDER DES GENERALS, DIE** • 1912
GENERALNAYA LINIYA see **STAROIE I NOVOIE** • 1929
GENERALS AND SOLDIERS see **SHOGUN TO SAMBO TO HEI** • 1942
GENERAL'S DAUGHTER, THE • 1911 • *Talmadge Norma* • USA
GENERAL'S DAUGHTER, THE see **PASA KIZI** • 1967
GENERAL'S DAUGHTER, THE see **DE TODOS MODOS JUAN TE LLAMAS** • 1976
GENERAL'S DAUGHTER, THE see **PUTRI SEORANG JENDERAL** • 1983
GENERALS OF TOMORROW (UKN) see **TOUCHDOWN, ARMY!** • 1938
GENERAL'S ONLY SON, THE • 1911 • Bouwmeester Theo • UKN
GENERAL'S SON, THE see **PASAZADE** • 1967
GENERALS WITHOUT BUTTONS (USA) see **GUERRE DES GOSSES, LA** • 1936
GENERATION • 1956 • Harris Hilary • USA
GENERATION • 1969 • Schaefer George • USA • TIME FOR GIVING, A (UKN)
GENERATION • 1985 • Tuchner Michael • TVM • USA
GENERATION, A (USA) see **POKOLENIE** • 1954
GENERATION, LA • 1964 • Shawqi Khalil • EGY
GENERATION DE LA GUERRE • 1971 • Fares Tewfik • ALG
GENERATION DU DESERT, LA • 1957 • Stephane Nicole • SHT • FRN • DESERT GENERATION, THE
GENERATION GAP • 1973 • Hickling Peter • UKN
GENERATION OF CONQUERORS see **POKOLENIYE POBEDITELI** • 1936
GENERATION SPONTANEE • 1909 • Cohl Emile • ANS • FRN • SPONTANEOUS GENERATION ○ GENERATIONS COMIQUES, LES
GENERATIONS COMIQUES, LES see **GENERATION SPONTANEE** • 1909
GENERATIONS OF RESISTANCE • 1980 • Davis Peter • USA
GENEROSITY see **AEDAL DAAD** • 1911
GENEROSITY OF MR. SMITH, THE • 1912 • Buckland Warwick? • UKN
GENEROUS COWBOYS • 1911 • *Bison* • USA
GENEROUS CUSTOMERS • 1910 • Melies Gaston • USA
GENEROUS EVENING see **SCHEDRYI VECHER** • 1980
GENESE, LA • 1973 • Alibert Pierre • ANM • FRN
GENESE D'UN REPAS • 1978 • Moullet Luc • DOC • FRN
GENESIS • 1966 • Merglova Jan • CZC
GENESIS • 1985 • Sen Mrinal • IND
GENESIS see **TOMORROW'S CHILD** • 1982
GENESIS: 4-9 • 1913 • Smalley Phillips • USA
GENESIS -A BAND IN CONCERT • 1976 • Maylam Tony • DOC • UKN
GENESIS I • 1968 • *Childs Reg* • CMP • USA
GENESIS II • 1969 • *Childs Reg* • CMP • USA
GENESIS II • 1973 • Moxey John Llewellyn • TVM • USA
GENESIS III • 1970 • *Childs Reg* • CMP • USA
GENESIS IV • 1971 • *Childs Reg* • CMP • USA
GENESUNG • 1956 • Wolf Konrad • GDR • RECOVERY
GENETIC CONTACT see **ANNA TO THE INFINITE POWER** • 1982
GENETICA EN CUBA, LA • 1967 • Villafuerte Santiago • DOC • CUB
GENEVIEVE • 1923 • Poirier Leon • FRN
GENEVIEVE • 1953 • Cornelius Henry • UKN
GENEVIEVE see **ENTRE LA MER ET L'EAU DOUCE** • 1967
GENGHIS KHAN • 1965 • Levin Henry • USA, YGS, FRG • DSCHINGIS KHAN ○ DZINGIS-KAN
GENGHIS KHAN see **GENGIS KHAN** • 1952
GENGHIS KHAN see **CHENGJI SIHAN** • 1985
GENGHIS KHAN AND HIS MONGOLS see **KING OF THE MONGOLS** • 1960
GENGIS KHAN • 1952 • Salvador Lou • PHL • GENGHIS KHAN ○ GHENGIS KHAN
GENIAL DETECTIVE PETER PEREZ, EL • 1952 • Delgado Agustin P. • MXC • PETER PEREZ DE PERALVILLO
GENIE, THE • 1953 • Comfort Lance • UKN
GENIE, THE • 1957 • Lewis Al • SHT • USA
GENIE DE FEU, LE • 1908 • Melies Georges • FRN • GENII OF FIRE, THE (USA)
GENIE DE L'INSTANT, LE • 1982 • Simoneau Yves • CND
GENIE DES CLOCHES, LES • 1908 • Melies Georges • FRN • FETE DU SONNEUR, LA ○ SPIRIT OF THE BELLS, THE
GENIE, DEUX ASSOCIES, UNE CLOCHE, UN (FRN) see **GENIO, DUE COMPARI, UN POLLO, UN** • 1976
GENIE WITH THE LIGHT TOUCH, THE • 1972 • Smith Paul J. • ANS • USA
GENII • 1969 • Uher Stefan • CZC • DEVILS
GENII OF DARKNESS (USA) see **NOSTRADAMUS, EL GENIO DE LAS TINIEBLAS** • 1960
GENII OF FIRE, THE (USA) see **GENIE DE FEU, LE** • 1908
GENII OF THE VASE, THE • 1914 • *Shields Ernest* • SHT • USA
GENIO ALEGRE, EL • 1937 • Delgado Fernando • SPN
GENIO DEL MALE, IL • 1912 • Lolli Alberto Carlo • ITL
GENIO, DUE COMPARI, UN POLLO, UN • 1976 • Damiani Damiano, Leone Sergio • ITL, FRN • GENIE, DEUX ASSOCIES, UNE CLOCHE, UN (FRN) ○ NOBODY'S THE GREATEST
GENIO Y FIGURA • 1952 • Mendez Fernando • MXC
GENITORI IN BLUE-JEANS • 1960 • Mastrocinque Camillo • ITL
GENIUS • 1970 • Markopoulos Gregory J. • USA
GENIUS, THE • 1911 • *American* • USA
GENIUS, THE • 1914 • Henderson Dell • USA
GENIUS, THE • 1917 • Gillstrom Arvid E. • SHT • USA
GENIUS, THE see **SUPERSABIO, EL** • 1948
GENIUS AT FORT LAPAWAI, THE • 1913 • *Bartlett Charles* • USA
GENIUS AT WORK • 1946 • Goodwins Leslie • USA • MASTER MINDS
GENIUS IN THE FAMILY, A (UKN) see **SO GOES MY LOVE** • 1946
GENIUS -PIERRE, THE see **PAWN OF FATE, THE** • 1916
GENJI KOZO • 1928 • Inagaki Hiroshi • JPN
GENJI MONOGATARI • 1951 • Yoshimura Kozaburo • JPN • TALE FROM GENJI, A ○ TALE OF GENJI, A
GENJI MONOGATARI • 1966 • Ichikawa Kon • JPN • TALE OF GENJI, THE
GENKAI-NADA • 1975 • Kara Juro • JPN • SEA OF GENKAI, THE
GENKAI TSUREZURE BUSHI • 1985 • Deme Masanobu • JPN • BALLAD OF GENKAI-SEA
GENNAMA TO BIJO TO SAN-AKUNIN • 1958 • Ichikawa Kon • JPN • MONEY AND THREE BAD MEN
GENNEI TOU VORRA, I • 1969 • Carayannis Costa • GRC, ITL • BRAVE BUNCH, THE
GENNEM KAMP TIL SEJR • 1911 • Gad Urban • FRG • THROUGH TRIALS TO VICTORY
GENNEM MORKE TIL LYS • 1913 • Davidsen Hjalmar • DNM
GENOA EXIT, THE see **EXIT GENUA** • 1989
GENOCIDE • 1963 • Lemaire Yvan • BLG
GENOCIDE • 1981 • Schwartzman Arnold • DOC • USA
GENOCIDE (USA) see **KONCHU DAISENSO** • 1968
GENOESE DRAGNET see **PROCESSO CONTRO IGNOTI** • 1952
GENOPSTANDELSEN see **EN OPSTANDELSE** • 1914
GENOSSE MUNCHHAUSEN • 1962 • Neuss Wolfgang • FRG
GENOU DE CLAIRE, LE • 1971 • Rohmer Eric • FRN • CLAIRE'S KNEE (UKN)
GENOVA A MANO ARMATA • 1977 • Lanfranchi Mario • ITL
GENOVEFFA DI BRABANTE • 1947 • Zeglio Primo • ITL
GENOVEVA • 1951 • Rabenalt Arthur M. • FRG, ITL • LEGGENDA DI GENOVEFFA, LA (ITL)
GENOVEVA DE BRABANTE • 1967 • Monter Jose Luis • SPN, ITL
GENRE MASCULIN • 1977 • Marboeuf Jean • FRN
GENROKU BISHONEN-KI • 1955 • Ito Daisuke • JPN • GENROKU'S HANDSOME YOUTH
GENROKU CHUSHINGURA PART I • 1941 • Mizoguchi Kenji • JPN • LOYAL 47 OF THE GENROKU ERA, THE (UKN) ○ LOYAL 47, THE (USA) ○ 47 RONIN, THE
GENROKU CHUSHINGURA PART II • 1942 • Mizoguchi Kenji • JPN
GENROKU JUSANNEN • 1931 • Inagaki Hiroshi • JPN
GENROKU ONNA • 1924 • *Tanaka Kinuyo* • JPN • WOMAN FROM THE GENROKU ERA, A ○ WOMAN OF THE GENROKU ERA, A
GENROKU'S HANDSOME YOUTH see **GENROKU BISHONEN-KI** • 1955
GENS D'ABITIBI • 1980 • Perrault Pierre, Gosselin Bernard • CND
GENS DE LA CAVE, LES • 1968 • Derkaoui Mustafa • SHT • PLN
GENS DE MATAPIT, LES • 1956 • Vilardebo Carlos • SHT • FRN
GENS DE PARTOUT, GENS DE NULLE PART • 1981 • Sarmiento Valeria • FRN • PEOPLE FROM EVERYWHERE, PEOPLE FROM NOWHERE
GENS DU MIL, LES • 1951 • Rouch Jean • FRN • CULTURE DU MIL, LA
GENS DU VOYAGE, LES • 1937 • Feyder Jacques • FRN • WANDERERS, THE
GENS QUI PLEURENT ET GENS QUI RIENT • 1900 • Melies Georges • FRN • CRYING AND LAUGHING (USA)
GENT FROM HONDURAS, THE • 1912 • *Errol Eileen* • USA
GENTE, LA • 1973 • de la Cerda Clemente • DOC • VNZ • FOLKS
GENTE ALEGRE • 1933 • Venturini Edward D.
GENTE BIEN • 1939 • Romero Manuel
GENTE CONMIGO • 1967 • Darnell Jorge • ARG • NATION WITH ME, A
GENTE COSI • 1950 • Cerchio Fernando • ITL • MISTRESS OF THE MOUNTAINS (USA)
GENTE DA PRAIA DE VIEIRA • 1976 • Campos Antonio • PRT
GENTE DA VIA • 1938 • Telmo Cottinelli • SHT • PRT

GENTE DEL METRO • 1976 • Morales Carlos • SPN • METRO PEOPLE
GENTE DEL PO • 1947 • Antonioni Michelangelo • DCS • ITL
GENTE DELL'ARIA • 1943 • Pratelli Esodo • ITL
GENTE DI RISPETTO • 1975 • Zampa Luigi • ITL • FLOWER IN HIS MOUTH, THE (USA)
GENTE D'ONORE • 1968 • Lulli Folco • ITL • PEOPLE OF HONOUR
GENTE EN BUENOS AIRES • 1974 • Landeck Eva • ARG • PEOPLE IN BUENOS AIRES
GENTE EN LA PLAYA • 1961 • Almendros Nestor • DCS • CUB
GENTE FELICE • 1957 • Loy Mino • ITL • BENVENUTO ONOREVOLE
GENTE PER BENE see **IMPIEGATA DI PAPA, L'** • 1933
GENTE SIN IMPORTANCIA • 1950 • Gonzalez Jose • SPN
GENTILEZZA DEL TOCCO, LA • 1988 • Calogero Francesco • ITL • GENTLE TOUCH, THE
GENTILHOMME COMMERCANT, LE • 1918 • Bernard Raymond • FRN
GENTILHOMME PAUVRE, LE • 1918-19 • du Plessis Armand • BLG
GENTILUOMO D'AMORE see **NEZ-DE-CUIR** • 1952
GENTLE ANNIE • 1944 • Marton Andrew • USA
GENTLE ARM, THE see **STREET CORNER** • 1953
GENTLE ART OF BURGLARY, THE • 1916 • Schrock Raymond L. • SHT • USA
GENTLE ART OF FISHING, THE • 1916 • Page Will • UKN
GENTLE ART OF MURDER, THE (UKN) see **CRIME NE PAIE PAS, LE** • 1962
GENTLE ART OF NORMAN MCLAREN, THE • McLaren Norman, Millar Gavin • UKN
GENTLE ART OF SEDUCTION, THE see **CHASSE A L'HOMME, LA** • 1964
GENTLE CONSPIRACY, THE • 1916 • Le Viness Carl M. • SHT • USA
GENTLE CORSICAN, THE • 1956 • Simmons Anthony • UKN
GENTLE CREATURE, A (UKN) see **FEMME DOUCE, UNE** • 1969
GENTLE CYCLONE, THE • 1926 • Van Dyke W. S. • USA
GENTLE DOCTOR, THE • 1921 • Paul Fred • UKN
GENTLE GANGSTER, THE • 1943 • Rosen Phil • USA
GENTLE GIANT • 1967 • Neilson James • USA
GENTLE GUNMAN, THE • 1952 • Dearden Basil, Relph Michael • UKN
GENTLE HABITS see **BRANDOS COSTUMES** • 1975
GENTLE INTRUDER, THE • 1917 • Kirkwood James • USA
GENTLE JULIA • 1923 • Lee Rowland V. • USA
GENTLE JULIA • 1936 • Blystone John G. • USA
GENTLE LOVE (UKN) see **TU SERAS TERRIBLEMENT GENTILLE** • 1968
GENTLE ONE, THE see **NEZNA** • 1968
GENTLE PEOPLE, THE • 1972 • *Mcbride Patsy* • USA
GENTLE PEOPLE, THE see **OUT OF THE FOG** • 1941
GENTLE PERSUASION see **ART OF GENTLE PERSUASION, THE** • 1970
GENTLE RAIN, THE • 1966 • Balaban Burt • USA, BRZ
GENTLE SAVAGE • 1978 • MacGregor Sean • USA
GENTLE SERGEANT, THE (UKN) see **THREE STRIPES IN THE SUN** • 1955
GENTLE SEX, THE • 1908 • *Essanay* • USA
GENTLE SEX, THE • 1943 • Howard Leslie, Elvey Maurice • UKN
GENTLE SEX, THE see **BUNDFALD** • 1957
GENTLE SINNERS • 1984 • Till Eric • CND
GENTLE STRANGERS • 1972 • Holmes Cecil • ASL
GENTLE TERROR, THE • 1962 • Marshall Frank • UKN
GENTLE THIEF OF LOVE see **UNDERBARA LOGNEN, DEN** • 1955
GENTLE TOUCH, THE see **GENTILEZZA DEL TOCCO, LA** • 1988
GENTLE TOUCH, THE (USA) see **FEMININE TOUCH, THE** • 1956
GENTLE TRAP, THE • 1960 • Saunders Charles • UKN
GENTLE VOLUNTEER, A • 1916 • Wilson Ben • SHT • USA
GENTLEMAN, THE • 1925 • Elliott William J. • UKN
GENTLEMAN AFTER DARK • 1942 • Marin Edwin L. • USA
GENTLEMAN AFTER MIDNIGHT see **IT'S LOVE I'M AFTER** • 1937
GENTLEMAN AT HEART, A • 1942 • McCarey Ray • USA • HELIOTROPE HARRY
GENTLEMAN ATT HYRA • 1940 • Arvedson Ragnar • SWD • GENTLEMAN FOR HIRE
GENTLEMAN AUF ZEIT • 1924 • Gerhardt Karl • FRG
GENTLEMAN BANDIT, THE • 1981 • Kaplan Jonathan • TVM • USA
GENTLEMAN BEGGAR, THE • 1905 • Collins Alf? • UKN
GENTLEMAN BURGLAR, THE • 1908 • Porter Edwin S. • USA
GENTLEMAN BURGLAR, THE • 1915 • Martin E. A. • USA
GENTLEMAN BURGLAR, THE • 1926 • Barnett Charles • UKN
GENTLEMAN BUSHRANGER, THE • 1921 • Smith Beaumont • ASL
GENTLEMAN CHAUFFEUR, THE (UKN) see **WHAT A MAN!** • 1930
GENTLEMAN DAKU • 1937 • *Biswas Anil (M)* • IND
GENTLEMAN DE COCODY, LE • 1965 • Christian-Jaque • FRN, ITL • DONNE, MITRA E DIAMANTI (ITL) ○ IVORY COAST ADVENTURE (UKN) ○ MAN FROM COCODY (USA)
GENTLEMAN D'EPSOM, LE • 1962 • Grangier Gilles • FRN, ITL
GENTLEMAN FOR A DAY, A • 1914 • *Benham Leland* • USA
GENTLEMAN FOR A DAY (UKN) see **UNION DEPOT** • 1932
GENTLEMAN FOR HIRE see **GENTLEMAN ATT HYRA** • 1940
GENTLEMAN FROM AMERICA, THE • 1923 • Sedgwick Edward • USA
GENTLEMAN FROM ARIZONA, THE • 1939 • Haley Earl • USA
GENTLEMAN FROM BLUE GULCH, THE see **CONVERSION OF FROSTY BLAKE, THE** • 1915
GENTLEMAN FROM CALIFORNIA, THE see **CALIFORNIANS, THE** • 1937
GENTLEMAN FROM DIXIE • 1942 • Herman Al • USA
GENTLEMAN FROM INDIANA, A • 1915 • Lloyd Frank • USA
GENTLEMAN FROM LOUISIANA, THE • 1936 • Pichel Irving • USA
GENTLEMAN FROM MISSISSIPPI, THE • 1914 • Sargent George L. • USA
GENTLEMAN FROM NOWHERE, THE • 1948 • Castle William • USA
GENTLEMAN FROM TEXAS, THE • 1946 • Hillyer Lambert • USA
GENTLEMAN GANGSTER see **GENTLEMANNAGANGSTERN** • 1941
GENTLEMAN GYPSY, THE • 1908 • Fitzhamon Lewin • UKN • TRIALS OF A GYPSY GENTLEMAN, THE
GENTLEMAN IN BLUE, THE • 1917 • *Kinematograph Concessions* • UKN
GENTLEMAN IN MUFTI, A • 1924 • Longford Raymond • ASL
GENTLEMAN IN THE HOUSE, THE see **HERR IM HAUS, DER** • 1940
GENTLEMAN JEKYLL AND DRIVER HYDE • 1950 • *International* • SHT • CND
GENTLEMAN JIM • 1942 • Walsh Raoul • USA
GENTLEMAN JOE • 1912 • *Lubin* • USA
GENTLEMAN JOE PALOOKA • 1946 • Endfield Cy • USA
GENTLEMAN JOE.. UCCIDI! • 1967 • Stegani Giorgio • ITL
GENTLEMAN MAYBE, A see **KANSKE EN GENTLEMAN** • 1935
GENTLEMAN MISBEHAVES, THE • 1946 • Sherman George • USA
GENTLEMAN OF ART, A • 1915 • Paton Stuart • USA
GENTLEMAN OF FASHION, A • 1913 • Baker George D. • USA
GENTLEMAN OF FORTUNE, A • 1912 • Fahrney Milton • USA
GENTLEMAN OF FORTUNE, THE • 1972 • Sery A. • USS
GENTLEMAN OF FRANCE, A • 1903 • Blackton J. Stuart • USA
GENTLEMAN OF FRANCE, A • 1921 • Elvey Maurice • UKN
GENTLEMAN OF LEISURE, A • 1914 • *Essanay* • USA
GENTLEMAN OF LEISURE, A • 1915 • Melford George • USA
GENTLEMAN OF LEISURE, A • 1916 • *Hippo* • USA
GENTLEMAN OF LEISURE, A • 1923 • Henabery Joseph • USA
GENTLEMAN OF NERVE, A • 1917 • De Haven Carter • SHT • USA
GENTLEMAN OF PARIS, A • 1927 • D'Arrast Harry D'Abbadie • USA
GENTLEMAN OF PARIS, A • 1931 • Hill Sinclair • UKN
GENTLEMAN OF QUALITY, A • 1919 • Young James • USA
GENTLEMAN OF THE ROAD -CAPTAIN STARLIGHT see **CAPTAIN STARLIGHT -GENTLEMAN OF THE ROAD** • 1911
GENTLEMAN OF THE ROOM see **KAMMARJUNKAREN** • 1914
GENTLEMAN OF THE STREETS see **MAN OF THE WORLD** • 1931
GENTLEMAN OF VENTURE • 1940 • Stein Paul L. • UKN • IT HAPPENED TO ONE MAN (USA)
GENTLEMAN OR THIEF? • 1912 • Cabanne W. Christy • USA
GENTLEMAN OR THIEF • 1914 • Henderson Dell • USA
GENTLEMAN PREFERRED, A • 1928 • Hotaling Arthur D. • USA
GENTLEMAN RANKER, THE • 1912 • Martinek H. O.? • UKN
GENTLEMAN RANKER, THE • 1913 • Aylott Dave • UKN • NOT GUILTY (USA) ○ RAISED FROM THE RANKS
GENTLEMAN RIDER, THE • 1919 • West Walter • UKN • HEARTS AND SADDLES
GENTLEMAN ROUGHNECK, A • 1925 • Jones Grover • USA
GENTLEMAN TRAMP, THE • 1975 • Patterson Richard • DOC • USA
GENTLEMAN UNAFRAID • 1923 • *Larkin George* • USA
GENTLEMAN WITH A BRIEF-CASE see **HERRE MED PORTFOLJ** • 1943
GENTLEMAN WITH GUNS • 1946 • Newfield Sam • USA
GENTLEMANNAGANGSTERN • 1941 • Hildebrand Weyler • SWD • GENTLEMAN GANGSTER
GENTLEMAN'S AGREEMENT • 1935 • Pearson George • UKN
GENTLEMAN'S AGREEMENT • 1947 • Kazan Elia • USA
GENTLEMAN'S AGREEMENT, A • 1915 • *Reeves Edith* • USA
GENTLEMAN'S AGREEMENT, A • 1918 • Smith David • USA
GENTLEMAN'S FATE • 1931 • LeRoy Mervyn • USA
GENTLEMAN'S GENTLEMAN, A • 1913 • Merwin Bannister • USA
GENTLEMAN'S GENTLEMAN, A • 1939 • Neill R. William • UKN
GENTLEMAN'S GENTLEMAN, A • 1941 • Geronimi Clyde • ANS • USA
GENTLEMEN, THE • 1987 • el Mihi Rafaat • EGY
GENTLEMEN ARE BORN • 1934 • Green Alfred E. • USA
GENTLEMEN BITTEN ZUR KASSE, DIE • 1965 • Olden John, Witt Claus Peter • MTV • FRG • GREAT BRITISH TRAIN ROBBERY, THE (USA) ○ POSTZUG-UBERFALL, DER
GENTLEMEN-GAUNER • 1920 • Zeyn Willy • FRG
GENTLEMEN GO BY, THE • 1948 • Newman Joan Widgey, Calthrop John • UKN
GENTLEMEN, I HAVE KILLED EINSTEIN see **ZABIL JSEM EINSTEINA, PANOVE** • 1969
GENTLEMEN IN ROOM 8 • 1951 • Hammid Alexander • USA
GENTLEMEN IN UNIFORM see **KRONANS KAVALJERER** • 1930
GENTLEMEN MARRY BRUNETTES • 1955 • Sale Richard • USA
GENTLEMEN OF NERVE • 1914 • Chaplin Charles • USA • SOME NERVE ○ CHARLIE AT THE RACES
GENTLEMEN OF THE NAVY see **FLOTTANS KAVALJERER** • 1949
GENTLEMEN OF THE NAVY (UKN) see **ANNAPOLIS FAREWELL** • 1935
GENTLEMEN OF THE NIGHT see **VENDICATORE MASCHERATO, IL** • 1964
GENTLEMEN OF THE PRESS • 1929 • Webb Millard • USA
GENTLEMEN OF THE WEST (UKN) see **HOODOO RANCH** • 1926
GENTLEMEN PREFER BLONDES • 1953 • Hawks Howard • USA
GENTLEMEN PREFER BLONDS • 1928 • St. Clair Malcolm • USA
GENTLEMEN PREFER NATURE GIRLS • 1963 • Wishman Doris • USA
GENTLEMEN PREFER SCOTCH • 1927 • Marshall George • SHT • USA
GENTLEMEN, THE BOYS see **PANI KLUCI** • 1975
GENTLEMEN THE CHORUS NO.1 • 1929 • *Bsfp* • SHT • UKN • CAMERA COCKTALES NO.3
GENTLEMEN THE CHORUS NO.2 • 1929 • *Bsfp* • SHT • UKN • MUSICAL MEDLEY NO.4
GENTLEMEN, WHO THREW THAT? • Urban Ivan, Stepanek Miroslav, Pojar Bretislav • ANS • CZC
GENTLY PASSED ANASTASIA see **DUIOS ANASTASIA TRECEA** • 1979
GENTLY WAS ANASTASIA PASSING see **DUIOS ANASTASIA TRECEA** • 1979
GENTRY SKYLARKING see **URI MURI** • 1949
GENTS IN A JAM • 1952 • Bernds Edward • SHT • USA
GENTS WITHOUT CENTS • 1944 • White Jules • SHT • USA
GENUINE • 1920 • Wiene Robert • FRG
GENUINE ENGLAND • 1976 • Ashton Dudley Shaw • DOC • UKN
GEO LE MYSTERIEUX • 1916 • Dulac Germaine • FRN • VRAIE RICHESSE, LA ○ MYSTERIOUS GEORGE ○ TRUE WEALTH
GEOGRAPHIE ET CINQ MEDIA, LA • 1970 • Moreau Michel • DCS • CND
GEOGRAPHY FILMS • 1944-49 • *Leacock Richard (Ph)* • DSS • USA
GEOGRAPHY LESSON, THE • 1931 • Grinde Nick • SHT • USA
GEOGRAPHY OF THE BODY • 1943 • Maas Willard • SHT • USA
GEOLE, LA • 1921 • Ravel Gaston
GEOMETRA PRINETTI SELVAGGIAMENTE OSVALDO • 1976 • Baldi Ferdinando • ITL
GEOMETRIE • 1966 • Beaudin Jean • SER • CND
GEOMETRISCHE EEND, DE • 1966 • van Maelder Louis • BLG
GEOPFERT.. • 1916 • Schmidthassler Walter • FRG
GEORDIE • 1955 • Launder Frank • UKN • WEE GEORDIE (USA)
GEORG • 1964 • Kaye Stanton • USA
GEORG ELSER -EINER AUS DEUTSCHLAND • 1989 • Brandauer Klaus Maria • FRG
GEORGE • 1963 • Leenhardt Roger • DCS • FRN
GEORGE! • 1970 • Bennett Wallace C. • USA, SWT
GEORGE AND JUNIOR see **HALF-PINT PIGMY** • 1948
GEORGE AND MARGARET • 1940 • King George • UKN
GEORGE AND MILDRED • 1980 • Frazer-Jones Peter • UKN
GEORGE AND ROSEMARY • 1987 • Snowden Alison, Fine David • ANM • CND
GEORGE AND THE STAR • 1985 • Potterton Gerald • MTV • CND • GEORGE ET L'ETOILE
GEORGE BARNWELL THE LONDON APPRENTICE • 1913 • Plumb Hay • UKN • IN THE TOILS OF THE TEMPTRESS (USA)
GEORGE BERNARD SHAW • 1957 • Ashton Dudley Shaw • SHT • UKN
GEORGE BIZET, COMPOSER OF CARMEN • 1938 • Fitzpatrick James A. • UKN
GEORGE BULLY • 1920 • Obal Max • FRG
GEORGE CLARK IN HIS FIRST CAR see **HIS FIRST CAR** • 1930
GEORGE DUMPSON'S PLACE • 1963 • Emshwiller Ed • SHT • USA
GEORGE ET L'ETOILE see **GEORGE AND THE STAR** • 1985
GEORGE FREDERICK HANDEL 1685-1759 • 1985 • Palmer Tony • UKN
GEORGE IN CIVVY STREET • 1946 • Varnel Marcel • UKN • REMEMBER THE UNICORN
GEORGE JESSEL AND HIS RUSSIAN ART CHOIR • 1931 • *Vitaphone Variety* • SHT • USA
GEORGE KASTRIOT -SKANDERBEG • Xhako Marianthi • DOC • ALB
GEORGE M. COHAN IN A LIBERTY LOAN APPEAL • 1918 • *Paramount* • SHT • USA
GEORGE MCKENNA STORY, THE • 1986 • Laneuville Eric • TVM • USA
GEORGE MOZART IN DOMESTIC TROUBLES • 1930 • *Balcon Michael (P)* • SHT • UKN
GEORGE QUI? • 1972 • Rosier Michele • FRN
GEORGE RAFT STORY, THE • 1961 • Newman Joseph M. • USA • SPIN OF A COIN (UKN)
GEORGE RANDALL AND BABE SCOTT IN THE IMPOSTER • 1932 • Hanna Pat • SHT • ASL
GEORGE ROBEY TURNS ANARCHIST • 1914 • *Burns Films* • UKN
GEORGE ROBEY'S DAY OFF • 1918 • Kinsella E. P., Morgan Horace • UKN
GEORGE STEVENS: A FILMAKER'S JOURNEY • 1984 • Stevens George Jr. • DOC • USA
GEORGE TAKES THE AIR (USA) see **IT'S IN THE AIR** • 1938
GEORGE WASHINGTON CARVER • 1940 • Parker Ben • USA
GEORGE WASHINGTON CARVER • 1959 • *Moss Carlton* • USA
GEORGE WASHINGTON COHEN • 1928 • Archainbaud George • USA
GEORGE WASHINGTON JONES • 1914 • France Charles H. • USA
GEORGE WASHINGTON, JR. • 1924 • St. Clair Malcolm • USA
GEORGE WASHINGTON SLEPT HERE • 1942 • Keighley William • USA
GEORGE WASHINGTON: THE FORGING OF A NATION • 1986 • Graham William A. • TVM • USA
GEORGE WASHINGTON'S ESCAPE • 1911 • Turner Otis • USA
GEORGE WHITE'S SCANDALS OF 1934 • 1934 • White George, Freeland Thornton, Lachman Harry • USA
GEORGE WHITE'S SCANDALS OF 1935 • 1935 • White George • USA
GEORGE WHITE'S SCANDALS OF 1945 • 1945 • Feist Felix E. • USA
GEORGES BRAQUE OU LE TEMPS DIFFERENT • 1974 • Rossif Frederic • DOC • FRN
GEORGES DANDIN see **DANDIN GYORGY** • 1955
GEORGES ET GEORGETTE • 1933 • Le Bon Roger, Schunzel Reinhold • FRN
GEORGES-ETIENNE CARTIER • 1962 • Howe John • CND
GEORGE'S FALSE ALARM • 1928 • Newfield Sam • SHT • USA
GEORGE'S ISLAND • 1990 • Donovan Paul • CND
GEORGE'S JOY RIDE • 1914 • Stow Percy • UKN
GEORGES-P. VANIER, SOLDAT, DIPLOMATE, GOUVERNEUR GENERAL • 1960 • Perron Clement • DCS • CND
GEORGE'S SCHOOL DAZE • 1927 • Newfield Sam • SHT • USA
GEORGETTE MEUNIER • 1988 • Stocklin Tania • SWT
GEORGI SAAKADZE PART I • 1942 • Chiaureli Mikhail • USS

GEORGI SAAKADZE PART II • 1943 • Chiaureli Mikhail • USS
GEORGIA • 1988 • Lewin Ben • ASL
GEORGIA see **FOUR FRIENDS** • 1981
GEORGIA COUNTY LOCKUP see **LUST FOR FREEDOM** • 1987
GEORGIA, GEORGIA • 1972 • Bjorkman Stig • SWD, USA
GEORGIA O'KEEFFE • 1947 • Rodakiewicz Henwar • USA
GEORGIA O'KEEFFE • 1977 • Adato Perry Miller • USA
GEORGIA PEACHES, THE • 1980 • Haller Daniel • TVM • USA
GEORGIA ROSE • 1930 • Gant Harry A. • USA
GEORGIA WEDDING, A • 1909 • Baker George D. • USA
GEORGIAN CHRONICLE OF THE NINETEENTH CENTURY • Rekhviashvili Aleksander • USS
GEORGIAN STATE DANCING COMPANY, THE • 1954 • Abuladze Tengiz, Chkheidze Revaz • DOC • USS
GEORGIA'S FRIENDS (UKN) see **FOUR FRIENDS** • 1981
GEORGIE AND THE DRAGON • 1951 • Cannon Robert • ANS • USA
GEORGINAS GRUNDE • 1974 • Schlondorff Volker • MTV • FRG, AUS • GEORGINA'S REASONS
GEORGINA'S REASONS see **GEORGINAS GRUNDE** • 1974
GEORGY GIRL • 1966 • Narizzano Silvio • UKN
GEPEITSCHT • 1919 • Boese Carl • FRG
GEPPO IL FOLLE • 1978 • Celentano Adriano • ITL
GERACAO BENDITA • 1972 • Bini Carlos • BRZ
GERAKS, THE see **GERATSITE** • 1958
GERALD CRANSTON'S LADY • 1924 • Flynn Emmett J. • USA
GERALD MANLEY HOPKINS • 1973 • Browne Peter Francis • SHT • UKN
GERALD MCBOING BOING • 1951 • Cannon Robert • ANS • USA
GERALD MCBOING BOING ON PLANET MOO • 1956 • Cannon Robert • ANS • USA
GERALD MCBOING BOING'S SYMPHONY • 1953 • Cannon Robert • ANS • USA
GERALD WILSON ALL-STAR ORCHESTRA • 1962 • Markas Gary • SHT • USA
GERALDINE • 1929 • Brown Melville • USA
GERALDINE • 1953 • Springsteen R. G. • USA
GERALDINE • 1987 • Fields Michael • USA
GERALDINE'S FIRST YEAR • 1922 • Cooper George A. • UKN
GERALD'S BUTTERFLY • 1911 • Bouwmeester Theo • UKN
GERALDTON • 1965 • McCullough Chris • DOC • ASL
GERANIUM • 1929 • Aylott Dave, Symmons E. F. • SHT • UKN
GERANIUM, A • 1911 • Brooke Van Dyke • USA
GERANIUM, THE • 1912 • *Dion Hector* • USA
GERARCHI SI MUORE • 1962 • Simonelli Giorgio C. • ITL
GERARD DE LA NUIT • 1955 • Hanoun Marcel • SHT • FRN
GERARD HAS HIS HAIR REMOVED WITH NAIR • 1967 • Warhol Andy • USA
GERARD MALANGA READS POETRY see **BUFFERIN** • 1966
GERATSITE • 1958 • Marinovich Anton • BUL • GERAKS, THE
GERDA FLOWERS POWERS • Lethem Roland • SHT • BLG
GERDABE GONAH • 1968 • Reis-Firouz Mehdi • IRN • WHIRLPOOL OF SIN, THE
GERDBADE ZENDEGI • 1968 • Fatemi Nezam • IRN • WHIRLWIND OF LIFE, THE
GERECHTIGKEIT • 1920 • Lux Stefan • FRG
GERETTET DURCH FUNKSPRUCH • 1923 • *Atlantik-Enterprises Inc.* • FRG
GERGASI • 1958 • *Shaw* • SNG
GERICHTSTAG • 1966 • Seggelke Herbert • FRG • TRIBUNAL
GERLA DI PAPA MARTIN, LA • 1909 • Caserini Mario • ITL
GERLA DI PAPA MARTIN, LA • 1940 • Bonnard Mario • ITL
GERLOVO EVENT see **GERLOVSKA ISTORYA** • 1971
GERLOVSKA ISTORYA • 1971 • Ostrovski Grisha • BUL • GERLOVO EVENT ○ INCIDENT AT GUERLOVO
GERM, THE • 1923 • McGreeney P. S. • USA
GERM GEM, A • 1916 • *Humphrey Orral* • SHT • USA
GERM IN THE KISS, THE • 1914 • *Powers* • USA
GERM OF MYSTERY, THE • 1916 • Daly William Robert • SHT • USA
GERMAINE • 1923 • Genina Augusto • ITL
GERMAINE GUEVREMONT, ROMANCIERE • 1958 • Patry Pierre • DCS • CND
GERMAN AIR-FORCE, THE see **FLIEGER.. FLIEGER.. KANONIERE!** • 1936
GERMAN BAND, THE • 1914 • *Lubin* • USA
GERMAN CALLING • 1942 • Lye Len • DCS • UKN
GERMAN DIARY, A see **DU BIST MEIN, EIN DEUTSCHES TAGEBUCH** • 1969
GERMAN MANPOWER • 1943 • Parrish Robert, Kanin Garson • DOC • USA
GERMAN SINGERS, THE • 1912 • *Lubin* • USA
GERMAN SISTERS, THE see **BLEIERNE ZEIT, DIE** • 1981
GERMAN SPY PERIL, THE • 1914 • Haldane Bert? • UKN
GERMAN STORY, THE see **DU UND MANCHER KAMARAD..** • 1956
GERMANIA, ANNO ZERO • 1947 • Rossellini Roberto • ITL, FRN, FRG • ALLEMAGNE, ANNEE ZERO (FRN) ○ GERMANY, YEAR ZERO ○ EVIL STREET
GERMANIA, SETTE DONNE A TESTA • 1970 • Nievo Stanis, Cavallina Paolo • ITL
GERMANIC LOVE see **GERMATIC LOVE** • 1916
GERMANIN • 1943 • Kimmich Max W. • FRG
GERMANS, THE • 1968 • Thorndike Andrew, Thorndike Annelie • DOC • GDR
GERMANS STRIKE AGAIN, THE see **YERMANI XANARHONTAI, I** • 1947
GERMANY • 1930 • *Holmes Burton* • USA
GERMANY -A REGIONAL GEOGRAPHY • 1964 • Rees Clive • DOC • UKN
GERMANY, BITTER LAND see **ALMANYA ACI VATAN** • 1980
GERMANY IN AUTUMN see **DEUTSCHLAND IM HERBST** • 1978
GERMANY -KEY TO EUROPE • 1953 • Dick Ronald • DCS • CND
GERMANY, PALE MOTHER see **DEUTSCHLAND, BLEICHE MUTTER** • 1980
GERMANY TODAY • 1923 • *Scott Walter K.* • DOC • USA
GERMANY, YEAR ZERO see **GERMANIA, ANNO ZERO** • 1947
GERMATIC LOVE • 1916 • Miller Rube • USA • GERMANIC LOVE
GERMINAL • 1913 • Capellani Albert • FRN
GERMINAL • 1963 • Allegret Yves • FRN, ITL, HNG • FURIA DEGLI UOMINI, LA (ITL)
GERMINATION D'UN HARICOT • 1928 • Dulac Germaine • DOC • FRN
GERMS AND MICROBES • 1916 • McKim Edwin • SHT • USA
GERN HAB' ICH DIE FRAUEN GEKILLT • 1966 • Soulanes Louis, Cardone Alberto, Reynolds Sheldon, Lynn Robert • AUS, FRN, ITL • CARNAVAL DES BARBOUZES, LE (FRN) ○ KILLER'S CARNIVAL (USA) ○ SPIE CONTRO IL MONDE
GERN HAB' ICH DIE FRAUEN GEKUSST • 1926 • Rahn Bruno • FRG • PAGANINI
GERN HAB' ICH DIE FRAU'N GEKUSST • 1934 • Emo E. W. • FRG • PAGANINI
GERO • 1927 • Ito Daisuke • JPN • SERVANT, THE
GERO NO KUBI • 1955 • Ito Daisuke • JPN • SERVANT'S NECK, THE
GEROI ARTIKI • 1934 • Troyanovsky Mark Antonovich, Shafran A. • USS • HEROES OF THE ARCTIC
GEROITE NA SHIPKA • 1955 • Vasiliev Sergei • BUL • HEROES OF SHIPKA ○ HEROS DE CHIPKA, LES
GERONIMO • 1939 • Sloane Paul • USA
GERONIMO • 1962 • Laven Arnold • USA
GERONIMO & SON • 1965 • Post Howard • ANS • USA
GERONIMO'S LAST RAID • 1912 • Hamilton G. P. • USA
GERONIMO'S REVENGE • 1962 • Keller Harry, Neilson James • MTV • USA
GERONTOKOROS, O • 1967 • Laskos Orestis • GRC • OLD BACHELOR, THE
GERT AND DAISY CLEAN UP • 1942 • Rogers Maclean • UKN
GERT AND DAISY'S WEEKEND • 1941 • Rogers Maclean • UKN
GERTIE GETS THE CASH • 1914 • *Roland Ruth* • USA
GERTIE ON TOUR • 1917 • *Mccay Winsor (P)* • ANS • USA
GERTIE THE DINOSAUR • Bray John R. • ANM • USA
GERTIE THE DINOSAUR • 1914 • McCay Winsor • USA • GERTIE THE TRAINED DINOSAUR
GERTIE THE TRAINED DINOSAUR see **GERTIE THE DINOSAUR** • 1914
GERTIE WAS A LADY see **STAR!** • 1968
GERTIE'S AWFUL FIX • 1916 • *Selby Gertrude* • SHT • USA
GERTIE'S BUSY DAY • 1916 • *Selby Gertrude* • SHT • USA
GERTIE'S GARTERS • 1916 • *Myers Harry* • SHT • USA
GERTIE'S GASOLINE GLIDE see **GABY'S GASOLINE GLIDE** • 1916
GERTIE'S JOY RIDE • 1915 • Frazee Edwin? • USA
GERTIE'S LATEST LOVE AFFAIR • 1916 • *Mutual* • USA
GERTRUD • 1964 • Dreyer Carl T. • DNM • GERTRUDE
GERTRUDE see **GERTRUD** • 1964
GERTRUDE AND ALICE IN PASSING • 1978 • Armatage Kay • CND
GERUCHT, HET • 1960 • Brusse Kees • NTH • RUMOUR, THE
GERUSALEMME LIBERATA • 1957 • Bragaglia Carlo Ludovico • ITL • MIGHTY CRUSADERS, THE (UKN) ○ MIGHTY INVADERS, THE (USA) ○ JERUSALEM SET FREE
GERUSALEMME LIBERATA, LA • 1911 • Guazzoni Enrico • ITL
GERUSALEMME LIBERATA, LA • 1917 • Guazzoni Enrico • ITL
GERVAISE • 1956 • Clement Rene • FRN
GESANGVEREIN SORGENFREI • 1931 • Wohlmuth Robert • FRG
GESCHEITERT • 1920 • Walther-Fein Rudolf • FRG
GESCHENKTE LOGE, DIE • 1928 • Guerra Armand • FRG
GESCHICHTE DER MAUD GREGAARDS, DIE see **HERRIN DER WELT 2, DIE** • 1919
GESCHICHTE DER NACHT • 1979 • Klopfenstein Clemens • DOC • SWT • STORY OF THE NIGHT
GESCHICHTE DER STILLEN MUHLE, DIE • 1914 • Oswald Richard • FRG
GESCHICHTE DER STILLEN MUHLE, DIE • 1951 • Oswald Richard • FRG
GESCHICHTE DES BARAK JOHNSON, DIE see **GESCHICHTE DES GRAUEN HAUSES 2, DIE** • 1921
GESCHICHTE DES GRAUEN HAUSES 1, DIE • 1921 • Lund Erik • FRG • MORD AUS ERSCHMAHTER LIEBE, DER
GESCHICHTE DES GRAUEN HAUSES 2, DIE • 1921 • Lund Erik • FRG • GESCHICHTE DES BARAK JOHNSON, DIE ○ MORD AUS VERWORFENHEIT, DER
GESCHICHTE DES GRAUEN HAUSES 3, DIE • 1921 • Lund Erik • FRG • MORD AUS VERZWIEFLUNG, DER
GESCHICHTE DES GRAUEN HAUSES 4, DIE • 1921 • Lund Erik • FRG • MORD AUS HABSUCHT, DER
GESCHICHTE DES PRINZEN ACHMED, DIE see **ABENTEUER DES PRINZEN ACHMED, DIE** • 1926
GESCHICHTE EINER EHE, DIE see **LIEBES DER BARONIN VON S., DIE** • 1924
GESCHICHTE EINER GEFALLENEN, DIE see **MARGARETE** • 1918
GESCHICHTE EINER JUNGEN LIEBE, DIE see **ANNEMARIE** • 1936
GESCHICHTE EINER KLEINEN PARISERIN, DIE • 1927 • Genina Augusto • FRG
GESCHICHTE EINER REICHEN ERBIN, DIE see **WINDSTARKE 9** • 1924
GESCHICHTE EINES CLOWNS, DIE see **DUDU, EIN MENSCHENSCHICKSAL** • 1924
GESCHICHTE EINES HUNDES, DIE see **KRAMBAMBULI** • 1940
GESCHICHTE EINES JUNGEN MADCHENS, DIE see **CLAIRE** • 1924
GESCHICHTE EINES LEBENS, DIE see **ANNELIE** • 1941
GESCHICHTE VOM ARMEN HASSAN, DIE • 1958 • Klein Gerhard • GDR • STORY OF POOR HASSAN, THE
GESCHICHTE VOM KLEINEN MUCK, DIE • 1953 • Staudte Wolfgang • GDR • STORY OF LITTLE MOOK, THE ○ LITTLE MOOK ○ LITTLE MUCK'S TREASURE
GESCHICHTEN AUS DEM DORF MAGINO • 1987 • Ogawa Shinsuke • DOC • JPN
GESCHICHTEN AUS DEM WIENERWALD • 1979 • Schell Maximilian • AUS, FRG • TALES FROM THE VIENNA WOODS
GESCHICHTEN JENER NACHT • 1967 • Carpentier Karl Heinz, Thein Ulrich, Vogel Frank, Klein Gerhard • GDR • STORIES OF THAT NIGHT ○ TALES OF THAT NIGHT
GESCHICHTEN VOM KUBELKIND • 1971 • Reitz Edgar, Stockl Ula • FRG
GESCHICHTSUNTERRICHT • 1973 • Straub Jean-Marie, Huillet Daniele • FRG • HISTORY LESSONS
GESCHIEDENE FRAU, DIE • 1926 • Janson Victor • FRG
GESCHIEDENE FRAU, DIE • 1953 • Jacoby Georg • FRG
GESCHIEDENEN, DIE • 1917 • Larsen Viggo • FRG
GESCHIEDENES FRAULEIN see **ICH HAB MICH SO AN DICH GEWOHNT** • 1952
GESCHLECHT DER ENGEL, DAS (FRG) see **SESSO DEGLI ANGELI, IL** • 1968
GESCHLECHT DER GRAFEN VON GHEYN, DAS • 1922 • Halm Alfred • FRG
GESCHLECHT DER SCHELME 1, DAS • 1917 • Halm Alfred • FRG
GESCHLECHT DER SCHELME 2, DAS • 1918 • Halm Alfred • FRG
GESCHLECHT DERER VON RINGWALL, DAS • 1918 • Biebrach Rudolf • FRG
GESCHLECHT IN FESSELN • 1928 • Dieterle William • FRG • SEX IN CHAINS (USA) ○ SEX IN FETTERS ○ GESCHLECHT IN FESSELN -DIE SEXUALNOT DER GEFANGEN ○ SEXES ENCHAINES, LES ○ CHAINES
GESCHLECHT IN FESSELN -DIE SEXUALNOT DER GEFANGEN see **GESCHLECHT IN FESSELN** • 1928
GESCHLOSSENE KETTE, DIE • 1920 • Stein Paul L. • FRG
GESCHMINKTE FRAU, DIE see **IM GLUTRAUSCH DER SINNE 2** • 1922
GESCHMINKTE JUGEND • 1929 • Boese Carl • FRG
GESCHMINKTE JUGEND • 1960 • Nosseck Max • FRG
GESCHOPF, DAS • 1924 • Philippi Siegfried • FRG
GESCHWADER FLEDERMAUS • 1958 • Engel Erich • GDR • FLEDERMAUS SQUADRON, THE
GESCHWINDIGKEIT • 1962 • Reitz Edgar • FRG
GESCHWISTER BARELLI • 1920 • Lowenbein Richard • FRG
GESCHWISTER LORRIS • 1915 • Larsen Viggo • FRG • DREI LORRIS, DIE
GESETZ DER LIEBE, DAS • 1945 • Schweikart Hans • FRG
GESETZ DER MINE, DAS • 1915 • May Joe • FRG
GESETZ DER SCHWARZEN BERGE, DAS • 1928 • Mengon Romano • FRG
GESETZ DER VATER, DAS • 1925 • *Problem-Film* • FRG
GESETZ DER WUSTE, DAS • 1920 • Sauer Fred • FRG
GESETZ OHNE GNADE • 1951 • Reinl Harald • FRG, AUS
GESICHT AM FENSTER, DAS • 1917 • Meinert Rudolf • FRG
GESICHT IM DUNKELN, DAS (FRG) see **A DOPPIA FACCIA** • 1969
GESICHT VON DER STANGE • 1961 • Ruehl Raimond • FRG
GESOLEI • 1923 • Ruttmann Walter • FRG
GESPENSTER • 1922 • Boese Carl • FRG • KONNEN TOTE LEBEN - - ?
GESPENSTER • 1939 • FRG • GHOSTS
GESPENSTER VON GARDEN HALL, DIE • 1919 • Wauer William • FRG
GESPENSTERSCHIFF, DAS • 1921 • Leni Paul • FRG
GESPENSTERSCHIFF, DAS see **SCHIFF OHNE HAFEN, DAS** • 1932
GESPENSTERSTUNDE, DIE • 1917 • Gad Urban • FRG
GESPENSTERUHR, DIE • 1915 • May Joe • FRG • BLAUE WASSER
GESPRENGTE GITTER • 1940-53 • Piel Harry • FRG
GESPRENGTE KETTEN • 1915 • *Andra Fern* • FRG
GESTANDNIS DER DREI, DAS • 1928 • Bauer James • FRG
GESTANDNIS DER GRUNEN MASKE, DAS • 1916 • Mack Max • FRG • GRUNE DAMON, DER
GESTANDNIS DER OLGA ORGINSKA, DAS • 1917 • Dessauer Siegfried • FRG
GESTANDNIS EINER SECHZEHNJAHRIGEN • 1961 • Tressler Georg • AUS
GESTANDNIS EINES MADCHENS, DAS • 1967 • Buchmann Jurgen • FRG • GIRL'S CONFESSION, A
GESTANDNIS UNTER VIER AUGEN • 1954 • Michel Andre • FRG
GESTAPO see **NIGHT TRAIN TO MUNICH** • 1940
GESTAPO'S LAST ORGY see **ULTIMA ORGIA DEL TERZO REICH, L'** • 1977
GESTARTES RENDEZ-VOUS • 1897 • Messter Oskar • FRG
GESTATTEN, MEIN NAME IST COX • 1955 • Jacoby Georg • FRG
GESTE, LE • 1912 • Perret Leonce • FRN
GESTE DE SEGOU, LA • 1989 • Coulibaly Sega • ANS • MLI
GESTEHEN SIE DR. CORDA! • 1958 • von Baky Josef • FRG • CONFESS DR. CORDA (USA)
GESTES ABSURDES • 1975-77 • Moreau Michel • DCS • CND
GESTES DU REPAS • 1958 • de Geneffe Fernand • BLG • WAYS OF EATING
GESTES DU SILENCE, LES • 1960 • Storck Henri • DOC • BLG
GESTICULADOR, EL see **IMPOSTOR, EL** • 1956
GESTIEFELTE KATER, DER • 1955 • Fredersdorf Herbert B. • FRG • PUSS 'N BOOTS (USA)
GESTO, IL • 1973 • Grottesi Marcello • ITL
GESTOHLENE GESICHT, DAS • 1931 • Schmidt Erich, Mayring Philipp L. • FRG
GESTOHLENE HERZ, DAS • 1934 • Reiniger Lotte • ANS • FRG • STOLEN HEART, THE
GESTOHLENE HOSE, DIE • 1956 • von Cziffra Geza • FRG
GESTOHLENE HOTEL, DAS • 1918 • Speyer Jaap • FRG
GESTOHLENE HOTEL, DAS • 1924 • *Deutsche Bioscop* • FRG
GESTOHLENE JAHR, DAS • 1951 • Frass Wilfred • FRG, AUS
GESTOHLENE MILLIONENREZEPT, DAS • 1921 • Wilhelm Carl • FRG
GESTOHLENE NASE, DIE • 1955 • Weiler Kurt • ANS • GDR • STOLEN NOSE, THE
GESTOHLENE PROFESSOR, DER • 1924 • Justitz Emil • FRG • VITUS THAVONS GENERALCOUP
GESTOHLENE SEELE, DIE • 1918 • Boese Carl • FRG
GESTORTE HOCHZEITSNACHT, DIE • 1916 • Heidemann Paul • FRG
GESTORTE HOCHZEITSNACHT, DIE • 1950 • Weiss Helmut • FRG • GUTE NACHT, MARY
GESTOS E FRAGMENTOS • 1983 • Santos Alberto Seixas • PRT
GESTRANDETE MENSCHEN • 1927 • Nehrke Kurt • FRG
GESTREIFTE DOMINO, DER • 1915 • Gartner Adolf • FRG
GESU DI NAZARETH (ITL) see **JESUS OF NAZARETH** • 1977
GESUCHT WIRD MAJORA • 1949 • Pfeiffer Hermann • FRG
GESUHNTE SCHULD • 1924 • *Waldorf-Film* • FRG
GESUNDE FRAU -GESUNDES VOLK • 1938 • FRG

GESUNKENEN, DIE • 1920 • Sauer Fred • FRG
GESUNKENEN, DIE • 1925 • Walther-Fein Rudolf, Dieterle William (U/c) • FRG • SUNKEN, THE (USA)
GESUZZA, LA SPOSA GARIBALDINA see **MILLE DI GARIBALDI, I** • 1933
GET A JOB • 1987 • Caslor Brad • ANS • CND
GET ALONG, LITTLE ZOMBIE • 1946 • Bernds Edward • SHT • USA
GET-AWAY, THE • 1941 • Buzzell Edward • USA
GET BACK • 1972 • Shebib Donald • CND • WINTER SUN
GET BUSY • 1924 • Roach Hal • SHT • USA
GET CARTER • 1970 • Hodges Mike • UKN
GET CHARLIE TULLY (USA) see **OOH.. YOU ARE AWFUL** • 1972
GET CHRISTIE LOVE! • 1974 • Graham William A. • USA
GET CRACKING • 1943 • Varnel Marcel • UKN
GET CRAZY • 1983 • Arkush Allan • USA
GET DOWN AND BOOGIE • 1975 • Witney William • USA • DARKTOWN STRUTTERS
GET 'EM ALL (USA) see **KENJU YO SARABA** • 1960
GET 'EM YOUNG • 1926 • Roach Hal • SHT • USA
GET GOING • 1943 • Yarbrough Jean • USA
GET HEP TO LOVE • 1942 • Lamont Charles • USA • SHE'S MY LOVELY (UKN)
GET IN AND GET OUT • 1914 • Weston Charles • UKN
GET IT MAN see **KUZIS STARI MOJ** • 1974
GET LOST • 1956 • Smith Paul J. • ANS • USA
GET LOST! LITTLE DOGGY • 1964 • Marcus Sid • ANS • USA
GET MARRIED MOTHER see **KAACHAN KEKKON SHIROYO** • 1962
GET MEAN • 1976 • Baldi Ferdinando • ITL • VENGEANCE OF THE BARBARIANS
GET OFF MY BACK (UKN) see **SYNANON** • 1965
GET OFF MY FOOT • 1935 • Beaudine William • UKN
GET ON WITH IT! see **DENTIST ON THE JOB** • 1961
GET ON YOUR MARKS see **LAVETE THESSIS** • 1973
GET OUT see **STORMY WEATHER** • 1935
GET OUT AND GET UNDER • 1914 • *Eclectic* • USA
GET OUT AND GET UNDER • 1914 • *Crystal* • USA
GET OUT AND GET UNDER • 1920 • Roach Hal ? • SHT • USA
GET OUT AND GET UNDER THE MOON • 1929 • Aylott Dave, Symmons E. F. • SHT • UKN
GET OUT OF HERE! see **FUERA DE AQUI!** • 1977
GET OUT OF IT see **STORMY WEATHER** • 1935
GET OUT OF MY ROOM • 1985 • Marin Cheech • USA
GET OUT OF TOWN see **GET OUTTA TOWN** • 1959
GET OUT YOUR BALLOON see **STEIG AUS DEINEM LUFTBALLON** • 1985
GET OUT YOUR HANDKERCHIEFS (USA) see **PREPAREZ VOS MOUCHOIRS** • 1978
GET OUTTA TOWN • 1959 • Davis Charles • USA • GANGSTER'S REVENGE ○ GET OUT OF TOWN
GET-RICH HALL AND FORD • 1911 • *Essanay* • USA
GET RICH QUICK • 1911 • *Thanhouser* • USA
GET RICH QUICK • 1913 • Lehrman Henry • USA
GET RICH QUICK • 1951 • Kinney Jack • ANS • USA
GET-RICH-QUICK BILLINGTON • 1913 • *Panzer Paul* • USA
GET-RICH-QUICK EDGAR • 1920 • Litson Mason N. • SHT • USA • FANS
GET RICH QUICK PORKY • 1937 • Clampett Robert • ANS • USA
GET-RICH-QUICK WALLINGFORD • 1916 • Niblo Fred • ASL
GET-RICH-QUICK WALLINGFORD • 1921 • Borzage Frank • USA
GET-RICH-QUICK WALLINGFORD see **NEW ADVENTURES OF GET-RICH-QUICK WALLINGFORD, THE** • 1931
GET RITA see **PUPA DEL GANGSTER, LA** • 1975
GET SMART, AGAIN! • 1989 • Nelson Gary • TVM • USA
GET THAT GIRL • 1931 • Crone George J. • USA
GET THAT GIRL (UKN) see **CARYL OF THE MOUNTAINS** • 1936
GET THAT GUITAR • 1965 • Bartsch Art • ANS • USA
GET THAT MAN • 1935 • Bennet Spencer Gordon • USA
GET THEE BEHIND ME see **VIA CRUCIS** • 1918
GET THEE TO A NUNNERY (UKN) see **FRATELLO HOMO, SORELLA BONA** • 1972
GET THERE SAFELY • 1973 • Henson Laurence • SHT • UKN
GET TO KNOW YOUR RABBIT • 1972 • De Palma Brian • USA
GET-TOGETHER, THE see **RIMPATRIATA, LA** • 1963
GET UP, DELFINA see **ISPRAVI SE, DELFINA** • 1978
GET VICTOR CORPUS -THE REBEL SOLDIER • 1987 • PHL
GET WET • 1966 • Canning William • CND • A L'EAU
GET WHAT YOU PAY FOR • 1970 • *Stacey Dist.* • USA • YOU GET WHAT YOU PAY FOR
GET YOUR DIPLOMA FIRST see **PASSE TON BAC D'ABORD** • 1979
GET YOUR HANDKERCHIEFS READY see **PREPAREZ VOS MOUCHOIRS** • 1978
GET YOUR MAN • 1921 • Hill George W., Howard William K. • USA
GET YOUR MAN • 1923 • Jeske George • SHT • USA
GET YOUR MAN • 1927 • Arzner Dorothy • USA
GET YOUR MAN • 1934 • King George • UKN
GET YOURSELF A COLLEGE GIRL • 1964 • Miller Sidney • USA • SWINGIN' SET, THE ○ WATUSI A GO-GO ○ GO-GO SET
GETAWAY, THE • 1914 • *Lubin* • USA
GETAWAY, THE • 1916 • *Pokes & Jabbs* • USA
GETAWAY, THE • 1917 • Cochrane George • SHT • USA
GETAWAY, THE • 1972 • Peckinpah Sam • USA
GETAWAY KATE • 1918 • Seitz George B. • SHT • USA
GETAWAY LIFE, THE see **DEROBADE, LA** • 1979
GETEILTE HIMMEL, DER • 1964 • Wolf Konrad • GDR • DIVIDED HEAVEN ○ DIVIDED SKY
GETEKENDE MENSEN • 1985 • Geelen Harry • DOC • NTH
GETSUYOBI NO YUKA • 1964 • Nakahira Ko • JPN • YUKA FROM MONDAY
GETTIN' BACK • 1974 • Crabtree Gary L. • DOC • USA
GETTIN' GLAMOUR • 1946 • Anderson Philip • SHT • USA
GETTING A HIRED GIRL • 1912 • *Cashman Harry* • USA
GETTING A MOTOR • 1929 • Aylott Dave, Symmons E. F. • SHT • UKN
GETTING A PATIENT • 1913 • Miller Ashley • USA
GETTING A START IN LIFE • 1915 • Mix Tom • USA
GETTING A SUIT PRESSED • 1914 • *Komic* • USA
GETTING ACQUAINTED • 1914 • Chaplin Charles • USA • FAIR EXCHANGE, A ○ HULLO EVERYBODY
GETTING AHEAD • 1965 • Post Howard • ANS • USA
GETTING ANDY'S GOAT • 1914 • France Charles H. • USA
GETTING ATMOSPHERE • 1912 • Bosworth Hobart • USA
GETTING AWAY FROM IT ALL • 1971 • Philips Lee • TVM • USA
GETTING AWAY WITH MURDER see **RICHTER UND SEIN HENKER, DER** • 1976
GETTING BACK TO NOTHING • 1970 • Burstall Tim • DOC • ASL
GETTING BY • 1916 • Robertson John S. • SHT • USA
GETTING DAD MARRIED • 1912 • *Eclair* • USA
GETTING DAD'S CONSENT • 1911 • Stow Percy • UKN
GETTING 'EM RIGHT • 1925 • *Larkin George* • USA
GETTING EVEN • Kerwin Harry E.
GETTING EVEN • 1909 • Griffith D. W. • USA
GETTING EVEN • 1911 • *Nestor* • USA
GETTING EVEN • 1911 • *Lubin* • USA
GETTING EVEN • 1912 • *Powers* • USA
GETTING EVEN • 1914 • *A.r. Films* • UKN
GETTING EVEN • 1914 • Hotaling Arthur D. • USA
GETTING EVEN • 1981 • Feldberg Mark • USA
GETTING EVEN • 1981 • Hart Harvey • CND • UTILITIES
GETTING EVEN see **HOSTAGE: DALLAS** • 1986
GETTING EVEN WITH EMILY • 1911 • *Essanay* • USA
GETTING EVIDENCE • 1906 • Porter Edwin S. • USA
GETTING FATHER'S CONSENT • 1909 • Coleby A. E. • UKN
GETTING FATHER'S GOAT • 1915 • *Kalem* • USA
GETTING GERTIE'S GARTER • 1927 • Hopper E. Mason • USA
GETTING GERTIE'S GARTER • 1945 • Dwan Allan • USA
GETTING HER MAN • 1924 • *Carew Ora* • USA
GETTING HIS CHANGE • 1907 • Hough Harold • UKN
GETTING HIS GOAT • 1915 • Harvey John • USA
GETTING HIS GOAT • 1920 • *Reelcraft* • SHT • USA
GETTING HIS GOAT • 1920 • Roach Hal • *Rolin* • SHT • USA
GETTING HIS GOAT see **PROPERTY MAN, THE** • 1914
GETTING HIS MAN • 1911 • Ince Thomas H. • USA
GETTING HIS OWN BACK • 1911 • *Essanay* • USA
GETTING HIS OWN BACK • 1913 • Calvert Charles? • UKN
GETTING HIS OWN BACK • 1914 • Plumb Hay? • UKN
GETTING HIS OWN BACK see **JOKER'S MISTAKE, THE** • 1912
GETTING IN WRONG • 1916 • Dillon John Francis • USA
GETTING INTO A SCRAPE • 1915 • *Ab* • USA
GETTING INTO HEAVEN • 1970 • Montoro Edward L. • USA
GETTING IT ON • 1983 • Olsen William • USA • AMERICAN VOYEUR
GETTING IT RIGHT • 1989 • Kleiser Randall • UKN, USA
GETTING L.A.'D • 1981 • Kidder Miles • USA
GETTING LUCKY • 1985 • SAF
GETTING MARRIED • 1911 • *Selig* • USA
GETTING MARRIED • 1913 • *Lubin* • USA
GETTING MARRIED • 1978 • Stern Steven Hilliard • TVM • USA
GETTING MARY MARRIED • 1912 • *Horner Violet* • USA
GETTING MARY MARRIED • 1919 • Dwan Allan • USA • MARRYING MARY (UKN)
GETTING OF WISDOM, THE • 1977 • Beresford Bruce • ASL
GETTING OFF • Dupree Hayes • USA
GETTING ON HIS NERVES • 1915 • Birch Cecil • UKN
GETTING ON THE BANDWAGON • 1957 • Parker Gudrun • CND
GETTING OVER • 1981 • Rollins Bernie • USA
GETTING PHYSICAL • 1984 • Stern Steven Hilliard • TVM • USA
GETTING REUBEN BACK • 1914 • Smalley Phillips • USA
GETTING RICH QUICK • 1912 • *Majestic* • USA
GETTING RID OF ALGY • 1914 • *Thanhouser* • USA
GETTING RID OF AUNT KATE • 1915 • Williams C. Jay • USA
GETTING RID OF HIS DOG • 1907 • Williamson James • UKN
GETTING RID OF HIS MOTHER-IN-LAW • 1914 • *Imp* • USA
GETTING RID OF NEPHEW • 1915 • *Ab* • USA
GETTING RID OF TROUBLE • 1912 • Henderson Dell • USA
GETTING RID OF UNCLE • 1910 • *Centaur* • USA
GETTING SAM HOME see **LAST OF THE SUMMER WINE: GETTING SAM HOME** • 1983
GETTING SISTER MARRIED • 1911 • *Briscoe Lottie* • USA
GETTING SMART see **TWO-FISTED** • 1935
GETTING SOLID WITH PAPA • 1914 • *Lubin* • USA
GETTING STARTED • 1979 • Condie Richard • ANS • CND
GETTING STRAIGHT • 1970 • Rush Richard • USA
GETTING THE AIR • 1930 • Meins Gus • SHT • USA
GETTING THE BEST OF DAD • 1913 • *Lubin* • USA
GETTING THE COIN • 1917 • *Pokes & Jabbs* • SHT • USA
GETTING THE EVIDENCE • 1913 • *Pilot* • USA
GETTING THE EVIDENCE • 1917 • *U.s.m.p.* • USA
GETTING THE GARDENER'S GOAT • 1915 • *Chamberlin Riley* • USA
GETTING THE GOODS ON FATHER • 1915 • *Empire* • USA
GETTING THE GOODS ON GERTIE • 1916 • *Morris Reggie* • SHT • USA
GETTING THE GRIP • 1913 • *Crystal* • USA
GETTING THE MONEY • 1912 • *Kalem* • USA
GETTING THE SACK • 1914 • Henderson Dell • USA
GETTING TO THE BALL GAME • 1914 • France Charles H. • USA
GETTING TOGETHER • 1976 • *Groome Malcolm* • USA
GETTING UP A PRACTISE • 1913 • Costello Maurice, Ranous William V. • USA
GETTING UP MADE EASY • 1903 • Stow Percy? • UKN
GETTING VIVIAN MARRIED • 1914 • *Crystal* • USA
GETTING WASTED • 1980 • Frizler Paul • USA
GETTO D'ACQUE, IL • 1914 • Genina Augusto • ITL
GETTY TEY • 1979 • Ndiaye Felix Samba • SNL
GETUPFTE KRAWATTE, DIE see **FALL CLIFFORD, DER** • 1917
GEURE YAKUZA EIGA • 1956 • Suzuki Seijun • JPN
GEVAARLIKE REIS • 1961 • SAF
GEVAARLIKE SPEL • 1962 • SAF
GEVATTER TOD • 1921 • Hanus Heinz • AUS • GODFATHER DEATH ○ DEATH
GEWALT • 1971 • Sanders Helma • FRG
GEWALT GEGEN RECHT • 1919 • Stein Paul L. • FRG
GEWALT UND GEWISSEN • 1967 • Stanzl Karl • AUS • FORCE AND CONSCIENCE
GEWEHR UBER, DAS • 1939 • von Alten Jurgen • FRG
GEWISSE ETWAS DER FRAUEN, DAS (FRG) see **COME IMPARAI AD AMARE LE DONNE** • 1966
GEWISSE UNTERSCHIED ODER DIE LINKE HAND DES JOSEF KONIG, DER • 1969 • Henner Ted • FRG
GEWISSEN, DAS • 1915 • Neuss Alwin • FRG
GEWISSEN, DAS • 1972 • Zeitler Karl Heinz • FRG, FRN, SPN
GEWISSEN DER WELT 1, DAS • 1921 • Hartwig Martin • FRG • TOTE HOTEL, DAS
GEWISSEN DER WELT 2, DAS • 1921 • Hartwig Martin • FRG • RAZZIA DER GERECHTIGKEIT
GEWISSEN DES ANDERN, DAS • 1917 • Hanus Emerich • FRG
GEWISSEN DES SEBASTIAN GEYER, DAS see **SCHUSS AM NEBELHORN, DER** • 1933
GEWISSER HERR GRAN, EIN • 1933 • Lamprecht Gerhard • FRG
GEWISSER JUDAS, EIN • 1958 • Werner • MTV • FRG
GEWITTER IM MAI • 1919 • Beck Ludwig • FRG
GEWITTER IM MAI • 1987 • Schwarzenberger Xaver • AUS, FRG • TEMPEST IN MAY
GEWITTERFLUG ZU CLAUDIA • 1937 • Waschneck Erich • FRG
GEWONDE, DE • 1966 • Noman Theo Van Haren • NTH • INJURED MAN, THE
GEZEICHNETE, DER • 1918 • von Woringen Paul • FRG
GEZEICHNETEN, DIE • 1921 • Dreyer Carl T. • FRG • LOVE ONE ANOTHER ○ STIGMATIZED ONE, THE ○ ELSKER HVERANDRE
GEZEICHNETEN, DIE (SWT) see **SEARCH, THE** • 1948
GEZI SHU • 1985 • Wu Ziniu • CHN • PIGEON TREE ○ DOVETREE
GHABA NUS EL LAIL • 1947 • Hassan Abdel Fattah • EGY • MIDNIGHT GHOST, THE
GHAHRAMAN-E-SHAHRE MA • 1968 • Fazeli Reza • IRN • HERO OF OUR TOWN, THE
GHALTA PUTLA • 1935 • Sarpotdar • IND
GHALT'AT ABB • 1952 • Barakat Henry • EGY • ERREUR D'UN PERE, L'
GHAMHA & SHADIHA • 1968 • Vand Ghasemi • IRN • SORROWS AND HAPPINESS
GHANCHAKKAR see **SHEIKCHILLI** • 1940
GHAR KA CHIRAG • 1967 • Bhambri Jagdev • IND • LAMP THAT LIGHTS THE HOME, THE
GHARAM FIL KARNAK • 1967 • Reda Aly • EGY • LOVE IN THE KARNAK
GHARAM TALEB • 1971 • Halim Hilmy • EGY • AMOUR D'ETUDIANT, UN
GHARAM WA INTIKAM • 1944 • Wahby Youssef • EGY • PASSION AND REVENGE
GHARAMIATE MAGNOUN • 1967 • Bakir Zoheir • EGY • ADVENTURES OF A FOOL
GHARAMU AL-MILLYUNIR • 1957 • Salem Atef • EGY • AMOURS DU MILLIONNAIRE, LES
GHARAONDA • 1977 • Bhimsain • IND • NEST, THE
GHARBAR • 1963 • Ivory James • IND, USA • HOUSEHOLDER, THE (USA)
GHARCHI RANI • 1968 • Rajdutta • IND
GHARE BHAIRE • 1983 • Ray Satyajit • IND • HOME AND THE WORLD, THE
GHARIB, EL • 1955 • el Sheikh Kamal, Wahab Fatin Abdel • EGY • STRANGER, THE (USA) ○ ETRANGER, L'
GHARIB AL SAGHIR, AL • 1962 • Nasser George • LBN • LITTLE STRANGER, THE ○ SMALL STRANGER, THE ○ PETIT ETRANGER, LE
GHARIBEH VA MEH • 1974 • Beyzai Bahram • IRN • STRANGER AND THE FOG, THE ○ GARIBEH VA MEH
GHASTLY ONES, THE • 1968 • Milligan Andy • USA
GHASTLY ORGIES OF COUNT DRACULA see **REINCARNATION OF ISABEL, THE** • 1973
GHATASHRADDHA • 1977 • Kasaravalli Girish • IND • RITUAL, A
GHAZAL • 1975 • Kimiyaei Massoud • IRN
GHAZIA MEN SONBAT • 1967 • Ziada El Sayad • EGY • DANCER FROM SONBAT
GHENGIS KHAN see **GENGIS KHAN** • 1952
GHETTO BLASTER, THE see **GHETTOBLASTERS** • 1989
GHETTO EXPERIMENTAL, LE • 1975 • Carre Jean-Michel, Schmedes Adam • DOC • FRN
GHETTO FREAKS see **SIGN OF AQUARIUS** • 1970
GHETTO SEAMSTRESS, THE • 1910 • *Yankee* • USA
GHETTO SHAMROCK, THE • 1926 • Ford Francis • USA
GHETTO TEREZIN see **DALEKA CESTA** • 1949
GHETTO WARRIORS see **BLACK GESTAPO** • 1975
GHETTOBLASTERS • 1989 • Stewart Alan • USA • GHETTO BLASTER, THE
GHEYSAR • 1970 • Kimiyaei Massoud • IRN
GHIAMAT ESHGHE • 1974 • Hessami Hooshang • IRN • RESURRECTION OF LOVE
GHIAUROV 50 • 1980 • Korabov Nicolai • BUL
GHIDORAH see **SANDAI KAIJU CHIKYU SAIDAI NO KESSEN** • 1965
GHIDRAH -THE THREE-HEADED MONSTER (USA) see **SANDAI KAIJU CHIKYU SAIDAI NO KESSEN** • 1965
GHODRATE-ESHGH • 1968 • Ekhart Robert • IRN • POWER OF LOVE, THE
GHOMAR BAZ • 1968 • Kassaei Abas • IRN • GAMBLER, THE
GHORBA, EL • 1971 • Tresgot Annie • ALG, FRN • PASSAGERS, LES (FRN) ○ PASSENGERS, THE ○ ELGHORBA
GHORBI-YE-SEVOM • 1967 • Malakouti • IRN • THIRD VICTIM, THE
GHOROUBE BOTPARASTAN • 1968 • Koushan Esmaeil • IRN • FAILURE OF IDOLATERS, THE
GHOSKS IS THE BUNK • 1939 • Fleischer Dave • ANS • USA
GHOSOGHAZAH • 1968 • Poorsaeid Esmaeil • IRN • RAINBOW
GHOST • 1960 • THL
GHOST • 1990 • Zucker Jerry • USA
GHOST see **KESHIN** • 1987
GHOST, A see **REVENANT, UN** • 1946
GHOST, THE • 1911 • Sennett Mack • USA
GHOST, THE • 1913 • *Victor* • USA

GHOST, THE • 1913 • Clifford William H. • *Domino* • USA
GHOST, THE • 1914 • Powell Frank • USA
GHOST, THE see **REVENANT, LE** • 1913
GHOST, THE see **REVENANTE, LA** • 1918
GHOST, THE see **FANTOME, LE** • 1936
GHOST, THE (USA) see **SPETTRO, LO** • 1962
GHOST AND DONA JUANITA, THE see **FANTASMA Y DONA JUANITA, EL** • 1944
GHOST AND MR. CHICKEN, THE • 1966 • Rafkin Alan • USA
GHOST AND MRS. MUIR, THE • 1947 • Mankiewicz Joseph L. • USA
GHOST AND THE CANDLE, THE see **REVENANT, LE** • 1903
GHOST APPEARS IN VALLEY • 1961 • JPN
GHOST BARON, THE see **SPOKBARONEN** • 1927
GHOST BEAUTY see **KAIDAN BOTAN DORO** • 1968
GHOST BREAKER, THE • 1914 • De Mille Cecil B., Apfel Oscar • USA
GHOST BREAKER, THE • 1922 • Green Alfred E. • USA
GHOST BREAKERS • 1940 • Marshall George • USA
GHOST BUSTER • 1952 • *Lamb Gil* • SHT • USA
GHOST BUSTERS see **SPOOK BUSTERS** • 1946
GHOST BUSTERS, THE • 1975 • Abbott Norman • MTV • USA
GHOST CAMERA, THE • 1933 • Vorhaus Bernard • UKN
GHOST CAN'T TAKE IT, THE see **UPIOR W PALACU** • 1960
GHOST CAT MANSION see **BOREI KAIBYO YASHIKI** • 1958
GHOST-CAT MANSION OF NABESHIMA see **NABESHIMA KAIBYODEN** • 1949
GHOST-CAT OF ARIMA PALACE see **KAIBYO ARIMA GOTEN** • 1953
GHOST-CAT OF GOJUSAN-TSUGI see **KAIBYO GOJUSAN-TSUGI** • 1956
GHOST-CAT OF KARAKURI TENJO see **KAIBYO KARAKURI TENJO** • 1958
GHOST-CAT OF OMA-GA-TSUJI see **KAIBYO OMA-GA-TSUJI** • 1954
GHOST-CAT OF OTAMA-GA-IKE see **KAIBYO OTAMA-GA-IKE** • 1960
GHOST-CAT OF YONAKI SWAMP see **KAIBYO YONAKI NUMA** • 1957
GHOST-CAT SWAMP OF HATRED see **KAIBYO NOROI NO NUMA** • 1968
GHOST-CAT WALL OF HATRED see **KAIBYO NOROI NO KABE** • 1958
GHOST CATCHERS • 1944 • Cline Eddie • USA
GHOST CHASE • 1988 • Emmerich Roland • USA
GHOST CHASERS • 1951 • Beaudine William • USA
GHOST CITY • 1921 • Bertram William • USA
GHOST CITY • 1932 • Fraser Harry L. • USA
GHOST CITY, THE • 1924 • Marchant Jay • SRL • USA
GHOST COMES HOME, THE • 1940 • Thiele Wilhelm • USA
GHOST CRAZY see **CRAZY KNIGHTS** • 1944
GHOST CREEPS, THE see **BOYS OF THE CITY** • 1940
GHOST DANCE • 1982 • Buffa Peter • USA
GHOST DANCE see **GHOSTDANCE** • 1984
GHOST DANCING • 1983 • Greene David • TVM • USA
GHOST DIVER • 1957 • Einfeld Richard, White Merrill G. • USA
GHOST FAKIRS, THE • 1915 • *Aubrey James* • USA
GHOST FEVER • 1984 • Madden Lee (Smithee Allan) • USA • BENNY AND BUFORD
GHOST FLOWER, THE • 1918 • Borzage Frank • USA
GHOST FOR SALE see **SPOKE TILL SALU** • 1939
GHOST FOR SALE, A • 1952 • Gover Victor M. • UKN
GHOST FROM THE POND see **KAIDAN HITOTSU-ME JIZO** • 1959
GHOST GIRL, THE • 1919 • *Drew Donna* • SHT • USA
GHOST GOES GEAR, THE • 1966 • Gladwish Hugh • UKN
GHOST GOES WEST, THE • 1935 • Clair Rene • UKN • FANTOME A VENDRE, LE (FRN)
GHOST GOES WILD, THE • 1947 • Blair George • USA
GHOST GUNMAN, THE see **PISTOLERO FANTASMA, EL** • 1967
GHOST GUNS • 1944 • Hillyer Lambert • USA
GHOST HOLIDAY, THE • 1907 • *Williams, Brown & Earle* • USA
GHOST HOUNDS • 1917 • *Ham & Bud* • SHT • USA
GHOST HOUSE, THE • 1917 • De Mille William C. • USA
GHOST HUNTER • 1975 • Migliaccio Flavio • BRZ
GHOST IN A CAB see **YUREI TAKUSHI** • 1956
GHOST IN LOVE, A (USA) see **ET SPOKELSE FORELSKER SEG** • 1947
GHOST IN THE CASTLE see **SPUK IM SCHLOSS** • 1944
GHOST IN THE GARRET, THE • 1921 • Jones F. Richard • USA
GHOST IN THE INVISIBLE BIKINI, THE • 1966 • Weis Don • USA • SLUMBER PARTY IN HORROR HOUSE ◦ BEACH PARTY IN A HAUNTED HOUSE ◦ BIKINI PARTY IN A HAUNTED HOUSE ◦ PAJAMA PARTY IN A HAUNTED HOUSE
GHOST IN THE NOONDAY SUN • 1973 • Medak Peter • UKN
GHOST IN THE TOWN see **PATTINATHIL BOOTHAM** • 1967
GHOST IN THE VILLAGE, THE • Hammer Erich • ANM • GDR
GHOST IN UNIFORM, THE • 1913 • *Thanhouser Kid* • USA
GHOST JESTERS, THE see **FANTASMAS BURLONES, LOS** • 1964
GHOST LOVE • 1956 • *Hwa Lili* • HKG
GHOST MUSIC OF SHAMISEN see **KAIDAN SHAMISEN-BORI** • 1962
GHOST OF A BARGAIN, THE • 1912 • *Rex* • USA
GHOST OF A CHANCE • 1987 • Taylor Don • TVM • USA
GHOST OF A CHANCE, A • 1968 • Darnley-Smith Jan • UKN
GHOST OF A CHANCE, A • 1973 • Hall Gorton • USA
GHOST OF A CHANCE, THE • 1916 • *Figman Max* • SHT • USA
GHOST OF A CHANCE, THE • 1919 • Webb Kenneth • SHT • USA
GHOST OF BINGVILLE INN, THE • 1915 • *Premier* • USA
GHOST OF BRAGEHUS see **SPOKET PA BRAGEHUS** • 1936
GHOST OF CHIBUSA ENOKI see **KAIDAN CHIBUSA ENOKI** • 1958
GHOST OF CHIDORI-GA-FUCHI see **KAIDAN CHIDORI-GA-FUCHI** • 1956
GHOST OF CRANLEIGH, THE see **GHOST OF GRANLEIGH, THE** • 1913
GHOST OF CROSSBONES CANYON, THE • 1953 • McDonald Frank • MTV • USA
GHOST OF CYPRESS SWAMP, THE • 1977 • McEveety Vincent • TVM • USA
GHOST OF DONKERGAT, THE see **SPOOK VAN DONKERGAT, DIE** • 1972
GHOST OF DRAGSTRIP HOLLOW, THE • 1959 • Hole William Jr. • USA • HAUNTED HOTROD, THE
GHOST OF FLIGHT 401, THE • 1978 • Stern Steven Hilliard • TVM • USA
GHOST OF FOLLY, THE • 1926 • Cline Eddie • SHT • USA
GHOST OF FRANKENSTEIN, THE • 1942 • Kenton Erle C. • USA
GHOST OF GOJUSAN-TSUGI see **KAIDAN GOJUSAN-TSUGI** • 1960
GHOST OF GRANLEIGH, THE • 1913 • Dawley J. Searle, Ridgely Richard? • USA • GHOST OF CRANLEIGH, THE
GHOST OF HIDDEN VALLEY • 1946 • Newfield Sam • USA
GHOST OF HONOR • 1957 • Sparber I. • ANS • USA
GHOST OF IWOJIMA, THE see **IWOJIMA** • 1959
GHOST OF JOHN HOLLING, THE (UKN) see **MYSTERY LINER** • 1934
GHOST OF KAGAMI-GA-FUCHI see **KAIDAN KAGAMI-GA-FUCHI** • 1959
GHOST OF KASANE-GA-FUCHI see **KAIDAN KASANE-GA-FUCHI** • 1957
GHOST OF KASANE-GA-FUCHI see **KAIDAN KASANE-GA-FUCHI** • 1960
GHOST OF LOVE see **FANTASMA D'AMORE** • 1980
GHOST OF MONK'S ISLAND, THE • 1967 • Summers Jeremy • SRL • UKN
GHOST OF MOTHER EVE, THE • 1914 • Edwin Walter • USA
GHOST OF MUDTOWN, THE • 1910 • *Pathe* • USA
GHOST OF OIWA see **KAIDAN OIWA NO BOREI** • 1961
GHOST OF OLD MORRO, THE • 1917 • Ridgely Richard • USA
GHOST OF RASHMON HALL, THE see **NIGHT COMES TOO SOON** • 1948
GHOST OF ROSY TAYLOR, THE • 1918 • Sloman Edward • USA
GHOST OF SACRAMENTO, THE see **DUCH ZAMCZYSKA SACRAMENTO** • 1962
GHOST OF SAGA MANSION see **KAIDAN SAGA YASHIKI** • 1953
GHOST OF ST. MICHAEL'S, THE • 1941 • Varnel Marcel • UKN
GHOST OF SAMARA, THE see **AFRIT SAMARA** • 1959
GHOST OF SEA VIEW MANOR, THE • 1913 • *Dragon* • USA
GHOST OF SELF, THE • 1913 • *Stonehouse Ruth* • USA
GHOST OF SLUMBER MOUNTAIN, THE • 1919 • Dawley Herbert M., O'Brien Willis • USA
GHOST OF SMILING JIM, THE • 1914 • *Ford Francis* • USA
GHOST OF SNAKE-GIRL see **KAIDAN HEBIONNA** • 1968
GHOST OF SNOW-GIRL PROSTITUTE see **KAIDAN YUKIJORO** • 1968
GHOST OF SULPHUR MOUNTAIN, THE • 1912 • Melies Gaston • USA
GHOST OF SUNSHINE MANSION, THE • Klingenberg Gerhard • GDR
GHOST OF THE CANYON, THE • 1920 • *Gibson Helen* • USA
GHOST OF THE CHINA SEAS • 1958 • Sears Fred F. • USA
GHOST OF THE CISCO KID see **GAY CABALLERO, THE** • 1940
GHOST OF THE DESERT, THE • 1917 • Horne James W. • SHT • USA
GHOST OF THE GIRL DIVER see **KAIDAN AMA YUREI** • 1960
GHOST OF THE GUEST, THE • 1943 • Nigh William • USA
GHOST OF THE HACIENDA, THE • 1913 • Ricketts Thomas • USA
GHOST OF THE HUNCHBACK see **KAIDAN SEMUSHI OTOKO** • 1965
GHOST OF THE JUNGLE, THE • 1916 • Hunt Jay • SHT • USA
GHOST OF THE MINE, THE • 1914 • *Eclair* • USA
GHOST OF THE MIRROR see **SHIH CHING YU-HUN**
GHOST OF THE ONE-EYED MAN see **KAIDAN KATAME OTOKO** • 1965
GHOST OF THE OPERA see **SPUK IM OPERNHAUS**
GHOST OF THE OVEN • 1910 • *Selig* • USA
GHOST OF THE RANCHO, THE • 1918 • Worthington William • USA
GHOST OF THE STRANGLER, THE see **ESPECTRO DEL ESTRANGULADOR, EL** • 1963
GHOST OF THE TOWN • 1952 • Sparber I. • ANS • USA
GHOST OF THE TWISTED OAKS, THE see **GHOST OF TWISTED OAKS, THE** • 1915
GHOST OF THE VARIETY, THE see **SPOGELSET I GRAVKAELDEREN** • 1910
GHOST OF THEIR ANCESTORS, THE • 1915 • *Nordisk* • DNM • GREAT INHERITANCE, THE
GHOST OF TOLSTON'S MANOR, THE • 1923 • Micheaux Oscar • USA
GHOST OF TWISTED OAKS, THE • 1915 • Olcott Sidney • USA • GHOST OF THE TWISTED OAKS, THE
GHOST OF WOLFPACK, THE see **TWIST OF SAND, A** • 1967
GHOST OF YESTERDAY • 1918 • *Selig* • USA
GHOST OF YOTSUYA, THE see **YOTSUYA KAIDAN** • 1949
GHOST OF YOTSUYA, THE see **YOTSUYA KAIDAN** • 1956
GHOST OF YOTSUYA, THE see **KAIDAN BANCHO SARAYASHIKI** • 1957
GHOST OF YOTSUYA, THE see **TOKAIDO YOTSUYA KAIDAN** • 1959
GHOST OF YOTSUYA, THE see **YOTSUYA KAIDAN** • 1959
GHOST OF YOTSUYA, THE see **KAIDAN OIWA NO BOREI** • 1961
GHOST OF YOTSUYA, THE see **YOTSUYA KAIDAN** • 1965
GHOST OF YOTSUYA, THE see **YOTSUYA KAIDAN -OIWA NO BOREI** • 1969
GHOST OF ZORRO • 1949 • Brannon Fred C. • USA
GHOST OF ZORRO • 1949 • Brannon Fred C. • SRL • USA
GHOST ON HOLIDAY, A see **SPOKE PA SEMESTER** • 1951
GHOST PARADE • 1931 • Sennett Mack • SHT • USA
GHOST PARTY see **HILLBILLYS IN A HAUNTED HOUSE** • 1967
GHOST PATROL • 1936 • Newfield Sam • USA
GHOST PATROL, THE • 1923 • Ross Nat • USA
GHOST REPORTER, THE see **SPOKREPORTERN** • 1941
GHOST RIDER, THE • 1925 • *Morrison Pete* • USA
GHOST RIDER, THE • 1935 • Levine Jack • USA
GHOST RIDER, THE • 1943 • Fox Wallace • USA
GHOST SHIP • 1952 • Sewell Vernon • UKN
GHOST SHIP see **YUREISEN** • 1957
GHOST SHIP see **MRTVA LADJA** • 1972
GHOST SHIP, THE • 1943 • Robson Mark • USA
GHOST SHIP, THE • 1986 • Potterton Gerald • MTV • CND
GHOST SHIP, THE see **REVANCHE DU MAUDIT, LA** • 1929
GHOST SHIPS • 1980 • Stoneman John • MTV • CND
GHOST SOLDIERS see **SUPERNATURALS, THE** • 1986
GHOST STEPS OUT, THE see **TIME OF THEIR LIVES, THE** • 1946
GHOST STORIES see **KWAIDAN** • 1964
GHOST STORY • 1972 • Moxey John Llewellyn • TVM • USA
GHOST STORY • 1974 • Weeks Stephen • UKN • MADHOUSE MANSION (USA)
GHOST STORY • 1981 • Irvin John • USA
GHOST STORY see **MAIN-MAIN HANTU** • 1990
GHOST STORY, THE • 1907 • Blackton J. Stuart • USA
GHOST STORY -BARABARA PHANTOM, A see **KAIDAN BARABARA YUREI** • 1968
GHOST STORY IN PASSAGE see **KAIDAN DOCHU** • 1958
GHOST STORY OF BOOBY TRAP see **KAIDAN OTOSHIANA** • 1968
GHOST STORY OF BROKEN DISHES AT BANCHO MANSION see **KAIDAN BANCHO SARAYASHIKI** • 1957
GHOST STORY OF DEVIL'S FIRE SWAMP see **KAIDAN ONIBI NO NUMA** • 1963
GHOST STORY OF FUNNY ACT IN FRONT OF TRAIN STATION see **KIGEKI EKIMAE KAIDAN** • 1964
GHOST STORY OF KAKUI STREET see **KAIDAN KAKUIDORI** • 1961
GHOST STORY OF PEONIES AND STONE LANTERNS, A see **KAIDAN BOTAN DORO** • 1968
GHOST STORY OF STONE LANTERNS AND CRYING IN THE NIGHT see **KAIDAN YONAKI-DORO** • 1962
GHOST STORY OF TWO TRAVELLERS see **KAIDAN DOCHU** • 1958
GHOST STORY OF WANDERER AT HONJO see **KAIDAN HONJO NANFUSHIGI** • 1957
GHOST STORY OF YOUTH see **SEISHUN KAIDAN** • 1955
GHOST TALES RETOLD • 1938 • Newman Widgey R. • UKN
GHOST TALKS, THE • 1929 • Seiler Lewis • USA
GHOST TALKS, THE • 1949 • White Jules • SHT • USA
GHOST THAT NEVER RETURNS, THE see **PRIVIDENIYE, KOTOROYE NE VOZVRASHCHAYETSA** • 1930
GHOST THAT WALKS ALONE, THE • 1944 • Landers Lew • USA
GHOST THAT WILL NOT RETURN, THE see **PRIVIDENIYE, KOTOROYE NE VOZVRASHCHAYETSA** • 1930
GHOST TOWN • 1936 • Fraser Harry L. • USA
GHOST TOWN • 1956 • Miner Allen H. • USA
GHOST TOWN • 1987 • Schmoeller David • USA
GHOST TOWN • 1988 • Governor Richard • USA
GHOST TOWN, THE see **GANDY GOOSE IN THE GHOST TOWN** • 1944
GHOST TOWN, THE see **PUEBLO FANTASMA, EL** • 1963
GHOST TOWN FROLICS • 1938 • Kline Lester • ANS • USA
GHOST TOWN GOLD • 1936 • Kane Joseph • USA
GHOST TOWN LAW • 1942 • Bretherton Howard • USA
GHOST TOWN RENEGADES • 1947 • Taylor Ray • USA
GHOST TOWN RIDERS • 1938 • Waggner George • USA
GHOST TRAIN see **YUREI RESSHA** • 1949
GHOST TRAIN, THE • 1927 • von Bolvary Geza • UKN, FRG
GHOST TRAIN, THE • 1931 • Forde Walter • UKN
GHOST TRAIN, THE • 1941 • Forde Walter • UKN
GHOST TRAIN, THE see **SPOOKTREIN, DE** • 1939
GHOST TRAIN MURDER, THE • 1959 • Maxwell Peter • UKN
GHOST VALLEY • 1932 • Allen Fred • USA
GHOST VALLEY RAIDERS • 1940 • Sherman George • USA
GHOST WAGON, THE • 1915 • Franz Joseph J. • USA
GHOST WALKS, THE • 1934 • Strayer Frank • USA
GHOST WALKS, THE • 1935 • Tennyson Walter • UKN
GHOST WANTED • 1940 • Jones Charles M. • ANS • USA
GHOST WARRIOR • 1985 • Carroll Larry • USA • SWORDKILL
GHOST WOMAN • Sin Ta • TWN
GHOST WRITER, THE • 1984 • Powell Tristram • TVM • USA
GHOST WRITERS • 1958 • Kneitel Seymour • ANS • USA
GHOSTBUSTERS • 1984 • Reitman Ivan • USA
GHOSTBUSTERS II • 1989 • Reitman Ivan • USA • LAST OF THE GHOSTBUSTERS, THE
GHOSTDANCE • 1984 • McMullen Ken • UKN • GHOST DANCE
GHOSTESSES • 1946 • Hughes Harry • UKN
GHOSTHOUSE • 1987 • Lenzi Umberto • ITL
GHOSTHOUSE 2 • 1988 • Newlin Martin • ITL • WITCHCRAFT ◦ WITCHERY
GHOSTKEEPER • 1981 • Makichuk James • CND
GHOSTLY AFFAIR, A • 1914 • Plumb Hay? • UKN
GHOSTLY FACE, THE • Yang Sai King • HKG • LEM MIEN KUEL
GHOSTLY INN, THE see **HALFWAY HOUSE, THE** • 1944
GHOSTLY TRAP, THE see **KAIDAN OTOSHIANA** • 1968
GHOSTRIDERS • 1986 • Stewart Alan • USA
GHOSTS • 1912 • *Macdonald Norman* • USA
GHOSTS • 1912 • Plumb Hay? • UKN
GHOSTS • 1913 • Bowman William J. • USA • WHO'S AFRAID?
GHOSTS • 1914 • Neame Elwin? • UKN
GHOSTS • 1915 • Nicholls George • USA
GHOSTS • 1917 • *Ebony* • SHT • USA
GHOSTS see **KOUZMA KRIOUTCHKOV** • 1914
GHOSTS see **GESPENSTER** • 1939
GHOSTS see **POWROT** • 1960
GHOSTS see **GHOSTS.. OF THE CIVIL DEAD** • 1988
GHOSTS, THE see **SPIRITISTEN** • 1914
GHOSTS AND FLYPAPERS • 1915 • Davis Ulysses • USA
GHOSTS AND THIEVES see **FANTASMI E LADRI** • 1959
GHOSTS AT CIRCLE X CAMP • 1912 • Melies Gaston • USA
GHOSTS BEFORE BREAKFAST see **VORMITTAGSPUK** • 1928
GHOSTS BEFORE NOON see **VORMITTAGSPUK** • 1928
GHOST'S BRIDE, THE • 1916 • *Puritan* • SHT • USA
GHOSTS DON'T DO IT • 1989 • Derek John • USA
GHOSTS FROM THE ATTIC see **STRASIDLA Z VIKYRE** • 1987
GHOSTS! GHOSTS! see **SPOKAR, DET SPOKAR, DET** • 1943
GHOST'S HOLIDAY, THE • 1907 • Fitzhamon Lewin • UKN
GHOSTS IN BUENOS AIRES see **FANTASMAS EN BUENOS AIRES** • 1942

GHOSTS IN ROME (USA) see **FANTASMI A ROMA** • 1961
GHOSTS IN THE CASTLE see **UPIOR W PALACU** • 1960
GHOSTS IN THE HOUSE see **FANTASMAS EN LA CASA** • 1958
GHOSTS IN THE NIGHT (UKN) see **GHOSTS ON THE LOOSE** • 1943
GHOSTS –ITALIAN STYLE see **QUESTI FANTASMI** • 1967
GHOSTS OF A RIVER • 1968 • Patry Pierre, Kasma Jacques • CND
GHOSTS OF BERKELEY SQUARE, THE • 1947 • Sewell Vernon • UKN
GHOSTS OF BUXLEY HALL, THE • 1980 • Bilson Bruce • USA
GHOSTS OF HANLEY HOUSE, THE • 1974 • *Baker Elsie* • TVM • UKN
GHOSTS OF ROME see **FANTASMI A ROMA** • 1961
GHOSTS.. OF THE CIVIL DEAD • 1988 • Hillcoat John • ASL • GHOSTS
GHOSTS OF TWO TRAVELERS AT TENAMONYA see **TENAMONYA YUREI DOCHU** • 1967
GHOSTS OF YESTERDAY • 1918 • Miller Charles • USA • TWO WOMEN
GHOSTS OF YESTERDAY • 1928 • Banfield George J., Eveleigh Leslie • SHS • UKN
GHOSTS ON PARADE see **YOKAI DAISENSO** • 1968
GHOSTS ON THE LOOSE • 1943 • Beaudine William • USA • GHOSTS IN THE NIGHT (UKN) ○ EAST SIDE KIDS MEET BELA LUGOSI, THE
GHOST'S SWORD, THE • Chang Ping-Han • HKG
GHOSTS THAT STILL WALK • 1977 • Flocker James T. • USA
GHOST'S VENGEANCE, A • HKG
GHOST'S WARNING, THE • 1911 • *Mcdermott Marc* • USA
GHOSTS WITH CHEESE see **FANTASMITAS CON QUESO** • 1970
GHOUL, THE • 1933 • Hunter T. Hayes • UKN
GHOUL, THE • 1975 • Francis Freddie • UKN
GHOUL IN SCHOOL, THE see **LYCANTHROPUS** • 1962
GHOULIES • 1985 • Bercovici Luca • USA
GHOULIES II • 1987 • Band Albert • USA
GHOULS, THE • 1988 • Roberts Vincent • USA
GHUDDI • 1979 • Zaki Syed Salahuddin • BNG • ROOTLESS, THE ○ KITE, THE
GHULAM ISHQ • 1978 • Shafaq Toryali • AFG • SLAVE OF LOVE, THE
GHUM BHANGAAR GAAN • 1964 • Dutt U. • IND
GHURUBA' • 1973 • Arafa Saad • EGY • ETRANGERS
GHURUBUN WA SHUROQ • 1970 • el Sheikh Kamal • EGY • AUBE ET CREPUSCULE
GIACCA VERDE, LA • 1979 • Giraldi Franco • ITL
GIACOBBE ED ESAU • 1963 • Landi Mario • ITL
GIACOBBE, L'UOMO CHE LOTTO CON DIO • 1965 • Baldi Marcello • ITL
GIACOMETTI • 1967 • Gill Michael • UKN
GIACOMO L'IDEALISTA • 1943 • Lattuada Alberto • ITL
GIALLO • 1933 • Camerini Mario • ITL
GIALLO AUTOMATICO • 1980 • Bozzetto Bruno • ANM • ITL
GIALLO MAPOLETANO • 1979 • Corbucci Sergio • ITL
GIAN BURRASCA • 1943 • Tofano Sergio • ITL
GIAN BURRASCA • 1983 • Pingitore Pier Francesco • ITL
GIANT • 1956 • Stevens George • USA
GIANT, THE see **MARED, EL** • 1964
GIANT, THE see **DEV ADAM** • 1968
GIANT BEHEMOTH, THE (USA) see **BEHEMOTH, THE SEA MONSTER** • 1959
GIANT CLAW, THE • 1957 • Sears Fred F. • USA • MARK OF THE CLAW, THE
GIANT FOR AMUAY, A see **GIGANTE PARA AMUAY, UN** • 1973
GIANT FROM THE UNKNOWN • 1958 • Cunha Richard E. • USA
GIANT GILA MONSTER, THE • 1959 • Kellogg Ray • USA
GIANT KILLER, THE • 1924 • Lantz Walter • ANS • USA
GIANT LAND • 1933 • Gillett Burt • ANS • USA
GIANT LEECHES, THE see **ATTACK OF THE GIANT LEECHES** • 1958
GIANT MONSTER see **NUITS DE RASPOUTINE, LES** • 1960
GIANT OF HIS RACE, A • 1921 • *Holmes Mabel* • USA
GIANT OF KYPSELA, THE see **GIGAS TIS KIPSELIS, O** • 1968
GIANT OF MARATHON, THE (UKN) see **BATTAGLIA DI MARATONA, LA** • 1959
GIANT OF METROPOLIS, THE (USA) see **GIGANTE DI METROPOLIS, IL** • 1961
GIANT OF NORWAY, THE • 1939 • Cahn Edward L. • USA • MAN WHO COULDN'T SAY NO, THE
GIANT OF THE EVIL ISLAND (USA) see **MISTERO DELL'ISOLA MALATESTA, IL** • 1965
GIANT OF THE LOST TOMB (UKN) see **MACISTE ALLA CORTE DELLO ZAR** • 1964
GIANT OF THE VALLEY OF KINGS see **MACISTE NELLA VALLE DEI RE** • 1960
GIANT OF THESSALY, THE (USA) see **GIGANTI DELLA TESSAGLIA, I** • 1960
GIANT POWDER • 1916 • McRae Henry • SHT • USA
GIANT SPIDER INVASION, THE • 1975 • Rebane Bill • USA • GREAT SPIDER INVASION, THE
GIANT WHEEL see **NAGARDOLA** • 1978
GIANT YMIR, THE see **20 MILLION MILES TO EARTH** • 1957
GIANTS A'FIRE (UKN) see **ROYAL MOUNTED PATROL, THE** • 1941
GIANTS OF ROME, THE see **GIGANTI DI ROMA, I** • 1964
GIANT'S TATTOO PARLOR, THE • Bass Howard • USA
GIANTS VS. YANKS • 1923 • McGowan Robert • SHT • USA
GIAPPONE PROIBITO see **PARADISO DELL'UOMO, IL** • 1962
GIARABUB • 1942 • Alessandrini Goffredo • ITL
GIARDINI DEL DIAVOLO, I • 1971 • Rizzo Alfredo • ITL
GIARDINO DEI FINZI-CONTINI, IL • 1970 • De Sica Vittorio • ITL, FRG • GARDEN OF THE FINZI-CONTINIS, THE (UKN)
GIARDINO DELLE DELIZIE, IL • 1968 • Agosti Silvano • ITL • GARDEN OF DELIGHTS, THE
GIARDINO DELLE ESPERIDI, IL • 1951 • Carpignano Vittorio • ITL
GIARRETTIERA COLT • 1967 • Rocco Gian Andrea • ITL • GARTER COLT
GIB MICH FREI • 1924 • Eriksen Erich • FRG
GIB MIR LIEBE • 1968 • Schlesinger Gunter • FRG • GIVE ME LOVE
GIBBI-WESTGERMANY • 1979 • Hauff Reinhard • FRG
GIBBONS: CANADA'S FIGHTING ELITE • 1987 • Jones Fred, Scott Ken • SHT • CND
GIBBSVILLE: THE TURNING POINT OF JIM MALLOY see **TURNING POINT OF JIM MALLOY, THE** • 1975
GIBBUNURI • 1986 • Bae Chang-Ho • SKR • SWEET DAYS OF YOUTH
GIBEL SENSATY • 1935 • Andrievski Alexander • USS • LOSS OF FEELING ○ LOSS OF SENSATION
GIBELTA NA ALEKASANDAR VILIKI • 1968 • Ikonomov Vladislav • BUL • FALL OF ALEXANDER THE GREAT, THE
GIBIER DE POTENCE • 1951 • Richebe Roger • FRN
GIBRALTAR • 1932 • Wright Basil • DOC • UKN
GIBRALTAR • 1938 • Ozep Fedor • FRN • IT HAPPENED IN GIBRALTAR
GIBRALTAR • 1963 • Gaspard-Huit Pierre • FRN, ITL, SPN • SPIONAGGIO A GIBILTERRA (ITL)
GIBRALTAR ADVENTURE • 1953 • Hill James • UKN • CLUE OF THE MISSING APE, THE
GIBSON GODDESS, THE • 1909 • Griffith D. W. • USA
GIBSON UPRIGHT, THE see **YOU FIND IT EVERYWHERE** • 1921
GID–AP, NAPOLEON • 1913 • *Essanay* • USA
GIDDAP • 1925 • *Sennett Mack (P)* • SHT • USA
GIDDH • 1984 • Ranga T. S. • IND • VULTURES
GIDDY AGE, THE • 1932 • Stafford Babe • SHT • USA
GIDDY GADGETS • 1962 • Kneitel Seymour • ANS • USA
GIDDY, GAY AND TICKLISH • 1915 • Cogley Nick • USA
GIDDY GIRL AND THE BUTTERFLY, THE • 1904 • *Cricks & Sharp* • UKN
GIDDY GOATS, THE • 1907 • Aylott Dave? • UKN
GIDDY GOLIGHTLY • 1917 • Mannering Cecil • UKN
GIDDY YAPPING • 1944 • Swift Howard • ANS • USA
GIDDYAP • 1959 • Babbitt Art • ANS • USA
GIDEON OF SCOTLAND YARD (USA) see **GIDEON'S DAY** • 1959
GIDEON'S DAY • 1959 • Ford John • UKN • GIDEON OF SCOTLAND YARD (USA)
GIDEON'S TRUMPET • 1980 • Collins Robert • TVM • USA
GIDGET • 1959 • Wendkos Paul • USA
GIDGET GETS MARRIED • 1972 • Swackhamer E. W. • TVM • USA
GIDGET GOES HAWAIIAN • 1961 • Wendkos Paul • USA
GIDGET GOES TO ROME • 1963 • Wendkos Paul • USA
GIDGET GROWS UP • 1970 • Sheldon James • TVM • USA
GIDGET'S SUMMER REUNION • 1985 • Bilson Bruce • TVM • USA
GIDGETTE GOES TO HELL • 1972 • Demme Jonathan (c/d) • USA
GIDSLET • 1913 • *Christensen Benjamin* • DNM
GIENEK • 1968 • Lomnicki Jan • DOC • PLN
GIERMEK • 1964 • Dulz Stanislaw • PLN • SHIELD–BEARER, THE
GIFLE, LA • 1974 • Pinoteau Claude • FRN, ITL • SCHIAFFO, LO (ITL) ○ SLAP, THE (USA)
GIFT • Stapp Philip • ANS • USA
GIFT • 1966 • Thomsen Knud Leif • DNM • VENOM (USA) ○ POISON
GIFT • 1973 • Brakhage Stan • USA
GIFT see **ANBALIPPU** • 1968
GIFT, THE • 1913 • Hulcup Jack • UKN • KISSING CUP
GIFT, THE • 1962 • Danska Herbert • USA
GIFT, THE • 1965 • Kelly Ron • CND
GIFT, THE • 1979 • Taylor Don • TVM • USA
GIFT, THE • 1984 • Jubenvill Ken • MTV • CND
GIFT, THE see **DAREK** • 1947
GIFT, THE see **CADEAU, LE** • 1961
GIFT, THE see **CADEAU, LE** • 1982
GIFT DER MEDICI, DAS • 1918 • Schmidthassler Walter • FRG
GIFT FOR HEIDI • 1958 • Templeton George • USA
GIFT FOR MUSIC • 1957 • Fyodorova Marina • USS
GIFT FROM A STRANGER • 1965 • Lofven Chris • SHT • ASL
GIFT FROM INDIA, A see **TOHFE HEND** • 1968
GIFT FROM SANTA CLAUS, A • 1909 • Porter Edwin S. • USA
GIFT GIRL, THE • 1917 • Julian Rupert • USA
GIFT IM WEIBE, DAS • 1919 • Decarli Bruno • FRG
GIFT IM ZOO • 1952 • Muller Hans • FRG
GIFT O' GAB • 1917 • Van Dyke W. S. • USA
GIFT OF FURY see **GREAT SANTINI, THE** • 1979
GIFT OF GAB, THE • 1934 • Freund Karl • USA
GIFT OF GAG • 1955 • Kneitel Seymour • ANS • USA
GIFT OF GOD, THE see **WEND KUUNI** • 1983
GIFT OF GREEN • 1946 • van Dongen Helen (c/d) • NTH
GIFT OF GREEN • 1952 • Flaherty David • USA
"GIFT OF HEALTH" LTD. see **AKTIEBOLAGET HALSANS GAVA** • 1916
GIFT OF LIFE, THE • 1982 • London Jerry • TVM • USA
GIFT OF LOVE • 1983 • Dewan Meera • DCS • IND
GIFT OF LOVE, THE • 1958 • Negulesco Jean • USA
GIFT OF LOVE, THE • 1978 • Chaffey Don • TVM • USA
GIFT OF LOVE: A CHRISTMAS STORY, THE • 1983 • Mann Delbert • TVM • USA
GIFT OF OSCAR, THE see **CADEAU D'OSCAR, LE** • 1965
GIFT OF THE BLACK FOLK, THE • 1977 • *Moss Carlton* • USA
GIFT OF THE FAIRIES, THE • 1917 • *Early Baby* • SHT • USA
GIFT OF THE MAGI • 1978 • Daniels Marc • TVM • USA
GIFT OF THE MAGI, THE • 1917 • Shaw Brinsley • USA
GIFT OF THE STORM, THE • 1913 • *Johnson Arthur* • USA
GIFT OF YOUTH, THE • 1909 • Blackton J. Stuart (Spv) • USA
GIFT SUPREME, THE • 1920 • Sellers Oliver L. • USA
GIFT UND LIEBE • 1924 • Linke Edmund • FRG
GIFT WRAPPED • 1952 • Freleng Friz • ANS • USA
GIFTAS • 1926 • Molander Olof • SWD • MARRIED LIFE
GIFTAS • 1957 • Henrikson Anders • SWD • OF LOVE AND LUST (USA) ○ MARRIED LIFE
GIFTAS VUXNAR DOTTRAR • 1933 • Wallen Sigurd • SWD • MARRIAGEABLE DAUGHTERS
GIFTED ONES, THE • 1959 • Haldane Don • CND
GIFTGAS • 1929 • Dubson Michael • FRG
GIFTPILEN • 1915 • Blom August • DNM • POISONOUS ARROW, THE
GIFTPLOMBE, DIE • 1918 • Wolff Carl Heinz • FRG
GIFTS FROM THE AIR • 1937 • *Mintz Charles (P)* • ANS • USA
GIFTS OF THE MAGI, THE see **DARY MAGOW** • 1972
GIFTS SNATCHED FROM NATURE • 1952 • Calotescu Virgil • DOC • RMN
GIFTSLANGEN ELLER PJERROTS SIDSTE OPTRAEDEN • 1913 • Davidsen Hjalmar • DNM
GIG, THE • 1985 • Gilroy Frank D. • USA
GIGANTE DE PEDRA, O • 1953 • Khouri Walter Hugo • BRZ
GIGANTE DI METROPOLIS, IL • 1961 • Scarpelli Umberto • ITL • GIANT OF METROPOLIS, THE (USA) ○ METROPOLIS
GIGANTE PARA AMUAY, UN • 1973 • de Witt George • DOC • VNZ • GIANT FOR AMUAY, A
GIGANTES INTERPLANETARIOS see **GIGANTES PLANETARIOS** • 1965
GIGANTES PLANETARIOS • 1965 • Crevenna Alfredo B. • MXC • GIGANTES INTERPLANETARIOS ○ PLANETARY GIANTS
GIGANTES Y CABEZUDOS • 1925 • Rey Florian • SPN
GIGANTI DEL CIELO, I • 1961 • *Petrosemolo Gaetano (P)* • DOC • ITL
GIGANTI DELLA TESSAGLIA, I • 1960 • Freda Riccardo • ITL, FRN • GEANT DE THESALIE, LE (FRN) ○ GIANT OF THESSALY, THE (USA) ○ ARGONAUTI, GLI ○ JASON AND THE GOLDEN FLEECE ○ ARGONAUTS, THE
GIGANTI DI ROMA, I • 1964 • Margheriti Antonio • ITL, FRN • GIANTS OF ROME, THE
GIGANTIC DEVIL, THE see **DIABLE GEANT OU LE MIRACLE DE LA MADONNE, LE** • 1902
GIGANTIC MARIONETTES • 1913 • Noy Wilfred? • UKN
GIGANTIS, THE FIRE MONSTER (USA) see **GOJIRA NO GYAKUSHYU** • 1955
GIGAS TIS KIPSELIS, O • 1968 • Karayannis Kostas • GRC • GIANT OF KYPSELA, THE
GIGGLE WATER • 1932 • Sweet Harry • SHT • USA
GIGI • 1948 • Audry Jacqueline • FRN
GIGI • 1958 • Minnelli Vincente • USA
GIGI AND THE FOUNTAIN OF YOUTH • ANM
GIGI GOES TO BAT see **GIGI GOES TO POT** • 1970
GIGI GOES TO POT • 1970 • Catah Sam S. • USA • GIGI GOES TO BAT
GIGLIO INFRANTO, IL • 1956 • Chili Giorgio W. • ITL
GIGOLETTE • 1921 • Pouctal Henri • FRN
GIGOLETTE • 1935 • Lamont Charles • USA • NIGHT CLUB (UKN)
GIGOLETTE • 1936 • Noe Yvan • FRN
GIGOLETTES • 1932 • Arbuckle Roscoe • USA
GIGOLETTES OF PARIS • 1933 • Martell Alphonse • USA
GIGOLO • 1926 • Howard William K. • USA
GIGOLO, LE • 1960 • Deray Jacques • FRN
GIGOLO, THE see **EINTANZER, DER** • 1978
GIGOLO – GIGOLET – CLASH – QUARRELLING see **GIGOLO – GIGOLET – NAGKAGULO – NAGKAGALIT** • 1968
GIGOLO – GIGOLET – NAGKAGULO – NAGKAGALIT • 1968 • de Guzman Ruben • PHL • GIGOLO – GIGOLET – CLASH – QUARRELLING
GIGOT • 1962 • Kelly Gene • USA
GIGUE MERVEILLEUSE, LA • 1909 • Melies Georges • FRN • MARVELOUS HIND LEG, THE
GIJS VAN GROENESTEIN, STRAATVEGER • 1976 • Grasveld Fons • DOC • NTH • PORTRAIT OF A ROADSWEEPER ○ ROADSWEEPER
GIL BLAS DE SANTILLANE see **AVENTURES DE GIL BLAS DE SANTILLANE, LES** • 1955
GIL VICENTE E O SEU TEATRO • 1966 • Ribeiro Antonio Lopes • PRT
GILA GILA • 1978 • Rojik Omar • MLY
GILBERT AND SULLIVAN see **STORY OF GILBERT AND SULLIVAN, THE** • 1953
GILBERT DYING TO DIE • 1915 • Elvey Maurice? • UKN
GILBERT GETS TIGER–ITIS • 1915 • Elvey Maurice? • UKN
GILBERT HARDING SPEAKING OF MURDER • 1953 • Dickson Paul • UKN
GILBERTO'S DREAM • 1980 • Pyke Roger • MTV • CND • REVE DE GILBERTO, LE
GILDA • 1946 • Vidor Charles • USA
GILDA LIVE • 1980 • Nichols Mike • USA
GILDED BUTTERFLY, THE • 1926 • Wray John Griffith • USA
GILDED CAGE, THE • 1915 • *Scott Betty* • USA
GILDED CAGE, THE • 1916 • Knoles Harley • USA
GILDED CAGE, THE • 1955 • Gilling John • UKN
GILDED DREAM, THE • 1920 • Sturgeon Rollin S. • USA
GILDED FOOL, THE • 1908 • *Essanay* • USA
GILDED FOOL, THE • 1915 • Lewis Edgar • USA
GILDED HIGHWAY, THE • 1926 • Blackton J. Stuart • USA
GILDED KID, THE • 1914 • Williams C. Jay • USA
GILDED LIFE, THE • 1917 • Weber Lois, Smalley Phillips • SHT • USA
GILDED LILIES • 1921 • Earle William P. S. • USA
GILDED LILY, THE • 1921 • Leonard Robert Z. • USA
GILDED LILY, THE • 1935 • Ruggles Wesley • USA
GILDED SPIDER, THE • 1916 • De Grasse Joseph • USA
GILDED YOUTH • 1915 • Julian Rupert • USA
GILDED YOUTH, A • 1917 • Sargent George L. • USA
GILDERSLEEVE ON BROADWAY • 1943 • Douglas Gordon • USA
GILDERSLEEVE'S BAD DAY • 1943 • Douglas Gordon • USA
GILDERSLEEVE'S GHOST • 1944 • Douglas Gordon • USA
GILDING THE LILY • 1937 • Miller David • SHT • USA
GILES' FIRST VISIT TO A HOSPITAL • 1909 • *Wrench Films* • UKN
GILES' FIRST VISIT TO LONDON • 1911 • Martinek H. O. • UKN
GILES HAS HIS FORTUNE TOLD • 1911 • Booth W. R.? • UKN
GILGAMESH • Collins Vincent • ANS • USA
GILGI EINE VON UNS • 1933 • Meyer Johannes • FRG
GILIAP • 1975 • Andersson Roy • SWD
GILL WOMAN see **GILL WOMEN OF VENUS** • 1967
GILL WOMEN, THE see **GILL WOMEN OF VENUS** • 1967
GILL WOMEN OF VENUS • 1967 • Bogdanovich Peter, Harrington Curtis • USA • VOYAGE TO THE PLANET OF PREHISTORIC WOMEN ○ GILL WOMEN, THE ○ GILL WOMAN
GILLEKOP • 1916 • Blom August • DNM
GILLIAGIN'S ACCIDENT POLICY • 1914 • *Ab* • USA
GILLS • 1914 • Burguet Charles • FRN
GILO COVIK • 1968 • Gluscevic Obrad • YGS • NAKED MAN, THE

GILSODDEUM • 1985 • Lim Kwon-Taek • SKR • GILSODOM
GILSODOM see **GILSODDEUM** • 1985
GILT EDGE STOCKS • 1913 • *Kalem* • USA
GIMBA • 1962 • Rangel Flavio • BRZ
GIMBO KI BETI • 1960 • *Naazi* • IND • DAUGHTER OF GIMBO
GIMME • 1923 • Hughes Rupert • USA
GIMME AN "F" • 1984 • Justman Paul • USA
GIMME MY QUARTERBACK • 1934 • Hays Jack • USA
GIMME SHELTER • 1970 • Maysles David, Maysles Albert, Zwerin Charlottę • USA
GIMPEI FROM KOINA see **KOINA NO GINPEI** • 1933
GIN NO BOOTS • 1967 • Ichimura Hirokazu • JPN • SILVER BOOTS
GIN-SHINJU see **SHIROGANE SHINJU** • 1956
GINA • 1974 • Arcand Denys • CND
GINA (USA) see **MORT EN CE JARDIN, LA** • 1956
GINECOLOGO DELLA MUTUA, IL • 1977 • D'Amato Joe • ITL • LADIES' DOCTOR
GINEPRO FATTO UOMO • 1964 • Bellocchio Marco • SHT • ITL
GINETTE RAVEL • 1969 • Woods Grahame • CND
GINEVRA DEGLI ALMIERI • 1935 • Brignone Guido • ITL
GING DA NICHT EBEN DAS GLUCK VORBEI? see **WIENER LIEBSCHAFTEN** • 1930
GINGA-TETSUDO NO YORU • 1985 • Sugii Gisaburo • JPN • NIGHT TRAIN FOR THE MILKY WAY, THE
GINGER • 1919 • George Burton • USA
GINGER • 1935 • Seiler Lewis • USA
GINGER • 1947 • Drake Oliver • USA
GINGER • 1971 • Schain Don • USA
GINGER see **RYZHIK** • 1960
GINGER see **ZUTA** • 1974
GINGER AND FRED (UKN) see **GINGER E FRED** • 1985
GINGER BREAD BOY, THE • 1934 • Lantz Walter, Nolan William • ANS • USA
GINGER E FRED • 1985 • Fellini Federico • ITL, FRN, FRG • GINGER AND FRED (UKN)
GINGER IN THE MORNING • 1973 • Wiles Gordon • USA
GINGER MEGGS • 1982 • Dawson Jonathan • ASL
GINGER MICK • 1920 • Longford Raymond • ASL
GINGER NUTT'S BEE-BOTHER • 1949 • Felstead Bert • UKN
GINGER NUTT'S CHRISTMAS • 1949 • Felstead Bert • UKN • CHRISTMAS CIRCUS
GINGER NUTT'S FOREST DRAGON see **FOREST DRAGON** • 1949
GINGER SEEKS A SOLUTION • 1914 • Kellino W. P. • UKN
GINGER SNAPS • 1929 • Lamont Charles • SHT • USA
GINGER VERSUS DYNAMITE see **JENGIBRE CONTRA DINAMITA** • 1939
GINGERBREAD • 1909 • Aylott Dave • UKN
GINGERBREAD COTTAGE, THE see **PERNIKOVA CHALOUPKA** • 1951
GINGERBREAD CUPID • 1912 • *Middleton Ed* • USA
GINGERBREAD HOUSE see **PERNIKOVA CHALOUPKA** • 1951
GINGERBREAD HOUSE see **WHOEVER SLEW AUNTIE ROO?** • 1971
GINGERBREAD HUT see **PERNIKOVA CHALOUPKA** • 1951
GINGERBREAD KINGDOM, THE • Wasilewski Zenon • ANM • PLN
GINGER'S REIGN • 1914 • King Burton L. • USA
GINGHAM GIRL, THE • 1920 • Davis James • SHT • USA
GINGHAM GIRL, THE • 1927 • Kirkland David • USA
GINGTSAT GUSI TSUKTSAP • 1988 • Chan Jackie • HKG • POLICE STORY PART II
GINGWAN GEI • 1988 • Chung Chi-Man Davi • HKG
GINK FROM KANKAKEE, THE • 1916 • *Humphrey Orral* • SHT • USA
GINK LANDS AGAIN, THE • 1916 • *Humphrey Orral* • SHT • USA
GINKO THE GEISHA see **SHUKUZU** • 1953
GINNEKO SAMON • 1928 • Inagaki Hiroshi • JPN
GINO • 1960 • Domnick Ottomar • FRG
GINPEI THE OUTLAW see **MOHOMONO GINPEI** • 1937
GINREI NO HATE • 1947 • Taniguchi Senkichi • JPN • TO THE END OF THE SILVER-CAPPED MOUNTAINS ○ SNOW TRAIL
GINREI NO ONJA • 1961 • Bansho Yoshiaki • JPN • STORM ON THE SILVERY PEAKS
GINSBERG • 1966 • Branaman Bob • USA
GINSBERG THE GREAT • 1927 • Haskin Byron • USA • BROADWAY KID, THE (UKN)
GINZA COSMETICS see **GINZA-GESHO** • 1951
GINZA FOR TWO OF US see **FUTARI NO GINZA** • 1967
GINZA-GESHO • 1951 • Naruse Mikio • JPN • GINZA COSMETICS
GINZA NO KOI NO MONOGATARI • 1962 • Kurahara Koreyoshi • JPN • LOVE IN GINZA
GINZA NO KOIBITOTACHI • 1961 • *Dan Reiko* • JPN • LOVERS OF GINZA (USA)
GINZA NO MOSA • 1960 • Ichikawa Kon • JPN • GINZA VETERAN, A
GINZA NO ONE-CHAN • 1959 • Sugie Toshio • JPN • THREE DOLLS IN GINZA
GINZA NO ONNA • 1955 • Yoshimura Kozaburo • JPN • WOMEN OF THE GINZA ○ WOMAN OF THE GINZA
GINZA NO YANAGI • 1932 • Gosho Heinosuke • JPN • WILLOWS OF GINZA ○ WILLOW TREE IN THE GINZA, A
GINZA SANSHIRO • 1950 • Ichikawa Kon • JPN • SANSHIRO AT GINZA ○ SANSHIRO OF GINZA
GINZA TAIKUTSU MUSUME • 1960 • Yamamoto Kajiro • JPN • GINZA TOMBOY
GINZA TOMBOY see **GINZA TAIKUTSU MUSUME** • 1960
GINZA VETERAN, A see **GINZA NO MOSA** • 1960
GINZAKKO MONOGATARI • 1961 • Inoue Umeji • JPN • THREE GINZA BOYS
GIOCARE D'AZZARDO • 1983 • Torrini Cinzia Th. • ITL • GAME OF CHANCE
GIOCATTOLO, IL • 1979 • Montaldo Giuliano • ITL
GIOCATTOLO DEE'AMORE, IL see **CENTO DI QUESTI GIORNI** • 1933
GIOCHI D'AMORE SUL FILO DI UNA LAMA • 1973 • Pellegrini Giuseppe • ITL
GIOCHI DE COLONIA • 1958 • Olmi Ermanno • DOC • ITL
GIOCHI DI FUOCO (ITL) see **JEU AVEC LE FEU, LE** • 1975
GIOCHI DI SOCIETA see **AI VOSTRI ORDINA, SIGNORA!** • 1939
GIOCHI EROTICI DI UNA FAMIGLIA PERBENE • 1976 • Degli Espinosa Francesco • ITL
GIOCHI PARTICOLARI • 1970 • Indovina Franco • ITL • SPECIAL GAMES ○ VOYEUR, LE
GIOCHI PROIBITI DELL'ARETINO PIETRO • 1972 • Regnoli Piero • ITL • TALES OF EROTICA
GIOCO AL MASSACRO • 1990 • Damiani Damiano • ITL • MASSACRE PLAY
GIOCO D'AZZARDO • 1943 • Bassi Parsifal • ITL • QUEL CARO DEMETRIO
GIOCO DEGLI INNAMORATI, IL (ITL) see **AMOUREUX DU FRANCE, LES** • 1963
GIOCO DELLA VITA, IL • 1970 • Borella Paolo • ITL
GIOCO DELLE SPIE, IL • 1966 • Bianchini Paolo • ITL, FRN • OUR MEN IN BAGDAD (USA) ○ SCUFFLE IN BAGDAD FOR X-27 ○ OUR MAN IN BAGDAD
GIOCO PER EVELINE, UN • 1971 • Avallone Marcello • ITL
GIOCO PERICOLOSO • 1942 • Malasomma Nunzio • ITL
GIOCONDA, LA • 1911 • Maggi Luigi • ITL
GIOCONDA, LA • 1953 • Solito Giacinto • ITL
GIOCONDA FARA SURIS • 1968 • Ursianu Malvina • RMN • GIOCONDA WITHOUT THAT SMILE ○ GIOCONDA WITHOUT A SMILE
GIOCONDA WITHOUT A SMILE see **GIOCONDA FARA SURIS** • 1968
GIOCONDA WITHOUT THAT SMILE see **GIOCONDA FARA SURIS** • 1968
GIOIA'S PHOTOS see **FOTO DI GIOIA, LE** • 1987
GIOIELLI DI MADAME DE..., I (ITL) see **MADAME DE..** • 1953
GION BAYASHI • 1953 • Mizoguchi Kenji • JPN • GION MUSIC FESTIVAL (UKN) ○ GION FESTIVAL MUSIC ○ GEISHA, A (USA) ○ GION MUSIC
GION FESTIVAL see **GION MATSURI** • 1933
GION FESTIVAL see **GION MATSURI** • 1968
GION FESTIVAL MUSIC see **GION BAYASHI** • 1953
GION MATSURI • 1933 • Mizoguchi Kenji • JPN • GION FESTIVAL
GION MATSURI • 1968 • Ito Daisuke, Yamanouchi Tetsuya • JPN • DAY THE SUN ROSE, THE (USA) ○ GION FESTIVAL
GION MUSIC see **GION BAYASHI** • 1953
GION MUSIC FESTIVAL (UKN) see **GION BAYASHI** • 1953
GION NO SHIMAI • 1936 • Mizoguchi Kenji • JPN • SISTERS OF THE GION (USA)
GIORDANO BRUNO • 1908 • Pastrone Giovanni • ITL
GIORDANO BRUNO • 1973 • Montaldo Giuliano • ITL
GIORGOBISTVE see **LISTOPAD** • 1968
GIORNATA BALORDA, LA • 1960 • Bolognini Mauro • ITL, FRN • CA S'EST PASSE A ROME (FRN) ○ FROM A ROMAN BALCONY (USA) ○ LOVE IS A DAY'S WORK ○ PICKUP IN ROME ○ DAY OF SIN, A ○ CRAZY DAY, A
GIORNATA NERA PER L'ARIETE • 1971 • Bazzoni Luigi • ITL • EVIL FINGERS (UKN)
GIORNATA PARTICOLARE, UNA • 1977 • Scola Ettore • ITL, CND • SPECIAL DAY, A (USA) ○ GREAT DAY, THE
GIORNATA SPESA BENE, UNA (ITL) see **JOURNEE BIEN REMPLIE, UNE** • 1973
GIORNI CANTATI, I • 1979 • Pietrangeli Paolo • ITL • SINGING DAYS, THE
GIORNI CONTATI, I • 1962 • Petri Elio • ITL • DAYS ARE NUMBERED, THE
GIORNI D'AMORE • 1955 • De Santis Giuseppe • ITL • DAYS OF LOVE
GIORNI D'AMORE SUL FILO DI LAMA • 1973 • Mollin M. • ITL
GIORNI DEL COMMISSARIO AMBROSIO, I • 1988 • Corbucci Sergio • ITL • DAYS OF INSPECTOR AMBROSIO, THE
GIORNI DELLA CHIMERA, I • 1975 • Corona Franco • ITL
GIORNI DELLA VIOLENZA, I • 1967 • Brescia Alfonso • ITL • DAYS OF VIOLENCE
GIORNI DELL'IRA, I • 1967 • Valerii Tonino • ITL, FRG • TOD RITT DIENSTAGS, DER (FRG) ○ DAY OF ANGER (UKN) ○ DAYS OF WRATH ○ DAY OF WRATH ○ GUN LAW
GIORNI DI FUOCO (ITL) see **WINNETOU II** • 1964
GIORNI DI FURORE • 1964 • Nahoum Isacco, Dolino Gianni, Canavero Giovanni, Canavero Alfieri, Serandrei Mario, De Santis Giuseppe, Visconti Luchino • DOC • ITL
GIORNI DI SANGUE • 1968 • Gicca Enzo • ITL
GIORNI FELICI • 1943 • Franciolini Gianni • ITL
GIORNI PIU BELLI, I • 1956 • Mattoli Mario • ITL
GIORNO ALLA FINE D'OTTOBRE, UN • 1978 • Spinola Paolo • ITL
GIORNO CALDO AL PARADISO SHOW • 1966 • Di Gianni Enzo • ITL
GIORNO COME OGNI GIORNO, UN • 1959 • Partesano Dino • DOC • ITL
GIORNO DA LEONI, UN • 1961 • Loy Nanni • ITL • DAY FOR LION-HEARTS, A
GIORNO DEI CRISTALLI, IL • 1978 • Battiato Giacomo • ITL
GIORNO DEL FURORE, IL • 1973 • Calenda Antonio • ITL, UKN • FURY (UKN) ○ ONE RUSSIAN SUMMER (USA) ○ UOMO, UN
GIORNO DEL GIUDIZIO, IL • 1971 • Gariazzo Mario • ITL • DRUMMER OF VENGEANCE
GIORNO DELLA CIVETTA, IL • 1967 • Damiani Damiano • ITL, FRN • MAFFIA FAIT LA LOI, LA (FRN) ○ DAY OF THE OWL, THE ○ MAFIA (USA) ○ MAFIA FAIT LA LOI, LA
GIORNO DELL'ASSUNTA, IL • 1977 • Russo Nino • ITL
GIORNO DI FESTA see **UOMO VENUTO DAL MARE, L'** • 1942
GIORNO DI NOZZE • 1942 • Matarazzo Raffaello • ITL
GIORNO E L'ORA, IL see **JOUR ET L'HEURE, LE** • 1963
GIORNO IN BARBAGIA, UN • 1958 • De Seta Vittorio • ITL
GIORNO IN CASERNA, UN see **ALLEGRO SQUADRONE, L'** • 1954
GIORNO IN EUROPA, UN • 1959 • Marsili Emilio • DOC • ITL
GIORNO IN PRETURA, UN • 1954 • Steno • ITL • DAY IN COURT, A (USA)
GIORNO NELLA VITA, UN • 1946 • Blasetti Alessandro • ITL • DAY OF LIFE, A
GIORNO PER GIORNO DISPERATAMENTE • 1961 • Giannetti Alfredo • ITL
GIORNO PIU CORTO, IL • 1963 • Corbucci Sergio • ITL • SHORTEST DAY, THE (USA)
GIORNO PRIMA, IL • 1987 • Montaldo Giuliano • ITL, CND • DAY BEFORE, THE
GIOTTO see **RACCONTO DA UN AFFRESCO** • 1940
GIOVANE ATTILA, IL see **TECNICA E IL RITO, LA** • 1971
GIOVANE CANAGLIA • 1958 • Vari Giuseppe • ITL, SPN
GIOVANE LEONE, IL (ITL) see **OH! QUE MAMBO** • 1959
GIOVANE NORMALE, IL • 1969 • Risi Dino • ITL • NORMAL YOUNG MAN, THE
GIOVANE TOSCANINI, IL • 1988 • Zeffirelli Franco • ITL, FRN • YOUNG TOSCANINI
GIOVANI MARITI • 1958 • Bolognini Mauro • ITL • YOUNG HUSBANDS (USA) ○ NEWLYWEDS
GIOVANI TIGRI, I • 1968 • Leonviola Antonio • ITL • YOUNG TIGERS, THE
GIOVANNA • 1956 • Pontecorvo Gillo • ITL
GIOVANNA D'ARCO • 1908 • Caserini Mario • ITL • JOAN OF ARC
GIOVANNA D'ARCO • 1913 • Oxilia Nino • ITL
GIOVANNA D'ARCO AL ROGO • 1954 • Rossellini Roberto • ITL, FRN • JOAN OF ARC AT THE STAKE ○ JOAN AT THE STAKE ○ JEANNE AU BUCHER
GIOVANNI • 1983 • Apon Annette • NTH
GIOVANNI DE MEDICI -THE LEADER see **CONDOTTIERI** • 1937
GIOVANNI DELLE BANDE NERE • 1910 • Caserini Mario • ITL
GIOVANNI DELLE BANDE NERE • 1957 • Grieco Sergio • ITL • VIOLENT PATRIOT, THE
GIOVANNI EPISCOPO see **DELITTO DI GIOVANNI EPISCOPO, IL** • 1947
GIOVANNINO • 1976 • Nuzzi Paolo • ITL
GIOVANNI'S GRATITUDE • 1913 • *Pickford Jack* • USA
GIOVANNIS RACHE • 1917 • Meinert Rudolf • FRG
GIOVANNONA COSCIALUNGA DISONORATA CON ONORE • 1973 • Martino Sergio • ITL
GIOVE IN DOPPIOPETTO • 1955 • Danza Daniele • ITL
GIOVEDI, IL • 1962 • Risi Dino • ITL • THURSDAY
GIOVENTU ALLA SBARRA • 1954 • Cerio Ferruccio • ITL
GIOVENTU DI NOTTE • 1962 • Sequi Mario • ITL, FRN
GIOVENTU DISPERATA see **RAGAZZO DAL CUORE DI FANGO** • 1957
GIOVENTU PERDUTA • 1948 • Germi Pietro • ITL • LOST YOUTH
GIOVENTU SUL BRENTA • 1961 • Casara Severino • ITL
GIOVINEZZA • 1952 • Pastina Giorgio • ITL
GIOVINEZZA GIOVINEZZA • 1969 • Rossi Franco • ITL • YOUTH MARCH (USA)
GIPERBOLOID INGENERA GARINA • 1965 • Gintsburg Alexander, Berdicevski Mikhail? • USS • HYPERBOLOID OF ENGINEER GARIN, THE ○ ENGINEER GARIN'S DEATH RAY
GIPFELSTURMER • 1933 • Wenzler Franz • FRG
GIPGO PULD BAM • 1985 • Bae Chang-Ho • SKR • DEEP BLUE NIGHT
GIPS-ROMANCA • 1960 • Urbanski Kazimierz • PLN • BIRTH OF A SCULPTURE
GIPSIES, THE see **CIKANI** • 1921
GIPSIES AT HOME see **CAMPEMENT DE BOHEMIENS** • 1896
GIPSIES IN IRELAND • 1911 • Olcott Sidney • USA
GIPSY see **TSYGAN** • 1967
GIPSY BLOOD • 1922 • Haldane Bert • UKN
GIPSY BLOOD see **GYPSY BLOOD** • 1931
GIPSY CAVALIER, A • 1922 • Blackton J. Stuart • UKN
GIPSY CHILD, THE • 1909 • Fitzhamon Lewin • UKN
GIPSY FORTUNE TELLER, THE • 1905 • Collins Alf? • UKN
GIPSY GIRL'S HONOUR, A • 1912 • Fitzhamon Lewin • UKN
GIPSY HATE • 1913 • Fitzhamon Lewin • UKN
GIPSY NAN • 1911 • Fitzhamon Lewin? • UKN
GIPSY TALISMAN, THE • 1912 • Cabanne W. Christy • USA
GIPSY TALISMAN, THE • 1914 • Henderson Dell • USA
GIR WHO CAME BACK, THE • 1923 • Forman Tom • USA
GIR WHO DIDN'T THINK, THE • 1917 • Haddock William F. • USA
GIR WHO WOULDN'T QUIT, THE • 1918 • Jones Edgar • USA
GIRA A.T.M., UNA • 1958 • Porter Julio • MXC
GIRAFFE, THE see **ZYRAFA** • 1966
GIRAFFE IN THE WINDOW, A see **ZIRAFA V OKNE** • 1968
GIRARA see **UCHU DAIKAIJU GUILALA** • 1967
GIRASOLI, I • 1969 • De Sica Vittorio • ITL, FRN • FLEURS DU SOLEIL, LES (FRN) ○ SUNFLOWER (USA) ○ SUNFLOWERS, THE
GIRDHAR GOPAL KI MIRA • 1949 • Roy Prafulla • IND
GIRDLE OF GOLD • 1952 • Tully Montgomery • UKN
GIRL, THE • 1987 • Mattsson Arne • SWD
GIRL, THE see **DEVOJKA** • 1965
GIRL, THE see **ELTAVOZOTT NAP** • 1968
GIRL, THE see **DEN MUSSO** • 1975
GIRL, A GUARD AND A GARRET, A • 1915 • MacMackin Archer • USA
GIRL, A GUITAR AND A TRUMPET, A see **KAERLIGHEDENS MELODI** • 1959
GIRL, A GUY AND A GOB, A • 1941 • Wallace Richard • USA • NAVY STEPS OUT, THE (UKN) ○ THREE GIRLS AND A GOB
GIRL ACROSS THE HALL, THE • 1914 • *Benham Harry* • USA
GIRL ACROSS THE WAY, THE • 1913 • Cabanne W. Christy • USA
GIRL AGAINST NAPOLEON, A see **CARMEN, LA DE RONDA** • 1959
GIRL ALASKA, THE • 1919 • Smith Albert I. • USA
GIRL ALONE, A • 1912 • Haldane Bert? • UKN
GIRL, AN ADVENTURE AND.. see **DZIEWCZYNA, PRZYGODA I..** • 1961
GIRL AND A SPY, A • 1911 • *Champion* • USA
GIRL AND HER MONEY, A • 1913 • Salter Harry • USA
GIRL AND HER TRUST, THE • 1912 • Griffith D. W. • USA
GIRL AND THE BACHELOR, THE • 1915 • *Moore Tom* • USA
GIRL AND THE BANDIT, THE • 1910 • *Kalem* • USA
GIRL AND THE BANDIT, THE • 1913 • *Frontier* • USA
GIRL AND THE BOY, THE see **FILLE ET LA GARCON, LA** • 1931
GIRL AND THE BRONCO BUSTER, THE • 1911 • Blache Alice • USA
GIRL AND THE BUGLER, THE (USA) see **ZVONYAT, OTKROYTE DVER** • 1965
GIRL AND THE BURGLAR, THE • 1911 • *Solax* • USA
GIRL AND THE CELLIST, THE see **DEMOISELLE ET LE VIOLONCELLISTE, LA** • 1964

GIRL AND THE CHAPERON, THE • 1912 • *Nestor* • USA
GIRL AND THE CHAUFFEUR, THE • 1911 • *Yankee* • USA
GIRL AND THE COWBOY, THE • 1912 • *Rawlinson Herbert* • USA
GIRL AND THE CRISIS, THE • 1917 • Mong William V. • USA
GIRL AND THE DEVIL, THE see **FLICKAN OCH DJAVULEN** • 1943
GIRL AND THE DINOSAUR, THE • 1918 • O'Brien Willis (Spvn) • ANS • USA
GIRL AND THE ECHO, THE see **DEVOCHKA I EKHO** • 1964
GIRL AND THE EXPLORER, THE • 1914 • Moore Tom • USA
GIRL AND THE FUGITIVE, THE • 1913 • *Essanay* • USA
GIRL AND THE GAMBLER, THE • 1913 • Grandon Francis J. • USA
GIRL AND THE GAMBLER, THE • 1939 • Landers Lew • USA • DOVE, THE
GIRL AND THE GAME, THE • 1916 • McGowan J. P. • SRL • USA
GIRL AND THE GANGSTER, THE • 1913 • *Blackwell Carlyle* • USA
GIRL AND THE GENERAL, THE (USA) see **RAGAZZA E IL GENERALE, LA** • 1966
GIRL AND THE GOLD MINE, THE • 1914 • Somers Dalton • UKN
GIRL AND THE GONDOLIER, THE • 1914 • *Kalem* • USA
GIRL AND THE GOOSE, THE see **SMART SEX, THE** • 1921
GIRL AND THE GORILLA, THE see **NABONGA** • 1944
GIRL AND THE GORILLA, THE see **ZAMBA** • 1949
GIRL AND THE GRAFT, THE • 1918 • Earle William P. S. • SHT • USA
GIRL AND THE GRAFTER, THE • 1913 • *Thanhouser* • USA
GIRL AND THE GREASER, THE • 1913 • *Kerrigan J. Warren* • USA
GIRL AND THE GUN, THE • 1912 • Dwan Allan • USA
GIRL AND THE HALF-BACK, THE • 1911 • *Fischer Margarita* • USA
GIRL AND THE HOBO, THE • 1914 • *Frontier* • USA
GIRL AND THE INVENTOR, THE • 1913 • *Reliance* • USA
GIRL AND THE JUDGE, THE • 1910 • *Vitagraph* • USA
GIRL AND THE JUDGE, THE • 1913 • Parker Lem B. • USA
GIRL AND THE JUDGE, THE • 1918 • O'Brien John B. • USA
GIRL AND THE LAW, THE • 1920 • Jaccard Jacques • SHT • USA
GIRL AND THE LEGEND, THE (USA) see **ROBINSON SOLL NICHT STERBEN** • 1957
GIRL AND THE MAIL BAG, THE • 1915 • Mix Tom • USA
GIRL AND THE MATINEE IDOL, THE • 1915 • Morrissey George • USA
GIRL AND THE MEN, THE see **MADCHEN UND DIE MANNER, DAS** • 1919
GIRL AND THE MISER, THE • 1914 • *Howley Irene* • USA
GIRL AND THE MOTOR BOAT, THE • 1911 • *Fuller Mary* • USA
GIRL AND THE MUMMY, THE • 1916 • *Hopper De Wolfe* • USA
GIRL AND THE OAK, THE see **DJEVOJCICA I HRAST** • 1954
GIRL AND THE OATH, THE • 1911 • *Champion* • USA
GIRL AND THE OUTLAW, THE • 1908 • Griffith D. W. • USA
GIRL AND THE OUTLAW, THE • 1913 • *Fuller Mary* • USA
GIRL AND THE PALIO, THE (USA) see **RAGAZZA DEL PALIO, LA** • 1957
GIRL AND THE PRESS PHOTOGRAPHER, THE see **PIGEN OG PRESSEFOTOGRAFEN** • 1962
GIRL AND THE REPORTER, THE • 1915 • Santschi Thomas • USA
GIRL AND THE RING, THE • 1917 • *Depp Harry* • USA
GIRL AND THE RIVER, THE see **EAU VIVE, L'** • 1956
GIRL AND THE SHERIFF, THE • 1911 • *Gardner Helen* • USA
GIRL AND THE SHERIFF, THE • 1912 • Christie Al • USA
GIRL AND THE SMUGGLER, THE • 1914 • *Wallace Irene* • USA
GIRL AND THE SPY, THE • 1915 • *Wilson Ben* • USA
GIRL AND THE STOWAWAY, THE • 1914 • Buel Kenean • USA
GIRL AND THE TENOR, THE • 1916 • Ellis Robert • SHT • USA
GIRL AND THE TIGER, THE • 1913 • *Clifford William* • USA
GIRL AND TWO BOYS, A • 1915 • *Beauty* • USA
GIRL ANGLE, THE • 1917 • Jones Edgar • USA
GIRL, ARTIST AND DOG • 1913 • *Majestic* • USA
GIRL AT BAY, A • 1919 • Mills Thomas R. • USA
GIRL AT DOJO TEMPLE, A see **MUSUME DOJIJI** • 1945
GIRL AT HIS SIDE, THE • 1914 • Eagle Oscar • USA
GIRL AT HOME, THE • 1917 • Neilan Marshall • USA
GIRL AT LANCING MILL, THE • 1913 • Buckland Warwick • UKN
GIRL AT LUNA PARK, THE see **KRITSI TOU LOUNA PARK, TO** • 1968
GIRL AT NOLAN'S, THE • 1915 • Davis Ulysses • USA
GIRL AT OLD MILL, THE • 1909 • *Kalem* • USA
GIRL AT THE BROOK, THE • 1913 • *Essanay* • USA
GIRL AT THE CUPOLA, THE • 1912 • *Williams Kathlyn* • USA
GIRL AT THE CURTAIN, THE • 1914 • *Bushman Francis X.* • USA
GIRL AT THE FAIR, THE see **KRITSI TOU LOUNA PARK, TO** • 1968
GIRL AT THE IRONING BOARD, THE • 1934 • Freleng Friz • ANS • USA
GIRL AT THE KEY, THE • 1912 • Miller Ashley • USA
GIRL AT THE KEY, THE • 1915 • *Edison* • USA
GIRL AT THE LOCK, THE • 1914 • Jones Edgar • USA
GIRL AT THE LODGE, THE • 1912 • Haldane Bert? • UKN
GIRL AT THE LUNCH COUNTER, THE • 1913 • Baker George D. • USA
GIRL AT WAR, A • 1913 • *Forde Virginia* • USA
GIRL BACK EAST, THE • 1911 • *Anderson Broncho Billy* • USA
GIRL BACK EAST, THE • 1913 • *Lubin* • USA
GIRL BACK HOME, THE • 1912 • Dwan Allan • USA
GIRL BANDIT, THE • 1914 • *Burbridge Jessie* • USA
GIRL BANDITS' HOODOO, THE • 1912 • *Coxen Ed* • USA
GIRL BEHIND THE BARRIER, THE • 1914 • Le Saint Edward J. • USA
GIRL BOY SCOUT, THE • 1914 • Batley Ethyle • UKN
GIRL BY THE ROADSIDE, THE • 1918 • Marston Theodore • USA
GIRL CALLED HATTER FOX, THE • 1977 • Schaefer George • TVM • USA
GIRL CALLED JULES, A (UKN) see **RAGAZZA DI NOME GIULIO, LA** • 1970
GIRL CALLED LOVE, A see **FILLE NOMMEE AMOUR, UNE** • 1968
GIRL CAN'T HELP IT, THE • 1956 • Tashlin Frank • USA
GIRL CAN'T STOP, THE (USA) see **CHIENS DANS LA NUIT, LES** • 1965
GIRL COMES TO TOWN, A see **FLICKA KOMMER TILL STAN, EN** • 1937
GIRL COWBOY, THE • 1919 • *Bison* • USA
GIRL CRAZY • 1929 • Sennett Mack • SHT • USA
GIRL CRAZY • 1932 • Seiter William A. • USA
GIRL CRAZY • 1943 • Taurog Norman • USA • WHEN THE GIRLS MEET THE BOYS
GIRL CRAZY see **WHEN THE BOYS MEET THE GIRLS** • 1965
GIRL DANCED INTO LIFE, THE see **ELETBE TANCOLTATOTT LANY** • 1964
GIRL DEPUTY, THE • 1912 • *Kalem* • USA
GIRL DETECTIVE, THE • 1915 • Horne James W. • USA
GIRL DETECTIVE, THE • 1916 • King Burton L. • SHT • USA
GIRL DETECTIVE'S RUSE, THE • 1913 • *Thanhouser* • USA
GIRL DIFFERENT FROM OTHERS, A • 1978 • el Din Kamal Salah • EGY
GIRL DIFFERENT FROM THE OTHERS, A see **ENA KORITSI ALLIOTIKO APO T'ALLA** • 1968
GIRL DIVER OF SPOOK MANSION see **AMA NO BAKEMONO YASHIKI** • 1959
GIRL DODGER, THE • 1919 • Storm Jerome • USA
GIRL DOWNSTAIRS see **ERWACHEN DES WEIBES, DAS** • 1927
GIRL DOWNSTAIRS, THE • 1938 • Taurog Norman • USA • AWAKENING OF KATRINA, THE ○ KATHERINE THE LAST
GIRL FEVER • 1961 • Petrushansky Yevsie, Price Sherman • USA
GIRL FIELD-MARSHAL, THE see **FELDMARESCIALLA, LA** • 1967
GIRL FOR HIRE see **GIRLS FOR HIRE** • 1970
GIRL FOR ME, A see **FLICKA FOR MEJ, EN** • 1943
GIRL FOR THE SUMMER see **SOMMARFLICKAN** • 1956
GIRL FOR THE SUMMER, A see **FILLE POUR L'ETE, UNE** • 1960
GIRL FRIEND, THE • 1935 • Buzzell Edward • USA
GIRL FRIENDS • 1978 • Weill Claudia • USA
GIRL FRIENDS, THE see **PODRUGI** • 1936
GIRL FRIENDS, THE (USA) see **AMICHE, LE** • 1955
GIRL-FRIENDS OF THE RICH, THE see **AMIGUITAS DE LOS RICOS, LAS** • 1968
GIRL FROM 5000 A.D., THE see **TERROR FROM THE YEAR 5000** • 1958
GIRL FROM A GOOD FAMILY see **DZIEWCZYNA Z DOBREGO DOMU** • 1962
GIRL FROM ALASKA, THE • 1942 • Grinde Nick • USA
GIRL FROM ANATOLIA, THE see **ANADOLU KIZI** • 1967
GIRL FROM ARIZONA, THE • 1910 • Golden Joseph A. • USA
GIRL FROM AVENUE A • 1940 • Brower Otto • USA
GIRL FROM BACKAFALL see **FLICKA FRAN BACKAFALL** • 1953
GIRL FROM BERYOZOVSK, THE see **DYEVOCHKA IZ BERYOZOVSKA** • 1975
GIRL FROM BEYOND, THE • 1918 • Wolbert William • USA
GIRL FROM BOHEMIA, THE • 1918 • McGill Lawrence • USA
GIRL FROM BUCHAREST see **DZIEWCZETA Z BUKARESZTU** • 1964
GIRL FROM CALGARY, THE • 1932 • Whitman Phil • USA
GIRL FROM CARTHAGE, THE see **AIN EL GHEZAL** • 1924
GIRL FROM CHICAGO, THE • 1916 • *Hulette Gladys* • SHT • USA
GIRL FROM CHICAGO, THE • 1927 • Enright Ray • USA
GIRL FROM CHICAGO, THE • 1933 • Micheaux Oscar • USA
GIRL FROM CHINA, THE (UKN) see **SHANGHAI LADY** • 1929
GIRL FROM CONEY ISLAND, THE see **JUST ANOTHER BLONDE** • 1926
GIRL FROM CORFU, THE • 1957 • Petropoulakis Yannis • GRC
GIRL FROM DENMARK, THE • 1970
GIRL FROM DOWNING STREET, THE • 1918 • Malins Geoffrey H. • UKN
GIRL FROM EVERYWHERE, THE • 1927 • Cline Eddie • SHT • USA
GIRL FROM FLANDERS, THE (USA) see **MADCHEN AUS FLANDERN, EIN** • 1956
GIRL FROM FRISCO, THE • 1915 • Horne James W. • USA
GIRL FROM FRISCO, THE • 1916-17 • SER • USA
GIRL FROM GAY PAREE, THE • 1927 • Stone Phil • USA
GIRL FROM GEORGIA, THE (UKN) see **HER SECRET** • 1933
GIRL FROM GOD'S COUNTRY • 1940 • Salkow Sidney • USA
GIRL FROM GOD'S COUNTRY, THE • 1921 • Shipman Nell, Van Tuyle Bert • USA
GIRL FROM GOLDEN RUN, THE • 1912 • *Bartlett Charles* • USA
GIRL FROM GUNSIGHT, THE • 1949 • Cowan Will • SHT • USA
GIRL FROM HAMBURG, THE see **FILLE DE HAMBOURG, LA** • 1958
GIRL FROM HAVANA • 1940 • Landers Lew • USA
GIRL FROM HAVANA, THE • 1929 • Stoloff Ben • USA
GIRL FROM HIS TOWN, THE • 1915 • Pollard Harry • USA
GIRL FROM HONG KONG (USA) see **BIS ZUM ENDE ALLER TAGE** • 1961
GIRL FROM IPANEMA see **GAROTA DE IPANEMA** • 1967
GIRL FROM IRELAND, THE (UKN) see **KATHLEEN MAVOURNEEN** • 1930
GIRL FROM JONES BEACH, THE • 1949 • Godfrey Peter • USA
GIRL FROM KIEV, THE • 1958 • Levchuk G. • USS
GIRL FROM LA MANCHA see **DULCINEA** • 1962
GIRL FROM LENINGRAD, THE see **FRONTOVYYE PODRUGI** • 1942
GIRL FROM LORRAINE, A (UKN) see **PROVINCIALE, LA** • 1981
GIRL FROM MANDALAY, THE • 1936 • Bretherton Howard • USA
GIRL FROM MANHATTAN, THE • 1948 • Green Alfred E. • USA
GIRL FROM MAXIM'S, THE • 1932 • Korda Alexander • UKN
GIRL FROM MEXICO, THE • 1939 • Goodwins Leslie • SHT • USA
GIRL FROM MEXICO, THE (UKN) see **MEXICALI ROSE** • 1929
GIRL FROM MISSOURI, THE • 1934 • Conway Jack • USA • ONE HUNDRED PERCENT PURE (UKN)
GIRL FROM MONTEREY, THE • 1943 • Fox Wallace • USA
GIRL FROM MONTMARTRE, THE • 1926 • Green Alfred E. • USA
GIRL FROM NOWHERE, THE • 1919 • Lucas Wilfred, Meredyth Bess • USA
GIRL FROM NOWHERE, THE • 1921 • Archainbaud George • USA
GIRL FROM NOWHERE, THE • 1928 • Edwards Harry J. • SHT • USA
GIRL FROM NOWHERE, THE see **SHOULD A GIRL MARRY?** • 1939
GIRL FROM OUT OF THIS WORLD, THE see **DREAMLAND CAPERS** • 1958
GIRL FROM OUTBACK, A • 1919 • ASL
GIRL FROM P.— A.T., THE see **GIRL FROM PUSSY CAT, THE** • 1969
GIRL FROM PARADISE see **FLICKAN FRAN PARADISET** • 1924
GIRL FROM PARMA, THE see **PARMIGIANA, LA** • 1963
GIRL FROM PETROVKA, THE • 1974 • Miller Robert Ellis • USA
GIRL FROM PODSKALI, THE see **DEVCE Z PODSKALI** • 1922
GIRL FROM PORCUPINE, THE • 1921 • Henderson Dell • USA
GIRL FROM PROSPERITY, THE • 1914 • Ince Ralph • USA
GIRL FROM PUSSY CAT, THE • 1969 • *American Film Dist. Corp.* • USA • GIRL FROM P.— A.T., THE
GIRL FROM RECTOR'S, THE • 1917 • *Mactammany Ruth* • USA
GIRL FROM RIO • 1939 • Hillyer Lambert • USA
GIRL FROM RIO, THE • 1927 • Terriss Tom • USA • LOLA (UKN)
GIRL FROM ROCKY POINT, THE • 1922 • Becker Fred G. • USA
GIRL FROM S.E.X. • 1982 • Vatelli Paul G. • USA
GIRL FROM S.I.N., THE • 1966 • Smith C. Davis • USA • GIRL FROM THE SECRET INNER NETWORK, THE
GIRL FROM SAN LORENZO, THE • 1950 • Abrahams Derwin • USA
GIRL FROM SCOTLAND YARD, THE • 1937 • Vignola Robert G. • USA
GIRL FROM SCOTLAND YARD, THE • 1948 • Barralet Paul • UKN • END OF ADVENTURE
GIRL FROM STARSHIP VENUS see **SEXPLORER, THE** • 1975
GIRL FROM STATE STREET, THE (UKN) see **STATE STREET SADIE** • 1928
GIRL FROM STORMY CROFT (USA) see **TOSEN FRAN STORMYRTORPET** • 1917
GIRL FROM TENTH AVENUE, THE • 1935 • Green Alfred E. • USA • MEN ON HER MIND (UKN)
GIRL FROM TEXAS, THE • 1914 • *Sterling Edythe* • USA
GIRL FROM TEXAS, THE (UKN) see **TEXAS, BROOKLYN AND HEAVEN** • 1948
GIRL FROM THE COUNTRY, A • 1912 • *Eclair* • USA
GIRL FROM THE COUNTRY, THE • 1912 • *Edison* • USA
GIRL FROM THE DEAD SEA, THE see **FILLE DE LA MER MORTE, LA** • 1966
GIRL FROM THE DEPARTMENT STORE, THE see **FLICKAN FRAN VARUHUSET** • 1933
GIRL FROM THE DISTANT RIVER, THE see **DEVUSHKA S DALEKOI REKI** • 1928
GIRL FROM THE EAST, THE • 1910 • *Nestor* • USA
GIRL FROM THE EAST, THE • 1915 • *Broncho* • USA
GIRL FROM THE FACTORY, A see **NACHALO** • 1971
GIRL FROM THE FAMILY OF MAN, THE • 1970 • Thornhill Michael • SHT • ASL
GIRL FROM THE GALLERY, THE see **FLICKAN FRAN TREDJE RADEN** • 1949
GIRL FROM THE HUONG RIVER, THE • 1987 • Minh Dang Nhat • VTN
GIRL FROM THE MARSH CROFT, A see **TOSEN FRAN STORMYRTORPET** • 1917
GIRL FROM THE MARSH CROFT, A see **TOSEN FRAN STORMYRTORPET** • 1947
GIRL FROM THE MATCH FACTORY see **TULITIKKUTEHTANN TYTTO** • 1989
GIRL FROM THE MOON, THE • 1961 • Podskalsky Zdenek • CZC
GIRL FROM THE MOON'S BRIDGE, THE see **TYTTO KUUNSILLALTA** • 1953
GIRL FROM THE MOUNTAIN VILLAGE, THE see **FLICKAN FRAN FJALLBYN** • 1948
GIRL FROM THE MOUNTAINS see **DEVCE Z HOR** • 1924
GIRL FROM THE MOUNTAINS see **DEVOJKA SA KOSMAJA** • 1972
GIRL FROM THE OUTSIDE, THE • 1919 • Barker Reginald • USA
GIRL FROM THE PROVINCES, THE see **PROVINCIALE, LA** • 1981
GIRL FROM THE REVUE see **GIRL VON DER REVUE, DAS** • 1928
GIRL FROM THE SECRET INNER NETWORK, THE see **GIRL FROM S.I.N., THE** • 1966
GIRL FROM THE SKY, THE • 1914 • Neame Elwin • UKN
GIRL FROM THE STARSHIP VENUS, THE • 1957 • Ford Derek • UKN
GIRL FROM THE STORMY CROFT, A see **TOSEN FRAN STORMYRTORPET** • 1917
GIRL FROM THE VILLAGE, THE see **FLICKAN FRAN BYN** • 1980
GIRL FROM THE WEST • 1923 • MacDonald Wallace • USA
GIRL FROM THUNDER MOUNTAIN, THE • 1914 • *Stonehouse Ruth* • USA
GIRL FROM TIM'S PLACE, THE • 1915 • *Fealy Maude* • USA
GIRL FROM TOBACCO ROW, THE • 1966 • Ormond Ron • USA
GIRL FROM TRIESTE, THE see **RAGAZZA DI TRIESTE, LA** • 1983
GIRL FROM WARD 17, THE see **KORITSI TOU 17, TO** • 1969
GIRL FROM WOOLWORTHS, THE • 1929 • Beaudine William • USA
GIRL GAME (USA) see **COPACABANA PALACE** • 1962
GIRL-GETTERS, THE (USA) see **SYSTEM, THE** • 1963
GIRL GLORY, THE • 1917 • Neill R. William • USA

GIRL GOD MADE FOR JONES, THE • 1917 • Baker Richard Foster • SHT • USA
GIRL GOES ON SHORE, A see **MADCHEN GEHT AN LAND, EIN** • 1938
GIRL GRABBERS, THE • 1968 • Nuchtern Simon • USA
GIRL GRIEF • 1932 • Parrott James • SHT • USA
GIRL HABIT, THE • 1931 • Cline Eddie • USA
GIRL HAPPY • 1965 • Sagal Boris • USA
GIRL HAS DISAPPEARED, A • 1966 • Kutz Kazimierz • PLN
GIRL HAS PLANS, THE see **LADY HAS PLANS, THE** • 1942
GIRL HATER, THE • 1915 • Morrisey Edward • USA
GIRL HE BROUGHT HOME, THE • 1915 • *Mcdermott J.* • USA
GIRL HE DIDN'T BUY, THE • 1928 • Fitzgerald Dallas M. • USA • BROADWAY BRIDE, A (UKN)
GIRL HE LEFT BEHIND, THE • 1912 • *Selig* • USA
GIRL HE LEFT BEHIND, THE • 1956 • Butler David • USA
GIRL HE LEFT BEHIND, THE see **ELIZABETH OF LADYMEAD** • 1949
GIRL HE LOVED, THE • 1940 • Pyriev Ivan • USS • LOVED ONE, THE
GIRL HUNTERS, THE • 1963 • Rowland Roy • UKN
GIRL I ABANDONED, THE see **WATASHIGA SUTETA ONNA** • 1969
GIRL I KNEW, THE • 1962 • Lebedev N. • USS
GIRL I LEFT BEHIND ME, THE • 1908 • *Kalem* • USA
GIRL I LEFT BEHIND ME, THE • 1915 • Carleton Lloyd B. • USA
GIRL I LOVED, THE • 1923 • De Grasse Joseph • USA
GIRL I LOVED, THE see **WAGA KOISESHI OTOME** • 1946
GIRL I MADE, THE (UKN) see **MADE ON BROADWAY** • 1933
GIRL IN 313 • 1940 • Cortez Ricardo • USA
GIRL IN 419, THE • 1933 • Hall Alexander, Somnes George • USA • DEAD ON ARRIVAL
GIRL IN A BIKINI see **POVERI MA BELLI** • 1956
GIRL IN A BOOT see **EINMAL KU' DAMM UND ZURUCK** • 1983
GIRL IN A DRESS-COAT see **FLICKAN I FRACK** • 1926
GIRL IN A DRESS-COAT see **FLICKAN I FRACK** • 1956
GIRL IN A MILLION • 1946 • Searle Francis • UKN
GIRL IN AUSTRALIA see **BELLO, ONESTO, EMIGRATO AUSTRALIA SPOSEREBBE COMPAESANA ILLIBATA** • 1971
GIRL IN BLACK, THE see **DYEVUSHKA V CHYORNOM** • 1968
GIRL IN BLACK, THE (USA) see **KORITSI META MAVRA, TO** • 1956
GIRL IN BLACK STOCKINGS, THE • 1957 • Koch Howard W. • USA
GIRL IN BLUE, THE • 1974 • *Selby David* • CND
GIRL IN BLUE, THE see **DIVKA V MODREM** • 1939
GIRL IN BLUE, THE see **U-TURN** • 1973
GIRL IN BOHEMIA, A • 1919 • Mitchell Howard M. • USA
GIRL IN DANGER • 1934 • Lederman D. Ross • USA • GIRL IN TROUBLE
GIRL IN DISTRESS (USA) see **JEANNIE** • 1941
GIRL IN EVERY PORT, A • 1928 • Hawks Howard • USA
GIRL IN EVERY PORT, A • 1952 • Erskine Chester • USA
GIRL IN GOLD BOOTS • 1968 • Mikels Ted V. • USA
GIRL IN HIS HOUSE, THE • 1918 • Mills Thomas R. • USA
GIRL IN HIS POCKET see **AMOUR DE POCHE, UN** • 1957
GIRL IN HIS ROOM, THE • 1922 • Jose Edward • USA • LOCKED OUT
GIRL IN LOVER'S LANE, THE • 1960 • Rondeau Charles R. • USA
GIRL IN LOWER 9, THE • 1916 • Madison Cleo, Mong William V. • SHT • USA
GIRL IN MOURNING, THE see **NINA DE LUTO, LA** • 1964
GIRL IN NUMBER 29, THE • 1920 • Ford John • USA
GIRL IN OVERALLS, THE (UKN) see **SWING SHIFT MAISIE** • 1943
GIRL IN PANTS, THE • 1914 • Smalley Phillips • USA
GIRL IN PAWN, THE (UKN) see **LITTLE MISS MARKER** • 1934
GIRL IN POSSESSION, THE • 1934 • Banks Monty • UKN
GIRL IN QUESTION, THE • 1914 • Pollard Harry? • USA
GIRL IN ROOM 2A, THE (USA) see **TERROR IN 2-A** • 1972
GIRL IN ROOM 13 • 1961 • Cunha Richard E. • USA, BRZ
GIRL IN ROOM 17, THE (UKN) see **VICE SQUAD** • 1953
GIRL IN ROOM 20, THE • 1945 • Williams Spencer • USA
GIRL IN THE ARMCHAIR, THE • 1912 • *Solax* • USA
GIRL IN THE AUTO, THE • 1912 • *Republic* • USA
GIRL IN THE BARRACKS see **FLICKA I KASERN** • 1955
GIRL IN THE BARRACKS, THE • 1910 • *Vitagraph* • USA
GIRL IN THE BIKINI, THE (USA) see **MANINA, LA FILLE SANS VOILE** • 1952
GIRL IN THE BOX, THE • 1918 • *Field Elinor* • USA
GIRL IN THE CAB, THE • 1932 • Scotto Aubrey • USA
GIRL IN THE CABOOSE, A • 1912 • *Kalem* • USA
GIRL IN THE CAGE • 1934 • Frenke Eugene • USA
GIRL IN THE CASE • 1914 • Costello Maurice, Gaillord Robert • USA
GIRL IN THE CASE • 1944 • Berke William • USA • SILVER KEY, THE (UKN)
GIRL IN THE CASE, THE • 1913 • *Calvert E. H.* • USA
GIRL IN THE CHECKERED COAT, THE • 1917 • De Grasse Joseph • USA
GIRL IN THE CROWD, THE • 1934 • Powell Michael • UKN
GIRL IN THE DARK see **FRIGHT** • 1971
GIRL IN THE DARK, THE • 1918 • Paton Stuart • USA
GIRL IN THE EMPTY GRAVE, THE • 1977 • Antonio Lou • TVM • USA
GIRL IN THE FILM, THE • 1911 • *Vitagraph* • USA
GIRL IN THE FLAT, THE • 1934 • Davis Redd • UKN
GIRL IN THE FRAME, THE • 1917 • *La Salle* • USA
GIRL IN THE GARRET, THE • 1917 • Cochrane George • SHT • USA
GIRL IN THE GINGHAM GOWN, THE • 1912 • *Champion* • USA
GIRL IN THE GLASS CAGE, THE • 1929 • Dawson Ralph • USA
GIRL IN THE GOLDEN KNICKERS, THE see **MUCHACHA DE LAS BRAGAS DE ORO, LA** • 1979
GIRL IN THE GOLDEN PANTIES, THE see **MUCHACHA DE LAS BRAGAS DE ORO, LA** • 1979
GIRL IN THE HEADLINES • 1963 • Truman Michael • UKN • MODEL MURDER CASE, THE (USA) ○ NOSE ON MY FACE, THE
GIRL IN THE HOUSE-BOAT, THE • 1913 • Miller Ashley • USA
GIRL IN THE KREMLIN, THE • 1957 • Birdwell Russell J. • USA
GIRL IN THE LIMOUSINE, THE • 1917 • Cochrane George • SHT • USA
GIRL IN THE LIMOUSINE, THE • 1924 • Semon Larry • USA
GIRL IN THE MIDDY, THE • 1914 • Williams C. Jay • USA
GIRL IN THE MIST • 1959 • Suzuki Hideo • JPN
GIRL IN THE MOON see **FRAU IM MOND, DIE** • 1929
GIRL IN THE NEWS, THE • 1940 • Reed Carol • UKN
GIRL IN THE NEXT ROOM, THE • 1912 • Golden Joseph A. • USA
GIRL IN THE NIGHT, THE • 1931 • Edwards Henry • UKN
GIRL IN THE PAINTING, THE see **PORTRAIT FROM LIFE** • 1948
GIRL IN THE PARK see **VISNJA NA TASMAJDANU** • 1968
GIRL IN THE PARK see **SANCTUARY OF FEAR** • 1979
GIRL IN THE PICTURE, THE • 1957 • Chaffey Don • UKN
GIRL IN THE PICTURE, THE • 1985 • Parker Cary • UKN
GIRL IN THE PULLMAN, THE • 1927 • Kenton Erle C. • USA • GIRL ON THE TRAIN, THE (UKN)
GIRL IN THE RAIN • 1927 • *Butler David* • USA
GIRL IN THE RAIN, THE • 1920 • Sturgeon Rollin S. • USA
GIRL IN THE RAIN, THE see **FLICKAN I REGNET** • 1955
GIRL IN THE RAIN, THE (UKN) see **DEVIL'S CAGE, THE** • 1928
GIRL IN THE RED VELVET SWING, THE • 1955 • Fleischer Richard • USA
GIRL IN THE RUMOUR, THE see **UWASA NO MUSUME** • 1935
GIRL IN THE SEARCHLIGHT see **PIGEN I SOGELYSET** • 1959
GIRL IN THE SHACK, THE • 1914 • *Marsh Mae* • USA
GIRL IN THE SHADE, THE see **HIKAGE NO KO** • 1957
GIRL IN THE SHOP WINDOW, THE see **RAGAZZA IN VETRINA, LA** • 1960
GIRL IN THE SHOW, THE • 1930 • Selwyn Edgar • USA • EVA THE FIFTH
GIRL IN THE TAXI, THE • 1921 • Ingraham Lloyd • USA
GIRL IN THE TAXI, THE • 1937 • Berthomieu Andre • UKN
GIRL IN THE TAXI, THE • 1938 • Bernhardt Curtis • USA
GIRL IN THE TENEMENT, THE • 1914 • Hastings Seymour • USA
GIRL IN THE TONNEAU, THE • 1932 • *Sennett Mack (P)* • SHT • USA
GIRL IN THE TRUNK, THE see **VALISE, LA** • 1973
GIRL IN THE WEB, THE • 1920 • Thornby Robert T. • USA • SHADOWED
GIRL IN THE WINDOW OPPOSITE see **FLICKAN I FONSTRET MITTEMOT** • 1942
GIRL IN THE WOODS • 1958 • Gries Tom • USA
GIRL IN TIN, THE see **RAGAZZA DI LATTA, LA** • 1970
GIRL IN TROUBLE • 1963 • Chase Brandon • USA
GIRL IN TROUBLE see **GIRL IN DANGER** • 1934
GIRL IN WHITE, THE • 1952 • Sturges John • USA • SO BRIGHT THE FLAME (UKN)
GIRL IS A GIRL, A see **PENN ENDRAAL PENN** • 1967
GIRL IS A GUN, A see **AVENTURE DE BILLY THE KID, UNE** • 1971
GIRL IS MINE, THE • 1950 • Deans Marjorie • UKN
GIRL ISN'T ALLOWED TO LOVE, A see **BARA IKUTABI** • 1955
GIRL KILLER, THE • 1967 • *Mahon Barry* • USA • SEX KILLER
GIRL LIKE ME, A see **ENA KORITSI ALLIOTIKO APO T'ALLA** • 1968
GIRL LIKE THAT, A • 1917 • Ford Hugh • USA • TURNING POINT, THE
GIRL LIKE THAT, A • 1917 • Henderson Dell • *Famous Players* • USA
GIRL LOVES BOY • 1937 • Mansfield Duncan • USA
GIRL MERCHANTS see **MARCHANDS DE FILLES** • 1957
GIRL MISSING • 1933 • Florey Robert • USA
GIRL MOST LIKELY, THE • 1957 • Leisen Mitchell • USA
GIRL MOST LIKELY TO.., THE • 1973 • Philips Lee • TVM • USA
GIRL MUST LIVE, A • 1939 • Reed Carol • UKN
GIRL NAMED EN, A see **EN TO IU ONNA** • 1971
GIRL NAMED JULIUS, A see **RAGAZZA DI NOME GIULIO, LA** • 1970
GIRL NAMED MARY, A • 1920 • Edwards Walter • USA
GIRL NAMED SILKE, A see **PIGEN SILKE** • 1971
GIRL NAMED SOONER, A • 1975 • Mann Delbert • USA
GIRL NAMED TAMIKO, A • 1962 • Sturges John • USA
GIRL NEXT DOOR, THE • 1910 • *Powers* • USA
GIRL NEXT DOOR, THE • 1913 • Fitzhamon Lewin • UKN
GIRL NEXT DOOR, THE • 1914 • *Frontier* • USA
GIRL NEXT DOOR, THE • 1914 • Finn Arthur • UKN
GIRL NEXT DOOR, THE • 1919 • Vignola Robert G. • USA
GIRL NEXT DOOR, THE • 1953 • Sale Richard • USA
GIRL NEXT DOOR, THE see **MENINA DO LADO, A** • 1988
GIRL NIHILIST, THE • 1908 • *Kalem* • USA
GIRL NO.217 see **CHELOVEK NO.217** • 1944
GIRL NYUYO, THE see **SHOJO NYUYO** • 1930
GIRL O' DREAMS, THE • 1918 • *American* • USA
GIRL O' MY DREAMS • 1934 • McCarey Ray • USA • LOVE RACE, THE (UKN)
GIRL O' THE WOODS, THE • 1913 • Salter Harry • USA
GIRL OF A GOOD FAMILY see **LIANGJIA FUNU** • 1985
GIRL OF FINLAND see **LAPUALAISMORSIAN** • 1967
GIRL OF GLENBEIGH, A • 1918 • Kerrigan J. M. • IRL
GIRL OF GOLD, THE • 1925 • Ince Ralph • USA
GIRL OF GOLD GULCH, THE • 1916 • Mix Tom • SHT • USA
GIRL OF HELL'S AGONY, THE • 1919 • Smith Cliff • USA
GIRL OF HIS DREAMS, THE • 1916 • Fahrney Milton • USA
GIRL OF LAST NIGHT, THE (USA) see **MADCHEN VON GESTERN NACHT, DAS** • 1938
GIRL OF LONDON, A • 1925 • Edwards Henry • UKN
GIRL OF LOST LAKE, THE • 1916 • Reynolds Lynn • USA
GIRL OF MY DREAMS, THE • 1918 • Chaudet Louis W. • USA
GIRL OF MY DREAMS (UKN) see **SWEETHEART OF SIGMA CHI, THE** • 1933
GIRL OF MY HEART • 1920 • Le Saint Edward J. • USA
GIRL OF MY HEART, THE • 1915 • Bantock Leedham • USA
GIRL OF PASSION • Efstratiadis Omiris • GRC
GIRL OF PICCADILLY, A see **MADEL VON PICCADILLY 1, DAS** • 1921
GIRL OF SEVENTEEN, A see **BINT SABATASHAR** • 1959
GIRL OF SHAME see **LIEBE KANN WIE GIFT SEIN** • 1958
GIRL OF STONE • 1982 • Markus Jindra • NTH
GIRL OF SUNSET PASS, THE • 1913 • *Williams Clara* • USA
GIRL OF THE BUSH, A • 1921 • Barrett Franklyn • ASL
GIRL OF THE CABARET, THE • 1913 • *Benham Harry* • USA
GIRL OF THE CAFES, A • 1914 • Kent Leon D. • USA
GIRL OF THE CORAL REEFS, THE • 1911 • *Yankee* • USA
GIRL OF THE DANCE HALL, THE • 1915 • Kent Leon D. • USA
GIRL OF THE DANCE HALLS, A • 1913 • *Frontier* • USA
GIRL OF THE GOLDEN WEST, THE • 1914 • De Mille Cecil B. • USA
GIRL OF THE GOLDEN WEST, THE • 1923 • Carewe Edwin • USA
GIRL OF THE GOLDEN WEST, THE • 1930 • Dillon John Francis • USA
GIRL OF THE GOLDEN WEST, THE • 1938 • Leonard Robert Z. • USA
GIRL OF THE GRASSLAND • 1955 • Xu Tao • CHN
GIRL OF THE GROVE, THE • 1912 • *Thanhouser* • USA
GIRL OF THE GYPSY CAMP, THE • 1915 • West Langdon • USA
GIRL OF THE HOUR, THE • 1917 • *Brenon Herbert* • SHT • USA
GIRL OF THE ISLANDS see **RED MORNING** • 1935
GIRL OF THE LIGHTHOUSE, THE • 1912 • *Bosworth Hobart* • USA
GIRL OF THE LIMBERLOST, A • 1924 • Meehan James Leo • USA
GIRL OF THE LIMBERLOST, A • 1934 • Cabanne W. Christy • USA
GIRL OF THE LIMBERLOST, THE • 1945 • Ferrer Mel • USA
GIRL OF THE MANOR, THE • 1912 • *Bush Pauline* • USA
GIRL OF THE MEIJI PERIOD, A see **MEIJI HARU AKI** • 1968
GIRL OF THE MOORS, THE (USA) see **MADCHEN VOM MOORHOF, DAS** • 1958
GIRL OF THE MOUNTAIN, THE • 1911 • *Vitagraph* • USA
GIRL OF THE MOUNTAINS, THE • 1912 • McRae Henry • USA
GIRL OF THE MUSIC HALL, THE • 1915 • Buel Kenean • USA
GIRL OF THE NIGHT • 1960 • Cates Joseph • USA
GIRL OF THE NIGHT, THE • 1915 • De Grasse Joseph • USA
GIRL OF THE NIGHT (UKN) see **BROADWAY DADDIES** • 1928
GIRL OF THE NILE, THE (USA) see **MUCHACHA DEL NILO, LA** • 1967
GIRL OF THE NORTHERN WOODS, THE • 1910 • *Thanhouser* • USA
GIRL OF THE OPEN ROAD, THE • 1914 • *Trunnelle Mabel* • USA
GIRL OF THE OZARKS • 1936 • Shea William • USA
GIRL OF THE PEOPLE, A • 1914 • *Fuller Mary* • USA
GIRL OF THE PINES, A • 1915 • *Maison Edna* • USA
GIRL OF THE PLAIN, THE see **YAYLA KIZI** • 1967
GIRL OF THE PLAINS, A • 1910 • *Bison* • USA
GIRL OF THE PORT • 1930 • Glennon Bert • USA • FIRE WALKER, THE
GIRL OF THE RANCH, THE see **ANGEL OF PARADISE RANCH, THE** • 1911
GIRL OF THE RANCHO • 1920 • Joos Therdo • SHT • USA
GIRL OF THE RANGE, THE • 1913 • *Frontier* • USA
GIRL OF THE RIO, THE • 1932 • Brenon Herbert • USA • DOVE, THE (UKN)
GIRL OF THE ROAD, THE see **FILLE DE LA ROUTE, LA** • 1962
GIRL OF THE SEA • 1920 • Kelley J. Winthrop • USA
GIRL OF THE SEASONS, THE • 1914 • *Princess* • USA
GIRL OF THE SEASONS, THE • 1915 • *Thanhouser* • USA
GIRL OF THE SECRET SERVICE, THE • 1915 • *Cunard Grace* • USA
GIRL OF THE SILVER BORDER • 1921 • Slavinsky Vladimir • CZC
GIRL OF THE SUNNY SOUTH, THE • 1913 • *American Kineto* • USA
GIRL OF THE TIMBER CLAIMS, THE • 1917 • Powell Paul • USA
GIRL OF THE WATER, THE see **FILLE DE L'EAU, LA** • 1924
GIRL OF THE WEST • 1916 • *Knickerbocker Star* • SHT • USA
GIRL OF THE WEST • 1925 • Neitz Alvin J. • USA
GIRL OF THE WEST, A • 1912 • *Vitagraph* • USA
GIRL OF THE WEST, THE • 1911 • *Anderson Broncho Billy* • USA
GIRL OF THE WEST, THE • 1920 • Moody Harry • SHT • USA
GIRL OF THE WOODS, A • 1909 • *Phoenix* • USA
GIRL OF THE YEAR, THE see **EDIE** • 1989
GIRL OF THE YEAR (UKN) see **PETTY GIRL, THE** • 1950
GIRL OF THIRTEEN • 1974 • Vrijman Jan • NTH
GIRL OF TODAY, A see **LOVE'S OPTION** • 1928
GIRL OF TODAY, THE • 1918 • Robertson John S. • USA
GIRL OF VALENCIA see **SCHMUGGLERBRAUT VON MALORCA, DIE** • 1929
GIRL OF YESTERDAY, A • 1915 • Dwan Allan • USA
GIRL ON A BALL, A see **DYEVOCHKA NA SHARYE** • 1967
GIRL ON A BROOM see **DIVKA NA KOSTETI** • 1971
GIRL ON A CHAIN GANG • 1966 • Gross Jerry • USA
GIRL ON A MOTORCYCLE • 1968 • Cardiff Jack • UKN, FRN • MOTOCYCLETTE, LA (FRN) ○ NAKED UNDER LEATHER
GIRL ON APPROVAL • 1962 • Frend Charles • UKN
GIRL ON THE BARGE, THE • 1929 • Sloman Edward • USA
GIRL ON THE BOARD, THE see **MADCHEN AUF DEM BRETT, DAS** • 1967
GIRL ON THE BOAT, THE • 1961 • Kaplan Henry • UKN
GIRL ON THE BRIDGE, THE • 1951 • Haas Hugo • USA • BRIDGE, THE
GIRL ON THE BROOMSTICK, THE (USA) see **DIVKA NA KOSTETI** • 1971
GIRL ON THE CANAL, THE (USA) see **PAINTED BOATS** • 1945
GIRL ON THE DIVING BOARD, THE see **MADCHEN AUF DEM BRETT, DAS** • 1967
GIRL ON THE FRONT PAGE, THE • 1936 • Beaumont Harry • USA
GIRL ON THE HILL, THE see **KATHLEEN** • 1941
GIRL ON THE LATE, LATE SHOW, THE • 1974 • Nelson Gary • TVM • USA
GIRL ON THE PIER, THE • 1953 • Comfort Lance • UKN
GIRL ON THE ROAD see **PETITS MATINS, LES** • 1961
GIRL ON THE ROOF • 1971 • Dimsey Ross • SHT • ASL
GIRL ON THE RUN • 1961 • Lee Joseph, Beckhard Arthur J. • USA
GIRL ON THE SPOT • 1946 • Beaudine William • USA • SERENADE FOR MURDER

GIRL ON THE STAIRS, THE • 1924 • Worthington William • USA
GIRL ON THE SWING, THE • 1989 • Hessler Gordon • USA
GIRL ON THE TRAIN, THE (UKN) see **GIRL IN THE PULLMAN, THE** • 1927
GIRL ON TRIPLE X, THE • 1910 • *Anderson Broncho Billy* • USA
GIRL OPPOSITE, THE see **FILLE D'EN FACE, LA** • 1968
GIRL OVERBOARD • 1929 • Ruggles Wesley • USA • PORT O' DREAMS (UKN) ○ SALVAGE
GIRL OVERBOARD • 1937 • Salkow Sidney • USA
GIRL PHILIPPA, THE • 1917 • Drew Sidney • USA
GIRL PROBLEM, THE • 1919 • Webb Kenneth • USA
GIRL PUSHER • 1968 • *Mitam Productions* • USA • GIRL PUSHERS
GIRL PUSHERS see **GIRL PUSHER** • 1968
GIRL RANCHERS, THE • 1913 • *Nestor* • USA
GIRL REFUGEE, THE (USA) see **PROSFYGOPOULA** • 1938
GIRL REPORTER, THE • 1910 • *Thanhouser* • USA
GIRL REPORTER, THE • 1913 • Smalley Phillips • USA
GIRL REPORTER'S BIG SCOOP, THE • 1912 • *Neason Hazel* • USA
GIRL REPORTER'S SCOOP, THE • 1917 • Kelsey Fred A. • SHT • USA
GIRL ROSEMARIE, THE see **MADCHEN ROSEMARIE, DAS** • 1958
GIRL RUSH, THE • 1931 • Christie Al • USA
GIRL RUSH, THE • 1944 • Douglas Gordon • USA
GIRL RUSH, THE • 1955 • Pirosh Robert • USA
GIRL SAID NO, THE • 1930 • Wood Sam • USA • FRESH FROM COLLEGE
GIRL SAID NO, THE • 1937 • Stone Andrew L. • USA
GIRL SCHOOL SCREAMERS see **GIRLS' SCHOOL SCREAMERS** • 1986
GIRL SCOUT, THE • 1910 • *Bison* • USA
GIRL SCOUT, THE see **GIRL SCOUT OR THE CANADIAN CONTINGENT IN THE BOER WAR, THE** • 1909
GIRL SCOUT OR THE CANADIAN CONTINGENT IN THE BOER WAR, THE • 1909 • Olcott Sidney • USA • GIRL SCOUT, THE
GIRL SCOUTS VS. THE COOKIE CREATURE • 1971 • *Rogers Susan* • SHT • USA
GIRL SELLERS, THE see **MARCHANDS DE FILLES** • 1957
GIRL SHERIFF, THE • 1912 • *Pathe* • USA
GIRL SHOCK • 1930 • Horne James W. • SHT • USA
GIRL SHY • 1924 • Newmeyer Fred, Taylor Sam • USA
GIRL-SHY COWBOY, THE • 1928 • Hough R. Lee • USA
GIRL SMUGGLERS • 1967 • Mahon Barry • USA
GIRL SPY, THE • 1909 • Olcott Sidney • USA
GIRL SPY BEFORE VICKSBURG, THE • 1910 • Olcott Sidney • USA
GIRL SPY IN MEXICO, A • 1913 • Fielding Romaine • *Lubin* • USA
GIRL SPY'S ATONEMENT, A • 1913 • *Phillips Norma* • USA
GIRL STAGE DRIVER, THE • 1914 • Cullison Webster • USA
GIRL STOWAWAY'S HEROISM, THE • 1911 • *Yankee* • USA
GIRL STRIKE LEADER, THE • 1910 • *Thanhouser* • USA
GIRL STRIKERS, THE • 1912 • *Kalem* • USA
GIRL STROKE BOY • 1971 • Kellett Bob • UKN • GIRL/BOY
GIRL STUDENT'S HOME, THE see **BEIT EL TALIBAT** • 1967
GIRL STUDENTS -IMPRESSIONS OF A TECHNICAL COLLEGE • 1965 • Junge Winifried • DOC • GDR
GIRL SWAPPERS, THE see **TWO AND TWO MAKE SIX** • 1962
GIRL THAT DIDN'T MATTER, THE • 1916 • *Landis Margaret* • SHT • USA
GIRL THAT I LOVE, THE see **WAGA KOISESHI OTOME** • 1946
GIRL THAT MADE THE TIME FLY, THE see **HOW TO MAKE TIME FLY** • 1906
GIRL, THE BODY AND THE PILL, THE • 1967 • Lewis Herschell G. • USA • PILL, THE
GIRL, THE CLOWN AND THE DONKEY, THE • 1913 • Seay Charles M. • USA
GIRL, THE COP, THE BURGLER, THE • 1914 • *Beery Wallace* • USA
GIRL, THE GOLD WATCH & DYNAMITE, THE • 1981 • Averback Hy • TVM • USA
GIRL, THE GOLD WATCH & EVERYTHING, THE • 1980 • Wiard William • TVM • USA
GIRL THIEF, THE • 1910 • *Kalem* • USA
GIRL THIEF, THE (USA) see **LOVE AT SECOND SIGHT** • 1934
GIRL TO BE KILLED see **HOLKA NA ZABITI** • 1975
GIRL TO KILL FOR, A • 1989 • Oliver Richard • USA
GIRL TO LIVE FOR, A see **OMRE BEDEL KIZ** • 1967
GIRL-TOY see **SON OF ALVIN** • 1984
GIRL TROUBLE • 1933 • Ray Bernard B. • USA
GIRL TROUBLE • 1934 • Cline Eddie • SHT • USA
GIRL TROUBLE • 1942 • Schuster Harold • USA
GIRL UNDER THE SHEET, THE see **RAGAZZA SOTTO IL LENZUOLO, LA** • 1961
GIRL VON DER REVUE, DAS • 1928 • Eichberg Richard • FRG • GIRL FROM THE REVUE
GIRL WAS YOUNG, THE (USA) see **YOUNG AND INNOCENT** • 1937
GIRL WHO CAME BACK, THE • 1918 • Vignola Robert G. • USA
GIRL WHO CAME BACK, THE • 1921 • Gordon Edward R. • UKN
GIRL WHO CAME BACK, THE • 1935 • Lamont Charles • USA
GIRL WHO CAME GIFT WRAPPED, THE • 1974 • Bilson Bruce • TVM • USA
GIRL WHO CAN COOK, THE • 1917 • *Meredith Lois* • SHT • USA
GIRL WHO COULDN'T GO WRONG, THE • 1915 • De Grasse Joseph • USA • WHEN A GOD PLAYED THE BADGER GAME
GIRL WHO COULDN'T GROW UP, THE • 1917 • Pollard Harry • USA
GIRL WHO COULDN'T QUITE, THE • 1950 • Lee Norman • UKN
GIRL WHO COULDN'T SAY NO, THE (USA) see **TENDERLY** • 1968
GIRL WHO DARED, THE • 1910 • *Defender* • USA
GIRL WHO DARED, THE • 1914 • *Fischer Margarita* • USA
GIRL WHO DARED, THE • 1920 • Smith Cliff • USA
GIRL WHO DARED, THE • 1944 • Bretherton Howard • USA
GIRL WHO DARED, THE see **PAID IN ADVANCE** • 1919
GIRL WHO DID NOT CARE, THE see **SEX LURE, THE** • 1916
GIRL WHO DIDN'T CARE, THE • 1916 • Durrant Fred W. • USA
GIRL WHO DIDN'T FORGET, THE • 1915 • Coyle Walter • USA
GIRL WHO DIDN'T TELL, THE • 1916 • Hill Robert F. • SHT • USA
GIRL WHO DISTRIBUTED HAPPINESS, THE see **KOFUKU O HAITATSU SURU MUSUME** • 1954
GIRL WHO DOESN'T KNOW, THE • 1917 • Bartlett Charles • USA
GIRL WHO FEARED DAYLIGHT, THE • 1916 • Henderson Lucius • SHT • USA
GIRL WHO FORGOT, THE • 1939 • Brunel Adrian • UKN • YOUNG PERSON IN PINK, THE
GIRL WHO GAVE IN, THE see **UNDERTOW, THE** • 1930
GIRL WHO HAD A SOUL, THE • 1915 • Henderson Lucius • USA
GIRL WHO HAD EVERYTHING, THE • 1953 • Thorpe Richard • USA
GIRL WHO JOINED THE BUSH RANGERS, THE • 1909 • Fitzhamon Lewin • UKN
GIRL WHO KEPT BOOKS, THE • 1915 • Miller Ashley • USA
GIRL WHO KNEW TOO MUCH, THE • 1969 • Lyon Francis D. • USA
GIRL WHO KNEW TOO MUCH, THE see **RAGAZZA CHE SAPEVA TROPPO, LA** • 1962
GIRL WHO LIKED PURPLE FLOWERS, THE see **LILA AKAC** • 1973
GIRL WHO LIVED IN STRAIGHT STREET, THE • 1914 • Buckland Warwick? • UKN
GIRL WHO LOST, THE • 1917 • Cochrane George • SHT • USA
GIRL WHO LOVES A SOLDIER, THE • 1916 • Butler Alexander • UKN
GIRL WHO MET SIMONE DE BEAUVOIR IN PARIS, THE • 1980 • Nicholson Arch • SHT • ASL
GIRL WHO MIGHT HAVE BEEN, THE • 1915 • *Kb* • USA
GIRL WHO MIGHT HAVE BEEN, THE • 1915 • Belmore Lionel • *Broadway Star* • USA
GIRL WHO PLAYED THE GAME, THE • 1914 • Buckland Warwick? • UKN
GIRL WHO RAN WILD, THE • 1922 • Julian Rupert • USA
GIRL WHO RODE IN THE PALIO, THE see **RAGAZZA DEL PALIO, LA** • 1957
GIRL WHO SPELLED FREEDOM, THE • 1986 • Wincer Simon • TVM • USA
GIRL WHO STAYED AT HOME, THE • 1919 • Griffith D. W. • USA
GIRL WHO STOLE THE EIFFEL TOWER, THE see **PARIS WHEN IT SIZZLES** • 1964
GIRL WHO TOOK THE WRONG TURNING, THE • 1915 • Bantock Leedham • UKN
GIRL WHO WANTED, THE • 1912 • *Republic* • USA
GIRL WHO WANTED TO LIVE, THE see **HER LIFE AND HIS** • 1917
GIRL WHO WATCHES THE MOUNTAIN, THE see **DAGLARI BEKLEYEN KIZ** • 1968
GIRL WHO WON, THE • 1916 • *Saunders Jackie* • SHT • USA
GIRL WHO WON OUT, THE • 1917 • Moore W. Eugene • USA
GIRL WHO WOULDN'T WORK, THE • 1925 • De Sano Marcel • USA
GIRL WHO WRECKED HIS HOME, THE • 1916 • Ward Albert • UKN
GIRL WITH A CHARACTER, A • 1939 • Yudin Konstantin • USS
GIRL WITH A JAZZ HEART, THE see **GIRL WITH THE JAZZ HEART, THE** • 1920
GIRL WITH A MELODY see **FLICKA MED MELODI** • 1954
GIRL WITH A PISTOL, THE (USA) see **RAGAZZA CON LA PISTOLA, LA** • 1967
GIRL WITH A SHELL, THE see **DIVKA S MUSLI** • 1979
GIRL WITH A SUITCASE (USA) see **RAGAZZA CON LA VALIGIA, LA** • 1961
GIRL WITH BAMBOO LEAVES see **SASABUE OMON** • 1969
GIRL WITH GOLDEN HAIR, THE see **CASQUE D'OR** • 1952
GIRL WITH GREEN EYES • 1964 • Davis Desmond • UKN • GIRL WITH THE GREEN EYES, THE
GIRL WITH GREEN EYES, THE see **GIRL WITH THE GREEN EYES, THE** • 1916
GIRL WITH HUNGRY EYES, THE • 1967 • Rotsler William • USA • GIRL WITH THE HUNGRY EYES, THE ○ FACE OF SIN, THE
GIRL WITH HYACINTHS see **FLICKA OCH HYACINTER** • 1950
GIRL WITH IDEAS, THE • 1937 • Simon S. Sylvan • USA • MIGHTIER THAN THE SWORD (UKN)
GIRL WITH NO REGRETS, THE • 1919 • Millarde Harry • USA
GIRL WITH THE CAMERA, THE • 1915 • *Premier* • USA
GIRL WITH THE CHAMPAGNE EYES, THE • 1918 • Franklin Chester M. • USA
GIRL WITH THE DEXTEROUS TOUCH, THE see **CHIN FEN SHEN-HSIEN SHOU** • 1975
GIRL WITH THE FABULOUS BOX, THE • 1969 • Nisbet Charles • USA
GIRL WITH THE GOLDEN EYES, THE (USA) see **FILLE AUX YEUX D'OR, LA** • 1961
GIRL WITH THE GOLDEN HAIR, THE see **HRYSOMALLOUSA** • 1979
GIRL WITH THE GREEN EYES, THE • 1916 • Blache Alice • USA • GIRL WITH GREEN EYES, THE
GIRL WITH THE GREEN EYES, THE see **GIRL WITH GREEN EYES** • 1964
GIRL WITH THE GUITAR, THE • 1958 • Fainzimmer Alexander • USS
GIRL WITH THE HAT BOX, THE see **DEVUSHKA S KOROBKOI** • 1927
GIRL WITH THE HUNGRY EYES, THE see **GIRL WITH HUNGRY EYES, THE** • 1967
GIRL WITH THE JAZZ HEART, THE • 1920 • Windom Lawrence C. • USA • GIRL WITH A JAZZ HEART, THE
GIRL WITH THE LANTERN, THE • 1912 • *Williams Kathlyn* • USA
GIRL WITH THE LONG HAIR, THE • Ho Fan • HKG
GIRL WITH THE MAGIC BOX, THE • 1965 • Mahon Barry • USA • MAGIC BOX, THE
GIRL WITH THE PISTOL, THE see **RAGAZZA CON LA PISTOLA, LA** • 1967
GIRL WITH THE RED FEATHER, THE • 1915 • Carleton Lloyd B. • USA
GIRL WITH THE RED HAIR, THE (USA) see **MEISJE MET HET RODE HAAT, HET** • 1981
GIRL WITH THE SKIN OF THE MOON, THE see **RAGAZZA DALLA PELLE DI LUNA, LA** • 1972
GIRL WITH THE THREE CAMELS, THE see **DIVKA SE TREMI VELBLOUDY** • 1967
GIRL WITH THREE CAMELS, A see **DIVKA SE TREMI VELBLOUDY** • 1967
GIRL WITHOUT A NAME see **FLICKA UTAN NAMN** • 1954
GIRL WITHOUT A ROOM • 1933 • Murphy Ralph • USA
GIRL WITHOUT A SOUL, THE • 1917 • Collins John H. • USA
GIRL WITHOUT AN ADDRESS, THE see **DEVUSHKA BEZ ADRESA** • 1957
GIRL WOMAN, THE • 1919 • Mills Thomas R. • USA
GIRL/BOY see **GIRL STROKE BOY** • 1971
GIRLFRIEND see **KANOJO** • 1926
GIRLFRIEND FROM HELL, THE • 1989 • Peterson Daniel M. • USA
GIRLFRIENDS • 1983 • De Renzy Alex • USA
GIRLFRIENDS, THE see **BICHES, LES** • 1968
GIRLFRIENDS AT THE FRONT see **FRONTOVYYE PODRUGI** • 1942
GIRLHOOD • 1961 • Estrin L. • USS
GIRLIES • 1910 • *American* • USA
GIRLIES AND GRUBBERS • 1919 • Pratt Gilbert • SHT • USA
GIRLIES BEHAVE • 1928 • Lamont Charles • SHT • USA
GIRLISH IMPULSE, A • 1911 • Salter Harry • USA
GIRLOGRAPHY • 1968 • Brandhild Arne • SWD
GIRLS • 1910 • *Bison* • USA
GIRLS • 1919 • Edwards Walter • USA
GIRLS • 1979 • Jaeckin Just • FRN, FRG, CND
GIRLS • 1985 • Levithan Nadav • ISR
GIRLS, THE see **BONNES FEMMES, LES** • 1960
GIRLS, THE see **DEVTCHATA** • 1962
GIRLS, THE see **FLICKORNA** • 1968
GIRLS, THE see **GEHENU LAMAI** • 1977
GIRLS ABOUT TOWN • 1931 • Cukor George • USA
GIRLS AMONG THE FLOWERS see **HANA NO NAKA NO MUSUMETACHI** • 1953
GIRLS AND BOYS see **DES GARCONS ET DES FILLES** • 1968
GIRLS AND DAD, THE • 1913 • *Nestor* • USA
GIRLS AND DADDY, THE • 1909 • Griffith D. W. • USA
GIRLS AND GUNPOWDER • 1920 • *Sunshine* • USA
GIRLS AND THE SINGLE SAILOR see **HOW TO PICK UP A GIRL** • 1967
GIRLS AND THE STUDENTS, THE see **GAKUSEI YARO TO MUSUMETACHI** • 1960
GIRLS AND THEIR NESHKA ROBEVA, THE see **NESHKA ROBEVA AND HER GIRLS** • 1985
GIRLS ARE FOR LOVING • 1973 • Schain Don • USA
GIRLS ARE WILLING, THE • 1959 • Axel Gabriel • DNM
GIRLS AT SEA • 1958 • Gunn Gilbert • UKN
GIRLS BEHIND BARS see **MADCHEN HINTER GITTERN** • 1949
GIRL'S BEST FRIEND, A • 1981 • Pachard Henri • USA
GIRL'S BEST FRIEND IS WALL STREET, A see **SHE KNEW ALL THE ANSWERS** • 1941
GIRL'S BEST YEARS, A • 1937 • Le Borg Reginald • SHT • USA
GIRL'S BRAVERY, A • 1912 • *Metcalfe Earl* • USA
GIRLS' CAMP see **MOASKAR EL BANAT** • 1967
GIRLS CAN PLAY • 1937 • Hillyer Lambert • USA
GIRLS COME FIRST • 1975 • McGrath Joseph • UKN
GIRLS COME TOO! • 1968 • *Monique Films* • USA • GIRLS TOO
GIRL'S CONFESSION, A see **GESTANDNIS EINES MADCHENS, DAS** • 1967
GIRL'S DECISION, A see **NINE POINTS OF THE LAW** • 1922
GIRLS DEMAND EXCITEMENT • 1931 • Felix Seymour • USA
GIRL'S DESIRE, A • 1922 • Divad David • USA
GIRL'S DIARY, THE • Chi James Lu • HKG
GIRLS DISAPPEAR see **DES FEMMES DISPARAISSENT** • 1959
GIRLS DON'T GAMBLE • 1920 • Butler Fred J. • USA
GIRLS' DORMITORY • 1936 • Cummings Irving • USA
GIRLS' DORMITORY see **DORTOIR DES GRANDES** • 1953
GIRLS' DORMITORY see **JOSHIRYO** • 1967
GIRL'S FOLLY, A • 1917 • Tourneur Maurice • USA
GIRLS FOR HIRE • 1970 • *Stacey Dist.* • USA • GIRL FOR HIRE
GIRLS FOR HIRE see **CHICAS DE ALQUILER** • 1973
GIRLS FOR MEN ONLY see **I LIKE BIRDS** • 1967
GIRLS FOR PLEASURE see **DOSSIER PROSTITUTION** • 1969
GIRLS FOR RENT • 1974 • Adamson Al • USA
GIRLS FOR THE MAMBO BAR, THE (UKN) see **MADCHEN FUR DIE MAMBO-BAR** • 1959
GIRLS FOR THE SUMMER see **RACCONTI D'ESTATE** • 1958
GIRLS FOR THE SUMMER (UKN) see **FILLE POUR L'ETE, UNE** • 1960
GIRLS FROM ARE see **FLICKORNA FRAN ARE** • 1920
GIRLS FROM ATLANTIS, THE see **MANNER SIND ZUM LIEBEN DA** • 1969
GIRLS FROM THE OLD TOWN, THE see **FLICKORNA FRAN GAMLA STA'N** • 1934
GIRLS FROM THUNDER STRIP, THE • 1966 • Hewitt David L. • USA
GIRLS FROM WILKO, THE see **PANNY Z WILKO** • 1979
GIRLS.. GIRLS!! see **BONNES FEMMES, LES** • 1960
GIRLS, GIRLS, GIRLS • 1944 • D'Arcy Harry • SHT • USA
GIRLS! GIRLS! GIRLS! • 1962 • Taurog Norman • USA
GIRLS, GIRLS (UKN) see **MADCHEN, MADCHEN** • 1967
GIRLS GONE WILD • 1929 • Seiler Lewis • USA
GIRLS GROWING UP • 1967 • *Halas John (P)* • ANS • UKN
GIRLS HE LEFT BEHIND, THE (UKN) see **GANG'S ALL HERE, THE** • 1943
GIRLS HE LEFT BEHIND HIM, THE • 1910 • *Thanhouser* • USA
GIRLS' HOTEL see **SYNDICATE VICE** • 1980
GIRLS IN 7C, THE • 1970 • *Distripix* • USA
GIRLS IN A FACTORY see **FLICKOR PA FABRIK** • 1935
GIRLS IN ACTION (UKN) see **OPERATION DAMES** • 1958
GIRLS IN ARMS see **OPERATION BULLSHINE** • 1959
GIRLS IN CHAINS • 1943 • Ulmer Edgar G. • USA

GIRLS IN ONE UMBRELLA, THE see **PARAPLUIE FANTASTIQUE, LE** • 1903
GIRLS IN PRISON • 1956 • Cahn Edward L. • USA
GIRLS IN THE HARBOUR see **FLICKOR I HAMN** • 1945
GIRLS IN THE NIGHT • 1953 • Arnold Jack • USA • LIFE AFTER DARK (UKN)
GIRLS IN THE OFFICE, THE • 1979 • Post Ted • TVM • USA
GIRLS IN THE SADDLE • 1969 • Mauro Ralph • USA
GIRLS IN THE SHADOWS see **SCHATTEN WERDEN LANGER, DIE** • 1962
GIRLS IN THE STREETS see **SCREAM IN THE STREETS, A** • 1972
GIRLS IN THE STREETS (USA) see **LONDON MELODY** • 1936
GIRLS IN THE SUN see **KORITSIA STON ILIO** • 1969
GIRLS IN UNIFORM see **MADCHEN IN UNIFORM** • 1931
GIRLS INDULGING IN A PILLOW FIGHT • 1901 • *Warwick Trading Co* • UKN
GIRLS JUST WANT TO HAVE FUN see **GIRLS JUST WANT TO HAVE FUN: THE MOVIE** • 1985
GIRLS JUST WANT TO HAVE FUN: THE MOVIE • 1985 • Metter Alan • USA • GIRLS JUST WANT TO HAVE FUN
GIRLS LED ASTRAY see **DETOURNEMENT DE MINEURES** • 1959
GIRL'S LOVE-LETTER, A • 1911 • Haldane Bert • UKN
GIRLS MARKED DANGER see **TRATTA DELLE BIANCHE, LA** • 1952
GIRLS MARKED DANGER see **TRAITE DES BLANCHES, LA** • 1965
GIRLS MEN FORGET • 1924 • Campbell Maurice • USA
GIRLS MOST LIKELY TO, THE (UKN) see **CLASS OF '74** • 1972
GIRLS NEVER TELL (UKN) see **HER FIRST ROMANCE** • 1951
GIRLS NEXT DOOR, THE • 1979 • Hong James • USA
GIRLS' NIGHT OUT see **GIRLS' NITE OUT** • 1983
GIRLS' NITE OUT • 1983 • Deubel Robert • USA • GIRLS' NIGHT OUT ○ SCAREMAKER, THE
GIRLS OF FRANCE, THE see **JEUNE FILLE DE FRANCE** • 1938
GIRLS OF GODIVA HIGH, THE • 1981 • Clark Jim* • USA • GOOD GIRLS OF GODIVA HIGH, THE ○ GODIVA GIRLS
GIRLS OF HUNTINGTON HOUSE, THE • 1973 • Kjellin Alf • TVM • USA
GIRLS OF IZU see **IZU NO MUSUMETACHI** • 1945
GIRLS OF LATIN QUARTER • 1960 • Travers Alfred • UKN
GIRLS OF NOWOLIPEK see **DZIEWCZETA Z NOWOLIPEK** • 1938
GIRLS OF PLEASURE ISLAND, THE • 1953 • Herbert F. Hugh, Ganzer Alvin • USA
GIRLS OF SAN FREDIANO, THE see **RAGAZZE DI SAN FREDIANO, LE** • 1955
GIRLS OF SMALAND see **FLICKORNA I SMALAND** • 1945
GIRLS OF SOLVIK, THE see **FLICKORNA PA SOLVIK** • 1926
GIRLS OF SPIDER ISLAND see **TOTER HING IM NETZ, EIN** • 1960
GIRLS OF THE BIG HOUSE • 1945 • Archainbaud George • USA
GIRLS OF THE GHETTO, THE • 1910 • *Thanhouser* • USA
GIRLS OF THE NIGHT (USA) see **FILLES DE NUIT** • 1958
GIRLS OF THE PIAZZA DI SPAGNA see **RAGAZZE DI PIAZZA DI SPAGNA, LE** • 1952
GIRLS OF THE RANGE, THE • 1910 • *Selig* • USA
GIRLS OF THE ROAD • 1940 • Grinde Nick • USA
GIRLS OF THE SPANISH STEPS, THE see **RAGAZZE DI PIAZZA DI SPAGNA, LE** • 1952
GIRLS OF THE VILLAGE, THE • 1917 • Sandground Maurice • UKN
GIRLS OF THE WHITE ORCHID • 1983 • Kaplan Jonathan • TVM • USA • DEATH RIDES TO OSAKA
GIRLS OF UPPAKRA, THE see **FLICKORNA PA UPPAKRA** • 1936
GIRLS ON A RAINY NIGHT • 1970 • Green Lou • USA
GIRLS ON F- STREET, THE • 1966 • Resnick Saul • USA • MAIDENS OF FETISH STREET ○ "F" STREET
GIRLS ON ICE • 1959 • Wu Chao-Ti • CHN
GIRLS ON PROBATION • 1938 • McGann William • USA
GIRLS ON THE BEACH, THE • 1965 • Witney William • USA • BEACH GIRLS
GIRLS ON THE LOOSE • 1958 • Henreid Paul • USA
GIRLS ON THE MOON see **NATURE GIRLS ON THE MOON** • 1960
GIRLS ON THE ROAD • 1972 • Schmidt Thomas • USA
GIRLS ON THE ROCKS • 1962 • Santos Anthony • USA
GIRLS ON TIGER REEF see **NUDES ON TIGER REEF** • 1965
GIRL'S OWN STORY, A • 1984 • Campion Jane • SHT • ASL
GIRLS PACKING SOAP see **VINOLIA SOAP** • 1897
GIRLS PLAYING LEAPFROG • 1898 • *Chard'S Vitagraph* • UKN
GIRLS PLEASE! • 1934 • Raymond Jack • UKN
GIRL'S PRISON • 1970 • *Kirt Films International* • USA
GIRLS' SCHOOL • 1938 • Brahm John • USA
GIRLS' SCHOOL • 1949 • *Biswas Anil (M)* • IND
GIRLS' SCHOOL • 1950 • Landers Lew • USA • DANGEROUS INHERITANCE (UKN)
GIRLS' SCHOOL see **NU-TZU HSUEH-HSAIO** • 1983
GIRLS' SCHOOL SCANDAL • 1969 • *Fleetan Films* • USA
GIRLS' SCHOOL SCREAMERS • 1986 • Finegan John P. • USA • GIRL SCHOOL SCREAMERS ○ DEATH LEGACY ○ PORTRAIT, THE
GIRLS' SCHOOL -VILE GAMES • Ezaki Mio • JPN
GIRL'S START, A see **LANY ELINDUL, EGY** • 1937
GIRL'S STRATAGEM, A • 1913 • Griffith D. W. • USA
GIRL'S TEARS, A see **LACRIMA DE FATA, O** • 1980
GIRLS THAT DO, THE • 1967 • Knight Sidney • USA
GIRLS TOO see **GIRLS COME TOO!** • 1968
GIRLS TOWN • 1942 • Halperin Victor Hugo • USA
GIRLS' TOWN • 1959 • Haas Charles • USA • INNOCENT AND THE DAMNED, THE
GIRLS UNDER 21 • 1940 • Nosseck Max • USA
GIRL'S WAR see **MADCHENKRIEG** • 1977
GIRLS WHO CRY OUT FOR LOVE (UKN) see **MADCHEN DIE NACH LIEBE SCHREIEN** • 1973
GIRLS WHO DARE • 1929 • Mattison Frank S. • USA
GIRLS WILL BE BOYS • 1911 • *Essanay* • USA
GIRLS WILL BE BOYS • 1913 • Smalley Phillips • USA
GIRLS WILL BE BOYS • 1931 • Watson William • USA
GIRLS WILL BE BOYS • 1934 • Varnel Marcel • UKN
GIRLS WITHOUT ROOMS (USA) see **FLAMMAN** • 1956
GIRLSAPOPPIN • 1964 • Good Knott • USA
GIRLTALK • 1988 • Davis Kate • USA
GIRLY see **MUMSY, NANNY, SONNY AND GIRLY** • 1969
GIRO • 1983 • Sigrist Hugo • SWT
GIRO CITY • 1982 • Francis Karl • UKN • AND NOTHING BUT THE TRUTH (USA)
GIRO DEL MONDO DEGLI INNAMORATI DI PEYNET • 1974 • Perfetto Cesare • ANM • ITL • TWO LOVERS AROUND THE WORLD
GIRO DEL MONDO IN 90 MINUTI, IL • 1967 • Carren H. • ITL
GIRO DI BOA • 1975 • Morandi Carlo • ITL
GIRO GIROTONDO.. CON IL SESSO E BELLO IL MONDO • 1976 • Brazzi Fabrizio • ITL
GIROLIMONI –IL MOSTRO DI ROMA • 1972 • Damiani Damiano • ITL • ASSASSINS OF ROME (USA)
GIRON • 1973 • Herrera Manuel • CUB
GIROTONDO DEGLI UNDICI LANCIERI • 1918 • D'Ambra Lucio • ITL
GIROVAGHI, I • 1956 • Fregonese Hugo • ITL
GISELE (UKN) see **ETREINTE, L'** • 1969
GISELLE • 1952 • Caldwell Henry • UKN
GISELLE • 1968 • Niebeling Hugo • FRG, USA
GISELLE • 1981 • Di Mello Victor • BRZ • HER SUMMER VACATION
GISELLE see **DANCERS** • 1987
GISHIKI • 1971 • Oshima Nagisa • JPN • CEREMONY, THE
GISMONDA see **LOVE'S CONQUEST** • 1918
GIST see **SARANSH** • 1984
GIT! • 1965 • Kadison Ellison • USA
GIT A HOSS • 1911 • *Standing Jack* • USA
GIT ALONG LIL' DUCKIE • 1955 • Tendlar Dave • ANS • USA
GIT ALONG, LITTLE DOGIES • 1937 • Kane Joseph • USA • SERENADE OF THE WEST (UKN)
GIT ALONG, LITTLE WIFIE • 1933 • Lamont Charles • SHT • USA
GITA SCOLASTICA, UNA • 1984 • Avati Pupi • ITL • SCHOOL OUTING, A
GITAN, LE • 1975 • Giovanni Jose • FRN, ITL • ZINGARO, LO ○ GYPSY, THE
GITANA • 1965 • Bollo Joaquin • SPN
GITANA BLANCA • 1965 • Seto Javier • SPN
GITANA BLANCA, LA • 1954 • Delgado Miguel M. • MXC
GITANA E EL REY, LA • 1945 • Bengoa Manuel • SPN
GITANA EN JALISCO, UNA • 1946 • Diaz Morales Jose • MXC
GITANA EN MEXICO, UNA • 1943 • Diaz Morales Jose • MXC
GITANA TENIAS QUE SER • 1953 • Baledon Rafael • SPN, MXC
GITANA Y EL CHARRO, LA • 1963 • Martinez Solares Gilberto • MXC, SPN, GTM • GYPSY-GIRL AND THE CHURL, THE
GITANELLA, LA • 1914 • Feuillade Louis • FRN
GITANELLA, LA • 1923 • Hugon Andre • FRN
GITANELLA, LA • 1940 • Delgado Fernando • SPN
GITANES • 1924 • de Baroncelli Jacques • FRN
GITANES • 1932 • de Baroncelli Jacques • FRN
GITANOS: ESCAPE FROM APARTHEID • 1976 • Hayers Sidney • USA • ESCAPE FROM APARTHEID ○ ONE AWAY
GITANOS ET PAPILLONS • 1954 • Gruel Henri • ANS • FRN
GITARREN DER LIEBE • 1954 • Jacobs Werner • FRG • GUITARS OF LOVE (USA)
GITTA ENTDECKT IHR HERZ • 1932 • Froelich Carl • FRG
GITTE IN APRIL • 1969 • Kristensen Hans • SHT • DNM
GIU IL SIPARIO • 1940 • Matarazzo Raffaello • ITL
GIU LA TESTA • 1971 • Leone Sergio • ITL • FISTFUL OF DYNAMITE, A (UKN) ○ DUCK, YOU SUCKER (USA)
GIU LE MANI.. CAROGNA • 1971 • Fidani Demofilo • ITL • DJANGO STORY
GIUBBE ROSSE • 1975 • D'Amato Joe • ITL
GIUDICATEMI • 1948 • Cristallini Giorgio • ITL • DRAMMA AL LUNA PARK
GIUDICE E I SUO BOIA, IL see **RICHTER UND SEIN HENKER, DER** • 1976
GIUDICE E LA MINORENNE, IL • 1974 • Nucci Franco • ITL
GIUDICE HALLER, IL see **CASO HALLER, IL** • 1933
GIUDITTA E OLOFERNE • 1929 • Negroni Baldassare • ITL
GIUDITTA E OLOFERNE • 1959 • Cerchio Fernando • ITL • HEAD OF A TYRANT (USA) ○ JUDITH AND HOLOPHERNES
GIUDIZIO DI MICHELANGELO, IL • 1949 • Pellegrini Glauco • SHT • ITL
GIUDIZIO UNIVERSALE, IL • 1961 • De Sica Vittorio • ITL, FRN • JUGEMENT DERNIER, LE (FRN) ○ LAST JUDGMENT, THE (USA)
GIUGNO '44 SBARCHEREMO IN NORMANDIA • 1968 • Klimovsky Leon • ITL, SPN • JUNE '44 LANDING IN NORMANDY
GIULIA E GIULIA • 1988 • Del Monte Peter • ITL • JULIA AND JULIA
GIULIANO DE' MEDICI • 1941 • Vajda Ladislao • ITL • CONGIURA DE' PAZZI, LA
GIULIANO L'APOSTATA • 1920 • Falena Ugo • ITL
GIULIETTA DEGLI SPIRITI • 1965 • Fellini Federico • ITL, FRN, FRG • JULIA UND DIE GEISTER (FRG) ○ JULIETTE DES ESPRITS (FRN) ○ JULIET OF THE SPIRITS (USA)
GIULIETTA E ROMEO • 1954 • Castellani Renato • ITL, UKN • ROMEO AND JULIET (UKN)
GIULIETTA E ROMEO • 1964 • Freda Riccardo • ITL, SPN • AMANTES DE VERONA, LOS (SPN) ○ ROMEO AND JULIET (USA)
GIULIO CESARE CONTRO I PIRATI • 1962 • Grieco Sergio • ITL • CAESAR AGAINST THE PIRATES (USA)
GIULIO CESARE IL CONQUISTATORE DELLE GALLIE • 1963 • Boccia Tanio • ITL • JULIUS CAESAR, CONQUEROR OF GAUL ○ CAESAR THE CONQUEROR
GIUMENTA VERDE, LA (ITL) see **JUMENT VERTE, LA** • 1959
GIUNGLA • 1942 • Malasomma Nunzio • ITL
GIUNSE RINGO E.. FU TEMPO DI MASSACRO • 1971 • Pinzauti Mario • ITL
GIUOCO DELLA VERITA, IL • 1974 • Massa Michele • ITL
GIURAMENTO D'AMORE • 1955 • Montero Roberto Bianchi • ITL
GIURO.. E IL UCCISE AD UNO AD UNO see **PILUK IL TIMIDO** • 1968
GIUSEPPE VENDUTO DAI FRATELLI (ITL) see **JOSEPH AND HIS BRETHREN** • 1962
GIUSEPPE VERDI • 1938 • Gallone Carmine • ITL • LIFE AND MUSIC OF GIUSEPPE VERDI, THE
GIUSEPPE VERDI • 1953 • Matarazzo Raffaello • ITL • LIFE AND MUSIC OF GIUSEPPE VERDI, THE (USA)
GIUSEPPE'S GOOD FORTUNE • 1912 • *Calvert E. H.* • USA
GIUSEPPINA • 1961 • Hill James • SHT • UKN
GIUSTIZIA see **PRIGIONIERO DI SANTA CRUZ, IL** • 1941
GIUSTIZIERE DEI MARE, IL • 1962 • Paolella Domenico • ITL, FRN • AVENGER OF THE SEVEN SEAS (USA) ○ EXECUTIONER ON THE SEAS, THE ○ EXECUTIONER ON THE HIGH SEAS, THE
GIUSTIZIERE DELLA MALA, IL see **GARDENIA** • 1979
GIUSTIZIERE DI DIO, IL • 1973 • Lattanzi Franco • ITL
GIUSTIZIERE DI MEZZOGIORNO, IL • 1975 • Amendola Mario • ITL
GIUSTIZIERE SFIDA LA CITTA, IL • 1975 • Lenzi Umberto • ITL • SYNDICATE SADISTS ○ ONE JUST MAN
GIV GUD EN CHANCE OM SONDAGEN • 1970 • Stangerup Henrik • DNM • GIVE GOD A CHANCE ON SUNDAYS
GIVE A DOG A BONE • 1967 • Cass Henry • UKN
GIVE A GIRL A BREAK • 1953 • Donen Stanley • USA
GIVE AND TAKE • 1928 • Beaudine William • USA
GIVE AND TAKE (UKN) see **SINGIN' IN THE CORN** • 1946
GIVE AND TYKE • 1957 • Hanna William, Barbera Joseph • ANS • USA
GIVE AWAY THE SHOW see **FIGOURATZIS, O** • 1968
GIVE 'EM AN INCH (UKN) see **HAUSFRAUEN –REPORT III** • 1972
GIVE 'EM HELL see **CA VA BARDER** • 1954
GIVE 'EM HELL, HARRY! • 1975 • Binder Steve?, Hunt Peter H.? • USA
GIVE 'EM WHAT THEY WANT • 1971 • Bryan James A. • USA
GIVE GOD A CHANCE ON SUNDAYS see **GIV GUD EN CHANCE OM SONDAGEN** • 1970
GIVE HER A RING • 1934 • Woods Arthur • UKN • GIVING YOU THE STARS
GIVE HER GAS • 1918 • Lyons Eddie, Moran Lee • SHT • USA
GIVE HER THE MOON (USA) see **CAPRICES DE MARIE, LES** • 1969
GIVE ME A BIT OF LOOOVE! see **DAME UN POCO DE AMOOOOR...!** • 1968
GIVE ME A CHILD see **CHILD IS BORN, A** • 1940
GIVE ME A COMPLAINT BOOK, PLEASE see **LET ME MAKE A COMPLAINT** • 1964
GIVE ME A LIGHT • 1909 • *Powhatan* • USA
GIVE ME A SAILOR • 1938 • Nugent Elliott • USA
GIVE ME FIVE see **QUA LA MANO** • 1980
GIVE ME FOOD see **VAT DE** • 1985
GIVE ME LIBERTY • 1937 • Eason B. Reeves • USA
GIVE ME LIBERTY • 1967 • Bakshi Ralph • ANS • USA
GIVE ME LOVE see **GIB MIR LIEBE** • 1968
GIVE ME TEN DESPERATE MEN see **DONNEZ-MOI DIX HOMMES DESESPERES** • 1961
GIVE ME THE STARS • 1944 • Rogers Maclean • UKN
GIVE ME THIS WOMAN see **CONSPIRATORS, THE** • 1944
GIVE ME YOUR EYES see **DONNE-MOI TES YEUX** • 1943
GIVE ME YOUR HEART • 1936 • Mayo Archie • USA • SWEET ALOES (UKN) ○ I GIVE MY HEART
GIVE ME YOUR PAW, FRIEND! see **DAY LAPU, DRUG!** • 1967
GIVE MY POOR HEART EASE: MISSISSIPPI DELTA BLUESMEN • 1975 • Ferris Bill, Ferris Josette • SHT • USA
GIVE MY REGARDS TO BROAD STREET • 1983 • Webb Peter • UKN
GIVE MY REGARDS TO BROADWAY • 1948 • Bacon Lloyd • USA • OFF TO BUFFALO
GIVE OUT, SISTERS • 1942 • Cline Eddie • USA
GIVE THE KIDS A BREAK • 1936 • Taylor Donald • UKN
GIVE TILL IT HURTS • 1937 • Feist Felix E. • SHT • USA
GIVE US A REST see **EMAK BAKIA** • 1926
GIVE US AIR see **DAYESH VOZDUKH** • 1924
GIVE US RADIO! see **DAESH RADIO!** • 1924
GIVE US THE MOON • 1944 • Guest Val • UKN
GIVE US THIS DAY • 1949 • Dmytryk Edward • UKN • SALT TO THE DEVIL (USA)
GIVE US THIS DAY see **INGEBORG HOLM** • 1913
GIVE US THIS NIGHT • 1936 • Hall Alexander • USA
GIVE US TOMORROW • 1980 • Winter Donovan • UKN
GIVE US WINGS • 1936 • Weiss Jiri • DOC • CZC
GIVE US WINGS • 1940 • Lamont Charles • USA
GIVE US YOUR HAND see **QUA LA MANO** • 1980
GIVEN WORD, THE see **PAGADOR DE PROMESSAS, O** • 1961
GIVING BECKY A CHANCE • 1917 • Estabrook Howard • USA
GIVING BILL A REST • 1913 • *Hotely Mae* • USA
GIVING THE BRIDE AWAY • 1919 • Roach Hal • SHT • USA
GIVING THEM FITS • 1915 • Roach Hal • USA
GIVING UP see **TUP AKKA LAKKO** • 1980
GIVING YOU THE STARS see **GIVE HER A RING** • 1934
GIVRES, LES • 1979 • Jaspard Alain • FRN
GIWAKU • 1983 • Nomura Yoshitaro • JPN • SUSPICION
GIYERA PATANI • 1968 • Villaflor Romy • PHL • MOCK WAR
GIZLI DUYGULAR • 1986 • Goren Serif • TRK • HIDDEN PASSIONS
GIZMO! • 1977 • Smith Howard • DOC • USA
GJURME TE BARDHA • 1981 • Kreyeziu Ekrem • YGS • BIJELI TRAGOVI ○ WHITE TRAIL, THE
GKN SPAT SYSTEM • 1966 • Erulkar Sarah • SHT • UKN
GLACE A TROIS FACES, LA • 1927 • Epstein Jean • FRN • GLASS WITH THREE FACES, THE ○ THREE-WAY MIRROR, THE ○ MIRROR WITH THREE FACES
GLACE AVEC DEUX BOULES, UNE • 1982 • Lara Christian • FRN
GLACIER FOX, THE see **KITAKITSUNE MONGATARI** • 1978
GLACIERS • 1942 • Decae Henri • SHT • FRN
GLACKENS CARTOONS • 1916 • Glackens W. L. • ASS • USA
GLAD DIG I DIN UNGDOM • 1939 • Lindberg Per • SWD • REJOICE WHILE YOU ARE YOUNG
GLAD EYE, THE • 1920 • Foss Kenelm • UKN
GLAD EYE, THE • 1927 • Elvey Maurice, Saville Victor • UKN
GLAD GUTT, EN • 1933 • Brunius John W. • SWD
GLAD RAG DOLL, THE • 1929 • Curtiz Michael • USA
GLAD RAGS • 1923 • Fay Hugh • USA
GLAD RAGS TO RICHES • 1933 • Lamont Charles • SHT • USA
GLAD TIDINGS • 1953 • Rilla Wolf • UKN

GLADA KALASET, DET • 1946 • Ekerot Bengt • SWD • GAY PARTY, THE
GLADA PARADEN • 1948 • Lingheim Emil A. • SWD • GAY PARADE
GLADE SKOMAKAREN, DEN • 1955 • Anderberg Torgny • SWD • MERRY SHOEMAKER, THE
GLADE SKRADDAREN, DEN • 1945 • Olsson Gunnar • SWD • GAY TAILOR, THE
GLADE VRINSK • 1975 • Bohwim Knut • NRW
GLADIADOR INVENCIBLE, EL • 1961 • Momplet Antonio • SPN, ITL • GLADIATORE INVINCIBILE, IL (ITL) ○ INVINCIBLE GLADIATOR, THE(USA)
GLADIATOR, THE • 1938 • Sedgwick Edward • USA
GLADIATOR, THE • 1986 • Ferrara Abel • TVM • USA
GLADIATOR OF ROME (USA) see **GLADIATORE DI ROMA, IL** • 1962
GLADIATORE CHE SFIDO L'IMPERO • 1965 • Paolella Domenico • ITL • CHALLENGE OF THE GLADIATOR (USA)
GLADIATORE DELLA TRACIA, IL see **SPARTACO** • 1952
GLADIATORE DI ROMA, IL • 1962 • Costa Mario • ITL • GLADIATOR OF ROME (USA) ○ BATTLES OF THE GLADIATORS
GLADIATORE INVINCIBILE, IL (ITL) see **GLADIADOR INVENCIBLE, EL** • 1961
GLADIATORERNA • 1969 • Watkins Peter • SWD • PEACE GAME, THE (UKN) ○ GLADIATORS
GLADIATORS see **GLADIATORERNA** • 1969
GLADIATORS, THE see **DEMETRIUS AND THE GLADIATORS** • 1954
GLADIATOR'S AFFIANCED BRIDE, THE • 1908 • *Tyler Walter* • UKN
GLADIATORS SEVEN (USA) see **SETTE GLADIATORI, I** • 1962
GLADIATRICI, LE • 1963 • Leoviola Antonio • ITL
GLADIOLA • 1915 • Collins John H. • USA
GLADSTONE: THE PROSTITUTE SCANDAL see **SECRET LIVES OF THE BRITISH PRIME MINISTERS: GLADSTONE, THE** • 1981
GLADYS' DAY DREAMS • 1917 • *Cahill Marie* • SHT • USA
GLAEDENS DAG • 1918 • Christian • DNM • DAY OF JOY ○ MISKENDT ○ NEGLECTED
GLAIVE ET LA BALANCE, LE • 1962 • Cayatte Andre • FRN, ITL • UNO DEI TRE (ITL) ○ TWO ARE GUILTY (USA)
GLAMADOR • 1957 • Colomb De Daunant Denys • FRN
GLAMIS CASTLE • 1926 • Elvey Maurice • UKN
GLAMOR BOY • 1938 • Goodwins Leslie • USA
GLAMOR FOR SALE • 1940 • Lederman D. Ross • USA • GLAMOUR FOR SALE
GLAMOR GIRL • 1947 • Dreifuss Arthur • USA • NIGHT CLUB GIRL ○ GLAMOUR GIRL
GLAMOROUS HOLLYWOOD • 1958 • Staub Ralph • SHT • USA
GLAMOROUS NIGHT • 1937 • Hurst Brian Desmond • UKN
GLAMOUR • 1931 • Hicks Seymour, Hughes Harry • UKN
GLAMOUR • 1934 • Wyler William • USA
GLAMOUR BOY • 1941 • Murphy Ralph • USA • HEARTS IN SPRINGTIME (UKN)
GLAMOUR BOY (UKN) see **MILLIONAIRE PLAYBOY, THE** • 1940
GLAMOUR FOR SALE see **GLAMOR FOR SALE** • 1940
GLAMOUR GIRL • 1938 • Woods Arthur • UKN
GLAMOUR GIRL see **GLAMOR GIRL** • 1947
GLANCE AT THE PUPIL OF THE SUN, A see **POGLED U ZJENICU SUNCA** • 1966
GLANCE TO THE PUPIL OF THE SUN see **POGLED U ZJENICU SUNCA** • 1966
GLANZ GEGEN GLUCK • 1923 • Trotz Adolf • FRG
GLANZ UND ELEND DER KURTISANEN • 1920 • Wiene Conrad, Ralph Louis • FRG • MORAL, DER MEISTER DES VERBRECHENS ○ QUEEN OF THE BOULEVARDS
GLANZ UND ELEND DER KURTISANEN • 1927 • Noa Manfred • FRG
GLANZ UND ENDE EINES KONIGS see **LUDWIG II** • 1955
GLAS • 1958 • Haanstra Bert • NTH • GLASS
GLAS DU PERE CESAIRE, LE • 1909 • *Gance Abel* • FRN
GLAS WASSER, DAS • 1960 • Kautner Helmut • FRG • GLASS OF WATER, A
GLAS WASSER, EIN • 1923 • Berger Ludwig • FRG • SPIEL DER KONIGIN, DAS
GLASBERGET • 1953 • Molander Gustaf • SWD • UNMARRIED
GLASERNE HIMMEL, DER • 1988 • Grosse Nina • FRG • GLASS SKY, THE ○ GLASS HEAVEN, THE
GLASERNE KUGEL, DIE • 1937 • Stanchina Peter • FRG • GLASS BALL, THE (USA)
GLASERNE TURM, DER • 1957 • Braun Harald • FRG • GLASS TOWER, THE (USA)
GLASERNE ZELLE, DIE • 1978 • Geissendorfer Hans W. • FRG • GLASS CELL, THE
GLASGOW 1980 • 1971 • Marzaroli Oscar • DCS • UKN
GLASGOW ENVIRONMENTAL IMPROVEMENT • 1975 • Gormley Charles • DOC • UKN
GLASGOW ORPHEUS CHOIR • 1951 • Hoellering George • UKN
GLASS • 1989 • Kennedy Chris • ASL
GLASS see **GLAS** • 1958
GLASS ALIBI, THE • 1940 • Wilder W. Lee • USA
GLASS BALL, THE see **SZKLANA KULA** • 1972
GLASS BALL, THE (USA) see **GLASERNE KUGEL, DIE** • 1937
GLASS-BEAD ROSARY, A see **PACIORKI JEDNEGO ROZANCA** • 1979
GLASS BEADS FROM THE SEA see **THALASSEIES I HANDRES, I** • 1967
GLASS-BOTTOM BOAT, THE • 1966 • Tashlin Frank • USA
GLASS CAGE, THE • 1955 • Tully Montgomery • UKN • GLASS TOMB, THE (USA)
GLASS CAGE, THE • 1964 • Santean Antonio • USA • DON'T TOUCH MY SISTER ○ DEN OF DOOM ○ BED OF FIRE
GLASS CAGE, THE (UKN) see **CAGE DE VERRE, LA** • 1964
GLASS CEILING see **TECHE DE VIDRIO** • 1982
GLASS CELL, THE see **GLASERNE ZELLE, DIE** • 1978
GLASS COFFIN • 1912 • *Eclair* • USA • CRYSTAL CASKET, THE
GLASS FROM THE ATTIC • 1988 • Kabelik Vladimir • DCS • CND
GLASS, GLASS, GLASS see **SKLO, SKLO, SKLO** • 1961
GLASS HAMMER, THE see **IF TOMORROW COMES** • 1971
GLASS HEAVEN, THE see **GLASERNE HIMMEL, DER** • 1988
GLASS HOUSE, THE • 1972 • Gries Tom • TVM • USA • TRUMAN CAPOTE'S THE GLASS HOUSE
GLASS HOUSES • 1922 • Beaumont Harry • USA
GLASS HOUSES • 1972 • Singer Alexander • USA
GLASS INDUSTRY, THE see **INDUSTRIE DU VERRE, L'**
GLASS KEY, THE • 1935 • Tuttle Frank • USA
GLASS KEY, THE • 1942 • Heisler Stuart • USA
GLASS MENAGERIE, THE • 1950 • Rapper Irving • USA
GLASS MENAGERIE, THE • 1973 • Harvey Anthony • TVM • USA
GLASS MENAGERIE, THE • 1987 • Newman Paul • USA
GLASS MOUNTAIN, THE • 1949 • Cass Henry, Anton Edoardo • UKN, ITL • MONTAGNA DI CRISTALLO, LA (ITL)
GLASS MOUNTAIN, THE see **SZKLANA GORA** • 1961
GLASS OF BEER, A see **PIKOLO VILAGOS, EGY** • 1955
GLASS OF GOAT'S MILK, A • 1909 • Stow Percy • UKN
GLASS OF WATER, A see **GLAS WASSER, DAS** • 1960
GLASS OF WINE, A see **GLASS VIN, ETT** • 1960
GLASS PISTOL, THE • 1914 • *Crystal* • USA
GLASS RABBIT see **GARASU NO USAGI** • 1979
GLASS SKY, THE see **GLASERNE HIMMEL, DER** • 1988
GLASS SLIPPER, THE • 1938 • Davis Mannie • ANS • USA
GLASS SLIPPER, THE • 1954 • Walters Charles • USA
GLASS SLIPPER, THE see **KHRUSTALNYY BASHMACHOK** • 1961
GLASS SPHINX, THE (USA) see **SFINGE D'ORO, LA** • 1967
GLASS TALE, THE • 1967 • Bedrich Vaclav • ANS • CZC
GLASS TOMB, THE (USA) see **GLASS CAGE, THE** • 1955
GLASS TOWER, THE (USA) see **GLASERNE TURM, DER** • 1957
GLASS VIN, ETT • 1960 • Werner Gosta • SHT • SWD • GLASS OF WINE, A
GLASS WALL, THE • 1953 • Shane Maxwell • USA
GLASS WALL, THE see **KANCHER DEYAL** • 1964
GLASS WEB, THE • 1953 • Arnold Jack • USA
GLASS WHISTLE, THE • 1970 • Tyrlova Hermina • ANS • CZC • WHISTLE, THE
GLASS WITH THREE FACES, THE see **GLACE A TROIS FACES, LA** • 1927
GLASS WOMAN • 1977 • Galal Nader • EGY
GLASS WORK OF TELEGAON, THE • 1915 • Phalke Dada • IND
GLASSMAKERS OF ENGLAND, THE • 1933 • Flaherty Robert • DCS • UKN
GLASTONBURY FAIR, THE • 1971 • Roeg Nicolas • SHT • UKN
GLASTONBURY FAYRE • 1973 • Neal Peter • UKN
GLATZKOPFBANDE, DIE • 1963 • Groschopp Richard • GDR
GLAUBE AN MICH • 1947 • von Cziffra Geza • AUS
GLAUBE SIEGT, DER • 1915 • Schonfeld Carl • FRG
GLAUBENSKETTEN • 1916 • Meinert Rudolf • FRG
GLEAM O'DAWN • 1922 • Dillon John Francis • USA
GLEAMING THE CUBE • 1988 • Clifford Graeme • USA
GLEASON'S NEW DEAL • 1933 • Horne James W. • SHT • USA
GLEBAE ADSCRIPTI • 1964 • Haupe Wlodzimierz • PLN
GLEE WORMS • 1936 • *Mintz Charles (P)* • ANS • USA
GLEEFUL GUARDIANS • 1916 • *Heinie & Louie* • USA
GLEISDREIECK • 1936 • Stemmle R. A. • FRG • ALARM AUF GLEIS B
GLEIWITZ CASE, THE see **FALL GLEIWITZ, DER** • 1961
GLEN AND RANDA • 1971 • McBride Jim • USA
GLEN FALLS SEQUENCE • 1946 • Crockwell Douglas • SHT • USA • GLENN FALLS SEQUENCE
GLEN GRAY AND HIS BAND • 1942 • Negulesco Jean • SHT • USA
GLEN OR GLENDA? • 1952 • Wood Edward D. Jr. • USA • I LED TWO LIVES ○ I CHANGED MY SEX ○ TRANSVESTITE ○ HE OR SHE
GLENDA • 1976 • SAF
GLENGARRY SCHOOLDAYS • 1922 • McRae Henry • CND, USA • CRITICAL AGE, THE (USA) ○ GOOD-FOR-NOTHIN', THE
GLENISTER OF THE MOUNTED • 1926 • Garson Harry • USA
GLENN FALLS SEQUENCE see **GLEN FALLS SEQUENCE** • 1946
GLENN GOULD: A PORTRAIT • 1985 • Till Eric (c/d) • MTV • CND
GLENN GOULD -OFF THE RECORD • 1960 • Koenig Wolf, Kroitor Roman • CND
GLENN GOULD -ON THE RECORD • 1960 • Koenig Wolf, Kroitor Roman • CND
GLENN MILLER STORY, THE • 1954 • Mann Anthony • USA
GLENROWAN AFFAIR • 1951 • Kathner Rupert • ASL
GLIKIA SIMORIA • 1983 • Nikolaidis Nikos • GRC • SWEET BUNCH
GLIMMERING • Thevenard Pierre • FRN
GLIMPSE OF A GARDEN • 1957 • Menken Marie • SHT • USA • GLIMPSE OF THE GARDEN
GLIMPSE OF AUSTRIA • 1938 • Fitzpatrick James • SHT • USA
GLIMPSE OF BYGONE DAYS, A • SHT • FRG
GLIMPSE OF LOS ANGELES, A • 1914 • Lucas Wilfred • DOC • USA
GLIMPSE OF PARADISE, A • 1934 • Ince Ralph • UKN
GLIMPSE OF THE CORNISH COAST, A • 1935 • Voller R. • UKN
GLIMPSE OF THE GARDEN see **GLIMPSE OF A GARDEN** • 1957
GLIMPSES FROM LIFE see **JIBON THEKEY NEYA** • 1969
GLIMPSES OF JAVA AND CEYLON • 1937 • Fitzpatrick James • SHT • USA
GLIMPSES OF LIFE see **TOREDEK AZ ELETROL** • 1981
GLIMPSES OF MODERN RUSSIA • 1930 • Bond Ralph • UKN
GLIMPSES OF NEW BRUNSWICK • 1938 • Fitzpatrick James • SHT • USA
GLIMPSES OF PERU • 1937 • Fitzpatrick James • SHT • USA
GLIMPSES OF THE MOON, THE • 1923 • Dwan Allan • USA
GLIMPSES OF WEST BENGAL • 1978 • Chandragupta Bansi • DOC • IND
GLINENI GOLUB • 1966 • Janic Tomo • YGS • CLAY PIGEON, THE
GLINKA • 1946 • Arnstam Leo • USS • GREAT GLINKA, THE (USA)
GLINKA see **KOMPOZITOR GLINKA** • 1952
GLINKA, MAN OF MUSIC see **KOMPOZITOR GLINKA** • 1952
GLISSANDO • 1985 • Daneliuc Mircea • RMN
GLISSEMENTS PROGRESSIFS DU PLAISIR, LES • 1973 • Robbe-Grillet Alain • FRN
GLITCH! • 1988 • Mastorakis Nico • USA
GLITTER see **DROP KICK, THE** • 1927
GLITTER see **I LIVE MY LIFE** • 1935
GLITTER DOME, THE • 1985 • Margolin Stuart • USA
GLITTERBALL, THE • 1976 • Cokliss Harley • USA
GLITTERING SWORD, THE • 1929 • Gow Ronald • UKN
GLITTERING YOU see **KIMI GA KAGAYAKU TOKI** • 1985
GLITZ • 1989 • Stern Sandor • USA
GLJIVA • 1972 • Grgic Zlatko • ANS • YGS • TOADSTOOLS
GLO FRIENDS SAVE CHRISTMAS, THE • 1986 • ANM • USA
GLO FRIENDS: THE MOVIE - THE QUEST • 1987 • ANM • USA • GLO FRIENDS: THE QUEST
GLO FRIENDS: THE QUEST see **GLO FRIENDS: THE MOVIE - THE QUEST** • 1987
GLOBAL AFFAIR, A • 1963 • Arnold Jack • USA
GLOBAL PANORAMA • 1971 • Dueck David B. • DOC • CND
GLOBAL QUIZ • 1955 • *Smith Pete* • SHT • USA
GLOBE OF DELIGHTS • 1971 • Wisbey Deanna • UKN
GLOBERO, EL • 1960 • Cardona Rene • MXC
GLOBKE TODAY • 1963 • Heynowski Walter • DOC • GDR
GLOBO DE CANTOLLA, EL • 1943 • Martinez Solares Gilberto • MXC
GLOCKE 1, DIE • 1917 • Hofer Franz • FRG
GLOCKE 2, DIE • 1921 • Hofer Franz • FRG
GLOCKE RUFT, DIE see **GLOCKEN LAUTEN UBERALL** • 1960
GLOCKEN DER KATHARINEKIRCHE, DIE • 1917 • Gartner Adolf • FRG
GLOCKEN LAUTEN UBERALL • 1960 • Antel Franz • AUS • GLOCKE RUFT, DIE
GLOCKENGIESSER VON TIROL, DER • 1956 • Haussler Richard • FRG
GLOCKERL VON BIRKENSTEIN, DAS • 1920 • Seitz Franz • FRG
GLOIRE A L'EAU • 1935 • Tessier Albert • DCS • CND
GLOIRE DE MON PERE, LE • 1989 • Robert Yves • FRN
GLOIRE DES CANAILLES, LA (FRN) see **DALLE ARDENNE ALL'INFERNO** • 1968
GLOIRE ROUGE • 1923 • Dieudonne Albert • FRN
GLOMDALSBRUDEN • 1925 • Dreyer Carl T. • NRW • BRIDE OF GLOMSDALE, THE ○ BRIDE OF GLOMDAL, THE
GLOOM CHASER, THE • 1928 • Lamont Charles • SHT • USA
GLOOM CHASERS, THE • 1935 • *Mintz Charles (P)* • ANS • USA
GLOOMY see **GRIS** • 1969
GLOOMY MORNING, A see **KHMUROE UTRO** • 1959
GLOOMY SUNDAY see **SOMBRE DIMANCHE** • 1948
GLOOSCAP COUNTRY • 1961 • Perry Margaret • DOC • CND
GLOOSKAP • 1972 • *Holt, Rinehart & Winston* • SHT • USA
GLORIA • 1916 • SAF
GLORIA • 1931 • Behrendt Hans • FRG
GLORIA • 1931 • Noe Yvan, Behrendt Hans • FRN
GLORIA • 1977 • Autant-Lara Claude • FRN
GLORIA • 1980 • Cassavetes John • USA
GLORIA, LA • 1912 • Negroni Baldassare • ITL
GLORIA, LA • 1916 • Mari Febo • ITL
GLORIA DE LA RAZA, LA • 1925 • Castillo Luis • BLV • GLORY OF THE RACE, THE
GLORIA DI SANGUE • 1919 • Lolli Alberto Carlo • ITL
GLORIA FATALIS • 1924 • *Munchener Filmindustrie* • FRG
GLORIA MAIRENA • 1952 • Lucia Luis • SPN
GLORIA MUNDI • 1969 • Kovasznai Gyorgy • ANS • HNG
GLORIA MUNDI • 1975 • Papatakis Nico • FRN
GLORIA SCOTT, THE • 1923 • Ridgwell George • UKN
GLORIANA • 1916 • Hopper E. Mason • USA
GLORIANNA'S GETAWAY • 1915 • *Burke Peggy* • USA
GLORIA'S ROMANCE • 1916 • Edwin Walter • SRL • USA
GLORIE see **O VECECH NADPRIROZENYCH** • 1958
GLORIFYING THE AMERICAN GIRL • 1929 • Webb Millard • USA • GLORIFYING THE SHOW GIRL
GLORIFYING THE SHOW GIRL see **GLORIFYING THE AMERICAN GIRL** • 1929
GLORIOUS ADVENTURE, THE • 1918 • Henley Hobart • USA
GLORIOUS ADVENTURE, THE • 1922 • Blackton J. Stuart • USA, UKN
GLORIOUS AVENGER • 1950 • *Franicoli Armando* • ITL
GLORIOUS BETTY • 1928 • Crosland Alan • USA
GLORIOUS CAMPAIGN, THE see **SPANILA JIZDA** • 1963
GLORIOUS DUST, THE see **DIVOTA PRASINE** • 1976
GLORIOUS FOOL, THE • 1922 • Hopper E. Mason • USA
GLORIOUS FOURTH • 1927 • Roach Hal • SHT • USA
GLORIOUS LADY, THE • 1919 • Irving George • USA • GLORIOUS YOUTH
GLORIOUS MARCH see **WSPANIALY MARSZ** • 1970
GLORIOUS MUD • 1983 • Keatley Philip • CND
GLORIOUS MUSKETEERS, THE • 1974 • Halas John • ANM • UKN, FRN, ITL • D'ARTAGNAN L'INTREPIDE (FRN)
GLORIOUS NIGHTS see **NOCHES DE GLORIA** • 1937
GLORIOUS SACRIFICE, THE (UKN) see **GLORY TRAIL, THE** • 1936
GLORIOUS SIXTH OF JUNE • 1934 • Cavalcanti Alberto • UKN
GLORIOUS SUNDAY see **DOMINGO DE GLORIA** • 1981
GLORIOUS SWITZERLAND • 1924 • *Holmes Burton* • DOC • USA
GLORIOUS SYDNEY OF TODAY • 1911 • Barrett Franklyn • DOC • ASL
GLORIOUS TIMES IN THE SPESSART see **HERRLICHE ZEITEN IM SPESSART** • 1967
GLORIOUS TRAIL, THE • 1928 • Rogell Albert S. • USA
GLORIOUS YOUTH see **GLORIOUS LADY, THE** • 1919
GLORIOUS YOUTH see **FASCINATING YOUTH** • 1926
GLORIOUS YOUTH see **EILEEN OF THE TREES** • 1928
GLORY • 1917 • King Burton L., Grandon Francis J. • USA
GLORY • 1956 • Butler David • USA
GLORY • 1989 • Zwick Edward • USA
GLORY see **SLAVA** • 1959
GLORY ALLEY • 1952 • Walsh Raoul • USA

GLORY AND MISERY OF HUMAN LIFE, THE see **IMMISELON IHANUUS JA KURJUUS** • 1988
GLORY BOY • 1973 • Sherin Edwin • USA • MY OLD MAN'S PLACE (UKN) ○ THERE'S NO PLACE LIKE HELL
GLORY BOYS, THE • 1982 • Ferguson Michael • TVM • USA, UKN
GLORY BRIGADE, THE • 1953 • Webb Robert D. • USA • BAPTISM OF FIRE
GLORY COMMAND see **MIDSHIPMAN JACK** • 1933
GLORY DAYS see **PLAIN CLOTHES** • 1988
GLORY ENOUGH FOR ALL • 1990 • Till Eric • CND
GLORY FOR ME see **BEST YEARS OF OUR LIVES, THE** • 1946
GLORY! GLORY! • 1989 • Anderson Lindsay • TVM • USA
GLORY GUYS, THE • 1965 • Laven Arnold • USA
GLORY OF CLEMENTINA, THE • 1915 • Miller Ashley • USA
GLORY OF CLEMENTINA, THE • 1922 • Chautard Emile • USA
GLORY OF LIGHT, THE • 1912 • *Solax* • USA
GLORY OF LOVE, THE see **WHILE PARIS SLEEPS** • 1923
GLORY OF THE BRASS BANDS, THE see **KDYBY TY MUSIKY NEBYLY** • 1963
GLORY OF THE RACE, THE see **GLORIA DE LA RAZA, LA** • 1925
GLORY OF YOLANDA, THE • 1917 • Bertsch Marguerite • USA
GLORY OF YOUTH, THE • 1915 • Gardner Louis B. • USA
GLORY ON THE SUMMIT see **YAMA NO SANKA: MOYURU WAKAMONO-TACHI** • 1962
GLORY STOMPERS, THE • 1967 • Lanza Anthony M. • USA
GLORY TO THE BULL see **BYKOWI CHWALA** • 1971
GLORY TRAIL, THE • 1936 • Shores Lynn • USA • GLORIOUS SACRIFICE, THE (UKN)
GLORY YEARS, THE • 1987 • Seidelman Arthur Allan • USA
GLOS SERCA • 1931 • Ordynski Ryszard • PLN
GLOS Z TAMTEGO SWIATA • 1962 • Rozewicz Stanislaw • PLN • VOICE FROM BEYOND
GLOSY • 1980 • Kijowski Janusz • PLN • VOICES
GLOVE, THE • 1913 • *Humphrey William* • USA
GLOVE, THE • 1978 • Hagen Ross • USA
GLOVE AFFAIR • 1939-43 • *Columbia* • SHT • USA
GLOVE TAPS • 1937 • Douglas Gordon • SHT • USA
GLOVED HAND, THE • 1911 • *Reliance* • USA
GLOVED HAND, THE see **SHADOWED** • 1946
GLOVES • 1914 • *Martin* • UKN
GLOVES OF PTAMES, THE • 1914 • Aylott Dave • UKN
GLOW LITTLE GLOW WORM GLOW • 1907 • Gilbert Arthur • UKN
GLOW WORM, THE • 1913 • Apfel Oscar • USA
GLOWA • 1953 • Borowczyk Walerian • SHT • PLN • HEAD, THE
GLOWING AUTUMN see **MOERU AKI** • 1978
GLOWING BRASIER, THE see **BRASIER ARDENT, LE** • 1922
GLOWING HEARTS see **GLUT IM HERZEN** • 1983
GLOWWORM, THE • 1930 • Fleischer Dave • ANS • USA
GLU, LA • 1913 • Capellani Albert • FRN
GLU, LA • 1926 • Fescourt Henri • FRN
GLU, LA • 1938 • Choux Jean • FRN
GLUCK AM RHEIN, DAS • 1921 • *Krafft-Lortzing Albert* • FRG
GLUCK AUF DEN LANDE • 1940 • Boese Carl • FRG • RURAL HAPPINESS (USA)
GLUCK AUS OHIO • 1951 • Paul Heinz • FRG
GLUCK BEI DEN FRAUEN • 1944 • Brauer Peter P. • FRG
GLUCK DER FRAU BEATE, DAS • 1918 • Rippert Otto • FRG
GLUCK IM SCHLOSS • 1933 • Preis Hasso • FRG
GLUCK IM WINKEL • 1927 • Rudolph Karl Heinz • FRG • DREI MADELS UND IHRE FREIER
GLUCK INS HAUS see **HAUS VOLL LIEBE, EIN** • 1954
GLUCK LIEGT AUF DER STRASSE, DAS • 1957 • Antel Franz • FRG
GLUCK MUSS MAN HABEN • 1953 • von Ambesser Axel • FRG • DREI VON DENEN MAN SPRICHT
GLUCK MUSST DU HABEN AUS DIESER WELT see **WER KUSST WEN?** • 1949
GLUCK UBER NACHT • 1932 • Neufeld Max • FRG
GLUCK UND GLAS see **GEFOLTERTE HERZEN 2** • 1920
GLUCK UND LIEBE IN MONACO • 1960 • Leitner Hermann • FRG
GLUCK UNTERWEGS • 1944 • Zittau Friedrich • FRG
GLUCK WOHNT NEBENAN, DAS • 1939 • Marischka Hubert • FRG
GLUCKHAFT SCHIFF, DAS see **NEULAND** • 1924
GLUCKLICHE REISE • 1933 • Abel Alfred • FRG
GLUCKLICHE REISE • 1954 • Engel Thomas • FRG
GLUCKLICHEN JAHRE DER THORWALDS, DIE • 1962 • Staudte Wolfgang, Olden John • FRG
GLUCKLICHEN MINUTEN DES GEORG HAUSER, DIE • 1974 • Mandavi Mansur • AUS • HAPPY MINUTES OF GEORG HAUSER, THE
GLUCKLICHER MENSCH, EIN • 1943 • Verhoeven Paul • FRG • SCHULE DES LEBENS
GLUCKLICHSTE EHE DER WELT, DIE • 1937 • Martin Karl Heinz • FRG • HAPPIEST MARRIED COUPLE IN VIENNA, THE (USA)
GLUCKSFALLE, DIE • 1920 • *Neumann Lotte* • FRG
GLUCKSFALLE, DIE see **GROSSTADTJUGEND** • 1928
GLUCKSJUNGE • 1918 • Larsen Viggo • FRG
GLUCKSKINDER • 1936 • Martin Paul • FRG
GLUCKSMUHLE, DIE • 1949 • Hanus Emerich • AUS
GLUCKSPILZE • 1934 • Stemmle R. A. • FRG
GLUCKSRITTER • 1957 • Rabenalt Arthur M. • FRG
GLUCKSSCHMIED, DER • 1919 • Czerny Ludwig • FRG
GLUCKSSCHMIEDE, DIE • 1916 • Salten Felix • FRG
GLUCKSZYLINDER, DER see **GOLDBLONDES MADCHEN, ICH SCHENK' DIR MEIN HERZ -ICH BIN JA SO VERLIEBT..** • 1932
GLUE-MY AFFAIR, A • 1913 • Borup C. • UKN
GLUED • 1912 • *Lubin* • USA
GLUHENDE BERGE-FLAMMENDES HERZ • 1930 • Seitz Franz • FRG
GLUHENDE GASSE, DIE • 1927 • Sugar Paul • FRG
GLUHENDE KAMMER, DIE • 1919 • Ziener Bruno • FRG
GLUMA NOVA CU FIER VECHI • 1965 • Calinescu Bob • ANS • RMN • NEW JOKE WITH SCRAP IRON, A ○ OLD IRON, NEW HUMOUR ○ NEW JOKE WITH OLD IRON, A
GLUMOV'S DIARY see **KINODNEVIK GLUMOVA** • 1923
GLURUMOV'S FILM DIARY see **KINODNEVIK GLUMOVA** • 1923
GLUT see **GLUT IM HERZEN** • 1983
GLUT IM HERZEN • 1983 • Koerfer Thomas • SWT • GLOWING HEARTS ○ GLUT
GLUTTON, THE • 1920 • *Franey William* • SHT • USA
GLUTTON'S NIGHTMARE, THE • 1901 • Stow Percy • UKN
GLUVI BARUT • 1989 • Cengic Bato • YGS • WET POWDER
GNAT, THE • 1926 • Smith Percy • UKN
GNAW: FOOD OF THE GODS II see **FOOD OF THE GODS II** • 1988
GNEZDO NA VETRU • 1981 • Neuland Olev • USS • NEST IN THE WIND ○ NEST OF WIND
GNIAZDO • 1974 • Rybkowski Jan • PLN • NEST, THE
GNIEZNO PORTAL, THE • 1957 • Jaworski Tadeusz • DOC • PLN
GNOME-MOBILE, THE • 1967 • Stevenson Robert • USA
GNOMES • 1980 • ANM • USA
GNOMES see **GARTENZWERGE, DIE** • 1962
GNOMES IN SPRING see **WIOSENNE PRZYGODY KRASNALA** • 1959
GNOSIS • 1972 • *Crocus Prod.* • USA
GO AND GET IT • 1920 • Neilan Marshall, Symonds Henry R. • USA
GO AND GET IT see **BUTTSUKE HONBAN** • 1958
GO AS YOU PLEASE • 1920 • Roach Hal • SHT • USA
GO ASK ALICE • 1972 • Korty John • TVM • USA
GO AWAY STOWAWAY • 1967 • Lovy Alex • ANS • USA
GO-BETWEEN, A see **ZEGEN** • 1988
GO-BETWEEN, THE • 1916 • Garwood William • SHT • USA
GO-BETWEEN, THE • 1970 • Losey Joseph • UKN
GO CHASE YOURSELF • 1938 • Cline Eddie • USA
GO CHASE YOURSELF • 1948 • White Jules • SHT • USA
GO CHEZ LES OISEAUX • 1939 • Grimault Paul • ANS • FRN
GO DOWN DEATH • 1944 • Williams Spencer • USA
GO EAST, YOUNG WOMAN • Barton J. • ANM • UKN
GO FLY A KITE • 1957 • Jones Charles M. • ANS • USA
GO FOR A TAKE • 1972 • Booth Harry • UKN
GO FOR BROKE! • 1951 • Pirosh Robert • USA
GO FOR BROKE • 1972 • *Ireland John* • ITL
GO FOR BROKE see **TOKKAN** • 1974
GO FOR BROKE see **SAVE THE DOG!** • 1988
GO FOR GOLD • 1984 • Fleming Stuart F. • SAF
GO FOR IT • 1976 • Rapp Paul • DOC • USA
GO FOR IT • 1983 • Clucher E. B. • ITL, USA
GO FOR THE GOLD • 1984 • Cooper Jackie • USA
GO FORWARD, FORWARD AND STILL FORWARD see **ZENSHIN ZENSHIN MATA ZENSHIN** • 1967
GO GET 'EM GARRINGER • 1919 • Traxler Ernest • USA
GO GET 'EM HAINES • 1936 • Newfield Sam • USA
GO GET 'EM HUTCH • 1922 • Seitz George B. • SRL • USA
GO GET 'EM POTTS • 1919 • SER • USA
GO GET HIM • 1921 • *Fairbanks William* • USA
GO-GETTER, THE • 1923 • Griffith D. W. • USA
GO GETTER, THE • 1937 • Berkeley Busby • USA
GO-GETTER, THE • 1955 • Goodwins Leslie, Jason Leigh • USA
GO GO AMIGO • 1965 • McKimson Robert • ANS • USA
GO GO BIG BEAT (USA) see **MODS AND ROCKERS** • 1964
GO GO BIG BEAT (USA) see **SWINGING U.K.** • 1964
GO GO BIG BEAT (USA) see **U.K. SWINGS AGAIN** • 1964
GO-GO-GIRL VOM BLOW-UP, DAS • 1969 • FRG
GO GO GO • 1963 • Menken Marie • SHT • USA
GO, GO, GO WORLD! (USA) see **PELO NEL MONDO, IL** • 1964
GO GO MANIA (USA) see **POP GEAR** • 1965
GO-GO SET see **GET YOURSELF A COLLEGE GIRL** • 1964
GO GO WAKADAISHO • 1967 • Iwauchi Katsumi • JPN • SKIING ON THE SUMMIT
GO HOG WILD see **HOG WILD** • 1980
GO INTO YOUR DANCE • 1935 • Mayo Archie, Florey Robert (U/c) • USA • CASINO DE PAREE (UKN)
GO, JOHNNY, GO • 1958 • Landres Paul • USA
GO KART GO! • 1964 • Darnley-Smith Jan • UKN
GO KIDS, THE see **FROG DREAMING** • 1985
GO, MAN, GO! • 1954 • Howe James Wong • USA
GO MASTERS, THE see **MIKAN NO TAIKYOKU** • 1982
GO NAKED IN THE WORLD • 1960' • MacDougall Ranald • USA
GO ON LIVING see **CONTINUAR A VIVER** • 1977
GO OUT INTO THE WORLD • 1950 • Hoving Hattum • NTH
GO SEE MOTHER.. FATHER IS WORKING see **VA VOIR MAMAN.. PAPA TRAVAILLE** • 1978
GO STRAIGHT • 1921 • Worthington William • USA
GO STRAIGHT • 1925 • O'Connor Frank • USA
GO TELL IT ON THE MOUNTAIN • 1985 • Lathan Stan • TVM • USA
GO TELL THE SPARTANS • 1978 • Post Ted • USA
GO TO BLAZES • 1930 • Edwards Harry J. • SHT • USA
GO TO BLAZES! • 1942 • Forde Walter • UKN
GO TO BLAZES • 1962 • Truman Michael • UKN
GO TO NOWHERE • 1966 • Ivanov-Vano Ivan • ANM • USS
GO TO SCHOOL, SON see **MATHE PEDI MOU GRAMATA** • 1981
GO TO THE LIGHT see **GO TOWARD THE LIGHT** • 1989
GO TO THE MOUNTAINS see **TIRARSE AL MONTE** • 1972
GO TO WORK, VAGABOND! see **VAI TRABALHAR VAGABUNDO!** • 1973
GO TOWARD THE LIGHT • 1989 • Robe Mike • USA • GO TO THE LIGHT
GO WEST • 1923 • Roach Hal • SHT • USA
GO WEST • 1925 • Keaton Buster • USA
GO WEST • 1940 • Buzzell Edward • USA • MARX BROTHERS GO WEST, THE (UKN)
GO WEST, BIG BOY • 1931 • *Terry Paul/ Moser Frank (P)* • ANS • USA
GO WEST, YOUNG GIRL • 1978 • Levi Alan J. • TVM • USA
GO WEST, YOUNG LADY • 1941 • Strayer Frank • USA
GO WEST, YOUNG MAN • 1919 • Beaumont Harry • USA
GO WEST, YOUNG MAN • 1936 • Hathaway Henry • USA
GO WEST, YOUNG WOMAN • 1920 • Christie Al, Sidney Scott • SHT • USA
GO WEST, YOUNG WOMAN, GO WEST • 1910 • *Selig* • USA
GO WITH MATT MONRO • 1967 • Tyrer Bertram • SHT • UKN
GOA DALLI C.I.D.999 • 1968 • Dorairaj B. • IND • C.I.D.999 FROM GOA
GOAD OF JEALOUSY, THE • 1916 • Hansel Howell?, McGill Lawrence? • SHT • USA
GOADED BY JEALOUSY • 1915 • Daly William Robert • USA
GOADED TO ANARCHY • 1905 • Paul Robert William • UKN
GOAL • 1936 • Barth-Moglia Luis • ARG
GOAL! see **GOAL! WORLD CUP 1966** • 1966
GOAL FOR THE YOUNG see **DEKKAI TAIYO** • 1967
GOAL IN THE CLOUDS (USA) see **ZIEL IN DEN WOLKEN** • 1938
GOAL KEEPER • 1937 • Timoshenko S. • USS
GOAL RUSH • 1946 • Sparber I. • ANS • USA
GOAL RUSH, THE • 1932 • *Iwerks Ub (P)* • ANS • USA
GOAL! WORLD CUP 1966 • 1966 • Dino Abidine, Devenish Ross • UKN, LCH • GOAL!
GOALIE'S ANXIETY AT THE PENALTY KICK, THE (USA) see **ANGST DES TORMANNS BIEN ELFMETER** • 1971
GOALKEEPER LIVES IN OUR STREET, THE see **BRANKAR BYDLI V NASI ULICI** • 1957
GOALKEEPER'S FEAR OF THE PENALTY, THE (UKN) see **ANGST DES TORMANNS BIEN ELFMETER** • 1971
GOAT • 1897 • *Paul R. W.* • UKN
GOAT, THE • 1914 • *Ab* • USA
GOAT, THE • 1915 • *Empire* • USA
GOAT, THE • 1917 • Gillstrom Arvid E. • SHT • USA
GOAT, THE • 1918 • Crisp Donald • USA
GOAT, THE • 1921 • Keaton Buster, St. Clair Malcolm • SHT • USA
GOAT, THE see **CHEVRE, LA** • 1981
GOAT AND THE HEDGEHOG, THE • Zykmund V., Vesela A. • ANM • CZC
GOAT AND THE LION, THE • 1957 • Lehky Vladimir • ANS • CZC
GOAT GETTER • 1925 • Rogell Albert S. • USA
GOAT GIRL OF BEAR CANYON, THE • 1912 • *Frontier* • USA
GOAT HORN, THE (USA) see **KOZUU POS** • 1972
GOBANCHO YUGIRIRO • 1963 • Tasaka Tomotaka • JPN • HOUSE OF SHAME, A
GOBBO, IL • 1960 • Lizzani Carlo • ITL, FRN • HUNCHBACK OF ROME, THE (USA) ○ BOSSU DE ROME, LE (FRN)
GOBEN NO TSUBAKI • 1965 • Nomura Yoshitaro • JPN • SCARLET CAMELIA
GOBI OUTPOST see **DESTINATION GOBI** • 1953
GOBITAL • 1975 • Brodeur Rene • CND
GOBLET OF LIFE AND DEATH, THE • 1912 • *Pathe* • USS
GOBLINS • 1987 • Short Robert • USA
GOBOTS: BATTLE OF THE ROCK LORDS • 1986 • Patterson Ray, Lusk Don, Zaslove Alan • ANM • USA
GOBOTS: THE ORIGINAL FULL LENGTH STORY • 1986 • ANM • USA
GOBS AND GALS • 1952 • Springsteen R. G. • USA • CRUISING CASANOVAS (UKN)
GOBS OF FUN • 1950 • Sparber I. • ANS • USA
GOBSECK • 1923 • Rist Preben • FRG
GOD AND HIS SERVANTS, A see **HERREN OZ HANS TJENERE** • 1959
GOD AND I see **DIOS Y YO** • 1973
GOD AND THE BABY • 1916 • Cochrane George • SHT • USA
GOD AND THE GYPSYMAN see **GUD FADER OCH TATTAREN** • 1954
GOD AND THE MAN • 1918 • Collins Edwin J. • UKN
GOD BALA see **DEV BALA** • 1938
GOD BLESS OUR RED, WHITE AND BLUE • 1918 • Wilson Rex • UKN
GOD BLESS THE BOMB see **WILD IN THE SKY** • 1972
GOD BLESS THE CHILD • 1988 • Elikann Larry • TVM • USA
GOD BLESS THE CHILDREN see **PSYCHIATRIST: GOD BLESS THE CHILDREN, THE** • 1970
GOD CALLS DORIAN see **DIO CHIAMATO DORIAN, IL** • 1970
GOD CREATED THEM, I KILL THEM see **DIO LI CREA, IO LI AMMAZZO** • 1968
GOD CREATES THEM AND THEN PUTS THEM TOGETHER see **DIO LI FA POI LI ACCOPPIA** • 1983
GOD DEVYATNADSATII • 1938 • Trauberg Ilya • USS • YEAR 1919, THE
GOD DIED IN VAIN • 1969 • Dukic Radivoje-Lola • YGS
GOD DISPOSES • 1912 • *Greenleaf Maurice* • USA
GOD, FATHERLAND AND AUTHORITY see **DEUS, PATRIA, AUTORIDADE** • 1976
GOD FORGIVES -I DON'T (USA) see **DIO PERDONA.. IO NO!** • 1967
GOD GAME, THE see **MAGUS, THE** • 1968
GOD GAVE HIM A DOG (UKN) see **BISCUIT EATER, THE** • 1940
GOD GAVE ME TWENTY CENTS • 1926 • Brenon Herbert • USA • FATE GAVE ME TWENTY CENTS
GOD, HOME, AUTHORITY see **DEUS, PATRIA, AUTORIDADE** • 1976
GOD IN THE GARDEN, THE • 1921 • Collins Edwin J. • UKN
GOD IS LOVE • 1913 • *Pathe* • USA
GOD IS LOVE • 1915 • *Mackley Arthur* • USA
GOD IS MY CO-PILOT • 1945 • Florey Robert • USA
GOD IS MY PARTNER • 1957 • Claxton William F. • USA
GOD IS NOT A FISH INSPECTOR • 1980 • Kroeker Allan • CND
GOD IS ON OUR SIDE see **ALLAH MANA** • 1954
GOD KARTICKEYA see **THIRUVARUTCHELVAR** • 1967
GOD KING, THE (UKN) see **SRI LANKA** • 1975
GOD KNOWS WHY BUT IT WORKS • 1976 • Noyce Phil • SHT • ASL • DR. K.
GOD LORD KRISHNA see **BHAGWAN SHRI KRISHNA** • 1950
GOD, MAN AND DEVIL • 1949 • Zeiden Joseph • USA
GOD NEEDS MAN (USA) see **DIEU A BESOIN DES HOMMES** • 1950
GOD OF CHANCE • 1913 • *Domino* • USA
GOD OF FORTUNE see **BHAGYADEVATHE** • 1968
GOD OF GAMBLERS • 1989 • Wong Ching • HKG
GOD OF GIRZAH, THE • 1913 • *Bison* • USA
GOD OF GOLD, THE • 1912 • Campbell Colin • USA
GOD OF LITTLE CHILDREN • 1917 • Ridgely Richard • USA
GOD OF LUCK, THE see **DIEU DU HASARD, LE** • 1919
GOD OF MANKIND • 1928 • Jones Grover • USA
GOD OF SIN see **GUNAHON KA DEVTA** • 1967
GOD OF TOMORROW, THE • 1913 • *Majestic* • USA
GOD OF WAR ADMIRAL YAMAMOTO AND THE COMBINED FLEET see **GUNSHIN YAMAMOTO GENSUI TO RENGO KANTAI**
GOD PULLS JOHANSSON'S HAIR see **VAR HERRE LUGGAR JOHANSSON** • 1944

GOD RIDES A HARLEY • 1988 • Stavrides Stavros C. • DOC • CND
GOD SELECTED HIS TRAVELERS see **HORA INCOGNITA, LA** • 1964
GOD SHIVA • 1955 • Haanstra Bert • DCS • NTH
GOD SHIVA DANCES see **JHANAK, JHANAK, PAYAL BAJE** • 1955
GOD SNAKE, THE see **DIOS SERPIENTE, EL** • 1970
GOD SPEAKS TODAY see **SUPREME SECRET, THE** • 1958
GOD TOLD ME TO see **DEMON** • 1976
GOD WHO TALKS, THE see **PESUM DEIVAM** • 1967
GOD WITHIN, THE • 1912 • Griffith D. W. • USA
GODA VANNER OCH TROGNA GRANNAR • 1938 • Hildebrand Weyler • SWD • GOOD FRIENDS AND FAITHFUL NEIGHBOURS
GODA VANNER OCH TROGNA GRANNAR • 1960 • Anderberg Torgny • SWD • GOOD FRIENDS AND FAITHFUL NEIGHBOURS
GODAN • 1962 • *Shankar Ravi (M)* • IND
GODARD'S PASSION (USA) see **PASSION** • 1982
GODCHILD, THE • 1974 • Badham John • TVM • USA
GODCHILDREN, THE • 1972 • Pearson Robert E. • USA
GODDAG BORN! • 1953 • Roos Jorgen • DOC • DNM
GODDAG DYR! • 1947 • Roos Jorgen, Mertz Albert • DOC • DNM
GODDELOSE STAD • 1958 • SAF
GODDESS, THE • 1915 • Ince Ralph • SRL • USA
GODDESS, THE • 1956 • Davies Valentine • USA
GODDESS, THE • 1958 • Cromwell John • USA
GODDESS, THE see **DEVI** • 1961
GODDESS BHAVANI see **BHAVANI** • 1967
GODDESS DURGA see **CHAMUNDESWARI** • 1937
GODDESS KALI see **MATA MAHAKALI** • 1968
GODDESS OF CHANCE, THE • 1917 • King Burton L. • SHT • USA
GODDESS OF LOST LAKE, THE • 1918 • Worsley Wallace • USA
GODDESS OF LOVE, THE • 1988 • Drake James R. • USA
GODDESS OF LOVE, THE see **VENERE DI CHERONEA, LA** • 1957
GODDESS OF LUCK (USA) see **NASIBANI DEVI** • 1927
GODDESS OF SAGEBRUSH GULCH, THE • 1912 • Griffith D. W. • USA
GODDESS OF SPRING, THE • 1934 • Jackson Wilfred • ANS • USA
GODDESS OF THE HOME see **GRIHA LAKSHMI** • 1959
GODDESS OF THE SEA • 1909 • *Le Lion* • FRN
GODDESS OF VENGEANCE see **KALI YUG, LA DEA DELLA VENDETTA** • 1963
GODDESS OF WAR, THE (USA) see **RANCHANDI** • 1929
GODE OG DET ONDE, DET • 1974 • Leth Jorgen • DNM • GOOD AND EVIL ○ GOOD AND THE BAD, THE
GODEFINGER • Logan Bob • FRN
GODELUREAUX, LES • 1960 • Chabrol Claude • FRN, ITL
GODEN K NESTROYEVOY • 1968 • Rogovoi Vladimir • USS • FIT FOR NON-COMBATANT DUTY
GODEN MOETEN HUN GETAL HEBBEN • 1971 • Jacobs Jos • BLG
GODFATHER see **DHARMATMA** • 1974
GODFATHER, THE • 1911 • *Reliance* • USA
GODFATHER, THE • 1972 • Coppola Francis Ford • USA
GODFATHER DEATH see **GEVATTER TOD** • 1921
GODFATHER MENDOZA see **COMPADRE MENDOZA, EL** • 1933
GODFATHER OF HARLEM (UKN) see **BLACK CAESAR** • 1973
GODFATHER OF HONG KONG see **TA E KOU** • 1972
GODFATHER, PART II, THE • 1974 • Coppola Francis Ford • USA
GODFATHER PART III, THE • 1990 • Coppola Francis Ford • USA
GODFATHER THE MASTER see **NINJA OPERATION 5: GODFATHER THE MASTER** • 1988
GODFORSAKEN HOLE see **SWIAT ZABITY DESKAMI** • 1962
GODHULI • 1978 • Karnad Girish, Karanth B. V. • IND • BOY WHO BECOMES AN ORPHAN, THE ○ TWILIGHT OF THE GODS
GODINI ZA LYUBOV • 1957 • Yankov Yanko • BUL • TOO LATE FOR LOVE?
GODISNJA DOBA • 1980 • Krelja Petar • YGS • FOUR SEASONS, THE ○ SEASONS, THE
GODIVA GIRLS see **GIRLS OF GODIVA HIGH, THE** • 1981
GODLESS GIRL, THE • 1929 • De Mille Cecil B. • USA
GODLESS MEN • 1921 • Barker Reginald • USA • BLACK PAWL
GODLY RELATIONS see **DEVIGA URAVU** • 1968
GODMOTHER, THE • 1912 • Ince Ralph • USA
GODMOTHERS, THE • Grefe William • USA
GODOVSHCHINA REVOLYUTSII • 1919 • Vertov Dziga • USS • ANNIVERSARY OF THE REVOLUTION
GODS AND THE DEAD, THE see **DEUSES E OS MORTOS, OS** • 1970
GOD'S BLOODY ACRE • 1975 • Kerwin Harry E. • USA
GODS CAN LAUGH, THE • 1948 • Williamson Cecil H. • UKN
GOD'S CHILD • 1921 • Cullison Webster • USA
GOD'S CLAY • 1919 • Rooke Arthur • UKN
GOD'S CLAY • 1928 • Cutts Graham • UKN
GOD'S COUNTRY • 1946 • Tansey Robert • USA
GOD'S COUNTRY • 1985 • Malle Louis • DOC • USA
GOD'S COUNTRY see **ALLAHA ADANAN TOPRAK** • 1967
GOD'S COUNTRY AND THE LAW • 1921 • Olcott Sidney • USA
GOD'S COUNTRY AND THE MAN • 1931 • McCarthy John P. • USA • ROSE OF THE RIO GRANDE
GOD'S COUNTRY AND THE MAN • 1937 • Bradbury Robert North • USA • AVENGING STRANGER, THE (UKN)
GOD'S COUNTRY AND THE WOMAN • 1916 • Sturgeon Rollin S. • USA
GOD'S COUNTRY AND THE WOMAN • 1937 • Keighley William • USA
GOD'S CRUCIBLE • 1917 • Reynolds Lynn • USA
GOD'S CRUCIBLE • 1920 • McRae Henry • CND, USA • FOREIGNER, THE
GOD'S EYE see **OJO DE DIOS, EL** • 1972
GOD'S GIFT see **WEND KUUNI** • 1983
GOD'S GIFT TO WOMEN • 1931 • Curtiz Michael • USA • TOO MANY WOMEN (UKN)
GOD'S GOOD MAN • 1919 • Elvey Maurice • UKN
GOD'S GREAT WILDERNESS • 1927 • Hartford David M. • USA
GOD'S GUN • 1976 • Parolini Gianfranco • ITL, ISR
GOD'S HALF ACRE • 1916 • Carewe Edwin • USA
GOD'S INN BY THE SEA • 1911 • Baker R. E. • USA
GOD'S ISLAND • 1980 • MacDonald Ramuna • CND
GOD'S LAW AND MAN'S • 1917 • Collins John H. • USA • WIFE BY PURCHASE, A
GOD'S LITTLE ACRE • 1958 • Mann Anthony • USA
GOD'S MAN • 1917 • Irving George • USA
GOD'S MANSION see **KHANEH-E-KHODA** • 1967
GODS MUST BE CRAZY, THE • 1981 • Uys Jamie • SAF
GODS MUST BE CRAZY II, THE • 1989 • Uys Jamie • SAF
GODS MUST WAIT, THE see **SANDCASTLES** • 1972
GODS OF FATE, THE • 1916 • Pratt Jack • USA
GODS OF THE PLAGUE see **GOTTER DER PEST** • 1969
GODS OF THE STREETS see **GATEGUTTER** • 1949
GOD'S OUTLAW • 1919 • Cabanne W. Christy • USA
GOD'S PAY DAY (?) see **WAGES OF SIN, THE** • 1922
GOD'S PRODIGAL • 1923 • Wynne Bert, Jose Edward • UKN
GOD'S RADIO PATROL see **FUNKSTREIFE GOTTES, DIE** • 1968
GODS REDEEM, THE • 1915 • Brooke Van Dyke • USA
GOD'S SERVANT see **SIERVO DE DIOS, EL** • 1968
GOD'S SPARROWS • 1970 • Carter Peter • CND
GOD'S STEPCHILDREN • 1938 • Micheaux Oscar • USA
GOD'S THUNDER (UKN) see **TONNERRE DE DIEU, LE** • 1965
GOD'S UNFORTUNATE • 1912 • Dwan Allan • USA
GOD'S WAR (UKN) see **KARIN INGMARSDOTTER** • 1920
GOD'S WAY • 1913 • Kirkland Hardee • USA
GOD'S WITNESS • 1915 • *La Badie Florence* • USA
GODSEND, THE • 1979 • Beaumont Gabrielle • UKN
GODSFORVALTEREN • 1914 • Davidsen Hjalmar • DNM
GODSJEREN • 1918 • Lauritzen Lau • DNM
GODSON, THE (USA) see **SAMOURAI, LE** • 1967
GODSPELL • 1973 • Greene David • USA
GODURIA, LA • 1976 • Loy Nanni • ITL
GODY MOLODYYE • 1959 • Mishurin Aleksey • USS • AGE OF YOUTH (USA) ○ TRAIN GOES TO KIEV, THE
GODZILLA 1985 • 1985 • Hashimoto Kohji, Kizer R. J. • JPN • GODZILLA: THE LEGEND IS REBORN ○ GOJIRO
GODZILLA FIGHTS THE GIANT MOTH see **MOSURA TAI GOJIRA** • 1964
GODZILLA, KING OF THE MONSTERS • 1956 • Morse Terry O., Honda Inoshiro • USA, JPN • GODZILLA (UKN) ○ GOJIRA (JPN)
GODZILLA NO GYAKUSHYU see **GOJIRA NO GYAKUSHYU** • 1955
GODZILLA NO MUSUKO see **GOJIRA NO MUSUKO** • 1967
GODZILLA RADON KINGGIDORAH see **KAIJU DAISENSO** • 1965
GODZILLA RAIDS AGAIN see **GOJIRA NO GYAKUSHYU** • 1955
GODZILLA TAI BIOLLANTE • 1989 • Omori Kazuki • JPN • GODZILLA VS. BIOLLANTE
GODZILLA TAI GAIGAN see **GOJIRA TAI GAIGAN** • 1972
GODZILLA TAI MOTHRA see **MOSURA TAI GOJIRA** • 1964
GODZILLA: THE LEGEND IS REBORN see **GODZILLA 1985** • 1985
GODZILLA (UKN) see **GODZILLA, KING OF THE MONSTERS** • 1956
GODZILLA VERSUS GIGAN see **GOJIRA TAI GAIGAN** • 1972
GODZILLA VERSUS HEDORA see **GOJIRA TAI HEDORA** • 1971
GODZILLA VERSUS MECHAGODZILLA see **GOJIRA TAI MEKAGOJIRA** • 1974
GODZILLA VERSUS MOTHRA see **MOSURA TAI GOJIRA** • 1964
GODZILLA VERSUS THE BIONIC MONSTER (UKN) see **GOJIRA TAI MEKAGOJIRA** • 1974
GODZILLA VERSUS THE COSMIC MONSTER (USA) see **GOJIRA TAI MEKAGOJIRA** • 1974
GODZILLA VERSUS THE GIANT MOTH see **MOSURA TAI GOJIRA** • 1964
GODZILLA VS. BIOLLANTE see **GODZILLA TAI BIOLLANTE** • 1989
GODZILLA VS. MEGALON see **GOJIRA TAI MEGALON** • 1973
GODZILLA VS. MONSTER ZERO see **SANDAI KAIJU CHIKYU SAIDAI NO KESSEN** • 1965
GODZILLA VS. THE SEA MONSTER (USA) see **NANKAI NO DAI KETTO** • 1966
GODZILLA VS. THE SEA MONSTER (USA) see **GOJIRA TAI MEGALON** • 1973
GODZILLA VS. THE SMOG MONSTER (USA) see **GOJIRA TAI HEDORA** • 1971
GODZILLA VS. THE THING (USA) see **MOSURA TAI GOJIRA** • 1964
GODZILLA, WAR OF THE MONSTERS see **GOJIRA TAI GAIGAN** • 1972
GODZILLA'S COUNTER ATTACK see **GOJIRA NO GYAKUSHYU** • 1955
GODZILLA'S REVENGE (USA) see **ORU KAIJU DAISHINGEKI** • 1969
GODZINA 11.15 -OPOWIESC O ZAMKU KROLEWSKIM W WARSZAWIE • 1971 • Perski Ludwik • DOC • PLN • AT 11.15 -THE STORY OF THE ROYAL CASTLE IN WARSAW
GODZINA BEZ SLONCA • 1954 • Komorowski Pawel • PLN • HOUR WITHOUT SUN, THE
GODZINA PASOMES ROZY see **GODZINA PASOWEJ ROZY** • 1963
GODZINA PASOWEJ ROZY • 1963 • Bielinska Halina • PLN, HNG • GODZINA PASOMES ROZY ○ HOUR OF THE ROSE, THE
GODZINA SZCZYTU • 1974 • Stawinski Jerzy Stefan • PLN • PEAK HOUR
GODZINA W • 1979 • Morgenstern Janusz • PLN
GODZINA ZA GODZINA • 1974 • Zaluski Roman • PLN • HOUR AFTER HOUR
GODZINY NADZIEI • 1956 • Rybkowski Jan • PLN • HOURS OF HOPE
GODZINY SZCZYTU • 1967 • Trzos-Rastawiecki Andrzej • DOC • PLN • RUSH HOURS
GOE TAM • 1968 • Choe Joemyong • SKR
GOED EN SNEL MACHINAAL MELKEN • 1966 • Geesink Joop • SHT • NTH
GOELETTES • 1968 • Gagne Jacques • DCS • CND
GOELETTES, LES • 1958-60 • Bonniere Rene • DCS • CND
GOEMONS • 1947 • Bellon Yannick • FRN
GOETHE -FILME DER UFA • 1932 • Wendhausen Fritz • FRG
GOETHE IN D ODER DIE BLUTNACHT AUF DEM SCHRECKENSTEIN ODER WIE ERWIN GESCHNONNECK EINE HAUPTROLLE .. • 1986 • Vosz Manfred • FRG
GOETHE LEBT..! • 1932 • Frowein Eberhard • FRG
GOETHE'S JUGENDGELIEBTE (USA) see **JUGENDGELIEBTE, DIE** • 1930
GOG • 1954 • Strock Herbert L. • USA
GOGGLE FISHING BEAR • 1949 • Lah Michael, Blair Preston • ANS • USA
GOGI RATIANI • 1928 • Mardzhanishvili Kote • USS
GOGLERBLOD see **TROLOS** • 1913
GOGLEREN see **ELSKOVS MAGT** • 1912
GOGOLA • Dave Balwant • IND
GOHA • 1958 • Baratier Jacques • FRN, TNS
GOHAR-E-SHABCHERAGH • 1967 • Koushan Esmaeil • IRN • BRIGHT GEM AT NIGHT
GOHIKI NO SHINSHI • 1966 • Gosha Hideo • JPN • CASH CALLS HELL
GOIN' ALL THE WAY • 1982 • Freedman Robert • USA
GOIN' COCONUTS • 1978 • Morris Howard • USA
GOIN' DOWN THE ROAD • 1970 • Shebib Donald • CND • ROUTE DE L'OUEST, LA ○ EN ROULANT MA BOULE ○ MARITIMERS ○ VOYAGE CHIMERIQUE, LE
GOIN' FISHIN' • 1940 • Cahn Edward L. • SHT • USA
GOIN' HOME • 1976 • Prentiss Chris • USA
GOIN' SOUTH • 1978 • Nicholson Jack • USA
GOIN' STRAIGHT • 1917 • Kelsey Fred A. • SHT • USA
GOIN' TO A GO-GO • 1967 • Constantino F. H. • PHL
GOIN' TO HEAVEN ON A MULE • 1934 • Freleng Friz • ANS • USA
GOIN' TO THE CHAPEL see **MONEY'S TIGHT** • 1988
GOIN' TO TOWN • 1935 • Hall Alexander • USA • HOW AM I DOING? ○ NOW I'M A LADY
GOIN' TO TOWN • 1944 • Goodwins Leslie • USA
GOING see **GAMAN** • 1977
GOING ALL OUT see **CORKY** • 1971
GOING ALL THE WAY • 1980 • Wilson Sandra • CND
GOING APE! • 1981 • Kronsberg Jeremy Joe • USA
GOING APE see **WHERE'S POPPA?** • 1970
GOING ASHORE see **STRANDHUGG** • 1949
GOING ASTRAY ON AN ORIENTATION COURSE see **BLOUDENI ORIENTACNIHO BEZCE** • 1985
GOING BACK see **DONUS** • 1973
GOING BANANAS • 1987 • Davidson Boaz • USA • MY AFRICAN ADVENTURE
GOING BERSERK • 1983 • Steinberg David • USA
GOING BYE BYE • 1934 • Rogers Charles • SHT • USA
GOING CRAZY • 1926 • Lamont Charles • SHT • USA
GOING CRAZY • 1981 • Madsen Olga • NTH
GOING CROOKED • 1926 • Melford George • USA
GOING DOWN • 1982 • Keenan Haydn • ASL
GOING DOWN FOR THE 3RD TIME • 1969 • Goetz Tommy • USA
GOING FOR BROKE • 1980 • McCowan George • CND • NEVER TRUST AN HONEST THIEF
GOING FOR FATHER • 1913 • *Eclair* • USA
GOING FOR THE GOLD: THE BILL JOHNSON STORY • 1985 • Taylor Don • TVM • USA • BILL JOHNSON STORY, THE
GOING GA-GA • 1928 • McCarey Leo, Horne James W. • SHT • USA
GOING GAY • 1933 • Gallone Carmine • UKN • KISS ME GOODBYE (USA)
GOING - GOING - GONE • 1915 • *Atla* • USA
GOING! GOING!! GONE!!! • 1915 • Collins Edwin J.? • UKN
GOING! GOING! GONE! • 1919 • Roach Hal • SHT • USA
GOING, GOING, GOSH! • 1952 • Jones Charles M. • ANS • USA
GOING GREAT • 1925 • Taurog Norman • SHT • USA
GOING HIGHBROW • 1935 • Florey Robert • USA
GOING HOLLYWOOD • 1933 • Walsh Raoul • USA
GOING HOME • 1971 • Leonard Herbert B. • USA
GOING HOME • 1972 • Mekas Adolfas • USA
GOING HOME • 1990 • Hare David • TVM • UKN
GOING HOME TO MOTHER • 1913 • *Lubin* • USA
GOING IN STYLE • 1979 • Brest Martin • USA
GOING MY WAY • 1944 • McCarey Leo • USA
GOING OF THE WHITE SWAN, THE • 1914 • Campbell Colin • USA
GOING ON 40 see **MIDDLE AGE CRAZY** • 1980
GOING PLACES • 1929 • Roberts Stephen • SHT • USA
GOING PLACES • 1939 • Enright Ray • USA
GOING PLACES • 1941 • *O'Brien Joseph/ Mead Thomas (P)* • SHS • USA
GOING PLACES • 1973 • Mapleston Charles • DCS • UKN
GOING PLACES see **VARIETY VIEWS NOS.94-102** • 1941
GOING PLACES see **VARIETY VIEWS NOS.103-115** • 1942
GOING PLACES (USA) see **VALSEUSES, LES** • 1974
GOING PLACES WITH GRAHAM MCNAMEE • 1938 • *O'Brien Joseph/ Mead Thomas (P)* • SHS • USA
GOING PLACES WITH GRAHAM MCNAMEE • 1939 • *O'Brien Joseph/ Mead Thomas (P)* • SHS • USA
GOING PLACES WITH GRAHAM MCNAMEE • 1940 • *O'Brien Joseph/ Mead Thomas (P)* • SHS • USA
GOING PLACES WITH LOWELL THOMAS • 1934 • Ford Charles E. • SHS • USA
GOING PLACES WITH LOWELL THOMAS • 1935 • Ford Charles E. • SHS • USA
GOING PLACES WITH LOWELL THOMAS • 1936 • Ford Charles E. • SHS • USA
GOING PLACES WITH LOWELL THOMAS • 1937 • Ford Charles E. • SHS • USA
GOING PLACES WITH LOWELL THOMAS • 1938 • Ford Charles E. • SHS • USA
GOING SANE • 1986 • Robertson Michael • ASL
GOING SOME • 1913 • *Penn M. O.* • USA
GOING SOME • 1914 • *White Pearl* • USA
GOING SOME • 1920 • Beaumont Harry • USA
GOING STEADY • 1958 • Sears Fred F. • USA
GOING STEADY see **YOTZ'IM KAVUA** • 1979
GOING STEADY: LEMON POPSICLE II (USA) see **YOTZ'IM KAVUA** • 1979
GOING STRAIGHT • 1916 • Franklin Sidney A., Franklin Chester M. • USA

GOING STRAIGHT • 1933 • Rawlins John* • UKN
GOING THE DISTANCE • 1979 • Cowan Paul • DOC • CND
GOING THE LIMIT • 1925 • Worne Duke • USA
GOING THE LIMIT • 1926 • Withey Chet • USA
GOING THE SAME WAY see **AYNI YOLUN YOLCUSU** • 1973
GOING THROUGH THE RYE • 1920 • *Vernon Bobby* • SHT • USA
GOING TO BED UNDER DIFFICULTIES (USA) see **DESHABILLAGE IMPOSSIBLE, LE** • 1900
GOING TO BLAZES • 1933 • Lantz Walter, Nolan William • ANS • USA
GOING TO CONGRESS • 1924 • Wagner Robert • SHT • USA
GOING TO MEET PAPA • 1913 • *Vitagraph* • USA
GOING TO PRESS • 1942 • Cahn Edward L. • SHT • USA
GOING TO THE DOGS • 1915 • *Powers* • USA
GOING TO THE DOGS • 1916 • Kernan Henry • SHT • USA
GOING TO THE "MAXIM" see **NU GAR JAG TILL MAXIM** • 1910
GOING TO TOWN (UKN) see **MA AND PA KETTLE GO TO TOWN** • 1950
GOING UNDERCOVER • 1988 • Clarke James Kenelm • USA • YELLOW PAGES
GOING UP • 1916 • Fahrney Milton • *Cub* • USA
GOING UP! • 1916 • Myll Louis • *Kleine* • SHT • USA
GOING UP • 1923 • Ingraham Lloyd • USA
GOING UP see **LIFT, DE** • 1983
GOING WEST TO MAKE GOOD • 1916 • Mix Tom • SHT • USA
GOING WILD • 1930 • Seiter William A. • USA
GOINGE, THE AKVAVIT CHAMPION see **GONGEHOVDINGEN** • 1961
GOINGEHOVDINGEN • 1953 • Ohberg Ake • SWD • CHIEF FROM GOINGE, THE
GOISSA • 1967 • Karayannis Kostas • GRC • CHARMER, THE
GOITIA, A GOD UNTO HIMSELF see **GOITIA, UN DIOS PARA SI MISMO** • 1989
GOITIA, UN DIOS PARA SI MISMO • 1989 • Lopez Diego • MXC • GOITIA, A GOD UNTO HIMSELF
GOJIRA (JPN) see **GODZILLA, KING OF THE MONSTERS** • 1956
GOJIRA NO GYAKUSHYU • 1955 • Oda Motoyoshi, Grimaldi Hugo • JPN • GIGANTIS, THE FIRE MONSTER (USA) ○ GODZILLA NO GYAKUSHYU ○ VOLCANO MONSTER, THE ○ RETURN OF GODZILLA, THE ○ GODZILLA RAIDS AGAIN ○ GODZILLA'S COUNTER ATTACK
GOJIRA NO MUSUKO • 1967 • Fukuda Jun • JPN • SON OF GODZILLA ○ GODZILLA NO MUSUKO
GOJIRA TAI GAIGAN • 1972 • Fukuda Jun • JPN • GODZILLA, WAR OF THE MONSTERS ○ WAR OF THE MONSTERS ○ CHIKIYU KOGERI MEIREI ○ GODZILLA TAI GAIGAN ○ GODZILLA VERSUS GIGAN
GOJIRA TAI HEDORA • 1971 • Banno Yoshimitsu • JPN • GODZILLA VS. THE SMOG MONSTER (USA) ○ GODZILLA VERSUS HEDORA
GOJIRA TAI MEGALON • 1973 • Fukuda Jun • JPN • GODZILLA VS. THE SEA MONSTER (USA) ○ GODZILLA VS. MEGALON
GOJIRA TAI MEKAGOJIRA • 1974 • Fukuda Jun • JPN • GODZILLA VERSUS THE COSMIC MONSTER (USA) ○ GODZILLA VERSUS THE BIONIC MONSTER (UKN) ○ GODZILLA VERSUS MECHAGODZILLA
GOJIRA TAI MOSURA see **MOSURA TAI GOJIRA** • 1964
GOJIRO see **GODZILLA 1985** • 1985
GOJU NO TU • 1944 • Gosho Heinosuke • JPN • FIVE-STORIED PAGODA, THE ○ PAGODA, THE
GOJUMAN-NIN NO ISAN • 1963 • Mifune Toshiro • JPN • LEGACY OF THE FIVE HUNDRED THOUSAND, THE ○ 500, 000 (USA) ○ HERITAGE OF FIVE HUNDRED THOUSAND PEOPLE, THE
GOKCE CICEK • 1973 • Akat Lutfu • TRK
GOKE, BODY SNATCHER FROM HELL see **KYUKETSUKI GOKEMIDORO** • 1968
GOKE THE VAMPIRE see **KYUKETSUKI GOKEMIDORO** • 1968
GOKUAKU BOZU • 1968 • Saeki Kiyoshi • JPN • EVIL PRIEST, THE
GOKUAKU BOZU HITOKIRI KAZOE UTA • 1968 • Harada Takashi • JPN • BALLAD OF MURDER
GOKUCHO NO KAOYAKU • 1968 • Furuhata Yasuo • JPN • BOSS IN JAIL
GOKUDO • 1968 • Yamashita Kosaku • JPN • FAST LIVER, THE
GOKUDO SHAIN YUKYO DEN • 1968 • Hasebe Toshiaki • JPN • ON GUARD FOR NONSENSE
GOKUHI ONNA GOMON • 1968 • Komori Haku • JPN • TOP SECRET OF TORTURING WOMEN
GOKUL • 1947 • Painter Vasant • IND • SHEPHERD
GOKUL CHA RAJA • 1950 • Gajbar Bal • IND • SHEPHERD KING, THE ○ KRISHNA
GOKUMON-TO • 1977 • Ichikawa Kon • JPN • ISLAND OF HORRORS (UKN) ○ DEVIL'S ISLAND, THE (USA)
GOKURAKU HANAYOMEJUKU • 1936 • Ogata Juzaburo • JPN • PARADISE OF NINETEEN BRIDES ○ PARADISE BRIDE'S SCHOOL, THE
GOL • 1982 • Kavur Omer • TRK • LAKE, THE
GOLA DEL LUPO, LA • 1923 • Lolli Alberto Carlo • ITL
GOLA PROFONDA NERA • 1977 • Zurli Guido • ITL • BLACK DEEP THROAT ○ QUEEN OF SEX
GOLA SUVEST • 1970 • Nikolov Milen • BUL • BARE CONSCIENCE
GOLAGHA • 1968 • Aghamaliyan Armaees • IRN
GOLAPI EKHON TRENE • 1977 • Hossain Amjad • BNG • GOLAPI'S NOW ON A TRAIN ○ ENDLESS TRAIL
GOLAPI'S NOW ON A TRAIN see **GOLAPI EKHON TRENE** • 1977
GOLD • Pakdivijit Chalong • THL
GOLD • 1914 • *Benham Harry* • USA
GOLD • 1917 • Jacoby Georg • FRG
GOLD • 1932 • Brower Otto • USA • VALLEY OF GOLD, THE (UKN)
GOLD • 1934 • Hartl Karl • FRG
GOLD • 1955 • Low Colin • CND
GOLD • Kaye Stanton • USA
GOLD • 1970 • Vyatich-Berezhnykh Damir • USS
GOLD • 1972 • Desloge Bill, Levis Bob • USA
GOLD • 1972 • Jay John, Kelly Ivan, O'Rahilly Ronan, Lambert Norman • USA
GOLD • 1974 • Hunt Peter • UKN
GOLD • 1982 • Potter Sally • UKN • GOLD DIGGERS, THE
GOLD see **KANE** • 1926
GOLD see **ZLOTO** • 1961
GOLD see **FORTY MILLION BUCKS** • 1978
GOLD see **KUNDAN** • 1987
GOLD AND DROSS • 1913 • *Nestor* • USA
GOLD AND DROSS • 1916 • *Puritan* • USA
GOLD AND GLITTER • 1912 • Griffith D. W. • USA
GOLD AND GRIT • 1925 • Thorpe Richard • USA
GOLD AND LEAD see **OR ET LE PLUMB, L'** • 1966
GOLD AND THE DROSS • 1916 • Gibbs B. C. • UKN
GOLD AND THE GILDED WAY • 1913 • Melies Gaston • USA
GOLD AND THE GIRL • 1925 • Mortimer Edmund • USA
GOLD AND THE GLORY, THE • 1989 • Auzins Igor • ASL • COOLANGATTA GOLD, THE
GOLD AND THE WOMAN • 1916 • Vincent James • USA
GOLD AND TWO MEN • 1913 • *Rex* • USA
GOLD AND WATER • 1913 • *Nestor* • USA
GOLD BAND, THE • 1916 • Bartlett Charles • SHT • USA
GOLD BAY ADVENTURE, THE see **DOBRODRUZSTVI NA ZLATE ZATOCE** • 1955
GOLD BIKINI • 1967 • De Leon Gerardo • PHL
GOLD, BLOOD, AND SUN see **ORO, SANGRE Y SOL** • 1925
GOLD BRAID see **FLYING FLEET, THE** • 1928
GOLD BRICK, THE • 1912 • *Beggs Lee* • USA
GOLD BRICK, THE • 1913 • France Charles H. • USA
GOLD-BRICKING CUPID • 1915 • Seiter William A. • USA
GOLD CHEVRONS • 1927 • *Big Three Prod.* • DOC • USA
GOLD CREEK MINING • 1913 • *Mace Fred* • USA
GOLD CURE, THE • 1919 • Collins John H. • USA • OH ANNICE
GOLD CURE, THE • 1925 • Kellino W. P. • UKN
GOLD, DESILVER ET CIE • 1916 • Burguet Charles • FRN
GOLD DIGGER OF WEEPAH, THE • 1927 • *Sennett Mack (P)* • SHT • USA
GOLD-DIGGERS see **GULDGRAVARNA** • 1959
GOLD DIGGERS, THE • 1923 • Beaumont Harry • USA
GOLD DIGGERS, THE see **GOLD** • 1982
GOLD DIGGER'S BALLAD, THE • 1959 • Burstall Tim • SHT • ASL
GOLD DIGGERS IN LAS VEGAS see **PAINTING THE CLOUDS WITH SUNSHINE** • 1951
GOLD DIGGERS OF BROADWAY • 1929 • Del Ruth Roy • USA
GOLD DIGGIN' WOODPECKER • 1972 • Smith Paul J. • ANS • USA
GOLD DREDGERS, THE see **HELL DIGGERS, THE** • 1921
GOLD DUST • 1916 • *Cossar John* • SHT • USA
GOLD DUST AND THE SQUAW, THE • 1915 • Mix Tom • USA
GOLD DUST BANDIT, THE • 1964 • Bartsch Art • ANS • USA
GOLD DUST GERTIE • 1931 • Bacon Lloyd • USA • WHY CHANGE YOUR HUSBAND? (UKN)
GOLD DUST OSWALD • 1935 • Lantz Walter, Nolan William • ANS • USA
GOLD EXPRESS, THE • 1955 • Fergusson Guy • UKN
GOLD FEVER • 1952 • Goodwins Leslie • USA
GOLD FEVER see **DUHUL AURULUI** • 1974
GOLD FISH, A see **RYBAR A ZLATA RYBKA** • 1951
GOLD FLOCKEN • 1975 • Schroeter Werner • FRG • FLOCONS D'OR
GOLD FOR THE CESARS see **ORO PER I CESARI** • 1963
GOLD FROM THE GUTTER see **ALT PAA ET KORT** • 1912
GOLD FROM THE SEA see **OR DES MERS, L'** • 1932
GOLD FROM WEEPAH • 1927 • Bertram William • USA
GOLD GETTERS, THE • 1935 • *Mintz Charles (P)* • ANS • USA
GOLD GHOST, THE • 1934 • Lamont Charles • SHT • USA
GOLD GRABBERS • 1922 • Ford Francis • USA
GOLD GUITAR, THE • 1966 • Todd J. Hunter • USA
GOLD HEELS • 1924 • Van Dyke W. S. • USA
GOLD HUNTERS, THE • 1925 • Hurst Paul C. • USA
GOLD HUNTERS, THE see **ALTIN AVCILARI** • 1968
GOLD IM DSCHAGGAGEBIET, DAS see **RECHT AUF SUNDE, DAS** • 1923
GOLD IN CLAY (USA) see **ORO ENTRE BARRO** • 1940
GOLD IN NEW FRISCO • 1939 • Verhoeven Paul • FRG
GOLD IN THE AUTO, THE • 1912 • *Republic* • USA
GOLD IN THE CROCK, THE • 1915 • *Jones Edgar* • USA
GOLD IS NOT ALL • 1910 • Griffith D. W. • USA
GOLD IS NOT ALL • 1913 • Lucas Wilfred • USA
GOLD IS SAD see **ORO ES TRISTE, EL** • 1973
GOLD IS WHERE YOU FIND IT • 1938 • Curtiz Michael • USA
GOLD IS WHERE YOU FIND IT • 1968 • Searle Francis • UKN
GOLD IS WHERE YOU FIND IT • 1970 • Bonniere Rene • CND
GOLD IS WHERE YOU LOSE IT • 1944 • White Jules • SHT • USA
GOLD LURE, THE see **LONE STAR RUSH, THE** • 1915
GOLD LUST, THE • 1911 • Dwan Allan • USA
GOLD LUST, THE • 1917 • *Big U* • SHT • USA
GOLD MADNESS • 1923 • Thornby Robert T. • USA • MAN FROM TEN STRIKE, THE
GOLD MEDALLION, THE • 1983 • *Porter Eric* • ANM • ASL
GOLD MESH BAG, THE • 1913 • *Grandin Ethel* • USA
GOLD MINE IN THE SKY • 1938 • Kane Joseph • USA
GOLD NECKLACE, A • 1910 • Griffith D. W. • USA
GOLD OF LONDON, THE see **ORO DI LONDRA, L'** • 1967
GOLD OF NAPLES see **ORO DI NAPOLI, L'** • 1954
GOLD OF THE AMAZON WOMEN • 1979 • Lester Mark L. • TVM • USA • QUEST FOR THE SEVEN CITIES
GOLD OF THE SEVEN SAINTS • 1961 • Douglas Gordon • USA
GOLD ON BLUE • 1978 • Holmes Cecil • SHT • ASL
GOLD RACKET, THE • 1937 • Gasnier Louis J. • USA
GOLD RAIDERS • 1951 • Bernds Edward • USA • THREE STOOGES GO WEST, THE (UKN)
GOLD RAIDERS • 1982 • Chalong D. P. • THL
GOLD RESERVE, THE • 1925 • Gardin Vladimir • USS
GOLD-RIMMED GLASSES, THE see **OCCHIALI D'ORO, GLI** • 1988
GOLD RING see **ZLOTE KOLO** • 1971
GOLD ROBBERS see **ESTOUFFADE A LA CARAIBE** • 1966
GOLD ROSE, THE see **ROSE D'OR, LA** • 1910
GOLD RUSH, THE • 1925 • Chaplin Charles • USA
GOLD RUSH DAZE • 1939 • Hardaway Ben, Dalton Cal • ANS • USA
GOLD RUSH MAISIE • 1940 • Marin Edwin L. • USA
GOLD SEEKERS, THE • 1910 • Griffith D. W. • USA
GOLD SHIP, THE • 1916 • Beal Frank • SHT • USA
GOLD, SILVER, BAD LUCK see **ORO, PLATA, MATA** • 1982
GOLD SPIDER, THE • 1910 • *Pathe* • FRN
GOLD SPIDER, THE see **GULDSPINDELN** • 1916
GOLD SQUAD • 1971 • SAF
GOLD STRIKE • 1950 • Cowan Will • SHT • USA
GOLD THAT GLITTERED, THE • 1917 • Mills Thomas R. • SHT • USA
GOLD THIEF, THE • 1914 • O'Sullivan Tony • USA
GOLD VON SAM COOPER, DAS • 1968 • Capitani Giorgio • FRG, ITL • OGNUNO PER SE (ITL) ○ RUTHLESS FOUR, THE (USA) ○ EACH MAN FOR HIMSELF ○ EVERYONE FOR HIMSELF ○ SAM COOPER'S GOLD ○ EACH ONE FOR HIMSELF
GOLD WING see **GOLDWING** • 1980
GOLDBERGS, THE see **MOLLY** • 1950
GOLDBLONDES MADCHEN, ICH SCHENK' DIR MEIN HERZ -ICH BIN JA SO VERLIEBT.. • 1932 • Bernauer Rudolf • FRG • GLUCKSZYLINDER, DER
GOLDDIGGERS IN PARIS • 1938 • Enright Ray • USA • GAY IMPOSTORS, THE (UKN)
GOLDDIGGERS OF '49 • 1936 • Avery Tex • ANS • USA
GOLDDIGGERS OF 1933 • 1933 • LeRoy Mervyn • USA
GOLDDIGGERS OF 1935 • 1935 • Berkeley Busby • USA
GOLDDIGGERS OF 1937 • 1936 • Bacon Lloyd • USA
GOLDELSE • 1918 • Mendel Georg Victor • FRG
GOLDEN AGE, THE see **SIECLE D'OR: L'ART DES PRIMITIFS FLAMANDS, UN** • 1953
GOLDEN AGE, THE (USA) see **AGE D'OR, L'** • 1930
GOLDEN AGE OF COMEDY, THE • 1958 • Youngson Robert • CMP • USA
GOLDEN ANTELOPE, THE see **ZOLOTAIA ANTILOPA** • 1954
GOLDEN APPLES see **JABLUNKA SE ZLATYMI JABLKY** • 1952
GOLDEN APPLES OF THE SUN • 1972 • McLean Barry Angus • CND • EVER AFTER ALL
GOLDEN ARMS see **BAZU TALAEI** • 1967
GOLDEN ARROW see **THREE MEN AND A GIRL** • 1949
GOLDEN ARROW, THE • 1936 • Green Alfred E. • USA
GOLDEN ARROW, THE (USA) see **FRECCIA D'ORO, LA** • 1962
GOLDEN ASS -THE TRIAL OF LUCIUS APULEIUS FOR WITCHCRAFT, THE see **ASINO D'ORO: PROCESSO PER FATTI STRANI CONTRO LUCIUS APULEIO CITTADINO ROMANO, L'** • 1970
GOLDEN AXE, THE • 1952 • Wilder William • SHT • USA
GOLDEN BALLOT, THE • 1920 • Miller Frank • UKN
GOLDEN BANGLES see **THANGA VALAYAL** • 1968
GOLDEN BAT see **OGON BATTO** • 1966
GOLDEN BED, THE • 1925 • De Mille Cecil B. • USA
GOLDEN BEETLE, THE • 1907 • *Pathe Freres* • FRN
GOLDEN BEETLE, THE (USA) see **SCARABEE D'OR, LE** • 1911
GOLDEN BIRD, THE see **LITTLE MISS HOOVER** • 1918
GOLDEN BLADE, THE • 1953 • Juran Nathan • USA
GOLDEN BOOT, THE • 1916 • Bowman William J. • SHT • USA
GOLDEN BOX, THE • 1970 • Davis Don • USA
GOLDEN BOY • 1939 • Mamoulian Rouben • USA
GOLDEN BOY IN BEIRUT see **ALTIN COCUK BEYRUTTA** • 1967
GOLDEN BRACKEN see **ZLATE KAPRADI** • 1963
GOLDEN BRAID • 1989 • Cox Paul • ASL
GOLDEN BREED, THE • 1968 • Davis Dale • DOC • USA
GOLDEN BUDDHA, THE • 1967 • *Chung Paul Chang* • HKG
GOLDEN BULLET, THE • 1917 • Kelsey Fred A. • SHT • USA
GOLDEN BUTTERFLY, THE see **GOLDENE SCHMETTERLING, DER** • 1926
GOLDEN CAGE, THE • 1933 • Campbell Ivar • UKN
GOLDEN CAGE, THE • 1975 • Kuyululu Ayten • ASL
GOLDEN CAGE, THE see **ARANYSARKANY** • 1966
GOLDEN CALF, THE • 1930 • Webb Millard • USA
GOLDEN CALF, THE • 1961 • Arvele Ritva • FNL
GOLDEN CALF, THE see **ZOLOTOY TELYONOK** • 1968
GOLDEN CARRIAGE, THE see **CARROSSE D'OR, LE** • 1952
GOLDEN CENTURY see **SIECLE D'OR: L'ART DES PRIMITIFS FLAMANDS, UN** • 1953
GOLDEN CHANCE, THE • 1913 • Nash Percy • UKN
GOLDEN CHANCE, THE • 1915 • Stather Frank • UKN
GOLDEN CHANCE, THE • 1916 • De Mille Cecil B. • USA
GOLDEN CHARIOTS • 1902 • Porter Edwin S. • USA
GOLDEN CHILD, THE • 1986 • Ritchie Michael • USA
GOLDEN CLAW, THE • 1915 • Barker Reginald • USA
GOLDEN CLAWS OF CAT GIRL • HKG
GOLDEN CLOUD, THE • 1913 • Kirkland Hardee • USA
GOLDEN COACH, THE see **CARROSSE D'OR, LE** • 1952
GOLDEN COCOON, THE • 1926 • Webb Millard • USA
GOLDEN COUPLE, THE see **OGON NO TOZOKO** • 1966
GOLDEN CROSS, THE • 1914 • *Fealy Maude* • USA
GOLDEN CURLS see **ZLATOVLASKA** • 1954
GOLDEN DAWN • 1930 • Enright Ray • USA
GOLDEN DAWN, THE • 1921 • Dewsbury Ralph • UKN
GOLDEN DAYS, THE see **ZLATE CASY** • 1978
GOLDEN DEER, THE • 1970 • ANS • JPN
GOLDEN DEMON, THE see **KONJIKI YASHA** • 1923
GOLDEN DEMON (USA) see **KONJIKI YASHA** • 1954
GOLDEN DISC, THE • 1958 • Sharp Don • UKN • INBETWEEN AGE, THE (USA)
GOLDEN DRAGON, SILVER SNAKE • Ho Godfrey • HKG
GOLDEN DREAMS • 1922 • Hampton Benjamin B. • USA
GOLDEN DREAMS see **ZLOTO** • 1961
GOLDEN DROSS • 1914 • *Reliance* • USA
GOLDEN DUSTMAN'S WALK, THE • 1905 • *Walturdaw* • UKN
GOLDEN EAGLE TRAIL, THE • 1917 • Horne James W. • SHT • USA
GOLDEN EARRINGS • 1947 • Leisen Mitchell • USA
GOLDEN EGGS, THE • 1941 • Jackson Wilfred • ANS • USA
GOLDEN EIGHTIES see **ANNEES 80, LES** • 1983
GOLDEN EYE, THE (UKN) see **MYSTERY OF THE GOLDEN EYE, THE** • 1948
GOLDEN EYES • 1968 • Sharma Kamal • IND
GOLDEN FERN, THE see **ZLATE KAPRADI** • 1963
GOLDEN FETTER, THE • 1917 • Le Saint Edward J. • USA
GOLDEN FISH, THE see **GOUDEN VIS, DE** • 1951
GOLDEN FISH, THE (USA) see **RYBAR A ZLATA RYBKA** • 1951

GOLDEN FISH, THE (USA) see **HISTOIRE D'UN POISSON ROUGE** • 1959
GOLDEN FLAME, THE • 1920 • Southwell Harry • ASL • HORDERN MYSTERY, THE
GOLDEN FLAME, THE • 1923 • *Hatton Dick* • USA
GOLDEN FLEECE, THE • 1918 • Hamilton G. P. • USA
GOLDEN FLEECING, THE • 1940 • Fenton Leslie • USA
GOLDEN FORTRESS, THE (UKN) see **SONAR KELLA** • 1975
GOLDEN GALLOWS, THE • 1922 • Scardon Paul • USA
GOLDEN GAMES, THE • 1975 • Barclay Robert • MTV • CND
GOLDEN GATE • 1981 • Wendkos Paul • TVM • USA
GOLDEN GATE MURDERS, THE • 1979 • Grauman Walter • TVM • USA • SPECTER ON THE BRIDGE
GOLDEN GATE TEARS see **CHINMEN NU** • 1941
GOLDEN GATES, THE • 1910 • *Champion* • USA
GOLDEN GATES, THE see **ZOLOTYE VOROTA** • 1969
GOLDEN GIFT, THE • 1922 • Karger Maxwell • USA
GOLDEN GIRL • 1951 • Bacon Lloyd • USA
GOLDEN GIRL see **DOKHTAR TALA** • 1968
GOLDEN GIRL see **GOLDENGIRL** • 1979
GOLDEN GLASSES, THE see **OCCHIALI D'ORO, GLI** • 1988
GOLDEN GLOVES • 1940 • Dmytryk Edward • USA
GOLDEN GLOVES • 1961 • Groulx Gilles • DCS • CND
GOLDEN GLOVES STORY, THE • 1950 • Feist Felix E. • USA
GOLDEN GLOVES (UKN) see **EX-CHAMP** • 1936
GOLDEN GOAL, THE • 1918 • Scardon Paul • USA
GOLDEN GOD, THE • 1914 • Fielding Romaine • USA
GOLDEN GOD, THE • 1917 • *Hanlon Alma* • USA
GOLDEN GODDESS, THE • 1916 • *Daw Marjorie* • USA
GOLDEN GODDESS OF RIO BENI see **GOLDENE GOTTIN VOM RIO BENI, DIE** • 1964
GOLDEN GOOSE, THE • 1914 • Ince Thomas H., Clifford William H. • USA
GOLDEN GOOSE, THE (USA) see **GOLDENE GANS, DIE**
GOLDEN GRAVE, THE see **ALTIN MEZAR** • 1968
GOLDEN GULLEN, THE • 1913 • Melies Gaston • USA
GOLDEN HAIR • 1912 • *Eclair* • USA
GOLDEN HAIR, THE • 1938 • Vyas Narottam • IND
GOLDEN HANDCUFFS, THE see **BANGARU SANKELLU** • 1968
GOLDEN HANDS • 1957 • Paradjanov Sergei • DOC • USS
GOLDEN HANDS OF KURIGAL • 1949 • Brannon Fred C. • USA
GOLDEN HARVEST • 1933 • Murphy Ralph • USA
GOLDEN HAWK, THE • 1952 • Salkow Sidney • USA
GOLDEN HEAD, THE • 1965 • Thorpe Richard • USA
GOLDEN HEAD OF THE AVENGER, THE see **ZOLOTAYA GOLOVA MSTITELYA** • 1989
GOLDEN HEART, THE • 1913 • *American* • USA
GOLDEN HEART, THE • 1917 • Sargent George L. • SHT • USA
GOLDEN HEART, THE see **ZLATE SRDECKO** • 1916
GOLDEN HEIST, THE see **INSIDE OUT** • 1975
GOLDEN HELMET (USA) see **CASQUE D'OR** • 1952
GOLDEN HEN, THE • 1946 • Davis Mannie • ANS • USA
GOLDEN HILLS see **ZLATYE GORI** • 1931
GOLDEN HOARD, THE • 1910 • *Nestor* • USA
GOLDEN HOARD OR BURIED ALIVE, THE • 1913 • *Vitagraph* • USA
GOLDEN HONEY • 1928 • Petrov Vladimir (c/d) • USS
GOLDEN HOOFS • 1941 • Shores Lynn • USA
GOLDEN HOPE, THE • 1920 • De Grasse Joseph • USA
GOLDEN HORDE, THE • 1951 • Sherman George • USA • GOLDEN HORDE OF GENGHIS KHAN, THE (UKN)
GOLDEN HORDE OF GENGHIS KHAN, THE (UKN) see **GOLDEN HORDE, THE** • 1951
GOLDEN HORT • 1966 • Franco Jesus
GOLDEN HOUR, THE (UKN) see **POT O' GOLD** • 1941
GOLDEN HUNCH • 1945 • *Nesbitt John* • SHT • USA
GOLDEN IDIOT, THE • 1917 • Berthelet Arthur • USA
GOLDEN IDOL, THE • 1954 • Beebe Ford • USA
GOLDEN ILSY, THE see **GOUDEN ILSY, DE** • 1957
GOLDEN IVORY • 1954 • Breakston George • UKN • WHITE HUNTRESS (USA)
GOLDEN KATHERINE see **ZLATA KATERINA** • 1934
GOLDEN KEY see **ZOLOTOI KLYUCHIK** • 1939
GOLDEN KEY, THE see **CAPTAIN'S PARADISE, THE** • 1953
GOLDEN KITE, THE see **ARANYSARKANY** • 1966
GOLDEN LADDER • 1957 • *Mckuen Rod* • SHT • USA
GOLDEN LADDER, THE • 1914 • *Kerrigan J. Warren* • USA
GOLDEN LADY, THE • 1974 • Larraz Jose R. • UKN, HKG
GOLDEN LADY (UKN) see **FIGHTING FRONTIERSMAN, THE** • 1946
GOLDEN LAKE, THE see **SPINNEN PART 1, DIE** • 1919
GOLDEN LIE, THE • 1909 • *Lubin* • USA
GOLDEN LIES • 1916 • *Washburn Bryant* • SHT • USA
GOLDEN LINK, THE • 1954 • Saunders Charles • UKN
GOLDEN LOTUS • 1973 • Li Han-Hsiang • HKG
GOLDEN LOUIS, THE • 1909 • Griffith D. W. • USA
GOLDEN MADONNA, THE • 1949 • Vajda Ladislao • UKN
GOLDEN MAGT see **MACHT DES GOLDES, DIE** • 1912
GOLDEN MAN see **ARANYEMBER, AZ** • 1917
GOLDEN MARIE (UKN) see **CASQUE D'OR** • 1952
GOLDEN MASK, THE (USA) see **SOUTH OF ALGIERS** • 1952
GOLDEN MISTRESS, THE • 1954 • Biberman Abner • USA
GOLDEN MOB see **OGON NO YARO-DOMO** • 1967
GOLDEN MOMENT, THE • 1980 • Sarafian Richard C. • TVM • USA • GOLDEN MOMENT: AN OLYMPIC LOVE STORY, THE
GOLDEN MOMENT: AN OLYMPIC LOVE STORY, THE see **GOLDEN MOMENT, THE** • 1980
GOLDEN MOUNTAINS see **ZLATYE GORI** • 1931
GOLDEN MOUNTAINS see **GULD OG GRLONNE SKOVE** • 1957
GOLDEN NEEDLES • 1974 • Pogostin S. Lee, Clouse Robert • USA • CHASE FOR THE GOLDEN NEEDLES, THE
GOLDEN NINJA WARRIOR • 1986 • Lai Joseph • HKG • GOLDEN NINJA WARRIORS
GOLDEN NINJA WARRIORS see **GOLDEN NINJA WARRIOR** • 1986
GOLDEN NYMPHS, THE see **HONEYMOON OF HORROR** • 1964
GOLDEN OPHELIA • 1975 • Martin Marcel • BLG
GOLDEN OYSTER • 1915 • Hotaling Arthur D. • USA
GOLDEN PATCH, THE • 1914 • *Selig* • USA
GOLDEN PATH, THE • 1945 • Pipinashvili Konstantin • USS
GOLDEN PATHWAY, THE • 1913 • Costello Maurice, Gaillord Robert • USA
GOLDEN PATSY, THE • 1962 • *Frobe Gert* • FRG
GOLDEN PAVEMENT, THE • 1915 • Hepworth Cecil M. • UKN
GOLDEN PEACOCK CASTLE see **OGON KUJYAKU-JO** • 1961
GOLDEN PEACOCK GARDEN see **OGON KUJYAKU-JO** • 1961
GOLDEN PILL, THE see **GOLDENE PILLE, DIE** • 1968
GOLDEN PINCE-NEZ, THE • 1922 • Ridgwell George • UKN
GOLDEN PIPPIN GIRL, THE • 1920 • Hunter A. C. • UKN • WHY MEN LEAVE HOME
GOLDEN PLAGUE, THE (USA) see **GOLDENE PEST, DIE** • 1954
GOLDEN POMEGRANATES, THE • 1924 • Paul Fred • UKN
GOLDEN POSITIONS, THE • 1970 • Broughton James • USA
GOLDEN PRINCE see **LOST EMPIRE, THE** • 1924
GOLDEN PRINCESS, THE • 1925 • Badger Clarence • USA
GOLDEN PRINCESS MINE, THE • 1913 • *Nestor* • USA
GOLDEN QUEENING, THE see **ZLATA RENETA** • 1965
GOLDEN RABBIT, THE • 1962 • MacDonald David • UKN
GOLDEN RAIDERS see **ESCAPE TO ATHENA** • 1979
GOLDEN RAINBOW, A • 1915 • *Rich Vivian* • USA
GOLDEN RAYS see **RAN RASA** • 1967
GOLDEN RENDEZVOUS • 1977 • Lazarus Ashley, Francis Freddie (U/c) • USA, SAF • NUCLEAR TERROR
GOLDEN RENNET, THE see **ZLATA RENETA** • 1965
GOLDEN RIVER, THE • 1983 • Grubcheva Ivanka • BUL
GOLDEN ROAD TO SAMARKAND, THE see **JADE ZARINE SAMARGHAND** • 1968
GOLDEN ROD, THE • 1912 • *Powers* • USA
GOLDEN ROSARY, THE • 1917 • Van Plack Tom • USA
GOLDEN RULE, THE • 1911 • *Reliance* • USA
GOLDEN RULE, THE • 1912 • *Barker Florence* • USA
GOLDEN RULE KATE • 1917 • Barker Reginald • USA
GOLDEN SALAMANDER, THE • 1950 • Neame Ronald • UKN
GOLDEN SANDS • 1984 • Gudmundsson Agust • ICL
GOLDEN SEA, THE see **SPINNEN PART 1, DIE** • 1919
GOLDEN SEAL, THE • 1983 • Zuniga Frank • USA
GOLDEN SECRET, THE • 1910 • Melies Gaston • USA
GOLDEN SECTION, THE see **ARANYMETSZES** • 1962
GOLDEN SHACKLES • 1928 • Fitzgerald Dallas M. • USA
GOLDEN SHAWL see **RAN SALU** • 1967
GOLDEN SHOVEL, THE see **ARANYASO** • 1914
GOLDEN SHOWER, THE • 1919 • Noble John W. • USA
GOLDEN SILENCE • 1923 • Hurst Paul C. • USA
GOLDEN SITA see **KANCHANA SITA** • 1977
GOLDEN SLING, THE see **ZLATNA PRACKA** • 1968
GOLDEN SMILE, THE see **GYLDNE SMIL, DEN** • 1935
GOLDEN SNARE, THE • 1921 • Hartford David M. • USA
GOLDEN SPARROW, THE see **BANGARU PICHIKA** • 1968
GOLDEN SPIDER, THE • 1915 • *Fuller Mary* • USA
GOLDEN SPURS • 1926 • West Walter • UKN
GOLDEN SPURS, THE • 1915 • Carleton Lloyd B. • USA
GOLDEN STALLION, THE • 1949 • Witney William • USA
GOLDEN STATE, THE • 1948 • *Paramount* • ANS • USA
GOLDEN STEPMOTHER, THE • 1966 • Brumberg Valentina, Brumberg Zinaida • ANS • USS
GOLDEN STRAIN, THE • 1925 • Schertzinger Victor • USA
GOLDEN SUPERMAN • 1968 • Yongil Park • SKR
GOLDEN SUPPER, THE • 1910 • Griffith D. W. • USA
GOLDEN TAIGA • 1935 • Schneiderov Vladimir • USS
GOLDEN TAIGA, THE • 1937 • Kazansky Gennadi, Ruf M. • USS
GOLDEN THING, THE see **GOLDENE DING, DAS** • 1971
GOLDEN THOUGHT, A • 1924 • *Mix Tom* • USA
GOLDEN THOUGHT, THE • 1917 • Mix Tom • SHT • USA
GOLDEN TOOTH, THE see **ZLATNIAT ZAB** • 1962
GOLDEN TOUCH, THE • 1935 • Disney Walt • ANS • USA
GOLDEN TOWN, THE see **ALTIN SHEER** • 1979
GOLDEN TRAIL, THE • 1915 • *Stanton Richard* • USA
GOLDEN TRAIL, THE • 1920 • Moomaw Lewis H., Hersholt Jean • USA
GOLDEN TRAIL, THE • 1927 • *Carter Dick* • USA
GOLDEN TRAIL, THE • 1940 • Herman Al • USA
GOLDEN TRAIL, THE (UKN) see **RIDERS OF THE WHISTLING SKULL, THE** • 1937
GOLDEN TRAIN, THE see **ZOLOTOI ESHELON** • 1961
GOLDEN TRAIN, THE see **TRENUL DE AUR** • 1988
GOLDEN TREASURE, THE • 1964 • Doukov Stoyan • ANM • BUL
GOLDEN TRIANGLE, THE • 1977 • Boonag Rome, Wu Ma • THL
GOLDEN TRIANGLE, THE • 1980 • Lee Lo • HKG
GOLDEN TWENTIES, THE • 1950 • *De Rochemont Richard (P)* • CMP • USA
GOLDEN VALLEY, THE see **SOLOTISTAJA DOLINA** • 1937
GOLDEN VIRGIN, THE (USA) see **STORY OF ESTHER COSTELLO, THE** • 1957
GOLDEN VISION, THE • 1968 • Loach Kenneth • MTV • UKN
GOLDEN VOYAGE OF SINBAD, THE • 1973 • Hessler Gordon • UKN • SINBAD'S GOLDEN VOYAGE
GOLDEN WALL, THE • 1918 • Henderson Dell • USA
GOLDEN WEB, THE • 1920 • Malins Geoffrey H. • UKN
GOLDEN WEB, THE • 1926 • Lang Walter • USA
GOLDEN WEDDING, THE • 1913 • *Beaumont Harry* • USA
GOLDEN WEDDING, THE • 1915 • Lloyd Frank • USA • THEIR GOLDEN WEDDING
GOLDEN WEST, THE • 1911 • *Australian Film Syndicate* • ASL
GOLDEN WEST, THE • 1919 • *Austral Photoplays* • ASL
GOLDEN WEST, THE • 1932 • Howard David • USA
GOLDEN WEST, THE • 1939 • Davis Mannie • ANS • USA
GOLDEN WOMAN, THE see **ZLATA ZENA** • 1920
GOLDEN YEARS see **ARANYKOR** • 1963
GOLDEN YEGGS • 1950 • Freleng Friz • ANS • USA
GOLDEN YOUTH (UKN) see **JUST SUPPOSE** • 1926
GOLDEN YUKON, THE • 1927 • Shipman Nell, Van Tuyle Bert • USA
GOLDENE ABGRUND, DER • 1927 • Bonnard Mario • FRG • WELT UND HALBWELT
GOLDENE BETT, DAS • 1912 • Schmidthassler Walter • FRG
GOLDENE BRUCKE, DIE • 1917 • Czerny Ludwig • FRG
GOLDENE BRUCKE, DIE • 1942 • Tourjansky Victor • FRG
GOLDENE BRUCKE, DIE • 1956 • Verhoeven Paul • FRG
GOLDENE BUCH, DAS • 1919 • von Antalffy Alexander • FRG
GOLDENE DING, DAS • 1971 • Reitz Edgar, Perakis Nikos, Stockl Ula, Brustellin Alf • FRG • GOLDEN THING, THE
GOLDENE FESSEL, DIE • 1944 • Thimig Hans • FRG
GOLDENE FLUT, DIE see **MANN OHNE NAMEN 4, DER** • 1920-21
GOLDENE FRIEDELCHEN, DAS • 1914-18 • Zelnik Friedrich • FRG
GOLDENE FRIEDELCHEN, DAS • 1916 • Hanus Emerich • FRG
GOLDENE GANS, DIE • 1944 • Reiniger Lotte • ANM • UKN
GOLDENE GANS, DIE • *Defa* • ANM • GDR • GOLDEN GOOSE, THE (USA)
GOLDENE GARTEN, DER • 1953 • Domnick Hans • FRG
GOLDENE GIFT, DAS see **DAMON DER WELT 3** • 1919
GOLDENE GLETSCHER, DER • 1932 • Kern August • FRG, SWT • HERRGOTTSGRENADIERE, DIE ○ GOLDFIEBER
GOLDENE GOTTIN VOM RIO BENI, DIE • 1964 • Martin Eugenio • FRG, FRN, SPN • GOLDEN GODDESS OF RIO BENI
GOLDENE HAAR, DAS • 1922 • Eichgrun Bruno • FRG
GOLDENE JURTE, DIE • 1961 • Kolditz Gottfried, Dordschpalam Rabschaa • GDR, MNG
GOLDENE KALB, DAS • 1917 • Biebrach Rudolf • FRG
GOLDENE KALB, DAS • 1924 • Felner Peter Paul • FRG
GOLDENE KLUB, DER • 1919 • Halm Alfred?, Sauer Fred? • FRG
GOLDENE KRONE, DIE • 1920 • Halm Alfred • FRG
GOLDENE KUGEL, DIE • 1921 • Wullner Robert • FRG
GOLDENE LUGE, DIE • 1919 • Lund Erik • FRG
GOLDENE MASKE, DIE • 1939 • Zerlett Hans H. • FRG
GOLDENE MAUER, DIE • 1920 • Kahn William? • FRG
GOLDENE MUMIE, DIE • 1918 • Eichberg Richard • FRG
GOLDENE NETZ, DAS • 1921 • Werckmeister Hans • FRG
GOLDENE PEST, DIE • 1921 • Ralph Louis • FRG
GOLDENE PEST, DIE • 1954 • Brahm John • FRG • GOLDEN PLAGUE, THE (USA)
GOLDENE PILLE, DIE • 1968 • Adloff Horst Manfred • FRG • GOLDEN PILL, THE
GOLDENE POL, DER • 1918 • Meinert Rudolf • FRG
GOLDENE SCHMETTERLING, DER • 1926 • Curtiz Michael • FRG • ROAD TO HAPPINESS, THE ○ GOLDEN BUTTERFLY, THE
GOLDENE SEE, DER see **SPINNEN PART 1, DIE** • 1919
GOLDENE SKORPION, DER • 1921 • Abter Adolf • FRG
GOLDENE SPINNE, DIE • 1943 • Engels Erich • FRG
GOLDENE STADT, DIE • 1942 • Harlan Veit • FRG
GOLDENES GESCHAFT, EIN • 1915 • Del Zopp Rudolf • FRG
GOLDENGIRL • 1979 • Sargent Joseph • USA • GOLDEN GIRL
GOLDENROD • 1977 • Hart Harvey • TVM • USA
GOLDFACE • 1967 • Albertini Bitto • ITL, SPN, VNZ • GOLDFACE IL FANTASTICO SUPERMAN (ITL) ○ GOLDFACE THE FANTASTIC SUPERMAN
GOLDFACE IL FANTASTICO SUPERMAN (ITL) see **GOLDFACE** • 1967
GOLDFACE THE FANTASTIC SUPERMAN see **GOLDFACE** • 1967
GOLDFELDER VON JACKSONVILLE, DIE • 1915 • Lowenbein Richard • FRG
GOLDFIEBER • 1919 • Schomburgk Hans • FRG
GOLDFIEBER see **GOLDENE GLETSCHER, DER** • 1932
GOLDFINGER • 1964 • Hamilton Guy • UKN
GOLDFISH, THE • 1924 • Storm Jerome • USA
GOLDFRAME • 1968 • Servais Raoul • ANS • BLG
GOLDIE • 1931 • Stoloff Ben • USA
GOLDIE AND THE BOXER • 1979 • Miller David • TVM • USA
GOLDIE AND THE BOXER GO TO HOLLYWOOD • 1981 • Miller David • TVM • USA
GOLDIE GETS ALONG • 1933 • St. Clair Malcolm • USA
GOLDIE LOCKS AND THE THREE BEARS • 1922 • Disney Walt • ANS • USA
GOLDILOCKS see **ZLATOVLASKA** • 1954
GOLDILOCKS see **GOLDILOCKS AND THE THREE BEARS** • 1982
GOLDILOCKS AND THE BEARS • 1934 • Cones James, Cones Nancy Ford • ANM • USA
GOLDILOCKS AND THE JIVIN' BEARS • 1944 • Freleng Friz • ANS • USA
GOLDILOCKS AND THE THREE BARES • 1963 • Lewis Herschell G. • USA • (GOLDILOCKS) THREE CHICKS
GOLDILOCKS AND THE THREE BEARS • 1917 • Moss Howard S. • ANS • USA
GOLDILOCKS AND THE THREE BEARS • 1934 • Lantz Walter, Nolan William • ANS • USA
GOLDILOCKS AND THE THREE BEARS • 1939 • Harman Hugh • ANS • USA
GOLDILOCKS AND THE THREE BEARS • 1982 • Cates Gilbert • MTV • USA • GOLDILOCKS
(GOLDILOCKS) THREE CHICKS see **GOLDILOCKS AND THE THREE BARES** • 1963
GOLDIMOUSE AND THE THREE CATS • 1960 • Freleng Friz • ANS • USA
GOLDIN'S LITTLE JOKE • 1902 • *Mutoscope & Biograph* • UKN
GOLDJUNGE • 1925 • *Mundator-Film* • FRG
GOLDMINE see **MINA DE ORO** • 1974
GOLDMINE VON SAR-KHIN, DIE see **JAGD NACH DEM TODE 4, DIE** • 1921
GOLDMOUTH • 1965 • Branaman Bob • USA
GOLDQUELLE, DIE • 1915 • Schonfeld Carl • FRG
GOLDRUNNER • Losee Richard • USA
GOLDSEEKER'S DAUGHTER, THE • 1909 • *Bison* • USA
GOLDSMITH'S SHOP, THE • 1988 • Anderson Michael • USA
GOLDSNAKE ANONIMA KILLERS • 1966 • Baldi Ferdinando • ITL, FRN, SPN • SUICIDE MISSION TO SINGAPORE (USA) ○ SINGAPUR, HORA CERO (SPN) ○ SINGAPORE, ZERO HOUR
GOLDSTEIN • 1965 • Kaufman Philip, Manaster Benjamin • USA
GOLDSUCHER, DIE • 1924 • *Frankl & Schmidt* • FRG
GOLDSUCHER VON ARKANSAS, DIE • 1964 • Martin Paul, Cardone Alberto • FRG, ITL, FRN • ALLA CONQUISTA DELL'ARKANSAS (ITL) ○ MASSACRE AT MARBLE CITY (UKN) ○ CHERCHEURS D'OR DE L'ARKANSAS, LES (FRN)
GOLDTAL, DAS • 1918 • *Enger Mogens* • FRG
GOLDTOWN GHOST RAIDERS • 1953 • Archainbaud George • USA
GOLDWHISKERS • 1964 • Learner Keith, Linnecar Vera • ANS • UKN

GOLDWING • 1980 • Thornton David • ANM • USA • GOLD WING

GOLDWOOD • 1975 • Shannon Kathleen • SHT • CND

GOLDWYN-BRAY PICTOGRAPHS • 1919-21 • *Goldwyn-Bray* • ASS • USA

GOLDWYN FOLLIES, THE • 1938 • Marshall George • USA

GOLDY: THE LAST OF THE GOLDEN BEARS • 1984 • Black Trevor • USA

GOLEM • 1980 • Szulkin Piotr • PLN

GOLEM, DER • 1914 • Galeen Henrik, Wegener Paul • FRG • MONSTER OF FATE, THE ○ GOLEM, THE

GOLEM, DER • 1916 • Gad Urban • DNM

GOLEM, LE • 1935 • Duvivier Julien • FRN, CZC • LEGEND OF PRAGUE, THE (UKN) ○ MAN OF STONE, THE ○ GOLEM, THE (USA)

GOLEM, LE • 1966 • Kerchbron Jean • FRN • GOLEM, THE (USA) ○ MASK OF THE GOLEM

GOLEM, THE see **GOLEM, DER** • 1914

GOLEM, THE (USA) see **GOLEM, WIE ER IN DIE WELT KAM, DER** • 1920

GOLEM, THE (USA) see **GOLEM, LE** • 1935

GOLEM, THE (USA) see **GOLEM, LE** • 1966

GOLEM AND THE DANCER see **GOLEM UND DIE TANZERIN, DER** • 1917

GOLEM AND THE DANCING GIRL, THE see **GOLEM UND DIE TANZERIN, DER** • 1917

GOLEM: HOW HE CAME INTO THE WORLD, THE see **GOLEM, WIE ER IN DIE WELT KAM, DER** • 1920

GOLEM UND DIE TANZERIN, DER • 1917 • Wegener Paul • FRG • GOLEM AND THE DANCING GIRL, THE ○ GOLEM AND THE DANCER

GOLEM, WIE ER IN DIE WELT KAM, DER • 1920 • Wegener Paul, Boese Carl • FRG • GOLEM: HOW HE CAME INTO THE WORLD, THE ○ GOLEM, THE (USA)

GOLEM'S DAUGHTER see **GOULVE, LA** • 1971

GOLEM'S LAST ADVENTURE, THE see **DORFSGOLEM, DER** • 1921

GOLF AND JAIL BIRDS • 1920 • *Century* • SHT • USA

GOLF BUG, THE • 1922 • Roach Hal • SHT • USA

GOLF CADDIE'S DOG, THE • 1912 • *Thanhouser* • USA

GOLF CHAMPION "CHICK" EVANS LINKS WITH SWEEDIE • 1914 • *Beery Wallace* • USA

GOLF CHUMP, THE • 1932 • Sweet Harry • SHT • USA

GOLF CHUMPS • 1939 • *Mintz Charles (P)* • ANS • USA

GOLF GAME AND THE BONNET, THE • 1913 • Baker George D. • USA

GOLF LATIN, LE • 1942 • Tedesco Jean • SHT • FRN

GOLF MAD • 1915 • *Horseshoe* • UKN

GOLF MISTAKES • 1937 • Feist Felix E. • SHT • USA

GOLF NUT, THE • 1927 • Edwards Harry J. • SHT • USA

GOLF NUTS • 1930 • *Terry Paul/ Moser Frank (P)* • ANS • USA

GOLF SPECIALIST, THE • 1930 • Brice Monte • SHT • USA

GOLF WIDOWS • 1928 • Kenton Erle C. • USA

GOLFA, UNA • 1957 • Demicheli Tulio • MXC

GOLFE NO ALGARVE • 1972 • Costa Jose Fonseca • SHT • PRT

GOLFER, THE • 1921 • Cline Eddie (c/d) • SHT • USA

GOLFER, THE • 1936 • *Lantz Walter (P)* • ANS • USA

GOLFERS, THE • 1929 • Sennett Mack • SHT • USA

GOLFING • 1913 • Hewitt G. Fletcher • UKN • COMIC GOLF

GOLFING EXTRAORDINARY, FIVE GENTLEMEN • 1896 • Acres Birt • UKN

GOLFO • 1912 • Bahatoris Costas • GRC

GOLFO, EL • 1968 • Escriva Vicente • SPN

GOLFO DE VIZCAYA • 1985 • Rebollo Javier • SPN • BAY OF BISCAY

GOLFO -GIRL OF THE MOUNTAINS • 1958 • Laskos G.

GOLFO QUE VIO UNA ESTRELLA, EL • 1953 • Iquino Ignacio F. • SPN

GOLFOS, LOS • 1959 • Saura Carlos • SPN • HOOLIGANS, THE ○ URCHINS, THE ○ SCOUNDRELS, THE ○ RIFF-RAFF

GOLGO 13 • 1974 • Sato Junya • IRN

GOLGOTA • 1966 • Dragan Mircea • RMN • GOLGOTHA

GOLGOTA • 1979 • Petrovski Meto • YGS • GOLGOTHA

GOLGOTHA • 1935 • Duvivier Julien • FRN • ECCE HOMO ○ BEHOLD THE MAN

GOLGOTHA see **GOLGOTA** • 1966

GOLGOTHA see **GOLGOTA** • 1979

GOLIA ALLA CONQUISTA DI BAGDAD • 1964 • Paolella Domenico • ITL • GOLIATH AT THE CONQUEST OF DAMASCUS (USA) ○ GOLIATH AT THE CONQUEST OF BAGDAD

GOLIA CONTRO IL CAVALIERE MASCHERATO see **GOLIA E IL CAVALIERE MASCHERATO** • 1964

GOLIA E IL CAVALIERE MASCHERATO • 1964 • Pierotti Piero • ITL • GOLIA CONTRO IL CAVALIERE MASCHERATO ○ HERCULES AND THE MASKED RIDER

GOLIAT CONTRA LOS GIGANTES (SPN) see **GOLIATH CONTRO I GIGANTI** • 1961

GOLIATH see **KARAMBOL** • 1964

GOLIATH AGAINST THE GIANTS (USA) see **GOLIATH CONTRO I GIGANTI** • 1961

GOLIATH AND THE BARBARIANS (USA) see **TERRORE DEI BARBARI, IL** • 1959

GOLIATH AND THE DRAGON (USA) see **VENDETTA DI ERCOLE, LA** • 1960

GOLIATH AND THE GIANTS see **GOLIATH CONTRO I GIGANTI** • 1961

GOLIATH AND THE GOLDEN CITY see **MACISTE ALLA CORTE DEL GRAN KHAN** • 1961

GOLIATH AND THE REBEL SLAVE (USA) see **GOLIATH E LA SCHIAVA RIBELLE** • 1963

GOLIATH AND THE SINS OF BABYLON (USA) see **MACISTE, L'EROE PIU GRANDE DEL MONDO** • 1963

GOLIATH AND THE VAMPIRES (USA) see **MACISTE CONTRO IL VAMPIRO** • 1961

GOLIATH AT THE CONQUEST OF BAGDAD see **GOLIA ALLA CONQUISTA DI BAGDAD** • 1964

GOLIATH AT THE CONQUEST OF DAMASCUS (USA) see **GOLIA ALLA CONQUISTA DI BAGDAD** • 1964

GOLIATH AWAITS • 1981 • Connor Kevin • TVM • USA

GOLIATH CONTRO I GIGANTI • 1961 • Malatesta Guido • ITL, SPN • GOLIAT CONTRA LOS GIGANTES (SPN) ○ GOLIATH AND THE GIANTS ○ GOLIATH AGAINST THE GIANTS (USA)

GOLIATH E LA SCHIAVA RIBELLE • 1963 • Caiano Mario • ITL, FRN • GOLIATH AND THE REBEL SLAVE (USA) ○ ARROW OF THE AVENGER (UKN)

GOLIATH II • 1960 • Reitherman Wolfgang • ANS • USA

GOLIGHTLY PUNISHED • 1914 • *Gaumont* • UKN

GOLLOCKS • 1975 • Abey Dennis • UKN

GOLLYWOG'S MOTOR ACCIDENT (USA) see **IN GOLLYWOG LAND** • 1912

GOLNAR • 1989 • Partovi Kambuzia • IRN

GOLOD.. GOLOD.. GOLOD • 1921 • Gardin Vladimir, Pudovkin V. I. • USS • HUNGER.. HUNGER.. HUNGER

GOLONDRINA, LA • 1938 • Contreras Torres Miguel • MXC • SWALLOW, THE (USA)

GOLOSHES OF FORTUNE • 1907 • DNM

GOLOWIN GEHT DURCH DIE STADT • 1940 • Stemmle R. A. • FRG

GOLPE DE ESTADO, EL see **BATALLA DE CHILE: PART 2** • 1976

GOLPE DE GARCIA see **QUEMA DE JUDAS, LA** • 1974

GOLPE DE MANO • 1969 • de la Loma Jose Antonio • SPN

GOLPE DE MIL MILLONES, UN • 1966 • Heusch Paolo • SPN, ITL, FRN • COLPO DA MILLE MILIARDI, UN (ITL) ○ STROKE OF A THOUSAND MILLIONS, A

GOLPEANDO EN LA SELVA • 1967 • Alvarez Santiago • DOC • CUB

GOLU HADAWATHA • 1968 • Peries Lester James • SLN • SILENCE OF THE HEART, THE

GOLUBOI EKSPRESS • 1929 • Trauberg Ilya • USS • CHINA EXPRESS ○ BLUE EXPRESS, THE

GOLUBOI LIED • 1970 • Sokolov Viktor • USS • BLUE ICE

GOLUBYE GORY ELY NEPRAVDOPODOBNAYA • 1983 • Shengelaya Eldar • USS • BLUE MOUNTAINS

GOLVEN • 1982 • Apon Annette • NTH • WAVES, THE

GOLYAKALIFA, A • 1917 • Korda Alexander • HNG • STORK CALIPH, THE

GOLYAMATA POBEDA • 1972 • Mirchev Vassil • BUL • GREAT VICTORY, THE

GOMAR, THE HUMAN GORILLA see **HORRIPLANTE BESTIA HUMANA, LA** • 1970

GOMBROWICZ O LA SEDUCCION • 1986 • Fischermann Alberto • ARG • GOMBROWICZ OR SEDUCTION

GOMBROWICZ OR SEDUCTION see **GOMBROWICZ O LA SEDUCCION** • 1986

GOMESU NO NA WA GOMESU: RYUSA • 1967 • Takahashi Osamu • JPN • WHO IS GOMEZ?

GOMMES, LES • 1969 • Deroisy Lucien • BLG, FRN

GOMMES, LES • 1972 • Robbe-Grillet Alain • FRN

GOMORRON BILL! • 1945 • Falk Lauritz, Winner Peter • SWD • GOOD MORNING BILL

GONDOLA • 1988 • Ito Chisei • JPN

GONDOLA, LA • 1942 • Pasinetti Francesco • ITL

GONDOLA DEL DIAVOLO, LA • 1946 • Campogalliani Carlo • ITL

GONDOLA DELLE CHIMERE, LA • 1935 • Genina Augusto • ITL, FRN • GONDOLE AUX CHIMERES, LA (FRN)

GONDOLA EYE, THE • 1963 • Hugo Ian • SHT • USA

GONDOLE AUX CHIMERES, LA (FRN) see **GONDOLA DELLE CHIMERE, LA** • 1935

GONDVISELES • 1987 • Erdoss Pal • HNG • TOLERANCE

GONE ARE THE DAYES • 1984 • Beaumont Gabrielle • TVM • USA

GONE ARE THE DAYS! • 1963 • Webster Nicholas • USA • MAN FROM C.O.T.T.O.N., THE ○ PURLIE VICTORIOUS ○ MAN FROM C.O.T.T.O.N. OR HOW I STOPPED WORRYING AND LEARNED TO LOVE THE BOLL WEEVIL, THE

GONE BATTY • 1954 • McKimson Robert • ANS • USA

GONE CURLING • 1963 • Howe John • CND

GONE IN 60 SECONDS • 1974 • Halicki H. B. • USA

GONE IN 60 SECONDS II -THE JUNKMAN • 1977 • Halicki H. B. • USA • JUNKMAN, THE

GONE TO CONEY ISLAND • 1910 • *Thanhouser* • USA

GONE TO EARTH • 1950 • Powell Michael, Pressburger Emeric • UKN • WILD HEART, THE (USA)

GONE TO GROUND • 1977 • Dobson Kevin • MTV • ASL

GONE TO SEED see **GANZ UND GAR VERWAHRLOSTES MADCHEN, EIN** • 1977

GONE TO THE COUNTRY • 1921 • Roach Hal • SHT • USA

GONE TO THE DOGS • 1928 • Merrick Fred V. • UKN

GONE TO THE DOGS • 1940 • Hall Ken G. • ASL

GONE TO THE DOGS see **GYPSY TRAIL, THE** • 1915

GONE UP NORTH FOR A WHILE • Maunder Paul • MTV • NZL

GONE WITH THE MIND • 1987 • Kuusi Janne • FNL

GONE WITH THE WEST • 1969 • Girard Bernard • USA • MAN WITHOUT MERCY ○ LITTLE MOON AND JUD MCGRAW ○ BRONCO BUSTERS

GONE WITH THE WIND • 1939 • Fleming Victor, Wood Sam (U/c), Cukor George (U/c) • USA

GONE WITH THE WIND see **RUZGAR GIBI GECTI** • 1968

GONG CRIED MURDER, THE • 1946 • Haines Ronald • UKN

GONG SHOW MOVIE, THE • 1980 • Barris Chuck • USA

GONGEHOVDINGEN • 1961 • Hovmand Annelise • DNM • GOINGE, THE AKVAVIT CHAMPION

GONIN NO HANZAISHA • 1959 • Ishii Teruo • JPN

GONIN NO KYODAI • 1939 • Yoshimura Kozaburo • JPN • FIVE BROTHERS AND SISTERS

GONIN NO SEKKOHEI • 1938 • Tasaka Tomotaka • JPN • FIVE SCOUTS

GONIN NO TOTSUGEKITAI • 1961 • Inoue Umeji • JPN • FIVE CHARGING SOLDIERS ○ LAST DITCH GLORY

GONIN NO YUKAINARO AIBO • 1930 • Tasaka Tomotaka • JPN

GONKA ZA SAMOGONKOJ • 1924 • Room Abram • SHT • USS • PURSUIT OF MOONSHINE, THE ○ MOONSHINERS, THE

GONKS GO BEAT • 1965 • Hartford-Davis Robert • UKN

GONUL KUSU • 1965 • Gulnar • TRK

GONULLU KAHRAMANLAR • 1968 • Basaran Tunc • TRK • VOLUNTEER HEROES

GONZA, THE SPEARMAN see **YARI NO GONZA** • 1985

GONZAGUE • 1922 • Diamant-Berger Henri • FRN

GONZAGUE • 1933 • Gremillon Jean • FRN • ACCORDEUR, L'

GONZAGUE • 1946 • Delacroix Rene • SHT • FRN

GONZALES' TAMALES • 1957 • Freleng Friz • ANS • USA

GONZALO ROIG • 1968 • Giral Sergio • SHT • CUB

GOO GOO EYES • 1903 • Porter Edwin S. • USA

GOO GOO GOLIATH • 1954 • Freleng Friz • ANS • USA

GOOD AFTERNOON • 1971 • Noyce Phil • DOC • ASL

GOOD AGAINST EVIL • 1977 • Wendkos Paul • TVM • USA

GOOD AGE, THE see **BEL AGE, LE** • 1958

GOOD AND BAD WOODCUTTERS, THE see **KUROI KIKORI TO SHIROI KIKORI** • 1959

GOOD AND EVIL • 1916 • Powers Francis • SHT • USA

GOOD AND EVIL • 1921 • *Doraine Lucy* • USA

GOOD AND EVIL see **GODE OG DET ONDE, DET** • 1974

GOOD AND GUILTY • 1962 • Kneitel Seymour • ANS • USA

GOOD AND NAUGHTY • 1926 • St. Clair Malcolm • USA

GOOD AND THE BAD, THE see **VARIA KATARA O DIHASMOS** • 1968

GOOD AND THE BAD, THE see **GODE OG DET ONDE, DET** • 1974

GOOD AND THE BAD, THE see **BON ET LES MECHANTS, LE** • 1976

GOOD AS GOLD • 1927 • Dunlap Scott R. • USA

GOOD BAD BOY • 1924 • Cline Eddie • SHT • USA

GOOD BAD GIRL, THE • 1931 • Neill R. William • USA

GOOD BAD GIRL, THE (UKN) see **INEZ FROM HOLLYWOOD** • 1924

GOOD BAD GUYS • 1940 • Cahn Edward L. • SHT • USA

GOOD BAD-MAN, THE • 1916 • Dwan Allan • USA • PASSING THROUGH

GOOD BAD MAN, THE see **PLOKHOY KHOROSHYI CHELOVEK** • 1974

GOOD-BAD WIFE, THE • 1920 • McCord Vera • USA

GOOD BED, A see **BON LIT, UN** • 1899

GOOD BEGINNING, THE • 1953 • Gunn Gilbert • UKN

GOOD BOY • 1976 • Reece Murray • MTV • NZL

GOOD BOY see **DOBAR DECKO** • 1981

GOOD BUSINESS DEAL, A • 1915 • Eason B. Reeves • USA

GOOD BUY • 1975 • Gross Yoram • ANS • ASL

GOOD-BY GIRLS! • 1923 • Storm Jerome • USA • DON'T GET EXCITED

GOOD BYE BRUCE LEE: HIS LAST GAME OF DEATH see **GOODBYE, BRUCE LEE** • 1975

GOOD-BYE FIRENZE! see **ARRIVEDERCI FIRENZE** • 1958

GOOD BYE, SEVILLA • 1955 • Iquino Ignacio F. • SPN

GOOD CATCH, A • 1903 • *Paul R. W.* • UKN

GOOD CATCH, A • 1912 • *Bushman Francis X.* • USA

GOOD CHEER • 1926 • Roach Hal • SHT • USA

GOOD CIDER • 1914 • *Lubin* • USA

GOOD CIGAR, A • 1911 • *Imp* • USA

GOOD COMPANIONS, THE • 1933 • Saville Victor • UKN

GOOD COMPANIONS, THE • 1957 • Thompson J. Lee • UKN

GOOD COMPANY see **LADY'S PROFESSION, A** • 1933

GOOD DAME • 1934 • Gering Marion • USA • GOOD GIRL (UKN)

GOOD DAY FOR A HANGING • 1958 • Juran Nathan • USA

GOOD DAY FOR FIGHTING, A see **CUSTER OF THE WEST** • 1968

GOOD DAY MR. H. • 1965 • Georgi Katja • ANM • GDR

GOOD DAY'S WORK, A • 1912 • *Powers* • USA

GOOD DEED see **UPKAR** • 1967

GOOD DEED DAILY • 1955 • Rasinski Connie • ANS • USA

GOOD DIE YOUNG, THE • 1954 • Gilbert Lewis* • UKN

GOOD EARTH, THE • 1936 • Franklin Sidney A., Fleming Victor (U/c) • USA

GOOD EGG, THE • 1939 • Jones Charles M. • ANS • USA

GOOD ELK, A • 1918 • Avery Charles • USA

GOOD EVENING • 1907 • Morland John • UKN

GOOD EVENING, JUDGE • 1916 • *Hamilton Lloyd V.* • SHT • USA

GOOD EVENING, MR. WALLENBERG see **WALLENBERG** • 1990

GOOD EXCUSE, A • 1914 • *Melies* • USA

GOOD FAIRY, THE • 1935 • Wyler William • USA

GOOD FAIRY, THE see **ZENMA** • 1951

GOOD FATHER, THE • 1986 • Newell Mike • UKN

GOOD FELLAS • 1990 • Scorsese Martin • USA

GOOD FELLOW, A • 1920 • Sanger Harry • SHT • USA

GOOD FELLOWS, THE • 1943 • Graham Jo • USA

GOOD FIGHT, THE • 1983 • Dore Mary, Sills Sam, Buckner Noel • DOC • USA

GOOD FINANCIAL SITUATION see **HIDARE UCHIWA** • 1935

GOOD FOR EVIL • 1911 • *Lubin* • USA

GOOD FOR EVIL • 1913 • *Lubin* • USA

GOOD FOR EVIL • 1913 • Calvert Charles? • UKN

GOOD FOR EVIL • 1913 • Kirkwood James • *Victor* • USA

GOOD-FOR-NOTHIN', THE see **GLENGARRY SCHOOLDAYS** • 1922

GOOD FOR NOTHING see **POLLY OF THE FOLLIES** • 1922

GOOD FOR NOTHING see **NIEDORAJDA** • 1937

GOOD-FOR-NOTHING see **ROKUDENASHI** • 1960

GOOD FOR NOTHING, THE • 1912 • Carleton Lloyd B. • USA

GOOD-FOR-NOTHING, THE • 1914 • *Anderson Broncho Billy* • USA

GOOD-FOR-NOTHING, THE • 1917 • Blackwell Carlyle • USA • GOOD FOR NOTHING, THE

GOOD FOR NOTHING, THE see **HIS NEW PROFESSION** • 1914

GOOD FOR NOTHING, THE see **GOOD-FOR-NOTHING, THE** • 1917

GOOD-FOR-NOTHING, THE see **TAUGENICHTS** • 1978

GOOD-FOR-NOTHING BRAT, THE • 1916 • Swickard Charles • SHT • USA

GOOD-FOR-NOTHING GALLAGHER • 1917 • Mong William V. • SHT • USA

GOOD-FOR-NOTHING JACK • 1913 • *Bison* • USA

GOOD FOR THE GOAT • 1913 • *Kalem* • USA

GOOD FOR THE GOUT • 1913 • Collins Edwin J.? • UKN

GOOD FOR YOU! see **OH OLSUN** • 1974

GOOD FORTUNE'S TARDY SMILE • 1914 • *Melies* • USA

GOOD FRIEND, THE • 1969 • Murakami Jimmy T. • ANS • USA

GOOD FRIENDS AND FAITHFUL NEIGHBOURS see **GODA VANNER OCH TROGNA GRANNAR** • 1938

GOOD FRIENDS AND FAITHFUL NEIGHBOURS see **GODA VANNER OCH TROGNA GRANNAR** • 1960

GOOD GIRL, BAD GIRL • 1984 • Ben Art • USA

GOOD GIRL SHOULD SOLVE HER OWN PROBLEMS, A see **BRA FLICKA REDER SIG SJALV** • 1913
GOOD GIRL (UKN) see **GOOD DAME** • 1934
GOOD GIRLS GO TO PARIS • 1939 • Hall Alexander • USA
GOOD GIRLS OF GODIVA HIGH, THE see **GIRLS OF GODIVA HIGH, THE** • 1981
GOOD GLUE STICKS (USA) see **COLLE UNIVERSELLE, LA** • 1907
GOOD GRACIOUS ANNABELLE • 1919 • Melford George • USA
GOOD GRACIOUS BOBBY • 1919 • *Vernon Bobby* • USA
GOOD GRACIOUS GRACE • 1919 • *Strand* • SHT • USA
GOOD GRIEF • 1972 • Jittlov Mike • ANS • USA
GOOD GUYS ALWAYS WIN, THE see **OUTFIT, THE** • 1973
GOOD GUYS AND THE BAD GUYS, THE • 1969 • Kennedy Burt • USA
GOOD GUYS WEAR BLACK • 1978 • Post Ted • USA
GOOD HEALTH IN SCOTLAND • 1943 • Russell Stanley • UKN
GOOD-HEARTED ANT, THE see **MRAV DOBRA SRCA** • 1965
GOOD HEAVENS! see **HIMMEL OCH PANNKAKA** • 1959
GOOD HOPE, THE see **OP HOOP VAN ZEGEN** • 1987
GOOD HOUSE DOG, A • 1914 • *Captain Kettle Films* • UKN
GOOD HOUSE DOG, A • 1916 • *Pyramid* • SHT • UKN
GOOD HOUSEWRECKING • 1933 • Sweet Harry • SHT • USA
GOOD HUMOR MAN, THE • 1950 • Bacon Lloyd • USA
GOOD IN HIM, THE • 1915 • Powell Paul • USA
GOOD IN THE WORST OF US, THE • 1913 • *Edison* • USA
GOOD IN THE WORST OF US, THE • 1913 • *Essanay* • USA
GOOD IN THE WORST OF US, THE • 1914 • *Eclair* • USA
GOOD IN THE WORST OF US, THE • 1915 • Humphrey William • USA
GOOD INDIAN, THE • 1913 • Duncan William • USA
GOOD INTENTION, THE • 1990 • August Bille • SWD
GOOD INTENTIONS • 1930 • Howard William K. • USA
GOOD INTENTIONS see **HOLD THAT BLONDE!** • 1945
GOOD JOKE, A • 1899 • Smith G. A. • UKN
GOOD JOKE, A • 1905 • *Walturdaw* • UKN
GOOD JOKE, A see **BONNE FARCE, UNE** • 1896
GOOD KICK OFF, A • 1910 • Fitzhamon Lewin? • UKN
GOOD KIDS, BAD KIDS • 1989 • Kia-Rostami Abbas • IRN
GOOD KING DAGOBERT, THE see **BON ROI DAGOBERT, LE** • 1963
GOOD LIFE, THE • 1975 • Davies John Howard • MTV • UKN
GOOD LIFE, THE (UKN) see **BELLE VIE, LA** • 1962
GOOD LITTLE BAD BOY, A • 1917 • Moore Vin • SHT • USA
GOOD LITTLE BOY AND THE BAD LITTLE BOY, THE • 1929 • Aylott Dave, Symmons E. F. • SHT • UKN
GOOD LITTLE BROWNIE • 1920 • *Sterling Merta* • SHT • USA
GOOD LITTLE DEVIL, A • 1914 • Porter Edwin S., Dawley J. Searle • USA
GOOD LITTLE MONKEYS, THE • 1935 • Harman Hugh • ANS • USA
GOOD LITTLE PAL, A • 1915 • Birch Cecil • UKN
GOOD-LOOKING GIRL AND YOUNG MAN WITH OWN MOTORCYCLE NEEDED see **SE SOLICITA MUCHACHA DE BUENA PRESENCIA Y JOVEN CON MOTO PROPIO** • 1977
GOOD LOSER, A • 1910 • *Pathe* • USA
GOOD LOSER, A • 1918 • Donaldson Dick • USA
GOOD LOVE AND THE BAD, THE • 1912 • Dwan Allan • USA
GOOD LUCK see **SPORTING LOVER, THE** • 1926
GOOD LUCK HORSESHOE, THE see **PODKOVA PRO STESTI** • 1946
GOOD LUCK IN OLD CLOTHES • 1918 • *Ebony* • SHT • USA
GOOD LUCK, MISS WYCKOFF • 1979 • Chomsky Marvin • USA • SIN, THE ○ SHAMING, THE
GOOD LUCK, MR. YATES • 1943 • Enright Ray • USA • RIGHT GUY
GOOD LUCK OF A "SOUSE", THE see **IL Y A DIEU POUR LES IVROGNES** • 1908
GOOD LUCK TO YOU see **HEROINE DU TRIANGLE D'OR, L'** • 1975
GOOD MAN'S HARD TO FIND, A see **HARD MAN'S GOOD TO FIND, A** • 1969
GOOD MARRIAGE, A (USA) see **BEAU MARIAGE, UN** • 1981
GOOD MEDICINE • 1929 • Pearce A. Leslie • USA
GOOD MEN AND BAD • 1923 • McCormick William Merrill • USA
GOOD MEN AND TRUE • 1922 • Paul Val • USA
GOOD MONDAY MORNING • 1982 • Sky Laura • DOC • CND
GOOD MORNIN' BLUES • 1978 • Lowe Walt • USA
GOOD MORNING • 1968 • Quist-Moller Fleming • ANS • DNM
GOOD MORNING see **OHAYO** • 1959
GOOD MORNING see **SUPROVAT** • 1977
GOOD MORNING AND GOODBYE! • 1967 • Meyer Russ • USA • LUST SEEKERS, THE
GOOD MORNING, BABILONIA • 1986 • Taviani Paolo, Taviani Vittorio • ITL, USA, FRN • GOOD MORNING BABYLON (USA)
GOOD MORNING BABYLON (USA) see **GOOD MORNING, BABILONIA** • 1986
GOOD MORNING BILL see **GOMORRON BILL!** • 1945
GOOD MORNING, BOYS • 1937 • Varnel Marcel • UKN • WHERE THERE'S A WILL (USA)
GOOD MORNING, DOCTOR (UKN) see **YOU BELONG TO ME** • 1941
GOOD MORNING, EVE! • 1934 • Mack Roy • SHT • USA
GOOD MORNING, HYACINTH AND JUNCTION • Burckhardt Rudy • SHT • USA
GOOD MORNING, JUDGE • 1913 • *Thanhouser* • USA
GOOD MORNING, JUDGE • 1916 • Ford Francis • SHT • USA
GOOD MORNING, JUDGE • 1922 • Roach Hal • SHT • USA
GOOD MORNING, JUDGE • 1928 • Seiter William A. • USA • BE YOURSELF
GOOD MORNING, JUDGE • 1943 • Yarbrough Jean • USA
GOOD MORNING, LITTLE COUNTESS see **BUENOS DIAS CONDESITA** • 1967
GOOD MORNING MADAM • 1925 • Bacon Lloyd • SHT • USA
GOOD MORNING, MISS DOVE • 1955 • Koster Henry • USA
GOOD MORNING NURSE • 1917 • Curtis Allen • SHT • USA
GOOD MORNING NURSE • 1920 • *Ovey George* • USA
GOOD MORNING, NURSE! • 1925 • *Sennett Mack (P)* • SHT • USA
GOOD MORNING PARIS see **BONJOUR PARIS** • 1953
GOOD MORNING POLAND • 1969 • Ford Aleksander • DOC • PLN
GOOD MORNING, TAIPEI see **TSAO'AN, T'AI-PEI** • 1979
GOOD MORNING TALES see **BUNA DIMINEATA POVESTE** • 1969
GOOD MORNING TEACHER see **GOOD MORNING TITSER** • 1968
GOOD MORNING TITSER • 1968 • Villaflor Romy • PHL • GOOD MORNING TEACHER
GOOD MORNING, VIETNAM • 1987 • Levinson Barry • USA
GOOD MOTHER, THE • 1988 • Nimoy Leonard • USA • PRICE OF PASSION, THE
GOOD MOTHERS see **MODREHJAELPEN** • 1942
GOOD MOUSE KEEPING • 1952 • Davis Mannie • ANS • USA
GOOD NATURED MAN, A • 1911 • *Yankee* • USA
GOOD NEIGHBOR NUDNIK • 1966 • Deitch Gene • ANS • USA
GOOD NEIGHBOR SAM • 1964 • Swift David • USA
GOOD NEIGHBOUR, THE see **KEDVES SZOMSZED, A** • 1979
GOOD NEIGHBOURS • Swingler Humphrey • UKN
GOOD NEWS • 1930 • Grinde Nick, MacGregor Edgar J. • USA
GOOD NEWS • 1947 • Walters Charles • USA
GOOD NEWS, BAD NEWS • 1974 • Leiterman Richard • DOC • CND
GOOD NEWS FOR JONES • 1911 • Aylott Dave? • UKN
GOOD NIGHT • 1898 • *Mutoscope & Biograph* • UKN
GOOD NIGHT • 1898 • Norton C. Goodwin • UKN
GOOD NIGHT ALIENS! • 1967 • Okamoto Tadashige • ANS • JPN
GOOD NIGHT, DARLING see **SLEEPLESS NIGHTS** • 1932
GOOD NIGHT ELMER • 1940 • Jones Charles M. • ANS • USA
GOOD NIGHT JUDGE • 1919 • *Depp Harry* • USA
GOOD NIGHT, NURSE • 1913 • *Mason Billy* • USA
GOOD NIGHT NURSE • 1918 • Arbuckle Roscoe • SHT • USA
GOOD NIGHT NURSE • 1920 • *Howell Alice* • SHT • USA
GOOD NIGHT, PAUL • 1918 • Edwards Walter • USA • GOODNIGHT PAUL
GOOD NIGHT, RUSTY • 1943 • Pal George • ANS • USA
GOOD NIGHT SOCRATES • 1962 • Hagmann Stuart • USA
GOOD NIGHT, TURK! • 1919 • Davis James • SHT • USA
GOOD NOOSE • 1962 • McKimson Robert • ANS • USA
GOOD OLD DAYS, THE • 1932 • De Mond Albert • SHT • USA
GOOD OLD DAYS, THE • 1939 • Neill R. William • UKN
GOOD OLD IRISH TUNES • 1941 • Rasinski Connie • ANS • USA
GOOD OLD SCHOOL DAYS (UKN) see **THOSE WERE THE DAYS** • 1940
GOOD OLD SCHOOLDAYS • 1930 • Foster John, Davis Mannie • ANS • USA
GOOD OLD SIWASH see **THOSE WERE THE DAYS** • 1940
GOOD OLD SOAK, THE • 1937 • Ruben J. Walter • USA • OLD SOAK, THE
GOOD OLD SUMMER TIME, THE • 1913 • *Brennan John E.* • USA
GOOD OLE COUNTRY MUSIC • 1956 • Pintoff Ernest • ANS • USA
GOOD OUT OF EVIL • 1915 • *Santa Barbara* • USA
GOOD PALS • 1914 • *Risser Marguerite* • USA
GOOD PALS • 1916 • *Pathe* • SHT • USA
GOOD PROVIDER, THE • 1922 • Borzage Frank • USA
GOOD PULL-UP, A • 1953 • Chaffey Don • UKN
GOOD QUEEN BESS • 1913 • Booth W. R.? • UKN
GOOD REFERENCES • 1920 • Neill R. William • USA
GOOD RESOLUTIONS • 1913 • Duncan William • USA
GOOD RIDDANCE • 1923 • Jeske George • SHT • USA
GOOD RIDDANCE see **SZABAD LELEGZET** • 1973
GOOD RIDDANCE (USA) see **BONS DEBARRAS, LES** • 1980
GOOD SAM • 1948 • McCarey Leo • USA
GOOD SAMARITAN, THE • 1903 • *Gaumont* • UKN
GOOD SAMARITAN, THE • 1913 • *Searchlight* • UKN
GOOD SCOUT • 1934 • *Iwerks Ub (P)* • ANS • USA
GOOD SCOUT BUSTER • 1928 • Newfield Sam • SHT • USA
GOOD SCOUTS • 1938 • King Jack • ANS • USA
GOOD SEA see **DOBRO MORJE** • 1958
GOOD SELL, A • 1912 • *Cosmoplitan* • UKN
GOOD SHEPHERD, THE • 1947 • Binney Josh • USA
GOOD SHEPHERDESS AND THE EVIL PRINCESS, THE see **BONNE BERGERE ET LA MECHANTE PRINCESSE, LA** • 1908
GOOD SHIP ROCK 'N RYE, THE • 1919 • Fishback Fred C. • SHT • USA
GOOD SKATE, A • 1916 • *Jockey* • USA
GOOD SNOOZE TONIGHT • 1963 • Kneitel Seymour • ANS • USA
GOOD SNUFF • 1912 • *Powers* • USA
GOOD SOLDIER, THE • 1981 • Billington Kevin • TVM • UKN
GOOD SOLDIER, THE see **BUON SOLDATO, IL** • 1982
GOOD SOLDIER SCHWEIK see **DOBRY VOJAK SVEJK** • 1926
GOOD SOLDIER SCHWEIK see **DOBRY VOJAK SVEJK** • 1931
GOOD SOLDIER SCHWEIK, THE see **OSUDY DOBREHO VOYAKA SVEJKA** • 1954
GOOD SOLDIER SCHWEIK, THE (USA) see **DOBRY VOJAK SVEIK** • 1929
GOOD SOLDIER SCHWEIK, THE (USA) see **BRAVE SOLDAT SCHWEJK, DER** • 1960
GOOD SOLDIER SCHWEIK PARTS I & 2, THE see **DOBRY VOJAK SVEJK** • 1957
GOOD SPIRITS • 1925 • Mayo Archie • SHT • USA
GOOD SPORT • 1931 • MacKenna Kenneth • USA
GOOD SPORT, A • 1913 • Williams C. Jay • USA
GOOD SPORT, A • 1984 • Antonio Lou • TVM • USA
GOOD STENOGRAPHER, THE • 1916 • *Myers Harry* • SHT • USA
GOOD STORIES • 1899 • Smith G. A. • UKN
GOOD STORY, A • 1901 • Smith G. A. • UKN
GOOD, THE BAD AND THE ANGEL, THE • 1969 • Lopez John • SHT • USA
GOOD, THE BAD AND THE BEAUTIFUL, THE • 1970 • Canton Robert • USA • CANDIDATE, THE
GOOD, THE BAD AND THE UGLY, THE (UKN) see **BUONO, IL BRUTO, IL CATTIVO** • 1967
GOOD THING GOING, A • 1979 • Nicholson Arch • TVM • ASL
GOOD TIME, A BAD GIRL, A see **GOOD TIME WITH A BAD GIRL, A** • 1967
GOOD TIME CHARLEY • 1927 • Curtiz Michael • USA
GOOD TIME FOR A DIME, A • 1941 • Lundy Dick • ANS • USA
GOOD TIME GIRL • 1948 • MacDonald David • UKN
GOOD TIME HENRY • 1934 • Horne James W. • SHT • USA
GOOD TIME SPOILED, A • 1914 • *Melies* • USA
GOOD TIME WITH A BAD GIRL, A • 1967 • *Mahon Barry* • USA • GOOD TIME, A BAD GIRL, A
GOOD TIMES • 1967 • Friedkin William • USA
GOOD TIMES AT THE RAINBOW BAR AND GRILL • 1986 • Bond Timothy • TVM • CND
GOOD TIMES, BAD TIMES • 1969 • Shebib Donald • DOC • CND
GOOD TIMES TWO • 1969 • Ryan Michael G. • DOC • NZL
GOOD TIMES, WONDERFUL TIMES • 1966 • Rogosin Lionel • USA, UKN
GOOD TO GO • 1986 • Novak Blaine • USA • SHORT FUSE
GOOD TONIC, A • 1912 • Wilson Frank? • UKN
GOOD TREE, A • 1984 • Walker Giles • MTV • CND
GOOD TRICK, A (USA) see **CHEVALIER DEMONTABLE ET LE GENERAL BOUM, LE** • 1901
GOOD TURN, A • 1911 • Salter Harry • USA
GOOD WIFE, THE (UKN) see **UMBRELLA WOMAN, THE** • 1986
GOOD WILL TO MEN • 1955 • Hanna William, Barbera Joseph • ANS • USA
GOOD WITHIN, THE • 1913 • Sullivan Frederick • USA
GOOD WOMAN, A • 1920 • Reicher Frank • USA
GOOD WOMAN, A see **LIANGJIA FUNU** • 1985
GOOD WOMAN, THE • 1916 • Mong William V. • SHT • USA
GOOD WOMEN • 1921 • Gasnier Louis J. • USA
GOODBYE • 1918 • Elvey Maurice • UKN
GOODBYE • 1949 • Shima Koji • JPN
GOODBYE • 1971 • Kanai Katsu • JPN
GOODBYE 1918 • 1918 • *Moore Mona* • SHT • UKN
GOODBYE AGAIN • 1933 • Curtiz Michael • USA
GOODBYE AGAIN • 1961 • Litvak Anatole • USA, FRN • AIMEZ-VOUS BRAHMS?
GOODBYE AGAIN see **OTRA VEZ ADIOS** • 1981
GOODBYE ALICIA see **ADIOS ALICIA** • 1977
GOODBYE & AMEN • 1978 • Damiani Damiano • ITL • UOMO DELLA C.I.A., THE ○ GOODBYE AND AMEN
GOODBYE AND AMEN see **GOODBYE & AMEN** • 1978
GOODBYE AND GOOD DAY! see **SAYONARA KONNICHIWA** • 1959
GOODBYE AND THANK YOU see **SALUUT EN DE KOST** • 1974
GOODBYE BILL • 1918 • Emerson John • USA
GOODBYE, BOYS see **DO SVIDANIYA, MALCHIKI** • 1965
GOODBYE, BROADWAY • 1938 • McCarey Ray • USA
GOODBYE, BRUCE LEE • 1975 • Lin Ping, Swartz Harold B. • HKG • GOOD BYE BRUCE LEE: HIS LAST GAME OF DEATH ○ HIS LAST GAME OF DEATH ○ LEGEND OF BRUCE LEE, THE
GOODBYE CHARLIE • 1964 • Minnelli Vincente • USA
GOODBYE, COLUMBUS • 1969 • Peerce Larry • USA
GOODBYE CRUEL WORLD • 1982 • Irving David • USA • UP THE WORLD
GOODBYE, DARLING see **TSAI-CHIEN, A-LANG** • 1970
GOODBYE DAVID see **ADIOS DAVID** • 1978
GOODBYE DOVES! see **PROSHCHAYTE, GOLUBI!** • 1961
GOODBYE EMMANUELLE • 1977 • Leterrier Francois • FRN
GOODBYE, FAREWELL • 1986 • Manttari Anssi • FNL
GOODBYE, FLICKMANIA! • 1979 • Harada Masato • JPN
GOODBYE, FRANKLIN HIGH • 1978 • MacFarland Mike • USA
GOODBYE, FRIENDS see **ISTEN VELETEK, BARATAINK** • 1987
GOODBYE GEMINI • 1970 • Gibson Alan • UKN
GOODBYE GIRL, THE • 1977 • Ross Herbert • USA
GOODBYE, GOOD DAY see **SAYONARA KONNICHIWA** • 1959
GOODBYE GRANADA! see **GRANADA ADDIO!** • 1968
GOODBYE IN THE MIRROR • 1965 • De Hirsch Storm • USA
GOODBYE KISS, THE • 1928 • Sennett Mack • USA • ROMANCE OF A BATHING GIRL, THE
GOODBYE LEGS • 1930 • Sennett Mack • SHT • USA
GOODBYE LITTLE GIRL see **ADIOS MUNECA** • 1987
GOODBYE LITTLE SISTER • 1908 • Gilbert Arthur • UKN
GOODBYE LOVE • 1933 • Humberstone H. Bruce • USA
GOODBYE, MISS TURLOCK • 1948 • Cahn Edward L. • SHT • USA
GOODBYE, MR. CHIPS • 1939 • Wood Sam • USA
GOODBYE, MR. CHIPS • 1969 • Ross Herbert • UKN
GOODBYE, MR. MOTH • 1942 • Lantz Walter • ANS • USA
GOODBYE MOSCOW see **SARABA MOSUKUWA GURENTAI** • 1968
GOODBYE MY DARLING see **SAYONARA MY DARLING** • 1968
GOODBYE, MY FANCY • 1951 • Sherman Vincent • USA
GOODBYE MY GIRL see **SHOJO-YO SAYONARA** • 1933
GOODBYE, MY LADY • 1956 • Wellman William A. • USA • BOY AND THE LAUGHING DOG, THE
GOODBYE MY LADY LOVE • 1924 • Fleischer Dave • ANS • USA
GOODBYE MY LADY LOVE • 1929 • Fleischer Dave • ANS • USA
GOODBYE MY LOVELY see **ADIOS PEQUENA** • 1985
GOODBYE, MY TEACHER see **LAO-SHIH, SZU-TI-YEH-K'A** • 1982
GOODBYE NEW YORK • 1984 • Kollek Amos • ISR, USA
GOODBYE, NORMA JEAN • 1976 • Buchanan Larry • ASL, USA
GOODBYE OPHELIA see **SBOHEM OFELIE** • 1980
GOODBYE PARADISE • 1982 • Schultz Carl • ASL
GOODBYE PEOPLE, THE • 1984 • Gardner Herb • USA
GOODBYE PORK PIE • 1981 • Murphy Geoff • NZL
GOODBYE, RAGGEDY ANN • 1971 • Cook Fielder • TVM • USA
GOODBYE SOLIDARITY see **ADJO SOLIDARITET** • 1984
GOODBYE SOUSA • 1973 • Ianzelo Tony • DOC • CND
GOODBYE STEAM see **ZEGNAJ PARO** • 1973
GOODBYE STORK see **ADIOS, CIGUENA, ADIOS** • 1970
GOODBYE, SUMMER • 1914 • Brooke Van Dyke • USA
GOODBYE SWEET MARIE • 1906 • Gilbert Arthur • UKN
GOODBYE TEHRAN see **KHODAHAFEZ TEHRAN** • 1967
GOODBYE TO ALL THAT • 1930 • Jeffrey R. E. • UKN
GOODBYE TO GLORY see **KONPEKI NO SORA TOKU** • 1960
GOODBYE TO THE DEVIL see **POZEGNANIE Z DIABLEM** • 1956
GOODBYE TO THE HILL see **PADDY** • 1969
GOODBYE TO THE PAST see **ROZSTANIE** • 1960
GOODDAY CAPTAIN see **CZESC KAPITANIE** • 1968

GOODE KNIGHT • 1934 • Stallings George • ANS • USA
GOODFELLOW'S CHRISTMAS EVE, A • 1911 • *Essanay* • USA
GOODHEART see **FAITH HEALER, THE** • 1921
GOODIE-GOODIE JONES • 1912 • *Selig* • USA
GOODIE THE GREMLIN • 1961 • Kneitel Seymour • ANS • USA
GOODIE'S GOOD DEED • 1963 • Kneitel Seymour • ANS • USA
GOODNESS! A GHOST • 1940 • D'Arcy Harry • SHT • USA
GOODNESS GRACIOUS OR MOVIES AS THEY SHOULDN'T BE • 1914 • Young James • USA
GOODNIGHT • 1907 • *Gaumont* • UKN
GOODNIGHT, CHILDREN • 1968 • Zilnik Zelimir • SHT • YGS
GOODNIGHT DARLING see **WELTERUSTEN SCHAT** • 1987
GOODNIGHT, GOD BLESS see **LUCIFER** • 1987
GOODNIGHT, MY LOVE • 1972 • Hyams Peter • TVM • USA
GOODNIGHT, NURSE • 1916 • Davey Horace • SHT • USA
GOODNIGHT PAUL see **GOOD NIGHT, PAUL** • 1918
GOODNIGHT, SWEET MARILYN • 1988 • Buchanan Larry • USA
GOODNIGHT SWEET NUDNIK • 1967 • Deitch Gene • ANS • USA
GOODNIGHT SWEETHEART • 1944 • Santley Joseph • USA
GOODNIGHT VIENNA • 1932 • Wilcox Herbert • UKN • MAGIC NIGHT (USA)
GOODRICH DIRT • 1915 • Carlson Wallace A. • SHS • USA
GOODTIME OUTLAWS, THE see **SMOKEY AND THE GOODTIME OUTLAWS** • 1978
GOODWILL TO ALL DOGS • 1960 • Halas John • ANS • UKN
GOODWIN SANDS, THE • 1948 • Hayward Rudall C. • UKN
GOODWIN SANDS, THE see **LADY FROM THE SEA, THE** • 1929
GOODY-GOODY JONES • 1912 • *Selig* • USA
GOOF BALLS see **GOOFBALLS** • 1987
GOOF ON THE ROOF • 1953 • White Jules • SHT • USA
GOOFBALLS • 1987 • Turner Brad • USA • GOOF BALLS
GOOFER TROUBLE • 1940 • Elvey Maurice • UKN
GOOFS AND SADDLES • 1937 • Lord Del • SHT • USA
GOOFY • 1932-53 • *Disney Walt (P)* • ASS • USA
GOOFY AGE, THE • 1924 • Roach Hal • SHT • USA
GOOFY AND WILBUR • 1939 • Huemer Dick • ANS • USA
GOOFY GAB • Baker Eddie • USA
GOOFY GARDENER • 1957 • Lovy Alex • ANS • USA
GOOFY GHOSTS • 1928 • Beaudine William • SHT • USA
GOOFY GOAT • 1931 • Esbaugh Ted • ANS • USA
GOOFY GONDOLAS • 1934 • *Mintz Charles (P)* • ANS • USA
GOOFY GOOFY GANDER • 1950 • Tytla Bill • ANS • USA
GOOFY GOPHERS • 1947 • Davis Arthur, Clampett Robert • ANS • USA
GOOFY GROCERIES • 1941 • Clampett Robert • ANS • USA
GOOFY GYMNASTICS • 1949 • Kinney Jack • ANS • USA
GOOFY MOVIES NOS.1-10 • 1934 • Smith Pete • SHS • USA
GOOFY NEWS VIEWS • 1945 • Marcus Sid • ANS • USA
GOOFY'S FREEWAY TROUBLE • 1965 • Clark Les • ANS • USA • FREEWAYPHOBIA NO.2
GOOFY'S GLIDER • 1940 • Kinney Jack • ANS • USA
GOOFYTONE NEWSREEL NO.1 • 1933 • Gullette George • SHT • USA
GOOFYTONE NEWSREEL NO.2 • 1933 • Gullette George • SHT • USA
GOOFYTONE NEWSREEL NO.3 • 1933 • Malkames Don • SHT • USA
GOOFYTONE NEWSREEL NO.4 • 1933 • Malkames Don • SHT • USA
GOOFYTONE NEWSREEL NO.5 • 1934 • Malkames Don • SHT • USA
GOOFYTONE NEWSREEL NO.6 • 1934 • Malkames Don • SHT • USA
GOOFYTONE NEWSREEL NO.7 • 1934 • Herrick F. Herrick • SHT • USA
GOOGOLPLEX • 1972 • Schwartz Lillian, Knowlton Kenneth • ANS • USA
GOON SHOW MOVIE, THE see **DOWN AMONG THE Z MEN** • 1952
GOON SONG, THE • 1966 • Bell Carl • ANS • USA
GOONA-GOONA • 1932 • *Roosevelt Andre/ Denis Armand (P)* • FRN
GOONEY GOLFERS • 1948 • Davis Mannie • ANS • USA
GOONEY IS BORN, A • 1971 • Smith Paul J. • ANS • USA
GOONEY'S GOOFY LANDING • 1970 • Smith Paul J. • ANS • USA
GOONIES, THE • 1985 • Donner Richard • USA
GOONLAND • 1938 • Fleischer Dave • ANS • USA
GOONS FROM THE MOON see **MIGHTY MOUSE IN GOONS FROM THE MOON** • 1951
GOOPI GYNE O BAGHI BYNE • 1969 • Ray Satyajit • IND • ADVENTURES OF GOOPI AND BAGHI, THE ○ GOOPY GYNE BAGHA BYNE ○ GOOPY AND BAGHA
GOOPY AND BAGHA see **GOOPI GYNE O BAGHI BYNE** • 1969
GOOPY BAGHA PHIRE ELO • 1990 • Ray Sandip • IND • RETURN OF GOOPY AND BAGHA, THE
GOOPY GEAR • 1931-32 • Ising Rudolf • ANS • USA
GOOPY GYNE BAGHA BYNE see **GOOPI GYNE O BAGHI BYNE** • 1969
GOOSE AND STUFFING • 1926 • Miller Frank • UKN
GOOSE AND THE GANDER, THE • 1935 • Green Alfred E. • USA
GOOSE BOXER, THE • Dai Shifu • HKG
GOOSE BOY, THE • 1951 • Ranody Laszlo, Nadasdy Kalman • HNG
GOOSE FLESH • 1927 • Taurog Norman • SHT • USA
GOOSE FLESH • 1981 • Murphy Maurice • ASL
GOOSE FLIES HIGH • 1938 • Foster John • ANS • USA
GOOSE GIRL, THE • 1911 • *Yankee* • USA
GOOSE GIRL, THE • 1915 • Thompson Frederick A., De Mille Cecil B. • USA
GOOSE GIRL, THE (USA) see **GANSEMAGD, DIE** • 1958
GOOSE GOES SOUTH, THE • 1941 • Hanna William, Barbera Joseph • ANS • USA
GOOSE HANGS HIGH, THE • 1925 • Cruze James • USA
GOOSE IN THE ROUGH • 1963 • Smith Paul J. • ANS • USA
GOOSE IS WILD, THE • 1963 • Smith Paul J. • ANS • USA
GOOSE STEP • 1939 • Newfield Sam • USA • HITLER -BEAST OF BERLIN (UKN) ○ BEASTS OF BERLIN
GOOSE STEPS OUT, THE • 1942 • Hay Will, Dearden Basil • UKN
GOOSE WOMAN, THE • 1925 • Brown Clarence • USA
GOOSE WOMAN, THE see **PAST OF MARY HOLMES, THE** • 1933
GOOSEBERRY PIE • 1943 • Pal George • ANS • USA
GOOSECREEK CLAIM, THE • 1911 • *Revier* • USA
GOOSELAND • 1926 • Cline Eddie • SHT • USA
GOPAK • 1931 • Chekanovsky • SHT • USS
GOPAL KRISHNA • 1928 • *Prabhat* • IND
GOPAL KRISHNA • 1938 • Damle V., Fatehlal S. • IND
GOPANNA THE HERDSMAN see **GOVALU GOPANNA** • 1968
GOPHER, THE • 1915 • Worthington William • USA
GOPHER, THE see **TOPO, EL** • 1971
GOPHER BROKE • 1958 • McKimson Robert • ANS • USA
GOPHER BROKE • 1969 • Smith Paul J. • ANS • USA
GOPHER GOOFY • 1942 • McCabe Norman • ANS • USA
GOPHER SPINACH • 1954 • Kneitel Seymour • ANS • USA
GOPHER TROUBLE • 1936 • Lantz Walter • ANS • USA
GOPINATH • 1948 • *Kapoor Raj* • IND
GOPINCHAND JASOOS • 1982 • *Kapoor Raj* • IND
GOR • 1987 • Kiersch Fritz • ITL
GORA • 1964 • Slesicki Wladyslaw • DOC • PLN • MOUNTAIN, THE ○ HILL, THE
GORA ZWANA KUBA • 1967 • Kidawa Janusz • DOC • PLN • HILL CALLED KUBA, THE
GORACA LINIA • 1965 • Jakubowska Wanda • PLN • HOT LINE, THE
GORACZKA • 1980 • Holland Agnieszka • PLN • FEVER
GORAKHNATH • 1951 • Irani Aspi • IND • MAYA MACHINDRA
GORANSSON'S BOY see **GORANSSONS POJKE** • 1941
GORANSSONS POJKE • 1941 • Hildebrand Weyler • SWD • GORANSSON'S BOY
GORATH see **YOSEI GORASU** • 1962
GORBALS STORY, THE • 1950 • MacKane David • UKN
GORD S. • 1978 • Zaritsky John • MTV • CND
GORDA ADORG • 1964-65 • Branaman Bob • USA
GORDEYEV FAMILY, THE (USA) see **FOMA GORDEEV** • 1959
GORDIAN, DER TYRANN • 1937 • Sauer Fred • FRG
GORDIAN KNOT, THE • 1911 • Baker R. E. • USA
GORDO AL AGUA • 1970 • *Zacarias* • MXC
GORDO DE NAVIDAD, EL • 1929 • Delgado Fernando • SPN
GORDON FREEMAN, NOVELTY ENTERTAINER • 1929 • *B.s.f.p.* • SHT • USA
GORDON HIGHLANDERS LEAVING FOR THE BOER WAR • 1899 • Paul Robert William • UKN
GORDON, IL PIRATO NERO • 1961 • Costa Mario • ITL • RAGE OF THE BUCCANEERS ○ GORDON THE BLACK PIRATE ○ BLACK PIRATE, THE ○ BLACK BUCCANEER, THE
GORDON JACOB • 1959 • Russell Ken • MTV • UKN
GORDON OF GHOST CITY • 1933 • Taylor Ray • SRL • USA
GORDON SISTERS BOXING • 1901 • Porter Edwin S. • USA
GORDON THE BLACK PIRATE see **GORDON, IL PIRATO NERO** • 1961
GORDON'S WAR • 1973 • Davis Ossie • USA
GORDOS E MAGROS • 1980 • Carneiro Mario • BRZ • FATS AND THINS
GORDURAS ALIMENTARES • 1954 • Mendes Joao • SHT • PRT
GORE-GORE GIRLS, THE • 1972 • Lewis Herschell G. • USA • BLOOD ORGY
GORE SARRI • 1913 • Arkatov Alexander • USS • SORROWS OF SARAH
GORE VIDAL'S BILLY THE KID see **BILLY THE KID** • 1988
GORE VIDAL'S LINCOLN • 1988 • Johnson Lamont • TVM • USA • LINCOLN
GORECHTO PLADNE • 1965 • Heskiya Zako • BUL • TORRID NOON ○ HOT NOON ○ HIGH NOON
GORGE BETWEEN LOVE AND HATE see **AIZO TOGE** • 1934
GORGE BETWEEN LOVE AND HATE see **AIENKYO** • 1937
GORGE OF FORGOTTEN STORIES, THE • 1975 • Keosayan Edmond • USS
GORGEOUS BIRD LIKE ME, A (UKN) see **BELLE FILLE COMME MOI, UNE** • 1972
GORGEOUS GEISHA, THE see **NIKUTAI NO SEISO** • 1964
GORGEOUS HUSSY, THE • 1936 • Brown Clarence • USA
GORGHI NEL FIUME see **STRADA FINISCE SUL FIUME, LA** • 1950
GORGO • 1961 • Lourie Eugene • UKN • NIGHT THE WORLD SHOOK, THE
GORGO, IL • 1918 • Ghione Emilio • ITL
GORGO VERSUS GODZILLA • 1962-69 • Carpenter John • SHT • USA
GORGON, THE • 1964 • Fisher Terence • UKN
GORGON CASE, THE see **SPRAWA GORGONIOWEJ** • 1977
GORGON, THE SPACE MONSTER • 1962-69 • Carpenter John • SHT • USA
GORGONA, LA • 1914 • Caserini Mario • ITL
GORGONA, LA • 1942 • Brignone Guido • ITL
GORGONES KE MANGES • 1968 • Dalianidis Ioannis • GRC • MERMAIDS AND WITCHES ○ MERMAIDS FOR LOVE
GORGONIOVA CASE see **SPRAWA GORGONIOWEJ** • 1977
GORGOPOTAMOS, O • 1968 • Maheras Ilias • GRC • RIVER, THE
GORILLA • 1955 • Romero George A. • SHT • USA
GORILLA • 1956 • Ottoson Lars Henrik, Nykvist Sven • SWD
GORILLA see **NABONGA** • 1944
GORILLA, THE • 1927 • Santell Alfred • USA
GORILLA, THE • 1930 • Foy Bryan • USA
GORILLA, THE • 1939 • Dwan Allan • USA
GORILLA AT LARGE • 1954 • Jones Harmon • USA
GORILLA HUNT, THE • 1926 • *Brubridge Ben* • DOC • USA • BURBRIDGE'S AFRICAN GORILLA HUNT
GORILLA HUNT, THE • 1939 • Iwerks Ub • ANS • USA
GORILLA MAN, THE • 1943 • Lederman D. Ross • USA
GORILLA MY DREAMS • 1948 • McKimson Robert • ANS • USA
GORILLA MYSTERY, THE • 1930 • Gillett Burt • ANS • USA
GORILLA OF SOHO, THE see **GORILLA VON SOHO, DER** • 1968
GORILLA SALUTES YOU, THE see **GORILLE VOUS SALUE BIEN, LE** • 1957
GORILLA SHIP • 1932 • Strayer Frank • USA
GORILLA STORY, THE • Hilton Arthur • USA
GORILLA VON SOHO, DER • 1968 • Vohrer Alfred • FRG • GORILLA OF SOHO, THE
GORILLA'S DANCE (USA) see **PLES GORILLA** • 1968
GORILLAS IN THE MIST • 1988 • Apted Michael • USA
GORILLE A MORDU L'ARCHEVEQUE, LE • 1962 • Labro Maurice • FRN • DEADLY DECOY, THE (USA) ○ BITE OF THE GORILLA, THE
GORILLE VOUS SALUE BIEN, LE • 1957 • Borderie Bernard • FRN • GORILLA SALUTES YOU, THE
GORILLES, LES • 1964 • Girault Jean • FRN
GORINE • 1971 • Ifticene Mohamed • ALG
GORIZONT • 1933 • Kuleshov Lev • USS • HORIZON -THE WANDERING JEW ○ HORIZON
GORIZONT • 1961 • Heifitz Josif • USS • HORIZON
GORJACE D ENEKI • 1935 • Heifitz Josif, Zarkhi Alexander • USS • RED ARMY DAYS ○ THOSE WERE THE DAYS! ○ HECTIC DAYS
GORKE TRAVE • 1965 • Mitrovic Zika • YGS, FRG • BITTEREKRAUTER (FRG) ○ BITTER GRASS, THE ○ BITTER HERBS
GORKIYE ZYORNA • 1967 • Gagiu Valeriu, Lysenko Vadim • USS • BITTER GRAINS ○ BITTER GRAIN
GORKY PARK • 1983 • Apted Michael • USA
GORKY TRILOGY, THE see **TRILOGIYA O GORKOM** • 1938-40
GORKY'S CHILDHOOD see **DETSTVO GORKOVO** • 1938
GORNO MARIONETTES, THE • 1928 • *Bsfp* • SHT • UKN • CAMERA COCKTALES NO.2
GOROD BOLSHOY SUDBY • 1961 • Kopalin Ilya • USS • MOSCOW STORY
GOROD PROSYPAYETSYA RANO • 1968 • Dolidze Siko • USS • CITY AWAKENS EARLY, THE
GOROD ZAZHIGAET OGNI • 1958 • Vengerov Vladimir • USS • LIGHTS GO ON IN THE CITY, THE
GOROD ZERO • 1989 • Shakhnazarov Karen • USS • ZERO CITY (UKN)
GORODA I GODY • 1973 • Zarkhi Alexander • USS • TOWNS AND YEARS ○ CITIES AND TIMES
GORODOK ANARA • 1976 • Kvirikadze Irakli • USS • ANARA QUARTER
GOROTSUKI • 1968 • Makino Masahiro • JPN • KICK-BOXER
GOROTSUKI INO • 1964 • Murano Tetsutaro • JPN • DEDICATED GUNMAN, THE
GORP • 1980 • Ruben Joseph • USA
GORUNMIYEN ADAM ISTANBULDA • 1956 • Akat Lutfu • TRK • INVISIBLE MAN IN ISTANBUL
GORY CREATURES, THE see **TERROR IS A MAN** • 1959
GORY HALLOWEEN, A • 1980 • Larry Sheldon • MTV • USA
GORY MURDER, THE • 1982 • HKG
GORY O ZMIERZCHU • 1970 • Zanussi Krzysztof • MTV • PLN • MOUNTAINS AT DUSK ○ HILLS AT DUSK
GORYACHI SNYEG • 1973 • Yegiazarov G. • USS • HOT SNOW
GORYCZ • 1962 • Wajzer Waclaw • ANS • PLN • BITTERNESS
GOSH • 1974 • Scheuer Tom • USA • ALICE GOODBODY
GOSH-DARN MORTGAGE, THE see **THAT GOSH-DARN MORTGAGE** • 1926
GOSKINO JOURNAL see **GOSKINO KALENDAR** • 1923-25
GOSKINO KALENDAR • 1923-25 • Vertov Dziga • SER • USS • GOSKINO JOURNAL
GOSLINGS see **HOUSATA** • 1979
GOSPEL • 1982 • Levick David, Rizenberg Frederick A. • USA
GOSPEL ACCORDING TO ST. MATTHEW, THE (UKN) see **VANGELO SECONDO MATTEO, IL** • 1964
GOSPEL ACCORDING TO VIC, THE (USA) see **HEAVENLY PURSUITS** • 1985
GOSPEL OF SOLENTINAME, THE see **EVANGELIO A SOLENTINAME** • 1979
GOSPEL ROAD, THE • 1973 • Elfstrom Robert • USA
GOSPODA MINISTARKA • 1958 • Skrigin Zorz • YGS
GOSPODA SKOTININY • 1927 • Roshal Grigori • USS • SKOTININS, THE
GOSPODIJICA DOKTOR -SPIJUNKA BEZ IMENA (YGS) see **FRAULEIN DOKTOR** • 1969
GOSSE DE LA BUTTE, UN • 1964 • Delbez Maurice • FRN
GOSSE DE PARIS • 1960 • Martin Marcel • SHT • FRN
GOSSE DE RICHE • 1920 • Hervil Rene, Burguet Charles, Mercanton Louis • FRN
GOSSE DE RICHE • 1938 • de Canonge Maurice • FRN
GOSSE EN OR, UN • 1938 • Pallu Georges • FRN • COEUR DE GOSSE
GOSSE SENSASS', UNE • 1956 • Bibal Robert • FRN
GOSSELINE, LA • 1923 • Feuillade Louis • FRN
GOSSES DE MISERE see **BAGNES D'ENFANTS** • 1933
GOSSES MENENT L'ENQUETE, LES • 1946 • Labro Maurice • FRN • ETRANGE MORT DE MONSIEUR CRAUQUAL, L' ○ CRIMINEL A PEUR DES GOSSES, LE ○ DRAME AU COLLEGE
GOSSETTE • 1922 • Dulac Germaine • FRN
GOSSIP • 1912 • *Powers* • USA
GOSSIP • 1923 • Baggot King • USA
GOSSIP • 1983 • Boyd Don • UKN
GOSSIP, THE • 1911 • Thompson Frederick A. • USA
GOSSIP COLUMNIST, THE • 1980 • Sheldon James • TVM • USA
GOSSIP DUCK, THE see **KACZKA-PLOTKA** • 1954
GOSSIP FROM THE FOREST • 1979 • Gibson Brian • TVM • UKN • GOSSIP FROM THE FRONT
GOSSIP FROM THE FRONT see **GOSSIP FROM THE FOREST** • 1979
GOSSIPER, THE (USA) see **CHRISMOSA, LA** • 1940
GOSSIPERS • 1905 • *Bitzer Billy (Ph)* • USA
GOSSIPING YAPVILLE • 1911 • *Essanay* • USA
GOSSIPY PLUMBER, THE • 1931 • Lamont Charles • SHT • USA
GOST O OSTROVA SVOBODY • 1963 • Karmen Roman • DOC • USS • GUEST FROM THE ISLAND OF FREEDOM, A ○ GUEST ON FREEDOM ISLAND
GOSTA BERLINGS SAGA • 1924 • Stiller Mauritz • SWD • ATONEMENT OF GOSTA BERLING, THE (UKN) ○ LEGEND OF GOSTA BERLING, THE ○ SAGA OF GOSTA BERLING, THE ○ STORY OF GOSTA BERLING, THE

GOSTI IZ GALAKSIJE • 1981 • Vukotic Dusan • YGS, CZC • VISITORS FROM THE ARCANA GALAXY ○ VISITORS FROM THE GALAXY
GOSUDARSTVENNI PRESTUPNIK • 1965 • Rozantsev Nikolai • USS • STATE CRIMINAL
GOT A MATCH? • 1912 • Sennett Mack • USA
GOT A PENNY BENNY • 1946 • Crouch William Forest • SHT • USA
GOT A PENNY STAMP? • 1908 • Stow Percy • UKN
GOT 'EM AGAIN • 1913 • Calvert Charles? • UKN
GOT IT MADE • 1973 • Clarke James Kenelm • UKN • COLORADO STONE ○ SWEET VIRGIN
GOT TO TELL IT: A TRIBUTE TO MAHALIA JACKSON • 1974 • Schwerin Jules • USA • MAHALIA JACKSON
GOTA DE SANGRE, LA • 1949 • Urueta Chano • MXC
GOTA DE SANGRE PARA MORIR AMANDO, UNA • 1973 • de la Iglesia Eloy • SPN
GOTA KANALEN • 1982 • Iveberg Hans • SWD • WHO PULLED THE PLUG?
GOTAMAH, THE BUDDHA • 1956 • Khanna Rajbana • IND
GOTCHA! • 1985 • Kanew Jeff • USA
GOTHAM see **DEAD CAN'T LIE, THE** • 1988
GOTHIC • 1987 • Russell Ken • UKN
GOTO, ISLAND OF LOVE see **GOTO, L'ILE D'AMOUR** • 1968
GOTO, L'ILE D'AMOUR • 1968 • Borowczyk Walerian • FRN • GOTO, ISLAND OF LOVE
GOTT ALLEIN DIE EHRE • 1927 • Peukert Leo • FRG
GOTT, MENSCH UND TEUFEL • *Urbach S.* • FRG
GOTT MIT UNS • 1964 • Di Giammatteo Fernaldo • ITL • DIO E CON NOI
GOTT MIT UNS • 1970 • Montaldo Giuliano • ITL, YGS • FIFTH DAY OF PEACE, THE (USA) ○ DIO E CON NOI ○ CRIME OF DEFEAT
GOTT SCHUTZT DIE LIEBENDEN • 1973 • Vohrer Alfred • FRG
GOTTA RUN! see **AJOLAHTO** • 1981
GOTTER DER PEST • 1969 • Fassbinder R. W. • FRG • GODS OF THE PLAGUE
GOTTER, MENSCHEN UND TIERE • 1925 • von Bolvary Geza • FRG • LIEBE DER BAJADERE, DIE
GOTTER VON TIBET see **LEBENDE BUDDHAS** • 1924
GOTTERDAMMERUNG (FRG) see **CADUTA DEGLI DEI, LA** • 1968
GOTTES ENGEL SIND UBERBALL • 1948 • Thimig Hans • AUS
GOTTES MUHLEN MAHLEN LANGSAM • 1939 • Medeolti J. • MILLS OF THE GODS, THE
GOTTESGEISSEL, DIE • 1919 • Curtiz Michael • AUS
GOTTESGERICHT • 1923 • *Wiking-Film* • FRG
GOTTIN, DIRNE UND WEIB • 1919 • Nootbaar Ernst • FRG
GOTTIN VOM RIO BENE, DIE see **MUNDO EXTRANO** • 1952
GOTTLICHE JETTE, DIE • 1937 • Waschneck Erich • FRG • DIVINE JETTA, THE (USA)
GOTZ VON BERLICHINGEN • 1955 • Stoger Alfred • FRG
GOTZ VON BERLICHINGEN ZUBENANNT MIT DER EISERNEN HAND • 1925 • Moest Hubert • FRG
GOTZENDAMMERUNG • 1920 • Noa Manfred • FRG • OPFER DER KEUSCHHEIT
GOTZENDAMMERUNG • 1922 • Berger Josef • FRG
GOUALEUSE, LA • 1938 • Rivers Fernand • FRN
GOUBBIAH see **GOUBBIAH MON AMOUR** • 1956
GOUBBIAH MON AMOUR • 1956 • Darene Robert • FRN, ITL • FUGA NEL SOLE (ITL) ○ GOUBBIAH ○ MON AMOUR ○ KISS OF FIRE
GOUDEN ILSY, DE • 1957 • van der Linden Charles Huguenot • DOC • NTH • GOLDEN ILSY, THE
GOUDEN VIS, DE • 1951 • Toonder Marten • ANM • NTH • GOLDEN FISH, THE
GOULUES, LES • 1975 • Pierson Claude • FRN
GOULVE, LA • 1971 • Mercier Mario, Fontana Bepi • FRN • EROTIC WITCHCRAFT (UKN) ○ GOLEM'S DAUGHTER ○ HOMO VAMPIRE
GOUMBE DES JEUNES NOCEURS, LA • 1966 • Rouch Jean • DOC • FRN
GOUPI MAINS-ROUGES • 1942 • Becker Jacques • FRN • IT HAPPENED AT THE INN (USA)
GOURD FAIRY, THE • Kuei Chih-Hung • HKG
GOURI • 1968 • Bhimsingh A. • IND
GOURMANDES DE SEXES, LES • 1978 • Love John • FRN
GOURMANDINES, LES • 1973 • Perol Guy • FRN • THREE INTO SEX WON'T GO ○ BIRD IN THE HAND, A
GOUROUSSE • 1956 • Regnier Michel • DCS • IVC
GOUT DE LA FARINE, LE • 1976 • Gosselin Bernard, Perrault Pierre • DOC • CND
GOUT DE LA PAIX, LE • 1974 • Dansereau Fernand, Rossignol Yolande • SHT • CND
GOUT DE LA VIOLENCE, LE • 1960 • Hossein Robert • FRN, FRG, ITL • HAUT FUR HAUT (FRG)
GOUTER DE BEBE, LE • 1896 • Lumiere Louis • FRN • REPAS DE BEBE, LE
GOUTTE DE SANG, LA • 1924 • Epstein Jean, Mariaud Maurice • FRN
GOUTY PATIENT, THE see **MALADE HYDROPHOPE, LE** • 1900
GOUVERNEUR, DER • 1939 • Tourjansky Victor • FRG
GOUVERNEUR DES TODES, DER • 1922 • Justitz Emil • FRG
GOVALU GOPANNA • 1968 • Rao C. S. • IND • GOPANNA THE HERDSMAN
GOVERNANTE, LA • 1974 • Grimaldi Gianni • ITL
GOVERNESS, THE • 1913 • Edwin Walter, Merwin Bannister • USA
GOVERNESS'S LOVE AFFAIR, THE see **NEW GOVERNESS, THE** • 1915
GOVERNMENT AGENTS VS. PHANTOM LEGION • 1951 • Brannon Fred C. • SRL • USA
GOVERNMENT GIRL • 1943 • Nichols Dudley • USA
GOVERNMENT INSPECTOR see **REVISOR** • 1933
GOVERNMENT RATIONS • 1910 • *Bison* • USA
GOVERNMENT TEST, THE • 1912 • *Lubin* • USA
GOVERNOR see **LATT SAHEB** • 1967
GOVERNOR, THE • 1912 • *Fuller Mary* • USA
GOVERNOR, THE • 1913 • Carleton Lloyd B. • USA
GOVERNOR, THE • 1977 • Brakhage Stan • SHT • USA
GOVERNOR BRADFORD • 1938 • Parry Hugh • UKN • GOVERNOR WILLIAM BRADFORD
GOVERNOR MAKER, THE • 1915 • *Clifford William* • USA
GOVERNOR WHO HAD A HEART, THE • 1912 • *Storey Edith* • USA
GOVERNOR WILLIAM BRADFORD see **GOVERNOR BRADFORD** • 1938
GOVERNOR'S BOSS, THE • 1915 • Davenport Charles E. • USA
GOVERNOR'S CLEMENCY, THE • 1912 • *Melies* • USA
GOVERNOR'S DAUGHTER, THE • 1909 • Olcott Sidney • USA
GOVERNOR'S DAUGHTER, THE • 1910 • *Thanhouser* • USA
GOVERNOR'S DAUGHTER, THE • 1912 • *Eclair* • USA
GOVERNOR'S DAUGHTER, THE • 1913 • Parker Lem B. • USA
GOVERNOR'S DAUGHTER, THE see **GUVERNORENS DATTER** • 1912
GOVERNOR'S DAUGHTERS, THE see **LANDSHOVDINGENS DOTTRAR** • 1915
GOVERNOR'S DECISION, THE • 1916 • Brenon Herbert • SHT • USA
GOVERNOR'S DOUBLE, THE • 1913 • Wright Fred E.? • USA
GOVERNOR'S GHOST, THE • 1914 • Davis Will S. • USA
GOVERNOR'S LADY, THE • 1915 • Melford George • USA
GOVERNOR'S LADY, THE • 1923 • Millarde Harry • USA
GOVERNOR'S PARDON, THE • 1910 • Salter Harry • USA
GOVERNOR'S ROMANCE, THE • 1913 • *Pilot* • USA
GOVERNOR'S VETO, THE • 1913 • *Eclair* • USA
GOVERNOR'S WIFE, THE see **NOOSE, THE** • 1928
GOW, THE HEAD HUNTER • 1928 • *Cooper Merian/ Schoedsack Ernest B.(Ph)* • USA
GOWN OF DESTINY, THE • 1918 • Reynolds Lynn • USA
GOWNS AND GIRLS • 1918 • *L-Ko* • SHT • USA
GOWRI • 1943 • *Kapoor Raj* • IND
GOYA • Arcady • SHT • FRN
GOYA • 1950 • Emmer Luciano • ITL • FESTA DI ISIDORA
GOYA • 1971 • Wolf Konrad • GDR, USS, BUL • GOYA ODER DER ARGE WEG ZUR ERKENNTNIS ○ GOYA, OR THE ROAD TO AWARENESS
GOYA • 1974 • Salvia Rafael J. • SPN
GOYA see **GOYA, HISTORIA DE UNA SOLEDAD** • 1970
GOYA, HISTORIA DE UNA SOLEDAD • 1970 • Quevedo Nino • SPN • GOYA
GOYA ODER DER ARGE WEG ZUR ERKENNTNIS see **GOYA** • 1971
GOYA, OR THE ROAD TO AWARENESS see **GOYA** • 1971
GOYESCAS • 1942 • Perojo Benito • SPN
GOYOKIN • 1969 • Gosha Hideo • JPN
GOYOSEN • 1927 • Kinugasa Teinosuke • JPN
GOYOUKIBA: KAMISORI HANZO JIGOKUZEME • 1973 • Masumura Yasuzo • JPN • POLICE FANG: RAZOR HANZO'S TORTURE IN HELL
GOZARESH • 1977 • Kia-Rostami Abbas • IRN • REPORT, THE
GOZASHT-E-BOZORG • 1967 • Amin-E-Amini • IRN • GREAT REMISSION, THE
GOZENCHO NO JIKANWARI • 1972 • Hani Susumu • JPN • MIDMORNING SCHEDULE ○ MORNING SCHEDULE ○ TIMETABLE
GOZYASLARIM • 1968 • Utku Umit • TRK • MY TEARS
GRA • 1968 • Kawalerowicz Jerzy • PLN • GAME, THE ○ PLAY
GRAA DAME, DEN • 1909 • Larsen Viggo • DNM • GRAY DAME, THE
GRAAL, LE see **LANCELOT DU LAC** • 1974
GRAB BAG BRIDE, A • 1917 • Hartman Ferris • USA
GRAB THE GHOST • 1920 • Goulding Alf, Roach Hal • SHT • USA
GRABBARNA I 57:AN • 1935 • Johansson Ivar • SWD • URCHINS IN NO.57
GRABBERS, THE see **SCAVENGERS, THE** • 1969
GRABENPLATZ 17 • 1958 • Engels Erich • FRG
GRABMAL DES UNBEKANNTEN SOLDATEN • 1935 • Oertel Curt • FRG
GRABMAL EINER GROSSEN LIEBE, DAS • 1928 • Osten Franz • FRG
GRABUGE, LE • 1968 • Luntz Edouard • FRN • HUNG UP
GRACE • 1982 • Kardash Virlana • UKN
GRACE A LA MUSIQUE • 1979 • Reichenbach Francois • MTV • FRN
GRACE KELLY • 1983 • Page Anthony • TVM • USA • GRACE KELLY STORY, THE
GRACE KELLY STORY, THE see **GRACE KELLY** • 1983
GRACE MOORE STORY, THE (UKN) see **SO THIS IS LOVE** • 1953
GRACE QUIGLEY • 1985 • Harvey Anthony • USA • ULTIMATE SOLUTION OF GRACE QUIGLEY, THE
GRACE'S GORGEOUS GOWNS • 1916 • *Delaney Bert* • SHT • USA
GRACIAS A DIOS Y LA REVOLUCION • 1981 • Tirado Wolfgang • NCR • THANKS TO GOD AND THE REVOLUTION
GRACIAS A LA VIDA • 1981 • Vasquez Angelina • FNL • THANKS BE TO LIFE
GRACIAS POR EL FUEGO • 1984 • Renan Sergio • ARG • THANKS FOR THE FIRE
GRACIE • 1978 • Barrie Scott • MTV • CND
GRACIE ALLEN MURDER CASE, THE • 1939 • Green Alfred E. • USA
GRACIE AT THE BAT • 1937 • Lord Del • SHT • USA
GRACIELA • 1956 • Torre-Nilsson Leopoldo • ARG
GRACIOUS LIVING see **VIE DE CHATEAU, LA** • 1966
GRAD • 1963 • Pavlovic Zivojin, Krakonjac Kokan • YGS • TOWN, THE
GRAD NIGHT • 1980 • Tenorio John • USA
GRADANIM IM5 • 1962 • Kolar Boris • ANS • YGS • CITIZEN IM5
GRADIVA • 1971 • Albertazzi Giorgio • ITL
GRADOSTROYITELI see **LYUBIT CHELOVYEKA** • 1972
GRADUADA, LA • 1971 • Ozores Mariano • SPN
GRADUATE, THE • 1967 • Nichols Mike • USA
GRADUATE FIRST see **PASSE TON BAC D'ABORD** • 1979
GRADUATE FROM THE COUNTRYSIDE see **HSIANG-HSIA PIYEH-SHENG** • 1976
GRADUATES, THE see **LICEENII** • 1987
GRADUATION see **BALLAGAS** • 1981
GRADUATION, THE see **PROWLER, THE** • 1981
GRADUATION DAY • 1968 • Shebib Donald • CND
GRADUATION DAY • 1981 • Freed Herb • USA
GRADUATION DAY IN BUGLAND • 1931 • Fleischer Dave • ANS • USA
GRADUATION EXERCISES • 1935 • *Mintz Charles (P)* • ANS • USA
GRADUATION PARTY see **FESTA DI LAUREA** • 1985
GRAF CHAGRON • 1924 • Volcker Hansjurgen • FRG • OBERST CHABERT
GRAF COHN • 1923 • Boese Carl • FRG
GRAF DOHNA UND SEINE MOWE • 1917 • *Bild-Und Film-Amt* • FRG
GRAF FESTENBERG • 1922 • Zelnik Friedrich • FRG
GRAF GREIF • 1925 • Wenter Adolf • FRG
GRAF IM PFLUGE, DER • 1922 • Moest Hubert • FRG
GRAF KOSTJA • 1925 • Robert Jacques • FRG
GRAF MICHAEL • 1918 • Halm Alfred • FRG
GRAF MICHAEL • 1923 • Zelnik Friedrich • FRG
GRAF PORNO UND SEINE MADCHEN • 1969 • FRG
GRAF STOCKELS BEKENNTNISSE • 1920 • Larsen Viggo • FRG
GRAF SYLVAINS RACHE • 1919 • Grunwald Willy • FRG
GRAF VON CAGLIOSTRO, DER • 1920 • Schunzel Reinhold • FRG • CAGLIOSTRO (USA) ○ COUNT CAGLIOSTRO
GRAF VON CARABAS, DER • 1935 • Reiniger Lotte • ANM • SWT • PUSS IN BOOTS ○ CARABAS
GRAF VON CHAROLAIS, DER • 1922 • Grune Karl • FRG • COUNT OF CHAROLAIS, THE
GRAF VON ESSEX, DER • 1922 • Felner Peter Paul • FRG
GRAF VON LUXEMBURG, DER • 1957 • Jacobs Werner • FRG
GRAFBEWAKER, DE • 1965 • Kumel Harry • BLG
GRAFEN POCCI -EINIGE KAPITEL ZUR GESCHICHTE EINER FAMILIE, DIE • 1968 • Syberberg Hans-Jurgen • DOC • FRG • POCCI COUNTS -SOME CHAPTERS IN THE HISTORY OF A FAMILY, THE
GRAFFITI • 1969 • *Ava Dist.* • USA
GRAFFITI BLACKBOARD see **RAKUGAKI KOKUBAN** • 1959
GRAFFITI BRIDGE • 1990 • Prince • USA
GRAFIKA CLOVEKU • 1957 • Kosmac France • YGS • OUTLINE OF MAN
GRAFIN DE CASTRO • 1916 • Gartner Adolf • FRG
GRAFIN DONELLI • 1924 • Pabst G. W. • FRG • COUNTESS DONELLI
GRAFIN KUCHENFEE • 1913 • Biebrach Rudolf • FRG
GRAFIN KUCHENFEE • 1917 • Biebrach Rudolf • FRG
GRAFIN LUKANI • 1916 • Burg Eugen • FRG
GRAFIN MARIZA • 1925 • Steinhoff Hans • FRG
GRAFIN MARIZA • 1932 • Oswald Richard • FRG
GRAFIN MARIZA • 1958 • Schundler Rudolf • FRG
GRAFIN MARUSCHKA • 1917 • Portegg R. • FRG
GRAFIN PLATTMAMSELL • 1926 • David Constantin J. • FRG
GRAFIN VON MONTE CHRISTO, DIE • 1919 • May Joe • FRG • COUNTESS OF MONTE CRISTO, THE
GRAFIN VON MONTE CHRISTO, DIE • 1932 • Hartl Karl • FRG • COUNTESS OF MONTE CRISTO, THE
GRAFIN VON NAVARRA, DIE • 1917 • Schmidthassler Walter • FRG
GRAFIN VON PARIS, DIE • 1922 • Buchowetzki Dimitri • FRG
GRAFIN WALEWSKA • 1920 • Rippert Otto • FRG
GRAFT • 1916 • Stanton Richard, Lessey George A. • SRL • USA
GRAFT • 1931 • Cabanne W. Christy • USA • DEAD LINE, THE
GRAFT see **FREEDOM OF THE PRESS** • 1928
GRAFT AND CORRUPTION see **CONFESSION** • 1957
GRAFT VERSUS LOVE • 1915 • *La Badie Florence* • USA
GRAFTERS • 1917 • Rosson Arthur • USA
GRAFTERS, THE • 1913 • Sullivan Frederick • USA
GRAFTING, THE see **PRZEKLADANIEC** • 1968
GRAHAM COUGHTRY IN IBIZA • 1971 • Owen Don • DOC • CND
GRAHAM MURDERS, THE see **BAD BLOOD** • 1980
GRAHAN • Prabhat Manjul • IND
GRAHANA • 1979 • Nagabharana T. S. • IND • ECLIPSE, THE
GRAIL, THE • 1915 • Worthington William • USA
GRAIL, THE • 1923 • Campbell Colin • USA
GRAIL, THE see **LANCELOT DU LAC** • 1974
GRAIN • 1936 • Preobrazhenskaya Olga, Pravov Ivan • USS
GRAIN DE BON SENS, UN • 1955 • *Image Jean (P)* • ANS • FRN
GRAIN DE SABLE, LE • 1964 • Kast Pierre • FRN, ITL, FRG • TRIANGOLO CIRCOLARE, IL (ITL) ○ UNMORALISCHEN, DIE (FRG) ○ CIRCULAR TRIANGLE, THE (USA) ○ TRIANGLE CIRCULAIRE, LE ○ TRIANGLE, LE
GRAIN DE SABLE, LE • 1982 • Meffre Pomme • FRN
GRAIN HANDLING IN CANADA • 1954 • Cote Guy-L. • DCS • CND
GRAIN OF DUST, A • 1915 • Carleton Lloyd B. • USA
GRAIN OF DUST, A • 1918 • Revier Harry • USA
GRAIN OF DUST, THE • 1928 • Archainbaud George • USA
GRAIN OF SAND, A • 1917 • Wilson Frank • UKN
GRAIN OF SUSPICION, A • 1916 • *Myers Harry* • SHT • USA
GRAIN OF THE VOICE • 1980 • Cantrill Arthur, Cantrill Corinne • DOC • ASL
GRAIN OF WHEAT, A see **HITOTSUBU NO MUGI** • 1958
GRAINE AU VENT • 1928 • Keroul Maurice • FRN
GRAINE AU VENT • 1943 • Gleize Maurice • FRN
GRAINE D'OR • 1973 • Bertolino Daniel • DCS • CND
GRAINS DE BEAUTE • 1931 • Caron Pierre • FRN
GRAJSKI BIKI • 1967 • Pogacnik Joze • YGS • STRONGHOLD OF TOUGHS ○ NOISY BULLS
GRAMAFON AVRAT • 1987 • Kurcenli Yusuf • TRK • GRAMOPHONE, THE
GRAMAPHONE SINGER • 1938 • *Biswas Anil (M)* • IND
GRAMBLING'S WHITE TIGER • 1981 • Brown George Stanford • TVM • USA • GRUMBLING WHITE TIGER, THE
GRAMINA'S LOVER see **AMANTE DI GRAMIGNA, L'** • 1968
GRAMMY AWARDS see **BEST ON RECORD, THE** • 1969
GRAMO VON BALET • 1966 • Schorm Evald • MTV • CZC
GRAMOOTVOD • 1962 • Dinov Todor • ANS • BUL • LIGHTNING ROD ○ LIGHTNING CONDUCTOR, THE
GRAMOPHONE, THE see **GRAMAFON AVRAT** • 1987
GRAMPS TO THE RESCUE • 1963 • Kneitel Seymour • ANS • USA
GRAMPY'S INDOOR OUTING • 1936 • Fleischer Dave • ANS • USA
GRAN • 1989 • Repina Nadezhda • USS • ON THE VERGE
GRAN AMOR DE BECQUER • 1946 • de Zavalia Alberto • ARG

GRAN AMOR DE CAPITAN BRANDO,EL see **AMOR DEL CAPITAN BRANDO, EL** • 1974
GRAN AMOR DEL CONDE DRACULA, EL • 1972 • Aguirre Javier • SPN • COUNT DRACULA'S GREAT LOVE ○ DRACULA'S GREAT LOVE (USA) ○ CEMETERY GIRLS ○ DRACULA'S VIRGIN LOVERS ○ GREAT LOVE OF COUNT DRACULA, THE
GRAN AUTOR, EL • 1953 • Crevenna Alfredo B. • MXC
GRAN BOLITTO • 1977 • Bolognini Mauro • ITL
GRAN CAIDA, LA • 1958 • Gonzalez De Leon Jose Luis • MXC, USA • BIG DROP, THE (USA)
GRAN CALAVERA, EL • 1949 • Bunuel Luis • MXC • GREAT MADCAP, THE (USA) ○ HAPPY SCOUNDREL, THE
GRAN CAMARADA, EL • 1939 • Blass Yago • ARG
GRAN CAMPEON, EL • 1949 • Urueta Chano • MXC
GRAN CASINO • 1946 • Bunuel Luis • MXC • EN EL VIEJO TAMPICO ○ IN OLD TAMPICO ○ TAMPICO
GRAN CIUDAD, UNA • 1973 • Cortes Joaquin • VNZ • BIG CITY, A
GRAN COARTADA, LA • 1962 • Madrid Jose Luis • SPN
GRAN COMORA • 1955 • Nediani Antonio • DOC • ITL
GRAN CRUCERO, EL • 1970 • Gutierrez Maesso Jose • SPN
GRAN CRUZ, LA • 1937 • Sevilla Raphael J. • MXC • HEAVY CROSS, THE (USA)
GRAN DESAFIO, EL • 1977 • Ruiz Jorge • SHT • BLV • GREAT CHALLENGE, THE
GRAN DIA, EL • 1956 • Gil Rafael • SPN, ITL
GRAN ESPECIALISTA SACANDO MUELAS EN EL HOTEL EUROPA • 1897 • Duran Manuel Trujillo • VNZ
GRAN ESPECTACULO, EL • 1955 • Zacarias Miguel • MXC, SPN
GRAN FAMILIA, LA • 1963 • Palacios Fernando • SPN
GRAN FIESTA, LA • 1977 • Fernandez Ramon • SPN
GRAN FIESTA, LA • 1987 • Zurinaga Marcos • PRC • BIG PARTY, THE (USA)
GRAN GALEOTO, EL • 1951 • Gil Rafael • SPN
GRAN GOPLE AL SERVICIO DE SU MAJESTAD BRITANICA see **COLPO MAESTRO AL SERVIZIO DI SUA MAESTA BRITANNICA** • 1967
GRAN HERENCIA, LA • Ruiz Jorge • DCS • BLV • GREAT HERITAGE, THE
GRAN HOTEL • 1944 • Delgado Miguel M. • MXC
GRAN MAKAKIKUS, EL • 1944 • Gomez Landero Humberto • MXC
GRAN MENTIRA, LA • 1956 • Gil Rafael • SPN
GRAN NOTICIA, LA • 1921 • Noriega Hope Carlos • MXC
GRAN PENSION LA ALEGRIA • 1942 • Irigoyen Julio • ARG
GRAN PILLO, EL • 1958 • Gazcon Gilberto • MXC
GRAN PREMIO • 1944 • Musso Giuseppe D., Scarpelli Umberto • ITL
GRAN PREMIO, EL • 1957 • Orellana Carlos • MXC
GRAN RUTA, LA • 1972 • Ayala Fernando • ARG • GREAT HIGHWAY, THE
GRAN SALTO AL VACIO, EL • 1979 • Alvarez Santiago • DOC • CUB
GRAN SECRETO, EL • 1943 • Remy Jacques • ARG
GRAN SENORA, UNA • 1959 • Amadori Luis Cesar • SPN
GRAN TAREA, LA • 1975 • Roncal Hugo • DCS • BLV
GRAN VARIETA • 1954 • Paolella Domenico • ITL
GRANA, LA (ITL) see **FRIC, LE** • 1959
GRANADA ADDIO! • 1968 • Girolami Marino • ITL • GOODBYE GRANADA!
GRANADA, GRANADA, MY GRANADA • 1967 • Karmen Roman • DOC • USS • GRANADA, MY GRANADA
GRANADA, MY GRANADA see **GRANADA, GRANADA, MY GRANADA** • 1967
GRANADEROS DEL AMOR • 1934 • Reinhardt John • USA • GRENADIERS OF LOVE
GRANATIERE DI POMERANIA, LA • 1920 • D'Ambra Lucio • ITL
GRANATOVYY BRASLET • 1965 • Room Abram • USS • GARNET BRACELET, THE (USA)
GRAND AMOUR, LE • 1968 • Etaix Pierre • FRN • GREAT LOVE, THE
GRAND AMOUR, LE see **HUBBU AL-KABIR, AL-** • 1968
GRAND AMOUR DE BEETHOVEN, UN • 1936 • Gance Abel • FRN • LIFE AND LOVES OF BEETHOVEN, THE (USA) ○ BEETHOVEN (UKN)
GRAND AMOUR DE JEUNE DESSAUER, LE see **TAMBOUR BATTANT** • 1933
GRAND BABY, THE • 1983 • Johnson Henry • USA
GRAND BABYLON HOTEL, THE • 1916 • Wilson Frank • UKN
GRAND BARRAGE, LE see **TEMPO SI E FERMATO, IL** • 1960
GRAND BAZAR, LE • 1973 • Zidi Claude • FRN
GRAND BIDULE, LE • 1967 • Andre Raoul • FRN • GREAT GIMMICK, THE
GRAND BLEU, LE • 1988 • Besson Luc • FRN • BIG BLUE, THE (UKN)
GRAND BLOND AVEC UNE CHAUSSURE NOIRE, LE • 1972 • Robert Yves • FRN • TALL BLOND MAN WITH ONE BLACK SHOE, THE (USA) ○ FOLLOW THAT GUY WITH THE ONE BLACK SHOE (UKN)
GRAND BLUFF, LE • 1933 • Champreux Maurice • FRN
GRAND BLUFF, LE • 1957 • Dally Patrice • FRN
GRAND BOUNCE • 1937 • Tourneur Jacques • SHT • USA
GRAND CANARY • 1934 • Cummings Irving • USA
GRAND CANYON • 1949 • Landres Paul • USA
GRAND CANYON • 1958 • Algar James • DOC • USA • GRAND CANYON SUITE
GRAND CANYON SUITE see **GRAND CANYON** • 1958
GRAND CANYON TRAIL • 1948 • Witney William • USA
GRAND CANYONSCOPE • 1954 • Nichols Charles • ANS • USA
GRAND CARNAVAL, LE • 1983 • Arcady Alexandre • FRN
GRAND CENTRAL MURDER • 1942 • Simon S. Sylvan • USA
GRAND CEREMONIAL, LE • 1968 • Jolivet Pierre-Alain • FRN • WEIRD WEIRDO (UKN)
GRAND CHEF, LE • 1959 • Verneuil Henri • FRN, ITL • NOI GANGSTERS (ITL) ○ GANGSTER BOSS (USA) ○ BIG CHIEF, THE
GRAND CHEMIN, LE • 1986 • Hubert Jean-Loup • FRN • GRAND HIGHWAY, THE (USA)
GRAND CHRISTMAS HARLEQUINADE • 1914 • Kellino W. P. • UKN
GRAND CINEMA • 1988 • Hedayat Hassan • IRN
GRAND CIRQUE, LE • 1949 • Peclet Georges • FRN
GRAND CIRQUE S'EN VA, LE • 1953 • de Gastyne Marco • SHT • FRN
GRAND COMBAT, LE • 1942 • Bernard-Roland • FRN
GRAND CONCERT, THE • 1960 • Halas John • ANS • UKN
GRAND CONCERT, THE see **BOLSHOI KONCERT** • 1951
GRAND-DAD • 1913 • *Harris Mildred* • USA
GRAND DADAIS, LE • 1967 • Granier-Deferre Pierre • FRN, FRG • ZEIT DER KIRSCHEN IST VORBEI, DIE (FRG) ○ VIRGIN YOUTH ○ BIG SOFTIE, THE
GRAND-DADDIE'S GRAND-DAUGHTER • 1914 • *Victor* • USA
GRAND DAY • 1989 • Ayyari Kianoush • IRN
GRAND DELIRE, LE • 1975 • Berry Dennis • FRN, FRG, ITL • PIERRE ET MARIE S'EN VONT ENSEMBLE
GRAND DEPART, LE • 1972 • Raysse Martial • FRN • BIG DEPARTURE, THE
GRAND DETOUR, LE • 1968 • Bedjaoui Ahmed • ALG
GRAND DUCHESS AND THE WAITER, THE • 1926 • St. Clair Malcolm • USA
GRAND DUEL, THE (USA) see **GRANDE DUELLO, IL** • 1973
GRAND DUEL IN MAGIC see **KAIRYU DAIKESSEN** • 1966
GRAND DUEL, LE (FRN) see **GRANDE DUELLO, IL** • 1973
GRAND DUKE AND MR. PIMM, THE see **LOVE IS A BALL** • 1962
GRAND DUKE'S FINANCES, THE see **FINANZEN DES GROSSHERZOGS, DIE** • 1924
GRAND DUKE'S FINANCES, THE see **FINANZEN DES GROSSHERZOGS, DIE** • 1934
GRAND ELAN, LE • 1939 • Christian-Jaque • FRN
GRAND EMBOUTEILLAGE, LE (FRN) see **BOTTLENECK** • 1979
GRAND ESCAPE, THE • 1946 • Baxter John • UKN
GRAND ESCOGRIFFE, LE • 1976 • Pinoteau Claude • FRN, ITL
GRAND EXIT • 1935 • Kenton Erle C. • USA
GRAND FANFARON, LE • 1976 • Clair Philippe • FRN, BLG
GRAND FILM ORDINAIRE, LE • 1970 • Frappier Roger • CND • GREAT ORDINARY MOVIE, THE ○ GRAND FILM ORDINAIRE OU JEANNE D'ARC N'EST PAS MORTE, SE PORTE BIEN, ET VIT AU QUEBEC, LE
GRAND FILM ORDINAIRE OU JEANNE D'ARC N'EST PAS MORTE, SE PORTE BIEN, ET VIT AU QUEBEC, LE see **GRAND FILM ORDINAIRE, LE** • 1970
GRAND FINALE • 1936 • Campbell Ivar • UKN
GRAND FOSSE, LE • 1980 • Ciampi Yves • FRN
GRAND FRERE, LE • 1982 • Girod Francis • FRN
GRAND GALA • 1952 • Campaux Francois • FRN
GRAND GUIGNOL • 1921 • Paul Fred • SER • UKN
GRAND GUIGNOL • 1987 • Marboeuf Jean • FRN
GRAND HARLEQUINADE • 1912 • Kellino W. P. • UKN
GRAND HIGHWAY, THE (USA) see **GRAND CHEMIN, LE** • 1986
GRAND HOOTER, THE • 1937 • Lord Del • SHT • USA
GRAND HOTEL..! • 1927 • Guter Johannes • FRG • HOTEL BOULEVARD
GRAND HOTEL • 1932 • Goulding Edmund • USA
GRAND HOTEL BABYLON, DAS • 1919 • Dupont E. A. • FRG
GRAND HOTEL DES PALMES • 1978 • Perlini Meme • ITL
GRAND HOTEL EXCELSIOR • 1983 • Castellano, Pipolo • ITL
GRAND HOTEL (FRN) see **MENSCHEN IM HOTEL** • 1959
GRAND HOTEL TO BIG INDIAN • 1906 • *Bitzer Billy (Ph)* • USA
GRAND ILLUSION • 1986 • Niskanen Tuija-Maija • FNL
GRAND ILLUSION (USA) see **GRANDE ILLUSION, LA** • 1937
GRAND JETE • 1966 • Dubelman Dick • USA
GRAND JEU, LE • 1933 • Feyder Jacques • FRN • GREAT GAME, THE
GRAND JEU, LE • 1954 • Siodmak Robert • FRN, ITL • GRANDE GIUOCO, IL (ITL) ○ FLESH AND THE WOMAN (USA) ○ CARD OF FATE (UKN) ○ FLESH AND WOMAN
GRAND JOURNAL ILLUSTRE, UN • 1927 • Greville Edmond T. • SHT • FRN
GRAND JOURNEY, THE see **TAIAN RYOKO** • 1968
GRAND JUNCTION CASE, THE • 1961 • Duffell Peter • UKN
GRAND JUNCTION HOTEL, THE • Beaudine William • SHT • USA
GRAND JURY • 1936 • Rogell Albert S. • USA
GRAND JURY • 1977 • Cain Christopher • USA
GRAND JURY SECRETS • 1939 • Hogan James P. • USA
GRAND LARCENY • 1922 • Worsley Wallace • USA
GRAND LARCENY • 1988 • Szwarc Jeannot • USA
GRAND MACHIN ET LE PETIT CHOSE, LE • 1910 • Cohl Emile • ANS • FRN
GRAND MAGIC CIRCUS, THE • 1973 • Marzaroli Oscar, Bushby Tom • UKN • ONCE UPON A TIME
GRAND MANAN • 1943 • Perry Margaret • DOC • CND
GRAND MANEUVER, THE (USA) see **GRANDES MANOEUVRES, LES** • 1955
GRAND MATIN, LE • 1975 • Guillemot Claude • SHT • FRN
GRAND MEAULNES, LE • 1967 • Albicocco Jean-Gabriel • FRN • WANDERER, THE (USA)
GRAND MELIES, LE • 1952 • Franju Georges • DOC • FRN • GREAT MELIES, THE
GRAND MOYENS, LES see **J'ETAIS UNE AVENTURIERE** • 1938
GRAND NATIONAL • 1988 • Laughlin Susan • ANM • UKN
GRAND NATIONAL NIGHT • 1953 • McNaught Bob • UKN • WICKED WIFE (USA)
GRAND NATIONAL STEEPLECHASE • 1898 • ASL
GRAND OCEAN, LE • 1974 • Millet Daniel, Millet Jean-Pierre • DOC • FRN
GRAND OEUVRE, LE • 1958 • Zuber • SHT • FRN
GRAND OLD FLAG, THE • 1913 • *Bison* • USA
GRAND OLD GIRL, THE • 1935 • Robertson John S. • USA • PORTRAIT OF LAURA BAYLES
GRAND OLD WOMAN see **WOMAN IN DISTRESS** • 1937
GRAND OLE OPRY • 1940 • McDonald Frank • USA
GRAND OLYMPICS, THE (USA) see **GRANDE OLYMPIADE, LA** • 1961
GRAND OPERA IN RUBEVILLE • 1914 • Miller Ashley • USA
GRAND PARADE, THE • 1930 • Newmeyer Fred • USA
GRAND PARSON, LE • 1981 • Arcady Alexandre • FRN
GRAND PASSION, THE • 1914 • *Princess* • USA
GRAND PASSION, THE • 1918 • Park Ida May • USA
GRAND PATRON, UN • 1951 • Ciampi Yves • FRN • PERFECTIONIST, THE (USA)
GRAND PAVOIS, LE • 1953 • Pinoteau Jack • FRN
GRAND PAYSAGE D'ALEXIS DROEVEN, LE • 1981 • Andrien Jean-Jacques • BLG, FRN • ENDLESS LAND OF ALEXIS DROEVEN, THE
GRAND-PERE • 1938 • Peguy Robert • FRN • FEMMES DE DEMAIN
GRAND-PERE MIRACLE • 1959 • Kazansky Gennadi • USS
GRAND PIANO, THE • 1979 • Pounchev Borislav • BUL
GRAND PRAIRIE, A WAY OF LIFE • 1981 • Dalen Zale R. • CND
GRAND PRIX • 1934 • Clowes St. John L. • UKN
GRAND PRIX • 1949 • Mason Bill • UKN
GRAND PRIX • 1966 • Frankenheimer John • USA
GRAND PRIX WINNER • 1968 • Bartsch Art • ANS • USA
GRAND PROMESSE, LA • 1950 • Lejtes Joseph • ISR
GRAND RAID, LE see **ALEXIS, GENTLEMAN-CHAUFFEUR** • 1937
GRAND REFRAIN, LE • 1936 • Mirande Yves • FRN
GRAND REMUE-MENAGE, LE • 1978 • Groulx Sylvie • CND
GRAND RENDEZ-VOUS, LE • 1949 • Dreville Jean • FRN • FRANKLIN ARRIVE
GRAND RESTAURANT, LE • 1967 • Besnard Jacques • FRN
GRAND REVE, LE see **ALTITUDE 3200** • 1938
GRAND ROCK, LE • 1967 • Garceau Raymond • CND
GRAND-RUE (FRN) see **CALLE MAYOR** • 1955
GRAND SABORDAGE, LE • 1972 • Perisson Alain • CND, FRN
GRAND-SAINT-BERNARD, LE • 1935 • Leherissey Jean • SHT • FRN
GRAND SECRET, LE • 1959 • Calderon Gerald • DOC • FRN
GRAND SEDUTTORE, IL (ITL) see **DON JUAN** • 1956
GRAND SEIGNEUR, UN • 1912 • Fescourt Henri • FRN
GRAND SEIGNEUR, UN see **BONS VIVANTS, LES** • 1966
GRAND SILENCE, LE • 1955 • Gout Pierre • SHT • FRN
GRAND SILENCE, LE (FRN) see **GRANDE SILENZIO, IL** • 1968
GRAND SLAM • 1933 • Dieterle William • USA
GRAND SLAM • 1978 • Hefin John • MTV • UKN
GRAND SLAM OPERA • 1936 • Lamont Charles • SHT • USA
GRAND SLAM (USA) see **AD OGNI COSTO** • 1967
GRAND SOIR, UN • 1976 • Reusser Francis • SWT, FRN • BIG NIGHT, THE ○ NIGHT OF THE REVOLUTION
GRAND SOUFFLE, LE • 1914 • Ravel Gaston • FRN
GRAND SUBSTITUTION, THE • 1965 • Yen Chen • HKG
GRAND SUD, LE • 1956 • Reichenbach Francois • SHT • FRN
GRAND THEFT AUTO • 1977 • Howard Ron • USA
GRAND TOUR '70: DESTINATION HOLY LAND • 1969 • De La Varre Andre Jr. • DOC • USA
GRAND TOUR, THE • 1972 • Fukushima Hal • ANS • JPN
GRAND TOUR -MANNED EXPLORATION OF THE OUTER PLANETS • 1973 • *Graphic* • USA
GRAND TOUR OF EASTERN EUROPE: BEHIND THE IRON CURTAIN • 1968 • De La Varre Andre Jr. • DOC • USA
GRAND TOUR OF LONDON AND PARIS (BY DAY AND BY NIGHT) • 1965 • De La Varre Andre Jr. • DOC • USA
GRAND TRUNK RAILROAD SCENES • 1900 • *Bitzer Billy (Ph)* • USA
GRAND UPROAR • 1933 • *Terry Paul/ Moser Frank (P)* • ANS • USA
GRAND UPROAR, THE • 1930 • Fleischer Dave • ANS • USA
GRAND VOYAGE, LE • 1973-74 • Valcour Pierre • DOC • CND
GRAND VOYAGE, LE • 1974 • Carriere Marcel • CND
GRAND VOYAGE, LE • 1981 • Tazi Abderrahmane • MRC
GRANDAD OF RACES • 1950 • De La Varre Andre • SHT • USA
GRANDAD RUDD • 1935 • Hall Ken G. • ASL
GRANDAD'S DREAM • 1967 • Voinov Konstantin • USS
GRANDAD'S EXILE • 1912 • Calvert Charles? • UKN
GRANDCHILD'S DEVOTION, A • 1906 • Fitzhamon Lewin • UKN
GRANDDADDY'S BOY • 1913 • MacGregor Norval • USA
GRANDDAD'S EXTRAVAGANCE • 1910 • *Centaur* • USA
GRANDDAUGHTER OF DRACULA see **NOCTURNA** • 1979
GRANDE ABBUFFATA, LA • 1973 • Ferreri Marco • ITL, FRN • GRANDE BOUFFE, LA (FRN) ○ BLOW-OUT (UKN)
GRANDE ADDIO, IL • 1957 • Polselli Renato • ITL
GRANDE ALERTE, LA see **MENACES** • 1939
GRANDE APPELLO, IL • 1936 • Camerini Mario • ITL • LAST ROLL-CALL, THE (USA) ○ RINNEGATO ○ ITALIA! ○ AFFRICA
GRANDE ARTE, A • 1989 • Salles Walter Jr. • BRZ • GREAT ART, THE
GRANDE ASSALTO, O • 1967 • Chadler C. Adolpho • BRZ • BIG ATTACK, THE
GRANDE ATTACCO, IL • 1978 • Lenzi Umberto • ITL, FRG, YGS • BIGGEST BATTLE, THE ○ BATTLE OF THE MARETHLINE ○ GREAT BATTLE, THE ○ BATTLE FORCE ○ GREATEST BATTLE, THE
GRANDE AURORA, LA • 1948 • Scotese Giuseppe Maria • ITL • GREAT DAWN, THE (USA)
GRANDE AVENTURE INDUSTRIELLE RACONTEE PAR EDOUARD SIMARD #1 & 2 • 1959 • DCS • CND
GRANDE AVVENTURA, LA • 1954 • Pisu Mario • ITL
GRANDE AVVENTURA DI SCARAMOUCHE, LA • 1970 • Pierotti Piero • ITL
GRANDE BAGARRE DE DON CAMILLO, LA (FRN) see **DON CAMILLO E L'ONOREVOLE PEPPONE** • 1955
GRANDE BAGARRE, LA (FRN) see **SOLDATO DI VENTURA, IL** • 1976
GRANDE BAISE, LA see **MES NUITS AVEC.. ALICE, PENELOPE, ARNOLD, MAUD ET RICHARD** • 1976
GRANDE BAISE II, LA • 1978 • FRN
GRANDE BARRIERA, LA • 1956 • Bolla Achille • DOC • ITL
GRANDE BARRIERE DE CORIL, LA • 1969 • Levie Pierre • BLG
GRANDE BATAILLE, LA • 1963 • Essid Hamadi • SHT • TNS
GRANDE BLEK, IL • 1988 • Piccioni Giuseppe • ITL • GREAT BLEK, THE
GRANDE BOUFFE, LA (FRN) see **GRANDE ABBUFFATA, LA** • 1973
GRANDE BOURGEOISE, LA (FRN) see **FATTI DI GENTE PER BENE** • 1974
GRANDE-BRETAGNE ET LES ETATS-UNITS DE 1896-1900 • 1968 • Allegret Marc • SHT • FRN
GRANDE BRETECHE, LA • 1943 • Calmettes Andre • FRN
GRANDE BRETECHE, LA • 1961 • Barma Claude • FRN

GRANDE CACCIA, LA • 1957 • Belgard Arnold, Capolino Edoardo • ITL, USA, UKN • EAST OF KILIMANJARO (USA) ○ BIG SEARCH, THE ○ TERRORE AL KILIMANGIARO
GRANDE CACCIA, LA see **ULTIME GRIDA DALLA SAVANA** • 1975
GRANDE CARAVANE, LA • 1934 • d'Esme Jean • DOC • FRN
GRANDE CASE, LA • 1949 • Dupont Jacques • SHT • FRN
GRANDE CHARTREUSE, LA • 1937 • Clement Rene • SHT • FRN
GRANDE CHEVAUCHEE DE ROBIN DES BOIS, LA (FRN) see **ARCIERE DI FUOCO, L'** • 1971
GRANDE CIDADE, A • 1966 • Diegues Carlos • BRZ • BIG CITY, THE
GRANDE CITE, LA • 1954 • Rouy • SHT • FRN • ANGKOR
GRANDE CLARTE, LA see **ANGES DU PECHES, LES** • 1943
GRANDE COLPO DEI 7 UOMINI D'ORO, IL • 1966 • Vicario Marco • ITL • SEVEN GOLDEN MEN STRIKE AGAIN (USA) ○ GREAT COUP OF THE 7 GOLDEN MEN
GRANDE COLPO DI SURCOUF, IL • 1967 • Bergonzelli Sergio • ITL, FRN, SPN • TONNERRE SUR L'OCEAN INDIEN (FRN) ○ VENGEANCE DU SURCOUF, LA
GRANDE CORRIDA, LA see **TARDE DE TOROS** • 1955
GRANDE DATE ,LA • Kamba Sebastien • SHT • CNG
GRANDE DEBAUCHE, LA • Baudricourt Michel • FRN
GRANDE DUELLO, IL • 1973 • Santi Giancarlo • ITL, FRG, FRN • DREI VATERUNSER FUR VIER HALUNKEN (FRG) ○ GRAND DUEL, THE (USA) ○ GRAND DUEL, LE (FRN) ○ BIG SHOWDOWN, THE ○ STORMRIDER
GRANDE ELIAS, O • 1950 • Duarte Arthur • PRT
GRANDE ENFILADE, LA • 1979 • Roy Jean-Claude • FRN
GRANDE EPREUVE, LA • 1927 • Hamman Joe, Raulet Georges • FRN
GRANDE EVASION, LA • 1974 • Gagne Jacques • DCS • CND
GRANDE EXTASE, LA • 1975 • Rhomm Patrice • FRN
GRANDE FAMILLE, LA see **A'ILA AL-KABIRA, AL-** • 1964
GRANDE FEIRA, A • 1961 • Pires Roberto • BRZ
GRANDE FILLE TOUTE SIMPLE, UNE • 1947 • Manuel Jacques • FRN • JUST A BIG SIMPLE GIRL
GRANDE FRIME, LA • 1976 • Zaphiratos Henri-T. • FRN • A NOUS LES MINETTES
GRANDE FROUSSE, LA • 1964 • Mocky Jean-Pierre • FRN • CITE DE L'INDICIBLE PEUR, LA ○ GREAT FEAR, THE
GRANDE GIUOCO, IL (ITL) see **GRAND JEU, LE** • 1954
GRANDE, GRANDE ERA A CIDADE • 1971 • Ceitil Rogerio, Antonio Lauro • PRT
GRANDE GUERRA, LA • 1959 • Monicelli Mario • ITL • GREAT WAR, THE
GRANDE IDEA, LA • 1959 • Crobu G. G. • ITL
GRANDE ILLISIONISTA, IL • 1983 • Tognola Jerko V. • SWT
GRANDE ILLUSION, LA • 1937 • Renoir Jean • FRN • GRAND ILLUSION (USA)
GRANDE INCONNUE, LA • 1939 • d'Esme Jean • DOC • FRN
GRANDE JAVA, LA • 1970 • Clair Philippe • FRN
GRANDE JOUISSANCE, LA • Baudricourt Michel • FRN
GRANDE LECHE, LA • 1978 • Bernard-Aubert Claude • FRN
GRANDE LECON, LA • 1940 • Peguy Robert • FRN
GRANDE LESSIVE, LA • 1968 • Mocky Jean-Pierre • FRN
GRANDE LEVRETTE, LA • 1978 • Bernard-Aubert Claude • FRN
GRANDE LUCE, LA • 1939 • Campogalliani Carlo • ITL • GREAT LIGHT, THE (USA) ○ MONTEVERGINE
GRANDE LUTTE DES MINEURS, LA • 1948 • Daquin Louis • SHT • FRN
GRANDE MAFFIA, LA • 1971 • Clair Philippe • FRN, ITL • GRANDE MAFIA, LA
GRANDE MAFIA, LA see **GRANDE MAFFIA, LA** • 1971
GRANDE MAGUET, LA • 1947 • Richebe Roger • FRN
GRANDE MARE, LA • 1930 • Bataille-Henri Jacques, Henley Hobart • FRN
GRANDE MARNIERE, LA • 1913 • Pouctal Henri • FRN
GRANDE MARNIERE, LA • 1943 • de Marguenat Jean • FRN
GRANDE MENTECAPTO, O • 1988 • Caldeira Oswalda • BRZ • GREAT MADMAN, THE
GRANDE MEUTE, LA • 1944 • de Limur Jean • FRN
GRANDE MOMENTO, O • 1959 • Santos Roberto • BRZ
GRANDE MOUILLE, LA • 1979 • Bernard-Aubert Claude • FRN
GRANDE NOTTE DI RINGO, LA • 1966 • Maffei Mario • ITL
GRANDE NOUBA, LA • 1973 • Caza Christian • FRN
GRANDE OLYMPIADE, LA • 1961 • Marcellini Romolo • DOC • ITL • GRAND OLYMPICS, THE (USA)
GRANDE OMBRA, LA • 1958 • Gora Claudio • ITL
GRANDE PAESE D'ACCIAIO, IL • 1960 • Olmi Ermanno • DOC • ITL
GRANDE PAGAILLE, LA (FRN) see **TUTTI A CASA** • 1960
GRANDE PALHACO, O • 1982 • Cobbett William • BRZ • GREAT CLOWN, THE
GRANDE PASSION, LA • 1929 • Hugon Andre • FRN
GRANDE PASSION, LA see **LIBERTE** • 1937
GRANDE PASTORALE, LA • 1943 • Clement Rene • DCS • FRN
GRANDE PAULETTE, LA • 1971 • Calderon Gerald • FRN
GRANDE PECHE • 1955 • Fabiani Henri • FRN
GRANDE PORTE, LA • 1973 • Soupart Andre • BLG
GRANDE RACKET, IL • 1976 • Castellari Enzo G. • ITL
GRANDE RECRE, LA • 1976 • Pierson Claude • FRN
GRANDE RELEVE, LA see **BANDERA, LA** • 1935
GRANDE RIBELLE, IL (ITL) see **MATHIAS SANDORFF** • 1962
GRANDE RINUNCIA, LA • 1951 • Vergano Aldo • ITL • SUOR TERESA
GRANDE RITORNO DI DJANGO, IL • 1987 • Rossati Nello • ITL • DJANGO STRIKES AGAIN
GRANDE RIVIERE, LA see **MISTACHIPU** • 1971
GRANDE SAUTERELLE, LA • 1967 • Lautner Georges • FRN, ITL, FRG • MADCHEN WIE DAS MEER, EIN (FRG) ○ BIG GRASSHOPPER, THE ○ SAUTERELLE ○ FEMMINA (ITL)
GRANDE SAUTERIE, LA • 1977 • Desvilles Jean • FRN
GRANDE SAVANA, LA • 1956 • Marcelli Elia • ITL
GRANDE SCROFA NERA, LA • 1972 • Ottoni Filippo • ITL
GRANDE SILENZIO, IL • 1936 • Zannini Giovanni • ITL
GRANDE SILENZIO, IL • 1968 • Corbucci Sergio • ITL, FRN • GRAND SILENCE, LE (FRN) ○ GREAT SILENCE, THE
GRANDE SPERANZA, LA • 1954 • Coletti Duilio • ITL • TORPEDO ZONE
GRANDE STRADA, LA • 1948 • Cottafavi Vittorio, Waszynski Michael • ITL • ODISSEA DI MONTECASSINO, L'
GRANDE STRADA AZZURRA, LA • 1957 • Pontecorvo Gillo • ITL, YGS • WIDE BLUE ROAD, THE (USA) ○ DENOMME SQUARCIO, UN ○ SQUARCIA ○ LUNGA STRADA AZZURRA, LA ○ LONG BLUE ROAD, THE ○ VELIKI PLAVI PUT
GRANDE TERRE, LA • 1955 • Vaudremont • SHT • FRN
GRANDE TORMENTA, LA • 1920 • Gallone Carmine • ITL
GRANDE TROUILLE, LA • 1974 • Grunstein Pierre • FRN
GRANDE VADROUILLE, LA • 1966 • Oury Gerard • FRN, UKN • DON'T LOOK NOW.. WE'RE BEING SHOT AT! (UKN) ○ DON'T LOOK NOW (USA)
GRANDE VALLATA, LA • 1961 • Dorigo Angelo • ITL
GRANDE VERGOGNA, LA • 1916 • Ghione Emilio • ITL
GRANDE VIE, LA • 1934 • Diamant-Berger Henri • FRN
GRANDE VIE, LA • 1950 • Schneider Henri • FRN
GRANDE VIE, LA (FRN) see **KUNSTSEIDENE MADCHEN, DAS** • 1960
GRANDE VIE TONIFIANTE DE LA FORET, LA • 1942-43 • Tessier Albert • DCS • CND
GRANDE VOLIERE, LA • 1947 • Peclet Georges • FRN
GRANDE XERIFE, O • 1972 • Zamuner Pio • BRZ
GRANDEE'S RING, THE • 1915 • *Beebe Earl* • USA
GRANDES AMIGOS • 1967 • Lucia Luis • SPN • GREAT FRIENDS
GRANDES CHASSES, LES • 1911 • Machin Alfred • SER • FRN
GRANDES ECLUSES, LES see **PICKING LOCKS** • 1937
GRANDES FAMILLES, LES • 1959 • de La Patelliere Denys • FRN • POSSESSORS, THE (USA)
GRANDES GUEULES, LES • 1965 • Enrico Robert • FRN, ITL • VAMPATA DI VIOLENZA, UNA (ITL) ○ WISE GUYS, THE (USA) ○ JAILBIRDS' VACATION
GRANDES JOUISSEUSES, LES • 1978 • Bernard-Aubert Claude • FRN • FRENCH EROTIC FANTASIES
GRANDES MANOEUVRES • 1896 • Melies Georges • FRN • MANOEUVRES OF THE FRENCH ARMY
GRANDES MANOEUVRES, LES • 1955 • Clair Rene • FRN, ITL • GRANDI MANOVRE (ITL) ○ SUMMER MANOEUVRES (UKN) ○ GRAND MANEUVER, THE (USA)
GRANDES MANOEUVRES DE L'ARMEE BELGE, LES • 1913 • Machin Alfred • BLG
GRANDES PERSONNES, LES • 1961 • Valere Jean • FRN, ITL • TIME OUT FOR LOVE (USA) ○ TASTE OF LOVE, A
GRANDES POMPEUSES, LES • Warren Ken • FRN
GRANDES VACANCES, LES • 1967 • Girault Jean • FRN, ITL • GRANDI VACANZE (ITL)
GRANDEUR ET DECADENCE see **DECADENCE ET GRANDEUR** • 1923
GRANDEUR ET DECADENCE see **FUSEE, LA** • 1933
GRANDEUR NATURE (FRN) see **LIFE SIZE** • 1973
GRANDEZA DE AMERICA, LA see **CRISTOBAL COLON** • 1943
GRANDFATHER • 1911 • *Walthall Henry B.* • USA
GRANDFATHER • 1913 • *Neason Hazel* • USA
GRANDFATHER see **FAD JAL** • 1979
GRANDFATHER, THE • 1912 • *West William* • USA
GRANDFATHER, THE • 1985 • Gharizadeh Majid • IRN
GRANDFATHER AUTOMOBILE see **DEDECEK AUTOMOBIL** • 1956
GRANDFATHER FOR SALE see **OUPA FOR SALE** • 1968
GRANDFATHER FROST see **MOROZKO** • 1965
GRANDFATHER SMALLWEED • 1928 • Croise Hugh • UKN
GRANDFATHER'S BIRTHDAY: OR, THE LAST ROLL CALL • 1908 • Coleby A. E. • UKN
GRANDFATHER'S CLOCK • 1912 • *Rex* • USA
GRANDFATHER'S CLOCK • 1934 • Gillett Burt, Tyer James • ANS • USA
GRANDFATHER'S FOLLIES • 1944 • Negulesco Jean • SHT • USA
GRANDFATHER'S GIFT • 1910 • *Lubin* • USA
GRANDFATHER'S OLD BOOTS • 1912 • Wilson Frank? • UKN
GRANDFATHER'S PILLS • 1908 • *Pathe* • FRN
GRANDFATHER'S ROMANCE • 1914 • *Eclair* • USA
GRANDFATHER'S TORMENTORS • 1905 • Cooper Arthur • UKN
GRANDFATHER'S TRAGIC DEATH • 1978 • Eliopoulou Vasiliki • GRC
GRANDHOTEL NEVADA • 1934 • Svitak • CZC
GRANDI CONDOTTIERI, I • 1966 • Baldi Marcello, Perez-Dolc Francesc • ITL
GRANDI MAGAZZINI • 1939 • Camerini Mario • ITL
GRANDI MAGAZZINI • 1987 • Castellano, Pipolo • ITL • BIG STORE
GRANDI MANOVRE (ITL) see **GRANDES MANOEUVRES, LES** • 1955
GRANDI PECCATORI, I • 1956 • Majano Anton Giulio • ITL
GRANDI VACANZE (ITL) see **GRANDES VACANCES, LES** • 1967
GRANDISON • 1979 • Kurz Achim • FRG
GRANDMA • 1911 • *Essanay* • USA
GRANDMA see **NONA, LA** • 1979
GRANDMA AND HER EIGHT GRANDCHILDREN IN THE FOREST see **MORMOR OG DE ATTE UNGENE I SKOGEN** • 1978
GRANDMA AND HER EIGHT GRANDCHILDREN IN THE TOWN see **MORMOR OG DE ATTE UNGENE I BYEN** • 1976
GRANDMA AND THE BAD BOYS • 1900 • Porter Edwin S. • USA
GRANDMA AND THE EIGHT CHILDREN (USA) see **MORMOR OG DE ATTE UNGENE I BYEN** • 1976
GRANDMA MOSES • 1950 • Hill Jerome • USA
GRANDMA THREADING HER NEEDLE • 1900 • Smith G. A. • UKN
GRANDMA'S BOY • 1922 • Newmeyer Fred • USA
GRANDMA'S BUOYS • 1936 • Goodwins Leslie • SHT • USA
GRANDMA'S GIRL • 1930 • Sennett Mack • SHT • USA
GRANDMA'S HOUSE • 1965 • Fleischner Bob • SHT • USA
GRANDMA'S HOUSE see **MIN FARMORS HUS** • 1984
GRANDMA'S HOUSE see **GRANDMOTHER'S HOUSE** • 1988
GRANDMA'S PET • 1932 • Lantz Walter, Nolan William • ANS • USA
GRANDMA'S READING GLASS • 1900 • Smith G. A. • UKN
GRANDMA'S SLEEPING DRAUGHT • 1912 • Stow Percy • UKN
GRANDMA'S TOO'FACHE • 1911 • *Comet* • USA
GRANDMOTHER • 1910 • *Kalem* • USA
GRANDMOTHER see **BABICKA** • 1920
GRANDMOTHER see **NAGYMAMA** • 1935
GRANDMOTHER see **BABICKA** • 1940
GRANDMOTHER see **YAABA** • 1988
GRANDMOTHER, THE • 1970 • Lynch David • SHT • USA
GRANDMOTHER, THE see **NAGYMAMA, A** • 1916
GRANDMOTHER, ILIKO, ILLARION AND ME see **YA BABUSHKA, ILIKO I ILLARION** • 1963
GRANDMOTHER LOVE • 1911 • *Solax* • USA
GRANDMOTHER SABELLA see **NONNA SABELLA, LA** • 1957
GRANDMOTHER'S ENCYCLOPAEDIA see **ENCYCLOPEDIE DE GRAND'MAMAN EN 13 VOLUMES, L'** • 1963
GRANDMOTHER'S EYEGLASSES see **LOUPE DE GRANDMAMAN, LA** • 1901
GRANDMOTHER'S GOAT • 1963 • Amalrik Leonid • ANS • USS
GRANDMOTHER'S HOUSE • 1988 • Rader Peter • USA • GRANDMA'S HOUSE
GRANDMOTHER'S REVOLUTION see **FARMORS REVOLUTION** • 1933
GRANDMOTHER'S STORY • 1908 • *Melies* • USA
GRANDMOTHER'S STORY OR TO THE LAND OF TOYS, A (USA) see **CONTE DE LA GRAND'MERE ET REVE DE L'ENFANT OU AU PAYS DES JOUETS** • 1908
GRANDMOTHER'S UMBRELLA (USA) see **BABUSKIN ZONTIK** • 1969
GRANDMOTHER'S WAR STORY • 1911 • Olcott Sidney • USA
GRANDMOTHER'S WOLF • 1900 • *Smith G. A. (P)* • UKN
GRANDPA • 1912 • *Reliance* • USA
GRANDPA AND THE BUTTERFLY • 1905 • Collins Alf? • UKN
GRANDPA CALLED IT ART • 1944 • Hart Walter • SHT • USA
GRANDPA GOES TO TOWN • 1940 • Meins Gus • USA
GRANDPA INVOLUNTARILY see **DEDECKEM PROTI SVE VULI** • 1939
GRANDPA IVAN • 1939 • Ivanov A. • ANS • USS
GRANDPA PLANTED A BEET see **ZASADIL DEDEK REPU** • 1945
GRANDPA SEWS ON A BUTTON • 1910 • *Gaumont* • UKN
GRANDPA'S BOY • 1927 • Lamont Charles • SHT • USA
GRANDPA'S FORTY WINKS see **IN THE LAND OF NOD** • 1908
GRANDPA'S PENSION DAY • 1908 • Cooper Arthur • UKN
GRANDPA'S REVENGE • 1906 • *Walturdaw* • UKN
GRANDPA'S SPECS • 1912 • *Powers* • USA
GRANDPA'S WILL • 1914 • Stow Percy • UKN
GRANDS, LES • 1916 • Denola Georges • FRN
GRANDS, LES • 1924 • Fescourt Henri • FRN
GRANDS, LES • 1936 • Gandera Felix, Bibal Robert • FRN
GRANDS CHEMINS, LES • 1963 • Marquand Christian • FRN, ITL • OF FLESH AND BLOOD (USA) ○ BARO, IL (ITL)
GRANDS ENFANTS, LES • 1980 • Tana Paul • CND
GRANDS ENFANTS, LES see **RETOUR DE L'IMMACULEE CONCEPTION, LE** • 1971
GRANDS FEUX • 1937 • Alexeieff Alexandre • SHT • FRN
GRANDS MOMENTS, LES • 1965 • Lelouch Claude • FRN
GRANDS MOMENTS DU MUNDIAL 78 • 1978 • Guillermou Jean-Louis • DOC • FRN
GRANDS MOYENS, LES • 1976 • Cornfield Hubert • FRN • MENTEUSES, LES
GRANDS SENTIMENTS FONT LES BONS GUEULETONS, LES • 1973 • Berny Michel • FRN
GRANDSON, THE see **HAFID, AL-** • 1974
GRANDUCHESSA SI DIVERTE, LA • 1940 • Gentilomo Giacomo • ITL
GRANDVIEW U.S.A. • 1984 • Kleiser Randall • USA
GRANE ELSTER • 1914 • May Joe • FRG
GRANGES BRULEES, LES • 1973 • Chapot Jean • FRN, ITL • MIA LEGGE, LA (ITL) ○ SUSPICION OF MURDER
GRANICA • 1938 • Lejtes Joseph • PLN
GRANICA • 1967 • Wionczek Roman • MTV • PLN • BORDER, THE
GRANICA • 1989 • Masirevic Zoran • YGS • BORDER, THE
GRANITE HOTEL • 1940 • Fleischer Dave • ANS • USA
GRANNY • 1913 • *Pilot* • USA
GRANNY • 1913 • O'Neil Barry • *Lubin* • USA
GRANNY • 1914 • Cabanne W. Christy • USA
GRANNY, THE see **BABICKA** • 1940
GRANNY GET YOUR GUN • 1940 • Amy George • USA
GRANNY TAKES OVER see **PATE KOLO U VOZU** • 1958
GRANNY'S OLD ARMCHAIR • 1913 • Kirkland Hardee • USA
GRANNY'S QUILTS • 1974 • Dalen Zale R. • CND
GRANO DE MOSTAZA, EL • 1962 • Saenz De Heredia Jose Luis • SPN
GRANPA see **DEDACEK** • 1968
GRANSFOLKEN • 1914 • Stiller Mauritz • SWD • PEOPLE OF THE BORDER ○ FRONTIER PEOPLE ○ BORDER FEUD, THE
GRANSLOTS • 1990 • Pettersson Lars-Goran • SWD • BORDER PLOT, THE
GRANT AND LINCOLN • 1911 • *Champion* • USA
GRANT, POLICE REPORTER • 1916-17 • USA
GRANTON TRAWLER • 1934 • Anstey Edgar, Grierson John • DOC • UKN
GRAPE DEALER'S DAUGHTER, THE • 1970 • Gutman Walter • USA
GRAPE NUTTY • 1949 • Lovy Alex • ANS • USA
GRAPES ARE RIPE, THE (USA) see **FROHLICHE WEINBERG, DER** • 1952
GRAPES OF PASSION see **AIYOKU** • 1966
GRAPES OF WRATH, THE • 1940 • Ford John • USA
GRAPH, THE see **WYKRES** • 1966
GRAPHIC SOUND • Antoine Jean, Janssens Jean • SHT • BLG
GRAPHIQUE DE BOSCOP, LE • 1976 • Dumoulin Georges, Sotha • FRN
GRAPHITY • Lethem Roland • SHT • BLG
GRASP OF GREED, THE • 1916 • De Grasse Joseph • USA • MR. MEESON'S WILL (UKN)
GRASP OF WIND, A • 1982 • Campbell Russell • NZL
GRASPING HAND, THE see **MAIN QUI ENTREINT, LA** • 1915
GRASS • 1968 • Le Grice Malcolm • UKN
GRASS: A NATION'S BATTLE FOR LIFE • 1925 • Schoedsack Ernest B., Cooper Merian C., Harrison Marguerite • USA • GRASS: THE EPIC OF A LOST TRIBE
GRASS COUNTY GOES DRY • 1914 • *Boulder Robert* • USA
GRASS DRYING • 1949 • Byass Nigel • UKN

GRASS IS ALWAYS GREENER OVER THE SEPTIC TANK, THE • 1978 • Day Robert • TVM • USA
GRASS IS GREENER, THE • 1961 • Donen Stanley • UKN
GRASS IS SINGING, THE • 1981 • Raeburn Michael • UKN, SWD • KILLING HEAT (USA)
GRASS ORPHAN, THE • 1922 • Crane Frank H. • UKN
GRASS: THE EPIC OF A LOST TRIBE see **GRASS: A NATION'S BATTLE FOR LIFE** • 1925
GRASS TOMB, THE • 1971 • Lee Doo-Yong • SKR
GRASS-WHISTLE see **MUGIBUE** • 1955
GRASS WIDOWERS • 1921 • Drury William • UKN
GRASSCUTTER, THE • 1989 • Mune Ian • NZL
GRASSHOPPER • 1975 • Vukotic Dusan • ANS • YGS
GRASSHOPPER, THE • 1970 • Paris Jerry • USA • PASSING OF EVIL, THE
GRASSHOPPER, THE see **KUZNECHIK** • 1980
GRASSHOPPER, THE (USA) see **POPPYGUNYA** • 1955
GRASSHOPPER AND THE ANT, THE • 1954 • Reiniger Lotte • ANS • UKN
GRASSHOPPER AND THE ANT, THE • 1988 • Papadatos Alekos • ANS • GRC
GRASSHOPPER AND THE ANT, THE see **CIGALE ET LA FOURMI, LA** • 1909
GRASSHOPPER AND THE ANT, THE see **CIGALE ET LA FOURMI, LA** • 1916-24
GRASSHOPPER AND THE ANT, THE see **JUGENDRAUSCH** • 1927
GRASSHOPPER AND THE ANT, THE see **CIGALE ET LA FOURMI, LA** • 1955
GRASSHOPPER AND THE ANT (USA) see **CIGALE ET LA FOURMI, LA** • 1897
GRASSHOPPER AND THE ANTS, THE • 1934 • Jackson Wilfred • ANS • USA
GRASSLANDS see **HEX** • 1973
GRASSVILLE GIRLS, THE • 1912 • *Mason Billy* • USA
GRASSY SHIRES, THE • 1944 • Anstey Edgar • DOC • UKN
GRATE IMPEERYUL SIRCUS, THE • 1914 • Martin E. A. • USA
GRATEFUL BADGER, THE (USA) see **BUNBUKU CHAGAMA** • 1958
GRATEFUL DEAD, THE • 1967 • Nelson Robert • SHT • USA
GRATEFUL DEAD, THE see **GRATEFUL DEAD MOVIE, THE** • 1977
GRATEFUL DEAD MOVIE, THE • 1977 • Garcia Jerry • DOC • USA • GRATEFUL DEAD, THE
GRATEFUL DOG, A • 1908 • *Warwick Trading Co.* • UKN
GRATEFUL GUS • 1958 • Tendlar Dave • ANS • USA
GRATEFUL OUTCAST, A • 1914 • Smalley Phillips • USA
GRATIEN GELINAS • 1966 • Bonniere Rene • DCS • CND
GRATITUDE • 1909 • *Essanay* • USA
GRATITUDE • 1910 • *Selig* • USA
GRATITUDE • 1913 • *Karr Darwin* • USA
GRATITUDE • 1914 • *Melies* • USA
GRATITUDE • 1915 • Physioc Wray • USA
GRATITUDE OF CONDUCTOR 786, THE • 1915 • *Gane Nolan* • USA
GRATITUDE OF WANDA, THE • 1913 • Reid Wallace • USA
GRATITUDE TO THE EMPEROR see **KO-ON** • 1927
GRATTICIELI • 1943 • Giannini Guglielmo • ITL
GRATUITES • 1927 • Gremillon Jean • SHT • FRN
GRAUE DAME, DIE see **SHERLOCK HOLMES** • 1937
GRAUE FRAU VON ALENCON, DIE • 1919 • *Bebe Tilly* • FRG
GRAUE HAUS, DAS see **MARIA, DIE GESCHICHTE EINES HERZENS** • 1926
GRAUE HERR, DER • 1915 • Larsen Viggo • FRG
GRAUE HUND, DER • 1922 • *Chateau-Filmwerke* • FRG
GRAUE MACHT, DIE • 1923 • Stranz Fred • FRG
GRAUEN, DAS • 1920 • Sauer Fred • FRG
GRAUSAME FREUDIN, DIE • 1932 • Lamac Carl • AUS, FRG
GRAUSAME JOB, DER (FRG) see **PEAU D'ESPION** • 1967
GRAUSIGE NACHTE • 1921 • Pick Lupu • FRG • HORRIBLE NIGHT
GRAUSIGEN UND SCHRECKLICHEN ABENTEUER EINES BEINAHE NORMALEN MENSCHEN, DIE see **BONDITIS** • 1967
GRAUSTARK • 1915 • Wright Fred E. • USA
GRAUSTARK • 1925 • Buchowetzki Dimitri • USA
GRAUZONE, DIE • 1977 • Murer Fredi M. • SWT
GRAVE, THE see **KIZGIN TOPRAK** • 1974
GRAVE AFFAIR, A • 1914 • *Gaumont* • UKN
GRAVE DESIRES see **BRIDES OF BLOOD** • 1968
GRAVE DIGGER'S AMBITIONS • 1913 • *Welt* • USA
GRAVE NEW WORLD • 1971 • Turner Steve • SHT • UKN
GRAVE OF THE SUN see **TAIYO NO HAKABA** • 1960
GRAVE OF THE VAMPIRE • 1972 • Hayes John • USA • SEED OF TERROR
GRAVE ROBBERS see **LADRON DE CADAVERES** • 1956
GRAVE ROBBERS FROM OUTER SPACE see **PLAN 9 FROM OUTER SPACE** • 1956
GRAVE TELLS ALL, THE see **SAIGO NO KIRIFUDA** • 1960
GRAVE UNDERTAKING, THE • 1917 • *Binns George* • SHT • USA
GRAVEDIGGER OF STORIES, THE see **ENTERRADOR DE CUENTOS, EL** • 1978
GRAVEDIGGER'S VOICE, THE see **VOZ DO COVEIRO, A** • 1943
GRAVESIDE STORY, THE see **COMEDY OF TERRORS, THE** • 1963
GRAVEYARD, THE see **PERSECUTION** • 1973
GRAVEYARD DISTURBANCE • 1987 • Bava Lamberto • ITL
GRAVEYARD OF CHRYSANTHEMUMS see **NOGIKU NO HAKA** • 1982
GRAVEYARD OF HORROR • 1971 • *Curran Bill* • MXC
GRAVEYARD OF HORROR see **DESCUARTIZADOR DE BINBROOK, EL** • 1971
GRAVEYARD OF THE FIREFLY, THE see **HOTARU NO HAKA** • 1988
GRAVEYARD OF YAKUZA, THE see **YAKUZA NO HAKABA** • 1976
GRAVEYARD SHIFT • 1986 • Ciccoritti Gerard • USA
GRAVEYARD SHIFT 2 see **GRAVEYARD SHIFT II: THE UNDERSTUDY** • 1989
GRAVEYARD SHIFT II: THE UNDERSTUDY • 1989 • Ciccoritti Gerard • USA • UNDERSTUDY, THE ○ GRAVEYARD SHIFT 2
GRAVEYARD TRAMPS see **INVASION OF THE BEE GIRLS** • 1973
GRAVITACIJA, ILI FANTASTICNA MLADOST CINOVNIKA BORISA HORVATA • 1968 • Ivanda Branko • YGS • GRAVITATION, OR THE FANTASTIC YOUTH OF BORIS HORVAT, THE CLERK
GRAVITATION, OR THE FANTASTIC YOUTH OF BORIS HORVAT, THE CLERK see **GRAVITACIJA, ILI FANTASTICNA MLADOST CINOVNIKA BORISA HORVATA** • 1968
GRAVITY AND SPACE • 1959 • Porter Eric • ANS • ASL
GRAVURE, LA • 1973 • Frappier Roger • DCS • CND
GRAVY • 1916 • *Drew Sidney* • SHT • USA
GRAVY TRAIN, THE • 1974 • Starrett Jack • TVM • USA • DION BROTHERS, THE
GRAY CLOUD'S DEVOTION • 1911 • *Bison* • USA
GRAY DAME, THE see **GRAA DAME, DEN** • 1909
GRAY DAWN, THE • 1922 • Howe Eliot? • USA • GREY DAWN, THE
GRAY GHOST, THE • 1917 • Paton Stuart • SRL • USA
GRAY HORIZON, THE • 1919 • Worthington William • USA
GRAY HORROR, THE • 1915 • *Smiley Joseph* • USA
GRAY HOUNDED HARE, THE • 1949 • McKimson Robert • ANS • USA
GRAY LADY, THE (UKN) see **GREY DAME, THE** • 1909
GRAY LADY DOWN • 1978 • Greene David • USA
GRAY MASK, THE • 1915 • Crane Frank H. • USA
GRAY MATTER see **BRAIN MACHINE, THE** • 1972
GRAY TOWERS MYSTERY, THE • 1919 • Noble John W. • USA • GREY TOWERS MYSTERY, THE
GRAY WOLF'S GHOST, THE • 1919 • Frame Park?, Franz Joseph J.? • USA • MARUJA
GRAY WOLF'S GRIEF • 1911 • *Powers* • USA
GRAY WOLF'S SQUAW • 1911 • *Yankee* • USA
GRAY WOLVES, THE • 1911 • *Selig* • USA
GRAYEAGLE • 1977 • Pierce Charles B. • USA
GRAZIE NONNA • 1975 • Girolami Marino • ITL • LOVER BOY (UKN)
GRAZIE, SIGNORE P.. • 1972 • Stefani Mauro • ITL
GRAZIE TANTE ARRIVEDERCI • 1977 • Ivaldi Mauro O. • ITL
GRAZIE, ZIA • 1967 • Samperi Salvatore • ITL • THANK YOU, AUNT (USA) ○ COME PLAY WITH ME ○ THANKS, AUNT
GRAZIE ZIO CI PROVO ANCH'IO • 1971 • Iquino Ignacio F. • ITL
GRAZIELLA • 1926 • Vandal Marcel • FRN
GRAZIELLA • 1955 • Bianchi Giorgio • ITL
GRE-NO-LI, NACKA & CO. • 1951 • Nycop Carl Adam, Engstrom Gert • SWD
GREASE • 1951 • Luff A. H. • UKN
GREASE • 1978 • Kleiser Randall • USA
GREASE 2 • 1982 • Birch Patricia • USA
GREASE PAINT INDIANS • 1913 • Haddock William F. • USA
GREASED LIGHTNING • 1919 • Storm Jerome • USA
GREASED LIGHTNING • 1928 • Taylor Ray • USA
GREASED LIGHTNING • 1977 • Schultz Michael • USA
GREASER, THE • 1915 • Walsh Raoul • USA
GREASER AND THE WEAKLING, THE • 1912 • Dwan Allan • USA
GREASER'S GAUNTLET, THE • 1908 • Griffith D. W. • USA
GREASER'S PALACE • 1972 • Downey Robert • USA
GREASER'S REVENGE, THE • 1914 • *Frontier* • USA
GREAT • 1975 • Godfrey Bob • ANS • UKN • GREAT ISAMBARD KINGDOM BRUNEL
GREAT ACCIDENT, THE • 1920 • Beaumont Harry • USA
GREAT ADVENTURE, THE • 1915 • Trimble Larry • UKN
GREAT ADVENTURE, THE • 1918 • Blache Alice • USA
GREAT ADVENTURE, THE • 1921 • Webb Kenneth • USA
GREAT ADVENTURE, THE • 1952 • Makovec Milos • CZC
GREAT ADVENTURE, THE see **ADVENTURERS, THE** • 1951
GREAT ADVENTURE, THE see **STORA AVENTYRET, DET** • 1953
GREAT ADVENTURE, THE (USA) see **RICHIAMO DEL LUPO, IL** • 1975
GREAT ADVENTURE OF LOVE see **KOI NO DAIBOKEN** • 1970
GREAT ADVENTURES OF CAPTAIN KIDD, THE • 1953 • Gould Charles, Abrahams Derwin • SRL • USA
GREAT ADVENTURES OF WILD BILL HICKOK, THE • 1938 • Wright Mack V., Nelson Sam • SRL • USA
GREAT ADVENTURES ON BOTTLE-GOURD ISLAND see **HYOKKORI HYOTAN JIMA** • 1967
GREAT AIR ROBBERY, THE • 1920 • Jaccard Jacques • USA
GREAT ALASKAN MYSTERY, THE • 1944 • Taylor Ray, Collins Lewis D. • SRL • USA • GREAT NORTHERN MYSTERY, THE (UKN)
GREAT ALBANIAN WARRIOR SKANDERBEG, THE see **VELIKII VOIN ALBANII SKANDERBEG** • 1953
GREAT ALLIGATOR, THE (USA) see **ALLIGATORS** • 1980
GREAT ALONE, THE • 1922 • Jaccard Jacques, Colwell James • USA
GREAT AMATEUR, THE see **STORE AMATOREN, DEN** • 1958
GREAT AMERICAN BEAUTY CONTEST, THE • 1973 • Day Robert • TVM • USA
GREAT AMERICAN BROADCAST, THE • 1941 • Mayo Archie • USA
GREAT AMERICAN COWBOY, THE • 1974 • Merrill Keith • DOC • USA
GREAT AMERICAN GAME, THE • 1917 • *Rhodes Billie* • USA
GREAT AMERICAN MUG, THE • 1945 • Endfield Cy • SHT • USA
GREAT AMERICAN PASTIME, THE • 1956 • Hoffman Herman • USA
GREAT AMERICAN PIE COMPANY, THE • 1935 • Grinde Nick • SHT • USA
GREAT AMERICAN RODEO, THE • 1974 • Merrill Keith • USA
GREAT AMERICAN TRAFFIC JAM, THE • 1980 • Frawley James • TVM • USA • GRIDLOCK
GREAT AMERICAN TRAGEDY, A • 1972 • Thompson J. Lee • TVM • USA
GREAT ANARCHIST MYSTERY, THE • 1912 • Raymond Charles • UKN
GREAT AND SMALL see **VELIKI I MALI** • 1956
GREAT ARCTIC SEAL HUNT see **SWILIN' RACKET, THE** • 1928
GREAT ARMORED CAR SWINDLE, THE (USA) see **BREAKING POINT, THE** • 1961
GREAT ART, THE see **GRANDE ARTE, A** • 1989
GREAT ASIA WAR AND THE INTERNATIONAL TRIBUNAL, THE see **DAITOWA SENSO TO KOKUSAI SAIBAN** • 1959
GREAT AUSTRALIAN BUSH, ITS WONDERS AND MYSTERY, THE • 1927 • *Bailey Edward Percy* • DOC • USA
GREAT AWAKENING, THE (UKN) see **NEW WINE** • 1941
GREAT BALLOON ADVENTURE, THE see **OLLY OLLY OXEN FREE** • 1978
GREAT BALLS OF FIRE • 1989 • McBride Jim • USA
GREAT BANK HOAX, THE see **SHENANIGANS** • 1977
GREAT BANK ROBBERY, THE • 1969 • Averback Hy • USA
GREAT BANK SENSATION, THE • 1915 • Noy Wilfred • UKN
GREAT BARGAIN SALE, THE • 1908 • Williamson James? • UKN
GREAT BARRIER, THE • 1937 • Rosmer Milton • UKN • SILENT BARRIERS (USA)
GREAT BATTLE, THE see **OSVOBOZHDENIE** • 1970
GREAT BATTLE, THE see **GRANDE ATTACCO, IL** • 1978
GREAT BATTLE OF EUROPE, THE (USA) see **VELIKAYA POBEDA SOVETSKOGO NARODA** • 1961
GREAT BATTLE OF THE VOLGA, THE (USA) see **VELIKAYA BITVA NA VOLGE** • 1963
GREAT BEGINNING, THE see **CHLEN PRAVITELSTAVA** • 1940
GREAT BET, THE (USA) see **GROSSE WETTE, DIE** • 1915
GREAT BETRAYAL, THE see **DAY OF TRIUMPH** • 1954
GREAT BIG BUNCH OF YOU, A • 1933 • Ising Rudolf • ANS • USA
GREAT BIG THING, A • 1966 • Till Eric • CND
GREAT BIG WORLD AND LITTLE CHILDREN see **WIELKA, WIELKA I NAJWIEKSZA** • 1962
GREAT BIRD MYSTERY, THE • 1932 • *Mintz Charles (P)* • ANS • USA
GREAT BLACK VS. WHITE PRIZE FIGHT, THE • 1910 • *Gaumont* • UKN
GREAT BLEK, THE see **GRANDE BLEK, IL** • 1988
GREAT BLONDINO, THE • 1967 • Nelson Robert • USA
GREAT BODHISATTVA PASS, THE see **DAIBOSATSU TOGE** • 1935
GREAT BODHISATTVA PASS, THE see **DAIBOSATSU TOGE** • 1957
GREAT BOGGS HAIR GROWER, THE • 1912 • *Majestic* • USA
GREAT BOOKIE ROBBERY, THE • 1985 • Cole Marcus, Joffe Mark • MTV • ASL
GREAT BOREDOM, THE • 1972 • Andonov Metodi • BUL
GREAT BRADLEY MYSTERY, THE • 1917 • Ridgely Richard • USA • WHOSE HAND?
GREAT BRAIN, THE • 1978 • Levin Sidney • USA
GREAT BRAIN ROBBERY, THE • Plymell Charles • ANS • USA
GREAT BRITISH TRAIN ROBBERY, THE (USA) see **GENTLEMEN BITTEN ZUR KASSE, DIE** • 1965
GREAT BULDIS, THE see **DVA, BOULDEJ, DVA** • 1930
GREAT BULL FIGHT • 1902 • Porter Edwin S. • USA
GREAT BULLION ROBBERY, THE • 1913 • Butler Alexander • UKN
GREAT BULLION ROBBERY, THE see **GREAT MAIL ROBBERY, THE** • 1927
GREAT CANADIAN SHOE-OFF, THE • 1972 • Lamothe Arthur • DCS • CND • A BON PIED, BON OEIL
GREAT CARGOES • 1935 • Rotha Paul • UKN
GREAT CARROT TRAIN ROBBERY, THE • 1969 • McKimson Robert • ANS • USA
GREAT CARUSO, THE • 1951 • Thorpe Richard • USA
GREAT CASH GIVEAWAY GETAWAY, THE • 1980 • O'Herlihy Michael • TVM • USA
GREAT CATCH, THE see **WIELKI POLOW** • 1961
GREAT CATHERINE • 1967 • Flemyng Gordon • UKN
GREAT CENTURY, THE • 1958 • Skanata Krsto • DOC • YGS
GREAT CHALLENGE, THE see **GRAN DESAFIO, EL** • 1977
GREAT CHANCE, THE see **VELKA PRILEZITOST** • 1950
GREAT CHASE, THE • 1962 • *Cort Harvey (P)* • CMP • USA
GREAT CHASE, THE (UKN) see **A TOUT CASSER** • 1968
GREAT CHEEZE MYSTERY, THE • 1941 • Davis Arthur • ANS • USA
GREAT CHEQUE FRAUD, THE • 1915 • Raymond Charles • UKN
GREAT CHESS MOVIE, THE see **JOUER SA VIE** • 1982
GREAT CHICAGO CONSPIRACY CIRCUS, THE see **CHICAGO 70** • 1970
GREAT CHRISTENING, THE • 1931 • NRW
GREAT CIRCLE • Napier-Bell J. B. • DOC • UKN
GREAT CIRCUS MYSTERY, THE • 1925 • Marchant Jay • USA
GREAT CITIZEN, A see **VELIKI GRAZHDANIN** • 1938
GREAT CITY, THE see **DAITOKAI RODOHEN** • 1930
GREAT CITY FIRE, THE • 1903 • *Warwick Trading Co* • UKN • LIFE OF AN ENGLISH FIREMAN, THE (USA)
GREAT CLOWN, THE see **MUHARRAJ EL KABIR, EL** • 1951
GREAT CLOWN, THE see **GRANDE PALHACO, O** • 1982
GREAT COGNITO, THE • 1983 • Vinton Will • ANS • USA
GREAT COMMANDMENT, THE • 1939 • Pichel Irving • USA
GREAT CONCERT see **BOLSHOI KONCERT** • 1951
GREAT CONSOLER, THE see **VELIKII UTESHITEL** • 1933
GREAT CONWAY, THE • 1940 • Reynolds S. E. • UKN
GREAT CORONA RACE, THE • 1916 • Stanton Richard • SHT • USA • SPEED KING, THE
GREAT COUP, A • 1919 • Dewhurst George • UKN
GREAT COUP OF THE 7 GOLDEN MEN see **GRANDE COLPO DEI 7 UOMINI D'ORO, IL** • 1966
GREAT COUPS OF HISTORY • 1970 • Darcus Jack • CND
GREAT CRUSADE, THE • 1936 • Watts Fred • UKN
GREAT DAN PATCH, THE • 1949 • Newman Joseph M. • USA • RIDE A RECKLESS MILE
GREAT DAWN, THE • 1938 • Chiaureli Mikhail • USS • THEY WANTED PEACE
GREAT DAWN, THE (USA) see **GRANDE AURORA, LA** • 1948
GREAT DAY • 1930 • Pollard Harry • USA
GREAT DAY • 1945 • Comfort Lance • UKN
GREAT DAY, THE • 1920 • Ford Hugh • USA
GREAT DAY, THE • 1952 • Burn Oscar • UKN
GREAT DAY, THE • 1969 • Ilic Dragoslav • YGS
GREAT DAY, THE see **GIORNATA PARTICOLARE, UNA** • 1977
GREAT DAY IN THE MORNING • 1956 • Tourneur Jacques • USA
GREAT DECEIT, THE • 1915 • Windom Lawrence C. • USA
GREAT DECEPTION, THE • 1926 • Higgin Howard • USA
GREAT DECIDE, THE • 1925 • Ruggles Wesley • SHT • USA

GREAT DECISION (UKN) see **MEN OF AMERICA** • 1932

GREAT DEFENDER, THE • 1934 • Bentley Thomas • UKN

GREAT DESIRE, THE see **CHRISTOPHER STRONG** • 1933

GREAT DETECTIVE, THE • 1915 • McKim Edwin • USA

GREAT DETECTIVE, THE • 1916 • *Hamilton Lloyd V.* • USA

GREAT DEVOTION, THE see **GREATER DEVOTION, THE** • 1914

GREAT DIAMOND MYSTERY, THE • 1924 • Clift Denison • USA

GREAT DIAMOND ROBBERY, THE • 1912 • *Vitagraph* • USA

GREAT DIAMOND ROBBERY, THE • 1914 • Arthur Daniel V. • USA

GREAT DIAMOND ROBBERY, THE • 1953 • Leonard Robert Z. • USA

GREAT DIAMOND ROBBERY, THE see **COLPO MAESTRO AL SERVIZIO DI SUA MAESTA BRITANNICA** • 1967

GREAT DICTATOR, THE • 1940 • Chaplin Charles • USA

GREAT DIRECT see **SEIKI NO DAIJAKUTEN** • 1968

GREAT DISCOVERY, THE • 1912 • *Solax* • USA

GREAT DISCOVERY, THE • 1913 • *Lubin* • USA

GREAT DIVIDE, THE • 1916 • Lewis Edgar • USA

GREAT DIVIDE, THE • 1924 • Barker Reginald • USA

GREAT DIVIDE, THE • 1930 • Barker Reginald • USA

GREAT DIVIDE, THE • 1951 • Sparling Gordon • DCS • CND

GREAT DOCUMENT, THE • 1980 • Filis Yannis • DOC • GRC

GREAT DRAUGHT, THE • 1912 • Campbell Colin • USA

GREAT DREAM, THE see **EMBRACERS, THE** • 1963

GREAT EARTH, THE see **BOLSHAYA ZEMLYA** • 1944

GREAT EASTERN STEEPLECHASE • 1925 • ASL

GREAT EASTERN STEEPLECHASE, OAKBANK HURDLES, OAKBANK CUP • 1915 • *Krischock H. (Ph)* • ASL

GREAT ECSTASY OF THE SCULPTOR STEINER, THE see **GROSSE EKSTASE DES BILDSCHNITZERS STEINER, DIE** • 1975

GREAT ECSTASY OF WOODCARVER STEINER, THE (UKN) see **GROSSE EKSTASE DES BILDSCHNITZERS STEINER, DIE** • 1975

GREAT ENERGY WASTE, THE • 1983 • Arioli Don • ANS • CND

GREAT ENTANGLEMENT, THE see **GROSSE VERHAU, DER** • 1970

GREAT ESCAPE 2, THE • 1988 • Wendkos Paul • MTV • USA • GREAT ESCAPE 2: THE UNTOLD STORY

GREAT ESCAPE 2: THE UNTOLD STORY see **GREAT ESCAPE 2, THE** • 1988

GREAT ESCAPE, THE • 1963 • Sturges John • USA

GREAT EVENTS AND ORDINARY PEOPLE see **DE GRANDS EVENEMENTS ET DES GENS ORDINAIRES** • 1979

GREAT EXPECTATIONS • 1917 • Vignola Robert G., Kaufman Joseph • USA

GREAT EXPECTATIONS • 1934 • Walker Stuart • USA

GREAT EXPECTATIONS • 1946 • Lean David • UKN

GREAT EXPECTATIONS • 1974 • Blom Per • SHT • NRW

GREAT EXPECTATIONS • 1975 • Hardy Joseph • TVM • UKN

GREAT EXPECTATIONS • 1982 • Tych Jean • ANM • ASL

GREAT EXPECTATIONS see **STORE FORVENTNINGER** • 1921

GREAT EXPECTATIONS – THE AUSTRALIAN STORY • 1986 • Burstall Tim • ASL • GREAT EXPECTATIONS – THE UNTOLD STORY

GREAT EXPECTATIONS – THE UNTOLD STORY see **GREAT EXPECTATIONS – THE AUSTRALIAN STORY** • 1986

GREAT EXPEDITION, THE • 1959 • Winter Donovan • UKN

GREAT EXPERIMENT, THE • 1915 • Santschi Thomas • USA

GREAT EXPERIMENT, THE • 1934 • *Mintz Charles (P)* • ANS • USA

GREAT EXPLORATIONS WITH JOHN GLENN –AFRICA • 1969 • Cominos N. H. • DOC • USA

GREAT FEAR, THE • 1915 • Dowlan William C. • USA

GREAT FEAR, THE see **VELIKI STRAH** • 1958

GREAT FEAR, THE see **GRANDE FROUSSE, LA** • 1964

GREAT FIGHT AT ALL–SERENO, THE • 1910 • Bouwmeester Theo? • UKN

GREAT FIGHT FOR THE CHAMPIONSHIP OF OUR COURT, THE • 1911 • *Urban Trading Co.* • UKN

GREAT FINALE TO ACT 1 (THE YEOMAN OF THE GUARD) • 1907 • Morland John • UKN

GREAT FISH OF MAUI, THE • 1968 • O'Neill Fred • ANS • NZL

GREAT FLAMARION, THE • 1945 • Mann Anthony • USA

GREAT FLIRTATION, THE • 1934 • Murphy Ralph • USA • I MARRIED AN ACTRESS

GREAT FOOL, THE see **DAKILANG TANGA** • 1968

GREAT FORCE, THE see **VELIKAYA SILA** • 1949

GREAT FRIENDS see **GRANDES AMIGOS** • 1967

GREAT GABBO, THE • 1929 • Cruze James • USA

GREAT GALEOTO, THE see **LOVERS?** • 1927

GREAT GAMBINI, THE • 1937 • Vidor Charles • USA

GREAT GAMBLE, THE • 1919 • Golden Joseph A. • SRL • USA

GREAT GAMBLER –AN IMAGE OF OUR TIME, THE see **DR. MABUSE, DER SPIELER 1** • 1922

GREAT GAME, A • 1909 • Porter Edwin S. • USA

GREAT GAME, THE • 1913 • *Warfield Irene* • USA

GREAT GAME, THE • 1918 • Coleby A. E. • UKN

GREAT GAME, THE • 1930 • Raymond Jack • UKN

GREAT GAME, THE • 1945 • Cass Henry • DCS • UKN

GREAT GAME, THE • 1953 • Elvey Maurice • UKN

GREAT GAME, THE see **GRAND JEU, LE** • 1933

GREAT GANTON MYSTERY, THE • 1913 • *Leonard Robert* • USA

GREAT GARRICK, THE • 1937 • Whale James • USA

GREAT GATSBY, THE • 1926 • Brenon Herbert • USA

GREAT GATSBY, THE • 1949 • Nugent Elliott • USA

GREAT GATSBY, THE • 1974 • Clayton Jack • USA

GREAT GAY ROAD, THE • 1920 • MacDonald Norman • UKN

GREAT GAY ROAD, THE • 1931 • Hill Sinclair • UKN

GREAT GENERATION, THE see **MAGY GENERACIO, A** • 1985

GREAT GEORGIA BANK HOAX, THE see **SHENANIGANS** • 1977

GREAT GERMAN NORTH SEA TUNNEL, THE • 1914 • Newman Frank • UKN

GREAT GILBERT AND SULLIVAN, THE (USA) see **STORY OF GILBERT AND SULLIVAN, THE** • 1953

GREAT GILDERSLEEVE, THE • 1942 • Douglas Gordon • USA

GREAT GIMMICK, THE see **GRAND BIDULE, LE** • 1967

GREAT GLINKA, THE (USA) see **GLINKA** • 1946

GREAT GLOVE FIGHT • 1900 • Williamson James • UKN

GREAT GLOVER, THE • 1939-43 • *Bridges Lloyd* • SHT • USA

GREAT GOBS • 1929 • Doane Warren • SHT • USA

GREAT GOD FEAR, THE • 1914 • *Marsh Mae* • USA

GREAT GOD GOLD • 1935 • Lubin Arthur • USA

GREAT GOLD ROBBERY, THE • 1913 • Elvey Maurice • UKN

GREAT GOLD SWINDLE, THE • 1984 • Power John • MTV • ASL

GREAT GRAND MOTHER • 1975 • Wheeler Anne • CND

GREAT GUNDOWN, THE • 1977 • Hunt Paul • USA

GREAT GUNDOWN, THE see **MACHISMO –40 GRAVES FOR 40 GUNS** • 1970

GREAT GUNS • 1927 • Disney Walt • ANS • USA

GREAT GUNS • 1932 • Lantz Walter, Nolan William • ANS • USA

GREAT GUNS • 1941 • Banks Monty • USA

GREAT GUY • 1936 • Blystone John G. • USA • PLUCK OF THE IRISH (UKN)

GREAT GUY AT HEART, A see **LAF U SRCU** • 1982

GREAT HANGMEN, THE see **SEYTANIN OGLU** • 1967

GREAT HARMONY, THE • 1913 • Dwan Allan • USA

GREAT HARVEST, THE • 1943 • Chambers Jack, Rotha Paul • DOC • UKN

GREAT HEART, THE • 1938 • Miller David • SHT • USA • FATHER DAMIEN

GREAT HEART OF THE WEST, THE • 1911 • Melies Gaston • USA

GREAT HEIGHT see **VYSOTA** • 1957

GREAT HERITAGE, THE see **GRAN HERENCIA, LA**

GREAT HIGHWAY, THE see **GRAN RUTA, LA** • 1972

GREAT HORA, THE • 1958 • Lotyanu Emil • SHT • USS

GREAT HOSPITAL MYSTERY, THE • 1937 • Tinling James • USA

GREAT HOTEL MURDER, THE see **GREAT HOTEL MYSTERY, THE** • 1935

GREAT HOTEL MYSTERY, THE • 1935 • Forde Eugene J. • USA • GREAT HOTEL MURDER, THE

GREAT HOUDINIS, THE • 1976 • Shavelson Melville • TVM • USA

GREAT HOUSE, THE see **CASA GRANDE, LA** • 1975

GREAT HUNGER DUEL, THE • 1922 • Graeme Kenneth • UKN

GREAT ICE RIP–OFF, THE • 1974 • Curtis Dan • TVM • USA

GREAT IDEA, A • 1935 • Schwarzwald Milton • SHT • USA

GREAT IMPERSONATION, THE • 1921 • Melford George • USA

GREAT IMPERSONATION, THE • 1935 • Crosland Alan • USA

GREAT IMPERSONATION, THE • 1942 • Rawlins John • USA

GREAT IMPOSTER, THE • 1918 • Thornton F. Martin • UKN

GREAT IMPOSTOR, THE • 1960 • Mulligan Robert • USA

GREAT INCIDENT see **VELKY PRIPAD** • 1946

GREAT INCIDENTS see **BAKUSHOYARO DAIJIKEN** • 1967

GREAT INHERITANCE, THE see **GHOST OF THEIR ANCESTORS, THE** • 1915

GREAT IS MY COUNTRY see **HOW BROAD IS OUR COUNTRY** • 1958

GREAT ISAMBARD KINGDOM BRUNEL see **GREAT** • 1975

GREAT JASPER • 1933 • Ruben J. Walter • USA

GREAT JESSE JAMES RAID, THE • 1953 • Le Borg Reginald • USA

GREAT JEWEL MYSTERY • 1905 • *Bitzer Billy (Ph)* • USA

GREAT JEWEL ROBBER, THE • 1950 • Godfrey Peter • USA • AFTER NIGHTFALL

GREAT JEWEL ROBBERY, THE • 1925 • Ince John • USA

GREAT JEWEL ROBBERY, THE (USA) see **KRADJA DRAGULJA** • 1959

GREAT JOHN L., THE • 1944 • Tuttle Frank • USA • MAN CALLED SULLIVAN, A (UKN)

GREAT JUNCTION HOTEL, THE • 1931 • Beaudine William • SHT • USA

GREAT K & A TRAIN ROBBERY, THE • 1926 • Seiler Lewis • USA

GREAT KALI'S VICTORY see **JAI MAHAKALI** • 1951

GREAT KIDNAPPING, THE see **POLIZIA STA A GUARDARE, LA** • 1973

GREAT KING, THE see **GROSSE KONIG, DER** • 1942

GREAT LAND, THE see **BOLSHAYA ZEMLYA** • 1944

GREAT LAND OF SMALL, THE see **C'EST PAS PARCE QU'ON EST PETIT QU'ON PEUT PAS ETRE GRAND** • 1987

GREAT LEAP, THE • 1914 • Cabanne W. Christy • USA

GREAT LESTER BOGGS, THE • 1975 • Thomason Harry • USA

GREAT LIE, THE • 1941 • Goulding Edmund • USA

GREAT LIFE, A see **BOLSHAYA ZHIZN** • 1940

GREAT LIGHT, THE (USA) see **GRANDE LUCE, LA** • 1939

GREAT LITTLE ARTIST, A • 1978 • Defalco Martin • MTV • CND

GREAT LOCOMOTIVE CHASE, THE • 1956 • Lyon Francis D. • USA • ANDREW'S RAIDER

GREAT LONDON MYSTERY, THE • 1920 • Raymond Charles • SRL • UKN

GREAT LONE LAND, THE • 1915 • Fielding Romaine • USA

GREAT LOVE, A • 1916 • Elfelt Clifford S. • USA

GREAT LOVE, A see **ETSI GENNITHIKE MIA MEGALI AGAPI** • 1968

GREAT LOVE, THE • 1918 • Griffith D. W. • USA

GREAT LOVE, THE • 1925 • Neilan Marshall • USA

GREAT LOVE, THE see **STORA KARLEKEN, DEN** • 1938

GREAT LOVE, THE see **GROSSE LIEBE, DIE** • 1942

GREAT LOVE, THE see **GRAND AMOUR, LE** • 1968

GREAT LOVE OF CAPTAIN BRANDO, THE see **AMOR DEL CAPITAN BRANDO, EL** • 1974

GREAT LOVE OF COUNT DRACULA, THE see **GRAN AMOR DEL CONDE DRACULA, EL** • 1972

GREAT LOVE SONGS, THE see **MEGALOS EROTIKOS, O** • 1972

GREAT LOVER, THE • 1920 • Lloyd Frank • USA

GREAT LOVER, THE • 1931 • Beaumont Harry • USA

GREAT LOVER, THE • 1949 • Hall Alexander • USA

GREAT LOVER, THE see **DON JUAN** • 1956

GREAT LOVER, THE see **TOKOH** • 1974

GREAT LOVES see **MEGALES AGAPES** • 1968

GREAT LURE OF PARIS, THE • 1913 • *Feature Photoplay Co* • SHT • USA

GREAT MACARTHY, THE • 1975 • Baker David • ASL

GREAT MADCAP, THE (USA) see **GRAN CALAVERA, EL** • 1949

GREAT MADMAN, THE see **GRANDE MENTECAPTO, O** • 1988

GREAT MAGIC see **MAHA MAYA** • 1945

GREAT MAIL ROBBERY, THE • 1927 • Seitz George B. • USA • GREAT BULLION ROBBERY, THE

GREAT MAN, THE • 1956 • Ferrer Jose • USA

GREAT MAN VOTES, THE • 1939 • Kanin Garson • USA

GREAT MANHUNT, THE see **STATE SECRET** • 1950

GREAT MANHUNT, THE (UKN) see **DOOLINS OF OKLAHOMA, THE** • 1949

GREAT MAN'S LADY, THE • 1942 • Wellman William A. • USA

GREAT MAN'S WHISKERS, THE • 1971 • Leacock Philip • TVM • USA

GREAT MARSHALL JEWEL CASE, THE • 1910 • *Defender* • USA

GREAT MCGINTY, THE • 1940 • Sturges Preston • USA • DOWN WENT MCGINTY (UKN)

GREAT MCGONAGALL, THE • 1974 • McGrath Joseph • UKN

GREAT MEADOW, THE • 1931 • Brabin Charles J. • USA

GREAT MEDDLER, THE • 1940 • Zinnemann Fred • SHT • USA

GREAT MEETING see **VELIKI MITING** • 1951

GREAT MELIES, THE see **GRAND MELIES, LE** • 1952

GREAT METROPOLIS: CHAPTER ON LABOUR, THE see **DAITOKAI RODOHEN** • 1930

GREAT MIKE, THE • 1944 • Fox Wallace • USA

GREAT MILL RACE, THE • 1975 • Crichton Robin • UKN

GREAT MINE DISASTER, THE (USA) see **HEROES OF THE MINE** • 1913

GREAT MISSOURI RAID, THE • 1950 • Douglas Gordon • USA

GREAT MISTAKE, A • 1910 • Rosenthal Joe • UKN

GREAT MR. HANDEL, THE • 1942 • Walker Norman • UKN

GREAT MR. NOBODY, THE • 1941 • Stoloff Ben • USA • BASHFUL HERO ○ STUFF OF HEROES

GREAT MOMENT, THE • 1921 • Wood Sam • USA

GREAT MOMENT, THE • 1944 • Sturges Preston • USA • GREAT WITHOUT GLORY ○ TRIUMPH OVER PAIN

GREAT MONKEY RIP–OFF, THE • 1979 • Stobart Thomas • USA

GREAT MONSTER YONGARY see **DAI KOESU YONGKARI** • 1967

GREAT MORGAN, THE • 1946 • Perrin Nat • USA

GREAT MOTOR BUS OUTRAGE, THE • 1915 • Noy Wilfred • UKN

GREAT MOUSE DETECTIVE, THE • 1986 • Musker John, Clements Ron, Michener Dave, Mattinson Burny • ANM • USA

GREAT MUPPET CAPER, THE • 1981 • Henson Jim • UKN

GREAT NEW YORK CON GAME, THE see **NEW YORK GAERI NO INAKKAPPE** • 1967

GREAT NIAGARA, THE • 1974 • Hale William • TVM • USA

GREAT NICKEL ROBBERY, THE • 1920 • Blystone John G. • SHT • USA

GREAT NIGHT, THE • 1922 • Mitchell Howard M. • USA

GREAT NIGHT BATHE, THE • 1980 • Zheljazkova Binka • BUL

GREAT NORTHERN MYSTERY, THE (UKN) see **GREAT ALASKAN MYSTERY, THE** • 1944

GREAT NORTHFIELD MINNESOTA RAID, THE • 1972 • Kaufman Philip • USA

GREAT OATH, THE see **BUYUK YEMIN** • 1967

GREAT OFFICE MYSTERY, THE • 1928 • *Banfield George J. (P)* • UKN

GREAT O'MALLEY, THE • 1937 • Dieterle William • USA • MAKING OF O'MALLEY

GREAT ONE, THE see **NIGHT WITH THE GREAT ONE, A** • 1969

GREAT ORDINARY MOVIE, THE see **GRAND FILM ORDINAIRE, LE** • 1970

GREAT ORE, THE see **BOLSHAYA RUDA** • 1964

GREAT OUTDOORS, THE • 1923 • Roach Hal • SHT • USA

GREAT OUTDOORS, THE • 1988 • Deutch Howard • USA • BIG COUNTRY

GREAT PALISADE, THE see **SOMA DAISAKU** • 1929

GREAT PANTS MYSTERY, THE • 1931 • Taurog Norman • SHT • USA

GREAT PATRIOTIC WAR, THE see **VELIKAYA OTECHESTVENNAYA** • 1965

GREAT PATSY TRIUMPH, THE see **NORMAL LOVE** • 1963

GREAT PEARL, THE • 1913 • *Lubin* • USA

GREAT PEARL TANGLE, THE • 1916 • Henderson Dell • SHT • USA

GREAT PHYSICIAN, THE • 1913 • Merwin Bannister • USA

GREAT PIE MYSTERY, THE • 1931 • Lord Del • SHT • USA

GREAT PIGGY BANK ROBBERY, THE • 1946 • Clampett Robert • ANS • USA

GREAT PLAINS, THE • 1957 • Kroitor Roman • CND

GREAT PLANE ROBBERY, THE • 1940 • Collins Lewis D. • USA

GREAT PLANE ROBBERY, THE • 1950 • Cahn Edward L. • USA

GREAT POISON MYSTERY, THE see **TRAGEDY OF BASIL GRIEVE, THE** • 1914

GREAT POLAND REGION, THE see **ZIEMIA WIELKOPOLSKA** • 1961

GREAT PONY RAID, THE • 1968 • Goode Frederic • UKN

GREAT POWER • 1929 • Rock Joseph • USA

GREAT POWER see **VELIKAYA SILA** • 1949

GREAT POWER RISING IN THE WORLD, A see **SHUSSE TAIKOKI** • 1938

GREAT PRETENDER, THE • 1989 • Webb Hans • SAF

GREAT PRINCE SHAN, THE • 1924 • Coleby A. E. • UKN

GREAT PROBLEM, THE • 1916 • Ingram Rex • USA

GREAT PROFILE, THE • 1940 • Lang Walter • USA

GREAT PUMPKIN PLOT, THE • SHT • USA

GREAT PYTHON ROBBERY, THE • 1914 • Finn Arthur • UKN

GREAT QUESTION, THE • 1915 • Ricketts Thomas • USA

GREAT QUESTION, THE • 1982 • Jamil Mohammed Shoukry • UKN, IRQ

GREAT RACE see **WIELKI BIEG** • 1988

GREAT RACE, THE • 1965 • Edwards Blake • USA

GREAT RADIAL MYSTERY, THE • 1914 • Craft William James • USA

GREAT RADIO MYSTERY, THE (UKN) see **TAKE THE STAND** • 1934

GREAT RADIUM MYSTERY, THE • 1919 • Hill Robert F., Broadwell Robert B. • SRL • USA • RADIUM MYSTERY, THE

GREAT RAILWAY ROBBERY, THE see **MISTAKEN ORDERS** • 1926
GREAT RED WAR, THE • 1916 • Batley Ethyle • UKN
GREAT REDEEMER, THE • 1920 • Brown Clarence, Tourneur Maurice (Spv) • USA
GREAT REMISSION, THE see **GOZASHT-E-BOZORG** • 1967
GREAT REWARD, THE • 1921 • Ford Francis • SRL • USA
GREAT RIDE, A • 1977 • Hulette Donald • USA • NIGHTMARE TRACKS ○ GREAT RIDE, THE
GREAT RIDE, THE see **GREAT RIDE, A** • 1977
GREAT RIVER FLOWS ON, THE see **DAHE BENLIU** • 1978
GREAT RIVIERA BANK ROBBERY, THE • 1979 • Megahy Francis • UKN • SEWERS OF GOLD ○ DIRTY MONEY
GREAT ROAD, THE see **VELIKY PUT** • 1927
GREAT ROAD, THE see **OINARU TABIJO** • 1960
GREAT ROAD, THE see **BOLSHAIA DOROGA** • 1963
GREAT ROCK 'N' ROLL SWINDLE, THE • 1980 • Temple Julien • UKN • ROCK 'N' ROLL SWINDLE, THE
GREAT ROCKY MOUNTAIN JAZZ PARTY, THE • 1977 • Lapenieks Vilis • DOC • USA
GREAT ROCKY MOUNTAIN RELAY RACE, THE • 1982 • Leiterman Richard • MTV • CND
GREAT ROMANCE, THE • 1919 • Otto Henry • USA
GREAT ROMANCE, THE see **FOREVER** • 1921
GREAT ROUND UP, THE • 1920 • Wright Mack V. • SHT • USA
GREAT RUBY, THE • 1915 • O'Neil Barry • USA
GREAT RUBY MYSTERY, THE • 1915 • Turner Otis • USA
GREAT RUPERT, THE • 1950 • Pichel Irving • USA
GREAT SACRIFICE, THE • 1912 • West Raymond B. • USA
GREAT SACRIFICE, THE (UKN) see **OPFERGANG** • 1944
GREAT SAFE TANGLE, THE • 1916 • *Stull Walter* • USA
GREAT ST. LOUIS BANK ROBBERY, THE • 1959 • Guggenheim Charles, Stix John • USA
GREAT ST. TRINIAN'S TRAIN ROBBERY, THE • 1966 • Launder Frank, Gilliat Sidney • UKN
GREAT SALOME DANCE, THE • 1908 • *Tyler Walter* • UKN
GREAT SANTINI, THE • 1979 • Carlino Lewis John • USA • ACE, THE ○ GIFT OF FURY
GREAT SCHNOZZLE, THE (UKN) see **PALOOKA** • 1934
GREAT SCOT • 1920 • *Murray Charles* • SHT • USA
GREAT SCOT ON WHEELS • 1911 • Stow Percy • UKN
GREAT SCOUT AND CATHOUSE THURSDAY, THE • 1976 • Taylor Don • USA • WILDCAT
GREAT SEA SCANDAL, THE • 1918 • Hutchinson Craig • SHT • USA
GREAT SEA SERPENT, THE • 1904 • Williamson James • UKN
GREAT SECLUSION see **VELKA SAMOTA** • 1959
GREAT SECRET, A • 1914 • Taylor William D.? • USA
GREAT SECRET, THE • 1910 • *Edison* • USA
GREAT SECRET, THE • 1917 • Cabanne W. Christy • SRL • USA
GREAT SENSATION, THE • 1925 • Marchant Jay • USA
GREAT SERVANT QUESTION, THE • 1904 • Fitzhamon Lewin • UKN
GREAT SHADOW, THE • 1920 • Knoles Harley • CND, USA
GREAT SILENCE, THE • 1915 • *Bushman Francis X.* • USA
GREAT SILENCE, THE see **GRANDE SILENZIO, IL** • 1968
GREAT SIN, THE see **BUYUK GUNAH** • 1968
GREAT SINNER, THE • 1949 • Siodmak Robert, Leroy Mervyn (U/c) • USA
GREAT SIOUX MASSACRE, THE • 1965 • Salkow Sidney • USA • GREAT SIOUX RAID, THE ○ CUSTER MASSACRE, THE ○ MASSACRE AT THE ROSEBUD
GREAT SIOUX RAID, THE see **GREAT SIOUX MASSACRE, THE** • 1965
GREAT SIOUX UPRISING, THE • 1953 • Bacon Lloyd • USA
GREAT SKI CAPER see **SNOW JOB** • 1972
GREAT SKYCOPTER RESCUE, THE • 1982 • Foldes Lawrence D. • USA
GREAT SMASH, THE • 1916 • *Smith Dick* • SHT • USA
GREAT SMOKEY ROADBLOCK, THE • 1976 • Leone John • USA • LAST OF THE COWBOYS, THE
GREAT SNAKES • 1920 • James Gerald, Quiribet Gaston • UKN
GREAT SOLITUDE • 1989 • Ozkan Yavuz • TRK
GREAT SOLITUDE see **VELKA SAMOTA** • 1959
GREAT SPACE CHASE, THE • 1979 • *Mighty Mouse* • ANM • USA
GREAT SPIDER INVASION, THE see **GIANT SPIDER INVASION, THE** • 1975
GREAT SPY CHASE, THE (USA) see **BARBOUZES, LES** • 1964
GREAT SPY MISSION, THE see **OPERATION CROSSBOW** • 1965
GREAT SPY RAID, THE • 1914 • Morgan Sidney • UKN
GREAT STAGECOACH ROBBERY, THE • 1945 • Selander Lesley • USA
GREAT STANLEY SECRET, THE • 1917 • USA
GREAT STEAM FAIR, THE • 1964 • Knight Derrick, Gladwell David • UKN
GREAT STEEPLECHASE, THE • 1912 • *Cooper Bigelow* • USA
GREAT STONE FACE, THE • 1968 • *Keaton Buster* • CMP • USA
GREAT STRENGTH see **VELIKAYA SILA** • 1949
GREAT STUFF • 1933 • Hiscott Leslie • UKN
GREAT SWINDLE, THE • 1941 • Collins Lewis D. • USA • MISSING EVIDENCE
GREAT SWORDSMEN OF JAPAN see **NIPPON KENGO-DEN** • 1945
GREAT TARWIN BANK ROBBERY, THE • 1959 • Cowan Tom • SHT • ASL
GREAT TASTE see **ODD TASTES** • 1968
GREAT TELEPHONE ROBBERY, THE • 1972 • Golan Menahem • ISR
GREAT TEMPTATION, A • 1906 • Hough Harold • UKN
GREAT TEMPTATION, THE see **PORTE DU LARGE, LA** • 1936
GREAT TEMPTATION OF THE PINK ELEPHANT, THE • 1969 • de Hert Robbe • BLG
GREAT TERROR, THE • 1922 • Ridgwell George • UKN
GREAT TEST, THE • 1928 • Ryder Alexandre • FRN
GREAT TEXAS DYNAMITE CHASE, THE • 1976 • Pressman Michael • USA • DYNAMITE WOMEN ○ DYNAMITE GIRLS
GREAT TIGER RUBY, THE • 1912 • Calvert Charles? • UKN
GREAT TOE MYSTERY, THE • 1914 • Avery Charles • USA
GREAT TORPEDO SECRET, THE • 1917 • Paton Stuart • SHT • USA
GREAT TOWEL ROBBERY, THE • 1913 • *Powers* • USA
GREAT TOY ROBBERY, THE • 1963 • Hale Jeffrey • ANS • CND
GREAT TRAIN HOLD-UP, THE • 1910 • *Melies* • USA
GREAT TRAIN ROBBERY, THE • 1903 • Porter Edwin S. • USA
GREAT TRAIN ROBBERY, THE • 1941 • Kane Joseph • USA
GREAT TRAIN ROBBERY, THE • 1966 • Goldscholl Morton, Goldscholl Mildred • ANM • USA
GREAT TRAIN ROBBERY, THE • 1979 • Crichton Michael • USA, UKN • FIRST GREAT TRAIN ROBBERY, THE (UKN)
GREAT TREASURE, THE • 1917 • Thayer Otis B. • SHT • USA
GREAT TROUBLES • 1961 • Brumberg Valentina, Brumberg Zinaida • ANS • USS
GREAT TRUNK MYSTERY, THE • 1908 • *W. B. & E.* • USA
GREAT TRUTH, THE • 1916 • *Plimpton Epic Pic.* • USA
GREAT TURF MYSTERY, THE • 1924 • West Walter • UKN
GREAT TURNING POINT, THE see **VELIKI PERELOM** • 1946
GREAT UNIVERSAL MYSTERY, THE • 1914 • Dwan Allan • USA
GREAT UNIVERSE, THE • 1955 • Klushantsev Pavel, Leschenko Nestor • USS
GREAT UNKNOWN, THE • 1913 • Lund O. A. C. • CND
GREAT UNKNOWN, THE see **VELKA NEZNAMA** • 1971
GREAT UNWASHED, THE • 1913 • *Ramo* • USA
GREAT VACUUM ROBBERY, THE • 1915 • Jones F. Richard • USA
GREAT VAN ROBBERY, THE • 1959 • Varnel Max • UKN
GREAT VARIETY, THE • 1965 • *Hollywood Mystery Films* • CMP • USA
GREAT VICTOR HERBERT, THE • 1939 • Stone Andrew L. • USA • VICTOR HERBERT
GREAT VICTORY, THE see **VELIKAYA POBEDA** • 1933
GREAT VICTORY, THE see **GOLYAMATA POBEDA** • 1972
GREAT VICTORY, WILSON OR THE KAISER?, THE • 1918 • Miller Charles • SHT • USA • WILSON OR THE KAISER?
GREAT WALDO PEPPER, THE • 1975 • Hill George Roy • USA
GREAT WALL, A see **GREAT WALL, THE** • 1986
GREAT WALL, THE • 1986 • Wang Cheng-Fang • USA, CHN • GREAT WALL IS A GREAT WALL, THE ○ GREAT WALL, A
GREAT WALL, THE see **MURAGLIA CINESE, LA** • 1958
GREAT WALL, THE see **SHIN NO SHIKOTEI** • 1963
GREAT WALL IS A GREAT WALL, THE see **GREAT WALL, THE** • 1986
GREAT WALL OF CHINA, THE • 1970 • Tuber Joel • UKN
GREAT WALL OF CHINA, THE see **SHIN NO SHIKOTEI** • 1963
GREAT WALLED CITY OF XAN, THE • Barwood Hal • ANS • USA
GREAT WALLENDAS, THE • 1978 • Elikann Larry • TVM • USA
GREAT WALTZ, THE • 1938 • Duvivier Julien, Fleming Victor (U/c), von Sternberg Josef (U/c) • USA
GREAT WALTZ, THE • 1972 • Stone Andrew L. • USA
GREAT WAR, THE see **GRANDE GUERRA, LA** • 1959
GREAT WARRIOR, THE see **VELIKII VOIN ALBANII SKANDERBEG** • 1953
GREAT WARRIOR SKANDERBEG, THE see **VELIKII VOIN ALBANII SKANDERBEG** • 1953
GREAT WATER PERIL, THE • 1918 • Roach Hal • SHT • USA
GREAT WATERS see **DA SHUI** • 1989
GREAT WELL, THE • 1924 • Kolker Henry • UKN • NEGLECTED WOMEN (USA)
GREAT WHALES • 1986 • Kool Allen • MTV • CND
GREAT WHILE IT LASTED • 1915 • Roach Hal • USA
GREAT WHITE • 1982 • Castellari Enzo G. • ITL
GREAT WHITE FLEET VISITS THE ANTIPODES, THE • 1908 • Perry Joseph H. • DOC • ASL
GREAT WHITE HOPE, THE • 1970 • Ritt Martin • USA
GREAT WHITE NORTH, THE • 1928 • Snow Sydney, Snow H. A. • USA • LOST IN THE ARCTIC ○ STELLA POLARIS
GREAT WHITE SHARK • 1986 • Kool Allen • CND
GREAT WHITE SILENCE, THE see **WITH CAPTAIN SCOTT, R.N., TO THE SOUTH POLE** • 1911
GREAT WHITE SILENCE, THE see **NINETY DEGREES SOUTH** • 1933
GREAT WHITE TOWER, THE see **SHIROI KYOTO** • 1966
GREAT WHITE TRAIL, THE • 1917 • Wharton Leopold • USA
GREAT WHITE WAY, THE • 1924 • Hopper E. Mason • USA • CAIN AND MABEL
GREAT WHO DOOD IT, THE • 1952 • Lantz Walter • ANS • USA
GREAT WITHOUT GLORY see **GREAT MOMENT, THE** • 1944
GREAT WORLD OF LITTLE CHILDREN, THE see **WIELKA, WIELKA I NAJWIEKSZA** • 1962
GREAT WRONG RIGHTED, A • 1908 • *Selig* • USA
GREAT WRONG RIGHTED, A • 1909 • *Lubin* • USA
GREAT WRONG RIGHTED, A • 1911 • *Yankee* • USA
GREAT YELLOWSTONE PARK HOLD-UP, THE • 1908 • *Kalem* • USA
GREAT ZIEGFELD, THE • 1936 • Leonard Robert Z. • USA
GREATER BARRIER, THE • 1915 • Thayer Otis B. • USA
GREATER CALL, THE • 1910 • *Essanay* • USA
GREATER CALL, THE • 1913 • Lund O. A. C. • USA
GREATER CHRISTIAN, THE • 1912 • *Rex* • USA
GREATER CLAIM, THE • 1921 • Ruggles Wesley • USA
GREATER COURAGE, THE • 1915 • *Essanay* • USA
GREATER COURAGE, THE • 1915 • *Big U* • USA
GREATER DEVOTION, THE • 1914 • Reid Wallace • USA • GREAT DEVOTION, THE
GREATER GLORY, THE • 1926 • Rehfeld Curt • USA • VIENNESE MELODY, THE
GREATER INFLUENCE, A • 1913 • Smalley Phillips • USA
GREATER LAW, THE • 1917 • Reynolds Lynn • USA
GREATER LAW, THE (UKN) see **LITTLE RED SCHOOLHOUSE, THE** • 1923
GREATER LOVE, THE • 1910 • Porter Edwin S. • USA
GREATER LOVE, THE • 1911 • *Reliance* • USA
GREATER LOVE, THE • 1912 • *Rex* • USA
GREATER LOVE, THE • 1912 • *Vitagraph* • USA
GREATER LOVE, THE • 1913 • *Nestor* • USA
GREATER LOVE, THE • 1913 • Dwan Allan • *American* • USA
GREATER LOVE, THE • 1914 • *Essanay* • USA
GREATER LOVE, THE • 1914 • Jones Edgar • *Lubin* • USA
GREATER LOVE, THE • 1914 • Marston Theodore • *Vitagraph* • USA
GREATER LOVE, THE • 1915 • Ince John • USA
GREATER LOVE, THE • 1919 • *King Mollie* • USA
GREATER LOVE, THE • 1919 • Malins Geoffrey H. • UKN
GREATER LOVE, THE see **WEAKNESS OF MAN, THE** • 1916
GREATER LOVE, THE see **STING OF THE LASH, THE** • 1921
GREATER LOVE, THE (UKN) see **RIDER OF THE PLAINS** • 1931
GREATER LOVE HATH NO MAN • 1911 • Blache Alice • USA
GREATER LOVE HATH NO MAN • 1913 • Butler Alexander? • UKN
GREATER LOVE HATH NO MAN • 1914 • Ridgely Richard • USA
GREATER LOVE HATH NO MAN • 1915 • *Corrigan Emmett* • USA
GREATER MOTIVE, THE • 1914 • Marston Theodore • USA
GREATER NEED, THE • 1916 • Dewsbury Ralph • UKN
GREATER OBLIGATION, THE • 1916 • Ashley Charles E. • SHT • USA
GREATER POWER, THE • 1915 • *Brunette Fritzie* • USA
GREATER POWER, THE • 1916 • *Griffith Harry S.* • SHT • USA
GREATER PROFIT, THE • 1921 • Worthington William • USA
GREATER PROMISE, A • 1936 • Korsh-Sablin Vladimir • USS
GREATER PUNISHMENT, THE • 1917 • Grandon Francis J. • SHT • USA
GREATER SINNER, THE • 1919 • Blume A. J. • USA
GREATER STRENGTH, THE • 1915 • Otto Henry • USA
GREATER THAN A CROWN • 1925 • Neill R. William • USA
GREATER THAN ART • 1915 • Collins John H. • USA
GREATER THAN FAME • 1920 • Crosland Alan • USA
GREATER THAN LOVE • 1920 • Stahl John M. • USA
GREATER THAN LOVE • 1921 • Niblo Fred • USA
GREATER THAN MARRIAGE • 1924 • Halperin Victor Hugo • USA
GREATER TREASURE, THE • 1914 • *Lubin* • USA
GREATER WAR, THE • 1926 • Raymond Jack • UKN
GREATER WEALTH • 1912 • Campbell Colin • USA
GREATER WILL, THE • 1915 • Knoles Harley • USA
GREATER WOMAN, THE • 1917 • Powell Frank • USA
GREATER WRONG, THE • 1916 • Terwilliger George W. • SHT • USA
GREATEST, THE • 1977 • Gries Tom • USA, UKN
GREATEST ADVERTISING CAMPAIGN THIS COUNTRY HAS EVER KNOWN • 1976 • Cavadini Alessandro, Cavadini Fabio • DOC • ASL
GREATEST AMERICAN HERO, THE • 1981 • Holcomb Rod • TVM • USA
GREATEST ATTACK, THE (UKN) see **TOUBIB, LE** • 1979
GREATEST BATTLE, THE see **GRANDE ATTACCO, IL** • 1978
GREATEST BATTLE ON EARTH, THE see **SANDAI KAIJU CHIKYU SAIDAI NO KESSEN** • 1965
GREATEST CHALLENGE OF ALL see **KIGEKI: IPPATSU SHOBU** • 1967
GREATEST CHILD IN THE WORLD, THE see **AAZAM TEFL FIL AALAM** • 1976
GREATEST GAME ON EARTH • 1955 • Brealey Gil • DOC • ASL
GREATEST GIFT, THE • 1918 • *Paramount* • SHT • USA
GREATEST GIFT, THE • 1974 • Sagal Boris • TVM • USA
GREATEST GIFT, THE see **IT'S A WONDERFUL LIFE** • 1946
GREATEST HOPE OF THE PEOPLE, THE • 1959 • Makhnach Leonid • DOC • USS
GREATEST IN THE WORLD, THE see **STORSTE I VERDEN, DET** • 1919
GREATEST KIDNAPPING IN THE WEST, THE see **PIU GRANDE RAPINA DEL WEST, LA** • 1967
GREATEST LOVE, THE • 1913 • *Majestic* • USA
GREATEST LOVE, THE • 1920 • Kolker Henry • USA
GREATEST LOVE, THE (USA) see **EUROPA '51** • 1952
GREATEST LOVE OF ALL, THE • 1925 • Beban George • USA
GREATEST MAN IN SIAM, THE • 1944 • Culhane James • ANS • USA
GREATEST MAN IN THE WORLD, THE • 1980 • Rosenblum Ralph • USA
GREATEST MENACE, THE • 1923 • Rogell Albert S. • USA
GREATEST OF THESE, THE • 1911 • Fitzhamon Lewin? • UKN
GREATEST OF THESE, THE • 1914 • *Francis Alec B.* • USA
GREATEST OF THESE, THE • 1926 • Barnett Charles • UKN
GREATEST OF THESE, THE • 1934 • Samuelson G. B. • UKN
GREATEST OF THESE IS CHARITY, THE • 1913 • *Nestor* • USA
GREATEST POWER, THE • 1917 • Carewe Edwin • USA
GREATEST QUESTION, THE • 1920 • Griffith D. W. • USA
GREATEST RESCUES OF EMERGENCY • 1978 • Cinader R. A. • USA
GREATEST SHOW ON EARTH, THE • 1952 • De Mille Cecil B. • USA
GREATEST SIN, THE • 1922 • *Nix Victor* • USA
GREATEST SNOW ON EARTH, THE • 1975 • Cardinal Roger • DCS • CND • PLUS GRANDES NEIGES DU MONDE, LES
GREATEST STORY EVER TOLD, THE • 1965 • Stevens George • USA • JESUS
GREATEST THING IN LIFE, THE • 1918 • Griffith D. W. • USA
GREATEST THING IN THE WORLD, THE • 1912 • *Wilder Marshall P.* • USA
GREATEST THING THAT ALMOST HAPPENED, THE • 1977 • Moses Gilbert • TVM • USA
GREATEST TRUTH, THE • 1921 • May Joe • FRG
GREATEST WILL, THE see **VONTADE MAIOR, UMA** • 1967
GREATEST WISH IN THE WORLD, THE • 1918 • Elvey Maurice • UKN
GREATHEART • 1921 • Ridgwell George • UKN
GRECIAN VASE, THE • 1913 • *Edison* • USA
GREECE AND ITS MAGNIFICENT HISTORICAL MONUMENTS • 1929 • *Foussianis A. A.* • DOC
GREED • 1917 • Marston Theodore • USA
GREED • 1924 • von Stroheim Erich • USA
GREED • 1980 • Schroeder Sebastian C. • MTV • SWT
GREED • 1982 • Nicholson Arch • DOC • ASL
GREED see **LUST FOR GOLD** • 1949
GREED AND GASOLINE • 1915 • *L-Ko* • USA
GREED FOR GOLD • 1913 • *Essanay* • USA
GREED FOR GOLD • 1913 • Grandon Francis J. • *Lubin* • USA

GREED IN THE SUN (USA) see **CENT MILLE DOLLARS AU SOLEIL** • 1963
GREED OF GOLD • 1912 • *Pathe* • USA
GREED OF GOLD see **DESERT GREED** • 1926
GREED OF OSMAN BEY, THE • 1913 • Ridgely Richard • USA
GREED OF WILLIAM HART, THE • 1948 • Mitchell Oswald • UKN • CRIMES OF THE BODY SNATCHERS ○ HORROR MANIACS (USA)
GREEDY BEE, THE see **TELHETETLEN MEHECSKE** • 1958
GREEDY BILLY • 1905 • Collins Alf? • UKN
GREEDY BOY'S DREAM, THE • 1949 • Massingham Richard • UKN
GREEDY FOR TWEETY • 1957 • Freleng Friz • ANS • USA
GREEDY GABBY GATOR • 1963 • Marcus Sid • ANS • USA
GREEDY GEORGE • 1913 • France Charles H. • USA
GREEDY GIRL, THE • 1908 • *Fitzhamon Lewin* • UKN
GREEDY HUMPTY DUMPTY • 1936 • Fleischer Dave • ANS • USA
GREEK COMMUNITY OF HEIDELBERG, THE • 1976 • Xanthopoulos Lefteris • DOC • GRC
GREEK CONNECTION, THE • 1974 • Carayannis Costa • GRC
GREEK INTERPRETER, THE • 1922 • Ridgwell George • UKN
GREEK MEETS GREEK • 1920 • Roach Hal • SHT • USA
GREEK MIRTHOLOGY • 1954 • Kneitel Seymour • ANS • USA
GREEK SCULPTURE • 1959 • Wright Basil, Ayrton Michael • DOC • UKN
GREEK STREET • 1930 • Hill Sinclair • UKN • LATIN LOVE (USA)
GREEK TESTAMENT • 1942 • Hasse Charles • DOC • UKN • SHRINE OF VICTORY, THE
GREEK TRAGEDY, A • 1986 • van Goethem Nicole • ANS • BLG
GREEK-TURK WAR IN ASIA MINOR • 1922 • *Pekras & Phelos* • DOC
GREEK TYCOON, THE • 1978 • Thompson J. Lee • USA
GREEKS HAD A WORD FOR THEM, THE • 1932 • Sherman Lowell • USA • THREE BROADWAY GIRLS
GREEKS HAD NO WORD FOR THEM ,THE • 1932 • De Mond Albert • SHT • USA
GREEN ALARM, THE • 1914 • Griffin Frank C. • USA
GREEN AND PLEASANT LAND • 1955 • Anderson Lindsay • DCS • UKN
GREEN APPLES • 1915 • MacMackin Archer • USA
GREEN ARCHER, THE • 1926 • Bennet Spencer Gordon • SRL • USA
GREEN ARCHER, THE • 1940 • Horne James W. • SRL • USA
GREEN ARCHER, THE see **GRUNE BOGENSCHUTZE, DER** • 1960
GREEN BACKS AND RED SKINS • 1915 • Fielding Romaine • USA
GREEN BERETS, THE • 1968 • Wayne John, Kellogg Ray • USA
GREEN BIRD, THE see **GRUNE VOGEL, DER** • 1979
GREEN BOOK, THE see **ZELENA KNIZKA** • 1948
GREEN BUDDHA, THE • 1954 • Lemont John • UKN
GREEN BUTTON, THE • Gurvich Irina • ANS • USS
GREEN CARAVAN, THE • 1922 • Collins Edwin J. • UKN
GREEN CARD • 1990 • Weir Peter • USA
GREEN CARNATION, THE see **TRIALS OF OSCAR WILDE, THE** • 1960
GREEN CARRIAGE, THE see **ZELYONAYA KARYETA** • 1967
GREEN CAT, THE • 1915 • Beggs Lee • USA
GREEN CAT, THE • 1922 • Roach Hal • SHT • USA
GREEN CHAINS see **ZELENIE TSEPOCHKI** • 1970
GREEN CLOAK, THE • 1915 • *Fenwick Irene* • USA
GREEN COCKATOO, THE see **FOUR DARK HOURS** • 1937
GREEN CORN • 1960 • Krska Vaclav • CZC
GREEN DESIRE • 1965 • Kuchar Mike • SHT • USA
GREEN DOLPHIN STREET • 1947 • Saville Victor • USA
GREEN DOOR, THE • 1917 • Mills Thomas R. • SHT • USA
GREEN DRAGON, THE • 1907 • Fitzhamon Lewin • UKN
GREEN EARTH, THE see **MIDORI NO DAICHI** • 1942
GREEN ELEVATOR, THE see **GRONNE HEISEN, DEN** • 1981
GREEN EXTERIOR AND RED INTERIOR see **VERDE POR FORA, VERMELHO POR DENTRO** • 1980
GREEN EYE OF THE YELLOW GOD, THE • 1913 • France Charles H. • USA
GREEN-EYED BLONDE, THE • 1957 • Girard Bernard • USA
GREEN-EYED DEVIL, THE • 1914 • Kirkwood James • USA
GREEN-EYED JOHNNY • 1919 • Dillon John Francis • SHT • USA
GREEN EYED MONSTER • 1912 • Dwan Allan • USA
GREEN-EYED MONSTER, THE • 1912 • *West William* • USA
GREEN-EYED MONSTER, THE • 1914 • *Clark Komic* • USA
GREEN-EYED MONSTER, THE • 1914 • Powell Paul • *Lubin* • USA
GREEN-EYED MONSTER, THE • 1915 • Birch Cecil • UKN
GREEN-EYED MONSTER, THE • 1916 • Edwards J. Gordon • USA
GREEN-EYED MONSTER, THE • 1921 • *Austin Jack* • USA
GREEN-EYED WOMAN, THE (UKN) see **TAKE A LETTER, DARLING** • 1942
GREEN EYES • 1916 • *Vim* • USA
GREEN EYES • 1916 • *Laemmle* • SHT • USA
GREEN EYES • 1918 • Neill R. William • USA
GREEN EYES • 1934 • Thorpe Richard • USA
GREEN EYES • 1976 • Erman John • TVM • USA
GREEN EYES AND BULLETS • 1917 • *Christie* • SHT • USA
GREEN FACTOR, THE see **GROENFAKTOR, DIE** • 1984
GREEN FIELDS • 1983 • Maslarov Plamen • USS
GREEN FIELDS see **GREENE FELDE** • 1937
GREEN FIELDS see **GREENFIELDS** • 1988
GREEN FINGERS • 1947 • Harlow John • UKN
GREEN FIRE • 1954 • Marton Andrew • USA
GREEN FLAME, THE • 1920 • Warde Ernest C. • USA
GREEN FLOOD see **ZOLDAR** • 1965
GREEN FOR DANGER • 1946 • Gilliat Sidney • UKN
GREEN FOR IRELAND • 1967 • Wooster Arthur G. • IRL
GREEN GHOST, THE see **SPECTRE VERT, LE** • 1930
GREEN GIRDLE • 1941 • Keene Ralph • DCS • UKN
GREEN GLASS BANGLES see **HARE KANCH KI CHOORIYAN** • 1967
GREEN GLOVE, THE • 1952 • Mate Rudolph • USA • GANTELET VERT, LE
GREEN GOD, THE • 1918 • Scardon Paul • USA
GREEN GODDESS, THE • 1923 • Olcott Sidney • USA
GREEN GODDESS, THE • 1930 • Green Alfred E. • USA
GREEN GRASS OF HOME, THE see **IARBA VERDE DE ACASA** • 1978
GREEN GRASS OF WYOMING • 1948 • King Louis • USA
GREEN GRASS WIDOWS • 1928 • Raboch Alfred • USA
GREEN GROW THE RUSHES • 1951 • Twist Derek • UKN • BRANDY ASHORE
GREEN HAT, THE see **OUTCAST LADY** • 1934
GREEN HELL • 1940 • Whale James • USA
GREEN HELL, THE see **GRUNE HOLLE, DIE** • 1931
GREEN HELMET, THE • 1961 • Forlong Michael • UKN
GREEN HORIZON, THE see **AFURIKA MONOGATARI** • 1981
GREEN HORIZONS see **ZELENE OBZORY** • 1962
GREEN HORIZONS see **AFURIKA MONOGATARI** • 1981
GREEN HORNET, THE • 1940 • Beebe Ford, Taylor Ray • SRL • USA
GREEN HORNET, THE see **FURY OF THE DRAGON** • 1966
GREEN HORNET STRIKES AGAIN, THE • 1940 • Beebe Ford, Rawlins John • SRL • USA
GREEN ICE • 1980 • Day Ernest • USA, UKN
GREEN IDOL, THE • 1915 • *Henabery J. E.* • USA
GREEN LEATHER NOTE CASE, THE • 1934 • Samuelson G. B. • UKN
GREEN LIFT, THE see **GRONA HISSEN** • 1944
GREEN LIGHT • 1937 • Borzage Frank • USA
GREEN LIGHT • 1965 • Azarov Vilen • USS
GREEN LIGHT FOR THE 1964 SUGAR CROP see **VIA LIBRE A LA ZAFRA DEL '64** • 1964
GREEN LIGHT TO JOY see **OYAKOGUSA** • 1967
GREEN LIGHT TO JOY (USA) see **CHICHIKO GUSA** • 1966
GREEN LINE, THE • 1944 • Donnelly Eddie • ANS • USA
GREEN LOVE • 1967 • Sremec Rudolf • DCS • YGS
GREEN MACHINE • 1976 • Ohlsson Terry • DOC • ASL
GREEN MAGIC (USA) see **MAGIA VERDE** • 1953
GREEN MAIDEN see **VERDE CONCELLA** • 1968
GREEN MAN, THE • 1956 • Day Robert • UKN
GREEN MANSIONS • 1959 • Ferrer Mel • USA
GREEN MANUELA, THE (UKN) see **GRUNE MANUELA, DIE** • 1923
GREEN MARE, THE (USA) see **JUMENT VERTE, LA** • 1959
GREEN MARE'S NEST, THE (UKN) see **JUMENT VERTE, LA** • 1959
GREEN MEN FROM OUTER SPACE see **GRONA GUBBAR FRAN Y.R.** • 1987
GREEN MIST, THE • 1924 • Paul Fred • UKN
GREEN MONKEY see **BLUE MONKEY** • 1987
GREEN MOUNTAIN see **GRUNE BERG, DER** • 1989
GREEN MOUNTAINS see **AOI SANMYAKU** • 1949
GREEN MURDER CASE, THE (UKN) see **NIGHT OF MYSTERY** • 1937
GREEN NATIVE COUNTRY see **MIDORI NO FURUSATO** • 1946
GREEN NECKLACE, THE see **GRONA HALSBANDET, DET** • 1912
GREEN ORCHARD, THE • 1916 • Weston Harold • UKN
GREEN PACK, THE • 1934 • Hunter T. Hayes • UKN
GREEN PASTURES, THE • 1936 • Keighley William, Connelly Marc • USA
GREEN PASTURES, THE see **VERDES PRADERAS, LAS** • 1979
GREEN PLANET, THE see **PLANETE VERTE, LA** • 1965
GREEN PROMISE, THE • 1949 • Russell William D. • USA • RAGING WATERS (UKN)
GREEN RAY, THE see **RAYON VERT, LE** • 1986
GREEN ROOM, THE (USA) see **CHAMBRE VERTE, LA** • 1978
GREEN ROOM SERIES, THE • 1919-20 • *Stage Women'S War Relief Fund* • SER • USA
GREEN ROSE, THE • 1914 • Buel Kenean • USA
GREEN SCARF, THE • 1954 • O'Ferrall George M. • UKN
GREEN SEX see **JUDAI NO AOI SEI** • 1968
GREEN SHADOW, THE • 1913 • Giblyn Charles • USA
GREEN SHADOW, THE see **MUSS 'EM UP** • 1936
GREEN SHOES, THE • 1968 • Brims Ian • UKN
GREEN SLIME, THE (USA) see **GAMMA SANGO UCHU DAISAKUSEN** • 1968
GREEN SPIDER, THE see **ZELYONYI PAUK** • 1916
GREEN SPOT MYSTERY, THE see **DETECTIVE LLOYD** • 1932
GREEN STOCKINGS • 1916 • North Wilfred • USA
GREEN STOCKINGS see **FLIRTING WIDOW, THE** • 1930
GREEN SWAMP, THE • 1916 • Sidney Scott • USA
GREEN TEMPTATION, THE • 1922 • Taylor William D. • USA
GREEN TERROR, THE • 1919 • Kellino W. P. • UKN
GREEN TIE ON THE LITTLE YELLOW DOG, THE • 1929 • Aylott Dave, Symmons E. F. • SHT • UKN
GREEN TORTOISE, THE see **TORTUGA VERDE, LA** • 1979
GREEN TREE, THE • 1965 • Roland Joseph, Zimmerman Ruth • ITL, USA
GREEN WALL, THE (USA) see **MURALLA VERDE, LA** • 1969
GREEN WIDOW see **VIHREA LESKI** • 1968
GREEN YEARS see **VERDES ANOS** • 1984
GREEN YEARS see **ZELENA LETA** • 1985
GREEN YEARS, THE • 1942 • Savchenko Igor • USS • YEARS OF YOUTH
GREEN YEARS, THE • 1946 • Saville Victor • USA
GREEN YEARS, THE see **VERDES ANOS, OS** • 1963
GREEN YEARS, THE see **ZOLDAR** • 1965
GREEN YEARS, THE see **TOSHIGORO** • 1968
GREENE FELDE • 1937 • Ulmer Edgar G., Ben-Ami Jacob • USA • GREEN FIELDS
GREENE MURDER CASE, THE • 1929 • Tuttle Frank • USA
GREENER YARD, THE • 1949 • Hannah Jack • ANS • USA
GREENFIELDS • 1988 • Yeshurun Isaac • ISR • GREEN FIELDS
GREENGAGE SUMMER, THE • 1961 • Gilbert Lewis* • UKN • LOSS OF INNOCENCE (USA)
GREENGROCERS II, THE see **VERDULEROS II, LOS** • 1987
GREENHIDE • 1926 • Chauvel Charles • ASL
GREENHORN, THE • 1913 • Giblyn Charles • USA
GREENHORN, THE • 1962 • Voinov Konstantin • USS
GREENHORN AND THE GIRL, THE • 1910 • *Lubin* • USA
GREENHOUSE, THE • 1985 • Serdaris Vangelis • GRC
GREENING OF THE NORTH, THE • 1982 • Muller John • DOC • CND
GREENLAND see **GRONLAND** • 1980
GREEN'S GOOSE • 1908 • Cooper Arthur • UKN
GREENSBASIS 13 • 1979 • SAF
GREENSLEEVES • Fayman Lynn • SHT • USA
GREENSTONE, THE • 1985 • Irvine Kevin • USA
GREENVILLE CODE, THE • 1916 • *Supreme* • USA
GREENWICH VILLAGE • 1944 • Lang Walter • USA
GREENWICH VILLAGE see **GREENWICH VILLAGE STORY** • 1963
GREENWICH VILLAGE STORY • 1963 • O'Connell Jack • USA • BIRTHPLACE OF THE HOOTENANNY ○ THEY LOVE AS THEY PLEASE ○ GREENWICH VILLAGE
GREETINGS • 1968 • De Palma Brian • USA
GREETINGS, ATOM! • Milchin L. • ANS • USS
GREETINGS, BAIT! • 1943 • Freleng Friz • ANS • USA
GREETINGS, FRIENDS see **SALUDOS AMIGOS** • 1942
GREETINGS FROM L.A. see **YOU CAN'T HURRY LOVE** • 1988
GREETINGS FROM WOLLOGONG • 1982 • Callaghan Mary • SHT • ASL
GREETINGS, IT IS I! see **ZDRAVSTVYI, ETO YA!** • 1965
GREETINGS MOSCOW! see **ZDRAVSTVAI MOSKVA** • 1945
GREETINGS TO MARIA see **SEDMINA** • 1969
GREETINGS TO THE SWALLOWS see **A POZDRAVUJTE VLASTOVKY** • 1972
GREFFE CARDIAQUE, LA • 1969 • Fournier Claude • DOC • CND
GREFFE CARDIAQUE, SYMPOSIUM DE MONTREAL, LA • 1969 • Fournier Claude • DCS • CND
GREG • 1976 • Noyce Phil • DCS • ASL
GREGOR MAROLD • 1918 • Kortner Fritz • AUS
GREGORIO • 1984 • *Chaski* • PRU
GREGORIO AND HIS ANGEL see **GREGORIO Y SU ANGEL** • 1966
GREGORIO Y SU ANGEL • 1966 • Martinez Solares Gilberto • MXC, USA • GREGORIO AND HIS ANGEL
GREGORY'S GIRL • 1980 • Forsyth Bill • UKN
GREGORY'S SHADOW • 1913 • *Solax* • USA
GREH see **AM ANFANG WAR ES SUNDE** • 1954
GREIFER, DER • 1930 • Eichberg Richard • FRG • NIGHT BIRDS
GREIFER, DER • 1958 • York Eugen • FRG
GREKH • 1916 • Protazanov Yakov, Asagaroff Georg • USS • SIN
GRELE DE FEU • 1951-55 • Tazieff Haroun • SHT • FRN
GRELL MYSTERY, THE • 1917 • Scardon Paul • USA
GRELUCHON DELICAT, LE • 1934 • Choux Jean • FRN • VALET DE COEUR, LE
GREMLINS • 1984 • Dante Joe • USA
GREMLINS 2: THE NEW BATCH • 1990 • Dante Joe • USA
GREMLINS, THE • 1942 • *Disney Walt (P)* • ANS • USA
GREMLOIDS • 1986 • Durham Todd • USA • HYPERSPACE
GRENADIERS OF LOVE see **GRANADEROS DEL AMOR** • 1934
GRENDEL GRENDEL GRENDEL • 1979 • Stitt Alexander • ANM • ASL
GRENFELL OF LABRADOR • 1976 • Macartney-Filgate Terence • CND
GRENOBLE LA VILLENEUVE, REINVENTER LA VILLE • 1974 • Regnier Michel • DOC • CND
GRENOBLE (USA) see **13 JOURS EN FRANCE** • 1968
GRENOUILLE ET LA BALEINE, LA see **TADPOLE AND THE WHALE** • 1988
GRENOUILLES QUI DEMANDENT UN ROI, LES • 1922 • Starevitch Ladislas • ANM • FRN • FROGS WHO WANTED A KING, THE (USA) ○ FROGLAND
GRENOUILLES QUI DEMANDENT UN ROI, LES • 1969 • Dagay Atilja • ANS • FRN • FROGS WHO WANTED A KING, THE (USA)
GRENS, DE • 1984 • de Winter Leon • NTH • FRONTIERS
GRENZFEUER • 1934 • Beck-Gaden Hanns • FRG
GRENZFEUER • 1939 • Lippl Alois J. • FRG
GRENZGANGERIN, DIE • 1983 • Rodl Josef • FRG
GRENZJAGER, DER • 1929 • Beck-Gaden Hanns • FRG
GRENZSTATION • 1951 • Hasso Harry • FRG
GRETA GARBAGE • 1972 • Cox Peter • SHT • ASL
GRETCHEN IN UNIFORM see **ARMEE GRETCHEN, EINE** • 1973
GRETCHEN SCHUBERT • 1926 • Moos Karl • FRG
GRETCHEN, THE GREENHORN • 1916 • Franklin Sidney A., Franklin Chester M. • USA
GRETE MINDE see **GRETE MINDE -DER WALD IST VOLLER WOLFE** • 1977
GRETE MINDE -DER WALD IST VOLLER WOLFE • 1977 • Genee Heidi • AUS, FRG • GRETE MINDE
GRETEL • 1973 • Armstrong Gillian • SHT • ASL
GRETEL AND LIESEL • 1931 • von Kaufmann Wilhelm
GRETEL ZIEHT DAS GROSSE LOS • 1933 • Boese Carl • FRG
GRETNA GREEN • 1909 • *Walturdaw* • UKN
GRETNA GREEN • 1912 • Melford George • UKN
GRETNA GREEN • 1915 • Heffron Thomas N., Ford Hugh • USA
GRETNA GREEN WEDDING, A • 1899 • *Paul R. W.* • UKN
GREVARNA PA SVANSTA • 1924 • Wallen Sigurd • SWD • COUNTS OF SVANSTA, THE
GREVE, LA • 1904 • Zecca Ferdinand • FRN
GREVE DES APACHES, LA • 1908 • Feuillade Louis • FRN
GREVE DES FORGERONS, LA • 1910 • Monca Georges • FRN
GREVE DES TRAVAILLEURS DE LIP, LA • 1974 • Marker Chris • FRN
GREVE SVENSSON • 1951 • Lingheim Emil A. • SWD • COUNT SVENSSON
GREVEN FRAN GRANDEN • 1949 • Kjellgren Lars-Eric • SWD • COUNT FROM THE LANE, THE
GREVENA • 1978 • Zaharopoulou Mika • DOC • GRC
GREVINDE CLARA • 1915 • Davidsen Hjalmar • DNM
GREVINDE HJERTELOS • 1915 • Holger-Madsen • DNM • BEGGAR PRINCESS, THE
GREVINDENS AERE • 1918 • Blom August • DNM • KNIPLINGER ○ LACE ○ COUNTESS'S HONOR, THE
GREY CAR GANG, THE see **BANDA DEL AUTOMOVIL GRIS, LA** • 1919
GREY CART, THE see **KORKARLEN** • 1921
GREY CONTRE X • 1939 • Maudru Pierre, Gragnon Alfred • FRN • INSPECTEUR GREY CONTRE X
GREY DAME, THE • 1909 • *Nordisk* • DNM • GRAY LADY, THE (UKN)
GREY DAWN see **KHMUROE UTRO** • 1959
GREY DAWN, THE see **GRAY DAWN, THE** • 1922

GREY DEVIL, THE • 1926 • Cohn Bennett • USA
GREY EAGLE'S LAST STAND • 1914 • *Darkfeather Mona* • USA
GREY EAGLE'S REVENGE • 1914 • *Kalem* • USA
GREY EYED DEMON see **SIVOOKY DEMON** • 1919
GREY FIERCE ONE, THE see **LYUTY** • 1974
GREY FOX, THE • 1981 • Borsos Philip • CND
GREY GARDENS • 1975 • Maysles Albert, Maysles David, Hovde Ellen, Meyer Muffie • DOC • USA
GREY GLOVE, THE • 1928 • Webb Dunstan • ASL
GREY GOLD see **OR GRIS, L'** • 1981
GREY KITE, THE • 1972 • Nijsten Maurice, Erkens Jo • SHT • NTH
GREY MATTER see **BRAIN MACHINE, THE** • 1972
GREY METROPOLIS, THE • 1953 • McIsaac Nigel • UKN
GREY MORNING see **MANHA CINZENTA** • 1969
GREY MOTOR CAR, THE see **BANDA DEL AUTOMOVIL GRIS, LA** • 1919
GREY OWL'S LITTLE BROTHER • 1932 • Sparling Gordon • DCS • CND • PETIT FRERE DE GREY OWL, LE
GREY OWL'S STRANGE GUESTS • 1934 • Sparling Gordon • DCS • CND
GREY PARASOL, THE • 1918 • Windom Lawrence C. • USA
GREY SENTINEL, THE • 1913 • King Burton L. • USA
GREY STREAK, THE • 1927 • *Barrymore William* • USA
GREY TOWERS MYSTERY, THE see **GRAY TOWERS MYSTERY, THE** • 1919
GREY VAN, THE see **CAMIONETA GRIS, LA** • 1990
GREY VULTURE, THE • 1926 • Sheldon Forrest • USA
GREY WILLOW IN BLOOM, THE • 1961 • Piesis Gunar • USS
GREYFRIARS BOBBY • 1961 • Chaffey Don • USA, UKN
GREYHOUND, THE • 1914 • McGill Lawrence • USA
GREYHOUND AND THE RABBIT, THE • 1940 • *Mintz Charles (P)* • ANS • USA
GREYHOUND LIMITED, THE • 1929 • Bretherton Howard • USA
GREYSKIN see **SIVOUSHKO** • 1962
GREYSTOKE see **GREYSTOKE: THE LEGEND OF TARZAN, LORD OF THE APES** • 1983
GREYSTOKE: THE LEGEND OF TARZAN, LORD OF THE APES • 1983 • Hudson Hugh • UKN • GREYSTOKE
GREYWATER PARK • 1924 • Paul Fred • UKN
GREZHNITSA • 1962 • Filippov Fyodor • USS • SINNER, THE
GRIBICHE • 1925 • Feyder Jacques • FRN • MOTHER OF MINE
GRIBOUILLE • 1937 • Allegret Marc • FRN • HEART OF PARIS (USA) ○ TREIZIEME JURE, LE
GRIBOUILLE REDEVIENT BOIREAU • 1912 • *Deed Andre* • FRN
GRIBUSHIN FAMILY, THE • 1923 • Rasumny Alexander • USS
GRICHEUX, LES • 1909 • Cohl Emile • ANS • FRN
GRID RULES • 1938 • Cahn Edward L. • SHT • USA
GRIDIRON FLASH • 1934 • Tryon Glenn • USA • LUCK OF THE GAME (UKN) ○ FOOTBALL FOOL, THE ○ KICK-OFF, THE
GRIDLEY'S WIFE • 1915 • Warren Giles R. • USA
GRIDLOCK see **GREAT AMERICAN TRAFFIC JAM, THE** • 1980
GRIDO, IL • 1957 • Antonioni Michelangelo • ITL • OUTCRY, THE (USA) ○ CRY, THE (UKN)
GRIDO DELLA CITTA, IL • 1950 • Risi Dino • SHT • ITL
GRIDO DELLA CITTA, IL • 1951 • De Caro Lucio • ITL
GRIDO DELLA TERRA, IL • 1948 • Coletti Duilio • ITL • EARTH CRIES OUT, THE (USA)
GRIECHE SUCHT GRIECHIN • 1966 • Thiele Rolf • FRG
GRIECHISCHE FEIGER • 1976 • Gotz Siggi • FRG • FRUIT IS RIPE, THE
GRIEF 81 • 1981 • Noel Jean-Guy • CND
GRIEF, LE see **GRIEVANCE, THE** • 1954
GRIEF IN BAGDAD • 1925 • Roach Hal • SHT • USA
GRIEF STREET • 1931 • Thorpe Richard • USA • STAGE WHISPERS (UKN)
GRIERSON • 1973 • Blais Roger • DOC • CND • MONSIEUR GRIERSON
GRIEVANCE, THE • 1954 • Parker Morten • SHT • CND • GRIEF, LE
GRIEVOUS BODILY HARM • 1987 • Joffe Mark • ASL • GBH: GREVIOUS BODILY HARM
GRIF STAROVO BORTZA • 1916 • Bauer Yevgeni • USS • GRIFFON OF AN OLD WARRIOR
GRIFF NACH DEN STERNEN • 1955 • Schroth Carl-Heinz • FRG • REACHING FOR THE STARS (USA)
GRIFF SWIMS THE CHANNEL • 1919 • Sandground Maurice • UKN
GRIFFE DU DESTIN, LA see **GRIFFE DU HASARD, LA** • 1937
GRIFFE DU HASARD, LA • 1937 • Pujol Rene • FRN • GRIFFE DU DESTIN, LA
GRIFFE ET LA DENT, LA • 1973 • Bel Francois, Vienne Gerard • DOC • FRN
GRIFFIN AND PHOENIX: A LOVE STORY • 1976 • Duke Daryl • TVM • USA • TODAY IS FOREVER
GRIFFINTOWN • 1972 • Regnier Michel • DCS • CND
GRIFFON OF AN OLD WARRIOR see **GRIF STAROVO BORTZA** • 1916
GRIFF'S LOST LOVE • 1919 • Sandground Maurice • UKN
GRIGORI RASPUTIN AND THE GREAT RUSSIAN REVOLUTION see **GRIGORI RASPUTIN I VELIKOR RUSSKOI** • 1917
GRIGORI RASPUTIN I VELIKOR RUSSKOI • 1917 • USS • GRIGORI RASPUTIN AND THE GREAT RUSSIAN REVOLUTION
GRIGORIS AFXENTIOU, A HERO LIVING IN OUR MEMORIES see **GRIGORIS AFXENTIOU, ENAS IROAS ME TO MNIMOSKOPIO** • 1973
GRIGORIS AFXENTIOU, ENAS IROAS ME TO MNIMOSKOPIO • 1973 • Filis Giorgos • GRC • GRIGORIS AFXENTIOU, A HERO LIVING IN OUR MEMORIES
GRIGSBY see **LAST GRENADE, THE** • 1970
GRIHA LAKSHMI • 1959 • Desai Raman B. • IND • GODDESS OF THE HOME
GRIHA LAKSHMI • 1967 • Ramakrishna P. S. • IND • LAKSHMI OF THE HOME
GRIHADAHA • 1936 • *Roy Bhimal (Ph)* • IND
GRIHAPRAVESH • 1978 • Bhattacharya Basu • IND • HOUSEWARMING, THE ○ HOUSE WARMING, THE
GRIHAYADHYA • 1982 • Dasgupta Buddhadeb • IND • CROSSROAD, THE
GRIJPSTRA & DE GIER • 1979 • Verstappen Wim • NTH • OUTSIDER IN AMSTERDAM
GRILLE, DIE • 1917 • Bolten-Baeckers Heinrich • FRG
GRILLER, DER • 1968 • Moorse Georg • FRG
GRILLON DU FOYER • 1933 • Boudrioz Robert • FRN
GRIM COMEDIAN, THE • 1921 • Lloyd Frank • USA
GRIM GAME, THE • 1919 • Willat Irvin V. • USA
GRIM JUSTICE • 1916 • Trimble Larry • UKN
GRIM MESSENGER, THE • 1915 • Ingraham Lloyd • USA
GRIM PASTURES • 1943 • Dunning George • ANS • USA • GRIM PASTURES, OR THE FIGHT FOR FODDER
GRIM PASTURES, OR THE FIGHT FOR FODDER see **GRIM PASTURES** • 1943
GRIM REAPER, THE see **ANTHROPOPHAGOUS** • 1980
GRIM REAPER, THE (USA) see **COMMARE SECCA, LA** • 1962
GRIM TOLL OF WAR, THE • 1913 • Melford George • USA
GRIMACE, LA • 1966 • Blier Bertrand • SHT • FRN
GRIMACES • 1968 • Ferro Gudmundur Gudmundsson • USA
GRIMACES see **GYERMEKBETEGSEGEK** • 1965
GRIMACI PARIZHI • 1924 • Vertov Dziga • USS • SCOWLS OF PARIS
GRIMALDI • 1914 • Vernon Charles • UKN
GRIMM'S FAIRY TALES • 1955 • FRG
GRIMM'S FAIRY TALES FOR ADULTS see **GRIMMS MARCHEN VON LUSTERNEN PARCHEN** • 1969
GRIMM'S FAIRY TALES (FOR ADULTS ONLY) see **GRIMMS MARCHEN VON LUSTERNEN PARCHEN** • 1969
GRIMM'S FAIRY TALES FOR LUSTING COUPLES see **GRIMMS MARCHEN VON LUSTERNEN PARCHEN** • 1969
GRIMMS MARCHEN VON LUSTERNEN PARCHEN • 1969 • Thiele Rolf • FRG • GRIMM'S FAIRY TALES (FOR ADULTS ONLY) ○ GRIMM'S FAIRY TALES FOR ADULTS ○ EROTIC ADVENTURES OF SNOW WHITE, THE ○ GRIMM'S FAIRY TALES FOR LUSTING COUPLES
GRIMPE-MOI DESSUS ET FAIS-MOI MAL • 1979 • Benazeraf Jose • FRN
GRIMSEY THE BELLHOP • 1917 • *Clark Alexander* • SHT • USA
GRIN AND BEAR IT • 1933 • Stevens George • SHT • USA
GRIN AND BEAR IT • 1954 • Hannah Jack • ANS • USA
GRIN AND SHARE IT • 1957 • Lah Michael • ANS • USA
GRIN AND WIN OR CONVERTED BY A BILLIKEN • 1909 • *Vitagraph* • USA
GRIND, THE • 1911 • *Imp* • USA
GRIND, THE • 1915 • De Grasse Joseph • USA
GRINGALET • 1946 • Berthomieu Andre • FRN
GRINGO • 1964 • Blasco Ricardo • SPN • DUELLO NEL TEXAS ○ GUNFIGHT AT RED SANDS
GRINGO • 1985 • Kowalski Lech • USA
GRINGO see **SPARA, GRINGO, SPARA** • 1968
GRINGO, THE • 1914 • Hart William S., Smith Cliff • USA
GRINGO, THE • 1916 • *Overland* • USA
GRINGO GETTA IL FUCILE • 1966 • Romero-Marchent Joaquin Luis • ITL
GRINGOS NON PERDONANO, I • 1965 • Cardone Alberto • ITL
GRINGUITA EN MEXICO, UNA • 1951 • Soler Julian • MXC
GRINNING FACE, THE see **GRINSENDE GESICHT, DAS** • 1921
GRINNING GRANGER, THE • 1920 • Maloney Leo • SHT • USA
GRINNING GUNS • 1927 • Rogell Albert S. • USA
GRINNING SKULL, THE • 1916 • Nicholls George • SHT • USA
GRINSENDE GESICHT, DAS • 1921 • Herzka Julius • AUS • MAN WHO LAUGHS, THE (USA) ○ GRINNING FACE, THE
GRIP • 1915 • Elvey Maurice • UKN
GRIP, THE • 1913 • Coleby A. E. • UKN
GRIP OF AMBITION, THE • 1914 • Wilson Frank • UKN
GRIP OF CIRCUMSTANCE, THE • 1914 • Calvert E. H. • USA
GRIP OF CRIME, THE • 1916 • Cochrane George • SHT • USA
GRIP OF DEATH, THE see **CENGKAMAN MAUT** • 1971
GRIP OF EVIL, THE • 1916 • Douglas W. A. S., Harvey Harry • SRL • USA
GRIP OF FEAR, THE (UKN) see **EXPERIMENT IN TERROR** • 1962
GRIP OF GOLD, THE • 1916 • Coyle Walter • SHT • USA
GRIP OF IRON, THE • 1913 • Charrington Arthur • UKN
GRIP OF IRON, THE • 1920 • Haldane Bert • UKN
GRIP OF JEALOUSY, THE • 1913 • *Hopkins Jack* • USA
GRIP OF JEALOUSY, THE • 1916 • De Grasse Joseph • USA
GRIP OF LOVE, THE • 1917 • Holubar Allen • SHT • USA
GRIP OF THE PAST, THE • 1914 • Collins Edwin J. • UKN
GRIP OF THE PAST, THE • 1914 • Smiley Joseph • USA
GRIP OF THE STRANGLER, THE • 1958 • Day Robert • UKN • HAUNTED STRANGLER, THE (USA) ○ STRANGLEHOLD
GRIP OF THE YUKON, THE • 1928 • Laemmle Ernst • USA
GRIP-SNATCHER, THE • 1912 • *Essanay* • USA
GRIPOTERIO, EL • 1971 • Sanchez Jose Ramon • ANS • SPN • GRIPOTERIUM, THE
GRIPOTERIUM, THE see **GRIPOTERIO, EL** • 1971
GRIPS, GRUNTS AND GROANS • 1937 • Black Preston • SHT • USA
GRIS • 1969 • Diez Antonio Gomez • SPN • GLOOMY
GRISBI (USA) see **TOUCHEZ PAS AU GRISBI** • 1953
GRISFESTEN • 1983 • Widerberg Bo • SWD, DNM
GRISJAKTEN • 1970 • Cornell Jonas • SWD • PIG HUNT, THE
GRISOU • 1938 • de Canonge Maurice • FRN • HOMMES SANS SOLEIL, LES
GRISSLY'S MILLIONS • 1944 • English John • USA
GRISSOM GANG, THE • 1971 • Aldrich Robert • USA
GRIST TO THE MILL • 1913 • *Warfield Irene* • USA
GRIT • 1924 • Tuttle Frank • USA
GRIT AND GRATITUDE • 1917 • Baker Graham • SHT • USA
GRIT OF A DANDY, THE • 1914 • von Herkomer Hubert • UKN
GRIT OF A JEW, THE • 1917 • Elvey Maurice • UKN
GRIT OF THE GIRL TELEGRAPHER, THE • 1912 • *Doone Larrie* • USA
GRIT OF THE GRINGO, THE • 1913 • *Nestor* • USA
GRIT WINS • 1929 • Levigard Josef • USA
GRITENME PIEDRAS AL CAMPO • 1956 • Delgado Miguel M. • MXC
GRITO, EL • 1968 • Aretche Leobardo Lopez, Joskowics Alfredo • MXC • SHOUT, THE
GRITO DE CELINA, EL • 1975 • David Mario • ARG • CELINA'S CRY
GRITO DE DOLORES, EL • 1908 • Haro Felipe De Jesus • MXC • SHOUT OF DOLORES, THE
GRITO DE LA CARNE, EL • 1950 • Soler Fernando • MXC
GRITO DE LA MUERTE, EL • 1958 • Mendez Fernando, San-Fernando Manuel (Us Vers) • MXC • LIVING COFFIN, THE (USA) ○ SCREAM OF DEATH ○ CRY OF DEATH
GRITO DEL PUEBLO, EL • 1978 • von Gunten Peter • DOC • SWT
GRITO EN EL NOCHE, EL • 1949 • Morayta Miguel • MXC
GRITO NA NOITE, UM • 1948 • Porfirio Carlos • PRT
GRITO SAGRADO, EL • 1954 • Amadori Luis Cesar • ARG
GRITOS A MEDIANOCHE • 1976 • Klimovsky Leon • SPN
GRITOS EN LA NOCHE • 1962 • Franco Jesus • SPN, FRN • AWFUL DR. ORLOFF, THE (USA) ○ HORRIBLE DR. ORLOFF, L' ○ DEMON DOCTOR, THE (UKN) ○ CRIES IN THE NIGHT
GRITTA OF THE CASTLE OF RATS see **GRITTA VOM RATTENSCHLOSS**
GRITTA VOM RATTENSCHLOSS • Brauer Jurgen • GDR • GRITTA OF THE CASTLE OF RATS
GRIVE, LA • 1968 • Bouguermouh Abderrahmane • ALG
GRIZZLY • 1976 • Girdler William • USA • KILLER GRIZZLY
GRIZZLY GOLFER • 1951 • Burness Pete • ANS • USA
GRIZZLY GULCH CHARIOT RACE, THE • 1915 • Mix Tom • USA
GROAN FROM A SOLITARY ISLAND see **KOTOU NO UMEKI** • 1968
GROBE ADELE, DIE • 1937 • Seitz Franz • FRG
GROCER'S REVENGE, THE • 1913 • French Charles K. • USA
GROCERY BOY, THE • 1932 • Jackson Wilfred • ANS • USA
GROCERY BOY, THE see **BAKALOGATOS, O** • 1968
GROCERY CLERK, THE • 1920 • Semon Larry • SHT • USA
GROCERY CLERK'S ROMANCE, THE • 1912 • Sennett Mack • USA
GROCERY GRAFTERS • 1917 • *Rolin* • SHT • USA
GROCK • 1931 • Boese Carl • FRG
GROCK • 1931 • Hamman Joe, Boese Carl • FRN
GROENFAKTOR, DIE • 1984 • SAF • GREEN FACTOR, THE
GROENLAND • 1949 • Languepin Jean-Jacques, Ichac Marcel • DCS • FRN
GROETNIS VIR DIE EERSTEMINISTER see **GROETNIS VIR DIE PRIME** • 1973
GROETNIS VIR DIE PRIME • 1973 • Retief Bertrand • SAF • GROETNIS VIR DIE EERSTEMINISTER
GROG • 1983 • Laudadio Francesco • ITL
GROGAN'S ALLEY • 1916 • *Eagle Film* • USA
GROMADA • 1950 • Kawalerowicz Jerzy, Sumerski Kazimierz • PLN • VILLAGE MILL, THE ○ RURAL COMMUNITY ○ COMMUNITY, THE ○ COMMUNE
GROMAIRE • 1967 • Reichenbach Francois • SHT • FRN
GRONA GUBBAR FRAN Y.R. • 1987 • Hatwig Hans • SWD • GREEN MEN FROM OUTER SPACE
GRONA HALSBANDET, DET • 1912 • Magnusson Charles • SWD • GREEN NECKLACE, THE
GRONA HISSEN • 1944 • Larsson Borje • SWD • GREEN LIFT, THE
GRONA HISSEN see **OPPAT MED GRONA HISSEN** • 1952
GRONKOBING GLADE GAVTYVE • 1925 • Lauritzen Lau • DNM
GRONLAND • 1980 • Roos Jorgen • DOC • DNM • GREENLAND
GRONLANDSFILMEN see **HVOR BJERGENE SEJLER** • 1954
GRONLANDSKE DIALEKTOPTAGELSER OG TROMMEDANSE FRA THULEDISTRIKTET • 1967 • Roos Jorgen • DOC • DNM
GRONNE HEISEN, DEN • 1981 • Saether Oddgeir • NRW • GREEN ELEVATOR, THE
GROOM PARTIE • 1979 • Kikoine Gerard • FRN
GROOM WORE SPURS, THE • 1951 • Whorf Richard • USA
GROOM'S DOOM, THE • 1914 • *L-Ko* • USA
GROOT WIT VOEL, DIE • 1956 • SAF
GROOVE ROOM • 1974 • Becker Vernon P. • UKN • WHAT THE SWEDISH BUTLER SAW
GROOVE TUBE, THE • 1974 • Shapiro Ken • USA
GROOVIE MOVIE • 1944 • Jason Will • SHT • USA
GROS BILL, LE • 1949 • Delacroix Rene, Bigras Jean-Yves • CND
GROS BRAS, LES • 1964 • Rigaud Francis • FRN
GROS CALIN • 1979 • Rawson Jean-Pierre • FRN, ITL
GROS COUP, LE • 1963 • Valere Jean • FRN, ITL • TRIANGOLO DEL DELITTO, IL (ITL)
GROS ET LE MAIGRE, LE • 1961 • Polanski Roman, Rousseau Jean-Pierre • FRN • FAT AND THE LEAN, THE (UKN)
GROS MALINS, LES • 1968 • Leboursier Raymond • FRN, ITL
GROS MORNE • 1967 • Giraldeau Jacques • DOC • CND
GROSS FOG • 1973 • Le Grice Malcolm • UKN
GROSS PARIS • 1974 • Grangier Gilles • FRN
GROSS SENSATIONS PROZESS, DER • 1923 • *Eisi-Film* • FRG
GROSS TENOR, DER • 1931 • Schwarz Hanns • FRG
GROSSALARM • 1938 • Jacoby Georg • FRG
GROSSE ABENTEUER, DAS • 1937 • Meyer Johannes • FRG
GROSSE ABENTEUERIN, DIE • 1928 • Wiene Robert • FRG
GROSSE ATTRAKTION, DIE • 1931 • Reichmann Max • FRG
GROSSE BLUFF, DER • 1933 • Jacoby Georg • FRG • SCHUSSE IN DER NACHT ○ BIG BLUFF, THE (USA)
GROSSE CAISSE, LA • 1966 • Joffe Alex • FRN
GROSSE CHANCE, DIE • 1934 • Janson Victor • FRG • EINMAL MOCHT ICH NOCH SO JUNG SEIN
GROSSE CHANCE, DIE • 1957 • Quest Hans • FRG
GROSSE CHEF, DER • 1921 • Obal Max • FRG
GROSSE COUP, DER • 1919 • Piel Harry • FRG
GROSSE DIEB, DER • 1922 • *Corder Colette* • FRG
GROSSE EKSTASE DES BILDSCHNITZERS STEINER, DIE • 1975 • Herzog Werner • FRG • GREAT ECSTASY OF WOODCARVER STEINER, THE (UKN) ○ GREAT ECSTASY OF THE SCULPTOR STEINER, THE
GROSSE FAHRT, DIE • 1931 • Walsh Raoul • FRG
GROSSE FALL, DER • 1945 • Anton Karl • FRG • IHR GROSSER FALL
GROSSE FREIHEIT NMR 7, DIE • 1944 • Kautner Helmut • FRG • PORT OF FREEDOM (UKN) ○ PALOMA, LA
GROSSE GEFAHR, DIE • 1915 • Sauer Fred • FRG
GROSSE GEHEIMNIS, DAS • 1920 • Gerdes Herbert • FRG

GROSSE GELEGENHEIT, DIE • 1925 • von Kabdebo Lorand • FRG • RAUB IN DER ZENTRALBANK
GROSSE GLUCK, DAS • 1967 • Antel Franz • AUS • LUCKY STRIKE, THE
GROSSE KONIG, DER • 1942 • Harlan Veit • FRG • GREAT KING, THE
GROSSE KRACH, DER • 1920 • Oswald Richard • FRG
GROSSE KUR, DIE • 1964 • Antel Franz • FRG, AUS
GROSSE LICHT, DAS • 1920 • Henning Hanna • FRG
GROSSE LIEBE, DIE • 1932 • Preminger Otto • AUS
GROSSE LIEBE, DIE • 1942 • Hansen Rolf • FRG • GREAT LOVE, THE
GROSSE LIEBE, EINE • 1949 • Bertram Hans • FRG
GROSSE LIEBESSPIEL, DAS • 1963 • Weidenmann Alfred • FRG, AUS • AND SO TO BED (USA)
GROSSE LOS, DAS see **MADCHEN MIT DEN FUNF NULLEN, DAS** • 1927
GROSSE LUGE, DIE • 1922 • Boese Carl • FRG
GROSSE MANDERIN, DER • 1949 • Stroux Karl H. • FRG
GROSSE NUMMER, DIE • 1942 • Anton Karl • FRG
GROSSE OPFER, DAS • 1918 • Stein Josef • FRG
GROSSE PAGAILLE, LA • 1969 • Steno • FRN
GROSSE PAUSE, DIE • 1927 • Froelich Carl • FRG
GROSSE PREIS, DER • 1922 • Tsotary Alfred • FRG
GROSSE PREIS, DER • 1944 • Anton Karl • FRG
GROSSE RAUSCH, DER • 1932 • Bernhardt Curtis • FRG
GROSSE REISE, DIE • 1961 • Dieterle William • MTV • FRG
GROSSE SCHATTEN, DER • 1942 • Verhoeven Paul • FRG
GROSSE SCHLAGERBUMMEL, DER see **O SOLE MIO** • 1960
GROSSE SCHULD, DIE • 1953 • Lehner Alfred • AUS, DNM
GROSSE SCHWEIGEN, DAS • 1915 • Biebrach Rudolf • FRG
GROSSE SEHNEN, DAS • 1925 • *Trans-Continental* • FRG
GROSSE SEHNSUCHT, DIE • 1930 • Sekely Steve • FRG
GROSSE SPIEL, DAS • 1942 • Stemmle R. A. • FRG
GROSSE SPIELER –EIN BILD DER ZEIT, DER see **DR. MABUSE, DER SPIELER 1** • 1922
GROSSE SPRUNG, DER • 1927 • Fanck Arnold • FRG • BIG JUMP, THE
GROSSE STAR–PARADE • 1954 • Martin Paul • FRG
GROSSE SUNDE, DIE (FRG) see **SUPREMA CONFESSIONE** • 1958
GROSSE SUNDERIN, DIE • 1913 • Biebrach Rudolf • FRG
GROSSE TETE, UNE • 1962 • de Givray Claude • FRN • GUERRE DES KARTS, LA
GROSSE TREIBJAGD, DIE (FRG) see **MERCENARIO, EL** • 1968
GROSSE UN DIE KLEINE WELT, DIE see **STRECKE, DIE** • 1927
GROSSE UNBEKANNTE 1, DIE • 1923 • Wolff Willi • FRG • KAKADU LEBERTRAN
GROSSE UNBEKANNTE 2, DIE • 1923 • Wolff Willi • FRG • DAME AUS LISSABON, DIE
GROSSE UNBEKANNTE, DER • 1919 • Piel Harry • FRG
GROSSE UNBEKANNTE, DER • 1927 • Noa Manfred • FRG • UNHEIMLICHE, DER
GROSSE UND DIE KLEINE WELT, DIE • 1921 • Mack Max • FRG
GROSSE UND DIE KLEINE WELT, DIE • 1936 • Riemann Johannes • FRG
GROSSE VERHAU, DER • 1970 • Kluge Alexander • FRG • GREAT ENTANGLEMENT, THE ○ BIG MESS, THE ○ BIG DUST–UP, THE
GROSSE VERSUCHUNG, DIE • 1952 • Hansen Rolf • FRG
GROSSE WAGNIS, DAS • 1919 • Moest Hubert • FRG
GROSSE WETTE, DIE • 1915 • Piel Harry • FRG • GREAT BET, THE (USA)
GROSSE WUNSCHKONZERT, DAS • 1960 • Rabenalt Arthur M. • AUS
GROSSE ZAPFENSTREICH, DER • 1952 • Hurdalek Georg • FRG
GROSSEN MANNES LIEBE, EINES • 1920 • Basch Felix • FRG
GROSSER GRAU–BLAUER VOGEL, EIN • 1970 • Schamoni Thomas • FRG • BIG GRAY–BLUE BIRD, A
GROSSFURSTIN ALEXANDRA • 1933 • Thiele Wilhelm • FRG
GROSSGLOCKNER HOCHALPEN–STRASSE, DIE • 1938 • FRG
GROSSI BESTONI, I (ITL) see **AMOUR CHEZ LES POIDS LOURDS, L'** • 1978
GROSSINDUSTRIELLE, DER • 1923 • Kaufmann Fritz • FRG
GROSSREINEMACHEN • 1935 • Lamac Carl • FRG • GENERAL HOUSECLEANING (USA)
GROSSTADTFIEBER • 1923 • *Alfas-Handels* • FRG
GROSSTADTFIEBER • 1925 • *Alfas-Handels* • FRG
GROSSTADTJUGEND • 1928 • Walther-Fein Rudolf • FRG • GLUCKSFALLE, DIE
GROSSTADTKAVALIERE see **KLEINE AUS DER KONFEKTION, DIE** • 1925
GROSSTADTKINDER • 1929 • Haase Arthur • FRG • ZWISCHEN SPREE UND PANKE
GROSSTADTMADELS 1 • 1921 • Neff Wolfgang • FRG
GROSSTADTMADELS 2 • 1921 • Neff Wolfgang • FRG
GROSSTADTMADELS 3 • 1921 • Neff Wolfgang • FRG
GROSSTADTMELODIE • 1943 • Liebeneiner Wolfgang • FRG
GROSSTADTNACHT • 1932 • Ozep Fedor • FRG
GROSSTADTNACHT • 1950 • Wolff Hans • AUS
GROSSTADTPIRATEN • 1930 • Schonlank Hans • FRG
GROSSTADTSCHMETTERLING • 1929 • Eichberg Richard • FRG • PAVEMENT BUTTERFLY
GROSSTE GAUNER DES JAHRHUNDERTS, DER • 1927 • Obal Max • FRG
GROSSTE LIEBE, DIE • 1928 • Grantham-Hayes H. C. • FRG
GROTE VERZOEKING VAN ST. ANTONIUS, DE • 1972 • Kempeneer H. • BLG
GROTE VIER, DE • 1947 • Geesink Joop • ANM • NTH • BIG FOUR IN CONFERENCE, THE
GROTESKEN IM SCHNEE • 1928 • Reiniger Lotte • ANS • FRG
GROTESQUE • 1988 • Tornatore Joe • USA
GROTESQUE CHICKEN, THE see **GALLINA VOGELBIRDAE** • 1963
GROTESQUES • 1908 • *Pathe* • FRN
GROTTE AUX SURPRISES, LA • 1904 • Melies Georges • FRN • GROTTO OF SURPRISES, THE (USA)
GROTTE DU DIABLE, LA • 1898 • Melies Georges • FRN
GROTTO OF SURPRISES, THE (USA) see **GROTTE AUX SURPRISES, LA** • 1904
GROTTO OF TORTURE, THE • 1912 • *Pathe* • USA
GROUCH, THE • 1912 • *Edison* • USA
GROUCH, THE (UKN) • 1913 • *Moore Owen* • USA
GROUCH, THE • 1916 • Beaumont Harry • SHT • USA
GROUCH, THE • 1918 • *Vitagraph* • SHT • USA
GROUCH, THE • 1918 • Apfel Oscar • *World* • USA
GROUCH, THE see **GROUSOUZES, HO** • 1961
GROUCH, THE ENGINEER • 1914 • McGowan J. P. • USA
GROUCHES AND SMILES • 1916 • Reynolds Lynn • SHT • USA
GROUCHO'S QUIET FOURTH • 1911 • *Yankee* • USA
GROUCHY • 1916 • *Wise Tom* • USA
GROUND CREW see **SKY GIANT** • 1938
GROUND FLOOR • 1989 • Minaiev Igor • USS
GROUND HOG PLAY • 1956 • Kneitel Seymour • ANS • USA
GROUND ZERO • 1973 • Flocker James T. • USA
GROUND ZERO • 1988 • Pattinson Michael, Myles Bruce • ASL
GROUND ZERO see **DEF–CON 4** • 1985
GROUNDLESS SUSPICION • 1913 • *Sawyer Laura* • USA
GROUNDS FOR DIVORCE • 1925 • Bern Paul • USA
GROUNDS FOR MARRIAGE • 1950 • Leonard Robert Z. • USA
GROUNDSTAR CONSPIRACY, THE • 1972 • Johnson Lamont • USA, CND
GROUP, THE • 1966 • Lumet Sidney • USA
GROUP, THE see **GRUPO** • 1970
GROUP GUIDANCE see **GROUP NO SHIDO** • 1956
GROUP INSTRUCTION see **GROUP NO SHIDO** • 1956
GROUP KAMIKAZE see **KAMIKAZE REN** • 1933
GROUP MARRIAGE • 1972 • Rothman Stephanie • USA
GROUP NO SHIDO • 1956 • Hani Susumu • DOC • JPN • GROUP GUIDANCE ○ GROUP INSTRUCTION
GROUP ONE • 1967 • Warhol Andy • USA
GROUP PORTRAIT WITH A LADY (USA) see **GRUPPENBILD MIT DAME** • 1977
GROUP THERAPY • 1966 • King Allan • CND
GROUPE EN EMBUSCADE, LE • 1971 • Beloufa Farouq • DOC • ALG
GROUPIE GIRL • 1970 • Ford Derek • UKN • BLOOD GROUPIE
GROUPIES • 1970 • Dorfman Ron, Nevard Peter • USA • ROCK '70
GROUSOUZES, HO • 1961 • Tzavellas Georges • GRC • OLD GROUCHY, THE ○ GROUCH, THE
GROV SPOG, EN • 1908 • *Holger-Madsen* • DNM • PRACTICAL JOKE AND A SAD END, A
GROVE, THE see **NAKED ZOO, THE** • 1970
GROVE, THE see **NAME FOR EVIL, A** • 1970
GROW UP IN ANGER see **QINGCHUN NUCHAO** • 1985
GROWING BETTER • 1923 • *Paton William* • USA
GROWING OLD see **OUDER WORDEN** • 1975
GROWING PAINS • 1928 • Mack Anthony • SHT • USA
GROWING PAINS • 1953 • Donnelly Eddie • ANS • USA
GROWING PAINS • 1980 • Revach Ze'Ev • ISR
GROWING PAINS • 1982 • Megahy Francis • TVM • UKN
GROWING PAINS see **HOMEWORK** • 1982
GROWING PAINS see **BAD MANNERS** • 1984
GROWING UP see **TAKEKURABE** • 1955
GROWING UP see **LITEN IDA** • 1981
GROWING UP AT PARADISE • 1977 • Wilson Sandra • CND
GROWING UP IN AMERICA • 1988 • Markson Morley • DOC • CND
GROWLER STORY, THE • 1957 • Ford John • SHT • USA
GROWN UP –AS FROM TODAY see **AB HEUTE ERWACHSEN**
GROWN–UP CHILDREN (USA) see **VZROSLYI DETI** • 1961
GROWN UP TOMORROW • 1981 • Schulz Bob • MTV • CND
GROWN–UPS • 1985 • Madden John • USA
GROWTH OF THE SOIL • 1929 • Sommerfeldt Gunnar
GROZA • 1934 • Petrov Vladimir • USS • THUNDERSTORM, THE ○ STORM, THE
GROZA NAD BYELOY • 1968 • Nemchenko Yevgyeni, Chaplin Stanislav • USS • THUNDERSTORM OVER THE BELAYA ○ STORM OVER THE BELAYA RIVER
GROZNA PRZYGODA KAPITANA PUSZKINA • 1964 • Laskowski Jan • ANS • PLN • TERRIBLE ADVENTURE OF CAPTAIN PUSHKIN, THE
GROZNY VEK see **IVAN GROZNI KINO–BALET** • 1977
GRUB STAKE, THE • 1923 • Van Tuyle Bert • USA • ROMANCE OF LOST VALLEY, THE
GRUB STAKE MORTGAGE, THE • 1912 • Dwan Allan • USA
GRUBE MORGENROT • 1948 • Schleif Wolfgang, Freund Erich • GDR
GRUBENKATASTROPHE, DIE • 1916 • *Weisse Hanni* • FRG
GRUDGE, THE • 1915 • Hart William S. • USA
GRUDGE, THE • 1917 • Mong William V. • SHT • USA
GRUESOME TWOSOME, A • 1945 • Clampett Robert • ANS • USA
GRUESOME TWOSOME, THE • 1967 • Lewis Herschell G. • USA
GRUFT MIT DEM RATSELSCHLOSS, DIE • 1964 • Gottlieb Franz J. • FRG • CURSE OF THE HIDDEN VAULT, THE (USA)
GRUMBLING WHITE TIGER, THE see **GRAMBLING'S WHITE TIGER** • 1981
GRUMP, THE see **BURBERO, IL** • 1987
GRUMPY • 1923 • De Mille William C. • USA
GRUMPY • 1930 • Cukor George, Gardner Cyril • USA
GRUN IST DIE HEIDE • 1932 • Behrendt Hans • FRG
GRUN IST DIE HEIDE • 1951 • Deppe Hans • FRG
GRUN IST DIE HEIDE • 1972 • Reinl Harald • FRG
GRUND • 1990 • Wilfert Mathias • FRG
GRUNE BERG, DER • 1989 • Murer Fredi M. • DOC • SWT • GREEN MOUNTAIN
GRUNE BOGENSCHUTZE, DER • 1960 • Roland Jurgen • FRG • GREEN ARCHER, THE
GRUNE DAMON, DER see **GESTANDNIS DER GRUNEN MASKE, DAS** • 1916
GRUNE DOMINO, DER • 1935 • Selpin Herbert • FRG
GRUNE HOCHZEIT • 1988 • Zschoche Hermann • GDR • JUST MARRIED
GRUNE HOLLE, DIE • 1931 • Bauer-Adamara • FRG • GREEN HELL, THE
GRUNE KAISER, DER • 1939 • Mundorf Paul • FRG
GRUNE LATERNE, DIE • 1930 • Heuberger Edmund • FRG
GRUNE MANN VON AMSTERDAM, DER • 1916 • Rippert Otto • FRG
GRUNE MANUELA, DIE • 1923 • Dupont E. A. • FRG • GREEN MANUELA, THE (UKN) ○ FILM AUS DEM SUEDEN, EIN
GRUNE MAPPE, DIE see **WENN DU ZU MIR HALST..** • 1962
GRUNE MONOKEL, DAS • 1929 • Meinert Rudolf • FRG
GRUNE PLAKAT, DAS • 1920 • Neff Wolfgang • FRG
GRUNE SALON, DER • 1944 • Barlog Boleslav • FRG
GRUNE SKARABAUS, DER • 1919 • *Paulig Albert* • FRG
GRUNE VAMPYR, DER • 1918 • Kahn William • FRG
GRUNE VOGEL, DER • 1979 • Szabo Istvan • FRG, HNG • GREEN BIRD, THE
GRUNEN TEUFEL VON MONTE CASSINO, DIE • 1958 • Reinl Harald • FRG
GRUNSTEIN VARIATION, THE see **GRUNSTEINVARIANTE, DIE**
GRUNSTEINVARIANTE, DIE • Wicki Bernhard • GDR • GRUNSTEIN VARIATION, THE
GRUNT! THE WRESTLING MOVIE • 1985 • Holzman Allan • FRG
GRUNYA KORNAKOVA • 1936 • Ekk Nikolai • USS • NIGHTINGALE, LITTLE NIGHTINGALE ○ NIGHTINGALE
GRUPO • 1970 • Cortez Cesar • VNZ • GROUP, THE
GRUPPENBILD MIT DAME • 1977 • Petrovic Aleksandar • FRG, FRN, YGS • PORTRAIT DE GROUPE AVEC DAME (FRN) ○ GROUP PORTRAIT WITH A LADY (USA)
GRUPPO DI FAMIGLIA IN UN INTERNO • 1974 • Visconti Luchino • ITL, FRN • CONVERSATION PIECE (USA) ○ VIOLENCE ET PASSION
GRUSS AUS DER TIEFE, EIN • 1915 • Hanus Emerich • FRG
GRUSS MIR DAS BLOND KIND AM RHEIN • 1925 • Boese Carl • FRG
GRUSS UND KUSS AUS DER WACHAU • 1950 • Schulz Fritz • AUS
GRUSS UND KUSS VERONIKA • 1933 • Boese Carl • FRG
GRUSTAINI BASHMACHOK see **KHRUSTALNYY BASHMACHOK** • 1961
GRY • 1970 • Lasota Grzegorz • PLN • PLAYS
GRY I ZABAWY • 1966 • Ziarnik Jerzy • DOC • PLN • GAMES
GRYNING • 1944 • Sucksdorff Arne • DCS • SWD • DAWN
GRZYBY • 1949 • Marczakowi Marta (c/d) • HNG
G'SCHICHTEN AUS DEM WIENERWALD • 1928 • Speyer Jaap • FRG
G'SCHICHTEN AUS DEM WIENERWALD • 1934 • Jacoby Georg • FRG • TALES FROM THE VIENNA WOODS (USA)
G'SCHICHTEN AUS DER STEIERMARK • 1929 • Lowenstein Hans Otto
GU • 1972 • Missen Vivian • ANS • BLG
GUACHA, LA • 1921 • Ferreyra Jose • ARG
GUADALAJARA • 1943 • Urueta Chano • MXC
GUADALAJARA EN VERANO • 1964 • Bracho Julio • MXC
GUADALAJARA ES MEXICO • 1975 • *Filicas Agrasanchez* • MXC
GUADALAJARA PUES • 1945 • de Anda Raul • MXC
GUADALCANAL DIARY • 1943 • Seiler Lewis • USA
GUADALUPE LA CHINACA • 1937 • Sevilla Raphael J. • MXC
GUAFU CUN • 1989 • Wang Wayne • CHN, HKG • WIDOW VILLAGE ○ VILLAGE OF WIDOWS
GUAGLIO see **PROIBITO RUBARE** • 1948
GUAGLIONE • 1956 • Simonelli Giorgio C. • ITL
GUAI AI VINTI! • 1955 • Matarazzo Raffaello • ITL
GUAMBIANOS • 1982 • Tirado Wolfgang, Reiter Jackie • DOC • UKN
GUANAJUATO DESTROYED see **GUANAJUATO DESTRUIDO** • 1902
GUANAJUATO DESTRUIDO • 1902 • Barragan Salvador Toscano • MXC • GUANAJUATO DESTROYED
GUANTES DE ORO • 1959 • Urueta Chano • MXC
GUAPA, RICA Y.. ESPECIAL • 1975 • Puig Jaime • SPN
GUAPO DEL 1900, UN • 1960 • Torre-Nilsson Leopoldo • ARG • TOUGH GUY OF 1900
GUAPO DEL 1900, UN • 1972 • Murua Lautaro • ARG • TOUGH GUY FROM 1900, A
GUAPO HEREDERO BUSCA ESPOSA • 1972 • Delgado Luis Maria • SPN
GUAPOS DEL PARQUE, LOS • 1905 • de Chomon Segundo • SPN
GUAPPARIA see **SERENATA TRAGICA** • 1951
GUAPPI, I • 1974 • Squitieri Pasquale • ITL • BLOOD BROTHERS
GUAPPI NON SI TOCCANO • 1979 • Bianchi Mario • ITL
GUARAIRA REPANO • 1977 • Fuentes Raul • DOC • VNZ
GUARANTEED RAINPROOF • 1914 • *Lubin* • USA
GUARANTEED VIRGIN see **ASSICURASI VERGINE** • 1967
GUARANTOR FOR ONE YEAR see **BURGSCHAFT FUER EIN JAHR** • 1980
GUARANY • 1948 • Freda Riccardo • ITL
GUARD 13 see **TRINACTY REVIR** • 1945
GUARD, THE see **STRACENA VARTA** • 1956
GUARD, THE see **HLIDAC** • 1970
GUARD, THE see **BEKCI** • 1985
GUARD ON THE BALTIC see **STRAZ NAD BALTYKIEM** • 1946
GUARD THAT GIRL! see **GUARD THE GIRL!** • 1935
GUARD THE GIRL! • 1935 • Hillyer Lambert • USA • GUARD THAT GIRL! ○ LADY BEWARE
GUARDAMI NUDA • 1972 • Alfaro Italo • ITL
GUARDATELE MA NON TOCCATELE • 1959 • Mattoli Mario • ITL
GUARDED LIPS see **LANDSFLYKTIGE, DE** • 1921
GUARDED VILLAGE 1944, THE see **VARTIOITU KYLA 1944** • 1978
GUARDIA DEL CORPO, LA • 1942 • Bragaglia Carlo Ludovico • ITL
GUARDIA, GUARDIA SCELTA, BRIGADIERE E MARESCIALLO • 1956 • Bolognini Mauro • ITL
GUARDIA, LADRO E CAMERIERA • 1958 • Steno • ITL
GUARDIAMARINAS, LOS • 1967 • Lazaga Pedro • SPN
GUARDIAN, THE • 1917 • Ashley Arthur • USA
GUARDIAN, THE • 1984 • Greene David • TVM • CND, USA
GUARDIAN, THE see **SKRBNIK** • 1974
GUARDIAN, THE see **SERAYDAR** • 1975
GUARDIAN ANGEL see **ANDJEO CUVAR** • 1986
GUARDIAN ANGEL, THE • 1912 • *Eclair* • USA
GUARDIAN ANGEL, THE see **SKYDDSANGELN** • 1990
GUARDIAN ANGELS • 1916 • Beaudine William • USA
GUARDIAN ANGELS • 1988 • Avildsen John G. • USA

GUARDIAN DEL PARAISO, EL • 1955 • Ruiz-Castillo Arturo • SPN
GUARDIAN EL PERRO SALVADOR • 1949 • Gomez Landero Humberto • MXC
GUARDIAN OF HONOUR, THE • 1921 • Paul Fred • UKN
GUARDIAN OF THE ABYSS • 1982 • Sharp Don • TVM • UKN
GUARDIAN OF THE ACCOLADE, THE • 1919 • Houry Henri • SHT • USA
GUARDIAN OF THE BANK, THE • 1908 • Coleby A. E. • UKN
GUARDIAN OF THE WILDERNESS • 1976 • O'Malley David • USA • MOUNTAIN MAN
GUARDIAN OF VIRTUE • 1914 • Protazanov Yakov • USS
GUARDIANS, THE see **FORMYDERNE** • 1978
GUARDIAN'S DILEMMA, THE • 1915 • Santschi Thomas • USA
GUARDIAN'S LUCK, A • 1912 • *Steppling John* • USA
GUARDIANS OF LOVE see **AI NO FUKEI** • 1929
GUARDIANS OF PHARE see **GARDIENS DU PHARE** • 1928
GUARDIANS OF THE FLOCKS, THE • 1915 • Jaccard Jacques • USA
GUARDIANS OF THE WILD • 1928 • McRae Henry • USA
GUARDIE E LADRI • 1951 • Monicelli Mario, Steno • ITL • COPS AND ROBBERS
GUARDING ANGEL, THE • 1909 • *Lubin* • USA
GUARDING BRITAIN'S SECRETS • 1914 • Calvert Charles • UKN • FIENDS OF HELL, THE
GUARDING PERMANENT PEACE see **NA STRAZY TRWALEGO POKOJU** • 1946
GUARD'S ALARM, THE • 1909 • *Urban-Eclipse* • USA
GUARD'S ALARUM, THE • 1908 • Booth W. R. • UKN
GUARDSMAN, THE • 1911 • Porter Edwin S. • USA
GUARDSMAN, THE • 1931 • Franklin Sidney A. • USA
GUARDSMAN, THE see **GARDEOFFIZIER, DER** • 1926
GUARIDA DEL BUITRE, LA • 1956 • Salvador Jaime • MXC
GUATEMALA • 1938 • FRG
GUAYANA ES.. • 1971 • Scheuren Jose Vicente • VNZ
GUBBEN KOMMER • 1939 • Lindberg Per • SWD • OLD MAN IS COMING, THE
GUBECZIANA • 1974 • Vukotic Dusan • ANS • YGS
GUBIJINSO • 1935 • Mizoguchi Kenji • JPN • FIELD POPPY, THE (UKN) ○ POPPIES (USA) ○ POPPY
GUBIJINSO • 1941 • Nakagawa Nobuo • JPN • POPPY
GUCCIONE • 1974 • Lynch Paul • CND
GUD FADER OCH TATTAREN • 1954 • Faustman Erik • SWD • GOD AND THE GYPSYMAN ○ TATTARBLOD
GUDERNES YNDLING • 1919 • Holger-Madsen • DNM • DIGTERKONGEN ○ TRIALS OF CELEBRITY ○ PENALTY OF FAME, THE
GUDRUN • 1963 • Anker • DNM • SUDDENLY, A WOMAN! (USA)
GUDUDE MOUSHAZHE • 1988 • Zhang Junzhao • CHN • LONER, THE
GUEMES –LA TIERRA EN ARMAS • 1972 • Torre-Nilsson Leopoldo • ARG • GUEMES –LAND IN ARMS
GUEMES –LAND IN ARMS see **GUEMES –LA TIERRA EN ARMAS** • 1972
GUENDALINA • 1957 • Lattuada Alberto • ITL, FRN
GUEPARD, LE (FRN) see **GATTOPARDO, IL** • 1963
GUEPARDO, EL • 1971 • Carretero Amaro • ANS • SPN • CHEETAH, THE
GUEPE, LA • 1987 • Carle Gilles • CND
GUEPES, LES • 1961 • Dhuit • SHT • FRN
GUEPIER, LE • 1975 • Pigaut Roger • FRN, ITL • HORNET'S NEST, THE
GUEPIOT, LE • 1981 • Pilissy Joska • FRN
GUERA DE LOS PASTELES, LA • 1978 • Cardona Rene • MXC
GUERA RODRIGUEZ, LA • 1976 • Cazals Felipe • MXC • FAIR RODRIGUEZ, THE
GUERA XOCHITL, LA • 1966 • Gonzalez Rogelio A. • MXC
GUERILLA, THE • 1908 • Griffith D. W. • USA
GUERILLA BRIGADE see **VSADNIKI** • 1939
GUERILLA FIGHTER, THE see **PADATIK** • 1973
GUERILLA GIRL see **GUERRILLA GIRL** • 1953
GUERILLA MENACE, THE • 1913 • *Bison* • USA
GUERILLAS see **SISSIT** • 1963
GUERILLAS IN PINK LACE see **GUERRILLAS IN PINK LACE** • 1964
GUERILLERA, LA • 1981 • Kast Pierre • FRN, SPN, PRT
GUERILLERO ET CELUI QUI N'Y CROYAIT PAS, LE • 1968 • d'Ormesson Antoine • FRN, ITL • GUERRILLERO, EL
GUERILLEROS, LES (FRN) see **BRIGANTI ITALIANI, I** • 1961
GUERISON DE L'OBESITE EN 5 MINUTES see **TRAITEMENT 706, LE** • 1910
GUERISSEUR, LE • 1953 • Ciampi Yves • FRN
GUERISSEURS, LES • 1988 • Bakaba Sijiri • IVC • ADUEFUE, THE LORDS OF THE STREET (UKN)
GUERISSEZ-NOUS DU MAL • 1972 • Garceau Raymond • DCS • CND
GUERITE, LA see **DOUANIERS ET CONTREBANDIERS** • 1905
GUERNICA • 1949 • Hessens Robert, Resnais Alain • FRN
GUERNICA • 1972 • Bottari Franco • ITL
GUERNICA • 1983 • Kosa Ferenc • HNG
GUERNICA see **ARBRE DE GUERNICA, L'** • 1975
GUERNSEY GRANITE • 1936 • Smith Brian • UKN
GUERRA ALLA GUERRA • 1946 • Marcellini Romolo • DOC • ITL
GUERRA CONJUGAL • 1974 • de Andrade Joaquim Pedro • BRZ • MATRIMONIAL WARFARE
GUERRA CONTINUA, LA • 1962 • Savona Leopoldo • ITL, FRN • DERNIERE ATTAQUE, LA (FRN) ○ WARRIORS FIVE (USA)
GUERRA DE DIOS, LA • 1953 • Gil Rafael • SPN • I WAS A PARISH PRIEST (USA)
GUERRA DE LOS MAGOS, LA (ARG) see **WIZARDS OF THE LOST KINGDOM** • 1984
GUERRA DE LOS PASTELES, LA • 1943 • Gomez Muriel Emilio • MXC
GUERRA DE PAPA, LA • 1977 • Mercero Antonio • SPN • DAD'S WAR ○ FATHER'S WAR
GUERRA DEI ROBOT, LA • 1978 • Brescia Alfonso • ITL • WAR OF THE ROBOTS (USA)
GUERRA DEI TOPLESS, LA • 1965 • Di Gianni Enzo • ITL • DONNE E DIAVOLI
GUERRA DEL CERDO, LA • 1975 • Torre-Nilsson Leopoldo • ARG • DIARIO DE LA GUERRA DEL CERDO ○ DIARY OF THE PIG WAR ○ PIG WAR, THE
GUERRA DEL CHACO, LA • 1936 • Bazoberry Jose Luis • DOC • BLV • WAR OF CHACO
GUERRA DEL FERRO, LA • 1983 • Lenzi Umberto • ITL, FRN • DOMINATORE DEL FERRO, IL ○ PADRONE DEL FERRO, IL ○ GUERRE DU FER, LA ○ IRON MASTER, THE ○ IRONMASTER, THE
GUERRA DES GAUCHOS, LA • 1942 • Demare Lucas • ARG • GAUCHO WAR
GUERRA DI TROIA, LA • 1961 • Ferroni Giorgio • ITL, FRN • WOODEN HORSE OF TROY, THE (UKN) ○ GUERRE DE TROIE, LA (FRN) ○ TROJAN HORSE, THE (USA) ○ TROJAN WAR, THE
GUERRA DO MIRANDUM, A • 1984 • Silva Fernando Matos • PRT
GUERRA E PACE (ITL) see **WAR AND PEACE** • 1956
GUERRA EMPIEZA EN CUBA, LA • 1957 • Mur Oti • SPN
GUERRA HA TERMINADO, LA • 1963 • Madrid Jose Luis • SPN
GUERRA IN TEMPO DI PACE see **MANOVRE D'AMORE** • 1941
GUERRA OLVIDADA, LA • 1967 • Alvarez Santiago • DOC • CUB • LAOS, THE FORGOTTEN WAR ○ FORGOTTEN WAR, THE
GUERRA OLVIDADO, LA see **MADINA BOE** • 1968
GUERRA SEGRETA, LA see **GUERRE SECRETE** • 1965
GUERRA SUCIA • 1984 • Cassado Alfredo • SPN • DIRTY WAR
GUERRE A LA DELINQUANCE see **DEFEATING DELINQUENCY** • 1951
GUERRE AMERE, LA see **COMME UN ECLAIR** • 1968
GUERRE AUX INDES • 1897 • Melies Georges • FRN
GUERRE AUX MOUCHES, LA • 1928 • O'Galop Marius • ANM • FRN
GUERRE AUX SAUTERELLES, LA • 1931 • Greville Edmond T. • SHT • FRN
GUERRE D'ALGERIE, LA • 1970 • Monnier Philippe, Courriere Yves • DOC • FRN
GUERRE DANS MON JARDIN, UNE • 1986 • Letourneau Diane • DOC • CND
GUERRE DE 1812, LA see **QUESTION OF IDENTITY: WAR OF 1812, A** • 1966
GUERRE DE CUBA ET L'EXPLOSION DU MAINE A LA HAVANE • 1898 • Melies Georges • FRN • BLOWING UP OF THE MAINE IN HAVANA HARBOUR, THE ○ QUAI DE LA HAVANE
GUERRE DE FEMMES • 1978 • Guerin Gerard • FRN
GUERRE DE PACIFICATION EN AMAZONIE, LA • 1976 • Billon Yves • DOC • FRN
GUERRE DE TROIE, LA (FRN) see **GUERRA DI TROIA, LA** • 1961
GUERRE DES BOUTONS, LA • 1961 • Robert Yves • FRN • WAR OF THE BUTTONS
GUERRE DES BOUTONS, LA see **GUERRE DES GOSSES, LA** • 1936
GUERRE DES ESPIONS, LA • Boyer Henri • FRN
GUERRE DES GOSSES, LA • 1936 • Daroy Jacques, Deslaw Eugene • FRN • GENERALS WITHOUT BUTTONS (USA) ○ GUERRE DES BOUTONS, LA ○ NOUS, LES GOSSES
GUERRE DES JEUNES, LA • 1969 • Haddad Moussa • ALG
GUERRE DES KARTS, LA see **GROSSE TETE, UNE** • 1962
GUERRE DES MOMIES, LA • 1974 • Heynowski Walter, Scheumann Gerhard • GDR
GUERRE DES PIANOS, LA • 1965 • Dansereau Jean, Labrecque Jean-Claude • DCS • CND
GUERRE DES POLICES, LA • 1979 • Davis Robin • FRN
GUERRE DES TUQUES, LA • 1985 • Melancon Andre • CND • DOG WHO STOPPED THE WAR, THE ○ CHATEAU DE NEIGE, LE ○ DOG THAT STOPPED THE WAR, THE
GUERRE DES VALSES, LA • 1933 • Ploquin Raoul, Berger Ludwig • FRN
GUERRE DU FER, LA see **GUERRA DEL FERRO, LA** • 1983
GUERRE DU FEU, LA (FRN) see **QUEST FOR FIRE** • 1981
GUERRE DU SILENCE, LA • 1959 • Lelouch Claude • DOC • FRN
GUERRE D'UN SEUL HOMME, LA • 1981 • Cozarinsky Edgardo • FRN • ONE MAN'S WAR
GUERRE EN DENTELLES • 1952 • Kast Pierre • FRN • JACQUES CALLOT, CORRESPONDANT DU GUERRE
GUERRE EN GRECE, LA • 1897 • Melies Georges • FRN
GUERRE EST FINIE, LA • 1966 • Resnais Alain • FRN, SWD • KRIGET AR SLUT (SWD) ○ WAR IS OVER, THE
GUERRE INCONNUE, LA • 1961 • Wolff Perry • DOC • FRN, USA • SMASHING OF THE REICH (USA)
GUERRE LONTAINE, LA • 1966 • Bonniere Rene • DOC • CND
GUERRE OUBLIEE, LA • 1988 • Boutet Richard • DOC • CND • FORGOTTEN WAR, THE ○ MEMORY FRAGMENTS
GUERRE PLANETARI • 1978 • Margheriti Antonio • ITL
GUERRE PLANETARI see **PIANETA DEGLI UOMINI SPENTI, IL** • 1961
GUERRE POPULAIRE AU LAOS, LA • 1969 • Ivens Joris (c/d) • DOC • FRN
GUERRE RUSSO-JAPONAISE, LA • 1904 • Nonguet Lucien • FRN
GUERRE SECRETE • 1965 • Christian-Jaque, Klinger Werner, Lizzani Carlo, Young Terence • FRN, FRG, ITL • SPIONE UNTER SICH (FRG) ○ DIRTY GAME, THE (UKN) ○ GUERRA SEGRETA, LA
GUERRERAS VERDES • 1976 • Torrado Ramon • SPN
GUERREROS Y CAUTIVAS • 1988 • Cozarinsky Edgardo • ARG, FRN, SWT • GUERRIERS ET CAPTIVES (FRN) ○ WARRIORS AND CAPTIVES
GUERRES CIVILES EN FRANCE • 1976 • Barat Francois, Nordon Vincent, Farges Joel • FRN
GUERRIERE DAL SENO NUDO, LE • 1974 • Young Terence • ITL, FRN, SPN • AMAZONES, LES (FRN) ○ AMAZONS, THE (UKN) ○ WAR GODDESS ○ AMAZZONI, LE
GUERRIERI • 1942 • Emmer Luciano, Gras Enrico • ITL
GUERRIERI DELL'ANNO 2072, I • 1984 • Fulci Lucio • ITL • WARRIORS OF YEAR 2072, THE
GUERRIERS ET CAPTIVES (FRN) see **GUERREROS Y CAUTIVAS** • 1988
GUERRILLA, LA • 1972 • Gil Rafael • SPN
GUERRILLA GIRL • 1953 • Christian John • USA • DAWN COMES LATE ○ GUERILLA GIRL
GUERRILLAS IN PINK LACE • 1964 • Montgomery George • USA, PHL • GUERILLAS IN PINK LACE
GUERRILLERA DE VILLA, LA • 1967 • Morayta Miguel • MXC, SPN • VILLA'S WOMAN GUERRILLA FIGHTER
GUERRILLERO, EL • 1930 • Buchs Jose • SPN
GUERRILLERO, EL see **GUERILLERO ET CELUI QUI N'Y CROYAIT PAS, LE** • 1968
GUERRILLEROS, LOS • 1962 • Ramirez Pedro L. • SPN • CAMPANAS DE AMANECER
GUESS WHAT!?! see **GUESS WHAT WE LEARNED IN SCHOOL TODAY?** • 1970
GUESS WHAT HAPPENED TO COUNT DRACULA? • 1970 • Merrick Laurence • USA
GUESS WHAT WE LEARNED IN SCHOOL TODAY? • 1970 • Avildsen John G. • USA • I AIN'T NO BUFFALO ○ GUESS WHAT!?!
GUESS WHO? • 1965 • Smith Paul J. • ANS • USA
GUESS WHO'S COMING? • 1969 • Hais Jai • USA
GUESS WHO'S COMING FOR BREAKFAST (UKN) see **NICHTEN DER FRAU OBERST, DIE** • 1968
GUESS WHO'S COMING TO DINNER • 1967 • Kramer Stanley • USA
GUESS WHO'S SLEEPING IN MY BED? • 1973 • Flicker Theodore J. • TVM • USA
GUESS WHO'S SLEEPING WITH US TONIGHT (UKN) see **RAT MAL, WER HEUT BEI UNS SCHLAFT..** • 1969
GUEST, THE • Gardner Frank • SHT • USA
GUEST, THE • 1976 • Devenish Ross • SAF • GUEST AT STEENKAMPSKRAAL, THE ○ BESOEKER, DIE
GUEST, THE see **OSPITE, L'** • 1971
GUEST, THE (USA) see **CARETAKER, THE** • 1963
GUEST AT DINNER, A see **UN OASPETE LA CINA** • 1987
GUEST AT STEENKAMPSKRAAL, THE see **GUEST, THE** • 1976
GUEST AT THE PARSONAGE, THE • 1912 • *Eclair* • USA
GUEST CAME, A see **DET KOM EN GAST** • 1947
GUEST FROM THE DARK, A see **NOCHNOI GOST** • 1957
GUEST FROM THE ISLAND OF FREEDOM, A see **GOST O OSTROVA SVOBODY** • 1963
GUEST HOUSE, THE (UKN) see **IN OLD CHEYENNE** • 1931
GUEST IN ONE'S HOME, A see **GAST I EGET HUS** • 1957
GUEST IN THE HOUSE, A • 1944 • Brahm John, De Toth Andre (U/c), Milestone Lewis (U/c) • USA
GUEST IN THE NIGHT see **NOCHNOI GOST** • 1957
GUEST IN THE NIGHT, A see **NOCNI HOST** • 1961
GUEST OF HONOUR • 1934 • King George • UKN
GUEST OF THE EVENING, THE • 1914 • Wilson Frank? • UKN
GUEST OF THE REGIMENT, THE • 1915 • Noy Wilfred • UKN
GUEST ON FREEDOM ISLAND see **GOST O OSTROVA SVOBODY** • 1963
GUEST PESTS • 1945 • Jason Will • SHT • USA
GUEST WIFE • 1945 • Wood Sam • USA
GUEST WORKERS see **GAESTEARBEJDERE** • 1973
GUESTLESS DINNER PARTY, THE see **STORE MIDDAG, DEN** • 1914
GUESTS ARE COMING (USA) see **JADA, GOSCIE, JADA** • 1962
GUESTS OF HONOUR • 1941 • Pitt • DOC • UKN
GUESTS OF HOTEL ASTORIA, THE • 1989 • Allemehzadeh Reza • NTH
GUESTS ON OUR LAND see **HOTES DE NOS TERRES, LES**
GUESTS WANTED • 1931 • Ceder Ralph • SHT • USA
GUET-APENS, LE • 1913 • Feuillade Louis • FRN
GUET-APENS A TANGER (FRN) see **AGGUATO A TANGERI** • 1958
GUET-APENS DANS LA FORET NOIRE see **FINANCE NOIRE** • 1940
GUEULE COMME LA MIENNE, UNE • 1959 • Dard Frederic • FRN
GUEULE D'AMOUR • 1937 • Gremillon Jean • FRN
GUEULE D'ANGE • 1955 • Blistene Marcel • FRN • PLEASURES AND VICES (USA)
GUEULE DE BOIS, LA see **VERLOREN MAANDAG** • 1973
GUEULE DE L'AUTRE, LA • 1979 • Tchernia Pierre • FRN
GUEULE DE L'EMPLOI, LA • 1973 • Rouland Jacques • FRN
GUEULE DU LOUP, LA • 1981 • Leviant Michel • FRN
GUEULE EN OR, UNE • 1936 • Colombier Piere • FRN
GUEULE OUVERTE, LA • 1973 • Pialat Maurice • FRN • MOUTH AGAPE, THE
GUEUX AU PARADIS, LES • 1945 • Le Henaff Rene • FRN • HOBOES IN PARADISE (USA)
GUEZIREH EL OSHAK • 1968 • Reda Hassan • EGY • ISLAND OF LOVERS
GUFF AND GUNPLAY • 1917 • Semon Larry • SHT • USA
GUGLIELMO OBERDAN • 1915 • Ghione Emilio • ITL
GUGLIELMO TELL • 1949 • Pastina Giorgio • ITL • ARCIERE DELLA FORESTA NERA, L'
GUGUSSE AND THE AUTOMATON (USA) see **GUGUSSE ET L'AUTOMATON** • 1897
GUGUSSE ET L'AUTOMATON • 1897 • Melies Georges • FRN • GUGUSSE AND THE AUTOMATON (USA) ○ CLOWN AND THE AUTOMATON
GUGUSTE ET BELZEBUTH • 1901 • Melies Georges • FRN • CLOWN VS. SATAN, THE (USA)
GUI DAO • 1980 • Dufaux Georges • DOC • CND • SUR LA VOIE
GUIA DE TURISTAS, LA • 1974 • *Henaine* • MXC
GUICHETS DU LOUVRE, LES • 1974 • Mitrani Michel • FRN • BLACK THURSDAY (USA) ○ GATES OF THE LOUVRE, THE
GUIDA • 1919 • Mari Febo • ITL
GUIDANCE TO THE INDULGENT see **DORAKU GOSHINAN** • 1928
GUIDE, THE • 1919 • Kenton Erle C. • SHT • USA
GUIDE, THE • 1965 • *Burman S. D. (M)* • IND
GUIDE, THE • 1965 • Danielewski Tad • USA, IND • SURVIVAL
GUIDE DOGS FOR THE BLIND • 1939 • Asquith Anthony • SHT • UKN
GUIDE FOR THE MARRIED MAN, A • 1967 • Kelly Gene • USA
GUIDE FOR THE MARRIED WOMAN, A • 1978 • Averback Hy • TVM • USA
GUIDE TO AMERICA see **SEX O'CLOCK NEWS, THE** • 1986
GUIDEBOOK TO MATRIMONY see **PORADNIK MATRYMONIALNY** • 1968
GUIDED MOUSE-ILLE • 1967 • Levitow Abe • ANS • USA

GUIDED MUSCLE • 1955 • Jones Charles M. • ANS • USA
GUIDERS, THE • 1916 • *Mcnish Frank E.* • USA
GUIDING CONSCIENCE see **LYKKEN** • 1916
GUIDING FATE • 1914 • O'Sullivan Tony • USA
GUIDING HAND, THE • 1914 • *Bauer Arthur* • USA
GUIDING HAND, THE • 1916 • Ellis Robert • SHT • USA
GUIDING HAND, THE • 1917 • Windom Lawrence C. • SHT • USA
GUIDING LIGHT, THE • 1913 • O'Neil Barry • USA
GUIDING LIGHT, THE • 1915 • Otto Henry • USA
GUIDO • 1979 • Michalak Richard • SHT • ASL
GUIDO DER ERSTE ODER DER GETAUSCHTE WURSTFABRIKANT • 1915 • Otto Paul • FRG
GUIDO IM PARADIES • 1915 • Otto Paul • FRG
GUIGNOLO, LE • 1980 • Lautner Georges • FRN, ITL
GUILALA see **UCHU DAIKAIJU GUILALA** • 1967
GUILD OF THE KUTNA HORA VIRGINS see **CECH PANEN KUTNOHORSKYCH** • 1938
GUILD OF THE MAIDENS OF KUTNA HORA see **CECH PANEN KUTNOHORSKYCH** • 1938
GUILD OF THE VIRGINS OF KUTNA see **CECH PANEN KUTNOHORSKYCH** • 1938
GUILE OF WOMEN • 1921 • Badger Clarence • USA
GUILLAUME TELL • 1896 • Reynaud Emile • FRN
GUILLAUME TELL • 1903 • Nonguet Lucien • FRN
GUILLAUME TELL see **WILHELM TELL –BERGEN IN FLAMMEN** • 1960
GUILLAUME TELL ET LE CLOWN • 1898 • Melies Georges • FRN • ADVENTURES OF WILLIAM TELL (USA) ○ WILLIAM TELL AND THE CLOWN
GUILLAUME TELL ET LE CLOWN see **AVENTURES DE GUILLAUME TELL** • 1898
GUILLOTINE • 1924 • Schamberg Guido • FRG
GUILT • 1931 • Fogwell Reginald • UKN
GUILT • 1976 • Gerinska Vesselina • BUL
GUILT see **TILLSAMMANS MED GUNILLA MANDAG KVALL OCH TISDAG** • 1965
GUILT, THE • 1915 • Smith Hamilton • USA
GUILT, THE see **CULPA, A** • 1981
GUILT IS MY SHADOW • 1950 • Kellino Roy • UKN • INTRUDER, THE
GUILT IS NOT MINE (USA) see **INGIUSTA CONDANNA, L'** • 1952
GUILT OF JANET AMES, THE • 1947 • Levin Henry • USA
GUILT OF SILENCE, THE • 1918 • Clifton Elmer • USA
GUILT OF STEPHEN ELDRIDGE, THE • 1916 • MacDonald J. Farrell • SHT • USA
GUILT OF VLADIMIR OLMER, THE see **VINA VLADIMIRA OLMERA** • 1956
GUILTLESS, THE see **GUNAHSIZLAR** • 1968
GUILTY • 1916 • McRae Henry • SHT • USA
GUILTY • 1918 • Lyons Eddie, Moran Lee • SHT • USA
GUILTY • 1920 • *Moranti Milburn* • USA
GUILTY • 1922 • *Miller Bill* • USA
GUILTY? • 1930 • Seitz George B. • USA
GUILTY? • 1956 • Greville Edmond T. • UKN, FRN • JE PLAIDE NON COUPABLE (FRN)
GUILTY see **THRU DIFFERENT EYES** • 1929
GUILTY, THE • 1947 • Reinhardt John • USA
GUILTY AS CHARGED (UKN) see **GUILTY AS HELL** • 1932
GUILTY AS HELL • 1932 • Kenton Erle C. • USA • GUILTY AS CHARGED (UKN) ○ RIDDLE ME THIS
GUILTY ASSIGNMENT see **BIG TOWN** • 1947
GUILTY BABY, THE • 1912 • *Diestel Lucy* • USA
GUILTY BY SUSPICION see **CRY IN THE DARK, A** • 1988
GUILTY BYSTANDER • 1950 • Lerner Joseph • USA
GUILTY CONSCIENCE • 1912 • *Solax* • USA
GUILTY CONSCIENCE • 1985 • Greene David • TVM • USA
GUILTY CONSCIENCE, A • 1921 • Smith David • USA • THOU ART THE MAN
GUILTY CONSCIENCE, THE • 1908 • Brooke Van Dyke • USA
GUILTY EGG, THE • 1918 • Lyons Eddie, Moran Lee • SHT • USA
GUILTY GENERATION, THE • 1931 • Lee Rowland V. • USA
GUILTY HAND, THE • 1913 • *Eclair* • USA
GUILTY HANDS • 1931 • Van Dyke W. S. • USA
GUILTY HOMICIDE see **HOMICIDIO CULPOSO**
GUILTY MAN, THE • 1918 • Willat Irvin V. • USA
GUILTY MELODY • 1936 • Pottier Richard • UKN
GUILTY MEN • 1945 • Daly Tom • DOC • CND
GUILTY NEIGHBORS • 1916 • *Hippo* • USA
GUILTY OF INNOCENCE: THE LENELL GETER STORY • 1987 • Heffron Richard T. • TVM • USA
GUILTY OF LOVE • 1920 • Knoles Harley • USA • THIS WOMAN –THIS MAN
GUILTY OF TREASON • 1949 • Feist Felix E. • USA • TREASON (UKN)
GUILTY ONE, THE • 1924 • Henabery Joseph • USA
GUILTY ONE, THE see **ALONG THE MALIBU** • 1916
GUILTY ONES, THE • 1916 • *Hardy Babe* • SHT • USA
GUILTY OR INNOCENT: THE SAM SHEPPARD MURDER CASE • 1975 • Lewis Robert Michael • TVM • USA
GUILTY OR NOT GUILTY • 1914 • *Anderson Mignon* • USA
GUILTY OR NOT GUILTY • 1932 • Ray Albert • USA
GUILTY OR NOT GUILTY • 1989 • Arvantis Dimitris • MTV • GRC
GUILTY PARTY, THE • 1912 • *Edison* • USA
GUILTY PARTY, THE • 1917 • Mills Thomas R. • USA
GUILTY PARTY, THE • 1962 • Harris Lionel • UKN
GUILTY SECRET, THE (USA) see **INTIMATE STRANGER, THE** • 1956
GUILTY THOUGH INNOCENT see **BEZ VINI VINOVATIYE** • 1945
GUILTY THOUGH INNOCENT see **SKYLDIG, IKKE SKYLDIG** • 1953
GUILTY TRAILS • 1938 • Waggner George • USA
GUILTY WIFE, THE • 1918 • *Grey Jane* • USA
GUINE-68 • 1968 • Simoes Quirino • SHT • PRT
GUINEA ENTERTAINER, THE • 1906 • Cooper Arthur • UKN
GUINEA PIG, THE • 1948 • Boulting Roy • UKN • OUTSIDER, THE (USA)
GUINEA-PIGS, THE see **PROEFKONIJNEN, DE** • 1980
GUINGUETTE • 1958 • Delannoy Jean • FRN, ITL
GUINJI WITH SEVEN FACES see **NANATSU NO KAWO NO GUINJI** • 1955
GUINNESS AT THE ALBERT HALL • 1966 • Williams Richard • UKN
GUINNESS BOOK OF RECORDS • 1968 • Bonniere Rene • DCS • CND
GUIRARA see **UCHU DAIKAIJU GUILALA** • 1967
GUIRLANDE MERVEILLEUSE, LA • 1903 • Melies Georges • FRN • MARVELLOUS WREATH, THE (USA) ○ MARVELLOUS HOOP, THE
GUITAR AND THE HOOTER, THE • Topouzanov Christo • ANS • BUL
GUITAR CRAZE • 1959 • Russell Ken • MTV • UKN
GUITAR MAKING • 1967 • Bonniere Rene • DCS • CND
GUITARE • 1973 • Lavoie Richard • CND
GUITARE AU POING • 1972 • Szuster Daniel • DOC • FRN
GUITARE ET LE JAZZ-BAND, LA • 1923 • Roudes Gaston • FRN
GUITARRA DE GARDEL, LA • 1949 • Klimovsky Leon • SPN
GUITARRAS DE MEDIANOCHE • 1957 • Baledon Rafael • MXC
GUITARRAS LLOREN GUITARRAS • 1964 • Delgado Miguel M. • MXC
GUITARS –FROM FLAMENCO TO JAZZ • 1962 • Markas Gary • SHT • USA
GUITARS OF LOVE (USA) see **GITARREN DER LIEBE** • 1954
GUL AGACI • 1967 • Aslan Mehmet • TRK • ROSE TREE, THE
GUL BABA • 1940 • Nadasdy Kalman • HNG
GUL BAKAWLI • 1960 • Dil Munshi • PKS
GUL HASAN • 1982 • Kurtiz Tuncel • TRK, SWD • HASAN THE ROSE
GUL SANOVAR • 1928 • *Kohinoor* • IND
GUL SANOVAR • 1934 • Masteri Homi • IND • FLOWER LAKE
GUL VE SEKER • 1968 • Seden Osman • TRK • SUGAR AND ROSES
GULA BILEN, DEN • 1963 • Mattsson Arne • SWD • YELLOW CAR, THE
GULA DIVISIONEN • 1954 • Olin Stig • SWD • YELLOW SQUADRON, THE
GULA KLINIKEN • 1942 • Johansson Ivar • SWD • YELLOW WARD
GULAG • 1985 • Young Roger • TVM • USA
GULBADAN • Hameed A. • PKS
GULBAKAVALI • 1947 • Modi Rustom • IND
GULBAKAVALI • 1955 • Desai Dhirubhai • IND
GULD OG GRLONNE SKOVE • 1957 • Axel Gabriel • DNM • GOLDEN MOUNTAINS
GULD TIL PRAERIENS SKRAPPE DRENGE • 1971 • Karlsson Finn • DNM
GULDEN MAGT see **MACHT DES GOLDES, DIE** • 1912
GULDET OG VORT HJERTE • 1913 • Holger-Madsen • DNM • VANSKELIGT VALG, ET ○ HEART'S VOICE, THE
GULDETS GIFT • 1916 • Holger-Madsen • DNM • POISON OF GOLD, THE ○ LERHJERTET ○ CLAY HEART, THE ○ TEMPTING OF MRS CHESTNEY, THE
GULDGRAVARNA • 1959 • Jarrel Bengt • SWD • GOLD-DIGGERS
GULDHORNENE • 1914 • van der Aa Kuhle Kai • DNM
GULDKALVEN • 1914 • Davidsen Hjalmar • DNM
GULDMONTEN see **ALT PAA ET KORT** • 1912
GULDREGN • 1988 • Kragh-Jacobsen Soren • DNM • SHOWER OF GOLD
GULDSPINDELN • 1916 • Magnussen Fritz • SWD • GOLD SPIDER, THE
GULEN GOZLER • 1977 • Egilmez Ertem • TRK • SMILING EYES
GULF BETWEEN, THE • 1916 • Bertram William • *Mustang* • SHT • USA
GULF BETWEEN, THE • 1916 • Sloman Edward • *Lubin* • SHT • USA
GULF BETWEEN, THE • 1918 • Physioc Wray • USA
GULF STREAM • 1939 • Alexeieff Alexandre • SHT • FRN
GULF STREAM • 1981 • MacKay Bruce • MTV • CND, USA
GULL! see **TRUT!** • 1944
GULL, THE see **TRUT!** • 1944
GULLE MINNAAR, DE • 1989 • Saks Mady • NTH
GULLI • 1926 • Shengelaya Nikolai, Push • USS
GULLIBLE CANARY, THE • 1942 • Geiss Alec • ANS • USA
GULLIVER • Gassman Vittorio • ITL
GULLIVER • 1976 • Ungria Alfonso • SPN
GULLIVER see **VOYAGE DE GULLIVER A LILLIPUT ET CHEZ LES GEANTS, LE** • 1902
GULLIVER CHEZ LES LILLIPUTIENS • 1923 • Mourlan Albert, Vilette Raymond • ANM • FRN • GULLIVER IN LILLIPUT
GULLIVER IN LILLIPUT • 1981 • Letts Barry • MTV • UKN, USA, AUS
GULLIVER IN LILLIPUT see **GULLIVER CHEZ LES LILLIPUTIENS** • 1923
GULLIVER IN THE LAND OF THE GIANTS • de Chomon Segundo
GULLIVER MICKEY • 1934 • Gillett Burt • ANS • USA
GULLIVER NO UCHU RYOKO see **GARIBAH NO UCHU RYOKO** • 1966
GULLIVERS REISEN • 1924 • AUS • GULLIVER'S TRAVELS
GULLIVER'S TRAVELS • *Hanna-Barbera* • ANM • USA
GULLIVER'S TRAVELS • 1939 • Fleischer Dave • ANM • USA
GULLIVER'S TRAVELS • 1977 • Hunt Peter • UKN, BLG
GULLIVER'S TRAVELS see **GULLIVERS REISEN** • 1924
GULLIVER'S TRAVELS AMONG THE LILLIPUTIANS AND THE GIANTS see **VOYAGE DE GULLIVER A LILLIPUT ET CHEZ LES GEANTS, LE** • 1902
GULLIVER'S TRAVELS BEYOND THE MOON (UKN) see **GARIBAH NO UCHU RYOKO** • 1966
GULLIVER'S TRAVELS: PART 2 • 1983 • Delgado Cruz • ANM • SPN • LAND OF THE GIANTS: GULLIVER'S TRAVELS PART 2
GULLIVER'S TRAVELS (USA) see **VOYAGE DE GULLIVER A LILLIPUT ET CHEZ LES GEANTS, LE** • 1902
GULLIVER'S TROUBLES • 1967 • Hubley John • ANS • USA
GULLS AND BUOYS • 1972 • Breer Robert • USA
GULLU GELIYOR GULLU • 1974 • Yilmaz Atif • TRK • GULLU IS COMING
GULLU IS COMING see **GULLU GELIYOR GULLU** • 1974
GULOCKY • 1983 • Zachar Jozef • CZC • MARBLES
GULSUSAN • 1985 • Olgac Bilge • TRK
GULT OG SORT see **SENSOMMER** • 1988
GULTEKIN • 1968 • Aslan Mehmet • TRK
GULVBEHANDLING • 1955 • Carlsen Henning • SHT • DNM
GUM see **UNIVERMAG** • 1922
GUM DROPS AND OVERALLS • 1919 • *Hampton Ruth* • SHT • USA
GUM MAN, THE • 1913 • *Missimer Howard* • USA
GUM RIOT, A • 1920 • *Mann Hank* • USA
GUMBALL RALLY, THE • 1976 • Bail Chuck • USA
GUMBASIA • 1955 • Clokey Art • ANS • USA
GUMBY'S ADVENTURES ON THE MOON • 1969 • Hoffman Roni • SHT • USA
GUMMI BARCHEN KUSST MAN NICHT • 1989 • Bannert Walter • FRG • REAL MEN DON'T EAT GUMMY BEARS
GUMMI TARZAN • 1981 • Kragh-Jacobsen Soren • DNM • RUBBER TARZAN
GUMNAM • 1983 • Yukol Prince Chatri • THL
GUMPS, THE • 1928 • Kenton Erle C., Taurog Norman, Grey Ray, Watson William, Corby Francis, Andrews Del, Kerr Robert, Kirkland David, Hutchinson Craig, Dawn Norman, Weber William • USA
GUMS • *Hall Terri* • USA
GUMSHOE • 1972 • Frears Stephen • UKN
GUMSHOE MAGOO • 1958 • Turner Gil • ANS • USA
GUN, THE • 1974 • Badham John • TVM • USA
GUN, THE see **SUO NOME FACEVA TREMARE.. INTERPOL IN ALLARME, IL** • 1973
GUN AND THE PULPIT, THE • 1974 • Petrie Daniel • TVM • USA
GUN BATTLE AT MONTEREY • 1957 • Hittelman Carl K., Franklin Sidney A. Jr. • USA
GUN BEFORE BUTTER • 1972 • Zadek Peter • FRG
GUN BEHIND THE MAN, THE • 1914 • *Brennan John* • USA
GUN BELT • 1953 • Nazarro Ray • USA
GUN BROTHERS • 1956 • Salkow Sidney • USA
GUN BUS see **GUNBUS** • 1987
GUN CODE • 1940 • Newfield Sam • USA
GUN CRAZY see **DEADLY IS THE FEMALE** • 1949
GUN DUEL IN DURANGO • 1957 • Salkow Sidney • USA • DUEL IN DURANGO
GUN FEVER • 1958 • Stevens Mark • USA
GUN FIGHT • 1961 • Cahn Edward L. • USA
GUN-FIGHTER, THE • 1911 • *Nestor* • USA
GUN FIGHTER, THE • 1915 • *Edwards Walter* • USA
GUN-FIGHTIN' GENTLEMAN, A • 1919 • Ford John • USA
GUN FOR A COWARD • 1957 • Biberman Abner • USA
GUN FROM NEVESINJE see **NEVESINJSKA PUSKA** • 1963
GUN FURY • 1953 • Walsh Raoul • USA
GUN GAME, THE • 1920 • Flaven Art • SHT • USA
GUN GLORY • 1957 • Rowland Roy • USA
GUN GOSPEL • 1927 • Brown Harry J. • USA
GUN GRIT • 1936 • Berke William • USA • PROTECTION RACKET (UKN)
GUN HAND, THE see **HE RIDES TALL** • 1964
GUN-HAND GARRISON • 1927 • Gordon Edward R. • USA
GUN HAWK, THE • 1963 • Ludwig Edward • USA
GUN IN HIS HAND • 1956 • Allen Lewis • MTV • USA
GUN IN HIS HAND, A • 1945 • Losey Joseph • SHT • USA
GUN IN THE HOUSE, A • 1981 • Nagy Ivan • TVM • USA
GUN JUSTICE • 1927 • Wyler William • SHT • USA
GUN JUSTICE • 1933 • James Alan • USA
GUN LAW • 1919 • Ford John • SHT • USA
GUN LAW • 1929 • De Lacy Robert?, Burch John? • USA • SWIFT LOVER, A (UKN)
GUN LAW • 1933 • Collins Lewis D. • USA
GUN LAW • 1938 • Howard David • USA
GUN LAW see **GIORNI DELL'IRA, I** • 1967
GUN LAW JUSTICE • 1949 • Hillyer Lambert • USA
GUN LORDS OF STIRRUP BASIN • 1937 • Newfield Sam • USA
GUN MAGIC • 1919 • Holt George • SHT • USA
GUN MAN, THE • 1911 • Dwan Allan • USA • GUNMAN, THE
GUN MEN OF PLUMAS, THE • 1914 • Franz Joseph J. • USA
GUN MOLL • 1938 • *Mckinney Nina Mae* • USA • GANG SMASHERS
GUN MOLL see **JIGSAW** • 1949
GUN MOLL see **MOME VERT-DE-GRIS, LA** • 1952
GUN MOLL see **PUPA DEL GANGSTER, LA** • 1975
GUN OF APRIL MORNING, THE see **CAPTAIN APACHE** • 1971
GUN PACKER, THE • 1919 • Ford John • SHT • USA
GUN PACKER, THE • 1938 • Fox Wallace • USA
GUN PLAY • 1935 • Herman Al • USA • INVISIBLE MESSAGE, THE (UKN) ○ LUCKY BOOTS
GUN POINT see **AT GUNPOINT** • 1955
GUN RANGER, THE • 1937 • Bradbury Robert North • USA
GUN RIDERS • 1970 • Adamson Al • USA • FIVE BLOODY DAYS TO TOMBSTONE ○ FIVE BLOODY GRAVES ○ LONELY MAN
GUN & ROSARY see **BARIL AT ROSARIO** • 1968
GUN RUNNER • 1949 • Hillyer Lambert • USA
GUN RUNNER • 1969 • Compton Richard • USA • GUNRUNNERS, THE
GUN RUNNER, THE • 1916 • SAF
GUN RUNNER, THE • 1928 • Lewis Edgar • USA
GUN RUNNER, THE (UKN) see **SANTIAGO** • 1956
GUN RUNNERS, THE • 1916 • Horne James W. • SHT • USA
GUN RUNNERS, THE • 1919 • Marshall George • SHT • USA
GUN RUNNERS, THE • 1958 • Siegel Don • USA
GUN-SHOT AT THE MOUNTAIN PASS see **VISTRIL V GORACH** • 1970
GUN SHOTS IN THE VALLEY OF JUGS • 1983 • LAO
GUN SHY • 1922 • Neitz Alvin J. • USA
GUN SMOKE • 1931 • Sloman Edward • USA • WESTERNER, THE
GUN SMOKE • 1945 • Bretherton Howard • USA
GUN SMOKE OVER THE GUADALOPE see **GUNSMOKE ON THE GUADALOPE** • 1935
GUN SMOKE (UKN) see **GUNSMOKE ON THE GUADALOPE** • 1935
GUN SMUGGLERS • 1948 • McDonald Frank • USA
GUN SMUGGLERS, THE • 1912 • *Blackwell Carlyle* • USA
GUN STREET • 1961 • Cahn Edward L. • USA
GUN TALK • 1947 • Hillyer Lambert • USA
GUN THAT SHOOK THE WEST, THE see **SOMETHING BIG** • 1972

GUN THAT WON THE WEST, THE • 1955 • Castle William • USA

GUN THE MAN DOWN see **ARIZONA MISSION** • 1956

GUN TO GUN • 1944 • Lederman D. Ross • SHT • USA

GUN TOWN • 1946 • Fox Wallace • USA

GUN WOMAN, THE • 1918 • Borzage Frank • USA

GUNAH • 1981 • Latif Engineer • AFG • FAULTS

GUNAHON KA DEVTA • 1967 • Sharma Devi • IND • GOD OF SIN

GUNAHSIZLAR • 1968 • Evin Semih • TRK • GUILTLESS, THE

GUNAN-BATOR • Davydov R. • ANS • USS

GUNAN IL GUERRIERO • 1983 • Prosperi Franco • ITL

GUNAN, KING OF THE BARBARIANS see **GUNANA RE BARBARO** • 1981

GUNAN, KING OF THE BARBARIANS see **SPADE DEI BARBARI, LE** • 1983

GUNAN NO.2 see **SPADE DEI BARBARI, LE** • 1983

GUNANA RE BARBARO • 1981 • Prosperi Franco • ITL • GUNAN, KING OF THE BARBARIANS ○ INVINCIBLE BARBARIAN, THE

GUNBOAT GINSBURG • 1930 • Sandrich Mark • SHT • USA

GUNBUS • 1987 • Perisic Zoran • YGS, UKN • SKY BANDITS ○ SKY PIRATES ○ GUN BUS

GUNDOWN • 1973 • King Philip • UKN

GUNES DOGGARKEN • 1985 • Goren Serif • TRK • RISING SUN, THE

GUNESE KOPRU • 1985 • Tokatli Erdogan • TRK • BRIDGE TO THE SUN

GUNESIN TUTULDUGU GUN • 1985 • Goren Serif • TRK • DAY OF THE ECLIPSE, THE

GUNESLI BATAKLIK • 1978 • Duru Sureyya • TRK • SUNNY SWAMP, THE

GUNEY OLUM SACIYOR • 1969 • Aslan Mehmet • TRK

GUNEY'S THE WALL see **MUR, LE** • 1983

GUNFIGHT, A • 1971 • Johnson Lamont • USA

GUNFIGHT AT COMANCHE CREEK • 1963 • McDonald Frank • USA

GUNFIGHT AT DODGE CITY, THE • 1959 • Newman Joseph M. • USA

GUNFIGHT AT INDIAN GAP • 1957 • Kane Joseph • USA

GUNFIGHT AT RED SANDS see **GRINGO** • 1964

GUNFIGHT AT SANDOVAL • 1961 • Keller Harry • MTV • USA

GUNFIGHT AT THE O.K. CORRAL • 1957 • Sturges John • USA

GUNFIGHT IN ABILENE • 1967 • Hale William • USA

GUNFIGHT ON SEVENTH STREET see **RANGEKI NO SHICHIBANGAI** • 1958

GUNFIGHTER see **FRONTIER LAW** • 1943

GUNFIGHTER, THE • 1917 • Hart William S. • USA

GUNFIGHTER, THE • 1923 • Reynolds Lynn • USA

GUNFIGHTER, THE • 1950 • King Henry • USA

GUNFIGHTERS • 1947 • Waggner George • USA • ASSASSIN, THE (UKN) ○ TWIN SOMBREROS

GUNFIGHTERS OF ABILENE • 1960 • Cahn Edward L. • USA

GUNFIGHTERS OF CASA GRANDE (USA) see **PISTOLEROS DE CASA GRANDE, LOS** • 1964

GUNFIGHTERS OF THE NORTHWEST • 1954 • Bennet Spencer Gordon • SRL • USA

GUNFIGHTER'S SON, THE • 1913 • Duncan William • USA

GUNFIRE • 1935 • Fraser Harry L. • USA

GUNFIRE • 1950 • Berke William • USA • FRANK JAMES RIDES AGAIN (UKN)

GUNFIRE AT INDIAN GAP • 1958 • Kane Joseph • USA

GUNG HO! • 1943 • Enright Ray • USA

GUNG HO • 1985 • Howard Ron • USA

GUNGA DIN • 1911 • *Powers* • USA

GUNGA DIN • 1939 • Stevens George • USA

GUNGALA, LA PANTERA NUDA • 1968 • Deodato Ruggero • ITL • GUNGALA, THE NAKED PANTHER

GUNGALA LA VERGINE DELLA GIUNGLA • 1967 • Ferrara Romano • ITL • GUNGALA THE VIRGIN OF THE JUNGLE

GUNGALA, THE NAKED PANTHER see **GUNGALA, LA PANTERA NUDA** • 1968

GUNGALA THE VIRGIN OF THE JUNGLE see **GUNGALA LA VERGINE DELLA GIUNGLA** • 1967

GUNGAN SUDENI KEMURI NASHI • 1950 • Sekigawa Hideo • JPN • WARSHIPS WITHOUT SMOKE

GUNGCAIL • 1978 • Amin Ruhul • BNG • SEAGULL

GUNHEAD see **GUNHED** • 1989

GUNHED • 1989 • Harada Masato • JPN • GUNHEAD

GUNKI HATAMEKU SHITANI • 1972 • Fukasaku Kinji • JPN • UNDER THE MILITARY FLAG

GUNLESS BAD MAN, THE • 1926 • Wyler William • SHT • USA

GUNMAKER OF MOSCOW, THE • 1913 • *Wilson Benjamin F.* • USA

GUNMAN, THE • 1914 • Walsh Raoul, Cabanne W. Christy • USA

GUNMAN, THE • 1952 • Collins Lewis D. • USA

GUNMAN, THE see **GUN MAN, THE** • 1911

GUNMAN CALLED NEBRASKA, A see **RINGO EN NEBRASKA** • 1965

GUNMAN FROM BRODIE, THE • 1941 • Bennet Spencer Gordon • USA

GUNMAN HAS ESCAPED, A • 1948 • Grey Richard M. • UKN

GUNMAN IN THE STREETS (UKN) see **TRAQUE, LE** • 1950

GUNMAN'S CODE • 1946 • Fox Wallace • USA

GUNMAN'S GOSPEL, THE • 1917 • Wells Raymond • SHT • USA

GUNMAN'S WALK • 1958 • Karlson Phil • USA

GUNMEN FROM LAREDO • 1959 • MacDonald Wallace • USA

GUNMEN OF ABILENE • 1950 • Brannon Fred C. • USA

GUNMEN OF THE RIO GRANDE (USA) see **SFIDA A RIO BRAVO** • 1965

GUNN • 1967 • Edwards Blake • USA

GUNNAR HEDES SAGA • 1923 • Stiller Mauritz • SWD • JUDGEMENT, THE (UKN) ○ BLIZZARD, THE (USA) ○ GUNNAR HEDE'S SAGA ○ OLD MANSION, THE

GUNNAR HEDE'S SAGA see **GUNNAR HEDES SAGA** • 1923

GUNNERS AND GUNS • 1935 • Hoyt Robert?, Callahan Jerry? • USA • GUNS AND GUNNERS (UKN)

GUNNING FOR JUSTICE • 1948 • Taylor Ray • USA

GUNNING FOR VENGEANCE • 1946 • Nazarro Ray • USA • JAIL BREAK (UKN) ○ JAILBREAK

GUNPLAY • 1951 • Selander Lesley • USA

GUNPOINT • 1966 • Bellamy Earl • USA

GUNPOINT see **AU BOUT DES FUSILS** • 1972

GUNPOINT see **SYOKSYKIERRE** • 1982

GUNPOINT! (UKN) see **AT GUNPOINT** • 1955

GUNPOWDER • 1987 • Warren Norman J. • UKN

GUNPOWDER AND LOVE see **KRUT OCH KARLEK** • 1957

GUNPOWDER PLOT, THE • 1900 • Hepworth Cecil M. • UKN

GUNPOWDER PRIMER • 1978 • Dinov Todor • BUL

GUNRUNNER, THE • 1984 • Castillo Nardo • CND

GUNRUNNERS, THE see **GUN RUNNER** • 1969

GUNS • 1980 • Kramer Robert • FRN

GUNS, THE see **FUZIS, OS** • 1964

GUNS, THE see **ARMAS, AS** • 1968

GUNS A'BLAZING see **LAW AND ORDER** • 1932

GUNS ACROSS THE VELDT • 1975 • Rennie Howard • SAF

GUNS AND FURY see **GUNS AND THE FURY, THE** • 1981

GUNS AND GREASERS • 1918 • Semon Larry • SHT • USA

GUNS AND GUITARS • 1936 • Kane Joseph • USA

GUNS AND GUNNERS (UKN) see **GUNNERS AND GUNS** • 1935

GUNS AND THE FURY, THE • 1981 • Zarindast Tony • MTV • USA • GUNS AND FURY

GUNS AND THE NIGHTINGALE see **KANONI KE T' AIDHONI, TO** • 1968

GUNS A'POPPIN • 1957 • White Jules • SHT • USA

GUNS AT BATASI • 1964 • Guillermin John • UKN

GUNS DON'T ARGUE • 1955 • Karn Bill, Hahn Richard • USA

GUNS FOR HIRE • 1932 • Collins Lewis D. • USA

GUNS FOR LIBERTY see **BANADIQ AL-HURIA** • 1962

GUNS FOR SAN SEBASTIAN (USA) see **CANONES DE SAN SEBASTIAN, LOS** • 1967

GUNS FOR THE DICTATOR (UKN) see **ARME A GAUCHE, L'** • 1965

GUNS, GIRLS AND GANGSTERS • 1958 • Cahn Edward L. • USA

GUNS IN THE AFTERNOON (UKN) see **RIDE THE HIGH COUNTRY** • 1962

GUNS IN THE DARK • 1937 • Newfield Sam • USA

GUNS IN THE HEATHER • 1969 • Butler Robert • UKN • SPY BUSTERS

GUNS IN THE TREES see **GUNS OF THE TREES** • 1961

GUNS OF A STRANGER • 1973 • Hinkle Robert • USA

GUNS OF AUGUST, THE • 1964 • Kroll Nathan • DOC • USA

GUNS OF BILLY KID • 1967 • San Juan Luis • PHL

GUNS OF DARKNESS • 1962 • Asquith Anthony • UKN

GUNS OF DIABLO • 1964 • Sagal Boris • MTV • USA • DAY OF RECKONING

GUNS OF FORT PETTICOAT, THE • 1957 • Marshall George • USA

GUNS OF HATE • 1948 • Selander Lesley • USA • GUNS OF WRATH

GUNS OF JUANA GALLO, THE see **JUANA GALLO** • 1960

GUNS OF JUSTICE see **COLORADO RANGER** • 1950

GUNS OF LOOS, THE • 1928 • Hill Sinclair • UKN

GUNS OF NAVARONE, THE • 1961 • Thompson J. Lee • USA, UKN

GUNS OF THE BLACK WITCH (USA) see **TERRORE DEI MARI, IL** • 1961

GUNS OF THE LAW • 1944 • Clifton Elmer • USA

GUNS OF THE MAGNIFICENT SEVEN • 1968 • Wendkos Paul • USA, SPN

GUNS OF THE PECOS • 1936 • Smith Noel • USA

GUNS OF THE TIMBERLAND • 1960 • Webb Robert D. • USA

GUNS OF THE TREES • 1961 • Mekas Jonas • USA • GUNS IN THE TREES

GUNS OF WRATH see **GUNS OF HATE** • 1948

GUNS OF WYOMING see **CATTLE KING** • 1963

GUNS OF ZANGARA • 1959 • *Stack Robert* • MTV • USA

GUNS, SIN AND BATHTUB GIN see **LADY IN RED, THE** • 1979

GUNSAULUS MYSTERY, THE • 1921 • Micheaux Oscar • USA

GUNSHIN YAMAMOTO GENSUI TO RENGO KANTAI • JPN • GOD OF WAR ADMIRAL YAMAMOTO AND THE COMBINED FLEET

GUNSHOT, THE • Lyubimov Pavel • USS

GUNSHOT IN THE FACTORY see **LAUKAUS TEEHTAALLA** • 1972

GUNSIGHT RIDGE • 1957 • Lyon Francis D. • USA

GUNSLINGER, THE • 1956 • Corman Roger • USA

GUNSLINGERS • 1950 • Fox Wallace • USA

GUNSMITH, THE • 1910 • *Powers* • USA

GUNSMOKE • 1947 • King Fred • USA • GUNSMOKE KILLERS

GUNSMOKE • 1953 • Juran Nathan • USA

GUNSMOKE IN TUCSON • 1958 • Carr Thomas • USA

GUNSMOKE KILLERS see **GUNSMOKE** • 1947

GUNSMOKE MESA • 1944 • Fraser Harry L. • USA

GUNSMOKE ON THE GUADALOPE • 1935 • Carre Bartlett • USA • GUN SMOKE OVER THE GUADALOPE ○ GUN SMOKE (UKN)

GUNSMOKE RANCH • 1937 • Kane Joseph • USA

GUNSMOKE: RETURN TO DODGE • 1987 • McEveety Vincent • TVM • USA

GUNSMOKE TRAIL • 1938 • Newfield Sam • USA

GUNSTLING VON SCHONBRUNN, DER • 1929 • Waschneck Erich • FRG

GUNTHER PLUSCHOWS FLIEGERSCHICKSAL see **IKARUS** • 1932

GUNTO NANBANSEN • 1950 • Inagaki Hiroshi • JPN

GUNUN ASH-SHABAB • 1972 • Shawqi Khalil • EGY • FOLIE DE JEUNESSE

GUQUKA • 1985 • SAF

GURAIDA • 1943 • *Tsuburaya Eiji (Ph)* • DOC • JPN

GURDEEP SINGH BAINS • 1977 • Shaffer Beverly • DOC • CND

GURENTAI JUNJOHA • 1963 • Masumura Yasuzo • JPN • DELINQUENTS OF PURE HEART

GURGLE, GURGLE, LITTLE BROOK • 1963 • Nosov P. • ANS • USS

GURI • 1979 • Darino Eduardo • URG, USA

GURI, FUTURE -PRESENT • Camacho Carlos Antonio • URG

GURIGANYA • 1972 • Ansara Martha • DOC • ASL

GURKA'S REVENGE, THE • 1914 • Coleby A. E. • UKN

GURKHAS OF NEPAL • 1985 • Sarin Vic • MTV • CND

GURTEL DER DOLLARFURSTIN, DER • 1916 • Schmidthassler Walter • FRG

GURTELSCHLOSS DER SENAHJA, DAS • 1918 • Hanus Emerich? • FRG

GURU, THE • 1969 • Ivory James • USA, IND

GURU BADUL • 1988 • Badul A. R. • MLY

GURU BHAKTI • 1961 • Kumar Rajendra • IND

GURU DAKSHINA • 1986 • Nihalani Dayal • IND • DISCIPLES' OFFERINGS TO THE PRIEST

GURU THE MAD MONK • 1970 • Milligan Andy • USA • GARU THE MAD MONK

GUS • 1976 • McEveety Vincent • USA

GUS AND THE ANARCHISTS • 1915 • Murphy J. A. • USA

GUS BROWN AND MIDNIGHT BREWSTER • 1985 • Fargo James • TVM • USA

GUS VAN AND HIS NEIGHBORS • 1934 • Schwarzwald Milton • SHT • USA

GUS VAN'S GARDEN PARTY • 1936 • Schwarzwald Milton • SHT • USA

GUS VAN'S MUSIC SHOPPE • 1935 • Schwarzwald Milton • SHT • USA

GUSANOS DE SEDA • 1976 • Rodriguez Francisco • SPN

GUSARSKAYA BALLADA • 1962 • Ryazanov Eldar • USS • BALLAD OF A HUSSAR, THE (USA) ○ HUSSAR'S BALLAD ○ HUSSAR BALLAD, THE

GUSHER, THE • 1913 • Sennett Mack • USA

GUSHU YIREN • 1987 • Tian Zhuangzhuang • CHN • TRAVELLING PLAYERS

GUSSIE, THE GRACEFUL LIFE GUARD • 1915 • *Burke Peggy* • USA

GUSSLE RIVALS JONAH • 1915 • Henderson Dell • USA

GUSSLE, THE GOLFER • 1914 • Henderson Dell • USA

GUSSLE TIED TO TROUBLE • 1915 • Avery Charles • USA

GUSSLE'S BACKWARD WAY • 1915 • Avery Charles • USA

GUSSLE'S DAY OF REST • 1915 • Henderson Dell • USA

GUSSLE'S WAYWARD PATH • 1915 • Avery Charles • USA

GUSSY RIDES A PONY • 1913 • *B & C* • UKN

GUSTAF WASA PARTS I & II • 1928 • Brunius John W. • SWD

GUSTAV ADOLF PAGE • 1960 • Hansen Rolf • AUS

GUSTAV EST MEDIUM see **GUSTAVE OU LE MEDIUM** • 1921

GUSTAV GEBHARDT'S GUTTER BAND • 1915 • *Cunningham Arthur* • USA

GUSTAV MOND.. DU GEHST SO STILLE • 1927 • Schunzel Reinhold • FRG

GUSTAVE MOREAU • 1961 • Kaplan Nelly • FRN

GUSTAVE OU LE MEDIUM • 1921 • Feuillade Louis • FRN • GUSTAV EST MEDIUM

GUSTAVUS AND THE HOLIDAY OF GOODWILL see **GUSZTAV ES A SZERETET UNNEPE** • 1966

GUSTAVUS (UKN) see **GUSZTAV-SOROZAJ** • 1960

GUSZTAV ES A SZERETET UNNEPE • 1966 • Jankovics Marcell • HNG • GUSTAVUS AND THE HOLIDAY OF GOODWILL

GUSZTAV-SOROZAJ • 1960 • Temesi Miklos, Dargay Attila, Jankovics Marcell, Nepp Jozsef • ASS • HNG • GUSTAVUS (UKN)

GUTE FEE, DIE • 1915 • Bolten-Baeckers Heinrich • FRG

GUTE NACHT, MARY see **GESTORTE HOCHZEITSNACHT, DIE** • 1950

GUTE PARTIE, DIE • 1917 • *Moja Hella* • FRG

GUTE RUF, DER • 1926 • Marodon Pierre • FRG

GUTE SIEBEN, DIE • 1940 • Liebeneiner Wolfgang • FRG

GUTEI KENKEI • 1931 • Gosho Heinosuke • JPN • SILLY YOUNGER BROTHER AND CLEVER ELDER BROTHER ○ STUPID YOUNG BROTHER AND WISE OLD BROTHER

GUTEN TAG, LIEBER TAG • 1960 • Klingenberg Gerhard • GDR

GUTEN TAG, SCHWIEGERMAMA • 1928 • Brandt Johannes • FRG

GUTIERRITOS • 1959 • Crevenna Alfredo B. • MXC

GUTS AND GLORY: THE RISE AND FALL OF OLIVER NORTH • 1989 • Robe Mike • TVM • USA

GUTTER see **DOBU** • 1954

GUTTER GIRLS (USA) see **YELLOW TEDDYBEARS, THE** • 1963

GUTTER MAGDALENE, THE • 1916 • Melford George • USA

GUTTER-SNIPES see **RANNSTENSUNGAR** • 1944

GUTTER TRASH • 1969 • Milligan Andy • USA • MALE & FEMALE SEXUALIS

GUTTERSNIPE, THE • 1915 • North Wilfred • USA

GUTTERSNIPE, THE • 1922 • Fitzgerald Dallas M. • USA

GUTTERSNIPES see **GATEGUTTER** • 1949

GUVERNORENS DATTER • 1912 • Blom August • DNM • GOVERNOR'S DAUGHTER, THE

GUV'NOR, THE • 1935 • Rosmer Milton • UKN • MR. HOBO (USA)

GUY, A GAL AND A PAL, A • 1945 • Boetticher Budd • USA

GUY AND GEYSER, THE • 1918 • Hutchinson Craig • SHT • USA

GUY CALLED CAESAR, A • 1962 • Marshall Frank • UKN

GUY COULD CHANGE, A • 1946 • Howard William K. • USA

GUY DE MAUPASSANT • 1982 • Drach Michel • FRN

GUY, EIGHT GIRLS, A see **MAN -EIGHT GIRLS, A** • 1968

GUY FAWKES • 1907 • *Walturdaw* • UKN

GUY FAWKES • 1923 • Elvey Maurice • UKN

GUY FAWKES AND THE GUNPOWDER PLOT • 1913 • Batley Ernest G. • UKN

GUY MANNERING • 1912 • *Dion Hector* • USA

GUY NAMED JOE, A • 1943 • Fleming Victor • USA

GUY OF WARWICK • 1926 • Paul Fred • UKN

GUY UPSTAIRS, THE • 1915 • MacMackin Archer • USA

GUY WHO CAME BACK, THE • 1951 • Newman Joseph M. • USA • GUY WHO SANK THE NAVY, THE

GUY WHO SANK THE NAVY, THE see **GUY WHO CAME BACK, THE** • 1951

GUYANA -CRIME OF THE CENTURY see **GUYANA EL CRIMEN DEL SIGLO** • 1979

GUYANA -CULT OF THE DAMNED see **GUYANA EL CRIMEN DEL SIGLO** • 1979

GUYANA EL CRIMEN DEL SIGLO • 1979 • Cardona Rene Jr. • MXC, SPN, PNM • GUYANA -CULT OF THE DAMNED ○ GUYANA -CRIME OF THE CENTURY

GUYANA TRAGEDY: THE STORY OF JIM JONES • 1980 • Graham William A. • TVM • USA

GUYRA GHOST MYSTERY, THE • 1921 • Cosgrove John • ASL

GUYS AND DOLLS • 1955 • Mankiewicz Joseph L. • USA

GUYS OF THE SEA see **UMI NO YARODOMO** • 1957

GUZIK • 1965 • Badzian Teresa • ANM • PLN • BUTTON, THE

GWANGI see **VALLEY OF GWANGI, THE** • 1969
GWEN see **GWEN, OU LE LIVRE DE SABLE** • 1984
GWEN FARRAR • 1926 • *De Forest Phonofilms* • SHT • UKN
GWEN FARRAR AND BILLY MAYERL • 1926 • *Deforest Phonofilms* • SHT • UKN
GWEN, OU LE LIVRE DE SABLE • 1984 • Laguionie Jean-Francois • ANM • FRN • GWEN
GWENDOLIN • 1914 • Vale Travers • USA
GWENDOLINE • 1984 • Jaeckin Just • FRN • PERILS OF GWENDOLINE IN THE LAND OF THE YIK YAK (USA) ○ PERILS OF GWENDOLINE, THE
GWENDOLYN, THE SEWING MACHINE GIRL • 1914 • *Ab* • USA
GWIAZDA PIOLUN • 1988 • Kluba Henryk • PLN • WORMWOOD STAR, THE
GWIAZDY MUSZA PLONAC • 1953 • Munk Andrzej, Lesiewicz Witold • DCS • PLN • STARS MUST SHINE, THE
GWIAZDZISTA ESKADRA • 1930 • Buczkowski Leonard • PLN • STAR SQUADRON, THE
GWYNCILLA, LEGEND OF THE DARK AGES • 1986 • Bausch Andy • LXM
GWYNETH OF THE WELSH HILLS • 1921 • Thornton F. Martin • UKN
GYAKUFUNSHA KAZOKU • 1984 • Ishii Sogo • JPN • CRAZY FAMILY, THE
GYAKUTEN RYOKO • 1969 • Segawa Shoji • JPN • TOPSY-TURVY JOURNEY (USA)
GYALOG A MENNYORSZAGBA • 1959 • Feher Imre • HNG • WALKING TO HEAVEN
GYARMAT A FOLD ALATT • 1951 • Fabri Zoltan (c/d) • HNG • COLONY BENEATH THE EARTH
GYCKLARNAS AFTON • 1953 • Bergman Ingmar • SWD • SAWDUST AND TINSEL (UKN) ○ NAKED NIGHT, THE (USA)
GYERMEKBETEGSEGEK • 1965 • Kardos Ferenc, Rozsa Janos • HNG • GRIMACES
GYERMEKEK, KONYVEK • 1962 • Meszaros Marta • DCS • HNG • CHILDREN, BOOKS
GYERTEK EL A NEVNAPOMRA • 1984 • Fabri Zoltan • HNG • HOUSE-WARMING, THE
GYILKOS A HAZBAN VAN, A • 1971 • Ban Robert • HNG • MURDERER IS IN THE HOUSE, THE
GYIMESI VADVIRAG • 1939 • Rathonyi August • WILDFLOWER OF GYIMES (USA)
GYLDNE SMIL, DEN • 1935 • Fejos Paul • DNM • GOLDEN SMILE, THE ○ SOURIRE D'OR, LE
GYLLENE UNGDOM • 1956 • Sinding Leif • NRW
GYM DANDY, A • 1927 • Newfield Sam • SHT • USA
GYM JAM • 1950 • Sparber I. • ANS • USA
GYM JAMS • 1938 • *Mintz Charles (P)* • ANS • USA
GYMBELLES AND BONEHEADS • 1919 • Smith Noel • SHT • USA
GYMKATA • 1985 • Clouse Robert • USA
GYMNASIUM JIM • 1922 • Del Ruth Roy • SHT • USA
GYMNASTIC RHYTHM • 1952 • *Smith Pete* • SHT • USA
GYMNASTICS • 1935 • Trego Charles T. • SHT • USA
GYMNASTICS -INDIAN CLUB PERFORMER • 1897 • Smith G. A. • UKN
GYMNASTIQUE • 1964 • Dansereau Jean • DOC • CND
GYMNASTS, THE • 1961 • Baillie Bruce • SHT • USA
GYOCHARO • 1955 • Yoo Myon-Mok • SKR • CROSSROADS
GYOEI NO MURE • 1984 • Somai Shinji • JPN • SEARCH FOR FISH
GYOJI • 1959 • Hani Susumu • DOC • JPN
GYONETSU NO SHIJIN TAKUBOKU • 1936 • Kumagai Hisatora • JPN • TAKUBOKU, THE PASSIONATE POET ○ JONETSU NO SHIJIN
GYONGYVIRAGTOL LOMBHULLASIG • 1954 • Homoki-Nagy Istvan • DOC • HNG • FROM BLOSSOM TIME TO AUTUMN LEAVES ○ FIGHT FOR LIFE ○ FROM BLOSSOM TIME TO AUTUMN FROST
GYOZO • 1982 • Szoreny Rezso • HNG
GYPPED IN EGYPT • 1930 • Foster John, Davis Mannie • ANS • USA
GYPPED IN THE PENTHOUSE • 1955 • White Jules • SHT • USA
GYPPO LOGGERS • 1957 • King Allan • CND
GYPSIES • 1936 • Schneider Eugene
GYPSIES • 1963 • Slesicki Wladyslaw • DOC • PLN
GYPSIES see **CIGANYOK** • 1962
GYPSY • 1937 • Neill R. William • UKN • TZIGANE
GYPSY • 1962 • LeRoy Mervyn • USA
GYPSY see **CIKANI** • 1921
GYPSY, THE • 1911 • Salter Harry • USA
GYPSY, THE see **GITAN, LE** • 1975
GYPSY AND THE GENTLEMAN, THE • 1958 • Losey Joseph • UKN
GYPSY ARTIST, THE • 1909 • *Bison* • USA
GYPSY BARON see **ZIGEUNERBARON, DER** • 1954
GYPSY BLOOD • 1931 • Lewis Cecil • UKN • CARMEN (USA) ○ GIPSY BLOOD
GYPSY BLOOD see **ZIGEUNERBLUT** • 1911
GYPSY BLOOD (USA) see **CARMEN** • 1918
GYPSY BRIDE, A • 1911 • Melies Gaston • USA
GYPSY BRIDE, THE • 1912 • *Champion* • USA
GYPSY CAMP VANISHES INTO THE BLUE, THE see **TABOR UHODIT V NEBO** • 1976
GYPSY CARAVAN see **DOM ZA VESANJE** • 1987
GYPSY COLT • 1953 • Marton Andrew • USA
GYPSY COURAGE • 1926 • Malins Geoffrey H., Parkinson H. B. • SHT • UKN
GYPSY FIDDLER, A • 1933 • *Terry Paul/ Moser Frank (P)* • ANS • USA
GYPSY FLIRT, THE • 1912 • Golden Joseph A. • USA
GYPSY FURY (USA) see **SINGOALLA** • 1949
GYPSY GAMBLER, THE • 1914 • *Darkfather Mona* • USA
GYPSY-GIRL AND THE CHURL, THE see **GITANA Y EL CHARRO, LA** • 1963
GYPSY GIRL (USA) see **SKY WEST AND CROOKED** • 1965
GYPSY GIRL'S LOVE, A • 1908 • *Kalem* • USA
GYPSY GIRL'S LOVE, A • 1910 • *Kalem* • USA
GYPSY HOLIDAY • 1945 • *Rasumny Mikhail* • SHT • USA
GYPSY JOE • 1916 • Badger Clarence, Campbell William • SHT • USA
GYPSY LAND • 1930 • Oumansky Alexander • UKN
GYPSY LIFE see **MIGHTY MOUSE IN GYPSY LIFE** • 1945
GYPSY LOVE • 1913 • *Patheplay* • USA
GYPSY LOVE see **CARMEN** • 1918
GYPSY LOVER, THE • 1909 • Fitzhamon Lewin • UKN
GYPSY MADCAP, A • 1914 • Ridgely Richard • USA
GYPSY MELODY • 1936 • Greville Edmond T. • UKN
GYPSY MOON • 1953 • *Reed Roland (P)* • USA
GYPSY MOTHS, THE • 1969 • Frankenheimer John • USA
GYPSY NIGHT • 1935 • Hecht Harold, Berne Josef • USA • OLD MILL STREAM, THE
GYPSY OF THE NORTH • 1928 • Pembroke Scott • USA
GYPSY PASSION • 1970 • *Able Film Co.* • USA
GYPSY PASSION see **MIARKA, LA FILLE A L'OURSE** • 1920
GYPSY PRINCE, THE • 1917 • Fahrney Milton • USA
GYPSY QUEEN, THE • 1913 • Sennett Mack • USA
GYPSY ROMANCE, THE • 1914 • Reid Wallace • USA
GYPSY ROMANCE, THE • 1926 • *Fairfax Thur* • USA
GYPSY TRAIL, THE • 1915 • Handworth Harry • USA • GONE TO THE DOGS
GYPSY TRAIL, THE • 1918 • Edwards Walter • USA
GYPSY WARRIORS, THE • 1978 • Antonio Lou • TVM • USA
GYPSY WAYS (USA) see **ZIGEUNERWEISEN** • 1940
GYPSY WILDCAT • 1944 • Neill R. William • USA
GYPSY'S BABY, THE • 1909 • Fitzhamon Lewin • UKN
GYPSY'S BRAND, THE • 1913 • *Kalem* • USA
GYPSY'S CURSE, THE • 1914 • Kellino W. P. • UKN
GYPSY'S JEALOUSY, A • 1909 • *Urban-Eclipse* • USA
GYPSY'S LOVE, A • 1912 • *Shamrock* • USA
GYPSY'S REGRET, THE • 1909 • *Powers* • USA
GYPSY'S REVENGE • 1907 • *Lubin* • USA
GYPSY'S REVENGE, THE • 1908 • Brooke Van Dyke • USA
GYPSY'S TRUST, THE • 1917 • Sloman Edward • USA
GYPSY'S WARNING, THE • 1913 • *Melies* • USA
GYROMORPHOSIS • 1958 • Hirsch Hy • SHT • NTH • CYROMORPHOSIS
GYROS: HANDLE WITH CARE • 1979 • Tichenor Harold • DOC • CND
GYROSCOPE, LE • Cantagrel Marc • DOC • FRN
GYULA VITEZ TELEN NYARON • 1971 • Bacskai-Lauro Istvan • HNG • KNIGHT OF THE TV SCREEN
GYUNYUYA FURANKI • 1956 • Nakahira Ko • JPN
GYURI see **CSEPLO GYURI** • 1978
GYURKOVICS, THE see **GYURKOVICSARNA** • 1920
GYURKOVICS GIRLS see **FLICKORNA GYURKOVICS** • 1926
GYURKOVICSARNA • 1920 • Brunius John W. • SWD • GYURKOVICS, THE

H

H-8 • 1958 • Tanhofer Nikola • YGS
H-A • 1975 • Kohanyi Julius • CND
H AND R • Siani Toni • USA
H BOMB • 1978 • Pakdivijit Chalong • THL • H-BOMB
H-BOMB see **H BOMB** • 1978
H COMME HORREUR see **ROSE ECORCHEE, LA** • 1970
H.E.A.L.T.H. • 1979 • Altman Robert • USA • HEALTH
H. FLEET, ROBBER see **ONE MORE TRAIN TO ROB** • 1971
H.G. WELLS COMEDIES • 1928 • Montagu Ivor • SER • UKN
H.G. WELLS' NEW INVISIBLE MAN see **HOMBRE QUE LOGRO SER INVISIBLE, EL** • 1957
H.G. WELLS' THE SHAPE OF THINGS TO COME • 1979 • McCowan George • CND • SHAPE OF THINGS TO COME, THE
H.M. PULMAN ESQ. • 1941 • Vidor King • USA
H.M.S. DEFIANT • 1962 • Gilbert Lewis* • UKN • DAMN THE DEFIANT! (USA) ○ BATTLE ABOARD THE DEFIANT
H.M.S. MINELAYER • 1941 • Cass Henry • DOC • UKN
H-MAN, THE (USA) see **BIYO TO EKITAININGEN** • 1958
H.O.G. see **HOUSE OF GOD, THE** • 1979
H.O.T.S. • 1979 • Sindell Gerald Seth • USA • HOTS
H.O.T.S. 2 • *Camp Coleen* • USA
H.R. PUFNSTUF see **PUFNSTUF** • 1970
H2O • 1929 • Steiner Ralph • USA
H25 • 1968 • Faenza Roberto • ITL
HA DA VENI'.. DON CALOGERO see **FILO D'ERBA, IL** • 1952
HA DESAPARECIDO UN PASAJERO • 1953 • Perla Alejandro • SPN
HA ENTRADO UN LADRON • 1948 • Gascon Jose • SPN
HA FATTO 13 see **HA FATTO TREDICI** • 1951
HA FATTO TREDICI • 1951 • Manzoni Carlo • ITL • HA FATTO 13 ○ I MADE 13
HA FATTO UNA SIGNORA, L' • 1938 • Mattoli Mario • ITL
HA! HA! HA! • 1934 • Fleischer Dave • ANS • USA
HA LLEGADO UN ANGEL • 1961 • Lucia Luis • SPN
HA MEGJON JOZSEF • 1975 • Kezdi-Kovacs Zsolt • HNG • WHEN JOSEPH RETURNS..
HA PASADO UN HOMBRE • 1955 • Seto Javier • SPN
HAAG, DEN • 1936 • van Neijenhoff Otto, Kal F. • NTH
HAAG HOLLAND, DEN see **DEN HAAG HOLLAND** • 1968
HAAK VRYSTAAT • 1970 • SAF
HAAKON VII • 1952 • Carlsen Henning (c/d) • SHT • DNM
HAAR JEET • 1939 • *Roy Bhimal (Ph)* • IND
HAAYO (FNL) see **BROLLOPSNATT, EN** • 1959
HA'AYT • 1981 • Yosha Yaki • ISR • VULTURE, THE
HAB' ICH NUR DEINE LIEBE • 1953 • von Borsody Eduard • AUS
HAB' MICH LIEB • 1942 • Braun Harald • FRG
HAB' SONNE IM HERZEN • 1953 • Waschneck Erich • FRG
HABABAM SINIFI UYANIYOR • 1977 • Egilmez Ertem • TRK • DEUCE CLASS AWAKES, THE
HABANERA • 1958 • Elorrieta Jose Maria • SPN
HABANERA, LA • 1937 • Sirk Douglas • FRG • CHEATED BY THE WINDS
HABARI NO TAKEKURABE • 1958 • Gosho Heinosuke • JPN • SKYLARK GROWING UP
HABATALES • 1960 • Halas John • ASS • UKN
HABEAS CORPUS • 1928 • Parrott James • SHT • USA
HABEN HA'OVED • 1968 • Shalhin Joseph, Steinhardt Alfred • ISR • PRODIGAL SON, THE
HABEN SIE FRITZCHEN NICHT GESEHEN? • 1918 • Grunwald Willy • FRG
HABIA UNA VEZ UN MARIDO • 1952 • Mendez Fernando • MXC
HABIB AL-UMR • 1946 • Barakat Henry • EGY • AMOUR DE MA VIE, L'
HABIBAT RIHALY • 1975 • Mazhar Ahmed • EGY • AIMEE D'UN AUTRE, L'
HABIBATI • 1973 • Barakat Henry • LBN • MA CHERIE
HABILITADO, EL • 1972 • Cedron Jorge • ARG • PROFIT-SHARER, THE
HABIT • 1921 • Carewe Edwin • USA
HABIT • 1966 • Wolman Dan • ISR
HABIT NE FAIT PAS LE MOINE, L' see **FABRICANT DE DIAMANTS, LE** • 1908
HABIT OF HAPPINESS, THE • 1916 • Dwan Allan • USA • LAUGH AND THE WORLD LAUGHS
HABIT RABBIT • 1963 • Hanna William, Barbera Joseph • ANS • USA
HABIT VERT, L' • 1937 • Richebe Roger • FRN
HABITACION PARA TRES • 1951 • de Lara Antonio • SPN
HABITANT GLORIEUX • 1982 • Lesaunier Daniel (c/d) • CND
HABITANT OF THE DESERT ISLE, THE (USA) see **ZITEL NEOBITAJEMOVO OSTROVA** • 1915
HABITANTES DE LA CASA DESHABITADA, LOS • 1946 • Delgras Gonzalo • SPN • INHABITANTS OF THE UNINHABITED HOUSE, THE
HABITANTES DE LA CASA DESHABITADA, LOS • 1959 • Ramirez Pedro L. • SPN
HABITANTES DE LA PRIMAVERA, LOS • 1971 • Blanco M., Odreman Mauricio • VNZ • INHABITANTS OF SPRING, THE
HABITAT 2000 • 1973 • Fox Beryl • DOC • CND
HABITS SANS DANGER see **SAFE CLOTHING** • 1949
HABITUAL SPRING, A • 1962 • Nicolaescu Sergiu • RMN • COMMON SPRING
HABLA, MUDITA • 1973 • Gutierrez Aragon Manuel • SPN • SPEAK, LITTLE MUTE ○ SPEAK, MUTE GIRL
HABLAMAS ESTA NOCHE • 1981 • Miro Pilar • SPN • LET'S TALK TONIGHT
HABRICHA EL HASHEMESH see **ESCAPE TO THE SUN** • 1972
HACE CIEN ANOS • 1950 • Obregon Antonio • SPN
HACELDAMA • 1919 • Duvivier Julien • FRN • PRIX DE SANG, LE
HACHA DIABOLICA, EL • 1964 • Diaz Morales Jose • MXC • DIABOLICAL HATCHET, THE ○ DIABOLICAL AXE, THE
HACHA PARA LA LUNA DE MIEL, UNA (SPN) see **ROSSO SEGNO DELLA FOLLIA, IL** • 1969
HACHIJIKAN NO KYOFU • 1957 • Suzuki Seijun • JPN
HACHIKO MONOGATARI • 1988 • Koyama Seijiro • JPN • STORY OF THE DOG HACHI, A
HACHININ NO HANAYOME • 1958 • Tasaka Katsuhiko • JPN • EIGHT BRIDES
HACHYYUHACHINENME NO TAIYO • 1941 • *Tsuburaya Eiji* • JPN
HACI BEKTAS VELI • 1967 • Ucak Fikret • TRK
HACI MURAD • 1967 • Baytan Natuk • TRK
HACI MURAT GELIYOR • 1968 • Baytan Natuk • TRK • HADJI MURAT IS COMING
HACIA LA GLORIA • 1931 • Camacho, Duran, Jiminez • BLV • TOWARDS GLORY
HACK AND SCHMIDT BOUT, THE • 1911 • *Essanay* • USA
HACK 'EM HIGH see **ASSAULT OF THE KILLER BIMBOS** • 1988
HACK O'LANTERN see **DEATH MASK** • 1987
HACK REBELLION, THE see **KONIKAPINA** • 1976
HACKSAW • 1971 • *Hunter Tab* • MTV • USA
HADA EN LA CIUDAD, UN • 1955 • Salvia Rafael J. • SPN
H'AD'A MA GANARU ABY • 1945 • Barakat Henry • EGY • FAUTE PATERNELLE, LA
HADAIRO NO TSUKI • 1957 • Sugie Toshio • JPN • SKIN COLOUR OF THE MOON
HADAKA DE KONBANWA • 1967 • Onishi Takanori • JPN • NAKED GOOD EVENING
HADAKA NO JUKYUSAI • 1970 • Shindo Kaneto • JPN • LIVE TODAY: DIE TOMORROW! ○ NINETEEN YEAR OLD MISFIT ○ NAKED NINETEEN YEAR OLD
HADAKA NO MACHI • 1937 • Uchida Tomu • JPN • NAKED TOWN, THE
HADAKA NO SHIMA • 1961 • Shindo Kaneto • JPN • NAKED ISLAND ○ ISLAND, THE
HADAKA NO TAISHO • 1958 • Horikawa Hiromichi • JPN • NAKED GENERAL
HADAKA NO TAIYO • 1958 • Ieki Miyoji • JPN • NAKED SUN
HADAKAKKO • 1961 • Tasaka Tomotaka • JPN • RUN GENTA RUN
HADAT'HA D'ATA LAYLA • 1954 • Barakat Henry • EGY • C'EST ARRIVE UNE CERTAIN NUIT
HADDA • 1985 • Aboulouakar Mohammed • MRC
HADDA PADDA • 1922 • Kamban Gudmundur • DNM
HADDOCK WITH AREPA • 1989 • Fernandez Gustavo • SHT • CLM, FRN
HADDUTA MISRIYA • 1982 • Shahin Youssef • EGY • EGYPTIAN STORY, AN ○ MEMOIRE, LA
HADHA HUWWA AL-HUBB see **HAZA HOWA EL HOB** • 1958
HADI JED • 1981 • Vlacil Frantisek • CZC • SNAKE POISON
HADIMRSKU DOESN'T KNOW see **TO NEZNATE HADIMRSKU** • 1931
HADITHA AL NASF METR • 1983 • Zikra Samir • SYR • HALF METER INCIDENT, THE
HADJI MURAT IS COMING see **HACI MURAT GELIYOR** • 1968
HADLEY'S REBELLION • 1984 • Walton Fred • USA
HADYBBUK • 1968 • Eldad Ilan, Friedman Shraga • ISR, FRG • DYBBUK, THE ○ BETWEEN TWO WORLDS
HAENDELIGT UHELD • 1971 • Balling Erik • DNM • ONE OF THOSE THINGS
HAERVAERK • 1977 • Roos Ole • DNM
HAEVNENS NAT • 1915 • Christensen Benjamin • DNM • NIGHT OF VENGEANCE (USA) ○ NIGHT OF REVENGE, THE ○ BLIND JUSTICE
HAEVNEREN • 1918 • Fonss Olaf • DNM
HAEVNET • 1911 • Blom August • DNM • BODES DER FOR, DET ○ VENGEANCE

HAFAT DOKHTAR BARYE HAFAT PESAR • 1968 • Motevaselani Mohamad • IRN • SEVEN GIRLS FOR SEVEN BOYS
HAFENBARON, DER • 1928 • Winar Ernest • FRG
HAFENBRAUT, DIE • 1927 • Neff Wolfgang • FRG
HAFENDROSCHKE "JUNGE LIEBE" see **SCHATTEN UBER ST. PAULI** • 1938
HAFENLORE 1, DIE • 1921 • Neff Wolfgang • FRG
HAFENLORE 2, DIE • 1921 • Neff Wolfgang • FRG
HAFENMELODIE • 1949 • Muller Hans • FRG
HAFID, AL- • 1974 • Salem Atef • EGY • GRANDSON, THE ○ PETIT-FILS, LE
HAFNARFJORDUR BEFORE AND NOW see **HAFNARFJORDUR FYRR OG NU** • 1968
HAFNARFJORDUR FYRR OG NU • 1968 • Hansen Gunnar Robertsson • DOC • ICL • HAFNARFJORDUR BEFORE AND NOW
HAFT SHAHR-E-ESHGH • 1967 • Mojtahedi Hamid • IRN • SEVEN CITIES OF LOVE
HAG IN A BLACK LEATHER JACKET • 1964 • Waters John* • USA
HAGAMAL VEHAYELED • 1968 • Takahashi Osamu • ISR, JPN • BOY AND A CAMEL, A
HAGAN • 1977 • Nord Victor • ISR • GARDEN, THE
HAGBARD AND SIGNE (USA) see **RODA KAPPAN, DEN** • 1967
HAGEDIS TEVEEL, EEN • 1960 • Verhoeven Paul* • NTH
HAGEN • 1980 • Wendkos Paul • TVM • USA
HAGGARD'S SHE -THE PILLAR OF FIRE (USA) see **DANSE DU FEU, LA** • 1899
HAGIBIS, NGA • 1970 • Enriquez Luis B. • PHL
HAGIOGRAPHIA • 1971 • Markopoulos Gregory J. • USA
HAGIVA • 1955 • Dickinson Thorold • ISR • HILL 24 DOESN'T ANSWER
HAGIZ, AL- • 1972 • Radi Mohamed • EGY • BARRIERE, LA
HAGLOULAH • 1968 • Perlov David • ISR • PILL, THE
HAGRINGEN • 1959 • Weiss Peter • SWD • MIRAGE
HAGYJATOK ROBINSONT • 1989 • Timar Peter • HNG • LEAVE ROBINSON ALONE! ○ ROBINSON
HAHA • 1929 • *Takamine Hideko* • JPN • MOTHER, THE
HAHA • 1963 • Shindo Kaneto • JPN • MOTHER, THE
HAHA • 1988 • Matsuyama Zenzo • JPN • MOTHER
HAHA NO CHIZU • 1942 • Shimazu Yasujiro • JPN • MOTHER'S MAD
HAHA NO HATSUKOI • 1954 • Hisamatsu Seiji • JPN • MOTHER'S FIRST LOVE
HAHA NO KYOKU • 1937 • Yamamoto Satsuo • JPN
HAHA O KOWAZUYA • 1934 • Ozu Yasujiro • JPN • MOTHER SHOULD BE LOVED, A ○ MOTHER OUGHT TO BE LOVED, A
HAHA O TAZUNETE SANBYAKURI • 1926 • Tasaka Tomotaka • JPN
HAHA SANNIN • 1958 • Hisamatsu Seiji • JPN • BOY AND THREE MOTHERS, A
HAHA TO KENJU • 1958 • Sekigawa Hideo • JPN • MOTHER AND GUN
HAHA TO KO • 1938 • Shibuya Minoru • JPN • MOTHER AND CHILD
HAHA, TSUMA, MUSUME see **MUSUME TSUMA HAHA** • 1960
HAHA WA SHINAZU • 1942 • Naruse Mikio • JPN • MOTHER NEVER DIES
HAHA YO, KIMI NO NA O KEGASU NAKARE • 1928 • Gosho Heinosuke • JPN • MOTHER, DO NOT SHAME YOUR NAME
HAHA-YO KOISHI • 1926 • Gosho Heinosuke • JPN • MOTHER'S LOVE, A ○ MOTHER, I MISS YOU
HAHAKOGUSA • 1942 • Tasaka Tomotaka • JPN • MOTHER-AND-CHILD GRASS
HAHAKOGUSA • 1959 • Yamamura So • JPN • MOTHER AND HER CHILDREN, A
HAHN IM KORB • 1937 • Paul Heinz • FRG
HAHN IM KORB, DER • 1925 • Jacoby Georg • FRG
HAHO, A TENGER • 1972 • Palasthy Gyorgy • HNG • JUNIOR JR. COMES
HAHO, OCSI! • 1971 • Palasthy Gyorgy • HNG • HI, JUNIOR! ○ TONY AND THE TICK-TOCK DRAGON
HAI-HSIA LIANG-AN • 1987 • Yu K'An-P'Ing • TWN • PEOPLE BETWEEN TWO CHINAS, THE
HAI HUN • 1957 • Xu Tao • CHN • SOUL OF THE SEA
HAI IL BONGIORNO DI TRINITA • 1977 • Baldi Ferdinando • ITL
HAI SBAGLIATO.. DOVEVI UCCIDERMI SUBITO! • 1973 • Bianchi Mario • ITL
HAI-SHUI CHENG LAN • 1988 • Liao Ch'Ing-Sung • TWN • WHEN THE OCEAN IS BLUE
HAI-T'AN-SHANG-TE YI T'IEN • 1983 • Yang Te-Ch'Ang • TWN • THAT DAY, ON THE BEACH
HAI-TANG • 1930 • Eichberg Richard • FRG • WEG ZUR SCHANDE, DER ○ ROAD TO DISHONOUR, THE
HAI-TANG • 1930 • Kemm Jean, Eichberg Richard • FRN
HAI-TE ERH-TZU • 1983 • Ch'Ing-Chieh Lin • TWN
HAI-YUAN CH'I-HAO • 1972 • Lo Wei • HKG • WANG YU'S SEVEN MAGNIFICENT FIGHTS ○ SEVEN MAGNIFICENT FIGHTS ○ SEAMAN NUMBER SEVEN
HAI ZI WANG • 1987 • Chen Kaige • CHN • KING OF THE CHILDREN ○ HAIZI WANG
HAIDHARI 3.30' APODRASATE • 1967 • Maheras Ilias • GRC • 3.30 ESCAPE FROM THE HAIDARI CAMP
HAIDO • 1967 • Dritsas Kostas • GRC
HAIDUCII • 1965 • Cocea Dinu • RMN • OUTLAWS, THE
HAIE UND KLEINE FISCHE • 1957 • Wisbar Frank • FRG • U BOAT 55
HAIFISCHFUTTERET, DER • Stranka Erwin • GDR • SHARK FEEDER, THE
HAIKEI TENNOHEIKA-SAMA • 1963 • Nomura Yoshitaro • JPN • DEAR EMPEROR
HAIKYO NO NAKA • 1923 • Mizoguchi Kenji • JPN • IN THE RUINS (USA) ○ AMONG THE RUINS
HAIL see **HAIL TO THE CHIEF** • 1973
HAIL AND FAREWELL • 1936 • Ince Ralph • UKN
HAIL BRITANNIA! • 1897 • *Paul R. W.* • UKN
HAIL BROTHER • 1935 • Jason Leigh • SHT • USA
HAIL COLUMBIA! • 1982 • Ferguson Graeme • CND
HAIL DAYS see **FAGYOSSZENTEK** • 1962
HAIL! HAIL! ROCK 'N' ROLL see **CHUCK BERRY HAIL! HAIL! ROCK 'N' ROLL** • 1987
HAIL, HERO! • 1969 • Miller David • USA
HAIL! MAFIA (USA) see **JE VOUS SALUE, MAFIA** • 1965
HAIL MARY see **JE VOUS SALUE MARIE** • 1984
HAIL MOTHERLAND! see **WITAJ OJCZYZNO!** • 1958
HAIL THE CONQUERING HERO • 1944 • Sturges Preston • USA
HAIL THE HERO • 1924 • Horne James W. • USA
HAIL, THE PRINCESS • 1930 • Roberts Stephen • SHT • USA
HAIL THE WOMAN • 1921 • Wray John Griffith • USA
HAIL TO FREEDOM see **VIVA LA LIBERTAD** • 1965
HAIL TO THE CHIEF • 1973 • Levinson Fred • USA • WASHINGTON, B.C. ○ HAIL
HAIL TO THE RANGERS • 1943 • Berke William • USA • ILLEGAL RIGHTS (UKN)
HAILSTONES AND HALIBUT BONES • 1964 • *Reade-Sterling Walter* • ANS • USA
HAIM SOUTINE • 1959 • Brabo • SHT • FRN
HAIMOUNE, EL • 1984 • Khemir Nacer • TNS, FRN • BALISEURS DU DESERT, LES (FRN)
HAINE • 1979 • Goult Dominique • FRN
HAINE, LA • 1914 • Pouctal Henri • FRN
HAINE DU SORCIER, LA • 1914 • Burguet Charles • FRN • HATE OF THE SORCERER, THE
HAIR • 1972 • Piwowski Marek • DOC • PLN
HAIR • 1979 • Forman Milos • USA
HAIR CARTOONS • 1915 • Marcus Sid • ANS • USA
HAIR CUT-UPS • 1953 • Donnelly Eddie • ANS • USA
HAIR IN THE SOUP, A see **COMME UN CHEVEU SUR LA SOUPE** • 1956
HAIR OF HER HEAD, THE • 1915 • Drew Sidney • USA
HAIR OF THE DOG • 1962 • Bishop Terry • UKN
HAIR OF THE DOG see **BRUN BITTER** • 1988
HAIR-RAISING EPISODE, A • 1915 • Batley Ernest G.? • UKN
HAIR-RAISING EPISODE IN ONE SPLASH • 1914 • Collins Edwin J.? • UKN
HAIR RAISING HARE • 1945 • Jones Charles M. • ANS • USA
HAIR-RAISING TALE, A • 1965 • Post Howard • ANS • USA
HAIR-RAISING TALE, A • 1970 • Elbogi Nala • SHT • UKN
HAIR RESTORER • 1907 • Fitzhamon Lewin • UKN
HAIR RESTORER, THE • 1909 • *Williams, Brown & Earle* • USA
HAIR RESTORER, THE see **LOTION MIRACULEUSE, LA** • 1907
HAIR RESTORER AND THE INDIANS, THE • 1911 • *Eytinge Harry* • USA
HAIR SOUP: OR, A DISGRUNTLED DINER • 1901 • *Paul R. W.* • UKN
HAIR TODAY, GONE TOMORROW • 1954 • Kneitel Seymour • ANS • USA
HAIR TRIGGER BAXTER • 1926 • Nelson Jack • USA
HAIR TRIGGER BURK • 1917 • Kelsey Fred A. • SHT • USA
HAIR-TRIGGER CASEY • 1936 • Fraser Harry L. • USA
HAIR TRIGGER CASEY see **IMMEDIATE LEE** • 1916
HAIR TRIGGER CASSIDY see **IMMEDIATE LEE** • 1916
HAIR TRIGGER STUFF • 1920 • Eason B. Reeves • USA
HAIRBREADTH ESCAPE OF JACK SHEPPARD, THE • 1900 • Booth W. R. • UKN
HAIRCUT • 1963 • Warhol Andy • USA
HAIRDRESSERS • 1971 • Rasker Frans • NTH
HAIRLESS HECTOR • 1941 • White Volney • ANS • USA
HAIRPIN TRAIL, THE • 1914 • Batley Ethyle? • UKN
HAIRPINS • 1920 • Niblo Fred • USA
HAIRS, THE see **KARVAT** • 1974
HAIRSPRAY • 1988 • Waters John* • USA
HAIRY APE, THE • 1944 • Santell Alfred • USA
HAIRY HERCULES • 1960 • Halas John, Batchelor Joy • ANS • UKN
HAIRY PISTOL, A see **KE NO HAETA KENJU** • 1968
HA'ISHA BACHEDER HASHENI • 1967 • Yeshurun Isaac • ISR • VARIATIONS ON A LOVE THEME ○ AHAVA LE ARBA YADAIYM
HAISHANG HUA • 1987 • Yeung Fan • HKG • IMMORTAL STORY
HAITAN • 1985 • Teng Wenji • CHN • AT THE BEACH
HAITATSU SARENAI SANTSU NO TEGAMI • 1979 • Nomura Yoshitaro • JPN • THREE LETTERS UNDELIVERED
HAITI EXPERIENCE see **UDENRIGSKORRESPONDENTEN** • 1983
HAITI EXPRESS • 1983 • Leth Jorgen • DNM
HAITI: J'ACCUSE • 1977 • Bertolino Daniel • DOC • CND
HAITI - QUEBEC • 1985 • Rached Tahani • MTV • CND
HAITOKU NO MESU • 1960 • Nomura Yoshitaro • JPN • DOCTORS CONDEMNED
HAIZAN NO UTA WA KANASHI • 1922 • Mizoguchi Kenji • JPN • FAILURE'S SONG IS SAD (USA) ○ SAD SONG OF THE DEFEATED, THE ○ SONG OF FAILURE, THE
HAIZI WANG see **HAI ZI WANG** • 1987
HAJDE DA SE VOLIMO JOS JEDAMPUT • 1989 • Crnobrnja Stanko • YGS • LET'S MAKE LOVE ONCE AGAIN
HAJDUCKA VREMENA • 1977 • Tadej Vladimir • YGS • DARE-DEVILS' TIME
HAJDUK • 1974 • Kardos Ferenc • HNG
HAJDUK • 1981 • Petkovic Aleksandar • YGS • OUTLAW, THE
HAJEN SOM VISSTE FOR MYCKET • 1989 • *Eriksson Anders* • SWD • SHARK WHO KNEW TOO MUCH, THE
HAJI-KARA • 1929 • Sharif-Zade • USS
HAJKA • 1978 • Pavlovic Zivojin • YGS • WITCH HUNT ○ MANHUNT, THE ○ PURSUIT ○ CHASE, THE
HAJNAL • 1971 • Szabo Istvan • DCS • HNG • DAWN
HAJNALI HAZTETOK • 1986 • Domolky Janos • HNG • ROOFS AT DAWN
HAJONAPLO • 1987 • Palasthy Gyorgy • HNG • SHIP'S REGISTER
HAJRA MOZDONY! • 1972 • Dargay Attila • HNG
HAK ASIKLARI • 1967 • Tengiz Asaf • TRK • LOVERS OF FAITH
HAK TAIYEUNG 731 • 1988 • Mou Tun-Fei • HKG • MAN BEHIND THE SUN
HAKAI • 1948 • Kinoshita Keisuke • JPN • APOSTASY
HAKAI • 1961 • Ichikawa Kon • JPN • OUTCAST, THE (UKN) ○ SIN, THE (USA) ○ OUTCASTS ○ BROKEN COMMANDMENT, THE
HAKANLARIN SAVASI • 1968 • Aslan Mehmet • TRK • BATTLE OF THE CHIEFS, THE
HAKARKA HA A DOM see **RED GROUND, THE** • 1954
HAKHOREFF HA'AKHARON • 1983 • Shelakh Rikl • ISR • LAST WINTER, THE
HAKIMO see **ESKIYA KANI** • 1968
HAKKARI'DE BIR MEVSIM • 1987 • Kiral Erden • TRK • SEASON IN HAKKARI, A
HAKKODA-SAN • 1976 • Moritani Shiro • JPN • MT.HAKKODA
HAKOIRI MUSUME • 1935 • Ozu Yasujiro • JPN • INNOCENT MAID, AN ○ YOUNG VIRGIN, THE
HAKON HAKONSEN • 1989 • Gaup Nils • NRW
HAKONE FUUNROKU • 1951 • Yamamoto Satsuo • JPN • STORM CLOUDS OVER MOUNT HAKONE ○ STORM CLOUDS OVER HAKONE
HAKO'S SACRIFICE • 1910 • *Vitagraph* • USA
HAKSUKOI SANNIN MUSUKO • 1955 • Aoyagi Nobuo • JPN • THREE BRIDGES FOR THREE SONS
HAKTOU TSAUHAN • 1989 • Hsu An-Hua • HKG
HAKU JA KOMACHI • 1958 • Hirozu Mitsuo • JPN
HAKUCHI • 1951 • Kurosawa Akira • JPN • IDIOT, THE
HAKUCHO MONOGATARI • 1956 • Horiuchi Masaru • JPN • STORY OF THE SWAN, THE
HAKUCHO NO SHIKAKU • 1978 • Murakawa Toru • JPN • BLIND SPOT UNDER THE SUN
HAKUCHU DODO • 1968 • Nomura Yoshitaro • JPN • THIEVES' HOLIDAY
HAKUCHU NO TORIMA • 1966 • Oshima Nagisa • JPN • VIOLENCE AT HIGH NOON ○ VIOLENCE AT NOON ○ PHANTOM KILLER
HAKUCHU NO ZANSATSU • 1967 • Umezu Meijiro • JPN • SLAUGHTER IN BROAD DAYLIGHT
HAKUFUJIN NO YOREN • 1956 • Toyeda • JPN • MYSTERIOUS LOVE OF MRS. WHITE
HAKUGIN-JO • 1960 • Saito Buichi • JPN • DUEL ON THE SILVER PEAK
HAKUGIN NO OZU • 1935 • Uchida Tomu • JPN • THRONE OF THE WHITE MAN ○ WHITE MAN'S THRONE, THE
HAKUJA DEN • 1958 • Yabushita Taiji, Okabe Kazuhiko • JPN • PANDA AND THE MAGIC SERPENT (USA) ○ WHITE SNAKE ENCHANTRESS, THE ○ MAGIC WHITE SERPENT, THE
HAKUJA-SHO • 1984 • Ito Toshiya • JPN • LEGEND OF THE WHITE SNAKE
HAKUJITSU-MU • 1980 • Takechi Tetsuji • JPN • DAYDREAM
HAKUJITSUMU • 1964 • Takechi Tetsuji • JPN • DAY-DREAM (USA)
HAKUMAT • 1988 • Chaudhry Haider • PKS
HAKUOKI • 1959 • Mori Issei • JPN
HAKUSEN-MIDARE KURO-KAMI • 1956 • *Azuma Chiyonosuke* • JPN • WHITE FAN, THE
HAL, EL • 1981 • el Maanouni Ahmed • MRC • TRANCES ○ TRANSES
HAL CHASE'S HOME RUN • 1911 • *Kalem* • USA
HAL KEMP AND HIS ORCHESTRA • 1941 • Negulesco Jean • SHT • USA
HAL ROACH COMEDY CARNIVAL • 1947 • Carr Bernard, Foster Harve • USA
HAL ROACH'S OUR GANG COMEDY see **OUR GANG COMEDY** • 1923-44
HAL SWAIN AND HIS SAX-O-FIVE • 1930 • *Balcon Michael (P)* • SHT • UKN
HALADEK • 1981 • Fazekas Lajos • HNG • NOT YET THE DAY
HALA'E AL SAYEDAT • 1960 • Wahab Fatin Abdel • EGY • HALLAQ AS-SAYIDAT ○ COIFFEUR POUR DAMES
HALAHAKA • 1981 • Nesher Avi • ISR • TROUPE, THE
HALAKA EL SAFKUDA, EL • 1949 • Lama Ibrahim • EGY • MISSING LINK, THE
HALALOS TAVSL • 1942 • Kalmar Laszlo • HNG
HALALRAITELT, A • 1989 • Zsombolyai Janos • HNG • ON DEATH ROW
HALALSENGO, A • 1917 • Curtiz Michael • HNG • DEATH BELL, THE
HALBBLUT • 1919 • Lang Fritz • FRG • HALF BREED, THE ○ HALF CASTE
HALBE-HALBE • 1978 • Brandner Uwe • FRG • FIFTY-FIFTY
HALBE UNSCHULD • 1920 • Kirsch John B. • FRG
HALBSEIDE • 1925 • Oswald Richard • FRG
HALBSTARKEN, DIE • 1956 • Tressler Georg • FRG • TEENAGE WOLF PACK (USA) ○ WOLFPACK (UKN) ○ WICKED ONES, THE
HALBWUCHSIGEN, DIE • 1929 • Heuberger Edmund • FRG
HALBZARTE, DIE • 1959 • Thiele Rolf • AUS
HALCON DE CASTILLA, EL • 1965 • Elorrieta Jose Maria • SPN
HALCON DEL DESIERTO, EL • 1965 • Lluch Miguel, Ross Red • SPN
HALCON SOLITARIO, EL • 1963 • Gomez Urquiza Zacarias • MXC
HALCON Y LA PRESA, EL (SPN) see **RESA DEI CONTI, LA** • 1967
HALDANE OF THE SECRET SERVICE • 1923 • Houdini Harry • USA
HALDY • 1963 • Kidawa Janusz • DOC • PLN • WASTE HEAPS
HALE AND HEARTY • 1922 • Roach Hal • SHT • USA
HALET I MUREN see **NAR ROSORNA SLA UT** • 1930
HALEURS DE BATEAUX, LES • 1896 • Melies Georges • FRN • TOWING A BOAT ON THE RIVER
HALF A BRIDE • 1928 • La Cava Gregory • USA
HALF A CENTURY OF SONGS (USA) see **CANZONI DI MEZZO SECOLO** • 1952
HALF A CHANCE • 1913 • Apfel Oscar • USA
HALF A CHANCE • 1920 • Thornby Robert T. • USA
HALF-A-DOLLAR BILL • 1924 • Van Dyke W. S. • USA
HALF A DOZEN EASY WAYS TO SAVE PETROL • 1980 • Robertson Michael • DOC • ASL
HALF A HERO • 1912 • Young James • USA
HALF A HERO • 1953 • Weis Don • USA
HALF A HOUSE • 1979 • Mack Brice • USA
HALF A LIFETIME • 1985 • Petrie Daniel • MTV • CND
HALF A LOAF see **YOKU** • 1958
HALF A LOAF OF KUNG FU • 1985 • Chen Chi Hua • HKG
HALF A MAN • 1925 • Sweet Harry • SHT • USA
HALF A MILLION • 1915 • McKim Edwin • USA

HALF A PINT see **PIKOLO VILAGOS, EGY** • 1955
HALF A ROGUE • 1916 • Otto Henry • USA
HALF A SINNER • 1934 • Neumann Kurt • USA • ALIAS THE DEACON
HALF A SINNER • 1940 • Christie Al • USA • EVERYTHING HAPPENS TO ANNE
HALF A SIXPENCE • 1967 • Sidney George • UKN, USA
HALF A TRUTH • 1922 • Hill Sinclair • UKN
HALF AN HOUR • 1920 • Knoles Harley • USA
HALF AN HOUR see **DOCTOR'S SECRET, THE** • 1930
HALF AND HALF • 1917 • *Depp Harry* • USA
HALF AND HALF • 1919 • Lyons Eddie, Moran Lee • SHT • USA
HALF ANGEL • 1936 • Lanfield Sidney • USA
HALF ANGEL • 1951 • Sale Richard • USA
HALF BACK, THE • 1917 • Turbett Ben • SHT • USA
HALF BACK BUSTER • 1928 • Newfield Sam • SHT • USA
HALF-BACK OF NOTRE DAME, THE • 1924 • *Sennett Mack (P)* • SHT • USA
HALF-BAKED ALASKA • 1965 • Marcus Sid • ANS • USA
HALF-BAKED RELATIONS • 1934 • Lamont Charles • SHT • USA
HALF BREED • 1973 • *Barker Lex* • YGS
HALF BREED, THE • 1908 • *Kalem* • USA
HALF BREED, THE • 1913 • *Pathe* • USA
HALF-BREED, THE • 1914 • *Bainbridge Sherman* • USA
HALF BREED, THE • 1916 • Dwan Allan • USA • CARQUENEZ WOODS, THE ○ HALF-BREED, THE
HALF BREED, THE • 1922 • Taylor Charles A. • USA
HALF-BREED, THE • 1952 • Gilmore Stuart • USA
HALF-BREED, THE see **HALVBLOD** • 1914
HALF-BREED, THE see **HALF BREED, THE** • 1916
HALF BREED, THE see **HALBBLUT** • 1919
HALF-BREED PARSON, THE • 1913 • *Bison* • USA
HALF-BREED SCOUT, THE • 1912 • *Bison* • USA
HALF-BREED SHERIFF, THE • 1913 • *Frontier* • USA
HALF-BREED'S ATONEMENT, THE • 1911 • *Powers* • USA
HALF BREED'S CONFESSION, THE • 1911 • *Champion* • USA
HALF BREED'S CONFESSION, THE • 1917 • *Paul Val* • SHT • USA
HALF-BREED'S DAUGHTER, THE • 1911 • *Christy Lillian* • USA
HALF-BREED'S PLAN, THE • 1911 • *Bison* • USA
HALF-BREED'S SACRIFICE, THE • 1912 • *Lubin* • USA
HALF BREED'S TREACHERY • 1910 • *Bison* • USA
HALF-BREED'S TREACHERY, THE • 1912 • *King Burton* • USA
HALF-BREED'S WAY, THE • 1912 • *Von Meter Harry* • USA
HALF CASTE see **HALBBLUT** • 1919
HALF DAY EXCURSION, THE • 1935 • Dean A. L. • UKN
HALF-EMPTY SADDLES • 1958 • Smith Paul J. • ANS • USA
HALF-FARE HARE • 1956 • McKimson Robert • ANS • USA
HALF FLAME, HALF BRINE • 1989 • Xia Gang • CHN
HALF HIS LIFE see **HALFTE DES LEBENS**
HALF HOLIDAY • 1931 • Stafford Babe • SHT • USA
HALF HUMAN (USA) see **JUJIN YUKI-OTOKO** • 1955
HALF LIFE • 1986 • O'Rourke Dennis • ASL
HALF LIFE see **DANCE OF THE DAMNED** • 1988
HALF MARRIAGE • 1929 • Cowen William J. • USA
HALF-MASTED SCHOONER • 1969 • MacKay Bruce • CND
HALF METER INCIDENT, THE see **HADITHA AL NASF METR** • 1983
HALF MILLION BRIBE, THE • 1916 • Jones Edgar • USA
HALF MOON STREET • 1986 • Swaim Bob • UKN
HALF-NAKED TRUTH, THE • 1932 • La Cava Gregory • USA
HALF OF HEAVEN see **MITAD DEL CIELO, LA** • 1985
HALF OPEN AND LUMPY • 1966-67 • Nelson Robert • SHT • USA
HALF ORPHANS, THE • 1913 • *Majestic* • USA
HALF PAST MIDNIGHT • 1948 • Claxton William F. • USA
HALF-PINT HERO, A • 1927 • Lamont Charles • SHT • USA
HALF PINT KID see **HARRIGAN'S KID** • 1943
HALF-PINT PALOMINO • 1953 • Lundy Dick • ANS • USA
HALF-PINT PIGMY • 1948 • Avery Tex • ANS • USA • GEORGE AND JUNIOR
HALF-PRICE HONEYMOON see **NASZUT FELARON** • 1936
HALF SHOT • 1912 • *Imp* • USA
HALF SHOT AT SUNRISE • 1930 • Sloane Paul • USA
HALF-SHOT SHOOTERS • 1936 • Black Preston • SHT • USA
HALF-SLAVE, HALF-FREE see **SOLOMON NORTHRUP'S ODYSSEY** • 1984
HALF THE ACTION • 1980 • Elliott B. Ron • USA
HALF-TRUTH see **ARDH SATYA** • 1983
HALF VIRGIN see **HANSHOJO** • 1953
HALF WAY TO HELL • 1961 • *Adamson Al* • USA
HALF WAY TO SHANGHAI • 1942 • Rawlins John • USA
HALF WIT, THE • 1916 • Melville Wilbert • SHT • USA
HALF-WITS HOLIDAY • 1947 • White Jules • SHT • USA
HALFBREED FOSTER SISTER, THE • 1912 • *Pathe* • USA
HALFBREED'S GRATITUDE, A • 1911 • Fitzhamon Lewin • UKN
HALFON HILL DOESN'T ANSWER • 1977 • Dayan Assaf, Alter Naftali • ISR
HALFTE DES LEBENS • Zschoche Hermann • GDR • HALF HIS LIFE
HALFWAY GIRL, THE • 1925 • Dillon John Francis • USA
HALFWAY HOUSE, THE • 1944 • Dearden Basil • UKN • GHOSTLY INN, THE
HALFWAY TO HEAVEN • 1929 • Abbott George • USA • HERE COMES THE BANDWAGON
HALFWAY TO HEAVEN see **MAYBE IT'S LOVE** • 1935
HALFWAY TO HELL • 1936 • Adamson Victor • USA
HALFWAY TO RENO • 1913 • *Benham Harry* • USA
HALFWIT, THE • 1913 • *Reliance* • USA
HALHATATLAN LEGIOS, A • 1971 • Somlo Tamas • HNG • IMMORTAL LEGIONARY, THE
HALHATATLANSAG • 1959 • Jancso Miklos • HNG • IMMORTALITY
HALIL THE BRIGAND see **ESKIYA HALIL** • 1968
HALIL, THE CROW-MAN see **KARGACI HALIL** • 1968
HALIMEDEN MEKTUP VAR • 1964 • Dogan Suha • TRK
HALIMUNAN HITAM • 1982 • Osman M. • MLY
HALKA • 1938 • Gardan Juliusz • PLN
HALKAS GELOBNIS • 1918 • Halm Alfred • FRG
HALL ALLA DORRAR OPPNA • 1973 • Ehlin Per-Arne • SWD • THERE'S A KEY TO EVERY DOOR ○ KEEP ALL DOORS OPEN
HALL OF FAME • 1948 • Parker Benjamin R. • SHT • USA
HALL OF KINGS • 1967 • Rasky Harry • MTV • USA
HALL OF LOST FOOTSTEPS, THE see **SAL ZTRACENYCH KROKU** • 1958
HALL OF MIRRORS • 1966 • Sonbert Warren • USA
HALL OF MIRRORS see **WUSA** • 1970
HALL OF MIRRORS, THE • 1982 • Hicks Scott • DOC • ASL
HALL PORTER'S INDISCRETION, THE • 1899 • *Warwick Trading Co.* • UKN
HALL ROOM BOYS • 1919-21 • *Cohn Productions* • SHS • USA
HALL-ROOM BOYS, THE • 1910 • *Walton Fred* • USA
HALL ROOM GIRLS, THE • 1913 • Smalley Phillips • USA
HALL ROOM GIRLS, THE • 1917 • Baker George D. • SHT • USA
HALL-ROOM RIVALS, THE • 1914 • Johnson Tefft • USA
HALLALI, L' • 1916 • de Baroncelli Jacques • FRN
HALLAQ AS-SAYIDAT see **HALA'E AL SAYEDAT** • 1960
HALLAQ DARB AL FUQHRA' • 1987 • Reggeb Mohammed • MRC • BARBER OF THE POOR QUARTER
HALLEBACK MANOR see **HALLEBACKS GARD** • 1961
HALLEBACKS GARD • 1961 • Blomgren Bengt • SWD • HALLEBACK MANOR
HALLELUJAH! • 1929 • Vidor King • USA
HALLELUJAH ANYHOW • 1990 • Jacobs Matthew • UKN
HALLELUJAH, I'M A BUM • 1933 • Milestone Lewis • USA • HALLELUJAH, I'M A TRAMP (UKN) ○ HEART OF NEW YORK ○ NEW YORK ○ LAZY BONES ○ HAPPY GO LUCKY ○ OPTIMIST, THE
HALLELUJAH, I'M A TRAMP (UKN) see **HALLELUJAH, I'M A BUM** • 1933
HALLELUJAH THE HILLS • 1963 • Mekas Adolfas • USA
HALLELUJAH TRAIL, THE • 1965 • Sturges John • USA
HALLES, LES • 1929 • Galitzine • SHT • FRN
HALLEY GENERATION, THE see **GENERACION HALLEY, LA** • 1986
HALLEY'S COMET • 1910 • FRN
HALLIDAY BRAND, THE • 1957 • Lewis Joseph H. • USA
HALLIG HOOGE • 1923 • *Solar-Film* • FRG • STOLZE FRAUEN
HALLMARK HALL OF FAME see **RESTING PLACE** • 1986
HALLMARKING • 1969 • Holmes Andrew • UKN
HALLO BABY see **HELLO BABY!** • 1975
HALLO BUDAPEST • 1933 • Vajda Ladislao • HNG • HELLO BUDAPEST (USA)
HALLO CAESAR! • 1926 • Schunzel Reinhold • FRG
HALLO, DIENSTMANN! • 1952 • Antel Franz • AUS
HALLO EVERYBODY • 1933 • Richter Hans • FRG
HALLO, FRAULEIN! • 1949 • Jugert Rudolf • FRG
HALLO HALLO! HIER SPRICHT BERLIN (FRG) see **ALLO BERLIN, ICI PARIS** • 1931
HALLO, HERE'S MEXICO • 1967 • Csoke Jozsef • DOC • HNG
HALLO, IT'S ME! see **ZDRAVSTVYI, ETO YA!** • 1965
HALLO JANINE • 1939 • Boese Carl • FRG
HALLO MOSCOW! see **ZDRAVSTVAI MOSKVA** • 1945
HALLO, NETTE • 1963 • Lisakovitch Viktor • DOC • USS
HALLO -SIE HABEN IHRE FRAU VERGUSSEN • 1949 • Walter Kurt E. • FRG
HALLO TAXI • 1958 • Kugelstadt Hermann • AUS
HALLO, TAXI see **HALO, TAKSI** • 1984
HALLO, TU POLSKIE RADIO LODZ • 1945 • Bohdziewicz Antoni • DOC • PLN • THIS IS POLISH RADIO LODZ SPEAKING
HALLO WARD! ...E FURONO VACANZE IS SANGUE (ITL) see **LLAMAN DE JAMAICA, MR. WARD** • 1967
HALLOJ I HIMMELSENGEN • 1965 • Balling Erik • DNM, FRG
HALLOOH SISTERS • 1990 • Runze Ottokar • FRG
HALLOW KIDS • 1987 • Miyagi Mariko • JPN
HALLOWEEN • 1931 • Huemer Dick, Marcus Sid • ANS • USA
HALLOWEEN • 1978 • Carpenter John • USA
HALLOWE'EN see **ZADNUSZKI** • 1961
HALLOWEEN II • 1981 • Rosenthal Rick • USA
HALLOWEEN III: SEASON OF THE WITCH • 1983 • Wallace Tommy Lee • USA
HALLOWEEN IV: THE RETURN OF MICHAEL MYERS • 1988 • Little Dwight H. • USA
HALLOWEEN PARTY see **NIGHT OF THE DEMONS** • 1988
HALLROOM BOYS • 1906 • *Bitzer Billy (Ph)* • USA
HALLS OF ANGER • 1970 • Bogart Paul • USA
HALLS OF MONTEZUMA • 1951 • Milestone Lewis • USA
HALLUCINATED ALCHEMIST, THE (USA) see **HALLUCINATION DE L'ALCHIMISTE, L'** • 1897
HALLUCINATION see **LIDERCNYOMAS** • 1920
HALLUCINATION see **HALLUCINATION GENERATION** • 1966
HALLUCINATION see **RUPTURE, LA** • 1970
HALLUCINATION DE L'ALCHIMISTE, L' • 1897 • Melies Georges • FRN • HALLUCINATED ALCHEMIST, THE (USA)
HALLUCINATION GENERATION • 1966 • Mann Edward • USA • HALLUCINATION
HALLUCINATIONER see **STUDIE II** • 1952
HALLUCINATIONS see **STUDIE II** • 1952
HALLUCINATIONS DU BARON DE MUNCHAUSEN, LES • 1911 • Melies Georges • FRN • HALLUCINATIONS OF BARON MUNCHAUSEN, THE (USA)
HALLUCINATIONS OF BARON MUNCHAUSEN, THE (USA) see **HALLUCINATIONS DU BARON DE MUNCHAUSEN, LES** • 1911
HALLUCINATIONS PHARMACEUTIQUES OU LE TRUC DU POTARD • 1908 • Melies Georges • FRN • TRUC DU POTARD, LE ○ PHARMACEUTICAL HALLUCINATIONS OR THE TRICK OF POTARD
HALLUCINATIONS SADIQUES • 1969 • Kormon Roy • FRN
HALLUCINATIONS SADIQUES • Bastide J.-P. • FRN
HALLUCINATORS, THE see **NAKED ZOO, THE** • 1970
HALO, THE see **O VECECH NADPRIROZENYCH** • 1958
HALO OF HEAT HAZE see **KAGERO-GASA** • 1959
HALO, TAKSI • 1984 • Radavanovic Vlasta • YGS • HALLO, TAXI
HALODHIA CHORAYA BAODHAN KHAI • 1988 • Barua Jahnu • IND • CATASTROPHE, THE
HALOTTLATO, A • 1978 • Moldovan Domokos • HNG • SEER OF THE DEAD, THE
HALSINGAR • 1923 • Larsson William • SWD • PEOPLE OF HALSINGLAND
HALSINGAR • 1933 • Johansson Ivar • SWD • PEOPLE OF HALSINGLAND
HALT, NICHT KUSSEN! • 1916 • Larsen Viggo • FRG
HALT, WHO GOES THERE? • 1967 • Culhane Shamus • ANS • USA
HALTA LENA OCH VINDOGDE PER • 1924 • Wallen Sigurd • SWD • LAME LENA AND CROSS-EYED PER
HALTA LENA OCH VINDOGDE PER • 1933 • Petschler Eric A. • SWD • LAME LENA AND CROSS-EYED PER
HALTA LENA OCH VINDOGDE PER see **LATA LENA OCH BLAOGDE PER** • 1947
HALTA LOTTA TAVERN see **HALTA LOTTAS KROG** • 1943
HALTA LOTTAS KROG • 1943 • Lundqvist Torsten • SWD • HALTA LOTTA TAVERN
HALTE.. POLICE! • 1948 • Severac Jacques • FRN
HALTED CAREER, A • 1914 • *Keystone* • USA
HALTED SYMPHONY, THE • 1916 • Broadwell Robert B. • SHT • USA
HALTENBANKEN • 1986 • Tuhus Oddvar Bull • NRW • BLOW OUT IN THE NORTH SEA
HALTEROFLIC • 1982 • Vallois Philippe • FRN
HALTET BEIDES GUT ZUSAMMEN • 1969 • Bottge Bruno J. • ANS • GDR • HOLD ON TO BOTH THINGS
HALTING HAND, THE • 1916 • *Big U* • SHT • USA
HALVAN RAKASTAA, PETER • 1973 • Kassila Matti • FNL • I WANT TO LOVE, PETER
HALVBLOD • 1914 • Sjostrom Victor • SWD • HALF-BREED, THE
HALVVAGS TILL HIMLEN • 1932 • Carlsten Rune, Windrow Stellan • SWD
HAM AN - • 1919 • *Henry Gale* • SHT • USA
HAM ACTORS, THE • 1915 • *Universal* • SHT • USA
HAM AGREES WITH SHERMAN • 1916 • *Hamilton Lloyd V.* • SHT • USA
HAM AMONG THE REDSKINS • 1915 • *Hamilton Lloyd V.* • USA
HAM AND DETECTIVE • 1915 • *Hamilton Lloyd V.* • USA
HAM AND EGGS • 1916 • *Ross Bud* • SHT • USA
HAM AND EGGS • 1933 • Lantz Walter, Nolan William • ANS • USA
HAM AND EGGS AT THE FRONT • 1927 • Del Ruth Roy • USA • HAM AND EGGS (UKN)
HAM AND EGGS (UKN) see **HAM AND EGGS AT THE FRONT** • 1927
HAM AND HATTIE • 1957 • *U.p.a.* • ASS • USA
HAM AND PREPAREDNESS • 1916 • *Hamilton Lloyd V.* • SHT • USA
HAM AND THE EXPERIMENTS • 1915 • Santell Alfred • USA
HAM AND THE HERMIT'S DAUGHTER • 1916 • *Hamilton Lloyd V.* • USA
HAM AND THE JITNEY BUS • 1915 • *Hamilton Lloyd V.* • USA
HAM AND THE MASKED MARVEL • 1916 • Edwards Harry J. • USA
HAM AND THE SAUSAGE FACTORY • 1915 • *Hamilton Lloyd V.* • USA
HAM AND THE VILLAIN FACTORY • 1914 • *Hamilton Lloyd V.* • USA
HAM ARTIST, THE see **FACE ON THE BARROOM FLOOR, THE** • 1914
HAM AT THE BEACH • 1915 • *Hamilton Lloyd V.* • USA
HAM AT THE FAIR • 1915 • *Hamilton Lloyd V.* • USA
HAM AT THE GARBAGE GENTLEMEN'S BALL • 1915 • Ward Chance E. • USA
HAM DARD • 1953 • *Biswas Anil (M)* • IND
HAM IN A ROLE, A • 1949 • McKimson Robert • ANS • USA
HAM IN THE DRUGSTORE • 1916 • *Hamilton Lloyd* • SHT • USA
HAM IN THE HAREM • 1915 • Ward Chance E. • USA
HAM IN THE NUT FACTORY • 1915 • *Hamilton Lloyd V.* • USA
HAM TAKES A CHANCE • 1916 • Beaudine William • SHT • USA
HAM THAT COULDN'T BE CURED, THE • 1942 • Lantz Walter • ANS • USA
HAM THE DIVER • 1916 • Beaudine William • SHT • USA
HAM THE EXPLORER • 1916 • *Hamilton Lloyd V.* • USA
HAM, THE FORTUNE-TELLER • 1916 • *Hamilton Lloyd V.* • SHT • USA
HAM, THE ICEMAN • 1914 • *Hamilton Lloyd V.* • USA
HAM, THE LINEMAN • 1914 • Neilan Marshall • USA
HAM, THE PIANO MOVER • 1914 • Neilan Marshall • USA
HAM WHAT WAS, THE • 1917 • Baker Richard Foster • SHT • USA
HAMAGURE NO KOMORIUTA • 1973 • Yoshimura Kozaburo • JPN • LULLABY OF HAMAGURE
HAMARA GHAR • 1965 • Abbas Khwaya Ahmad • IND
HAMARA SHAHER • 1985 • Patwardhan Anand • IND • BOMBAY OUR CITY
HAMARI BAAT • 1943 • *Kapoor Raj* • IND
HA'MATARAH TIRAN • 1968 • Nussbaum Raphael • ISR, FRG • SINAI COMMANDOS (USA) ○ 6-TAGE-KRIEG, DER (FRG) ○ SCHATTEN UBER TIRAN-KOMMANDO SINAI ○ MISSION TIRAN
HAMATEUR NIGHT • 1939 • Avery Tex • ANS • USA
HAMATI KOMBOLA ZORRIA • 1952 • Rafla Hilmy • EGY • MY MOTHER-IN-LAW IS AN ATOMIC BOMB
HAMATI MALAK • 1960 • Karama Issa • EGY
HAMBONE AND HILLIE • 1984 • Watts Roy • USA • ADVENTURES OF HAMBONE AND HILLIE, THE
HAMBRE • 1938 • Palacios Fernando • MXC
HAMBRE NUESTRA DE CADA DIA, EL • 1959 • Gonzalez Rogelio A. • MXC
HAMBURG • 1961 • Roos Jorgen • DOC • DNM
HAMBURG ALTONA • 1989 • Mihletic Vedran, Mitrovic Mladen, Krencer Dragutin • YGS
HAMBURG -CITY OF VICE (UKN) see **POLIZEIREVIER DAVIDSWACHE (ST. PAULI)** • 1964
HAMBURG DISEASE, THE see **HAMBURGER KRANKEIT, DIE** • 1980
HAMBURG OFF-LIMITS see **POLIZEIREVIER DAVIDSWACHE (ST. PAULI)** • 1964

HAMBURG: WELTSTRASSE SEE • 1938 • Ruttmann Walter • DOC • FRG • WELTSTRASSE SEE -WELTHAFEN HAMBURG
HAMBURGER see **HAMBURGER -THE MOTION PICTURE** • 1986
HAMBURGER HILL • 1987 • Irvin John • USA
HAMBURGER KRANKEIT, DIE • 1980 • Fleischmann Peter • FRG, FRN • MALADIE DE HAMBOURG, LA (FRN) ○ HAMBURG DISEASE, THE
HAMBURGER -THE MOTION PICTURE • 1986 • Marvin Mike • USA • HAMBURGER
HAME KHELNE DO • 1962 • *Biswas Anil (M)* • IND
HAME'AHEV • 1985 • Bat-Adam Michal • ISR • LOVER, THE
HAMELIN • 1967 • Delgado Luis Maria • SPN
HAMFAT ASAR • 1965 • Jordan Larry • ANS • USA
HAMFAT'S SUCCESS • 1912 • *Eclair* • USA
HAMILCHAMA AL HASHALOM • 1967 • Dassin Jules • DOC • ISR • SURVIVAL 67 ○ SURVIVAL
HAMILTON IN THE MUSIC FESTIVAL • 1961 • Halas John • ANS • UKN
HAMILTON THE MUSICAL ELEPHANT • 1961 • Halas John • ANS • USA
HAMIS IZABELLA, A • 1968 • Bacskai-Lauro Istvan • HNG • FAKE ISABELLA, THE
HAMLES • 1960 • Skolimowski Jerzy • SHT • PLN • PETIT HAMLET, LE
HAMLET • 1907 • Melies Georges • FRN • HAMLET, PRINCE OF DENMARK
HAMLET • 1908 • Blackton J. Stuart • USA
HAMLET • 1910 • *Lux* • FRN
HAMLET • 1910 • Barker Will • UKN
HAMLET • 1910 • Blom August • DNM
HAMLET • Desfontaines Henri? • FRN
HAMLET • 1912 • Raymond Charles • UKN
HAMLET • 1913 • Plumb Hay • UKN
HAMLET • 1914 • *Williams Eric* • UKN
HAMLET • 1914 • Young James • USA
HAMLET • 1915 • Kellino W. P. • UKN
HAMLET • 1920 • Gade Svend, Schall Heinz • FRG
HAMLET • 1948 • Olivier Laurence • UKN
HAMLET • 1960 • Wirth Franz Peter • MTV • FRG
HAMLET • 1964 • Colleran Bill • USA
HAMLET • 1969 • Richardson Tony • UKN
HAMLET • Coronado Celestino • UKN
HAMLET • 1970 • Wood Peter • USA
HAMLET • 1971 • Bonniere Rene • CND
HAMLET • 1980 • *Jacobi Derek* • MTV • UKN
HAMLET • 1987 • Kaurismaki Aki • FNL
HAMLET • 1990 • Zeffirelli Franco • UKN
HAMLET see **AMLETO** • 1910
HAMLET see **BLOOD FOR BLOOD** • 1927
HAMLET see **GAMLET** • 1964
HAMLET AT ELSINORE • 1964 • Saville Philip • UKN, DNM
HAMLET GOES BUSINESS see **HAMLET LIIKEMAAILMASSA** • 1988
HAMLET IM DORF MRDUSA DONJA see **PREDSTAVA HAMLETA U MRDUSI DONJOJ** • 1974
HAMLET LIIKEMAAILMASSA • 1988 • Kaurismaki Aki • FNL • HAMLET GOES BUSINESS
HAMLET MADE OVER • 1916 • Metcalfe Earl • SHT • USA
HAMLET, PRINCE OF DENMARK see **HAMLET** • 1907
HAMLET RAZY PIEC • 1966 • Perski Ludwik • DOC • PLN • HAMLET TIMES FIVE
HAMLET TIMES FIVE see **HAMLET RAZY PIEC** • 1966
HAMLET (USA) see **AMLETO** • 1908
HAMLET (USA) see **AMLETO** • 1914
HAMLET (USA) see **AMLETO** • 1917
HAMLET (USA) see **KHUN-E-NAHAK** • 1928
HAMLET (USA) see **KHOON-KA-KHOON** • 1935
HAMLET (USA) see **KHOON-E-NAHAG** • 1953
HAMLET (USA) see **HAMLIE** • 1965
HAMLET'S CASTLE see **SHAKESPEARE OG KRONBERG** • 1951
HAMLIE • 1965 • Bishop Terry • GHN • HAMLET (USA)
HAMMAM AL-MALAT'ILI see **HAMMAN EL MALATIHI** • 1973
HAMMAN EL MALATIHI • 1973 • Abu Saif Salah • EGY • HAMMAM AL-MALAT'ILI ○ BAINS DE MALATILI, LES
HAMMARFORSENS BRUS • 1948 • Frisk Ragnar • SWD • ROAR OF HAMMER RAPIDS, THE
HAMMER • Moll Bruno • SWT
HAMMER • 1972 • Clark Bruce • USA
HAMMER, THE • 1915 • *Gibson Margaret* • USA
HAMMER AGAINST WITCHES, A see **KLADIVO NA CARODEJNICE** • 1969
HAMMER FOR THE WITCHES see **KLADIVO NA CARODEJNICE** • 1969
HAMMER OR ANVIL see **NAKOVAINA ILLI TCHOUK** • 1972
HAMMER THE TOFF • 1952 • Rogers Maclean • UKN
HAMMERER'S CHASE, THE see **CACADA DO MALHADEIRO, A** • 1968
HAMMERHEAD • 1967 • Dlz • PHL
HAMMERHEAD • 1968 • Miller David • UKN
HAMMERHEAD JONES • 1987 • Ingria Robert Michael • USA
HAMMERHEAD JONES: DEATH MATCH • Ingria Robert Michael • USA
HAMMERSMITH IS OUT • 1972 • Ustinov Peter • UKN, USA, MXC
HAMMETT • 1980 • Wenders Wim • USA
HAMMOND MYSTERY, THE (UKN) see **UNDYING MONSTER, THE** • 1942
HAMNAREN • 1915 • Stiller Mauritz • SWD • REVENGER, THE ○ AVENGER, THE
HAMNDEN AR LJUV • 1915 • Hansen Edmond • SWD • REVENGE IS SWEET
HAMNSTAD • 1948 • Bergman Ingmar • SWD • PORT OF CALL
HAMOON • 1989 • Mehrjui Dariush • IRN
HAMPELMANN, DER • 1917 • Moest Hubert • FRG
HAMPELMANN, DER • 1930 • Emo E. W. • FRG • PUPPET, THE
HAMPELMANN, DER • 1938 • Martin Karl Heinz • FRG
HAMPELMANNS GLUCKSTAG • *Ponto Erich* • FRG
HAMPELS ABENTEUER • 1915 • Oswald Richard • FRG
HAMPI • 1960 • Rouch Jean • DCS • FRN
HAMPTON see **MURDER OF FRED HAMPTON, THE** • 1971
HAMPTON COURT PALACE • 1926 • Cann Bert • UKN
HAMRAAZ • 1967 • Chopra B. R. • IND • MY SECRET
HAMRAHI see **HUMRAHI** • 1945
HAM'S BUSY DAY • 1916 • Edwards Harry J. • SHT • USA
HAM'S EASY EATS • 1915 • *Hamilton Lloyd V.* • USA
HAM'S HARROWING DUEL • 1915 • *Hamilton Lloyd V.* • USA
HAM'S STRATEGY • 1916 • *Hamilton Lloyd V.* • USA
HAM'S WATERLOO • 1916 • Edwards Harry J. • SHT • USA
HAM'S WHIRLWIND FINISH • 1916 • *Hamilton Lloyd V.* • USA
HAMSAFAR • 1974 • *Vossoughi Behrooz* • IRN • VOYAGE COMPANION, THE
HAMSIN see **KHAMSIN** • 1982
HAMSTER, THE see **KRECEK** • 1946
HAMSTER OF HAPPINESS, THE • 1979 • Ashby Hal • USA • SECOND-HAND HEARTS
HAMZA'S SUITCASE see **SHANTET HAMZA** • 1967
HAN CHRISTIAN ANDERSEN (USA) see **MR. H.C. ANDERSEN** • 1950
HAN DE WIT • 1989 • Ranzijn Joost • NTH
HAN GLOMDE HENNEALDRIG • 1952 • Spafford Robert B., Lindberg Sven • SWD • LONG SEARCH, THE (USA) ○ MEMORY OF LOVE
HAN, HON OCH PENGARNA • 1936 • Henrikson Anders • SWD • HE, SHE AND THE MONEY
HAN, HUN OG HAMLET • 1933 • Lauritzen Lau • DNM
HAN MATADO A TONGOLELE • 1948 • Gavaldon Roberto • MXC
HAN MATADO A UN CADAVER • 1960 • Salvador Julio • SPN
HAN ROBADO UNA ESTRELLA • 1961 • Seto Javier • SPN
HAN SOM KLARA BOVEN • 1935 • Soderholm Oscar • SWD
HANA • 1941 • Yoshimura Kozaburo • JPN • BLOSSOM ○ FLOWER
HANA • 1967 • Kuri Yoji • ANS • JPN • FLOWER, THE
HANA HIRAKU • 1948 • Ichikawa Kon • JPN • FLOWER BLOOMS, A
HANA ICHIMOMME • 1985 • Ito Toshiya • JPN • LIFE WITH SENILITY
HANA NO BOJO • 1958 • Suzuki Hideo • JPN • FLOWER, THE
HANA NO DAISHOGAI • 1959 • Shima Koji • JPN • VARIOUS FLOWERS
HANA NO KODOKAN • 1953 • Mori Issei • JPN • RISE OF KODOKAN, THE
HANA NO KOIBITOTACHI • 1968 • Saito Takeichi • JPN • SWEET INTERNS, THE
HANA NO NAGADOSU • 1954 • Kinugasa Teinosuke • JPN • END OF A PROLONGED JOURNEY
HANA NO NAKA NO MUSUMETACHI • 1953 • Yamamoto Kajiro • JPN • GIRLS AMONG THE FLOWERS
HANA NO OEDO MUSEKININ • 1965 • Yamamoto Kajiro • JPN • SAMURAI JOKER
HANA NO SUGAO • 1949 • Shibuya Minoru • JPN • FACE OF A FLOWER
HANA NO UTAGE • 1967 • Ichimura Hirokazu • JPN • FALLING BLOSSOMS
HANA NO YOSHIWARA HYAKUNIN-GIRI • 1960 • Uchida Tomu • JPN • MURDER IN YOSHIWARA
HANA NO YUKYO-DEN • 1958 • Yasuda Kimiyoshi • JPN
HANA NOREN • 1959 • Toyoda Shiro • JPN
HANA O KUU MUSHI • 1967 • Nishimura Shogoro • JPN • BURNING NATURE
HANA SAKU MINATO • 1943 • Kinoshita Keisuke • JPN • BLOSSOMING PORT, THE
HANA TO ARASHI TO GANG • 1961 • Ishii Teruo • JPN • FLOWER, STORM AND GANG
HANA TO DOTO • 1964 • Suzuki Kiyonori • JPN
HANA TO KAIJITSU • 1967 • Morinaga Kenjiro • JPN • SUNLIGHT AND SHADOWS
HANA TO MOGURA • 1969 • Okamoto Tadanari • ANS • JPN • FLOWERS AND MOLES
HANA TO NAMIDA TO HONOO • 1970 • Inoue Umeji • JPN • PERFORMERS, THE (USA)
HANA TO RYU • 1962 • Masuda Toshio • JPN • MAN WITH A DRAGON TATTOO
HANAFUDA TOSEI • 1967 • Narusawa Masashige • JPN • CARDS ARE MY LIFE
HANAKOGO NO UTA • 1937 • Gosho Heinosuke • JPN • SONG OF A FLOWER BASKET ○ SONG OF THE FLOWER BASKET
HANAKURABE TANUKI DOCHU • 1961 • Tanaka Tokuzo • JPN • TANUKI VAGABONDS
HANAMUKO NO NEGOTO • 1934 • Gosho Heinosuke • JPN • BRIDEGROOM TALKS IN HIS SLEEP, A ○ SLEEPING WORDS OF THE BRIDEGROOM
HANANE KADIET EL YOM • 1944 • Salim Kamel • EGY • PROBLEM OF THE DAY, THE
HANANO IROMICHI • 1967 • Ogawa Kinya • JPN • LOVE TECHNIQUE OF FLOWERS
HANAOKA SEISHU NO TSUMA • 1967 • Masumura Yasuzo • JPN • WIFE OF SEISHU HANAOKA, THE ○ SEISHU HANAOKA'S WIFE
HANAORI • 1968 • Kawamoto Kihachiro • ANS • JPN • BREAKING OF BRANCHES IS FORBIDDEN ○ BREAKING BRANCHES IS FORBIDDEN ○ TEARING OF BRANCHES PROHIBITED
HANARE GOZE, ORIN • 1978 • Shinoda Masahiro • JPN • BANISHED (USA) ○ ORIN, A BLIND WOMAN ○ BALLAD OF ORIN, THE ○ BANISHED ORIN ○ MELODY IN GRAY
HANAREBA ONNANAREBA • 1952 • *Yamada Isuzu* • JPN • BECAUSE OF MOTHER BECAUSE OF WOMAN
HANASAKA JIJII • 1923 • Kinugasa Teinosuke • JPN
HANAUMA BAY • 1985 • Wallace Tommy Lee • USA • MADE IN HAWAII
HANAUTA OJOSAN • 1938 • Shibuya Minoru • JPN • HUMMING GIRL, A
HANAYAHANARU SHOTAI • 1968 • Yamamoto Kunihiko • JPN • LAVISH INVITATION, A
HANAYOME BOSHUCHU • 1957 • Nomura Yoshitaro • JPN
HANAYOME NO MINE, CHOGOLISA • 1959 • Horiba Nobuyo • JPN • CHOGOLISA, THE BRIDE'S PEAK
HANAYOME NO NEGOTO • 1933 • Gosho Heinosuke • JPN • SLEEPING WORDS OF THE BRIDE ○ BRIDE TALKS IN HER SLEEP, THE
HANAYOME RIKKOHO • 1957 • Harada Hasuo • JPN
HANAYOME-SAN WA SEKAI ICHI • 1959 • Shindo Kaneto • JPN • BRIDE FROM JAPAN, THE ○ WORLD'S BEST BRIDE, THE
HANAYOME SANJUSO • 1958 • Honda Inoshiro • JPN
HANAYOME WA DOKONI IRU • 1956 • Nomura Yoshitaro • JPN • LOOK FOR YOUR BRIDE
HAND, THE • 1960 • Cass Henry • UKN
HAND, THE • 1977 • Godfrey Bob • ANS • UKN
HAND, THE • 1981 • Stone Oliver • USA
HAND, THE see **RUKA** • 1964
HAND, THE see **MAIN, LA** • 1969
HAND ACROSS THE CRADLE • 1911 • *Nestor* • USA
HAND AM VORHANG, DIE • 1915 • Mack Max • FRG
HAND AT THE WINDOW, THE • 1915 • Weston Charles • UKN
HAND AT THE WINDOW, THE • 1918 • Wells Raymond • USA
HAND BAG, THE • 1912 • *Finch Flora* • USA
HAND BELL, THE • 1909 • *Gaumont* • FRN
HAND DES SCHICKSALS • 1919 • Zwingenburg L. M. • AUS
HAND DES WURGERS, DIE • 1920 • Eichgrun Bruno • FRG
HAND IN HAND • 1960 • Leacock Philip • UKN • STAR AND THE CROSS, THE
HAND IN HAND see **KEZENFOGVA** • 1963
HAND IN HAND see **CODO CON CODO** • 1967
HAND IN THE TRAP, THE see **MANO EN LA TRAMPA, LA** • 1961
HAND INVISIBLE, THE • 1919 • Hoyt Harry O. • USA
HAND ME A COUNT see **FLY MEJ EN GREVE** • 1959
HAND-ME-DOWN SUIT, A see **UBRANIE PRAWIE NOWE** • 1963
HAND MOVIE • 1968 • Rainer Yvonne • SHT • USA
HAND OF A CHILD, THE • 1913 • Noy Wilfred • UKN
HAND OF A DEAD MAN, THE see **MANO DE UN HOMBRE MUERTO, EL** • 1963
HAND OF ADAM, THE • 1975 • Grigor Murray • DCS • UKN
HAND OF DEATH • 1962 • Nelson Gene • USA • FIVE FINGERS OF DEATH
HAND OF DESTINY, THE • 1912 • *Pathe* • USA
HAND OF DESTINY, THE • 1913 • *Kalem* • USA
HAND OF DESTINY, THE • 1914 • Mackenzie Donald • USA
HAND OF FATE, THE • 1908 • *Lubin* • USA
HAND OF FATE, THE • 1910 • *Vitagraph* • USA
HAND OF FATE, THE • 1912 • *Gordon Phyllis* • USA
HAND OF FATE, THE • 1913 • *Essanay* • USA
HAND OF FATE, THE • 1914 • *Hollister Alice* • USA
HAND OF FATE, THE • 1920 • Angeles Bert • SHT • USA
HAND OF GOD, THE • 1915 • Lambart Harry • USA
HAND OF HORROR, THE • 1914 • Seay Charles M. • USA
HAND OF IRON, THE • 1914 • West Langdon • USA
HAND OF LUCK see **LYOGKAYA RUKA** • 1967
HAND OF MYSTERY, THE • 1912 • *Sorelle William* • USA
HAND OF NAHAWEE, THE • 1915 • Warren Giles R. • USA
HAND OF NIGHT, THE • 1966 • Goode Frederic • UKN • BEAST OF MOROCCO
HAND OF PERIL, THE • 1916 • Tourneur Maurice • USA
HAND OF POWER, THE • 1970 • Vohrer Alfred • FRG
HAND OF PROVIDENCE, THE • 1910 • *Atlas* • USA
HAND OF PROVIDENCE, THE • 1913 • *Crystal* • USA
HAND OF THE ARTIST, THE • 1906 • Booth W. R. • UKN
HAND OF THE GALLOWS see **BANDE DES SCHRECKENS, DIE** • 1960
HAND OF THE HEIRESS, THE • 1910 • *Lubin* • USA
HAND OF THE HUN, THE • 1917 • Pastrone Giovanni • ITL
HAND OF THE LAW • 1913 • *Warner'S Features* • USA
HAND OF THE LAW, THE • 1915 • Taylor Edward C. • USA
HAND OF THE SKELETON, THE see **MAIN DU SQUELETTE, LA** • 1915
HAND OF UNCLE SAM, THE • 1910 • *Kerrigan J. Warren* • USA
HAND ORGAN MAN, THE • 1909 • Olcott Sidney • USA
HAND-PAINTED ABSTRACTION • 1933 • McLaren Norman, McAllister Stewart • ANS • UKN
HAND PRINT MYSTERY, THE • 1914 • Vignola Robert G. • USA
HAND THAT ROCKS THE CRADLE, THE • 1914 • *Stonehouse Ruth* • USA
HAND THAT ROCKS THE CRADLE, THE • 1917 • Weber Lois, Smalley Phillips • USA
HAND THAT RULES THE WORLD, THE • 1914 • *August Edwin* • USA
HAND-TINTING • 1967 • Wieland Joyce • SHT • USA
HAND TO HAND see **MANO A MANO** • 1932
HANDAYA • 1980 • Thotawatte Titus • SLN
HANDCUFF MYSTERY SOLVED, THE • 1905 • *Walturdaw* • UKN
HANDCUFFED • 1929 • Worne Duke • USA
HANDCUFFED ANGEL, THE see **KELEPCELI MELEK** • 1967
HANDCUFFED FOR LIFE • 1913 • *Solax* • USA
HANDCUFFS see **TEJO MUYO** • 1969
HANDCUFFS see **LISICE** • 1970
HANDCUFFS OR KISSES • 1921 • Archainbaud George • USA
HANDE • 1928 • Simon Stella, Bandy Miklos • SHT • FRG • HANDS (USA) ○ BALLET OF HANDS
HANDE AUS DEM DUNKEL • 1933 • Waschneck Erich • FRG
HANDE HOCH • 1942 • Weidenmann Alfred • FRG
HANDE HOCH 1 • 1921 • Neff Wolfgang • FRG
HANDE HOCH 2 • 1921 • Neff Wolfgang • FRG
HANDE HOCH, HIER EDDY POLO • 1928 • Lasko Leo • FRG
HANDELEN MED MENNESKELIV • 1915 • Davidsen Hjalmar • DNM
HANDFUL OF CLOUDS, A (UKN) see **DOORWAY TO HELL, THE** • 1930
HANDFUL OF DUST • 1973 • Keenan Haydn, Kuyululu Ayten • SHT • ASL
HANDFUL OF DUST, A • 1988 • Sturridge Charles • UKN, USA
HANDFUL OF GRAIN • 1959 • Khan Mehboob • IND
HANDFUL OF JELLY BABIES, A • 1977 • Turkiewicz Sophia • SHT • USA
HANDFUL OF LOVE, A see **HANDFULL KARLEK, EN** • 1973
HANDFUL OF PARADISE, A see **BIR AVUC CENNET** • 1985
HANDFUL OF RICE, A see **MAN OCH KVINNA** • 1939
HANDFUL OF SKY, A see **BIR AVUC GOKYUZU** • 1987
HANDFUL OF TIME, A see **HANDFULL TID, EN** • 1988
HANDFULL KARLEK, EN • 1973 • Sjoman Vilgot • SWD • HANDFUL OF LOVE, A
HANDFULL TID, EN • 1988 • Asphaug Martin • NRW • FISTFUL OF TIME, A ○ HANDFUL OF TIME, A

HANDGUN • 1983 • Garnett Tony • USA • DEEP IN THE HEART
HANDICAP, THE • 1912 • *King Burton* • USA
HANDICAP, THE • 1925 • *Phil Goldstone Prod.* • USA
HANDICAP DER LIEBE, DAS • 1921 • Hartwig Martin • FRG
HANDICAP OF BEAUTY, THE • 1915 • *Falstaff* • USA
HANDICAP PICTURES see **HANDICAPBILLEDER** • 1986
HANDICAPBILLEDER • 1986 • Korst Stine • DCS • DNM • HANDICAP PICTURES
HANDICAPPED FUTURE see **BEHINDERTE ZUKUNFT** • 1971
HANDKUSS, DER • 1979 • Seiler Alexander J. • SWT
HANDLAR OM KARLEK, DET see **MELODI OM VAREN, EN** • 1943
HANDLE WITH CARE • 1912 • *Quirk Billy* • USA
HANDLE WITH CARE • 1914 • *Royal* • USA
HANDLE WITH CARE • 1922 • Rosen Phil • USA
HANDLE WITH CARE • 1932 • Butler David • USA
HANDLE WITH CARE • 1935 • Davis Redd • UKN • LOOK OUT MR. HAGGIS
HANDLE WITH CARE • 1952 • Hughes Geoffrey • UKN
HANDLE WITH CARE • 1958 • Friedkin David • USA • MOCK TRIAL
HANDLE WITH CARE • 1964 • McCarthy John K. • USA
HANDLE WITH CARE • 1972 • *Mark Robert*
HANDLE WITH CARE • 1986 • Cox Paul • DOC • ASL
HANDLE WITH CARE see **ONE WILD NIGHT** • 1938
HANDLE WITH CARE see **CITIZEN'S BAND** • 1977
HANDLEBARS • 1933 • White Jules • SHT • USA
HANDLER DER VIER JAHRESZEITEN, DER • 1971 • Fassbinder R. W. • FRG • MERCHANT OF THE FOUR SEASONS, THE ○ MERCHANT OF FOUR SEASONS, THE
HANDLING • 1946 • Mulholland Donald • SHT • CND • TRAVAIL MANUEL
HANDLING SHIPS • 1946 • Halas John, Batchelor Joy • ANM • UKN
HANDMAIDENS OF GOD, THE see **SERVANTES DU BON DIEU, LES** • 1978
HANDMAID'S TALE, THE • 1989 • Schlondorff Volker • FRG, USA
HANDS • Shaw-Smith David • DSS • IRL
HANDS • 1961 • Heyer John • SHT • ASL
HANDS, THE see **CHERIA, TA** • 1962
HANDS ACROSS THE BORDER • 1926 • Kirkland David • USA
HANDS ACROSS THE BORDER • 1944 • Kane Joseph • USA
HANDS ACROSS THE OCEAN • 1946 • Myers Gordon • UKN
HANDS ACROSS THE ROCKIES • 1941 • Hillyer Lambert • USA
HANDS ACROSS THE SEA • 1912 • Mervale Gaston • ASL
HANDS ACROSS THE SEA IN '76 • 1911 • Slavin James • USA
HANDS ACROSS THE TABLE • 1935 • Leisen Mitchell • USA
HANDS DOWN • 1918 • Julian Rupert • USA
HANDS IN HARMONY • 1950 • Blais Roger • DCS • CND • NEIL CHOTEM AU CLAVIER
HANDS IN HARMONY see **TALKING HANDS** • 1936
HANDS IN THE DARK • 1917 • McRae Henry • SHT • USA
HANDS INVISIBLE • 1914 • *Powers* • USA
HANDS, KNEES AND BUMPS A DAISY • 1969 • Dunning George • ANM • UKN
HANDS OF A KILLER (UKN) see **PIANETI CONTRO DI NOI, I** • 1961
HANDS OF A STRANGER • 1962 • Arnold Newt • USA • ANSWER, THE
HANDS OF A STRANGER • 1987 • Elikann Larry • TVM • USA
HANDS OF A STRANGLER see **MAINS D'ORLAC, LES** • 1959
HANDS OF A WIZARD, THE • 1908 • Booth W. R. • UKN
HANDS OF CORMAC JOYCE • 1972 • Cook Fielder • TVM • USA, ASL
HANDS OF MAN, THE • Sefranka Bruno • CZC
HANDS OF MENACE (UKN) see **TERROR TRAIL** • 1946
HANDS OF NARA, THE • 1922 • Garson Harry • USA
HANDS OF ORLAC, THE (UKN) see **MAINS D'ORLAC, LES** • 1959
HANDS OF ORLAC, THE (USA) see **ORLACS HANDE** • 1925
HANDS OF ORLAC (UKN) see **MAD LOVE** • 1935
HANDS OF SPACE • 1961 • SAF
HANDS OF STEEL • 1986 • Dolman Martin • ITL • FISTS OF STEEL
HANDS OF THE FLAG • 1901 • *Mitchell & Kenyon* • UKN
HANDS OF THE RIPPER • 1971 • Sasdy Peter • UKN
HANDS OFF • 1921 • Marshall George • USA
HANDS OFF • 1927 • Laemmle Ernst • USA
HANDS OFF GRETEL! (UKN) see **HANSEL UND GRETEL VERLIEFEN SICH IM WALD** • 1970
HANDS OFF THE LOOT see **TOUCHEZ PAS AU GRISBI** • 1953
HANDS ON THE CITY see **MANI SULLA CITTA, LE** • 1963
HANDS ON THE TOWN see **MANI SULLA CITTA, LE** • 1963
HANDS OVER THE CITY (USA) see **MANI SULLA CITTA, LE** • 1963
HANDS TO WORK see **MANOS A LA OBRA**
HANDS UP • 1917 • Browning Tod • USA
HANDS UP • 1918 • Horne James W., Gasnier Louis J.(Spv) • SRL • USA
HANDS UP • 1920 • *West Billy* • SHT • USA
HANDS UP! • 1926 • Badger Clarence • USA
HANDS UP! see **RECE DO GORY** • 1967
HANDS UP!: OR, CAPTURED BY HIGHWAYMEN • 1904 • Collins Alf • UKN
HANDS (USA) see **HANDE** • 1928
HANDSCHIFT DES INKA, DIE • 1925 • Bock-Stieber Gernot • FRG
HANDSOME see **POGI** • 1967
HANDSOME ANTONIO see **BELL'ANTONIO, IL** • 1960
HANDSOME ARNE AND ROSA see **SMUKKE-ARNE OG ROSA** • 1967
HANDSOME AUGUSTA see **STILIGA AUGUSTA** • 1946
HANDSOME BOY TRYING TO RULE THE WORLD see **TENKA O NERU BISHONEN** • 1955
HANDSOME BRUTE, THE • 1925 • Eddy Robert • USA
HANDSOME DOZEN, THE see **POGI DOZEN, THE** • 1967
HANDSOME DRAGOON'S MATCH, THE • 1970 • Sequens Jiri • CZC
HANDSOME HARRY MINDS THE SHOP • 1914 • *Melies* • USA
HANDSOME PRIEST, THE see **PRETE BELLO, IL** • 1990
HANDSOME STRANGER see **CHAAN PARDESSE** • 1981
HANDSOME, THE UGLY, THE STUPID, THE see **BELLO, IL BRUTO, IL CRETINO, IL** • 1967
HANDSOMER MAN, THE • 1911 • *Vitagraph* • USA
HANDSWORTH SONGS • 1987 • Akomfrah John • UKN
HANDVOLL HELDEN, EINE see **LETZTE KOMPANIE, DIE** • 1967
HANDVOLL NOTEN, EINE • 1961 • Schneidereit Otto, Spiess Helmut • GDR
HANDVOLL RIS, EN see **MAN OCH KVINNA** • 1939
HANDVOLL ZARTLICHKEIT, EINE • 1972 • van Ackeren Robert • FRG
HANDWRITTEN • 1959 • Boultenhouse Charles • SHT • USA
HANDY ANDY • 1921 • Wynne Bert • UKN
HANDY ANDY • 1934 • Butler David • USA • MERRY ANDREW
HANDY ANDY THE CLUMSY SERVANT • 1901 • *Paul R. W.* • UKN
HANDY HENRY • 1917 • Drew Sidney • SHT • USA
HANDY MAN, THE • 1918 • Parrott Charles • SHT • USA
HANDY MAN, THE • 1920 • Forde Walter • UKN
HANDY MAN, THE • 1923 • Kerr Robert • USA
HANDY MAN AROUND THE HOUSE, A • 1919 • *Briggs Comedies* • SHT • USA
HANDYMAN, THE see **HOMME A TOUT FAIRE, L'** • 1980
HANECH'SHEKET see **AHAVA BANAMAL** • 1967
HANEDA HATSU 7H 50 • 1958 • Masuda Toshio • JPN
HANG 'EM HIGH • 1968 • Post Ted • USA
HANG LOOSE • 1970 • *Rap* • USA
HANG ON COWBOY • 1916 • Fielding Romaine • SHT • USA
HANG ON, DOGGY see **TECI, TECI, KUZA MOJ** • 1977
HANG-SHENG, MY SON see **WO ERH HAN-SHENG** • 1985
HANG TOUGH see **HOTSHOT** • 1987
HANG UP! • 1989 • Chan Pauline • SHT • ASL
HANG-UP, THE • 1969 • Hayes John • USA
HANG YOUR HAT ON THE WIND • 1969 • Lansburgh Larry • USA
HANGAR 18 • 1980 • Conway James L. • USA • INVASION FORCE
HANGED MAN, THE • 1965 • Siegel Don • TVM • USA
HANGED MAN, THE • 1974 • Caffey Michael • TVM • USA
HANGED MAN, THE • 1976 • Zeillemakers Meino • NTH
HANGED MAN'S FARM see **FERME DU PENDU, LA** • 1945
HANGGANAN NG MATATAPANG • 1967 • Amigo Rey • PHL • END OF THE BRAVE
HANGI HORA • 1968 • Jayakody Rohini • SLN • HIDE AND SEEK
HANGING A PICTURE • 1915 • *Williams Eric* • UKN
HANGING BY A THREAD • 1979 • Fenady George • TVM • USA
HANGING FIRE • 1926 • Roberts Stephen • SHT • USA
HANGING JUDGE, THE • 1918 • Edwards Henry • UKN
HANGING JUDGE, THE see **LIFE AND TIMES OF JUDGE ROY BEAN, THE** • 1972
HANGING LAMP, THE • 1908 • *Pathe* • FRN
HANGING OF JAKE ELLIS, THE • 1969 • Hearn J. Van • USA • CALICO QUEEN, THE
HANGING ON A KNIFE see **KAPIT SA PATALIM** • 1984
HANGING ON TO THIN AIR see **DRZANJE ZA VAZDUH** • 1985
HANGING OUT THE CLOTHES: OR, MASTER, MISTRESS AND MAID • 1898 • Smith G. A. • UKN
HANGING RAIN • 1935 • Heale Patrick K. • UKN
HANGING STOCKINGS ON A CHRISTMAS TREE see **NIGHT BEFORE CHRISTMAS, THE** • 1905
HANGING TREE • 1958 • Godfrey Bob • SHT • UKN
HANGING TREE, THE • 1959 • Daves Delmer • USA
HANGING WOMAN, THE • 1971 • Davidson John • SPN
HANGMAN • 1964 • Goldman Les, Julian Paul • ANS • USA
HANGMAN, THE • 1959 • Curtiz Michael • USA
HANGMAN, THE see **VERDUGO, EL** • 1964
HANGMAN, THE see **MAJSTER KAT** • 1965
HANGMAN OF LONDON, THE see **HENKER VON LONDON, DER** • 1963
HANGMAN OF ST. MARIEN, THE see **HENKER VON SANKT MARIEN, DER** • 1920
HANGMAN OF VENICE, THE see **BOIA DI VENEZIA, IL** • 1964
HANGMAN WAITS, THE • 1947 • Barr-Smith A. • UKN
HANGMANS HOUSE • 1928 • Ford John • USA
HANGMAN'S KNOT • 1952 • Huggins Roy • USA
HANGMAN'S NOOSE see **OCTOBER MAN, THE** • 1947
HANGMAN'S WHARF • 1950 • Williamson Cecil H. • UKN
HANGMEN • 1987 • Ingvordsen J. Christian • USA
HANGMEN ALSO DIE • 1943 • Lang Fritz • USA • LEST WE FORGET
HANGMEN, WOMEN AND SOLDIERS (USA) see **HENKER, FRAUEN UND SOLDATEN** • 1935
HANGOVER see **BAKSMALLA** • 1973
HANGOVER SQUARE • 1945 • Brahm John • USA
HANGSA – MITHUN • 1968 • Chowdhury Partha Pratim • IND • DUCK AND SWAN
HANGUP • 1974 • Hathaway Henry • USA • SUPER DUDE
HANGYABOLY • 1971 • Fabri Zoltan • HNG • ANT'S NEST
HANGYAKU • 1967 • Matsuo Akinori • JPN • DEBT OF BLOOD, THE
HANGYAKUJI • 1961 • Ito Daisuke • JPN • CONSPIRATOR, THE
HANIBALOVE ALPE • 1969 • Grgic Zlatko, Kolar Boris, Zaninovic Ante • ANS • YGS, FRG • LIGHTHOUSE KEEPING
HANIN • 1971 • Francis Yussif • SHT • EGY • NOSTALGIE
HANIN AL-ARD • 1971 • Jamil Mohammed Shoukry • SHT • IRQ • NOSTALGIE DE LA TERRE ○ AMOUR DE LA TERRE
HANJO see **HANNYO** • 1961
HANK • 1977 • Haldane Don • MTV • CND
HANK AND MARY WITHOUT APOLOGIES • 1970 • Higgins Dick • SHT • USA
HANK, HENNERY AND FRIEND • 1976 • SAF
HANK WILLIAMS "THE SHOW HE NEVER GAVE" • 1982 • Acomba David • CND
HANKA • 1955 • Vorkapich Slavko • YGS
HANKY PANKY • 1982 • Poitier Sidney • USA
HANKY PANKY CARDS • 1907 • Booth W. R. • UKN
HANLON: IN DEFENCE OF MINNIE DEAN • 1984 • Tourell Wayne • TVM • NZL • DEFENCE OF MINNIE DEAN, THE
HANNA • 1989 • Mann Michael • USA
HANNA see **HANNA K** • 1983
HANNA AMON • 1951 • Harlan Veit • FRG
HANNA I SOCIETEN • 1940 • Olsson Gunnar • SWD • HANNA IN SOCIETY
HANNA IN SOCIETY see **HANNA I SOCIETEN** • 1940
HANNA K • 1983 • Costa-Gavras • FRN • HANNA
HANNA MONSTER, DARLING see **HANNA MONSTER, LIEBLING** • 1988
HANNA MONSTER, LIEBLING • 1988 • Berger Christian • AUS • HANNA MONSTER, DARLING
HANNAH AND HER SISTERS • 1985 • Allen Woody • USA
HANNAH DUSTIN • 1908 • Olcott Sidney • USA
HANNAH LEE see **OUTLAW TERRITORY** • 1953
HANNAH, QUEEN OF THE VAMPIRES see **CRYPT OF THE LIVING DEAD** • 1973
HANNAH WON'T YOU OPEN THAT DOOR • 1909 • *Warwick Trading Co.* • UKN
HANNAH'S HENPECKED HUSBAND • 1915 • *Hasting Carey L.* • USA
HANNA'S WAR • 1988 • Golan Menahem • USA • HANNA'S WAR ○ INNOCENT HEROES
HANNA'S WAR see **HANNA'S WAR** • 1988
HANNE • 1975 • van der Heijden Maartje • SHT • NTH
HANNELES HIMMELFAHRT • 1922 • Gad Urban • FRG
HANNELES HIMMELFAHRT • 1934 • von Harbou Thea • FRG
HANNEMANN, ACH HANNEMANN • 1919 • *Bender Henry* • FRG
HANNERL • 1952 • Marischka Ernst • AUS • ICH TANZE MIR DIR IN DEN HIMMEL HINEIN
HANNERL UND IHRE LIEBHABER • 1921 • Basch Felix • FRG
HANNERL UND IHRE LIEBHABER • 1935 • Hochbaum Werner • AUS
HANNERL VOM ROLANDSBOGEN, DAS • 1928 • Neff Wolfgang • FRG
HANNIBAL • 1973 • Koller Xavier • SWT
HANNIBAL see **ANNIBALE** • 1959
HANNIBAL BROOKS • 1969 • Winner Michael • UKN
HANNIBAL TANAR UR • 1956 • Fabri Zoltan • HNG • PROFESSOR HANNIBAL
HANNIE CAULDER • 1971 • Kennedy Burt • UKN
HANNIGAN'S HAREM • 1913 • *Patheplay* • USA
HANNO CAMBIATO FACCIO • 1971 • Farina Corrado • ITL • THEY'VE CHANGED FACES
HANNO RAPITO UN UOMO • 1937 • Righelli Gennaro • ITL
HANNO RUBATO UN TRAM • 1955 • Bonnard Mario • ITL
HANNYO • 1961 • Nakamura Noboru • JPN • WOMEN OF TOKYO ○ HANJO
HANOI HILTON see **HANOI HOTEL, THE** • 1987
HANOI HOTEL, THE • 1987 • Chetwynd Lionel • USA • HANOI HILTON
HANOI, MARTES TRECE • 1967 • Alvarez Santiago • DOC • CUB • HANOI, TUESDAY 13TH (UKN)
HANOI, TUESDAY 13TH (UKN) see **HANOI, MARTES TRECE** • 1967
HANOSHRIM • 1984 • Hirshorn Marian • DOC • DNM
HANOVER STREET • 1979 • Hyams Peter • USA
HANRAN • 1954 • Saburi Shin • JPN • REBELLION
HANRAN • 1959 • Masumura Yasuzo • JPN • CAST-OFF, THE
HANS AND GRETHE see **HANS OG GRETHE** • 1913
HANS AND HIS BOSS • 1915 • Ransom Charles • USA
HANS BRINKER • 1979 • Scheerer Robert • USA • HANS BRINKER AND THE SILVER SKATES ○ SILVER SKATES, THE ○ HANS BRINKER OF THE SILVER SKATES
HANS BRINKER AND THE SILVER SKATES see **HANS BRINKER** • 1979
HANS BRINKER OF THE SILVER SKATES see **HANS BRINKER** • 1979
HANS BRINKER, OR, THE SILVER SKATES • 1962 • Foster Norman • USA, SWD
HANS BROLLOPSNATT • 1916 • Stiller Mauritz • SWD • HIS WEDDING NIGHT ○ ADVENTURE, THE ○ AVENTYRET
HANS CHRISTIAN AND THE GEOGRAPHIC SOCIETY • 1980 • Forsberg Lars Lennart • MTV • SWD
HANS CHRISTIAN ANDERSEN • 1952 • Vidor Charles • USA • HANS CHRISTIAN ANDERSEN.. AND THE DANCER
HANS CHRISTIAN ANDERSEN.. AND THE DANCER see **HANS CHRISTIAN ANDERSEN** • 1952
HANS CHRISTIAN ANDERSEN FAIRY TALES • 1952 • Brooks Thor L. • SHS • DNM
HANS DIE SKIPPER • 1953 • SAF
HANS EN DIE ROINEK • 1961 • SAF
HANS ENGELSKA FRU • 1927 • Molander Gustaf • SWD • HIS ENGLISH WIFE
HANS FADERS BROTT • 1915 • Magnussen Fritz • SWD • HIS FATHER'S CRIME
HANS FORSTE HONORAR see **FORSTE HONORAR, DET** • 1912
HANS GODE GENIUS • 1920 • Blom August • DNM • MOD STJERNERNE ○ HIS GUARDIAN ANGEL
HANS, HEIN UND HENNY • 1914 • Biebrach Rudolf • FRG
HANS, HET LEVEN VOOR DE DOOD • 1983 • van Gasteren Louis A. • DOC • NTH • HANS, LIFE BEFORE DEATH
HANS HUSTRUS FORFLUTNA • 1915 • Stiller Mauritz • SWD • HIS WIFE'S PAST
HANS IM GLUCK • 1936 • Herlth Robert, Rohrig Walter • FRG
HANS IM GLUCK • 1938 • Richter Hans • SWT
HANS IM GLUCK • 1949 • Hamel Peter • FRG
HANS IN ALLEN GASSEN • 1930 • Froelich Carl • FRG
HANS IN BALANS • 1970 • Zwartjes Frans • SHT • NTH
HANS KAERESTE • 1916 • Davidsen Hjalmar • DNM
HANS KLUNGE • 1928 • Hylten-Cavallius Ragnar • SWD
HANS LE MARIN • 1948 • Villiers Francois • FRN • WICKED CITY, THE (USA)
HANS, LIFE BEFORE DEATH see **HANS, HET LEVEN VOOR DE DOOD** • 1983
HANS LIVS MATCH • 1932 • Branner Per-Axel • SWD • HIS GREATEST MATCH
HANS MAJESTAT FAR VANTA • 1931 • Berthels Theodor • SWD
HANS MAJESTAT FAR VANTA • 1945 • Edgren Gustaf • SWD • HIS MAJESTY WILL HAVE TO WAIT
HANS MAJESTATS RIVAL • 1943 • Hildebrand Weyler • SWD • HIS MAJESTY'S RIVAL
HANS MEMLING • 1938 • Cauvin Andre • BLG
HANS' MILLIONS • 1911 • *Essanay* • USA

HANS NADS TESTAMENTE • 1919 • Sjostrom Victor • SWD • HIS GRACE'S LAST TESTAMENT (UKN) ○ HIS GRACE'S WILL (USA) ○ WILL OF HIS GRACE, THE
HANS NADS TESTAMENTE • 1940 • Lindberg Per • SWD • HIS GRACE'S WILL
HANS OFFICIELLA FASTMO • 1944 • Jerring Nils • SWD • HIS OFFICIAL FIANCEE
HANS OG GRETHE • 1913 • *Dreyer Carl T.(Sc)* • DNM • HANS AND GRETHE
HANS OHNE TUREN UND FUNSTER, DAS • 1921 • Feher Friedrich • FRG
HANS RIGTIGE KONE • 1917 • Holger-Madsen • DNM • HIS REAL WIFE ○ WHICH IS WHICH
HANS ROCKLE UND DER TEUFEL • 1975 • Kratzert Hans • GDR
HANS STAUB • 1978 • Dindo Richard • DOC • SWT
HANS STORE CHANCE • 1915 • Davidsen Hjalmar • DNM
HANS TRUTZ IM SCHLARAFFENLAND • 1917 • Wegener Paul • FRG
HANS VANSKELIGSTE ROLLE • 1912 • Blom August • DNM • HIS MOST DIFFICULT PART
HANS WESTMAR • 1933 • Wenzler Franz • FRG • HORST WESSEL
HANSA VILAK • 1980 • Bandaranayake Dharmasiri • SLN
HANSEATEN • 1925 • Lamprecht Gerhard • FRG
HANSEL AND GRETEL • 1909 • Dawley J. Searle • USA
HANSEL AND GRETEL • 1923 • *Century* • SHT • USA
HANSEL AND GRETEL • 1933 • *Terry Paul/ Moser Frank (P)* • ANS • USA
HANSEL AND GRETEL • 1934 • Cones James, Cones Nancy Ford • ANM • USA
HANSEL AND GRETEL • 1954 • Paul John • ANM • USA
HANSEL AND GRETEL • 1954 • Reiniger Lotte • ANS • UKN
HANSEL AND GRETEL • 1982 • Frawley James • MTV • USA
HANSEL AND GRETEL • 1987 • Talan Len • UKN, ISR
HANSEL AND GRETEL see **HANSEL UND GRETEL** • 1924
HANSEL AND GRETEL see **MIGHTY MOUSE IN HANSEL AND GRETEL** • 1952
HANSEL AND GRETEL see **JAS I MALGOSIA** • 1959
HANSEL AND GRETEL see **HANSEL UND GRETEL VERLIEFEN SICH IM WALD** • 1970
HANSEL AND GRETEL see **IVICA I MARICA** • 1979
HANSEL AND GRETEL GET LOST IN THE WOODS see **HANSEL UND GRETEL VERLIEFEN SICH IM WALD** • 1970
HANSEL AND GRETEL (USA) see **HANSEL UND GRETEL** • 1954
HANSEL UND GRETEL • 1924 • AUS • STORY OF HANSEL AND GRETEL, THE (UKN) ○ HANSEL AND GRETEL
HANSEL UND GRETEL • 1954 • Janssen Walter • FRG • HANSEL AND GRETEL (USA)
HANSEL UND GRETEL VERLIEFEN SICH IM WALD • 1970 • Gottlieb Franz J. • FRG • HANDS OFF GRETEL! (UKN) ○ HANSEL AND GRETEL ○ HANSEL AND GRETEL GET LOST IN THE WOODS
HANSHOJO • 1953 • *Hidari Sachiko* • JPN • HALF VIRGIN
HANSOM CAB, THE see **AMAKAKI, TO** • 1957
HANSOM CABMAN, THE • 1924 • Edwards Harry J. • USA • BE CAREFUL
HANSOM DRIVER, THE • 1913 • Sennett Mack • USA
HANSOME SERGE see **BEAU SERGE, LE** • 1958
HANSU KURISHITAN ANDERUSAN NO SEKAI • 1968 • Yabuki Kimio • ANM • JPN • WORLD OF HANS CHRISTIAN ANDERSEN, THE (USA)
HANSWURST VON RIGA, DER • 1921 • Prechtl Hanns • FRG
HANTISE, LA • 1912 • Feuillade Louis • FRN
HANTU RIMAU • 1959 • Rao B. N., Krishnan L., Noor S. Roomai • MLY
HANTU SIANG • Badul A. R. • MLY
HANUL DINTRE DEALURI • 1988 • Nicolae Cristiana • RMN • INN AMONG THE HILLS, THE
HANUMAN JANMAN • 1925 • *Hindustan* • IND • BIRTH OF HANUMAN
HANUMAN JANMAN • 1953 • Nene Raja • IND • BIRTH OF HANUMAN
HANUMAN PATEL VIJAY • 1951 • Wadia Homi • IND
HANUMAN VIJAY • 1929 • *British India Film Co* • IND • HANUMAN'S VICTORY
HANUMAN'S VICTORY see **HANUMAN VIJAY** • 1929
HANUMAN'S VICTORY see **JAI HANUMAN** • 1944
HANUMAN'S VICTORY see **JAI HANUMAN** • 1948
HANUSSEN • 1955 • Fischer O. W., Marischka Georg • FRG
HANUSSEN • 1988 • Szabo Istvan • HNG, FRG
HANYATT-HOMLOK • 1984 • Revesz Gyorgy • HNG • HELTER-SKELTER
HANYE • 1983 • *Xu Huanshan* • CHN • CHILLY NIGHT
HANZAI ROKUGOCHI • 1960 • Murayama Mitsuo • JPN
HAP-KI-DO • 1973 • Huang Feng • HKG
HAPAX LEGOMENA I: NOSTALGIA • 1971 • Frampton Hollis • USA
HAPAX LEGOMENA II: POETIC JUSTICE • 1971 • Frampton Hollis • USA
HAPAX LEGOMENA III: CRITICAL MASS • 1972 • Frampton Hollis • USA
HAPAX LEGOMENA IV: TRAVELLING MATTE • 1972 • Frampton Hollis • USA
HAPAX LEGOMENA V: ORDINARY MATTER • 1972 • Frampton Hollis • USA
HAPAX LEGOMENA VI: REMOTE CONTROL • 1972 • Frampton Hollis • USA
HAPAX LEGOMENA VII: SPECIAL EFFECTS • 1972 • Frampton Hollis • USA
HA'PENNY BREEZE • 1950 • Worth Frank, Sharp Don (U/c) • UKN
HAPISHANE GELINI • 1968 • Erakalin Ulku • TRK • PRISON'S BRIDE, THE
HAPLESS END? OR HOW NUMBSKULL EMPTYBROOK WON THE HAND OF SUCH A BEAUTIFUL AND RICH LADY see **HAY ENDKO? ELI KUINKA UUNO TURHAPURO SAI NIIN KAUNIIN JA RIKKAAN VAIMON** • 1977
HAPLESS HAPPENINGS • 1916 • *Heinie & Louie* • USA
HAPPENING • 1967 • Boureau Marc • FRN
HAPPENING, THE see **IT'S WHAT'S HAPPENING** • 1967
HAPPENING, THE see **YEH-CH'IH** • 1980
HAPPENING DER VAMPIRE see **GEBISSEN WIRD NUR NACHTS -HAPPENING DER VAMPIRE** • 1971
HAPPENING IN AFRICA see **AFRICA EROTICA** • 1970
HAPPENING IN CALCUTTA • 1980 • Chandragupta Bansi • DOC • IND
HAPPENING IN WHITE • 1970 • Sachs Gunther • DOC
HAPPENINGS • Godfrey Bob • ANS • UKN
HAPPENINGS I • 1962-64 • Saroff Raymond • SHT • USA
HAPPENINGS II • 1962-64 • Saroff Raymond • SHT • USA
HAPPIDROME • 1943 • Brandon Phil • UKN
HAPPIER MAN, THE • 1915 • *Cummings Irving* • USA
HAPPIEST DAYS OF YOUR LIFE, THE • 1950 • Launder Frank • UKN
HAPPIEST MAN ON EARTH, THE • 1940 • Miller David • SHT • USA
HAPPIEST MARRIED COUPLE IN VIENNA, THE (USA) see **GLUCKLICHSTE EHE DER WELT, DIE** • 1937
HAPPIEST MILLIONAIRE, THE • 1967 • Tokar Norman • USA
HAPPIEST TIME, THE see **MOOISTE TIJD.., DE** • 1963
HAPPILY BURIED • 1939 • Feist Felix E. • SHT • USA
HAPPILY EVER AFTER • 1978 • Scheerer Robert • TVM • USA
HAPPILY EVER AFTER see **C'ERA UNA VOLTA** • 1967
HAPPILY EVER AFTER see **FELIZES PARA SEMPRE** • 1984
HAPPILY UNMARRIED • 1976 • Wheeler Anne • CND
HAPPINESS • 1917 • Barker Reginald • USA
HAPPINESS • 1923 • Vidor King • USA
HAPPINESS see **STCHASTIE** • 1934
HAPPINESS see **SHIAWASE** • 1974
HAPPINESS see **KOFUKU** • 1982
HAPPINESS A LA MODE • 1919 • Edwards Walter • USA
HAPPINESS AHEAD • 1928 • Seiter William A. • USA
HAPPINESS AHEAD • 1934 • LeRoy Mervyn • USA
HAPPINESS C.O.D. • 1935 • Lamont Charles • USA
HAPPINESS CAGE, THE see **MIND SNATCHERS, THE** • 1972
HAPPINESS FOR SALE see **GEKAUFTE GLUCK, DAS** • 1989
HAPPINESS FOR TWO see **SRECA U DVOJE** • 1969
HAPPINESS FOR YOU: SENTIMENTAL BOY see **KIMI NI SHIAWASE O: SENTIMENTAL BOY** • 1967
HAPPINESS IN LOVE see **PREMALO PRAMADAM** • 1967
HAPPINESS IN TWENTY YEARS (UKN) see **BONHEUR DANS 20 ANS, LE** • 1971
HAPPINESS IS A CURIOUS CATCH see **LYKKEN ER EN UNDERLIG FISK** • 1989
HAPPINESS IS A THREE LEGGED DOG • 1967 • Airey Anthony • SHT • ASL
HAPPINESS OF ASYA, THE see **ISTORIA ASI KHYACHINOI, KOTORAYA LYUBILA, DANE VYSHLA ZAMUKH** • 1966
HAPPINESS OF THREE WOMEN, THE • 1917 • Taylor William D. • USA
HAPPINESS OF THREE WOMEN, THE • 1954 • Elvey Maurice • UKN • WISHING WELL (USA)
HAPPINESS OF US ALONE see **NAMONAKU MAZUSHIKU UTSUKUSHIKU** • 1961
HAPPINESS PREFERRED see **OUTCAST, THE** • 1936
HAPPINESS REMEDY, THE • 1931 • Cozine Ray • SHT • USA
HAPPINESS (USA) see **BONHEUR, LE** • 1964
HAPPY • 1934 • Zelnik Friedrich • UKN
HAPPY • 1983 • Philips Lee • TVM • USA
HAPPY ACCIDENT, A • 1909 • *Edison* • USA
HAPPY ALCOHOLIC, THE • 1984 • Francis Karl • UKN
HAPPY ALEXANDER see **ALEXANDRE LE BIENHEUREUX** • 1968
HAPPY AND LUCKY • 1938 • Rasinski Connie • ANS • USA
HAPPY ANNIVERSARY • Chaudhri Amin • USA
HAPPY ANNIVERSARY • 1959 • Miller David • USA
HAPPY ANNIVERSARY see **HEUREUX ANNIVERSAIRE** • 1962
HAPPY AS CAN BE • 1958 • Gold Jack • SHT • UKN
HAPPY AS THE GRASS WAS GREEN • 1973 • Davis Charles • USA • HAZEL'S PEOPLE
HAPPY ASYA see **ISTORIA ASI KHYACHINOI, KOTORAYA LYUBILA, DANE VYSHLA ZAMUKH** • 1966
HAPPY AWAKENING, THE • 1915 • *Alhambra* • USA
HAPPY BIGAMIST see **YIWA LIANGQI** • 1987
HAPPY BIRTHDAY • 1938 • *Mintz Charles (P)* • ANS • USA
HAPPY BIRTHDAY • 1975 • Mehrjui Dariush • IRN
HAPPY BIRTHDAY • 1979 • Bozzetto Bruno • ANM • ITL
HAPPY BIRTHDAY • 1988 • Marshall Andrew, Renwick David • USA
HAPPY BIRTHDAY BLACKIE • 1963 • Leacock Richard • DOC • USA
HAPPY BIRTHDAY, DAVY • 1970 • Fontaine Richard • USA
HAPPY BIRTHDAY, GEMINI • 1980 • Benner Richard • USA
HAPPY BIRTHDAY, MARILYN! see **BOLDOG SZULETESNAPOT MARILYN!** • 1981
HAPPY BIRTHDAY TO ME • 1981 • Thompson J. Lee • USA, CND
HAPPY BIRTHDAY, WANDA JANE • 1971 • Robson Mark • USA
HAPPY BIRTHDAZE • 1943 • Gordon Dan • ANS • USA
HAPPY BUTTERFLY • 1934 • *Mintz Charles (P)* • ANS • USA
HAPPY CANARY, THE see **VESELAYA KANAREIKA** • 1929
HAPPY CIRCUS, THE see **VESELY CIRKUS** • 1951
HAPPY CIRCUS DAYS • 1942 • Rasinski Connie • ANS • USA
HAPPY CLOWN, THE see **TOBO, THE HAPPY CLOWN** • 1965
HAPPY COBBLERS, THE • 1952 • Davis Mannie • ANS • USA
HAPPY COERSION, A • 1914 • *Lester Louise* • USA
HAPPY DAY • 1975 • Voulgaris Pantelis • GRC
HAPPY DAYS • 1920 • *West Billy* • SHT • USA
HAPPY DAYS • 1929 • Stoloff Ben • USA
HAPPY DAYS • 1936 • *Iwerks Ub (P)* • ANS • USA
HAPPY DAYS AND LONELY NIGHTS • 1929 • Aylott Dave, Symmons E. F. • SHT • UKN
HAPPY DAYS ARE HERE AGAIN • 1936 • Lee Norman • UKN • HAPPY DAYS REVUE ○ STAGE FOLK
HAPPY DAYS ARE HERE AGAIN • 1975 • Weisz Frans • NTH
HAPPY DAYS ARE HERE AGAIN see **CHASING RAINBOWS** • 1930
HAPPY DAYS REVUE see **HAPPY DAYS ARE HERE AGAIN** • 1936
HAPPY DAZE • 1919 • Reisner Charles F. • SHT • USA
HAPPY DEATHDAY • 1969 • Cass Henry • UKN
HAPPY DIN DON see **HUANLE DINGDANG** • 1985
HAPPY DIVORCE, A see **LYKKELIG SKILSMISSE, EN** • 1974
HAPPY DOLLARS see **THEY JUST HAD TO GET MARRIED** • 1933
HAPPY DUSTMAN PLAY GOLF, THE • 1914 • Kellino W. P. • UKN
HAPPY DUSTMEN, THE • 1913 • Kellino W. P. • UKN
HAPPY DUSTMEN'S CHRISTMAS, THE • 1914 • Kellino W. P. • UKN
HAPPY END • 1966 • Lipsky Oldrich • CZC • STASTNY KONEC
HAPPY END • 1969 • Donev Donyo • ANS • BUL
HAPPY END see **HAPPY ENDING** • 1958
HAPPY END see **LIETO FINE** • 1983
HAPPY-END AM ATTERSEE see **HAPPY-END AM WORTHERSEE** • 1964
HAPPY-END AM WORTHERSEE • 1964 • Hollmann Hans • FRG, AUS • HAPPY-END AM ATTERSEE
HAPPY END OF A PERFECT DAY • 1914 • *American* • USA
HAPPY ENDING • 1958 • Mimica Vatroslav • ANS • YGS • HAPPY END
HAPPY ENDING • 1968 • Jones Glyn • UKN
HAPPY ENDING see **HAPPY LANDING** • 1938
HAPPY ENDING see **NIGHT OF NIGHTS, THE** • 1940
HAPPY ENDING, THE • 1924 • Cooper George A. • UKN
HAPPY ENDING, THE • 1931 • Webb Millard • UKN
HAPPY ENDING, THE • 1969 • Brooks Richard • USA
HAPPY ENDINGS • 1982 • Black Noel • TVM • USA
HAPPY ENDINGS • 1983 • Thorpe Jerry • TVM • USA
HAPPY EVENT • 1939 • Brunner Patrick • UKN
HAPPY EVENT IN THE POORLUCK FAMILY, A • 1911 • Fitzhamon Lewin • UKN
HAPPY EVER AFTER • 1932 • Stevenson Robert, Martin Paul • UKN
HAPPY EVER AFTER • 1954 • Zampi Mario • UKN • TONIGHT'S THE NIGHT (USA) ○ O'LEARY NIGHT
HAPPY FAMILY • 1946 • Haines Ronald • UKN
HAPPY FAMILY • 1970 • Soloviev Sergei • USS
HAPPY FAMILY see **NINDU SAMSARAM** • 1968
HAPPY FAMILY see **SRECNA PORODICA** • 1981
HAPPY FAMILY, A • 1899 • *Warwick Trading Co.* • UKN
HAPPY FAMILY, A • 1912 • *Imp* • USA
HAPPY FAMILY, A • 1935 • *Mintz Charles (P)* • ANS • USA
HAPPY FAMILY, THE • 1936 • Rogers Maclean • UKN
HAPPY FAMILY, THE • 1952 • Box Muriel • UKN • MR. LORD SAYS NO (USA) ○ LIVE AND LET LIVE
HAPPY FAMILY, THE (UKN) see **MERRY FRINKS, THE** • 1934
HAPPY FAMILY LIFE see **FAMILIENGLUCK** • 1975
HAPPY FANNY FIELDS AND THE FOUR LITTLE DUTCHMEN • 1913 • *Selsior* • UKN
HAPPY GEARS, THE • 1912 • *Starevitch Ladislas (P)* • USS
HAPPY GHOST II • 1985 • Chisium Clifton Ko • CHN
HAPPY GIGOLO, THE see **PASSION HOTEL**
HAPPY GIPSIES..! see **SKUPLJACI PERJA** • 1967
HAPPY GO DUCKY • 1958 • Hanna William, Barbera Joseph • ANS • USA
HAPPY GO LOOPY • 1960 • Hanna William, Barbera Joseph • ANS • USA
HAPPY-GO-LOVELY • 1951 • Humberstone H. Bruce • UKN
HAPPY-GO-LUCKY • 1914 • Young James • USA
HAPPY GO LUCKY • 1943 • Bernhardt Curtis • USA
HAPPY GO LUCKY • 1947 • Rasinski Connie • ANS • USA
HAPPY GO LUCKY see **HALLELUJAH, I'M A BUM** • 1933
HAPPY-GO-LUCKY STATION-MASTER, A see **NONKI EKICHO**
HAPPY-GO-NUTTY • 1944 • Avery Tex • ANS • USA
HAPPY HARMONIES • 1934-37 • *Harman Hugh/ Ising Rudolf (P)* • ASS • USA
HAPPY HAROLD'S HOLIDAY • 1911 • *Walturdaw* • UKN
HAPPY HAUNTING GROUNDS • 1940 • *Terry Paul (P)* • ANS • USA
HAPPY HAWAII • 1928 • *Holmes Burton* • DOC • USA
HAPPY HOBOES • 1933 • Stallings George, Rufle George • ANS • USA
HAPPY HOBO'S HELP • 1911 • *Nestor* • USA
HAPPY HOLIDAY • 1978 • Sanderson Jon • USA
HAPPY HOLIDAYS • 1940 • *Mintz Charles(P)* • ANS • USA
HAPPY HOLLAND • 1952 • Donnelly Eddie • ANS • USA
HAPPY HOME, THE • 1913 • *Pathe* • USA
HAPPY HOMECOMING, COMRADE see **KALI PATRITHA, SYNTROFE** • 1987
HAPPY HOOKER, THE • 1975 • Sgarro Nicholas • USA
HAPPY HOOKER GOES TO HOLLYWOOD, THE • 1980 • Roberts Alan • USA
HAPPY HOOKER GOES TO WASHINGTON, THE • 1977 • Levey William A. • USA
HAPPY HOOLIGAN AND HIS AIRSHIP see **TWENTIETH CENTURY TRAMP, THE** • 1902
HAPPY HOOLIGAN APRIL-FOOLED • 1901 • Porter Edwin S. • USA
HAPPY HOOLIGAN EARNS HIS DINNER • 1903 • *Bitzer Billy (Ph)* • USA
HAPPY HOOLIGAN IN DR. JEKYLL AND MR. ZIP • 1920 • Nolan William • ANS • USA
HAPPY HOOLIGAN SURPRISED • 1901 • Porter Edwin S. • USA
HAPPY HOOLIGAN TURNS BURGLAR • 1902 • Porter Edwin S. • SHT • USA
HAPPY HOUR see **SOUR GRAPES** • 1987
HAPPY HOUSE, THE • 1915 • *Tabor Richard* • USA
HAPPY IN THE MORNING • 1938 • Jackson Pat • DCS • UKN
HAPPY IS THE BRIDE • 1958 • Boulting Roy • UKN
HAPPY JACK, A HERO • 1910 • Powell Frank • USA
HAPPY JOURNEY see **STASTNOU CESTU** • 1943
HAPPY LAND • 1943 • Pichel Irving • USA
HAPPY LANDING • 1934 • *Monogram* • USA • AIR PATROL (UKN)
HAPPY LANDING • 1938 • Del Ruth Roy • USA • HAPPY ENDING
HAPPY LANDING • 1949 • *Terry Paul (P)* • ANS • USA
HAPPY LANDING (UKN) see **FLYING HIGH** • 1931
HAPPY MAN, THE • 1906 • Cooper Arthur • UKN
HAPPY MAN, THE • 1961 • Topaldgikov Stefan • ANS • BUL
HAPPY MASQUERADER, THE • 1916 • Ricketts Thomas • SHT • USA
HAPPY MINUTES OF GEORG HAUSER, THE see **GLUCKLICHEN MINUTEN DES GEORG HAUSER, DIE** • 1974
HAPPY MOTHER'S DAY see **QUINT CITY, U.S.A.** • 1963
HAPPY MOTHER'S DAY, LOVE GEORGE • 1973 • McGavin Darren • USA • RUN, STRANGER, RUN

HAPPY MOTHER'S DAY, MRS. FISHER see **QUINT CITY, U.S.A.** • 1963
HAPPY NAT'S DILEMMA • 1917 • *Sloane W. J.* • SHT • USA
HAPPY NEW YEAR • 1987 • Avildsen John G. • USA
HAPPY NEW YEAR see **SRECNA NOVA** • 1960
HAPPY NEW YEAR! see **BUEK!** • 1979
HAPPY NEW YEAR 1949 see **SRECNA NOVA** • 1986
HAPPY NEW YEAR, A • 1910 • *Walturdaw* • UKN
HAPPY NEW YEAR CAPER, THE see **BONNE ANNEE, LA** • 1973
HAPPY NEW YEAR (USA) see **BONNE ANNEE, LA** • 1973
HAPPY OLD YEAR see **FELIZ AND VELHO** • 1988
HAPPY ONES DIE TWICE, THE see **SRETNI UMIRU DVAPUT** • 1967
HAPPY PAIR, A • 1915 • Wilson Ben • USA
HAPPY PAIR, THE • 1921 • Paul Fred • UKN
HAPPY PILGRIMAGE see **YAJIKITA DOCHUKI** • 1958
HAPPY POLO • 1932 • *Van Beuren* • ANS • USA
HAPPY PRINCE, THE • 1974 • Mills Michael • CND
HAPPY PRISONER, THE • 1924 • Croise Hugh • UKN
HAPPY RASCALS, THE • 1926 • Miller Frank • SER • UKN
HAPPY RASCALS, THE • 1926 • Miller Frank • UKN
HAPPY RETURNS • 1919 • Dillon John Francis • SHT • USA
HAPPY ROAD, THE • 1956 • Kelly Gene • USA
HAPPY SCENES FROM ANIMAL LIFE see **GAUDEAMUS** • 1912
HAPPY SCENES OF THE LIFE OF THE ANIMALS see **GAUDEAMUS** • 1912
HAPPY SCOUNDREL, THE see **GRAN CALAVERA, EL** • 1949
HAPPY SCOUTS • 1938 • Kopietz Fred • ANS • USA
HAPPY SHITS see **LYCKLIGA SKITAR** • 1970
HAPPY SINCE I MET YOU • 1981 • Taylor Baz • MTV • UKN
HAPPY SONG • 1923 • Shimizu Hiroshi • JPN
HAPPY SQUIRRELS • ANS • USS
HAPPY SUNDAY, A see **DOMINGO FELIZ, UN** • 1988
HAPPY THANKSGIVING, A • 1911 • *Reliance* • USA
HAPPY THIEVES, THE • 1962 • Marshall George • USA • OLDEST CONFESSION, THE ○ ONCE A THIEF
HAPPY THO MARRIED • 1935 • Ripley Arthur • SHT • USA
HAPPY THOUGH MARRIED • 1919 • Niblo Fred • USA
HAPPY TIME, THE • 1952 • Fleischer Richard • USA
HAPPY TIMES see **INSPECTOR GENERAL, THE** • 1949
HAPPY TOGETHER • 1988 • Damski Mel • USA
HAPPY TOGETHER see **SEUNG GIN HO** • 1989
HAPPY TOTS, THE • 1939 • Harrison Ben • ANS • USA
HAPPY TOTS' EXPEDITION, THE • 1940 • Harrison Ben • ANS • USA
HAPPY VALLEY • 1952 • Donnelly Eddie • ANS • USA
HAPPY VESTKOPING see **LYCKLIGA VESTKOPING** • 1937
HAPPY VINEYARD, THE see **FROHLICHE WEINBERG, DER** • 1927
HAPPY VINEYARD, THE see **FROHLICHE WEINBERG, DER** • 1952
HAPPY WANDERER, THE (USA) see **FROHLICHE WANDERER, DER** • 1955
HAPPY WARRIOR, THE • 1917 • Thornton F. Martin • UKN
HAPPY WARRIOR, THE • 1925 • Blackton J. Stuart • USA
HAPPY WARRIORS • 1933 • White Jules • SHT • USA
HAPPY WE see **TVA KILLAR OCH EN TJEJ** • 1983
HAPPY WORLD OF HELO, THE see **MUNDO ALEGRE DE HELO, O** • 1967
HAPPY YEARS, THE • 1950 • Wellman William A. • USA • ADVENTURES OF YOUNG DINK STOVER ○ YOUR ONLY YOUNG TWICE
HAPPY YOU AND MERRY ME • 1936 • Fleischer Dave • ANS • USA
HAPPYEND NERO • 1974 • Battaglia Enzo • ITL
HAPPY'S MISHAPS • 1915 • *Eclectic* • USA
HAPURA, DIE TOTE STADT 1 • 1921 • Heiland Heinz Karl • FRG • KAMPF UM DAS MILLIONENTESTAMENT, DER
HAPURA, DIE TOTE STADT 2 • 1921 • Heiland Heinz Karl • FRG • STREIT UM DIE RUINEN, DER
HAPUSLAH AIRMATAMU • 1975 • Amin M. • MLY • WIPE AWAY YOUR TEARS ○ TEARS AND SORROW
HAQIQA AL-ARIYA, AL- • 1963 • Salem Atef • EGY • VERITE TOUTE NUE, LA
HAR BORJAR AVENTYRET • 1965 • Donner Jorn • SWD • ADVENTURE STARTS HERE
HAR DU SET ALICE? • 1981 • Wielopolska Brita • DNM • HAVE YOU SEEN ALICE?
HAR HAR DU DITT LIV • 1966 • Troell Jan • SWD • HERE'S YOUR LIFE (USA) ○ HERE IS YOUR LIFE
HAR HAR MAHADEV • 1950 • Desai Jayant • IND
HAR JEG RET TIL AT TAGE MIT EGET LIV • 1917 • Holger-Madsen • DNM • FLUGTEN FRA LIVET ○ FLIGHT FROM LIFE, THE ○ CAN WE ESCAPE ○ BEYOND THE BARRICADE
HAR KOMMER BARSARKARNA • 1965 • Mattsson Arne • SWD, YGS • TWO VIKINGS, THE
HAR KOMMER PIPPI LANGSTRUMP • 1972 • Hellbom Olle • SWD
HAR KOMMER VI • 1947 • Zacharias John, Lagerwall Sture • SWD • HERE WE COME
HARA GOURI • 1923 • *Lotus* • IND
HARA-KIRI • 1928 • Iribe Marie-Louise • FRN
HARA-KIRI see **BATTLE, THE** • 1934
HARACIMA DOKUNMA • 1965 • Kazankaya Hasan • TRK
HARAGAN DE LA FAMILIA, EL • 1940 • Amadori Luis Cesar • ARG
HARAGASHIONNA • 1968 • Wakamatsu Koji • JPN • WOMB TO LET, A
HARAKARA • 1975 • Yamada Yoji • JPN • BRETHREN
HARAKIRI • 1919 • Lang Fritz • FRG
HARAKIRI see **SEPPUKU** • 1962
HARALD HANDFASTE • 1947 • Faustman Erik • SWD
HARALDS KUHNSTE ABENTEUER see **LUFTFAHRT UBER DEN OZEAN, DIE** • 1924
HARAM, AL- • 1964 • Barakat Henry • EGY • PECHE, LE
HARAM ALEK • 1953 • Karama Issa • EGY • SHAME ON YOU
HARANGOK ROMABA MENTEK, A • 1958 • Jancso Miklos • HNG • BELLS HAVE GONE TO ROME, THE
HARANGOK VAROSA -VESZPREM • 1966 • Meszaros Marta • SHT • HNG • VESZPREM -CITY OF BELLS ○ CITY OF BELLS, THE
HARAP ALB see **DE-AS FI HARAP ALB** • 1965
HARAPOS FERJ • 1939 • Keleti Marton • HNG • BITING HUSBAND (USA)
HARB AL BATROL LAN TAKA'A • 1974 • Ben Baraka Sohail • MRC • PETROLEUM WAR WILL NOT TAKE PLACE, THE
HARBINGER OF PEACE, THE • 1912 • *Brower Robert* • USA
HARBOR IN THE HEART OF EUROPE see **PRISTAV V SRDCI EUROPY** • 1939-40
HARBOR ISLAND • 1912 • Parker Lem B. • USA
HARBOR LIGHT YOKOHAMA (USA) see **KIRI NI MUSEBU YORU** • 1968
HARBOR LIGHTS • 1963 • Dexter Maury • USA
HARBOR LIGHTS see **HAVENLICHTEN** • 1960
HARBOR OF HAPPINESS, THE • 1916 • Brooke Van Dyke • SHT • USA
HARBOR OF LOVE, THE • 1914 • MacGregor Norval • USA
HARBOR OF MISSING MEN, THE • 1950 • Springsteen R. G. • USA
HARBOR PATROL • 1924 • *Ferguson Al* • USA
HARBOUR • 1978 • Semler Dean • DOC • ASL
HARBOUR, THE • 1963 • Stoyanov Yuli • DOC • BUL
HARBOUR, THE • 1966 • Jonsson Thorsteinn • SHT • ICL
HARBOUR BEAT • 1989 • Elfick David • ASL
HARBOUR DRIFT see **JENSEITS DER STRASSE** • 1929
HARBOUR IN THE FOG see **KIRI NO MINATO** • 1923
HARBOUR LIGHTS, THE • 1914 • Nash Percy • UKN
HARBOUR LIGHTS, THE • 1923 • Terriss Tom • UKN
HARBOUR OF DESIRE see **JOEN NO CHIMATA** • 1922
HARBOUR OF DESIRE see **PORT DU DESIR, LE** • 1954
HARBOUR OF FICKLE WINDS see **MINATO NO UWAKIKAZE** • 1936
HARBOUR OF LOVE see **AHAVA BANAMAL** • 1967
HARBOUR OF NO RETURN see **KAERAZARU HATOBA** • 1966
HARBOUR RATS see **UMI NO YARODOMO** • 1957
HARBOUR WOMAN see **MUJER DEL PUERTO, LA** • 1933
HARCERZE NA ZLOCIE • 1953 • Has Wojciech J. • DCS • PLN • SCOUTS AT A RALLY
HARCMODOR • 1980 • Darday Istvan • HNG • STRATAGEM
HARD AND FAST MARRIAGE, A see **SVATBA JAKO REMEN** • 1967
HARD ASFALT • 1985 • Skagen Solve • NRW • HARD ASPHALT
HARD ASPHALT see **HARD ASFALT** • 1985
HARD BARGAIN see **THIEVES' HIGHWAY** • 1949
HARD BLOW see **MOCNE UDERZENIE** • 1967
HARD BLOW -OPUS 2 see **MOCNE UDERZENIE -OPUS 2** • 1967
HARD BOILED • 1919 • Schertzinger Victor • USA • HARD-BOILED
HARD BOILED • 1925 • McCarey Leo • SHT • USA
HARD BOILED • 1926 • Blystone John G. • USA
HARD-BOILED see **HARD BOILED** • 1919
HARD-BOILED EGG, THE • 1916 • Kingsley Pierce • USA
HARD BOILED EGG, THE • 1948 • Rasinski Connie • ANS • USA
HARD-BOILED HAGGERTY • 1927 • Brabin Charles J. • USA
HARD BOILED MAHONEY • 1947 • Beaudine William • USA
HARD-BOILED TENDERFOOT, A • 1924 • Roach Hal • SHT • USA
HARD BOILED YEGGS • 1930 • Buzzell Edward • SHT • USA
HARD CASE AND FIST • 1987 • Zarindast Tony • USA • HARDCASE AND FIST
HARD CASH • 1910 • *Imp* • USA
HARD CASH • 1913 • Seay Charles M. • USA
HARD CASH • 1921 • Collins Edwin J. • UKN
HARD CHARGER see **TINY LUND: HARD CHARGER** • 1969
HARD CHOICES • 1986 • King Rick • USA
HARD CIDER • 1914 • Wright Walter • USA
HARD CIDER • 1920 • *Franey William* • SHT • USA
HARD CONTRACT • 1969 • Pogostin S. Lee • USA
HARD COUNTRY • 1980 • Greene David • USA
HARD COVER see **BEST SELLER** • 1987
HARD DAGS NAT, EN • 1987 • Rygard Elisabeth • SHT • DNM • HARD DAY'S NIGHT, A
HARD DAY AT THE OFFICE, A • 1977 • Sens Al • ANS • CND
HARD DAY FOR ARCHIE, A • 1983 • McBride Jim • USA
HARD DAYS see **DIAS DIFICILES** • 1987
HARD DAYS -HARD NIGHTS • 1990 • Konigstein Horst • FRG
HARD DAY'S NIGHT, A • 1964 • Lester Richard • UKN • BEATLES: A HARD DAY'S NIGHT
HARD DAY'S NIGHT, A see **HARD DAGS NAT, EN** • 1987
HARD DRIVER see **LAST AMERICAN HERO, THE** • 1973
HARD, FAST AND BEAUTIFUL • 1951 • Lupino Ida • USA
HARD FEELINGS • 1962 • Kachanov R. • ANS • USS
HARD FEELINGS • 1981 • Duke Daryl • CND
HARD FISTS • 1927 • Wyler William • USA
HARD GUY • 1941 • Clifton Elmer • USA • PROFESSIONAL BRIDE (UKN)
HARD HITTIN' HAMILTON • 1924 • Thorpe Richard • USA
HARD HOMBRE, THE • 1931 • Brower Otto • USA
HARD JOB, A • 1916 • Currier Frank • SHT • USA
HARD KLANG • 1952 • Mattsson Arne • SWD • DULL CLANG, A
HARD KNOCKS • 1924 • Roach Hal • SHT • USA
HARD KNOCKS • 1980 • McLennan Don • ASL
HARD KNOCKS AND LOVE TAPS • 1921 • Del Ruth Roy • SHT • USA
HARD KNOX • 1984 • Werner Peter • TVM • USA
HARD KNUCKLE • 1987 • Marinos Lex • ASL
HARD LABOR ON THE RIVER DOURO see **DOURO, FAINA FLUVIAL** • 1931
HARD LABOUR • 1936 • *Wise Vic* • SHT • UKN
HARD LIFE see **UKHABY ZHIZNI** • 1928
HARD LIFE, A see **VITA DIFFICILE, UNA** • 1961
HARD LIFE OF AN ADVENTURER, THE see **TEZKY ZIVOT DOBRODRUHA** • 1941
HARD LITTLE NUT, A see **KRYEPKI ORYESHEK** • 1968
HARD LOVE, A see **TROUDNA LYUBOV** • 1974
HARD LUCK • 1917 • Hotaling Arthur D. • SHT • USA
HARD LUCK • 1918 • MacQuarrie Murdock • SHT • USA
HARD LUCK • 1919 • Sidney Scott • SHT • USA
HARD LUCK • 1921 • Cline Eddie, Keaton Buster • SHT • USA
HARD LUCK BILL • 1912 • Fahrney Milton • USA
HARD LUCK BILL • 1913 • *Potel Victor* • USA
HARD LUCK DAME see **DANGEROUS** • 1935
HARD MAN, THE • 1957 • Sherman George • USA
HARD MAN'S GOOD TO FIND, A • 1969 • Bergue Jacques • USA • GOOD MAN'S HARD TO FIND, A ○ NIGHT SHIFT
HARD NIGHT, A • 1970 • *Pri* • UKN
HARD NUT TO CRACK, A see **KRYEPKI ORYESHEK** • 1968
HARD ON THE TRAIL see **HARD TRAIL** • 1969
HARD PART BEGINS, THE • 1973 • Lynch Paul • CND
HARD RAIN • 1989 • Yates Peter • USA
HARD RAIN see **DOSHABURI** • 1957
HARD RIDE, THE • 1971 • Topper Burt • USA
HARD ROAD, THE • 1915 • Myers Harry • USA
HARD ROAD, THE • 1970 • Graver Gary • USA
HARD ROCK see **GALLOPING ACE, THE** • 1924
HARD ROCK BREED, THE • 1918 • Wells Raymond • USA
HARD ROCK HARRIGAN • 1935 • Howard David • USA
HARD SHOULDER • 1989 • Kilroy Mark • IRL
HARD SOAP, HARD SOAP • 1977 • Chinn Robert C. • USA
HARD STEEL • 1942 • Walker Norman • UKN • WHAT SHALL IT PROFIT
HARD SUMMER, A see **VIZIVAROSI NYAR** • 1965
HARD SWING, THE • 1962 • Putnam Michael • USA
HARD TICKET TO HAWAII • 1987 • Sidaris Andy • USA
HARD TIME FAMILY see **FLUGJAHR, DAS** • 1982
HARD TIMES • 1909 • Stow Percy • UKN
HARD TIMES • 1915 • Bentley Thomas • UKN
HARD TIMES • 1975 • Hill Walter • USA • STREETFIGHTER, THE (UKN)
HARD TIMES see **FUKEIKI JIDAI** • 1930
HARD TIMES see **NA PRZELAJ** • 1971
HARD TIMES FOR DRACULA see **TEMPI DURI PER I VAMPIRI** • 1959
HARD TIMES FOR DRACULA see **TIEMPOS DUROS PARA DRACULA** • 1976
HARD TIMES FOR VAMPIRES see **TEMPI DURI PER I VAMPIRI** • 1959
HARD TIMES IN HARDSCRAPPLE • 1917 • Santell Alfred • USA
HARD TO BE A GOD see **TRUDNO BYT BOGOM** • 1988
HARD TO BEAT • 1909 • Porter Edwin S. • USA
HARD TO GET • 1929 • Beaudine William • USA
HARD TO GET • 1938 • Enright Ray • USA • HEAD OVER HEELS
HARD TO HANDLE • 1933 • LeRoy Mervyn • USA
HARD TO HOLD • 1984 • Peerce Larry • USA
HARD TO KILL • 1990 • Malmuth Bruce • USA
HARD TO SWALLOW see **JAGODE U GRLU** • 1985
HARD TRAIL • 1969 • Corarito Greg • USA • HARD ON THE TRAIL
HARD TRAVELING • 1986 • Bessie Dan • USA
HARD TRUTH, THE see **HARDE SANDHED, DEN** • 1980
HARD WASH • 1896 • *Bitzer Billy (Ph)* • USA
HARD WAY, THE • 1916 • Heffron Thomas N. • SHT • USA
HARD WAY, THE • 1916 • West Walter • UKN
HARD WAY, THE • 1943 • Sherman Vincent • USA
HARD WAY, THE • 1980 • Dryhurst Michael • UKN, IRL
HARD WILLS see **HARDA VILJOR** • 1922
HARD-WON HAPPINESS see **TRUDNOE SCHASTE** • 1958
HARD WORD, THE • 1966 • Robertson Michael • SHT • ASL
HARDA BANDAGE • 1960 • *Gunwall Per (Edt)* • SWD
HARDA LEKEN, DEN • 1956 • Kjellgren Lars-Eric • SWD • TOUGH GAME, THE
HARDA VILJOR • 1922 • Brunius John W. • SWD • IRON WILLS (USA) ○ HARD WILLS
HARDBODIES • 1984 • Griffiths Mark • USA
HARDBODIES 2 • 1986 • Griffiths Mark • USA
HARDBOILED • 1929 • Ince Ralph • USA • REAL GIRL, A (UKN)
HARDBOILED CANARY, THE • 1941 • Stone Andrew L. • USA • MAGIC IN MUSIC ○ THERE'S MAGIC IN MUSIC
HARDBOILED ROSE • 1929 • Weight F. Harmon • USA
HARDCASE • 1971 • Moxey John Llewellyn • TVM • USA
HARDCASE AND FIST see **HARD CASE AND FIST** • 1987
HARDCORE • 1977 • Clarke James Kenelm • UKN
HARDCORE • 1979 • Schrader Paul • USA • HARDCORE LIFE, THE
HARDCORE LIFE, THE see **HARDCORE** • 1979
HARDCOVER see **I, MADMAN** • 1988
HARDE SANDHED, DEN • 1980 • Clante Carsten • DNM • HARD TRUTH, THE
HARDER BOYS! • Zingarelli • CLM
HARDER THEY COME, THE • 1973 • Henzell Perry • JMC
HARDER THEY FALL, THE • 1956 • Robson Mark • USA
HARDEST WAY, THE • 1912 • *Eclair* • USA
HARDEST WAY, THE • 1913 • *Siegmann George* • USA
HARDHAT AND LEGS • 1980 • Philips Lee • TVM • USA
HARDI LES GARS! • 1931 • Champreux Maurice • FRN • FACTEUR DU TOUR DE FRANCE, LE
HARDII PARDAILLAN • 1963 • Borderie Bernard • FRN, ITL • ARMI DELLA VENDETTA, LE (ITL)
HARDING'S HERITAGE • 1913 • *Patheplay* • USA
HARDLY A CRIMINAL see **APENA UN DELINCUENTE** • 1947
HARDLY WORKING • 1981 • Lewis Jerry • USA
HARDROCK DOME • 1917 • *Messmer Otto (P)* • ASS • USA
HARDROCK ZOMBIES • 1984 • Shah Krishna • USA
HARDSHIP OF MILES STANDISH, THE • 1940 • Freleng Friz • ANS • USA
HARDSHIPS OF YOUNG BOHACEK, THE see **UTRPENI MLADEHO BOHACKA** • 1969
HARDUP FAMILY'S BLUFF, THE • 1913 • *Pathe* • USA
HARDWARE • 1989 • Stanley Richard • UKN
HARDWARE WARS • 1977 • Fosselius Ernie • SHT • USA
HARDWORKING CLERK, THE see **KOSHIBEN GANBARE** • 1931
HARDYS RIDE HIGH, THE • 1939 • Seitz George B. • USA
HARE-ABIAN NIGHTS • 1959 • Harris Ken • ANS • USA
HARE AND HEDGEHOG • 1964 • Gurvich Irina • ANS • USS
HARE AND THE HOUNDS, THE • 1940 • Donnelly Eddie • ANS • USA
HARE AND THE TORTOISE, THE • 1916 • Daly William Robert • SHT • USA
HARE BRAINED HYPNOTIST, THE • 1942 • *Schlesinger Leon (P)* • ANS • USA
HARE-BRAINED HYPNOTIST, THE • 1942 • Freleng Friz • ANS • USA

HARE BREADTH FINISH, A • 1957 • Rasinski Connie • ANS • USA
HARE-BREADTH HURRY • 1963 • Jones Charles M. • ANS • USA
HARE BRUSH • 1955 • Freleng Friz • ANS • USA
HARE CENSUS, THE see **PREBROYVANE NA DIVITE ZAITSI** • 1973
HARE CONDITIONED • 1945 • Jones Charles M. • ANS • USA
HARE-DO • 1948 • Freleng Friz • ANS • USA
HARE DO • 1949 • Freleng Friz • ANS • USA
HARE FORCE • 1944 • Freleng Friz • ANS • USA
HARE GROWS IN MANHATTAN, A • 1947 • Freleng Friz • ANS • USA
HARE KANCH KI CHOORIYAN • 1967 • Sahu Kishore • IND • GREEN GLASS BANGLES
HARE KRISHNA • 1966 • Mekas Jonas • USA
HARE-LESS WOLF • 1958 • Freleng Friz • ANS • USA
HARE LIFT • 1953 • Freleng Friz • ANS • USA
HARE MAIL, THE • 1931 • Lantz Walter, Nolan William • ANS • USA
HARE REMOVER • 1945 • Tashlin Frank • ANS • USA
HARE RIBBIN • 1944 • Clampett Robert • ANS • USA
HARE SPLITTER • 1948 • Freleng Friz • ANS • USA
HARE TONIC • 1945 • Jones Charles M. • ANS • USA
HARE TRIGGER • 1932 • Freleng Friz • ANS • USA
HARE-TRIMMED • 1953 • Freleng Friz • ANS • USA • HARE TRIMMED
HARE TRIMMED see **HARE-TRIMMED** • 1953
HARE-UM SCARE-UM • 1939 • Hardaway Ben, Dalton Cal • ANS • USA
HARE-WAY TO THE STARS • 1958 • Jones Charles M. • ANS • USA
HARE WE GO • 1950 • Freleng Friz • ANS • USA
HAREDEVIL HARE • 1948 • Jones Charles M. • ANS • USA
HAREEMU OHGEN LEMON POPSICLE 6 • 1984 • Wolman Dan • ISR, FRG • UP YOUR ANCHOR -LEMON POPSICLE VI ○ EIS AM STIEL, 6 TEIL ○ ESKIMO LIMON 6 ○ UP YOUR ANCHOR
HAREKOSODE • 1961 • Yasuda Kimiyoshi • JPN • CLEAR WEATHER
HAREM • 1985 • Joffe Arthur • FRN • D'ARDENELLE
HAREM • 1986 • Hale William • TVM • USA • HAREM: THE LOSS OF INNOCENCE
HAREM, L' • 1967 • Ferreri Marco • ITL • HER HAREM (USA) ○ HAREM, THE
HAREM, LE • 1979 • FRN
HAREM, THE see **HAREM, L'** • 1967
HAREM BUNCH, OR WAR AND PEACE, THE see **HAREM BUNCH, OR WAR AND PIECE, THE** • 1969
HAREM BUNCH, OR WAR AND PIECE, THE • 1969 • Hunt Paul • USA • HAREM BUNCH, OR WAR AND PEACE, THE ○ DESERT ODYSSEY
HAREM CAPTIVES, THE • 1912 • *Pathe* • USA
HAREM GIRL • 1952 • Bernds Edward • USA
HAREM HANGUPS • 1970 • *Able Film Co.* • USA
HAREM HOLIDAY (UKN) see **HARUM SCARUM** • 1965
HAREM KEEPER OF THE OIL SHEIKS see **ILSA, HAREM KEEPER OF THE OIL SHEIKS** • 1975
HAREM KNIGHT, A • 1926 • Cline Eddie • SHT • USA
HAREM ROMANCE, A • 1917 • Donovan Frank P. • USA
HAREM-SCAREM • 1920 • Williamson Robin E. • SHT • USA
HAREM SCAREM • 1927 • Disney Walt • ANS • USA
HAREM SCAREM DEACON, THE • 1916 • Curtis Allen • SHT • USA
HAREM SKIRT, THE • 1911 • *Tress Henry (P)* • UKN
HAREM SKIRT, THE • 1911 • *Kerrigan J. Warren* • USA
HAREM SONO DESERTI, GLI • 1956 • Colacurci Antonio • DOC • ITL • TURCHIA
HAREM: THE LOSS OF INNOCENCE see **HAREM** • 1986
HAREMETS PERLE • 1915 • Lind Alfred • DNM
HAREMS AND HOOKUM • 1919 • Pratt Gilbert • SHT • USA
HAREM'S CAGE • 1986 • Kamal Hussein • EGY
HAREMSEVENTYR, ET • 1914 • Holger-Madsen • DNM • ADVENTURE IN A HAREM, AN
HAREMSLIEBCHEN • 1925 • *Symphon* • FRG
HARES AND THE FROGS, THE (USA) see **LIEVRE ER LES GRENOUILLES, LA** • 1969
HARESUGATA ICHIBAN MATOI • 1956 • Kono Juichi • JPN
HARI DARSHUAN • 1953 • Desai Raman B. • IND • AUDIENCE WITH GOD
HARI-HAR BHAKTI • 1955 • Raghuvir C. • IND • DEVOTEE TO THE GOD
HARI HONDAL BARGADAR • 1981 • Benegal Shyam • IND • SHARE CROPPER
HARI NG NINJA • 1969 • Gaudite Solano • PHL
HARI NG SLUMS • 1968 • Gaudite Solano • PHL • KING OF THE SLUMS
HARI NG YABANG • 1968 • Marquez Artemio • PHL • KING OF BOASTFULNESS
HARIA • 1959 • Kumar Rajendra • IND
HARIB, AL- • 1973 • el Sheikh Kamal • EGY • FUGITIF, LE
HARIB MINA AL-HAYAT • 1963 • Salem Atef • EGY • FUGITIF DE LA VIE, LE
HARICOT, LE • 1962 • Sechan Edmond • FRN
HARIKOMI • 1958 • Namura Yoshitaro • JPN • CHASE, THE
HARIS, AL- • 1966 • Shawqi Khalil* • IRQ • VEILLEUR DE NUIT, LE
HARISCHANDRA • 1932 • IND
HARISCHANDRA • 1951 • *Studio X* • IND
HARISCHANDRA • 1959 • Desai Dhirubhai • IND
HARISHCHANDRA • 1912 • Phalke Dada • IND • KING HARISHCHANDRA ○ RAJA HARISHCHANDRA
HARISHCHANDRA • 1935 • Ghosh Prafulla • IND
HARJEET • 1940 • *Sircar B. N. (P)* • IND
HARK see **ONE MORE TRAIN TO ROB** • 1971
HARKA • 1941 • Arevalo Carlos • SPN
HARLAN COUNTY, U.S.A. • 1976 • Kopple Barbara • DOC • USA
HARLEKIN • 1931 • Reiniger Lotte • ANS • FRG • HARLEQUIN
HARLEKIN, DER • 1919 • Rex Eugen • FRG
HARLEKIN ES SZERELMESE • 1966 • Feher Imre • HNG • HARLEQUIN AND HIS LOVER
HARLEM • 1943 • Gallone Carmine • ITL
HARLEM AFTER MIDNIGHT • 1934 • Micheaux Oscar • USA
HARLEM BOUND • 1935 • Schwarzwald Milton • SHT • USA
HARLEM DYNAMITE • 1947 • Malkames Don • SHT • USA
HARLEM FOLLIES • 1950 • *Herald* • USA
HARLEM GLOBETROTTERS, THE • 1951 • Brown Phil, Jason Will • USA
HARLEM GLOBETROTTERS ON GILLIGAN'S ISLAND, THE • 1981 • Baldwin Peter • TVM • USA
HARLEM HOTSHOTS • 1940 • *Horne Lena* • SHT • USA
HARLEM IS HEAVEN • 1932 • *Robinson Bill* • SHT • USA • HARLEM RHAPSODY
HARLEM JAZZ FESTIVAL • 1955 • Kohn Joseph • USA
HARLEM NIGHTS • 1989 • Murphy Eddie • USA
HARLEM ON THE PRAIRIE • 1938 • Newfield Sam • USA
HARLEM ON THE PRAIRIE • 1939 • Buell Jed • USA
HARLEM RHAPSODY see **HARLEM IS HEAVEN** • 1932
HARLEM RHYTHM • 1947 • Malkames Don • SHT • USA
HARLEM RIDES THE RANGE • 1939 • Kahn Richard C. • USA
HARLEM ROCK 'N' ROLL (UKN) see **ROCK 'N' ROLL REVUE** • 1956
HARLEM STORY see **COOL WORLD, THE** • 1964
HARLEM WEDNESDAY • 1958 • Hubley John • ANS • USA
HARLEMANIA • 1938 • *Basie Count* • SHT • USA
HARLEQUIN • 1979 • Wincer Simon • ASL • DARK FORCES (USA)
HARLEQUIN see **HARLEKIN** • 1931
HARLEQUIN, THE see **ARLEKIN** • 1960
HARLEQUIN, THE see **ARLEKIN** • 1969
HARLEQUIN AND HIS LOVER see **HARLEKIN ES SZERELMESE** • 1966
HARLEQUIN NIMBO, THE • 1947-50 • Wasilewski Zenon • ANM • PLN
HARLEQUINADE • 1906 • Fitzhamon Lewin • UKN
HARLEQUINADE • 1908 • Cooper Arthur • UKN
HARLEQUINADE, THE • 1910 • Rains Fred • UKN
HARLEQUINADE, THE • 1915 • *Union Jack* • UKN
HARLEQUINADE, THE see **HERE WE ARE AGAIN** • 1913
HARLEQUINADE LET LOOSE, A • 1912 • Plumb Hay? • UKN
HARLEQUINADE -WHAT THEY FOUND IN THE LAUNDRY BASKET • 1901 • Williamson James • UKN
HARLEQUIN'S LOVE STORY, THE • 1907 • *Pathe Freres* • FRN
HARLIS • 1975 • van Ackeren Robert • FRG • RED HOT IN BED (UKN)
HARLOT • 1965 • Warhol Andy • USA
HARLOW • 1965 • Douglas Gordon • USA
HARLOW • 1965 • Segal Alex • USA
HARLOW HANDICAP, THE • 1914 • *Anderson Mignon* • USA
HARM MACHINE, THE see **AGENT FOR H.A.R.M.** • 1966
HARMADIK NEKIFUTAS • 1973 • Bacso Peter • HNG • LAST CHANCE, THE ○ THIRD BEGINNING, THE
HARMLESS FLIRTATION, A • 1911 • *Powers* • USA
HARMLESS FLIRTATION, A • 1915 • *Ovey George* • USA
HARMLESS LUNATIC'S ESCAPE, THE • 1908 • Fitzhamon Lewin? • UKN
HARMLESS ONE, THE • 1913 • Fielding Romaine • USA
HARMON OF MICHIGAN • 1941 • Barton Charles T. • USA
HARMONESTS AND MIGUELITO VALDES' ORCHESTRA, THE • 1950 • *Universal* • SHT • USA
HARMONIA • 1947 • Has Wojciech J. • DCS • PLN • HARMONY
HARMONICA see **HARMONIKU** • 1978
HARMONIE • 1977 • Klein Bonnie • DOC • CND
HARMONIE see **TOUBIB, LE** • 1979
HARMONIES DE PARIS • 1927 • Derain Lucy • FRN
HARMONIKAR • 1953 • *Stallich Jan (Ph)* • SHT • CZC
HARMONIKU • 1978 • Noer Arifin C. • INN • HARMONICA
HARMONIUM IN CALIFORNIA • 1979 • Fortier Bob • MTV • CND
HARMONY • 1965 • Ratz Gunter • ANM • GDR
HARMONY see **HARMONIA** • 1947
HARMONY ABROAD • 1965 • Winter Donovan • SHT • UKN
HARMONY AND DISCORD • 1913 • *Frontier* • USA
HARMONY AND DISCORD • 1916 • *Armstrong Billy* • SHT • USA
HARMONY AT HOME • 1930 • MacFadden Hamilton • USA • SHE STEPS OUT
HARMONY BOYS, THE • 1929 • Santley Joseph • SHT • USA
HARMONY HEAVEN • 1929 • Hitchcock Alfred, Polo Eddie, Bentley Thomas, Brandt Edward • UKN
HARMONY IN A FLAT • 1916 • Schrock Raymond L. • SHT • USA
HARMONY INN (UKN) see **HOME IN SAN ANTONE** • 1949
HARMONY LANE • 1935 • Santley Joseph • USA • MINSTREL CARNIVAL
HARMONY LANE • 1954 • Gill Byron • UKN
HARMONY PARADE (UKN) see **PIGSKIN PARADE** • 1936
HARMONY ROW • 1933 • Thring F. W. • ASL
HARMONY TRAIL • 1944 • Tansey Robert • USA • WHITE STALLION (UKN)
HARMS CASE, THE see **SLUCAJ HARMS** • 1987
HARNESS, THE • 1971 • Sagal Boris • TVM • USA
HARNESS FEVER • 1976 • Chaffey Don • ASL • BORN TO RUN (USA)
HARNESS THE HUAI RIVER • 1952 • Shih Mei • CHN
HARNESS THE WIND • 1978 • Goldsmith Sidney • ANM • CND
HARNESSED LIGHTNING • 1948 • Moore Harold James • SHT • USA
HARNESSED RHYTHM • 1936 • Tourneur Jacques • SHT • USA
HARO • 1977 • Behat Gilles • FRN
HAROLD AND MAUDE • 1971 • Ashby Hal • USA
HAROLD AND THE PURPLE CRAYON • 1957 • Piel David • ANS • USA
HAROLD LAND - RED MITCHELL QUINTET • 1962 • Binder Steve • SHT • USA
HAROLD LLOYD'S FUNNY SIDE OF LIFE • 1966 • CMP • USA • FUNNY SIDE OF LIFE, THE
HAROLD LLOYD'S WORLD OF COMEDY • 1962 • *Lloyd Harold* • CMP • USA
HAROLD PREVENTS A CRIME • 1912 • Wilson Frank? • UKN
HAROLD ROBBINS' THE BETSY see **BETSY, THE** • 1978
HAROLD ROBBIN'S THE PIRATE see **PIRATE, THE** • 1978
HAROLD TEEN • 1928 • LeRoy Mervyn • USA
HAROLD TEEN • 1934 • Roth Murray • USA • DANCING FOOL, THE (UKN)
HAROLD, THE LAST OF THE SAXONS • 1919 • Drew Sidney Mrs. • SHT • USA
HAROLD THE NURSE GIRL • 1916 • Currier Frank • SHT • USA
HAROLD'S BAD MAN • 1915 • Mix Tom • USA
HAROLD'S BURGLAR • 1914 • *Crystal* • USA
HAROLD'S TOUPEE • 1914 • *Simon Louis* • USA
HAROM CSILLAG • 1960 • Jancso Miklos, Varkonyi Zoltan, Wiedermann Karoly • HNG • THREE STARS (USA)
HAROM NYUL, A • 1972 • Dargay Attila • HNG • THREE HARES
HAROM SARKANY, A • 1936 • Vajda Ladislao • HNG • THREE SPINSTERS, THE
HAROUN AND GHAROUN • 1967 • Fatemi Nezam • IRN
HARP IN HOCK, A • 1927 • Hoffman Renaud • USA • SAMARITAN, THE
HARP KING, THE • 1920 • *Wilkie Nan* • UKN
HARP OF BURMA, THE see **BIRUMA NO TATEGOTO** • 1956
HARP OF TARA, THE • 1914 • West Raymond B. • USA
HARPER • 1966 • Smight Jack • USA • MOVING TARGET, THE (UKN)
HARPER MYSTERY, THE • 1913 • Trimble Larry • UKN
HARPER VALLEY P.T.A. • 1978 • Bennett Richard • USA
HARPOON • 1948 • Scott Ewing • USA
HARPS AND HALOS • 1917 • *Fisher Bud(Anm)* • ANM • USA
HARPY • 1970 • Freedman Jerrold • TVM • USA
HARRAD EXPERIMENT, THE • 1973 • Post Ted • USA
HARRAD SUMMER • 1974 • Stern Steven Hilliard • USA • STUDENT UNION
HARRASSED HERO, THE • 1954 • Elvey Maurice • UKN
HARRER CASE, THE see **FALL HARRER, DER** • 1986
HARRI! HARRI! see **YON SYLISSA** • 1977
HARRIED AND HURRIED • 1965 • Larriva Rudy • ANS • USA
HARRIET AND THE PIPER • 1920 • Bracken Bertram • USA
HARRIET CRAIG • 1950 • Sherman Vincent • USA
HARRIF, EL • 1983 • Khan Mohamed • EGY • STREET PLAYER
HARRIGAN • 1907 • Gilbert Arthur • UKN
HARRIGAN'S CHILD see **HARRIGAN'S KID** • 1943
HARRIGAN'S KID • 1943 • Reisner Charles F. • USA • HARRIGAN'S CHILD ○ HALF PINT KID
HARRIS DOWN UNDER see **DANGER DOWN UNDER** • 1988
HARRIS IN THE SPRING • 1937 • Goodwins Leslie • SHT • USA
HARRISON AND HARRISON see **HARRISON ES HARRISON** • 1917
HARRISON ES HARRISON • 1917 • Korda Alexander • HNG • HARRISON AND HARRISON
HARRY AND HARRIET see **FRAU NAMENS HARRY, EIN** • 1990
HARRY AND SON • 1983 • Newman Paul • USA
HARRY AND THE BUTLER see **HARRY OG KAMMERTJENEREN** • 1961
HARRY AND THE HENDERSONS • 1987 • Dear William • USA • BIGFOOT AND THE HENDERSONS (UKN)
HARRY AND TONTO • 1974 • Mazursky Paul • USA
HARRY AND WALTER GO TO NEW YORK • 1976 • Rydell Mark • USA
HARRY BLACK see **HARRY BLACK AND THE TIGER** • 1958
HARRY BLACK AND THE TIGER • 1958 • Fregonese Hugo • USA • HARRY BLACK
HARRY HAPPY • 1963 • Kneitel Seymour • ANS • USA
HARRY HILL AUF WELLE 1000 • 1926 • Arnheim Valy • FRG
HARRY HILL CONTRA SHERLOCK HOLMES see **DETEKTIVDUELL, DAS** • 1920
HARRY HILL, DER HERR DER WELT • 1923 • Batz Lorenz • FRG
HARRY HILL IM BANNE DER TODESSTRAHLEN • 1925 • Arnheim Valy • FRG
HARRY HILLS JAGD AUF DEN TOD 1 • 1924 • Batz Lorenz • FRG
HARRY HILLS JAGD AUF DEN TOD 2 • 1924 • Batz Lorenz • FRG
HARRY HOOTON • 1970 • Cantrill Arthur, Cantrill Corinne • ASL
HARRY IN YOUR POCKET • 1973 • Geller Bruce • USA • HARRY NEVER HOLDS
HARRY JAMES AND THE MUSIC MAKERS • 1943 • Cowan Will • SHT • USA
HARRY LAUDER IN A HURRY • 1908 • Collins Alf? • UKN
HARRY LAUDER SONGS • 1931 • Pearson George • SER • UKN
HARRY MUNTER • 1969 • Grede Kjell • SWD • GAY HARRY
HARRY NEVER HOLDS see **HARRY IN YOUR POCKET** • 1973
HARRY OG KAMMERTJENEREN • 1961 • Christensen Bent • DNM • HARRY AND THE BUTLER
HARRY PALMER RETURNS see **FUNERAL IN BERLIN** • 1966
HARRY PARRY AND HIS RADIO RHYTHM CLUB SEPTET • 1943 • Shepherd Horace • SHT • UKN
HARRY PEELS SCHWERSTER SIEG see **REITER OHNE KOPF 3, DER** • 1921
HARRY TATE GRIMACES • 1899 • *Warwick Trading Co.* • UKN
HARRY TATE IMPERSONATIONS • 1899 • *Warwick Trading Co.* • UKN
HARRY THE FOOTBALLER • 1911 • Fitzhamon Lewin • UKN
HARRY THE SWELL • 1915 • Martinek H. O. • UKN
HARRY, THIS IS SALLY see **WHEN HARRY MET SALLY** • 1989
HARRY THOMPSON'S IMITATIONS OF SOUSA • 1901 • Porter Edwin S. • USA
HARRY TRACY see **HARRY TRACY, DESPERADO** • 1981
HARRY TRACY, DESPERADO • 1981 • Graham William A. • CND • HARRY TRACY
HARRY TRUMAN: PLAIN SPEAKING • 1977 • Petrie Daniel • MTV • USA
HARRY WATSON'S PONY TUMBLING ACT • 1902 • *Warwick Trading Co.* • UKN
HARRY'S GAME see **BELFAST ASSASSIN** • 1982
HARRY'S GAME: THE MOVIE see **BELFAST ASSASSIN** • 1982
HARRY'S HAPPY HONEYMOON • 1916 • *Yorke Jay* • USA
HARRY'S HONGKONG • 1987 • London Jerry • TVM • USA
HARRY'S LESSON • 1913 • *Majestic* • USA
HARRY'S PIG • 1917 • *La Pearl Harry* • SHT • USA
HARRY'S WAR • 1981 • Merrill Keith • USA
HARRY'S WATERLOO • 1914 • *Benham Harry* • USA

HART OF LONDON, THE • 1970 • Chambers Jack* • DOC • CND
HART OF THE DREADFUL WEST, THE see **PERFECTLY FIENDISH FLANAGAN OR THE HART OF THE DREADFUL WEST** • 1918
HART TO HART • 1979 • Mankiewicz Tom • TVM • USA
HARTE MANNER -HEISSE LIEBE • 1956 • Cap Frantisek • FRG, ITL • RAGAZZA DELLA SALINA, LA (ITL) ○ SAND, LOVE AND SALT (USA) ○ SALZ UND BROT ○ MADCHEN UND MANNER
HARTIGAN • Perry Hart • SHT • USA
HARTLEY FAMILY OF VANCOUVER, THE • 1972 • Long Jack • CND
HARTLEY WONDERS, THE • 1903 • *Urban Trading Co.* • UKN
HARTNEY MERWIN'S ADVENTURE • 1915 • Martin E. A. • USA
HARTORRIHTRA, I • 1967 • Karayannis Kostas • GRC • FORTUNE-TELLER, THE
HARU ICHIBAN • 1966 • Ichimura Hirokazu • JPN • SPRING BREEZE
HARU KORO NO HANA NO EN • 1958 • Kinugasa Teinosuke • JPN • SYMPHONY OF LOVE ○ SPRING BOUQUET, A ○ SPRING BANQUET, A
HARU KURU ONI • 1989 • Kobayashi Akira • JPN • DEMONS IN SPRING
HARU NO KANE • 1985 • Kurahara Koreyoshi • JPN • SPRING BELL
HARU NO KOTEKI • 1953 • Nakamura Noboru • JPN • SPRING DREAM
HARU NO KYOEN • 1947 • Yamamoto Kajiro • JPN
HARU NO MEZAME • 1947 • Naruse Mikio • JPN • SPRING AWAKENING ○ SPRING AWAKENS
HARU NO SASAYAKI • 1952 • Toyoda Shiro • JPN • WHISPER OF SPRING
HARU NO TAWAMURE • 1949 • Yamamoto Kajiro • JPN • SPRING FLIRTATION ○ SPRING CAPRICE
HARU NO TODOROKI • 1952 • *Mikuni Rentaro* • JPN • ROARS OF SPRING
HARU NO USHIO • 1950 • Nakamura Noboru • JPN • SPRING TIDE
HARU NO UZIMAKI • 1954 • *Kyo Machiko* • JPN • WHIRLPOOL OF SPRING
HARU NO YUME • 1960 • Kinoshita Keisuke • JPN • SPRING DREAMS
HARU O MATSU HITOBITO • 1959 • Nakamura Noboru • JPN • WAITING FOR SPRING ○ THOSE WHO WAIT FOR SPRING
HARU TO MISUME • 1932 • Tasaka Tomotaka • JPN • SPRING AND A GIRL
HARU WA GOFUJIN KARA • 1932 • Ozu Yasujiro • JPN • SPRING COMES WITH THE LADIES ○ SPRING COMES FROM THE LADIES
HARUBIYORI • 1967 • Oba Hideo • JPN • FORGIVING HEART, THE
HARUKANARI HAHA NO KUNI • 1950 • Ito Daisuke • JPN • MOTHERLAND FAR FAR AWAY, THE
HARUKANARU OTOKO • 1957 • Taniguchi Senkichi • JPN
HARUKANARU SORO • 1981 • Sato Junya • JPN • LONG WAY FOR A MOTOR CAR, A
HARUKANARU YAMA NO YOBIGOE • 1979 • Yamada Yoji • JPN • ECHO OF THE FAR MOUNTAIN
HARUKOMA NO UTA • 1985 • Koyama Seijiro • JPN • BALLAD OF PONY
HARUM SCARUM • 1965 • Nelson Gene • USA • HAREM HOLIDAY (UKN)
HARUM-SCARUM FAMILY, A see **SZELEBURDI CSALAD** • 1982
HARUN AL RASCHID • 1924 • Curtiz Michael • AUS
HARUN AL-RASHID'S FAVOURITE see **HARUN RESID'IN GOZDESI** • 1967
HARUN RESID'IN GOZDESI • 1967 • Yilmaz Atif • TRK • HARUN AL-RASHID'S FAVOURITE
HARUO NO TONDA SORA • 1977 • Yamada Tengo • JPN • SKY WHERE HARUO FLEW, THE
HARURANMAN • 1968 • Chiba Yasuki • JPN • DEVILS-IN-LAW
HARVARD, HERE I COME • 1942 • Landers Lew • USA • HERE I COME (UKN)
HARVARD-PRAMIE, DIE • 1917 • Philippi Siegfried • FRG
HARVEST • 1915 • *Ritchie Franklin* • USA
HARVEST • 1962 • Van Dyke Willard • DOC • USA
HARVEST • 1980 • Walker Giles • MTV • CND
HARVEST see **JULIKA, DIE** • 1936
HARVEST see **URODZAJ** • 1959
HARVEST: 3000 YEARS see **MIRT SOST SHI AMIT** • 1972
HARVEST, THE • 1911 • *Reliance* • USA
HARVEST, THE • 1913 • *Nestor* • USA
HARVEST, THE see **VOZVRASHCHENIE VASSILIYA BORTNIKOVA** • 1953
HARVEST DAYS (UKN) see **MOUNTAIN RHYTHM** • 1942
HARVEST FOR TOMORROW • 1950 • Cole Lionel • UKN
HARVEST GOLD • 1945 • Murphy Mervyn • ASL
HARVEST HANDS • 1923 • Roach Hal • SHT • USA
HARVEST HELP • 1940 • Wright Basil • DOC • UKN
HARVEST IN THE COOPERATIVE DOSZA see **ARAT AZ OROSHAZI DOZSA** • 1953
HARVEST MELODY • 1943 • Newfield Sam • USA
HARVEST MONTH see **ELOKUU** • 1956
HARVEST MOON, THE • 1920 • Dawley J. Searle • USA
HARVEST OF DESPAIR • 1986 • Nowytski Slavko • DOC • CND
HARVEST OF FLAME, THE • 1913 • Reid Wallace, Neilan Marshall (U/c) • USA
HARVEST OF GOLD, THE • 1916 • Horne James W. • SHT • USA
HARVEST OF HATE • 1979 • Thornhill Michael • TVM • ASL
HARVEST OF HATE see **VARMLANNINGARNA** • 1921
HARVEST OF HATE, THE • 1929 • McRae Henry • USA
HARVEST OF MY LAI, THE • 1970 • Ophuls Marcel • MTV • FRG
HARVEST OF REGRETS, THE • 1914 • *Foster Morris* • USA
HARVEST OF SIN • 1913 • Edwards Walter • USA
HARVEST OF SIN, THE • 1912 • Collins Edwin J.? • UKN
HARVEST OF TEARS, A see **PRESSENS MAGT** • 1913
HARVEST ROMANCE, A • 1914 • *Millers 101 Ranch* • USA
HARVEST SHALL COME, THE • 1941 • Anderson Max • DOC • UKN
HARVEST THUNDER see **VINTAGE, THE** • 1957
HARVEST TIME • 1940 • Rasinski Connie • ANS • USA
HARVEST (USA) see **REGAIN** • 1937
HARVESTER, THE • 1927 • Meehan James Leo • USA
HARVESTER, THE • 1936 • Santley Joseph • USA
HARVEY • 1950 • Koster Henry • USA
HARVEY • 1970 • *Stacey Dist.* • USA
HARVEY GIRLS, THE • 1945 • Sidney George • USA
HARVEY MIDDLEMAN, FIREMAN • 1965 • Pintoff Ernest • USA
HARVEY SWINGS • 1970 • *Jo-Jo Productions* • USA
HARVEY'S GIRL see **HOW TO SUCCEED WITH GIRLS** • 1964
HARY JANOS see **JANOS HARY** • 1964
HAS ANYBODY HERE SEEN CANADA? • 1979 • Kramer John • DOC • CND
HAS ANYBODY HERE SEEN KELLY? • 1926 • Fleischer Dave • ANS • USA
HAS ANYBODY HERE SEEN KELLY? see **HI, GOOD LOOKIN'** • 1944
HAS ANYBODY HERE SEEN KELLY? (UKN) see **ANYBODY HERE SEEN KELLY?** • 1928
HAS ANYBODY SEEN MY GAL? • 1952 • Sirk Douglas • USA
HAS BEEN, THE • 1915 • *Arey Wayne* • USA
HAS MAN THE RIGHT TO KILL? • 1919 • *Popular Film Co.* • USA
HAS THE WORLD GONE MAD! • 1923 • Dawley J. Searle • USA
HASAMBA • 1970 • Silberg Joel • ISR
HASAN-AGA'S WIFE see **HASANAGINICA** • 1967
HASAN THE ROSE see **GUL HASAN** • 1982
HASANAGINICA • 1967 • Popovic Mica • YGS • WIFE OF HASAN-AGA, THE ○ HASAN-AGA'S WIFE
HASARD ET LA VIOLENCE, LE • 1974 • Labro Philippe • FRN, ITL
HASARD ET L'AMOUR, LE • 1913 • Linder Max • FRN
HASAYARIM • 1967 • Shagrir Micha • ISR • PATROL, THE ○ SCOUTS, THE
HASCHEN IN DIE GRUBE • 1968 • Fritz Roger • FRG
HASCHISCH • 1968 • Soutter Michel • SWT • HASHISH
HASCHISCH, DAS PARADIES DER HOLLE • 1921 • Bruck Reinhard • FRG
HASEENA 420 • 1988 • Butt Mahmood • PKS
HASEK'S EXEMPLARY CINEMATOGRAPH see **VZORNY KINEMATOGRAF JAROSLAVA HASKA** • 1955
HASEMANNS TOCHTER • 1920 • Bolten-Baeckers Heinrich • FRG
HASENBRATEN, DER • 1915 • Sauer Fred • FRG
HASENKLEIN KANN NICHTS DAFUR • 1932 • Neufeld Max • FRG • DRUNTER UND DRUBER?
HASH AND HAVOC • 1916 • Semon Larry • SHT • USA
HASH AND HEARTS • 1917 • *Greater Pictures* • SHT • USA
HASH HOUSE BLUES • 1931 • *Mintz Charles (P)* • ANS • USA
HASH HOUSE COUNT, THE • 1913 • *Brennan John* • USA
HASH HOUSE FRAUD, A • 1915 • Frazee Edwin • USA
HASH HOUSE HERO see **STAR BOARDER, THE** • 1914
HASH HOUSE MASHERS • 1915 • Cogley Nick, Frazee Edwin • USA
HASH HOUSE MYSTERY, THE • 1917 • Myers Harry • SHT • USA
HASH HOUSE ROMANCE, A • 1917 • *Three C* • USA
HASH SHOP, THE • 1930 • Lantz Walter, Nolan William • ANS • USA
HASHECHOUNA SHELANOU • 1968 • Zohar Uri • ISR • FISH, FOOTBALL AND GIRLS
HASHER, THE • 1920 • *Franey William* • SHT • USA
HASHER'S DELIRIUM • 1906 • *Gaumont* • FRN
HASHER'S DELIRIUM, THE see **SONGE D'UN GARCON DE CAFE, LE** • 1910
HASHI NO NAI KAWA • 1969 • Imai Tadashi • JPN • RIVER WITHOUT A BRIDGE PARTS 1 & 2, THE ○ BRIDGE ACROSS NO RIVER ○ RIVER WITHOUT BRIDGES
HASHIMOTO SAN • 1959 • Tendlar Dave, Kuwahara Bob • ANS • USA
HASHIMURA TOGO • 1917 • De Mille William C. • USA
HASHISH see **HASCHISCH** • 1968
HASHOTER AZULAI • 1971 • Kishon Ephraim • ISR • POLICEMAN, THE (USA) ○ COP, THE
HASHTOMIN ROOZE HAFTEH • 1973 • Radjaian Hossein • IRN • EIGHTH DAY OF THE WEEK, THE
HASINA 420 • 1988 • PKS • BEAUTY 420
HASIP AND NASIP see **HASIP ILE NASIP** • 1976
HASIP ILE NASIP • 1976 • Yilmaz Atif • TRK • HASIP AND NASIP
HASLO "KORN" • 1968 • Podgorski Waldemar • PLN • PASSWORD "KORN"
HASS • 1920 • Noa Manfred • FRG
HASS OHNE GNADE • 1962 • Lothar Ralph • FRG
HASS UND LIEBE see **WELT IN FLAMMEN 1, DIE** • 1923
HASSAN AND NAYIMA see **HASSAN WA NAIMA** • 1958
HASSAN ET NAIMA see **HASSAN WA NAIMA** • 1958
HASSAN TERRE S'EVADE • 1975 • Badie Mustapha • ALG
HASSAN TERRO • 1967 • Hamina Mohamed Lakhdar • ALG • "TERRORIST" HASSAN, THE ○ HASSAN-TERVO
HASSAN-TERVO see **HASSAN TERRO** • 1967
HASSAN WA NAIMA • 1958 • Barakat Henry • EGY • HASSAN ET NAIMA ○ HASSAN AND NAYIMA
HASSLE IN A CASTLE • 1966 • Smith Paul J. • ANS • USA
HASSLICHE MADCHEN, DAS • 1933 • Koster Henry • FRG
HAST DU GELIEBT AM SCHONEN RHEIN • 1927 • Bauer James • FRG
HASTA CIERTO PUNTO • 1984 • Alea Tomas Gutierrez • CUB • UP TO A POINT
HASTA DESPUES DE LA MUERTE • 1919 • Vollrath Ernesto • MXC
HASTA EL VIENTO TIENE MIEDO • 1968 • Enrique Taboada Carlos • MXC • EVEN THE WIND IS AFRAID
HASTA LA VICTORIA SIEMPRE • 1967 • Alvarez Santiago • DOC • CUB • TILL VICTORY ALWAYS ○ ALWAYS UNTIL VICTORY
HASTA QUE EL MATRIMONIO NOS SEPARE • 1976 • Lazaga Pedro • SPN
HASTA QUE LLOVIO EN SAYULA • 1940 • Contreras Torres Miguel • MXC
HASTA QUE PERDIO JALISCO • 1945 • de Fuentes Fernando • MXC
HASTHANDLARENS FLICKOR • 1954 • Holmsen Egil • SWD • TIME OF DESIRE (USA)
HASTY EXIT, A • 1914 • *Royal* • USA
HASTY HARE, THE • 1952 • Jones Charles M. • ANS • USA
HASTY HAZING, A • 1917 • Chaudet Louis W. • SHT • USA
HASTY HEART • 1983 • Speer Martin • USA
HASTY HEART, THE • 1949 • Sherman Vincent • UKN
HASTY JILTING, A • 1913 • *Frontier* • USA
HASTY JUDGEMENT, A • 1914 • *Melies* • USA
HASTY MARRIAGE see **ELSIETETT HAZASSAG** • 1968
HASTY MARRIAGE, THE • 1931 • Pratt Gilbert • SHT • USA
HAT, THE • 1912 • *Charleson Mary* • USA
HAT, THE • 1962 • Kneitel Seymour • ANS • USA
HAT, THE • 1964 • Hubley John, Hubley Faith • ANS • USA
HAT, THE see **KAPELUSZ** • 1962
HAT, THE see **SESIR** • 1976
HAT, THE (USA) see **SOMBRERO, EL** • 1964
HAT BAGATELL • 1988 • ANT • HNG • SIX BAGATELLES
HAT BOX MYSTERY, THE • 1947 • Hillyer Lambert • USA
HAT CHECK GIRL • 1932 • Lanfield Sidney • USA • EMBASSY GIRL (UKN)
HAT CHECK HONEY • 1944 • Cline Eddie • USA
HAT, COAT AND GLOVE • 1934 • Miner Worthington • USA
HAT DANCE • 1898 • *Cinematograph Co.* • UKN
HAT HET BOLDOGSAG • 1939 • De Toth Andre • HNG • SIX WEEKS OF HAPPINESS
HAT OF FORTUNE • 1908 • *Lubin* • USA
HAT OF THE WORK BRIGADE LEADER, THE see **HUT ES BRIGADIERS, DER**
HAT ON A STICK see **SHAPKA NA TOYAGA** • 1972
HAT PARADE see **PARADE DE CHAPEAUX** • 1936
HAT WITH MANY SURPRISES, THE (USA) see **CHAPEAU A SURPRISES, LE** • 1901
HATACHI NO KOI (JPN) see **AMOUR A VINGT ANS, L'** • 1962
HATARA KENDARE • 1967 • Perera L. M. • SLN • FOUR HOROSCOPES
HATARAKU IKKA • 1939 • Naruse Mikio • JPN • WHOLE FAMILY WORKS, THE
HATARI! • 1962 • Hawks Howard • USA
HATASVADADASZOK • 1983 • Szurdi Miklos • HNG • MIDNIGHT REHEARSAL
HATCH UP YOUR TROUBLES • 1949 • Hanna William, Barbera Joseph • ANS • USA
HATCHET, THE • 1969 • Muresan Mircea • RMN
HATCHET FOR A HONEYMOON (USA) see **ROSSO SEGNO DELLA FOLLIA, IL** • 1969
HATCHET MAN, THE • 1932 • Wellman William A. • USA • HONOURABLE MR. WONG, THE (UKN)
HATCHET MURDERS, THE see **PROFONDO ROSSO** • 1975
HATE • 1917 • Hall Walter • USA
HATE • 1922 • Karger Maxwell • USA
HATE BAJARE • 1967 • Sinha Tapan • IND • AT THE MARKET-PLACE
HATE FOR HATE (UKN) see **ODIO PER ODIO** • 1967
HATE IN PARADISE see **TEA LEAVES IN THE WIND** • 1938
HATE OF THE SORCERER, THE see **HAINE DU SORCIER, LA** • 1914
HATE SHIP, THE • 1929 • Walker Norman • UKN
HATE THAT WITHERS, THE • 1914 • *Kalem* • USA
HATE TO LOVE • 1982 • Pacheco Bruno-Lazaro • SHT • CND
HATE TRAIL, THE • 1922 • Morante Milburn • USA
HATE (USA) see **ODIO** • 1939
HATE YOUR NEIGHBOUR see **ODIA IL PROSSIMO TUO** • 1968
HATED K.P., THE • 1919 • *Miller-Hodkinson* • SHT • USA
HATEFUL BONDAGE, A • 1914 • Fitzhamon Lewin? • UKN
HATEFUL GOD, THE • 1914 • *Kb* • USA
HATER OF MEN • 1917 • Miller Charles • USA
HATER OF WOMEN, THE • 1912 • *Quirk Billy* • USA
HATERS, THE • 1912 • Dwan Allan • USA
HATESHINAKI JONETSU • 1949 • Ichikawa Kon • JPN • PASSION WITHOUT LIMITS, THE ○ ENDLESS PASSION, THE ○ PASSION WITHOUT END
HATESHINAKI YOKUBO • 1958 • Imamura Shohei • JPN • ENDLESS DESIRE, THE
HATFIELDS AND THE MCCOYS, THE • 1975 • Ware Clyde • TVM • USA
HATFUL OF DREAMS, A • 1944 • Pal George • ANS • USA
HATFUL OF RAIN, A • 1957 • Zinnemann Fred • USA
HATFUL OF RAIN, A • 1968 • Moxey John Llewellyn • TVM • USA
HATFUL OF TROUBLE, A • 1915 • *Farrington Frank* • USA
HATHA YOGA • 1981 • Maurice Andre • DOC • FRN
HATHAT DEKHA • 1967 • Dutta Nityananda • IND • UNEXPECTED ENCOUNTER
HATHOLDAS ROZSAKERT • 1979 • Ranody Laszlo • HNG • ROSE GARDEN OF SIX ACRES
HATI BATU • 1971 • Amin M. • MLY • CRUEL HEART
HATI BUKAN KRISTAL • 1989 • Alauddin Raja Ahmad • MLY • EAR IS NOT A CRYSTAL, THE
HATIFA • 1960 • Hartmann Siegfried • GDR
HATIM TA • 1956 • *Shakila* • IND
HA'TIMHONI • 1970 • Wolman Dan • ISR, USA • DREAMER, THE
HATIMTAI-KI-BETI • 1955 • *Citra* • IND
HATMAKER, THE see **FANTOMES DU CHAPELIER, LES** • 1981
HATOBA NO TAKA • 1967 • Nishimura Shogoro • JPN • LONE HAWK OF THE WATER FRONT
HATOBUE O FUKU ONNA • 1932 • Tasaka Tomotaka • JPN
HATRED see **MOLLENARD** • 1937
HATRED see **NENAVIST** • 1978
HATRED see **ODIO** • 1980
HATRED FOR HATRED see **ODIO PER ODIO** • 1967
HATS AND HAPPINESS • 1912 • *Powers* • USA
HATS DOWN! • 1960 • Topaldgikov Stefan • BUL
HATS IS HATS • 1915 • Van Wally • USA
HATS OFF • 1927 • Yates Hal • USA
HATS OFF • 1936 • Petroff Boris L. • USA
HATS OFF TO RHYTHM see **EARL CARROLL SKETCHBOOK** • 1946
HATSUHARA TANUKI GOTEN • 1959 • Kimura Keigo • JPN • ENCHANTED PRINCESS, THE
HATSUKOI • 1926 • Gosho Heinosuke • JPN • FIRST LOVE

HATSUKOI JIGOKU-HEN • 1968 • Hani Susumu • JPN • NANAMI: INFERNO OF FIRST LOVE ○ INFERNO OF FIRST LOVE, THE
HATSUKOI MONDO • 1950 • Shibuya Minoru • JPN • FIRST LOVE QUESTIONS AND ANSWERS
HATSUKOI MONOGATARI • 1957 • Maruyama Seiji • JPN • STORY OF FIRST LOVE, THE
HATSUKOI SENGEN • 1968 • Umezu Meijiro • JPN • IF I WERE A STAR
HATTA MARRI • 1932 • Stafford Babe • SHT • USA
HATTER AND HIS DOG, THE • 1914 • *Captain Kettle* • UKN
HATTER'S BALL, THE see **HATTMAKARENS BAL** • 1928
HATTER'S CASTLE • 1941 • Comfort Lance • UKN
HATTER'S GHOSTS, THE see **FANTOMES DU CHAPELIER, LES** • 1981
HATTIE, THE HAIR HEIRESS • 1915 • *Keyes Francis* • USA
HATTIE'S NEW HAT • 1913 • *Lubin* • USA
HATTMAKARENS BAL • 1928 • Persson Edvard • SWD • HATTER'S BALL, THE
HATTOGOL VIJAY • Gupta Bula Das, Goswami Raghunath • IND • HATTOGOL'S VICTORY
HATTOGOL'S VICTORY see **HATTOGOL VIJAY**
HATTON GARDEN ROBBERY, THE • 1915 • Batley Ethyle • UKN
HATTON OF HEADQUARTERS • 1917 • MacDonald Donald • SHT • USA • ODD TRICK, THE
HATTYUDAL • 1964 • Keleti Marton • HNG • VILLA NEGRA
HAUBENLERCHE, DIE see **WENN MENSCHEN REIF ZUR LIEBE WERDEN** • 1927
HAUGHTY PRETTY GIRL, THE • 1981 • Kim Soo-Yong • SKR
HAUL IN ONE, A • 1956 • Sparber I. • ANS • USA
HAUNTED • 1915 • *Superba* • USA
HAUNTED • 1916 • *E.& R. Jungle Film* • SHT • USA
HAUNTED • 1976 • De Gaetano Michael A. • USA
HAUNTED • 1982 • Glenister John, Flemyng Gordon • MTV • UKN
HAUNTED see **NIGHT OF THE DEMON** • 1957
HAUNTED AND HOUNDED • 1916 • Horkheimer H. M., Horkheimer E. D. • SHT • USA
HAUNTED AND THE HUNTED, THE (UKN) see **DEMENTIA 13** • 1963
HAUNTED ATTIC, THE • 1915 • *Edwards John* • USA
HAUNTED BACHELOR, THE • 1912 • *Eclair* • USA
HAUNTED BARN • 1931 • ASL
HAUNTED BEDROOM, THE • 1907 • Booth W. R. • UKN
HAUNTED BEDROOM, THE • 1913 • Ridgely Richard • USA
HAUNTED BEDROOM, THE • 1919 • Niblo Fred • USA
HAUNTED BELL, THE • 1916 • Otto Henry • SHT • USA
HAUNTED BRIDE, THE • 1913 • Smalley Phillips, Weber Lois • USA
HAUNTED BY CONSCIENCE • 1910 • *Kalem* • USA
HAUNTED BY HER PAST • 1987 • Pressman Michael • TVM • USA
HAUNTED BY HIMSELF • 1917 • *Payson Blanche* • SHT • USA
HAUNTED BY HIS MOTHER-IN-LAW • 1913 • Wilson Frank? • UKN
HAUNTED BY THE COPS • 1909 • *Pathe* • FRN
HAUNTED CAFE • 1911 • *Messter-Film* • FRG
HAUNTED CASTLE see **HIROKU KAIBYODEN** • 1969
HAUNTED CASTLE, THE • 1897 • Smith G. A. • UKN
HAUNTED CASTLE, THE • 1908 • *Pathe* • FRN
HAUNTED CASTLE, THE • 1922 • *Educational* • SHT • USA
HAUNTED CASTLE, THE • 1969 • Tanaka Tokuzo • JPN
HAUNTED CASTLE, THE see **CHATEAU HANTE, LE** • 1897
HAUNTED CASTLE, THE see **SPUKSCHLOSS IM SPESSART, DAS** • 1959
HAUNTED CASTLE, THE (USA) see **MANOIR DU DIABLE, LE** • 1896
HAUNTED CASTLE AT DUDINCI, THE see **ZACARANI DVORAC U DUDINCINA** • 1951
HAUNTED CASTLE (USA) see **SCHLOSS VOGELOD** • 1921
HAUNTED CAT, THE • 1951 • Donnelly Eddie • ANS • USA
HAUNTED CAVE see **AMA NO BAKEMONO YASHIKI** • 1959
HAUNTED CHATEAU, THE see **CHATEAU HANTE, LE** • 1897
HAUNTED CITY, THE see **KISERTET LUBLON** • 1977
HAUNTED CURIOSITY SHOP, THE • 1901 • Booth W. R. • UKN
HAUNTED ENGLAND • 1961 • Winner Michael • UKN
HAUNTED GOLD • 1933 • Wright Mack V. • USA
HAUNTED HARBOR • 1944 • Bennet Spencer Gordon, Grissell Wallace A. • SRL • USA
HAUNTED HAT, THE • 1915 • Louis Will • USA
HAUNTED HEARTS • 1915 • *Madison Cleo* • USA
HAUNTED HEARTS • 1919 • *West Billy* • SHT • USA
HAUNTED HEIRESS, A • 1925 • *Marian Edna* • SHT • USA
HAUNTED HILLS • 1924 • *Bemis Jim* • SHT • USA
HAUNTED HOMESTEAD, THE • 1927 • Wyler William • SHT • USA
HAUNTED HONEYMOON • 1987 • Wilder Gene • UKN
HAUNTED HONEYMOON, THE • 1925 • Roach Hal • SHT • USA
HAUNTED HONEYMOON (USA) see **BUSMAN'S HONEYMOON** • 1940
HAUNTED HOTEL, THE • 1906 • Blackton J. Stuart • USA
HAUNTED HOTEL, THE • 1918 • Rains Fred • UKN
HAUNTED HOTROD, THE see **GHOST OF DRAGSTRIP HOLLOW, THE** • 1959
HAUNTED HOUSE • 1939 • Henabery Joseph • SHT • USA
HAUNTED HOUSE • 1940 • McGowan Robert • USA • BLAKE MURDER MYSTERY, THE (UKN)
HAUNTED HOUSE see **BHUTIO MAHAL** • 1932
HAUNTED HOUSE see **RUMAH PUAKA** • 1957
HAUNTED HOUSE, THE • 1899 • *Lubin* • USA
HAUNTED HOUSE, THE • 1911 • *Imp* • USA
HAUNTED HOUSE, THE • 1913 • *Kalem* • USA
HAUNTED HOUSE, THE • 1913 • *Patheplay* • USA
HAUNTED HOUSE, THE • 1913 • *American* • USA
HAUNTED HOUSE, THE • 1917 • Parker Albert • USA
HAUNTED HOUSE, THE • 1918 • Frazee Edwin • SHT • USA
HAUNTED HOUSE, THE • 1921 • Cline Eddie, Keaton Buster • SHT • USA
HAUNTED HOUSE, THE • 1922 • Kenton Erle C. • SHT • USA
HAUNTED HOUSE, THE • 1925 • *Terry Paul (P)* • ANS • USA
HAUNTED HOUSE, THE • 1928 • Christensen Benjamin • USA
HAUNTED HOUSE, THE • 1928 • Disney Walt, Iwerks Ub • ANS • USA
HAUNTED HOUSE, THE • 1929 • Iwerks Ub • ANS • USA
HAUNTED HOUSE, THE see **MAISON EN HANTEE, LA** • 1907
HAUNTED HOUSE, THE see **HSIUNG CHAI** • 1977
HAUNTED HOUSE, THE (UKN) see **AU SECOURS!** • 1923
HAUNTED HOUSE OF HORROR, THE • 1969 • Armstrong Michael • UKN • HORROR HOUSE (USA) ○ DARK, THE
HAUNTED HOUSE OF WILD ISLE, THE • 1915 • *Nilsson Anna Q.* • USA
HAUNTED HOUSEBOAT, THE • 1904 • Collins Alf • UKN
HAUNTED HOUSECLEANING • 1960 • Rasinski Connie • ANS • USA
HAUNTED HOUSES AND CASTLES OF GREAT BRITAIN • 1926 • *Banfield George J.(P)* • SER • UKN
HAUNTED INN, THE • 1910 • *Cosmopolitan* • USA
HAUNTED ISLAND • 1928 • Hill Robert F. • SRL • USA
HAUNTED ISLAND, THE • 1911 • *Powers* • USA
HAUNTED LIFE OF A DRAGON-TATTOOED LASS, THE see **KAIDAN NOBORIRYU** • 1970
HAUNTED MAN, THE • 1909 • *Duskes* • FRG
HAUNTED MAN, THE • 1966 • Willis Stanley • UKN
HAUNTED MINE, THE • 1946 • Abrahams Derwin • USA
HAUNTED MIRROR, THE • 1916 • Middleton Edwin • USA
HAUNTED MIRROR, THE see **STRASZNY DWOR** • 1936
HAUNTED MOUSE • 1965 • Jones Charles M. • ANS • USA
HAUNTED MOUSE, THE • 1941 • Avery Tex • ANS • USA
HAUNTED NIGHT, THE • 1957 • Pintoff Ernest • ANS • USA
HAUNTED OAK, THE • 1904 • Fitzhamon Lewin • UKN
HAUNTED PAJAMAS, THE • 1917 • Balshofer Fred J. • USA
HAUNTED PALACE • 1949 • Fisher Richard • UKN
HAUNTED PALACE, THE • 1963 • Corman Roger • USA
HAUNTED PICTURE GALLERY, THE • 1899 • Smith G. A. • UKN
HAUNTED PLANET see **TERRORE NELLO SPAZIO** • 1965
HAUNTED RANCH • 1943 • Tansey Robert • USA
HAUNTED RANCH, THE see **HAUNTED RANGE, THE** • 1926
HAUNTED RANGE, THE • 1926 • Hurst Paul C. • USA • HAUNTED RANCH, THE
HAUNTED ROCKER, THE • 1912 • *Young Clara Kimball* • USA
HAUNTED ROOM, THE • 1911 • *C.g.p.c.* • FRN
HAUNTED SCENE PAINTER, THE • 1904 • Booth W. R.? • UKN
HAUNTED SENTINEL TOWER, THE • 1911 • *Edison* • USA
HAUNTED SHIP, THE • 1927 • Sheldon Forrest • USA
HAUNTED SHIP, THE • 1930 • Foster John, Davis Mannie • ANS • USA
HAUNTED SPOOKS • 1920 • Goulding Alf, Roach Hal • SHT • USA
HAUNTED STATION, THE • 1915 • Davis James • USA
HAUNTED STRANGLER, THE (USA) see **GRIP OF THE STRANGLER, THE** • 1958
HAUNTED STUDIO, THE • Hempel Johannes • ANM • GDR
HAUNTED SUMMER • 1989 • Passer Ivan • USA
HAUNTED: THE FERRYMAN • 1986 • Irvin John • UKN
HAUNTED TRAILS • 1949 • Hillyer Lambert • USA
HAUNTED VALLEY • 1923 • Marshall George • SRL • USA
HAUNTERS OF THE DEEP • 1985 • Bogle Andrew • USA
HAUNTING, THE • 1963 • Wise Robert • UKN
HAUNTING CASTLE IN SALZKAMMERGUT, THE see **SPUKSCHLOSS IM SALZKAMMERGUT** • 1965
HAUNTING EYE, THE • 1915 • *Premier* • USA
HAUNTING FEAR, THE • 1915 • Vignola Robert G. • USA
HAUNTING MEMORY, THE • 1915 • *Harris Joseph* • USA
HAUNTING OF CASTLE MONTEGO, THE see **CASTLE OF EVIL** • 1966
HAUNTING OF HAMILTON HIGH, THE • 1986 • Pittman Bruce • CND
HAUNTING OF HEWIE DOWKER, THE • 1976 • Rubie Howard • MTV • ASL
HAUNTING OF JULIA, THE • 1976 • Loncraine Richard • UKN, CND • FULL CIRCLE
HAUNTING OF M, THE • 1979 • Thomas Anna • UKN
HAUNTING OF PENTHOUSE D, THE • 1974 • Kaplan Henry • USA
HAUNTING OF ROSALIND, THE • 1973 • *Sarandon Susan* • USA
HAUNTING OF SARAH HARDY, THE • 1989 • *Bergen Polly* • USA
HAUNTING OF SILAS P. GOULD, THE • 1915 • Neame Elwin • UKN
HAUNTING PASSION, THE • 1983 • Korty John • TVM • USA
HAUNTING SEASON see **HUNTING SEASON** • 1982
HAUNTING SHADOWS • 1920 • King Henry • USA • HOUSE OF A THOUSAND CANDLES, THE
HAUNTING SYMPHONY, THE • 1916 • *Wilbur Crane* • SHT • USA
HAUNTING WINDS • 1915 • Le Viness Carl M. • USA
HAUNTS • 1977 • Freed Herb • USA • VEIL, THE
HAUNTS FOR HIRE • 1916 • *Bray-Gilbert* • USA • HAUNTS FOR RENT
HAUNTS FOR RENT see **HAUNTS FOR HIRE** • 1916
HAUNTS OF THE VERY RICH • 1972 • Wendkos Paul • TVM • USA
HAUPT DER MEDUSA, DER • 1919 • AUS • HEAD OF MEDUSA, THE
HAUPT DES JUAREZ, DAS • 1920 • Guter Johannes • FRG
HAUPTDARSTELLER, DER • 1978 • Hauff Reinhard • FRG • MAIN ACTOR, THE (UKN) ○ LEADING MAN, THE
HAUPTLEHRER HOFER • 1975 • Lilienthal Peter • FRG • SCHOOLMASTER HOFER
HAUPTMANN FLORIAN VON DER MUHLE • 1968 • Wallroth Werner W. • GDR • CAPTAIN FLORIAN OF THE MILL
HAUPTMANN-STELLVERTRETER, DER • 1915 • Ostermayr Peter • FRG
HAUPTMANN UND SEIN HELD, DER • 1955 • Nosseck Max • FRG
HAUPTMANN VON KOLN, DER • 1956 • Dudow Slatan • GDR • CAPTAIN OF COLOGNE, THE
HAUPTMANN VON KOPENICK, DER • 1907 • *Freund Karl (Ph)* • FRG
HAUPTMANN VON KOPENICK, DER • 1926 • Dessauer Siegfried • FRG • CAPTAIN OF KOPENICK, THE
HAUPTMANN VON KOPENICK, DER • 1931 • Oswald Richard • FRG • CAPTAIN OF KOPENICK, THE
HAUPTMANN VON KOPENICK, ER • 1956 • Kautner Helmut • FRG • CAPTAIN FROM KOPENICK, THE (USA)
HAUPTSACHE GLUCKLICH • 1941 • Lingen Theo • FRG
HAURI • 1987 • Matula Julius • CZC • SHARPIES
HAUS AM KROGEL, DAS • 1927 • Winar Ernest • FRG
HAUS AM MEER, DAS • 1924 • Kaufmann Fritz • FRG
HAUS AM MEER, DAS • 1972 • Hauff Reinhard • FRG
HAUS DER FRAUEN • 1977 • Zanussi Krzysztof • FRG • HOUSE OF WOMEN
HAUS DER LEIDENSCHAFTEN, DAS • 1916 • Reinert Robert • FRG
HAUS DER LUGE, DAS • 1925 • Pick Lupu • FRG • ARME, KLEINE HEDWIG ○ WILDENTE, DIE ○ WILD DUCK, THE
HAUS DER QUALEN, DAS • 1921 • Wilhelm Carl • FRG
HAUS DER TAUSEND FREUDEN, DAS • 1967 • Summers Jeremy • FRG, SPN • CASA DE LAS MIL MUNECAS, LA (SPN) ○ HOUSE OF A THOUSAND DOLLS(USA) ○ HOUSE OF A THOUSAND PLEASURES, THE ○ HOUSE OF 1000 DOLLS
HAUS DER UNSCULD, DAS • 1920 • *Mara Lya* • FRG
HAUS DER VERRUFENEN, DAS • 1922 • Dessauer Siegfried • FRG • FRAU MIT DEN ZEHN MASKEN 4, DIE
HAUS DES LEBENS • 1952 • Hartl Karl • FRG
HAUS DES YOGHI, DAS see **YOGHI, DER** • 1916
HAUS GEGENUBER, DAS • 1918 • Meinert Rudolf • FRG
HAUS IM DUNKELN, DAS • 1924 • Bock-Stieber Gernot • FRG
HAUS IN DER DRAGONERGASSE, DAS • 1921 • Oswald Richard • FRG
HAUS IN DER KARPFENGASSE, DAS • 1964 • Hoffmann Kurt • FRG
HAUS IN MONTEVIDEO, DAS • 1951 • Goetz Curt, von Maertens Valerie • FRG
HAUS IN MONTEVIDEO, DAS • 1963 • Kautner Helmut • FRG
HAUS NR.7 • 1923 • *Trautmann-Ewest-Film* • FRG
HAUS NUMMER 17 • 1928 • von Bolvary Geza • FRG
HAUS OHNE FENSTER, DAS see **HUND VON BASKERVILLE 6, DER** • 1920
HAUS OHNE FENSTER UND TUREN, DAS • 1914 • Rye Stellan • FRG • HOUSE WITHOUT WINDOWS OR DOORS, THE
HAUS OHNE LACHEN, DAS • 1923 • Lamprecht Gerhard • FRG
HAUS OHNE MANNER, DAS • 1928 • Randolf Rolf • FRG
HAUS VOLL LIEBE, EIN • 1954 • Schweikart Hans • FRG, AUS • GLUCK INS HAUS
HAUS ZUM MOND, DAS • 1920 • Martin Karl Heinz • FRG
HAUSDAME AUS BESTER FAMILIE GESUCHT • 1915 • Schmidthassler Walter • FRG
HAUSER'S MEMORY • 1970 • Sagal Boris • USA
HAUSFRAUEN REPORT • 1971 • Schroeder Eberhard • FRG • ON THE SIDE (UKN)
HAUSFRAUEN -REPORT II • 1971 • Schroeder Eberhard • FRG • MOST GIRLS WILL (UKN)
HAUSFRAUEN -REPORT III • 1972 • Schroeder Eberhard • FRG • GIVE 'EM AN INCH (UKN)
HAUSTYRANN, DER • 1959 • Deppe Hans • FRG
HAUSU • 1977 • Obayashi Nobuhiko • JPN • HOUSE
HAUT COMME TROIS POMMES • 1935 • Vajda Ladislao, Ramelot Pierre • FRN • VILLAGE EN FOLIE, LE
HAUT FUR HAUT (FRG) see **GOUT DE LA VIOLENCE, LE** • 1960
HAUT LE VENT • 1942 • de Baroncelli Jacques • FRN • AIR NATAL
HAUT LES MAINS • 1912 • Feuillade Louis • FRN
HAUTE INFIDELITE (FRN) see **ALTA INFEDELTA** • 1964
HAUTE LISSE • 1956 • Gremillon Jean • SHT • FRN
HAUTES SOLITUDES, LES • 1973 • Garrel Philippe • FRN
HAUTES VARIETES (FRN) see **CIBLES VIVANTES** • 1960
HAUTS-LIEUX DE LA REVOLUTION, LES • 1963 • Bouchouchi Youssef • SHT • ALG
HAVAI KHATAULA • 1946 • Khan A. M., Alam Sultan • IND
HAVALERNES SANG • 1984 • Hastrup Jannik • DNM • SONG OF THE WHALES
HAVANA • 1990 • Pollack Sydney • USA
HAVANA 61 see **HAWANA 61** • 1961
HAVANA ROSE • 1951 • Beaudine William • USA
HAVANA WIDOWS • 1933 • Enright Ray • USA
HAVE A CIGAR • 1914 • Calvert Charles? • UKN
HAVE A GOOD TRIP see **STASTNOU CESTU** • 1974
HAVE A HEART • 1934 • Butler David • USA
HAVE A HEART see **SENORITA FROM THE WEST** • 1945
HAVE A NICE WEEKEND! • 1975 • Walters Michael • USA
HAVE ANOTHER • 1919 • *Parsons William* • SHT • USA
HAVE BIKINI WILL TRAVEL • 1962 • Kunz Werner • SWT • LET'S GO NATIVE
HAVE FIGURE, WILL TRAVEL • 1963 • Overton Alan • CND
HAVE GUN -CAN'T TRAVEL • 1967 • Smith Paul J. • ANS • USA
HAVE GUN, WILL TRAVEL see **QUATTRO DELL'AVE MARIA, I** • 1968
HAVE I EVER LIED TO YOU BEFORE? • 1976 • Spotton John • CND
HAVE IT OUT, MY BOY, HAVE IT OUT! • 1911 • Coleby A. E. • UKN
HAVE IT YOUR OWN WAY see **DANCE, GIRL, DANCE** • 1940
HAVE ROCKET, WILL TRAVEL • 1959 • Rich David Lowell • USA
HAVE SOME MORE MEAT • 1915 • Birch Cecil • UKN
HAVE SOME SPINACH? see **COZ TAKHLE DAT SI SPENAT?** • 1976
HAVE YOU A MATCH? • 1913 • Calvert Charles? • UKN
HAVE YOU CALLED A DOCTOR? • 1974 • Gauzner V. • USS
HAVE YOU EVER BEEN NORTH OF PRINCESS STREET? • 1972 • Raymont Peter • DOC • CND
HAVE YOU EVER WONDERED • 1947 • Barclay David • SHT • USA
HAVE YOU FORGOTTEN? see **AMATHAKA VUNADA?** • 1967
HAVE YOU GOT ANY CASTLES? • 1938 • Tashlin Frank • ANS • USA
HAVE YOU HEARD ABOUT TILLIE? • 1916 • Smith David • SHT • USA
HAVE YOU HEARD OF THE SAN FRANCISCO MIME TROUPE? • 1968 • Lenzer Don, Wardenburg Fred • DOC • USA
HAVE YOU SEEN ALICE? see **HAR DU SET ALICE?** • 1981
HAVE YOU SEEN DRUM RECENTLY? • 1989 • Schadeberg Jurgen • SAF

HAVE YOU SEEN MY GIRL? • 1915 • *Thistle* • USA
HAVE YOU SEEN THE BAREFOOT GOD? see **KIMI WA HADASHI NO KAMI O MITAKA** • 1985
HAVE YOU SOLD YOUR DOZEN ROSES? • 1957 • Greene Philip, Willis Alan • USA
HAVE YOU THOUGHT OF TALKING TO THE DIRECTOR? • 1962 • Baillie Bruce • SHT • USA
HAVEN see **SARANA** • 1967
HAVEN OF REFUGE, THE • 1911 • *Selig* • USA
HAVENLICHTEN • 1960 • Servais Raoul • ANS • BLG • HARBOR LIGHTS
HAVET OG MENNESKENE • 1970 • Aagaard Sigfred • DNM
HAVET STIGER • 1990 • Einarson Oddvar • NRW • RISING TIDE
HAVETS DJAVUL • 1937 • Fejos Paul • DCS • DNM, SWD • SEA DEVIL, THE
HAVETS HUSMAEND • 1954 • Carlsen Henning • SHT • DNM
HAVETS MELODI • 1934 • Wilhelm Prins, Brunius John W. • SWD • MELODY OF THE SEA ○ FRAN YTTERSTA SKAREN ○ FROM THE UTTERMOST ISLANDS
HAVETS SON • 1949 • Husberg Rolf • SWD • SON OF THE SEA
HAVINCK • 1987 • Weisz Frans • NTH
HAVING A GOOD TIME • 1913 • *Essanay* • USA
HAVING A LOVELY TIME • 1970 • Bentley Robert • UKN
HAVING A WILD WEEKEND (USA) see **CATCH US IF YOU CAN** • 1965
HAVING BABIES • 1976 • Day Robert • TVM • USA
HAVING BABIES II • 1977 • Michaels Richard • TVM • USA
HAVING BABIES III • 1978 • Cooper Jackie • TVM • USA
HAVING IT ALL • 1982 • Zwick Edward • TVM • USA
HAVING LIED ONLY ONCE • Bortko V. • USS
HAVING THEIR PICTURE TAKEN • 1913 • *Powers* • USA
HAVING WONDERFUL CRIME • 1945 • Sutherland A. Edward • USA
HAVING WONDERFUL TIME • 1938 • Santell Alfred • USA
HAVIS AMANDA -THE BELLE OF HELSINKI • 1983 • Ruutsalo Eino • DOC • FNL
HAVLANDET • 1985 • Glomm Lasse • NRW • NORTHERN LIGHTS
HAVOC • 1925 • Lee Rowland V. • USA
HAVOC see **THUNDERING DAWN** • 1923
HAVOC see **UNHEIL, DAS** • 1972
HAVOC, THE • 1916 • Berthelet Arthur • USA
HAVRE • 1986 • Berto Juliet • FRN
HAVRE SAC • 1963 • Lepeuve Monique • SHT • FRN
HAVSGAMAR • 1945 • Ohberg Ake • SWD
HAVSGAMARNA • 1915 • Sjostrom Victor • SWD • SEA VULTURES ○ SEA EAGLE
HAWAA ALAL TARIK • 1968 • Helmy Hussein • EGY • EVE AT THE CROSSROADS
HAWAA WAL KERD • 1968 • Mustafa Niazi • EGY • EVE AND THE MONKEY
HAWAI-MAREI-OKI KAISEN • 1942 • Yamamoto Kajiro • JPN • WAR AT SEA FROM HAWAII TO MALAYA, THE ○ BATTLE OF HAWAII ○ BATTLES OF HAWAII AND MALAY OFF SHORE, THE
HAWAI NO YORU • 1954 • Makino Masahiro • JPN
HAWAII • 1966 • Hill George Roy • USA
HAWAII BEACH BOY see **BLUE HAWAII** • 1961
HAWAII CALLS • 1938 • Cline Eddie • USA
HAWAII FIVE-O • 1968 • Freeman Leonard • TVM • USA
HAWAII FIVE-O: V FOR VASHON • 1972 • Dubin Charles S. • TVM • USA
HAWAIIAN AYE AYE • 1964 • Chiniquy Gerry • ANS • USA
HAWAIIAN BIRDS • 1936 • Fleischer Dave • ANS • USA
HAWAIIAN BUCKAROO • 1938 • Taylor Ray • USA
HAWAIIAN CAPERS • 1937 • Schwarzwald Milton • SHT • USA
HAWAIIAN HEAT • 1984 • Vejar Mike • USA
HAWAIIAN HOLIDAY • 1937 • Sharpsteen Ben • ANS • USA
HAWAIIAN LOVE • 1913 • *Champion* • USA
HAWAIIAN LULLABY • 1968 • ANM • NTH
HAWAIIAN NIGHTS • 1939 • Rogell Albert S. • USA
HAWAIIAN NIGHTS (UKN) see **DOWN TO THEIR LAST YACHT** • 1934
HAWAIIAN NUTS • 1917 • Beaudine William • USA
HAWAIIAN PINEAPPLE • 1930 • *Terry Paul/ Moser Frank (P)* • ANS • USA
HAWAIIAN REVELLERS, THE • 1928 • *De Forest Phonofilms* • SHT • UKN • MUSIC WITHOUT WORDS ○ MUSICAL MEDLEY NO.4
HAWAIIAN RHYTHM • 1940 • Ceballos Larry • SHT • USA
HAWAIIAN THIGH • 1965 • Felderman Bob • USA
HAWAIIANS, THE • 1970 • Gries Tom • USA • MASTER OF THE ISLANDS (UKN)
HAWANA 61 • 1961 • Hoffman Jerzy, Skorzewski Edward • DCS • PLN • HAVANA 61
HAWID GHARAM • 1955 • Barakat Henry • EGY • RENDEZ-VOUS D'AMOUR
HAWK, THE • 1917 • Scardon Paul • USA
HAWK, THE see **TRAIL OF THE HAWK** • 1935
HAWK, THE (UKN) see **RIDE HIM, COWBOY** • 1932
HAWK, THE (USA) see **GAVILAN, EL** • 1939
HAWK AND THE HERMIT, THE • 1915 • *Davenport Dorothy* • USA
HAWK ISLAND see **MIDNIGHT MYSTERY** • 1930
HAWK OF POWDER RIVER, THE • 1948 • Taylor Ray • USA
HAWK OF THE CARIBBEAN, THE see **SPARVIERO DEI CARAIBI, LO** • 1963
HAWK OF THE HILLS • 1929 • Bennet Spencer Gordon • USA
HAWK OF THE NORTH see **DOKUGANRYU MASAMUNE** • 1959
HAWK OF THE WILDERNESS • 1938 • Witney William, English John • SRL • USA
HAWK OF WILD RIVER • 1952 • Sears Fred F. • USA
HAWK THE SLAYER • 1980 • Marcel Terry • UKN
HAWKEN • 1986 • Pierce Charles B. • USA
HAWKERS, THE see **MAGLIARI, I** • 1959
HAWKEYE AND THE CHEESE MYSTERY • 1914 • *Powers* • USA
HAWKEYE, COASTGUARD • 1912 • Plumb Hay • UKN
HAWKEYE, HALL PORTER • 1914 • Plumb Hay • UKN
HAWKEYE HAS TO HURRY • 1913 • Plumb Hay • UKN
HAWKEYE, KING OF THE CASTLE • 1915 • Plumb Hay • UKN
HAWKEYE LEARNS TO PUNT • 1911 • Fitzhamon Lewin • UKN
HAWKEYE MEETS HIS MATCH • 1913 • Plumb Hay • UKN
HAWKEYE RIDES IN A POINT-TO-POINT • 1913 • Plumb Hay? • UKN
HAWKEYE, SHOWMAN • 1912 • Plumb Hay • UKN
HAWKEYE TO THE RESCUE • 1913 • *Nestor* • USA
HAWKEYE'S GREAT CAPTURE • 1913 • *Moran Lee* • USA
HAWKINS AND WATKINS • 1932 • *Sennett Mack (P)* • SHT • USA
HAWKINS' HAT • 1910 • *Lubin* • USA
HAWKINS MOVES • 1912 • *Powers* • USA
HAWKINS ON MURDER • 1973 • Taylor Jud • TVM • USA • DEATH AND THE MAIDEN
HAWKINS' ROOMER, THE • 1913 • *Powers* • USA
HAWKS • 1988 • Miller Robert Ellis • UKN
HAWKS see **NIGHTHAWKS** • 1980
HAWKS, THE • 1969 • Tully Montgomery • UKN
HAWKS, THE see **NEAMUL SOIMARESTILOR** • 1965
HAWKS AND SPARROWS (USA) see **UCCELLACCI E UCCELLINI** • 1966
HAWKS AND THE SPARROWS, THE see **UCCELLACCI E UCCELLINI** • 1966
HAWK'S NEST, THE • 1928 • Christensen Benjamin • USA
HAWK'S TRAIL, THE • 1920 • Van Dyke W. S. • SRL • USA
HAWLEYS OF HIGH STREET • 1933 • Bentley Thomas • UKN
HAWMPS! • 1976 • Camp Joe • USA
HAWTHORNE OF THE U.S.A. • 1919 • Cruze James • USA • HAWTHORNE THE ADVENTURER
HAWTHORNE THE ADVENTURER see **HAWTHORNE OF THE U. S.A.** • 1919
HAXAN • 1921 • Christensen Benjamin • DNM, SWD • WITCHCRAFT THROUGH THE AGES (UKN) ○ HEKSEN
HAXAN • 1955 • Michel Andre • SWD, FRN • SORCIERE, LA (FRN) ○ BLONDE WITCH ○ SORCERESS, THE ○ WITCH
HAXNATTEN • 1937 • Bauman Schamyl • SWD • WITCHES' NIGHT
HAY ALGUIEN DETRAS DE LA PUERTA • 1960 • Demicheli Tulio • SPN
HAY ANGELES CON ESPUELAS • 1955 • Mendez Fernando • MXC
HAY ANGELES SIN ALAS • 1971 • *Prods. Raul De Anda* • MXC
HAY ENDKO? ELI KUINKA UUNO TURHAPURO SAI NIIN KAUNIIN JA RIKKAAN VAIMON • 1977 • Kokkonen Ere • FNL • HAPLESS END? OR HOW NUMBSKULL EMPTYBROOK WON THE HAND OF SUCH A BEAUTIFUL AND RICH LADY
HAY FEVER • 1920 • Hayes Ward • SHT • USA
HAY FOOT, STRAW FOOT • 1919 • Storm Jerome • USA
HAY GANNINUNI • 1959 • Wahab Fatin Abdel • EGY • ILS VONT ME RENDRE FOU! ○ J'EN DEVIENS FOU!
HAY HO! • 1913 • Stow Percy • UKN
HAY LUGAR PARA DOS • 1948 • Galindo Alejandro • MXC
HAY MUERTOS QUE NO HACEN RUIDO • 1946 • Gomez Landero Humberto • MXC • THERE ARE DEAD THAT ARE SILENT
HAY QUE EDUCAR A PAPA • 1970 • Lazaga Pedro • SPN
HAY QUE EDUCAR AL NINO • 1940 • Amadori Luis Cesar • ARG
HAY QUE MATAR A B • 1974 • Borau Jose Luis • SPN • "B" MUST BE KILLED ○ B MUST DIE
HAY RIDE, THE • 1937 • Davis Mannie, Gordon George • ANS • USA
HAY RUBE • 1954 • Smith Paul J. • ANS • USA
HAY UN CAMINO A LA DERECHA • 1953 • Rovira Beleta Francisco • SPN
HAY UN NINO EN SU FUTURO • 1951 • Cortes Fernando • MXC
HAYACHINE NO FU • 1983 • Haneda Sumiko • JPN • TRADITIONAL DANCE AT HYACHINE VILLAGE
HAYAKURYO SANDO GASA • 1960 • Nakagawa Nobuo • JPN
HAYALLERIN, ASKIM VE SEN • 1987 • Yilmaz Atif • TRK • MY DREAMS, MY LOVE AND YOU
HAYAT ACILARI • 1967 • Aykanat Orhan • TRK • PAINS OF LIFE
HAYAT AL NAHEL • 1985 • Jurdi Hisham • LBN • LIFE OF THE BEES
HAYAT AL-YAWMIYYA FI QARIA SURIYYA, AL- • 1974 • Amiralai Omar • SYR • VIE QUOTIDIENNE DANS UN VILLAGE SYRIEN, LA ○ EVERYDAY LIFE IN A SYRIAN VILLAGE ○ HAYATT AL YAWMIYAH FI GARIAH SURIYAH, AL
HAYAT HERGUN YENIDEN BASLAR • 1978 • Refig Halit • TRK • EACH DAY LIFE BEGINS ANEW
HAYAT HILWA, AL- • 1966 • Halim Hilmy • EGY • VIE EST DOUCE, LA
HAYAT KHIFA, EL • 1968 • Mesnaoui Ahmed, Tazi Mohamed • MRC • VAINCRE POUR VIVRE ○ WIN TO LIVE
HAYAT OU MAUT • 1955 • el Sheikh Kamal • EGY • LIFE OR DEATH ○ HAYATUN AW MAWT ○ VIE OU MORT
HAYATA DONUS • 1967 • Duru Sureyya • TRK • ZENGIN VE SERSERI ○ BACK TO LIFE ○ RICH AND IDLE
HAYATI • 1970 • Wahab Fatin Abdel • EGY • MA VIE
HAYATI AL-KHASSA • 1974 • Marzouk Said • EGY • JE VEUX UNE SOLUTION ○ I WANT A SOLUTION
HAYATOZUKO NO HANRAN • 1957 • Matsuda Sadatsugu • JPN
HAYATT AL YAWMIYAH FI GARIAH SURIYAH, AL see **HAYAT AL-YAWMIYYA FI QARIA SURIYYA, AL-** • 1974
HAYATUN AW MAWT see **HAYAT OU MAUT** • 1955
HAYAUCHIINU • 1967 • Murano Tetsutaro • JPN • QUICK DRAW DOG
HAYCART CROSSES HADLEY GREEN • 1895 • Acres Birt • UKN
HAYDN see **ESZTERHAZA MUZSIKUSA, HAYDN** • 1960
HAYDUT see **ESKIYA HALIL** • 1968
HAYE MERA DIL • 1968 • Ved • IND • ALAS! MY HEART
HAYFOOT • 1942 • Guiol Fred • USA
HAYFOOT, STRAWFOOT • 1926 • Pratt Gilbert, Moffitt Jefferson • SHT • USA
HAYL-MOSKAU • 1932 • Schmidgof • USS
HAYSEED, THE • 1919 • Arbuckle Roscoe • USA
HAYSEED ROMANCE • 1935 • Lamont Charles • SHT • USA
HAYSEEDS, THE • 1933 • Smith Beaumont • ASL
HAYSEEDS' BACKBLOCKS SHOW, THE • 1917 • Smith Beaumont • ASL
HAYSEED'S BARGAIN, THE • 1908 • *Urban* • USA
HAYSEEDS COME TO TOWN (SYDNEY), THE • 1917 • Smith Beaumont • ASL
HAYSEEDS' MELBOURNE CUP, THE • 1918 • Smith Beaumont • ASL
HAYSTACK, THE see **MEULE, LA** • 1962
HAYSTACKS AND STEEPLES • 1916 • Badger Clarence, Lund Bert • SHT • USA
HAYWIRE • 1980 • Tuchner Michael • TVM • USA
HAZ, A • 1963 • Olah Gabor • HNG • HOUSE, THE
HAZ A SZIKLAK ALATT • 1958 • Makk Karoly • HNG • HOUSE UNDER THE ROCKS, THE
HAZ LA LOCA Y NO LA GUERRA • 1977 • Truchado Jose • SPN
HAZ-PUSH • 1928 • Bek-Nazarov Amo • DOC • USS • KHAZ-PUSH
HAZA HOWA EL HOB • 1958 • Abu Saif Salah • EGY • HADHA HUWWA AL-HUBB ○ C'EST CA, L'AMOUR!
HAZAAR-RATEN • 1953 • IND
HAZAFELE • 1974 • Kovacs Andras • HNG • HOMEWARD
HAZAL see **HAZEL** • 1980
HAZARD • 1948 • Marshall George • USA
HAZARD • 1959 • Stobart Thomas • UKN
HAZARD OF HEARTS, A • 1987 • Hough John • TVM • UKN
HAZARD OF YOUTH, THE • 1913 • Terwilliger George W. • USA
HAZARDOUS COURTSHIP, A • 1915 • Louis Will • USA
HAZARDOUS VALLEY • 1927 • Neitz Alvin J. • USA
HAZARDS AND HOME RUNS • 1917 • Semon Larry • SHT • USA
HAZARDS OF HELEN, THE • 1914-17 • McGowan J. P., Davis James • SRL • USA
HAZARD'S PEOPLE • 1976 • Szwarc Jeannot • TVM • USA
HAZASOKIK AZ URAM • 1913 • Curtiz Michael • HNG • MY HUSBAND LIES
HAZEL • 1980 • Ozzenturk Ali • TRK • HAZAL
HAZEL KIRKE • 1912 • Apfel Oscar • USA
HAZEL KIRKE • 1916 • Wharton Leopold, Wharton Theodore • USA
HAZEL, THE HEARTBREAKER • 1910 • *Bison* • USA
HAZEL'S PEOPLE see **HAPPY AS THE GRASS WAS GREEN** • 1973
HAZERS HAZED, THE • 1912 • *Thanhouser* • USA
HAZING, THE • 1978 • Curtis Douglas • USA • CURIOUS CASE OF THE CAMPUS CORPSE, THE ○ CAMPUS CORPSE, THE
HAZING A NEW SCHOLAR • 1910 • *Defender* • USA
HAZING IN HELL see **PLEDGE NIGHT** • 1988
HAZING THE HONEYMOONERS • 1914 • *Gaumont* • USA
HAZOBABAS, O • 1968 • Laskos Orestis • GRC • ADMIRING FATHER, AN ○ SIMPLE FATHER, THE
HAZUGSAG NELKUL • 1945 • Gertler Viktor • HNG • WITHOUT LIES
HAZUKASHII GIKO • 1967 • Mukoi Hiroshi • JPN • SHAMEFUL TECHNIQUE
HAZUKASHII YUME • 1927 • Gosho Heinosuke • JPN • INTIMATE DREAM ○ SHAMEFUL DREAM
HE see **EL** • 1952
HE see **ON** • 1961
HE ALMOST ELOPED • 1916 • Christie Al • SHT • USA
HE ALMOST LANDS AN ANGEL • 1916 • Beery Wallace • SHT • USA
HE AND HIMSELF • 1913 • *Nestor* • USA
HE AND HIS SISTER see **ON A JEHO SESTRA** • 1931
HE AND LIFE see **KARE TO JINSEI** • 1929
HE AND SHE • 1898 • *British Mutoscope & Biograph* • UKN
HE AND SHE • 1970 • Cimber Matt • USA • MAN AND WIFE
HE AND SHE see **KANOJO TO KARE** • 1963
HE AND SHE see **EKINOS KI EKINI** • 1967
HE AND SHE see **ASSOLUTO NATURALE, L'** • 1969
HE ANSWERED THE AD • 1913 • Angeles Bert • USA
HE ASKED FOR IT • 1940 • D'Arcy Harry • SHT • USA
HE ATTENDED THE MEETING • 1913 • Collins Edwin J.? • UKN
HE BECAME A REGULAR • 1916 • Clements Roy • SHT • USA
HE BECOMES A COP • 1916 • Beery Wallace • SHT • USA
HE BRINGS LUCK see **LYOGKAYA RUKA** • 1967
HE CALLED HER IN • 1913 • Dwan Allan • USA
HE CANNOT GET A WORD IN EDGEWAYS • 1906 • Martin J. H.? • UKN
HE CAN'T MAKE IT STICK • 1943 • Sommer Paul, Hubley John • ANS • USA
HE CHANGED HIS MIND • 1914 • *Lubin* • USA
HE COMES UP SMILING • 1918 • Dwan Allan • USA
HE COOKED HIS GOOSE • 1952 • White Jules • SHT • USA
HE COULD NOT LOSE HER • 1913 • *Eclair* • USA
HE COULDN'T DANCE, BUT HE LEARNED • 1909 • *Vitagraph* • USA
HE COULDN'T EXPLAIN • 1915 • Hotaling Arthur D. • USA
HE COULDN'T FOOL HIS MOTHER-IN-LAW • 1915 • Curtis Allen • USA
HE COULDN'T FOOL HIS WIFE • 1918 • Curtis Allen • SHT • USA
HE COULDN'T GET UP IN THE MORNING • 1917 • *Mckee Raymond* • SHT • USA
HE COULDN'T LOSE • 1913 • *Thanhouser* • USA
HE COULDN'T SAY NO • 1938 • Seiler Lewis • USA • LARGER THAN LIFE
HE COULDN'T SUPPORT HIS WIFE • 1915 • Curtis Allen • USA
HE COULDN'T TAKE IT • 1933 • Nigh William • *Monogram* • USA • ONE OF THE MANY (UKN) ○ PROCESS SERVER, THE ○ BORN TOUGH
HE CURED HIS GOUT • 1915 • *Joker* • USA
HE DANCED HIMSELF TO DEATH • 1914 • Ince Ralph • USA
HE DID ADMIRE HIS BOOTS • 1911 • Wilson Frank? • UKN
HE DID AND HE DIDN'T • 1916 • Arbuckle Roscoe • SHT • USA • LOVE AND LOBSTERS
HE DID AND HE DIDN'T • 1919 • Seiter William A. • USA
HE DID HIS BEST • 1929 • Pearce A. Leslie • USA
HE DID IT FOR THE BEST • 1913 • Kellino W. P. • UKN
HE DID IT HIMSELF • 1917 • Walsh James O., Taylor Rex, Richmond J. A. • SHT • USA
HE DID NOT WANT TO KILL see **ON NYE KHOTEL UBIVAT** • 1967

HE DIDN'T LIKE THE TUNE • 1911 • *Yankee* • USA
HE DIDN'T WANT TO DO IT • 1916 • Leigh J. L. V. • UKN
HE DIED AFTER THE WAR (USA) see **TOKYO SENSO SENGO HIWA** • 1970
HE DIED AND HE DIDN'T • 1916 • Miller Rube • SHT • USA
HE DIED WITH HIS EYES OPEN see **ON NE MEURT QUE DEUX FOIS** • 1986
HE DOESN'T CARE TO BE PHOTOGRAPHED • 1912-14 • Cohl Emile • ANS • USA
HE DONE HIS DUTY • 1937 • Lamont Charles • SHT • USA
HE DOOD IT AGAIN • 1943 • Donnelly Eddie • ANS • USA
HE ELOPED WITH HER FATHER • 1910 • Fitzhamon Lewin? • UKN
HE FELL IN A CABARET • 1915 • Frazee Edwin? • USA
HE FELL IN LOVE WITH HIS MOTHER-IN-LAW • 1913 • *Joker* • USA
HE FELL IN LOVE WITH HIS MOTHER-IN-LAW • 1913 • Angeles Bert • *Vitagraph* • USA
HE FELL IN LOVE WITH HIS WIFE • 1909 • *Vitagraph* • USA
HE FELL IN LOVE WITH HIS WIFE • 1916 • Taylor William D. • USA
HE FELL IN THE PARK • 1915 • Lyons Eddie • USA
HE FELL ON THE BEACH • 1917 • Christie Al • USA
HE FORGOT TO REMEMBER • 1926 • Roach Hal • SHT • USA
HE FORGOT TO REMEMBER • 1944 • Yates Hal • SHT • USA
HE FOUGHT FOR THE U.S.A. • 1911 • *Essanay* • USA
HE FOUND A STAR • 1941 • Carstairs John Paddy • UKN
HE GAVE A MILLION • 1914 • *Lubin* • USA
HE GOT HIMSELF A WIFE • 1915 • Stanley George C. • USA
HE GOT HIS • 1918 • Jackson Harry • SHT • USA
HE GOT MORE THAN HE BARGAINED FOR • 1899 • *Mutoscope & Biograph* • UKN
HE GOT RID OF THE MOTHS • 1910 • *Lubin* • USA
HE GOT THERE AFTER ALL • 1917 • Jackson Harry • SHT • USA
HE GYMNE TAXIARCHIA (GRC) see **NAKED BRIGADE, THE** • 1965
HE HAD A GUESS COMING • 1913 • Henderson Dell • USA
HE HAD BUT FIFTY CENTS • 1912 • *Imp* • USA
HE HAD 'EM BUFFALOED • 1917 • Beaudine William • SHT • USA
HE HAD TO CAMOUFLAGE • 1917 • Ruggles Wesley • SHT • USA
HE HAS TAKEN HIM FOR ANOTHER • 1957 • Li Han-Hsiang • HKG
HE HIRED THE BOSS • 1943 • Loring Thomas Z. • USA
HE IS COMING • 1970 • *Cosmos Films* • USA
HE IS MY BROTHER • 1976 • Dmytryk Edward • USA
HE KILLED HIS FAMILY AND WENT TO THE MOVIES see **MATOU A FAMILIA E FOI AO CINEMA** • 1989
HE KILLS NIGHT AFTER NIGHT AFTER NIGHT see **NIGHT AFTER NIGHT AFTER NIGHT** • 1970
HE KISSED THE BRIDE see **THEY ALL KISSED THE BRIDE** • 1942
HE KNEW TOO MUCH (UKN) see **DEVIL'S MATE** • 1933
HE KNEW WOMEN • 1930 • Herbert F. Hugh, Shores Lynn • USA
HE KNOWS YOU'RE ALONE • 1981 • Mastroianni Armand • USA • BLOOD WEDDING
HE LAUGHED LAST • 1956 • Edwards Blake • USA
HE LAUGHS LAST • 1920 • Robbins Jess • SHT • USA
HE LEADS, OTHERS FOLLOW • 1919 • Roach Hal • SHT • USA
HE LEARNED ABOUT WOMEN • 1933 • Corrigan Lloyd • USA
HE LEARNED ABOUT WOMEN see **TELLING THE WORLD** • 1928
HE LEARNED JU-JITSU -SO DID THE MISSUS • 1905 • Martin J. H.? • UKN
HE LEARNS THE TRICK OF MESMERISM • 1909 • *Pathe* • FRN
HE LEFT ON A BRIGHT CLEAR DAY see **WYSZEDL W JASNY POGODNY DZIEN** • 1973
HE LEFT ON A CLEAR FINE DAY see **WYSZEDL W JASNY POGODNY DZIEN** • 1973
HE LEFT ONE FINE DAY see **WYSZEDL W JASNY POGODNY DZIEN** • 1973
HE LIKES THINGS UPSIDE DOWN • 1912-14 • Cohl Emile • ANS • USA
HE LIVES BY NIGHT • 1982 • Liang Puzhi • HKG
HE LIVES ON • 1949 • Grigorov Roumen • DOC • RMN
HE LOVED AN ACTRESS see **STARDUST** • 1937
HE LOVED HER NOT • 1930 • Marshall George • SHT • USA
HE LOVED HER SO • 1918 • Hotaling Arthur D. • SHT • USA
HE LOVED HER SO see **TWENTY MINUTES OF LOVE** • 1914
HE LOVED LIKE HE LIED • 1920 • St. Clair Malcolm • SHT • USA
HE LOVED THE LADIES • 1916 • Davey Horace • USA
HE LOVED THE LADIES • 1929 • Pearce A. Leslie • USA
HE LOVES AND SHE LOVES • 1929 • Aylott Dave, Symmons E. F. • SHT • UKN
HE LOVES THE LADIES • 1914 • Sennett Mack • USA
HE LOVES TO BE AMUSED • 1912-14 • Cohl Emile • ANS • USA
HE LOVES TO WATCH THE FLIGHT OF TIME • 1913 • Cohl Emile • ANS • USA
HE MADE HIS MARK • 1914 • Murphy J. A. • USA
HE MADE ME LOVE HIM • 1916 • *Moser Frank (Anm)* • ANS • USA
HE MAID ME • 1916 • Lyons Eddie, Moran Lee • USA
HE MAKES ME FEEL LIKE DANCIN' • 1983 • Ardolino Emile • DOC • USA
HE MALE VAMP, A • 1920 • Watson William • SHT • USA
HE-MAN see **BARAKO** • 1967
HE-MAN AND SHE-RA: A CHRISTMAS SPECIAL • 1986 • Hayes Frank • ANM • USA
HE-MAN AND SHE-RA: THE SECRET OF THE SWORD* • 1985 • Lamore Marsh, Reed Bill, Wetzler Gwen, Friedman Ed, Kachivas Lou • ANM • USA • SECRET OF THE SWORD, THE
HE-MAN SEAMAN • 1962 • Bartsch Art • ANS • USA
HE-MAN'S COUNTRY, A • 1926 • Hatton Richard • USA
HE MARRIED HER ANYHOW • 1914 • *Franey William* • USA
HE MARRIED HIS WIFE • 1919 • *Roberts Edith* • SHT • USA
HE MARRIED HIS WIFE • 1940 • Del Ruth Roy • USA
HE MATADO A UN HOMBRE • 1963 • Bracho Julio • MXC
HE MENT WELL • 1917 • Jackson Harry • SHT • USA
HE MET A FRENCH GIRL see **THIS IS THE NIGHT** • 1932
HE MET THE CHAMPION • 1910 • *Essanay* • USA
HE MURDERED HIS WIFE see **ENGLIMA STO KAVOURI** • 1973
HE MUST BE ACCUSED • 1963 • Lisakovitch Viktor • USS
HE MUST HAVE A WIFE • 1912 • Henderson Dell • USA
HE NEARLY WON OUT • 1914 • *Lubin* • USA
HE NEVER FOUND OUT • 1914 • *Lubin* • USA
HE NEVER GIVES UP see **WANG-YANG-CHUNG-TE YI-T'IAO CH'UAN** • 1980
HE NEVER KNEW • 1913 • *Rex* • USA
HE NEVER KNEW • 1914 • Ince Ralph • USA
HE NEVER KNEW • 1915 • *Ramona* • USA
HE NEVER SAID A WORD • 1914 • *Nestor* • USA
HE NEVER TOUCHED ME • 1917 • Semon Larry • SHT • USA
HE OR SHE see **GLEN OR GLENDA?** • 1952
HE POSES FOR HIS PORTRAIT • 1912-14 • Cohl Emile • ANS • USA
HE RAN ALL THE WAY • 1951 • Berry John • USA
HE RIDES TALL • 1964 • Springsteen R. G. • USA • GUN HAND, THE
HE RUINS HIS FAMILY REPUTATION • 1913 • Cohl Emile • ANS • USA
HE SAID HE COULD ACT • 1914 • Hotaling Arthur D. • USA
HE SCARED THE GIRLS OFF see **SCARE THEIR PANTS OFF** • 1968
HE SHANG • 1988 • Xia Jun • CHN • RIVER ELEGY
HE, SHE AND IT • 1920 • France Charles H. • SHT • USA
HE, SHE AND THE MONEY see **HAN, HON OCH PENGARNA** • 1936
HE, SHE OR IT? (UKN) see **POUPEE, LA** • 1958
HE SHOOTS, HE SCORES see **LANCE ET COMPTE** • 1987
HE SLEPT WELL • 1913 • Cohl Emile • ANS • USA
HE SNOOPS TO CONQUER • 1944 • Varnel Marcel • UKN
HE STAYED FOR BREAKFAST • 1940 • Hall Alexander • USA
HE STUBS HIS TOE • 1910 • *Essanay* • USA
HE SWORE OFF SMOKING • 1912 • *Wordsworth William* • USA
HE TAKES PATIENCE BUT DOESN'T NEGLECT • 1979 • Hafez Hassan • EGY
HE TAKES WELL AT PARTIES • 1915 • *Pathe Exchange* • USA
HE THAT LAUGHS LAST • 1913 • *Sun Films* • UKN
HE THAT WILL STEAL A PIN.. see **OD RZEMYCZKA..** • 1961
HE, THE DOLPHIN see **ELE, O BOTO** • 1988
HE THOUGHT HE WENT TO WAR • 1916 • *France Charles H.* • USA
HE TRIED ON HANDCUFFS • 1909 • *Vitagraph* • USA
HE TRUMPED HER ACE • 1930 • *Sennett Mack (P)* • SHT • USA
HE, TU M'ENTENDS! • 1979 • Victor Renaud • FRN
HE WAITED • 1913 • Thompson Frederick A. • USA
HE WAITS FOREVER • 1914 • *Lubin* • USA
HE WALKED BY NIGHT • 1948 • Werker Alfred L., Mann Anthony (U/c) • USA
HE WALKS LIKE A TIGER see **KING OF KUNG FU** • 1973
HE WALKS THROUGH THE FIELDS see **HOU HALACH BASADOT** • 1967
HE WANTED A BABY • 1909 • *Lubin* • USA
HE WANTED CHICKENS • 1914 • *Lubin* • USA
HE WANTED HIS PANTS • 1914 • *Lubin* • USA
HE WANTED TO BE BRAVE • 1963 • Kurchevsky V., Serebryakov N. • ANS • USS
HE WANTED TO BE KING see **ITHELE NA YINI VASILIAS** • 1967
HE WANTED TO PROPOSE, BUT.. • 1912 • Wilson Frank? • UKN
HE WANTED WORK • 1914 • *Lubin* • USA
HE WANTS WHAT HE WANTS WHEN HE WANTS IT • 1913 • Cohl Emile • ANS • USA
HE WAS A CZECH MUSICIAN see **TO BYL CESKY MUZIKANT** • 1940
HE WAS A MILLIONAIRE • 1911 • *Solax* • USA
HE WAS A TRAVELLING MAN • 1915 • *Wheeler George H.* • USA
HE WAS BAD • 1914 • Hevener Jerold T. • USA
HE WAS BORN, HE SUFFERED, HE DIED • 1974 • Brakhage Stan • USA
HE WAS CALLED ROBERT see **YEVO ZOVUT ROBERT** • 1967
HE WAS HER MAN • 1934 • Bacon Lloyd • USA
HE WAS HER MAN • 1937 • Freleng Friz • ANS • USA
HE WAS MY FRIEND see **A FOST PRIETENUL MEU** • 1961
HE WAS NO LADY • 1919 • Wulze Harry • SHT • USA
HE WAS NOT ILL, ONLY UNHAPPY • 1912-14 • Cohl Emile • ANS • USA
HE WAS ONLY A BATHING SUIT SALESMAN • 1915 • Myers Harry • USA
HE WAS ONLY FEUDIN' • 1943 • Edwards Harry J. • SHT • USA
HE WAS SO FOND OF ANIMALS • 1913 • Fitzhamon Lewin • UKN
HE WASN'T ENGAGED AT THE OFFICE • 1906 • Jeapes Harold? • UKN
HE WENT AND WON • 1916 • *Hardy Oliver* • USA
HE WENT TO SEE THE DEVIL PLAY • 1908 • *Vitagraph* • USA
HE WHO DIED OF LOVE see **QUE MURIO DE AMOR, EL** • 1945
HE WHO GETS RAPPED • 1925 • Ruggles Wesley • SHT • USA
HE WHO GETS SLAPPED • 1924 • Sjostrom Victor • USA
HE WHO GETS SMACKED • 1925 • Bacon Lloyd • SHT • USA
HE WHO HESITATES • 1919 • Beaudine William • USA
HE WHO LAUGHS LAST • 1910 • *Vitagraph* • USA
HE WHO LAUGHS LAST • 1911 • *Kalem* • USA
HE WHO LAUGHS LAST • 1914 • *Komic* • USA
HE WHO LAUGHS LAST • 1925 • Nelson Jack • USA
HE WHO LAUGHS LAST LAUGHS BEST • 1908 • *Essanay* • USA
HE WHO LEAVES IN THE RAIN see **KTO ODZHDZA V DAZDI** • 1977
HE WHO LIVED JUDO see **SUGATA SANSHIRO** • 1955
HE WHO MUST DIE (USA) see **CELUI QUI DOIT MOURIR** • 1956
HE WHO RIDES A TIGER • 1965 • Crichton Charles • UKN
HE WHO SHOOTS FIRST (UKN) see **DJANGO SPARA PER PRIMO** • 1966
HE WHO SINGS MEANS NO EVIL see **TKO PJEVA, ZLO NE MISLI** • 1971
HE WHO TAKES WHAT ISN'T HIS'N • 1913 • Stow Percy • UKN
HE WINKED AND WON • 1917 • *Hardy Oliver* • USA
HE WINS • 1918 • Perez Marcel • USA
HE WOKE UP IN TIME • 1914 • *Lubin* • USA
HE WON A RANCH • 1914 • *Lubin* • USA
HE WORE A WIG • 1914 • *Lubin* • USA
HE WOULD A-WOOING GO • 1936 • Field Mary • UKN
HE WOULD ACT • 1915 • Kellino W. P. • UKN
HE WOULD A'HUNTING GO • 1913 • Nicholls George • USA
HE WOULD FISH • 1909 • *Anglo-American* • UKN
HE WOULD FIX THINGS • 1913 • Miller Ashley • USA
HE WOULD SPEAK • 1912 • Stow Percy • UKN
HE WOULDN'T STAY DOWN • 1915 • Parrott Charles • USA
HE WOULDN'T TIP • 1916 • *Burns Neal* • USA
HE WOULDN'T WEAR GLASSES • 1916 • *Figman Max* • SHT • USA
HE WROTE A BOOK • 1916 • Garwood William • SHT • USA
HE WROTE POETRY? • 1916 • Ellis Robert • SHT • USA
HEAD • 1968 • Rafelson Bob • USA
HEAD see **DOPE** • 1968
HEAD see **WILD RIDERS** • 1971
HEAD, THE see **GLOWA** • 1953
HEAD, THE see **RAS, AR-** • 1976
HEAD, THE (USA) see **NACKTE UND DER SATAN, DIE** • 1959
HEAD FOR BUSINESS, A • 1911 • Salter Harry • USA
HEAD FOR THE DEVIL, A see **NACKTE UND DER SATAN, DIE** • 1959
HEAD FOR THE HILLS see **SOD SISTERS** • 1969
HEAD GUY, THE • 1930 • Guiol Fred • SHT • USA
HEAD HUNTERS see **CAZADORES DE CABEZAS** • 1960
HEAD HUNTERS, THE • 1913 • *Bison* • USA
HEAD HUNTERS OF MALEKULA see **CANNIBALS OF THE SOUTH SEAS** • 1912
HEAD HUNTERS OF THE SOUTH SEAS • 1922 • Johnson Martin E. • DOC • USA
HEAD LADY • 1968 • Elliott B. Ron • USA • HEAD MISTRESS, THE ○ HEADMISTRESS
HEAD MAKES, THE HEAD DRAWS, THE • Todorov Dimiter • ANS • USA
HEAD MAN, THE • 1928 • Cline Eddie • USA • BOSS OF LITTLE ARCADY, THE
HEAD MEN, THE • 1963 • Biggs Julian, Howe John • CND
HEAD MISTRESS, THE see **HEAD LADY** • 1968
HEAD NURSE • 1974 • *Harris Rachel* • USA
HEAD OF A TYRANT (USA) see **GIUDITTA E OLOFERNE** • 1959
HEAD OF JANUS, THE see **JANUSKOPF, DER** • 1920
HEAD OF MEDUSA, THE see **HAUPT DER MEDUSA, DER** • 1919
HEAD OF MEDUSA, THE see **MEDUSAN PAA** • 1974
HEAD OF PANCHO VILLA, THE see **CABEZA DE PANCHO VILLA, LA** • 1955
HEAD OF THE FAMILY • 1933 • Daumery John • UKN
HEAD OF THE FAMILY, THE • 1916 • Wilson Ben • SHT • USA
HEAD OF THE FAMILY, THE • 1922 • Haynes Manning • UKN
HEAD OF THE FAMILY, THE • 1928 • Boyle Joseph C. • USA
HEAD OF THE FAMILY, THE (USA) see **PADRE DI FAMIGLIA, IL** • 1967
HEAD OF THE HOUSE • 1952 • *Leacock Richard (Ph)* • DOC • USA
HEAD OF THE HOUSE, THE • 1916 • Horkheimer H. M., Horkheimer E. D. • SHT • USA
HEAD OF THE HOUSE PLAYS ACCORDION, THE • 1949 • Kassila Matti • FNL
HEAD OF THE RIBBON COUNTER, THE • 1913 • *Benham Harry* • USA
HEAD OFFICE • 1986 • Finkleman Ken • USA
HEAD OFICE • 1936 • Brown Melville • UKN
HEAD ON • 1980 • Grant Michael • CND • FATAL ATTRACTION (USA)
HEAD OVER HEELS • 1922 • Schertzinger Victor, Bern Paul • USA
HEAD OVER HEELS • 1925 • Del Ruth Roy • SHT • USA
HEAD OVER HEELS • 1937 • Hale Sonnie • UKN • HEAD OVER HEELS IN LOVE (USA)
HEAD OVER HEELS • 1979 • Silver Joan Micklin • USA • CHILLY SCENES OF WINTER
HEAD OVER HEELS see **HARD TO GET** • 1938
HEAD OVER HEELS IN LOVE (USA) see **HEAD OVER HEELS** • 1937
HEAD RAG HOP • 1970 • Turner Peter • SHT • UKN
HEAD SCAPE • 1972 • Furukawa Taku • ANS • JPN
HEAD SET • 1978 • USA
HEAD SPOON • 1971 • Furukawa Taku • ANS • JPN
HEAD START, MEETING THE COMPUTER CHALLENGE see **ORDINATEUR ET TETE** • 1984
HEAD THAT WOULDN'T DIE, THE see **BRAIN THAT WOULDN'T DIE, THE** • 1962
HEAD WAITER, THE • 1914 • *Joker* • USA
HEAD WAITER, THE • 1914 • *Thanhouser* • USA
HEAD WAITER, THE • 1920 • Semon Larry • SHT • USA
HEAD WAITER, THE see **SERVICE FOR LADIES** • 1927
HEAD WELL-SCREWED ON, A • 1961 • Fyodorova Marina • USS
HEAD WIND, A see **VETER V LITSO** • 1929
HEAD WINDS • 1925 • Blache Herbert • USA • OVERBOARD
HEAD WOUND, THE see **FEJLOVES** • 1968
HEADDRESSES OF DIFFERENT PERIODS see **HISTOIRE D'UN CHAPEAU** • 1910
HEADFILM • Lawder Standish D. • SHT • USA
HEADFUL OF LOVE, A • 1969 • *Distripix* • USA
HEADHUNTER • 1988 • Schaeffer Franky • USA
HEADIN' EAST • 1937 • Scott Ewing • USA
HEADIN' FOR BROADWAY • 1980 • Brooks Joseph • USA
HEADIN' FOR DANGER • 1928 • Bradbury Robert North • USA • ASKING FOR TROUBLE (UKN)
HEADIN' FOR GOD'S COUNTRY • 1943 • Morgan William • USA
HEADIN' FOR THE RIO GRANDE • 1936 • Bradbury Robert North • USA
HEADIN' FOR TROUBLE • 1931 • McGowan J. P. • USA

HEADIN' HOME • 1920 • Windom Lawrence C. • USA
HEADIN' NORTH • 1921 • Bartlett Charles • USA
HEADIN' NORTH • 1930 • McCarthy John P. • USA
HEADIN' SOUTH • 1918 • Rosson Arthur • USA
HEADIN' THROUGH • 1924 • Maloney Leo, Williamson Bob • USA
HEADIN' WEST • 1922 • Craft William James • USA
HEADIN' WEST • 1946 • Nazarro Ray • USA • CHEAT'S LAST THROW, THE (UKN)
HEADIN' WESTWARD • 1928 • McGowan J. P. • USA
HEADING FOR HEAVEN • 1947 • Collins Lewis D. • USA
HEADING FOR TROUBLE • 1947 • Yates Hal • SHT • USA
HEADING SOUTH see **CAMINO DEL SUR, EL** • 1987
HEADLESS EYES • 1971 • Bateman Kent • USA
HEADLESS GHOST, THE • 1959 • Scott Peter Graham • UKN
HEADLESS HORSEMAN, THE • 1922 • Venturini Edward D. • USA
HEADLESS HORSEMAN, THE • 1934 • Iwerks Ub • ANS • USA
HEADLESS HORSEMAN, THE • 1973 • Vainshtok Vladimir • USS
HEADLESS MOTHS • 1921 • Leonard Robert Z. • USA
HEADLESS RIDER, THE (USA) see **JINETE SIN CABEZA, EL** • 1956
HEADLESS WARRIOR, THE • Gautama Sisworo • INN
HEADLEYS AT HOME, THE • 1938 • Beute Chris • USA • AMONG THOSE PRESENT (UKN)
HEADLIGHTS IN THE FOG see **FARI NELLA NEBBIA** • 1942
HEADLINE • 1943 • Harlow John • UKN
HEADLINE CRASHER • 1937 • Goodwins Leslie • USA
HEADLINE HUNTERS • 1955 • Witney William • USA
HEADLINE HUNTERS • 1968 • Ingrams Jonathan • UKN
HEADLINE HUNTRESS see **CHANGE OF HEART** • 1938
HEADLINE SHOOTER see **HEADLINE SHOOTERS** • 1933
HEADLINE SHOOTERS • 1933 • Brower Otto • USA • EVIDENCE IN CAMERA (UKN) ○ HEADLINE SHOOTER
HEADLINE WOMAN, THE • 1935 • Nigh William • USA • WOMAN IN THE CASE, THE (UKN)
HEADLINERS, THE • 1915 • Kelsey Fred A. • USA
HEADLINES • 1925 • Griffith Edward H. • USA
HEADLINES OF DESTRUCTION (USA) see **JE SUIS UN SENTIMENTAL** • 1955
HEADMAN, THE see **HOVDINGEN** • 1984
HEADMAN'S REVENGE, THE • 1913 • Collins Edwin J.? • UKN
HEADMASTER, THE • 1921 • Foss Kenelm • UKN
HEADMASTER'S DIARY, A • 1975 • Frumin B. • USS
HEADMISTRESS see **HEAD LADY** • 1968
HEADMISTRESS, THE see **SIT EL NAZRA, EL** • 1968
HEADQUARTERS STATE SECRET (USA) see **SOLDATENSENDER CALAIS** • 1960
HEADS • 1969 • Gidal Peter • UKN
HEADS see **HLAVY** • 1979
HEADS AND TAILS see **ORZEL I RESZKA** • 1974
HEADS I KILL YOU, TAILS YOU'RE DEAD • 1972 • Carnimeo Giuliano • ITL
HEADS I WIN • 1963 • Robin Georges • SHT • UKN
HEADS OR TAILS • 1912 • *Cosmopolitan* • UKN
HEADS OR TAILS • 1914 • *B & C* • UKN
HEADS OR TAILS • 1978 • Zielinska Ida Eva • CND
HEADS OR TAILS see **PILE OU FACE** • 1980
HEADS OR TAILS see **PISMO-GLAVA** • 1984
HEADS THAT ARE CUT see **CABEZAS CORTADAS** • 1970
HEADS UP • 1925 • Garson Harry • USA
HEADS UP • 1930 • Schertzinger Victor • USA
HEADS UP see **SINGLE HANDED** • 1923
HEADS WE GO • 1933 • Banks Monty • UKN • CHARMING DECEIVER, THE (USA)
HEADS WIN • 1919 • Kendall Preston • USA
HEADS YOU LOSE • 1974 • Grossman J. • UKN
HEADSTAND see **KOPFSTAND** • 1981
HEADSTAND, MADAM! see **KOPFSTAND, MADAM!** • 1967
HEALER, THE • 1935 • Barker Reginald • USA
HEALERS, THE • 1915 • *Reliance* • USA
HEALERS, THE • 1974 • Gries Tom • TVM • USA
HEALING • 1977 • Lasry Pierre • CND
HEALING FAITH, THE • 1910 • *Lubin* • USA
HEALING WATER, THE see **BUDOSVIZ** • 1966
HEALTH see **H.E.A.L.T.H.** • 1979
HEALTH BY THE YEAR • 1915 • *De Angelis Jefferson* • USA
HEALTH CLUB see **TOXIC AVENGER, THE** • 1985
HEALTH FARM, THE • 1936 • Davis Mannie, Gordon George • ANS • USA
HEALTH FOR THE NATION see **HEALTH OF A NATION** • 1939
HEALTH-GIVING WATERS OF TISZA, THE see **ELTETO TISZA-VIZ** • 1954
HEALTH IN INDUSTRY • 1938 • Watt Harry • DOC • UKN
HEALTH IN WAR • 1940 • Jackson Pat • DCS • UKN
HEALTH OF A NATION • 1939 • Monck John • DOC • UKN • HEALTH FOR THE NATION ○ FORTY MILLION PEOPLE
HEALTH ROAD, THE • 1916 • Holubar Allen • SHT • USA
HEALTH SPA, THE • 1978 • Dia Claire • USA
HEALTHY AND HAPPY • 1919 • Smith Noel • SHT • USA
HEALTHY LUST AND FUN see **SALUT I FORCA AL CANUT** • 1979
HEALTHY NEIGHBORHOOD, A • 1913 • Sennett Mack • USA
HEALTHY, WEALTHY AND DUMB • 1938 • Lord Del • SHT • USA
HEAP BIG CHIEF • 1919 • Roach Hal • SHT • USA
HEAP BIG HEPCAT • 1960 • Smith Paul J. • ANS • USA
HEAP, HEP INJUNS • 1950 • Sparber I. • ANS • USA
HEAR 'EM AND WEEP • 1933 • Santley Joseph • SHT • USA
HEAR 'EM RAVE • 1918 • Roach Hal • SHT • USA
HEAR ME GOOD • 1957 • McGuire Don • USA
HEAR MY SONG • 1967 • De Witt Elmo • SAF • HOOR MY LIED
HEAR NO EVIL • 1914 • *Essanay* • USA
HEAR NO EVIL • 1982 • Falk Harry • TVM • USA
HEAR NO EVIL see **FLESH AND FURY** • 1952
HEAR THAT TRUMPET TALK see **CRIMSON CANARY, THE** • 1945
HEAR THE PIPERS CALLING • 1918 • Watts Tom • UKN
HEARD IN COURT • 1909 • *Warwick Trading Co.* • UKN
HEARD OVER THE 'PHONE • 1908 • Porter Edwin S. • USA
HEARSAY see **SEE CHINA AND DIE** • 1982
HEARSE, THE • 1980 • Bowers George • USA
HEARST AND DAVIES AFFAIR, THE • 1985 • Rich David Lowell • TVM • USA
HEART • 1987 • Lemmo James • USA
HEART see **KOKORO** • 1973
HEART, THE • 1964 • Kidawa Janusz • DOC • PLN
HEART, THE see **KOKORO** • 1955
HEART AND HAND see **HOUSE DIVIDED, A** • 1932
HEART AND SOUL • 1917 • Edwards J. Gordon • USA
HEART AND SOUL • 1987 • Stephan Bernhard • GDR
HEART AND SOUL see **NON-CONFORMIST PARSON, A** • 1919
HEART AND SOUL see **MISCHIEF** • 1985
HEART AND SOUL (USA) see **CUORE** • 1948
HEART AWAKENED, A • 1915 • Terwilliger George W. • USA
HEART BANDIT, THE • 1924 • Apfel Oscar • USA
HEART BEAT • 1979 • Byrum John • USA • HEARTBEAT
HEART BEAT see **SZIVDOBOGAS** • 1961
HEART BEAT see **COL CUORE IN GOLA** • 1967
HEART BEAT FRESCO • 1966 • de la Parra Pim • NTH • HEARTBEAT FRESCO
HEART BEATS • 1915 • Adolfi John G. • USA
HEART BEATS AGAIN, THE see **SERDTSYE BETSYA YNOV** • 1956
HEART BEATS ANEW, THE see **SERDTSYE BETSYA YNOV** • 1956
HEART BEEPS • 1981 • Arkush Allan • USA • HEARTBEEPS
HEART BENEATH, THE • 1919 • *Hart Neal* • SHT • USA
HEART BOWED DOWN, THE • 1906 • Gilbert Arthur • UKN
HEART BREAKER, THE • 1915 • Johnston Lorimer • USA
HEART BREAKERS, THE • 1916 • *Saunders Jackie* • SHT • USA
HEART BROKERS, THE • 1913 • O'Neil Barry • USA
HEART BURN • 1942 • D'Arcy Harry • SHT • USA
HEART BUSTER, THE • 1924 • Conway Jack • USA
HEART CONDITION • 1990 • Parriott James • USA
HEART EXPOSED, THE see **COEUR DECOUVERT, LE** • 1988
HEART FARM, THE see **MAN WHO WANTED TO LIVE FOREVER, THE** • 1970
HEART FOR A SONG, THE see **SRDCE ZA PISNICKU** • 1933
HEART FOR HEART see **SZIUEL SZIVERT** • 1939
HEART IN MOURNING see **CORACAO DE LUTO** • 1968
HEART IN PAWN, A • 1919 • Worthington William • USA • SHADOWS
HEART IN RAGS, A • 1912 • McRae Henry • USA
HEART INTO HEARTS see **SAMYAN SAN SEIGAI** • 1989
HEART IS A LONELY HUNTER, THE • 1968 • Miller Robert Ellis • USA
HEART KNOWS NO FRONTIERS, THE see **CUORI SENZA FRONTIERE** • 1950
HEART LIKE A WHEEL see **BORN TO WIN** • 1983
HEART LINE, THE • 1921 • Thompson Frederick A. • USA
HEART MENDERS, THE • 1916 • *Hamilton Lloyd V.* • SHT • USA
HEART MUST KEEP SILENCE, THE see **HERZ MUSS SCHWEIGEN, DAS** • 1944
HEART O' THE HILLS • 1919 • Franklin Sidney A. • USA
HEART O' THE WEST see **HEARTS OF THE WEST** • 1925
HEART OF A BANDIT, THE • 1915 • O'Sullivan Tony • USA
HEART OF A BOSS, THE • 1912 • *Lubin* • USA
HEART OF A CHAMPION • 1915 • *Darcy Les* • ASL
HEART OF A CHAMPION: THE RAY MANCINI STORY • 1985 • Michaels Richard • TVM • USA
HEART OF A CHILD • 1958 • Donner Clive • UKN
HEART OF A CHILD, THE • 1913 • *Thanhouser Kid* • USA
HEART OF A CHILD, THE • 1915 • Shaw Harold • UKN
HEART OF A CHILD, THE • 1920 • Smallwood Ray C. • USA
HEART OF A CHILD (USA) see **CORAZON DE NINO** • 1939
HEART OF A CLOWN see **KLOVNEN** • 1926
HEART OF A CLOWN, THE • 1909 • Porter Edwin S. • USA
HEART OF A COSSACK, THE • 1912 • Makarenko Mr. • USA
HEART OF A COWARD, THE • 1926 • Worne Duke • USA
HEART OF A COWBOY, THE • 1909 • Anderson G. M. • USA
HEART OF A COWBOY, THE • 1910 • *Defender* • USA
HEART OF A CRACKSMAN • 1913 • Robards Willis, Reid Wallace • USA
HEART OF A CROOK, THE • 1914 • *Kb* • USA
HEART OF A DOLL, THE • 1913 • *Gaumont* • USA
HEART OF A DOLL, THE • 1916 • *Fairbanks Madeline* • SHT • USA
HEART OF A FISHERGIRL, THE • 1910 • Fitzhamon Lewin • UKN
HEART OF A FOLLIES GIRL, THE • 1928 • *Dove Billie* • USA
HEART OF A FOOL see **IN THE HEART OF A FOOL** • 1920
HEART OF A FOOL, THE • 1913 • *Garwood William* • USA
HEART OF A FOOL, THE • 1916 • Davenport Harry • SHT • USA
HEART OF A FRIEND see **SYERDTSE DRUGA** • 1967
HEART OF A GAMBLER, THE • 1913 • *Essanay* • USA
HEART OF A GIRL • 1918 • Adolfi John G. • USA
HEART OF A GYPSY MAID, THE • 1913 • Collins Edwin J.? • UKN
HEART OF A HEATHEN, THE • 1913 • *Powers* • USA
HEART OF A HERO, THE • 1916 • Chautard Emile • USA • NATHAN HALE
HEART OF A JEWESS, THE • 1913 • Smalley Phillips, Weber Lois • USA
HEART OF A LION, THE • 1918 • Lloyd Frank • USA
HEART OF A MAGDALENE, THE • 1914 • *Maison Edna* • USA
HEART OF A MAN • 1920 • *Coburn Wallace* • SHT • USA
HEART OF A MAN, THE • 1912 • *Case Helen* • USA
HEART OF A MAN, THE • 1912 • Southwell Gilbert • UKN
HEART OF A MAN, THE • 1915 • Thayer Otis B. • USA
HEART OF A MAN, THE • 1959 • Wilcox Herbert • UKN
HEART OF A MERMAID, THE • 1916 • Henderson Lucius • SHT • USA
HEART OF A MOTHER (UKN) see **SERDTSE MATERI** • 1966
HEART OF A NATION, THE (UKN) see **WE AMERICANS** • 1928
HEART OF A NATION (UKN) see **UNTEL PERE ET FILS** • 1940
HEART OF A PAINTED WOMAN, THE • 1915 • Blache Alice • USA
HEART OF A PEDDLER, THE • 1916 • *Supreme* • USA
HEART OF A PROUD WOMAN, THE see **KOKORO OGORERU ONNA** • 1930
HEART OF A RACE TOUT • 1909 • Boggs Frank • USA
HEART OF A ROSE, THE • 1910 • Porter Edwin S. • USA
HEART OF A ROSE, THE • 1913 • *Rosenfeld Sidney* • USA
HEART OF A ROSE, THE • 1919 • Denton Jack • UKN
HEART OF A SAVAGE, THE • 1911 • Griffith D. W. • USA
HEART OF A SHOW GIRL, THE • 1916 • Worthington William • SHT • USA
HEART OF A SIOUX, THE • 1910 • *Lubin* • USA
HEART OF A SIREN • 1925 • Rosen Phil • USA • HEART OF A TEMPTRESS
HEART OF A SOLDIER, THE • 1912 • *Kerrigan J. Warren* • USA
HEART OF A TEMPTRESS see **HEART OF A SIREN** • 1925
HEART OF A TEXAN, THE • 1922 • Hurst Paul C. • USA
HEART OF A TIGRESS, THE • 1915 • MacGregor Norval • USA
HEART OF A TRAMP, THE • 1912 • *Nestor* • USA
HEART OF A TYRANT see **ZSARNOK SZIVE AVAGY BOCCACCIO MAGYARORSZAGON, A** • 1981
HEART OF A VAGABOND, THE • 1915 • Mitchell Bruce • USA
HEART OF A VAQUERO • 1913 • *Nestor* • USA
HEART OF A WAIF, THE • 1915 • Seay Charles M. • USA
HEART OF A WOLF see **TRAP, THE** • 1922
HEART OF A WOMAN • 1914 • *Little Anna* • USA
HEART OF A WOMAN, THE • 1912 • Buckland Warwick? • UKN
HEART OF A WOMAN, THE • 1920 • Pratt Jack • USA
HEART OF ALASKA • 1924 • McCracken Harold • USA
HEART OF AN ACTRESS see **AME D'ARTISTE** • 1925
HEART OF AN ACTRESS, THE • 1910 • *Yankee* • USA
HEART OF AN ACTRESS, THE • 1913 • *Joyce Alice* • USA
HEART OF AN ACTRESS, THE • 1915 • Morgan George • USA
HEART OF AN ACTRESS, THE (UKN) see **HER BODY IN BOND** • 1918
HEART OF AN ARTIST • 1982 • Leiterman Richard • MTV • CND
HEART OF AN ARTIST • 1983 • Shatalow Peter • CND
HEART OF AN ARTIST, THE • 1913 • *White Pearl* • USA
HEART OF AN INDIAN, THE • 1916 • *Buffalo* • SHT • USA
HEART OF AN INDIAN MOTHER, THE • 1911 • *Kalem* • USA
HEART OF AN OUTCAST, THE see **KARDIA ENOS ALITI, I** • 1968
HEART OF ARIZONA, THE • 1938 • Selander Lesley • USA
HEART OF AYMARA see **CORAZON AYMARA** • 1925
HEART OF BIG DAN • 1920 • *Lowell John* • SHT • USA
HEART OF BONITA, THE • 1916 • Reynolds Lynn • SHT • USA
HEART OF BRITAIN • 1970 • Vas Robert • UKN • HUMPHREY JENNINGS
HEART OF BRITAIN, THE • 1941 • Jennings Humphrey • DOC • UKN • THIS IS ENGLAND (USA)
HEART OF BROADWAY, THE • 1928 • Worne Duke • USA • RESTLESS YOUTH (UKN)
HEART OF CARITA, THE • 1914 • *Johnston J. W.* • USA
HEART OF CERISE, THE • 1915 • De Grasse Joseph • USA
HEART OF DIXIE • 1988 • Anderson Martin • USA
HEART OF DRAGON see **FIRST MISSION, THE**
HEART OF ESMERALDA, THE • 1912 • Ranous William V. • USA
HEART OF EZRA GREER, THE • 1917 • Chautard Emile • USA
HEART OF FLAME • 1915 • Ricketts Thomas • USA
HEART OF GENERAL ROBERT E. LEE, THE • 1928 • Neill R. William • SHT • USA
HEART OF GIPSY, THE • 1919 • Miller Charles • USA
HEART OF GLASS (USA) see **HERZ AUS GLAS** • 1976
HEART OF GOLD • 1917 • Sargent George L. • USA
HEART OF GOLD • 1919 • Vale Travers • USA
HEART OF GOLD see **ZLATE SRDECKO** • 1916
HEART OF GOLD, A • 1915 • Ricketts Thomas • USA
HEART OF GYPSY, THE • 1912 • *Imp* • USA
HEART OF HERNANDA, THE • 1913 • *Powers* • USA
HEART OF HIROSHIMA, THE see **AI TO SHI NO KIROKU** • 1966
HEART OF HUMANITY • 1919 • Holubar Allen • USA
HEART OF JABEZ FLINT, THE • 1915 • *Hunt Jay* • USA
HEART OF JENNIFER, THE • 1915 • Kirkwood James • USA
HEART OF JIM BRICE, THE • 1915 • Costello Maurice • USA
HEART OF JOHN BARLOW, THE • 1911 • *Ayres Sydney* • USA
HEART OF JOHN GRIMM, THE • 1912 • *Mitchell Ralph* • USA
HEART OF JUANITA, THE • 1919 • Middleton George E. • USA
HEART OF KATHLEEN, THE • 1913 • Spencer Richard V. • USA
HEART OF LINCOLN, THE • 1915 • Ford Francis • USA
HEART OF MAGGIE MALONE, THE • 1914 • Le Saint Edward J. • USA
HEART OF MARY ANN, THE • 1917 • Stonehouse Ruth • SHT • USA
HEART OF MARYLAND, THE • 1915 • Brenon Herbert • USA
HEART OF MARYLAND, THE • 1921 • Terriss Tom • USA
HEART OF MARYLAND, THE • 1927 • Bacon Lloyd • USA
HEART OF MIDLOTHIAN, THE • 1914 • Wilson Frank • UKN
HEART OF MIDNIGHT • 1988 • Chapman Matthew • USA
HEART OF MRS. ROBINS, THE • 1913 • Brooke Van Dyke • USA
HEART OF NASONIA, THE • 1919 • *Doraldina* • USA
HEART OF NEW YORK see **HALLELUJAH, I'M A BUM** • 1933
HEART OF NEW YORK, THE • 1916 • MacNamara Walter • USA
HEART OF NEW YORK, THE • 1932 • LeRoy Mervyn • USA
HEART OF NICHETTE, THE • 1911 • *Dalberg Camilla* • USA
HEART OF NORA FLYNN, THE • 1916 • De Mille Cecil B. • USA
HEART OF O YAMA, THE • 1908 • Griffith D. W. • USA
HEART OF OAK • 1910 • Fitzhamon Lewin • UKN
HEART OF PARIS (USA) see **GRIBOUILLE** • 1937
HEART OF PARO, THE • 1915 • Santschi Thomas • USA
HEART OF PAULA, THE • 1916 • *Ulrich Lenore* • USA
HEART OF RACHEL, THE • 1918 • Hickman Howard • USA
HEART OF REALITY see **KOKORO NO JITSUGETSU** • 1931
HEART OF ROMANCE, THE • 1918 • Millarde Harry • USA
HEART OF SALOME, THE • 1927 • Schertzinger Victor • USA
HEART OF SCOTLAND • 1961-62 • *Grierson John (P)* • DOC • UKN
HEART OF SHOW BUSINESS, THE • 1957 • Staub Ralph • DOC • USA
HEART OF SISTER ANN, THE • 1915 • Shaw Harold • UKN
HEART OF SMILING JOE, THE • 1914 • *Frontier* • USA
HEART OF SOLOMON, THE see **SERDCE SOLOMONA** • 1932
HEART OF SONNY JIM, THE • 1914 • Johnson Tefft • USA

HEART OF SPAIN • 1937 • Kline Herbert • DOC • USA
HEART OF STEEL • 1983 • Wrye Donald • TVM • USA
HEART OF STONE see **KALTE HERZ, DAS** • 1950
HEART OF STONE see **ZANKYO MUJO** • 1968
HEART OF TARA, THE • 1916 • Bowman William J. • USA
HEART OF TESSA, THE • 1910 • *Capitol* • USA
HEART OF TEXAS RYAN, THE • 1917 • Martin E. A. • USA • SINGLE SHOT PARKER
HEART OF THE BLUE RIDGE, THE • 1915 • Young James • USA
HEART OF THE FOREST, A • 1913 • Ince Ralph • USA
HEART OF THE FOREST, THE see **CORAZON DEL BOSQUE** • 1978
HEART OF THE GOLDEN WEST • 1942 • Kane Joseph • USA
HEART OF THE HILLS • 1914 • Edwin Walter • *Victor* • USA
HEART OF THE HILLS • 1919 • De Grasse Joseph • USA
HEART OF THE HILLS, THE • 1914 • Reid Wallace • *Rex* • USA
HEART OF THE HILLS, THE • 1916 • Ridgely Richard • USA
HEART OF THE HURRICANE, THE see **IM HERZEN DER HURRICAN** • 1980
HEART OF THE KING'S JESTER, THE • 1911 • *Vitagraph* • USA
HEART OF THE LAW, THE • 1913 • *Calvert E. H.* • USA
HEART OF THE MATTER, THE • 1953 • O'Ferrall George M. • UKN
HEART OF THE MOUNTAINS, THE see **KOKORO NO SANMYAKU** • 1966
HEART OF THE NIGHT see **KALB EL LEIL** • 1989
HEART OF THE NIGHT, THE see **CORAZON DE LA NOCHE, EL** • 1983
HEART OF THE NIGHT WIND, THE • 1914 • Edwin Walter • USA
HEART OF THE NORTH • 1938 • Seiler Lewis • USA
HEART OF THE NORTH, THE • 1921 • Revier Harry • USA
HEART OF THE PRINCESS MARSARI, THE • 1915 • *Snow Marguerite* • USA
HEART OF THE RIO GRANDE, THE • 1942 • Morgan William • USA
HEART OF THE ROCKIES • 1937 • Kane Joseph • USA
HEART OF THE ROCKIES • 1951 • Witney William • USA
HEART OF THE SHERIFF, THE • 1915 • Mix Tom • USA
HEART OF THE STAG • 1983 • Firth Michael • NZL
HEART OF THE SUNSET • 1918 • Powell Frank • USA
HEART OF THE WEST • 1936 • Bretherton Howard • USA
HEART OF THE WEST see **HEARTS OF THE WEST** • 1925
HEART OF THE WILDS • 1918 • Neilan Marshall • USA
HEART OF THE YUKON, THE • 1927 • Van Dyke W. S. • USA • RAW COUNTRY, THE
HEART OF TWENTY, THE • 1920 • Kolker Henry • USA
HEART OF VALESKA, THE • 1913 • Miller Ashley • USA
HEART OF VIRGINIA • 1948 • Springsteen R. G. • USA
HEART OF VIRGINIA KEEP, THE • 1916 • Baker Richard Foster • SHT • USA
HEART OF WETONA, THE • 1919 • Franklin Sidney A. • USA
HEART OF YOUTH, THE • 1920 • Vignola Robert G. • USA
HEART OF YOUTH, THE see **FIRST LOVE** • 1921
HEART PUNCH, THE • 1914 • Paton Stuart • USA
HEART PUNCH, THE • 1919 • *Willard Jess* • SHT • USA
HEART PUNCH, THE • 1932 • Eason B. Reeves • USA
HEART RAIDER, THE • 1923 • Ruggles Wesley • USA • ARMS AND THE GIRL, THE
HEART REBELLIOUS, THE • 1914 • *Ince John Edward Jr.* • USA
HEART RECLAIMED, A • 1912 • *Rex* • USA
HEART ROYAL (UKN) see **SPORT OF KINGS** • 1947
HEART SINGS, THE • 1958 • Melik-Avekyan G. • USS
HEART SNATCHER, THE • 1920 • Del Ruth Roy, McLean K. G. • SHT • USA
HEART SONG (USA) see **ONLY GIRL, THE** • 1932
HEART SPECIALIST, THE • 1922 • Urson Frank • USA
HEART STRATEGY • 1917 • *Anderson Claire* • USA
HEART STRINGS • 1917 • Holubar Allen • USA
HEART STRINGS • 1920 • Edwards J. Gordon • USA
HEART THAT BROKE FROM PAIN, THE see **KARDIA POU LIYISE TON PONO** • 1968
HEART THAT GOES DING DING, THE see **DUANG DUANG MYEE TAI ATHAI** • 1982
HEART THAT IS MADE OF STONE, THE see **PATTHAR KE SANAM** • 1968
HEART THAT SEES, THE • 1913 • *Baggot King* • USA
HEART.. THE HEART, THE see **SYERDTSE.. SYERDTSE** • 1977
HEART THIEF, THE • 1927 • Chrisander Nils • USA
HEART THIEF (USA) see **HERZENSCHLIEB** • 1938
HEART THROBS • 1913 • Miller Charles? • USA
HEART TO HEART • 1928 • Beaudine William • USA
HEART TO HEART (USA) see **CONFIDENCES POUR CONFIDENCES** • 1978
HEART TO HEARTS see **SAMYAN SEIGAI** • 1988
HEART TO LET, A • 1921 • Dillon Eddie • USA
HEART TO WIN see **RICKY 1** • 1986
HEART TREMORS see **SZIVZUR** • 1982
HEART TROUBLE • 1915 • Coyle Walter • USA
HEART TROUBLE • 1919 • *Lyons Eddie* • SHT • USA
HEART TROUBLE • 1928 • Langdon Harry • USA
HEART TROUBLE see **HER NIGHT OF ROMANCE** • 1924
HEART TRUMP IN TOKYO FOR OSS 117 see **ATOUT COEUR A TOKYO POUR OSS 117** • 1966
HEART WITHIN, THE • 1957 • Eady David • UKN
HEART WRECKER, THE • 1916 • Ridgwell George • SHT • USA
HEARTACHES • 1915 • Kaufman Joseph • USA
HEARTACHES • 1916 • Carleton Lloyd B. • SHT • USA
HEARTACHES • 1947 • Wrangell Basil • USA
HEARTACHES • 1981 • Shebib Donald • CND
HEARTBALM see **CROSSROADS OF NEW YORK, THE** • 1922
HEARTBEAT • 1946 • Wood Sam • USA
HEARTBEAT • 1949 • Menzies William Cameron • SHT • USA
HEARTBEAT see **ANGELE** • 1934
HEARTBEAT see **CHAMADE, LA** • 1968
HEARTBEAT see **DAKKET QALB** • 1976
HEARTBEAT see **HEART BEAT** • 1979
HEARTBEAT FRESCO see **HEART BEAT FRESCO** • 1966
HEARTBEAT (USA) see **SCHPOUNTZ, LE** • 1937
HEARTBEATS OF LONG AGO • 1911 • Griffith D. W. • USA
HEARTBEEPS see **HEART BEEPS** • 1981
HEARTBOUND • 1925 • Lambert Glen • USA
HEARTBREAK • 1931 • Werker Alfred L. • USA
HEARTBREAK see **ARRACHE-COEUR, L'** • 1980
HEARTBREAK GIRL, THE • *Wayne Heather* • USA
HEARTBREAK HOTEL • 1988 • Columbus Chris • USA
HEARTBREAK KID, THE • 1972 • May Elaine • USA
HEARTBREAK MOTEL see **RED NECK COUNTY** • 1975
HEARTBREAK RIDGE • 1955 • Dupont Jacques • FRN
HEARTBREAK RIDGE • 1986 • Eastwood Clint • USA
HEARTBREAKER • 1983 • Zuniga Frank • USA
HEARTBREAKER, DIE • 1983 • Bringmann Peter F. • FRG • HEARTBREAKERS, THE
HEARTBREAKERS • 1985 • Roth Bobby • USA
HEARTBREAKERS, THE see **HEARTBREAKER, DIE** • 1983
HEARTBROKEN SHEP • 1913 • Lytton L. Rogers, Young James • USA
HEARTBURN • 1934 • Horne James W. • SHT • USA
HEARTBURN • 1986 • Nichols Mike • USA
HEARTEASE • 1919 • Beaumont Harry • USA
HEARTFARM see **MAN WHO WANTED TO LIVE FOREVER, THE** • 1970
HEARTH LIGHTS • 1913 • *Hale Alan* • USA
HEARTLAND • 1979 • Pearce Richard • USA
HEARTLAND REGGAE • 1980 • Lewis J. P. • DOC • CND
HEARTLESS GRIEF • 1986 • Sokurov Alexander • USS
HEARTLESS HUSBANDS • 1925 • Bracken Bertram • USA
HEARTLESS MOTHER, A • 1908 • Fitzhamon Lewin • UKN
HEARTS • 1913 • *Walpole Stanley* • USA
HEARTS see **COEURS NEUFS** • 1969
HEARTS ABLAZE • 1915 • Johnston Lorimer • USA
HEARTS ADRIFT • 1914 • Porter Edwin S. • USA
HEARTS AFLAME • 1923 • Barker Reginald • USA
HEARTS AND ARMOUR (USA) see **ARMI E GLI AMORI, LE** • 1983
HEARTS AND CLUBS • 1915 • *Cub* • USA
HEARTS AND CLUBS • 1915 • McCray Roy • *Joker* • USA
HEARTS AND CLUBS • 1920 • Davis James • SHT • USA
HEARTS AND CROSSES • 1913 • *Eclair* • USA
HEARTS AND DIAMONDS • 1912 • Dawley J. Searle • USA
HEARTS AND DIAMONDS • 1914 • Baker George D. • USA
HEARTS AND DIAMONDS • 1920 • Beaudine William • USA
HEARTS AND DIAMONDS see **HEARTS OR DIAMONDS?** • 1918
HEARTS AND DIAMONDS see **ORLOW, DER** • 1927
HEARTS AND DOLLARS (USA) see **TATIANA** • 1924
HEARTS AND FACES see **AS A MAN LIVES** • 1923
HEARTS AND FISTS • 1926 • Ingraham Lloyd • USA
HEARTS AND FLAGS • 1911 • *Edison* • USA
HEARTS AND FLAMES • 1915 • Edwards Harry J. • USA
HEARTS AND FLOUR • 1917 • Smith Dick • SHT • USA
HEARTS AND FLOWERS • 1914 • *Victor* • USA
HEARTS AND FLOWERS • 1914 • *Essanay* • USA
HEARTS AND FLOWERS • 1914 • *Cosmos* • USA
HEARTS AND FLOWERS • 1915 • Siegmann George • USA
HEARTS AND FLOWERS • 1919 • Cline Eddie • SHT • USA
HEARTS AND FLOWERS FOR TORA see **OTOKO WA TSURAIYO, TORAJIRO AJISAI NO KOI** • 1983
HEARTS AND GLOWERS • 1960 • Taras Martin B. • ANS • USA
HEARTS AND GUTS see **DAS TRIPAS CORACAO** • 1982
HEARTS AND HAMMERS • 1920 • Edwards Harry J. • SHT • USA
HEARTS AND HARPOONS • 1917 • *Sparkle* • SHT • USA
HEARTS AND HATS • 1919 • *Strand* • SHT • USA
HEARTS AND HOOFS • 1913 • *Garwood William* • USA
HEARTS AND HORSES • 1913 • Dwan Allan, Reid Wallace • USA
HEARTS AND LET US • 1918 • Lyons Eddie, Moran Lee • SHT • USA
HEARTS AND MASKS • 1914 • Campbell Colin • USA
HEARTS AND MASKS • 1921 • Seiter William A. • USA
HEARTS AND MINDS • 1967 • Petty Bruce • ANS • ASL
HEARTS AND MINDS • 1974 • Davis Peter • DOC • USA
HEARTS AND MINDS see **UOMO DA RISPETTARE, UN** • 1972
HEARTS AND PLANETS • 1915 • Parrott Charles • USA
HEARTS AND POLITICS • 1910 • *Lubin* • USA
HEARTS AND ROSES • 1915 • Totten Joseph Byron • USA
HEARTS AND SADDLES • 1917 • Mix Tom, Eddy Robert • SHT • USA
HEARTS AND SADDLES see **GENTLEMAN RIDER, THE** • 1919
HEARTS AND SKIRTS • 1912 • *Nestor* • USA
HEARTS AND SOLES • 1956 • Duncan Alma • ANM • CND
HEARTS AND SPANGLES • 1926 • O'Connor Frank • USA
HEARTS AND SPARKS • 1916 • Parrott Charles • SHT • USA
HEARTS AND SPURS • 1925 • Van Dyke W. S. • USA
HEARTS AND SWORDS • 1914 • *Sterling* • USA
HEARTS AND SWORDS • 1915 • *Glaum Louise* • USA
HEARTS AND THE CIRCUS see **IRON TEST, THE** • 1919
HEARTS AND THE HIGHWAY • 1915 • North Wilfred • USA
HEARTS ARE THUMPS • 1937 • Douglas Gordon • SHT • USA • HEARTS ARE TRUMPS
HEARTS ARE TRUMP • 1910 • *Lubin* • USA
HEARTS ARE TRUMPS • 1914 • *Pathe* • USA
HEARTS ARE TRUMPS • 1920 • Ingram Rex • USA
HEARTS ARE TRUMPS see **HEARTS ARE THUMPS** • 1937
HEARTS ARE TRUMPS see **HJERTER ER TRUMF** • 1975
HEARTS ASLEEP • 1919 • Hickman Howard • USA
HEART'S COMMAND, THE see **KAK VELIT SYERDTSYE** • 1968
HEART'S CRUCIBLE, A • 1916 • *Madison Cleo* • USA
HEART'S DESIRE • 1917 • Grandon Francis J. • USA
HEART'S DESIRE • 1935 • Stein Paul L. • UKN • MY HEART'S DELIGHT
HEART'S DESIRE (UKN) see **MICHAEL** • 1924
HEARTS DIVIDED • 1936 • Borzage Frank • USA
HEARTS ENTANGLED • 1913 • *White Pearl* • USA
HEARTS FULL OF LOVE see **KARDIES POU XEROUN N' AGAPOUN** • 1967
HEART'S HAVEN • 1922 • Hampton Benjamin B. • USA
HEART'S HIGHWAY, THE • 1914 • *Eclair* • USA
HEART'S HUNGER • 1915 • Morgan George • USA
HEARTS IN ARMOUR see **ARMI E GLI AMORI, LE** • 1983
HEARTS IN BONDAGE • 1936 • Ayres Lew • USA
HEARTS IN CONFLICT • 1912 • *Imp* • USA
HEARTS IN DIXIE • 1929 • Van Buren A. H., Sloane Paul • USA
HEARTS IN EXILE • 1915 • Young James • USA
HEARTS IN EXILE • 1929 • Curtiz Michael • USA
HEARTS IN HOCK • 1919 • Parrott Charles • SHT • USA
HEARTS IN LOVE (USA) see **VERLIEBTE HERZEN** • 1939
HEARTS IN REUNION (UKN) see **REUNION** • 1936
HEARTS IN SHADOW • 1915 • Eason B. Reeves • USA
HEARTS IN SPRINGTIME (UKN) see **GLAMOUR BOY** • 1941
HEARTS IN THE STORM see **CUORI NELLA TORMENTA** • 1984
HEART'S KINGDOM see **SOLTAN GHALBHA** • 1968
HEART'S MELODY see **MELODIE DES HERZENS** • 1929
HEART'S MEMORIES, THE see **PAMYAT SERDTSA** • 1958
HEART'S MUSIC, THE see **HUDBA SRDCI** • 1934
HEARTS O' THE RANGE • 1921 • Morante Milburn • USA
HEARTS OF AGE, THE • 1934 • Vance William, Welles Orson • SHT • USA
HEARTS OF FIRE • 1987 • Marquand Richard • UKN
HEARTS OF GOLD • 1910 • *Powers* • USA
HEARTS OF GOLD • 1910 • *Nestor* • USA
HEARTS OF GOLD • 1914 • *Paget Alfred* • USA
HEARTS OF GOLD • 1915 • Malins Geoffrey H. • UKN
HEARTS OF HUMANITY • 1932 • Cabanne W. Christy • USA
HEARTS OF HUMANITY • 1936 • Baxter John • UKN • CRYPT, THE
HEARTS OF ITALY • 1911 • *Powers* • USA
HEARTS OF LIEUTENANTS see **LOJNANTSHJARTAN** • 1942
HEARTS OF LOVE • 1918 • Haydon J. Charles • USA
HEARTS OF MEN • 1912 • *Mason William* • USA
HEARTS OF MEN • 1914 • Farnum Marshall • USA
HEARTS OF MEN • 1915 • Vekroff Perry N. • USA • SCHOOL BELLS
HEARTS OF MEN • 1919 • Beban George • USA
HEARTS OF MEN • 1928 • Hogan James P. • USA
HEARTS OF MEN, THE • 1912 • Collins Edwin J. • UKN
HEARTS OF MEN, THE see **HUNS WITHIN OUR GATES** • 1918
HEARTS OF OAK • 1914 • Physioc Wray • USA
HEARTS OF OAK • 1924 • Ford John • USA
HEARTS OF OAK • 1933 • Wetherell M. A., Hewett Graham • UKN
HEARTS OF STEEL see **STALOWE SERCA** • 1948
HEARTS OF THE BRADYS, THE • 1915 • *Ayres Sydney* • USA
HEARTS OF THE DARK • 1913 • *Hunt Irene* • USA
HEARTS OF THE FIRST EMPIRE • 1913 • *Humphrey William* • USA
HEARTS OF THE FOREST • 1914 • Kendall Preston • USA
HEARTS OF THE FOUR, THE see **FOUR HEARTS** • 1945
HEARTS OF THE JUNGLE • 1915 • Grandon Francis J. • USA
HEARTS OF THE NORTHLAND • 1913 • *Imp* • USA
HEARTS OF THE WEST • 1910 • *Champion* • USA
HEARTS OF THE WEST • 1925 • *Cuneo Lester* • USA • HEART O' THE WEST ○ HEART OF THE WEST
HEARTS OF THE WEST • 1975 • Zieff Howard • USA • HOLLYWOOD COWBOY
HEARTS OF THE WOODS • 1921 • Calnek Roy • USA
HEARTS OF THE WORLD • 1918 • Griffith D. W. • USA, UKN
HEARTS OF WOMEN • 1914 • Humphrey William, Johnson Tefft • USA
HEARTS OF YOUTH • 1920 • Miranda Thomas N., Webb Millard • USA
HEARTS OR DIAMONDS? • 1918 • King Henry • USA • HEARTS AND DIAMONDS
HEART'S REVENGE, A • 1918 • Lund O. A. C. • USA
HEART'S RIGHT • 1977 • Emes Ian • UKN
HEARTS THAT ARE HUMAN • 1915 • *Big U* • USA
HEARTS THAT ARE HUMAN • 1915 • Bramble A. V. • UKN
HEARTS THAT MEET see **HJARTAN SOM MOTAS** • 1914
HEARTS TO LET • 1915 • Humphrey William • USA
HEART'S TRIBUTE, THE • 1916 • Plaissetty Rene • SHT • USA
HEARTS TRUMP DIAMONDS see **LADY IN JEWELS, THE** • 1925
HEARTS UNDER OILSKINS • 1911 • *Powers* • USA
HEARTS UNITED • 1914 • *Sawyer* • USA
HEARTS UNITED • 1914 • Milligan N. E. • *Liberty* • USA
HEARTS UNITED • 1915 • *Reliance* • USA
HEARTS UNKNOWN • 1912 • *Solax* • USA
HEARTS UP! • 1920 • Paul Val • USA
HEART'S VOICE, THE see **GULDET OG VORT HJERTE** • 1913
HEARTSEASE • 1913 • Lytton L. Rogers, Young James • USA
HEARTSEASE • 1919 • Beaumont Harry • USA
HEARTSICK AT SEA • 1917 • *Russell Dan* • SHT • USA
HEARTSONG • 1917 • *Lukas Paul* • HNG
HEARTSOUNDS • 1984 • Jordan Glenn • TVM • USA
HEARTSTRINGS • 1914 • Giblyn Charles • USA
HEARTSTRINGS • 1923 • Greenwood Edwin • UKN
HEARTWORN HIGHWAYS • 1981 • Szalapski James • DOC • USA
HEARTY GREETING FROM THE EARTH see **SRDECNY POZDRAV ZE ZEMEKOULE** • 1983
HEAT • 1972 • Morrissey Paul • USA
HEAT • 1987 • Richards R. M. • USA
HEAT see **ZNOI** • 1963
HEAT, THE see **UPAL** • 1964
HEAT AND DUST • 1982 • Ivory James • USA
HEAT AND LUST see **SWEDISH SEX CLINIC** • 1981
HEAT AND LUST: DIARY OF A SEX THERAPIST see **SWEDISH SEX CLINIC** • 1981
HEAT AND MUD see **NETSUDEICHI** • 1950
HEAT AND SUNLIGHT • 1986 • Nilsson Rob • USA
HEAT AT MIDNIGHT see **ESPIONS A L'AFFUT** • 1966
HEAT HAZE see **KAGERO** • 1969
HEAT LIGHTNING • 1934 • LeRoy Mervyn • USA
HEAT LINE, THE see **LIGNE DE CHALEUR, LA** • 1988
HEAT OF ANGER • 1971 • Taylor Don • TVM • USA
HEAT OF DESIRE (USA) see **PLEIN SUD** • 1981
HEAT OF MADNESS • 1966 • Wuest Harry • USA
HEAT OF MIDNIGHT see **ESPIONS A L'AFFUT** • 1966
HEAT OF THE SUMMER (USA) see **CHALEURS D'ETE** • 1959
HEAT (USA) see **...Y EL DEMONIO CREO A LOS HOMBRES** • 1960
HEAT WAVE • 1935 • Elvey Maurice • UKN • CODE, THE
HEAT WAVE • 1974 • Jameson Jerry • TVM • USA
HEAT WAVE, THE • 1911 • Wilson Frank? • UKN
HEAT WAVE, THE see **ZNOI** • 1963
HEAT WAVE ISLAND see **KAGERO** • 1969

HEATED VENGEANCE see **JUNGLE, THE** • 1985
HEATHCLIFF MOVIE: HEATHCLIFF AND ME, THE see **HEATHCLIFF -THE MOVIE** • 1986
HEATHCLIFF -THE MOVIE • 1986 • Bianchi Bruno • ANM • USA • HEATHCLIFF MOVIE: HEATHCLIFF AND ME, THE
HEATHEN HOLES see **HEIDENLOCHER** • 1986
HEATHENS OF KUMMEROW AND THEIR MERRY PRANKS, THE see **HEIDEN VON KUMMEROW UND IHRE LUSTIGEN STREICHE, DIE** • 1967
HEATHER AND YON • 1944 • Edwards Harry J. • SHT • USA
HEATHER (USA) see **WRZOS** • 1938
HEATHERS • 1989 • Lehmann Michael • USA • LETHAL ATTRACTION
HEATING POWDER • 1908 • *Lubin* • USA
HEAT'S OFF, THE • 1967 • Bakshi Ralph • ANS • USA
HEAT'S ON, THE • 1943 • Ratoff Gregory • USA • TROPICANA (UKN)
HEATWAVE • 1981 • Noyce Phil • ASL
HEATWAVE see **HOT AND COLD** • 1989
HEATWAVE LASTED FOUR DAYS, THE • 1975 • Jackson Douglas • CND
HEATWAVE (USA) see **HOUSE ACROSS THE LAKE, THE** • 1954
HEAVE AWAY MY JOHNNY • 1948 • Halas John, Batchelor Joy • ANS • UKN
HEAVE-HO! see **HEJ RUP!** • 1934
HEAVE TWO • 1933 • Goodwins Leslie • SHT • USA
HEAVEN • 1987 • Keaton Diane • USA
HEAVEN see **OURANOS** • 1963
HEAVEN see **NIGHT IN HEAVEN, A** • 1983
HEAVEN, THE see **PARADISO, IL** • 1912
HEAVEN AND EARTH • 1990 • Kadokawa Haruki • JPN
HEAVEN AND EARTH see **SORCIER DU CIEL, LE** • 1948
HEAVEN AND EARTH see **LANGIT AT LUPA** • 1967
HEAVEN AND EARTH see **HIMMEL UND ERDE** • 1982
HEAVEN AND EARTH see **HIMMEL UND ERDE** • 1989
HEAVEN AND HELL see **JANNA WAR NARR** • 1953
HEAVEN AND HELL see **TENGOKU TO JIGOKU** • 1963
HEAVEN AND HELL see **PIEKLO I NIEBO** • 1966
HEAVEN AND HELL see **HIMMEL OG HELVEDE** • 1988
HEAVEN AND ITS AFFAIRS see **CIEL ET SES AFFAIRES, LE** • 1967
HEAVEN AND OCEAN! -STOMPA AT SEA see **HIMMEL OG HAV! -STOMPA TIL SJOS** • 1967
HEAVEN AVENGES • 1912 • Griffith D. W. • USA
HEAVEN BOUND (UKN) see **BIG TIME OR BUST** • 1934
HEAVEN CAN WAIT • 1943 • Lubitsch Ernst • USA
HEAVEN CAN WAIT • 1978 • Beatty Warren, Henry Buck • USA
HEAVEN CAN'T WAIT see **HOT PURSUIT** • 1983
HEAVEN DESCENDS see **JHUK GAYA AASMAN** • 1968
HEAVEN & EARTH MAGIC FEATURE see **NUMBER 12** • 1943-58
HEAVEN FELL THAT NIGHT (UKN) see **BIJOUTIERS DU CLAIR DE LUNE, LES** • 1958
HEAVEN FOR A DRUNKARD see **YOPPARAI TENGOKU** • 1962
HEAVEN FOR JENNY see **DRIFTWOOD** • 1948
HEAVEN HELP US • 1985 • Dinner Michael • USA • CATHOLIC BOYS (UKN)
HEAVEN HELP US FROM OUR FRIENDS see **THAT LUCKY TOUCH** • 1975
HEAVEN IS FOR ME see **LANGIT AY PARA SA AKIN, ANG** • 1968
HEAVEN IS ROUND THE CORNER • 1944 • Rogers Maclean • UKN
HEAVEN KNOWS, MR. ALLISON • 1957 • Huston John • UKN, USA
HEAVEN LINKED WITH LOVE see **TENGOKU NI MUSUBU KOI** • 1933
HEAVEN ON A SHOESTRING see **NIGHT OF NIGHTS, THE** • 1940
HEAVEN ON EARTH • 1927 • Rosen Phil • USA
HEAVEN ON EARTH • 1931 • Mack Russell • USA
HEAVEN ON EARTH • 1960 • Spafford Robert B. • ITL, USA
HEAVEN ON EARTH • 1966 • *Davis Film Dist.* • USA
HEAVEN ON EARTH • 1986 • Kroeker Allan • CND, UKN
HEAVEN ON EARTH see **LANGIT SA LUPA, ANG** • 1968
HEAVEN ON ONE'S HEAD see **CIEL SUR LA TETE, LE** • 1964
HEAVEN ONLY KNOWS see **MONTANA MIKE** • 1947
HEAVEN OVER THE MARSHES see **CIELO SULLA PALUDE** • 1949
HEAVEN SCENT • 1956 • Jones Charles M. • ANS • USA
HEAVEN SENT (UKN) see **DROLE DE PAROISSIEN, UN** • 1963
HEAVEN SHIP see **HIMMELSKIBET** • 1917
HEAVEN WILL PROTECT A WOIKING GOIL • 1916 • *Powell Russ* • USA
HEAVEN WILL PROTECT THE WORKING GIRL • 1914 • *Joker* • USA
HEAVEN WITH A BARBED WIRE FENCE • 1939 • Cortez Ricardo • USA
HEAVEN WITH A GUN • 1969 • Katzin Lee H. • USA
HEAVEN WITH NO LOVE see **PUKOTINA RAJA** • 1961
HEAVENLY ASSIGNMENT see **HEAVENLY BODIES** • 1963
HEAVENLY BODIES • 1963 • Meyer Russ • USA • HEAVENLY ASSIGNMENT
HEAVENLY BODIES • 1985 • Dane Lawrence • CND
HEAVENLY BODY, THE • 1943 • Hall Alexander • USA
HEAVENLY DAYS • 1944 • Estabrook Howard • USA
HEAVENLY DAZE • 1948 • White Jules • SHT • USA
HEAVENLY DESIRE • 1979 • Jaacovi Jaacov • USA
HEAVENLY GIFT • 1972 • Ben-Artzi Gad • ISR
HEAVENLY HOSTS see **MENNYEI SEREGEK** • 1984
HEAVENLY KID, THE • 1985 • Medoway Cary • USA
HEAVENLY METAL see **METALL DES HIMMELS** • 1934
HEAVENLY MUSIC • 1943 • Berne Josef • SHT • USA
HEAVENLY PLAY, THE see **HIMLASPELET** • 1942
HEAVENLY PURSUITS • 1985 • Gormley Charles • UKN • GOSPEL ACCORDING TO VIC, THE (USA) ○ JUST ANOTHER MIRACLE
HEAVENLY PUSS • 1949 • Hanna William, Barbera Joseph • ANS • USA
HEAVENLY STAR • 1972 • Holleb Alan • SHT • USA
HEAVENLY TWINS, THE • 1907 • Fitzhamon Lewin • UKN
HEAVENLY TWINS, THE • 1912 • Batley Ernest G. • UKN
HEAVENLY TWINS AT LUNCH, THE • 1903 • Porter Edwin S. • USA
HEAVENLY TWINS AT ODDS, THE • 1903 • Porter Edwin S. • USA
HEAVENLY VOICE, THE • 1912 • *Johnson Arthur* • USA
HEAVENLY WIDOW, THE • 1913 • *Fraunholz Fraunie* • USA
HEAVENS ABOVE! • 1963 • Boulting John • UKN
HEAVENS CALL, THE see **NEBO ZOVYOT** • 1959
HEAVEN'S GATE • 1980 • Cimino Michael • USA • JOHNSON COUNTY WAR
HEAVEN'S GATE see **OUR LITTLE GIRL** • 1935
HEAVEN'S HEROES • 1986 • *Ralphe David* • USA
HEAVENS! MY HUSBAND! • 1932 • Stafford Babe • SHT • USA
HEAVEN'S TOUCH • 1983 • Evans Warren • USA
HEAVILY MARRIED • 1937 • Hutton Clayton • UKN
HEAVY CROSS, THE (USA) see **GRAN CRUZ, LA** • 1937
HEAVY CURSE OF A SPLIT, THE see **VARIA KATARA O DIHASMOS** • 1968
HEAVY INDUSTRIES • 1936 • Elder John C. • DOC • UKN
HEAVY LOAD • 1976 • Vincent Chuck • USA
HEAVY LOAD, A see **LOURD CHARGEMENT, UN** • 1898
HEAVY MELON, THE see **VARI PEPONI, TO** • 1976
HEAVY METAL • 1981 • Potterton Gerald • ANM • CND • METAL HURLANT
HEAVY METAL (USA) see **RIDING HIGH** • 1980
HEAVY SEAS • 1923 • Roach Hal • SHT • USA
HEAVY THUNDER see **BLOOD AND GUTS** • 1978
HEAVY TRAFFIC • 1973 • Bakshi Ralph • ANM • USA
HEAVY VILLAINS • 1915 • Baker George D. • USA
HEAVY WATER • 1960 • Jordan Larry, Collins Jess • SHT • USA
HEBA THE SNAKE WOMAN • 1915 • *Excel* • UKN
HEBI HIME-SAMA • 1940 • Kinugasa Teinosuke • JPN • SERPENT PRINCESS, THE ○ MISS SNAKE PRINCESS ○ SNAKE PRINCESS, THE
HEBIHIME DOUCHUH • 1949 • Kimura Keigo, Marune Santaro • JPN • PRINCESS SNAKE'S TRAVELS ○ SNAKE PRINCESS
HEBIMUSUME TO HAKUHATSUKI • 1968 • Yuasa Noriaki • JPN • SNAKE GIRL AND THE SILVER-HAIRED WITCH, THE
HEBREW FUGITIVE, THE • 1908 • *Lubin* • USA
HEBREW LESSON, THE • 1973 • Mankowitz Wolf • IRL
HEC RAMSEY see **CENTURY TURNS, THE** • 1971
HEC RAMSEY: SCAR TISSUE • 1974 • McLaglen Andrew V. • TVM • USA
HEC RAMSEY: THE MYSTERY OF THE GREEN FEATHER • 1972 • Daugherty Herschel • TVM • USA
HEC RAMSEY: THE MYSTERY OF THE YELLOW ROSE • 1973 • Benton Douglas • TVM • USA
HECATE • 1982 • Schmid Daniel • SWT, FRN • HECATE, MAITRESSE DE LA NUIT
HECATE, MAITRESSE DE LA NUIT see **HECATE** • 1982
HECC, A • 1989 • Gardos Peter • HNG, FRG • JUST FOR KICKS
HECHO VIOLENTO • 1958 • Forque Jose Maria • SPN
HECKLE AND JECKLE IN KING TUT'S TOMB • 1950 • *Terrytoon* • ANS • USA
HECKLE AND JECKLE, THE TALKING MAGPIES • 1946-56 • *Terry Paul (P)* • ASS • USA
HECKLER, THE • 1940 • Lord Del • SHT • USA
HECKLERS, THE • 1966 • Strick Joseph • MTV • UKN
HECKLING HARE, THE • 1941 • Avery Tex • ANS • USA
HECTIC DAYS see **GORJACE D ENEKI** • 1935
HECTIC HONEYMOON • 1938 • Yarbrough Jean • SHT • USA
HECTOR • 1983 • Ferre Carlos Perez • SPN • HECTOR, THE STIGMA OF FEAR
HECTOR • 1988 • *Urbanus* • BLG
HECTOR AND MILLIE SAVE UNCLE TOM • 1974 • McGill Chris • SHT • ASL
HECTOR LE FORTICHE see **ETTORE LO FUSTO** • 1972
HECTOR SERVADAC'S ARK see **NA KOMETE** • 1970
HECTOR THE MIGHTY see **ETTORE LO FUSTO** • 1972
HECTOR, THE STIGMA OF FEAR see **HECTOR** • 1983
HECTOR'S HECTIC LIFE • 1948 • Tytla Bill • ANS • USA
HECTOR'S INHERITANCE • 1911 • *Solax* • USA
HEDDA • 1975 • Nunn Trevor • UKN
HEDDA GABBLER • 1917 • Powell Frank • USA
HEDDA GABBLER • 1919 • Pastrone Giovanni • ITL
HEDDA GABBLER • 1924 • Eckstein Franz • FRG
HEDDA GABBLER • 1979 • Decorte Jan • BLG
HEDE BLOD, DET • 1911 • Gad Urban • DNM
HEDGE BETWEEN, THE • 1914 • *Rex* • USA
HEDGE OF HEART'S DESIRE • 1916 • King Burton L. • SHT • USA
HEDGEHOG FRIENDSHIP see **IGELFREUNDSCHAFT** • 1962
HEDGEHOG IN THE FOG • Norshtein Yuri • ANM • USS • HEDGEHOG IN THE MIST
HEDGEHOG IN THE MIST see **HEDGEHOG IN THE FOG**
HEDGEHOG'S WAR, THE • 1980 • Grubcheva Ivanka • BUL
HEDONIST HYPNOTIST • 1970 • *Stacey Dist.* • USA
HEDONISTIC PLEASURES • 1969 • De Priest Ed • USA
HEDWIC: THE COOL LAKES OF DEATH • 1985 • Russell Ken • UKN
HEDWIG, THE COOL LAKES OF DEATH • 1982 • van Brakel Nouchka • NTH
HEDY • 1965 • Warhol Andy • USA • HEDY THE SHOPLIFTER ○ 14 YEAR OLD GIRL, THE
HEDY THE SHOPLIFTER see **HEDY** • 1965
HEE • 1969 • Adriaense P. • BLG
HEEL OF ITALY, THE see **YELLOW CAESAR, THE** • 1941
HEEL OF THE LAW, THE • 1916 • Tucker George Loane • SHT • USA
HEEL TAPS see **LADY IN HIGH HEELS, THE** • 1925
HEELS, THE see **CRAPULAS, LOS** • 1981
HEER • 1956 • *Biswas Anil (M)* • IND
HEGIRE, L' • 1969 • Bouchouchi Youssef • ALG
HEI HSI-YI • 1981 • Ch'U Yuan • HKG • BLACK LIZARD
HEI NO NAKA NO KORINAI MENMEN • 1988 • Morisaki Higashi • JPN • STUBBORN GUYS BEHIND THE WALLS
HEI PAO SHIJIAN • 1985 • Huang Jianxin • CHN • BLACK CANNON AFFAIR, THE ○ BLACK CANNON INCIDENT, THE ○ HEIPAO SHIJIAN
HEI SHAN LU • 1990 • Zhou Xiaowen • CHN
HEI TIKI • 1935 • Markey Alexander • USA • PRIMITIVE PASSIONS (UKN)
HEIDELBERGER ROMANZE • 1951 • Verhoeven Paul • FRG
HEIDEMARIE • 1956 • Kugelstadt Hermann • SWT
HEIDEMELODIE • 1956 • Erfurth Ulrich • FRG
HEIDEN VON KUMMEROW UND IHRE LUSTIGEN STREICHE, DIE • 1967 • Jacobs Werner • FRG • HEATHENS OF KUMMEROW AND THEIR MERRY PRANKS, THE
HEIDENLOCHER • 1986 • Paulus Wolfram • AUS, FRG • HEATHEN HOLES
HEIDEPRINZESSCHEN, DAS • 1918 • Mendel Georg Victor • FRG
HEIDEROSLEIN • 1926 • Becker Carl • FRG
HEIDESCHULMEISTER UWE KARSTEN • 1933 • Wolff Carl Heinz • FRG
HEIDESCHULMEISTER UWE KARSTEN • 1954 • Deppe Hans • FRG
HEIDESOMMER • 1945 • York Eugen • FRG • VERLIEBTER SOMMER
HEIDI • 1937 • Dwan Allan • USA
HEIDI • 1965 • Jacobs Werner • AUS
HEIDI • 1974 • Wyndham-Davis June • MTV • UKN
HEIDI see **SON TORNATA PER TE** • 1953
HEIDI AND PETER see **HEIDI UND PETER** • 1954
HEIDI KEHRT HEIM • 1967 • Mann Delbert • FRG, USA • HEIDI (USA)
HEIDI UND PETER • 1954 • Schnyder Franz • SWT • HEIDI AND PETER
HEIDI (USA) see **HEIDI KEHRT HEIM** • 1967
HEIDI'S SONG • 1982 • Taylor Robert • ANM • USA
HEIDO • 1979 • Scarpelli Giacomo, Scavolini Daniele • ITL
HEIEN • 1930 • Ivens Joris • NTH • PILE DRIVING
HEIFER, THE see **VAQUILLA, LA** • 1985
HEIGHT see **VYSOTA** • 1957
HEIGHT A see **V RAIONYE VYSOTY A** • 1941
HEIGHT OF AMBITION • 1952 • *Hall Cameron* • SHT • UKN
HEIGHT OF BATTLE, THE see **SENKA NO HATE** • 1950
HEIGHTS, THE see **VYSOTA** • 1957
HEIGHTS OF DANGER • 1953 • Bradford Peter • UKN
HEIGHTS OF HAZARDS, THE • 1915 • Lambart Harry • USA
HEILIGE BERG, DER • 1926 • Fanck Arnold • FRG • HOLY MOUNTAIN, THE ○ WRATH OF THE GODS
HEILIGE ERBE, DAS • 1957 • Solm Alfred • AUS • WER DIE HEIMAT LIEBT
HEILIGE FEUER, DAS • 1943 • Steinhoff Hans • FRG
HEILIGE FLAMME, DIE • 1931 • Viertel Berthold • FRG
HEILIGE HASS 1, DER • 1921 • Noa Manfred • FRG
HEILIGE HASS 2, DER • 1921 • Noa Manfred • FRG • FLUCHT VOR DEM TODE, DIE
HEILIGE LUGE, DIE • 1927 • Holger-Madsen • FRG
HEILIGE LUGE, DIE • 1955 • Liebeneiner Wolfgang • FRG
HEILIGE ODER DIRNE • 1929 • Berger Martin • FRG • NEBENBUHLERIN
HEILIGE SCHWEIGEN, DAS • 1930 • Beck-Gaden Hanns • FRG
HEILIGE SIMPLICIA, DIE see **LEGENDE VON DER HEILIGEN SIMPLICIA, DIE** • 1920
HEILIGE UND IHR NARR, DIE • 1928 • Dieterle William • FRG • SAINT AND HER FOOL, THE (USA) ○ SAINTE ET LE FOU, LA
HEILIGE UND IHR NARR, DIE • 1957 • Ucicky Gustav • AUS
HEILIGE ZIEL, DAS • 1942 • Nomura Kosho, Ofuna Shokiku • FRG, JPN
HEILIGEN DREI BRUNNEN, DIE • 1930 • Bonnard Mario • FRG • SYMPHONIE DER BERGE
HEIMAT • 1938 • Froelich Carl • FRG • MAGDA
HEIMAT • 1984 • Reitz Edgar • FRG • HOMELAND
HEIMAT AM RHEIN • 1933 • Sauer Fred • FRG
HEIMAT -DEINE LIEDER • 1959 • May Paul • FRG
HEIMAT DER GORALEN, DIE • 1938 • FRG
HEIMAT FUR HEIMATLOSE see **HOME FOR THE HOMELESS** • 1981
HEIMAT IN NOT see **STERBENDE VOLKER 1** • 1922
HEIMAT RUFT, DIE • 1937 • Sirk Douglas • FRG • HOME IS CALLING
HEIMAT UND FREMDE • 1913 • May Joe • FRG
HEIMATERDE • 1941 • Deppe Hans • FRG
HEIMATGLOCKEN • 1952 • Kugelstadt Hermann • FRG
HEIMATLAND • 1955 • Antel Franz • AUS
HEIMATLOS • 1958 • Fredersdorf Herbert B. • FRG
HEIMATLOSEN, DIE • 1924 • *Neutral-Film* • FRG
HEIMKEHR • 1928 • May Joe • FRG • HOMECOMING
HEIMKEHR • 1941 • Rohrig Walter, Ucicky Gustav • FRG • HOMECOMING
HEIMKEHR DES ODYSSEUS, DIE • 1918 • Biebrach Rudolf • FRG
HEIMKEHR DES ODYSSEUS, DIE • 1922 • Obal Max • FRG
HEIMKEHR INS GLUCK • 1933 • Boese Carl • FRG
HEIMLICH EHEN • 1956 • von Wangenheim Gustav • GDR
HEIMLICH, STILL UND LEISE • 1953 • Deppe Hans • FRG
HEIMLICHE GRAFIN, DIE • 1942 • von Bolvary Geza • FRG
HEIMLICHE SUNDER • 1926 • Seitz Franz • FRG
HEIMLICHEN BRAUTE, DIE • 1944 • Meyer Johannes • FRG
HEIMLICHES RENDEZVOUS • 1949 • Hoffmann Kurt • FRG
HEIMLICHKEITEN • 1968 • Staudte Wolfgang • FRG, BUL • SECRETS
HEIMWEH • 1927 • Righelli Gennaro • FRG • HOMESICKNESS ○ EXILED
HEIMWEH • 1937 • von Alten Jurgen • FRG • HOMESICKNESS
HEIMWEH.. DORT WO DIE BLUMEN BLUH'N • 1957 • Antel Franz • AUS
HEIMWEH NACH DER ZUKUNFT • 1967 • Heynowski Walter, Scheumann Gerhard • GDR
HEIMWEH NACH DEUTSCHLAND • 1954 • Redetzki Bernhard • FRG
HEIMWEH NACH DIR • 1952 • Stemmle R. A. • FRG
HEINIE AND THE 400 • 1916 • *Rolin* • USA
HEINIE AND THE MAGIC MAN • 1916 • *Rolin* • USA
HEINIE'S MILLIONS • 1915 • *Starlight* • USA
HEINIE'S OUTING • 1915 • *Sterling* • USA
HEINRICH • 1977 • Sanders Helma • FRG • HEINRICH VON KLEIST
HEINRICH HEINES ERSTE LIEBE • 1922 • Christa Eva • FRG
HEINRICH PENTHESILEA VON KLEIST • 1983 • Neuenfel Max • FRG
HEINRICH VON KLEIST see **HEINRICH** • 1977

HEINTJE -EIN HERZ GEHT AUF REISEN • 1969 • Jacobs Werner • FRG
HEINTJE -EINMAL WIRD DIE SONNE WIEDER SCHEINEN • 1970 • Hinrich Hans • FRG
HEINTJE, MIN BEDSTE VEN • 1970 • Jacobs Werner • FRG
HEINZ IM MOND • 1934 • Stemmle R. A. • FRG
HEINZELMANNCHEN • 1956 • Kobler Erich • FRG • SHOEMAKER AND THE ELVES, THE (USA) ○ BROWNIE
HEINZE'S RESURRECTION • 1913 • Sennett Mack • USA
HEIPAO SHIJIAN see **HEI PAO SHIJIAN** • 1985
HEIR APPARENT, THE • 1912 • *Mcdermott Marc* • USA
HEIR BEAR • 1953 • Lundy Dick • ANS • USA
HEIR CONDITIONED • 1955 • Freleng Friz • ANS • USA
HEIR-LOONS • 1925 • Jones Grover • USA
HEIR OF MARS, THE see **PASNYOK MARSA** • 1914
HEIR OF THE AGES, THE • 1917 • Le Saint Edward J. • USA
HEIR OF THE BROKEN O, THE • 1918 • Bradbury Robert North • SHT • USA
HEIR OF THE E. Z. RANCH, THE • 1916 • *Cub* • USA
HEIR OF THE MILITARY ROAD, THE • Krumin Varis • USS
HEIR TO GENGHIS KHAN, THE see **POTOMOK CHINGIS-KHAN** • 1928
HEIR TO JENGHIZ KHAN, THE see **POTOMOK CHINGIS-KHAN** • 1928
HEIR TO THE HOORAH see **EVER SINCE EVE** • 1934
HEIR TO THE HOORAH, THE • 1916 • De Mille William C. • USA • HEIR TO THE HURRAH, THE
HEIR TO THE HURRAH, THE see **HEIR TO THE HOORAH, THE** • 1916
HEIR TO TROUBLE • 1935 • Bennet Spencer Gordon • USA
HEIRATE MICH, CHERI • 1964 • von Ambesser Axel • FRG, AUS
HEIRATEN -ABER WEN? • 1938 • Boese Carl • FRG • FALSCHE KATZE, DIE
HEIRATEN VERBOTEN! • 1957 • Paul Heinz • FRG
HEIRATSANNONCEN • 1925 • Kaufmann Fritz • FRG
HEIRATSFALLE, DIE • 1927 • Eckstein Franz • FRG
HEIRATSFIEBER • 1928 • Walther-Fein Rudolf • FRG
HEIRATSINSTITUT IDA & CO. • 1937 • Janson Victor • FRG
HEIRATSKANDIDATEN • 1958 • Kugelstadt Hermann • FRG, AUS
HEIRATSNEST, DAS • 1927 • Walther-Fein Rudolf • FRG
HEIRATSSCHWINDLER • 1925 • Boese Carl • FRG
HEIRATSSCHWINDLER • 1937 • Selpin Herbert • FRG • ROTE MUTZE, DIE
HEIRATSSCHWINDLER, DER • 1922 • Neff Wolfgang • FRG
HEIRESS, THE • 1911 • Porter Edwin S. • USA
HEIRESS, THE • 1913 • *Steppling John* • USA
HEIRESS, THE • 1949 • Wyler William • USA
HEIRESS, THE • 1965 • Hooper Tobe • SHT • USA
HEIRESS AND THE CROOK, THE • 1914 • *Counselman Mildred* • USA
HEIRESS AT "COFFEE DAN'S", THE • 1917 • Dillon Eddie • USA
HEIRESS FOR A DAY • 1918 • Dillon John Francis • USA
HEIRESS FOR TWO, AN • 1915 • Christie Al • USA
HEIRESS OF DRACULA, THE see **VAMPYROS LESBOS -DIE ERBIN DES DRACULA** • 1971
HEIRESSES, THE see **OROKSEG** • 1980
HEIRLOOM MYSTERY, THE • 1936 • Rogers Maclean • UKN
HEIRLOOMS • 1920 • *Henry Gale* • SHT • USA
HEIRS • 1969 • Vasslinov Ivan • ANS • BUL
HEIRS see **OROKOSOK** • 1970
HEIRS, THE • 1960 • Levchuk Timofey • USS
HEIRS, THE see **ERBEN, DIE** • 1982
HEISS WEHT DER WIND • 1964 • Olsen Rolf • FRG, AUS • MEIN FREUND SHORTY
HEISSBLUTIG • 1979 • Frank Hubert • AUS • HOT-BLOODED
HEISSE ERNTE • 1956 • Konig Hans H. • FRG
HEISSE SEX IN BANGKOK • 1974 • Dietrich Erwin C. • SWT • HOT SEX IN BANGKOK
HEISSE SPUR KAIRO-LONDON (FRG) see **SFINGE SORRIDE PRIMA DI MORIRE STOP -LONDRA, LA** • 1964
HEISSE SPUR ST. PAULI see **FLUCHTWEG ST. PAULI - GROSSALARM FUR DIE DAVIDSWACHE** • 1971
HEISSE TOD, DER • 1969 • Franco Jesus • FRG, ITL, SPN • 99 MUJERES (SPN) ○ 99 DONNE (ITL) ○ 99 WOMEN (USA) ○ PROSTITUTES IN PRISON ○ 99 FRAUEN
HEISSE WARE • 1959 • May Paul • FRG
HEISSER HAFEN HONGKONG • 1962 • Roland Jurgen • FRG, ITL • SEGRETO DI BUDDA, IL (ITL) ○ HONG KONG HOT HARBOR (USA) ○ SECRETS OF BUDDHA (UKN) ○ HOT HONG KONG HARBOUR
HEISSER HERBST, EIN • 1988 • Zanke Susanne • AUS • HOT AUTUMN, A
HEISSER SAND AUF SYLT • 1968 • Macc Jerzy, Savage Peter • FRG • NEW LIFE STYLE, THE (USA) ○ HOT SAND ON SYLT ○ JUST TO BE LOVED
HEISSER SOMMER • 1968 • Hasler Joachim • GDR • HOT SUMMER
HEISSES BLUT • 1911 • Gad Urban • FRG • BURNING BLOOD
HEISSES BLUT • 1936 • Jacoby Georg • FRG
HEISSES PFLASTER FUR SPIONE (FRG) see **DA BERLINO L'APOCALISSE** • 1967
HEISSES PFLASTER KOLN • 1967 • Hofbauer Ernst • FRG • WALK THE HOT STREETS (UKN) ○ HOT PAVEMENTS OF COLOGNE
HEISSES SPIEL FUR HARTE MANNER (FRG) see **REBUS** • 1968
HEIST, THE • 1972 • McDougall Don • TVM • USA
HEIST, THE see **TEMPS DES LOUPS -TEMPO DI VIOLENZA, LE** • 1970
HEIST, THE (UKN) see **$ DOLLARS** • 1971
HEISTERS, THE • 1970 • Hooper Tobe • SHT • USA
HEITAI GOKUDO • 1968 • Saeki Kiyoshi • JPN • PROFLIGATE SOLDIER, A
HEITAI YAKUZA • 1965 • Masumura Yasuzo • JPN • HOODLUM SOLDIER, THE
HEITAI YAKUZA GODATSU • 1968 • Tanaka Tokuzo • JPN • HOODLUM SOLDIER AND 100,000 DOLLARS, THE
HEITAI YAKUZA NAGURIKOMI • 1967 • Tanaka Tokuzo • JPN • HOODLUM FLAG BEARER, THE
HEITAI YAKUZA: ORE NI MAKASERO • 1967 • Tanaka Tokuzo • JPN • OUTLAW SOLDIERS: LET ME HANDLE IT ○ ORE NI MAKASERO
HEJ, BYSTRA WODA • 1959 • Kallwejt Tadeusz • PLN • HI, CLEAR WATER
HEJ DU GLADA SOMMAR • 1965 • Larsson Borje • SWD • SALTA GUBBAR OCH SEXTANTER ○ SAILORS AND SEXTANTS
HEJ RUP! • 1934 • Fric Martin • CZC • HEAVE-HO!
HEJ, STINE! • 1971 • Roos Lise • DNM • HEY, STINE!
HEJ TE ELEVEN FA.. • 1963 • Jancso Miklos • SHT • HNG • LIVING TREE ○ OLD FOLK SONG, AN
HEJA ROLAND! • 1966 • Widerberg Bo • SWD • THIRTY TIMES YOUR MONEY ○ BLAND SUNAR OCH MODS
HEKAYET NUS EL LAIL • 1964 • Karama Issa • EGY • TALE OF MIDNIGHT, A
HEKAYET THALASS BANAT • 1968 • Zulficar Mahmoud • EGY • STORY OF THREE GIRLS, THE
HEKKUS LETTEM • 1972 • Fejer Tamas • HNG • I'VE BECOME A COP
HEKSEN see **HAXAN** • 1921
HEKSEN OG CYKLISTEN • 1909 • Larsen Viggo • DNM • WITCH AND THE BICYCLIST, THE (USA) ○ WITCH AND THE CYCLIST, THE ○ WITCH AND THE BICYCLE, THE ○ BICYCLE AND THE WITCH
HEKSENE FRA DEN FORSTENEDE SKOG • 1977 • Greve Bredo • NRW • WITCHES FROM THE STONED FOREST ○ HEKSESABBAT ○ WITCHES
HEKSESABBAT see **HEKSENE FRA DEN FORSTENEDE SKOG** • 1977
HEKSNETTER • 1954 • Sinding Leif • NRW
HELD ALLER MADCHENTRAUME, DER • 1929 • Land Robert • FRG
HELD BY A CHILD • 1914 • Aylott Dave • UKN
HELD BY BANDITS • 1908 • *Kalem* • USA
HELD BY THE ENEMY • 1917 • Forrester M. F. • SHT • USA
HELD BY THE ENEMY • 1920 • Crisp Donald • USA
HELD BY THE LAW • 1927 • Laemmle Edward • USA
HELD DES TAGES, DER • 1921 • Bach Rudi • FRG
HELD DES UNTERSEEBOOTES, EIN • 1915 • Schmidthassler Walter • FRG
HELD EINER NACHT (FRG) see **HRDJA JEDNO NOCI** • 1935
HELD FOR DAMAGES • 1916 • Harvey John • SHT • USA
HELD FOR MURDER (UKN) see **HER MAD NIGHT** • 1932
HELD FOR RANSOM • 1908 • *Lubin* • USA
HELD FOR RANSOM • 1913 • Apfel Oscar • USA
HELD FOR RANSOM • 1913 • Wilson Frank? • UKN
HELD FOR RANSOM • 1914 • *l.s.p.* • USA
HELD FOR RANSOM • 1938 • Bricker Clarence • USA
HELD IN TRUST • 1920 • Ince John • USA
HELD IN TRUST • 1949 • Williamson Cecil H. • UKN
HELD MEINER TRAUME, DER • 1960 • Rabenalt Arthur M. • FRG • HERO OF MY DREAMS, THE
HELD TO ANSWER • 1923 • Shaw Harold • USA
HELD TO RANSOM • 1906 • Cooper Arthur • UKN
HELD UP FOR THE MAKIN'S • 1920 • Eason B. Reeves • SHT • USA
HELDEN • 1958 • Wirth Franz Peter • FRG • ARMS AND THE MAN (USA)
HELDEN -HIMMEL UND HOLLE (FRG) see **SETTE CONTRO LA MORTE** • 1965
HELDEN IN EEN SCHOMMELSTOEL • 1963 • Weisz Frans • NTH • HEROES IN A ROCKING CHAIR
HELDEN SIND MUDE, DIE (FRG) see **HEROS SONT FATIGUES, LES** • 1955
HELDENLEBEN DES ERFINDERS DER U-BOOTE WILHELM BAUER, DAS see **HOCH KLINGT DAS LIED VOM U-BOOT-MANN** • 1917
HELDENTUM NACH LADENSCHLUSS • 1955 • Seitz Franz* • FRG
HELDINNEN • 1960 • Haugk Dietrich • FRG
HELDORADO • 1946 • Witney William • USA • HELLDORADO
HELE DORP WEET, DIE • 1961 • SAF
HELE, ON LETI! • 1985 • Tintera Tomas • CZC • LOOK, HE'S FLYING!
HELEN AND FERNANDA see **HELENA Y FERNANDA** • 1970
HELEN GRAYSON'S STRATEGY • 1917 • McDermott John • SHT • USA
HELEN INTERVENES • 1915 • *Badgley Helen* • USA
HELEN KELLER.. THE MIRACLE CONTINUES • 1983 • Gibson Alan • TVM • UKN, USA
HELEN MORGAN STORY, THE • 1957 • Curtiz Michael • USA • BOTH ENDS OF THE CANDLE (UKN)
HELEN OF FOUR GATES • 1920 • Hepworth Cecil M. • UKN
HELEN OF THE CHORUS • 1916 • Ridgwell George • SHT • USA
HELEN OF TROY • 1955 • Wise Robert • USA
HELEN OF TROY see **PRIVATE LIFE OF HELEN OF TROY, THE** • 1927
HELEN OF TROY see **SKONA HELENA** • 1951
HELEN OF TROY see **AMANTE DI PARIDE, L'** • 1955
HELEN OF TROY see **LEONE DI TEBE, IL** • 1964
HELEN, QUEEN OF THE NAUTCH GIRLS • 1973 • Ivory James • DOC • IND
HELENA 1 • 1924 • Noa Manfred • FRG • RAUB DER HELENA, DER
HELENA 2 • 1924 • Noa Manfred • FRG • UNTERGANG TROJAS, DER
HELENA IN SYDNEY • 1967 • Cowan Tom • SHT • ASL
HELENA Y FERNANDA • 1970 • Diamante Julio • SPN, FRN • NEUROSIS ○ HELEN AND FERNANDA
HELENE • 1936 • Benoit-Levy Jean, Epstein Marie • FRN
HELENE see **ORDONNANCE, L'** • 1933
HELENE LA BELLE see **BELLE HELENE, LA** • 1957
HELENE OF THE NORTH • 1915 • Dawley J. Searle • USA
HELENE, OU LE MALENTENDU • 1972 • Laguionie Jean-Francois • ANS • FRN
HELENE, REINE DE TROIE see **LEONE DI TEBE, IL** • 1964
HELEN'S BABIES • 1915 • *Benham Harry* • USA
HELEN'S BABIES • 1924 • Seiter William A. • USA
HELEN'S MARRIAGE • 1912 • Sennett Mack, Henderson Dell • USA
HELEN'S STRATAGEM • 1914 • *Johnstone Lamar* • USA
HELGA • 1967 • Bender Erich F. • FRG • VOM WERDEN DES MENSCHLICHEN LEBENS
HELGA see **THREE WHO LOVED** • 1931
HELGA AND MICHAEL see **HELGA UND MICHAEL** • 1968
HELGA, LA LOUVE DE STILBERG • 1979 • Garnier Alain • FRN
HELGA UND MICHAEL • 1968 • Bender Erich F. • FRG • MICHAEL AND HELGA (USA) ○ HELGA AND MICHAEL
HELGALEIN • 1969 • Ballmann Herbert • FRG
HELICOPTER, THE • 1944 • Donnelly Eddie • ANS • USA
HELICOPTER, THE see **HELIKOPTER** • 1962
HELICOPTER CANADA • 1967 • Boyko Eugene • DOC • CND
HELICOPTER HOLYLAND • 1970 • Barclay Robert • MTV • CND
HELICOPTER INVADERS see **HELICOPTER SPIES, THE** • 1967
HELICOPTER SPIES, THE • 1967 • Sagal Boris • USA • HELICOPTER INVADERS
HELICOPTERE S'EN CHARGERA, L' • 1951 • Masson Jean • SHT • FRN
HELIGA LOGNEN, DEN • 1944 • Frisk Ragnar • SWD • HOLY LIE
HELIKOPTER • 1962 • Nehrebecki Wladyslaw • ANS • PLN • HELICOPTER, THE
HELIOGABALE • 1910 • Calmettes Andre • FRN
HELIOPLASTICS see **HELIOPLASTYKA** • 1966
HELIOPLASTYKA • 1966 • Brzozowski Jaroslaw • DOC • PLN • HELIOPLASTICS
HELIOTROPE • 1920 • Baker George D. • USA
HELIOTROPE HARRY see **GENTLEMAN AT HEART, A** • 1942
HELL • Raamat Rein • ANM • USS
HELL see **INFERNO, L'** • 1909
HELL see **JIGOKU** • 1960
HELL see **HOLLE, DIE** • 1971
HELL see **TI-YU** • 1975
HELL AND HEAVEN see **PIEKLO I NIEBO** • 1966
HELL AND HIGH WATER • 1933 • McNutt William Slavens, Jones Grover • USA • CAP'N JERICHO (UKN)
HELL AND HIGH WATER • 1954 • Fuller Samuel • USA
HELL AND HIGH WATER see **KILLING AT HELL'S GATE** • 1981
HELL AND THE WAY OUT • 1926 • *Shields James K.* • DOC • USA
HELL AT THE AGE OF TEN see **ENFER A DIX ANS, L'** • 1968
HELL BELOW • 1932 • Conway Jack • USA • PIGBOATS
HELL BELOW, THE (UKN) see **CAIDS, LES** • 1972
HELL BELOW ZERO • 1931 • UKN
HELL BELOW ZERO • 1954 • Robson Mark • UKN
HELL BENT • 1918 • Ford John • USA
HELL-BENT FOR ELECTION • 1943 • Jones Charles M. • ANS • USA
HELL BENT FOR FRISCO • 1931 • Paton Stuart • USA
HELL BENT FOR GLORY (UKN) see **LAFAYETTE ESCADRILLE** • 1958
HELL-BENT FOR HEAVEN • 1926 • Blackton J. Stuart • USA • HYPOCRITE, THE
HELL BENT FOR LEATHER • 1960 • Sherman George • USA
HELL BENT FOR LOVE • 1934 • Lederman D. Ross • USA • NO SPEED LIMIT
HELL-BENT HARRY • 1919 • Kennedy Aubrey M. • USA
HELL BENT KID, THE see **FIEND WHO WALKED THE WEST, THE** • 1958
HELL BLOWN UP see **VZORVANNY AD** • 1967
HELL BOATS • 1969 • Wendkos Paul • UKN • MTB: MALTA WORLD WAR 2 ○ M.T.B.
HELL BOUND • 1931 • Lang Walter • USA
HELL BOUND • 1957 • Hole William Jr. • USA
HELL CAMP see **OPPOSING FORCE** • 1986
HELL CANYON OUTLAWS • 1957 • Landres Paul • USA • TALL TROUBLE, THE (UKN)
HELL CAT, THE • 1918 • Barker Reginald • USA
HELL CAT, THE • 1934 • Rogell Albert S. • USA
HELL COMES TO FROGTOWN • 1988 • Jackson Donald G., Kizer R. J. • USA
HELL CREATURES, THE see **INVASION OF THE SAUCER-MEN** • 1957
HELL DIGGERS, THE • 1921 • Urson Frank • USA • GOLD DREDGERS, THE
HELL DIVERS • 1931 • Hill George W. • USA
HELL DRIVERS • 1957 • Endfield Cy • UKN
HELL DRIVERS • 1990 • Mulcahy Russell • USA
HELL FACE see **ROSTRO INFERNAL** • 1961
HELL FIGHTERS OF THE EAST • 1972 • Chang Ch'Eh • HKG • HELLFIGHTERS OF THE EAST ○ FOUR RIDERS
HELL FIRE • 1986 • Murray William • USA • PRIMAL SCREAM
HELL-FIRE AUSTIN • 1932 • Sheldon Forrest • USA
HELL FOR SURE see **SEGURA EST EL INFIERNO** • 1986
HELL HARBOR • 1930 • King Henry • USA
HELL HAS NO DOORS • Lateef Ahmed • SHT • USA
HELL HATH NO FURY • 1917 • Bartlett Charles • USA
HELL HOLE see **HELLHOLE** • 1985
HELL IN FRAUENSEE see **DREI FRAUEN VON URBAN HELL, DIE** • 1928
HELL IN KOREA (USA) see **HILL IN KOREA, A** • 1956
HELL IN NORMANDY (UKN) see **TESTA DI SBARCO PER OTTO IMPLACABILI** • 1968
HELL IN THE HEAVENS • 1934 • Blystone John G. • USA
HELL IN THE PACIFIC • 1966 • DOC • USA
HELL IN THE PACIFIC • 1968 • Boorman John • USA, JPN • TAIHEIYO NO JIGOKU (JPN) ○ TWO SOLDIERS EAST AND WEST ○ ENEMY, THE
HELL IN TOWN see **NELLA CITTA L'INFERNO** • 1958
HELL IS A CITY • 1960 • Guest Val • UKN
HELL IS EMPTY • 1967 • Ainsworth John, Knowles Bernard • UKN, CZC
HELL IS FOR HEROES • 1962 • Siegel Don • USA
HELL IS SOLD OUT • 1951 • Anderson Michael • UKN
HELL ISLAND see **SLAUGHTERHOUSE ROCK** • 1988
HELL, LIVE see **INFERNO IN DIRETTA** • 1985
HELL MORGAN'S GIRL • 1917 • De Grasse Joseph • USA
HELL NIGHT • 1981 • Desimone Tom • USA
HELL NO LONGER see **MEPRIS N'AURA QU'UN TEMPS, LE** • 1970
HELL OF A ROW, A see **HUS I HELVETE** • 1974
HELL OF LOST PILOTS, THE (USA) see **PARADIS DES PILOTES PERDUS, LE** • 1948

HELL ON DEVIL'S ISLAND • 1957 • Nyby Christian • USA
HELL ON EARTH (USA) see **NIEMANDSLAND** • 1931
HELL ON FRISCO BAY • 1955 • Tuttle Frank • USA • DARKEST HOUR, THE
HELL ON THE BATTLEGROUND • 1988 • Prior David A. • USA
HELL ON WHEELS • 1967 • Zens Will • USA
HELL PRISON see **DIARIO SEGRETO DI UN CARCERE FEMMINILE** • 1973
HELL RACER see **DEATH DRIVER** • 1979
HELL RACERS see **DEATH DRIVER** • 1979
HELL RAIDERS • 1965 • Buchanan Larry • MTV • USA
HELL RAIDERS • 1985 • Samtani Gope
HELL RAIDERS OF THE DEEP (USA) see **SETTE DELL'ORSA MAGGIORE, I** • 1953
HELL RIDERS • 1985 • Bryan James • USA
HELL RIVER see **PARTIZAN** • 1974
HELL ROARIN' REFORM • 1919 • Le Saint Edward J. • USA
HELL SCREEN • 1968 • Toyoda Shiro • JPN
HELL SHIP, THE • 1920 • Dunlap Scott R. • USA
HELL SHIP, THE see **ELD OMBORD** • 1922
HELL-SHIP MORGAN • 1936 • Lederman D. Ross • USA • HELL SHIP MORGAN
HELL SHIP MORGAN see **HELL-SHIP MORGAN** • 1936
HELL SHIP MUTINY • 1957 • Sholem Lee, Williams Elmo • USA
HELL SO FEARED BY ALL see **INFIERNO DE TODOS TAN TEMIDO, EL** • 1979
HELL SOLDIER • 1986 • Gallagher John A. • USA
HELL SQUAD • 1958 • Topper Burt • USA
HELL SQUAD • 1984 • Hartford Ken • USA
HELL TO ETERNITY • 1960 • Karlson Phil • USA
HELL TO HELL • 1989 • Khan Mumtaz Ali • PKS
HELL TO MACAO see **SIGILLO DI PECHINO, IL** • 1966
"HELL TO PAY" AUSTIN • 1916 • Powell Paul • USA • LOVE IN THE WEST ○ HELL-TO-PAY AUSTIN
HELL-TO-PAY AUSTIN see **"HELL TO PAY" AUSTIN** • 1916
HELL TOWN • 1985 • Medford Don • TVM • USA
HELL TOWN see **BORN TO THE WEST** • 1938
HELL UNLIMITED • 1936 • McLaren Norman, Biggar Helen • ANS • UKN
HELL UP IN HARLEM • 1973 • Cohen Larry • USA
HELL WITH HEROES, THE • 1968 • Sargent Joseph • USA • TIME FOR HEROES, A ○ RUN HERO RUN
HELLBENDERS, THE (USA) see **CRUDELI, I** • 1966
HELLBOUND: HELLRAISER II see **HELLRAISER II: HELLBOUND** • 1989
HELLCAMP see **OPPOSING FORCE** • 1986
HELLCAT, THE • 1928 • Hughes Harry • UKN • WILD CAT HETTY
HELLCATS, THE • 1968 • Slatzer Robert F. • USA
HELLCATS OF THE NAVY • 1957 • Juran Nathan • USA
HELLDORADO • 1935 • Cruze James • USA
HELLDORADO see **HELDORADO** • 1946
HELLE • 1971 • Vadim Roger • FRN
HELLE BROTHERS, THE • 1975 • Sinke Digna • SHT • NTH
HELLE FOR HELENE • 1959 • Axel Gabriel • DNM
HELLE FOR LYKKE • 1969 • Henriksen Finn • DNM • BRIDEGROOM OF HAPPINESS
HELLEGAT • 1980 • Le Bon Patrick • BLG
HELLER IN PINK TIGHTS • 1960 • Cukor George • USA • HELLER WITH A GUN
HELLER WAHN • 1983 • von Trotta Margarethe • FRG, FRN • SHEER MADNESS ○ FRIENDS AND HUSBANDS
HELLER WITH A GUN see **HELLER IN PINK TIGHTS** • 1960
HELLES MADCHEN, EIN • 1916 • *Glassner Erika* • FRG
HELLEVISION • 1939 • *Roadshow Attraction* • CMP • USA
HELLFIGHTERS • 1969 • McLaglen Andrew V. • USA
HELLFIGHTERS OF THE EAST see **HELL FIGHTERS OF THE EAST** • 1972
HELLFIRE • 1949 • Springsteen R. G. • USA
HELLFIRE CLUB, THE • 1961 • Baker Robert S. • UKN
HELLGATE • 1953 • Warren Charles Marquis • USA
HELLGATE • 1989 • Levey William A. • USA, SAF
HELLHOLE • 1985 • De Moro Pierre • USA • HELL HOLE
HELLHOUNDS OF ALASKA (UKN) see **BLUTIGEN GEIER VON ALASKA, DIE** • 1973
HELLHOUNDS OF THE WEST • 1922 • *Hatton Dick* • USA
HELLINGER'S LAW • 1981 • Penn Leo • TVM • USA
HELLION, THE • 1919 • Cox George L. • USA
HELLION, THE • 1924 • Mitchell Bruce • USA
HELLIONS, THE • 1961 • Annakin Ken • UKN, SAF
HELLISH BRAIN, THE see **BLUE DEMON CONTRA CEREBROS INFERNALES** • 1968
HELLISH SPIDERS see **ARANAS INFERNALES** • 1966
HELLO AGAIN • 1987 • Perry Frank • USA
HELLO ALOHA • 1952 • Kinney Jack • ANS • USA
HELLO AND GOODBYE • 1973 • Melnikov Vitali • USS
HELLO, ANNAPOLIS • 1942 • Barton Charles T. • USA • PERSONAL HONOUR (UKN)
HELLO BABY • 1925 • McCarey Leo • SHT • USA
HELLO BABY! • 1975 • Bergenstrahle Johan • SWD • HALLO BABY
HELLO! BEAUTIFUL (UKN) see **POWERS GIRLS, THE** • 1942
HELLO, BILL • 1909 • *Phoenix* • USA
HELLO BILL • 1915 • *L-Ko* • USA
HELLO BILL! • 1915 • *Kleine* • USA • FIXER, THE
HELLO BUDAPEST see **KISZTIHAND BUDAPEST** • 1975
HELLO BUDAPEST (USA) see **HALLO BUDAPEST** • 1933
HELLO, CAPITALIST! see **BONJOUR CAPITALISTE..** • 1982
HELLO CAPTAIN • 1978 • Aziz Mohamed Abdel • EGY
HELLO, CENTRAL! • 1912 • *Buckley May* • USA
HELLO CENTRAL, GIVE ME HEAVEN • 1913 • *Fearnley Jane* • USA
HELLO CHEYENNE • 1928 • Forde Eugene J. • USA
HELLO CHILDREN see **ZDRAVSTVYITE DETI** • 1962
HELLO CUBANS see **SALUT LES CUBAINS** • 1963
HELLO, DOLLY! • 1969 • Kelly Gene • USA
HELLO DOWN THERE • 1969 • Arnold Jack • USA • SUB-A-DUB-DUB
HELLO ELEPHANT (USA) see **BUONGIORNO ELEFANTE** • 1952
HELLO, EVERYBODY • 1933 • Seiter William A. • USA
HELLO EXCHANGE • 1916 • Storrie Kelly • UKN
HELLO, FRISCO, HELLO • 1943 • Humberstone H. Bruce • USA
HELLO GIRL OF COYOTE CAMP • 1914 • *Premier* • USA
HELLO GOD • 1958 • Marshall William • USA
HELLO GOD! • 1988 • Bae Chang-Ho • SKR
HELLO GOODBYE • 1925 • Taurog Norman • SHT • USA
HELLO -GOODBYE • 1970 • Negulesco Jean • UKN
HELLO, HELLO see **ALLO, ALLO** • 1961
HELLO HOLLYWOOD • 1925 • Taurog Norman • SHT • USA
HELLO, HOW AM I • 1939 • Fleischer Dave • ANS • USA
HELLO, LIFE! see **ZDRAVSTVUJ, ZIZN!** • 1962
HELLO LITTLE GIRL HELLO • 1908 • Gilbert Arthur • UKN
HELLO LONDON • 1958 • Smith Sidney* • UKN
HELLO MABEL • 1914 • *Normand Mabel* • USA
HELLO MARS • 1922 • Goulding Alf • SHT • USA
HELLO MARY LOU: PROM NIGHT II • 1987 • Pittman Bruce • CND • PROM NIGHT 2: HELLO MARY LOU
HELLO MR. KIVI see **PAIVAA, HERRA KIVI** • 1983
HELLO MOM see **SHE'S A SWEETHEART** • 1945
HELLO MUNICH • 1968 • Papic Krsto • SHT • YGS
HELLO NAPOLEON • 1931 • Edwards Harry J. • SHT • USA
HELLO OUT THERE • 1949 • Whale James • USA
HELLO PARDNERS • 1923 • Kenton Erle C. • SHT • USA
HELLO, PROSPERITY • 1934 • Lamont Charles • SHT • USA
HELLO RADIO see **RADIO PARADE** • 1933
HELLO RUSSIA • 1930 • Edwards Harry J. • SHT • USA
HELLO SAILOR • 1927 • Sandrich Mark • SHT • USA
HELLO, SATCHMO! • 1965 • Spata Jan • DCS • CZC
HELLO SISTER • 1930 • Lang Walter • USA
HELLO SISTER • 1933 • Crosland Alan • USA • CLIPPED WINGS (UKN)
HELLO SISTER! • 1933 • Werker Alfred L. • USA
HELLO SUCKER • 1941 • Cline Eddie • USA
HELLO SWEETHEART • 1935 • Banks Monty • UKN
HELLO, TEACHER • 1918 • Roach Hal • SHT • USA
HELLO, TELEVISION • 1930 • Sennett Mack • SHT • USA
HELLO THAR • 1930 • Buzzell Edward • SHT • USA
HELLO.. THERE'S SOMEONE CALLED GIULIANA FOR YOU see **PRONTO.. C'E UNA CERTA GIULIANA PER TE** • 1967
HELLO TROUBLE • 1913 • *Stine Charles* • USA
HELLO TROUBLE • 1918 • Parrott Charles • SHT • USA
HELLO TROUBLE • 1932 • Hillyer Lambert • USA
HELLO UNCLE • 1920 • Roach Hal • SHT • USA
HELLO, VERA see **SZEVASZ, VERA** • 1967
HELLO! WEST INDIES • 1943 • Page John • UKN
HELLO, YOUNG LOVERS • 1981 • Brocka Lino • PHL
HELLRAISER • 1987 • Barker Clive • UKN, USA
HELLRAISER II: HELLBOUND • 1989 • Randel Anthony • UKN • HELLBOUND: HELLRAISER II
HELL'S 400 • 1926 • Wray John Griffith • USA • JUST AND UNJUST
HELL'S ANGELS • 1930 • Hughes Howard • USA
HELL'S ANGELS '69 • 1969 • Madden Lee • USA
HELL'S ANGELS FOREVER • 1982 • Chase Richard, Gast Leon, Keating Kelvin • USA
HELL'S ANGELS ON WHEELS • 1967 • Rush Richard • USA • LEADER OF THE PACK, THE
HELL'S BELLES • 1970 • Dexter Maury • USA • BOSTON WARRIORS
HELL'S BELLES see **WOMEN EVERYWHERE** • 1930
HELL'S BELLS • 1929 • *Disney Walt (P)* • ANS • USA
HELL'S BELLS see **CAMPANA DEL INFIERNO, LA** • 1973
HELL'S BLOODY DEVILS • 1967 • Adamson Al • USA • SMASHING THE CRIME SYNDICATE (UKN) ○ OPERATION M ○ FAKERS, THE
HELL'S BOARDER see **HELL'S BORDER** • 1922
HELL'S BORDER • 1922 • *Fairbanks William* • USA • HELL'S BOARDER
HELL'S BOSS see **MEIDO NO KAOYAKU** • 1957
HELL'S BRIGADE • 1980 • Klimovsky Leon • ITL • HELL'S BRIGADE: THE FINAL ASSAULT ○ ATTACK FORCE NORMANDY
HELL'S BRIGADE: THE FINAL ASSAULT see **HELL'S BRIGADE** • 1980
HELL'S CARGO • 1939 • Huth Harold • UKN • DANGEROUS CARGO (USA)
HELL'S CARGO see **BELOW THE SEA** • 1933
HELL'S CARGO see **ALERTE EN MEDITERRANEE** • 1938
HELL'S CARGO (USA) see **MCGLUSKY THE SEA ROVER** • 1935
HELL'S CHOSEN FEW • 1968 • Hewitt David L. • USA
HELL'S CRATER • 1918 • Pearson W. B. • USA
HELL'S CREATURES see **MARCA DEL HOMBRE LOBO, LA** • 1968
HELL'S CROSSROADS • 1957 • Adreon Franklin • USA
HELL'S END • 1918 • McLaughlin J. W. • USA
HELL'S FIRE • 1934 • Iwerks Ub • ANS • USA • VULCAN ENTERTAINS
HELL'S FIVE HOURS • 1958 • Copeland Jack L. • USA
HELL'S FURY GORDON • 1920 • De La Mothe Leon • USA
HELL'S GATE see **JIGOKUMON** • 1953
HELL'S HALF ACRE • 1919 • Kennedy Aubrey M. • USA
HELL'S HALF ACRE • 1954 • Auer John H. • USA
HELL'S HEADQUARTERS • 1932 • Stone Andrew L. • USA
HELL'S HEELS • 1930 • Lantz Walter, Nolan William • ANS • USA
HELL'S HEROES • 1930 • Wyler William • USA
HELL'S HEROES • 1940 • Wyler William • USA
HELL'S HIGHROAD • 1925 • Julian Rupert • USA
HELL'S HIGHWAY • 1932 • Brown Rowland • USA • LIBERTY ROAD
HELL'S HIGHWAY see **VIOLENT ROAD** • 1958
HELL'S HINGES • 1916 • Hart William S., Swickard Charles • USA
HELL'S HOLE • 1923 • Flynn Emmett J. • USA • PAYDAY ○ AVALANCHE
HELL'S HORIZON • 1955 • Gries Tom • USA
HELL'S HOUSE • 1932 • Higgin Howard • USA
HELL'S ISLAND • 1930 • Sloman Edward • USA
HELL'S ISLAND • 1955 • Karlson Phil • USA • SOUTH SEAS FURY ○ LOVE IS A WEAPON
HELL'S ISLAND see **PAKLENI OTOK** • 1980
HELL'S KITCHEN • 1939 • Dupont E. A., Seiler Lewis • USA
HELL'S KITCHEN see **DEVIL'S PARTY, THE** • 1938
HELL'S KITCHEN see **ANKOKUGAI SAIGO NO HI** • 1962
HELL'S KITCHEN (UKN) see **TENTH AVENUE** • 1928
HELL'S LONG ROAD • 1963 • Roberti Charles • ITL
HELL'S OASIS • 1920 • Hart Neal • USA
HELL'S OUTPOST • 1954 • Kane Joseph • USA
HELL'S PLAYGROUND • 1967 • Clark Jesse • USA • RIOT AT LAUDERDALE
HELL'S RIVER see **MAN FROM HELL'S RIVER, THE** • 1922
HELL'S TATTOOERS see **TOKUGAWA IREZUMISHI: SEME JIGOKU** • 1970
HELL'S VALLEY • 1931 • Neitz Alvin J. • USA
HELL'S WORM see **JIGOKU NO MUSHI** • 1938
HELLSEHER, DER see **MEIN HERZ SEHNT SICH NACH LIEBE** • 1931
HELLSEHERIN, DIE see **SOMNABUL** • 1929
HELLSHIP BRONSON • 1928 • Henabery Joseph • USA
HELLSTROM CHRONICLE, THE • 1971 • Green Walon • USA
HELLYYS • 1972 • Donner Jorn • FNL, SWD • TENDERNESS ○ OHMET ○ KRAPULA
HELLZAPOPPIN! • 1941 • Potter H. C. • USA
HELMETS see **SLJEMOVI** • 1967
HELP • 1916 • Drew Sidney • SHT • USA
HELP! • 1920 • *Henry Gale* • SHT • USA
HELP! • 1954 • Alvey Glenn H. Jr. • SHT • ITL
HELP! • 1965 • Lester Richard • UKN
HELP! see **AU SECOURS!** • 1923
HELP see **LEAVE IT TO ME** • 1933
HELP see **SEGITSEG** • 1970
HELP, DE DOKTER VERZUIPT! • 1974 • van der Heyde Nikolai • NTH • HELP, THE DOCTOR'S DROWNING!
HELP FOR MOTHERS see **MODREHJAELPEN** • 1942
HELP! HELP! • 1912 • Sennett Mack, Henderson Dell • USA
HELP! HELP! • 1915 • *Chamberlain Riley* • USA
HELP! HELP! • 1916 • *Stull Walter* • USA
HELP, HELP, HELP! • 1916 • Semon Larry • SHT • USA
HELP, HELP, HYDROPHOBIA! • 1913 • Lehrman Henry, Sennett Mack (Spv) • USA
HELP! HELP! POLICE! • 1917 • *Mason Billy* • USA
HELP! HELP! POLICE! • 1919 • Dillon Eddie • USA
HELP, HE'S DROWNING see **SPASITYE UTOPAYUSHCHEVO** • 1968
HELP, I'M AN HEIRESS see **SEGITSEG OROKOLTEM!** • 1937
HELP, I'M INVISIBLE see **HILFE, ICH BIN UNSICHTBAR** • 1951
HELP! I'VE INHERITED see **SEGITSEG OROKOLTEM!** • 1937
HELP ME, COMRADE! see **AYUDEME UD, COMPADRE!** • 1968
HELP ME DARLING see **AMORE MIO AIUTAMI** • 1969
HELP ME DREAM (USA) see **AIUTAMI A SOGNARE** • 1980
HELP, MURDER, POLICE • 1914 • *Starlight Comedy* • USA
HELP! MY SNOWMAN'S BURNING DOWN • 1964 • Davidson Carson • SHT • USA
HELP ONE ANOTHER • 1924 • Roach Hal • SHT • USA
HELP! POLICE! • 1909 • *Lubin* • USA
HELP, THE DOCTOR'S DROWNING! see **HELP, DE DOKTER VERZUIPT!** • 1974
HELP, VENGOS! see **VOITHIA O VENGOS** • 1967
HELP WANTED • 1911 • Powell Frank • USA
HELP WANTED • 1915 • *Meredith Lois* • USA
HELP WANTED • 1918 • Drew Sidney, Drew Sidney Mrs. • SHT • USA
HELP WANTED • 1939 • Zinnemann Fred • SHT • USA
HELP WANTED FEMALE • 1968 • Perkins Harold • USA
HELP WANTED: KIDS • 1986 • Greenwalt David • TVM • USA
HELP WANTED -MALE! • 1920 • King Henry • USA • LEONA GOES A-HUNTING
HELP WANTED: MALE • 1982 • Wiard William • TVM • USA
HELP YOURSELF • 1920 • Ballin Hugo • USA • TRIMMED WITH RED
HELP YOURSELF • 1932 • Daumery John • UKN
HELPFUL AL • 1925 • Lamont Charles • SHT • USA
HELPFUL GENIE, THE • 1951 • Rasinski Connie • ANS • USA
HELPFUL HOGAN • 1923 • La Cava Gregory • SHT • USA
HELPFUL SISTERHOOD, A • 1914 • Brooke Van Dyke • USA
HELPING GRANDMA • 1931 • McGowan Robert • SHT • USA
HELPING HAND see **MAIN SECOURABLE, LE** • 1908
HELPING HAND, A • 1913 • Buckland Warwick • UKN
HELPING HAND, THE • 1908 • Griffith D. W. • USA
HELPING HAND, THE • 1912 • *Imp* • USA
HELPING HAND, THE • 1913 • *Majestic* • USA
HELPING HAND, THE • 1913 • *Ramo* • USA
HELPING HAND, THE • 1917 • *Connelly Bobby* • USA
HELPING HANDS • 1941 • Cahn Edward L. • SHT • USA
HELPING HIM OUT • 1911 • Golden Joseph A. • USA
HELPING HIMSELF see **HIS NEW PROFESSION** • 1914
HELPING JOHN • 1912 • *Cooper Bigelow* • USA
HELPING MOTHER • 1914 • *Weber Lois* • USA
HELPING PAW, A • 1941 • Marcus Sid • ANS • USA
HELPLESS HIPPO • 1954 • Rasinski Connie • ANS • USA
HELPLESS MAN • 1911 • *Reliance* • USA
HELPLESS TASTE, THE see **SAN-CHIAO HSI-T'I** • 1982
HELPMATES • 1931 • Parrott James • SHT • USA
HELSINKI 62 see **HELSINKY 62** • 1962
HELSINKI - NAPOLI - ALL NIGHT LONG • 1987 • Kaurismaki Mika • FNL, FRG
HELSINKY 62 • 1962 • Schorm Evald • DOC • CZC • HELSINKI 62
HELTER SKELTER • 1929 • Lamont Charles • SHT • USA
HELTER SKELTER • 1949 • Thomas Ralph • UKN
HELTER SKELTER • 1955 • Smith Paul J. • ANS • USA
HELTER SKELTER • 1976 • Gries Tom • TVM • USA
HELTER-SKELTER see **HANYATT-HOMLOK** • 1984
HELTER SWELTER • 1950 • Kneitel Seymour • ANS • USA
HELWA WA CHAKIA • 1968 • Karama Issa • EGY • PRETTY AND TERRIBLE
HEM FRAN BABYLON • 1941 • Sjoberg Alf • SWD • HOME FROM BABYLON
HEM HAYU ASAR • 1960 • Dienar Baruch • ISR • THEY WERE TEN (USA)
HEMAT I NATTEN see **YON SYLISSA** • 1977
HEMBRA • 1970 • Ardavin Cesar • SPN
HEMINGWAY • Canel Fausto • CUB
HEMINGWAY'S ADVENTURES OF A YOUNG MAN (UKN) see **ADVENTURES OF A YOUNG MAN** • 1962
HEMLIGA SVENSSON • 1933 • Bauman Schamyl • SWD • SECRET AGENT SVENSSON
HEMLIGHETEN • 1983 • Hartleb Rainer, Lindqvist Staffan • SWD • SECRETS
HEMLIGT GIFTERMAL, ETT • 1912 • Sjostrom Victor • SWD • SECRET MARRIAGE, A
HEMLOSA, DE see **UTSTOTTA, DE** • 1931

HEMMELIGHEDSFULDE TRAKTAT, DEN • 1912 • Lind Alfred • DNM
HEMMELIGHEDSFULDE X, DET • 1913 • Christensen Benjamin • DNM • MYSTERIOUS X, THE
HEMMUNGSLOS see **SCHICKSAL EINER MILLIARDARSTOCHTER, DAS** • 1923
HEMMUNGSLOSE MANON (FRG) see **MANON 70** • 1968
HEMPAS BAR • 1978 • Thelestam Lars G. • SWD • HOME IS THE SAILOR ○ TRIUMPH TIGER '57
HEMSLAVINNOR • 1933 • Widestedt Ragnar • SWD • HOUSEMAIDS
HEMSLAVINNOR see **VI HEMSLAVINNOR** • 1942
HEMSOBORNA • 1919 • Barcklind Carl • SWD • PEOPLE OF HEMSO
HEMSOBORNA • 1944 • Wallen Sigurd • SWD • PEOPLE OF HEMSO, THE
HEMSOBORNA • 1955 • Mattsson Arne • SWD • PEOPLE OF HEMSO, THE
HEMTREVNAD I KASERN • 1942 • Rodin Gosta • SWD
HEN AND HORSES, THE • 1966 • Gedris Marionas Vintzo • USS
HEN AND THE CHANGELINGS, THE • Bottge Bruno J. • GDR
HEN FRUIT • 1914 • *Melies* • USA
HEN FRUIT • 1930 • Lantz Walter • ANS • USA
HEN HOP • 1942 • McLaren Norman • ANS • CND
HEN HOUSE HERO, A • 1912 • *Weston Mildred* • USA
HEN IN THE WIND, A see **KAZE NO NAKA NO MENDORI** • 1948
HEN-PECKED see **PETHEROPLIKTOS** • 1968
HEN WILL SQUAWK AGAIN, A see **NIWATORI WA FUTATABI NAKU** • 1954
HEN WITH THE WRONG CHICKS, THE see **HENNE MIT DEN FALSCHEN HUHNCHEN, DIE**
HENANPUP, THE • 1916 • *Powers* • SHT • USA
HENCRAKE WITCH • 1913 • *Summit* • USA
HENDERSON MONSTER, THE • 1980 • Hussein Waris • TVM • USA
HENDES AERE see **FOR SIT LANDS AERE** • 1915
HENDES HELT • 1917 • Holger-Madsen • DNM • VOGT DIG FOR DINE VENNER
HENDES MODERS LOFTE • 1916 • Holger-Madsen • DNM • DODENS KONTRAKT ○ SUPER SHYLOCK, A
HENDES NAADE • 1925 • Blom August • DNM
HENDRICKS' DIVORCE, THE • 1913 • *Majestic* • USA
HENDRIK CONSCIENCE • 1964 • Kumel Harry • BLG
HENGAMEH • 1968 • Khachikian Samouel • IRN
HENHOUSE HENERY • 1949 • McKimson Robert • ANS • USA
HENKEL –EIN DEUTSCHES WERK IN SEINER ARBEIT • 1938 • Ruttmann Walter • FRG
HENKER, DER see **STAATSANWALT KLAGT AN, DER** • 1928
HENKER, FRAUEN UND SOLDATEN • 1935 • Meyer Johannes • FRG • HANGMEN, WOMEN AND SOLDIERS (USA)
HENKER VON LONDON, DER • 1963 • Zbonek Edwin • FRG • MAD EXECUTIONERS, THE (USA) ○ HANGMAN OF LONDON, THE
HENKER VON SANKT MARIEN, DER • 1920 • Freisler Fritz • FRG • HANGMAN OF ST. MARIEN, THE
HENLEY REGATTA • 1896 • Acres Birt • UKN
HENLEY REGATTA • 1898 • Hepworth Cecil M. • UKN
HENNE MIT DEN FALSCHEN HUHNCHEN, DIE • *Bottge Bruno J. (P)* • ANS • GDR • HEN WITH THE WRONG CHICKS, THE
HENNES KUNGLIG HOGHET • 1916 • Magnussen Fritz • SWD • HER ROYAL HIGHNESS
HENNES LILLA MAJESTAT • 1925 • Wallen Sigurd • SWD • HER LITTLE MAJESTY
HENNES LILLA MAJESTAT • 1939 • Bauman Schamyl • SWD • HER LITTLE MAJESTY
HENNES MELODI • 1940 • Brooks Thor L. • SWD • HER MELODY
HENNES MERGET KONGELIGE HOYHET • 1968 • Berg Arnljot • NRW • HENNES MYCKET KUNGLIGA HOGHET ○ HER VERY ROYAL HIGHNESS
HENNES MYCKET KUNGLIGA HOGHET see **HENNES MERGET KONGELIGE HOYHET** • 1968
HENNESSY • 1975 • Sharp Don • UKN • FIFTH OF NOVEMBER, THE
HENO Y ENSILAJE • 1962 • Giral Sergio • DOC • CUB
HENPECK GETS A NIGHT OFF • 1914 • Henderson Dell • USA
HENPECKED • 1930 • Lantz Walter, Nolan William • ANS • USA
HENPECKED AND PECKED HENS • 1920 • Morante Milburn • USA
HENPECKED BURGLAR, THE • 1913 • *Fraunholz Fraunie* • USA
HENPECKED DUCK • 1941 • Clampett Robert • ANS • USA
HENPECKED HINDOO, THE • 1905 • Collins Alf • UKN
HENPECKED HOBOES • 1946 • Avery Tex • ANS • USA
HENPECKED HOD CARRIER, THE • 1913 • *Chamberlin Riley* • USA
HENPECKED HUSBAND • 1905 • *Bitzer Billy (Ph)* • USA
HENPECKED HUSBAND, THE • 1906 • Collins Alf? • UKN
HENPECKED IKE • 1912 • *Lyons Ed* • USA
HENPECKED ROOSTER • 1944 • Kneitel Seymour • ANS • USA
HENPECKED SMITH • 1915 • *Welford Dallas* • USA
HENPECKED (UKN) see **BLONDIE IN SOCIETY** • 1941
HENPECK'S DOUBLE • 1912 • Aylott Dave? • UKN
HENPECK'S HOLIDAY • 1913 • *Sphinx Film* • UKN
HENPECK'S NIGHTMARE • 1914 • *Waterwheel* • UKN
HENRETTELSEN • 1903 • Elfelt Peter • DNM
HENRETTELSEN see **MARTIN** • 1980
HENRI • 1985 • Labonte Francois • CND
HENRI BARBUSSE • 1958 • Lods Jean • DCS • FRN
HENRI GAUDIER-BRZESKA • 1968 • Cantrill Arthur, Cantrill Corinne • DOC • UKN
HENRI ROUSSEAU LE DOUANIER • 1950 • Lo Duca Joseph-Marie • SHT • FRN
HENRI STORCK, EYEWITNESS • 1988 • de Hert Robbe • DOC • BLG
HENRIETTA MARIA: OR, THE QUEEN OF SORROW • 1923 • Greenwood Edwin • UKN
HENRIETTA'S HAIR • 1913 • France Charles H. • USA
HENRIETTA'S HOLIDAY see **FETE A HENRIETTE, LA** • 1953
HENRIETTE see **FETE A HENRIETTE, LA** • 1953
HENRIETTE JACOBY • 1918 • Oswald Richard • FRG
HENRIQUE, O NAVEGADOR • 1960 • Mendes Joao • PRT
HENRY • 1955 • Anderson Lindsay • DCS • UKN
HENRY • 1966 • Sens Al • ANS • CND
HENRY see **FLAMBEREDE HJERTER** • 1986
HENRY 9 TILL 5 • 1970 • Godfrey Bob • ANS • UKN
HENRY ALDRICH, BOY SCOUT • 1944 • Bennett Hugh • USA • HENRY –BOY SCOUT (UKN)
HENRY ALDRICH, EDITOR • 1942 • Bennett Hugh • USA
HENRY ALDRICH FOR PRESIDENT • 1941 • Bennett Hugh • USA
HENRY ALDRICH GETS GLAMOR • 1943 • Bennett Hugh • USA • HENRY GETS GLAMOUR (UKN)
HENRY ALDRICH HAUNTS A HOUSE • 1943 • Bennett Hugh • USA • HENRY HAUNTS A HOUSE (UKN)
HENRY ALDRICH PLAYS CUPID • 1944 • Bennett Hugh • USA • HENRY PLAYS CUPID (UKN)
HENRY ALDRICH SWINGS IT • 1943 • Bennett Hugh • USA • HENRY SWINGS IT (UKN)
HENRY ALDRICH'S LITTLE SECRET • 1944 • Bennett Hugh • USA • HENRY'S LITTLE SECRET (UKN)
HENRY AND DIZZY • 1942 • Bennett Hugh • USA • MR. ALDRICH'S BOY
HENRY AND JUNE • 1990 • Kaufman Philip • USA
HENRY B. WALTHALL IN RETRIBUTION • 1928 • Mayo Archie • SHT • USA
HENRY –BOY SCOUT (UKN) see **HENRY ALDRICH, BOY SCOUT** • 1944
HENRY BUSSE AND HIS ORCHESTRA • 1940 • Negulesco Jean • SHT • USA
HENRY COTTON: THIS GAME OF GOLF • 1974 • Raeburn Michael • SHT • UKN
HENRY DAVID THOREAU: THE BEAT OF A DIFFERENT DRUMMER • 1972 • Macartney-Filgate Terence • DOC • CND
HENRY FORD'S AMERICA • 1977 • Brittain Don • DOC • CND
HENRY GELDZAHLER • 1965 • Warhol Andy • USA
HENRY GETS GLAMOUR (UKN) see **HENRY ALDRICH GETS GLAMOR** • 1943
HENRY GOES ARIZONA • 1939 • Marin Edwin L. • USA • SPATS TO SPURS (UKN)
HENRY HAUNTS A HOUSE (UKN) see **HENRY ALDRICH HAUNTS A HOUSE** • 1943
HENRY IV see **ENRICO IV** • 1984
HENRY IV, PART I • 1979 • Giles David • MTV • UKN
HENRY IV, PART II • 1979 • Giles David • MTV • UKN
HENRY, KING OF NAVARRE • 1924 • Elvey Maurice • UKN
HENRY LIMPET see **INCREDIBLE MR. LIMPET, THE** • 1964
HENRY MILLER ODYSSEY, THE • 1974 • Snyder Robert • DOC • USA
HENRY MOORE • 1951 • Read John • UKN
HENRY MOORE • 1968 • Kohanyi Julius • SHT • CND
HENRY MOORE AT THE TATE GALLERY • 1970 • Lassally Walter (c/d) • SHT • UKN
HENRY PLAYS CUPID (UKN) see **HENRY ALDRICH PLAYS CUPID** • 1944
HENRY, PORTRAIT OF A SERIAL KILLER • 1987 • McNaughton John • USA
HENRY STANLEY, THE LION KILLER see **RAINY, THE LION KILLER** • 1914
HENRY STEPS OUT • 1940 • Newman Widgey R. • UKN
HENRY SWINGS IT (UKN) see **HENRY ALDRICH SWINGS IT** • 1943
HENRY THE EIGHTH see **THREEFOLD TRAGEDY, THE** • 1922
HENRY, THE RAINMAKER • 1949 • Yarbrough Jean • USA
HENRY V • 1945 • Olivier Laurence • UKN • KING HENRY V
HENRY V • 1979 • Giles David • MTV • UKN
HENRY V • 1989 • Branagh Kenneth • UKN
HENRY VIII • 1911 • Parker Louis N. • UKN
HENRY VIII • 1978 • Billington Kevin • MTV • UKN
HENRY VIII see **ROYAL FLESH** • 1968
HENRY VIII AND HIS SIX WIVES • 1972 • Hussein Waris • UKN
HENRYK'S SISTER • 1988 • Peres Ruth • ISR
HENRY'S ANCESTORS • 1917 • Drew Sidney, Drew Sidney Mrs. • SHT • USA
HENRY'S BACK ROOM see **HENRYS BAKVAERELSE** • 1981
HENRYS BAKVAERELSE • 1981 • Lepre Gianni • NRW • HENRY'S BACK ROOM
HENRY'S LITTLE KID • 1916 • Christie Al • SHT • USA
HENRY'S LITTLE SECRET (UKN) see **HENRY ALDRICH'S LITTLE SECRET** • 1944
HENRY'S NIGHT IN • 1969 • *Kline Barbara* • USA
HENRY'S SOCIAL SPLASH • 1934 • Horne James W. • SHT • USA
HENRY'S THANKSGIVING • 1916 • Drew Sidney • SHT • USA
HENS, THE see **DAJAJ, AD-** • 1976
HEN'S DUCKLING, THE • 1915 • *Reliance* • USA
HENSHITSUSHA • 1967 • Yamamoto Shinya • JPN • DEGENERATE, A
HENSO-KYOKU • 1975 • Nakahira Yasushi • JPN • VARIATION
HENST MAESTOSO AUSTRIA • 1956 • Kugelstadt Hermann • AUS
HENTAI • 1966 • Shiga Takashi • JPN • ABNORMAL
HENTAI SHOJO • 1968 • Yamamoto Shinya • JPN • ABNORMAL VIRGIN
HENTAIMA • 1967 • Seki Koji • JPN • ABNORMAL CRIMINAL
HENTAIZUMA • 1968 • Tsuzuki Yohnosuke • JPN • ABNORMAL WIFE, AN
HEP CAT, THE • 1942 • Clampett Robert • ANS • USA
HEP CAT SYMPHONY • 1949 • Kneitel Seymour • ANS • USA
HEP MOTHER HUBBARD • 1956 • Rasinski Connie • ANS • USA
HEPATICA see **YUKIWARISO** • 1951
HEPCAT, THE • 1946 • Davis Mannie • ANS • USA
HEPHAESTUS PLAGUE, THE see **BUG** • 1975
HER ACCIDENTAL HUSBAND • 1923 • Fitzgerald Dallas M. • USA
HER ACTOR FRIEND • 1926 • *Sennett Mack (P)* • SHT • USA
HER ADOPTED FATHER • 1912 • *Kahn Eleanor* • USA
HER ADOPTED FATHER • 1915 • MacMackin Archer • USA
HER ADOPTED FATHERS • 1911 • *Selig* • USA
HER ADOPTED MOTHER • 1915 • *Big U* • USA
HER ADOPTED PARENTS • 1910 • *Vitagraph* • USA
HER ADVENTUROUS NIGHT • 1946 • Rawlins John • USA • SHE MEANT NO HARM
HER ALIBI • 1915 • *Borzage Frank* • USA
HER ALIBI • 1989 • Beresford Bruce • USA
HER AMBITION • 1912 • *Powers* • USA
HER AMBITION • 1926 • Lamont Charles • SHT • USA
HER AMBITIOUS AMBITION • 1918 • *Diamond* • SHT • USA
HER AMERICAN HUSBAND • 1918 • Hopper E. Mason • USA
HER AMERICAN PRINCE • 1916 • Turner D. H. • USA
HER AND SHE AND HIM (USA) see **CLAUDE ET GRETA** • 1970
HER ANNIVERSARIES • 1917 • Drew Sidney, Drew Sidney Mrs. • SHT • USA
HER ANSWER • 1915 • *Leslie Lilie* • USA
HER ARTISTIC TEMPERAMENT • 1911 • Salter Harry • USA
HER ATONEMENT • 1911 • *Powers* • USA
HER ATONEMENT • 1913 • Melville Wilbert • USA
HER ATONEMENT • 1915 • *Wiggins Lillian* • USA
HER AVIATOR • 1918 • *Chatterdon Arthur* • USA
HER AWAKENING • 1911 • Griffith D. W. • USA
HER AWAKENING • 1912 • Plumb Hay • UKN
HER AWAKENING • 1914 • *Princess* • USA
HER AWAKENING • 1914 • Cabanne W. Christy • *Majestic* • USA
HER AWAKENING • 1916 • *Speed* • SHT • UKN
HER AWFUL FIX • 1918 • *Rhodes Billie* • SHT • USA
HER BACHELOR GUARDIAN • 1912 • Martinek H. O. • UKN
HER BAD QUARTER OF AN HOUR • 1916 • Van Deusen Courtlandt • SHT • USA
HER BANDIT SWEETHEART • 1914 • *Farley Dot* • USA
HER BANK ACCOUNT • 1918 • *Rhodes Billie* • USA
HER BAREBACK CAREER • 1917 • Blystone John G. • SHT • USA
HER BARGAIN • 1915 • Ayres Sydney • USA
HER BARGAIN DAY • 1920 • Ireland Frederick J. • SHT • USA
HER BASHFUL BEAU • 1930 • Newfield Sam • SHT • USA
HER BATTLE FOR EXISTENCE • 1910 • *Thanhouser* • USA
HER BEAR ESCAPE • 1919 • *Christie* • USA
HER BELOVED ENEMY • 1917 • Warde Ernest C. • USA
HER BELOVED VILLAIN • 1920 • Wood Sam • USA • VEGLIONE, LA
HER BENNY • 1920 • Bramble A. V. • UKN
HER BETTER NATURE • 1912 • *Eclipse* • USA
HER BETTER SELF • 1912 • Haldane Bert? • UKN
HER BETTER SELF • 1916 • Cunard Grace • SHT • USA
HER BETTER SELF • 1917 • Vignola Robert G. • USA
HER BIG ADVENTURE • 1926 • Ince John • USA
HER BIG BROTHER • 1914 • *Hauck Roy* • USA
HER BIG NIGHT • 1926 • Brown Melville • USA • BIG NIGHT, THE
HER BIG SCOOP • 1914 • Vale Travers • USA
HER BIG STORY • 1913 • Dwan Allan • USA
HER BIKINI NEVER GOT WET • 1962 • Hakim Gaston • USA • DRY BIKINI, THE
HER BIRTHDAY • 1911 • *Imp* • USA
HER BIRTHDAY KNIGHT • 1917 • *Depp Harry* • SHT • USA
HER BIRTHDAY PRESENT • 1913 • Lehrman Henry, Sennett Mack (Spv) • USA
HER BIRTHDAY PRESENT • 1914 • *Premier* • USA
HER BIRTHDAY PRESENT • 1914 • Crisp Donald • *Majestic* • USA
HER BIRTHDAY ROSES • 1912 • *Republic* • USA
HER BIRTHDAY SURPRISE • 1911 • *Yankee* • USA
HER BITTER CUP • 1916 • Madison Cleo, King Joe • USA
HER BITTER LESSON • 1912 • Kirkland Hardee • USA
HER BITTER LESSON • 1914 • Vignola Robert G. • USA
HER BLEEDING HEART • 1916 • Pratt Jack • USA
HER BLIGHTED LOVE • 1918 • Wright Walter • SHT • USA
HER BODY IN BOND • 1918 • Leonard Robert Z. • USA • HEART OF AN ACTRESS, THE (UKN)
HER BODYGUARD • 1933 • Beaudine William • USA
HER BOHEMIAN PARTY • 1918 • Avery Charles • USA
HER BOUNTY • 1914 • Dwan Allan?, De Grasse Joseph? • USA
HER BOY • 1912 • *Gordon Julia Swayne* • USA
HER BOY • 1913 • Melville Wilbert • USA
HER BOY • 1915 • Wilson Frank • UKN
HER BOY • 1918 • Irving George • USA
HER BOYS • 1912 • *Essanay* • USA
HER BRAVE HERO • 1914 • *Belmont Baldy* • USA
HER BRAVE RESCUER • 1913 • *Wiggins Lillian* • USA
HER BREATH OF FAITH • 1911 • Porter Edwin S. • USA
HER BRIDAL NIGHTMARE • 1920 • Christie Al • SHT • USA
HER BROTHER • 1912 • *Vitagraph* • USA
HER BROTHER • 1914 • *Frontier* • USA
HER BROTHER see **OTOTO** • 1960
HER BROTHER see **OTOTO** • 1976
HER BROTHER'S PARD • 1914 • *Ammex* • USA
HER BROTHER'S PARTNER • 1912 • *Champion* • USA
HER BROTHER'S PHOTOGRAPH • 1911 • *Edison* • USA
HER BROTHER'S TUTOR • 1912 • Collins Edwin J.? • UKN
HER BURGLAR • 1912 • *Pollard Harry* • USA
HER BURIED PAST • 1915 • Kelsey Fred A. • USA
HER CANDY KID • 1917 • *Anderson Claire* • USA
HER CAPTIVE • 1911 • *Bison* • USA
HER CARDBOARD LOVER • 1942 • Cukor George • USA
HER CARDBOARD LOVER see **CARDBOARD LOVER, THE** • 1928
HER CAREER • 1915 • King Burton L. • USA
HER CAVE MAN see **STONE AGE, THE** • 1917
HER CELLULOID HERO • 1916 • Christie Al • SHT • USA
HER CHANCE • 1916 • MacDonald Donald • SHT • USA
HER CHILD see **HER UNBORN CHILD** • 1930
HER CHILDREN • 1914 • Shaw Harold • UKN
HER CHILD'S HONOR • 1911 • Salter Harry • USA
HER CHOICE • 1911 • *Reliance* • USA
HER CHOICE • 1912 • Ince Ralph • USA
HER CHOICE • 1915 • Price Albert G. • USA
HER CHUM'S BROTHER • 1911 • Olcott Sidney • USA
HER CIRCUS KNIGHT see **CIRCUS GIRL, THE** • 1916
HER CIRCUS NIGHT • 1917 • Wright Walter • SHT • USA
HER CITY BEAU • 1917 • Wilson Millard K. • SHT • USA
HER CODE OF HONOR • 1919 • Stahl John M. • USA • CODE OF HONOR ○ CALL OF THE HEART
HER COLLEGE EXPERIENCE • 1915 • *Darkfeather Mona* • USA
HER CONDONED SIN • 1917 • Griffith D. W. • USA

HER CONDONED SIN see **JUDITH OF BETHULIA** • 1914
HER CONFESSION • 1915 • *La Badie Florence* • USA
HER CONVERT • 1915 • O'Sullivan Tony • USA
HER CONVICT BROTHER • 1912 • *Neason Alice* • USA
HER CORNER IN HEARTS • 1912 • *Rich Vivian* • USA
HER COUNTRY COUSIN • 1915 • Ransom Charles • USA
HER COUNTRY FIRST • 1918 • Young James • USA
HER COUNTRY'S CALL • 1917 • Ingraham Lloyd • USA
HER COUSIN BILL • 1914 • *Crystal* • USA
HER COUSIN FRED • 1912 • Salter Harry • USA
HER COWBOY LOVER • 1910 • *Powers* • USA
HER COWBOY LOVER • 1911 • *Vitagraph* • USA
HER CRIME WAS LOVE see **POSTMEISTER, DER** • 1940
HER CROOKED CAREER • 1917 • Christie Al • SHT • USA
HER CROSS • 1919 • Bramble A. V. • UKN
HER CROWNING GLORY • 1911 • *Bunny John* • USA
HER CROWNING GLORY • 1913 • Buckland Warwick? • UKN
HER DAD, THE CONSTABLE • 1911 • Baker R. E. • USA
HER DAD'S PISTOL • 1910 • *Powers* • USA
HER DANCING PARTNER • 1922 • Cooper George A. • UKN
HER DANGEROUS PATH • 1923 • Clements Roy • SER • USA
HER DARING, TEARING WAYS • 1917 • Moore Vin • SHT • USA
HER DARKEST HOUR • 1911 • Ince Thomas H. • USA
HER DARKEST HOUR • 1912 • *Thanhouser* • USA
HER DEBT OF HONOR see **DEBT OF HONOR, A** • 1916
HER DEBT OF HONOUR • 1910 • Haldane Bert? • UKN
HER DECISION • 1918 • Conway Jack • USA
HER DEFIANCE • 1916 • *Madison Cleo* • SHT • USA
HER DEVOTED SON • 1915 • *Liberty* • USA
HER DEVOTION see **KENSHIN** • 1961
HER DIARY • 1912 • *Powers* • USA
HER DIARY • 1912 • *Vitagraph* • USA
HER DILEMMA (UKN) see **CONFESSIONS OF A CO-ED** • 1931
HER DISENGAGEMENT RING • 1918 • *Rhodes Billie* • USA
HER DOCTOR see **JEJI LEKAR** • 1933
HER DOG GONE DOG • 1917 • *Rhodes Billie* • SHT • USA
HER DOG-GONE WEDDING • 1920 • Williams Harry • SHT • USA
HER DOGGY • 1914 • Reehm George E. • USA
HER DOLLY'S REVENGE • 1909 • *Lux* • USA
HER DONKEY LOVE • 1917 • *Triangle* • USA
HER DORMANT LOVE • 1915 • O'Sullivan Tony • USA
HER DOUBLE CROSS • 1917 • *Paramount* • USA
HER DOUBLE LIFE • 1916 • Edwards J. Gordon • USA • IN THE LIGHT
HER DREAM MAN • 1916 • Reynolds Lynn • SHT • USA
HER DREAM OF LIFE • 1916 • Beal Frank • SHT • USA
HER DREAMS OF YESTERDAY • 1913 • *Excelsior* • USA
HER DRESSMAKER'S BILLS • 1912 • *White Pearl* • USA
HER DUMMY HUSBAND • 1915 • *Eclair* • USA
HER DUTY • 1914 • *Princess* • USA
HER EASTER HAT • 1915 • *Allen Estelle* • USA
HER ECONOMIC INDEPENDENCE • 1917 • Drew Sidney, Drew Sidney Mrs. • SHT • USA
HER EDUCATION • 1912 • Parker Lem B. • USA
HER ELEPHANT MAN • 1920 • Dunlap Scott R. • USA
HER ENLISTED MAN see **RED SALUTE** • 1935
HER ER BANERNE • 1948 • Christensen Theodor • DNM
HER ESCAPE • 1914 • De Grasse Joseph • USA
HER EXCELLENCY, THE GOVERNOR • 1917 • Parker Albert? • USA
HER EXCELLENCY THE GOVERNOR • 1935 • Walker Stuart • USA
HER EXCLUSIVE HAT • 1911 • *Lubin* • USA
HER FACE • 1912 • *Mcdermott Marc* • USA
HER FACE VALUE • 1921 • Heffron Thomas N. • USA
HER FACE WAS HER FORTUNE • 1909 • *Lubin* • USA
HER FACE WAS HER FORTUNE • 1913 • Williams C. Jay • USA
HER FAIRY GODFATHER • 1913 • *Majestic* • USA
HER FAIRY PRINCE • 1915 • *Wickey Violet* • USA
HER FAITH IN THE FLAG • 1913 • Thornby Robert T. • USA
HER FAITHFUL COMPANIONS • 1914 • Fitzhamon Lewin • UKN
HER FAITHFUL HEART • 1911 • Melies Gaston • USA
HER FAITHFUL YUMA SERVANT • 1913 • *Gebhardt George* • USA
HER FALLEN HERO • 1914 • *Kalem* • USA
HER FAME AND SHAME • 1917 • Griffin Frank C. • SHT • USA
HER FATAL HAND • 1915 • Aylott Dave? • UKN
HER FATAL MILLIONS • 1923 • Beaudine William • USA
HER FATAL MISTAKE • 1910 • *American* • USA
HER FATAL SHOT • 1918 • *Jaxon* • USA
HER FATHER • 1913 • *Lubin* • USA
HER FATHER • 1915 • *Lewis Ralph* • USA
HER FATHER SAID NO • 1927 • McKeown Jack • USA
HER FATHER, THE SHERIFF • 1912 • *Republic* • USA
HER FATHER'S DAUGHTER • 1913 • *Laughlin Anna* • USA
HER FATHER'S DAUGHTER • 1940 • Dickinson Desmond • UKN
HER FATHER'S GOLD • 1916 • Moore W. Eugene • USA
HER FATHER'S GUILT • 1914 • *Bison* • USA
HER FATHER'S HAT • 1912 • *Vitagraph* • USA
HER FATHER'S KEEPER • 1917 • Dwan Allan (Spv) • USA
HER FATHER'S PHOTOGRAPH • 1911 • Martinek H. O. • UKN
HER FATHER'S PICTURE • 1915 • *Whitman Velma* • USA
HER FATHER'S PRIDE • 1910 • Griffith D. W. • USA
HER FATHER'S SECRETARY • 1911 • *Yankee* • USA
HER FATHER'S SILENT PARTNER • 1914 • Crisp Donald • USA
HER FATHER'S SIN • 1910 • *Solax* • USA
HER FATHER'S SON • 1916 • Taylor William D. • USA
HER FATHER'S STATION • 1917 • Frazee Edwin • SHT • USA
HER FATHER'S STORY • 1913 • *Broncho* • USA
HER FAVORITE PATIENT • 1945 • Stone Andrew L. • USA • BEDSIDE MANNER
HER FAVORITE TUNE • 1909 • *Phoenix* • USA
HER FAVOURITE HUSBAND • 1950 • Soldati Mario • UKN • TAMING OF DOROTHY, THE (USA)
HER FEATHERED NEST • 1916 • *Murray Charles* • SHT • USA
HER FICKLE FORTUNE • 1917 • *Triangle* • USA
HER FIGHTING CHANCE • 1914 • Ricketts Thomas • USA
HER FIGHTING CHANCE • 1917 • Carewe Edwin • USA
HER FILMLAND HERO • 1915 • Franklin Sidney A., Franklin Chester M. • USA
HER FINAL CHOICE • 1913 • *Reliance* • USA
HER FINAL RECKONING • 1918 • Chautard Emile • USA
HER FINANCIAL FRENZY • 1916 • *Myers Harry* • SHT • USA
HER FINISH TOUCH • 1917 • *Anderson Claire* • SHT • USA
HER FIREMAN • 1913 • *Garwood William* • USA
HER FIRST ADVENTURE • 1908 • *Bitzer Billy (Ph)* • USA
HER FIRST AFFAIR (USA) see **PREMIER RENDEZ-VOUS** • 1941
HER FIRST AFFAIRE • 1932 • Dwan Allan • UKN
HER FIRST APPEARANCE • 1910 • Porter Edwin S. • USA
HER FIRST ARREST • 1914 • *Powers* • USA
HER FIRST ASSIGNMENT • 1912 • *Powers* • USA
HER FIRST ATTEMPT see **LOTTIE'S PANCAKES** • 1907
HER FIRST BEAU • 1916 • Cline Eddie • SHT • USA
HER FIRST BEAU • 1941 • Reed Theodore • USA
HER FIRST BISCUITS • 1909 • Griffith D. W. • USA
HER FIRST CAKE • 1906 • Williamson James • UKN
HER FIRST CHOICE • 1912 • *Bison* • USA
HER FIRST EGG • 1931 • *Terry Paul/ Moser Frank (P)* • ANS • USA
HER FIRST ELOPEMENT • 1920 • Wood Sam • USA
HER FIRST EXPERIENCE (USA) see **IHR ERSTES ERLEBNIS** • 1939
HER FIRST FALSE HARE • 1919 • Parrott Charles • USA
HER FIRST GAME • 1917 • Drew Sidney, Drew Sidney Mrs. • SHT • USA
HER FIRST HUSBAND • 1915 • Nash Percy? • UKN
HER FIRST KISS • 1919 • Griffin Frank C. • SHT • USA
HER FIRST LESSON • 1914 • *Williams Nellie* • USA
HER FIRST LONG DRESS • 1910 • *Selig* • USA
HER FIRST LOVE see **FIRST LOVE** • 1921
HER FIRST LOVE AFFAIR see **FORSTE KAERLIGHED, DEN** • 1912
HER FIRST MATE • 1933 • Wyler William • USA
HER FIRST MISTAKE • 1918 • Wright Walter • SHT • USA
HER FIRST OFFENCE • 1913 • *Lubin* • USA
HER FIRST PANCAKE see **LOTTIE'S PANCAKES** • 1907
HER FIRST ROMANCE • 1940 • Dmytryk Edward • USA • RIGHT MAN, THE
HER FIRST ROMANCE • 1951 • Friedman Seymour • USA • GIRLS NEVER TELL (UKN) ○ ROMANTIC AGE, THE
HER FIVE-FOOT HIGHNESS • 1920 • Franklin Harry L. • USA
HER FLING • 1918 • Park Ida May • USA
HER FLOWERS • 1908 • *Pathe* • FRN
HER FORGOTTEN DANCING SHOES • 1912 • *Vitagraph* • USA
HER FORGOTTEN PAST • 1933 • Ford Wesley • USA
HER FRACTURED VOICE • 1917 • *U.s.m.p.* • USA
HER FRIEND BROWN • 1918 • *Rhodes Billie* • USA
HER FRIEND, THE BAD MAN • 1913 • *Nestor* • USA
HER FRIEND THE BANDIT • 1914 • Chaplin Charles, Normand Mabel • USA • MABEL'S FLIRTATION ○ THIEF CATCHER, A
HER FRIEND, THE BUTLER • 1913 • *Lyons Eddie* • USA
HER FRIEND THE CHAUFFEUR • 1917 • Christie Al • SHT • USA
HER FRIEND, THE DOCTOR • 1912 • *Nestor* • USA
HER FRIEND, THE DOCTOR • 1916 • Christie Al • SHT • USA
HER FRIEND THE ENEMY • 1907 • Fitzhamon Lewin? • UKN
HER FRIEND, THE ENEMY • 1918 • *Field Elinor* • USA
HER FRIEND, THE MILKMAN • 1915 • Lyons Eddie • USA
HER GALLANT KNIGHTS • 1913 • *La Badie Florence* • USA
HER GAME • 1919 • Crane Frank H. • USA
HER GENEROUS WAY • 1909 • Salter Harry • USA
HER GETHSEMANE • 1915 • Smith David • USA
HER GIFT • 1912 • *Johnson Arthur* • USA
HER GILDED CAGE • 1922 • Wood Sam • USA
HER GOLDEN HAIR WAS HANGING DOWN HER BACK • 1925 • Butler Alexander • UKN
HER GOOD NAME • 1917 • *Southern Jean* • USA
HER GRANDCHILD • 1912 • *Costello Maurice* • USA
HER GRANDMOTHER'S WEDDING DRESS • 1914 • Lessey George A. • USA
HER GRANDPARENTS • 1915 • Powell Frank • USA
HER GRAVE MISTAKE • 1914 • *Mcquarrie Murdock* • USA
HER GREAT AMBITION (UKN) see **CHORUS KID, THE** • 1928
HER GREAT CHANCE • 1912 • *Melies* • USA
HER GREAT CHANCE • 1918 • Maigne Charles • USA
HER GREAT DILEMMA • 1917 • MacDonald Donald?, Coldeway Anthony W.? • SHT • USA
HER GREAT HOUR • 1916 • Taylor Stanner E. V. • USA
HER GREAT INVENTION • 1916 • Ellis Robert • USA
HER GREAT MATCH • 1915 • *Kane Gail* • USA
HER GREAT MISTAKE • 1917 • *Walcamp Marie* • SHT • USA
HER GREAT MISTAKE • 1925 • Butler Alexander • UKN
HER GREAT MOMENT see **INTERLOPER, THE** • 1918
HER GREAT PART • 1916 • Reynolds Lynn, Paul Val • SHT • USA
HER GREAT PRICE • 1916 • Carewe Edwin • USA
HER GREAT SCOOP • 1914 • Costello Maurice, Gaillord Robert • USA
HER GREATER GIFT see **ARTISTIC TEMPERAMENT, THE** • 1919
HER GREATEST LOVE • 1917 • Edwards J. Gordon • USA
HER GREATEST LOVE see **SUO PIU GRANDE AMORE, IL** • 1958
HER GREATEST PERFORMANCE • 1916 • Paul Fred • UKN
HER GREATEST STORY • 1916 • Reynolds Lynn • SHT • USA
HER GUARDIAN • 1911 • Noy Wilfred • UKN
HER GUARDIAN • 1913 • Parker Lem B. • USA
HER GUARDIAN • 1917 • *World* • USA
HER HALF BROTHER see **PALS OF THE WEST** • 1922
HER HAND • 1914 • O'Sullivan Tony • USA
HER HAPPINESS • 1915 • Beaumont Harry • USA
HER HAREM (USA) see **HAREM, L'** • 1967
HER HEART IN HER THROAT see **UNSEEN, THE** • 1945
HER HEART'S DEPTH • 1912 • *Powers* • USA
HER HEART'S DESIRE • 1917 • Campbell Colin • SHT • USA
HER HEART'S REFUGE • 1912 • *Lubin* • USA
HER HELPING HAND • 1918 • *Strand* • USA
HER HERITAGE • 1914 • Pollard Harry • USA
HER HERITAGE • 1919 • Merwin Bannister • UKN
HER HERO • 1911 • Brooke Van Dyke • USA
HER HERO • 1915 • *Royal* • USA
HER HERO • 1917 • *Rhodes Billie* • SHT • USA
HER HERO MAID • 1916 • Davey Horace • SHT • USA
HER HERO'S PREDICAMENT • 1913 • *Nestor* • USA
HER HIDDEN LIFE • 1915 • Reehm George E. • USA
HER HIDDEN PAST see **ONNA KEIZU** • 1961
HER HIGHER AMBITION • 1914 • *Frontier* • USA
HER HIGHER DESTINY see **AS MAN MADE HER** • 1917
HER HIGHNESS AND THE BELLBOY • 1945 • Thorpe Richard • USA
HER HONOR THE GOVERNOR • 1926 • Withey Chet • USA • SECOND MRS. FENWAY, THE
HER HONOR, THE MARE • 1943 • Sparber I. • ANS • USA
HER HONOR THE MAYOR • 1920 • Cazeneuve Paul • USA
HER HORRID HONEYMOON • 1914 • *Lubin* • USA
HER HOUR • 1913 • *Carlyle Francis* • USA
HER HOUR • 1917 • Cowl George • USA
HER HOUR OF RETRIBUTION • 1914 • Brett B. Harold • UKN
HER HOUR OF TRIUMPH • 1912 • *Russell Martha* • USA
HER HUMBLE MINISTRY • 1911 • Salter Harry • USA
HER HUSBAND • 1914 • Marston Theodore • USA
HER HUSBAND AND MY WIFE • 1913 • *Apollo* • USA
HER HUSBAND LIES • 1937 • Ludwig Edward • USA • LOVE TRAP, THE
HER HUSBANDS • 1914 • *Lyons Eddie* • USA
HER HUSBAND'S AFFAIRS • 1947 • Simon S. Sylvan • USA
HER HUSBAND'S DECEPTION • 1911 • *American* • USA
HER HUSBAND'S FAITH • 1916 • Carleton Lloyd B. • SHT • USA
HER HUSBAND'S FRIEND • 1913 • Kirkland Hardee • USA
HER HUSBAND'S FRIEND • 1914 • Vignola Robert G. • USA
HER HUSBAND'S FRIEND • 1920 • Niblo Fred • USA
HER HUSBAND'S HONOR • 1915 • *Pemberton Henry* • USA
HER HUSBAND'S HONOR • 1916 • *Wilson Ben* • USA
HER HUSBAND'S HONOR • 1918 • King Burton L. • USA
HER HUSBAND'S PICTURE • 1913 • *Lubin* • USA
HER HUSBAND'S SECRET • 1925 • Lloyd Frank • USA • JUDGMENT
HER HUSBAND'S SECRETARY • 1937 • McDonald Frank • USA
HER HUSBAND'S SON • 1915 • Brabin Charles J. • USA
HER HUSBAND'S TRADEMARK • 1922 • Wood Sam • USA
HER HUSBAND'S WIFE • 1913 • Johnson Arthur • USA
HER HUSBAND'S WIFE • 1916 • Abramson Ivan • *Ivan Film* • USA
HER HUSBAND'S WIFE • 1916 • Christie Al • *Nestor* • USA
HER HUSBAND'S WIFE see **MANN SEINER FRAU, DER** • 1925
HER HUSKY HERO • 1927 • Taurog Norman • SHT • USA
HER IDOL • 1915 • Smiley Joseph • USA
HER IMAGINARY LOVER • 1933 • King George • UKN
HER INDIAN BROTHER • 1913 • *Kalem* • USA
HER INDIAN GUARDIAN • 1912 • *Comet* • USA
HER INDIAN HERO • 1912 • *Gebhardt George* • USA
HER INDIAN MOTHER • 1910 • Olcott Sidney • USA • INDIAN MOTHER, THE
HER INDISCRETIONS • 1927 • *Hamilton Mahlon* • USA
HER INNOCENT MARRIAGE • 1913 • Dwan Allan, Reid Wallace • USA
HER INSPIRATION • 1911 • *Lubin* • USA
HER INSPIRATION • 1915 • McGlynn Frank • USA
HER INSPIRATION • 1919 • Thornby Robert T. • USA • KATE OF KENTUCKY
HER INVISIBLE HUSBAND • 1916 • Moore Matt • SHT • USA
HER IRON WILL • 1917 • Taylor Russell • SHT • USA
HER JOKE ON BELMONT • 1913 • *Crystal* • USA
HER JUNGLE LOVE • 1938 • Archainbaud George • USA
HER KID SISTER • 1912 • Smalley Phillips • USA
HER KIND OF MAN • 1946 • De Cordova Frederick • USA
HER KINGDOM OF DREAMS • 1919 • Neilan Marshall • USA
HER LADY FRIEND • 1913 • *White Pearl* • USA
HER LADYSHIP • 1914 • *Selig* • USA
HER LADYSHIP'S PAGE • 1912 • *Benham Harry* • USA
HER LANDLORD LOVER • 1929 • Hutton Clayton • UKN
HER LAST AFFAIRE • 1935 • Powell Michael • UKN
HER LAST CHANCE • 1914 • Avery Charles • USA
HER LAST FLIRTATION • 1915 • Davis Ulysses • USA
HER LAST HOPE • 1914 • *Warner'S Features* • USA
HER LAST PEARL see **ANO NAMI NO HATEMADE III** • 1962
HER LAST RESORT • 1912 • *Bison* • USA
HER LAST SHOT • 1912 • *Vitagraph* • USA
HER LAST TRIP • 1939 • Jennings Humphrey • DCS • UKN • S.S. IONIAN
HER LEGACY • 1913 • Balshofer Fred J. • USA
HER LESSON • 1910 • *Centaur* • USA
HER LESSON • 1915 • *Regent* • USA
HER LESSON • 1916 • *Anderson Broncho Billy* • SHT • USA
HER LESSON • 1917 • Drew Sidney, Drew Sidney Mrs. • SHT • USA
HER LIFE AND HIS • 1917 • Sullivan Frederick • USA • GIRL WHO WANTED TO LIVE, THE
HER LIFE AS A MAN • 1984 • Miller Robert Ellis • TVM • USA
HER LIFE IN LONDON • 1915 • West R. Harley • UKN
HER LIFE'S STORY • 1912 • *Powers* • USA
HER LIFE'S STORY • 1914 • De Grasse Joseph • USA
HER LITTLE DARLING • 1913 • *Crystal* • USA
HER LITTLE MAJESTY see **HENNES LILLA MAJESTAT** • 1925
HER LITTLE MAJESTY see **HENNES LILLA MAJESTAT** • 1939
HER LITTLE PET • 1913 • Wilson Frank • UKN
HER LITTLE SLIPPER • 1911 • *Pathe* • USA
HER LONELY SOLDIER • 1919 • Nash Percy • UKN
HER LORD AND MASTER • 1912 • *Powers* • USA
HER LORD AND MASTER • 1921 • Jose Edward • USA
HER LOVE COTTAGE (UKN) see **MASKED ANGEL** • 1928
HER LOVE LETTERS • 1914 • *Benham Harry* • USA
HER LOVE STORY • 1924 • Dwan Allan • USA
HER LOVER'S BROTHER (UKN) see **TRAPPED IN TIA JUANA** • 1932
HER LOVER'S HONOUR • 1909 • Martinek H. O. • UKN
HER LOVER'S VOICE • 1913 • *Imp* • USA
HER LOVING RELATIONS • 1916 • Smith David • SHT • USA
HER LUCK IN LONDON • 1914 • Elvey Maurice • UKN
HER LUCKLESS SCHEME • 1916 • *Abbott Gypsy* • SHT • USA
HER LUCKY DAY • 1920 • *Howell Alice* • SHT • USA
HER LUCKY LEAP • 1925 • Luddy Edward I. • USA
HER LUCKY NIGHT • 1945 • Lilley Edward • USA

HER MAD ADVENTURE (UKN) see **ONE SPLENDID HOUR** • 1929
HER MAD BARGAIN • 1921 • Carewe Edwin • USA
HER MAD NIGHT • 1932 • Hopper E. Mason • USA • HELD FOR MURDER (UKN)
HER "MAIL" PARENT • 1912 • Plumb Hay? • UKN
HER MAJESTY • 1922 • Irving George • USA
HER MAJESTY, LOVE • 1931 • Dieterle William • USA
HER MAN • 1918 • Ince Ralph • USA
HER MAN • 1924 • *Fairbanks William* • USA
HER MAN • 1930 • Garnett Tay • USA
HER MAN GILBEY (USA) see **ENGLISH WITHOUT TEARS** • 1944
HER MAN O' WAR • 1926 • Urson Frank • USA
HER MARBLE HEART • 1916 • Jones F. Richard • SHT • USA
HER MARKET VALUE • 1925 • Powell Paul • USA
HER MARRIAGE LINES • 1917 • Wilson Frank • UKN
HER MARRIAGE VOW • 1924 • Webb Millard • USA
HER MARTYRDOM • 1915 • *Johnson Arthur* • USA
HER MASTER • 1911 • *Selig* • USA
HER MASTERFUL MAN • 1912 • *Essanay* • USA
HER MASTER'S VOICE • 1936 • Santley Joseph • USA
HER MATERNAL RIGHT • 1916 • Thornby Robert T.?, Ince John? • USA
HER MELODY see **HENNES MELODI** • 1940
HER MENACING PAST • 1915 • *Anderson Mignon* • USA
HER MERRY MIX-UP • 1917 • *Gibson Margaret* • USA
HER MESSAGE TO HEAVEN • 1916 • *Laemmle* • SHT • USA
HER MISCHIEVOUS BROTHER • 1912 • *Punch* • USA
HER MISTAKE • 1918 • Steger Julius • USA
HER MOMENT • 1918 • Beal Frank • USA • WHY BLAME ME?
HER MOONSHINE LOVER • 1914 • *Lyons Eddie* • USA
HER MORNING DIP • 1906 • Collins Alf • UKN
HER MOTHER INTERFERES • 1911 • Sennett Mack • USA
HER MOTHER WAS A LADY • 1914 • Ince John • USA
HER MOTHER'S AMBITION • 1913 • *Patheplay* • USA
HER MOTHER'S DAUGHTER • 1915 • Powell Paul • USA
HER MOTHER'S FIANCEE • 1911 • *Yankee* • USA
HER MOTHER'S IMAGE • 1911 • *Bellamy George* • UKN
HER MOTHER'S LOVE • 1911 • *Reliance* • USA
HER MOTHER'S NECKLACE • 1914 • Crisp Donald • USA
HER MOTHER'S OATH • 1913 • Griffith D. W. • USA
HER MOTHER'S PICTURE • 1913 • *Solax* • USA
HER MOTHER'S SECRET • 1915 • *Lubin* • USA
HER MOTHER'S SECRET • 1915 • Thompson Frederick A. • *Fox* • USA
HER MOTHER'S SWEETHEART • 1916 • Ridgwell George • SHT • USA
HER MOTHER'S VOICE • 1915 • *Royal* • USA
HER MOTHER'S WEAKNESS • 1914 • O'Sullivan Tony • USA
HER MOTHER'S WEDDING GOWN • 1910 • *Vitagraph* • USA
HER MOUNTAIN HOME see **EASTERN GIRL, THE** • 1912
HER MOVIE MADNESS • 1918 • Kerr Robert • SHT • USA
HER MUSICAL BEAUS • 1915 • *Superba* • USA
HER MUSICAL COOK • 1915 • Douglass James • USA
HER MYSTERIOUS ESCORT • 1915 • Dowlan William C. • USA
HER NAKED SOUL • 1916 • Windom Lawrence C. • SHT • USA
HER NAME IS VASFIYE see **ADI VASFIYE** • 1985
HER NAMELESS(?) CHILD • 1915 • Elvey Maurice • UKN
HER NATURE DANCE • 1917 • Campbell William • SHT • USA
HER NAUGHTY CHOICE • 1917 • Curtis Allen • SHT • USA
HER NAUGHTY EYES • 1916 • *Howell Alice* • SHT • USA
HER NAUGHTY WINK • 1920 • Blystone John G. • SHT • USA
HER NEARLY HUSBAND • 1920 • Sidney Scott • USA
HER NEIGHBOR • 1913 • *Thanhouser* • USA
HER NEIGHBORS NEXT DOOR • 1914 • Vale Travers • USA
HER NERVE • 1913 • *Horner Violet* • USA
HER NEW BEAU • 1913 • Sennett Mack • USA
HER NEW CHAUFFEUR • 1913 • *Rex* • USA
HER NEW HAT • 1914 • Smalley Phillips • USA
HER NEW JOB • 1915 • *Farley Dot* • USA
HER NEW YORK • 1917 • Lund O. A. C. • USA
HER NEWSBOY FRIEND • 1908 • *Vitagraph* • USA
HER NIGHT OF NIGHTS • 1922 • Henley Hobart • USA
HER NIGHT OF ROMANCE • 1924 • Franklin Sidney A. • USA • HEART TROUBLE ○ ONE NIGHT
HER NIGHT OUT • 1920 • Davey Horace • SHT • USA
HER NIGHT OUT • 1932 • McGann William • UKN
HER NOVEL IDEA • 1920 • *Supreme Comedies* • USA
HER OATH OF VENGEANCE • 1915 • Grandon Francis J. • USA
HER OBSESSION • 1917 • Drew Sidney • SHT • USA
HER ODD TASTES • 1969 • *Jordan Marsha* • USA
HER OFFICIAL FATHERS • 1917 • Clifton Elmer, Henabery Joseph • USA
HER OLD LOVE • 1912 • *Crystal* • USA
HER OLD SWEETHEART • 1912 • Hale Albert W. • USA
HER OLD TEACHER • 1914 • O'Sullivan Tony • USA
HER ONE MISTAKE • 1918 • Le Saint Edward J. • USA
HER ONE REDEEMING FEATURE • 1915 • Buckland Warwick • UKN
HER ONLY BOY • 1913 • *Lubin* • USA
HER ONLY PAL • 1912 • Fitzhamon Lewin • UKN
HER ONLY SON • 1912 • Plumb Hay? • UKN
HER ONLY SON • 1913 • Parker Lem B. • USA
HER ONLY SON • 1914 • Lawrence Gerald • UKN • WIDOW'S SON, A
HER ONLY WAY • 1918 • Franklin Sidney A. • USA • WHAT MIGHT HAVE BEEN
HER OTHER SELF • 1915 • Sloman Edward • USA
HER OWN BLOOD • 1915 • King Burton L. • USA
HER OWN COUNTRY • 1912 • Dwan Allan • USA
HER OWN FREE WILL • 1924 • Scardon Paul • USA
HER OWN HOME • 1914 • *Fowler Lottye* • USA
HER OWN MONEY • 1922 • Henabery Joseph • USA
HER OWN PEOPLE • 1917 • Sidney Scott • USA
HER OWN RIVAL • 1914 • *English Films* • UKN
HER OWN STORY • 1922 • *Deane Sydney* • USA
HER OWN STORY • 1926 • Ford Francis • USA
HER OWN WAY • 1915 • Blache Herbert • USA
HER PAINTED HERO • 1915 • Jones F. Richard • USA
HER PAINTED PEDIGREE • 1916 • *Mcquire Paddy* • SHT • USA
HER PANELLED DOOR (USA) see **WOMAN WITH NO NAME, THE** • 1950
HER PARTNER • 1916 • Wolbert William • SHT • USA
HER PEIGNOIR • 1917 • Pitt Charles • SHT • USA
HER PENALTY • 1921 • Bruun Einar J. • UKN
HER PERFECT HUSBAND • 1916 • Drew Sidney • SHT • USA
HER PERFECT HUSBAND • 1920 • *Baker Eddie* • USA
HER PERILOUS RIDE • 1917 • Campbell Colin • SHT • USA
HER PET • 1911 • Sennett Mack, Henderson Dell • USA
HER PHONY LOVERS • 1915 • *Jupiter* • USA
HER PHOTOGRAPH • 1910 • Golden Joseph A. • USA
HER POLISHED FAMILY • 1912 • *Edison* • USA
HER PONY'S LOVE • 1913 • Fitzhamon Lewin • UKN
HER PORTRAIT • 1910 • *Powers* • USA
HER PRESENT • 1913 • *Lubin* • USA
HER PREY • 1915 • Worthington William • USA
HER PRICE • 1918 • Lawrence Edmund • USA
HER PRIMITIVE MAN • 1917 • D'Elba Henri • SHT • USA
HER PRIMITIVE MAN • 1944 • Lamont Charles • USA
HER PRIMITIVE MATE (UKN) see **NO PLACE TO GO** • 1927
HER PRIMITIVE MODEL • 1914 • Vale Travers • USA
HER PRISONER • 1911 • *Bison* • USA
HER PRIVATE AFFAIR • 1929 • Stein Paul L. • USA
HER PRIVATE HELL • 1968 • Warren Norman J. • UKN
HER PRIVATE HUSBAND • 1920 • Griffin Frank C. • SHT • USA
HER PRIVATE LIFE • 1929 • Korda Alexander • USA
HER PRIVATE SECRETARY • 1910 • *Powers* • USA
HER PROPER PLACE • 1915 • West Langdon • USA
HER PURCHASE PRICE • 1919 • Hickman Howard • USA
HER RAGGED KNIGHT • 1914 • Salter Harry • USA
HER REALIZATION • 1915 • *Anderson Broncho Billy* • USA
HER "REALLY" MOTHER • 1914 • Pollard Harry • USA
HER REDEMPTION • 1924 • Phillips Bertram • UKN • GAYEST OF THE GAY, THE
HER RELATIONS • 1912 • Stow Percy • UKN
HER RENUNCIATION • 1915 • Morgan George • USA
HER REPUTATION • 1923 • Wray John Griffith • USA
HER REPUTATION • 1931 • Morgan Sidney • UKN
HER REPUTATION (UKN) see **BROADWAY BAD** • 1933
HER RESALE VALUE • 1933 • Eason B. Reeves • USA
HER RETURN • 1915 • *Anderson Broncho Billy* • USA
HER RETURN see **JEJ POWROT** • 1974
HER RIGHT TO HAPPINESS • 1913 • *Marshall Boyd* • USA
HER RIGHT TO LIVE • 1917 • Scardon Paul • USA
HER RIVAL'S NECKLACE • 1907 • *Warwick Trading Co.* • UKN
HER ROMANCE • 1910 • *Powers* • USA
HER ROMANCE • 1921 • Paul Fred • UKN
HER ROMEO • 1915 • Hotaling Arthur D. • USA
HER ROSARY • 1913 • Apfel Oscar • USA
HER ROYAL HIGHNESS • 1913 • Miller Ashley • USA
HER ROYAL HIGHNESS see **HENNES KUNGLIG HOGHET** • 1916
HER RUSTIC HERO • 1915 • Christie Al • USA
HER RUSTIC ROMEO • 1918 • *Rhodes Billie* • USA
HER SACRIFICE • 1911 • Griffith D. W. • USA
HER SACRIFICE • 1912 • Haldane Bert? • UKN
HER SACRIFICE • 1914 • Campbell Colin • USA
HER SACRIFICE • 1926 • Lucas Wilfred • USA
HER SACRIFICE (UKN) see **BLIND DATE** • 1934
HER SALVATION • 1917 • *King Joe* • SHT • USA
HER SAVINGS SAVED • 1918 • Edwards Henry • UKN
HER SCOOP see **KANOJO NO TOKUDANE** • 1952
HER SCRAMBLED AMBITIONS • 1917 • Walsh James O. • USA
HER SCREEN IDOL • 1918 • *Sterling Ford* • SHT • USA
HER SECOND CHANCE • 1926 • Hillyer Lambert • USA
HER SECOND HUSBAND • 1918 • Henderson Dell • USA
HER SECRET • 1912 • *Anderson Mignon* • USA
HER SECRET • 1915 • *Grandin Ethel* • USA
HER SECRET • 1917 • Vekroff Perry N. • USA
HER SECRET • 1919 • Jensen Frederick S. • UKN
HER SECRET • 1933 • Millais Warren • USA • GIRL FROM GEORGIA, THE (UKN)
HER SECRET see **HIMITSU** • 1953
HER SECRET LIFE • 1987 • Kulik Buzz • TVM • USA • CODENAME: DANCER
HER SECRET STILL • 1920 • Moore Vin • SHT • USA
HER SECRETARIES • 1913 • Smalley Phillips • USA
HER SHATTERED IDOL • 1915 • O'Brien John B. • USA
HER SICK FATHER • 1913 • *Lubin* • USA
HER SIDESHOW SWEETHEART • 1914 • *Lubin* • USA
HER SILENT SACRIFICE • 1917 • Jose Edward • USA
HER SISTER • 1911 • Porter Edwin S. • USA
HER SISTER • 1914 • Le Saint Edward J. • USA
HER SISTER • 1917 • O'Brien John B. • USA
HER SISTER see **TEMPTATIONS OF A SHOP GIRL** • 1927
HER SISTER FROM PARIS • 1925 • Franklin Sidney A. • USA
HER SISTER'S GUILT • 1916 • *Triumph* • USA
HER SISTER'S HONOUR see **KID SISTER, THE** • 1927
HER SISTER'S SECRET • 1913 • *Cruze James* • USA
HER SISTER'S SECRET • 1946 • Ulmer Edgar G. • USA
HER SISTER'S SILENCE • 1912 • Coleby A. E.? • UKN
HER SISTER'S SIN • 1916 • Ford Francis • SHT • USA
HER SLIGHT MISTAKE • 1915 • Mix Tom • USA
HER SLUMBERING CONSCIENCE • 1915 • Physioc Wray • USA
HER SOCIAL VALUE • 1921 • Storm Jerome • USA
HER SOLDIER SWEETHEART • 1910 • Olcott Sidney • USA
HER SON • 1911 • *Kalem* • USA
HER SON • 1920 • West Walter • UKN
HER SON see **SONNEN** • 1914
HER SOUL REVEALED • 1915 • Reehm George E. • USA
HER SOUL'S INSPIRATION • 1917 • Conway Jack • USA
HER SOUL'S SONG • 1916 • Carleton Lloyd B. • SHT • USA
HER SPANISH COUSINS • 1914 • Lessey George A. • USA
HER SPEEDY AFFAIR • 1915 • Davey Horace • USA
HER SPLENDID FOLLY • 1933 • O'Connor William A. • USA
HER SPOILED BOY • 1911 • Melies Gaston • USA
HER SPOILED BOY • 1912 • *Schaefer Anne* • USA
HER SPOONEY AFFAIR • 1918 • *Rhodes Billie* • USA
HER STEADY CARFARE • 1916 • Davey Horace • SHT • USA
HER STEPCHILDREN • 1915 • *Perley Charles* • USA
HER STEPMOTHER • 1913 • *Champion* • USA
HER STORY • 1920 • Butler Alexander • UKN
HER STRANGE DESIRE (USA) see **POTIPHAR'S WIFE** • 1931
HER STRANGE EXPERIENCE • 1917 • Ryder Maxwell • SHT • USA
HER STRANGE WEDDING • 1917 • Melford George • USA
HER STURDY OAK • 1921 • Heffron Thomas N. • USA
HER SUITOR'S SUIT • 1914 • Buckland Warwick? • UKN
HER SUMMER HERO • 1928 • Dugan James • USA
HER SUMMER VACATION see **GISELLE** • 1981
HER SUNKISSED HERO • 1916 • *Burns Neal* • SHT • USA
HER SUPREME SACRIFICE • 1913 • *Pyramid* • USA
HER SUPREME SACRIFICE • 1915 • Buel Kenean • USA
HER SURRENDER • 1916 • Abramson Ivan • USA
HER SWEET REVENGE • 1910 • *Vitagraph* • USA
HER SWEETEST MEMORY • 1913 • *Vitagraph* • USA
HER SWEETHEART see **CHRISTOPHER BEAN** • 1933
HER TEDDY BEAR • 1912 • Raymond Charles? • UKN
HER TEMPORARY HUSBAND • 1923 • McDermott John • USA
HER TEMPTATION • 1917 • Stanton Richard • USA
HER TENDER FEET • 1919 • Parrott Charles • USA
HER TERRIBLE ORDEAL • 1910 • Griffith D. W. • USA
HER TERRIBLE PERIL • 1910 • *Bison* • USA
HER TERRIBLE TIME • 1918 • *Rhodes Billie* • USA
HER "THING".. VIBRATIONS see **VIBRATIONS** • 1969
HER THREE MOTHERS • 1915 • Giblyn Charles • USA
HER THREE PROPOSALS • 1911 • *Champion* • USA
HER TORPEDOED LOVE • 1917 • Griffin Frank C. • SHT • USA
HER TRIP TO NEW YORK • 1914 • *Essanay* • USA
HER TUTORS • 1913 • *Eclair* • USA
HER TWELVE MEN • 1954 • Leonard Robert Z. • USA
HER TWIN BROTHER • 1914 • *Meredyth Bess* • USA
HER TWO JEWELS • 1913 • *Thanhouser* • USA
HER TWO SONS • 1911 • Salter Harry • USA
HER UNBORN CHILD • 1930 • McGrath Charles, Ray Albert • USA • HER CHILD
HER UNCLE • 1915 • Tucker George Loane • UKN
HER UNCLE JOHN • 1912 • *Lubin* • USA
HER UNCLE'S CONSENT • 1912 • *Lubin* • USA
HER UNCLE'S WILL • 1910 • *Vitagraph* • USA
HER UNCLE'S WILL • 1911 • *Solax* • USA
HER UNMARRIED LIFE • 1918 • Blystone John G. • SHT • USA
HER UNWILLING HUSBAND • 1920 • Scardon Paul • USA
HER VANISHED YOUTH • 1916 • Kelsey O. C. • SHT • USA
HER VERY ROYAL HIGHNESS see **HENNES MERGET KONGELIGE HOYHET** • 1968
HER VICTORY ETERNAL • 1914 • Martin E. A. • USA
HER VISITOR • 1912 • *White Pearl* • USA
HER VOCATION • 1915 • Castle James W. • USA
HER WAY • 1911 • Porter Edwin S. • *Rex* • USA
HER WAY • 1913 • Kirkland Hardee • USA
HER WAY • 1914 • *Princess* • USA
HER WAY OF LOVE see **EE PUT** • 1929
HER WAYWARD PARENTS • 1917 • MacGregor Norval • SHT • USA
HER WAYWARD SISTER • 1916 • Greene Clay M. • USA
HER WAYWARD SON • 1914 • De Grasse Joseph • USA
HER WEAKLING BROTHER • 1915 • Ince John • USA
HER WEDDING BELL • 1913 • Kirkwood James?, O'Sullivan Tony? • USA
HER WEDDING DAY • 1916 • Gerrard Douglas • SHT • USA
HER WEDDING DRESS see **WEDDING DRESS, THE** • 1912
HER WEDDING NIGHT • 1915 • Daly William Robert • USA
HER WEDDING NIGHT • 1930 • Tuttle Frank • USA
HER WEDDING RING • 1911 • Merwin Bannister • USA
HER WEEK OF ANGUISH • 1912 • *Eclair* • USA
HER WHIRLWIND WEDDING • 1918 • *Novak Eva* • SHT • USA
HER WHOLE DUTY • 1912 • *Champion* • USA
HER WILD OAT • 1927 • Neilan Marshall • USA
HER WINNING PUNCH • 1915 • Parrott Charles • USA
HER WINNING WAY • 1910 • *Melies* • USA
HER WINNING WAY • 1919 • *Strand* • SHT • USA
HER WINNING WAY • 1921 • Henabery Joseph • USA
HER WONDERFUL DAY • 1915 • Garber Herbert • USA
HER WONDERFUL LIE see **ADDIO, MIMI** • 1947
HER WONDERFUL SECRET • 1916 • Kelley J. Winthrop • SHT • USA • ANGEL UNAWARES, AN
HER WOODEN LEG • 1913 • Hotaling Arthur D. • USA
HER WORDS CAME TRUE • 1911 • *Selig* • USA
HER YESTERDAY • 1912 • *Powers* • USA
HER YOUNGER SISTER • 1914 • Cooley Frank • USA
HER ZAMAN KALBIMDESIN • 1967 • Sagiroglu Duygu • TRK • YOU ARE ALWAYS IN MY HEART
HERACLIO BERNAL see **RAYO DE SINALOA, EL** • 1935
HERAKLES • 1962 • Herzog Werner • SHT • FRG
HERB ALPERT AND THE TIJUANA BRASS BAND DOUBLE FEATURE • 1966 • Hubley John, Hubley Faith • ANS • USA
HERB THE VERB • 1974 • Jelly Chris • UKN
HERBE SAUVAGE, L' • 1978 • Duparc Henri • IVC
HERBERT KAUFMAN'S WEEKLY • 1920 • SER • USA
HERBERT VON KARAJAN • 1966 • Reichenbach Francois • SHT • FRN
HERBERTS SUNDE • 1915 • Del Zopp Rudolf • FRG
HERBIE ANYONE LIVED IN A PRETTY HOMETOWN • 1965 • Lucas George • SHT • USA
HERBIE GOES BANANAS • 1980 • McEveety Vincent • USA
HERBIE GOES TO MONTE CARLO • 1977 • McEveety Vincent • USA
HERBIE RIDES AGAIN (UKN) see **LOVE BUG RIDES AGAIN, THE** • 1972
HERBST MELODIE see **LIEBESERWACHEN** • 1936
HERBSTMANOVER • 1926 • Neff Wolfgang • FRG
HERBSTMANOVER • 1935 • Jacoby Georg • FRG • FALL MANOEUVRES (USA)
HERBSTMILCH • 1988 • Vilsmaier Joseph • FRG • AUTUMN MILK (UKN)
HERBSTSONATE • 1978 • Bergman Ingmar • FRG, SWD • HOSTSONATEN (SWD) ○ AUTUMN SONATA (USA)
HERBSTSTURME • 1919 • Matull Kurt • FRG
HERBSTZAUBER • 1923 • *Hess Emil* • FRG
HERBSTZEIT AM RHEIN • 1928 • Philippi Siegfried • FRG

HERCEGNO PONGYOLABAN, A • 1914 • Curtiz Michael • HNG • PRINCESS PONGYOLA
HERCULE • 1937 • Esway Alexander, Carlo-Rim • FRN • INCORRUPTIBLE, L'
HERCULE A LA CONQUETE DE L'ATLANTIDE see **ERCOLE ALLA CONQUISTA DI ATLANTIDE** • 1961
HERCULE CONTRE MOLOCH see **ERCOLE CONTRO MOLOCH** • 1964
HERCULE CONTRE ROME (FRN) see **ERCOLE CONTRO ROMA** • 1964
HERCULE ET LA REINE DE LYDIE (FRN) see **ERCOLE E LA REGINA DI LIDIA** • 1959
HERCULES • 1983 • Cozzi Luigi • ITL, USA
HERCULES AGAINST MOLOCH see **ERCOLE CONTRO MOLOCH** • 1964
HERCULES AGAINST ROME (USA) see **ERCOLE CONTRO ROMA** • 1964
HERCULES AGAINST THE BARBARIANS (USA) see **MACISTE NELL'INFERNO DII GENGHIS KHAN** • 1964
HERCULES AGAINST THE MONGOLS (USA) see **MACISTE CONTRO I MONGOLI** • 1964
HERCULES AGAINST THE MOON MEN (USA) see **MACISTE E LA REGINA DI SAMAR** • 1964
HERCULES AGAINST THE SONS OF THE SUN (USA) see **ERCOLE CONTRO I FIGLI DEL SOLE** • 1964
HERCULES AND THE BIG STICK see **DOUZE TRAVAUX D'HERCULE, LES** • 1910
HERCULES AND THE BLACK PIRATES (USA) see **SANSONE CONTRO IL CORSARO NERO** • 1962
HERCULES AND THE CAPTIVE WOMEN see **ERCOLE ALLA CONQUISTA DI ATLANTIDE** • 1961
HERCULES AND THE CONQUEST OF ATLANTIS see **ERCOLE ALLA CONQUISTA DI ATLANTIDE** • 1961
HERCULES AND THE HAUNTED WOMEN see **ERCOLE ALLA CONQUISTA DI ATLANTIDE** • 1961
HERCULES AND THE HAUNTED WORLD see **ERCOLE AL CENTRO DELLA TERRA** • 1961
HERCULES AND THE HYDRA see **AMORI DI ERCOLE, GLI** • 1960
HERCULES AND THE MASKED RIDER see **GOLIA E IL CAVALIERE MASCHERATO** • 1964
HERCULES AND THE PRINCESS OF TROY • 1964 • Antonini Alfredo • ITL
HERCULE AND THE QUEEN OF LIDIA see **ERCOLE E LA REGINA DI LIDIA** • 1959
HERCULES AND THE QUEEN OF SHEBA (USA) see **ERCOLE E LA REGINA DI LIDIA** • 1959
HERCULES AND THE TEN AVENGERS see **TRIONFO DI ERCOLE, IL** • 1964
HERCULES AND THE TREASURE OF THE INCAS (USA) see **SANSONE E IL TESORO DEGLI INCAS** • 1964
HERCULES AND THE TYRANTS OF BABYLON (USA) see **ERCOLE CONTRO I TIRANNI DI BABILONIA** • 1964
HERCULES AT THE CENTRE OF THE EARTH (UKN) see **ERCOLE AL CENTRO DELLA TERRA** • 1961
HERCULES ATTACKS see **ERCOLE CONTRO MOLOCH** • 1964
HERCULES CHALLENGE see **ERCOLE CONTRO MOLOCH** • 1964
HERCULES CHALLENGES SAMSON see **ERCOLE SFIDA SANSONE** • 1964
HERCULES CONQUERS ATLANTIS see **ERCOLE ALLA CONQUISTA DI ATLANTIDE** • 1961
HERCULES CONTRA LOS HIJOS DEL SOL (SPN) see **ERCOLE CONTRO I FIGLI DEL SOLE** • 1964
HERCULES GOES BANANAS see **HERCULES IN NEW YORK** • 1970
HERCULES II see **ADVENTURES OF HERCULES, THE** • 1984
HERCULES IN NEW YORK • 1970 • Seidelman Arthur Allan • USA • HERCULES THE MOVIE ○ HERCULES GOES BANANAS
HERCULES IN THE CENTRE OF THE EARTH see **ERCOLE AL CENTRO DELLA TERRA** • 1961
HERCULES IN THE DESERT (USA) see **VALLE DELL'ECO TONANTE, LA** • 1964
HERCULES IN THE HAUNTED WORLD (USA) see **ERCOLE AL CENTRO DELLA TERRA** • 1961
HERCULES IN THE REGIMENT • 1909 • *Pathe* • USA
HERCULES IN THE VALE OF WOE (USA) see **MACISTE CONTRO ERCOLE NELLA VALLE DEI GUAI** • 1962
HERCULES, MACISTE, SAMSON AND URSUS VS. THE UNIVERSE see **ERCOLE, SANSONE, MACISTE E URSUS: GLI INVINCIBILE** • 1965
HERCULES OF THE DESERT see **VALLE DELL'ECO TONANTE, LA** • 1964
HERCULES' PILLS see **PILLOLE D'ERCOLE, LE** • 1960
HERCULES, PRISONER OF EVIL (USA) see **URSUS IL TERRORE DEI KIGHISI** • 1964
HERCULES, SAMSON AND ULYSSES (USA) see **ERCOLE SFIDA SANSONE** • 1964
HERCULES THE ATHLETE see **VERDENS HERKULES** • 1908
HERCULES THE AVENGER • 1965 • *Park Reg* • ITL
HERCULES THE INVINCIBLE (USA) see **ERCOLE L'INVINCIBILE** • 1963
HERCULES THE MOVIE see **HERCULES IN NEW YORK** • 1970
HERCULES (UKN) see **FATICHE DI ERCOLE, LE** • 1957
HERCULES UNCHAINED (UKN) see **ERCOLE E LA REGINA DI LIDIA** • 1959
HERCULES VS. KING FU (USA) see **SCHIAFFONI E KARATI** • 1974
HERCULES VS. MOLOCH see **ERCOLE CONTRO MOLOCH** • 1964
HERCULES VS. THE GIANT WARRIORS (USA) see **TRIONFO DI ERCOLE, IL** • 1964
HERCULES VS. ULYSSES see **ULISSE CONTRO ERCOLE** • 1961
HERD, THE see **SURU** • 1979
HERD OF DRUMS • 1985 • SAF
HERDEIROS, OS • 1970 • Diegues Carlos • BRZ • INHERITORS, THE
HERDERS, THE • 1911 • *Selig* • USA
HERDSMAN, THE • 1967 • Shamshiev Bolotbek • SHT • USS
HERDSMAN, THE • 1982 • Xie Jin • CHN
HERE AND THERE • 1916 • *Stull Walter* • SHT • USA
HERE AND THERE • 1936 • Baxter John • UKN
HERE AND THERE • 1964 • Heynowski Walter • DOC • GDR
HERE AND THERE see **ATCHI WA KOTCHI** • 1962
HERE ARE LIONS see **ZDE JSOU LVI** • 1958
HERE ARE SOME MIRACLES see **NO MIRACLE AT ALL** • 1965
HERE ARE THE LADIES • 1971 • Quested John • USA
HERE AT THE WATER'S EDGE • 1960 • Hurwitz Leo T. • DOC • USA
HERE, BENEATH THE NORTH STAR see **TAALLA POHJANTAHDEN ALLA** • 1968
HERE COME THE BOOGIE MEN see **YOU'LL FIND OUT** • 1940
HERE COME THE CO-EDS • 1945 • Yarbrough Jean • USA
HERE COME THE GIRLS • 1918 • Roach Hal • SHT • USA
HERE COME THE GIRLS • 1953 • Binyon Claude • USA
HERE COME THE HUGGETTS • 1948 • Annakin Ken • UKN • WEDDING BELLS
HERE COME THE JETS • 1959 • Fowler Gene Jr. • USA
HERE COME THE LITTLES • 1985 • Deyries Bernard • ANM • LXM
HERE COME THE MARINES • 1952 • Beaudine William • USA
HERE COME THE NELSONS • 1952 • De Cordova Frederick • USA • MEET THE NELSONS
HERE COME THE SEVENTIES • 1970-72 • Fox Beryl • SER • CND
HERE COME THE SPIDERS see **THE SPIDERS NO DAISODO** • 1968
HERE COME THE TIGERS • 1978 • Cunningham Sean S. • USA • MANNY'S ORPHANS
HERE COME THE WAVES • 1944 • Sandrich Mark • USA
HERE COMES A POLICEMAN see **STRICTLY ILLEGAL** • 1935
HERE COMES CARTER • 1936 • Clemens William • USA • VOICE OF SCANDAL, THE (UKN)
HERE COMES CHARLIE • 1926 • Taurog Norman • SHT • USA
HERE COMES COOKIE • 1935 • McLeod Norman Z. • USA • PLOT THICKENS, THE (UKN) ○ SOUP TO NUTS
HERE COMES DODIE • 1970 • *Mj Productions* • USA
HERE COMES ELMER • 1943 • Santley Joseph • USA • HITCHHIKE TO HAPPINESS (UKN)
HERE COMES EVERYBODY • 1973 • Whitmore John • DOC • USA
HERE COMES HAPPINESS • 1941 • Smith Noel • USA
HERE COMES KELLY • 1943 • Beaudine William • USA
HERE COMES MR. JORDAN • 1941 • Hall Alexander • USA • MR. JORDAN COMES TO TOWN
HERE COMES MR. ZERK • 1943 • White Jules • SHT • USA
HERE COMES PRECIOUS • 1927 • Rodney Earle • SHT • USA
HERE COMES THE BAND • 1935 • Sloane Paul • USA
HERE COMES THE BANDWAGON see **HALFWAY TO HEAVEN** • 1929
HERE COMES THE BRIDE • 1915 • *Clayton Ethel* • USA
HERE COMES THE BRIDE • 1919 • Robertson John S. • USA
HERE COMES THE BRIDE • *Morris David* • USA
HERE COMES THE BRIDE see **BRIDE, THE** • 1973
HERE COMES THE CAVALRY • 1941 • Lederman D. Ross • SHT • USA
HERE COMES THE GROOM • 1918 • *Vernon Bobby* • USA
HERE COMES THE GROOM • 1934 • Sedgwick Edward • USA
HERE COMES THE GROOM • 1951 • Capra Frank • USA
HERE COMES THE HURRICANE see **ALLA VIENE EL TEMPORAL** • 1988
HERE COMES THE NASHVILLE SOUND • 1966 • Kane Joseph • USA • COUNTRY BOY
HERE COMES THE NAVY • 1934 • Bacon Lloyd • USA • HEY SAILOR
HERE COMES THE SUN • 1945 • Baxter John • UKN
HERE COMES TROUBLE • 1936 • Seiler Lewis • USA
HERE COMES TROUBLE • 1948 • Guiol Fred • USA
HERE HE COMES • 1926 • Corby Travers • USA
HERE I AM • 1962 • Baillie Bruce • USA
HERE I AM A STRANGER • 1939 • Del Ruth Roy • USA
HERE I COME (UKN) see **HARVARD, HERE I COME** • 1942
HERE IS A FOUNTAIN see **KOKO NI IZUMI ARI** • 1955
HERE IS A MAN see **DEVIL AND DANIEL WEBSTER, THE** • 1941
HERE IS A SPRING see **KOKO NI IZUMI ARI** • 1955
HERE IS CANADA • 1972 • Ianzelo Tony • DOC • CND
HERE IS CUBA see **YA -KUBA** • 1962
HERE IS MY HEART • 1934 • Tuttle Frank • USA
HERE IS OUR HOUSE • 1974 • Sokolov Viktor • USS
HERE IS PARADISE • 1934 • Hurley Frank • DOC • ASL
HERE IS THE LAND • 1937 • Hawes Stanley • DOC • UKN
HERE IS YOUR LIFE see **HAR HAR DU DITT LIV** • 1966
HERE KIDDIE KIDDIE • 1960 • Hanna William, Barbera Joseph • ANS • USA
HERE, MUKHTAR! see **COME HERE, MUKHTAR!** • 1964
HERE REMAINS A MEMORY • 1965 • Buckley Anthony • DOC • ASL
HERE SHE GOES AND THERE SHE GOES • 1913 • Noy Wilfred • UKN
HERE THEY COME DOWN THE STREET see **PARADE** • 1952
HERE TO STAY • 1976 • Bonniere Rene • CND
HERE TODAY, GONE TAMALE • 1959 • Freleng Friz • ANS • USA
HERE TODAY.. WHERE TOMORROW? • 1985 • Belec Marilyn A. • CND
HERE UPON WE'RE BOTH AGREED • 1907 • Morland John • UKN
HERE WALKS TRAGEDY • 1957 • Uher Stefan • CZC
HERE WE ARE AGAIN • 1913 • Collins Edwin J. • UKN • HARLEQUINADE, THE
HERE WE COME see **HAR KOMMER VI** • 1947
HERE WE COME GATHERING • 1945 • Delmaine Barry • UKN
HERE WE GO AGAIN • 1942 • Dwan Allan • USA
HERE WE GO AGAIN (UKN) see **PRIDE OF THE BOWERY** • 1940
HERE WE GO AROUND THE MULBERRY BUSH • 1967 • Donner Clive • UKN
HERE, WHERE WE LIVE see **TU GDZIE ZYJEMY** • 1962
HERE WILL I NEST • 1941 • Turner Melburn E. • CND
HEREC KTEREHO NENI VIDET • 1971 • Bocek Jaroslav • CZC • INVISIBLE ACTOR, THE
HEREDE EL INFIERNO see **ANGEL DEL INFIERNO** • 1958
HEREDERO EN APUROS • 1956 • Iglesias Miguel • SPN
HEREDITARY FOOLS • 1975 • Mustafa Niazi • EGY
HEREDITY • 1912 • Griffith D. W. • USA
HEREDITY • 1915 • Humphrey William • USA
HEREDITY • 1918 • Earle William P. S. • USA • BLOOD OF THE TREVORS
HEREDITY IN MAN • 1937 • Durden J. V. • UKN
HEREJE, EL (SPN) see **ERETICO, L'** • 1958
HERENCIA, LA • 1964 • Alventosa Ricardo • ARG • INHERITANCE, THE (USA)
HERENCIA DE LA LLORONA, LA • 1946 • Magdaleno Mauricio • MXC • HERITAGE OF THE CRYING WOMAN, THE
HERENCIA MACABRA • 1940 • Bohr Jose • MACABRE LEGACY, A (USA)
HERENCIA MALDITA • 1963 • Ortega Juan J. • MXC
HERENCIA TRAGICA • 1958 • Urueta Chano • MXC
HERE'S A FINE HOW D'YE DO • 1907 • Morland John • UKN
HERE'S A HOW-D'YE-DO • 1906 • Gilbert Arthur • UKN
HERE'S FREEDOM! see **ITT A SZABADSAG!** • 1990
HERE'S GEORGE • 1932 • Davis Redd • UKN
HERE'S HEALTH UNTO HIS MAJESTY • 1902 • Moss Hugh • UKN
HERE'S LAS VEGAS see **SPREE** • 1967
HERE'S LOOKING AT YOU • 1974 • Gordon Lee • DOC • CND
HERE'S LUCK • 1931 • Roberts Stephen • SHT • USA
HERE'S NUDNIK • 1965 • Deitch Gene • ANS • USA
HERE'S THE GANG • 1935 • Schwarzwald Milton • SHT • USA
HERE'S THE KNIFE, DEAR: NOW USE IT see **NIGHTMARE** • 1963
HERE'S THE PLACE FOR US • 1973 • Bukovsky E. • USS
HERE'S TO GOOD OLD JAIL • 1938 • Donnelly Eddie • ANS • USA
HERE'S TO HARRY'S GRANDFATHER! • 1970 • Rubbo Michael • CND • SUMMER'S NEARLY OVER
HERE'S TO ROMANCE • 1935 • Green Alfred E. • USA
HERE'S TO THE GIRLS see **OJOSAN KANPAI** • 1949
HERE'S TO THE MEMORY • 1947 • Howells Jack • DOC • UKN
HERE'S TO YOU MR. ROBINSON • 1976 • Tammer Peter, Patterson Garry • DOC • ASL
HERE'S YOUR ANSWER • 1947 • Parker Benjamin R. • SHT • USA
HERE'S YOUR CHANCE • 1980 • GRC
HERE'S YOUR HAT • 1913 • *Essanay* • USA
HERE'S YOUR LIFE (USA) see **HAR HAR DU DITT LIV** • 1966
HERE'S YOUR MEN • 1922 • Maloney Leo, Beebe Ford • USA
HERETIC, THE see **EXORCIST II: THE HERETIC** • 1977
HERETIC, THE see **HERETIK** • 1987
HERETIK • 1987 • Stojan Andrej • YGS • HERETIC, THE
HEREWARD THE WAKE • 1924 • *Regent Films* • SHT • UKN
HERFRA MIN VERDEN GAR • 1976 • Thomsen Christian Braad • DNM • WELL-SPRING OF MY WORLD ○ WELLSPRING OF MY YOUTH
HERFSLAND • 1979 • SAF
HERGOTTSSCHNITZER VON AMMERGAU, DER • 1952 • Reinl Harald • FRG
HERGUN OLMEKTENSE • 1964 • Ceylan Ferit • TRK
HERHANGI BIR KADIN • 1982 • Goren Serif • TRK • ANY WOMAN
HERIDA LUMINOSA, LA • 1956 • Demicheli Tulio • MXC, SPN
HERITAGE • 1915 • Leonard Robert Z. • USA
HERITAGE • 1920 • Roubert William L. • USA
HERITAGE • 1935 • Chauvel Charles • ASL
HERITAGE • 1939 • Scott J. Booth • CND
HERITAGE • 1977 • Friel Deirdre • MTV • IRL
HERITAGE • 1979 • Bourke Terry • MTV • ASL
HERITAGE see **KARAMI-AI** • 1962
HERITAGE see **ODKAZ** • 1965
HERITAGE see **SLAEGTEN** • 1978
HERITAGE see **ARVEN** • 1979
HERITAGE see **DEDISCINA** • 1985
HERITAGE ,L' • 1920 • de Baroncelli Jacques • FRN
HERITAGE, L' • 1960 • Devlin Bernard • CND
HERITAGE, L' • 1975 • Bouamari Mohamed • ALG
HERITAGE, THE • 1913 • *Majestic* • USA
HERITAGE, THE see **INHERITANCE, THE** • 1970
HERITAGE, THE see **OROKSEG** • 1980
HERITAGE.. AFRICA • 1988 • Ansah • GHN
HERITAGE DE CENT MILLIONS, UN • 1924 • du Plessis Armand • FRN
HERITAGE DE LA CHOUETTE, L' • 1988 • Marker Chris • FRN • OWL'S LEGACY, THE (UKN)
HERITAGE DE VIOLENCE, L' • Delannoy Jean • FRN
HERITAGE DU CROISSANT, L' • 1950 • Leenhardt Roger • DCS • FRN
HERITAGE OF A CENTURY, THE • 1915 • *Davenport Dorothy* • USA
HERITAGE OF BJORNDAL, THE see **ERBE VON BJORNDAL, DAS** • 1960
HERITAGE OF DRACULA, THE see **VAMPYROS LESBOS -DIE ERBIN DES DRACULA** • 1971
HERITAGE OF EVE, THE • 1913 • Barker Reginald? • USA
HERITAGE OF FIVE HUNDRED THOUSAND PEOPLE, THE see **GOJUMAN-NIN NO ISAN** • 1963
HERITAGE OF HAMILTON CLEEK, THE • 1914 • Lessey George A. • USA
HERITAGE OF HATE, THE • 1916 • George Burton • USA
HERITAGE OF THE CRYING WOMAN, THE see **HERENCIA DE LA LLORONA, LA** • 1946
HERITAGE OF THE DESERT • 1933 • Hathaway Henry • USA
HERITAGE OF THE DESERT • 1939 • Selander Lesley • USA
HERITAGE OF THE DESERT, THE • 1924 • Willat Irvin V. • USA
HERITAGE OF THE PLAINS see **BORN TO THE WEST** • 1938
HERITAGE OF VALOR • 1916 • Curtis Allen • SHT • USA
HERITAGE REGAINED • 1949 • Coffey Frank • DOC • ASL
HERITIER, L' • 1973 • Labro Philippe • FRN, ITL • EREDE, L' (ITL) ○ INHERITOR, THE
HERITIER DES MONDESIR, L' • 1939 • Valentin Albert • FRN • C'EST UN MYSTERE
HERITIER DU BAL TABARIN, L' • 1933 • Kemm Jean • FRN
HERITIERES, LES (FRN) see **OROKSEG** • 1980
HERITIERS, LES • 1959 • Laviron Jean • FRN
HERITIERS DE LA VIOLENCE, LES • 1977 • Vamos Thomas • CND
HERITIERS DE L'ONCLE JAMES, LES • 1924 • Machin Alfred • FRN

HERKULES MAIER • 1927 • Esway Alexander • FRG

HERKULESFURDOI EMLEK • 1977 • Sandor Pal • HNG • STRANGE MASQUERADE (USA) ○ IMPROPERLY DRESSED ○ STRANGE ROLE, A

HERLOCK SHOLMES IN BE-A-LIVE CROOK • 1930 • *A.s.f.i.* • SHT • UKN • ANNA WENT WRONG

HERMAN • 1989 • Gustavson Erik F. • NRW

HERMAN AND KATNIP • 1953-59 • *Paramount* • ASS • USA

HERMAN SLOBBE see **BLIND KIND 2** • 1966

HERMAN TEIRLINCK • 1953 • Storck Henri • DOC • BLG

HERMAN THE CATOONIST • 1953 • Sparber I. • ANS • USA

HERMANA ALEGRIA, LA • 1954 • Lucia Luis • SPN

HERMANA BLANCA, LA • 1960 • Davison Tito • MXC

HERMANA IMPURA, LA • 1947 • Morayta Miguel • MXC

HERMANA MENOR • 1952 • Viladomat Domingo • SPN

HERMANA SAN SULPICIO, LA • 1927 • Rey Florian • SPN

HERMANA SAN SULPICIO, LA • 1934 • Rey Florian • SPN

HERMANA SAN SULPICIO, LA • 1952 • Lucia Luis • SPN

HERMANAS KARAMBAZO, LAS • 1959 • Alazraki Benito • MXC

HERMANAS X, LAS • 1962 • Curiel Federico • MXC

HERMANN DER CHERUSKER: DIE SCHACHT IM TEUTOBURGER WALD see **MASSACRO DELLA FORESTA NERA, IL** • 1966

HERMANN UND DOROTHEA VON HEUTE see **LIEBESLEUTE** • 1935

HERMANNCHEN, DAS • 1936 • Paul Heinz • FRG • NEE, NEE, WAS ES NICH' ALLES GIBT

HERMANNS ERZAHLUNGEN • 1926 • Stanke Kurt • FRG

HERMANNSSCHLACHT, DIE • 1924 • Konig Leo? • FRG

HERMANO JUAN, EL • 1941 • Momplet Antonio • ARG

HERMANO PEDRO, EL • 1964 • Contreras Torres Miguel • MXC, GTM

HERMANOS BARRIGAN, LOS • 1963 • Crevenna Alfredo B. • MXC

HERMANOS CARTAGENA, LOS • 1985 • Agazzi Paolo • BLV • BROTHERS CARTAGENA, THE

HERMANOS CENTELLA, LOS • 1966 • Fernandez Fernando • MXC

HERMANOS CORSOS, LOS • 1955 • Fleider Leo • ARG • CORSICAN BROTHERS, THE

HERMANOS DE SANGRE • 1972 • *Carmel* • MXC

HERMANOS DEL HIERRO, LOS • 1961 • Rodriguez Ismael • MXC • MY SON, THE HERO (USA)

HERMANOS DEL VIENTO, LOS • 1975 • Bojorquez Alberto • MXC

HERMANOS DIABLO, LOS • 1959 • Mendez Fernando, Urueta Chano • MXC

HERMANOS, LOS • Semper Gabriela • CLM • BROTHERS, THE

HERMANOS MUERTE, LOS • 1964 • Baledon Rafael • MXC

HERMAN'S HERD • 1949 • Cowan Will • SHT • USA

HERMELINMANTEL, DER • 1915 • Schmidthassler Walter • FRG

HERMENEGILDE • 1976 • Lavoie Richard • DOC • CND • HERMENEGILDE, VISION D'UN PIONNIER DU CINEMA QUEBECOIS 1908-73

HERMENEGILDE, VISION D'UN PIONNIER DU CINEMA QUEBECOIS 1908-73 see **HERMENEGILDE** • 1976

HERMES BIRD • 1979 • Broughton James • USA

HERMIN UND DIE SIEBEN AUFRECTEN • 1935 • Wisbar Frank • FRG

HERMIT, THE • 1912 • *Mason Billy* • USA

HERMIT, THE • 1914 • Ricketts Thomas • USA

HERMIT, THE see **SYNDIG KAERLIGHED** • 1915

HERMIT CRAB, THE see **EREMITKRAFTEN** • 1965

HERMIT DOCTOR OF GAYA, THE see **STRONGER THAN DEATH** • 1920

HERMIT IN STORMY WEATHER see **ENSLINGEN I BLASVADER** • 1959

HERMIT JOHANNES see **ENSLINGEN JOHANNES** • 1957

HERMIT OF BIRD ISLAND, THE • 1915 • *Metcalfe Earl* • USA

HERMIT OF THE ROCKIES • 1910 • *Champion* • USA

HERMITE, L' • Renier Gerard • FRN

HERMIT'S GOLD, THE • 1911 • Dwan Allan • USA

HERMIT'S HOARD, THE • 1917 • *American* • USA

HERMIT'S RUSE, THE • 1913 • *Williams George* • USA

HERMIT'S SECRET, THE • 1914 • *Hall Lindsley J.* • USA

HERMIT'S WIFE see **ENSLIGENS HUSTRU** • 1916

HERMOSO IDEAL • 1947 • Galindo Alejandro • MXC

HERNAMSARIN • 1967 • Oddsson Reynir • DOC • ICL • OCCUPATION YEARS, THE ○ YEARS OF OCCUPATION

HERNCRAKE WITCH, THE • 1912 • Melford Mark • UKN

HERNING • 1965 • Thorsen Jens Jorgen, Maruni Novi • DNM

HERO, THE • 1911 • *Imp* • USA

HERO, THE • 1914 • Thompson Frederick A. • USA

HERO, THE • 1917 • Gillstrom Arvid E. • SHT • USA

HERO, THE • 1923 • Gasnier Louis J. • USA • HIS BROTHER'S WIFE

HERO, THE • 1960 • Brahm John • MTV • USA

HERO, THE • 1983 • Giesbrecht Johnny • CND

HERO, THE see **SATURDAY'S HERO** • 1951

HERO, THE see **NAYAK** • 1966

HERO, THE see **BLOOMFIELD** • 1969

HERO, THE see **HJALTEN** • 1989

HERO AIN'T NOTHIN' BUT A SANDWICH, A • 1977 • Nelson Ralph • USA

HERO -ALMOST, A • 1911 • *Lubin* • USA

HERO AMONG MEN, A • 1913 • *Lubin* • USA

HERO AND LEANDER • 1910 • *Ambrosio* • ITL

HERO AND THE TERROR • 1982 • Tannen William • USA

HERO AT LARGE • 1980 • Davidson Martin • USA

HERO BUNKER • 1971 • Andrews George • GRC

HERO BY PROXY, A • 1916 • Beery Wallace • SHT • USA

HERO-CAPTAIN KORKORAN see **HRDINNY KAPITAN KORKORAN** • 1934

HERO COMMANDOS • Rosenberg Andy • USA

HERO COWARD, THE • 1913 • Wharton Theodore • USA

HERO ENGINEER, THE • 1910 • *Kalem* • USA

HERO FOR A DAY • 1939 • Young Harold • USA

HERO FOR A DAY • 1953 • Davis Mannie • ANS • USA

HERO FOR A MINUTE, A • 1917 • Kerr Robert • SHT • USA

HERO FOR A NIGHT see **HRDJA JEDNO NOCI** • 1935

HERO FOR A NIGHT, A • 1927 • Craft William James • USA • FLYING NUT, THE

HERO HIRARAL • 1988 • Mehta Ketan • IND

HERO IN SPITE OF HIMSELF, A • 1910 • Stow Percy • UKN

HERO IN SPITE OF HIMSELF, A see **HJALTE MOT SIN VILJA** • 1915

HERO IN THE FAMILY • 1986 • Damski Mel • TVM • USA

HERO 'N EVERYTHING, A • 1920 • Curtis Allen • SHT • USA

HERO OF BABYLON, THE see **EROE DI BABILONIA, L'** • 1963

HERO OF BUNCO HILL, THE • 1917 • Peacocke Leslie T. • SHT • USA

HERO OF E.Z. RANCH, THE • 1916 • Fahrney Milton • USA

HERO OF HEROES • 1971 • Wu Ming-Hsiung • HKG

HERO OF LIAO YANG • 1904 • *Bitzer Billy (Ph)s* • USA

HERO OF LITTLE ITALY, THE • 1913 • *Sweet Blanche* • USA

HERO OF MY DREAMS, THE see **HELD MEINER TRAUME, DER** • 1960

HERO OF OUR TIME, A see **ZAPISKI PECHORINA** • 1967

HERO OF OUR TIMES, A • 1969 • Ferrater-Mora J. • USA

HERO OF OUR TOWN, THE see **GHAHRAMAN-E-SHAHRE MA** • 1968

HERO OF PINE RIDGE, THE (UKN) see **YODELIN' KID FROM PINE RIDGE** • 1937

HERO OF ROME (USA) see **COLOSSO DI ROMA, IL** • 1964

HERO OF SUBMARINE D-2, THE • 1916 • Scardon Paul • USA

HERO OF THE BIG SNOWS, A • 1926 • Raymaker Herman C. • USA

HERO OF THE COASTGUARD • 1979 • Sirchanda Siri • THL

HERO OF THE DARDANELLES, A • 1915 • Rolfe Alfred • ASL • STORMING OF GALLIPOLI, THE

HERO OF THE HOUR, THE • 1913 • *De Forrest Charles* • USA

HERO OF THE HOUR, THE • 1917 • Wells Raymond • USA

HERO OF THE NORTH, THE • 1914 • *Sawyer* • USA

HERO OF THE TOWN see **ISSHIN TASUKE -TENKA NO ICHIDAIJI** • 1958

HERO OF THE TRENCHES, A • 1915 • Thornton F. Martin? • UKN

HERO OF THE YEAR see **BOHATER ROKU** • 1986

HERO ON HORSEBACK, A • 1927 • Andrews Del • USA

HERO TRACK WALKER, THE • 1911 • *Kalem* • USA

HERO WITH A KNIFE see **KAMALI ZEYBEK** • 1964

HEROD THE GREAT (USA) see **ERODE IL GRANDE** • 1958

HERODIADE • 1910 • Jasset Victorin • USA

HEROE A LA FUERZA • 1963 • Delgado Miguel M. • MXC • PARPADO CAIDO, EL

HEROE DE NACOZARI, EL • 1933 • Calles Guillermo • MXC

HEROE DESCONOCIDO, EL • 1981 • Pastor Julian • MXC

HEROES • 1977 • Kagan Jeremy Paul • USA

HEROES, THE • 1916 • *Plump & Runt* • USA

HEROES, THE see **INVINCIBLE SIX, THE** • 1970

HEROES AND HUSBANDS • 1922 • Withey Chet • USA

HEROES AND SINNERS (USA) see **HEROS SONT FATIGUES, LES** • 1955

HEROES ARE BORN TWICE • 1978 • Dehni Salah • SYR

HEROES ARE MADE see **KAK ZAKALYALAS STAL** • 1942

HEROES ARE SILENT, THE see **HRDINOVE MLCI** • 1946

HEROES ARE TIRED, THE see **HEROS SONT FATIGUES, LES** • 1955

HEROES AT LEISURE • 1939 • Trego Charles T. • SHT • USA

HEROES BY CHANCE see **YAREBA YARERUZE ZENIN SHUGO** • 1968

HEROES DE MAR • 1978 • Duran Rojas Fernando • MXC • TEMPESTAD

HEROES DEL 95 • 1946 • Alfonso Raul • SPN

HEROES DEL AIRE • 1957 • Torrado Ramon • SPN

HEROES DEL BARIO, LOS • 1936 • Vidal Armando

HEROES DIE YOUNG • 1960 • Shepard Gerald S. • USA

HEROES FOR SALE • 1933 • Wellman William A. • USA

HEROES IN A ROCKING CHAIR see **HELDEN IN EEN SCHOMMELSTOEL** • 1963

HEROES IN BLUE • 1927 • Worne Duke • USA

HEROES IN BLUE • 1939 • Watson William • USA

HEROES IN HELL see **EROI ALL'INFERNO** • 1974

HEROES IN YELLOW AND BLUE see **HJALTAR I GULT OCH BLATT** • 1940

HEROES OF FREEDOM • 1980 • Sami Asrul • INN

HEROES OF SHIPKA see **GEROITE NA SHIPKA** • 1955

HEROES OF TELEMARK, THE • 1965 • Mann Anthony • UKN • UNKNOWN BATTLE, THE

HEROES OF THE ALAMO • 1937 • Fraser Harry L. • USA

HEROES OF THE ARCTIC see **GEROI ARTIKI** • 1934

HEROES OF THE BLUE AND THE GRAY • 1912 • *Francis Evelyn* • USA

HEROES OF THE CROSS • 1909 • Perry Joseph H. • ASL

HEROES OF THE FLAMES • 1931 • Hill Robert F. • SRL • USA

HEROES OF THE HILLS • 1938 • Sherman George • USA

HEROES OF THE MARNE (USA) see **HEROS DE LA MARNE, LE** • 1938

HEROES OF THE MINE • 1913 • Pearson George • UKN • GREAT MINE DISASTER, THE (USA)

HEROES OF THE MINE • 1932 • Newman Widgey R. • UKN

HEROES OF THE MUTINY • 1911 • Ranous William V. • USA

HEROES OF THE NIGHT • 1927 • O'Connor Frank • USA

HEROES OF THE PLAINS • 1917 • *Big U* • SHT • USA

HEROES OF THE RANGE • 1936 • Bennet Spencer Gordon • USA

HEROES OF THE REGIMENT see **BONNIE SCOTLAND** • 1935

HEROES OF THE SADDLE • 1940 • Witney William • USA

HEROES OF THE SEA • 1918 • *Darling Kitty* • SHT • UKN

HEROES OF THE SEA • 1941 • Braun Vladimir • USS

HEROES OF THE STREET • 1922 • Beaudine William • USA

HEROES OF THE WEST • 1932 • Taylor Ray • SRL • USA

HEROES OF THE WEST COAST see **VASTKUSTENS HJALTAR** • 1940

HEROES, ONE AND ALL • 1913 • *Myers Harry* • USA

HEROES SIN FAMA • 1940 • Soffici Mario • ARG

HEROES THREE • 1911 • *Edison* • USA

HEROES THREE see **WARRIORS THREE**

HEROES TWO see **TEMPLE OF THE DRAGON** • 1974

HEROIC AMBROSE • 1918 • *Swain Mack* • SHT • USA

HEROIC COWARD, THE • 1910 • *Yankee* • USA

HEROIC DAUGHTER OF ISLAM, THE see **ISLAMIYETIN KAHRAMAN KIZI** • 1968

HEROIC DAYS, THE • 1960 • Mason Bill • UKN

HEROIC EVENTS, THE see **CHIANG-HU HAN-TZU** • 1976

HEROIC HAROLD • 1913 • Smalley Phillips • USA

HEROIC LOVER, THE • 1929 • Smith Noel • USA • WHIRLWIND LOVER, THE (UKN)

HEROIC MISSION -THE FIREMEN 2 see **MISSIONE EROICA -I POMPIERI 2** • 1987

HEROIC PURGATORY see **RENGOKU EROICA** • 1970

HEROIC RESCUE, A • 1913 • Seay Charles M. • USA

HEROIC TIMES see **DALIAS IDOK** • 1983

HEROICO BONIFACIO, EL • 1951 • Cahen Enrique • ARG

HEROIN • 1968 • Thiel Heinz, Brandt Horst E. • GDR

HEROIN GANG, THE • 1968 • Hutton Brian G. • USA • SOL MADRID

HEROINA • 1965 • Melendez Jeronimo Melendez • USA

HEROINA • 1972 • de la Torre Raul • ARG • HEROINE

HEROINE see **HEROINA** • 1972

HEROINE see **CAPTIVE** • 1985

HEROINE DE L'ENFANCE, L' • 1975 • Lagrange Yvan • FRN

HEROINE DU TRIANGLE D'OR, L' • 1975 • Lamour Marianne • DOC • FRN • GOOD LUCK TO YOU

HEROINE OF '76, A • 1911 • Porter Edwin S. • USA

HEROINE OF 101 RANCH, THE • 1910 • *Columbia* • USA

HEROINE OF MAFEKING, THE • 1909 • *Selig* • USA

HEROINE OF MONS, THE • 1914 • Noy Wilfred • UKN

HEROINE OF PAWNEE JUNCTION, THE • 1910 • *Yankee* • USA

HEROINE OF PIONEER DAYS, A • 1912 • *Comet* • USA

HEROINE OF SAN JUAN, THE • 1916 • Ford Francis • SHT • USA

HEROINE OF THE PLAINS, THE • 1912 • *Bison* • USA

HEROINE OF THE REVOLUTION, A • 1911 • *Solax* • USA

HEROINES DU MAL, LES • 1978 • Borowczyk Walerian • FRN • THREE IMMORAL WOMEN (UKN) ○ HEROINES OF EVIL (USA)

HEROINES OF EVIL (USA) see **HEROINES DU MAL, LES** • 1978

HEROINE'S STORY see **NAIKA SAMBAD** • 1967

HEROIQUE MONSIEUR BONIFACE, L' • 1949 • Labro Maurice • FRN • SYMPATHETIQUE MONSIEUR BONIFACE, LE

HEROIS DO MAR • 1949 • Garcia Fernando • PRT

HEROISM see **EROICA** • 1958

HEROISME DE PADDY, L' • 1916 • Gance Abel • FRN

HEROISMUS EINER FRANZOSIN • 1913 • Biebrach Rudolf • FRG

HERON -A REPTILE BIRD?, THE • 1968 • Bostan Ion • DOC • RMN

HERON AND THE CRANE, THE see **CRANE AND HERON**

HERO'S BROTHER, THE see **BRAT GEROYA** • 1940

HEROS DE CHIPKA, LES see **GEROITE NA SHIPKA** • 1955

HEROS DE LA MARNE, LE • 1938 • Hugon Andre • FRN • JEAN LEFRANCOIS, HEROS DE LA MARNE ○ HEROES OF THE MARNE (USA)

HEROS DE L'AIR, LES • 1962 • Laurent, Mitry Jean • SHT • FRN

HEROS DE L'YSER, LES • 1915 • Perret Leonce • FRN

HERO'S FALL, A • 1917 • Avery Charles • USA

HERO'S ISLAND • 1962 • Stevens Leslie • USA • LAND WE LOVE, THE

HEROS MODESTES, LES • 1935 • Mesnier Paul • FRN

HEROS N'ONT PAS FROID AUX ORIELLES, LES • 1978 • Nemes Charles • FRN

HERO'S REWARD • 1962 • Kneitel Seymour • ANS • USA

HERO'S REWARD, A • 1913 • *Brennan John E.* • USA

HEROS SANS RETOUR (FRN) see **MARSCHIER UND KREPIER** • 1962

HEROS SONT FATIGUES, LES • 1955 • Ciampi Yves • FRN, FRG • HELDEN SIND MUDE, DIE (FRG) ○ HEROES AND SINNERS (USA) ○ HEROES ARE TIRED, THE

HERO'S TEARS, A • Li Tan Yeong • HKG

HERO'S WAY see **KURSUN ATA ATA BITER** • 1985

HERO'S WORLD, THE see **DONYAYE GHAHREMANAN** • 1967

HEROSTRATUS • 1967 • Levy Don • UKN

HERR ARNES PENGAR • 1919 • Stiller Mauritz • SWD • THREE WHO WERE DOOMED (USA) ○ SNOWS OF DESTINY (UKN) ○ SIR ARNE'S TREASURE ○ TREASURE OF ARNE, THE

HERR ARNES PENNIGAR • 1954 • Molander Gustaf • SWD • SIR ARNE'S TREASURE

HERR ASSESSOR, DER • 1917 • Heidemann Paul • FRG

HERR AUF BESTELLUNG, DER • 1930 • von Bolvary Geza • FRG

HERR AUF SCHLOSS BRASSAC (FRG) see **TONNERRE DE DIEU, LE** • 1965

HERR AUS DEM ZUCHTHAUS, DER • 1921 • Philippi Siegfried • FRG

"HERR BARON", DER • 1915 • Basch Felix • FRG

HERR BUROVORSTEHER, DER • 1931 • Behrendt Hans • FRG

HERR COLLINS AVENTYR • 1943 • Henrikson Anders • SWD • MR. COLLINS' ADVENTURES

HERR DER BESTIEN, DER • 1921 • Wendt Ernst • FRG

HERR DER LIEBE, DER • 1919 • Lang Fritz • FRG • MASTER OF LOVE, THE

HERR DER NACHT, DER • 1926 • Wolff Carl Heinz • FRG

HERR DER UNTERWELT, DER • 1922 • Stein Josef • FRG

HERR DER WELT • 1951 • Liebeneiner Wolfgang • FRG

HERR DER WELT 1, DER • 1917 • Reinert Robert • FRG

HERR DER WELT 2, DER • 1918 • Reinert Robert • FRG • LEBENDE TOTE, DER

HERR DER WELT, DER • 1934 • Piel Harry • FRG • MASTER OF THE WORLD ○ RULER OF THE WORLD

HERR DES LEBENS, DER • 1920 • Fleck Jacob, Fleck Luise • AUS

HERR DES TODES, DER • 1914 • Obal Max • FRG • MASTER OF DEATH, THE

HERR DES TODES, DER • 1926 • Steinhoff Hans • FRG

HERR DOKTOR • 1917 • Feuillade Louis • FRN

HERR FINANZDIREKTOR, DER • 1931 • Friedmann-Friedrich Fritz • FRG

HERR FLEISCHER'S ALBUM see **ALBUM FLEISCHERA** • 1963

HERR GENERALDIREKTOR, DER • 1925 • Wendhausen Fritz • FRG • DEVOTION

HERR HUSASSISTENEN • 1939 • Arvedson Ragnar • SWD • MR. HOUSEKEEPER

HERR IM HAUS, DER • 1940 • Helbig Heinz • FRG • GENTLEMAN IN THE HOUSE, THE

HERR IMPRESARIO, DER • 1921 • Peukert Leo • FRG

HERR KAMMERSANGER, DER see **LOCKENDE ZIEL, DAS** • 1930
HERR KOBIN GEHT AUF ABENTEUER • 1934 • Deppe Hans • FRG
HERR LANDRAT, DER • 1922 • Bolten-Baeckers Heinrich • FRG
HERR MEETS HARE • 1945 • Freleng Friz • ANS • USA
HERR MEISTER UND FRAU MEISTERIN • 1928 • Mann Alfred Theodor • FRG
HERR OHNE WOHNUNG, DER • 1925 • Bolten-Baeckers Heinrich • FRG
HERR OHNE WOHNUNG, DER • 1934 • Emo E. W. • AUS
HERR PAPA, DER • 1922 • Bolten-Baeckers Heinrich • FRG
HERR PUNTILA AND HIS SERVANT MATTI see **HERR PUNTILA UND SEIN KNECHT MATTI** • 1955
HERR PUNTILA UND SEIN KNECHT MATTI • 1955 • Cavalcanti Alberto • AUS • MR. PUNTILA AND HIS VALET MATTI ○ PUNTILA ○ HERR PUNTILA AND HIS SERVANT MATTI
HERR SANDERS LEBT GEFAHRLICH • 1943 • Stemmle R. A. • FRG
HERR SENATOR, DER • 1934 • Sauer Fred • FRG • FLIEGENDE AHNFRAU, DIE
HERR STORMS FORSTE MONOCLE see **MIN FORSTE MONOCLE** • 1911
HERR TARTUFF see **TARTUFF** • 1925
HERR UBER LEBEN UND TOD • 1919 • Pick Lupu • FRG
HERR UBER LEBEN UND TOD • 1955 • Vicas Victor • FRG • MASTER OVER LIFE AND DEATH
HERR UND DIENER • 1917 • Gartner Adolf • FRG
HERR UND HUND • 1963 • Van Den Berg • FRG
HERR VOM ANDERN STERN, DER • 1948 • Hilpert Heinz • FRG • MAN FROM ANOTHER STAR, THE
HERR VOM FINANZAMT, DER • 1928 • Philippi Siegfried • FRG
HERRA HUU –JESTAPA JEPULIS, PENIKAT SIPULIKS • 1974 • Talaskivi Jaakko • FNL • HOLY JUMPING JIMMINY! SAID MR. WHO
HERRA LAHTINEN LAHTEE LIPETTIIN • 1939 • Tapiovaara Nyrki • FNL • MR. LAHTINEN TAKES FRENCH LEAVE
HERRA PUNTILA JA HANEN RENKINSA MATTI • 1979 • Langbacka Ralf • FNL, SWD • MR. PUNTILA AND HIS SERVANT MATTI
HERRADURA, LA • 1957 • Artero Antonio • SHT • SPN
HERRE MED PORTFOLJ • 1943 • Arvedson Ragnar • SWD • GENTLEMAN WITH A BRIEF–CASE
HERREN, DIE • 1965 • Seitz Franz*, Thiele Rolf, Weidenmann Alfred • FRG
HERREN DER MEERE • 1922 • Korda Alexander • AUS • MASTERS OF THE SEA
HERREN MIT DER WEISSEN WESTE, DIE • 1970 • Staudte Wolfgang • FRG • THOSE GENTLEMEN WHO HAVE A CLEAN SHEET
HERREN OZ HANS TJENERE • 1959 • Skouen Arne • NRW • MASTER AND HIS SERVANTS, THE ○ GOD AND HIS SERVANTS, A
HERREN VOM MAXIM • 1932 • Boese Carl • FRG
HERREN VOM MAXIM, DIE • 1920 • Boese Carl • FRG
HERRENPARTIE • 1964 • Staudte Wolfgang • GDR, YGS • MEN'S OUTING
HERRENREITERIN, DIE (FRG) see **PADRONA E SERVITA, LA** • 1976
HERRENVOLK see **NADLIDE** • 1946
HERRERO, EL • 1943 • Pereda Ramon • MXC
HERRGOTT AM WEGE, DER • 1918 • Seitz Franz? • FRG
HERRGOTTSGRENADIERE, DIE see **GOLDENE GLETSCHER, DER** • 1932
HERRGOTTSSCHNITZER VON OBERAMMERGAU, DER • 1930 • Seitz Franz • FRG
HERRIN DER WELT 1, DIE • 1919 • May Joe • FRG • FREUNDIN DES GELBEN MANNES, DIE
HERRIN DER WELT 2, DIE • 1919 • May Joe • FRG • GESCHICHTE DER MAUD GREGAARDS, DIE
HERRIN DER WELT 3, DIE • 1919 • May Joe • FRG • RABBI VON KUANG–FU, DER
HERRIN DER WELT 4, DIE • 1919 • Krafft Uwe Jens • FRG • KONIG MAKOMBE
HERRIN DER WELT 5, DIE • 1919 • Krafft Uwe Jens • FRG • OPHIR, DIE STADT DER VERGANGENHEIT
HERRIN DER WELT 6, DIE • 1919 • May Joe • FRG • FRAU MIT DEN MILLIARDEN, DIE
HERRIN DER WELT 7, DIE • 1919 • May Joe • FRG • WOHLTATERIN DER MENSCHHEIT, DIE
HERRIN DER WELT 8, DIE • 1919 • May Joe • FRG • RACHE DER MAUD FERGUSSON, DIE
HERRIN DER WELT, DIE • 1919 • May Joe, Krafft Uwe Jens • SER • FRG • MISTRESS OF THE WORLD
HERRIN DER WELT (FRG) see **MISTERO DEI TREI CONTINENTI, IL** • 1959
HERRIN IHRER TAT • 1919 • Bach Rudi • FRG
HERRIN UND IHR KNECHT, DIE • 1929 • Oswald Richard • FRG
HERRIN VOM SALZERHOF, DIE see **WETTERLEUCHTEN AM DACHSTEIN** • 1953
HERRIN VOM SOLDERHOF, DIE • 1955 • von Alten Jurgen • FRG
HERRIN VON ATLANTIS, DIE • 1932 • Pabst G. W. • FRG • MISTRESS OF ATLANTIS, THE ○ LOST ATLANTIS
HERRIN VON CAMPINA, DIE see **UNMOGLICHE FRAU, DIE** • 1936
HERRIN VON MONBIJOU, DIE • 1924 • Zelnik Friedrich • FRG
HERRING BELT, THE • 1964 • Kohanyi Julius • CND
HERRING HUNT • 1953 • Biggs Julian • CND
HERRING MURDER CASE, THE • 1931 • Fleischer Dave • ANS • USA
HERRING MURDER MYSTERY, THE • 1943 • Roman Don • ANS • USA
HERRING ON THE TRAIL, A • 1913 • Wilson Frank? • UKN
HERRINGBONE CLOUDS see **IWASHIGUMO** • 1958
HERRLICHE ZEITEN • 1950 • Neumann Gunther, Ode Erik, Aeckerle Fritz, Vietzke Hans • FRG • 50 JAHRE –HEITER BETRACHTET
HERRLICHE ZEITEN IM SPESSART • 1967 • Hoffmann Kurt • FRG • GLORIOUS TIMES IN THE SPESSART ○ SPESSART ROCKETS
HERRLICHES DASEIN, EIN • 1974 • Staudte Wolfgang • FRG
HERRN FILIP COLLINS ABENTEUER • 1925 • Guter Johannes • FRG
HERRN JOSEFS LETZTE LIEBE • 1959 • Kugelstadt Hermann • FRG
HERRSCHER, DER • 1937 • Harlan Veit • FRG • RULER, THE (USA)
HERRSCHER OHNE KRONE • 1957 • Braun Harald • FRG • KING IN SHADOW
HERS TO HOLD • 1943 • Ryan Frank • USA
HERSELF • 1918 • Nash Percy • UKN
HERSENSCHIMMEN see **MIND SHADOWS** • 1988
HERSEYE RAGMEN • 1987 • Oguz Orhan • TRK • DESPITE EVERYTHING
HERZ AM RHEIN, DAS • 1925 • Lisson Heinrich • FRG
HERZ AUS GLAS • 1976 • Herzog Werner • FRG • HEART OF GLASS (USA)
HERZ BLEIBT ALLEIN, EIN • 1955 • von Bolvary Geza • FRG • MEIN LEOPOLD
HERZ DAME see **GEHEIMNIS DER SECHS SPIELKARTEN 6, DAS** • 1921
HERZ DER KONIGIN, DAS see **HERZ EINER KONIGIN, DAS** • 1940
HERZ DER LILIAN THORLAND, DAS • 1924 • Neff Wolfgang • FRG
HERZ DES CASANOVA, DAS • 1919 • Lund Erik • FRG
HERZ DES MAHARADSCHA, DAS see **EMERALD OF THE EAST** • 1928
HERZ EINER KONIGIN, DAS • 1940 • Froelich Carl • FRG • HERZ DER KONIGIN, DAS
HERZ GEHT VOR ANKER • 1940 • Stockel Joe • FRG
HERZ IST TRUMP • 1934 • Boese Carl • FRG
HERZ KEHRT HEIM, EIN • 1956 • York Eugen • FRG
HERZ KONIG see **GEHEIMNIS DER SECHS SPIELKARTEN 5, DAS** • 1921
HERZ MODERN MOBLIERT • 1940 • Lingen Theo • FRG
HERZ MUSS SCHWEIGEN, DAS • 1944 • Ucicky Gustav • FRG • HEART MUST KEEP SILENCE, THE
HERZ OHNE GNADE • 1958 • Tourjansky Victor • FRG
HERZ OHNE HEIMAT • 1940 • Linnekogel Otto • FRG
HERZ SCHLAGT FUR ERIKA, EIN • 1956 • Reinl Harald • FRG
HERZ SPIELT FALSCH, EIN • 1953 • Jugert Rudolf • FRG
HERZ UND EINE SEELE, EIN see **...UND WER KUSST MICH?** • 1956
HERZ VOLL MUSIK, EIN • 1955 • Stemmle R. A. • FRG
HERZ VOM HOCHLAND, DAS • 1920 • Oberlander Hans • FRG
HERZ VON ST. PAULI, DAS • 1957 • York Eugen • FRG
HERZBLATT, ODER WIE SAG ICH'S MEINER TOCHTER • 1969 • Vohrer Alfred • FRG • HONEY BUN, OR HOW TO TELL MY DAUGHTER
HERZBLUT 1 see **IM SCHATTEN DES GLUCKS** • 1919
HERZBLUT 2 see **GEHEIMNIS DER ALTEN TRUHE, DAS** • 1919
HERZBUBE • 1972 • Skolimowski Jerzy • FRG, USA • KING, QUEEN, KNAVE (USA) ○ SEX, LOVE, MURDER
HERZEN IM STURM • 1922 • Paul Peter • AUS
HERZEN IM STURM • 1951 • von Alten Jurgen • FRG
HERZEN OHNE ZIEL • 1928 • Ucicky Gustav, Perojo Benito • FRG
HERZENSCHLIEB • 1938 • Boese Carl • FRG • HEART THIEF (USA)
HERZENSDIEB, DER see **WIE EIN DIEB IN DER NACHT** • 1945
HERZENSFREUD –HERZENSLIED • 1940 • Marischka Hubert • FRG
HERZENSPHOTOGRAPH, DER • 1928 • Reichmann Max • FRG
HERZKONIG • 1947 • Weiss Helmut • FRG • WALZER INS GLUCK, EIN
HERZL see **THUS SPAKE THEODOR HERZL** • 1967
HERZLICH WILLKOMMEN • 1990 • Bohm Hark • FRG • CROSSING BORDERS
HERZOG FERRANTES ENDE • 1922 • Wegener Paul • FRG
HERZOG HANSL • 1930 • Neufeld Max • FRG
HERZOG VON ALERIA, DER • 1923 • Schall Heinz • FRG
HERZOG VON REICHSTADT, DER • 1931 • Tourjansky Victor • FRG
HERZOGIN SATANELLA • 1919 • Curtiz Michael • AUS • SATAN'S MEMOIRS (USA)
HERZOGIN VON LANGEAIS, DIE see **LIEBE** • 1927
HERZTRUMPT • 1920 • Dupont E. A. • FRG
HE'S A COCKEYED WONDER • 1950 • Godfrey Peter • USA • FREDDIE THE GREAT
HE'S A DEVIL • 1916 • Christie Al • SHT • USA
HE'S A HERO see **YUNG–CH'UN TA–HSIUNG** • 1978
HE'S A LAWYER • 1913 • Dillon Eddie • USA
HE'S A LEGEND see **YUNG–CH'UN TA–HSIUNG** • 1978
HE'S A LEGEND, HE'S A HERO • 1977 • Chen Wah, Chang Chee • HKG • STORY OF THE DRAGON, THE
HE'S A LEGEND, HE'S A HERO see **YUNG–CH'UN TA–HSIUNG** • 1978
HE'S A PRINCE see **REGULAR FELLOW, A** • 1925
HE'S AT IT AGAIN • 1971 • Lubowski Rudolf • FRG
HE'S BEAR • 1915 • Hotaling Arthur D. • USA
HE'S FIRED, SHE'S HIRED • 1984 • Daniels Marc • TVM • USA
HE'S GOT 'EM • 1910 • *Warwick* • UKN
HE'S IN AGAIN • 1915 • Fahrney Milton • USA
HE'S IN AGAIN • 1917 • *Jaxon* • USA
HE'S IN AGAIN • 1919 • Parrott Charles • USA
HE'S MY GIRL • 1987 • Beaumont Gabrielle • USA • PULLING IT OFF
HE'S MY GUY • 1943 • Cline Eddie • USA
HE'S MY HUSBAND AND I'LL KILL HIM WHEN I LIKE see **MARITO E MIO E L'AMMAZZO QUANDO MI PARE, IL** • 1967
HE'S MY PAL • 1924 • Seiler Lewis • SHT • USA
HE'S MY PAL see **LONE COWBOY, THE** • 1933
HE'S NOT YOUR SON • 1984 • Taylor Don • TVM • USA
HESAP GUNU • 1967 • Okcugil Nejat • TRK • JUDGMENT DAY, THE
HESITANT MARKSMAN, THE • 1957 • Toman Ivo • CZC
HESITATING HOUSES • 1926 • *Sennett Mack (P)* • SHT • USA
HESITATING LOVE • 1932 • Horne James W. • SHT • USA
HESOKURI SHACHO • 1955 • Chiba Yasuki • JPN • PRESIDENT'S BOSS, THE
HESPER OF THE MOUNTAINS • 1916 • North Wilfred • USA
HEST PA SOMMERFERIE • 1959 • Henning-Jensen Astrid • DNM
HESTEN • 1943 • Henning-Jensen Bjarne • DNM • HORSES
HESTEN PAA KONGENS NYTORV • 1941 • Henning-Jensen Bjarne • DOC • DNM
HESTER STREET • 1974 • Silver Joan Micklin • USA
HET AR MIN LANGTAN • 1956 • Logardt Bengt • SWD • MY HOT DESIRE
HET SNO • 1968 • Axelman Torbjorn • SWD • HOT SNOW
HETA FROM NISKAVUORI see **NISKAVUOREN HETA** • 1952
HETA OF NISKAVUORI FARM see **NISKAVUOREN HETA** • 1952
HETERODYNE • 1967 • Frampton Hollis • SHT • USA
HETEROSEXUAL, THE see **BICHES, LES** • 1968
HETEROSEXUAL (UKN) see **JULIETTE DE SADE** • 1969
HETS • 1944 • Sjoberg Alf • SWD • TORMENT (USA) ○ FRENZY
HETSZAZEVES SZERELEM • 1921 • *Lukas Paul* • HNG
HEUBODENGEFLUSTER • 1967 • Olsen Rolf • FRG • WHISPERING IN THE HAYLOFT
HEULENDE WOLF, DER • 1919 • *Auen Carl* • FRG
HEURE DE LA LIBERATION A SONNE, L' see **SAAT EL TAHRIR DAKKAT BARRA YA ISTI'MAR** • 1974
HEURE DE LA VERITE, L' • 1964 • Calef Henri • FRN, ISR • HOUR OF TRUTH (USA)
HEURE DU DESTIN, L' see **VERTIGES** • 1946
HEURE DU REVE, L' • 1914 • Perret Leonce • FRN
HEURE EXQUISE see **NUIT DE DECEMBRE** • 1939
HEURE EXQUISE, L' • 1980 • Allio Rene • FRN
HEURE PRES DE TOI, UNE • 1932 • Lubitsch Ernst • FRN
HEURE TRAGIQUE, L' • 1914 • Pouctal Henri • FRN
HEURES, LES • 1909 • Feuillade Louis • FRN
HEURES BRULANTES DE PLAISIR, LES • 1974 • Bastia Jean • FRN
HEURES CHAUDES • 1959 • Felix Louis • FRN • HOT HOURS (USA)
HEUREUSE AVENTURE, L' • 1935 • Georgesco Jean • FRN • DEPARTS
HEUREUSE INTERVENTION • 1919 • Florey Robert • SWT
HEUREUX ANNIVERSAIRE • 1962 • Etaix Pierre, Carriere Jean-Claude • SHT • FRN • ANNIVERSARY, THE (UKN) ○ HAPPY ANNIVERSARY
HEUREUX QUI COMME ULYSSE • 1970 • Colpi Henri • FRN
HEUT' KOMMT'S DRAUF AN • 1933 • Gerron Kurt • FRG
HEUT' WACHT DIE WELT SONNTAG FUR MICH see **KAISERWALZER** • 1932
HEUT' SPIELT DER STRAUSS • 1928 • Wiene Conrad • FRG
HEUT TANZT MARRIETT • 1928 • Zelnik Friedrich • FRG • SWEETHEART
HEUT WAR ICH BEI DER FRIEDA • 1928 • Philippi Siegfried • FRG
...HEUTE ABEND BEI MIR • 1934 • Boese Carl • FRG
HEUTE BLAU UND MORGEN BLAU • 1957 • Philipp Harald • FRG • VERRUCKTE FAMILIE, EINE
HEUTE HEIRATET MEIN MANN • 1956 • Hoffmann Kurt • FRG
HEUTE IST DER SCHONSTE TAG IN MEINEM LEBEN • 1936 • Oswald Richard • AUS
HEUTE KUNDIGT MIR MEIN MANN • 1962 • Goldbaum Peter, Nussgruber Rudolf • FRG
HEUTE NACHT –EVENTUELL • 1930 • Emo E. W. • FRG
HEUTE NACHT ODER NIE • 1972 • Schmid Daniel • SWT • TONIGHT OR NEVER
HEUTE NACHT PASSIERT'S • 1953 • Antel Franz • FRG
HEUTE UBER 40 SIND, DIE • 1960 • Jung-Alsen Kurt • FRG
HEVISBERY GOCHA • 1964 • Sanishvili Nikolai • USS
HEVSUR BALLAD, THE see **KHEVSURSKAYA BALLADA** • 1965
HEVSURSKAIA BALLADA see **KHEVSURSKAYA BALLADA** • 1965
HEX • 1973 • Garen Leo • USA • GRASSLANDS
HEX WITH SEX, THE see **TO HEX WITH SEX** • 1969
HEXAGONAL'S ROCKERS • 1978 • Namiand Gilbert • FRN • NEW WAVE FRENCH CONNECTION
HEXE, DIE • 1921 • Eckstein Franz • FRG • WITCH, THE
HEXE, DIE • 1954 • Ucicky Gustav • FRG • WITCH, THE
HEXE VON LOLARUH, DIE • 1921 • Wildenhain Felix • FRG
HEXE VON NORDEROOG, DIE • 1919 • Moest Hubert • FRG
HEXEN • 1949 • Schott-Schobinger Hans • AUS
HEXEN • 1954 • Spiess Helmut • GDR
HEXEN BIS AUFS BLUT GEQUALT see **BRENN, HEXE, BRENN** • 1969
HEXEN: GESCHANDET UND ZU TODE GEQUALT • 1972 • Hoven Adrian • FRG • WITCHES: VIOLATED AND TORTURED TO DEATH (USA) ○ MARK OF THE DEVIL, PART II
HEXEN VON SALEM, DIE (GDR) see **SORCIERES DE SALEM, LES** • 1957
HEXENGOLD • 1920 • Eriksen Erich • FRG
HEXENLIED, DAS • 1919 • Burg Eugen • FRG • WITCH'S SONG, THE
HEXENTOTER VON BLACKMOOR, DER (FRG) see **PROCESO DE LAS BRUJAS, EL** • 1970
HEXER, DER • 1932 • Lamac Carl • FRG, AUS
HEXER, DER • 1964 • Vohrer Alfred • FRG • MYSTERIOUS MAGICIAN, THE (USA) ○ MAGICIAN, THE ○ WIZARD, THE
HEXLEIN VON GROSS–TORNAU, DAS • 1918 • von Woringen Paul • FRG
HEY BABE! see **BABE!** • 1980
HEY BABU RIBA • 1986 • Acin Jovan • YGS
HEY BOY! HEY GIRL! • 1959 • Rich David Lowell • USA
HEY BOY! HEY GIRL • 1967 • Villaflor Romy • PHL
HEY, BUDDY! see **AIBO** • 1966
HEY DIDDLE DIDDLE • 1930 • Marshall George • SHT • USA
HEY DIDDLE DIDDLE • 1935 • *Terry Paul/ Moser Frank (P)* • ANS • USA
HEY DOCTOR • 1918 • Blystone John G. • SHT • USA
HEY GOOD LOOKIN' • 1983 • Bakshi Ralph • ANM • USA
HEY! HEY! COWBOY • 1927 • Reynolds Lynn • USA
HEY, HEY FEVER • 1935 • Harman Hugh • ANS • USA
HEY! HEY! U.S.A.! • 1938 • Varnel Marcel • UKN
HEY, I'M ALIVE! • 1975 • Schiller Lawrence • TVM • USA
HEY JO • 1975 • Suissa Daniele J. • MTV • CND
HEY, JOE • 1989 • Asgari-Nasab Manoochehr • IRN
HEY, LET'S TWIST! • 1961 • Garrison Greg • USA
HEY, MAESTRO! • 1987 • Managadze Noda • USS
HEY MARCEL • 1983 • Tammer Peter • DOC • ASL
HEY NANNY NANNY • 1934 • Holmes Ben • USA
HEY, PINEAPPLE! see **PINEAPPLE BUTAI** • 1960

HEY, ROOKIE • 1944 • Barton Charles T. • USA
HEY, RUBE! • 1928 • Seitz George B. • USA • HIGH STAKES (UKN)
HEY RUBE! see **WILD WEST SHOW, THE** • 1928
HEY SAILOR see **HERE COMES THE NAVY** • 1934
HEY, STINE! see **HEJ, STINE!** • 1971
HEY THERE! • 1918 • Roach Hal • SHT • USA
HEY THERE, IT'S YOGI BEAR • 1964 • Hanna William, Barbera Joseph • ANM • USA
HEY! WHAT'S OUR LIFE LIKE?! • 1975 • Gorkovenko Yu. • USS
HEYA • 1967 • Kuri Yoji • ANS • JPN • ROOM, THE
HI, BEAUTIFUL! • 1944 • Goodwins Leslie • USA • PASS TO ROMANCE (UKN) ○ BE IT EVER SO HUMBLE
HI, BUDDY! • 1943 • Young Harold • USA
HI, CLEAR WATER see **HEJ, BYSTRA WODA** • 1959
HI-DE-HO • 1937 • Mack Roy • SHT • USA
HI DI HO • 1947 • Binney Josh • USA
HI DIDDLE DIDDLE • 1927 • Edwards J. Steven • UKN
HI DIDDLE DIDDLE • 1943 • Stone Andrew L. • USA • DIAMONDS AND CRIME ○ TRY AND FIND IT
HI FEATHERTOP AT THE FAIR • 1911 • *Essanay* • USA
HI-FI • 1987 • Blazevski Vladimir • YGS
HI-FI A GOGO • 1958 • Rocamora Pierre-A. • FRN
HI-FI JINX • 1962 • Kneitel Seymour • ANS • USA
HI GANG! • 1941 • Varnel Marcel • UKN
HI, GAUCHO! • 1935 • Atkins Thomas • USA
HI, GOOD LOOKIN' • 1944 • Lilley Edward • USA • HAS ANYBODY HERE SEEN KELLY?
HI HI LONDON • 1969 • JPN
HI-JACK • 1957 • Williamson Cecil H. • UKN • ACTION STATIONS
HI-JACK HIGHWAY (USA) see **GAS-OIL** • 1955
HI-JACKED • 1950 • Newfield Sam • USA
HI-JACKERS, THE • 1963 • O'Connolly Jim • UKN
HI-JACKING RUSTLERS • 1926 • Cohn Bennett • USA • FLAMING WEST, THE (USA)
HI, JUNIOR! see **HAHO, OCSI!** • 1971
HI MO TSUKI MO • 1969 • Nakamura Noboru • JPN • THROUGH DAYS AND MONTHS
HI, MOM! • 1970 • De Palma Brian • USA
HI NEIGHBOR! • 1934 • Meins Gus • SHT • USA
HI, NEIGHBOR • 1942 • Lamont Charles • USA
HI NELLIE! • 1934 • LeRoy Mervyn • USA
HI NO ATARU SAKAMICHI • 1958 • Tasaka Tomotaka • JPN • STREET IN THE SUN
HI NO ATARU SAKAMICHI • 1967 • Nishikawa Katsumi • JPN • SLOPE IN THE SUN, A
HI NO BARA • 1948 • Nakamura Noboru • JPN • SCARLET ROSE
HI NO HATE • 1954 • Yamamoto Satsuo • JPN • TO THE END OF THE SUN ○ END OF THE SUN
HI NO TORI • 1979 • Ichikawa Kon • JPN • PHOENIX, THE ○ FIREBIRD
HI-RIDERS, THE see **HIGH RIDERS** • 1977
HI-RISE WISE GUYS • 1970 • Smith Paul J. • ANS • USA
HI-SEAS HI-JACKER • 1963 • Marcus Sid • ANS • USA
HI! STOP THOSE BARRELS • 1908 • Fitzhamon Lewin • UKN
HI WA SHIZUMAZU • 1954 • Nakamura Noboru • JPN • SUN NEVER SETS, THE
HI WA SHIZUMI, HI WA NOBORU • 1972 • Kurahara Koreyoshi • JPN • SUNSET, SUNRISE
HI YA, CHARACTER see **HI'YA, CHUM** • 1943
HI' YA, SAILOR • 1943 • Yarbrough Jean • USA
HI-YO SILVER! • 1940 • Witney William, English John • USA
HIAWANDA'S CROSS • 1913 • *Fielding Romaine* • USA
HIAWATHA • 1903 • Rosenthal Joe • UKN, CND • HIAWATHA, THE MESSIAH OF THE OJIBWAY
HIAWATHA • 1909 • Ranous William V. • USA
HIAWATHA • 1913 • *Moore F. E. (P)* • USA
HIAWATHA • 1913 • *Kinemacolor* • USA
HIAWATHA • 1952 • Neumann Kurt • USA
HIAWATHA, THE MESSIAH OF THE OJIBWAY see **HIAWATHA** • 1903
HIAWATHA'S RABBIT HUNT • 1941 • Freleng Friz • ANS • USA
HIBANA • 1922 • Kinugasa Teinosuke • JPN • SPARK
HIBANA • 1956 • Kinugasa Teinosuke • JPN • SPARK
HIBERNATUS • 1969 • Molinaro Edouard • FRN, ITL • LOUIS DE FUNES E IL NONNO SURGELATO (ITL)
HIBOTAN BAKUTO • 1968 • Yamashita Kosaku • JPN • RED PEONY GAMBLER, THE
HIBOTAN BAKUTO, ISSHUKU IPPAN • 1968 • Suzuki Noribumi • JPN • WOMAN GAMBLER, KANTO AFFAIR
HIBOTAN BAKUTO -ORYU SANJO • 1970 • Kato Yasushi • JPN • WOMAN GAMBLER: ORYU COMES
HIBOTANBAKUTO -OINICHI ITADAKIMASU • 1971 • Kato Yasushi • JPN • WOMAN GAMBLER -DEATH FOR THE WICKED
HIBOU ET LE CORBEAU, LE • 1973 • Hoedeman Co • ANS • CND • OWL AND THE RAVEN -AN ESKIMO LEGEND, THE
HIBOU ET LE LEMMING, LE • 1971 • Hoedeman Co • ANS • CND • OWL AND THE LEMMING -AN ESKIMO LEGEND, THE
HIC-CUP PUP • 1954 • Hanna William, Barbera Joseph • ANS • USA
HIC-CUPS THE CHAMP • 1932 • *Mintz Charles (P)* • ANS • USA
HIC NAIR GENTLEMAN CAMBRIOLEUR • 1911 • Novelli Enrico • ITL
HIC SUNT LEONES see **ZDE JSOU LVI** • 1958
HICBIR GECE • 1989 • Ileri Selim • TRK
HICCUP HOUND • 1963 • Kneitel Seymour • ANS • USA
HICHU NO HI • 1968 • Shindo Takae • JPN • SECRET OF SECRETS
HICK, THE • 1921 • Taurog Norman, Semon Larry • SHT • USA
HICK, A SLICK AND A CHICK, A • 1948 • Davis Arthur • ANS • USA
HICK CHICK, THE • 1946 • Avery Tex • ANS • USA
HICK MANHATTAN • 1918 • Justice Martin • USA
HICKEY AND BOGGS • 1972 • Culp Robert • USA
HICKORY HILL • 1968 • Leacock Richard • DOC • USA
HICKORY HIRAM • 1918 • Frazee Edwin • SHT • USA
HICKS IN NIGHTMARELAND • 1915 • Barre Raoul • ANS • USA
HICKSVILLE EPICURE, THE • 1913 • Henderson Dell • USA
HICKSVILLE TRAGEDY TROUPE, THE • 1915 • *Kalem* • USA
HICKTOWN RIVALS, THE • 1915 • *Joker* • USA
HICKVILLE TO BROADWAY • 1921 • Harbaugh Carl • USA
HICKVILLE'S DIAMOND MYSTERY • 1915 • *Carney Augustus* • USA
HICKVILLE'S FINEST • 1914 • *Ab* • USA
HICRAN GECESI • 1968 • Seden Osman • TRK • NIGHT OF SORROW, THE
HIDARE UCHIWA • 1935 • Gosho Heinosuke • JPN • GOOD FINANCIAL SITUATION ○ LEFT-HANDED FAN ○ LIFE OF LUXURY, A
HIDAVATAS • 1969 • Jankovics Marcell • HNG • INAUGURATION
HIDDEN, THE • 1987 • Sholder Jack • USA
HIDDEN, THE see **RAHSIA** • 1987
HIDDEN ACES • 1927 • Mitchell Howard M. • USA
HIDDEN AGENDA • 1990 • Loach Kenneth • UKN
HIDDEN AND SEEKING • 1971 • Werner Peter • USA
HIDDEN BADGE, THE • 1919 • Holt George • SHT • USA
HIDDEN BANK ROLL, THE • 1913 • *Lubin* • USA
HIDDEN BONDS, THE • 1912 • *Rex* • USA
HIDDEN CHILDEN, THE • 1917 • Apfel Oscar • USA
HIDDEN CITY • 1915 • Ford Francis • USA
HIDDEN CITY • 1987 • Poliakoff Stephen • UKN
HIDDEN CITY see **CIDADE OCULTA** • 1986
HIDDEN CITY (UKN) see **DARKEST AFRICA** • 1936
HIDDEN CLUE, THE • 1914 • *Mills Thomas R.* • USA
HIDDEN CODE, THE • 1920 • Le Strange Richard • USA
HIDDEN COLOUR see **COLOR ESCONDIDO** • 1987
HIDDEN CRIME • 1915 • *Hunt Irene* • USA
HIDDEN DANGER • 1948 • Taylor Ray • USA
HIDDEN DANGER, THE • 1917 • *Darkfeather Mona* • SHT • USA
HIDDEN DANGERS • 1920 • Bertram William • SRL • USA • VANISHING MASK, THE ○ MOODS OF EVIL ○ BLACK CIRCLE, THE
HIDDEN DEATH • 1914 • Melies Gaston • FRN
HIDDEN ENEMY • 1940 • Bretherton Howard • USA
HIDDEN EVIDENCE • 1934 • Hillyer Lambert • SHT • USA
HIDDEN EYE, THE • 1945 • Whorf Richard • USA
HIDDEN FACE, THE • 1916 • Middleton Edwin • SHT • USA
HIDDEN FACE, THE • 1965 • Dromgoole Patrick • UKN
HIDDEN FACE, THE see **ROSTRO OCULTO, EL** • 1964
HIDDEN FEAR • 1957 • De Toth Andre • USA
HIDDEN FEAR see **MAN OUTSIDE** • 1986
HIDDEN FIRE, THE • 1990 • Kavosh Habib • IRN
HIDDEN FIRES • 1913 • Tucker George Loane • USA
HIDDEN FIRES • 1918 • Irving George • USA
HIDDEN FLAME, THE see **FLAMME CACHEE, LA** • 1919
HIDDEN FORTRESS, THE see **KAKUSHI TORIDE NO SAN-AKUNIN** • 1958
HIDDEN GEM see **SANGAWUNU MENIKE** • 1967
HIDDEN GOLD • 1932 • Rosson Arthur • USA
HIDDEN GOLD • 1940 • Selander Lesley • USA
HIDDEN GUN, THE see **VIEUX FUSIL, LE** • 1975
HIDDEN GUNS • 1956 • Gannaway Albert C. • USA
HIDDEN HAND, THE • 1918 • Vincent James • SRL • USA
HIDDEN HAND, THE • 1942 • Stoloff Ben • USA
HIDDEN HAND, THE see **IT IS FOR ENGLAND** • 1916
HIDDEN HEART, THE • 1953 • Beaudine William • USA
HIDDEN HOARD, THE • 1908 • Fitzhamon Lewin • UKN
HIDDEN HOMICIDE • 1959 • Young Tony • UKN
HIDDEN IN THE FOG see **I DIMMA DOLD** • 1953
HIDDEN KNOWLEDGE see **SKJULT VIDEN** • 1978
HIDDEN LAW, THE • 1916 • *Clifford William* • USA
HIDDEN LETTERS, THE • 1914 • Brooke Van Dyke • USA
HIDDEN LIFE, THE see **VERBORGEN LEVEN, HET** • 1920
HIDDEN LIGHT • 1920 • Schomer Abraham S. • USA
HIDDEN LIGHT, THE • 1912 • *Rex* • USA
HIDDEN LITTLE HOUSES • Munteanu Stefan • ANM • RMN
HIDDEN LOOT • 1925 • Bradbury Robert North • USA
HIDDEN LOVE, A • 1913 • *White Pearl* • USA
HIDDEN MASTER, THE • 1940 • Lee Sammy • SHT • USA
HIDDEN MENACE, THE • 1925 • Hutchison Charles • USA
HIDDEN MENACE (USA) see **STAR OF THE CIRCUS** • 1938
HIDDEN MESSAGE, THE • 1914 • *Reliance* • USA
HIDDEN MINE, THE • 1911 • *Anderson Broncho Billy* • USA
HIDDEN NATION, THE see **NACION CLANDESTINA, LA** • 1989
HIDDEN PASSIONS see **GIZLI DUYGULAR** • 1986
HIDDEN PEARLS • 1918 • Melford George • USA
HIDDEN PIT, THE • 1919 • *Lowell John* • SHT • USA
HIDDEN PLEASURES see **PLACERES OCULTOS, LOS** • 1977
HIDDEN POWER • 1939 • Collins Lewis D. • USA • POWER TO KILL, THE
HIDDEN PROFILE see **KAZE NO SHISEN** • 1963
HIDDEN REALITY, THE see **SKJULTE VIRKELIGHED, DEN** • 1987
HIDDEN RIVER see **RIO ESCONDIDO** • 1947
HIDDEN ROOM, THE (USA) see **OBSESSION** • 1948
HIDDEN ROOM OF 1000 HORRORS, THE see **TELL-TALE HEART, THE** • 1960
HIDDEN SCAR, THE • 1916 • O'Neil Barry • USA
HIDDEN SECRET see **FIRST YANK INTO TOKYO** • 1945
HIDDEN SECRET (UKN) see **YANK IN INDO-CHINA, A** • 1952
HIDDEN SPRING, THE • 1917 • Hopper E. Mason • USA
HIDDEN THOUGHTS see **NATURAL ENEMIES** • 1979
HIDDEN TRAIL, THE • 1912 • Ince Thomas H. • USA
HIDDEN TREASURE • 1911 • Wilson Frank? • UKN
HIDDEN TREASURE, THE • 1908 • *Selig* • USA
HIDDEN TREASURE, THE • 1912 • *American* • USA
HIDDEN TREASURE, THE • 1915 • *Alhambra* • USA
HIDDEN TREASURE, THE see **DOKTOR NIKOLA** • 1909
HIDDEN TREASURE RANCH • 1913 • *Kerrigan J. Warren* • USA
HIDDEN TRUTH, THE • 1919 • Steger Julius • USA
HIDDEN TRUTH, THE see **BERCANDA DALAM DUKA** • 1981
HIDDEN UNDER CAMPFIRE • 1910 • *Walturdaw* • UKN
HIDDEN VALLEY • 1932 • Bradbury Robert North • USA
HIDDEN VALLEY, THE • 1916 • Warde Ernest C. • USA
HIDDEN VALLEY, THE see **LAND UNKNOWN, THE** • 1957
HIDDEN VALLEY DAYS • 1948 • Crouch William Forest • SHT • USA
HIDDEN VALLEY OUTLAWS • 1944 • Bretherton Howard • USA
HIDDEN WAY, THE • 1926 • De Grasse Joseph • USA
HIDDEN WEALTH • 1912 • Waller Wallett • UKN
HIDDEN WITNESS, THE • 1913 • *Hollister Alice* • USA
HIDDEN WITNESS, THE • 1914 • Martinek H. O. • UKN
HIDDEN WOMAN, THE • 1922 • Dwan Allan • USA
HIDDEN WOMAN, THE see **ESCONDIDA, LA** • 1955
HIDE AND GO SHRIEK • 1987 • Schoolnik Stuart • USA • CLOSE YOUR EYES AND PRAY
HIDE AND GO SIDNEY • 1960 • Bartsch Art • ANS • USA
HIDE AND PEAK • 1956 • Tendlar Dave • ANS • USA
HIDE AND SEEK • 1912 • *Reliance* • USA
HIDE AND SEEK • 1913 • Nicholls George, Sennett Mack (Spv) • USA
HIDE AND SEEK • 1922 • Walker Martin • UKN
HIDE AND SEEK • 1932 • Fleischer Dave • ANS • USA
HIDE AND SEEK • 1963 • Endfield Cy • UKN
HIDE AND SEEK • 1972 • Eady David • UKN
HIDE AND SEEK • 1984 • Bonniere Rene • MTV • CND
HIDE AND SEEK see **KURRAGOMMA** • 1963
HIDE AND SEEK see **HANGI HORA** • 1968
HIDE AND SEEK see **LICKERISH QUARTET, THE** • 1970
HIDE AND SEEK see **PIEDRA LIBRE** • 1976
HIDE AND SEEK see **HIDE'N SEEK** • 1980
HIDE AND SEEK, DETECTIVES • 1918 • Cline Eddie • SHT • USA
HIDE AND SHRIEK • 1938 • Douglas Gordon • SHT • USA
HIDE AND SHRIEK • 1955 • Kneitel Seymour • ANS • USA
HIDE AND SHRIEK see **AMERICAN GOTHIC** • 1988
HIDE IN PLAIN SIGHT • 1979 • Caan James • USA
HIDE-OUT • 1930 • Barker Reginald • USA
HIDE-OUT • 1934 • Van Dyke W. S. • USA
HIDEAWAY • 1937 • Rosson Richard • USA • HOUSE IN THE COUNTRY
HIDEAWAY see **PIILOPIRTTI** • 1978
HIDEAWAY GIRL • 1937 • Archainbaud George • USA
HIDEAWAYS, THE see **FROM THE MIXED-UP FILES OF MRS. BASIL E. FRANKWEILER** • 1973
HIDEG NAPOK • 1966 • Kovacs Andras • HNG • COLD DAYS (UKN)
HIDEKO NO SHASHO-SAN • 1941 • Naruse Mikio • JPN • HIDEKO THE BUS CONDUCTOR
HIDEKO THE BUS CONDUCTOR see **HIDEKO NO SHASHO-SAN** • 1941
HIDE'N SEEK • 1980 • Wolman Dan • ISR • HIDE AND SEEK
HIDEOUS SUN DEMON, THE • 1959 • Clarke Robert, Cassarino Thomas, Bontross Thomas • USA • BLOOD ON HIS LIPS (UKN) ○ TERROR FROM THE SUN ○ SUN DEMON, THE
HIDEOUT • 1949 • Ford Philip • USA
HIDEOUT, THE • 1956 • Scott Peter Graham • UKN
HIDEOUT, THE see **PLANQUE, LA** • 1961
HIDEOUT, THE (USA) see **SMALL VOICE, THE** • 1948
HIDEOUT IN THE ALPS (USA) see **DUSTY ERMINE** • 1936
HIDER IN THE HOUSE • 1989 • Patrick Matthew • USA
HIDING FROM THE LAW • 1915 • *Coombs Guy* • USA
HIDING IN HOLLAND • 1919 • *Universal* • SHT • USA
HIDING MAN, THE see **HOMBRE OCULTO, EL** • 1970
HIDING OF BLACK BILL, THE • 1918 • Smith David • SHT • USA
HIDING OUT • 1987 • Giraldi Bob • USA • ADULT EDUCATION
HIDING PLACE, THE • 1975 • Collier James F. • USA
HIENA, LA • 1974 • Madrid Jose Luis • SPN
HIER, AUJOURD'HUI, DEMAIN see **MINI-MIDI** • 1968
HIER, AUJOURD'HUI ET DEMAIN • 1970 • Diagne Costa • GUN • YESTERDAY, TODAY AND TOMORROW
HIER, AUJOURD'HUI ET DEMAIN (FRN) see **IERI, OGGI, DOMANI** • 1963
HIER BIN ICH, HIER BLEIB ICH • 1959 • Jacobs Werner • FRG
HIERBA SALVAJE • 1978 • Delgado Luis Maria • SPN
HIEROGLYPHIC, THE • 1912 • *Keefe Zena* • USA
HIERONYMUS • 1971 • Savoldelli Reto Andrea • DOC • SWT
HIER'S ONS WEER • 1950 • SAF
HIGANBANA • 1958 • Ozu Yasujiro • JPN • EQUINOX FLOWER
HIGASHI KARA KITA OTOKO • 1961 • Inoue Umeji • JPN • MAN FROM THE EAST, THE (USA)
HIGASHI SHINAKI • 1968 • Isomi Tadahiko • JPN • EAST CHINA SEA, THE
HIGE NO CHIKARA • 1931 • Naruse Mikio • JPN • BEARD OF STRENGTH ○ STRENGTH OF A MOUSTACHE, THE
HIGGENSES VS. JUDSONS • 1911 • Salter Harry • USA
HIGGINS FAMILY, THE • 1938 • Meins Gus • USA
HIGGINS FAMILY, THE see **MEET THE MISSUS** • 1940
HIGH • 1968 • Kent Larry • CND • IN (USA)
HIGH AIR • 1956 • Dwan Allan • SHT • USA
HIGH AND DIZZY • 1920 • Roach Hal • SHT • USA
HIGH AND DIZZY • 1950 • Yates Hal • SHT • USA
HIGH AND DRY (USA) see **MAGGIE, THE** • 1953
HIGH AND HANDSOME • 1925 • Garson Harry • USA • WINNING HIS STRIPES
HIGH AND HAPPY see **HIT PARADE OF 1947** • 1947
HIGH AND LOW • 1913 • Dwan Allan • USA
HIGH AND LOW see **DU HAUT EN BAS** • 1933
HIGH AND LOW see **TENGOKU TO JIGOKU** • 1963
HIGH AND THE FLIGHTY, THE • 1956 • McKimson Robert • ANS • USA
HIGH AND THE MIGHTY, THE • 1954 • Wellman William A. • USA
HIGH ANXIETY • 1977 • Brooks Mel • USA
HIGH ARCTIC -LIFE IN THE LAND • 1958 • Muir Dalton • DOC • CND
HIGH ASHBURY • 1967 • Warhol Andy • USA
HIGH-BALLIN' • 1978 • Carter Peter • CND • HIGH BALLIN'
HIGH BALLIN' see **HIGH-BALLIN'** • 1978
HIGH BARBAREE • 1947 • Conway Jack • USA
HIGH BEER PRESSURE • 1936 • Goodwins Leslie • SHT • USA
HIGH-BORN CHILD AND THE BEGGAR, THE • 1913 • *Lawrence Adelaide* • USA
HIGH BRIGHT SUN, THE • 1964 • Thomas Ralph • UKN • MCGUIRE GO HOME (USA)
HIGH BROW STUFF • 1924 • Wagner Robert • SHT • USA
HIGH BUT NOT DRY • 1967 • Culhane Shamus • ANS • USA
HIGH CARD • 1982 • Gough Bill • MTV • CND

HIGH-CLASS NONSENSE • 1917 • *Hutton Lucille* • USA
HIGH COMMAND, THE • 1937 • Dickinson Thorold • UKN
HIGH COMMISSIONER, THE (USA) see **NOBODY RUNS FOREVER** • 1968
HIGH CONQUEST • 1946 • Allen Irving • USA
HIGH COST OF FLIRTING • 1915 • Bertram William • USA
HIGH COST OF LIVING, THE • 1912 • *Solax* • USA
HIGH COST OF LIVING, THE • 1912 • *Edison* • USA
HIGH COST OF LIVING, THE • 1912 • Arnaud M. • *Eclair*
HIGH COST OF LIVING, THE • 1917 • Drew Sidney • SHT • USA
HIGH COST OF LOVING, THE • 1958 • Ferrer Jose • USA • BAY THE MOON
HIGH COST OF REDUCTION, THE • 1913 • Henderson Dell • USA
HIGH COST OF STARVING, THE • 1917 • Peacocke Leslie T. • SHT • USA
HIGH COST OF WEDDINGS, THE • 1918 • *Field Elinor* • USA
HIGH COUNTRY • 1979 • Miller George* • ASL
HIGH COUNTRY • 1984 • Hughes Bill • MTV • ASL • MAN FROM THE HIGH COUNTRY, THE
HIGH COUNTRY, THE • 1981 • Hart Harvey • CND • FIRST HELLO, THE
HIGH CRIME (USA) see **POLIZIA INCRIMINA, LA LEGGE ASSOLVE, LA** • 1973
HIGH C'S • 1930 • Horne James W. • SHT • USA
HIGH DIVER, THE • 1909 • *Kalem* • USA
HIGH DIVER'S CURSE, THE • 1916 • *Russell Dan* • SHT • USA
HIGH DIVER'S LAST KISS, A • 1918 • Smith Noel • SHT • USA
HIGH DIVING AT HIGHGATE • 1903 • *Paul R. W.* • UKN
HIGH DIVING HARE • 1949 • Freleng Friz • ANS • USA
HIGH EXPLOSIVE • 1943 • McDonald Frank • USA
HIGH EXPLOSIVE see **SUNSET STRIP CASE, THE** • 1938
HIGH FIDELITY • 1975 • Starkiewicz Antoinette • ANS • UKN
HIGH FINANCE • 1917 • Turner Otis • USA
HIGH FINANCE • 1933 • King George • UKN
HIGH FLIERS • 1916 • Myers Harry • SHT • USA
HIGH FLIES THE HAWK see **PISEN O SLETU** • 1949
HIGH FLIGHT • 1957 • Gilling John • UKN
HIGH FLIGHT see **WYSOKIE LOTY** • 1978
HIGH FLYER, THE • 1926 • Brown Harry J. • USA
HIGH FLYERS • 1937 • Cline Eddie • USA
HIGH FLYIN' GEORGE • 1927 • Newfield Sam • SHT • USA
HIGH-FLYING BRIDE see **SORA KAKERU HANAYOME** • 1959
HIGH FLYING SPY • 1972 • McEveety Vincent • TVM • USA
HIGH FURY (USA) see **WHITE CRADLE INN** • 1947
HIGH GAME • 1908 • Coleby A. E. • UKN
HIGH GEAR • 1924 • Mayo Archie • SHT • USA
HIGH GEAR • 1931 • Stevens George • SHT • USA
HIGH GEAR • 1933 • Jason Leigh • USA • BIG THRILL, THE (UKN)
HIGH GEAR JEFFREY • 1921 • Sloman Edward • USA
HIGH GRADER, THE • 1914 • *Reliance* • USA
HIGH GRADERS, THE • 1913 • *Nestor* • USA
HIGH GRASS CIRCUS • 1978 • Ianzelo Tony, Schioler Tolken • DOC • CND
HIGH HAND, THE • 1915 • Taylor William D. • USA
HIGH HAND, THE • 1926 • Maloney Leo • USA
HIGH HAT • 1927 • Creelman James Ashmore • USA • BEHIND THE SCENES
HIGH HAT • 1929 • Santley Joseph • SHT • USA
HIGH HAT • 1937 • Sanforth Clifford • USA
HIGH HAZARD • 1935 • Watson Stanley • UKN
HIGH HEELS • 1921 • *Granger Elsa* • ASL
HIGH HEELS • 1921 • Kohlmar Lee • USA • CHRISTINE OF THE YOUNG HEART
HIGH HEELS see **TACOS ALTOS** • 1986
HIGH HEELS, TRUE LOVE • 1981 • Frank Dimitri Frenkel • NTH
HIGH HEELS (USA) see **DOCTEUR POPAUL** • 1972
HIGH HELL • 1958 • Balaban Burt • UKN
HIGH HONOUR, A • 1974 • Karelov Yevgyeni • USS
HIGH HOPES • 1988 • Leigh Mike • UKN • WINTER
HIGH ICE • 1980 • Jones Eugene S. • TVM • USA • S.O.S. AVALANCHE
HIGH IMPACT WELDING • 1984 • Rodgers Bob • DOC • CND
HIGH INFIDELITY see **ALTA INFEDELTA** • 1964
HIGH-JACK'N THE SHOW • 1938 • Schwarzwald Milton • SHT • USA
HIGH JINKS IN SOCIETY • 1949 • Hill Robert Jordan • UKN
HIGH JINX, A • 1925 • Seiler Lewis • SHT • USA
HIGH JUMP • 1959 • Grayson Godfrey • UKN
HIGH JUMPER see **HOJDHOPPAR'N** • 1980
HIGH KUKUS • 1973 • Broughton James • USA
HIGH LIFE • 1914 • Williams C. Jay • USA
HIGH LIFE BELOW STAIRS • 1900 • *Paul R. W.* • UKN
HIGH LIFE HITS SLIPPERY SAM • 1914 • *Essanay* • USA
HIGH-LIFE TAYLOR • 1908 • Melies Georges • FRN • SIDESHOW WRESTLERS (?)
HIGH LONESOME • 1950 • Le May Alan • USA
HIGH MIDNIGHT • 1979 • Haller Daniel • TVM • USA
HIGH-MINDED see **UYARNTHA MANITHAN** • 1968
HIGH MOUNTAIN RANGERS • 1987 • Conrad Robert • TVM • USA
HIGH MOUNTAIN VENTURE • 1973 • Matthews Ross • ASL
HIGH NOON • 1952 • Zinnemann Fred • USA
HIGH NOON see **GORECHTO PLADNE** • 1965
HIGH NOON, PART TWO: THE RETURN OF WILL KANE • 1980 • Jameson Jerry • TVM • USA
HIGH NOTE • 1960 • Jones Charles M. • ANS • USA
HIGH OLD TIME, A • 1899 • *Warwick Trading Co.* • UKN
HIGH OLD TIME, A • 1914 • *Mina* • USA
HIGH OVER THE BORDERS • 1942 • Jacoby Irving • DCS • CND
HIGH PAVEMENT see **MY SISTER AND I** • 1948
HIGH PERIL see **KEY, THE** • 1934
HIGH PLAINS DRIFTER • 1973 • Eastwood Clint • USA
HIGH PLAY • 1917 • Sloman Edward • USA
HIGH POCKETS • 1919 • Lowry Ira M. • USA
HIGH-POWERED • 1945 • Berke William • USA
HIGH-POWERED RIFLE, THE • 1960 • Dexter Maury • USA
HIGH PRESSURE • 1931 • LeRoy Mervyn • USA
HIGH PRICE OF PASSION, THE • 1986 • Elikann Larry • TVM • USA
HIGH PRIESTESS OF SEXUAL WITCHCRAFT • 1973 • Buchanan Beau • USA
HIGH RANK see **VYSOKOYE ZVANIYE** • 1973
HIGH RIDE • 1982 • Avalon Phillip • DOC • ASL
HIGH RIDERS • 1977 • Clark Greydon • USA • HI-RIDERS, THE
HIGH RISE • 1972 • Stone Danny • USA
HIGH RISE • 1989 • Robinson Bruce • UKN
HIGH RISK • 1976 • O'Steen Sam • TVM • USA
HIGH RISK • 1981 • Raffill Stewart • USA
HIGH ROAD, THE • 1915 • Noble John W. • USA
HIGH ROAD, THE (UKN) see **LADY OF SCANDAL, THE** • 1930
HIGH ROAD TO CHINA • 1982 • Hutton Brian G. • USA
HIGH ROLLERS, THE • 1921 • Roach Hal • SHT • USA
HIGH ROLLING • 1977 • Auzins Igor • ASL • HIGH ROLLING IN A HOT CORVETTE
HIGH ROLLING IN A HOT CORVETTE see **HIGH ROLLING** • 1977
HIGH SCHOOL • 1940 • Nicholls George Jr. • USA
HIGH SCHOOL • 1969 • Wiseman Frederick • DOC • USA
HIGH SCHOOL see **STUDENT AFFAIRS** • 1987
HIGH SCHOOL BIG SHOT • 1959 • Rapp Joel • USA • YOUNG SINNERS (UKN)
HIGH SCHOOL CAESAR • 1960 • Ireland O'Dale • USA
HIGH SCHOOL CONFIDENTIAL • 1958 • Arnold Jack • USA • YOUNG HELLIONS ○ YOUNG KILLERS
HIGH SCHOOL GIRL • 1935 • Wilbur Crane • USA
HIGH SCHOOL GIRL'S REVOLT, THE see **JOGAKUSEI GERILLA** • 1970
HIGH SCHOOL HELLCATS • 1959 • Bernds Edward • USA • SCHOOL FOR VIOLENCE (UKN)
HIGH SCHOOL HERO • 1927 • Butler David • USA • JUST LADS (UKN)
HIGH SCHOOL HERO • 1946 • Dreifuss Arthur • USA
HIGH SCHOOL HONEYMOON see **TOO SOON TO LOVE** • 1960
HIGH SCHOOL SPIRITS • 1988 • Schaertl Michael L. • USA • HIGH SPIRITS
HIGH SCHOOL STUDENT AND WOMAN TEACHER: MERCILESS YOUTH see **KOUKOUSEI TO ONNA KYOUSHI: HIJOU NO SEI SHUN** • 1962
HIGH SCHOOL, U.S.A. • 1983 • Amateau Rod • TVM • USA
HIGH SCHOOL (USA) see **TERZA LICEO** • 1954
HIGH SEA BLUES • 1926 • Roberts Stephen • SHT • USA
HIGH SEAS • 1929 • Clift Denison • UKN
HIGH SEAS HIJACK • 1976 • Bushelman John • USA
HIGH SEASON • 1987 • Peploe Clare • UKN
HIGH SEASON see **NACKT UND HEISS AUF MYKONOS** • 1979
HIGH SIERRA • 1941 • Walsh Raoul • USA
HIGH SIGN, THE • 1916 • *Stull Walter* • SHT • USA
HIGH SIGN, THE • 1917 • Clifton Elmer • USA
HIGH SIGN, THE • 1921 • Cline Eddie, Keaton Buster • SHT • USA
HIGH SOCIETY • 1924 • Roach Hal • SHT • USA
HIGH SOCIETY • 1932 • Rawlins John* • UKN
HIGH SOCIETY • 1955 • Beaudine William • USA • BOWERY BOYS
HIGH SOCIETY • 1956 • Walters Charles • USA
HIGH SOCIETY see **SOCIAL LION, THE** • 1930
HIGH SOCIETY BLUES • 1930 • Butler David • USA
HIGH SOCIETY LIMITED see **FEINE GESELLSCHAFT BESCHRANKTE HAFTUNG** • 1982
HIGH SOCIETY (UKN) see **SCANDAL** • 1929
HIGH SPEED • 1916 • Wilson Millard K. • SHT • USA
HIGH SPEED • 1917 • Sargent George L., Clifton Elmer • USA
HIGH SPEED • 1920 • Miller Charles • USA
HIGH SPEED • 1924 • Blache Herbert • USA
HIGH SPEED • 1932 • Lederman D. Ross • USA
HIGH SPEED • 1953 • *Lassally Walter (Ph)* • SHT • UKN
HIGH SPEED CHALLENGE see **OTOKO NO CHOSEN** • 1968
HIGH SPEED FLIGHT: PART 1: APPROACHING THE SPEED OF SOUND • 1957 • De Normanville Peter • DOC • UKN
HIGH SPEED LEE • 1923 • Murphy Dudley • USA
HIGH SPIRITS • 1988 • Jordan Neil • UKN, USA, IRL
HIGH SPIRITS see **HIGH SCHOOL SPIRITS** • 1988
HIGH SPOTS • 1927 • Roberts Stephen • SHT • USA
HIGH SPOTS ON BROADWAY • 1914 • Sennett Mack • USA
HIGH SPY see **THIGH SPY** • 1967
HIGH STAKE, A see **HJERTERNES KAMP** • 1912
HIGH STAKES • 1918 • Hoyt Arthur • USA
HIGH STAKES • 1931 • Sherman Lowell • USA
HIGH STAKES • 1987 • Kent Larry • CND
HIGH STAKES (UKN) see **HEY, RUBE!** • 1928
HIGH STAKES (UKN) see **TWO-FISTED STRANGER** • 1946
HIGH STEAKS • 1962 • Deitch Gene • ANS • USA
HIGH STEEL • 1965 • Owen Don • CND • CHARPENTIER DU CIEL
HIGH STEPPERS • 1926 • Carewe Edwin • USA
HIGH STRUNG • 1928 • Sandrich Mark • SHT • USA
HIGH TENSION • 1936 • Dwan Allan • USA • TROUBLEMAKERS
HIGH TENSION (USA) see **SANT HANDER INTE HAR** • 1950
HIGH TERRACE, THE • 1956 • Cass Henry • UKN
HIGH TIDE • 1918 • Hamilton G. P. • USA
HIGH TIDE • 1922 • Roach Hal • SHT • USA
HIGH TIDE • 1947 • Reinhardt John • USA
HIGH TIDE • 1987 • Armstrong Gillian • ASL
HIGH TIDE see **MARE ALTA** • 1968
HIGH TIDE see **OSEKA** • 1968
HIGH TIDE AT NOON • 1957 • Leacock Philip • UKN
HIGH TIDE IN NEWFOUNDLAND • 1953 • McLean Grant • DOC • CND
HIGH TIME • 1960 • Edwards Blake • USA
HIGH TOR • 1956 • *Crosby Bing* • MTV • USA
HIGH TREASON • 1929 • Elvey Maurice • UKN
HIGH TREASON • 1951 • Boulting Roy • UKN
HIGH TREASON see **HOCHVERRAT** • 1929
HIGH TREASON see **EPI ESKHATI PRODHOSIA** • 1968
HIGH TREASON see **ESHATI PRODOSIA** • 1970
HIGH TREASON (USA) see **ROCKS OF VALPRE, THE** • 1935
HIGH UP see **VYSOTA** • 1957
HIGH VELOCITY • 1977 • Kramer Remi • USA
HIGH VENTURE (UKN) see **PASSAGE WEST** • 1951
HIGH VERMILION (UKN) see **SILVER CITY** • 1951
HIGH VOLTAGE • 1929 • Higgin Howard • USA • WANTED (UKN)
HIGH VOLTAGE see **VISOKI NAPON** • 1981
HIGH WALL • 1947 • Bernhardt Curtis • USA
HIGH WALL, THE see **VYSOKA ZED** • 1964
HIGH, WIDE AND HANDSOME • 1937 • Mamoulian Rouben • USA
HIGH, WILD AND FREE • 1968 • Eastman Gordon • DOC • USA
HIGH WIND IN JAMAICA, A • 1965 • Mackendrick Alexander • UKN
HIGH WINDOW, THE (UKN) see **BRASHER DOUBLOON, THE** • 1947
HIGH YELLOW • 1965 • Buchanan Larry • USA
HIGHBINDERS, THE • 1910 • *Lubin* • USA
HIGHBINDERS, THE • 1915 • Browning Tod • USA
HIGHBINDERS, THE • 1926 • Terwilliger George W. • USA
HIGHBROW LOVE • 1913 • Henderson Dell • USA
HIGHER AND HIGHER • 1943 • Whelan Tim • USA
HIGHER COURT • Franks Hercs • DOC • USS
HIGHER DESTINY, THE • 1916 • Brabin Charles J. • SHT • USA
HIGHER DUTY, THE • 1913 • *Lamon Isabel* • USA
HIGHER EDUCATION • 1986 • Sheppard John • CND
HIGHER IMPULSE, THE • 1914 • *Eclair* • USA
HIGHER JUSTICE, THE • 1913 • Apfel Oscar • USA
HIGHER LAW, THE • 1911 • Nicholls George • USA
HIGHER LAW, THE • 1913 • *Imp* • USA
HIGHER LAW, THE • 1913 • Fielding Romaine • *Lubin* • USA
HIGHER LAW, THE • 1914 • *Majestic* • USA
HIGHER LAW, THE • 1914 • Giblyn Charles • *Bison* • USA
HIGHER LAW, THE (UKN) see **Nth COMMANDMENT, THE** • 1923
HIGHER MERCY, THE • 1912 • Ranous William V. • USA
HIGHER POWER, A • 1912 • *Champion* • USA
HIGHER POWER, A • 1916 • Batley Ethyle • UKN
HIGHER PRINCIPLE, A see **VYSSI PRINCIP** • 1960
HIGHER THAN A KITE • 1943 • Lord Del • SHT • USA
HIGHER THE FEWER, THE • 1911 • *Thanhouser* • USA
HIGHER THOUGHT, THE • 1912 • *Majestic* • USA
HIGHER TOLL, THE • 1911 • *Kalem* • USA
HIGHER VOICE, THE • 1916 • *Rancho* • USA
HIGHEST BID, THE • 1916 • Russell William • USA
HIGHEST BIDDER, THE • 1913 • *Lubin* • USA
HIGHEST BIDDER, THE • 1915 • *Empire* • USA
HIGHEST BIDDER, THE • 1921 • Worsley Wallace • USA
HIGHEST HONOUR see **HIGHEST HONOUR: A TRUE STORY, THE** • 1984
HIGHEST HONOUR: A TRUE STORY, THE • 1984 • Maxwell Peter • ASL, JPN • SOUTHERN CROSS ○ HIGHEST HONOUR
HIGHEST LAW, THE • 1921 • Ince Ralph • USA
HIGHEST TRUMP, THE • 1919 • Young James • USA
HIGHFLYTE'S AEROPLANE • 1910 • *Pathe* • FRN
HIGHLAND CRAFTS • 1973 • Marzaroli Oscar • DCS • UKN
HIGHLAND DOCTOR • 1943 • Mander Kay • UKN
HIGHLAND FLING • 1936 • Haynes Manning • UKN
HIGHLAND HEART OF NOVA SCOTIA • 1964 • Perry Margaret • DOC • CND
HIGHLAND HOLIDAY • 1972 • Marzaroli Oscar • DCS • UKN
HIGHLAND ROBBERS' FOLK DANCE, THE see **ZBOJNICKI** • 1955
HIGHLAND WINTER • 1984 • Scholes Roger • DOC • ASL
HIGHLANDER • 1985 • Mulcahy Russell • USA
HIGHLANDER, THE • 1911 • Bouwmeester Theo • UKN
HIGHLANDERS' DEFIANCE, THE • 1910 • *Selig* • USA
HIGHLANDS • 1971 • Marzaroli Oscar • DCS • UKN
HIGHLANDS OF SCOTLAND • 1936 • Elder John C. • DOC • UKN
HIGHLIGHTS AND SHADOWS • 1916 • *Clifford William* • SHT • USA
HIGHLIGHTS OF FARNBOROUGH 1952 • 1952 • De Normanville Peter • DOC • UKN
HIGHLIGHTS OF RADIO • 1952 • *S & R Productions* • SHT • UKN
HIGHLY DANGEROUS • 1950 • Baker Roy Ward • UKN
HIGHLY IRREGULAR see **WIFE TAKES A FLYER, THE** • 1942
HIGHPOINT • 1980 • Carter Peter • CND
HIGHS • 1976 • Brakhage Stan • SHT • USA
HIGHSCHOOL GIRLS see **KUO-CHUNG NU-SHENG** • 1989
HIGHWAY 13 • 1949 • Berke William • USA
HIGHWAY 301 • 1950 • Stone Andrew L. • USA
HIGHWAY, THE see **MOTOR HIGHWAY, THE** • 1975
HIGHWAY DRAGNET • 1954 • Juran Nathan • USA
HIGHWAY GIRL • 1975 • Compton Richard • USA • RETURN TO MACON COUNTY ○ RETURN TO MACON COUNTY LINE
HIGHWAY NUMBER 15 • 1965 • Czurko Edward • SHT • PLN
HIGHWAY OF FATE, THE • 1916 • Hill Robert F. • SHT • USA
HIGHWAY OF HATE, THE see **LEOFOROS TOU MISOUS, I** • 1968
HIGHWAY OF HOPE, THE • 1917 • Estabrook Howard • USA
HIGHWAY OF LOVE, THE see **KOI NO HIGHWAY** • 1967
HIGHWAY ONE • 1977 • Otton Steve • ASL
HIGHWAY PATROL • 1938 • Coleman C. C. Jr. • USA
HIGHWAY PICKUP (UKN) see **CHAIR DE POULE** • 1964
HIGHWAY QUEEN, THE (UKN) see **MALKAT HAKVISH** • 1972
HIGHWAY RACKETEERS see **TIP-OFF GIRLS** • 1938
HIGHWAY RUNNERY • 1965 • Larriva Rudy • ANS • USA
HIGHWAY SINGS, THE see **SILNICE SPIVA** • 1937
HIGHWAY SNOBBERY • 1936 • *Mintz Charles (P)* • ANS • USA
HIGHWAY SNOBBERY • 1964 • Kneitel Seymour • ANS • USA
HIGHWAY TO BATTLE • 1961 • Morris Ernest • UKN
HIGHWAY TO FREEDOM (UKN) see **JOE SMITH, AMERICAN** • 1942
HIGHWAY TO HELL • 1990 • de Jong Ate • USA
HIGHWAY TO HELL see **DANGER PATROL** • 1937
HIGHWAY TOURING see **TURISMO DE CARRETERA** • 1968
HIGHWAY WEST • 1941 • McGann William • USA
HIGHWAYMAN, THE • 1915 • Van Wally • USA
HIGHWAYMAN, THE • 1951 • Selander Lesley • USA
HIGHWAYMAN, THE • 1987 • Heyes Douglas • TVM • USA
HIGHWAYMAN HAL • 1913 • Plumb Hay? • UKN

HIGHWAYMAN RIDES, THE see **BILLY THE KID** • 1930
HIGHWAYMAN'S HONOUR, A • 1914 • von Herkomer Siegfried • UKN
HIGHWAYMAN'S SHOES • 1913 • *Eclair* • USA
HIGHWAYS BY NIGHT • 1942 • Godfrey Peter • USA
HIHYU MONOGATARI • 1975 • Suzuki Seijun • JPN
HIJA DE DRACULA, LA • 1971 • Franco Jesus • SPN
HIJA DE FRANKENSTEIN, LA see **SANTO CONTRA LA HIJA DE FRANKENSTEIN** • 1971
HIJA DE JUAN SIMON, LA • 1935 • Saenz De Heredia Jose Luis, Bunuel Luis (U/c) • SPN
HIJA DE JUAN SIMON, LA • 1955 • Delgras Gonzalo • SPN
HIJA DE LA OTRA, LA • 1950 • Orona Vicente • MXC
HIJA DEL CIELO, LA • 1943 • Ortega Juan J. • MXC
HIJA DEL CORREGIDOR, LA • 1925 • Buchs Jose • SPN
HIJA DEL ENGANO, LA • 1951 • Bunuel Luis • MXC • DAUGHTER OF DECEIT (USA) ○ DON QUINTIN, EL AMARGAO
HIJA DEL MAR, LA • 1953 • Momplet Antonio • SPN
HIJA DEL MINISTRO, LA • 1951 • Mendez Fernando • MXC
HIJA DEL PANADERO, LA • 1949 • Rodriguez Joselito • MXC
HIJA DEL PAYASO, LA • 1945 • Rodriguez Joselito • MXC
HIJA DEL PENAL, LA • 1935 • Maroto Eduardo G. • SPN
HIJA DEL PENAL, LA • 1949 • Soler Fernando • MXC
HIJA DEL REGIMENTO, LA • 1944 • Salvador Jaime • MXC
HIJA DEL SOL, LA see **PASIONES INFERNALES** • 1966
HIJA DEL VIEJITO GUARDAFARO, LA • 1939 • Irigoyen Julio • ARG
HIJACK • 1973 • Horn Leonard • TVM • USA
HIJACK • 1975 • Forlong Michael • UKN
HIJACK see **THIS IS A HIJACK** • 1973
HIJACK TO HELL • 1986 • Power John • ASL
HIJACKED TO HELL see **NO TIME TO DIE** • 1985
HIJACKING A BRASS BAND see **UNOS MORAVANKY** • 1982
HIJACKING OF THE ACHILLE LAURO, THE • 1988 • Collins Robert • TVM • USA • TERROR SQUAD
HIJAS CASADERAS • 1954 • Martinez Solares Gilberto • MXC
HIJAS DE DON LAUREANO, LAS • 1972 • *De Anda Raul* • MXC
HIJAS DE ELENA, LAS • 1963 • Cardona Rene Jr. • MXC, CLM
HIJAS DE ELENA, LAS • 1963 • Ozores Mariano • SPN
HIJAS DEL AMAPOLO, LAS • 1960 • Martinez Solares Gilberto • MXC
HIJAS DEL CID, LA see **SPADA DEL CID, LA** • 1962
HIJAS DEL ZORRO, LAS • 1963 • Curiel Federico • MXC
HIJAZO DE MI VIDAZA • 1971 • *Oro* • MXC
HIJI TOSHI • 1960 • Suzuki Hideo • JPN • FORBIDDEN SCOOP ○ HIJO TOSHI
HIJIRI KANNON DAIBOSATSU • 1976 • Wakamatsu Koji • JPN • EROS STERNA
HIJIRIMEN ONNA DAIMYO • 1959 • Mori Masaki • JPN
HIJO AAJA BHOLI • NPL • YESTERDAY, TODAY AND TOMORROW
HIJO DE ALMA GRANDE, EL • 1974 • *Filmicas Agrasanchez* • MXC
HIJO DE CRUZ DIABLO, EL • 1941 • Orona Vicente • MXC
HIJO DE GABINO BARRERA, EL • 1964 • Cardona Rene • MXC
HIJO DE HURACAN RAMIREZ, EL • 1965 • Rodriguez Joselito • MXC
HIJO DE JESSE JAMES, EL (SPN) see **SOLO CONTRO TUTTI** • 1965
HIJO DE LA CALLE, EL • 1949 • Torres-Rios Leopoldo • ARG
HIJO DE LA NOCHE, EL • 1949 • Gascon Jose • SPN
HIJO DE LOS POBRES, EL • 1974 • *Filmadora Chapultepec* • MXC
HIJO DE NADIE, EL • 1945 • Contreras Torres Miguel • MXC
HIJO DEL BANDIDO, EL • 1948 • Aguilar Rolando • MXC
HIJO DEL BARRIO, EL • 1940 • Ferreyra Jose • ARG
HIJO DEL CAPITAN BLOOD, EL • 1962 • Demicheli Tulio • SPN, ITL, USA • FIGLIO DEL CAPITANO BLOOD, IL (ITL) ○ SON OF CAPTAIN BLOOD, THE(USA)
HIJO DEL CHARRO NEGRO, EL • 1960 • Martinez Arturo • MXC
HIJO DEL CRACK, EL • 1953 • Torre-Nilsson Leopoldo, Torres-Rios Leopoldo • ARG • SON OF THE STAR, THE
HIJO DEL DIABLO, EL • 1965 • Gomez Urquiza Zacarias • MXC • SON OF THE DEVIL, THE ○ DEVIL'S SON, THE
HIJO DEL PISTOLERO, EL (SPN) see **SON OF A GUNFIGHTER** • 1965
HIJO DEL PUEBLO, EL • 1973 • *Cima* • MXC
HIJO DESOBEDIENTE, EL • 1945 • Gomez Landero Humberto • MXC
HIJO TOSHI see **HIJI TOSHI** • 1960
HIJOS AJENOS, LOS • 1958 • Rodriguez Roberto • MXC
HIJOS ARTIFICIALES, LOS • 1943 • Momplet Antonio • ARG
HIJOS ARTIFICIALES, LOS • 1952 • Soler Fernando • MXC
HIJOS DE DON VENANCIO, LOS • 1944 • Pardave Joaquin • MXC
HIJOS DE FIERRO, LOS • 1972 • Solanas Fernando • MTV • ARG, FRN, FRG • SONS OF FIERRO
HIJOS DE FRANCISCO EL HOMBRE • 1976 • Contreras Fernando • DOC • CLM
HIJOS DE LA CALLE, LOS • 1950 • Rodriguez Roberto • MXC
HIJOS DE LA MALA VIDA • 1946 • Delgado Agustin P. • MXC
HIJOS DE LA OSCURIDAD • 1950 • Portas Rafael E. • MXC
HIJOS DE ...., LOS • 1977 • Delgado Luis Maria • SPN
HIJOS DE LOS RICOS, LOS see **ACA LAS TORTAS** • 1951
HIJOS DE MARIA MORALES, LOS • 1952 • de Fuentes Fernando • MXC
HIJOS DE NADIE, LOS • 1952 • Vejar Carlos • MXC
HIJOS DE RANCHO GRANDE, LOS • 1956 • Bustillo Oro Juan • MXC
HIJOS DE SATANAS, LOS • 1971 • *Brooks* • MXC
HIJOS DE SCARAMOUCHE, LA • 1974 • Martinez Celeiro Francisco • SPN
HIJOS DEL CONDENADO, LOS • 1964 • Mariscal Alberto • MXC
HIJOS DEL DIA Y DE LA NOCHE, LOS see **BANDA J.S. CRONACA CRIMINALE DEL FAR WEST, LA** • 1972
HIJOS DEL DIVORCIO, LOS • 1957 • de la Serna Mauricio • MXC • CHILDREN OF DIVORCE
HIJOS DEL OTRO, LOS • 1947 • Catrani Catrano • ARG
HIJOS DEL SUBDESARROLLO, LOS • 1975 • Alvarez Carlos • CLM • CHILDREN OF UNDERDEVELOPMENT
HIJOS QUE YO SONE, LOS • 1964 • Gavaldon Roberto • MXC
HIJOSEN • 1958 • Makino Masahiro • JPN
HIJOSEN NO ONNA • 1933 • Ozu Yasujiro • JPN • WOMEN ON THE FIRING LINE ○ DRAGNET GIRL
HIKA • 1951 • Yamamoto Kajiro • JPN • ELEGY
HIKAGE NO KO • 1957 • *Yamada Isuzu* • JPN • GIRL IN THE SHADE, THE
HIKARI • 1928 • Uchida Tomu • JPN • RAY, A
HIKARI NO TATSU ONNA • 1920 • Murata Minoru • JPN • WOMAN STANDING IN THE LIGHT, A
HIKARITOKAGE • 1946 • *Hara Setsuko* • JPN • LIGHT AND SHADOW
HIKARU ONNA • 1988 • Somai Shinji • JPN • BRILLIANT WOMAN, THE
HIKARU UMI • 1963 • Nakahira Ko • JPN • BRIGHT SEA
HIKAYAT AL-UMR KULLUH • 1965 • Halim Hilmy • EGY • HISTOIRE D'UNE VIE
HIKAYAT HUBB • 1959 • Halim Hilmy • EGY • HISTOIRE D'AMOUR
HIKAYAT MIN BALADNA • 1969 • Halim Hilmy • EGY • RECIT DE NOTRE PAYS, UN
HIKAYATU BINT ISMAHA MARMAR • 1972 • Barakat Henry • EGY • HISTOIRE D'UNE FILLE NOMMEE MARMAR
HIKEN • 1963 • Inagaki Hiroshi • JPN • YOUNG SWORDSMAN
HIKEN AGEHA NO CHO • 1962 • Ito Daisuke • JPN
HIKEN YABURI • 1969 • Ikehiro Kazuo • JPN • BROKEN SWORDS
HIKING IS HERR MULLER'S HOBBY see **WANDERN IST HERRN MULLERS LUST** • 1973
HIKING WITH MADEMOISELLE • 1933 • Nakhimoff Edward • UKN
HIKINIGE • 1966 • Naruse Mikio • JPN • MOMENT OF TERROR ○ HIT AND RUN
HIKISAKARETA SEISO • 1967 • Tanaka Tokuzo • JPN • NIGHT FLIGHT
HIKISAKARETA SHOJO • 1968 • Nishihara Giichi • JPN • TORN VIRGIN, A
HIKKOSHI FUFU • 1928 • Ozu Yasujiro • JPN • COUPLE ON THE MOVE, A ○ TWO ON THE MOVE
HIKO SHOJO • 1963 • Urayama Kirio • JPN • EACH DAY I CRY
HIKO SHONEN • 1964 • Kawabe K. • JPN • JUVENILE DELINQUENTS ○ CLASSROOM JUNGLE
HIKOKI WA NAZE TOBUKA • 1943 • *Tsuburaya Eiji (Ph)* • JPN
HIKUIDORI • 1927 • Kinugasa Teinosuke • JPN • CASSOWARY
HILARIO CONDORI • 1980 • Agazzi Paolo • BLV
HILARIO CONDORI: CAMPESINO • 1980 • Agazzi Paolo • BLV
HILARIOUS POSTERS, THE (USA) see **AFFICHES EN GOGUETTE, LES** • 1906
HILARITY ON BOARD SHIP • 1902 • Smith G. A. • UKN
HILARIUS • 1976 • Bokor Pierre • MTV • RMN
HILARY OF THE HILLS • 1915 • *Bondhill Gertrude* • USA
HILDA CRANE • 1956 • Dunne Philip • USA • MANY LOVES OF HILDA CRANE, THE
HILDA OF HERON COVE • 1913 • Martin E. A. • USA
HILDA OF THE MOUNTAINS • 1913 • *Nestor* • USA
HILDA OF THE SLUMS • 1915 • Davis Ulysses • USA
HILDA ROUTS THE ENEMY • 1915 • Birch Cecil • UKN
HILDA WAKES • 1913 • *Blanchard Eleanor* • USA
HILDA WARREN AND DEATH see **HILDE WARREN UND DER TOD** • 1917
HILDA WAS A GOODLOOKER • 1986 • Thew Anna • USA
HILDA'S BUSY DAY • 1915 • Birch Cecil • UKN
HILDA'S HUSKY HELPER • 1916 • *Cooper Claude* • USA
HILDA'S LOVERS • 1911 • Haldane Bert? • UKN
HILDE PETERSEN POSTLAGERND • 1935 • Janson Victor • FRG
HILDE UND DIE 4 PS • 1936 • Paul Heinz • FRG
HILDE WARREN UND DER TOD • 1917 • May Joe • FRG • HILDA WARREN AND DEATH
HILDUR AND THE MAGICIAN • 1969 • Jordan Larry • USA
HILFE, ICH BIN UNSICHTBAR • 1951 • Emo E. W. • FRG • ALAS, I'M INVISIBLE ○ HELP, I'M INVISIBLE
HILFE, ICH LIEBE ZWILLINGE • 1969 • Weck Peter • FRG
HILFE, MICH LIEBT EINE JUNGFRAU • 1969 • Rabenalt Arthur M. • FRG, FRN • VIRGINS ON THE VERGE
HILFE, SIE LIEBT MICH • 1956 • Cap Frantisek • FRG
HILFE! UEBERFALL! • 1931 • Meyer Johannes • FRG
HILFERUF, DER • 1916 • Gartner Adolf • FRG • BANKNOTENFALSCHER, DIE
HILJA, MAITOTYTTO • 1953 • Sarkka Toivo • FNL
HILL 24 DOESN'T ANSWER see **HAGIVA** • 1955
HILL 171 see **HILL 171: TOUR OF DUTY**
HILL 171: TOUR OF DUTY • *Miller Robert* • USA • HILL 171
HILL 203 see **NIHYAKUSAN KOCHI** • 1981
HILL, THE • 1965 • Lumet Sidney • UKN
HILL, THE see **GORA** • 1964
HILL BILLY, THE • 1918 • Ford John • USA
HILL BILLY, THE • 1924 • Hill George W. • USA • VALLEY OF THE WOLF
HILL BILLY, THE (UKN) see **SCARLET DROP, THE** • 1918
HILL CALLED KUBA, THE see **GORA ZWANA KUBA** • 1967
HILL FARM, THE • 1988 • Baker Mark • ANM • UKN
HILL FOLKS • 1912 • *Gem* • USA
HILL IN KOREA, A • 1956 • Amyes Julian • UKN • HELL IN KOREA (USA)
HILL OF DEATH see **KOZARA** • 1962
HILL ON THE DARK SIDE OF THE MOON, A see **BERGET PA MANENS BAKSIDA** • 1983
HILL TILLIES • 1936 • Meins Gus • SHT • USA
HILL TRIBE, THE • 1979 • Yugala Prince • THL
HILLBILLING AND COOING • 1956 • Kneitel Seymour • ANS • USA
HILLBILLY, THE • 1935 • Lantz Walter • ANS • USA
HILLBILLY ARTIST • 1945 • *Mead Thomas (P)* • SHT • USA
HILLBILLY BLITZKRIEG • 1942 • Mack Roy • USA
HILLBILLY GOAT • 1937 • Goodwins Leslie • SHT • USA
HILLBILLY HARE • 1950 • McKimson Robert • ANS • USA
HILLBILLYS IN A HAUNTED HOUSE • 1967 • Yarbrough Jean • USA • GHOST PARTY
HILLCREST MYSTERY, THE • 1918 • Fitzmaurice George • USA
HILLMAN, THE see **IN THE BALANCE** • 1917
HILL'S ANGELS (UKN) see **NORTH AVENUE IRREGULARS, THE** • 1979
HILLS ARE CALLING, THE • 1914 • Hepworth Cecil M. • UKN
HILLS AT DUSK see **GORY O ZMIERZCHU** • 1970
HILLS HAVE EYES, THE • 1977 • Craven Wes • USA
HILLS HAVE EYES II, THE • 1985 • Craven Wes • USA
HILLS OF DONEGAL, THE • 1947 • Argyle John F. • UKN
HILLS OF GLORY, THE • 1916 • Bertram William • SHT • USA
HILLS OF HATE • 1921 • *Hoxie Jack* • USA
HILLS OF HATE • 1926 • Longford Raymond • ASL
HILLS OF HOME • 1948 • Wilcox Fred M. • USA • MASTER OF LASSIE
HILLS OF KENTUCKY • 1927 • Bretherton Howard • USA
HILLS OF OKLAHOMA • 1950 • Springsteen R. G. • USA
HILLS OF OLD WYOMING • 1937 • Watt Nate • USA
HILLS OF PEACE, THE • 1914 • *Church Fred* • USA
HILLS OF PERIL • 1927 • Hillyer Lambert • USA
HILLS OF SILENCE, THE • 1914 • *Bison* • USA
HILLS OF STRIFE, THE • 1913 • Ince John • USA
HILLS OF THE BRAVE (UKN) see **PALOMINO, THE** • 1950
HILLS OF UTAH • 1951 • English John • USA
HILLS OF WYOMIN', THE • 1936 • Fleischer Dave • ANS • USA
HILLS RUN RED, THE (UKN) see **FIUME DI DOLLARI, UN** • 1967
HILLSBORO STORY, THE see **DIVORCE** • 1945
HILLSIDE STRANGLERS, THE see **CASE OF THE HILLSIDE STRANGLERS, THE** • 1988
HILLY BILLY • 1951 • Cowan Will • SHT • USA
HILLY FIELDS see **CHYLE POLA** • 1970
HILM LAYLA • 1949 • Badrakan Salaheddine • EGY • DREAM OF A NIGHT ○ HULMU LAILATUN ○ REVE D'UNE NUIT, LA
HILMANPAIVAT • 1954 • Kassila Matti • FNL • HILMA'S BIRTHDAY
HILMA'S BIRTHDAY see **HILMANPAIVAT** • 1954
HILTON HANOI see **PILOTEN IM PYJAMA** • 1968
HIM WHO HAS • 1931 • Elliot Grace • USA
HIMAKATHARA • 1982 • Wickremaratne Dharmasiri • SLN • DEVIL BIRD
HIMALA • 1983 • Bernal Ishmael • PHL
HIMALAYA • 1950 • Ichac Marcel • DCS • FRN
HIMALAYA NO MAO • 1956 • Kono Juichi • JPN
HIMALAYA PASSION CRUELLE • 1952 • Languepin Jean-Jacques • FRN
HIMALAYAN EPIC see **DRAME A LA NANDA DEVI** • 1951
HIMATSCHAL, DER THRON DER GOTTER • 1931 • Dyhrenfuss G. O. • FRG • WEISSE TOD IN HIMALAYA, DER
HIMATSURI • 1985 • Yanagimachi Mitsuo • JPN • FIRE FESTIVAL
HIMAWARI MUSUME • 1953 • *Mifune Toshiro* • JPN • SUNFLOWER GIRL
HIMBEERSPIESE, DIE • 1915 • Del Zopp Rudolf • FRG
HIMEGOTO • 1967 • Takagi Takeo • JPN • SECRETS
HIMEYURI LILY TOWER see **HIMEYURI NO TO** • 1953
HIMEYURI LILY TOWER see **HIMEYURI NO TO** • 1982
HIMEYURI NO TO • 1953 • Imai Tadashi • JPN • YOUNG GIRLS OF OKINAWA, THE ○ TOWER OF LILIES, THE ○ HIMEYURI LILY TOWER
HIMEYURI NO TO • 1982 • Imai Tadashi • JPN • HIMEYURI LILY TOWER
HIMGHAR • 1987 • Ray Sandip • IND • FROZEN HOMES
HIMIKO • 1974 • Shinoda Masahiro • JPN
HIMITSU • 1953 • Hisamatsu Seiji • JPN • HER SECRET
HIMLASPELET • 1942 • Sjoberg Alf • SWD • ROAD TO HEAVEN, THE ○ HEAVENLY PLAY, THE ○ PATH THAT LEADS TO HEAVEN, THE
HIMMEL, AMOR UND ZWIRN • 1960 • Erfurth Ulrich • FRG
HIMMEL AUF ERDEN • 1935 • Emo E. W. • AUS
HIMMEL AUF ERDEN, DER • 1927 • Schirokauer Alfred • FRG
HIMMEL IST NIE AUSVERKRAUT, DER • 1955 • Weidenmann Alfred • FRG
HIMMEL OCH PANNKAKA • 1959 • Ekman Hasse • SWD • GOOD HEAVENS!
HIMMEL OG HAVI -STOMPA TIL SJOS • 1967 • Christensen Nils Reinhardt • NRW • HEAVEN AND OCEAN! -STOMPA AT SEA
HIMMEL OG HELVEDE • 1988 • Arnfred Morten • DNM • HEAVEN AND HELL
HIMMEL OG HELVETE • 1969 • Vennerod Oyvind • NRW
HIMMEL OHNE STERNE • 1955 • Kautner Helmut • FRG • SKY WITHOUT STARS (USA)
HIMMEL UBER BERLIN, DER • 1987 • Wenders Wim • FRG • WINGS OF DESIRE (UKN) ○ SKY ABOVE BERLIN, THE
HIMMEL UND ERDE • 1982 • Pilz Michael • DOC • AUS • HEAVEN AND EARTH
HIMMEL UND ERDE • 1989 • Samir • SWT • HEAVEN AND EARTH
HIMMEL, WIR ERBEN EIN SCHLOSS • 1943 • Brauer Peter P. • FRG
HIMMELBLAUE ABENDKLEID, DAS • 1941 • Engels Erich • FRG
HIMMELEKSPRESSEN • 1964 • Lund-Sorensen Sune • DNM
HIMMELFAHRTSKOMMANDO EL ALAMEIN (FRG) see **COMMANDOS** • 1968
HIMMELHUNDE • 1942 • von Norman Roger • FRG
HIMMELSKIBET • 1917 • Holger-Madsen • DNM • FOURTEEN MILLION LEAGUES FROM EARTH ○ 400 MILLION MILES FROM EARTH ○ TRIP TO MARS, A ○ SHIP TO HEAVEN, A ○ AIRSHIP, THE ○ SKY SHIP ○ SHIP OF HEAVEN, THE ○ HEAVEN SHIP
HIMMELSKONIGIN, DIE • 1919 • Wilhelm Carl • FRG
HIMMLISCHE WALZER, DER • 1948 • von Cziffra Geza • AUS
HIMMO KING OF JERUSALEM • 1988 • Guttman Amos • ISR
HIMO • 1965 • Sekigawa Hideo • JPN • PROCURER, THE
HIMO TO KUSARI • 1968 • Funada Sei • JPN • ROPE AND CHAIN
HIMOTSUKI SHOJO • 1968 • Sakao Masanao • JPN • VIRGIN WITH AN ENCUMBRANCE
HIMS ANCIENT AND MODERN • 1922 • Roberts Edward D. • UKN
HIMSELF AS HERSELF • 1967 • Markopoulos Gregory J. • USA
HIN OCH SMALANNINGEN • 1927 • Petschler Eric A. • SWD • DEVIL AND THE MAN FROM SMALAND, THE

HIN OCH SMALANNINGEN • 1949 • Johansson Ivar • SWD
HIN UND HER • 1950 • Lingen Theo • FRG
HINANGO KITA SA LUSAK • 1967 • Torres Mar S. • PHL • I TOOK YOU FROM THE MIRE
HINCHA, EL • 1957 • Elorrieta Jose Maria • SPN
HIND, THE see **ALAGEYIK** • 1958
HINDENBERG, THE • 1975 • Wise Robert • USA
HINDERED see **BEHINDERT** • 1973
HINDI SA IYO ANG MUNDO, BABY PORCUNA • 1978 • Zialcita Danny L. • PHL • WORLD IS NOT YOURS, BABY PORCUNA, THE
HINDISTAN CEVIZI • 1967 • Seden Osman • TRK • COCOANUT, THE
HINDLE WAKES • 1918 • Elvey Maurice • UKN
HINDLE WAKES • 1927 • Elvey Maurice • UKN • FANNY HAWTHORNE (USA)
HINDLE WAKES • 1931 • Saville Victor • UKN
HINDLE WAKES • 1952 • Crabtree Arthur • UKN • HOLIDAY WEEK (USA)
HINDOO CHARM, THE • 1913 • Costello Maurice • USA
HINDOO CURSE, THE (UKN) see **HINDOO'S CURSE, THE** • 1912
HINDOO DAGGER, THE • 1909 • Griffith D. W. • USA
HINDOO FAKIR • 1902 • Porter Edwin S. • USA
HINDOO JUGGLERS • 1900 • Booth W. R. • UKN
HINDOOS AND HAZARDS • 1918 • Semon Larry • SHT • USA
HINDOO'S CHARM, THE • 1912 • *Lubin* • USA
HINDOO'S CURSE, THE • 1912 • Ranous William V. • USA • HINDOO CURSE, THE (UKN)
HINDOO'S PRIZE, THE • 1912 • *Prescott Vivian* • USA
HINDOO'S REVENGE, THE • 1916 • *Lily* • SHT • USA
HINDOO'S TREACHERY, THE • 1910 • Aylott Dave • UKN
HINDRANCE • Moretti Pierre • ANS • CND
HINDU, THE • 1953 • Ferrin Frank • USA • SABAKA (UKN)
HINDU HINDOO, THE • 1917 • *Binns George* • SHT • USA
HINDU IMAGE, THE see **MYSTERY OF THE HINDU IMAGE, THE** • 1914
HINDU PRINCE, THE • 1911 • *Solax* • USA
HINDU TOMB, THE see **INDISCHE GRABMAL I-II, DAS** • 1921
HINDUSTAN HAMARA • 1950 • Zils Paul • IND • OUR INDIA (USA)
HINEINI • 1936 • Nordhaus Gosta • FRG
HINEMOA • 1913 • *Melies* • USA
HINEMOA • 1919 • *Austral Photoplays* • ASL
HININ KAKUMEI • 1967 • Adachi Masao • JPN • CONTRACEPTIVE REVOLUTION
HINKU AND VINKU • 1964 • Partanen Heikki • SER • FNL
HINODE NO SAKEBI • 1967 • Fujita Shigeo • JPN • CRYING FOR THE SUN
HINOKI BUTAI • 1946 • Toyoda Shiro • JPN • CYPRESS BOARDS
HINOTORI • 1948 • *Hasegawa Kazu* • JPN • FIRE BIRD
HINOTORI 2772 see **HINOTORI 2772 AI NO COSMOZONE** • 1980
HINOTORI 2772 AI NO COSMOZONE • 1980 • Sugiyama Taku • JPN • SPACE FIREBIRD 2772 ○ HINOTORI 2772 ○ SPACE FIREBIRD ○ PHOENIX 2772
HINTER DEN ROTEN MAUERN VON LICHTERFELDE see **KADETTEN** • 1931
HINTER KLOSTERMAUERN • 1928 • Seitz Franz • FRG
HINTER KLOSTERMAUERN • 1952 • Reinl Harald • FRG
HINTER VERSCHLOSSENEN TUREN • 1989 • Schmid Anka • SWT • BEHIND LOCKED DOORS
HINTER VERSCHLOSSENENTUREN • 1918 • von Woringen Paul • FRG
HINTERHOEFE DER LIEBE • 1968 • Dietrich Erwin C. • FRG • BACKYARD OF LOVE
HINTERTREPPE, DIE • 1921 • Jessner Leopold, Leni Paul • FRG • BACKSTAIRS
HINTON, DINTON AND MERE • 1929 • Aylott Dave, Symmons E. F. • SHT • UKN
HINTONJARO SZERELEM • 1954 • Ranody Laszlo • HNG • LOVE TRAVELS BY COACH
HINTON'S DOUBLE • 1917 • Warde Ernest C. • USA
HINTS ON HORSEMANSHIP • 1924 • Benstead Geoffrey • SER • UKN
HINUNTER • 1936 • Nordhaus Gosta • FRG
HIOB • 1918 • *Von Winterstein Eduard* • FRG
HIP ACTION • 1933 • Marshall George • SHT • USA
HIP, HEP AND 21 see **HIP, HOT AND 21** • 1967
HIP, HIP, HURRA! • 1987 • Grede Kjell • SWD, DNM, NRW • HIP, HIP, HURRAH!
HIP, HIP, HURRAH! see **HIP, HIP, HURRA!** • 1987
HIP, HIP–HURRY! • 1958 • Jones Charles M. • ANS • USA
HIP HIP HYPNOTISM • 1920 • *Ovey George* • USA
HIP HIP OLE • 1964 • Kneitel Seymour • ANS • USA
HIP, HOT AND 21 • 1967 • Berry Dale • USA • HIP, HEP AND 21
HIPNOS FOLLIA DI UN MASSACRO • 1967 • Bianchini Paolo • ITL, SPN • MASSACRE MANIA (USA) ○ HYPNOS (SPN)
HIPNOSIS see **NUR TOTE ZEUGEN SCHWEIGEN** • 1963
HIPNOTIZADOR, EL • 1939 • Helu Antonio • MXC
HIPOCITA • 1949 • Morayta Miguel • MXC
HIPOLITO EL DE SANTA • 1949 • de Fuentes Fernando • MXC
HIPOPOTAMO, EL • 1971 • Carretero Amaro • ANS • SPN • HIPPOTAMUS, THE
HIPOTESIS DEL CUADRO ROBADO • 1978 • Ruiz Raul • FRN • HYPOTHESIS OF THE STOLEN PAINTING ○ HYPOTHESE DU TABLEAU VOLE, L' ○ HYPOTHESIS OF A STOLEN PAINTING
HIPOTEZA • 1972 • Zanussi Krzysztof • MTV • PLN • HYPOTHESIS
HIPPETY HOPPER • 1949 • McKimson Robert • ANS • USA
HIPPIE GIRLS, THE see **LOVING AND LAUGHING** • 1971
HIPPIE HOLLYWOOD: THE ACID-BLASTING FREAKS see **MONDO HOLLYWOOD** • 1967
HIPPIE REVOLT, THE • 1967 • Beatty Edgar • USA • SOMETHING'S HAPPENING
HIPPIES OF KAWACHI see **KAWACHI FUTEN ZOKU** • 1968
HIPPO • 1980 • SAF
HIPPOCAME, L' see **HIPPOCAMPE GEOLOGIQUE, L'** • 1933
HIPPOCAMPE GEOLOGIQUE, L' • 1933 • Painleve Jean • SHT • FRN • SEA HORSE, THE (UKN) ○ HIPPOCAME, L'
HIPPOCRATES see **HIPPOCRATES TACHI** • 1981
HIPPOCRATES AND DEMOCRACY • 1973 • *Daudoulaki Katia* • GRC
HIPPOCRATES TACHI • 1981 • Omori Kazuki • JPN • HIPPOCRATES
HIPPODROME (USA) see **GELIEBTE BESTIE** • 1959
HIPPONE-LA-ROYALE • 1952 • Leherissey Jean • SHT • FRN
HIPPOPOTAMUS WHO WAS AFRAID OF VACCINATION, THE • 1967 • Amalrik Leonid • USS
HIPPOTAMUS, THE see **HIPOPOTAMO, EL** • 1971
HIPPYDROME TIGER • 1968 • Lovy Alex • ANS • USA
HIPS HIPS HOORAY • 1934 • Sandrich Mark • USA
HIRAK RAJARDESHE • 1978 • Ray Satyajit • IND • IN THE LAND OF KING HIRAK ○ KINGDOM OF DIAMONDS, THE
HIRAM AND ZEKE MASQUERADE • 1914 • *Frontier* • USA
HIRAM BUYS AN AUTO • 1913 • Campbell Colin • USA
HIRAM GREEN, DETECTIVE • 1913 • Seay Charles M. • USA
HIRAM NA KAMAY • Cayado Tony • PHL • CLUTCHING HAND, THE
HIRAM'S BRIDE • 1909 • Olcott Sidney • USA
HIRAM'S HOTEL • 1914 • *Brennan John E.* • USA
HIRAM'S INHERITANCE • 1915 • Curtis Allen • USA
HIRATE MIKI • 1951 • *Yamamura So* • JPN • MIKI THE SWORDSMAN
HIRCIN KADIN • 1967 • Erakalin Ulku • TRK • SHREW, THE
HIRED AND FIRED • 1916 • *Vim* • USA
HIRED AND FIRED • 1916 • Beery Wallace • *Universal* • SHT • USA
HIRED AND FIRED • 1916 • Dillon John Francis • *Vogue* • SHT • USA
HIRED AND FIRED • 1920 • *Hackett Lillian* • SHT • USA
HIRED AND FIRED • 1922 • Roach Hal • SHT • USA
HIRED AND FIRED • 1929 • Taurog Norman • SHT • USA
HIRED DRESS SUIT, THE • 1913 • *Majestic* • USA
HIRED GIRL, THE • 1915 • Ingraham Lloyd • USA
HIRED GUN see **LAST GUNFIGHTER, THE** • 1959
HIRED GUN, THE • 1957 • Nazarro Ray • USA
HIRED HAND, THE • 1971 • Fonda Peter • USA
HIRED HUSBAND • 1947 • Yates Hal • SHT • USA
HIRED KILLER, THE (USA) see **TECNICA DI UN OMICIDIO** • 1966
HIRED MAN, THE • 1918 • Schertzinger Victor • USA
HIRED, TIRED AND FIRED • 1916 • Hunt Jay • SHT • USA
HIRED, TIRED, FIRED • 1908 • *Essanay* • USA
HIRED WIFE • 1934 • Melford George • USA • MARRIAGE OF CONVENIENCE (UKN)
HIRED WIFE • 1940 • Seiter William A. • USA
HIRELING, THE • 1973 • Bridges Alan • UKN
HIREN OKARU KAMPEI • 1956 • Sazaki Ko • JPN
HIRMAN, AL- • 1953 • Salem Atef • EGY • PRIVATION, LA
HIRNBRENNEN • 1982 • Huber Leopold • AUS, SWT • BRAIN-STORM
HIROKU KAIBYODEN • 1969 • Tanaka Tokuzo • JPN • HAUNTED CASTLE
HIROKU ONNA RO • 1968 • Inoue Akira • JPN • WOMEN'S PRISON
HIROKU ONNADERA • 1969 • Tanaka Tokuzo • JPN • SECRETS OF A WOMEN'S TEMPLE
HIROKU ONNAGURA • 1968 • Mori Issei • JPN • YOSHIWARA STORY, THE
HIRONDELLE ET LA MESANGE, L' • 1921 • Antoine Andre • FRN
HIROSHIMA • 1953 • Sekigawa Hideo • JPN
HIROSHIMA 28 • Lung Kong • HKG
HIROSHIMA HEARTACHE see **SONO YO WA WASURENAI** • 1962
HIROSHIMA MON AMOUR • 1959 • Resnais Alain • FRN, JPN • 24-JIKAN NO JOJI (JPN)
HIROSHIMA NAGASAKI • 1983 • Hayakawa Masami • JPN • WHAT THE ATOMIC BOMB BROUGHT
HIRSEKORN • 1931 • Marton Andrew • FRG
HIRSEKORN GREIFT EIN • 1931 • Bernauer Rudolf • AUS
HIRSIZ KIZ • 1968 • Inanoglu Turker • TRK • THIEF, THE
HIRSIZ PRENSES • 1967 • Pecen Nevzat • TRK • THIEVING PRINCESS, THE
HIRT VON MARIA SCHNEE, DER • 1919 • Raffay Iwa • FRG
HIRTTAMATTOMAT • 1972 • Pasanen Spede, Loiri Vesa-Matti • FNL • UNHANGED, THE
HIRUSAGARI NO AIBIKI • 1967 • Mukoi Hiroshi • JPN • AFTERNOON RENDEZVOUS
HIRYU NO KEN • 1937 • Inagaki Hiroshi • JPN • MATCHLESS SWORD ○ SWORD OF FLYING DRAGON
HIRYU TEKKAMEN • 1958 • Mori Masaki • JPN
HIS ACTRESS DAUGHTER • 1912 • Haldane Bert? • UKN
HIS AFFAIR (UKN) see **THIS IS MY AFFAIR** • 1937
HIS AFFIANCED WIFE • 1915 • *Fisher George* • USA
HIS ALIBI see **CREAM PUFF ROMANCE, A** • 1916
HIS AND HERS • 1961 • Hurst Brian Desmond • UKN
HIS AND HIS see **HONEYMOON HOTEL** • 1964
HIS APOLOGIES • 1935 • Newman Widgey R. • UKN
HIS ATHLETIC WIFE • 1913 • *Forbes Gertrude* • USA
HIS AUNT EMMA • 1913 • Smalley Phillips • USA
HIS AUTO RUINATION • 1916 • Fishback Fred C. • SHT • USA
HIS AUTO'S MAIDEN TRIP • 1912 • Henderson Dell • USA
HIS AWFUL DAUGHTER • 1913 • Smalley Phillips • USA
HIS AWFUL DOWNFALL • 1917 • *Adams Rex* • SHT • USA
HIS AWFUL VENGEANCE • 1914 • *Reliance* • USA
HIS BABY • 1916 • Davey Horace • SHT • USA
HIS BABY DOLL • 1917 • *Anderson Claire* • USA
HIS BABY'S SHIRT • 1910 • *Powers* • USA
HIS BACHELOR DADDIES • 1930 • Beaudine Harold • SHT • USA
HIS BACHELOR DINNER • 1915 • *Reliance* • USA
HIS BACK AGAINST THE WALL • 1922 • Lee Rowland V. • USA
HIS BAD POLICY • 1917 • *Triangle* • USA
HIS BELOVED VIOLIN • 1915 • MacQuarrie Murdock • USA
HIS BEST FRIEND • 1911 • *Solax* • USA
HIS BEST FRIEND • 1913 • O'Neil Barry • USA
HIS BEST FRIEND (USA) see **SIEN BESTER FREUND** • 1929
HIS BEST FRIEND (USA) see **SEIN BESTER FREUND** • 1937
HIS BEST GIRL • 1916 • Goulding Alf • USA
HIS BEST GIRL • 1921 • Parrott Charles, Roach Hal • SHT • USA
HIS BEST GIRL AFTER ALL • 1911 • *Lubin* • USA
HIS BEST LITTLE GIRL'S BROTHER • 1911 • *Selig* • USA
HIS BEST MAN (UKN) see **TIMES SQUARE PLAYBOY** • 1936
HIS BETTER ELF • 1958 • Smith Paul J. • ANS • USA
HIS BETTER HALF • 1920 • *Finch Flora* • SHT • USA
HIS BETTER HALF • 1927 • Taurog Norman • SHT • USA
HIS BETTER SELF • 1911 • *Selig* • USA
HIS BETTER SELF • 1911 • Blache Alice • *Solax* • USA
HIS BETTER SELF • 1912 • Balshofer Fred J. • USA
HIS BETTER SELF • 1913 • *Frontier* • USA
HIS BETTER SELF • 1913 • Johnson Arthur • *Lubin* • USA
HIS BIG CHANCE • 1914 • *Ogle Charles* • USA
HIS BIG PAL see **TOUGH GUY, THE** • 1926
HIS BIRTHDAY • 1911 • Golden Joseph A. • USA
HIS BIRTHDAY GIFT • 1915 • Reehm George E. • USA
HIS BIRTHDAY GIFT • 1916 • *Rolma* • SHT • USA
HIS BIRTHDAY JACKET • 1912 • *Essanay* • USA
HIS BIRTHRIGHT • 1918 • Worthington William • USA
HIS BITTER FATE • 1917 • *Binns George* • USA
HIS BITTER HALF • 1950 • Freleng Friz • ANS • USA
HIS BITTER LESSON • 1915 • Batley Ethyle • UKN
HIS BITTER PILL • 1916 • Fishback Fred C. • SHT • USA
HIS BLOOMING BLOOMERS • 1918 • *Diamond* • SHT • USA
HIS BLOWOUT • 1916 • Dillon John Francis • SHT • USA
HIS BLUSHING BRIDE • 1916 • *Leary Nolan* • USA
HIS BODY FOR RENT • 1919 • Lyons Eddie, Moran Lee • SHT • USA
HIS BODY GUARD • 1915 • Hotaling Arthur D. • USA
HIS BOGUS BOAST • 1917 • Williamson Robin E. • SHT • USA
HIS BOGUS UNCLE • 1911 • Salter Harry • USA
HIS BOMB POLICY • 1917 • Parrott Charles • SHT • USA
HIS BONDED WIFE • 1918 • Brabin Charles J. • USA
HIS BRAND • 1913 • *Julian Rupert* • USA
HIS BRAVE DEFENDER • 1901 • Paul Robert William • UKN
HIS BREACH OF DISCIPLINE • 1910 • *Edison* • USA
HIS BREAD AND BUTTER • 1916 • Cline Eddie, Mann Hank • SHT • USA
HIS BRIDAL FRIGHT • 1940 • Lord Del • SHT • USA
HIS BRIDAL NIGHT • 1919 • Webb Kenneth • USA
HIS BRIDAL SWEET • 1934 • Goulding Alf • SHT • USA
HIS BROTHER • 1913 • *Bison* • USA
HIS BROTHER BILL • 1914 • Ince John • USA
HIS BROTHER FROM BRAZIL see **ADAM AND EVIL** • 1927
HIS BROTHER WILLIE • 1912 • *Powers* • USA
HIS BROTHER'S BLOOD • 1914 • Carleton Lloyd B. • USA
HIS BROTHER'S DEBT • 1915 • Otto Henry • USA
HIS BROTHER'S DOUBLE • 1911 • *Lubin* • USA
HIS BROTHER'S GHOST • 1945 • Newfield Sam • USA
HIS BROTHER'S KEEPER • 1913 • *Nestor* • USA
HIS BROTHER'S KEEPER • 1915 • *Kb* • USA
HIS BROTHER'S KEEPER • 1915 • O'Sullivan Tony • *Ab* • USA
HIS BROTHER'S KEEPER • 1916 • Daly William Robert • SHT • USA
HIS BROTHER'S KEEPER • 1921 • North Wilfred • USA
HIS BROTHER'S KEEPER • 1939 • Neill R. William • UKN
HIS BROTHER'S KEEPER see **PHILIP HOLDEN -WASTER** • 1916
HIS BROTHER'S PAL • 1916 • Wilson Ben • SHT • USA
HIS BROTHER'S REDEMPTION • 1916 • *Lily* • USA
HIS BROTHER'S SIN • 1916 • *Lily* • SHT • USA
HIS BROTHER'S WIFE • 1914 • Clark Jack J. • USA
HIS BROTHER'S WIFE • 1915 • Buckland Warwick • UKN
HIS BROTHER'S WIFE • 1916 • Knoles Harley • USA
HIS BROTHER'S WIFE • 1936 • Van Dyke W. S. • USA • LADY OF THE TROPICS (UKN)
HIS BROTHER'S WIFE see **HERO, THE** • 1923
HIS BROTHER'S WIVES • 1913 • *Nestor* • USA
HIS BUDDY • 1919 • *Morrison Pete* • SHT • USA
HIS BUDDY'S WIFE • 1925 • Terriss Tom • USA • HIS PAL'S WIFE
HIS BUNKIE • 1915 • Belmore Lionel • USA
HIS BURGLAR BROTHER • 1912 • Coleby A. E.? • UKN
HIS BUSTED TRUST • 1916 • Cline Eddie • SHT • USA
HIS BUSY DAY • 1917 • *Triangle* • USA
HIS BUSY DAY • 1918 • Rains Fred • UKN
HIS BUSY DAY • 1918 • Roach Hal • SHT • USA
HIS BUSY HOLIDAY see **NIPPER'S BUSY HOLIDAY** • 1915
HIS BUTLER'S SISTER • 1943 • Borzage Frank • USA
HIS CALL see **YEVO PRIZYV** • 1925
HIS CANNIBAL WIFE • 1917 • *La Salle* • USA
HIS CAPTIVE • 1915 • Lloyd Frank • USA
HIS CAPTIVE WOMAN • 1929 • Fitzmaurice George • USA • STRANDED IN PARADISE
HIS CAREER • 1912 • *Powers* • USA
HIS CHANCE TO MAKE GOOD • 1912 • *Duncan William* • USA
HIS CHANGE OF HEART • 1914 • Reehm George E. • USA
HIS CHEAP WATCH • 1907 • Mottershaw Frank • UKN
HIS CHILDREN • 1913 • O'Neil Barry • USA
HIS CHILDREN'S CHILDREN • 1923 • Wood Sam • USA
HIS CHILD'S CAPTIVE • 1910 • *Lubin* • USA
HIS CHINESE FRIEND • 1913 • Melies Gaston • USA
HIS CHOICE • 1913 • von Herkomer Hubert • UKN
HIS CHORUS GIRL WIFE • 1911 • Salter Harry • USA
HIS CHORUS GIRL WIFE • 1913 • *Nicholls George* • USA
HIS CHORUS GIRL WIFE • 1914 • Miller Ashley • USA
HIS CHUM, THE BARON • 1913 • Nicholls George, Sennett Mack (Spv) • USA
HIS CODE OF HONOR • 1913 • *Myers Harry* • USA
HIS COLLEGE PROXY • 1918 • *Burns Neal* • SHT • USA
HIS COLLEGE WIFE • 1915 • MacMackin Archer • USA
HIS COMING-OUT PARTY • 1917 • Beaudine William • SHT • USA
HIS COMRADE'S WIFE • 1914 • Ridgely Richard • USA
HIS CONQUERED SELF • 1915 • *Balboa* • USA
HIS CONSCIENCE • 1911 • Bouwmeester Theo • UKN
HIS CONSCIENCE • 1913 • *Lubin* • USA
HIS CONSCIENCE • 1913 • *Frontier* • USA
HIS CONSCIOUS CONSCIENCE • 1916 • Semon Larry • SHT • USA
HIS CONVERT • 1915 • Ridgely Richard • USA
HIS CONVICT BRIDE • 1918 • Gavin John F. • ASL
HIS COOK LADY • 1912 • *Majestic* • USA
HIS COOL NERVE • 1917 • *Mccoy Harry* • USA
HIS COOLING COURTSHIP • 1915 • *Lane Lupino* • UKN
HIS COUNTRY (UKN) see **SHIP COMES IN, A** • 1928

HIS COUNTRY'S BIDDING see **CALL, THE** • 1914
HIS COUNTRY'S HONOUR • 1914 • Calvert Charles • UKN • AVIATOR SPY, THE (USA)
HIS CRAZY JOB • 1913 • *Lyons Eddie* • USA
HIS CRIMINAL CAREER • 1915 • Reehm George E. • USA
HIS CRIMINAL CAREER • 1917 • *Triangle* • USA
HIS CROOKED CAREER • 1913 • Sennett Mack • USA
HIS CROOKED CAREER • 1917 • *Schade Fritz* • SHT • USA
HIS CRUCIBLE • 1915 • *Craig Nell* • USA
HIS CURIOSITY • 1917 • Drew Sidney, Drew Sidney Mrs. • SHT • USA
HIS DAREDEVIL QUEEN see **MABEL AT THE WHEEL** • 1914
HIS DARK CHAPTER see **WHAT A MAN!** • 1930
HIS DARKER SELF • 1924 • Noble John W. • USA
HIS DATE WITH GWENDOLINE • 1913 • *Pathe* • USA
HIS DAUGHTER • 1911 • Griffith D. W. • USA
HIS DAUGHTER • 1912 • *Mcdermott Marc* • USA
HIS DAUGHTER • 1913 • Kirkwood James • USA
HIS DAUGHTER AND HIS GOLD • 1906 • Fitzhamon Lewin • UKN
HIS DAUGHTER IS PETER (USA) see **SEINE TOCHTER IST DER PETER** • 1936
HIS DAUGHTER PAYS • 1918 • Trinchera Paul • USA
HIS DAUGHTERS • 1909 • *Maufacturers Film Agency* • UKN
HIS DAUGHTER'S BRACELET • 1911 • *Pathe* • USA
HIS DAUGHTER'S CHOICE • 1912 • *Art Films* • UKN
HIS DAUGHTER'S DILEMMA • 1916 • Dewsbury Ralph • UKN
HIS DAUGHTER'S LEGACY • 1910 • *Pantograph* • USA
HIS DAUGHTER'S LOYALTY • 1912 • *Powers* • USA
HIS DAUGHTER'S SECOND HUSBAND • 1916 • *Medusa Film* • USA
HIS DAUGHTER'S VOICE • 1907 • Booth W. R. • UKN
HIS DAY • 1912 • *Adolfi John* • USA
HIS DAY OF DOOM • 1918 • *Triangle* • USA
HIS DAY OF FREEDOM • 1913 • *Reliance* • USA
HIS DAY OF GLORY see **SUA GIORNATA DI GLORIA, LA** • 1968
HIS DAY OF REST • 1908 • *Bitzer Billy (Ph)* • USA
HIS DAY OUT • 1918 • Gillstrom Arvid E. • SHT • USA
HIS DEADLY CALM • 1917 • Drew Sidney, Drew Sidney Mrs. • SHT • USA
HIS DEADLY UNDERTAKING • 1917 • *Triangle Komedy* • USA
HIS DEAREST FOES • 1914 • *Essanay* • USA
HIS DEAREST POSSESSION • 1919 • Edwards Henry • UKN
HIS DEBT • 1919 • Worthington William • USA • DEBT, THE
HIS DESPERATE DEED • 1915 • O'Sullivan Tony • USA
HIS DESTINY • 1928 • Hart Neal • CND • NORTH OF 49 DEGREES (USA)
HIS DETERMINATION REWARDED • 1912 • *Eclair* • USA
HIS DISENGAGEMENT RING • 1918 • *Bevan Billy* • SHT • USA
HIS DISGUISED PASSION • 1917 • *Millican Bob* • SHT • USA
HIS DIVORCED WIFE • 1919 • Gerrard Douglas • USA
HIS DOCTOR'S ORDERS • 1914 • Franey William • USA
HIS DOG • 1927 • Brown Karl • USA
HIS DOG-GONE LUCK • 1914 • *Lyons Eddie* • USA
HIS DOLL WIFE • 1915 • Smallwood Ray C. • USA
HIS DOMINANT PASSION • 1914 • *Baird Leah* • USA
HIS DOUBLE • 1911 • *Tress Henry (P)* • UKN
HIS DOUBLE • 1912 • *Solax* • USA
HIS DOUBLE • 1915 • *Terriss Feature* • USA
HIS DOUBLE DID IT • 1915 • *C.k.* • USA
HIS DOUBLE EXPOSURE • 1919 • *Strand* • SHT • USA
HIS DOUBLE FLIVVER • 1917 • *Triangle* • USA
HIS DOUBLE LIFE • 1917 • Drew Sidney, Drew Sidney Mrs. • SHT • USA
HIS DOUBLE LIFE • 1918 • *Griffith Ray* • SHT • USA
HIS DOUBLE LIFE • 1933 • Hopkins Arthur, De Mille William C. • USA
HIS DOUBLE SURPRISE • 1913 • *Gem* • USA
HIS DOUBLE TREASURE • 1911 • *Yankee* • USA
HIS DREAM • 1911 • *Reliance* • USA
HIS DREAM FULFILLED • 1914 • *Melies* • USA
HIS DRESS REHEARSAL • 1914 • *Frontier* • USA
HIS DRESS SHIRT • 1911 • *Pickford Mary* • USA
HIS DRESS SUIT • 1912 • *Majestic* • USA
HIS DUKESHIP, MR. JACK • 1916 • Williams C. Jay • SHT • USA
HIS DUMB WIFE • 1911 • *Solax* • USA
HIS DUTY • 1909 • Griffith D. W., Powell Frank • USA
HIS DUTY • 1910 • *Powers* • USA
HIS DUTY • 1912 • Rains Fred • UKN
HIS EAR FOR MUSIC • 1917 • Drew Sidney, Drew Sidney Mrs. • SHT • USA
HIS EGYPTIAN AFFINITY • 1915 • Christie Al • USA
HIS EMERGENCY WIFE • 1915 • *Hale Alan* • USA
HIS ENEMY • 1913 • Brabin Charles J. • USA
HIS ENEMY • 1914 • *Princess* • USA
HIS ENEMY THE LAW • 1918 • Wells Raymond • USA
HIS ENEMY'S FRIEND • 1922 • Maloney Leo, Beebe Ford • USA
HIS ENGLISH WIFE see **HANS ENGELSKA FRU** • 1927
HIS ERROR • 1930 • Roberts Stephen • SHT • USA
HIS EX MARKS THE SPOT • 1940 • White Jules • SHT • USA
HIS EXCELLENCY • 1914 • Powell Paul • USA
HIS EXCELLENCY • 1952 • Hamer Robert • UKN
HIS EXCELLENCY see **YEVO PREVOSHODITIELSTVO** • 1927
HIS EXCELLENCY see **EXCELLENSEN** • 1944
HIS EXCELLENCY see **JEHO EXCELENCE**
HIS EXCELLENCY'S ADJUDANT • 1972 • Tashkov Yevgyeni • USS
HIS EXCITING NIGHT • 1938 • Meins Gus • USA
HIS EXONERATION • 1911 • *Lubin* • USA
HIS EXTRA BIT • 1918 • *Davenport Dorothy* • SHT • USA
HIS FAIRY GODMOTHER • 1915 • Van Wally • SHT • USA
HIS FAITH IN HUMANITY • 1914 • *Garwood William* • USA
HIS FAITHFUL FURNITURE • 1911 • *Lux* • FRN
HIS FAITHFUL SERVANT • 1913 • *Rex* • USA
HIS FALSE FRIEND • 1916 • *Puritan* • USA
HIS FAMILY TREE • 1917 • Curtis Allen • SHT • USA
HIS FAMILY TREE • 1935 • Vidor Charles • USA
HIS FATAL BEAUTY • 1917 • Beaudine William • SHT • USA
HIS FATAL BITE • 1920 • *Gayety* • USA
HIS FATAL FATE • 1918 • *Marks Lou* • SHT • USA
HIS FATAL MOVE • 1917 • *Bacon Lloyd* • USA
HIS FATAL SHOT • 1915 • Physioc Wray • USA
HIS FATE'S REHEARSAL • 1912 • *Prior Herbert* • USA
HIS FATHER • 1913 • *Frontier* • USA
HIS FATHER'S BUGLE • 1912 • *Kelly Louise* • USA
HIS FATHER'S CHOICE • 1912 • *Hotely Mae* • USA
HIS FATHER'S CRIME see **HANS FADERS BROTT** • 1915
HIS FATHER'S DEPUTY • 1913 • Duncan William • USA
HIS FATHER'S FOOTSTEPS • 1915 • Sterling Ford, Parrott Charles • USA
HIS FATHER'S HOUSE • 1911 • *Nestor* • USA
HIS FATHER'S HOUSE • 1914 • *Moreno Antonio* • USA
HIS FATHER'S RIFLE • 1915 • Le Saint Edward J. • USA
HIS FATHER'S SIN • 1915 • Kellino W. P. • UKN
HIS FATHER'S SON • 1912 • *Thanhouser* • USA
HIS FATHER'S SON • 1912 • *Vitagraph* • USA
HIS FATHER'S SON • 1914 • *Kerrigan J. Warren* • USA
HIS FATHER'S SON • 1917 • Baker George D. • USA
HIS FATHER'S VOICE: MRS. KELLY • 1913 • Booth W. R.? • UKN
HIS FATHER'S WIFE • 1913 • *Thompson Dave* • USA
HIS FATHER'S WIFE • 1919 • Crane Frank H. • USA
HIS FAVORITE PASTIME • 1914 • Nicholls George • USA • BARE HEAD, THE
HIS FEROCIOUS PAL (UKN) see **FEROCIOUS PAL, THE** • 1934
HIS FIGHT • 1914 • Campbell Colin • USA
HIS FIGHTING BLOOD • 1915 • Santschi Thomas • USA
HIS FIGHTING BLOOD • 1935 • English James W. • USA
HIS FINAL BLOW OUT • 1917 • Mann Hank • SHT • USA
HIS FIREMAN'S CONSCIENCE • 1914 • O'Sullivan Tony • USA
HIS FIRST AND LAST APPEARANCE • 1912 • *Powers* • USA
HIS FIRST AUTO • 1912 • *Lubin* • USA
HIS FIRST CAR • 1930 • Banks Monty • UKN • GEORGE CLARK IN HIS FIRST CAR
HIS FIRST CASE • 1913 • *American* • USA
HIS FIRST CASE • 1914 • *Shumway L. C.* • USA
HIS FIRST CASE • 1933 • Horne James W. • SHT • USA
HIS FIRST CIGAR, PROBABLY THE LAST • 1902 • Smith G. A. • UKN
HIS FIRST COMMAND • 1929 • La Cava Gregory • USA
HIS FIRST COMMISSION • 1911 • *Edison* • USA
HIS FIRST EXPERIENCE • 1913 • Hotaling Arthur D. • USA
HIS FIRST EXPERIMENT IN CHEMISTRY • 1908 • *Warwick Trading Co.* • UKN
HIS FIRST FALSE STEP • 1916 • Campbell William • SHT • USA
HIS FIRST FLAME • 1927 • Edwards Harry J. • USA
HIS FIRST GIRL • 1909 • Baker George D. • USA
HIS FIRST JOB • 1908 • Melies Georges • FRN
HIS FIRST KODAK • 1913 • *Rice Herbert* • USA
HIS FIRST LONG TROUSERS • 1911 • *Selig* • USA
HIS FIRST LOVE • 1914 • *Majestic* • USA
HIS FIRST LOVE • 1918 • Drew Sidney, Drew Sidney Mrs. • SHT • USA
HIS FIRST MONOCLE see **MIN FORSTE MONOCLE** • 1911
HIS FIRST PATIENT • 1911 • *Imp* • USA
HIS FIRST PATIENT see **FORSTE HONORAR, DET** • 1912
HIS FIRST PERFORMANCE • 1913 • France Charles H. • USA
HIS FIRST PLACE • 1910 • *Warwick* • UKN
HIS FIRST RIDE • 1914 • *Selig* • USA
HIS FIRST SILK HAT • 1906 • Mottershaw Frank • UKN
HIS FIRST SKATE • 1912 • *Lubin* • USA
HIS FIRST SOVEREIGN • 1912 • Melford Mark • UKN
HIS FIRST TOOTH • 1916 • Drew Sidney • SHT • USA
HIS FIRST TOP HAT • 1907 • Martin J. H.? • UKN
HIS FIRST TRIP • 1911 • *Brower Robert* • USA
HIS FIRST VALENTINE • 1910 • *Edison* • USA
HIS FIRST VISIT TO WARSAW • 1908 • *Fertner Antoni* • PLN
HIS FISHY FOOTSTEPS • 1917 • *Jaxon* • USA
HIS FLESH AND BLOOD • 1914 • *Whitman Features* • USA
HIS FLIRTING WAYS • 1917 • Christie Al • SHT • USA
HIS FOOT-HILL FOLLY • 1917 • *Griffith Ray* • USA
HIS FOREIGN WIFE • 1927 • McCarthy John P. • USA
HIS FORGOTTEN WIFE • 1924 • Seiter William A. • USA • LOST
HIS FRIEND JIMMY • 1913 • *Nestor* • USA
HIS FRIEND, THE BURGLAR • 1911 • Salter Harry • USA
HIS FRIEND, THE CAPTAIN • 1915 • *Pathe Exchange* • USA
HIS FRIEND, THE ELEPHANT • 1916 • Christie Al • USA
HIS FRIEND, THE UNDERTAKER • 1913 • *Nestor* • USA
HIS FRIEND'S TIP • 1919 • Lyons Eddie, Moran Lee • SHT • USA
HIS FRIEND'S WIFE • 1911 • Baker R. E. • USA
HIS GENEROSITY • 1918 • Drew Sidney, Drew Sidney Mrs. • SHT • USA
HIS GIRL FRIDAY • 1940 • Hawks Howard • USA
HIS GIRLIE • 1911 • *Lubin* • USA
HIS GLORIOUS NIGHT • 1929 • Barrymore Lionel • USA • BREATH OF SCANDAL
HIS GLORIOUS ROMANCE (UKN) see **COME ON COWBOYS!** • 1924
HIS GOLDEN GRAIN • 1915 • Davis Ulysses • USA
HIS GOLDEN HOME • 1916 • Clements Roy • SHT • USA
HIS GOLDEN ROMANCE • 1918 • Van Deusen Courtlandt • SHT • USA
HIS GOOD INTENTIONS • 1912 • *Nestor* • USA
HIS GOOD NAME • 1915 • Reynolds Lynn • USA
HIS GOOD NAME see **TRIFLING WITH HONOR** • 1923
HIS GRACE GIVES NOTICE • 1924 • Kellino W. P. • UKN
HIS GRACE GIVES NOTICE • 1933 • Cooper George A. • UKN
HIS GRACE'S LAST TESTAMENT (UKN) see **HANS NADS TESTAMENTE** • 1919
HIS GRACE'S WILL see **HANS NADS TESTAMENTE** • 1940
HIS GRACE'S WILL (USA) see **HANS NADS TESTAMENTE** • 1919
HIS GRANDCHILD • 1914 • Miller Ashley • USA
HIS GRANDSON • 1913 • *All-British Films* • UKN
HIS GRATITUDE • 1914 • *Imp* • USA
HIS GREAT ADVENTURE (USA) see **SU GRAN AVENTURA** • 1938
HIS GREAT CHANCE • 1923 • *Burns Sandy* • USA
HIS GREAT MOMENT see **SENTENCE OF DEATH, THE** • 1927
HIS GREAT OPPORTUNITY • 1914 • Buckland Warwick? • UKN
HIS GREAT SACRIFICE • 1911 • *Atlas* • USA
HIS GREAT SACRIFICE • 1911 • *Yankee* • USA
HIS GREAT TRIUMPH • 1916 • Nigh William • USA • NOTORIOUS GALLAGHER
HIS GREAT UNCLE'S SPIRIT • 1912 • *Ober George* • USA
HIS GREATEST BATTLE • 1925 • Horner Robert J. • USA
HIS GREATEST GAMBLE • 1934 • Robertson John S. • USA • FAMILY MAN
HIS GREATEST MATCH see **HANS LIVS MATCH** • 1932
HIS GREATEST ROLE see **SENECHAL LE MAGNIFIQUE** • 1957
HIS GREATEST SACRIFICE • 1921 • Edwards J. Gordon • USA
HIS GREATEST VICTORY • 1913 • Lessey George A. • USA
HIS GUARDIAN ANGEL • 1915 • *Fuller Mary* • USA
HIS GUARDIAN ANGEL • 1916 • *Palette Eugene* • SHT • USA
HIS GUARDIAN ANGEL see **HANS GODE GENIUS** • 1920
HIS GUARDIAN AUTO • 1915 • *Cruze James* • USA
HIS GUIDING ANGEL • 1915 • *Clary Charles* • USA
HIS GUIDING SPIRIT • 1914 • Martin E. A. • USA
HIS GYPSY SWEETHEART • 1910 • *Powers* • USA
HIS HAIR RAISING TALE • 1951 • Freleng Friz • ANS • USA
HIS HALTED CAREER • 1914 • Wright Walter • USA
HIS HAND AND SEAL • 1915 • MacDonald J. Farrell • USA
HIS HAND SLIPPED see **SE LE PASO LA MANO** • 1952
HIS HARD JOB • 1916 • Currier Frank • SHT • USA
HIS HEART, HIS HAND AND HIS SWORD • 1914 • Johnston Lorimer, Hamilton G. P. • USA
HIS HELL-REVOLVER see **YATSUNO KENJU WA JIGOKUDAZE** • 1958
HIS HEREAFTER • 1916 • Jones F. Richard • SHT • USA
HIS HEROINE • 1913 • *Thanhouser* • USA
HIS, HERS see **TEU, TUA** • 1981
HIS, HERS AND THEIRS see **YOURS, MINE AND OURS** • 1968
HIS HIDDEN PURPOSE • 1918 • *Conklin Chester* • SHT • USA
HIS HIDDEN SHAME • 1918 • *Keystone* • SHT • USA
HIS HIDDEN TALENT • 1917 • *Triangle* • USA
HIS HIGHNESS • 1916 • Foote Mr. • UKN
HIS HIGHNESS THE JANITOR • 1916 • Curtis Allen • SHT • USA
HIS HOME COMING • 1915 • Lessey George A. • USA
HIS HOME SWEET HOME • 1919 • Semon Larry • SHT • USA
HIS HONOR THE MAYOR • 1913 • Thompson Frederick A. • USA
HIS HONOUR AT STAKE • 1912 • Haldane Bert? • UKN
HIS HOODOO • 1913 • Dillon Eddie • USA
HIS HOUR • 1924 • Vidor King • USA
HIS HOUR OF MANHOOD • 1914 • Barker Reginald? • USA
HIS HOUR OF TRIUMPH • 1913 • Tucker George Loane • USA
HIS HOUSE IN ORDER • 1920 • Ford Hugh • USA
HIS HOUSE IN ORDER • 1928 • Ayrton Randle • UKN
HIS HOUSE IN ORDER OR THE WIDOW'S QUEST • 1913 • North Wilfred • USA
HIS HOUSEHOLD BUTTERFLY • 1917 • *Triangle* • USA
HIS HUNTING TRIP • 1910 • *Essanay* • USA
HIS I.O.U. • 1915 • *Thanhouser* • USA
HIS IDEAL OF POWER • 1913 • *August Edwin* • USA
HIS IMAGINARY CRIME • 1910 • *Bison* • USA
HIS IMAGINARY FAMILY • 1913 • *Ostriche Muriel* • USA
HIS INDIAN BRIDE • 1910 • *Champion* • USA
HIS INDIAN GUARDIAN • 1916 • *Sunset* • USA
HIS INDIAN NEMESIS • 1914 • *Kalem* • USA
HIS INDIAN WIFE • 1916 • *Hiawatha* • SHT • USA
HIS INNOCENT DUPE see **SJAELETYVEN** • 1915
HIS INSPIRATION • 1913 • Cabanne W. Christy? • USA
HIS INSPIRATION • 1914 • *Moore Tom* • USA
HIS IVORY DOME • 1916 • Walsh James O. • USA
HIS IVORY WEDDING ANNIVERSARY • 1919 • *Klever Pictures* • SHT • USA
HIS JAZZ BRIDE • 1926 • Raymaker Herman C. • USA
HIS JONAH DAY • 1920 • Robbins Jess • SHT • USA
HIS JUNGLE SWEETHEART • 1915 • Warren Giles R. • USA
HIS JUST DESERTS • 1914 • Lawrence Gerald • UKN
HIS KID SISTER • 1914 • Davis Ulysses • USA
HIS KIND OF WOMAN • 1951 • Farrow John, Fleischer Richard (U/c) • USA
HIS LADY see **WHEN A MAN LOVES** • 1927
HIS LADY (UKN) see **WHEN A MAN LOVES** • 1920
HIS LAND • 1987 • Collier James F. • USA
HIS LAST ADVENTURE (UKN) see **BATTLING BUCKAROO** • 1932
HIS LAST APPEAL • 1914 • Martin E. A. • USA
HIS LAST BET • 1913 • *Thanhouser* • USA
HIS LAST BOW • 1923 • Ridgwell George • UKN
HIS LAST BULLET • 1928 • *Hoxie Al* • USA
HIS LAST BURGLARY • 1910 • Griffith D. W. • USA
HIS LAST BURGLARY • 1911 • Bouwmeester Theo • UKN
HIS LAST CALL • 1914 • Johnson Tefft • USA
HIS LAST CENT • 1911 • *Costello Maurice* • USA
HIS LAST CHANCE • 1914 • Crane Frank H. • USA
HIS LAST CROOKED DEAL • 1911 • *Champion* • USA
HIS LAST CROOKED DEAL • 1913 • *King Henry* • USA
HIS LAST DEAL • 1913 • *Majestic* • USA
HIS LAST DEAL • 1915 • *Wilson Tom* • USA
HIS LAST DEFENCE • 1919 • Wilmer Geoffrey • UKN
HIS LAST DOLLAR • 1910 • Griffith D. W.?, Powell Frank? • USA
HIS LAST DOLLAR • 1914 • *Higgins David* • USA
HIS LAST FALSE STEP • 1919 • Jones F. Richard • SHT • USA
HIS LAST FIGHT • 1913 • Ince Ralph • USA
HIS LAST FLING • 1935 • Lamont Charles • SHT • USA
HIS LAST GAMBLE • 1913 • *White Pearl* • USA
HIS LAST GAME • 1909 • *Imp* • USA
HIS LAST GAME OF DEATH see **GOODBYE, BRUCE LEE** • 1975
HIS LAST HAUL • 1928 • Neilan Marshall • USA • PIOUS CROOKS (UKN) ○ LAST HAUL, THE
HIS LAST LAUGH • 1916 • Wright Walter • SHT • USA
HIS LAST PARADE • 1911 • *Lubin* • USA
HIS LAST PERFORMANCE • 1915 • *Big U* • USA
HIS LAST PILL • 1917 • *Compson Betty* • SHT • USA
HIS LAST RACE • 1923 • Eason B. Reeves, Mitchell Howard M. • USA
HIS LAST SCENT • 1916 • Avery Charles • USA
HIS LAST SERENADE • 1915 • Lloyd Frank • USA
HIS LAST TRICK • 1915 • Lloyd Frank • USA
HIS LAST TWELVE HOURS (USA) see **E PIU FACILE CHE UN CAMMELLO** • 1950

HIS LAST WILL see **DALEKA JEST DROGA** • 1963
HIS LAST WISH • 1915 • Morrisey Edward • USA
HIS LATE EXCELLENCY see **SELIGE EXZELLENZ, DIE** • 1927
HIS LEADING LADY • 1916 • *Rancho* • USA
HIS LESSON • 1912 • Griffith D. W. • USA
HIS LESSON • 1915 • *Siegmann George* • USA
HIS LESSON • 1917 • Smith David • SHT • USA
HIS LIFE • 1912 • *August Edwin* • USA
HIS LIFE FOR HIS EMPEROR • 1913 • Humphrey William • USA
HIS LITTLE GIRL • 1909 • *Lubin* • USA
HIS LITTLE INDIAN MODEL • 1912 • *Gray Betty* • USA
HIS LITTLE LORDSHIP • 1915 • Watts Tom • UKN
HIS LITTLE PAGE • 1914 • Brooke Van Dyke • USA
HIS LITTLE PAL • 1914 • *Greeson Elsie* • USA
HIS LITTLE PARTNER • 1912 • *Nestor* • USA
HIS LITTLE ROOM-MATE • 1917 • De Haven Carter • SHT • USA
HIS LITTLE SISTER • 1909 • *Wrench Films* • UKN
HIS LITTLE SISTER • 1912 • *Lubin* • USA
HIS LITTLE SON WAS WITH HIM ALL THE TIME • 1910 • Stow Percy • UKN
HIS LITTLE SPIRIT • 1917 • Drew Sidney • SHT • USA
HIS LITTLE STORY • 1916 • Moore Matt • SHT • USA
HIS LITTLE WIFE • 1916 • Beaumont Harry • SHT • USA
HIS LORDSHIP • 1910 • *Powers* • USA
HIS LORDSHIP • 1915 • Tucker George Loane • UKN
HIS LORDSHIP • 1916 • McKim Edwin • SHT • USA
HIS LORDSHIP • 1932 • Powell Michael • UKN
HIS LORDSHIP • 1936 • Mason Herbert • UKN • MAN OF AFFAIRS (USA) ○ MAN OF AFFAIRES ○ NELSON TOUCH, THE
HIS LORDSHIP, BILLY SMOKE • 1913 • Thornby Robert T. • USA
HIS LORDSHIP GOES TO PRESS • 1938 • Rogers Maclean • UKN
HIS LORDSHIP REGRETS • 1938 • Rogers Maclean • UKN
HIS LORDSHIP, THE VALET • 1912 • *Northrup Harry* • USA
HIS LORDSHIP'S DILEMMA • 1915 • *Fields W.c.* • USA
HIS LORDSHIP'S HUNTING TRIP • 1911 • *Bison* • USA
HIS LORDSHIP'S ROMANCE • 1913 • *Patheplay* • USA
HIS LORDSHIP'S WHITE FEATHER • 1912 • Blache Alice • USA
HIS LOSING DAY • 1915 • *Ab* • USA
HIS LOST LOVE • 1909 • Griffith D. W. • USA
HIS LOVE FIGHT • 1917 • Mann Hank • SHT • USA
HIS LOVE OF CHILDREN • 1912 • Kirkwood James • USA
HIS LOVING SPOUSE • 1914 • Henderson Dell • USA
HIS LOYAL HIGHNESS (UKN) see **HIS ROYAL HIGHNESS** • 1932
HIS LUCKLESS LOVE • 1915 • Henderson Dell • USA
HIS LUCKY BLUNDER • 1920 • Morris Charles • SHT • USA
HIS LUCKY DAY • 1914 • *Crystal* • USA
HIS LUCKY DAY • 1916 • Currier Frank • SHT • USA
HIS LUCKY DAY • 1929 • Cline Eddie • USA
HIS LUCKY DAY • 1934 • Christie Al • USA
HIS LUCKY VACATION • 1915 • Davey Horace • USA
HIS LYING HEART • 1916 • Sterling Ford, Avery Charles • SHT • USA
HIS MADONNA • 1912 • *Barker Florence* • USA
HIS MAIDEN AUNT • 1913 • Martinek H. O.? • UKN
HIS MAJESTY AND CO • 1935 • Kimmins Anthony • UKN
HIS MAJESTY BUNKER BEAN • 1918 • Taylor William D. • USA
HIS MAJESTY, BUNKER BEAN • 1925 • Beaumont Harry • USA
HIS MAJESTY BUNKER BEAN (UKN) see **BUNKER BEAN** • 1936
HIS MAJESTY DICK TURPIN • 1916 • Ford Francis • SHT • USA • BEHIND THE MASK
HIS MAJESTY MR. JONES see **PRIMA COMMUNIONE** • 1950
HIS MAJESTY O'KEEFE • 1954 • Haskin Byron • UKN
HIS MAJESTY THE AMERICAN • 1919 • Henabery Joseph • USA
HIS MAJESTY THE KING • 1915 • *Hulette Gladys* • USA
HIS MAJESTY THE OUTLAW • 1924 • Jaccard Jacques • USA
HIS MAJESTY, THE SCARECROW OF OZ • 1914 • MacDonald J. Farrell • USA • NEW WIZARD OF OZ, THE
HIS MAJESTY WILL HAVE TO WAIT see **HANS MAJESTAT FAR VANTA** • 1945
HIS MAJESTY'S DATES see **MIT CSINALT FELSEGED 3 – 5 – 19?** • 1964
HIS MAJESTY'S FIELD MARSHALL see **C. A. K. POLNI MARSALEK** • 1930
HIS MAJESTY'S GUESTS STEAL A HOLIDAY • 1910 • *Barker Will (P)* • UKN
HIS MAJESTY'S RIVAL see **HANS MAJESTATS RIVAL** • 1943
HIS MARRIAGE FAILURE • 1917 • *Binns George H.* • USA
HIS MARRIAGE MIXUP • 1935 • Black Preston • SHT • USA
HIS MARRIAGE WOW • 1925 • *Sennett Mack (P)* • SHT • USA
HIS MARRIED LIFE • 1916 • *West Billy* • SHT • USA
HIS MASTERPIECE • 1909 • Merwin Bannister • USA
HIS MASTERPIECE • 1912 • *Selig* • USA
HIS MASTERPIECE • 1915 • *Johnson Emory* • USA
HIS MASTERPIECE • 1916 • Ricketts Thomas • SHT • USA
HIS MASTER'S BREATH • 1920 • Fishback Fred C. • SHT • USA
HIS MASTER'S SON • 1911 • *Essanay* • USA
HIS MASTER'S VOICE • 1904 • *Warwick Trading Co.* • UKN
HIS MASTER'S VOICE • 1910 • Martinek H. O. • UKN
HIS MASTER'S VOICE • 1919 • *Vernon Bobby* • USA
HIS MASTER'S VOICE • 1925 • Hoffman Renaud • USA
HIS MATRIMONIAL MOANS • 1918 • *Barks Lou* • SHT • USA
HIS MEAL TICKET • 1921 • Cline Eddie • SHT • USA
HIS MERRY MIX-UP • 1917 • *Christie* • USA
HIS MERRY MIX-UP • 1917 • Parrott Charles • *Fox* • SHT • USA
HIS MESSAGE • 1912 • Ince Thomas H. • USA
HIS MEXICAN BRIDE • 1909 • *Centaur* • USA
HIS MEXICAN SWEETHEART • 1912 • *Pathe* • USA
HIS MIDDLE NAME WAS TROUBLE • 1915 • *Banner* • USA
HIS MILITARY FIGURE • 1917 • Jackson Harry • SHT • USA
HIS MIND'S TRAGEDY • 1911 • *Powers* • USA
HIS MIS-STEP • 1920 • Davey Horace • SHT • USA
HIS MISJUDGEMENT • 1911 • *Conness Robert* • USA
HIS MISTAKE • 1912 • *Hawley Ormi* • USA
HIS MISTRESS • 1984 • Rich David Lowell • TVM • USA
HIS MODEL WIFE • 1917 • *Ham Harry* • USA
HIS MORAL CODE • 1916 • Calvert E. H. • SHT • USA
HIS MOST DIFFICULT PART see **HANS VANSKELIGSTE ROLLE** • 1912
HIS MOTHER • 1910 • *Champion* • USA
HIS MOTHER • 1911 • *Vitagraph* • USA
HIS MOTHER • 1912 • Olcott Sidney • USA
HIS MOTHER-IN-LAW'S VISIT • 1913 • France Charles H. • USA
HIS MOTHER'S BIRTHDAY • 1913 • *Shay W. E.* • USA
HIS MOTHER'S BOY • 1916 • Kelsey Fred A. • SHT • USA
HIS MOTHER'S BOY • 1917 • Schertzinger Victor • USA • MOTHER'S BOY
HIS MOTHER'S HOME • 1914 • Physioc Wray • USA
HIS MOTHER'S HOPE • 1912 • *Lessey George* • USA
HIS MOTHER'S HOUSE see **SIN MORS HUS** • 1973
HIS MOTHER'S HYMN • 1911 • *Solax* • USA
HIS MOTHER'S LETTER • 1910 • *Powers* • USA
HIS MOTHER'S LOVE • 1913 • *Imp* • USA
HIS MOTHER'S NECKLACE • 1910 • Bouwmeester Theo • UKN
HIS MOTHER'S PICTURE • 1912 • *Nilsson Anna Q.* • USA
HIS MOTHER'S PORTRAIT • 1915 • Borzage Frank • USA
HIS MOTHER'S PORTRAIT: OR, THE SOLDIER'S VISION • 1900 • Fitzhamon Lewin • UKN
HIS MOTHER'S SACRIFICE • 1915 • Batley Ethyle • UKN
HIS MOTHER'S SCARF • 1911 • Griffith D. W. • USA
HIS MOTHER'S SHROUD • 1912 • *Vitagraph* • USA
HIS MOTHER'S SON • 1912 • Cabanne W. Christy • USA
HIS MOTHER'S SON • 1913 • Griffith D. W. • USA
HIS MOTHER'S SONG • 1913 • *Shay W. E.* • USA
HIS MOTHER'S THANKSGIVING • 1910 • Porter Edwin S. • USA
HIS MOTHER'S TRUST • 1914 • Crisp Donald • USA
HIS MOUSE FRIDAY • 1951 • Hanna William, Barbera Joseph • ANS • USA
HIS MOVE • 1905 • *Bitzer Billy (Ph)* • USA
HIS MOVIE MUSTACHE • 1917 • *Vim* • USA
HIS MUSICAL CAREER • 1914 • Chaplin Charles • USA • MUSICAL TRAMPS ○ PIANO MOVERS, THE
HIS MUSICAL SNEEZE • 1919 • White Jack • SHT • USA
HIS MUSICAL SOUL • 1912 • *Solax* • USA
HIS MYSTERIOUS ADVENTURE (USA) see **SEINE FRAU, DIE UNBEKANNTE** • 1923
HIS MYSTERIOUS NEIGHBOR • 1915 • Otto Henry • USA
HIS MYSTERIOUS PROFESSION • 1915 • MacMackin Archer • USA
HIS MYSTERY GIRL • 1923 • Hill Robert F. • USA • ALL FOR THE LOVE OF GLORIA ○ NO QUESTIONS ASKED
HIS NAME IS BLAZEJ REJDAK see **NAZYWA SIE BLAZEJ REJDAK, MIESZKA W ROZNICY, W JEDRZEJOWSKIM POWIECIE** • 1969
HIS NAME IS ROBERT see **YEVO ZOVUT ROBERT** • 1967
HIS NAME IS SUKHE-BATOR see **YEVO ZOVUT SUKHE-BATOR** • 1942
HIS NAME WAS FEDOR • 1963 • Lisakovitch Viktor • DOC • USS
HIS NAME WAS KING (USA) see **LO CHIAMAVANO KING** • 1971
HIS NAME WAS MADRON (UKN) see **MADRON** • 1970
HIS NAUGHTY NIGHT • 1920 • *Banks Monty* • SHT • USA
HIS NAUGHTY THOUGHT • 1917 • Fishback Fred C. • SHT • USA
HIS NAUGHTY WIFE • 1919 • Heerman Victor • SHT • USA
HIS NEIGHBOR'S PANTS • 1914 • *Warner'S Features* • USA
HIS NEIGHBOR'S WIFE • 1912 • *Powers* • USA
HIS NEIGHBOR'S WIFE • 1913 • Porter Edwin S. • USA
HIS NEIGHBOR'S WIFE • 1916 • Davey Horace • SHT • USA
HIS NEMESIS • 1914 • McGowan J. P. • USA
HIS NEPHEW'S SCHEME • 1913 • Seay Charles M. • USA
HIS NEW AUTOMOBILE • 1915 • Lessey George A. • USA
HIS NEW FAMILY • 1910 • *Edison* • USA
HIS NEW JOB • 1914 • *Sterling* • USA
HIS NEW JOB • 1915 • Chaplin Charles • USA
HIS NEW LID • 1910 • Powell Frank?, Griffith D. W.? • USA
HIS NEW MAMA • 1910 • Fitzhamon Lewin? • UKN
HIS NEW MAMMA • 1924 • Del Ruth Roy • SHT • USA
HIS NEW PROFESSION • 1914 • Chaplin Charles • USA • GOOD FOR NOTHING, THE ○ HELPING HIMSELF
HIS NEW STENOGRAPHER • 1928 • *Sennett Mack (P)* • SHT • USA
HIS NEW WIFE • 1911 • *Imp* • USA
HIS NEW YORK WIFE • 1926 • Kelley Albert • USA
HIS NIBS • 1921 • La Cava Gregory • USA
HIS NIECE FROM IRELAND • 1913 • Johnson Arthur • USA
HIS NIGHT OUT • 1914 • *Joker* • USA
HIS NIGHT OUT • 1915 • *Ab* • USA
HIS NIGHT OUT • 1935 • Nigh William • USA
HIS NIGHT OUT see **THEIR NIGHT OUT** • 1933
HIS NIMBLE TWIST • 1918 • *Triangle* • USA
HIS NINE LIVES • 1918 • *Triangle* • USA
HIS NOBS, THE DUKE • 1915 • *Nestor* • USA
HIS NOBS THE PLUMBER • 1913 • *Mace Fred* • USA
HIS NOISY STILL • 1920 • Del Ruth Roy • SHT • USA
HIS OBLIGATION • 1915 • Bertram William • USA
HIS OFF DAY • 1938 • Rasinski Connie • ANS • USA
HIS OFFICIAL FIANCEE • 1919 • Vignola Robert G. • USA
HIS OFFICIAL FIANCEE see **HANS OFFICIELLA FASTMO** • 1944
HIS OLD-FASHIONED DAD • 1913 • *Leonard Robert* • USA
HIS OLD-FASHIONED DAD • 1917 • *Gilfether Daniel* • USA
HIS OLD-FASHIONED MOTHER • 1913 • Dwan Allan • USA
HIS OLD PAL'S SACRIFICE • 1914 • *West Charles H.* • USA
HIS ONE AND ONLY • 1916 • *Hippo* • USA
HIS ONE NIGHT STAND • 1917 • *Triangle* • USA
HIS ONLY CHANCE • 1918 • *Conant Captain* • ASL
HIS ONLY CHILD • 1910 • *Essanay* • USA
HIS ONLY DAUGHTER • 1910 • Bouwmeester Theo? • UKN
HIS ONLY FATHER • 1919 • Roach Hal • SHT • USA
HIS ONLY FRIEND • 1909 • Fitzhamon Lewin • UKN
HIS ONLY PAIR • 1902 • *Paul R. W.* • UKN
HIS ONLY PAIR OF TROUSERS • 1907 • Coleby A. E.? • UKN
HIS ONLY PANTS • 1915 • Lyons Eddie • USA
HIS ONLY SON • 1912 • Fahrney Milton, Conway Jack • USA
HIS OTHER SELF • 1912 • *Baggot King* • USA
HIS OTHER WIFE • 1921 • Nash Percy • UKN
HIS OTHER WOMAN (UKN) see **DESK SET, THE** • 1957
HIS OWN BLOOD • 1913 • *August Edwin* • USA
HIS OWN FAULT • 1912 • Sennett Mack • USA
HIS OWN HERO • 1915 • Henderson Dell • USA
HIS OWN HOME TOWN • 1918 • Schertzinger Victor • USA
HIS OWN LAW • 1920 • Read J. Parker • USA
HIS OWN LAW • 1924 • *Barry Wesley* • USA
HIS OWN LAWYER • 1925 • Buckingham Thomas • USA
HIS OWN MEDICIN • 1919 • *Parsons Smiling Bill* • SHT • USA
HIS OWN NEMESIS • 1916 • Chaudet Louis W. • SHT • USA
HIS OWN PEOPLE • 1918 • Earle William P. S. • USA
HIS OWN STORY • 1916 • Lessey George A. • SHT • USA
HIS PAIR OF PANTS • 1912 • *Lubin* • USA
HIS PAJAMA GIRL • 1920 • Edwards Harry J. • USA
HIS PAL'S GAL • 1920 • Ridgwell George • SHT • USA
HIS PAL'S REQUEST • 1913 • *Madison Cleo* • USA
HIS PAL'S WIFE see **HIS BUDDY'S WIFE** • 1925
HIS PARISIAN WIFE • 1919 • Chautard Emile • USA
HIS PARTNER'S SACRIFICE • 1915 • French Charles K. • USA
HIS PARTNER'S SHARE • 1912 • *Melies* • USA
HIS PARTNER'S SHARE • 1912 • *Bison* • USA
HIS PARTNER'S WIFE • 1912 • *Republic* • USA
HIS PEASANT PRINCESS • 1915 • Castle James W. • USA
HIS PEOPLE • 1925 • Sloman Edward • USA • PROUD HEART ○ JEW, THE
HIS PERFECT DAY • 1917 • *Triangle* • USA
HIS PERFECT DAY • 1917 • Drew Sidney • *Drew* • SHT • USA
HIS PEST FRIEND • 1938 • Goodwins Leslie • SHT • USA
HIS PHANTOM BURGLAR • 1915 • Aylott Dave? • UKN
HIS PHANTOM SWEETHEART • 1915 • Ince Ralph • USA
HIS PICTURE • 1916 • Garwood William • SHT • USA
HIS PICTURE IN THE PAPERS • 1916 • Emerson John • USA
HIS POOR LITTLE GIRL • 1915 • Morrisey Edward • USA
HIS PRECIOUS LIFE • 1917 • Raymaker Herman C. • SHT • USA
HIS PREHISTORIC BLUNDER • 1922 • Hutchinson Craig • USA
HIS PREHISTORIC PAST • 1914 • Chaplin Charles • USA • DREAM, A ○ KING CHARLIE ○ CAVEMAN, THE
HIS PRICELESS TREASURE • 1913 • Curtis Allen • USA
HIS PRIDE AND SHAME • 1916 • Sterling Ford, Parrott Charles • SHT • USA
HIS PRIOR CLAIM • 1914 • *Ab* • USA
HIS PRIVATE LIFE • 1926 • Arbuckle Roscoe • USA
HIS PRIVATE LIFE • 1928 • Tuttle Frank • USA
HIS PRIVATE SECRETARY • 1933 • Whitman Phil • USA
HIS PRIVATE WIFE • 1920 • *Conklin Chester* • USA
HIS PROMISE • 1916 • *Utah* • SHT • USA
HIS PUNCTURED REPUTATION • 1918 • *Franey William* • SHT • USA
HIS PUNISHMENT • 1912 • French Charles K. • USA
HIS PUNISHMENT • 1914 • *Majestic* • USA
HIS PUPPY LOVE • 1921 • Reisner Charles F. • SHT • USA
HIS QUAKER GIRL • 1918 • *Rhodes Billie* • USA
HIS REAL CHARACTER • 1915 • Franz Joseph J. • USA
HIS REAL WIFE see **HANS RIGTIGE KONE** • 1917
HIS REDEMPTION • 1913 • *Lubin* • USA
HIS REFORMATION • 1909 • *Anderson Broncho Billy* • USA
HIS REFORMATION • 1914 • Holmes-Gore Arthur • UKN
HIS REGENERATION • 1915 • Anderson G. M., Chaplin Charles • USA
HIS RESPONSIBILTY • 1914 • *Hunt Irene* • USA
HIS REST DAY • 1927 • Cooper George A. • UKN
HIS RETURN • 1915 • Walsh Raoul • USA
HIS RETURN • 1916 • Madison Cleo • SHT • USA
HIS REVENGE • 1910 • *Powers* • USA
HIS REWARD • 1913 • *Lubin* • USA
HIS REWARD • 1914 • Sullivan Frederick • USA
HIS RISE AND TUMBLE • 1917 • *Triangle* • USA
HIS RISE TO FAME • 1927 • McEveety Bernard F. • USA • RISING TO FAME (UKN)
HIS RIVAL • 1916 • Drew Sidney • SHT • USA
HIS ROBE OF HONOR • 1918 • Ingram Rex • USA
HIS ROMANCE • 1911 • *Yankee* • USA
HIS ROMANCE • 1911 • *Yankee* • USA
HIS ROMANTIC WIFE • 1913 • *Crystal* • USA
HIS ROMANY WIFE • 1915 • *Hale Alan* • USA
HIS ROYAL HIGHNESS • 1911 • *Imp* • USA
HIS ROYAL HIGHNESS • 1918 • Blackwell Carlyle • USA
HIS ROYAL HIGHNESS • 1932 • Thring F. W. • ASL • HIS LOYAL HIGHNESS (UKN)
HIS ROYAL NIBS • 1918 • *Evans Charles* • SHT • USA
HIS ROYAL PANTS • 1914 • *Nestor* • USA
HIS ROYAL SHYNESS • 1932 • Pearce A. Leslie • SHT • USA
HIS ROYAL SLYNESS • 1919 • Roach Hal • SHT • USA
HIS SACRIFICE • 1913 • *American* • USA
HIS SACRIFICE • 1913 • *Thanhouser* • USA
HIS SAD AWAKENING • 1915 • Ransom Charles • USA
HIS SALAD DAYS • 1918 • Rains Fred • UKN
HIS SAVING GRACE • 1917 • *Sutherland Eddie* • USA
HIS SCARLET CLOAK see **AKAI JINBAORI** • 1958
HIS SCARLET PAST • 1919 • *Strand* • SHT • USA
HIS SECOND CHANCE • 1913 • *Britannia* • UKN
HIS SECOND CHILDHOOD • 1914 • Avery Charles • USA
HIS SECOND CHILDHOOD • 1914 • Calvert Charles? • UKN
HIS SECOND CHOICE • 1911 • *Nestor* • USA
HIS SECOND LOVE • 1912 • *Pathe* • USA
HIS SECOND WIFE • 1910 • *Imp* • USA
HIS SECOND WIFE • 1911 • *Yankee* • USA
HIS SECOND WIFE • 1912 • *Powers* • USA
HIS SECOND WIFE • 1913 • Ince Ralph • USA
HIS SECRET • 1913 • Powell Frank • USA
HIS SECRET • 1916 • Hertz Aleksander • PLN
HIS SECRET SIN • 1912 • Coleby A. E.? • UKN
HIS SECRETARY • 1912 • *Ogle Charles* • USA
HIS SECRETARY • 1925 • Henley Hobart • USA
HIS SENSE OF DUTY • 1912 • Barker Reginald • USA
HIS SENSE OF DUTY • 1914 • *Melies* • USA
HIS SERGEANT'S STRIPES • 1910 • Melies Gaston • USA
HIS SERVANT • 1914 • Lund O. A. C. • USA
HIS SICK FRIEND • 1910 • Salter Harry • USA
HIS SIDE PARD • 1912 • *Nestor* • USA
HIS SILENT RACKET • 1933 • *Chase Charley* • SHT • USA
HIS SILVER BACHELORHOOD • 1913 • Brooke Van Dyke • USA
HIS SINGULAR LESSON • 1915 • Coyle Walter • USA

HIS SISTER • 1913 • *Selig* • USA
HIS SISTER • 1913 • *Rex* • USA
HIS SISTER-IN-LAW • 1910 • Griffith D. W., Powell Frank • USA
HIS SISTER LUCIA • 1913 • *American* • USA
HIS SISTER'S CHAMPION • 1916 • Collins John H. • USA
HIS SISTER'S CHILDREN • 1911 • *Vitagraph* • USA
HIS SISTER'S HONOUR • 1914 • Haldane Bert? • UKN
HIS SISTER'S KIDDIES • 1915 • *Badgley Helen* • USA
HIS SISTER'S KIDS • 1913 • Thornby Robert T. • USA
HIS SISTER'S SWEETHEART • 1911 • Blache Alice • USA
HIS SMASHING CAREER • 1915 • *Sterling Ford* • USA
HIS SMASHING CAREER • 1917 • *Ritchie Billie* • SHT • USA
HIS SMOTHERED LOVE • 1918 • Cline Eddie • SHT • USA
HIS SOB STORY • 1914 • *Wilson Ben* • USA
HIS SOCIAL RISE • 1917 • *Triangle* • USA
HIS SON • 1911 • *Reliance* • USA
HIS SON • 1911 • Haldane Bert? • UKN
HIS SON-IN-LAW • 1913 • *Swayne Marian* • USA
HIS SOUL MATE • 1915 • *Clayton Ethel* • USA
HIS SPANISH WIFE • 1910 • *Lubin* • USA
HIS SPEEDY FINISH • 1917 • *Perrin Jack* • USA
HIS "SPRING OVERCOAT" • 1912 • *Cines* • ITL
HIS SQUAW • 1912 • Giblyn Charles • USA
HIS STEP-MOTHER • 1912 • *Trunnelle Mabel* • USA
HIS STOLEN FORTUNE • 1914 • *Bushman Francis X.* • USA
HIS STRENGTH OF MIND • 1918 • Drew Sidney, Drew Sidney Mrs. • SHT • USA
HIS STRENUOUS HONEYMOON • 1914 • *Lyons Eddie* • USA
HIS STRENUOUS VISIT • 1916 • *Myers Harry* • SHT • USA
HIS STUBBORN WAY • 1911 • *Lubin* • USA
HIS SUDDEN RECOVERY • 1914 • *Lubin* • USA
HIS SUDDEN RIVAL • 1917 • *Dillon Jack* • USA
HIS SUICIDE • 1914 • Hevener Jerold T. • USA
HIS SUPERFICIAL WIFE • 1915 • *Edwards Walter* • USA
HIS SUPERIOR OFFICER • 1904 • Fitzhamon Lewin • UKN
HIS SUPREME MOMENT • 1925 • Fitzmaurice George • USA
HIS SUPREME MOMENT see **SPORTING VENUS, THE** • 1925
HIS SUPREME SACRIFICE see **CALL OF THE EAST, THE** • 1922
HIS SWEETHEART • 1917 • Crisp Donald • USA
HIS SWEETHEART WHEN A BOY • 1907 • Cooper Arthur? • UKN
HIS SWEETHEART'S BIRTHDAY • 1908 • *Norwood* • USA
HIS TAKING WAYS • 1914 • Wright Walter • USA
HIS TAKING WAYS • 1917 • *Dillon Jack* • USA
HIS TALE IS TOLD • 1944 • Edwards Harry J. • SHT • USA
HIS TALENTED WIFE • 1914 • Parrott Charles • USA
HIS TEMPER-MENTAL MOTHER-IN-LAW • 1916 • *L-Ko* • SHT • USA
HIS TEMPORARY AFFAIR (UKN) see **EX-BAD BOY** • 1931
HIS TEMPORARY WIFE • 1920 • Levering Joseph • USA
HIS TERRIBLE LESSON • 1911 • Melies Gaston • USA
HIS THANKLESS JOB • 1917 • *Bacon Lloyd* • USA
HIS THREE BRIDES • 1915 • Metcalfe Earl • USA
HIS THRIFTY WIFE • 1912 • *Essanay* • USA
HIS TICKLISH JOB • 1917 • Parrott Charles • SHT • USA
HIS TIGER LADY • 1928 • Henley Hobart • USA • NIGHT OF MYSTERY, A
HIS TIME WILL COME • 1956 • Begalin Mazhit • USS
HIS TIRED UNCLE • 1913 • North Wilfred • USA
HIS TRADE • 1912 • *Lubin* • USA
HIS TRUST • 1911 • Griffith D. W. • USA
HIS TRUST see **DARING CHANCES** • 1924
HIS TRUST FULFILLED • 1911 • Griffith D. W. • USA
HIS TRYSTING PLACE • 1914 • Chaplin Charles • USA • FAMILY HOUSE, THE ○ FAMILY HOME
HIS TURNING POINT • 1915 • *Joy Leatrice* • USA
HIS TWIN • 1915 • *Royal* • USA
HIS TWIN BROTHER • 1913 • *Barnett Chester* • USA
HIS TWO CHILDREN • 1909 • *Bison* • USA
HIS TWO DAUGHTERS see **KOHLHIESELS TOCHTER** • 1920
HIS TWO LOVES see **PUCCINI** • 1953
HIS TWO PATIENTS • 1915 • *Benham Harry* • USA
HIS UNCLE DUDLEY • 1917 • Jones F. Richard, O'Brien Don • SHT • USA
HIS UNCLE'S DECEPTION • 1914 • *Melies* • USA
HIS UNCLE'S HEIR • 1913 • Lewis Edgar • USA
HIS UNCLE'S WARD • 1916 • *Mason Sydney* • SHT • USA
HIS UNCLE'S WILL • 1914 • *Leonard Robert* • USA
HIS UNCLE'S WIVES • 1913 • *Darnell Jean* • USA
HIS UNCONSCIOUS CONSCIENCE • 1917 • *Fay Hugh* • SHT • USA
HIS UNDESIRABLE RELATIVES • 1913 • Williams C. Jay • USA
HIS UNKNOWN GIRL • 1914 • Lambart Harry • USA
HIS UNKNOWN RIVAL • 1915 • Allen Frederick J. • UKN
HIS UNLUCKY JOB • 1921 • Enright Ray (c/d) • SHT • USA
HIS UNLUCKY NIGHT • 1928 • *Sennett Mack (P)* • SHT • USA
HIS UNTIMELY VISIT • 1910 • *Pantograph* • USA
HIS UNWITTING CONQUEST • 1914 • Physioc Wray • USA
HIS UPS AND DOWNS • 1913 • Sennett Mack • USA
HIS VACATION • 1910 • *Selig* • USA
HIS VACATION • 1911 • *Nestor* • USA
HIS VACATION • 1912 • *Lubin* • USA
HIS VACATION • 1913 • *Victor* • USA
HIS VACATION • 1914 • *Crystal* • USA
HIS VAMPY WAYS • 1919 • *Hall Walter* • SHT • USA
HIS VINDICATION (USA) see **KING'S OUTCAST, THE** • 1915
HIS VINEGAR BATH • 1918 • *Bret Tom* • USA
HIS VOCATION • 1915 • *De Carlton Grace* • USA
HIS WAITING CAREER • 1916 • *West Billy* • SHT • USA
HIS WARD'S LOVE • 1909 • Griffith D. W. • USA
HIS WARD'S SCHEME • 1915 • Morrisey Edward • USA
HIS WASHING DAY • 1905 • Cooper Arthur • UKN
HIS WATERY WATERLOO • 1917 • Donovan Frank P. • USA
HIS WAY OF WINNING HER • 1913 • *Mace Fred* • USA
HIS WEAK MOMENT • 1933 • Edwards Harry J. • SHT • USA
HIS WEAKNESS • 1912 • *Powers* • USA
HIS WEAKNESS CONQUERED • 1913 • *August Edwin* • USA
HIS WEDDED WIFE • 1914 • Humphrey William • USA
HIS WEDDING DAY • 1912 • *Majestic* • USA
HIS WEDDING DAY • 1914 • *Sterling Ford* • USA • FATAL WEDDING, THE
HIS WEDDING EVE • 1912 • *Santschi Thomas* • USA
HIS WEDDING MORN • 1908 • Coleby A. E. • UKN
HIS WEDDING NIGHT • 1916 • Christie Al • SHT • USA
HIS WEDDING NIGHT • 1917 • Arbuckle Roscoe • SHT • USA
HIS WEDDING NIGHT see **HANS BROLLOPSNATT** • 1916
HIS WEDDING PROMISE • 1916 • *Myers Harry* • SHT • USA
HIS WEEKEND • 1932 • Cline Eddie • SHT • USA
HIS WEEK'S PAY • 1910 • Stow Percy • UKN
HIS WESTERN WAY • 1912 • *Fielding Romaine* • USA
HIS WHITE LIE • 1916 • Coyle Walter • SHT • USA
HIS WICKED EYES • 1919 • Hutchinson Craig • SHT • USA
HIS WIDOW • 1913 • Hotaling Arthur D. • USA
HIS WIDOW'S MIGHT • 1917 • *Banks Monty* • USA
HIS WIFE • 1911 • *Nestor* • USA
HIS WIFE • 1914 • *Lubin* • USA
HIS WIFE • 1915 • Platt George Foster • USA
HIS WIFE AND HIS WORK • 1914 • Davis Ulysses • USA
HIS WIFE GOT ALL THE CREDIT • 1917 • Baker Graham • SHT • USA
HIS WIFE KNEW ABOUT IT • 1915 • Drew Sidney • USA
HIS WIFE'S AFFAIR see **NIGHT WATCH, THE** • 1928
HIS WIFE'S AFFINITY • 1913 • *Solax* • USA
HIS WIFE'S ALLOWANCE • 1916 • Smith David • SHT • USA
HIS WIFE'S BIRTHDAY • 1911 • *Urban Trading Co.* • UKN
HIS WIFE'S BIRTHDAY • 1919 • *Strand* • SHT • USA
HIS WIFE'S BIRTHDAY PRESENT • 1913 • *Kinemacolor* • USA
HIS WIFE'S BROTHER • 1910 • Bouwmeester Theo? • UKN
HIS WIFE'S BROTHER • 1912 • Coleby A. E. • UKN
HIS WIFE'S BURGLAR • 1913 • *Nestor* • USA
HIS WIFE'S BURGLAR • 1914 • Seay Charles M. • USA
HIS WIFE'S CALLER • 1920 • Blystone John G. • SHT • USA
HIS WIFE'S CHILD • 1913 • Salter Harry • USA
HIS WIFE'S FAMILY • 1914 • *Joker* • USA
HIS WIFE'S FLIRTATION • 1914 • *Sterling Ford* • USA
HIS WIFE'S FRIEND • 1918 • Wright Walter • SHT • USA
HIS WIFE'S FRIEND • 1920 • De Grasse Joseph • USA • WHITE ROCK, THE
HIS WIFE'S FRIENDS • 1913 • *Essanay* • USA
HIS WIFE'S GOOD NAME • 1916 • Ince Ralph • USA
HIS WIFE'S HABIT • 1970 • Houck Joy N. Jr. • USA • WOMEN AND BLOODY TERROR
HIS WIFE'S HERO • 1917 • Baker Graham • SHT • USA
HIS WIFE'S HUSBAND • 1915 • *Nestor* • USA
HIS WIFE'S HUSBAND • 1920 • Edwards Harry J. • SHT • USA
HIS WIFE'S HUSBAND • 1922 • Cooper George A. • UKN
HIS WIFE'S HUSBAND • 1922 • Webb Kenneth • USA
HIS WIFE'S HUSBAND see **MAZ SWOJEJ ZONY** • 1961
HIS WIFE'S INSURANCE • 1911 • *Solax* • USA
HIS WIFE'S JEALOUSY • 1912 • *Pathe* • USA
HIS WIFE'S LOVER see **ZEIN WEIB'S LIEBENIK** • 1931
HIS WIFE'S MISTAKE • 1916 • Arbuckle Roscoe • SHT • USA • WRONG MR. STOUT, THE
HIS WIFE'S MONEY • 1920 • Ince Ralph • USA
HIS WIFE'S MOTHER • 1909 • Griffith D. W. • USA
HIS WIFE'S MOTHER • 1912 • *Lubin* • USA
HIS WIFE'S MOTHER • 1916 • Drew Sidney • SHT • USA
HIS WIFE'S MOTHER • 1932 • Hughes Harry • UKN
HIS WIFE'S NEW LID • 1915 • Metcalfe Earl • USA
HIS WIFE'S OLD SWEETHEART • 1912 • *Pathe* • USA
HIS WIFE'S PAST • 1915 • *Blair Ruth* • USA
HIS WIFE'S PAST see **HANS HUSTRUS FORFLUTNA** • 1915
HIS WIFE'S PET • 1914 • Henderson Dell • USA
HIS WIFE'S RELATIVES • 1913 • *Vitagraph* • USA
HIS WIFE'S RELATIVES • 1917 • Chaudet Louis W. • SHT • USA
HIS WIFE'S SECRET • 1911 • *Tapley Rose* • USA
HIS WIFE'S SECRET • 1915 • *Anderson Broncho Billy* • USA
HIS WIFE'S STORY • 1915 • MacDonald J. Farrell • USA
HIS WIFE'S STRATAGEM • 1912 • Smalley Phillips • USA
HIS WIFE'S SWEETHEART • 1915 • Louis Will • USA
HIS WIFE'S SWEETHEARTS • 1910 • *Sennett Mack* • USA
HIS WIFE'S VISITOR • 1909 • Griffith D. W. • USA
HIS WIFE'S VISITOR • 1916 • *Gayety* • USA
HIS WILD OATS • 1916 • Sterling Ford, Badger Clarence • SHT • USA
HIS WINNING WAY • 1914 • *Princess* • USA
HIS WINNING WAY • 1917 • *Three C* • USA
HIS WOMAN • 1920 • Terwilliger George W. • SHT • USA
HIS WOMAN • 1931 • Sloman Edward • USA
HIS WOMAN see **THOSE WHO DANCE** • 1930
HIS WONDERFUL LAMP • 1913 • Collins Edwin J.? • UKN
HIS WOODEN LEG • 1916 • Davey Horace • SHT • USA
HIS WOODEN WEDDING • 1924 • McCarey Leo • SHT • USA
HIS WORD • 1915 • *Empire* • USA
HIS WORK OR HIS WIFE • 1909 • Stow Percy • UKN
HIS WORLD OF DARKNESS • 1916 • Wilson Ben • SHT • USA
HIS WORSHIP MR. MONTREAL: THE LIFE AND TIMES OF CAMILLIEN HOUDE • 1976 • Brittain Don, Canell Marrin, Duncan Robert • CND
HIS YANKEE GIRL • 1910 • *Powers* • USA
HIS YOUNG WIFE (USA) see **MISERIE DEL SIGNOR TRAVET, LE** • 1946
HIS YOUNGER BROTHER • 1911 • *Thanhouser* • USA
HIS YOUNGER BROTHER • 1913 • Calvert Charles? • UKN
HIS YOUNGER BROTHER • 1914 • *Frontier* • USA
HIS YOUNGER SISTER see **ANI IMOTO** • 1977
HIS YOUTHFUL FANCY • 1920 • Kenton Erle C. • SHT • USA
HISBISCUS TOWN see **FURONG ZHEN** • 1985
HISHAKAKU TO KIRATSUNE see **JINSEI GEKIJO -HISHAKAKU TO KIRATSUNE** • 1968
HISN, AL- • 1977 • Abdes-Salam Shadi • EGY • CITADELLE, LA
HISS AND MAKE UP • 1943 • Freleng Friz • ANS • USA
HISSHOKA • 1945 • Mizoguchi Kenji, Tasaka Tomotaka, Makino Masahiro, Shimazu • JPN • SONG OF VICTORY ○ HISSYO KA ○ VICTORY SONG
HISSYO KA see **HISSHOKA** • 1945
HIST! AT SIX O'CLOCK • 1916 • Christie Al • SHT • USA
HIST! SPIES • 1917 • Drew Sidney, Drew Sidney Mrs. • SHT • USA
HISTIRE GEOLOGIQUE DE LA CHAINE DES ALPES • 1958 • Painleve Jean • SHT • FRN
HISTOIRE A SUIVRE.. • 1986 • Beaudry Diane • MTV • CND
HISTOIRE COMIQUE see **FELICIE NANTEUIL** • 1942
HISTOIRE COMME UNE AUTRE, UNE • 1981 • Driessen Paul • ANM • CND • SAME OLD STORY, THE
HISTOIRE D'ADELE H., L' • 1975 • Truffaut Francois • FRN • STORY OF ADELE H., THE (USA)
HISTOIRE D'ADRIEN • 1980 • Denis Jean-Pierre • FRN
HISTOIRE D'AIMER see **HOMME QUI ME PLAIT, L'** • 1969
HISTOIRE D'ALLER PLUS LOIN • 1974 • Kanapa Jerome, Paul Bernard • DOC • FRN
HISTOIRE D'AMOUR, UNE • 1951 • Lefranc Guy • FRN • YOUNG LOVE
HISTOIRE D'AMOUR, UNE see **MARIE, LEGENDE HONGROISE** • 1932
HISTOIRE D'AMOUR, UNE see **LIEBELEI** • 1933
HISTOIRE D'AMOUR, UNE see **HIKAYAT HUBB** • 1959
HISTOIRE DE BICYCLETTES • 1953 • Roussel Emile • SHT • FRN
HISTOIRE DE CHANTER • 1946 • Grangier Gilles • FRN
HISTOIRE DE CHAPEAUX see **HISTOIRE D'UN CHAPEAU** • 1910
HISTOIRE DE CIVILISATION OCCIDENTALE • 1972 • Lamothe Arthur • DOC • CND
HISTOIRE DE FEMMES, UNE see **WIVES' TALE, A** • 1980
HISTOIRE DE FRANCE • 1933 • Masson Jean • SHS • FRN
HISTOIRE DE LA COMMUNICATION, UNE • 1965 • Hebert Pierre • ANS • CND
HISTOIRE DE LA POMME • 1982 • Renaud France Y. Y. • CND
HISTOIRE DE LA PRESSE AU QUEBEC • 1975 • Valcour Pierre • DCS • CND
HISTOIRE DE L'OEIL, L' (BLG) see **SIMONA** • 1974
HISTOIRE DE LOURDES • 1932 • Dekeukeleire Charles • BLG
HISTOIRE DE MINNA GLAESENS • 1913 • Machin Alfred • NTH
HISTOIRE DE MON AMOUR see **QISSAT HUBBI** • 1955
HISTOIRE DE NOTRE TERRE • 1970 • Cherif Hachemi • SHT • ALG
HISTOIRE DE PAUL • 1975 • Feret Rene • FRN
HISTOIRE DE PECHE • 1945 • Palardy Jean • DCS • CND
HISTOIRE DE PECHE • 1975 • Chabot Jean • DOC • CND
HISTOIRE DE PERLES see **BEAD GAME, THE** • 1977
HISTOIRE DE PIN-UP GIRLS • 1950 • Gibaud Marcel • SHT • FRN
HISTOIRE DE PUCE • 1909 • Feuillade Louis • FRN
HISTOIRE DE RIRE • 1941 • L'Herbier Marcel • FRN • FOOLISH HUSBANDS (USA)
HISTOIRE DE SINGES • 1949 • de Gastyne Marco • SHT • FRN
HISTOIRE DE VENT, UNE • 1988 • Ivens Joris • FRN, NTH • TALE OF THE WIND
HISTOIRE DE WAHARI • 1971 • Blanchet Vincent, Monod Jean • DOC • FRN
HISTOIRE DE WHISKY, UNE • 1961 • Regnier Michel • DCS • CND
HISTOIRE D'EAU • 1959 • Truffaut Francois, Godard Jean-Luc • SHT • FRN
HISTOIRE D'ELEPHANTS, UNE • 1958 • Rossif Frederic • SHT • FRN
HISTOIRE DES MOUVEMENTS DE JEUNESSE AU QUEBEC • 1976 • Valcour Pierre • DCS • CND
HISTOIRE DES SCHTROUMPFS • 1964 • Ryssack Eddy • ANS • BLG
HISTOIRE DES TREIZE see **LIEBE** • 1927
HISTOIRE D'O • 1959-61 • Anger Kenneth • FRN • STORY OF O, THE
HISTOIRE D'O, L' • 1975 • Jaeckin Just • FRN • STORY OF O, THE (USA)
HISTOIRE D'O (CHAPITRE II) • 1984 • Rochat Eric • FRN
HISTOIRE D'Q • 1975 • Kahn David • SWT • STORY OF Q, THE
HISTOIRE DU CAPORAL • 1983 • Baronnet Jean • FRN
HISTOIRE DU COSTUME • 1939 • Clement Rene • SHT • FRN
HISTOIRE DU FUTUR ANTERIEUR • 1969 • Cassendo Frank • SHT • FRN • STORY OF PREVIOUS FUTURE
HISTOIRE DU PALAIS IDEAL • 1954 • Baratier Jacques • FRN
HISTOIRE DU SOLDAT INCONNU • 1932 • Storck Henri • DOC • BLG • SOLDAT INCONNU, LE
HISTOIRE D'UN CHAPEAU • 1910 • Cohl Emile • ANS • FRN • HEADDRESSES OF DIFFERENT PERIODS ○ HISTOIRE DE CHAPEAUX
HISTOIRE D'UN CRIME • 1901 • Zecca Ferdinand • FRN
HISTOIRE D'UN CRIME • 1908 • Nonguet Lucien • FRN
HISTOIRE D'UN CRIME, L' see **INCENDAIRES, LES** • 1906
HISTOIRE D'UN FILM • 1954 • Herwig Hans • SHT • FRN
HISTOIRE D'UN GRAND PEUPLE • 1968 • Cherif Hachemi, Ifticene Mohamed • ALG
HISTOIRE D'UN HERITAGE, L' • 1961 • Shawqi Khalil • SHT • EGY
HISTOIRE D'UN OISEAU QUI N'ETAIT PAS POUR LE CHAT • 1975 • Peche Jean-Jacques, Mertens Pierre • BLG
HISTOIRE D'UN PAIN, L' • 1947 • Lavoie Hermenegilde • DCS • CND
HISTOIRE D'UN PETIT GARCON DEVENU GRAND • 1963 • Reichenbach Francois • SHT • FRN
HISTOIRE D'UN POISSON ROUGE • 1959 • Sechan Edmond • SHT • FRN • GOLDEN FISH, THE (USA) ○ STORY OF A GOLDEN FISH
HISTOIRE D'UN VALET DE CHAMBRE • 1912 • Perret Leonce • FRN
HISTOIRE D'UNE BIBITE • 1963 • Hebert Pierre • ANS • CND
HISTOIRE D'UNE CHAISE see **CHAIRY TALE, A** • 1957
HISTOIRE D'UNE FILLE NOMMEE MARMAR see **HIKAYATU BINT ISMAHA MARMAR** • 1972
HISTOIRE D'UNE VIE see **HIKAYAT AL-UMR KULLUH** • 1965
HISTOIRE EN GRIS • 1963 • Hebert Pierre • ANS • CND
HISTOIRE ENTRE MILLE, UNE • 1931 • de Rieux Max • FRN
HISTOIRE IMMORTELLE • 1968 • Welles Orson • FRN • IMMORTAL STORY
HISTOIRE SIMPLE, UNE • 1978 • Sautet Claude • FRN, FRG • SIMPLE STORY, A
HISTOIRE TRES BONNE ET TRES JOYEUSE DE COLINOT TROUSSE-CHEMISE, L' see **COLINOT TROUSSE CHEMISE** • 1973
HISTOIRES D'A • 1973 • Belmont Charles, Issartel Marielle • DOC • FRN
HISTOIRES D'AMERIQUE • 1989 • Akerman Chantal • BLG, FRN • AMERICAN STORIES FOOD FAMILY AND PHILOSOPHY

HISTOIRES DE FEMMES see **MENSONGES** • 1945
HISTOIRES DE LA REVOLUTION • 1970 • Mazif Sid-Ali, Laradji Rabah, Bedjaoui Ahmed • ALG
HISTOIRES DE Q • 1974 • Davy Jean-Francois • FRN, BLG, ITL • PRICKLY PROBLEMS ○ FRENCH TICKLER ○ STORY OF Q, THE ○ Q
HISTOIRES E CLOWN • Image Jean • ANM • FRN
HISTOIRES EXTRAORDINAIRES • 1949 • Faurez Jean • FRN • UNUSUAL TALES ○ ASYLUM OF HORROR
HISTOIRES EXTRAORDINAIRES • 1968 • Vadim Roger, Malle Louis, Fellini Federico • FRN, ITL • SPIRITS OF THE DEAD (USA) ○ TALES OF MYSTERY (UKN) ○ TROIS HISTOIRES EXTRAORDINAIRES D'EDGAR POE ○ THREE STRANGE STORIES OF EDGAR POE ○ STRANGE TALES ○ TRE PASSI NEL DELIRIO ○ STORIE STRAORDINARIE
HISTOIRES EXTRAORDINAIRES see **FUNF UNHEIMLICHE GESCHICHTEN** • 1933
HISTOIRES INSOLITES • 1974 • Chabrol Claude • MTV • FRN
HISTORIA COTIDIANA, LA • 1971 • Veitia Hector • DOC • CUB
HISTORIA DE AMOR, UNA • 1968 • Grau Jorge • SPN • LOVE STORY, A
HISTORIA DE BIENVENIDO, LA • 1964 • Fenollar Augusto • SPN
HISTORIA DE LAGARTOS • 1989 • Bustamente Juan Carlos • CHL • LIZARD STORIES
HISTORIA DE LISBOA POR IMAGENS • 1953 • Ribeiro Antonio Lopes • SHT • PRT
HISTORIA DE LOS REYES, UNA • 1988 • Marichal Poli • ANS • PRC • STORY OF THE MAGI, A
HISTORIA DE TRES HERMANAS • 1979 • Walerstein Mauricio • VNZ
HISTORIA DE UN AMOR • 1955 • Gavaldon Roberto • MXC
HISTORIA DE UN BALLET • 1960 • Massip Jose • DOC • CUB • HISTORY OF A BALLET, THE
HISTORIA DE UN BANCO DE VENEZUELA, LA • 1978 • Blanco Javier • DCS • VNZ • HISTORY OF A BANK IN VENEZUELA, THE
HISTORIA DE UN CANALLA • 1963 • Bracho Julio • MXC
HISTORIA DE UN CORAZON • 1950 • Bracho Julio • MXC
HISTORIA DE UN DOCUMENTO • 1971 • Menendez Oscar • MXC
HISTORIA DE UN GRAN AMOR • 1942 • Bracho Julio • MXC
HISTORIA DE UN HOMBRE • 1961 • Pamplona Clemente • SPN
HISTORIA DE UN MARIDO INFIEL • 1954 • Galindo Alejandro • MXC
HISTORIA DE UN ROBLE SOLO • 1982 • Caiozzi Silvio • CHL • STORY OF A SOLITARY ROBLES
HISTORIA DE UNA ABRIFIO DE MINK • 1954 • Gomez Muriel Emilio • MXC
HISTORIA DE UNA BATALLA • 1962 • Gomez Manuel Octavio • DOC • CUB • HISTORY OF A BATTLE ○ STORY OF A BATTLE
HISTORIA DE UNA CHICA SOLA • 1969 • Grau Jorge • SPN
HISTORIA DE UNA ESCALERA • 1950 • Iquino Ignacio F. • SPN
HISTORIA DE UNA TRAICION • 1972 • Nieves Conde Jose Antonio • SPN
HISTORIA DEL 1900 • 1949 • del Carril Hugo • ARG
HISTORIA DEL HIMNO NACIONAL see **MEXICANOS AL GRITO DE GUERRA** • 1943
HISTORIA DEL P.R.I. • 1972 • MXC • HISTORY OF THE P.R.I.
HISTORIA DEL TANGO, LA • 1950 • *Lamas Fernando* • ARG
HISTORIA DI UNA MALA MUJER • 1948 • Saslavsky Luis • ARG • LADY WINDERMERE'S FAN
HISTORIA DI UNA NOCHE • 1941 • Saslavsky Luis • ARG
HISTORIA EN DOS ALDEAS • 1950 • del Amo Antonio • SPN
HISTORIA ESTRICTAMENTE INMORAL, UNA see **CHELY** • 1976
HISTORIA JEDNOGO MYSLIWCA • 1958 • Drapella Hubert • PLN • STORY OF A FIGHTER PLANE, THE
HISTORIA NATURAE • 1967 • Svankmajer Jan • ANS • CZC
HISTORIA OFFICIAL, LA • 1984 • Puenzo Luis • ARG • OFFICIAL STORY, THE (USA) ○ OFFICIAL VERSION, THE (UKN) ○ OFFICIAL HISTORY
HISTORIA PERVERSA, UNA (SPN) see **UNA SULL'ALTRA** • 1969
HISTORIA WSPOLCZESNA • 1961 • Jakubowska Wanda • PLN • IT HAPPENED YESTERDAY ○ CONTEMPORARY HISTORY ○ CONTEMPORARY STORY
HISTORIA Y LA VIDA EXTRATERRESTRE, LA • 1975 • Atienza Juan G., Saavedra Alvaro • SPN
HISTORIA ZOLTEJ CIZEMKI • 1962 • Checinski Sylwester • PLN • STORY OF THE YELLOW BOOTEE, THE ○ YELLOW SLIPPERS, THE (USA)
HISTORIAS DE CIUDAD: ALGUIEN SE ACERCA • 1990 • Cervantes Ramon • MXC • CITY STORIES: SOMEONE'S COMING
HISTORIAS DE LA FERIA • 1957 • Rovira Beleta Francisco • SPN
HISTORIAS DE LA FIESTA • 1965 • Ozores Mariano • SPN
HISTORIAS DE LA RADIO • 1955 • Saenz De Heredia Jose Luis • SPN
HISTORIAS DE LA REVOLUCION • 1960 • Alea Tomas Gutierrez • CUB
HISTORIAS DE LA TELEVISION • 1965 • Saenz De Heredia Jose Luis • SPN
HISTORIAS DE MADRID • 1956 • Comas Ramon • SPN
HISTORIAS DEL CHUQUIAGO • 1976 • Eguino Antonio • BLV • STORIES FROM THE CHUQUIAGO ○ CHUQUIAGO
HISTORIAS PROHIBIDAS DE PULGARCITO • 1979 • Leduc Paul • DOC • MXC • FORBIDDEN TALES OF TOM THUMB
HISTORIAS SELVAGEMS • 1977 • Campos Antonio • PRT
HISTORICAL DAYS see **HISTORYCZNE DNI** • 1947
HISTORICAL FAN see **EVENTAIL ANIME, L'** • 1909
HISTORICAL ODDITIES • 1955 • *Smith Pete* • SHT • USA
HISTORIE FIKOVEHO LISTO • 1938 • *Hammid Alexander* • CZC • HISTORY OF THE FIG LEAF
HISTORIEN OM BARBARA • 1967 • Kjaerulff-Schmidt Palle • DNM • STORY OF BARBARA, THE
HISTORIEN OM EN MAND • 1944 • Roos Jorgen, Mertz Albert • DOC • DNM • STORY OF A MAN
HISTORIEN OM EN MODER • 1912 • Blom August • DNM • MODERS KAERLIGHED, EN ○ LIFE OF A MOTHER, THE
HISTORIEN OM EN MODER • 1979 • Weeke Claus • DNM • STORY OF A MOTHER
HISTORIEN OM ET FALL see **JULIA, JULIA -HISTORIEN OM ET FALL** • 1981
HISTORIEN OM ET SLOT J.F. WILLUMSEN • 1951 • Roos Jorgen • DOC • DNM • WILLUMSEN
HISTORIEN OM KIM SKOV • 1981 • Jorgensen Hans-Henrik • DNM • STORY OF KIM SKOV, THE
HISTORIEN OM LASSE OG GEIR • 1975 • Wam Svend • NRW • STORY OF LASSE AND GEIR, THE ○ LASSE OG GEIR
HISTORIES OF THE CHIVALROUS see **KYOKAKU RETSUDEN** • 1968
HISTORY • 1970 • Gehr Ernie • USA
HISTORY see **REKISHI** • 1940
HISTORY see **STORIA, LA** • 1986
HISTORY, AGE OF NUCLEAR MADNESS, THE see **REKISHI, KAKU KYORAN NO JIDAI** • 1984
HISTORY BEHIND WALLS see **KABE NO NAKANO HIMEGOTO** • 1965
HISTORY BOOK • Hastrup Jannik • ANM • DNM
HISTORY IS MADE AT NIGHT • 1937 • Borzage Frank • USA
HISTORY LESSONS see **GESCHICHTSUNTERRICHT** • 1973
HISTORY MAN, THE • 1981 • Knights Robert • MTV • UKN
HISTORY OF A BALLET, THE see **HISTORIA DE UN BALLET** • 1960
HISTORY OF A BANK IN VENEZUELA, THE see **HISTORIA DE UN BANCO DE VENEZUELA, LA** • 1978
HISTORY OF A BATTLE see **HISTORIA DE UNA BATALLA** • 1962
HISTORY OF A BUTTERFLY -A ROMANCE OF INSECT LIFE, THE • 1910 • Williamson James • UKN
HISTORY OF A LOAF • 1908 • *Spencer C. (P)* • ASL
HISTORY OF A STRUGGLE • 1977 • Cinema Action • UKN
HISTORY OF ADVENTURE • 1964 • Bass Saul • SHT • USA
HISTORY OF ALBERTFALVA, A see **ALBERTFALVAI TORTENET** • 1955
HISTORY OF ARMS see **TAPUM, LA STORIA DELLE ARMI** • 1958
HISTORY OF BEER • 1956 • Kawamoto Kihachiro • ANS • JPN
HISTORY OF BRUTALITY TO WOMEN, A • 1983 • Lee Doo-Yong • SKR
HISTORY OF CANBERRA • 1927 • ASL
HISTORY OF COAL, THE • Szabos Szabolcs • ANS • HNG
HISTORY OF COSTUME, A see **KOSTIMIRANI RENDEZ-VOUS** • 1965
HISTORY OF DHRUVA see **DHRUVA CHARITRA** • 1921
HISTORY OF INVENTIONS • 1960 • *Halas John (P)* • ANS • UKN
HISTORY OF INVENTIONS, THE see **STORIE DELLE INVENZIONI, LA** • 1959
HISTORY OF LU TING, THE see **LU TING CHI** • 1979
HISTORY OF MR. POLLY, THE • 1949 • Pelissier Anthony • UKN
HISTORY OF MOTION IN MOTION, THE • 1967 • Vanderbeek Stan • USA
HISTORY OF MOTOR RACING, A • 1964 • Mason Bill • DOC • UKN
HISTORY OF NUMBERS, THE see **SZAMOK TORTENETE, A** • 1962
HISTORY OF POSTWAR JAPAN AS TOLD BY A BAR HOSTESS see **NIPPON SENGOSHI -MADAMU ONBORO NO SEIKATSU** • 1970
HISTORY OF THE BLUE MOVIE, A • 1970 • De Renzy Alex • USA
HISTORY OF THE BURNING YEARS, THE see **POVEST PLAMENNYKH LET** • 1960
HISTORY OF THE CINEMA • 1956 • Halas John • ANS • UKN
HISTORY OF THE CIVIL WAR see **ISTORIYA GRAZHDENSKOI VOINI** • 1921
HISTORY OF THE ENGLISH WOOL TRADE • 1945-52 • Napier-Bell J. B. • DOC • UKN
HISTORY OF THE FIG LEAF see **HISTORIE FIKOVEHO LISTO** • 1938
HISTORY OF THE HELICOPTER, THE • 1951 • Erulkar Sarah • DOC • UKN
HISTORY OF THE JAPANESE UNDERWORLD, A see **NIPPON ANKOKUSHI: NASAKE MUYO** • 1968
HISTORY OF THE P.R.I. see **HISTORIA DEL P.R.I.** • 1972
HISTORY OF THE VATICAN, THE see **VATICANO DE PIO XII, EL** • 1941
HISTORY OF THE WORLD IN THREE MINUTES FLAT, THE • 1980 • Mills Michael • ANS • CND
HISTORY OF THE WORLD PART 1 • 1980 • Brooks Mel • USA
HISTORY OF WALTON, THE • 1953 • Daborn John • UKN
HISTORY OF WRITING, THE • 1948 • Martin-Jones John • DOC • UKN
HISTORY ON THE RUN: THE MEDIA AND THE '79 ELECTION • 1979 • Raymont Peter • DOC • UKN
HISTORY REPEATS ITSELF • 1910 • *Edison* • USA
HISTORYCZNE DNI • 1947 • Bossak Jerzy • DOC • PLN • HISTORICAL DAYS
HISTRIA, HERACLEA AND SWANS • 1968 • Bostan Ion • DOC • RMN
HIT! • 1973 • Furie Sidney J. • USA
HIT, THE • 1984 • Frears Stephen • UKN
HIT AND RUM • 1935 • Holmes Ben • SHT • USA
HIT AND RUN • 1924 • Sedgwick Edward • USA
HIT AND RUN • 1957 • Haas Hugo • USA
HIT AND RUN • Spry Robin • CND
HIT AND RUN • 1982 • Braverman Charles • USA • REVENGE SQUAD ○ TAXI
HIT AND RUN see **GAZOLAS** • 1955
HIT AND RUN see **HIKINIGE** • 1966
HIT-AND-RUN DRIVER • 1935 • Cahn Edward L. • SHT • USA
HIT HIM AGAIN • 1918 • Roach Hal • SHT • USA
HIT HIM AGAIN see **FATAL MALLET, THE** • 1914
HIT LADY • 1974 • Wynn Tracey Keenan • USA
HIT LIST • 1988 • Lustig William • USA
HIT MAN • 1972 • Armitage George • USA • STREET WARRIOR
HIT MAN, THE see **MEAN JOHNNY BURROWS** • 1976
HIT MAN, THE (UKN) see **SCOUMOUNE, LA** • 1973
HIT ME AGAIN (UKN) see **SMARTY** • 1934
HIT OF THE SHOW • 1928 • Ince Ralph • USA
HIT OR MISS • 1919 • Henderson Dell • USA
HIT PARADE, THE see **HIT PARADE OF 1937** • 1937
HIT PARADE OF 1937 • 1937 • Meins Gus • USA • I'LL REACH FOR A STAR ○ HIT PARADE, THE
HIT PARADE OF 1941, THE • 1940 • Auer John H. • USA
HIT PARADE OF 1943 • 1943 • Rogell Albert S. • USA • CHANGE OF HEART
HIT PARADE OF 1947 • 1947 • McDonald Frank • USA • HIGH AND HAPPY
HIT PARADE OF 1951 • 1950 • Auer John H. • USA • SONG PARADE
HIT TEAM, THE see **COMPANY OF KILLERS** • 1968
HIT THE DECK • 1930 • Reed Luther • USA
HIT THE DECK • 1955 • Rowland Roy • USA
HIT THE HAY • 1946 • Lord Del • USA
HIT THE HIGH SPOTS • 1924 • Roach Hal • SHT • USA
HIT THE ICE • 1943 • Lamont Charles, Kenton Erle C. (U/c) • USA • OH, DOCTOR ○ PARDON MY SKI
HIT THE ROAD • 1941 • May Joe • USA
HIT THE SADDLE • 1937 • Wright Mack V. • USA
HIT-THE-TRAIL HOLLIDAY • 1918 • Neilan Marshall • USA
HIT TUNE JAMBOREE • 1942 • Le Borg Reginald • SHT • USA
HIT TUNE SERENADE • 1943 • Le Borg Reginald • SHT • USA
HITCH-HIKE see **AUTOSTOP** • 1977
HITCH HIKE LADY • 1936 • Scotto Aubrey • USA • EVENTFUL JOURNEY (UKN)
HITCH HIKE TO HEAVEN • 1935 • Strayer Frank • USA • FOOTLIGHTS AND SHADOWS (UKN)
HITCH-HIKE TO HELL • 1978 • Berwick Irvin • USA • KIDNAPPED CO-ED
HITCH HIKER, THE • 1933 • Gillstrom Arvid E. • USA
HITCH-HIKER, THE • 1953 • Lupino Ida • USA • DIFFERENCE, THE
HITCH HIKERS • 1947 • Rasinski Connie • ANS • USA
HITCH-HIKERS, THE • 1984 • SAF
HITCH IN TIME, A • 1978 • Darnley-Smith Jan • UKN
HITCHED • 1971 • Sagal Boris • TVM • USA • WESTWARD THE WAGON (UKN)
HITCHER, THE • 1985 • Harmon Robert • USA
HITCHHIKE! • 1974 • Hessler Gordon • TVM • USA • CRISSCROSS
HITCHHIKE TO HAPPINESS • 1945 • Santley Joseph • USA
HITCHHIKE TO HAPPINESS (UKN) see **HERE COMES ELMER** • 1943
HITCHHIKER, THE • 1939 • Donnelly Eddie • ANS • USA
HITCHHIKER, THE • 1971 • Sefer Amos • ISR
HITCHHIKERS, THE • 1971 • Sebastian Ferdinand, Sebastian Beverly • USA
HITCHIN' POSTS • 1920 • Ford John • USA • LAND OF PROMISE, THE (UKN)
HITCHY-COO • 1916 • Aylott Dave? • UKN
HITCHY-KOO • 1913 • Collins Edwin J.? • UKN
HITLER • 1962 • Heisler Stuart • USA • WOMEN OF NAZI GERMANY
HITLER, A CAREER (USA) see **HITLER, EINE KARRIERE** • 1977
HITLER, A FILM FROM GERMANY see **HITLER: EIN FILM AUS DEUTSCHLAND** • 1977
HITLER -ATTENTATER MAURICE B • 1979 • Herman Villi, Sturm Hans, Meienberg Niklaus • SWT
HITLER -BEAST OF BERLIN (UKN) see **GOOSE STEP** • 1939
HITLER, CONNAIS PAS • 1962 • Blier Bertrand • FRN
HITLER -DEAD OR ALIVE • 1943 • Grinde Nick • USA
HITLER: EIN FILM AUS DEUTSCHLAND • 1977 • Syberberg Hans-Jurgen • FRG • HITLER, A FILM FROM GERMANY ○ OUR HITLER
HITLER, EINE KARRIERE • 1977 • Fest Joachim C., Herrendorfer Christian • FRG • HITLER, A CAREER (USA)
HITLER FROM AROUND THE CORNER see **HITLER IZ NASEG SOKAKA** • 1975
HITLER GANG, THE • 1944 • Farrow John • USA
HITLER IZ NASEG SOKAKA • 1975 • Tadej Vladimir • YGS • HITLER FROM AROUND THE CORNER
HITLER LIVES? • 1945 • Siegel Don • SHT • USA
HITLER: THE LAST TEN DAYS (UKN) see **ULTIMI DIECI GIORNI DI HITLER, GLI** • 1973
HITLERJUNGE QUEX • 1933 • Steinhoff Hans • FRG
HITLERJUNGE QUEX • 1935 • Stemmle R. A. • FRG
HITLER'S CHILDREN • 1943 • Dmytryk Edward • USA
HITLER'S EXECUTIONERS (USA) see **NURNBERGER PROZESS, DER** • 1958
HITLER'S GOLD see **INSIDE OUT** • 1975
HITLER'S HANGMAN see **HITLER'S MADMAN** • 1943
HITLER'S MADMAN • 1943 • Sirk Douglas • USA • HITLER'S HANGMAN
HITLER'S S.S.: PORTRAIT IN EVIL • 1985 • Goddard Jim • TVM • USA • HITLER'S S.S.: PORTRAIT OF EVIL
HITLER'S S.S.: PORTRAIT OF EVIL see **HITLER'S S.S.: PORTRAIT IN EVIL** • 1985
HITLER'S SON • 1978 • Amateau Rod • USA, FRG
HITMAN see **AMERICAN COMMANDOS** • 1985
HITO HADA KANNON • 1937 • Kinugasa Teinosuke • JPN • SACRED PROTECTOR, THE
HITO NO ISSHO, PARTS I, II & III • 1928 • Mizoguchi Kenji • JPN • LIFE OF MAN, THE (USA) ○ LIFE OF A MAN ○ MAN'S LIFE, A
HITO NO YO NO SUGATA • 1928 • Gosho Heinosuke • JPN • SITUATION OF THE HUMAN WORLD, THE ○ MAN'S WORLDLY APPEARANCE
HITO O KUTTA HANASHI • 1925 • Yamamoto Kajiro • JPN
HITOHADA KUJAKU • 1958 • Mori Issei • JPN
HITOHIRA NO YUKI • 1985 • Negishi Kichitaro • JPN • SNOWDROP, A
HITOKIRI • 1969 • Gosha Hideo • JPN • TENCHU
HITORI MUSUKO • 1930 • Ozu Yasujiro • JPN • ONLY SON, THE
HITORI NERU YO NO KONATSU • 1955 • Aoyagi Nobuo • JPN • TEARS OF THE GEISHA KONATSU
HITORI OKAMI • 1968 • Ikehiro Kazuo • JPN • LONE STALKER, THE
HITOTSUBU NO MUGI • 1958 • Yoshimura Kozaburo • JPN • GRAIN OF WHEAT, A ○ ONE GRAIN OF BARLEY

HITOZUMATSUBAKI • 1967 • Ichimura Hirokazu • JPN • WIFE CAMELIA
HITS AND MISSES • 1919 • *Gayety* • USA
HITS OF THE NINETIES • 1949 • Parker Benjamin R. • SHT • USA
HITS OF TODAY • 1934 • Schwarzwald Milton • SHT • USA
HITTEBARNET • 1916 • Holger-Madsen • DNM • FOUNDLING OF FATE, THE
HITTER, THE • 1979 • Leitch Christopher • USA
HITTIN' THE TRAIL • 1937 • Bradbury Robert North • USA
HITTING A NEW HIGH • 1937 • Walsh Raoul • USA
HITTING HOME • 1988 • Spry Robin • CND • OBSESSED
HITTING THE HEADLINES (UKN) see **YOKEL BOY** • 1942
HITTING THE HIGH SPOTS • 1918 • Swickard Charles • USA
HITTING THE JACKPOT (UKN) see **BLONDIE HITS THE JACKPOT** • 1949
HITTING THE TRAIL • 1918 • Henderson Dell • USA
HITTING THE TRAIL TO HALLELUJAH LAND • 1931-32 • Ising Rudolf • ANS • USA
HIVER • 1964 • Kamler Piotr, Voisin Andre • FRN
HIVER 54, L'ABBE PIERRE • 1989 • Amar Denis • FRN
HIVER 60 • 1983 • Michel Thierry • BLG
HIVER, L' • 1970 • Hanoun Marcel • FRN, BLG
HIVER AU CANADA, L' see **WINTER IN CANADA** • 1953
HIVER BLEU, L' • 1980 • Blanchard Andre • CND • BLUE WINTER
HIVER BRULANT, UN • 1971 • Carle Gilles • CND
HIVER EN FROID MINEUR, L' • 1969 • Labrecque Jean-Claude • DCS • CND
HIVERNALE see **OVERVINTRINGEN** • 1965
HIWA NG LAGIM • 1970 • Cruz Jose Miranda • PHL • HIWAGA NG LAGIM? ○ MYSTERY AND TERROR
HIWAGA NG LAGIM? see **HIWA NG LAGIM** • 1970
HIWAGA SA BALETE DRIVE • 1988 • Gallaga Peque • PHL • BALETE DRIVE HORROR STORY
HIWAR • 1972 • el Sheikh Kamal • EGY • DIALOGUE
HIWAY HECKLERS • 1968 • Smith Paul J. • ANS • USA
HI'YA, CHUM • 1943 • Young Harold • USA • EVERYTHING HAPPENS TO US (UKN) ○ HI YA, CHARACTER
HIYAMESHI TO OSAN TO CHAN • 1965 • Tasaka Tomotaka • JPN • OSAN
HIZUNDA JOYOKU • 1967 • Kuroiwa Matsutaro • JPN • DISTORTED DESIRE
HJAELP OS • 1961 • Barfod Bent • DNM
HJAELPEN • 1911 • Dinesen Robert • DNM
HJALPSAMMA HERRN • 1954 • Eiworth Roland • SWD
HJALTAR I GULT OCH BLATT • 1940 • Bauman Schamyl • SWD • HEROES IN YELLOW AND BLUE
HJALTAR MOT SIN VILJA • 1948 • Husberg Rolf • SWD, DNM • CALLE OG PALLE
HJALTE MOT SIN VILJA • 1915 • Hansen Edmond • SWD • HERO IN SPITE OF HIMSELF, A
HJALTEN • 1989 • Fagerstrom-Olsson Agneta • SWD • HERO, THE
HJARTAN SOM MOTAS • 1914 • Sjostrom Victor • SWD • MEETING HEARTS ○ HEARTS THAT MEET
HJARTATS ROST • 1930 • Carlsten Rune • SWD • VOICE OF THE HEART
HJARTATS TRIUMF • 1929 • Molander Gustaf • SWD • TRIUMPH OF THE HEART
HJARTER KNEKT • 1950 • Ekman Hasse • SWD • JACK OF HEARTS
HJEMLIG HUGGE • 1983 • Arnfred Morten • SHT • DNM • DOMESTIC COSINESS
HJERT AND TECTOR see **HJERT OCH TECTOR** • 1976
HJERT OCH TECTOR • 1976 • Abrahamsen Christer • SWD • HJERT AND TECTOR
HJERTE AF GULD, ET see **HJERTETS GULD** • 1912
HJERTEBETVINGEREN • 1917 • Lauritzen Lau • DNM
HJERTER ER TRUMF • 1975 • Brydesen Lars • DNM • HEARTS ARE TRUMPS
HJERTERNES KAMP • 1912 • Blom August • DNM • HIGH STAKE, A
HJERTESTORME • 1915 • Blom August • DNM
HJERTETS GULD • 1912 • Blom August • DNM • HJERTE AF GULD, ET ○ FAITHFUL UNTO DEATH
HJERTETYVEN • 1943 • Roos Jorgen, Mertz Albert • DOC • DNM • THIEF OF HEARTS, THE
HJULSAGA, EN • *Ekman Gosta* • SWD • TALE OF WHEELS
HLAVY • 1979 • Sis Peter • ANS • CZC • HEADS
HLEDAM DUM HOLUBI • 1985 • Plivova-Simkova Vera • CZC • I'M LOOKING FOR A PIGEON HOUSE
HLIDAC • 1970 • Renc Ivan • CZC • WATCHMAN, THE ○ GUARD, THE
HLIDAC C.47 • 1937 • Rovensky Josef • CZC • WATCHMAN NO.47
HLINAK • 1972 • Zahradnik Jan • SWT • CLAY ELF, THE
HNOKE KHAN SU GA MU HMAR PIN • 1982 • Nyunt Win • BRM • POUTING AND BEGUILING
HO! • 1968 • Enrico Robert • FRN, ITL • HO! CRIMINAL FACE ○ CRIMINAL FACE ○ STORIA DI UN CRIMINALE (ITL)
HO AMATA UNA DIVA • 1957 • De Marchi Luigi • ITL
HO! CRIMINAL FACE see **HO!** • 1968
HO FATTO SPLASH • 1980 • Nichetti Maurizio • ITL
HO GIURATO DI UCCIDERTI see **VENGANZA, LA** • 1957
HO PERDUTO MIA MOGLIE see **FINALEMENT SOLI** • 1942
HO PERDUTO MIO MARITO! • 1937 • Guazzoni Enrico • ITL
HO PIANTO PER TE • 1954 • Rippo Gino • ITL • CRUDELE MENZOGNA
HO RITROVATO MIO FIGLIO • 1954 • Piccon Elio • ITL
HO SCELTO L'AMORE • 1953 • Zampi Mario • ITL
HO SOGNATO IL PARADISO • 1950 • Pastina Giorgio • ITL • STREETS OF SORROW (USA)
HO TANTO VOGLIA DI CANTARE! • 1944 • Mattoli Mario • ITL
HO TENTATO DI VIVERE see **CONTRORAPINA** • 1979
HO UNA MOGLIE PAZZA, PAZZA, PAZZA (ITL) see **RELAXE-TOI, CHERIE** • 1964
HO VINTO LA LOTTERIA DI CAPODANNO • 1990 • Parenti Neri • ITL • I WON THE NEW YEAR LOTTERY
HO VISTO BRILLARE LE STELLE • 1940 • Guazzoni Enrico • ITL • HO VISTO BRILLARE UNA STELLA
HO VISTO BRILLARE UNA STELLA see **HO VISTO BRILLARE LE STELLE** • 1940
HOA-BINH • 1970 • Coutard Raoul • FRN • PEACE
HOAGY CARMICHAEL • 1939 • Roush Leslie • SHT • USA
HOARDED ASSETS • 1918 • Scardon Paul • USA
HOARDER, THE • 1969 • Lambart Evelyn • ANS • CND
HOARY LEGENDS OF THE CAUCASUS, THE see **ASHIK KERIB** • 1987
HOAX • 1972 • Anderson Robert** • USA
HOAX, THE • 1972 • *Ewing Bill* • USA
HOAX HOUSE, THE • 1916 • Webster Harry Mcrae • SHT • USA
HOAXING THE PROFESSOR • 1906 • *Cricks & Sharp* • UKN
HOAXTERS, THE • 1953 • *Schary Dore (P)* • DOC • USA
HOB WA KHYANA • 1968 • Bedeir El Sayed • EGY • LOVE AND TREASON
HOBBIES • 1941 • Labrousse Georges • SHT • USA
HOBBIT, THE • 1977 • Rankin Arthur Jr. • ANM • USA
HOBBLE SKIRT, THE • 1910 • *Imp* • USA
HOBBLED HEARTS • 1917 • *Dillon Jack* • USA
HOBBS IN A HURRY • 1918 • King Henry • USA
HOBBY • 1967 • Szczechura Daniel • ANS • PLN
HOBBY • 1978 • Schlumpf Hans-Ulrich • DOC • SWT
HOBBY FAMILY, THE see **EVERYBODY'S HOBBY** • 1939
HOBBY HORSE LAFFS • 1942 • McCabe Norman • ANS • USA
HOBGOBLIN, THE see **KLABAUTERMANN, DER** • 1924
HOBGOBLINS • 1921 • Roach Hal • SHT • USA
HOBO, THE • 1912 • *Bosworth Hobart* • USA
HOBO, THE • 1917 • Gillstrom Arvid E. • SHT • USA
HOBO, THE see **HORNY HOBO** • 1969
HOBO AND THE CIRCUS, THE • Chatterton Bob • SHT • USA
HOBO AND THE HOBBLE SKIRT, THE • 1913 • *Roland Ruth* • USA
HOBO AND THE MYTH, THE • 1913 • *Roland Ruth* • USA
HOBO BOBO • 1947 • McKimson Robert • ANS • USA
HOBO BOUND • 1946 • *Mead Thomas (P)* • SHT • USA
HOBO CLUB, THE • 1912 • *Lubin* • USA
HOBO COWBOY, THE • 1911 • Melies Gaston • USA
HOBO GADGET BAND • 1939 • Hardaway Ben, Dalton Cal • ANS • USA
HOBO IMPOSTER, THE • 1916 • *Jockey* • USA
HOBO LUCK • 1911 • *Pathe* • USA
HOBO NERVE • 1915 • *Novelty* • USA
HOBO OVER PIZEN CITY, THE • 1920 • Ridgwell George • SHT • USA
HOBO PHILOSOPHER, A • 1914 • *Melies* • USA
HOBO RAID, THE • 1917 • Santell Alfred • SHT • USA
HOBOES • 1915 • *Starlight* • USA
HOBOES, THE see **LANDSTREICHER, DIE** • 1937
HOBOES IN PARADISE (USA) see **GUEUX AU PARADIS, LES** • 1945
HOBOKEN TO HOLLYWOOD • 1926 • *Sennett Mack (P)* • SHT • USA
HOBO'S CHRISTMAS, A • 1987 • Mackenzie Will • TVM • USA
HOBO'S DREAM • 1908 • *Lubin* • USA
HOBO'S DREAM OF WEALTH, THE • 1910 • *Pantograph* • USA
HOBO'S HOLIDAY • 1963 • Kneitel Seymour • ANS • USA
HOBO'S INVENTION, THE • 1915 • *Royal* • USA
HOBO'S REDEMPTION, THE • 1912 • *Reid Hal* • USA
HOBO'S REST CURE, THE • 1912 • *Selig* • USA
HOBO'S ROUNDUP, THE • 1911 • *American* • USA
HOBSON'S CHOICE • 1920 • Nash Percy • UKN
HOBSON'S CHOICE • 1931 • Bentley Thomas • UKN
HOBSON'S CHOICE • 1954 • Lean David • UKN
HOBSON'S CHOICE • 1983 • Cates Gilbert • TVM • USA
HOCH DROBEN AUF DEM BERG • 1957 • von Bolvary Geza • FRG
HOCH KLINGT DAS LIED VOM U-BOOT-MANN • 1917 • Matull Kurt • FRG • HELDENLEBEN DES ERFINDERS DER U-BOOTE WILHELM BAUER, DAS
HOCH KLINGT DER RADETZKYMARSCH • 1958 • von Bolvary Geza • AUS
HOCHBAHNKATASTROPHE, DIE • 1921 • Arnheim Valy • FRG
HOCHELAGA • 1972 • Labrecque Jean-Claude • DCS • CND
HOCHLAND • 1920 • Brachvogel Heinz Udo • FRG
HOCHMUT KOMMT VOR DEM KNALL • 1960 • Jung-Alsen Kurt • GDR • PRIDE COMES BEFORE THE FALL
HOCHSPANNUNG 100.000 VOLT! see **BLITZZENTRALE, DIE** • 1921
HOCHSTAPLER • 1921 • Funck Werner • FRG
HOCHSTAPLER WIDER WILLEN • 1924 • von Bolvary Geza • FRG • DOPPELGANGER DES HERRN SCHNEPFE, DER
HOCHSTAPLERIN, DIE • 1927 • Berger Martin • FRG
HOCHSTAPLERIN, DIE • 1943 • Anton Karl • FRG
HOCHSTAPLERIN DER LIEBE • 1954 • Konig Hans H. • AUS
HOCHSTE GUT EINER FRAU IST IHR SCHWEIGEN, DAS • 1981 • Pinkus Gertrud • DOC • SWT • MOST VALUABLE ASSET OF A WOMAN IS HER SILENCE, THE
HOCHSTE WURF, DER • 1915 • Del Zopp Rudolf • FRG
HOCHTOURIST, DER • 1931 • Zeisler Alfred • FRG
HOCHTOURIST, DER • 1942 • Schlissleder Adolf • FRG
HOCHTOURIST, DER • 1961 • Erfurth Ulrich • FRG
HOCHVERRAT • 1929 • Meyer Johannes • FRG • HIGH TREASON
HOCHZEIT AM NEUSIEDLER SEE • 1963 • Olsen Rolf • AUS
HOCHZEIT AM WOLFGANGSEE • 1934 • Behrendt Hans • FRG
HOCHZEIT AUF BARENHOF • 1942 • Froelich Carl • FRG
HOCHZEIT AUF IMMENHOF • 1956 • von Collande Volker • FRG
HOCHZEIT AUF REISEN • 1953 • Verhoeven Paul • FRG
HOCHZEIT DER CASSILDA MEDIADORES, DIE • 1917 • *Neumann Lotte* • FRG
HOCHZEIT DES FIGARO, DIE • 1968 • Hess Joachim • MTV • FRG • MARRIAGE OF FIGARO, THE (USA) ○ FIGAROS HOCHZEIT
HOCHZEIT IM EXCENTRICCLUB, DIE • 1917 • May Joe • FRG • WEDDING IN THE ECCENTRIC CLUB, THE
HOCHZEIT IM HEU • 1951 • Rabenalt Arthur M. • FRG, AUS
HOCHZEIT MIT ERIKA • 1949 • von Borsody Eduard • AUS
HOCHZEIT MIT HINDERNISSEN • 1939 • Seitz Franz • FRG
HOCHZEIT VON LANNECKEN, DIE • 1964 • Carow Heiner • GDR • LANNEKEN WEDDING, THE
HOCHZEIT VON VALENI, DIE see **SKLAVEN DER LIEBE** • 1924
HOCHZEITRISE, DIE • 1939 • Ritter Karl • FRG • WEDDING JOURNEY, THE (USA)
HOCHZEITSHOTEL, DAS • 1944 • Boese Carl • FRG
HOCHZEITSMORGEN, EIN • 1920 • Seitz Franz • FRG
HOCHZEITSNACHT • 1941 • Boese Carl • FRG
HOCHZEITSNACHT IM PARADIES • 1950 • von Bolvary Geza • FRG
HOCHZEITSNACHT IM PARADIES • 1962 • Martin Paul • AUS
HOCHZEITSNACHT IM REGEN • 1969 • Seemann Horst • GDR • WEDDING NIGHT IN THE DRIZZLE ○ WEDDING NIGHT IN THE RAIN
HOCHZEITSREISE • 1969 • Gregan Ralf • FRG
HOCHZEITSREISE ZU DRITT • 1932 • Schmidt Erich, May Joe • FRG, AUS • WENN ICH EINMAL EINE DUMMHEIT MACHE..
HOCHZEITSREISE ZU DRITT • 1939 • Marischka Hubert • FRG
HOCHZEITSTRAUM, EIN • 1936 • Engel Erich • FRG • THUNDER LIGHTNING AND SUNSHINE (USA)
HOCK KEYS - JEAN POESY FIGHT • 1912 • ASL
HOCKEY • 1981 • Tuhus Oddvar Bull • NRW • ICE-HOCKEY ○ HOCKEY FEVER ○ HOCKEYFEBER
HOCKEY, LE • 1963-64 • Portugais Louis • DCS • CND
HOCKEY -CANADA'S NATIONAL GAME • 1932 • Sparling Gordon • DCS • CND
HOCKEY CHAMP, THE • 1939 • King Jack • ANS • USA
HOCKEY CHAMPIONS • 1933 • Sparling Gordon • DCS • CND
HOCKEY FEVER see **HOCKEY** • 1981
HOCKEY HOMICIDE • 1945 • Kinney Jack • ANS • USA
HOCKEY NIGHT • 1984 • Shapiro Paul • CND
HOCKEY PLAYERS • 1965 • Goldin R. • USS
HOCKEY STARS' SUMMER • 1951 • Sparling Gordon • DCS • CND
HOCKEYFEBER see **HOCKEY** • 1981
HOCKZEITSGLOCKEN • 1954 • Wildhagen Georg • FRG
HOCU ZIVJETI • 1983 • Mikuljan Miroslav • YGS • I WANT TO LIVE
HOCUS POCUS • 1949 • White Jules • SHT • USA
HOCUS POCUS POWWOW • 1968 • Lovy Alex • ANS • USA
HOCUSSING OF CIGARETTE, THE • 1924 • Croise Hugh • UKN
HOD CARRIER'S MILLION, THE • 1917 • *Cooper Claude* • USA
HODAG • Huber Larry • ANS • USA
HODDLE STREET SUITE • 1977 • Dunkley-Smith John • ASL
HODGE PODGE • 1913 • *Howe Lyman H. (P)* • USA
HODIME SE K SOBE, MILACKU? • 1975 • Schulhoff Petr • CZC • DARLING, ARE WE A GOOD MATCH..?
HODINA MODRYCH SLONU • Cvrcek Radim, Rozkopal Zdenek • CZC • HOUR OF THE BLUE ELEPHANTS, THE
HODJA FRA PJORT • 1986 • Wielopolska Brita • DNM • HODJA FROM PJORT
HODJA FROM PJORT see **HODJA FRA PJORT** • 1986
HOEDOWN • 1950 • Nazarro Ray • USA
HOEN DANU • 1927 • Uchida Tomu • JPN • CANNON SMOKE AND RAIN OF SHELLS
HOF OHNE LACHEN, DER • 1923 • *Schonfeld Gisela* • FRG
HOFFMAN • 1970 • Rakoff Alvin • UKN
HOFFMANNS ERZAHLUNGEN • 1911 • Kolm Anton, Fleck Luise • AUS, HNG • TALES OF HOFFMANN
HOFFMANNS ERZAHLUNGEN • 1916 • Oswald Richard • FRG • TALES OF HOFFMANN (USA)
HOFFMANNS ERZAHLUNGEN • 1924 • Neufeld Max • AUS • TALES OF HOFFMANN
HOFFMANNS ERZAHLUNGEN • 1958 • Fischer Heinz • GDR
HOFFMANNS ERZAHLUNGEN • 1970 • Kaslik Vaclav • FRG
HOFFMANOVY POVIDKY • 1962 • Kaslik Vaclav • CZC • TALES OF HOFFMANN, THE
HOFFMEYER'S LEGACY • 1912 • Sennett Mack • USA
HOFFNUNG AUF SEGEN see **FAHRT INS VERDERBEN, DIE** • 1924
HOFFNUNG SYMPHONY ORCHESTRA, THE • 1965 • Whitaker Harold • ANS • UKN
HOFFNUNGSLOSER FALL, EIN • 1939 • Engel Erich • FRG
HOFINTRIGE, EN • 1912 • Blom August • DNM • COURT INTRIGUE, A
HOFJAGD IN ISCHL see **ZWEI HERZEN UND EIN THRON** • 1955
HOFKONZERT, DAS • 1936 • Sirk Douglas • FRG
HOFRAT GEIGER, DER • 1947 • Wolff Hans • AUS • MARIANDL
HOG WILD • 1930 • Parrott James • SHT • USA • AERIAL ANTICS
HOG WILD • 1980 • Rose Les • CND • GO HOG WILD
HOGAN OUT WEST • 1915 • Avery Charles • USA
HOGAN, THE PORTER • 1915 • Avery Charles • USA
HOGAN VS. SCHMIDT • 1912 • *Lubin* • USA
HOGAN'S ALLEY • 1912 • *O'Connor Edward* • USA
HOGAN'S ALLEY • 1914 • *Pathe* • USA
HOGAN'S ALLEY • 1925 • Del Ruth Roy • USA
HOGAN'S ANNUAL SPREE • 1914 • Avery Charles • USA
HOGAN'S ARISTOCRATIC DREAM • 1915 • Avery Charles • USA
HOGAN'S MUSSY JOB • 1915 • Avery Charles • USA
HOGAN'S ROMANCE UPSET • 1915 • Avery Charles • USA
HOGAN'S WILD OATS • 1915 • Avery Charles • USA
HOGAR, DULCE HOGAR • 1941 • Barth-Moglia Luis • ARG
HOGARAKA NI AYUME • 1930 • Ozu Yasujiro • JPN • WALK CHEERFULLY
HOGARTH • 1976 • Bennett Edward • UKN
HOGE VELUWE, DE • 1968 • Crama Nico • SHT • NTH
HOGFJALLETS DOTTER • 1914 • Sjostrom Victor • SWD • DAUGHTER OF THE HIGH MOUNTAIN ○ DAUGHTER OF THE MOUNTAIN
HOGHEBAZAN • 1967 • Safaei Reza • IRN • IMPOSTORS, THE
HOGHET SINGLAR • 1928 • Hylten-Cavallius Ragnar • SWD
HOGO FOGO HOMOLKA • 1971 • Papousek Jaroslav • CZC
HOGRE ANDAMAL • 1921 • Carlsten Rune • SWD • FOR HIGH ENDS
HOGS AND WARSHIPS see **BUTA TO GUNKAN** • 1961
HOGSTA VINSTEN • 1915 • Hansen Edmond • SWD • FIRST PRIZE
HOGSTA VINSTEN • 1916 • Klercker Georg • SWD • FIRST PRIZE, THE
HOGUERAS EN LA NOCHE • 1937 • Porchet Arturo • USS
HOGY ALLUNK, FIATALEMBER? • 1963 • Revesz Gyorgy • HNG • WELL, YOUNG MAN?
HOGY SZALADNAK FAK • 1966 • Zolnay Pal • HNG • SZAK, A ○ SACK, THE

HOGYAN FELEJTSUK EL ELETUNK LEGNAGYOBB SZERELMET? • 1980 • Szasz Peter • HNG • HOW TO FORGET THE GREATEST LOVE OF ONE'S LIFE?
HOHE LIED DER LIEBE, DAS • 1922 • Schall Heinz • FRG
HOHE LIED DER LIEBE, DAS see **MANON LESCAUT** • 1919
HOHE SCHULE • 1934 • Engel Erich • FRG • GEHEIMNIS DES CARLO CAVELLI, DAS ○ SECRETS OF CAVELLI, THE ○ COLLEGE
HOHEIT DARF NICHT KUSSEN see **LIEBLING DER WELT** • 1949
HOHEIT LASSEN BITTEN • 1954 • Verhoeven Paul • FRG
HOHEIT RADIESCHEN • 1923 • *Danny Kaden-Film* • FRG
HOHEIT TANZT WALZER • 1926 • Freisler Fritz • FRG
HOHEIT TANZT WALZER • 1935 • Neufeld Max • AUS
HOHEIT VATER UND SON see **WIR VON GOTTES GNADEN.. HOHEIT VATER UND SOHN** • 1918
HOHELIED DER KRAFT, DAS • 1930 • Fischinger Oskar • ANS • FRG • HYMN OF ENERGY, THE
HOHELIED DER KRAFT, DAS • 1930 • Paringer Lorenz • FRG
HOHEN UND TIEFEN • 1915 • *Morena Erna* • FRG
HOHENFEUER • 1985 • Murer Fredi M. • SWT • ALPINE FIRE
HOHENFIEBER • 1924 • Bock-Stieber Gernot • FRG
HOHENLUFT • 1917 • Biebrach Rudolf • FRG
HOHERE BEFEHL, DER • 1935 • Lamprecht Gerhard • FRG
HOHERE TOCHTER • 1927 • Lowenbein Richard • FRG
HOHOEMU HINSEI • 1930 • Gosho Heinosuke • JPN • SMILING CHARACTER, A ○ SMILING LIFE, A
HOHOEMU NIKKATSU • 1932 • Yamamoto Kajiro • JPN • SMILING NIKKATSU
HOI POLLOI • 1935 • Lord Del • SHT • USA
HOIST ON HIS OWN PETARD • 1912 • Henderson Dell • USA
HOJAS • 1970 • Solas Humberto • CUB • LEAVES
HOJDHOPPAR'N • 1980 • Molin Lars • SWD • HIGH JUMPER
HOJE, ESTREIA • 1967 • Lopes Fernando • SHT • PRT
HOJT SPIL • 1913 • Blom August • DNM • FORFEJLET SPRING, ET ○ DASH FOR LIBERTY, A
HOKEN see **MORDVAPEN TILL SALU** • 1963
HOKKAI YUKYODEN • 1967 • Takamori Ryuichi • JPN • OUTLAWS OF THE NORTHERN SEA
HOKKAIDO MONOGATARI • 1968 • Sugihara Fumiharu • JPN • HOKKAIDO STORY
HOKKAIDO NO DAISHIZEN • 1957 • Iwasu Vichisa • JPN • NATURE OF HOKKAIDO, THE
HOKKAIDO STORY see **HOKKAIDO MONOGATARI** • 1968
HOKUM HOTEL • 1932 • Foster John, Bailey Harry • ANS • USA
HOKUS FOCUS • 1933 • Sandrich Mark • SHT • USA
HOKUSAI • 1953 • Teshigahara Hiroshi • SHT • JPN
HOKUSAI AN ANIMATED SKETCHBOOK • 1978 • White Tony • UKN
HOKUSAI MANGA • 1982 • Shindo Kaneto • JPN • HOKUSAI, UKIYOE MASTER
HOKUSAI, UKIYOE MASTER see **HOKUSAI MANGA** • 1982
HOKUSPOKUS • 1930 • Ucicky Gustav • FRG
HOKUSPOKUS • 1953 • Hoffmann Kurt • FRG
HOKUSPOKUS -ODER WIE LASSE ICH MEINEN MANN VERSCHWINDEN • 1966 • Hoffmann Kurt • FRG
HOL VOLT, HOL NEM VOLT.. • 1987 • Gazdag Gyula • HNG • HUNGARIAN FAIRY TALE, A
HOLA, MUCHACHO! • 1961 • Mariscal Ana • SPN
HOLCROFT COVENANT, THE • 1985 • Frankenheimer John • USA
HOLD ANYTHING • 1930 • Harman Hugh, Ising Rudolf • ANS • USA
HOLD AUTUMN IN YOUR HAND see **SOUTHERNER, THE** • 1944
HOLD BACK THE DAWN • 1941 • Leisen Mitchell • USA
HOLD BACK THE NIGHT • 1956 • Dwan Allan • USA
HOLD BACK THE SEA see **LAGE LANDEN, DE** • 1961
HOLD BACK TOMORROW • 1955 • Haas Hugo • USA
HOLD 'EM JAIL • 1932 • Taurog Norman • USA
HOLD 'EM NAVY • 1937 • Neumann Kurt • USA • THAT NAVY SPIRIT (UKN)
HOLD 'EM YALE! • 1928 • Griffith Edward H. • USA • AT YALE
HOLD 'EM, YALE • 1935 • Lanfield Sidney • USA • UNIFORM LOVERS (UKN)
HOLD 'ER SHERIFF • 1926 • Roberts Stephen • SHT • USA
HOLD 'ER SHERIFF • 1931 • Sennett Mack • USA
HOLD EVERYBODY • 1926 • Ray Albert • USA
HOLD EVERYTHING • 1926 • Roach Hal • SHT • USA
HOLD EVERYTHING • 1930 • Del Ruth Roy • USA
HOLD FAST • 1916 • Myll Louis • SHT • USA
HOLD FAST • 1927 • Sandrich Mark • SHT • USA
HOLD HANDS see **DOSTE TA HERIA** • 1970
HOLD HIGH THE TORCH see **COURAGE OF LASSIE** • 1946
HOLD IT! • 1938 • Fleischer Dave • ANS • USA
HOLD ME TIGHT • 1920 • Summerville Slim, Lord Del • SHT • USA
HOLD ME TIGHT • 1933 • Butler David • USA
HOLD ME WHILE I'M NAKED • 1966 • Kuchar George • SHT • USA
HOLD MY BABY • 1925 • Roach Hal • SHT • USA
HOLD MY HAND • 1938 • Freeland Thornton • UKN
HOLD MY HAND I'M DYING • 1989 • Ryan Terence • UKN, SAF, USA
HOLD ON! • 1966 • Lubin Arthur • USA • THERE'S NO PLACE LIKE SPACE
HOLD ON, HEART see **AGUENTA CORACAO** • 1984
HOLD ON, SWINDLE! see **SE SEGURA, MALANDRO!** • 1979
HOLD ON TO BOTH THINGS see **HALTET BEIDES GUT ZUSAMMEN** • 1969
HOLD ON TO YOUR HATS • 1967 • Pojar Bretislav • ANM • CZC • HOLD YOUR HATS
HOLD STILL • 1926 • Beaudine Harold • USA
HOLD THAT BABY • 1949 • Le Borg Reginald • USA
HOLD THAT BEAR • 1927 • Sandrich Mark • SHT • USA
HOLD THAT BLONDE! • 1945 • Marshall George • USA • GOOD INTENTIONS
HOLD THAT CO-ED • 1938 • Marshall George • USA • HOLD THAT GIRL (UKN)
HOLD THAT DREAM see **HOLD THE DREAM** • 1986
HOLD THAT GHOST • 1941 • Lubin Arthur • USA
HOLD THAT GIRL • 1934 • MacFadden Hamilton • USA
HOLD THAT GIRL (UKN) see **HOLD THAT CO-ED** • 1938
HOLD THAT HYPNOTIST • 1957 • Jewell Austen • USA • OUT OF THIS WORLD
HOLD THAT KISS • 1938 • Marin Edwin L. • USA
HOLD THAT LINE • 1952 • Beaudine William • USA
HOLD THAT LION • 1926 • Beaudine William • USA • HUNTING TROUBLE ○ LADIES FIRST
HOLD THAT LION • 1947 • White Jules • SHT • USA
HOLD THAT POSE • 1927 • Cline Eddie • SHT • USA
HOLD THAT POSE • 1950 • Kinney Jack • ANS • USA
HOLD THAT ROCK • 1956 • Lovy Alex • ANS • USA
HOLD THAT WOMAN! • 1940 • Newfield Sam • USA
HOLD THE DREAM • 1986 • Sharp Don • MTV • UKN, USA • HOLD THAT DREAM
HOLD THE KETCHUP • 1977 • Kish Albert • DOC • CND
HOLD THE LAND • 1949 • Collings Geoffrey • ASL
HOLD THE LION, PLEASE • 1942 • Jones Charles M. • ANS • USA
HOLD THE LION PLEASE • 1951 • Sparber I. • ANS • USA
HOLD THE PRESS • 1933 • Rosen Phil • USA
HOLD THE WIRE • 1936 • Fleischer Dave • ANS • USA
HOLD TIGHT TO THE SATELLITE (UKN) see **A PIED, A CHEVAL ET EN SPOUTNIK** • 1958
HOLD UP • 1929 • Santley Joseph • SHT • USA
HOLD UP • 1972 • Lorente German • FRN
HOLD-UP • 1986 • Arcady Alexandre • CND • QUICK CHANGE
HOLD-UP, THE • Hempel Johannes • ANM • GDR
HOLD-UP, THE • 1911 • Blache Alice • USA
HOLD-UP, THE • 1915 • *Ovey George* • USA
HOLD UP, THE • 1933 • Brice Monte • SHT • USA
HOLD-UP A LA MILANAISE (FRN) see **AUDACE COLPI DEI SOLITI IGNOTI** • 1959
HOLD-UP A SAINT-TROP' • 1960 • Felix Louis • FRN • PLAY-BOYS, LES
HOLD-UP AU CRAYON, LE • 1971 • Reichenbach Francois • FRN
HOLD-UP EN MUSIQUE see **GANG DES PIANOS A BRETELLES, LE** • 1952
HOLD-UP IN BUCKEYE CANYON, THE • 1912 • *Comet* • USA
HOLD-UP POUR LAURA see **CINQUANTE BRIQUES POUR JO** • 1967
HOLD YOUR BREATH • 1924 • Christie Al • SHT • USA
HOLD YOUR BREATH • 1924 • Sidney Scott • USA
HOLD YOUR HAT • 1926 • Roberts Stephen • SHT • USA
HOLD YOUR HATS see **HOLD ON TO YOUR HATS** • 1967
HOLD YOUR HORSES • 1921 • Hopper E. Mason • USA
HOLD YOUR MAN • 1929 • Flynn Emmett J. • USA
HOLD YOUR MAN • 1932 • Wood Sam • USA
HOLD YOUR TEMPER • 1933 • White Sam • SHT • USA
HOLD YOUR TEMPER • 1943 • French Lloyd • SHT • USA
HOLDING HIS OWN • 1911 • *Essanay* • USA
HOLDING THE FORT • 1912 • *Mcleod Elsie* • USA
HOLDUDVAR, A • 1969 • Meszaros Marta • HNG • BINDING SENTIMENTS ○ BINDING TIES
HOLDUP IN A COUNTRY GROCERY STORE • 1904 • Porter Edwin S. • USA
HOLDUP MAN, THE • 1920 • Ridgwell George • SHT • USA
HOLDUP OF ROCKY MT. EXPRESS • 1906 • *Bitzer Billy (Ph)* • USA
HOLE, THE • 1962 • Hubley John, Hubley Faith • ANS • USA
HOLE, THE see **ANA** • 1957
HOLE, THE see **ONIBABA** • 1964
HOLE, THE see **DUPKATA** • 1967
HOLE, THE see **RUPA** • 1971
HOLE, THE (UKN) see **TROU, LE** • 1960
HOLE IDEA, THE • 1955 • McKimson Robert • ANS • USA
HOLE IN THE EARTH see **DZIURA W ZIEMI** • 1970
HOLE IN THE FOREHEAD, A see **BUCO IN FRONTE, UN** • 1968
HOLE IN THE GARDEN WALL, THE • 1914 • *Julian Rupert* • USA
HOLE IN THE GROUND, A • 1917 • Richmond J. A. • SHT • USA
HOLE IN THE GROUND, A • 1963 • McNaughton Bruce • ASL
HOLE IN THE GROUND, A see **DZIURA W ZIEMI** • 1970
HOLE IN THE HEAD, A • 1959 • Capra Frank • USA
HOLE IN THE MOON, A see **HOR BALEVANA** • 1965
HOLE IN THE WALL, THE • 1914 • *Melies* • USA
HOLE IN THE WALL, THE • 1919 • *Nestor* • SHT • USA
HOLE IN THE WALL, THE • 1921 • Karger Maxwell • USA
HOLE IN THE WALL, THE • 1929 • Florey Robert • USA
HOLE IN THE WALL, THE see **AGUJERO EN LA PARED, EL** • 1982
HOLE LOT OF TROUBLE, A • 1970 • Searle Francis • UKN
HOLI • 1984 • Mehta Ketan • IND • FESTIVAL OF FIRE, THE
HOLIDAY • 1930 • Griffith Edward H. • USA
HOLIDAY • 1938 • Cukor George • USA • FREE TO LIVE (UKN) ○ UNCONVENTIONAL LINDA
HOLIDAY • 1957 • Taylor John • DCS • UKN
HOLIDAY see **CHHUTI** • 1967
HOLIDAY see **V DYEN PRAZDNIKA** • 1980
HOLIDAY, THE see **VILLEGGIATURA, LA** • 1973
HOLIDAY, THE see **LOMA** • 1976
HOLIDAY AFFAIR • 1949 • Hartman Don • USA
HOLIDAY AM WORTHERSEE • 1956 • Schott-Schobinger Hans • FRG, AUS
HOLIDAY AT SCHOOL • 1946 • CND
HOLIDAY CAMP • 1947 • Annakin Ken • UKN
HOLIDAY FOR A DOG see **PRAZDNINY PRO PSA** • 1981
HOLIDAY FOR DRUMSTICKS • 1949 • Davis Arthur • ANS • USA
HOLIDAY FOR HENRIETTA (USA) see **FETE A HENRIETTE, LA** • 1953
HOLIDAY FOR HOMICIDE • 1978 • Shebib Donald • CND
HOLIDAY FOR LOVERS • 1959 • Levin Henry • USA
HOLIDAY FOR SHOESTRINGS • 1946 • Freleng Friz • ANS • USA
HOLIDAY FOR SINNERS • 1952 • Mayer Gerald • USA • DAYS BEFORE LENT
HOLIDAY HIGHLIGHTS • 1940 • Avery Tex • ANS • USA
HOLIDAY HOOKERS see **NATALE IN CASA D'APPUNTAMENTO** • 1976
HOLIDAY HOTEL (USA) see **HOTEL DE LA PLAGE, L'** • 1978
HOLIDAY HUSBAND, THE • 1920 • Hunter A. C. • UKN
HOLIDAY IN BRITAIN see **JUTALOMUTAZAS** • 1975
HOLIDAY IN HAVANA • 1949 • Yarbrough Jean • USA
HOLIDAY IN ISTANBUL see **ISTANBUL TATILI** • 1968
HOLIDAY IN MEXICO • 1946 • Sidney George • USA
HOLIDAY IN SPAIN (UKN) see **SCENT OF MYSTERY** • 1960
HOLIDAY IN TOKYO, A see **TOKYO NO KYUJITSU** • 1958
HOLIDAY INN • 1942 • Sandrich Mark • USA
HOLIDAY ISLAND (USA) see **VACANZE A ISCHIA** • 1957
HOLIDAY LAND • 1934 • *Mintz Charles(P)* • ANS • USA
HOLIDAY LOVERS • 1932 • Harrison Jack • UKN
HOLIDAY NIGHT • 1954 • Ozerov Yury • USS
HOLIDAY OF HOPE • 1962 • Ganev Hristo • DOC • BUL
HOLIDAY OF ST. JORGEN, THE see **PRAZDNIK SVYATOVO IORGENE** • 1930
HOLIDAY ON SYLT see **URLAUB AUF SYLT** • 1957
HOLIDAY ON THE BUSES • 1973 • Izzard Bryan • UKN
HOLIDAY RHYTHM • 1950 • Scholl Jack • USA
HOLIDAY WEEK (USA) see **HINDLE WAKES** • 1952
HOLIDAY WITH SURPRISES see **NACIALOTO NA EDNA VACANZIA** • 1966
HOLIDAYS • 1963 • Junge Winifried • DOC • GDR
HOLIDAYS see **UNNEPNAPOK** • 1967
HOLIDAY'S END • 1937 • Carstairs John Paddy • UKN
HOLIDAYS IN HELL see **IGAZA FI GEHANNAM** • 1949
HOLIDAYS IN THE SOUTH see **FERIAS NO SUL** • 1967
HOLIDAYS ON THE COSTA SMERALDA see **VACANZE SULLA COSTA SMERALDA** • 1968
HOLIDAYS ON THE RIVER YARRA • 1990 • Berkeley Leo • ASL
HOLIDAYS WITH AN ANGEL see **DOVOLENA S ANDELEM** • 1952
HOLIDAYS WITH PAY • 1948 • Blakeley John E. • UKN
HOLKA NA ZABITI • 1975 • Herz Juraj • CZC • GIRL TO BE KILLED
HOLLAND • 1968 • van Nie Rene • DCS • NTH
HOLLAND DAYS • 1934 • *Terry Paul/ Moser Frank (P)* • ANS • USA
HOLLAND SUBMARINE TORPEDO BOAT • 1904 • *Bitzer Billy (Ph)* • USA
HOLLAND -TERRA CULINARIS • 1972 • Erends Ronny • DOC • NTH
HOLLAND TERRA FERTILIS • 1968 • Erends Ronny • SHT • NTH
HOLLANDMADEL • 1953 • Hubler-Kahla J. A. • FRG
HOLLE, DIE • 1971 • Lenica Jan • ANS • FRG • HELL ○ ENFER, L'
HOLLE DER JUNGFRAUEN, DIE • 1927 • Dinesen Robert • FRG
HOLLE DER LIEBE • 1926 • Rahn Bruno • FRG
HOLLE VON CAYENNE, DIE see **FLUCHT AUS DER HOLLE** • 1928
HOLLE VON MACAO, DIE (FRG) see **SIGILLO DI PECHINO, IL** • 1966
HOLLE VON MANITOBA, DIE • 1965 • Reynolds Sheldon • FRG, SPN • LUGAR LLAMADA "GLORY", UN (SPN) ○ PLACE CALLED GLORY, A (USA)
HOLLE VON MONTMARTRE, DIE • 1928 • Reiber Willy • FRG
HOLLENJAGD AUF HEISSE WARE (FRG) see **NEW YORK CHIAMA SUPERDRAGO** • 1966
HOLLENMASCHINE, DIE • 1920 • Arnheim Valy • FRG
HOLLENREITER, DER • 1922 • Arnheim Valy • FRG
HOLLENSPUK IN 6 AKTEN, EIN see **KURFURSTENDAMM** • 1920
HOLLENTEMPO • 1933 • Ralph Louis • FRG
HOLLISCHE MACHT, DIE • 1922 • Wiene Robert • FRG
HOLLOW, THE • 1975 • Nierenberg George T. • USA
HOLLOW IMAGE • 1979 • Chomsky Marvin • TVM • USA
HOLLOW-MY-WEANIE, DR. FRANKENSTEIN • 1969 • USA • FRANKENSTEIN DE SADE
HOLLOW OF HER HAND, THE see **IN THE HOLLOW OF HER HAND** • 1918
HOLLOW POINT see **IN SELF DEFENSE** • 1987
HOLLOW TREE, THE • 1913 • *Pathe* • USA
HOLLOW TRIUMPH • 1948 • Sekely Steve • USA • SCAR, THE (UKN)
HOLLOWAY'S TREASURE • 1924 • Hill Sinclair • UKN
HOLLOWHEAD AS A MAGICIAN • 1912 • *C.g.p.c.* • FRN
HOLLY AND THE IVY, THE • 1952 • O'Ferrall George M. • UKN
HOLLY HOUSE, THE • 1916 • Sloman Edward • SHT • USA
HOLLYWOOD • 1923 • Cruze James • USA
HOLLYWOOD AIR FORCE see **WEEKEND WARRIORS** • 1986
HOLLYWOOD AIRFORCE BASE see **WEEKEND WARRIORS** • 1986
HOLLYWOOD AND VINE • 1945 • Thurn-Taxis Alexis • USA • DAISY (THE DOG) GOES HOLLYWOOD (UKN) ○ DAISY GOES HOLLYWOOD
HOLLYWOOD BABIES • 1933 • *Mintz Charles (P)* • ANS • USA
HOLLYWOOD BARN DANCE • 1947 • Ray Bernard B. • USA
HOLLYWOOD BLUE • 1970 • *Osco Bill/ Ziehm Howard (P)* • DOC • USA
HOLLYWOOD BOULEVARD • 1937 • Florey Robert • USA
HOLLYWOOD BOULEVARD • 1976 • Dante Joe, Arkush Allan • USA
HOLLYWOOD BOUND • 1923 • Lamont Charles • SHT • USA
HOLLYWOOD BOWL • 1938 • Perkins Elmer • ANS • USA
HOLLYWOOD BRONC BUSTERS • 1956 • Staub Ralph • SHT • USA
HOLLYWOOD CANINE CANTEEN • 1946 • McKimson Robert • ANS • USA
HOLLYWOOD CANTEEN • 1944 • Daves Delmer • USA
HOLLYWOOD CAPERS • 1935 • King Jack • ANS • USA
HOLLYWOOD CAVALCADE • 1939 • Cummings Irving, St. Clair Malcolm (U/c) • USA • FALLING STARS
HOLLYWOOD CHAINSAW HOOKERS • 1988 • Ray Fred Olen • USA • HOLLYWOOD HOOKERS
HOLLYWOOD COP • 1987 • Shervan Amir • USA
HOLLYWOOD COWBOY • 1937 • Scott Ewing • USA • WINGS OVER WYOMING ○ LOOKING FOR TROUBLE
HOLLYWOOD COWBOY see **HEARTS OF THE WEST** • 1975
HOLLYWOOD DAFFY • 1946 • Freleng Friz • ANS • USA
HOLLYWOOD DAREDEVILS • 1943 • Lewyn Louis • SHT • USA
HOLLYWOOD DETOUR, A • 1942 • Tashlin Frank • ANS • USA
HOLLYWOOD DIET • 1932 • *Terry Paul/ Moser Frank (P)* • ANS • USA

HOLLYWOOD DOUBLE, A • 1932 • *Sennett Mack (P)* • SHT • USA
HOLLYWOOD DREAMING • 1987 • Wilson Jim • USA • MOVIE MAKERS, THE ○ SMART ALEC
HOLLYWOOD ES ASI • 1944 • Delano Jorge • CHL
HOLLYWOOD EXTRA! • 1936 • Feist Felix E. • SHT • USA
HOLLYWOOD EXTRA, A see **LIFE AND DEATH OF 9413, A HOLLYWOOD EXTRA, THE** • 1928
HOLLYWOOD EXTRA GIRL • 1935 • Moulton • SHT • USA
HOLLYWOOD FATHERS • 1954 • Staub Ralph • SHT • USA
HOLLYWOOD FUN FESTIVAL • 1952 • Staub Ralph • SHT • USA
HOLLYWOOD GADABOUT • 1935 • Lewyn Louis • SHT • USA
HOLLYWOOD GHOST STORIES • 1986 • Forsher James • USA
HOLLYWOOD GLAMOUR ON ICE • 1957 • Staub Ralph • SHT • USA
HOLLYWOOD GOES CRAZY • 1932 • *Mintz Charles (P)* • ANS • USA
HOLLYWOOD GRADUATION • 1938 • Davis Arthur • ANS • USA
HOLLYWOOD GROWS UP • 1954 • Staub Ralph • SHT • USA
HOLLYWOOD HALFBACKS • 1931 • Lamont Charles • SHT • USA
HOLLYWOOD HANDICAP • 1938 • Keaton Buster • SHT • USA
HOLLYWOOD HANDICAP, THE • 1932 • Lamont Charles • SHT • USA
HOLLYWOOD HAPPENINGS • 1931 • Sennett Mack • SHT • USA
HOLLYWOOD HARRY • 1985 • Forster Robert • USA
HOLLYWOOD HERO, A • 1927 • Edwards Harry J. • SHT • USA
HOLLYWOOD HIGH • 1976 • Wright Patrick • USA
HOLLYWOOD HIGH PART II • 1981 • Byrd Caruth C., Thornberg Lee • USA
HOLLYWOOD HOBBIES • 1939 • Sidney George • SHT • USA
HOLLYWOOD! HOLLYWOOD! see **THAT'S ENTERTAINMENT PART 2** • 1976
HOLLYWOOD HONEYMOON • Yates Hal • SHT • USA
HOLLYWOOD HOODLUM • 1934 • Eason B. Reeves • USA • WHAT PRICE FAME? (UKN)
HOLLYWOOD HOOKERS see **HOLLYWOOD CHAINSAW HOOKERS** • 1988
HOLLYWOOD HOT TUBS • 1984 • Vincent Chuck • USA
HOLLYWOOD HOTEL • 1938 • Berkeley Busby • USA
HOLLYWOOD IN DEBLATSCHKA PESCARA • 1965 • Schamoni Ulrich • SHT • FRG
HOLLYWOOD KID, THE • 1924 • Del Ruth Roy • USA
HOLLYWOOD KIDS • 1932 • Lamont Charles • SHT • USA
HOLLYWOOD KNIGHT • 1979 • Worth David • USA
HOLLYWOOD KNIGHTS, THE • 1980 • Mutrux Floyd • USA
HOLLYWOOD LUCK • 1932 • Arbuckle Roscoe • USA
HOLLYWOOD MAN • 1976 • Starrett Jack • USA • DEATH THREAT ○ NO ONE CRIES FOREVER
HOLLYWOOD MATADOR, THE • 1942 • Lantz Walter • ANS • USA
HOLLYWOOD MEATCLEAVER MASSACRE see **MEATCLEAVER MASSACRE** • 1977
HOLLYWOOD NUDES see **HOLLYWOOD NUDES REPORT** • 1963
HOLLYWOOD NUDES REPORT • 1963 • Mahon Barry • USA • HOLLYWOOD REPORT, OR HOW GIRLS MAKE NUDIE MOVIES ○ HOLLYWOOD NUDES
HOLLYWOOD ON TRIAL • 1976 • Helpern David Jr. • DOC • USA
HOLLYWOOD OR BUST • 1956 • Tashlin Frank • USA
HOLLYWOOD OUTTAKES • 1979 • *Schwarz Richard (P)* • USA
HOLLYWOOD OUTTAKES • 1984 • Goldstein Bruce • CMP • USA
HOLLYWOOD PARTY • 1934 • Boleslawski Richard (U/c), Dwan Allan (U/c), Goulding Edmund (U/c), Rowland Roy (U/c) • USA
HOLLYWOOD PARTY IN TECHNICOLOR • 1937 • Rowland Roy • SHT • USA
HOLLYWOOD PICNIC • 1937 • *Mintz Charles (P)* • ANS • USA
HOLLYWOOD PINK • *Bleu Bunny* • USA
HOLLYWOOD PREMIERE • 1933 • Roth Murray • USA
HOLLYWOOD REPORT, OR HOW GIRLS MAKE NUDIE MOVIES see **HOLLYWOOD NUDES REPORT** • 1963
HOLLYWOOD REPORTER, THE • 1926 • Mitchell Bruce • USA
HOLLYWOOD REVUE, THE (UKN) see **HOLLYWOOD REVUE OF 1929, THE** • 1929
HOLLYWOOD REVUE OF 1929 see **WIR SCHALTEN UM AUF HOLLYWOOD** • 1931
HOLLYWOOD REVUE OF 1929, THE • 1929 • Reisner Charles F. • USA • HOLLYWOOD REVUE, THE (UKN)
HOLLYWOOD RHAPSODY see **LIFE AND DEATH OF 9413, A HOLLYWOOD EXTRA, THE** • 1928
HOLLYWOOD ROUND-UP • 1938 • Scott Ewing • USA
HOLLYWOOD RUNAROUND • 1932 • Lamont Charles • SHT • USA
HOLLYWOOD SCOUT • 1945 • Anderson Philip • SHT • USA
HOLLYWOOD SCREEN TEST • 1937 • Simon S. Sylvan • SHT • USA
HOLLYWOOD SHOWER OF STARS • 1955 • *Columbia* • SHT • USA
HOLLYWOOD SHUFFLE • 1987 • Townsend Robert • USA
HOLLYWOOD SPEAKS • 1932 • Buzzell Edward • USA
HOLLYWOOD STADIUM MYSTERY • 1938 • Howard David • USA • STADIUM MURDERS, THE
HOLLYWOOD STAR, A • 1929 • Sennett Mack • SHT • USA
HOLLYWOOD STARS ON PARADE • 1954 • *Columbia* • SHT • USA
HOLLYWOOD STEPS OUT • 1941 • Avery Tex • ANS • USA
HOLLYWOOD STORY • 1951 • Castle William • USA
HOLLYWOOD STRANGLER, THE see **DON'T ANSWER THE PHONE!** • 1980
HOLLYWOOD STRANGLER MEETS THE SKID ROW SLASHER • 1982 • Steckler Ray Dennis • USA
HOLLYWOOD SUPERSTAR see **DINAH EAST** • 1970
HOLLYWOOD SWEEPSTAKES • 1939 • Harrison Ben • ANS • USA
HOLLYWOOD TEN, THE • 1970 • Burke Martyn • DOC • CND
HOLLYWOOD -THE SECOND STEP • 1936 • Feist Felix E. • USA
HOLLYWOOD THEME SONG, A • 1930 • Beaudine William • SHT • USA
HOLLYWOOD THRILL MAKERS • 1953 • Ray Bernard B. • USA
HOLLYWOOD THROUGH A KEYHOLE see **CHEVAUX D'HOLLYWOOD, LES** • 1964
HOLLYWOOD TROUBLE • 1935 • Townley Jack • SHT • USA
HOLLYWOOD VARIETIES • 1950 • Landres Paul • USA
HOLLYWOOD VICE SQUAD • 1986 • Spheeris Penelope • USA
HOLLYWOOD WIVES • 1985 • Day Robert • MTV • USA
HOLLYWOOD YOU NEVER SEE, THE • 1935 • *De Mille Cecil* • SHT • USA
HOLLYWOOD ZAP • 1986 • Cohen David • USA
HOLLYWOOD'S WORLD OF FLESH • 1963 • Frost R. L. • USA • WORLD OF FLESH
HOLNAP MAJD HOLNAP see **MAJD HOLNAP** • 1980
HOLOCAUST • 1978 • Chomsky Marvin • MTV • USA
HOLOCAUST see **OLOKAFTOMA** • 1970
HOLOCAUST 2000 • 1978 • De Martino Alberto • ITL, UKN • CHOSEN, THE
HOLOCAUST - SIKHS • 1986 • Singh Hardev • CND
HOLSTEIN • 1978 • Owen Don • CND
"HOLT-HUP" ISTANTANEA DI UNA RAPINA • 1974 • Lorente German • ITL
HOLT OF THE SECRET SERVICE • 1941 • Horne James W. • SRL • USA
HOLT VIDEK • 1971 • Gaal Istvan • HNG • DEAD LANDSCAPE ○ DEAD COUNTRY, THE ○ DEAD AREA
HOLTAK VISSZAJARNAK, A • 1968 • Wiedermann Karoly • HNG • DEAD COME BACK, THE
HOLTPONT • 1983 • Peterffy Andras • HNG • DEAD END
HOLUBICE • 1960 • Vlacil Frantisek • CZC • WHITE DOVE, THE ○ DOVE
HOLY DEVIL, THE see **SVYATOI CHORT** • 1917
HOLY FAMILY, THE • 1972 • van den Brink Jan • DOC • NTH
HOLY FAMILY, THE • 1981 • Kerbosch Roeland • DOC • NTH
HOLY FAMILY, THE see **PYHA PERHE** • 1976
HOLY INNOCENTS, THE see **SANTOS INOCENTES, LOS** • 1984
HOLY JUMPING JIMMINY! SAID MR. WHO see **HERRA HUU - JESTAPA JEPULIS, PENIKAT SIPULIKS** • 1974
HOLY LIE see **HELIGA LOGNEN, DEN** • 1944
HOLY MATRIMONY • 1943 • Stahl John M. • USA
HOLY MOUNTAIN, THE see **HEILIGE BERG, DER** • 1926
HOLY MOUNTAIN, THE see **MONTANA SAGRADA, LA** • 1972
HOLY OFFICE, THE see **SANTO OFICIO, EL** • 1972
HOLY ORDERS • 1917 • Coleby A. E., Rooke Arthur • UKN
HOLY PILGRIMAGE see **TEERTH YATRA** • 1958
HOLY PILGRIMAGE -KAMRUP, THE see **DEBITIRTHA-KAMRUP** • 1967
HOLY SAINT, THE (USA) see **ANNEE SAINTE, L'** • 1976
HOLY SINNER, THE • 1929 • *Worldart Film Co.* • USA
HOLY SINNER, THE see **SVATA HRISNICE** • 1970
HOLY SMOKE • 1963 • Borowczyk Walerian • ANS • FRN
HOLY SPIRITS see **KHOMSAN** • 1990
HOLY TERROR see **ALICE, SWEET ALICE** • 1977
HOLY TERROR, A • 1931 • Cummings Irving • USA
HOLY TERROR, THE • 1929 • Mack Anthony • SHT • USA
HOLY TERROR, THE • 1937 • Tinling James • USA
HOLY TERROR, THE see **BEBERT ET L'OMNIBUS** • 1963
HOLY YEAR 1950 • 1950 • Muto Anthony
HOLZ HACKEN • 1978 • Michalak Richard • SHT • ASL
HOLZAPEL WEISSE ALLES • 1932 • Janson Victor • FRG
HOMA KE EMA • 1967 • Dimopoulos Aris • GRC • EARTH AND BLOOD
HOMA VAFTIKE KOKKINO, TO • 1965 • Georgiadis Vassilis • GRC • TERRE SANGLANTE ○ BLOOD ON THE LAND
HOMAGE • 1915 • Worthington William • USA
HOMAGE A M. BELL see **FOR YOU MR. BELL** • 1972
HOMAGE AT SIESTA TIME see **HOMENAJE A LA HORA DE LA SIESTA** • 1964
HOMAGE TO ADRIANA see **HOMENAJE PARA ADRIANA** • 1968
HOMAGE TO CHAGALL -THE COLOURS OF LOVE • 1976 • Rasky Harry • DOC • CND
HOMAGE TO FRANCOIS COUPERIN • 1964 • Stapp Philip • ANS • USA
HOMAGE TO JEAN TINGUELY'S HOMAGE TO NEW YORK • 1960 • Breer Robert • SHT • USA
HOMAGE TO TARZAN see **HOMENAJE A TARZAN** • 1970
HOMARD, LE • 1913 • Perret Leonce • FRN
HOMBORI see **HOMBROI** • 1949
HOMBRA DE MODA, EL • 1980 • Mendez-Leite Fernando • SPN • FASHIONABLE MAN, THE ○ MAN IN VOGUE, THE
HOMBRE • 1967 • Ritt Martin • USA
HOMBRE • 1970 • de la Cerda Clemente • VNZ • MAN
HOMBRE • 1975 • *Cine Vision* • MXC
HOMBRE ACOSADO • 1950 • Lazaga Pedro • SPN
HOMBRE COMO LOS DEMAS, UN • 1974 • Maso Pedro • SPN
HOMBRE CUANDO ES HOMBRE, EL • 1982 • Sarmiento Valeria • CRC, CHL • MAN WHEN HE'S A MAN, A
HOMBRE DE CARACAS, EL • 1968 • Xiol Juan • SPN
HOMBRE DE LA AMETRALLODORA, EL • 1960 • Urueta Chano • MXC
HOMBRE DE LA DILIGENCIA ,EL • 1963 • Elorrieta Jose Maria • SPN, ITL • FURIA DEGLI APACHE, LA ○ FURY OF THE APACHES ○ APACHE FURY
HOMBRE DE LA ESQUINA ROSADA • 1961 • Mujica Rene • ARG
HOMBRE DE LA FURIA, EL • 1965 • Orozco Fernando • MXC, VNZ • MAS ALLA DE ORINOCO
HOMBRE DE LA ISLA, EL • 1959 • Escriva Vicente • SPN
HOMBRE DE LA LEGION, EL (SPN) see **UOMO DELLA LEGIONE, L'** • 1940
HOMBRE DE LA MANDOLINA, EL • 1983 • Ortega Gonzalo Martinez • MXC • MAN WITH THE MANDOLIN, THE
HOMBRE DE LA MASCARA DE HIERRO, EL • 1943 • Aurelio Galindo Marco • MXC
HOMBRE DE LOS HONGOS, EL • 1976 • Gavaldon Roberto • MXC
HOMBRE DE LOS MUNECOS, EL • 1943 • Iquino Ignacio F. • SPN
HOMBRE DE MAISINICU, EL • 1973 • Perez Manuel • CUB • MAN FROM MAISINICU, THE
HOMBRE DE MARRAKECH, EL see **HOMME DE MARRAKECH, L'** • 1966
HOMBRE DE MUNDO, EL • 1948 • Tamayo Manuel • SPN
HOMBRE DE NEGOCIOS, UN • 1945 • Lucia Luis • SPN
HOMBRE DE PAPEL, EL • 1963 • Rodriguez Ismael • MXC • PAPER MAN, THE
HOMBRE DE TOLEDO, EL • 1966 • Martin Eugenio • SPN, ITL, FRG • UOMO DI TOLEDO, L' ○ CAPTAIN FROM TOLEDO (UKN)
HOMBRE DE UNA SOLA NOTE, UN • 1988 • Pineda Frank • NCR • MAN WITH ONLY ONE NOTE, THE
HOMBRE DEL ALAZAN, EL • 1958 • Gonzalez Rogelio A. • MXC
HOMBRE DEL EXPRESO DE ORIENTE, EL • 1961 • Moro Francesco De Borja • SPN
HOMBRE DEL PARAGUAS BLANCAS, EL • 1958 • Romero-Marchent Joaquin Luis • SPN
HOMBRE DEL PUENTE, EL • 1975 • *Conacine* • MXC
HOMBRE DEL PUNO DE ORO, EL • 1966 • Balcazar Jaime Jesus • SPN, ITL • UOMO DAL PUGNO D'ORO, L' (ITL) ○ MAN WITH THE GOLDEN FIST, THE
HOMBRE DEL RIO MALO, EL (SPN) see **...E CONTINUAVANO A FREGARSI IL MILIONE DI DOLLARI** • 1971
HOMBRE DEL SABADO, EL • 1947 • Torres-Rios Leopoldo • ARG
HOMBRE DEL VALLE MALDITO, EL (SPN) see **UOMO DELLA VALLE MALEDETTA, L'** • 1964
HOMBRE EN LA TRAMPA • 1968 • Cervera Pascual • SPN
HOMBRE EN LA TRAMPA, UN • 1963 • Baledon Rafael • MXC
HOMBRE EN MI VIDA • 1932 • Beaudine William • USA
HOMBRE IMPORTANTE, EL see **ANIMAS TRUJANO, EL HOMBRE IMPORTANTE** • 1961
HOMBRE INQUIETO, EL • 1954 • Salvador Jaime • MXC
HOMBRE INVISIBLE ATACA, EL • 1967 • Mentasti Martin Rodriguez • ARG • INVISIBLE MAN ATTACKS, THE
HOMBRE LLAMADO FLOR DE OTONO, UN • 1978 • Olea Pedro • SPN • FLOWER OF AUTUMN ○ FLOR DE OTONO
HOMBRE LLAMADO LOLA, UN • 1977 • Lazaga Pedro • SPN
HOMBRE MAIO, EL • 1930 • McGann William • SPN
HOMBRE MIRANDO AL SUDESTE • 1986 • Subiela Eliseo • ARG • MAN FACING SOUTHEAST (USA) ○ MAN LOOKING SOUTHEAST
HOMBRE O DEMONIO (MXC) see **MAD EMPRESS, THE** • 1939
HOMBRE OCULTO, EL • 1970 • Ungria Alfonso • SPN • MAN IN HIDING, THE ○ HIDING MAN, THE
HOMBRE PELIGROSO, UN • 1935 • Kahn Richard C. • MXC • DANGEROUS MAN, A (USA)
HOMBRE PELIGROSO, UN • 1964 • Martinez Arturo? • MXC
HOMBRE PERSEGUIDO POR UN OVNI, EL • 1975 • Olaria Juan Carlos • SPN
HOMBRE PROPONE.., EL • 1964 • Chavira J. Alfonso • MXC
HOMBRE QUE ASESINO, EL • 1931 • Buchowetzki Dimitri, de Battle Carlos • SPN
HOMBRE QUE GANO LA RAZON, EL • 1986 • Agresti Alejandro • ARG
HOMBRE QUE HIZO EL MILAGRO, EL • 1958 • Sandrini Luis • ARG • MAN WHO CREATED A MIRACLE, THE
HOMBRE QUE LOGRO SER INVISIBLE, EL • 1957 • Crevenna Alfredo B. • MXC • INVISIBLE MAN IN MEXICO (UKN) ○ NEW INVISIBLE MAN, THE (USA) ○ H.G. WELLS' NEW INVISIBLE MAN ○ MAN WHO BENEFITS BY BEING INVISIBLE, THE
HOMBRE QUE MATO A BILLY EL NINO, EL (SPN) see **...E DIVENNE IL PIU SPIETATO BANDITO DEL SUD** • 1967
HOMBRE QUE ME GUSTA, EL • 1958 • Demicheli Tulio • MXC
HOMBRE QUE PERDIO EL TREN, EL • 1958 • Klimovsky Leon • SPN
HOMBRE QUE QUISO SER POBRE, EL • 1955 • Salvador Jaime • MXC
HOMBRE QUE SE QUISO MATAR • 1941 • Gil Rafael • SPN
HOMBRE QUE SE QUISO MATAR, EL • 1970 • Gil Rafael • SPN
HOMBRE QUE SE REIA DEL AMOR, EL • 1932 • Perojo Benito • SPN
HOMBRE QUE SUPO AMAR, EL • 1976 • Picazo Miguel • SPN
HOMBRE QUE VIAJABA DESPACITO, EL • 1957 • Romero-Marchent Joaquin Luis • SPN
HOMBRE QUE VINO DEL ODIO, EL • 1970 • Klimovsky Leon • SPN
HOMBRE QUE VINO DEL UMMO, EL • 1970 • Demicheli Tulio • SPN, FRG, ITL • DRACULA JAGD FRANKENSTEIN (FRG) ○ MONSTRUOS DEL TERROR, LOS ○ OPERACION TERROR ○ ASSIGNMENT TERROR ○ DRACULA VS. FRANKENSTEIN (UKN) ○ MAN WHO CAME FROM UMMO, THE ○ FRG ○ DRACULA HUNTS FRANKENSTEIN
HOMBRE QUE YO QUIERO, EL • 1978 • Porto Juan Jose • SPN
HOMBRE SIN HONOR • 1944 • Iquino Ignacio F. • SPN
HOMBRE SIN PATRIA, EL • 1922 • Contreras Torres Miguel • MXC • MAN WITHOUT A COUNTRY, THE
HOMBRE SIN ROSTRO, EL • 1950 • Bustillo Oro Juan • MXC • MAN WITHOUT A FACE, THE
HOMBRE SOLO NO VALE NADA, UN • 1949 • Lugones Mario C. • ARG
HOMBRE.. UNA CIUDAD, UN • 1980 • Hildalgo Joaquin • SPN • MAN.. A CITY, A
HOMBRE VA POR EL CAMINO, UN • 1949 • Mur Oti • SPN
HOMBRE VINO A MATAR, UN • 1968 • Klimovsky Leon • SPN, ITL • UOMO VENUTO PER UCCIDERE, L' (ITL) ○ MAN CAME TO KILL, A ○ RATTLER KID
HOMBRE Y EL FUEGO, EL • 1970 • Carretero Amaro • ANS • SPN • MAN AND FIRE
HOMBRE Y EL MONSTRUO, EL • 1958 • Baledon Rafael • MXC • MAN AND THE MONSTER, THE (USA)
HOMBRE Y LA BESTIA, EL • 1962 • MXC • MAN AND THE BEAST, THE
HOMBRE Y LA BESTIA, EL • 1972 • Soler Julian • MXC • MAN AND THE BEAST, THE
HOMBRE Y LA BESTIA, EL see **EXTRANO CASO DEL HOMBRE Y LA BESTIA, EL** • 1951
HOMBRE Y UN COLT, UN • 1967 • Demicheli Tulio • SPN, ITL • UOMO E UNA COLT, UN (ITL)

HOMBRES CONTRA HOMBRES • 1953 • Momplet Antonio • SPN
HOMBRES DE LUPE ALVIREZ, LOS • 1966 • Martinez Arturo • MXC
HOMBRES DE ROCA • 1965 • de Anda Raul Jr. • MXC
HOMBRES DEL AIRE • 1939 • Martinez Solares Gilberto • MXC
HOMBRES DEL MAL TIEMPO 1968 • 1968 • Saderman Alejandro • CUB
HOMBRES DEL MAR • 1938 • Urueta Chano • MXC • MEN OF THE SEA (USA)
HOMBRES DEL MAR • 1977 • Demare Lucas • VNZ • SEAMEN
HOMBRES LAS PREFIEREN VIUDAS, LOS • 1970 • Klimovsky Leon • SPN
HOMBRES NO LLORAN, LOS • 1971 • *Estudios America* • MXC
HOMBRES PIENSAN SOLO EN ESO, LOS • 1977 • Cahen Enrique • VNZ, ARG • MEN THINK ONLY ABOUT THAT
HOMBRES SIN ALMA • 1950 • Orol Juan • MXC
HOMBROI • 1949 • Rouch Jean • DCS • FRN • HOMBORI
HOME • 1911 • Merwin Bannister • USA
HOME • 1915 • Elvey Maurice • UKN
HOME • 1916 • Miller Charles • USA
HOME • 1919 • Weber Lois • USA
HOME • 1977 • Templeman Connie • UKN
HOME see **DOM** • 1958
HOME AGAIN • 1912 • *Imp* • USA
HOME AGAIN • 1915 • *Tincher Fay* • USA
HOME AGAIN • 1959 • Jacoby Irving • SHT • USA
HOME AGAIN MY CHERRY BLOSSOM • 1907 • Gilbert Arthur • UKN
HOME AGAIN MY CHERRY BLOSSOM • 1909 • *Warwick Trading Co.* • UKN
HOME ALONE • 1990 • Columbus Chris • USA
HOME AND ABROAD see **DES PARDES** • 1978
HOME AND AWAY • 1956 • Sewell Vernon • UKN
HOME AND AWAY • 1974 • Alexander Mike • UKN
HOME AND MOTHER • 1912 • *Davenport Dorothy* • USA
HOME AND REFUGE see **YON SYLISSA** • 1977
HOME AND THE WORLD, THE see **GHARE BHAIRE** • 1983
HOME AT HONG KONG see **CHIA TSAI HSIANG-KANG** • 1984
HOME AT LAST, A • 1909 • *Vitagraph* • USA
HOME AT SEVEN • 1952 • Richardson Ralph • UKN • MURDER ON MONDAY (USA)
HOME BEAUTIFUL, THE • 1913 • Stow Percy • UKN
HOME BEFORE DARK • 1958 • LeRoy Mervyn • USA
HOME BEFORE MIDNIGHT • 1980 • Walker Pete • UKN
HOME BONER • 1939 • D'Arcy Harry • SHT • USA
HOME BREAKER, THE see **HOMEBREAKER, THE** • 1919
HOME BREAKERS, THE • 1915 • Wright Walter • USA
HOME BREAKERS, THE • 1916 • Bracken Bertram • SHT • USA
HOME BREAKING HOUND, A • 1915 • Parrott Charles • USA
HOME BREW • 1919 • *Christie* • USA
HOME BREW • 1920 • *Century* • SHT • USA
HOME BREW see **FIRESIDE BREWER, A** • 1920
HOME CANNING • 1948 • Yates Hal • SHT • USA
HOME-CASTLES see **KASHTI-KREPOSTI** • 1966
HOME COMFORTS • 1916 • Storrie Kelly • UKN
HOME COMING • 1915 • Calvert E. H. • USA
HOME-COMING SONG (USA) see **CANCION DEL REGRESO, LA** • 1940
HOME CONSTRUCTION • 1926 • Sanderson Challis, Newman Widgey R. • UKN
HOME CURE, THE • 1915 • Drew Sidney • USA
HOME DE NEO, L' • 1988 • Abril Albert • SPN • NEON MAN, THE
HOME DEFENCE • 1917 • De Vonde Chester M. • SHT • USA
HOME DEFENSE • 1943 • King Jack • ANS • USA
HOME EARLY • 1939 • Rowland Roy • SHT • USA
HOME FIRES • 1983 • King Allan, Till Eric • SER • CND
HOME FIRES • 1987 • Uno Michael Toshiyuki • TVM • USA
HOME FOLKS • 1912 • Griffith D. W. • USA
HOME FOR CHRISTMAS see **JOULUKSI KOTIIN** • 1974
HOME FOR GENTLE SOULS, A • 1980 • Mihailov Evgeniy • BUL
HOME FOR TANYA, A (USA) see **OTCHII DOM** • 1959
HOME FOR THE HOLIDAYS • 1972 • Moxey John Llewellyn • TVM • USA
HOME FOR THE HOLIDAYS see **THREE LITTLE VAGABONDS** • 1913
HOME FOR THE HOMELESS • 1981 • Dueck David B. • CND • HEIMAT FUR HEIMATLOSE
HOME FREE • 1972 • Eckert John M. • CND
HOME FREE • 1976 • Yates Rebecca, Salzman Glen • CND
HOME FREE see **VISITORS, THE** • 1972
HOME FREE ALL • 1983 • Bird Stewart • USA
HOME FROM BABYLON see **HEM FRAN BABYLON** • 1941
HOME FROM HANGING, A see **DOM ZA VESANJE** • 1987
HOME FROM HOME • 1939 • Smith Herbert • UKN
HOME FROM HOME • 1982 • Heaven Simon • DOC • UKN
HOME FROM THE CLUB • 1903 • *Warwick Trading Co.* • UKN
HOME FROM THE HILL • 1960 • Minnelli Vincente • USA
HOME FROM THE SEA • 1962 • Peries Lester James • SHT • SLN
HOME FROM THE SEA see **KOKYO** • 1972
HOME FRONT, THE • 1940 • Hawes Stanley • DCS • CND
HOME FRONT, THE • 1980 • Harris Harry • TVM • USA
HOME GUARD, THE • 1941 • Davis Mannie • ANS • USA
HOME GUARD, THE • 1941 • Taylor Donald • UKN • CITIZEN'S ARMY
HOME IN INDIANA • 1944 • Hathaway Henry • USA
HOME IN OKLAHOMA • 1946 • Witney William • USA
HOME IN SAN ANTONE • 1949 • Nazarro Ray • USA • HARMONY INN (UKN)
HOME IN WYOMIN' • 1942 • Morgan William • USA
HOME INFLUENCE • 1920 • Mannering Cecil • UKN
HOME IS BEST AFTER ALL • 1911 • *Lubin* • USA
HOME IS CALLING see **HEIMAT RUFT, DIE** • 1937
HOME IS THE HERO • 1959 • Cook Fielder • UKN • SINS OF THE FATHER
HOME IS THE SAILOR see **HEMPAS BAR** • 1978
HOME IS WHERE THE HEART IS • 1987 • Bromfield Rex • USA
HOME IS WHERE THE HEART IS see **SQUARE DANCE** • 1987
HOME JAMES • 1918 • Sautell Albert A. • SHT • USA
HOME JAMES • 1928 • Beaudine William • USA
HOME-KEEPING HEARTS • 1921 • Ellis Carlyle • USA
HOME LIFE • 1962 • Rasinski Connie • ANS • USA
HOME MADE • 1927 • Hines Charles • USA
HOME-MADE CAR, THE • 1964 • Hill James • SHT • UKN
HOME MADE HOME • 1951 • Kinney Jack • ANS • USA
HOME MADE MAN, A • 1928 • Taurog Norman • SHT • USA
HOME-MADE MINCE PIE • 1910 • *Thanhouser* • USA
HOME-MADE PIES • 1916 • *Stull Walter* • USA
HOME MAID • 1944 • Jason Will • SHT • USA
HOME MAKER, THE • 1925 • Baggot King • USA
HOME MELODY, A • 1910 • *Vitagraph* • USA
HOME MOVIE • 1969 • Cantrill Arthur, Cantrill Corinne • ASL
HOME MOVIES • 1940 • Wrangell Basil • SHT • USA
HOME MOVIES • 1980 • De Palma Brian • USA
HOME NATIONAL COUNCIL 1943 see **KRAJOWA RADA NARODOWA 1943** • 1945
HOME OF A MARRIED WOMAN'S PARENTS see **MAITIGHAR** • 1960
HOME OF OUR OWN, A • 1975 • Day Robert • USA
HOME OF SILENCE, THE • 1915 • *Farrington Reenie* • USA
HOME OF THE BLIZZARD see **DR. MAWSON IN THE ANTARCTIC** • 1913
HOME OF THE BRAVE • 1949 • Robson Mark • USA
HOME OF THE BRAVE • 1960 • Hart Harvey • MTV • CND
HOME OF THE BRAVE • 1986 • Anderson Laurie • USA
HOME OF THE BUFFALO • 1934 • Oliver Bill • DOC • CND
HOME OF THE ICEBERG • 1948 • Parker Benjamin R. • SHT • USA
HOME OF YOUR OWN, A • 1964 • Lewis Jay • UKN
HOME ON THE PRAIRIE • 1939 • Townley Jack • USA
HOME ON THE RAGE • 1938 • Lord Del • SHT • USA
HOME ON THE RAILS • 1982 • Driessen Paul • ANM • NTH, CND
HOME ON THE RANGE • 1933 • Willett Paul B. • USA
HOME ON THE RANGE • 1935 • Jacobson Arthur • USA • CODE OF THE WEST
HOME ON THE RANGE • 1940 • Ising Rudolf • ANS • USA
HOME ON THE RANGE • 1944-45 • Jodoin Rene, McLaren Norman • ANS • CND
HOME ON THE RANGE • 1946 • Springsteen R. G. • USA
HOME ON THE RANGE • 1982 • Scrine Gil • DCS • ASL
HOME RULE • 1920 • *Conklin Chester* • USA
HOME RUN AMBROSE • 1918 • Fredericks Walter S. • SHT • USA
HOME RUN BAKER'S DOUBLE • 1914 • Buel Kenean • USA
HOME RUN BILL • 1919 • *Mason Billy* • SHT • USA
HOME RUN ON THE KEYS • 1936 • USA
HOME SECRETARY, THE see **MINISTERN** • 1971
HOME SPUN • 1913 • *Travers Richard C.* • USA
HOME SPUN FOLKS see **HOMESPUN FOLKS** • 1920
HOME STRETCH, THE • 1920 • Roach Hal • SHT • USA
HOME STRETCH, THE • 1921 • Nelson Jack • USA
HOME STRIKE-BREAKERS, THE • 1912 • *Imp* • USA
HOME STRUCK • 1927 • Ince Ralph • USA
HOME STUFF • 1921 • Kelley Albert • USA
HOME SWEET HOME • 1911 • Golden Joseph A. • USA
HOME SWEET HOME • 1912 • *Lubin* • USA
HOME SWEET HOME • 1913 • O'Neil Barry • USA
HOME SWEET HOME • 1914 • Griffith D. W. • USA
HOME SWEET HOME • 1917 • Noy Wilfred • UKN
HOME SWEET HOME • 1921 • Parkinson H. B. • SHT • UKN
HOME SWEET HOME • 1933 • Cooper George A. • UKN
HOME SWEET HOME • 1945 • Blakeley John E. • UKN
HOME SWEET HOME • 1970 • Zwartjes Frans • SHT • NTH
HOME SWEET HOME • 1972 • de Kermadec Liliane • FRN
HOME SWEET HOME • 1973 • Lamy Benoit • BLG • FETE A JULES, LA
HOME SWEET HOME • 1980 • Mills Michael (c/d) • SER • CND
HOME SWEET HOME • 1980 • Pena Nettie • USA
HOME SWEET HOMEWRECKER • 1962 • Smith Paul J. • ANS • USA
HOME, SWEET HOMICIDE • 1946 • Bacon Lloyd • USA
HOME SWEET NUDNIK • 1965 • Deitch Gene • ANS • USA
HOME SWEET SWAMPY • 1962 • Kneitel Seymour • ANS • USA
HOME TALENT • 1921 • Sennett Mack • USA
HOME TO DANGER • 1951 • Fisher Terence • UKN
HOME TO OUR MOUNTAINS (IL TROVATORE) • 1906 • Gilbert Arthur • UKN
HOME TO STAY • 1978 • Mann Delbert • TVM • USA
HOME TOWN see **FURUSATO** • 1930
HOME TOWN GIRL, THE • 1919 • Vignola Robert G. • USA
HOME TOWN OLYMPICS • 1936 • *Terry Paul/ Moser Frank (P)* • ANS • USA
HOME TOWN STORY • 1951 • Pierson Arthur • USA
HOME TOWNERS, THE • 1928 • Foy Bryan • USA
HOME TRAIL, THE • 1918 • Wolbert William • USA
HOME TRAIL, THE • 1927 • Wyler William • SHT • USA
HOME TRIP see **POROZHNII REIS** • 1963
HOME TWEET HOME • 1950 • Freleng Friz • ANS • USA
HOME WANTED • 1919 • Johnson Tefft • USA
HOME WITH A SECRET • 1963 • Lofven Chris • SHT • ASL
HOME WITHOUT MOTHER • 1906 • Martin J. H.? • UKN
HOME WORK • 1935 • Goulding Alf • SHT • USA
HOME WORK • 1942 • D'Arcy Harry • SHT • USA
HOME WRECKERS, THE • 1917 • Chaudet Louis W. • SHT • USA
HOMEBODIES • 1974 • Yust Larry • USA
HOMEBOUND see **KOTIA PAIN** • 1989
HOMEBOUND ESCAPE FROM THE PAST see **KOTIA PAIN** • 1989
HOMEBOY • 1989 • Seresin Michael • USA
HOMEBOYS • 1978 • Yahruas Bill • DOC • USA
HOMEBREAKER, THE • 1919 • Schertzinger Victor • USA • HOME BREAKER, THE
HOMECOMING • 1948 • LeRoy Mervyn • USA
HOMECOMING • 1979 • Carle Gilles • MTV • CND
HOMECOMING • 1990 • Majdzadeh Hassan • IRN
HOMECOMING see **HEIMKEHR** • 1928
HOMECOMING see **HEIMKEHR** • 1941
HOMECOMING see **KIKYO** • 1964
HOMECOMING, THE • 1912 • *Eclair* • USA
HOMECOMING, THE • 1973 • Hall Peter • UKN, USA
HOMECOMING, THE see **IGNOTAS CAME BACK HOME** • 1956
HOMECOMING, THE see **POVRATAK** • 1966
HOMECOMING, THE see **HOMECOMING: A CHRISTMAS STORY, THE** • 1971
HOMECOMING: A CHRISTMAS STORY, THE • 1971 • Cook Fielder • TVM • USA • HOMECOMING, THE
HOMECOMING BALLAD, THE see **BALADA DEL REGRESO, LA** • 1974
HOMECOMING NIGHT see **NIGHT OF THE CREEPS** • 1986
HOMECOMING OF HENRY, THE • 1915 • Young James • USA
HOMECOMING OF JIM, THE • 1920 • Miller Ashley • SHT • USA
HOMECOMING SONG • 1983 • Smaragdis Ianis • GRC
HOMEFRONT see **MORGAN STEWART'S COMING HOME** • 1987
HOMELAND see **LO PAIS** • 1974
HOMELAND see **HEIMAT** • 1984
HOMELAND OF ELECTRICITY, THE • 1968 • Shepitko Larissa • DCS • USS
HOMELESS • 1916 • Tucker George Loane • SHT • USA
HOMELESS FLEA, THE • 1940 • Ising Rudolf • ANS • USA
HOMELESS HARE • 1950 • Jones Charles M. • ANS • USA
HOMELESS ONES, THE • 1954 • Goldsmith Sidney • ANM • CND
HOMELESS PUP, THE • 1937 • Gordon George • ANS • USA
HOMELY GIRL • 1936 • Koster Henry • USA
HOMELY SISTERS, THE see **NAMIDA GAWA** • 1967
HOMEM AS DIREITAS, UM • 1944 • do Canto Jorge Brum • PRT
HOMEM CELEBRE, O • 1974 • Faria Miguel • BRZ
HOMEM DA CAPA PRETA, O • 1986 • Rezende Sergio • BRZ • MAN IN THE BLACK CAPE, THE
HOMEM DO CORPO FECHADO, O • 1972 • Magalhaes Schubert • BRZ
HOMEM DO PAU BRASIL, O • 1981 • de Andrade Joaquim Pedro • BRZ • MAN OF THE BRAZILIAN LOG, THE ○ MAN OF THE BRAZIL-TREE, THE
HOMEM DO RIBATEJO, UM • 1946 • Campos Henrique • PRT
HOMEM E O TRABALHO, O • 1960 • Spiguel Miguel • SHT • PRT
HOMEM E SUA JAULA, UM • 1969 • Campos Fernando Cony • BRZ • MAN AND HIS PRISON, A
HOMEM E UMA OBRA, UM • 1950 • Mendes Joao • SHT • PRT
HOMEM LOBO, O • 1971 • Rossi Raffaello • BRZ • WOLF MAN, THE
HOMEM NU, O • 1968 • Santos Roberto • BRZ • NAKED MAN, THE
HOMEM QUE VIROU SUCO, O • 1981 • de Andrade Joao Batista • BRZ • MAN WHO TURNED UP JUICE, THE
HOMEMADE MOVIE • 1990 • Watanabe Fumiki • JPN
HOMEMADE MOVIES • 1922 • Grey Ray, Meins Gus • SHT • USA
HOMEMAKER, THE • 1919 • Dewhurst George • UKN
HOMENAJE A LA HORA DE LA SIESTA • 1964 • Torre-Nilsson Leopoldo • ARG • FOUR WOMEN FOR ONE HERO (UKN) ○ HOMAGE AT SIESTA TIME
HOMENAJE A TARZAN • 1970 • Ruiz Rafael • ANM • SPN • CAZADORA INCONSCIENTE, LA ○ UNCONSCIOUS HUNTER, THE ○ HOMAGE TO TARZAN
HOMENAJE PARA ADRIANA • 1968 • Picazo Miguel • SPN • HOMAGE TO ADRIANA
HOMER • 1970 • Trent John • USA
HOMER AND EDDIE • 1989 • Konchalovsky Andrei • USA
HOMER COMES HOME • 1920 • Storm Jerome • USA
HOMER ON THE RANGE • 1964 • Post Howard • ANS • USA
HOMER, THE HORSE WHO COULDN'T TALK • 1958 • Bunin Louis • ANM • USA
HOMER'S ODYSSEY • 1909 • *Special* • USA • ULYSSES
HOMER'S ODYSSEY (USA) see **ODISSEA, L'** • 1911
HOMES FOR ALL • 1947 • DOC • UKN • THIS MODERN AGE NO.1
HOMESDALE • 1971 • Weir Peter • DOC • ASL
HOMESICK • 1928 • Lehrman Henry • USA
HOMESICKNESS see **HEIMWEH** • 1927
HOMESICKNESS see **HEIMWEH** • 1937
HOMESICKNESS see **KYOSHU** • 1988
HOMESPUN FOLKS • 1920 • Wray John Griffith • USA • HOME SPUN FOLKS
HOMESPUN HERO, A • 1920 • Beaudine William • SHT • USA
HOMESPUN TRAGEDY, A • 1913 • Finley Ned, Castle James W. • USA
HOMESPUN VAMP, A • 1922 • O'Connor Frank • USA
HOMESTEAD RACE, THE • 1913 • *American* • USA
HOMESTEADER, THE • 1915 • *Gibson Margaret* • USA
HOMESTEADER, THE • 1922 • Micheaux Oscar • USA
HOMESTEADER DROOPY • 1954 • Avery Tex • ANS • USA
HOMESTEADERS, THE • 1953 • Collins Lewis D. • USA
HOMESTEADERS' FEUD, THE • 1917 • Horne James W. • SHT • USA
HOMESTEADERS OF PARADISE VALLEY • 1947 • Springsteen R. G. • USA
HOMESTRETCH, THE • 1947 • Humberstone H. Bruce • USA
HOMETOWN see **DOON PO SA AMIN** • 1968
HOMETOWN see **FURUSATO** • 1984
HOMETOWN U.S.A. • 1979 • Baer Max • USA
HOMETOWN (USA) see **FURUSATO** • 1922
HOMETOWN (USA) see **FURUSATO** • 1930
HOMEWARD see **HAZAFELE** • 1974
HOMEWARD BORNE • 1957 • Hiller Arthur • MTV • USA
HOMEWARD BOUND • 1923 • Ince Ralph • USA • LIGHT TO LEEWARD, THE
HOMEWARD BOUND • 1980 • Michaels Richard • TVM • USA
HOMEWARD IN DARKNESS see **YON SYLISSA** • 1977
HOMEWARD IN THE NIGHT see **YON SYLISSA** • 1977
HOMEWARD TRAIL, THE see **WALLOP, THE** • 1921
HOMEWORK • 1982 • Beshears James • USA • GROWING PAINS
HOMEWORK • 1989 • Kia-Rostami Abbas • IRN
HOMICIDAL • 1961 • Castle William • USA
HOMICIDE • 1948 • Jacoves Felix • USA
HOMICIDE see **REQUISITOIRE, LE** • 1930

HOMICIDE see **DEATH SCREAM** • 1975
HOMICIDE BUREAU • 1939 • Coleman C. C. Jr. • USA
HOMICIDE FOR THREE • 1948 • Blair George • USA • INTERRUPTED HONEYMOON, AN (UKN)
HOMICIDE PATROL • 1956 • Doniger Walter • USA
HOMICIDE SECTION: COUNTERSTROKE see **DIVISION HOMICIDIOS** • 1978
HOMICIDE SQUAD, THE • 1931 • Cahn Edward L., Melford George • USA • LOST MEN (UKN)
HOMICIDES PART II • Kuei Chih-Hung, Sun Chung, Hua Shan • HKG
HOMICIDE'S WEAPON, THE • 1917 • *American* • USA
HOMICIDIO CULPOSO • Bolivar Cesar • VNZ • GUILTY HOMICIDE
HOMICIDIO EN CHICAGO • 1968 • Zabalza Jose Maria • SPN
HOMLOCK SHERMES • 1913 • *White Pearl* • USA
HOMMAGE A ALBERT EINSTEIN • 1955 • Lods Jean • DCS • FRN
HOMMAGE A AUGUST SANDER • 1977 • Schnabel Pavel • DCS • FRG
HOMMAGE A DEBUSSY • 1967 • L'Herbier Marcel • SHT • FRN
HOMMAGE A DON HELDER CAMARA • 1971 • Buchet Jean-Marie • BLG
HOMMAGE A GEORGES BIZET • 1943 • Cuny Louis • FRN
HOMMAGE A NOTRE PAYSANNERIE • 1938 • Tessier Albert • DCS • CND
HOMMAGE TO RAMEAU • 1967 • Whitney John • SHT • USA
HOMME, L' • 1945 • Margaritis Gilles • SHT • FRN
HOMME, L' see **RAJAR, AR-** • 1968
HOMME A ABATTRE, L' • 1936 • Mathot Leon • FRN • MARKED MAN, THE
HOMME A ABATTRE, UN • 1967 • Condroyer Philippe • FRN, SPN • MAN TO KILL, A
HOMME A FEMMES, L' • 1960 • Cornu Jacques-Gerard • FRN
HOMME A LA BARBICHE, L' • 1932 • Valray Louis • SHT • FRN
HOMME A LA BUICK, L' • 1967 • Grangier Gilles • FRN
HOMME A LA CAGOULE NOIRE, L' see **BETE AUX SEPT MANTEAUX, LA** • 1936
HOMME A LA GRILLE, L' • 1918 • Protazanov Yakov • USS
HOMME A LA MER, UN • 1948 • Loew Jacques • SHT • FRN
HOMME A LA MER, UN • 1973 • Hella Patrick • BLG
HOMME A LA PIPE, L' • 1962 • Leenhardt Roger • DCS • FRN
HOMME A LA TETE EN CAOUTCHOUC, L' • 1902 • Melies Georges • FRN • MAN WITH THE RUBBER HEAD, THE (USA) ○ INDIA RUBBER HEAD, THE ○ SWELLED HEAD, A
HOMME A LA TRAINE, L' • 1986 • Beaudin Jean • CND
HOMME A LA VALISE, L' • 1984 • Akerman Chantal • FRN
HOMME A L'HISPANO, L' • 1926 • Duvivier Julien • FRN
HOMME A L'HISPANO, L' • 1932 • Epstein Jean • FRN • MAN IN THE HISPANO-SUIZA, THE
HOMME A L'IMPERMEABLE, L' • 1957 • Duvivier Julien • FRN, ITL • MAN IN THE RAINCOAT, THE (UKN)
HOMME A L'OREILLE CASSEE, L' • 1934 • Boudrioz Robert • FRN
HOMME A MA TAILLE, UN • 1983 • Carducci Annette • FRN, FRG
HOMME A TOUT FAIRE, L' • 1980 • Lanctot Micheline • CND • HANDYMAN, THE
HOMME A VENDRE, UN see **CAPTIF, LE** • 1957
HOMME AIMANTE, L' • 1907 • Feuillade Louis • FRN
HOMME AMOUREUX, UN • 1986 • Kurys Diane • FRN, ITL, USA • MAN IN LOVE, A
HOMME ATLANTIQUE, L' • 1981 • Duras Marguerite • FRN
HOMME AU CERVEAU GREFFE, L' • 1971 • Doniol-Valcroze Jacques • FRN, ITL, FRG • UOMO DAL CERVELLO TRAPIANTATO L' (ITL) ○ MAN WITH THE BRAIN GRAFT, THE ○ MAN WITH THE TRANSPLANTED BRAIN, THE
HOMME AU CHAPEAU DE SOIE, L' • 1983 • Linder Maud • DOC • FRN
HOMME AU CHAPEAU ROND, L' • 1946 • Billon Pierre • FRN • ETERNAL HUSBAND, THE (USA)
HOMME AU CRANE RASE, L' see **MAN DIE ZIJN HAAR KORT LIET KNIPPEN** • 1966
HOMME AU FOULARD A POIS, L' • 1916 • Feyder Jacques • FRN
HOMME AU GANTS BLANCS, L' • 1908 • Capellani Albert • FRN • MAN WITH THE WHITE GLOVES, THE
HOMME AU PILON, L' • 1969 • Tolbi Abdelaziz • ALG
HOMME AUX CENT TRUCS, L' • 1901 • Melies Georges • FRN • CONJURER WITH A HUNDRED TRICKS, THE (USA)
HOMME AUX CENT VISAGES, L' (FRN) see **MATTATORE, IL** • 1960
HOMME AUX CLEFS D'OR, L' • 1956 • Joannon Leo • FRN • MAN WITH THE GOLDEN KEYS (USA)
HOMME AUX FIGURES DE CIRE, L' see **FIGURES DE CIRE** • 1912
HOMME AUX MAINS D'AGILE, L' • 1949 • Mathot Leon • FRN
HOMME AUX MILLE INVENTIONS, L' • 1910 • Melies Georges • FRN • MAN WITH A THOUSAND INVENTIONS, THE
HOMME AUX NERFS D'ACIER, L' (FRN) see **SUO NOME FACEVA TREMARE.. INTERPOL IN ALLARME, IL** • 1973
HOMME AUX OISEAUX, L' • 1952 • Devlin Bernard, Palardy Jean • SHT • CND • BIRD FANCIER, THE
HOMME AUX TROIS MASQUES, L' • 1921 • Navarre Rene • FRN
HOMME BLESSE, L' • 1983 • Chereau Patrice • FRN
HOMME BRUN, L' • 1980 • Charles Freddy • BLG
HOMME, CETTE DUALITE, L' • 1958 • Lemaire Yvan • SHT • BLG • MAN, THAT DUAL PERSONALITY
HOMME CLOUE, L' • 1913 • Protazanov Yakov • USS
HOMME COMME IL FAUT, UN • 1909 • Melies Georges • FRN
HOMME D'A COTE, UN • 1982 • Truffaut Francois • FRN
HOMME DANS LA LUMIERE, L' • 1954 • Tavano Fred • SHT • FRN
HOMME DANS LA LUNE, L' • 1898 • Melies Georges • FRN • ASTRONOMER'S DREAM, THE (UKN) ○ TRIP TO THE MOON, A (USA) ○ LUNE A UN METRE, LA ○ MAN IN THE MOON, THE ○ REVE DE L'ASTRONOME, LE
HOMME DANS LA TOUR, L' see **MAN IN THE PEACE TOWER, THE** • 1951
HOMME DE COMPAGNE, L' • 1916 • Feyder Jacques • FRN
HOMME DE DAMAS, L' see **HOMMES DE PROIE, LES** • 1937
HOMME DE DESIR, L' • 1970 • Delouche Dominique • FRN • MAN OF DESIRE, THE
HOMME DE JOIE, L' • 1950 • Grangier Gilles • FRN
HOMME DE LA JAMAIQUE, L' • 1950 • de Canonge Maurice • FRN
HOMME DE LA NOUVELLE-ORLEANS, L' • 1958 • Rowe Thomas L. • SHT • FRN • TAILGATE MAN FROM NEW ORLEANS
HOMME DE LA NUIT, L' • 1946 • Jayet Rene • FRN
HOMME DE LA NUIT, L' see **CARREFOUR** • 1938
HOMME DE LA TOUR EIFFEL, L' see **MAN ON THE EIFFEL TOWER, THE** • 1949
HOMME DE L'INTERPOL, L' • 1965 • Boutel Maurice • FRN
HOMME DE LONDRES, L' • 1943 • Decoin Henri • FRN
HOMME DE MA VIE, L' • 1951 • Lefranc Guy • FRN, ITL • UOMO DELLA MIA VITA, L' (ITL)
HOMME DE MARRAKECH, L' • 1966 • Deray Jacques • FRN, ITL, SPN • SAQUEADORES DEL DOMINGO, LOS (SPN) ○ UOMO DI CASABLANCA, L' (ITL) ○ HOMBRE DE MARRAKECH, EL ○ THAT MAN GEORGE (USA) ○ OUR MAN IN MARRAKESH
HOMME DE MYKONOS, L' • 1965 • Gainville Rene • FRN, ITL, BLG
HOMME DE NEW YORK, L' • 1967 • Camus Marcel • FRN
HOMME DE NULLE PART, L' • 1936 • Chenal Pierre • FRN • LATE MATHIAS PASCAL, THE (USA) ○ MAN FROM NOWHERE, THE
HOMME DE PEINE, L' • 1911 • Carre Michel • FRN
HOMME DE PROIE, L' • 1912 • Feuillade Louis • FRN
HOMME DE RIO, L' • 1963 • de Broca Philippe • FRN, ITL • UOMO DI RIO, L' (ITL) ○ THAT MAN FROM RIO (USA) ○ MAN FROM RIO, THE
HOMME DE SUERTE, UN • 1930 • Perojo Benito • SPN
HOMME DE TETES, UN • 1898 • Melies Georges • FRN • FOUR TROUBLESOME HEADS, THE (USA) ○ MANY-HEADED MAN
HOMME DE TROP, UN • 1967 • Costa-Gavras • FRN, ITL • 13° UOMO, IL (ITL) ○ ONE MAN TOO MANY ○ SHOCK TROOPS
HOMME DE TROP A BORD, UN • 1935 • Le Bon Roger, Lamprecht Gerhard • FRN
HOMME DES CINQ SAISONS, L' see **TREFLE A CINQ FEUILLES, LE** • 1971
HOMME DES POISONS, L' • 1916 • Feuillade Louis • FRN
HOMME D'ISTAMBUL, L' (FRN) see **COLPO GROSSO A GALATA BRIDGE** • 1965
HOMME DU FLEUVE, L' • 1973 • Prevost Jean-Pierre • FRN
HOMME DU JOUR, L' • 1935 • Duvivier Julien • FRN • MAN OF THE HOUR (USA)
HOMME DU LAC, L' • 1962 • Garceau Raymond • DCS • CND • LAKE MAN, THE
HOMME DU LARGE, L' • 1920 • L'Herbier Marcel • FRN • MAN OF THE WIDE-OPEN SPACES, THE ○ MAN OF THE OPEN SEAS
HOMME DU MINNESOTA, L' (FRN) see **MINNESOTA CLAY** • 1965
HOMME DU NIGER, L' • 1939 • de Baroncelli Jacques • FRN • FORBIDDEN LOVE (USA)
HOMME DU SUD, L' (FRN) see **SOUTHERNER, THE** • 1944
HOMME DU TRAIN 117, L' • 1923 • Maudru Charles • FRN
HOMME EN COLERE, L' • 1978 • Pinoteau Claude • FRN, CND • LABYRINTH
HOMME EN FUITE, L' • 1981 • Edelstein Simon • SWT • MAN ON THE RUN, A
HOMME EN HABIT, UN • 1931 • Guissart Rene, Bossis Robert • FRN
HOMME EN MARCHE, L' • 1952 • Lallier, Rivoalen • SHT • FRN
HOMME EN OR, UN • 1934 • Dreville Jean • FRN • MAN AND HIS WOMAN, A (USA)
HOMME EST MORT, UN • 1972 • Deray Jacques • FRN, ITL • FUNERALE A LOS ANGELES (ITL) ○ OUTSIDE MAN, THE (USA)
HOMME EST SATISFAIT, L' • 1906 • Melies Georges • SHT • FRN • WHO LOOKS, PAYS (USA) ○ MAN IS SATISFIED, THE ○ HONNEUR EST SATISFAIT, L'
HOMME ET FEMME see **MAN OCH KVINNA** • 1939
HOMME ET LA BETE, L' • 1953 • de Gastyne Marco • SHT • FRN
HOMME ET LA POUPEE, L' • 1922 • Mariaud Maurice • FRN • MAN AND THE DOLL, THE
HOMME ET L'ALIMENTATION, L' • 1967 • Portugais Louis • DCS • CND
HOMME ET LE FROID, L' • 1970 • Regnier Michel • DOC • CND
HOMME ET LE GEANT -UNE LEGENDE ESQUIMO, L' • 1975 • Hoedeman Co • ANS • CND • MAN AND THE GIANT -AN ESKIMO LEGEND, THE
HOMME ET LE SOL AU CANADA FRANCAIS, L' • Lavoie Hermenegilde • DCS • CND
HOMME ET LE SPORT, L' • 1977 • Reichenbach Francois • MTV • FRN
HOMME ET L'ENFANT, L' • 1956 • Andre Raoul • FRN, ITL • CREATURE DEL MALE (ITL) ○ MAN AND CHILD
HOMME ET L'HIVER AU CANADA FRANCAIS, L' • Lavoie Hermenegilde • DCS • CND
HOMME ET SON BOSS, UN • 1970 • Lamothe Arthur, Borremans Guy • CND
HOMME ET SON PECHE, UN • 1948 • Gury Paul • CND • MAN AND HIS SIN, A
HOMME ET UNE FEMME, UN • 1966 • Lelouch Claude • FRN • MAN AND A WOMAN, A (UKN)
HOMME ET UNE FEMME: VINGT ANS DEJA, UN • 1985 • Lelouch Claude • FRN • MAN AND A WOMAN: 20 YEARS LATER, A (USA)
HOMME ETALON, L' • Bernard-Aubert Claude • FRN
HOMME FRAGILE, L' • 1980 • Clouzot Claire • FRN
HOMME GIFLE, L' • 1912 • Fescourt Henri • FRN
HOMME HEUREUX, UN • 1932 • Bideau Antonin • FRN
HOMME INUSABLE, L' • 1923 • Bernard Raymond • FRN
HOMME INVISIBLE, L' • 1909 • Zecca Ferdinand • FRN • INVISIBLE THIEF, AN
HOMME LE PLUS SEXY DU MONDE, L' • de Nesle Robert • FRN
HOMME LIBRE, UN • 1972 • Muller Roberto • FRN
HOMME MARCHE DANS LA VILLE, UN • 1949 • Pagliero Marcello • FRN
HOMME MOUCHE, L' • 1902 • Melies Georges • FRN • HUMAN FLY, THE (USA)
HOMME MULTIPLIE, L' • 1969 • Dufaux Georges, Godbout Jacques • DCS • CND
HOMME MYSTERIEUX, L' • 1933 • Tourneur Maurice • FRN • OBSESSION (USA)
HOMME NOIR, L' • 1924 • Machin Alfred • FRN
HOMME, NOTRE AMI, L' • 1955 • de Gastyne Marco • SHT • FRN
HOMME NU, L' • 1911 • Desfontaines Henri • FRN
HOMME NU, UN see **NU COMME UN VER** • 1933
HOMME-ORCHESTRE, L' • 1900 • Melies Georges • FRN • ONE-MAN BAND, THE (USA)
HOMME-ORCHESTRE, L' • 1969 • Korber Serge • FRN, ITL • BEATO FRA LE DONNE (ITL) ○ HOMME ORCHESTRE, L'
HOMME ORCHESTRE, L' see **HOMME-ORCHESTRE, L'** • 1969
HOMME PASSA, UN • 1918 • Roussell Henry • FRN
HOMME PERDU, UN see **CABANE AUX SOUVENIRS, LA** • 1946
HOMME PRESSE, L' • 1976 • Molinaro Edouard • FRN, ITL • MAN IN A HURRY (USA) ○ HURRIED MAN, THE (UKN)
HOMME PROTEE, L' • 1899 • Melies Georges • FRN • LIGHTNING CHANGE ARTIST (USA) ○ CHAMELEON MAN, THE
HOMME QUI A VENDU SA TETE, L' see **GAIETES DE LA FINANCE, LES** • 1935
HOMME QUI AIMAIT LES TRAINS, L' • 1984 • Manuel Pierre • BLG
HOMME QUI AIMANT LES FEMMES, L' • 1977 • Truffaut Francois • FRN • MAN WHO LOVED WOMEN, THE (UKN) ○ MAN WHO LOVED LOVE, THE (USA)
HOMME QUI ASSASSINA, L' • 1917 • Andreani Henri • FRN
HOMME QUI ASSASSINA, L' • 1930 • Tarride Jean, Bernhardt Curtis • FRN
HOMME QUI CHERCHE LA VERITE, L' • 1939 • Esway Alexander • FRN
HOMME QUI DORT, UN • 1973 • Perec Georges, Queysanne Bernard • FRN, TNS • MAN WHO SLEEPS, A
HOMME QUI JOUE AVEC LE FEU, L' • 1942 • de Limur Jean • FRN
HOMME QUI ME PLAIT, L' • 1969 • Lelouch Claude • FRN, ITL • TIPO CHE MI PAICE, UN (ITL) ○ LOVE IS A FUNNY THING (USA) ○ MAN I LIKE, A (UKN) ○ HISTOIRE D'AIMER ○ AGAIN A LOVE STORY ○ MAN I LOVE, A
HOMME QUI MENT, L' (FRN) see **MUZ KTORY LUZE** • 1968
HOMME QUI NE SAIT PAS DIRE NON, L' • 1932 • Hilpert Heinz • FRN
HOMME QUI N'ETAIT PAS LA, L' • 1986 • Feret Rene • FRN
HOMME QUI PERDIT SON OMBRE, L' see **RAGOL EL LAZI FAKAD ZILLOH, EL** • 1968
HOMME QUI REVIENT DE LOIN, L' • 1949 • Castanier Jean • FRN • MAN WHO RETURNED FROM AFAR, THE
HOMME QUI RIT, L' • 1909 • FRN • MAN WHO LAUGHS, THE
HOMME QUI TRAHIT LA MAFIA, L' • 1967 • Gerard Charles • FRN, ITL • CALIBRO 38 (ITL)
HOMME QUI VALAIT DES MILLIARDS, L' • 1967 • Boisrond Michel • FRN, ITL • UOMO CHE VALEVA MILIARDI, L' (ITL) ○ MILLION DOLLAR MAN (UKN)
HOMME QUI VENDAIT SON AME, L' • 1943 • Paulin Jean-Paul • FRN • HOMME QUI VENDAIT SON AME AU DIABLE, L' ○ MAN WHO SOLD HIS SOUL, THE
HOMME QUI VENDAIT SON AME AU DIABLE, L' see **HOMME QUI VENDAIT SON AME, L'** • 1943
HOMME QUI VENDIT SON AME AU DIABLE, L' • 1920 • Caron Pierre • FRN • MAN WHO SOLD HIS SOUL TO THE DEVIL, THE
HOMME QUI VIENT DE LA NUIT, L' • 1970 • Dague Jean-Claude • FRN
HOMME QUI VOULAIT VIOLER LE MONDE ENTIER, L' see **BLACK LOVE** • 1974
HOMME RENVERSE, L' • 1988 • Dion Yves • CND
HOMME SANS COEUR, L' • 1936 • Joannon Leo • FRN
HOMME SANS NOM, L' • 1942 • Mathot Leon • FRN
HOMME SANS NOM, UN • 1932 • Le Bon Roger, Ucicky Gustav • FRN
HOMME SANS TETE, L' • 1912 • Cohl Emile • ANS • FRN
HOMME SANS VISAGE, L' • 1918 • Feuillade Louis • FRN
HOMME SANS VISAGE, L' • 1974 • Franju Georges • FRN, ITL • SHADOWMAN (UKN) ○ NUITS ROUGES ○ MAN WITHOUT A FACE, THE
HOMME SE PENCHE SUR SON PASSE, UN • 1958 • Rozier Willy • FRN, FRG • SCHWARZER STERN IN WEISSEN NACHT (FRG)
HOMME SUR LA VOIE, UN see **CZLOWIEK NA TORZE** • 1956
HOMME TRAHI, L' • 1953 • Kapps Walter • FRN
HOMME TRAQUE, L' • 1946 • Bibal Robert • FRN
HOMME TRAQUE, L' • 1969 • Tolbi Abdelaziz • ALG
HOMME VOILE, L' (FRN) see **VEILED MAN, THE** • 1987
HOMMES, LES • 1973 • Vigne Daniel • FRN, ITL • REGOLAMENTO DI CONTI (ITL)
HOMMES BLEUS, LES see **BAROUD** • 1931
HOMMES D'AUJOURD'HUI • 1952 • Fradetal Marcel • SHT • FRN
HOMMES D'AUJOURD'HUI • 1953 • Mitry Jean • SHT • FRN
HOMMES D'AUJOURD'HUI, LES • 1928 • Puchalski Eduard • PLN
HOMMES DE JOIE POUR FEMMES VICIEUSES • 1974 • Chevalier Pierre • FRN
HOMMES DE LA BALEINE, LES • 1956 • Ruspoli Mario • SHT • FRN
HOMMES DE LA COTE, LES • 1934 • Pellenc Andre • FRN
HOMMES DE LA CROIX BLEUE, LES see **BLEKITNY KRZYZ** • 1956
HOMMES DE LA WAHGI, LES • 1963 • Villeminot Jacques • SHT • FRN
HOMMES DE L'ACIER, LES • 1948 • Tedesco Jean • SHT • FRN
HOMMES DE LAS VEGAS, LES (FRN) see **LAS VEGAS, 500 MILLONES** • 1968
HOMMES DE PROIE, LES • 1937 • Rozier Willy • FRN • HOMME DE DAMAS, L'

HOMMES DU CHAMPAGNE, LES • 1950 • Leenhardt Roger • DCS • FRN

HOMMES DU PETROLE, LES • 1961 • Heinrich, Chapot • SHT • FRN

HOMMES EN BLANC, L' • 1955 • Habib Ralph • FRN • DOCTORS, THE (USA) ○ MEN IN WHITE

HOMMES ENTRE EUX • 1976 • Terry Norbert • FRN

HOMMES ET BETES • 1946 • Mineur Jean • SHT • FRN

HOMMES ET LES AUTRES, LES • 1954 • Guerra Ruy • SHT • FRN

HOMMES ET LOUPS (FRN) see **UOMINI E LUPI** • 1956

HOMMES FIERS • 1953 • Degelin Emile, de Boe Gerard • BLG

HOMMES NE PENSENT QU'A CA! • 1945 • Robert Yves • FRN

HOMMES NOUVEAUX, LES • 1922 • Violet Edouard-Emile, Donatien E. B. • FRN

HOMMES NOUVEAUX, LES • 1936 • L'Herbier Marcel • FRN

HOMMES OUBLIES, LES • 1935 • Ryder Alexandre • FRN

HOMMES OUBLIES, LES • 1957 • Bellon Yannick, Villeminot Jacques • FRN

HOMMES PREFERENT LES GROSSES, LES • 1981 • Poire Jean-Marie • FRN

HOMMES QUI FONT LA PLUIE, LES • 1951 • Rouch Jean • FRN • FAISEURS DE PLUIE, LES ○ RAINMAKERS ○ YENENDI

HOMMES QUI VIENNENT DU CIEL, LES • 1971-74 • Floquet Francois • DOC • CND

HOMMES SANS NOM, LES • 1937 • Vallee Jean • FRN

HOMMES SANS PEUR, LES • 1941 • Noe Yvan • FRN

HOMMES SANS SOLEIL, LES see **GRISOU** • 1938

HOMMES VEULENT VIVRE!, LES • 1961 • Moguy Leonide • FRN, ITL • UOMINI VOGLIONO VIVERE, GLI (ITL) ○ CRIME DU DOCTEUR CHARDIN, LE ○ MAN WANTS TO LIVE! ○ MEN WANT TO LIVE

HOMMOKU YAWA • 1924 • Murata Minoru • JPN • NIGHT TALES OF HOMMOKU

HOMO AUGENS • 1972 • Zaninovic Ante • YGS

HOMO EROTICUS • 1971 • Vicario Marco • ITL • MAN OF THE YEAR (USA)

HOMO HOMINI • Bedrich Vaclav • SHT • CZC

HOMO IMMANIS • 1919 • Czinner Paul • AUS • UNMENSCH, DER

HOMO SAPIENS • 1959 • Popescu-Gopo Ion • ANS • RMN

HOMO SAPIENS • 1978 • Mariani Fiorella • ITL

HOMO SUM • 1919 • von Klodnicki Octav • FRG

HOMO VAMPIRE see **GOULVE, LA** • 1971

HOMO VARSOVIENSIS • 1965 • Wionczek Roman • MTV • PLN

HOMOLKA A TOBOLKA • 1972 • Papousek Jaroslav • CZC • HOMOLKA AND TOBOLKA

HOMOLKA AND TOBOLKA see **HOMOLKA A TOBOLKA** • 1972

HOMOMAN, L' • 1964 • Lefebvre Jean-Pierre • SHT • CND

HOMOMANIA • Darino Eduardo • URG

HOMUNCULUS • 1916-17 • Rippert Otto • SER • FRG • HOMUNKULUS DER FUHRER

HOMUNCULUS • 1917 • Magnussen Fritz • SWD

HOMUNCULUS 1 • 1916 • Rippert Otto • FRG

HOMUNCULUS 2 • 1916 • Rippert Otto • FRG • GEHEIMNISVOLLE BUCH, DAS

HOMUNCULUS 3 • 1916 • Rippert Otto • FRG • LIEBESTRAGODIE DES HOMUNCULUS, DIE

HOMUNCULUS 4 • 1916 • Rippert Otto • FRG • RACHE DES HOMUNCULUS, DIE

HOMUNCULUS 5 • 1917 • Rippert Otto • FRG • VERNICHTUNG DER MENSCHHEIT, DIE

HOMUNCULUS 6 • 1917 • Rippert Otto • FRG • ENDE DES HOMUNCULUS, DAS

HOMUNKULUS DER FUHRER see **HOMUNCULUS** • 1916-17

HON DANSADE EN SOMMAR • 1951 • Mattsson Arne • SWD • SHE ONLY DANCED ONE SUMMER ○ ONE SUMMER OF HAPPINESS ○ SOMMARDANSEN

HON, DEN ENDA • 1926 • Molander Gustaf • SWD • SHE, THE ONLY ONE ○ SHE'S THE ONLY ONE

HON ELLER INGEN • 1934 • Rodin Gosta • SWD • SHE OR NO ONE

HON, HAN OCH ANDERSSON • 1926 • Edgren Gustaf • SWD • SHE, HE AND ANDERSSON

HON KOM SOM EN VIND • 1952 • Faustman Erik • SWD • SHE CAME LIKE A WIND ○ FABIAN OCH FLICKAN

HON. MR. JAP VAN WINKLE, THE • 1919 • *Chester C. L. (P)* • USA

HON SEGRADE • 1916 • Sjostrom Victor • SWD • SHE WAS VICTORIOUS ○ SHE CONQUERED

HON TRODDE DET VAR HAN • 1943 • Branner Per-Axel • SWD • SHE THOUGHT IT WAS HIM ○ TJUVARNAS KONUNG

HON. WILLIAM'S DONAH, THE • 1914 • Neame Elwin • UKN

HONDO • 1953 • Farrow John • USA

HONDO AND THE APACHES • 1967 • Katzin Lee H. • MTV • USA

HONDURAS HURRICANE • 1938 • *Captain And The Kids* • ANS • USA

HONEM QUE COMPROU O MUNDO, O • 1968 • Coutinho Eduardo • BRZ • MAN WHO BUYS THE WORLD, THE

HONENUKI • 1967 • Fukuda Seiichi • JPN • MUTILATION

HONEST, DECENT AND TRUE • 1985 • Blair Les • TVM • UKN

HONEST FINDER, THE see **TROUBLE IN PARADISE** • 1932

HONEST FORGER, THE • 1944 • *O'Brien Joseph/ Mead Thomas (P)* • USA

HONEST HUTCH • 1920 • Badger Clarence • USA

HONEST INJUN • 1926 • Taurog Norman • SHT • USA

HONEST JOHN (UKN) see **RHYTHM ROUND-UP** • 1945

HONEST LOVE AND TRUE • 1938 • Fleischer Dave • ANS • USA

HONEST MAN, AN • 1918 • Borzage Frank • USA

HONEST NEWSBOY'S REWARD, AN • 1908 • *Lubin* • USA

HONEST THIEF, THE • 1918 • Seitz George B. • SHT • USA

HONEST THIEVES • 1917 • *Depp Harry* • USA

HONEST YOUNG MAN, AN • 1913 • *Thanhouser* • USA

HONESTLY AND CHEATINGLY see **PA HEDER OCH SKOJ** • 1956

HONESTY IS THE BEST POLICY • 1908 • Porter Edwin S. • USA

HONESTY IS THE BEST POLICY • 1926 • Engholm F. W. • UKN

HONESTY -THE BEST POLICY • 1926 • Bennett Chester, Ray Albert • USA

HONESTY'S STRANGE REWARD • 1906 • *Pathe* • FRN

HONEY • 1930 • Ruggles Wesley • USA • COME OUT OF THE KITCHEN

HONEY • 1966 • Denby Jerry • USA • HONEY HEAT

HONEY • 1981 • Angelucci Gianfranco • ITL, SPN

HONEY BEE, THE • 1920 • Julian Rupert • USA

HONEY BOY see **HONEYBOY** • 1982

HONEY BUN, OR HOW TO TELL MY DAUGHTER see **HERZBLATT, ODER WIE SAG ICH'S MEINER TOCHTER** • 1969

HONEY COMB, A • 1965 • Kotowski Jerzy • ANM • PLN

HONEY HARVESTER • 1949 • Hannah Jack • ANS • USA

HONEY HEAT see **HONEY** • 1966

HONEY HONEYMOON • 1967 • de Jesus Ding M. • PHL

HONEY, I SHRUNK THE KIDS • 1989 • Johnston Joe • USA

HONEY-MOUSERS, THE • 1956 • McKimson Robert • ANS • USA

HONEY PIE • 1976 • USA

HONEY POT, THE • 1967 • Mankiewicz Joseph L. • UKN, USA, ITL • IT COMES UP MURDER ○ ANYONE FOR VENICE?

HONEY & WEST • 1968 • Feleo Ben • PHL

HONEY WOLVES, THE see **HONUNGSVARGAR** • 1989

HONEYBABY see **HONEYBABY, HONEYBABY** • 1974

HONEYBABY, HONEYBABY • 1974 • Schultz Michael • USA • BEIRUT CONTRACT ○ HONEYBABY

HONEYBOY • 1982 • Berry John • TVM • USA • HONEY BOY

HONEYBUGS' FIRST QUARREL, THE • 1912 • *Essanay* • USA

HONEYBUN • 1974 • Romero Eddie • USA • HOW TO TELL MY DAUGHTER?

HONEYBUN see **HONNEPONNETJE** • 1988

HONEYBUNCH see **HONNEPONNETJE** • 1988

HONEYCHILE • 1951 • Springsteen R. G. • USA

HONEYCOMB (USA) see **MADRIGUERA, LA** • 1969

HONEYLAND • 1935 • Ising Rudolf • ANS • USA

HONEYLAND • 1986 • Kovach June • SWT

HONEYLESS HONEYMOON, THE • 1917 • Jackson Harry • SHT • USA

HONEYMOON • 1928 • Golden Robert • USA

HONEYMOON • 1947 • Keighley William • USA • TWO MEN AND A GIRL (UKN)

HONEYMOON • 1959 • Powell Michael • SPN • LUNA DE MIEL

HONEYMOON • 1980 • Panoussopoulos George • GRC

HONEYMOON • 1989 • Lieberman Robert • USA

HONEYMOON see **SMEKMANAD** • 1972

HONEYMOON see **HONNING MANE** • 1978

HONEYMOON see **MEDENI MJESEC** • 1984

HONEYMOON see **MITSUGETSU** • 1984

HONEYMOON see **LUNE DE MIEL** • 1986

HONEYMOON see **MEDENI MESEC** • 1989

HONEYMOON, THE • 1899 • *Riley Brothers* • UKN

HONEYMOON, THE • 1917 • Giblyn Charles • USA

HONEYMOON, THE • 1956 • Kosheverova Nadezhda • USS

HONEYMOON, THE see **VOYAGE DE NOCES, LE** • 1976

HONEYMOON ADVENTURE, A • 1931 • Elvey Maurice • UKN • FOOTSTEPS IN THE NIGHT (USA)

HONEYMOON AHEAD • 1945 • Le Borg Reginald • USA • ROMANCE, INCORPORATED

HONEYMOON AHEAD (USA) see **ADAM'S APPLE** • 1928

HONEYMOON AT NIAGARA FALLS • 1906 • Porter Edwin S. • USA

HONEYMOON BABY, THE • 1915 • Drew Sidney • USA

HONEYMOON BLUES • Bernds Edward • SHT • USA

HONEYMOON BRIDGE • 1935 • Lord Del • SHT • USA

HONEYMOON CAR • 1916 • *Myers Harry* • SHT • USA

HONEYMOON DEFERRED • 1940 • Landers Lew • USA

HONEYMOON DEFERRED • 1951 • Camerini Mario • UKN

HONEYMOON EXPRESS, THE • 1926 • Flood James • USA

HONEYMOON: FIRST, SECOND AND THIRD CLASS, THE • 1904 • Fitzhamon Lewin • UKN

HONEYMOON FLATS • 1928 • Webb Millard • USA

HONEYMOON FOR THREE • 1935 • Mittler Leo • UKN

HONEYMOON FOR THREE • 1941 • Bacon Lloyd • USA

HONEYMOON FOR THREE, A • 1910 • *Essanay* • USA

HONEYMOON FOR THREE, A • 1915 • Elvey Maurice • UKN

HONEYMOON HARDSHIPS • 1924 • Ceder Ralph • SHT • USA

HONEYMOON HARMONY (UKN) see **LEAVE IT TO LESTER** • 1930

HONEYMOON HATE • 1927 • Reed Luther • USA

HONEYMOON HORROR • 1982 • Preston Harry • USA

HONEYMOON HOTEL • 1925 • Wallace Richard • SHT • USA

HONEYMOON HOTEL • 1934 • Duval Earl • ANS • USA

HONEYMOON HOTEL • 1964 • Levin Henry • USA • HIS AND HIS

HONEYMOON HOTEL see **UNDER NEW MANAGEMENT** • 1946

HONEYMOON IN A BALLOON see **VOYAGE DE NOCES EN BALLON** • 1908

HONEYMOON IN BALI • 1939 • Griffith Edward H. • USA • HUSBANDS OR LOVERS (UKN) ○ HUSBANDS AND LOVERS ○ MY LOVE FOR YOURS ○ ARE HUSBANDS NECESSARY?

HONEYMOON IN DEVON, A • 1932 • *Watts Dodo* • SHT • UKN

HONEYMOON IN PARADISE • 1985 • Lemoine Michel • FRN

HONEYMOON IS OVER, THE • 1970 • *Stacey Dist.* • USA

HONEYMOON, ITALIAN STYLE (UKN) see **VIAGGIO DI NOZZE ALL'ITALIANA** • 1965

HONEYMOON KILLERS, THE • 1970 • Kastle Leonard • USA

HONEYMOON LANE • 1931 • Craft William James • USA

HONEYMOON LIMITED • 1935 • Lubin Arthur • USA

HONEYMOON LODGE • 1943 • Lilley Edward • USA

HONEYMOON LODGING, THE • 1913 • *Francis Evelyn* • USA

HONEYMOON MACHINE, THE • 1961 • Thorpe Richard • USA

HONEYMOON MERRY-GO-ROUND see **OLYMPIC HONEYMOON** • 1936

HONEYMOON OF HORROR • 1964 • Meyer Irwin • USA • ORGY OF THE GOLDEN NUDES ○ GOLDEN NYMPHS, THE

HONEYMOON OF TERROR • 1961 • Peri • USA • ECSTASY ON LOVERS ISLAND ○ ECSTASY OF LOVERS

HONEYMOON PACT, THE • 1915 • North Wilfred • USA

HONEYMOON RANCH • 1920 • Townley Robin H. • USA

HONEYMOON ROLL, THE • 1915 • Seiter William A. • USA

HONEYMOON SQUABBLE, A • 1925 • Watson William • USA

HONEYMOON SURPRISE, THE • 1917 • Peacocke Leslie T. • SHT • USA

HONEYMOON SWEDISH STYLE see **PILSKA JULIA PA BROLLOPSRESAN** • 1982

HONEYMOON THROUGH SNOW TO SUNSHINE ,A • 1910 • Hotaling Arthur D. • USA

HONEYMOON TRIO • 1931 • Arbuckle Roscoe • USA

HONEYMOON TRIP, THE see **BROLLOPSRESAN** • 1936

HONEYMOON WITH A STRANGER • 1969 • Peyser John • TVM • USA

HONEYMOON WITHOUT TROUBLES see **CHAHR ASSAL BIDOUN EZAAG** • 1968

HONEYMOON ZEPPELIN • 1930 • Sennett Mack • USA

HONEYMOONERS, THE • 1911 • *Snow Marguerite* • USA

HONEYMOONERS, THE • 1912 • *Lubin* • USA

HONEYMOONERS, THE • 1912 • *Champion* • USA

HONEYMOONERS, THE • 1914 • Baker George D. • *Vitagraph* • USA

HONEYMOONERS, THE • 1914 • Salter Harry • *Victor* • USA

HONEYMOONERS, THE • 1915 • MacMackin Archer • USA

HONEYMOONERS, THE • 1917 • *Derr George* • SHT • USA

HONEYMOONIACS • 1929 • Roberts Stephen • SHT • USA

HONEYMOONING • 1919 • *De Haven Carter* • SHT • USA

HONEYMOON'S OVER, THE • 1939 • Forde Eugene J. • USA

HONEYPOT, THE • 1920 • Granville Fred Leroy • UKN

HONEY'S MONEY • 1962 • Freleng Friz • ANS • USA

HONEYSUCKLE ROSE • 1941 • Murray Warren • SHT • USA

HONEYSUCKLE ROSE • 1980 • Schatzberg Jerry • USA • ON THE ROAD AGAIN

HONEYSUCKLE (USA) see **MADRESELVA** • 1939

HONG GAOLIANG • 1987 • Zhang Yimou • CHN • RED SORGHUM

HONG KONG • 1951 • Foster Lewis R. • USA • BOMBS OVER CHINA

HONG KONG 1941 • 1985 • Liang Puzhi • HKG

HONG KONG AFFAIR • 1958 • Heard Paul F. • USA

HONG KONG CONFIDENTIAL • 1958 • Cahn Edward L. • USA

HONG KONG GRAFFITI see **NUREN FENGQING HUA** • 1985

HONG KONG, HONG KONG see **NAN YU NU** • 1984

HONG KONG HOT HARBOR (USA) see **HEISSER HAFEN HONGKONG** • 1962

HONG KONG NIGHTS • 1935 • Hopper E. Mason • USA

HONG-KONG UN ADDIO • 1963 • Polidoro Gian Luigi • ITL

HONG YU • 1975 • Cui Wei • CHN • CRIMSON RAIN

HONGHU CHIWEIDUI • 1961 • Xie Tian, Chen Fangqian, Xu Feng • CHN • RED GUARDS OF LAKE HONG

HONGKONG 73 • 1974 • Ch'U Yuan • HKG

HONGKONG EMMANUELLE • Man Hwa • HKG

HONJITSU KYUSHIN • 1952 • Shibuya Minoru • JPN • NO CONSULTATION TODAY ○ DOCTOR'S DAY OFF, THE ○ NO CONSULTATION TO BE HELD

HONJO NANA FUSHIGI • 1957 • *Shintoho* • JPN • SEVEN WONDERS OF HONJO, THE

HONK YOUR HORN • 1930 • Goulding Alf • USA

HONKA JA GRANIITTI • 1977 • Szintai Istvan • FNL, HNG • PINE AND GRANITE

HONKERS, THE • 1972 • Ihnat Steve • USA

HONKEY DONKEY • 1934 • Meins Gus • SHT • USA • HONKY-DONKEY

HONKIN SATSUJIN JIKEN • 1975 • Takabayashi Yoichi • JPN • MURDER CASE OF HONKIN, THE

HONKON NO HOSHI • 1962 • Chiba Yasuki • JPN • STAR OF HONG KONG (USA)

HONKON NO SHIROIBARA • 1965 • Fukuda Jun • JPN • WHITE ROSE OF HONG KONG (USA)

HONKON NO YORU • 1961 • Chiba Yasuki • JPN • NIGHT IN HONG KONG, A

HONKY • 1972 • Graham William A. • USA

HONKY-DONKEY see **HONKEY DONKEY** • 1934

HONKY TONK • 1929 • Bacon Lloyd • USA

HONKY TONK • 1941 • Conway Jack • USA

HONKY TONK • 1974 • Taylor Don • TVM • USA

HONKY TONK FREEWAY • 1980 • Schlesinger John • USA

HONKYTONK MAN • 1983 • Eastwood Clint • USA

HONKYTONK NIGHTS • 1979 • Webb Charles • USA

HONNEPONNETJE • 1988 • van Hemert Ruud • NTH • HONEYBUN ○ HONEYBUNCH

HONNETE HOMME, UN • 1963 • Kyrou Ado • ANS • FRN • HONORABLE MAN, AN

HONNEUR D'ARTISTE • 1917 • Kemm Jean • FRN

HONNEUR DE L'AUTRE, L' • 1927 • Marodon Pierre • FRN

HONNEUR DE L'HOMME ROUGE, L' • 1912 • Roudes Gaston • FRN

HONNEUR DU CORSAIRE, L' • 1908 • Jasset Victorin • FRN

HONNEUR DU CORSE, L' • 1906 • Blache Alice • FRN

HONNEUR D'UN CAPITAINE, L' • 1982 • Schoendoerffer Pierre • FRN

HONNEUR D'UN PERE, L' • 1906 • Zecca Ferdinand • FRN

HONNEUR EST SATISFAIT, L' see **HOMME EST SATISFAIT, L'** • 1906

HONNEUR ET L'ARGENT, L' • 1912 • Perret Leonce • FRN

HONNEURS DE LA GUERRE, LES • 1961 • Dewever Jean • FRN

HONNING MANE • 1978 • August Bille • DNM • HONEYMOON ○ IN MY LIFE

HONNO • 1966 • Shindo Kaneto • JPN • LOST SEX (UKN) ○ IMPOTENCE ○ INSTINCT

HONOLULU • 1939 • Buzzell Edward • USA

HONOLULU LU • 1941 • Barton Charles T. • USA

HONOLULU - TOKYO - HONG KONG • 1963 • Chiba Yasuki • JPN, HKG

HONOLULU WILES • 1930 • *Mintz Charles (P)* • ANS • USA

HONOO TO ONNA • 1967 • Yoshida Yoshishige • JPN • IMPASSE

HONOR • 1929 • Shirvanzada A.

HONOR AMONG LOVERS • 1931 • Arzner Dorothy • USA • SEX IN BUSINESS

HONOR AMONG MEN • 1924 • Clift Denison • USA

HONOR AMONG THIEVES see **ADIEU L'AMI** • 1968

HONOR AND THE SWORD • 1912 • *Hawley Ormi* • USA

HONOR BETRAYED see **FEAR** • 1988

HONOR BOUND • 1920 • Jaccard Jacques • USA

HONOR BOUND • 1928 • Green Alfred E. • USA

HONOR BOUND • 1989 • Szwarc Jeannot • USA

HONOR BRIGHT • 1988 • Kagan Jeremy Paul • USA
HONOR FIRST • 1922 • Storm Jerome • USA
HONOR MILITAR • 1919 • Berra Fernando Orozco • MXC • MILITARY HONOR
HONOR OF A PUGILIST, THE • 1912 • *Powers* • USA
HONOR OF A SOLDIER, THE • 1913 • *Prior Herbert* • USA
HONOR OF AN OUTLAW, THE • 1917 • Kelsey Fred A. • SHT • USA
HONOR OF BILL JACKSON, THE • 1915 • *Ideal* • USA
HONOR OF HIS FAMILY, THE • 1910 • Griffith D. W. • USA
HONOR OF HIS HOUSE, THE • 1918 • De Mille William C. • USA • HONOR OF THE HOUSE
HONOR OF KENNETH MCGRATH, THE • 1915 • Ayres Sydney • USA
HONOR OF LADY BEAUMONT, THE • 1913 • *Tennant Barbara* • USA
HONOR OF MARY BLAKE, THE • 1916 • Stevens Edwin • USA
HONOR OF MEN, THE • 1917 • Marshall George • SHT • USA
HONOR OF MEN, THE • 1919 • *Hart Neal* • SHT • USA
HONOR OF THE CAMP, THE • 1915 • King Burton L. • USA
HONOR OF THE DISTRICT ATTORNEY, THE • 1915 • Eason B. Reeves • USA
HONOR OF THE FAMILY • 1931 • Bacon Lloyd • USA
HONOR OF THE FAMILY, THE • 1912 • *Rex* • USA
HONOR OF THE FIRM, THE • 1912 • *Eclair* • USA
HONOR OF THE FLAG, THE • 1911 • Melies Gaston • USA
HONOR OF THE FORCE • 1914 • *Lubin* • USA
HONOR OF THE FORCE, THE • 1913 • France Charles H. • USA
HONOR OF THE HOUSE see **HONOR OF HIS HOUSE, THE** • 1918
HONOR OF THE HUMBLE, THE • 1914 • Salter Harry • USA
HONOR OF THE LAW, THE • 1914 • Vale Travers • USA
HONOR OF THE MOUNTED • 1932 • Fraser Harry L. • USA • BEYOND THE BORDER (UKN)
HONOR OF THE MOUNTED, THE • 1914 • Dwan Allan • USA
HONOR OF THE ORMSBYS, THE • 1915 • Henderson Dell? • USA
HONOR OF THE PRESS • 1932 • Eason B. Reeves • USA • SCOOP, THE (UKN)
HONOR OF THE RANGE • 1934 • James Alan • USA
HONOR OF THE RANGE, THE • 1920 • Beebe Ford (c/d) • SRL • USA
HONOR OF THE RANGE, THE • 1920 • Maloney Leo • SHT • USA
HONOR OF THE REGIMENT, THE • 1913 • Lucas Wilfred • USA
HONOR OF THE SLUMS, THE • 1909 • Brooke Van Dyke • USA
HONOR OF THE TRIBE, THE • 1912 • *Bison* • USA
HONOR OF THE TRIBE, THE • 1916 • *Buffalo* • SHT • USA
HONOR OF THE WEST • 1939 • Waggner George • USA
HONOR OF THIEVES, THE • 1909 • Griffith D. W. • USA
HONOR REDEEMED • 1914 • *Melies* • USA
HONOR SYSTEM, THE • 1913 • *Blackwell Carlyle* • USA
HONOR SYSTEM, THE • 1917 • *Fact Films* • USA
HONOR SYSTEM, THE • 1917 • Walsh Raoul • *Fox* • USA
HONOR THY COUNTRY • 1916 • Wilson Ben • SHT • USA
HONOR THY FATHER • 1912 • *Majestic* • USA
HONOR THY FATHER • 1912 • *Lubin* • USA
HONOR THY FATHER • 1915 • Vignola Robert G. • USA
HONOR THY FATHER • 1971 • Wendkos Paul • TVM • USA
HONOR THY HUSBAND • 1915 • Reynolds Lynn • USA
HONOR THY MOTHER • 1913 • *Melies* • USA
HONOR THY NAME • 1916 • Giblyn Charles • USA
HONOR TO DIE, THE • 1915 • *Jolivet Rita* • USA
HONORABLE ALGERNON, THE • 1913 • Brooke Van Dyke • USA
HONORABLE ALGY, THE • 1916 • West Raymond B. • USA
HONORABLE CAD, AN • 1919 • Terwilliger George W. • USA
HONORABLE CAT STORY • 1961 • Rasinski Connie • ANS • USA
HONORABLE CATHERINE, L' • 1942 • L'Herbier Marcel • FRN • SOLANGE
HONORABLE FAMILY PROBLEM • 1962 • Kuwahara Bob • ANS • USA
HONORABLE FRIEND • 1915 • Melford George • USA
HONORABLE FRIEND, THE • 1916 • Le Saint Edward J. • USA
HONORABLE LADIES OF PARDUBICE, THE see **POCESTNE PANI PARDUBICKE** • 1944
HONORABLE MAN, AN see **HONNETE HOMME, UN** • 1963
HONORABLE MR. BUGGS, THE • 1927 • Jackman Fred • SHT • USA
HONORABLE SOCIETE ,L' • 1978 • Weinberger Anielle • FRN
HONORABLE STANISLAS AGENT SECRET, L' • 1963 • Dudrumet Jean-Charles • FRN, ITL • SPIONAGGIO SENZA FRONTIERE (ITL) ○ RELUCTANT SPY, THE (USA)
HONORABLES CABALLEROS QUE DEJO LA GUERRA, LOS • 1977 • Rodriguez Oziel • VNZ • HONOURABLE GENTLEMEN LEFT BY THE WAR, THE ○ INNOCENT TRAP
HONORABLES SINVERGUENZAS • 1960 • Gamboa Jose Luis • SPN
HONORABLY DISCHARGED • 1917 • Kelsey Fred A. • SHT • USA
HONORARY CONSUL, THE see **BEYOND THE LIMIT** • 1983
HONORE DE MARSEILLE • 1956 • Regamey Maurice • FRN
HONOR'S ALTAR • 1916 • West Raymond B.? • USA
HONOR'S CROSS • 1918 • Worsley Wallace • USA
HONOUR see **NAMUS** • 1926
HONOUR see **KEHORMATAN** • 1974
HONOUR ABOVE ALL (UKN) see **BLUE DANUBE, THE** • 1928
HONOUR AMONG THIEVES • 1912 • Aylott Dave? • UKN
HONOUR AMONG THIEVES • 1915 • Batley Ernest G. • UKN
HONOUR AMONG THIEVES • 1916 • Noy Wilfred • UKN
HONOUR AMONG THIEVES see **WEEDS** • 1987
HONOUR AMONG THIEVES (UKN) see **TOUCHEZ PAS AU GRISBI** • 1953
HONOUR AND GLORY see **BECSULET ES DICSOSEG** • 1951
HONOUR AND GLORY see **CEST A SLAVA** • 1968
HONOUR GUARD, THE see **WOLF LAKE** • 1978
HONOUR IN PAWN • 1916 • Weston Harold • UKN
HONOUR OF THE FAMILY see **AILE SEREFI** • 1977
HONOUR THY FATHER • 1976 • Perris Anthony • MTV • CND
HONOUR THY FATHER • 1984 • SAF
HONOURABLE EVENT, THE • 1913 • Trimble Larry • UKN
HONOURABLE GENTLEMEN LEFT BY THE WAR, THE see **HONORABLES CABALLEROS QUE DEJO LA GUERRA, LOS** • 1977
HONOURABLE MEMBER, AN • 1982 • Brittain Don • MTV • CND
HONOURABLE MEMBER FOR OUTSIDE LEFT, THE • 1925 • Hill Sinclair • UKN
HONOURABLE MR. WONG, THE (UKN) see **HATCHET MAN, THE** • 1932
HONOURABLE MURDER, AN • 1960 • Grayson Godfrey • UKN
HONOURABLE RENE LEVESQUE, THE • 1966 • Fox Beryl • DOC • CND
HONOURABLE WAY, THE see **TIMIOS DROMOS** • 1968
HONOURING THE RUSSIAN FLAG • 1913 • Protazanov Yakov • USS
HONOURS EASY • 1935 • Brenon Herbert • UKN
HONOURS EVEN • 1908 • Collins Alf? • UKN
HONRADEZ DE LA CERRADURA, LA • 1950 • Escobar Luis • SPN
HONRADEZ ES UN ESTORBO, LA • 1937 • Bustillo Oro Juan • MXC
HONRARAS A TUS PADRES • 1936 • Orol Juan • MXC
HONRYU • 1926 • Gosho Heinosuke • JPN • RAPID STREAM, A ○ TORRENT, A
HONTE DE LA FAMILLE, LA • 1969 • Balducci Richard • FRN
HONTE DE LA JUNGLE, LA see **TARZOON, LA HONTE DE LA JUNGLE** • 1974
HONUNGSVARGAR • 1989 • Olofsson Christina • SWD • HONEY WOLVES, THE
HONZIKOVA CESTA • 1956 • Vosmik Milan • CZC
HOO-HA • Rapaport Monroe • SHT • USA
HOO-RAY KIDS, THE • 1929 • Harman Bobby • SER • UKN
HOOCH • 1976 • Mann Edward • USA
HOODED MOB, THE see **AFTER DARK** • 1923
HOODLUM, THE • 1919 • Franklin Sidney A. • USA • RAGAMUFFIN, THE (UKN)
HOODLUM, THE • 1951 • Nosseck Max • USA
HOODLUM EMPIRE • 1952 • Kane Joseph • USA
HOODLUM FLAG BEARER, THE see **HEITAI YAKUZA NAGURIKOMI** • 1967
HOODLUM PRIEST, THE • 1961 • Kershner Irvin • USA
HOODLUM PRIEST, THE (USA) see **YAKUZA BOZU** • 1967
HOODLUM SAINT, THE • 1945 • Taurog Norman • USA
HOODLUM SOLDIER, THE see **HEITAI YAKUZA** • 1965
HOODLUM SOLDIER AND 100,000 DOLLARS, THE see **HEITAI YAKUZA GODATSU** • 1968
HOODLUM SOLDIER DESERTS AGAIN, THE see **SHIN HEITAI YAKUZA** • 1966
HOODLUMS, THE see **PERRO GANCHO, EL** • 1969
HOODLUM'S HONOR see **GANOVENEHRE** • 1966
HOODMAN BLIND • 1913 • Gordon James • USA
HOODMAN BLIND • 1923 • Ford John • USA
HOODMAN BLIND see **MAN OF SORROW, A** • 1916
HOODOO, THE • 1910 • *Pathe* • FRN
HOODOO, THE • 1910 • Golden Joseph A. • USA
HOODOO, THE • 1914 • *Joker* • USA
HOODOO ALARM CLOCK, THE • 1910 • *Imp* • USA
HOODOO ANN • 1916 • Ingraham Lloyd, Griffith D. W. (U/c) • USA
HOODOO HAT, THE • 1912 • *Roland Ruth* • USA
HOODOO LETTER, THE • 1912 • *Eclair* • USA
HOODOO PEARLS, THE • 1913 • Sullivan Frederick • USA
HOODOO RANCH • 1926 • Bertram William • USA • GENTLEMEN OF THE WEST (UKN)
HOODOO UMBRELLA, THE • 1913 • Angeles Bert • USA
HOODOOED • 1912 • *Lubin* • USA
HOODOOED • 1920 • Parrott Charles • SHT • USA
HOODOOED ON HIS WEDDING DAY • 1913 • *Roland Ruth* • USA
HOODOOED STORY, THE • 1917 • Windom Lawrence C. • SHT • USA
HOODOO'S BUSY DAY, THE • 1915 • *Duncan Bud* • USA
HOODWINK • 1982 • Whatham Claude • ASL
HOOEY HEROES • 1917 • *Heinie & Louie* • SHT • USA
HOOF MARKS • 1927 • Wright Tenny • USA
HOOFBEATS OF VENGEANCE • 1929 • McRae Henry • USA
HOOFS AND GOOFS • 1957 • White Jules • SHT • USA
HOOK, THE • 1962 • Seaton George • USA
HOOK AND HAND • 1914 • Blache Alice • USA
HOOK AND LADDER • 1924 • Sedgwick Edward • USA
HOOK AND LADDER • 1932 • McGowan Robert • SHT • USA
HOOK AND LADDER HOKUM • 1933 • Stallings George, Tashlin Frank • ANS • USA
HOOK AND LADDER NO.9 • 1927 • Weight F. Harmon • USA • PENDULUM, THE (UKN)
HOOK AND LADDER NUMBER ONE • 1932 • *Terry Paul/ Moser Frank (P)* • ANS • USA
HOOK, LINE AND SINKER • 1922 • Roach Hal • SHT • USA
HOOK, LINE AND SINKER • 1930 • Cline Eddie • USA
HOOK, LINE AND SINKER • 1939 • Donnelly Eddie • ANS • USA
HOOK, LINE AND SINKER • 1969 • Marshall George • USA
HOOK, LINE AND STINKER • 1958 • Jones Charles M. • ANS • USA
HOOK LINE AND STINKER • 1969 • Smith Paul J. • ANS • USA
HOOK LION AND STINKER • 1950 • Hannah Jack • ANS • USA
HOOKED • 1913 • *Crystal* • USA
HOOKED, THE see **VICIADOS, OS** • 1968
HOOKED AND ROOKED • 1952 • White Jules • SHT • USA
HOOKED AT THE ALTAR • 1926 • *Sennett Mack (P)* • SHT • USA
HOOKED BEAR • 1956 • Hannah Jack • ANS • USA
HOOKED GENERATION, THE • 1969 • Grefe William • USA • FLORIDA CONNECTION, THE ○ EVERGLADE KILLINGS, THE ○ ALLIGATOR ALLEY
HOOKERS, THE • 1967 • Horthy Jalo Miklos • USA
HOOKERS CONVENTION • 1979 • USA
HOOKERS ON DAVIE • 1984 • Dale Holly, Cole Janis • DOC • CND
HOOKS AND FEELERS • 1983 • Read Melanie • NZL
HOOKS AND JABS • 1933 • Gillstrom Arvid E. • SHT • USA
HOOKY SPOOKY • 1957 • Kneitel Seymour • ANS • USA
HOOLA BOOLA • 1941 • Pal George • ANS • USA
HOOLIGAN ASSISTS THE MAGICIAN • 1900 • Porter Edwin S. • USA
HOOLIGANS see **POBEL** • 1978
HOOLIGANS, THE see **GOLFOS, LOS** • 1959
HOOLIGAN'S ATTACK ON THE HIGHWAY • 1902 • *Warwick Trading Co.* • UKN
HOOLIGAN'S CHRISTMAS DREAM • 1903 • *Biograph* • USA
HOOP-LA • 1919 • Chaudet Louis W. • USA
HOOP-LA • 1933 • Lloyd Frank • USA
HOOP-SKIRTS, MY DEAR • 1912 • *Power William H.* • USA
HOOP VAN HET VADERLAND, DE • 1982 • Sinke Digna • DOC • NTH
HOOPER • 1978 • Needham Hal • USA
HOOR-E-BAGHDAD • 1963 • *Darasing* • IND
HOOR-E-SAMANDER • 1936 • Desai Dhirubhai • IND
HOOR MY LIED see **HEAR MY SONG** • 1967
HOORAY FOR HOLLYWOOD! • 1976 • CMP • USA
HOORAY FOR LOVE • 1935 • Lang Walter • USA
HOORAY FOR SANDBOX LAND • 1965 • Newland Marvin • DOC • CND
HOOSEGOW, THE • 1929 • Parrott James • SHT • USA
HOOSIER HOLIDAY • 1943 • McDonald Frank • USA • FARMYARD FOLLIES (UKN)
HOOSIER ROMANCE, A • 1918 • Campbell Colin • USA
HOOSIER SCHOOLBOY, THE • 1937 • Nigh William • USA • YESTERDAY'S HERO (UKN)
HOOSIER SCHOOLMASTER, THE • 1914 • *Figman Max* • USA
HOOSIER SCHOOLMASTER, THE • 1924 • Sellers Oliver L. • USA
HOOSIER SCHOOLMASTER, THE • 1935 • Collins Lewis D. • USA • SCHOOLMASTER, THE (UKN)
HOOSIERS • 1987 • Anspaugh David • USA • BEST SHOT (UKN)
HOOT MAN see **HOOT MON!** • 1919
HOOT MON! • 1919 • Roach Hal • SHT • USA • HOOT MAN
HOOT TOOT • 1918 • Davis James • SHT • USA
HOOTCH COUNTY BOYS, THE see **RED NECK COUNTY** • 1975
HOOTENANNY HOOT • 1963 • Nelson Gene • USA
HOOTIE'S BLUES • 1978 • Becker Bart, Farrell Mike • DCS • USA
HOOTS MON! • 1939 • Neill R. William • UKN
HOOVER VS. THE KENNEDYS: THE SECOND CIVIL WAR • 1987 • O'Herlihy Michael • TVM • USA
HOOVERIZING • 1918 • *U.s.m.p.* • USA
HOOVU MULLU • 1968 • Seshagiri Rao A. V. • IND • FLOWER AND THORN
HOP AND GO • 1943 • McCabe Norman • ANS • USA
HOP-FROG • 1912 • Desfontaines Henri • SHT • FRN
HOP HARRIGAN • 1946 • Abrahams Derwin • SRL • USA
HOP-HEAD'S DREAM • 1914 • *Ab* • USA
HOP, LOOK AND LISTEN • 1948 • Freleng Friz • ANS • USA
HOP O' MY THUMB • 1912 • *Gaumont* • FRN
HOP-PICKERS, THE see **STARCI NA CHMELU** • 1964
HOP, SKIP AND A CHUMP • 1942 • Freleng Friz • ANS • USA
HOP SMUGGLERS, THE • 1914 • *Hunt Irene* • USA
HOP, THE BELL HOP • 1919 • Parrott Charles • SHT • USA
HOP, THE DEVIL'S BREW • 1916 • Smalley Phillips, Weber Lois • USA
HOPALONG CASSIDY • 1935 • Bretherton Howard • USA • HOPALONG CASSIDY ENTERS
HOPALONG CASSIDY ENTERS see **HOPALONG CASSIDY** • 1935
HOPALONG CASSIDY RETURNS • 1936 • Watt Nate • USA
HOPALONG CASUALTY • 1960 • Jones Charles M. • ANS • USA
HOPALONG RIDES AGAIN • 1937 • Selander Lesley • USA
HOPE • 1912 • *Mccoy Gertrude* • USA
HOPE • 1913 • *Eyton Bessie* • USA
HOPE • 1919 • Wilson Rex • USA • SWEETHEARTS
HOPE see **NADEJE** • 1963
HOPE see **AASRA** • 1967
HOPE see **UMUT** • 1970
HOPE, THE • 1920 • Blache Herbert • USA
HOPE AND GLORY • 1987 • Boorman John • UKN
HOPE AND OTHER POEMS: WLADYSAW BRONIEWSKI see **NADZIEJA I INNE WIERSZE: WLADYSLAW BRONIEWSKI** • 1962
HOPE AND PAIN see **DAUNTAUN HIROZU** • 1988
HOPE AVENUE see **VIALE DELLE SPERANZA** • 1953
HOPE BAR -THE LAST TO CLOSE see **BAR ESPERANCA -O ULTIMO QUE FECHA** • 1982
HOPE CHEST, THE • 1918 • Clifton Elmer • USA
HOPE DIAMOND MYSTERY, THE • 1921 • Paton Stuart • SRL • USA
HOPE FOR TOMORROW • 1990 • Srisuparb Somohing • THL • CHILLI AND HAM
HOPE FOSTER'S MOTHER • 1914 • Belmore Lionel • USA
HOPE IS NOT DEAD YET see **NOZOMI NAKI NI ARAZU** • 1949
HOPE NAMED BOLIVIA, A see **ESPERANZA LLAMADA BOLIVIA, UNA**
HOPE OF BLUE SKY see **KIBO NO AOZORA** • 1960
HOPE OF HIS SIDE, THE see **WHERE'S GEORGE?** • 1935
HOPE OF YOUTH, THE see **KIBO NO SEISHUN** • 1942
HOPE SEEMS INFINITE • 1972 • Saks Ron • ANS • USA
HOPEAA RAJAN TAKAA • 1963 • Niskanen Mikko • FNL • SILVER FROM ACROSS THE BORDER
HOPEFUL DONKEY, THE • 1943 • Davis Mannie • ANS • USA
HOPELESS DAWN, THE • 1913 • Campbell Colin • USA
HOPELESS GAME, THE • 1914 • Myers Harry • USA
HOPELESS ONES, THE see **UMUTSUZLAR** • 1971
HOPELESS ONES, THE (USA) see **SZEGENYLEGENYEK (NEHEZELETUEK)** • 1965
HOPELESS PASSION, A • 1911 • Wilson Frank? • UKN
HOPELESSLY LOST • 1972 • Daneliya Georgi • USS
HOPES AND DREAMS • 1969 • Mehdi Al Rachid • SDN
HOPES FOR TOMORROW see **ESOK MASIH ADA** • 1979
HOPES GONE WITH THE WIND see **ELPIDHES POU NAVAYISAN** • 1968
HOPES OF BELINDA, THE • 1913 • *Karr Darwin* • USA
HOPES OF BLIND ALLEY, THE • 1914 • Dwan Allan • USA
HOPI LEGEND, A • 1913 • Reid Wallace • USA • PUEBLO ROMANCE, A
HOPI RAIDER, THE • 1914 • *Kalem* • USA

HOPKINS' DOG-GONE LUCK • 1912 • *Nestor* • USA
HOPLA PA SENGEKANTEN • 1976 • Hilbard John • DNM • DANISH ESCORT GIRLS ○ JUMPIN' AT THE BEDSIDE ○ ESCORT GIRLS
HOPPER, THE • 1918 • Heffron Thomas N. • USA
HOPPITY GOES TO TOWN (UKN) see **MR. BUG GOES TO TOWN** • 1941
HOPPITY POP • 1946 • McLaren Norman • ANS • USA
HOPPLA, HERR LEHRER • 1920 • *Kiesslich Curt Wolfram* • FRG
HOPPLA -JETZT KOMMT EDDIE • 1958 • Klinger Werner • FRG
HOPPSAN! • 1955 • Olin Stig • SWD • MONSTRET
HOPPY AND LUCKY • 1952 • McKimson Robert • ANS • USA
HOPPY DAZE • 1961 • McKimson Robert • ANS • USA
HOPPY SERVES A WRIT • 1943 • Archainbaud George • USA
HOPPY'S HOLIDAY • 1947 • Archainbaud George • USA
HOPSCOTCH • 1980 • Neame Ronald • UKN, USA
HOPU-SAN • 1951 • Yamamoto Kajiro • JPN
HOR BALEVANA • 1965 • Zohar Uri • ISR • HOLE IN THE MOON, A
HOR, VAR DER IKKE EN, SOM LO? • 1978 • Carlsen Henning • DNM • DID SOMEBODY LAUGH?
HORA BRUJA, LA • 1985 • de Arminan Jaime • SPN • WITCHING HOUR, THE
HORA CERO: OPERACION ROMMEL • 1968 • Klimovsky Leon • SPN, ITL • ZERO HOUR: OPERATION ROMMEL ○ BULLET FOR ROMMEL, A ○ OPERACION ROMMEL ○ URLO DEI GIGANTI, L'
HORA DA ESTRELA, A • 1986 • Amaral Suzana • BRZ • HOUR OF THE STAR, THE
HORA-DANCE, THE • Bostan Elisabeta, Bostan Ion • SHT • RMN
HORA DE AMOR, UMA • 1964 • Fraga Augusto • PRT
HORA DE LA VERDAD, LA • 1944 • Foster Norman • MXC • HOUR OF TRUTH, THE
HORA DE LOS HORNOS, LA • 1968 • Getino Octavio, Solanas Fernando • DOC • ARG • HOUR OF THE FURNACES, THE (USA)
HORA DE LOS NINOS, LA • 1969 • Ripstein Arturo • MXC • CHILDREN'S HOUR
HORA DEL BURRO, LA • 1978 • Rodriguez Oziel • VNZ • DONKEY'S HOUR
HORA DEL JAGUAR, LA • 1977 • Crevenna Alfredo B. • MXC
HORA DEL SOL, LA • 1975 • Kuhn Rodolfo • ARG • HOUR OF THE SUN
HORA DEL TIGRE, LA • Lugo Alfredo • VNZ
HORA E VEZ DE AUGUSTO MATRAGA, A • 1965 • Santos Roberto • BRZ • TIME AND HOUR OF AUGUSTO MATRAGA, THE
HORA H, A • 1938 • do Canto Jorge Brum • SHT • PRT
HORA INCOGNITA, LA • 1964 • Ozores Mariano • SPN • DIOS ELIJIO SUS VIAJEROS ○ GOD SELECTED HIS TRAVELERS ○ UNKNOWN HOUR, THE
HORA Y MEDIA DE BALAZOS • 1956 • Galindo Alejandro • MXC
HORACE 62 • 1962 • Versini Andre • FRN
HORACE COMEDIES • 1919 • Rooke Arthur • SER • UKN
HORACE EARNS A HALO • 1919 • Rooke Arthur • UKN
HORACE OF PUTNEY • 1923 • *Thespian Productions* • UKN
HORACE'S TRIUMPH • 1919 • Rooke Arthur • UKN
HORACIJEV USPON I PAD • 1969 • Grgic Zlatko, Kolar Boris, Zaninovic Ante • ANS • YGS, FRG • RISE AND FALL OF HORATIO, THE
HORAFA FAMILY, THE see **IKOGENIA HORAFA** • 1968
HORAFUKI TAIKOKI • 1964 • Furusawa Kengo • JPN • SANDAL KEEPER, THE (USA)
HORAS DE AGONIA • 1956 • Delgado Miguel M. • MXC
HORAS DE MARIA, AS • 1977 • de Macedo Antonio • PRT • MARIA'S HOURS
HORAS INCIERTAS • 1951 • Elorrieta Jose Maria • SPN
HORAS PROHIBIDAS, LAS • 1968 • Xiol Juan • SPN
HORATIO see **ORAZI E CURIAZI** • 1961
HORATIO HORNBLOWER see **CAPTAIN HORATIO HORNBLOWER R.N.** • 1951
HORATIO SPARKINS • 1913 • Brooke Van Dyke • USA
HORATIO'S DECEPTION • 1920 • Mannering Cecil • UKN
HORDERN MYSTERY, THE see **GOLDEN FLAME, THE** • 1920
HORDUBAL BROTHERS, THE see **HORDUBALOVE** • 1937
HORDUBALOVE • 1937 • Fric Martin • CZC • HORDUBAL BROTHERS, THE ○ HORDUBALS, THE
HORDUBALS, THE see **HORDUBALOVE** • 1937
HORECKA • 1958 • Jires Jaromil • SHT • CZC • FEVER
HORETA TSUYOMI • 1968 • Mizukawa Junzo • JPN • MAYOR'S SECRET, THE
HORI, MA PANENKO! • 1967 • Forman Milos • CZC • FIREMEN'S BALL, THE (USA) ○ FIREMAN'S BALL, THE (UKN) ○ THERE'S A FIRE, MY DOLLY! ○ LIKE A HOUSE ON FIRE ○ SONG OF THE FIREMAN ○ FIRE! FIRE!
HORIS MARTYRES • 1984 • Papamalis Nikos • GRC • WITHOUT WITNESSES
HORIZON see **GORIZONT** • 1933
HORIZON see **GORIZONT** • 1961
HORIZON see **HORIZONT** • 1971
HORIZON, L' • 1967 • Rouffio Jacques • FRN
HORIZON, THE • 1966 • Kidawa Janusz • DOC • PLN
HORIZON, THE • 1989 • Mollagholipoor Rasoul • IRN
HORIZON, THE see **CHIHEISEN** • 1984
HORIZON -THE WANDERING JEW see **GORIZONT** • 1933
HORIZONS • 1953 • *Blais Roger (P)* • SER • CND
HORIZONS • 1983 • Norman Ron • USA
HORIZONS see **AFAQ** • 1973
HORIZONS DE QUEBEC • 1948 • Devlin Bernard • DCS • CND
HORIZONS NOIRS see **SVARTA HORISONTER** • 1936
HORIZONS NOUVEAUX • 1961 • Gillet • SHT • FRN
HORIZONS OF QUEBEC • 1952 • Garceau Raymond • DCS • CND • QUEBEC XXe SIECLE
HORIZONS SAN FIN • 1952 • Dreville Jean • FRN • ENDLESS HORIZONS
HORIZONS WEST • 1952 • Boetticher Budd • USA • TEXAS MAN, THE
HORIZONT • 1971 • Gabor Pal • HNG • HORIZON
HORIZONTAL see **HORIZONTALE** • 1924
HORIZONTAL LIEUTENANT, THE • 1962 • Thorpe Richard • USA
HORIZONTAL-VERTICAL ORCHESTRA see **HORIZONTAL-VERTIKAL ORCHESTER** • 1921
HORIZONTAL-VERTIKAL ORCHESTER • 1921 • Eggeling Viking • SWD • HORIZONTAL-VERTICAL ORCHESTRA
HORIZONTALE • 1924 • Eggeling Viking • FRG • HORIZONTAL
HORIZONTE ANGOLANO • 1973 • Mendes Joao • SHT • PRT
HORIZONTE TE HAPURA • 1968 • Gjika Viktor • ALB • BROAD HORIZONS
HORIZONTES DE LUZ • 1960 • Klimovsky Leon • SPN
HORIZONTES DE SANGRE • 1960 • Ortega Juan J. • MXC
HORIZONTES NUEVOS • 1931 • Howard David • USA
HORKA KASE • 1988 • Urban Radovan • CZC • HOT PROBLEM, A
HORKA LASKA • 1958 • Mach Josef • CZC • LOST CANNON, THE
HORKA ZIMA • 1972 • Kachyna Karel • CZC • HOT WINTER
HORLA, LE • 1966 • Pollet Jean-Daniel • SHT • FRN
HORLOGE MAGIQUE, L' (FRN) see **WUNDERUHR, DIE** • 1928
HORLOGER DE ST. PAUL, L' • 1973 • Tavernier Bertrand • FRN • WATCHMAKER OF ST. PAUL, THE (UKN) ○ CLOCKMAKER, THE ○ CLOCKMAKER OF ST. PAUL, THE (USA)
HORMIGA NEGRA • 1977 • Defilippi Ricardo • ARG
HORN see **TOM HORN** • 1979
HORN-A-PLENTY • 1970 • *Kirt Films International* • USA
HORN BLOWS AT MIDNIGHT, THE • 1945 • Walsh Raoul • USA
HORN I NORR, ETT • 1950 • Sucksdorff Arne • DCS • SWD • LIVING STREAM, THE
HORNERO, EL ZORRO Y LA LUNA LLENA, EL • 1977 • Darino Eduardo • ANM • URG • BIRD, THE FOX AND THE FULL MOON, THE
HORNETS, THE • 1968 • Wenceslao Jose Pepe • PHL
HORNET'S NEST • 1923 • West Walter • UKN
HORNET'S NEST • 1970 • Karlson Phil • USA • VALOR OF WAR, THE
HORNET'S NEST, A • 1913 • France Charles H. • USA
HORNET'S NEST, THE • 1919 • Young James • USA
HORNET'S NEST, THE • 1955 • Saunders Charles • UKN
HORNET'S NEST, THE see **GUEPIER, LE** • 1975
HORNIKOVA RUZE • 1974 • Brdecka Jiri • ANM • CZC
HORNING IN • 1965 • Post Howard • ANS • USA
HORNSEY FILM, THE • 1969 • Holland Patricia • UKN
HORNY HOBO • 1969 • *Fleetan Films* • USA • THORNY HOBOES ○ HOBO, THE
HORO ZANMAI • 1928 • Inagaki Hiroshi • JPN • WANDERING GAMBLER, THE
HOROKI • 1954 • Hisamatsu Seiji • JPN • FORSAKEN
HOROKI • 1962 • Naruse Mikio • JPN • RECORDING OF WANDERING, A ○ WANDERER'S NOTEBOOK, A ○ LONELY LANE
HOROSCOPE see **976 EVIL** • 1988
HOROSCOPE, L' • 1978 • Girault Jean • FRN • FAIS GAFFE A LA MARCHE
HOROSCOPE FOR A CHILD • 1970 • Benegal Shyam • DCS • IND
HOROSCOPE OF JESUS CHRIST, THE see **JEZUS KRISZTUS HOROSZKOPJA** • 1988
HOROSCOPE SEPTEMBER • 1972 • *Project 7* • ANS • USA
HOROSCOPE (USA) see **HOROSKOP** • 1969
HOROSCOPO, EL • 1972 • Lazaga Pedro • SPN
HOROSKOP • 1969 • Draskovic Boro • YGS • HOROSCOPE (USA)
HOROUCI SRDCE • 1962 • Vavra Otakar • CZC • PASSIONATE HEART, THE ○ ARDENT HEART, THE ○ BURNING HEART, THE
HORRIBLE CAUCHEMAR, UN • 1901 • Zecca Ferdinand • SHT • FRN • HORRIBLE NIGHTMARE, A
HORRIBLE CAUCHEMAR, UN • 1916-24 • Lortac • ANS • FRN
HORRIBLE DR. HICHCOCK, THE (USA) see **ORRIBILE SEGRETO DEL DR. HICHCOCK, L'** • 1962
HORRIBLE DR. ORLOFF, L' see **GRITOS EN LA NOCHE** • 1962
HORRIBLE EXAMPLE, THE • 1913 • Seay Charles M. • USA
HORRIBLE HOUSE ON THE HILL, THE see **PEOPLETOYS** • 1974
HORRIBLE HYDE • 1915 • Hansel Howell? • USA
HORRIBLE MIDNIGHT see **JIGOKU NO GOZEN NIJI** • 1958
HORRIBLE MILL WOMEN, THE see **MULINO DELLE DONNE DI PIETRA, IL** • 1960
HORRIBLE NIGHT see **GRAUSIGE NACHTE** • 1921
HORRIBLE NIGHTMARE, A see **HORRIBLE CAUCHEMAR, UN** • 1901
HORRIBLE PROFESSION, THE (UKN) see **SURSIS POUR UN ESPION** • 1964
HORRIBLE SECRET OF DR. HICHCOCK, THE see **ORRIBILE SEGRETO DEL DR. HICHCOCK, L'** • 1962
HORRIBLE SEXY VAMPIRE, THE (USA) see **VAMPIRO DE LA AUTOPISTA, EL** • 1970
HORRIDO • 1924 • Meyer Johannes • FRG
HORRIFYING NEIGHBOURS, THE see **HORRIPILANTES VECINOS, LOS** • 1979
HORRIPILANTES VECINOS, LOS • 1979 • Lovera Nestor • VNZ • HORRIFYING NEIGHBOURS, THE
HORRIPLANTE BESTIA HUMANA, LA • 1970 • Cardona Rene • MXC • NIGHT OF THE BLOODY APES ○ GOMAR, THE HUMAN GORILLA
HORROR • 1963 • De Martino Alberto • SPN, ITL • BLANCHEVILLE MONSTER, THE (USA)
HORROR • 1965 • Hintsch Gyorgy • HNG
HORROR! see **CHILDREN OF THE DAMNED** • 1963
HORROR, THE • Pollard Bud • USA
HORROR AND SEX see **HORROR Y SEXO** • 1970
HORROR AT 37000 FEET • 1972 • Rich David Lowell • TVM • USA • STONES
HORROR CASTLE (USA) see **VERGINE DI NORIMBERGA, LA** • 1963
HORROR CASTLE (WHERE THE BLOOD FLOWS) see **VERGINE DI NORIMBERGA, LA** • 1963
HORROR CHAMBER OF DR. FAUSTUS, THE (USA) see **YEUX SANS VISAGE, LES** • 1959
HORROR CREATURES OF THE PREHISTORIC PLANET see **HORROR OF THE BLOOD MONSTERS** • 1970
HORROR DREAM • 1947 • Peterson Sidney, Hirsch Hy • SHT • USA
HORROR EXPRESS (USA) see **PANICO EN EL TRANSIBERIANO** • 1972
HORROR FILM 1 • 1970 • Le Grice Malcolm • UKN
HORROR FILM 2 • 1972 • Le Grice Malcolm • UKN
HORROR FROM BEYOND, THE see **BLOOD THIRST** • 1965
HORROR HIGH • 1973 • Stouffer Larry • USA • TWISTED BRAIN
HORROR HOSPITAL • 1973 • Balch Anthony • UKN • COMPUTER KILLERS (USA)
HORROR HOTEL (USA) see **CITY OF THE DEAD** • 1960
HORROR HOUSE (USA) see **HAUNTED HOUSE OF HORROR, THE** • 1969
HORROR ISLAND • 1941 • Waggner George • USA
HORROR: L'ASSASSINO HA LE ORE CONTATE (ITL) see **COPLAN SAUVE SA PEAU** • 1967
HORROR MANIACS (USA) see **GREED OF WILLIAM HART, THE** • 1948
HORROR MOVIE • 1981 • Murphy Maurice • ASL
HORROR OF A DEFORMED MAN see **KYOFU NIKEI NINGEN** • 1969
HORROR OF AN UGLY WOMAN see **KAIDAN KASANEGAFUCHI** • 1970
HORROR OF CHICAGO, THE see **TERRIBLE DE CHICAGO, EL** • 1968
HORROR OF DARKNESS • 1965 • Almond Paul • MTV • CND
HORROR OF DEATH, THE see **ASPHYX, THE** • 1972
HORROR OF DRACULA (USA) see **DRACULA** • 1958
HORROR OF FRANKENSTEIN, THE • 1970 • Sangster Jimmy • UKN
HORROR OF IT ALL, THE • 1964 • Fisher Terence • UKN
HORROR OF MALFORMED MEN see **KYOFU NIKEI NINGEN** • 1969
HORROR OF PARTY BEACH, THE • 1964 • Tenney Del • USA • INVASION OF THE ZOMBIES
HORROR OF SNAPE ISLAND (USA) see **TOWER OF EVIL** • 1972
HORROR OF THE BLOOD MONSTERS • 1970 • Adamson Al • USA • SPACE MISSION OF THE LOST PLANET ○ VAMPIRE MEN OF THE LOST PLANET ○ HORROR CREATURES OF THE PREHISTORIC PLANET ○ FLESH CREATURES OF THE RED PLANET ○ FLESH CREATURES, THE
HORROR OF THE RED PLANET see **WIZARD OF MARS** • 1964
HORROR OF THE STONE WOMEN see **MULINO DELLE DONNE DI PIETRA, IL** • 1960
HORROR OF THE ZOMBIES (USA) see **BUQUE MALDITO, EL** • 1974
HORROR ON SNAPE ISLAND see **TOWER OF EVIL** • 1972
HORROR PLANET (USA) see **INSEMINOID** • 1982
HORROR RISES FROM THE TOMB (USA) see **ESPANTO SURGE DE LA TUMBA, EL** • 1972
HORROR SHOW see **HOUSE 3: THE HORROR SHOW** • 1989
HORROR STAR • 1981 • Vane Norman Thaddeus • USA • FRIGHTMARE ○ BODY SNATCHERS, THE
HORROR STORY • 1972 • Gallego Manuel Esteba • SPN
HORROR THAT HORRIFIES see **BHOOT BUNGLA** • 1965
HORROR Y SEXO • 1970 • Cardona Rene • MXC • HORROR AND SEX
HORRORES DEL BOSQUE NEGRO, LOS see **LOBA, LA** • 1964
HORRORITUAL • 1972 • *Atwater Barry* • SHT • USA
HORRORS OF BURKE AND HARE, THE (USA) see **BURKE AND HARE** • 1971
HORRORS OF DRINK, THE see **DRUNKARD'S CONVERSION, THE** • 1901
HORRORS OF FRANKENSTEIN • Brzezinski Tony • SHT • USA
HORRORS OF SORTS: TANYA'S ISLAND see **TANYA'S ISLAND** • 1980
HORRORS OF SPIDER ISLAND see **TOTER HING IM NETZ, EIN** • 1960
HORRORS OF THE BLACK FOREST see **LOBA, LA** • 1964
HORRORS OF THE BLACK MUSEUM • 1959 • Crabtree Arthur • UKN • CRIME IN THE MUSEUM OF HORRORS (USA)
HORRORS OF THE BLACK ZOO see **BLACK ZOO** • 1963
HORS-D'OEUVRE • 1960 • Lamb Derek (c/d) • ANS • CND
HORS D'OEUVRES • 1961 • Low Colin • CND
HORS-LA-LOI, LES • 1969 • Fares Tewfik • ALG • LAWLESS, THE
HORS-MOUANE • 1986 • Dinel Pierre • DOC • CND
HORSE • 1965 • Warhol Andy • USA
HORSE see **UMA** • 1941
HORSE, LA • 1969 • Granier-Deferre Pierre • FRN, ITL, FRG • CLAN DEGLI UOMINI VIOLENTI, IL (ITL)
HORSE, THE see **KON** • 1968
HORSE, THE see **KONJ** • 1972
HORSE! A HORSE!, A • 1916 • Stow Percy • UKN
HORSE AND CARRIAGE (USA) see **AMAXAKI, TO** • 1957
HORSE AND MRS. GRUNDY, A • 1911 • Fitzhamon Lewin • UKN
HORSE AND POLISH AFFAIRS, THE see **KON A SPRAWA POLSKA** • 1967
HORSE ATE THE HAT, THE see **CHAPEAU DE PAILLE D'ITALIE, UN** • 1927
HORSE CALLED COMANCHE, A see **TONKA** • 1958
HORSE CALLED JESTER, A • 1979 • Fairbairn Kenneth • UKN
HORSE CALLED NIJINSKY, A • 1972 • Durden-Smith Jo • DOC • UKN
HORSE CARRIAGE FROM MYSORE see **MYSORE TONGA** • 1968
HORSE COLLARS see **HORSES' COLLARS** • 1935
HORSE COPS • 1931 • Foster John, McManus J. J. • ANS • USA
HORSE DRAWN MAGIC • 1979 • Henaut Dorothy Todd • DOC • CND • HORSE-DRAWN MAGIC
HORSE-DRAWN MAGIC see **HORSE DRAWN MAGIC** • 1979
HORSE FEATHERS • 1932 • McLeod Norman Z. • USA
HORSE FLY OPERA • 1941 • Donnelly Eddie • ANS • USA
HORSE HARE • 1960 • Freleng Friz • ANS • USA
HORSE IN THE GREY FLANNEL SUIT, THE • 1968 • Tokar Norman • USA
HORSE LAUGHS see **CAPALLOLOGY** • 1974
HORSE MANIAC, THE see **KIGEKI-KEIBA HISSHOHO** • 1967
HORSE, MY HORSE see **AT** • 1982

HORSE OF ANOTHER COLOR, A • 1915 • *Essanay* • USA
HORSE OF OXUMAIRE, THE see **CAVALO DE OXUMAIRE, O** • 1961
HORSE ON BILL, A • 1913 • Henderson Dell • USA
HORSE ON BROADWAY, A • 1926 • *Frank S. Mattison Prod.* • USA
HORSE ON FRED, A • 1913 • *Mace Fred* • USA
HORSE ON SOPHIE, A • 1914 • *Essanay* • USA
HORSE ON THE MERRY-GO-ROUND, THE • 1938 • Iwerks Ub • ANS • USA
HORSE OVER TEA KETTLE • 1962 • Breer Robert • ANS • USA
HORSE PLAY • 1924 • Lantz Walter • ANS • USA
HORSE PLAY • 1937 • Yarbrough Jean • SHT • USA
HORSE PLAY • 1967 • Smith Paul J. • ANS • USA
HORSE PLAY see **HORSEPLAY** • 1973
HORSE RACE AT HAWLEY'S RANCH, THE • 1913 • *Frontier* • USA
HORSE RACES • 1905 • Barragan Salvador Toscano • MXC
HORSE REBELLION, THE see **PULAKAPINA** • 1977
HORSE SENSE • 1924 • Hayes Ward • USA
HORSE SENSE • 1938 • Newman Widgey R. • UKN
HORSE SENSE • 1944 • Bird Richard • UKN
HORSE SHOER'S GIRL, THE • 1910 • *Powers* • USA
HORSE SHOES • 1927 • Bruckman Clyde • USA
HORSE SHOO • 1964 • Hanna William, Barbera Joseph • ANS • USA
HORSE SOLDIERS, THE • 1959 • Ford John • USA
HORSE STEALER: OR, A CASUAL ACQUAINTANCE, THE • 1905 • Green Tom • UKN
HORSE THAT ATE THE BABY, THE • 1906 • Stow Percy • UKN
HORSE THAT CRIED, THE see **DOROGOI TSENOI** • 1957
HORSE THAT WOULDN'T STAY HITCHED, THE • 1913 • *Brennan John* • USA
HORSE, THE WOMAN AND THE GUN, THE see **AT AVRAT SILAH** • 1966
HORSE THIEF • 1905 • *Bitzer Billy (Ph)* • USA
HORSE THIEF see **DAOMAZEI** • 1985
HORSE THIEF, THE • 1911 • *Powers* • USA
HORSE THIEF, THE • 1912 • *Pathe* • USA
HORSE THIEF, THE • 1912 • Dwan Allan • USA
HORSE THIEF, THE • 1913 • Lucas Wilfred • USA
HORSE THIEF, THE • 1914 • Davis Ulysses • USA
HORSE THIEF'S BIGAMY, THE • 1911 • Dwan Allan • USA
HORSE THIEF'S DAUGHTER, THE • 1912 • *Nestor* • USA
HORSE THIEVES, THE • 1912 • *Pathe* • USA
HORSE THIEVES OF BAR X RANCH, THE • 1912 • *Champion* • USA
HORSE TRADER, THE • 1914 • *Royal* • USA
HORSE TRADER, THE • 1926 • Wyler William • SHT • USA
HORSE TRADER, THE see **TRICK OF HEARTS, A** • 1928
HORSE WITH THE FLYING TAIL, THE • 1961 • Lansburgh Larry • DOC • USA
HORSE WITHOUT A HEAD, THE • 1963 • Chaffey Don • UKN
HORSE WRANGLER, THE • 1914 • Adolfi John G. • USA
HORSEBREAKER, THE see **DOMADOR, THE** • 1978
HORSEFLESH see **SPORTING BLOOD** • 1931
HORSEFLY FLEAS, A • 1948 • McKimson Robert • ANS • USA
HORSEHOOFS • 1931 • *Carey Harry* • USA
HORSEMAN see **BAKURO ICHIDAI** • 1963
HORSEMAN OF DIVINE PROVIDENCE, THE see **JINETE DE LA DIVINA PROVIDENCIA, EL** • 1989
HORSEMAN OF THE PLAINS, A • 1928 • Stoloff Ben • USA
HORSEMAN, THE WOMAN AND THE MOTH, THE • 1968 • Brakhage Stan • SHT • USA
HORSEMASTERS, THE • 1961 • Fairchild William • UKN
HORSEMEN, THE • 1951 • Yudin Konstantin • USS
HORSEMEN, THE • 1971 • Frankenheimer John • USA
HORSEMEN OF THE REVOLUTION see **VSADNIKI REVOLUTSII** • 1968
HORSEMEN OF THE SIERRAS • 1949 • Sears Fred F. • USA • REMEMBER ME (UKN)
HORSENSCHIMMEN see **MIND SHADOWS** • 1988
HORSEPLAY • 1933 • Sedgwick Edward • USA
HORSEPLAY • 1973 • Straiton John S. • ANS • CND • HORSE PLAY
HORSES see **UMA** • 1941
HORSES see **HESTEN** • 1943
HORSES see **ETO LOSHADI** • 1965
HORSES AND THEIR ANCESTORS • 1962 • Hubley John • ANS • USA
HORSES ARE BORN SUCH see **CAVALLI SI NASCE** • 1988
HORSES' COLLARS • 1935 • Bruckman Clyde • SHT • USA • HORSE COLLARS
HORSE'S EGG see **KUDREMOTTE** • 1977
HORSES IN WINTER • 1988 • Raxlen Rick, Vallely Patrick • CND
HORSE'S MOUTH, THE • 1959 • Neame Ronald • UKN
HORSE'S MOUTH, THE (USA) see **ORACLE, THE** • 1953
HORSES OF DEATH • 1972 • Dunning George • ANM • UKN
HORSES OF THE VERCORS, THE see **CHEVAUX DE VERCORS, LES** • 1943
HORSE'S TALE, A • 1954 • Smith Paul J. • ANS • USA
HORSESHOE, THE • 1912 • *Selig* • USA
HORSESHOE, THE see **PODKOVA PRO STESTI** • 1946
HORSESHOE COMEDIES • 1920 • Goldin Sidney M. • SER • UKN
HORSESHOE -FOR LUCK, A • 1914 • Drew Sidney • USA
HORSESHOE FOR LUCK, A see **PODKOVA PRO STESTI** • 1946
HORSESHOE LUCK • 1915 • *United Film Service* • USA
HORSESHOE LUCK • 1924 • Franz Joseph J. • USA
HORSEY • 1926 • Parkinson H. B. • SER • UKN
HORSIE see **QUEEN FOR A DAY** • 1951
HORSING AROUND • 1957 • White Jules • SHT • USA
HORSING AROUND • 1973 • Pindal Kaj • ANS • CND
HORSKE VOLANI SOS • 1929 • Marten Leo, Studecky • CZC • SOS IN THE MOUNTAINS
HORST WESSEL see **HANS WESTMAR** • 1933
HORTOBAGY • 1936 • Hoellering George • HNG
HORTON HATCHES THE EGG • 1942 • Clampett Robert • ANS • USA
HORTON HEARS A WHO • 1971 • Jones Charles M. • ANS • USA
HORU -MUNAKATA SHIKO NO SEKAI • 1975 • Yanagawa Takeo • DOC • JPN • WOOD-BLOCK PRINTING -THE WORLD OF SHIKO MUNAKATA
HORVATOV IZBOR • 1985 • Galic Eduard • YGS • HORVAT'S CHOICE
HORVAT'S CHOICE see **HORVATOV IZBOR** • 1985
HORYU-JI • 1958 • Hani Susumu • DOC • JPN • HORYUJI TEMPLE ○ HORYU TEMPLE
HORYU TEMPLE see **HORYU-JI** • 1958
HORYUJI TEMPLE see **HORYU-JI** • 1958
HOSE, DIE • 1927 • Behrendt Hans • FRG • ROYAL SCANDAL ○ TROUSERS, THE
HOSEKRAEMMEREN • 1971 • Thomsen Knud Leif • DNM
HOSEN DES RITTERS VON BREDOW, DIE • 1973 • Petzold Konrad • GDR
HOSHI WA MIDARE TOBU • 1924 • Ito Daisuke • JPN
HOSHIKAGE NO HATOBA • 1968 • Nishimura Shogoro • JPN • STARDUST WHARF
HOSHIYO NAGEKUNA: SHORI NO OTOKO • 1967 • Masuda Toshio • JPN • MAN OF VICTORY, THE
HOSPEDE DO QUARTO NO.13, O • 1946 • Duarte Arthur • PRT, SPN • HUESPEDE DEL CUARTO NO.13, EL (SPN)
HOSPITAL • 1971 • Erends Ronny • DCS • NTH
HOSPITAL • 1971 • Wiseman Frederick • DOC • USA
HOSPITAL, THE • Pogacnik Joze • DCS • YGS
HOSPITAL, THE • 1971 • Hiller Arthur • USA
HOSPITAL BABY, THE • 1912 • *Essanay* • USA
HOSPITAL DE URGENCIA • 1956 • Santillan Antonio • SPN
HOSPITAL GENERAL • 1956 • Arevalo Carlos • SPN
HOSPITAL HOAX, A • 1912 • *Brennan John E.* • USA
HOSPITAL HOSPITALITY • 1939 • Christy William • UKN
HOSPITAL MASSACRE see **X-RAY** • 1981
HOSPITAL OF TERROR see **NURSE SHERRI** • 1978
HOSPITAL OF TRANSFIGURATION, THE see **SZPITAL PRZEMIENIENIA** • 1978
HOSPITAL ROMANCE, A • 1913 • *Reliance* • USA
HOSPITAL (UKN) see **SZPITAL** • 1962
HOSPITALIKY • 1937 • Fleischer Dave • ANS • USA
HOSPITALS DON'T BURN DOWN • 1977 • Trenchard-Smith Brian • DOC • ASL
HOSPITALS, THE WHITE MAFIA see **BISTURI, LA MAFIA BIANCA** • 1973
HOSSZU AZ UT HAZAIG • 1960 • Mariassy Felix • HNG • IT IS A LONG WAY HOME
HOSSZU VAGTA (HNG) see **LONG RIDE, THE** • 1983
HOST, THE • 1923 • Bacon Lloyd • SHT • USA
HOST, THE • 1988 • Densham Pen • USA
HOST TO A GHOST • 1941 • Lord Del • SHT • USA
HOST TO A GHOST • 1947 • Yates Hal • SHT • USA
HOSTAGE • Walsh Aisling • SHT • IRL
HOSTAGE • 1983 • Shields Frank • ASL, FRG • HOSTAGE: THE CHRISTINE MARESCH STORROY ○ SAVAGE ATTRACTION (USA)
HOSTAGE • 1987 • Mohr Hanro, Rubens Percival? • USA, SAF
HOSTAGE • 1988 • Levin Peter • TVM • USA
HOSTAGE, THE • 1913 • *Patheplay* • USA
HOSTAGE, THE • 1917 • Thornby Robert T. • USA
HOSTAGE, THE • 1956 • Huth Harold • UKN
HOSTAGE, THE • 1967 • Doughton Russell S. Jr. • USA
HOSTAGE, THE see **THREE JUMPS AHEAD** • 1923
HOSTAGE: DALLAS • 1986 • Little Dwight H. • USA • GETTING EVEN
HOSTAGE FLIGHT • 1985 • Stern Steven Hilliard • TVM • USA • TERROR IN THE SKY
HOSTAGE HEART, THE • 1977 • McEveety Bernard • TVM • USA
HOSTAGE OF THE EMBASSY, THE see **MYSTISKE SELSKABSDAME** • 1916
HOSTAGE OF THE NORTH • 1915 • *Edwards Walter* • USA
HOSTAGE STORY, A see **TUSZTORTENET** • 1988
HOSTAGE: THE CHRISTINE MARESCH STORROY see **HOSTAGE** • 1983
HOSTAGE TOWER, THE • 1980 • Guzman Claudio • TVM • USA
HOSTAGES • 1943 • Tuttle Frank • USA
HOSTAGES • 1975 • Eady David • UKN
HOSTAGES, THE • 1979 • Cardona Rene • MXC
HOSTAGES, THE see **OTAGES, LES** • 1939
HOSTAGES, THE (USA) see **GANG DES OTAGES, LE** • 1972
HOSTERIA DEL CABALLITO BLANCO, LA • 1948 • Perojo Benito • ARG
HOSTESS ALSO HAS A COUNT, THE see **FRAU WIRTIN HAT AUCH EINEN GRAFEN** • 1968
HOSTESSES DU SEXE, LES • 1976 • Philippe-Gerard Didier • FRN
HOSTILE COUNTRY • 1950 • Carr Thomas • USA • OUTLAW FURY
HOSTILE GUNS • 1967 • Springsteen R. G. • USA
HOSTILE LOVERS see **DUSMAN ASIKLAR** • 1967
HOSTILE WIND, THE • 1956 • Kalatozov Mikhail • USS
HOSTILE WITNESS • 1968 • Milland Ray • UKN
HOSTILE WITNESS see **TERRORIST ON TRIAL: THE UNITED STATES VS. SALIM AJAMI** • 1988
HOSTILITE see **FEELING OF HOSTILITY, THE** • 1948
HOSTSONATEN (SWD) see **HERBSTSONATE** • 1978
HOSZAKADAS • 1974 • Kosa Ferenc • HNG • SNOW-FALL
HOT ACTS OF LOVE see **AMOUR AUX TROUSSES, L'** • 1974
HOT AIR see **TWENTY MILLION SWEETHEARTS** • 1934
HOT AIR ACES • 1949 • Sparber I. • ANS • USA
HOT AIR SALESMAN, THE • 1937 • Fleischer Dave • ANS • USA
HOT AND ADOLESCENTS see **CHALEURS** • 1970
HOT AND BLUE (UKN) see **JEUX POUR COUPLES INFIDELES** • 1972
HOT AND BOTHERED • 1930 • Buzzell Edward • SHT • USA
HOT AND BOTHERED • 1931 • Lamont Charles • SHT • USA
HOT AND COLD • 1933 • Lantz Walter, Nolan William • ANS • USA
HOT AND COLD • 1989 • Kotcheff Ted • USA • HEATWAVE
HOT AND COLD PENGUIN • 1955 • Lovy Alex • ANS • USA
HOT AND DEADLY • 1981 • Hong Elliot • USA • RETRIEVERS, THE
HOT AND HAPPY • 1935 • Sparling Gordon • DCS • CND
HOT AND HECTIC • 1945 • Cowan Will • SHT • USA
HOT -AND HOW! • 1930 • Roberts Stephen • SHT • USA
HOT AND NAKED see **QUAND LES FILLES SE DECHAINENT** • 1973
HOT AND SEXY (UKN) see **BADEMEISTER REPORT** • 1974
HOT ANGEL, THE • 1958 • Parker Joe • USA
HOT APPLICATIONS • 1917 • Clements Roy • SHT • USA
HOT AUTUMN, A see **HEISSER HERBST, EIN** • 1988
HOT BED, THE • 1965 • Epstein Harry • USA
HOT BED OF SEX (UKN) see **ALLA RICERCA DEL PIACERE** • 1972
HOT BLOOD • 1956 • Ray Nicholas • USA • TAMBOURINE
HOT BLOOD • 1989 • Blot Philippe • FRN
HOT BLOOD see **WILD ONE, THE** • 1953
HOT BLOOD see **PETER UND SABINE** • 1968
HOT BLOOD see **DELI KAN** • 1982
HOT-BLOODED see **HEISSBLUTIG** • 1979
HOT BLOODED GALS see **SOCK IT TO ME BABY** • 1968
HOT BLOODED WOMAN • 1965 • Berry Dale • USA
HOT BLUE see **JEUX POUR COUPLES INFIDELES** • 1972
HOT BOARDING HOUSE • 1970 • Shamblin Gene • USA
HOT BOX • 1972 • Viola Joe • USA, PHL
HOT BRIDGE • 1930 • Sandrich Mark • SHT • USA
HOT BUBBLEGUM see **SHIFSHUF NAIM** • 1981
HOT BUBBLEGUM: LEMON POPSICLE III see **SHIFSHUF NAIM** • 1981
HOT CAKES FOR TWO • 1926 • *Sennett Mack (P)* • SHT • USA
HOT CAR GIRL • 1958 • Kowalski Bernard • USA
HOT CARGO • 1946 • Landers Lew • USA
HOT CARS • 1956 • McDougall Don • USA
HOT CAT? see **KUUMA KISSA?** • 1968
HOT CENTRE OF THE WORLD, THE • 1970 • Burstall Tim • SHT • ASL
HOT CHANNELS • 1973 • Benjamin R. G. • USA
HOT CHILD IN THE CITY • 1987 • Florea John • USA
HOT CHILI see **HOT SUMMER** • 1985
HOT CHOCOLATE • 1941 • Berne Josef • SHT • USA • COTTONTAIL
HOT CIRCUIT • 1972 • Glicker Paul, Lerner Richard • USA
HOT CORNER MURDER see **YOMMANNIN NO MOKUGEKISHA** • 1960
HOT COWGIRLS see **LIPPS AND MCCAINE** • 1978
HOT CRIME, A see **ATSUI HANKO** • 1968
HOT CROSS BUNNY • 1948 • McKimson Robert • ANS • USA
HOT CURVES • 1930 • Taurog Norman • USA
HOT DALLAS NIGHTS • 1981 • Kendrick Tony • USA
HOT DAYS see **ZILE FIERBINTI** • 1976
HOT DIGGITY DOG • 1967 • Smith Paul J. • ANS • USA
HOT DOG • 1920 • Fishback Fred C. • SHT • USA
HOT DOG • 1928 • Disney Walt • ANS • USA
HOT DOG • 1930 • Fleischer Dave • ANS • USA
HOT DOG • 1983 • Markle Peter • USA • HOT DOG.. THE MOVIE
HOT DOG CARTOONS • 1925 • Bray John R. • ANM • USA
HOT DOG CARTOONS • 1926-27 • Lantz Walter, Geronimi Clyde • ASS • USA
HOT DOG.. THE MOVIE see **HOT DOG** • 1983
HOT DOGGIE • 1925 • Rodney Earle • USA
HOT DOGS • 1916 • *Stull Walter* • SHT • USA
HOT DOGS • 1919 • *West Billy* • SHT • USA
HOT DOGS • 1980 • Fournier Claude • CND • CHIENS-CHAUDS, LES ○ CLEAN-UP SQUAD, THE
HOT DOGS see **MABEL'S BUSY DAY** • 1914
HOT DOGS ON ICE • 1938 • *Mintz Charles (P)* • ANS • USA
HOT ENOUGH FOR JUNE • 1963 • Thomas Ralph • UKN • AGENT 8 3/4 (USA)
HOT EROTIC DREAMS • 1967 • Shuman Mort • USA
HOT, FAST AND LOOSE • 1973 • Avery Dwayne • USA • BOOBY TRAP
HOT FEET • 1931 • Lantz Walter, Nolan William • ANS • USA
HOT FINISH see **MABEL AT THE WHEEL** • 1914
HOT FINISH, A • 1914 • *Imp* • USA
HOT FINISH, A • 1915 • *Rieger Marjorie* • USA
HOT FOOT • 1943 • Holmes Ben • SHT • USA
HOT FOOT LIGHTS • 1945 • Swift Howard • ANS • USA
HOT-FOOT ROMANCE, A • 1915 • *Ab* • USA
HOT FOR HOLLYWOOD • 1930 • Lantz Walter, Nolan William • ANS • USA
HOT FOR PARIS • 1929 • Walsh Raoul • USA
HOT FRUSTRATIONS see **TRAITE DES BLANCHES, LA** • 1965
HOT GIRLS FOR MEN ONLY (USA) see **I LIKE BIRDS** • 1967
HOT HANDS OF LOVE • 1966 • *Novak Harry H.* • USA
HOT, HARD AND MEAN see **BLACK MAMA, WHITE MAMA** • 1973
HOT-HEAD, THE see **FLAMING HOUR, THE** • 1922
HOT HEADS AND COLD FEET • 1915 • *Heinie & Louie* • USA
HOT HEELS • 1924 • Roach Hal • SHT • USA
HOT HEELS • 1928 • Craft William James • USA • PAINTING THE TOWN ○ PATENTS PENDING
HOT HEIR • 1931 • Kellino W. P. • UKN
HOT HEIRESS, THE • 1931 • Badger Clarence • USA
HOT HOLLOWS see **PASSION IN HOT HOLLOWS** • 1969
HOT HONG KONG HARBOUR see **HEISSER HAFEN HONGKONG** • 1962
HOT HORSE see **ONCE UPON A HORSE** • 1958
HOT HOURS (USA) see **HEURES CHAUDES** • 1959
HOT HOUSE see **HOTHOUSE** • 1951-53
HOT HOUSE, THE • 1970 • West Al • USA
HOT ICE • 1952 • Hume Kenneth • UKN
HOT ICE • 1955 • White Jules • SHT • USA
HOT IN PARADISE see **TOTER HING IM NETZ, EIN** • 1960
HOT KISS • 1969 • Goetz Tommy • USA
HOT LEAD • 1951 • Gilmore Stuart • USA
HOT LEAD see **TASTE OF HOT LEAD, A** • 1969
HOT LEAD AND COLD FEET • 1978 • Butler Robert • USA
HOT LEATHERETTE • 1966-67 • Nelson Robert • SHT • USA
HOT LEGS • 1980 • Chinn Robert C. • USA
HOT LIGHTNING • 1927 • Roberts Stephen • SHT • USA
HOT LINE • 1970 • Goetz Tommy • USA
HOT LINE, THE see **GORACA LINIA** • 1965
HOT LINE, THE see **ROUBLE A DEUX FACES, LE** • 1969
HOT LIPS • 1978 • USA
HOT LIPS FOR HOT HEADS • 1970 • *Mitam Productions* • USA
HOT LITTLE GIRL, THE see **SHIBIRE-KURAGE** • 1972

HOT LUCK • 1928 • Lamont Charles • SHT • USA
HOT LUNCH • Perkins Harold • USA
HOT MARSHLAND, THE see **NETSUDEICHI** • 1950
HOT MILLIONS • 1968 • Till Eric • UKN, USA
HOT MONEY • 1935 • Horne James W. • SHT • USA
HOT MONEY • 1936 • McGann William • USA
HOT MONEY GIRL (USA) see **TREASURE OF SAN TERESA, THE** • 1959
HOT MONTH OF AUGUST, THE (USA) see **ZESTOS MENAS AUGOUSTOS, HO** • 1966
HOT MOVES • 1985 • Sotos Jim • USA
HOT NEON see **LINDA LOVELACE FOR PRESIDENT** • 1975
HOT NEWS • 1928 • Badger Clarence • USA
HOT NEWS • 1936 • Kellino W. P. • UKN
HOT NEWS • 1953 • Bernds Edward • USA
HOT NEWS see **SCANDAL FOR SALE** • 1932
HOT NIGHT, A see **ATSUI YORU** • 1969
HOT NIGHTS IN FRANKFURT see **IN FRANKFURT SIND DIE NACHTE HEISS** • 1966
HOT NIGHTS ON THE CAMPUS • 1966 • Orlando Tony • USA • NIGHTS ON THE CAMPUS
HOT NOCTURNE see **BLUES IN THE NIGHT** • 1941
HOT NOON • 1953 • Smith Paul J. • ANS • USA
HOT NOON see **GORECHTO PLADNE** • 1965
HOT OFF THE PRESS • 1922 • Roach Hal • SHT • USA
HOT OFF THE PRESS • 1935 • Herman Al • USA
HOT ON ICE • 1938 • Veer Willard V., Lieb Tom • SHT • USA
HOT ON SIN ISLAND see **IT'S HOT ON SIN ISLAND** • 1964
HOT ONES, THE (UKN) see **CORVETTE SUMMER** • 1978
HOT OR COLD • 1928 • Roberts Stephen • SHT • USA
HOT PAINT • 1988 • Larry Sheldon • TVM • USA
HOT PANTS HOLIDAY • 1972 • Mann Edward • USA
HOT PAPRIKA • 1935 • Black Preston • SHT • USA
HOT PAVEMENTS OF COLOGNE see **HEISSES PFLASTER KOLN** • 1967
HOT PEARL see **HOT PEARL SNATCH, THE** • 1966
HOT PEARL SNATCH, THE • 1966 • *Dash Pauly* • USA • PERILOUS PEARLS OF PAULINE, THE ○ HOT PEARL
HOT PEARLS (UKN) see **BLONDE FROM SINGAPORE, THE** • 1941
HOT PEPPER • 1933 • Blystone John G. • USA
HOT PICKLES • 1910 • Fitzhamon Lewin • UKN
HOT PIE • 1906 • Collins Alf? • UKN
HOT PLAYMATES see **CARNALITA** • 1974
HOT POTATO • 1976 • Williams Oscar • USA
HOT POTATO see **PATATA BOLLENTE, LA** • 1979
HOT PROBLEM, A see **HORKA KASE** • 1988
HOT PROPERTY • 1983 • Brocka Lino • PHL
HOT PROPERTY see **TAKE ME HIGH** • 1973
HOT PURSUIT • 1981 • West James I.
HOT PURSUIT • 1983 • Forrest Stanley • USA, NTH • YAB-YUM OP STELTEN (NTH) ○ HEAVEN CAN'T WAIT
HOT PURSUIT • 1987 • Lisberger Steven • USA
HOT RACKETS • 1979 • McCallum Robert • USA
HOT-REAL • 1988 • Szabo Ildiko • HNG • DAMN REAL
HOT RESORT • 1985 • Robins John • USA
HOT RHYTHM • 1944 • Beaudine William • USA
HOT ROCK, THE • 1972 • Yates Peter • USA • HOW TO STEAL A DIAMOND IN FOUR UNEASY LESSONS (UKN)
HOT ROD • 1950 • Collins Lewis D. • USA
HOT ROD • 1979 • Armitage George • TVM • USA • REBEL OF THE ROAD
HOT ROD ACTION • 1969 • McCabe Gene • DOC • USA
HOT ROD AND REEL • 1959 • Jones Charles M. • ANS • USA
HOT ROD GANG • 1958 • Landers Lew • USA • FURY UNLEASHED (UKN)
HOT ROD GIRL • 1956 • Martinson Leslie H. • USA
HOT ROD HUCKSTER • 1954 • Smith Paul J. • ANS • USA
HOT ROD HULLABALOO • 1966 • Naud William T. • USA
HOT ROD RUMBLE • 1957 • Martinson Leslie H. • USA
HOT RODS • 1953 • Donnelly Eddie • ANS • USA
HOT RODS TO HELL • 1967 • Brahm John • USA • 52 MILES TO MIDNIGHT ○ 52 MILES TO TERROR
HOT SAND ON SYLT see **HEISSER SAND AUF SYLT** • 1968
HOT SANDS • 1934 • *Terry Paul/ Moser Frank (P)* • ANS • USA
HOT SATURDAY • 1932 • Seiter William A. • USA
HOT SCOTS • 1948 • Bernds Edward • SHT • USA
HOT SEX IN BANGKOK see **HEISSE SEX IN BANGKOK** • 1974
HOT SEX TRAMP see **MASTER BEATER, THE** • 1969
HOT SHOTS • 1956 • Yarbrough Jean • USA
HOT SHOTS • *Jordan Jennifer* • USA
HOT SKIN see **HOT SKIN AND COLD CASH** • 1965
HOT SKIN AND COLD CASH • 1965 • Mahon Barry • USA • HOT SKIN
HOT SNAKE • 1976 • Duran Fernando • MXC
HOT SNOW see **HET SNO** • 1968
HOT SNOW see **GORYACHI SNYEG** • 1973
HOT SOUP • 1927 • Sandrich Mark • SHT • USA
HOT SPELL • 1958 • Mann Daniel, Cukor George (U/c) • USA
HOT SPELL, THE • 1936 • Davis Mannie, Gordon George • ANS • USA
HOT SPLASH • 1987 • Ingrassia James • USA
HOT SPOT • 1932 • Lord Del • SHT • USA
HOT SPOT • 1989 • Figgis Mike • UKN
HOT SPOT • 1990 • Hopper Dennis • USA
HOT SPOT (UKN) see **I WAKE UP SCREAMING** • 1941
HOT SPUR • 1968 • Frost R. L. • USA • NAKED SPUR, THE ○ FIERY SPUR ○ LONGEST SPUR, THE
HOT STEEL • 1940 • Cabanne W. Christy • USA
HOT STREAK see **JINXED** • 1982
HOT STUFF • 1912 • Sennett Mack • USA
HOT STUFF • 1914 • *Joker* • USA
HOT STUFF • 1915 • *Aubrey James* • USA
HOT STUFF • 1924 • Roach Hal • SHT • USA
HOT STUFF • 1929 • LeRoy Mervyn • USA
HOT STUFF • 1956 • White Jules • SHT • USA
HOT STUFF • 1971 • Grgic Zlatko • ANS • CND • FEU? PAS POUR LES HOMMES, LE
HOT STUFF • 1979 • Deluise Dom • USA
HOT STUFF (USA) see **PAURA IN CITTA** • 1976
HOT SUMMER • 1985 • Sachs William • USA • HOT CHILI
HOT SUMMER see **HEISSER SOMMER** • 1968
HOT SUMMER GAME, A • 1965 • Bruner James • USA • IT'S ALL IN THE GAME
HOT SUMMER IN BAREFOOT COUNTY • 1974 • Zens Will • USA
HOT SUMMER NIGHT • 1956 • Friedkin David • USA • CAPITAL OFFENSE
HOT SUMMER NIGHT, A • 1982 • Weisz Frans • NTH
HOT SUMMER WEEK • 1973 • Schmidt Thomas • USA
HOT T-SHIRTS • 1979 • Vincent Chuck • USA
HOT TAMALE • 1920 • *Rube Christian* • USA
HOT TAMALE • 1930 • Foster John • ANS • USA
HOT TARGET • 1985 • Lewiston Denis • NZL
HOT THRILLS see **HOT THRILLS AND WARM CHILLS** • 1967
HOT THRILLS AND WARM CHILLS • 1967 • Berry Dale • USA • HOT THRILLS
HOT TIME IN A COLD QUARTER, A • 1909 • *Walturdaw* • UKN
HOT TIME IN ATLANTIC CITY, A • 1909 • *Lubin* • USA
HOT TIME IN SNAKEVILLE, A • 1914 • *Potel Victor* • USA
HOT TIME IN THE OLD TOWN TONIGHT, A • 1930 • Fleischer Dave • ANS • USA
HOT TIME ON ICE • 1967 • Smith Paul J. • ANS • USA
HOT TIMES • 1929 • Roberts Stephen • SHT • USA
HOT TIMES • 1974 • McBride Jim • USA • ADVENTURES OF ARCHIE, THE
HOT TIP • 1935 • McCarey Ray, Sistrom William • USA • LEANDER CLICKS
HOT TO TROT • 1988 • Dinner Michael • USA
HOT TOMORROWS • 1977 • Brest Martin • USA
HOT TOUCH, THE • 1981 • Vadim Roger • CND • FRENCH KISS
HOT TURKEY • 1930 • *Terry Paul/ Moser Frank (P)* • ANS • USA
HOT VACATION see **OATSUI KYUKA** • 1968
HOT WATER • 1924 • Taylor Sam, Newmeyer Fred • USA
HOT WATER • 1937 • Strayer Frank • USA • JONES FAMILY IN HOT WATER, THE ○ TOO MUCH LIMELIGHT
HOT WATER see **JUNIOR** • 1985
HOT WATER AND VEGETABUEL • 1928 • *De Forest Phonofilm* • SHT • UKN
HOT WATER, COLD WATER see **EAU CHAUDE, L'EAU FRETTE, L'** • 1976
HOT WHEELS see **KUUMAT KUNDIT** • 1976
HOT WIND see **NEPPU** • 1934
HOT WIND see **NEPPU** • 1943
HOT WIND see **GARM HAVA** • 1973
HOT WIND see **KHAMSIN** • 1982
HOT WINDS see **GARM HAVA** • 1973
HOT WINTER see **HORKA ZIMA** • 1972
HOT WIRE • 1980 • Dobbs Frank Q. • USA • HOTWIRE
HOT WIRES • 1931 • Sweet Harry • USA
HOT YEARS, THE see **TOPLE GODINE** • 1966
HOTARU NO HAKA • 1988 • Takahata Isao • ANM • JPN • GRAVEYARD OF THE FIREFLY, THE
HOTARUBI • 1958 • Gosho Heinosuke • JPN • FIREFLY LIGHT ○ FIREFLIES ○ FIREFLY'S LIGHT
HOTBED OF SIN (USA) see **BOITE DE NUIT** • 1951
HOTCH-POTCH • 1989 • Zaluski Roman • PLN
HOTCHA MELODY • 1935 • *Mintz Charles (P)* • ANS • USA
HOTEL • 1967 • Quine Richard • USA
HOTEL • 1983 • London Jerry • TVM • USA
HOTEL, THE see **CIGARRA NO ES UN BICHO, LA** • 1963
HOTEL ADION • 1955 • von Baky Josef • FRG
HOTEL ADVENTURE see **AVENTYR PA HOTELL** • 1934
HOTEL ALLOTRIA • 1956 • Bender Ludwig • FRG • SAISON IN OBERBAYERN
HOTEL ANCHOVY • 1934 • Christie Al • USA
HOTEL APEX • 1952 • Kees Weldon • SHT • USA
HOTEL AT OSAKA see **OSAKA NO YADO** • 1954
HOTEL BERLIN • 1945 • Godfrey Peter • USA
HOTEL BLUE STAR, THE see **HOTEL MODRA HVEZDA** • 1941
HOTEL BON PLAISIR • Barny Michel • FRN
HOTEL BOULEVARD see **GRAND HOTEL..!** • 1927
HOTEL-CHATEAU • 1970 • Carriere Marcel • DOC • CND
HOTEL COLONIAL • 1987 • Torrini Cinzia Th. • ITL, USA
HOTEL CONTINENTAL • 1932 • Cabanne W. Christy • USA
HOTEL DE FRANCE • 1986 • Chereau Patrice • FRN
HOTEL DE HOBO • 1915 • *Ck* • USA
HOTEL DE LA GARE, L' • 1914 • Feuillade Louis • FRN
HOTEL DE LA MUERTE see **SANTO EN EL HOTEL DE LA MUERTE** • 1961
HOTEL DE LA PAIX • 1983 • Schlondorff Volker • FRN
HOTEL DE LA PLAGE, L' • 1978 • Lang Michel • FRN • HOLIDAY HOTEL (USA)
HOTEL DE LOS CHIFLADOS, EL • 1938 • Helu Antonio • MXC
HOTEL DE VERANO • 1943 • Cardona Rene • MXC
HOTEL DER TOTEN GASTE • 1965 • Itzenpilz Eberhard • FRG, SPN
HOTEL DES AMERIQUES • 1981 • Techine Andre • FRN
HOTEL DES ETUDIANTS • 1932 • Tourjansky Victor • FRN
HOTEL DES INVALIDES • 1952 • Franju Georges • DCS • FRN
HOTEL DES VOYAGEURS DE COMMERCE, L' • 1906 • Melies Georges • FRN • ROADSIDE INN, A
HOTEL DICK • 1989 • Gordon Stuart • USA
HOTEL DISGRACE, A • 1917 • *Bacon Lloyd* • USA
HOTEL DU BONHEUR see **FUNDUQ AS-SAADA** • 1971
HOTEL DU LAC • 1985 • Foster Giles • TVM • UKN
HOTEL DU LIBRE ECHANGE, L' • 1934 • Allegret Marc • FRN
HOTEL DU NORD • 1938 • Carne Marcel • FRN
HOTEL DU PARADIS • 1987 • Bokova Jana • UKN
HOTEL DU PLAISIR • Kessler Christian • FRN
HOTEL DU SILENCE, L' • 1908 • Cohl Emile • ANS • FRN
HOTEL ELECTRICO, EL • 1906 • de Chomon Segundo • SPN • ELECTRIC HOTEL, THE (USA)
HOTEL EMPOISONNE L' • 1897 • Melies Georges • FRN • BADLY MANAGED HOTEL, A
HOTEL FOR MEN • 1969 • Heinz John • SHT • USA
HOTEL FOR STRANGERS see **HOTEL PRO CIZINCE** • 1966
HOTEL FOR WOMEN • 1939 • Ratoff Gregory • USA • ELSA MAXWELL'S HOTEL FOR WOMEN
HOTEL HAYWIRE • 1937 • Archainbaud George • USA
HOTEL HONEYMOON • 1912 • Blache Alice • USA
HOTEL IMPERIAL • 1927 • Stiller Mauritz • USA
HOTEL IMPERIAL • 1939 • Florey Robert • USA
HOTEL LONDON • 1989 • Jamal Ahmad A. • UKN
HOTEL MAGNEZIT • 1980 • Tarr Bela • SHT • HNG
HOTEL MEDUSA • 1919 • von Woringen Paul • FRG
HOTEL MEUBLE • 1981 • Lobet Marc • BLG, FRN
HOTEL MIX-UP, A • 1917 • *West Billy* • USA
HOTEL MIX-UP, THE • 1908 • *Melies* • USA
HOTEL MIXUP see **MABEL'S STRANGE PREDICAMENT** • 1914
HOTEL MODRA HVEZDA • 1941 • Fric Martin • CZC • HOTEL BLUE STAR, THE
HOTEL MONTEREY • 1972 • Akerman Chantal • USA
HOTEL MOUSE, THE • 1923 • Paul Fred • UKN
HOTEL MYSTERY, THE • 1902 • *Paul R. W.* • UKN
HOTEL NEW HAMPSHIRE, THE • 1983 • Richardson Tony • USA
HOTEL NUPTIAL • 1979 • USA
HOTEL OF FREE LOVE (UKN) see **PENSION DU LIBRE AMOUR, LA** • 1973
HOTEL OF THE STARS • 1981 • Carlsen Jon Bang • DNM
HOTEL PACIFIC see **DVOJI SVET V HOTELU PACIFIK** • 1975
HOTEL PARADAISO • 1966 • Glenville Peter • UKN, USA, FRN • PARADISO, HOTEL DU LIBRE-EXCHANGE (FRN)
HOTEL PARADIS • 1916 • Dinesen Robert • DNM • HOTEL PARADISO
HOTEL PARADISO see **HOTEL PARADIS** • 1916
HOTEL POLAN AND ITS GUESTS • Seemann Horst • GDR
HOTEL POTEMKIN • 1924 • Neufeld Max • AUS
HOTEL PRO CIZINCE • 1966 • Masa Antonin • CZC • HOTEL FOR STRANGERS
HOTEL RESERVE • 1944 • Comfort Lance, Greene Max • UKN
HOTEL ROOM see **CAMERA D'ALBERGO** • 1980
HOTEL SACHA • 1939 • Engel Erich • FRG
HOTEL SAHARA • 1951 • Annakin Ken • UKN
HOTEL ST. PAULI • 1988 • Vennerod Petter, Wam Svend • NRW
HOTEL SPLENDIDE • 1932 • Powell Michael • UKN
HOTEL SUNRISE • 1937 • Gaal Bela • HNG
HOTEL TERMINUS -THE LIFE AND TIMES OF KLAUS BARBIE • 1988 • Ophuls Marcel • DOC • USA
HOTEL VARIETY • 1932 • Cannon Raymond • USA • PASSING SHOW, THE (UKN)
HOTEL VILLA GOERNE • 1981 • Cortes Busi • MXC
HOTEL ZUM GOLDENEN ENGEL • 1922 • Bolten-Baeckers Heinrich • FRG
HOTELGEHEIMNISSE • 1928 • Feher Friedrich • FRG
HOTELL KAKBRINKEN • 1946 • Bauman Schamyl • SWD
HOTELL PARADISETS HEMLIGHET • 1931 • Schneevoigt George • SWD • SECRET OF THE PARADISE HOTEL
HOTELMAN'S HOLIDAY see **EKIMAE RYUKAN** • 1958
HOTELPORTIER, DER • 1941 • Haller Hermann • SWT
HOTELRATTE, DIE see **LIEBE UND DIEBE** • 1928
HOTELRATTEN • 1927 • Speyer Jaap • FRG
HOTES DE NOS TERRES, LES • Gaudard Lucette • FRN • GUESTS ON OUR LAND
HOTHEAD • 1963 • Mann Edward • USA
HOTHEAD • 1971 • Vuco Vuk • YGS
HOTHEAD see **COUP DE TETE** • 1978
HOTHOUSE • 1951-53 • Whitney John • ANS • USA • HOT HOUSE
HOTHOUSE VENUS, A see **SKLENIKOVA VENUSA** • 1985
HOTLINE • 1982 • Jameson Jerry • TVM • USA • REACHOUT
HOTLIPS JASPER • 1944 • Pal George • ANS • USA
HOTOTOGISU • 1932 • Gosho Heinosuke • JPN • CUCKOO
HOTOVO, JEDEM • 1947 • Hofman Eduard • ANS • CZC • WE'RE OFF! ○ ALL ABOARD
HOTPOT • 1929 • Aylott Dave, Symmons E. F. • SHT • USA
HOTS see **H.O.T.S.** • 1979
HOTS 3 see **REVENGE OF THE CHEERLEADERS** • 1976
HOTSHOT • 1987 • King Rick • USA • HANG TOUGH ○ STRIKING CHANCE
HOTSPRINGS HOLIDAY (USA) see **ONSEN GERIRA DAI SHOGEKI** • 1968
HOTSPRING'S HOTSHOP see **DAISHOGEKI** • 1968
HOTSY FOOTSY • 1952 • Hurtz William • ANS • USA
HOTSY-TOTSY • 1925 • Cline Eddie • SHT • USA
HOTTA HAYATO • 1933 • Ito Daisuke • JPN
HOTTENTOT, THE • 1922 • Horne James W., Andrews Del • USA
HOTTENTOT, THE • 1929 • Del Ruth Roy • USA
HOTTENTOT AND THE GRAMOPHONE, THE • 1908 • Fitzhamon Lewin? • UKN
HOTTER AFTER DARK • 1967 • *Maggrore Tony* • USA
HOTTER THAN HAITI • 1931 • Edwards Harry J. • SHT • USA
HOTTER THAN HOT • 1929 • Foster Lewis R. • SHT • USA
HOTTER THAN SNOW • 1985 • SAF
HOTTEST SHOW IN TOWN, THE • 1974 • Kronhausen Phyllis, Kronhausen Eberhard • SWD, SWT
HOTWIRE see **HOT WIRE** • 1980
HOU DIE BLINKKANT BO • 1960 • SAF
HOU HALACH BASADOT • 1967 • Millo Joseph • ISR • HE WALKS THROUGH THE FIELDS
HOU HSING K'OU SHOU • 1979 • Chang Sen • HKG • SNAKE IN THE MONKEY'S SHADOW
HOUAT • 1963 • Magrou Alain • SHT • FRN
HOUBU DUIYUAN • 1983 • Wu Ziniu • CHN • CANDIDATE
HOUDAILLE: DAYS OF COURAGE, DAYS OF RAGE • 1981 • Sky Laura • DOC • CND
HOUDINI • 1953 • Marshall George • USA
HOUDINI see **MASTER MYSTERY, THE** • 1919
HOUEN ZO • 1953 • van der Horst Herman • DOC • NTH • STEADY NOW ○ STEADY!
HOULA-HOULA • 1959 • Darene Robert • FRN, ITL
HOUND ABOUT THAT • 1961 • Kneitel Seymour • ANS • USA
HOUND AND THE RABBIT, THE • 1937 • Ising Rudolf • ANS • USA
HOUND-DOG MAN • 1959 • Siegel Don • USA
HOUND FOR POUND • 1963 • Kneitel Seymour • ANS • USA
HOUND FOR TROUBLE, A • 1951 • Jones Charles M. • ANS • USA
HOUND HUNTERS • 1947 • Avery Tex • ANS • USA
HOUND OF BLACKWOOD CASTLE, THE see **HUND VON BLACKWOOD CASTLE, DER** • 1968
HOUND OF SILVER CREEK, THE • 1928 • Paton Stuart • USA
HOUND OF THE BASKERVILLES, THE • 1921 • Elvey Maurice • UKN

HOUND OF THE BASKERVILLES, THE • 1931 • Gundrey V. Gareth • UKN
HOUND OF THE BASKERVILLES, THE • 1939 • Lanfield Sidney • USA
HOUND OF THE BASKERVILLES, THE • 1959 • Fisher Terence • UKN
HOUND OF THE BASKERVILLES, THE • 1972 • Crane Barry • TVM • USA • SHERLOCK HOLMES: HOUND OF THE BASKERVILLES
HOUND OF THE BASKERVILLES, THE • 1978 • Morrissey Paul • UKN
HOUND OF THE BASKERVILLES, THE • 1983 • Hickox Douglas • UKN
HOUND OF THE BASKERVILLES, THE see **HUND VON BASKERVILLE, DER** • 1929
HOUND OF THE BASKERVILLES, THE (USA) see **CHIEN DE BASKERVILLE, LE** • 1914
HOUND OF THE BASKERVILLES, THE (USA) see **HUND VON BASKERVILLE, DER** • 1914
HOUND OF THE BASKERVILLES, THE (USA) see **HUND VON BASKERVILLE 3, DER** • 1915
HOUND OF THE BASKERVILLES, THE (USA) see **HUND VON BASKERVILLE, DER** • 1936
HOUND OF THE DEEP • 1926 • Hurley Frank • ASL • PEARLS OF THE SOUTH SEAS
HOUND THAT THOUGHT HE WAS A RACCOON, THE • 1960 • McGowan Tom • USA
HOUNDABOUT • 1959 • Kneitel Seymour • ANS • USA
HOUNDED • 1914 • *Wilson Ben* • USA
HOUNDED (UKN) see **JOHNNY ALLEGRO** • 1949
HOUNDING THE HARES • 1948 • Donnelly Eddie • ANS • USA
HOUNDS OF NOTRE DAME, THE • 1980 • Dalen Zale R. • CND
HOUNDS OF SPRING, THE • 1979 • Josephson Erland • SWD
HOUNDS OF WAR see **BROTHERS** • 1983
HOUNDS OF ZAROFF, THE (UKN) see **MOST DANGEROUS GAME, THE** • 1932
HOUP-LA! • 1928 • Miller Frank • UKN • LION TAMER, THE
HOUR AFTER HOUR see **GODZINA ZA GODZINA** • 1974
HOUR AND THE MAN, THE • 1914 • *Bushman Francis X.* • USA
HOUR BEFORE DAWN, AN • 1913 • Dawley J. Searle • SHT • USA
HOUR BEFORE THE DAWN, THE • 1944 • Tuttle Frank • USA
HOUR BEFORE THE RENDEZVOUS, THE • 1965 • Brumberg Valentina, Brumberg Zinaida • ANS • USS • HOUR UNTIL THE MEETING, AN
HOUR FOR LUNCH, AN • 1939 • Rowland Roy • SHT • USA
HOUR GLASS, THE • 1972 • Popescu-Gopo Ion • ANM • RMN
HOUR GLASS, THE see **DIAMONDS AND PEARLS** • 1918
HOUR OF 13, THE • 1952 • French Harold • USA, UKN
HOUR OF CONFINEMENT see **TOQUE DE QUEDA** • 1978
HOUR OF DANGER, THE • 1914 • *Kalem* • USA
HOUR OF DEATH, THE see **OLUM SAATI** • 1967
HOUR OF DECISION • 1957 • Pennington-Richards C. M. • UKN
HOUR OF FATE, THE • 1911 • *Reliance* • USA
HOUR OF FEAR, THE (UKN) see **TWO O'CLOCK IN THE MORNING** • 1929
HOUR OF FREEDOM, AN • 1915 • Johnson Arthur • USA
HOUR OF GLORY (USA) see **SMALL BACK ROOM, THE** • 1948
HOUR OF JUSTICE, THE see **ORA TIS DHIKEOSINIS, I** • 1967
HOUR OF PERIL, AN • 1912 • *Rex* • USA
HOUR OF RECKONING, THE • 1914 • *Broncho* • USA
HOUR OF RECKONING, THE • 1927 • Ince John • USA
HOUR OF TERROR, AN • 1909 • *World* • USA
HOUR OF TERROR, AN • 1912 • *American* • USA
HOUR OF TERROR, AN • 1913 • Smalley Phillips • USA
HOUR OF TERROR, AN • 1914 • *Ab* • USA
HOUR OF TERROR, AN • 1917 • Moore Matt • SHT • USA
HOUR OF THE ASSASSIN • 1987 • Llosa Luis • USA, PRU
HOUR OF THE BLUE ELEPHANTS, THE see **HODINA MODRYCH SLONU**
HOUR OF THE FULL MOON, THE see **CHAS POLNOLUNIYA** • 1989
HOUR OF THE FURNACES, THE (USA) see **HORA DE LOS HORNOS, LA** • 1968
HOUR OF THE GUN • 1967 • Sturges John • USA • LAW AND TOMBSTONE, THE
HOUR OF THE LIBERATION HAS SOUNDED, THE see **SAAT EL TAHRIR DAKKAT BARRA YA ISTI'MAR** • 1974
HOUR OF THE ROSE, THE see **GODZINA PASOWEJ ROZY** • 1963
HOUR OF THE STAR, THE see **HORA DA ESTRELA, A** • 1986
HOUR OF THE SUN, THE see **HORA DEL SOL, LA** • 1975
HOUR OF THE TRIAL see **I PROVNINGENS STUND** • 1915
HOUR OF THE WOLF (UKN) see **VARGTIMMEN** • 1968
HOUR OF TRIAL see **I PROVNINGENS STUND** • 1915
HOUR OF TRIAL, THE • 1920 • Coleby A. E. • UKN
HOUR OF TRUTH, THE see **HORA DE LA VERDAD, LA** • 1944
HOUR OF TRUTH (USA) see **HEURE DE LA VERITE, L'** • 1964
HOUR OF WRATH see **ORA TIS ORGIS, I** • 1968
HOUR OF YOUTH, THE • 1914 • *Thanhouser* • USA
HOUR STRIKES TEN, THE • 1974 • Barakat • EGY
HOUR UNTIL THE MEETING, AN see **HOUR BEFORE THE RENDEZVOUS, THE** • 1965
HOUR WITH CHEKHOV, AN see **CHINY I LIUDI** • 1929
HOUR WITHOUT SUN, THE see **GODZINA BEZ SLONCA** • 1954
HOURGLASS SANATORIUM, THE (USA) see **SANATORIUM POD KLEPSYDRA** • 1973
HOURS BETWEEN, THE (UKN) see **TWENTY-FOUR HOURS** • 1931
HOURS OF HOPE see **GODZINY NADZIEI** • 1956
HOURS OF LONELINESS see **OBVIOUS SITUATION, AN** • 1930
HOURS OF LOVE, THE see **ORE DELL'AMORE, LE** • 1963
HOUSATA • 1979 • Smyczek Karel • CZC • GOSLINGS
HOUSE • 1955 • Eames Charles, Eames Ray • USA
HOUSE • 1986 • Miner Steve • USA
HOUSE see **DOM** • 1958
HOUSE see **HAUSU** • 1977
HOUSE see **BAAN** • 1986
HOUSE 2: THE SECOND STORY • 1987 • Wiley Ethan • USA
HOUSE 3: THE HORROR SHOW • 1989 • Isaac James • USA • HORROR SHOW
HOUSE, THE • 1962 • Manupelli George • SHT • USA
HOUSE, THE see **HUIS, DE** • 1962
HOUSE, THE see **HAZ, A** • 1963
HOUSE, THE see **CASA, LA** • 1974
HOUSE, THE see **KUCA** • 1976
HOUSE, THE see **HUSID** • 1983
HOUSE ACROSS THE BAY, THE • 1940 • Mayo Archie • USA
HOUSE ACROSS THE LAKE, THE • 1954 • Hughes Ken • UKN • HEATWAVE (USA)
HOUSE ACROSS THE STREET, THE • 1914 • *Leonard Robert* • USA
HOUSE ACROSS THE STREET, THE • 1949 • Bare Richard L. • USA
HOUSE ACROSS THE STREET, THE (USA) see **MAISON D'EN FACE, LA** • 1936
HOUSE AND MASTER see **DOM I KHOZYAIN** • 1967
HOUSE AND THE BRAIN, THE • 1973 • *Charles Keith* • USA
HOUSE AT THE BRIDGE, THE • 1908 • *Lubin* • USA
HOUSE AT THE CROSSROADS, THE • 1959 • Bahna Vladimir • CZC
HOUSE AT THE EDGE OF THE PARK, THE see **CASA AI CONFINI DEL PARCO, LA** • 1980
HOUSE AT THE END OF THE CEMETERY, THE see **QUELLA VILLA ACCANTO AL CIMITERO** • 1982
HOUSE AT THE END OF THE WORLD see **MONSTER OF TERROR** • 1965
HOUSE AT THE TERMINUS, THE see **TAM NA KONECNE** • 1957
HOUSE BEHIND THE CEDARS, THE • 1927 • Micheaux Oscar • USA
HOUSE BEHIND THE HEDGE, THE (UKN) see **UNKNOWN TREASURES** • 1926
HOUSE BOAT, THE • 1916 • *Conklin Chester* • SHT • USA
HOUSE BOAT ELOPEMENT, A • 1913 • *Powers* • USA
HOUSE BROKEN • 1936 • Hankinson Michael • UKN
HOUSE BROKEN • 1987 • Lawrence Denny • ASL
HOUSE BUILDER UPPER, THE • 1938 • Fleischer Dave • ANS • USA
HOUSE BUILT UPON SAND, THE • 1917 • Morrisey Edward • USA
HOUSE BUSTERS • 1952 • Rasinski Connie • ANS • USA
HOUSE BY THE CEMETERY, THE see **QUELLA VILLA ACCANTO AL CIMITERO** • 1982
HOUSE BY THE LAKE, THE (USA) see **DEATH WEEKEND** • 1976
HOUSE BY THE RIVER • 1950 • Lang Fritz • USA
HOUSE CALLS • 1978 • Zieff Howard • USA
HOUSE CAT, THE • 1948 • Felstead Bert • UKN
HOUSE CAT, THE see **MAN'S WOMAN** • 1917
HOUSE CLEANING • 1912 • *Lubin* • USA
HOUSE CLEANING • 1933 • *Mintz Charles (P)* • ANS • USA
HOUSE CLEANING BLUES • 1937 • Fleischer Dave • ANS • USA
HOUSE-CLEANING HORRORS • 1918 • Lyons Eddie, Moran Lee • SHT • USA
HOUSE CLEANING TIME • 1929 • Foster John • ANS • USA
HOUSE DEMOLISHED AND REBUILT, A • 1901 • Blache Alice • FRN
HOUSE DISCORDANT, THE • 1914 • *Leonard Robert* • USA
HOUSE DIVIDED, A • 1913 • *Bison* • USA
HOUSE DIVIDED, A • 1913 • *Solax* • USA
HOUSE DIVIDED, A • 1919 • Blackton J. Stuart • USA
HOUSE DIVIDED, A • 1932 • Wyler William • USA • HEART AND HAND
HOUSE DIVIDED, THE • 1913 • *Patheplay* • USA
HOUSE FOR TWO, A see **DUM PRO DVA** • 1988
HOUSE FOR WOMEN, A see **CASA DE MUJERES** • 1977
HOUSE FULL see **DR. JOSSER K.C.** • 1931
HOUSE FULL OF HAPPINESS, A see **KET EMELET BOLDOGSAG** • 1960
HOUSE HUNTING • 1913 • *Majestic* • USA
HOUSE HUNTING see **MAKE ME AN OFFER** • 1980
HOUSE HUNTING MICE • 1948 • Jones Charles M. • ANS • USA
HOUSE I LIVE IN, THE • 1945 • *Leroy Mervyn (P)* • DCS • USA
HOUSE I LIVE IN, THE see **DOM, V KOTOROM YA ZHIVU** • 1957
HOUSE IN A MESS, A see **LUDA KUCA** • 1981
HOUSE IN BAYSWATER, A • 1960 • Russell Ken • MTV • UKN
HOUSE IN MARSH ROAD, THE • 1960 • Tully Montgomery • UKN • INVISIBLE CREATURE (USA) ○ HOUSE ON MARSH ROAD, THE
HOUSE IN NAPLES • 1969 • Savage Peter • USA
HOUSE IN NIGHTMARE PARK, THE • 1973 • Sykes Peter • UKN • NIGHT OF THE LAUGHING DEAD ○ CRAZY HOUSE ○ NIGHTMARE PARK
HOUSE IN ORDER • 1936 • Sparling Gordon • CND • MAISON EN ORDRE, LA
HOUSE IN RUE RAPP, THE • 1946 • Haines Ronald • UKN
HOUSE IN SUBURBIA, THE • 1913 • Trimble Larry • USA
HOUSE IN THE COUNTRY see **HIDEAWAY** • 1937
HOUSE IN THE DESERT, THE • 1947 • Oyserman Ben • ISR
HOUSE IN THE FIELDS, THE see **CASA DINTRE CIMPURI** • 1980
HOUSE IN THE JUNGLE, A • 1969 • Power John • DOC • ASL
HOUSE IN THE SNOW DRIFTS, THE see **DOM V SUGROBAKH** • 1928
HOUSE IN THE SOUTH, THE see **CASA DEL SUR, LA** • 1974
HOUSE IN THE SQUARE, THE • 1951 • Baker Roy Ward • UKN, USA • I'LL NEVER FORGET YOU (USA) ○ MAN OF TWO WORLDS ○ JOURNEY TO THE PAST
HOUSE IN THE SUBURBS, A see **DUM NA PREDMESTI** • 1933
HOUSE IN THE TREE, THE • 1913 • *Majestic* • USA
HOUSE IN THE WILDERNESS see **DOM NA PUSTKOWIU** • 1949
HOUSE IN THE WOODS, THE • 1913 • *Hawley Ormi* • USA
HOUSE IN THE WOODS, THE • 1957 • Munden Maxwell • UKN
HOUSE IN THE WOODS, THE see **MAISON DES BOIS, LA** • 1971
HOUSE IS BLACK, THE see **KHANEH SIAH AST** • 1962
HOUSE IS NOT A HOME, A • 1964 • Rouse Russell • USA
HOUSE NEAR THE PRADO, THE • 1969 • Hearn J. Van • USA
HOUSE NEXT DOOR, THE • 1914 • O'Neil Barry • USA
HOUSE NO.8 • 1986 • Volev Nikolai • DOC • BUL
HOUSE NO.44 • 1955 • *Burman S. D. (M)* • IND
HOUSE NUMBER 17 see **HUSET NR.17** • 1949
HOUSE OF 72 TENANTS • 1974 • Ch'U Yuan • HKG
HOUSE OF 1000 DOLLS see **HAUS DER TAUSEND FREUDEN, DAS** • 1967
HOUSE OF 1000 PLEASURES • 1977 • Margheriti Antonio • ITL
HOUSE OF 1000 WOMEN, THE see **2000 WOMEN** • 1944
HOUSE OF A THOUSAND CANDLES • 1936 • Lubin Arthur • USA
HOUSE OF A THOUSAND CANDLES, THE • 1915 • Heffron Thomas N. • USA
HOUSE OF A THOUSAND CANDLES, THE see **HAUNTING SHADOWS** • 1920
HOUSE OF A THOUSAND DOLLS(USA) see **HAUS DER TAUSEND FREUDEN, DAS** • 1967
HOUSE OF A THOUSAND DREAMS • 1969 • *Hunt Paul* • USA
HOUSE OF A THOUSAND PLEASURES, THE see **HAUS DER TAUSEND FREUDEN, DAS** • 1967
HOUSE OF A THOUSAND RELATIONS, THE • 1915 • Myers Harry • USA
HOUSE OF A THOUSAND SCANDALS, THE • 1915 • Ricketts Thomas • USA
HOUSE OF A THOUSAND TREMBLES, THE • 1922 • *Star Comedy* • SHT • USA
HOUSE OF BAMBOO • 1955 • Fuller Samuel • USA
HOUSE OF BENTLEY, THE • 1915 • Ingraham Lloyd • USA
HOUSE OF BERNARDA ALBA • Lorca • ISR
HOUSE OF BERNARDA ALBA, THE see **CASA DE BERNARDA ALBA, LA** • 1987
HOUSE OF BLACKMAIL • 1953 • Elvey Maurice • UKN
HOUSE OF BONDAGE, THE • 1913 • West Raymond B. • USA
HOUSE OF BONDAGE, THE • 1914 • Kingsley Pierce • USA
HOUSE OF CARDS • 1917 • Blache Alice • USA
HOUSE OF CARDS • 1947 • Vogel Joseph, Whitney John, Whitney James • SHT • USA
HOUSE OF CARDS • 1969 • Guillermin John • USA
HOUSE OF CARDS see **DESIGNING WOMEN** • 1934
HOUSE OF CARDS see **AKASH KUSUM** • 1965
HOUSE OF CARDS see **KARTYAVAR** • 1968
HOUSE OF CARDS, A • 1915 • Kent Leon D. • USA
HOUSE OF CARDS, THE • 1909 • Porter Edwin S. • USA
HOUSE OF CATS, THE • 1966 • *Harris Jerry* • USA
HOUSE OF CHANCE (UKN) see **CHEATING BLONDES** • 1933
HOUSE OF CONNELLY, THE (UKN) see **CAROLINA** • 1934
HOUSE OF CRAZIES (USA) see **ASYLUM** • 1972
HOUSE OF DANGER • 1934 • Hutchison Charles • USA
HOUSE OF DARK SHADOWS see **DARK SHADOWS** • 1970
HOUSE OF DARKENED WINDOWS, THE • 1925 • *Brownlee Lark* • USA
HOUSE OF DARKNESS • 1948 • Mitchell Oswald • UKN
HOUSE OF DARKNESS, THE • 1913 • Griffith D. W. • USA
HOUSE OF DARKNESS, THE • 1914 • *Lubin* • USA
HOUSE OF DEATH • 1916 • Protazanov Yakov • USS
HOUSE OF DEATH see **PEE-MAK**
HOUSE OF DECEIT, THE (UKN) see **MARRY THE GIRL** • 1928
HOUSE OF DISCORD, THE • 1913 • Kirkwood James • USA
HOUSE OF DISTEMPERLY, THE • 1914 • Evans Fred, Evans Joe • UKN
HOUSE OF DR. BELHOMME, THE • 1946 • Smith Maurice Digby • UKN
HOUSE OF DR. EDWARDES, THE see **SPELLBOUND** • 1945
HOUSE OF DOOM see **OJOS AZULES DE LA MUNECA ROTA, LOS** • 1973
HOUSE OF DOOM (UKN) see **BLACK CAT, THE** • 1934
HOUSE OF D'OR, THE • 1914 • Powell Paul • USA
HOUSE OF DRACULA • 1945 • Kenton Erle C. • USA
HOUSE OF DRAGON GIRLS, THE see **HOUSE OF THE RED DRAGON** • 1969
HOUSE OF DREAMS • 1933 • Frenguelli Tony • UKN
HOUSE OF DREAMS • 1963 • Berry Robert • USA
HOUSE OF ERRORS • 1942 • Ray Bernard B. • USA
HOUSE OF EVIL • 1974 • Glenn Bill • TVM • USA
HOUSE OF EVIL see **EVIL, THE** • 1978
HOUSE OF EVIL see **HOUSE ON SORORITY ROW** • 1983
HOUSE OF EVIL, THE • 1968 • Hill Jack, Ibanez Juan • MXC • MACABRE SERENADE ○ DANCE OF DEATH
HOUSE OF EXORCISM, THE see **CASA DELL'EXORCISMO, LA** • 1975
HOUSE OF FATE (UKN) see **MUSS 'EM UP** • 1936
HOUSE OF FEAR • 1939 • May Joe • USA
HOUSE OF FEAR, THE • 1914 • Ince John • USA
HOUSE OF FEAR, THE • 1915 • Daly Arnold, Miller Ashley • *Gold Rooster* • USA
HOUSE OF FEAR, THE • 1915 • Paton Stuart • *Imp* • USA
HOUSE OF FEAR, THE • 1945 • Neill R. William • USA
HOUSE OF FEAR, THE see **MANOIR DE LA PEUR, LE** • 1927
HOUSE OF FLAME • 1979 • Kawamoto Kihachiro • ANS • JPN
HOUSE OF FLICKERS • 1925 • Del Ruth Roy (c/d) • SHT • USA
HOUSE OF FOLLY see **DARSKAPENS HUS** • 1951
HOUSE OF FORTESCUE, THE • 1916 • Wilson Frank • UKN
HOUSE OF FRANKENSTEIN • 1945 • Kenton Erle C. • USA • DEVIL'S BROOD, THE ○ DOOM OF DRACULA ○ DESTINY ○ CHAMBER OF HORRORS
HOUSE OF FREAKS see **CASTELLO DELLE DONNE MALEDETTE, IL** • 1973
HOUSE OF FRIGHT see **MASCHERA DEL DEMONIO, LA** • 1960
HOUSE OF FRIGHT (USA) see **TWO FACES OF DR. JEKYLL, THE** • 1960
HOUSE OF GAMES • 1987 • Mamet David • USA
HOUSE OF GHOSTS see **BEIT AL ASHBAH** • 1952
HOUSE OF GLASS, THE • 1918 • Chautard Emile • USA
HOUSE OF GOD, THE • 1979 • Wrye Donald • USA • H.O.G.
HOUSE OF GOLD, THE • 1918 • Carewe Edwin • USA
HOUSE OF GOLDEN WINDOWS, THE see **HOUSE OF THE GOLDEN WINDOWS, THE** • 1916
HOUSE OF HANGING • 1980 • Ichikawa Kon • JPN
HOUSE OF HASHIMOTO • 1960 • Rasinski Connie • ANS • USA
HOUSE OF HATE, THE • 1918 • Seitz George B. • SRL • USA
HOUSE OF HIS MASTER, THE • 1912 • Parker Lem B. • USA
HOUSE OF HOOKERS, THE • 1970 • *Able Film Co.* • USA
HOUSE OF HORROR, THE • 1915 • Physioc Wray • USA
HOUSE OF HORROR, THE • 1929 • Christensen Benjamin • USA
HOUSE OF HORRORS • 1946 • Yarbrough Jean • USA • JOAN MEDFORD IS MISSING (UKN)

HOUSE OF INSANE WOMEN see **EXORCISM'S DAUGHTER** • 1974
HOUSE OF INTRIGUE, THE • 1919 • Ingraham Lloyd • USA
HOUSE OF INTRIGUE, THE (USA) see **LONDRA CHIAMA POLO NORD** • 1957
HOUSE OF JOZEF MATUS, THE see **DOM JOZEF MATUSA** • 1978
HOUSE OF LIES, THE • 1916 • Taylor William D. • USA
HOUSE OF LIGHT, THE see **CHAMBRE BLANCHE, LA** • 1969
HOUSE OF LOST SOULS, THE see **DUM ZTRACENYCH DUSI** • 1967
HOUSE OF LOVERS (UKN) see **POT-BOUILLE** • 1957
HOUSE OF MADAME LULU, THE see **CASA DE MADAME LULU, LA** • 1968
HOUSE OF MADNESS see **MANSION DE LA LOCURA, LA** • 1971
HOUSE OF MAGIC • 1937 • *Lantz Walter (P)* • ANS • USA
HOUSE OF MARNEY, THE • 1926 • Hepworth Cecil M. • UKN
HOUSE OF MENACE see **KIND LADY** • 1935
HOUSE OF MIRRORS, THE • 1916 • Farnum Marshall • USA
HOUSE OF MIRTH, THE • 1918 • Capellani Albert • USA
HOUSE OF MORTAL SIN • 1975 • Walker Pete • UKN • CONFESSIONAL, THE ○ CONFESSIONAL MURDERS, THE ○ CONFESSION AT DEATH'S DOOR, THE
HOUSE OF MYSTERY • 1916 • *Gilmore Paul* • SHT • USA
HOUSE OF MYSTERY • 1931 • Neumann Kurt • SHT • USA
HOUSE OF MYSTERY • 1934 • Nigh William • USA
HOUSE OF MYSTERY • 1961 • Sewell Vernon • UKN • UNSEEN, THE
HOUSE OF MYSTERY, THE • 1911 • *Pathe* • USA
HOUSE OF MYSTERY, THE • 1913 • Noy Wilfred • UKN
HOUSE OF MYSTERY, THE • 1917 • *Cossar John* • SHT • USA
HOUSE OF MYSTERY, THE • 1920 • *Vosburgh Harold* • USA
HOUSE OF MYSTERY, THE • 1938 • Collins Lewis D. • USA
HOUSE OF MYSTERY, THE see **ANTRE DES ESPRITS, L'** • 1901
HOUSE OF MYSTERY (UKN) see **NIGHT MONSTER, THE** • 1943
HOUSE OF MYSTERY (USA) see **AT THE VILLA ROSE** • 1939
HOUSE OF "NO CHILDREN" • 1912 • *Comet* • USA
HOUSE OF NUMBERS • 1957 • Rouse Russell • USA
HOUSE OF OLD WOMEN, THE see **DOM STARYCH KOBIET** • 1956
HOUSE OF PAIN AND PLEASURE • 1969 • Rotsler William • USA
HOUSE OF PARADISE, THE see **CASA DEL PARAISO, LA** • 1981
HOUSE OF PEACE • 1911 • *Solax* • USA
HOUSE OF PERDITION (USA) see **CASA DE PERDICION** • 1954
HOUSE OF PERIL, THE • 1922 • Foss Kenelm • UKN
HOUSE OF PLEASURE (UKN) see **FRAU WIRTIN HAT AUCH EINE NICHTE** • 1968
HOUSE OF PLEASURE (USA) see **PLAISIR, LE** • 1951
HOUSE OF PRETENSE, THE • 1913 • *De Lespine Edgena* • USA
HOUSE OF PRIDE, THE • 1912 • *Bushman Francis X.* • USA
HOUSE OF PSYCHOTIC WOMEN, THE see **OJOS AZULES DE LA MUNECA ROTA, LOS** • 1973
HOUSE OF REFUGE see **BONDAGE** • 1933
HOUSE OF REVELATION, THE • 1916 • Brabin Charles J. • SHT • USA
HOUSE OF RICORDI (USA) see **CASA RICORDI** • 1954
HOUSE OF ROTHSCHILD, THE • 1934 • Werker Alfred L. • USA
HOUSE OF SCANDAL, THE • 1917 • *Triangle* • USA
HOUSE OF SCANDAL, THE • 1928 • Baggot King • USA
HOUSE OF SECRETS • 1957 • Green Guy • UKN • TRIPLE DECEPTION (USA)
HOUSE OF SECRETS, THE • 1917 • Ellis Robert • SHT • USA
HOUSE OF SECRETS, THE • 1929 • Lawrence Edmund • USA
HOUSE OF SECRETS, THE • 1936 • Reed Roland • USA
HOUSE OF SETTLEMENT (UKN) see **MR. SOFT TOUCH** • 1949
HOUSE OF SEVEN CORPSES, THE see **HOUSE OF THE SEVEN CORPSES, THE** • 1973
HOUSE OF SEVEN JOYS see **WRECKING CREW, THE** • 1968
HOUSE OF SHADOWS see **CASA DE LAS SOMBRAS, LA** • 1976
HOUSE OF SHAME see **OLGA'S HOUSE OF SHAME** • 1964
HOUSE OF SHAME, A see **GOBANCHO YUGIRIRO** • 1963
HOUSE OF SHAME, THE • 1928 • King Burton L. • USA
HOUSE OF SILENCE, THE • 1915 • Reehm George E. • USA
HOUSE OF SILENCE, THE • 1918 • Crisp Donald • USA
HOUSE OF SILENCE, THE • 1937 • Neilson-Baxter R. K. • UKN
HOUSE OF SILENCE, THE see **VOCE DEL SILENZIO, LA** • 1952
HOUSE OF SILENCE (USA) see **TYSTNADENS HUS** • 1933
HOUSE OF SIN (UKN) see **MENTEURS, LES** • 1961
HOUSE OF SOLOMON see **SOLOMON IN SOCIETY** • 1922
HOUSE OF STORKS, THE see **MAISON DES CIGOGNES, LA**
HOUSE OF STRANGE LOVES, THE (USA) see **ONNA UKIYO BURO** • 1968
HOUSE OF STRANGERS • 1949 • Mankiewicz Joseph L. • USA
HOUSE OF SURPRISE, THE • 1916 • *Junior John* • SHT • USA
HOUSE OF SVEND DYRING, THE • 1908 • DNM
HOUSE OF TAO LING, THE (UKN) see **DANGEROUS MILLIONS** • 1946
HOUSE OF TEARS, THE • 1915 • Carewe Edwin • USA
HOUSE OF TEMPERLEY, THE • 1913 • Shaw Harold • UKN
HOUSE OF TERRIBLE SCANDALS, THE • 1917 • Lehrman Henry, Kirkland David • SHT • USA
HOUSE OF TERROR • 1972 • Goncharoff Sergei • USA • FIVE AT THE FUNERAL, THE
HOUSE OF TERROR, THE see **CASA DEL TERROR, LA** • 1959
HOUSE OF TERRORS see **KAIDAN SEMUSHI OTOKO** • 1965
HOUSE OF THE ANGEL, THE see **CASA DEL ANGEL, LA** • 1957
HOUSE OF THE ARROW, THE • 1930 • Hiscott Leslie • UKN
HOUSE OF THE ARROW, THE • 1940 • French Harold • UKN • CASTLE OF CRIMES
HOUSE OF THE ARROW, THE • 1953 • Anderson Michael • UKN
HOUSE OF THE BLACK DEATH • 1965 • Daniels Harold • USA • WIDDERBURN HORROR, THE ○ NIGHT OF THE BEAST ○ BLOOD OF THE MAN-DEVIL ○ BLOOD OF THE MAN BEAST
HOUSE OF THE BRICK DOLLS, THE see **BRICK DOLLHOUSE, THE** • 1967
HOUSE OF THE DAMNED • 1963 • Dexter Maury • USA
HOUSE OF THE DARK STAIRWAY see **CASA CON LA SCALA NEL BUIO, LA** • 1983
HOUSE OF THE DEAD • 1980 • Allmendinger Knute • USA
HOUSE OF THE DEAD see **ALIEN ZONE** • 1975
HOUSE OF THE DOVES, THE see **CASA DE LAS PALOMAS, LA** • 1971
HOUSE OF THE FRIGHTS see **CASA DE LOS ESPANTOS, LA** • 1961
HOUSE OF THE GOLDEN WINDOWS, THE • 1916 • Melford George • USA • HOUSE OF GOLDEN WINDOWS, THE
HOUSE OF THE LIVING DEAD, THE • 1973 • Austin Ray • SAF • DOCTOR MANIAC ○ SKADUWEES OOR BRUGPLASS
HOUSE OF THE LONG SHADOWS • 1983 • Walker Pete • UKN
HOUSE OF THE LOST COURT, THE • 1915 • Brabin Charles J. • USA
HOUSE OF THE LUTE see **YU-HUO FEN CH'IN** • 1980
HOUSE OF THE OGRE, THE see **CASA DEL OGRO, LA** • 1938
HOUSE OF THE RAVENS, THE see **CASA DE LOS CUERVOS, LA** • 1941
HOUSE OF THE RED DRAGON • 1969 • Donne John • USA • HOUSE OF DRAGON GIRLS, THE
HOUSE OF THE RISING SUN • 1985 • Vincent Chuck • USA
HOUSE OF THE RISING SUN • 1987 • Gold Gregg • USA
HOUSE OF THE SEVEN CORPSES, THE • 1973 • Harrison Paul • USA • HOUSE OF SEVEN CORPSES, THE ○ SEVEN TIMES DEATH
HOUSE OF THE SEVEN GABLES, THE • 1910 • Dawley J. Searle • USA
HOUSE OF THE SEVEN GABLES, THE • 1940 • May Joe • USA
HOUSE OF THE SEVEN HAWKS, THE • 1959 • Thorpe Richard • UKN, USA
HOUSE OF THE SEVEN TOMBS, THE see **CASA DE LAS SIETE TUMBAS, LA** • 1982
HOUSE OF THE SLEEPING VIRGINS, THE see **NEMURERU BIJO** • 1968
HOUSE OF THE SPANIARD, THE • 1936 • Denham Reginald • UKN
HOUSE OF THE THREE GIRLS, THE (USA) see **DREIMADERLHAUS, DAS** • 1958
HOUSE OF THE TOLLING BELLS, THE • 1920 • Blackton J. Stuart • USA
HOUSE OF THREE DEUCES, THE • 1916 • Ellis Robert • USA
HOUSE OF TOMORROW, THE • 1949 • Avery Tex • ANS • USA
HOUSE OF TOYS, THE • 1920 • Cox George L. • USA
HOUSE OF TRENT, THE • 1933 • Walker Norman • UKN • TRENT'S FOLLY
HOUSE OF TROY, THE see **IN GAY MADRID** • 1930
HOUSE OF UNCLAIMED WOMEN see **SMASHING BIRD I USED TO KNOW, THE** • 1969
HOUSE OF UNREST, THE • 1931 • Gordon Leslie H. • UKN
HOUSE OF USHER • 1969 • Hunter Richard • SHT • USA
HOUSE OF USHER, THE see **FALL OF THE HOUSE OF USHER, THE** • 1960
HOUSE OF WAX • 1953 • De Toth Andre • USA
HOUSE OF WHIPCORD • 1974 • Walker Pete • UKN
HOUSE OF WHISPERS, THE • 1920 • Warde Ernest C. • USA
HOUSE OF WOMEN • 1962 • Doniger Walter, Wilbur Crane • USA • LADIES OF THE MOB
HOUSE OF WOMEN see **KVINNOHUSET** • 1953
HOUSE OF WOMEN see **HAUS DER FRAUEN** • 1977
HOUSE OF WOODEN BLOCKS, THE see **TSUMIKI NO HAKO** • 1968
HOUSE OF YOUTH, THE • 1924 • Ince Ralph • USA
HOUSE ON 56TH STREET, THE • 1933 • Florey Robert • USA
HOUSE ON 92ND STREET, THE • 1945 • Hathaway Henry • USA • NOW IT CAN BE TOLD
HOUSE ON A HILL, THE • 1949 • Harvey Maurice • DOC • UKN
HOUSE ON A VOLCANO, THE • 1928 • Bek-Nazarov Amo • USS
HOUSE ON BARE MOUNTAIN, THE • 1962 • Frost R. L. • USA • NIGHT ON BARE MOUNTAIN
HOUSE ON BEAVER STREET, THE • 1970 • *Able Film Co.* • USA
HOUSE ON CARROLL STREET, THE • 1987 • Yates Peter • USA • JIGSAW
HOUSE ON CEDAR HILL, THE • 1926 • Moss Carlton • USA
HOUSE ON CHELOUCHE STREET, THE • 1973 • Mizrahi Moshe • ISR
HOUSE ON CHIMNEY SQUARE see **DOM NA TRUBNOI** • 1928
HOUSE ON E STREET, THE • 1915 • *Regent* • USA
HOUSE ON FRONT STREET • 1979 • Schulz Bob • MTV • CND
HOUSE ON FRONT STREET, THE • 1977 • Jonas George • CND
HOUSE ON GARIBALDI STREET, THE • 1979 • Collinson Peter • TVM • USA • EICHMANN
HOUSE ON GREENAPPLE ROAD, THE • 1970 • Day Robert • TVM • USA
HOUSE ON HAUNTED HILL • 1958 • Castle William • USA
HOUSE ON HOCUM HILL, THE • 1916 • MacMackin Archer • USA • HOUSE ON HOKUM HILL, THE
HOUSE ON HOKUM HILL, THE see **HOUSE ON HOCUM HILL, THE** • 1916
HOUSE ON MARSH ROAD, THE see **HOUSE IN MARSH ROAD, THE** • 1960
HOUSE ON SKULL MOUNTAIN, THE • 1974 • Honthaner Ron • USA
HOUSE ON SORORITY ROW • 1983 • Rosman Mark • USA • HOUSE OF EVIL ○ SEVEN SISTERS
HOUSE ON STRAW HILL, THE see **EXPOSE** • 1975
HOUSE ON TELEGRAPH HILL • 1951 • Wise Robert • USA
HOUSE ON THE DUNE, THE (USA) see **MAISON DANS LA DUNE, LA** • 1934
HOUSE ON THE EDGE OF THE PARK, THE see **CASA AI CONFINI DEL PARCO, LA** • 1980
HOUSE ON THE FRONT LINE, THE (USA) see **NA SEMI VETRAKH** • 1962
HOUSE ON THE HILL see **QUARANTINED** • 1970
HOUSE ON THE HILL, THE • 1910 • *Edison* • USA
HOUSE ON THE HILL, THE • 1914 • Johnson Tefft • USA
HOUSE ON THE HILL, THE • 1916 • *Supreme* • USA
HOUSE ON THE MARSH, THE • 1920 • Paul Fred • UKN
HOUSE ON THE SAND • 1967 • Zarindast Tony • USA
HOUSE ON THE WASTELANDS see **DOM NA PUSTKOWIU** • 1949
HOUSE ON THE WATERFRONT, THE see **PORT DU DESIR, LE** • 1954
HOUSE ON TRUBNAYA SQUARE, THE see **DOM NA TRUBNOI** • 1928
HOUSE ON WHEELS, A • 1966 • Buchvarova Radka • BUL
HOUSE OPPOSITE, THE • 1917 • Wilson Frank • UKN
HOUSE OPPOSITE, THE • 1931 • Summers Walter • UKN
HOUSE OUTSIDE THE CEMETERY, THE see **QUELLA VILLA ACCANTO AL CIMITERO** • 1982
HOUSE PARTY • 1990 • Hudlin Reginald • USA
HOUSE PARTY, THE • 1915 • *Vokes Harry* • USA
HOUSE PARTY AT CARSON MANOR, THE • 1915 • *Jewett Ethel* • USA
HOUSE SAFE FOR TIGERS, A see **MA VART HUS FORSKONASFRAN TIGRAR** • 1973
HOUSE SURROUNDED, THE (USA) see **OMRINGADE HUSET, DET** • 1922
HOUSE THAT BLED TO DEATH, THE • 1985 • Clegg Tom • TVM • UKN
HOUSE THAT CRIED MURDER, THE see **BRIDE, THE** • 1973
HOUSE THAT DINKY BUILT, THE • 1925 • Lantz Walter • ANS • USA
HOUSE THAT DRIPPED BLOOD, THE • 1970 • Duffell Peter • UKN
HOUSE THAT JACK BUILT, THE • 1900 • Smith G. A. • UKN
HOUSE THAT JACK BUILT, THE • 1911 • *Lubin* • USA
HOUSE THAT JACK BUILT, THE • 1912 • Dwan Allan • USA
HOUSE THAT JACK BUILT, THE • 1916 • Davenport Charles E. • SHT • USA
HOUSE THAT JACK BUILT, THE • 1918 • *Vernon Bobby* • USA
HOUSE THAT JACK BUILT, THE • 1939 • Marcus Sid • ANS • USA
HOUSE THAT JACK BUILT, THE • *Koenig Wolf/mckay Jim (P)* • ANS • CND
HOUSE THAT JACK BUILT, THE • 1969 • Tunis Ron • ANS • CND
HOUSE THAT JACK MOVED, THE • 1915 • *Ashley Arthur* • USA
HOUSE THAT JAZZ BUILT, THE • 1921 • Stanlaws Penrhyn • USA
HOUSE THAT JERRY BUILT, THE • 1913 • Wilson Frank? • UKN
HOUSE THAT SCREAMED, THE (USA) see **RESIDENCIA, LA** • 1969
HOUSE THAT VANISHED, THE (UKN) see **SCREAM.. AND DIE!** • 1973
HOUSE THAT WENT CRAZY, THE • 1914 • Jackson Harry • USA
HOUSE THAT WOULD NOT DIE, THE • 1970 • Moxey John Llewellyn • TVM • USA • HOUSE THAT WOULDN'T DIE, THE ○ AMMIE, COME HOME
HOUSE THAT WOULDN'T DIE, THE see **HOUSE THAT WOULD NOT DIE, THE** • 1970
HOUSE TO LET • 1906 • Martin J. H.? • UKN
HOUSE TOP ROMANCE, A • 1912 • *Republic* • USA
HOUSE TRICKS • 1946 • Kneitel Seymour • ANS • USA
HOUSE UNDER THE ROCKS, THE see **HAZ A SZIKLAK ALATT** • 1958
HOUSE WARMERS • 1929 • Harman Bobby • UKN
HOUSE WARMING • 1954 • Chu Shih-Ling • HKG
HOUSE WARMING, THE see **GRIHAPRAVESH** • 1978
HOUSE-WARMING, THE see **GYERTEK EL A NEVNAPOMRA** • 1984
HOUSE WHERE DEATH LIVED, THE see **DELUSION** • 1981
HOUSE WHERE DEATH LIVES, THE see **DELUSION** • 1981
HOUSE WHERE EVIL DWELLS, THE • 1982 • Connor Kevin • USA
HOUSE WHERE HELL FROZE OVER, THE see **KEEP MY GRAVE OPEN** • 1975
HOUSE WHERE I LIVE, THE see **DOM, V KOTOROM YA ZHIVU** • 1957
HOUSE WITH AN ATTIC (USA) see **DOM S MEZONINOM** • 1961
HOUSE WITH CLOSED SHUTTERS, THE • 1910 • Griffith D. W. • USA
HOUSE WITH NOBODY IN IT, THE • 1915 • Garrick Richard • USA
HOUSE WITH THE DARK STAIRCASE, THE see **CASA CON LA SCALA NEL BUIO, LA** • 1983
HOUSE WITH THE DRAWN SHADES, THE • 1915 • Wilson Ben • USA
HOUSE WITH THE TALL PORCH, THE • 1912 • *Mcallister Jessie* • USA
HOUSE WITH THE YELLOW CARPET, THE see **CASA DEL TAPPETO GIALLO, LA** • 1983
HOUSE WITHOUT A CHRISTMAS TREE, THE • 1972 • Bogart Paul • TVM • USA
HOUSE WITHOUT A KEY • 1926 • Bennet Spencer Gordon • SRL • USA
HOUSE WITHOUT BOUNDARIES, THE see **CASA SIN FRONTERAS, LA** • 1971
HOUSE WITHOUT CHILDREN, THE • 1919 • Brodsky Samuel • USA
HOUSE WITHOUT FRONTIERS, THE (USA) see **CASA SIN FRONTERAS, LA** • 1971
HOUSE WITHOUT WINDOWS see **DOM BEZ OKIEN** • 1962
HOUSE WITHOUT WINDOWS OR DOORS, THE see **HAUS OHNE FENSTER UND TUREN, DAS** • 1914
HOUSE WRECKERS, THE • 1917 • *Nestor* • USA
HOUSEBOAT • 1958 • Shavelson Melville • USA
HOUSEBOAT MYSTERY, THE • 1914 • Brett B. Harold • UKN
HOUSEBREAKERS, THE • 1914 • Dillon Eddie • USA
HOUSECLEANING • 1919 • Kellette John William • SHT • USA
HOUSEFUL OF BLISS, A see **KET EMELET BOLDOGSAG** • 1960
HOUSEHOLDER, THE (USA) see **GHARBAR** • 1963
HOUSEKEEPER, THE • 1912 • *Powers* • USA
HOUSEKEEPER, THE (USA) see **JUDGEMENT IN STONE, A** • 1986

HOUSEKEEPER OF CIRCLE C, THE • 1913 • *Mackley Arthur* • USA

HOUSEKEEPER'S DAUGHTER, THE • 1939 • Roach Hal • USA

HOUSEKEEPING • 1916 • *Myers Harry C.* • USA

HOUSEKEEPING • 1987 • Forsyth Bill • USA • SYLVIE'S ARK

HOUSEKEEPING UNDER COVER • 1915 • *Osterman Kathryn* • USA

HOUSEMAID, THE • 1915 • *Loveridge Margaret* • USA

HOUSEMAIDS see **HEMSLAVINNOR** • 1933

HOUSEMASTER • 1938 • Brenon Herbert • UKN

HOUSES IN THAT ALLEY • 1978 • Hawal Kasim • IRQ

HOUSES OF GLASS • 1915 • *Roland Ruth* • USA

HOUSES THAT ARE FORTS see **KASHTI-KREPOSTI** • 1966

HOUSES WITHOUT FENCES • 1974 • Stoyanov Georgi • BLG

HOUSEWARMING, THE see **GRIHAPRAVESH** • 1978

HOUSEWIFE • 1934 • Green Alfred E. • USA

HOUSEWIFE, THE • 1974 • Bennett Cathy • CND • MENAGERE, LA

HOUSEWIFE HERMAN • 1938 • Donnelly Eddie • ANS • USA

HOUSEWIVES AND BARTENDERS • 1968 • *Mitam Productions* • USA

HOUSEWIVES ON CALL • 1967 • *Mitam Productions* • USA

HOUSING • Espinosa Julio Garcia • CUB

HOUSING • 1920 • Miller Frank • UKN

HOUSING AND NATURE see **ASUMINEN JA LUONTO** • 1966

HOUSING PROBLEM, THE • 1946 • Davis Mannie • ANS • USA

HOUSING PROBLEMS • 1935 • Anstey Edgar, Elton Arthur • DOC • UKN

HOUSLE A SEN • 1947 • Krska Vaclav • CZC • VIOLIN AND THE DREAM, THE

HOUSLOVY KONCERT • 1962 • Jires Jaromil (c/d) • SHT • CZC • VIOLIN CONCERT, THE

HOUSTON SISTERS, THE • 1926 • *De Forest Phonofilms* • SHT • UKN • MUSICAL MEDLEY NO.5

HOUSTON STORY, THE • 1956 • Castle William • USA

HOUSTON TEXAS • 1956 • Reichenbach Francois • DCS • FRN

HOUSTON, TEXAS, U.S.A. • 1979 • Reichenbach Francois • DOC • FRN

HOUSTON: THE LEGEND OF TEXAS • 1986 • Levin Peter • TVM • USA

HOUSTON, WE'VE GOT A PROBLEM • 1974 • Doheny Lawrence • TVM • USA

HOVDINGEN • 1984 • Kristiansen Terje • NRW • CHIEFTAIN, THE ○ HEADMAN, THE

HOVDINGENS SON AR DOD • 1938 • Fejos Paul • DCS • SWD • CHIEF'S SON IS DEAD, THE

HOVEDJAEGERNE • 1971 • Christensen Bent • DNM

HOVERBUG • 1970 • Darnley-Smith Jan • UKN

HOW A BRITISH BULLDOG SAVED THE UNION JACK • 1906 • *Walturdaw* • UKN

HOW A BURGLAR FEELS • 1907 • Martin J. H.? • UKN

HOW A HORSESHOE UPSET A HAPPY FAMILY • 1912 • *O'Connor Edward* • USA

HOW A HOUSE WAS BUILT FOR A KITTEN • 1963 • Kachanov R. • ANS • USS

HOW A HOUSEKEEPER LOST HER CHARACTER • 1913 • Rains Fred • UKN

HOW A MAN LOVES see **WOMAN HE LOVED, THE** • 1922

HOW A MAP IS MADE see **COMO SE HACE UNA MAPA** • 1978

HOW A MOSQUITO OPERATES • 1910 • McCay Winsor • ANS • USA • STORY OF A MOSQUITO, THE ○ MOSQUITO, THE

HOW A SOLDIER DESERTED THE FORCES see **KAK SOLDAT OT VOYSKA OTSTAL** • 1968

HOW A SOLDIER REMAINED AT HOME see **KAK SOLDAT OT VOYSKA OTSTAL** • 1968

HOW A SPARROW LOOKED FOR BRAINS • 1971 • *Aleksandr Dovzhenko Studio* • USS

HOW ABOUT US? see **HVAD MED OS?** • 1963

HOW ABOUT YOU • 1917 • *Fact Films* • USA

HOW ALGY CAPTURED A WILD MAN • 1911 • *Selig* • USA

HOW ALLOPATH CONQUERED BONEOPATH • 1915 • *Luna* • USA

HOW AM I DOING? see **GOIN' TO TOWN** • 1935

HOW AN AEROPLANE FLIES • Napier-Bell J. B. • DOC • UKN

HOW ARCHIBALD CAUGHT THE LION • 1913 • *Diamond Films* • UKN

HOW ARE ALL THE BOYS? see **BATTLING ORIOLES, THE** • 1924

HOW 'ARRY SOLD HIS SEEDS • 1912 • Raymond Charles • UKN

HOW AUNTIE WAS FOOLED • 1911 • *Powers* • USA

HOW AWFUL ABOUT ALLAN • 1970 • Harrington Curtis • TVM • USA

HOW BABY CAUGHT COLD • 1906 • Stow Percy • UKN

HOW BAXTER BUTTED IN • 1925 • Beaudine William • USA

HOW BEAVER STOLE FIRE • 1972 • Leaf Caroline • ANS • USA

HOW BELLA WAS WON • 1911 • *Edison* • USA

HOW BETTY CAPTURED THE OUTLAW • 1911 • *Kalem* • USA

HOW BETTY MADE GOOD • 1913 • Duncan William • USA

HOW BETTY WON THE SCHOOL • 1911 • *Normand Mabel* • USA

HOW BILL 'ARRIS TOOK THE DARDANELLES • 1915 • *Excel* • UKN

HOW BILL SQUARED IT FOR HIS BOSS • 1914 • *Komic* • USA

HOW BILLY GOT HIS RAISE • 1915 • Curtis Allen • USA

HOW BILLY KEPT HIS WORD • 1914 • Wilson Frank? • UKN

HOW BOBBIE CALLED HER BLUFF • 1914 • Seay Charles M. • USA

HOW BOBBY JOINED THE CIRCUS • 1912 • *Edison* • USA

HOW BRIDGES ARE BORN see **KESONCI** • 1965

HOW BRIDGET'S LOVER ESCAPED (USA) see **MARIAGE DE VICTORINE, LE** • 1907

HOW BROAD IS OUR COUNTRY • 1958 • Karmen Roman • DOC • USS • GREAT IS MY COUNTRY

HOW BROWN BROUGHT HOME THE GOOSE • 1905 • Collins Alf? • UKN

HOW BROWN GOT MARRIED • 1909 • *Lubin* • USA

HOW BURKE AND BURKE MADE GOOD • 1914 • Lambart Harry • USA

HOW CALLAHAN CLEANED UP LITTLE HELL • 1915 • Santschi Thomas • USA

HOW CECIL PLAYED THE GAME • 1913 • Collins Edwin J.? • UKN

HOW CHAMPIONSHIPS ARE WON -AND LOST • 1910 • *Corbett James J.* • USA

HOW CHARLIE'S GAME WAS SPOILED • 1911 • *Tress Henry (P)* • UKN

HOW CHIEF PONGO WON HIS BRIDE • 1913 • Melies Gaston • USA • HOW CHIEF TE PONGO WON HIS BRIDE

HOW CHIEF TE PONGO WON HIS BRIDE see **HOW CHIEF PONGO WON HIS BRIDE** • 1913

HOW CHILDREN PAINT see **JAK SI DETI MALUJI** • 1958

HOW CISSY MADE GOOD • 1915 • Baker George D. • USA

HOW CLARENCE GOT HIS • 1914 • *Melies* • USA

HOW COME? • 1949 • Barclay David • SHT • USA

HOW COME NOBODY'S ON OUR SIDE • 1975 • Michaels Richard • USA • CAPERS

HOW COOPERATIVES WORK see **TAK GOSPODARZA SPOLDZIELCY** • 1951

HOW COULD IT HAPPEN see **A ESLI ETO LYUBOV?** • 1961

HOW COULD WILLIAM TELL? • 1919 • La Cava Gregory • ANS • USA • JERRY ON THE JOB

HOW COULD YOU, CAROLINE? • 1918 • Thompson Frederick A. • USA

HOW COULD YOU, JEAN? • 1918 • Taylor William D. • USA

HOW COULD YOU UNCLE? • 1918 • Sandground Maurice • UKN

HOW DEATH CAME TO EARTH • 1971 • Patel Ishu • ANS • CND

HOW DID A NICE GIRL LIKE YOU GET INTO THIS BUSINESS? (USA) see **WIE KOMMT EIN SO REIZENDES MADCHEN WIE SIE ZU DIESEM GEWERBE?** • 1969

HOW DID IT FINISH? • 1913 • Miller Ashley • USA

HOW DO I KNOW IT'S SUNDAY? • 1934 • Freleng Friz • ANS • USA

HOW DO I LOVE THEE? • 1970 • Gordon Michael • USA

HOW DO, IT'S ME! see **ZDRAVSTVYI, ETO YA!** • 1965

HOW DO YOU DO see **LAUGH YOUR BLUES AWAY** • 1943

HOW DO YOU DO, CHILDREN? see **ZDRAVSTVYITE DETI** • 1962

HOW DO YOU DOOO? (UKN) see **HOW DOOO YOU DO?** • 1945

HOW DO YOU DRIVE? • 1958 • Blais Roger • DCS • CND

HOW DO YOU FEEL? • 1916 • Chaudet Louis W. • SHT • USA

HOW DO YOU LIKE THEM BANANAS? • 1966 • Rogosin Lionel • SHT • USA

HOW DOCTOR CUPID WON OUT • 1915 • Christie Al • USA

HOW DR. NICOLA PROCURED THE CHINESE CANE see **DR. NICOLA** • 1909

HOW DOES IT FEEL • 1976 • Csaky Mick • UKN

HOW DOOO YOU DO? • 1945 • Murphy Ralph • USA • HOW DO YOU DOOO? (UKN)

HOW DRY I AM • 1919 • Roach Hal • SHT • USA

HOW DUCKS ARE FATTENED • 1899 • *Bitzer Billy (Ph)* • USA

HOW EARLY SAVED THE FARM • 1915 • *Early Baby* • USA

HOW EVE HELPED THE WAR FUND • 1918 • Leigh J. L. V. • UKN

HOW FAR AND YET HOW NEAR see **JAK DALEKA STAD, JAK BLISKO** • 1971

HOW FAR FROM HERE, HOW NEAR see **JAK DALEKA STAD, JAK BLISKO** • 1971

HOW FATHER ACCOMPLISHED HIS WORK • 1912 • *Wadsworth William* • USA

HOW FATHER KILLED THE CAT • 1906 • Stow Percy • UKN

HOW FATHER WON OUT • 1914 • *Shield Ernest* • USA

HOW FATTY GOT EVEN • 1913 • *Nestor* • USA

HOW FATTY MADE GOOD • 1913 • *Mack Hughie* • USA

HOW FILMY WON HIS SWEETHEART • 1913 • *Chamberlin Riley* • USA

HOW FINE HOW FRESH THE ROSES WERE see **KAK KHOROSHI, KAK SVEZHI BYLI ROZI** • 1913

HOW FRECKLES WON HIS BRIDE • 1913 • *Pollard Harry* • USA

HOW FUNNY CAN SEX BE (USA) see **SESSO MATTO** • 1973

HOW GAS IS MADE • 1935 • Anstey Edgar • DOC • UKN

HOW GIRLS LOVE MEN TODAY see **JET GENERATION** • 1968

HOW GOD CAME TO SONNY BOY • 1914 • King Burton L. • USA

HOW GOOD THE WHITES ARE! see **COME SONO BUONI I BIANCI** • 1988

HOW GRANDPA CHANGED TILL NOTHING WAS LEFT see **JAK STARECEK MENIL AZ VYMENIL** • 1952

HOW GREEN IS MY SPINACH • 1950 • Kneitel Seymour • ANS • USA

HOW GREEN SAVED HIS MOTHER-IN-LAW • 1914 • *Joker* • USA

HOW GREEN SAVED HIS WIFE • 1914 • *Joker* • USA

HOW GREEN WAS MY VALLEY • 1941 • Ford John • USA

HOW HE LIED TO HER HUSBAND • 1931 • Lewis Cecil • UKN

HOW HE LIED TO HER HUSBAND • 1957 • Berezantseva Tatyana • USS

HOW HE LOST HIS TROUSERS • 1914 • *Lubin* • USA

HOW HE MADE GOOD • 1912 • *Bison* • USA

HOW HE MADE GOOD • 1912 • *American* • USA

HOW HE MISSED HIS TRAIN (USA) see **REVEIL D'UN MONSIEUR PRESSE, LE** • 1901

HOW HE PAPERED THE ROOM • 1912 • *Bunny John* • USA

HOW HE REDEEMED HIMSELF • 1911 • *Champion* • USA

HOW HE WON • 1913 • *Komic* • USA

HOW HE WON HER • 1912 • *Majestic* • USA

HOW HE WON HER • 1913 • *Powers* • USA

HOW HELEN GOT EVEN • 1915 • Crisp Donald, Siegmann George • USA

HOW HELEN WAS ELECTED • 1912 • Parker Lem B. • USA

HOW HERODES WAS BEHEADED BY THE HIPPIES see **DE COMO HERODES FUE DEGOLLADO POR LOS HIPPIES** • 1972

HOW HEROES ARE MADE • 1914 • Parrott Charles • USA

HOW HIGH IS UP? • 1940 • Lord Del • SHT • USA

HOW HIRAM WON OUT • 1913 • Sennett Mack • USA

HOW HOPKINS RAISED THE RENT • 1911 • *Solax* • USA

HOW HUBBY GOT A RAISE • 1910 • Powell Frank • USA

HOW HUBBY MADE GOOD • 1910 • *Essanay* • USA

HOW HUMAN LIFE BEGINS • 1923 • *Brown Herman Jacob* • DOC • USA

HOW I BECAME BLACK see **WIE ICH EIN NEGER WURDE** • 1970

HOW I BEGAN • 1926 • Sanderson Challis, Newman Widgey R. • SHT • UKN

HOW I COOK-ED PEARY'S RECORD • 1909 • Booth W. R. • UKN • UP THE POLE

HOW I GOT INTO COLLEGE • 1989 • Holland Savage Steve • USA

HOW I HUNTED LIONS see **JAK POLOWALEM NA LWA** • 1967

HOW I LEARNED TO LOVE WOMEN see **COME IMPARAI AD AMARE LE DONNE** • 1966

HOW I LOST THE WAR see **COME PERSI LA GUERRA** • 1947

HOW I PLAY GOLF • 1931 • Marshall George • SHS • USA

HOW I SPENT MY SUMMER VACATION • 1967 • Hale William • TVM • USA • DEADLY ROULETTE (UKN)

HOW I STARTED THE SECOND WORLD WAR see **JAK ROZPETALEM DRUGA WOJNE SWIATOWA** • 1969

HOW I STOLE A MILLION see **JAK SE KRADE MILION** • 1967

HOW I UNLEASHED THE SECOND... see **JAK ROZPETALEM DRUGA WOJNE SWIATOWA** • 1969

HOW I WAS SYSTEMATICALLY DESTROYED BY AN IDIOT see **KAKO SAM SISTEMATSK UNISTEN OD IDIOTA** • 1984

HOW I WON THE BELT • 1914 • Strather Frank • UKN

HOW I WON THE V.C. • 1910 • *Walturdaw* • UKN

HOW I WON THE WAR • 1967 • Lester Richard • UKN

HOW IDA GOT A HUSBAND • 1915 • *Kalem* • USA

HOW IS IT DONE? • 1913 • Wilson Frank? • UKN

HOW ISAACS WON THE CUP • 1906 • Hough Harold • UKN

HOW IT FEELS TO BE RUN OVER • 1900 • Hepworth Cecil M. • UKN

HOW IT HAPPENED • 1913 • Duncan William • USA

HOW IT HAPPENED • 1917 • *Pokes & Jabbs* • USA

HOW IT HAPPENED • 1925 • Butler Alexander • UKN

HOW IT HAPPENED see **COMO SUCEDIO** • 1974

HOW IT IS DONE • 1904 • *Mutoscope & Biograph* • UKN

HOW IT WORKED • 1913 • *Komic* • USA

HOW IT WORKED • 1917 • *Pokes & Jabbs* • USA

HOW IZZY STUCK TO HIS POST • 1914 • *Reliance* • USA

HOW IZZY WAS SAVED • 1914 • *Reliance* • USA

HOW JACK GOT EVEN WITH BUD • 1912 • *Champion* • USA

HOW JACK WON OUT • 1912 • *Reliance* • USA

HOW JIM PROPOSED • 1912 • *Kalem* • USA

HOW JOHANNA SAVED THE HOME • 1914 • *Farley Dot* • USA

HOW JOHN CAME HOME • 1915 • Drew Sidney • USA

HOW JONES GOT A NEW SUIT • 1908 • Coleby A. E. • UKN

HOW JONES LOST HIS ROLL • 1905 • Porter Edwin S. • SHT • USA

HOW JONES PAID HIS DEBTS • 1909 • *Urban-Eclipse* • USA

HOW JONES SAW THE BALL GAME • 1912 • *Imp* • USA

HOW JONES SAW THE CARNIVAL • 1908 • *Vitagraph* • USA

HOW JONES SAW THE DERBY • 1905 • Raymond Charles? • UKN

HOW KICO WAS BORN see **KAKO SE RIDIO KICO** • 1951

HOW KIKO WAS BORN see **KAKO SE RIDIO KICO** • 1951

HOW KITCHENER WAS BETRAYED • 1921 • Nash Percy • UKN

HOW KUTASEK AND KUTILKA GOT UP IN THE MORNING see **KUTASEK A KUTILKA JAK RANO VASTAVALI** • 1952

HOW LIEUTENANT PIMPLE CAPTURED THE KAISER • 1914 • Evans Fred, Evans Joe • UKN

HOW LIEUTENANT ROSE R.N. SPIKED THE ENEMY GUNS • 1915 • Stow Percy • UKN

HOW LONE WOLF DIED • 1914 • Farnum Marshall • USA

HOW LONG • 1976 • SAF

HOW LONG DOES MAN MATTER? see **MEDDIG EL AZ EMBER?** • 1967

HOW LOVE CAME • 1916 • Calvert Charles? • UKN

HOW LOVE CONQUERED HYPNOTISM see **STRANGE CASE OF PRINCESS KAHN, THE** • 1914

HOW MAN LEARNED TO FLY see **JAK SE CLOVEK NAUCIL LETAT** • 1958

HOW MANY ROADS see **LOST MAN, THE** • 1969

HOW MANY TIMES • 1969 • Shiffen Arlo • USA

HOW MARY DECIDED • 1911 • Coleby A. E. • UKN • RESULT OF A PICNIC, THE (USA)

HOW MARY MET THE COWPUNCHERS • 1911 • Melies Gaston • USA

HOW MCDOUGAL TOPPED THE SCORE • 1924 • *Gordon Leslie* • ASL

HOW MEN LOVE WOMEN • 1915 • Moran Percy • UKN

HOW MEN PROPOSED • 1913 • *Crystal* • USA

HOW MIKE GOT THE SOAP IN HIS EYES • 1903 • *Bitzer Billy (Ph)* • USA

HOW MILLIE BECAME AN ACTRESS • 1911 • *Ince Ralph* • USA

HOW MOLLY AND POLLY GO PA'S CONSENT • 1912 • Haldane Bert? • UKN

HOW MOLLY MADE GOOD • 1915 • McGill Lawrence • USA • HOW MOLLY MALONE MADE GOOD

HOW MOLLY MALONE MADE GOOD see **HOW MOLLY MADE GOOD** • 1915

HOW MOSHA CAME BACK • 1914 • *Crystal* • USA

HOW MOTION PICTURES ARE MADE • 1914 • Sennett Mack • DOC • USA

HOW MRS. MURRAY SAVED THE AMERICAN ARMY • 1911 • Dawley J. Searle • USA

HOW MUCH I LOVE YOU see **GAANO KITA KAMAHAL** • 1968

HOW MUCH LAND DOES A MAN NEED • 1979 • Kroeker Allan • CND

HOW MUCH LOVING DOES A NORMAL COUPLE NEED? • 1967 • Meyer Russ • USA • CONJUGAL CABIN ○ COMMON LAW CABIN! ○ COMMON-LAW CABIN

HOW MUCH WOOD WOULD A WOODCHUCK CHUCK? • 1976 • Herzog Werner • FRG

HOW NED GOT THE RAISE • 1912 • *Mcalvoy Thomas* • USA

HOW NICE, THE WORLD OF LOVE • 1977 • el Elmi Yehia • EGY

HOW NOT TO LOSE YOUR HEAD WHILE SHOTFIRING • 1973 • Dunning George • ANM • UKN

HOW NOT TO ROB A DEPARTMENT STORE (USA) see **CENT BRIQUES ET DES TUILES** • 1965

HOW NOT TO SUCCEED IN BUSINESS • 1975 • Halas John • ANS • UKN
HOW NOW BOING BOING • 1954 • Cannon Robert • ANS • USA
HOW NOW, SWEET EROS? see **IMAGO** • 1970
HOW OLD IS ANN? • 1903 • Porter Edwin S. • USA
HOW ONE PEASANT KEPT TWO GENERALS see **HOW ONE PEASANT SUPPORTED TWO GENERALS** • 1966
HOW ONE PEASANT SUPPORTED TWO GENERALS • 1966 • Ivanov-Vano Ivan, Danilevich V. • ANS • USS • HOW ONE PEASANT KEPT TWO GENERALS
HOW PATRICK'S EYES WERE OPENED • 1912 • *Edison* • USA
HOW PIMPLE SAVED KISSING CUP • 1913 • Evans Fred, Evans Joe • UKN
HOW PIMPLE WON THE DERBY • 1914 • Evans Fred, Evans Joe • UKN
HOW POETS ENJOY LIFE see **JAK BASNIKUN CHUTNA ZIVOT** • 1987
HOW POTTS BACKED THE WINNER • 1909 • Coleby A. E. • UKN
HOW PRETTY CHA CHA CHA! see **QUE LINDO CHA CHA CHA!** • 1954
HOW PUNY POTTER BECAME STRONG • 1911 • Coleby A. E. • UKN
HOW RASTUS GETS HIS TURKEY • 1910 • Golden Joseph A. • USA
HOW RASTUS GOT HIS PORK CHOPS • 1908 • *Lubin* • USA
HOW RICHARD HARRIS BECAME KNOWN AS DEADWOOD DICK • 1915 • Paul Fred, MacBean L. C. • UKN
HOW ROBINSON WAS CREATED • 1961 • Ryazanov Eldar • USS
HOW ROMEO AND JULIET FELL IN LOVE see **KAKO SU SE VOLELI ROMEO I JULIJA** • 1967
HOW RULERS LIVE see **VLASTELI BYTA** • 1932
HOW SCROGGINS FOUND THE COMET • 1910 • Aylott Dave • UKN
HOW SHALL THEY HEAR? • 1959 • Holmes Cecil • DOC • ASL
HOW SHE FOOLED AUNTIE • 1915 • *Moore Matt* • USA
HOW SHE HATED MEN • 1918 • *Vera Lillian* • SHT • USA
HOW SHE MARRIED • 1912 • *Imp* • USA
HOW SHE TRIUMPHED • 1911 • Griffith D. W. • USA
HOW SHE WON HIM • 1910 • *Vitagraph* • USA
HOW SHORTY KEPT HIS PROMISE • 1913 • Ford Francis • USA
HOW SHORTY KEPT HIS WORD • 1912 • *Bison* • USA
HOW SHORTY WON OUT • 1912 • *Prescott Vivian* • USA
HOW SIMPKINS DISCOVERED THE NORTH POLE • 1908 • *Vitagraph* • USA
HOW SIR ANDREW LOST HIS VOTE • 1911 • *Mcdermott Marc* • USA
HOW SLEEP THE BRAVE • 1981 • Swift Lyndon James • USA • ONCE UPON A TIME IN VIETNAM ○ COMBAT ZONE ○ FORGOTTEN PARALLEL, THE
HOW SLIPPERY SAM SAW THE SHOW • 1915 • Clements Roy • USA
HOW SMILER RAISED THE WIND • 1912 • Aylott Dave • UKN
HOW SORROWFUL see **AYA NI KANASHIKI** • 1956
HOW SPOTTED DUFF SAVED THE SQUIRE • 1914 • Kellino W. P. • UKN
HOW SPRIGGINS TOOK LODGERS • 1911 • *Edison* • USA
HOW SPRY I AM • 1942 • White Jules • SHT • USA
HOW STARRY WAS MY NIGHT see **CHE POR-SETARE BOOD SHABAM** • 1977
HOW STARS ARE MADE • 1916 • *Howell Alice* • SHT • USA
HOW STATES ARE MADE • 1912 • *Vitagraph* • USA
HOW STEVE MADE GOOD • 1912 • *Conway Jack* • USA
HOW SWEET IS HER VALLEY • 1974 • Brummer Alois • FRG
HOW SWEET IT IS! • 1968 • Paris Jerry • USA
HOW TALES COME TO LIFE • 1956 • Boyadgieva Lada • DOC • BUL
HOW TALKIES TALK • 1934 • Carter Donald • UKN
HOW TASTY WAS MY LITTLE FRENCHMAN see **COMO ERA GOSTOSO O MEU FRANCES** • 1971
HOW TEXAS GOT LEFT • 1911 • *Sais Marin* • USA
HOW THE ARFUL DODGER SECURED A MEAL • 1908 • Coleby A. E. • UKN
HOW THE BERLIN WORKER LIVES see **WIE DER BERLINER ARBEITER WOHNT** • 1930
HOW THE BOYS FOUGHT THE INDIANS • 1912 • *Boss Yale* • USA
HOW THE BULLDOG PAID THE RENT • 1909 • Raymond Charles? • UKN
HOW THE BURGLAR TRICKED THE BOBBY • 1901 • Hepworth Cecil M. • UKN
HOW THE CAT AND DOG SCRUBBED THE FLOOR • ANS • CZC
HOW THE CAUSE WAS WON • 1912 • *Harte Betty* • USA
HOW THE COSTER SOLD THE SEEDS • 1908 • *Warwick Trading Co.* • UKN
HOW THE DACHSHUND OPERATES see **JAK DZIALA JAMNICZEK** • 1971
HOW THE DAY WAS SAVED • 1913 • Dillon Eddie • USA
HOW THE DOCTOR MADE GOOD • 1911 • *Powers* • USA
HOW THE "DUKE OF LEISURE" REACHED HIS WINTER HOME • 1912 • *Selig* • USA
HOW THE DUTCH BEAT THE IRISH • 1901 • Porter Edwin S. • USA
HOW THE EARTH WAS CARPETED • 1914 • Miller Ashley • USA
HOW THE EGG WENT ON A RAMBLE • 1969 • Kluge Josef • ANS • CZC
HOW THE ELECTOR WILL VOTE see **KAK BUDET GOLOSOVAT'IZBIRATEL'** • 1937
HOW THE ELEPHANT GOT HIS TRUNK • 1925 • Lantz Walter • ANS • USA
HOW THE F-100 GOT ITS TAIL see **F-100** • 1956
HOW THE GIRLS GOT EVEN • 1911 • *Champion* • USA
HOW THE GRINCH STOLE CHRISTMAS • 1966 • Jones Charles M. • ANS • USA
HOW THE HELL ARE YOU? • 1972 • Soul Veronika • ANS • CND
HOW THE HUNGRY MAN WAS FED • 1911 • *Edison* • USA
HOW THE KID WENT OVER THE RANGE • 1914 • *Reliance* • USA
HOW THE LANDLORD COLLECTED HIS RENTS • 1909 • *Edison* • USA
HOW THE LOSER WON • 1909 • *Phoenix* • USA
HOW THE MOLE GOT HIS OVERALLS see **JAK KRTEK KE KALHOTKAM PRISEL** • 1957
HOW THE MOLE GOT HIS TROUSERS see **JAK KRTEK KE KALHOTKAM PRISEL** • 1957
HOW THE OFFICE BOY SAW THE BALL GAME • 1906 • Porter Edwin S. • USA
HOW THE OLD MAN CAUGHT THE OMNIBUS (USA) see **STOP THAT BUS!** • 1903
HOW THE PLAY WAS ADVERTISED • 1912 • *Pathe* • USA
HOW THE POOR HELP THE POOR • 1905 • Collins Alf? • UKN
HOW THE PUPPY TORE HIS TROUSERS see **JAK SI PEJSEK ROZTRHL KALHOTY** • 1951
HOW THE RANGER WAS CURED • 1912 • *Nestor* • USA
HOW THE RHINOCEROS GOT HIS SKIN • 1938 • Sutiev V. • ANS • USS
HOW THE SERVICE IS! see **COMO ESTA EL SERVICIO!** • 1968
HOW THE SPIRIT OF '76 WAS PAINTED • 1913 • *Pilot* • USA
HOW THE SQUIRE WAS CAPTURED • 1911 • *Edison* • USA
HOW THE STEEL WAS TEMPERED see **KAK ZAKALYALAS STAL** • 1942
HOW THE STORY GREW • 1911 • *Lubin* • USA
HOW THE TELEPHONE CAME TO TOWN • 1911 • *Edison* • USA
HOW THE TENDERFOOT MADE GOOD • 1910 • *Champion* • USA
HOW THE TRAMPS TRICK THE MOTORIST • 1905 • Fitzhamon Lewin • UKN
HOW THE WEST WAS WON • 1962 • Hathaway Henry, Ford John, Marshall George • USA
HOW THE WORLD WORKS see **JAK JE SVET ZARIZEN** • 1956
HOW THEY GOT THE VOTE • 1912 • Miller Ashley • UKN, USA
HOW THEY MADE A MAN OF BILLY BROWN • 1909 • Chart Jack • UKN
HOW THEY OUTWITTED FATHER • 1913 • Williams C. Jay • USA
HOW THEY STOPPED THE RUN ON THE BANK • 1911 • Turner Otis • USA
HOW THEY STRUCK OIL • 1914 • Henderson Dell • USA
HOW THEY WORK IN CINEMA • 1911 • *Eclair* • FRN
HOW THINGS DO DEVELOP • 1914 • Plumb Hay? • UKN
HOW TIMES DO CHANGE • 1916 • Christie Al • SHT • USA
HOW TO DIE see **KAKO UMRETI** • 1972
HOW TO AVOID FRIENDSHIP • 1964 • *Snyder William L. (P)* • ANS • USA
HOW TO BE A DETECTIVE • 1936 • Feist Felix E. • SHT • USA
HOW TO BE A DETECTIVE • 1952 • Kinney Jack • ANS • USA
HOW TO BE A HOSTESS • 1959 • *Halas John (P)* • UKN
HOW TO BE A SAILOR • 1944 • Kinney Jack • ANS • USA
HOW TO BE HAPPY THOUGH MARRIED • 1917 • Kelsey Fred A. • SHT • USA
HOW TO BE HAPPY THOUGH MARRIED • 1919 • *Strand* • SHT • USA
HOW TO BE LOVED (USA) see **JAK BYC KOCHANA** • 1962
HOW TO BE LUCKY • 1910 • *Pathe* • USA
HOW TO BE THE WORST OF OFFICE WORKERS see **SARARIIMAN AKUTO JUTSU** • 1968
HOW TO BE VERY, VERY POPULAR • 1955 • Johnson Nunnally • USA
HOW TO BEAT THE HIGH COST OF LIVING • 1980 • Scheerer Robert • TVM • USA • MONEYBALL
HOW TO BEHAVE • 1936 • Ripley Arthur • SHT • USA
HOW TO BREAK 90 • 1933 • Marshall George • SHS • USA
HOW TO BREAK 90 AT CROQUET • 1935 • Marcus Lee • SHT • USA
HOW TO BREAK A QUARTERHORSE • 1965 • Keatley Philip • CND
HOW TO BREAK UP A HAPPY DIVORCE • 1976 • Paris Jerry • USA
HOW TO BUILD AN IGLOO • 1949 • Wilkinson Douglas • DCS • CND • COMMENT CONSTRUIRE VOTRE IGLOU
HOW TO CATCH A MAN (UKN) see **TAKT OG TONE I HIMMELSENGEN** • 1971
HOW TO CLEAN HOUSE • 1948 • Roberts Charles E. • SHT • USA
HOW TO COMMIT MARRIAGE • 1969 • Panama Norman • USA
HOW TO DANCE • 1953 • Kinney Jack • ANS • USA
HOW TO DO ANYTHING AT ALL WITH GIRLS • 1968 • *Abrams & Parisi* • USA • ANYTHING WITH GIRLS
HOW TO DO IT AND WHY OR CUTEY AT COLLEGE • 1914 • Van Wally • USA
HOW TO EAT • 1939 • Rowland Roy • SHT • USA
HOW TO EDUCATE A WIFE • 1924 • Bell Monta • USA
HOW TO FATTEN CHICKENS see **POUR EPATER LES POULES**
HOW TO FIGHT WITH YOUR WIFE • 1975 • Fox Beryl • DOC • CND
HOW TO FIGURE INCOME TAX • 1938 • Rowland Roy • SHT • USA
HOW TO FILL A WILD BIKINI see **HOW TO STUFF A WILD BIKINI** • 1965
HOW TO FIND A WIFE FOR A FARMER see **AKATON MIES** • 1983
HOW TO FIRE A LEWIS GUN • 1918 • Fleischer Max • SHT • USA
HOW TO FIRE A STOKES MORTAR • 1918 • Fleischer Max • SHT • USA
HOW TO FISH • 1942 • Kinney Jack • ANS • USA
HOW TO FORGET THE GREATEST LOVE OF ONE'S LIFE? see **HOGYAN FELEJTSUK EL ELETUNK LEGNAGYOBB SZERELMET?** • 1980
HOW TO FRAME A FIGG • 1971 • Rafkin Alan • USA
HOW TO FURNISH A FLAT see **JAK ZARIDITI BYT** • 1959
HOW TO FURNISH AN APARTMENT see **JAK ZARIDITI BYT** • 1959
HOW TO GET AHEAD IN ADVERTISING • 1989 • Robinson Bruce • UKN
HOW TO GET RID OF HELENA see **JAK SE ZBAVIT HELENKY** • 1967
HOW TO GROW BETTER BANANAS • 1976 • Barron J. O. • SHT • UKN
HOW TO HANDLE WOMEN • 1928 • Craft William James • USA • PRINCE OF K'NUTS, THE (UKN) ○ FRESH EVERY HOUR ○ THREE DAYS ○ PRINCE OF PEANUTS, THE ○ MEET THE PRINCE
HOW TO HAVE AN ACCIDENT AT WORK • 1959 • Nichols Charles • ANS • USA
HOW TO HAVE AN ACCIDENT IN THE HOME • 1956 • Nichols Charles • ANS • USA
HOW TO HAVE GOOD CHILDREN • 1966 • Macourek Milos • ANS • CZC
HOW TO HOLD YOUR HUSBAND -BACK • 1941 • Hines Johnny • SHT • USA
HOW TO KEEP A HUSBAND • 1914 • *Prescott Vivian* • USA
HOW TO KEEP COOL • 1953 • Rasinski Connie • ANS • USA
HOW TO KEEP DOGS • 1928 • Sewell George • DOC • UKN
HOW TO KEEP SLIM see **JAK NA TO** • 1963
HOW TO KEEP THE RED LAMP BURNING (USA) see **BONS VIVANTS, LES** • 1966
HOW TO KILL 400 DUPONTS see **ARRIVA DORELLIK** • 1967
HOW TO KILL A LADY see **GEHEIMNIS DER GELBEN MONCHE, DAS** • 1966
HOW TO KILL A MOTHER-IN-LAW see **COMO MATAR UMA SOGRA** • 1980
HOW TO KILL A PLAYBOY see **COMO MATAR UM PLAY-BOY** • 1968
HOW TO MAKE £2000 • 1914 • *Heron Andrew (P)* • UKN
HOW TO MAKE A BIG HIT see **OOANA SHOBU** • 1968
HOW TO MAKE A DIRTY MOVIE • 1968 • *Fleetan Films* • USA • HOW TO MAKE A SEX MOVIE
HOW TO MAKE A DOLL • 1967 • Lewis Herschell G. • USA
HOW TO MAKE A LINO-CUT • 1938 • Hurrie William, Richardson Violet J. • UKN
HOW TO MAKE A MONSTER • 1958 • Strock Herbert L. • USA
HOW TO MAKE A SEX MOVIE see **HOW TO MAKE A DIRTY MOVIE** • 1968
HOW TO MAKE IT • 1968 • Corman Roger • USA • WHAT'S IN IT FOR HARRY? ○ TARGET: HARRY
HOW TO MAKE LOVE TO A NEGRO WITHOUT GETTING TIRED see **COMMENT FAIRE L'AMOUR AVEC UN NEGRE SANS SE FATIGUER** • 1988
HOW TO MAKE TIME FLY • 1906 • Martin J. H.? • UKN • GIRL THAT MADE THE TIME FLY, THE
HOW TO MARKET BETTER BANANAS • 1976 • Barron J. O. • SHT • UKN
HOW TO MARRY A MILLIONAIRE • 1953 • Negulesco Jean • USA
HOW TO MURDER A PLAYBOY see **COMO MATAR UM PLAY-BOY** • 1968
HOW TO MURDER A RICH UNCLE • 1957 • Patrick Nigel, Varnel Max • UKN
HOW TO MURDER YOUR WIFE • 1965 • Quine Richard • USA
HOW TO OPERATE BEHIND ENEMY LINES • 1942 • Ford John • USA
HOW TO PICK UP A GIRL • 1967 • Reid Ernest • CND • SEX AND THE SINGLE SAILOR (USA) ○ GIRLS AND THE SINGLE SAILOR ○ SINGLE SAILOR ○ EROTIKOS ○ LOVE AND THE SINGLE SAILOR
HOW TO PICK UP GIRLS! • 1978 • Persky Bill • TVM • USA
HOW TO PLAY BASEBALL • 1942 • Kinney Jack • ANS • USA
HOW TO PLAY FOOTBALL • 1944 • Kinney Jack • ANS • USA
HOW TO PLAY GOLF • 1944 • Kinney Jack • ANS • USA
HOW TO PULL OUT A WHALE'S TOOTH see **JAK VYTRHNOUT VELRYBE STOLICKU** • 1980
HOW TO RAISE A BABY • 1938 • Rowland Roy • SHT • USA
HOW TO READ • 1938 • Rowland Roy • SHT • USA
HOW TO READ AN ARMY MAP • 1918 • Fleischer Max • SHT • USA
HOW TO RELAX • 1954 • Rasinski Connie • ANS • USA
HOW TO ROB A BANK (UKN) see **NICE LITTLE BANK THAT SHOULD BE ROBBED, A** • 1958
HOW TO SAVE A MARRIAGE (AND RUIN YOUR LIFE) • 1968 • Cook Fielder • USA
HOW TO SCORE • 1978 • Enders Robert • DCS • UKN
HOW TO SCORE WITH GIRLS • 1980 • Lowell Ogden • USA
HOW TO SEDUCE A PLAYBOY (USA) see **BEL AMI 2000 ODER: WIE VERFUHRT MAN EINEN PLAYBOY?** • 1966
HOW TO SEDUCE A WOMAN • 1974 • Martin Charles • USA
HOW TO SEDUCE A WOMAN see **COMO SEDUCIR A UNA MUJER** • 1967
HOW TO SHOOT ROSEMARIES see **JAK SE TOCI ROZMARYNY** • 1977
HOW TO SLEEP • 1935 • Grinde Nick • SHT • USA
HOW TO SLEEP • 1953 • Kinney Jack • ANS • USA
HOW TO SMUGGLE A HERNIA ACROSS THE BORDER • 1949 • Lewis Jerry • USA
HOW TO START A FIRE see **CONSTRUIRE EN FEU** • 1926
HOW TO START THE DAY • 1937 • Rowland Roy • SHT • USA
HOW TO STEAL A DIAMOND IN FOUR UNEASY LESSONS (UKN) see **HOT ROCK, THE** • 1972
HOW TO STEAL A HUNDRED KILOS OF DIAMONDS IN RUSSIA see **COME RUBARE UN QUINTALE DI DIAMANTI IN RUSSIA** • 1967
HOW TO STEAL A MILLION • 1966 • Wyler William • USA
HOW TO STEAL A MILLION see **JAK SE KRADE MILION** • 1967
HOW TO STEAL A MILLION see **KAYFA TESRAK MILLIONAIRE** • 1968
HOW TO STEAL AN AIRPLANE • 1971 • Martinson Leslie H. • TVM • USA • ONLY ONE DAY LEFT BEFORE TOMORROW ○ ONE DAY BEFORE TOMORROW
HOW TO STEAL THE CROWN OF ENGLAND see **COME RUBARE LA CORONA D'INGHILTERRA** • 1967
HOW TO STEAL THE WORLD • 1968 • Roley Sutton • TVM • USA
HOW TO STOP A MOTOR CAR • 1902 • Stow Percy • UKN
HOW TO STUFF A WILD BIKINI • 1965 • Asher William • USA • HOW TO FILL A WILD BIKINI
HOW TO STUFF A WOODPECKER • 1960 • Smith Paul J. • ANS • USA
HOW TO SUB-LET • 1939 • Rowland Roy • SHT • USA
HOW TO SUCCEED IN BUSINESS WITHOUT REALLY TRYING • 1967 • Swift David • USA

HOW TO SUCCEED WITH GIRLS • 1964 • Biery Edward A. • USA • HARVEY'S GIRL

HOW TO SUCCEED WITH GIRLS see **PEEPING PHANTOM, THE** • 1964

HOW TO SUCCEED WITH SEX • 1970 • Gordon Bert I. • USA • HOW TO SUCCEED WITH THE OPPOSITE SEX ○ TOM CAT

HOW TO SUCCEED WITH THE OPPOSITE SEX see **HOW TO SUCCEED WITH SEX** • 1970

HOW TO SWIM • 1942 • Kinney Jack • ANS • USA

HOW TO TAKE A VACATION • 1941 • Roush Leslie • SHT • USA

HOW TO TELL MY DAUGHTER? see **HONEYBUN** • 1974

HOW TO TRAIN A DOG • 1936 • Ripley Arthur • SHT • USA

HOW TO TRAP A WOODPECKER • 1971 • Smith Paul J. • ANS • USA

HOW TO UNDRESS IN PUBLIC WITHOUT UNDUE EMBARRASSMENT • 1965 • Bennett Compton • UKN

HOW TO USE THE TELEPHONE • 1948 • Law Michael • UKN

HOW TO VOTE • 1936 • Feist Felix E. • SHT • USA

HOW TO WAKE PRINCESSES see **JAK SE BUDI PRINCEZNY** • 1977

HOW TO WATCH FOOTBALL • 1938 • Rowland Roy • SHT • USA

HOW TOMMY SAVED HIS FATHER • 1912 • *Casey Kenneth* • USA

HOW TOMMY WON THE VICTORIA CROSS • 1899 • *Warwick Trading Co.* • UKN

HOW TONY BECAME A HERO • 1911 • *Champion* • USA

HOW VANDYCK WON HIS WIFE • 1912 • Haldane Bert? • UKN

HOW WAR CAME • 1941 • Fennell Paul • ANS • USA

HOW WASHINGTON CROSSED THE DELAWARE • 1912 • Dawley J. Searle • USA

HOW WE BEAT THE EMDEN • 1915 • Rolfe Alfred • ASL

HOW WE FOUGHT THE EMDEN see **FATE OF THE EMDEN, THE** • 1915

HOW WE STOLE THE ATOMIC BOMB see **COME RUBAMMO LA BOMBA ATOMICA** • 1967

HOW WET WAS MY OCEAN • 1940 • Donnelly Eddie • ANS • USA

HOW, WHEN AND WITH WHOM see **COME, QUANDO, PERCHE** • 1968

HOW, WHEN, WHY? see **COME, QUANDO, PERCHE** • 1968

HOW, WHY AND FOR WHAT IS A GENERAL ASSASSINATED see **COMO, PORQUE Y PARA QUE SE ASESINA A UN GENERAL?** • 1971

HOW WIDE IS SIXTH AVENUE • 1962 • Burckhardt Rudy • SHT • USA

HOW WIFEY WON OUT • 1915 • *Mina* • USA

HOW WILLIE RAISED TOBACCO • 1911 • *Edison* • USA

HOW WILLINGLY YOU SING • 1975 • Patterson Garry • ASL

HOW WILLY JOINED BARNUM BILL • 1913 • Kellino W. P. • UKN

HOW WINKY FOUGHT FOR A BRIDE • 1914 • Birch Cecil • UKN

HOW WINKY WHACKED THE GERMANS • 1914 • Birch Cecil • UKN

HOW WOMEN LOVE • 1910 • *Powers* • USA

HOW WOMEN LOVE • 1913 • *Crystal* • USA

HOW WOMEN LOVE • 1922 • Webb Kenneth • USA

HOW WOMEN WIN • 1911 • *Powers* • USA

HOW YOU WOMEN ARE see **COMO SOIS LA MUJERES** • 1968

HOW YUKONG MOVED THE MOUNTAINS (UKN) see **COMMENT YUKONG DEPLACA LES MONTAGNES** • 1976

HOWA WE HEYA • 1964 • Wahab Fatin Abdel • EGY

HOWARD • 1957 • Haldane Don • SHT • CND

HOWARD: A NEW BREED OF HERO see **HOWARD THE DUCK** • 1986

HOWARD CASE, THE • 1936 • Richardson Frank • UKN

HOWARD IN PARTICULAR • 1979 • Egoyan Atom • CND

HOWARD THE DUCK • 1986 • Huyck Willard • USA • HOWARD: A NEW BREED OF HERO

HOWARDS OF VIRGINIA, THE • 1940 • Lloyd Frank • USA • TREE OF LIBERTY, THE (UKN)

HOWDY BROADWAY • 1929 • *Ruby Ellalee* • USA

HOWDY DUKE • 1927 • Taurog Norman • SHT • USA

HOWDY MATE • 1931 • Edwards Harry J. • SHT • USA

HOWL, THE (USA) see **URLO, L'** • 1968

HOWLIN' JONES • 1913 • Duncan William • USA

HOWLING 2, THE see **HOWLING II.. YOUR SISTER IS A WEREWOLF** • 1984

HOWLING 3: THE MARSUPIALS see **HOWLING III, THE** • 1987

HOWLING, THE • 1981 • Dante Joe • USA

HOWLING II.. YOUR SISTER IS A WEREWOLF • 1984 • Mora Philippe • USA, ITL, FRN • HOWLING 2, THE

HOWLING III, THE • 1987 • Mora Philippe • ASL • HOWLING 3: THE MARSUPIALS ○ MARSUPIALS: THE HOWLING 3, THE

HOWLING IN THE WOODS, A • 1971 • Petrie Daniel • TVM • USA

HOWLING IV: THE ORIGINAL NIGHTMARE • 1988 • Hough John • USA

HOWLING LIONS AND CIRCUS QUEENS • 1919 • Moore Vin • SHT • USA

HOWLING MILLER, THE see **ULVOVA MYLLARI** • 1983

HOWLING SUCCESS • 1954 • Rasinski Connie • ANS • USA

HOWLING SUCCESS, A • 1919 • *Nat. Film Corp. Of America* • USA

HOW'S ABOUT IT? • 1943 • Kenton Erle C. • USA • SOLID SENDERS

HOW'S CHANCES • 1934 • Kimmins Anthony • UKN • DIPLOMATIC LOVER, THE

HOW'S CROPS? • 1934 • Stallings George • ANS • USA • BROWNIE'S VICTORY GARDEN

HOW'S MY BABY? • 1930 • Roberts Stephen • SHT • USA

HOW'S YOUR HUSBAND? • 1919 • Lyons Eddie, Moran Lee • SHT • USA

HOW'S YOUR POOR WIFE? • 1917 • Kellino W. P. • UKN

HOWZER • 1972 • *Desiante Peter* • USA

HOY CANTO PARA TI • 1950 • Land Kurt • ARG

HOY COMIENZA LA VIDA • 1935 • Segura Juan Jose • MXC

HOY COMO AYER • 1965 • Ozores Mariano • SPN

HOY NO PASAMOS LISTA • 1950 • Alfonso Raul • SPN

HOYAT GWAN TSOI LEI • 1990 • Ou Dingping • HKG

HOYDEN, THE • 1911 • Salter Harry • USA

HOYDEN, THE • 1916 • Smith David • SHT • USA

HOYDEN'S AWAKENING, THE • 1913 • Parker Lem B. • USA

HOYO • 1954 • Makino Masahiro • JPN • LAST EMBRACE

HR. TELL OG SON • 1930 • Lauritzen Lau • DNM

HRA NA KRALE • 1967 • Jires Jaromil • CZC • KING GAME, THE

HRA O JABLKO • 1976 • Chytilova Vera • CZC • APPLE GAME, THE

HRA O ZIVOT • 1956 • Weiss Jiri • CZC • LIFE WAS THE STAKE (UKN) ○ NO MIDDLE ROAD ○ LIFE AT STAKE ○ LIFE WAS AT STAKE

HRABINA COSEL • 1968 • Antczak Jerzy • PLN • COUNTESS COSEL (UKN)

HRAFNINN FLYGUR • 1983 • Gunnlaugsson Hrafn • ICL, SWD • REVENGE OF THE BARBARIANS ○ WHEN THE RAVEN FLIES ○ RAVEN FLIES, THE ○ RAVEN, THE

HRAJEME SI • 1957 • Hofman Eduard • ANS • PLN • LET'S PLAY

HRANJENIK • 1970 • Mimica Vatroslav • YGS • MAN ON OTHER PEOPLE'S CARE, THE ○ FOSTERLING, THE

HRATKY S CERTEM • 1956 • Mach Josef • CZC • PLAYING WITH THE DEVIL

HRDINA JEDNO NOCI see **HRDJA JEDNO NOCI** • 1935

HRDINNY KAPITAN KORKORAN • 1934 • Cikan Miroslav • CZC • HERO-CAPTAIN KORKORAN

HRDINOVE MLCI • 1946 • Cikan Miroslav • CZC • HEROES ARE SILENT, THE

HRDJA JEDNO NOCI • 1935 • Fric Martin • CZC, FRG • HELD EINER NACHT (FRG) ○ HERO FOR A NIGHT ○ HRDINA JEDNO NOCI ○ JRDINA JEDNE NOCI

HRICHY LASKY • 1929 • Lamac Carl • CZC

HRIMA ITAN VROMIKO, TO • 1967 • Kosteletos Odisseas • GRC • MONEY WAS DIRTY, THE ○ DIRTY MONEY

HRISNA KREV • 1929 • Trivas Victor • CZC • SINFUL BLOOD

HRNEC NAFOUKANEC • 1961 • Hofman Eduard • ANS • PLN

HRNECKU VARI • 1953 • Bedrich Vaclav • CZC • WONDER POT, THE

HROMATA TIS IRIDOS, TA see **CHROMATA TIS IRIDOS, TA** • 1973

HRONIKO TIS KIRIAKIS • 1974 • Kanellopoulos Takis • GRC • SUNDAY CHRONICLE, A

HRST PLNA VODY see **HRST VODY** • 1971

HRST VODY • 1971 • Kadar Jan, Klos Elmar • CZC, USA • SOMETHING IS DRIFTING ON THE WATER ○ NECO NESE VODA ○ ZMITANA ○ ADRIFT ○ HRST PLNA VODY ○ TOUHA ZVANA ANADA ○ ANADA

HRY A SNY • 1958 • Vosmik Milan • CZC

HRYSOMALLOUSA • 1979 • Lykouresis Tonis • GRC • GIRL WITH THE GOLDEN HAIR, THE

HSI-HSUEH JEN-MO • 1976 • Fu Ch'I • HKG • BLOOD, THE

HSI, NOU, AI, LUEH • 1970 • Pai Ching Jui, Hu King, Li Hsing, Li Han-Hsiang • TWN • FOUR MOODS (USA) ○ HSI NU AI LE

HSI NU AI LE see **HSI, NOU, AI, LUEH** • 1970

HSI-PIEH HAI-AN • 1987 • Wan Jen • TWN • FAREWELL TO THE CHANNEL, A

HSI SHIH • 1966 • Li Han-Hsiang • HKG

HSI-YU CHI • 1960 • SER • HKG • JOURNEY TO THE WEST, THE ○ MONKEY

HSIA-LIU SHE-HUI • 1977 • Kao Pao Shu • HKG • LOW SOCIETY

HSIA NU • 1968 • Hu King • HKG • TOUCH OF ZEN, A ○ GALLANT GIRL, THE

HSIANG-CHIAO T'IEN-T'ANG • 1989 • Wang T'Ung • TWN • BANANA PARADISE

HSIANG-HSIA PIYEH-SHENG • 1976 • Ch'En Yao-Ch'I • HKG • GRADUATE FROM THE COUNTRYSIDE

HSIAO CHENG KU-SHIH • 1979 • Li Hsing • HKG • STORY OF A SMALL TOWN, THE

HSIAO CH'UAN YI CHAO • 1979 • Chan Jackie • HKG • FEARLESS HYENA, THE

HSIAO HU-LU • 1982 • Yang Chia-Hun • TWN • UNSINKABLE MISS CALABASH

HSIAO SHANTUNG TAO HSIANGKANG • 1975 • Lo Wei • HKG • SHANTUNG MAN IN HONGKONG

HSIAO SHIH-YI LANG • 1978 • Ch'U Yuan • HKG • SWORDSMAN AND ENCHANTRESS

HSIAO T'AO-FAN • 1983 • Chang P'Ei-Ch'Eng • TWN • LITTLE PRISONER, THE

HSIN CHING-WU MEN • 1976 • Lo Wei • HKG • NEW FIST OF FURY, THE

HSIU-HUA TA TAO • 1978 • Ch'U Yuan • HKG • CLAN OF AMAZONS

HSIUNG CHAI • 1977 • Li Han-Hsiang • HKG • HAUNTED HOUSE, THE

HSIUNG PANG • 1981 • Yu Yunk'Ang • HKG

HSU LAO-HU AND THE WHITE WIDOW see **HSU LAO-HU YU PAI KUA-FU** • 1980

HSU LAO-HU YU PAI KUA-FU • 1980 • Li Han-Hsiang • HKG • HSU LAO-HU AND THE WHITE WIDOW

HSUEH-SHENG-CHICH AI • 1982 • Lin Ch'Ing-Chieh • TWN • STUDENT DAYS

HSUEH TI TZU • 1975 • Ho Meng-Hua • HKG • FLYING GUILLOTINE, THE

HSUEH TSAI SHAO • 1987 • Tam Patrick • TWN • SNOW IS BURNING

HSUEH YING-WU • 1980 • Hua Shan • HKG • BLOODY PARROT

HTHES, SIMERA, AVRIO • 1979 • Karayannis Kostas • GRC • YESTERDAY, TODAY, TOMORROW

HU-MAN • 1975 • Laperrousaz Jerome • FRN • PLEURS

HU-YUEH-TE KU-SHIH • 1982 • Hsu An-Hua • HKG • STORY OF WOO-VIET, THE ○ STORY OF WU-VIET, THE

HUA MU-LAN • 1965 • Yueh Feng • HKG • LADY GENERAL, THE (USA)

HUA T'IEN-T'SO • 1961 • Yen Chun • HKG • BRIDENAPPING

HUAJIE SHIDAI • 1985 • Chen Anqi • HKG • MY NAME AIN'T SUZIE

HUAN YEN • 1979 • Chung-Hsun T'U • TWN • YOUR SMILING FACE

HUANG FEI-HUNG YU LU A-TS'AI • 1978 • Liu Chia-Liang • HKG • CHALLENGE OF THE MASTERS, THE ○ SHAOLIN CHALLENGES NINJA

HUANG-SE KU-SHIH • 1988 • Wang Hsiao-Ti, Chin Kuo-Chao, Zhang Aijia • TWN • GAME THEY CALL SEX, THE

HUANG-T'IEN HOU-T'U • 1981 • Pai Ching-Jui • TWN • COLDEST WINTER IN PEKING, THE

HUANG TUDI • 1985 • Chen Kaige • CHN • YELLOW EARTH

HUANLE DINGDANG • 1985 • Hui Michael • HKG • HAPPY DIN DON

HUANLE YINGXIONG • 1988 • Wu Ziniu • CHN • JOYOUS HEROES, THE

HUAPANGO • 1937 • Bustillo Oro Juan • MXC

HUB BAHDALA, EL • 1951 • Abu Saif Salah • EGY • LOVE IS A SCANDAL ○ HUBB BAHDHALA, AL-

HUB ILAL ABAD • 1958 • Shahin Youssef • EGY • FOREVER YOURS ○ HUBBUN 'ILA AL-ABAD

HUBAL • 1974 • Poreba Bohdan • PLN • MAJOR HUBAL

HUBB AD'-D'A'I • 1970 • Barakat Henry • EGY • AMOUR PERDU

HUBB AL-LADHI KAN, AL- • 1971 • Badrakhan Ali • EGY • AMOUR QUI FUT, L'

HUBB BAHDHALA, AL- see **HUB BAHDALA, EL** • 1951

HUBB FI BAGHDAD • 1986 • Al-Rawi Abdel-Hadi • IRQ • LOVE IN BAGHDAD

HUBB WA KARATI • 1973 • Al-Yassiri Fiasal • SYR • AMOUR ET KARATE

HUBBI AL-WAHID • 1960 • el Sheikh Kamal • EGY • MON SEUL AMOUR

HUBBIE'S SURPRISE • 1914 • *Royal* • USA

HUBBU AL-KABIR, AL- • 1968 • Barakat Henry • LBN • GRAND AMOUR, LE

HUBBUN 'ILA AL-ABAD see **HUB ILAL ABAD** • 1958

H'UBBUN LA ANSAHU • 1963 • Arafa Saad • EGY • INOUBLIABLE AMOUR

HUBBUN TAHTA AL-MAT'AR • 1975 • Kamal Hussein • EGY • LOVE IN THE RAIN

HUBBUN WA IDAM • 1956 • el Sheikh Kamal • EGY • AMOUR ET PEINE CAPITALE

HUBBY BUYS A BABY • 1913 • Thompson Frederick A. • USA

HUBBY DOES THE WASHING • 1912 • *Quirk Billy* • USA

HUBBY GETS HIS • 1915 • *Zenith Films* • USA

HUBBY GOES TO THE RACES • 1912 • Wilson Frank? • UKN

HUBBY MINDS THE BABY • 1912 • *Reliance* • USA

HUBBY PUTS ONE OVER • 1916 • Curtis Allen • *Joker* • SHT • USA

HUBBY PUTS ONE OVER • 1916 • Greene Clay M. • *Lubin* • SHT • USA

HUBBY TO THE RESCUE • 1914 • Dillon Eddie • USA

HUBBY'S BEANO • 1914 • Storrie Kelly • UKN

HUBBY'S CARE • 1915 • *Joker* • USA

HUBBY'S CHICKEN • 1916 • *Myers Harry* • SHT • USA

HUBBY'S DAY AT HOME • 1911 • *Kalem* • USA

HUBBY'S ESCAPADE • 1916 • *Hippo* • USA

HUBBY'S HOLIDAY • 1917 • *Burns Neal* • SHT • USA

HUBBY'S JOB • 1913 • Sennett Mack, Lehrman Henry • USA

HUBBY'S LATEST ALIBI • 1928 • *Sennett Mack (P)* • SHT • USA

HUBBY'S LETTER • 1912 • Fitzhamon Lewin? • UKN

HUBBY'S NEW COAT • 1913 • *White Pearl* • USA

HUBBY'S NIGHT OFF • 1914 • *Roland Ruth* • USA

HUBBY'S NIGHT OUT • 1913 • *Crystal* • USA

HUBBY'S NIGHT OUT • 1917 • *Compson Betty* • SHT • USA

HUBBY'S POLLY • 1913 • *Panzer Paul* • USA

HUBBY'S PRESENT • 1916 • *Judy* • USA

HUBBY'S QUIET LITTLE GAME • 1926 • *Sennett Mack (P)* • SHT • USA

HUBBY'S RELATIVES • 1916 • *Myers Harry C.* • SHT • USA

HUBBY'S SCHEME • 1911 • *Carney Augustus* • USA

HUBBY'S TOOTHACHE • 1913 • North Wilfred • USA

HUBBY'S VACATION • 1908 • *Lubin* • USA

HUBBY'S WEEK-END TRIP • 1928 • *Sennett Mack (P)* • SHT • USA

HUBERT AND ARTHUR • 1914 • *Williams Eric* • UKN

HUBERTUSJAGD • 1959 • Kugelstadt Hermann • FRG

HUBSCHER ALS DIE ANDERE, EINE • 1961 • von Ambesser Axel • FRG

HUCK AND TOM • 1918 • Taylor William D. • USA

HUCKLEBERRY FINN • 1920 • Taylor William D. • USA

HUCKLEBERRY FINN • 1931 • Taurog Norman • USA

HUCKLEBERRY FINN • 1974 • Thompson J. Lee • USA

HUCKLEBERRY FINN • 1975 • Totten Robert • TVM • USA

HUCKLEBERRY FINN see **ADVENTURES OF HUCKLEBERRY FINN, THE** • 1938

HUCKLEBERRY FINN see **ADVENTURES OF HUCKLEBERRY FINN, THE** • 1960

HUCKSTERS, THE • 1947 • Conway Jack • USA

HUD • 1963 • Ritt Martin • USA

HUD • 1986 • Lokkeberg Vibeke • NRW • SKIN ○ WILD ONE, THE

HUDBA SRDCI • 1934 • Innemann Svatopluk • CZC • HEART'S MUSIC, THE

HUDBA Z MARSU • 1954 • Kadar Jan, Klos Elmar • CZC • MUSIC FROM MARS ○ MUSIC ON MARS

HUDDLE • 1932 • Wood Sam • USA • IMPOSSIBLE LOVER, THE (UKN)

HUDODELCI • 1987 • Slak Franci • YGS • FELONS, THE

HUDSON'S BAY • 1940 • Pichel Irving • USA

HUDUD • 1984 • Laham Doreid • SYR • BORDERS

HUDUD AL MULTAHIBA, AL • 1986 • Hadad Saheb • IRQ • FLAMING BORDERS

HUDUTLARIN KANUNU • 1966 • Akat Lutfu • TRK • LAW OF SMUGGLING, THE

HUE AND CRY • 1947 • Crichton Charles • UKN

HUELLA • 1940 • Barth-Moglia Luis • ARG • TRIAL (USA)

HUELLA DE LUZ • 1943 • Gil Rafael • SPN

HUELLA DE UNOS LABIOS, LA • 1951 • Bustillo Oro Juan • MXC

HUELLA DEL CHACAL, LA • 1955 • Salvador Jaime • MXC

HUELLA MACABRA, LA • 1962 • Crevenna Alfredo B. • MXC • MACABRE MARK, THE

HUELLAS • 1988 • Lugo Ledith • PRC • IMPRINTS

HUELLAS DEL DESTINO • 1957 • Bosch Juan • SPN

HUELLAS DEL PASADO • 1950 • Crevenna Alfredo B. • MXC

HUERCO, EL • 1963 • Robles Mario • VNZ

HUERTO DEL FRANCES, EL • 1977 • Molina Jacinto • SPN

HUESO, EL • 1968 • Gimenez-Rico Antonio • SPN • BONE, THE
HUESPED DE LA TINIEBLAS, EL • 1948 • del Amo Antonio • SPN
HUESPEDE DE LA MARQUESA, LOS • 1951 • Salvador Jaime • MXC
HUESPEDE DEL CUARTO NO.13, EL (SPN) see **HOSPEDE DO QUARTO NO.13, O** • 1946
HUEY see **BLACK PANTHERS** • 1968
HUEY LONG • 1985 • Burns Ken • DOC • USA
HUEY'S DUCKY DADDY • 1953 • Sparber I. • ANS • USA
HUEY'S FATHER'S DAY • 1959 • Kneitel Seymour • ANS • USA
HUFF AND PUFF • 1956 • Potterton Gerald, Munro Grant • ANS • CND
HUFRA, AL- • 1969 • Siddik Khalid • SHT • KWT • FOSSE, LE
HUG BUG, THE • 1926 • Roach Hal • SHT • USA
HUG IN A SECRET ROOM see **MISSHITSU NO HOYO** • 1967
HUG OF HELL see **JIGOKU NO AIBU** • 1967
HUGE • Arnold Steven • USA
HUGE ADVENTURES OF TREVOR, A CAT, THE • 1986 • Taylor John* • ANM • ASL
HUGGERS see **CRAZY MOON** • 1986
HUGGETTS ABROAD, THE • 1949 • Annakin Ken • UKN
HUGH MACDIARMID, A PORTRAIT • 1964 • Tait Margaret • UKN
HUGH MACDIARMID: NO FELLOW TRAVELLERS • 1972 • Marzaroli Oscar • DCS • UKN
HUGHES AND HARLOW: ANGELS IN HELL • 1978 • Buchanan Larry • USA • ANGELS IN HELL
HUGHES AUFRAY • 1986 • Prefontaine Michel • MTV • CND
HUGHEY OF THE CIRCUS • 1915 • Van Wally • USA
HUGHEY THE PROCESS SERVER • 1916 • Van Wally • SHT • USA
HUGHIE AT THE VICTORY DERBY • 1919 • Pearson George • SHT • UKN
HUGO AND JOSEFIN see **HUGO OCH JOSEFIN** • 1967
HUGO AND JOSEPHINE see **HUGO OCH JOSEFIN** • 1967
HUGO ARCHITECTE • 1964-69 • Rohmer Eric • MTV • FRN
HUGO, DER WEIBERSCHRECK • 1968 • Albin Hans • FRG
HUGO OCH JOSEFIN • 1967 • Grede Kjell • SWD • HUGO AND JOSEFIN ○ HUGO AND JOSEPHINE
HUGO THE HIPPO • 1975 • Feigenbaum Bill • ANM • HNG, USA
HUGO THE HUNCHBACK • 1910 • *Selig* • USA
HUGO, THE RISKY FELLOW see **HUGONG PANGAHAS** • 1967
HUGO VAN GROOT • 1912 • Machin Alfred • NTH
HUGON THE MIGHTY • 1918 • Sturgeon Rollin S. • USA
HUGONG PANGAHAS • 1967 • Espiritu Romy • PHL • HUGO, THE RISKY FELLOW
HUGS AND HUBBUB • 1917 • Baker Graham • SHT • USA
HUGS AND KISSES see **PUSS & KRAM** • 1967
HUGS AND MUGS • 1950 • White Jules • SHT • USA
HUGUENOT, LE • 1909 • Feuillade Louis • FRN
HUIA • 1975 • Taylor Denis, Steven Geoff, Dadson Philip • NZL • TEST PICTURES
HUIDA, LA • 1955 • Isasi Antonio • SPN
HUIDA EN LA FRONTERA • 1966 • Torres Manuel • SPN
HUIDA HACIA LA MUERTE • 1967 • Bollo Joaquin • SPN
HUILOR • 1938 • Alexeieff Alexandre • SHT • FRN
HUIS, DE • 1962 • van Gasteren Louis A. • NTH • HOUSE, THE ○ HUIS, HET
HUIS, HET see **HUIS, DE** • 1962
HUIS-CLOS • 1954 • Audry Jacqueline • FRN • VICIOUS CIRCLE ○ NO EXIT
HUIS CLOS see **NO EXIT** • 1962
HUIS OP HORINGS • 1963 • SAF
HUIS VOOR AFBRAAK • 1966 • de Poorter R. • BLG
HUIT HOMMES DANS LA CHATEAU • 1942 • Pottier Richard • FRN
HUIT JEUNES FILLES A MARIER see **JEUNES FILLES A MARIER** • 1935
HUIT JOURS DE BONHEUR see **NUITS DE VENISE** • 1931
HUIT MILLIONS DE DOT • 1918 • Bergerat Theo • FRN
HUIT TEMOINS • 1965 • Godbout Jacques • DOC • CND
HUITIEME JOUR, LE • 1959 • Hanoun Marcel • FRN
HUITIEME MERVEILLE, LA • 1964 • Misonne Claude • DOC • BLG
HUK! • 1956 • Barnwell John • USA
HUKM AZ-ZAMAN • 1952 • Barakat Henry • EGY • EXIGENCE DES TEMPS, L'
HUKMU KARAKUCH • 1953 • Wahab Fatin Abdel • EGY • REGNE DE KARAKOCHE, LE
HULA • 1927 • Fleming Victor • USA
HULA-HOPP, GONNY • 1959 • Paul Heinz • FRG
HULA HULA HUGHIE • 1917 • Davis James • SHT • USA
HULA HULA LAND • 1917 • *Armstrong Billy* • SHT • USA
HULA HULA LAND • 1949 • Davis Mannie • ANS • USA
HULA HULAS AND HOKUS POKUS • 1918 • Hall Walter • SHT • USA
HULA LA LA • 1951 • McCollum Hugh • SHT • USA
HULDA FROM HOLLAND • 1916 • O'Brien John B. • USA
HULDA OF HOLLAND • 1913 • Dawley J. Searle • USA
HULDA RASMUSSEN • 1911 • Gad Urban • FRG • WHEN PASSION BLINDS HONESTY ○ DYREKOBT GLIMMER
HULDA THE SILENT • 1916 • Turner Otis • SHT • USA
HULDA'S LOVERS • 1908 • *Bitzer Billy (Ph)* • USA
HULDE VERSTEEG MD • 1970 • SAF
HULING BARAHA • 1968 • Pangilinana Johnny • PHL • LAST CARD
HULL OF A MESS, A • 1942 • Sparber I. • ANS • USA
HULLA KESA • 1980 • Parkkinnen Tapio • FNL • FUNNY SUMMER, THE
HULLABA-LULU • 1944 • Kneitel Seymour • ANS • USA
HULLABALOO • 1940 • Marin Edwin L. • USA
HULLABALOO • 1955 • Ordynsky Vassily, Segel Yakov • USS
HULLABALOO OVER GEORGIE AND BONNIE'S PICTURES • 1978 • Ivory James • USA
HULLO ELEPHANT see **BUONGIORNO ELEFANTE** • 1952
HULLO EVERYBODY see **GETTING ACQUAINTED** • 1914
HULLO, HULLO see **ALLO, ALLO** • 1961
HULLO MARMADUKE • 1924 • Smith Beaumont • ASL
HULLO! WHO'S YOUR LADY FRIEND? • 1917 • Kellino W. P. • UKN
HULM AL BARRI, AL • 1985 • Rached Mustapha • SYR • WILD DREAM
HULMU LAILATUN see **HILM LAYLA** • 1949
HULUNKENGEIGER, DER • 1922 • Bauer James • FRG
HULYESEG NEM AKADALY • 1985 • Xantus Janos • HNG • IDIOTS MAY APPLY
HUM DONO • 1962 • Jeet Amar • IND
HUM PANCHHI EL DAL KE • 1957 • Rao Sadashiv • IND
HUM TUM AUR WOH • 1938 • *Biswas Anil (M)* • IND
HUMAIN, TROP HUMAIN • 1972 • Malle Louis • DOC • FRN • HUMAN CONDITION, A (UKN) ○ HUMAN, TOO HUMAN
HUMAN AMPHIBIAN, THE see **CHELOVEK AMPHIBIA** • 1962
HUMAN BAIT see **BAIT, THE** • 1921
HUMAN BEAST, THE see **HUMAN DESIRE** • 1954
HUMAN BEAST, THE (USA) see **BETE HUMAINE, LA** • 1938
HUMAN BEAST, THE (USA) see **BESTIA HUMANO, LA** • 1964
HUMAN BEING, A see **NINGEN** • 1962
HUMAN BEING, THE see **NINGEN** • 1925
HUMAN BEING AND WAR see **SENSO TO NINGEN** • 1970
HUMAN BULLET, A see **NIKUDAN** • 1968
HUMAN CACTUS, THE • 1916 • Julian Rupert • SHT • USA
HUMAN CARGO • 1929 • Edwards J. Steven • UKN
HUMAN CARGO • 1936 • Dwan Allan • USA
HUMAN CATOS, THE • 1916 • Wilson Elsie Jane • USA
HUMAN CAULDRON, THE • 1916 • Lambart Harry • SHT • USA
HUMAN CLAY • 1918 • Physioc Wray • USA
HUMAN CLAY, THE see **BARRO HUMANO, EL** • 1955
HUMAN COLLATERAL • 1920 • Windom Lawrence C. • USA
HUMAN COMEDY, THE • 1943 • Brown Clarence • USA
HUMAN CONDITION, A (UKN) see **HUMAIN, TROP HUMAIN** • 1972
HUMAN CONDITION, THE see **POSTAVA K PODPIRANI** • 1963
HUMAN DESIRE • 1954 • Lang Fritz • USA • HUMAN BEAST, THE
HUMAN DESIRE, THE • 1919 • North Wilfred • USA
HUMAN DESIRES • 1924 • George Burton • UKN
HUMAN DESTINIES see **JOHAN ULFSTJERNA** • 1923
HUMAN DRIFTWOOD • 1916 • Chautard Emile, Tourneur Maurice • USA
HUMAN DUPLICATORS, THE • 1965 • Grimaldi Hugo • USA, ITL • SPAZIALE K.1
HUMAN DUTCH, THE see **ALLEMAN** • 1963
HUMAN EXPERIMENTS • 1979 • Goodell Gregory • USA • BEYOND THE GATE
HUMAN FACE IS A MONUMENT, THE • 1965 • Vanderbeek Stan • USA
HUMAN FACE OF CARACAS, THE see **ROSTRO HUMANO DE CARACAS, EL** • 1973
HUMAN FACE OF JAPAN, THE • 1982 • Howes Oliver • DOC • ASL
HUMAN FACE OF THE PACIFIC, THE • 1984 • Howes Oliver (c/d) • DOC • ASL
HUMAN FACTOR, THE • 1975 • Dmytryk Edward • UKN, ITL
HUMAN FACTOR, THE • 1979 • Preminger Otto • UKN
HUMAN FEELINGS • 1978 • Pintoff Ernest • TVM • USA
HUMAN FISH, THE • 1933 • Bruckman Clyde • SHT • USA
HUMAN FLAME, THE • 1917 • *Leonard Robert* • SHT • USA
HUMAN FLY, THE • 1896 • Paul Robert William • UKN • UPSIDE DOWN
HUMAN FLY, THE (USA) see **HOMME MOUCHE, L'** • 1902
HUMAN FOLLY • 1968 • Sibianu Gheorghe • ANM • RMN • HUMAN FOOLISHNESS
HUMAN FOOLISHNESS see **HUMAN FOLLY** • 1968
HUMAN GAMBLE, THE • 1916 • Carleton Lloyd B. • SHT • USA
HUMAN HEARTS • 1910 • Reid Hal • USA
HUMAN HEARTS • 1912 • Turner Otis • USA
HUMAN HEARTS • 1914 • Baggot King • USA
HUMAN HEARTS • 1922 • Baggot King • USA
HUMAN HIGHWAY • 1982 • Stockwell Dean, Young Neil • USA
HUMAN HOUNDS • 1916 • *Plump & Runt* • SHT • USA
HUMAN HOUND'S TRIUMPH, A • 1915 • Parrott Charles • USA
HUMAN IMPERFECTIONS see **TINIMBANG KA NGUNI'T KULANG** • 1974
HUMAN INSTINCT • 1979 • Cheyaroon Permpol • THL
HUMAN INVESTMENT, THE • 1915 • *Hawley Ormi* • USA
HUMAN JUNGLE, THE • 1954 • Newman Joseph M. • USA
HUMAN KINDNESS • 1913 • Dwan Allan • USA
HUMAN LANDSCAPE see **MANNISKAN LANDSCAP** • 1964
HUMAN LAW • 1926 • Elvey Maurice • UKN
HUMAN LIFE IN YOUR HANDS see **ZYCIE LUDZKIE W TWOIM REKU** • 1951
HUMAN MARKET • 1983 • Kim Hyo-Chon • SKR
HUMAN MENACE, THE • 1915 • Lucas Wilfred • USA
HUMAN MONSTER, THE (USA) see **DARK EYES OF LONDON, THE** • 1939
HUMAN NATURE • 1912 • *Republic* • USA
HUMAN OCTOPUS, THE • 1915 • *Edwards Walter* • USA
HUMAN OCTOPUS, THE see **PULPO HUMANO, EL** • 1933
HUMAN ORCHID, THE • 1916 • Field C. C. • USA
HUMAN PASSIONS • 1919 • Tyrol Jacques • USA
HUMAN PATTERNS see **NINGEN MOYO** • 1949
HUMAN PENDULUM, THE • 1916 • McRae Henry • SHT • USA
HUMAN PROMISE see **NINGEN NO YAKUSOKU** • 1985
HUMAN PYRAMID, THE see **PYRAMIDE DE TRIBOULET, LA** • 1899
HUMAN REVOLUTION see **NINGEN KAKUMEI** • 1973
HUMAN REVOLUTION, PART II see **ZOKU NINGEN KAKUMEI** • 1975
HUMAN REVOLUTION: SEQUEL see **ZOKU NINGEN KAKUMEI** • 1975
HUMAN SABOTAGE (UKN) see **MURDER IN THE BIG HOUSE** • 1942
HUMAN SACRIFICE, THE • 1911 • *Reliance* • USA
HUMAN SAILBOAT • 1942 • *O'Brien Joseph/ Mead Thomas (P)* • SHT • USA
HUMAN SIDE, THE • 1934 • Buzzell Edward • USA
HUMAN SOUL, THE • 1914 • *Balboa* • USA
HUMAN SPARROWS (UKN) see **SPARROWS** • 1926
HUMAN STUFF • 1920 • Eason B. Reeves • USA
HUMAN TARANTULA, THE see **NEMURI KYOSHIRO HITOHADAGUMO** • 1968
HUMAN TARGET • 1973 • Rubie Howard • MTV • ASL
HUMAN TARGET, THE • 1918 • Wells Jack • SHT • USA
HUMAN TARGETS • 1932 • McGowan J. P. • USA
HUMAN TERROR, THE • 1924 • *Francis Alec B.* • USA
HUMAN THEATRE see **JINSEI GEKIJO** • 1983
HUMAN TIGER, THE • 1918 • *Sedgwick Eileen* • SHT • USA
HUMAN, TOO HUMAN see **HUMAIN, TROP HUMAIN** • 1972
HUMAN TORCH, THE • 1963 • Glut Don • SHT • USA
HUMAN TORNADO see **DOLEMITE** • 1975
HUMAN TORNADO, THE • 1925 • Wilson Ben • USA
HUMAN TORNADO, THE • 1976 • Roquemore Cliff • USA
HUMAN TORPEDO, THE • 1911 • *Hopkins Jack* • USA
HUMAN TORPEDOES see **SETTE DELL'ORSA MAGGIORE, I** • 1953
HUMAN TORPEDOES see **NINGEN GYORAI SHUTSUGEKISU** • 1955
HUMAN TORPEDOES see **AH KAITEN TOKUBETSU KOGEKITAI** • 1968
HUMAN TORPEDOES ATTACK see **NINGEN GYORAI SHUTSUGEKISU** • 1955
HUMAN VAPOUR, THE see **GASU NINGEN DAIICHIGO** • 1960
HUMAN VOICE, THE see **VOICE, THE** • 1967
HUMAN VULTURE, THE • 1913 • *Patheplay* • USA
HUMAN WALL, THE see **NINGEN NO KABE** • 1959
HUMAN WOLVES see **OKAMI TO BUTA TO NINGEN** • 1964
HUMAN WOMAN see **MENSCHENFRAUEN** • 1980
HUMAN WRECKAGE • 1923 • Wray John Griffith • USA
HUMAN ZOO see **NINGEN DOBUTSUEN** • 1961
HUMANETTES • 1930-31 • Jason Leigh • ASS • USA
HUMANIDAD • 1933 • Maugard Adolfo Best • SHT • MXC
HUMANISME, L' see **HUMANISME, VICTOIRE DE L'ESPRIT, L'** • 1956
HUMANISME, VICTOIRE DE L'ESPRIT, L' • 1956 • Haesaerts Paul • BLG • HUMANISME, L'
HUMANITY • 1917 • Anderson G. M. • USA
HUMANITY • 1933 • Dillon John Francis • USA
HUMANITY AND PAPER BALLOONS see **NINJO KAMIFUSEN** • 1937
HUMANITY IN THE ROUGH • 1914 • Warren Edward • USA
HUMANITY: OR, ONLY A JEW • 1913 • Lawson John, Haldane Bert • UKN
HUMANITY THROUGH THE AGES (USA) see **CIVILISATION A TRAVERS LES AGES, LA** • 1907
HUMANITY'S HOPE • 1948 • Sen Fou • CHN
HUMANIZING MR. WINSBY • 1916 • *Chesebro George N.* • USA
HUMANOID, THE (USA) see **UMANOIDE, L'** • 1979
HUMANOID DEFENDER • 1985 • Satlof Ron • USA
HUMANOID WOMAN see **CHEREZ TERNII K ZVEZDAM** • 1981
HUMANOIDS FROM THE DEEP • 1980 • Peeters Barbara • USA • HUMANOIDS OF THE DEEP ○ MONSTER
HUMANOIDS OF THE DEEP see **HUMANOIDS FROM THE DEEP** • 1980
HUMAN'S PROMISE see **NINGEN NO YAKUSOKU** • 1985
HUMANWOMEN see **MENSCHENFRAUEN** • 1980
HUMBERTO CIRCUS, THE see **CIRKUS HUMBERTO** • 1978
HUMBLE AND DESPISED, THE see **TAPINOS KE KATAFRONEMENOS** • 1968
HUMBLE HERO, A • 1912 • *Selig* • USA
HUMBLE MAN AND THE SINGER, THE see **DEMUTIGE UND DIE SANGERIN, DER** • 1925
HUMBLE ONE, THE • 1960 • Borisov A. • USS
HUMBREGOLO, EL • Portabella Pedro
HUMBUG, THE see **LOVE CAPTIVE, THE** • 1934
HUMBUGS AND HUSBANDS • 1918 • Semon Larry • SHT • USA
HUMDINGER, THE • 1926 • Taurog Norman • SHT • USA
HUMDRUM BROWN • 1918 • Ingram Rex • USA
HUMEUR A L'HUMEUR, L' • 1990 • Perusse Michele • DOC • CND
HUMEUR VAGABONDE, L' • 1971 • Luntz Edouard • FRN
HUMILITY • 1917 • Pratt Jack • USA
HUMMEL-HUMMEL see **KLEINER GOLDENER BERG, EIN** • 1936
HUMMING BIRD, THE • 1924 • Olcott Sidney • USA
HUMMING GIRL, A see **HANAUTA OJOSAN** • 1938
HUMMING WIRES see **OVERLAND TELEGRAPH, THE** • 1929
HUMMINGBIRD • 1968 • Cueri Charles • SHT • USA • SHAFFER JAMES P.
HUMO DE MARIHUANA • 1968 • Demare Lucas • ARG • MARIHUANA SMOKE
HUMO EN LOS OJOS • 1946 • Gout Alberto • MXC
HUMONGOUS • 1982 • Lynch Paul • CND
HUMOR OVER STRINGS see **UMOR PE SFORI** • 1954
HUMORESKA • 1939 • Vavra Otakar • CZC • HUMORESQUE ○ HUMOROUS SKETCH
HUMORESQUE • 1920 • Borzage Frank • USA
HUMORESQUE • 1929 • Aylott Dave, Symmons E. F. • SHT • UKN
HUMORESQUE • 1946 • Negulesco Jean • USA
HUMORESQUE see **ZHUMORESKI** • 1925
HUMORESQUE see **HUMORESKA** • 1939
HUMORISMO NEGRO see **UMORISMO NERO** • 1965
HUMOROUS PHASES OF A FUNNY FACE • 1906 • Blackton J. Stuart • USA • HUMOROUS PHASES OF FUNNY FACES
HUMOROUS PHASES OF FUNNY FACES see **HUMOROUS PHASES OF A FUNNY FACE** • 1906
HUMOROUS SKETCH see **HUMORESKA** • 1939
HUMOUR NOIR see **UMORISMO NERO** • 1965
HUMOURS OF A RIVER PICNIC, THE • 1906 • Green Tom? • UKN
HUMOURS OF AMATEUR GOLF, THE • 1906 • *Urban Trading Co.* • UKN
HUMP-BACKED WOMAN, THE see **KAMBUR** • 1973
HUMPBACKED HORSE, THE • 1976 • Ivanov-Vano Ivan • ANM • USS
HUMPHREY JENNINGS see **HEART OF BRITAIN** • 1970
HUMPHREY TAKES A CHANCE (UKN) see **JOE PALOOKA IN HUMPHREY TAKES A CHANCE** • 1950
HUMPTY DUMPTY • 1935 • *Iwerks Ub (P)* • ANS • USA
HUMPTY DUMPTY CIRCUS • 1908 • *Kalem* • ANS • USA
HUMPTY DUMPTY CIRCUS, THE • 1914 • *Humpty Dumpty* • UKN
HUMPTY DUMPTY R.A. • 1915 • *Humpty Dumpty Films* • UKN
HUMRAHI • 1945 • Roy Bimal • IND • HAMRAHI

HUMUNQUS HECTOR • 1976 • Festa Campanile Pasquale • ITL
HUN, HAN OG HAMLET • 1921 • Lauritzen Lau • DNM
HUN WITHIN, THE • 1918 • Withey Chet • USA • PERIL WITHIN, THE
HUNAN GIRL XIAOXAIO see **XIANGNU XIAOXIAO** • 1985
HUNCH, THE • 1921 • Baker George D. • USA • TEMPTING LUCK
HUNCH, THE • 1967 • Erulkar Sarah • UKN
HUNCHBACK, THE • 1909 • Brooke Van Dyke • USA
HUNCHBACK, THE • 1911 • Coleby A. E. • UKN
HUNCHBACK, THE • 1913 • *Moore Tom* • USA
HUNCHBACK, THE • 1914 • Cabanne W. Christy • USA
HUNCHBACK, THE • 1914 • Wilson Frank • UKN
HUNCHBACK, THE see **AHDAB, EL** • 1947
HUNCHBACK, THE see **KAMBOURIS, O** • 1967
HUNCHBACK AND THE DANCER, THE see **BUCKLIGE UND DIE TANZERIN, DER** • 1920
HUNCHBACK FIDDLER • 1909 • *Pathe* • FRN
HUNCHBACK OF CEDAR LODGE, THE • 1914 • *Balboa* • USA
HUNCHBACK OF ENMEI-IN, THE see **ENMEI-IN NO SEMUSHIOTOKO** • 1924
HUNCHBACK OF NOTRE DAME see **NOTRE DAME DE PARIS** • 1957
HUNCHBACK OF NOTRE DAME, THE • 1923 • Worsley Wallace • USA
HUNCHBACK OF NOTRE DAME, THE • 1939 • Dieterle William • USA
HUNCHBACK OF NOTRE DAME, THE • 1977 • Cooke Alan • MTV • UKN
HUNCHBACK OF NOTRE DAME, THE • 1982 • Tuchner Michael • TVM • UKN
HUNCHBACK OF NOTRE DAME, THE see **BADSHAH DAMPATI** • 1953
HUNCHBACK OF NOTRE DAME, THE (USA) see **NOTRE DAME DE PARIS** • 1911
HUNCHBACK OF ROME, THE (USA) see **GOBBO, IL** • 1960
HUNCHBACK OF THE MORGUE, THE (USA) see **JOROBADO DE LA MORGUE, EL** • 1972
HUNCHBACK OF UCLA, THE see **BIG MAN ON CAMPUS** • 1989
HUNCHBACK PONY, THE see **KONEK-GORBUNOK** • 1947
HUNCHBACK ROBBER, THE see **PENYAMUN SI BONGKOK** • 1972
HUNCHBACK'S ROMANCE, THE • 1915 • Goldin Sidney M. • USA
HUND VON BASKERVILLE 1, DER • 1914 • Oswald Richard • FRG
HUND VON BASKERVILLE 2, DER • 1914 • Oswald Richard • FRG
HUND VON BASKERVILLE 3, DER • 1915 • Oswald Richard • FRG • HOUND OF THE BASKERVILLES, THE (USA) ○ UNHEIMLICHE ZIMMER, DAS
HUND VON BASKERVILLE 5, DER • 1920 • Zeyn Willy • FRG • DR. MACDONALDS SANATORIUM
HUND VON BASKERVILLE 6, DER • 1920 • Zeyn Willy? • FRG • HAUS OHNE FENSTER, DAS
HUND VON BASKERVILLE, DER • 1914 • Meinert Rudolf • FRG • HOUND OF THE BASKERVILLES, THE (USA)
HUND VON BASKERVILLE, DER • 1929 • Oswald Richard • FRG • HOUND OF THE BASKERVILLES, THE
HUND VON BASKERVILLE, DER • 1936 • Lamac Carl • FRG • HOUND OF THE BASKERVILLES, THE (USA)
HUND VON BLACKWOOD CASTLE, DER • 1968 • Vohrer Alfred • FRG • HOUND OF BLACKWOOD CASTLE, THE
HUNDE! WOLLT IHR EWIG LEBEN? • 1959 • Wisbar Frank • FRG • DOGS, DO YOU WANT TO LIVE FOREVER ○ BATTLE INFERNO
HUNDEMAMACHEN • 1919 • Biebrach Rudolf • FRG
HUNDERT TAGE • 1935 • Wenzler Franz • FRG, ITL
HUNDERTTAUSENDE UNTER ROTEN FAHNEN • 1929 • Blum Victor • DOC • FRG • HUNDREDS OF THOUSANDS UNDER RED FLAGS
HUNDRA • 1983 • Cimber Matt • USA, SPN
HUNDRA DRAGSPEL OCH EN FLICKA • 1946 • Frisk Ragnar • SWD • HUNDRED ACCORDIONS AND ONE GIRL, A
HUNDRED ACCORDIONS AND ONE GIRL, A see **HUNDRA DRAGSPEL OCH EN FLICKA** • 1946
HUNDRED DAYS AFTER CHILDHOOD, A see **STO DNEI POSLE DETSTVA** • 1975
HUNDRED DAYS WITH THE SHIP "BULGARIA", A • 1955 • Stoyanov Yuli • DOC • BUL
HUNDRED DOLLAR BILL, THE • 1913 • *Majestic* • USA
HUNDRED FOR ONE, A • 1941 • Rappaport Herbert • USS
HUNDRED HORSEMEN, THE see **CENTO CAVALIERI, I** • 1965
HUNDRED HORSES TOWARDS A HUNDRED BANKS, A see **STO KONI DO STU BRZEGOW** • 1978
HUNDRED HOUR HUNT, THE (USA) see **EMERGENCY CALL** • 1952
HUNDRED MONSTERS, THE see **YOKAI HYAKU MONOGATARI** • 1968
HUNDRED POUND WINDOW, THE • 1943 • Hurst Brian Desmond • UKN
HUNDRED THOUSAND CHILDREN, A • 1955 • Anderson Lindsay • DCS • UKN
HUNDRED TO ONE • 1933 • West Walter • UKN
HUNDRED TRICKS, A • 1906 • *Pathe* • FRN
HUNDREDS OF THOUSANDS UNDER RED FLAGS see **HUNDERTTAUSENDE UNTER ROTEN FAHNEN** • 1929
HUNDREDTH CHANCE, THE • 1920 • Elvey Maurice • UKN
HUNDRETH SUMMER, THE • 1964 • Macartney-Filgate Terence • DOC • CND
HUNDSTAGE • 1944 • von Cziffra Geza • FRG
HUNDSTAGE • 1958 • Houwer Rob • SHT • NTH • DOG DAYS
HUNENREPORT • 1972 • Fronz Fritz • AUS, FRG • REPORT ON PROSTITUTION
HUNG CHU'A HSIAO TZU • 1975 • Chang Ch'Eh • HKG • DISCIPLES OF SHAOLIN
HUNG HAI-ARH • 1975 • Chang Ch'Eh • HKG • FANTASTIC MAGIC BABY, THE
HUNG HSI-KUAN • 1977 • Liu Chia-Liang • HKG • EXECUTIONERS FROM SHAOLIN
HUNG LOU MENG • 1966 • Wang Ping • CHN • DREAM OF THE RED CHAMBER, THE (USA)
HUNG LOU MENGHSING • 1977 • Ch'lu Kang-Chien • HKG • DREAM OF THE RED CHAMBER '77
HUNG SIK LEUNG DJE CHING • 1960 • Xie Jin • CHN • RED DETACHMENT OF WOMEN, THE
HUNG TU-TZU • 1958 • Pan Lei • HKG • RED BEARD
HUNG UP see **GRABUGE, LE** • 1968
HUNG WEN-TING SAN P'O PAI LIEN CHIAO • 1980 • Lo Lieh • HKG • CLAN OF THE WHITE LOTUS
HUNG WITHOUT EVIDENCE • 1925 • Butler Alexander • UKN
HUNG YING TAO • 1976 • Chang Hsing-Yen • HKG • RED TASSELLED SWORD, THE
HUNGARIAN FAIRY TALE, A see **HOL VOLT, HOL NEM VOLT..** • 1987
HUNGARIAN GOULASH • 1930 • *Terry Paul/ Moser Frank (P)* • ANS • USA
HUNGARIAN NABOB, A see **MAGYAR NABOB -KARPATHY ZOLTAN, EGY** • 1966
HUNGARIAN NABOB, THE • 1915 • *Mailes Charles H.* • USA
HUNGARIAN NIGHTS • Janson Victor • FRG
HUNGARIAN REQUIEM • 1990 • Makk Karoly • HNG
HUNGARIAN RHAPSODY see **UNGARISCHE RHAPSODIE** • 1913
HUNGARIAN RHAPSODY see **UNGARISCHE RHAPSODIE** • 1928
HUNGARIAN RHAPSODY (USA) see **MAGYAR RAPSZODIA** • 1978
HUNGARIAN VILLAGE, A see **ISTENMEZEJEN** • 1974
HUNGARIANS ON THE PRAIRIE see **MAGYAROK A PRERIN** • 1980
HUNGARIANS (UKN) see **MAGYAROK** • 1978
HUNGARN IN FLAMMEN • 1957 • Erdelyi • DOC • HNG • REVOLT IN HUNGARY
HUNGARY TODAY • 1965 • Csoke Jozsef • DOC • HNG
HUNGER • 1932 • Hurwitz Leo T. • DOC • USA
HUNGER see **FAIM, LA** • 1973
HUNGER see **MINESTRONE, IL** • 1980
HUNGER, THE • 1982 • Scott Anthony • USA
HUNGER, DER KOCH UND DAS PARADIES, DER • 1982 • Keusch Erwin, Saurer Karl • SWT • HUNGER, THE COOK AND PARADISE
HUNGER FOR LOVE see **FOME DE AMOR** • 1968
HUNGER.. HUNGER.. HUNGER see **GOLOD.. GOLOD.. GOLOD** • 1921
HUNGER IN WALDENBURG see **UNSER TAGLICHES BROT** • 1929
HUNGER KNOWS NO LAW • 1914 • *Novak Jane* • USA
HUNGER OF THE BLOOD, THE • 1921 • Watt Nate • USA
HUNGER OF THE HEART, THE • 1913 • *Patheplay* • USA
HUNGER OF THE WORLD, THE see **FAIM DU MONDE, LA** • 1958
HUNGER PAINS • 1935 • *Granger Dorothy* • SHT • USA
HUNGER PROPHET, THE see **PROFETA DA FOME, O** • 1970
HUNGER STRAITS see **KIGA KAIGYO** • 1965
HUNGER STRIFE • 1960 • Hannah Jack • ANS • USA
HUNGER STRIKE, THE • 1913 • *B & C* • UKN • 'TWAS ONLY A DREAM
HUNGER STRIKE, THE • 1916 • *Payne Edmund* • SHT • UKN
HUNGER, THE COOK AND PARADISE see **HUNGER, DER KOCH UND DAS PARADIES, DER** • 1982
HUNGER (USA) see **SVALT** • 1966
HUNGERJAHRE • 1980 • Bruckner Jutta • FRG • YEARS OF HUNGER
HUNGERNDE MILLIONARE • 1919 • Wauer William • FRG
HUNGER'S CURSE • 1910 • Haldane Bert? • UKN
HUNGRY ACTORS, THE • 1914 • *Stewart Roy* • USA
HUNGRY BESTIALITY see **UETA JUHYOKU** • 1968
HUNGRY BOARDERS, THE • 1915 • *Aubrey James* • USA
HUNGRY COUNTRYMAN, THE see **SANDWICHES, THE** • 1899
HUNGRY DOG, THE • 1960 • Halas John • ANS • UKN
HUNGRY EYES • 1918 • Julian Rupert • USA
HUNGRY FOR LOVE see **ADUA E LE COMPAGNE** • 1960
HUNGRY FOR LOVE see **FOME DE AMOR** • 1968
HUNGRY FOR SEX (UKN) see **LIEBESSPIELE JUNGER MADCHEN** • 1972
HUNGRY GOAT, THE • 1943 • Gordon Dan • ANS • USA
HUNGRY HANK AT THE FAIR • 1915 • *Royal* • USA
HUNGRY HEART • 1988 • Acquisto Luigi • ASL
HUNGRY HEART, A • 1917 • Chautard Emile • *Peerless* • USA
HUNGRY HEART, THE • 1917 • Vignola Robert G. • *Paramount* • USA
HUNGRY HEARTS • 1911 • *Vitagraph* • USA
HUNGRY HEARTS • 1916 • *Hardy Oliver* • SHT • USA
HUNGRY HEARTS • 1922 • Hopper E. Mason • USA
HUNGRY HILL • 1947 • Hurst Brian Desmond • UKN
HUNGRY HOBOES • 1928 • Disney Walt • ANS • USA
HUNGRY I REUNION • 1981 • Cohen Thomas A. • USA
HUNGRY KOOK GOES BAZOOK • SHT • USA
HUNGRY LIONS AND TENDER HEARTS • 1920 • Del Ruth Roy, St. Clair Malcolm • SHT • USA
HUNGRY LIONS IN A HOSPITAL • 1918 • White Jack • SHT • USA
HUNGRY MAN, THE • 1970 • *Inter-Continental Film Dist.* • USA
HUNGRY MINDS • 1948 • Daly Tom • DOC • CND
HUNGRY MOTOR-CAR, THE • 1910 • *Lux* • FRN
HUNGRY PAIR, A • 1911 • *Essanay* • USA
HUNGRY PETS see **PLEASE DON'T EAT MY MOTHER!** • 1972
HUNGRY SOLDIERS, THE • 1914 • *Powers* • USA
HUNGRY SWAMP see **EHES INGOVANY** • 1989
HUNGRY WIVES see **JACK'S WIFE** • 1973
HUNGRY WOLF, THE • 1942 • Harman Hugh • ANS • USA
HUNGRY WOLVES, THE see **AC KURTLAR** • 1969
HUNGRY'S HAPPY DREAM • 1916 • Hedlund Guy • SHT • USA
HUNK • 1987 • Bassoff Lawrence • USA
HUNKY AND SPUNKY • 1938-39 • Fleischer Dave • ASS • USA
HUNKY AND SPUNKY • 1938 • Fleischer Dave • ANS • USA
HUNS, THE (USA) see **REGINA DEI TARTARI, LA** • 1960
HUNS AND HYPHENS • 1918 • Semon Larry • SHT • USA
HUNS OF THE NORTH SEA • 1914 • Morgan Sidney • UKN
HUNS WITHIN OUR GATES • 1918 • *Caine Derwent Hall* • USA • HEARTS OF MEN, THE
HUNT see **SHIKAR** • 1968
HUNT, THE • 1915 • Sterling Ford, Parrott Charles • USA
HUNT, THE • 1924 • Marshall George • SHT • USA
HUNT, THE see **JAKTEN** • 1959
HUNT, THE see **CACA, A** • 1963
HUNT, THE see **CAZA, LA** • 1965
HUNT, THE see **JAKTEN** • 1965
HUNT FOR A COLLAR, THE • 1910 • Booth W. R. • UKN
HUNT FOR RED OCTOBER, THE • 1989 • McTiernan John • USA
HUNT THE MAN DOWN • 1950 • Archainbaud George • USA • SEVEN WITNESSES
HUNT TO KILL see **WHITE BUFFALO, THE** • 1976
HUNTED • 1952 • Crichton Charles • UKN • STRANGER IN BETWEEN, THE (USA)
HUNTED • 1971 • Crane Peter • UKN
HUNTED see **JAGAD** • 1945
HUNTED see **ADHIKI KATARA** • 1968
HUNTED, THE • 1948 • Bernhard Jack • USA
HUNTED, THE see **PARANOMI, I** • 1958
HUNTED, THE see **FIGURES IN A LANDSCAPE** • 1970
HUNTED, THE see **TOUCH ME NOT** • 1973
HUNTED BY HAWKEYE • 1913 • Plumb Hay • UKN
HUNTED DOWN • 1912 • *Bison* • USA
HUNTED DOWN • 1914 • *United Artists* • USA
HUNTED IN HOLLAND • 1961 • Williams Derek • UKN
HUNTED LADY, THE • 1977 • Lang Richard • TVM • USA
HUNTED MAN, THE • 1917 • McDermott John • SHT • USA
HUNTED MEN • 1930 • McGowan J. P. • USA
HUNTED MEN • 1938 • King Louis • USA
HUNTED PEOPLE see **GEHETZTE MENSCHEN** • 1932
HUNTED THROUGH THE EVERGLADES • 1911 • Olcott Sidney • USA
HUNTED (UKN) see **VIGILANTES RIDE, THE** • 1943
HUNTED WOMAN, THE • 1916 • Drew Sidney • USA
HUNTED WOMAN, THE • 1925 • Conway Jack • USA
HUNTER • 1971 • Horn Leonard • TVM • USA
HUNTER see **LOVEC**
HUNTER, THE • 1931 • Lantz Walter, Nolan William • ANS • USA
HUNTER, THE • 1959 • Beresford Bruce • SHT • ASL
HUNTER, THE • 1979 • Kulik Buzz • USA
HUNTER BAJ • Khan A. M. • IND
HUNTER FROM LALVAR see **OKHOTNIK IZ LALVARA** • 1967
HUNTER IN THE DARK • 1979 • Gosha Hideo • JPN
HUNTER OF FORTUNES, A • 1915 • Marston Theodore • USA • FORTUNE HUNTER, A
HUNTER OF THE SUN see **TAIYO NO KARYUDO** • 1970
HUNTER OF THE UNKNOWN see **AGENTE 3S3 MASSACRO AL SOLE** • 1966
HUNTERS, THE • 1958 • Powell Dick • USA
HUNTERS, THE see **DREAMSLAYER** • 1974
HUNTERS, THE see **KINIGI, I** • 1976
HUNTERS ARE FOR KILLING • 1970 • Kowalski Bernard • TVM • USA
HUNTERS ARE THE HUNTED, THE see **JAGDSZENEN AUS NIEDERBAYERN** • 1970
HUNTER'S BLOOD • 1986 • Hughes Robert C. • USA
HUNTERS BOLD • 1924 • Roach Hal • SHT • USA
HUNTER'S CROSSING • 1985 • Page Teddy • USA
HUNTER'S DIARY, THE see **RYOJIN NIKKI** • 1964
HUNTER'S DREAM, THE • 1911 • *Kalem* • USA
HUNTERS OF THE DEEP • 1955 • *Gries Tom (P)* • DOC • USA
HUNTERS OF THE GOLDEN COBRA see **PREDATORI DEL COBRA D'ORO, I** • 1982
HUNTERS OF THE REEF • 1978 • Singer Alexander • TVM • USA
HUNTIN' TROUBLE • 1924 • Maloney Leo, Williamson Bob • USA
HUNTING • 1915 • *Ross Budd* • USA
HUNTING • 1989 • Howson Frank • ASL
HUNTING A HUSBAND • 1915 • Davis Ulysses • USA
HUNTING ACCIDENT, THE • 1978 • Lotyanu Emil • USS • SHOOTING PARTY, THE (USA)
HUNTING AFRICAN ANIMALS see **TRAILING BIG GAME IN AFRICA** • 1923
HUNTING BIG GAME IN AFRICA • 1909 • Boggs Frank • USA
HUNTING BIG GAME IN AFRICA WITH GUN AND CAMERA • 1922 • *Snow Sydney (Ph)* • DOC • USA
HUNTING FLIES see **POLOWANIE NA MUCHY** • 1969
HUNTING IN SIBERIA (USA) see **ZVEROLOVY** • 1959
HUNTING IN THE BIALOWIEZA FOREST see **POLOWANIE W BIALOWIEZY** • 1935
HUNTING KANGAROOS BY MOTOR CAR • 1916 • ASL
HUNTING OF THE HAWK, THE • 1917 • Fitzmaurice George • USA
HUNTING PARTY, THE • 1971 • Medford Don • USA, UKN
HUNTING RIFLE see **RYOJU** • 1961
HUNTING SCENE see **JACHTTAFEREEL** • 1971
HUNTING SCENES FROM BAVARIA (USA) see **JAGDSZENEN AUS NIEDERBAYERN** • 1970
HUNTING SCENES FROM LOWER BAVARIA see **JAGDSZENEN AUS NIEDERBAYERN** • 1970
HUNTING SEASON • 1982 • Kroeker Allan • CND • HAUNTING SEASON
HUNTING SEASON, THE • 1935 • Gillett Burt, Palmer Tom • ANS • USA
HUNTING THE HUNTER • 1929 • Roberts Stephen • SHT • USA
HUNTING THE RARE SNOW GOOSE • 1950 • Blais Roger • DCS • CND
HUNTING THE TEDDY BEAR see **TARTARIN DE TARASCON OU UNE CHASSE A L'OURS** • 1908
HUNTING TIGERS IN INDIA • 1929 • Dyott George M., Meehan James Leo • DOC • USA
HUNTING TIME see **AV ZAMANI** • 1987
HUNTING TROUBLE • 1933 • Horne James W. • SHT • USA
HUNTING TROUBLE see **HOLD THAT LION** • 1926
HUNTING WITH A GUN • 1930 • Oliver Bill • DOC • CND
HUNTINGTOWER • 1927 • Pearson George • UKN
HUNTRESS, THE • 1923 • Reynolds Lynn • USA
HUNTRESS OF MEN, THE • 1916 • Henderson Lucius • USA
HUNTSMAN, THE • 1920 • Blystone John G. • SHT • USA
HUNTSMAN, THE • 1972 • Jackson Douglas • CND
HUNTSMEN, THE see **KINIGI, I** • 1976
HUNZA -THE HIMALAYAN SHANGRI-LA • 1962 • Sulistrowski Zygmunt • DOC • USA

HUO LONG • 1985 • Li Han-Hsiang • CHN • LAST EMPEROR, THE
HUOSHAO YUANMINGYUAN • 1983 • Li Han-Hsiang • HKG, CHN • BURNING OF YUANMINGYUAN, THE ◦ BURNING OF THE IMPERIAL PALACE
HUR-E-BAGHDAD • 1946 • *Pande Leela* • IND
HUR TOKIGT SOM HELST • 1949 • *Svensk Talfilm* • SWD
HURACAN RAMIREZ • 1952 • Rodriguez Roberto • MXC
HURACAN RAMIREZ Y LA MONJITA • 1972 • *Cinema Roma* • MXC
HURDES, LAS • 1932 • Bunuel Luis • SPN • TIERRA SANS PAIN ◦ LAND WITHOUT BREAD ◦ UNPROMISED LAND ◦ TERRE SANS PAIN
HURDY GURDY • 1929 • McCarey Leo • SHT • USA
HURDY GURDY • 1930 • Lantz Walter, Nolan William • ANS • USA
HURDY GURDY, THE • 1958 • Sakellarios Alekos • GRC
HURDY GURDY HARE • 1950 • McKimson Robert • ANS • USA
HURLEMENTS see **SURAKH** • 1973
HURLEVENT • 1986 • Rivette Jacques • FRN • WUTHERING HEIGHTS
HURLING • 1936 • Miller David • SHT • USA
HURON CONVERTS, THE • 1915 • *Henabery Joseph* • USA
"HURONEN", DIE • 1921 • Marischka Ernst • AUS
HURONS DE LORETTE, LES • 1955 • Lavoie Hermenegilde • DCS • CND
HURRA, DIE SCHULE BRENNT • 1970 • Jacobs Werner • FRG
HURRA! DIE SCHWEDINNEN SIND DA • 1978 • Gottlieb Franz J. • FRG
HURRA -EIN JUNGE! • 1931 • Jacoby Georg • FRG
HURRA -EIN JUNGE! • 1953 • Marischka Ernst • FRG
HURRA FOR OS • 1963 • Hasselbalch Hagen • DNM • MEET THE DANES
HURRA FOR ANDERSENS • 1966 • Andersen Knut • NRW
HURRA FOR DE BLA HUSARER • 1971 • Reenberg Annelise • DNM • HURRAY FOR THE BLUE HUSSARS ◦ HUSSAR HONEYMOON
HURRA! ICH BIN PAPA • 1939 • Hoffmann Kurt • FRG • HURRAH! I'M A PAPA (USA)
HURRA-TA-TA • 1975 • Bohwim Knut • NRW
HURRA, WIR SIND MAL WIDER JUNGGESELLEN • 1971 • Philipp Harald • FRG
HURRAH FOR ADVENTURE! see **DES VACANCES EN OR** • 1969
HURRAH FOR DEATH see **VIVA LA MUERTE** • 1970
HURRAH FOR SOLDIERS, A • 1962-63 • Baillie Bruce • SHT • USA
HURRAH! ICH LIEBE! • 1928 • Thiele Wilhelm • FRG • HURRAH! I'M ALIVE! ◦ FALSCHE WITTWE, DIE
HURRAH! I'M A PAPA (USA) see **HURRA! ICH BIN PAPA** • 1939
HURRAH! I'M ALIVE! see **HURRAH! ICH LIEBE!** • 1928
HURRAY FOR BETTY BOOP • 1980 • *Dalton Dan (P)* • CMP • USA • BETTY BABY
HURRAY FOR THE BLUE HUSSARS see **HURRA FOR DE BLA HUSARER** • 1971
HURRICANE • 1930 • Ince Ralph • USA
HURRICANE • 1974 • Jameson Jerry • TVM • USA
HURRICANE • 1979 • Troell Jan • USA • FORBIDDEN PARADISE
HURRICANE see **BAOFENG-ZHOUYU** • 1961
HURRICANE see **CICLON** • 1963
HURRICANE, THE • 1926 • *Lake Alice* • USA
HURRICANE, THE • 1937 • Ford John, Heisler Stuart (U/c) • USA
HURRICANE AT PILGRIM HALL • 1953 • Bare Richard L. • USA
HURRICANE DRUMMER, THE • 1967 • *Watari Tetsuya* • JPN
HURRICANE EXPRESS • 1932 • Schaefer Armand, McGowan J. P. • USA
HURRICANE EXPRESS, THE • 1932 • Schaefer Armand, McGowan J. P. • SRL • USA
HURRICANE HAL • 1925 • Russell Bernard D. • USA
HURRICANE HORSEMAN • 1925 • Eddy Robert • USA
HURRICANE HORSEMAN • 1931 • Schaefer Armand • USA • MEXICAN, THE (UKN)
HURRICANE HUTCH • 1921 • Seitz George B. • SRL • USA
HURRICANE HUTCH IN MANY ADVENTURES • 1924 • Hutchison Charles • UKN
HURRICANE IN GALVESTON • 1913 • Vidor King (c/d) • USA
HURRICANE ISLAND • 1951 • Landers Lew • USA
HURRICANE KID, THE • 1925 • Sedgwick Edward • USA
HURRICANE RANGER, THE see **TRIPLE ACTION** • 1925
HURRICANE ROSY see **TEMPORALE ROSY** • 1979
HURRICANE SMITH • 1941 • Vorhaus Bernard • USA • DOUBLE IDENTITY
HURRICANE SMITH • 1952 • Hopper Jerry • USA
HURRICANE'S GAL • 1922 • Holubar Allen • USA
HURRIED MAN, THE (UKN) see **HOMME PRESSE, L'** • 1976
HURRY CALL, A • 1932 • Sandrich Mark • SHT • USA
HURRY, CHARLIE, HURRY • 1941 • Roberts Charles E. • USA
HURRY, DOCTOR • 1925 • *Sennett Mack (P)* • SHT • USA
HURRY DOCTOR • 1931 • Fleischer Dave • ANS • USA
HURRY, HE'S COMING see **UTEKAJME, UZ IDE** • 1988
HURRY! HURRY! • 1957 • Menken Marie • SHT • USA
HURRY, HURRY see **DEPRISA, DEPRISA** • 1980
HURRY! KURAMA! see **SHIPPU! KURAMA TENGU** • 1956
HURRY SUNDOWN • 1967 • Preminger Otto • USA
HURRY TOMORROW • 1976 • Cohen Richard, Rafferty Kevin • DOC • USA
HURRY UP OR I'LL BE 30 • 1973 • Jacoby Joseph • USA • FRIEND, THE
HURRY UP, PLEASE • 1908 • *Pathe* • FRN
HURRY WEST • 1921 • Roach Hal • SHT • USA
HURRYING ON THE WAVES see **BEGUSHCHAYA PO VOLNAM** • 1967
HURTING, THE see **PSYCHO FROM TEXAS** • 1982
HURUB SAGHIRA • 1983 • Baghdadi Marun • LBN • LITTLE WARS ◦ SMALL WARS
HURVINEK CIRCUS, THE see **CIRKUS HURVINEK** • 1955
HURVINEK'S CIRCUS see **CIRKUS HURVINEK** • 1955
HUS I HELVETE • 1974 • Stromdahl Erik • SWD • HELL OF A ROW, A
HUSAREN, HERAUS • 1937 • Jacoby Georg • FRG
HUSARENFIEBER • 1925 • Jacoby Georg • FRG
HUSARENLIEBE • 1926 • Boese Carl • FRG
HUSARENLIEBE • 1932 • Wolff Carl Heinz • FRG
HUSARENMANOVER see **IHR KORPORAL** • 1956
HUSASSISTENTEN • 1914 • Holger-Madsen • DNM • NAAR FRUEN SKIFTER PIGE
HUSBAND see **KANAVAN** • 1968
HUSBAND, THE see **GATTE, DER** • 1989
HUSBAND AND HOW TO TRAIN "IT", A • 1907 • Hough Harold • UKN
HUSBAND AND WIFE • 1916 • O'Neil Barry • USA
HUSBAND AND WIFE see **MARITO E MOGLIE** • 1952
HUSBAND AND WIFE see **FUFU** • 1953
HUSBAND AND WIFE see **PATI PATNI** • 1967
HUSBAND FOR ANNA, A see **MARITO PER ANNA ZACCHEO, UN** • 1953
HUSBAND FOR CATERINA, A see **MATRIMONIO DI CATERINA, IL** • 1982
HUSBAND FOR SALE see **KIGEKI, OTTO URIMASU** • 1968
HUSBAND FOR SUSY, A see **RANGON ALUL** • 1960
HUSBAND HUNTER • 1918 • Marshall George • SHT • USA
HUSBAND HUNTER • 1920 • Durrant Fred W. • UKN
HUSBAND HUNTER, THE • 1920 • Mitchell Howard M. • USA • MYRA MEETS HIS FAMILY
HUSBAND HUNTERS • 1927 • Adolfi John G. • USA
HUSBAND UNDER THE BED see **MAZ POD LOZKIEM** • 1967
HUSBAND WON BY ELECTION, A • 1913 • Eagle Oscar • USA
HUSBANDS • 1970 • Cassavetes John • USA
HUSBANDS AND HUMBUGS • 1918 • *Semon Lawrence* • SHT • USA
HUSBANDS AND LOVERS • 1924 • Stahl John M. • USA
HUSBANDS AND LOVERS see **HONEYMOON IN BALI** • 1939
HUSBANDS AND WIVES • 1920 • Levering Joseph • USA
HUSBANDS AND WIVES see **ZANHA-VA SHOHARHA** • 1967
HUSBANDS ARE SO JEALOUS • 1934 • Samuelson G. B. • UKN
HUSBAND'S AWAKENING, A • 1912 • Johnson Arthur • USA
HUSBAND'S AWAKENING, A • 1913 • *Lubin* • USA
HUSBANDS BEWARE • 1907 • Hough Harold • UKN
HUSBANDS BEWARE • 1956 • White Jules • SHT • USA
HUSBAND'S CHASTITY, A see **OTTO NO TEISO** • 1937
HUSBAND'S EXPERIMENT, THE • 1914 • *Ab* • USA
HUSBANDS FOR RENT • 1927 • Lehrman Henry • USA
HUSBAND'S HOLIDAY • 1931 • Milton Robert • USA
HUSBANDS IN TOWN see **MARITI IN CITTA** • 1957
HUSBAND'S JEALOUS WIFE, A • 1910 • *Thanhouser* • USA
HUSBAND'S LOVE, A • 1914 • Cooper Toby • UKN
HUSBAND'S MISTAKE, A • 1910 • *Bison* • USA
HUSBAND'S MISTAKE, A • 1913 • *Kerrigan J. Warren* • USA
HUSBANDS OR LOVERS? see **NJU** • 1924
HUSBANDS OR LOVERS (UKN) see **HONEYMOON IN BALI** • 1939
HUSBANDS' REUNION • 1933 • Marshall George • SHT • USA
HUSBAND'S SACRIFICE, A • 1910 • *Powers* • USA
HUSBAND'S TRICKS, A • 1913 • Humphrey William • USA
HUSBANDS WANTED • 1911 • *Swayne Marian* • USA
HUSBANDS WANTED • 1924 • Mayo Archie • SHT • USA
HUSBAND'S WIFE, A • 1918 • *Sunshine* • SHT • USA
HUSE TIL MENNESKER • 1972 • Roos Jorgen • DOC • DNM
HUSET I SKOGEN • 1978 • Thorstenson Espen • NRW
HUSET NR.17 • 1949 • Stevens Gosta • SWD • HOUSE NUMBER 17
HUSH • 1921 • Garson Harry • USA
HUSH-A-BYE MURDER see **MY LOVER, MY SON** • 1970
HUSH.. HUSH, SWEET CHARLOTTE • 1964 • Aldrich Robert • USA • WHAT EVER HAPPENED TO COUSIN CHARLOTTE
HUSH LITTLE BABY DON'T YOU CRY • 1984 • Hawks Don • USA
HUSH MONEY • 1921 • Maigne Charles • USA
HUSH MONEY • 1931 • Lanfield Sidney • USA
HUSH MY MOUSE • 1946 • Jones Charles M. • ANS • USA
HUSHABYE BABY • 1915 • *Coronet* • UKN
HUSHED HOUR, THE • 1920 • Mortimer Edmund • USA
HUSHING THE SCANDAL • 1915 • Henderson Dell • USA
HUSID • 1983 • Edvardsson Egill • ICL • HOUSE, THE
HUSKING BEE, THE • 1911 • *Walker Lillian* • USA
HUSKORS, ET • 1914 • Holger-Madsen • DNM • LYSTENSTYRET ◦ ENOUGH OF IT
HUSKS • 1916 • Humphrey William • SHT • USA
HUSKS OF LOVE • 1916 • Mong William V. • SHT • USA
HUSKY • 1951 • *Sovexportfilms* • ANS • USS
HUSN KA CHOR • 1953 • Wadia J. B. H. • IND
HUSSAR BALLAD, THE see **GUSARSKAYA BALLADA** • 1962
HUSSAR HONEYMOON see **HURRA FOR DE BLA HUSARER** • 1971
HUSSARDS, LES • 1955 • Joffe Alex • FRN
HUSSARDS AND GRISETTES • 1901 • Blache Alice • FRN
HUSSAR'S BALLAD see **GUSARSKAYA BALLADA** • 1962
HUSSARS OF FEHERVARI (USA) see **FEHERVARI HUSZAROK** • 1939
HUSSITE WARRIOR, THE see **JAN ZIZKA A TROCHOVA** • 1954
HUSSY • 1980 • Chapman Matthew • UKN
HUSSY, THE (USA) see **DROLESSE, LA** • 1979
HUSTINGS REVISITED, THE • 1963 • Watson Patrick • DOC • CND
HUSTLE • 1976 • Aldrich Robert • USA
HUSTLE AND HARMONY • 1917 • Kernan Henry • SHT • USA
HUSTLED WEDDING, A • 1911 • Wilson Frank? • UKN
HUSTLER, THE • 1921 • Parrott Charles, Roach Hal • SHT • USA
HUSTLER, THE • 1961 • Rossen Robert • USA
HUSTLER OF MUSCLE BEACH, THE • 1980 • Kaplan Jonathan • TVM • USA
HUSTLER SQUAD • 1976 • Gallardo Cesar Chat • PHL, USA • DIRTY HALF DOZEN
HUSTLER SQUAD see **DOLL SQUAD, THE** • 1973
HUSTLIN' HAWK • 1923 • Pembroke Percy • SHT • USA
HUSTLING • 1975 • Sargent Joseph • TVM • USA
HUSTLING ADVERTISER, A • 1909 • *Essanay* • USA
HUSTLING FOR HEALTH • 1919 • Roach Hal • SHT • USA
HUSTRU FOR EN DAG • 1933 • Rodin Gosta • SWD
HUSTRUER • 1975 • Breien Anja • NRW • WIVES
HUSTRUER TI AR ETTER • 1985 • Breien Anja • NRW • WIVES, TEN YEARS AFTER
HUSZ EVRE EGYMASTOL • 1962 • Feher Imre • HNG • TRUTH CANNOT BE HIDDEN
HUSZ ORA • 1964 • Fabri Zoltan • HNG • TWENTY HOURS (UKN)
HUSZAR A TELBEN • 1917 • Curtiz Michael • HNG
HUSZARSERELEM • 1935 • Sekely Steve • HNG
HUT see **ALOUNAK** • 1968
HUT, DER • 1965 • Herbst Helmut • FRG
HUT AB, WENN DU KUSST • 1972 • Losansky Rolf • GDR
HUT ES BRIGADIERS, DER • Brandt • GDR • HAT OF THE WORK BRIGADE LEADER, THE
HUT NO. E.W. 2106 V • 1915 • Del Zopp Rudolf • FRG
HUT ON SYCAMORE GAP, THE • 1915 • King Burton L. • USA
HUTANG DARAH • 1971 • Kadarisman S. • MLY • BLOOD DEBT
HUTCH OF THE U.S.A. • 1924 • Chapin James • USA • HUTCH -U.S.A.
HUTCH STIRS 'EM UP • 1923 • Crane Frank H. • UKN
HUTCH -U.S.A. see **HUTCH OF THE U.S.A.** • 1924
HUTET EUCH VOR LEICHTEN FRAUEN • 1929 • Philippi Siegfried • FRG
HUTET EURE TOCHTER • 1922 • Goldin Sidney M. • AUS
HUTET EURE TOCHTER • 1962 • Houwer Rob, Hart Wolf, Schedereit Karl, Kruttner Walter, Blackwood Michael, Spieker Franz-Josef, Hauff Eberhard • FRG • GELBE WAGEN, DER ◦ ZEHNTAUSEND
HUTTE D'ACAJOU, LA • 1926 • Vorins Henri • FRN
HUTTERITES, THE • 1963 • Low Colin • DOC • CND
HUUH HUUH • 1965 • Le Bon Patrick • SHT • NTH
HUYENDO DE SI MISMO • 1953 • Fortuny Juan • SPN
HUYENDO DEL SISMO • 1970 • Plasencia Arturo • VNZ • ESCAPING FROM THE EARTHQUAKE
HVAD ER I BANGE FOR? see **ER I BANGE?** • 1971
HVAD MED OS? • 1963 • Carlsen Henning • DNM • EPILOGUE (USA) ◦ HOW ABOUT US?
HVAD VIL DE HA? • 1956 • Henrickson Jens, Neergaard Preben • DNM
HVEM EIER TYSSEDAL • 1976 • Skagen Solve, Wadman Malte • DOC • NRW • WHO OWNS TYSSEDAL?
HVEM ER GENTLEMANTYVEN • 1915 • Holger-Madsen • DNM • STRAKOFF THE ADVENTURER
HVEM ER HAN? see **ENSOM KVINDE, EN** • 1914
HVEM HAR BESTEMT..? • 1978 • Vennerod Petter, Wam Svend • NRW • SAYS WHO?
HVEM MYRDER HVEM • 1977 • Vilstrup Li • DNM • WHO'S MURDERING WHOM?
HVEM VAR FORBRYDEREN? • 1912 • Blom August • DNM • SAMVITTIGHEDSNAG ◦ AT THE 11TH HOUR
HVER ER..? • 1983 • Gunnlaugsson Hrafn • ICL
HVERT SYVENDE SEKUND • 1948 • Holst Per • DNM
HVEZDA • 1969 • Hanibal Jiri • CZC • STAR, THE
HVEZDA BETLEMSKA • 1969 • Tyrlova Hermina • ANS • CZC • STAR OF BETHLEHEM, THE
HVEZDA JEDE NA JIH • 1957 • Lipsky Oldrich • CZC • STAR GOES SOUTH, THE
HVEZDA Z POSLEDNI STACE • 1939 • Slavicek Jiri • CZC • STAR OF THE ONE-NIGHT STANDS, THE
HVEZDA ZVANA PELYNEK • 1964 • Fric Martin • CZC • STAR NAMED WORMWOOD, A
HVIDE DAME, DEN • 1913 • Holger-Madsen • DNM • WHITE GHOST, THE
HVIDE DJOEVEL, DEN • 1916 • Holger-Madsen • DNM • DJOEVELENS PROTEGE ◦ DEVIL'S PROTEGE, THE ◦ WHITE DEVIL, THE ◦ CAUGHT IN THE TOILS
HVIDE HINGST, DEN • 1962 • Watt Harry • DNM • BOY WHO LOVED HORSES, THE
HVIDE SLAVEHANDEL I, DEN • 1910 • Blom August • DNM • WHITE SLAVE, THE
HVIDE SLAVEHANDEL II, DEN • 1911 • Blom August • DNM • IN THE HANDS OF IMPOSTORS
HVIDE SLAVEHANDEL III, DEN • 1912 • Gad Urban • DNM • BERYGTEDE HUS, DET ◦ NINA ◦ NINA, IN THE HANDS OF THE IMPOSTORS
HVIDE SLAVEHANDES, DET • 1907 • Larsen Viggo • DNM
HVIDE SLAVEHANDES SIDSTOFFER, DEN • 1910 • Lind Alfred • DNM
HVIS LILLE PIGE ER DU? • 1963 • Balling Erik • DNM • WHOSE LITTLE GIRL ARE YOU?
HVITT LANDSKAP • 1984 • Lepre Gianni • NRW • LANDSCAPE IN WHITE
HVO SOM ELSKER SIN FADER • 1915 • Holger-Madsen • DNM • WHO SO LOVETH HIS FATHER'S HONOR ◦ FAKLEN
HVOR BJERGENE SEJLER • 1954 • Henning-Jensen Bjarne • DOC • DNM • IN THE COUNTRY OF ICEBERGS ◦ WHERE MOUNTAINS FLOAT ◦ GRONLANDSFILMEN
HVOR ER DE TYSKE STUDENTER? • 1960 • Mertz Albert • DNM
HVOR ER LIGET, MOLLER? • 1970 • Kaas Preben • DNM
HVOR ER MAGTEN BLEVET AR? • 1968 • Carlsen Henning • DNM
HVOR SORGERNE GLEMMES • 1916 • Holger-Madsen • DNM • SOSTER CECILIES OFFER ◦ SISTER CECILIA
HVOR VEJENE MODES • 1948 • Hasselbalch Hagen • DNM
HVORDAN DET VIDERE GIK DEN GRIMME AELLING • 1981 • Hastrup Jannik • ANM • DNM • FURTHER ADVENTURES OF THE UGLY DUCKLING, THE
HVORFOR GOR DE DET? • 1970 • Kronhausen Phyllis, Kronhausen Eberhard • DNM
HVORLEDES DR. NICOLA ERHVERVEDE DEN KINESISKE STOK see **DR. NICOLA** • 1909
HWA NYEO CHON • 1985 • Kim Gi • SKR • FIRE WOMAN VILLAGE
HY MAKER'S SKITS 'N' SKETCHES • 1936 • *Universal* • SHT • USA
HY RUTABAGA • 1973 • Pojar Bretislav • ANM • CZC
HYAKUMAN-NIN NO MUSUMETACHI • 1963 • Gosho Heinosuke • JPN • MILLION GIRLS, A
HYAKUMAN-RYO NO TSUBO • 1935 • Yamanaka Sadao • JPN • MILLION RYO MONEY POT, THE
HYANEN DER LUST see **WEG, DER ZUR VERDAMMNIS FUHRT 2, DER** • 1919
HYANEN DER NACHT • 1924 • *Bob Gotz-Film* • FRG
HYANEN DER WELT 1 • 1921 • Stranz Fred • FRG • OPFER DER HYANEN

HYANEN DER WELT 2 • 1921 • Stranz Fred • FRG • EINSAME INSEL, DIE
HYAPPATSU HYAKUCHU • 1968 • Fukuda Jun • JPN • BOOTED BABE, BUSTED BOSS ○ OOGON NO ME
HYAS, LE • 1929 • Painleve Jean • SHT • FRN
HYBRID • 1967 • Chambers Jack* • DOC • CND
HYBRID see **JENA IN CASSAFORTE, UNA** • 1967
HYDE AND GO TWEET • 1960 • Freleng Friz • ANS • USA
HYDE AND HARE • 1955 • Freleng Friz • ANS • USA
HYDE AND SNEAK • 1962 • Smith Paul J. • ANS • USA
HYDE PARK • 1934 • Faye Randall • UKN
HYDE PARK CORNER • 1935 • Hill Sinclair • UKN
HYDE SISTERS, THE • 1928 • *British Sound Film Prod.* • SHT • UKN • MUSICAL MEDLEY NO.3
HYDRA • 1936 • Hewer H. R. • UKN
HYDRAULICS • 1940 • Elton Ralph • UKN
HYDRO, THE • 1920 • Sandground Maurice • UKN
HYDROCEPHALES, LES • 1965 • Stephane Nicole • FRN
HYDROTHERAPIE FANTASTIQUE • 1909 • Melies Georges • FRN • DOCTOR'S SECRET, THE (USA) ○ SECRET DU MEDECIN, LE ○ SECRET DU DOCTEUR, LE
HYENA IN THE STRONG-BOX, A see **JENA IN CASSAFORTE, UNA** • 1967
HYENA OF LONDON, THE see **JENA DI LONDRA, LA** • 1964
HYENA'S LAUGH • 1927 • Lantz Walter, Geronimi Clyde • ANS • USA
HYENA'S SUN see **SHAMS WA ADH-DHIBA, ASH-** • 1976
HYGEIA AT THE SOLITO • 1917 • Smith David • SHT • USA
HYGIENE IS HALF HEALTH • Pogacnik Joze • DCS • YGS
HYIUCH HAGDI • 1985 • Dotan Shimon • ISR • SMILE OF THE LAMB, THE
HYMENEE • 1946 • Couzinet Emile • FRN
HYMN IN PRAISE OF THE SUN • 1960 • Jordan Larry • SHT • USA
HYMN OF ENERGY, THE see **HOHELIED DER KRAFT, DAS** • 1930
HYMN OF PEACE, THE see **HYMNE DE PAIX** • 1966
HYMN OF THE NATIONS see **HYMN TO THE NATIONS** • 1946
HYMN TO A TIRED MAN see **NIHON NO SEISHUN** • 1968
HYMN TO HER • 1974 • Brakhage Stan • USA
HYMN TO THE NATIONS • 1946 • Hammid Alexander • DOC • USA • TOSCANINI: HYMN TO THE NATIONS ○ HYMN OF THE NATIONS
HYMNE DE PAIX • 1966 • Marzouk Said • SHT • EGY • HYMN OF PEACE, THE
HYOHEKI • 1958 • Masumura Yasuzo • JPN • PRECIPICE, THE
HYOKKORI HYOTAN JIMA • 1967 • Yabushita Taiji • ANM • JPN • GREAT ADVENTURES ON BOTTLE-GOURD ISLAND ○ MADCAP ISLAND, THE
HYORAKU YUME MONOGATARI • 1943 • *Tsuburaya Eiji (Ph)* • JPN
HYORYU • 1982 • Moritani Shiro • JPN • WRECKAGE
HYORYU SHITAI • 1959 • Sekigawa Hideo • JPN • DEAD DRIFTER, A
HYOTAN SUZUME • 1957 • Yokoyama Ryuichi • ANM • JPN • SPARROW IN A GOURD, THE
HYOTEN • 1966 • Yamamoto Satsuo • JPN • FREEZING POINT
HYP-NUT-TIST, THE • 1935 • Fleischer Dave • ANS • USA
HYPER AUTO EROTIC ART HAYASHI • Borowczyk Walerian • FRN
HYPER SAPIEN: PEOPLE FROM ANOTHER STAR • 1986 • Hunt Peter • UKN, CND
HYPERBOLOID OF ENGINEER GARIN, THE see **GIPERBOLOID INGENERA GARINA** • 1965
HYPERION • 1973 • Veroiu Mircea • RMN
HYPERSPACE see **GREMLOIDS** • 1986
HYPNO AND TRANCE • 1915 • Ransom Charles • USA
HYPNOS (SPN) see **HIPNOS FOLLIA DI UN MASSACRO** • 1967
HYPNOSE • 1919 • *Hanussen Eric Jan* • FRG
HYPNOSIS (USA) see **NUR TOTE ZEUGEN SCHWEIGEN** • 1963
HYPNOTIC CHAIR, THE • 1912 • *Majestic* • USA
HYPNOTIC COLLECTOR, THE • 1913 • *Pilot* • USA
HYPNOTIC CURE, THE • 1909 • *Lubin* • USA
HYPNOTIC DETECTIVE, THE • 1912 • *Selig* • USA
HYPNOTIC EYE, THE • 1960 • Blair George • USA
HYPNOTIC EYES • 1933 • *Terry Paul/ Moser Frank (P)* • ANS • USA
HYPNOTIC HICK • 1953 • Patterson Don • ANS • USA
HYPNOTIC MONKEY, THE • 1915 • Santell Alfred • SHT • USA
HYPNOTIC NELL • 1912 • *Roland Ruth* • USA
HYPNOTIC PORTRAIT, THE • 1922 • Graeme Kenneth • UKN
HYPNOTIC POWER • 1914 • *Sterling Ford* • USA
HYPNOTIC SPRAY, THE • 1909 • *Gaumont* • UKN
HYPNOTIC SUGGESTION • 1909 • Aylott Dave • UKN
HYPNOTIC VIOLINIST, THE • 1914 • *Warner'S Features* • SHT • USA
HYPNOTIC WIFE, THE • 1909 • *Pathe* • FRN
HYPNOTISED • 1933 • Sennett Mack • USA
HYPNOTISEUR, DER • 1914 • Fleck Luise, Fleck Jacob • AUS • SVENGALI
HYPNOTISING THE HYPNOTIST see **HYPNOTIST, THE** • 1911
HYPNOTISM • 1910 • *Lux* • FRN
HYPNOTISM IN HICKVILLE • 1913 • *Carney Augustus* • USA
HYPNOTIST, THE • 1911 • *Turner Florence* • USA • HYPNOTISING THE HYPNOTIST
HYPNOTIST, THE • 1912 • *Lubin* • USA
HYPNOTIST, THE • 1921 • Fleischer Dave • ANS • USA
HYPNOTIST, THE • 1957 • Tully Montgomery • UKN • SCOTLAND YARD DRAGNET (USA)
HYPNOTIST, THE • 1960 • *Halas John (P)* • ANS • UKN
HYPNOTIST, THE (UKN) see **LONDON AFTER MIDNIGHT** • 1927
HYPNOTIST AND THE CONVICT, THE • 1911 • Bouwmeester Theo?, Booth W. R.? • UKN
HYPNOTIST AT WORK, A see **MAGNETISEUR, LE** • 1897
HYPNOTIST'S JOKE, THE • 1908 • Cooper Arthur? • UKN
HYPNOTIST'S REVENGE, THE • 1907 • *Biograph* • USA
HYPNOTIST'S REVENGE, THE • 1909 • Melies Georges • FRN
HYPNOTIZED • 1910 • *Thanhouser* • USA
HYPNOTIZED • 1912 • *Duncan William* • USA
HYPNOTIZED • 1913 • *Crystal* • USA
HYPNOTIZED • 1932 • Sennett Mack • USA
HYPNOTIZED • 1952 • Davis Mannie • ANS • USA
HYPNOTIZING A HYPNOTIST • 1911 • *Farley Dot* • USA
HYPNOTIZING MAMIE • 1913 • *Roland Ruth* • USA
HYPO-CHONDRI-CAT • 1950 • Jones Charles M. • ANS • USA
HYPOCHONDRIAC, THE • 1917 • Drew Sidney, Drew Sidney Mrs. • SHT • USA
HYPOCRISY • 1916 • Buel Kenean • USA
HYPOCRITE, THE • 1913 • *Moore Owen* • USA
HYPOCRITE, THE • 1921 • Micheaux Oscar • USA
HYPOCRITE, THE see **HELL-BENT FOR HEAVEN** • 1926
HYPOCRITES • 1915 • Weber Lois • USA
HYPOCRITES, THE • 1916 • Tucker George Loane • UKN • MORALS OF WEYBURY, THE
HYPOCRITES, THE • 1923 • Giblyn Charles • UKN
HYPOTHEFE BETA • 1967 • Meunier Jean-Charles • ANS • FRN • HYPOTHESIS BETA
HYPOTHERMIA • 1984 • Nicolle Douglas • DOC • CND
HYPOTHESE DU TABLEAU VOLE, L' see **HIPOTESIS DEL CUADRO ROBADO** • 1978
HYPOTHESIS see **HYPOTHEZY** • 1963
HYPOTHESIS see **HIPOTEZA** • 1972
HYPOTHESIS BETA see **HYPOTHEFE BETA** • 1967
HYPOTHESIS OF A STOLEN PAINTING see **HIPOTESIS DEL CUADRO ROBADO** • 1978
HYPOTHESIS OF THE STOLEN PAINTING see **HIPOTESIS DEL CUADRO ROBADO** • 1978
HYPOTHEZY • 1963 • Silhan Vladimir • SHT • CZC • HYPOTHESIS
HYPPOLIT A LAKAJ • 1931 • Sekely Steve • HNG
HYSTERIA • 1964 • Francis Freddie • UKN
HYSTERICAL • 1982 • Bearde Chris • USA
HYSTERICAL HIGHSPOTS IN AMERICAN HISTORY • 1941 • Lantz Walter • ANS • USA
HYSTERICAL HISTORY • 1953 • Kneitel Seymour • ANS • USA

I

I see **JAG** • 1966
I -A GROUPIE see **ICH -EIN GROUPIE** • 1970
I, A LOVER (USA) see **JEG -EN ELSKER** • 1966
I, A MAN • 1967 • Warhol Andy • USA
I A MARQUIS see **JEG -EN MARKI** • 1967
I, A NEGRO (UKN) see **MOI, UN NOIR** • 1957
I, A NOBLEMAN (USA) see **JEG -EN MARKI** • 1967
I, A PUSSY • 1970 • *Able Film Co.* • USA
I A VIRGIN see **BADARNA** • 1968
I A VIRGIN see **JAG EN OSKULD** • 1968
I -A WOMAN see **JAG -EN KVINNA (I)** • 1965
I, A WOMAN -3 see **TRE SLAGS KAERLIGHED** • 1970
I -A WOMAN (II) see **JAG -EN KVINNA (II)** • 1968
I -A WOMAN PART TWO: MARRIAGE see **JAG -EN KVINNA (II)** • 1968
I ACCUSE • 1916 • Haddock William F. • USA
I ACCUSE! • 1958 • Ferrer Jose • UKN
I ACCUSE see **J'ACCUSE** • 1919
I ACCUSE MY PARENTS • 1944 • Newfield Sam • USA
I ACCUSE (UKN) see **J'ACCUSE** • 1937
I ACCUSE (UKN) see **LIFE OF EMILE ZOLA, THE** • 1937
I ADORE YOU • 1933 • King George • UKN
I, AGAINST SOCIETY see **AKO LABAN SA LIPUNAN** • 1967
I AIM AT THE STARS • 1960 • Thompson J. Lee • UKN
I AIN'T GOT NOBODY • 1932 • Fleischer Dave • ANS • USA
I AIN'T NO BUFFALO see **GUESS WHAT WE LEARNED IN SCHOOL TODAY?** • 1970
I AM A CAMERA • 1955 • Cornelius Henry • UKN
I AM A CAT see **WAGAHAI WA NEKO DE ARU** • 1936
I AM A CAT see **WAGAHAI WA NEKO DEARU** • 1974
I AM A CRIMINAL • 1938 • Nigh William • USA
I AM A CRIMINAL see **SOY UN DELINCUENTE** • 1976
I AM A DANCER (UKN) see **DANSEUR: RUDOLPH NUREYEV, UN** • 1972
I AM A DETECTIVE • 1972 • Kalatozishvili Georgi • USS
I AM A FUGITIVE see **I AM A FUGITIVE FROM A CHAIN GANG** • 1932
I AM A FUGITIVE FROM A CHAIN GANG • 1932 • LeRoy Mervyn • USA • I AM A FUGITIVE
I AM A FUGITIVE FROM A WHITE SLAVE GANG (UKN) see **TRAITE DES BLANCHES, LA** • 1965
I AM A GIRL WITH THE DEVIL IN MY BODY see **JSEM DEVCE S CERTEM V TELE** • 1933
I AM A LITTER BASKET • 1959 • Ritchie James • UKN
I AM A NYMPHOMANIAC see **JE SUIS UNE NYMPHOMANE** • 1971
I AM A SOLDIER, MOTHER see **YA SOLDAT, MAMA** • 1967
I AM A SON OF AMERICA.. AND I'M INDEBTED TO IT see **DE AMERICA SOY HIJO.. Y A ELLA ME DEBO** • 1972
I AM A THIEF • 1935 • Florey Robert • USA
I AM A WOMAN III see **TRE SLAGS KAERLIGHED** • 1970
I AM AFRAID (USA) see **IO HO PAURA** • 1977
I AM ALLADIN see **MAIN HOON ALLADIN** • 1965
I AM AN ANTISTAR see **ICH BIN EIN ANTISTAR** • 1976
I AM AN E.S.P. see **SONO UN FENOMENO PARANORMALE** • 1985
I AM AN OLD TREE • 1975 • Rubbo Michael • CND
I AM ANNA MAGNANI see **IO SONO ANNA MAGNANI** • 1979
I AM AVAILABLE (UKN) see **DESAXEES, LES** • 1972
I AM BLUSHING see **JAG RODNAR** • 1980
I AM CHICANO AND A SEEKER OF JUSTICE see **SOY CHICANO Y JUSTICIERO** • 1974
I AM CHICANO AND MEXICAN see **SOY CHICANO Y MEXICANO** • 1974
I AM CUBA see **YA -KUBA** • 1962
I AM CURIOUS -BLUE see **JAG AR NYFIKEN -BLA** • 1968
I AM CURIOUS -TAHITI • 1970 • Tobalina Carlos • USA
I AM CURIOUS -YELLOW (UKN) see **JAG AR NYFIKEN -GUL** • 1967
I AM DREAMING OF MUSIC • 1986 • Koulev Henri • DOC • BUL
I AM FIRE AND ICE see **JAG AR ELD OCH LUFT** • 1944
I AM FOR EXCITEMENT see **I AM FOR SALE** • 1968
I AM FOR SALE • 1968 • *Barr Andrea* • USA • I AM FOR EXCITEMENT
I AM FORTUNATE see **NANE BHAGYAVATHI** • 1968
I AM FRIGID.. WHY? (UKN) see **JE SUIS FRIGIDE.. POURQUOI?** • 1972
I AM FURIOUS • 1969 • Patrick Alain • USA • JE SUIS FURIEUX
I AM GUILTY • 1921 • Nelson Jack • USA
I AM HERE • 1972 • Fujieda Ryuji • ANS • JPN
I AM HIS FIANCEE • 1970 • Trakhtenberg Naum • USS • I'M HIS FIANCEE
I AM INDISPENSABLE see **NENANTE NENE** • 1968
I AM LEGEND see **OMEGA MAN, THE** • 1971
I AM LIVING (UKN) see **MAIN ZINDA HOON** • 1988
I AM LONELY see **KIMSESIZIM** • 1967
I AM MARIA see **JAG AR MARIA** • 1979
I AM NOT AFRAID • 1939 • Wilbur Crane • USA
I AM NOT MYSELF see **JA NEJSEM JA** • 1985
I AM ON FIRE see **JA GORE** • 1967
I AM PHOTOGENIC see **SONO FOTOGENICO** • 1980
I AM SANDRA see **SANDRA -THE MAKING OF A WOMAN** • 1970
I AM SARTANA: YOUR ANGEL OF DEATH see **SONO SARTANA IL VOSTRO BECCHINO** • 1969
I AM SEBASTIAN OTT (USA) see **ICH BIN SEBASTIAN OTT** • 1939
I AM SEXY see **TENTATIONS DE MARIANNE, LES** • 1972
I AM SNUB-NOSED BUT I CAN SMELL (USA) see **SOY CHATO, PERO LAS HUELO** • 1939
I AM SOMEBODY • Barke Lothar • ANS • GDR
I AM SORRY see **SUTFONGDIK NUIYAN** • 1989
I AM SUZANNE • 1934 • Lee Rowland V. • USA
I AM THE CHEESE • 1983 • Jiras Robert • USA
I AM THE COMPETENT see **NENE MONAGANNI** • 1968
I AM THE LAW • 1922 • Carewe Edwin • USA
I AM THE LAW • 1938 • Hall Alexander • USA • OUTSIDE THE LAW
I AM THE LAW see **PREFETTO DI FERRO, IL** • 1977
I AM THE MAN • 1924 • Abramson Ivan • USA
I AM THE ONE see **MAIN WOHI HOON** • 1967
I AM THE WALRUS • Ostrow Philip • SHT
I AM THE WOMAN • 1921 • Ford Francis • USA
I AM TIEN-SHAN • 1972 • Poplavskaya Irina • USS
I AM TOKICHIRO see **BAKU WA TOUKICHIROH** • 1955
I AM TWENTY see **MNE DVADTSAT LET** • 1961-63
I AM TWENTY YEARS OLD see **MNE DVADTSAT LET** • 1961-63
I AM TWO YEARS OLD see **WATASHI WA NISAI** • 1962
I AM WITH YOU see **JAG AR MED EDER..** • 1948
I AND MY LOVE see **GALIA** • 1966
I, AND MY LOVERS see **GALIA** • 1966
I AS IN ICARUS see **I.. COMME ICARE** • 1979
I ASK FOR THE FLOOR see **JA PRASU SLOVA** • 1975
I BECAME A CRIMINAL (USA) see **THEY MADE ME A FUGITIVE** • 1947
I BEDZIE MIAL DOM • 1978 • Petelski Czeslaw, Petelska Ewa • PLN • WE WILL HAVE A HOME
I BEHELD HIS GLORY • 1952 • Coyle John T. • USA
I BELIEVE • 1918 • *Cosmofotofilm* • USA
I BELIEVE see **MAN WITHOUT A SOUL, THE** • 1916
I BELIEVE IN YOU • 1952 • Dearden Basil, Relph Michael • UKN
I BELIEVED IN YOU • 1934 • Cummings Irving • USA • DISILLUSION
I BOG STVOTI KAFANSKU PEVACICU • 1972 • Zivanovic Jovan • YGS • AND GOD CREATED THE CAFE SINGER
I BOMBED PEARL HARBOR (USA) see **TAIHEIYO NO ARASHI** • 1960
I BRIST PA BEVIS • 1943 • Frisk Ragnar • SWD • LACK OF EVIDENCE
I BURY THE LIVING • 1958 • Band Albert • USA
I CALL FIRST see **WHO'S THAT KNOCKING AT MY DOOR?** • 1967
I CAME A STRANGER see **FREMD BIN ICH EINGEZOGEN** • 1978
I CAN EXPLAIN • 1922 • Baker George D. • USA • STAY HOME
I CAN GET IT FOR YOU WHOLESALE • 1951 • Gordon Michael • USA • THIS IS MY AFFAIR (UKN) ○ ONLY THE BEST
I CAN HARDLY WAIT • 1943 • White Jules • SHT • USA
I CANNOT LIVE WITHOUT YOU see **SENSIZ YASAYAMAM** • 1980
I CANNOT SAY THAT PERSON'S NAME see **SONO HITO NO NA WA IENAI** • 1951
I CAN'T ESCAPE FROM YOU • 1936 • Fleischer Dave • ANS • USA
I CAN'T FORGIVE YOU see **SENI AFFEDEMEN** • 1967
I CAN'T GET STARTED • 1986 • Fisher Rodney • TVM • ASL
I CAN'T GIVE YOU ANYTHING BUT LOVE • 1929 • Aylott Dave, Symmons E. F. • SHT • UKN
I CAN'T GIVE YOU ANYTHING BUT LOVE, BABY • 1940 • Rogell Albert S. • USA
I CAN'T.. I CAN'T • 1969 • Haggard Piers • IRL • WEDDING NIGHT (USA)
I CAN'T READ ENGLISH • 1908 • *Essanay* • USA
I CAN'T REMEMBER • 1949 • Yates Hal • SHT • USA
I CARRY THE WORLD see **PASAN KO ANG DAIGDIG** • 1988
I CHANGED MY SEX see **GLEN OR GLENDA?** • 1952
I CHEATED THE LAW • 1949 • Cahn Edward L. • USA
I CLAUDIUS • 1937 • von Sternberg Josef • UKN
I COLORADOS see **COLORADOS, I** • 1967
I COMMAND THE PARADE see **PREHLIDCE VELIM JA** • 1969
I.. COMME ICARE • 1979 • Verneuil Henri • FRN • I AS IN ICARUS
I CONFESS • 1953 • Hitchcock Alfred • USA
I CONFESS • 1988 • Ron Zohara • ISR
I CONQUER THE SEA • 1936 • Halperin Victor Hugo • USA
I COULD GO ON SINGING • 1962 • Neame Ronald • UKN • LONELY STAGE, THE
I COULD NEVER HAVE SEX WITH ANY MAN WHO HAS SO LITTLE REGARD FOR MY HUSBAND • 1973 • McCarty Robert • USA
I COVER BIG TOWN • 1947 • Thomas William C. • USA • I COVER THE UNDERWORLD
I COVER CHINATOWN • 1936 • Foster Norman • USA

I COVER THE UNDERWORLD • 1955 • Springsteen R. G. • USA
I COVER THE UNDERWORLD see **I COVER BIG TOWN** • 1947
I COVER THE WAR • 1937 • Lubin Arthur • USA
I COVER THE WATERFRONT • 1933 • Cruze James • USA • FRISCO WATERFRONT
I CRAVE YOU BODY • 1961 • Lutz Abe • USA • I CRAVE YOUR..
I CRAVE YOUR.. see **I CRAVE YOU BODY** • 1961
I CRIED TOO see **MAN HAM GERYE KARDAM** • 1968
I CROSSED THE COLOR LINE see **BLACK KLANSMAN, THE** • 1966
I DAG BORJAR LIVET • 1939 • Bauman Schamyl • SWD • LIFE BEGINS TODAY
I DAG GIFTER SIG MIN MAN • 1943 • Arvedson Ragnar • SWD • MY HUSBAND IS GETTING MARRIED TODAY
I DEAL IN DANGER • 1966 • Grauman Walter • MTV • USA
I DEMAND PAYMENT • 1938 • Sanforth Clifford • USA
I DEN GRONNE SKOV • 1968 • Kjaerulff-Schmidt Palle • DNM • IN A GREEN FOREST ○ IN A GREEN WOOD
I DEN STORE PYRAMIDE • 1974 • Roos Jorgen • DOC • DNM • INSIDE THE GREAT PYRAMID
I, DESIRE • 1982 • Moxey John Llewellyn • TVM • USA
I DID IT! see **SONO STATO IO!** • 1937
I DID IT, MAMA • 1909 • Griffith D. W. • USA
I DID LIVE BUT.. see **IKITEWA MITAKEREDO** • 1984
I DID NOT KILL BOB NEVILLE • 1978 • Zaritsky John • MTV • CND
I DID NOT LIVE LONG see **NIE POZYLEM DLUGO** • 1967
I DIDN'T DO IT • 1945 • Varnel Marcel • UKN
I DIED A THOUSAND TIMES • 1955 • Heisler Stuart • USA • JAGGED EDGE
I DIED A THOUSAND TIMES see **STEEL JUNGLE, THE** • 1956
I DIMMA DOLD • 1953 • Kjellgren Lars-Eric • SWD • HIDDEN IN THE FOG
I DIN FARS LOMME • 1972 • Roos Lise • DNM • IN YOUR DAD'S POCKET ○ IN DADDY'S POCKET
I DISCOVERED HEAVEN see **NAAN KANDA SWARGAM** • 1960
I DISMEMBER MAMA • 1972 • Leder Paul • USA • POOR ALBERT AND LITTLE ANNIE ○ CRAZED
I DISSENT • 1969 • Boyadgieva Lada • BUL
I DLA WAS SWIECI SLONCE • 1956 • Poreba Bohdan • DOC • PLN • SUN SHINES FOR YOU TOO, THE
I DO • 1921 • Newmeyer Fred, Taylor Sam • SHT • USA
I DO see **WE WHO ARE YOUNG** • 1940
I DO! see **MENG** • 1984
I DO LIKE A JOKE • 1916 • Wilson Frank • UKN
I DO LIKE TO BE BESIDE THE SEASIDE • 1925 • Butler Alexander • UKN
I DO VOODOO • 1970 • *Stacey Dist.* • USA
I DO WHAT I LIKE • 1969 • Szemes Marianne • DOC • HNG
I DO WHAT I WILL see **JEG ER SGU' MIN EGEN** • 1967
I DODENS VANTRUM • 1946 • Ekman Hasse • SWD • IN DEATH'S WAITING ROOM ○ INTERLUDE
I DODJE PROPAST SVETA • 1969 • Petrovic Aleksandar • YGS • BICE SKORO PROPAST SVETA ○ IT RAINS IN MY VILLAGE
I DOIDE DENYAT see **I DOYDE DENYAT** • 1974
I DON'T CARE GIRL, THE • 1952 • Bacon Lloyd • USA
I DON'T CARE IF THERE'S A GIRL THERE • 1909 • *Warwick Trading Co.* • UKN
I DON'T GIVE A DAMN see **DON'T GIVE A DAMN** • 1987
I DON'T KNOW YOU, BUT I LOVE YOU (USA) see **ICH KENN' DICH NICHT UND LIEBE DICH** • 1933
I DON'T LIKE MONDAYS see **NIE LUBIE PONIEDZIALKU** • 1971
I DON'T PROTEST, I LOVE see **IO NON PROTESTO, IO AMO** • 1967
I DON'T REMEMBER • 1935 • Black Preston • SHT • USA
I DON'T SCARE • 1956 • Sparber I. • ANS • USA
I DON'T SELL MY HEART see **DHEN POULAO TIN KARDIA MOU** • 1967
I DON'T THINK! • 1914 • *B & C* • UKN
I DON'T THINK IT'S MEANT FOR US • 1971 • Shannon Kathleen • DOC • CND
I DON'T UNDERSTAND YOU ANYMORE • 1980 • Corbucci Sergio • ITL
I DON'T WANT TO BE A MAN see **ICH MOCHTE KEIN MANN SEIN** • 1919
I DON'T WANT TO BE BORN • 1975 • Sasdy Peter • UKN • DEVIL WITHIN HER, THE (USA) ○ IT LIVES WITHIN HER ○ MONSTER, THE ○ BABY, THE ○ SHARON'S BABY
I DON'T WANT TO GET MARRIED see **NU VREAU SA MA INSOR** • 1960
I DON'T WANT TO HEAR ANYTHING see **NECHNI NIC STYSET** • 1978
I DON'T WANT TO MAKE HISTORY • 1936 • Fleischer Dave • ANS • USA
I DOOD IT • 1943 • Minnelli Vincente • USA • BY HOOK OR BY CROOK (UKN)
I DOYDE DENYAT • 1974 • Dyulgerov Georgi • BLG • THERE CAME THE DAY ○ AND THE DAY CAME ○ I DOIDE DENYAT
I DREAM ABOUT COLOURS see **SZINES TINTAKROL ALMODOM** • 1981
I DREAM OF JEANNE • 1970 • Marquez Artemio • PHL
I DREAM OF JEANNIE • 1952 • Dwan Allan • USA • I DREAM OF JEANNIE WITH THE LIGHT BROWN HAIR
I DREAM OF JEANNIE: 15 YEARS LATER • 1985 • Asher William • TVM • USA
I DREAM OF JEANNIE WITH THE LIGHT BROWN HAIR • 1940 • Ceballos Larry • SHT • USA
I DREAM OF JEANNIE WITH THE LIGHT BROWN HAIR see **I DREAM OF JEANNIE** • 1952
I DREAM TOO MUCH • 1935 • Cromwell John • USA
I DREAMED OF YOU see **ICH HAB' VON DIR GETRAUMT** • 1944
I DREAMT I DWELT IN HARLEM • 1941 • Snody Robert R. • SHT • USA
I DRINK YOUR BLOOD • 1970 • Durston David E. • USA
I DUR OCH SKUR • 1953 • Olin Stig • SWD • IN MAJOR AND SHOWERS
I EAT CANNIBALS • 1987 • Nicolaou Ted • USA
I EAT YOUR SKIN • 1964 • Tenney Del • USA • VOODOO BLOOD BATH ○ ZOMBIES
I EATS MY SPINACH • 1933 • Fleischer Dave • ANS • USA
I ELFTE TIMMEN • 1916 • Magnussen Fritz • SWD • AT THE ELEVENTH HOUR
I ENTRUST MY WIFE TO YOU (USA) see **RAD BIZOM A FELESEGEM** • 1939
I ESCAPED FROM DEVIL'S ISLAND • 1973 • Witney William • USA, MXC • ESCAPE DE LA ISLA DEL DIABLO (MXC)
I ESCAPED FROM THE GESTAPO • 1943 • Young Harold • USA • NO ESCAPE
I EVEN MET HAPPY GYPSIES (USA) see **SKUPLJACI PERJA** • 1967
I EVEN MET SOME HAPPY GYPSIES see **SKUPLJACI PERJA** • 1967
I.F.1 NE REPOND PLUS • 1932 • Hartl Karl • FRN
I.F.O. • 1986 • Lommel Ulli • USA
I.F. STONE'S WEEKLY • 1973 • Bruck Jerry Jr. • DOC • USA
I FAILED BUT.. see **RAKUDAI WA SHITA KEREDO** • 1930
I FEAR NO FOE • 1909 • *Warwick Trading Co.* • UKN
I FEEL IT COMING • 1969 • Knight Sidney • USA • SOLDIER'S WIFE
I FEEL IT RISING • 1976 • Antonero Luis F. • USA
I FEEL LIKE A FEATHER IN THE BREEZE • 1936 • Fleischer Dave • ANS • USA
I FELL IN LOVE • 1989 • Barjatiyas • IND
"I" FILM see **IK-FILM** • 1929
I FIRST WANTED TO FIND THE TRUTH see **JEG VILLE FORST FINDE SANDHEDEN** • 1987
I FLUNKED BUT.. see **RAKUDAI WA SHITA KEREDO** • 1930
I FLY FOR KICKS see **NANIKA OMOROI KOTO NAIKA** • 1963
I FORCE YOU TO LIVE • 1977 • Kirsten Ralf • GDR
I FORGIVE THE WORDS see **JA PRASU SLOVA** • 1975
I FOUND A DOG • 1949 • Landers Lew • SHT • USA
I FOUND STELLA PARRISH • 1935 • LeRoy Mervyn • USA
I, FRANCIS SKORINA see **YA, FRANCIS SKORINA** • 1970
I GAVE MY HEART TO A TURK see **BIR TURK'E GONUL VERDIM** • 1969
I GET DIZZY WHEN I DO THAT TWOSTEP DANCE • 1908 • Gilbert Arthur • UKN
I GIVE MY HEART • 1935 • Varnel Marcel • UKN • LOVES OF MADAME DUBARRY, THE (USA) ○ DUBARRY, THE
I GIVE MY HEART see **GIVE ME YOUR HEART** • 1936
I GIVE MY LIFE see **PORT-ARTHUR** • 1936
I GIVE MY LOVE • 1934 • Freund Karl • USA
I GO, I SEE AND SHOOT see **VADO, VEDO E SPARA** • 1968
I GO TO THE SUN see **IDE KU SLONCU** • 1955
I GO TOWARDS THE SUN see **IDE KU SLONCU** • 1955
I GOPHER YOU • 1954 • Freleng Friz • ANS • USA
I GOT A NAME see **LAST AMERICAN HERO, THE** • 1973
I GOT A ROBE • 1944-45 • Ladouceur Jean-Paul • ANS • CND
I GOT PLENTY OF MUTTON • 1944 • Tashlin Frank • ANS • USA
I GRADUATED BUT.. see **DAIGAKU WA DETA KEREDA** • 1929
I GULT OCH BLATT • 1942 • Ahrle Elof • SWD • IN BLUE AND YELLOW
I HAD A FEELING I WAS DEAD see **ICH DACHTE, ICH WARE TOT** • 1974
I HAD MY BROTHER'S WIFE see **SUSUZ YAZ** • 1963
I HAD SEVEN DAUGHTERS (UKN) see **J'AVAIS SEPT FILLES** • 1954
I HAIL FROM CHILDHOOD see **YA RODOM IZ DYETSTVA** • 1967
I HATE ACTORS (USA) see **JE HAIS LES ACTEURS** • 1986
I HATE BLONDES see **ODIO LE BIONDE** • 1980
I HATE BUT LOVE see **NIKUI ANCHIKUSHO** • 1962
I HATE HORSES see **BREEZING HOME** • 1937
I HATE ISTANBUL see **ISTANBULU SEVMIYORUM** • 1968
I HATE MY BABY see **ODIO MI CUERPO** • 1973
I HATE TO LOSE • 1977 • Rubbo Michael • CND
I HATE WOMEN • 1934 • Scotto Aubrey • USA
I HATE YOUR GUTS see **INTRUDER, THE** • 1961
I HAVE A CRISIS see **ESTOY EN CRISIS** • 1983
I HAVE A NEW MASTER (UKN) see **ECOLE BUISSONIERE, L'** • 1948
I HAVE A STRANGER'S FACE see **TANIN NO KAO** • 1966
I HAVE AN EGG see **JA MAM JAJKO** • 1966
I HAVE LIVED • 1933 • Thorpe Richard • USA
I HAVE LOST TOBY • 1909 • *Urban-Eclipse* • USA
I HAVE NO MOUTH BUT I MUST SCREAM see **AND NOW THE SCREAMING STARTS!** • 1973
I HAVE SEEN DEATH see **YO HE VISTO LA MUERTE** • 1967
I HAVE THE RIGHT TO KILL see **OLDURMEK HAKKIMDIR** • 1968
I HAVE THE SUN IN MY BACK see **ORE NO SENAKA NI HI GA ATARU** • 1963
I HAVE TWO MUMMIES AND TWO DADDIES see **IMAM DVIJE MAME I DVA TATE** • 1968
I HAVE YOU ALWAYS IN MY HEART see **S' EHO PANDA STI KARDIA MOU** • 1967
I HAVEN'T GOT A HAT • 1934 • Freleng Friz • ANS • USA
I HEAR YOU CALLING ME • 1919 • Coleby A. E. • UKN
I HEARD • 1933 • Fleischer Dave • ANS • USA
I HEARD THE OWL CALL MY NAME • 1973 • Duke Daryl • TVM • USA
I HIRED A CONTRACT KILLER • 1990 • Kaurismaki Aki • FNL
I HUVET PA EN GAMMAL GUBBE • 1968 • Danielsson Tage • SWD • OUT OF AN OLD MAN'S HEAD ○ IN AN OLD MAN'S HEAD
I + I • 1981 • Hyytiainen Pekka • FNL
I, JAMES LEWIS see **THIS WOMAN IS MINE** • 1941
I, JANE DOE • 1948 • Auer John H. • USA • DIARY OF A BRIDE (UKN)
I JIZN', I SLIOZY, I LYUBOV • 1983 • Gubenko Nikolai • USS • AND LIFE AND TEARS AND LOVE
I JOMFRUENS TEGN • 1973 • Karlsson Finn • DNM
I, JUSTICE see **JA SPRAVEDLNOST** • 1967
I-KATI ELIMNYANA • 1976 • SAF
I KILL, YOU KILL see **IO UCCIDO, TU UCCIDI** • 1965
I KILLED see **JAG DRAPTE** • 1943
I KILLED EINSTEIN see **ZABIL JSEM EINSTEINA, PANOVE** • 1969
I KILLED EINSTEIN, GENTLEMEN see **ZABIL JSEM EINSTEINA, PANOVE** • 1969
I KILLED FACUNDO see **YO MATE A FACUNDO** • 1975
I KILLED GERONIMO • 1950 • Hoffman John • USA
I KILLED LUCIO FLAVIO see **EU MATEI LUCIO FLAVIO** • 1980
I KILLED RASPUTIN (UKN) see **J'AI TUE RASPOUTINE** • 1967
I KILLED THAT MAN • 1941 • Rosen Phil • USA
I KILLED THE COUNT • 1938 • Zelnik Friedrich • UKN • WHO IS GUILTY?
I KILLED WILD BILL HICKOK • 1956 • Talmadge Richard • USA
I KISS YOUR HAND, MADAME (USA) see **ICH KUSSE IHRE HAND, MADAME** • 1929
I KNEW HER WELL see **IO LA CONOSCEVO BENE** • 1965
I KNOW AN OLD LADY WHO SWALLOWED A FLY • 1962 • Lamb Derek • ANS • CND
I KNOW EVERYBODY AND EVERYBODY'S RACKET • 1933 • Brice Monte • SHT • USA
I KNOW I PLAYED EVERY NOTE see **ITZHAK PERLMAN, VIRTUOSO VIOLINIST** • 1978
I KNOW I'M GOING TO LOVE YOU see **EU SEI QUE VOU TE AMAR** • 1986
I KNOW MY FIRST NAME IS STEPHEN • 1989 • Elikann Larry • USA
I KNOW THAT YOU KNOW THAT I KNOW (USA) see **IO SO CHE TU SAI CHE IO SO** • 1983
I KNOW WHERE I'M GOING • 1945 • Powell Michael, Pressburger Emeric • UKN
I KNOW WHY THE CAGED BIRD SINGS • 1979 • Cook Fielder • USA
I KNOW YOU see **LOOK BEFORE YOU LOVE** • 1948
I KNOW YOU ARE THE MURDERER • 1971 • Schulhoff Petr • CZC
I KRONANS KLADER • 1915 • Klercker Georg • SWD • IN UNIFORM
I LAGENS NAMN • 1987 • Sundvall Kjell • SWD • IN THE NAME OF THE LAW
I LAPPBJORNENS RIKE • 1940 • Wesslen Stig • SWD
I LED TWO LIVES see **GLEN OR GLENDA?** • 1952
I LIFT UP MY FINGER AND SAY TWEET TWEET • 1929 • Aylott Dave, Symmons E. F. • SHT • UKN
I LIKE BABIES AND INFINKS • 1937 • Fleischer Dave • ANS • USA
I LIKE BATS • Warchol Grzegorz • PLN
I LIKE BIRDS • 1967 • Walker Pete • UKN • HOT GIRLS FOR MEN ONLY (USA) ○ GIRLS FOR MEN ONLY ○ FOR MEN ONLY
I LIKE GIRLS WHO DO • 1974 • Billian Hans • FRG
I LIKE IT see **A ME MI PLACE** • 1985
I LIKE IT THAT WAY • 1934 • Lachman Harry • USA
I LIKE MONEY (USA) see **MR. TOPAZE** • 1961
I LIKE MOUNTAIN MUSIC • 1933 • Fleischer Dave • ANS • USA
I LIKE MOUNTAIN MUSIC • 1933 • Ising Rudolf • *Warner* • ANS • USA
I LIKE TO SEE THE WHEELS TURN • 1981 • Walker Giles • MTV • CND
I LIKE YOUR NERVE • 1931 • McGann William • USA
I LIVE FOR LOVE • 1935 • Berkeley Busby • USA • I LIVE FOR YOU (UKN) ○ ROMANCE IN A GLASS HOUSE
I LIVE FOR YOU (UKN) see **I LIVE FOR LOVE** • 1935
I LIVE FOR YOUR DEATH see **VIVO PER LA TUA MORTE** • 1968
I LIVE HERE • 1973 • Harmon Paul • SHT • ASL
I LIVE IN FEAR (USA) see **IKIMONO NO KIROKU** • 1955
I LIVE IN GROSVENOR SQUARE • 1945 • Wilcox Herbert • UKN • YANK IN LONDON, A (USA)
I LIVE MY LIFE • 1935 • Van Dyke W. S. • USA • GLITTER
I LIVE ON DANGER • 1942 • White Sam • USA
I LIVE WITH ME DAD • 1987 • Maloney Paul • ASL
I LIVED A LIE see **I PASSED FOR WHITE** • 1960
I LIVED WITH YOU • 1933 • Elvey Maurice • UKN
I LIVETS BRANDING • 1915 • Holger-Madsen • DNM • CROSSROADS OF LIFE, THE
I LIVETS VAR, ELLER FORSTA ALSKARINNAN • 1912 • Garbagny Paul • SWD • IN THE SPRING OF LIFE, OR HIS FIRST LOVE
I LOST MY HEART IN HEIDELBERG see **STUDENT'S ROMANCE, THE** • 1935
I LOVE see **YA LYUBLYU** • 1936
I LOVE A BAND LEADER • 1945 • Lord Del • USA • MEMORY FOR TWO (UKN)
I LOVE A LASSIE • 1907 • Gilbert Arthur • UKN
I LOVE A LASSIE • 1925 • Fleischer Dave • ANS • USA
I LOVE A LASSIE • 1931 • Pearson George • SHT • UKN
I LOVE A MAN IN UNIFORM • 1984 • McBrearty Don • MTV • CND
I LOVE A MYSTERY • 1945 • Levin Henry • USA
I LOVE A MYSTERY • 1967 • Stevens Leslie • USA
I LOVE A PARADE • 1933 • Ising Rudolf • ANS • USA
I LOVE A SOLDIER • 1944 • Sandrich Mark • USA
I LOVE BLUE see **JEG ELSKER BLAT** • 1968
I LOVE CHARLES ALBERT • 1918 • *Brady Edward* • SHT • USA
I LOVE CHILDREN, BUT! • 1952 • Barclay David • SHT • USA
I LOVE DOLLAR • 1985 • van der Keuken Johan • DOC • NTH
I LOVE MARIA see **TIEJIA WUDI MALIYA** • 1988
I LOVE MELVIN • 1952 • Weis Don • USA
I LOVE MEXICO • 1970 • Soule Thayer • DOC • USA
I LOVE MY HUSBAND, BUT! • 1946 • Barclay David • SHT • USA
I LOVE MY MOTHER-IN-LAW, BUT! • 1948 • Barclay David • SHT • USA
I LOVE MY WIFE • 1970 • Stuart Mel • USA
I LOVE MY WIFE, BUT! • 1947 • Barclay David • SHT • USA
I LOVE N.Y. • 1987 • Bozzacchi Gianni • USA
I LOVE THAT MAN • 1933 • Brown Harry J. • USA
I LOVE THE NURSES • 1914 • Hartigan P. C. • USA
I LOVE TO BE A SAILOR • 1931 • Pearson George • SHT • UKN
I LOVE TO SINGA • 1936 • Avery Tex • ANS • USA
I LOVE TROUBLE • 1947 • Simon S. Sylvan • USA
I LOVE YOU • 1913 • *Majestic* • USA
I LOVE YOU • 1918 • Edwards Walter • USA
I LOVE YOU • 1987 • Ferreri Marco • ITL, FRN
I LOVE YOU see **IO TI AMO** • 1968
I LOVE YOU see **S'AGAPO** • 1970
I LOVE YOU see **EU TE AMO** • 1981

I LOVE YOU see **TE AMO** • 1986
I LOVE YOU AGAIN • 1940 • Van Dyke W. S. • USA
I LOVE YOU, ALICE B. TOKLAS! • 1968 • Averback Hy • USA
I LOVE YOU, GOODBYE • 1974 • O'Steen Sam • TVM • USA
I LOVE YOU, I DON'T (UKN) see **JE T'AIME MOI NON PLUS** • 1976
I LOVE YOU, I HATE YOU • 1968 • Hart David • UKN • OTHER PEOPLE, THE ○ SLEEP IS LOVELY
I LOVE YOU, I KILL YOU see **ICH LIEBE DICH, ICH TOTE DICH** • 1970
I LOVE YOU, I LOVE YOU see **JE T'AIME, JE T'AIME** • 1967
I LOVE YOU, I LOVE YOU NOT see **AMO NON AMO** • 1979
I LOVE YOU JUST FOR FUN • 1988 • Gusner Iris • GDR
I LOVE, YOU LOVE see **JAG ALSKAR, DU ALSKAR** • 1968
I LOVE, YOU LOVE see **JA MILUJEM, TY MILUJES** • 1980
I LOVE, YOU LOVE (USA) see **IO AMO, TU AMI** • 1960
I LOVE YOU, ME NO LONGER (USA) see **JE T'AIME MOI NON PLUS** • 1976
I LOVE YOU, NO MATTER WHAT I AM see **SERE CUALQUIER COSA PERO TE QUIERO** • 1986
I LOVE YOU ROSA (UKN) see **ANI OHEV OTACH ROSA** • 1971
I LOVE YOU TO DEATH • 1989 • Kasdan Lawrence • USA
I LOVE YOU, YOU VIXEN see **JAG ALSKAR DIG, ARGBIGGA** • 1946
I LOVED A SOLDIER • 1936 • Hathaway Henry • USA
I LOVED A WOMAN • 1933 • Green Alfred E. • USA • RED MEAT
I LOVED YOU.. see **YA VAS LYUBIL..** • 1968
I LOVED YOU WEDNESDAY • 1933 • King Henry, Menzies William Cameron • USA
I LOVENS TEGN • 1976 • Hedman Werner • DNM
I MADE 13 see **HA FATTO TREDICI** • 1951
I, MADMAN • 1988 • Takacs Tibor • USA • HARDCOVER
I-MAN • 1986 • Allen Corey • TVM • USA
I, MARQUIS DE SADE • 1967 • Hilliard Richard • USA • I, THE MARQUIS
I MARRIED A CENTERFOLD • 1984 • Werner Peter • TVM • USA
I MARRIED A COMMUNIST • 1949 • Stevenson Robert • USA • WOMAN ON PIER 13, THE (UKN) ○ WOMAN AT PIER THIRTEEN, THE
I MARRIED A DOCTOR • 1936 • Mayo Archie • USA
I MARRIED A MONSTER FROM OUTER SPACE • 1958 • Fowler Gene Jr. • USA
I MARRIED A NAZI see **MAN I MARRIED, THE** • 1940
I MARRIED A PRIEST see **ME CASE CON UN CURA** • 1968
I MARRIED A SHADOW (USA) see **J'AI ESPOUSE UNE OMBRE** • 1983
I MARRIED A SOLDIER see **IN THE MEANTIME, DARLING** • 1944
I MARRIED A SPY (USA) see **SECRET LIVES** • 1937
I MARRIED A VAMPIRE • 1986 • Raskin Jay • USA
I MARRIED A WEREWOLF (UKN) see **LYCANTHROPUS** • 1962
I MARRIED A WITCH • 1942 • Clair Rene • USA • MA FEMME EST UNE SORCIERE (FRN)
I MARRIED A WOMAN • 1958 • Kanter Hal • USA
I MARRIED ADVENTURE • 1940 • *Johnson Osa (P)* • CMP • USA
I MARRIED AN ACTRESS see **GREAT FLIRTATION, THE** • 1934
I MARRIED AN ANGEL • 1942 • Van Dyke W. S. • USA
I MARRIED FOR LOVE see **SZERELEMBOEL NOESUELTEM** • 1938
I MARRIED TOO YOUNG see **MARRIED TOO YOUNG** • 1962
I MARRIED WYATT EARP • 1982 • O'Herlihy Michael • TVM • USA
I MARRIED YOU FOR FUN (USA) see **TI HO SPOSATO PER ALLEGRIA** • 1967
I MARRIED YOU FOR GAIETY see **TI HO SPOSATO PER ALLEGRIA** • 1967
I, MAUREEN • 1978 • Manatis Janine • CND
I MET A MURDERER • 1939 • Kellino Roy • UKN
I MET HIM IN PARIS • 1937 • Ruggles Wesley • USA
I MET MY LOVE AGAIN • 1938 • Logan Joshua, Ripley Arthur • USA
I MINNENAS BAND • 1916 • Klercker Georg • SWD • TIED TO ONE'S MEMORIES
I MISS YOU, HUGS AND KISSES • 1978 • Markowitz Murray • CND, USA • DROP DEAD DEAREST ○ LEFT FOR DEAD
I, MOBSTER • 1958 • Corman Roger • USA • MOBSTER, THE (UKN)
I, MONSTER • 1972 • Weeks Stephen • UKN
I MORGEN ER DET SLUT • 1987 • Aagaard Sigfred • DNM • TOMORROW IT'S OVER
I MORGEN MIN ELSKEDE • 1971 • Karlsson Finn • DNM • TOMORROW MY LOVE
I MORKASTE SMALAND • 1943 • Bauman Schamyl • SWD • IN THE DARKEST CORNER OF SMALAND
I MORKRETS BOJOR • 1917 • Klercker Georg • SWD • IN THE CHAINS OF DARKNESS
I MURDERED A MAN see **NOTORIOUS GENTLEMAN, THE** • 1935
I.N.R.I. • 1923 • Wiene Robert • FRG • CROWN OF THORNS
I NATT ELLER ALDRIG • 1941 • Molander Gustaf • SWD • TONIGHT OR NEVER
I NEED • 1967 • Sebastian Ferdinand • USA • I NEED A MAN.. ANY MAN ○ I NEED A MAN
I NEED A MAN see **I NEED** • 1967
I NEED A MAN.. ANY MAN see **I NEED** • 1967
I NEED A MAN LIKE YOU TO MAKE MY DREAMS COME TRUE • 1987 • Stermac Daria, Paakspuu Kalli • SHT • CND
I NEED A WOMAN see **ADAMSSON I SVERIGE** • 1966
I NEED MORE STAFF • 1973 • Crombie Donald • SHT • ASL
I NEVER CHANGES MY ATTITUDE • 1937 • Fleischer Dave • ANS • USA
I NEVER FORGET THE WIFE • 1907 • *Warwick Trading Co.* • UKN
I NEVER PROMISED YOU A ROSE GARDEN • 1977 • Page Anthony • USA
I NEVER SAID A WORD • 1912 • *Nestor* • USA
I NEVER SANG FOR MY FATHER • 1970 • Cates Gilbert • USA • STRANGERS
I NEVER WAS IN VIENNA see **NUNCA ESTUVE EN VIENA** • 1987
I NIKTO DRUGOY • 1968 • Shulman Iosif • USS • AND NO ONE ELSE
I NOD OCH LUST • 1938 • Johansson Ivar • SWD
I ONLY ARSKED! • 1958 • Tully Montgomery • UKN
I ONLY HAVE EYES FOR YOU • 1937 • Avery Tex • ANS • USA
I ONLY WANT YOU TO LOVE ME see **ICH WILL DOCH NUR, DASS IHR MICH LIEBT** • 1976
I OUGHT TO BE IN PICTURES • 1982 • Ross Herbert • USA
I OWE YOU $10 • 1912 • *Nestor* • USA
I PARADIS.. • 1941 • Lindberg Per • SWD • IN PARADISE
I PASSED BUT.. see **DAIGAKU WA DETA KEREDA** • 1929
I PASSED FOR WHITE • 1960 • Wilcox Fred M. • USA • I LIVED A LIE
I PICKED YOU FROM THE GUTTER see **PINULOT KA LANG SA LUPA** • 1988
I, PIERRE RIVIERE see **MOI, PIERRE RIVIERE, AYANT EGORGE MA MERE, MA SOEUR ET MA FRERE** • 1977
I PLANT THE WIND IN MY CITY see **SIEMBRO VIENTO EN MI CIUDAD** • 1979
I PLEAD NOT GUILTY see **ORKIZOME IME ATHOA** • 1968
I PROMISE TO PAY • 1937 • Lederman D. Ross • USA
I PROMISE TO PAY see **PAYROLL** • 1961
...I PROTECT MYSELF AGAINST MY ENEMIES! see **...DAI NEMICI MI GUARDO IO!** • 1968
I PROVNINGENS STUND • 1915 • Sjostrom Victor • SWD • AT THE MOMENT OF TRIAL ○ HOUR OF TRIAL ○ HOUR OF THE TRIAL
I.Q.S. • 1967 • Salvia Rafael J. • SPN
I QUIT • 1917 • Curtis Allen • SHT • USA
I REACH FOR YOUR HAND see **LET'S SHAKE HANDS** • 1963
I REMEMBER • Khamraev Ali • USS
I REMEMBER ALL, RICARDS see **YA VSYE POMNYU, RICHARD** • 1967
I REMEMBER LOVE • 1981 • Meisel Norbert • USA
I REMEMBER MAMA • 1948 • Stevens George • USA
I REMEMBER NUDNIK • 1967 • Deitch Gene • ANS • USA
I RESIGN FROM THE WORLD • 1966 • Skanata Krsto • DOC • YGS
I RING DOORBELLS • 1946 • Strayer Frank • USA
I RO HA NI HO HE TU • 1960 • Nakamura Noboru • JPN • OF MEN AND MONEY
I ROK OCH DANS • 1954 • Gamlin Yngve, Blomgren Bengt • SWD • IN SMOKE AND DANCING
I ROSLAGENS FAMN • 1945 • Bauman Schamyl • SWD • IN THE BEAUTIFUL PROVINCE OF ROSLAGEN
I SAILED TO TAHITI WITH AN ALL GIRL CREW • 1969 • Bare Richard L. • USA
I SAW HER FIRST see **YO LA VI PRIMERO** • 1974
I SAW HIM FIRST • 1912 • *Roland Ruth* • USA
I SAW THE KILLER see **KYATSU O NIGASUNE** • 1956
I SAW THE SHADOW • 1966 • Iimura Takahiko • SHT • JPN
I SAW WHAT YOU DID • 1965 • Castle William • USA
I SAW WHAT YOU DID • 1987 • Walton Fred • USA
I SEE A DARK STRANGER • 1946 • Launder Frank • UKN • ADVENTURESS, THE (USA)
I SEE A SOLDIER see **KORITSI TOU STRATIOTI, TO** • 1970
I SEE EVERYBODY NAKED see **VEDO NUDO** • 1969
I SEE ICE • 1938 • Kimmins Anthony • UKN
I SEE THE SUN • 1965 • Gogoberidze Lana • USS
I SEE THIS LAND FROM AFAR see **AUS DER FERNE SEHE ICH DIESES LAND** • 1978
I SEED THE WINDS see **JE SEME A TOUT VENT** • 1952
I SELL ANYTHING • 1934 • Florey Robert • USA
I SELL MY SKIN DEARLY see **VENDO CARA LA PELLE** • 1968
I SENT A LETTER TO MY LOVE (USA) see **CHERE INCONNUE** • 1980
I SHALL BLOW YOU ALL UP -INSPECTOR BLOOMFIELD'S CASE NO.1 see **ICH SPRENG EUCH ALLE IN DIE LUFT -INSPEKTOR BLOMFIELDS FALL NR.1** • 1968
I SHALL LIVE AGAIN (USA) see **VIVIRE OTRA VEZ** • 1939
I SHALL MARRY ONLY YOU see **NINNE PELLADUTHA** • 1968
I SHALL NOT FORGET see **WASURERU MONOKA** • 1968
I SHALL NOT YIELD • 1918 • Ivanovsky Alexander • USS
I SHALL RETURN (UKN) see **AMERICAN GUERRILLA IN THE PHILIPPINES, AN** • 1950
I SHAN'T BE LONG • 1942 • Vavra Otakar • CZC
I SHOT BILLY THE KID • 1950 • Berke William • USA
I SHOT JESSE JAMES • 1949 • Fuller Samuel • USA
I SHOULD HAVE STOOD IN BEDLAM • 1949 • Lewis Jerry • SHT • USA
I SHOULD SAY SO! • 1914 • Aylott Dave • UKN
I SHOULD WORRY • 1914 • *Royal* • USA
I SIGN IN BLOOD see **IMZAM KANLA YAZILIR** • 1970
I SING, I CRY see **WO KO, WO CH'I** • 1980
I SING OF PEACE • 1961 • Gass Karl • DOC • GDR
I-SKI LOVE-SKI YOU-SKI • 1936 • Fleischer Dave • ANS • USA
I SKRZYPCE PRZESTALY GRAC • 1988 • Ramati Alexander • PLN, USA • AND THE VIOLINS STOPPED PLAYING ○ AND THE FIDDLE FELL SILENT
I SKYTTENS TEGN • 1978 • Hedman Werner • DNM • AGENT 69 JENSEN I SKYTTENS TEGN ○ EMMANUELLE IN DENMARK ○ AGENT 69
I SLAGBJORNENS SPAR • 1931 • Utterstrom Johan, Utterstrom Sven • DOC • SWD • SILVERTIP
I SLEPT WITH A GHOST see **YO DORMI CON UN FANTASMA** • 1947
I SOM HAR INTRADEN.. • 1945 • Mattsson Arne • SWD • YOU WHO ARE ABOUT TO ENTER
I SPIT ON YOUR GRAVE • 1981 • Zarchi Meir • USA • DAY OF THE WOMAN
I SPIT ON YOUR GRAVE (USA) see **J'IRAI CRACHER SUR VOS TOMBES** • 1959
I SPY • 1933 • Dwan Allan • UKN • MORNING AFTER, THE (USA)
I SPY, I SPY see **OUR MAN IN MARRAKESH** • 1966
I STAND ACCUSED • 1938 • Auer John H. • USA
I STAND ACCUSED see **ACT OF MURDER, AN** • 1948
I STAND CONDEMNED (USA) see **MOSCOW NIGHTS** • 1935
I START COUNTING • 1969 • Greene David • UKN
I STARTED TO GROW LATER • 1963 • Zaninovic Stejpan • DOC • YGS
I STILL PUT OFF FORGETTING YOU see **VSE OTLAGAM DA TE ZABRAVYA** • 1990
I STJERNERNE STAAR DET SKREVET • 1914 • Davidsen Hjalmar • DNM
I STOLE A MILLION • 1939 • Tuttle Frank • USA
I SURRENDER DEAR • 1931 • Sennett Mack • USA
I SURRENDER, DEAR • 1948 • Dreifuss Arthur • USA
I SURVIVED CERTAIN DEATH see **PREZIL JSEM SVOU SMRT** • 1960
I SURVIVED MY DEATH see **PREZIL JSEM SVOU SMRT** • 1960
I-TAI CHIEN-WANG • 1969 • Kwok Nan-Hung • HKG • KING OF SWORDSMEN (USA) ○ SWORDSMAN OF ALL SWORDSMAN
I TAKE THESE MEN • 1983 • Peerce Larry • TVM • USA
I TAKE THIS OATH • 1940 • Newfield Sam • USA
I TAKE THIS WOMAN • 1931 • Gering Marion, Vorkapich Slavko • USA
I TAKE THIS WOMAN • 1939 • Van Dyke W. S., von Sternberg Josef (U/c) • USA
I TAW A PUDDY TAT • 1948 • Freleng Friz • ANS • USA
I THANK A FOOL • 1962 • Stevens Robert • UKN, USA
I THANK YOU • 1941 • Varnel Marcel • UKN
I THE ABORIGINAL • 1961 • Holmes Cecil • DOC • ASL
I, THE BODY see **MORIANERNA** • 1965
I THE COUNTESS • 1988 • Popzlatev Peter • BUL
I.. THE DOCTOR see **ANA AL DOCTOR** • 1968
I THE DOLEFUL GOD see **JA TRUCHLIVY BUH** • 1969
I, THE EXECUTIONER see **MINAGOROSHI NO REIKA** • 1968
I, THE JURY • 1953 • Essex Harry • USA
I, THE JURY • 1982 • Heffron Richard T. • USA
I THE JUSTICE see **JA SPRAVEDLNOST** • 1967
I, THE MARQUIS see **I, MARQUIS DE SADE** • 1967
I THE SAD GOD see **JA TRUCHLIVY BUH** • 1969
I, THE WORST OF ALL see **YO, LA PEOR DE TODAS** • 1990
I THINK OF YOU OFTEN • 1983 • Barrie Scott • SHT • CND
I THINK WE'RE BEING FOLLOWED • 1967 • Day Robert • USA
I.. THOU.. AND SHE (USA) see **IO.. TU.. Y..** • 1933
I THOUGHT YOU LOVED ME AS I LOVED YOU • 1922 • *Parkinson H. B. (P)* • SHT • UKN
I TO CE PROCI • 1985 • Dizdarevic Nenad • YGS • THAT TO WILL PASS
I TOLD YOU SO • 1977 • Emes Ian • UKN
I TOO HAVE A HEART see **BENIMDE KALBIM VAR** • 1968
I TOOK YOU FROM THE MIRE see **HINANGO KITA SA LUSAK** • 1967
I TVILLINGERNES TEGN • 1975 • Hedman Werner • DNM • IN THE SIGN OF GEMINI ○ SEXUAL FANTASIES
I TY ZOSTANIESZ INDIANINEM • 1962 • Nalecki Konrad • PLN
I TYRENS TEGN • 1974 • Hedman Werner • DNM
I UNGDOMMENS MAKT • 1980 • Skolmen Roar • NRW • IN THE POWER OF YOUTH ○ JUNIOR HEADS
I VIDEL SEM DALJINE MEGLENE I KALNE • 1964 • Bourek Zlatko • ANS • YGS • FAR AWAY I SAW MIST AND MUD ○ FOG AND MUD
I, VOR PITTFALKS, UNIVERSAL CONFIDENCE MAN • 1967 • Williams Richard • ANS • UKN
I WAKE UP SCREAMING • 1941 • Humberstone H. Bruce • USA • HOT SPOT (UKN)
I WALK ABOUT MOSCOW see **YA SHAGAYU PO MOSKVE** • 1964
I WALK ALONE • 1948 • Haskin Byron • USA
I WALK AROUND MOSCOW see **YA SHAGAYU PO MOSKVE** • 1964
I WALK THE LINE • 1970 • Frankenheimer John • USA
I WALK TO THE SUN see **IDE KU SLONCU** • 1955
I WALKED WITH A ZOMBIE • 1943 • Tourneur Jacques • USA
I WANNA BE A LIFEGUARD • 1936 • Fleischer Dave • ANS • USA
I WANNA BE A SAILOR • 1937 • Avery Tex • ANS • USA
I WANNA HOLD YOUR HAND • 1978 • Zemeckis Robert • USA
I WANNA MINK • 1960 • Halas John • ANS • UKN
I WANNA PLAY HOUSE • 1936 • Freleng Friz • ANS • USA
I WANT A DIVORCE • 1940 • Murphy Ralph • USA
I WANT A HUSBAND • 1919 • Hertz Aleksander • PLN
I WANT A HUSBAND see **MAN SHOHAR MIKHAM** • 1968
I WANT A SOLUTION see **HAYATI AL-KHASSA** • 1974
I WANT HER DEAD see **W** • 1974
I WANT HIM DEAD see **LO VOGLIO MORTO** • 1968
I WANT LOVE AND TENDERNESS • 1978 • Hafez Nagdi • EGY
I WANT MORE • 1970 • Beap Jack • USA • SOCK IT TO ME WITH FLESH
I WANT MORE see **YUAN WANG AI TA JEN!** • 1976
I WANT MY DINNER • 1903 • *Bitzer Billy (Ph)* • USA
I WANT MY MAN • 1925 • Hillyer Lambert • USA
I WANT MY MUMMY • 1966 • Post Howard • ANS • USA
I WANT TO BE A LADY • 1919 • *Joy Gloria* • SHT • USA
I WANT TO BE A MOTHER • 1937 • Roland George • USA
I WANT TO BE A SHELLFISH see **WATASHI WA KAI NI NARITAI** • 1959
I WANT TO BE A WOMAN (UKN) see **CAMBIO DE SEXO** • 1977
I WANT TO BE AN ACTRESS • 1937 • *Mintz Charles (P)* • ANS • USA
I WANT TO BE AN ENGINEER • 1983 • Shaffer Beverly • DOC • CND • NOUS SOMMES LES INGENIEURES
I WANT TO BE SWEDEN'S REMBRANDT -OR DIE! see **JAG SKALL BLI SVERIGES REMBRANDT -ELLER DO!** • 1990
I WANT TO CRY I WON'T CRY see **CUANDO QUIERO LLORAR NO LLORO** • 1972
I WANT TO FORGET • 1918 • Kirkwood James • USA
I WANT TO GET MARRIED see **MARRY ME** • 1949
I WANT TO GO HOME (UKN) see **JE VEUX RENTRER A LA MAISON** • 1989
I WANT TO GO TO SCHOOL • 1959 • Krish John • UKN
I WANT TO KEEP MY BABY! • 1976 • Thorpe Jerry • TVM • USA
I WANT TO KNOW WHY I HAVE WINGS see **VREAU SA STIU DE CE AM ARIPI** • 1984
I WANT TO LIVE! • 1958 • Wise Robert • USA
I WANT TO LIVE • 1983 • Rich David Lowell • TVM • USA
I WANT TO LIVE see **ICH WILL LEBEN** • 1976
I WANT TO LIVE see **HOCU ZIVJETI** • 1983
I WANT TO LOVE, PETER see **HALVAN RAKASTAA, PETER** • 1973
I WANT WHAT I WANT • 1972 • Dexter John • UKN

I WANT YOU • 1951 • Robson Mark • USA
I WANT YOU! • 1969 • Catah Sam S. • USA
I WANT YOU TO SEE MY GIRL • 1909 • *Warwick Trading Co.* • UKN
I WANTED THE TROUSERS see **VOLEVO I PANTALONI** • 1990
I WANTED TO LIVE see **ICH WOLLTE LEBEN** • 1982
I WANTED WINGS • 1941 • Leisen Mitchell • USA
I WAS A COMMUNIST FOR THE F.B.I. • 1951 • Douglas Gordon • USA
I WAS A CONVICT • 1939 • Scotto Aubrey • USA
I WAS A CRIMINAL see **CAPTAIN OF KOEPENICK** • 1942
I WAS A DANCER • 1949 • Richardson Frank • UKN
I WAS A FIREMAN see **FIRES WERE STARTED** • 1943
I WAS A GOOD LITTLE GIRL UNTIL I MET YOU • 1916 • *Tress Henry* • SHT • UKN
I WAS A KAPO see **BYLEM KAPO** • 1965
I WAS A MAIL ORDER BRIDE • 1982 • Chomsky Marvin • TVM • USA
I WAS A MALE SEX BOMB see **MONSIEUR DE COMPAGNIE, UN** • 1964
I WAS A MALE WAR BRIDE • 1949 • Hawks Howard • USA • YOU CAN'T SLEEP HERE (UKN)
I WAS A MAN • 1967 • Mahon Barry • USA
I WAS A NINETY-POUND WEAKLING • 1959 • Koenig Wolf, Dufaux Georges • DCS • CND
I WAS A PARISH PRIEST (USA) see **GUERRA DE DIOS, LA** • 1953
I WAS A PRISONER IN KOREA see **BAMBOO PRISON, THE** • 1954
I WAS A PRISONER ON DEVIL'S ISLAND • 1941 • Landers Lew • USA
I WAS A SHOPLIFTER • 1950 • Lamont Charles • USA • SHOPLIFTER
I WAS A SPY • 1933 • Saville Victor • UKN
I WAS A TEENAGE ALIEN • 1980 • Cooper Bob • USA
I WAS A TEENAGE APEMAN • 1959 • Glut Don • SHT • USA
I WAS A TEENAGE BIRDMAN • 1962 • *Delta Sf Film Group* • SHT • UKN
I WAS A TEENAGE BOY see **WILLY MILLY** • 1985
I WAS A TEENAGE CAVEMAN see **TEENAGE CAVEMAN** • 1958
I WAS A TEENAGE FRANKENSTEIN • 1957 • Strock Herbert L. • USA • TEEENAGE FRANKENSTEIN (UKN)
I WAS A TEENAGE GORILLA see **KONGA** • 1961
I WAS A TEENAGE RUMPOT • 1960 • Kuchar George, Kuchar Mike • SHT • USA
I WAS A TEENAGE SEX MUTANT • 1988 • Decoteau David • USA
I WAS A TEENAGE THUMB • 1963 • Jones Charles M. • ANS • USA
I WAS A TEENAGE TV TERRORIST • 1987 • Singer Stanford • USA • AMATEUR HOUR
I WAS A TEENAGE VAMPIRE • 1959 • Glut Don • SHT • USA
I WAS A TEENAGE VAMPIRE see **MY BEST FRIEND IS A VAMPIRE** • 1988
I WAS A TEENAGE WEREWOLF • 1957 • Fowler Gene Jr. • USA • BLOOD OF THE WEREWOLF
I WAS A ZOMBIE FOR THE F.B.I. • 1984 • Penczner Marius • USA
I WAS AN ADVENTURESS • 1940 • Ratoff Gregory • USA
I WAS AN AMERICAN SPY • 1951 • Selander Lesley • USA
I WAS BORN BUT.. see **UMARETE WA MITA KEREDO** • 1932
I WAS BORN GREEK • 1968 • King Allan, Brayne Bill • CND
I WAS BORN IN JERUSALEM see **ANI YERUSHALMI** • 1971
I WAS DYING ANYWAY, SIGNS OF SUICIDE • 1977 • Mankiewicz Francis • SHT • CND
I WAS FIFTEEN see **DEN SOMMEREN JEG FYLTE 15** • 1974
I WAS FRAMED • 1942 • Lederman D. Ross • USA
I WAS HAPPY HERE • 1965 • Davis Desmond • UKN • TIME LOST AND TIME REMEMBERED (USA) ○ PASSAGE OF LOVE
I WAS KAPO see **BYLEM KAPO** • 1965
I WAS MEANT FOR YOU • 1913 • O'Sullivan Tony • USA
I WAS MONTY'S DOUBLE • 1958 • Guillermin John • UKN • MONTY'S DOUBLE
I WAS NINETEEN see **ICH WAR NEUNZEHN** • 1967
I WASN'T SCARED • 1977 • Walker Giles • MTV • CND
I WILL • 1919 • Herrick Hubert, Foss Kenelm • UKN
I WILL FIGHT NO MORE FOREVER • 1975 • Heffron Richard T. • TVM • USA
I WILL GO LIKE A WILD HORSE see **J'IRAI COMME UN CHEVAL FOU** • 1973
I WILL.. I WILL.. FOR NOW • 1976 • Panama Norman • USA
I WILL IF YOU WILL (UKN) see **INFERMIERA, L'** • 1975
I WILL MAKE NO MORE BORING ART • 1988 • MacGillivray William D. • DOC • CND
I WILL REPAY • 1916 • *Clayton Marguerite* • SHT • USA
I WILL REPAY • 1917 • Earle William P. S. • USA • MUNICIPAL REPORT, A
I WILL REPAY • 1923 • Kolker Henry • UKN • SWORDS AND THE WOMAN (USA)
I WILL REPAY • 1984 • SAF
I WILL REPAY see **ANOTHER SCANDAL** • 1924
I WILL RETURN see **VRATICU SE** • 1957
I WISH I HAD A GIRL • 1912 • *Imp* • USA
I WISH I HAD WINGS • 1933 • Ising Rudolf • ANS • USA
I WISH I WAS A DOVE see **VOLIO BIH DA SAM GOLUB** • 1989
I WISH I WERE IN DIXIE • 1969 • Goetz Tommy • USA
I WISH TO SPEAK see **JA PRASU SLOVA** • 1975
I WISHED ON THE MOON • 1935 • Fleischer Dave • ANS • USA
I WON THE NEW YEAR LOTTERY see **HO VINTO LA LOTTERIA DI CAPODANNO** • 1990
I WONDER WHO'S KILLING HER NOW? • 1976 • Stern Steven Hilliard • USA
I WONDER WHO'S KISSING HER NOW • 1931 • Fleischer Dave • ANS • USA
I WONDER WHO'S KISSING HER NOW • 1947 • Bacon Lloyd • USA
I WONDER WHY • 1965 • Segal Steve, Ables Fred • SHT • USA
I WON'T DANCE see **JUST THE WAY YOU ARE** • 1984
I WON'T FORGET THAT NIGHT see **SONO YO WA WASURENAI** • 1962
I WON'T LOVE YOU see **NIE BEDE CIE KOCHAC** • 1974
I WON'T WAIT TILL TOMORROW see **NEM VAROK HOLNAPIG** • 1967
I WOULD LIKE TO MARRY YOU • 1907 • Morland John • UKN
I WOULDN'T BE IN YOUR SHOES • 1948 • Nigh William • USA
I YAM LOVE SICK • 1938 • Fleischer Dave • ANS • USA
I YAM WHAT I YAM • 1933 • Fleischer Dave • ANS • USA
I, YOU, THEY see **JE, TU, ELLES** • 1971
I, ZORBA • 1987 • Wise Robert • USA
IACOB • 1988 • Daneliuc Mircea • RMN
IAN AND SYLVIA ON THE TRAIL OF "98" • 1973 • Barclay Robert • MTV • CND
IANKO THE MUSICIAN see **NOWY JANKO MUZYKANT** • 1960
IARBA VERDE DE ACASA • 1978 • Gulea Stere • RMN • GREEN GRASS OF HOME, THE
IAWA • 1953 • Flornoy Bertrand • DOC • FRN
IB AND LITTLE CHRISTINA • 1908 • Stow Percy • UKN
IBANEZ' TORRENT see **TORRENT, THE** • 1924
IBARAGI UKON • 1939 • Inagaki Hiroshi • JPN
IBERICAS F.C., LAS • 1971 • Maso Pedro • SPN
IBIS • 1975 • Kimiyaei Massoud • IRN
IBIS ROUGE, L' • 1975 • Mocky Jean-Pierre • FRN
IBM CLOSE-UP • 1968 • Kroitor Roman, Ferguson Graeme • CND
IBM PUPPET SHOWS • 1965 • Eames Charles, Eames Ray • SHT • USA
IBN AN-NIL see **IBN EL NIL** • 1951
IBN EL NIL • 1951 • Shahin Youssef • EGY • SON OF THE NILE, THE ○ IBN AN-NIL ○ NILE'S SON, THE
IBN HAMIDU • 1956 • Wahab Fatin Abdel • EGY • FILS D'AMIDOU, LE
IBO AND GULSAH see **IBO ILE GULSAH** • 1978
IBO ILE GULSAH • 1978 • Yilmaz Atif • TRK • IBO AND GULSAH
IBONG ADARNA • 1941 • Salumbides Vicente • PHL
IBRET • 1971 • Goren Serif, Guney Yilmaz • TRK • EXAMPLE, THE
IBU MERTUA KU • Ramlee P. • MLY • MY MOTHER-IN-LAW
IBUN SARUTOBI SASUKE • 1965 • Shinoda Masahiro • JPN • SAMURAI SPY ○ SARUTOBI
IBUNDA • 1986 • Karya Teguh • INN • MOTHER
ICAROS • 1973 • Lilienthal Peter • FRG
ICARUS • 1960 • De Palma Brian • USA
ICARUS • 1967 • Afanasjew Jerzy, Zitzman Jerzy • ANS • PLN
ICARUS MONTGOLFIER WRIGHT • 1962 • Engel Jules • ANS • USA
ICARUS XB-1 see **IKARIE XB-1** • 1963
ICE • 1970 • Kramer Robert • USA
ICE • 1984 • Weldon John • ANM • CND
ICE see **IS** • 1970
ICE ACES • 1948 • Barclay David • SHT • USA
ICE AGE see **EISZEIT** • 1975
ICE ANTICS • 1939 • Miller David • SHT • USA
ICE-BREAKER KRASSNIN, THE see **PODVIG VO IDACH** • 1928
ICE-BREAKING see **ISEN BRYDES** • 1947
ICE-CAPADES • 1941 • Santley Joseph • USA
ICE-CAPADES REVUE • 1942 • Vorhaus Bernard • USA • RHYTHM HITS THE ICE (UKN)
ICE CARNIVAL, THE • 1941 • Donnelly Eddie • ANS • USA
ICE CASTLES • 1978 • Wrye Donald • USA
ICE COLD COCOS • 1926 • Lord Del • SHT • USA
ICE COLD IN ALEX • 1958 • Thompson J. Lee • UKN • DESERT ATTACK (USA)
ICE CONTINENT, THE see **CONTINENTE DI GHIACCIO, IL** • 1975
ICE CREAM JACK, THE • 1907 • Collins Alf • UKN
ICE-CREAM MAN, THE • 1984 • Prohmvitake Pakorn • THL
ICE CREAM SODA • 1968 • Meyering Kees • SHT • NTH
ICE FLOOD, THE • 1926 • Seitz George B. • USA
ICE FOLLIES OF 1939, THE • 1939 • Schunzel Reinhold • USA
ICE-HOCKEY see **HOCKEY** • 1981
ICE HOUSE, THE • 1969 • McGowan Stuart E. • USA • LOVE IN COLD BLOOD ○ PASSION PIT, THE
ICE MAN'S BRIDE, AN • 1917 • *Keystone* • SHT • USA
ICE MAN'S LUCK • 1929 • Lantz Walter • ANS • USA
ICE PALACE • 1960 • Sherman Vincent • USA
ICE PALACE, THE see **IS-SLOTTET** • 1986
ICE PIRATES • 1984 • Raffill Stewart • USA
ICE POND • 1939 • Davis Mannie • ANS • USA
ICE RUNNER, THE • 1989 • Coleman Clifford • USA
ICE SCREAM • 1957 • Kneitel Seymour • ANS • USA
ICE STATION ZEBRA • 1968 • Sturges John • USA
ICEBIRDS see **ISFUGLE** • 1983
ICEBOUND • 1924 • De Mille William C. • USA
ICEBOX MURDERS, THE • 1986 • *Taylor Jack* • USA
ICED BULLET, THE • 1917 • Barker Reginald • USA
ICELAND • 1942 • Humberstone H. Bruce • USA • KATINA (UKN)
ICELANDIC SHOCK STATION, THE see **STELLA I ORLOFI** • 1987
ICEMAN • 1984 • Schepisi Fred • USA
ICEMAN AND THE ARTIST, THE • 1916 • *Hamilton Lloyd V.* • SHT • USA
ICEMAN COMETH, THE • 1973 • Frankenheimer John • USA
ICEMAN COMETH, THE see **GAPDUNG KEIHAP** • 1989
ICEMAN DUCKETH, THE • 1964 • Monroe Phil • ANS • USA
ICEMAN'S BALL, THE • 1932 • Sandrich Mark • SHT • USA
ICEMAN'S REVENGE, THE • 1913 • *Majestic* • USA
ICH BEI TAG UND DU BEI NACHT • 1932 • Berger Ludwig • FRG
ICH BIN AUCH NUR EINE FRAU • 1962 • Weidenmann Alfred • FRG • ONLY A WOMAN (USA)
ICH BIN AUF DER WELT, UM GLUCKLICH ZU SEIN see **MADCHEN IN WEISS** • 1936
ICH - BIN - DU.. • 1920 • Bauer James • FRG
ICH BIN EIN ANTISTAR • 1976 • von Praunheim Rosa • FRG • I AM AN ANTISTAR
ICH BIN EIN ELEFANT, MADAME • 1968 • Zadek Peter • FRG • I'M AN ELEPHANT, MADAME (UKN)
ICH BIN GLEICH WIEDER DA • 1939 • Brauer Peter P. • FRG
ICH BIN SEBASTIAN OTT • 1939 • Forst Willi • FRG • I AM SEBASTIAN OTT (USA)
ICH BITTE UM VOLLMACHT • 1944 • Leiter Karl • FRG
ICH BLEIB' BEI DIR • 1931 • Meyer Johannes • FRG • MARYS START IN DIE EHE
ICH BRAUCHE DICH • 1944 • Schweikart Hans • FRG
ICH DACHTE, ICH WARE TOT • 1974 • Gremm Wolfgang • FRG • I HAD A FEELING I WAS DEAD
ICH, DAS ABENTEUER HEUTE EINE FRAU ZU SEIN • 1973 • vom Bruck Roswitha • FRG • CLIMAX (UKN)
ICH DENKE OFT AN PIROSCHKA • 1955 • Hoffmann Kurt • FRG
ICH DIENTE UM DICH • 1923 • *Ebert-Film* • FRG
ICH DZIEN POWSZEDNI • 1963 • Scibor-Rylski Aleksander • PLN • THEIR EVERYDAY LIFE ○ EVERYDAY
ICH -EIN GROUPIE • 1970 • Williams Fred • FRG, SWT • ME, A GROUPIE ○ I -A GROUPIE
ICH FUR DICH -DU FUR MICH • 1934 • Froelich Carl • FRG
ICH GEH' AUS UND DU BLEIBST DA • 1931 • Behrendt Hans • FRG
ICH GLAUB' NIE MEHR AN EINE FRAU • 1930 • Reichmann Max • FRG
ICH GLAUBE AN DICH • 1945 • Hansen Rolf • FRG • MATHILDE MOHRING
ICH HAB DICH LIEB • 1926 • Krause Karl Otto • FRG
ICH HAB MEIN HERZ IM AUTOBUS VERLOREN • 1929 • Gambino Domenico M., Campogalliani Carlo • FRG
ICH HAB MEIN HERZ IN HEIDELBERG VERLOREN • 1926 • Bergen Arthur • FRG
ICH HAB' MEIN HERZ IN HEIDELBERG VERLOREN • 1952 • Neubach Ernst • FRG
ICH HAB MICH SO AN DICH GEWOHNT • 1952 • von Borsody Eduard • FRG • GESCHIEDENES FRAULEIN
ICH HAB' VON DIR GETRAUMT • 1944 • Staudte Wolfgang • FRG • I DREAMED OF YOU
ICH HABE DICH GELIEBT BIS IN DEN TOD • 1918 • *Fichtner Erwin* • FRG
ICH HABE IM MAI VON DER LIEBE GETRAUMT • 1927 • Seitz Franz • FRG
ICH HABE SIE GUT GEKANNT (FRG) see **IO LA CONOSCEVO BENE** • 1965
ICH HASSE BLONDINEN see **ODIO LE BIONDE** • 1980
ICH HATT' EINEN KAMERADEN • 1923 • *Sing-Film* • FRG
ICH HATT' EINEN KAMERADEN • *Gebuhr Otto* • FRG
ICH HATT' EINEN KAMERADEN • 1926 • Wiene Conrad • FRG
ICH HATTE EINST EIN SCHONES VATERLAND • 1928 • Mack Max • FRG
ICH HEIRATE HERRN DIREKTOR • 1960 • Liebeneiner Wolfgang • AUS
ICH HEIRATE MEINE FRAU • 1934 • Riemann Johannes • FRG
ICH HEIRATE MEINE FRAU see **IHR LETZTES LIEBESABENTEUER** • 1927
ICH HEIRATE MEINEN MANN • 1931 • Emo E. W. • FRG
ICH HEISSE NIKI • 1952 • Jugert Rudolf • FRG
ICH KANN NICHT LANGER SCHWEIGEN • 1962 • Wiedermann Jochen • FRG • TRAGEDY OF SILENCE, THE
ICH KAUF MIR LIEBER EINEN TIROLERHUT • 1965 • Billian Hans • FRG
ICH KENN' DICH NICHT UND LIEBE DICH • 1933 • von Bolvary Geza • FRG • I DON'T KNOW YOU, BUT I LOVE YOU (USA)
ICH KENNE DICH NICHT MEHR see **UN-ERHORTE FRAU, DIE** • 1936
ICH KLAGE AN • 1919 • Illes Eugen • FRG
ICH KLAGE AN • 1941 • Liebeneiner Wolfgang • FRG • I'M ACCUSING
ICH KUSSE IHRE HAND, MADAME • 1929 • Land Robert • FRG • I KISS YOUR HAND, MADAME (USA)
ICH LASSE DICH NICHT • 1919 • Eriksen Erich • FRG
ICH LEBE FUR DICH • 1929 • Dieterle William • FRG • TRIUMPH OF LOVE (USA) ○ TRIOMPHE DE LA VIE, LE
ICH LIEBE ALLE FRAUEN • 1935 • Lamac Carl • FRG
ICH LIEBE DICH • 1925 • Stein Paul L. • FRG
ICH LIEBE DICH • 1938 • Selpin Herbert • FRG
ICH LIEBE DICH, ICH TOTE DICH • 1970 • Brandner Uwe • FRG • I LOVE YOU, I KILL YOU
ICH MACH' DICH GLUCKLICH • 1949 • von Szlatinay Alexander • FRG
ICH MOCHT' SO GERN MIR DIR ALLEIN SEIN • 1937 • Martin Karl Heinz • FRG • MILLIONARE
ICH MOCHTE KEIN MANN SEIN • 1919 • Lubitsch Ernst • FRG • I DON'T WANT TO BE A MAN
ICH ODER DU • 1919 • *Lux-Film* • FRG
ICH PUTI RAZOSHCHLIS • 1932 • Fedorov • USS
ICH SCHLAFE MIT MEINEM MORDER • 1971 • Becker Wolfgang • FRG • DEAD SEXY
ICH SCHWORE UND GELOBE • 1960 • von Radvanyi Geza • FRG
ICH SEHNE MICH NACH DIR • 1934 • Riemann Johannes • FRG
ICH SING' MICH IN DEIN HERZ HINEIN • 1934 • Kampers Fritz • FRG
ICH SPRENG EUCH ALLE IN DIE LUFT -INSPEKTOR BLOMFIELDS FALL NR.1 • 1968 • Zehetgruber Rudolf • FRG • I SHALL BLOW YOU ALL UP -INSPECTOR BLOOMFIELD'S CASE NO.1
ICH SPURE DEINE HAUT • 1968 • Schlesinger Gunter • FRG • TOUCH ME (UKN)
ICH SUCHE DICH • 1956 • Fischer O. W. • FRG
ICH SUCHE EINEN MANN • 1966 • Weidenmann Alfred • FRG
ICH TANZE MIR DIR IN DEN HIMMEL HINEIN see **HANNERL** • 1952
ICH UND DIE KAISERIN • 1932 • Hollander Friedrich • FRG
ICH UND DU • 1953 • Weidenmann Alfred • FRG
ICH UND MEIN FRAU • 1953 • von Borsody Eduard • AUS
ICH UND MEINE SCHWEIGERSOHNE • 1956 • Jacoby Georg • FRG
ICH VERTRAUE DIR MEINE FRAU AN • 1943 • Hoffmann Kurt • FRG
ICH VERWEIGERE DIE AUSSAGE • 1939 • Linnekogel Otto • FRG
ICH WAR EIN HASSLICHES MADCHEN • 1955 • Liebeneiner Wolfgang • FRG
ICH WAR IHM HORIG • 1958 • Becker Wolfgang • FRG
ICH WAR JACK MORTIMER • 1935 • Froelich Carl • FRG
ICH WAR NEUNZEHN • 1967 • Wolf Konrad • GDR • I WAS NINETEEN ○ NINETEEN
ICH WAR ZU HEIDELBERG STUDENT • 1927 • Neff Wolfgang • FRG

ICH WARTE AUF DICH • 1952 • von Collande Volker • FRG
ICH WARTE AUF DICH see **FALL RAINIER, DER** • 1942
ICH WEISS, WOFUR ICH LEBE • 1955 • Verhoeven Paul • FRG
ICH WERDE DICH AUF HANDEN TRAGEN • 1943 • Hoffmann Kurt • FRG
ICH WERDE DICH AUF HANDEN TRAGEN • 1958 • Harlan Veit • FRG
ICH WILL DICH LIEBE LEHREN • 1932 • Hilpert Heinz • FRG
ICH WILL DOCH NUR, DASS IHR MICH LIEBT • 1976 • Fassbinder R. W. • FRG • I ONLY WANT YOU TO LOVE ME
ICH WILL LEBEN • 1976 • Eggers Jorg A. • AUS • I WANT TO LIVE
ICH WILL NICHT WISSEN, WER DU BIST • 1932 • von Bolvary Geza • FRG
ICH WOLLTE LEBEN • 1982 • Ninaus Alfred, Ninaus Ruth • AUS • I WANTED TO LIVE
ICH ZAHLE TAGLICH MEIN SORGEN • 1960 • Martin Paul • FRG
ICHAAT AL-HUBB • 1960 • Wahab Fatin Abdel • EGY • RUMEUR D'AMOUR
ICHABOD AND MR. TOAD • 1949 • Algar James, Kinney Jack, Geronimi Clyde • ANM • USA • ADVENTURES OF ICHABOD AND MR. TOAD, THE
ICHHAPURAN • 1969 • Sen Mrinal • IND • WISH-FULFILMENT
ICHIBAN UTSUKUSHIKU • 1944 • Kurosawa Akira • JPN • MOST BEAUTIFUL, THE ○ MOST BEAUTIFULLY
ICHIJOJI NO KETTO • 1941 • Inagaki Hiroshi • JPN • DUEL AT ICHIJOJI TEMPLE
ICHIJOJI NO KETTO • 1955 • Inagaki Hiroshi • JPN • DUEL AT ICHIJOJI TEMPLE ○ SAMURAI (PART II)(USA)
ICHINICHI 240 JIKAN • 1970 • Teshigahara Hiroshi • SHT • JPN • ONE DAY, 240 HOURS
ICI, AILLEURS • 1961 • Vilardebo Carlos • SHT • FRN
ICI ET AILLEURS • 1977 • Godard Jean-Luc, Mieville Anne-Marie • FRN
ICI L'ON PECHE • 1941 • Jayet Rene • FRN
ICI NAIT LA FANTAISIE • Misonne Claude • DOC • BLG
ICICLE THIEF (UKN) see **LADRI DI SAPONETTE** • 1989
ICKLE MEETS PICKLE • 1942 • Rasinski Connie • ANS • USA
ICLI KIZ FUNDA • 1967 • Karamanbey Cetin • TRK • FUNDA, THE SENSIBLE GIRL
ICOGRADA CONGRESS • 1966 • Halas John • UKN
ICONOCKAUT • 1975 • Nunes Jose Maria • SPN
ICONOCLAST, THE • 1910 • Griffith D. W. • USA
ICONOCLAST, THE • 1913 • West Raymond B. • USA
ICONOSTASIS see **IKONOSTASAT** • 1968
ICY BREASTS (USA) see **SEINS DE GLACE, LES** • 1974
ID AL-MAIRUN • 1967 • Shahin Youssef • SHT • EGY • FETE DU MAYROUN, LA ○ MYRON
I'D CLIMB THE HIGHEST MOUNTAIN • 1931 • Fleischer Dave • ANS • USA
I'D CLIMB THE HIGHEST MOUNTAIN • 1951 • King Henry • USA
I'D GIVE MY LIFE • 1936 • Marin Edwin L. • USA • NOOSE
I'D LIKE A SHAVE see **CHCIALBYM SIE OGOLIC** • 1967
I'D LIKE A WORD WITH YOU • 1979 • Robinson Peter • UKN
I'D LIKE TO SHAVE see **CHCIALBYM SIE OGOLIC** • 1967
I'D LOVE TO FALL ASLEEP AND WAKE UP IN MY MAMMY'S ARMS • 1922 • *Parkinson H. B. (P)* • SHT • UKN
I'D LOVE TO TAKE ORDERS FROM YOU • 1936 • Avery Tex • ANS • USA
I'D RATHER BE RICH • 1964 • Smight Jack • USA
I'D RATHER WALK • 1984 • Dalen Zale R. • MTV • CND
IDA REGENYE • 1934 • Sekely Steve • HNG
IDADE DA TERRA, A • 1981 • Rocha Glauber • BRZ • AGE OF THE EARTH, THE ○ AGE DE LA TERRE, L'
IDAHO • 1925 • Hill Robert F. • SRL • USA
IDAHO • 1942 • Kane Joseph • USA
IDAHO KID, THE • 1936 • Hill Robert F. • USA
IDAHO RED • 1929 • De Lacy Robert • USA
IDAHO TRANSFER • 1975 • Fonda Peter • USA • DERANGED
IDA'S CHRISTMAS • 1912 • Brooke Van Dyke • USA
IDATEN KICHIJI • 1927 • Ito Daisuke • JPN
IDE DO SLONCA see **IDE KU SLONCU** • 1955
IDE KU SLONCU • 1955 • Wajda Andrzej • SHT • PLN • MARCH TOWARDS THE SUN ○ I GO TOWARDS THE SUN ○ IDE DO SLONCA ○ TOWARDS THE SUN ○ I GO TO THE SUN ○ INTO THE SUN ○ I WALK TO THE SUN
IDEA, THE see **IDEE, L'** • 1934
IDEA DEMONSTRATIONS • 1972 • Parr Mike • ASL
IDEA DI UN'ISOLA • 1970 • Rossellini Roberto • MTV • ITL
IDEA FISSA, L' • 1964 • Puccini Gianni, Guerrini Mino • ITL • LOVE AND MARRIAGE (USA)
IDEA GIRL • 1946 • Jason Will • USA
IDEAL • 1965 • Pojar Bretislav • ANS • CZC
IDEAL see **BHAVANA** • 1984
IDEAL HUSBAND, AN • 1948 • Korda Alexander • UKN
IDEAL HUSBAND, AN see **IDEALNY MUZH** • 1981
IDEAL LODGER, THE see **IDEALE UNTERMIETER, DER** • 1956
IDEAL SEPTIMY • 1938 • Kubasek Vaclav • CZC • SEPTIMA'S IDEAL
IDEAL WOMAN see **AADARSHA NAARI** • 1983
IDEAL WOMAN, THE (USA) see **FEMME IDEALE, LA** • 1933
IDEALE BRAUTPAAR, DAS • 1954 • Stemmle R. A. • FRG
IDEALE FRAU, DIE • 1959 • von Baky Josef • FRG
IDEALE GATTIN, DIE • 1914 • Ewers Hans H. • FRG
IDEALE UNTERMIETER, DER • 1956 • Schmidt Wolf • FRG • IDEAL LODGER, THE
IDEALER GATTE, EIN • 1935 • Selpin Herbert • FRG
IDEALIST • 1977 • Pretnar Igor • YGS
IDEALNY MUZH • 1981 • Georgiev Viktor • USS • IDEAL HUSBAND, AN
IDEE, L' • 1934 • Bartosch Berthold • ANS • FRN • IDEA, THE
IDEE A L'EAU, UNE see **IRRESISTIBLE REBELLE, L'** • 1940
IDEE DE FRANCOISE, L' • 1923 • Saidreau Robert • FRN
IDEE FOLLE, UNE • 1932 • de Vaucorbeil Max • FRN
IDEES FIXES (FRN) see **VARIATIONS ON THE SAME THEME** • 1978
IDEGEN ARCOK • 1974 • Szoreny Rezso • HNG • STRANGE FACES
IDEIGLENES PARADICSOM • 1981 • Kovacs Andras • HNG • TEMPORARY PARADISE

IDEL ADEL ADEL • 1945 • Henrikson Anders • SWD • NOTHING BUT OLD NOBILITY
IDEMO DALJE • 1983 • Sotra Zdravko • YGS • LET'S GO ON
IDENTICAL IDENTITIES • 1913 • *Calvert E. H.* • USA
IDENTIFICATION see **AZONOSITAS** • 1976
IDENTIFICATION, THE • 1914 • McGowan J. P. • USA
IDENTIFICATION DES VEHICULES • 1966 • Rivard Fernand • DCS • CND
IDENTIFICATION OF A WOMAN see **IDENTIFICAZIONE DI UNA DONNA** • 1982
IDENTIFICATIONS MARKS -NONE see **RYSOPIS** • 1964
IDENTIFICAZIONE DI UNA DONNA • 1982 • Antonioni Michelangelo • ITL, FRN • IDENTIFICATION OF A WOMAN
IDENTIFYING FEATURES: VERY HANDSOME see **SEGNI PARTICOLARI: BELLISSIMO** • 1984
IDENTIKIT • 1974 • Patroni Griffi Giuseppe • ITL • DRIVER'S SEAT, THE (USA)
IDENTITE • 1973 • Dong Jean-Marie • GBN
IDENTITE JUDICAIRE • 1950 • Bromberger Herve • FRN • MONSIEUR MURDERER
IDENTITY, THE • 1986 • Hatamikia Ebrahim • IRN
IDENTITY CRISIS • 1989 • Van Peebles Melvin • USA
IDENTITY PARADE (UKN) see **LINE-UP, THE** • 1934
IDENTITY UNKNOWN • 1945 • Colmes Walter, Bretherton Howard? • USA
IDENTITY UNKNOWN • 1960 • Marshall Frank • UKN
IDI AMIN DADA • 1974 • Schroeder Barbet • DOC • FRN • GENERAL IDI AMIN DADA (USA) ○ GENERAL AMIN (UKN) ○ GENERAL IDI AMIN DADA: AUTOPORTRAIT
IDI AMIN -MY PEOPLE LOVE ME • 1975 • Burke Martyn • DOC • CND
IDI I SMOTRI • 1986 • Klimov Elem • USS • COME AND SEE (UKN)
IDILIO DE ESTACION, UN • 1978 • Uset Anibal E. • ARG • SEASONAL IDYLL, A
IDILIO EN MALLORCA • 1942 • Neufeld Max • SPN
IDILLIO • 1978 • Risi Nelo • MTV • ITL • INFINITO DI GIACOMO LEOPARDI, L'
IDILLIO 1848 see **AMO TE SOLA** • 1935
IDILLIO A BUDAPEST • 1941 • Ansoldi Giorgio, Varriale Gabriele • ITL • DUCA E FORSE UNA DUCHESSA, UN
IDILLIO TRAGICO • 1912 • Negroni Baldassare • ITL
IDIOT, DER see **IRRENDE SEELEN** • 1921
IDIOT, L' • 1945 • Lampin Georges • FRN
IDIOT, THE • 1914 • Crisp Donald • *Majestic* • USA
IDIOT, THE • 1914 • Vale Travers • *Ab* • USA
IDIOT, THE see **DUMMKOPF, DER** • 1920
IDIOT, THE see **HAKUCHI** • 1951
IDIOT, THE (USA) see **NASTASIA FILIPOVNA** • 1958
IDIOT A PARIS, UN • 1967 • Korber Serge • FRN • IDIOT IN PARIS
IDIOT IN LOVE, AN see **CHIJIN NO AI** • 1960
IDIOT IN LOVE, AN see **CHIJIN NO AI** • 1967
IDIOT IN PARIS see **IDIOT A PARIS, UN** • 1967
IDIOT OF THE MOUNTAINS, THE • 1909 • Bouwmeester Theo? • UKN
IDIOT OF XEENEMUNDE, THE • 1964 • Balik Jaroslav • CZC
IDIOTS DE LUXE • 1945 • White Jules • SHT • USA
IDIOT'S DELIGHT • 1938 • Brown Clarence • USA
IDIOTS MAY APPLY see **HULYESEG NEM AKADALY** • 1985
IDLE BOAST, THE • 1911 • *Lubin* • USA
IDLE CLASS, THE • 1921 • Chaplin Charles • USA
IDLE HANDS • 1920 • Reicher Frank • USA
IDLE RICH, THE • 1915 • *L-Ko* • USA
IDLE RICH, THE • 1915 • Ransom Charles • *Edison* • USA
IDLE RICH, THE • 1921 • Karger Maxwell • USA • JUNK
IDLE RICH, THE • 1929 • De Mille William C. • USA
IDLE ROOMERS • 1944 • Lord Del • SHT • USA
IDLE TONGUES • 1924 • Hillyer Lambert • USA • DOCTOR NYE
IDLE WIVES • 1916 • Weber Lois, Smalley Phillips • USA
IDLER see **NAMAKEMONO** • 1927
IDLER, THE • 1914 • *Reliance* • USA
IDLER, THE • 1914 • Johnson Tefft • *Vitagraph* • USA
IDLER, THE • 1915 • Carleton Lloyd B. • USA
IDLERS AT WORK see **IDLERS THAT WORK** • 1949
IDLERS OF THE FERTILE VALLEY see **TEMBELIDES TIS EFORIS KILADAS, I** • 1976
IDLERS THAT WORK • 1949 • Anderson Lindsay • DCS • UKN • IDLERS AT WORK
IDO ABLAKAI, AZ • 1969 • Fejer Tamas • HNG • WINDOWS OF TIME, THE
IDO KEREKE, AZ • 1961 • Jancso Miklos • SHT • HNG • WHEELS OF TIME, THE
IDO VAN see **MEGALL AZ IDO** • 1981
IDO ZERO DAISAKUSEN • 1969 • Honda Inoshiro • JPN • LATITUDE ZERO
IDOL see **IDOLAT** • 1972
IDOL, THE • 1915 • Bertram William • USA
IDOL, THE • 1966 • Petrie Daniel • UKN
IDOL DANCER, THE • 1920 • Griffith D. W. • USA
IDOL OF BONANZA CAMP, THE • 1913 • *Gaden Alexander* • USA
IDOL OF FATE, THE • 1915 • MacGregor Norval • USA
IDOL OF PARIS • 1948 • Arliss Leslie • UKN
IDOL OF PARIS, THE • 1914 • Elvey Maurice • UKN
IDOL OF THE CROWD • 1944 • *O'Brien Joseph/ Mead Thomas (P)* • USA
IDOL OF THE CROWDS • 1937 • Lubin Arthur • USA
IDOL OF THE HOUR, THE • 1913 • *Snow Marguerite* • USA
IDOL OF THE NORTH, THE • 1921 • Neill R. William • USA • TEASER, THE
IDOL OF THE STAGE, THE • 1916 • Garrick Richard • USA
IDOL ON PARADE • 1959 • Gilling John • UKN
IDOL WORSHIPPER, THE • 1912 • *Cornwall Blanche* • USA
IDOLAT • 1972 • Chavdarov Georgi • BUL • IDOL
IDOLATORS • 1917 • Edwards Walter • USA
IDOLATRADA • 1984 • Gomes Paulo Augusto • BRZ • IDOLISED
IDOLE, L' • 1924 • Bieganski Victor • PLN
IDOLE, L' • 1947 • Esway Alexander • FRN
IDOLE DES FOULES, L' see **FATINAT AL-JAMAHIR** • 1964
IDOLE DES JEUNES, L' • 1974 • Lagrange Yvan • FRN
IDOLES, LES • 1963 • Karmitz Marin • SHT • FRN

IDOLES, LES • 1968 • Marc'O • FRN
IDOLI CONTROLUCE • 1966 • Battaglia Enzo • ITL
IDOLISED see **IDOLATRADA** • 1984
IDOLMAKER, THE • 1980 • Hackford Taylor • USA
IDOLO, EL • 1949 • Chenal Pierre • CHL
IDOLO DA BOLA, O • 1952 • Marques Carlos • SHT • PRT
IDOLO DEL TANGO, EL • 1949 • Canziani Hector • ARG
IDOLO MALDITO, EL • 1971 • *Nova* • MXC
IDOLOS • 1943 • Rey Florian • SPN
IDOLOS DE LA RADIO • 1935 • Morera Eduardo
IDOLS • 1916 • Cullison Webster • USA
IDOL'S EYE, THE • 1910 • *Imp* • USA
IDOLS IN THE DUST (UKN) see **SATURDAY'S HERO** • 1951
IDOLS OF CLAY • 1915 • Leonard Robert Z. • USA
IDOLS OF CLAY • 1920 • Fitzmaurice George • USA
IDOMENEO • 1990 • Kreihsl Michael • AUS
IDU DANI • 1968 • Dragic Nedeljko • YGS, ITL • PASSING DAYS ○ DAYS ELAPSE, THE ○ DAY COMES, THE
IDU DANI • 1971 • Hadzic Fadil • YGS • DAYS ARE PASSING
IDU NA GROZU • 1965 • Mikailyan Sergei • USS • INTO THE STORM
IDYL, THE see **IDYLL, THE** • 1948
IDYL OF HAWAII, AN • 1912 • *American* • USA
IDYL OF THE HILLS, AN • 1915 • De Grasse Joseph • USA
IDYLL, THE • 1948 • Lee Francis • ANS • USA • IDYL, THE
IDYLL IN A TUNNEL see **IDYLLE SOUS UN TUNNEL** • 1901
IDYLLE • 1897 • Blache Alice • FRN
IDYLLE • 1972 • Ledoux Patrick • BLG
IDYLLE A LA FERME • 1912 • Linder Max • FRN
IDYLLE A LA PLAGE • 1931 • Storck Henri • SHT • BLG
IDYLLE AU CAIRE • 1933 • Heymann Claude, Schunzel Reinhold • FRN
IDYLLE AU CHATEAU see **DANS LA VIE TOUT S'ARRANE** • 1949
IDYLLE INTERROMPUE • 1897-98 • Blache Alice • FRN
IDYLLE SOUS UN TUNNEL • 1901 • Zecca Ferdinand • FRN • IDYLL IN A TUNNEL
IDYLLE TRAGIQUE, UNE • 1921 • Ravel Gaston • FRN
IEMAND SOOS JY see **SOMEONE LIKE YOU** • 1978
IEMITSU TO HIKOZA TO ISSHIN TASUKE • 1961 • Sawashima Chu • JPN • SHOGUN AND THE FISHMONGER
IERAISHAN see **YEI RAI SHAN** • 1951
IERI, OGGI, DOMANI • 1953 • Rolvy Sasy • ITL
IERI, OGGI, DOMANI • 1963 • De Sica Vittorio • ITL, FRN • YESTERDAY, TODAY AND TOMORROW (USA) ○ IERI, OGGI E DOMANI ○ HIER, AUJOURD'HUI ET DEMAIN (FRN)
IERI, OGGI E DOMANI see **IERI, OGGI, DOMANI** • 1963
IEVGENY ONYEGIN • 1958 • Tikhomirov Roman • USS • EUGENE ONEGIN
IF • 1916 • Kinder Stuart • UKN
IF.. • 1968 • Anderson Lindsay • UKN • CRUSADERS
IF A BODY MEETS A BODY • 1945 • White Jules • SHT • USA
IF A COMRADE CALLS • 1963 • Ivanov Alexander • USS
IF A MAN ANSWERS • 1962 • Levin Henry • USA
IF A PICTURE TELLS A STORY • 1924 • Quiribet Gaston • UKN
IF A THOUSAND CLARINETS see **KDYBY TISIC KLARINETU** • 1964
IF A WOMAN LOVES see **KADIN SEVERSE** • 1968
IF ALL THE GUYS IN THE WORLD (USA) see **SI TOUS LES GARS DU MONDE** • 1955
IF ALL THE WOMEN IN THE WORLD see **KISS THE GIRLS AND MAKE THEM DIE** • 1966
IF ALL THE WOMEN IN THE WORLD see **AN OLES IYINEKES TOU KOSMOU** • 1967
IF AT FIRST YOU DON'T SUCCEED • 1914 • Martin E. A. • USA
IF BUSINESS INTERFERES..? see **STEPPIN' OUT** • 1925
IF CATS COULD SING • 1950 • Donnelly Eddie • ANS • USA
IF DEW FALLS RAIN FOLLOWS see **DRIVER DAGG FALLER REGN** • 1946
IF DREAMS CAME TRUE • 1912 • *Rex* • USA
IF DREAMS CAME TRUE OR WHO'D HAVE THUNK IT? • 1913 • *Mack Hughie* • USA
IF ENGLAND WERE INVADED see **RAID OF 1915, THE** • 1914
IF EVER I SEE YOU AGAIN • 1978 • Brooks Joseph • USA
IF EVERY GUY IN THE WORLD see **SI TOUS LES GARS DU MONDE** • 1955
IF FATE WILL PART US see **KADER AYIRSA BILE** • 1968
IF FOUR WALLS TOLD • 1922 • Paul Fred • UKN
IF HE HOLLERS, LET HIM GO • 1968 • Martin Charles • USA
IF I DIDN'T MISS YOU • 1929 • Aylott Dave, Symmons E. F. • SHT • UKN
IF I DON'T AGREE MUST I GO AWAY? • 1969 • Pearson Peter • CND
IF I GROW UP • Szoboszlay Peter • ANM • HNG
IF I HAD A GIRL see **KEBY SOM MAL DIEVCA** • 1976
IF I HAD A GUN see **KEBY SOM MAL PUSKU** • 1972
IF I HAD A MILLION • 1932 • Roberts Stephen, Cruze James, Seiter William A., Taurog Norman, Lubitsch Ernst, Humberstone H. Bruce • USA
IF I HAD A MILLION • 1973 • *Schuck John* • MTV • USA
IF I HAD FOUR DROMEDARIES see **SI J'AVAIS QUATRE DROMADAIRES** • 1966
IF I HAD MY WAY • 1940 • Butler David • USA
IF I HAD TO DO IT ALL OVER AGAIN see **SI C'ETAIT A REFAIRE** • 1975
IF I LOSE YOU see **SENI KAYBEDERESEN** • 1961
IF I LOVE YOU? see **LIUBLIU LITEBIA?** • 1934
IF I MARRY AGAIN • 1925 • Dillon John Francis • USA
IF I SHOULD PLANT A TINY SEED OF LOVE • 1909 • *Warwick Trading Co.* • UKN
IF I WAS A DADDY see **KDYBYCH BYL TATOU** • 1939
IF I WERE A BIRDIE see **KEBY SOM BOL VTACKOM**
IF I WERE A SPY see **SI J'ETAIS UN ESPION** • 1966
IF I WERE A STAR see **HATSUKOI SENGEN** • 1968
IF I WERE BOSS • 1938 • Rogers Maclean • UKN
IF I WERE FOR REAL see **CHIA-JU WO SHIH CHEN-TE** • 1981
IF I WERE FREE • 1933 • Nugent Elliott • USA • BEHOLD WE LIVE (UKN)
IF I WERE KING • 1920 • Edwards J. Gordon • USA
IF I WERE KING • 1938 • Lloyd Frank • USA
IF I WERE KING (USA) see **WENN ICH KONIG WARI** • 1934
IF I WERE QUEEN • 1922 • Ruggles Wesley • USA

IF I WERE RICH • 1936 • Faye Randall • UKN
IF I WERE SINGLE • 1927 • Del Ruth Roy • USA
IF I WERE THE ONLY GIRL • 1916 • *Tress Henry* • SHT • UKN
IF I WERE YOUNG AGAIN • 1914 • Grandon Francis J. • USA
IF I'M LUCKY • 1946 • Seiler Lewis • USA • YOU'RE FOR ME
IF IT AIN'T STIFF, IT AIN'T WORTH A ... • 1977 • Abson Nick • DOC • UKN
IF IT DON'T CONCERN YOU LET IT ALONE • 1908 • *Essanay* • USA
IF IT WERE A DREAM see **YUME DE ARITAI** • 1962
IF IT WERE EVER THUS • 1911 • *Reliance* • USA
IF IT WERE NOT FOR POLLY • 1914 • Henderson Dell • USA
IF IT WEREN'T FOR MUSIC see **KDYBY TY MUSIKY NEBYLY** • 1963
IF IT'S TUESDAY, IT STILL MUST BE BELGIUM • 1987 • Sweeney Bob • TVM • USA
IF IT'S TUESDAY, THIS MUST BE BELGIUM • 1969 • Stuart Mel • USA
IF LOOKS COULD KILL • 1987 • Vincent Chuck • USA
IF LOOKS COULD KILL • 1990 • Dear William • USA
IF LOVE BE TRUE • 1909 • *Lubin* • USA
IF MARRIAGE FAILS • 1925 • Ince John • USA
IF MATCHES STRUCK • 1922 • Quiribet Gaston • UKN
IF MUSIC BE THE FOOD OF LOVE see **NEDTUR** • 1979
IF MY COUNTRY SHOULD CALL • 1916 • De Grasse Joseph • USA
IF MY WIFE CHEATS ME see **KARIM BENI ALDATIRSA** • 1967
IF NO TRAIN COMES • 1966 • Zahariev Edward • BUL
IF ONE COULD SEE INTO THE FUTURE • 1911 • *Ambrosio* • ITL
"IF ONLY" JIM • 1921 • Jaccard Jacques • USA
IF PIGS HAD WINGS see **PORCI CON LE ALI** • 1977
IF THE CAP FITS • 1947 • Hughes Ken • DCS • UKN
IF THE GODS LAUGH see **FIGHTING LOVE** • 1927
IF THE HORSEMEN.. see **SI LES CAVALIERS..**
IF THE HUNS CAME TO MELBOURNE • 1916 • Coates George • ASL
IF THE MAN IN THE MOON WERE A COON • 1908 • *Walturdaw* • UKN
IF THE WIND FRIGHTENS YOU see **SI LE VENT TE FAIT PEUR** • 1959
IF THERE WAS NO MUSIC see **KDYBY TY MUSIKY NEBYLY** • 1963
IF THERE WAS NOT A PARTING see **AYRILIK OLMASAYDI** • 1967
IF THESE WALLS COULD SPEAK • 1965 • Harmon Bill • SER • ASL
IF THEY TELL YOU I FELL see **SI TE DICEN QUE CAI** • 1989
IF THINGS WERE DIFFERENT • 1980 • Lewis Robert • TVM • USA
IF THIS BE LOVE see **A ESLI ETO LYUBOV?** • 1961
IF THIS BE SIN (USA) see **THAT DANGEROUS AGE** • 1949
IF THIS ISN'T LOVE • 1934 • Jason Leigh • SHT • USA
IF THOU WERT BLIND • 1917 • Thornton F. Martin • UKN
IF TOMORROW COMES • 1971 • McCowan George • TVM • USA • GLASS HAMMER, THE
IF TOMORROW COMES • 1986 • London Jerry • MTV • USA
IF WAR COMES TOMORROW • 1938 • Berezko G., Antsi-Polovski, Karmazinski N.
IF WAR COMES TOMORROW • 1938 • Dzigan Yefim • DOC • USS
IF WE ALL WERE ANGELS (USA) see **WENN WIR ALLE ENGEL WAREN** • 1936
IF WE KNEW THEN see **AFTERSHOCK** • 1989
IF WE LIVED TOGETHER see **SI VIVIERAMOS JUNTOS** • 1982
IF WE MEET AGAIN see **SI VOLVEMOS A VERNOS** • 1967
IF WE ONLY KNEW • 1913 • Griffith D. W. • USA
IF WE SEE EACH OTHER AGAIN see **SI VOLVEMOS A VERNOS** • 1967
IF WILLIAM PENN CAME TO LIFE • 1907 • *Lubin* • USA
IF WINTER COMES • 1923 • Millarde Harry • USA
IF WINTER COMES • 1947 • Saville Victor • USA
IF WOMEN ONLY KNEW • 1921 • Griffith Edward H. • USA
IF WOMEN WERE POLICEMEN • 1908 • Stow Percy • UKN
IF YOU BELIEVE IT, IT'S SO • 1922 • Forman Tom • USA
IF YOU COULD ONLY COOK • 1935 • Seiter William A. • USA
IF YOU COULD SEE WHAT I HEAR • 1981 • Till Eric • CND
IF YOU DON'T STOP IT YOU'LL GO BLIND • 1975 • Levy Bob, Brasselle Keefe • USA • YOU MUST BE JOKING
IF YOU DREAM AND WAKE UP see **KUNG MANGARAP KA'T MAGISING** • 1977
IF YOU FEEL LIKE SINGING (UKN) see **SUMMER STOCK** • 1950
IF YOU GOT THE FEELIN' • 1973 • Dominic John • USA
IF YOU HAD A WIFE LIKE THIS • 1907 • *Bitzer Billy (Ph)* • USA
IF YOU KNEW ELIZABETH • 1957 • Frankenheimer John • MTV • USA
IF YOU KNEW SUSIE • 1948 • Douglas Gordon • USA
IF YOU KNOW WHAT I MEAN • 1982 • *Houwer Rob (P)* • ANM • NTH • MR. BUMBLE
IF YOU LIKE IT see **SUKI NAREBA KOSO** • 1928
IF YOU LOVE ME see **AISUREBAKOSO** • 1955
...IF YOU MEET SARTANA PRAY FOR YOUR DEATH see **...SE INCONTRI SARTANA PREGA PER LA TUA MORTE** • 1968
IF YOU ONLY KNEW • 1946 • Gould Dave • SHT • USA
IF YOU PLAY WITH CRAZY BIRDS see **SPIELST DU MIT SCHRAGEN VOGELN** • 1968
IF YOU SEE A CAT.. see **JESLI UJRZYSZ KOTA FRUWAJACEGO PO NIEBIE** • 1972
IF YOU STAND BY ME see **WENN DU ZU MIR HALST..** • 1962
IF YOU TOUCH ME see **ORENI SAWARUTO ABUNAINE**
IF YOU WANT A DIVORCE, YOU HAVE ONE! see **KDYZ ROZVOD, TAK ROZVOD!** • 1982
IF YOU WANT TO BE HAPPY see **YESLI KHOCHESH BYT SCHASTLIVYM** • 1974
IF YOU WANT TO KNOW WHO WE ARE • 1907 • Morland John • UKN
IF YOU WANT TO LIVE.. SHOOT! see **SE VUOI VIVERE.. SPARA!** • 1968
IF YOUR HOME IS DEAR TO YOU see **YESLI DOROG TEBYE TVOY DOM** • 1967
IF YOUTH BUT KNEW • 1926 • Cooper George A. • UKN
IF YOUTH ONLY KNEW.. see **SI JEUNESSE SAVAIT..** • 1947

IFIGENIA • 1977 • Cacoyannis Michael • GRC • IPHIGENIA
IFIGENIA • 1979 • Sozio Silvia Manrique • VNZ
IFIGENIA • 1987 • Feo Ivan • VNZ
IFRITA HANIM • 1948 • Barakat Henry • EGY • DIABLESSE, LA
IFRITU 'IMRA'ATI see **AFRIT MERATI** • 1968
IFTIRA • 1968 • Utku Umit • TRK • SLANDER
IFTITAH'IYYATUN LI AL-BINA • 1974 • Nahhass Hashim An- • SHT • EGY • OUVERTURE POUR LA CONSTRUCTION
IGA NO SUIGETSU • 1958 • Watanabe Kunio • JPN • AMBUSH AT IGU PASS
IGAZ-E? • 1963 • Rozsa Janos • HNG • LOVE?
IGAZA FI GEHANNAM • 1949 • Zulficar Izzeddine • EGY • HOLIDAYS IN HELL ○ AGAZA FI GAHANIM ○ VACANCES EN ENFER
IGDENBU • 1930 • Bek-Nazarov Amo • USS
IGELFREUNDSCHAFT • 1962 • Zschoche Hermann • GDR, CZC • HEDGEHOG FRIENDSHIP
IGEN • 1964 • Revesz Gyorgy • HNG • YES
'IGH ART • 1915 • Birch Cecil • UKN
IGLOO • 1932 • Scott Ewing • USA
IGLOO FOR TWO, AN • 1955 • Rasinski Connie • ANS • USA
IGMAN MARCH, THE see **IGMANSKI MARS** • 1984
IGMANSKI MARS • 1984 • Sotra Zdravko • YGS • IGMAN MARCH, THE
IGNACE • 1937 • Colombier Piere • FRN
IGNATZ'S ICY INJURY • 1916 • *Armstrong Bill* • SHT • USA
IGNORANCE • 1916 • Fitzgerald J. A. • USA
IGNORANCE • 1922 • *Metcalfe Earl* • USA
IGNOTAS CAME BACK HOME • 1956 • Rasumny Alexander • USS • HOMECOMING, THE
IGOR AND THE LUNATICS • 1985 • Parolini Billy • USA
IGOR BULICHOV see **EGOR BULYCHOV** • 1953
IGOROTA see **IGOROTA, THE LEGEND OF THE TREE OF LIFE** • 1967
IGOROTA, THE LEGEND OF THE TREE OF LIFE • 1967 • Nepomuceno Luis • PHL • LEGEND OF THE TREE OF LIFE, THE ○ IGOROTA
IGORROTES, CROCODILES AND A HAT BOX • 1916 • Dillon John Francis • USA
IGRA • 1962 • Vukotic Dusan • SHT • YGS • GAME, THE (USA) ○ PLAY
IGRA BYEZ NICHYEY • 1967 • Kavtaradze Yuri • USS • GAME WITHOUT A DRAW
IGREK-17 • 1972 • Tsancov Villy • BUL • Y-SEVENTEEN ○ Y 17
IGROK • 1972 • Batalov Alexei • USS, CZC • GAMBLER, THE
IGUANA DALLA LINGUA DI FUOCO, L' • 1971 • Freda Riccardo • ITL
IGY JOTTEM • 1964 • Jancso Miklos • HNG • MY WAY HOME (UKN)
IHEN KUROTE-GUMI • 1937 • Ito Daisuke • JPN
IHLATHI LEZIMANGA • 1985 • SAF
IHMEMIES • 1979 • Peippo Antti • FNL • MIRACLE MAN, THE ○ WONDERMAN
IHMISET • 1948 • Vaala Valentin • FNL
IHOLIDE • 1985 • SAF
IHR 106 GEBURTSTAG • 1958 • Luders Gunther • FRG
IHR BESTER SCHUSS • 1916 • Biebrach Rudolf • FRG
IHR DUNKLER PUNKT • 1928 • Guter Johannes • FRG
IHR ERSTES ERLEBNIS • 1939 • von Baky Josef • FRG • HER FIRST EXPERIENCE (USA)
IHR ERSTES RENDEZVOUS • 1955 • von Ambesser Axel • FRG, AUS
IHR FEHLTRITT • 1923 • Asagaroff Georg • FRG
IHR GEBURTSTAG see **MOBILMACHUNG IN DER KUCHE 2** • 1915
IHR GLUCK VERKENNEN, DIE • 1920 • Illes Eugen • FRG
IHR GROSSER FALL see **GROSSE FALL, DER** • 1945
IHR GROSSES GEHEIMNIS • 1918 • May Joe? • FRG
IHR GROSSTER ERFOLG • 1934 • Meyer Johannes • FRG • THERESE KRONES
IHR JUNGE • 1918 • Eckstein Franz • FRG
IHR JUNGE • 1931 • Feher Friedrich • FRG, AUS, CZC • WENN DIE GEIGEN KLINGEN
IHR KORPORAL • 1956 • Emo E. W. • FRG, AUS • HUSARENMANOVER
IHR LASST DEN ARMEN SCHULDIG WERDEN.. • 1918 • Eckstein Franz • FRG
IHR LEIBHUSAR • 1937 • Marischka Hubert • FRG, AUS, HNG
IHR LEIBREGIMENT • 1955 • Deppe Hans • FRG
IHR LETZTE FILM • 1920 • *Hofmann Ernst* • FRG
IHR LETZTER FEHLER see **VERGESST MIR MEINE TRAUDEL NICHT** • 1957
IHR LETZTES LIEBESABENTEUER • 1927 • Reichmann Max • FRG • ICH HEIRATE MEINE FRAU
IHR PRIVATSEKRETAR • 1940 • Klein Charles • FRG
IHR RECHT • 1920 • *Wolter Hilde* • FRG
IHR SCHLECHTER RUF • 1921 • Eckstein Franz • FRG
IHR SCHONSTER TAG • 1962 • Verhoeven Paul • FRG
IHR SPORT • 1919 • Biebrach Rudolf • FRG
IHR UNTER OFFIZIER • 1915 • Halm Alfred • FRG
IHRE DURCHLAUCHT, DIE VERKAUFERIN • 1933 • Hartl Karl • FRG
IHRE GROSSE PRUFUNG • 1954 • Jugert Rudolf • FRG
IHRE HAUT ZU MARKTE TRAGEN, DIE • 1962 • Zbonek Edwin • FRG • DEUTSCHLAND, DEINE STERNCHEN
IHRE HOHEIT BEFIEHLT • 1931 • Schwarz Hanns • FRG
IHRE HOHEIT DIE TANZERIN • 1922 • Eichberg Richard • FRG
IHRE LETZTE DUMMHEIT • 1924 • Arvay Richard • FRG
IHRE MAJESTAT DIE LIEBE • 1930 • May Joe • FRG
II RALLY INTERNACIONAL BNU • 1972 • de Almeida Manuel Faria • SHT • PRT
III-ES, A • 1919 • Korda Alexander • HNG • NUMBER III ○ IN ROOM III ○ IN NO.III ○ THIRD, THE
III-ES, A • 1937 • Sekely Steve • HNG • III-ES SZOBABAN ○ IN ROOM III ○ THIRD ROOM, THE
III-ES SZOBABAN see **III-ES, A** • 1937
III PLAN DE DESARROLLO ECONOMICO Y SOCIAL • 1972 • Aguirre Javier • SHT • SPN
IJA OMINIRA • 1979 • Balogun Ola • NGR • FIGHT FOR FREEDOM
IJO NA HANNO: MONZETSU • 1967 • Nishihara Giichi • JPN • FALLING UNCONSCIOUS

IJO, PAPA! see **JO, PAPA** • 1975
IJO TAIKEN HAKUSHO: JOTAI SEIKEI • 1967 • Mukoi Hiroshi • JPN • PLASTIC BODY SURGERY
IJO TAIKEN HOKUKU HAKUSHO: AOI BOKO • 1967 • Shindo Takae • JPN • REPORT ON ABNORMAL EXPENSES: BLUE VIOLATION
IJOH BOHKOHZAI • 1968 • Okuwaki Toshio • JPN • ABNORMAL VIOLATION
IJSSALON, DE • 1985 • Frank Dimitri Frenkel • NTH
IJYO SEI HANZAI • 1968 • Seki Koji • JPN • ABNORMAL SEX CRIMES
IK-FILM • 1929 • Ivens Joris (c/d) • NTH • "I" FILM
IK KOM WAT LATER NAAR MADRA • 1966 • Ditvoorst Adriaan • NTH
IK KOM WAT LATER TILL MADRA • 1965 • Ditvoorst Adriaan • SHT • NTH • THAT WAY TO MADRA
IKALUOKKA • 1976 • Honkasalo Pirjo, Lehto Pekka • DOC • FNL • THEIR AGE
IKANARU HOSHI NO MOTONI • 1962 • Toyoda Shiro • JPN • UNDER WHAT STARS
IKARI NO KOTO • 1958 • Mizuki Yoko • JPN • SEVEN FORGOTTEN MEN
IKARI NO MACHI • 1950 • Naruse Mikio • JPN • TOWN OF ANGER ○ ANGRY STREET, THE
IKARI NO UMI • 1944 • Imai Tadashi • JPN • CRUEL SEA, THE ○ ANGRY SEA, THE
IKARIA XB-1 see **IKARIE XB-1** • 1963
IKARIE XB-1 • 1963 • Polak Jindrich • CZC • VOYAGE TO THE END OF THE UNIVERSE (USA) ○ ICARUS XB-1 ○ IKARIA XB-1
IKARUS • 1932 • Pluschow Gunther • FRG • GUNTHER PLUSCHOWS FLIEGERSCHICKSAL
IKARUS, IM HOHENFLUG DER LEIDENSCHAFTEN • 1918 • Froelich Carl • FRG • ADLER VON FLANDERN, DER
IKASAMA BAKUCHI • 1968 • Ozawa Shigehiro • JPN • FAKE GAME, THE
IKAW AT ANG GABI • 1979 • Zialcita Danny L. • PHL
IKAW AY AKIN • 1978 • Bernal Ishmael • PHL • YOU ARE MINE
IKAW AY AKIN, AKO AY SA IYO • 1968 • Torres Mar S. • PHL • YOU'RE MINE, I'M YOURS
IKE see **IKE: THE WAR YEARS** • 1978
IKE CAPTURES A FORT • 1915 • *Federal* • USA
IKE GOES TO THE FRONT • 1915 • *Federal* • USA
IKE IN GETTYSBURG • 1986 • Jarrott Charles • MTV • USA
IKE STOPS A BATTLE • 1915 • *Federal* • USA
IKE THE WAR CORRESPONDENT • 1915 • *Federal* • USA
IKE: THE WAR YEARS • 1978 • Shavelson Melville, Sagal Boris • TVM • USA • IKE
IKE WITH THE GERMAN ARMY • 1915 • *Federal* • USA
IKEBANA • 1953-57 • Teshigahara Hiroshi • SHT • JPN
IKERU NINGYO • 1929 • Uchida Tomu • JPN • LIVING DOLL, A
IKERU SHIKABANE • 1917 • Tanaka Eizo • JPN • LIVING CORPSE, THE
IKH ZNALI TOLKO V LITSO • 1967 • Timonishin Anton • USS • KNOWN ONLY BY SIGHT
IKHTIAR, AL- see **EKHTIAR, AL** • 1970
IKI ARKADAS • 1976 • Goren Serif • TRK • TWO FRIENDS
IKI TEN O TSUKU • 1926 • Tasaka Tomotaka • JPN
IKIMONO NO KIROKU • 1955 • Kurosawa Akira • JPN • I LIVE IN FEAR (USA) ○ RECORDING OF A LIVING BEING ○ RECORD OF A LIVING BEING ○ WHAT THE BIRDS KNEW
IKINOKOTTA SHINSENGUMI • 1932 • Kinugasa Teinosuke • JPN • SURVIVING SHINSENGUMI, THE
IKIRU • 1952 • Kurosawa Akira • JPN • LIVING ○ TO LIVE ○ DOOMED
IKIRYO • 1927 • Ito Daisuke • JPN • EVIL SPIRIT
IKISI DE CESURDU • 1963 • *Guney Yilmaz* • TRK • BRAVE MEN, THE
IKITEIRU GAZO • 1948 • Chiba Yasuki • JPN • LIVING PORTRAIT
IKITEIRU MAGOROKU • 1943 • Kinoshita Keisuke • JPN • MAGOROKU IS STILL ALIVE ○ LIVING MAGOROKU, THE
IKITEITA NORAINU • 1961 • Masuda Toshio • JPN
IKITEWA MITAKEREDO • 1984 • Inoue Kazuo • JPN • I DID LIVE BUT..
IKITOSHI IKERUMONO • 1934 • Gosho Heinosuke • JPN • EVERYTHING THAT LIVES ○ LIVING, THE
IKITOSHI IKERUMONO • 1955 • *Mikuni Rentaro* • JPN • EVERYTHING THAT LIVES
IKOGENIA HORAFA • 1968 • Asimakopoulos Kostas • GRC • FAMILY PORTRAIT, A ○ HORAFA FAMILY, THE
IKONOSTASAT • 1968 • Hristov Hristo, Dinov Todor • BUL • ICONOSTASIS
IKPUCK THE IGLOO DWELLER • 1934 • Finnie Richard S. • DOC • CND
IL A ETE PERDU UNE MARIEE • 1932 • Joannon Leo • FRN
IL AIME LE BRUIT • 1912-14 • Cohl Emile • ANS • USA
IL AUT QU'UNE PORTE SOIT OUVERTE OU FERME • 1949 • Cuny Louis • FRN
IL BI E IL BA • 1985 • Nichetti Maurizio • ITL
IL CAPITANO (UKN) see **KANONEN-SERENADE** • 1958
IL EST CHARMANT • 1931 • Mercanton Louis • FRN • PARIS, JE T'AIME
IL EST MINUIT DR. SCHWEITZER • 1952 • Haguet Andre • FRN • STORY OF DOCTOR SCHWEITZER, THE
IL ETAIT TROIS FLIBUSTIERS (FRN) see **MOSCHETTIERI DEL MARE, I** • 1962
IL ETAIT UN CHAISE see **CHAIRY TALE, A** • 1957
IL ETAIT UN FOIS TROIS FLIBUSTIERS, see **MOSCHETTIERI DEL MARE, I** • 1962
IL ETAIT UN PETIT NAVIRE • 1943 • Palardy Jean • DCS • CND
IL ETAIT UN VIEUX SAVANT • Misonne Claude • ANM • BLG
IL ETAIT UNE FOIS • 1933 • Perret Leonce • FRN
IL ETAIT UNE FOIS DANS L'EST • 1973 • Brassard Andre • CND • ONCE UPON A TIME IN THE EAST
IL ETAIT UNE FOIS DES GENS HEUREUX: LES PLOUFFE see **PLOUFFE, LES** • 1981
IL ETAIT UNE FOIS LA CHATTE MOUILLEE • 1976 • Hustaix Lucien • FRN
IL ETAIT UNE FOIS LES ANNEES 60 • 1971 • Jelot-Blanc Jean-Jacques, Rancurel Jean-Louis • FRN

IL ETAIT UNE FOIS.. L'ESPACE(1-12) • 1981 • Barille Albert • ANM • FRN
IL ETAIT UNE FOIS UN FLIC • 1972 • Lautner Georges • FRN, ITL • C'ERA UNA VOLTA UN COMMISSARIO (ITL) ○ FLIC STORY (UKN)
IL ETAIT UNE FOIS UN HOMOSEXUEL • 1979 • Terry Norbert • FRN
IL ETAIT UNE GUERRE • 1958 • Portugais Louis • CND
IL ETAIT UNE MONTAGNE • Muntcho Monique • FRN
IL FAUT CHERCHER POUR APPRENDRE • 1981 • Bonin Laurier • MTV • CND
IL FAUT, IL FAUT see **LAZAM LAZAM** • 1971
IL FAUT QU'UNE BIBLIOTHEQUE SOIT OUVERTE OU FERMEE • 1957 • Garceau Raymond • DCS • CND
IL FAUT TUER BIRGITT HAAS • 1981 • Heynemann Laurent • FRN, FRG • BIRGIT HAAS MUST BE KILLED (USA)
IL FAUT VIVRE DANGEREUSEMENT • 1975 • Makovski Claude • FRN
IL MAESTRO • 1989 • Hansel Marion • BLG • MAESTRO
IL MISTERIO DEL 2o PIANO see **CASA SENZA TEMPO, LA** • 1943
IL NE FAUT PAS JOUER AVEC LE FEU • 1929 • Colombier Piere • FRN
IL NE FAUT PAS MOURIR • 1968 • Lefebvre Jean-Pierre • CND • IL NE FAUT PAS MOURIR POUR CA ○ DON'T LET IT KILL YOU ○ NO GOOD TO DIE FOR THAT
IL NE FAUT PAS MOURIR POUR CA see **IL NE FAUT PAS MOURIR** • 1968
IL NE SUFFIT PAS QUE DIEU SOIT AVEC LES PAUVRES • 1976 • Alawiya Burhan, Thabet Lutfi • EGY
IL N'Y A PAS DE FUMEE SANS FEU • 1972 • Cayatte Andre • FRN, ITL • NON C'E FUMO SENZA FUOCO (ITL) ○ WHERE THERE'S SMOKE (USA)
IL N'Y PAS D'OUBLI • 1975 • Gonzalez Rodrigo, Mallet Marilu, Fajardo Jorge • CND • THERE IS NO FORGETTING
IL PARADISO TERRESTRE see **A CHACUN SON PARADIS** • 1951
IL PLEUT BERGER • 1961 • Lanoe Henri • SHT • FRN
IL PLEUT DANS MA MAISON • 1969 • Larouche Pierre, Lamy Benoit • BLG
IL PLEUT SUR SANTIAGO see **LLUEVE SOBRE SANTIAGO** • 1975
IL PLEUT TOUJOURS OU C'EST MOUILLE • 1974 • Simon Jean-Daniel • FRN
IL S'ENFLA SI BIEN • 1956-57 • Devlin Bernard • SHT • CND
IL SONT FOUS LES SORCIERS • 1978 • Lautner Georges • FRN
IL SUFFIT D'AIMER • 1960 • Darene Robert • FRN, ITL • BERNADETTE OF LOURDES (USA) ○ BERNADETTE DE LOURDES ○ IT IS ENOUGH TO LOVE
IL SUFFIT D'UNE FOIS • 1946 • Feix Andree • FRN
IL TROVATORE • 1914 • Simone Charles • USA
IL Y A DES JOURS.. ET DES LUNES • 1990 • Lelouch Claude • FRN
IL Y A DES PIEDS AU PLAFOND • 1912 • Gance Abel • FRN
IL Y A DIEU POUR LES IVROGNES • 1908 • Melies Georges • FRN • GOOD LUCK OF A "SOUSE", THE
IL Y A LONGTEMPS, O AMOUR! see **ZAMAN YA HUBB** • 1971
IL Y A LONGTEMPS QUE JE T'AIME • 1979 • Tacchella Jean-Charles • FRN • IT'S A LONG TIME THAT I'VE LOVED YOU ○ SOUPCON
IL Y A UN HOMME CHEZ NOUS see **FI BAYTINA RAJUL** • 1960
IL Y AUN TRAIN TOUTES LES HEURES • 1961 • Cavens Andre • BLG
IL Y EUT UN SOIR, IL Y EUT UN MATIN • 1963 • Patry Pierre • SHT • CND
ILA AYN • 1957 • Nasser George • LBN • WHERE TO? ○ WHITHER? ○ TOWARDS THE UNKNOWN
ILAL ABAD • 1961 • Salim Kamel • EGY • FOREVER
IL'ALLONT-Y DISPARAITRE? • 1976-77 • Brault Michel, Gladu Andre • DCS • CND
ILDPROVE, EN • 1915 • Holger-Madsen • DNM • TERRIBLE ORDEAL, A
ILE AU TRESOR, L' • 1986 • Ruiz Raul • FRN
ILE AUX COQUELICOTS, L' • 1970 • Matalon Eddy • FRN
ILE AUX COUDRES • 1939 • Tessier Albert • DCS • CND
ILE AUX FEMMES NUES, L' • 1952 • Lepage Henri • FRN • NAKED IN THE WIND (USA) ○ NAKED IN THE MIND
ILE AUX FILLES PERDUES, L' (FRN) see **PRIGIONIERE DELL'ISOLA DEL DIAVOLO, LE** • 1962
ILE AUX GRUES, TERRE DE SERENITE • 1939 • Tessier Albert • DCS • CND
ILE AUX NUAGES, L' see **EVENTAIL, L'** • 1947
ILE AUX OIES, L' • 1966 • Lavoie Richard • DCS • CND
ILE AUX OISEAUX, L' • 1958 • de Gastyne Marco • FRN
ILE D'AMOUR, L' • 1927 • Durand Jean • FRN
ILE D'AMOUR, L' • 1943 • Cam Maurice • FRN
ILE DE CALYPSO: OU, ULYSSE ET LE GEANT POLYPHEME, L' • 1905 • Melies Georges • FRN • ULYSSES AND THE GIANT POLYPHEMUS (USA) ○ MYSTERIOUS ISLAND, THE
ILE DE LA SOLITUDE, L' • 1936 • de Gastyne Marco • FRN
ILE DE ORLEANS • 1938 • Crawley Budge, Crawley Judith • DOC • CND
ILE DE PAIX, L' • 1969 • Cauvin Andre • BLG
ILE DE PAQUES • 1935 • Storck Henri, Ferno John • DOC • BLG • EASTER ISLAND
ILE DE SAINT-LAURENT, UNE • 1958 • Garceau Raymond • DCS • CND
ILE DE SEIN, L' • 1958 • Vogel Raymond • SHT • FRN
ILE D'EPOUVANTE • 1913 • *Eclipse* • FRN • ISLAND OF TERROR
ILE DES DESESPERES, L' • 1955 • Sassy Jean-Paul • FRN
ILE DES DRAGONS, L' • 1973 • Ronet Maurice • DOC • FRN • VERS L'ILE DRAGON
ILE DES PASSIONS, L' • 1982 • Regis Jack • FRN, SPN • ISLAND OF PASSION ○ PASSION ISLAND ○ SAMANKA
ILE DES VEUVES, L' • 1936 • Heymann Claude • FRN
ILE D'ORLEANS see **ILE FLEURIE, L'** • 1939
ILE D'ORLEANS, L' • Lavoie Hermenegilde • DCS • CND
ILE D'ORLEANS, RELIQUAIRE D'HISTOIRE • 1939 • Tessier Albert • DCS • CND
ILE D'OUESSANT, L' see **ENEZ EUSSA** • 1961
ILE DU BOUT DU MONDE, L' • 1958 • Greville Edmond T. • FRN • TEMPTATION ISLAND (UKN) ○ TEMPTATION (USA)
ILE DU DIABLE, L' • 1899 • Melies Georges • FRN
ILE ENCHANTEE, L' • 1927 • Roussell Henry • FRN
ILE FLEURIE, L' • 1939 • Tessier Albert • DCS • CND • ILE D'ORLEANS
ILE JAUNE, L' • 1974 • Cousineau Jacques • CND
ILE MYSTERIEUSE, L' • 1943 • Rigal Andre • ANS • FRN
ILE MYSTERIEUSE, L' • 1973 • Colpi Henri, Bardem Juan Antonio • FRN, ITL • ISOLA MISTERIOSA E IL CAPITANO NEMO, L' (ITL) ○ MYSTERIOUS ISLAND, THE (USA) ○ MYSTERIOUS ISLAND OF CAPTAIN NEMO, THE ○ ISLA MISTERIOSA, LA
ILEGAL, LA • 1980 • MXC • ILLEGAL ALIEN WOMAN, THE
ILEGITIMA, LA • 1955 • Urueta Chano • MXC
ILEKSEN • 1978 • O'Rourke Dennis • UKN • ELECTION
ILES, LES • 1982 • Azimi Iradj • FRN, FRG
ILES DE LA MADELEINE • 1952 • Palardy Jean • DCS • CND
ILES DE LA MADELEINE, LES • 1956 • Proulx Maurice • DCS • CND
ILES DE LA MADELEINE: LA PECHE COTIERE • 1965-66 • Garceau Raymond • DCS • CND
ILES DE LA MADELEINE: LA PECHE HAUTIERE • 1965-66 • Garceau Raymond • DCS • CND
ILES DE LA MADELEINE: LES PETONCLES • 1965-66 • Garceau Raymond • DCS • CND
ILES DE LA MADELEINE: LES USINES A POISSON • 1965-66 • Garceau Raymond • DCS • CND
ILES DE LA MADELEINE: TOURISME ET TRANSPORTS • 1965-66 • Garceau Raymond • DCS • CND
ILES ENCHANTEES, LES • 1964 • Vilardebo Carlos • FRN, PRT • ILHAS ENCANTADAS, AS (PRT)
ILHA DAS MAOS DE FADA, A • 1957 • Garcia Fernando • SHT • PRT
ILHA DE MOCAMBIQUE • 1971 • Spiguel Miguel • SHT • PRT
ILHA DE MORAES, A see **ILHA DOS AMORES, A** • 1978
ILHA DOS AMORES, A • 1978 • Rocha Paulo • PRT, JPN • KOI NO UKISHIMA (JPN) ○ ISLAND OF LOVES, THE ○ ILHA DE MORAES, A
ILHA QUE NASCE DO MAR, A • 1956 • Garcia Fernando • SHT • PRT
ILHA VERDE, A • 1954 • Campos Henrique • SHT • PRT
ILHAS CRIOULAS DE CABO VERDE, AS • 1947 • Ribeiro Antonio Lopes • SHT • PRT
ILHAS ENCANTADAS, AS (PRT) see **ILES ENCHANTEES, LES** • 1964
ILIAC PASSION, THE see **PROMETHEUS BOUND -THE ILLIAC PASSION** • 1966
ILIKIA TIS THALASSAS, I • 1979 • Papayiannidis Takis • DOC • GRC • AGE OF THE SEA, THE
ILIOS TOU THANATOU, O • 1978 • Dimopoulos Dinos • GRC • SUN OF DEATH, THE
ILK ASKIM • 1967 • Ergun Nuri • TRK • MY FIRST LOVE
ILK VE SON • 1968 • Un Memduh • TRK • FIRST AND THE LAST, THE
I'LL BE GLAD WHEN YOU'RE DEAD YOU RASCAL YOU • 1932 • Fleischer Dave • ANS • USA
I'LL BE GOOD, OLD MAN! • 1978 • Schulhoff Petr • CZC
I'LL BE HOME FOR CHRISTMAS • 1984 • McKenzie Brian • DOC • ASL
I'LL BE SEEING YOU • 1944 • Dieterle William, Cukor George (U/c) • USA • DOUBLE FURLOUGH
I'LL BE SKIING YA • 1947 • Sparber I. • ANS • USA
I'LL BE SUING YOU • 1934 • Meins Gus • SHT • USA
I'LL BE THERE • 1927 • Yaconelli Frank • USA
I'LL BE THERE see **OUT ALL NIGHT** • 1927
I'LL BE WAITING see **ORE WA MATTERU-ZE** • 1957
I'LL BE YOUR SWEETHEART • 1945 • Guest Val • UKN
I'LL BE YOURS • 1947 • Seiter William A. • USA
I'LL BUILD IT MYSELF • 1946 • Yates Hal • SHT • USA
I'LL BUY YOU see **ANATA KAIMASU** • 1956
I'LL CRY ALONE see **OBI O TOKU NATSUKO** • 1965
I'LL CRY TOMORROW • 1955 • Mann Daniel • USA
I'LL DEFEND YOU MY LOVE see **DIFENDO IL MIO AMORE** • 1956
I'LL DIE FOR MAMA • 1979 • Chopra Yash
I'LL DIE TO LIVE -GUSTAV MAHLER see **STERBEN WERD' ICH, UM ZU LEBEN (GUSTAV MAHLER)** • 1987
ILL-FATED LOVE see **AMOR DE PERDICAO** • 1977
I'LL FIND A WAY • 1978 • Shaffer Beverly • SHT • CND
I'LL FIX IT • 1934 • Neill R. William • USA
I'LL FIX THAT • 1941 • Roberts Charles E. • SHT • USA
I'LL FOLLOW IN YOUR STEPS see **SEGUIRE TUS PASOS** • 1968
I'LL GET BY • 1950 • Sale Richard • USA
I'LL GET HER FIRST • 1916 • Clements Roy • SHT • USA
I'LL GET HIM YET • 1919 • Clifton Elmer • USA
I'LL GET THERE SOMEHOW • 1984 • Zaritsky John • MTV • CND
I'LL GET YOU FOR THIS (UKN) see **LUCKY NICK CAIN** • 1951
I'LL GET YOU (USA) see **ESCAPE ROUTE** • 1952
I'LL GIVE A MILLION • 1938 • Lang Walter • USA
I'LL GIVE A MILLION see **DARO UN MILIONE** • 1935
I'LL GO AND LIVE BY MYSELF see **VADO A VIVERE DA SOLO** • 1983
I'LL GO.. I'LL KILL HIM AND COME BACK see **VADO.. L'AMMAZZO E TORNO** • 1967
I'LL LOVE YOU ALWAYS • 1935 • Bulgakov Leo • USA
I'LL MARRY SIMON LE BON see **SPOSERO' SIMON LE BON** • 1985
I'LL MEET YOU IN HEAVEN see **MAXIE** • 1985
ILL MET BY MOONLIGHT • 1956 • Powell Michael, Pressburger Emeric • UKN • NIGHT AMBUSH (USA)
I'LL NAME THE MURDERER • 1936 • Johnston Raymond K. • USA
I'LL NEVER CROW AGAIN • 1941 • Fleischer Dave • ANS • USA
I'LL NEVER FORGET HIS FACE see **DHEN THA XEHASO POTE TIN MORFI TOU** • 1968
I'LL NEVER FORGET THE SONG OF NAGASAKI see **NAGASAKI NO UTA WA WASUREJI** • 1952
I'LL NEVER FORGET YOU (USA) see **HOUSE IN THE SQUARE, THE** • 1951
I'LL NEVER FORGOT WHAT'S 'IS NAME • 1967 • Winner Michael • UKN
I'LL NEVER HEIL AGAIN • 1941 • White Jules • SHT • USA
I'LL NEVER LOVE AGAIN see **ARTIK SEVMIYECEGIM** • 1968
ILL OMEN see **ZNAK BEDY** • 1986
I'LL ONLY MARRY A SPORT • 1909 • *Lubin* • USA
I'LL REACH FOR A STAR see **HIT PARADE OF 1937** • 1937
I'LL REMEMBER APRIL • 1945 • Young Harold • USA
I'LL SAVE MY LOVE see **TWO LOVES** • 1961
I'LL SAY HE FORGOT • 1920 • *Harlan Otis* • USA
I'LL SAY SO • 1918 • Walsh Raoul • USA
I'LL SEE YOU IN HELL (USA) see **TI ASPETTERO ALL'INFERNO** • 1960
I'LL SEE YOU IN MY DREAMS • 1951 • Curtiz Michael • USA
I'LL SEE YOU IN SEPTEMBER • 1967 • Silos Raul T. • PHL
I'LL SELL MY LIFE see **I'LL SET MY LIFE** • 1941
I'LL SET MY LIFE • 1941 • Clifton Elmer • USA • I'LL SELL MY LIFE
I'LL SHOW YOU THE TOWN • 1925 • Pollard Harry • USA
ILL-STARRED BABBIE • 1915 • *Saunders Jackie* • USA
I'LL STICK TO YOU • 1933 • Hiscott Leslie • UKN
I'LL TAKE MANHATTAN • 1987 • Hickox Douglas, Michaels Richard • MTV • USA
I'LL TAKE MILK • 1946 • Yates Hal • SHT • USA
I'LL TAKE ROMANCE • 1937 • Griffith Edward H. • USA
I'LL TAKE SWEDEN • 1965 • De Cordova Frederick • USA
I'LL TAKE VANILLA • 1922 • Roach Hal • SHT • USA
I'LL TAKE VANILLA • 1934 • Parrott Charles, Dunn Eddie • SHT • USA
I'LL TAKE YOU HOME AGAIN, KATHLEEN • 1929 • Aylott Dave, Symmons E. F. • SHT • UKN
I'LL TELL DEMIREL see **DEMIREL'E SOYLERIM** • 1967
I'LL TELL THE WORLD • 1934 • Sedgwick Edward • USA
I'LL TELL THE WORLD • 1945 • Goodwins Leslie • USA
I'LL TELL THE WORLD see **BOOB, THE** • 1926
I'LL TRY TONIGHT see **STASERA MI BUTTO** • 1968
I'LL TURN TO YOU • 1946 • Faithfull Geoffrey • UKN
I'LL WAIT FOR YOU • 1941 • Sinclair Robert B. • USA • MEN OF THE CITY
I'LL WAIT FOR YOU IN HELL see **TI ASPETTERO ALL'INFERNO** • 1960
I'LL WALK BESIDE YOU • 1943 • Rogers Maclean • UKN
ILL WIND, AN • 1912 • *Rex* • USA
ILL WIND, AN • 1914 • *Sterling* • USA
ILLEGAL • 1932 • McGann William • UKN
ILLEGAL • 1955 • Allen Lewis • USA
ILLEGAL, THE see **ALAMBRISTA!** • 1978
ILLEGAL ABORTION • 1966 • Spry Robin • DOC • CND
ILLEGAL ALIEN • 1982 • *Keller Gregory (P)* • USA
ILLEGAL ALIEN WOMAN, THE see **ILEGAL, LA** • 1980
ILLEGAL CARGO (USA) see **CARGAISON BLANCHE** • 1957
ILLEGAL DIVORCE, THE (UKN) see **SECOND HAND WIFE** • 1933
ILLEGAL ENTRY • 1949 • De Cordova Frederick • USA
ILLEGAL IMMIGRANT, THE see **FEIFA YIMIN** • 1985
ILLEGAL RIGHTS (UKN) see **HAIL TO THE RANGERS** • 1943
ILLEGAL TRAFFIC • 1938 • King Louis • USA
ILLEGALLY YOURS • 1988 • Bogdanovich Peter • USA
ILLEGALS, THE • 1948 • Levin Meyer
ILLIAC PASSION, THE see **PROMETHEUS BOUND -THE ILLIAC PASSION** • 1966
ILLICIT • 1931 • Mayo Archie • USA
ILLICIT CARGO see **OUTSIDE THE THREE MILE LIMIT** • 1940
ILLICIT DESIRE • 1973 • Li Han-Hsiang • HKG
ILLICIT INTERLUDE (USA) see **SOMMARLEK** • 1951
ILLICIT LIQUOR SELLER, THE • 1916 • SAF
ILLICIT RENDEZVOUS see **NURETA AIBIKI** • 1967
ILLIKO, ILLARION, GRANDMOTHER AND ME see **YA BABUSHKA, ILIKO I ILLARION** • 1963
ILLUMINATED TEXTS • 1983 • Elder Bruce • CND
ILLUMINATION • 1912 • Reid Hal • USA
ILLUMINATION see **ILLUMINATIONS** • 1963
ILLUMINATIONS • 1963 • Reichenbach Francois • SHT • FRN • ILLUMINATION
ILLUMINATIONS • 1976 • Cox Paul • ASL
ILLUMINATIONS see **ILUMINACJA** • 1973
ILLUMINATIONS, LES • 1958 • Gruel Henri • ANS • FRN • METROPOLITAIN
ILLUSION • 1929 • Mendes Lothar • USA
ILLUSION • 1941 • Tourjansky Victor • FRG
ILLUSION • 1980 • Staikov Lyudmil • BUL
ILLUSION see **MAYA** • 1936
ILLUSION see **ILUZIJA** • 1967
ILLUSION see **MAYA** • 1982
ILLUSION, THE • 1985 • Haji-Miri Sa'Id • IRN
ILLUSION IN MOLL • 1952 • Jugert Rudolf • FRG
ILLUSION IS A GANGSTER GIRL see **GANGSTERMEISJE, HET** • 1967
ILLUSION OF BEING A MILLIONAIRE, THE see **MILIONARIO POR ILUSION** • 1973
ILLUSION OF BLOOD see **YOTSUYA KAIDAN** • 1965
ILLUSION OF LOVE • 1929 • *Ho John* • USA
ILLUSION ON THE FIELD ROAD, THE see **CHIMERA NA POLNEJ DRODZE** • 1970
ILLUSION TRAVELS BY STREETCAR, THE see **ILUSION VIAJA EN TRANVIA, LA** • 1953
ILLUSION ZU DRITT • 1927 • Heitau Heinz • FRG
ILLUSIONIST, THE • 1983 • Stelling Jos • NTH
ILLUSIONNISTE DOUBLE ET LA TETE VIVANTE, L' • 1900 • Melies Georges • FRN • TRIPLE CONJURER AND THE LIVING HEAD, THE (USA)
ILLUSIONNISTE FIN DE SIECLE, L' • 1899 • Melies Georges • FRN • IMPRESSIONNISTE FIN DE SIECLE, L' ○ UP-TO-DATE CONJUROR, AN
ILLUSIONNISTE MONDAIN, L' • 1901 • Zecca Ferdinand • FRN • MUNDANE ILLUSIONIST, THE
ILLUSIONNISTE RENVERSANT • 1903 • Blache Alice • FRN
ILLUSIONS • 1962 • Belson Jordan • SHT • USA
ILLUSIONS • 1972 • CMP • USA • THRESHOLD 9 ILLUSIONS
ILLUSIONS • 1982 • Grauman Walter • TVM • USA
ILLUSIONS see **FOIRE AUX CHIMERES, LA** • 1946
ILLUSIONS see **BAD TIMING** • 1980
ILLUSIONS D'AMOUR see **AWHAM AL-HUBB** • 1970
ILLUSIONS FANTAISISTES, LES • 1909 • Melies Georges • FRN • WHIMSICAL ILLUSIONS

ILLUSIONS FANTASMAGORIQUES • 1898 • Melies Georges • FRN • FAMOUS BOX TRICK, THE (USA) ○ FANTASMAGORICAL ILLUSIONS

ILLUSIONS FANTASTIQUES see **CREATIONS SPONTANEES** • 1898

ILLUSIONS FUNAMBULESQUES • 1903 • Melies Georges • FRN • 20TH CENTURY ILLUSTRATIONIST, THE (UKN) ○ EXTRAORDINARY ILLUSIONS (USA)

ILLUSORY SUMMER OF '68, THE • 1984 • Paskaljevic Goran • YGS

ILLUSTRATED MAN, THE • 1969 • Smight Jack • USA

ILLUSTRATED PROVERBS • 1912 • Thornton F. Martin • UKN

ILLUSTRATIVE WORDS • 1969 • Patel Ishu • ANS • IND

ILLUSTRE ATTRICE CICALA FORMICA, L' • 1920 • D'Ambra Lucio • ITL

ILLUSTRE MACHEFER, L' • 1914 • Feuillade Louis • FRN

ILLUSTRE MAURIN, L' • 1933 • Hugon Andre • FRN

ILLUSTRIOUS CORPSES see **CADAVERI ECCELLENTI** • 1976

ILLUSTRIOUS ENERGY • 1987 • Narbey Leon • NZL

ILLUSTRIOUS PRINCE, THE • 1919 • Worthington William • USA

ILOMBE • 1978 • Gavarry Christian • FRN, GBN

ILONA • 1922 • Dinesen Robert • FRG

ILS.. • 1970 • Simon Jean-Daniel • FRN • THEM

ILS APPELLENT CA UN ACCIDENT • 1981 • Delon Nathalie • FRN • THEY CALL THAT AN ACCIDENT

ILS ETAIENT 5 PERMISSIONNAIRES • 1940 • Caron Pierre • FRN

ILS ETAIENT CINQ • 1951 • Pinoteau Jack • FRN

ILS ETAIENT NEUF CELIBATAIRES • 1939 • Guitry Sacha • FRN • NINE BACHELORS (USA)

ILS ONT FAIT DE MOI UN ASSASSIN see **JAALLUNI MUJRIMAN** • 1954

ILS ONT TUE JAURES • 1962 • Bellsolell Jean-Paul • DOC • FRN

ILS ONT VINGT ANS • 1950 • Delacroix Rene • FRN

ILS SONT DANS LES VIGNES • 1951 • Vernay Robert • FRN • LOVE IN THE VINEYARD

ILS SONT FOUS CES NORMANDS see **CHENE D'ALLOUVILLE, LE** • 1980

ILS SONT FOUS CES SORCIERS • 1978 • Lautner Georges • FRN

ILS SONT GRANDS CES PETITS • 1979 • Santoni Joel • FRN

ILS SONT NUS • 1966 • Pierson Claude • CND, FRN • WE ARE ALL NAKED (USA) ○ DAYS OF DESIRE (UKN)

ILS VONT ME RENDRE FOU! see **HAY GANNINUNI** • 1959

ILS Y VIENNENT TOUS, AU CINEMA • 1917 • Heuze Andre, Diamant-Berger Henri • FRN

ILSA, HAREM KEEPER OF THE OIL SHEIKS • 1975 • Edmonds Don • CND, USA • HAREM KEEPER OF THE OIL SHEIKS

ILSA, LA TIGRESSE DU GOULAG • 1977 • Lafleur Jean • CND • TIGRESS OF SIBERIA, THE ○ ISLA, THE TIGRESS OF SIBERIA

ILSA, SHE-WOLF OF THE S.S. • 1973 • Edmonds Don • CND, USA

ILUMINACJA • 1973 • Zanussi Krzysztof • PLN • ILLUMINATIONS

ILUMINADO, EL • 1982 • Guedez Jesus Enrique • VNZ

ILUSION VIAJA EN TRANVIA, LA • 1953 • Bunuel Luis • MXC • ILLUSION TRAVELS BY STREETCAR, THE ○ RUNAWAY STREETCAR, THE ○ STREETCAR, THE

ILUSTRATE CU FLORI DE CIMP • 1974 • Blaier Andrei • RMN • POSTCARDS WITH FLOWERS

ILUSTRE PEREA, EL • 1943 • Buchs Jose • SPN

ILUZIJA • 1967 • Papic Krsto • YGS • ILLUSION

ILYA MUROMETS • 1956 • Ptushko Alexander • USS • EPIC HERO AND THE BEAST, THE (UKN) ○ SWORD AND THE DRAGON, THE(USA) ○ ILYA MUROMETZ

ILYA MUROMETZ see **ILYA MUROMETS** • 1956

ILYICH ZASTAVA see **MNE DVADTSAT LET** • 1961-63

ILYINSKIYE O MAYAKOVSKOM • 1973 • Yutkevich Sergei • MTV • USS

ILYITCH SQUARE see **MNE DVADTSAT LET** • 1961-63

ILZA CERAMICS see **CERAMIKA ILZECKA** • 1951

IM 6 STOCK • 1961 • Olden John • FRG

IM 100-KILOMETER-TEMPO • 1918 • Arnheim Valy • FRG

I'M A BIG SHOT NOW • 1936 • Freleng Friz • ANS • USA

I'M A CIVILIAN HERE MYSELF • 1945 • *Benchley Robert* • SHT • USA

I'M A FATHER • 1934 • Horne James W. • SHT • USA

I'M A FUGITIVE see **SOY UN PROFUGO** • 1946

I'M A MAN • 1978 • Vidor King • SHT • USA

I'M A MONKEY'S UNCLE • 1948 • White Jules • SHT • USA

I'M A SNIPER • 1943-46 • Monkman John • DOC • UKN

I'M A STRANGER • 1952 • Williams Brock • UKN

I'M A STRANGER HERE MYSELF • 1974 • Halpern David M. • USA

IM ABGRUND DES HASSES • 1921 • Werckmeister Hans • FRG

I'M ACCUSING see **ICH KLAGE AN** • 1941

I'M AFRAID see **IO HO PAURA** • 1977

I'M AFRAID TO COME HOME IN THE DARK • 1930 • Fleischer Dave • ANS • USA

I'M AFRAID TO GO HOME IN THE DARK • 1909 • *Warwick Trading Co.* • UKN

I'M ALIVE • 1977 • Kohanyi Julius • CND

I'M ALL RIGHT, JACK • 1959 • Boulting John • UKN

I'M ALMOST NOT CRAZY: JOHN CASSAVETES -THE MAN AND HIS WORK • 1984 • Ventura • DOC • USA

I'M AN ELEPHANT, MADAME (UKN) see **ICH BIN EIN ELEFANT, MADAME** • 1968

I'M AN EXPLOSIVE • 1933 • Brunel Adrian • UKN

I'M ANGRY FOR YOUR SAKE • 1967 • Szemes Marianne • DOC • HNG • I'M SORRY FOR YOUR SAKE

IM AUTO DURCH ZWEI WELTEN • 1931 • Stinnes Clarenore, Soderstrom Carl A. • FRG

IM BAHNWARTERHAUSL • 1919 • Bolten-Baeckers Heinrich • FRG

IM BANNE DER BERGE • 1931 • Osten Franz • FRG • ALMENRAUSCH

IM BANNE DER FRAU see **GEHEIMNIS DER GLADIATORENWERKE 1, DAS** • 1920

IM BANNE DER HYPNOSE see **AUGEN** • 1919

IM BANNE DER KRALLE • 1925 • Froelich Carl • AUS

IM BANNE DER LEIDENSCHAFTEN • 1914 • Schmidthassler Walter • FRG

IM BANNE DER MADONNA • 1950 • Greville Edmond T. • FRG, FRN

IM BANNE DER SCHULD • *Eichberg Richard* • FRG

IM BANNE DER VERGANGENHEIT • 1915 • Piel Harry • FRG

IM BANNE DES ANDERN • 1920 • Brunner Rolf • FRG

IM BANNE DES EULENSPIEGELS • 1932 • Wisbar Frank • FRG

IM BANNE DES MONTE MIRACOLO • 1944 • Trenker Luis • FRG

IM BANNE DES SCHWEIGENS • 1916 • Henning Hanna • FRG

IM BANNE DES UNHEIMLICHEN • 1968 • Vohrer Alfred • FRG • IN THE GRIP OF THE SINISTER ONE

IM BANNE FREMDEN WILLENS • 1915 • Dessauer Siegfried • FRG

IM BLICKPUNKT -LANDWIRTSCHAFT • 1967 • Muller Heinz • GDR • CENTRE OF ATTENTION -FARMING

I'M BULLET-PROOF see **BANA KURSUN ISLEMEZ** • 1967

I'M BURNING see **JA GORE** • 1967

I'M CALLED CHATA AGUAYO see **ME LLAMAN LA CHATA AGUAYO** • 1988

I'M COLD • 1954 • Avery Tex • ANS • USA • SOME LIKE IT HOT ○ CHILLY WILLY

I'M COMING, DOC • 1975 • USA

I'M CRAZY ABOUT YOU see **TE QUIERO CON LOCURA** • 1935

I'M CRAZY TO BE MARRIED • 1915 • *Starlight* • USA

I'M DANCING AS FAST AS I CAN • 1982 • Hofsiss Jack • USA

IM DEM GROSSEN AUGENBLICK see **IM GROSSEN AUGENBLICK** • 1911

IM DIENSTE DER LIEBE • 1919 • Sauer Fred • FRG

IM DIENSTE DER MENSCHLICHKEIT • 1938 • Ruttmann Walter • FRG

IM DIENSTE DER TODESGOTTIN see **THUG, DER** • 1916

I'M DRAWING THEIR FIRE ON MYSELF • 1964 • Kolosov Sergei • USS

I'M EIGHTY IN THE MORNING • 1929 • Aylott Dave, Symmons E. F. • SHT • UKN

IM FASCHING DER SINNE • 1920 • Kayser Charles Willy • FRG • FASCHING DER SINNE

IM FEUER DER SCHIFFSKANONEN • 1915 • Schmidthassler Walter • FRG

I'M FIVE • 1967 • Topouzanov Christo • ANM • BUL

I'M FOR THE HIPPOPOTAMUS see **IO STO CON GLI IPPOPOTAMI** • 1980

I'M FOREVER BLOWING BUBBLES • 1930 • Fleischer Dave • ANS • USA

IM FOTOATELIER • 1932 • Valentin Karl • FRG

I'M FREE see **ANA HURRA** • 1959

I'M FROM ARKANSAS • 1944 • Landers Lew • USA

I'M FROM CHILDHOOD see **YA RODOM IZ DYETSTVA** • 1967

I'M FROM MISSOURI • 1939 • Reed Theodore • USA

I'M FROM THE BLACK SEA • 1944 • Macheret Alexander • USS

I'M FROM THE CITY • 1938 • Holmes Ben • USA

IM GEHEIMDIENST • 1931 • Ucicky Gustav • FRG • IN THE EMPLOY OF THE SECRET SERVICE (USA)

I'M GETTING MYSELF A YACHT • 1981 • Corbucci Sergio • ITL

I'M GLAD MY BOY GREW TO BE A SOLDIER • 1915 • Beal Frank • USA

IM GLANZE IHRER KRONEN • 1968 • Puhl Reginald • DOC • FRG • IN THE GLORY OF THEIR CROWNS

IM GLUTRAUSCH DER SINNE 1 • 1922 • Zeyn Willy • FRG

IM GLUTRAUSCH DER SINNE 2 • 1922 • Zeyn Willy • FRG • GESCHMINKTE FRAU, DIE

I'M GOING TO BE FAMOUS • 1982 • Leder Paul • USA

I'M GONNA GIT YOU SUCKA • 1989 • Wayans Keenen Ivory • USA

IM GROSSEN AUGENBLICK • 1911 • Gad Urban • FRG • IM DEM GROSSEN AUGENBLICK

I'M HAPPY see **SON CONTENTO** • 1984

IM HAUSE DES KOMMERZIENRATS • 1917 • Mendel Georg Victor • FRG

IM HEIDEKRUG • 1934 • Boese Carl • FRG

I'M HERE BELLETT see **WATASHII WA BELLETT** • 1964

IM HERZEN DES HURRICAN • 1980 • Bohm Hark • FRG • HEART OF THE HURRICANE, THE

IM HERZEN LIEBE TRAGEN, DIE • 1918 • Beck Ludwig • FRG

IM HIMMEL IST DOCH JAHRMARKT • 1969 • Losansky Rolf • GDR

I'M HIS FIANCEE see **I AM HIS FIANCEE** • 1970

IM-HO-TEP see **MUMMY, THE** • 1932

I'M HOMESICK, THAT'S ALL • 1945 • Crouch William Forest • SHT • USA

IM HOTEL "ZUR SUSSEN NACHTIGALL" • 1928 • Lowenstein Hans Otto • AUS • MADAME WAGT EINEN SEITENSPRUNG

I'M IN THE ARMY NOW • 1936 • Fleischer Dave • ANS • USA

I'M JUMPING OVER PUDDLES AGAIN (UKN) see **UZ ZASE SKACU PRES KALUZE** • 1970

I'M JUST A JITTERBUG • 1939 • Lovy Alex • ANS • USA

I'M JUST A KID • Savoie Michael • DCS • CND

I'M JUST A LUCKY SO-AND-SO • 1946 • Gould Dave • SHT • USA

I'M JUST CURIOUS • 1944 • Kneitel Seymour • ANS • USA

I'M JUST WILD ABOUT JERRY • 1965 • Jones Charles M. • ANS • USA

IM KAMPF MIT DEM BERGE • 1921 • Fanck Arnold • FRG

IM KAMPF MIT DER UNTERWELT • 1931 • Aldini Carlo • FRG

IM KAMPF UM DIAMANTENFELDER • 1921 • Schomburgk Hans • FRG

IM KRUG ZUM GRUNEN KRANZE • 1925 • Lisson Heinrich • FRG

IM KRUG ZUM GRUNEN KRANZE see **FUNF KARNICKEL, DIE** • 1953

IM LANDE DER KONIGIN VON SABA • 1935 • Helfritz Hans • FRG • IN THE LAND OF THE QUEEN OF SHEBA

IM LAUF DER ZEIT • 1976 • Wenders Wim • FRG • KING OF THE ROAD (USA) ○ KINGS OF THE ROAD ○ IN THE COURSE OF TIME

IM LEBENSWIRBEL • 1916 • Schall Heinz • FRG

IM LETZTEN AUGENBLICK • 1920 • Boese Carl • FRG

IM LETZTEN AUGENBLICK • 1923 • Reicher Ernst • FRG

I'M LIKE THAT TOO see **SADAN ER JEG OSSE** • 1979

I'M LOOKING FOR A PIGEON HOUSE see **HLEDAM DUM HOLUBI** • 1985

IM LUXUSZUG • 1927 • Schonfelder Erich • FRG

IM NAMEN DES TEUFELS • 1962 • Carstairs John Paddy • FRG, UKN • DEVIL'S AGENT, THE (UKN)

IM NAMEN DES VOLKES • 1939 • Engels Erich • FRG

I'M NO ANGEL • 1933 • Ruggles Wesley • USA

I'M NO COUNTERFEITER • 1913 • Davis Will S. • USA

I'M NOBODY'S SWEETHEART NOW • 1940 • Lubin Arthur • USA

I'M NOT FEELING MYSELF TONIGHT • 1976 • McGrath Joseph • UKN

I'M NOT GOING TO EAT • 1961 • Goldberger Kurt • DOC • CZC

I'M NOT STAYING WITH YOU ANYMORE see **IO CON TE NON CI STO' PIU'** • 1984

I'M OFF TO PHILADELPHIA • 1909 • *Warwick Trading Co.* • UKN

I'M ON MY WAY • 1919 • Roach Hal • SHT • USA

I'M ON MY WAY • 1961 • Pavlovsky V. • USS

I'M POOR BUT ANGRY see **SIROMA SAM AL' SAM BESAN** • 1971

I'M POOR BUT STUPID see **SIROMA SAM AL' SAM BESAN** • 1971

IM PRATER BLUHN WIEDER DIE BAUME • 1929 • Emo E. W. • FRG

IM PRATER BLUH'N WIEDER DIE BAUME • 1958 • Wolff Hans • FRG

I'M PURE MEXICAN see **SOY PURO MEXICANO** • 1942

IM RAUSCHE DER LEIDENSCHAFT • 1923 • Schamberg Guido • FRG

IM RAUSCHE DER MILLIARDEN • 1922 • Berger Josef • FRG

IM RAUSCHE DER MILLIARDEN see **FLUCH DER MENSCHHEIT 2, DER** • 1920

IM REICHE DER FLAMMEN • 1919 • Heiland Heinz Karl • FRG

IM REICHE DES SILBERNEN LOWEN • 1965 • Gottlieb Franz J. • FRG, SPN

I'M SCARED • 1981 • Hyytiainen Pekka • FNL

IM SCHATTEN DER ANDEREN • 1924 • *Deutsche Mutoscop* • FRG

IM SCHATTEN DER EHE • 1923 • *Dusseldofer Film-Manufaktur* • FRG

IM SCHATTEN DER MOSCHEE • 1923 • Hall Walter • FRG

IM SCHATTEN DER VERGANGENHEIT • 1922 • Wenter Adolf • FRG

IM SCHATTEN DES BERGES • 1940 • Lippl Alois J. • FRG

IM SCHATTEN DES GLUCKS • 1919 • *Smolowa Sibyl* • FRG • HERZBLUT 1

IM SCHATTEN DES KARAKORUM • 1955 • Schuhmacher Eugen • FRG • SHADOW OF KARAKORUM, THE

IM SCHATTEN DES MEERES • 1912 • Stark Kurt • FRG • SCHATTEN DES MEERES ○ IN THE SHADOW OF THE SEA

IM SCHATTEN GEHEN, DIE • 1921 • Schall Heinz • FRG

IM SCHATTEN LEBEN, DIE • 1917 • Eichberg Richard • FRG

IM SCHLOSS DER BLUTIGEN BEGIERDE • 1968 • Hoven Adrian • FRG • IN THE CASTLE OF BLOODY DESIRES ○ CASTLE OF LUST (USA) ○ IN THE CASTLE OF BLOODY LUST

IM SCHULDBUCH DES HASSES • 1920 • Del Zopp Rudolf • FRG

IM SCHWARZEN ROSSL • 1961 • Antel Franz • AUS

IM SENDERAUM • 1938 • Valentin Karl • FRG

IM SINGENDEN ROSSL AM KONIGSEE • 1963 • Antel Franz • AUS

I'M SO SLEEPY • 1911 • Stow Percy • UKN

IM SONDERAUFTRAG • 1959 • Thiel Heinz • GDR

IM SONNENSCHEIN • 1936 • Gallone Carmine • AUS • THANK YOU, MADAME (USA) ○ OPERNRING

I'M SORRY • 1965 • Hafela Courtney • USA

I'M SORRY FOR YOUR SAKE see **I'M ANGRY FOR YOUR SAKE** • 1967

I'M SPEAKING TO CARACAS see **YO HABLO A CARACAS** • 1978

IM STAHLNETZ DES DR. MABUSE • 1961 • Reinl Harald • FRG, FRN, ITL • PHANTOM MEETS THE RETURN OF DR. MABUSE, THE ○ RETOUR DU DOCTEUR MABUSE, LE ○ F.B.I. CONTRO DR. MABUSE ○ PHANTOM FIEND ○ RETURN OF DR. MABUSE, THE ○ IN THE STEEL NET OF DR. MABUSE

I'M STEPPING OUT see **COM LICENCA, EU VOU A LUTA** • 1986

I'M STILL ALIVE • 1940 • Reis Irving • USA

IM STILLEN OZEAN • 1924 • *Danny Kaden-Film* • FRG

IM STRUDEL DER GROSSTADT • 1921 • *Weisse Hanni* • FRG

IM TAL IST SCHON DER FRUHLING.. see **SOHNE DES HERRN GASPARY, DIE** • 1948

IM TEMPEL DER VENUS see **MIT MEINEN AUGEN** • 1944

I'M THANKFUL FOR WHAT I'VE GOT • 1987 • Cochrane Fiona • SHT • ASL

I'M THE ANGEL OF DEATH see **AZRAIL BENIM** • 1968

I'M THE HERO see **EROE SONO IO, L'** • 1951

IM TROMMELFEUER DER WESTFRONT • 1936 • Kaiser Charles W. • FRG

I'M WEARING MY HEART AWAY FOR YOU • 1909 • *Warwick Trading Co.* • UKN

IM WEISSEN ROSSL • 1926 • Oswald Richard • FRG

IM WEISSEN ROSSL • 1935 • Lamac Carl • AUS

IM WEISSEN ROSSL • 1952 • Forst Willi • FRG

IM WEISSEN ROSSL • 1960 • Jacobs Werner • FRG, AUS • WHITE HORSE INN, THE (USA)

IM WERDER BLUHEN DIE BAUME • 1928 • Sauer Fred • FRG

IM WIRBEL DES LEBENS • 1919 • Lund Erik • FRG

I'M YOUR HUSBAND • 1916 • Peacocke Leslie T. • SHT • USA

IM ZEICHEN DER SCHLANGE • 1922 • Stein Josef • FRG

IM ZEICHEN DER SCHULD • 1918 • Eichberg Richard • FRG

IM ZEICHEN DES KREUZES • 1983 • MTV • FRG • DUE TO AN ACT OF GOD

IM ZEICHEN DES VERTRAUENS • 1938 • Ruttmann Walter • FRG

IM ZWINGER • 1964 • Schamoni Peter • SHT • FRG

IMA HITOTABI NO • 1947 • Gosho Heinosuke • JPN • ONCE MORE ○ ONE MORE TIME

IMA KNUTT GETS A BITE • 1916 • Watt Nate • USA

IMA LJUBAVI NEMA LJUBAVI • 1968 • Rajic Nikola • YGS • WITH LOVE OR WITHOUT LOVE
IMA SIMP -DETECTIVE • 1915 • *Balboa* • USA
IMA SIMP, GOAT • 1915 • *Balboa* • USA
IMA SIMP ON THE JOB • 1915 • *Balboa* • USA
IMA VAMP • 1920 • Lascelle Ward • SHT • USA
IMA VAMP, FAIRYLAND AND MEMORIES • 1920 • Lascelle Ward • USA
IMA WA NAMONAI OTOKO DAGA • 1958 • Murayama Shinji • JPN • TRUMPET OF VICTORY
IMAGE • 1964 • Shaye Robert • SHT • USA
IMAGE • 1974 • Lemaitre Maurice • FRN
IMAGE see **OMOKAGE** • 1948
IMAGE see **MONDO HOLLYWOOD** • 1967
IMAGE, L' • 1925 • Feyder Jacques • FRN
IMAGE, THE • 1968 • Armstrong Michael • SHT • UKN
IMAGE, THE • 1976 • Metzger Radley H. • USA
IMAGE, THE see **IMAGEN, LA** • 1974
IMAGE BEFORE MY EYES • 1981 • Waletzky Josh • DOC
IMAGE BY IMAGES I-IV • 1954-56 • Breer Robert • SHS • USA
IMAGE, FLESH AND VOICE • 1969 • Emshwiller Ed • USA
IMAGE-IMAGE • 1981 • Laguionie Jean-Francois • ANS • FRN
IMAGE IN THE SNOW • 1943-48 • Maas Willard, Menken Marie • SHT • USA • IMAGES IN THE SNOW
IMAGE MAKER, THE • 1917 • Moore W. Eugene • USA
IMAGE MAKERS, THE • 1979 • Kish Albert • DOC • CND
IMAGE OF A MOTHER, THE see **MABUTA NO HAHA** • 1931
IMAGE OF BRUCE LEE • 1978 • Yeung Kuen • HKG
IMAGE OF DEATH • 1978 • Dobson Kevin • MTV • ASL
IMAGE OF FATE, THE • 1911 • *Imp* • USA
IMAGE OF LOVE, THE • 1964 • Stoumen Louis Clyde • DOC • USA
IMAGE OF MYTHICAL CHARACTER • 1988 • Theos Dimosthenis • GRC
IMAGE OF THE PAST, AN • 1915 • Browning Tod • USA
IMAGE ONE: AN EVENT • 1963 • Sharits Paul J. • SHT • USA
IMAGE WIFE see **RIKO NA OYOME-SAN** • 1958
IMAGEMAKER, THE • 1986 • Weiner Hal • USA
IMAGEN, LA • 1974 • Carbonell Maria L. • VNZ • IMAGE, THE
IMAGEN DE CARACAS • 1968 • Robles Mario, Borges Jacobo • VNZ • IMAGES OF CARACAS
IMAGEN DE VENEZUELA • 1968 • Gonzalez Daniel, Camacho Carlos Antonio, Angola Carlos, Arrieta Nelson, Bichier Jean-Jacques, Guedez Jesus Enrique • VNZ • IMAGES OF VENEZUELA
IMAGENS • 1973 • Filho Luis Rosemberg • BLG • IMAGES
IMAGENS DE PORTUGAL • 1933 • Contreiras Anibal • SHT • PRT
IMAGES • 1955 • Bail Rene • CND
IMAGES • 1970 • Kohanyi Julius • CND
IMAGES • 1970 • Raggett Hugh • UKN
IMAGES • 1972 • Altman Robert • USA, IRL
IMAGES see **IMAGENS** • 1973
IMAGES A PROPOS DE "ENLUMINURES AUTOUR DES MINUTES DU PROCES DE GILLES DE RAIS" • 1975 • Lancelot Martine • FRN • ETRANGE HISTOIRE DE GILLES DE RAIS, L'
IMAGES AND ALTMAN • 1972 • Stuart Falcon • UKN
IMAGES B.C. • 1984 • Nicolle Douglas • MTV • CND
IMAGES DE BAUDELAIRE • 1959 • Touchard Pierre-Aime • SHT • FRN
IMAGES DE CHINE • 1973 • Carriere Marcel • DOC • CND
IMAGES DE LA FOLIE • 1950 • Fulchignoni Enrico • FRN
IMAGES DE LA GASPESIE • 1972 • Labrecque Jean-Claude • DCS • CND
IMAGES DE LA VIE QUEBECOIS • 1979 • Lavoie Richard • SER • CND
IMAGES DE NOEL EN PAYS DU QUEBEC • 1954 • Rivard Fernand, Desmarteau Charles • DCS • CND
IMAGES DE SOLOGNE • 1959 • de Roubaix Paul • SHT • FRN
IMAGES DES MONDES PERDUS • 1959 • Lifchitz Philippe • SHT • FRN
IMAGES D'ETHIOPIE • 1948 • Pichonnier Paul, Pichonnier Jean • BLG
IMAGES D'HIER ET D'AUJOURD'HUI • 1960 • Leduc • SHT • FRN
IMAGES D'OSTENDE • 1930 • Storck Henri • DOC • BLG
IMAGES DU DEBAT • 1979 • Ruiz Raul • FRN • IMAGES OF DEBATE
IMAGES EN NEGATIF • 1956 • Deslaw Eugene • SHT • FRN
IMAGES FANTASTIQUES • Crama Nico • SHT • NTH
IMAGES IN THE SNOW see **IMAGE IN THE SNOW** • 1943-48
IMAGES (JEUX) • 1953 • Bail Rene • CND
IMAGES MATHEMATIQUES DE LA LUTTE POUR LA VIE • 1937 • Painleve Jean • SHT • FRN
IMAGES MATHEMATIQUES DE LA QUATRIEME DIMENSION • 1937 • Painleve Jean • SHT • FRN
IMAGES MEDIEVALES • 1949 • Novik William • SHT • FRN • PICTURES OF THE MIDDLE AGES
IMAGES OF A RELIEF • 1979 • von Trier Lars • DNM
IMAGES OF AN OLD WORLD see **OBRAZY STAREHO SVETA** • 1972
IMAGES OF CANADA • 1972 • Robertson George C. • SER • CND
IMAGES OF CARACAS see **IMAGEN DE CARACAS** • 1968
IMAGES OF DEBATE see **IMAGES DU DEBAT** • 1979
IMAGES OF LIGHT AND CURVE • 1958 • Jakob Dennis, Hora Jon • USA
IMAGES OF PRODUCTIVITY • 1964 • Harrington Curtis • SHT • USA
IMAGES OF VENEZUELA see **IMAGEN DE VENEZUELA** • 1968
IMAGES POUR BACH • 1972 • Jabely Jean • ANS • FRN
IMAGES POUR BAUDELAIRE • 1958 • Kast Pierre • SHT • FRN
IMAGES POUR DEBUSSY • 1952 • Mitry Jean • SHT • FRN
IMAGES PREHISTORIQUES • 1955 • Arcady • SHT • FRN
IMAGES STONE B.C. • 1979 • Long Jack • CND
IMAGES SUR LES MUSIQUES FRANCAISES • Guillon Madelaine • FRN
IMAGI NINGTHEM • 1982 • Sharma Abiram Syam • IND • MY SON, MY PRECIOUS
IMAGINACION AL PODER, LA • 1971 • de la Cerda Clemente • VNZ • IMAGINATION IN POWER
IMAGINARY ELOPEMENT, AN • 1911 • *Imp* • USA
IMAGINARY KNIGHT, THE see **CAVALIERE INESISTENTE, IL** • 1970
IMAGINARY LOVE SCENE, AN • 1902 • *Mutoscope & Biograph* • UKN
IMAGINARY PARADISE see **KUSO TENGOKU** • 1968
IMAGINARY PATIENT, AN see **MALADE IMAGINAIRE, LE** • 1897
IMAGINARY SWEETHEART (UKN) see **PROFESSIONAL SWEETHEART** • 1933
IMAGINARY VOYAGE, AN • 1964 • Popescu Mircea • RMN
IMAGINARY VOYAGE, THE see **VOYAGE IMMAGINAIRE, LE** • 1925
IMAGINATION • 1910 • *Essanay* • USA
IMAGINATION • 1912 • *Solax* • USA
IMAGINATION • 1943 • Wickersham Bob • ANM • USA
IMAGINATION • 1969 • Kuri Yoji • ANS • JPN
IMAGINATION see **KALPANA** • 1946
IMAGINATION see **DOUBLE LIFE, A** • 1948
IMAGINATION IN POWER see **IMAGINACION AL PODER, LA** • 1971
IMAGINATIVE WILLIE • 1911 • *Powers* • USA
IMAGINE • 1972 • Lennon John, Ono Yoko • UKN, USA
IMAGINE MY EMBARRASSMENT • 1928 • Yates Hal • SHT • USA
IMAGINE ONE EVENING FOR DINNER see **METTI, UNA SERA A CENA** • 1969
IMAGINE ROBINSON see **TU IMAGINES ROBINSON** • 1968
IMAGINE THE SOUND • 1981 • Mann Ron • DOC • CND
IMAGINI VIVE (CIO CHE DI ME HANNO LASCIATO) • 1976 • Giannarelli Ansano • MTV • ITL
IMAGO • 1970 • Bosnick Ned • USA • HOW NOW, SWEET EROS? ○ TO BE FREE
IMALI • 1984 • SAF
IMAM DVIJE MAME I DVA TATE • 1968 • Golik Kreso • YGS • I HAVE TWO MUMMIES AND TWO DADDIES ○ TOO MANY PARENTS
IMAMIN GAZABI • 1967 • Yalinkilic Yavuz • TRK • WRATH OF THE IMAM, THE
IMAR THE SENATOR • 1914 • *Garwood William* • USA
IMBARCO A MEZZANOTTE • 1952 • Losey Joseph • USA, ITL • STRANGER ON THE PROWL (USA) ○ ENCOUNTER
IMBECILES ET LES AUTRES, LES • 1977 • Pavel Samy • BLG
IMBOSCATA, L' • 1916 • Ghione Emilio • ITL
IMBRAT'URIYYAT MIN • 1972 • Kamal Hussein • EGY • EMPIRE DE M., L'
IMBROGLIONI, GLI • 1963 • Fulci Lucio • ITL, SPN
IMCOMPARABLE see **ADWITIYA** • 1968
IMERES TOU '36 • 1972 • Angelopoulos Theo • GRC • DAYS OF '36 (USA) ○ MERES TOU 1936 ○ JOURS DE 36
IMI HAGENERALIT • 1979 • Silberg Joel • ISR • MY MOTHER THE GENERAL
IMIE OJCA • 1969 • Slesicki Wladyslaw • PLN • FATHER'S NAME
IMITATEUR, L' • 1930 • Diamant-Berger Henri • FRN
IMITATION GENERAL • 1958 • Marshall George • USA
IMITATION OF CHRIST • 1970 • Warhol Andy • USA
IMITATION OF LIFE • 1934 • Stahl John M. • USA
IMITATION OF LIFE • 1959 • Sirk Douglas • USA
IMITATIONS • 1915 • Otto Henry • USA
IMMACOLATA AND CONCETTA: THE OTHER JEALOUSY see **IMMACOLATA E CONCETTA** • 1979
IMMACOLATA E CONCETTA • 1979 • Piscicelli Salvatore • ITL • IMMACOLATA AND CONCETTA: THE OTHER JEALOUSY
IMMACULATE CONCEPTION OF BABY BUMP, THE see **SINFUL LIFE, A** • 1989
IMMACULATE ROAD, THE • 1960 • Mate Rudolph • USA
IMMAGINE DELL'ALTRA, L' • 1918 • Serena Gustavo • ITL
IMMAGINI DI UN CONVENTO • 1979 • D'Amato Joe • ITL
IMMAGINI POPOLARI SICILIANE PROFANE • 1952 • Birri Fernando, Verdone Mario • DOC • ITL
IMMAGINI POPOLARI SICILIANE SACRE • 1952 • Birri Fernando, Verdone Mario • DOC • ITL
IMMATURE PUNTER • 1898 • Hepworth Cecil M. • UKN
IMMEDIATE DISASTER (USA) see **STRANGER FROM VENUS, A** • 1954
IMMEDIATE FAMILY • 1989 • Kaplan Jonathan • USA
IMMEDIATE LEE • 1916 • Borzage Frank • USA • HAIR TRIGGER CASSIDY ○ HAIR TRIGGER CASEY
IMMEDIATE POSSESSION • 1931 • Varney-Serrao Arthur • UKN
IMMENSEE • 1943 • Harlan Veit • FRG • CARNIVAL
IMMENSITA, L' • 1967 • De Fina P. V. Oscar • ITL • RAGAZZA DEL PAIP'S, LA ○ IMMENSITY, THE ○ PAIP'S GIRL
IMMENSITY, THE see **IMMENSITA, L'** • 1967
IMMENSO E ROSSO • 1975 • Andrei Marcello • ITL
IMMER ARGER MIT DEM BETT • 1961 • Schundler Rudolf • FRG • MEINE FRAU DAS CALL GIRL
IMMER ARGER MIT DEN PAUKERN • 1968 • Vock Harald • FRG • ALWAYS TROUBLE WITH TEACHER
IMMER BEI VOLLMUND • 1970 • Lubowski Rudolf • FRG
IMMER DIE MADCHEN • 1959 • Remond Fritz • AUS
IMMER NUR DU • 1941 • Anton Karl • FRG
IMMER WENN DER TAG BEGINNT • 1957 • Liebeneiner Wolfgang • FRG
IMMER WENN ES NACHT WIRD • 1961 • Bove Hans Dieter • FRG • LOVE FEAST, THE (USA) ○ ALWAYS WHEN NIGHT FALLS
IMMER WENN ICH GLUCKLICH BIN see **WALZERLANGE** • 1938
IMMER WILL ICH DIR GEHOREN • 1960 • Assmann Arno • FRG
IMMIGRANT, THE • 1917 • Chaplin Charles • SHT • USA
IMMIGRANT, THE • 1919 • Hollywood Edwin L. • USA
IMMIGRANT, THE • 1978 • Levi Alan J. • TVM • USA
IMMIGRANT, THE • 1990 • Hatamikia Ebrahim • IRN
IMMIGRANT CHRONICLE • 1978 • Turkiewicz Sophia • MTV • ASL
IMMIGRANTS, THE • 1915 • Melford George • USA
IMMIGRANTS, THE see **METANASTES, I** • 1976
IMMIGRANT'S VIOLIN, THE • 1912 • Turner Otis • USA
IMMIGRE, L' • 1959 • Devlin Bernard • SHT • CND
IMMISELON IHANUUS JA KURJUUS • 1988 • Kassila Matti • FNL • GLORY AND MISERY OF HUMAN LIFE, THE
IMMORAL see **IMMORALE, L'** • 1980
IMMORAL, THE • 1965 • *Joseph Brenner Associates* • SWD
IMMORAL CHARGE see **SERIOUS CHARGE** • 1959
IMMORAL GIRLS OF THE NAKED WEST see **IMMORAL WEST -AND HOW IT WAS LOST, THE** • 1962
IMMORAL MAN, THE see **IMMORALE, L'** • 1967
IMMORAL MR. TEAS, THE • 1958 • Meyer Russ • USA
IMMORAL MOMENT, THE (USA) see **DENONCIATION, LA** • 1962
IMMORAL RELATIONSHIP see **MIDARETA KANKEI** • 1967
IMMORAL TALES see **CONTES IMMOREAUX** • 1974
IMMORAL WEST, THE see **IMMORAL WEST -AND HOW IT WAS LOST, THE** • 1962
IMMORAL WEST -AND HOW IT WAS LOST, THE • 1962 • Meyer Russ • USA • IMMORAL GIRLS OF THE NAKED WEST ○ WILD GIRLS OF THE NAKED WEST ○ NAKED WEST -AND HOW IT WAS LOST, THE ○ NAKED GIRLS OF THE GOLDEN WEST ○ IMMORAL WEST, THE
IMMORALE, L' • 1967 • Germi Pietro • ITL, FRN • BEAUCOUP TROP POUR UN SEUL HOMME (FRN) ○ TOO MUCH FOR ONE MAN ○ CLIMAX, THE (USA) ○ IMMORAL MAN, THE
IMMORALE, L' • 1980 • Mulot Claude • FRN • CONFESSIONS OF A PROSTITUTE ○ IMMORAL
IMMORALITA, L' • 1978 • Pirri Massimo • ITL
IMMORTAL see **AMAR** • 1948
IMMORTAL, THE • 1969 • Sargent Joseph • TVM • USA
IMMORTAL ALAMO, THE • 1911 • Melies Gaston • USA
IMMORTAL BACHELOR, THE • 1979 • Fondato Marcello • ITL
IMMORTAL BATTALION (USA) see **WAY AHEAD, THE** • 1944
IMMORTAL BLACKSMITH, THE • 1944 • Lee Sammy • SHT • USA
IMMORTAL FLAME, THE • 1916 • Abramson Ivan • USA
IMMORTAL FRANCE (USA) see **UNTEL PERE ET FILS** • 1940
IMMORTAL GARRISON, THE (USA) see **BESSMERTNYI GARNIZON** • 1956
IMMORTAL GENTLEMAN • 1935 • Newman Widgey R. • UKN
IMMORTAL GOOSE, THE • 1909 • Raymond Charles? • UKN
IMMORTAL HERITAGE, THE • 1980 • Carne Marcel • FRN
IMMORTAL JAPAN • 1954 • Abe Yutaka • JPN
IMMORTAL LAND, THE • 1958 • Wright Basil • DOC • UKN
IMMORTAL LEGIONARY, THE see **HALHATATLAN LEGIOS, A** • 1971
IMMORTAL LOVE see **EIEN NO HITO** • 1961
IMMORTAL LOVE see **NESMRTELNA LASKA** • 1961
IMMORTAL MAN, THE see **OLUMSUZ ADAMLAR** • 1968
IMMORTAL MELODIES (USA) see **UNSTERBLICHE MELODIEN** • 1935
IMMORTAL MONSTER, THE see **CALTIKI IL MOSTRO IMMORTALE** • 1959
IMMORTAL PITCHER see **FUMETSU NO NEKKYU** • 1955
IMMORTAL SERGEANT, THE • 1943 • Stahl John M. • USA
IMMORTAL STORY see **HISTOIRE IMMORTELLE** • 1968
IMMORTAL STORY see **HAISHANG HUA** • 1987
IMMORTAL STORY see **NIEMORALNA HISTORIA** • 1990
IMMORTAL STUPA • 1961 • *Roy Bhimal (P)* • IND
IMMORTAL SWAN, THE • 1935 • Nakhimoff Edward • UKN
IMMORTAL VAGABOND, THE (USA) see **UNSTERBLICHE LUMP, DER** • 1930
IMMORTAL WOMAN, THE see **IMMORTELLE, L'** • 1963
IMMORTAL WOMAN, THE see **OLUMSUZ KADIN** • 1967
IMMORTAL YOUTH see **BESMRTNA MLADOST** • 1948
IMMORTALE, L' see **IMMORTELLE, L'** • 1963
IMMORTALITA see **IMMORTALITA, CAMILLO TORRES, UN PRETE GUERRIGLIERO** • 1970
IMMORTALITA, CAMILLO TORRES, UN PRETE GUERRIGLIERO • 1970 • Breccia Paolo • ITL • IMMORTALITA ○ IMMORTALITY
IMMORTALITY • 1958 • Tovstonogov G., Chiginsky A. • USS
IMMORTALITY see **KHULUD** • 1948
IMMORTALITY see **HALHATATLANSAG** • 1959
IMMORTALITY see **IMMORTALITA, CAMILLO TORRES, UN PRETE GUERRIGLIERO** • 1970
IMMORTALIZER, THE • 1989 • Bender Joel • USA
IMMORTALS, THE see **NEMURITORII** • 1974
IMMORTALS OF BONNIE SCOTLAND see **LIFE OF ROBERT BURNS, THE** • 1926
IMMORTALS OF BONNIE SCOTLAND see **LIFE OF SIR WALTER SCOTT, THE** • 1926
IMMORTELLE, L' • 1963 • Robbe-Grillet Alain • FRN, ITL, TRK • IMMORTALE, L' ○ IMMORTAL WOMAN, THE
IMMORTELLES, LES • 1963 • Kyrou Ado • FRN
IMMOVABLE GUEST, THE • 1919 • *Finch Flora* • SHT • USA
IMOGEN CUNNINGHAM -PHOTOGRAPHER • 1970 • Korty John • DCS • USA
IMOHTO • 1974 • Fujita Toshiya • JPN • MY SISTER
IMOLATION A HAMLET • Mitrotti Mario • VNZ
IMOTO NO SHI • 1921 • Kinugasa Teinosuke • JPN • DEATH OF MY SISTER, THE
IMP, THE • 1920 • Ellis Robert • USA
IMP, THE • 1981 • Yu Yunk'Ang • HKG
IMP, THE see **SORORITY BABIES IN THE SLIMEBALL BOWL-O-RAMA** • 1988
IMP ABROAD, THE • 1914 • *Victor* • USA
IMP IN THE BODY, THE see **CON EL DIABLO EN EL CUERPO** • 1954
IMP IN THE BOTTLE, THE • 1950 • *Pyramid Prods.* • SHT • USA
IMP IN THE BOTTLE, THE see **LIEBE, TOD UND TEUFEL** • 1934
IMP OF THE BOTTLE, THE • 1909 • *Edison* • USA
IMP ROMANCE, AN • 1913 • *Imp* • USA
IMPACIENCIA DEL CORAZON • 1958 • Davison Tito • MXC
IMPACT • 1933 • Marshall George • SHT • USA
IMPACT • 1949 • Lubin Arthur • USA
IMPACT • 1963 • Maxwell Peter • UKN
IMPACT • 1989 • Nel Frans • SAF
IMPALEMENT, THE • 1910 • Griffith D. W. • USA
IMPANGO • 1982 • SAF
IMPASSE • 1945 • Dard Pierre • FRN
IMPASSE • 1956 • Bonnardot Jean-Claude • FRN
IMPASSE • 1962 • Kitts Robert • UKN
IMPASSE • 1969 • Benedict Richard • USA
IMPASSE see **HONOO TO ONNA** • 1967
IMPASSE DES DEUX ANGES • 1948 • Tourneur Maurice • FRN
IMPASSE DES VERTUS • 1955 • Mere Pierre • FRN • LOVE AT NIGHT (USA) ○ SEX AT NIGHT
IMPASSE D'UN MATIN, L' • 1964 • Desvilles • SHT • FRN
IMPASSIVE FOOTMAN, THE • 1932 • Dean Basil • UKN • WOMAN IN CHAINS (USA) ○ WOMAN IN BONDAGE

IMPATIENCE • 1928 • Dekeukeleire Charles • BLG
IMPATIENT HEART, THE • 1971 • Badham John • TVM • USA
IMPATIENT MAIDEN • 1932 • Whale James • USA
IMPATIENT PATIENT, THE • 1925 • Templeman Harcourt • UKN
IMPATIENT PATIENT, THE • 1942 • McCabe Norman • ANS • USA
IMPATIENT YEARS, THE • 1944 • Cummings Irving • USA
IMPECCABLE HENRI, L' • 1948 • Tavano Charles-Felix • FRN • IMPECCABLE MONSIEUR HENRI, L'
IMPECCABLE MONSIEUR HENRI, L' see **IMPECCABLE HENRI, L'** • 1948
IMPEDIMENT, THE • 1911 • Haldane Bert? • UKN
IMPERATIF, L' • 1982 • Zanussi Krzysztof • FRN, FRG • IMPERATIVE (USA)
IMPERATIVE (USA) see **IMPERATIF, L'** • 1982
IMPERATORE DI CAPRI, L' • 1949 • Comencini Luigi • ITL
IMPERATRICE ET MOI, L' see **MOI ET L'IMPERATRICE** • 1932
IMPERCEPTIBLE TRANSMUTATIONS (USA) see **TRANSMUTATIONS IMPERCEPTIBLES** • 1904
IMPERFECT ANGEL (USA) see **SCHMUTZIGER ENGEL** • 1958
IMPERFECT LADIES see **IT'S A GREAT LIFE** • 1929
IMPERFECT LADY, THE • 1947 • Allen Lewis • USA • MRS. LORING'S SECRET (UKN)
IMPERFECT LADY, THE (UKN) see **PERFECT GENTLEMAN, THE** • 1935
IMPERFECT LOVER, THE • 1921 • West Walter • UKN
IMPERFECT LOVER, THE • 1925 • Mayo Archie • SHT • USA
IMPERFECT MURDER (UKN) see **DELITTO QUASI PERFETTO** • 1966
IMPERFECT PERFECTORS • 1910 • *Atlas* • USA
IMPERIAL GRACE, THE (USA) see **KO-ON** • 1927
IMPERIAL GUARD CAVALRY • 1976 • Hall Russell • UKN • COUNT PUSHKIN VODKA
IMPERIAL JAPANESE DANCE • 1894 • *Edison* • USA
IMPERIAL JAPANESE EMPIRE, THE see **DAINIPPON TEIKOKU** • 1983
IMPERIAL OIL see **MOLECULES** • 1966
IMPERIAL REGIO CAPESTRO • 1915 • Lolli Alberto Carlo • ITL
IMPERIAL SUNSET • 1969 • Koenig Joseph, Lipsett Arthur • SHT • CND
IMPERIAL VENUS (USA) see **VENUS IMPERIALE** • 1962
IMPERIO DE DRACULA, EL • 1966 • Curiel Federico • MXC • MUJERES DE DRACULA, LAS ○ EMPIRE OF DRACULA (USA) ○ WOMEN OF DRACULA, THE
IMPERIO DE LA FORTUNAM, EL • 1986 • Ripstein Arturo • MXC • EMPIRE OF FORTUNE, THE
IMPERO DEL SOLE, L' • 1956 • Craveri Mario, Gras Enrico, Moser Giorgio • DOC • ITL • EMPIRE IN THE SUN (USA)
IMPERSONATING THE POLICEMAN LODGER • 1910 • Bouwmeester Theo? • UKN
IMPERSONATION, THE • 1916 • *Gerber Neva* • USA
IMPERSONATION OF TOM, THE • 1915 • Mix Tom • USA
IMPERSONATOR, THE • 1914 • France Charles H. • USA
IMPERSONATOR, THE • 1961 • Shaughnessy Alfred • UKN
IMPERSONATOR'S JOKE, THE • 1908 • *Essanay* • USA
IMPETUOUS JIM • 1913 • *Punch* • USA
IMPETUOUS YOUTH (UKN) see **GEIGER VON FLORENZ, DER** • 1926
IMPIEGATA DI PAPA, L' • 1933 • Blasetti Alessandro • ITL • PAPA, VOGLIO IMPIEGARMI! ○ GENTE PER BENE
IMPIEGATE STRADALI, L' • 1976 • Landi Mario • ITL • BATTON STORY
IMPIEGATO, L' • 1959 • Puccini Gianni • ITL • EMPLOYEE, THE
IMPINDISO • 1985 • SAF
IMPLACABLE DESTINY see **LOVE ME AND THE WORLD IS MINE** • 1928
IMPLOSION • 1966 • Fraikin Marcel • BLG
IMPONENTE, EL • 1972 • *Prods. Leo* • MXC
IMPORTANCE OF BEING ANOTHER MAN'S WIFE, THE • 1914 • Wilson Frank? • UKN
IMPORTANCE OF BEING EARNEST, THE • 1952 • Asquith Anthony • UKN
IMPORTANCE OF BEING SEXY, THE see **COME BACK PETER** • 1969
IMPORTANCE OF BEING SEXY, THE see **LOVING AND LAUGHING** • 1971
IMPORTANCE OF KEEPING PERFECTLY STILL, THE • 1977 • Pattinson Michael • SHT • ASL
IMPORTANCE OF NOT BEING NOTICED, THE see **IMPORTANTE E NON FARSI NOTARE, L'** • 1980
IMPORTANCE OF WOOD, THE • 1982 • van Vuure Jan • DOC • NTH
IMPORTANT BUSINESS • 1944 • Jason Will • SHT • USA
IMPORTANT, C'EST D'AIMER, L' • 1974 • Zulawski Andrzej • FRN, ITL, FRG • MOST IMPORTANT THING: LOVE, THE (USA)
IMPORTANT MAN, THE (USA) see **ANIMAS TRUJANO, EL HOMBRE IMPORTANTE** • 1961
IMPORTANT PEOPLE • 1934 • Brunel Adrian • UKN
IMPORTANT WITNESS, THE • 1933 • Newfield Sam • USA
IMPORTANTE E NON FARSI NOTARE, L' • 1980 • Guerrieri Romolo • ITL • IMPORTANCE OF NOT BEING NOTICED, THE
IMPORTANZA DI AVERE UN CAVALLO, L' • 1972 • Santesso Walter • MTV • ITL
IMPORTED BRIDEGROOM, THE • 1989 • Berger Pamela • USA
IMPOSIBLE PARA UNA SOLTERONA • 1975 • Romero-Marchent Rafael • SPN
IMPOSIBRANTE • 1968 • Guzman Patricio • SPN
IMPOSSIBILA IUBIRE • 1984 • Vaeni Constantin • RMN • IMPOSSIBLE LOVE
IMPOSSIBILE, L' • 1981 • Brocani Franco • ITL
IMPOSSIBILITE DE S'ENTENDRE see **MAFISH TAFAHUM** • 1962
IMPOSSIBLE see **NYE MOZHET BYTI** • 1976
IMPOSSIBLE, L' see **MUSTAHIL, AL-** • 1964
IMPOSSIBLE AVEU, L' • 1935 • Guarino Joseph • FRN
IMPOSSIBLE BALANCING FEAT, AN (USA) see **EQUILIBRE IMPOSSIBLE, L'** • 1902
IMPOSSIBLE CATHERINE • 1919 • O'Brien John B. • USA
IMPOSSIBLE CONVICTS • 1905 • *Bitzer Billy (Ph)* • USA
IMPOSSIBLE DINNER, THE (USA) see **DINER IMPOSSIBLE, LE** • 1904
IMPOSSIBLE HAPPENS, THE see **IMPOSSIVEL ACONTECE, O** • 1969
IMPOSSIBLE HOUR, THE • Leth Jorgen • DNM
IMPOSSIBLE LOVE see **IMPOSSIBILA IUBIRE** • 1984
IMPOSSIBLE LOVER, THE (UKN) see **HUDDLE** • 1932
IMPOSSIBLE LOVERS, THE • 1906 • Mottershaw Frank • UKN
IMPOSSIBLE MAN, THE • 1920 • Goodwins Fred • UKN
IMPOSSIBLE MAP, THE • 1947 • Lambart Evelyn • ANS • CND
IMPOSSIBLE MARRIAGE, AN see **LIVETS GOGLESPIL** • 1916
IMPOSSIBLE MONSIEUR PIPELET, L' • 1955 • Hunebelle Andre • FRN • MONSIEUR PIPELET
IMPOSSIBLE MRS. BELLEW, THE • 1922 • Wood Sam • USA
IMPOSSIBLE OBJECT see **QUESTO IMPOSSIBILE OGGETTO** • 1973
IMPOSSIBLE OBJET, L'(FRN) see **QUESTO IMPOSSIBILE OGGETTO** • 1973
IMPOSSIBLE ON SATURDAY (USA) see **PAS QUESTION LE SAMEDI** • 1965
IMPOSSIBLE PAS FRANCAIS • 1974 • Lamoureux Robert • FRN
IMPOSSIBLE POSSUM • 1954 • Lundy Dick • ANS • USA
IMPOSSIBLE SPY, THE • 1987 • Goddard Jim • TVM • USA, UKN
IMPOSSIBLE SUSAN • 1918 • Ingraham Lloyd • USA
IMPOSSIBLE TASK, AN see **KOUNIA POU SE KOUNAGE** • 1967
IMPOSSIBLE VOYAGE, AN see **VOYAGE A TRAVERS L'IMPOSSIBLE, LE** • 1904
IMPOSSIBLE WOMAN, THE • 1919 • Milton Meyrick • UKN
IMPOSSIBLE YEARS, THE • 1968 • Gordon Michael • USA
IMPOSSIVEL ACONTECE, O • 1969 • Chadler C. Adolpho • BRZ • IMPOSSIBLE HAPPENS, THE
IMPOSTER, THE • 1926 • Withey Chet • USA
IMPOSTER, THE • 1929 • Fogwell Reginald • UKN
IMPOSTER, THE • 1943 • Duvivier Julien • USA • STRANGE CONFESSION ○ IMPOSTOR, THE
IMPOSTER, THE • 1955 • Osone Tatsuo • JPN
IMPOSTER, THE • 1984 • Pressman Michael • TVM • USA
IMPOSTER, THE see **IMPOSTOR, THE** • 1918
IMPOSTOR, EL • 1936 • Kirkland David • MXC
IMPOSTOR, EL • 1956 • Fernandez Emilio • MXC • GESTICULADOR, EL
IMPOSTOR, THE • 1910 • *Bison* • USA
IMPOSTOR, THE • 1911 • *Thanhouser* • USA
IMPOSTOR, THE • 1912 • *Nestor* • USA
IMPOSTOR, THE • 1912 • *Lubin* • USA
IMPOSTOR, THE • 1913 • *Broncho* • USA
IMPOSTOR, THE • 1913 • Barker Reginald • USA
IMPOSTOR, THE • 1914 • *Komic* • USA
IMPOSTOR, THE • 1914 • Carleton Lloyd B. • *Lubin* • USA
IMPOSTOR, THE • 1915 • Capellani Albert • USA
IMPOSTOR, THE • 1918 • Henderson Dell • USA • IMPOSTER, THE
IMPOSTOR, THE • 1975 • Abroms Edward M. • TVM • USA
IMPOSTOR, THE see **TAILOR-MADE MAN, A** • 1931
IMPOSTOR, THE see **IMPOSTER, THE** • 1943
IMPOSTORS • 1981 • Rappaport Mark • USA
IMPOSTORS, THE see **HOGHEBAZAN** • 1967
IMPOSTORS, THE see **IMPOSZTOROK** • 1969
IMPOSZTOROK • 1969 • Mariassy Felix • HNG • IMPOSTORS, THE
IMPOT ET TOUT.. ET TOUT • 1968 • Poirier Anne-Claire • DOC • CND
IMPOTENCE see **HONNO** • 1966
IMPOTENCE see **XALA** • 1974
IMPOTENT, THE • 1980 • Dayan Assaf • ISR
IMPOTENT, THE see **FUNOSHA** • 1967
"IMP"PROBABLE MR. WEE GEE, THE • 1966 • Price Sherman • USA
IMPRACTICABLE JOURNEY, AN • 1905 • *Pathe Freres* • FRN
IMPRACTICAL JOKER, THE • 1937 • Fleischer Dave • ANS • USA
IMPRECATEUR, L' • 1976 • Bertucelli Jean-Louis • FRN, SWT • ACCUSER, THE
IMPREGNATION see **JUTAI** • 1967
IMPRESE DI UNA SPADA LEGGENDARIA, LE • 1957 • McDonald Frank, Juran Nathan • USA
IMPRESJE CHOPINOWSKIE • 1970 • Perski Ludwik • DOC • PLN • IMPRESSIONS OF CHOPIN
IMPRESSIO • 1970 • Suo-Anttila Seppo • ANS • FNL • IMPRESSION
IMPRESSION see **IMPRESSIO** • 1970
IMPRESSION AND PRE-IMPRESSION IN FRANCE • 1979 • Kohanyi Julius • MTV • CND
IMPRESSIONEN AUS EINEM THEATER • 1957 • Oertel Curt • FRG
IMPRESSIONNISTE FIN DE SIECLE, L' see **ILLUSIONNISTE FIN DE SIECLE, L'** • 1899
IMPRESSIONNISTES, LES • See Jean-Claude • SHT • FRN
IMPRESSIONS • 1932 • Jakubowska Wanda • DOC • PLN
IMPRESSIONS 1670-1970 • 1970 • Chapman Christopher • DOC • CND
IMPRESSIONS DE NEW YORK • 1955 • Reichenbach Francois • SHT • FRN
IMPRESSIONS DE PARIS • 1967 • Reichenbach Francois • SHT • FRN
IMPRESSIONS OF APRIL see **STEMMING I APRIL** • 1947
IMPRESSIONS OF CHOPIN see **IMPRESJE CHOPINOWSKIE** • 1970
IMPREVISIBLES NOUVEAUTES • 1961 • Rossif Frederic • FRN • UNFORESEEABLE NOVELTIES
IMPREVISTO, L' • 1919 • Caserini Mario • ITL
IMPREVISTO, L' • 1941 • Simonelli Giorgio C. • ITL
IMPREVISTO, L' • 1961 • Lattuada Alberto • ITL, FRN • IMPREVU, L' (FRN) ○ UNEXPECTED, THE
IMPREVU, L' • 1916 • Perret Leonce • FRN
IMPREVU, L' • 1965 • Amadon Alpha • SHT • FRN
IMPREVU, L' (FRN) see **IMPREVISTO, L'** • 1961
IMPRINTS see **HUELLAS** • 1988
IMPROBABLE YARN OF MCQUIRK, THE • 1916 • Walsh Phil • SHT • USA
IMPROMPTU • 1932 • McGann William • UKN
IMPROMPTU see **KACAMAK** • 1987
IMPROMPTU BATH, THE • 1899 • *Haydon & Urry* • UKN
IMPRONTA, L' • 1920 • Rosa Silvio Laurenti • ITL
IMPROPAGANDA • 1919 • Harrison Saul • SHT • USA
IMPROPER CHANNELS • 1981 • Till Eric • CND • PROPER CHANNELS
IMPROPER CONDUCT (USA) see **MAUVAISE CONDUITE** • 1984
IMPROPER DUCHESS, THE • 1936 • Hughes Harry • UKN
IMPROPER ONES, THE see **UANSTAENDIGE, DE** • 1983
IMPROPERLY DRESSED see **HERKULESFURDOI EMLEK** • 1977
IMPROVING THE ODDS • 1983 • Dodd Thomas • MTV • CND
IMPROVISATIONS IN BLACK AND WHITE • 1952 • *Bruel Axel (P)* • SHT • DNM
IMPROVISATIONS NO.1 • 1948 • Belson Jordan • SHT • USA
IMPROVVISAMENTE UN GIORNO • 1974 • Ausino Carlo • ITL
IMPROVVISAMENTE UNA SERA, UN AMORE (ITL) see **GALETS D'ETRETAT, LES** • 1971
IMPRUDENCIA • 1944 • Soler Julian • MXC
IMPRUDENT LOVER, THE see **UBETAENKSOMME ELSKER, DEN** • 1983
IMPUDENT GIRL, AN (UKN) see **EFFRONTEE, L'** • 1985
IMPUDENT LOVER, THE see **UBETAENKSOMME ELSKER, DEN** • 1983
IMPULSE • 1913 • *Majestic* • USA
IMPULSE • 1922 • MacGregor Norval • USA
IMPULSE • 1955 • De La Tour Charles, Endfield Cy (U/c) • UKN
IMPULSE • 1984 • Baker Graham* • USA
IMPULSE • 1989 • Locke Sondra • USA
IMPULSE see **WANT A RIDE, LITTLE GIRL?** • 1974
IMPULSES • 1965 • Davis James* • SHT • USA
IMPULSES see **THIRTEENTH COMMANDMENT, THE** • 1920
IMPULSION 7 • 1971 • Avedis Howard • USA
IMPULSIVE KILLER see **SHODO SATSUJIN, MUSUKO YO** • 1979
IMPULSOS OPTICOS EN PROGRESION GEOMETRICA • 1971 • Aguirre Javier • SHT • SPN • OPTICAL IMPULSES IN GEOMETRIC PROGRESSION
IMPUMELELO • 1983 • SAF
IMPURE, THE see **WILD RIDERS** • 1971
IMPURE THOUGHTS • 1985 • Simpson Michael A. • USA
IMPURES, LES • 1954 • Chevalier Pierre • FRN
IMPURITY see **YOGORE** • 1967
IMPUSCATURI PE PORTATIV • 1967 • Grigoriu Cezar • RMN • SHOTS ON THE STAVE
IMPUTATO ALZATEVI! • 1939 • Mattoli Mario • ITL
IMPUTAZIONE DI OMICIDIO PER UNO STUDENTE • 1972 • Bolognini Mauro • ITL
IMRA'A ACHIQA • 1974 • Fahmy Ashraf • EGY • WOMAN IN LOVE, A
IMRA'A FI AT-TARIQ • 1958 • Zulficar Izzeddine • EGY • FEMME SUR LA ROUTE, UNE
IMRA'ATI MUDIR AM see **MERATI MOUDIR AME** • 1966
IMRA'ATUN SAIYI'ATA AS-SUMA • 1972 • Barakat Henry • EGY • FEMME DE MAUVAISE REPUTATION, UNE
IMRAATY MAJNUNA see **MERATI MAGNOUNA.. MAGNOUNA..** • 1968
IMUS • 1973 • Kuri Yoji • ANS • JPN
IMUSI • 1985 • SAF
IMZAM KANLA YAZILIR • 1970 • Aslan Mehmet • TRK • I SIGN IN BLOOD
IN A BOX • 1969 • Noyes Eliot • ANS • CND
IN A CARTOON STUDIO see **MAKING 'EM MOVE** • 1931
IN A CERTAIN WAY see **DE CIERTA MANERA** • 1977
IN A CLOCK STORE see **CLOCK STORE, THE** • 1931
IN A COLT'S SHADOW (UKN) see **ALL'OMBRA DI UNA COLT** • 1965
IN A FANTASTIC VISION see **V BLOUZNENI** • 1928
IN A FAR COUNTRY • 1981 • Manatis Janine • MTV • CND
IN A FOG • 1916 • *Emerald* • SHT • USA
IN A FULL MOON NIGHT see **IN UNA NOTTE DI CHIARO DI LUNA** • 1990
IN A GARDEN • 1912 • *Chamberlain Riley* • USA
IN A GLASS CAGE see **TRAS EL CRISTAL** • 1985
IN A GREEN FOREST see **I DEN GRONNE SKOV** • 1968
IN A GREEN WOOD see **I DEN GRONNE SKOV** • 1968
IN A HEMPEN BAG • 1909 • Griffith D. W. • USA
IN A JACKPOT • 1915 • Lyons Eddie • USA
IN A JAPANESE GARDEN • 1915 • Platt George Foster • USA
IN A JAPANESE GARDEN • 1928 • Freund Karl • UKN
IN A JAPANESE TEA GARDEN • 1913 • Dawley J. Searle • USA
IN A LONELY PLACE • 1950 • Ray Nicholas • USA • BEHIND THIS MASK
IN A LOOKING GLASS • 1916 • Windom Lawrence C. • SHT • USA
IN A LOTUS GARDEN • 1931 • Paul Fred • UKN
IN A MIST • 1959 • Groot Rens • ANS • NTH
IN A MOMENT OF TEMPTATION • 1927 • Carle Philip • USA
IN A MONASTERY GARDEN • 1929 • Brunel Adrian • SHT • UKN
IN A MONASTERY GARDEN • 1932 • Elvey Maurice • UKN
IN A MONASTERY GARDEN see **REVELATION** • 1924
IN A MOST NOBLE MANNER • 1986 • Stoyanov Yuli • DOC • BUL
IN A NUT-SHELL • 1981 • Pieters Guido • NTH
IN A NUTSHELL • 1971 • Mills Michael, Arioli Don, Drew Les • SHT • CND
IN A PERSIAN GARDEN • 1914 • *Bright Mildred* • USA
IN A PIG'S EYE • 1934 • Holmes Ben • USA
IN A PINCH • 1919 • *De Haven Carter* • SHT • USA
IN A PROHIBITION TOWN • 1914 • France Charles H. • USA
IN A PROHIBITION TOWN • 1916 • Humphrey Orral • USA
IN A ROMAN GARDEN • 1913 • MacDonald Mr. • USA
IN A SECRET GARDEN see **OF LOVE AND DESIRE** • 1963
IN A SHALLOW GRAVE • 1988 • Bowser Kenneth • USA
IN A STRANGE LAND see **STRANGERS IN A STRANGE LAND** • 1913
IN A TRAP see **W MATNI** • 1965
IN A VILLAGE see **DE SFASURAREA** • 1954
IN A WAREHOUSE see **KURA NO NAKA** • 1982
IN A WAY see **DE CIERTA MANERA** • 1977
IN A WILD MOMENT (USA) see **MOMENT D'EGAREMENT, UN** • 1978
IN A WOMAN'S POWER • 1913 • Brenon Herbert • USA
IN A YEAR OF 13 MOONS (USA) see **IN EINEM JAHR MIT 13 MONDEN** • 1978
IN A YEAR WITH 13 MOONS see **IN EINEM JAHR MIT 13 MONDEN** • 1978

IN ADAM'S CLOTHES AND A LITTLE IN EVE'S TOO see **AATAMIN PUVUSSA JA VAHAN EEVANKIN** • 1971
IN ADAM'S DRESS AND A LITTLE IN EVE'S TOO see **AATAMIN PUVUSSA JA VAHAN EEVANKIN** • 1971
IN AFTER YEARS • 1912 • *Johnson Arthur* • USA
IN AFTER YEARS • 1913 • Kirkwood James • USA
IN AFTER YEARS • 1917 • Martin E. A. • SHT • USA
IN AGAIN, OUT AGAIN • 1917 • Christie Al • *Nestor* • SHT • USA
IN AGAIN –OUT AGAIN • 1917 • Emerson John • *Douglas Fairbanks Film Corp.* • USA
IN AGGUATO • 1915 • Negroni Baldassare • ITL
IN ALL INTIMACY see **IN ALLE STILTE** • 1978
IN ALL THINGS MODERATION • 1914 • Crampton Howard • USA
IN ALLE STILTE • 1978 • Boumans Ralf • BLG • IN ALL INTIMACY
IN AMORE SI PECCA IN DUE • 1954 • Cottafavi Vittorio • ITL
IN AN ENCHANTED CIRCLE see **W ZAKLETYM KREGU** • 1968
IN AN OLD MAN'S HEAD see **I HUVET PA EN GAMMAL GUBBE** • 1968
IN AN OLD TRUNK • 1914 • *Eclair* • USA
IN AND OUT • 1914 • *Essanay* • USA
IN AND OUT • 1914 • *Sterling* • USA
IN AND OUT • 1915 • *Banner* • USA
IN AND OUT • 1917 • Seiter William A. • USA
IN AND OUT • 1918 • *French George* • USA
IN AND OUT • 1920 • *Franey William* • USA
IN AND OUT • 1920 • Semon Larry • SHT • USA
IN AND OUT • 1990 • Snowden Alison, Fine David • ANS • CND
IN AND OUT OF SOCIETY • 1915 • *L-Ko* • USA
IN ANOTHER GIRL'S SHOES • 1917 • Samuelson G. B., Butler Alexander • UKN
IN ANOTHER'S NEST • 1913 • Dwan Allan • USA
IN ARCADIA • 1916 • Van Deusen Courtlandt • SHT • USA
IN ARIZONA • 1910 • *Nestor* • USA
IN AUTUNNO UN ANNO DOPO • 1970 • Vallone Raf • ITL
IN BABY'S GARDEN • 1915 • *Hastings Carey L.* • USA
IN BAD • 1918 • Sloman Edward • USA
IN BAD ALL AROUND • 1919 • Watson William • SHT • USA
IN BED –IN BAD • 1917 • De Vonde Chester M. • SHT • USA
IN BERMUDA • 1914 • Dawley J. Searle • USA
IN BETWEEN • 1955 • Brakhage Stan • SHT • USA
IN BETWEEN • 1978 • Mekas Jonas • USA
IN BLOSSOM TIME • 1911 • Olcott Sidney • USA
IN BLOSSOM TIME • 1912 • *Thanhouser* • USA
IN BLUE AND YELLOW see **I GULT OCH BLATT** • 1942
IN BONDAGE see **FAITH** • 1919
IN BORROWED PLUMES • 1920 • Sandground Maurice • UKN
IN BORROWED PLUMES • 1926 • Halperin Victor Hugo • USA • BORROWED PLUMES (UKN)
IN BORROWED PLUMES • 1928 • Malins Geoffrey H. • UKN
IN BRIDAL ATTIRE • 1914 • Beggs Lee • USA
IN BROAD DAYLIGHT • 1971 • Day Robert • TVM • USA
IN BROAD DAYLIGHT see **W BIALY DZIEN** • 1980
IN BROAD DAYLIGHT (UKN) see **BROAD DAYLIGHT** • 1922
IN BRONCHO LAND • 1926 • Ricks Archie • USA
IN BROTHERLY YUGOSLAVIA see **W BRATNIEJ JUGOSLAWII** • 1946
IN CALIENTE • 1935 • Bacon Lloyd • USA
IN CAMPAGNA, CHE PASSIONE! see **ARIA DI PAESE** • 1933
IN CAMPAGNA E CADUTA UNA STELLA • 1940 • De Filippo Eduardo • ITL
IN CAPO AL MONDO see **CHI LAVORI E PERDUTO** • 1963
IN CASE YOU'RE CURIOUS • 1951 • Barclay David • SHT • USA
IN CASTLE OR COTTAGE (USA) see **IN COTTAGE AND CASTLE** • 1911
IN CELEBRATION • 1974 • Anderson Lindsay • MTV • UKN, CND
IN CELLAR COOL • 1929 • Aylott Dave, Symmons E. F. • SHT • UKN
IN CERCA DI FELICITA • 1943 • Gentilomo Giacomo • ITL • CANTO DELL'AMORE, IL
IN CHINA see **V KITAI** • 1941
IN CINDERELLA'S SHOES • 1916 • Millarde Harry • USA
IN COLD BLOOD • 1967 • Brooks Richard • USA
IN CONFERENCE • 1931 • Cline Eddie • SHT • USA
IN CONTINUO • 1972 • Gilic Vlatko • SHT • YGS
IN CONVICT GARB • 1913 • Webster Harry Mcrae • USA
IN COTTAGE AND CASTLE • 1911 • Stow Percy • UKN • IN CASTLE OR COTTAGE (USA)
IN COUNTRY • 1989 • Jewison Norman • USA
IN COUNTRY see **CEASE FIRE** • 1985
IN CROWD, THE see **DANCE PARTY** • 1987
IN CUPID'S REALM • 1908 • *Vitagraph* • USA
IN DADDY'S POCKET see **I DIN FARS LOMME** • 1972
IN DANGER AND DISTRESS, COMPROMISE MEANS DEATH see **IN GEFAHR UND GROSSTER NOT BRINGT DER MITTELWEG DEN TOD** • 1975
IN DANGER AND GREATEST DISTRESS, THE MIDDLE COURSE BRINGS DEATH see **IN GEFAHR UND GROSSTER NOT BRINGT DER MITTELWEG DEN TOD** • 1975
IN DANGEROUS COMPANY • 1988 • Preuss Reuben • USA
IN DANGER'S HOUR • 1914 • *Bauer Arthur* • USA
IN DARKNESS WAITING see **STRATEGY OF TERROR** • 1969
IN DEATH'S SHADOW • 1913 • *Crystal* • USA
IN DEATH'S WAITING ROOM see **I DODENS VANTRUM** • 1946
IN DECEMBER THE ROSES WILL BLOOM AGAIN see **CHOICES OF THE HEART** • 1983
IN DEEP • 1925 • Lamont Charles • SHT • USA
IN DEFENCE OF MADRID see **DEFENCE OF MADRID, THE** • 1936
IN DEFENSE OF KIDS • 1982 • Reynolds Gene • TVM • USA
IN DEFIANCE OF THE LAW • 1914 • Campbell Colin • USA
IN DEN GOLDFELDERN VON NEVADA • 1920 • Neff Wolfgang • FRG
IN DEN KRALLEN DER OCHRANA • 1916 • *Szalit Julius* • FRG
IN DEN KRALLEN DER SCHULD • 1924 • *Richard Frieda* • FRG • MUTTERSORGEN
IN DEN KRALLEN DES VAMPYRES see **FRAUENSCHONHEIT UNTER DEM SEZIERMESSER, EINE** • 1920
IN DEN STERNEN STEHT ES GESCHRIEBEN • 1925 • Reiber Willy • FRG
IN DER FREMDE • 1975 • Saless Sohrab Shahid • IRN, FRG • FAR FROM HOME
IN DER HEIMAT, DA GIBT'S EIN WIEDERSEHN! • 1926 • Schunzel Reinhold, Mittler Leo • FRG
IN DER HOLLE IST NOCH PLATZ • 1961 • von Theumer Ernst Ritter • FRG • THERE IS STILL ROOM IN HELL (USA) ○ SEX AGENT
IN DER NACHT.. • 1915 • Hanus Emerich • FRG
IN DER NACHT • 1931 • Ruttmann Walter • FRG, SWT • IN THE NIGHT
IN DER ROTT • 1938 • FRG
IN DER SCHLINGE DES INDERS see **MACHT DES BLUTES 2** • 1921
IN DER SOMMERFRISCH'N • 1920 • Prager Wilhelm • FRG
IN DER TIEFE DES SCHACHTS • 1912 • May Joe • FRG
IN DER WERKSTATT –NUREMBERG JAZZ COLLEGIUM • 1970 • Reinhardt Hannes • SHT • FRG
IN DESERT AND JUNGLE see **W PUSTYNI I W PUSZCZY** • 1972
IN DESERT AND WILDERNESS see **W PUSTYNI I W PUSZCZY** • 1972
IN DESPERATION see **DESPERACJA** • 1989
IN DICKENS LAND • 1913 • Pearson George • DCS • UKN
IN DIE LENTE VAN ONS LIEFDE • 1967 • Wiesner Louis • SAF • IN THE SPRING OF OUR LOVE
IN DIPLOMATIC CIRCLES • 1913 • O'Sullivan Tony • USA
IN DIS–A–COUNTREE • 1912 • *Buckley May* • USA
IN DISAGREEMENT see **U RASKO–RAKU** • 1968
IN DOUBLE HARNESS • 1915 • Moore Tom • USA
IN DRACULA'S CASTLE • 1973 • Totten Robert • USA • MYSTERY IN DRACULA'S CASTLE
IN DREAMLAND (USA) see **NEL PAESE DEI SOGNI** • 1906
IN DREAMY JUNGLETOWN • 1916 • *Macmillan Violet* • SHT • USA
IN DRY TERRITORY • 1912 • *Nestor* • USA
IN DUBIOUS BATTLE • 1988 • Kershner Irvin • USA
IN DUE SI SOFFRE MEGLIO • 1943 • Malasomma Nunzio • ITL
IN DUTCH • 1914 • *Brennan John E.* • USA
IN DUTCH • 1918 • Blystone John G. • SHT • USA
IN DUTCH • 1931 • Foster John, Bailey Harry • ANS • USA
IN DUTCH • 1946 • Nichols Charles • ANS • USA
IN DUTCH WITH A DUCHESS • 1915 • *Superba* • USA
IN EARLY ARIZONA • 1938 • Levering Joseph • USA • UNWELCOME VISITORS (UKN)
IN EINEM JAHR MIT 13 MONDEN • 1978 • Fassbinder R. W. • FRG • IN A YEAR OF 13 MOONS (USA) ○ IN THE YEAR OF 13 MOONS ○ IN A YEAR WITH 13 MOONS
IN EINEM KUHLEN GRUNDE • 1921 • Agerty Max • FRG
IN EINEM KUHLEN GRUNDE see **MUHLE IM SCHWARZWALD, DIE** • 1934
IN EINER FREMDEN STADT • 1963 • Hess Joachim • MTV • FRG
IN EINER KLEINEN KONDITOREI • 1930 • Wohlmuth Robert • FRG • WAS KLEINE MADCHEN TRAUMEN
IN ENEMY COUNTRY • 1968 • Keller Harry • USA
IN EVERY WOMAN'S LIFE • 1924 • Cummings Irving • USA
IN EVERY WOMAN'S LIFE see **MY BILL** • 1938
IN EXILE • 1912 • *Selig* • USA
IN EXILE • 1970 • Carter Peter • CND
IN FACCIA AL DESTINO • 1913 • Negroni Baldassare • ITL
IN FADING LIGHT • 1990 • Martin Murray • UKN
IN FAIRYLAND • 1912 • Booth W. R.? • UKN
IN FAMIGLIA SI SPARA (ITL) see **BARBOUZES, LES** • 1964
IN FAST COMPANY • 1924 • Horne James W. • USA
IN FAST COMPANY • 1946 • Lord Del • USA
IN FATE'S CYCLE • 1914 • Marston Theodore • USA
IN FATE'S GRIP • 1913 • Weston Charles • UKN
IN FEAR OF HIS PAST • 1914 • *Alden Mary* • USA
IN FIECARE ZI MI–E DOR DE TINE • 1988 • Vitandis Gheorghe • RMN • YOU ARE ALWAYS IN MY HEART
IN FLAGRANTI • 1944 • Schweikart Hans • FRG
IN FLOWERS PALED • 1911 • *Reliance* • USA
IN FOLLY'S TRAIL • 1920 • Sturgeon Rollin S. • USA
IN FONDO ALLA PISCINA • 1971 • Martin Eugenio • ITL
IN FOR LIFE • 1970 • *Stacey Dist.* • USA
IN FOR LIFE see **CADENA PERPETUA** • 1978
IN FOR THIRTY DAYS • 1919 • Cullison Webster • USA
IN FOR TREATMENT see **OPNAME** • 1979
IN FORMER DAYS see **IN JENEN TAGEN** • 1947
IN FRANKFURT SIND DIE NACHTE HEISS • 1966 • Olsen Rolf • AUS • CALL GIRLS OF FRANKFURT (USA) ○ HOT NIGHTS IN FRANKFURT ○ PLAYGIRLS OF FRANKFURT
IN FRIENDSHIP'S NAME • 1912 • *Powers* • USA
IN FRONT OF THE GALLOWS see **BROSTA STIN AGHONI (MIA SFERA YIA MENA)** • 1968
IN FULL CRY • 1921 • Bruun Einar J. • UKN
IN GAY MADRID • 1930 • Leonard Robert Z. • USA • HOUSE OF TROY, THE
IN GEFAHR UND GROSSTER NOT BRINGT DER MITTELWEG DEN TOD • 1975 • Kluge Alexander, Reitz Edgar • FRG • IN DANGER AND DISTRESS, COMPROMISE MEANS DEATH ○ IN DANGER AND GREATEST DISTRESS, THE MIDDLE COURSE BRINGS DEATH ○ BLIND ALLEY
IN GEHEIMER MISSION • 1938 • von Alten Jurgen • FRG
IN GINOCCHIO DA TE • 1964 • Fizzarotti Ettore Maria • ITL
IN GIRUM IMUS NOCTE ET CONSUMIMUR IGNI • 1978 • Debord Guy • FRN
IN GOD WE TRUST • 1913 • Martin E. A. • USA
IN GOD WE TRUST (OR GIMME THAT PRIME TIME RELIGION) • 1979 • Feldman Marty • USA
IN GOD'S CARE • 1912 • *Pathe* • USA
IN GOD'S NAME • Sharif-Zade • USS
IN GOD'S NAME • 1974 • Davison Bill • UKN
IN GOLD WE TRUST • 1990 • Pakdivijit Chalong • THL
IN GOLDEN DAYS • 1908 • *Essanay* • USA
IN GOLLYWOG LAND • 1912 • Booth W. R., Thornton F. Martin • UKN • GOLLYWOG'S MOTOR ACCIDENT (USA)
IN GOOD COMPANY • 1984 • Frost Harvey • MTV • CND
IN HAMBURG SIND DIE NACHTE LANG • 1955 • Michel Max • FRG
IN HARM'S WAY • 1965 • Preminger Otto • USA
IN HER BROTHER'S DEFENCE • 1912 • *Majestic* • USA
IN HER DADDIE'S FOOTSTEPS • 1915 • *Grandin Ethel* • USA
IN HER MOTHER'S FOOTSTEPS • 1915 • *Leslie Lilie* • USA
IN HER SLEEP • 1914 • *Ostriche Muriel* • USA
IN HIGH GEAR • 1924 • Bradbury Robert North • USA
IN HIGH LIFE • 1914 • *Edison* • USA
IN HIGH SOCIETY • 1915 • *Hamilton Lloyd V.* • USA
IN HIGH SPEED • 1917 • *Price Kate* • SHT • USA
IN HIS BROTHER'S PLACE • 1919 • Franklin Harry L. • USA
IN HIS FATHER'S FOOTSTEPS • 1912 • *West William* • USA
IN HIS FATHER'S FOOTSTEPS • 1915 • Rowland Eugene • USA
IN HIS GRIP • 1921 • Calvert Charles • UKN
IN HIS MIND'S EYE • 1915 • Giblyn Charles • USA
IN HIS OWN TRAP • 1916 • Wilson Ben • SHT • USA
IN HIS PRIME • 1972 • Storm Esben • SHT • ASL
IN HIS STEPS • 1936 • Brown Karl • USA • SINS OF THE CHILDREN
IN HOC SIGNO VINCES • 1913 • Oxilia Nino • ITL
IN HOLLAND • 1929 • Taurog Norman • SHT • USA
IN HOLLYWOOD see **JONES FAMILY IN HOLLYWOOD, THE** • 1939
IN HOLLYWOOD WITH POTASH AND PERLMUTTER • 1924 • Green Alfred E. • USA • SO THIS IS HOLLYWOOD (UKN)
IN HONOR BOUND • 1912 • *Leonard Marion* • USA
IN HONOR'S WEB • 1919 • Scardon Paul • USA
IN HOT BLOOD • 1968 • Landwehr Joel • USA
IN HOT PURSUIT • 1987 • Travis John • USA
IN HUMANITY'S CAUSE • 1911 • *Eclair* • USA
IN HUMBLE GUISE • 1915 • *Balboa* • USA
IN INDIA • Richly Zsolt • ANS • HNG
IN ITALIA SI CHIAMA AMORE • 1963 • Sabel Virgilio • DOC • ITL
IN JENEN TAGEN • 1947 • Kautner Helmut • FRG • SEVEN JOURNEYS (USA) ○ IN FORMER DAYS
IN JEST AND EARNEST • 1911 • Fitzhamon Lewin • UKN
IN JUDGEMENT OF.. • 1918 • Davis Will S. • USA
IN JUNGLE WILDS • 1914 • *Bison* • USA
IN JUNGLE WILDS • 1916 • Chaudet Louis W. • SHT • USA
IN JUST ONE LIFETIME see **BARE ET LIV –HISTORIEN OM FRIDTJOF NANSEN** • 1968
IN KEEPING WITH THE LAW see **TORVENYSERTES NELKUL** • 1988
IN KETTEN DER LEIDENSCHAFT see **LEIDENSWEG EINES ACHTZEHNJAHRIGEN, DER** • 1920
IN KEY • 1976 • Thoms Albie • SHT • ASL
IN KLUIS • 1978 • Gruyaert Jan • BLG • ENCLOSURE, THE
IN LABOUR see **BUNBEN** • 1968
IN LAMPLIGHT LAND • 1935 • Pal George • ANS • NTH
IN–LAWS, THE • 1979 • Hiller Arthur • USA
IN–LAWS ARE OUT • 1934 • White Sam • SHT • USA
IN LEASH • 1915 • *Swayne Marian* • USA
IN LEOPARD LAND • 1915 • Santschi Thomas • USA
IN LETZTE MINUTE • 1939 • Kirchhoff Friedrich • FRG
IN LETZTE SEKUNDE • 1916 • Schmidthassler Walter • FRG
IN LIEU OF DAMAGES • 1914 • Ridgely Richard • USA
IN LIFE'S CYCLE • 1910 • Griffith D. W. • USA
IN LIKE FLINT • 1967 • Douglas Gordon • USA
IN LIKE FLYNN • 1985 • Lang Richard • TVM • USA
IN LINE OF DUTY • 1931 • Glennon Bert • USA
IN LITTLE ITALY • 1909 • Griffith D. W. • USA
IN LITTLE ITALY • 1912 • *Bosworth Hobart* • USA
IN LONDON'S TOILS • 1913 • Butler Alexander? • UKN
IN LOVE see **ENAMORADA** • 1946
IN LOVE see **V LYUBLENNYE** • 1970
IN LOVE see **STRANGERS IN LOVE** • 1983
IN LOVE AND WAR • 1913 • *Patheplay* • USA
IN LOVE AND WAR • 1913 • Dwan Allan • *Bison* • USA • CALL TO ARMS, THE
IN LOVE AND WAR • 1958 • Dunne Philip • USA
IN LOVE AND WAR • 1987 • Aaron Paul • TVM • USA • LOVE AND WAR
IN LOVE AT 40 • 1935 • Ripley Arthur • SHT • USA
IN LOVE CANCER • 1987 • Robertson Jenny • ANM • ASL
IN LOVE IN AUSTRIA see **VERLIEBT IN OSTERRICH** • 1967
IN LOVE WITH A FIREMAN • 1916 • Beaudine William • USA
IN LOVE WITH A PICTURE GIRL • 1909 • Stow Percy • UKN
IN LOVE WITH A SUFFRAGETTE • 1914 • *Lux* • USA
IN LOVE WITH AN ACTRESS • 1911 • Wilson Frank? • UKN
IN LOVE WITH AN OLDER WOMAN • 1982 • Bender Jack • TVM • USA
IN LOVE WITH COPENHAGEN see **FORELSKET I KOBENHAVN** • 1960
IN LOVE WITH LIFE • 1934 • Strayer Frank • USA • RE–UNION (UKN)
IN LOVE WITH LOVE • 1924 • Lee Rowland V. • USA
IN LOVE WITH SEX • 1974 • Pierson Claude • CND, FRN, ITL
IN LOVE'S LABORATORY • 1917 • Griffith Edward H.? • USA
IN LOVE'S OWN WAY • 1915 • Ince John • USA
IN MAJOR AND SHOWERS see **I DUR OCH SKUR** • 1953
IN MEMORIAM • 1977 • Brasso Enrique • SPN
IN MEMORIAM LASZLO MESZAROS see **MESZAROS LASZLO EMLEKERE** • 1968
IN MEMORY OF SERGEI ORDZHONIKIDZYE see **PAMYATI SERGO ORDZHONIKIDZYE** • 1937
IN MEXICO • 1916 • *Falstaff* • USA
IN MIZZOURA • 1914 • *Mcintosh Burr* • USA
IN MIZZOURA • 1919 • Ford Hugh • USA
IN MONTEZUMA FROM "THE BELLE OF MAYFAIR" • 1906 • Gilbert Arthur • UKN
IN.. MORAL, EL • 1976 • Canalejas Jose A. • SPN
IN MOTHER'S FOOTSTEPS see **FOLLOWING MOTHER'S FOOTSTEPS** • 1911
IN MRS. PANKHURST'S FOOTSTEPS see **MODERNA SUFFRAGETTEN, DEN** • 1913
IN MUNCHEN STEHT EIN HOFBRAUHAUS • 1952 • Breuer Siegfried • FRG
IN MY GONDOLA • 1936 • *Mintz Charles (P)* • ANS • USA
IN MY HEART, ON MY MIND, ALL DAY LONG • 1922 • *Parkinson H. B. (P)* • SHT • UKN
IN MY HOUSE I'M BOSS see **EN MI CASA MANDO YO** • 1968
IN MY LIFE see **HONNING MANE** • 1978
IN MY MERRY OLDSMOBILE • 1931 • Fleischer Dave • ANS • USA
IN MY SLEEP I SEE CLEARLY see **ES QUAN DORMO QUE HI VEIG CLAR** • 1988

IN MY THOUGHTS, I'M YEARNING FOR YOU • Khrzhanovsky Andrei • ANM • USS
IN MYSTERIOUS WAYS • 1914 • *Lubin* • USA
IN 'N OUT • 1986 • Franco Ricardo • SPN • ST. JUDE OF THE BORDER
IN NAME DER MENSCHLICHKEIT see **PROZESS, DER** • 1948
IN NAME ONLY • 1939 • Cromwell John • USA • KIND MEN MARRY, THE ○ MEMORY OF LOVE
IN NAME ONLY • 1969 • Swackhamer E. W. • TVM • USA
IN NAMEN DES KAISERS • 1925 • Dinesen Robert • FRG
IN NAMEN DES KONIGS • 1923 • Schonfelder Erich • FRG
IN NAMEN DES VOLKES • 1975 • Runze Ottokar • FRG • IN THE NAME OF THE PEOPLE
IN NEIGHBORING KINGDOMS • 1910 • Humphrey William • USA
IN NEW GUINEA WILDS • 1929 • Jackson William J. • ASL
IN NO.III see **III-ES, A** • 1919
IN NOME DEL PADRE see **NEL NOME DEL PADRE** • 1971
IN NOME DEL PAPA RE • 1977 • Magni Luigi • ITL • IN THE NAME OF THE POPE KING
IN NOME DEL POPOLO ITALIANO • 1971 • Risi Dino • ITL • IN THE NAME OF THE ITALIAN PEOPLE
IN NOME DELLA LEGGE • 1949 • Germi Pietro • ITL • IN THE NAME OF THE LAW ○ MAFIA
IN NORTHERN FORESTS • 1911 • *Vitagraph* • USA
IN OLD AMARILLO • 1951 • Witney William • USA
IN OLD ARIZONA • 1909 • *Selig* • USA
IN OLD ARIZONA • 1929 • Walsh Raoul, Cummings Irving • USA
IN OLD CALIENTE • 1939 • Kane Joseph • USA
IN OLD CALIFORNIA • 1910 • Griffith D. W. • USA
IN OLD CALIFORNIA • 1929 • King Burton L. • USA
IN OLD CALIFORNIA • 1942 • McGann William • USA
IN OLD CALIFORNIA, WHEN THE GRINGOES CAME • 1911 • Boggs Frank • USA
IN OLD CHEYENNE • 1931 • Paton Stuart • USA • GUEST HOUSE, THE (UKN)
IN OLD CHEYENNE • 1941 • Kane Joseph • USA
IN OLD CHICAGO • 1938 • King Henry, Humberstone H.bruce • USA
IN OLD COLORADO • 1941 • Bretherton Howard • USA
IN OLD FLORIDA • 1911 • Olcott Sidney • USA
IN OLD HEIDELBERG see **OLD HEIDELBERG** • 1915
IN OLD ITALY • 1914 • Ince Thomas H., Spencer Richard V. • USA
IN OLD KENTUCKY • 1909 • Griffith D. W. • USA
IN OLD KENTUCKY • 1920 • Neilan Marshall, Green Alfred E. • USA
IN OLD KENTUCKY • 1927 • Stahl John M. • USA
IN OLD KENTUCKY • 1935 • Marshall George • USA
IN OLD MADRID • 1911 • Ince Thomas H. • USA
IN OLD MAZUMA • 1931 • Ross Nat • SHT • USA
IN OLD MEXICO • 1915 • *Reliance* • USA
IN OLD MEXICO • 1938 • Venturini Edward D. • USA
IN OLD MISSOURI • 1940 • McDonald Frank • USA
IN OLD MONTANA • 1939 • Johnston Raymond K. • USA
IN OLD MONTEREY • 1939 • Kane Joseph • USA
IN OLD NEW MEXICO • 1945 • Rosen Phil • USA • CISCO KID IN OLD NEW MEXICO, THE (UKN)
IN OLD OKLAHOMA see **WAR OF THE WILDCATS** • 1943
IN OLD PANAMA • 1913 • *Imp* • USA
IN OLD SACRAMENTO • 1946 • Kane Joseph • USA • FLAME OF SACRAMENTO
IN OLD SANTA FE • 1934 • Howard David • USA
IN OLD SIBERIA see **KATORGA** • 1928
IN OLD TAMPICO see **GRAN CASINO** • 1946
IN OLD TENNESSEE • 1912 • *Baggot King* • USA
IN OLD TOWN • 1912 • *Majestic* • USA
IN OLD VIENNA • 1956 • *Rottinger Heinz* • AUS, USA
IN OLD VIRGINIA • 1914 • Ince John • USA
IN OLDEN DAYS (USA) see **ALTRI TEMPI** • 1952
IN ONE LIFETIME • 1968 • Nicholson Arch, Tammer Peter • DOC • ASL
IN ONION THERE IS STRENGTH • 1916 • Curtis Allen • SHT • USA
IN OUR ALLEY • 1906 • Collins Alf? • UKN
IN OUR CAVES • Topaldgikov Stefan • BUL
IN OUR HANDS • 1959 • Sarma V. L. • SHT • UNN
IN OUR HANDS • 1984 • DOC • USA
IN OUR LAND BULLETS ARE BEGINNING TO FLOWER • Malmer Lennart, Romare Ingela • DOC • SWD
IN OUR TIME • 1933 • Ginever Aveling • UKN
IN OUR TIME • 1944 • Sherman Vincent • USA
IN OUR TIME see **KUANG-YIN-TE KUSHIH** • 1983
IN OUR WATER • 1982 • Switzgable Meg • DOC • USA
IN PADUREA LUI ION • 1969 • Petringenaru Adrian • ANS • RMN • IN THE FOREST OF ION (USA)
IN PAPER PLANES see **NA PAPIRNATIH AVIONIH** • 1967
IN PARADISE see **I PARADIS..** • 1941
IN PARADISE see **W RAJU** • 1962
IN PARIS A.W.O.L. • 1936 • Reed Roland • USA • LET'S PRETEND WE'RE SWEETHEARTS (UKN)
IN PARIS PARKS • 1954 • Clarke Shirley • USA
IN PASSING see **EN PASSANT** • 1943
IN PAWN • 1914 • Somers Dalton • UKN
IN PAYMENT FULL • 1912 • Porter Edwin S. • USA
IN PAYMENT OF THE PAST • 1917 • King Burton L. • SHT • USA
IN PEACE AND WAR • 1914 • Noy Wilfred • UKN
IN PEACEFUL HOLLOW • 1913 • *Nestor* • USA
IN PENOMBRA • 1919 • Falena Ugo • ITL
IN PERIL OF HIS LIFE • 1913 • *Kalem* • USA
IN PERIL OF THE SEA • 1913 • Tucker George Loane • USA
IN PERIL OF THEIR LIVES • 1912 • *Kalem* • USA
IN PERIL'S PATH • 1914 • *Hastings Carey L.* • USA
IN PERSON • 1935 • Seiter William A. • USA
IN PIENO SOLE (ITL) see **PLEIN SOLEIL** • 1960
IN POSSESSION • 1985 • Guest Val • UKN
IN POVERTY'S POWER • 1918 • *Roland Ruth* • SHT • USA
IN PRAISE OF HANDS • 1974 • Winkler Donald • MTV • CND
IN PRAISE OF JAMES CARABINE see **BLARNEY** • 1926
IN PRAISE OF LOVE • 1975 • Rakoff Alvin • MTV • UKN
IN PRAISE OF OLDER WOMEN • 1978 • Kaczender George • CND, USA
IN PREHISTORIC DAYS see **BRUTE FORCE** • 1913
IN PURSUIT OF ADAM see **W POGONI ZA ADAMEM** • 1969
IN PURSUIT OF D.B. COOPER see **PURSUIT OF D.B. COOPER, THE** • 1981
IN PURSUIT OF FASHION • 1910 • Fitzhamon Lewin • UKN
IN PURSUIT OF POLLY • 1918 • Withey Chet • USA • PURSUIT OF POLLY
IN PURSUIT OF THE YELLOW SHIRT see **W POGONI ZA ZOLTA KOSZULKA** • 1954
IN QUARANTINE • 1912 • *Steppling John* • USA
IN QUEST OF A STORY • 1914 • Reehm George E. • USA
IN QUEST OF HEALTH • 1907 • Cooper Arthur • UKN
IN QUEST OF THE GOLDEN PRINCE see **LOST EMPIRE, THE** • 1924
IN RAW COLOR • 1915 • Frank Alexander F. • USA
IN REAL LIFE • 1914 • *Essanay* • USA
IN RED DOG TOWN • 1915 • *Ab* • USA
IN REMEMBRANCE • 1914 • *Selig* • USA
IN RETREAT see **EN RETIRADA** • 1984
IN ROOM 202 • 1920 • *Supreme Comedies* • USA
IN ROOM 303 • 1947 • Yates Hal • SHT • USA
IN ROOM III see **III-ES, A** • 1919
IN ROOM III see **III-ES, A** • 1937
IN ROSIE'S ROOM (UKN) see **ROSIE THE RIVETER** • 1944
IN ROUGH STYLE (USA) see **A LO MACHO** • 1939
IN SACHEN TIMPE • 1934 • Wolff Carl Heinz • FRG
IN SAIGON: SOME MAY LIVE see **SOME MAY LIVE** • 1967
IN SARA'S EYES • 1977 • Stevens Carter • USA
IN SAT LA NOI • 1951 • Iliu Victor, Georgescu Jean • RMN • OUR VILLAGE
IN SCHULD VERSTRICKT • 1915 • *Speyer Eva* • FRG
IN SCHWEBENDER PEIN • 1915 • Del Zopp Rudolf • FRG
IN SEARCH OF A GOLDEN SKY • 1983 • Sellier Charles E. Jr. • USA • CHILDREN OF THE NORTH WOODS
IN SEARCH OF A GOLDEN SKY • 1986 • Richard Jefferson • USA
IN SEARCH OF A HERO • 1926 • Worne Duke • USA
IN SEARCH OF A HOUSE see **GECEKONDU PESINDE** • 1967
IN SEARCH OF A HUSBAND • 1915 • Noy Wilfred • UKN
IN SEARCH OF A SINNER • 1920 • Kirkland David • USA
IN SEARCH OF A THRILL • 1923 • Apfel Oscar • USA
IN SEARCH OF A WIFE • 1915 • Worthington William • USA
IN SEARCH OF ALICE see **ALICENTE ANWESHANAM** • 1989
IN SEARCH OF AMERICA • 1970 • Bogart Paul • TVM • USA
IN SEARCH OF ANCIENT ASTRONAUTS • 1975 • Landsburg Alan • DOC • USA
IN SEARCH OF ANNA • 1979 • Storm Esben • ASL
IN SEARCH OF ARCADY • 1919 • Bracken Bertram • USA
IN SEARCH OF BACCHUS • 1913 • *Kinemacolor* • USA
IN SEARCH OF BIG FOOT • 1976 • Crowley Lawrence, Miller William F. • DOC • USA
IN SEARCH OF DEV • 1984 • Sandford Gerry, Ryan Stephen • IRL
IN SEARCH OF DRACULA • 1972 • Floyd Calvin • SWD
IN SEARCH OF FAMINE see **AKALER SANDHANE** • 1980
IN SEARCH OF FARLEY MOWAT • 1981 • Thomson Andy • MTV • CND
IN SEARCH OF GREGORY • 1970 • Wood Peter • UKN, ITL • ALLA RICERCA DI GREGORY (ITL)
IN SEARCH OF HAPPINESS see **V POISKACH RADOSTI** • 1939
IN SEARCH OF HISTORIC JESUS • 1979 • Schellerup Henning • USA
IN SEARCH OF HOME • 1953 • Blais Roger • DCS • CND • FAMILLE DE CHOIX, UNE
IN SEARCH OF INNOCENCE see **A LA RECHERCHE DE L'INNOCENCE** • 1963
IN SEARCH OF JEWISH AMSTERDAM • 1976 • Bregstein Philo • NTH
IN SEARCH OF LOVE • 1928 • Ra Un-Gya • KOR
IN SEARCH OF NOAH'S ARK • 1976 • Conway James L. • DOC • USA
IN SEARCH OF QUIET • 1913 • *Moore Matt* • USA
IN SEARCH OF THE BOWHEAD WHALE • 1974 • Mason William • DOC • CND
IN SEARCH OF THE CASTAWAYS • 1961 • Stevenson Robert • USA, UKN • CASTAWAYS, THE
IN SEARCH OF THE LAST GOOD MAN • 1990 • Campbell Peg • SHT • CND
IN SEARCH OF THE MIRACULOUS • 1967 • Malanga Gerard • USA
IN SEARCH OF THE SUN see **SONNENSUCHER, DIE** • 1958
IN SEARCH OF TREASURE see **EM BUSCA DO TESOURO** • 1967
IN SELF-DEFENCE • 1914 • *Henley Hobart* • USA
IN SELF DEFENSE • 1947 • Bernhard Jack • USA
IN SELF DEFENSE • 1987 • Green Bruce Seth • TVM • USA • HOLLOW POINT
IN SELF DEFENSE see **EN DEFENSA PROPIA** • 1917
IN SELF DEFENSE (USA) see **LANDSFLYKTIGE, DE** • 1921
IN SEPTEMBER see **EN SEPTIEMBRE** • 1981
IN SHERIDAN'S DAYS • 1924 • *Regent Films* • SHT • UKN
IN SILENCE • 1965 • Kidawa Janusz • DOC • PLN
IN SLAVERY DAYS • 1913 • Turner Otis • USA
IN SLUMBERLAND • 1917 • Willat Irvin V. • USA
IN SMOKE AND DANCING see **I ROK OCH DANS** • 1954
IN SOAK • 1914 • *Eclectic* • USA
IN SOCIETY • 1921 • *Roberts Edith* • USA
IN SOCIETY • 1944 • Yarbrough Jean • USA
IN SOCIETY AND OUT • 1916 • Jackson Harry • SHT • USA
IN SOFT IN A STUDIO • 1916 • Roach Hal • SHT • USA
IN SONG AND DANCE • 1964 • Robinson Lee • DOC • ASL
IN SPITE OF ALL • 1912 • *Diamond Films* • UKN
IN SPITE OF ALL • 1915 • Miller Ashley • USA
IN SPITE OF DANGER • 1935 • Hillyer Lambert • USA • DEVIL'S CARGO
IN SPITE OF EVERYTHING see **TROTZ ALLEDEM** • 1972
IN SPITE OF HIM • 1915 • Kaufman Joseph • USA
IN SPITE OF THE EVIDENCE • 1914 • *Selig* • USA
IN SPITE OF THE LAW see **TVERS IGJENNOM LOV** • 1979
IN SPRING ONE PLANTS ALONE • 1980 • Ward Vincent • NZL
IN STRANGE COMPANY (UKN) see **FIRST AID** • 1931
IN STUMPLAND • 1917 • *Juvenile* • USA
IN SUCH TREPIDATION I SHALL CREEP OFF TONIGHT TO THE EVIL BATTLE see **ZU BOSER SCHLACHT SCHLEICH' ICH HEUT NACHT SO BANG** • 1970
IN SUMMER AT FIVE O'CLOCK see **KESALLA KELLO 5** • 1963
IN SUMMER WE MUST LOVE • 1974 • *Kamel Madiha* • EGY
IN SUNNY ITALY • 1911 • *Yankee* • USA
IN SUNNY SPAIN • 1914 • *Imp* • USA
IN SWIFT WATER • 1912 • Salter Harry • USA
IN TANDEM • 1974 • Kowalski Bernard • TVM • USA • MOVIN' ON
IN TANGLED WEBS • 1914 • *Patheplay* • USA
IN TAXI 23 • 1914 • *Lyons Eddie* • USA
IN TEMPERANCE • 1913 • *Kalem* • USA
IN TEMPERANCE TOWN • 1913 • *Nestor* • USA
IN TEUFELSKRALLEN • 1915 • Del Zopp Rudolf • FRG
IN THAT VILLAGE DOWN THAT VALLEY UP THE HILL • 1929 • Aylott Dave, Symmons E. F. • SHT • UKN
IN THE AFRICAN JUNGLE • 1917 • Martin E. A. • SHT • USA
IN THE AFTERMATH: ANGELS NEVER SLEEP • 1987 • Colpaert Carl • USA, JPN • ANGELS NEVER SLEEP
IN THE AFTERNOON OF WAR • 1981 • Francis Karl • UKN • MOUSE AND THE WOMAN, THE ○ AFTERNOON OF WAR
IN THE AISLES OF THE WILD • 1912 • Griffith D. W. • USA
IN THE AMAZON JUNGLE • 1915 • Chaudet Louis W. • USA
IN THE ARCTIC NIGHT • 1911 • Trimble Larry • USA
IN THE ARMS OF THE BOMBAY NIGHT see **BOMBAI RAAT KI BAHON MEIN** • 1967
IN THE ARTIST'S STUDIO • 1986 • Tosheva Nevena • DOC • BUL
IN THE ASSASSIN'S SIGHTS see **NA MIRA DO ASSASSINO** • 1968
IN THE AUTUMN ALL WILL BE DIFFERENT see **SYKSYLLA KAIKKI ON TOISIN** • 1978
IN THE BACKGROUND • 1915 • Powell Paul • USA
IN THE BAD LANDS • 1909 • Boggs Frank • USA
IN THE BAG • 1932 • Edwards Harry J. • SHT • USA
IN THE BAG • 1932 • Foster John, Rufle George • ANS • USA
IN THE BAG • 1956 • Hannah Jack • ANS • USA
IN THE BAGGAGE COACH AHEAD • 1911 • *Edison* • USA
IN THE BALANCE • 1912 • *Republic* • USA
IN THE BALANCE • 1917 • Scardon Paul • USA • HILLMAN, THE
IN THE BARBER SHOP (USA) see **SALON DE COIFFURE** • 1908
IN THE BATTLE'S SMOKE • 1913 • *Pilot* • USA
IN THE BEAUTIFUL PROVINCE OF ROSLAGEN see **I ROSLAGENS FAMN** • 1945
IN THE BEGINNING • 1975 • Gill Michael • MTV • UKN
IN THE BEGINNING see **BIBLE!** • 1974
IN THE BELLY OF THE DRAGON (UKN) see **DANS LE VENTRE DRAGON** • 1988
IN THE BIESZCZADY HILLS see **W BIESZCZADACH** • 1966
IN THE BIG CITY see **V BOLSHOI GORODE** • 1927
IN THE BISHOP'S CARRIAGE • 1913 • Porter Edwin S., Dawley J. Searle • USA
IN THE BISHOP'S CARRIAGE see **SHE COULDN'T HELP IT** • 1921
IN THE BLACK HILLS • 1910 • *Nestor* • USA
IN THE BLACK MOUNTAINS • 1941 • Shengelaya Nikolai • USS
IN THE BLOOD • 1913 • *Smalley Phillips* • USA
IN THE BLOOD • 1915 • *Regent* • USA
IN THE BLOOD • 1915 • Noy Wilfred • UKN
IN THE BLOOD • 1923 • West Walter • UKN
IN THE BOARDING HOUSE • 1915 • *Ab* • USA
IN THE BOGIE MAN'S CAVE (USA) see **CUISINE DE L'OGRE, LA** • 1908
IN THE BONDS OF PASSION see **SKAEBNES VEJE** • 1913
IN THE BORDER STATES • 1910 • Griffith D. W. • USA
IN THE CANDLELIGHT • 1914 • *Garwood William* • USA
IN THE CASTLE OF BLOODY DESIRES see **IM SCHLOSS DER BLUTIGEN BEGIERDE** • 1968
IN THE CASTLE OF BLOODY LUST see **IM SCHLOSS DER BLUTIGEN BEGIERDE** • 1968
IN THE CELLAR • 1960 • Halas John • ANS • UKN
IN THE CHAINS OF DARKNESS see **I MORKRETS BOJOR** • 1917
IN THE CHORUS • 1911 • *Thanhouser* • USA
IN THE CIRCLE OF PEACE see **W KREGU CISZY** • 1960
IN THE CIRCLE OF SILENCE see **W KREGU CISZY** • 1960
IN THE CIRCUS ARENA • 1952 • Varlamov Leonid • USS
IN THE CLAW OF THE LAW • 1915 • *Voss Fatty* • USA
IN THE CLAWS OF THE EAGLE • 1989 • PHL
IN THE CLUB see **W KLUBIE** • 1963
IN THE CLUTCH OF THE SPIDER see **DANS LES GRIFFES DE L'ARAIGNEE** • 1920
IN THE CLUTCHES OF A VAPOR BATH • 1911 • *Bunny John* • USA
IN THE CLUTCHES OF MILK • 1917 • Hutchinson Craig • SHT • USA
IN THE CLUTCHES OF THE GANG • 1914 • Sennett Mack, Nicholls George • USA
IN THE CLUTCHES OF THE GANGSTERS • 1914 • *Kb* • USA
IN THE CLUTCHES OF THE HINDU • 1920 • *Gaumont* • SRL • USA
IN THE CLUTCHES OF THE HUN • 1915 • Evans Joe? • UKN
IN THE CLUTCHES OF THE KU KLUX KLAN • 1913 • Olcott Sidney • USA • IN THE POWER OF THE KU KLUX KLAN
IN THE CLUTCHES OF THE VILLAIN • 1914 • *Asher Max* • USA
IN THE COILS OF THE PYTHON • 1913 • *Bainbridge Sherman* • USA
IN THE COMMISSION RANKS • 1911 • *Nestor* • USA
IN THE COMMUNITY OF THE SPIRIT OF THE WILDERNESS see **W GROMADZIE DUCHA PUSZCZY** • 1957
IN THE CONSERVATORY • 1914 • *Princess* • USA
IN THE COOL OF THE DAY • 1963 • Stevens Robert • UKN, USA
IN THE CORNER • 1985 • Egoyan Atom • MTV • CND
IN THE COUNTRY • 1967 • Kramer Robert • USA
IN THE COUNTRY OF ICEBERGS see **HVOR BJERGENE SEJLER** • 1954
IN THE COUNTRY OF THE AVALANCHES • 1931 • Dolidze Siko • USS

IN THE COUNTRY OF THE CANNIBALS • 1958 • Dinov Todor • ANS • BUL • CANNIBAL COUNTRY
IN THE COURSE OF TIME see **IM LAUF DER ZEIT** • 1976
IN THE COW COUNTRY • 1914 • Edwards Walter? • USA
IN THE CURRENT OF LIFE • Xhako Marianthi • DOC • ALB
IN THE CUSTODY OF STRANGERS • 1982 • Greenwald Robert • TVM • USA
IN THE CYCLE OF LIFE • 1913 • *Powers* • USA
IN THE CZAR'S NAME • 1910 • *Yankee* • USA
IN THE DARK • 1915 • *Clayton Ethel* • USA
IN THE DARK • 1916 • *Serial Film* • USA
IN THE DARK • 1918 • *Vernon Bobbie* • SHT • USA
IN THE DARK • 1928 • Miller Frank • UKN
IN THE DARK see **ENTRE TINIEBLAS** • 1983
IN THE DARK VALLEY • 1910 • *Kalem* • USA
IN THE DARKEST CORNER OF SMALAND see **I MORKASTE SMALAND** • 1943
IN THE DAYLIGHT • 1914 • Ricketts Thomas • USA
IN THE DAYS see **NAINA PAIVINA** • 1955
IN THE DAYS OF '49 • 1911 • Griffith D. W. • USA
IN THE DAYS OF BUFFALO BILL • 1922 • Laemmle Edward • USA • DAYS OF BUFFALO BILL, THE
IN THE DAYS OF CHIVALRY • 1911 • Dawley J. Searle • USA
IN THE DAYS OF DANIEL BOONE • 1923 • Craft William James, Messenger Frank, Marchant Jay • SRL • USA • DANIEL BOONE
IN THE DAYS OF FANNY • 1915 • Marston Theodore • USA
IN THE DAYS OF GOLD • 1911 • Bosworth Hobart • USA
IN THE DAYS OF HIS YOUTH • 1914 • *Smalley Phillips* • USA
IN THE DAYS OF OLD • 1914 • *Eclair* • USA
IN THE DAYS OF ROBIN HOOD • 1913 • Thornton F. Martin • UKN
IN THE DAYS OF SAINT PATRICK • 1920 • Whitten Norman • UKN
IN THE DAYS OF SLAVERY • 1914 • *Edison* • USA
IN THE DAYS OF STRUGGLE see **V DNI BORBI** • 1920
IN THE DAYS OF THE COVERED WAGON • 1924 • *Ford Francis* • USA
IN THE DAYS OF THE GUILLOTINE • 1914 • *Melies* • USA
IN THE DAYS OF THE PADRES • 1914 • *Domino* • USA
IN THE DAYS OF THE SIX NATIONS • 1911 • *Republic* • USA
IN THE DAYS OF THE STRUGGLE see **V DNI BORBI** • 1920
IN THE DAYS OF THE THUNDERING HERD • 1914 • Campbell Colin • USA
IN THE DAYS OF THE TRAJAN • 1913 • Johnston Lorimer • USA
IN THE DAYS OF TRAFALGAR see **BLACK-EYED SUSAN** • 1914
IN THE DAYS OF WARS • 1913 • *Wilbur Crane* • USA
IN THE DAYS OF WITCHCRAFT • 1909 • *Edison* • USA
IN THE DAYS OF WITCHCRAFT • 1913 • Huntley Fred W. • USA
IN THE DEAD MAN'S ROOM • 1913 • Calvert Charles? • UKN
IN THE DEAD O' NIGHT • 1916 • Gerrard Douglas • SHT • USA
IN THE DEPTHS OF THE NIGHT see **NA BOCA DA NOITE** • 1971
IN THE DEVIL'S BOWL see **DEVIL'S BOWL, THE** • 1923
IN THE DEVIL'S DOGHOUSE • 1934 • Holmes Ben • SHT • USA
IN THE DEVIL'S GARDEN (USA) see **ASSAULT** • 1971
IN THE DEVIL'S THROAT (USA) see **NA GARGANTA DO DIABLO** • 1960
IN THE DIPLOMATIC SERVICE • 1916 • Bushman Francis X. • USA
IN THE DOG HOUSE • 1934 • Ripley Arthur • SHT • USA
IN THE DOGHOUSE • 1961 • Conyers Darcy • UKN • VET IN THE DOGHOUSE
IN THE DRAGON'S CLAWS • 1915 • *Shumway L. C.* • USA
IN THE DREDGER'S CLAW • 1914 • *Lubin* • USA
IN THE DRINK • 1943 • Hughes Harry • UKN
IN THE EARLY DAYS • 1911 • *Nestor* • USA
IN THE ELEMENTAL WORLD • 1913 • *Ab* • USA
IN THE EMPLOY OF THE SECRET SERVICE (USA) see **IM GEHEIMDIENST** • 1931
IN THE END • 1913 • *Nestor* • USA
IN THE ENVIRONMENT OF LIQUIDS AND NASALS A PARASITIC VOWEL SOMETIMES DEVELOPS • 1975 • Landow George • USA
IN THE EYE OF THE LAW • 1914 • *Leonard Robert* • USA
IN THE FACE OF THE WORLD see **UROK ISTORIJI** • 1957
IN THE FACTORY see **W FABRYCE** • 1951
IN THE FALL see **IN THE FALLS** • 1983
IN THE FALL EVERYTHING IS DIFFERENT see **SYKSYLLA KAIKKI ON TOISIN** • 1978
IN THE FALL OF '55 EDEN CRIED see **EDEN CRIED** • 1967
IN THE FALL OF '64 • 1914 • Ford Francis • USA
IN THE FALLS • 1983 • Kroeker Allan • CND • IN THE FALL
IN THE FANGS OF JEALOUSY • 1914 • *Eclair* • USA
IN THE FAR EAST • 1937 • Marion David
IN THE FIRELIGHT • 1913 • Ricketts Thomas • USA
IN THE FIRST ARMED UNIT • NKR
IN THE FIRST DEGREE • 1927 • Rosen Phil • USA
IN THE FLAMES OF SUNRISE see **ARUNODOYER AGNISHAKHI** • 1972
IN THE FLAMES OF THE REVOLUTION • 1967 • Keko Endri • DOC • ALB
IN THE FLAT ABOVE • 1912 • Young James • USA
IN THE FOG • 1916 • *Dudley Edwin* • USA
IN THE FOG see **BLIND ADVENTURE** • 1933
IN THE FOOTHILLS OF THE PIRIN MOUNTAINS • 1958 • Stoyanov Yuli • DOC • BUL
IN THE FOREST • 1978 • Mulloy Phil • UKN
IN THE FOREST, IN THE SITES see **DO LESICKA NA CEKANOU** • 1966
IN THE FOREST OF ION (USA) see **IN PADUREA LUI ION** • 1969
IN THE FRENCH STYLE • 1963 • Parrish Robert • USA, FRN • A LA FRANCAISE (FRN)
IN THE FRONT LINE see **NA LINII OGNYA -OPERATORY KINOKHRONIKI** • 1941
IN THE FROZEN NORTH • 1910 • *Selig* • USA
IN THE FURNACE FIRE • 1912 • Thompson Frederick A. • USA
IN THE FUTURE • 1932 • Thring F. W. (c/d) • ASL
IN THE GAMBLER'S WEB • 1914 • Jones Edgar • USA
IN THE GARDEN • 1913 • France Charles H. • USA
IN THE GARDEN FAIR • 1912 • Thompson Frederick A. • USA
IN THE GLARE OF THE LIGHTS • 1914 • *Bushman Francis X.* • USA
IN THE GLITTER PALACE • 1977 • Butler Robert • TVM • USA
IN THE GLOAMING • 1919 • Collins Edwin J. • UKN
IN THE GLORY OF THEIR CROWNS see **IM GLANZE IHRER KRONEN** • 1968
IN THE GOLDEN HARVEST TIME • 1910 • *Selig* • USA
IN THE GOOD OLD DAYS • 1910 • Fitzhamon Lewin • UKN
IN THE GOOD OLD DAYS • 1919 • Lyons Eddie, Moran Lee • SHT • USA
IN THE GOOD OLD SUMMER TIME • 1913 • *Vitagraph* • USA
IN THE GOOD OLD SUMMERTIME • 1927 • Fleischer Dave • ANS • USA
IN THE GOOD OLD SUMMERTIME • 1930 • Fleischer Dave • ANS • USA
IN THE GOOD OLD SUMMERTIME • 1949 • Leonard Robert Z. • USA
IN THE GOOD OLD TIMES • 1905 • Cooper Arthur • *Alpha Trading Co.* • UKN • POOR OLD MR. AND MRS. BROWN IN THE STOCKS
IN THE GOOD OLD TIMES • 1905 • Williamson James • *Williamson* • UKN
IN THE GORGE • 1971 • Duletic Vojko • YGS
IN THE GOVERNMENT SERVICE • 1912 • *Republic* • USA
IN THE GOVERNOR'S KEEPING • 1916 • *Supreme* • USA
IN THE GRASP OF THE LAW • 1915 • Lloyd Frank • USA
IN THE GRAY OF THE DAWN • 1910 • *Reliance* • USA
IN THE GRAZING COUNTRY • 1901 • *Bitzer Billy (Ph)* • USA
IN THE GREASE! • 1925 • Roach Hal • SHT • USA
IN THE GREAT BIG WEST • 1911 • *Champion* • USA
IN THE GREAT NORTHWEST • 1910 • *Selig* • USA
IN THE GREEN ROOM • 1901 • Smith G. A. • UKN
IN THE GRIP OF A CHARLATAN • 1913 • *Joyce Alice* • USA
IN THE GRIP OF DEATH • 1913 • Martinek H. O.? • UKN
IN THE GRIP OF POLAR ICE • 1917 • Hurley Frank • DOC • ASL • ENDURANCE
IN THE GRIP OF SPIES • 1914 • Martinek H. O. • UKN
IN THE GRIP OF THE LOBSTER • 1966 • Smith Jack** • USA
IN THE GRIP OF THE MANIAC see **MISS MUERTE** • 1966
IN THE GRIP OF THE SINISTER ONE see **IM BANNE DES UNHEIMLICHEN** • 1968
IN THE GRIP OF THE SPIDER see **NELLA STRETTA MORSA DEL RAGNO** • 1971
IN THE GRIP OF THE SULTAN • 1915 • Bary Leon • UKN
IN THE GRIP OF THE VAMPIRE • 1912 • *Gaumont* • FRN
IN THE GROOVE • 1941 • Ceballos Larry • SHT • USA
IN THE HANDS OF A BRUTE • 1914 • Olcott Sidney • USA
IN THE HANDS OF IMPOSTORS see **HVIDE SLAVEHANDEL II, DEN** • 1911
IN THE HANDS OF THE BLACK HANDS • 1913 • Dillon Eddie • USA
IN THE HANDS OF THE ENEMY • 1908 • *Essanay* • USA
IN THE HANDS OF THE ENEMY • 1910 • Bouwmeester Theo? • UKN
IN THE HANDS OF THE ENEMY • 1915 • *Foster Morris* • USA
IN THE HANDS OF THE JURY • 1915 • Vignola Robert G. • USA
IN THE HANDS OF THE LAW • 1917 • *Meredith Lois* • USA
IN THE HANDS OF THE LONDON CROOKS • 1913 • Butler Alexander? • UKN
IN THE HANDS OF THE SPOILERS • 1916 • Bary Leon • UKN
IN THE HAREM OF HASCHEM • 1913 • Nicholls George • USA
IN THE HAUNTS OF FEAR • 1913 • *Graybill Joseph* • USA
IN THE HAUNTS OF RIP VAN WINKLE • 1906 • *Bitzer Billy (Ph)* • USA
IN THE HEADLINES • 1929 • Adolfi John G. • USA
IN THE HEART OF A FOOL • 1920 • Dwan Allan • USA • HEART OF A FOOL
IN THE HEART OF A SHELL • 1916 • Matthews H. C. • SHT • USA
IN THE HEART OF KOSMET • 1954 • Strbac Milenko • YGS
IN THE HEART OF NEW YORK • 1916 • Wilson Ben • SHT • USA
IN THE HEART OF THE CATSKILLS • 1906 • *Bitzer Billy (Ph)* • USA
IN THE HEART OF THE CEDAR • 1983 • von Puttkamer Peter • DOC • CND
IN THE HEART OF THE FOREST see **CORAZON DEL BOSQUE** • 1978
IN THE HEART OF THE HILLS • 1915 • King Burton L. • USA
IN THE HEART OF THE SIERRAS • 1911 • *Bison* • USA
IN THE HEART OF THE WOODS • 1915 • *Rich Vivian* • USA
IN THE HEAT OF THE NIGHT • 1967 • Jewison Norman • USA
IN THE HILLS BEYOND • 1915 • Ayres Sydney • USA
IN THE HILLS OF KENTUCKY • 1914 • Jones Edgar • USA
IN THE HILLS OF KENTUCKY • 1916 • *Buffalo* • USA
IN THE HOLLOW OF AN OAK • 1914 • *Frontier* • USA
IN THE HOLLOW OF HER HAND • 1918 • Maigne Charles • USA • HOLLOW OF HER HAND, THE
IN THE HOT LANDS • 1911 • Melies Gaston • USA
IN THE HOUR OF DISASTER • 1916 • Fielding Romaine • SHT • USA
IN THE HOUR OF HIS NEED • 1913 • Buckland Warwick? • UKN
IN THE HOUR OF HIS NEED • 1925 • *Loeb Mitchell* • USA
IN THE HOUSE OF BREDE • 1975 • Schaefer George • UKN
IN THE HOUSE OF THE CHIEF • 1916 • Heffron Thomas N. • SHT • USA
IN THE ICY OCEAN • 1952 • Zguridi Alexander • DOC • USS
IN THE JUNGLE • 1917 • Moss Howard S. • ANM • USA
IN THE JUNGLE • 1960 • Halas John • ANS • UKN
IN THE JUNGLE see **W DZUNGLI** • 1957
IN THE JUNGLE WILDS • 1915 • *Bison* • USA
IN THE JURY ROOM • 1915 • Fleming Carroll • USA
IN THE KIEV ZONE see **NA KIYEVSKOM NAPRAVYENII** • 1968
IN THE KING OF PRUSSIA • 1983 • De Antonio Emile • USA
IN THE KINGDOM OF DREAMS (USA) see **NEL REGNO DEI SOGNI**
IN THE KINGDOM OF FAIRYLAND • 1903 • *Lubin* • USA
IN THE KING'S SERVICE • 1915 • Santschi Thomas • USA
IN THE LABYRINTH • 1966 • Liikala Bob • USA
IN THE LABYRINTH OF MEMORY see **V BLUDISKU PAMATI** • 1985
IN THE LAND OF A THOUSAND AND ONE NIGHTS see **W KRAINIE TYSIACA I JEDNEJ NOCY** • 1969
IN THE LAND OF ARCADIA • 1914 • North Wilfred • USA
IN THE LAND OF FIRE • 1913 • *Melies* • USA
IN THE LAND OF KING HIRAK see **HIRAK RAJARDESHE** • 1978
IN THE LAND OF NOD • 1908 • Cooper Arthur • SHT • UKN • GRANDPA'S FORTY WINKS
IN THE LAND OF NOD • 1909 • *Pathe* • FRN
IN THE LAND OF THE CACTUS • 1911 • *American* • USA
IN THE LAND OF THE CACTUS • 1913 • *Fielding Romaine* • USA
IN THE LAND OF THE FROGS • 1942 • Rubino Antonio • ANS • ITL
IN THE LAND OF THE GOLD MINES • 1908 • FRN
IN THE LAND OF THE HEAD HUNTERS • 1914 • Curtis Edward Sheriff • USA
IN THE LAND OF THE OTTER • 1915 • *Storm Jerome* • USA
IN THE LAND OF THE QUEEN OF SHEBA see **IM LANDE DER KONIGIN VON SABA** • 1935
IN THE LAND OF THE SAD FAIRY TALE see **W KRAINIE SMUJNEJ BAJKI** • 1959
IN THE LAND OF THE SETTING SUN • 1919 • *Hersholt Jean* • USA • MARTYRS OF YESTERDAY
IN THE LAND OF THE TORTILLA • 1916 • MacMackin Archer • USA
IN THE LAND OF THE VAMPIRES • 1935 • Starevitch Ladislas • ANM • FRN
IN THE LAND OF TOYS see **V KUROLNOI STRANE** • 1940
IN THE LAPS OF THE GODS • 1916 • MacDonald Donald • SHT • USA
IN THE LAST STRIDE • 1916 • Keith Martyn • ASL
IN THE LATIN QUARTER • 1914 • Belmore Lionel • USA
IN THE LIGHT see **HER DOUBLE LIFE** • 1916
IN THE LINE OF DUTY • 1915 • *Warner Marion* • USA
IN THE LINE OF DUTY • 1987 • Chung Chi-Man Davi • HKG
IN THE LITTLE HOUSE UNDER EMAUZY see **V TOM DOMECKU POD EMAUZY** • 1933
IN THE LONG AGO • 1913 • Campbell Colin • USA
IN THE LONG RUN • 1912 • *Davenport Dorothy* • USA
IN THE MANSION OF LONELINESS • 1915 • Cooley Frank • USA
IN THE MATTER OF KAREN ANN QUINLAN • 1977 • Jordan Hal • TVM • USA
IN THE MEANTIME, DARLING • 1944 • Preminger Otto • USA • I MARRIED A SOLDIER
IN THE MEANTIME IT'S MIDDAY see **EINSTWEILEN WIRD ES MITTAG** • 1988
IN THE MESH OF HER HAIR • 1914 • *Woodruff Eleanor* • USA
IN THE MESH OF THE NET • 1915 • *Balboa* • USA
IN THE MIDDLE OF SUMMER see **W SRODKU LATA** • 1975
IN THE MIDDLE OF THE NIGHT see **MIDT OM NATTEN** • 1984
IN THE MIDNIGHT HOUR see **MIDNIGHT HOUR, THE** • 1985
IN THE MIDST OF AFRICAN WILDS • 1915 • Carleton Lloyd B. • USA
IN THE MIDST OF THE JUNGLE • 1913 • *Selig* • USA
IN THE MINISTER'S KEEPING • 1915 • *Premier* • USA
IN THE MISSION SHADOWS • 1910 • Melies Gaston • USA
IN THE MIST OR THE LOST BRIDE see **NATTENS GAADE** • 1914
IN THE MONEY • 1934 • Strayer Frank • USA
IN THE MONEY • 1958 • Beaudine William • USA
IN THE MONTH OF MAY • 1970 • Khutsiev Marlen • USS
IN THE MOOD • 1987 • Robinson Phil Alden • USA • WOO-WOO KID, THE
IN THE MOONLIGHT • 1914 • Ricketts Thomas • USA
IN THE MOON'S RAY • 1914 • *Bushman Francis X.* • USA
IN THE MOUNTAINS see **TAM NA HORACH** • 1920
IN THE MOUNTAINS OF ALA-TAU see **V GORACH ALA-TAU** • 1944
IN THE MOUNTAINS OF KENTUCKY • 1910 • *Vitagraph* • USA
IN THE MOUNTAINS OF VIRGINIA • 1913 • Hamilton G. P.? • USA
IN THE MOUNTAINS OF YUGOSLAVIA see **V GORAKH YUGOSLAVII** • 1946
IN THE MOVIES • 1916 • *Emerald* • SHT • USA
IN THE MOVIES • 1922 • Parrott Charles • USA
IN THE N.Y. SUBWAY • 1903 • *Bitzer Billy (Ph)* • USA
IN THE NAME OF LIFE see **VO IMYA ZHIZNI** • 1947
IN THE NAME OF LOVE • 1925 • Higgin Howard • USA
IN THE NAME OF OUR MOTHERLAND see **VO IMYA RODINI** • 1943
IN THE NAME OF SPORT • 1990 • Peeva Adela • BUL
IN THE NAME OF THE FATHER see **NEL NOME DEL PADRE** • 1971
IN THE NAME OF THE FATHERLAND see **VO IMYA RODINI** • 1943
IN THE NAME OF THE FUHRER see **AU NOM DU FUHRER** • 1978
IN THE NAME OF THE ITALIAN PEOPLE see **IN NOME DEL POPOLO ITALIANO** • 1971
IN THE NAME OF THE LAW • 1916 • Nowland Eugene • SHT • USA
IN THE NAME OF THE LAW • 1922 • Johnson Emory • USA • MIDNIGHT CALL
IN THE NAME OF THE LAW see **IN NOME DELLA LEGGE** • 1949
IN THE NAME OF THE LAW see **KANUN NAMINA** • 1968
IN THE NAME OF THE LAW see **I LAGENS NAMN** • 1987
IN THE NAME OF THE PEOPLE see **IN NAMEN DES VOLKES** • 1975
IN THE NAME OF THE PEOPLE see **U IME NARODA** • 1987
IN THE NAME OF THE POPE KING see **IN NOME DEL PAPA RE** • 1977
IN THE NAME OF THE PRINCE OF PEACE • 1914 • Dawley J. Searle • USA
IN THE NAME OF THE QUEEN • 1898 • *Paul R. W.* • UKN
IN THE NAME OF THE REVOLUTION • 1964 • Gabay Gennadiy • USS
IN THE NAME OF THE SON see **EN EL NOMBRE DEL HIJO** • 1987
IN THE NAVY see **ABBOTT AND COSTELLO IN THE NAVY** • 1941

IN THE NEW WORLD see **EN UN MUNDO NUEVO** • 1971
IN THE NEXT ROOM • 1930 • Cline Eddie • USA
IN THE NICK • 1960 • Hughes Ken • UKN
IN THE NICK OF TIME • 1908 • *Selig* • USA
IN THE NICK OF TIME • 1910 • *Edison* • USA
IN THE NICK OF TIME • 1911 • *Solax* • USA
IN THE NICK OF TIME • 1911 • Rolfe Alfred • ASL
IN THE NICK OF TIME • 1912 • Emerson W. D. • USA
IN THE NICK OF TIME • 1913 • *Thanhouser* • USA
IN THE NICK OF TIME • 1914 • *Reliance* • USA
IN THE NICK OF TIME • 1914 • Middleton Edwin • *Ab* • USA
IN THE NICK OF TIME • 1940 • Hall Ken G. • ASL
IN THE NICK OF TIME see **LET GEORGE DO IT** • 1938
IN THE NICK OF TIME see **V HO DINE DVANASTE** • 1959
IN THE NICOTINE • 1961 • Kneitel Seymour • ANS • USA
IN THE NIGHT • 1913 • *Eclair* • USA
IN THE NIGHT • 1916 • Myers Harry • SHT • USA
IN THE NIGHT • 1920 • Richardson Frank • UKN
IN THE NIGHT see **IN DER NACHT** • 1931
IN THE NIGHT (UKN) see **GANG'S ALL HERE, THE** • 1941
IN THE NIGHT WATCH see **VEILLE D'ARMES** • 1925
IN THE NIKITSKY BOTANICAL GARDEN • 1952 • Ozerov Yury • USS
IN THE NORTH WOODS • 1912 • Griffith D. W. • USA
IN THE NORTHERN WOODS • 1912 • *Imp* • USA
IN THE NORTHLAND • 1914 • Ince Thomas H. • USA
IN THE OLD ATTIC • 1914 • Thompson Frederick A. • USA
IN THE OLD DAYS YOU COULD LAUGH see **VROEGER KON JE LACHEN** • 1982
IN THE OLD DUTCH TIMES • 1913 • *Neill Richard* • USA
IN THE OPEN • 1914 • *American* • USA
IN THE OUTSKIRTS OF THE CITY see **VAROS PEREMEN, A** • 1957
IN THE PACIFIC • 1957 • Zguridi Alexander • DOC • USS
IN THE PALACE OF THE KING • 1915 • Wright Fred E. • USA
IN THE PALACE OF THE KING • 1923 • Flynn Emmett J. • USA
IN THE PALMY DAYS • 1915 • *Mina* • USA
IN THE PARADISE OF UNKNOWN PAPUA see **WITH THE HEADHUNTERS IN PAPUA** • 1923
IN THE PARADISE OF UNMARRIED WOMEN see **NO PARAISO DAS SOLTEIRONAS** • 1969
IN THE PARK • 1915 • Chaplin Charles • USA • CHARLIE ON THE SPREE
IN THE PARK • 1933 • Sherman Frank, Rufle George • ANS • USA
IN THE PATH OF PERIL • 1917 • Morton Walter • USA
IN THE PERGAMON MUSEUM • 1962 • Bottcher Jurgen • DOC • GDR
IN THE PHOTOGRAPH see **KOD FOTOGRAFA** • 1959
IN THE PILLORY see **U POZERNOVO STOLBA** • 1924
IN THE PLUMBER'S GRIP • 1915 • *Harris James* • USA
IN THE PODHALE REGION see **NA PODHALU** • 1967
IN THE POPE'S EYE see **PAP'OCCHIO, IL** • 1980
IN THE POWER OF A HYPNOTIST • 1913 • Olcott Sidney, Hunter T. Hayes • USA • IN THE POWER OF THE HYPNOTIST
IN THE POWER OF BLACKLEGS • 1913 • *Joyce Alice* • USA
IN THE POWER OF THE HYPNOTIST see **IN THE POWER OF A HYPNOTIST** • 1913
IN THE POWER OF THE KU KLUX KLAN see **IN THE CLUTCHES OF THE KU KLUX KLAN** • 1913
IN THE POWER OF YOUTH see **I UNGDOMMENS MAKT** • 1980
IN THE PRIME OF LIFE see **EKSPEDITRICEN** • 1911
IN THE PRIME OF LIFE see **LEGSZEBB FERFIKOR** • 1972
IN THE PROMISED LAND • 1970 • Bonniere Rene • SHT • CND
IN THE PYTHON'S DEN see **FOR EAST IS EAST** • 1913
IN THE RAIN • 1985 • Dad Seyfollah • IRN
IN THE RANKS • 1913 • Ford Francis • USA
IN THE RANKS • 1914 • Nash Percy • UKN
IN THE RANKS • 1916 • *Stull Walter* • SHT • USA
IN THE REALM OF THE SENSES (USA) see **AI NO CORRIDA** • 1976
IN THE REAR OF THE ENEMY • 1942 • Schneider Eugene
IN THE RED RAYS OF THE SLEEPING SUN see **AKAI YUKI NO TERASARETE** • 1925
IN THE REDMAN'S COUNTRY • 1913 • *Bison* • USA
IN THE RIGHT OF WAY • 1911 • *Melies* • USA
IN THE RING • 1916 • *Pokes & Jabbs* • USA
IN THE RIVER see **EN EL RIO** • 1961
IN THE ROOM WOMEN COME AND GO TALKING TO MICHELANGELO • 1970 • Leszczynski Witold • SWD
IN THE RUINS OF BA'ALBAK • 1936 • Costi George • LBN
IN THE RUINS (USA) see **HAIKYO NO NAKA** • 1923
IN THE SAGE BRUSH COUNTRY • 1915 • Hamilton G. P.? • USA
IN THE SAME BOAT • 1913 • *Arling Charles* • USA
IN THE SAN FERNANDO VALLEY • 1912 • *Nestor* • USA
IN THE SANDS OF THE DESERT see **W PIASKACH PUSTYNI** • 1962
IN THE SEA • 1948 • Beadle Ernest • USA
IN THE SEASON OF BUDS • 1910 • Griffith D. W. • USA
IN THE SECRET SERVICE • 1913 • McRae Henry • USA
IN THE SECRET STATE • 1985 • Morahan Christopher • UKN
IN THE SERPENT'S POWER • 1910 • *Selig* • USA
IN THE SERVICE OF THE KING • 1909 • Fitzhamon Lewin • UKN
IN THE SERVICE OF THE STATE • 1912 • *Lubin* • USA
IN THE SERVICE OF THE STATE • 1916 • Horne James W. • SHT • USA
IN THE SEVEN WINDS • Rostotsky Stanislav • USS
IN THE SEVEN WINDS see **NA SEMI VETRAKH** • 1962
IN THE SHADE OF THE OLD APPLE SAUCE • 1931 • Fleischer Dave • ANS • USA
IN THE SHADE OF THE OLD APPLE TREE • 1930 • Fleischer Dave • ANS • USA
IN THE SHADOW • 1913 • Lackaye James • USA
IN THE SHADOW • 1915 • Handworth Harry • USA
IN THE SHADOW OF A COLT see **ALL'OMBRA DI UNA COLT** • 1965
IN THE SHADOW OF ASSINIBOINE • 1936 • Oliver Bill • DOC • CND
IN THE SHADOW OF BIG BEN • 1914 • Wilson Frank? • UKN
IN THE SHADOW OF DARKNESS • 1913 • Haldane Bert? • UKN
IN THE SHADOW OF DEATH see **V TYENI SMYERTI** • 1972
IN THE SHADOW OF DISGRACE • 1914 • Ridgely Richard • USA
IN THE SHADOW OF FEAR • 1988 • Karapidis Giorgos • GRC
IN THE SHADOW OF KILIMANJARO • 1986 • Patel Raju • USA, UKN, KNY
IN THE SHADOW OF MOUNT SHASTA • 1910 • *Selig* • USA
IN THE SHADOW OF NIGHT • 1917 • *Shay William* • SHT • USA
IN THE SHADOW OF PRISON BARS see **RISTIKON VARJOSSA** • 1945
IN THE SHADOW OF THE AGES • Topaldgikov Stefan • BUL
IN THE SHADOW OF THE FACTORY see **TEHTAAN VARJOSSA** • 1969
IN THE SHADOW OF THE MOSQUE • 1914 • *Eclair* • USA
IN THE SHADOW OF THE MOUNTAINS • 1913 • Lessey George A. • USA
IN THE SHADOW OF THE PAST see **TINE ZABUTYKH PREDKIV** • 1965
IN THE SHADOW OF THE PINES • 1911 • *Bosworth Hobart* • USA
IN THE SHADOW OF THE POLE • 1928 • Finnie Richard S. • DOC • CND
IN THE SHADOW OF THE ROCKIES • 1918 • Thayer Otis B. • SHT • USA
IN THE SHADOW OF THE ROPE • 1912 • Nash Percy • UKN
IN THE SHADOW OF THE SEA see **IM SCHATTEN DES MEERES** • 1912
IN THE SHADOW OF THE SUN • 1981 • Jarman Derek • UKN
IN THE SHADOW OF THE SUN see **A LA SOMBRE DEL SOL** • 1978
IN THE SHADOW OF THE WIND see **FOUS DE BASSAN, LES** • 1986
IN THE SHENANDOAH VALLEY • 1908 • *Selig* • USA
IN THE SHUFFLE • 1916 • Ricketts Thomas • SHT • USA
IN THE SIGN OF GEMINI see **I TVILLINGERNES TEGN** • 1975
IN THE SIGN OF THE SERPENT see **SEMNUL SARPELUI** • 1981
IN THE SIGNAL BOX • 1922 • Parkinson H. B. • UKN
IN THE SIXTIES • 1964 • Mills Peter • UKN
IN THE SKIN WITH ME • Moberly Luke • USA
IN THE SMUGGLER'S GRIP • 1913 • Collins Edwin J. • UKN
IN THE SOUP • 1914 • *Lubin* • USA
IN THE SOUP • 1920 • *Rube Christian* • USA
IN THE SOUP • 1936 • Edwards Henry • UKN
IN THE SOUTH CHINA COUNTRYSIDE see **DEL-KINA TAJAIN** • 1957
IN THE SOUTH SEAS • 1913 • *Rex* • USA
IN THE SOUTH SEAS WITH MR. AND MRS. PINCHOT see **SOUTH SEAS** • 1930
IN THE SOUTHERN HILLS • 1914 • *Domino* • USA
IN THE SOUTHLAND • 1913 • Nicholls George • USA
IN THE SOWING • 1912 • *Early Baby* • USA
IN THE SPIDER'S GRIP (USA) see **DANS LES GRIFFES DE L'ARAIGNEE** • 1920
IN THE SPIDER'S WEB • 1914 • *Majestic* • USA
IN THE SPIDER'S WEB • 1924 • Boudrioz Robert
IN THE SPIRIT • 1990 • Seacat Sandra • USA
IN THE SPRING OF LIFE, OR HIS FIRST LOVE see **I LIVETS VAR, ELLER FORSTA ALSKARINNAN** • 1912
IN THE SPRING OF OUR LOVE see **IN DIE LENTE VAN ONS LIEFDE** • 1967
IN THE SPRINGTIME OF LIFE see **NA PRIMAVERA DA VIDA** • 1926
IN THE STEEL NET OF DR. MABUSE see **IM STAHLNETZ DES DR. MABUSE** • 1961
IN THE STEPPE • 1951 • Ulyantsev A., Buneyev Boris • USS
IN THE STEPS OF OUR ANCESTORS • 1961 • Zguridi Alexander • DOC • USS
IN THE STEPS OF THE BUDDHA • Hettiarachi P. • DCS • SLN
IN THE STORM see **U OLUJI** • 1952
IN THE STORM see **EN LA TORMENTA** • 1980
IN THE STRETCH • 1914 • *Scovelle Phil* • USA
IN THE SULTAN'S GARDEN • 1911 • *Baggot King* • USA
IN THE SULTAN'S POWER • 1909 • Boggs Frank • USA
IN THE SUMMERTIME • 1906 • Fitzhamon Lewin • UKN
IN THE SUMMERTIME see **DURANTE L'ESTATE** • 1971
IN THE SUNLIGHT • 1915 • Ricketts Thomas • USA
IN THE SUNSET COUNTRY • 1915 • Cooley Frank • *Mustang* • USA
IN THE SUNSET COUNTRY • 1915 • King Burton L. • *Bison* • USA
IN THE SUNSHINE • 1958 • Khamraev Ali • USS
IN THE SWEET DRY AND DRY • 1920 • *Pioneer Film* • SHT • USA
IN THE SWEET PIE AND PIE • 1941 • White Jules • SHT • USA
IN THE SWIM • 1919 • Perez Marcel • USA
IN THE SWITCH TOWER • 1915 • Edwards Walter • USA
IN THE TALL GRASS COUNTRY • 1910 • Melies Gaston • USA
IN THE TALL WHEAT-FIELDS • 1971 • Millionshchikov L. • USS
IN THE TALONS OF AN EAGLE • 1917 • Grandon Francis J. • USA
IN THE TENNESSEE HILLS • 1915 • Miller Charles • USA
IN THE TENTS OF THE ASRA • 1912 • *Bosworth Hobart* • USA
IN THE TEPEE'S LIGHT • 1911 • *Reliance* • USA
IN THE TIDE • 1912 • *Republic* • USA
IN THE TIME OF REBELLION • 1908 • *Norwood* • USA
IN THE TIMES OF DON PORFIRIO see **EN TIEMPOS DE DON PORFIRIO** • 1939
IN THE TOILS • 1913 • *Adams Lionel* • USA
IN THE TOILS OF THE BLACKMAILER • 1913 • Butler Alexander? • UKN
IN THE TOILS OF THE DEVIL • 1913 • *Milano* • ITL
IN THE TOILS OF THE TEMPTRESS (USA) see **GEORGE BARNWELL THE LONDON APPRENTICE** • 1913
IN THE TOWN OF "S" see **V GORODE "S"** • 1966
IN THE TRACES OF THE BALL • 1966 • Csoke Jozsef • DOC • HNG
IN THE TRAP see **EN LA TRAMPA** • 1978
IN THE TWILIGHT • 1915 • Ricketts Thomas • USA
IN THE VALE OF SORROW • 1915 • *Beauty* • USA
IN THE VALLEY • 1915 • *Huling Lorraine* • USA
IN THE VILLAIN'S POWER • 1917 • O'Brien Willis • USA
IN THE VOID • 1969 • Bijlsma Ronald • ANS • NTH
IN THE WAKE OF A STRANGER • 1959 • Eady David • UKN
IN THE WAKE OF THE BOUNTY • 1933 • Chauvel Charles • ASL
IN THE WARDEN'S GARDEN • 1915 • *Domino* • USA
IN THE WATCHES OF THE NIGHT • 1909 • Griffith D. W. • USA
IN THE WATCHES OF THE NIGHT • 1913 • *Leonard Marion* • USA
IN THE WATER • 1923 • *Mack Donald* • USA
IN THE WEB • 1910 • *Columbia* • USA
IN THE WEB OF THE GRAFTERS • 1916 • MacQuarrie Murdock • USA
IN THE WEB OF THE SPIDER • 1917 • Ellis Robert • SHT • USA
IN THE WEE WEE HOURS.. • 1987 • Ben-Meir • SHT • USA
IN THE WEST • 1923 • Holt George • USA
IN THE WHITE CITY see **DANS LA VILLE BLANCHE** • 1983
IN THE WILD see **VADON** • 1988
IN THE WILD MOUNTAINS see **YE SHAN** • 1985
IN THE WILD WEST • 1910 • *Bison* • USA
IN THE WILD WEST • 1919 • *Jester* • SHT • USA
IN THE WILD WEST see **NA DZIKIM ZACHODZIE** • 1970
IN THE WILDERNESS • 1910 • *Selig* • USA
IN THE WILDS OF AFRICA • 1913 • *Carlyle Grace* • USA
IN THE WINDOW RECESS • 1909 • Griffith D. W. • USA
IN THE WIND'S EYE • 1989 • Jozani Massoud Jafari • IRN
IN THE WINGS see **DERYNE, HOL VAN?** • 1975
IN THE WINKING OF AN EYE see **KISAPMATA** • 1981
IN THE WOLA CLUB see **W KLUBIE NA WOLI** • 1963
IN THE WOLF'S FANGS • 1914 • *Clifford William* • USA
IN THE WOOD SHED SHE SAID SHE WOULD • 1929 • Aylott Dave, Symmons E. F. • SHT • UKN
IN THE WOODS see **RASHOMON** • 1950
IN THE WORLD'S MOUTH see **NA BOCA DO MUNDO** • 1980
IN THE WRONG FLAT • 1913 • *Solax* • USA
IN THE YEAR 2000 • 1912 • Blache Alice • USA
IN THE YEAR 2014 • 1914 • *Asher Max* • USA
IN THE YEAR 2889 • 1966 • Buchanan Larry • USA • YEAR 2889 ○ 2889
IN THE YEAR OF 13 MOONS see **IN EINEM JAHR MIT 13 MONDEN** • 1978
IN THE YEAR OF THE APE see **APINAN VUONNA** • 1983
IN THE YEAR OF THE PIG • 1969 • De Antonio Emile • DOC • USA
IN THE YEAR OF THE RUBBLE-CLEARING WOMAN see **RAMA DAMA -IM JAHR DE TRUMMERFRAU** • 1990
IN THE ZOO • 1933 • Lantz Walter, Nolan William • ANS • USA
IN THEIR HOUR OF NEED • 1913 • *Thanhouser* • USA
IN THEIR PRIME see **TAMEN ZHENG NIANQING** • 1987
IN THESE DAYS see **NAINA PAIVINA** • 1955
IN THIS CORNER • 1948 • Reisner Charles F. • USA
IN THIS CORNER • 1982 • Brocka Lino • PHL
IN THIS NEW WAY OF LIFE NOTHING IS LIKE THE PAST • 1977 • Acevedo Josefina • SHT • VNZ
IN THIS OUR LIFE • 1942 • Huston John • USA
IN THIS TOWN THERE ARE NO THIEVES see **EN ESTE PUEBLO NO HAY LADRONES** • 1965
IN THIS WAY WHICH IS SO USUAL NOWADAYS see **PA DETTA NUMERA VANLIGA SATT** • 1916
IN THREE HOURS • 1913 • *Coxen Ed* • USA
IN TIME FOR PRESS • 1911 • Melies Gaston • USA
IN TIME OF PERIL • 1912 • *Thanhouser* • USA
IN TIME OF PESTILENCE • 1951 • Halas John • ANS • UKN
IN TIME WITH INDUSTRY see **TRADE TATTOO** • 1937
IN TOO DEEP see **MACK THE KNIFE** • 1989
IN TOW • 1914 • Vidor King • SHT • USA
IN TOWN TONIGHT • 1935 • Smith Herbert • UKN
IN TRE VERSO L'AVVENTURA • 1971 • Passalacqua Pino • ITL
IN TREASON'S GRASP • 1917 • Ford Francis • USA
IN TREUE STARK • 1926 • Brandt Heinrich • FRG
IN TROUBLE WITH EVE (USA) see **TROUBLE WITH EVE** • 1960
IN TRUST • 1915 • Eason B. Reeves • USA
IN TUDOR DAYS • 1924 • *Regent Films* • SHT • UKN
IN TUNE • 1914 • Hamilton G. P.? • USA
IN TUNE WITH THE WILD • 1914 • Martin E. A. • USA
IN TWO MINDS • 1967 • Loach Kenneth • MTV • UKN
IN UN GIORNO PIENO DI SOLE • 1970 • Negri Giulio Giuseppe • ITL
IN UNA NOTTE DI CHIARO DI LUNA • 1990 • Wertmuller Lina • ITL, FRN • IN A FULL MOON NIGHT
IN UNIFORM see **I KRONANS KLADER** • 1915
IN (USA) see **HIGH** • 1968
IN VACANZA AL MARE see **RAGAZZE AL MARE** • 1956
IN VENICE • 1933 • *Terry Paul/ Moser Frank (P)* • ANS • USA
IN VIAGGIO CON PAPA' • 1983 • Sordi Alberto • ITL • TRAVEL WITH DADDY
IN WALKED CHARLEY • 1932 • Doane Warren • SHT • USA
IN WALKED MARY • 1920 • Archainbaud George • USA
IN WAR TIME • 1910 • *Imp* • USA
IN WHICH ANNIE GIVES IT THOSE ONES • 1989 • Krishen Pradip • IND
IN WHICH WE LIVE • 1943 • Massingham Richard • UKN
IN WHICH WE SERVE • 1942 • Coward Noel, Lean David • UKN
IN WIEN HAB' ICH EINMAL EIN MADEL GELIEBT • 1930 • Schonfelder Erich • FRG
IN WILD MAN'S LAND • 1914 • *Majestic* • USA
IN WOLF'S CLOTHING • 1912 • Wilson Frank? • UKN
IN WOLF'S CLOTHING • 1914 • *Joyce Alice* • USA
IN WONDERLAND • 1931 • Lantz Walter, Nolan William • ANS • USA
IN WRONG • 1914 • *Crystal* • USA
IN WRONG • 1915 • *Atlas* • USA
IN WRONG • 1915 • *Royal* • USA
IN WRONG • 1918 • *Jaxon* • USA
IN WRONG • 1919 • Kirkwood James • USA
IN WRONG see **BETWEEN SHOWERS** • 1914
IN WRONG RIGHT • 1917 • *Triangle* • USA
IN WRONG WRIGHT • 1920 • Russell Albert • SHT • USA
IN YAKUTIA see **W JAKUCJI** • 1969
IN YOUR DAD'S POCKET see **I DIN FARS LOMME** • 1972

IN YOUR GARDEN • 1938 • Alderson John • UKN
IN ZULULAND • 1915 • Louis Will • USA
INA-BUSHI • 1940 • Kamei Fumio • JPN • INA SONG, THE
INA KA NG ANAK MO • 1979 • Brocka Lino • PHL
INA RAY HUTTON AND HER ORCHESTRA • 1943 • Roush Leslie • SHT • USA
INA SONG, THE see **INA-BUSHI** • 1940
INACCESIBLE, LA • 1920 • Buchs Jose • SPN
INADMISSABLE EVIDENCE • 1968 • Page Anthony • UKN
INAFFERRABILE 12, L' • 1950 • Mattoli Mario • ITL • DOUBLE TROUBLE
INAFFERRABILE E INVINCIBILE MR. INVISIBILE, L' • 1970 • Margheriti Antonio • ITL, SPN, FRG • INVENCIBLE HOMBRE INVISIBLE, EL (SPN) ○ INVINCIBLE INVISIBLE MAN, THE ○ SUPER INVISIBLE MAN ○ INVINCIBLE MR. INVISIBLE ○ MR. SUPER INVISIBLE ○ MR. INVISIBLE ○ MISTER UNSICHTBAR
INAINTE DE TACERE • 1979 • Visarion Alexa • RMN • AHEAD OF THE SILENCE
INAKAPPE TAISHO • 1971 • *Toho* • ANS • JPN
INASSOUVIE, L' (FRN) see **AMORE A ROMA, UN** • 1960
INASSOUVIES, LES (FRN) see **DE SADE 70** • 1969
INAUGURACAO DO ESTADIO NACIONAL • 1947 • Ribeiro Antonio Lopes • SHT • PRT
INAUGURACAO DO SEMINARIO DOS OLIVAIS • 1934 • Vieira Manuel Luis • SHT • PRT
INAUGURATION see **HIDAVATAS** • 1969
INAUGURATION DE LA STATUE, L' • 1913 • Linder Max • FRN • MAX ET L'INAUGURATION DE LA STATUE
INAUGURATION DE L'EXPOSITION UNIVERSELLE • 1900 • Lumiere Louis • FRN
INAUGURATION OF THE COMMONWEALTH • 1901 • Perry Joseph H. • DOC • ASL
INAUGURATION OF THE PLEASURE DOME • 1954 • Anger Kenneth • USA • LORD SHIVA'S DREAM
INAY • 1977 • Brocka Lino • PHL
INAZUMA • 1952 • Naruse Mikio • JPN • LIGHTNING
INAZUMA • 1967 • Oba Hideo • JPN • FLASH OF LIGHTNING, A
INAZUMA KAIDO • 1957 • Mori Issei • JPN
INAZUMA KOTENGU • 1958 • Matsumura Shoji • JPN • SCROLL'S SECRET, THE (USA)
INAZUMA-ZOSHI • 1952 • Inagaki Hiroshi • JPN • LIGHTNING ADVANCE
INBAD THE COUNT • 1912 • Christie Al • USA
INBAD THE SAILOR • 1915 • *Bray J. R. (P)* • USA
INBAD THE SAILOR • 1923 • *Sennett Mack (P)* • SHT • USA
INBAD THE SAILOR • 1924 • Stoloff Ben, Carruth Clyde • SHT • USA
INBAD THE SAILOR • 1935 • *Cammer Joseph* • USA
INBETWEEN AGE, THE (USA) see **GOLDEN DISC, THE** • 1958
INBREKER, DE • 1972 • Weisz Frans • NTH • FRAME UP, THE ○ BURGLAR, THE
INCA see **KINGS OF THE SUN** • 1963
INCANTESIMO TRAGICO • 1951 • Sequi Mario • ITL • OLIVIA ○ TRAGIC SPELL
INCANTEVOLE NEMICA, L' • 1953 • Gora Claudio • ITL
INCANTO DELLA FORESTA, L' • 1957 • Ancillotto Alberto • DOC • ITL • SONG OF THE FOREST (UKN)
INCANTO DI MEZZANOTTE • 1940 • Baffico Mario • ITL • LADRO DI STELLE
INCARNATION OF KRISHNA see **SHREE KRISHNAVTAR** • 1922
INCARNATION OF KRISHNA see **KRISHNAVATAR** • 1932
INCARNATION OF VISHNU see **VISHNU AVATAR** • 1921
INCARNATION (USA) see **PUNARJANMA** • 1926
INCATENATA, L' • 1921 • Genina Augusto • ITL
INCATENATA DAL DESTINO • 1956 • Di Gianni Enzo • ITL
INCE CUMALI • 1967 • Duru Yilmaz • TRK • CUMALI, THE THIN ONE
INCENDAIRES, LES • 1906 • Melies Georges • FRN • HISTOIRE D'UN CRIME, L' ○ DESPERATE CRIME, A
INCENDARIO DI ROMA, L' • 1963 • Malatesta Guido • ITL
INCENDIARY see **MORDBRANNERSKAN** • 1926
INCENDIARY BLONDE • 1945 • Marshall George • USA
INCENDIARY INDIANS • 1911 • *Pathe* • USA
INCENDIARY OF EUROPE, THE see **BRANDSTIFTER EUROPAS, DIE** • 1926
INCENDIARY'S DAUGHTER, THE • 1923 • Cervenkova Thea • CZC
INCENSE FOR THE DAMNED • 1970 • Hartford-Davis Robert • UKN • BLOODSUCKERS (USA) ○ DOCTORS WEAR SCARLET ○ BLOODSUCKER
INCENSURATI, GLI • 1961 • Giaculli Francesco • ITL
INCENSURATO PROVATA DISONESTA CARRIERA ASSICURATA CERCASI • 1972 • Baldi Marcello • ITL
INCERTIDUMBRE • 1936 • Sociar Tridro
INCEST see **CARMILLA** • 1968
INCESTE, L' • 1973 • Franco Jesus
INCESTUEUSES, LES • 1976 • Benazeraf Jose • FRN
INCESTUOUS, THE see **FUXI FUXI** • 1989
INCHES • Scott Steve • USA
INCHIESTA, L' • 1971 • Amico Gianni • MTV • ITL • INQUIRY, THE
INCHIESTA, L' • 1987 • Damiani Damiano • ITL • INQUIRY, THE (USA) ○ ENQUIRY, THE
INCHIESTA SU UN DELITTO DELLA POLIZIA (ITL) see **ASSASSINS DE L'ORDRE, LES** • 1970
INCHON • 1980 • Young Terence • USA, SKR • OPERATION INCHON
INCIDENT • 1948 • Beaudine William • USA
INCIDENT, THE • 1967 • Peerce Larry • USA
INCIDENT AT CRESTRIDGE • 1981 • Taylor Jud • TVM • USA • INCIDENT IN CRESTRIDGE ○ LADY WITH A BADGE
INCIDENT AT GUERLOVO see **GERLOVSKA ISTORYA** • 1971
INCIDENT AT MIDNIGHT • 1963 • Harrison Norman • UKN
INCIDENT AT OWL CREEK see **RIVIERE DU HIBOU, LA** • 1961
INCIDENT AT PHANTOM HILL • 1966 • Bellamy Earl • USA • FACELESS MEN, THE
INCIDENT AT RAVEN'S GATE • 1988 • De Heer Rolf • ASL
INCIDENT AT RESTIGOUCHE • 1984 • Obomsawin Alanis • CND • EVENEMENTS DE RESTIGOUCHE, LES
INCIDENT AT THE TELEGRAPH OFFICE • 1941 • Kozintsev Grigori • SHT • USS
INCIDENT CLOS, L' • 1989 • Thorn Jean-Pierre • FRN
INCIDENT FROM DON QUIXOTE see **AVENTURES DE DON QUICHOTTE** • 1908
INCIDENT IN A GLASS BLOWERS SHOP • Bauer Byron • SHT • USA
INCIDENT IN AN ALLEY • 1962 • Cahn Edward L. • USA
INCIDENT IN BENDERATH see **ZWISCHENFALL IN BENDERATH** • 1956
INCIDENT IN CRESTRIDGE see **INCIDENT AT CRESTRIDGE** • 1981
INCIDENT IN SAIGON (USA) see **TRANSIT A SAIGON** • 1962
INCIDENT IN SAN FRANCISCO • 1970 • Medford Don • TVM • USA
INCIDENT IN SHANGHAI • 1938 • Carstairs John Paddy • UKN
INCIDENT IN THE BOER WAR, AN • 1900 • Green George • UKN
INCIDENT INDEPENDANT DE NOTRE VOLONTE, UN • 1977 • Huisman Michel • BLG
INCIDENT ON A DARK STREET • 1972 • Kulik Buzz • TVM • USA
INCIDENT ON A VOLCANO see **SLUCHAI V VULKANYE** • 1941
INCIDENT ON BRIGHTON PIER, AN • 1900 • Smith G. A. • UKN
INCIDENTS IN THE LIFE OF LORD NELSON • 1905 • Jeapes Harold? • UKN
INCIDENTS OF THE GREAT EUROPEAN WAR • 1914 • Pearson George • UKN
INCILI CAVUS • 1968 • Hancer Nisan • TRK • PEARLED SERGEANT, THE
INCINERATOR OF CADAVERS see **SPALOVAC MRTVOL** • 1968
INCITATION AU PLAISIR • 1981 • Turbay Max • FRN
INCLINATIONS • 1966 • Haas Eva, Haas Guido • SHT • SWT
INCOGNITO • 1913 • *Kerrigan J. Warren* • USA
INCOGNITO • 1914 • *General* • USA
INCOGNITO • 1915 • MacMackin Archer • USA
INCOGNITO • 1916 • Dinesen Robert • DNM
INCOGNITO • 1933 • Gerron Kurt • FRN • SON ALTESSE VOYAGE
INCOGNITO • 1958 • Dally Patrice • FRN
INCOGNITO • 1967 • Dlz • PHL
INCOME TAX COLLECTORS, THE • 1923 • Kenton Erle C. • SHT • USA
INCOME TAX SAPPY • 1954 • White Jules • SHT • USA
INCOMING FRESHMAN see **INCOMING FRESHMEN** • 1979
INCOMING FRESHMEN • 1979 • Lewald Eric, Morgan Glenn • USA • INCOMING FRESHMAN
INCOMPARABLE BELLAIRS, THE • 1914 • Shaw Harold • UKN • INCOMPARABLE MISTRESS BELLAIRS, THE (USA)
INCOMPARABLE MISTRESS BELLAIRS, THE (USA) see **INCOMPARABLE BELLAIRS, THE** • 1914
INCOMPATIBILITY • 1913 • Stow Percy • UKN
INCOMPETENT, THE • 1914 • *Ince John* • USA
INCOMPETENT HERO, AN • 1914 • Arbuckle Roscoe, Dillon Eddie • USA
INCOMPETENT THIEF, THE • 1909 • *Walturdaw* • UKN
INCOMPLETE, THE • 1967 • Doicheva Zdenka • ANS • BUL
INCOMPRESO • 1966 • Comencini Luigi • ITL • VITA COL FIGLIO ○ MISUNDERSTOOD
INCONFIDENTES, OS • 1972 • de Andrade Joaquim Pedro • BRZ • CONGIURA, LA ○ CONSPIRATORS, THE
INCONNU DE HONG-KONG, L' • 1964 • Poitrenaud Jacques • FRN • STRANGER FROM HONG-KONG (USA)
INCONNU DE SHANDIGOR, L' • 1967 • Roy Jean-Louis • SWT • UNKNOWN MAN OF SHANDIGOR, THE ○ UNKNOWN FROM SHANDIGOR, THE ○ UNKNOWN OF SHANDIGOR, THE
INCONNU D'UN SOIR, L' • 1948 • Bromberger Herve, Neufeld Max • FRN, AUS
INCONNUE, L' • 1913 • Jasset Victorin • FRN
INCONNUE, L' • 1917 • de Baroncelli Jacques • FRN
INCONNUE, L' • 1966 • Weisz Claude • SHT • FRN • UNKNOWN, THE
INCONNUE DE MONTE CARLO, L' • 1938 • Berthomieu Andre • FRN • DAME DE MONTE CARLO, LA
INCONNUE DE MONTREAL, L' • 1950 • Devaivre Jean • FRN, CND • SON COPAIN
INCONNUE DES SIX JOURS, L' • 1927 • Painleve Jean, Sti Rene • SHT • FRN
INCONNUE NO.13, L' • 1948 • Paulin Jean-Paul • FRN
INCONNUS AUX PETITS PIEDS, LES • 1978 • Gobbi Sergio • FRN
INCONNUS DANS LA MAISON, LES • 1941 • Decoin Henri • FRN • STRANGERS IN THE HOUSE
INCONNUS DE LA TERRE, LES • 1962 • Ruspoli Mario • DOC • FRN
INCONSTANT, L' • 1931 • Rigaud Andre, Behrendt Hans • FRN • JE SORS ET TU RESTES LA ○ AMOUR DISPOSE, L'
INCONSTANT, THE • 1910 • *Powers* • USA
INCONSTANT YOUTH see **ADDIO GIOVINEZZA!** • 1927
INCONTRI CON GLI UMANOIDI • 1979 • Ricci Tonino • ITL
INCONTRI DI NOTTE • 1943 • Malasomma Nunzio • ITL
INCONTRI DI UN GIORNO • 1947 • Gallo Vittorio • ITL • DAY'S ENCOUNTERS, A
INCONTRI MOLTO RAVVICINATI see **INCONTRI MOLTO.. RAVVICINATI DEL QUARTO TIPO** • 1978
INCONTRI MOLTO.. RAVVICINATI DEL QUARTO TIPO • 1978 • Gariazzo Mario • ITL • VERY CLOSE ENCOUNTERS OF THE FOURTH KIND ○ INCONTRI MOLTO RAVVICINATI ○ COMING OF ALIENS, THE
INCONTRO • 1971 • Schivazappa Piero • ITL
INCONTRO D'AMORE • 1975 • Liberatore Ugo • ITL
INCONTRO D'AMORE A BALI • 1970 • Liberatore Ugo • ITL
INCONVENIENT INFANT, AN • 1925 • Templeman Harcourt • UKN
INCORRIGIBLE • Mattsson Arne • SWD
INCORRIGIBLE, L' • 1975 • de Broca Philippe • FRN
INCORRIGIBLE, LA • 1930 • Mittler Leo • SPN
INCORRIGIBLE BARBARA see **UNVERBESSERLICHE BARBARA, DIE** • 1977
INCORRIGIBLE DUKANE, THE • 1915 • Durkin James • USA
INCORRIGIBLES, THE • 1913 • *Heron Andrew (P)* • UKN
INCORRUPTIBLE, L' see **HERCULE** • 1937
INCORRUPTIBLE CROWN, THE • 1915 • Wilson Frank • UKN
INCREASING WARDROBE, AN see **DESHABILLAGE IMPOSSIBLE, LE** • 1900
INCREDIBILE ATTESTA, L' • 1956 • Loy Mino • ITL
INCREDIBILE STORIA DI MARTA DUBOIS, L' • 1972 • Scandelari Jacques • ITL
INCREDIBLE AND SAD TALE OF LATIN AMERICA AND THE HEARTLESS CONQUISTADORS, THE • 1989 • Cabal Ricardo • SHT • CLM
INCREDIBLE CHESTY (72-32-36) MORGAN AND HER DEADLY WEAPONS, THE • 1974 • Wishman Doris • USA • DEADLY WEAPONS
INCREDIBLE CLOSET MONSTER, THE see **MONSTER IN THE CLOSET** • 1986
INCREDIBLE FACE OF DR. B., THE (USA) see **ROSTRO INFERNAL** • 1961
INCREDIBLE, FANTASTIC, EXTRAORDINARY see **INCRIVEL, FANTASTICO, EXTRAORDINARIO** • 1969
INCREDIBLE FLORIDAS • 1972 • Weir Peter • DCS • ASL
INCREDIBLE HULK, THE • 1978 • Johnson Kenneth • TVM • USA
INCREDIBLE HULK RETURNS, THE • 1988 • Corea Nick • TVM • USA • RETURN OF THE INCREDIBLE HULK
INCREDIBLE INVASION, THE see **INVASION SINIESTRA** • 1968
INCREDIBLE JEWEL ROBBERY, THE • 1959 • Leisen Mitchell • MTV • USA
INCREDIBLE JOURNEY, THE • 1963 • Markle Fletcher • USA
INCREDIBLE JOURNEY OF DOCTOR MEG LAUREL, THE • 1979 • Green Guy • TVM • USA
INCREDIBLE KUNG FU MISSION, THE • 1982 • Chang Hsin-Yi • HKG
INCREDIBLE MACHINE, THE • 1975 • Rosten Irwin • DOC • USA
INCREDIBLE MELTING MAN, THE • 1977 • Sachs William • USA
INCREDIBLE MR. CHADWICK, THE • 1980 • Mann Daniel • USA
INCREDIBLE MR. LIMPET, THE • 1964 • Lubin Arthur • USA • BE CAREFUL HOW YOU WISH ○ HENRY LIMPET ○ MR. LIMPET
INCREDIBLE MR. WILLIAMS see **AMAZING MR. WILLIAMS** • 1940
INCREDIBLE ONE, THE • Ovtcharov Sergei • USS
INCREDIBLE PETRIFIED WORLD, THE • 1958 • Warren Jerry • USA
INCREDIBLE PRAYING MANTIS, THE see **DEADLY MANTIS, THE** • 1957
INCREDIBLE ROCKY MOUNTAIN RACE, THE • 1978 • Conway James L. • TVM • USA
INCREDIBLE SARAH, THE • 1976 • Fleischer Richard • UKN, USA
INCREDIBLE SEX-RAY MACHINE, THE • 1978 • *Digart Uschi* • USA
INCREDIBLE SEX REVOLUTION, THE • 1965 • Zugsmith Albert • USA
INCREDIBLE SHRINKING MAN, THE • 1957 • Arnold Jack • USA
INCREDIBLE SHRINKING WOMAN, THE • 1981 • Schumacher Joel • USA
INCREDIBLE STORY, AN see **NEVEROYATNA ISTORIA** • 1964
INCREDIBLE STRANGER, THE • 1942 • Tourneur Jacques • SHT • USA
INCREDIBLE TORTURE SHOW, THE • 1977 • Reed Joel M. • USA • BLOODSUCKING FREAKS
INCREDIBLE TRANSPLANT, THE see **INCREDIBLE TWO-HEADED TRANSPLANT, THE** • 1971
INCREDIBLE TWO-HEADED TRANSPLANT, THE • 1971 • Lanza Anthony M. • USA • INCREDIBLE TRANSPLANT, THE
INCREDIBLE VOYAGE OF STINGRAY, THE • 1965 • Patillo Alan, Elliott David, Kelly John • ANM • UKN
INCREDIBLE WEREWOLF MURDERS, THE see **MALTESE BIPPY, THE** • 1969
INCREDIBLY STRANGE CREATURES, THE see **INCREDIBLY STRANGE CREATURES WHO STOPPED LIVING AND BECAME CRAZY MIXED-UP ZOMBIES, THE** • 1964
INCREDIBLY STRANGE CREATURES WHO STOPPED LIVING AND BECAME CRAZY MIXED-UP ZOMBIES, THE • 1964 • Steckler Ray Dennis • USA • TEENAGE PYSCHO MEETS BLOODY MARY ○ INCREDIBLY STRANGE CREATURES, THE
INCREVABLE, L' • 1959 • Boyer Jean • FRN
INCRIMINATING LETTER, THE • 1913 • *Essanay* • USA
INCRIVEIS IN THIS CRAZY WORLD see **INCRIVEIS NESTE MUNDO LOUCO, OS** • 1967
INCRIVEIS NESTE MUNDO LOUCO, OS • 1967 • Junior Brancato • BRZ • INCRIVEIS IN THIS CRAZY WORLD
INCRIVEL, FANTASTICO, EXTRAORDINARIO • 1969 • Chadler C. Adolpho • BRZ • INCREDIBLE, FANTASTIC, EXTRAORDINARY
INCUBO see **PAURA, LA** • 1954
INCUBO, L' • 1917 • Palermi Amleto • ITL
INCUBO E FINITO, L' see **OPERAZIONE MITRA** • 1955
INCUBO SULLA CITTA CONTAMINATA see **NIGHTMARE CITY** • 1980
INCUBUS • 1965 • Stevens Leslie • USA
INCUBUS • 1981 • Hough John • CND
INCUBUS see **RAGAZZA CHE SAPEVA TROPPO, LA** • 1962
INCUBUS see **MORTE ACCAREZZA A MEZZANOTTE, LA** • 1972
INDAGINE SU UN CITTADINA AL DI SOPRA DI OGNO SOSPETTO • 1970 • Petri Elio • ITL • INVESTIGATION INTO A CITIZEN ABOVE SUSPICION ○ INVESTIGATION OF A PRIVATE CITIZEN ○ INVESTIGATION OF A CITIZEN ABOVE SUSPICION
INDAGINE SU UN DELITTO PERFETTO • 1979 • Rosati Giuseppe • ITL • PERFECT CRIME, THE
INDAGINE SU UN PARA ACCUSATO DI OMICIDA (ITL) see **DERNIER SAUT, LE** • 1969
INDAMA NUHIBB see **ENDAMA NOVHEA** • 1967
INDE 69, L' see **INDE FANTOME, L'** • 1969
INDE AU FEMININ, L' • 1972 • Chardeaux Francois • DOC • FRN
INDE FANTOME, L' • 1969 • Malle Louis • DOC • FRN • PHANTOM INDIA (USA) ○ REFLEXION SUR UN VOYAGE ○ LOUIS MALLE'S INDIA ○ INDE 69, L'
INDECENCES • Regis Jack • FRN
INDECENT DESIRES • 1968 • Silverman Louis • USA

INDECENT EXPOSURE • 1981 • McCallum Robert • USA
INDECENT OBSESSION, AN • 1985 • Marinos Lex • ASL
INDECENT (USA) see **SCHWARZE NYLONS -HEISSE NACHTE** • 1958
INDECISIVE YEARS see **KRISTOVE ROKY** • 1967
INDEKS • 1978 • Kijowski Janusz • PLN • INDEX
INDELA • 1985 • SAF
INDELIBLE STAIN, THE • 1912 • *Santschi Thomas* • USA
INDEPENDENCE • 1976 • Huston John • DCS • USA
INDEPENDENCE • 1987 • Patterson John • TVM • USA
INDEPENDENCE B'GOSH • 1918 • Harrison Saul • SHT • USA
INDEPENDENCE DAY • 1981 • Roth Bobby • USA
INDEPENDENCE DAY • 1983 • Mandel Robert • USA • FOLLOW YOUR DREAMS ○ LOVE, HONOR AND OBEY
INDEPENDENCE OF SUSAN, THE • 1914 • Ricketts Thomas • USA
INDEPENDENCE OR DEATH see **INDEPENDENCIA OU MORTE** • 1972
INDEPENDENCIA OU MORTE • 1972 • Coimbra Carlos • BRZ • INDEPENDENCE OR DEATH
INDEPENDENT WOMAN, AN • 1915 • *Reliance* • USA
INDESIDERABILI, GLI see **CON LA RABBIA AGLI OCCHI** • 1976
INDESIDERABILI, LE see **DONNE SENZA NOME** • 1950
INDESIRABLE, L' • 1933 • de Ruelle Emile • FRN
INDESTRUCTIBLE MAN, THE • 1956 • Pollexfen Jack • USA
INDESTRUCTIBLE MR. JENKS, THE • 1913 • *Roland Ruth* • SHT • USA
INDESTRUCTIBLE MRS. TALBOT, THE see **LADY CONSENTS, THE** • 1936
INDESTRUCTIBLE WIFE, THE • 1919 • Maigne Charles • USA
INDEX see **INDEKS** • 1978
INDEX, THE see **KARTOTEKA** • 1966
INDEX HANS RICHTER • 1969 • Markopoulos Gregory J. • USA
INDI RACE: BAKUSO • 1967 • Teshigahara Hiroshi • DOC • JPN • INDIANAPOLIS CAR RACE ○ EXPLOSION COURSE ○ BAKUSO
INDIA • 1960 • Rossellini Roberto • DOC • ITL, FRN
INDIA • 1975 • Faria Antonio • PRT
INDIA • 1976 • Noonan Chris (c/d) • DSS • ASL
INDIA -14 YEARS AFTER • 1960 • King Allan • CND
INDIA 67 • 1967 • Sukhdev S. • DOC • IND • INDIA 1967
INDIA 1967 see **INDIA 67** • 1967
INDIA, LA • 1974 • *Conacine* • MXC
INDIA, A FILHA DO SOL • 1982 • Barreto Fabio • BRZ • INDIA, DAUGHTER OF THE SUN
INDIA BONITA, LA • 1939 • Helu Antonio • MXC • PRETTY INDIAN GIRL, THE (USA)
INDIA, DAUGHTER OF THE SUN see **INDIA, A FILHA DO SOL** • 1982
INDIA FAVOLOSA • 1955 • Macchi Giulio • DOC • ITL
INDIA FOREVER • 1986 • Vulchanov Rangel • DOC • BUL
INDIA ON PARADE • 1937 • Fitzpatrick James • SHT • USA
INDIA RUBBER HEAD, THE see **HOMME A LA TETE EN CAOUTCHOUC, L'** • 1902
INDIA SONG • 1975 • Duras Marguerite • FRN
INDIA SPEAKS • 1933 • *Futter Walter (P)* • USA
INDIA TRIP, THE • 1972 • Davies Bill • CND
INDIA UNVEILED • 1985 • Prakash Sanjeev • IND
INDIA VISTA DA ROSELLINI, L' • 1959 • Rossellini Roberto • MTV • ITL
INDIAN, THE • 1909 • *Selig* • USA
INDIAN, THE • 1914 • *West Charles* • USA
INDIAN, THE • 1916 • Miles David • SHT • USA
INDIAN, THE see **INDIO, EL** • 1938
INDIAN ADVENTURE see **INDIAN TORTENET** • 1961
INDIAN AGENT • 1948 • Selander Lesley • USA
INDIAN AGENT, THE • 1914 • *Darkfeather Mona* • USA
INDIAN AMBUSCADE, THE • 1914 • *Kalem* • USA
INDIAN AND THE CHILD, THE • 1912 • *Anderson Broncho Billy* • USA
INDIAN AND THE COWGIRL, THE • 1910 • *Bison* • USA
INDIAN ATTACK IN DEATH PASS see **INDIANENOVERVAL IN DE DODENPAS** • 1967
INDIAN BLOOD • 1910 • *Lubin* • USA
INDIAN BLOOD • 1912 • *Pathe* • USA
INDIAN BLOOD • 1913 • *Bison* • USA
INDIAN BLOOD • 1914 • *Kalem* • USA
INDIAN BRAVE'S CONVERSION, AN • 1911 • *Yankee* • USA
INDIAN BROTHERS, THE • 1911 • Griffith D. W. • USA
INDIAN CHANGELING, THE • 1915 • *Reliance* • USA
INDIAN CHIEF AND THE SIEDLITZ POWDER, THE • 1901 • Hepworth Cecil M. • UKN
INDIAN CHILD'S GRATITUDE, THE • 1916 • *Utah* • USA
INDIAN CLASSICAL SCHOOL OF MUSIC, AN see **DHRUPAD** • 1983
INDIAN CORN • 1972 • Smith Paul J. • ANS • USA
INDIAN DIAMOND, AN • 1915 • Crane Frank H. • USA
INDIAN DON JUAN, AN • 1913 • *Patheplay* • USA
INDIAN DRAMA • 1910-12 • Melies Gaston • USA
INDIAN DURBAR • 1937-40 • *Cardiff Jack (Ph)* • DCS • UKN
INDIAN ECLIPSE, AN • 1914 • *Nestor* • USA
INDIAN FANTASY • 1957 • Gross Anthony, Hoppin Hector • ANM • UKN • INDIAN PHANTASY
INDIAN FATE • 1914 • *Kalem* • USA
INDIAN FIGHTER, THE • 1955 • De Toth Andre • USA
INDIAN FIGUEREDO, THE see **INDIO FIGUEREDO, EL** • 1973
INDIAN FLUTE, THE • 1911 • *Vitagraph* • USA
INDIAN FORTUNE TELLER, THE • 1911 • *Champion* • USA
INDIAN GIRL'S AWAKENING, AN • 1910 • *Essanay* • USA
INDIAN GIRL'S ROMANCE, THE • 1910 • *Lubin* • USA
INDIAN HERO, AN • 1911 • *Bison* • USA
INDIAN IDYL, AN • 1912 • *Pathe* • USA
INDIAN ISHMAIL, AN • 1912 • *Bison* • USA
INDIAN JEALOUSY • 1912 • Dwan Allan • USA
INDIAN LAND GRAB, THE • 1910 • *Champion* • USA
INDIAN LEGEND, AN • 1911 • *Bison* • USA
INDIAN LEGEND, AN • 1912 • Giblyn Charles • USA
INDIAN LOVE AFFAIR, AN • 1911 • *Bison* • USA
INDIAN LOVE CALL see **ROSE MARIE** • 1936
INDIAN LOVE CULT • 1970 • USA
INDIAN LOVE LYRICS, THE • 1923 • Hill Sinclair • UKN
INDIAN MAIDEN'S CHOICE, AN • 1910 • *Bison* • USA
INDIAN MAIDEN'S LESSON, THE • 1911 • Barker Reginald? • USA
INDIAN MAID'S ELOPEMENT, AN • 1912 • *Bison* • USA
INDIAN MAID'S SACRIFICE, THE • 1911 • *Joyce Alice* • USA
INDIAN MAID'S STRATEGY, AN • 1913 • *Darkfeather Mona* • USA
INDIAN MAID'S VENGEANCE, THE • 1916 • *Buffalo* • SHT • USA
INDIAN MAID'S WARNING, THE • 1913 • *Roland Ruth* • USA
INDIAN MARTYR, AN • 1911 • *Bison* • USA
INDIAN MASSACRE, THE • 1912 • Ince Thomas H. • USA
INDIAN MORNING see **UTRO INDIA** • 1959
INDIAN MOTHER, THE see **HER INDIAN MOTHER** • 1910
INDIAN MUTINY, THE • 1912 • Thompson Frederick A. • USA
INDIAN NEMESIS, AN • 1911 • *Bison* • USA
INDIAN NEMESIS, AN • 1913 • *Dudley Charles* • USA
INDIAN OCEAN • 1946 • Field Mary • DOC • UKN
INDIAN OUTCAST, AN • 1912 • *Bison* • USA
INDIAN PAINT • 1967 • Foster Norman • USA
INDIAN PETE'S GRATITUDE • 1910 • *Lanning Frank* • USA
INDIAN PHANTASY see **INDIAN FANTASY** • 1957
INDIAN PRINCESS, THE • 1910 • *Nestor* • USA
INDIAN PUDDING • 1930 • *Terry Paul/ Moser Frank (P)* • ANS • USA
INDIAN RAIDERS, THE • 1910 • *Selig* • USA
INDIAN RAIDERS, THE • 1912 • *Reid Wallace* • USA
INDIAN ROMEO AND JULIET • 1912 • Trimble Larry • USA
INDIAN RUNNER'S ROMANCE, THE • 1909 • Griffith D. W. • USA
INDIAN RUSTLERS, THE • 1911 • *Bison* • USA
INDIAN SCARF, THE (USA) see **INDISCHE TUCH, DAS** • 1963
INDIAN SCOUT (UKN) see **DAVY CROCKETT, INDIAN SCOUT** • 1950
INDIAN SCOUT'S VENGEANCE, THE • 1910 • Olcott Sidney • USA
INDIAN SERENADE • 1937 • *Mintz Charles (P)* • ANS • USA
INDIAN SIGNS • 1943 • Roberts Charles E. • SHT • USA
INDIAN SORCERER, THE (USA) see **FAKIR DE SINGAPOUR, LE** • 1908
INDIAN SPIRIT GUIDE, THE • 1969 • Baker Richard • MTV • UKN
INDIAN SQUAW'S SACRIFICE, THE • 1910 • *Defender* • USA
INDIAN STORY see **INDIAN TORTENET** • 1961
INDIAN STORY, AN • 1982 • Bose Tapan K. • DOC • IND
INDIAN SUFFRAGETTES, THE • 1914 • *Darkfeather Mona* • USA
INDIAN SUMMER • 1912 • *Solax* • USA
INDIAN SUMMER • 1913 • Parker Lem B. • USA
INDIAN SUMMER • 1973 • Nikolov Milen • BUL
INDIAN SUMMER • 1987 • Forder Timothy • UKN
INDIAN SUMMER see **BALJE LJETO** • 1971
INDIAN SUMMER see **PRIMA NOTTE DI QUIETE, LA** • 1972
INDIAN SUMMER see **DIXIE LANES** • 1988
INDIAN SUMMER see **SENSOMMER** • 1988
INDIAN SUMMER, AN • 1912 • Griffith D. W. • *Ab* • USA
INDIAN SUMMER OF DRY VALLEY JOHNSON, THE • 1917 • Justice Martin • USA
INDIAN SUMMER (UKN) see **JUDGE STEPS OUT, THE** • 1949
INDIAN SUNBEAM, AN • 1912 • Anderson G. M. • USA
INDIAN TEMPLES • 1937-40 • *Cardiff Jack (Ph)* • DCS • UKN
INDIAN TERRITORY • 1950 • English John • USA
INDIAN TOMB, THE see **INDISCHE GRABMAL I-II, DAS** • 1921
INDIAN TOMB, THE see **INDISCHE GRABMAL, DAS** • 1938
INDIAN TOMBSTONE, THE (UKN) see **INDISCHE GRABMAL I-II, DAS** • 1921
INDIAN TORTENET • 1961 • Jancso Miklos • SHT • HNG • INDIAN ADVENTURE ○ INDIAN STORY
INDIAN TRAIL, THE • 1916 • *Utah* • USA
INDIAN TRAILER, THE • 1909 • *Anderson Broncho Billy* • USA
INDIAN TRAPPER'S PRIZE, AN • 1911 • *Bison* • USA
INDIAN TRAPPER'S VINDICATION, THE • 1915 • *Reliance* • USA
INDIAN UPRISING • 1952 • Nazarro Ray • USA
INDIAN UPRISING AT SANTA FE, THE • 1912 • *Blackwell Carlyle* • USA
INDIAN VENDETTA, AN • 1912 • Fitzhamon Lewin • UKN
INDIAN VESTAL, AN • 1911 • *Bosworth Hobart* • USA
INDIAN VILLAGE see **INDISK BY** • 1951
INDIAN WARPATH, THE • 1916 • *Buffalo* • SHT • USA
INDIAN WHOOPEE • 1933 • Davis Mannie • ANS • USA
INDIAN WIFE'S DEVOTION, AN • 1909 • *Selig* • USA
INDIAN WOMAN'S PLUCK, THE • 1912 • Wilson Frank? • UKN
INDIAN YOUTH -AN EXPLORATION • 1968 • Benegal Shyam • DCS • IND
INDIANA JONES AND THE LAST CRUSADE • 1988 • Spielberg Steven • USA
INDIANA JONES AND THE TEMPLE OF DOOM • 1983 • Spielberg Steven • USA
INDIANAPOLIS see **TO PLEASE A LADY** • 1950
INDIANAPOLIS CAR RACE see **INDI RACE: BAKUSO** • 1967
INDIANAPOLIS SPEEDWAY • 1939 • Bacon Lloyd • USA • DEVIL ON WHEELS (UKN) ○ ROARING CROWD, THE
INDIANENOVERVAL IN DE DODENPAS • 1967 • van der Linden H. J. • NTH • INDIAN ATTACK IN DEATH PASS
INDIANER, DER • 1988 • Schubel Rolf • DOC • FRG • RED INDIAN, THE
INDIANO, EL • 1954 • Soler Fernando • MXC, SPN
INDIAN'S AMBITIONS, AN • 1911 • *Bison* • USA
INDIAN'S APPRECIATION, AN • 1911 • *Lubin* • USA
INDIANS ARE COMING, THE • 1930 • McRae Henry • SRL • USA
INDIANS ARE STILL FAR AWAY, THE (UKN) see **INDIENS SONT ENCORE LOIN, LES** • 1977
INDIAN'S BRIDE, AN • 1909 • *Bison* • USA
INDIAN'S FRIENDSHIP, AN • 1912 • *Anderson Broncho Billy* • USA
INDIANS GAMBLING FOR FURS -IS IT WAR OR PEACE? • 1903 • Rosenthal Joe • UKN, CND
INDIAN'S GRATITUDE, AN • 1910 • *Pathe* • USA
INDIAN'S GRATITUDE, AN • 1912 • *Fielding Romaine* • USA
INDIAN'S GRATITUDE, AN • 1913 • Morty Frank • USA
INDIAN'S HONOR, AN • 1908 • *Vitagraph* • USA
INDIAN'S HONOR, AN • 1913 • Montgomery Frank E., Conway Jack • USA
INDIAN'S HONOR, AN • 1914 • *Downs Rex* • USA
INDIAN'S LAMENT, THE • 1917 • McRae Henry • SHT • USA
INDIAN'S LOVE, AN • 1911 • *Powers* • USA
INDIAN'S LOVE, AN • 1911 • *Bison* • USA
INDIAN'S LOYALTY, AN • 1913 • Griffith D. W.? • USA
INDIAN'S MISTAKE, AN • 1911 • *Bison* • USA
INDIANS, MY BROTHERS see **INDIENS, NOS FRERES** • 1933
INDIAN'S NARROW ESCAPE, THE • 1915 • *Anderson Broncho Billy* • USA
INDIAN'S RECOMPENSE, AN • 1912 • Thornton F. Martin • UKN
INDIAN'S ROMANCE, AN • 1908 • Mottershaw Frank • UKN
INDIAN'S SACRIFICE, AN • 1911 • *Essanay* • USA
INDIAN'S SACRIFICE, THE • 1911 • *Lubin* • USA
INDIAN'S SECRET, THE • 1913 • *Bison* • USA
INDIAN'S TEST, AN • 1910 • *Bison* • USA
INDIC, L' • 1983 • Leroy Serge • FRN
INDICT AND CONVICT • 1974 • Sagal Boris • TVM • USA
INDIEN - EUROPA see **FLUG UM DEN ERDBALL 2, DER** • 1925
INDIEN PARLE, L' • 1967 • Carriere Marcel • DOC • CND
INDIENS DU SAINT-MAURICE • Tessier Albert • DCS • CND
INDIENS KAPLOB MED TIDEN • 1967 • Solbjerghoj Paul, Garnier Derck • ANS • DNM
INDIENS, MES FRERES see **INDIENS, NOS FRERES** • 1933
INDIENS, NOS FRERES • 1933 • Titayna • DOC • FRN • INDIANS, MY BROTHERS ○ INDIENS, MES FRERES
INDIENS SONT ENCORE LOIN, LES • 1977 • Moraz Patricia • SWT • INDIANS ARE STILL FAR AWAY, THE (UKN)
INDIFFERENTI, GLI • 1964 • Maselli Francesco • ITL, FRN • TIME OF INDIFFERENCE (USA) ○ DEUX RIVALES, LES (FRN) ○ TIME FOR INDIFFERENCE
INDIGESTAO • 1926 • Vieira Manuel Luis • PRT
INDIGESTION: OU, CHIRURGIE FIN DE SIECLE, UNE • 1902 • Melies Georges • FRN • UP-TO-DATE SURGERY (USA) ○ SURE CURE FOR INDIGESTION
INDIGOFARVNING I GAMLE DAGE • 1949 • Lassen Hans • DNM
INDIO • 1971 • *Rodas* • MXC
INDIO • 1990 • Margheriti Antonio • ITL
INDIO, EL • 1938 • Vargas De La Maza Armando • MXC • INDIAN, THE
INDIO BLACK, SAI CHE TI DICO: SEI UN GRAN FIGLIO DI.. • 1970 • Parolini Gianfranco • ITL • BOUNTY HUNTERS, THE (UKN) ○ ADIOS, SABATA (USA)
INDIO FIGUEREDO, EL • 1973 • Roche Luis Armando • SHT • VNZ • INDIAN FIGUEREDO, THE
INDIOS A NORD-OVEST • 1964 • De Marchi Luigi • ITL
INDISCHE GRABMAL, DAS • 1938 • Eichberg Richard • FRG • INDIAN TOMB, THE
INDISCHE GRABMAL, DAS • 1959 • Lang Fritz • FRG, ITL, FRN • SEPOLCRO INDIANO, IL (ITL) ○ TOMBEAU HINDOU, LE (FRN) ○ JOURNEY TO THE LOST CITY
INDISCHE GRABMAL I, DAS • 1921 • May Joe • FRG • SENDUNG DES JOGHI, DIE
INDISCHE GRABMAL I-II, DAS • 1921 • May Joe • FRG • MYSTERIES OF INDIA, THE (USA) ○ INDIAN TOMBSTONE, THE (UKN) ○ INDIAN TOMB, THE ○ ABOVE THE LAW ○ HINDU TOMB, THE
INDISCHE GRABMAL II, DAS • 1921 • May Joe • FRG • TIGER VON ESCHNAPUR, DER
INDISCHE NACHTE • 1920 • *Andersen Iven* • FRG
INDISCHE RACHE • 1920 • Jacoby Georg, Lasko Leo • FRG
INDISCHE TOD, DER • 1915 • Hanus Emerich • FRG
INDISCHE TUCH, DAS • 1963 • Vohrer Alfred • FRG • INDIAN SCARF, THE (USA)
INDISCREET • 1931 • McCarey Leo • USA
INDISCREET • 1958 • Donen Stanley • USA, UKN
INDISCREET CORINNE • 1917 • Dillon John Francis • USA
INDISCREET LETTERS • 1909 • *Le Lion* • FRN
INDISCREET STAIRCASE, THE see **INDISCREET STAIRWAY** • 1966
INDISCREET STAIRWAY • 1966 • Ren-Mart • USA • UP THE NAUGHTY STAIRCASE ○ INDISCREET STAIRCASE, THE
INDISCRET, L' • 1969 • Reichenbach Francois • FRN, FRG
INDISCRET AUX BAINS DE MER, L' • 1897 • Melies Georges • FRN • PEEPING TOM AT THE SEASIDE
INDISCRETES, LES • 1955 • Andre Raoul • FRN
INDISCRETION • 1915 • Jones Edgar • USA
INDISCRETION • 1916 • *Grandin Ethel* • SHT • USA
INDISCRETION • 1917 • North Wilfred • USA
INDISCRETION • 1921 • Davis Will S. • USA
INDISCRETION, L' • 1982 • Lary Pierre • FRN
INDISCRETION (UKN) see **CHRISTMAS IN CONNECTICUT** • 1945
INDISCRETION (UKN) see **STAZIONE TERMINI** • 1953
INDISCRETIONS OF AN AMERICAN WIFE (USA) see **STAZIONE TERMINI** • 1953
INDISCRETIONS OF BETTY, THE • 1910 • *Vitagraph* • USA
INDISCRETIONS OF EVE • 1932 • Lewis Cecil • UKN • NEW YEAR'S EVE
INDISCRETS, LES • 1896 • Melies Georges • FRN • PEEPING TOMS, THE
INDISK BY • 1951 • Sucksdorff Arne • DCS • SWD • INDIAN VILLAGE
INDISKRETE FRAU, DIE • 1927 • Boese Carl • FRG
INDISPENSABLE SINNER, THE see **NEOBHODIMIYAT GRESHNIK** • 1971
INDIVIDUALLY YOURS • 1974 • Haig Don • CND
INDIZIENBEWEIS • 1928 • Jacoby Georg • FRG
INDLU YEDIMONI • 1985 • SAF
INDOHANA YOLAHLEKO • 1985 • SAF
INDOLENTES, LOS • 1977 • Estrada Jose • MXC
INDOMABILE ANGELICA, L' (ITL) see **INDOMPTABLE ANGELIQUE** • 1967
INDOMABLE, EL • 1965 • Baledon Rafael • MXC
INDOMITABLE LENI PEICKERT, THE see **UNBEZAHMBARE LENI PEICKERT, DIE** • 1969
INDOMITABLE TEDDY ROOSEVELT, THE • 1983 • Engle Harrison • DOC • USA
INDOMPTABLE ANGELIQUE • 1967 • Borderie Bernard • FRN, ITL, FRG • INDOMABILE ANGELICA, L' (ITL) ○ UNBEZAHMBARE ANGELIQUE (FRG)
INDONESIA CALLING • 1946 • Ivens Joris • SHT • ASL
INDONESIAN FAMILY, AN see **RODZINA INDONEZYJSKA** • 1973
INDOOR OUTING • 1944 • Sparber I. • ANS • USA

INDOVINA CHI VIENE A MERENDA • 1969 • Ciorciolini Marcello • ITL

INDRA LEELA • 1954 • Sharma Rajendra • IND • DRAMA OF GOD

INDRA SABHA • 1932 • *Kajjan* • IND

INDROGABLES, LES • 1972 • Beaudin Jean • SHT • CND

INDUCED SYNDROME see **PLAGUE** • 1978

INDULTO, EL • 1960 • Saenz De Heredia Jose Luis • SPN

INDUNILA • 1968 • Rajapakse Kingsley • SLN • DARK BLUE

INDUSTRIA CERVEJEIRA EM PORTUGAL -2, A • 1968 • Vasconcelos Antonio-Pedro • SHT • PRT

INDUSTRIA CHAVE • 1960 • Mendes Joao • SHT • PRT

INDUSTRIA DEL MATRIMONIO, LA • 1964 • Ayala Fernando • ARG

INDUSTRIA PARA EL CAMPO, UNA • 1967 • Aguirre Javier • SHT • SPN

INDUSTRIAL BRITAIN • 1933 • Flaherty Robert, Elton Arthur, Wright Basil • DCS • UKN

INDUSTRIAL CANADA • 1957 • Cote Guy-L. • DCS • CND • CANADA INDUSTRIEL, LE

INDUSTRIAL SAVOY • 1974 • de Pedro Manuel • DCS • VNZ

INDUSTRIAL SPY see **SANGYO SUPAI** • 1968

INDUSTRIAL SPY FREE-FOR-ALL see **CRAZY DAYO TENKA MUTEKI** • 1967

INDUSTRIAL SYMPHONY see **PHILIPS RADIO** • 1931

INDUSTRIAS REGIONAIS • 1959 • Ribeiro Antonio Lopes • SHT • PRT

INDUSTRIE DE LA TAPISSERIE ET DU MEUBLE SCULPTE, L' • 1935 • Storck Henri • DOC • BLG

INDUSTRIE DU VERRE, L' • Gaudard Lucette • FRN • GLASS INDUSTRY, THE

INDUSTRIE DU VERRE, L' • 1913 • Burel Leonce-Henry • SHT • FRN

INDUSTRIE LOURDE, L' • 1962 • Saleh Tewfik • SHT • EGY

INDUSTRIE LOURDE, L' • 1964 • Shawqi Khalil • SHT • EGY

INDYUKI • 1958 • Mikalowskus V. • USS • TURKEYS

INEBRIATED PHOTOGRAPHER, THE • 1898 • *Cinematograph Co.* • UKN

INELIGIBLE FOR TRIAL • 1969 • Krasnopolsky Vladimir, Uskov Valeri • USS

INES DE CASTRO • 1944 • de Barros Jose Leitao, Garcia Vinolas Manuel Augusto • PRT • DEAD QUEEN, THE

INESFREE see **INNISFREE** • 1989

INESORABILI, GLI • 1951 • Mastrocinque Camillo • ITL • SICILIAN STORY

INEVITABLE, THE • 1913 • Wilson Frank? • UKN

INEVITABLE, THE • 1915 • Coyle Walter • USA

INEVITABLE, THE • 1917 • Goetz Ben • USA • DRAGONFLY, THE

INEVITABLE, THE • 1918 • Edwards Henry • UKN

INEVITABLE MONSIEUR DUBOIS, L' • 1943 • Billon Pierre • FRN

INEVITABLE PENALTY, THE • 1915 • Winter Percy • USA

INEVITABLE RETRIBUTION, THE • 1915 • O'Sullivan Tony • USA

INEXHAUSTIBLE CAB, THE • 1899 • Smith G. A. • UKN

INEXPERIENCED ANGLER, THE • 1909 • Wilson Frank? • UKN

INEZ FROM HOLLYWOOD • 1924 • Green Alfred E. • USA • GOOD BAD GIRL, THE (UKN)

INFAME, LA • 1953 • Zacarias Miguel • MXC

INFAME ACCUSA • 1952 • Vari Giuseppe • ITL

INFAMIA ARABA • 1912 • Caserini Mario • ITL

INFAMIE • 1922 • Waldmann Emil • FRG

INFAMIE D'UNE AUTRE, L' • 1914 • de Morlhon Camille • FRN

INFAMOUS, THE see **AERELOSE, DEN** • 1916

INFAMOUS CONDUCT • 1966 • Martin Richard • UKN

INFAMOUS DON MIGUEL, THE • 1913 • *Cooper Marian* • USA

INFAMOUS LADY, THE • 1928 • Barkas Geoffrey, Barringer Michael • UKN

INFAMOUS MISS REVELL, THE • 1921 • Fitzgerald Dallas M. • USA

INFAMOUS YEARS, THE see **ANOS INFAMES, LOS** • 1975

INFAMY AT SEA see **DECKS RAN RED, THE** • 1958

INFANT AT SNAKEVILLE, THE • 1911 • *Anderson Broncho Billy* • USA

INFANT HEART SNATCHER, AN • 1914 • *Thanhouser* • USA

INFANTILE ADULTS see **VZROSLYI DETI** • 1961

INFANTRYMAN'S BRIDE, THE see **JAAKARIN MORSIAN** • 1939

INFANZIA, VOCAZIONE E PRIMA ESPERIENZE DI GIACOMO CASANOVA, VENEZIANO • 1969 • Comencini Luigi • ITL • CASANOVA

INFATUATION • 1915 • *Fischer Margarita* • USA

INFATUATION • 1925 • Cummings Irving • USA

INFATUATION • 1930 • Geneen Sasha • UKN

INFATUATION • 1989 • Djarot Slamet Rahardjo • INN

INFATUATION see **½-DUAN QING** • 1985

INFEDELI, LE • 1952 • Monicelli Mario, Steno • ITL • UNFAITHFULS, THE (USA) ○ UNFAITHFUL, THE

INFELICE • 1915 • Paul Fred, MacBean L. C. • UKN

INFERENCE EN OPTIQUE • 1957 • Tavano Fred • SHT • FRN

INFERIOR DECORATOR • 1948 • Hannah Jack • ANS • USA

INFERIOR DECORATOR • 1965 • Post Howard • ANS • USA

INFERIOR SEX, THE • 1920 • Henabery Joseph • USA

INFERMIERA, L' • 1975 • Rossati Nello • ITL • SECRETS OF A SENSUOUS NURSE, THE (USA) ○ I WILL IF YOU WILL (UKN) ○ SENSUOUS NURSE, THE ○ NURSE, THE

INFERMIERA DI MIO PADRE, L' • 1975 • Bianchi Mario • ITL

INFERMIERA DI NOTTE, L' • 1979 • Laurenti Mariano • ITL

INFERMIERE, L' • 1914 • Pouctal Henri • FRN

INFERMIERI DELLA MUTUA, GLI • 1969 • Orlandini Giuseppe • ITL

INFERNAL ANGELS see **CANALLAS, LOS** • 1968

INFERNAL CAKEWALK, THE see **CAKE-WALK INFERNAL, LE** • 1903

INFERNAL CAULDRON, THE see **CHAUDRON INFERNAL, LE** • 1903

INFERNAL CAULDRON AND THE PHANTASMAL VAPOURS, THE see **CHAUDRON INFERNAL, LE** • 1903

INFERNAL IDOL, THE see **CRAZE** • 1973

INFERNAL LAIR, THE see **ANTRE INFERNALE, L'** • 1905

INFERNAL MACHINE • 1933 • Varnel Marcel • USA

INFERNAL MACHINE, THE see **MACCHINA AMMAZZACATTIVI, LA** • 1948

INFERNAL MEAL, THE see **REPAS INFERNAL, LE** • 1901

INFERNAL PIG, THE • 1913 • *Handworth Octavia* • USA

INFERNAL RAY, THE see **RAGGIO INFERNALE, IL** • 1967

INFERNAL STREET • 1973 • Shen Jiang • HKG

INFERNAL TRIANGLE, AN • 1913 • Humphrey William • USA

INFERNAL TRIANGLE, THE • 1935 • Douglas Gordon • SHT • USA

INFERNAL TRIO, THE (USA) see **TRIO INFERNAL** • 1974

INFERNO • 1920 • Czinner Paul • AUS • SPIEL MIT DEM TEUFER, DAS

INFERNO • 1953 • Baker Roy Ward • USA

INFERNO • 1979 • Argento Dario • ITL • INFERNO '80

INFERNO '80 see **INFERNO** • 1979

INFERNO, L' • 1909 • De Liguoro Giuseppe • ITL • DANTE'S INFERNO (USA) ○ HELL

INFERNO, L' • 1910 • *Helios* • ITL • DANTE'S INFERNO (USA)

INFERNO A CARACAS (ITL) see **FUNF VOR ZWOLF IN CARACAS** • 1966

INFERNO ADDOSSO, L' • 1959 • Vernuccio Gianni • ITL • LOVE NOW.. PAY LATER (USA) ○ ACCOMPLICES, THE ○ SIN NOW.. PAY LATER

INFERNO DEI MORTI-VIVENTI • 1981 • Mattei Bruno • ITL, SPN • ZOMBIE CREEPING FLESH

INFERNO DEL DESERTO, L' • 1969 • Loy Nanni • ITL

INFERNO DELL'AMORE, L' (ITL) see **LIEBESHOLLE** • 1928

INFERNO DES VERBRECHENS see **DR. MABUSE, DER SPIELER 2** • 1922

INFERNO DI PIGALLE, L' (ITL) see **DESERT DE PIGALLE, LE** • 1957

INFERNO -EIN SPIEL VON MENSCHEN UNSERER ZEIT see **DR. MABUSE, DER SPIELER 2** • 1922

INFERNO GIALLO • 1943 • von Radvanyi Geza • ITL

INFERNO IN DIRETTA • 1985 • Deodato Ruggero • ITL • CUT AND RUN ○ HELL, LIVE

INFERNO IN PARADISE • 1976 • Forsyth Ed • MTV • USA

INFERNO IN SAFEHAVEN see **BLOODSCAPE** • 1989

INFERNO IN SPACE • 1954 • Morse Hollingsworth • MTV • USA

INFERNO -MEN OF OUR TIME see **DR. MABUSE, DER SPIELER 2** • 1922

INFERNO -MENSCHEN DER ZEIT see **DR. MABUSE, DER SPIELER 2** • 1922

INFERNO NEL PACIFICO • 1967 • Medori Alfredo • ITL

INFERNO OF A PIT see **ANAJIGOKU** • 1968

INFERNO OF FIRST LOVE, THE see **HATSUKOI JIGOKU-HEN** • 1968

INFERNO OF FLESH see **NIKUJIGOKU** • 1967

INFERNO OF NAKED WOMEN see **RAJO JIGOKU** • 1968

INFERNO OF THE FLESH see **GENDAI KUNOICHI NIKU JIGOKU** • 1968

INFERNO THUNDERBOLT • 1986 • Ho Godfrey • HKG

INFIDEL, THE • 1922 • Young James • USA

INFIDELE, L' see **KHAINA, AL-** • 1965

INFIDELES, LES • 1972 • Lara Christian • FRN • ADULTERESS, THE

INFIDELIDAD • 1938 • Maicon Boris • MXC

INFIDELITY • 1917 • Miller Ashley • USA

INFIDELITY • 1987 • Rich David Lowell • TVM • USA

INFIDELITY see **DR. RAMEAU** • 1915

INFIDELITY AMERICAN STYLE • 1967 • Johnsen S. N. • USA

INFIDELITY IN DUPLICATE see **ONTROUW IN DUPLO** • 1969

INFIDELITY (UKN) see **CLEMENCEAU CASE, THE** • 1915

INFIDELITY (UKN) see **ALTRI TEMPI** • 1952

INFIDELITY (UKN) see **AMANT DE CINQ JOURS, L'** • 1960

INFIELES, LAS • 1953 • Galindo Alejandro • MXC

INFIERNO DE ALMAS • 1958 • Alazraki Benito • MXC

INFIERNO DE LOS POBRES, EL • 1950 • Orol Juan • MXC

INFIERNO DE TODOS TAN TEMIDO, EL • 1979 • Olhovich Sergio • MXC • HELL SO FEARED BY ALL

INFIERNO TAN TEMIDO, EL • 1980 • de la Torre Raul • ARG • THAT MUCH-DREADED HELL

INFIERNO, TUYA ES LA VICTORIA • 1971 • Franco Jesus • SPN

INFIJAR, EL • 1986 • Hajjar Rafik • LBN • EXPLOSION, THE

INFILTRATOR, THE (USA) see **SERIE NOIRE** • 1954

INFINIE TENDRESSE, UNE • 1969 • Jallaud Pierre • FRN

INFINITE • 1977 • Popescu-Gopo Ion • ANM • RMN • INFINITY

INFINITELY TRANSPARENT BLUE see **KAGIRI NAKU TOMEI NI CHIKAI BLUE** • 1978

INFINITO DI GIACOMO LEOPARDI, L' see **IDILLIO** • 1978

INFINITY see **INFINITE** • 1977

INFIRMES MOTEURS CEREBRAUX • 1973 • Gagne Jacques • DCS • CND

INFIRMIERE DE NUIT, L' • 1966 • Patry Pierre • DCS • CND

INFIRMIERE N'A PAS DE CULOTTE, L' • 1980 • Leroi Francis • FRN

INFIRMIERE RURALE, L' see **COUNTRY NURSE** • 1951

INFIRMIERES PERVERSES • 1978 • Honaro Rene • FRN

INFIRMIERES TRES COMPLAISANTES • 1980 • Baudricourt Michel • FRN

INFIRMIERES TRES SPECIALES • 1976 • Bernard-Aubert Claude • FRN

INFLAMMATION OF NIGHT see **YORU NO TADARE** • 1967

INFLATION • 1928 • Richter Hans • SHT • FRG

INFLATION • 1933 • Myers Zion • SHT • USA

INFLUENCE OF A CHILD, THE • 1913 • *Lawrence Adelaide* • USA

INFLUENCE OF BRONCHO BILLY, THE • 1913 • *Anderson Broncho Billy* • USA

INFLUENCE OF SYMPATHY • 1913 • Salter Harry • USA

INFLUENCE OF THE UNKNOWN, THE • 1913 • Cabanne W. Christy? • USA

INFLUENTIAL AGENT, THE see **AGENT A LE BRAS LONG, L'** • 1908

INFONIE INACHEVEE, L' • 1973 • Frappier Roger • DOC • CND

INFORMATION • 1966 • Frampton Hollis • USA

INFORMATION KID see **FAST COMPANIONS** • 1932

INFORMATION MACHINE, THE • 1957 • Eames Charles, Eames Ray • ANS • USA

INFORMATION RECEIVED • 1961 • Lynn Robert • UKN

INFORMATIQUE EN ALGERIE • 1973 • Rachedi Ahmed • SHT • ALG

INFORME GENERAL • 1977 • Portabella Pedro • SPN

INFORMER, THE • 1912 • Griffith D. W. • USA

INFORMER, THE • 1914 • Barker Reginald? • USA

INFORMER, THE • 1929 • Robison Arthur • UKN

INFORMER, THE • 1935 • Ford John • USA

INFORMER, THE see **MOURSHED, EL** • 1989

INFORMERS, THE • 1963 • Annakin Ken • UKN • UNDERWORLD INFORMERS (USA) ○ SNOUT, THE

INFORTUNADO FORTUNATO, EL • 1952 • Cahen Enrique • ARG

INFORTUNES DE LA VERTU, LES(FRN) see **MARQUIS DE SADE: JUSTINE** • 1968

INFORTUNES D'UN EXPLORATEUR, LES • 1900 • Melies Georges • FRN • MESAVENTURES D'UN EXPLORATEUR ○ MISFORTUNES OF AN EXPLORER

INFRA-MAN • 1976 • Hua-Shan • HKG

INFRA SUPERMAN, THE see **SUPER INFRAMAN, THE** • 1975

INFRASEXUM • 1969 • Tobalina Carlos • USA

INGA -I HAVE LUST (UKN) see **JAG EN OSKULD** • 1968

INGA (USA) see **JAG EN OSKULD** • 1968

INGAGI • 1930 • McKee Grace • USA

INGANNI • 1985 • Faccini Luigi • ITL • DECEPTIONS

INGANNO • 1953 • Brignone Guido • ITL

INGE BLIVER VOKSEN • 1954 • Roos Jorgen • DOC • DNM

INGE LARSEN • 1923 • Steinhoff Hans • FRG

INGE OG STEN SPOR' (KAERLIGHEDENS SPROG) • 1970 • Wickman Torgny • DNM

INGE UND DIE MILLIONEN • 1933 • Engel Erich • FRG

INGEBORG • 1960 • Liebeneiner Wolfgang • FRG

INGEBORG HOLM • 1913 • Sjostrom Victor • SWD • GIVE US THIS DAY

INGEGERD BREMSSEN CASE, THE see **FALLET INGEGERD BREMSSEN** • 1942

INGEN MANS KVINNA • 1953 • Kjellgren Lars-Eric • SWD • NO MAN'S WOMAN

INGEN MORGONDAG • 1957 • Mattsson Arne • SWD • NO TOMORROW

INGEN ROSER, TAKK • 1979 • Erlsbo Leif • NRW • DO ME A FAVOUR

INGEN SA TOKIG SOM JAG • 1955 • Faustman Erik • SWD • NO ONE IS CRAZIER THAN I AM ○ KARLEK PA TURNE

INGEN TID TIL KOERTERN • 1957 • Hovmand Annelise • DNM • NO TIME FOR TENDERNESS

INGEN VAG TILLBAKA • 1947 • Adolphson Edvin • SWD • NO WAY BACK

INGENIEURS ,LES • 1957 • Palardy Jean • DCS • CND

INGENIEURS DE LA MER, LES • 1952 • Renaud • SHT • FRN

INGENIOUS JOHANSSON see **PAHITTIGA JOHANSSON** • 1951

INGENIOUS REVENGE, AN • 1908 • Coleby A. E. • UKN

INGENIOUS SAFE DEPOSIT, AN • 1909 • Stow Percy • UKN

INGENJOR ANDREES LUFTFARD • 1983 • Troell Jan • SWD, NRW, FRG • FLIGHT OF THE EAGLE, THE ○ ANDREES LUFTFARD

INGENTING OVANLIGT • 1957 • Weiss Peter • SHT • SWD • NOTHING UNUSUAL

INGENU, L' • 1971 • Carbonnaux Norbert • FRN

INGENUA, L' • 1975 • Baldanello Gianfranco • ITL

INGENUE LIBERTINE, L' see **MINNE L'INGENUE LIBERTINE** • 1950

INGENUE LIBERTINE, UNE see **EROTICAS VACACIONES DE STELA, LAS** • 1978

INGENUITY • 1912 • *Casey Kenneth* • USA

INGENUO, L' • 1919 • Falena Ugo • ITL

INGHILTERRA NUDA • 1969 • De Sisti Vittorio • ITL • NAKED ENGLAND (UKN)

INGILIZ KEMAL • 1968 • Egilmez Ertem • TRK • KEMAL, THE ENGLISHMAN

INGILIZ KEMAL LAWRENS'E KARIS • 1949 • Akat Lutfu • TRK

INGILIZ KEMALIN OGLO • 1968 • Seden Osman • TRK • SON OF KEMAL, THE ENGLISHMAN, THE

INGILOSI YOKUFA • 1979 • SAF

INGINOCCHIATI STRANIERO.. I CADAVERI NON FANNO OMBRA! • 1970 • Fidani Demofilo • ITL

INGIUSTA CONDANNA, L' • 1952 • Masini Giuseppe • ITL • QUELLI CHE NON MUOIONO ○ GUILT IS NOT MINE (USA)

INGLORIOUS BASTARDS, THE see **QUEL MALEDETTO TRENO BLINDATO** • 1978

INGMAR BERGMAN • 1972 • Bjorkman Stig • DOC • SWD

INGMAR BERGMANIN MA AILMA • 1976 • Donner Jorn • DOC • FNL • THREE SCENES WITH INGMAR BERGMAN ○ TRE SCENER MED INGMAR BERGMAN

INGMAR INHERITANCE, THE see **INGMARSARVET** • 1925

INGMARSARVET • 1925 • Molander Gustaf • SWD • INGMAR INHERITANCE, THE

INGMARSSONERNA • 1919 • Sjostrom Victor • SWD • SON OF INGMAR, THE ○ SONS OF INGMAR, THE

INGO VS. FLOYD see **MASTARNAS MATCH** • 1959

INGOMAR • 1908 • Porter Edwin S. • USA

INGOMAR OF THE HILLS • 1915 • *Essanay* • USA

INGORGO, L' see **BOTTLENECK** • 1979

INGORGO, UNA STORIA IMPOSSIBILE, L' see **BOTTLENECK** • 1979

INGRAT, L' see **NAMRUD, AL-** • 1956

INGRATE, THE • 1908 • Griffith D. W. • USA

INGRATE, THE • 1912 • *Lane Adele* • USA

INGRATE, THE • 1913 • *Nestor* • USA

INGRATE, THE • 1913 • *Majestic* • USA

INGRATE, THE • 1914 • Pollard Harry? • USA

INGRATE, THE • 1915 • Martinek H. O. • UKN

INGRATITUDE • 1909 • *World Films* • USA

INGRATITUDE, L' • 1969 • Fettar Sid-Ali • ALG

INGRATITUDE OF LIZ TAYLOR • 1915 • Le Saint Edward J. • USA

INGRESSO CENTESIMI 10 • 1956 • Ferronetti Ignazio • ITL

INGRID -DIE GESCHICHTE EINES FOTOMODELLS • 1955 • von Radvanyi Geza • FRG

INGRID SULLA STRADA • 1973 • Rondi Brunello • ITL

INHABITANT OF A DESERT ISLE see **ZITEL NEOBITAJEMOVO OSTROVA** • 1915

INHABITANTS OF SPRING, THE see **HABITANTES DE LA PRIMAVERA, LOS** • 1971

INHABITANTS OF THE UNINHABITED HOUSE, THE see **HABITANTES DE LA CASA DESHABITADA, LOS** • 1946

INHERIT THE WIND • 1960 • Kramer Stanley • USA

INHERIT THE WIND • 1988 • Greene David • TVM • USA

INHERITANCE • 1915 • Easton Clem • USA
INHERITANCE • 1920 • Noy Wilfred • UKN
INHERITANCE • 1964 • Irvin John • DCS • UKN
INHERITANCE, THE • 1911 • *Edison* • USA
INHERITANCE, THE • 1964 • Mayer Harold • DOC • USA
INHERITANCE, THE • 1970 • Okeyev Tolomush • USS • HERITAGE, THE
INHERITANCE, THE see **KARAMI-AI** • 1962
INHERITANCE, THE see **DAG DOKTER** • 1978
INHERITANCE, THE (USA) see **UNCLE SILAS** • 1947
INHERITANCE, THE (USA) see **HERENCIA, LA** • 1964
INHERITANCE, THE (USA) see **EREDITA FERRAMONTI, L'** • 1975
INHERITED PASSIONS • 1916 • Hamilton G. P. • USA
INHERITED TAINT, THE • 1911 • *Vitagraph* • USA
INHERITOR, THE see **HERITIER, L'** • 1973
INHERITORS, THE see **GAIETY GIRL, THE** • 1924
INHERITORS, THE see **HERDEIROS, OS** • 1970
INHERITORS, THE see **EREDITA FERRAMONTI, L'** • 1975
INHERITORS, THE (USA) see **ERBEN, DIE** • 1982
INHIBITION • 1976 • Poeti Paolo • ITL • INHIBITIONS ○ CARINE
INHIBITIONS see **INHIBITION** • 1976
INHUMAINE, L' • 1923 • L'Herbier Marcel • FRN • INHUMAN WOMAN, THE (UKN) ○ NEW ENCHANTMENT, THE ○ LIVING DEAD MAN, THE ○ FUTURISMO
INHUMAN FATHER, AN • 1907 • Martin J. H.? • UKN
INHUMAN WOMAN, THE (UKN) see **INHUMAINE, L'** • 1923
INHUMANOIDS: THE EVIL THAT LIES WITHIN • 1986 • ANM • USA
INIBIZIONI DEL DOTTOR GAUDENZI VEDOVA COL COMPLESSO DELLA BUONANIMA • 1971 • Grimaldi Gianni • ITL
INICIACION DE UN SHAMAN • 1979 • Held Raul • DOC • VNZ
INICIACION EN EL AMOR, LA • 1976 • Aguirre Javier • SPN
INIT SA MAGDAMAG • 1983 • Guillen Laurice • PHL • PASSIONS IN THE NIGHT
INITIAL BROOCH, THE • 1916 • Batley Ethyle • UKN
INITIAL KICK see **POCETNI UDARAC** • 1990
INITIATION • 1967 • Belanger Fernand • CND
INITIATION • 1971 • Shead Garry • ASL
INITIATION • 1987 • Pearce Michael • ASL
INITIATION, L' • 1969 • Heroux Denis • CND • INITIATION, THE
INITIATION, THE • 1968 • Wellburn William • USA
INITIATION, THE • 1982 • Stewart Larry • USA
INITIATION, THE see **INITIATION, L'** • 1969
INITIATION, THE see **INIZIAZIONE, L'** • 1987
INITIATION A LA DANSE DES POSSEDEES • 1948 • Rouch Jean • DCS • FRN
INITIATION A LA MORT see **MAGICIENS, LES** • 1975
INITIATION A L'ART • 1945 • Blais Roger • DCS • CND
INITIATION OF SARAH, THE • 1978 • Day Robert • TVM • USA
INIZIAZIONE, L' • 1987 • Mingozzi Gianfranco • ITL, FRN • INITIATION, THE
INJU • 1977 • Kato Tai • JPN • OBSESSION
INJUN TROUBLE • 1938 • Clampett Robert • ANS • USA
INJUN TROUBLE • 1951 • Donnelly Eddie • ANS • USA
INJUN TROUBLE • 1969 • McKimson Robert • ANS • USA
INJURED BOY see **WAKAMONO TACHI NO YORU TO HIRU** • 1963
INJURED MAN, THE see **GEWONDE, DE** • 1966
INJUSTICE! MY LORD! see **YUAN WANG AI TA JEN!** • 1976
INJUSTICE OF JUSTICE, THE • 1916 • *Laemmle* • SHT • USA
INJUSTICE OF MAN, THE • 1911 • *Walthall William* • USA
INJUSTICE (UKN) see **ROAD GANG** • 1936
INK SPOTS, THE • 1955 • Cowan Will • SHT • USA
INKADA • 1981 • SAF
INKEDAMA • 1975 • Sabela Simon • SAF • ORPHAN, THE
INKEY AND CO • 1913 • Lepard Ernest • UKN
INKEY AND CO -GLAD EYE • 1913 • Lepard Ernest • UKN
INKEY AND CO IN BUSINESS • 1913 • Lepard Ernest • UKN
INKI • Jones Charles M. • ASS • USA
INKI • 1973 • Moorse Georg • FRG
INKI AND THE LION • 1941 • Jones Charles M. • ANS • USA
INKI AND THE MYNAH BIRD • 1942 • Jones Charles M. • ANS • USA
INKI AT THE CIRCUS • 1947 • Jones Charles M. • ANS • USA
INKLINGS • 1927 • Fleischer Dave • ASS • USA
INKOGNITO • 1936 • Schneider-Edenkoben Richard • FRG
INKOGNITO IM PARADIES • 1950 • Stockel Joe • FRG
INKRAKTARNA • 1974 • Wickman Torgny • SWD, UKN • LET US PLAY SEX ○ SWEDISH SEX GAMES ○ INTRUDERS, THE ○ INTRUDER, THE
INKUNZI • 1976 • SAF
INLAWFULL • 1937 • Yarbrough Jean • SHT • USA
INLED MIG I FRESTELSE • 1933 • Rodin Gosta • SWD
INMACULADA • 1950 • Bracho Julio • MXC
INMACULADA, LA • 1939 • Gasnier Louis J. • SPN
INMATE TRAINING, PARTS 1 AND 2 • 1967 • Pearson Peter • DOC • CND
INMATES: A LOVE STORY • 1981 • Green Guy • TVM • USA
INMON: SHOJO ZUMA KANTSU • 1967 • Mukoi Kan • JPN • OBSCENE FAMILY INSIGNIA
INMORALES, LOS • 1974 • Balcazar Alfonso • SPN
INN AMONG THE HILLS, THE see **HANUL DINTRE DEALURI** • 1988
INN AT OSAKA, AN see **OSAKA NO YADO** • 1954
INN AT SPESSART, THE see **WIRTSHAUS IM SPESSART, DAS** • 1958
INN FOR TROUBLE • 1960 • Pennington-Richards C. M. • UKN
INN IN OSAKA, AN see **OSAKA NO YADO** • 1954
INN IN TOKYO, AN see **TOKYO NO YADO** • 1935
INN OF DEATH, THE • 1908 • Brooke Van Dyke • USA
INN OF EVIL see **INOCHI BONIFURO** • 1970
INN OF "GOOD REST", THE see **AUBERGE DU BON REPOS, L'** • 1903
INN OF OSAKA see **OSAKA NO YADO** • 1954
INN OF THE BLUE MOON, THE • 1918 • O'Brien John B. • USA
INN OF THE CRUEL DOLLS, THE see **RASTHAUS DER GRAUSAMEN PUPPEN, DAS** • 1967
INN OF THE DAMNED • 1975 • Bourke Terry • ASL
INN OF THE FLYING DRAGON, THE see **FLYGANDE DRAKEN, DEN** • 1980
INN OF THE FRIGHTENED PEOPLE (USA) see **REVENGE** • 1971
INN OF THE SIXTH HAPPINESS • 1958 • Robson Mark • UKN
INN OF THE WINGED GODS, THE • 1914 • *Kerrigan J. Warren* • USA
INN ON DARTMOOR, THE (USA) see **WIRTSHAUS VON DARTMOOR, DAS** • 1964
INN ON THE HEATH, THE • 1914 • Melford Jakidawdra • UKN
INN ON THE RIVER, THE (USA) see **GASTHAUS AN DER THEMSE, DAS** • 1962
INN WAY OUT, THE • 1968 • Short Anthony • SHT • UKN
INN WHERE NO MAN RESTS, THE (USA) see **AUBERGE DU BON REPOS, L'** • 1903
INNAMORATA, L' • 1921 • Genina Augusto • ITL
INNAMORATI, GLI • 1955 • Bolognini Mauro • ITL • WILD LOVE (USA) ○ YOUTH IN LOVE
INNAMORATO PAZZO • 1982 • Castellano, Pipolo • ITL
INNANZI A LUI TREMAVA TUTTA ROMA see **DAVANTI A LUI TREMAVA TUTTA ROMA** • 1946
INNEN & AUSSEN • 1983 • Schoenherr H. H. K. • SWT
INNER AND OUTER SPACE • 1960 • Breer Robert • ANS • USA
INNER BRUTE, THE • 1915 • *Lorenz John* • USA
INNER CHAMBER, THE • 1915 • Melville Wilbert • USA
INNER CHAMBER, THE • 1921 • Jose Edward • USA
INNER CIRCLE, THE • 1912 • Griffith D. W. • USA
INNER CIRCLE, THE • 1946 • Ford Philip • USA
INNER CIRCLE, THE see **PILGRIM LADY, THE** • 1947
INNER CONSCIENCE, THE • 1914 • *Majestic* • USA
INNER EYE, THE • 1974 • Ray Satyajit • SHT • IND
INNER GLOW, THE • 1916 • Davenport Harry • SHT • USA
INNER LIFE see **ZYCIE WENETRZNE** • 1988
INNER MAN, THE • 1922 • Smith Hamilton • USA
INNER MIND, THE • 1911 • *Clary Charles* • USA
INNER MIND, THE • 1916 • *Lily* • USA
INNER RING, THE • 1920 • Terwilliger George W. • SHT • USA
INNER SANCTUM • 1948 • Landers Lew • USA
INNER SCAR (USA) see **CICATRICE INTERIEURE, LA** • 1971
INNER SHRINE, THE • 1917 • Reicher Frank • USA
INNER SOUL, THE • 1916 • Kent Leon D. • SHT • USA
INNER STATE • 1983 • Tchorzewski Krzysztof • PLN
INNER STRUGGLE, THE • 1916 • Sloman Edward • USA
INNER VOICE, THE • 1920 • Neill R. William • USA
INNERDALEN 1984 • 1980 • Einarson Oddvar • DOC • NRW
INNERSPACE • 1987 • Dante Joe • USA
INNERTUBE ANTICS • 1944 • Gordon George • ANS • USA
INNERVIEW, THE • 1973 • Beymer Richard • USA
INNI RAHILA • 1955 • Zulficar Izzeddine • EGY • DEPART TRAGIQUE ○ JE PARS
INNISFREE • 1989 • Guerin Jose Luis • DOC • SPN • INESFREE
INNOCENCE • 1913 • *Panzer Paul* • USA
INNOCENCE • 1917 • Kirkwood James • USA
INNOCENCE • 1923 • Le Saint Edward J. • USA
INNOCENCE see **INNOCENT** • 1918
INNOCENCE see **PANENSTVI** • 1937
INNOCENCE see **INOCENCIA** • 1982
INNOCENCE IS BLISS (UKN) see **MISS GRANT TAKES RICHMOND** • 1949
INNOCENCE OF LIZETTE, THE • 1917 • Kirkwood James • USA
INNOCENCE OF RUTH, THE • 1916 • Collins John H. • USA
INNOCENCE UNPROTECTED • 1942 • Dragoljub • YGS
INNOCENCE UNPROTECTED see **NEVINOST BEZ ZASTITE** • 1968
INNOCENCES IMPUDIQUES • Roy Jean-Claude • FRN
INNOCENT • 1918 • Fitzmaurice George • USA • INNOCENCE
INNOCENT • 1921 • Elvey Maurice • UKN
INNOCENT see **NIGHT MESSAGE, THE** • 1924
INNOCENT see **AMAYAKUDU** • 1968
INNOCENT see **PALMANAM** • 1968
INNOCENT, L' • 1937 • Cammage Maurice • FRN • BOUQUETS FROM NICHOLAS (USA)
INNOCENT, THE • 1985 • Mackenzie John • UKN
INNOCENT, THE • 1987 • el Tayeb Atif • EGY
INNOCENT, THE see **NIRDOSHI** • 1967
INNOCENT, THE (USA) see **INNOCENTE, L'** • 1976
INNOCENT ADVENTURESS, THE • 1919 • Vignola Robert G. • USA
INNOCENT AFFAIR, AN • 1948 • Bacon Lloyd • USA • DON'T TRUST YOUR HUSBAND
INNOCENT AND THE DAMNED, THE see **GIRLS' TOWN** • 1959
INNOCENT AND THE DAMNED, THE see **ASPEN** • 1977
INNOCENT BRIDEGROOM, AN • 1913 • *Crystal* • USA
INNOCENT BURGLAR, AN • 1915 • *Marshall Boyd* • USA
INNOCENT BURGLAR, THE • 1911 • *Costello Maurice* • USA
INNOCENT BUT AWKWARD • 1914 • Drew Sidney • USA
INNOCENT BYSTANDERS • 1972 • Collinson Peter • UKN
INNOCENT CHEAT, THE • 1921 • Wilson Ben • USA
INNOCENT CONSPIRACY, AN • 1913 • *Pilot* • USA
INNOCENT CROOK, AN • 1916 • *Burns Sammy* • USA
INNOCENT DAD • 1913 • *Imp* • USA
INNOCENT DAD • 1914 • *Brennan John E.* • USA
INNOCENT DELILAH, AN • 1914 • Davis Ulysses • USA
INNOCENT EYE, THE • 1958 • Schlesinger John • UKN
INNOCENT GAMES • 1970 • Baltrushaitis A. • USS
INNOCENT GRAFTER, AN • 1912 • Dwan Allan • USA
INNOCENT HEROES see **HANNA'S WAR** • 1988
INNOCENT HUSBANDS • 1925 • McCarey Leo • SHT • USA
INNOCENT IN THE CITY, AN see **BIGONAHI DAR SHAHR** • 1968
INNOCENT INFORMER, AN • 1913 • Miller Ashley • USA
INNOCENT KIDNAPPER, AN • 1915 • *Banner* • USA
INNOCENT LIE, THE • 1916 • Olcott Sidney • USA
INNOCENT LOVE • 1928 • *Glass Gaston* • USA
INNOCENT LOVE, AN • 1982 • Young Roger • TVM • USA
INNOCENT MAGDALENE, AN • 1916 • Dwan Allan • USA
INNOCENT MAID, AN see **HAKOIRI MUSUME** • 1935
INNOCENT MAN, AN • 1989 • Yates Peter • USA
INNOCENT MEETING • 1959 • Grayson Godfrey • UKN
INNOCENT PREY • 1984 • Eggleston Colin • ASL
INNOCENT REVENGE • 1985 • SAF
INNOCENT SALLY see **DIRTY MIND OF YOUNG SALLY, THE** • 1972
INNOCENT SANDWICHMAN, THE • 1915 • *Novelty* • USA
INNOCENT SEX see **TEENAGE INNOCENCE**
INNOCENT SINNER, AN • 1915 • Buel Kenean • USA
INNOCENT SINNER, THE • 1917 • Walsh Raoul • USA
INNOCENT SINNER, THE see **UNINVITED GUEST, THE** • 1924
INNOCENT SINNERS • 1917 • *Binns George H.* • SHT • USA
INNOCENT SINNERS • 1958 • Leacock Philip • UKN
INNOCENT SORCERERS (USA) see **NIEWINNI CZARODZIEJE** • 1959
INNOCENT THEFT, AN • 1912 • *Casey Kenneth* • USA
INNOCENT THIEF, AN • 1914 • *Captain Kettle* • UKN
INNOCENT THIEF, AN • 1915 • Seay Charles M. • USA
INNOCENT TRAITOR, AN • 1915 • *Arey Wayne* • USA
INNOCENT TRAP see **HONORABLES CABALLEROS QUE DEJO LA GUERRA, LOS** • 1977
INNOCENT VAMPIRE, AN • 1916 • Ellis Robert • USA
INNOCENT VAMPIRE, AN • 1917 • *Triangle* • USA
INNOCENT VICTIM see **JACKSON COUNTY JAIL** • 1976
INNOCENT VICTIM, AN • 1914 • Hotaling Arthur D. • USA
INNOCENT VILLAIN, AN • 1915 • Wulze Harry • USA
INNOCENT VILLAIN, AN • 1917 • *Turpin Ben* • USA
INNOCENT WITCH, AN see **OSOREZAN NO ONNA** • 1965
INNOCENTE, L' • 1976 • Visconti Luchino • ITL, FRN • INNOCENT, THE (USA) ○ INTRUDER, THE
INNOCENTE CASIMIRO, L' • 1945 • Campogalliani Carlo • ITL
INNOCENTI PAGANO, GLI • 1953 • Capuano Luigi • ITL
INNOCENTS, LES • 1988 • Techine Andre • FRN
INNOCENTS, THE • 1961 • Clayton Jack • UKN
INNOCENTS, THE see **NEVINATKA** • 1929
INNOCENTS ABROAD see **JUNGEN AUSREISSERINNEN, DIE** • 1971
INNOCENTS ABROAD, THE • 1982 • Salce Luciano • TVM • USA
INNOCENTS AUX MAINS SALES, LES • 1975 • Chabrol Claude • FRN, FRG, ITL • DIRTY HANDS (USA) ○ INNOCENTS WITH DIRTY HANDS
INNOCENTS IN PARIS • 1953 • Parry Gordon • UKN
INNOCENTS OF CHICAGO, THE • 1932 • Lane Lupino • UKN • WHY SAPS LEAVE HOME (USA) ○ MILKY WAY, THE
INNOCENTS OF PARIS • 1929 • Wallace Richard • USA
INNOCENT'S PROGRESS • 1918 • Borzage Frank • USA
INNOCENTS WITH DIRTY HANDS see **INNOCENTS AUX MAINS SALES, LES** • 1975
INNOCENZA E TURBAMENTO • 1974 • Dallamano Massimo • ITL
INNOCULATING HUBBY • 1916 • *Burns Neal* • SHT • USA
INNOMINATO, L' • 1909 • Caserini Mario • ITL
INNS AND OUTS • 1918 • Evans Fred, Evans Joe • UKN
INNU-ASI see **TERRE DE L'HOMME** • 1980
INNU ASI see **TERRE DE L'HOMME** • 1980
INOCENCIA • 1982 • Lima Walter Jr. • BRZ • INNOCENCE
INOCENTE, EL • 1955 • Gonzalez Rogelio A. • MXC
INOCENTE, EL see **PENA DE MUERTE** • 1961
INOCENTE, LA • 1970 • *Zodiaco* • MXC
INOCENTES, LOS • 1960 • Baledon Rafael • MXC
INOCENTES, LOS • 1962 • Bardem Juan Antonio • SPN
INOCHI ARU KAGIRI • 1947 • Kusuda • JPN • AS LONG AS WE LIVE
INOCHI ARUKAGHIRI • 1946 • Yamamura So • JPN • FOR LIFE
INOCHI BONIFURO • 1970 • Kobayashi Masaki • JPN • AT THE RISK OF MY LIFE ○ INN OF EVIL
INOCHI KARETEMO • 1968 • Takamori Tatekazu • JPN • THIS LOVE FOREVER
INOCHI O KAKERU OTOKO • 1958 • Kato Bin • JPN • MAN WHO STAKES HIS LIFE, A
INOCHISHIRAZU NO AITSU • 1967 • Matsuo Akinori • JPN • RECKLESS ONE, THE
INONDATION, L' • 1924 • Delluc Louis • FRN
INONDATIONS • 1969 • Al-Ktari Naceur • MTV • TNS
INOUBLIABLE AMOUR see **H'UBBUN LA ANSAHU** • 1963
INQUEST • 1931 • Samuelson G. B. • UKN
INQUEST • 1939 • Boulting Roy • UKN
INQUEST see **VORUNTERSUCHUNG** • 1931
INQUIETACOES DE UMA MULHER CASADA • 1980 • Salva Alberto • BRZ • ANXIETIES OF A MARRIED WOMAN
INQUIETUDES DE DIANE, LES • 1986 • Leduc Jacques • MTV • CND
INQUIETUDES DE SHANTI ANDIA, LAS • 1946 • Ruiz-Castillo Arturo • SPN
INQUIETUDINE • 1946 • Carpignano Vittorio, Cordero Emilio • ITL
INQUILAB • 1935 • *Kapoor Raj* • IND
INQUILAB • 1984 • *Bachan Amitabh* • IND • JUSTICE
INQUILINA DEL PIANO DI SOPRA, L' • 1977 • Baldi Ferdinando • ITL
INQUILINO, EL • 1958 • Nieves Conde Jose Antonio • SPN
INQUIRING MIND, THE • 1960 • Bairstow David • DOC • CND
INQUIRY, THE see **INCHIESTA, L'** • 1971
INQUIRY, THE (USA) see **INCHIESTA, L'** • 1987
INQUISICION • 1976 • Molina Jacinto • SPN • INQUISITION (USA)
INQUISIDOR, EL • 1974 • Arias Bernardo • ARG, PRU • INQUISITOR, THE
INQUISIT VISIT, THE • 1961 • Kneitel Seymour • ANS • USA
INQUISITION (USA) see **INQUISICION** • 1976
INQUISITIVE BERTIE • 1906 • Hough Harold • UKN • BERTIE AT THE GYMNASIUM
INQUISITIVE BOOTS, THE • 1905 • Fitzhamon Lewin • UKN
INQUISITIVE IKE • 1914 • Elvey Maurice? • UKN
INQUISITIVE LETTER, THE • 1961 • Tyrlova Hermina • ANM • CZC
INQUISITIVE VISITORS AT THE DYE WORKS • 1905 • Green Tom? • UKN
INQUISITOR, THE see **INQUISIDOR, EL** • 1974
INQUISITOR, THE see **GARDE A VUE** • 1982
INQULBAD • 1937 • Bose Debaki • IND
INRAN • 1968 • Mukoi Hiroshi • JPN • LEWD ONES, THE
INS AND THE OUTS, THE (USA) see **UNS ET LES AUTRES, LES** • 1981
INS BLAUE LEBEN (FRG) see **CASTELLI IN ARIA** • 1939
INS BLAUWEISSE HIMMELBEIT • 1976 • Brummer Alois • FRG

INSAAN JAG UTHA • 1959 • *Burman S. D. (M)* • IND
INSACIABLE • 1978 • Bo Armando • ARG • INSATIABLE
INSACIABLE, LA • 1946 • Ortega Juan J. • MXC
INSAF • 1937 • *Biswas Anil (M)* • IND
INSAISISSABLE FREDERIC, L' • 1945 • Pottier Richard • FRN
INSAN IKI KERE YASAR • 1968 • Gulyuz Aram • TRK • YOU ONLY LIVE TWICE
INSANE CHRONICLE see **BLAZNOVA KRONIKA** • 1964
INSANE HEIRESS, THE • 1910 • *Yankee* • USA
INSANITY • 1968 • Kiisk Kaliu • USS
INSANITY • *Stamp Terence*
INSANITY see **STRIP-TEASE** • 1976
INSANIYAT • 1955 • Vasan S. S. • IND
INSATIABLE • 1980 • Daniels Godfrey • USA
INSATIABLE see **INSACIABLE** • 1978
INSATIABLE 2 • 1984 • Daniels Godfrey • USA
INSATIABLE, L' • Lewis James H. • FRN
INSATIABLE, THE see **AHORTAGOS, O** • 1968
INSATIABLE ALICIA AND THE MARQUIS see **MARQUES, LA MENOR Y EL TRAVESTI, EL** • 1982
INSATIABLE BEE, THE see **TELHETETLEN MEHECSKE** • 1958
INSATIABLES, THE (UKN) see **INSAZIABILI, GLI** • 1969
INSATISFAITE, L' • 1971 • Pallardy Jean-Marie • FRN • UNSATISFIED, THE (UKN)
INSAZIABILI, GLI • 1969 • De Martino Alberto • ITL, FRG • INSATIABLES, THE (UKN) ○ FEMMINE INSAZIABILI
INSAZIABILI, LE (ITL) see **TANT D'AMOUR PERDU** • 1958
INSCRIPTION, THE • 1914 • Jones Edgar • USA
INSCRUTABLE DREW, INVESTIGATOR • 1926 • Coleby A. E. • SER • UKN
INSECT see **BLUE MONKEY** • 1987
INSECT, THE see **NIPPON KONCHUKI** • 1963
INSECT TO INJURY • 1956 • Tendlar Dave • ANS • USA
INSECT WOMAN • Yung Kim Kee • SKR
INSECT WOMAN, THE (USA) see **NIPPON KONCHUKI** • 1963
INSECTS, THE • 1963 • Murakami Jimmy T. • ANS • UKN
INSECTS, THE (USA) see **AVIACIONNAJA NEDELJA NASEKOMYCH** • 1912
INSEGNANTE, L' • 1975 • Cicero Nando • ITL
INSEGNANTE BALLA.. CON TUTTA LA CLASSE, L' • 1979 • Carnimeo Giuliano • ITL
INSEGNANTE VA IN COLLEGIO, L' • 1978 • Laurenti Mariano • ITL
INSEGNANTE VIENE A CASA, L' • 1978 • Tarantini Michele Massimo • ITL
INSEKTSOMMER • 1976 • Andersen Knut • NRW
INSEL, DIE • 1934 • Steinhoff Hans • FRG
INSEL, DIE • 1974 • Wenders Wim • SHT • FRG • ISLAND, THE
INSEL DER 1,000 FREUDEN, DIE • 1977 • Frank Hubert • FRG • SEX FEVER ON AN ISLAND OF 1,000 DELIGHTS ○ SEX FEVER ○ SEX SLAVES
INSEL DER AMAZONEN • 1960 • Meyer Otto • FRG • SEVEN DARING GIRLS (USA)
INSEL DER DAMONEN, DIE • 1933 • Dalsheim Friedrich • FRG • BLACK MAGIC
INSEL DER GEZEICHNETEN, DIE • 1920 • Delmont Joseph • FRG
INSEL DER GLUCKLICHEN, DIE • 1919 • Coenen Josef • FRG
INSEL DER SCHWANE • 1983 • Zschoche Hermann • GDR • ISLAND OF SWANS ○ SWAN ISLAND
INSEL DER SELIGEN, DIE • 1913 • Reinhardt Max • FRG • ISLE OF THE BLESSED, THE
INSEL DER SILBERREIHER, DIE see **OSTROV STRIBRNYCH VOLAVEK** • 1976
INSEL DER TRAUME, DIE • 1925 • Stein Paul L. • FRG • ANSTANDIGE FRAU, EINE ○ ISLE OF DREAMS, THE
INSEL DER VERBOTENEN KUSSE, DIE • 1926 • Jacoby Georg • FRG
INSEL DER VERSCHOLLENEN, DIE • 1921 • Gad Urban • FRG
INSEL OHNE MORAL • 1950 • von Collande Volker • FRG
INSEMINOID • 1982 • Warren Norman J. • UKN • HORROR PLANET (USA)
INSEPARABLES, THE • 1929 • Millar Adelqui, Stafford John • UKN
INSERTS • 1975 • Byrum John • UKN
INSHAVOGUE • 1911 • *Yankee* • USA
INSIANG • 1977 • Brocka Lino • PHL
INSIDE A GIRLS' DORMITORY (USA) see **DORTOIR DES GRANDES** • 1953
INSIDE A NUDE PARTY • 1966 • *De Cenzie Peter* • USA
INSIDE AMY see **MOGLIETTINA, LA** • 1975
INSIDE DAISY CLOVER • 1965 • Mulligan Robert • USA
INSIDE DESIREE COUSTEAU • 1979 • Gucci Leon • USA
INSIDE DETROIT • 1955 • Sears Fred F. • USA
INSIDE EDGES • 1975 • Emshwiller Ed • USA
INSIDE FACTS • 1915 • Stanton Richard • USA
INSIDE FIGHTING CANADA • 1942 • Beveridge Jane Marsh • DOC • CND
INSIDE FRANCE • 1944 • Daly Tom • DOC • CND
INSIDE INFORMATION • 1934 • Hill Robert F. • USA
INSIDE INFORMATION • 1939 • Lamont Charles • USA
INSIDE INFORMATION • 1957 • Tully Montgomery • UKN
INSIDE INFORMATION (UKN) see **LONE PRAIRIE, THE** • 1943
INSIDE JENNIFER WELLES • 1977 • Welles Jennifer • USA
INSIDE JOB • 1946 • Yarbrough Jean • USA
INSIDE JOB, AN • 1988 • Hickey Aidan • SHT • IRL
INSIDE JOB (UKN) see **ALPHA CAPER, THE** • 1973
INSIDE LOOKING OUT • 1977 • Cox Paul • ASL
INSIDE MAN, THE see **SLAGSKAMPEN** • 1984
INSIDE MARILYN CHAMBERS • 1976 • Mitchell Jim • DOC • USA
INSIDE MOVES • 1980 • Donner Richard • USA
INSIDE NORTH VIETNAM • 1967 • Greene Felix • DOC • USA
INSIDE OF THE CUP, THE • 1921 • Capellani Albert • USA
INSIDE OF THE WHITE SLAVE TRAFFIC, THE • 1913 • *London Samuel H.* • USA
INSIDE OUT • Shamshum George • LBN
INSIDE OUT • 1971 • Parker Graham • CND
INSIDE OUT • 1975 • Duffell Peter • UKN, FRG • GOLDEN HEIST, THE ○ HITLER'S GOLD
INSIDE OUT • 1986 • Taicher Robert • USA
INSIDE OUT see **VIE A L'ENVERS, LA** • 1964
INSIDE SEKA • 1980 • Yontz Seka, Yontz Ken • USA
INSIDE STORY • 1938 • Cortez Ricardo • USA
INSIDE STORY, THE • 1948 • Dwan Allan • USA
INSIDE STRAIGHT • 1951 • Mayer Gerald • USA
INSIDE THE COFFEE PLANTATION see **CAFETAL ADENTRO** • 1989
INSIDE THE EARTH • 1910 • *Pathe* • FRN
INSIDE THE GREAT PYRAMID see **I DEN STORE PYRAMIDE** • 1974
INSIDE THE KREMLIN see **IZ GLUBINY STOLETIY** • 1961
INSIDE THE LABYRINTH • 1986 • DOC • UKN
INSIDE THE LAW • 1942 • MacFadden Hamilton • USA
INSIDE THE LINES • 1918 • Hartford David M. • USA
INSIDE THE LINES • 1930 • Pomeroy Roy J. • USA
INSIDE THE MAFIA • 1959 • Cahn Edward L. • USA
INSIDE THE ROOM • 1935 • Hiscott Leslie • UKN
INSIDE THE THIRD REICH • 1982 • Chomsky Marvin • TVM • USA
INSIDE THE U.S.S.R. • 1961 • Stepanova Lidiya, Zenyakin Arkadij • USS
INSIDE THE WALLS OF FOLSOM PRISON • 1951 • Wilbur Crane • USA • STORY OF FOLSOM, THE
INSIDE TIP, AN • 1915 • *Foster Morris* • USA
INSIDENT OF PARADYSSTRAND • 1973 • SAF
INSIDIOUS DR. FU MANCHU, THE see **RETURN OF DR. FU MANCHU, THE** • 1930
INSIEME • 1979 • Loy Nanni • ITL
INSIGNE MYSTERIEUX, L' • 1923 • Desfontaines Henri • FRN
INSIGNIFICANCE • 1985 • Roeg Nicolas • UKN
INSINUATION • 1922 • Wilson Margery • USA
INSOLENT L' • 1972 • Roy Jean-Claude • FRN • INSOLENT, THE
INSOLENT, THE see **INSOLENT L'** • 1972
INSOLENT MATADOR, THE • 1960 • Halas John • ANS • UKN
INSOLITA Y ESPECTACULAR MARCHA DE CHUCHO EL ESENIO Y SU COMBO LATINO-AMERICANOS • 1972 • Odreman Mauricio • VNZ • CHUCHO AND THE LATIN-AMERICANS
INSOLITO EMBARAZO DE LOS MARTINEZ, EL • 1975 • Aguirre Javier • SPN
INSOMNIA • 1916 • Metcalfe Earl • SHT • USA
INSOMNIA IS GOOD FOR YOU • 1957 • Arliss Leslie • UKN
INSOMNIA (UKN) see **INSOMNIE** • 1965
INSOMNIAC, THE • 1971 • Giesler Rodney • UKN
INSOMNIE • 1965 • Etaix Pierre • SHT • FRN • INSOMNIA (UKN)
INSOUMIS, L' • 1964 • Cavalier Alain • FRN, ITL
INSOUMIS, LES see **FIGHT FOR US** • 1989
INSOUMISES, LES • 1955 • Gaveau Rene • FRN • QUATRE VEUVES, LES
INSPAN • 1953 • SAF
INSPECTEUR AIME LA BAGARRE, L' • 1956 • Devaivre Jean • FRN
INSPECTEUR CONNAIT LA MUSIQUE, L' • 1955 • Josipovici Jean • FRN • BLUES
INSPECTEUR GREY • 1936 • de Canonge Maurice • FRN
INSPECTEUR GREY CONTRE X see **GREY CONTRE X** • 1939
INSPECTEUR LA BAVURE • 1980 • Zidi Claude • FRN
INSPECTEUR LAVARDIN • 1986 • Chabrol Claude • FRN
INSPECTEUR SERGIL • 1946 • Daroy Jacques • FRN
INSPECTEUR TAHAR, L' • 1969 • Riad Mohamed Slimane • ALG
INSPECTION see **WIZJA LOKALNA** • 1965
INSPECTOR, EL see **CALTZONZIN INSPECTOR** • 1972
INSPECTOR, THE • 1937 • Newman Widgey R. • UKN
INSPECTOR, THE • 1961 • Dunne Philip • UKN • LISA
INSPECTOR, THE see **REVISOR** • 1933
INSPECTOR, THE see **INSPEKTOR** • 1965
INSPECTOR AND THE NIGHT, THE see **INSPECTORAT I NOSHTA** • 1963
INSPECTOR CALLS, AN • 1954 • Hamilton Guy • UKN
INSPECTOR CHOCOLATE see **SHENTAN ZHUGULI** • 1987
INSPECTOR CLOUSEAU • 1968 • Yorkin Bud • UKN
INSPECTOR GENERAL, THE • 1949 • Koster Henry • USA • HAPPY TIMES
INSPECTOR GENERAL, THE see **REVISOR** • 1933
INSPECTOR GENERAL, THE see **REVIZOR** • 1952
INSPECTOR GOES HOME, THE see **INSPEKTOR SE VRACA KUCI** • 1959
INSPECTOR HORNLEIGH • 1939 • Forde Eugene J. • UKN
INSPECTOR HORNLEIGH GOES TO IT • 1941 • Forde Walter • UKN • MAIL TRAIN (USA)
INSPECTOR HORNLEIGH ON HOLIDAY • 1939 • Forde Walter • UKN
INSPECTOR IS KILLED, THE • 1973 • *Conte Richard* • ITL
INSPECTOR LO GATTO see **COMMISSARIO LO GATTO, IL** • 1987
INSPECTOR MAIGRET (USA) see **MAIGRET TEND UN PIEGE** • 1957
INSPECTOR MASK • 1950-56 • Kolar Boris, Kostelac Nicola, Mimica Vatroslav, Vrbanic Ivo • ASS • YGS
INSPECTOR PIMPLE • 1914 • Evans Fred, Evans Joe • UKN
INSPECTOR RETURNS HOME, THE see **INSPEKTOR SE VRACA KUCI** • 1959
INSPECTOR VICTOR CONTRA ARSENIO LUPIN, EL • 1945 • Peon Ramon • MXC
INSPECTOR WEARS SKIRTS II, THE • 1989 • Chin Wellson • HKG
INSPECTORAT I NOSCTTA see **INSPECTORAT I NOSHTA** • 1963
INSPECTORAT I NOSHTA • 1963 • Vulchanov Rangel • BUL • INSPECTOR AND THE NIGHT, THE ○ INSPECTORAT I NOSCTTA
INSPECTOR'S BIRTHDAY, THE • 1903 • Collins Alf • UKN
INSPECTOR'S DOUBLE, THE • 1916 • Beaudine William • SHT • USA
INSPECTOR'S STORY, THE • 1913 • O'Neil Barry • USA
INSPECTOR'S WIFE, THE • 1918 • *Jaxon* • USA
INSPEKCJA PANA ANATOLA • 1959 • Rybkowski Jan • PLN • MR. ANATOL'S INSPECTION
INSPEKTOR • 1965 • Djukanovic Milo • YGS • INSPECTOR, THE
INSPEKTOR SE VRACA KUCI • 1959 • Mimica Vatroslav • ANS • YGS • INSPECTOR RETURNS HOME, THE ○ INSPECTOR GOES HOME, THE
INSPIRACE • 1949 • Zeman Karel • ANS • CZC • INSPIRATION (USA)
INSPIRATION • 1915 • *Munson Audrey* • USA
INSPIRATION • 1928 • McEveety Bernard F. • USA • LOVE'S TEST (UKN)
INSPIRATION • 1930 • Brown Clarence • USA
INSPIRATION (USA) see **INSPIRACE** • 1949
INSPIRATIONS • 1982 • Sherman Joe • USA
INSPIRATIONS OF HARRY LARRABEE, THE • 1917 • Bracken Bertram • USA
INSTALLMENT COLLECTOR, THE • 1908 • *Essanay* • USA
INSTALLMENT PLAN, THE • 1912 • *Majestic* • USA
INSTALLMENT PLAN, THE • 1917 • De Vonde Chester M. • SHT • USA
INSTALLMENT PLAN MARRIAGE, THE • 1913 • *Crystal* • USA
INSTANT COFFEE see **FISCHIA IL SESSO** • 1974
INSTANT FILM #2 • Brittin Charles • SHT • USA
INSTANT FRENCH • 1965 • Bairstow David • DOC • CND
INSTANT IN THE WIND, AN • 1988 • Rademakers Fons • BLG
INSTANT JUSTICE see **MARINE ISSUE** • 1986
INSTANT NYMPHO, 3+3 + SEX • 1970 • USA
INSTANT PICTURES (USA) see **POLAROID** • 1978
INSTANT PRES D'ELLE, UN • 1974 • Benoit Denyse • CND
INSTANT SEX • 1980 • Godfrey Bob • ANS • UKN
INSTANT SUCCESS see **OVERNIGHT SUCCESS** • 1970
INSTANTANEOUS NERVE POWDER • 1909 • *Pathe* • FRN
INSTANTANES A JUAN-LES-PINS • 1953 • Mariaud Robert • SHT • FRN
INSTANTES DISPERSOS • 1972 • Barrero Jose Antonio • SHT • SPN
INSTINCT see **HONNO** • 1966
INSTINCT, L' • 1916 • Pouctal Henri • FRN
INSTINCT, L' • 1930 • Mathot Leon • FRN
INSTINCT DE FEMME • Othnin-Girard Claude • FRN
INSTINCT EST MAITRE, L' • 1916 • Feyder Jacques • FRN
INSTINCT OF MALE AND FEMALE see **MESU-OSU NO HONNO** • 1967
INSTITUT AGRONOMIQUE • 1967 • Ifticene Mohamed • SHT • ALG
INSTITUTE FOR REVENGE • 1979 • Annakin Ken • TVM • USA
INSTITUTEUR, L' see **MUALLIM, AL-** • 1974
INSTITUTION, THE see **ANSTALT, DIE** • 1978
INSTITUTIONAL QUALITY • 1969 • Landow George • USA
INSTITUTS FAMILIAUX see **JOURNEES D'ETUDES** • 1960
INSTRUCTION BY CORRESPONDENCE • 1909 • *Vitagraph* • USA
INSTRUCTION PERIOD see **JIDAI NO KYOJI** • 1932
INSTRUCTIONAL STEAMER 'RED STAR' see **INSTRUKTORII PAROKHOD 'KRASNAIA ZVEZDA'** • 1920
INSTRUCTIVE STORY see **SHIDO MONOGATARI** • 1941
INSTRUCTOR, THE • 1983 • Bendell Don • USA
INSTRUKTORII PAROKHOD 'KRASNAIA ZVEZDA' • 1920 • Vertov Dziga • USS • INSTRUCTIONAL STEAMER 'RED STAR'
INSTRUMENTS OF FATE • 1915 • Batley Ethyle • UKN
INSTRUMENTS OF THE ORCHESTRA • 1946 • Mathieson Muir • DOC • UKN
INSTRUMENTS OF THE ORCHESTRA • 1971 • Large Brian • SHT • UKN
INSULT • 1932 • Lachman Harry • UKN
INSULTIN' THE SULTAN • 1934 • *Iwerks Ub (P)* • ANS • USA
INSULTING THE SULTAN • 1920 • Roach Hal • SHT • USA
INSURANCE AGENT, THE • 1913 • Johnson Arthur • USA
INSURANCE FRAUD, AN • 1919 • Carlton Frank • UKN
INSURANCE INVESTIGATOR • 1951 • Blair George • USA
INSURANCE MAN, THE • 1985 • Eyre Richard • UKN
INSURANCE MAN FROM INGERSOLL, THE • 1976 • Pearson Peter • MTV • CND
INSURANCE NIGHTMARE, THE • 1915 • Ward Chance E. • USA
INSURANCE SWINDLERS, THE • 1916 • Stanton Richard • SHT • USA
INSURE YOUR WIFE see **ASEGURA A SU MUJER** • 1935
INSURED FOR LIFE • 1960 • *Halas John (P)* • ANS • UKN
INSURGENT MEXICO see **KRASNYE KOLOKOLA** • 1981
INSURGENT SENATOR, THE • 1912 • *Phillips Augustus* • USA
INSURGENTE, EL • 1940 • Sevilla Raphael J. • MXC
INSURING CUTEY • 1915 • Van Wally • USA
INSURRECCION DE LA BURGUESIA, LA see **BATALLA DE CHILE: PART 1** • 1974
INSURRECTION, THE • 1915 • Terwilliger George W. • USA
INSURRECTION OF THE BOURGEOISE see **BATALLA DE CHILE: PART 1** • 1974
INSURRECTO, THE • 1911 • *Kalem* • USA
INTA HABIBI • 1956 • Shahin Youssef • EGY • YOU ARE MY LOVE
INTA UMRY • 1964 • Salman Mohammed • LBN • TU ES MA VIE
INTABA YEGOLIDE • 1985 • SAF
INTEGRAL VIBRANTE DE ALEJANDRO OTERO • 1973 • Cosmi Carlo • SHT • VNZ • ARTIST ALEXANDER OTERO, THE
INTEGRATION • 1960 • Garceau Raymond • DCS • CND
INTEGRITY OF THE HONOURABLE, THE see **SALAMAT AL JALIL** • 1985
INTELEKTUALISTA • 1969 • Giersz Witold • ANS • PLN • INTELLECTUALS, THE
INTELLECTUALS, THE see **INTELEKTUALISTA** • 1969
INTELLIGENCE MEN, THE • 1965 • Asher Robert • UKN • SPYLARKS (USA)
INTENT TO KILL • 1958 • Cardiff Jack • UKN
INTENTIONS OF MURDER see **AKAI SATSUI** • 1964
INTENZIONE, L' • 1975 • Masi Marco • ITL
INTER NOS see **OKKAR A MILLI** • 1982
INTER RAIL • 1981 • Svensson Birgitta • SWD
INTERCEPTED GETAWAY, AN • 1914 • *Majestic* • USA
INTERCEPTED GIFT, AN • 1915 • *Alhambra* • USA
INTERCEPTED VENGEANCE, AN • 1915 • Davis Ulysses • USA
INTERDIT, L' • 1976 • Maheu Pierre • DOC • CND
INTERDIT AU PUBLIC • 1949 • Pasquali Alfred • FRN
INTERDIT AUX MOINS DE 13 ANS • 1982 • Bertucelli Jean-Louis • FRN
INTERDIT DE SEJOUR • 1954 • de Canonge Maurice • FRN • PRICE OF LOVE, THE

INTERESADAS, LAS • 1952 • Gonzalez Rogelio A. • MXC
INTERESSEN DER BANK KONNEN NICHT DIE INTERESSEN SEIN, DIE LINA BRAAKE HAT see **LINA BRAAKE** • 1975
INTERESTING STORY, AN • 1904 • Williamson James • UKN
INTERFACE • 1984 • Anderson Andy • USA
INTERFERENCE • 1929 • Mendes Lothar, Pomeroy Roy J. • USA
INTERFERENCE see **EASY LIVING** • 1949
INTERFERENCE see **INTERFERENS** • 1982
INTERFERENCE OF BRONCHO BILLY, THE • 1914 • *Anderson Broncho Billy* • USA
INTERFERENS • 1982 • Leth Jorgen • DNM • INTERFERENCE
INTERFERIN' GENT, THE • 1927 • Thorpe Richard • USA
INTERGALACTIC ZOO • 1964 • Goldscholl Morton, Goldscholl Mildred • ANS • USA
INTERGIRL • 1989 • Todorovsky Petr • USS
INTERIM • 1951 • Brakhage Stan • SHT • USA
INTERIM BALANCE see **VERNI ZUSTANEME** • 1945
INTERIOR • Munteanu Stefan • ANM • RMN
INTERIOR 29 see **ESKINITA 29** • 1968
INTERIOR DECORATOR • 1942 • Beauchamp Clem • SHT • USA
INTERIOR MECHANISM see **MECANISMO INTERIOR** • 1971
INTERIOR OF A CONVENT see **INTERNO DI UN CONVENTO** • 1977
INTERIOR OF A RAILWAY CARRIAGE –BANK HOLIDAY, THE • 1901 • Hepworth Cecil M. • UKN
INTERIORS • 1978 • Allen Woody • USA
INTERLOPER, THE • 1918 • Apfel Oscar • USA • HER GREAT MOMENT
INTERLUDE • 1957 • Sirk Douglas • USA
INTERLUDE • 1967 • Billington Kevin • UKN • WHEN TOMORROW COMES
INTERLUDE see **I DODENS VANTRUM** • 1946
INTERLUDE BY CANDLELIGHT see **TUSSENSPEL BIJ KAARSLICHT** • 1959
INTERLUDIUM ELECTRONICUM • 1964 • Hoving Hattum • SHT • NTH
INTERMEDE • 1965 • Labrecque Jean-Claude • DCS • CND
INTERMEZZO • 1919 • Muller-Hagen Carl? • FRG
INTERMEZZO • 1936 • Molander Gustaf • SWD
INTERMEZZO • 1936 • von Baky Josef • FRG
INTERMEZZO • 1939 • Ratoff Gregory • USA • ESCAPE TO HAPPINESS (UKN) ○ INTERMEZZO, A LOVE STORY
INTERMEZZO • 1974 • Popescu-Gopo Ion • ANM • RMN
INTERMEZZO, A LOVE STORY see **INTERMEZZO** • 1939
INTERMEZZO CRIMINAL • 1953 • Barth-Moglia Luis • ARG
INTERMEZZO EINER EHE IN SIEBEN TAGEN see **SOLL MAN HEIRATEN?** • 1925
INTERMISSION • 1971 • *Harvey Marshall/rogers Bob/boyd Steve (P)* • SHT • USA
INTERMITTENT PORTRAYAL see **OCANA, UN RETRATO INTERMITENTE** • 1978
INTERNADO PARA SENORAS • 1943 • Martinez Solares Gilberto • MXC
INTERNAL AFFAIRS • 1989 • Figgis Mike • USA
INTERNATIONAL AFFAIR, AN • 1950 • *Austin John* • SHT • UKN
INTERNATIONAL AIRPORT • 1985 • Dubin Charles S., Chaffey Don • TVM • USA
INTERNATIONAL BALLET COMPETITION –VARNA • 1964 • Tosheva Nevena • DOC • BUL
INTERNATIONAL COUNTERFEITERS • 1957 • *Howard Gordon* • FRG
INTERNATIONAL CRIME • 1938 • Lamont Charles • USA
INTERNATIONAL EUCHARISTIC CONGRESS • 1926 • *Fox Film Corp.* • DOC • USA
INTERNATIONAL EXCHANGE • 1905 • Fitzhamon Lewin • UKN
INTERNATIONAL FESTIVAL IN EDINBURGH, THE • 1956 • Stiopul Savel • DOC • RMN
INTERNATIONAL GORILLEY • 1990 • Mohammad Jan • PKS
INTERNATIONAL HEART BREAKER, AN • 1911 • *Fuller Mary* • USA
INTERNATIONAL HOTEL (USA) see **VIPS, THE** • 1963
INTERNATIONAL HOUSE • 1933 • Sutherland A. Edward • USA
INTERNATIONAL HOUSE • 1966 • Wolman Dan • ISR
INTERNATIONAL JAZZ FESTIVAL • 1962 • Ledoux Patrick • SHT • BLG
INTERNATIONAL LADY • 1941 • Whelan Tim • USA
INTERNATIONAL MARRIAGE, AN • 1916 • Lloyd Frank • USA
INTERNATIONAL PROSTITUTION see **BRIGADE CRIMINELLE** • 1980
INTERNATIONAL REVELS • 1940 • Ceballos Larry • SHT • USA
INTERNATIONAL REVUE • 1936 • Harris Buddy • UKN
INTERNATIONAL ROMANCE, AN • 1912 • Cox George L. • USA
INTERNATIONAL SETTLEMENT • 1938 • Forde Eugene J. • USA
INTERNATIONAL SMORGASBROAD • 1965 • Mahon Barry • USA • SMORGASBROAD
INTERNATIONAL SMUGGLING GANG see **KOKUSAI MITSUYUDAN** • 1944
INTERNATIONAL SNEAK, AN • 1917 • Fishback Fred C.?, Cline Eddie? • SHT • USA
INTERNATIONAL SPIES, THE (USA) see **LIEUTENANT DARING AND THE PLANS OF THE MINEFIELDS** • 1912
INTERNATIONAL SPY see **SPY RING** • 1938
INTERNATIONAL SPY see **SMASHING THE SPY RING** • 1939
INTERNATIONAL SPY, THE • 1917 • Howard George Bronson • SHT • USA
INTERNATIONAL SQUADRON • 1941 • Mendes Lothar • USA • FLIGHT PATROL
INTERNATIONAL TOURNEE OF ANIMATION see **TOURNEE TITLES** • 1981
INTERNATIONAL VELVET • 1967 • Warhol Andy • USA
INTERNATIONAL VELVET • 1978 • Forbes Bryan • UKN
INTERNATIONAL WOODPECKER • 1957 • Smith Paul J. • ANS • USA
INTERNATIONAL WOOLMARK, THE • 1965 • Broun M. L. • DCS • UKN
INTERNATIONAL YEAR OF DISABLED PERSONS • 1981 • Ricketson James • ASL
INTERNATIONAL ZONE • 1943 • Moguy Leonide • USA
INTERNATIONALE • 1933 • Alexandrov Grigori • USS
INTERNECINE PROJECT, THE • 1974 • Hughes Ken • UKN, FRG • MANIPULATOR, THE
INTERNEES OF KAMPALI see **SHIROI HADA TO KIIROI TAICHO** • 1961
INTERNES CAN'T TAKE MONEY • 1937 • Santell Alfred • USA • YOU CAN'T TAKE MONEY (UKN)
INTERNO BERLINESE • 1985 • Cavani Liliana • ITL, FRG • BERLIN AFFAIR ○ AFFAIRE BERLINESE ○ BERLIN INTERIOR ○ LEIDENSCHAFTEN
INTERNO DI UN CONVENTO • 1977 • Borowczyk Walerian • ITL • SEX LIFE IN A CONVENT (USA) ○ BEHIND CONVENT WALLS (UKN) ○ WITHIN THE CLOISTER ○ BEHIND THE CONVENT WALLS ○ INTERIOR OF A CONVENT
INTERNS, THE • 1962 • Swift David • USA
INTERPLANETARY REVOLUTION see **MEZHPLANETNAYA REVOLUTSIYA** • 1924
INTERPLANETARY TOURISTS see **ASTRONAUTAS, LOS** • 1960
INTERPLANETARY WEDDING, AN see **MATRIMONIO INTERPLANETARIO, UN** • 1910
INTERPLAY • 1970 • Viola Albert T. • USA • PART-TIME VIRGINS (UKN)
INTERPOL • 1957 • Gilling John • UKN • PICKUP ALLEY (USA)
INTERPOL CODE 8 • 1965 • *Mihashi Tatsuya* • JPN
INTERPOL CONTRE X • 1960 • Boutel Maurice • FRN
INTERPOL STRIPTEASE see **MANI IN ALTO** • 1961
INTERPRETACJE • 1965 • Brzozowski Jaroslaw • DOC • PLN • INTERPRETATIONS
INTERPRETATIONS see **INTERPRETACJE** • 1965
INTERRARANG • 1969 • Biagetti Giuliano • ITL
INTERROGATION, THE see **PRZESLUCHANIE** • 1981
INTERROGATION OF THE STATUE OF LIBERTY see **C'EST LA VIE RROSE –EIN JUNGGESELLENSPIEL** • 1977
INTERROGATION OF THE WITNESSES • 1987 • Scholz Gunther • GDR
INTERROGATORIO, L' • 1970 • De Sisti Vittorio • ITL
INTERRUPTED BATH, AN • 1908 • Coleby A. E. • UKN
INTERRUPTED BATHERS • 1902 • Porter Edwin S. • USA
INTERRUPTED COURTSHIP, AN • 1910 • *Electrograff* • USA
INTERRUPTED COURTSHIP, AN • 1913 • *Hotely Mae* • USA
INTERRUPTED COURTSHIP, THE • 1899 • *Warwick Trading Co.* • UKN
INTERRUPTED ELOPEMENT, AN • 1911 • *Swayne Marian* • USA
INTERRUPTED ELOPEMENT, AN • 1912 • Sennett Mack • USA
INTERRUPTED ELOPEMENT, AN • 1913 • *Majestic* • USA
INTERRUPTED FLIGHT see **PRZERWANY LOT** • 1964
INTERRUPTED GAME, AN • 1911 • Lehrman Henry, Sennett Mack (Spv) • USA
INTERRUPTED HONEYMOON, AN • 1905 • Fitzhamon Lewin • UKN
INTERRUPTED HONEYMOON, AN • 1910 • *Essanay* • USA
INTERRUPTED HONEYMOON, AN • 1917 • Avery Charles • USA
INTERRUPTED HONEYMOON, AN (UKN) see **HOMICIDE FOR THREE** • 1948
INTERRUPTED HONEYMOON, THE • 1913 • Haldane Bert? • UKN
INTERRUPTED HONEYMOON, THE • 1913 • Young James • USA
INTERRUPTED HONEYMOON, THE • 1916 • Noy Wilfred • UKN
INTERRUPTED HONEYMOON, THE • 1936 • Hiscott Leslie • UKN
INTERRUPTED HONEYMOON, THE see **CHARMANT VOYAGE DE NOCES** • 1899
INTERRUPTED JOURNEY, THE • 1949 • Birt Daniel • UKN • CORD, THE
INTERRUPTED JOY RIDE, THE • 1909 • *Edison* • USA
INTERRUPTED MELODY • 1955 • Bernhardt Curtis • USA
INTERRUPTED MESSAGE, THE • 1900 • *Bitzer Billy (Ph)* • USA
INTERRUPTED NAP, AN • 1914 • *Lubin* • SHT • USA
INTERRUPTED PICNIC • 1902 • Porter Edwin S. • USA
INTERRUPTED PICNIC, AN • 1898 • Hepworth Cecil M. • UKN
INTERRUPTED PICNIC, THE • 1906 • *Mitchell & Kenyon* • UKN
INTERRUPTED PRIZE FIGHT, THE • 1902 • *Warwick Trading Co.* • UKN
INTERRUPTED REHEARSAL, THE • 1938 • Hopwood R. A. • UKN
INTERRUPTED REHEARSAL: OR, MURDER WILL OUT, AN • 1901 • *Paul R. W.* • UKN
INTERRUPTED SEANCE, AN • 1914 • *Browning Tod* • USA
INTERRUPTED SOLITUDE • 1974 • Emshwiller Ed • USA
INTERRUPTED SUICIDE, AN • 1913 • *Champion* • USA
INTERRUPTED TRACKS see **UNTERBROCHENE SPUR, DIE** • 1982
INTERRUPTED WEDDING, AN • 1912 • *Kalem* • USA
INTERRUPTED WEDDING, THE • 1912 • *Comet* • USA
INTERRUPTED WEDDING, THE see **LADY FROM HELL, THE** • 1926
INTERRUPTED WEDDING BELLS • 1913 • Miller Ashley • USA
INTERSECTION • 1970 • Noyce Phil • SHT • ASL
INTERSTATE EIGHT-OARED CHAMPIONSHIP FOR KING'S CUP • 1925 • ASL
INTERSTATE FOOTBALL • 1923 • *Krischock H. (Ph)* • ASL
INTERSTATE YACHT RACE • 1922 • *Murphy Fred E. (Ph)* • ASL
INTERVAL • 1965 • Roos Ole • DNM
INTERVAL • 1972 • Mann Daniel • USA, MXC • INTERVALO
INTERVAL BETWEEN ACTS see **ENTR'ACTE** • 1924
INTERVAL FOR ROMANCE see **STREET SINGER, THE** • 1937
INTERVALO see **INTERVAL** • 1972
INTERVENTION IN THE FAR EAST see **VOLOCHAYEVSKIYE DNI** • 1938
INTERVIEW • 1979 • Leaf Caroline, Soul Veronika • CND
INTERVIEW see **MUQABALA** • 1972
INTERVIEW see **INTERVISTA** • 1987
INTERVIEW, THE • 1961 • Pintoff Ernest • ANS • USA
INTERVIEW, THE • 1970 • Sen Mrinal • IND
INTERVIEW WITH IVAN SHUSIKOV, AN • 1977 • Sens Al • SHT • CND
INTERVIEWS ON PERSONAL PROBLEMS see **NESKOLKO INTERVYU PO LICHNYM VOPROSAM** • 1980
INTERVIEWS ON PLANAS see **ENTREVISTA SOBRE PLANAS** • 1973
INTERVIEWS WITH MY LAI VETERANS • 1970 • Strick Joseph • DOC • USA
INTERVISTA • 1987 • Fellini Federico • ITL • FEDERICO FELLINI'S INTERVISTA (USA) ○ INTERVIEW
INTERVISTA CON SALVADOR ALLENDE • 1973 • Rossellini Roberto • MTV • ITL
INTERZONE • 1987 • Sarafian Deran • USA
INTIKAM MELEGI –KADIN HAMLET • 1977 • Erksan Metin • TRK • ANGEL OF VENGEANCE –THE FEMALE HAMLET, THE
INTILL HELVETETS PORTAR • 1948 • Gentele Goran • SWD • UNTO THE GATES OF HELL
INTIM–REPORT • 1968 • Sharon Rubin, Mock Joachim, van Encke Jorg • FRG • INTIMATE REPORT (UKN)
INTIMACY • 1966 • Stoloff Victor • USA • DECEIVERS, THE
INTIMACY • 1975 • Sarne Mike • UKN, BRZ • INTIMIDADE
INTIMACY see **INTIMIDAD** • 1989
INTIMACY IN A BATHROOM see **INTIMIDADES EN UN CUARTO DE BANO** • 1989
INTIMACY OF PARKS, THE see **INTIMIDAD DE LOS PARQUES, LA** • 1964
INTIMATE see **NAZDIKIAN** • 1986
INTIMATE AGONY • 1982 • Wendkos Paul • TVM • USA
INTIMATE BETRAYAL • 1987 • Lewis Robert Michael • USA
INTIMATE CHRONICLE see **CRONICA INTIMA** • 1978
INTIMATE CONFESSIONS OF A CHINESE COURTESAN • 1973 • Ch'U Yuan • HKG
INTIMATE CONFESSIONS OF STELLA see **EROTICAS VACACIONES DE STELA, LAS** • 1978
INTIMATE CONTACT • 1987 • Hussein Waris • TVM • UKN
INTIMATE DESIRES OF WOMEN, THE • 1973 • Gottlieb Franz J. • FRG
INTIMATE DIARY OF ARTISTS' MODELS • 1964 • Wolk Larry • USA • DIARY OF ARTISTS AND MODELS ○ DIARY OF A MODEL ○ ARTIST'S MODELS
INTIMATE DREAM see **HAZUKASHII YUME** • 1927
INTIMATE ENCOUNTERS • 1986 • Nagy Ivan • TVM • USA • ENCOUNTERS IN THE NIGHT
INTIMATE GAMES • 1976 • Gates Tudor • UKN
INTIMATE INTERLUDE, AN • 1928 • *Whelan Albert* • SHT • UKN
INTIMATE LIGHTNING (UKN) see **INTIMNI OSVETLENI** • 1965
INTIMATE MOMENTS see **MADAME CLAUDE 2** • 1981
INTIMATE POWER see **POUVOIR INTIME** • 1983
INTIMATE REFLECTIONS • 1975 • Boyd Don • UKN
INTIMATE RELATIONS • 1937 • Hutton Clayton • UKN
INTIMATE RELATIONS • 1953 • Frank Charles H. • UKN • DISOBEDIENT
INTIMATE REPORT (UKN) see **INTIM–REPORT** • 1968
INTIMATE RESTAURANT, THE see **RESTAURANT INTIM** • 1950
INTIMATE STRANGER • 1947 • Darling Roy • ASL
INTIMATE STRANGER, THE • 1956 • Losey Joseph • UKN • GUILTY SECRET, THE (USA) ○ FINGER OF GUILT
INTIMATE STRANGERS • 1977 • Moxey John Llewellyn • TVM • USA • BATTERED
INTIMATE STRANGERS • 1986 • Miller Robert Ellis • TVM • USA
INTIMIDAD • 1989 • Rotberg Dana • MXC • INTIMACY
INTIMIDAD DE LOS PARQUES, LA • 1964 • Antin Manuel • ARG • INTIMACY OF PARKS, THE
INTIMIDADE see **INTIMACY** • 1975
INTIMIDADES DE UNA PROSTITUTA • 1972 • Bo Armando • ARG • SEX IS THE NAME OF THE GAME (UKN)
INTIMIDADES EN UN CUARTO DE BANO • 1989 • Hermosillo Jaime Humberto • MXC • INTIMACY IN A BATHROOM
INTIMIDATOR, THE see **TOWN BULLY, THE** • 1988
INTIMITA PROIBITA DI UNA GIOVANE SPOSA • 1970 • Brazzi Oscar • ITL
INTIMITATEN • 1944 • Martin Paul • FRG • DREIMAL KLINGELN
INTIMNI OSVETLENI • 1965 • Passer Ivan • CZC • INTIMATE LIGHTNING (UKN)
INTO AUSTRALIA'S UNKNOWN • 1915 • Hurley Frank • DOC • ASL
INTO HER KINGDOM • 1926 • Gade Svend • USA
INTO NO MAN'S LAND • 1928 • Wheeler Cliff • USA • SECRET LIE, THE (UKN)
INTO SOCIETY AND OUT • 1914 • *Essanay* • USA
INTO THE BLUE • Catling Darrell • DCS • UKN
INTO THE BLUE • 1951 • Wilcox Herbert • UKN • MAN IN THE DINGHY (USA)
INTO THE DARK • 1915 • King Burton L. • USA
INTO THE DARKNESS • 1912 • *Rex* • USA
INTO THE DARKNESS • 1986 • Parkinson Michael • UKN
INTO THE DEPTHS • 1914 • *Hollister Alice* • USA
INTO THE DESERT • 1912 • *Snow Marguerite* • USA
INTO THE FIRE see **LEGEND OF WOLF LODGE, THE** • 1988
INTO THE FOOTHILLS • 1914 • *Eclair* • USA
INTO THE GENUINE • 1912 • *Winterhoff Carl* • USA
INTO THE HANDS OF PEASANTS see **W CHLOPSKIE RECE** • 1946
INTO THE HOMELAND • 1987 • Glatter Lesli Linka • TVM • USA
INTO THE JAWS OF DEATH • 1910 • *Edison* • USA
INTO THE JUNGLE • 1912 • *Kalem* • USA
INTO THE LIGHT • 1911 • *Yankee* • USA
INTO THE LIGHT • 1913 • Nicholls George • USA
INTO THE LIGHT • 1915 • *Novak Jane* • USA
INTO THE LIGHT • 1916 • Batley Ethyle • UKN
INTO THE LIGHT • 1919 • Bradbury Robert North • USA
INTO THE LIGHT • 1975 • Koltsov Vitali • USS
INTO THE LIGHT see **WISE GUY, THE** • 1926
INTO THE LION'S PIT • 1914 • *August Edwin* • USA
INTO THE NET • 1924 • Seitz George B. • SRL • USA
INTO THE NIGHT • 1928 • Worne Duke • USA
INTO THE NIGHT • 1984 • Landis John • USA
INTO THE NIGHT (UKN) see **WISE GUY, THE** • 1926
INTO THE NORTH • 1913 • Wharton Theodore • USA
INTO THE NORTHLAND • 1916 • Daly William Robert • SHT • USA
INTO THE PRIMITIVE • 1916 • Heffron Thomas N. • USA
INTO THE RIVER • 1919 • *Brent Evelyn* • SHT • USA

INTO THE SHADOW • 1909 • *Vitagraph* • USA
INTO THE STORM see **IDU NA GROZU** • 1965
INTO THE STRAIGHT • 1949 • McCreadie Tom O. • ASL
INTO THE SUN see **IDE KU SLONCU** • 1955
INTO THE SUNSET • 1976 • Lotyanu Emil • DOC • USS
INTO THE UNKNOWN • 1954 • Fancey E. J. • UKN
INTO THE WILDERNESS • 1914 • *Eclair* • USA
INTO THIN AIR • 1985 • Young Roger • TVM • USA • BRIAN WALKER, PLEASE CALL HOME
INTO YOUR DANCE • 1935 • Freleng Friz • ANS • USA
INTOARCEREA DIN IAD • 1984 • Margineanu Nicolae • RMN • RETURN FROM HELL
INTOARCEREA LUI VODA LAPUSNEANU • 1980 • Ursianu Malvina • RMN • RETURN OF KING LAPUSNEANU, THE
INTOCCABILI, GLI • 1969 • Montaldo Giuliano • ITL, USA • MACHINE GUN MCCAIN (USA) ○ UNTOUCHABLES, THE
INTOLERANCE • 1916 • Griffith D. W. • USA
INTOXICATED see **ALS IN EEN ROES** • 1987
INTOXICATED ARTIST, THE • 1899 • *Warwick Trading Co.* • UKN
INTOXICATION see **RAUSCH** • 1919
INTR-O DIMINEATA • Veroiu Mircea • SHT • RMN • ONE MORNING
INTR-O DIMINEATA • 1960 • Marcus Manole • RMN • ONE MORNING
INTRACTABLE SPAIN • 1962 • Stern J., Stern K.
INTRAMUROS (PHL) see **WALLS OF HELL, THE** • 1964
INTRANSIGENTS, THE see **NEPRIMIRIMITE** • 1964
INTRE OGLINZI PARALELE • 1978 • Veroiu Mircea • RMN • BETWEEN OPPOSITE MIRRORS ○ BETWEEN PARALLEL MIRRORS ○ BETWEEN FACING MIRRORS
INTRECCIO, L' • 1970 • Young Terence • ITL
INTREPID DAVY • 1911 • *Vitagraph* • USA
INTREPID MR. TWIGG, THE • 1969 • Francis Freddie • SHT • UKN
INTREPIDE, L' • 1975 • Girault Jean • FRN
INTRIGA • 1943 • Roman Antonio • SPN
INTRIGA EN EL ESCENARIO • 1953 • Catalan Feliciano • SPN
INTRIGANTE, L' • 1939 • Couzinet Emile • FRN • BELLE BORDELAISE, LA
INTRIGANTES, LES • 1954 • Decoin Henri • FRN
INTRIGO, L' • 1964 • Sala Vittorio, Marshall George • ITL, FRN • DARK PURPOSE (USA)
INTRIGO A DELFI • 1979 • Bergonzelli Sergio • ITL
INTRIGO A LOS ANGELES • 1964 • Ferrara Romano • ITL
INTRIGO A PARIGI (ITL) see **MONSIEUR** • 1964
INTRIGUE • 1916 • Lloyd Frank • USA
INTRIGUE • 1917 • Robertson John S. • USA
INTRIGUE • 1947 • Marin Edwin L. • USA
INTRIGUE • 1988 • Drury David • TVM • USA
INTRIGUE, THE • 1912 • *Imp* • USA
INTRIGUE, THE • 1914 • *Balboa* • USA
INTRIGUE AND LOVE see **KABALE UND LIEBE** • 1959
INTRIGUE AND LOVE see **UKLADY A LASKA** • 1972
INTRIGUE IN PARIS see **MISS V FROM MOSCOW** • 1943
INTRIGUE OF THE YAGYU FAMILY, THE see **YAGYU ICHIZOKU NO IMBOU** • 1977
INTRIGUEN DER MADAME DE LA POMMERAYE, DIE • 1921 • Wendhausen Fritz • FRG
INTRIGUERS, THE • 1914 • Smiley Joseph • USA
INTRIGUES DE SYLVIA COUSKI, LES • 1973 • Arrieta Adolfo • FRN
INTRODUCE ME • 1925 • Crone George J. • USA
INTRODUCING.. JANET • 1981 • Yates Rebecca, Salzman Glen • CND
INTRODUCING THE DIAL • 1935 • *Grierson John (P)* • DOC • UKN
INTRODUCTION see **VSTUPLENIE** • 1962
INTRODUCTION A LA HUSSARDE • Thierry Alain • FRN
INTRODUCTION TO ARNOLD SCHOENBERG'S ACCOMPANIMENT FOR A CINEMATOGRAPHIC SCENE see **EINLEITUNG ZU ARNOLD SCHOENBERG BEGLEIT MUSIK EINER LICHTSPIELSCENE** • 1969
INTRODUCTION TO ERICA • 1956 • Stewart Paul • USA
INTRODUCTION TO JAZZ • 1953 • Sanders Denis • SHT • USA
INTRODUCTION TO JET ENGINE, AN • 1959 • Jodoin Rene • ANS • CND • COMMENT FONCTIONNE LE MOTEUR A JET
INTRODUCTION TO MARRIAGE see **KEKKON-GAKU NYUMON** • 1930
INTRODUCTION TO THE ENEMY see **VIETNAM JOURNEY** • 1974
INTRODUCTION TO VIOLENCE • 1971 • Onazama • DOC • JPN
INTRODUCTIONS • 1975 • Desvilles Jean • FRN
INTRODUCTIONS EXTRAORDINARY • 1906 • Martin J. H.? • UKN
INTRODUCTORY SPEECH IS BY.., THE see **UVODNI SLOVO PRONESE** • 1964
INTROSPECTION • 1947 • Arledge Sarah • SHT • USA
INTRUDER • 1988 • Spiegel Scott • USA • LAST CHECKOUT, THE ○ NIGHT CREW
INTRUDER, THE • 1909 • *World* • USA
INTRUDER, THE • 1913 • *Solax* • USA
INTRUDER, THE • 1913 • North Wilfred, Costello Maurice • *Vitagraph* • USA
INTRUDER, THE • 1914 • Cabanne W. Christy • *Majestic* • USA
INTRUDER, THE • 1914 • Reid Wallace • *Nestor* • USA
INTRUDER, THE • 1916 • *Essanay* • SHT • USA
INTRUDER, THE • 1916 • Ridgwell George • *Bison* • USA
INTRUDER, THE • 1928 • *Compton Juliette* • SHT • UKN
INTRUDER, THE • 1933 • Ray Albert • USA
INTRUDER, THE • 1953 • Hamilton Guy • UKN
INTRUDER, THE • 1961 • Corman Roger • USA • STRANGER, THE (UKN) ○ I HATE YOUR GUTS ○ SHAME
INTRUDER, THE • 1966 • Skanata Krsto • DOC • YGS
INTRUDER, THE • 1980 • Eustace David F. • MTV • CND
INTRUDER, THE • 1987 • Burnama Jopi
INTRUDER, THE see **INVADER, THE** • 1936
INTRUDER, THE see **GUILT IS MY SHADOW** • 1950
INTRUDER, THE see **DAKHIL, EL** • 1967
INTRUDER, THE see **INKRAKTARNA** • 1974
INTRUDER, THE see **INNOCENTE, L'** • 1976
INTRUDER, THE see **INTRUSA, A** • 1981
INTRUDER BEHIND THE SCENES, AN see **INTRUS DANS LA LOGE DES FIGURANTES, UN** • 1900
INTRUDER IN THE DUST • 1949 • Brown Clarence • USA
INTRUDER WITHIN, THE • 1981 • Carter Peter • TVM • USA
INTRUDERS, THE • 1947 • Donnelly Eddie • ANS • USA
INTRUDERS, THE • 1967 • Graham William A. • TVM • USA • DEATH DANCE AT MADELIA
INTRUDERS, THE • 1969 • Robinson Lee • ASL
INTRUDERS, THE see **INKRAKTARNA** • 1974
INTRUDERS, THE see **RALLARBLOD** • 1978
INTRUS, L' • 1973 • Berckmans Jean-Pierre • BLG
INTRUS, L' • 1983 • Jouannet Irene • FRN
INTRUS, LES • 1971 • Gobbi Sergio • FRN • MENACE (UKN)
INTRUS DANS LA LOGE DES FIGURANTES, UN • 1900 • Melies Georges • FRN • INTRUDER BEHIND THE SCENES, AN
INTRUSA, A • 1981 • Christensen Carlos Hugo • BRZ, ARG • INTRUDER, THE
INTRUSA, L' • 1955 • Matarazzo Raffaello • ITL
INTRUSA, LA • 1953 • Morayta Miguel • MXC
INTRUSE, L' • 1913 • Feuillade Louis • FRN
INTRUSION AT LOMPOC, THE • 1912 • Dwan Allan • USA
INTRUSION OF ISABEL, THE • 1919 • Ingraham Lloyd • USA
INTRUSO, EL • 1944 • Magdaleno Mauricio • MXC
INTUNECARE • Tatos Alexandru • RMN • GATHERING CLOUDS
INUBUE • 1977 • Nakajima Sadao • JPN • DOGFLUTE
INUGAMI FAMILY, THE see **INUGAMI-KE NO ICHIZOKU** • 1976
INUGAMI-KE NO ICHIZOKU • 1976 • Ichikawa Kon • JPN • INUGAMI FAMILY, THE
INUGAMIKE NO TATARI • 1977 • Ito Toshiya • JPN • CURSE OF INAGAMI, THE
INUNDACOES NO VALE DO TEJO • 1939 • Coelho Jose Adolfo • SHT • PRT
INUNDADOS, LOS • 1962 • Birri Fernando • ARG • FLOODED OUT
INUPIATUN • 1981 • Tichenor Harold • MTV • CND
INUTILES, LOS • 1963 • Castellon Alfredo • SHT • SPN
INVADER, THE • 1913 • *Lubin* • USA
INVADER, THE • 1936 • Brunel Adrian • UKN • OLD SPANISH CUSTOM, AN (USA) ○ INTRUDER, THE
INVADERS, THE • 1909 • Stow Percy • UKN
INVADERS, THE • 1912 • Ince Thomas H., Ford Francis • USA
INVADERS, THE • 1913 • Melford George • USA
INVADERS, THE • 1929 • McGowan J. P. • USA
INVADERS, THE • 1977 • May Nick • UKN
INVADERS, THE see **INVASORI, GLI** • 1961
INVADERS, THE (USA) see **49TH PARALLEL** • 1941
INVADERS FROM MARS • 1953 • Menzies William Cameron • USA
INVADERS FROM MARS • 1985 • Hooper Tobe • USA
INVADERS FROM OUTER SPACE, THE see **INVASORES DEL ESPACIO, LOS** • 1967
INVADERS FROM SPACE see **YUSEI OJI** • 1959
INVADERS FROM SPACE see **ATOMIC RULERS OF THE WORLD** • 1964
INVADERS FROM SPACE see **ATTACK FROM SPACE** • 1964
INVADERS FROM THE DEEP see **STINGRAY: INVADERS FROM THE DEEP** • 1964
INVADERS FROM THE PLANETS see **KOTETSU NO KYOJIN - KAISEIJIN NO MAJYO** • 1957
INVADERS FROM THE SPACE SHIP see **YUSEI OJI** • 1959
INVADERS OF THE LOST GOLD see **SAFARI SENZA RITORNO** • 1981
INVANDRARNA • 1970 • Troell Jan • SWD • NEW LAND, THE (USA) ○ UNTO A NEW LAND ○ NYBYGGARNA ○ SETTLERS, THE
INVASION • 1965 • Bridges Alan • UKN
INVASION • 1968 • Santiago Hugo • ARG
INVASION see **TATARJARAS** • 1917
INVASION see **NASHESTIVIYE** • 1945
INVASION 1700 (USA) see **COL FERRO E COL FUOCO** • 1962
INVASION 1775...1975, L' • 1976 • Godbout Jacques • DCS • CND
INVASION, L' • 1970 • Allegret Yves • FRN, ITL • INVASIONE, L' (ITL)
INVASION, LA • 1977 • Marmol Julio Cesar • VNZ • INVASION, THE
INVASION, THE • 1973 • *Dullea Keir* • MTV • USA
INVASION, THE see **INVASIONE, L'** • 1964
INVASION, THE see **INWAZJA** • 1970
INVASION, THE see **INVASION, LA** • 1977
INVASION BY THE ATOMIC ZOMBIES see **NIGHTMARE CITY** • 1980
INVASION DE LOS MUERTOS, LA • 1972 • Cardona Rene • MXC • INVASION OF THE DEAD, THE
INVASION DE LOS VAMPIROS, LA • 1961 • Morayta Miguel • MXC • INVASION OF THE VAMPIRES, THE (USA)
INVASION DE LOS ZOMBIES ATOMICAS, LA see **NIGHTMARE CITY** • 1980
INVASION EARTH 2150 A.D. see **DALEKS' INVASION OF EARTH 2150 A.D.** • 1966
INVASION EARTH: THEY CAME FROM OUTER SPACE • 1988 • Skotak Bob • USA
INVASION FORCE • 1989 • Baldwin Tom • USA
INVASION FORCE see **HANGAR 18** • 1980
INVASION FROM A PLANET see **UCHU KAISOKU-SEN** • 1961
INVASION FROM INNER EARTH • 1977 • Rebane Ito • USA
INVASION FROM THE MOON see **MUTINY IN OUTER SPACE** • 1965
INVASION FROM THE SOUTH • 1956 • Howe John • DOC • CND
INVASION: ITS POSSIBILITIES • 1909 • *Urban Charles* • UKN
INVASION NORTEAMERICANA, LA • 1914 • MXC
INVASION OF BRITAIN, THE (USA) see **VICTORY AND PEACE** • 1918
INVASION OF CAROLS ENDERS, THE • 1974 • Curtis Dan • TVM • USA
INVASION OF JOHNSON COUNTY, THE • 1976 • Jameson Jerry • TVM • USA
INVASION OF MARS see **ANGRY RED PLANET, THE** • 1959
INVASION OF PLANET X see **KAIJU DAISENSO** • 1965
INVASION OF PRIVACY, THE • 1982 • Damski Mel • TVM • USA
INVASION OF THE ANIMAL PEOPLE (USA) see **RYMDINVASION I LAPPLAND** • 1958
INVASION OF THE ASTRO-MONSTER(S) see **KAIJU DAISENSO** • 1965
INVASION OF THE ASTROS see **KAIJU DAISENSO** • 1965
INVASION OF THE ATOMIC ZOMBIES see **NIGHTMARE CITY** • 1980
INVASION OF THE BEE GIRLS • 1973 • Sanders Denis • USA • GRAVEYARD TRAMPS
INVASION OF THE BLOOD FARMERS • 1971 • Adlum Ed • USA • BLOOD FARMERS
INVASION OF THE BODY SNATCHERS • 1956 • Siegel Don • USA • THEY CAME FROM ANOTHER WORLD ○ SLEEP NO MORE
INVASION OF THE BODY SNATCHERS • 1978 • Kaufman Philip • USA
INVASION OF THE BODY STEALERS (USA) see **BODY STEALERS, THE** • 1969
INVASION OF THE BODYSUCKERS see **BLUE MONKEY** • 1987
INVASION OF THE DEAD, THE see **INVASION DE LOS MUERTOS, LA** • 1972
INVASION OF THE FLESH EATERS see **APOCALISSE DOMANI** • 1980
INVASION OF THE FLYING SAUCERS see **EARTH VS. THE FLYING SAUCERS** • 1956
INVASION OF THE GARGON see **TEEN-AGERS FROM OUTER SPACE** • 1959
INVASION OF THE HELL CREATURES (UKN) see **INVASION OF THE SAUCER-MEN** • 1957
INVASION OF THE LOVE DRONES • 1975 • Hamlin Jerome • USA
INVASION OF THE NEPTUNE MEN (USA) see **UCHU KAISOKU-SEN** • 1961
INVASION OF THE SAUCER-MEN • 1957 • Cahn Edward L. • USA • INVASION OF THE HELL CREATURES (UKN) ○ SPACEMEN SATURDAY NIGHT ○ HELL CREATURES, THE
INVASION OF THE STAR CREATURES • 1962 • Ve Sota Bruno • USA • STAR CREATURES, THE
INVASION OF THE THUNDERBOLT PAGODA, THE • Cohen Ira • SHT • USA
INVASION OF THE VAMPIRES, THE (USA) see **INVASION DE LOS VAMPIROS, LA** • 1961
INVASION OF THE ZOMBIES see **HORROR OF PARTY BEACH, THE** • 1964
INVASION OF THE ZOMBIES (USA) see **SANTO CONTRA LOS ZOMBIES** • 1961
INVASION PACIFIQUE, L' see **QUEBEC USA** • 1962
INVASION QUARTET • 1961 • Lewis Jay • UKN
INVASION SINIESTRA • 1968 • Ibanez Juan, Hill Jack • MXC, USA • INCREDIBLE INVASION, THE ○ SINISTER INVASION ○ ALIEN TERROR
INVASION U.S.A. • 1952 • Green Alfred E. • USA
INVASION U.S.A. • 1985 • Zito Joseph • USA
INVASION UFO • 1980 • Anderson Gerry, Lane David, Tomblin David • UKN • U.F.O. -INVASION U.F.O.
INVASIONE, L' • 1964 • Bazzoni Camillo • SHT • ITL • INVASION, THE
INVASIONE, L' (ITL) see **INVASION, L'** • 1970
INVASIONEN • 1969 • Svenstedt Carl-Henrik, Borje Stefania • SHT • SWD
INVASORE, L' • 1943 • Giannini Nino • ITL
INVASORES DEL ESPACIO, LOS • 1967 • Ziener Guillermo • SPN • INVADERS FROM OUTER SPACE, THE
INVASORI, GLI • 1961 • Bava Mario • ITL, FRN • RUEE DES VIKINGS, LA (FRN) ○ ERIK THE CONQUEROR (USA) ○ FURY OF THE VIKINGS ○ INVADERS, THE
INVENCIBLE HOMBRE INVISIBLE, EL (SPN) see **INAFFERRABILE E INVINCIBILE MR. INVISIBILE, L'** • 1970
INVENCIBLES, LAS • 1963 • Curiel Federico • MXC
INVENCIBLES, LOS (SPN) see **INVINCIBILI SETTE, GLI** • 1964
INVENTAIRE D'UNE COLONIE • 1965-66 • Garceau Raymond • DCS • CND
INVENTAIRE LAUSANNOIS • 1982 • Yersin Yves • DOC • SWT
INVENTEUR, L' • 1910 • Carre Michel • FRN
INVENTEUR ACHARNE, UN see **ORIGINAL LOCATAIRE, UN**
INVENTEURS AU QUEBEC, LES • Ferrand Carlos • MTV • CND
INVENTEZ • 1986 • Ferrand Carlos • MTV • CND
INVENTIAMO L'AMORE • 1938 • Mastrocinque Camillo • ITL
INVENTING TROUBLE • 1915 • Kellino W. P. • UKN
INVENTION, L' • 1967 • Patris Gerard, Ferrari L. • SHT • FRN
INVENTION CONVENTION • 1953 • Sparber I. • ANS • USA
INVENTION DU MONDE, L' • 1952 • Zimbacca Michel, Bedouin Jean-Louis • FRN
INVENTION DU PROFESSEUR MECANICAS • 1916-24 • Lortac • ANS • FRN
INVENTION FOR DESTRUCTION see **VYNALEZ ZKAZY** • 1958
INVENTION OF DESTRUCTION see **VYNALEZ ZKAZY** • 1958
INVENTION OF THE ADOLESCENT, THE • 1967 • Watson Patricia • CND
INVENTION OF THE DOOR, THE • 1972 • Pittman Oscar • ANS • USA
INVENTIONS OF AN IDIOT • 1909 • *Lubin Sigmund* • USA
INVENTIVE LOVE see **ELSKOVS OPFINFSOMHED** • 1913
INVENTOR, THE • 1910 • *Pathe* • USA
INVENTOR, THE see **ERFINDER, DER** • 1981
INVENTOR CRAZYBRAINS AND HIS WONDERFUL AIRSHIP (USA) see **DIRIGEABLE FANTASTIQUE OU LE CAUCHEMAR D'UN INVENTEUR, LE** • 1906
INVENTOR OF SHOES (USA) see **IZUMITELJ CIPELA** • 1967
INVENTORS, THE • 1918 • *Fisher Bud (Anm)* • ANS • USA
INVENTORS, THE • 1934 • Christie Al • USA
INVENTOR'S GALVANIC FLUID, THE see **LIQUID ELECTRICITY** • 1907
INVENTOR'S MODEL, THE • 1910 • *Essanay* • USA
INVENTOR'S PERIL, THE • 1915 • Smiley Joseph • USA
INVENTOR'S SECRET, THE • 1911 • *Cines* • ITL
INVENTOR'S SECRET, THE • 1911 • Sennett Mack • USA
INVENTOR'S SKETCH, THE • 1913 • Lessey George A. • USA
INVENTOR'S SON, THE • 1911 • Bouwmeester Theo, Miles David? • UKN
INVENTOR'S WIFE, THE • 1914 • *Johnson Arthur* • USA

INVENTORY see **STAN POSIADANIA** • 1989
INVENZIONE DELLA CROCE, L' • 1949 • Emmer Luciano, Gras Enrico • ITL • LEGEND OF THE TRUE CROSS ○ PIERO DELLA FRANCESCA
INVENZIONE DI MOREL, L' • 1974 • Greco Emidio • ITL
INVERARY • 1907 • Gilbert Arthur • UKN
INVERGORDON SMELTER, THE • 1972 • Marzaroli Oscar • DCS • UKN
INVERNO TI FARA TORNARE, L' (ITL) see **AUSSI LONGUE ABSENCE, UNE** • 1961
INVESTIGACION CRIMINAL • 1970 • Bosch Juan • SPN
INVESTIGADOR CAPULINA, EL • 1973 • *Panorama* • MXC
INVESTIGATING MAGISTRATE AND THE FOREST, THE • 1976 • Vulchanov Rangel • BUL • INVESTIGATING MAGISTRATE AND THE WOOD, THE
INVESTIGATING MAGISTRATE AND THE WOOD, THE see **INVESTIGATING MAGISTRATE AND THE FOREST, THE** • 1976
INVESTIGATION, THE see **SI JOLI VILLAGE, UN** • 1978
INVESTIGATION CONTINUES, THE see **SLYEDSTVIYE PRODOLZHAYETSYA** • 1967
INVESTIGATION INTO A CITIZEN ABOVE SUSPICION see **INDAGINE SU UN CITTADINA AL DI SOPRA DI OGNO SOSPETTO** • 1970
INVESTIGATION OF A CITIZEN ABOVE SUSPICION see **INDAGINE SU UN CITTADINA AL DI SOPRA DI OGNO SOSPETTO** • 1970
INVESTIGATION OF A PRIVATE CITIZEN see **INDAGINE SU UN CITTADINA AL DI SOPRA DI OGNO SOSPETTO** • 1970
INVESTIGATION OF MURDER, AN (UKN) see **LAUGHING POLICEMAN, THE** • 1973
INVESTMENT, THE • 1914 • Carleton Lloyd B. • USA
INVESTMENT PICTURE, THE • 1980 • Bittman Roman • DOC • CND
INVIATI SPECIALI • 1943 • Marcellini Romolo • ITL • CORRISPONDENTI DE GUERRA ○ AMANTI FRA DUE GUERRE
INVIERNO EN MALLORCA, UN see **JURTZENKA** • 1969
INVIGORATING ELECTRICITY • 1910 • Fitzhamon Lewin? • UKN
INVINCIBILE CAVALIERE MASCHERATO, L' • 1964 • Lenzi Umberto • ITL, FRN • INVINCIBLE MASKED RIDER, THE (USA) ○ TERROR OF THE BLACK MASK
INVINCIBILE SUPERMAN, L' • 1968 • Bianchini Paolo • ITL
INVINCIBILI DIECI GLADIATORI, GLI • 1965 • Iquino Ignacio F. • ITL
INVINCIBILI FRATELLI MACISTE, GLI • 1965 • Mauri Roberto • ITL • INVINCIBLE BROTHERS MACISTE, THE (USA) ○ MACISTE BROTHERS, THE
INVINCIBILI SETTE, GLI • 1964 • De Martino Alberto • ITL, SPN • INVENCIBLES, LOS (SPN) ○ SECRET SEVEN, THE (USA) ○ INVINCIBLE SEVEN, THE
INVINCIBILI TRE, GLI • 1965 • Parolini Gianfranco • ITL, TNS • THREE AVENGERS, THE (USA) ○ INVINCIBLE THREE, THE
INVINCIBLE see **NEPOBEDIMYIE** • 1942
INVINCIBLE, THE see **BRUCE LEE THE INVINCIBLE** • 1980
INVINCIBLE ARMOUR, THE • *Huang Cheng Li* • HKG
INVINCIBLE BAD NAMES see **AKUMYO MUTEKI** • 1965
INVINCIBLE BARBARIAN, THE see **GUNANA RE BARBARO** • 1981
INVINCIBLE BOXER see **KING BOXER** • 1971
INVINCIBLE BROTHERS MACISTE, THE (USA) see **INVINCIBILI FRATELLI MACISTE, GLI** • 1965
INVINCIBLE FROM HELL, THE • 1981 • Sin Wee Kyun • HKG
INVINCIBLE GLADIATOR, THE(USA) see **GLADIADOR INVENCIBLE, EL** • 1961
INVINCIBLE INVISIBLE MAN, THE see **INAFFERRABILE E INVINCIBILE MR. INVISIBILE, L'** • 1970
INVINCIBLE IRON PALM, THE see **WU-TI T'IEH SHA CHANG** • 1973
INVINCIBLE KUNG FU LEGS, THE see **LEG FIGHTERS, THE** • 1980
INVINCIBLE LOVE see **KONIGSKINDER** • 1962
INVINCIBLE LOVERS • 1988 • Tsiolis Stavros • GRC
INVINCIBLE MASKED RIDER, THE (USA) see **INVINCIBILE CAVALIERE MASCHERATO, L'** • 1964
INVINCIBLE MR. INVISIBLE see **INAFFERRABILE E INVINCIBILE MR. INVISIBILE, L'** • 1970
INVINCIBLE OBSESSED FIGHTER • King John • HKG
INVINCIBLE ONE, THE see **FUJIMINA AITSU** • 1967
INVINCIBLE ONES, THE see **MAGLUP EDILEMEYENLER** • 1976
INVINCIBLE POLE FIGHTER, THE • Liu Chia-Liang • HKG • EIGHT DIAGRAM POLE FIGHTER, THE ○ INVINCIBLE POLE FIGHTERS, THE
INVINCIBLE POLE FIGHTERS, THE see **INVINCIBLE POLE FIGHTER, THE**
INVINCIBLE SEVEN, THE see **INVINCIBILI SETTE, GLI** • 1964
INVINCIBLE SHAOLIN KUNG FU • Ko Shih Hao • HKG • SECRET SHAOLIN KUNG FU, THE
INVINCIBLE SIX, THE • 1970 • Negulesco Jean • USA, IRN • HEROES, THE
INVINCIBLE SLEUTH, AN • *Cines* • SHT • ITL
INVINCIBLE SPACEMAN see **ATOMIC RULERS OF THE WORLD** • 1964
INVINCIBLE SUPER CHAN • Sun Yang • HKG
INVINCIBLE SWORD, THE see **PEDANG SAKTI** • 1971
INVINCIBLE SWORD, THE see **SPADE DEI BARBARI, LE** • 1983
INVINCIBLE THREE, THE see **INVINCIBILI TRE, GLI** • 1965
INVINCIBLE WATARI • 1970 • *Chang Kong* • HKG
INVINGATORUL • 1981 • Marascu Todur • RMN • WINNER, THE
INVISIBILI, GLI • 1988 • Squitieri Pasquale • ITL • INVISIBLE ONES, THE
INVISIBILITY • 1909 • Hepworth Cecil M., Fitzhamon Lewin • UKN
INVISIBLE, THE • 1912 • *Eclair* • USA
INVISIBLE ACTOR, THE see **HEREC KTEREHO NENI VIDET** • 1971
INVISIBLE ADVERSARIES see **UNSICHTBARE GEGNER** • 1977
INVISIBLE ADVERSARY see **UNSICHTBARE GEGNER** • 1977
INVISIBLE AGENT • 1942 • Marin Edwin L. • USA
INVISIBLE ARMADA, THE see **USYNLIGE HAER, DEN** • 1945
INVISIBLE ARMY, THE • Jacobsen Johan • DNM
INVISIBLE ASSASSIN, THE see **ASESINO INVISIBLE, EL** • 1964
INVISIBLE ASSET, THE • 1963 • Harrison Norman • UKN
INVISIBLE AVENGER • 1958 • Howe James Wong, Sledge John • USA • BOURBON STREET SHADOWS
INVISIBLE BATMAN, THE • 1985 • *Gunadi Etore* • ITL
INVISIBLE BATTALION, THE see **NEVIDNI BATALJON** • 1968
INVISIBLE BOND, THE • 1920 • Maigne Charles • USA • SEE-SAW, THE
INVISIBLE BOY, THE • 1908 • Aylott Dave • UKN
INVISIBLE BOY, THE • 1957 • Hoffman Herman • USA
INVISIBLE CLAWS OF DR. MABUSE, THE see **UNSICHTBAREN KRALLEN DES DR. MABUSE, DIE** • 1962
INVISIBLE CREATURE (USA) see **HOUSE IN MARSH ROAD, THE** • 1960
INVISIBLE CYCLIST • 1912 • *Pathe* • FRN
INVISIBLE DIVORCE, THE • 1920 • Deverich Nat C., Mills Thomas R. • USA
INVISIBLE DR. MABUSE, THE (USA) see **UNSICHTBAREN KRALLEN DES DR. MABUSE, DIE** • 1962
INVISIBLE DOG, THE • 1909 • Booth W. R. • UKN
INVISIBLE ENEMY • 1938 • Auer John H. • USA
INVISIBLE ENEMY, THE • 1916 • *E.k.o. Film Co.* • USA
INVISIBLE FAMILY, THE see **INVISIBLE PEOPLE, THE** • 1903
INVISIBLE FEAR, THE • 1921 • Carewe Edwin • USA
INVISIBLE FLUID, THE • 1908 • McCutcheon Wallace • USA
INVISIBLE FOE, THE • 1913 • *Kalem* • USA
INVISIBLE GHOST, THE • 1941 • Lewis Joseph H. • USA • PHANTOM KILLER, THE
INVISIBLE GOVERNMENT, THE • 1913 • Eagle Oscar • USA
INVISIBLE HAND, THE • 1920 • Bowman William J. • SRL • USA
INVISIBLE HANDS • 1913 • *Lux* • USA
INVISIBLE HORROR, THE see **UNSICHTBAREN KRALLEN DES DR. MABUSE, DIE** • 1962
INVISIBLE INFORMER, THE • 1946 • Ford Philip • USA
INVISIBLE INK • 1913 • *Fraunholz Fraunie* • USA
INVISIBLE INK • 1921 • Fleischer Dave • ANS • USA
INVISIBLE INVADERS • 1959 • Cahn Edward L. • USA
INVISIBLE KID, THE • 1988 • Crouse Avery • USA
INVISIBLE KILLER, THE • 1939 • Newfield Sam • USA
INVISIBLE MAN see **TOMEI NINGEN** • 1954
INVISIBLE MAN see **TOMEI KAIJIN** • 1958
INVISIBLE MAN see **MARDE-NAMAREI** • 1967
INVISIBLE MAN, THE • 1933 • Whale James • USA
INVISIBLE MAN, THE • 1975 • Lewis Robert Michael • TVM • USA
INVISIBLE MAN, THE see **UNSICHTBARE, DER** • 1963
INVISIBLE MAN ATTACKS, THE see **HOMBRE INVISIBLE ATACA, EL** • 1967
INVISIBLE MAN -DR. EROS see **TOMEININGEN EROHAKASE** • 1968
INVISIBLE MAN GOES THROUGH THE CITY, AN see **UNSICHTBARER GEHT DURCH DIE STADT, EIN** • 1933
INVISIBLE MAN IN ISTANBUL see **GORUNMIYEN ADAM ISTANBULDA** • 1956
INVISIBLE MAN IN MEXICO (UKN) see **HOMBRE QUE LOGRO SER INVISIBLE, EL** • 1957
INVISIBLE MAN RETURNS, THE • 1940 • May Joe • USA
INVISIBLE MAN'S REVENGE, THE • 1944 • Beebe Ford • USA
INVISIBLE MEN, THE see **INVISIBLES, LOS** • 1961
INVISIBLE MENACE, THE • 1938 • Farrow John • USA • WITHOUT WARNING
INVISIBLE MESSAGE, THE (UKN) see **GUN PLAY** • 1935
INVISIBLE MR. UNMEI, THE • 1951 • Breakston George, Stahl C. Ray • USA, JPN
INVISIBLE MONSTER, THE • 1950 • Brannon Fred C. • SRL • USA • PHANTOM RULER
INVISIBLE MOUSE, THE • 1947 • Hanna William, Barbera Joseph • ANS • USA
INVISIBLE ONES, THE see **INVISIBILI, GLI** • 1988
INVISIBLE PEOPLE, THE • 1903 • Duncan F. Martin • UKN • INVISIBLE FAMILY, THE
INVISIBLE POWER, THE • 1914 • Melford George • USA
INVISIBLE POWER, THE • 1921 • Lloyd Frank • USA • ALIBI, THE
INVISIBLE POWER (UKN) see **WASHINGTON MERRY-GO-ROUND** • 1932
INVISIBLE RAY, THE • 1920 • Pollard Harry • SRL • USA
INVISIBLE RAY, THE • 1936 • Hillyer Lambert • USA
INVISIBLE RAY, THE see **PARIS QUI DORT** • 1924
INVISIBLE REVENGE, THE • 1925 • *Fox* • ANS • USA
INVISIBLE SABRE, THE • *Chen Man-Ling* • HKG
INVISIBLE SIVA, THE (USA) see **SIVA L'INVISIBLE** • 1904
INVISIBLE STRANGER see **ASTRAL FACTOR** • 1976
INVISIBLE STRIPES • 1940 • Bacon Lloyd • USA
INVISIBLE SWORDSMAN see **TOMEI KENSHI** • 1970
INVISIBLE TEENAGER, THE • 1962 • Glut Don • SHT • USA
INVISIBLE TERROR, THE (USA) see **UNSICHTBARE, DER** • 1963
INVISIBLE THIEF, AN see **HOMME INVISIBLE, L'** • 1909
INVISIBLE THIEF (USA) see **INVISIBLES, LES** • 1905
INVISIBLE WALL see **ME NO KABE** • 1958
INVISIBLE WALL, THE • 1947 • Forde Eugene J. • USA
INVISIBLE WALL, THE see **OSYNLIGA MUREN, DEN** • 1944
INVISIBLE WEB, THE • 1917 • Baker Richard Foster • SHT • USA
INVISIBLE WEB, THE • 1921 • Rule Beverly C. • USA
INVISIBLE WOMAN, THE • 1941 • Sutherland A. Edward • USA
INVISIBLE WOMAN, THE • 1982 • Levi Alan J. • TVM • USA
INVISIBLE WOMAN, THE see **FEMME INVISIBLE, LA** • 1933
INVISIBLE WONDERS OF THE GREAT BARRIER REEF • 1961 • Monkman Noel • DOC • ASL
INVISIBLE WRESTLER, THE • 1911 • *Lux* • USA
INVISIBLES, LES • 1905 • Velle Gaston, Moreau Gabriel • FRN • INVISIBLE THIEF (USA)
INVISIBLES, THE see **PROKLETI DOMU HAJNU** • 1988
INVISIBLES, LOS • 1961 • Salvador Jaime • MXC • INVISIBLE MEN, THE
INVITACION, LA • 1982 • Antin Manuel • ARG • INVITATION, THE
INVITATA, L' • 1969 • De Seta Vittorio • ITL, FRN • INVITEE, L' (FRN) ○ UNINVITED, THE (USA)
INVITATION • 1951 • Reinhardt Gottfried • USA
INVITATION • 1981 • Ruiz Raul • DCS • FRN
INVITATION, L' • 1973 • Goretta Claude • SWT, FRN • INVITATION, THE (UKN)
INVITATION, THE see **INVITACION, LA** • 1982
INVITATION, THE (UKN) see **INVITATION, L'** • 1973
INVITATION A LA CHASSE • 1974 • Chabrol Claude • MTV • FRN
INVITATION AND AN ATTACK, AN • 1915 • Brabin Charles J. • USA
INVITATION AU VOYAGE • 1982 • Del Monte Peter • FRN, ITL, FRG
INVITATION AU VOYAGE, L' • 1927 • Dulac Germaine • FRN
INVITATION TO A GUNFIGHTER • 1964 • Wilson Richard • USA
INVITATION TO A MURDER see **FLIGHT FROM DESTINY** • 1941
INVITATION TO DEATH see **WOMAN IN GREEN, THE** • 1945
INVITATION TO HAPPINESS • 1939 • Ruggles Wesley • USA
INVITATION TO HAPPINESS see **KOFUKU ENO SHOTAI** • 1947
INVITATION TO HELL • 1982 • Murphy Michael J. • USA
INVITATION TO HELL • 1984 • Craven Wes • TVM • USA
INVITATION TO JAIL, AN see **KANGOKU ENO SHOTAI** • 1967
INVITATION TO LUST • 1966 • Wertheim Ron • USA
INVITATION TO MAGIC • 1956 • Baim Harold • UKN
INVITATION TO MONTE CARLO • 1959 • Lloyd Euan • DOC • UKN
INVITATION TO MURDER • 1959 • Lynn Robert • UKN
INVITATION TO PROSPERITY • 1960 • Mallinson John • UKN
INVITATION TO RUIN • 1968 • Richter Kurt • USA
INVITATION TO THE DANCE • 1956 • Kelly Gene • USA, UKN
INVITATION TO THE DANCE (USA) see **AUFFORDERUNG ZUM TANZ** • 1935
INVITATION TO THE ENCHANTED TOWN see **SENNIN BURAKU** • 1960
INVITATION TO THE INSIDE see **ZAPROSZENIE DO WNETRZA** • 1978
INVITATION TO THE ROYAL WEDDING, AN • 1972 • Rasky Harry • CND
INVITATION TO THE WALTZ • 1935 • Merzbach Paul • UKN
INVITATION TO THE WEDDING • 1983 • Brooks Joseph • UKN
INVITE DE LA DERNIERE HEURE, L' see **INVITE DE LA ONZIEME HEURE, L'** • 1945
INVITE DE LA ONZIEME HEURE, L' • 1945 • Cloche Maurice • FRN • INVITE DE LA DERNIERE HEURE, L' ○ ZOO
INVITE DU MARDI, L' • 1949 • Deval Jacques • FRN • DU THE POUR MONSIEUR JOSE
INVITE MONSIEUR A DINER • 1933 • Autant-Lara Claude • FRN
INVITE SURPRISE, L' • 1989 • Lautner Georges • FRN
INVITED OUT • 1917 • Jackson Harry • SHT • USA
INVITED PEOPLE • 1981 • Ha Won Choi • SKR
INVITEE, L' (FRN) see **INVITATA, L'** • 1969
INVITES DE M. LATOURTE, LES • 1904 • Melies Georges • FRN • SIMPLE SIMON'S SURPRISE PARTY (USA) ○ BONNE SURPRISE, UNE
INVITO A PRANZO, UN • 1908 • Guazzoni Enrico • ITL
INVITO ALLO SPORT • 1979 • Quilici Folco • ITL
INVOCATION OF MY DEMON BROTHER (UKN) see **ZAP** • 1969
INVOCATIONS • 1983 • Shah Sanjiv • IND
INWAZJA • 1970 • Schabenbeck Stefan • ANM • PLN • INVASION, THE
INYAH, THE JUNGLE GODDESS see **FORBIDDEN ADVENTURE** • 1934
INYAKANYAKA • 1977 • SAF
INYEMBEZI ZAMI • 1983 • SAF
INYOKA • 1984 • SAF
INYYE NYNCHYE VREMENA • 1968 • Chiaureli Mikhail • USS • TIMES ARE DIFFERENT NOW ○ OTHER TIMES
IO, AMLETO • 1953 • Simonelli Giorgio C. • ITL
IO AMO, TU AMI • 1960 • Blasetti Alessandro • ITL, FRN • J'AIME, TU AIMES (FRN) ○ I LOVE, YOU LOVE (USA) ○ ANTOLOGIA UNIVERSALE DELL'AMORE
IO BACIO.. TU BACI • 1961 • Vivarelli Piero • ITL
IO, CATERINA • 1958 • Palella Oreste • ITL
IO, CHIARA E LO SCURO • 1983 • Ponzi Maurizio • ITL • ME, CHIARA AND LO SCURO
IO CON TE NON CI STO' PIU' • 1984 • *Guerritore Monica* • ITL • I'M NOT STAYING WITH YOU ANYMORE
IO CRISTINA STUDENTESSA DEGLI SCANDALI • 1971 • Bergonzelli Sergio • ITL
IO DONNA • 1971 • Cardone Alberto • ITL
IO DONNA, TU DONNA see **COMINCERA TUTTO UN MATTINO** • 1979
IO E CATARINA • 1981 • Sordi Alberto • ITL, FRN
IO E DIO • 1970 • Squitieri Pasquale • ITL
IO E L'IPPOPOTAMO see **IO STO CON GLI IPPOPOTAMI** • 1980
IO E LUI • 1973 • Salce Luciano • ITL
IO E MIA SORELLA • 1988 • Verdone Carlo • ITL • ME AND MY SISTER
IO, EMMANUELLE • 1969 • Canevari Cesare • ITL • MAN FOR EMMANUELLE, A (UKN)
IO HO PAURA • 1977 • Damiani Damiano • ITL • I AM AFRAID (USA) ○ I'M AFRAID
IO, IO, IO.. E GLI ALTRI • 1966 • Blasetti Alessandro • ITL • CONFERENZA CON PROIEZIONI ○ ME, ME, ME.. AND NO OTHERS
IO LA CONOSCEVO BENE • 1965 • Pietrangeli Antonio • ITL, FRN, FRG • ICH HABE SIE GUT GEKANNT (FRG) ○ AMOUR TEL QU'IL EST, L' (FRN) ○ I KNEW HER WELL
IO, MAMMETA E TU • 1958 • Bragaglia Carlo Ludovico • ITL • ME, MOTHER AND YOU
IO MONACA, PER TRE CAROGNE E SETTE PECCATRICI • 1972 • del Amo Antonio • ITL
IO MUOIO DISPERATA see **ANIMALI PAZZI** • 1939
IO NON GRATTO.. RUBO! see **FURTO E L'ANIMA DEL COMMERCIO, IL** • 1971
IO NON PERDONA.. UCCIDO • 1968 • Romero-Marchent Rafael • ITL
IO NON PROTESTO, IO AMO • 1967 • Baldi Ferdinando • ITL • I DON'T PROTEST, I LOVE
IO NON SCAPPO.. FUGGO • 1970 • Prosperi Franco • ITL
IO NON SPEZZO.. ROMPO • 1971 • Corbucci Bruno • ITL
IO NON VEDO, TU NON PARLI, LUI NON SENTE • 1971 • Camerini Mario • ITL
IO PIACCIO • 1955 • Bianchi Giorgio • ITL • VIA DEL SUCCESSO CON LE DONNE, LA

IO SEMIRAMIDE • 1963 • Zeglio Primo • ITL • SLAVE QUEEN OF BABYLON (USA) ○ SEMIRAMIS
IO SO CHE TU SAI CHE IO SO • 1983 • Sordi Alberto • ITL • I KNOW THAT YOU KNOW THAT I KNOW (USA)
IO SONO ANNA MAGNANI • 1979 • Vermorcksen Chris • BLG • ANNA MAGNANI: UN FILM D'AMOUR ○ I AM ANNA MAGNANI
IO SONO IL CAPATAZ • 1951 • Simonelli Giorgio C. • ITL
IO SONO LA PRIMULA ROSSA • 1954 • Simonelli Giorgio C. • ITL • SANCULOTTO, IL
IO SONO MIA • 1978 • Scandurra Sofia • ITL
IO SONO UN AUTACHICO • 1977 • Moretti Nanni • ITL
IO SONO UN SENTIMENTALE (ITL) see **JE SUIS UN SENTIMENTAL** • 1955
IO STO CON GLI IPPOPOTAMI • 1980 • Zingarelli Italo • ITL • IO E L'IPPOPOTAMO ○ I'M FOR THE HIPPOPOTAMUS
IO, SUO PADRE • 1939 • Bonnard Mario • ITL
IO T'AMERO SEMPRE see **T'AMERO SEMPRE** • 1933
IO T'HO INCONTRATA A NAPOLI • 1946 • Francisci Pietro • ITL
IO TI AMO • 1968 • Margheriti Antonio • ITL • I LOVE YOU
IO TIGRO, TU TIGRI, EGLI TIGRA • 1978 • Capitani Giorgio, Pozzetto Renato • ITL
IO, TU, LORO E GLI ALTRI • 1984 • Clucher E. B. • ITL • DOUBLE TROUBLE
IO.. TU.. Y.. • 1933 • Reinhardt John • I.. THOU.. AND SHE (USA)
IO UCCIDO, TU UCCIDI • 1965 • Puccini Gianni • ITL, FRN • I KILL, YOU KILL
IOANNIS O VIEOS • 1972 • Marketaki Tonia • GRC • BITTERNESS OF THE JEWISH SCAPEGOAT, THE ○ VIOLENT JOHN ○ IOANNIS OFVIEOS
IOANNIS OFVIEOS see **IOANNIS O VIEOS** • 1972
IOKO OKUMURA see **OKUMURA IOKO** • 1940
IOLANTA • 1963 • Gorikker Vladimir • USS
IOLA'S PROMISE • 1912 • Griffith D. W. • USA
IOLE THE CHRISTIAN • 1915 • King Burton L. • USA
ION MARIN'S LETTER TO SCINTEIA • 1949 • Iliu Victor • RMN
IONA, THE WHITE SQUAW • 1909 • *Bison* • USA
IOWA UNDER FIRE • 1924 • *Pictorial Sales Bureau* • DOC • USA
IPADUNAY AIYE? • 1967 • Ramanathan S. • SLN • WHY WERE WE EVER BORN?
IPANEMA TODA NUA • 1972 • Giachetta Libero Miguel • BRZ
IPC IN TRIPOLI • 1955 • Nasser George • SHT • LBN
IPCRESS FILE, THE • 1965 • Furie Sidney J. • UKN
IPEKCE • 1987 • Olgac Bilge • TRK
IPHIGENIA see **IFIGENIA** • 1977
IPHUTHA • 1985 • SAF
IPNOS KE THANATOS • 1975 • Aristopoulos Konstantinos • GRC • SLEEP AND DEATH
IPNOSI (ITL) see **NUR TOTE ZEUGEN SCHWEIGEN** • 1963
IPOGIA DIADROMI • 1984 • Doxiadis Apostolos • GRC • UNDERGROUND PASSAGE
IPPATSU DAIBOKEN • 1968 • Yamada Yoji • JPN • MILLION DOLLAR CHASE
IPPOCAMPO, L' • 1943 • Rosmino Gian Paolo • ITL
IPPODROMI ALL'ALBA • 1950 • Blasetti Alessandro • DOC • ITL
IPPON GATANA DOHYOIRI • 1931 • Inagaki Hiroshi • JPN • SWORD AND THE SUMO RING, A
IPPON GATANA DOHYOIRI • 1934 • Kinugasa Teinosuke • JPN • SWORD AND THE SUMO RING, A
IPPON GATANA DOHYOIRI • 1957 • Makino Masahiro • JPN
IPPON GATANA DOHYOIRI • 1960 • Yasuda Kimiyoshi • JPN • SWORD AND THE SUMO RING, A
IPU'S DEATH see **MOARTEA LUI IPU** • 1972
IQA • 1970 • Maleh Nabil • SHT • SYR • RYTHMES ○ RHYTHM, A
IQAB, AL- • 1947 • Barakat Henry • EGY • PUNITION, LA
IQABO • 1985 • SAF
IQHAWE • 1980 • SAF
IQHAWE II • 1984 • SAF
IR POR LANA • 1976 • Diez Miguel Angel • SHT • SPN
IRA DE DIOS, LA • 1971 • *Aurora* • MXC
IRA DI ACHILLE, L' • 1962 • Girolami Marino • ITL • FURY OF ACHILLES (USA) ○ ACHILLES (UKN)
IRA DI DIO, L' • 1968 • Cardone Alberto • ITL, SPN • WRATH OF GOD, THE
IRACEMA • 1976 • Bodansky Jorge • BRZ
IRADIDDIO, LO • 1963 • Zac Pino • ANS • ITL
IRAN • 1971 • Lelouch Claude • DCS • FRN
IRAN, UN PRINTEMPS EN HIVER • 1980 • Akika Ali • DOC • FRN
IRANY HOLLANDIA • 1986 • van Oostrum Hilde • DOC • NTH, HNG • TRAIN TO HOLLAND
IRAQI WORK SONG, AN • 1977 • Al-Tohamy Foa'Ad • IRQ
IRAQIAN WOMAN, THE • 1978 • Hajjar Rafik • IRQ
IRASHAIMASEN • 1954 • Mizuko Harumi • JPN
IRATAN IRACEMA • 1984 • Guilherme Paulo • PRT
IRE A SANTIAGO • 1964 • Gomez Sara • DOC • CUB
IRELAND • 1975 • Kelly Ron • DOC • CND
IRELAND AND ISRAEL • 1912 • *Champion* • USA
IRELAND: BEHIND THE WIRE • 1974 • Berwick Street Collective • UKN
IRELAND IN REVOLT • 1921 • *Chicago Tribune* • DOC • USA
IRELAND, ISLE OF SPORT • 1961 • Fairbairn Kenneth • IRL
IRELAND OR BUST • 1932 • *Terry Paul/ Moser Frank (P)* • ANS • USA
IRELAND THE OPPRESSED • 1912 • Olcott Sidney • USA
IRELAND -THE TEAR AND THE SMILE • 1960 • Van Dyke Willard • DOC • USA
IRELAND'S BORDER LINE (USA) see **BLARNEY** • 1938
IRENE • 1926 • Green Alfred E. • USA
IRENE • 1940 • Wilcox Herbert • USA
IRENE D'OR • 1923 • Zelnik Friedrich • FRG
IRENE ET SA FOLIE • 1980 • Queysanne Bernard • FRN
IRENE IN NOTEN • 1953 • Emo E. W. • AUS, YGS
IRENE, IRENE • 1975 • Del Monte Peter • ITL
IRENE LATOUR, CONTORTIONIST • 1901 • *Warwick Trading Co.* • UKN
IRENE NEGLUDOV • 1919 • Tourjansky Victor • USS
IRENE, THE ONION EATER'S DAUGHTER • 1914 • *Victor* • USA
IRENE'S BUSY DAY • 1914 • *Victor* • USA
IRENES FEHLTRITT • 1919 • *Widal Maria* • FRG
IRENE'S INFATUATION • 1912 • *Bunny John* • USA
IREZUMI • 1966 • Masumura Yasuzo • JPN • SPIDER GIRL ○ SPIDER TATTOO
IREZUMI ICHIDAI • 1966 • Suzuki Kiyonori • JPN • WHITE TIGER TATTOO (USA)
IREZUMI MUZAN • 1968 • Sekigawa Hideo • JPN • TATTOOED TEMPTRESS
IREZUMI (SPIRIT OF TATTOO) (USA) see **SEKKA TOMURAI ZASHI IREZUMI** • 1981
IRGENDWO IN BERLIN • 1946 • Lamprecht Gerhard • GDR • SOMEWHERE IN BERLIN (USA)
IRGENDWO IN EUROPA (FRG) see **VALAHOL EUROPABAN** • 1947
IRHAM DUMU'I • 1954 • Barakat Henry • EGY • PITIE POUR MES LARMES
IRHAM H'UBB • 1958 • Barakat Henry • EGY • PITIE POUR MON AMOUR
IRINA KIRSANOVA • 1915 • Bauer Yevgeni • USS
IRIS • 1915 • Hepworth Cecil M. • UKN
IRIS • 1968 • Greenberg David • ISR
IRIS • 1985 • Isaac Tony • NZL
IRIS • 1987 • Saks Mady • NTH
IRIS see **SLAVE OF VANITY, A** • 1920
IRIS AND THE LIEUTENANT see **IRIS OCH LOJTNANTSHJARTA** • 1946
IRIS BLEU, L' • 1919 • de Morlhon Camille • FRN
IRIS OCH LOJTNANTSHJARTA • 1946 • Sjoberg Alf • SWD • IRIS (UKN) ○ IRIS AND THE LIEUTENANT
IRIS PERDUE ET RETROUVEE • 1933 • Gasnier Louis J. • FRN
IRIS (UKN) see **IRIS OCH LOJTNANTSHJARTA** • 1946
IRISCHE TRAGODIE see **MEIN LEBEN FUR IRLAND** • 1941
IRISH AND PROUD OF IT • 1936 • Pedelty Donovan • UKN
IRISH AND PROUD OF IT (UKN) see **KING KELLY OF THE U.S.A.** • 1934
IRISH BOY, THE • 1910 • *Lubin* • USA
IRISH DESTINY • 1925 • Eppel I. J. • UKN • IRISH MOTHER, AN
IRISH EYES • 1918 • Dowlan William C. • USA
IRISH EYES see **PADDY O'HARA** • 1917
IRISH EYES ARE SMILING • 1944 • Ratoff Gregory • USA
IRISH FOR LUCK • 1936 • Woods Arthur • UKN • MEET THE DUCHESS
IRISH GIRL, THE • 1917 • Kerrigan J. M. • IRL
IRISH GIRL'S LOVE, AN • 1912 • Olcott Sidney • USA
IRISH GRINGO, THE • 1935 • Thompson William L. • USA
IRISH HEARTS • 1911 • *Atlas* • USA
IRISH HEARTS • 1927 • Haskin Byron • USA
IRISH HEARTS • 1934 • Hurst Brian Desmond • UKN • NORAH O'NEALE (USA)
IRISH HERO, AN • 1909 • *Vitagraph* • USA
IRISH HONEYMOON, THE • 1911 • Olcott Sidney • USA
IRISH IMMIGRANT, THE • 1926 • Croise Hugh • UKN
IRISH IN AMERICA, THE • 1915 • Olcott Sidney • USA
IRISH IN US, THE • 1935 • Bacon Lloyd • USA
IRISH JIG • 1898 • *Levi,jones & Co* • UKN
IRISH LUCK • 1925 • Heerman Victor • USA
IRISH LUCK • 1939 • Bretherton Howard • USA • AMATEUR DETECTIVE (UKN)
IRISH MELODY • 1950 • Barralet Paul • UKN
IRISH MOTHER, AN see **IRISH DESTINY** • 1925
IRISH REBEL, THE • 1916 • *Kalem* • USA
IRISH STEW • 1930 • *Terry Paul/ Moser Frank (P)* • ANS • USA
IRISH SWEEPSTAKES • 1934 • *Terry Paul/ Moser Frank (P)* • ANS • USA
IRISH TOUCHSTONE, AN • 1968 • Gordon Lee • DOC • CND, IRL
IRISH WHISKEY REBELLION • 1972 • Erskine Chester • USA
IRISHMAN, THE • 1978 • Crombie Donald • ASL
IRISHMAN AND THE BUTTON, THE • 1902 • Smith G. A. • UKN
IRITH IRITH • 1985 • Alter Naftali • ISR
IRMA • 1977 • SAF
IRMA IN WONDERLAND • 1916 • Warrenton Lule • SHT • USA
IRMA LA DOUCE • 1963 • Wilder Billy • USA
IRMA LA MALA • 1936 • Sevilla Raphael J. • MXC
IRMAK • 1973 • Akat Lutfu • TRK • RIVER, THE
IRMAOS SEM CORAGEM, OS see **DESEMPREGADOS, OS** • 1972
IRO • 1962 • Iimura Takahiko • SHT • JPN
IRO • 1966 • Murayama Shinji • JPN • SPOILS OF THE NIGHT (USA) ○ NIGHT HUNTER
IRO NO MICHIZURE • 1967 • Mukoi Hiroshi • JPN • COMPANIONS OF LOVE
IRO NO TEHAI-SHI • 1967 • Yamashita Osamu • JPN • LOVE AFFAIR BROKER, THE
IRODORARERU KUCHIBIRU • 1929 • Toyoda Shiro • JPN • PAINTED LIPS
IROGOKUDOH • 1968 • Komori Haku • JPN • LUSTFUL BRUTE
IROKEZAKARI • 1968 • Sawa Kenji • JPN • BLOOM OF VOLUPTUOUSNESS
IROKURUI • 1968 • Sawa Kenji • JPN • EROTOMANIAC, AN
IRON AGE, THE (USA) see **ETA DEL FERRO, L'** • 1964
IRON AND STEEL • 1914 • Costello Maurice, Gaillord Robert • USA
IRON ANGEL • 1964 • Kennedy Ken • USA
IRON ANGEL see **ENGEL AUS EISEN** • 1981
IRON ANGELS • 1988 • *Saiju Hideki*
IRON ARM see **BRASONG BAKAL** • 1968
IRON ARM'S REMORSE • 1910 • *Pantograph* • USA
IRON BREAD • 1970 • Pei Vivian • THL
IRON-CARRIER, THE see **JARNBARAREN** • 1911
IRON-CLAD LOVER, THE • 1910 • *Thanhouser* • USA
IRON CLAW, THE • 1916 • Jose Edward, Seitz George B. • SRL • USA • LAUGHING MASK, THE
IRON CLAW, THE • 1941 • Horne James W. • SRL • USA
IRON COLLAR, THE see **SHOWDOWN** • 1963
IRON CROSS, THE see **EISERNE KREUZ, DER** • 1914
IRON CROSS, THE see **CRUZ DE FERRO, A** • 1967
IRON CROWN, THE see **CORONA DI FERRO, LA** • 1941
IRON CURTAIN, THE • 1948 • Wellman William A. • USA • BEHIND THE IRON CURTAIN
IRON DRAGON STRIKES BACK, THE • Siu Kwai • HKG
IRON DUKE, THE • 1935 • Saville Victor • UKN • WELLINGTON
IRON DUKE, THE see **SECRET LIVES OF THE BRITISH PRIME MINISTERS: THE IRON DUKE, THE** • 1983
IRON EAGLE • 1986 • Furie Sidney J. • USA
IRON EAGLE II see **IRON EAGLE II: BATTLE BEYOND THE FLAG** • 1989
IRON EAGLE II: BATTLE BEYOND THE FLAG • 1989 • Furie Sidney J. • USA • IRON EAGLE II
IRON EARTH, COPPER SKY see **YER DEMIR, GOK BAKIR** • 1987
IRON FAN AND MAGIC SWORD • 1970 • *Shaw* • HKG
IRON FIST • 1926 • McGowan J. P. • USA
IRON FIST ADVENTURE, THE • 1986 • Lee Sean • HKG
IRON FIST OF KWANGTUNG see **CANTON IRON KUNG FU**
IRON FIST (UKN) see **AWAKENING OF JIM BURKE, THE** • 1935
IRON FISTS see **PANJE-E-AHANIN** • 1968
IRON FLOOD, THE see **ZHELYEZNY POTOK** • 1967
IRON FLOWER, THE see **VASVIRAG** • 1957
IRON GATE see **BAB EL HADID** • 1957
IRON GLOVE, THE • 1954 • Castle William • USA • KISS AND THE SWORD, THE
IRON HAND, THE • 1916 • Davis Ulysses • USA
IRON HAND, THE see **ELDEST SON RULES, THE** • 1912
IRON HEART, THE • 1917 • Fitzmaurice George • USA
IRON HEART, THE • 1920 • Clift Denison, Cazeneuve Paul • USA
IRON HEEL, THE • 1912 • *Mcdonald Norman* • USA
IRON HEEL, THE see **JELOZNAYA PUYATA** • 1919
IRON HELMET, THE • 1910 • *Walturdaw* • UKN
IRON HELMET, THE (USA) see **ZELEZNY KLOBOUK** • 1960
IRON HORSE, THE • 1924 • Ford John • USA
IRON HORSE, THE • 1968 • Yuan Chiu-Feng • HKG
IRON JUSTICE • 1915 • Morgan Sidney • UKN
IRON MAIDEN, THE • 1962 • Thomas Gerald • UKN • SWINGIN' MAIDEN, THE (USA)
IRON MAJOR, THE • 1943 • Enright Ray • USA
IRON MAN • 1931 • Browning Tod • USA
IRON MAN • 1951 • Pevney Joseph • USA
IRON MAN, THE • 1925 • Bennett Whitman • USA
IRON MAN, THE • 1930 • Foster John • ANS • USA
IRON MASK, THE • 1929 • Dwan Allan • USA
IRON MASTER, THE • 1911 • Porter Edwin S. • USA
IRON MASTER, THE • 1913 • Cabanne W. Christy • USA
IRON MASTER, THE • 1914 • Vale Travers • USA
IRON MASTER, THE • 1933 • Franklin Chester M. • USA
IRON MASTER, THE see **PADRONE DELLE FERRIERE, IL** • 1919
IRON MASTER, THE see **GUERRA DEL FERRO, LA** • 1983
IRON MISTRESS, THE • 1952 • Douglas Gordon • USA
IRON MITT, THE • 1916 • Dillon John Francis • SHT • USA
IRON MOUNTAIN TRAIL • 1953 • Witney William • USA
IRON NAG, THE • 1925 • *Sennett Mack (P)* • SHT • USA
IRON NECK see **IRON NECK LI**
IRON NECK LI • Chang Jen Chieh • HKG • IRON NECK
IRON OX: THE TIGER KILLER see **T'IEH NIU FU HU** • 1973
IRON OX, THE TIGER'S KILLER see **T'IEH NIU FU HU** • 1973
IRON PETTICOAT, THE • 1956 • Thomas Ralph • UKN, USA • NOT FOR MONEY
IRON PREFECT, THE see **PREFETTO DI FERRO, IL** • 1977
IRON RIDER, THE • 1920 • Dunlap Scott R. • USA
IRON RING see **KANAWA** • 1972
IRON RING, THE • 1917 • Archainbaud George • USA
IRON RIVALS, THE • 1916 • McRae Henry • SHT • USA
IRON ROAD, THE (UKN) see **BUCKSKIN FRONTIER** • 1943
IRON SHERIFF, THE • 1957 • Salkow Sidney • USA
IRON STAIR, THE • 1920 • Thornton F. Martin • UKN • BRANDED SOUL, THE (USA)
IRON STAIR, THE • 1933 • Hiscott Leslie • UKN
IRON STRAIN, THE • 1916 • Barker Reginald • USA
IRON SWORDSMAN, THE (USA) see **CONTE UGOLINO, IL** • 1950
IRON TEST, THE • 1919 • Hurst Paul C., Bradbury Robert North • SRL • USA • HEARTS AND THE CIRCUS
IRON TO GOLD • 1922 • Durning Bernard J. • USA
IRON TRAIL, THE • 1913 • McRae Henry • USA
IRON TRAIL, THE • 1921 • Neill R. William • USA
IRON TRIANGLE, THE • 1988 • Weston Eric • USA
IRON WARRIOR • 1986 • Brescia Alfonso • ITL
IRON WILL, THE • 1916 • MacDonald J. Farrell • SHT • USA
IRON WILLS (USA) see **HARDA VILJOR** • 1922
IRON WOMAN, THE • 1916 • Harbaugh Carl • USA
IRON WOMAN, THE see **THAT'S MY UNCLE** • 1935
IRONIA DEL DINERO, LA • 1954 • Neville Edgar • SPN
IRONIE DU DESTIN, L' • 1924 • Kirsanoff Dimitri • FRN • IRONY OF FATE, THE
IRONIE DU SORT, L' • 1925 • Monca Georges, Keroul Maurice • FRN
IRONIE DU SORT, L' • 1974 • Molinaro Edouard • FRN
IRONMASTER, THE • 1913 • Barker Reginald? • USA
IRONMASTER, THE see **GUERRA DEL FERRO, LA** • 1983
IRONS OF WRATH • 1987 • Millar Gavin • UKN
IRONSIDE • 1967 • Goldstone James • TVM • USA
IRONWEED • 1987 • Babenco Hector • USA
IRONY OF FATE • 1910 • Salter Harry • USA
IRONY OF FATE, THE • 1912 • Haldane Bert? • UKN
IRONY OF FATE, THE • 1912 • Young James • USA
IRONY OF FATE, THE • 1975 • Ryazanov Eldar • USS
IRONY OF FATE, THE see **IRONIE DU DESTIN, L'** • 1924
IRONY OF JUSTICE, THE • 1916 • Hansel Howell?, McGill Lawrence? • SHT • USA
IROQUOIS TRAIL, THE • 1950 • Karlson Phil • USA • TOMAHAWK TRAIL, THE (UKN)
IROWANA • 1967 • Kataoka Hitoshi • JPN • TRAP OF LUST
IRRE VON SCHLOSS IHORRINGHUUS, DIE • 1920 • Weigert August • FRG
IRRECONCILABLE, THE • 1980 • Thomopoulos Andreas • GRC
IRRECONCILABLE DIFFERENCES • 1984 • Shyer Charles • USA
IRRENDE SEELEN • 1921 • Froelich Carl • FRG • SKLAVEN DER SINNE ○ IDIOT, DER

IRRESISTIBLE • 1982 • Brown Edwin Scott • USA
IRRESISTIBLE see **BELLE MA POVERE** • 1957
IRRESISTIBLE CATHERINE, L' • 1955 • Pergament Andre • FRN
IRRESISTIBLE FLAPPER, THE • 1919 • Wilson Frank • UKN
IRRESISTIBLE LOVER, THE • 1927 • Beaudine William • USA
IRRESISTIBLE MAN, THE (USA) see **UNWIDERSTEHLICHE, DER** • 1937
IRRESISTIBLE REBELLE, L' • 1940 • Le Chanois Jean-Paul • FRN • IDEE A L'EAU, UNE
IRRESPONSIBLE SYD • 1915 • De Gray Sidney • USA
IRRFAHRT INS GLUCK • 1914 • Hamburger • FRG
IRRGARTEN DER LEIDENSCHAFT (FRG) see **PLEASURE GARDEN, THE** • 1926
IRRIGATION • 1980 • Gordon Lee • DOC • CND, USA
IRRIGATION: THE ORD RIVER SCHEME AND THE M.I.A. • 1973 • Howes Oliver • DOC • ASL
IRRITABLE MODEL, AN see **MODELE IRASCIBLE, UN** • 1897
IRRLICHT • 1919 • Lund Erik • FRG
IRRLICHTER see **LIEBE DER BRUDER ROTT, DIE** • 1929
IRRTUM DES HERZENS • 1939 • Hoffmann Bernd • FRG
IRRUNGEN • 1919 • Biebrach Rudolf • FRG
IRRWEGE DER LIEBE • 1918 • Stein Josef • FRG
IRRWEGE DER LIEBE • 1927 • Lisson Heinrich • FRG
IRU MALARGAL • 1967 • Thirulokachander A. S. • IND • TWO FLOWERS
IRWIN ALLEN'S PRODUCTION OF FIRE! see **FIRE!** • 1977
IRYUHIN–NASHI • 1959 • Murayama Shinji • JPN • LOST ARTICLES
IS • 1970 • Lindman • MTV • SWD • ICE
IS A MOTHER TO BLAME? • 1922 • Sheldon Roy • USA
IS ANNA ANDERSON ANASTASIA? see **ANASTASIA –DIE LETZTE ZARENTOCHTER** • 1956
IS ANY GIRL SAFE? • 1916 • Jaccard Jacques • USA
IS ANYBODY DOING ANYTHING ABOUT IT? • 1967 • Crombie Donald • SHT • ASL
IS CHRISTMAS A BORE? • 1915 • Drew Sidney • USA
IS CONAN DOYLE RIGHT? • 1923 • Harvey John Joseph • SHT • USA
IS DIVORCE A FAILURE? • 1923 • Worsley Wallace • USA • WHEN CIVILIZATION FAILED
IS EVERYBODY HAPPY? • 1928 • Yates Hal • SHT • USA
IS EVERYBODY HAPPY? • 1929 • Mayo Archie • USA
IS EVERYBODY HAPPY? • 1941 • Ceballos Larry • SHT • USA
IS EVERYBODY HAPPY? • 1943 • Barton Charles T. • USA
IS HE ELIGIBLE? • 1912 • *Edison* • USA
IS IT A SIN? see **KASALANAN KAYA?** • 1968
IS IT A WOMAN'S WORLD? • 1956 • Haldane Don • SHT • CND
IS IT EASY TO BE YOUNG • Podnieks Yu. • DOC • USS
IS IT YOU? • 1987 • Jaglom Henry • USA
IS IT YOUR HAT? • 1912 • *Pathe* • USA
IS LIFE BEAUTIFUL? see **VIDA E BELAI?, A** • 1982
IS LIFE WORTH LIVING? • 1921 • Crosland Alan • USA
IS LOVE EVERYTHING? • 1924 • Cabanne W. Christy • USA
IS MARRIAGE A FAILURE? (UKN) see **FOOLISH MATRONS, THE** • 1921
IS MARRIAGE SACRED? • 1916-17 • SER • USA
IS MARRIAGE THE BUNK? • 1925 • McCarey Leo • SHT • USA
IS MATRIMONY A FAILURE? • 1922 • Cruze James • USA
IS MONEY ALL? • 1917 • Baldwin Ruth Ann • SHT • USA
IS MONEY EVERTHING? • 1923 • Lyons Glen • USA
IS MY FACE RED? • 1932 • Seiter William A. • USA
IS MY PALM READ? see **IS MY PALM RED?** • 1933
IS MY PALM RED? • 1933 • Fleischer Dave • ANS • USA • IS MY PALM READ?
IS PARIS BURNING? (UKN) see **PARIS BRULE–T–IL?** • 1966
IS–SLOTTET • 1986 • Blom Per • NRW • ICE PALACE, THE
IS THAT IT? • 1987 • Trust Wilf • UKN
IS THAT NICE? • 1926 • Andrews Del • USA
IS THE BAGPIPE AN INSTRUMENT? • 1979 • Shopov Assen • BUL
IS THERE A DOCTOR IN THE MOUSE? • 1964 • Jones Charles M. • ANS • USA
IS THERE ANYBODY THERE? • 1976 • Maxwell Peter • MTV • ASL
IS THERE ANYTHING WRONG IN THAT? • 1929 • Aylott Dave, Symmons E. F. • SHT • UKN
IS THERE JUSTICE? • 1931 • Paton Stuart • USA
IS THERE ONE WHO UNDERSTANDS ME? • 1981 • O'Mordha Sean • IRL
IS THERE SEX AFTER DEATH? • 1971 • Abel Alan, Abel Jeanne • USA
IS THERE SEX AFTER MARRIAGE? • 1974 • Robinson Richard • USA
IS THIS A RECORD? • 1973 • Turpin • SHT • UKN
IS THIS TRIP REALLY NECESSARY? see **IS YOUR TRIP REALLY NECESSARY?** • 1969
IS YOUR DAUGHTER SAFE? • 1927 • King Louis, Lee Leon • USA
IS YOUR HONEYMOON REALLY NECESSARY? • 1953 • Elvey Maurice • UKN
IS YOUR SWEETHEART FALSE? • 1919 • *Strand* • USA
IS YOUR TRIP REALLY NECESSARY? • 1969 • Benoit Ben • USA • IS THIS TRIP REALLY NECESSARY? ○ BLOOD OF THE IRON MAIDEN ○ TRIP TO TERROR
IS ZAT SO? • 1927 • Green Alfred E. • USA
ISAAC LITTLE–FEATHERS • 1985 • Rose Les • CND • DRASTIC MEASURES
ISAACS AS A BROKER'S MAN • 1913 • Calvert Charles? • UKN
ISABEL • 1968 • Almond Paul • CND
ISABEL AUF DER TREPPE • 1984 • Unterberg Hannelore • GDR • ISABEL ON THE STAIRS
ISABEL DE SOLIS REINA DE GRANADA • 1931 • Buchs Jose • SPN
ISABEL IS DEATH see **TATU BOLA** • 1972
ISABEL ON THE STAIRS see **ISABEL AUF DER TREPPE** • 1984
ISABELL, A DREAM • 1958 • Cozzi Luigi • ITL
ISABELLA D'ARAGON • 1910 • Pasquali Ernesto Maria • ITL
ISABELLA DUCHESSA DEI DIAVOLI • 1969 • Corbucci Bruno • ITL
ISABELLE A PEUR DES HOMMES • 1957 • Gourguet Jean • FRN
ISABELLE AND LUST see **ISABELLE DEVANT LE DESIR** • 1974
ISABELLE AUX DOMBES • 1951 • Pialat Maurice • SHT • FRN
ISABELLE DEVANT LE DESIR • 1974 • Berckmans Jean-Pierre • FRN, BLG • ISABELLE AND LUST
ISABELLE EBERHARDT • 1990 • Pringle Ian • FRN
ISABELLE ET LA LOCOMOTIVE • 1972 • Ledoux Patrick • BLG
ISABEL'S CHOICE • 1981 • Green Guy • TVM • USA
ISADORA • 1968 • Reisz Karel • UKN • LOVES OF ISADORA, THE
ISADORA DUNCAN, THE BIGGEST DANCER IN THE WORLD • 1966 • Russell Ken • MTV • UKN
ISADORE A LA DEVEINE • 1919 • Florey Robert • SHT • SWT
ISADORE SUR LE LAC • 1919 • Florey Robert • SHT • SWT
ISALAMUSI • 1984 • SAF
ISANG LIBONG MUKHA • 1968 • Marquez Artemio • PHL • ONE THOUSAND FACES
ISAYAN • 1980 • Aksoy Orhan • TRK • REVOLT, THE
ISBAN ISRAEL • 1920 • SAF
ISCHIA L'ISOLA FIORITA • 1956 • Heusch Paolo • DOC • ITL
ISCHIA OPERAZIONE AMORE • 1966 • Sala Vittorio • ITL
ISEN BRYDES • 1947 • Roos Jorgen • DOC • DNM • ICE–BREAKING
ISEZAKICHO BLUES see **ISEZAKICHO BURUSU** • 1968
ISEZAKICHO BURUSU • 1968 • Murayama Shinji • JPN • ISEZAKICHO BLUES
ISFUGLE • 1983 • Kragh-Jacobsen Soren • DNM • ICEBIRDS ○ THUNDERBIRDS
ISH GABIBBLE • 1913 • *Solax* • USA
ISH RACHAEL • 1975 • Mizrahi Moshe • ISR • RACHEL'S MAN
ISHAM JONES AND HIS ORCHESTRA • 1934 • Mack Roy • SHT • USA
ISHI GASSEN • 1955 • *Yamada Isuzu* • JPN • STONE BATTLE
ISHI OF THE FISH MARKET see **NINKYO KASHI NO ISHIMATSU** • 1967
ISHI, THE LAST OF HIS TRIBE • 1978 • Miller Robert Ellis • TVM • USA
ISHIMATSU FROM MORI see **MORI NO ISHIMATSU** • 1949
ISHIMATSU OF MORI see **MORI NO ISHIMATSU** • 1949
ISHIMATSU OF THE FOREST see **MORI NO ISHIMATSU** • 1949
ISHIMATSU TRAVELS WITH GHOSTS see **MORI NO ISHIMATSU YUREI DOCHU** • 1959
ISHINAKA SENSEI GYOJOKI • 1950 • Naruse Mikio • JPN • CONDUCT REPORT OF PROFESSOR ISHINAKA ○ CONDUCT REPORT ON PROFESSOR ISHINAWA
ISHINAKA SENSEI GYOJOKI • 1966 • Maruyama Seiji • JPN • BIG WIND FROM TOKYO (USA)
ISHQ PAR ZOR NAHIN • 1970 • *Burman S. D. (M)* • IND
ISHQ WA DOSTI • 1946 • Latif Reshid • IND, AFG • LOVE AND FRIENDSHIP
ISHTAR • 1987 • May Elaine • USA
ISHWAR BHAKTI • 1951 • Gunjal Dada • IND • DEVOTEE TO ISHWAR
ISI NERAKA • 1960 • Sulong Jamil • MLY • SINNERS TO HELL
ISIDOR HUBER UND DIE FOLGEN • 1972 • Graf Urs, Graf Marlies • SWT
ISIDRO EL LABRADOR • 1963 • Salvia Rafael J. • SPN • ISIDRO THE PEASANT
ISIDRO THE PEASANT see **ISIDRO EL LABRADOR** • 1963
ISIGANGI • 1981 • SAF
ISIMANGA • 1976 • SAF
ISINAMUVA • 1985 • SAF
ISIPHO SEZWE • 1985 • SAF
ISIQHWAGA • 1982 • SAF
ISIS • 1910 • *Pathe* • SHT • FRN
ISIS • 1973 • Hurley Maury • USA
ISIS AU 8 • 1972 • Chartrand Alain • CND
ISITHIXO SEGOLIDE • 1984 • SAF
ISITWALANDWE: THE STORY OF THE SOUTH AFRICAN FREEDOM CHARTER • 1980 • Feinberg Barry • UKN
ISIVUMELWANO • 1978 • Sabela Simon • SAF • ISUVUMELWANO
ISKANDARYA LIH? see **ISKINDIRIA.. LEH?** • 1978
ISKANJA • 1980 • Klopcic Matjaz • YGS • TRAZANJA ○ SEARCH
ISKENDRIA KAMAN WAKAMAN • 1989 • Shahin Youssef • EGY, FRN • ALEXANDRIA MORE AND MORE
ISKHOD • 1968 • Bobrovsky Anatoli, Buntar Zhamian Ghiin • USS, MNG • OUTCOME, THE
ISKINDIRIA.. LEH? • 1978 • Shahin Youssef • EGY • ISKANDARYA LIH? ○ ALEXANDRIA, POURQUOI? ○ ALEXANDRIA, WHY? ○ ASKNDRIE.. LIE?
ISKOLAKERULOK • 1989 • Kardos Ferenc • HNG • TRUANTS
ISKUSAVANJE DAVOLA • 1989 • Nikolic Zivko • YGS, FRN • TEMPTING THE DEVIL
ISLA, LA • 1974 • *I.p.a.* • MXC
ISLA, LA • 1979 • Doria Alejandro • ARG • ISLAND, THE
ISLA CON TOMATE, UNA • 1962 • Leblanc Tony • SPN
ISLA DE LA DESESPERACION, LA • 1971 • *Avant* • MXC
ISLA DE LA MUERTE, LA (SPN) see **GEHEIMNIS DER TODESINSEL, DAS** • 1967
ISLA DE LA PASION, LA • 1941 • Fernandez Emilio • MXC • PASSION ISLAND (USA) ○ ISLAND OF PASSION, THE
ISLA DE LOS DINOSAUROS, LA • 1966 • Portillo Rafael • MXC, USA • ISLAND OF THE DINOSAURS, THE ○ DINOSAUR ISLAND
ISLA DE LOS HOMBRES SOLOS, LA • 1973 • *Churubusco Azteca* • MXC
ISLA DE LOS MUERTOS, LA see **SNAKE PEOPLE** • 1968
ISLA DE MUJERES • 1952 • *Baledon Rafael* • MXC
ISLA DE SAL • 1964 • de la Cerda Clemente • VNZ • ISLAND OF SALT
ISLA DEL TESORO • 1969 • Gomez Sara • DOC • CUB
ISLA DEL TESORO, LA see **TREASURE ISLAND** • 1972
ISLA MALDITA, LA • 1934 • Maicon Boris • MXC
ISLA MISTERIOSA, LA see **ILE MYSTERIEUSE, L'** • 1973
ISLA PARA DOS • 1958 • Davison Tito • MXC
ISLA, THE TIGRESS OF SIBERIA see **ILSA, LA TIGRESSE DU GOULAG** • 1977
ISLAMIYETIN KAHRAMAN KIZI • 1968 • Arikan Kayahan • TRK • HEROIC DAUGHTER OF ISLAM, THE
ISLAND • 1975 • Cox Paul • SHT • ASL
ISLAND • 1988 • Cox Paul • ASL
ISLAND, THE • 1980 • Ritchie Michael • USA
ISLAND, THE see **HADAKA NO SHIMA** • 1961
ISLAND, THE see **ON** • 1966
ISLAND, THE see **VIOLENZA AL SOLE** • 1969
ISLAND, THE see **INSEL, DIE** • 1974
ISLAND, THE see **ISLA, LA** • 1979
ISLAND, THE see **SHENGSI XIAN** • 1985
ISLAND, THE see **ADA** • 1987
ISLAND AFFAIR see **BREVI AMORE A PALMA DI MAJORCA** • 1959
ISLAND AT THE TOP OF THE WORLD, THE • 1974 • Stevenson Robert • USA
ISLAND CAPTIVES • 1937 • Kershner Glenn • USA
ISLAND CHRONICLE see **PAD ITALIJA** • 1982
ISLAND CLAWS • 1980 • Cardenas Hernan • USA • NIGHT OF THE CLAW
ISLAND COMEDY, AN • 1911 • *Mcdermott Marc* • USA
ISLAND ESCAPE (UKN) see **NO MAN IS AN ISLAND** • 1962
ISLAND FLING, THE • 1946 • Tytla Bill • ANS • USA
ISLAND FROG • Chung Jin-Woo • SKR
ISLAND FUSE • 1971 • Cantrill Arthur, Cantrill Corinne • DOC • ASL
ISLAND IN FLIGHT • 1930 • Rasumny Alexander • USS
ISLAND IN THE SKY • 1938 • Leeds Herbert I. • USA
ISLAND IN THE SKY • 1953 • Wellman William A. • USA
ISLAND IN THE SNOW see **ZEMLYA SANNIKOVA** • 1973
ISLAND IN THE SUN • 1957 • Rossen Robert • USA, UKN
ISLAND JESS • 1914 • Tudor F. C. S. • UKN
ISLAND LOVE SONG • 1986 • Sarin Vic • MTV • CND
ISLAND LURE, THE • 1976 • Bonniere Rene • SHT • CND
ISLAND MEN see **WEST OF KERRY** • 1938
ISLAND NATION, AN see **OUR ISLAND NATION** • 1937
ISLAND NATION: JAPAN, AN • 1949 • *De Rochemont Louis (P)* • DCS • USA
ISLAND OF ADVENTURE, THE • 1982 • Squire Anthony • UKN
ISLAND OF ADVENTURE, THE see **LIGHT OF VICTORY, THE** • 1919
ISLAND OF BLOOD • 1986 • Naud William T. • USA • WHODUNNIT?
ISLAND OF CRIME (UKN) see **SEQUESTRO DI PERSONA** • 1968
ISLAND OF DEATH • 1975 • Mastorakis Nico • GRC • CRAVING FOR LUST, A
ISLAND OF DEATH see **QUIEN PUEDE MATAR A UN NINO?** • 1975
ISLAND OF DESIRE, THE • 1917 • Turner Otis • USA
ISLAND OF DESIRE (UKN) see **LOVE TRADER, THE** • 1930
ISLAND OF DESIRE (USA) see **SATURDAY ISLAND** • 1951
ISLAND OF DESPAIR, THE • 1926 • Edwards Henry • UKN
ISLAND OF DR. MOREAU, THE • 1977 • Taylor Don • USA
ISLAND OF DR. MOREAU, THE see **ISLAND OF LOST SOULS** • 1933
ISLAND OF DOOM • 1933 • Timoshenko S. • USS
ISLAND OF DOOMED MEN • 1940 • Barton Charles T. • USA • DEAD MAN'S ISLE
ISLAND OF DREAMS • 1982 • Burton Geoff • ASL
ISLAND OF FLAME, THE see **CUBA SEGODNYA** • 1960
ISLAND OF FORGOTTEN SINS, THE • 1941 • Diamant-Berger Henri
ISLAND OF GREAT HOPES, AN see **WYSPA WIELKICH NADZIEI** • 1957
ISLAND OF HAPPINESS see **ONNEN SAARI** • 1955
ISLAND OF HAPPINESS, THE • 1916 • Leggett J. Alexander • USA
ISLAND OF HORRORS (UKN) see **GOKUMON–TO** • 1977
ISLAND OF INTRIGUE, THE • 1919 • Otto Henry • USA
ISLAND OF LIONS, THE • 1913 • Whitman Frank • USA
ISLAND OF LIVING HORROR see **BRIDES OF BLOOD** • 1968
ISLAND OF LOST MEN • 1939 • Neumann Kurt • USA
ISLAND OF LOST SOULS • 1933 • Kenton Erle C. • USA • ISLAND OF DR. MOREAU, THE
ISLAND OF LOST WOMEN • 1959 • Tuttle Frank • USA
ISLAND OF LOVE • 1963 • Da Costa Morton • USA • NOT ON YOUR LIFE
ISLAND OF LOVE • *Hunter Diane* • USA
ISLAND OF LOVE XANAVA • Sulistrowski Zygmunt • USA
ISLAND OF LOVERS see **GUEZIREH EL OSHAK** • 1968
ISLAND OF LOVES, THE see **ILHA DOS AMORES, A** • 1978
ISLAND OF MONGOOSES, THE see **MONGUZOK SZIGETEN, A** • 1959
ISLAND OF MONTE CRISTO (UKN) see **SWORD OF VENUS** • 1952
ISLAND OF MUTANTS see **ISOLA DEGLI UOMINI PESCE, L'** • 1979
ISLAND OF MUTATIONS see **ISOLA DEGLI UOMINI PESCE, L'** • 1979
ISLAND OF NAKED SCANDAL see **SHIMA TO RATAI JIKEN** • 1931
ISLAND OF NEVER WAS, THE • 1916 • Miller Rube • USA
ISLAND OF PASSION see **ILE DES PASSIONS, L'** • 1982
ISLAND OF PASSION, THE see **ISLA DE LA PASION, LA** • 1941
ISLAND OF PERVERSITY, THE • 1913 • Miller Ashley • USA
ISLAND OF PROCIDA, THE (USA) see **ISOLA DI MONTECRISTO, L'** • 1950
ISLAND OF REGENERATION, THE • 1915 • Davenport Harry • USA
ISLAND OF ROMANCE, THE • 1922 • Wright Humberston • UKN
ISLAND OF ROSES • 1957 • Gass Karl • DOC • GDR
ISLAND OF SALT see **ISLA DE SAL** • 1964
ISLAND OF SHAME (UKN) see **YOUNG ONE, THE** • 1960
ISLAND OF SILVER HERONS, THE see **OSTROV STRIBRNYCH VOLAVEK** • 1976
ISLAND OF SISTER TERESA, THE see **MYSTERIOUS ISLAND OF BEAUTIFUL WOMEN** • 1979
ISLAND OF SURPRISE, THE • 1916 • Scardon Paul • USA
ISLAND OF SWANS see **INSEL DER SCHWANE** • 1983
ISLAND OF TERROR • 1965 • Fisher Terence • UKN • NIGHT OF THE SILICATES ○ NIGHT THE CREATURES CAME ○ SILICATES, THE ○ CREEPERS, THE ○ NIGHT THE SILCATES CAME
ISLAND OF TERROR see **ILE D'EPOUVANTE** • 1913
ISLAND OF THE ALIVE • 1986 • Cohen Larry • USA • IT'S ALIVE III: ISLAND OF THE ALIVE

ISLAND OF THE BIG CLOTH • 1969 • McConnell Edward • DCS • UKN
ISLAND OF THE BLUE DOLPHINS • 1964 • Clark James B. • USA
ISLAND OF THE BURNING DAMNED (USA) see **NIGHT OF THE BIG HEAT** • 1967
ISLAND OF THE BURNING DOOMED see **NIGHT OF THE BIG HEAT** • 1967
ISLAND OF THE DAMNED (USA) see **QUIEN PUEDE MATAR A UN NINO?** • 1975
ISLAND OF THE DEAD see **DODES "O", DE** • 1913
ISLAND OF THE DEAD see **GEHEIMNIS DER TODESINSEL, DAS** • 1967
ISLAND OF THE DINOSAURS, THE see **ISLA DE LOS DINOSAUROS, LA** • 1966
ISLAND OF THE DOOMED (USA) see **GEHEIMNIS DER TODESINSEL, DAS** • 1967
ISLAND OF THE FISH MEN, THE see **ISOLA DEGLI UOMINI PESCE, L'** • 1979
ISLAND OF THE FISHERMEN, THE see **ISOLA DEGLI UOMINI PESCE, L'** • 1979
ISLAND OF THE LAST ZOMBIES, THE see **REGINA DEI CANNIBALI, LA** • 1979
ISLAND OF THE LIVING DEAD see **ZOMBI 2** • 1979
ISLAND OF THE LOST • 1967 • Browning Ricou, Florea John • USA • DANGEROUS ISLAND ○ LOST ISLAND
ISLAND OF THE MONGOOSES, THE see **MONGUZOK SZIGETEN, A** • 1959
ISLAND OF THE SAVAGE SEX SLAVES see **TANZERINNEN FUR TANGER** • 1977
ISLAND OF THE SILVER HERONS see **OSTROV STRIBRNYCH VOLAVEK** • 1976
ISLAND OF THE SNAKE PEOPLE see **SNAKE PEOPLE** • 1968
ISLAND OF THE TWILIGHT PEOPLE see **TWILIGHT PEOPLE** • 1972
ISLAND OF TURTLES • 1958 • Monkman Noel • DOC • ASL
ISLAND OF WISDOM, THE • 1920 • Keith Anthony • UKN
ISLAND ON THE CONTINENT see **SZIGET A SZARAZFOLDON** • 1968
ISLAND PEOPLE • 1940 • Leacock Philip • DOC • UKN
ISLAND PRINCESS, THE see **PRINCIPESSA DELLE CANARIE, LA** • 1956
ISLAND RESCUE (USA) see **APPOINTMENT WITH VENUS** • 1951
ISLAND ROMANCE, AN • 1913 • Collins Edwin J.? • UKN
ISLAND SINNER, THE (USA) see **PECCATRICE DELL'ISOLA, LA** • 1953
ISLAND SONS • 1987 • Levi Alan J. • TVM • USA
ISLAND TARGET • 1945 • Smart Ralph • DCS • ASL
ISLAND TRADER • 1970 • Rubie Howard • ASL
ISLAND WIVES • 1922 • Campbell Webster • USA
ISLAND WOMAN • 1958 • Berke William • USA
ISLAND WOMAN see **SHIMA NO ONNA** • 1920
ISLANDER, THE • 1978 • Krasny Paul • TVM • USA
ISLANDERS, THE • Holmes J. B. • DOC • UKN
ISLANDERS, THE • 1939 • Harvey Maurice • DOC • UKN
ISLANDERS, THE • 1965 • Robertson George C. • CND
ISLANDERS, THE • 1967 • Holmes Cecil • DOC • ASL
ISLANDS see **VERFUHRUNG AM MEER** • 1963
ISLANDS IN THE STREAM • 1977 • Schaffner Franklin J. • USA
ISLANDS OF THE WEST • 1973 • Forsyth Bill • DCS • UKN
ISLANDS ON THE LAGOON see **ISOLE DELLA LAGUNA** • 1947
ISLAS MARIAS • 1950 • Fernandez Emilio • MXC
ISLE OF ABANDONED HOPE, THE • 1914 • *Bison* • USA
ISLE OF CONQUEST, THE • 1919 • Jose Edward • USA • BROKEN BARRIER, THE ○ BY RIGHT OF CONQUEST
ISLE OF CONTENT, THE • 1915 • Nicholls George • USA
ISLE OF DESTINY • 1940 • Clifton Elmer • USA
ISLE OF DESTINY, THE • 1920 • *Character Pictures* • USA
ISLE OF DOUBT • 1922 • Smith Hamilton • USA
ISLE OF DREAMS, THE see **INSEL DER TRAUME, DIE** • 1925
ISLE OF ESCAPE • 1930 • Bretherton Howard • USA
ISLE OF FORGOTTEN SINS • 1943 • Ulmer Edgar G. • USA • MONSOON
ISLE OF FORGOTTEN WOMEN • 1927 • Seitz George B. • USA • FORGOTTEN WOMEN (UKN)
ISLE OF FURY • 1936 • McDonald Frank • USA
ISLE OF HOPE, THE • 1925 • Nelson Jack • USA
ISLE OF INTRIGUE • 1931 • Harwood A. R. • SHT • ASL
ISLE OF INTRIGUE, THE • 1918 • Ford Francis • USA
ISLE OF LEVANT • 1957 • *Kunz Werner (P)* • SWT, DNM
ISLE OF LIFE, THE • 1916 • George Burton • USA
ISLE OF LOST MEN • 1928 • Worne Duke • USA
ISLE OF LOST SHIPS, THE • 1923 • Tourneur Maurice • USA
ISLE OF LOST SHIPS, THE • 1929 • Willat Irvin V. • USA
ISLE OF LOVE, THE • 1916 • Middleton Edwin • USA
ISLE OF LOVE, THE • 1922 • Balshofer Fred J. • USA
ISLE OF MAN T.T. 1950 • 1950 • Hughes Geoffrey • DOC • UKN
ISLE OF MISSING MEN • 1942 • Oswald Richard • USA
ISLE OF MYSTERY, THE (UKN) see **COMBAT** • 1927
ISLE OF OBLIVION (USA) see **OSTROV ZABVENNYA** • 1917
ISLE OF PINGO PONGO, THE • 1938 • Avery Tex • ANS • USA
ISLE OF RETRIBUTION, THE • 1926 • Hogan James P. • USA
ISLE OF RHUM, THE • 1971 • Mylne Christopher • DCS • UKN
ISLE OF SIN (USA) see **FLITTERWOCHEN IN DER HOLLE** • 1960
ISLE OF SINNERS (UKN) see **DIEU A BESOIN DES HOMMES** • 1950
ISLE OF SUNKEN GOLD • 1927 • Webb Harry S. • SRL • USA
ISLE OF THE BLESSED, THE see **INSEL DER SELIGEN, DIE** • 1913
ISLE OF THE DEAD • 1945 • Robson Mark • USA
ISLE OF THE DEAD see **LITTLE PHANTASY ON A 19TH CENTURY PAINTING, A** • 1946
ISLE OF THE DEAD (USA) see **DODES "O", DE** • 1913
ISLE OF THE FISH MEN see **SCREAMERS** • 1979
ISLE OF THE LION see **OROSZLAN UGRANI KESZUL, AZ** • 1969
ISLE OF THE SNAKE PEOPLE see **SNAKE PEOPLE** • 1968
ISLE OF VANISHING MEN, THE • 1924 • Alder William F. • DOC • USA
ISLEROS, LOS • 1952 • Demare Lucas • ARG
ISLES FEROE, LES see **FOROYAR FAEROERNE** • 1960
ISMAEL BEY • 1914 • Volkov Alexander • USS
ISMAEL RIVERA: PORTRAIT IN PUERTO RICAN see **ISMAEL RIVERA: RETRATO EN BORICUA** • 1989
ISMAEL RIVERA: RETRATO EN BORICUA • 1989 • Trigo Enrique • DOC • PRC • ISMAEL RIVERA: PORTRAIT IN PUERTO RICAN
ISMAIL YASSIN, BULISS HARBI • 1958 • Wahab Fatin Abdel • EGY • ISMAIL YASSIN M.P.
ISMAIL YASSIN DANS LA MARINE see **ISMAIL YASSIN FI AL-'USTUL** • 1958
ISMAIL YASSIN DANS LA POLICE see **ISMAIL YASSIN FI AL-BULISS** • 1955
ISMAIL YASSIN DANS L'ARMEE see **ISMAIL YASSIN FI AL-JAYSH** • 1955
ISMAIL YASSIN FI AL-BULISS • 1955 • Wahab Fatin Abdel • EGY • ISMAIL YASSIN DANS LA POLICE
ISMAIL YASSIN FI AL-JAYSH • 1955 • Wahab Fatin Abdel • EGY • ISMAIL YASSIN DANS L'ARMEE
ISMAIL YASSIN FI AL-'USTUL • 1958 • Wahab Fatin Abdel • EGY • ISMAIL YASSIN DANS LA MARINE
ISMAIL YASSIN M.P. see **ISMAIL YASSIN, BULISS HARBI** • 1958
ISMAIL YASSIN AND THE GHOST see **AFRITET ISMAIL YASSINE** • 1954
ISMAIL YASSINE AS TARZAN see **ISMAIL YASSINE TARAZANE** • 1958
ISMAIL YASSINE TARAZANE • 1958 • Mustafa Niazi • EGY • ISMAIL YASSINE AS TARZAN
ISMERETLEN ISMEROS • 1988 • Rozsa Janos • HNG • LITTLE ALIEN, THE
ISMERI A SZANDI-MANDIT? • 1969 • Gyarmathy Livia • HNG • DO YOU KNOW "SUNDAY-MONDAY"?
ISMIK HARAMI • 1958 • Wahab Fatin Abdel • EGY • AU VOLEUR!
ISN'T IT LOVELY TO BE IN LOVE • 1909 • *Warwick Trading Co.* • UKN
ISN'T IT ROMANTIC? • 1948 • McLeod Norman Z. • USA
ISN'T IT SHOCKING? • 1973 • Badham John • TVM • USA
ISN'T IT WARM? • 1918 • *Depp Harry* • SHT • USA
ISN'T IT WONDERFUL! • 1914 • Armstrong Charles • UKN
ISN'T LIFE A BITCH? see **CHIENNE, LA** • 1931
ISN'T LIFE TERRIBLE? • 1925 • McCarey Leo • SHT • USA
ISN'T LIFE WONDERFUL • 1924 • Griffith D. W. • USA
ISN'T LIFE WONDERFUL! • 1953 • French Harold • UKN • UNCLE WILLIE'S BICYCLE SHOP
ISN'T LOVE CUCKOO • 1925 • *Sennett Mack (P)* • SHT • USA
ISO NGESO • 1984 • SAF
ISO VAALEE • 1983 • Kerttula Veikko • FNL • BOMBSHELL, THE ○ BIG BLOND
ISOBEL • 1920 • Carewe Edwin • USA • ISOBEL OR THE TRAIL'S END ○ TRAIL'S END, THE
ISOBEL OR THE TRAIL'S END see **ISOBEL** • 1920
ISOGASHII NIKUTAI • 1967 • Matsubara Jiro • JPN • BUSY BODY
ISOKA • 1979 • SAF
ISOLA see **PRINCIPESSA DELLE CANARIE, LA** • 1956
ISOLA, L' see **VIOLENZA AL SOLE** • 1969
ISOLA BELLA • 1961 • Grimm Hans • FRG
ISOLA BIANCA, L' • 1950 • Risi Dino • SHT • ITL
ISOLA DEGLI UOMINI PESCE, L' • 1979 • Martino Sergio • ITL • ISLAND OF THE FISH MEN, THE ○ SOMETHING WAITS IN THE DARK ○ ISLAND OF THE FISHERMEN, THE ○ ISLAND OF MUTANTS ○ ISLAND OF MUTATIONS ○ SCREAMERS ○ FISH MEN, THE
ISOLA DEL SOGNO, L' • 1947 • Remani Ernesto • ITL • AMORI E CANZONI
ISOLA DEL TESORO, L' • 1973 • Bianchi Andrea • ITL
ISOLA DELLA SALUTE, L' • 1954 • Heusch Paolo • DOC • ITL
ISOLA DELLE DONNE SOLE, L' (ITL) see **POSSEDEES, LES** • 1955
ISOLA DELLE SVEDESI, L' • 1969 • Amadio Silvio • ITL • TWISTED GIRLS (UKN)
ISOLA DELL'INCANTO, L' see **ALESSANDRO, SEI GRANDE!** • 1941
ISOLA DI ARTURO, L' • 1962 • Damiani Damiano • ITL • ARTURO'S ISLAND
ISOLA DI MONTECRISTO, L' • 1950 • Sequi Mario • ITL • ISLAND OF PROCIDA, THE (USA)
ISOLA DI SMERALDO, L' • 1957 • Lavino Ermanno • DOC • ITL
ISOLA MISTERIOSA E IL CAPITANO NEMO, L' (ITL) see **ILE MYSTERIEUSE, L'** • 1973
ISOLA TENEBROSA, L' • 1916 • Campogalliani Carlo • ITL
ISOLATED HOUSE, THE • 1915 • *Victory Films* • UKN
ISOLATION • 1982 • van Elst Gerrit • NTH
ISOLATION THERMIQUE, L' • 1958 • Lavoie Hermenegilde • DOC • CND
ISOLDE • 1988 • Rex Jytte • DNM
ISOLE DE FUOCO • 1954 • De Seta Vittorio • ITL
ISOLE DELLA LAGUNA • 1947 • Emmer Luciano, Gras Enrico • ITL • ISLANDS ON THE LAGOON
ISOLE DELL'AMORE, LE • 1970 • De Martino Pino • ITL
ISOLES, LES see **SERGENT X, LE** • 1931
ISOTOPES IN MEDICAL SCIENCE see **IZOTOPOK A GYOGYASZATBAN** • 1959
ISPANIYA • 1939 • Shub Esther • USS • SPAIN
ISPAVLENNOMU VERIT • 1959 • Zhilin Viktor • USS • CERTIFIED CORRECT
ISPETTORE SPARA A VISITA, L' (ITL) see **MONOCLE RIT JAUNE, LE** • 1964
ISPETTORE VARGAS, L' • 1940 • Franciolini Gianni • ITL • SBARRA, LA
ISPRAVI SE, DELFINA • 1978 • Djurcinov Aleksandar • YGS • GET UP, DELFINA ○ STAND UP STRAIGHT, DELPHINE
ISPYTANIE VERNOSTI • 1954 • Pyriev Ivan • USS • TEST OF FIDELITY
ISRAEL • 1918 • Antoine Andre • FRN
ISRAEL see **MOISSON DE L'ESPOIR, LES** • 1969
ISRAEL, AN 5727 see **COMME UN ECLAIR** • 1968
ISRAEL, AN ADVENTURE • 1957 • Hammid Alexander (c/d) • USA
ISRAEL.. TERRE RETROUVEE • 1956 • de Gastyne Marco • SHT • FRN
ISRAEL WHY? see **POURQUOI ISRAEL?** • 1973
ISRAELI BOY • 1955 • Broyde Ruth • DOC • ISR
ISSA LE TISSERAND • 1985 • Ouedraogo Idrissa • SHT • BRK • ISSA THE WEAVER
ISSA THE WEAVER see **ISSA LE TISSERAND** • 1985
ISSA VALLEY, THE see **DOLINA ISSY** • 1983
ISSATSU TASHO KEN • 1929 • Ito Daisuke • JPN
ISSHIN TASUKE • 1930 • Inagaki Hiroshi • JPN • PERSONAL AID
ISSHIN TASUKE EDOKKO MATSURI • 1967 • Yamashita Kosaku • JPN • OUR CHIVALROUS FISH-PEDDLER
ISSHIN TASUKE -OTOKO NO NAKA NO OTOKO IPPIKI • 1959 • Sawashima Chu • JPN • BRAVEST FISHMONGER
ISSHIN TASUKE -TENKA NO ICHIDAIJI • 1958 • Sawashima Chu • JPN • HERO OF THE TOWN
ISSUN BOSHI • 1959 • *Toei* • ANS • JPN • MIGHTY DWARF, THE
IST ARBEIT SCHANDE? see **SCHNEIDERKOMTESS, DIE** • 1922
IST EDDY POLO SCHULDIG? • 1928 • Lasko Leo • FRG
IST GERALDINE KEIN ENGEL? • 1963 • Perrin Steve • AUS
IST MAMA NICHT FABELHAFT? • 1958 • Beauvais Peter • FRG
IST MEIN MAN NICHT FABELHAFT? • 1933 • Jacoby Georg • FRG
ISTANA YANG HILANG • 1961 • Umboh Wim • INN • LOST PALACE, THE
ISTANBUL • 1957 • Pevney Joseph • USA
ISTANBUL • 1964 • Pialat Maurice • SHT • FRN
ISTANBUL • 1989 • Arehn Mats • SWD
ISTANBUL 44 • 1967 • Kazankaya Hasan • TRK
ISTANBUL 65 see **COLPO GROSSO A GALATA BRIDGE** • 1965
ISTANBUL EXPRESS • 1968 • Irving Richard • TVM • USA
ISTANBUL KALDIRIMLARI • 1968 • Dinler Mehmet • TRK • STREETS OF ISTANBUL, THE
ISTANBUL SOKAKLARINDA • 1931 • Ertugrul Muhsin • TRK
ISTANBUL TATILI • 1968 • Inanoglu Turker • TRK • HOLIDAY IN ISTANBUL
ISTANBULDA CUMB US VAR • 1968 • Gultekin Sirri • TRK • MERRY-MAKING IN ISTANBUL
ISTANBULU SEVMIYORUM • 1968 • Erakalin Ulku • TRK • I HATE ISTANBUL
ISTEN ES EMBER ELOTT • 1968 • Makk Karoly • HNG, YGS • BEFORE GOD AND MAN
ISTEN HOZTA, ORNAGY UR! • 1969 • Fabri Zoltan • HNG • TOTH FAMILY, THE
ISTEN OSZI CSILLAGA • 1962 • Kovacs Andras • HNG • AUTUMN STAR
ISTEN VELETEK, BARATAINK • 1987 • Simo Sandor • HNG • GOODBYE, FRIENDS
ISTENMEZEJEN • 1974 • Elek Judit • HNG • HUNGARIAN VILLAGE, A
ISTID see **EISZEIT** • 1975
ISTITUTO GRIMALDI see **NESSUNO TORNO INDIETRO** • 1943
ISTORIA ASI KHYACHINOI, KOTORAYA LYUBILA, DANE VYSHLA ZAMUKH • 1966 • Konchalovsky Andrei • USS • STORY OF ASI, WHO LOVED BUT DID NOT MARRY, THE ○ ASYA'S HAPPINESS ○ HAPPINESS OF ASYA, THE ○ HAPPY ASYA
ISTORIA ODNOGO KOLZA • 1948 • Dolin Boris • USS • TALE OF A LINK, THE
ISTORIES MIAS KERITRAS • 1981 • Vergitsis Nikos • GRC • STORIES OF A BEEHIVE
ISTORIYA GRAZHDENSKOI VOINI • 1921 • Vertov Dziga • USS • HISTORY OF THE CIVIL WAR
'ISTORY AND 'ORTICULTURE • 1938 • Alderson John • UKN
ISTRUTTORIA E CHIUSA, DIMENTICHI, L' • 1971 • Damiani Damiano • ITL • TANTE SBARRE
ISTVAN, A KIRALY • 1984 • Koltay Gabor • HNG • STEPHEN, THE KING
ISTVAN SZONYI • 1959 • Kollanyi Agoston • HNG
ISU • 1962 • Kuri Yoji • ANS • JPN • CHAIR, THE
ISUVUMELWANO see **ISIVUMELWANO** • 1978
IT • 1927 • Badger Clarence, von Sternberg Josef • USA
IT! • 1966 • Leder Herbert J. • USA • CURSE OF THE GOLEM
IT see **IT! THE TERROR FROM BEYOND SPACE** • 1958
IT see **ES** • 1965
IT AIN'T CITY MUSIC • 1973 • Davenport Tom • USA
IT AIN'T EASY • 1972 • Hurley Maury • USA
IT AIN'T HAY • 1943 • Kenton Erle C. • USA • MONEY FOR JAM (UKN)
IT AIN'T NO SIN see **BELLE OF THE NINETIES** • 1934
IT ALL CAME OUT IN THE WASH • 1912 • Costello Maurice • USA
IT ALL CAME TRUE • 1940 • Seiler Lewis • USA
IT ALL COMES OUT IN THE END • 1970 • *Jo-Jo Dist.* • USA
IT ALL DEPENDS • 1915 • O'Neil Barry? • USA
IT ALL DEPENDS ON YOU • 1929 • Aylott Dave, Symmons E. F. • SHT • UKN
IT ALL GOES TO SHOW • 1969 • Searle Francis • SHT • UKN
IT ALMOST HAPPENED • 1915 • Davey Horace • USA
IT ALWAYS ENDS THAT WAY (USA) see **TERMINA SIEMPRE ASI** • 1940
IT ALWAYS HAPPENS • 1935 • Lord Del • SHT • USA
IT ALWAYS RAINS ON SUNDAYS • 1947 • Hamer Robert • UKN
IT ALWAYS STOPS RAINING see **IT LOOKS LIKE RAIN** • 1945
IT BEGAN IN SPAIN see **ZACZELO SIE W HISZPANII** • 1950
IT BEGAN ON THE CLYDE • 1946 • Annakin Ken • DCS • UKN
IT BEGAN ON THE VISTULA • 1966 • Piekalkiewicz Janusz • UKN • ZACZELO SIE NAD WISLA ○ UNFINISHED WAR, THE ○ POLISH PASSION
IT CAME BY FREIGHT • 1914 • *Royal* • USA
IT CAME FROM BENEATH THE SEA • 1955 • Gordon Robert • USA
IT CAME FROM HOLLYWOOD • 1982 • Solt Andrew, Leo Malcolm • USA
IT CAME FROM OUTER SPACE • 1953 • Arnold Jack • USA
IT CAME FROM THE LAKE see **MONSTER** • 1979
IT CAME UPON A MIDNIGHT CLEAR • 1984 • Hunt Peter H. • TVM • USA
IT CAME WITHOUT WARNING see **WITHOUT WARNING** • 1980
IT CAN BE DONE • 1921 • Smith David • USA
IT CAN BE DONE • 1929 • Newmeyer Fred • USA

IT CAN BE DONE.. AMIGO • 1974 • *Spencer Bud* • ITL
IT CAN'T BE! see **NYE MOZHET BYT!** • 1976
IT CAN'T BE DONE • 1918 • Goldin Sidney M. • SHT • USA
IT CAN'T BE DONE • 1948 • *Nesbitt John* • SHT • USA
IT CAN'T BE TRUE • 1916 • Hutchinson Craig • SHT • USA
IT CAN'T HAPPEN HERE see **ES NALUNK LEHTETLEN** • 1965
IT CAN'T LAST FOREVER • 1937 • MacFadden Hamilton • USA
IT COMES UP LOVE • 1943 • Lamont Charles • USA • DATE WITH AN ANGEL, A (UKN) ○ ON THE BEAM
IT COMES UP MURDER see **HONEY POT, THE** • 1967
IT CONCERNS US ALL see **DET GAELDER OS ALLE!** • 1949
IT CONQUERED THE EARTH see **IT CONQUERED THE WORLD** • 1956
IT CONQUERED THE WORLD • 1956 • Corman Roger • USA • IT CONQUERED THE EARTH
IT COULD HAPPEN TO YOU • 1937 • Rosen Phil • USA
IT COULD HAPPEN TO YOU • 1939 • Werker Alfred L. • USA
IT COULD HAPPEN TO YOU • 1952 • Barclay David • SHT • USA
IT COULDN'T HAPPEN HERE • 1988 • Bond Jack • UKN
IT COULDN'T HAPPEN TO A NICER GUY • 1974 • Howard Cy • TVM • USA
IT COULDN'T HAVE HAPPENED • 1936 • Rosen Phil • USA
IT CURED HUBBY • 1914 • *Lubin* • USA
IT DEPENDS ON US TOO.. see **RAJTUNK IS MULIK** • 1960
IT DID LOOK SUSPICIOUS • 1911 • *Vitagraph* • USA
IT DIDN'T WORK OUT RIGHT • 1916 • Hill Robert F. • SHT • USA
IT DOESN'T PAY • 1912 • *Rex* • USA
IT DOESN'T PAY • 1915 • Physioc Wray • USA
IT DON'T MEAN A THING • 1967 • Quist-Moller Fleming • SHT • DNM
IT DROPPETH AS THE GENTLE RAIN • 1963 • Beresford Bruce • SHT
IT FELL FROM THE FLAME BARRIER see **FLAME BARRIER, THE** • 1958
IT FELL FROM THE SKY see **ALIEN DEAD, THE** • 1980
IT FURTHERS ONE TO HAVE SOMEWHERE TO GO • 1971 • Gibbons Geoffrey • ANS • UKN
IT GROWS ON TREES • 1952 • Lubin Arthur • USA
IT HAD TO BE YOU • 1947 • Hartman Don, Mate Rudolph • USA
IT HAD TO HAPPEN • 1936 • Del Ruth Roy • USA
IT HAPPENED see **PULNOCNI PRIHODA** • 1960
IT HAPPENED ALL NIGHT • 1941 • Roberts Charles E. • USA
IT HAPPENED ALL NIGHT (USA) see **AFFAIRE D'UNE NUIT, L'** • 1960
IT HAPPENED AT LAKEWOOD MANOR see **PANIC AT LAKEWOOD MANOR** • 1977
IT HAPPENED AT THE BEACH • 1913 • *Powers* • USA
IT HAPPENED AT THE FANTASTIC TIHANY CIRCUS see **SUCEDIO EN EL FANTASTICO CIRCO TIHANY** • 1981
IT HAPPENED AT THE INN (USA) see **GOUPI MAINS-ROUGES** • 1942
IT HAPPENED AT THE MILITIA STATION • 1963 • Azarov Vilen • USS
IT HAPPENED AT THE WORLD'S FAIR • 1963 • Taurog Norman • USA
IT HAPPENED EVERY THURSDAY • 1953 • Pevney Joseph • USA
IT HAPPENED HERE • 1964 • Brownlow Kevin, Mollo Andrew • UKN
IT HAPPENED IN ADEN see **C'EST ARRIVE A ADEN** • 1956
IT HAPPENED IN ATHENS • 1962 • Marton Andrew • USA
IT HAPPENED IN BERLIN see **TATORT BERLIN** • 1957
IT HAPPENED IN BROAD DAYLIGHT (USA) see **ES GESCHAH AM HELLICHTEN TAG** • 1958
IT HAPPENED IN BROOKLYN • 1947 • Whorf Richard • USA
IT HAPPENED IN DONBAS see **ETA BYLO V DONBASE** • 1945
IT HAPPENED IN EUROPE see **VALAHOL EUROPABAN** • 1947
IT HAPPENED IN FLATBUSH • 1942 • McCarey Ray • USA
IT HAPPENED IN GIBRALTAR see **GIBRALTAR** • 1938
IT HAPPENED IN HAVERSTRAW • 1913 • *Komic* • USA
IT HAPPENED IN HOLLYWOOD • 1931 • Ceder Ralph • SHT • USA
IT HAPPENED IN HOLLYWOOD • 1937 • Lachman Harry • USA • ONCE A HERO (UKN)
IT HAPPENED IN HOLLYWOOD • 1972 • Locke Peter • USA
IT HAPPENED IN HOLLYWOOD (UKN) see **ANOTHER FACE** • 1935
IT HAPPENED IN HONOLULU • 1916 • Reynolds Lynn • USA
IT HAPPENED IN JAVA • 1913 • Melies Gaston • USA
IT HAPPENED IN KALOMA see **IT'S A DATE** • 1940
IT HAPPENED IN LEICESTER SQUARE • 1949 • Benstead Geoffrey • UKN
IT HAPPENED IN NEW YORK • 1935 • Crosland Alan • USA
IT HAPPENED IN PARIS • 1919 • Hartford David M. • USA
IT HAPPENED IN PARIS • 1935 • Wyler Robert, Reed Carol • UKN
IT HAPPENED IN PARIS see **LADY IN QUESTION, THE** • 1940
IT HAPPENED IN PARIS (UKN) see **DESPERATE ADVENTURE, A** • 1938
IT HAPPENED IN PARIS (USA) see **C'EST ARRIVE A PARIS** • 1952
IT HAPPENED IN PENKOVO see **DELO BYLO V PENKOVE** • 1957
IT HAPPENED IN PIKERSVILLE • 1916 • Hevener Jerold T. • SHT • USA
IT HAPPENED IN ROME see **SOUVENIR D'ITALIE** • 1957
IT HAPPENED IN ROOM 7 • 1917 • Peacocke Leslie T. • SHT • USA
IT HAPPENED IN SNAKEVILLE • 1915 • Clements Roy • USA
IT HAPPENED IN SOHO • 1948 • Chisnell Frank • UKN
IT HAPPENED IN SPAIN • 1935 • D'Arrast Harry D'Abbadie • USA • THREE-CORNERED HAT, THE
IT HAPPENED IN THE PARK (USA) see **VILLA BORGHESE** • 1953
IT HAPPENED IN THE STREET see **TOVA SE SLUCHI NA ULITSATA** • 1956
IT HAPPENED IN THE WEST • 1911 • *Selig* • USA
IT HAPPENED IN TOKYO see **KAWA NO ARU SHITAMACHI NO HANASHI** • 1955
IT HAPPENED IN TOKYO see **TWENTY PLUS TWO** • 1961
IT HAPPENED ON FIFTH AVENUE • 1947 • Del Ruth Roy • USA
IT HAPPENED ON FRIDAY • 1915 • Christie Al • USA
IT HAPPENED ON THE NEW YEAR DAY see **PRZYGODA NOWOROCZNA** • 1963
IT HAPPENED ON THIS DAY see **DOGODILO SE NA DANASNJI DAN** • 1987
IT HAPPENED ON WASH DAY • 1915 • Hotaling Arthur D. • USA
IT HAPPENED ONE CHRISTMAS • 1977 • Wrye Donald • TVM • USA
IT HAPPENED ONE DAY • 1934 • Parrott Charles, Dunn Eddie • SHT • USA
IT HAPPENED ONE DAY see **THIS SIDE OF HEAVEN** • 1932
IT HAPPENED ONE NIGHT • 1934 • Capra Frank • USA
IT HAPPENED ONE NIGHT see **YOU CAN'T RUN AWAY FROM IT** • 1956
IT HAPPENED ONE SUMMER see **STATE FAIR** • 1944
IT HAPPENED ONE SUNDAY • 1944 • Lamac Carl • UKN
IT HAPPENED OUT WEST • 1923 • *Farnum Franklyn* • USA
IT HAPPENED OUT WEST • 1937 • Bretherton Howard • USA • MAN FROM THE BIG CITY, THE (UKN)
IT HAPPENED THUS • 1912 • *Moore Owen* • USA
IT HAPPENED TO ADELE • 1917 • Brooke Van Dyke • USA
IT HAPPENED TO CRUSOE • 1941 • *Mintz Charles (P)* • ANS • USA
IT HAPPENED TO JANE • 1959 • Quine Richard • USA • THAT JANE FROM MAINE ○ TWINKLE AND SHINE
IT HAPPENED TO ONE MAN (USA) see **GENTLEMAN OF VENTURE** • 1940
IT HAPPENED TO US • 1972 • Rothschild Amalie • USA
IT HAPPENED TO YOU • Youngson Robert • SHT • USA
IT HAPPENED TOMORROW • 1943 • Clair Rene • USA • C'EST ARRIVE DEMAIN
IT HAPPENED WHILE HE FISHED • 1915 • Davey Horace • USA
IT HAPPENED YESTERDAY see **HISTORIA WSPOLCZESNA** • 1961
IT HAPPENS EVERY SPRING • 1949 • Bacon Lloyd • USA
IT HAPPENS IN ROMA (USA) see **ULTIMI CINQUE MINUTI, GLI** • 1955
IT HELPS TO BE MADE • 1966 • King John • DOC • NZL
IT HURTS ONLY WHEN I LAUGH (UKN) see **ONLY WHEN I LAUGH** • 1981
IT IS A LONG WAY HOME see **HOSSZU AZ UT HAZAIG** • 1960
IT IS BETTER TO LIVE see **LIVING IS BETTER** • 1956
IT IS ENOUGH TO LOVE see **IL SUFFIT D'AIMER** • 1960
IT IS FOR ENGLAND • 1916 • Cohen Lawrence • UKN • HIDDEN HAND, THE
IT IS HARD TO PLEASE HIM, BUT IT IS WORTH IT • 1912-14 • Cohl Emile • ANS • USA
IT IS MY MUSIC see **DET AR MIN MUSIK** • 1942
IT IS NEVER TOO LATE TO MEND • 1911 • Lincoln W. J. • ASL
IT IS NEVER TOO LATE TO MEND • 1913 • Seay Charles M. • USA
IT IS NEVER TOO LATE TO MEND • 1925 • Butler Alexander • UKN
IT IS NOT GOOD THAT MAN SHOULD BE ALONE see **NO ES BUENO QUE EL HOMBRE ESTE SOLO** • 1972
IT IS NOT ORANGES -BUT HORSES see **DET ER IKKE APPELSINER -DET ER HESTE** • 1967
IT IS SIN.. BUT I LIKE IT see **ES PECADO PERO ME GUSTA** • 1979
IT IS THE LAW • 1924 • Edwards J. Gordon • USA
IT IS UNBELIEVABLE see **EDDINI AKHLAK** • 1953
IT ISN'T BEING DONE THIS SEASON • 1921 • Sargent George L. • USA
IT ISN'T BUT • 1978 • Milosevic Mica • YGS
IT ISN'T DONE • 1937 • Hall Ken G. • ASL
IT LIVES AGAIN • 1978 • Cohen Larry • USA • IT'S ALIVE 2
IT LIVES BY NIGHT see **BAT PEOPLE, THE** • 1974
IT LIVES WITHIN HER see **I DON'T WANT TO BE BORN** • 1975
IT LOOKS LIKE RAIN • 1945 • Burnford Paul • SHT • USA • IT ALWAYS STOPS RAINING
IT MADE HIM MAD • 1913 • *Vitagraph* • USA
IT MAKES A DIFFERENCE • 1917 • Baldwin Ruth Ann • SHT • USA
IT MAY BE YOU • 1915 • Louis Will • USA
IT MAY BE YOUR DAUGHTER • 1916 • *Moral Uplift Society* • USA
IT MAY COME TO THIS • 1914 • *White Pearl* • USA
IT MAY COME TO THIS • 1920 • Ross Jack • UKN
IT MAY HAPPEN TO YOU • 1937 • Bucquet Harold S. • SHT • USA
IT MEANS THAT TO ME (USA) see **ME FAIRE CA A MOI..** • 1961
IT MIGHT BE YOU • 1946 • Gordon Michael S. • DOC • UKN
IT MIGHT HAPPEN TO YOU • 1920 • Santell Alfred • USA
IT MIGHT HAPPEN TO YOU • 1925 • Herrick F. Herrick • USA
IT MIGHT HAVE BEEN • 1910 • *Lubin* • USA
IT MIGHT HAVE BEEN • 1913 • Nicholls George • USA
IT MIGHT HAVE BEEN SERIOUS • 1915 • *Dillon Jack* • USA
IT MOVES see **SE MUEVE** • 1977
IT MUST BE LOVE • 1926 • Green Alfred E. • USA
IT MUST BE LOVE • 1940 • Rasinski Connie • ANS • USA
IT MUST NOT BE FORGOTTEN see **OB ETOM ZABY VAT NELZYA** • 1954
IT MUST NOT HAPPEN AGAIN • 1948 • USA • EVA BRAUN AND HITLER STORY
IT NEARLY HAPPENED • 1916 • Curtis Allen • SHT • USA • FIFTY-FIFTY
IT NEVER CAME see **KAKHONO ASHENI** • 1963
IT NEVER COULD HAPPEN • 1916 • *Travers Richard C.* • SHT • USA
IT NEVER GOT BY • 1916 • Drew Sidney • SHT • USA
IT ONLY HAPPENS TO OTHERS (USA) see **CA N'ARRIVE QU'AUX AUTRES** • 1971
IT ONLY TAKES 5 MINUTES see **ROTTEN APPLE, THE** • 1963
IT OUGHT TO BE A CRIME • 1931 • Ray Albert • SHT • USA
IT PAYS TO ADVERTISE • 1919 • Crisp Donald • USA
IT PAYS TO ADVERTISE • 1931 • Tuttle Frank • USA
IT PAYS TO ADVERTISE see **ANNONSERA** • 1936
IT PAYS TO BE FUNNY • 1947 • Pollard Bud • USA
IT PAYS TO BE KIND • 1912 • *Gibson Dorothy* • USA
IT PAYS TO EXERCISE • 1918 • Jones F. Richard • SHT • USA
IT PAYS TO WAIT • 1912 • Dwan Allan • USA
IT RAINED ALL DAY THE NIGHT I LEFT see **DEUX AFFREUX SUR LE SABLE** • 1979
IT RAINS IN MY VILLAGE see **I DODJE PROPAST SVETA** • 1969
IT RAINS ON OUR LOVE (USA) see **DET REGNAR PA VAR KARLEK** • 1946
IT SEEMED LIKE A GOOD IDEA AT THE TIME • 1975 • Trent John • CND
IT SHOULD HAPPEN TO YOU • 1954 • Cukor George • USA • NAME FOR HERSELF, A
IT SHOULDN'T HAPPEN TO A DOG • 1945 • Yates Hal • SHT • USA
IT SHOULDN'T HAPPEN TO A DOG • 1946 • Leeds Herbert I. • USA
IT SHOULDN'T HAPPEN TO A VET • 1976 • Till Eric • UKN • ALL THINGS BRIGHT AND BEAUTIFUL (USA)
IT SOUNDED LIKE A KISS • 1916 • Chaudet Louis W. • SHT • USA
IT STALKED THE OCEAN FLOOR see **MONSTER FROM THE OCEAN FLOOR** • 1954
IT STARTED AT MIDNIGHT see **SCHWEIK'S NEW ADVENTURES** • 1943
IT STARTED IN NAPLES • 1960 • Shavelson Melville • USA
IT STARTED IN PARADISE • 1952 • Bennett Compton • UKN • FANFARE FOR FIGLEAVES
IT STARTED IN SPAIN see **ZACZELO SIE W HISZPANII** • 1950
IT STARTED IN THE ALPS (USA) see **ARUPUSU NO WADADAISHO** • 1966
IT STARTED IN TOKYO (UKN) see **TWENTY PLUS TWO** • 1961
IT STARTED LIKE THIS see **ETO NACHINADOS TAK..** • 1956
IT STARTED WITH A KISS • 1959 • Marshall George • USA
IT STARTED WITH ADAM see **IT STARTED WITH EVE** • 1941
IT STARTED WITH EVE • 1941 • Koster Henry • USA • ALMOST AN ANGEL ○ IT STARTED WITH ADAM
IT TAKES A GOOD MAN TO DO THAT • 1929 • Aylott Dave, Symmons E. F. • SHT • UKN
IT TAKES A THIEF see **CHALLENGE, THE** • 1960
IT TAKES ALL KINDS • 1969 • Davis Eddie • ASL, USA • IT TAKES ALL KINDS, TO CATCH A THIEF
IT TAKES ALL KINDS, TO CATCH A THIEF see **IT TAKES ALL KINDS** • 1969
IT TAKES GASOLINE TO WIN A GIRL • 1909 • *Phoenix* • USA
IT TAKES TWO • 1988 • Beaird David • USA • MY NEW CAR
IT! THE TERROR FROM BEYOND SPACE • 1958 • Cahn Edward L. • USA • IT, THE VAMPIRE FROM BEYOND SPACE ○ IT ○ IT, THE VAMPIRE FROM OUTER SPACE
IT, THE VAMPIRE FROM BEYOND SPACE see **IT! THE TERROR FROM BEYOND SPACE** • 1958
IT, THE VAMPIRE FROM OUTER SPACE see **IT! THE TERROR FROM BEYOND SPACE** • 1958
IT TOLLS FOR THEE • 1962 • Fuller Samuel • MTV • USA
IT WAS A FAINT DREAM see **ASAKI YUMEMISHI** • 1974
IT WAS A GAY BALL NIGHT see **ES WAR EINE RAUSCHENDE BALLNACHT** • 1939
IT WAS A LOVER AND HIS LASS • 1975 • Hallstrom Lasse • SWD
IT WAS A QUARTER AND WILL SOON BE HALF PAST see **BYLO CTVRT A BUDE PUL** • 1968
IT WAS ALL FOR SALE see **IT'S ALL FOR SALE** • 1969
IT WAS CALLED S.N. see **SE LLAMABA S.N.** • 1978
IT WAS EVENING AND IT WAS MORNING see **DIT WAS AAND EN DIT WAS MORE** • 1978
IT WAS I (USA) see **SONO STATO IO!** • 1937
IT WAS IN MAY see **DET VAR I MAJ** • 1915
IT WAS LIKE THIS • 1915 • Otto Henry • USA
IT WAS NIGHT IN ROME see **ERA NOTTE A ROMA** • 1960
IT WAS NOT IN VAIN see **NIJE BILO UZALUD** • 1957
IT WAS SOME PARTY • 1914 • Dillon Eddie • USA
IT WAS THE FIRST OF MAY • 1922 • Cervenkova Thea • CZC
IT WAS TO BE • 1915 • Kaufman Joseph • USA
IT WASN'T EASY.. • 1978 • Crama Nico • DOC • CND, NTH
IT WASN'T GOING TO HAPPEN TO ME • 1975 • Ricketson James • DOC • ASL
IT WASN'T POISON AFTER ALL • 1913 • Williams C. Jay • USA
IT WILL ALL BE OVER TONIGHT see **DNES VECER VSECHNO SKONCI** • 1954
IT WILL BE CALLED COLOMBIA see **Y SE LLAMARIA COLOMBIA** • 1978
IT WILL HAPPEN TOMORROW see **DOMANI ACCADRA** • 1988
IT WILL RAIN TENDERLY • Tulyakhodzhaev Nazim • ANM • USS
IT WON'T RUB OFF, BABY! see **SWEET LOVE, BITTER** • 1967
IT WOULD HAVE BEEN TERRIBLE • 1958 • Strbac Milenko • YGS
IT WOULD SERVE 'EM RIGHT • 1953 • Barclay David • SHT • USA
ITALIA! see **GRANDE APPELLO, IL** • 1936
ITALIA 61 • 1961 • Lenica Jan, Zamecznic W. • ANS • PLN • ITALY 61
ITALIA A MANO ARMATA • 1976 • Girolami Marino • ITL • SPECIAL COP IN ACTION
ITALIA E DI MODA, L' • 1963 • Bramieri Gino, Rondi Gian Luigi • ITL
ITALIA IN PATAGONIA • 1958 • Guerrasio Guido • DOC • ITL
ITALIA INPIGIAMA (COSTUMI SESSUALI DELLA TRIBU ITALIANE), L' • 1977 • Guerrasio Guido • ITL
ITALIA K2 • 1955 • Baldi Marcello • DOC • ITL
ITALIA NI NOTTE N.1 • 1964 • De Marchi Luigi • DOC • ITL • ITALIAN SEXY SHOW
ITALIA NON E UN PAESA POVERE, L' • 1960 • Taviani Paolo, Taviani Vittorio, Ivens Joris • ITL • ITALY IS NOT A POOR COUNTRY
ITALIA PICCOLA • 1957 • Soldati Mario • ITL
ITALIA PROIBITA • 1963 • Biagi Enzo, Giordani Brando, Giordani Sergio • DOC • ITL
ITALIA S'E ROTTA, L' • 1976 • Steno • ITL
ITALIA ULTIMO ATTO? • 1977 • Pirri Massimo • ITL
ITALIA VISTA DAL CIELO, L' • 1978 • Quilici Folco • MTV • ITL

ITALIAN, THE • 1915 • Barker Reginald • USA
ITALIAN, THE • 1979 • Schreibman Myrl A. • USA
ITALIAN BARBER, THE • 1911 • Griffith D. W. • USA
ITALIAN BLOOD • 1911 • Griffith D. W. • USA
ITALIAN BRIDE, THE • 1913 • *Pathe* • USA
ITALIAN BROTHERS see **FRATELLI D'ITALIA** • 1990
ITALIAN CONNECTION, THE (USA) see **MALA ORDINA, LA** • 1972
ITALIAN FRIENDSHIP • 1912 • *Powers* • USA
ITALIAN GIRL FROM KIPSELA, AN see **MIA ITALIDHA AP' TI KIPSELI** • 1968
ITALIAN HOLIDAY • 1961 • De La Varre Andre Jr. • DOC • USA
ITALIAN IN ALGIERS, THE • 1969 • Genini Lusatti • ANS • ITL
ITALIAN IN AMERICA, AN see **ITALIANO IN AMERICA, UN** • 1967
ITALIAN IN WARSAW, AN • 1964 • Lenartowicz Stanislaw • PLN
ITALIAN JOB, THE • 1969 • Collinson Peter • UKN
ITALIAN LOVE • 1913 • *Cummings Irving* • USA
ITALIAN LOVE • 1914 • *Beauty* • USA
ITALIAN LOVE • 1914 • *Essanay* • USA
ITALIAN LOVE STORY, AN • 1909 • *Bison* • USA
ITALIAN MACHINE, THE • 1976 • Cronenberg David • CND
ITALIAN NIGHT see **NOTTE ITALIANA** • 1988
ITALIAN ROMANCE, AN • 1912 • *Champion* • USA
ITALIAN SECRET SERVICE • 1968 • Comencini Luigi • ITL
ITALIAN SEXY SHOW see **ITALIA NI NOTTE N.1** • 1964
ITALIAN SHERLOCK HOLMES • 1910 • *Yankee* • USA
ITALIAN STALLION see **PARTY AT KITTY AND STUDS** • 1970
ITALIAN STRAW HAT, THE see **CHAPEAU DE PAILLE D'ITALIE, UN** • 1927
ITALIAN TAXI DRIVER IN NEW YORK see **TASSINARO A NEW YORK, UN** • 1988
ITALIAN TRANSPLANT see **TRASPIANTO, IL** • 1970
ITALIAN WOMAN, AN see **OGGETTI SMARRITI** • 1979
ITALIAN WOMEN AND LOVE see **ITALIANE E L'AMORE, LE** • 1961
ITALIANA IN ALGERI, L' • 1968 • Luzzati Emmanuele • ANM • ITL
ITALIANAMERICAN • 1974 • Scorsese Martin • DCS • USA
ITALIANE E L'AMORE, LE • 1961 • Vancini Florestano, Musso Carlo, Risi Nelo, Nelli Piero, Macchi Giulio, Baldi Gian Vittorio, Mazzetti Lorenza, Maselli Francesco, Questi Giulio, Ferreri Marco, Mingozzi Gianfranco • ITL • LATIN LOVERS (USA) ○ ITALIAN WOMEN AND LOVE
ITALIANI ALL'INFERNO • 1960 • Novaro Enrico • DOC • ITL
ITALIANI COME NOI • 1964 • Prunas Pasquale • DOC • ITL
ITALIANI E LE VACANZE, GLI • 1964 • Ratti Filippo M. • DOC • ITL
ITALIANI! E SEVERAMENTE PROIBITO SERVIRSI DELLA TOILETTE DURANTE LE FERMATE • 1969 • Sindoni Vittorio • ITL
ITALIANI SI DIVERTONO COSI, GLI • 1963 • Vernuccio Gianni • ITL
ITALIANI SONO MATTI, GLI • 1958 • Coletti Duilio, Delgado Luis Maria • ITL
ITALIANO, BRAVA GENTE • 1964 • De Santis Giuseppe • ITL, USS • ONI SHLI NA VOSTOK (USS) ○ ATTACK AND RETREAT (USA) ○ ITALIANS, GOOD PEOPLE ○ THEY WENT TO VOSTOK ○ THEY HEADED FOR THE EAST
ITALIANO HA 50 ANNI, L' • 1962 • Trapani Francomaria • DOC • ITL
ITALIANO IN AMERICA, UN • 1967 • Sordi Alberto • ITL • ITALIAN IN AMERICA, AN
ITALIANS, GOOD PEOPLE see **ITALIANO, BRAVA GENTE** • 1964
ITALIAN'S GRATITUDE, AN • 1911 • *Solax* • USA
ITALIEN DES ROSES, L' • 1972 • Matton Charles • FRN
ITALIENISCHES CAPRICCIO • 1961 • Pellegrini Glauco • GDR
ITALIENRIESE -LIEBE INBEGRIFFEN • 1958 • Becker Wolfgang • FRG
ITALY • 1974 • Fruet William • CND
ITALY 61 see **ITALIA 61** • 1961
ITALY 1943 see **CONSPIRACY OF HEARTS** • 1960
ITALY IS NOT A POOR COUNTRY see **ITALIA NON E UN PAESA POVERE, L'** • 1960
ITALY: YEAR ONE (UKN) see **ANNO UNO** • 1974
ITAMAE • 1959 • Hani Susumu • DOC • JPN
ITARAF, AL- • 1964 • Arafa Saad • EGY • CONFESSION, LA
ITARNITAK • 1960 • Lavoie Richard, Panvion A. H. • DCS • CND
ITAZU • 1988 • Goto Toshio • JPN
ITAZURA • 1959 • Nakamura Noboru • JPN • LOVE LETTERS ○ JOKE, THE
ITAZURA • 1967 • Yamamoto Shinya • JPN • MISCHIEF
ITAZURA KOZO • 1935 • Yamamoto Kajiro • JPN • TRICKS OF AN ERRAND BOY
ITCH, THE • 1965 • Post Howard • ANS • USA
ITCH IN TIME, AN • 1943 • Clampett Robert • ANS • USA
ITCHING FOR REVENGE • 1915 • *Voss Fatty* • USA • SHOT IN A BAR-ROOM
ITCHING HOUR, THE • 1931 • Foster Lewis R. • SHT • USA
ITCHING PALMS • 1923 • Horne James W. • USA
ITCHY FINGERS see **SHEN T'OU MIAO T'AN SHOU TUO-TUO** • 1980
ITEL A BALATON • 1932 • Fejos Paul • HNG • VERDICT OF LAKE BATALON, THE ○ STORM AT BATALON
ITELET • 1970 • Kosa Ferenc • HNG • JUDGEMENT
ITEM 72-D • 1969 • Summer Edward T. • SHT • USA
ITHELE NA YINI VASILIAS • 1967 • Theodoropoulos Angelos • GRC • HE WANTED TO BE KING
ITIM • 1977 • De Leon Mike • PHL • BLACK
ITINERAIRE BIS • 1981 • Drillaud Christian • FRN
ITINERAIRE D'UN ENFANT GATE • 1988 • Lelouch Claude • FRN
ITINERAIRE MARIN, L' • 1962 • Rollin Jean • FRN
ITINERANT ACTOR, AN see **TABIYAKUSHA** • 1940
ITINERANT WEDDING, AN • 1913 • *Patheplay* • USA
I'TIRAFATU ZAWJ • 1964 • Wahab Fatin Abdel • EGY • AVEUX D'UN MARI, LES
ITL see **CIEL SUR LA TETE, LE** • 1964
ITL see **SUSANNE -DIE WIRTIN VON DER LAHN** • 1967
ITL see **TURM DER VERBOTENEN LIEBE, DER** • 1968
ITL see **COMMENT DETRUIRE LA REPUTATION DU PLUS CELEBRE AGENT SECRET DU MONDE** • 1973
ITL see **FIN DE SEMANA PARA LOS MUERTOS** • 1974
IT'LL PASS • 1982 • Arens Agna • SHT • NTH
IT'LL WORK OUT see **LOSER SIG, DET** • 1977
ITO ANG AKING KASAYSAYAN • 1967 • de Villa Jose • PHL • THIS IS MY LIFE
ITO ANG DIGMAAN • 1968 • Gaudite Solano • PHL • THIS IS WAR
ITO ANG KARATE • 1967 • Diaz Leody M. • PHL • THIS IS KARATE
ITO ANG PILIPINO • 1967 • Gallardo Cesar Chat • PHL • THIS IS A FILIPINO
ITO, THE BEGGAR BOY • 1910 • *Vitagraph* • USA
ITOHABU NO AKAI YANE • 1977 • Kumagai Isao • JPN • RED ROOF OF EATOHARB, THE
ITOHAN MONOGATARI • 1957 • Ito Daisuke • JPN
ITOSHINO WAGAKO • 1926 • Gosho Heinosuke • JPN • MY BELOVED CHILD ○ MY LOVING CHILD
IT'S A 2'6" ABOVE THE GROUND WORLD • 1972 • Thomas Ralph • UKN • LOVE BAN, THE
IT'S A BARE BARE WORLD • 1964 • Lang W. • UKN
IT'S A BARE WORLD see **MY BARE LADY** • 1962
IT'S A BEAR • 1913 • *Crystal* • USA
IT'S A BEAR • 1914 • *Edison* • USA
IT'S A BEAR • 1916 • Smith David • SHT • USA
IT'S A BEAR • 1919 • Windom Lawrence C. • USA
IT'S A BEAR • 1924 • Roach Hal • SHT • USA
IT'S A BEAR see **JUST A BEAR** • 1931
IT'S A BET • 1935 • Esway Alexander • UKN • SAFE BET, A
IT'S A BIG COUNTRY • 1951 • Weis Don, Hartman Don, Vidor Charles, Brown Clarence, Sturges John, Thorpe Richard, Wellman William A. • USA
IT'S A BIKINI WORLD • 1967 • Rothman Stephanie • USA
IT'S A BIRD • 1919 • *Mann Harry* • SHT • USA
IT'S A BOY • 1914 • *Sterling* • USA
IT'S A BOY • 1920 • Smith Noel • SHT • USA
IT'S A BOY • 1923 • Roach Hal • SHT • USA
IT'S A BOY • 1933 • Whelan Tim • UKN
IT'S A CINCH • 1918 • *Fazenda Louise* • SHT • USA
IT'S A CINCH • 1932 • Arbuckle Roscoe • USA
IT'S A COP • 1934 • Rogers Maclean • UKN
IT'S A CRIME • 1957 • Low Colin, Munro Grant, Koenig Wolf • ANS • CND • C'EST CRIMINAL
IT'S A CRUEL WORLD • 1918 • Curtis Allen • SHT • USA
IT'S A DATE • 1940 • Seiter William A. • USA • IT HAPPENED IN KALOMA
IT'S A DIFFERENT GIRL AGAIN • 1907 • Morland John • UKN
IT'S A DIFFERENT GIRL AGAIN • 1909 • *Warwick Trading Co.* • UKN
IT'S A DOG'S LIFE • 1942 • Wilmot Robert • SHT • USA
IT'S A DOG'S LIFE • 1955 • Hoffman Herman • USA • BAR SINISTER, THE ○ WILDFIRE
IT'S A DOG'S LIFE see **VITA DA CANI** • 1950
IT'S A FIASCO, GENTLEMEN • 1970 • Pojar Bretislav, Stepanek Miroslav • ANM • CZC
IT'S A FUNNY, FUNNY WORLD • 1979 • Shissel Ziv • ISR
IT'S A GIFT • 1923 • Roach Hal • SHT • USA
IT'S A GIFT • 1934 • McLeod Norman Z. • USA • BACK PORCH
IT'S A GRAND LIFE • 1953 • Blakeley John E. • UKN
IT'S A GRAND OLD NAG • 1947 • Clampett Robert • ANS • USA
IT'S A GRAND OLD WORLD • 1937 • Smith Herbert • UKN
IT'S A GREAT DAY • 1956 • Warrington John • UKN
IT'S A GREAT FEELING • 1949 • Butler David • USA
IT'S A GREAT LIFE • 1918 • *Steiner William* • SHT • USA
IT'S A GREAT LIFE • 1920 • Hopper E. Mason • USA • EMPIRE BUILDERS
IT'S A GREAT LIFE • 1929 • Wood Sam • USA • IMPERFECT LADIES ○ COTTON AND SILK
IT'S A GREAT LIFE • 1936 • Cline Eddie • USA • FROM LITTLE ACORNS
IT'S A GREAT LIFE • 1943 • Strayer Frank • USA
IT'S A GREAT LIFE see **TOLLER HECHT AUF KRUMMEN TOUREN** • 1961
IT'S A GREEK LIFE • 1936 • Gordon Dan • ANS • USA
IT'S A HAP-HAP-HAPPY DAY • 1941 • Fleischer Dave • ANS • USA
IT'S A HARD LIFE • 1919 • Roach Hal • SHT • USA
IT'S A HAVE • 1906 • Collins Alf? • UKN
IT'S A HOBBY FOR HARVEY • 1980 • Lank Barry • SHT • CND
IT'S A JOKE, SON • 1947 • Stoloff Ben • USA
IT'S A KING • 1932 • Raymond Jack • UKN
IT'S A LIVING • 1958 • Hoskins Win • ANS • USA
IT'S A LONG, LONG WAY TO TIPPERARY • 1914 • Elvey Maurice • UKN
IT'S A LONG TIME THAT I'VE LOVED YOU see **IL Y A LONGTEMPS QUE JE T'AIME** • 1979
IT'S A LONG WAY TO TIPPERARY • 1914 • Dean George • ASL
IT'S A LOVELY DAY • 1949 • Felstead Bert • UKN
IT'S A LOVELY DAY TOMORROW • 1975 • Goldschmidt John • MTV • UKN
IT'S A MAD CANGACO see **DEU A LOUCA NO CANGACO** • 1969
IT'S A MAD, MAD, MAD, MAD WORLD • 1963 • Kramer Stanley • USA
IT'S A MAD, MAD WORLD see **FIGUI BIREN** • 1987
IT'S A MAD WORLD see **AALAM MODHEK GEDDAN** • 1968
IT'S A MEAN OLD WORLD • 1977 • English John W. • DOC • USA
IT'S A PANIC • 1935 • Mack Roy • SHT • USA
IT'S A PARTY • 1987 • Campbell Peg • SHT • CND
IT'S A PIPE • 1926 • Marshall George • SHT • USA
IT'S A PLEASURE • 1945 • Seiter William A. • USA
IT'S A REAL PARADISE see **C'EST UN VRAI PARADIS**
IT'S A SHAME • 1914 • *Lubin* • USA
IT'S A SHAME TO TAKE THE MONEY • 1913 • *Belmont Claude* • USA
IT'S A SICK, SICK, SICK WORLD • 1965 • Scarpati Antonio • USA • SICK, SICK, SICK WORLD ○ SICK, SICK WORLD
IT'S A SICK, SICK WORLD see **TABU N.2** • 1965
IT'S A SMALL WORLD • 1935 • Cummings Irving • USA
IT'S A SMALL WORLD • 1950 • Castle William • USA
IT'S A SMALL WORLD • 1951 • Gilbert Lewis* • UKN
IT'S A WILD LIFE • 1918 • Pratt Gilbert, Roach Hal • SHT • USA
IT'S A WISE CHILD • 1931 • Leonard Robert Z. • USA
IT'S A WOMAN'S WORLD see **SHIN ONNA ONNA ONNA MONOGATARI** • 1964
IT'S A WONDERFUL DAY • 1949 • Wilson Hal • UKN
IT'S A WONDERFUL LIFE • 1946 • Capra Frank • USA • GREATEST GIFT, THE
IT'S A WONDERFUL WORLD • 1939 • Van Dyke W. S. • USA
IT'S A WONDERFUL WORLD • 1956 • Guest Val • UKN
IT'S A WONDROUS, WONDROUS, WONDROUS, WONDROUS WORLD see **SHONEN JACK TO MAHOTSUKAI** • 1967
IT'S ADAM'S FAULT see **C'EST LA FAUTE D'ADAM** • 1957
"IT'S ALIVE" • 1968 • Buchanan Larry • USA
IT'S ALIVE • 1973 • Cohen Larry • USA
IT'S ALIVE 2 see **IT LIVES AGAIN** • 1978
IT'S ALIVE III: ISLAND OF THE ALIVE see **ISLAND OF THE ALIVE** • 1986
IT'S ALL ADAM'S FAULT see **C'EST LA FAUTE D'ADAM** • 1957
IT'S ALL FOR SALE • 1969 • Duffy Kevin • USA • IT WAS ALL FOR SALE
IT'S ALL GREEK TO ME see **VAMPING VENUS** • 1928
IT'S ALL HAPPENING • 1963 • Sharp Don • UKN • DREAM MAKER, THE
IT'S ALL IN THE GAME • 1982 • Siegel Don • USA
IT'S ALL IN THE GAME see **HOT SUMMER GAME, A** • 1965
IT'S ALL IN THE STARS • 1946 • Rasinski Connie • ANS • USA
IT'S ALL IN YOUR MIND • 1938 • Ray Bernard B. • USA
IT'S ALL OVER see **A BANNA** • 1980
IT'S ALL OVER TOWN • 1963 • Hickox Douglas • UKN
IT'S ALL TRUE • 1942 • Welles Orson, Foster Norman • USA
IT'S ALL UP WITH AUNTIE see **DET ER NAT MED FRU KNUDSEN** • 1971
IT'S ALL WRONG • 1916 • Clements Roy • SHT • USA
IT'S ALL WRONG • 1917 • *Myers Harry* • USA
IT'S ALL YOURS • 1938 • Nugent Elliott • USA
IT'S ALRIGHT MA • 1967 • Thomopoulos Andreas • UKN
IT'S ALWAYS FAIR WEATHER • 1955 • Kelly Gene, Donen Stanley • USA
IT'S ALWAYS SUNDAY • 1955 • Dwan Allan • SHT • USA
IT'S ALWAYS THE WOMAN • 1916 • Noy Wilfred • UKN
IT'S AN ADVENTURE, CHARLIE BROWN • 1983 • Melendez Bill • ANM • USA
IT'S AN ILL WIND • 1915 • *Falstaff* • USA
IT'S AN ILL WIND • 1939 • Hardaway Ben, Dalton Cal • ANS • USA
IT'S BAD TO MIX see **PATATA BOLLENTE, LA** • 1979
IT'S BEST TO BE NATURAL • 1913 • Stow Percy • UKN
IT'S BETTER TO PULL AT THE SAME END see **VE DVOU SE TO LEPE TAHNE** • 1928
IT'S CALLED MURDER BABY • 1982 • Weston Sam • USA • DIXIE RAY: HOLLYWOOD STAR
IT'S CALM HERE see **MESTA TUT TIKHIYE** • 1967
IT'S CHEAPER TO BE MARRIED • 1917 • Curtis Allen • SHT • USA
IT'S DEATH FOR ME TO LOVE YOU see **KAMATAYAN KO, ANG IBIGIN KA** • 1968
IT'S EASY TO BECOME A FATHER • 1929 • Schonfelder Erich • FRG
IT'S EASY TO MAKE MONEY • 1919 • Carewe Edwin • USA
IT'S EASY TO REMEMBER • 1935 • Fleischer Dave • ANS • USA
IT'S FINISHED see **A BANNA** • 1980
IT'S FOR THE BIRDIES • 1962 • Kneitel Seymour • ANS • USA
IT'S FOR THE BIRDS • 1967 • Bakshi Ralph • ANS • USA
IT'S FOREVER SPRINGTIME (USA) see **E PRIMAVERA** • 1949
IT'S GONNA BE ALL RIGHT • 1971 • Steed Judy • CND
IT'S GOOD TO BE ALIVE • 1974 • Landon Michael • TVM • USA
IT'S GOT ME AGAIN • 1931 • Ising Rudolf • ANS • USA
IT'S GREAT TO BE ALIVE • 1933 • Werker Alfred L. • USA
IT'S GREAT TO BE CRAZY • 1918 • Peacocke Leslie T. • SHT • USA
IT'S GREAT TO BE MARRIED • 1916 • Peacocke Leslie T. • SHT • USA
IT'S GREAT TO BE YOUNG • 1946 • Lord Del • USA
IT'S GREAT TO BE YOUNG • 1956 • Frankel Cyril • UKN
IT'S GREEK TO ME-OW • 1961 • Deitch Gene • ANS • USA
IT'S HANDY WHEN PEOPLE DON'T DIE • 1980 • McArdle Tom • IRL
IT'S HAPPINESS THAT COUNTS • 1918 • Phillips Bertram • UKN
IT'S HARD BEING A MAN see **OTOKO WA TSURAIYO** • 1969
IT'S HARD TO BE GOD see **TRUDNO BYT BOGOM** • 1988
IT'S HARD TO BE GOOD • 1948 • Dell Jeffrey • UKN
IT'S HARD TO RECOGNIZE A PRINCESS • 1968 • Pojar Bretislav • ANS • CND
IT'S HEARTTHROB THAT WE PLAY see **WAN DE JIU SHI XINTIAO** • 1989
IT'S HOT IN HELL see **SINGE EN HIVER, UN** • 1962
IT'S HOT IN PARADISE (USA) see **TOTER HING IM NETZ, EIN** • 1960
IT'S HOT ON SIN ISLAND • 1964 • Marshall Peter • USA • HOT ON SIN ISLAND
IT'S HUMMER TIME • 1950 • McKimson Robert • ANS • USA
IT'S IN THE AIR • 1935 • Reisner Charles F. • USA • LET FREEDOM RING
IT'S IN THE AIR • 1938 • Kimmins Anthony • UKN • GEORGE TAKES THE AIR (USA)
IT'S IN THE BAG • 1936 • Beaudine William • UKN
IT'S IN THE BAG • 1943 • Mason Herbert • UKN
IT'S IN THE BAG • 1945 • Wallace Richard • USA • FIFTH CHAIR, THE (UKN)
IT'S IN THE BAG (UKN) see **AFFAIRE EST DANS LE SAC, L'** • 1932
IT'S IN THE BLOOD • 1938 • Gerrard Gene • UKN
IT'S IN THE STARS • 1938 • Miller David • SHT • USA
IT'S JUST BETTER • 1981 • Shaffer Beverly • MTV • CND
IT'S JUST MY LUCK • 1908 • Cooper Arthur • UKN
IT'S JUST THE WAY IT IS • 1943 • *Two Cities* • SHT • UKN

IT'S LIVING THAT COUNTS see **LO QUE IMPORTA ES VIVIR** • 1987
IT'S LONG SINCE THE CHRYSANTHEMUMS BLOOMED IN THE GARDENS see **OTVECELI NA DAVNO CHRISANTEMY V SADO** • 1916
IT'S LOVE AGAIN • 1936 • Saville Victor • UKN
IT'S LOVE I'M AFTER • 1937 • Mayo Archie • USA • GENTLEMAN AFTER MIDNIGHT
IT'S LOVE THAT MAKES THE WORLD GO ROUND • 1913 • Stow Percy • UKN
IT'S MAGIC (UKN) see **ROMANCE ON THE HIGH SEAS** • 1948
IT'S ME • 1976 • Zwartjes Frans • NTH
IT'S ME HERE, BELLETT see **WATASHII WA BELLETT** • 1964
IT'S MINE see **MOJE, NIE DAM** • 1964
IT'S MONDAY, AT LAST see **VEGRE, HETFO** • 1971
IT'S MORNING see **UZ JE RANO** • 1956
IT'S MY FAULT see **SHIN ONO GA TSUMI** • 1926
IT'S MY LIFE TO LIVE • 1980 • Auzins Igor • MTV • ASL
IT'S MY LIFE (UKN) see **VIVRE SA VIE** • 1962
IT'S MY MODEL see **DET AR MIN MODELL** • 1946
IT'S MY TURN • 1980 • Weill Claudia • USA
ITS NAME WAS ROBERT see **CALL ME ROBERT**
IT'S NEVER TO LATE • 1916 • Hancock H. E. • SHT • USA
IT'S NEVER TOO LATE • 1956 • McCarthy Michael • UKN
IT'S NEVER TOO LATE see **DET AR ALDRIG FOR SENT** • 1956
IT'S NEVER TOO LATE see **POTE DHEN INE ARGA** • 1968
IT'S NEVER TOO LATE TO MEND • 1917 • Aylott Dave • UKN
IT'S NEVER TOO LATE TO MEND • 1922 • Wynn George • UKN
IT'S NEVER TOO LATE TO MEND • 1937 • MacDonald David • UKN
IT'S NEVER TOO LATE TO START AGAIN • 1961 • Lacko Jan • CZC
IT'S NICE ISN'T IT? see **EJA NAIKA** • 1981
IT'S NICE TO HAVE A MOUSE AROUND THE HOUSE • 1965 • Freleng Friz • ANS • USA
IT'S NIFTY TO BE THRIFTY • 1944 • Kneitel Seymour • ANS • USA
IT'S NO LAUGHING MATTER • 1915 • Weber Lois • USA
IT'S NO USE CRYING OVER SPILT MILK • 1900 • Cooper Arthur • UKN
IT'S NOON see **MAHIRU NARI** • 1978
IT'S NOT ALL PAINTING AND DRAWING, YOU KNOW • 1971 • Jones Ian • UKN
IT'S NOT ALL TRUE see **NEM TUDO E VERDADE** • 1986
IT'S NOT CRICKET • 1937 • Ince Ralph • UKN
IT'S NOT CRICKET • 1949 • Roome Alfred, Rich Roy • UKN
IT'S NOT EASY TO GET MARRIED see **POP CIRA I POP SPIRA** • 1965
IT'S NOT ENOUGH TO BE A MOTHER see **NO BASTA SER MADRE** • 1937
IT'S NOT JUST YOU, MURRAY • 1964 • Scorsese Martin • SHT • USA
IT'S NOT MY BODY • 1970 • Wertheim Ron • USA
IT'S NOT REALLY OUR FAULT THAT WE MOUNTAIN DWELLERS ARE WHERE WE ARE see **WIE BERGLER IN DEN BERGEN SIND EIGENTLICH NICHT SCHULD, DASS WIR DA SIND** • 1975
IT'S NOT SIZE THAT COUNTS see **PERCY'S PROGRESS** • 1974
IT'S NOT THE SIZE THAT COUNTS! (USA) see **PERCY'S PROGRESS** • 1974
IT'S NOT TOO LATE see **POKA .NE. POZDNO** • 1958
IT'S NOTHING MUMMY, JUST A GAME see **NO ES NADA MAMA, SOLO UN JUEGO** • 1974
IT'S ON THE RECORD • 1937 • Schwarzwald Milton • SHT • USA
IT'S ONLY A MACHINE see **SNOMOBILE** • 1973
IT'S ONLY A QUESTION OF TIME • 1975 • Beauman Nicholas • SHT • ASL
IT'S ONLY MONEY • 1962 • Tashlin Frank • USA
IT'S ONLY MONEY see **DOUBLE DYNAMITE** • 1951
IT'S PINK BUT IS IT MINK? • 1975 • McKimson Robert • ANS • USA
IT'S RAIN AND SHINE TOGETHER see **VERI AZ ORDOG A FELESEGET** • 1978
IT'S RAINING SOLDIERS • 1953-54 • Devlin Bernard • DCS • CND
IT'S RICE –AUSTRALIAN • 1968 • Murray John B. • DOC • ASL
IT'S SAM SMALL AGAIN see **SAM SMALL LEAVES TOWN** • 1937
IT'S SHOWTIME • 1976 • *Weintraub Fred (P)* • CMP • USA • PAWS, JAWS AND CLAWS
IT'S SNOW • 1974 • Thomas Gayle • ANM • CND
IT'S SO EASY • 1966 • Crombie Donald • DOC • ASL
IT'S SO SIMPLE • 1968 • Szemes Marianne • DOC • HNG
IT'S SPRING AGAIN see **ZENOBIA** • 1939
IT'S THAT MAN AGAIN • 1943 • Forde Walter • UKN
IT'S THE CATS • 1926 • Fleischer Dave • ANS • USA
IT'S THE CAT'S • 1934 • Ray Albert • SHT • USA
IT'S THE EASTER BEAGLE, CHARLIE BROWN • 1974 • Roman Phil • ANS • USA
IT'S THE FAULT OF PARADISE see **TUTTA COLPA DEL PARADISO** • 1985
IT'S THE NATURAL THING TO DO • 1939 • Fleischer Dave • ANS • USA
IT'S THE OLD ARMY GAME • 1926 • Sutherland A. Edward • USA
IT'S THE ONLY WAY TO GO • 1969 • Austin Ray • SHT • UKN
IT'S TIME FOR EVERYBODY • 1954 • Cannon Robert • ANS • USA
IT'S TIME –THE GOUGH AND BOB SHOW • 1973 • Dimsey Ross • DOC • ASL
IT'S TOUGH TO BE A BIRD • 1969 • Kimball Ward • ANS • USA
IT'S TOUGH TO BE FAMOUS • 1932 • Green Alfred E. • USA
IT'S TRAD, DAD • 1962 • Lester Richard • UKN • RING–A–DING RHYTHM (USA)
IT'S UP TO YOU • 1941 • Kazan Elia • DOC • USA
IT'S UP TO YOU see **OSS EMELLAN** • 1969
IT'S VERY TRYING • 1914 • *Royal* • USA
IT'S WHAT'S HAPPENING • 1967 • Silverstein Elliot • USA • HAPPENING, THE
IT'S WHEN WE ARE YOUNG, WE'RE GROWING OLD • 1973 • Thorstenson Espen • SHT • NRW
IT'S WINNING THAT COUNTS • 1975 • Woods Grahame • CND
IT'S YOU I WANT • 1936 • Ince Ralph • UKN
IT'S YOUR MONEY • 1982 • Reusch Peter • MTV • CND
IT'S YOUR MOVE • 1945 • Yates Hal • SHT • USA
IT'S YOUR MOVE (USA) see **SEI SIMPATICHE CAROGNE** • 1968
IT'S YOUR THING • 1970 • Cargiulo Mike • DOC • USA
ITSKY, THE INVENTOR • 1915 • Williams C. Jay • USA
ITSUWARERU SEISO • 1951 • Yoshimura Kozaburo • JPN • CLOTHES OF DECEPTION ○ UNDER SILK GARMENTS ○ DECEIVING COSTUME
ITT A SZABADSAG! • 1990 • Vajda Peter • HNG • HERE'S FREEDOM!
ITTO • 1934 • Benoit-Levy Jean, Epstein Marie • FRN, MRC
ITTORYU SHINAN • 1936 • Ishibashi Seiichi • JPN • TEACHING OF THE ITTOU STYLE, THE ○ FIRST CLASS TEACHING
ITZHAK PERLMAN, VIRTUOSO VIOLINIST • 1978 • Nupen Christopher • UKN • I KNOW I PLAYED EVERY NOTE
IUBELEI • 1944 • Petrov Vladimir • USS • JUBILEE
IUBIRILE UNEI BLONDE • 1988 • Nicoara Radu • RMN • LOVES OF A BLONDE, THE
IUMORESKI see **ZHUMORESKI** • 1925
IUNOST' MIRA • 1949 • Ovanesova Arscia • USS, HNG • YOUTH OF THE WORLD, THE ○ WORLD YOUTH FESTIVAL ○ YUNOST MIRA
IVALLO THE GREAT • 1963 • Vulcev Nikola • BUL
IVAN • 1932 • Dovzhenko Alexander • USS
IVAN AND ALEXANDRA • 1988 • Nichev Ivan • BUL
IVAN AND THE WITCH BABA–YAGA • ANS • USS
IVAN FRANKO • 1956 • Levchuk Timofey • USS
IVAN FYODOROV, THE FIRST PRINTER • 1941 • Levkoev G. • USS
IVAN GROZNI KINO–BALET • 1977 • Derbenev Vadim, Grigorovich Yuri • USS • IVAN THE TERRIBLE ○ GROZNY VEK
IVAN GROZNYI • 1945-47 • Eisenstein Sergei • USS • IVAN THE TERRIBLE PARTS 1, 2 & 3
IVAN, IL FIGLIO DEL DIAVOLO BIANCO • 1954 • Brignone Guido • ITL • IVAN, SON OF THE WHITE DEVIL ○ IVAN (USA)
IVAN IL TERRIBILE • 1915 • Guazzoni Enrico • ITL
IVAN KONDAREN • 1973 • Korabov Nicolai • BUL
IVAN KUPALA'S EVE • 1968 • Ilyenko Yury • USS • ON THE EVE OF IVAN KUPALA'S DAY
IVAN MAKAROVICH • 1968 • Dobrolyubov Igor • USS
IVAN NIKULIN –RUSSIAN SAILOR see **RUSSIAN SAILOR –IVAN NIKULIN** • 1944
IVAN PAVLOV see **AKADEMIK IVAN PAVLOV** • 1949
IVAN, SON OF THE WHITE DEVIL see **IVAN, IL FIGLIO DEL DIAVOLO BIANCO** • 1954
IVAN THE TERRIBLE • 1979 • Ohrimenko L. • USS
IVAN THE TERRIBLE see **KRYLYA KHOLOPAL** • 1926
IVAN THE TERRIBLE see **IVAN GROZNI KINO–BALET** • 1977
IVAN THE TERRIBLE PART 1 • 1945 • Eisenstein Sergei • USS
IVAN THE TERRIBLE PART 2 • 1946 • Eisenstein Sergei • USS • BOYARS' PLOT, THE
IVAN THE TERRIBLE PART 3 • 1947 • Eisenstein Sergei • USS • BATTLES OF IVAN, THE
IVAN THE TERRIBLE PARTS 1, 2 & 3 see **IVAN GROZNYI** • 1945-47
IVAN (USA) see **IVAN, IL FIGLIO DEL DIAVOLO BIANCO** • 1954
IVAN VASILYEVICH see **IVAN VASILYEVICH MENJAET PROFESSIJU** • 1973
IVAN VASILYEVICH MENJAET PROFESSIJU • 1973 • Gaidai Leonid • USS • IVAN VASSILIEVICH CHANGES HIS PROFESSION ○ IVAN VASILYEVICH
IVAN VASSILIEVICH CHANGES HIS PROFESSION see **IVAN VASILYEVICH MENJAET PROFESSIJU** • 1973
IVANHOE • 1913 • Bantock Leedham • UKN • REBECCA THE JEWESS (USA)
IVANHOE • 1913 • Brenon Herbert • UKN, USA
IVANHOE • 1952 • Thorpe Richard • USA, UKN
IVANHOE • 1982 • Camfield Douglas • TVM • UKN
IVANNA • 1960 • Ivchenko Viktor • USS
IVANNA • 1970 • Merino Jose Luis • SPN, ITL • SCREAM OF THE DEMON LOVER ○ KILLERS OF THE CASTLE OF BLOOD ○ BLOOD CASTLE
IVANOVO DETSTVO • 1962 • Tarkovsky Andrei • USS • MY NAME IS IVAN (USA) ○ IVAN'S CHILDHOOD ○ YOUNGEST SPY, THE ○ DETSTVO IVANA ○ CHILDHOOD OF IVAN
IVANOVS, THE • 1975 • Saltykov Alexei • USS
IVAN'S CHILDHOOD see **IVANOVO DETSTVO** • 1962
IVAS • 1940 • Ivanov-Vano Ivan • ANS • USS
I'VE ALWAYS LOVED YOU • 1946 • Borzage Frank • USA • CONCERTO (UKN)
I'VE ALWAYS WANTED TO CALL YOU MY SWEETHEART • 1929 • Aylott Dave, Symmons E. F. • SHT • UKN
I'VE BECOME A COP see **HEKKUS LETTEM** • 1972
I'VE BEEN AROUND • 1935 • Cahn Philip • USA
I'VE COME ABOUT THE SUICIDE • 1988 • Turkiewicz Sophia • ASL
I'VE CRIED ALL MY LIFE see **OMRUNCE AGLADIM** • 1967
I'VE GOT A HORSE • 1938 • Smith Herbert • UKN
I'VE GOT RINGS ON MY FINGERS • 1929 • Fleischer Dave • ANS • USA
I'VE GOT SIXPENCE • 1944-45 • Ladouceur Jean-Paul • ANS • CND
I'VE GOT THIS PROBLEM • 1966 • Clasky Ron • USA
I'VE GOT TO LIVE see **MAN MASTE JU LEVA** • 1978
I'VE GOT TO SING A TORCH SONG • 1933 • Palmer Tom • ANS • USA
I'VE GOT YER NUMBER • 1916 • Curtis Allen • SHT • USA
I'VE GOT YOU, YOU'VE GOT ME BY THE CHIN HAIRS (USA) see **JE TE TIENS, TU ME TIENS PAR LA BARBICHETTE** • 1978
I'VE GOT YOUR NUMBER • 1934 • Enright Ray • USA
I'VE GOTTA HORSE • 1965 • Hume Kenneth • UKN • WONDERFUL DAY
I'VE HEARD THE MERMAIDS SINGING • 1987 • Rozema Patricia • CND • CHANT DES SIRENES, LE
I'VE LIVED BEFORE • 1956 • Bartlett Richard • USA
I'VE LOST A TOOTH see **NIE MAM JUZ ZEBA** • 1964
I'VE LOVED A MURDERER see **BIR KATIL SEVDIM** • 1967
I'VE LOVED A SAVAGE WOMAN see **VAHSI BIR ERKEK SEVDIM** • 1968
I'VE MARRIED FOR LOVE see **SZERELEMBOEL NOESUELTEM** • 1938
I'VE NEVER SEEN ANYTHING LIKE IT • 1967 • Sens Al • ANS • CND
IVICA I MARICA • 1979 • Stalter Pavao • ANS • YGS • HANSEL AND GRETEL
IVO see **FLUCHTVERSUCH** • 1976
IVORY APE, THE • 1980 • Kotani Tom • TVM • USA
IVORY COAST ADVENTURE (UKN) see **GENTLEMAN DE COCODY, LE** • 1965
IVORY HAND, THE • 1915 • Noy Wilfred • UKN
IVORY-HANDLED GUN, THE • 1935 • Taylor Ray • USA
IVORY HUNTER (USA) see **WHERE NO VULTURES FLY** • 1951
IVORY SNUFF BOX, THE • 1915 • Tourneur Maurice • USA
IVRAIE, L' • 1913 • Jasset Victorin • FRN
IVROGNE, L' see **METHYSTAKOS, O** • 1950
IVROGNES, LES • 1896 • Melies Georges • FRN • DRUNKARDS, THE
IVY • 1947 • Wood Sam • USA
IVY AND THE OAK, THE • 1916 • MacDonald Donald • SHT • USA
IVY LEAGUE KILLERS • 1962 • Davidson William • CND • FAST ONES, THE
IVY'S DEVELOPEMENT • 1914 • Neame Elwin • UKN
IWAN KOSCHULA • 1914 • Oswald Richard • FRG
IWASHIGUMO • 1958 • Naruse Mikio • JPN • HERRINGBONE CLOUDS ○ SUMMER CLOUDS
IWISA • 1981 • SAF
IWOJIMA • 1959 • Uno Jukichi • JPN • GHOST OF IWOJIMA, THE
IX OLYMPISCHE WINTERSPIELE 1964 IN INNSBRUCK • 1964 • Hermann Theo • AUS • NINTH WINTER OLYMPIC GAMES 1964, THE
IX SESJA KRN • 1946 • Bossak Jerzy • DOC • PLN • 9TH SESSION OF THE HOME NATIONAL COUNCIL
IXE 13 • 1971 • Godbout Jacques • CND
IZ GLUBINY STOLETIY • 1961 • Morgenshtern V. • USS • INSIDE THE KREMLIN
IZ JIZNI OTDYKHAIOUCHTCHIKH • 1980 • Gubenko Nikolai • USS
IZA NENI • 1933 • Sekely Steve • HNG
IZAKAYA CHOJI • 1984 • Furuhata Yasuo • JPN • CHOJI, A TAVERN MASTER
IZBAVITELJ • 1977 • Papic Krsto • YGS • REDEEMER, THE ○ RAT SAVIOUR, THE
IZBRANNYE • 1983 • Soloviev Sergei • USS • ELECT, THE
IZDAJNIK • 1963 • Rakonjac Kokan • YGS • TRAITOR, THE
IZGONEN OT RAYA • 1967 • Dinov Todor • ANS • BUL • DRIVEN OUT OF PARADISE ○ EXPELLED FROM PARADISE
IZGUBLJENA OLOVKA • 1960 • Skubonja Fedor • YGS • MISSING PENCIL, THE
IZGUBLJENI ZAVICAJ • 1981 • Babaja Ante • YGS • LOST HOMELAND, THE
IZHORSK BATTALION, THE • 1972 • Kazansky Gennadi • USS
IZIDUPHUNGA • 1977 • SAF
IZIGEBENGU • 1984 • SAF
IZIN • 1975 • Gursu Temel • TRK • LEAVE
IZIPHUKUPHUKU • 1983 • SAF
IZLAZ 19 • 1989 • Djordjevic Mladomir Purisa • YGS • EXIT 19
IZMEDJU STRAHA I DUZNOSTI • 1977 • Duletic Vojko • YGS • BETWEEN FEAR AND DUTY
IZMEDJU USANA I CASE • 1968 • Vunak Dragutin • YGS, ITL • BETWEEN THE GLASS AND THE LIP ○ IZMEDU USANA I CASE ○ BETWEEN LIPS AND GLASS
IZMEDU USANA I CASE see **IZMEDJU USANA I CASE** • 1968
IZMYENA • 1967 • Sabirov Takhir • USS • BETRAYAL
IZOTOPOK A GYOGYASZATBAN • 1959 • Jancso Miklos • SHT • HNG • ISOTOPES IN MEDICAL SCIENCE
IZPIT • 1971 • Dyulgerov Georgi • BUL • EXAM ○ TEST, THE
IZPITI PO NIKOYE VREME • 1974 • Grubcheva Ivanka • BUL • EXAMS AT AN IN APPROPRIATE TIME ○ EXAMS AT ANY OLD TIME
IZRAZI JA • 1969 • Jovanovic Jovan • YGS • EXPRESSIVE I, THE
IZU DANCER see **IZU NO ODORIKO** • 1967
IZU DANCER, THE see **IZU NO ODORIKO** • 1933
IZU NO MUSUMETACHI • 1945 • Gosho Heinosuke • JPN • GIRLS OF IZU
IZU NO ODORIKO • 1933 • Gosho Heinosuke • JPN • DANCING GIRLS OF IZU ○ IZU DANCER, THE ○ DANCER OF IZU
IZU NO ODORIKO • 1954 • Nomura Yoshitaro • JPN • DANCING GIRLS OF IZU
IZU NO ODORIKO • 1960 • Kawazu Yoshiro • JPN • DANCING GIRLS OF IZU
IZU NO ODORIKO • 1963 • Nishikawa Katsumi • JPN • DANCING GIRLS OF IZU
IZU NO ODORIKO • 1967 • Onchi Hideo • JPN • IZU DANCER
IZUKO E • 1954 • Ohba Hideo • JPN
IZUMI • 1956 • Kobayashi Masaki • JPN • FOUNTAINHEAD, THE ○ FOUNTAIN, THE ○ SPRING, THE
IZUMITELJ CIPELA • 1967 • Grgic Zlatko • ANS • YGS • INVENTOR OF SHOES (USA) ○ SHOE INVENTOR, THE
IZVOR ZIVOTA • 1969 • Majdak Nikola, Sajtinac Borislav • ANS • YGS • SPRING OF LIFE, THE
IZVRNUTA PRICA • 1972 • Grgic Zlatko • ANS • YGS • DOUBLE TROUBLE
IZZY AND HIS RIVAL • 1914 • *Reliance* • USA
IZZY AND MOE • 1985 • Cooper Jackie • TVM • USA • IZZY AND MOE, THE BOOTLEG BUSTERS
IZZY AND MOE, THE BOOTLEG BUSTERS see **IZZY AND MOE** • 1985
IZZY AND THE BANDIT • 1914 • *Komic* • USA
IZZY AND THE DIAMOND • 1914 • *Reliance* • USA
IZZY GETS THE WRONG BOTTLE • 1914 • *Reliance* • USA
IZZY THE DETECTIVE • 1914 • *Davidson Max* • USA
IZZY THE OPERATOR • 1914 • *Reliance* • USA
IZZY'S NIGHT OUT • 1914 • *Davidson Max* • USA

J

J 3, LES • 1945 • Richebe Roger • FRN

J.A. MARTIN PHOTOGRAPHE • 1976 • Beaudin Jean • FRN, CND • J.A. MARTIN PHOTOGRAPHER

J.A. MARTIN PHOTOGRAPHER see **J.A. MARTIN PHOTOGRAPHE** • 1976

J.A.T.P. • 1950 • Mili Gjon • SHT • USA

J. AND S. –HISTORIA CRIMINAL DEL FAR WEST (SPN) see **BANDA J.S. CRONACA CRIMINALE DEL FAR WEST, LA** • 1972

J. AND S. – STORIA CRIMINALE DEL FAR WEST see **BANDA J. S. CRONACA CRIMINALE DEL FAR WEST, LA** • 1972

J.C. • 1972 • McGaha William • USA

J.D.'S REVENGE • 1976 • Marks Arthur • USA

J. EDGAR HOOVER • 1987 • Collins Robert • USA

J. EDGAR HOOVER see **PRIVATE FILES OF J. EDGAR HOOVER, THE** • 1978

J.F.K. AND MR. K. • 1963 • Sheppard Gordon H. • DOC • CND

J.H. SQUIRES' CELESTE OCTET • 1928 • *De Forest Phonofilms* • SHT • UKN • MUSICAL MEDLEY NO.2

J.J. GARCIA • 1984 • Randall John • USA

J.J. STARBUCK • 1988 • Allen Corey • TVM • USA

J–MEN FOREVER • 1979 • Patterson Richard • USA

J.O.E. AND THE COLONEL • 1985 • Satlof Ron • TVM • USA

J.R. see **WHO'S THAT KNOCKING AT MY DOOR?** • 1967

J.S. BACH –FANTASY IN G MINOR see **JOHANN SEBASTIAN BACH: FANTASIA G–MOLL** • 1965

J.S. BROWN –O ULTIMO HEROI • 1982 • Frazao Jose • BRZ • J.S. BROWN –THE LAST HERO

J.S. BROWN –THE LAST HERO see **J.S. BROWN –O ULTIMO HEROI** • 1982

J.TH. ARNFRED • 1974 • Roos Jorgen • DOC • DNM

J.W. COOP • 1972 • Robertson Cliff • USA

JA GORE • 1967 • Majewski Janusz • SHT • PLN • I'M BURNING ○ I AM ON FIRE

JA, JA, DIE FRAUN SIND MEINE SCHWACHE SEITE • 1929 • Heuberger Edmund • FRG

JA, JA, DIE LIEBE IN TIROL • 1955 • von Bolvary Geza • FRG

JA, JA, MEIN GENERAL! BUT WHICH WAY TO THE FRONT (UKN) see **WHICH WAY TO THE FRONT?** • 1970

JA MAM JAJKO • 1966 • Brzozowski Andrzej • PLN • I HAVE AN EGG

JA MILUJEM, TY MILUJES • 1980 • Hanak Dusan • CZC • I LOVE, YOU LOVE

JA NEJSEM JA • 1985 • Vorlicek Vaclav • CZC • I AM NOT MYSELF

JA PRASU SLOVA • 1975 • Panfilov Gleb • USS • I WISH TO SPEAK ○ I ASK FOR THE FLOOR ○ MAY I TAKE THE FLOOR? ○ PROSHU SLOVA ○ I FORGIVE THE WORDS ○ MAY I HAVE THE FLOOR?

JA SAM • 1959 • Zukowska Jadwiga • PLN • ME ALONE

JA SE FAZEM AUTOMOVEIS EM PORTUGAL see **EM PORTUGAL JA SE FAZEM AUTOMOVEIS** • 1938

JA, SO EIN MADCHEN MIT SECHZEHN • 1959 • Grimm Hans • FRG

JA SPRAVEDLNOST • 1967 • Brynych Zbynek • CZC • I THE JUSTICE ○ I, JUSTICE

JA, TREU IST DIE SOLDATENLIEBE • 1932 • Jacoby Georg • FRG

JA TRUCHLIVY BUH • 1969 • Kachlik Antonin • CZC • I THE DOLEFUL GOD ○ I THE SAD GOD

JA, VI ELSKER • 1983 • Skagen Solve, Wadman Malte, Szepesy Andrew • NRW • LAST GLEAMING

JAAHYVAISET see **AVSKEDET** • 1980

JAAHYVAISET PRESIDENTILLE • 1987 • Kassila Matti • FNL • FAREWELL TO THE PRESIDENT

JAAKARIN MORSIAN • 1939 • Orko Risto • FNL • SOLDIER'S BRIDE (USA) ○ INFANTRYMAN'S BRIDE, THE

JAAL • 1952 • *Burman S. D. (M)* • IND

JAAL • 1967 • Bhattacharjee Moni • IND • COUNTERFEIT

JAALLUNI MUJRIMAN • 1954 • Salem Atef • EGY • ILS ONT FAIT DE MOI UN ASSASSIN

JAAN PEHCHAN • 1950 • *Kapoor Raj* • IND

JAANE BHI DO YAARON • 1983 • Shah Kundan • IND

JAAR VAN DE KREEFT, HET • 1975 • Curiel Herbert • NTH • YEAR OF THE CANCER

JAB YAAD KISIKI AATI HAI • 1967 • Saigal Naresh • IND • WHEN MEMORIES ARE STIRRED UP

JABABIRA, AL • 1965 • Chams Hassib • LBN • COLOSSI, THE

JABALKATA • 1963 • Dinov Todor, Doukov Stoyan • ANM • BUL • APPLE, THE

JABBERWALK see **THIS IS AMERICA** • 1977

JABBERWOCKY • 1974 • Svankmajer Jan • ANM • CZC

JABBERWOCKY • 1977 • Gilliam Terry • UKN

JABEZ'S CONQUEST • 1915 • *Craig Nell* • USA

JABLONOVA PANNA • 1974 • Pojar Bretislav • ANM • CZC • APPLE TREE MAIDEN, THE

JABLONSKI • 1972 • Dolgoy Reevan • CND

JABLUNKA SE ZLATYMI JABLKY • 1952 • Hofman Eduard • ANS • CZC • APPLE TREE WITH GOLDEN APPLES, THE ○ GOLDEN APPLES

JACARE • 1943 • Ford Charles E. • USA

JACARE, KILLER OF THE AMAZON • 1942 • Buck Frank • USA

J'ACCUSE • 1919 • Gance Abel • FRN • I ACCUSE

J'ACCUSE • 1937 • Gance Abel • FRN • THAT THEY MAY LIVE (USA) ○ I ACCUSE (UKN)

JACEK AND HIS DOG see **JACEK I JEGO PIES** • 1966

JACEK I JEGO PIES • 1966 • Wator Edward • ANS • PLN • JACEK AND HIS DOG ○ JACK AND HIS DOG

JACHT DER SIEBEN SUNDEN, DIE • 1928 • Fleck Jacob, Fleck Luise • FRG • YACHT OF THE SEVEN SINS

JACHTTAFEREEL • 1971 • Ockersen Thijs • NTH • HUNTING SCENE

JACHYME HOD TO DO STROJE • 1973 • Podskalsky Zdenek • CZC • JOACHIM, PUT IT IN THE MACHINE

JACHYMOV • 1934 • Hammid Alexander • DCS • CZC

JACK • 1916 • Borzage Frank • SHT • USA

JACK • 1925 • Saidreau Robert • FRN

JACK • 1960 • Heyer John • SHT • ASL

JACK • 1977 • Halldoff Jan • SWD • WHAT THE HELL, JACK!

JACK AHOY! • 1934 • Forde Walter • UKN

JACK AND HIS DOG see **JACEK I JEGO PIES** • 1966

JACK AND JILL • 1917 • Taylor William D. • USA

JACK AND JILL see **JACK 'N' JILL** • 1980

JACK AND JILL: A POSTSCRIPT • 1970 • Adams Phillip, Robinson Brian • ASL

JACK AND JILL II • 1984 • Vincent Chuck • USA

JACK AND JIM (USA) see **JACQUES ET JIM** • 1903

JACK AND JINGLES • 1912 • *Selig* • USA

JACK AND MIKE • 1986 • Bender Jack • TVM • USA

JACK AND OLD MAC • 1956 • Justice Bill • ANS • USA

JACK AND THE BEAN STALK • 1913 • *Benham Leland* • USA

JACK AND THE BEANSTALK • 1902 • Porter Edwin S. • USA

JACK AND THE BEANSTALK • 1903 • *Lubin* • USA

JACK AND THE BEANSTALK • 1912 • *Carnahan Thomas Jr.* • UKN

JACK AND THE BEANSTALK • 1912 • Dawley J. Searle • USA • JACK, THE GIANT KILLER

JACK AND THE BEANSTALK • 1917 • Franklin Chester M., Franklin Sidney A. • USA

JACK AND THE BEANSTALK • 1922 • Disney Walt • ANS • USA

JACK AND THE BEANSTALK • 1924 • Goulding Alf • SHT • USA

JACK AND THE BEANSTALK • 1931 • Fleischer Dave • ANS • USA

JACK AND THE BEANSTALK • 1933 • *Iwerks Ub (P)* • ANS • USA

JACK AND THE BEANSTALK • 1952 • Yarbrough Jean • USA

JACK AND THE BEANSTALK • 1954 • Reiniger Lotte • ANS • UKN • JACK THE GIANT KILLER

JACK AND THE BEANSTALK • 1970 • Mahon Barry • USA

JACK AND THE BEANSTALK • 1982 • Johnson Lamont • MTV • USA

JACK AND THE FAIRIES • 1912 • Kinder Stuart • UKN

JACK AND THE SOLDIER • 1979 • Pringle Ian • ASL

JACK AND THE WITCH (USA) see **SHONEN JACK TO MAHOTSUKAI** • 1967

JACK ARMSTRONG • 1947 • Fox Wallace • SRL • USA

JACK CHANTY • 1915 • Figman Max • USA

JACK, EL DESTRIPADOR DE LONDRES • 1971 • Madrid Jose Luis • SPN, ITL • SETTE CADAVERI PER SCOTLAND YARD (ITL) ○ JACK THE RIPPER ○ JACK, THE MANGLER OF LONDON

JACK EL NEGRO (SPN) see **BLACK JACK** • 1949

JACK FAT AND JIM SLIM AT CONEY ISLAND • 1910 • *Vitagraph* • USA

JACK FINA AND HIS ORCHESTRA • 1949 • *Universal* • SHT • USA

JACK FLASH • 1981 • Hayers Sidney • MTV

JACK FROST • 1923 • Parrott Charles • USA

JACK FROST • 1934 • *Iwerks Ub (P)* • ANS • USA

JACK FROST see **MOROZKO** • 1965

JACK IN THE BOX • 1912 • *Westbrook Virginia* • SHT • USA

JACK IN THE LETTERBOX • 1908 • Fitzhamon Lewin • UKN

JACK JAGGS AND DUM DUM (USA) see **TOM TIGHT ET DUM DUM** • 1903

JACK JOHNSON • 1971 • Cayton William • DOC • USA

JACK KENARD, COWARD • 1915 • Seay Charles M. • USA

JACK KNIFE MAN, THE • 1920 • Vidor King • USA

JACK LE RAMONEUR • 1906 • Melies Georges • FRN • CHIMNEY SWEEP (USA) ○ PETIT RAMONEUR, LE

JACK LOGAN'S DOG • 1910 • *Powers* • USA

JACK LONDON • 1942 • Santell Alfred • USA • ADVENTURES OF JACK LONDON

JACK LONDON LA MIA GRANDE AVVENTURA • 1973 • D'Alessandro Angelo • ITL • AVVENTURA DEL GRANDE NORD, L'

JACK LONDON'S KLONDIKE FEVER • 1980 • Carter Peter • CND • KLONDIKE FEVER

JACK LONDON'S TALES OF THE FISH PATROL • 1923 • USA • TALES OF THE FISH PATROL

JACK LONDON'S TALES OF THE KLONDIKE • 1980 • Pearson Peter (c/d) • SER • CND

JACK LONDON'S TALES OF THE KLONDIKE: SCORN OF WOMEN • 1981 • Fournier Claude • CND

JACK MASON'S LAST DEED • 1911 • Melies Gaston • USA • JACK WILSON'S LAST DEED

JACK MCCALL, DESPERADO • 1953 • Salkow Sidney • USA

JACK MEETS HIS WATERLOO • 1913 • *Kerrigan J. Warren* • USA

JACK MORTIMER • 1962 • Kehlmann Michael • MTV • FRG

JACK 'N' JILL • 1980 • Vincent Chuck • USA • JACK AND JILL

JACK 'N' JILL 2 • 1981 • Vincent Chuck • USA • DESIRES OF A NAUGHTY NYMPHO

JACK O' CLUBS • 1924 • Hill Robert F. • USA

JACK O' HEARTS • 1926 • Hartford David M. • USA

JACK OF ALL TRADES • 1936 • Hulbert Jack, Stevenson Robert • UKN • TWO OF US, THE (USA)

JACK OF ALL TRADES see **ENAS VENGOD GIA OLES TIS DOULIES** • 1969

JACK OF DIAMONDS • 1912 • Dwan Allan • USA • QUEEN OF HEARTS

JACK OF DIAMONDS • 1949 • Sewell Vernon • UKN

JACK OF DIAMONDS • 1967 • Taylor Don • USA, FRG

JACK OF HEARTS • 1985 • Scott Cynthia • MTV • CND

JACK OF HEARTS see **HJARTER KNEKT** • 1950

JACK OF HEARTS, THE • 1919 • Eason B. Reeves • SHT • USA

JACK OF SPADES see **WALET PIKOWY** • 1960

JACK O'LANTERN see **CONDEMNED TO DEATH** • 1932

JACK PERRYS EHEGLUCK ODER DAS GESTANDNIS AM HOCHZEITSABEND • 1918 • Trautmann Ludwig • FRG

JACK POT • 1940 • Rowland Roy • SHT • USA

JACK RABBIT AND THE BEANSTALK • 1943 • Freleng Friz • ANS • USA

JACK RIDER, THE • 1921 • Seeling Charles R. • USA

JACK, SAM AND PETE • 1919 • Moran Percy • UKN

JACK SHEPPARD • 1912 • Nash Percy • UKN

JACK SHEPPARD • 1923 • Taylor Henry C. • UKN

JACK SHEPPARD (USA) see **ROBBERY OF THE MAIL COACH** • 1903

JACK SLADE • 1953 • Schuster Harold • USA • SLADE (UKN)

JACK SPRATT AND THE SCALES OF LOVE • 1915 • *Potel Victor* • SHT • USA

JACK SPRATT AS A BLACKLEG WAITER • 1914 • Cooper Toby • UKN

JACK SPRATT AS A BRICKLAYER • 1914 • Cooper Toby • UKN

JACK SPRATT AS A BUS CONDUCTOR • 1914 • Cooper Toby • UKN

JACK SPRATT AS A DUDE • 1914 • Cooper Toby • UKN

JACK SPRATT AS A GARDENER • 1914 • Cooper Toby • UKN

JACK SPRATT AS A POLICEMAN • 1914 • Cooper Toby • UKN

JACK SPRATT AS A SPECIAL CONSTABLE • 1914 • Cooper Toby • UKN

JACK SPRATT AS A WAR LORD • 1914 • Cooper Toby • UKN

JACK SPRATT AS A WOUNDED PRUSSIAN • 1914 • Cooper Toby • UKN

JACK SPRATT'S PARROT • 1915 • Cooper Toby? • UKN

JACK SPRATT'S PARROT AS THE ARTFUL DODGER • 1916 • Cooper Toby? • UKN

JACK SPRATT'S PARROT GETTING HIS OWN BACK • 1916 • Cooper Toby? • UKN

JACK SPRATT'S PARROT PUTTING THE LID ON IT • 1916 • Cooper Toby? • UKN

JACK SPURLOCK, PRODIGAL • 1918 • Harbaugh Carl • USA

JACK STRAW • 1920 • De Mille William C. • USA

JACK TAR • 1915 • Haldane Bert • UKN

JACK THE GIANT KILLER • 1933 • Fryer Bryant • ANS • CND

JACK THE GIANT KILLER • 1962 • Juran Nathan • USA

JACK, THE GIANT KILLER see **JACK AND THE BEANSTALK** • 1912

JACK THE GIANT KILLER see **JACK AND THE BEANSTALK** • 1954

JACK THE HANDYMAN • 1912 • Southwell Gilbert • UKN

JACK THE HANDYMAN • 1915 • *Horseshoe* • UKN

JACK THE KISSER • 1907 • Porter Edwin S. • USA

JACK THE MAN–APE see **EVOLUTION OF MAN, THE** • 1920

JACK, THE MANGLER OF LONDON see **JACK, EL DESTRIPADOR DE LONDRES** • 1971

JACK THE RIDER see **TZAK O KAVALLARIS** • 1979

JACK THE RIPPER • 1959 • Baker Robert S. • UKN

JACK THE RIPPER • 1978 • Franco Jesus • FRG

JACK THE RIPPER • 1988 • Wickes David • TVM • UKN

JACK THE RIPPER see **JACK, EL DESTRIPADOR DE LONDRES** • 1971

JACK TILLMAN: THE SURVIVALIST • 1987 • Shore Sig • USA • SURVIVALIST, THE

JACK TRENT INVESTIGATES • 1957 • Negus Olive • UKN

JACK UND JENNY • 1963 • Vicas Victor • FRG

JACK WILSON'S LAST DEED see **JACK MASON'S LAST DEED** • 1911

JACKA V.C. • 1978 • Buesst Nigel (c/d) • DOC • ASL

JACKAL OF NAHUELTORO, THE (UKN) see **CHACAL DE NAHUELTORO, EL** • 1969

JACKAL OF TULA METSI, THE see **JAKKALS VAN TULA METSI, DIE** • 1967

JACKALS • 1986 • Grillo Gary • USA • AMERICAN JUSTICE

JACKALS, THE • 1967 • Webb Robert D. • SAF

JACKALS OF A GREAT CITY • 1916 • Le Saint Edward J. • SHT • USA

JACKAROO, THE • 1917 • Hurst Paul C. • SHT • USA

JACKASS MAIL • 1942 • McLeod Norman Z. • USA

JACKBOOT MUTINY see **ES GESCHAH AM 20 JULI** • 1955

JACKE WIE HOSE • 1953 • Kubat Eduard • GDR

JACKEROO, THE • 1961 • Mason Richard • UKN

JACKEROO OF COOLABONG, THE • 1920 • Lucas Wilfred • ASL

JACKI • 1977 • Andrees Angelica • GDR

JACKIE • 1921 • Ford John • USA

JACKIE AND THE BEANSTALK • 1929 • Harman Bobby • UKN

JACKIE CHAN VERSUS JIMMY WANG YU see **KILLER METEORS, THE** • 1984

JACKIE CHAN'S POLICE STORY see **POLICE STORY** • 1986

JACKIE COOPER'S CHRISTMAS • 1931 • Reisner Charles F. • SHT • USA • CHRISTMAS PARTY, THE

JACKIE MCLEAN ON MARS • 1980 • Levis Ken • DOC • USA

JACKIE ROBINSON STORY, THE • 1950 • Green Alfred E. • USA

JACKIE'S NIGHTMARE • 1929 • Harman Bobby • UKN

JACKNIFE • 1988 • Jones David • USA

JACKO THE ARTIST see **BEAUX–ARTS DE JOCKO, LES** • 1909

JACKPOT • 1960 • Tully Montgomery • UKN

JACKPOT • 1975 • Young Terence • UKN

JACKPOT 2 • 1982 • Kaurismaki Mika • FNL

JACKPOT, THE • 1950 • Lang Walter • USA

JACKPOT CLUB, THE • 1914 • *Frazer Robert* • USA

JACKPOT IN BANGKOK FOR OSS 117 see **BANCO A BANGKOK** • 1964

JACKPOT JITTERS • 1949 • Beaudine William • USA • JIGGS AND MAGGIE IN JACKPOT JITTERS (UKN)

JACK'S AWAKENING • 1914 • *Barker* • UKN

JACK'S BACK • 1988 • Herrington Rowdy • USA • RED RAIN

JACK'S BIRTHDAY • 1909 • *Essanay* • USA

JACK'S BURGLAR • 1912 • *Melies* • USA

JACK'S CHRYSANTHEMUM • 1913 • Young James • USA

JACK'S PALS • 1915 • Grandon Francis J. • USA

JACK'S RETURN • 1905 • Collins Alf? • UKN

JACK'S RETURN • 1910 • *Actophone* • USA

JACK'S RIVAL • 1904 • Collins Alf? • UKN

JACK'S SHACK • 1934 • *Terry Paul/ Moser Frank (P)* • ANS • USA

JACK'S SISTER • 1911 • Haldane Bert • UKN

JACK'S THE BOY • 1932 • Forde Walter • UKN • NIGHT AND DAY (USA)

JACK'S UMBRELLA • 1911 • *Hopkins Jack* • USA

JACK'S WIFE • 1973 • Romero George A. • USA • HUNGRY WIVES ○ SEASON OF THE WITCH

JACK'S WORLD • 1912 • Dwan Allan • USA • MAN'S WORD, A

JACKSON COUNTY JAIL • 1976 • Miller Michael • USA • INNOCENT VICTIM

JACKSON FIVE, THE • 1972 • *Halas John (P)* • ASS • UKN
JACKSTRAWS • 1916 • Mayo Melvin • SHT • USA
JACKTOWN • 1962 • Martin William • USA
JACKY VISITS THE ZOO • 1962 • Ransen Mort • CND
JACOB see **TORRES SNORTEVOLD** • 1940
JACOB SMITAREN • 1983 • Du Rees Goran, Olofsson Christina • SWD • WHERE WERE YOU, JACOB?
JACOB THE LIAR (USA) see **JAKOB DER LUGNER** • 1975
JACOB TWO-TWO MEETS THE HOODED FANG • 1977 • Flicker Theodore J. • CND
JACOBO TIMERMAN: PRISONER WITHOUT A NAME, CELL WITHOUT A NUMBER see **PRISONER WITHOUT A NAME, CELL WITHOUT A NUMBER** • 1983
JACOB'S LADDER • 1979 • Ricketson James • DOC • ASL
JACOB'S LADDER • 1990 • Lyne Adrian • USA
JACOB'S LADDER see **JACOBS STEGE** • 1942
JACOBS STEGE • 1942 • Molander Gustaf • SWD • JACOB'S LADDER
JACOTTE see **JACQUES ET JACOTTE** • 1936
JACQUELINE • 1956 • Baker Roy Ward • UKN
JACQUELINE • 1959 • Liebeneiner Wolfgang • FRG
JACQUELINE BOUVIER KENNEDY • 1981 • Gethers Steve • TVM • USA
JACQUELINE E GLI UOMINI • 1967 • Pinoteau Jack • ITL
JACQUELINE ET L'AMOUR see **VOYAGES DE NOCES** • 1932
JACQUELINE KENNEDY'S ASIAN JOURNEY • 1962 • Seitzer Leo • USA
JACQUELINE, OR BLAZING BARRIERS • 1923 • Henderson Dell • USA • BLAZING BARRIERS
JACQUELINE SUSANN'S ONCE IS NOT ENOUGH • 1974 • Green Guy • USA • ONCE IS NOT ENOUGH
JACQUELINE SUSANN'S VALLEY OF THE DOLLS • 1981 • Grauman Walter • TVM • USA
JACQUERIE, LA • 1911 • Bourgeois Gerard • FRN
JACQUES BREL IS ALIVE AND WELL AND LIVING IN PARIS • 1974 • Heroux Denis • CND, FRN
JACQUES CALLOT, CORRESPONDANT DU GUERRE see **GUERRE EN DENTELLES** • 1952
JACQUES COPEAU • 1963 • Leenhardt Yvonne • SHT • FRN
JACQUES ET JACOTTE • 1936 • Peguy Robert • FRN • JACOTTE
JACQUES ET JIM • 1903 • Melies Georges • FRN • JACK AND JIM (USA) ○ COMICAL CONJURING
JACQUES ET NOVEMBRE • 1985 • Beaudry Jean, Bouvier Francois • CND
JACQUES FEYDER ET SON CHEF D'OEUVRE • 1974 • Antoine Raymond, van der Hagen Charles • DOC • BLG
JACQUES GRAND'MAISON • 1968 • Dansereau Fernand • DCS • CND
JACQUES-HENRI LARTIGUE • 1980 • Reichenbach Francois • MTV • FRN
JACQUES LANDAUZE • 1919 • Hugon Andre • FRN
JACQUES MESRINE • 1983 • Palud Herve • FRN
JACQUES OF THE SILVER NORTH • 1919 • MacGregor Norval • USA
JACQUES PREVERT • Pozner Andre • DOC
JACQUES, THE WOLF • 1913 • *Lund Oscar* • USA
JACQUES-YVES COUSTEAU'S WORLD WITHOUT SUN see **MONDE SANS SOLEIL, LE** • 1964
JAD • 1976 • Cenevski Kiril • YGS • MISERY
JADA, GOSCIE, JADA • 1962 • Zalewski Gerard, Rutkiewicz Jan, Drobaczynski Romuald • PLN • GUESTS ARE COMING (USA)
JADARABALE • 1968 • Dorairaj B. • IND • COBWEB
JADE • 1934 • Samuelson G. B. • UKN
JADE BOX, THE • 1930 • Taylor Ray • SRL • USA
JADE CASKET, THE see **COFFRET DE JADE, LE** • 1921
JADE CLAW • 1979 • Hwa I Hung, Pal Ming • HKG • CRYSTAL FIST
JADE CUP, THE • 1926 • Crane Frank H. • USA
JADE DRAGON CONNECTION • 1987 • Leder Paul • USA
JADE HEART, THE • 1915 • Aylott Dave • UKN
JADE JUNGLE see **ARMED RESPONSE** • 1986
JADE LOVE • 1984 • Chang Yi • TWN
JADE MASK, THE • 1945 • Rosen Phil • USA • CHARLIE CHAN AND THE JADE MASK
JADE NECKLACE, THE • 1917 • Terwilliger George W. • SHT • USA
JADE PUSSYCAT, THE see **SILKEN PUSSYCAT, THE** • 1977
JADE TIGER see **PAI-YU LAO-HU** • 1977
JADE ZARINE SAMARGHAND • 1968 • Motii Nasser Malak • IRN • GOLDEN ROAD TO SAMARKAND, THE
JADEH TABAH KARAN • 1968 • Zarindast Mohamad • IRN • CRIMINALS' ROAD
JADU-I-KANGAN • 1940 • Vakil Nanubhai • IND
JADU-I-KISMET • 1944 • IND
JADUGARIN • 1937 • *Yadav Balasaheb* • IND • ENCHANTRESS
JADUI-ANGOOTHI • 1948 • Khan A. M. • IND • MAGIC RING
JADUI BANSARI • 1948 • *Prakash* • IND • MAGIC FLUTE
JADUI-CHITRA • 1948 • Zaveri Jaswant C. • IND • MAGIC PICTURE
JADUI-E-PUTLI • 1946 • *Mohan* • IND • MAGIC DOLL
JADUI-SHEHANAI • 1948 • Siddiqui Naseem • IND • MAGIC ORCHESTRA
JADUI-SINDOOR • 1948 • Siddiqui Naseem • IND • MAGIC MARK
JADWIGA L'S 24 HOURS see **DWADZIESCIA CZTERY GODZINY JADWIGI L.** • 1967
JAFFERY • 1916 • Irving George • USA
JAG • 1966 • Kylberg Peter • SWD • I
JAG ALSKAR DIG, ARGBIGGA • 1946 • Ohberg Ake • SWD • I LOVE YOU, YOU VIXEN
JAG ALSKAR DIG, KARLSSON • 1947 • Lauritzen Lau Jr., Zacharias John • SWD
JAG ALSKAR, DU ALSKAR • 1968 • Bjorkman Stig • SWD • I LOVE, YOU LOVE
JAG AR ELD OCH LUFT • 1944 • Henrikson Anders • SWD • I AM FIRE AND ICE
JAG AR MARIA • 1979 • Wedel Karsten • SWD • I AM MARIA
JAG AR MED BARN • 1979 • Hallstrom Lasse • SWD • FATHER TO BE
JAG AR MED EDER.. • 1948 • Stevens Gosta • SWD • I AM WITH YOU
JAG AR NYFIKEN -BLA • 1968 • Sjoman Vilgot • SWD • I AM CURIOUS -BLUE
JAG AR NYFIKEN -GUL • 1967 • Sjoman Vilgot • SWD • I AM CURIOUS -YELLOW (UKN)
JAG DRAPTE • 1943 • Molander Olof • SWD • I KILLED
JAG -EN ALSKARE (SWD) see **JEG -EN ELSKER** • 1966
JAG -EN KVINNA (I) • 1965 • Ahlberg Mac • SWD, DNM • JEG -EN KVINDE (DNM) ○ I -A WOMAN
JAG -EN KVINNA (II) • 1968 • Ahlberg Mac • SWD, DNM • JEG -EN KVINDE II (DNM) ○ I -A WOMAN (II) ○ JAG -EN KVINNA II: AKTENSKAPET ○ I -A WOMAN PART TWO: MARRIAGE
JAG -EN KVINNA II: AKTENSKAPET see **JAG -EN KVINNA (II)** • 1968
JAG EN MARKIS -MED UPPDRAG ATT ALSKA (SWD) see **JEG - EN MARKI** • 1967
JAG EN OSKULD • 1968 • Sarno Joe • SWD, USA • INGA -I HAVE LUST (UKN) ○ INGA (USA) ○ I A VIRGIN
JAG GIFTA MIG -ALDRIG • 1932 • Berglund Erik, Hugo Per • SWD
JAG HETER EBON LUNDIN • 1972 • Oscarsson Per • SWD • MY NAME IS EBON LUNDIN
JAG HETER STELIOS see **KOCKSGATAN 48** • 1972
JAG RODNAR • 1980 • Sjoman Vilgot • SWD • I AM BLUSHING
JAG SKALL BLI SVERIGES REMBRANDT -ELLER DO! • 1990 • Guner Goran • SWD • I WANT TO BE SWEDEN'S REMBRANDT -OR DIE!
JAG VILL LIGGA MED DIN AYSKARE MAMMA • 1978 • Whyte Andrew • SWD • SWEDISH CONFESSIONS ○ KARLEKSSVINGEL ○ KARLEKSVIRVELN
JAGA WA HASHITTA • 1970 • Nishimura Kiyoshi • JPN • CREATURE CALLED MAN, THE
JAGAD • 1945 • Palm Bengt • SWD • HUNTED
JAGAD AV VARGARNA see **LAILA** • 1937
JAGARPLUTONEN see **PA LIV OCH DOD** • 1943
JAGD AUF BLAUE DIAMANTEN • 1966 • SAF • DIAMOND WALKERS, THE
JAGD AUF MENSCHEN • 1926 • Malasomma Nunzio • FRG
JAGD AUF RAUBFISCHE • 1938 • FRG
JAGD AUF SCHURKEN 1 see **ACHTGROSCHENMADEL 1, DAS** • 1921
JAGD AUF SCHURKEN 2 see **ACHTGROSCHENMADEL 2, DAS** • 1921
JAGD IN TRAKEHNEN • 1938 • FRG
JAGD NACH DEM GLUCK • 1920 • Freisler Fritz • AUS
JAGD NACH DEM GLUCK, DIE • 1930 • Gliese Rochus • FRG
JAGD NACH DEM STIEFEL, DIE • 1962 • Petzold Konrad • GDR
JAGD NACH DEM TODE 1, DIE • 1920 • Gerhardt Karl • FRG
JAGD NACH DEM TODE 2, DIE • 1920 • Wiene Robert, Brandt Johannes • FRG • VERBOTENE STTADT, DIE
JAGD NACH DEM TODE 3, DIE • 1921 • Gerhardt Karl • FRG • MANN IM DUNKEL, DER
JAGD NACH DEM TODE 4, DIE • 1921 • Gerhardt Karl • FRG • GOLDMINE VON SAR-KHIN, DIE
JAGD NACH DER BRAUT, DIE • 1927 • Jacoby Georg • FRG
JAGD NACH DER FRAU, DIE • 1922 • Ziener Bruno • FRG
JAGD NACH DER MILLION, DIE • 1930 • Obal Max • FRG • CHASE FOR MILLIONS, THE
JAGD NACH WAHRHEIT, DIE • 1921 • Grune Karl • FRG
JAGDAUSFLUG NACH BERLIN, EIN • 1917 • Heidemann Paul • FRG
JAGDSZENEN AUS NIEDERBAYERN • 1970 • Fleischmann Peter • FRG • HUNTING SCENES FROM BAVARIA (USA) ○ HUNTERS ARE THE HUNTED, THE ○ HUNTING SCENES FROM LOWER BAVARIA
JAGER, DIE • 1982 • Makk Karoly • FRG
JAGER AUS KURPFALZ, DER • 1933 • Behr Carl • FRG
JAGER VOM ROTECK, DER • 1955 • Kugelstadt Hermann • FRG
JAGER VON DER RISS, DER • 1930 • Seitz Franz • FRG
JAGER VON FALL, DER • 1918 • Beck Ludwig • FRG
JAGER VON FALL, DER • 1926 • Seitz Franz • FRG
JAGER VON FALL, DER • 1936 • Deppe Hans • FRG
JAGER VON FALL, DER • 1957 • Ucicky Gustav • FRG
JAGERBLUT • 1922 • Seitz Franz • FRG
JAGERSTATTER CASE, THE see **FALL JAGERSTATTER, DER** • 1972
JAGGA DAKU • 1960 • Chandrakant • IND • BANDIT, THE
JAGGED EDGE • 1985 • Marquand Richard • USA
JAGGED EDGE see **I DIED A THOUSAND TIMES** • 1955
JAGGER BREAKS ALL RECORDS • 1909 • Gobbett T. J.? • UKN
JAGIRDAR • 1937 • *Biswas Anil (M)* • IND
JAGO HUA SAVERA • 1958 • Kardar Ajay • BNG • DAY SHALL DAWN
JAGODE U GRLU • 1985 • Karanovic Srdjan • YGS • HARD TO SWALLOW
JAGS AND JEALOUSY • 1916 • Beaudine William • SHT • USA
JAGTE RAHO • 1956 • Mitre Shanbhu, Maitra Amit • IND • UNDER COVER OF NIGHT ○ KEEP AWAKE
JAGTEN PAA GENTLEMANROVEREN • 1910 • Blom August • DNM
JAGTERS, DIE • 1960 • SAF
JAGUAR • 1953-71 • Rouch Jean • DOC • FRN
JAGUAR • 1956 • Blair George • USA
JAGUAR • 1967 • Domolky Janos • HNG
JAGUAR • 1980 • Brocka Lino • PHL
JAGUAR DE OBSIDIANA, EL see **PALOMILLA, LA** • 1976
JAGUAR LIVES • 1978 • Pintoff Ernest • USA
JAGUAR TRAP, THE • 1915 • Santschi Thomas • USA
JAGUAR'S CLAWS, THE • 1917 • Neilan Marshall • USA
JAGUAR'S TRAIL, THE • 1920 • *Coburn Wallace* • SHT • USA
JAGUEY DE LAS RUINAS, EL • 1944 • Martinez Solares Gilberto • MXC
JAGWAL • Ghimiray Tulshi • NPL • WAITING, THE
JAHANAM • 1971 • Amin M. • MLY • DAMNATION!
JAHR, DAS • 1948 • Oertel Curt • FRG
JAHR DES HERRN, DAS • 1950 • Stoger Alfred • AUS • KRAFT DER LIEBE ○ WALLNERBUB, DER
JAHRE VERGEHEN, DIE • 1944 • Rittau Gunther • FRG • SENATOR, DER
JAHRESZEITEN DES LIEBENS, DIE • 1915 • Hofer Franz • FRG
JAHRMARKT DES LEBENS • 1927 • Balogh Bela • FRG
JAHRTAUSENDE SEHEN AUF EUCH HERAB • 1933 • Oertel Curt • FRG
J'AI 17 ANS • 1945 • Berthomieu Andre • FRN • MY FIRST LOVE (USA)
JAI BABA FELUNATH • 1977 • Ray Satyajit • IND • ELEPHANT GOD, THE ○ JOI BABA FELUNATH
JAI BHIM • 1949 • Mane Anant • IND • BHIM'S VICTORY
J'AI ESPOUSE UNE OMBRE • 1983 • Davis Robin • FRN • I MARRIED A SHADOW (USA)
JAI HANUMAN • 1944 • *Prafulls Pics* • IND • HANUMAN'S VICTORY
JAI HANUMAN • 1948 • Thakur Ramchandra • IND • HANUMAN'S VICTORY
J'AI HUIT ANS • 1958 • Mauro-Humberto • BRZ
JAI MAHADEV • 1953 • Thakur Ramchandra • IND • MAHADEV'S VICTORY
JAI MAHAKALI • 1951 • Desai Dhirubhai • IND • GREAT KALI'S VICTORY
J'AI MON VOYAGE see **QUAND C'EST PARTI, C'EST PARTI** • 1973
J'AI PAS DE CULOTTE • Schreiner Charlie • FRN
J'AI PEUR POUR MON ENFANT see **QALBY ALA WALADI** • 1952
J'AI QUELQUE CHOSE A NOUS DIRE • 1930 • Allegret Marc • SHT • FRN
J'AI RENCONTRE DEUX JEUNE FILLES • 1962 • Khalifa Omar • SHT • TNS
J'AI RENCONTRE LE PERE NOEL • 1984 • Gion Christian • FRN
JAI SHANKAR • 1951 • Ishwarla • IND • SHANKAR'S VICTORY
J'AI TANT DANSE • 1944 • Dunning George • ANS • CND
J'AI TOUT DONNE see **JOHNNY DAYS** • 1971
J'AI TRES ENVIE • 1977 • Baudricourt Michel • FRN
J'AI TUE see **CARREFOUR DU CRIME** • 1947
J'AI TUE RASPOUTINE • 1967 • Hossein Robert • FRN, ITL • TONNERRE SUR SAINT-PETERSBURG ○ I KILLED RASPUTIN (UKN) ○ RASPUTIN (USA) ○ THUNDER OVER ST. PETERSBURG
J'AI UN HANNETON DANS MON PANTALON • 1906 • Blache Alice • FRN
J'AI UNE IDEE • 1934 • Richebe Roger • FRN
J'AI VOULU RIRE COMME LES AUTRES • 1979 • Dubois Bernard • FRN, ITL
JAIDER -DER EINSAME JAGER • 1970 • Vogeler Volker • FRG
JAIDER'S GANG see **BANDA DE JAIDER, LA** • 1974
JAIL, THE • 1972 • Anderson Michael, Jacobs Paul, Landau Saul, Yahruas Bill • DOC • USA
JAIL BAIT • 1937 • Lamont Charles • SHT • USA
JAIL BAIT • 1954 • Wood Edward D. Jr. • USA
JAIL BAIT (USA) see **WILDWECHSEL** • 1972
JAIL BIRD see **OLTRE LA PORTA** • 1983
JAIL BIRD, THE • 1921 • Roach Hal • SHT • USA
JAIL BIRDS • 1914 • Hamilton G. P.? • USA
JAIL BIRDS • 1923 • Brouett Albert • UKN
JAIL BIRDS • 1932 • *Iwerks Ub (P)* • ANS • USA
JAIL BIRDS • 1934 • *Terry Paul/ Moser Frank (P)* • ANS • USA
JAIL BREAK, THE • 1946 • Donnelly Eddie • ANS • USA
JAIL BREAK (UKN) see **GUNNING FOR VENGEANCE** • 1946
JAIL BREAK (UKN) see **A CAVALLO DELLA TIGRE** • 1961
JAIL BREAKERS, THE • 1929 • Terry Paul • ANS • USA
JAIL BUSTERS • 1955 • Beaudine William • USA
JAIL HOSTESS • 1942 • *O'Brien Joseph/ Mead Thomas (P)* • SHT • USA
JAIL HOUSE BLUES • 1942 • Rogell Albert S. • USA
JAIL KEYS MADE HERE • 1970 • Boltin Lee • SHT • USA
JAIL YAATRA • 1947 • *Kapoor Raj* • IND
JAILBAIT see **JAILBAIT BABYSITTER** • 1977
JAILBAIT BABYSITTER • 1977 • Stevens Carter • USA • JAILBAIT
JAILBIRD • 1971 • Pearse John • SHT • UKN
JAILBIRD see **SWEET HUNTERS** • 1969
JAILBIRD, THE • 1913 • Collins Edwin J.? • UKN
JAILBIRD, THE • 1920 • Ingraham Lloyd • USA • JAILBIRDS
JAILBIRD IN BORROWED FEATHERS • 1910 • Bouwmeester Theo? • UKN
JAILBIRD; OR, THE BISHOP AND THE CONVICT, THE • 1905 • Raymond Charles? • UKN
JAILBIRDS • 1916 • *Hamilton Lloyd V.* • SHT • USA
JAILBIRDS • 1939 • Mitchell Oswald • UKN
JAILBIRDS see **JAILBIRD, THE** • 1920
JAILBIRDS' LAST FLIGHT, THE • 1916 • *Armstrong Bill* • SHT • USA
JAILBIRDS (UKN) see **PARDON US** • 1931
JAILBIRDS' VACATION see **GRANDES GUEULES, LES** • 1965
JAILBREAK • 1936 • Grinde Nick • USA • MURDER IN THE BIG HOUSE (UKN)
JAILBREAK see **NUMBERED MEN** • 1930
JAILBREAK see **GUNNING FOR VENGEANCE** • 1946
JAILBREAK (USA) see **GAOLBREAK** • 1962
JAILBREAKER, THE • 1919 • Parrott Charles • SHT • USA
JAILBREAKERS • 1959 • Grasshoff Alex • USA
JAILED • 1916 • Roach Hal • USA
JAILED AND BAILED • 1923 • Roach Hal • SHT • USA
JAILHOUSE BLUES • 1929 • Smith Basil • SHT • USA
JAILHOUSE ROCK • 1957 • Thorpe Richard • USA
JAIME • 1974 • Reis Antonio • PRT
J'AIME TOUTES LES FEMMES • 1935 • Lamac Carl • FRN
J'AIME, TU AIMES (FRN) see **IO AMO, TU AMI** • 1960
JAIN • 1967 • Komori Haku • JPN • SNAKY ADULTERY
JAIT-RE-JAIT • 1977 • Patel Jabbar • IND • VICTORY, THE
JAJAUMA NARASHI • 1966 • Sugie Toshio • JPN • TAMING OF THE SHREW, THE
JAJE • 1960 • Mimica Vatroslav • ANS • YGS • EGG, THE (USA)
JAJE • 1973 • Grgic Zlatko • ANS • YGS • EGG, THE
JAK BASNIKUN CHUTNA ZIVOT • 1987 • Klein Dusan • CZC • HOW POETS ENJOY LIFE
JAK BYC KOCHANA • 1962 • Has Wojciech J. • PLN • HOW TO BE LOVED (USA)

JAK DALEKA STAD, JAK BLISKO • 1971 • Konwicki Tadeusz • PLN • HOW FAR FROM HERE, HOW NEAR ○ SO NEAR AND YET SO FAR ○ SO FAR, SO NEAR ○ HOW FAR AND YET HOW NEAR
JAK DOSTAT TATINKA DO POLEPSOVNY • 1979 • Polednakova Marie • CZC • DADDY'S GOT TO GO TO THE REFORM SCHOOL
JAK DZIALA JAMNICZEK • 1971 • Antonisz Julian • PLN • HOW THE DACHSHUND OPERATES
JAK JE SVET ZARIZEN • 1956 • Hofman Eduard • ANS • PLN • HOW THE WORLD WORKS
JAK KRTEK KE KALHOTKAM PRISEL • 1957 • Miler Zdenek • ANS • CZC • HOW THE MOLE GOT HIS OVERALLS ○ HOW THE MOLE GOT HIS TROUSERS
JAK LIDE ZAJALI POHYB • 1962 • Vosahlik Bohumil • CZC • RECORDING OF MOVEMENT, THE
JAK NA TO • 1963 • Brdecka Jiri • ANM • CZC • HOW TO KEEP SLIM
JAK PEJSEK A KOCICKOU PSALI PSANI • 1954 • Hofman Eduard • ANS • PLN • PUPPY AND KITTEN WRITE A LETTER, THE
JAK PEJSEK A KOLICKA MYLI PODLAHU • 1950 • Hofman Eduard • ANS • PLN • PUPPY AND THE KITTEN WASH THE FLOOR, THE
JAK PEJSEK S KOCICKOU DELALI DORT • 1951 • Hofman Eduard • ANS • PLN • PUPPY AND THE KITTEN MAKE A CAKE, THE
JAK POLOWALEM NA LWA • 1967 • Nehrebecki Wladyslaw • ANS • PLN • HOW I HUNTED LIONS
JAK ROZPETALEM DRUGA WOJNE SWIATOWA • 1969 • Chmielewski Tadeusz • PLN • HOW I STARTED THE SECOND WORLD WAR ○ HOW I UNLEASHED THE SECOND... ○ JAK ROZPETALEM IL WOJNE SWIATOWA, JAK ZAKONCZYLEM IL WOJNE SWIATOWA
JAK ROZPETALEM IL WOJNE SWIATOWA, JAK ZAKONCZYLEM IL WOJNE SWIATOWA see **JAK ROZPETALEM DRUGA WOJNE SWIATOWA** • 1969
JAK SE BUDI PRINCEZNY • 1977 • Vorlicek Vaclav • CZC • HOW TO WAKE PRINCESSES
JAK SE CLOVEK NAUCIL LETAT • 1958 • Brdecka Jiri • ANS • CZC • COMIC HISTORY OF AVIATION, A ○ HOW MAN LEARNED TO FLY
JAK SE KRADE MILION • 1967 • Balik Jaroslav • CZC • HOW TO STEAL A MILLION ○ HOW I STOLE A MILLION
JAK SE MOUDRY ARISTOTELES STAL JESTE MOUDREJSIM • 1970 • Brdecka Jiri • ANM • CZC • WISE ARISTOTLE GETS STILL WISER ○ ARISTOTLE
JAK SE TOCI ROZMARYNY • 1977 • Plivova-Simkova Vera • CZC • HOW TO SHOOT ROSEMARIES
JAK SE ZBAVIT HELENKY • 1967 • Gajer Vaclav • CZC • HOW TO GET RID OF HELENA
JAK SI DETI MALUJI • 1958 • Jerabek Jiri • CZC • CHARM OF CHILDREN'S DRAWINGS, THE ○ HOW CHILDREN PAINT
JAK SI PEJSEK ROZTRHL KALHOTY • 1951 • Hofman Eduard • ANS • PLN • HOW THE PUPPY TORE HIS TROUSERS
JAK STARECEK MENIL AZ VYMENIL • 1952 • Trnka Jiri • ANS • CZC • HOW GRANDPA CHANGED TILL NOTHING WAS LEFT
JAK VYTRHNOUT VELRYBE STOLICKU • 1980 • Polednakova Marie • CZC • HOW TO PULL OUT A WHALE'S TOOTH
JAK ZARIDITI BYT • 1959 • Pojar Bretislav • ANM • CZC • HOW TO FURNISH AN APARTMENT ○ HOW TO FURNISH A FLAT
JAKALSDRAAI SE MENSE • 1975 • SAF
JAKARTA • 1988 • Kaufman Charles • USA • TRIANGLE INVASION
JAKARTA JAKARTA • 1978 • Prijono Ami • INN
JAKE SPEED • 1986 • Lane Andrew • USA
JAKE THE PLUMBER • 1927 • Luddy Edward I. • USA
JAKE'S DAUGHTER • 1910 • Bouwmeester Theo? • UKN
JAKE'S HOODOO • 1914 • *Younge Lucille* • USA
JAKIRI VALIENTE • 1968 • Gallardo Cesar Chat • PHL
JAKKALS VAN TULA METSI, DIE • 1967 • Conradie Franz • SAF • JACKAL OF TULA METSI, THE
JAKKO • 1941 • Buch Fritz Peter • FRG
JAKKU TO MAME NO KI • 1974 • Sugii Gisaburo • JPN
JAKO GIFT • 1985 • Olmer Vit • CZC • LIKE POISON
JAKO ZAJICI • 1981 • Smyczek Karel • CZC • LIKE RABBITS ○ LIKE HARES
JAKOB DER LUGNER • 1975 • Beyer Frank • GDR • JACOB THE LIAR (USA)
JAKOMAN AND TETSU see **JAKOMAN TO TETSU** • 1949
JAKOMAN AND TETSU see **JAKOMAN TO TETSU** • 1964
JAKOMAN TO TETSU • 1949 • Taniguchi Senkichi • JPN • JAKOMAN AND TETSU ○ YAKOMAN TO TETSU
JAKOMAN TO TETSU • 1964 • Fukasaku Kinji • JPN • JAKOMAN AND TETSU
JAKTEN • 1959 • Lochen Erik • NRW • HUNT, THE
JAKTEN • 1965 • Gamlin Yngve • SWD • HUNT, THE
JAKUB • 1976 • Koval Ota • CZC
JALAN JALAN: A JOURNEY TO SUDANESE JAVA see **WET EARTH AND WARM PEOPLE** • 1971
JALEA REAL • 1981 • Mira Carlos • SPN • ROYAL JELLY
JALIM JADUGARIN • 1929 • *Sharada* • IND • ENCHANTRESS, THE (USA)
JALISCO CANTA EN SEVILLA • 1948 • de Fuentes Fernando • MXC, SPN
JALISCO NEVER LOSES (USA) see **JALISCO NUNCA PIERDE** • 1937
JALISCO NUNCA PIERDE • 1937 • Urueta Chano • MXC • JALISCO NEVER LOSES (USA)
JALKEEN SYNTIINLANKEEMUKSEN • 1953 • Laine Edvin • FNL • AFTER THE FALL OF MAN
JALMARI JA HULDA • 1971 • Katainen Elina • FNL
JALNA • 1935 • Cromwell John • USA
JALOPY • 1953 • Beaudine William • USA
JALOPY OF THE SKIES • 1946 • Timoshenko S. • USS
JALOUSIE • 1922 • Bieganski Victor • PLN
JALOUSIE 1976 see **VOYAGE DE NOCES, LE** • 1976
JALOUSIE DU BARBOUILLE, LA • 1927 • Cavalcanti Alberto • FRN • JEALOUSY OF THE SCRIBBLER, THE
JALOUX COMME UN TIGRE • 1964 • Cowl Darry, Delbez Maurice • FRN
JALSAGHAR • 1958 • Ray Satyajit • IND • MUSIC ROOM, THE
JALTE BADAN • 1973 • Sagar Ramanand • IND • BURNING BODY
JALTI NISHANI • 1957 • *Biswas Anil (M)* • IND
JAM AND JEALOUSY • 1914 • *Joker* • USA
JAM AND JELLY SESSION • 1955 • Moore J. Stanley • CND
JAM DOWN • 1980 • Bonn Emmanuel • DOC • FRN
JAM NOW IN SEASON • 1906 • Collins Alf? • UKN
JAM SESSION • 1942 • Berne Josef • SHT • USA
JAM SESSION • 1944 • Barton Charles T. • USA
JAM SESSION • 1951 • Neurisse Pierre • SHT • FRN
JAMAI SASTHI • 1931 • *Madan Theatres* • IND
JAMAICA see **JAMAICA RUN** • 1953
JAMAICA INN • 1939 • Hitchcock Alfred • UKN
JAMAICA INN • 1985 • Clark Lawrence Gordon • TVM • UKN
JAMAICA RUN • 1953 • Foster Lewis R. • USA • JAMAICA
JAMAICAN GOLD see **FORTY MILLION BUCKS** • 1978
JAMAICANS IN LONDON • 1970 • N'Gakane Lionel • SHT • UKN
JAMAIS AVANT LE MARIAGE • 1982 • Ceccaldi Daniel • FRN
JAMAIS DEUX SANS TROIS • 1951 • Berthomieu Andre • FRN
JAMAIS LE DIMANCHE see **POTE TIN KYRIAKI** • 1959
JAMAIS PLUS TOUJOURS • 1975 • Bellon Yannick • FRN
JAMBES EN L'AIR, LES see **CESAR GRANDBLAISE** • 1970
JAMBES EN L'AIR A BANGKOK • 1974 • Sala Henri • FRN
JAMBON D'ARDENNES • 1977 • Lamy Benoit • BLG, FRN
JAMBOREE • 1944 • Santley Joseph • USA
JAMBOREE • 1949 • Bilcock David Sr. • DOC • ASL
JAMBOREE • 1957 • Lockwood Roy • USA • DISC JOCKEY JAMBOREE (UKN)
JAMBOREE see **SON OF KONG** • 1933
JAMBOREE (UKN) see **ROOKIES ON PARADE** • 1941
JAMBUL • 1953 • Dzigan Yefim • USS
JAMES AT 15 • 1977 • Hardy Joseph • TVM • USA
JAMES BANDE 00 SEXE • Baudricourt Michel • FRN
JAMES BATMAN • 1967 • Marquez Artemio • PHL
JAMES BOYS IN MISSOURI • 1908 • *Essanay* • USA
JAMES BROTHERS, THE (UKN) see **TRUE STORY OF JESSE JAMES, THE** • 1956
JAMES BROTHERS OF MISSOURI, THE • 1950 • Brannon Fred C. • USA
JAMES DEAN: PORTRAIT OF A FRIEND • 1976 • Butler Robert • TVM • USA
JAMES DEAN STORY, THE • 1957 • Altman Robert, George George W. • DOC • USA
JAMES DEAN, THE FIRST AMERICAN TEENAGER • 1975 • Connolly Ray • UKN • FIRST AMERICAN TEENAGER, THE
JAMES ENSOR • 1971 • Haesaerts Paul • BLG
JAMES JOYCE'S ULYSSES see **ULYSSES** • 1967
JAMES JOYCE'S WOMEN • 1985 • Pearce Michael • ASL
JAMES LEE'S WIFE • 1913 • *Weber Lois* • USA
JAMES MICHENER'S DYNASTY • 1976 • Philips Lee • TVM • USA
JAMES OU PAS • 1971 • Soutter Michel • SWT
JAMES RAMSAY MACDONALD see **SECRET LIVES OF THE BRITISH PRIME MINISTERS: MACDONALD, THE** • 1983
JAMES TONT OPERAZIONE D.U.E. • 1966 • Corbucci Bruno • ITL
JAMES TONT, OPERAZIONE U.N.O. • 1965 • Corbucci Bruno, Grimaldi Gianni • ITL
JAMESTOWN • 1923 • Hollywood Edwin L. • USA
JAMESTOWN BALOOS • 1957 • Breer Robert • SHT • USA
JAMESTOWN EXPOSITION • 1907 • *Bitzer Billy (Ph)* • USA
JAMIE • 1963 • Howe John • CND
JAMIE 21 • 1973 • SAF
JAMILA EL GAZAIRIA • 1958 • Shahin Youssef • EGY • JAMILA, THE ALGERIAN GIRL ○ GAMILA AL-GAZA'IRIYYA ○ DJAMILA ○ GAMILA BOHRAID
JAMILA, THE ALGERIAN GIRL see **JAMILA EL GAZAIRIA** • 1958
JAMILYA • 1970 • Poplavskaya Irina • USS
JAMMIN' THE BLUES • 1944 • Mili Gjon • SHT • USA
JAMMING WITH GENE KRUPA • 1959 • *Mineo Sal* • SHT • USA
JAMUNA PULINEY • 1933 • Ganguly P. N. • IND
JAN AMOS COMENIUS see **PUTOVANI JANA AMOSE** • 1983
JAN ARIMA NO SHUGEKI • 1959 • Ito Daisuke • JPN
JAN BARUJAN • 1931 • Uchida Tomu • JPN • JEAN VALJEAN
JAN CIMBURA • 1941 • Cap Frantisek • CZC
JAN GARBER AND HIS ORCHESTRA • 1941 • Negulesco Jean • SHT • USA
JAN HUS • 1954 • Vavra Otakar • CZC
JAN KONSTANTIN • 1961 • Schorm Evald • CZC
JAN OF THE BIG SNOWS • 1922 • Seay Charles M. • USA
JAN ON THE BARGE • 1987 • Dziuba Helmut • GDR
JAN PETRO'S RETURN see **NAVRAT JANA PETRU** • 1985
JAN RAP EN ZIJN MAAT • 1989 • Schenkkan Ine • NTH • TOUGH
JAN ROHAC OF DUBA see **JAN ROHAC Z DUBE** • 1947
JAN ROHAC Z DUBE • 1947 • Borsky Vladimir • CZC • WARRIORS OF FAITH ○ JAN ROHAC OF DUBA
JAN UND DIE SCHWINDLERIN • 1944 • Weissbach Hans • FRG
JAN VEDDER'S DAUGHTER • 1913 • Miller Ashley • USA
JAN ZIZKA A TROCHOVA • 1954 • Vavra Otakar • CZC • HUSSITE WARRIOR, THE
JANA ARANYA see **DAHANA-ARANJA** • 1976
JANA, DAS MADCHEN AUS DEM BOHMERWALD • 1935 • Land Robert, Synek Emil • AUS, CZC
JANAK NANDINI • 1938 • Burma Phani • IND • BIRTH OF NANDINI
JANAM JANMAKE PHERE • 1957 • Desai Manoo • IND
JANAYAT • 1981 • Shafaq Toryali • AFG • CRIMINALS
JANDRO • 1964 • Coll Julio • SPN
JANE • 1914 • *Essanay* • USA
JANE • 1915 • Lloyd Frank • USA
JANE • 1962 • Pennebaker D. A., Dryden Hope • USA
JANE AND THE LOST CITY • 1988 • Marcel Terry • UKN
JANE AND THE STRANGER • 1910 • Salter Harry • USA
JANE AUSTEN IN MANHATTAN • 1980 • Ivory James • TVM • USA
JANE B. PAR AGNES V. • 1988 • Varda Agnes • FRN
JANE BLEIBT JANE • 1977 • Bockmayer Walter, Buhrmann Rolf • FRG • JANE FOREVER
JANE DOE • 1982 • Nagy Ivan • TVM • USA
JANE EYRE • 1910 • ITL
JANE EYRE • 1910 • Marston Theodore • USA
JANE EYRE • 1914 • Crane Frank H. • *Imp* • USA
JANE EYRE • 1914 • Faust Martin J. • *Garrison* • USA
JANE EYRE • 1915 • Vale Travers • USA
JANE EYRE • 1921 • Ballin Hugo • USA
JANE EYRE • 1934 • Cabanne W. Christy • USA
JANE EYRE • 1944 • Stevenson Robert • USA
JANE EYRE • 1968 • Lois Giorgos • GRC
JANE EYRE • 1970 • Mann Delbert • TVM • UKN
JANE EYRE • 1983 • Amyes Julian • MTV • UKN
JANE FOREVER see **JANE BLEIBT JANE** • 1977
JANE GOES A'WOOING • 1919 • Melford George • USA
JANE GRAY • 1911 • Caserini Mario • ITL
JANE MARRIES • 1913 • *Imp* • USA
JANE OF THE DUNES • 1913 • Ridgely Richard • USA
JANE OF THE MOTH-EATEN FARM • 1913 • Tucker George Loane • USA
JANE OF THE SOIL • 1915 • *Drew Lillian* • USA
JANE ON THE WARPATH • 1906 • Collins Alf? • UKN
JANE SHORE • 1908 • *Gaumont* • UKN
JANE SHORE • 1911 • Powell Frank • UKN
JANE SHORE • 1915 • Haldane Bert, Thornton F. Martin • UKN • STRIFE ETERNAL, THE (USA)
JANE SHORE • 1922 • Collins Edwin J. • UKN
JANE STEPS OUT • 1938 • Stein Paul L. • UKN
JANE, THE JUSTICE • 1914 • Pollard Harry • USA
JANE WAS WORTH IT • 1915 • Baker George D. • USA
JANEK'S FEEDING TROUGH see **KARMNIK JANKOWY** • 1952
JANE'S BASHFUL HERO • 1916 • Baker George D. • SHT • USA
JANE'S BROTHER, THE PARANOIAC • 1913 • Tucker George Loane • USA
JANE'S CHOICE • 1916 • Moore Matt • SHT • USA
JANE'S DECLARATION OF INDEPENDENCE • 1915 • Giblyn Charles • USA
JANE'S ENGAGEMENT PARTY • 1926 • Newfield Sam • SHT • USA
JANES GODE VEN see **STORSTE I VERDEN, DET** • 1919
JANE'S HONEYMOONS • 1926 • Lamont Charles • SHT • USA
JANE'S HUSBAND • 1916 • Baker George D. • SHT • USA
JANE'S LOVERS • 1914 • *Shields Ernest* • USA
JANE'S PREDICAMENT • 1926 • Newfield Sam • SHT • USA
JANE'S SEXUAL AWAKENING see **SWEET SEXUAL AWAKENING**
JANE'S SLEUTH • 1927 • Newfield Sam • SHT • USA
JANE'S WATERLOO • 1913 • Smiley Joseph • USA
JANET AND JOHN -GROW UP! • 1974 • Duff Euan • UKN
JANET OF THE CHORUS • 1915 • Brooke Van Dyke • USA
JANET'S FLIRTATION • 1911 • Fitzhamon Lewin? • UKN
JANGADA, LA see **OCHOCIENTAS MIL LEGUAS POR EL AMAZONAS** • 1958
JANGADA -EN BRASILIANSK RAPSODI see **VILDARNA VID DODENS FLOD** • 1958
JANGADERO • 1961 • Guggenheim • USA
JANGAM • 1985 • I Du-Yong • SKR • FIRST SON
JANGAN AMBIL NYAWAKU • 1981 • Sophiaan Sophan • INN • DON'T LET ME DIE
JANGAN KAU TANGISI • 1972 • Timoer Ratno • MLY • DON'T YOU CRY
JANGAN TINGGAL DAKU • 1971 • Ramlee P. • MLY • DON'T LEAVE ME
JANGLE, JANGLE, SOUND THE BELLS see **JHANAK, JHANAK, PAYAL BAJE** • 1955
JANGO • 1929 • *Davenport Daniel* • DOC • USA
JANGO • 1984 • Tendler Silvio • BRZ
JANICE • 1973 • Strick Joseph • USA
JANICE MEREDITH • 1924 • Hopper E. Mason • USA • BEAUTIFUL REBEL, THE
JANIE • 1944 • Curtiz Michael • USA
JANIE • 1970 • Bravman Jack • USA
JANIE CANUCK • 1982 • Lavut Martin • CND
JANIE GET YOUR GUN • 1965 • Smith Paul J. • ANS • USA
JANIE GETS MARRIED • 1946 • Sherman Vincent • USA
JANIKSEN VUOSI • 1977 • Jarva Risto • FNL • YEAR OF THE HARE, THE
JANINE • 1961 • Pialat Maurice • SHT • FRN
JANIS • 1974 • Alk Howard, Findlay Seaton • DOC • CND
JANITOR, THE • 1914 • *Reliance* • USA
JANITOR, THE • 1914 • Lehrman Henry • *Keystone* • USA
JANITOR, THE • 1916 • Beery Wallace • SHT • USA
JANITOR, THE (UKN) see **EYEWITNESS** • 1981
JANITOR FALSELY ACCUSED, THE • 1908 • *Lubin* • USA
JANITOR IN TROUBLE, A see **TRIBULATIONS D'UN CONCIERGE** • 1896
JANITOR'S BOTTLE, THE • 1909 • *Edison* • USA
JANITOR'S BUSY DAY, THE • 1916 • Christie Al • SHT • USA
JANITOR'S FALL, A • 1918 • *Triangle* • USA
JANITOR'S FLIRTATION, THE • 1914 • Seay Charles M. • USA
JANITOR'S FORTUNE, THE • 1914 • *Frontier* • USA
JANITOR'S JOYFUL JOB, A • 1915 • *Hardy Oliver* • USA
JANITOR'S QUIET LIFE, THE • 1913 • Seay Charles M. • USA
JANITOR'S REVENGE, THE • 1914 • *Ab* • USA
JANITOR'S SON, THE • 1914 • *Frontier* • USA
JANITOR'S VENDETTA, A • 1916 • Beaudine William • SHT • USA
JANITOR'S VENGEANCE, A • 1917 • *Depp Harry* • USA
JANITOR'S WIFE'S TEMPTATION, A • 1915 • Henderson Dell • USA
JANITZIO • 1934 • Navarro Carlos • MXC
JANKEN • 1970 • Forsberg Lars Lennart • SWD • YANKEE, THE
JANKEN MUSUME • 1955 • Sugie Toshio • JPN • SO YOUNG SO BRIGHT (USA) ○ THREE KINDS OF GIRLS
JANKO THE MUSICIAN see **NOWY JANKO MUZYKANT** • 1960
JANMASHTAMI • 1950 • Bhatt Nanabhai • IND • BIRTH OF ASHTANNI
JANNA WAR NARR • 1953 • Fawzi Hussein • EGY • HEAVEN AND HELL
JANNE VANGMAN AND THE BIG COMET see **JANNE VANGMAN OCH DEN STORA KOMETEN** • 1955
JANNE VANGMAN I FARTEN • 1953 • Olsson Gunnar • SWD • JANNE VANGMAN IS BUSY
JANNE VANGMAN IS BUSY see **JANNE VANGMAN I FARTEN** • 1953

JANNE VANGMAN OCH DEN STORA KOMETEN • 1955 • Palm Bengt • SWD • JANNE VANGMAN AND THE BIG COMET
JANNE VANGMAN ON NEW ADVENTURES see **JANNE VANGMAN PA NYA AVENTYR** • 1949
JANNE VANGMAN PA NYA AVENTYR • 1949 • Olsson Gunnar • SWD • JANNE VANGMAN ON NEW ADVENTURES
JANNE VANGMANS BRAVADER • 1948 • Olsson Gunnar • SWD • EXPLOITS OF JANNE VANGMAN
JANNIE TOTSIENS • 1970 • Rautenbach Jans • SAF
JANOS • 1980 • Kohanyi Julius • CND
JANOS HARY • 1964 • Szinetar Miklos • HNG • HARY JANOS
JANOS PATKAI, SCULPTEUR • 1981 • Ruiz Raul • DCS • FRN
JANOS TORNYAI • 1962 • Meszaros Marta • SHT • HNG • TORNYAI JANOS
JANOS VITEZ • 1939 • Gaal Bela • HNG • JOHN, THE HERO (USA)
JANOS VITEZ • 1973 • Jankovics Marcell • ANM • HNG • JOHNNIE CORNCOB ○ CHILDE JOHN
JANOSIK • 1921 • Siakel Jaroslav, Horlivy Frantisek • CZC
JANOSIK • 1935 • Fric Martin • CZC
JANOSIK • 1953 • Haupe Wlodzimierz, Bielinska Halina • PLN
JANOSIK I • 1962 • Bielik Palo • CZC
JANOSIK II • 1963 • Bielik Palo • CZC
JANSSONS FRESTELSE • 1928 • Wallen Sigurd • SWD • JANSSON'S TEMPTATION
JANSSONS FRESTELSE • 1936 • Rodin Gosta • SWD • JANSSON'S TEMPTATION
JANSSON'S TEMPTATION see **JANSSONS FRESTELSE** • 1928
JANSSON'S TEMPTATION see **JANSSONS FRESTELSE** • 1936
JANUARY MAN, THE • 1989 • O'Connor Pat • USA
JANUARY UPRISING IN KIEV IN 1918 (UKN) see **ARSENAL** • 1928
JANUS-FACED see **JANUSKOPF, DER** • 1920
JANUSKOPF • 1972 • Maetzig Kurt • GDR
JANUSKOPF, DER • 1920 • Murnau F. W. • FRG • DR. JEKYLL AND MR. HYDE (UKN) ○ HEAD OF JANUS, THE ○ JANUS-FACED ○ LOVE'S MOCKERY
JANWAR • 1965 • IND
JANYEONMON • 1985 • Jeong Jin-U • SKR • MA-NIM, THE
JAP STANDARD BEARER, THE • 1904 • *Urban Trading Co.* • UKN
JAP THE GIANT KILLER • 1904 • *Cricks & Sharp* • UKN
JAP VERSUS RUSSIAN • 1904 • *Paul R. W.* • UKN
JAPAN • 1975 • Kelly Ron • DOC • CND
JAPAN -DAS DORFCHEN FURUYASHIKI • 1984 • Ogawa Shinsuke • DOC • JPN
JAPAN D'HIER ET D'AUJOURD'HUI • 1959 • Kast Pierre • SHT • FRN
JAPAN FOR SALE see **NIPPON-ICHI NO URAGIRIOTOKO** • 1968
JAPAN OF FANTASY see **JAPON DE FANTAISIE** • 1909
JAPAN: THE THIRD SUPERSTATE • 1967 • Baker David • DOC • ASL
JAPANERIN, DIE • 1918 • Dupont E. A. • FRG
JAPANESE ACROBATS • 1904 • Porter Edwin S. • USA
JAPANESE ARE HERE, THE see **NIHONJIN KOKONI-ARI** • 1968
JAPANESE BRAVERY -AN INCIDENT IN THE WAR • 1904 • *Gaumont* • UKN
JAPANESE BUTTERFLIES • 1908 • *Pathe* • FRN
JAPANESE COURTSHIP, A • 1913 • *Majestic* • USA
JAPANESE CRIMINAL HISTORY -VIOLATION AT NOON see **NIHON HANZAISHI HAKUCHU NON BOHKOHKI** • 1968
JAPANESE DEMON, A see **SATORI** • 1973
JAPANESE FANTASY, A see **JAPON DE FANTAISIE** • 1909
JAPANESE GRANDMOTHERS see **NIPPON NO OBACHAN** • 1962
JAPANESE HISTORY OF SEX CUSTOMS -DOUBLE SUICIDE see **NIHON SEI FUZOKUSHI MURISHINJA** • 1968
JAPANESE HOUSE • 1955 • Peterson Sidney • USA
JAPANESE IDYL, A • 1912 • *Rex* • USA
JAPANESE INSECT STORY see **NIPPON KONCHUKI** • 1963
JAPANESE JUDO COMMONLY KNOWN AS JIU JITSU • 1913 • Melies Gaston • DOC • USA
JAPANESE LANTERNS • 1935 • Gillett Burt, Eshbaugh Ted • ANS • USA
JAPANESE MAGIC • 1912 • Kinder Stuart • UKN
JAPANESE MAGIC see **JAPON DE FANTAISIE** • 1909
JAPANESE MASK, THE • 1915 • *Pathe* • SHT • FRN
JAPANESE NIGHTINGALE, A • 1918 • Fitzmaurice George • USA
JAPANESE PEACH BOY, A • 1910 • *Morin Pilar* • USA
JAPANESE SPY, THE • 1910 • *Kalem* • USA
JAPANESE SUMMER: DOUBLE SUICIDE see **MURI SHINJU NIHON NO NATSU** • 1967
JAPANESE SWORDMAKER, THE • 1913 • *Melies* • USA
JAPANESE SWORDS: THE WORK OF KOUHEI MIYAIRI see **NIHONTOU: MIYAIRI KOUHEI NO WAZA** • 1976
JAPANESE TRAGEDY, A see **NIHON NO HIGEKI** • 1945
JAPANESE TRAGEDY, A see **NIHON NO HIGEKI** • 1953
JAPANESE WAR BRIDE • 1952 • Vidor King • USA
JAPANESE WEDDING, A • 1913 • Melies Gaston • DOC • USA
JAPANESE WIFE, THE see **MOGLIE GIAPPONESE, LA** • 1968
JAPANESE YOUTH see **NIHON NO SEISHUN** • 1968
JAPANISCHE MASKE 1, DIE • 1922 • Heiland Heinz Karl • FRG • BANDITENNEST AUF DEM ADLERSTEIN, DAS
JAPANISCHE MASKE 2, DIE • 1923 • Heiland Heinz Karl • FRG
JAPAN'S HISTORY OF SEX CUSTOMS -THE BREASTS see **NIHON MARUHI FUZOKUSHI CHIBUSA** • 1968
JAPON, LE • 1982 • Reichenbach Francois • DOC • FRN • JAPON DE FRANCOIS REICHENBACH, LE ○ JAPON INSOLITE, LE
JAPON DE FANTAISIE • 1909 • Cohl Emile • ANS • FRN • JAPAN OF FANTASY ○ JAPANESE MAGIC ○ JAPANESE FANTASY, A
JAPON DE FRANCOIS REICHENBACH, LE see **JAPON, LE** • 1982
JAPON INSOLITE, LE see **JAPON, LE** • 1982
JAPONAISERIES • 1904 • Velle Gaston • FRN
JAPONESESNO ESPERAN, LOS • 1977 • Gonzalez Rogelio A. • MXC
JAPOTEURS • 1942 • Kneitel Seymour • ANS • USA
JAQUE A LA DAMA • 1978 • Rodriguez Francisco • SPN
JAR, THE • 1984 • Toscano Bruce • USA
JAR OF CRANBERRY SAUCE, A • 1910 • *Edison* • USA
JARDIM DAS ESPUMAS, O • 1970 • Filho Luis Rosemberg • BRZ
JARDIM DE ALAH • 1988 • Neves David • BRZ • GARDEN OF ALLAH
JARDIM ZOOLOGICO • 1954 • Mendes Joao • SHT • PRT
JARDIN DE LA DELICIAS, EL • 1970 • Saura Carlos • SPN • GARDEN OF DELIGHTS, THE
JARDIN DE TIA ISABEL, EL • 1971 • Cazals Felipe • MXC • AUNT ELIZABETH'S GARDEN ○ GARDEN OF AUNT ELIZABETH, THE
JARDIN DES HESPERIDES, LE • 1975 • Robiolles Jacques • FRN
JARDIN DES SUPPLICES, LE • 1976 • Gion Christian • FRN
JARDIN DU LUXEMBOURG • 1929 • Franken Mannus, Ankersmit H. J. • NTH
JARDIN PUBLIC, UN • 1954 • Paviot Paul • SHT • FRN
JARDIN QUI BASCULE, LE • 1974 • Gilles Guy • FRN
JARDINIER, LE • 1981 • Sentier Jean-Pierre • FRN
JARDINIER, LE see **ARROSEUR ARROSE, L'** • 1895
JARDINIER BRULANT DES HERBES • 1896 • Melies Georges • FRN • GARDENER BURNING WEEDS
JARDINIER D'ARGENTEUIL, LE • 1966 • Le Chanois Jean-Paul • FRN, FRG • BLUTEN, GAUNER UND DIE NACHT VON NIZZA (FRG)
JARDINIER ET LE PETIT ESPIEGLE, LE see **ARROSEUR ARROSE, L'** • 1895
JARDINS D'ARABIE • 1963 • Pialat Maurice • SHT • FRN
JARDINS DE LISBOA • 1941 • Coelho Jose Adolfo • SHT • PRT
JARDINS DE PARIS • 1961 • de Vaucorbeil Max • SHT • FRN
JARDINS DE PARIS, LES • 1948 • Resnais Alain • DOC • FRN
JARDINS D'HIVER, LES • 1976 • Dufaux Georges • DOC • CND
JARDINS DU DIABLE, LES see **COPLAN SAUVE SA PEAU** • 1967
JARED FAIRFAX'S MILLIONS • 1915 • *Kalem* • USA
JARGUS LAPIN • 1960 • Medved Jozef • CZC
JARHA FI AL-HAIT • 1977 • Farhati Jalili • MRC • CRACK IN THE WALL, A
JARISKATSIS see **OTETS SOLDATA** • 1965
JARL THE WIDOWER see **ANKEMAN JARL** • 1945
JARMAK CUDOW • 1966 • Hoffman Jerzy • DOC • PLN • MARKET OF MIRACLES
JARNAC'S TREACHEROUS BLOW see **COUP DE JARNAC, UN** • 1909
JARNBARAREN • 1911 • Linden Gustaf M. • SWD • IRON-CARRIER, THE
JARNETS MAN • 1935 • Olsson Gunnar • SWD
JARNI VODY • 1968 • Krska Vaclav • CZC • SPRING WATERS ○ SPRING FLOODS
JAROSLAW DABROWSKI • 1975 • Poreba Bohdan • PLN
JARR FAMILY DISCOVERS HARLEM, THE • 1915 • Davenport Harry • USA
JARRETT • 1973 • Shear Barry • TVM • USA
J'ARROSE MES GALONS • 1936 • Pujol Rene, Damont Jacques • FRN
JARRS VISIT ARCADIA, THE • 1915 • Davenport Harry • USA
JARVANY • 1975 • Gabor Pal • HNG • EPIDEMIC
JARZEBINA CZERWONA • 1969 • Petelska Ewa, Petelski Czeslaw • PLN • RED ROWANBERRIES ○ ROWAN TREE, THE
JAS I MALGOSIA • 1959 • Hoffman Jerzy, Skorzewski Edward • SHT • PLN • HANSEL AND GRETEL
JASAMINE FRECKEL'S LOVE AFFAIR • 1921 • Ramster P. J. • ASL
JASCHA HEIFETZ MASTER CLASS • 1962 • Hammid Alexander, Thompson Francis • USA
JASEI NO IN • 1920 • Kurihara Kisaburo • JPN • LASCIVIOUSNESS OF THE VIPER, THE ○ OBSCENITY OF THE VIPER ○ MALICIOUSNESS OF THE SNAKE'S EVIL, THE
JASHUMON NO ONNA • 1924 • Kinugasa Teinosuke • JPN • WOMAN'S HERESY, A
JASMIN • 1988 • Ariffin Kamarul • MLY
JASMIN II • 1988 • Ariffin Kamarul • MLY
JASMINE • 1912 • Buckland Warwick? • UKN
JASMIN'S SWEET LOVE see **YASEMININ TATLI ASKI** • 1968
JASNY DZIEN WOLNOSCI • 1962 • Forbert Wladyslaw • PLN • CLEAR DAY OF LIBERTY
JASON AND THE ARGONAUTS • 1963 • Chaffey Don • UKN • JASON AND THE GOLDEN FLEECE
JASON AND THE GOLDEN FLEECE see **GIGANTI DELLA TESSAGLIA, I** • 1960
JASON AND THE GOLDEN FLEECE see **JASON AND THE ARGONAUTS** • 1963
JASOO • 1935 • Lindtberg Leopold, Lesch W. • SWT
JASPER • 1942-46 • *Pal George (P)* • ASS • USA
JASPER AND THE BEANSTALK • 1945 • Pal George • ANS • USA
JASPER AND THE HAUNTED HOUSE • 1942 • Pal George • ANS • USA
JASPER AND THE WATERMELONS • 1942 • Pal George • ANS • USA
JASPER GOES FISHING • 1943 • Pal George • ANS • USA
JASPER GOES HUNTING • 1943 • Pal George • ANS • USA
JASPER IN A JAM • 1946 • Pal George • ANS • USA
JASPER LANDRY'S WILL see **UNCLE JASPER'S WILL** • 1922
JASPER TELL • 1945 • Pal George • ANS • USA
JASPER'S BOOBY TRAP • 1945 • Pal George • ANS • USA
JASPER'S DERBY • 1946 • Pal George • ANS • USA
JASPER'S MINSTRELS • 1945 • Pal George • ANS • USA
JASPER'S MUSIC LESSON • 1943 • Pal George • ANS • USA
JASPER'S PARADISE • 1944 • Pal George • ANS • USA
JASSY • 1947 • Knowles Bernard • UKN
JATAGAN MALA • 1953 • Makavejev Dusan • SHT • YGS
JATSZANI KELL see **LILY IN LOVE** • 1985
JAULA SIN SECRETOS, LA • 1962 • Navarro Agustin • ARG
JAUNE EN PERIL, LE see **SAD SONG OF YELLOW SKIN** • 1970
JAUNE LE SOLEIL • 1971 • Duras Marguerite • FRN
JAVA, UNE • 1927 • de Size Jean, Roussell Henry • FRN
JAVA, UNE • 1938 • Orval Claude • FRN • JAVA BLEUE, LA
JAVA BLEUE, LA see **JAVA, UNE** • 1938
JAVA DES OMBRES, LA • 1983 • Goupil Romain • FRN, FRG
JAVA HEAD • 1923 • Melford George • USA
JAVA HEAD • 1934 • Ruben J. Walter, Dickinson Thorold (U/c) • UKN
JAVA SEAS (UKN) see **EAST OF JAVA** • 1935
J'AVAIS SEPT FILLES • 1954 • Boyer Jean • FRN, ITL • SETTE PECCATI DI PAPA, I (ITL) ○ MY SEVEN LITTLE SINS (USA) ○ I HAD SEVEN DAUGHTERS (UKN)
JAVANESE DANCERS • 1913 • Melies Gaston • DOC • USA
JAVANESE DANCING • 1953-54 • Devlin Bernard • DCS • CND
JAVOR, A • 1987 • Ban Robert • HNG • JAVOR, THE
JAVOR, THE see **JAVOR, A** • 1987
JAWAHARLAL NEHRU • 1982 • Benegal Shyam • DOC • IND, USS
JAWANI • 1942 • *Biswas Anil (M)* • IND
JAWANI-KI-RAAT • 1939 • *Sircar B. N. (P)* • IND
JAWLOCK JONES • 1914 • *Captain Kettle Films* • UKN
JAWS • 1975 • Spielberg Steven • USA
JAWS 2 • 1978 • Szwarc Jeannot • USA
JAWS 3-D • 1983 • Alves Joe • USA
JAWS 4 see **JAWS -THE REVENGE** • 1987
JAWS AL-ARBARA • 1949 • Wahab Fatin Abdel • EGY • MARI DES QUATRE, LE
JAWS OF DEATH, THE • 1976 • Grefe William • USA • MAKO: THE JAWS OF DEATH
JAWS OF HELL (USA) see **BALACLAVA** • 1928
JAWS OF HELL (USA) see **BALACLAVA** • 1930
JAWS OF JUSTICE • 1933 • Bennet Spencer Gordon • USA
JAWS OF JUSTICE, THE • 1919 • Holt George • SHT • USA
JAWS OF SATAN • 1981 • Claver Bob • USA • KING COBRA
JAWS OF STEEL • 1927 • Enright Ray • USA
JAWS OF THE DRAGON • 1976 • Harris Jack C. • HKG
JAWS OF THE JUNGLE • 1936 • *Kendis J. D. (P)* • USA
JAWS -THE REVENGE • 1987 • Sargent Joseph • USA • JAWS 4
JAY BIRD, THE see **JAYBIRD, THE** • 1920
JAY LENO'S AMERICAN DREAM • 1986 • Wohl Ira • USA
JAYBIRD, THE • 1920 • Rosen Phil • SHT • USA • JAY BIRD, THE
JAYHAWKERS, THE • 1959 • Frank Melvin • USA
JAYNE MANSFIELD: A SYMBOL OF THE 50'S see **JAYNE MANSFIELD STORY, THE** • 1980
JAYNE MANSFIELD -AN AMERICAN TRAGEDY • 1981 • Winters David • USA
JAYNE MANSFIELD STORY, THE • 1980 • Lowry Dick • TVM • USA • JAYNE MANSFIELD: A SYMBOL OF THE 50'S
JAYWALKER, THE • 1956 • Cannon Robert • ANS • USA
JAZBO SHERIFF, THE • 1918 • Hotaling Arthur D. • SHT • USA
JAZOL • 1985 • Cenevski Kiril • YGS • KNOT, THE ○ CVOR
JAZOO • 1968 • Camie John • SHT • USA
JAZU MUSUME NI EIKO ARE • 1958 • Yamamoto Kajiro • JPN • RISE AND FALL OF A JAZZ GIRL, THE
JAZU MUSUME TANJO • 1957 • Sunohara Masahisa • JPN • JAZZ GIRL TANJO
JAZZ • Cruze James • USA
JAZZ #1 • Gurvin Abe • SHT • USA
JAZZ A PARIS, LE • 1965 • Keigel Leonard • SHT • FRN
JAZZ AGE, THE • 1929 • Shores Lynn • USA
JAZZ ALL AROUND see **MIDT I EN JAZZTID** • 1969
JAZZ AND JAILBIRDS • 1919 • Howe J. A. • SHT • USA
JAZZ AUF BURG SCHWANECK • 1960 • van der Linden Charles Huguenot • SHT • FRG
JAZZ BALL • 1956 • *Paramount* • CMP • USA
JAZZ BAND • 1978 • Avati Pupi • ITL
JAZZ BANDITS, THE • 1920 • Del Ruth Roy • SHT • USA
JAZZ BOY, THE see **JAZZGOSSEN** • 1958
JAZZ BRIDE, THE (UKN) see **COMPANIONATE MARRIAGE, THE** • 1928
JAZZ CINDERELLA • 1930 • Pembroke Scott • USA • LOVE IS LIKE THAT (UKN)
JAZZ COCKTAIL • 1951 • *Universal* • CMP • USA
JAZZ COMEDY see **VESYOLYE REBYATA** • 1934
JAZZ CRUSADERS • 1962 • Binder Steve • SHT • USA
JAZZ CRUSADERS, THE • 1962 • Markas Gary • SHT • USA
JAZZ DANCE • 1954 • Tilton Roger • SHT • USA
JAZZ EN POEZIE • 1966 • van Gasteren Louis A. • SHT • NTH
JAZZ EXPATRIATES • 1980 • Van Davis Jeffrey, Croissant Claus • DOC • FRG
JAZZ FESTIVAL • 1949-56 • Corsan Well • CMP • USA
JAZZ FESTIVAL • 1968 • *Universal* • SHT • USA
JAZZ FOOL, THE • 1928 • Disney Walt, Iwerks Ub • ANS • USA
JAZZ FROM STUDIO 61 • 1959 • Genns Karl • SHT • USA
JAZZ GIRL, THE • 1926 • Mitchell Howard M. • USA
JAZZ GIRL TANJO see **JAZU MUSUME TANJO** • 1957
JAZZ HEAVEN • 1929 • Brown Melville • USA
JAZZ HOOFER: THE LEGENDARY BABY LAURENCE • 1981 • Hancock Bill • USA
JAZZ HOUNDS, THE • 1922 • *Reol Productions* • USA
JAZZ IN BELGIUM see **THREE DAYS IN APRIL** • 1972
JAZZ IN EXILE • 1978 • France Chuck • DCS • USA
JAZZ IN PIAZZA • 1974 • Adriano Pino • ITL
JAZZ IN POLAND see **JAZZ W POLSCE** • 1964
JAZZ IS A CHILD • 1962 • Binder Steve • SHT • USA
JAZZ IS OUR RELIGION • 1972 • Jeremy John • UKN
JAZZ-JAMBOREE NOS.1-3 • 1953 • Roulleau Edgar • SHS • FRN
JAZZ KREML • 1957 • Schamoni Peter • SHT • FRG
JAZZ MAD • 1928 • Weight F. Harmon • USA • SYMPHONY, THE
JAZZ MAD • 1931 • *Terry Paul/ Moser Frank (P)* • ANS • USA
JAZZ MAD see **ZIS BOOM BAH** • 1941
JAZZ MAMAS • 1929 • Sennett Mack • SHT • USA
JAZZ ME BABY see **ZERO GIRLS** • 1965
JAZZ MONKEY, THE • 1919 • Campbell William • SHT • USA
JAZZ-O-RAMA • 1953 • *Yates Pictures* • CMP • USA
JAZZ OF LIGHTS • 1954 • Hugo Ian • SHT • USA
JAZZ ON A BRIGHT SUMMER'S DAY • 1979 • Molsner Torben • SHT • DNM
JAZZ ON A SUMMER'S DAY • 1958 • Stern Bert • USA
JAZZ PAINTED PORTRAITS • Wasylewski Andrzej • SER • PLN
JAZZ PARENTS see **MAD WHIRL, THE** • 1925
JAZZ RHYTHM • 1930 • *Mintz Charles (P)* • ANS • USA
JAZZ SCRAPBOOK • 1982 • Buesst Nigel • DOC • ASL
JAZZ SINGER, THE • 1927 • Crosland Alan • USA
JAZZ SINGER, THE • 1953 • Curtiz Michael • USA

JAZZ SINGER, THE • 1980 • Fleischer Richard • USA
JAZZ STRINGER, THE • 1928 • Noble Joe, Noble George • ANS • UKN
JAZZ: THE INTIMATE ART • 1968 • Drew Robert • USA
JAZZ TRIPTYCH see **TRYPTYK JAZZOWY** • 1960
JAZZ W POLSCE • 1964 • Majewski Janusz • SHS • PLN • MODERN POLISH JAZZ GROUPS ○ JAZZ IN POLAND
JAZZ WAITER see **CAUGHT IN A CABARET** • 1914
JAZZBANDITEN • 1959 • Ulrich Bodo • FRG
JAZZBOAT • 1960 • Hughes Ken • UKN
JAZZED HONEYMOON, A • 1919 • Roach Hal • SHT • USA
JAZZGOSSEN • 1958 • Ekman Hasse • SWD • JAZZ BOY, THE
JAZZING FOR BLUE JEAN • Temple Julien • UKN
JAZZING WITH SOCIETY see **CAUGHT IN A CABARET** • 1914
JAZZLAND • 1928 • Fitzgerald Dallas M. • USA
JAZZMAN • 1983 • Shakhnazarov Karen • USS
JAZZMANIA • 1923 • Leonard Robert Z. • USA
JAZZTIME • 1929 • Jeffrey R. E. • UKN
JAZZY JANITOR, A • 1920 • Watson William • SHT • USA
JD AND THE SALT FLAT KID • 1978 • Grasshoff Alex • USA
JE • 1960 • Portugais Louis • DCS • CND
JE BRULE DE PARTOUT • 1978 • Franco Jesus • FRN
JE CHANTE • 1938 • Stengel Christian • FRN
JE CRIE! JE JOUIS! • 1978 • Bernard-Aubert Claude • FRN
JE HAIS LES ACTEURS • 1986 • Krawczyk Gerard • FRN • I HATE ACTORS (USA)
JE HAIS LES BLONDES (FRN) see **ODIO LE BIONDE** • 1980
JE KA MI ODER DEIN GLUCK IST GANZ VON DIESER WELT • 1979 • Holenstein Roman • DOC • SWT
JE L'AI ETE TROIS FOIS • 1953 • Guitry Sacha • FRN
JE LE VOULAIS • 1917 • Rasumny Alexander • USS
JE ME SOUVIENS • 1984 • Kinsey Nicholas • MTV • CND
JE ME SOUVIENS see **DON'T FORGET** • 1979
JE N'AI QUE TOI see **MALISH GHIRAK** • 1958
JE N'AI QUE TOI AU MONDE • 1949 • de Meyst E. G., Magnin William • FRN
JE N'AIME QUE TOI • 1949 • Montazel Pierre • FRN • C'EST TOI QUE J'AIME
JE N'AVOUERAI PAS see **LAN ATARIF** • 1961
JE NE SAIS PAS.. MOI NON PLUS • 1972 • van Gasteren Louis A. • MTV • NTH
JE NE SAIS RIEN MAIS JE DIRAI TOUT • 1973 • Richard Pierre • FRN
JE PARLE D'AMOUR • 1978 • Hartmann-Clausset Madeleine • FRN
JE PARS see **INNI RAHILA** • 1955
JE PLAIDE NON COUPABLE (FRN) see **GUILTY?** • 1956
JE REVE D'ETRE UN IMBECILE HEUREUX see **DEUX IMBECILES HEUREUX** • 1975
JE REVIENDRAI A KANDARA • 1956 • Vicas Victor • FRN
JE REVIENDRAI PAR LA FENETRE see **PAR LA FENETRE** • 1947
JE SEME A TOUT VENT • 1952 • Kast Pierre • FRN • I SEED THE WINDS
JE SERAI SERIEUX COMME LE PLAISIR see **SERIEUX, COMME LE PLAISIR** • 1975
JE SERAI SEULE APRES MINUIT • 1931 • de Baroncelli Jacques • FRN
JE SORS ET TU RESTES LA see **INCONSTANT, L'** • 1931
JE SUIS A PRENDRE! • 1978 • Leroi Francis • FRN
JE SUIS AVEC TOI • 1943 • Decoin Henri • FRN
JE SUIS EN MEME TEMPS MAUDIT ET CLASSIQUE • 1978 • Simoneau Guy • MTV • CND
JE SUIS FRIGIDE.. POURQUOI? • 1972 • Pecas Max • FRN • I AM FRIGID.. WHY? (UKN) ○ SHE SHOULD HAVE STAYED IN BED ○ COMMENT LE DESIR VIENT AUX FILLES
JE SUIS FURIEUX see **I AM FURIOUS** • 1969
JE SUIS L'AMOUR see **ANA AL-HUBB** • 1953
JE SUIS LE SEIGNEUR DU CHATEAU • 1989 • Wargnier Regis • FRN
JE SUIS LOIN DE TOI MIGNONNE • 1976 • Fournier Claude • CND
JE SUIS PIERRE RIVIERE • 1975 • Lipinska Christine • FRN
JE SUIS SEULE see **ANA WAHDI** • 1952
JE SUIS TIMIDE MAIS JE ME SOIGNE • 1978 • Richard Pierre • FRN
JE SUIS UN HOMME PERDU • 1932 • Greville Edmond T. • SHT • FRN
JE SUIS UN MOUCHARD • 1952 • Chanas Rene • FRN
JE SUIS UN SENTIMENTAL • 1955 • Berry John • FRN, ITL • IO SONO UN SENTIMENTALE (ITL) ○ HEADLINES OF DESTRUCTION (USA)
JE SUIS UNE NYMPHOMANE • 1971 • Pecas Max • FRN • I AM A NYMPHOMANIAC
JE SUIS VICIEUSE MAIS JE ME SOIGNE • Baudricourt Michel • FRN
JE T'ADORE, MAIS POURQUOI? • 1931 • Colombier Piere • FRN • RADIEUX-CONCERT
JE T'AI ECRIT UNE LETTRE D'AMOUR see **CHERE INCONNUE** • 1980
JE T'AI OFFERT MA VIE see **WAHABTAK HAYATI** • 1956
JE T'AIME • 1974 • Duceppe Pierre • CND
JE T'AIME, JE T'AIME • 1967 • Resnais Alain • FRN, SPN • I LOVE YOU, I LOVE YOU
JE T'AIME, MA CHERIE! see **AHIBBAK YA HILWA**
JE T'AIME MOI NON PLUS • 1976 • Gainsbourg Serge • FRN, FRG • I LOVE YOU, ME NO LONGER (USA) ○ I LOVE YOU, I DON'T (UKN)
JE T'AIME, TU DANSES • 1974 • Weyergans Francois • BLG
JE T'ATTENDRAI see **MAQUILLAGE** • 1932
JE T'ATTENDRAI see **DESERTEUR, LE** • 1939
JE TE CONFIE MA FEMME • 1933 • Guissart Rene • FRN
JE TE TIENS, TU ME TIENS PAR LA BARBICHETTE • 1978 • Yanne Jean • FRN • I'VE GOT YOU, YOU'VE GOT ME BY THE CHIN HAIRS (USA)
JE TE VERRAI • 1957 • Barakat Henry • EGY
JE TIRE MA REVERENCE see **MISSION A TANGIER** • 1949
JE, TU, ELLES • 1971 • Foldes Peter • FRN • I, YOU, THEY
JE, TU, IL, ELLE • 1975 • Akerman Chantal • BLG
JE TU SUCE, TU ME SUCES, IL ME SUCE • 1980 • Benazeraf Jose • FRN
JE VAIS CRAQUER • 1980 • Leterrier Francois • FRN
JE VEUX RENTRER A LA MAISON • 1989 • Resnais Alain • FRN • I WANT TO GO HOME (UKN)
JE VEUX UNE SOLUTION see **HAYATI AL-KHASSA** • 1974
JE VOUS AIME • 1980 • Berri Claude • FRN
JE VOUS AIME • 1990 • Panfilov Gleb • USS
JE VOUS AIMERAI TOUJOURS • 1932 • Camerini Mario • FRN
JE VOUS FERAI AIMER LA VIE • 1978 • Korber Serge • FRN
JE VOUS SALUE, MAFIA • 1965 • Levy Raoul J. • FRN, ITL • DA NEW YORK: MAFIA UCCIDE! (ITL) ○ HAIL! MAFIA (USA)
JE VOUS SALUE MARIE • 1984 • Godard Jean-Luc • FRN, SWT • HAIL MARY
JE VOUS Y PRRRRENDS! • 1897-98 • Blache Alice • FRN
JEALOUS • 1989 • Nivelli Mickey • USA
JEALOUS BUMBLE BEE, THE see **ZAZDROSNY TRZMIEL** • 1965
JEALOUS CAVALIER, THE • 1910 • Noy Wilfred? • UKN
JEALOUS DOLL: OR, THE FRUSTRATED ELOPEMENT, THE • 1909 • Stow Percy • UKN
JEALOUS FOOLS see **JEALOUS HUSBANDS** • 1923
JEALOUS GEORGE • 1911 • *Selig* • USA
JEALOUS GUY, A • 1916 • Semon Larry • SHT • USA
JEALOUS HUSBAND, A • 1913 • Johnson Arthur • USA
JEALOUS HUSBAND, A • 1914 • *Sterling Ford* • USA
JEALOUS HUSBAND, THE • 1910 • Rains Fred • UKN
JEALOUS HUSBAND, THE • 1911 • Sennett Mack • USA
JEALOUS HUSBANDS • 1923 • Tourneur Maurice • USA • JEALOUS FOOLS
JEALOUS JAMES • 1914 • *Lubin* • USA
JEALOUS JOLTS • 1917 • Miller Rube • SHT • USA
JEALOUS LOVER • 1933 • *Terry Paul/ Moser Frank (P)* • ANS • USA
JEALOUS OLD MAID • 1908 • Brooke Van Dyke • USA
JEALOUS PAINTER, THE • 1898 • Williamson James • UKN
JEALOUS PROFESSORS, THE • 1910 • *Lux* • USA
JEALOUS RAGE, THE • 1912 • Dwan Allan • USA
JEALOUS SEX see **AWFUL TRUTH, THE** • 1925
JEALOUS WAITER, THE • 1913 • Lehrman Henry, Sennett Mack (Spv) • USA
JEALOUS WIFE, A • 1910 • *Powers* • USA
JEALOUS WIFE, THE • 1904 • Collins Alf • UKN
JEALOUS WIFE, THE see **ZILIARA, I** • 1968
JEALOUSY • 1897 • *Paul R. W.* • UKN
JEALOUSY • 1910 • *Columbia* • USA
JEALOUSY • 1911 • *Turner Florence* • USA
JEALOUSY • 1912 • *Walthall William* • USA
JEALOUSY • 1913 • *Mitchell Doris* • USA
JEALOUSY • 1915 • *Starlight* • USA
JEALOUSY • 1915 • *Thanhouser* • USA
JEALOUSY • 1915 • Melville Wilbert • *Lubin* • USA
JEALOUSY • 1916 • Davis Will S. • USA
JEALOUSY • 1929 • de Limur Jean • USA
JEALOUSY • 1931 • Samuelson G. B. • UKN
JEALOUSY • 1934 • Neill R. William • USA • SPRING THREE THOUSAND ONE HUNDRED
JEALOUSY • 1945 • Machaty Gustav • USA
JEALOUSY • 1963 • Dinov Todor • ANS • BUL
JEALOUSY • 1984 • Bloom Jeffrey • TVM • USA
JEALOUSY see **EIFERSUCHT** • 1925
JEALOUSY see **SHITTO** • 1949
JEALOUSY see **GELOSIA** • 1953
JEALOUSY see **ZAZDROSC** • 1967
JEALOUSY see **ZWARTZIEK** • 1974
JEALOUSY A LA CARTE • 1916 • Miller Rube • USA
JEALOUSY AND GIANT POWDER • 1914 • *Imp* • USA
JEALOUSY AND MEDICINE see **ZAZDROSC I MEDYCYNA** • 1939
JEALOUSY AND THE MAN • 1909 • Griffith D. W. • USA
JEALOUSY, ITALIAN STYLE (USA) see **DRAMMA DELLA GELOSIA -TUTTI I PARTICOLARI IN CRONACA** • 1970
JEALOUSY OF JANE, THE • 1913 • *Gail Jane* • USA
JEALOUSY OF MIGUEL AND ISABELLA, THE • 1913 • Duncan William • USA
JEALOUSY OF THE SCRIBBLER, THE see **JALOUSIE DU BARBOUILLE, LA** • 1927
JEALOUSY ON THE RANCH • 1912 • *Pathe* • USA
JEALOUSY (UKN) see **EMERGENCY WEDDING** • 1950
JEALOUSY, WHAT ART THOU? • 1915 • *Wilson Ben* • USA
JEALOUSY'S FIRST WIFE • 1916 • Le Viness Carl M. • SHT • USA
JEALOUSY'S FOOLS • 1915 • Reehm George E. • USA
JEALOUSY'S TRAIL • 1913 • *American* • USA
JEAN AND THE CALICO DOLL • 1910 • *Vitagraph* • USA
JEAN AND THE WAIF • 1910 • *Vitagraph* • USA
JEAN BELIVEAU • 1972 • Barclay Robert • MTV • CND
JEAN CARIGNAN, VIOLONEUX • 1975 • Gosselin Bernard • DOC • CND
JEAN CHOUAN • 1925 • Luitz-Morat • FRN
JEAN COCTEAU • 1949 • Roos Jorgen • DOC • DNM
JEAN COCTEAU FAIT DU CINEMA • 1925 • Cocteau Jean • SHT • FRN
JEAN COTON • 1953 • Allegret Marc • SHT • FRN • FILM DE JEAN, LE
JEAN D'AGREVE • 1922 • Leprince Rene • FRN
JEAN DE FLORETTE • 1985 • Berri Claude • FRN
JEAN DE FLORETTE 2e PARTIE see **MANON DES SOURCES** • 1985
JEAN DE LA LUNE • 1931 • Choux Jean • FRN
JEAN DE LA LUNE • 1948 • Achard Marcel • FRN
JEAN DE LA LUNE • 1977 • Villiers Francois • MTV • FRN
JEAN DE POUDRE • 1912 • Tourneur Maurice • FRN • JEAN LA POUDRE
JEAN DRAPEAU • 1968 • Bonniere Rene • DCS • CND
JEAN EFFEL • 1948 • *Resnais Alain (Ed)* • FRN
JEAN ET LOULOU see **EPOUX SCANDALEUX, LES** • 1935
JEAN-FRANCOIS XAVIER DE.. • 1970 • Audy Michel • CND
JEAN GALMOT, AVENTURIER • 1990 • Maline Alain • FRN
JEAN GASCON • 1971 • Bonniere Rene • DCS • CND
JEAN GENET • Bourseiller Antoine • DOC • FRN
JEAN-GINA B. • 1984 • Graff Philippe, Rolin Diane • BLG, FRN, NTH
JEAN GOES FISHING • 1910 • *Vitagraph* • USA
JEAN GOES FORAGING • 1910 • *Vitagraph* • USA
JEAN INTERVENES • 1912 • *Turner Florence* • USA
JEAN-JACQUES ROUSSEAU • 1958 • Leenhardt Roger, Vivet Jean-Paul • DCS • FRN
JEAN-JACQUES SERVAN-SCHREIBER • 1972 • Bonniere Rene • DCS • CND
JEAN JAURES • 1959 • Lods Jean • DCS • FRN
JEAN KOLBASINK THE HAIRDRESSER see **YAGODKI LYUBVI** • 1926
JEAN LA FRANCAISE see **JOANA A FRANCESA** • 1973
JEAN LA POUDRE see **JEAN DE POUDRE** • 1912
JEAN LE MANCHOT • 1911 • Carre Michel • FRN
JEAN LEFRANCOIS, HEROS DE LA MARNE see **HEROS DE LA MARNE, LE** • 1938
JEAN-LUC GODARD • 1964 • Doniol-Valcroze Jacques • FRN
JEAN-LUC PERSECUTE • 1965 • Goretta Claude • MTV • SWT
JEAN MILO OU LE VOYAGE DU FIGURATIF A L'ABSTRAIT • 1961 • Haesaerts Luc • DCS • BLG
JEAN O' THE HEATHER • 1916 • Olcott Sidney • USA
JEAN OF THE GUTTER see **JEANNE OF THE GUTTER** • 1919
JEAN OF THE JAIL • 1912 • *Joyce Alice* • USA
JEAN OF THE WILDERNESS • 1914 • *Foster Morris* • USA
JEAN-PAUL BELMONDO • 1965 • Lelouch Claude • DOC • FRN
JEAN PERRON, SELLIER • 1975 • Plamondon Leo • DOC • CND
JEAN PIAGET • 1977 • Goretta Claude • SWT • EPISTEMOLOGY OF JEAN PIAGET, THE
JEAN-PIERRE POITEVIN • 1968 • Dansereau Fernand • DCS • CND
JEAN RENOIR LE PATRON • 1966 • Rivette Jacques • DOC • FRN
JEAN RESCUES • 1911 • *Turner Florence* • USA
JEAN RICHARD, LE • 1958-60 • Bonniere Rene • DCS • CND
JEAN-ROBERT OUELLETTE • 1968 • Dansereau Fernand • DCS • CND
JEAN ST. GERMAIN.. ILLIMITE • 1981 • Lavoie Richard • CND
JEAN TARIS, CHAMPION DE NATATION • 1931 • Vigo Jean • SHT • FRN • JEAN TARIS, SWIMMING CHAMPION (USA) ○ TARIS, ROI DE L'EAU ○ TARIS CHAMPION DE NATATION ○ TARIS OU LA NATATION
JEAN TARIS, SWIMMING CHAMPION (USA) see **JEAN TARIS, CHAMPION DE NATATION** • 1931
JEAN, THE FAITHFUL • 1915 • Reehm George E. • USA
JEAN VALJEAN • 1909 • *Vitagraph* • USA
JEAN VALJEAN see **JAN BARUJAN** • 1931
JEANNE • 1934 • Marret Georges • FRN
JEANNE AU BUCHER see **GIOVANNA D'ARCO AL ROGO** • 1954
JEANNE D'ARC • 1900 • Melies Georges • FRN • JOAN OF ARC (USA)
JEANNE D'ARC • 1908 • Capellani Albert • FRN • JOAN OF ARC (USA)
JEANNE D'ARC • 1972 • Panfilov Gleb • USS
JEANNE DIELMAN, 23, QUAI DU COMMERCE 1080 BRUXELLES • 1976 • Akerman Chantal • BLG, FRN
JEANNE DORE • 1915 • Mercanton Louis • FRN
JEANNE DORE • 1917 • Bernard Raymond • FRN
JEANNE DORE • 1938 • Bonnard Mario • ITL
JEANNE EAGELS • 1957 • Sidney George • USA
JEANNE MOREAU • 1966 • Reichenbach Francois • SHT • FRN
JEANNE OF THE GUTTER • 1919 • Brenon Herbert • USA • JEAN OF THE GUTTER
JEANNE OF THE MARSHES (UKN) see **BEHIND MASKS** • 1921
JEANNE OF THE WOODS • 1915 • Henderson Lucius • USA
JEANNETTE BOURGOGNE • 1938 • Gourguet Jean • FRN
JEANNIE • 1941 • French Harold • UKN • GIRL IN DISTRESS (USA)
JEANNOT LA FRIME see **FREDDY** • 1978
JEANNOT L'INTREPIDE • 1950 • Image Jean • ANM • FRN • JOHNNY THE GIANT KILLER (USA) ○ JOHNNY AND THE WICKED GIANT
JEANNOU • 1943 • Poirier Leon • FRN
JEANS AND T-SHIRT see **JEANS E UNA MAGLIETTA, UN** • 1984
JEANS E UNA MAGLIETTA, UN • 1984 • Laurenti Mariano • ITL • JEANS AND T-SHIRT
JEAN'S EVIDENCE • 1913 • Trimble Larry • UKN
JEAN'S PLAN • 1946 • Hammond William C. • UKN
JEANS TONIC • 1983 • Patient Michel • FRN
JECA E A FREIRA, O • 1968 • Mazzaropi Amacio • BRZ • RUSTIC AND THE NUN, THE
JED HOLCOMB'S PRIZE BOX • 1913 • *Nestor* • USA
JEDANAESTA ZAPOVEST • 1970 • Kljakovic Vanca • YGS • ELEVENTH COMMANDMENT, THE
JEDDA • 1955 • Chauvel Charles • ASL • JEDDA THE UNCIVILIZED (USA)
JEDDA THE UNCIVILIZED (USA) see **JEDDA** • 1955
JEDE FRAU HAT EIN GEHEIMNIS • 1934 • Obal Max • FRG
JEDE FRAU HAT EIN SUSSES GEHEIMNIS see **ABENTEUER GEHT WEITER, DAS** • 1939
JEDE FRAU HAT ETWAS • 1930 • Mittler Leo • FRG
JEDE MENGE KOHLE • 1982 • Winkelmann Adolf • FRG • ANY AMOUNT OF COAL
JEDE NACHT IN EINEM ANDERN BETT • 1957 • Verhoeven Paul • FRG
JEDE STUNDE VERLETZT UND DIE LEUTE TOTET • 1963 • Lilienthal Peter • FRG
JEDEN DZIEN W POLSCE • 1949 • Has Wojciech J. • DCS • PLN • ONE DAY IN POLAND
JEDEN PLUS JEDEN • 1971 • Gebski Jozef, Halor Antoni • PLN • ONE PLUS ONE
JEDEN STRIBRNY • 1977 • Balik Jaroslav • CZC • ONE SILVER PIECE
JEDENACTE PRIKAZANI • 1925 • Kubasek Vaclav • CZC • ELEVENTH COMMANDMENT, THE
JEDENACTE PRIKAZANI • 1935 • Fric Martin • CZC • ELEVENTH COMMANDMENT, THE
JEDER FRAGT NACH ERIKA • 1931 • Zelnik Friedrich • FRG
JEDER FUR SICH UND GOTT GEGEN ALLE • 1974 • Herzog Werner • FRG • ENIGMA OF KASPER HAUSER, THE (UKN) ○ LEGEND OF KASPER HAUSER, THE ○ MYSTERY OF KASPER HAUSER, THE (USA) ○ EVERY MAN FOR HIMSELF AND GOD AGAINST ALL ○ KASPER HAUSER

JEDER STIRBT FUR SICH ALLEIN • 1976 • Vohrer Alfred • FRG • WE ALL DIE ALONE
JEDERMANN • 1961 • Reinhardt Gottfried • AUS • EVERYMAN (USA) ○ SALZBURG EVERYMAN, THE
JEDERMANNS FRAU • 1924 • Korda Alexander • FRG • EVERYBODY'S WOMAN ○ JEDERMANNS WEIB
JEDERMANNS WEIB see **JEDERMANNS FRAU** • 1924
JEDNA Z MILIONU • 1935 • Slavinsky Vladimir • CZC • ONE IN A MILLION
JEDNOG DANA LJUBAV • 1969 • Saranovic Radomir • YGS • ONE DAY OF LOVE
JED'S LITTLE ELOPEMENT • 1915 • *Lyons Eddie* • USA
JED'S TRIP TO THE FAIR • 1916 • Christie Al • SHT • USA
JEEP, THE • 1938 • Fleischer Dave • ANS • USA
JEEP-HERDERS • 1949 • Talmadge Richard • USA
JEEPERS CREEPERS • 1939 • Clampett Robert • ANS • USA
JEEPERS CREEPERS • 1939 • McDonald Frank • USA • MONEY ISN'T EVERYTHING (UKN)
JEEPERS CREEPERS' CAR CHASE • 1965 • Glut Don • SHT • USA
JEEPNEY KING • 1968 • Santiago Pablo • PHL
JEET • 1949 • *Biswas Anil (M)* • IND
JEET-KUNE-DO – THE KILLER PUNCH OF BRUCE LEE see **CHIEH-CH'UAN-TAO** • 1976
JEEVAN REKHA • *Rnfc* • NPL • LINE OF LIFE, THE
JEEVAN SANGEET • 1968 • Mukherjee Arabinda • IND • SONG OF LIFE, THE
JEEVAN SATHI • 1939 • *Biswas Anil (M)* • IND
JEEVANAMSAM • 1968 • Rajagopal Malliyam • IND • ALIMONY
JEEVIKAN ANUVADHIKKU • 1967 • Thomas P. A. • IND • LET ME LIVE
JEEVITHA BANDHAM • 1968 • Gopinath M. S. • IND • EXISTING LOVE
JEEVITHALU • 1968 • Murthy P. S. • IND • LIVES
JEEWAN JYOTI • 1953 • *Burman S. D. (M)* • IND
JEFE, EL • 1958 • Ayala Fernando • ARG • CHIEF, THE ○ BOSS, THE
JEFE MAXIMO, EL • 1940 • de Fuentes Fernando • MXC • BIG BOSS, THE
JEFF • 1968 • Herman Jean • FRN, ITL • ADDIO JEFF (ITL)
JEFF GORDON SPACCA TUTTO (ITL) see **CES DAMES S'EN MELENT** • 1964
JEFFRIES-CORBETT FIGHT (RESTAGED) • 1903 • *Bitzer Billy (Ph)* • USA
JEFFRIES JR. • 1924 • McCarey Leo • SHT • USA
JEFFRIES ON HIS RANCH • 1910 • *Yankee* • USA
JEFF'S DOWNFALL • 1912 • Haldane Bert? • UKN
JEG ELSKER BLAT • 1968 • Methling Sven • DNM • I LOVE BLUE
JEG -EN ELSKER • 1966 • Nyberg Borje • DNM, SWD • JAG – EN ALSKARE (SWD) ○ I, A LOVER (USA)
JEG -EN KVINDE (DNM) see **JAG -EN KVINNA (I)** • 1965
JEG -EN KVINDE II (DNM) see **JAG -EN KVINNA (II)** • 1968
JEG -EN MARKI • 1967 • Ahlberg Mac, Guldbrandsen Peer • DNM, SWD • JAG EN MARKIS -MED UPPDRAG ATT ALSKA (SWD) ○ I, A NOBLEMAN (USA) ○ I A MARQUIS ○ RELUCTANT SADIST, THE
JEG ER SGU' MIN EGEN • 1967 • Balling Erik • DNM • I DO WHAT I WILL
JEG ET HUS MIG BYGGE VIL • 1955 • Carlsen Henning • SHT • DNM
JEG HAR ELSKET OG LEVET • 1940 • Schneevoigt George • DNM
JEG SA JESUS DO • 1975 • Fyrsting Ib • DNM
JEG VILLE FORST FINDE SANDHEDEN • 1987 • Carlsen Jon Bang • DNM • I FIRST WANTED TO FIND THE TRUTH
JEGO WIELKA MILOSC • 1936 • Krawicz Mecislas, Perzanowska S. • PLN
JEHANNE • 1956 • Enrico Robert • FRN
JEHO EXCELENCE • Novak Ilya • CZC • HIS EXCELLENCY
JEJ POWROT • 1974 • Orzechowski Witold • PLN • HER RETURN
JEJAK BERTAPAK • 1979 • Sulong Jamil • MLY • SYNDICATE, THE
JEJAKA-JEJAKA • 1986 • INN
JEJI LEKAR • 1933 • Slavinsky Vladimir • CZC • HER DOCTOR
JEKYLL • 1969 • Albertazzi Giorgio • MTV • ITL
JEKYLL AND HYDE see **SKAEBNESVANGRE OPFINDELSE, DEN** • 1910
JEKYLL AND HYDE PORTFOLIO, THE • 1971 • Haims Eric Jeffrey • USA
JEKYLL AND HYDE.. TOGETHER AGAIN • 1982 • Belson Jerry • USA
JEKYLL EXPERIMENT, THE see **DR. JEKYLL'S DUNGEON OF DEATH** • 1979
JEKYLL'S INFERNO see **TWO FACES OF DR. JEKYLL, THE** • 1960
JELBESZED • 1975 • Luttor Mara • HNG • RECOVERY
JELENIDO • 1972 • Bacso Peter • HNG • PRESENT INDICATIVE
JELENLET • 1965 • Jancso Miklos • SHT • HNG • PRESENCE, THE
JELF'S • 1915 • Tucker George Loane • UKN • MAN OF HIS WORD, A (USA)
JELLY FISH, THE • 1926 • Roberts Stephen (c/d) • SHT • USA
JELLYFISH, THE • 1918 • *Parson William* • SHT • USA
JELOZNAYA PUYATA • 1919 • Gardin Vladimir • USS • IRON HEEL, THE
JEMIMA AND JOHNNY • 1966 • Ngakane Lionel • UKN
JEMIMA AND THE EDITOR • 1912 • Fitzhamon Lewin • UKN
JEMIOLA • 1974 • Szpakowicz Piotr • PLN • MISTLETOE, A
J'EN DEVIENS FOU! see **HAY GANNINUNI** • 1959
JEN HSIA JEN • 1984 • Wu Ma • HKG • DEAD AND THE DEADLY, THE
JEN SI TAK TROCHU PISKNOUT • 1981 • Smyczek Karel • CZC • JUST A LITTLE WHISTLE ○ JUST TO WHISTLE A BIT
JENA DI LONDRA, LA • 1964 • Mancini Gino • ITL • HYENA OF LONDON, THE
JENA IN CASSAFORTE, UNA • 1967 • Canevari Cesare • ITL • HYENA IN THE STRONG-BOX, A ○ HYBRID
JENA PIU NE HA NE VUOLE, LA • 1970 • Isgro Emilio • ITL
JENARO, EL DE LOS CATORCE • 1974 • Ozores Mariano • SPN
JENATSCH • 1987 • Schmid Daniel • SWT
JENCHINA U CHETVERO JEJEU MUJCHINE • 1983 • Pupa Algimantas • USS • WOMAN AND HER FOUR MEN, A
JENGIBRE CONTRA DINAMITA • 1939 • *Cantinflas* • SHT • MXC • GINGER VERSUS DYNAMITE
JENIFER HALE • 1937 • Mainwaring Bernerd • UKN
JENKINS AND THE DONKEY • 1912 • *Cines* • ITL
JENKINS' JINX • 1916 • Greene Clay M. • SHT • USA
JENKINS-PERKINS WAR, THE • 1912 • *Solax* • USA
JENKS AND HIS MOTOR BOAT • 1912 • *Comet* • USA
JENKS AND THE JANITOR • 1914 • Seay Charles M. • USA
JENKS BECOMES A DESPERATE CHARACTER • 1913 • Henderson Dell • USA
JENKS' DAY OFF • 1910 • *Thanhouser* • USA
JENNIE GERHARDT • 1933 • Gering Marion • USA
JENNIE LEES HA UNA NUOVA PISTOLA (SPN) see **SFIDA A RIO BRAVO** • 1965
JENNIE (UKN) see **PORTRAIT OF JENNIE** • 1948
JENNIE, WIFE/CHILD • 1965 • Landis James, Cohen Robert Carl • USA • TENDER GRASS
JENNIFER • 1953 • Newton Joel • USA
JENNIFER • 1964 • De Palma Brian • SHT • USA
JENNIFER • 1978 • Mack Brice • USA • JENNIFER (THE SNAKE GODDESS)
JENNIFER see **LEVRES DE SANG** • 1974
JENNIFER: A WOMAN'S STORY • 1979 • Green Guy • TVM • USA
JENNIFER ON MY MIND • 1971 • Black Noel • USA
JENNIFER (THE SNAKE GODDESS) see **JENNIFER** • 1978
JENNY • 1936 • Carne Marcel • FRN
JENNY • 1958 • van Hemert Willy • NTH, FRG
JENNY • 1970 • Bloomfield George • USA • AND JENNY MAKES THREE
JENNY • 1977 • Carlsen Jon Bang • DCS • DNM
JENNY BE GOOD • 1920 • Taylor William D. • USA
JENNY BUMMEL DURCH DIE MANNER • 1929 • Speyer Jaap • FRG
JENNY KISSED ME • 1986 • Trenchard-Smith Brian • ASL
JENNY LAMOUR (USA) see **QUAI DES ORFEVRES** • 1947
JENNY LIND • 1931 • Robison Arthur • FRN
JENNY LIND (UKN) see **LADY'S MORALS, A** • 1930
JENNY OMROYD OF OLDHAM • 1920 • Etheridge Frank • UKN
JENNY STIEHLT EUROPA • 1932 • Piel Harry • FRG
JENNY UND DER HERR IM FRACK • 1941 • Martin Paul • FRG
JENNY'S DIARY • 1975 • Donner Clive • SHT • UKN
JENNY'S PEARLS • 1913 • Lehrman Henry, Sennett Mack (Spv) • USA
JENNY'S WAR • 1985 • Gethers Steve • TVM • USA
JENS LANGKNIV • 1940 • *Henning-Jensen Bjarne* • DNM
JENS MANSSON I AMERIKA • 1947 • Janzon Bengt • SWD • JENS MANSSON IN AMERICA
JENS MANSSON IN AMERICA see **JENS MANSSON I AMERIKA** • 1947
JEN'S PLACE • 1982 • Yates Rebecca, Salzman Glen • CND
JENSEITS DER GRENZE see **EDELWEISS** • 1923
JENSEITS DER KLOSTERMAUERN • *Morsbach K.* • FRG
JENSEITS DER STRASSE • 1929 • Mittler Leo • FRG • HARBOUR DRIFT
JENSEITS DES RHEINS (FRG) see **PASSAGE DU RHIN, LE** • 1960
JENSEITS DES STROMES • 1922 • Czerny Ludwig • FRG • BEYOND THE RIVER
JENSEITS VON GUT UND BOSE • 1921 • Sauer Fred • FRG • AUS DEN TIEFEN DER GROSSTADT
JENSEITS VON GUT UND BOSE see **OLTRE IL BENE E IL MALE** • 1977
JENTESPRANGET • 1973 • Thomsen Knud Leif • NRW • LINA'S WEDDING
JEOPARDY • 1952 • Sturges John • USA
JEPHTAH'S DAUGHTER • 1909 • Blackton J. Stuart (Spv) • USA
JEPHTAH'S DAUGHTER • 1913 • MacDonald J. Farrell • USA
JEPPE OF THE HILL • 1981 • Holst Per • DNM
JERBO, EL • 1971 • Carretero Amaro • ANS • SPN • JERBOA, THE
JERBOA, THE see **JERBO, EL** • 1971
JEREMELU • 1965 • Levine Naomi • SHT • USA
JEREMIAH JOHNSON • 1972 • Pollack Sydney • USA • SAGA OF JEREMIAH JOHNSON, THE ○ CROW KILLER, THE
JEREMY • 1973 • Barron Arthur • USA
JERICHO • 1937 • Freeland Thornton • UKN • DARK SANDS (USA)
JERICHO • 1945 • Calef Henri • FRN • BEHIND THESE WALLS ○ DERRIERE CES MURS
JERICHO • 1989 • Cammell Donald • USA
JERICHO MILE, THE • 1979 • Mann Michael • TVM • USA
JERK, THE • 1979 • Reiner Carl • USA
JERK A ISTAMBUL • 1967 • Rigaud Francis • FRN, ITL • CENTO MILIONI PER MORIRE (ITL) ○ BAROUDEURS, LES ○ PUNCH-UP IN ISTANBUL
JERK, TOO, THE • 1984 • Schultz Michael • TVM • USA
JERKY TURKEY • 1945 • Avery Tex • ANS • USA
JERKY TURKEY • 1968 • Smith Paul J. • ANS • USA
JERNBANENS DATTER • 1911 • Blom August • DNM • DAUGHTER OF THE RAILWAY, THE
JEROME BOSCH • 1963 • Weyergans Francois • SHT • FRN
JEROME PERREAU • 1935 • Gance Abel • FRN • QUEEN AND THE CARDINAL, THE (USA) ○ JEROME PERREAU, HEROS DES BARRICADES
JEROME PERREAU, HEROS DES BARRICADES see **JEROME PERREAU** • 1935
JEROMIN • 1953 • Lucia Luis • SPN
JERRICO THE WONDER CLOWN see **THREE RING CIRCUS** • 1954
JERRY • 1924 • Gallone Carmine • ITL
JERRY -A GRANDE PARADA • 1967 • Barros Carlos Alberto De Souza • BRZ • JERRY -THE BIG BOASTER
JERRY AND HIS PAL • 1917 • Fahrney Milton • SHT • USA
JERRY AND JUMBO • 1953 • Hanna William, Barbera Joseph • ANS • USA
JERRY AND THE BANDITS • 1916 • Fahrney Milton • USA
JERRY AND THE BLACKHANDERS • 1916 • Fahrney Milton • USA
JERRY AND THE BULLY • 1917 • Fahrney Milton • USA
JERRY AND THE BURGLARS • 1917 • Fahrney Milton • SHT • USA
JERRY AND THE COUNTERFEITERS • 1916 • *Ovey George* • USA
JERRY AND THE GOLDFISH • 1951 • Hanna William, Barbera Joseph • ANS • USA
JERRY AND THE GUNMAN • 1915 • *Ovey George* • USA
JERRY AND THE LION • 1950 • Hanna William, Barbera Joseph • ANS • USA
JERRY AND THE MOONSHINERS • 1916 • Fahrney Milton • USA
JERRY AND THE OUTLAWS • 1917 • Fahrney Milton • USA
JERRY AND THE SMUGGLERS • 1916 • Fahrney Milton • USA
JERRY AND THE VAMPIRE • 1917 • Bartlett Charles • USA
JERRY AT THE WALDORF • 1917 • Fahrney Milton • USA
JERRY BUILDERS, THE • 1930 • Banks Monty • UKN
JERRY-BUILT HOUSE, THE • 1906 • Fitzhamon Lewin • UKN
JERRY FOR SHORT see **LITTLE DUCHESS, THE** • 1917
JERRY-GO-ROUND • 1965 • Levitow Abe • ANS • USA
JERRY GRAY AND THE BAND OF THE DAY • 1950 • *Universal* • SHT • USA
JERRY IN MEXICO • 1916 • *Ovey George* • USA
JERRY IN THE MOVIES • 1916 • Fahrney Milton • USA
JERRY IN YODEL LAND • 1917 • Fahrney Milton • USA
JERRY JERRY QUITE CONTRARY • 1966 • Jones Charles M. • ANS • USA
JERRY JOINS THE ARMY • 1917 • Fahrney Milton • USA
JERRY LAND CACCIATORE DI SPIE (ITL) see **WARTELISTE ZUR HOLLE** • 1967
JERRY LAND, SPY-HUNTER see **WARTELISTE ZUR HOLLE** • 1967
JERRY LIVINGSTON AND HIS TALK OF THE TOWN MUSIC • 1939 • French Lloyd • SHT • USA
JERRY ON THE FARM • 1917 • *Ovey George* • USA
JERRY ON THE JOB • 1916-17 • La Cava Gregory, Hoban W. C. • ASS • USA
JERRY ON THE JOB see **HOW COULD WILLIAM TELL?** • 1919
JERRY ON THE RAILROAD • 1917 • *Ovey George* • USA
JERRY SHIPS A CIRCUS • 1916 • Hoban W. C. • ANS • USA
JERRY TAKES GAS • 1917 • Bartlett Charles • SHT • USA
JERRY -THE BIG BOASTER see **JERRY -A GRANDE PARADA** • 1967
JERRY THE GIANT • 1926 • Selander Lesley, Sandrich Mark • SHT • USA
JERRY, THE JANITOR • 1916 • *Reserve Photoplays* • SER • USA
JERRY TO THE RESCUE • 1915 • *Ovey George* • USA
JERRY TRIES AGAIN • 1917 • *Ovey George* • SHT • USA
JERRY'S BEST FRIEND • 1917 • Bartlett Charles • SHT • USA
JERRY'S BIG DEAL • 1917 • Fahrney Milton • USA
JERRY'S BIG DOINGS • 1916 • Fahrney Milton • USA
JERRY'S BIG GAME • 1916 • Fahrney Milton • USA
JERRY'S BIG HAUL • 1916 • Fahrney Milton • USA
JERRY'S BIG LARK • 1916 • Fahrney Milton • USA
JERRY'S BIG MYSTERY • 1917 • Fahrney Milton • USA
JERRY'S BIG RAID • 1917 • Fahrney Milton • SHT • USA
JERRY'S BIG STUNT • 1917 • Fahrney Milton • USA
JERRY'S BOARDING HOUSE • 1917 • Fahrney Milton • SHT • USA
JERRY'S BRILLIANT SCHEME • 1917 • Fahrney Milton • USA
JERRY'S BUSY DAY • 1915 • Fahrney Milton • USA
JERRY'S CELEBRATION • 1916 • Fahrney Milton • SHT • USA
JERRY'S COUSIN • 1951 • Hanna William, Barbera Joseph • ANS • USA
JERRY'S DIARY • 1949 • Hanna William, Barbera Joseph • ANS • USA
JERRY'S DOUBLE HEADER • 1916 • Fahrney Milton • SHT • USA
JERRY'S ELOPEMENT • 1916 • Fahrney Milton • USA
JERRY'S EUGENIC MARRIAGE • 1917 • *Ovey George* • USA
JERRY'S FINISHED TOUCH • 1917 • *Ovey George* • USA
JERRY'S GENTLE NURSING • 1917 • Fahrney Milton • USA
JERRY'S GETAWAY • 1917 • *Ovey George* • USA
JERRY'S HOPELESS TANGLE • 1917 • Fahrney Milton • USA
JERRY'S JAM • 1917 • *Ovey George* • USA
JERRY'S LUCKY DAY • 1917 • Fahrney Milton • SHT • USA
JERRY'S MASTER STROKE • 1917 • Fahrney Milton • SHT • USA
JERRY'S MILLIONS • 1916 • Fahrney Milton • USA
JERRY'S MOTHER-IN-LAW • 1913 • Young James • USA
JERRY'S PERFECT DAY • 1916 • Fahrney Milton • USA
JERRY'S PICNIC • 1917 • Fahrney Milton • USA
JERRY'S RED HOT TRAIL • 1917 • Fahrney Milton • USA
JERRY'S REVENGE • 1915 • Fahrney Milton • USA
JERRY'S ROMANCE • 1917 • *Ovey George* • SHT • USA
JERRY'S RUNNING FIGHT • 1917 • Fahrney Milton • SHT • USA
JERRY'S SOFT SNAP • 1917 • Fahrney Milton • USA
JERRY'S STAR BOUT • 1917 • Fahrney Milton • USA
JERRY'S STRATAGEM • 1916 • Fahrney Milton • USA
JERRY'S TRAIL • 1917 • *Ovey George* • USA
JERRY'S TRIPLE ALLIANCE • 1917 • *Ovey George* • SHT • USA
JERRY'S UNCLE'S NAMESAKE • 1914 • Drew Sidney, Young James • USA
JERRY'S VICTORY • 1917 • Bartlett Charles • SHT • USA
JERRY'S WHIRLWIND FINISH • 1917 • Fahrney Milton • USA
JERRY'S WINNING WAY • 1916 • Fahrney Milton • SHT • USA
JERSEY SKEETER, A • 1902 • *Biograph* • USA
JERUSALEM • 1926 • Molander Gustaf • SWD
JERUSALEM • 1937-40 • *Cardiff Jack (Ph)* • DCS • UKN
JERUSALEM • 1973 • Fox Beryl • DOC • CND
JERUSALEM FILE, THE • 1971 • Flynn John • USA, ISR • JERUSALEM, JERUSALEM
JERUSALEM IN THE TIME OF CHRIST • 1908 • *Kalem* • USA
JERUSALEM, JERUSALEM see **JERUSALEM FILE, THE** • 1971
JERUSALEM SET FREE see **GERUSALEMME LIBERATA** • 1957
JERY'S DOUBLE CROSS • 1917 • Bartlett Charles • SHT • USA
JES' CALL ME JIM • 1920 • Badger Clarence • USA
JES' PLAIN DOG • 1910 • *Imp* • USA

JESIEN • 1956 • Borowczyk Walerian • SHT • PLN
JESIENNY DZIEN • 1969 • Kutz Kazimierz • MTV • PLN • AUTUMN DAY, AN
JESLI UJRZYSZ KOTA FRUWAJACEGO PO NIEBIE • 1972 • Szczechura Daniel • ANS • PLN • IF YOU SEE A CAT..
JESS • 1912 • *Thanhouser* • USA
JESS • 1914 • *Wilson Ednamae* • USA
JESS OF THE HILL COUNTRY • 1916 • *Nichols Marguerite* • SHT • USA
JESS OF THE MOUNTAIN COUNTRY • 1914 • *World* • USA
JESSE • 1988 • Jordan Glenn • USA
JESSE AND JAMES • 1931 • *Terry Paul/ Moser Frank (P)* • ANS • USA
JESSE AND LESTER: TWO BROTHERS IN A PLACE CALLED TRINITY see **JESSE E LESTER DUE FRATELLI IN UN POSTO CHIAMATO TRINITA** • 1972
JESSE AND LESTER (UKN) see **JESSE E LESTER DUE FRATELLI IN UN POSTO CHIAMATO TRINITA** • 1972
JESSE E LESTER DUE FRATELLI IN UN POSTO CHIAMATO TRINITA • 1972 • Genta Renzo • ITL • JESSE AND LESTER (UKN) ○ JESSE AND LESTER: TWO BROTHERS IN A PLACE CALLED TRINITY
JESSE JAMES • 1927 • Ingraham Lloyd • USA • OUTLAW RIDER, THE (UKN)
JESSE JAMES • 1939 • King Henry • USA
JESSE JAMES AS THE OUTLAW • 1921 • Coates Franklin B. • USA
JESSE JAMES AT BAY • 1941 • Kane Joseph • USA
JESSE JAMES JR. • 1942 • Sherman George • USA • SUNDOWN FURY
JESSE JAMES MEETS FRANKENSTEIN'S DAUGHTER • 1966 • Beaudine William • USA • JESSE JAMES VS. FRANKENSTEIN'S DAUGHTER
JESSE JAMES RIDES AGAIN • 1947 • Brannon Fred C., Carr Thomas • SRL • USA
JESSE JAMES UNDER THE BLACK FLAG • 1921 • Coates Franklin B. • USA
JESSE JAMES VS. FRANKENSTEIN'S DAUGHTER see **JESSE JAMES MEETS FRANKENSTEIN'S DAUGHTER** • 1966
JESSE JAMES VS. THE DALTONS • 1954 • Castle William • USA
JESSE JAMES' WOMEN • 1954 • Barry Donald • USA
JESSE OWENS STORY, THE • 1984 • Irving Richard • TVM • USA
JESSICA • 1962 • Negulesco Jean • USA, FRN, ITL • SAGE-FEMME, LE CURE ET LE BON DIEU, LA (FRN)
JESSICA see **MISS JESSICA IS PREGNANT** • 1970
JESSICA'S FIRST PRAYER • 1908 • Aylott Dave? • UKN
JESSICA'S FIRST PRAYER • 1921 • Wynne Bert • UKN
JESSIE • 1981 • Forbes Bryan • TVM
JESSIE AND SUPERMAN see **KDO CHCE ZABIT JESSI?** • 1966
JESSIE, THE STOLEN CHILD • 1909 • Brooke Van Dyke • USA
JESSIE'S GIRLS see **JESSI'S GIRLS** • 1975
JESSI'S GIRLS • 1975 • Adamson Al • USA • WANTED WOMEN ○ JESSIE'S GIRLS
JESS'S DIDACTIC NICKELODEON see **FORTY AND ONE NIGHTS, THE** • 1963
JESSY • 1961 • Rilla Wolf • DOC • UKN
JEST, THE • 1921 • Paul Fred • UKN
JEST OF GOD, A see **RACHEL, RACHEL** • 1968
JEST OF HONOR • 1934 • Stallings George • ANS • USA
JEST OF JEALOUSY, THE • 1915 • *Marion Frances* • USA
JEST OF TALKY JONES, THE • 1918 • *Holloway Carol* • SHT • USA
JESTEM PRZECIW • 1985 • Trzos-Rastawiecki Andrzej • PLN • OBJECTION
JESTER • 1908 • Porter Edwin S. • USA
JESTER, THE • 1916 • *Essanay* • SHT • USA
JESTER AND THE QUEEN, THE see **SASEK A KRALOVNA** • 1987
JESTER'S JOKE, THE • 1912 • Booth W. R. • UKN • MERRY JESTER, THE
JESTER'S TALE, THE see **BLAZNOVA KRONIKA** • 1964
JESUS • 1979 • Sykes Peter, Krish John • UKN, ISR • STORY OF JESUS, THE
JESUS see **KING OF KINGS** • 1961
JESUS see **GREATEST STORY EVER TOLD, THE** • 1965
JESUS CHRIST, SUPERSTAR • 1973 • Jewison Norman • USA
JESUS CHRIST'S HOROSCOPE see **JEZUS KRISZTUS HOROSZKOPJA** • 1988
JESUS DE MONTREAL • 1988 • Arcand Denys • CND
JESUS DE NAZARETH • 1942 • Diaz Morales Jose • MXC
JESUS LA CAILLE see **M'SIEUR LA CAILLE** • 1955
JESUS, MARIA Y JOSE • *Murray Guillermo* • MXC • JESUS, MARY AND JOSEPH
JESUS, MARY AND JOSEPH see **JESUS, MARIA Y JOSE**
JESUS OF NAZARETH • 1928 • *Van Loan Philip* • USA
JESUS OF NAZARETH • 1977 • Zeffirelli Franco • TVM • USA, ITL • GESU DI NAZARETH (ITL) ○ LIFE OF JESUS, THE
JESUS OF NAZARETH see **FROM THE MANGER TO THE CROSS** • 1912
JESUS OF OTTAKRING see **JESUS VON OTTAKRING** • 1976
JESUS TRIP, THE • 1971 • Mayberry Russ • USA
JESUS VON OTTAKRING • 1976 • Pellert Wilhelm • AUS • JESUS OF OTTAKRING
JESUS WANTED see **CERCASI GESU** • 1982
JESUSITA EN CHIHUAHUA • 1942 • Cardona Rene • MXC
JESUS'S BOYS • 1982 • Rosma Juha • SHT • FNL
JET • 1959 • Falk Lauritz • SWD
JET ATTACK • 1958 • Cahn Edward L. • USA • THROUGH HELL TO GLORY (UKN)
JET CAGE, THE • 1962 • Freleng Friz • ANS • USA
JET F-104 DASSYUTSU SEYO • 1968 • Murayama Mitsuo • JPN • F-104, BAIL OUT
JET GENERATION • 1968 • Schmidt Eckhardt • FRG • WIE MADCHEN HEUTE MANNER LIEBEN ○ HOW GIRLS LOVE MEN TODAY
JET JOB • 1952 • Beaudine William • USA
JET LAG (USA) see **VERTIGO IN MANHATTAN** • 1980
JET MEN OF THE AIR (UKN) see **AIR CADET** • 1951
JET OVER THE ATLANTIC • 1960 • Haskin Byron • USA
JET PILOT • 1957 • von Sternberg Josef, Hughes Howard (U/c) • USA
JET PINK • 1967 • Chiniquy Gerry • ANS • USA
JET PROPELLED • 1966 • *Short Ramsey (P)* • UKN
JET PROPULSION • Chambers Jack • DOC • UKN
JET SEX see **UND SIE GENIESSEN DIE LIEBE** • 1976
JET SEX see **CANDI GIRL** • 1977
JET STORM • 1959 • Endfield Cy • UKN • KILLING URGE ○ JET STREAM
JET STREAM see **JET STORM** • 1959
J'ETAIS, JE SUIS, JE SERAI • 1974 • Heynowski Walter, Scheumann Gerhard • GDR
J'ETAIS UNE AVENTURIERE • 1938 • Bernard Raymond • FRN • GRAND MOYENS, LES
J'ETAIS VENU POUR UN AN • 1977 • Lesaunier Daniel • MTV • CND
JETEE, LA • 1962 • Marker Chris • FRN • PIER, THE ○ JETTY, THE ○ RUNWAY, THE
JETEE ET PLAGE DE TROUVILLE (2e PARTIE) • 1896 • Melies Georges • FRN • BEACH AND PIER AT TROUVILLE PART 2
JETSONS MEET THE FLINTSTONES, THE see **FLINTSTONES: THE JETSONS MEET THE FLINTSTONES** • 1987
JETTATORE • 1919 • Eichberg Richard • FRG
JETTATORE • 1940 • Herrera Luis Bayon
JETTCHEN GEBERT • 1918 • Oswald Richard • FRG
JETTE ET PLAGE DE TROUVILLE 1er PARTIE • 1896 • Melies Georges • FRN • BEACH AND PIER AT TROUVILLE PART ONE
JETTY, THE see **JETEE, LA** • 1962
JETZT DREHT DIE WELT SICH NUR UM DICH • 1964 • Liebeneiner Wolfgang • AUS
JETZT SCHLAGTS 13 • 1950 • Emo E. W. • AUS • ES SCHLAGT DREIZEHN
JETZT UND IN DER STUNDE MEINES TODES • 1963 • Petzold Konrad • GDR
JEU • 1974 • Gray Reginald • FRN • PASSANT, LE
JEU 1 • 1962 • Reichenbach Francois, Sanders Dirk • SHT • FRN • JEUX
JEU AVEC LE FEU, LE • 1975 • Robbe-Grillet Alain • FRN, ITL • GIOCHI DI FUOCO (ITL)
JEU BRUTAL, UN • 1982 • Brisseau Jean-Claude • FRN
JEU DANGEREUX, UN • 1976 • Melancon Andre • SHT • CND
JEU DE CHAQUE JOUR, LE see **LUBATU KULLI YUM** • 1971
JEU DE COUDES • 1979 • Driessen Paul • ANM • CND
JEU DE LA PUCE, LE • 1970 • Desvilles • SHT • FRN
JEU DE LA VERITE, LE • 1961 • Hossein Robert • FRN
JEU DE LA VIE, LE see **POP GAME** • 1967
JEU DE L'HIVER, LE • 1962 • Dansereau Jean, Gosselin Bernard • DCS • CND
JEU DE L'OIE, LE • 1981 • Ruiz Raul • SHT • FRN • SNAKES AND LADDERS
JEU DE MAINS, JEU DE VILAINS • 1989 • *Ferreol Andrea* • SWT, FRN
JEU DE MASSACRE • 1967 • Jessua Alain • FRN • KILLING GAME, THE (USA) ○ COMIC STRIP HERO ○ ALL WEEKEND LOVERS
JEU DE SOLITAIRE, LE • 1975 • Adam Jean-Francois • FRN • GAME OF SOLITAIRE, THE
JEU D'ENFANT, UN • 1990 • Kane Pascal • FRN
JEU DES PROPOSITIONS, LE • 1966 • Hebert Pierre • ANS • CND
JEU DU RENARD, LE • 1990 • Caprile Anne • FRN
JEU ETERNEL, LE • 1971 • Maleh Nabil • SYR • ECUME, L'
JEU SI SIMPLE, UN • 1964 • Groulx Gilles • DCS • CND
JEUDI -A CHEVAL SUR L'ARGENT • 1978 • Leduc Jacques • DCS • CND
JEUDI ON CHANTERA COMME DIMANCHE • 1966 • Storck Henri • DOC • BLG
JEUDI ON CHANTERA COMME DIMANCHE • 1968 • de Heusch Luc • BLG, FRN • SONGS ON THURSDAY AS WELL AS ON SUNDAY
JEUGDDAG • 1929 • Ivens Joris • SHT • NTH • DAY OF YOUTH (USA) ○ DAYS OF YOUTH
JEUNE COUPLE, UN • 1968 • Gainville Rene • FRN • YOUNG COUPLE, A (USA)
JEUNE FILLE, LA see **YOUNG ONE, THE** • 1960
JEUNE FILLE ASSASSINEE, LA • 1974 • Vadim Roger • FRN, ITL, FRG • VITA BRUCIATA, UNA (ITL) ○ CHARLOTTE: A GIRL MURDERED ○ CHARLOTTE
JEUNE FILLE AU JARDIN • 1936 • Kirsanoff Dimitri • SHT • FRN
JEUNE FILLE AUX CONTES, LA see **KORITSI ME TA PARAMYTHIA** • 1957
JEUNE FILLE DE FRANCE • 1938 • Allegret Marc, Allegret Yves • DCS • FRN • GIRLS OF FRANCE, THE
JEUNE FILLE D'UNE NUIT, LA • 1934 • Le Bon Roger, Schunzel Reinhold • FRN
JEUNE FILLE EFFRAYEE, LA see **QUELQU'UN A TUE** • 1933
JEUNE FILLE ET UN MILLION,UNE • 1932 • Ellis Fred, Neufeld Max • FRN • DESIR 22
JEUNE FILLE LIBRE LE SOIR see **BABYSITTER, LA** • 1975
JEUNE FILLE SAVAIT, UNE • 1947 • Lehmann Maurice • FRN
JEUNE FILLE, UN SEUL AMOUR, UNE (FRN) see **KATJA** • 1959
JEUNE FILLES AUJOURD'HUI see **MATURAREISE** • 1943
JEUNE FILLES DE PARIS • 1936 • Vermorel Claude • FRN • VIE N'EST PAS UN ROMAN, LA
JEUNE FILLES DEVANT L'AMOUR see **ENFANTS DE PARIS** • 1936
JEUNE FILLES EN UNIFORME (FRN) see **MADCHEN IN UNIFORM** • 1958
JEUNE FOLLE, LA • 1952 • Allegret Yves, Sigurd Jacques • FRN • DESPERATE DECISION (USA) ○ REVENGE AT DAYBREAK
JEUNE HOMME, UN see **AINE DES FERCHAUX, L'** • 1963
JEUNE HOMME ET LA MORT, LE • 1953 • Anger Kenneth • FRN
JEUNE HOMME ET LE LION, LE • 1976 • Delannoy Jean • MTV • FRN, UKN, CND • YOUNG MAN AND THE LION, THE
JEUNE HOMME HONORABLE, UN see **AINE DES FERCHAUX, L'** • 1963
JEUNE HOMME QUI SE TUE, UN see **CHOURINETTE** • 1933
JEUNE MAGICIEN, LE • 1987 • Dziki Waldemar • CND, PLN • YOUNG MAGICIAN, THE
JEUNE MARIE, LE • 1982 • Stora Bernard • FRN
JEUNE MORTE, LA • 1965 • Faraldo Claude • FRN, PRT
JEUNE PATRIARCHE • 1957 • Bourguignon Serge • FRN
JEUNE PROIE POUR MAUVAIS GARCONS • 1977 • Terry Norbert • FRN
JEUNE SAIT PAS LIRE • 1985 • Payer Roch Christophe • MTV • CND • ETRE ANALPHABETE A 20 ANS
JEUNES, LES • 1965-66 • Garceau Raymond • DCS • CND
JEUNES FILLES A L'UNIVERSITE see **BANATUN FI AL-GAMI'A** • 1969
JEUNES FILLES A MARIER • 1935 • Vallee Jean • FRN • HUIT JEUNES FILLES A MARIER
JEUNES FILLES DE BONNE FAMILLE, LES see **SAINTES NITOUCHES, LES** • 1962
JEUNES FILLES EN DETRESSE • 1939 • Pabst G. W. • FRN • LOI SACREE, LA
JEUNES FILLES IMPUDIQUES • 1973 • Rollin Jean • FRN
JEUNES FILLES MODERNES see **BINT AL-YUM** • 1956
JEUNES GENS A MARIER • 1912 • Cohl Emile • ANS • FRN
JEUNES KIDNAPPES, LES • 1969 • Cardinal Roger • DCS • CND
JEUNES LOUPS, LES • 1968 • Carne Marcel • FRN, ITL • YOUNG WOLVES, THE ○ YOUNG BREED
JEUNES MARIES • 1953 • Grangier Gilles • FRN, ITL • SPOSATA IERI (ITL)
JEUNES ROMANCIERS, LES • 1963-64 • Fournier Claude • DCS • CND
JEUNES TIMIDES • 1941 • Allegret Yves • FRN • DEUX TIMIDES, LES
JEUNESSE • 1923 • Madzelewski Eugenjusz • PLN
JEUNESSE • 1934 • Lacombe Georges • FRN
JEUNESSE, UNE • 1983 • Mizrahi Moshe • FRN • YOUTH
JEUNESSE ANNEE 0 • 1964 • Portugais Louis • DOC • CND
JEUNESSE AU SOLEIL • 1965 • Nasri Samir • LBN
JEUNESSE D'ABORD • 1935 • Stelli Jean, Heymann Claude • FRN • EMPEREUR DES VACHES, L' ○ CETTE PETITE EST PARFAITE
JEUNESSE DE FRANCE • 1968 • Allegret Marc • SHT • FRN
JEUNESSE RURALE • 1957 • Proulx Maurice • DCS • CND
JEUNESSES DU MONDE • 1936 • Masson Jean • SHT • FRN
JEUNESSES MUSICALES • 1956 • Jutra Claude • DOC • CND
JEUX • 1979 • Ruiz Raul • FRN • GAMES
JEUX see **JEU 1** • 1962
JEUX D'ADULTES (FRN) see **PADRE DI FAMIGLIA, IL** • 1967
JEUX DANGEREUX • 1958 • Chenal Pierre • FRN, ITL • DANGEROUS GAMES (USA)
JEUX DE CARTES • 1916 • Cohl Emile • ANS • FRN
JEUX DE CARTES • 1959 • Lacam Henri • ANS • FRN • GAME OF CARDS
JEUX DE FEMMES • 1945 • Cloche Maurice • FRN • FIANCEES EN LOCATION
JEUX DE JEROLAS • 1967 • Carle Gilles • DOC • CND
JEUX DE LA COMTESSE DOLINGEN DE GRATZ, LES • 1981 • Binet Catherine • FRN
JEUX DE LA XXI OLYMPIADE • 1976 • Labrecque Jean-Claude • CND
JEUX DE L'AMOUR, LES • 1960 • de Broca Philippe • FRN • LOVE GAME, THE (USA) ○ PLAYING AT LOVE
JEUX DE LANGUE • 1977 • Leroi Francis • FRN
JEUX DE LANGUE PARTICULIERS • Baudricourt Michel • FRN
JEUX DE L'ETE ET DE LA MER • 1936 • Storck Henri • DOC • BLG
JEUX DE L'HUMOUR ET DU HASARD, LES see **MON COEUR ET SES MILLIONS** • 1931
JEUX D'ENFANTS • 1913 • Fescourt Henri • FRN
JEUX D'ENFANTS • 1946 • Painleve Jean • SHT • FRN
JEUX DES ANGES, LES • 1964 • Borowczyk Walerian • ANS • FRN • GAMES OF THE ANGELS, THE (USA)
JEUX DES REFLETS DE LA VITESSE • 1923 • Chomette Henri • FRN
JEUX DU QUEBEC 1967 • 1967 • Bobet Jacques • CND
JEUX DU QUEBEC: CINQ ANS APRES • 1976 • Cardinal Roger • DCS • CND
JEUX EROTIQUES DE NUIT • 1979 • Vadim Roger • FRN, USA • NIGHT GAMES (USA)
JEUX IMTIMES A DOMICILE • Nauroy Alain C. • FRN
JEUX INTERDITS • 1948 • Clement Rene • FRN • FORBIDDEN GAMES (USA) ○ SECRET GAME, THE (UKN) ○ SECRET GAMES
JEUX PARTICULIERS • 1980 • Baudricourt Michel • FRN
JEUX POUR COUPLES INFIDELES • 1972 • Desvilles Jean • FRN • HOT AND BLUE (UKN) ○ EXECUTIVE HOUSEWIVES ○ HOT BLUE
JEUX SONT FAIT, LES • 1947 • Delannoy Jean • FRN • CHIPS ARE DOWN, THE (USA) ○ DIE IS CAST, THE (UKN) ○ JIG IS UP, THE
JEUX SONT FAUTS, LES • 1979 • Renaud France Y. Y. • CND
JEUX UNIVERSITAIRES • 1969 • Bouguermouh Abderrahmane • ALG
JEW, THE see **HIS PEOPLE** • 1925
JEW AT WAR, A see **DAVID GORELICK** • 1931
JEW OF MESTRI, THE see **KAUFMANN VON VENEDIG, DER** • 1923
JEW SUSS • 1934 • Mendes Lothar • UKN • POWER (USA)
JEW SUSS see **JUD SUSS** • 1940
JEWEL • 1915 • Smalley Phillips, Weber Lois • USA
JEWEL see **CHAPTER IN HER LIFE, A** • 1923
JEWEL, THE • 1933 • Denham Reginald • UKN
JEWEL, THE • 1960 • ANS • HNG
JEWEL, THE • 1972 • *I.p.a.* • MXC
JEWEL, THE see **BIJOU, LE** • 1947
JEWEL CASE, THE see **SOLVDAASEN MED JUVELERNE** • 1910
JEWEL IN PAWN, A • 1917 • Conway Jack • USA
JEWEL IN THE CROWN, THE • 1984 • O'Brien Jim, Morahan Christopher • MTV • UKN
JEWEL OF ALLAH, THE • 1914 • *Payne Edna* • USA
JEWEL OF DEATH, THE • 1917 • Fahrney Milton • SHT • USA
JEWEL OF THE NILE • 1985 • Teague Lewis • USA
JEWEL OF THE PACIFIC • 1932 • Hurley Frank • DOC • ASL
JEWEL ROBBERY • 1932 • Dieterle William • USA
JEWEL SONG, THE see **FACING THE MUSIC** • 1933
JEWEL THIEF • 1967 • Anand Vijay • IND
JEWEL THIEVES, THE • 1909 • Fitzhamon Lewin • UKN
JEWEL THIEVES OUTWITTED, THE • 1913 • Wilson Frank • UKN

JEWEL THIEVES RUN TO EARTH BY SEXTON BLAKE, THE • 1910 • *Gaumont* • UKN
JEWELLED DAGGER OF FATE, THE • 1915 • *Reliance* • USA
JEWELLED NIGHTS • 1925 • Carbasse Louise • ASL
JEWELLED SLIPPERS, THE • 1913 • *Corrigan Thomas* • USA
JEWELLER'S TERROR, THE see **JUVELERERNES SKROEK** • 1915
JEWELS, THE • 1912 • *Shaw Harold M.* • USA
JEWELS AND FINE CLOTHES • 1912 • Moss Hugh • UKN
JEWELS AND JIMJAMS • 1915 • Aylott Dave • UKN • DEFECTIVE DETECTIVE, THE
JEWEL'S DARL • 1987 • Wells Peter • SHT • NZL
JEWELS OF A SACRIFICE see **JEWELS OF SACRIFICE** • 1913
JEWELS OF ALLAH, THE • 1911 • *Thanhouser* • USA
JEWELS OF BRANDENBURG • 1947 • Forde Eugene J. • USA
JEWELS OF DESIRE • 1927 • Powell Paul • USA
JEWELS OF SACRIFICE • 1913 • Dwan Allan • USA • JEWELS OF A SACRIFICE
JEWISH GAUCHOS, THE see **GAUCHOS JUDIOS, LOS** • 1975
JEWISH PRUDENCE • 1927 • Roach Hal • SHT • USA
JEW'S CHRISTMAS, THE • 1913 • Smalley Phillips, Weber Lois • USA
JEWS IN POLAND • 1957 • Ladowicz B. • PLN
JEZDEC FORMULE RISK • 1973 • Kachlik Antonin • CZC • DRIVER OF THE RISK CATEGORY ○ RISKY DRIVER, THE
JEZEBEL • 1938 • Wyler William • USA
JEZEBEL see **JOYS OF JEZEBEL, THE** • 1970
JEZEBELS, THE • 1975 • Hill Jack • USA • SWITCHBLADE SISTERS ○ PLAYGIRL GANG
JEZERO • 1950 • Dukic Radivoje-Lola • YGS
JEZIORO BODENSKI • 1985 • Zaorski Janusz • PLN • BODENSEE
JEZIORO OSOBLIWOSCI • 1973 • Batory Jan • PLN • CURIO LAKE
JEZUS KRISZTUS HOROSZKOPJA • 1988 • Jancso Miklos • HNG • HOROSCOPE OF JESUS CHRIST, THE ○ JESUS CHRIST'S HOROSCOPE
JHANAK, JHANAK, PAYAL BAJE • 1955 • Shantaram Rajaram • IND • JANGLE, JANGLE, SOUND THE BELLS ○ GOD SHIVA DANCES
JHANSI-KI-RANI • 1953 • Modi Sohrab • IND • TIGER AND THE FLAME, THE ○ QUEEN OF JHANSI
JHOMAR CHOR • 1986 • Nayyar Sharif • PKS • BRIDE'S THIEF
JHUK GAYA AASMAN • 1968 • Tandon Lekh • IND • HEAVEN DESCENDS
JI-JINS ARRIVED, THE see **LLEGARON LOS JI-JINS** • 1971
JIA • 1957 • Chen Xihe, Ye Ming • CHN • FAMILY
JIATING SHENSHEN • 1989 • Shi Shujun • CHN
JIBAN MARAN • 1939 • *Sircar B. N. (P)* • IND
JIBAN MRITYU • 1967 • Nag Hiren, Roy Biswanath • IND • MATTER OF LIFE AND DEATH, A
JIBARITO RAFAEL, EL • 1966 • Soler Julian • MXC, PRC
JIBARO • 1985 • Torres Daniel • CUB • WILD DOG
JIBON THEKEY NEYA • 1969 • Raihan Zahir • BNG, PKS • GLIMPSES FROM LIFE
JIBUN NO ANA NO NAKADE • 1955 • Uchida Tomu • JPN • EACH WITHIN HIS SHELL
JIDAI NO KYOJI • 1932 • Inagaki Hiroshi • JPN • INSTRUCTION PERIOD
JIDAIYA NO NYOBO • 1983 • Morisaki Higashi • JPN • WIFE IN THE ANTIQUE SHOP, A
JIDOSHA DOROBO • 1964 • Wada Yoshinori • JPN • CAR THIEF
JIG IS UP, THE see **JEUX SONT FAIT, LES** • 1947
JIGGS AND MAGGIE IN COURT • 1948 • Beaudine William, Cline Eddie • USA
JIGGS AND MAGGIE IN JACKPOT JITTERS (UKN) see **JACKPOT JITTERS** • 1949
JIGGS AND MAGGIE IN SOCIETY • 1948 • Cline Eddie • USA
JIGGS AND MAGGIE OUT WEST • 1950 • Beaudine William • USA
JIGGS AND THE SOCIAL LION • 1920 • Morris Reggie • SHT • USA
JIGGS IN SOCIETY • 1920 • Morris Reggie • SHT • USA
JIGOKU • 1960 • Nakagawa Nobuo • JPN • SINNERS TO HELL ○ HELL
JIGOKU-HEN • 1969 • Toyoda Shiro • JPN • PORTRAIT OF HELL
JIGOKU NO AIBU • 1967 • Tsurumaki Jiro • JPN • HUG OF HELL
JIGOKU NO GOZEN NIJI • 1958 • Sekigawa Hideo • JPN • HORRIBLE MIDNIGHT
JIGOKU NO KIFUJIN • 1949 • Oda Motoyoshi • JPN • LADY FROM HELL
JIGOKU NO MAGARIKADO • 1959 • Kurahara Koreyoshi • JPN • TURNING IN HELL, A
JIGOKU NO MUSHI • 1938 • Inagaki Hiroshi • JPN • HELL'S WORM
JIGOKU NO YOJIMBO • 1955 • *Mikuni Rentaro* • JPN • BODYGUARD OF HELL
JIGOKUBANA • 1957 • Ito Daisuke • JPN • FLOWERS OF HELL
JIGOKUMON • 1953 • Kinugasa Teinosuke • JPN • GATE OF HELL (USA) ○ HELL'S GATE
JIGSAW • 1944 • Cass Henry • DCS • UKN
JIGSAW • 1949 • Markle Fletcher • USA • GUN MOLL
JIGSAW • 1962 • Guest Val • UKN
JIGSAW • 1968 • Goldstone James • USA
JIGSAW • 1971 • Graham William A. • TVM • USA • MAN ON THE MOVE
JIGSAW • 1979 • Pinoteau Claude • CND
JIGSAW • 1982 • Rose Robina • UKN
JIGSAW • 1989 • Gracie Marc • ASL
JIGSAW see **HOUSE ON CARROLL STREET, THE** • 1987
JIGSAW MAN, THE • 1982 • Young Terence • USA
JIGSAW MURDERS • 1989 • Mundhra Jag • USA
JIHI SHINCHO • 1927 • Mizoguchi Kenji • JPN • LIKE THE CHANGING HEART OF A BIRD ○ CUCKOO (USA)
JIKAN NO KYOFU see **DAI SANJI SEKAI TAISEN-YONJI-ICHI JIKAN NO KYOFU** • 1960
JIKEN • 1977 • Nomura Yoshitaro • JPN • ACCIDENT, THE
JILL • 1977 • Guevara Enrique • SPN
JILL AND THE OLD FIDDLE • 1915 • Plumb Hay • UKN
JILL JOHNSON • 1977 • Armatage Kay • CND
JILLALI 1 • 1965 • Kuypers Rik • BLG
JILT, THE • 1909 • Griffith D. W. • USA
JILT, THE • 1915 • Otto Henry • USA
JILT, THE • 1922 • Cummings Irving • USA • EXILED
JILTED • 1912 • *Snow Marguerite* • USA
JILTED • 1987 • Bennett Bill • ASL
JILTED IN JAIL • 1917 • Clements Roy • SHT • USA
JILTED JANET • 1918 • Ingraham Lloyd • USA
JILTED JOKER, THE • 1911 • *Essanay* • USA
JILTED WOMAN'S REVENGE, A • 1908 • Raymond Charles? • UKN
JIM • 1914 • Grandon Francis J. • *Selig* • USA
JIM • 1914 • Ricketts Thomas • *American* • USA
JIM • 1980 • Crombie Donald • DOC • ASL
JIM see **WHAT A WIFE LEARNED** • 1923
JIM ALL-ALONE • 1912 • Buckland Warwick? • UKN
JIM AND JOE • 1911 • Reid Hal • USA
JIM AND MUGGINS TOUR TORONTO! • 1978 • Kennedy Michael • CND
JIM AND THE PIRATES see **JIM OCH PIRATERNA BLOM** • 1987
JIM BENTLEY'S ADVENTURE • 1912 • *American* • USA
JIM BLUDSO • 1912 • *Mcgowan J. P.* • USA
JIM BLUDSO • 1917 • Lucas Wilfred, Browning Tod • USA
JIM BOUGNE BOXEUR • 1923 • Diamant-Berger Henri • FRN
JIM BRIDGER'S INDIAN BRIDE • 1910 • *Kalem* • USA
JIM BUCK see **PORTRAIT OF A HIT MAN** • 1978
JIM CAMERON'S WIFE • 1914 • Barker Reginald?, Hart William S.? • USA
JIM COMES TO JO'BURG • 1949 • SAF
JIM CORWEY IST TOT • 1921 • *Vernon Hedda* • FRG
JIM CROW • 1912 • Peguy Robert • FRN
JIM, DER MANN MIT DER NARBE see **MANN, DER SEINEN MORDER SUCHT, DER** • 1931
JIM GOLDEN POKER • 1970 • Narzisi Gianni • ITL
JIM GRIMSBY'S BOY • 1916 • Barker Reginald • USA
JIM HANVEY, DETECTIVE • 1937 • Rosen Phil • USA
JIM IL PRIMO • 1964 • Bergonzelli Sergio • ITL • KILLER'S CANYON (UKN) ○ LAST GUN, THE
JIM JAR JANITOR, A • 1928 • *Sennett Mack (P)* • SHT • USA
JIM JEFFRIES-JIM SHARKEY FIGHT • 1899 • *Bitzer Billy (Ph)* • USA
JIM LA HOULETTE • 1926 • Rimsky Nicolas, Lion Roger • FRN
JIM LA HOULETTE • 1935 • Berthomieu Andre • FRN • JIM LA HOULETTE, ROI DES VOLEURS
JIM LA HOULETTE, ROI DES VOLEURS see **JIM LA HOULETTE** • 1935
JIM OCH PIRATERNA BLOM • 1987 • Alfredson Hans • SWD • JIM AND THE PIRATES
JIM OF THE MOUNTED POLICE • 1911 • Fitzhamon Lewin • UKN
JIM PIERSALL STORY, THE see **FEAR STRIKES OUT** • 1957
JIM PLAYS BERKELEY • 1971 • Pilafian Peter • DOC • USA
JIM REGAN'S LAST RAID • 1914 • *Broncho* • USA
JIM SHVANTE -SVANETIS MARILI see **SOL SVANETII** • 1930
JIM SLOCUM NO.46393 • 1916 • Cummings Robert • SHT • USA
JIM STIRLING'S ARCHITECTURE • 1973 • Parks Ron • DOC • UKN
JIM TAKES A CHANCE • 1913 • *American* • USA
JIM, THE BURGLAR • 1913 • Hotaling Arthur D. • USA
JIM THE CONQUEROR • 1927 • Seitz George B. • USA
JIM THE FIREMAN • 1914 • Haldane Bert? • UKN
JIM THE MAN • 1967 • Katz Max • USA
JIM, THE MAN WITH THE SCAR see **MANN, DER SEINEN MORDER SUCHT, DER** • 1931
JIM, THE MULE BOY • 1911 • *Edison* • USA
JIM, THE PENMAN • 1915 • Ford Hugh • USA
JIM THE PENMAN • 1921 • Webb Kenneth • USA
JIM THE PENMAN • 1947 • Chisnell Frank • UKN
JIM THE RANCHMAN • 1910 • *Selig* • USA
JIM THE SCORPION • 1915 • Martinek H. O. • UKN
JIM THE SIGNALMAN • 1906 • Martin J. H.? • UKN
JIM THE WORLD'S GREATEST see **STORY OF A TEENAGER** • 1976
JIM THORPE -ALL AMERICAN • 1951 • Curtiz Michael • USA • MAN OF BRONZE (UKN)
JIM WEBB, SENATOR • 1914 • *Imp* • USA
JIM WEST, GAMBLER • 1915 • *Shumway L. C.* • USA
JIMI HENDRIX • 1973 • Head John, Weis Gary, Boyd Joe • DOC • USA
JIMINY CRICKETS • 1925 • Wallace Richard • SHT • USA
JIMMIE AS A HYPNOTIST • 1912 • *Gaumont* • FRN
JIMMIE HIGGINS • 1933 • Tasin Georgi
JIMMIE LUNCEFORD AND HIS DANCE ORCHESTRA • 1936 • Henabery Joseph • SHT • USA
JIMMIE PULLS THE TRIGGER • 1912 • FRN
JIMMIE THE PORTER • 1914 • MacGregor Norval • USA
JIMMIE'S DOGGONE LUCK • 1919 • *Strand* • SHT • USA
JIMMIE'S JOB • 1911 • *Kelly Paul* • USA
JIMMIE'S MILLIONS • 1925 • Hogan James P. • USA • JIMMY'S MILLIONS
JIMMY • 1913 • *Shirley Thomas* • USA
JIMMY • 1914 • Ince Thomas H., Spencer Richard V. • USA
JIMMY • 1915 • Oliver Guy • USA
JIMMY • 1916 • Bramble A. V., Stannard Eliot • UKN
JIMMY • 1984 • Kardash Virlana • USA
JIMMY see **PETIT JIMMY, LE** • 1930
JIMMY AND JOE AND THE WATER SPOUT • 1905 • Stow Percy • UKN
JIMMY AND SALLY • 1933 • Tinling James • USA
JIMMY B. & ANDRE • 1980 • Green Guy • TVM • USA
JIMMY BOY • 1935 • Baxter John • UKN
JIMMY BRUITEUR see **PETIT JIMMY, LE** • 1930
JIMMY DALE, ALIAS "THE GREY SEAL" • 1917 • Webster Harry Mcrae • SRL • USA
JIMMY DORSEY AND HIS ORCHESTRA • 1938 • French Lloyd • SHT • USA
JIMMY DORSEY AND HIS ORCHESTRA • 1940 • Roush Leslie • SHT • USA
JIMMY DORSEY AND HIS ORCHESTRA • 1948 • Cowan Will • SHT • USA
JIMMY DORSEY'S VARIETIES • 1952 • Cowan Will • SHT • USA
JIMMY, EIN SCHICKSAL VON MENSCH UND TIER • 1922 • Speyer Jaap • FRG
JIMMY FRESH WINNING A SQUAW • 1917 • *Cook Frank B.* • USA
JIMMY GETS THE PENNANT • 1917 • Moss Howard S. • ANM • USA
JIMMY GLOVER CONDUCTING HIS FAMOUS ORCHESTRA • 1900 • *Gibbos' Bio-Tableaux* • UKN
JIMMY HAYES AND MURIEL • 1914 • Mix Tom • USA
JIMMY KELLY AND THE KIDNAPPER • 1914 • *Joker* • USA
JIMMY LESTER, CONVICT AND GENTLEMAN • 1912 • Buckland Warwick? • UKN
JIMMY ON THE JOB • 1915 • MacMackin Archer • USA
JIMMY REARDON see **NIGHT IN THE LIFE OF JIMMY REARDON, A** • 1988
JIMMY SMITH TRIO • 1962 • Binder Steve • SHT • USA
JIMMY, THE BOY WONDER • 1966 • Lewis Herschell G. • USA
JIMMY THE C. • 1978 • Picker Jimmy • SHT • USA
JIMMY THE GENT • 1934 • Curtiz Michael • USA
JIMMY THE KID • 1983 • Nelson Gary • USA
JIMMY THE TIGER see **TZIMIS O TIGRIS** • 1966
JIMMY WITHERSPOON & PENNY BRIGHT • 1966-67 • Nelson Robert • SHT • USA
JIMMY'S DECEPTION • 1913 • *Powers* • USA
JIMMY'S FINISH • 1913 • *Kalem* • USA
JIMMY'S MILLIONS see **JIMMIE'S MILLIONS** • 1925
JIMMY'S MISFORTUNE • 1912 • *Pate Gwendolyn* • USA
JIMPUREN see **KAMIKAZE REN** • 1933
JIM'S ATONEMENT • 1912 • *Fischer Margarita* • USA
JIM'S ATONEMENT • 1913 • *Forde Eugenia* • USA
JIM'S COLLEGE DAYS • 1913 • *Majestic* • USA
JIM'S FOLKS • 1918 • Van Tuyle Bert • SHT • USA
JIM'S PARTNER • 1912 • *Pathe* • USA
JIM'S REWARD • 1913 • Melville Wilbert • USA
JIM'S VINDICATION • 1912 • Duncan William • USA
JIM'S VINDICATION • 1914 • Collins John H. • USA
JIM'S WIFE • 1912 • *Edison* • USA
JIMSON JOINS THE ANARCHISTS • 1911 • Rains Fred • UKN
JIMSON JOINS THE PIECANS • 1911 • Rains Fred • UKN
JINANBO KARASU • 1955 • Hirozu Mitsuo • JPN • JINANBOU GARASU ○ SECOND SON CROW
JINANBOU GARASU see **JINANBO KARASU** • 1955
JINCHOGE • 1966 • Chiba Yasuki • JPN • DAPHNE
JINETE, EL • 1953 • Orona Vicente • MXC
JINETE DE LA DIVINA PROVIDENCIA, EL • 1989 • Blancarte Oscar • MXC • HORSEMAN OF DIVINE PROVIDENCE, THE
JINETE ENMASCARADO, EL • 1960 • Munoz Manuel • MXC
JINETE FANTASMA, EL • 1946 • Portas Rafael E. • MXC
JINETE FANTASMA, EL see **PISTOLERO FANTASMA, EL** • 1967
JINETE JUSTICIERO EN RETANDO A LA MUERTE, EL • 1965 • Cardona Rene • MXC
JINETE NEGRO, EL • 1958 • Urueta Chano • MXC
JINETE NEGRO, EL • 1960 • Gonzalez Rogelio A. • MXC
JINETE SIN CABEZA, EL • 1956 • Urueta Chano • MXC • HEADLESS RIDER, THE (USA)
JINETE SOLITARIO, EL • 1958 • Baledon Rafael • MXC
JINETE SOLITARIO EN EL VALLE DE LOS BUITRES, EL • 1958 • Baledon Rafael • MXC
JINETE SOLITARIO EN EL VALLE DE LOS DESAPARECIDOS, EL • 1958 • Baledon Rafael • MXC
JINETES DE LA BRUJA, LOS • 1965 • Orona Vicente • MXC • EN EL VIEJO GUANAJUATO ○ RIDERS OF THE WITCH, THE ○ WITCH'S RIDERS, THE ○ BEWITCHED RIDERS, THE
JINETES DE LA LLANURA • 1964 • Mariscal Alberto • MXC
JINETES DEL TERROR, LOS (SPN) see **TERRORE DEI MANTELLI ROSSI, IL** • 1963
JING • 1988 • Li Yalin • CHN • WELL, THE
JINGCHA GUSHI see **POLICE STORY** • 1986
JINGI NAKI TATAKAI • 1972 • Fukasaku Kinji • JPN • YAKUZA PAPERS, THE
JINGI NAKI TATAKAI, CHOJO SAKUSEN • 1973 • Fukasaku Kinji • JPN • FIGHT BETWEEN YAKUZA FAMILIES
JINGLE BELLES • 1941 • Le Borg Reginald • SHT • USA
JINGLE BELLS • 1927 • Lantz Walter • ANS • USA
JINGLE BELLS • 1931 • *Terry Paul/ Moser Frank (P)* • ANS • USA
JINGLE JANGLE JINGLE • 1947 • Hopper Jerry • SHT • USA
JINGY • 1968 • Reyes Efren • PHL
JINKEE • 1969 • Torres Mar S. • PHL
JINKO EISEN TO JINRUI NO HAMETSU • 1958 • Ishii Teruo • JPN • SPACESHIP OF HUMAN DESTRUCTION ○ SUPER GIANT 5 (USA)
JINKS AND THE BARBER • 1914 • Murphy J. A. • USA
JINKS, THE GROUCH • 1909 • *Lubin* • USA
JINKYO • 1924 • Mizoguchi Kenji • JPN • THIS DUSTY WORLD (USA) ○ WORLD DOWN HERE, THE ○ DUSTY WORLD ○ DUSTY PLACE ○ WORLD DOWN THERE, THE
JINRUIGAKU NYUMON • 1966 • Imamura Shohei • JPN • PORNOGRAPHERS: INTRODUCTION TO ANTHROPOLY, THE ○ AMORISTS, THE ○ PORNOGRAPHER, THE
JINSEI GEKIJO • 1936 • Uchida Tomu • JPN • THEATRE OF LIFE
JINSEI GEKIJO • 1952 • Saburi Shin • JPN • THEATRE OF LIFE
JINSEI GEKIJO • 1983 • Fukasaku Kinji • JPN • HUMAN THEATRE
JINSEI GEKIJO -HISHAKAKU TO KIRATSUNE • 1968 • Uchida Tomu • JPN • HISHAKAKU TO KIRATSUNE ○ KAKU AND TSUNE
JINSEI GEKIJO SEISHUN-HEN • 1958 • Sugie Toshio • JPN • THEATRE OF LIFE
JINSEI NO AI • 1923 • Ushihara Kiyohiko • JPN • LOVE OF LIFE
JINSEI NO ONIMOTSU • 1935 • Gosho Heinosuke • JPN • BURDEN OF LIFE
JINSEI O MITSUMETE • 1923 • Kinugasa Teinosuke • JPN
JINSEI TOMBOGAERI • 1946 • Imai Tadashi • JPN • LIFE IS LIKE A SOMERSAULT ○ SOMERSAULT OF LIFE
JINX • 1919 • Schertzinger Victor • USA
JINX JOINS THE TEMPERANCE CLUB • 1911 • Sennett Mack • USA
JINX JUMPER, THE • 1917 • Dwan Allan (Spv) • USA

JINX MONEY • 1948 • Beaudine William • USA
JINX ON JENKS, THE • 1915 • Dillon Eddie • USA
JINXED • 1982 • Siegel Don • USA • STRYKE AND HYDE ○ HOT STREAK
JINX'S BIRTHDAY PARTY • 1912 • Henderson Dell • USA
JINY VZDUCH • 1939 • Fric Martin • CZC • FRESH AIR ○ ANOTHER AIR
JINYE XINGGUANG CANLAN • 1988 • Hsu An-Hua • HKG
JIPNYUM • 1977 • Choi In-Hyon • KOR • CONCENTRATION
J'IRAI COMME UN CHEVAL FOU • 1973 • Arrabal Fernando • FRN • I WILL GO LIKE A WILD HORSE
J'IRAI CRACHER SUR VOS TOMBES • 1959 • Gast Michel • FRN • I SPIT ON YOUR GRAVE (USA)
JIRAIKA GUMI • 1928 • Ikeda Tomiyasu • JPN
JIRI TRNKA'S PUPPETS see **LOUTKY JIRIHO TRNKY** • 1955
JIRINA SEJBALOVA • 1961 • Makovec Milos • CZC
JIRO MONOGATARI • 1955 • Shimizu Hiroshi • JPN
JIRO MONOGATARI • 1988 • Morikawa Tokihisa • JPN • STORY OF JIRO, THE
JIROCHI THE CHIVALROUS see **ZOKU JIROCHI FUJI** • 1960
JIROCHO'S TRAVELS see **NAGURI KOMI KOSHUJI** • 1953
JIROKICHI GOSHI • 1951 • Ito Daisuke • JPN
JIRUBA TETSU • 1950 • Kosugi Isamu • JPN • TETSU JIRUBA
JIS DESH MEN GANGA BEHIT • 1961 • *Kapoor Raj (P)* • IND • WHERE THE GANGES FLOWS
JISHIN RETTO • 1980 • Ohmori Kenjiro • JPN • EARTHQUAKE 7.9 ○ MEGAFORCE 7.9
JITNEY DRIVER'S ROMANCE, THE • 1916 • Curtis Allen • SHT • USA
JITNEY ELOPEMENT, A • 1915 • Chaplin Charles • USA • MARRIED IN HASTE
JITNEY JACK AND GASOLINA • 1916 • *Powers* • SHT • USA
JITNEY SUBMARINE, THE • 1915 • *Atla* • USA
JITTERBUG FOLLIES • 1939 • Gross Milt • ANS • USA
JITTERBUG JIVE • 1950 • Tytla Bill • ANS • USA
JITTERBUG KNIGHTS • 1939 • Marcus Sid • ANS • USA
JITTERBUGS • 1943 • St. Clair Malcolm • USA
JITTERS, THE • 1938 • Goodwins Leslie • SHT • USA
JITTERS THE BUTLER • 1932 • Sandrich Mark • SHT • USA
JITTERUMBA • 1947 • Cowan Will • SHT • USA
JITTERY JESTER • 1958 • Smith Paul J. • ANS • USA
JIVARO • 1954 • Ludwig Edward • USA • LOST TREASURE OF THE AMAZON (UKN)
JIVE • 1979 • Downey Robert • USA
JIVE BUSTERS • 1944 • Collins Lewis D. • SHT • USA
JIVE JUNCTION • 1943 • Ulmer Edgar G. • USA • SWING HIGH (UKN)
JIVE TURKEY • 1976 • Brame Bill • USA
JIVEASP • 1975 • Kooris Richard • DOC • USA
JIVIN' AND JAMMIN' • 1948 • *Pattinson-Knight C. (P)* • SHT • UKN
JIVIN' IN BE BOP • 1947 • Williams Spencer?, Anderson Leonard? • USA
JIVIN' JAM SESSION • 1942 • Le Borg Reginald • SHT • USA
JIWA REMAJA • 1975 • Sulong Jamil • MLY • RESTLESS YOUTH
JIWHALA • 1968 • Gabale Ram • IND
JIYAGAOKA FUJIN • 1960 • Saeki Kozo • JPN
JIYU GAKKU • 1951 • Shibuya Minoru, Yoshimura Kozaburo • JPN • SCHOOL OF FREEDOM ○ FREEDOM SCHOOL
JIZDNI HLIDKA • 1936 • Binovec Vaclav • CZC • MOUNTED PATROL, THE
JIZN I SMERT Q.S. POUCHKINA • 1910 • Goncharov Vasili M. • USS • LIFE AND DEATH OF PUSHKIN, THE
J'ME MARIE, J'ME MARIE PAS • 1973 • Dansereau Mireille • DOC • CND
JMENUJI SE FIFINKA • 1953 • *Stallich Jan (Ph)* • SHT • CZC
JO • 1971 • Girault Jean • FRN • GAZEBO, THE ○ JOE -THE BUSY BODY
JO AS A HAZNAL • 1935 • Zsoldos Andor, Schulz Fritz • FATHER KNOWS BEST (USA)
JO HIBBARD'S CLAIM • 1913 • Barker Reginald? • USA
JO JO DANCER, YOUR LIFE IS CALLING • 1986 • Pryor Richard • USA
JO LA ROMANCE • 1948 • Grangier Gilles • FRN • CELLE QUE J'AIME
JO, PAPA • 1975 • de Arminan Jaime • JPN • BLOODY HELL, DAD! ○ IJO, PAPA!
JO THE CROSSING SWEEPER • 1910 • *Walturdaw* • UKN
JO THE CROSSING SWEEPER • 1918 • Butler Alexander • UKN
JO, THE WANDERER'S BOY • 1912 • Buckland Warwick? • UKN
JOACHIM, PUT IT IN THE MACHINE see **JACHYME HOD TO DO STROJE** • 1973
JOACHIM'S DICTIONARY (UKN) see **DICTIONNAIRE DE JOACHIM, LE** • 1965
JOAN AT THE STAKE see **GIOVANNA D'ARCO AL ROGO** • 1954
JOAN LUI: BUT ONE DAY I AM COMING THERE BY MONDAY see **JOAN LUI: MA UN GIORNO NEL PAESE ARRIVO IO DI LUNEDI'** • 1985
JOAN LUI: MA UN GIORNO NEL PAESE ARRIVO IO DI LUNEDI' • 1985 • Celentano Adriano • ITL • JOAN LUI: BUT ONE DAY I AM COMING THERE BY MONDAY
JOAN MEDFORD IS MISSING (UKN) see **HOUSE OF HORRORS** • 1946
JOAN MIRO • 1948 • Aurel Jean • SHT • FRN
JOAN OF ARC • 1948 • Fleming Victor • USA
JOAN OF ARC • Heliczer Piero • USA
JOAN OF ARC see **GIOVANNA D'ARCO** • 1908
JOAN OF ARC see **MADCHEN JOHANNA, DAS** • 1935
JOAN OF ARC AT THE STAKE see **GIOVANNA D'ARCO AL ROGO** • 1954
JOAN OF ARC OF MONGOLIA • 1989 • Ottinger Ulrike • FRG
JOAN OF ARC (USA) see **JEANNE D'ARC** • 1900
JOAN OF ARC (USA) see **JEANNE D'ARC** • 1908
JOAN OF FLANDERS see **WAR BRIDES** • 1916
JOAN OF OZARK see **JOAN OF THE OZARKS** • 1942
JOAN OF PARIS • 1942 • Stevenson Robert • USA
JOAN OF PLATTSBURG • 1918 • Tucker George Loane, Humphrey William • USA
JOAN OF THE ANGELS (USA) see **MATKA JOANNA OD ANIOLOW** • 1961
JOAN OF THE CATTLELANDS see **STRAIGHT SHOOTING** • 1917
JOAN OF THE OZARKS • 1942 • Santley Joseph • USA • QUEEN OF SPIES (UKN) ○ JOAN OF OZARK
JOAN OF THE WOODS • 1918 • Vale Travers • USA
JOAN THE FRENCHWOMAN see **JOANA A FRANCESA** • 1973
JOAN THE WOMAN • 1916 • De Mille Cecil B. • USA
JOAN (UKN) see **CARRY IT ON** • 1970
JOANA A FRANCESA • 1973 • Diegues Carlos • BRZ • JOANNA FRANCESA (USA) ○ JEAN LA FRANCAISE ○ JOAN THE FRENCHWOMAN
JOANNA • 1925 • Carewe Edwin • USA
JOANNA • 1968 • Sarne Mike • UKN
JOANNA • 1969 • SAF
JOANNA FRANCESA (USA) see **JOANA A FRANCESA** • 1973
JOAO see **JOAO EN HET MES** • 1972
JOAO AND THE KNIFE see **JOAO EN HET MES** • 1972
JOAO EN HET MES • 1972 • Sluizer George • BRZ, BLG • JOAO AND THE KNIFE ○ JOAO
JOAO PATAO • 1940 • do Canto Jorge Brum • PRT
JOAQUIN MURIETA • 1970 • Bellamy Earl • TVM • USA
JOAQUIN MURRIETA • 1938 • Wilcox Fred M. • SHT • USA
JOAQUIN MURRIETA see **MURIETA** • 1965
JOB, A see **BAARA** • 1979
JOB, THE see **POSTO, IL** • 1961
JOB, THE see **STOTEN** • 1961
JOB A PLEIN TEMPS, UNE • 1977 • Melancon Andre • SHT • CND
JOB AND THE GIRL, THE • 1911 • *American* • USA
JOB AND THE JEWELS, THE • 1915 • Mackley Arthur • USA
JOB FOR A GOB, A • 1955 • Kneitel Seymour • ANS • USA
JOB FOR LIFE, A • 1917 • *Dudley Charles* • USA
JOB IN A MILLION • 1937 • Cherry Evelyn Spice • DOC • UKN
JOB LAZADASA • 1983 • Gyongyossy Imre, Kabay Barna • HNG • REVOLT OF JOB, THE
JOBARD A TUE SA BELLE-MERE • 1911 • Cohl Emile • ANS • FRN
JOBARD AMOUREUX TIMIDE • 1911 • Cohl Emile • ANS • FRN
JOBARD CHANGE DE BONNE • 1911 • Cohl Emile • ANS • FRN
JOBARD CHAUFFEUR see **JOBARD FIANCE PAR INTERIM** • 1911
JOBARD EST DEMANDE EN MARIAGE • 1911 • Cohl Emile • ANS • FRN
JOBARD FIANCE PAR INTERIM • 1911 • Cohl Emile • ANS • FRN • JOBARD CHAUFFEUR
JOBARD GARCON DE RECETTES • 1911 • Cohl Emile • ANS • FRN
JOBARD NE PEUT PAS RIRE • 1911 • Cohl Emile • ANS • FRN
JOBARD NE PEUT PAS VOIS LES FEMMES TRAVAILLER • 1911 • Cohl Emile • ANS • FRN
JOBARD PORTEFAIX PAR AMOUR • 1911 • Cohl Emile • ANS • FRN
JOBBE-KHANEH • 1975 • Farmanara Bahman • IRN • MEMORY ROOM
JOBLESS SAMURAI see **RONINGAI** • 1928
JOBLOT RECRUITS, THE • 1914 • *Essanay* • USA
JOBMAN • 1989 • Roodt Darrell • SAF
JOBS AND MEN see **DELA Y LYUDI** • 1932
JOBSON'S LUCK • 1913 • Martinek H. O. • UKN
JOCASTE • 1924 • Ravel Gaston
JOCELYN • 1922 • Poirier Leon • FRN
JOCELYN • 1933 • Guerlais Pierre • FRN
JOCELYN • 1951 • de Casembroot Jacques • FRN
JOCHI NO SHIGEMI • 1968 • Ogawa Kinya • JPN • BUSH OF LOVE FOOLERY, A
JOCHUKKO • 1955 • Tasaka Tomotaka • JPN • MAID'S KID, THE
JOCK PETERSEN (USA) see **PETERSEN** • 1974
JOCKEY, THE • 1914 • Lyndhurst F. L. • UKN
JOCKEY, THE • 1919 • Kenton Erle C. • USA
JOCKEY PAR AMOUR see **MAX JOCKEY PAR AMOUR** • 1912
JOCKO • 1982 • Donaldson Roger • SHS • NZL
JOCKO MUSICIEN • 1903 • Blache Alice • FRN
JOCKS • 1987 • Carver Steve • USA • ROAD TRIP
JOCOND, LE • 1914 • Feuillade Louis • FRN
JOCONDE, LA • 1958 • Gruel Henri • SHT • FRN
JOCONDES, LES • 1982 • Pillault Jean-Daniel • FRN
JOCULAR WINDS • 1913 • Dwan Allan • USA
JOCULAR WINDS OF FATE, THE • 1912 • Young James • USA
JODAI NO CHOKOKU • 1950 • Mizuki • SHT • JPN • COMICAL SCULPTURE
JODELN IS KA SUND • 1974 • Lommel Ulli • FRG
JODY • Tucker Glenn • USA
JOE • 1924 • Smith Beaumont • ASL
JOE • 1970 • Avildsen John G. • USA • GAP, THE
JOE ALBANY.. A JAZZ LIFE • 1980 • Langer Carole • DOC • USA
JOE AND ETHEL TURP CALL ON THE PRESIDENT • 1939 • Sinclair Robert B. • USA • CALL ON THE PRESIDENT, A
JOE AND MAXI • 1977 • Gold Joel, Cohen Maxi • USA
JOE AND PETUNIA • 1968 • Spargo Nicholas • ANS • UKN
JOE AND ROSIE • 1975 • Lavut Martin • DOC • CND
JOE AND ROXY • 1957 • Haldane Don • SHT • CND
JOE BATTLE see **BRANNIGAN** • 1975
JOE BOKO • 1915-16 • *Carlson Wallace A./ Bray J.r. (P)* • ASS • USA
JOE BULLET • 1974 • SAF
JOE BUTTERFLY • 1957 • Hibbs Jesse • USA
JOE CALIGULA • 1966 • Benazeraf Jose • FRN
JOE, CERCATI UN POSTO PER MORIRE • 1968 • Carnimeo Giuliano • ITL • JOE.. FIND A PLACE TO DIE (UKN) ○ FIND A PLACE TO DIE ○ JOE.. LOOK FOR A PLACE TO DIE ○ CERCATI UN POSTO PER MORIRE
JOE COCKER -MAD DOGS AND ENGLISHMEN see **MAD DOGS AND ENGLISHMEN** • 1971
JOE DAKOTA • 1957 • Bartlett Richard • USA
JOE DANCER see **BIG BLACK PILL, THE** • 1981
JOE DANCER VOL.1 see **BIG BLACK PILL, THE** • 1981
JOE DEBBS • 1919 • *Lang Fritz* • SER • FRG
JOE DEXTER see **OESTE NEVADA JOE** • 1965
JOE DOMINO • 1968 • de Jesus Ding M. • PHL
JOE DOPE HELPS CAUSE INFLATION • 1944 • MacKay Jim • ANS • CND
JOE E MARGHERITO see **ARRIVANO JOE E MARGHERITO** • 1974
JOE EGG see **DAY IN THE DEATH OF JOE EGG, A** • 1972
JOE, EL IMPLACABLE (SPN) see **NAVAJO JOE** • 1966
JOE ET LA SORCIERE TSETSEBOSSE • Image Jean • ANM • FRN
JOE.. FIND A PLACE TO DIE (UKN) see **JOE, CERCATI UN POSTO PER MORIRE** • 1968
JOE GLOW, THE FIREFLY • 1941 • Jones Charles M. • ANS • USA
JOE HARKIN'S WARD • 1915 • *Farrington Rene* • USA
JOE HILL • 1971 • Widerberg Bo • SWD, USA • BALLAD OF JOE HILL, THE
JOE IL RUSSO • 1936 • Matarazzo Raffaello • ITL
JOE KIDD • 1972 • Sturges John • USA
JOE LEAHY'S NEIGHBOURS • 1988 • Connolly Bob, Anderson Robyn • DOC • ASL
JOE L'IMPLACABILE • 1967 • Margheriti Antonio • ITL • DINAMITE JOE
JOE.. LOOK FOR A PLACE TO DIE see **JOE, CERCATI UN POSTO PER MORIRE** • 1968
JOE LOUIS STORY, THE • 1953 • Gordon Robert • USA
JOE MACBETH • 1955 • Hughes Ken • UKN, USA
JOE MARTIN TURNS THEM LOOSE • 1915 • De Rosselli Rex, Bourgeois Paul • USA
JOE MURGATROYD SAYS • 1929 • Aylott Dave, Symmons E. F. • SHT • UKN
JOE NAVIDAD • 1966 • Pink Sidney • SPN, USA • CHRISTMAS KID, THE (USA)
JOE O TROMEROS • 1955 • Dimopoulos Dinos • GRC • JOE THE TERRIBLE
JOE PALOOKA see **PALOOKA** • 1934
JOE PALOOKA, CHAMP • 1946 • Le Borg Reginald • USA
JOE PALOOKA IN FIGHTING MAD see **FIGHTING MAD** • 1948
JOE PALOOKA IN HUMPHREY TAKES A CHANCE • 1950 • Yarbrough Jean • USA • HUMPHREY TAKES A CHANCE (UKN)
JOE PALOOKA IN THE BIG FIGHT • 1949 • Endfield Cy • USA • BIG FIGHT, THE
JOE PALOOKA IN THE COUNTERPUNCH • 1949 • Le Borg Reginald • USA
JOE PALOOKA IN THE KNOCKOUT • 1947 • Le Borg Reginald • USA
JOE PALOOKA IN THE SQUARED CIRCLE • 1950 • Le Borg Reginald • USA • SQUARED CIRCLE, THE (UKN)
JOE PALOOKA IN TRIPLE CROSS • 1951 • Le Borg Reginald • USA • TRIPLE CROSS, THE (UKN)
JOE PALOOKA IN WINNER TAKE ALL • 1948 • Le Borg Reginald • USA • WINNER TAKE ALL (UKN)
JOE PALOOKA MEETS HUMPHREY • 1950 • Yarbrough Jean • USA
JOE PANTHER • 1976 • Krasny Paul • USA
JOE PETIT BOUM-BOUM • 1972 • Image Jean • ANM • FRN
JOE PRING • 1989 • Salvador Augusto • PHL
JOE REICHMAN AND HIS ORCHESTRA • 1940 • Negulesco Jean • SHT • USA
JOE SLAUGHTER • 1983 • SAF
JOE SMITH, AMERICAN • 1942 • Thorpe Richard • USA • HIGHWAY TO FREEDOM (UKN)
JOE -THE BUSY BODY see **JO** • 1971
JOE THE PIRATE • 1912 • *Imp* • USA
JOE THE TERRIBLE see **JOE O TROMEROS** • 1955
JOE THEISS SAXOTETTE • 1929 • *Bsfp* • SHT • UKN • MUSICAL MEDLEY NO.1
JOE VALACHI: A SEGRETI DI COSA NOSTRA see **COSA NOSTRA** • 1972
JOE VALACHI (ITL) see **COSA NOSTRA** • 1972
JOE VALLI AND CHARLIE ALBERT IN LONG LOST SON • 1932 • Hanna Pat • SHT • ASL
JOE VERSUS THE VOLCANO • 1990 • Shanley John Patrick • USA
JOEMBER • 1970 • Macskassy Gyula, Varnai Gyorgy • ANS • HNG • ASSISTANCE
JOEN • 1947 • Shibuya Minoru • JPN • PASSION FIRE
JOEN • 1959 • Kinugasa Teinosuke • JPN • TORMENTED FLAME ○ AFFAIR, THE
JOEN • 1967 • Yoshida Yoshishige • JPN • AFFAIR, THE
JOEN NO CHIMATA • 1922 • Mizoguchi Kenji • JPN • HARBOUR OF DESIRE ○ CITY OF DESIRE ○ TOWN OF FIRE
JOEN NO HATOBA • 1951 • *Kyo Machiko* • JPN • PIER OF PASSION
JOEN NO SABAKU • 1967 • Matsubara Jiro • JPN • DESERT OF DESIRE
JOE'S BED-STUDY BARBER SHOP: WE CUT HEADS • 1983 • Lee Spike • USA
JOE'S DEVOTION • 1915 • *Navajo* • USA
JOE'S LUNCHEON WAGON • 1934 • *Terry Paul/ Moser Frank (P)* • ANS • USA
JOE'S PARTNER, BILL • 1915 • French Charles K. • USA
JOE'S RETRIBUTION • 1914 • *Premier* • USA
JOE'S REWARD • 1912 • *Dion Hector* • USA
JOE'S WEDDING • 1909 • *Urban-Eclipse* • USA
JOEY • 1975 • *Gibson Brian (P)* • UKN
JOEY • 1986 • Ellison Joseph • USA
JOEY see **MAKING CONTACT** • 1986
JOEY AND HIS TROMBONE • 1915 • Castle James W. • USA
JOEY AND SAM • 1965 • Benson Roy • UKN
JOEY BOY • 1965 • Launder Frank • UKN
JOEY KNOWS A VILLAIN • 1960 • Richards James • SHT • UKN
JOEY LEADS THE WAY • 1960 • Richards James • SHT • UKN
JOEY THE SHOWMAN • 1916 • Evans Joe • SHT • UKN
JOEY WALKS IN HIS SLEEP • 1916 • Evans Joe • SHT • UKN
JOEY'S 21ST BIRTHDAY • 1915 • Evans Joe • UKN
JOEY'S APACHE MANIA • 1916 • Evans Joe • SHT • UKN
JOEY'S AUNT • 1916 • Evans Joe • SHT • UKN
JOEY'S AUTOMATIC FURNITURE • 1916 • Evans Joe • SHT • UKN
JOEY'S BLACK DEFEAT • 1916 • Evans Joe • SHT • UKN
JOEY'S DREAM • 1916 • Evans Joe • SHT • USA

JOEY'S HIGH JINKS • 1916 • Evans Joe • SHT • UKN
JOEY'S LIAR METER • 1916 • Evans Joe • SHT • UKN
JOEY'S NIGHT ESCAPADE • 1916 • Evans Joe • SHT • UKN
JOEY'S NO ASS • 1960 • Richards James • SHT • UKN
JOEY'S PERMIT • 1916 • Evans Joe • SHT • UKN
JOEY'S PLUCK • 1916 • Evans Joe • SHT • UKN
JOFROI • 1933 • Pagnol Marcel • FRN • WAYS OF LOVE (USA)
JOFU TO JOFU • 1967 • Watanabe Mamoru • JPN • FANCY MAN AND A FANCY WOMAN, A
JOG ALONG • 1946 • Gould Dave • SHT • USA
JOGAKUSEI GERILLA • 1970 • Adachi Masao • JPN • HIGH SCHOOL GIRL'S REVOLT, THE
JOGASHIMA • 1924 • Ito Daisuke • JPN
JOGASHIMA NO AME • 1950 • Tanaka Shigeo • JPN • JOUGASAKI NO AME ○ JOUGASAKI'S RAIN
JOGHI, DER see **YOGHI, DER** • 1916
JOGO DE MAO, O • 1984 • Rutler Monique • PRT
JOGO PERIGOSO see **JUEGO PELIGROSO** • 1966
JOGOKU NO HANAMICHI • 1960 • Makino Masahiro • JPN
JOG'S TROT • 1976 • Papadopoulos John • SHT • ASL
JOH-OU BACHI see **JOOBACHI** • 1978
JOHAN • 1921 • Stiller Mauritz, Nordeen Arthur • SWD
JOHAN AT SNIPPEN see **JOHAN PA SNIPPEN** • 1956
JOHAN AT SNIPPEN WINS THE GAME see **JOHAN PA SNIPPEN TAR HEM SPELET** • 1957
JOHAN, CARNET INTIME HOMOSEXUEL • 1976 • Vallois Philippe • FRN
JOHAN EKBERG • 1964 • Troell Jan • DCS • SWD
JOHAN PA SNIPPEN • 1956 • Frisk Ragnar • SWD • JOHAN AT SNIPPEN
JOHAN PA SNIPPEN TAR HEM SPELET • 1957 • Jarrel Bengt • SWD • JOHAN AT SNIPPEN WINS THE GAME
JOHAN SEBASTIAN BACH • 1961 • Wrestler Philip • UKN
JOHAN STRAUSS see **WALTZ KING, THE** • 1963
JOHAN ULFSTJERNA • 1923 • Brunius John W. • SWD • HUMAN DESTINIES
JOHAN ULFSTJERNA • 1936 • Edgren Gustaf • SWD
JOHANES DOKTOR FAUST • 1958 • Radok Emil • ANS • CZC • FAUST
JOHANN • 1943 • Stemmle R. A. • FRG
JOHANN BAPTISTE LINGG • 1920 • Teuber Arthur • FRG
JOHANN MOUSE • 1953 • Hanna William, Barbera Joseph • ANS • USA
JOHANN SEBASTIAN BACH: FANTASIA G-MOLL • 1965 • Svankmajer Jan • ANM • CZC • JOHANN SEBASTIAN BACH -FANTASY IN G MINOR ○ J.S. BACH -FANTASY IN G MINOR ○ BACH'S FANTASY IN G MINOR ○ FANTASY IN G MINOR -JOHANN SEBASTIAN BACH
JOHANN SEBASTIAN BACH -FANTASY IN G MINOR see **JOHANN SEBASTIAN BACH: FANTASIA G-MOLL** • 1965
JOHANN STRAUSS -DER KONIG OHNE KRONE • 1987 • Antel Franz • AUS, GDR, FRG • JOHANN STRAUSS -THE KING WITHOUT A CROWN
JOHANN STRAUSS, K. UND K. HOFBALLMUSIKDIREKTOR • 1932 • Wiene Conrad • FRG • KAISER WALZER ○ VIENNESE WALTZ
JOHANN STRAUSS -THE KING WITHOUT A CROWN see **JOHANN STRAUSS -DER KONIG OHNE KRONE** • 1987
JOHANN THE COFFIN MAKER • 1928 • Florey Robert • USA
JOHANNA ENLISTS • 1918 • Taylor William D. • USA
JOHANNA, THE BARBARIAN • 1914 • Baker George D. • USA
JOHANNAS TRAUM • 1975 • Schroeter Werner • FRG
JOHANNES FILS DE JOHANNES • 1919 • Hugon Andre • FRN
JOHANNES GOTH • 1920 • Gerhardt Karl • FRG
JOHANNES' HEMMELIGHED • 1986 • Sandgren Ake • DNM • JOHN'S SECRET
JOHANNES JORGENSEN I ASSISSI • 1950 • Roos Jorgen • DOC • DNM
JOHANNES JORGENSEN I SVENDBORG • 1954 • Roos Jorgen • DOC • DNM
JOHANNES KEPLER • 1975 • Vogel Frank • GDR
JOHANNES LARSEN • 1957 • Roos Jorgen • DOC • DNM
JOHANNES UND DIE 13 SCHONHEITSKONIGINNEN • 1951 • Stoger Alfred • FRG
JOHANNES V. JENSEN • 1947 • Roos Jorgen • DOC • DNM
JOHANNISFEUER • 1939 • Rabenalt Arthur M. • FRG • ST. JOHN'S FIRE (USA)
JOHANNISNACHT • 1918 • Attenberger Toni • FRG
JOHANNISNACHT • 1933 • Reiber Willy • FRG
JOHANNISNACHT • 1956 • Reinl Harald • FRG
JOHANNISTRAUM • 1919 • Justitz Emil • FRG
JOHANSSON AND VESTMAN see **JOHANSSON OCH VESTMAN** • 1946
JOHANSSON OCH VESTMAN • 1946 • Molander Olof • SWD • JOHANSSON AND VESTMAN
JOHAR IN BOMBAY • 1967 • Sohni Shantilal • IND
JOHN AND JULIE • 1955 • Fairchild William • UKN
JOHN AND MARSHA • Weiner Peter • ANS • USA
JOHN AND MARY • 1969 • Yates Peter • USA
JOHN AND MARY see **SAILOR TAKES A WIFE, THE** • 1945
JOHN AND THE MAGIC MUSIC MAN • 1977 • Scott Ciarin • SHT • UKN
JOHN AND THE MISSUS • 1987 • Pinsent Gordon • CND
JOHN AND YOKO: A LOVE STORY • 1985 • Stern Sandor • TVM • USA • JOHN AND YOKO: THE COMPLETE STORY
JOHN AND YOKO: THE COMPLETE STORY see **JOHN AND YOKO: A LOVE STORY** • 1985
JOHN ARTHUR'S TRUST • 1912 • *Johnson Arthur* • USA
JOHN BARLEYCORN • 1914 • Bosworth Hobart • USA
JOHN BATES' SECRET • 1917 • *Bush Pauline* • SHT • USA
JOHN BAXTER'S WARD • 1911 • *Powers* • USA
JOHN BOUSALL OF THE U.S. SECRET SERVICE • 1913 • Martin E. A. • USA
JOHN BREWSTER'S WIFE • 1916 • *Cooke Ethyle* • SHT • USA
JOHN BROWN'S HEIR • 1911 • Porter Edwin S. • USA
JOHN BULL'S ANIMATED SKETCH-BOOK • 1916 • Dyer Anson • ANM • UKN
JOHN BULL'S FIRESIDE see **JOHN BULL'S HEARTH** • 1903
JOHN BULL'S HEARTH • 1903 • Smith G. A. • UKN • JOHN BULL'S FIRESIDE
JOHN BURNS OF GETTYSBURG • 1913 • *Buel Kenean* • USA
JOHN CAT • 1984 • Koenig Wolf • CND
JOHN CHILCOTE, M.P. see **MASQUERADER, THE** • 1922
JOHN CITIZEN • 1927 • Newman Widgey R. • UKN
JOHN COLEMAN'S KID • 1913 • *Leslie Rolf* • UKN
JOHN COLTER'S ESCAPE • 1912 • *Selig* • USA
JOHN COLTRANE QUARTET, THE • 1964 • Moore Richard • SHT • USA
JOHN DOE, DYNAMITE (UKN) see **MEET JOHN DOE** • 1941
JOHN DOUGH AND THE CHERUB • 1910 • *Selig* • USA
JOHN ERICSSON -SEGRAGEN VID HAMPTON ROADS • 1937 • Edgren Gustaf • SWD • JOHN ERICSSON -THE VICTOR AT HAMPTON ROADS
JOHN ERICSSON -THE VICTOR AT HAMPTON ROADS see **JOHN ERICSSON -SEGRAGEN VID HAMPTON ROADS** • 1937
JOHN ERMINE OF THE YELLOWSTONE • 1917 • Ford Francis • USA • JOHN ERMINE OF YELLOWSTONE
JOHN ERMINE OF YELLOWSTONE see **JOHN ERMINE OF THE YELLOWSTONE** • 1917
JOHN F. KENNEDY: YEARS OF LIGHTNING, DAYS OF DRUMS • 1966 • Herschensohn Bruce • USA • YEARS OF LIGHTNING, DAYS OF DRUMS
JOHN FORREST FINDS HIMSELF • 1920 • Edwards Henry • UKN
JOHN GILPIN • 1908 • Stow Percy • UKN
JOHN GILPIN • 1951 • Halas John • ANS • UKN
JOHN GILPIN'S RIDE • 1908 • Fitzhamon Lewin • UKN
JOHN GLAYDE'S HONOR • 1915 • Irving Henry George • USA
JOHN GLUECKSTADT • 1975 • Miehe Ulf • FRG
JOHN GOLDFARB, PLEASE COME HOME! • 1965 • Thompson J. Lee • USA
JOHN GRAHAM'S GOLD • 1910 • *Lubin* • USA
JOHN HALIFAX, GENTLEMAN • 1910 • Marston Theodore • USA
JOHN HALIFAX, GENTLEMAN • 1915 • Pearson George • UKN
JOHN HALIFAX, GENTLEMAN • 1938 • King George • UKN
JOHN HARDY'S INVENTION • 1910 • *Powers* • USA
JOHN HENRY AND THE INKY-POO • 1946 • Pal George • ANS • USA
JOHN HENRY CALLING • 1926 • Sanderson Challis, Newman Widgey R. • SER • UKN
JOHN HERIOT'S WIFE • 1920 • Doxat-Pratt B. E., Binger Maurits H. • UKN
JOHN HIRSCH: A PORTRAIT OF A MAN AND A THEATRE • 1965 • Ransen Mort • DOC • CND
JOHN IL BASTARDO see **JOHNNY IL BASTARDO** • 1967
JOHN KIM BELL • 1984 • Azzopardi Anthony • MTV • CND
JOHN LAIR'S RENFRO VALLEY BARN DANCE • 1966 • Johnson William R. • USA • RENFREW VALLEY BARN DANCE
JOHN LAW AND THE MISSISSIPPI BUBBLE • 1978 • Condie Richard • ANS • CND
JOHN LEYTON TOUCH, THE • 1961 • *Viscount Films* • SHT • UKN
JOHN LINWORTH'S ATONEMENT • 1914 • Wilson Frank? • UKN
JOHN LOVES MARY • 1949 • Butler David • USA
JOHN LYMAN, PEINTRE • 1959 • Dansereau Fernand • DCS • CND
JOHN MANLEY'S AWAKENING • 1913 • Miller Ashley • USA
JOHN MEADE'S WOMAN • 1937 • Wallace Richard • USA • MAN AND A WOMAN, A
JOHN MOVIE • 1983 • Carmona Jean-Claude • FRN • LEGENDE D'UN SIECLE, LA
JOHN NEEDHAM'S DOUBLE • 1916 • Weber Lois, Smalley Phillips • USA
JOHN OAKHURST, GAMBLER • 1911 • *Bosworth Hobart* • USA
JOHN OF THE FAIR • 1952 • McCarthy Michael • UKN
JOHN O'HARA'S GIBBSVILLE see **TURNING POINT OF JIM MALLOY, THE** • 1975
JOHN OSBORNE'S TRIUMPH • 1917 • MacQuarrie Murdock • SHT • USA
JOHN PAUL JONES • 1959 • Farrow John • USA
JOHN PAWKSON'S BRUTALITY • 1915 • Collins Edwin J.? • UKN
JOHN PELLET'S DREAM • 1916 • Julian Rupert • SHT • USA
JOHN PETTICOATS • 1919 • Hillyer Lambert • USA
JOHN RANCE, GENTLEMAN • 1914 • Brooke Van Dyke • USA
JOHN READ AND LOUISE BRYANT STORY, THE see **REDS** • 1981
JOHN REED see **REED, MEXICO INSURGENTE** • 1971
JOHN ROOL • 1916 • Meinert Rudolf • FRG
JOHN SMITH • 1922 • Heerman Victor • USA • ON PROBATION
JOHN SMITH WAKES UP • 1940 • Weiss Jiri • UKN
JOHN STEINBECK'S EAST OF EDEN see **EAST OF EDEN** • 1982
JOHN STERLING, ALDERMAN • 1912 • *Baggot King* • USA
JOHN SULLIVAN STORY, THE • 1980 • Stevens David • MTV • ASL
JOHN T. ROCKS AND THE FLIVVER • 1915 • *Anderson Mignon* • USA
JOHN THE BASTARD see **JOHNNY IL BASTARDO** • 1967
JOHN, THE HERO • 1972 • Jankovics Marcell, Nepp Jozsef, Ternovszky Bela • ANM • HNG
JOHN, THE HERO (USA) see **JANOS VITEZ** • 1939
JOHN THE SOLDIER OF VENGEANCE see **JUAN SOLDADO, O VENGANZA** • 1939
JOHN, THE TENANT see **ARENDAS ZSIDO, AZ** • 1917
JOHN THE WAGONER • 1913 • *Nestor* • USA
JOHN THE YOUNGER BROTHER see **JON AZ OCSEM** • 1919
JOHN TOBIN'S SWEETHEART • 1913 • Baker George D. • USA
JOHN TOM LITTLE BEAR • 1917 • Smith David • SHT • USA
JOHN TRAVOLTA.. DA UN INSOLITO DESTINO • 1979 • Parenti Neri • ITL
JOHN WILLIE AT BLACKPOOL • 1913 • *Sphinx Films* • UKN • SMIFFY AT BLACKPOOL
JOHN WILLIE, COME ON • 1909 • *Warwick Trading Co.* • UKN
JOHNNIE • 1920 • *Selznick* • SHT • USA
JOHNNIE CORNCOB see **JANOS VITEZ** • 1973
JOHNNIE FROM JONESBORO • 1914 • *Frontier* • USA
JOHNNIE, GO GET 'EM • 1918 • *Christie* • USA
JOHNNIE MAE GIBSON: F.B.I. • 1986 • Duke Bill • TVM • USA
JOHNNIE WATERS THE GARDEN • 1911 • *Solax* • USA
JOHNNIE'S BIRTHDAY • 1916 • Douglass James • USA
JOHNNY A DENNIS A ALFRED • 1976-77 • Brault Michel, Gladu Andre • DCS • CND
JOHNNY ALLEGRO • 1949 • Tetzlaff Ted • USA • HOUNDED (UKN)
JOHNNY AND THE INDIANS • 1909 • *Centaur* • USA
JOHNNY AND THE WICKED GIANT see **JEANNOT L'INTREPIDE** • 1950
JOHNNY ANGEL • 1945 • Marin Edwin L. • USA
JOHNNY APOLLO • 1940 • Hathaway Henry • USA • DANCE WITH THE DEVIL
JOHNNY APPLESEED • 1948 • Jackson Wilfred • ANS • USA
JOHNNY BANCO • 1967 • Allegret Yves • FRN, ITL, FRG • JONNY BANCO -GELIEBTER TAUGENICHTS (FRG)
JOHNNY BE GOOD • 1988 • Smith Bud • USA • QUARTERBACK SNEAK
JOHNNY BELINDA • 1948 • Negulesco Jean • USA
JOHNNY BELINDA • 1982 • Harvey Anthony • TVM • USA
JOHNNY BLADE • 1987 • Freed Herb • USA
JOHNNY BULL • 1986 • Weill Claudia • TVM • USA
JOHNNY CASH! see **JOHNNY CASH: THE MAN, HIS WORLD, HIS MUSIC** • 1970
JOHNNY CASH: THE MAN, HIS WORLD, HIS MUSIC • 1970 • Elfstrom Robert • USA • JOHNNY CASH!
JOHNNY COME LATELY • 1943 • Howard William K. • USA • JOHNNY VAGABOND (UKN)
JOHNNY COMES FLYING HOME • 1946 • Stoloff Ben • USA
JOHNNY CONCHO • 1956 • McGuire Don • USA
JOHNNY COOL • 1968 • Asher William • USA
JOHNNY DANGEROUSLY • 1984 • Heckerling Amy • USA
JOHNNY DARK • 1954 • Sherman George • USA
JOHNNY DAYS • 1971 • Reichenbach Francois • DOC • FRN • JOHNNY HALLYDAY PAR FRANCOIS REICHENBACH ○ J'AI TOUT DONNE ○ JOHNNY HALLYDAY
JOHNNY DIAMINI • 1985 • SAF
JOHNNY DO OR DIE • 1968 • Marquez Artemio • PHL
JOHNNY DOESN'T LIVE HERE ANY MORE • 1944 • May Joe • USA • AND SO THEY WERE MARRIED
JOHNNY DOUGHBOY • 1942 • Auer John H. • USA
JOHNNY EAGER • 1941 • LeRoy Mervyn • USA
JOHNNY FEDORA AND ALICE BLUE BONNET • 1946 • Kinney Jack • ANS • USA
JOHNNY FIRECLOUD • 1975 • Castleman William Allen • USA
JOHNNY FRENCHMAN • 1945 • Frend Charles • UKN
JOHNNY GET YOUR GUN • 1919 • Crisp Donald • USA
JOHNNY GET YOUR HAIR CUT • 1926 • Mayo Archie, Eason B. Reeves • USA
JOHNNY GETS HIS GUN see **STRAIGHT FROM THE SHOULDER** • 1936
JOHNNY GOES DUCKING • 1913 • *Brennan John* • USA
JOHNNY GOT HIS GUN • 1971 • Trumbo Dalton • USA
JOHNNY GUITAR • 1954 • Ray Nicholas • USA
JOHNNY GUNMAN • 1957 • *Brooks Martin* • USA
JOHNNY HALLYDAY see **JOHNNY DAYS** • 1971
JOHNNY HALLYDAY PAR FRANCOIS REICHENBACH see **JOHNNY DAYS** • 1971
JOHNNY HAMLET see **QUELLA SPORCA STORIA DEL WEST** • 1968
JOHNNY HANDSOME • 1989 • Hill Walter • USA
JOHNNY HOLIDAY • 1949 • Goldbeck Willis • USA
JOHNNY IL BASTARDO • 1967 • Crispino Armando • ITL • JOHN THE BASTARD ○ JOHN IL BASTARDO
JOHNNY IN THE CLOUDS (USA) see **WAY TO THE STARS, THE** • 1945
JOHNNY LARSEN • 1979 • Arnfred Morten • DNM
JOHNNY MINOTAUR • 1971 • *Koulizakis Nikos* • GRC
JOHNNY NOBODY • 1961 • Patrick Nigel • UKN
JOHNNY NORSE • 1964 • Siegel Don • USA
JOHNNY NORTH see **KILLERS, THE** • 1964
JOHNNY O'CLOCK • 1947 • Rossen Robert • USA
JOHNNY O'KEEFE -THE WILD ONE • 1983 • Thoms Albie • DOC • ASL
JOHNNY ON THE RUN • 1953 • Gilbert Lewis*, Harris Vernon, Latham Patricia • UKN
JOHNNY ON THE SPOT • 1912 • *Reliance* • USA
JOHNNY-ON-THE-SPOT • 1916 • *Jockey* • USA
JOHNNY-ON-THE-SPOT • 1919 • Franklin Harry L. • USA
JOHNNY ON THE SPOT • 1954 • Rogers Maclean • UKN
JOHNNY ONE-EYE • 1950 • Florey Robert • USA
JOHNNY ORO • 1966 • Corbucci Sergio • ITL • RINGO AND HIS GOLDEN PISTOL
JOHNNY OUR see **JOHNNY UNSER** • 1980
JOHNNY RATON • 1969 • Escriva Vicente • SPN
JOHNNY RENO • 1966 • Springsteen R. G. • USA
JOHNNY RING AND THE CAPTAIN'S SWORD • 1921 • Stevens Norman L. • USA
JOHNNY ROCCO • 1958 • Landres Paul • USA
JOHNNY SMITH AND POKER HUNTAS • 1938 • Avery Tex • ANS • USA
JOHNNY SOKKO AND HIS GIANT ROBOT see **VOYAGE INTO SPACE** • 1965
JOHNNY STOOL PIGEON • 1949 • Castle William • USA
JOHNNY STURMGEWEHR • 1989 • Mamin Ueli • SWT
JOHNNY THE BARBER • 1915 • Dillon John Francis • USA
JOHNNY THE GIANT KILLER (USA) see **JEANNOT L'INTREPIDE** • 1950
JOHNNY THE MUSICIAN see **NOWY JANKO MUZYKANT** • 1960
JOHNNY TIGER • 1966 • Wendkos Paul • USA
JOHNNY TIGER see **JOHNNY TIGRE** • 1967
JOHNNY TIGRE • 1967 • Marquez Carlito • PHL • JOHNNY TIGER
JOHNNY TOUGH • 1983 • SAF
JOHNNY TREMAIN • 1957 • Stevenson Robert • USA
JOHNNY TROUBLE • 1957 • Auer John H. • USA
JOHNNY UNSER • 1980 • Polak Robert, Fink Tone • AUS • JOHNNY OUR
JOHNNY VAGABOND (UKN) see **JOHNNY COME LATELY** • 1943
JOHNNY, WE HARDLY KNEW YE • 1977 • Cates Gilbert • TVM • USA
JOHNNY WEST IL MANCINO • 1965 • Parolini Gianfranco • ITL, FRN, SPN
JOHNNY, YOU'RE WANTED • 1956 • Sewell Vernon • UKN
JOHNNY YUMA • 1966 • Guerrieri Romolo • ITL
JOHNNY'S GUN • 1907 • Fitzhamon Lewin • UKN
JOHNNY'S JUMBLE • 1916 • MacMackin Archer • SHT • USA
JOHNNY'S RIM • 1907 • Mottershaw Frank • UKN

JOHNNY'S WEEK END • 1930 • Watson William • USA

JOHN'S NEW SUIT OR WHY HE DIDN'T GO TO CHURCH • 1908 • *Vitagraph* • USA

JOHN'S SECRET see **JOHANNES' HEMMELIGHED** • 1986

JOHN'S WIFE (USA) see **FEMME DE JEAN, LA** • 1974

JOHNSON AT THE WEDDING • 1911 • Bouwmeester Theo • UKN

JOHNSON – BURNS FIGHT • 1908 • *Higgins Ernest (Ph)* • ASL

JOHNSON COUNTY WAR see **HEAVEN'S GATE** • 1980

JOHNSON'S STRANGE ALE • 1911 • Rains Fred • UKN

JOHNSTOWN FLOOD, THE • 1926 • Cummings Irving • USA • FLOOD, THE (UKN)

JOHNSTOWN FLOOD, THE • 1946 • Rasinski Connie • ANS • USA

JOHNSTOWN MONSTER, THE • 1971 • Pooley Olaf • UKN

JOI BABA FELUNATH see **JAI BABA FELUNATH** • 1977

JOI–UCHI see **JOIUCHI –HAIRYOZUMA SHIMATSU** • 1967

JOIAS DO ALTO ALENTEJO • 1959 • Ribeiro Antonio Lopes • SHT • PRT

JOIE DE REVIVRE, LA • 1947 • Storck Henri • DOC • BLG

JOIE DE VIVRE • 1934 • Hoppin Hector, Gross Anthony • ANS • FRN

JOIE DE VIVRE, LA • 1946 • Tedesco Jean • SHT • FRN

JOIE DE VIVRE AU QUEBEC • 1974 • Danis Aime • DCS • CND

JOIN OUR RANKS • 1959 • Panfilov Gleb • DOC • USS

JOIN THE CIRCUS • 1923 • Roach Hal • SHT • USA

JOIN THE MARINES • 1937 • Staub Ralph • USA

JOINING THE ARMY • 1900 • *Paul R. W.* • UKN

JOINING UP • 1928 • Croise Hugh • UKN

JOINT VENTURE • 1978 • Damiano Gerard? • USA

JOINT WIPERS • 1932 • Foster John, Stallings George • ANS • USA

JOINT'S BATTLE, THE see **BATALLA DEL PORRO, LA** • 1982

JOISSANCES • Baudricourt Michel • FRN

JOIUCHI –HAIRYOZUMA SHIMATSU • 1967 • Kobayashi Masaki • JPN • SAMURAI REBELLION ○ REBELLION ○ JOI–UCHI

JOKAI SENHIME GOTEN • *Leo Production* • ANM • JPN

JOKE see **SCHERZO** • 1983

JOKE, A • 1967 • Donev Donyo • ANM • BUL

JOKE, THE see **ITAZURA** • 1959

JOKE, THE see **ZERT** • 1968

JOKE IN JERKS, A • 1914 • Aylott Dave? • UKN

JOKE OF DESTINY, A (USA) see **SCHERZO** • 1983

JOKE OF DESTINY, LYING IN WAIT AROUND THE CORNER LIKE A BANDIT, A see **SCHERZO** • 1983

JOKE ON GRANDMA, A • 1901 • Porter Edwin S. • USA

JOKE ON HOWLING WOLF, A • 1913 • Sturgeon Rollin S. • USA

JOKE ON JANE, A • 1914 • *Beauty* • USA

JOKE ON JANE, THE • 1914 • *Kalem* • USA

JOKE ON THE GARDENER, A see **PRACTICAL JOKE, A** • 1898

JOKE ON THE JOKER, A • 1914 • *Crystal* • USA

JOKE ON THE JOKER, THE • 1911 • Sennett Mack • USA

JOKE ON THE MOTORIST, A • 1904 • *Warwick Trading Co* • UKN

JOKE ON THE SHERIFF, A • 1913 • *Crystal* • USA

JOKE ON YELLENTOWN, THE • 1914 • Mackley Arthur • USA

JOKE THAT FAILED, THE • 1904 • Stow Percy • UKN

JOKE THAT FAILED, THE • 1917 • Wilson Frank • UKN

JOKE THAT FAILED, THE • 1921 • Paul Fred, Raymond Jack • UKN

JOKE WASN'T ON BEN BOLT, THE • 1913 • *Eldridge Charles* • USA

JOKEI see **JOKYO** • 1960

JOKER • 1976 • Yeshurun Isaac • ISR

JOKER • 1985 • SAF

JOKER, THE • 1931 • Waschneck Erich • FRN

JOKER, THE • 1987 • Patzak Peter • FRG • LETHAL OBSESSION

JOKER, THE see **KING, QUEEN, JOKER** • 1921

JOKER, THE see **JOKEREN** • 1928

JOKER, THE see **BROMISTA, EL** • 1980

JOKER, THE (USA) see **FARCEUR, LE** • 1960

JOKER IS WILD, THE • 1957 • Vidor Charles • USA • ALL THE WAY

JOKEREN • 1928 • Jacoby Georg • DNM • SPIEL GLUCKSRITTERN UND SCHONEN FRAUEN, EIN ○ JOKER, THE

JOKERS, THE • 1966 • Winner Michael • UKN

JOKER'S MISTAKE, THE • 1912 • Booth W. R. • UKN • GETTING HIS OWN BACK

JOKES MY FOLKS NEVER TOLD ME • 1979 • Woolery Gerry • USA

JOKING BRICKLAYERS, THE • 1914 • *Pathe* • USA

JOKO INVOCA DIO.. E MUORI • 1968 • Margheriti Antonio • ITL, FRG • VENGEANCE (UKN)

JOKO LE SINGE • 1916-24 • Lortac • ANS • FRN

JOKYO • 1960 • Ichikawa Kon, Yoshimura Kozaburo, Masumura Yasuzo • JPN • WOMAN'S TESTAMENT, A ○ CODE OF WOMEN ○ JOKEI ○ WOMEN'S SCROLL

JOKYO ICHIDAI • 1958 • Ichikawa Seiichiro • JPN • UNDEFEATED WOMAN

JOKYOSHI NO HIMITSU • 1967 • Kimata Akitaka • JPN • SECRET OF A WOMAN TEACHER

JOKYU AISHI • 1930 • Gosho Heinosuke • JPN • SAD STORY OF A BARMAID

JOLANDA, LA FIGLIA DEL CORSARO NERO • 1953 • Soldati Mario • ITL

JOLANTA –DEN GACKANDE SUGGAN • 1945 • Bolander Hugo • SWD • JOLANTA –THE ELUSIVE SOW

JOLANTA –THE ELUSIVE SOW see **JOLANTA –DEN GACKANDE SUGGAN** • 1945

JOLI COEUR, LE • 1983 • Perrin Francis • FRN

JOLI MAI, LE • 1963 • Marker Chris, Lhomme Pierre • DOC • FRN

JOLI MONDE • 1935 • Le Henaff Rene • FRN

JOLIE BERGERE, LA see **RA'IA AL-HASNA', AR-** • 1972

JOLIFOU INN • 1955 • Low Colin • ANS • CND

JOLIGUD: CHRONICLES FROM THE SALADILLO NEIGHBOURHOOD see **JOLIGUD: CRONICAS DE EL SALADILLO** • 1989

JOLIGUD: CRONICAS DE EL SALADILLO • 1989 • Pradelli Augusto • VNZ • JOLIGUD: CHRONICLES FROM THE SALADILLO NEIGHBOURHOOD

JOLLIER, THE • 1911 • *Stanley Frederick* • USA

JOLLY • 1923 • Gallone Carmine • ITL

JOLLY BAD FELLOW, A • 1963 • Chaffey Don • UKN • THEY ALL DIED LAUGHING (USA)

JOLLY BILL OF THE ROLLICKING R • 1911 • Dwan Allan • USA • SLOPPY BILL OF THE ROLLICKING R

JOLLY, CLOWN DA CIRCO • 1923 • Camerini Mario • ITL

JOLLY, DER TEUFELSKERL • 1921 • Seitz Franz • FRG

JOLLY FARMERS, THE • 1930 • Jeffrey R. E. • UKN

JOLLY FELLOW, THE • 1988 • Koulev Henri • ANM • BUL

JOLLY FELLOWS, THE see **VESYOLYE REBYATA** • 1934

JOLLY FISH • 1932 • Foster John, Stallings George • ANS • USA

JOLLY GENIE, THE • 1962 • Barry Wesley E. • USA

JOLLY GOOD COMPANY • 1909 • *Warwick Trading Co* • UKN

JOLLY GOOD FELLOW, A • 1913 • *Reliance* • USA

JOLLY GOOD FELONS • 1934 • Stallings George • ANS • USA

JOLLY GOOD FURLOUGH, A • 1943 • Gordon Dan • ANS • USA

JOLLY GREEN • 1970 • Coutard Raoul • SHT • FRN

JOLLY JILTER, THE • 1927 • Cline Eddie • SHT • USA

JOLLY LITTLE ELVES • 1934 • Lantz Walter, Nolan William • ANS • USA

JOLLY MAKES A HASH OF THINGS • 1915 • *Ward Lily* • UKN

JOLLY MUSICIANS, THE see **VESYOLY MUSIKANTY** • 1937

JOLLY OLD COUPLE, A • 1900 • Smith G. A. • UKN

JOLLY OLD HIGGINS (UKN) see **EARL OF PUDDLESTONE** • 1940

JOLLY TARS • 1926 • Taurog Norman • SHT • USA

JOLLY TARS, THE • 1917 • *Pokes & Jabbs* • SHT • USA

JOLLY THE CLOWN • 1957 • Kneitel Seymour • ANS • USA

JOLLY TRIO'S DREAM • 1909 • *Pathe* • FRN

JOLLY WHIRL, THE see **SINGERIES HUMAINES** • 1910

JOLLYBOY'S DREAM • 1914 • Aylott Dave • UKN

JOLLY'S LITTLE BIT • 1915 • *Pyramid* • UKN

JOLSON SINGS AGAIN • 1949 • Levin Henry • USA

JOLSON STORY, THE • 1946 • Green Alfred E., Lewis Joseph H. • USA

JOLT, THE • 1921 • Marshall George • USA

JOLT FOR GENERAL GERM, A • 1931 • Fleischer Dave • ANS • USA

JOLT FOR THE JANITOR, A • 1913 • France Charles H. • USA

JOLTED JUSTICE • 1917 • Miller Rube • SHT • USA

JOLTS AND JEWELRY • 1917 • Semon Larry • SHT • USA

JOLTS OF JEALOUSY • 1914 • *Eclectic* • USA

JOM • 1982 • Samb Ababacar • SNL • JOM: OU, L'HISTOIRE D'UN PEUPLE ○ DIGNITY

JOM: OU, L'HISTOIRE D'UN PEUPLE see **JOM** • 1982

JON see **JON –KERTOMUS MAAILMAN LOPUSTA** • 1982

JON –A STORY ABOUT THE END OF THE WORLD see **JON –KERTOMUS MAAILMAN LOPUSTA** • 1982

JON AZ OCSEM • 1919 • Curtiz Michael • HNG • JOHN THE YOUNGER BROTHER

JON –KERTOMUS MAAILMAN LOPUSTA • 1982 • Pyhala Jaakko • FNL • JON –A STORY ABOUT THE END OF THE WORLD ○ JON

JON ODDUR AND JON BJARNI • 1982 • Bertelsson Thrainn • ICL

JON SCHUELER: PORTRAIT OF AN ARTIST • 1972 • Black John • DCS • UKN

JONAH, A • 1914 • Dillon Eddie • USA

JONAH MAN: OR, THE TRAVELLER BEWITCHED, THE • 1904 • Fitzhamon Lewin, Hepworth Cecil M. • UKN • BEWITCHED TRAVELER, THE (USA)

JONAH WHO WILL BE 25 IN THE YEAR 2000 (USA) see **JONAS –QUI AURA 25 ANS L'AN 2000** • 1976

JONAS • 1957 • Domnick Ottomar • FRG

JONAS, DEJME TOMU VE STREDU • 1985 • Sis Vladimir • CZC • JONAS, FOR INSTANCE, ON WEDNESDAY

JONAS, FOR INSTANCE, ON WEDNESDAY see **JONAS, DEJME TOMU VE STREDU** • 1985

JONAS –QUI AURA 25 ANS L'AN 2000 • 1976 • Tanner Alain • SWT • JONAH WHO WILL BE 25 IN THE YEAR 2000 (USA)

JONATHAN LIVINGSTONE SEAGULL • 1973 • Bartlett Hall • USA

JONATHAN (USA) see **JONATHAN, VAMPIRE STERBEN NICHT** • 1970

JONATHAN, VAMPIRE STERBEN NICHT • 1970 • Geissendorfer Hans W. • FRG • JONATHAN (USA)

JONATHANA AND THE WITCH see **JONATHANA UND DIE HEXE** • 1986

JONATHANA UND DIE HEXE • 1986 • Neuberger Bernd • AUS, FRG • JONATHANA AND THE WITCH

JONES AND HIS NEW NEIGHBORS • 1909 • Griffith D. W. • USA

JONES AND THE LADY BOOK AGENT • 1909 • Griffith D. W. • USA

JONES' AUTO, THE • 1916 • *Drew Sidney* • SHT • USA

JONES' BIRTHDAY • 1907 • Hough Harold • UKN

JONES' BURGLAR • 1909 • Griffith D. W. • USA

JONES' BURGLAR TRAP • 1914 • *Crystal* • USA

JONES BUYS CHINA • 1910 • Rains Fred • UKN

JONES DRESSES FOR THE PAGEANT • 1910 • Rains Fred • UKN

JONES FAMILY IN BIG BUSINESS, THE see **BIG BUSINESS** • 1937

JONES FAMILY IN HOLLYWOOD, THE • 1939 • St. Clair Malcolm • USA • IN HOLLYWOOD

JONES FAMILY IN HOT WATER, THE see **HOT WATER** • 1937

JONES FAMILY IN QUICK MILLIONS • 1939 • St. Clair Malcolm • USA • QUICK MILLIONS

JONES GETS ARRESTED • 1909 • *Bison* • USA

JONES GOES SHOPPING • 1913 • Williams C. Jay • USA

JONES' HYPNOTIC EYE • 1915 • Smith David • USA

JONES' JONAH DAY • 1913 • *Brennan John* • USA

JONES JUNIOR: OR, MONEY FOR NOTHING • 1910 • Rains Fred • UKN

JONES KEEPS HOUSE • 1917 • Smith David • SHT • USA

JONES' LOTTERY PRIZE • 1910 • Rains Fred • UKN

JONES' MISTAKE • 1912 • Collins Edwin J. • UKN

JONES' NIGHTMARE • 1911 • Rains Fred • UKN • LOBSTER STILL PURSUED HIM, THE

JONES' PATENT MOTOR • 1906 • Cooper Arthur • UKN

JONES RESURRECTED • 1912 • *Crystal* • USA

JONES TESTS HIS WIFE'S COURAGE • 1910 • Wilson Frank? • UKN

JONES' WEDDING DAY • 1912 • *Imp* • USA

JONES' WEDDING DAY • 1914 • Hale Albert W. • USA

JONESES HAVE AMATEUR THEATRICALS, THE • 1909 • Griffith D. W. • USA

JONETSU NO FUCHIN • 1926 • Tasaka Tomotaka • JPN • RISE AND FALL OF LOVE

JONETSU NO ICHIYA • 1929 • Gosho Heinosuke • JPN • ONE NIGHT OF PASSION ○ NIGHT OF PASSION ○ NETSUJO NO ICHIYA

JONETSU NO SHIJIN see **GYONETSU NO SHIJIN TAKUBOKU** • 1936

JONGARA see **TSUGARU JONGARA–BUSHI** • 1973

JONGE HARTEN • 1936 • van der Linden Charles Huguenot • NTH • YOUNG HEARTS

JONGENS, JONGENS WAT EEN MEID • 1966 • de la Parra Pim • NTH

JONGLEUR, LE • 1980 • Vamos Thomas • CND

JONGLEUR EMERITE, UN • 1912 • Cohl Emile • ANS • FRN

JONI • 1980 • Collier James F. • USA

JONIKO: ALASKA BOY see **JONIKO AND THE KUSH TA KA** • 1969

JONIKO AND THE KUSH TA KA • 1969 • Beebe Ford • USA • JONIKO: ALASKA BOY ○ FRONTIER ALASKA

JONKER DIAMOND • 1936 • Tourneur Jacques • SHT • USA

JONNY BANCO –GELIEBTER TAUGENICHTS (FRG) see **JOHNNY BANCO** • 1967

JONNY, HAUTE–COUTURE • 1935 • de Poligny Serge • FRN

JONNY & JESSY • 1973 • Andersen Wies • BLG

JONNY, JUNGE MANN FUR SCHONE STUNDEN • 1973 • Weidenmann Alfred • FRG

JONNY RETTET NEBRADOR • 1953 • Jugert Rudolf • FRG

JONQUE, LA • 1964 • Guillemot Claude • SHT • FRN

JONQUIERE • 1969 • Dansereau Fernand • DCS • CND

JONS UND ERDME • 1959 • Vicas Victor • FRG, ITL • DONNA DELL'ALTRO, LA (ITL)

JONSSON GANG ON MAJORCA, THE see **JONSSONLIGAN PA MALLORCA** • 1989

JONSSON GANG TURNS UP AGAIN, THE see **JONSSONLIGAN DYKKER UPP IGEN** • 1987

JONSSONLIGAN DYKKER UPP IGEN • 1987 • Ekman Mikael • SWD • JONSSON GANG TURNS UP AGAIN, THE

JONSSONLIGAN PA MALLORCA • 1989 • Ekman Mikael • SWD • JONSSON GANG ON MAJORCA, THE

JONUBE SHAHR • 1959 • Ghaffary Farrokh • IRN • SOUTHERN TEHERAN

JOOBACHI • 1978 • Ichikawa Kon • JPN • QUEEN BEE ○ JOH–OU BACHI

JORD • 1986 • Wam Svend, Vennerod Petter • NRW • EARTH

JORDAN CHANCE, THE • 1978 • Irving Jules • TVM • USA

JORDAN IS A HARD ROAD • 1915 • Dwan Allan • USA

JORDEN ER FLAD • 1976 • Stangerup Henrik • DNM • EARTH IS FLAT, THE

JORDEN ER VORES MOR • 1987 • Elsass Peter • DOC • DNM • EARTH IS OUR MOTHER, THE

JORDEN RUNT MED FANNY HILL • 1973 • Ahlberg Mac • SWD • AROUND THE WORLD WITH FANNY HILL

JORDENS HAEVN see **OMSTRIDTE JORD, DEN** • 1915

JORGE, A BRAZILIAN see **JORGE UM BRASILEIRO** • 1988

JORGE UM BRASILEIRO • 1988 • Thiago Paulo • BRZ • JORGE, A BRAZILIAN

JORINDE AND JORINGEL • Hempel Johannes • ANM • GDR

JORINDE AND JORINGEL • 1922 • Raboldt Toni • ANM • FRG

JORIS IVEN'S CHINA see **COMMENT YUKONG DEPLACA LES MONTAGNES** • 1976

JORNADA DE MUERTE (SPN) see **DEATH JOURNEY** • 1976

JOROBADO, EL • 1943 • Salvador Jaime • MXC • ENRIQUE DE LAGARDERE

JOROBADO DE LA MORGUE, EL • 1972 • Aguirre Javier • SPN • HUNCHBACK OF THE MORGUE, THE (USA)

JORUND SMED (NRW) see **DIT VINDARNA BAR** • 1948

JORY • 1971 • Fons Jorge • MXC, USA

JOS CARBONE • 1975 • Tremblay Hugues • CND

JOS OVAJ PUT • 1984 • Kresoja Dragan • YGS • JUST ONCE MORE

J'OSE • 1984 • Bonmariage Manu • BLG

JOSE COLLINS DRAMAS, THE • 1923 • Bentley Thomas • SER • UKN

JOSE DO TELHADO • 1945 • Miranda Armando • PRT

JOSE LUCIANO'S VISIT see **VISITACIONES DE JOSE LUCIANO, LAS** • 1982

JOSE MARIA • 1963 • Forn Josep Maria • SPN

JOSE TORRES COHORT • 1959 • Teshigahara Hiroshi • SHT • JPN

JOSE TORRES, PART II • 1965 • Teshigahara Hiroshi • DOC • JPN

JOSEF DRENTERS • 1960 • King Allan • CND

JOSEF KAJETAN TYL • 1925 • Innemann Svatopluk • CZC

JOSEF KILLIAN see **POSTAVA K PODPIRANI** • 1963

JOSEF UND SEINE BRUDER • 1922 • Froelich Carl • FRG • JOSEPH AND HIS BRETHREN

JOSEFINE: DAS LIEBESTOLLE KATZCHEN • 1972 • von Cziffra Geza • FRG • SCHOOL FOR VIRGINS (UKN)

JOSEFINE MUTZENBACHER 2 TEIL: MEINE 365 LIEBHABER • 1971 • Nachmann Kurt • FRG • DON'T GET YOUR KNICKERS IN A TWIST (UKN) ○ MEINE 365 LIEBHABER

JOSEI KAZOKU • 1963 • Misumi Kenji • JPN • FEMININE FAMILY ○ WOMEN FAMILY

JOSEI NI KANSURU JUNISHO • 1954 • Ichikawa Kon • JPN • TWELVE CHAPTERS ABOUT WOMEN ○ TWELVE CHAPTERS ON WOMEN

JOSEI NO KAKUGO • 1940 • Shibuya Minoru • JPN • WOMAN'S RESOLUTION, A

JOSEI NO SHORI • 1946 • Mizoguchi Kenji • JPN • VICTORY OF WOMEN, THE (UKN) ○ WOMEN'S VICTORY (USA)

JOSEI WA TSUYOSHI • 1924 • Mizoguchi Kenji • JPN • WOMEN ARE STRONG (USA) ○ STRONG IS THE FEMALE

JOSELITO VAGABUNDO • 1965 • Morayta Miguel • MXC, SPN

JOSEPH AND HIS BRETHREN • 1915 • Parker Louis N. • USA

JOSEPH AND HIS BRETHREN • 1962 • Gross Aline, Gross Yoram • ANM • ISR
JOSEPH AND HIS BRETHREN • 1962 • Rapper Irving, Ricci Luciano • USA, ITL • GIUSEPPE VENDUTO DAI FRATELLI (ITL) ○ SOLD INTO EGYPT ○ STORY OF JOSEPH AND HIS BRETHREN, THE ○ JOSEPH SOLD BY HIS BROTHERS
JOSEPH AND HIS BRETHREN see **JOSEF UND SEINE BRUDER** • 1922
JOSEPH AND HIS BROTHERS • 1979 • Hively Jack • MTV • USA
JOSEPH AND ZOLIKHA see **YOSEF-VA-ZOLIKHA** • 1968
JOSEPH ANDREWS • 1977 • Richardson Tony • UKN
JOSEPH CHARBONNEAU, SIXIEME EVEQUE DE MONTREAL • 1975 • Valcour Pierre • DCS • CND
JOSEPH DESA see **RELUCTANT SAINT, THE** • 1962
JOSEPH ET MARIE • 1979 • Berzosa Jose-Maria • DOC • FRN • MOTS ET LES GESTES, LES
JOSEPH GREER AND HIS DAUGHTER see **WHAT FOOLS MEN** • 1925
JOSEPH HAYDN see **ESZTERHAZA MUZSIKUSA, HAYDN** • 1960
JOSEPH HOWE: THE TRIBUNE OF NOVA SCOTIA • 1961 • Biggs Julian • CND
JOSEPH IN THE LAND OF EGYPT • 1914 • Moore W. Eugene • USA
JOSEPH IN THE LAND OF EGYPT • 1932 • Roland George • USA
JOSEPH KILIAN (USA) see **POSTAVA K PODPIRANI** • 1963
JOSEPH MANES • 1952 • Pojar Bretislav • DCS • CZC
JOSEPH OF RYYSYRANTA see **RYYSYRANNAN JOOSEPPI** • 1955
JOSEPH SCHMIDT STORY, THE see **LIED GEHT UM DIE WELT, EIN** • 1933
JOSEPH SOLD BY HIS BROTHERS see **JOSEPH AND HIS BRETHREN** • 1962
JOSEPH TERMINI • 1926 • *Deforest Phonofilms* • SHT • UKN
JOSEPH THE DREAMER see **BAAL CHACHALOMOT** • 1959
JOSEPHA • 1981 • Frank Christopher • FRN
JOSEPHINE • 1980 • Leiterman Richard • DOC • CND
JOSEPHINE AND HER LOVERS • 1910 • Fitzhamon Lewin? • UKN
JOSEPHINE AND MEN • 1955 • Boulting Roy • UKN
JOSEPHINE EARLE • 1929 • *Bsfp* • SHT • UKN • MUSICAL MEDLEY NO.4
JOSEPHINE VENDUE PAR SES SOEURS • 1913 • Denola Georges • FRN
JOSEPHSONN • 1977 • Hassler Jurg • DOC • SWT
JOSEPT TU M'ENERVES • 1936 • Kapps Walter • FRN
JOSETTE • 1936 • Christian-Jaque • FRN
JOSETTE • 1938 • Dwan Allan • USA
JOSH AND CINDY'S WEDDING TRIP • 1911 • *Edison* • USA
JOSHIDAISEI NO KINJIRARETA HANAZONO • 1967 • Ogawa Kinya • JPN • FORBIDDEN FLOWER GARDEN
JOSHIGAKUSEI GOKUHI NIKKI • 1968 • Shindo Takae • JPN • SECRET DIARY OF A GIRL STUDENT
JOSHIGAKUSEI SEI NO MEIRO • 1968 • Ogawa Kinya • JPN • LABYRINTH OF SEX, A
JOSHIRYO • 1967 • Mukoi Hiroshi • JPN • GIRLS' DORMITORY
JOSHOKU NO MOTSURE • 1968 • Sakao Masanao • JPN • ENTANGLEMENT OF LUST
JOSH'S SUICIDE • 1911 • Lehrman Henry, Sennett Mack (Spv) • USA
JOSHU TO TOMONI • 1957 • Hisamatsu Seiji • JPN • WOMEN IN PRISON
JOSHUA • 1977 • Spangler Larry • USA • BLACK RIDER, THE
JOSHUA, A NIGERIAN PORTRAIT • 1962 • King Allan • CND
JOSHUA AND THE BLOB • 1972 • Lange John C. • ANS • USA
JOSHUA IN A BOX • 1970 • Lange John C. • ANS • USA
JOSHUA THEN AND NOW • 1985 • Kotcheff Ted • CND
JOSIE'S CASTLE • 1972 • *Fielding Tom* • USA
JOSIE'S CONEY ISLAND NIGHTMARE see **CONEY ISLAND NIGHTMARE, A** • 1914
JOSIE'S DECLARATION OF INDEPENDENCE • 1914 • Beggs Lee • USA
JOSIE'S LEGACY • 1914 • Beggs Lee • USA
JOSLAT • 1920 • Fejos Paul • HNG • PROPHECY
JOSSELYN'S WIFE • 1919 • Hickman Howard • USA
JOSSELYN'S WIFE • 1926 • Thorpe Richard • USA
JOSSER IN THE ARMY • 1932 • Lee Norman • UKN
JOSSER JOINS THE NAVY • 1932 • Lee Norman • UKN
JOSSER, K.C. • 1929 • Croise Hugh • UKN
JOSSER ON THE FARM • 1934 • Hunter T. Hayes • UKN
JOSSER ON THE RIVER • 1932 • Lee Norman • UKN
JOSSER P.C. see **P.C. JOSSER** • 1931
JOSTOJOEI SHOHAR • 1968 • Vahdat Nosratolah • IRN • LOOKING FOR A HUSBAND
JOSZEF KATUS • 1966 • Verstappen Wim • NTH • MINDER GELUKKIGE TERUGKEER VAN JOSZEF KATUS NAAR HET LAND VAN REMBRANDT, DE
JOTA DANCED BY THE BEAUTIFUL ROMERO • 1905 • Barragan Salvador Toscano • MXC
JOTAI • 1964 • Onchi Hideo • JPN • CALL OF FLESH, THE
JOTAI JOHATSU • 1967 • Fukuda Seiichi • JPN • WOMAN'S BODY VANISHES
JOTAI NO DORONUMA • 1968 • Mukoyama Katsuhito • JPN • QUICKSAND OF THE FEMALE BODY, THE
JOTAI NO IZUMI • 1959 • Nakagawa Nobuo • JPN • CONDITION OF A FOUNTAIN
JOTAI SAMBASHI • 1959 • Ishii Teruo • JPN • RED PIERS
JOTAI WA KANASHIKU • 1957 • Inagaki Hiroshi • JPN • GEISHA IN THE OLD CITY, A
JOTAI ZANGYAKUZO • 1967 • Sakao Masanao • JPN • CRUEL MAP OF WOMEN'S BODIES
JOUDOUCHKA GOLOVLEF • 1934 • Ivanovsky Alexander • USS
JOUE AVEC DODO, IL • 1912-14 • Cohl Emile • ANS • USA
JOUER SA VIE • 1982 • Carle Gilles, Coudari Camille • DOC • CND • GREAT CHESS MOVIE, THE
JOUET, LE • 1976 • Veber Francis • FRN • TOY, THE (USA)
JOUET CRIMINEL, LE • 1969 • Arrieta Adolfo • FRN, SPN
JOUETS ANCIENS, LES • 1976 • Dansereau Fernand, Rossignol Yolande • DCS • CND
JOUETS ANIMES, LES • 1912 • Cohl Emile • ANS • FRN • JOUJOUX SAVANTS, LES
JOUETS VIVANTS, LES • 1908 • de Chomon Segundo • FRN • LIVING TOYS, THE
JOUEUR, LE • 1938 • Daquin Louis, Lamprecht Gerhard • FRN
JOUEUR, LE • 1958 • Autant-Lara Claude • FRN, ITL • GAMBLER, THE
JOUEUR DE QUILLES, LE • 1968 • Lajournade Jean-Pierre • FRN
JOUEUR D'ECHECS, LE • Bunuel Juan • MTV • FRN
JOUEUR D'ECHECS, LE • 1926 • Bernard Raymond • FRN • CHESS PLAYER, THE (USA)
JOUEUR D'ECHECS, LE • 1938 • Dreville Jean • FRN • CHESS PLAYER, THE (USA) ○ DEVIL IS AN EMPRESS, THE
JOUEURS D'ONDES, LES • 1952 • Bonniere Rene • DCS • FRN
JOUEUSE D'ORGUE, LA • 1924 • Burguet Charles • FRN
JOUEUSE D'ORGUE, LA • 1936 • Roudes Gaston • FRN
JOUG, LE • 1919 • Ravel Gaston • FRN
JOUGASAKI NO AME see **JOGASHIMA NO AME** • 1950
JOUGASAKI'S RAIN see **JOGASHIMA NO AME** • 1950
JOUIR! • 1978 • Kikoine Gerard • FRN
JOUISSANCES • 1974 • Davy Jean-Francois • FRN
JOUISSANCES see **SUPREMES JOUISSANCES** • 1977
JOUISSANCES A DOMICILE • 1985 • Lemoine Michel • FRN • JOUISSANCES ROULANTES ○ MOBILE-HOME GIRLS
JOUISSANCES ASIATIQUES • 1979 • Bernard-Aubert Claude • FRN
JOUISSANCES PERVERSES • 1979 • Leroi Francis • FRN
JOUISSANCES PROFONDES • Baudricourt Michel • FRN
JOUISSANCES ROULANTES see **JOUISSANCES A DOMICILE** • 1985
JOUISSANCES TRES SPECIALES • 1978 • Baudricourt Michel • FRN
JOUISSEUSES, LES • 1974 • Hustaix Lucien • FRN
JOUISSEUSES DE HONG KONG, LES • Warren Ken • FRN
JOUJOU • 1916 • Negroni Baldassare • ITL
JOUJOUX SAVANTS, LES see **JOUETS ANIMES, LES** • 1912
JOULUKSI KOTIIN • 1974 • Pakkasvirta Jaakko • FNL • HOME FOR CHRISTMAS
JOULUKUU • 1969 • von Bagh Peter • SHT • FNL • DECEMBER
JOUR A PARIS, UN • 1957 • Moky Michel • FRN
JOUR APRES JOUR • 1962 • Perron Clement • DCS • CND • DAY AFTER DAY
JOUR AVEC VOUS, UN • 1951 • Legrand Jean-Rene • FRN
JOUR COMME LES AUTRES, UN • 1953 • Rouquier Georges • SHT • FRN
JOUR COMME LES AUTRES, UN • 1958 • Bordry Paul • FRN
JOUR COMME UN AUTRE, UN • 1974 • Suter Daniel • SWT • DAY LIKE ANY OTHER DAY, A
JOUR DANS MA VIE, UN see **YUM MIN UMRI** • 1960
JOUR DE FETE • 1948 • Tati Jacques • FRN • BIG DAY, THE
JOUR DE FETE • 1949 • Strick Joseph • DCS • FRN • VILLAGE FAIR, THE (UKN)
JOUR DE GLOIRE, LE • 1976 • Besnard Jacques • FRN, FRG
JOUR DE MARCHE A TROUVILLE • 1896 • Melies Georges • FRN • MARKET DAY (TROUVILLE)
JOUR DE NOCES • 1930 • Gleize Maurice • FRN
JOUR DE NOCES • 1971 • Goretta Claude • MTV • FRN • WEDDING DAY, THE
JOUR DE PAQUES see **BELLE EQUIPE, LA** • 1936
JOUR DES PARQUES, LE see **RUPTURE, LA** • 1970
JOUR DES ROIS, LE • 1990 • Treilhou Marie-Claude • FRN
JOUR D'ETE, UN • 1933 • Lacombe Georges • FRN
JOUR DRAG, LE • 1970 • Gagne Jacques • DCS • CND
JOUR DU FORAIN, LE • 1987 • Derkaoui, Kettani • MRC • DAY OF THE HAWKER
JOUR DU FROTTEUR, LE • 1932 • Cavalcanti Alberto • FRN
JOUR DU SEIGNEUR, LE • 1980 • Bedel Jean-Pierre • MTV • CND
JOUR DU TERME, LE • 1904 • Blache Alice • FRN
JOUR EN SUEDE, UN • 1952 • Demarne Pierre • SHT • FRN
JOUR ET LA NUIT, LE see **SUZANNE ET SES BRIGANDS** • 1948
JOUR ET L'HEURE, LE • 1963 • Clement Rene • FRN, ITL • DAY AND THE HOUR, THE (USA) ○ GIORNO E L'ORA, IL ○ VIVIAMO OGGI ○ TODAY WE LIVE
JOUR ET NUIT • Menoud Jean-Bernard • SWT
JOUR, LA FETE, UN • 1974 • Sisser Pierre • FRN • BIG BAZAR
JOUR LES TEMOINS DISPARAITRONT • 1980 • Buyens Frans • DOC • BLG
JOUR OU LE CLOWN PLEURA, LE • 1974 • Lewis Jerry • FRN • DAY THE CLOWN CRIED, THE
JOUR QUELQUE PART, UN • 1971 • Derkaoui Mustafa • SHT • FRN
JOUR "S..", LE • 1984 • Lefebvre Jean-Pierre • CND
JOUR SANS EVIDENCE, UN • 1970 • Patry Yvan • CND
JOUR SANS LENDEMAIN see **YAWMUN BILA GHAD** • 1961
JOUR SE LEVE, LE • 1939 • Carne Marcel • FRN • DAYBREAK (USA)
JOUR SE LEVE ET LES CONNERIES COMMENCENT, LE • 1981 • Mulot Claude • FRN
JOUR VIENDRA, UN • 1933 • Veber Serge, Lamprecht Gerhard • FRN • TOUT ARRIVE
JOURNAL • 1973 • Akerman Chantal • BLG
JOURNAL ANIME, LE • 1908 • Cohl Emile • ANS • FRN • ANIMATED JOURNAL, THE ○ MON JOURNAL
JOURNAL DE LA RESISTANCE • 1945 • FRN
JOURNAL DE M. BONNAFOUS • 1971 • Swaim Bob • SHT • FRN
JOURNAL D'UN COMBAT, LE • 1965 • Gilles Guy • DCS • FRN
JOURNAL D'UN CURE DE CAMPAGNE, LE • 1950 • Bresson Robert • FRN • DIARY OF A COUNTRY PRIEST (USA)
JOURNAL D'UN FOU • 1963 • Coggio Roger • FRN
JOURNAL D'UN JEUNE TRAVAILLEUR • 1973 • Ifticene Mohamed • ALG
JOURNAL D'UN SCELERAT • 1950 • Rohmer Eric • SHT • FRN
JOURNAL D'UN SUBSTITUT DE CAMPAGNE EN EGYPTE see **YAWMIYYAT NAIB FI AL-ARYAF** • 1968
JOURNAL D'UN SUICIDE, LE • 1971 • Stanojevic Stanislav • FRN
JOURNAL D'UNE FEMME DE CHAMBRE, LE • 1963 • Bunuel Luis • FRN, ITL • DIARIO DI UNA CAMERIERA, IL (ITL) ○ DAIRY OF A CHAMBERMAID (USA)
JOURNAL D'UNE FEMME DE CHAMBRE, LE (FRN) see **DIARY OF A CHAMBERMAID** • 1946
JOURNAL D'UNE FEMME EN BLANC, LE • 1964 • Autant-Lara Claude • FRN, ITL • WOMAN IN WHITE, A (USA)
JOURNAL D'UNE JEUNE FILLE • Kikoine Gerard • FRN
JOURNAL D'UNE MAISON DE CORRECTION, LE • 1980 • Cachoux Georges • FRN
JOURNAL EROTIQUE D'UN BUCHERON, LE • 1973 • Pallardy Jean-Marie • FRN • EROTIC DIARY
JOURNAL FOLICHON, LE • 1910 • Cohl Emile • ANS • FRN
JOURNAL I-III • 1979 • Dindo Richard • DOC • SWT
JOURNAL INACHEVE • 1982 • Mallet Marilu • CND • UNFINISHED DIARY
JOURNAL INTIME D'UNE NYMPHOMANE, LE • 1972 • de Nesle Robert • FRN • DIARY OF A NYMPHOMANIAC (UKN)
JOURNAL OF A CRIME • 1934 • Keighley William • USA
JOURNAL OF THE ORANGE FLOWER see **KARATACHI NIKKI** • 1959
JOURNAL TOMBE A CINQ HEURES, LE • 1942 • Lacombe Georges • FRN
JOURNALIST see **ZHURNALIST** • 1967
JOURNALIST, THE • 1979 • Thornhill Michael • ASL
JOURNALIST, THE see **VASHA ZNAKOMAYA** • 1927
JOURNALIST, THE see **NOVINAR** • 1979
JOURNALIST'S TALE, A • 1985 • Godfrey Bob • ANS • UKN
JOURNEE A L'EXPOSITION PROVINCIALE DE QUEBEC, UNE • 1942 • Proulx Maurice • DCS • CND
JOURNEE A L'UNIVERSITE DE PAIX, UNE • 1969 • Cauvin Andre • BLG
JOURNEE AVEC JACQUES HELIAN ET SON ORCHESTRE, UNE • 1947-51 • Verneuil Henri • SHT • FRN
JOURNEE AVEC LES SCOUTS • Lavoie Hermenegilde • DCS • CND
JOURNEE BIEN REMPLIE, UNE • 1973 • Trintignant Jean-Louis • FRN, ITL • GIORNATA SPESA BENE, UNA (ITL) ○ FULL DAY'S WORK, A (USA) ○ WELL-FILLED DAY, A
JOURNEE DANS LA VIE DE RAMIKELLE, UNE • 1973 • Sens Al • ANS • CND
JOURNEE DANS LES PARCS NATIONAUX, UNE • 1979 • Beaudin Jean • CND
JOURNEE DE FLAMBEAU, LA see **FLAMBEAU CHIEN PERDU** • 1916
JOURNEE DE GREVE • 1909 • Jasset Victorin • FRN
JOURNEE D'UN-NON GREVISTE, LA • 1908 • Feuillade Louis • FRN
JOURNEE EN AFRIQUE, UNE • 1933 • Gross Anthony • ANS • FRN
JOURNEE EN TAXI, UNE • 1981 • Menard Robert • CND
JOURNEE NATURELLE • 1947 • Resnais Alain • FRN • VISITE A MAX ERNST
JOURNEES D'ETUDES • 1960 • Tessier Albert • DCS • CND • INSTITUTS FAMILIAUX
JOURNEY • 1972 • Almond Paul • CND • DETOUR
JOURNEY • 1980 • Yossifova Iskra, Petrova Malina • BUL
JOURNEY see **PUTESHESTVIYE** • 1967
JOURNEY see **TABIJI** • 1967
JOURNEY see **TABIJI** • 1987
JOURNEY, THE • 1958 • Litvak Anatole • USA • SOME OF US MAY DIE
JOURNEY, THE • 1965 • Robertson George C. • CND
JOURNEY, THE • 1972 • Cox Paul • SHT • ASL
JOURNEY, THE • 1989 • Kia-Rostami Abbas • IRN
JOURNEY, THE see **TABIJI** • 1953
JOURNEY, THE see **LASSIE'S GREAT ADVENTURE** • 1963
JOURNEY, THE see **RESAN** • 1967
JOURNEY, THE see **PODROZ** • 1970
JOURNEY, THE see **PUTOVANJE** • 1972
JOURNEY, THE see **YATRA** • 1988
JOURNEY, THE (UKN) see **VIAGGIO, IL** • 1974
JOURNEY AHEAD • 1947 • Mills Peter • UKN
JOURNEY AMONG WOMEN • 1977 • Cowan Tom • ASL
JOURNEY BACK TO OZ • 1971 • Sutherland Hal • ANM • USA
JOURNEY BENEATH THE DESERT (USA) see **ANTINEA, L'AMANTE DELLA CITTA SEPOLTA** • 1961
JOURNEY BEYOND THE STARS see **2001: A SPACE ODYSSEY** • 1968
JOURNEY BEYOND THREE SEAS see **PARDESI** • 1957
JOURNEY ENDS see **YATHRAYUDE ANTHYAM** • 1988
JOURNEY FOR JEREMY • 1949 • Hill James • UKN
JOURNEY FOR MARGARET • 1942 • Van Dyke W. S. • USA
JOURNEY FOR THREE • 1950 • Forlong Michael • NZL
JOURNEY FROM BERLIN see **WORKING TITLE: JOURNEYS FROM BERLIN/1971** • 1971
JOURNEY FROM DARKNESS • 1975 • Goldstone James • TVM • USA
JOURNEY FROM ETSA • 1957 • Biggs Julian • CND
JOURNEY FROM THE EAST • 1956 • Sturt George • UKN
JOURNEY FROM THE SHADOWS • 1938 • Weiss Jiri • DOC • CZC
JOURNEY FROM ZERO • 1961 • Blais Roger • DCS • CND • LONGUE RANDONEE, LA
JOURNEY HOME, THE • 1990 • Voizard Marc • SHT • CND
JOURNEY IN BOSCAVIA see **VOYAGE EN BOSCAVIE** • 1958
JOURNEY IN THE COSMOS • 1966 • Doukov Stoyan, Trayanov Anton • ANS • BUL • TRIP IN SPACE, A
JOURNEY INSIDE MY BRAIN see **UTAZAS A KOPONYAM KORUL** • 1970
JOURNEY INTO APRIL see **PUTESHESTVIE APRELY** • 1963
JOURNEY INTO AUTUMN (UKN) see **KVINNODROM** • 1955
JOURNEY INTO BEYOND see **REISE IN JENSEITS -DIE WELT DES UBERNATURLICHEN** • 1975
JOURNEY INTO CHILDHOOD • 1970 • Karsakbaev Abdulla • USS
JOURNEY INTO DARKNESS • 1967 • Trainor James • ASL
JOURNEY INTO DARKNESS • 1969 • Hill James, Sasdy Peter • ANT • UKN
JOURNEY INTO FEAR • 1942 • Foster Norman, Welles Orson (U/c) • USA
JOURNEY INTO FEAR • 1975 • Mann Daniel • USA, CND
JOURNEY INTO LIGHT • 1951 • Heisler Stuart • USA

JOURNEY INTO MEDICINE • 1946 • Van Dyke Willard • DOC • USA
JOURNEY INTO MIDNIGHT • 1969 • Gibson Alan, Baker Richard • ANT • UKN
JOURNEY INTO NOWHERE • 1963 • Scully Dennis • UKN • MURDER BY AGREEMENT
JOURNEY INTO PREHISTORY, A see **CESTA DO PRAVEKU** • 1955
JOURNEY INTO PRIMEVAL TIMES, A see **CESTA DO PRAVEKU** • 1955
JOURNEY INTO SELF • 1969 • *Mcgraw Bill (P)* • DOC • USA
JOURNEY INTO SOLITUDE see **TABI NO OMOSA** • 1972
JOURNEY INTO SPRING • Keene Ralph • DOC • UKN
JOURNEY INTO THE BEYOND see **REISE IN JENSEITS -DIE WELT DES UBERNATURLICHEN** • 1975
JOURNEY INTO THE NIGHT see **GANG IN DIE NACHT, DER** • 1920
JOURNEY INTO THE UNKNOWN see **REISE IN JENSEITS -DIE WELT DES UBERNATURLICHEN** • 1975
JOURNEY INTO THE UNKNOWN, A see **WYCIECZKA W NIEZNANE** • 1968
JOURNEY INTO YESTERDAY see **PORTRAIT FROM LIFE** • 1948
JOURNEY OF A PRESIDENT AND HIS SECRETARY see **DOTEI SHACHO TO ONNA-HISHO** • 1959
JOURNEY OF A STONE see **SAFARE SANG** • 1977
JOURNEY OF A THOUSAND AND ONE NIGHTS see **MATATABI SEN ICHIYA** • 1936
JOURNEY OF DEATH see **NORTH OF HUDSON BAY** • 1923
JOURNEY OF EIGHT CHILDREN see **NAOHACHI KODOMO TABI** • 1934
JOURNEY OF HOPE see **REISE DER HOFFNUNG** • 1989
JOURNEY OF LOVE see **KAZE NO BOJO** • 1970
JOURNEY OF LOVE (USA) see **BUON VIAGGIO POVER'UOMO** • 1951
JOURNEY OF NATTY GANN, THE • 1985 • Kagan Jeremy Paul • USA • NATTY GANN
JOURNEY OF O, THE • 1975 • Friedman David F. • USA
JOURNEY OF ROBERT F. KENNEDY, THE see **UNFINISHED JOURNEY OF ROBERT F. KENNEDY, THE** • 1969
JOURNEY OF STRETCHERS see **MASSA HA'ALUNKOT** • 1977
JOURNEY OF THE CHARIOT see **THER THIRUVIZHU** • 1968
JOURNEY OF VINCENC MOSTEK AND SIMON PESL OF VLCNOV TO PRAGUE 1969 A.D., THE see **CESTA DO PRAHY VINCENCE MOSTEK A SIMONA PESLA Z VLCNOZA L.P. 1969** • 1969
JOURNEY OF YOUTH see **SEISHUN MUSEN RYOKO** • 1958
JOURNEY OUT see **RESAN BORT** • 1945
JOURNEY OUT OF DARKNESS • 1967 • Trainor James • ASL
JOURNEY OUT OF THE CITY, THE see **WYCIECZKA Z MIASTA** • 1968
JOURNEY ROUND MY SKULL, A see **UTAZAS A KOPONYAM KORUL** • 1970
JOURNEY THAT SHOOK THE WORLD, THE see **JULES VERNE'S ROCKET TO THE MOON** • 1967
JOURNEY THROUGH FILMLAND • 1921 • Smith Beaumont • DOC • USA
JOURNEY THROUGH ROSEBUD • 1972 • Gries Tom • USA
JOURNEY THROUGH SAND see **REIS DOOR HET ZAND** • 1982
JOURNEY THROUGH SPACE AND TIME • 1939 • Waller Fred • USA
JOURNEY THROUGH THE BLACK SUN • 1975 • Austin Ray, Katzin Lee H. • MTV • UKN • SPACE 1999: JOURNEY THROUGH THE BLACK SUN
JOURNEY THROUGH THE DARK ZONE • 1989 • Bilson Danny • USA
JOURNEY THROUGH THE PAST • 1972 • Young Neil • USA
JOURNEY TO A BROKEN HEART • 1971 • Tammer Peter • DOC • ASL
JOURNEY TO A PRIMEVAL AGE see **CESTA DO PRAVEKU** • 1955
JOURNEY TO AMERICA, THE • 1987 • Carlsen Jon Bang • DNM
JOURNEY TO ANOTHER CITY see **PUTESHESTVIE V DRUGOI GOROD** • 1968
JOURNEY TO CYTHERA see **TAXIDI STA KYTHERA** • 1984
JOURNEY TO FREEDOM • 1957 • Dertano Robert C. • USA
JOURNEY TO HELL -THE LUCKY 9 COMMANDOS • 1968 • Garces Armando, Herrera S. • PHL
JOURNEY TO ITALY see **VIAGGIO IN ITALIA** • 1953
JOURNEY TO JERUSALEM, A • 1968 • Mindlin Michael Jr. • DOC • USA
JOURNEY TO NO END • 1977 • Hoffman Sonia • SHT • ASL
JOURNEY TO NOWHERE • 1963 • SAF
JOURNEY TO NOWHERE, A • 1916 • *Vitagraph* • SHT • USA
JOURNEY TO NOWHERE, THE see **VIAJE A NINGUNA PARTE, EL** • 1986
JOURNEY TO PRIMEVAL TIMES, A see **CESTA DO PRAVEKU** • 1955
JOURNEY TO SHILOH • 1968 • Hale William • USA
JOURNEY TO STRANGE LANDS, A • 1960 • Stiopul Savel • RMN
JOURNEY TO SUNDEVIT see **RIE REISE NACH SUNDEVIT** • 1966
JOURNEY TO THE 4TH PLANET see **ANGRY RED PLANET, THE** • 1959
JOURNEY TO THE BEGINNING OF TIME (USA) see **CESTA DO PRAVEKU** • 1955
JOURNEY TO THE CENTER OF THE EARTH • 1959 • Levin Henry • USA
JOURNEY TO THE CENTER OF THE EARTH • 1988 • Lemorande Rusty • USA
JOURNEY TO THE CENTER OF TIME • 1967 • Hewitt David L. • USA • TIME WARP
JOURNEY TO THE CENTRE OF THE EARTH • 1976 • Slapczynski Richard • ANM • ASL
JOURNEY TO THE CENTRE OF THE EARTH (USA) see **VOYAGE AU CENTRE DE LA TERRE** • 1909
JOURNEY TO THE DAY • 1960 • Frankenheimer John • MTV • USA
JOURNEY TO THE END OF NIGHT • 1982 • Tammer Peter • DOC • ASL
JOURNEY TO THE FAR SIDE OF THE SUN see **DOPPELGANGER** • 1969
JOURNEY TO THE LOST CITY see **INDISCHE GRABMAL, DAS** • 1959
JOURNEY TO THE MIDDLE OF THE EARTH, A see **VOYAGE AU CENTRE DE LA TERRE** • 1909
JOURNEY TO THE MOON see **REHLA ILAL KAMAR** • 1959
JOURNEY TO THE NORTH see **KITAGUNI NO RYOJO** • 1967
JOURNEY TO THE NORTH POLE, A • 1903 • Paul Robert William • UKN
JOURNEY TO THE PAST see **HOUSE IN THE SQUARE, THE** • 1951
JOURNEY TO THE PLACE OF ACCIDENT see **PUTOVANJE NA MJESTO NESRECE** • 1972
JOURNEY TO THE SEVENTH PLANET • 1961 • Pink Sidney • USA, DNM
JOURNEY TO THE STARS • 1961 • Wilson John • USA
JOURNEY TO THE UNKNOWN • 1969 • *Miles Vera* • MTV • UKN, USA
JOURNEY TO THE WEST, THE see **HSI-YU CHI** • 1960
JOURNEY TO VIENNA see **REISE NACH WIEN, DIE** • 1973
JOURNEY TO YOU, THE see **RESAN TILL DEJ** • 1953
JOURNEY TOGETHER • 1945 • Boulting John • UKN
JOURNEY TOWARDS BIRTH, A • 1988 • MacDalland Maria • ANM • DNM
JOURNEY WITH A CINE CAMERA, A • 1952 • Schneiderov Vladimir • DOC • USS
JOURNEY WITH FATHER see **RESA MED FAR** • 1968
JOURNEY WITH GHOST ALONG TOKKAIDO ROAD see **ALONG WITH GHOSTS** • 1969
JOURNEY WITH JACOB see **UTAZAS JAKABBAL** • 1972
JOURNEY WITHOUT RETURN see **REISE OHNE WIEDERKEHR** • 1990
JOURNEY'S END • 1915 • *Royal* • USA
JOURNEY'S END • 1918 • Vale Travers • USA
JOURNEY'S END • 1930 • Whale James • UKN, USA
JOURNEY'S END, THE • 1915 • Chaudet Louis W. • USA
JOURNEY'S END, THE • 1921 • Ballin Hugo • USA
JOURNEY'S ENDING, THE • 1913 • Taylor Stanner E. V. • USA
JOURNEYS FROM BERLIN see **WORKING TITLE: JOURNEYS FROM BERLIN/1971** • 1971
JOURNEYS IN MY LAND see **VIAGENS NA MINHA TERRA** • 1980
JOURNEYS LAND (UKN) see **REISENS INS LANDESINNERE** • 1988
JOURS DE 36 see **IMERES TOU '36** • 1972
JOURS DE NOTRE VIE, LES • 1981 • Rabinowicz Maurice • BLG, FRN
JOURS DE TOURMENTES • 1983 • Zoumbara Paul • BRK • DAYS OF TORMENT
JOURS DE VOLOTCHAIEV, LES see **VOLOCHAYEVSKIYE DNI** • 1938
JOURS D'OCTOBRE, LES see **OCTIABR' DNI** • 1958
JOURS ET NUITS see **AYYAMUN WA LAYALI** • 1955
JOURS GRIS, LES • 1974 • Azimi Iradj • FRN
JOURS HEUREUX, LES • 1941 • de Marguenat Jean • FRN
JOUSIAMPUJA • 1983 • Kassila Taavi • FNL • ARCHER, THE
JOVANA LUKINA • 1980 • Nikolic Zivko • YGS
JOVANKA AND THE OTHERS see **JOVANKA E LE ALTRE** • 1960
JOVANKA E LE ALTRE • 1960 • Ritt Martin • ITL, USA • FIVE BRANDED WOMEN (USA) ○ JOVANKA AND THE OTHERS
JOVEN, LA see **YOUNG ONE, THE** • 1960
JOVEN CASADA, LA • 1975 • Camus Mario • SPN
JOVEN DE 16 ANOS, UNA • 1962 • Martinez Solares Gilberto • MXC
JOVEN DEL CARRITO, EL • 1958 • Cardona Rene • MXC
JOVEN JUAREZ, EL • 1954 • Gomez Muriel Emilio • MXC
JOVEN MANCORNADORA, LA • 1959 • de la Serna Mauricio • MXC
JOVEN REBELDE, EL • 1961 • Espinosa Julio Garcia • CUB • YOUNG REBEL, THE
JOVENCITO DRACULA, EL • 1975 • Benito Carlos • SPN
JOVENES AMANTES, LOS • 1970 • Alazraki Benito • MXC
JOVENES, LOS • 1960 • Alcoriza Luis • MXC • YOUTHS, THE
JOVENES VIEJOS, LOS • 1961 • Kuhn Rodolfo • ARG • SAD YOUNG MEN, THE
JOVENES Y BELLAS • 1961 • Cortes Fernando • MXC
JOVENS PRA FRENTE • 1968 • Diniz Alcino • BRZ • UNCONVENTIONAL YOUTH
JOVIAL EXPRESSIONS • 1905 • Green Tom? • UKN
JOVIAL FLUID, THE • 1913 • Kellino W. P. • UKN
JOVIAL MONKS IN THE REFECTORY, THE • 1898 • *Paul R. W.* • UKN
JOVIAL MONKS NO.1, THE • 1899 • Williamson James • UKN
JOVIAL MONKS NO.2 -TIT FOR TAT, THE • 1899 • Williamson James • UKN
JOVITA see **JOWITA** • 1967
JOWITA • 1967 • Morgenstern Janusz • PLN • YOVITA (USA) ○ JOVITA
JOY • 1977 • *Mitchell Sharon* • USA
JOY • 1983 • Bergon Serge • FRN, CND
JOY see **ZONNETJE** • 1920
JOY AND LIGHT see **UITZICHT OP DE HEMEL** • 1961
JOY AND THE DRAGON • 1916 • King Henry • USA
JOY GIRL, THE • 1927 • Dwan Allan • USA
JOY GIRLS see **SHUNPU-DEN** • 1965
JOY HOUSE, THE (USA) see **FELINS, LES** • 1964
JOY IN THE MORNING • 1965 • Segal Alex • USA
JOY OF EFFORT, THE • 1973 • Bittman Roman • DOC • CND
JOY OF FATE, A • 1917 • *Triangle* • USA
JOY OF FLYING see **FREUDE AM FLIEGEN** • 1977
JOY OF FOOLING AROUND, THE • 1979 • du Bois Pierre • FRN
JOY OF FREEDOM, THE • 1917 • Drew Sidney, Drew Sidney Mrs. • SHT • USA
JOY OF JESABELLE, THE see **JOYS OF JEZEBEL, THE** • 1970
JOY OF LETTING GO, THE • 1976 • Gregory John • USA
JOY OF LIVING • 1938 • Garnett Tay • USA
JOY OF LIVING see **FUTURES VEDETTES** • 1955
JOY OF LIVING: THE ART OF RENOIR • 1952 • Oser Jean • USA
JOY OF LOVE, THE see **BLAHO LASKY** • 1966
JOY OF SEX, THE • 1984 • Coolidge Martha • USA
JOY PARADE, THE (UKN) see **LIFE BEGINS IN COLLEGE** • 1937
JOY RIDE • 1935 • Hughes Harry • UKN
JOY RIDE • 1958 • Bernds Edward • USA
JOY RIDE, THE • 1912 • *Powers* • USA
JOY RIDE, THE • 1913 • *Patheplay* • USA
JOY RIDER, THE • 1921 • Roach Hal • SHT • USA
JOY RIDERS, THE • 1913 • *Joker* • USA
JOY RIDERS, THE • 1917 • Clark Frank, Dunham Phil • SHT • USA
JOY SCOUTS • 1939 • Cahn Edward L. • SHT • USA
JOY STICKS see **VIDEO MADNESS** • 1983
JOY STREET • 1929 • Cannon Raymond • USA
JOY TILL MORNING • Kachlik Antonin • CZC
JOY TONIC • 1929 • Lamont Charles • SHT • USA
JOYAS DEL DIABLO, LA • 1968 • Elorrieta Jose Maria • SPN, CND, TNS
JOYAS DEL PECADO, LAS • 1949 • Crevenna Alfredo B. • MXC
JOYAUX DE LA MER DE CORAIL • 1973-74 • Valcour Pierre • DOC • CND
JOYCE AT 34 • 1972 • Weill Claudia, Chopra Joyce • SHT • USA
JOYCE OF THE NORTH WOODS • 1913 • Miller Ashley • USA
JOYCE'S STRATEGY • 1916 • *Fair Joyce* • SHT • USA
JOYEUSE PRISON, LA • 1956 • Berthomieu Andre • FRN
JOYEUSES, LES • Frederic Jean-Jacques • FRN
JOYEUSES COLONIES DE VACANCES, LES • 1979 • Gerard Michel • FRN
JOYEUSES NOCES DE SAINT-LOLO, LES • 1913 • Fescourt Henri • FRN
JOYEUSES PAQUES • 1984 • Lautner Georges • FRN
JOYEUX COMPERES • Pierson Claude • FRN
JOYEUX CONSCRIT, LES see **BATAILLE DU FEU, LA** • 1948
JOYEUX FAUX PROPHETE RUSSE, LE • 1904 • Melies Georges • FRN • FAKE RUSSIAN PROPHET, THE (USA)
JOYEUX LURONS, LES • 1972 • Gerard Charles • FRN
JOYEUX MICROBES, LES • 1909 • Cohl Emile • ANS • FRN • JOYOUS MICROBES, THE ○ MAGIC CARTOONS ○ MERRY MICROBES, THE
JOYEUX NOEL see **QUAI DES ORFEVRES** • 1947
JOYEUX PELERINS, LES • 1950 • Pasquali Alfred • FRN
JOYEUX TROMBLONS, LES • 1974-75 • Storck Henri • DOC • BLG
JOYFUL AND TRIUMPHANT • 1965 • Kavanagh Brian • DOC • ASL
JOYFUL WISDOM, THE see **GAI SAVOIR, LE** • 1967
JOYLESS STREET, THE (UKN) see **FREUDLOSE GASSE, DIE** • 1925
JOYO • 1960 • Misumi Kenji • JPN • PATTERNS OF LOVE
JOYOKU NO KUROZUISEN • 1967 • Wakamatsu Koji • JPN • BLACK NARCISSUS OF DESIRE
JOYOUS ADVENTURES OF ARISTIDE PUJOL, THE • 1920 • Miller Frank • UKN
JOYOUS HEROES, THE see **HUANLE YINGXIONG** • 1988
JOYOUS LIAR, THE • 1919 • Warde Ernest C. • USA
JOYOUS MICROBES, THE see **JOYEUX MICROBES, LES** • 1909
JOYOUS TROUBLEMAKERS, THE • 1920 • Edwards J. Gordon • USA
JOYRIDE • 1977 • Ruben Joseph • USA
JOYRIDE TO NOWHERE • 1978 • von Theumer Ernst Ritter • FRG
JOYRIDERS • 1989 • Walsh Aisling • UKN, IRL
JOYS ELOPE, THE • 1916 • *International Film Service* • SHT • USA
JOYS OF A JEALOUS WIFE, THE • 1913 • Costello Maurice • USA
JOYS OF GEORGETTE • 1969 • *Distripix* • USA
JOYS OF JEZEBEL, THE • 1970 • Stootsberry A. P. • USA • JOY OF JESABELLE, THE ○ JEZEBEL
JOYS OF PERSECUTION, THE • 1911 • *Powers* • USA
JOYS OF THE FATHER OF HIS COUNTRY, THE see **SLASTI OTCE VLASTI** • 1968
JOYS OF TORTURE, THE see **TOKUGAWA ONNA KEIBATSUSHI** • 1968
JOYSTICKS see **VIDEO MADNESS** • 1983
JOYU • 1947 • Kinugasa Teinosuke • JPN • ACTRESS
JOYU • 1956 • Shindo Kaneto • JPN • ACTRESS, AN
JOYU SUMAKO NO KOI • 1947 • Mizoguchi Kenji • JPN • LOVES OF SUMAKO THE ACTRESS, THE (USA) ○ LOVES OF ACTRESS SUMAKO, THE ○ LOVE OF SUMAKO THE ACTRESS, THE
JOYU TO SHIJIN see **JOYU TO SHINJI** • 1935
JOYU TO SHINJI • 1935 • Naruse Mikio • JPN • ACTRESS AND THE POET, THE ○ JOYU TO SHIJIN
JOZEF KOSTRZEVSKI • 1969 • Czurko Edward • SHT • PLN
JR. STAR TREK • 1969 • Emshwiller Peter • SHT • USA
JRDINA JEDNE NOCI see **HRDJA JEDNO NOCI** • 1935
JSEM DEVCE S CERTEM V TELE • 1933 • Anton Karl • CZC • I AM A GIRL WITH THE DEVIL IN MY BODY
J'SORS AVEC LUI PIS JE L'AIME • 1977 • Beaudry Jean • CND
JSOUC NA RECE MLYNAR JEDEN • 1971 • Brdecka Jiri • ANM • CZC • THERE WAS A MILLER ON THE RIVER
J'TE DIS QU'ELLE T'A FAIT DE L'OEIL see **ET MOI J'TE DIS QU'ELLE T'A FAIT DE L'OEIL** • 1935
JU-JITSU • 1907 • Collins Alf • UKN
JU-JITSU TO THE RESCUE • 1913 • Raymond Charles • UKN • SELF DEFENCE
JUAN A LAS OCHO, PABLO A LAS DIEZ • 1973 • Bosch Juan • SPN
JUAN AND JUANITA • 1912 • Melville Wilbert • USA
JUAN AND JUNIOR IN A DIFFERENT WORLD see **JUAN Y JUNIOR EN UN MONDO DIFERENTE** • 1970
JUAN CARIZZA see **DON MANUEL, DER BANDIT** • 1929
JUAN CHARRASQUEADO • 1947 • Cortazar Ernesto • MXC
JUAN COLORADO • 1965 • Zacarias Miguel • MXC
JUAN GLOBO • 1949 • Amadori Luis Cesar • ARG
JUAN GUERRERO • 1963 • Morayta Miguel • MXC
JUAN JOSE • 1917 • de Banos Ricardo • SPN
JUAN JOSE • 1929 • Guarino Joseph • FRN
JUAN JOSE see **LIFE** • 1928
JUAN MOREIRA • 1909 • Gallo Mario • ARG
JUAN MOREIRA • 1948 • Barth-Moglia Luis • ARG
JUAN MOREIRA • 1973 • Favio Leonardo • ARG
JUAN NEGRO • 1978 • Cardona Mario • DOC • CRC

JUAN PEDRO EL DALLADOR see **LEY DE UNA RAZA, LA** • 1967
JUAN PISTOLAS • 1935 • Curwood Robert • MXC
JUAN PISTOLAS • 1966 • Cardona Rene Jr. • MXC
JUAN POLAINAS • 1960 • Cardona Rene • MXC
JUAN QUE REIA • 1976 • Galettini Carlos • ARG • JUAN WHO LAUGHED
JUAN SIN MIEDO • 1938 • Segura Juan Jose • MXC
JUAN SIN MIEDO • 1960 • Gazcon Gilberto • MXC
JUAN SOLDADO • 1919 • Castilla Enrique • MXC
JUAN SOLDADO, O VENGANZA • 1939 • Gasnier Louis J. • SPN • JOHN THE SOLDIER OF VENGEANCE
JUAN VICENTE GOMEZ • 1975 • de Pedro Manuel • DOC • VNZ
JUAN WHO LAUGHED see **JUAN QUE REIA** • 1976
JUAN Y JUNIOR EN UN MONDO DIFERENTE • 1970 • Olea Pedro • SPN • JUAN AND JUNIOR IN A DIFFERENT WORLD
JUANA GALLO • 1960 • Zacarias Miguel • MXC • GUNS OF JUANA GALLO, THE
JUANILLO, PAPA Y MAMA • 1956 • Alberto Juan, Salvador Julio • SPN
JUANITA • 1913 • *Darkfeather Mona* • USA
JUANITA • 1935 • Caron Pierre • FRN
JUANITA BANANA • 1968 • de Villa Jose • PHL • ANG MAGKAIBANG DAIDIGNI JUANITA BANANA
JUANITO • 1959 • Palacios Fernando • SPN
JUANTOPOCHO • 1977 • Bolivar Cesar • VNZ
JUAREZ • 1939 • Dieterle William • USA
JUAREZ Y MAXIMILIANO • 1933 • Contreras Torres Miguel • MXC
JUARI • 1968 • Prakash Suraj • IND • GAMBLER
JUBAL • 1956 • Daves Delmer • USA
JUBIABA • 1988 • dos Santos Nelson Rodrigues • BRZ
JUBILATION STREET see **KANKO NO MACHI** • 1944
JUBILAUMS-PREIS, DER • 1917 • Neuss Alwin • FRG
JUBILE D'ARGENT DES FRERES MARISTES D'ALMA • 1952 • Lavoie Hermenegilde • DOC • CND
JUBILEE • 1965 • Andronikashvili O. • ANS • USS
JUBILEE • 1978 • Jarman Derek • UKN
JUBILEE see **IUBELEI** • 1944
JUBILEE, THE see **JUBILEUSZ** • 1962
JUBILEE CHRONICLE see **KRONIKA JUBILEUSZOWA** • 1959
JUBILEE STORY see **KRONIKA JUBILEUSZOWA** • 1959
JUBILEE TRAIL • 1954 • Kane Joseph • USA
JUBILEE WINDOW • 1935 • Pearson George • UKN
JUBILEJ G. IKLA see **JUBILEJ GOSPODINA IKLA** • 1955
JUBILEJ GOSPODINA IKLA • 1955 • Mimica Vatroslav • YGS • MR. IKL'S JUBILEE ○ JUBILEJ G. IKLA
JUBILEUSZ • 1962 • Karabasz Kazimierz • DCS • PLN • JUBILEE, THE
JUBILO • 1919 • Badger Clarence • USA
JUBILO, JR. • 1924 • McGowan Robert • SHT • USA
JUCKLINS, THE • 1920 • Melford George • USA • FIGHTING SCHOOLMASTER, THE (UKN)
JUD SUSS • 1940 • Harlan Veit • FRG • JEW SUSS
JUDA • 1972 • Gilic Vlatko • SHT • YGS
JUDAH see **CHEATER, THE** • 1920
JUDAI NO AOI SEI • 1968 • Inoue Yoshio • JPN • GREEN SEX
JUDAI NO SEITEN • 1953 • Shima Koji • JPN • TEENAGER'S SEX MANUAL
JUDAI NO YUWAKU • 1954 • *Wakao Ayako* • JPN • TEMPTATIONS OF TEENAGERS
JUDAS • 1918 • Curtiz Michael • HNG • DUDAS
JUDAS • 1930 • Ivanov-Barkov Yevgeni • USS
JUDAS • 1936 • Ojeda Manuel R. • MXC
JUDAS, EL • 1952 • Iquino Ignacio F. • SPN
JUDAS CITY • Tamijian • USA
JUDAS GOAT see **XTRO** • 1982
JUDAS MONEY see **JUDASPENGAR** • 1915
JUDAS' SILVER • 1988 • Ovcharov Svetoslav • BUL
JUDAS.., TOMA TUS MONEDAS • 1971 • Ramirez Pedro L. • SPN
JUDAS VON TIROL, DER • 1933 • Osten Franz • FRG • EWIGE VERRAT, DER
JUDAS WAS A WOMAN (UKN) see **BETE HUMAINE, LA** • 1938
JUDASPENGAR • 1915 • Sjostrom Victor • SWD • TRAITOR'S REWARD ○ JUDAS MONEY
JUDD FOR THE DEFENSE • 1970 • Hart Harvey • TVM • USA
JUDE • 1983 • Klausner Drew • USA
JUDE VON PRAG, DER • 1915 • *Sandten Thea* • FRG
JUDEL GRA NA SKRZYPKACH see **YIDL MITN FIDL** • 1937
JUDEX • 1916 • Feuillade Louis • SRL • FRN • PLUS GRAND SUCCES DE RENE CRESTE, LE
JUDEX • 1963 • Franju Georges • FRN, ITL • UOMO IN NERO, L' (ITL)
JUDEX 34 • 1933 • Champreux Maurice • FRN
JUDGE, THE • 1916 • *Murray Charles* • SHT • USA
JUDGE, THE • 1949 • Clifton Elmer • USA • GAMBLERS, THE (UKN)
JUDGE, THE • 1986 • Maslarov Plamen • BUL
JUDGE, THE see **DOMAREN** • 1960
JUDGE ALTON B. PARKER • 1904 • *Bitzer Billy (Ph)* • USA
JUDGE AND HIS HANGMAN, THE see **RICHTER UND SEIN HENKER, DER** • 1976
JUDGE AND JAKE WYLER, THE • 1972 • Rich David Lowell • TVM • USA
JUDGE AND JEOPARDY see **KUBI** • 1968
JUDGE AND THE ASSASSIN, THE (USA) see **JUGE ET L'ASSASSIN, LE** • 1975
JUDGE AND THE SINNER, THE see **JUGENDRICHTER, DER** • 1960
JUDGE AND THE WOMAN, THE see **NAME THE MAN** • 1924
JUDGE BROWN SERIES • 1919 • SER • USA
JUDGE BROWN'S JUSTICE • 1918 • Vidor King • SHS • USA
JUDGE DEE • 1974 • Kagan Jeremy Paul • TVM • USA • JUDGE DEE IN THE MONASTERY MURDERS
JUDGE DEE IN THE MONASTERY MURDERS see **JUDGE DEE** • 1974
JUDGE DUNN'S DECISION • 1914 • Le Saint Edward J. • USA
JUDGE FOR A DAY • 1935 • Fleischer Dave • ANS • USA
JUDGE HARDY AND SON • 1939 • Seitz George B. • USA
JUDGE HARDY'S CHILDREN • 1938 • Seitz George B. • USA
JUDGE HER NOT • 1921 • Hall George Edwardes • USA
JUDGE HORTON AND THE SCOTTSBORO BOYS • 1976 • Cook Fielder • TVM • USA
JUDGE JEFFERSON REMEMBERS • 1945 • Haines Ronald • UKN
JUDGE NOT • 1920 • Bruun Einar J. • UKN
JUDGE NOT OR THE WOMAN OF MONA DIGGINGS • 1915 • Leonard Robert Z. • USA
JUDGE NOT THAT YE BE NOT JUDGED • 1909 • Brooke Van Dyke • USA
JUDGE OF BODRUM, THE see **BODRUM HAKIMI** • 1977
JUDGE OF ZALAMEA, THE see **RICHTER VON ZALAMEA, DER** • 1955
JUDGE PIMPLE • 1915 • Evans Fred, Evans Joe • UKN
JUDGE PRIEST • 1934 • Ford John • USA
JUDGE RUMMY IN BEAR FACTS • 1920 • La Cava Gregory • ANS • USA
JUDGE SIMPKINS' SUMMER COURT • 1911 • *Essanay* • USA
JUDGE STEPS OUT, THE • 1949 • Ingster Boris • USA • INDIAN SUMMER (UKN)
JUDGE THE WILD QUEEN • 1968 • Doucette Albert J. • USA
JUDGE YE NOT IN HASTE • 1910 • *Yankee* • USA
JUDGED BY APPEARANCES • 1914 • Plumb Hay? • UKN
JUDGED BY APPEARANCES • 1916 • Croise Hugh • UKN
JUDGED BY HIGHER POWER • 1911 • *Champion* • USA
JUDGEMENT • 1909 • Olcott Sidney • USA
JUDGEMENT • 1916 • Batley Ernest G. • UKN
JUDGEMENT • 1922 • *Moore Joe* • USA
JUDGEMENT • 1989 • Sachs William • USA
JUDGEMENT see **ITELET** • 1970
JUDGEMENT see **PRESUDA** • 1978
JUDGEMENT, THE • 1913 • *Domino* • USA
JUDGEMENT, THE • 1985 • SAF
JUDGEMENT, THE see **RECKLESS DISREGARD** • 1985
JUDGEMENT, THE (UKN) see **GUNNAR HEDES SAGA** • 1923
JUDGEMENT AT NUREMBERG • 1961 • Kramer Stanley • USA
JUDGEMENT BOOK, THE • 1935 • Hutchison Charles • USA
JUDGEMENT DAY • 1978 • Cutaia Jon • USA
JUDGEMENT IN STONE, A • 1986 • Rawi Ousama • CND • HOUSEKEEPER, THE (USA)
JUDGEMENT OF BUDDHA, THE • 1913 • *Melies* • USA
JUDGEMENT OF HISTORY, THE see **PERED SUDOM ISTORII** • 1966
JUDGEMENT OF MEN, THE • 1915 • *Victor* • USA
JUDGEMENT OF SOLOMON, THE • 1909 • Blackton J. Stuart (Spv) • USA
JUDGEMENT OF THE DEEP, THE • 1913 • *Lubin* • USA
JUDGEMENT OF THE GUILTY • 1916 • Conway Jack • USA
JUDGEMENT OF THE SEA, THE • 1912 • *Melies* • USA
JUDGEMENTS OF THE MIGHTY DEEP, THE • 1910 • *Edison* • USA
JUDGE'S FRIEND, THE (UKN) see **MIJN VRIEND** • 1980
JUDGES OF THE BIBLE, THE see **JUECES DE LA BIBLIA, LOS** • 1964
JUDGE'S SON, THE • 1913 • *Broncho* • USA
JUDGE'S STORY, THE • 1911 • *Eline Marie* • USA
JUDGE'S VINDICATION, THE • 1913 • Apfel Oscar • USA
JUDGE'S WARD, THE • 1909 • *Lubin* • USA
JUDGE'S WHISKERS, THE • 1909 • *Vitagraph* • USA
JUDGE'S WIFE, THE • 1914 • Taylor William D. • USA
JUDGMENT see **HER HUSBAND'S SECRET** • 1925
JUDGMENT AT NUREMBERG • 1959 • Hill George Roy • MTV • USA
JUDGMENT DAY, THE see **HESAP GUNU** • 1967
JUDGMENT DEFERRED • 1952 • Baxter John • UKN
JUDGMENT HOUSE, THE • 1917 • Blackton J. Stuart • USA
JUDGMENT IN BERLIN • 1988 • Penn Leo • USA
JUDGMENT IN THE SUN see **OUTRAGE** • 1964
JUDGMENT OF GOD, THE see **JUGEMENT DE DIEU, LE** • 1949
JUDGMENT OF THE HILLS • 1927 • Meehan James Leo • USA
JUDGMENT OF THE MAD see **SUD SUMASSHEDSHICH** • 1962
JUDGMENT OF THE PEOPLE • 1947 • Karmen Roman • USS • NUREMBERG
JUDGMENT OF THE STORM • 1924 • Andrews Del • USA
JUDGMENT (UKN) see **OPENING NIGHT, THE** • 1927
JUDITH • 1922 • Monca Georges • FRN
JUDITH • 1966 • Mann Daniel • USA, UKN, ISR • CONFLICT
JUDITH AND HOLOPHERNES see **GIUDITTA E OLOFERNE** • 1959
JUDITH AND WERNER see **JUDITH OG WERNER** • 1981
JUDITH ET HOLOPHERNE • 1909 • Feuillade Louis • FRN
JUDITH OF BETHULIA • 1914 • Griffith D. W. • USA • HER CONDONED SIN
JUDITH OF THE CUMBERLANDS • 1916 • McGowan J. P. • USA
JUDITH OG WERNER • 1981 • Rex Jytte • DNM • JUDITH AND WERNER
JUDITH TERPEAUVE • 1979 • Chereau Patrice • FRN • JUDITH THERPAUVE ○ FEMME DANGEREUSE, UNE
JUDITH THERPAUVE see **JUDITH TERPEAUVE** • 1979
JUDITH TRACHTENBERG • 1920 • Galeen Henrik • FRG
JUDO CHAMP see **ARASHI NO KUDOKEN** • 1958
JUDO CHAMPION see **MINAMI TAIHEIYO NO WAKADAISHO** • 1967
JUDO-JINKS • 1953-54 • Devlin Bernard • DCS • CND
JUDO, KARATE MATADOR • 1967 • Gaudite Solano • PHL
JUDO KUDOS • 1968 • Bartsch Art • ANS • USA
JUDO SAGA see **SUGATA SANSHIRO** • 1945
JUDO SAGA see **SUGATA SANSHIRO** • 1965
JUDO SAGA II see **ZOKU SUGATA SANSHIRO** • 1945
JUDO SCHOOL EXPULSION LETTER see **KODOKAN HAMONJO** • 1968
JUDO SHOWDOWN (USA) see **YAWARA SEMPU DOTO NO TAIKETSU** • 1966
JUDOKA AGENT SECRET • 1966 • Zimmer Pierre • FRN, ITL • CARNET PER UN MORTO (ITL)
JUDOU • 1990 • Zhang Yimou • HKG
JUDY • 1970 • Hanson David W. • USA
JUDY BUYS A HORSE • 1939 • Comfort Lance • UKN
JUDY FORGOT • 1915 • Hunter T. Hayes • USA
JUDY GOES TO TOWN (UKN) see **PUDDIN' HEAD** • 1941
JUDY OF ROGUES' HARBOR • 1920 • Taylor William D. • USA
JUDY'S LITTLE NO-NO • 1969 • Price Sherman • USA • LET'S DO IT
JUE XIANG • 1985 • Zhang Zeming • CHN • SWAN SONG
JUECES DE LA BIBLIA, LOS • 1964 • Perez-Dolc Francesc • SPN, ITL • JUDGES OF THE BIBLE, THE
JUEGO DE AMOR PROHIBIDO • 1975 • de la Iglesia Eloy • SPN
JUEGO DE HOMBRES • 1964 • Gamboa Jose Luis • SPN • GAME OF MEN
JUEGO DE LA GUITARRA, EL • 1971 • *A.a.mexicanos* • MXC
JUEGO DE LA OCA, EL • 1965 • Summers Manuel • SPN
JUEGO DE LA VERDAD, EL • 1963 • Forque Jose Maria • SPN
JUEGO DE NAIPES • 1969 • Gijon Salvador • ANS • SPN • GAME OF CARDS
JUEGO DE NINOS • 1958 • Cahen Enrique • SPN
JUEGO DE NINOS see **SIMITRIO** • 1960
JUEGO DE PELOTA, EL see **ULAMA, EL** • 1985
JUEGO DEL ADULTERIO, EL • 1973 • Romero-Marchent Joaquin Luis • SPN
JUEGO DEL AMOR Y DEL AZAR, EL • 1944 • Torres-Rios Leopoldo • ARG
JUEGO DIABOLICO • 1958 • Fernandez Fernando • MXC • DIABOLIC GAME
JUEGO DIABOLICO • 1964 • *Farell Raul* • MXC
JUEGO HISTORICO, UN • 1971 • Fraga Jorge • DOC • CUB
JUEGO MAS DIVERTIDO, EL • 1988 • Martinez Lazaro Emilio • SPN • FUNNIEST GAME, THE
JUEGO PELIGROSO • 1966 • Ripstein Arturo, Alcoriza Luis • MXC, BRZ • JOGO PERIGOSO
JUEGO SUCIO EN PANAMA • 1974 • Demicheli Tulio • SPN
JUEGO Y LA VIDA, EL • 1977 • Jordan Josefina • DOC • VNZ • PLAY AND LIFE
JUEGOS DE SOCIEDAD • 1973 • Merino Jose Luis • SPN • SOCIETY'S GAMES
JUEGOS PELIGROSOS • 1964 • Balbuena Silvio F. • SPN
JUERGAS DEL SENORITO, LAS • 1972 • Balcazar Alfonso • SPN
JUEVES MILAGRO, LOS • 1957 • Berlanga Luis Garcia • SPN • ON THURSDAYS A MIRACLE ○ THURSDAYS, MIRACLE
JUEX PRECOCES (FRN) see **ROSSETTO, IL** • 1960
JUEZ DE LA SOGA, EL • 1972 • *Rosas Priego* • MXC
JUEZ SANGRIENTO, EL see **PROCESO DE LAS BRUJAS, EL** • 1970
JUG O' RUM • 1911 • *Powers* • USA
JUG OF BREAD, A LOAF OF WINE, AND LEWIS CARROLL IN A BARREL, A • 1968 • Dentino John • SHT • USA
JUGADOR, EL • 1947 • Klimovsky Leon • ARG
JUGADOR, EL • 1952 • Orona Vicente • MXC
JUGADOR DE AJEDREZ, EL • 1980 • Bunuel J. • MXC
JUGANDO A MORIR • 1966 • Gan Jose H. • SPN
JUGANDO CON LA MUERTE see **TARGET EAGLE** • 1982
JUGANDOSE LA VIDA • 1959 • Martinez Arturo • MXC
JUGAR CON FUEGO • 1978 • Larraz Jose R. • SPN
JUGAR, JUGAR VAMOS A MATAR • 1979 • San Miguel Santiago • VNZ, SPN • PLAY AND THRILL, WE WILL KILL
JUGE, LE • 1919 • Bergerat Theo • FRN
JUGE, LE • 1969 • Girault Jean • FRN
JUGE, LE • 1983 • Lefebvre Philippe • FRN
JUGE ET L'ASSASSIN, LE • 1975 • Tavernier Bertrand • FRN • JUDGE AND THE ASSASSIN, THE (USA)
JUGE FAYARD DIT "LE SHERIF", LE • 1977 • Boisset Yves • FRN • SHERIFF, LE
JUGEMENT DE DIEU, LE • 1949 • Bernard Raymond • FRN • JUDGMENT OF GOD, THE
JUGEMENT DE MINUIT, LE • 1932 • Esway Alexander, Charlot Andre • FRN • MYSTERE DE LA DAME BLONDE, LE ○ VENGEUR, LE
JUGEMENT DE SALOMON • 1916 • de Baroncelli Jacques • FRN
JUGEMENT DERNIER, LE • 1945 • Chanas Rene • FRN
JUGEMENT DERNIER, LE • 1971 • Le Bon Patrick • BLG
JUGEMENT DERNIER, LE • 1972 • Masse Francis • FRN
JUGEMENT DERNIER, LE (FRN) see **GIUDIZIO UNIVERSALE, IL** • 1961
JUGEMENT DES PIERRES, LE • 1914 • Poirier Leon • FRN
JUGEMENT DIVIN, LE • 1917 • Protazanov Yakov • USS
JUGEMENT DU FAUVE, LE • 1913-18 • Durand Jean • FRN
JUGEMENT DU GARDE CHAMPETRE • 1908 • Melies Georges • FRN • FORESTER'S REMEDY, THE (?)
JUGEND • 1920 • Eichberg Richard • FRG
JUGEND • 1922 • Sauer Fred • FRG
JUGEND • 1938 • Harlan Veit • FRG • YOUTH (USA)
JUGEND, DIE • 1917 • von Woringen Paul • FRG
JUGEND DER KONIGIN LUISE, DIE see **KONIGIN LUISE 1** • 1927
JUGEND PHOTOGRAPHIERT • 1961 • Schamoni Peter • SHT • FRG • JUGEND SIEHT SICH SELBST
JUGEND SIEHT SICH SELBST see **JUGEND PHOTOGRAPHIERT** • 1961
JUGEND UND TOLLHEIT • 1912 • Gad Urban • FRG, DNM • UNGDOM OG DAARSKAB (DNM)
JUGEND VON HEUTE • 1938 • Brauer Peter P. • FRG • YOUTH OF TODAY (USA)
JUGEND VON MORGEN see **KAMPF DER TERTIA, DER** • 1928
JUGENDGELIEBTE, DIE • 1930 • Tintner Hans • FRG • GOETHE'S JUGENDGELIEBTE (USA) ○ FRIEDERIKE VON SESENHEIM
JUGENDLIEBE • 1919 • Moest Hubert • FRG
JUGENDLIEBE • 1944 • von Borsody Eduard • FRG
JUGENDRAUSCH • 1927 • Asagaroff Georg, Starevitch Ladislas • FRG • EVA AND THE GRASSHOPPER (USA) ○ GRASSHOPPER AND THE ANT, THE ○ NEMESIS
JUGENDRICHTER, DER • 1960 • Verhoeven Paul • FRG • JUDGE AND THE SINNER, THE
JUGENDSUNDEN • 1929 • Wolff Carl Heinz • FRG
JUGENDTRAGODIE • 1929 • Trotz Adolf • FRG
JUGEZ-LES BIEN see **EN VOTRE AME ET CONSCIENCE** • 1960
JUGGERNAUT • 1936 • Edwards Henry • UKN
JUGGERNAUT • 1969 • Boyko Eugene • SHT • CND
JUGGERNAUT • 1974 • Lester Richard • UKN • TERROR ON THE BRITANNIC
JUGGERNAUT, THE • 1915 • Ince Ralph • USA
JUGGINS' MOTOR • 1903 • Williamson James • UKN
JUGGINS' MOTOR SKATES • 1909 • Stow Percy • UKN
JUGGLER • 1898 • *Cinematograph Co* • UKN
JUGGLER, THE • 1953 • Dmytryk Edward • USA

JUGGLER OF OUR LADY, THE • 1957 • Kouzel Al • ANS • USA
JUGGLING JUSTICE • 1916 • Ellis Robert • USA
JUGGLING MAD • 1913 • Kellino W. P. • UKN
JUGGLING ON THE BRAIN • 1910 • Bouwmeester Theo • UKN
JUGGLING THE TRUTH • 1915 • *Burns Bobby* • USA
JUGGLING WITH FATE • 1913 • Duncan William • USA
JUGNU • 1973 • *Burman S. D. (M)* • IND
JUGNU • 1987 • *Siddiqui Arifa* • PKS
JUGUEMOS EN EL MUNDO • 1972 • Avellaneda Maria Herminia • ARG • LET'S PLAY IN THE WORLD
JUGUETES ROTOS • 1966 • Summers Manuel • SPN
JUHA • 1937 • Tapiovaara Nyrki • FNL
JUHO VESAINEN • 1974 • Katajisto Heikko • FNL
JUHYO NO YOROMEKI • 1968 • Yoshida Yoshishige • JPN • FLICKER OF THE SILVER THAW ○ AFFAIR IN THE SNOW
JUICE • 1975 • USA
JUICHININ NO SAMURAI • 1967 • Kudo Eiichi • JPN • ELEVEN SAMURAI
JUICIO DE ARCADIO, EL • 1965 • Enrique Taboada Carlos • MXC
JUICIO DE FALDAS • 1969 • Saenz De Heredia Jose Luis • SPN
JUICIO DE MARTIN CORTES, EL • 1973 • Galindo Alejandro • MXC • TRIAL OF MARTIN CORTES, THE
JUICIO FINAL • 1955 • Ochoa Jose • SPN
JUIF ERRANT, LE • 1904 • Melies Georges • FRN • WANDERING JEW, THE (USA)
JUIF ERRANT, LE • 1926 • Luitz-Morat • FRN
JUIF POLONAIS, LE • 1925 • Southwell Harry • FRN • POLISH JEW, THE
JUIF POLONAIS, LE • 1931 • Kemm Jean • FRN
JUJI HOKA • 1939 • Toyoda Shiro • JPN • CROSSFIRE
JUJIN YUKI-OTOKO • 1955 • Honda Inoshiro, Crane Kenneth L. • JPN • HALF HUMAN (USA) ○ MONSTER SNOWMAN ○ SNOWMAN ○ ABOMINABLE SNOWMAN, THE
JUJIRO • 1928 • Kinugasa Teinosuke • JPN • SHADOWS OF THE YOSHIWARA ○ SHADOWS OF YOSHIWARA ○ CROSSWAYS ○ CROSSROADS
JUKE BAR • 1990 • Barry Martin • ANS • CND
JUKE BOX JAMBOREE • 1942 • Lovy Alex • ANS • USA
JUKE BOX JENNY • 1942 • Young Harold • USA
JUKE BOX QUEEN, THE • 1967 • Reyes Efren • PHL
JUKE BOX RHYTHM • 1959 • Dreifuss Arthur • USA
JUKE BOX, URLI D'AMORE • 1959 • Morassi Mauro • ITL
JUKE GIRL • 1942 • Bernhardt Curtis • USA
JUKE JOINT • 1947 • Williams Spencer • USA
JUKTI, TAKKO AAR GAPPO • 1974 • Ghatak Ritwik • IND • REASON, DEBATE AND A TALE
JUKU-SAI NO HARU • 1933 • Gosho Heinosuke • JPN • SPRING OF A NINETEEN YEAR OLD ○ NINETEENTH SPRING, THE
JUKU WA HANAZAKARI • 1958 • Mori Masaki • JPN
JUKYUSAI NO CHIZU • 1979 • Yanagimachi Mitsuo • JPN • MAP FOR 19 YEARS OLD, A ○ NINETEEN YEAR OLD'S PLAN, A
JULCHEN UND JETTCHEN: DIE VERLIEBTEN APOTHEKERSTOCHTER • 1980 • Dietrich Erwin C. • SWT • COME PLAY WITH ME 3
JULEFROKOSTEN • 1976 • Henriksen Finn • DNM • WHAT A CHRISTMAS PARTY
JULES AND JIM (UKN) see **JULES ET JIM** • 1961
JULES ET JIM • 1961 • Truffaut Francois • FRN • JULES AND JIM (UKN)
JULES LE MAGNIFIQUE • 1976 • Moreau Michel • DOC • CND
JULES OF THE STRONG HEART • 1918 • Crisp Donald • USA
JULES VERNE • Arcady • SHT • FRN
JULES VERNE AS A CHILD see **PETIT JULES VERNE, LE** • 1907
JULES VERNE'S ROCKET TO THE MOON • 1967 • Sharp Don • UKN • THOSE FANTASTIC FLYING FOOLS (USA) ○ ROCKET TO THE MOON ○ P.T. BARNUM'S ROCKET TO THE MOON ○ BLAST OFF! ○ JOURNEY THAT SHOOK THE WORLD, THE
JULESBURG • 1956 • Foster Harve • MTV • USA
JULIA • 1977 • Zinnemann Fred • USA
JULIA AND JULIA see **GIULIA E GIULIA** • 1988
JULIA, ANNA, GENOWEFA • 1968 • Sokolowska Anna • PLN • JULIE, ANNE, GENEVIEVE
JULIA, DU BIST ZAUBERHAFT • 1962 • Weidenmann Alfred • AUS, FRN • ADORABLE JULIA (FRN) ○ ADORABLE JULIE ○ SEDUCTION OF JULIA, THE
JULIA ET LES HOMMES • Rothemund Sigi • FRN
JULIA JUBILERAR • 1938 • Lauritzen Lau Jr., O'Fredericks Alice • SWD
JULIA, JULIA -A FAIRYTALE see **JULIA, JULIA -ET EVENTYR** • 1981
JULIA, JULIA -ET EVENTYR • 1981 • Wam Svend, Vennerod Petter • NRW • JULIA, JULIA -A FAIRYTALE
JULIA, JULIA -HISTORIEN OM ET FALL • 1981 • Wam Svend, Vennerod Petter • NRW • JULIA, JULIA -THE STORY OF A DOWNFALL ○ STORY OF A DOWNFALL, THE ○ HISTORIEN OM ET FALL
JULIA, JULIA -THE STORY OF A DOWNFALL see **JULIA, JULIA -HISTORIEN OM ET FALL** • 1981
JULIA LEBT • 1963 • Vogel Frank • GDR • JULIA LIVES
JULIA LIVES see **JULIA LEBT** • 1963
JULIA MISBEHAVES • 1948 • Conway Jack • USA
JULIA UND DIE GEISTER (FRG) see **GIULIETTA DEGLI SPIRITI** • 1965
JULIA (USA) see **ES WAR NICHT DIE NACHTIGALL** • 1974
JULIA VREVSKAYA see **YULIYA VREVSKAYA** • 1978
JULIA Y EL CELACANTO • 1959 • Momplet Antonio • SPN
JULIAN MARCHLEWSKI • 1950 • Perski Ludwik • DOC • PLN
JULIANA DO AMOR PERDIDO • 1970 • Ricardo Sergio • BRZ • LOST LOVE JULIANA
JULIANA IN SEVENTY TURBULENT YEARS see **JULIANA IN ZEVENTIG BEWOGEN JAREN** • 1979
JULIANA IN ZEVENTIG BEWOGEN JAREN • 1979 • Kohlhaas Anton • NTH • JULIANA IN SEVENTY TURBULENT YEARS
JULIANWALE • 1953 • *Biswas Anil (M)* • IND
JULIE • 1956 • Stone Andrew L. • USA
JULIE, ANNE, GENEVIEVE see **JULIA, ANNA, GENOWEFA** • 1968
JULIE DARLING • 1982 • Nicolas Paul • CND, FRG
JULIE DE CARNEILHAN • 1949 • Manuel Jacques • FRN
JULIE ETAIT BELLE • 1976 • Saurel Jacques-Rene • FRN • ETE PAS COMME LES AUTRES, UN ○ SAGES ET LES FOUS, LES
JULIE IS NO ANGEL! • 1967 • Crane Larry • USA • JULIE'S NO ANGEL
JULIE LA ROUSSE • 1959 • Boissol Claude • FRN • JULIE THE REDHEAD (USA)
JULIE O'BRIAN • 1981 • Shaffer Beverly • MTV • CND
JULIE POT-DE-COLLE • 1977 • de Broca Philippe • FRN • JULIE POT DE COLLE
JULIE POT DE COLLE see **JULIE POT-DE-COLLE** • 1977
JULIE THE REDHEAD (USA) see **JULIE LA ROUSSE** • 1959
JULIE'S NO ANGEL see **JULIE IS NO ANGEL!** • 1967
JULIET AND HER ROMEO • 1923 • Phillips Bertram • UKN
JULIET BUYS A BABY see **JULIETA COMPRA UN HIJO** • 1935
JULIET BUYS A SON see **JULIETA COMPRA UN HIJO** • 1935
JULIET OF THE SPIRITS (USA) see **GIULIETTA DEGLI SPIRITI** • 1965
JULIET OR THE KEY OF DREAMS see **JULIETTE OU LA CLE DES SONGES** • 1951
JULIETA COMPRA UN HIJO • 1935 • King Louis • USA • JULIET BUYS A BABY ○ JULIET BUYS A SON
JULIETA ENGANA A ROMEO • 1964 • Zabalza Jose Maria • SPN
JULIETTA • 1953 • Allegret Marc • FRN
JULIETTE? • 1973 • Pilard Philippe • FRN
JULIETTE DE SADE • 1969 • Sabatini Lorenzo • ITL • HETEROSEXUAL (UKN) ○ MADEMOISELLE DE SADE E I SOUI VIZI
JULIETTE DES ESPRITS (FRN) see **GIULIETTA DEGLI SPIRITI** • 1965
JULIETTE DU COTE DES HOMMES • 1981 • Bories Claudine • DOC • FRN
JULIETTE E JULIETTE (ITL) see **JULIETTE ET JULIETTE** • 1973
JULIETTE ET JULIETTE • 1973 • Forlani Remo • FRN, ITL • JULIETTE E JULIETTE (ITL)
JULIETTE ET L'AIR DU TEMPS • 1976 • Gilson Rene • FRN
JULIETTE OU LA CLE DES SONGES • 1951 • Carne Marcel • FRN • JULIET OR THE KEY OF DREAMS
JULIKA, DIE • 1936 • von Bolvary Geza • AUS • ERNTE ○ HARVEST
JULIO BEGINS IN JULY see **JULIO COMIENZA EN JULIO** • 1978
JULIO COMIENZA EN JULIO • 1978 • Caiozzi Silvio • CHL • JULIO BEGINS IN JULY
JULIUS CAESAR • 1908 • Ranous William V.? • USA
JULIUS CAESAR • 1909 • *Itala* • ITL
JULIUS CAESAR • 1911 • *Benson Frank* • UKN
JULIUS CAESAR • 1926 • Cooper George A. • UKN
JULIUS CAESAR • 1945 • Bennett Compton • SHT • UKN
JULIUS CAESAR • 1950 • Bradley David • USA
JULIUS CAESAR • 1953 • Deane Charles • UKN
JULIUS CAESAR • 1953 • Mankiewicz Joseph L. • USA
JULIUS CAESAR • 1970 • Burge Stuart • UKN
JULIUS CAESAR • 1978 • Wise Herbert • TVM • UKN
JULIUS CAESAR, CONQUEROR OF GAUL see **GIULIO CESARE IL CONQUISTATORE DELLE GALLIE** • 1963
JULIUS SIZZER • 1931 • Luddy Edward I. • SHT • USA
JULOT, DER APACHE • 1921 • Delmont Joseph • FRG
JULOTTA • 1937 • Roosling Gosta • SWD • CHRISTMAS MORN
JULY 14TH (USA) see **QUATORZE JUILLET** • 1932
JULY 22ND see **22 LIPCA** • 1949
JULY DAYS • 1923 • Roach Hal • SHT • USA
JULY PORK BELLIES see **FOR PETE'S SAKE** • 1974
JULY RAIN see **LYULSKI DOZHD** • 1967
JULY SHOWER, A see **LYULSKI DOZHD** • 1967
JUMBLE SALE • 1974 • Abnudi Atiat Al- • SHT • UKN
JUMBLES AND JOKERS • 1918 • Howe J. A. • SHT • USA
JUMBO see **BILLY ROSE'S JUMBO** • 1962
JUMEAU, LE • 1984 • Robert Yves • FRN
JUMEAUX DE BRIGHTON, LES • 1936 • Heymann Claude • FRN
JUMEAUX SYMETRIQUES, LES • 1970 • Moreau Michel • DCS • CND
JUMENT VAPEUR, LA • 1978 • Bunuel Joyce • FRN • DIRTY DISHES (USA)
JUMENT VERTE, LA • 1959 • Autant-Lara Claude • FRN, ITL • GIUMENTA VERDE, LA (ITL) ○ GREEN MARE'S NEST, THE (UKN) ○ GREEN MARE, THE (USA) ○ BEDROOM VENDETTA
JUMP • 1968 • Jonsson Thorsteinn • SHT • ICL
JUMP • 1971 • Manduke Joe • USA • FURY ON WHEELS
JUMP • 1972 • Keeshen Jim • ANS • USA
JUMP, CHUMP, JUMP • 1938 • Lord Del • SHT • USA
JUMP FOR GLORY • 1937 • Walsh Raoul • UKN • WHEN THIEF MEETS THIEF (USA)
JUMP INTO HELL • 1955 • Butler David • USA
JUMP TO GLORY see **SALTO A LA GLORIA** • 1959
JUMP YOUR JOB • 1922 • Roach Hal • SHT • USA
JUMPIN' AT THE BEDSIDE see **HOPLA PA SENGEKANTEN** • 1976
JUMPIN' JACK FLASH • 1986 • Marshall Penny • USA
JUMPIN' JIVE • 1941 • Ceballos Larry • SHT • USA
JUMPIN' JUPITER • 1955 • Jones Charles M. • ANS • USA
JUMPIN' NIGHT IN THE GARDEN OF EDEN, A • 1988 • Goldman Michael • USA
JUMPING • 1984 • Tezuka Osamu • ANS • JPN
JUMPING ASH see **T'IAO HUI** • 1977
JUMPING BEANS • 1922 • Fleischer Dave • ANS • USA
JUMPING BEANS • 1930 • *Terry Paul/ Moser Frank (P)* • ANS • USA
JUMPING FOR JOY • 1956 • Carstairs John Paddy • UKN
JUMPING JACKS • 1952 • Taurog Norman • USA
JUMPING JACKS AND JAIL BIRDS • 1918 • Howe J. A. • SHT • USA
JUMPING JEALOUSY • 1917 • *Myers Harry* • USA
JUMPING LEGS, SWINGING WINGS • 1963 • Kollanyi Agoston • HNG
JUMPING OVER PUDDLES AGAIN see **UZ ZASE SKACU PRES KALUZE** • 1970
JUMPING THE CLAIM see **LIFE UNDER THE SOUTHERN CROSS** • 1911
JUMPING THE PUDDLES AGAIN see **UZ ZASE SKACU PRES KALUZE** • 1970
JUMPING WITH TOY • 1957 • Tendlar Dave • ANS • USA
JUMPS AND JEALOUSY • 1916 • Semon Larry • SHT • USA
JUN • 1981 • Yokoyama Hiroto • JPN
JUN-AI MONOGATARI • 1957 • Imai Tadashi • JPN • STORY OF PURE LOVE, A
JUN SHOJO SHIRABE • 1968 • Ogawa Kinya • JPN • RESEARCH INTO A TRUE VIRGIN
JUNACY • 1967 • Halladin Danuta • DOC • PLN • BRAVE FELLOWS
JUNAK MARKOS see **YUNAK MARKO** • 1953
JUNANASAI NO DANGAI • 1957 • Harada Hasuo • JPN
JUNANGE • 1932 • Yamamoto Kajiro • JPN • ORDEAL
JUNCTION 88 • 1940 • *Sissle Noble* • USA
JUNCTION CITY • 1952 • Nazarro Ray • USA
JUNE • Cornell Joseph, Brakhage Stan • SHT • USA • TOWERHOUSE
JUNE '44 LANDING IN NORMANDY see **GIUGNO '44 SBARCHEREMO IN NORMANDIA** • 1968
JUNE BRIDE • 1948 • Windust Bretaigne • USA
JUNE BRIDE, A • 1935 • *Terry Paul/ Moser Frank (P)* • ANS • USA
JUNE DAYS • 1961 • Kachlik Antonin • CZC
JUNE FRIDAY • 1915 • McRae Duncan • USA
JUNE MADNESS • 1917 • Henley Hobart • SHT • USA
JUNE MADNESS • 1920 • Roach Hal • SHT • USA
JUNE MADNESS • 1922 • Beaumont Harry • USA
JUNE MARKS • 1966 • Shebib Donald • CND
JUNE MOON • 1931 • Sutherland A. Edward • USA
JUNE NIGHT see **JUNINATT** • 1965
JUNE TE SONE • 1967 • Pethkar Yeshwant • IND
JUNE'S BIRTHDAY PARTY • 1905 • Porter Edwin S. • USA
JUNG MUSS MAN SEIN • 1916 • Albes Emil • FRG
JUNGBRUNNEN • 1952 • Oertel Curt • FRG
JUNGE ADLER • 1944 • Weidenmann Alfred • FRG
JUNGE BARON NEUHAUS, DER • 1934 • Ucicky Gustav • FRG
JUNGE DAME AUS GUTER FAMILIE, EINE • 1919 • *Abel Alfred* • FRG
JUNGE DAME VON WELT, EINE • 1919 • Halm Alfred • FRG
JUNGE ENGLANDER, DER • 1958 • Kolditz Gottfried • GDR
JUNGE FRAU, DER • 1935 • Lamac Carl • FRG
JUNGE GOETHE, DER see **SOHN DER GOTTER, DER** • 1918
JUNGE HERZEN • 1944 • Barlog Boleslav • FRG
JUNGE LEUTE BRAUCHEN LIEBE • 1961 • von Cziffra Geza • AUS
JUNGE LIEBE • 1928 • Schwarz Hanns • FRG
JUNGE LORD, DER • 1965 • Sellner Gustav Rudolf • FRG • YOUNG LORD, THE (USA)
JUNGE MAMA • 1921 • Krafft Uwe Jens • FRG
JUNGE MEDARDUS, DER • 1923 • Curtiz Michael, Kolowrat Sascha • AUS
JUNGE MONCH, DER • 1978 • Achternbusch Herbert • FRG • YOUNG MONK, THE
JUNGE SCHRIE MORD, EIN (FRG) see **BOY CRIED MURDER, THE** • 1966
JUNGE SUNDERIN, DIE • 1960 • Jugert Rudolf • FRG
JUNGE TORLESS, DER • 1966 • Schlondorff Volker • FRG, FRN • DESARROIS DE L'ELEVE TORLESS, LES (FRN) ○ YOUNG TORLESS (USA)
JUNGEN AUSREISSERINNEN, DIE • 1971 • Boos Walter • FRG • RUNAWAY GIRLS ○ INNOCENTS ABROAD
JUNGEN VOM KRANICHSEE, DIE • 1950 • Pohl Arthur • GDR • BOYS FROM THE LAKE OF CRANES, THE
JUNGENS • 1941 • Stemmle R. A. • FRG
JUNGER FRUHLING • 1986 • Leidenfrost Alexander • AUS • YOUNG SPRING
JUNGER MANN, DER ALLES KANN • 1957 • Engel Thomas • FRG
JUNGES BLUT • 1926 • Noa Manfred • FRG
JUNGES GEMUSE • 1956 • Reisch Gunter • GDR • FRESH VEGETABLES
JUNGES HERZ VOLL LIEBE • 1953 • May Paul • FRG
JUNGES MADCHEN -EINE JUNGER MANN, EIN see **KNOCK OUT** • 1935
JUNGFERN VOM BISCHOFSBERG • 1943 • Brauer Peter P. • FRG
JUNGFRAU AUF DEM DACH, DIE • 1954 • Preminger Otto • FRG
JUNGFRAU AUS ZWEITER HAND • 1967 • von Rathony Akos • FRG • SECOND-HAND VIRGIN
JUNGFRAU GEGEN MONCH • 1934 • Emo E. W. • FRG
JUNGFRAU VOM KYNAST, DIE • 1921 • Moest Hubert • FRG
JUNGFRAUEN REPORT • 1972 • Franco Jesus • FRG
JUNGFRAUEN VON BUMSHAUSEN, DIE • 1969 • Billian Hans • FRG • RUN, VIRGIN, RUN (UKN)
JUNGFRAUENKRIEG • 1957 • Kugelstadt Hermann • AUS
JUNGFRU PA JUNGFRUSUND • 1949 • Arvedson Ragnar • SWD • MAID FROM JUNGFRUSUND, THE
JUNGFRUKALLAN • 1960 • Bergman Ingmar • SWD • VIRGIN SPRING, THE (UKN)
JUNGGESELLENFALLE • 1953 • Bottger Fritz • FRG
JUNGLA NERA (ITL) see **ESCLAVE BLANC, L'** • 1936
JUNGLE • 1937-40 • *Cardiff Jack (Ph)* • DCS • UKN
JUNGLE see **UNTAMED** • 1929
JUNGLE, THE • 1914 • Thomas Augustus • USA
JUNGLE, THE • 1952 • Berke William • USA
JUNGLE, THE • 1985 • Murphy Edward • USA • HEATED VENGEANCE
JUNGLE ADVENTURE see **AFRICAN HOLIDAY** • 1937
JUNGLE ADVENTURE CAMPA, CAMPA see **DJUNGELAVENTYRET CAMPA, CAMPA** • 1976
JUNGLE ADVENTURES • 1921 • *Johnson Martin* • DOC • USA • MARTIN JOHNSON'S JUNGLE ADVENTURES
JUNGLE ASSAULT • 1988 • Prior David A. • USA
JUNGLE ATTACK see **CROSSWIND** • 1951
JUNGLE BLOCK see **CHIZU NO NAI MACHI** • 1960
JUNGLE BOOK, THE • 1967 • Reitherman Wolfgang • ANM • USA
JUNGLE BOOK, THE (UKN) see **RUDYARD KIPLING'S JUNGLE BOOK** • 1942
JUNGLE BOY • 1955 • Cerf Norman A. • USA

JUNGLE BOY see **VANASARA** • 1968
JUNGLE BRIDE • 1933 • Hoyt Harry O., Kelley Albert • USA
JUNGLE BURGER see **TARZOON, LA HONTE DE LA JUNGLE** • 1974
JUNGLE CAPTIVE • 1944 • Young Harold • USA • WILD JUNGLE CAPTIVE (UKN)
JUNGLE CAT • 1960 • Algar James • DOC • USA
JUNGLE CAT see **ALAMID** • 1967
JUNGLE CAVALCADE • 1941 • *Bonafield Jay (Ed)* • CMP • USA
JUNGLE CHILD, THE • 1916 • Edwards Walter • USA
JUNGLE CONQUEST • 1943 • Heyer John • DOC • ASL
JUNGLE CURE, THE • 1916 • *E & R Jungle Film* • SHT • USA
JUNGLE DANCE see **DJUNGELDANSEN** • 1937
JUNGLE DRUMS • 1943 • Gordon Dan • ANS • USA
JUNGLE DRUMS OF AFRICA • 1953 • Brannon Fred C. • SRL • USA
JUNGLE D'UNE GRAND VILLE • 1929 • Marten Leo, Viel Marguerite • FRN, CZC • BIG CITY JUNGLE ○ DZUNGLE VELKOMESTA
JUNGLE EMPEROR, THE see **JUNGLE TATEI**
JUNGLE EN FOLIE, LA • 1952 • Lalande Claude • FRN • MONSIEUR DUPONT HOMME BLANC ○ SORCIER BLANC, LE ○ TOUBAB, LE
JUNGLE FEVER see **EUR WEG FUHRT DURCH DIE HOLLE** • 1984
JUNGLE FIGHTERS (USA) see **LONG AND THE SHORT AND THE TALL, THE** • 1960
JUNGLE FIRE see **SELVA DE FUEGO, LA** • 1945
JUNGLE FLASHLIGHT, THE • 1916 • *Clifford William* • SHT • USA
JUNGLE FLIGHT • 1947 • Newfield Sam • USA
JUNGLE FOOL • 1929 • Foster John, Davis Mannie • ANS • USA
JUNGLE GANGSTER • 1946 • Parker Benjamin R. • SHT • USA
JUNGLE GENTLEMAN, A • 1919 • Fishback Fred C. • SHT • USA
JUNGLE GENTS • 1954 • Bernds Edward • USA
JUNGLE GIRL • 1941 • Witney William, English John • SRL • USA
JUNGLE GIRL see **BOMBA AND THE JUNGLE GIRL** • 1952
JUNGLE GIRL AND THE SLAVER see **LIANE, DIE WEISSE SKLAVIN** • 1957
JUNGLE GODDESS • 1922 • Conway James • SRL • USA
JUNGLE GODDESS • 1949 • Collins Lewis D. • USA
JUNGLE GODDESS (USA) see **LUANA, LA FIGLIA DELLA FORESTA VERGINE** • 1968
JUNGLE GODS • 1927 • *Von Hoffman Carl* • USA
JUNGLE GOLD • 1944 • Bennet Spencer Gordon, Grissell Wallace A. • USA • PERILS OF THE DARKEST JUNGLE
JUNGLE HEADHUNTERS • 1951 • *Lesser Julian (P)* • DOC • USA
JUNGLE HEAT • 1927 • Roberts Stephen • SHT • USA
JUNGLE HEAT • 1957 • Koch Howard W. • USA
JUNGLE HEAT • 1984 • Trikonis Gus • USA • DANCE OF THE DWARFS
JUNGLE HELL • 1932 • Meehan James Leo • USA
JUNGLE HELL • 1956 • Cerf Norman A. • USA
JUNGLE HERO, THE • 1916 • Hunt Jay • SHT • USA
JUNGLE HOLOCAUST see **CANNIBAL HOLOCAUST** • 1980
JUNGLE INTERLUDE see **SUNANO UE NO SHOKUBUTSUGUN** • 1964
JUNGLE ISLAND (UKN) see **WOLVES OF THE SEA** • 1937
JUNGLE JAM • 1931 • Foster John, Rufle George • ANS • USA
JUNGLE JAZZ • 1930 • Foster John, Bailey Harry • ANS • USA
JUNGLE JIM • 1937 • Beebe Ford, Smith Cliff • SRL • USA
JUNGLE JIM • 1948 • Berke William • USA
JUNGLE JIM IN THE FORBIDDEN LAND • 1952 • Landers Lew • USA • JUNGLE JIM IN THE LAND OF THE GIANTS ○ FORBIDDEN LAND, THE
JUNGLE JIM IN THE LAND OF THE GIANTS see **JUNGLE JIM IN THE FORBIDDEN LAND** • 1952
JUNGLE JINGLES • 1929 • Lantz Walter • ANS • USA
JUNGLE JITTERS • 1934 • *Iwerks Ube (P)* • ANS • USA
JUNGLE JITTERS • 1938 • Freleng Friz • ANS • USA
JUNGLE JIVE • 1944 • Culhane James • ANS • USA
JUNGLE JUMBLE • 1932 • Lantz Walter, Nolan William • ANS • USA
JUNGLE JUSTICE • 1915 • Daly William Robert • USA
JUNGLE JUSTICE • 1953 • Eason B. Reeves • USA
JUNGLE JUVENILES • 1937 • Haeseler John A. • SHT • USA
JUNGLE JUVENILES NO.2 • 1938 • Haeseler John A. • SHT • USA
JUNGLE KING • 1939 • Ghadiali Nari • IND
JUNGLE LINE • 1978 • Hoffman Sonia • DOC • ASL
JUNGLE LOVERS, THE • 1915 • Carleton Lloyd B. • USA
JUNGLE MADNESS • 1967 • Duga Don • ANS • USA
JUNGLE MAN • 1941 • Fraser Harry L. • USA
JUNGLE MAN-EATERS • 1954 • Sholem Lee • USA
JUNGLE MANHUNT • 1951 • Landers Lew • USA
JUNGLE MASTER, THE • 1914 • McRae Henry • USA
JUNGLE MASTER, THE • 1985 • Fidani Demofilo • ITL
JUNGLE MENACE • 1937 • Melford George, Fraser Harry L. • SRL • USA
JUNGLE MOON MEN • 1955 • Gould Charles • USA
JUNGLE MYSTERY, THE • 1932 • Taylor Ray • SRL • USA
JUNGLE OF CHANG (USA) see **MAN OCH KVINNA** • 1939
JUNGLE OUTCASTS, THE • 1916 • Swickard Charles • SHT • USA
JUNGLE PALS • 1923 • Seiler Lewis, Stoloff Ben • SHT • USA
JUNGLE PATROL • 1948 • Newman Joseph M. • USA
JUNGLE PRINCESS • 1923 • *Hansen Juanita* • USA
JUNGLE PRINCESS, THE • 1936 • Thiele Wilhelm • USA
JUNGLE QUEEN • 1945 • Taylor Ray, Collins Lewis D. • SRL • USA
JUNGLE QUEEN • 1956 • Ghadiali Nari • IND
JUNGLE QUEEN, THE • 1915 • McRae Henry • USA
JUNGLE QUEEN'S JEWELS, THE see **DJUNGELDROTTNINGENS SMYCKE** • 1917
JUNGLE RAIDERS • 1945 • Selander Lesley • SRL • USA
JUNGLE RAIDERS see **CAPTAIN YANKEE AND THE JUNGLE RAIDERS** • 1984
JUNGLE RAMPAGE see **RAMPAGE** • 1963
JUNGLE REVENGE, A • 1915 • Santschi Thomas • USA
JUNGLE RHYTHM • 1928 • Disney Walt, Iwerks Ub • ANS • USA
JUNGLE SAMARITAN, THE • 1914 • MacGregor Norval • USA
JUNGLE SEX see **BLACK BUNCH, THE** • 1972
JUNGLE SIREN • 1942 • Newfield Sam • USA
JUNGLE STAMPEDE • 1950 • Breakston George • USA
JUNGLE STOCKADE, THE • 1915 • Santschi Thomas • USA
JUNGLE STREET • 1961 • Saunders Charles • UKN • JUNGLE STREET GIRLS (USA)
JUNGLE STREET GIRLS (USA) see **JUNGLE STREET** • 1961
JUNGLE TALES OF TARZAN see **TARZAN THE MIGHTY** • 1928
JUNGLE TATEI • Tezuka Osamu • ANM • JPN • KIMBO, THE WHITE LION ○ JUNGLE EMPEROR, THE
JUNGLE TERROR see **FIREBALL JUNGLE** • 1968
JUNGLE TRACK • 1959 • Zguridi Alexander • DOC • USS
JUNGLE TRAGEDY, A • 1917 • *Walcamp Marie* • SHT • USA
JUNGLE TRAIL, THE • 1919 • Stanton Richard • USA
JUNGLE TRAIL OF THE SON OF TARZAN • 1923 • Revier Harry, Flaven Art • USA
JUNGLE TREACHERY • 1917 • Hodge Rex, Pearson W. B. • SHT • USA
JUNGLE TREASURE (USA) see **OLD MOTHER RILEY'S JUNGLE TREASURE** • 1951
JUNGLE WARFARE • 1943 • Halas John, Batchelor Joy • ANS • UKN
JUNGLE WARRIORS see **EUR WEG FUHRT DURCH DIE HOLLE** • 1984
JUNGLE WOLF • 1986 • Ordonez Charles • USA
JUNGLE WOMAN • 1926 • Hurley Frank • ASL, UKN
JUNGLE WOMAN • 1944 • Le Borg Reginald • USA
JUNGLE WOMAN, THE see **NABONGA** • 1944
JUNGLING AUS DER KONFEKTION, DER • 1926 • Lowenbein Richard • FRG
JUNI • *Shahi Angshumala* • NPL • NAME OF A GIRL
JUNINATT • 1965 • Liedholm Lars-Erik • SWD • JUNE NIGHT
JUNINATTEN • 1940 • Lindberg Per • SWD • NIGHT IN JUNE, A
JUNININ NO SHASHIN-KA • 1953-57 • Teshigahara Hiroshi • DCS • JPN • TWELVE PHOTOGRAPHERS
JUNIO 44, DESEMBARCAREMOS EN NORMANDIA • 1968 • Klimovsky Leon • SPN
JUNIOR • 1985 • Hawley Jim • USA • HOT WATER
JUNIOR ADVENTURERS • Magiton Isaac • USS
JUNIOR ARMY • 1942 • Landers Lew • USA • CADETS ON PARADE (UKN)
JUNIOR BONNER • 1972 • Peckinpah Sam • USA
JUNIOR COMMUTERS see **VLAKARI** • 1988
JUNIOR CURSILLO • 1968 • Diaz Leody M. • PHL
JUNIOR G-MEN • 1940 • Beebe Ford, Rawlins John • SRL • USA
JUNIOR G-MEN OF THE AIR • 1942 • Taylor Ray, Collins Lewis D. • SRL • USA
JUNIOR HEADS see **I UNGDOMMENS MAKT** • 1980
JUNIOR JIVE BOMBERS • 1944 • Prinz Leroy • SHT • USA
JUNIOR JR. COMES see **HAHO, A TENGER** • 1972
JUNIOR MISS • 1945 • Seaton George • USA
JUNIOR OFFICER, THE • 1912 • *Bosworth Hobart* • USA
JUNIOR PARTNER, THE • 1913 • *La Badie Florence* • USA
JUNIOR PROM • 1946 • Dreifuss Arthur • USA
JUNIOR YEAR HIGH SCHOOL see **TERZA LICEO** • 1954
JUNJO • 1930 • Naruse Mikio • JPN • PURE LOVE
JUNJO NIJUSO • 1967 • Umezu Meijiro • JPN • LOVERS' DUET
JUNK see **IDLE RICH, THE** • 1921
JUNK HOUSE see **ASHGHALDOUNI** • 1973
JUNK MAN, THE • 1918 • Roach Hal • SHT • USA • JUNKMAN, THE
JUNK PLAYGROUND, THE see **SKRAMMELLEGEPLADSEN** • 1966
JUNK SHOP, THE see **SBERNE SUROVOSTI** • 1965
JUNKER HINRICHS VERBOTENE LIEBE • 1925 • *Ufa* • FRG
JUNKER HINRICHS VERBOTENE LIEBE see **ZUR SACHE SCHATZCHEN** • 1968
JUNKET 89 • 1970 • Plummer Peter • UKN
JUNKIE see **WAI DIP** • 1990
JUNKIE DOG see **CANINABUS** • 1979
JUNKMAN, THE see **JUNK MAN, THE** • 1918
JUNKMAN, THE see **GONE IN 60 SECONDS II -THE JUNKMAN** • 1977
JUNO AND THE PAYCOCK • 1929 • Hitchcock Alfred • UKN • SHAME OF MARY BOYLE, THE (USA)
JUNO MAKES FRIENDS • 1957 • Woodhouse Barbara • UKN
JUNOON • 1978 • Benegal Shyam • IND • POSSESSED ○ OBSESSION
JUNQUEIRA • 1983 • Hauser Cristina • SHT • PRT
JUNTOS, PERO NO REVUELTOS • 1938 • Rivero Fernando A. • MXC • UNITED BUT NOT MIXED (USA)
JUPITER • 1971 • Prevost Jean-Pierre • FRN
JUPITER SMITTEN • 1910 • *Gaumont* • FRN
JUPITER'S DARLING • 1954 • Sidney George • USA
JUPITER'S THIGH see **ON A VOLE LA CUISSE DE JUPITER** • 1979
JUPITER'S THUNDERBOLTS OR THE HOME OF THE MUSES see **TONNERRE DE JUPITER, LE** • 1903
JURAME • 1961 • Ochoa Jose • SPN
JURAMENTO DE LAGARDERE, EL • 1954 • Klimovsky Leon • ARG
JURAMENTO DE SANGRE • 1960 • Peon Ramon • MXC
JUREBAVARD, UN • 1947-51 • Verneuil Henri • SHT • FRN
JURKO THE OUTLAW see **ZBOJNIK JURKO**
JURNAIL SINGH • 1987 • PKS
JUROR NUMBER SEVEN • 1915 • Wilson Ben • USA
JURTZENKA • 1969 • Camino Jaime • SPN • INVIERNO EN MALLORCA, UN ○ WINTER IN MALLORCA
JURY GOES ROUND AND ROUND, THE • *Vague Vera* • SHT • USA
JURY OF FATE, THE • 1917 • Browning Tod • USA
JURY OF HER PEERS, A • 1981 • Heckel Sally • SHT • USA
JURY OF ONE see **VERDICT, LE** • 1974
JURY OF THE JUNGLE (UKN) see **FURY OF THE JUNGLE** • 1934
JURYMAN, THE • 1987 • Chapman Michael • USA
JURY'S EVIDENCE • 1936 • Ince Ralph • UKN
JURY'S SECRET, THE • 1938 • Sloman Edward • USA
JURY'S VERDICT, THE • 1913 • *Patheplay* • USA
JUS' PASSIN' THROUGH • 1923 • Parrott Charles • SHT • USA
JUS PRIMAE NOCTIS • 1972 • Festa Campanile Pasquale • ITL
JUSQU'A LA NUIT • 1984 • Martiny • FRN
JUSQU'A LA VICTOIRE • 1970 • Godard Jean-Luc, Gorin Jean-Pierre • DOC • FRN • 'TIL VICTORY (USA) ○ TILL VICTORY
JUSQU'A PLUS SOIF • 1961 • Labro Maurice • FRN
JUSQU'AU BATEAU see **MEHRI TO PLIO** • 1968
JUSQU'AU BOUT DU MONDE • 1962 • Villiers Francois • FRN • FILO DI SPERANZA, UN (ITL)
JUSQU'AU COEUR • 1968 • Lefebvre Jean-Pierre • CND • RIGHT TO THE HEART
JUSQU'AU COU • 1964 • Heroux Denis • CND
JUSQU'AU DERNIER • 1956 • Billon Pierre • FRN
JUSQU'AU FOND DU PETIT TROU • Henco Jess • FRN
JUSQU'AU SOIR OU LA LIGNE DES JOURS.. • 1966 • Fares Tewfik • ALG
JUSQUES AU FEU EXCLUSIVEMENT • 1971 • Ginsey • SHT • FRN
JUSSUF EL FANIT, DER WUSTENRAUBER • 1922 • Gerhardt Karl, Stein Josef • FRG
JUST, THE • 1969 • Kidawa Janusz • DOC • PLN
JUST A BAD KID • 1912 • *Thanhouser* • USA
JUST A BEAR • 1931 • Stafford Babe • SHT • USA • IT'S A BEAR
JUST A BIG SIMPLE GIRL see **GRANDE FILLE TOUTE SIMPLE, UNE** • 1947
JUST A BIT OF LIFE • 1914 • Morrisey Edward • USA
JUST A BOY • 1912 • *Solax* • USA
JUST A CLOWN • 1934 • *Terry Paul/ Moser Frank (P)* • ANS • USA
JUST A FEW THINGS • 1916 • Beery Wallace • SHT • USA
JUST A FIRE-FIGHTER • 1913 • *Gail Jane* • USA
JUST A GAME see **RIEN QU'UN JEU** • 1983
JUST A GIGOLO • 1931 • Conway Jack • USA • DANCING PARTNER, THE (UKN)
JUST A GIGOLO • 1932 • Fleischer Dave • ANS • USA
JUST A GIGOLO (USA) see **SCHONER GIGOLO -ARMER GIGOLO** • 1978
JUST A GIRL • 1913 • Weston Charles • UKN • ONLY A GIRL
JUST A GIRL • 1916 • Butler Alexander • UKN
JUST A GOOD GUY • 1924 • Roach Hal • SHT • USA
JUST A KID • 1914 • O'Sullivan Tony • USA
JUST A LARK • 1915 • *Rea Isabel* • USA
JUST A LITTLE BULL • 1940 • Donnelly Eddie • ANS • USA
JUST A LITTLE GIRL see **PROSTO DYEVOCHKA** • 1967
JUST A LITTLE INCONVENIENCE • 1977 • Flicker Theodore J. • TVM • USA
JUST A LITTLE NOTE • 1970 • Noyce Phil (c/d) • SHT • ASL
JUST A LITTLE PIECE OF CLOTH • 1906 • Martin J. H.? • UKN
JUST A LITTLE WHISTLE see **JEN SI TAK TROCHU PISKNOUT** • 1981
JUST A MINUTE • 1924 • Roach Hal • SHT • USA
JUST A MOTHER • 1923 • *Gurleigh Burtram* • USA
JUST A NOTE • 1914 • Hotaling Arthur D. • USA
JUST A NUT • 1914 • Weston Charles • UKN
JUST A PAIN IN THE PARLOR • 1932 • Marshall George • SHT • USA
JUST A PAL • 1930 • Taurog Norman • SHT • USA
JUST A SHABBY DOLL • 1913 • *Thanhouser* • USA
JUST A SONG AT TWILIGHT • 1914 • *Cummings Dick* • USA
JUST A SONG AT TWILIGHT • 1917 • King Carleton S. • USA
JUST A SONG AT TWILIGHT • 1922 • King Carleton S. • USA
JUST A WIFE • 1920 • Hickman Howard • USA
JUST A WOLF AT HEART • 1962 • Hanna William, Barbera Joseph • ANS • USA
JUST A WOMAN • 1912 • *Powers* • USA
JUST A WOMAN • 1918 • Steger Julius • USA
JUST A WOMAN • 1925 • Cummings Irving • USA
JUST A WOMAN see **DOCTEUR FRANCOISE GAILLAND** • 1975
JUST ACROSS THE STREET • 1952 • Pevney Joseph • USA
JUST AN OLD SWEET SONG • 1976 • Miller Robert Ellis • TVM • USA
JUST AND UNJUST see **HELL'S 400** • 1926
JUST ANOTHER BLONDE • 1926 • Santell Alfred • USA • GIRL FROM CONEY ISLAND, THE
JUST ANOTHER MIRACLE see **HEAVENLY PURSUITS** • 1985
JUST ANOTHER MISSING KID • 1981 • Zaritsky John • MTV • CND
JUST ANOTHER MURDER • 1935 • Sennett Mack • USA
JUST ANOTHER WAR see **UOMINI CONTRO** • 1970
JUST AROUND THE CORNER • 1921 • Marion Frances • USA
JUST AROUND THE CORNER • 1938 • Cummings Irving • USA
JUST AS HE THOUGHT • 1916 • Humphrey Orral • SHT • USA
JUST AS I AM • 1915 • Campbell Colin • USA
JUST AS I AM see **AS GOD MADE HER** • 1920
JUST AS IT HAPPENED • 1915 • Bartlett Charles • USA
JUST AS THE CLOCK STRUCK NINE • 1911 • *Essanay* • USA
JUST ASK FOR DIAMOND • 1988 • Bayley Stephen • UKN • FALCON'S MALTESER, THE
JUST ASK JUPITER • 1938 • Davis Mannie • ANS • USA
JUST BEFORE DAWN • 1946 • Castle William • USA • EXPOSED BY THE CRIME DOCTOR
JUST BEFORE DAWN • 1981 • Lieberman Jeff • USA
JUST BEFORE NIGHTFALL (UKN) see **JUSTE AVANT LA NUIT** • 1971
JUST BELOW PAR • 1968 • Wallace Stephen • DOC • ASL
JUST BETWEEN FRIENDS • 1986 • Burns Allan • USA
JUST BETWEEN US • 1961 • *Pax Films* • USA
JUST BOYS • 1914 • *Ab* • USA
JUST BROWN'S LUCK • 1913 • Sennett Mack • USA
JUST CALL ME LUCKY see **CALL ME LUCKY** • 1973
JUST CISSY'S LITTLE WAY • 1913 • Johnson Arthur • USA
JUST CRAZY ABOUT HORSES • 1978 • Lovejoy Tim • DOC • USA
JUST DANDY • 1928 • Roberts Stephen • SHT • USA
JUST DECEPTION, A • 1917 • Coleby A. E. • UKN
JUST DENNIS: THE MOVIE • 1988 • *Windom William* • USA
JUST DOGS • 1932 • Gillett Burt • ANS • USA
JUST DROPPED IN • 1919 • Roach Hal • SHT • USA
JUST DUCKY • 1953 • Hanna William, Barbera Joseph • ANS • USA

JUST FOR A KID • 1916 • Dillon John Francis • USA
JUST FOR A SONG • 1930 • Gundrey V. Gareth • UKN
JUST FOR FUN • 1963 • Flemyng Gordon • UKN
JUST FOR FUN, JUST FOR PLAY see **KALEIDOSKOP VALESKA GERT –NUR ZUM SPASS NUR ZUM SPIEL** • 1977
JUST FOR HER • 1911 • *Imp* • USA
JUST FOR KICKS see **URUSAI IMOTOTACHI** • 1961
JUST FOR KICKS see **HECC, A** • 1989
JUST FOR LUCK • 1913 • *Imp* • USA
JUST FOR THE HELL OF IT • 1968 • Lewis Herschell G. • USA
JUST FOR TONIGHT • 1918 • Giblyn Charles • USA
JUST FOR TONIGHT • 1935 • Heale Patrick K. • UKN
JUST FOR YOU • 1952 • Nugent Elliott • USA
JUST FOR YOU • 1955 • Carreras Michael • UKN
JUST FOR YOU • 1964 • Hickox Douglas • UKN • DISK–O–TEK HOLIDAY (USA)
JUST GOLD • 1913 • Griffith D. W. • USA
JUST HARD LUCK • 1913 • *Majestic* • USA
JUST HATS • 1912 • *Quirk Billy* • USA
JUST HER LUCK • 1916 • MacDonald Donald • SHT • USA
JUST HIS LUCK • 1911 • *Nestor* • USA
JUST HIS LUCK • 1912 • *Selig* • USA
JUST HOME MADE • 1918 • *Strand* • USA • JUST HOME MAID
JUST HOME MAID see **JUST HOME MADE** • 1918
JUST IMAGINATION • 1916 • Myll Louis • SHT • USA
JUST IMAGINE • 1930 • Butler David • USA
JUST IN TIME • 1906 • Fitzhamon Lewin • UKN
JUST IN TIME • 1907 • Williamson James? • UKN
JUST IN TIME • 1912 • *Bison* • USA
JUST IN TIME • 1913 • *Smalley Phillips* • USA
JUST IN TIME • 1914 • *B & C* • UKN
JUST IN TIME • 1915 • Nash Percy? • UKN
JUST IN TIME FOR DINNER • 1911 • *Comet* • USA
JUST JANE • 1913 • *Robinson Gertrude* • USA
JUST JIM • 1915 • Lund O. A. C. • USA
JUST JOE • 1960 • Rogers Maclean • UKN
JUST KEEP A THOUGHT FOR ME • 1922 • Parkinson H. B. • SHT • UKN • KEEP A LITTLE THOUGHT FOR ME
JUST KIDDING • 1917 • *Rhodes Billie* • SHT • USA
JUST KIDS • 1911 • *Powers* • USA
JUST KIDS • 1913 • *Punch* • USA
JUST KIDS • 1913 • Henderson Dell • *Ab* • USA
JUST KIDS • 1913 • Lehrman Henry • *Keystone* • USA
JUST KIDS • 1914 • *Eclair* • USA
JUST KIDS • 1915 • *Thanhouser Kidlet* • USA
JUST KITTY • 1916 • Hill Robert F. • SHT • USA
JUST LADS (UKN) see **HIGH SCHOOL HERO** • 1927
JUST LIKE A GIRL • 1906 • *Warwick Trading Co.* • UKN
JUST LIKE A MOTHER • 1913 • Haldane Bert? • UKN
JUST LIKE A WOMAN • 1908 • *Essanay* • USA
JUST LIKE A WOMAN • 1912 • Griffith D. W. • USA
JUST LIKE A WOMAN • 1915 • Santschi Thomas • USA
JUST LIKE A WOMAN • 1923 • Beal Scott R., McClung Hugh • USA
JUST LIKE A WOMAN • 1938 • Stein Paul L. • UKN • SWEET RACKET
JUST LIKE A WOMAN • 1966 • Fuest Robert • UKN
JUST LIKE AMERICA see **TISZTA AMERIKA** • 1987
JUST LIKE AT HOME see **OLYAN, MINT OTTHON** • 1978
JUST LIKE DAD • 1918 • *Christie* • USA
JUST LIKE FRIENDS see **FOR VANSKAPS SKULL** • 1965
JUST LIKE HEAVEN • 1930 • Neill R. William • USA
JUST LIKE HIS WIFE • 1915 • *Mutual* • USA
JUST LIKE KIDS • 1915 • Hotaling Arthur D. • USA
JUST LIKE THE WEST • 1912 • *Imp* • USA
JUST LIKE WEATHER see **MEIGUO XIN** • 1987
JUST LOOK AT JAKE • 1915 • *Clayton Ethel* • USA
JUST LUCK • 1912 • *Morey Harry T.* • USA
JUST MAINE FOLK • 1912 • *Lubin* • USA
JUST MAN, THE see **JUSTICERO, EL** • 1967
JUST MARRIED • 1912 • *Lubin* • USA
JUST MARRIED • 1928 • Strayer Frank • USA
JUST MARRIED • 1987 • Schmulevich Michael • USA
JUST MARRIED see **GRUNE HOCHZEIT** • 1988
JUST ME AND MY LITTLE GIRLIE • 1976 • Blagg Linda • SHT • ASL
JUST ME AND YOU • 1978 • Erman John • USA • JUST YOU AND ME
JUST MICKEY • 1930 • Disney Walt • ANS • USA • FIDDLIN' AROUND
JUST MOTHER • 1914 • *Oakley Laura* • USA
JUST MY LUCK • 1933 • Raymond Jack • UKN
JUST MY LUCK • 1936 • Heinz Ray • USA
JUST MY LUCK • 1957 • Carstairs John Paddy • UKN
JUST NEIGHBORS • 1919 • Roach Hal • SHT • USA
JUST NOBODY • 1913 • *Lubin* • USA
JUST NUTS • 1915 • Roach Hal • USA
JUST OFF BROADWAY • 1924 • *Gilbert John* • USA
JUST OFF BROADWAY • 1929 • O'Connor Frank • USA
JUST OFF BROADWAY • 1942 • Leeds Herbert I. • USA • TWELVE MEN IN A BOX
JUST ONCE • 1968 • Perris Anthony • CND
JUST ONCE MORE see **CHANS** • 1962
JUST ONCE MORE see **JOS OVAJ PUT** • 1984
JUST ONE LIFE see **BARE ET LIV –HISTORIEN OM FRIDTJOF NANSEN** • 1968
JUST ONE MORE CHANCE • 1932 • Fleischer Dave • ANS • USA
JUST ONE MORE TIME • 1963 • Megahy Francis • UKN
JUST ONE OF THE GUYS • 1985 • Gottlieb Lisa • USA
JUST ONE OF THOSE WEDNESDAYS • 1964 • Hersko Janos • HNG
JUST ONE WORD • 1929 • Santley Joseph • SHT • USA
JUST OUT OF COLLEGE • 1912 • *Lubin* • USA
JUST OUT OF COLLEGE • 1915 • Irving Henry George • USA
JUST OUT OF COLLEGE • 1921 • Green Alfred E. • USA
JUST OUT OF REACH • 1979 • Blagg Linda • DOC • ASL
JUST OUTSIDE THE DOOR • 1920 • Irving George • USA
JUST PALS • 1920 • Ford John • USA
JUST PALS • 1932 • Stoloff Ben • SHT • USA
JUST PEGGY • 1918 • Lipman J. A. • ASL
JUST PEOPLE see **SAMO LJUDI** • 1957
JUST PLAIN FOLKS • 1908 • Baker George D. • USA
JUST PLAIN FOLKS • 1916 • Dowlan William C. • SHT • USA
JUST PLAIN FOLKS • 1918 • *Vernon Bobby* • SHT • USA
JUST PLAIN FOLKS • 1925 • Bradbury Robert North • USA
JUST PLANE BEEP • 1965 • Larriva Rudy • ANS • USA
JUST PRETENDING • 1912 • *Hackett Albert* • USA
JUST PUNISHMENT, A • 1914 • Le Saint Edward J. • USA
JUST RAMBLING ALONG • 1918 • Roach Hal • SHT • USA
JUST RETRIBUTION • 1915 • *Hawley Ormi* • USA
JUST REWARD, A • 1909 • *Lubin* • USA
JUST ROUTINE • 1967 • Inman Jeff • SHT • UKN
JUST SHOW PEOPLE • 1913 • Brooke Van Dyke • USA
JUST SMILE • 1911 • *Reliance* • USA
JUST SMITH • 1933 • Walls Tom • UKN • NEVER COME BACK
JUST SPOOKS • 1925 • Lantz Walter • ANS • USA
JUST SQUAW • 1919 • Middleton George E. • USA
JUST STARTING see **PRAVE ZACINAME** • 1946
JUST SUPPOSE • 1920 • *Mattison Frank S.* • USA
JUST SUPPOSE • 1926 • Webb Kenneth • USA • GOLDEN YOUTH (UKN)
JUST SUPPOSE • 1948 • Barclay David • SHT • USA
JUST SYLVIA • 1918 • Vale Travers • USA
JUST TELL ME WHAT YOU WANT • 1979 • Lumet Sidney • USA
JUST THE JOB • 1974 • Duffell Peter • UKN
JUST THE TWO OF US • 1975 • Peeters Barbara • USA
JUST THE WAY YOU ARE • 1984 • Molinaro Edouard • USA • I WON'T DANCE
JUST THIS ONCE • 1951 • Weis Don • USA
JUST TO BE LOVED see **HEISSER SAND AUF SYLT** • 1968
JUST TO WHISTLE A BIT see **JEN SI TAK TROCHU PISKNOUT** • 1981
JUST TONY • 1922 • Reynolds Lynn • USA
JUST TOO LATE • 1912 • *Nestor* • USA
JUST TOO LATE • 1919 • *Klever Pictures* • SHT • USA
JUST TRAMPS • 1915 • *Pathe Exchange* • USA
JUST TRAVELIN' • 1927 • Carpenter Horace B. • USA
JUST TWO LITTLE GIRLS • 1911 • *Nestor* • USA
JUST US • 1986 • Glenn Gordon • ASL
JUST VERDICT, A • 1912 • *Lubin* • USA
JUST WE TWO • 1934 • Horne James W. • SHT • USA
JUST WHAT BOBBY WANTED • 1917 • Seay Charles M. • SHT • USA
JUST WHAT I NEEDED • 1955 • Barclay David • SHT • USA
JUST WILLIAM • 1939 • Cutts Graham • UKN
JUST WILLIAM'S LUCK • 1947 • Guest Val • UKN
JUST YET BUT NOT QUITE • 1916 • Hutchinson Craig • SHT • USA
JUST YOU AND ME see **JUST ME AND YOU** • 1978
JUST YOU AND ME, KID • 1979 • Stern Leonard • USA
JUSTE AVANT LA NUIT • 1971 • Chabrol Claude • FRN, ITL • JUST BEFORE NIGHTFALL (UKN)
JUSTE DROIT, LE • 1979 • Poljinsky Serge, Zadeh Sandra • FRN
JUSTICA DO CEU • 1952 • Manuel Vitor • PRT
JUSTICE • 1910 • *Nestor* • USA
JUSTICE • 1914 • Wilson Frank • UKN
JUSTICE • 1917 • Elvey Maurice • UKN
JUSTICE see **PRAVDA** • 1962
JUSTICE see **INQUILAB** • 1984
JUSTICE A LA CARTE • 1916 • Robertson John S. • SHT • USA
JUSTICE AND CARYL CHESSMAN • 1960 • Reynolds Quentin, Spiegel Ed • USA
JUSTICE D'ABORD • 1921 • Protazanov Yakov • FRN
JUSTICE DENIED • 1990 • Cowan Paul • CND
JUSTICE EST FAITE • 1951 • Cayatte Andre • FRN • LET JUSTICE BE DONE (UKN) ○ JUSTICE IS DONE (USA)
JUSTICE ET LA VENGEANCE POURSUIVANT LE CRIME • 1905 • *Melies Georges (P)* • FRN
JUSTICE FOR SALE (UKN) see **NIGHT COURT** • 1932
JUSTICE FOR SELWYN see **PRIPAD PRO SELWYN** • 1968
JUSTICE IN THE FAR NORTH • 1910 • Salter Harry • USA
JUSTICE IS DONE (USA) see **JUSTICE EST FAITE** • 1951
JUSTICE OF MANITOU • 1912 • *Pathe* • USA
JUSTICE OF SOCIETY, THE see **SAMHALLETS DOM** • 1912
JUSTICE OF THE DESERT • 1912 • *Vitagraph* • USA
JUSTICE OF THE FAR NORTH • 1925 • Dawn Norman • USA • ESKIMO, THE
JUSTICE OF THE RANGE • 1935 • Selman David • USA
JUSTICE OF THE SAGE • 1912 • Dwan Allan • USA
JUSTICE OF THE WILD • 1913 • *Nestor* • USA
JUSTICE TAKES A HOLIDAY • 1933 • Bennet Spencer Gordon • USA
JUSTICE VICTORIOUS see **RETTEN SEJRER** • 1917
JUSTICERO, EL • 1967 • dos Santos Nelson Pereira • BRZ • JUST MAN, THE ○ JUSTICIER, LE
JUSTICES • 1978 • Cayatte Andre • FRN
JUSTICIA DE LOS VILLALOBOS, LA • 1959 • Zambrano Enrique • CUB, MXC
JUSTICIA DE PANCHO VILLA, LA • 1939 • Aguila Guz, Calles Guillermo • MXC
JUSTICIA DEL COYOTE ,LA • 1954 • Romero-Marchent Joaquin Luis • SPN
JUSTICIA DEL GAVILAN VENGADOR, LA • 1956 • Salvador Jaime • MXC
JUSTICIA DEL LOBO, LA • 1951 • Orona Vicente • MXC
JUSTICIA ES MENOR DE EDAD, LA • 1970 • *Cinema Marte* • MXC
JUSTICIER, LE • 1909 • Jasset Victorin • FRN
JUSTICIER, LE see **JUSTICERO, EL** • 1967
JUSTICIERE, LA • 1913 • Bourgeois Gerard • FRN
JUSTICIERE, LA • 1913 • Jasset Victorin • FRN
JUSTICIERE, LA • 1925 • Gleize Maurice • FRN
JUSTICIERO VENGADOR, EL • 1960 • Munoz Manuel • MXC
JUSTIFIABLE DECEPTION, A • 1915 • Batley Ethyle • UKN
JUSTIFIED • 1909 • *Essanay* • USA
JUSTIFIED • 1915 • Otto Henry • USA
JUSTIN CASE • 1988 • Edwards Blake • TVM • USA
JUSTIN DE MARSEILLE • 1934 • Tourneur Maurice • FRN • MA BELLE MARSEILLE
JUSTINE • 1967 • Johnsen S. N. • USA • JUSTINE: THE EROTIC EXCESS OF EVIL
JUSTINE • 1969 • Cukor George, Strick Joseph (U/c) • USA
JUSTINE • 1976 • Mackinnon Stuart, Myers Clive, Perkins Nigel • UKN
JUSTINE see **MARQUIS DE SADE: JUSTINE** • 1968
JUSTINE see **CRUEL PASSION** • 1977
JUSTINE AND JULIET see **MARQUIS DE SADE: JUSTINE** • 1968
JUSTINE DE SADE • 1970 • Pierson Claude • CND, FRN, ITL • VIOLATION OF JUSTINE, THE ○ SADE'S JUSTINE
JUSTINE + JULIETTE • 1974 • Ahlberg Mac • SWD
JUSTINE OVVERO LE DISAVVENTURE DELLA VERTU (ITL) see **MARQUIS DE SADE: JUSTINE** • 1968
JUSTINE: THE EROTIC EXCESS OF EVIL see **JUSTINE** • 1967
JUSTINIAN AND THEODORA • 1911 • Turner Otis • USA
JUSTINIAN'S HUMAN TORCHES (USA) see **TORCHES HUMAINES** • 1908
JUSTLY PUNISHED • 1914 • *Melies* • USA
JUTAI • 1948 • Shibuya Minoru • JPN
JUTAI • 1967 • Kimata Akitaka • JPN • IMPREGNATION
JUTALOMUTAZAS • 1975 • Darday Istvan • HNG • HOLIDAY IN BRITAIN ○ PRIZE TRIP, THE
JUTNUTS, THE • 1989 • DNM
JUTRO • 1967 • Djordjevic Purisa • YGS • MORNING
JUTRO MEKSYK • 1965 • Scibor-Rylski Aleksander • PLN • MEXICO TOMORROW ○ MEXICO, SOON ○ TOMORROW MEXICO
JUTRO PREMIERA • 1946 • *Kawalerowicz Jerzy* • PLN • MORNING PREMIERE
JUTRO PREMIERA • 1962 • Morgenstern Janusz • PLN • PREMIERE TOMORROW ○ OPENING TOMORROW
JUULIA • 1964 • Makinen Aito, Elstela Esko • FNL • ONNELLISET LEIKIT
JUVE CONTRE FANTOMAS • 1914 • Feuillade Louis • SRL • FRN • JUVE VS. FANTOMAS ○ FANTOMAS II
JUVE VS. FANTOMAS see **JUVE CONTRE FANTOMAS** • 1914
JUVELERERNES SKROEK • 1915 • Christian • DNM • LAST ADVENTURE OF THE SKELETON'S HAND, THE ○ SKELETHAANDENS SIDSTE BEDRIFT ○ SKELETHAANDEN ○ JEWELLER'S TERROR, THE ○ SKELETON'S HAND, THE
JUVENATRIX: A CLASSIC TALE OF HORROR see **REJUVENATOR, THE** • 1988
JUVENILE BARBERS, THE • 1906 • Barker Will • UKN
JUVENILE COMEDIAN, A • 1904 • *Urban Trading Co.* • UKN
JUVENILE COURT • 1938 • Lederman D. Ross • USA
JUVENILE COURT • 1973 • Wiseman Frederick • DOC • USA
JUVENILE DELINQUENTS see **HIKO SHONEN** • 1964
JUVENILE DELINQUENTS see **SHAONIAN FAN** • 1985
JUVENILE DREAMS see **SUENOS JUVENILES** • 1968
JUVENILE FIREMEN, THE • 1910 • *Wrench Films* • UKN
JUVENILE HYPNOTIST, A • 1911 • Booth W. R. • UKN • JUVENILE PRANKS
JUVENILE JUNGLE • 1958 • Witney William • USA
JUVENILE JURY • 1946 • Crouch William Forest • SHT • USA
JUVENILE KIDNAPPERS, THE • 1913 • *Frontier* • USA
JUVENILE LIAISON • 1975 • Broomfield Nicholas, Churchill Joan • UKN
JUVENILE LOVE AFFAIR, A • 1912 • *Costello Dolores* • USA
JUVENILE PASSION see **KURUTTA KAJITSU** • 1956
JUVENILE PRANKS see **JUVENILE HYPNOTIST, A** • 1911
JUVENILE SCIENTIST, A • 1907 • Booth W. R. • UKN
JUVENIZER, THE see **CHUNG–SHEN TA SHIH** • 1981
JUVENTUD A LA INTEMPERIE • 1961 • Iquino Ignacio F. • SPN • UNSATISFIED, THE (USA)
JUVENTUD DESENFRENADA • 1956 • Diaz Morales Jose • MXC
JUVENTUD, DIVINO TESORO • 1977 • Larraz Jose R. • SPN • MENAGE A TROIS
JUVENTUD DROGADA • 1977 • Truchado Jose • SPN
JUVENTUD REBELDE • 1961 • Soler Julian • MXC
JUVENTUD SE IMPONE, LA • 1964 • Soler Julian • MXC • NUEVA OLA, LA
JUVENTUD SIN LEY • 1965 • Martinez Solares Gilberto • MXC • REBELDES A GO GO
JUVENTUDE • 1950 • dos Santos Nelson Pereira • SHT • BRZ
JUVENTUDE E TERNURA • 1968 • Teixeira Aurelio • BRZ • YOUTH AND TENDERNESS
JUWELENMARDER, DIE • 1928 • Garai-Arvai • FRG
JUX WILL ER SICH MACHEN, EINEN • 1928 • Brandt Johannes • FRG
JUXBARON, DER • 1926 • Wolff Willi • FRG
JUYAKU NO ISU • 1958 • Kakei Masanori • JPN • POST AS DIRECTOR, THE
JUYUSHI ASH–SHAMS • 1975 • Abdes-Salam Shadi • EGY • ARMEES DU SOLEIL, LES
JUZGADO PERMANENTE • 1953 • Romero-Marchent Joaquin Luis • SPN
JUZNA PATEKA • 1983 • Crvenkovski Steva • YGS • SOUTHERN TRAIL, THE ○ SOUTHERN COURSE, THE ○ JUZNA STAZA
JUZNA STAZA see **JUZNA PATEKA** • 1983
JWALA • 1987 • Anand Gul • IND
JWAR BHATA • 1944 • *Biswas Anil (M)* • IND
JY IS MY LEIFLING • 1968 • De Villiers Dirk • SAF • YOU ARE MY DARLING
J'Y SUIS, J'Y RESTE • 1953 • Labro Maurice • FRN
JYOJI ZANKOKUSHI • 1968 • Yamashita Osamu • JPN • CRUEL HISTORY OF AFFAIRS
JYOTAI • 1969 • Masumura Yasuzo • JPN • VIXEN
JYOTAI KAIKA • 1968 • Okuwaki Toshio • JPN • FLORESCENCE OF A WOMAN'S BODY
JYOTI • 1969 • *Burman S. D. (M)* • IND
JYRTDAN • 1970 • *Aslanov Elchin* • ANM • USS
JY'S LIEFLIK VANAAND • 1962 • SAF

K

K 1 GREIFT EIN! • 1933 • Heuberger Edmund • FRG
K–2 • 1988 • Weiner Hal • USA
K 2 • 1989 • Dobray Gyorgy • HNG • PROS.. 2 ○ PROS.. 2: A FILM ABOUT PROSTITUTION –LADIES OF THE NIGHT

K-9 • 1989 • Daniel Rod • USA
K-9000: A SPACE ODDITY • 1968 • Mitchell Robert, Swarthe Robert • ANS • USA
K.O. • 1968 • Muresan Mircea • RMN • KNOCK-OUT
K.O. • 1978 • Renyi Tamas • HNG
K -A FILM ABOUT PROSTITUTION (RAKOCZI SQUARE) see **K -FILM A PROSTITUALTAKROL (RAKOCZI TER)** • 1988
K.C.I. BEYOND THE THREE R'S • 1982 • Barrie Scott • CND
K.D. LANG'S ODYSSEY IN JAPAN • 1985 • Barclay Robert • MTV • CND
K -DAS HAUS DES SCHWEIGENS • 1951 • Hinrich Hans • FRG
K.E.B. • 1973 • Are Vasco • ITL
K -FILM A PROSTITUALTAKROL (RAKOCZI TER) • 1988 • Dobray Gyorgy • HNG • K -A FILM ABOUT PROSTITUTION (RAKOCZI SQUARE)
K.G.B. CONNECTION, THE • 1981 • Burke Martyn • DOC • CND
K.I.A. KILLED IN ACTION see **EYE OF THE EAGLE II** • 1989
K NOVOMU BEREGU • 1955 • Lukov Leonid • USS • TOWARDS THE NEW BANK ◦ TOWARD NEW SHORES
K.O. SUZETTE • 1969 • *Landow Suzzan* • USA
K.O. VA E UCCIDI • 1966 • Ferrero Carlo • ITL
K.SH.E. • 1932 • Shub Esther • USS • KOMOSOL, PATRON OF ELECTRIFICATION ◦ KOMOSOL, LEADER OF ELECTRIFICATION
K SVYETU • 1968 • Shilenko B., Lapoknysh Vasil, Ilyinski N. • USS • TOWARDS THE LIGHT
K -THE UNKNOWN • 1924 • Pollard Harry • USA
K.U.K. BALLETTMADEL, DAS • 1926 • Neufeld Max • AUS • ROYAL BALLET GIRL, THE (USA) ◦ BALLETTERHERZOG, DER ◦ VIRTUE
K. UND K. FELDMARSCHALL • 1956 • Emo E. W. • AUS
K. UND K. FELDMARSCHALL, DER see **FALSCHE FELDMARSCHALL, DER** • 1930
K VOPROSU O PEREMIRII S FINLJANDIEJ • 1945 • Raizman Yuli • DOC • USS • A PROPOS OF THE TRUCE WITH FINLAND
K.Y.T.E.S. HOW WE DREAM OURSELVES • 1985 • Saltzman Deepa Mehta • DOC • CND
K9 BAASPATROLLIEHOND • 1972 • SAF
K13 S13 see **ABENTEUER EINES ZEHNMARKSCHEINES, DIE** • 1926
KA-KE-KI-KU • 1958-60 • Bonniere Rene • DCS • CND
KAACHAN KEKKON SHIROYO • 1962 • Gosho Heinosuke • JPN • GET MARRIED MOTHER ◦ MOTHER, GET MARRIED
KAACHAN TO JUICHI-NIN NO KODOMO • 1966 • Gosho Heinosuke • JPN • OUR WONDERFUL YEARS ◦ MOTHER AND ELEVEN CHILDREN
KAADU • 1974 • Karnad Girish • IND • FOREST, THE
KAADU KUDRE • 1978 • Kambar Chandrashekhar • IND • WILD HORSE, THE
KAAGAZ KE PHOOL • 1959 • Dutt Guru • IND
KAASAN NAGAIKI SHITENE • 1962 • Kawazu Yoshiro • JPN • MAMA I NEED YOU
KAATHAL VAHANAM • 1968 • Thirumugam A. • IND • VEHICLE OF LOVE
KAATHAVARAAYAN • 1959 • Ramanna • IND
KAATIL • 1953 • Akat Lutfu • TRK
KABADAYI • 1968 • Figenli Yavuz • TRK • BULLY, THE
KABAKA • Red Raymond • SHT • PHL
KABALA • 1982 • Rozsa Janos • HNG • MASCOT
KABALE UND LIEBE • 1959 • Hellberg Martin • GDR • INTRIGUE AND LOVE
KABALE UND LIEBE see **LUISE MILLERIN** • 1922
KABALE UND LIEBE IM ZIRKUS see **LIEBE IST DER FRAUEN MACHT, DIE** • 1924
KABARET • 1964 • Kijowicz Miroslaw • ANS • PLN • CABARET
KABE ATSUKI HEYA • 1953 • Kobayashi Masaki • JPN • THICK WALLED ROOM, THE ◦ ROOM WITH THICK WALLS
KABE NO NAKANO HIMEGOTO • 1965 • Wakamatsu Koji • JPN • HISTORY BEHIND WALLS ◦ AFFAIRS IN THE WALLS
KABINE 27 see **FRAU UBER BORD** • 1945
KABINETT DES DR. CALIGARI, DAS • 1919 • Wiene Robert • FRG • CABINET OF DR. CALIGARI, THE (USA) ◦ CABINET DES DR. CALIGARI, DAS
KABINETT DES DR. LARIFARI, DAS • 1930 • Wohlmuth Robert • FRG
KABINETT DES DR. SEGATO, DAS • 1923 • *Aafa, Althoff-Ambos-Film* • FRG • CABINET OF DR. SEGATO, THE
KABIR SAHEB • 1938 • *Kohinoor* • IND
KABOCHA • 1928 • Ozu Yasujiro • JPN • PUMPKIN
KABOCHA SODOKI • 1926 • Tasaka Tomotaka • JPN
KABULIWALA • 1961 • Gupta Hemen • IND
KABURITSUKI JINSEI • 1968 • Kumashiro Tatsumi • JPN • FRONT ROW
KABZAA • Bhatt Mahesh • IND
KACAK • 1968 • Ceylan Ferit • TRK • FUGITIVE, THE
KACAKLAR • 1971 • Guney Yilmaz • TRK • FUGITIVES, THE
KACAMAK • 1987 • Sabuncu Basar • TRK • IMPROMPTU
KACHUSHA • 1914 • Hosoya K. • JPN • KATUSHA
KACZKA-PLOTKA • 1954 • Nehrebecki Wladyslaw • ANS • PLN • GOSSIP DUCK, THE
KACZMAREK • 1928 • Wilhelm Carl • FRG
KACZMAREK see **MUSKETIER KACZMAREK** • 1917
KAD BUDEM MRTAV I BEO • 1968 • Pavlovic Zivojin • YGS • WHEN I AM DEAD AND WHITE
KAD CUJES ZVONA • 1969 • Vrdoljak Antun • YGS • WHEN THE BELLS START RINGING ◦ WHEN YOU HEAR THE BELLS TOLL ◦ WHEN YOU HEAR THE BELLS
KAD DODJE LAV • 1973 • Hladnik Bostjan • YGS • WHEN THE LION COMES ◦ KO PRIDE LEV
KAD GOLUBOVI POLETE • 1968 • Radavanovic Vlasta • YGS • WHEN PIGEONS FLY
KAD PROJECE KASNI see **KUR PRANVERA VONOHET** • 1980
KAD ZRIJU JAGODE see **KO ZORIJO JAGODE** • 1979
KADAICHA see **STONES OF DEATH** • 1988
KADAICHA: THE DEATH STONE see **STONES OF DEATH** • 1988
KADAPATHAKA CHAYA • 1988 • Obeysekara Vasantha • SLN
KADARWATI • 1985 • Sophiaan Sophan • INN
KADDISCH • 1924 • Licho Adolf Edgar • FRG • TOTENGEBET, DAS
KADDU BEYKAT • 1975 • Faye Safi • SNL • NEWS FROM THE VILLAGE ◦ PEASANT LETTER
KADE PO DOZDOT see **KUDA POSLE KISE?** • 1967
KADER AYIRSA BILE • 1968 • Duru Sureyya • TRK • IF FATE WILL PART US
KADER BAGI • 1967 • Inanoglu Turker • TRK • LINK OF FATE, THE
KADER BOYLE ISTEDI • 1968 • Akat Lutfu • TRK • FATE WILLED IT SO
KADETTEN • 1931 • Jacoby Georg • FRG • HINTER DEN ROTEN MAUERN VON LICHTERFELDE ◦ BOYS IN UNIFORM
KADETTEN • 1939 • Ritter Karl • FRG
KADETTKAMRATER • 1939 • Hildebrand Weyler • SWD • FELLOW CADETS
KADHDHAB, AL- • 1975 • Abu Saif Salah • EGY • LIAR, THE
KADIN ASLA UNUTMAZ • 1968 • Aksoy Orhan • TRK • WOMAN NEVER FORGETS, A
KADIN DUSMANI • 1967 • Engin Ilhan • TRK • WOMAN HATER, THE
KADIN INTIKAMI • 1968 • Engin Ilhan • TRK • WOMAN'S REVENGE, A
KADIN SEVERSE • 1968 • Erakalin Ulku • TRK • IF A WOMAN LOVES
KADINIM • 1967 • Olgac Bilge • TRK • MY WOMAN
KADININ ADI YOK • 1987 • Yilmaz Atif • TRK • WOMAN HAS NO NAME
KADISSIYA, EL see **QADISSIA, AL-** • 1981
KADOYNG • 1972 • Shand Ian • UKN
KADUN LAKAISIJAT • 1989 • Soinio Olli • FNL • STREET-SWEEPERS
KADZHANA • 1936 • Pipinashvili Konstantin • USS
KAERANU SASABUE • 1926 • Gosho Heinosuke • JPN • BAMBOO LEAF FLUTE OF NO RETURN ◦ NO RETURN
KAERAZARU HATOBA • 1966 • Ezaki Mio • JPN • HARBOUR OF NO RETURN
KAERE FAMILIE, DEN see **KARA FAMILJEN, DEN** • 1962
KAERE IRENE • 1971 • Thomsen Christian Braad • DNM • DEAR IRENE (UKN)
KAERE LEGETOJ, DET • 1968 • Axel Gabriel • DNM • DANISH BLUE (UKN) ◦ POPULAR TOY, THE
KAEREZARU HIBI • 1978 • Fujita Toshiya • JPN • DAYS OF NO RETURN
KAERLIGHED GOR BLIND • 1912 • Blom August • DNM • LOVE IS BLIND
KAERLIGHED MOD BETALING (DNM) see **FUR ZWEI GROSCHEN ZARTLICHKEIT** • 1957
KAERLIGHED PA KREDIT • 1955 • Henning-Jensen Astrid • DNM • LOVE ON CREDIT
KAERLIGHED PA RULLERSKOJTER • 1943 • Roos Jorgen, Mertz Albert • DOC • DNM
KAERLIGHED UDEN STOP • 1988 • Kristensen Hans • DNM • LOVE WITHOUT END ◦ LOVE ON A NON-STOP
KAERLIGHEDENS MELODI • 1959 • Christensen Bent • DNM • GIRL, A GUITAR AND A TRUMPET, A ◦ FORMULA FOR LOVE
KAERLIGHEDENS STYRKE • 1911 • Blom August • DNM • POWER OF LOVE, THE
KAERLIGHEDENS TRIUMF • 1914 • Holger-Madsen • DNM • ROMANCE OF A WILL, THE ◦ TESTAMENTET
KAERLIGHEDS VAEDDEMAALET • 1914 • Blom August • DNM • WAGER, THE
KAERLIGHEDSLAENGEL • 1915 • Blom August • DNM • PUKKELRYGGEDE, DEN ◦ CRIPPLE GIRL, THE
KAERLIGHEDSOEN • 1924 • Sandberg Anders W. • DNM • AMAZING ELOPEMENT, THE
KAERLIGHEDSPEKULANTEN • 1917 • Lauritzen Lau • DNM
KAETTE KITA YOPPARAI • 1968 • Oshima Nagisa • JPN • THREE RESURRECTED DRUNKARDS ◦ SINNER IN PARADISE ◦ DRUNK THAT CAME BACK, THE
KAETTEKITA GOKUDO • 1968 • Yamashita Kosaku • JPN • RETURN OF THE OUTLAW
KAFAR • 1976 • Sen Mrinal • IND
KAFER AUF EXTRATOUR, EIN • 1973 • Zehetgruber Rudolf • FRG • BEETLE IN OVERDRIVE, A
KAFER GEHT AUFS GANZE, EIN • 1971 • Zehetgruber Rudolf • FRG
KAFER GIBT VOLLGAS, EIN • 1972 • Zehetgruber Rudolf • FRG, SWT • BEETLE GOES FLAT OUT, A
KAFERI AN KHATIATAK • 1933 • *Mair Aziza* • EGY • PAY FOR YOUR SINS
KAFFEEHAUS, DAS • 1970 • Fassbinder R. W. • MTV • FRG
KAFFIR'S GRATITUDE, THE • 1916 • *Clifford William* • SHT • USA
KAFFIR'S SKULL, THE • 1914 • Adolfi John G. • USA
KAFKAS KARTALI • 1968 • Atadeniz Yilmaz • TRK • EAGLE OF CAUCASUS, THE
KAFR KASSEM • 1974 • Alawiya Burhan • SYR, LBN • KAFR QASIM
KAFR QASIM see **KAFR KASSEM** • 1974
KAFUKU • 1937 • Naruse Mikio • JPN • LEARN FROM EXPERIENCE
KAGAJ KE PHOOL • 1959 • *Burman S. D. (M)* • IND
KAGAMI NO NAKKA NO RAZO • 1963 • Nakamura Noboru • JPN
KAGAYAKU SHOWA • 1928 • Shimazu Yasujiro • JPN • BRILLIANT SHOWA PERIOD, THE
KAGE NO KURUMA • 1970 • Nomura Yoshitaro • JPN • SHADOW WITHIN, THE
KAGEMUSHA • 1980 • Kurosawa Akira • JPN • SHADOW WARRIOR, THE
KAGENAKI KOL • 1958 • Suzuki Seijun • JPN
KAGERO • 1969 • Shindo Kaneto • JPN • HEAT WAVE ISLAND ◦ HEAT HAZE
KAGERO EZU • 1959 • Kinugasa Teinosuke • JPN • STOP THE OLD FOX
KAGERO-GASA • 1959 • Misumi Kenji • JPN • HALO OF HEAT HAZE
KAGERO-ZA • 1982 • Suzuki Seijun • JPN • THEATRE TROUPE KAGERO
KAGI • 1959 • Ichikawa Kon • JPN • ODD OBSESSIONS (UKN) ◦ KEY, THE (USA)
KAGI • 1974 • Kumashiro Tatsumi • JPN • KEY
KAGI NO KAGI • 1964 • Taniguchi Senkichi • JPN
KAGIRI NAKU TOMEI NI CHIKAI BLUE • 1978 • Murakami Ryu • JPN • INFINITELY TRANSPARENT BLUE
KAGIRIARU HI O AINI IKITE • 1967 • Tanaka Shigeo • JPN • SUITORS, THE
KAGIRINAKI ZENSHIN • 1937 • Uchida Tomu • JPN • UNENDING ADVANCE
KAGUYAHIMI • 1935 • *Tsuburaya Eiji (Ph)* • JPN
KAHAN-HAI-MANZIL • 1940 • *Devi Illa* • IND
KAHAN KAHAN SE GUZAR GAVA • 1981 • Sathyu M. S. • IND • WHAT WE HAVE ALL BEEN THROUGH ◦ MANY PHASES OF LIFE, THE
KAHDEKSAN SURMANLUOTIA • 1972 • Niskanen Mikko • MTV • FNL • EIGHT FATAL BULLETS ◦ EIGHT DEADLY SHOTS
KAHDEKSAS VELJES • 1971 • Pasanen Spede • FNL • EIGHTH BROTHER, THE
KAHER EL ZAMAN • 1986 • el Sheikh Kamal • EGY • CONQUEROR OF TIME
KAHIN AURCHAL • 1968 • Anand Vijay • IND • ELSEWHERE
KAHIN DIN KAHIN RAAT • 1968 • Darshan • IND • SOMEWHERE DAY, SOMEWHERE NIGHT
KAHLE SANGER, DER • 1967 • Schamoni Ulrich • MTV • FRG
KAHN DER FROHLICHEN LEUTE, DER • 1950 • Hinrich Hans • FRG
KAHREDEN KURSUN • 1965 • Atadeniz Yilmaz • TRK
KAHUNA • 1981 • Sillman Frank • USA
KAHVECI GUZELI • 1968 • Aslan Muzaffer • TRK • BEAUTIFUL COFFEE-SELLER, THE
KAIBIGAN KONG STO. NINO • 1967 • de Guzman Armando • PHL • MY FRIEND, THE SAINT
KAIBYO ARIMA GOTEN • 1953 • Arai Ryohei • JPN • GHOST-CAT OF ARIMA PALACE
KAIBYO GOJUSAN-TSUGI • 1956 • Kato Bin • JPN • GHOST-CAT OF GOJUSAN-TSUGI
KAIBYO KARAKURI TENJO • 1958 • Fukada Kinnosuke • JPN • GHOST-CAT OF KARAKURI TENJO
KAIBYO KOSHINUKE DAISODO • 1954 • Saito Torajiro • JPN • WEAK-KNEED FROM FEAR OF GHOST-CAT
KAIBYO NOROI NO KABE • 1958 • Misumi Kenji • JPN • GHOST-CAT WALL OF HATRED
KAIBYO NOROI NO NUMA • 1968 • Ishikawa Yoshihiro • JPN • CURSED POND, THE ◦ GHOST-CAT SWAMP OF HATRED
KAIBYO OKAZAKI SODO • 1954 • Kato Bin • JPN • TERRIBLE GHOST-CAT OF OKAZAKI
KAIBYO OMA-GA-TSUJI • 1954 • Kato Bin • JPN • GHOST-CAT OF OMA-GA-TSUJI
KAIBYO OTAMA-GA-IKE • 1960 • Ishikawa Yoshihiro • JPN • GHOST-CAT OF OTAMA-GA-IKE
KAIBYO RANBU • 1956 • Igayama Masamitsu • JPN • PHANTOM CAT, THE ◦ MANY GHOST-CATS
KAIBYO YONAKI NUMA • 1957 • Tasaka Katsuhiko • JPN • GHOST-CAT OF YONAKI SWAMP ◦ NECROMANCY
KAICHO-ON • 1981 • Hashiura Masato • JPN • SOUND OF THE TIDE, THE
KAIDAN see **KWAIDAN** • 1964
KAIDAN AMA YUREI • 1960 • Katono Goro • JPN • GHOST OF THE GIRL DIVER
KAIDAN BANCHO SARAYASHIKI • 1957 • Kono Juichi • JPN • GHOST STORY OF BROKEN DISHES AT BANCHO MANSION ◦ GHOST OF YOTSUYA, THE
KAIDAN BARABARA YUREI • 1968 • Ogawa Kinya • JPN • GHOST STORY -BARABARA PHANTOM, A ◦ DISMEMBERED GHOST
KAIDAN BOTAN DORO • 1968 • Yamamoto Satsuo • JPN • GHOST STORY OF PEONIES AND STONE LANTERNS, A ◦ MY BRIDE IS A GHOST ◦ BOTANDORO ◦ GHOST BEAUTY ◦ BRIDE FROM HELL, THE ◦ BOTAN DORO ◦ BRIDE FROM HADES, THE
KAIDAN CHIBUSA ENOKI • 1958 • Katono Goro • JPN • GHOST OF CHIBUSA ENOKI
KAIDAN CHIDORI-GA-FUCHI • 1956 • Koishi Eiichi • JPN • GHOST OF CHIDORI-GA-FUCHI ◦ SWAMP, THE
KAIDAN DOCHU • 1958 • Sawashima Tadashi • JPN • LADY WAS A GHOST, THE ◦ GHOST STORY IN PASSAGE ◦ GHOST STORY OF TWO TRAVELLERS
KAIDAN FUKAGAWA JOWA • 1952 • Inuzuka Minoru • JPN • TRAGIC GHOST STORY OF FUKAGAWA
KAIDAN GOJUSAN-TSUGI • 1960 • Uchide Kokichi • JPN • GHOST OF GOJUSAN-TSUGI
KAIDAN HEBIONNA • 1968 • Nakagawa Nobuo • JPN • FEAR OF THE SNAKE WOMAN ◦ GHOST OF SNAKE-GIRL
KAIDAN HITOTSU-ME JIZO • 1959 • Fukada Kinnosuke • JPN • GHOST FROM THE POND
KAIDAN HONJO NANFUSHIGI • 1957 • Katono Goro • JPN • GHOST STORY OF WANDERER AT HONJO ◦ SEVEN MYSTERIES
KAIDAN IJIN YUREI • 1963 • Kobayashi Satoru • JPN • CAUCASIAN GHOST
KAIDAN IRO-ZANGE-KYOREN ONNA SHISHO • 1957 • Kurahashi Ryosuke • JPN • DANCING MISTRESS
KAIDAN KAGAMI-GA-FUCHI • 1959 • Mori Masaki • JPN • GHOST OF KAGAMI-GA-FUCHI
KAIDAN KAKUIDORI • 1961 • Mori Issei • JPN • GHOST STORY OF KAKUI STREET
KAIDAN KASANE-GA-FUCHI • 1957 • Nakagawa Nobuo • JPN • GHOST OF KASANE-GA-FUCHI ◦ DEPTHS, THE
KAIDAN KASANE-GA-FUCHI • 1960 • Yasuda Kimiyoshi • JPN • GHOST OF KASANE-GA-FUCHI
KAIDAN KASANEGAFUCHI • 1970 • Yasuda Kimiyoshi • JPN • HORROR OF AN UGLY WOMAN ◦ MASSEUR'S CURSE
KAIDAN KATAME OTOKO • 1965 • Kobayashi Tsuneo • JPN • CURSE OF THE ONE-EYED CORPSE ◦ GHOST OF THE ONE-EYED MAN
KAIDAN NOBORIRYU • 1970 • Ishii Teruo • JPN • BLIND WOMAN'S CURSE, THE (USA) ◦ TATTOOED SWORDSWOMAN ◦ HAUNTED LIFE OF A DRAGON-TATTOOED LASS, THE
KAIDAN OIWA NO BOREI • 1961 • Kato Tai • JPN • GHOST OF YOTSUYA, THE ◦ GHOST OF OIWA
KAIDAN ONIBI NO NUMA • 1963 • Kato Bin • JPN • GHOST STORY OF DEVIL'S FIRE SWAMP

KAIDAN OTOSHIANA • 1968 • Shima Koji • JPN • GHOSTLY TRAP, THE ○ PIT OF DEATH, THE ○ GHOST STORY OF BOOBY TRAP

KAIDAN SAGA YASHIKI • 1953 • Arai Ryohei • JPN • GHOST OF SAGA MANSION

KAIDAN SEMUSHI OTOKO • 1965 • Sato Hajime • JPN • GHOST OF THE HUNCHBACK ○ HOUSE OF TERRORS

KAIDAN SHAMISEN-BORI • 1962 • Uchide Kokichi • JPN • GHOST MUSIC OF SHAMISEN

KAIDAN YONAKI-DORO • 1962 • Tasaka Katsuhiko • JPN • GHOST STORY OF STONE LANTERNS AND CRYING IN THE NIGHT

KAIDAN YUKIJORO • 1968 • Tanaka Tokuzo • JPN • GHOST OF SNOW-GIRL PROSTITUTE ○ YUKIONNA, WOMAN OF THE SNOW ○ YUKIONNA ○ SNOW GHOST

KAIDAN ZANKOKU MONOGATARI • 1968 • Hase Kazuo • JPN • CURSE OF THE BLOOD ○ CRUEL GHOST LEGEND

KAIGENREI • 1972 • Yoshida Yoshishige • JPN • COUP D'ETAT

KAIGENREI NO YORU • 1981 • Yamashita Kosaku • JPN • NIGHT UNDER MARTIAL LAW, THE

KAIGUN • 1943 • Tasaka Tomotaka • JPN • NAVY

KAIGUN • 1963 • Murayama Shinji • JPN • NAVY, THE

KAIGUN BAKUGEKITAI • 1940 • Kimura Keigo • DOC • JPN • NAVAL BOMBER FLEET, THE ○ NAVY BOMBERS

KAIGUN TOKUBETSU SHONEN HEI • 1972 • Imai Tadashi • JPN • SPECIAL BOY SOLDIERS OF THE NAVY ○ ETERNAL CAUSE ○ NAVY'S SPECIAL BOY SAILORS

KAIGYAKU SAN ROSHI • 1930 • Inagaki Hiroshi • JPN • THREE JESTING RONIN

KAII UTSUNOMIYA TSURITENJO • 1956 • Nakagawa Nobuo • JPN • WEIRD DEATH TRAP AT UTSUNOMIYA

KAIJIN • 1929 • Murata Minoru • JPN • ASHES ○ KAJIN

KAIJU DAISENSO • 1965 • Honda Inoshiro • JPN • INVASION OF THE ASTRO-MONSTER(S) ○ GODZILLA RADON KINGGIDORAH ○ INVASION OF PLANET X ○ MONSTER ZERO (USA) ○ BATTLE OF THE ASTROS ○ INVASION OF THE ASTROS

KAIJU OJI • 1968 • Tsuchiya Keinosuke • JPN • MONSTER PRINCE

KAIJU SOSHINGEKI • 1968 • Honda Inoshiro • JPN • DESTROY ALL MONSTERS (USA) ○ OPERATION MONSTERLAND ○ MARCH OF THE MONSTERS, THE ○ ATTACK OF THE MARCHING MONSTERS

KAIKOKO DANJI • 1926 • Mizoguchi Kenji • JPN • CHILDREN OF THE SEA (USA) ○ BOYS FROM THE SEA, THE ○ BOY FROM THE NAVY, THE

KAIKOKUKI • 1928 • Kinugasa Teinosuke • JPN • TALES FROM A COUNTRY BY THE SEA

KAIKUJA ERAMAASSA • 1986 • Lehtinen Virke • DOC • FNL • ECHOES OF THE WILDERNESS

KAIKYO • 1983 • Moritani Shiro • JPN • TUNNEL BELOW THE STRAIT ○ STRAIT

KAILAN MAHUHUGASAN ANG KASALANAN • 1989 • PHL

KAILANMA'Y DI KA MAG-IISA • 1968 • Crisostomo Fely • PHL • NEVER WILL YOU BE ALONE

KAIN • 1918 • Schmidthassler Walter • FRG

KAIN • 1975 • Schonherr Dietmar • BLG, AUS, FRG

KAIN DEL PLANETA OSCURO • 1982 • Broderick John, Stout Bill • ARG, USA • KAIN OF THE DARK PLANET ○ WARRIOR AND THE SORCERESS, THE

KAIN OF THE DARK PLANET see **KAIN DEL PLANETA OSCURO** • 1982

KAINSZEICHEN, DAS • 1919 • Oswald Richard • FRG

KAINTUCK • 1912 • Reid Hal • USA

KAINTUCKY BILL • 1914 • *Kalem* • USA

KAINUU 39 • 1978 • Honkasalo Pirjo, Lehto Pekka • FNL • TWO FORCES

KAIPAUS • 1974 • Bergholm Eija-Elina • FNL • LONGING

KAIRAKU NO WANA • 1967 • Fukada Kinnosuke • JPN • TRAP OF PLEASURE

KAIROUAN • 1973 • Ben Ammar Abdul Latif • SHT • TNS

KAIRYU • 1959 • Horiuchi Manao • JPN

KAIRYU DAIKESSEN • 1966 • Yamauchi Tetsuya • JPN • MAGIC SERPENT (USA) ○ GRAND DUEL IN MAGIC ○ FROGGO AND DROGGO

KAISANSHIKI • 1967 • Fukasaku Kinji • JPN • BREAK-UP, THE

KAISE KAHOON • 1964 • *Burman S. D. (M)* • IND

KAISEN NO ZENYA • 1943 • Yoshimura Kozaburo • JPN • ON THE EVE OF WAR ○ NIGHT BEFORE THE WAR, THE

KAISER, THE see **KAISER, BEAST OF BERLIN, THE** • 1918

KAISER, BEAST OF BERLIN, THE • 1918 • Julian Rupert • USA • KAISER, THE

KAISER CAPTURES PIMPLE, THE • 1915 • Evans Fred, Evans Joe • UKN

KAISER CASE, THE (USA) see **CAUSA KAISER** • 1932

KAISER DER SAHARA, DER see **MANN OHNE NAMEN 2, DER** • 1920-21

KAISER UND DAS WASCHERMADEL, DER • 1957 • Neubach Ernst • AUS

KAISER VON KALIFORNIEN, DER • 1936 • Trenker Luis • FRG • EMPEROR OF CALIFORNIA, THE

KAISER WALZER see **JOHANN STRAUSS, K. UND K. HOFBALLMUSIKDIREKTOR** • 1932

KAISER WAS THERE, A • 1918 • Avery Charles • SHT • USA

KAISER WILHELMS GLUCK UND ENDE • 1919 • Achsel Willy • FRG

KAISERAUGST • 1976 • DOC • SWT

KAISERBALL • 1956 • Antel Franz • AUS

KAISERIN, DIE • 1927 • Zelnik Friedrich • FRG

KAISERIN ELISABETH VON OESTERREICH • 1920 • Raffe Rolf • FRG

KAISERIN VON CHINA, DIE • 1953 • Sekely Steve • FRG

KAISERJAGER • 1956 • Forst Willi • AUS

KAISERLIEBCHEN • 1931 • Tintner Hans • FRG

KAISERMANOVER • 1954 • Antel Franz • AUS

KAISER'S DREAM, THE • 1914 • *Captain Kettle* • UKN

KAISER'S FINISH, THE • 1918 • Harvey John Joseph, Saum Clifford P. • USA

KAISER'S LACKEY, THE see **UNTERTAN, DER** • 1951

KAISER'S LAST SQUEAL, THE see **YANKEE DOODLE IN BERLIN** • 1919

KAISER'S PRESENT, THE • 1915 • Aylott Dave • UKN

KAISER'S SHADOW, THE • 1918 • Neill R. William • USA • KAISER'S SHADOW OR THE TRIPLE CROSS, THE

KAISER'S SHADOW OR THE TRIPLE CROSS, THE see **KAISER'S SHADOW, THE** • 1918

KAISER'S SPIES, THE • 1914 • Raymond Charles • UKN

KAISERSCHNITT -EINE OPERETTE • 1978 • Kaiser Alfred • AUS • CAESARIAN -AN OPERETTA

KAISERWALZER • 1932 • Zelnik Friedrich • FRG • HEUT' MACHT DIE WELT SONNTAG FUR MICH ○ AUDIENZ IN ISCHL

KAISERWALZER • 1953 • Antel Franz • AUS

KAISHAIN SEIKATSU • 1930 • Ozu Yasujiro • JPN • LIFE OF AN OFFICE WORKER

KAITEI 30,000 MAIRU • 1970 • *Okuda Sadahiro (Anm)* • ANM • JPN • 30,000 MILES UNDER THE SEA

KAITEI DAISENSO • 1966 • Sato Hajime • JPN • TERROR BENEATH THE SEA (USA) ○ WATER CYBORG(S)

KAITEI GUNKAN • 1963 • Honda Inoshiro • JPN • ATORAGON, THE FLYING SUPERSUB ○ ATRAGON THE FLYING SUB ○ ATROGON (USA) ○ ATORAGON ○ UNDERWATER WARSHIP

KAITEI KARA KITA ONNA • 1959 • Kurahara Koreyoshi • JPN • WOMEN FROM THE BOTTOM OF THE SEA

KAITO JIBAKO see **KAITO ZIVACO** • 1967

KAITO, RUBY • 1989 • Wada Makoto • JPN • RUBY, THE THIEF

KAITO SAYAMARO • 1928 • *Tsuburaya Eiji (Ph)* • JPN • SAYAMARO THE GREAT THIEF

KAITO SHIRO ZUKEN • 1935 • Inagaki Hiroshi • JPN • WHITE HOOD

KAITO ZIVACO • 1967 • Tsuboshima Takashi • JPN • MONSIEUR ZIVACO ○ KAITO JIBAKO

KAIZOKU BAHANSEN • 1960 • Sawashima Tadashi • JPN • PIRATES

KAIZOKU RONINGAI • 1958 • Inagaki Hiroshi • JPN

KAIZUKOSEN • 1951 • Inagaki Hiroshi • JPN • PIRATES

KAJA, I'LL KILL YOU see **KAJA, UBIT CU TE!** • 1967

KAJA, UBIT CU TE! • 1967 • Mimica Vatroslav • YGS • KAYA, I'LL KILL YOU ○ KAJA, I'LL KILL YOU ○ KAYA (USA)

KAJAN GAR TILL SJOSS • 1943 • Husberg Rolf • SWD • KAJAN GOES TO SEA

KAJAN GOES TO SEA see **KAJAN GAR TILL SJOSS** • 1943

KAJIN see **KAIJIN** • 1929

KAJIRINAKI HODO • 1934 • Naruse Mikio • JPN • STREET WITHOUT END

KAJITSU NO NAI MORI • 1964 • Tomimoto Sokichi • JPN • FOREST OF NO ESCAPE

KAK BUDET GOLOSOVAT'IZBIRATEL' • 1937 • Yutkevich Sergei • USS • HOW THE ELECTOR WILL VOTE

KAK KHOROSHI, KAK SVEZHI BYLI ROZI • 1913 • Protazanov Yakov • USS • HOW FINE HOW FRESH THE ROSES WERE

KAK KUBYSKIN STAL KINOAKTEROM • 1915 • Tourjansky Victor • USS

KAK MOLODY MY BYLI • 1985 • Belikov Mikhail • USS • WE WERE SO YOUNG.. ○ WHEN WE WERE YOUNG

KAK SOLDAT OT VOYSKA OTSTAL • 1968 • Meliava Tamaz • USS • HOW A SOLDIER DESERTED THE FORCES ○ HOW A SOLDIER REMAINED AT HOME

KAK VELIT SYERDTSYE • 1968 • Kimyagarov Boris • USS • AS THE HEART COMMANDS ○ HEART'S COMMAND, THE

KAK ZAKALYALAS STAL • 1942 • Donskoi Mark • USS • HOW THE STEEL WAS TEMPERED ○ HEROES ARE MADE

KAKA MALA WACHAVA • 1967 • Paranjpe Raja • IND

KAKA YO • Kamba Sebastien • SHT • CNG • KAYAKO

KAKABAKABA KA BA? • 1981 • De Leon Mike • PHL • WILL YOUR HEART BEAT FASTER?

KAKADU LEBERTRAN see **GROSSE UNBEKANNTE 1, DIE** • 1923

KAKADU UND KIEBITZ • 1920 • Schonfelder Erich • FRG

KAKAV DEDA TAKAV UNUK • 1984 • Calic Zoran • YGS • LIKE GRANDFATHER, LIKE GRANDSON

KAKAZSKAYA PLENNITZA • 1967 • Gaidai Leonid • USS • KIDNAPPING -CAUCASIAN STYLE ○ PRISONER OF THE CAUCASUS ○ CAUCASIAN CAPTIVE ○ CAPTIVE GIRL OF THE CAUCASUS OR NEW ADVENTURES OF SHURIK ○ CAUCASIAN PRISONER, THE

KAKHONO ASHENI • 1963 • Raihan Zahir • BNG • IT NEVER CAME

KAKI MONYET • 1985-89 • Osman Aziz M. • MTV • MLY

KAKITA AKANISHI see **AKANISHI KAKITA** • 1936

KAKKA • 1940 • Imai Tadashi • JPN • GENERAL, THE ○ YOUR HIGHNESS

KAKKIENTRUPPEN • 1977 • Girolami Marino • ITL

KAKO • 1961 • Nakamura Noboru • JPN • ESTUARY, THE

KAKO JE PROPAO ROKENROL • 1989 • Pezo Zoran, Slavica Vladimir, Gajic Goran • YGS • RISE AND FALL OF ROCK'N'ROLL, THE

KAKO SAM SISTEMATSK UNISTEN OD IDIOTA • 1984 • Sijan Slobodan • YGS • HOW I WAS SYSTEMATICALLY DESTROYED BY AN IDIOT

KAKO SE RIDIO KICO • 1951 • Vukotic Dusan • ANS • YGS • HOW KICO WAS BORN ○ HOW KIKO WAS BORN

KAKO SU SE VOLELI ROMEO I JULIJA • 1967 • Zivanovic Jovan • YGS • HOW ROMEO AND JULIET FELL IN LOVE ○ ROMEO AND JULIET OF TODAY

KAKO UMRETI • 1972 • Stamenkovic Miomir • YGS • HOW TO DIE

KAKOLI • 1989 • Behzad Ferial • IRN • CRESTED BIRD, THE

KAKS TAVALLISTA LAHTISTA • 1960 • Salminen Ville • FNL

KAKSI • 1972 • Kurkvaara Maunu • FNL • TWO

KAKSI VIHTORIA • 1939 • Tapiovaara Nyrki • FNL • TWO HENPECKED HUSBANDS

KAKU AND TSUNE see **JINSEI GEKIJO -HISHAKAKU TO KIRATSUNE** • 1968

KAKUK MARCI • 1973 • Revesz Gyorgy • HNG • MARTIN CUCKOO

KAKUSHI TORIDE NO SAN-AKUNIN • 1958 • Kurosawa Akira • JPN • THREE BAD MEN IN A HIDDEN FORTRESS ○ HIDDEN FORTRESS, THE

KAKUTE KAMIKAZE WA FUKU • 1944 • Marune Santaro • JPN • THUS BLOWS THE DIVINE WIND ○ THUS THE DIVINE WIND ARRIVES

KAL AAJ AUR KAL • 1971 • Kapoor Prithviraj • IND

KALA • 1958 • Hieng Andrej, Golik Kreso • YGS

KALA BAZAR • 1960 • *Burman S. D. (M)* • IND

KALA PANI • 1958 • *Burman S. D. (M)* • IND

KALA PATHAR • 1978 • Chopra Yash • IND

KALAA, EL • 1988 • Chouikh • ALG • CITADEL, THE (UKN)

KALAAGH • 1977 • Beyzai Bahram • IRN • CROW, THE ○ KALAGH

KALABALIKEN I BENDER • 1983 • Arehn Mats • SWD

KALABOG EN BOSYO • 1959 • Cayado Tony • PHL

KALAGH see **KALAAGH** • 1977

KALAHARI • 1961 • SAF

KALALIUVIT • 1970 • Roos Jorgen • DOC • DNM • ER DU GRONLAENDER

KALAMAZOO • 1975 • Hopkin Rob • SHT • UKN

KALAMAZOO • 1986 • Forcier Andre • CND

KALAMITA • 1978 • Chytilova Vera • CZC • CALAMITY

KALAMITATEN • 1961 • Woesthoff Alwin • FRG

KALAPANA, 1964 • 1965 • Charlot Martin • DOC • USA

KALAU BERPAUT DI-DAHAN RAPOH • 1970 • Rojik Omar • MLY • LOVE IN DANGER

KALB EL LEIL • 1989 • el Tayeb Atif • EGY • HEART OF THE NIGHT

KALBIMDEKI YABANCI • 1968 • Gultekin Sirri • TRK • STRANGER IN MY HEART, THE

KALD MIG MIRIAM • 1968 • Henning-Jensen Astrid • DNM

KALDA RUBY, THE • 1920 • Harbaugh Carl • SHT • USA

KALDE SPOR • 1962 • Skouen Arne • NRW • COLD TRACKS

KALEIDOSCOPE • 1935 • Lye Len • ANS • UKN

KALEIDOSCOPE • 1961 • Eames Charles, Eames Ray • USA

KALEIDOSCOPE • 1966 • Smight Jack • USA, UKN • BANK BREAKER, THE

KALEIDOSCOPE • 1967 • Markson Morley • SHT • CND • MAN AND COLOUR -KALEIDOSCOPE

KALEIDOSCOPE, THE see **CHAALCHITRA** • 1981

KALEIDOSKOP see **KALEIDOSKOP VALESKA GERT -NUR ZUM SPASS NUR ZUM SPIEL** • 1977

KALEIDOSKOP VALESKA GERT -NUR ZUM SPASS NUR ZUM SPIEL • 1977 • Schlondorff Volker • FRG • NUR ZUM SPASS NUR ZUM SPIEL ○ KALEIDOSKOP ○ FOR FUN -FOR PLAY ○ ONLY FOR FUN, ONLY FOR PLAY ○ JUST FOR FUN, JUST FOR PLAY

KALEMITES VISIT GIBRALTAR, THE • 1912 • Olcott Sidney • DOC • USA

KALGOORLIE CUP • 1921 • *Murphy Fred E. (Ph)* • ASL

KALI • 1967 • Gerstein Cassandra M. • SHT • USA

KALI PATRITHA, SYNTROFE • 1987 • Xanthopoulos Lefteris • GRC • HAPPY HOMECOMING, COMRADE

KALI YUG, DEESE DE LA VENGEANCE (FRN) see **KALI YUG, LA DEA DELLA VENDETTA** • 1963

KALI YUG (FRG) see **KALI YUG, LA DEA DELLA VENDETTA** • 1963

KALI YUG, LA DEA DELLA VENDETTA • 1963 • Camerini Mario • ITL, FRN, FRG • KALI YUG, DEESE DE LA VENGEANCE (FRN) ○ KALI YUG (FRG) ○ KALI-YUG, THE GODDESS OF REVENGE ○ GODDESS OF VENGEANCE

KALI-YUG, THE GODDESS OF REVENGE see **KALI YUG, LA DEA DELLA VENDETTA** • 1963

KALIA MARDAN • 1934 • Rajopadhyaya • IND • MURALIWALA

KALIA MARDAN see **KALYA MARDAN** • 1919

KALIBER FUNF KOMMA ZWEI • 1920 • Zeyn Willy • FRG

KALIF STORCH • 1935 • Reiniger Lotte • ANS • FRG

KALIGHAT -PLACE OF PILGRIMAGE see **MAHATIRTHA KALIGHAT** • 1967

KALIMAN • 1970 • *Kali* • MXC

KALIMAN EN EL MUNDO DE HUMANON • 1974 • *Kali* • MXC

KALIMATU AL-HAQ • 1953 • Wahab Fatin Abdel • EGY • PAROLE VRAIE, LA

KALIN ORELAT • 1950 • Borozanov Boris • BUL • KALIN THE EAGLE

KALIN THE EAGLE see **KALIN ORELAT** • 1950

KALINA KRASNAYA • 1974 • Shukshin Vassili • USS • RED SNOW-BALL TREE, THE

KALININ, STAROST OF RUSSIA see **VSEROSSIISKII STAROSTA KALININ** • 1920

KALININ, THE ELDER STATESMAN OF ALL RUSSIA see **VSEROSSIISKII STAROSTA KALININ** • 1920

KALINSKY JUSTICE • 1971 • Bonniere Rene • CND

KALISOCHINA ADHRUSHTAM • 1968 • Viswanath K. • IND • GAINS OF FORTUNE

KALIYA MARDAN see **KALYA MARDAN** • 1919

KALIYALLA KALLYANAM • 1968 • Raj A. B. • IND

KALIYUGAYA • 1982 • Peries Lester James • SLN • CHANGING VILLAGE PART 2 ○ TIME OF KALI, THE

KALKA • 1988 • Rana Shahid • PKS • BLACK HAND

KALKMALERIER • 1954 • Roos Jorgen • DOC • DNM • FRESCOS IN DANISH CHURCHES ○ MURALS

KALKOOT • 1935 • Kale D. K. • IND • KISMAT-KI-BHUL-SUDHA

KALLE KARLSSON FRAN JULARBO • 1952 • Johansson Ivar • SWD • KALLE KARLSSON FROM JULARBO

KALLE KARLSSON FROM JULARBO see **KALLE KARLSSON FRAN JULARBO** • 1952

KALLE PA SPANGEN • 1939 • Lingheim Emil A. • SWD

KALLE STROPP, GRODAN BOLL OCH DERAS VANNER • 1955 • Funck Hasse

KALLE UTTER • 1925 • Swanstrom Karin • SWD

KALLELSEN • 1974 • Nykvist Sven • SWD • VOCATION, THE

KALLUM KANIYAGUM • 1968 • Shankar K. • IND • STONE WILL ALSO TURN INTO FRUIT, THE

KALOS ILTHE TO DHOLLARIO • 1967 • Sakellarios Alekos • GRC • WELCOME DOLLARS

KALOSZE SZCZESCIA • 1958 • Bohdziewicz Antoni • PLN • LUCKY GALOSHES

KALPANA • 1946 • Shankar Uday • IND • IMAGINATION

KALPIKE LIVA see **KALPIKI LIRA, I** • 1955

KALPIKI LIRA, I • 1955 • Tzavellas Georges • GRC • COUNTERFEIT COIN, THE (USA) ○ FALSE POUND STERLING, THE ○ FALSE COIN, THE ○ KALPIKE LIVA

KALSOMMERFUGLEN • 1948 • Knudsen Erik R. • DNM

KALT, KALTER, AM KALTESTEN! • 1938 • Rikli Martin • FRG • FROZEN AIR

KALTE HAM SKARVEN, DE • 1964 • Gustavson Erik F. • NRW

KALTE HERZ, DAS • 1923 • Sauer Fred • FRG • PAKT MIT DEM SATAN, DER ○ COLD HEART, THE

KALTE HERZ, DAS • 1930 • *Mercedes-Film* • FRG • COLD HEART, THE

KALTE HERZ, DAS • 1950 • Verhoeven Paul • GDR • COLD HEART, THE ○ HEART OF STONE

KALTE HERZ, DAS see **WIRTSHAUS IM SPESSART, DAS** • 1923

KALTE MAMSELL, DIE • 1933 • Boese Carl • FRG

KALTE PARADIES, DAS • 1986 • Safarik Bernard • SWT

KALTES FIEBER • 1984 • Rusnack Joseph • FRG • COLD FEVER

KALTGESTELLT • 1980 • Sinkel Bernard • FRG • PUT ON ICE

KALU DIYA DHARA • 1974 • Abeysekera Tissa • SLN • FALL OF BLACK WATER

KALVARIA • 1960 • Meszaros G. • HNG • CALVARY

KALWARIA see **PAMIATKA Z KALWARII** • 1958

KALYA MARDAN • 1919 • Phalke Dada • IND • CHILDHOOD OF KRISHNA, THE ○ KALIYA MARDAN ○ KALIA MARDAN ○ SLAYING OF THE SERPENT, THE

KALYUG • 1980 • Benegal Shyam • IND • MACHINE AGE, THE

KAM CERT NEMUZE • 1959 • Podskalsky Zdenek • CZC • WHERE THE DEVIL CANNOT GO (USA) ○ OUT OF REACH OF THE DEVIL

KAM NECHODI INSPEKTOR • 1964 • Kudelka Ladislav • CZC • WHERE THE INSPECTOR DOES NOT GO

KAM S NIM? • 1922 • Wasserman Vaclav • CZC • WHERE TO PUT IT?

KAMA SUTRA '71 • 1970 • *Variety Films* • USA

KAMA SUTRA RIDES AGAIN • 1972 • Godfrey Bob • ANS • UKN

KAMA SUTRA (USA) see **KAMASUTRA –VOLLENDUNG DER LIEBE** • 1969

KAMAELEONEN see **MAANEPRINSESSEN** • 1916

KAMAHL • 1979 • Blagg Linda • DOC • ASL

KAMAL • 1949 • *Burman S. D. (M)* • IND

KAMALI ZEYBEGIN INTIKAMI • 1967 • Akinci Nuri • TRK • REVENGE OF KAMALI ZEYBEK, THE

KAMALI ZEYBEK • 1964 • Akinci Nuri • TRK • HERO WITH A KNIFE

KAMALI ZEYBEK CAKIRCALIYA KARSI • 1967 • Akinci Nuri • TRK • KAMALI ZEYBEK VS. CAKIRCALI

KAMALI ZEYBEK VS. CAKIRCALI see **KAMALI ZEYBEK CAKIRCALIYA KARSI** • 1967

KAMARAD DO DESTE • 1988 • Soukup Jaroslav • CZC • FRIEND IN NEED, A

KAMARATKY • 1978 • Uher Stefan • CZC • FRIENDS, THE

KAMASUTRA –PERFECTION OF LOVE see **KAMASUTRA –VOLLENDUNG DER LIEBE** • 1969

KAMASUTRA (UKN) see **KAMASUTRA –VOLLENDUNG DER LIEBE** • 1969

KAMASUTRA –VOLLENDUNG DER LIEBE • 1969 • Jaeger Kobi • DOC • FRG • KAMA SUTRA (USA) ○ KAMASUTRA (UKN) ○ KAMASUTRA –PERFECTION OF LOVE

KAMASZVAROS • 1962 • Meszaros Marta • DCS • HNG • TOWN IN THE AWKWARD AGE, A

KAMATA KOSHINKYOKU • 1983 • Fukasaku Kinji • JPN • KAMATA MOVIE MARCH

KAMATA MOVIE MARCH see **KAMATA KOSHINKYOKU** • 1983

KAMATAYAN KO, ANG IBIGIN KA • 1968 • Cayado Tony • PHL • IT'S DEATH FOR ME TO LOVE YOU

KAMBOURIS, O • 1967 • Georgiou George • GRC • HUNCHBACK, THE

KAMBUR • 1973 • Yilmaz Atif • TRK • HUMP-BACKED WOMAN, THE

KAMELDAMEN • 1969 • Vemmer Mogens • DNM

KAMELEONTERNA • 1970 • Axelman Torbjorn • SWD • CHAMELEONS, THE

KAMELIEN DAME, DIE see **DAME AUX CAMELIAS, LA** • 1981

KAMEN A ZIVOT • 1966 • Seko Garik • ANS • CZC • STONE AND LIFE

KAMENNI TSVETOK • 1946 • Ptushko Alexander • USS • STONE FLOWER, THE

KAMENNY GOST • 1967 • Gorikker Vladimir • USS • STONE GUEST, THE

KAMENNY KRYEST • 1968 • Osyka Leonid • USS • STONE CROSS, THE

KAMENOM ZAROBLJENI • 1959 • Boskovic Bosko • YGS

KAMER MET UITZICHT • 1966 • Gruyaert Jan • BLG

KAMERAD HEDWIG • 1945 • Lamprecht Gerhard • FRG

KAMERADEN • 1919 • Guter Johannes • FRG

KAMERADEN • 1941 • Schweikart Hans • FRG

KAMERADEN see **ALLES UM EINE FRAU** • 1935

KAMERADEN AUF SEE • 1938 • Paul Heinz • FRG • COMRADES AT SEA (USA)

KAMERADSCHAFT • 1931 • Pabst G. W. • FRG • COMRADESHIP

KAMERAJAGD AUF SEEHUNDE • 1937 • Schulz Ulrich K. T. • FRG • SEALS

KAMERATER • 1982 • Andersen Knut • NRW • FRIENDS ○ FOR TORS SKYLD

KAMET CONQUERED: AN EPIC ADVENTURE ON THE ROOF OF THE WORLD • 1932 • Smythe F. S. • UKN

KAMI • 1982 • Yeoh Patrick • MLY

KAMI E NO MICHI • 1928 • Gosho Heinosuke • JPN • ROAD TO GOD ○ WAY TO THE GOD, THE

KAMI NINGYO HARU NO SASAYAKI • 1926 • Mizoguchi Kenji • JPN • PAPER DOLL'S WHISPER OF SPRING, A (USA) ○ KAMININGYO HARU NO SASAYAKI

KAMI-SHIBAI • 1956 • Boisrobert Gilles • FRN

KAMIENNE NIEBO • 1959 • Petelska Ewa, Petelski Czeslaw • PLN • SKY IS OUR ROUTE, THE ○ SKY IS OUR ROOF, THE ○ SKY OF STONE, A

KAMIGAMI NO FUKAKI YOKUBO • 1968 • Imamura Shohei • JPN • KURAGEJIMA –LEGENDS FROM A SOUTHERN ISLAND ○ DEEP DESIRE OF GODS ○ PROFOUND DESIRE OF THE GODS, THE ○ KURAGEJIMA: TALES FROM A SOUTHERN ISLAND ○ KURAGEJIMA

KAMIKAZE • 1962 • Wolff Perry • DOC • USA, FRN

KAMIKAZE • 1982 • Gremm Wolfgang • FRG • KAMIKAZE '89

KAMIKAZE • 1986 • Grousset Didier • FRN

KAMIKAZE '89 see **KAMIKAZE** • 1982

KAMIKAZE GROUP see **KAMIKAZE REN** • 1933

KAMIKAZE REN • 1933 • Mizoguchi Kenji • JPN • GROUP KAMIKAZE ○ MEIJI SAMURAI ○ SHIMPU-REN ○ SHIMPU GROUP, THE ○ KAMIKAZE GROUP ○ JIMPUREN

KAMIKAZE –SUICIDE SOLDIER, THE see **MINAMI-TAIHEIYO NAMI TAKASHI** • 1962

KAMIKAZEN –LAST NIGHT IN MILAN see **KAMIKAZEN –ULTIMA NOTTE A MILANO** • 1988

KAMIKAZEN –ULTIMA NOTTE A MILANO • 1988 • Salvatores Gabriele • ITL • KAMIKAZEN –LAST NIGHT IN MILAN

KAMILLA • 1981 • Lokkeberg Vibeke • NRW

KAMILLA OG TYVEN • 1988 • Salomonsen Grete • NRW • STORY OF KAMILLA, THE ○ CAMILLA AND THE THIEF

KAMING TAGA BUNDOK • 1968 • Carlos Luciano B. • PHL • WE, THE MOUNTAIN PEOPLE

KAMING TAGA ILOG • 1968 • Carlos Luciano B. • PHL • WE, THE RIVER PEOPLE

KAMININGYO HARU NO SASAYAKI see **KAMI NINGYO HARU NO SASAYAKI** • 1926

KAMIONAT • 1980 • Hristov Hristo • BUL • LORRY, THE

KAMISAKA SHIRO NO HANZAI • 1957 • *Hidari Sachiko* • JPN • CRIME OF SHIRO KAMISAKA, THE

KAMISAMA NO KOIBITO • 1968 • Nomura Yoshitaro • JPN • ANGEL'S LOVER

KAMISAMA NO KURETA AKAMBO • 1979 • Maeda Yoichi • JPN • BABY GIVEN BY GOD, A

KAMISORI • 1923 • Shimazu Yasujiro • JPN • RAZOR, THE

KAMITSUKARETA KAOYAKU • 1958 • Nakamura Noboru • JPN • COUNTRY BOSS

KAMLA • 1946 • *Desai Lila* • IND

KAMLATA • 1935 • Kabuli A. R. • IND

KAMMARJUNKAREN • 1914 • Stiller Mauritz • SWD • CHAMBERLAIN, THE ○ GENTLEMAN OF THE ROOM

KAMMENA TETKA • 1960 • Karpas Jan • ANS • CZC • STONE AUNTIE, THE

KAMMERMUSIK • 1925 • Froelich Carl • FRG

KAMMERSANGER, DER • 1920 • Zeyn Willy • FRG

KAMMERSPIL • 1966 • Gammeltoft Ole • DNM

KAMO • 1965 • Sekigawa Hideo • JPN • DUPE, THE

KAMO TO NEGI • 1968 • Taniguchi Senkichi • JPN • BAMBOOZLERS, THE

KAMONG SENTOSA • 1952 • Eason B. Reeves • USA

KAMO'S LAST FEAT • 1974 • Kevorkov S., Melik-Avekyan G. • USS

KAMOURASKA • 1973 • Jutra Claude • CND, FRN

KAMPEN MOD KRAEFTEN • 1947 • Dreyer Carl T. • SHT • DNM • STRUGGLE AGAINST CANCER, THE

KAMPEN MOD URETTEN • 1949 • Palsbo Ole • DNM

KAMPEN OM BARNET • 1914 • Davidsen Hjalmar • DNM

KAMPEN OM EN REMBRANDT • 1915 • Hansen Edmond • SWD • FIGHT FOR THE REMBRANDT PAINTING, THE

KAMPEN OM HANS HJARTA • 1916 • Stiller Mauritz • SWD • BATTLE FOR HIS HEART, THE ○ FIGHT FOR HIS HEART, THE ○ STRUGGLE FOR HIS HEART, THE

KAMPEN OM MARDOLA • 1972 • Einarson Oddvar • DOC • NRW • MARDOLA CONTEST, THE

KAMPEN OM TUNGTVANNET see **BATAILLE DE L'EAU LOURDE, LA** • 1947

KAMPF • 1932 • Schonfelder Erich • FRG

KAMPF, DER see **KAMPFER** • 1935

KAMPF DER GESCHLECHTER • 1926 • Brandt Heinrich • FRG

KAMPF DER GESCHLECHTER, DER • 1919 • Delmont Joseph • FRG

KAMPF DER TERTIA • 1953 • Ode Erik • FRG

KAMPF DER TERTIA, DER • 1928 • Mack Max • FRG • JUGEND VON MORGEN

KAMPF DES DONALD WESTHOF, DER • 1927 • Wendhausen Fritz • FRG • TRIAL OF DONALD WESTHOF, THE

KAMPF DES UNABHANGIGEN GEGEN DES KOMMERZIELLEN FILM see **STURM UBER LA SARRAZ** • 1929

KAMPF GEGEN BERLIN, DER • 1925 • Reichmann Max • FRG

KAMPF IN DEN LUTEN, DER • 1919 • Arnheim Valy • FRG

KAMPF MIT DEM DRACHEN, DER • 1930 • Siodmak Robert • SHT • FRG

KAMPF MIT DEM DRACHEN, DER • 1935 • Seitz Franz • FRG • FIGHT WITH THE DRAGON (USA)

KAMPF UM BLOND • 1932 • Speyer Jaap • FRG • MADCHEN, DIE SPURLOS VERSCHWINDEN

KAMPF UM DAS FLUSSIGE GOLD: OL see **STADT ANATOL** • 1936

KAMPF UM DAS MILLIONENTESTAMENT, DER see **HAPURA, DIE TOTE STADT 1** • 1921

KAMPF UM DEN BAR, DER • 1933 • Sauer Fred • FRG

KAMPF UM DEN JUWELENSCHMUCK • 1923 • *West-Deutsche Film-Ges* • FRG

KAMPF UM DEN MANN, DER • 1927 • Werckmeister Hans • FRG

KAMPF UM DIE EHE 1, DER • 1919 • Zeyn Willy • FRG • WENN IN DER EHE DIE LEIBE STIRBT

KAMPF UM DIE EHE 2, DER • 1919 • Zeyn Willy • FRG • FEINDLICHE GATTEN

KAMPF UM DIE FRAU • 1932 • von Maydell Fr. • FRG, FNL • TUNDRA, DIE

KAMPF UM DIE SCHOLLE • 1925 • Waschneck Erich • FRG

KAMPF UM EIN KIND • 1975 • Engstrom Ingemo • FRG

KAMPF UM KARTHAGO, DER see **SALAMMBO** • 1925

KAMPF UM ROM, TEIL 1: KOMM NUR, MEIN LIEBSTES VOGELEIN • 1969 • Siodmak Robert • FRG, ITL, RMN • STRUGGLE FOR ROME, THE ○ BATTLE FOR ROME

KAMPF UM ROM, TEIL 2: DER VERRAT • 1969 • Siodmak Robert • FRG, ITL, RMN

KAMPF UMS GLUCK • 1988 • Giger Bernhard • SWT • FIGHT FOR HAPPINESS

KAMPF UMS ICH, DER • 1922 • Brandt Heinrich • FRG

KAMPF UMS LEBEN • 1929 • *Morel Sybill* • FRG

KAMPF UMS MATTERHORN, DER • 1928 • Bonnard Mario, Malasomma Nunzio • FRG • STRUGGLE FOR THE MATTERHORN

KAMPF UMS MATTERHORN, DER • 1934 • Bonnard Mario, Malasomma Nunzio • FRG • STRUGGLE FOR THE MATTERHORN

KAMPF UNTER DEM MEERESSPIEGEL, DER • 1919 • Batz Lorenz • FRG

KAMPFENDE GEWALTEN ODER WELT OHNE KRIEG • 1920 • Bernhardt Fritz • FRG • WELT OHNE KRIEG (AUS DEN GEHEIMDOKUMENTEN DES PROF. DR. BARNEY)

KAMPFENDE HERZEN • 1921 • Lang Fritz • FRG • VIER UM DIE FRAU ○ FOUR AROUND A WOMAN

KAMPFENDE WELTEN see **KINDER DER FINSTERNIS 2** • 1921

KAMPFER • 1935 • von Wangenheim Gustav • USS • KAMPF, DER

KAMPFGESCHWADER LUTZOW • 1941 • Bertram Hans • FRG

KAMPON NI SATANAS • 1970 • Isidro Mar B. • PHL • DISCIPLE OF SATAN

KAMPUCHEA EXPRESS see **ANGKOR** • 1982

KAMPUCHEA, MORT ET RESURRECTION • 1980 • Heynowski Walter, Scheumann Gerhard • GDR

KAMPUS BIRU • 1976 • Prijono Ami • INN

KAMRATER I VAPENROCKEN • 1938 • Bauman Schamyl • SWD • COMRADES IN UNIFORM

KAMRATHUSTRU see **LIVET GAR VIDARE** • 1941

KAMSISH • 1965 • Issa Sayyed • SHT • EGY

KAN • 1985 • Goren Serif • TRK • BLOOD, THE

KAN DAVASI • 1967 • Gorec Ertem • TRK • VENDETTA

KAN DOKTORN KOMMA? • 1942 • Husberg Rolf • SWD • CAN YOU COME DOCTOR?

KAN GOVDEYI GOTURDU • 1965 • Atadeniz Yilmaz • TRK

K'AN-HAI-TE JIH-TZU • 1983 • Wang T'Ung • TWN • FLOWER IN THE RAINY NIGHT, A

KAN KAERLIGHED KURERES? • 1924 • Lauritzen Lau • DNM

KAN NG HARAGAN, ANG • 1967 • Gallardo Cesar Chat • PHL • FAMILY OF THE RECKLESS

KAN SU GIBI AKACAK • 1969 • Atadeniz Yilmaz • TRK

KANAL • 1957 • Wajda Andrzej • PLN • THEY LOVED LIFE ○ SEWER

KANAL • 1979 • Kiral Erden • TRK • CANAL, THE

KANAN KIRI O.K. • 1989 • INN

KANARIFUGLEN • 1973 • Bang-Hansen Pal • NRW • CANARY BIRD, THE

KANASHIKI HAKUCHI • 1924 • Mizoguchi Kenji • JPN • SONG OF THE SAD IDIOT (USA) ○ SAD IDIOT, THE

KANASHIMI NO BELLADONNA • 1973 • Yamamoto Eiichi • ANM • JPN • BELLADONNA

KANASHIMI WA ONNA DAKENI • 1958 • Shindo Kaneto • JPN • ONLY WOMEN HAVE TROUBLE ○ SORROW IS ONLY FOR WOMEN

KANASHITI KOTABA • 1952 • Mizuko Harumi • JPN • SAD SPEECH

KANAT AYYAM • 1970 • Halim Hilmy • EGY • THERE WERE DAYS

KANAVAN • 1968 • Neelakantan P. • IND • HUSBAND

KANAWA • 1972 • Shindo Kaneto • JPN • IRON RING

KANAYAN YARA • 1968 • Arikan Kayahan • TRK • BLEEDING WOUND, THE

KANCHANA SITA • 1977 • Aravindan G. • IND • GOLDEN SITA

KANCHENJUNGHA • 1962 • Ray Satyajit • IND • KANGCHENJUNGA

KANCHER DEYAL • 1964 • Raihan Zahir • BNG • GLASS WALL, THE

KANCHHI • 1986 • *Shrestha Shiva* • NPL • YOUNGEST ONE

KANCHO IMADA SHISEZU • 1942 • Yoshimura Kozaburo • JPN • SPY ISN'T DEAD YET, THE ○ SPY HAS NOT YET DIED, THE ○ YET SPIES HAVEN'T DIED

KANDHAN KARUNAI • 1967 • Nagarajan A. P. • IND • KARTICK'S BLESSING

KANDIDAAT, DIE • 1968 • Rautenbach Jans • SAF • CANDIDATE, THE

KANDIDAT, DER • 1980 • Schlondorff Volker, Kluge Alexander • DOC • FRG • CANDIDATE, THE

KANDIL OM HASHEM • 1968 • Atia Kamal • EGY • LAMP OF HASHEM, THE

KANDOO • 1974 • Goleh Freydoon • IRN • BEEHIVE

KANDY PERAHERA • 1971 • Peries Lester James • SHT • SLN • PROCESSION OF KANDY, THE

KANDYLAND • 1987 • Schnitzer Robert Allen • USA

KANE • 1926 • Mizoguchi Kenji • JPN • MONEY (USA) ○ GOLD ○ KIN

KANE see **BROTHER JOHN** • 1972

KANE AND ABEL • 1985 • Kulik Buzz • TVM • USA

KANEC STARYCH CASU • 1989 • Menzel Jiri • CZC • END OF OLD TIMES, THE (UKN)

KANGAROO • 1915-20 • *Bray John R. (P)* • ANS • USA

KANGAROO • 1952 • Milestone Lewis • ASL, USA

KANGAROO • 1986 • Burstall Tim • ASL

KANGAROO, THE • 1914 • *World* • USA

KANGAROO, THE see **KENGURU, A** • 1975

KANGAROO COURTING • 1954 • Burness Pete • ANS • USA

KANGAROO KID, THE • 1938 • Harrison Ben • ANS • USA

KANGAROO KID, THE • 1950 • Selander Lesley • USA

KANGAROO STEAK • 1930 • *Terry Paul/ Moser Frank (P)* • ANS • USA

KANGCHENJUNGA see **KANCHENJUNGHA** • 1962

KANGELOPORTA, I • 1979 • Makris Dimitris • GRC • DOOR WITH BARS, THE

KANGO FIRE BRIGADE, THE • 1914 • Cooper Toby • UKN

KANGOKU ENO SHOTAI • 1967 • Inoue Akira • JPN • INVITATION TO JAIL, AN

KANHAIYA • 1959 • *Kapoor Raj* • IND

KANHASSHU KENKAJIN • 1958 • Mori Masaki • JPN

KANIKOSEN • 1953 • Yamamura So • JPN • CRAB-CANNING SHIP ○ CRAB-CANNING BOAT

KANIMIN SON DAMLASINA KADAR • 1970 • Figenli Yavuz • TRK

KANINE ARISTOCRATS • 1945 • *Mead Thomas (P)* • SHT • USA

KANINMANNEN • 1990 • Larsson Stig • SWD • RABBIT MAN, THE

KANJUT SAR • 1961 • Guerrasio Guido • DOC • ITL • MONTAGNA CHE HA IN VETTA UN LAGO, LA

KANKA DO POHADKY • 1981 • Koval Ota • CZC • BLOT IN THE FAIRY-TALE, A

KANKAMBA • 1980 • Alassane Moustapha • NGR

KANKAN-MUSHI WA UTAU • 1931 • Tasaka Tomotaka • JPN

KANKANDA DEIVAM • 1967 • Gopalakrishnan K. S. • IND • LIVING DEITY

KANKO NO MACHI • 1944 • Kinoshita Keisuke • JPN • JUBILATION STREET ○ CHEERING TOWN

KANKON SOSAI • 1959 • Ichikawa Kon • JPN • EARTHLY RITUALS

KANKU • 1970 • Rathod Kantilal • IND

KANLI BUGDAY • 1965 • Ceylan Ferit • TRK

KANLI HAYAT • 1967 • Gorec Ertem • TRK • BLOODY LIFE
KANLI OBA • 1968 • Peyda Huseyin • TRK • BLOODY CAMP, THE
KANLI TAKIP • 1967 • Figenli Yavuz • TRK • BLOODY CHASE, THE
KANNAKAMBARA • 1976 • Kshirsagar Shridar • IND
KANNAN EN KATHALAN • 1968 • Neelakantan P. • IND • KANNAN MY LOVER
KANNAN MY LOVER see **KANNAN EN KATHALAN** • 1968
KANNESHWARA RAMA • 1976 • Sathyu M. S. • IND • LEGENDARY OUTLAW, THE
KANNIBAL CAPERS • 1935 • *Mintz Charles (P)* • ANS • USA
KANOJO • 1926 • Gosho Heinosuke • JPN • GIRLFRIEND ○ SHE
KANOJO NO TOKUDANE • 1952 • *Kyo Machiko* • JPN • HER SCOOP
KANOJO NO UNMEI • 1924 • Kinugasa Teinosuke • JPN • SHE HAS LIVED HER DESTINY ○ KANOJO TO UNMEI
KANOJO TO KARE • 1963 • Hani Susumu • JPN • SHE AND HE ○ HE AND SHE
KANOJO TO UNMEI see **KANOJO NO UNMEI** • 1924
KANONADA • 1964 • Vabalas Raimondas, Zhebrunas Arunas • USS • CANNONADE
KANONEN-SERENADE • 1958 • Staudte Wolfgang • FRG, ITL • PEZZO, CAPOPEZZO E CAPITANO (ITL) ○ ALWAYS VICTORIOUS (USA) ○ IL CAPITANO (UKN) ○ MUZZLE, THE
KANONI KE T' AIDHONI, TO • 1968 • Kambanelis Iakovos, Kambanelis Giorgos • GRC • GUNS AND THE NIGHTINGALE
KANPAI MIAI KEKKON • 1958 • Mizuko Harumi • JPN • TOAST TO MARRIAGE, A
KANRAKU NO ONNA • 1924 • Mizoguchi Kenji • JPN • WOMAN OF PLEASURE (USA)
KANSAN, THE • 1943 • Archainbaud George • USA • WAGON WHEELS (UKN)
KANSAS • 1988 • Stevens David • USA
KANSAS CITY BOMBER • 1972 • Freedman Jerrold • USA
KANSAS CITY CONFIDENTIAL • 1953 • Karlson Phil • USA • SECRET FOUR, THE (UKN)
KANSAS CITY KITTY • 1944 • Lord Del • USA
KANSAS CITY MASSACRE, THE • 1975 • Curtis Dan • TVM • USA
KANSAS CITY PRIME, THE see **PRIME CUT** • 1972
KANSAS CITY PRINCESS • 1934 • Keighley William • USA
KANSAS CYCLONE • 1941 • Sherman George • USA
KANSAS PACIFIC • 1953 • Nazarro Ray • USA
KANSAS RAIDERS • 1950 • Enright Ray • USA
KANSAS SALOON SMASHERS • 1901 • Porter Edwin S. • USA
KANSAS TERRITORY • 1952 • Collins Lewis D. • USA
KANSAS TERRORS • 1939 • Sherman George • USA
KANSIN see **VENTO D'AFRICA** • 1949
KANSIPAIKKA • 1968 • Tolonen Asko • SHT • FNL • DECK PASSAGE
KANSKE EN DIKTARE • 1933 • Marmstedt Lorens • SWD • POET MAYBE, A
KANSKE EN GENTLEMAN • 1935 • Arvedson Ragnar, Ibsen Tancred • SWD • GENTLEMAN MAYBE, A
KANSKE EN GENTLEMAN • 1951 • Frisk Ragnar • SWD
KANTA TO KUROSIBI SENSEI • 1957 • Harada Hasuo • JPN
KANTARO TSUKIYO UTA • 1952 • *Otowa Nobuko* • JPN • SONG OF MATCHLESS MOONLIGHT, THE
KANTI NIGAR • 1968 • Erakalin Ulku • TRK • BLOODY NIGAR
KANTO • 1923 • Mizoguchi Kenji • DOC • JPN
KANTO MO HIROUGOZANSU • 1967 • Noguchi Haruyasu • JPN • STORM OF KANTO, A
KANTO MUSHOGAERI • 1967 • Takeda Kazunari • JPN • TO KILL A KILLER
KANTO ONNA TOBAKUSHI • 1968 • Inoue Yoshio • JPN • WOMAN CHAMPION, THE
KANTO ONNA YAKUZA • 1968 • Inoue Akira • JPN • DUEL AT THE QUARRY
KANTOR IDEAL • 1932 • Fric Martin • CZC, FRG • BETRAGEN UNGENUGEND (FRG) ○ CONDUCT UNSATISFACTORY ○ MASTER IDEAL
KANTOROWITZ • 1923 • Ruttmann Walter • FRG
KANTSUBAKI • 1921 • Inoue Masao • JPN • WINTER CAMELLIA
KANTUS, THE FINAL VOYAGE • 1989 • Norden Francisco • FRN, CLM
KANUN NAMINA • 1968 • Gulyuz Aram • TRK • IN THE NAME OF THE LAW
KANUNSUZ TOPRAK • 1967 • Olgac Bilge • TRK • LAWLESS LAND
KANZENNARU KEKKON • 1967 • Yamamoto Shinya • JPN • PERFECT MARRIAGE
KAO • 1960 • Shima Koji • JPN • FACE, THE
KAO • 1965 • Kuri Yoji • ANS • JPN • FACE, THE
KAO NO NAI ONNA • 1959 • Murayama Shinji • JPN • DISMEMBERED CORPSE
KAOS see **XAOS** • 1984
KAOYAKU • 1957 • Nakamura Noboru • JPN • BOSS, THE
KAPA • 1971 • Grgic Zlatko • ANS • YGS • CAP, THE
KAPAG PUSO NA ANG SALOP PART II • 1989 • PHL
KAPAL KINDALA • 1933 • *Sircar B. N. (P)* • IND
KAPALKUNDALA • 1939 • *Sircar B. N. (P)* • IND
KAPELLMEISTERS PFLEGEKIND • 1915 • Bolten-Baeckers Heinrich • FRG
KAPELUSZ • 1962 • Majewski Janusz • PLN • HAT, THE
KAPELUSZ PANA ANATOLA • 1958 • Rybkowski Jan • PLN • MR. ANATOL'S HAT
KAPETAN ARBANAS MARKO • 1968 • Bourek Zlatko • ANS • YGS • CAPTAIN ARBANAS MARKO
KAPETAN FANTIS BASTOUNIS, O • 1968 • Sakellarios Alekos • GRC • KNAVE OF SPADES ○ CAPTAIN FANTIS
KAPETAN LESI • 1960 • Mitrovic Zika • YGS • CAPTAIN LESI
KAPETAN MIKULA MALI • 1974 • Gluscevic Obrad • YGS
KAPG PUSO'Y SINUGATAN • 1967 • Crisostomo Fely • PHL • WHEN THE HEART IS WOUNDED
KAPHETZOU • 1961 • Sakellarios Alekos • GRC • FORTUNE TELLER, THE (USA) ○ COFFEE FORTUNE TELLER, THE
KAPI, VODE, RATNICI • 1962 • Pavlovic Zivojin, Rakonjac Kokan, Babac Marko • YGS • RAINDROPS, WATERS, WARRIORS
KAPISKIE LIUDI • 1944 • Alexandrov Grigori • USS • THOSE FROM THE CASPIAN ○ MEN OF THE CASPIAN ○ KASPICHY
KAPIT SA PATALIM • 1984 • Brocka Lino • PHL • HANGING ON A KNIFE
KAPITAL UND LIEBE • 1915 • Karfiol William • FRG
KAPITAN, DER • 1971 • Hoffmann Kurt • FRG
KAPITAN DABAC • 1959 • Bielik Palo • CZC • CAPTAIN DABAC
KAPITAN HANSENS ABENTEUER • 1918 • Piel Harry • FRG
KAPITAN KORDA • 1979 • Pinkava Josef • CZC • CAPTAIN KORDA
KAPITANE BLEIBEN AN BORD • 1959 • Hellberg Martin • GDR • CAPTAINS DO NOT LEAVE THE SHIP
KAPITANSKAIA DOTSHKA • 1958 • Kaplunovsky Vladimir • USS • CAPTAIN'S DAUGHTER, THE
KAPLAN VON SAN LORENZO, DER • 1953 • Ucicky Gustav • FRG • MEA CULPA
KAPO • 1960 • Pontecorvo Gillo • FRN, ITL, YGS
KAPOTE KLENE KE I DONATI • 1967 • Tegopoulos Apostolos • GRC • SOMETIMES EVEN THE BRAVE CRY
KAPPA NO PATARO • 1957 • *Toei Doga* • ANS • JPN • ADVENTURES OF A WATER IMP
KAPPA NO YOMEI-TORI • 1958 • *National Farm Cinema* • ANS • JPN • KAPPA TAKES A BRIDE
KAPPA TAKES A BRIDE see **KAPPA NO YOMEI-TORI** • 1958
KAPTAJN KLYDE OG HANS VENNER VENDER TILBAGE • 1981 • Klein Jesper • DNM • RETURN OF CAPTAIN KLYDE, THE
KAPTEIN CAPRIVI • 1972 • SAF
KAPTEIN MARIA • 1978 • Richter Dagmar • NRW • CAPTAIN MARIA
KAPT'N BAY-BAY • 1953 • Kautner Helmut • FRG, AUS
KAPT'N RAUHBEIN AUS ST. PAULI see **KAT'N RAUHBEIN AUS ST. PAULI** • 1971
KAPURUSH O MAHAPURUSH • 1965 • Ray Satyajit • IND • COWARD AND THE HOLY MAN, THE (UKN) ○ COWARD AND THE GREAT MAN, THE ○ COWARD AND THE SAINT, THE (USA)
KAPUT LAGER LA FINE DELLA SS • 1978 • Solvay Paolo • ITL
KAPUTTE KINO, DAS • 1971 • Schoenherr H. H. K. • SWT
KAPUZINERGRUFT, DIE • 1971 • Schaaf Johannes • FRG
KAPWA WALANG PANGINOON • 1968 • Castillo Celso Ad. • PHL • BOTH WITH NO MASTERS
KAPY SELAN ALLA • 1967 • Niskanen Mikko • FNL • SKIN SKIN (UKN) ○ UNDER YOUR SKIN
KAR A KENZINERT • 1964 • Ban Frigyes • HNG • CAR CRAZY
KAR PAPAY • 1952 • Agradoot • IND
KARA see **RED MORNING** • 1935
KARA ATMACA • 1967 • Kan Kemal • TRK • BLACK HAWK, THE
KARA ATMACANIN INTIKAMI • 1968 • Hancer Nisan • TRK • REVENGE OF THE BLACK HAWK, THE
KARA BAHTIM • 1968 • Ucanoglu Yucel • TRK • MY DARK CHANCE
KARA BATTALIN ACISI • 1968 • Heper Alp Zeki • TRK • PAIN OF KARA BATTAL, THE
KARA CARSAFLI GELIN • 1976 • Duru Sureyya • TRK • DARK-VEILED BRIDE, THE
KARA DAVUT • 1967 • Basaran Tunc • TRK • BLACK DAVUT
KARA DUVAKLI GELIN • 1967 • Dinler Mehmet • TRK • BLACK VEILED BRIDE, THE
KARA FAMILJEN, DEN • 1962 • Balling Erik • SWD, DNM • KAERE FAMILIE, DEN ○ DEAR FAMILY
KARA GOZLUM EFKARLANMA • 1968 • Gultekin Sirri • TRK • DON'T GET BLUE, MY DARK-EYED ONE
KARA GUNES • 1968 • Kan Kemal • TRK • DARK SUN
KARA KAFA • 1980 • Yurtsever Korhan • TRK • BLACK HEAD
KARA KARTAL • 1967 • Hancer Nisan • TRK • BLACK EAGLE, THE
KARA LEKEN, DEN • 1959 • Fant Kenne • SWD • LOVE GAME, THE ○ BELOVED GAME, THE
KARA OFKE • 1968 • Ucanoglu Yucel • TRK • BITTER RAGE
KARA PENCE • 1968 • Aslan Mehmet • TRK • DARK CLAW
KARA PLNA BOLESTI • 1985 • Parnicky Stanislav • CZC • BALLAD OF WRETCHES, A
KARA SAHIN • 1964 • Akinci Nuri • TRK
KARA SEVDA • 1968 • Havaeri Seyfi • TRK • DARK LOVE
KARA SEVDALI BULUT • 1987 • Ozer Muammer • TRK • CLOUD IN LOVE, THE
KARA SLAKTEN • 1933 • Molander Gustaf • SWD • DEAR RELATIVES
KARA YAZIM • 1968 • Havaeri Seyfi • TRK • MY DARK FATE
KARABOTAN • 1926 • Nomura H. • JPN • COLLAR BUTTON
KARACAOGLANIN KARA SEVDASI • 1959 • Yilmaz Atif • TRK • KARACAOGLAN'S MAD LOVE
KARACAOGLAN'S MAD LOVE see **KARACAOGLANIN KARA SEVDASI** • 1959
KARACHI • 1988 • Einarson Oddvar • NRW
KARAGEORGE • 1910 • Barry Jules • FRN, YGS
KARAGHIOZIS • 1975 • Voudouri Lena • GRC
KARAKKAZE YARO • 1960 • Masumura Yasuzo • JPN • AFRAID TO DIE
KARAKORAM • 1936 • Ichac Marcel • DOC • FRN
KARAKORUM • 1956 • Horiba Nobuyo • JPN
KARAKURI MUSUME • 1927 • Gosho Heinosuke • JPN • TRICKY GIRL ○ FAKE GIRL
KARAMANEH • 1924 • Paul Fred • UKN
KARAMAT ZAWJATI see **KARAMET ZAWGATY** • 1967
KARAMAZOF see **MORDER DIMITRI KARAMASOFF, DER** • 1931
KARAMBOL • 1964 • Mariassy Felix • HNG • GOLIATH
KARAMBOL • 1966 • Sharlandgiev Ljobomir • BUL • CARAMBOL
KARAMBOLAGE • 1983 • Kino Kitty • AUS • CANNON
KARAMET ZAWGATY • 1967 • Wahab Fatin Abdel • EGY • MY WIFE'S HONOUR ○ KARAMAT ZAWJATI
KARAMI-AI • 1962 • Kobayashi Masaki • JPN • INHERITANCE, THE ○ ENTANGLEMENT, THE ○ HERITAGE
KARAMOJA • 1954 • Treutle William B., Treutle William B. Mrs. • DOC • USA
KARAMOJA • 1962 • Root Alan, Root Joan • DCS • UKN • TEAR FOR KARAMOJA, A
KARANLIK YOLLAR • 1968 • Ceylan Ferit • TRK • DARK STREETS
KARAOGLAN VS. THE GREEN DRAGON see **KARAOGLAN YESIL EJDER** • 1967
KARAOGLAN YESIL EJDER • 1967 • Yalaz Suat • TRK • KARAOGLAN VS. THE GREEN DRAGON
KARATACHI NIKKI • 1959 • Gosho Heinosuke • JPN • JOURNAL OF THE ORANGE FLOWER ○ TRIFOLIATE ORANGE DIARY, THE
KARATE see **KARATE, THE HAND OF DEATH** • 1961
KARATE, THE see **GEKITOTSU SATSUJINKEN** • 1973
KARATE CHAMPIONS, THE • 1968 • Rowe George • PHL
KARATE COMMANDOS • 1968 • Herrera Armando A. • PHL
KARATE EXPERT, THE see **KARATISTA** • 1967
KARATE FIGHTERS • 1968 • Garces Armando • PHL
KARATE GHOSTBUSTER • Lo Wei • HKG
KARATE IN TANGIERS FOR AGENT Z-7 see **MARK DONEN AGENTE Z 7** • 1966
KARATE KID • 1967 • Cruz Abraham • PHL
KARATE KID, THE • 1984 • Avildsen John G. • USA
KARATE KID II, THE • 1986 • Avildsen John G. • USA
KARATE KID III, THE • 1989 • Avildsen John G. • USA
KARATE KILL see **KILL OR BE KILLED** • 1980
KARATE KILLER, THE • 1974 • *Mahler Howard*
KARATE KILLERS, THE • 1967 • Shear Barry • USA
KARATE OLYMPIA • 1976 • SAF
KARATE QUEEN see **REYNA NG KARATE** • 1967
KARATE, SAMURAI AND LOVE see **KARATE, SAMURAI, AT PAGIBIG** • 1968
KARATE, SAMURAI, AT PAGIBIG • 1968 • Gaudite Solano • PHL • KARATE, SAMURAI AND LOVE
KARATE, THE HAND OF DEATH • 1961 • Holt Joel • USA • KARATE
KARATE WAR see **DIGMAAN SA KARATE** • 1967
KARATE WARRIOR • 1988 • De Angelis Fabrizio • ITL • FIST OF POWER
KARATE WARRIORS • 1981 • Yamaguchi Kazuhiko • JPN
KARATECA AZTECA, EL • 1974 • *Henaine* • MXC
KARATISTA • 1967 • Garces Armando • PHL • KARATE EXPERT, THE
KARAWANA • 1964 • Nehrebecki Wladyslaw • ANS • PLN • CARAVAN, THE
KARAYUKI-SAN • 1975 • Imamura Shohei • JPN • KARAYUKI-SAN, THE MAKING OF A PROSTITUTE
KARAYUKI-SAN, THE MAKING OF A PROSTITUTE see **KARAYUKI-SAN** • 1975
KARBID UND SAUERAMPFER • 1963 • Beyer Frank • GDR • CARBIDE AND SORREL
KARD, A • 1977 • Domolky Janos • HNG • SWORD, THE
KARD ES KOCKA • 1959 • Feher Imre • HNG • SWORD AND DICE
KARDAMOM TOWN see **FOLK OG ROVERE I KARDEMOMME BY** • 1988
KARDES KAVGASI • 1967 • Inanoglu Turker • TRK • BROTHERLY FEUD
KARDESIM BENIM • 1983 • Colgecen Nesli • TRK • MY BROTHER
KARDIA ENOS ALITI, I • 1968 • Tegopoulos Apostolos • GRC • HEART OF AN OUTCAST, THE
KARDIA POU LIYISE TON PONO • 1968 • Papakostas Giorgos • GRC • HEART THAT BROKE FROM PAIN, THE ○ WOUNDED HEART, A
KARDIES POU XEROUN N' AGAPOUN • 1967 • Thalassinos Errikos • GRC • HEARTS FULL OF LOVE
KARDO, THE CATMAN see **KARDONG PUSA** • 1968
KARDONG KIDLAT • *Illang-Ilang Prod.* • PHL
KARDONG PUSA • 1968 • Reyes Efren • PHL • KARDO, THE CATMAN
KARE JOHN • 1964 • Lindgren Lars-Magnus • SWD • DEAR JOHN
KARE TO JINSEI • 1929 • Ushihara Kiyohiko • JPN • HE AND LIFE
KAREINARU ICHIZOKU • 1973 • Yamamoto Satsuo • JPN • FAMILY, THE
KAREL CAPEK'S TALES see **CAPKOVY POVIDKY** • 1947
KAREL HAVLICEK BOROVSKY • 1925 • Lamac Carl, Pistek Theodor • CZC
KAREL HAVLICEK BOROVSKY • 1931 • Innemann Svatopluk • CZC
KAREL HYNEK MACHA • 1937 • Molas Zet • CZC
KAREN, THE LOVEMAKER see **AFRICA EROTICA** • 1970
KARGACI HALIL • 1968 • Yalinkilic Yavuz • TRK • HALIL, THE CROW-MAN
KARIERA • 1948 • Stekly Karel • CZC • CAREER, THE
KARIERA • 1955 • Koecher J. • PLN • CAREER, THE
KARIERA PAVLA CAMRDY • 1931 • Krnansky M. J. • CZC • PAVEL CAMRDA'S CAREER
KARIM • 1971 • Thiam Momar • SNL
KARIM BENI ALDATIRSA • 1967 • Gulyuz Aram • TRK • IF MY WIFE CHEATS ME
KARIN DAUGHTER OF INGMAR (USA) see **KARIN INGMARSDOTTER** • 1920
KARIN DAUGHTER OF MAN see **KARIN MANSDOTTER** • 1954
KARIN, INGMAR'S DAUGHTER see **KARIN INGMARSDOTTER** • 1920
KARIN INGMARSDOTTER • 1920 • Sjostrom Victor • SWD • KARIN DAUGHTER OF INGMAR (USA) ○ GOD'S WAR (UKN) ○ KARIN, INGMAR'S DAUGHTER
KARIN MANSDOTTER • 1954 • Sjoberg Alf • SWD • KARIN DAUGHTER OF MAN ○ ERIK XIV
KARIN UN CORPO CHE BRUCIA (ITL) see **BAL DES VOYOUS, LE** • 1968
KARINA THE DANCER see **MAISON DU MALTAIS, LA** • 1927
KARINO • 1975 • Batory Jan • JPN
KARIUS OG BAKTUS • 1955 • Caprino Ivo • NRW
KARJOLSTEINEN • 1978 • Andersen Knut • NRW • TURN OF THE ROAD, THE
KARL FOR SIN HATT • 1940 • Bauman Schamyl • SWD • TVA HJARTAN OCH EN KOJA ○ ABLE MAN, AN
KARL FREDRIK REGERAR • 1934 • Edgren Gustaf • SWD • KARL FREDRIK REIGNS
KARL FREDRIK REIGNS see **KARL FREDRIK REGERAR** • 1934

KARL I KOKET, EN • 1954 • Husberg Rolf • SWD • MAN IN THE KITCHEN, A
KARL MARX • 1963 • Roshal Grigori • USS
KARL MARX • 1977 • Petty Bruce • ANS • ASL
KARL MARX STREET • 1965 • Bottcher Jurgen • DOC • GDR
KARL MAY • 1975 • Syberberg Hans-Jurgen • FRG
KARL RAUMT AUF see **GANZER KERL, EIN** • 1935
KARL VALENTIN, DER SONDERLING • 1929 • Jerven Walter • FRG
KARL VALENTINS HOCHZEIT • 1912 • Ansfelder • FRG
KARL XII • 1925 • Brunius John W. • SWD • CHARLES XII
KARLA • 1969 • Sarno Joe • USA
KARLA'S MARRIAGES see **KARLINE MANZELSTVA** • 1981
KARLAS TANTE • 1915 • Larsen Viggo • FRG
KARLCHEN AUF DER BRAUTSCHAU • 1919 • Albes Emil • FRG
KARLEK • 1952 • Molander Gustaf • SWD • LOVE
KARLEK 1-1000 • 1967 • Olsson Lennart • SWD • LOVE 1-1000
KARLEK 65 • 1965 • Widerberg Bo • SWD • LOVE 65 (UKN)
KARLEK EFTER NOTER • 1935 • Husberg Rolf, Rodin Gosta • SWD • LOVE FROM MUSIC
KARLEK MASTE VI HA • 1930 • Bergman Gustaf • SWD • WE MUST HAVE LOVE
KARLEK OCH ALLSANG • 1944 • Andersson Fredrik • SWD
KARLEK OCH DYNAMIT • 1933 • Lund O. A. C. • SWD • SOMMARNATTER I SKARGARDEN ○ LOVE AND DYNAMITE
KARLEK OCH JOURNALISTIK • 1916 • Stiller Mauritz • SWD • LOVE AND JOURNALISM (UKN) ○ LOVE AND THE JOURNALIST
KARLEK OCH KASSABRIST • 1932 • Molander Gustaf • SWD • LOVE AND DEFICIT
KARLEK OCH LANDSTORM • 1931 • Lindlof John, Bauman Schamyl • SWD • LOVE AND VETERAN RESERVES
KARLEK OCH STATISTIK • Lindgren Lars-Magnus • SHT • SWD • LOVE AND STATISTICS
KARLEK OCH STORTLOPP • 1946 • Husberg Rolf • SWD • LOVE AND DOWNHILL SKIING
KARLEK OCH VANSKAP • 1941 • Sinding Leif • NRW
KARLEK PA TURNE see **INGEN SA TOKIG SOM JAG** • 1955
KARLEK -SA GOR VI BREV TILL INGE OCH STEEN • 1972 • Wickman Torgny • SWD
KARLEK, SOLSKEN OCH SANG • 1948 • Gunwall Per • SWD • MED KARLEK, SOLSKEN OCH SANG ○ LOVE, SUNSHINE AND SONG
KARLEK STARKARE AN HAT • 1914 • Sjostrom Victor • SWD • LOVE STRONGER THAN HATE ○ LOVE STRONGER THAN HATRED
KARLEKEN • 1980 • Kallifatides Theodor • SWD • LOVE
KARLEKEN SEGRAR • 1916 • Klercker Georg • SWD • LOVE WILL CONQUER
KARLEKEN SEGRAR • 1949 • Molander Gustaf • SWD • LOVE WILL CONQUER
KARLEKENS BROD • 1953 • Mattsson Arne • SWD • BREAD OF LOVE, THE
KARLEKENS DECIMALER • 1960 • Ekman Hasse • SWD • DECIMALS OF LOVE, THE
KARLEKENS IRRFARDER • 1915 • Magnussen Fritz • SWD
KARLEKENS OGON • 1922 • Brunius John W. • SWD • EYES OF LOVE, THE
KARLEKENS SPRAK • 1969 • Wickman Torgny • SWD • LANGUAGE OF LOVE (UKN)
KARLEKENS SPRAK 2 • 1974 • Wickman Torgny • SWD, FRG • MORE ABOUT THE LANGUAGE OF LOVE ○ LANGUAGE OF LOVE 2
KARLEKS SOMMAR, EN • 1979 • Arehn Mats • SWD • SUMMER'S LOVE, A
KARLEKSBARN see **LINJE SEX** • 1958
KARLEKSEXPRESSEN • 1932 • Marmstedt Lorens • SWD • LOVE EXPRESS, THE
KARLEKSHISTORIA, EN • 1969 • Andersson Roy • SWD • SWEDISH LOVE STORY, A
KARLEKSLIVETS OFFER • 1944 • Lingheim Emil A., Alw Gabriel • SWD
KARLEKSNATT VID ORESUND, EN • 1931 • Cederstrand Solve, Widestedt Ragnar • SWD • NIGHTS OF LOVE ON ORESUND
KARLEKSSVINGEL see **JAG VILL LIGGA MED DIN AYSKARE MAMMA** • 1978
KARLEKSVIRVELN see **JAG VILL LIGGA MED DIN AYSKARE MAMMA** • 1978
KARLI KIPPE • 1962 • Georgi Klaus, Georgi Katja • ANS • GDR • CHARLEY BUTT ○ CIGARETTE CHARLIE
KARLINE MANZELSTVA • 1981 • Kavciak Vladimir • CZC • KARLA'S MARRIAGES
KARLOVY VARY • 1934 • Hammid Alexander • DCS • CZC
KARLSSON • 1989 • Alexandersson Hakan • SWD
KARLSSON BROTHERS, THE see **BRODERNA KARLSSON** • 1974
KARLSSON ON THE ROOF • 1975 • Hellbom Olle • SWD
KARMA • 1933 • Freer-Hunt J. L. • UKN, IND
KARMA • 1985 • Minh Ho Quong • USA, VTN
KARMA • 1988 • I Du-Yong • SKR • UP
KARMILA • 1975 • Prijono Ami • INN
KARMNIK JANKOWY • 1952 • Has Wojciech J. • SHT • PLN • JANEK'S FEEDING TROUGH
KARNAK, AL • 1976 • Badrakhan Ali • EGY
KARNAL • 1983 • Diaz-Abaya Marilou • PHL
KARNAVALNAYA NOCH • 1956 • Ryazanov Eldar • USS • CARNIVAL IN MOSCOW (USA) ○ CARNIVAL NIGHT
KARNEVAL • 1908 • *Holger-Madsen* • DNM • BANK DIRECTOR, THE ○ CARNIVAL
KARNEVAL • 1961 • Olsson Lennart • SWD • CARNIVAL
KARNEVAL, ANDEO I PRAH • 1990 • Vrdoljak Antun • YGS • CARNIVAL, ANGEL AND DUST
KARNEVAL DER LIEBE • 1943 • Martin Paul • FRG
KARNEVAL IN WEISS • 1952 • Albin Hans, Sokal H. R. • FRG
KARNEVAL UND LIEBE • 1934 • Lamac Carl • AUS
KARNIVAL KID, THE • 1928 • Disney Walt, Iwerks Ub • ANS • USA
KARO 1O see **GEHEIMNIS DER SECHS SPIELKARTEN 1, DAS** • 1920
KAROL • 1966 • Szczechura Daniel • ANS • PLN
KAROL LIR • 1969 • Kozintsev Grigori • USS • KING LEAR ○ KORAL LIR
KAROLY-BAKAK • 1918 • Korda Zoltan (c/d) • HNG
KARPER, DE • 1966 • Brosens Albert • NTH
KARPURAM • 1967 • Shanmugam C. N. • IND • CAMPHOR
KARRIAR • 1938 • Bauman Schamyl • SWD • CAREER
KARRIERE • 1930 • Trotz Adolf • FRG
KARRIERE • 1966 • Gaspard-Huit Pierre • FRG, FRN • CAREER
KARRIERE IN PARIS • 1951 • Klaren Georg C. • GDR
KARSAVITSA • 1969 • Zhebrunas Arunas • USS • BEAUTIFUL GIRL, THE ○ BEAUTY, A
KARSH, THE SEARCHING EYE • 1986 • Rasky Harry • MTV • CND
KARST • 1965 • Tucker Roger • SHT • UKN
KARTAL EFE • 1967 • Arikan Kayahan • TRK • MASTER EAGLE
KARTENLEGERIN, DIE • 1922 • *Polini Bella* • FRG
KARTHAUZI, A • 1916 • Curtiz Michael • HNG • CARTHUSIAN, THE
KARTICK'S BLESSING see **KANDHAN KARUNAI** • 1967
KARTKA Z PODROZY • 1983 • Dziki Waldemar • PLN • POSTCARD FROM A JOURNEY
KARTOFFELSUPP, KARTOFFELSUPP see **SCHON IST DIE MANOVERZEIT** • 1938
KARTOFLER • 1944 • Palsbo Ole • DNM • POTATO, THE
KARTOTEKA • 1966 • Giersz Witold • ANS • PLN • CARD-INDEX, THE ○ FILE, THE ○ INDEX, THE
KARTUNE • 1952-53 • *Paramount* • ASS • USA
KARTYAVAR • 1968 • Hintsch Gyorgy • HNG • HOUSE OF CARDS
KARUMAKKARAYO • 1980 • Abeysekera Tissa • SLN
KARUMEN JUNJOSU • 1952 • Kinoshita Keisuke • JPN • CARMEN'S PURE LOVE
KARUMEN KOKYO NI KAERU • 1951 • Kinoshita Keisuke • JPN • CARMEN COMES HOME
KARUSEL • 1971 • Schweitzer Mikhail • USS • MERRY-GO-ROUND, THE ○ ROUNDABOUT, THE ○ CAROUSEL
KARUSELLEN • 1923 • Buchowetzki Dimitri • SWD • MERRY-GO-ROUND ○ LIVING TARGET, THE
KARUSELLEN • 1942 • Ibsen Tancred • SWD
KARUSELLEN GAR • 1940 • Wallen Sigurd • SWD • MERRY-GO-ROUND IN FULL SWING, THE
KARUSELLEN I FJALLEN • 1955 • Frisk Ragnar • SWD • MERRY-GO-ROUND IN THE MOUNTAINS
KARUSSEL • 1937 • Elling Alwin • FRG
KARUSSEL DES LEBENS • 1919 • Jacoby Georg • FRG • LAST PAYMENT (USA)
KARUSSEL DES LEBENS, DAS • 1923 • Buchowetzki Dimitri • FRG
KARUSSEL DES TODES, DAS • 1928 • Paul Heinz • FRG • MERRY-GO-ROUND OF FATE, THE
KARUSSELL see **KORHINTA** • 1955
KARUTHA RATRIKAL • 1967 • Mahesh • IND • DARK NIGHTS
KARUZELA LOWICKA • 1958 • Hoffman Jerzy, Skorzewski Edward • DCS • PLN • LOWICZ MERRY-GO-ROUND, THE ○ CARNIVAL OF LOWICZ, THE
KARVAT • 1974 • Huunonen Seppo • FNL • HAIRS, THE ○ OBSESSION
KARWAE HAIYAT • 1935 • *Sircar B. N. (P)* • IND
KARZAN, IL FAVOLOSO UOMO DELLA GIUNGLA • 1971 • Fidani Demofilo • ITL • KARZAN, THE FABULOUS JUNGLE MAN ○ MOST FANTASTIC AND MARVELOUS ADVENTURE IN THE JUNGLE
KARZAN, THE FABULOUS JUNGLE MAN see **KARZAN, IL FAVOLOSO UOMO DELLA GIUNGLA** • 1971
KA'S, AL • 1986 • Damak Mohammed • TNS • CUP, THE
KASAKI • 1961 • Pronin Vassily • USS • COSSACKS, THE ○ KHAZAKKI ○ KAZAKI
KASALANAN KAYA? • 1968 • Enriquez Luis B. • PHL • IS IT A SIN?
KASAR • 1974 • Jires Jaromil • SHT • CZC • SAFE-CRACKER, THE
KASARI • 1958 • Blumenfeld Pavel • CZC • SAFE-BREAKERS
KASCHEMMENADEL • 1921 • Hartwig Martin • FRG
KASCHEMMENGRAFIN • 1922 • Neff Wolfgang • FRG
KASEBIER ODER DIE GESTOHLENE SCHLACHT • 1972 • Stranka Erwin • GDR
KASEKI • 1975 • Kobayashi Masaki • JPN • FOSSILS
KASEKI NO MORI • 1973 • Shinoda Masahiro • JPN • PETRIFIED FOREST, THE
KASERNENZAUBER • 1930 • Boese Carl • FRG
KASHI TO KODOMO • 1962 • Teshigahara Hiroshi • JPN • PITFALL, THE (USA) ○ CHEAP SWEET AND A KID ○ OTOSHI ANA
KASHIMA PARADISE • 1973 • Deswarte Benie, Le Masson Yann • DOC • FRN
KASHIMANADA NO ONNA • 1959 • Yamamura So • JPN • MAIDENS OF KASHIMA SEA
KASHINATH • 1943 • *Sircar B. N. (P)* • IND
KASHKAI: DERNIERS NOMADES D'IRAN, LES • 1971-74 • Bertolino Daniel • DOC • CND
KASHMIR • 1981 • Falzon Albert • DOC • ASL
KASHMIRI RUN • 1969 • Peyser John • SPN, USA • TIBETANA
KASHMIRI WATERWAYS • 1981 • Falzon Albert • DOC • ASL
KASHTANKA • 1925 • Preobrazhenskaya Olga • USS
KASHTANKA • 1952 • Tsekhanovsky M. M. • ANM • USS
KASHTI-KREPOSTI • 1966 • Doukov Stoyan • ANM • BUL • HOUSES THAT ARE FORTS ○ HOME-CASTLES
KASIMIR • 1978 • USA
KASIMPASALI • 1965 • Akinci Nuri • TRK
KASIMPASALI RECEP • 1965 • Akinci Nuri • TRK
KASKADER • 1971 • Giersz Witold • ANS • PLN • STUNTMAN, THE
KASKARA • 1974 • O. Dore • FRG
KASKENADES VAN DR. KWAK • 1948 • SAF
KASMARAN • 1988 • Rahardjo Slamet • INN
KASPAR HAUSER • 1915 • Matull Kurt • FRG • TRAGODIE DES KASPAR HAUSER, DIE
KASPAREK KOUZELNIKEM • 1927 • Kokeisl • CZC • PUNCH THE MAGICIAN
KASPER HAUSER see **JEDER FUR SICH UND GOTT GEGEN ALLE** • 1974
KASPER IN DE ONDERWERELD • 1979 • van der Heyden Jef • BLG
KASPICHY see **KAPISKIE LIUDI** • 1944
KASR EL MALOUN, EL • 1962 • Reda Hassan • EGY • ACCURSED CASTLE, THE
KASR EL SHAWK • 1967 • el Imam Hassan • EGY
KASSBACH • 1979 • Patzak Peter • AUS
KASSEN STEMMER • 1976 • Langberg Ebbe • DNM
KASSENREVISION • 1918 • Stein Josef • FRG
KASSET GHARAM • 1946 • Salim Kamel • EGY • STORY OF LOVE
KASSETTE, DIE • 1917 • Wolff Carl Heinz • FRG
KASSETTENLIEBE • 1982 • Lyssy Rolf • SWT • CASSETTE LOVE AFFAIRS
KASSIERE, DE • 1989 • Verbong Ben • NTH • CASHIER, THE ○ LILY WAS HERE
KASSO DEN • 1978 • Coulibaly Sega • MLI • PRISONNIER, LE ○ PRISONER, THE
KASTELYOK LAKOI • 1966 • Elek Judit • SHT • HNG • OCCUPANTS OF MANOR HOUSE ○ TENANTS OF CASTLES
KASTILYONG BUHANGIN • 1981 • O'Hara Mario • PHL • SAND CASTLE
KASTRULLRESAN • 1950 • Mattsson Arne • SWD • SAUCEPAN JOURNEY, THE
KASTURI • 1978 • Dutt Bimal • IND
KASTUS KALINOVSKY • 1928 • Gardin Vladimir • USS
KASZEBE • 1970 • Ber Ryszard • PLN
KATAHRISIS EXOUSIAS • 1970 • Tsiolis Stavros • GRC • ABUSE
KATAK ET KUTUK SE RACONTENT ET CHANTENT • 1971 • Lavoie Richard • DCS • CND
KATAKOMBY • 1940 • Fric Martin • CZC • CATACOMBS
KATAKU • 1979 • Kawamoto • JPN • THIS WORLD
KATAKU NO HITO • 1985 • Fukasaku Kinji • JPN • MAN IN A HURRY
KATALA • 1989 • Bodrov Sergei, Buravski Alexander • USS • GAMBLER, THE
KATANALOTIKI KINONIA • 1971 • Carayannis Costa • GRC • CONSUMER SOCIETY
KATARA INE O HORISMOS • 1968 • Thalassinos Errikos • GRC • PARTING IS A MALEDICTION
KATARA TIS MANAS, I • 1961 • Georgiadis Vassilis • GRC • PROMISE, THE
KATARAMENI AGAPI • 1968 • Kosteletos Odisseas • GRC • CURSED LOVE
KATARAMENI ORA • 1968 • Doukas Kostas • GRC • EVIL EYE
KATARIN • 1977 • Satariano Cecil • MLT
KATARINA A JEJI DETI • 1970 • Gajer Vaclav • CZC • KATHERINE AND HER CHILDREN ○ CATHERINE AND HER DAUGHTERS
KATARSIS see **SFIDA AL DIAVOLO** • 1965
KATARYNKA • 1956 • Bielinska Halina • PLN
KATASKOPI STO SARONIKO • 1968 • Tallas Gregg R. • GRC • OPERATION SKYBOLT ○ SPIES IN SARONIKO ○ ASSIGNMENT SKYBOLT
KATASTOPHE EINES VOLKES, DIE • 1920 • *Marbeck Ria* • FRG
KATAYOKU DAKE NO TENSHI • 1985 • Masuda Toshio • JPN • ANGEL WITH ONE WING, AN
KATCHEM KATE • 1912 • Sennett Mack • USA
KATCHEN FUR ALLES • 1949 • von Rathony Akos • FRG
KATE AND ANNA MCGARRIGLE • 1981 • Leaf Caroline • CND
KATE AND THE CROCODILE • Plivova-Simkova Vera • CZC
KATE BLISS AND THE TICKER TAPE KID • 1978 • Kennedy Burt • TVM • USA
KATE IN THE CALL BOX • 1929 • Aylott Dave, Symmons E. F. • SHT • UKN
KATE MCSHANE • 1975 • Chomsky Marvin • TVM • USA
KATE MORRIS, VICE-PRESIDENT • 1984 • Suissa Daniele J. • MTV • CND
KATE OF KENTUCKY see **HER INSPIRATION** • 1919
KATE PLUS TEN • 1938 • Denham Reginald • UKN • QUEEN OF CRIME (USA)
KATE THE COP • 1913 • Hotaling Arthur D. • USA
KATE WATERS OF THE SECRET SERVICE • 1914 • Giblyn Charles • USA
KATE, WON'T YOU ROLLER SKATE? • 1909 • *Warwick Trading Co* • UKN
KATEI NIKKI • 1938 • Yamamoto Satsuo • JPN • FAMILY DIARY
KATEI NO JIJYO • 1962 • Yoshimura Kozaburo • JPN • THEIR LEGACY
KATEI SEIKATSU • 1978 • Tichenor Harold • DOC • CND
KATER LAMPE • 1936 • Harlan Veit • FRG
KATERINA ISMAILOVA see **KATERINA ISMAYLOVA** • 1966
KATERINA ISMAYLOVA • 1966 • Shapiro Mikhail • USS • LADY MACBETH OF MTSENSK (UKN) ○ KATERINA ISMAILOVA ○ KATERINA IZMAYLOVA
KATERINA IZMAYLOVA see **KATERINA ISMAYLOVA** • 1966
KATE'S AFFINITIES • 1916 • Curtis Allen • SHT • USA • KATE'S LOVER'S KNOT
KATE'S LOVER'S KNOT see **KATE'S AFFINITIES** • 1916
KATE'S REDEMPTION • 1909 • *Empire Films* • UKN
KATE'S SECRET • 1986 • Seidelman Arthur Allan • TVM • USA
KATHA • 1982 • Pranjpye Sai • IND • STORY
KATHAL PARAVAI • 1967 • Seshagiri Rao A. V. • IND • LOVE BIRD
KATHARINA DIE GROSSE • 1920 • Schunzel Reinhold • FRG
KATHARINA DIE LETZTE • 1935 • Koster Henry • AUS • KATHERINE THE LAST ○ CATHERINE THE LAST
KATHARINA KARASCHKIN • 1917 • Eichberg Richard • FRG
KATHARINA KNIE • 1929 • Grune Karl • FRG
KATHE KOLLWITZ -PICTURES OF A LIFE • 1987 • Kirsten Ralf • GDR
KATHERINE • 1974 • Davies John Michael • UKN
KATHERINE • 1975 • Kagan Jeremy Paul • TVM • USA
KATHERINE AND HER CHILDREN see **KATARINA A JEJI DETI** • 1970
KATHERINE AND THE HANGMAN • 1966 • Latallo Katarzyna • ANM • PLN
KATHERINE REED STORY, THE • 1965 • Altman Robert • SHT • USA

KATHERINE THE LAST see **KATHARINA DIE LETZTE** • 1935

KATHERINE THE LAST see **GIRL DOWNSTAIRS, THE** • 1938

KATHLEEN • 1941 • Bucquet Harold S. • USA • GIRL ON THE HILL, THE

KATHLEEN MAVOURNEEN • 1906 • Porter Edwin S. • USA

KATHLEEN MAVOURNEEN • 1911 • *Yankee* • USA

KATHLEEN MAVOURNEEN • 1913 • Brabin Charles J. • *Edison* • USA

KATHLEEN MAVOURNEEN • 1913 • Brenon Herbert • *Imp* • USA

KATHLEEN MAVOURNEEN • 1919 • Brabin Charles J. • USA

KATHLEEN MAVOURNEEN • 1930 • Ray Albert • USA • GIRL FROM IRELAND, THE (UKN)

KATHLEEN MAVOURNEEN • 1937 • Lee Norman • UKN • KATHLEEN (USA)

KATHLEEN, THE IRISH ROSE • 1914 • *Fealy Maude* • USA

KATHLEEN (USA) see **KATHLEEN MAVOURNEEN** • 1937

KATHODOS TON ENNEA • 1984 • Siopachas Christos • GRC • DESCENT OF THE NINE

KATHY O' • 1958 • Sher Jack • USA

KATHY KARUKS IS A GRIZZLY BEAR • 1976 • Pearson Peter • MTV • CND

KATHY'S LOVE AFFAIR see **COURTNEYS OF CURZON STREET, THE** • 1947

KATI AND THE WILD CAT • 1955 • Kollanyi Agoston • HNG

KATI BORI NA KANOUME EMIS I DHIO • 1972 • Zois Kostis • GRC • WE COULD DO SOMETHING TOGETHER

KATI KOURASMENA PALLIKARIA • 1967 • Dimopoulos Dinos • GRC • RETIRED PLAYBOY, A

KATIA • 1938 • Tourneur Maurice • FRN

KATIA see **KATJA** • 1959

KATIA THE BEAUTY see **KRASAVICE KATA** • 1919

KATIE DID IT • 1951 • De Cordova Frederick • USA

KATIE: PORTRAIT OF A CENTERFOLD • 1978 • Greenwald Robert • TVM • USA

KATIGOROUMENI, APOLOYISOU • 1968 • Katsimitsoulias Andreas • GRC • ACCUSED PLEADS NOT GUILTY, THE

KATIJUBATO • 1986 • Fink Tone • AUS

KATINA (UKN) see **ICELAND** • 1942

KATINKA • 1918 • Otto Paul • FRG

KATINKA • 1987 • von Sydow Max • SWD, DNM, UKN

KATIP • 1968 • Erakalin Ulku • TRK • USKUDARA GIDERKEN ○ ON THE WAY TO USKUDAR ○ SECRETARY, THE

KATIRCILAR • 1987 • Goren Serif • TRK • MULE DRIVERS, THE

KATIRCIYANI • 1967 • Yalinkilic Yavuz • TRK

KATIUSCIA • 1923 • Rosa Silvio Laurenti • ITL

KATJA • 1959 • Siodmak Robert • FRG, FRN • JEUNE FILLE, UN SEUL AMOUR, UNE (FRN) ○ ADORABLE SINNER (USA) ○ MAGNIFICENT SINNER ○ KATIA

KATJUSCHA MASLOVA see **AUFERSTEHUNG** • 1923

KATKA • 1949 • Kadar Jan • CZC • CATHY ○ KATYA ○ KITTY

KATKA BUMAZHNYI RANET see **KATKA BUMAZHNYR ANYOT** • 1926

KATKA BUMAZHNYR ANYOT • 1926 • Ermler Friedrich, Johanson Eduard • USS • KATKA'S REINETTE APPLES ○ KATKA BUMAZHNYI RANET

KATKA'S REINETTE APPLES see **KATKA BUMAZHNYR ANYOT** • 1926

KATMANDU (ITL) see **CHEMINS DE KATMANDOU, LES** • 1969

KAT'N RAUHBEIN AUS ST. PAULI • 1971 • Olsen Rolf • FRG • KAPT'N RAUHBEIN AUS ST. PAULI

KATNIP COLLEGE • 1938 • Hardaway Ben, Dalton Cal • ANS • USA

KATNIP'S BIG DAY • 1959 • Kneitel Seymour • ANS • USA

KATNIPS OF 1940 • 1934 • *Mintz Charles (P)* • ANS • USA

KATO HAYABUSA SENTOTAI • 1944 • Yamamoto Kajiro • JPN • GENERAL KATO'S FALCON FIGHTERS

KATOK I SKRIPKA • 1961 • Tarkovsky Andrei • USS • VIOLIN AND ROLLER (USA) ○ VIOLIN AND THE ROLLER, THE ○ STEAMROLLER AND THE VIOLIN, THE ○ ROLLER AND THE VIOLIN, THE

KATORGA • 1928 • Raizman Yuli • USS • PENAL SERVITUDE ○ FORCED LABOUR ○ CONVICT LABOUR ○ IN OLD SIBERIA ○ PRISON

KATRINA • 1943 • Edgren Gustaf • SWD

KATRINA • 1969 • SAF

KATRINA DEAD • 1967 • Warhol Andy • USA

KATS IS KATS • 1920 • La Cava Gregory • ANS • USA

KATTORNA • 1965 • Carlsen Henning • SWD • CATS, THE

KATU (HOW I LIVED AS EVE) see **KATU (THE FRENCH GIRL AND THE NUDISTS)** • 1964

KATU (THE FRENCH GIRL AND THE NUDISTS) • 1964 • Sulistrowski Zygmunt • USA, BRZ • KATU (HOW I LIVED AS EVE)

KATUPEILIN TAKANA • 1948 • Saakka Toivo • FNL • BEHIND THE STREET MIRROR

KATUSHA see **KACHUSHA** • 1914

KATUTURA • 1974 • Schweizer Ulrich • DOC • SWT

KATY • 1983 • Moro Jose Luis Santiago • MXC, SPN • KATY CATERPILLAR

KATY CATERPILLAR see **KATY** • 1983

KATY DIDD see **DEAD GAME** • 1923

KATYA see **KATKA** • 1949

KATYUSHA • 1964 • Lisakovitch Viktor • DOC • USS

KATZ & CARASSO • 1971 • Golan Menahem • ISR

KATZ' IM SACK, DIE • 1934 • Eichberg Richard • FRG

KATZ UND MAUS • 1967 • Pohland Hansjurgen • FRG, PLN • KOT I MYSZ (PLN) ○ CAT AND MOUSE (USA)

KATZELMACHER • 1969 • Fassbinder R. W. • FRG

KATZENJAMMER KIDS, THE • 1912 • *Mohler Guy* • USA

KATZENJAMMER KIDS, THE • 1916-24 • Stallings George • ASS • USA

KATZENJAMMER KIDS NO.2: THEY GO TOBOGGANING, THE • 1912 • *Selig* • USA

KATZENJAMMER KIDS NO.3: THEY PLAN A TRIP TO GERMANY, THE • 1912 • *Selig* • USA

KATZENJAMMER KIDS NO.4: THEY ENTERTAIN COMPANY • 1912 • *Selig* • USA

KATZENJAMMER KIDS NO.5: THEY GO TO SCHOOL • 1912 • *Selig* • USA

KATZENJAMMER KIDS NO.6: SCHOOL DAYS, THE • 1912 • *Selig* • USA

KATZENJAMMER KIDS NO.7: UNWILLING SCHOLARS, THEY CORRUPT THE SCHOOL, THE • 1912 • *Selig* • USA

KATZENJAMMER KIDS NO.8: THE ARRIVAL OF COUSIN OTTO, THE • 1912 • *Selig* • USA

KATZENSTEG, DER • 1915 • Mack Max • FRG

KATZENSTEG, DER • 1927 • Lamprecht Gerhard • FRG • BETRAYAL

KATZENSTEG, DER • 1937 • Buch Fritz Peter • FRG • CAT'S PATH, THE

KAUAPISHIT MIAM KUAKUATSHEU ETENTAKUESS see **CARCAJOU ET LE PERIL BLANC** • 1971-77

KAUF DIR EINEN BUNTEN LUFT BALLON • 1961 • von Cziffra Geza • FRG, AUS

KAUFMANN VON VENEDIG, DER • 1923 • Felner Peter Paul • FRG • JEW OF MESTRI, THE ○ MERCHANT OF VENICE, THE

KAUFT MARIETT-AKTIEN • 1922 • von Antalffy Alexander • FRG

KAUHUKAKARA • 1971 • Pasanen Spede • FNL • ENFANT TERRIBLE, L'

KAUKASIERIN, DIE • 1917 • *Landa Max* • FRG

KAULE • 1967 • Bar Rainer • GDR

KAUNIS MUISTO • 1977 • Strandberg Per-Olof • FNL • BEAUTIFUL MEMORY

KAUPUNGISSA ON TULEVAISUUS • 1967 • Jarva Risto • SHT • FNL • TOWN IS OUR FUTURE, THE

KAUSALYA PARINAYAM • 1937 • Iyer C. S. V. • IND

KAUTSCHUK • 1938 • von Borsody Eduard • FRG

KAVALER ZOLOTOI ZVEZDY • 1950 • Raizman Yuli • USS • KNIGHT OF THE GOLD STAR, THE ○ CAVALIER OF THE GOLD STAR ○ DREAM OF A COSSACK

KAVALIER VOM WEDDING, DER • 1926 • Neff Wolfgang • FRG

KAVALIERE • 1923 • Stranz Fred? • FRG

KAVALIERE VON KURFURSTENDAMM • 1932 • Mengon Romano • FRG

KAVALIERS, DIE • 1966 • SAF

KAVALKARAN • 1967 • Neelakantan P. • IND • WATCHMAN, THE

KAVARNA ASTORIA • 1989 • Pogacnik Joze • YGS • CAFFE ASTORIA

KAVIARMAUSCHEN, DAS • 1919 • Dammann Gerhard • FRG

KAVIARPRINZESSIN, DIE • 1929 • Lamac Carl • FRG

KAVIK, THE WOLF DOG see **COURAGE OF KAVIK, THE WOLF DOG, THE** • 1980

KAWA, ANO URAGIRI GA OMOKU • 1967 • Mori Kota • JPN • RIVER -POEM OF WRATH, THE

KAWA NO ARU SHITAMACHI NO HANASHI • 1955 • Kinugasa Teinosuke • JPN • IT HAPPENED IN TOKYO ○ STORY OF A RIVER DOWNTOWN, THE

KAWA NO UE NO TAIYO • 1934 • Uchida Tomu • JPN

KAWACHI FUTEN ZOKU • 1968 • Chiba Yasuki • JPN • HIPPIES OF KAWACHI

KAWACHI ICHIDAI • 1966 • Suzuki Seijun • JPN

KAWACHI YUKYODEN • 1967 • Takamori Ryuichi • JPN • TROUGHS OF KAWACHI

KAWAITA HANA • 1964 • Shinoda Masahiro • JPN • PALE FLOWER

KAWAITA MIZUUMI • 1960 • Shinoda Masahiro • JPN • YOUTH IN FURY ○ DRY LAKE

KAWANAKAJIMA KASSEN • 1941 • Kinugasa Teinosuke • JPN • BATTLE AT KAWANAKAJIMA ○ BATTLE OF KAWANAKAJIMA, THE

KAWANO HOTORIDE • 1963 • *Kayama Yuzo* • JPN • BORN IN SIN (USA)

KAWIN LARI • 1975 • Karya Teguh • INN • ELOPEMENT, THE

KAYA, I'LL KILL YOU see **KAJA, UBIT CU TE!** • 1967

KAYA (USA) see **KAJA, UBIT CU TE!** • 1967

KAYAKO see **KAKA YO**

KAYFA TESRAK MILLIONAIRE • 1968 • Hafez Magdy • EGY • HOW TO STEAL A MILLION

KAYNTIKORTTINI • 1964 • Kivikoski Erkko • FNL • VISITING CARD, THE ○ MY CALLING CARD

KAYTOS-KUKKA • 1966 • Partanen Heikki • SHT • FNL • FLOWER FOR CONDUCT, A

KAZABLAN • 1974 • Golan Menahem • ISR

KAZAHANA • 1959 • Kinoshita Keisuke • JPN • SNOW FLURRY

KAZAKHSTAN FRONT, THE see **TEBYE FRONT** • 1943

KAZAKHSTAN FRONTU see **TEBYE FRONT** • 1943

KAZAKI see **KASAKI** • 1961

KAZAKS -MINORITE NATIONALE -SINKIANG, LES • 1977 • Ivens Joris (c/d) • SHT • FRN

KAZAN • 1921 • Bracken Bertram • USA

KAZAN • 1949 • Jason Will • USA

KAZAN, THE FEARLESS (UKN) see **OUTLAWS' HIGHWAY** • 1934

KAZDA KORUNA DOBRA • 1961 • Brynych Zbynek • CZC • EVERY PENNY COUNTS

KAZDEMU WOLNO KOCHAC • 1933 • Krawicz Mecislas, Warnecki J. • PLN

KAZDY DEN ODVAHU • 1964 • Schorm Evald • CZC • COURAGE FOR EVERYDAY LIFE ○ ODVAHU PRO VSEDNI DEN ○ EVERYDAY COURAGE ○ COURAGE FOR EVERY DAY

KAZDY MLADY MUZ • 1965 • Juracek Pavel • CZC • EVERY YOUNG MAN

KAZE FUTATABI • 1952 • Toyoda Shiro • JPN • WIND ONCE MORE

KAZE NI SOYOGU ASHI • 1951 • Sunohara Masahisa • JPN • REEDS THAT RUSTLE IN THE WIND

KAZE NO ARU MICHI • 1959 • Nishikawa Katsumi • JPN

KAZE NO BOJO • 1970 • Nakamura Noboru • JPN • JOURNEY OF LOVE

KAZE NO KO • 1949 • Yamamoto Kajiro • JPN • WIND OF HONOUR

KAZE NO NAKA NO KODOMO see **KAZE NO NAKA NO KODOMOTACHI** • 1937

KAZE NO NAKA NO KODOMOTACHI • 1937 • Shimizu Hiroshi • JPN • CHILDREN IN THE WIND ○ KAZE NO NAKA NO KODOMO

KAZE NO NAKA NO MENDORI • 1948 • Ozu Yasujiro • JPN • HEN IN THE WIND, A

KAZE NO SHISEN • 1963 • Kawazu Yoshiro • JPN • HIDDEN PROFILE

KAZE TACHINU • 1955 • Shima Koji • JPN • AUTUMN INTERLUDE

KAZE TO ONNA TO TABIGARASU • 1958 • Kato Tai • JPN • WIND WOMAN AND WANDERER

KAZIMIERZ THE GREAT see **KAZIMIERZ WIELKI** • 1975

KAZIMIERZ WIELKI • 1975 • Petelska Ewa, Petelski Czeslaw • PLN • KAZIMIERZ THE GREAT ○ KING CASIMIR THE GREAT

KAZOKU • 1942 • Shibuya Minoru • JPN • FAMILY, A

KAZOKU • 1971 • Yamada Yoji • JPN • WHERE SPRING COMES LATE ○ FAMILY, A

KAZOKU KAIGI • 1954 • Nakamura Noboru • JPN • FAMILY CONFERENCE

KAZUKO GAME see **KAZUKO GEEMU** • 1983

KAZUKO GEEMU • 1983 • Morita Yoshimitsu • JPN • FAMILY GAME ○ KAZUKO GAME

KAZZAM INTERNATIONAL • 1976 • Petty Bruce • ANS • ASL

KDE JE MISA? • 1954 • Hofman Eduard • ANS • CZC • WHERE IS MISHA? ○ WHERE'S MISHA?

KDE REKY MAJI SLUNCE • 1961 • Krska Vaclav • CZC • DAY THE TREES WILL BLOOM, THE

KDO CHCE ZABIT JESSI? • 1966 • Vorlicek Vaclav, Macourek Milos • CZC • WHO WANTS TO KILL JESSIE? ○ WHO WOULD KILL JESSIE? ○ WHO KILLED JESSIE? ○ JESSIE AND SUPERMAN ○ WHO SAVES JESSIE?

KDO HLEDA ZLATE DNO • 1975 • Menzel Jiri • CZC • WHO SEEKS A HANDFUL OF GOLD ○ WHO LOOKS FOR GOLD ○ WHO SEEKS THE GOLD BOTTOM

KDO NEKI TAM POJE see **KO TO TAMO PEVA?** • 1981

KDO SETRI, TEN JEDE • 1954 • Hofman Eduard • ANS • PLN

KDO SVE NEBE NEUNESE • 1959 • Schorm Evald • SHT • CZC • TOO MUCH TO CARRY

KDYBY TISIC KLARINETU • 1964 • Rohac Jan, Svitacek Vladimir • CZC • IF A THOUSAND CLARINETS ○ THOUSAND CLARINETS, A

KDYBY TY MUSIKY NEBYLY • 1963 • Forman Milos • CZC • WHY DO WE NEED ALL THE BRASS BANDS? (USA) ○ GLORY OF THE BRASS BANDS, THE ○ IF IT WEREN'T FOR MUSIC ○ IF THERE WAS NO MUSIC

KDYBYCH BYL TATOU • 1939 • Cikan Miroslav • CZC • IF I WAS A DADDY

KDYZ MA SVATEK DOMINIKA • 1967 • Valasek Jan • CZC • DOMINIKA'S NAME-DAY

KDYZ ROZVOD, TAK ROZVOD! • 1982 • Skalsky Stepan • CZC • IF YOU WANT A DIVORCE, YOU HAVE ONE!

KDYZ STRUNY LKAJI • 1930 • Feher Friedrich • CZC • WHEN THE STRINGS WEEP ○ WHEN THE VIOLIN SIGHS

KDYZ V RAJI PRSELO • 1987 • Pivonkova Magda • CZC • WHEN IT RAINED IN PARADISE

KE ARTEKO EGUNAK • 1989 • Ezeiza Antxon • SPN • DAYS OF SMOKE

KE ARTEKO EGUNAK see **DIAS DE HUMO** • 1989

KE GHAR KE DERA • 1985 • Rimal Pradeep • NPL • OF A HOUSE AND A RENTED FLAT

KE I PENTE ISAN KOLASMENES • 1968 • Kazan Lakis • GRC • AND THE FIVE WERE PUNISHED ○ DAMNED, THE

KE NO HAETA KENJU • 1968 • Yamatoya Jiku • JPN • HAIRY PISTOL, A

KE TUMI? • 1967 • Chakravarty Shyam • IND • WHERE ARE YOU?

KEAN • 1910 • *Blom August* • DNM

KEAN • 1921 • Biebrach Rudolf • FRG

KEAN • 1923 • Volkov Alexander • FRN • DESORDRE ET GENIE

KEAN • 1940 • Brignone Guido • ITL

KEAN, GENIO E SREGOLATEZZA • 1957 • Gassman Vittorio, Rosi Francesco (U/c) • ITL • KEAN, GENIUS OR SCOUNDREL

KEAN, GENIUS OR SCOUNDREL see **KEAN, GENIO E SREGOLATEZZA** • 1957

KEANE OF KALGOORIE • 1912 • Gavin John F. • ASL

KEATON'S COP • 1989 • Burge Robert • USA

KEBECKOOTUT • 1975 • Valcour Pierre • DOC • CND

KEBY SOM BOL VTACKOM • Slivka Ondrej • ANM • CZC • IF I WERE A BIRDIE

KEBY SOM MAL DIEVCA • 1976 • Uher Stefan • CZC • IF I HAD A GIRL

KEBY SOM MAL PUSKU • 1972 • Uher Stefan • CZC • IF I HAD A GUN

KECHINBO NAGAYA • 1927 • Uchida Tomu • JPN

KEDAMONO NO KEN • 1965 • Gosha Hideo • JPN • SAMURAI GOLD SEEKERS

KEDAMONO NO TORU MICHI • 1959 • Sekigawa Hideo • JPN • BEAST'S PASSAGE

KEDAMONO NO YADO • 1951 • Osone Tatsuo • JPN • DEN OF BEASTS

KEDERLI GUNLERIM • 1967 • Aksoy Orhan • TRK • MY SORROWFUL DAYS

KEDVES SZOMSZED, A • 1979 • Kezdi-Kovacs Zsolt • HNG • GOOD NEIGHBOUR, THE

KEECHAK VADH • 1951 • *Manik* • IND

KEEFER • 1978 • Shear Barry • TVM • USA

KEEFMAN • 1977 • van Leeuwen Wouter • SHT • NTH

KEEGANS, THE • 1976 • Badham John • TVM • USA

KEELER AFFAIR, THE see **CHRISTINE KEELER AFFAIR, THE** • 1964

KEEP, THE • 1983 • Mann Michael • UKN

KEEP A LITTLE THOUGHT FOR ME see **JUST KEEP A THOUGHT FOR ME** • 1922

KEEP ALL DOORS OPEN see **HALL ALLA DORRAR OPPNA** • 1973

KEEP AN EYE ON AMELIA (UKN) see **OCCUPE-TOI D'AMELIE** • 1949

KEEP AWAKE see **JAGTE RAHO** • 1956

KEEP COOL • Nelson Barrie • ANS • USA

KEEP 'EM FLYING • 1941 • Lubin Arthur • USA

KEEP 'EM GROWING • 1943 • Davis Mannie • ANS • USA

KEEP 'EM HOME • 1922 • St. Clair Malcolm • SHT • USA

KEEP 'EM ROLLING • 1934 • Archainbaud George • USA • RODNEY

KEEP 'EM SAILING • 1942 • Wrangell Basil • SHT • USA

KEEP 'EM SLUGGING • 1943 • Cabanne W. Christy • USA

KEEP FIT • 1937 • Kimmins Anthony • UKN
KEEP FROZEN • 1977 • Enoksen Ivar • SHT • NRW
KEEP GOING • 1926 • Harvey John • USA
KEEP IN STYLE • 1934 • Fleischer Dave • ANS • USA
KEEP IT CLEAN • 1952 • Barclay David • SHT • USA
KEEP IT CLEAN • 1956 • Paltenghi David • UKN
KEEP IT COOL • 1954 • Cowan Will • SHT • USA
KEEP IT COOL (UKN) see **LET'S ROCK** • 1958
KEEP IT DARK • 1915 • Cooper Toby • UKN
KEEP IT IN THE FAMILY • 1973 • Kent Larry • CND
KEEP IT QUIET • 1934 • Hiscott Leslie • UKN
KEEP IT UP DOWNSTAIRS • 1976 • Young Robert • UKN
KEEP IT UP JACK! • 1974 • Ford Derek • UKN
KEEP LAUGHING • 1932 • Arbuckle Roscoe • USA
KEEP ME IN see **TUCK ME IN** • 1970
KEEP MOVING • 1915 • *Watson & Bickel* • USA
KEEP MOVING! • 1916 • Myll Louis • SHT • USA
KEEP MY GRAVE OPEN • 1975 • Brownrigg S. F. • USA • HOUSE WHERE HELL FROZE OVER, THE
KEEP OF MY GRASS • 1972 • *Wood Gary* • USA
KEEP OFF! KEEP OFF! • 1975 • Berman Shelley • USA
KEEP OFF THE GRASS see **RIGHT THAT FAILED, THE** • 1922
KEEP ON ROCKIN" see **SWEET TORONTO** • 1972
KEEP ON SMOKING, LADANYI see **TE CSAK PIPALJ LADANYI** • 1938
KEEP ON WALKING see **CAMMINACAMMINA** • 1983
KEEP OUR LADS HOME GOING see **KEEP THE HOME FIRES BURNING** • 1916
KEEP QUIET • 1912 • *Majestic* • USA
KEEP SHOOTING • 1942 • D'Arcy Harry • SHT • USA
KEEP SMILING • 1918 • *Field Elinor* • USA
KEEP SMILING • 1925 • Pratt Gilbert, Austin Albert • USA
KEEP SMILING • 1938 • Banks Monty • UKN, USA • SMILING ALONG (USA)
KEEP SMILING • 1938 • Leeds Herbert I. • USA • MISS FIX-IT (UKN)
KEEP TALKING, BABY • 1961 • Lefranc Guy • FRN
KEEP THE COOL BABY • 1967 • Harriton Chuck • ANS • USA
KEEP THE HOME FIRES BURNING • 1916 • Batley Ethyle • UKN • KEEP OUR LADS HOME GOING
KEEP TO THE RIGHT • 1920 • *Taliaferro Mabel* • USA
KEEP TO YOUR TRADE see **SKOMAKARE BLIV VID DIN LAST** • 1915
KEEP WAITING FOR ME see **ESPERAME MUCHO** • 1982
KEEP WALKING see **CAMMINACAMMINA** • 1983
KEEP YOUNG • 1955 • *O'Brien Dave* • SHT • USA
KEEP YOUR EYE ON PAISLEY • 1975 • Gormley Charles • DOC • UKN
KEEP YOUR FINGERS CROSSED see **CATCH ME A SPY** • 1971
KEEP YOUR GRIN UP • 1955 • Sparber I. • ANS • USA
KEEP YOUR MOUTH SHUT • 1944 • McLaren Norman, Dunning George • ANS • CND
KEEP YOUR POWDER DRY • 1944 • Buzzell Edward • USA • THERE WERE THREE OF US
KEEP YOUR SEATS PLEASE • 1936 • Banks Monty • UKN
KEEPER, THE • 1976 • Drake Tom • CND
KEEPER OF PROMISES, THE see **PAGADOR DE PROMESSAS, O** • 1961
KEEPER OF THE BEES • 1947 • Sturges John • USA
KEEPER OF THE BEES, THE • 1925 • Meehan James Leo • USA
KEEPER OF THE BEES, THE • 1935 • Cabanne W. Christy • USA
KEEPER OF THE DOOR • 1919 • Elvey Maurice • UKN
KEEPER OF THE FLAME • 1942 • Cukor George • USA
KEEPER OF THE FLOCK, THE • 1915 • *Brunette Fritzie* • USA
KEEPER OF THE GATE, THE • 1917 • Gerrard Douglas • SHT • USA
KEEPER OF THE LIGHT, THE • 1909 • Dawley J. Searle • USA
KEEPER OF THE LIGHT, THE • 1914 • *Ostriche Muriel* • USA
KEEPER OF THE LIONS • 1937 • *Lantz Walter (P)* • ANS • USA
KEEPERS see **SPOOK WHO SAT BY THE DOOR, THE** • 1973
KEEPERS, THE see **BRAIN EATERS, THE** • 1958
KEEPERS, THE (UKN) see **TETE CONTRE LES MURS, LA** • 1958
KEEPERS OF THE EARTH, THE see **BRAIN EATERS, THE** • 1958
KEEPERS OF THE FLOCK • 1913 • Brabin Charles J. • UKN
KEEPERS OF THE NIGHT (USA) see **NACHTWACHE** • 1949
KEEPERS OF YOUTH • 1931 • Bentley Thomas • UKN
KEEPING A HUSBAND • 1914 • *Ostriche Muriel* • USA
KEEPING AN EYE ON FATHER • 1912 • *Francis Alec B.* • USA
KEEPING COMPANY • 1930 • Buzzell Edward • SHT • USA
KEEPING COMPANY • 1940 • Simon S. Sylvan • USA
KEEPING FIT • 1942 • Lubin Arthur • SHT • USA
KEEPING HIS WORD • 1910 • *Imp* • USA
KEEPING HUSBANDS HOME • 1913 • Angeles Bert • USA
KEEPING IN SHAPE • 1942 • Roush Leslie • SHT • USA
KEEPING IT DARK • 1915 • Davey Horace • USA
KEEPING MABEL HOME • 1911 • *Trunnelle Mabel* • USA
KEEPING MAN INTERESTED • 1922 • Cooper George A. • UKN
KEEPING ON • 1982 • Kopple Barbara • TVM • USA
KEEPING TRACK • 1986 • Spry Robin • CND
KEEPING UP APPEARANCES • 1913 • Smiley Joseph • USA
KEEPING UP WITH HUBBY • 1913 • *Kinemacolor* • USA
KEEPING UP WITH KRAZY • 1962 • Deitch Gene • ANS • USA
KEEPING UP WITH THE JONES • 1915 • *Palmer H. J. (P)* • ASS • USA
KEEPNG UP WITH LIZZIE • 1921 • Ingraham Lloyd • USA
KEEPS RAININ' ALL THE TIME • 1934 • Fleischer Dave • ANS • USA
KEETJE TIPPEL • 1975 • Verhoeven Paul* • NTH • CATHY TIPPEL
KEGYELET • 1967 • Szabo Istvan • SHT • HNG • PIETY
KEHOE'S MARIMBA BAND • 1944 • *Columbia* • SHT • USA
KEHORMATAN • 1974 • Sandy Bobby • INN • HONOUR
KEHRAUS • 1984 • Muller H. Ch., Polt G. • FRG • CLEAN SWEEP
KEHRE ZURUCK! ALLES VERGEBEN! • 1915 • Mack Max • FRG
KEHRE ZURUCK! ALLES VERGEBEN! • 1929 • Schonfelder Erich • FRG
KEIHO 177 JO-FUJO KYOHAKU BOKOZAI • 1968 • Sakao Masanao • JPN • ARTICLE 177 OF THE CRIMINAL LAW
KEIJI MONOGATARI • 1982 • Watanabe Yusuke • JPN • DETECTIVE STORY
KEIKO • 1979 • Gagnon Claude • JPN
KEIMENDE SAAT • 1922 • Schall Heinz • FRG
KEIMENDES LEBEN see **FRAUEN, HUTET EURE MUTTERSCHAFT!** • 1925
KEIMENDES LEBEN 1 • 1918 • Jacoby Georg • FRG
KEIMENDES LEBEN 2 • 1918 • Jacoby Georg • FRG
KEIMENDES LEBEN 3 see **MORAL UND SINNLICHKEIT** • 1919
KEIN AERGER MIT CLEOPATRA • 1960 • Schneider Helmut • GDR
KEIN AUSKOMMEN MIT DEM EINKOMMEN • 1957 • Fredersdorf Herbert B. • FRG
KEIN, EIN HUND, EIN VAGABUND, EIN • 1934 • Rabenalt Arthur M. • FRG • VEILLEICHT WAR'S NUR EIN TRAUM ○ CHILD, A DOG, A VAGABOND, A
KEIN ENGEL IST SO REIN • 1950 • Weiss Helmut • FRG
KEIN ENGEL IST SO REIN • 1960 • Becker Wolfgang • FRG
KEIN HUSUNG • 1954 • Pohl Arthur • GDR
KEIN PLATZ FUR LIEBE • 1947 • Deppe Hans • GDR • NO PLACE FOR LOVE
KEIN PLATZ FUR WILDE TIERE • 1956 • Grzimek Bernard, Grzimek Michael • FRG • NO ROOM FOR WILD ANIMALS
KEINE ANGST, LIEBLING, ICH PASS SCHON AUF! • 1970 • Strahl Erwin • FRG
KEINE ANGST VOR GROSSEN TIEREN • 1953 • Erfurth Ulrich • FRG
KEINE ANGST VOR LIEBE • 1933 • Steinhoff Hans • FRG
KEINE ANGST VOR SCHWIEGERMUTTERN • 1954 • Engels Erich • FRG
KEINE FEIER OHNE MEYER • 1932 • Boese Carl • FRG
KEINE ZEIT FUR SCHWACHE STUNDEN • 1957 • Jugert Rudolf • AUS
KEINE ZEIT FUR TRANEN • 1984 • Bohm Hark • FRG • NO TIME FOR TEARS
KEINEN TAG OHNE DICH • 1933 • Behrendt Hans • FRG • WOVON SOLL DER SCHORNSTEIN RAUCHEN
KEINEN TAG OHNE DICH see **SO'N WINDHUND!** • 1931
KEIRAKU HICHO • 1928 • Kinugasa Teinosuke • JPN
KEIRIN SHONIN GYOJOKI • 1964 • Nishimura • JPN
KEIRO'S CAT • 1905 • Collins Alf • UKN • PUSSY'S BREAKFAST
KEISATSU-KAN • 1933 • Uchida Tomu • JPN
KEISATSU-KAN TO BORYOKU-DAN • 1959 • Ichikawa Kon • JPN • POLICE AND SMALL GANGSTERS
KEISATSU NIKKI • 1955 • Hisamatsu Seiji • JPN • POLICE DIARY
KEITH OF THE BORDER • 1918 • Smith Cliff • USA
KEITSIK • 1989 • Chan Jackie • HKG • MR. CANTON AND LADY ROSE ○ MIRACLE
KEJARLAH DAKU.. KAU KUTANGKAP • 1985 • Umam Chaerul • INN • RAMADHAN & RAMONA
KEJKLOVACKA • ANS • CZC
KEJSAREN • 1978 • Hagelback Josta • SWD • EMPEROR, THE
KEJSARN AV PORTUGALLIEN • 1944 • Molander Gustaf • SWD • EMPEROR OF PORTUGAL, THE
KEK BALVANY, A • 1931 • Lazar Lajos • HNG • BLUE IDOL, THE
KEKEDASHI JIDAI • 1947 • Saeki • JPN • TENDERFOOT DAYS
KEKKON • 1947 • Kinoshita Keisuke • JPN • MARRIAGE
KEKKON-GAKU NYUMON • 1930 • Ozu Yasujiro • JPN • INTRODUCTION TO MARRIAGE
KEKKON KOSHINKYOKU • 1951 • Ichikawa Kon • JPN • WEDDING MARCH
KEKKON NIJUSO • 1927 • Tasaka Tomotaka • JPN • DOUBLE MARRIAGE
KEKKON NO SEITAI • 1941 • Imai Tadashi • JPN • MARRIED LIFE ○ SITUATION OF MARRIAGE, THE
KEKKON SHIKI KEKKON SHIKI • 1963 • Nakamura Noboru • JPN • MARRIAGE CEREMONY
KEKKON SHIMASU • 1969 • Nakamura Noboru • JPN • MARRIAGE JAPANESE STYLE
KEKKON SHINAI ONNA • 1987 • Gosha Hideo • JPN • WOMAN WHO WOULDN'T MARRY, A
KEKKON SODAN • 1965 • Nakahira Ko • JPN • MARRIAGE CONSULTATION
KEKVERCSEK ERDEJEBEN, A • 1954 • Homoki-Nagy Istvan • HNG • FOREST OF THE FALCONS
KELANA • 1972 • Kadarisman S. • MLY
KELCY GETS HIS MAN • 1927 • Wyler William • SHT • USA
KELEKIS 50 YEARS IN THE CHIPS • 1982 • Lank Barry • SHT • CND
KELEPCELI MELEK • 1967 • Dinler Mehmet • TRK • HANDCUFFED ANGEL, THE
KELI MANDALA • 1990 • Nihalsingha D. B. • SLN
KELLNERIN ANNA, DIE • 1940 • Brauer Peter P. • FRG
KELLO • 1984 • Manttari Anssi • FNL • CLOCK, THE
KELLY • 1981 • Chapman Christopher • CND
KELLY AND ME • 1957 • Leonard Robert Z. • USA
KELLY COUNTRY • 1972 • Cooper Stuart • DOC • ASL
KELLY FROM THE EMERALD ISLE • 1913 • Warren Edward • USA
KELLY GANG, THE • 1910 • ASL • NED KELLY THE IRONCLAD BUSHRANGER ○ KELLY GANG OF OUTLAWS, THE ○ BAIL UP
KELLY GANG, THE • 1917 • *Mills Frank* • ASL
KELLY GANG, THE • 1920 • Southwell Harry • ASL
KELLY GANG OF OUTLAWS, THE see **KELLY GANG, THE** • 1910
KELLY IS MY NAME see **DARK HORSE, THE** • 1946
KELLY OF THE SECRET SERVICE • 1936 • Hill Robert F. • USA
KELLY TAKES HIS MISSUS TO SOUTHEND • 1913 • *Martin'S* • UKN
KELLY THE SECOND • 1936 • Meins Gus • USA
KELLY, U.S.A. • 1911 • *Atlas* • USA
KELLY'S GHOST • 1914 • *Crystal* • USA
KELLY'S HEROES • 1970 • Hutton Brian G. • USA, YGS • WARRIORS, THE
KELLYS OF TOBRUK, THE • 1942 • Kathner Rupert • ASL
KELP INDUSTRY, THE • 1913 • Sennett Mack • DOC • USA
KELUARGA SI COMAT • 1974 • Sattar Aziz • MLY • COMAT AND FAMILY
KELVANEY see **ROGUE COP** • 1954
KEMAL THE BOMB see **BOMBA KEMAL** • 1967
KEMAL, THE ENGLISHMAN see **INGILIZ KEMAL** • 1968
KEMANA HATI KAN KU BAWA • 1979 • Amir Yusaini • MLY • LOST HEART
KEMBANG KERTAS • 1985 • Rahardjo Slamet • INN • PAPER FLOWERS
KEMBANG LAYU • 1970 • Kadarisman S. • MLY • WITHERED
KEMBARA SENIMAN JALANAN • 1985 • MLY • WAYSIDE SINGERS
KEMBER SIAM • 1988 • Badul A. R. • MLY
KEMEK • 1970 • Gershuny Theodore • ITL, FRG
KEMEKO NO UTA • 1968 • Tanaka Yasuyoshi • JPN • ADORABLE IMP
KEMENYKALAP ES KRUMPLIORR • 1978 • Bacskai-Lauro Istvan • HNG • TOP HAT AND SPUDS NOSE
KEMIRA -DIARY OF A STRIKE • 1984 • Zubrycki Tom • DOC • ASL
KEMONO NO NEMURI • 1960 • Suzuki Seijun • JPN
KEMONOMICHI • 1965 • Sugawa Eizo • JPN • BEAST ALLEY (USA) ○ WAY OF THE BEAST, THE
KEMPO SAMURAI see **DOJO YABURI** • 1964
KEMPY see **WISE GIRLS** • 1929
KEMURI • 1925 • Ito Daisuke • JPN • SMOKE
KEN • 1964 • Misumi Kenji • JPN • SWORD, THE
KEN HALL • 1978 • Salvat Keith • DOC • ASL
KEN-KIESSE • 1982 • Mweze Nganguka • DCS • ZRE, FRN
KEN MURRAY SHOOTING STARS • 1979 • Murray Ken • USA
KEN WA SABAKU • 1924 • Ito Daisuke • JPN
KEN WA SHITTEITA • 1958 • Uchide Kokichi • JPN • SWORD AND LOVE
KENDENUP TODAY • 1923 • ASL
KENDO KIDS see **CHU-CHIEN SHAO-NIEN** • 1983
KENGO ARAKI MATAEMON • 1938 • Ito Daisuke • JPN • SWORDSMAN MATAEMON ARAKI
KENGURU, A • 1975 • Zsombolyai Janos • HNG • KANGAROO, THE
KENILWORTH • 1909 • Blackton J. Stuart (Spv) • USA
KENILWORTH CASTLE AND AMY ROBSART • 1926 • Elvey Maurice • UKN
KENJU NO OLITE • 1960 • JPN
KENJU YO SARABA • 1960 • Sugawa Eizo • JPN • GET 'EM ALL (USA)
KENKA ELEGY see **KENKA SEREJII** • 1966
KENKA SEREJII • 1966 • Suzuki Seijun • JPN • KENKA ELEGY ○ ELEGY FOR A QUARREL
KENKA TARO • 1960 • Masuda Toshio • JPN • TOUGH GUY
KENNEDY SQUARE • 1916 • Drew Sidney • USA
KENNEDY THE GREAT • 1939 • Roberts Charles E. • SHT • USA
KENNEDY'S CASTLE • 1938 • Goodwins Leslie • SHT • USA
KENNEL MURDER CASE, THE • 1933 • Curtiz Michael • USA
KENNER • 1968 • Sekely Steve • USA • YEAR OF THE CRICKET
KENNST DU DAS LAND • 1931 • David Constantin J. • FRG, ITL • SALTARELLO
KENNWORT MACHIN • 1939 • Waschneck Erich • FRG
KENNWORT: REIHER • 1964 • Jugert Rudolf • FRG
KENNY & CO. • 1976 • Coscarelli Don • USA
KENNY ROGERS AS THE GAMBLER • 1980 • Lowry Dick • USA • GAMBLER, THE
KENNY ROGERS AS THE GAMBLER, PART II -THE ADVENTURE CONTINUES • 1983 • Lowry Dick • TVM • USA
KENNY ROGERS AS THE GAMBLER PART III: THE LEGEND CONTINUES • 1987 • Lowry Dick • TVM • USA
KENNY'S LOVE • 1987 • Woods Rowan • SHT • ASL
KENO BATES, LIAR • 1915 • Hart William S., Smith Cliff • USA
KENRANTARU SATSUJIN • 1951 • Kato Bin • JPN • BRILLIANT MURDER
KENSETSU NO HITOBITO • 1935 • Ito Daisuke • JPN • PEOPLE'S BUILDING
KENSHIN • 1961 • Tanaka Shigeo • JPN • HER DEVOTION
KENSINGTON MYSTERY, THE • 1924 • Croise Hugh • UKN • AFFAIR OF DARTMOOR TERRACE, THE
KENT CHRONICLES, THE see **BASTARD, THE** • 1978
KENT OIL REFINERY, THE • 1954 • Pickering Peter, Ingram John, Holmes J. B. • DOC • UKN
KENT STATE • 1981 • Goldstone James • TVM • USA
KENT THE FIGHTING MAN • 1916 • Coleby A. E. • UKN
KENTAUROK • 1979 • Zalakevicius Vitautus, Szabo Gyula • HNG, USS, CZC • CENTAURS, THE ○ KENTAVRY
KENTAVRY see **KENTAUROK** • 1979
KENTERING • 1932 • Hin Jan • NTH • TURN OF THE TIDE
KENTISH INDUSTRIES • 1913 • Pearson George • DOC • UKN
KENTON'S HEIR • 1913 • *Carlyle Francis* • USA
KENTUCKIAN, THE • 1908 • McCutcheon Wallace • USA
KENTUCKIAN, THE • 1955 • Lancaster Burt • USA
KENTUCKIANS, THE • 1921 • Maigne Charles • USA
KENTUCKY • 1938 • Butler David • USA
KENTUCKY BELLE • 1931 • Lantz Walter, Nolan William • ANS • USA
KENTUCKY BLUE STREAK • 1935 • Johnston Raymond K. • USA • BLUE STREAK, THE (UKN)
KENTUCKY BROTHERS • 1917 • *Puritan* • USA
KENTUCKY CINDERELLA, A • 1917 • Julian Rupert • USA
KENTUCKY COLONEL, THE • 1920 • Seiter William A. • USA
KENTUCKY COURAGE see **LITTLE SHEPHERD OF KINGDOM COME, THE** • 1928
KENTUCKY DAYS • 1923 • Soloman David • USA
KENTUCKY DERBY, THE • 1922 • Baggot King • USA • SUBURBAN HANDICAP, THE ○ THEY'RE OFF
KENTUCKY EPISODE, AN • 1915 • Reehm George E. • USA
KENTUCKY FEUD • 1905 • *Bitzer Billy (Ph)* • USA
KENTUCKY FEUD, A • 1912 • *Rex* • USA
KENTUCKY FEUD, THE • 1913 • Russell Martha • USA
KENTUCKY FOES • 1913 • *Hale Alan* • USA
KENTUCKY FRIED MOVIE, THE • 1977 • Landis John • USA
KENTUCKY GENTLEMAN, A • 1914 • *Kerrigan J. Warren* • USA
KENTUCKY GIRL • 1912 • Buel Kenean • USA
KENTUCKY GIRL, A • 1911 • *Yankee* • USA

KENTUCKY GIRL, A • 1915 • *French Charles K.* • USA
KENTUCKY HANDICAP • 1926 • Brown Harry J. • USA
KENTUCKY IDYL, A • 1915 • Jaccard Jacques • USA
KENTUCKY JUBILEE • 1951 • Ormond Ron • USA
KENTUCKY KERNELS • 1934 • Stevens George • USA • TRIPLE TROUBLE (UKN)
KENTUCKY LUCK see **RACING ROMANCE** • 1926
KENTUCKY MINSTRELS • 1934 • Baxter John • UKN
KENTUCKY MOONSHINE • 1938 • Butler David • USA • THREE MEN AND A GIRL (UKN)
KENTUCKY PIONEER, A • 1910 • *Selig* • USA
KENTUCKY PLANTER, A • 1909 • *Bison* • USA
KENTUCKY PRIDE • 1925 • Ford John • USA
KENTUCKY RIFLE • 1956 • Hittelman Carl K. • USA
KENTUCKY ROMANCE, A • 1914 • *Kb* • USA
KENTUCKY WOMAN • 1982 • Doniger Walter • TVM • USA
KENYA • 1962 • Leacock Richard (c/d) • DOC • USA • KENYA, SOUTH AFRICA
KENYA -COUNTRY OF TREASURE see **SYNDICATE, THE** • 1968
KENYA, SOUTH AFRICA see **KENYA** • 1962
KENZI • 1947 • Ivernel Vicky • FRN, MRC • MON TRESOR
KEOMA • 1976 • Castellari Enzo G. • ITL • VIOLENT BREED, THE (UKN)
KEPI, LE • 1905 • Blache Alice • FRN
KEPT • 1968 • Anders Jan • USA
KEPT HUSBANDS • 1931 • Bacon Lloyd • USA
KEPVADASZOK • 1985 • Szurdi Andras, Szurdi Miklos • HNG • PICTURE HUNTERS, THE
KERANDA JINGGA • 1970 • Rojik Omar • MLY • CRIMSON COFFIN
KEREC THE KEEN-WITTED • 1969 • Gale Joze • YGS
KERESZTELO • 1968 • Gaal Istvan • HNG • BAPTISM ○ CHRISTENING PARTY
KERL LIEBT MICH -UND DAS SOLL ICH GLAUBEN, DER • 1959 • Gosov Marran • FRG
KERMES see **KIRMES** • 1960
KERMESSE • 1958 • Martinez Solares Gilberto • MXC
KERMESSE AUX CHANSONS • 1947-51 • Verneuil Henri • SHT • FRN
KERMESSE FANTASTIQUE • 1947 • Geesink Joop • ANM • NTH
KERMESSE HEROIQUE, LA • 1935 • Feyder Jacques • FRN • CARNIVAL IN FLANDERS (UKN)
KERMESSE ROUGE, LA • 1946 • Mesnier Paul • FRN
KERNEL NUTT • 1916 • Williams C. Jay, Dickson Charles • SHS • USA
KERNEL NUTT AND HIGH SHOES • 1916 • Williams C. Jay • SHT • USA
KERNEL NUTT AND PRINCE TANGO • 1916 • Dickson Charles • SHT • USA
KERNEL NUTT FLIRTS WITH WIFIE • 1916 • Williams C. Jay • SHT • USA
KERNEL NUTT IN MEXICO • 1916 • Williams C. Jay • SHT • USA
KERNEL NUTT, THE FOOTMAN • 1916 • Williams C. Jay • SHT • USA
KERNEL NUTT, THE JANITOR • 1916 • Williams C. Jay • SHT • USA
KERNEL NUTT, THE PIANO TUNER • 1916 • Dickson Charles • SHT • USA
KERNEL NUTT WINS A WIFE • 1916 • Williams C. Jay • SHT • USA
KERNEL NUTT'S $100 BILL • 1916 • Williams C. Jay • SHT • USA
KERNEL NUTT'S MUSICAL SHIRT • 1916 • Williams C. Jay • SHT • USA
KERNELS OF CORN • 1948 • Moore Harold James • SHT • USA
KEROUAC • 1985 • Antonelli John • DOC • USA
KERRI CHEARTON IN JUNGLE-TUNGLE • 1930 • *Asfi* • SHT • UKN
KERRY GOW, THE • 1912 • Olcott Sidney • USA
KERTES HAZAK UTCAJA • 1962 • Fejer Tamas • HNG • LOVE IN THE SUBURB ○ GARDEN SUBURB
KES • 1969 • Loach Kenneth • UKN
KESA AND MORITO see **KESA TO MORITO** • 1939
KESA TO MORITO • 1939 • Inagaki Hiroshi • JPN • KESA AND MORITO
KESAKAPINA • 1969 • Pakkasvirta Jaakko • FNL • SUMMER REBELLION
KESALLA KELLO 5 • 1963 • Kivikoski Erkko • FNL • IN SUMMER AT FIVE O'CLOCK ○ THIS SUMMER AT 5
KESAN MAKU • 1975 • Tolonen Asko • FNL • TASTE OF SUMMER, A
KESERU IGAZSAG • 1956 • Varkonyi Zoltan • HNG • BITTER TRUTH
KESERU MEZESHETEK • 1939 • Balogh Bela • HNG • BITTER HONEYMOON (USA)
KESHER HAURANIUM see **A CHI TOCCA...TOCCA!** • 1978
KESHIN • 1987 • Higashi Yoichi • JPN • GHOST
KESHTYE NOAH • 1968 • Parvisi Khosrow • IRN • NOAH'S SHIP
KESONCI • 1965 • Tanovic Bakir • YGS • HOW BRIDGES ARE BORN
KESSEN • 1944 • Yoshimura Kozaburo, Hagiyama Teruo • JPN • DECISIVE BATTLE
KESSEN NANKAI NO DAIKAIJU • 1970 • Honda Inoshiro • JPN • YOG -MONSTER FROM SPACE (USA) ○ NANKAI NO DAIKAIJU ○ SPACE AMOEBA
KESSEN NO OZORA E • 1943 • Watanabe Kunio • JPN • TOWARD THE DECISIVE BATTLE IN THE SKY
KESYTTOMAT VELJEKSET • 1970 • Kivikoski Erkko • FNL • BROTHERS, THE ○ VELJEKSET
KET ARCKEP • 1965 • Kovacs Andras • DCS • HNG • TWO PORTRAITS
KET BORS OKROCSKE • 1955 • Macskassy Gyula • ANS • HNG • TWO LITTLE MAGIC OXEN ○ MAGIC OXEN ○ TWO MAGIC BULLS, THE
KET ELHATAROZAS • 1976 • Gyongyossy Imre, Kabay Barna • HNG • QUITE ORDINARY LIFE, A ○ TWO DECISIONS
KET EMELET BOLDOGSAG • 1960 • Hersko Janos • HNG • HOUSE FULL OF HAPPINESS, A ○ HOUSEFUL OF BLISS, A
KET FELIDO A POKOLBAN • 1961 • Fabri Zoltan • HNG • LAST GOAL, THE (UKN) ○ TWO HALF-TIMES IN HELL ○ ELEVEN MEN
KET FENYKEP • 1975 • Suranyi Andras • HNG • TWO PHOTOGRAPHS
KET FOGOLY • 1939 • Sekely Steve • HNG • TWO PRISONERS
KET LANY AZ UTCAN • 1939 • De Toth Andre • HNG • TWO GIRLS OF THE STREET
KET VALLOMAS • 1957 • Keleti Marton • HNG • TWO CONFESSIONS
KETAREV ASSZONY • 1920 • von Bolvary Geza • HNG
KETCHAM AND KILLEM • 1913 • *Mace Fred* • USA
KETIKA MUSIM SEMI TIBA • 1987 • Sandy Bobby • INN • WHEN SPRING COMES
KETLELKU ASSZORY, A • 1917 • Korda Alexander • HNG • WOMAN WITH TWO SOULS, THE
KETO AND KOTE • 1954 • Tabliashvili V.
KETSZER KETTO NEHA 5 • 1954 • Revesz Gyorgy • HNG • TWO TIMES TWO ARE SOMETIMES FIVE
KETSZIVU FERFI, A • 1916 • Korda Alexander • HNG • MAN WITH TWO HEARTS, THE ○ DOUBLE-HEARTED MAN, A
KETTE DER SCHULD, DIE • 1921 • Osten Franz • FRG
KETTE KLIRRT, DIE • 1923 • Stein Paul L. • FRG
KETTE VON PERLEN UND ABENTEUERN, EINE see **WHITECHAPEL** • 1920
KETTEVALT MENNYEZET • 1981 • Gabor Pal • HNG • WASTED LIVES
KETTLE CREEK see **MOUNTAIN JUSTICE** • 1930
KETTLES IN THE OZARKS, THE • 1956 • Lamont Charles • USA
KETTLES ON OLD MACDONALD'S FARM, THE • 1957 • Vogel Virgil W. • USA
KETTO • 1967 • Masuda Toshio • JPN • ENDLESS DUEL, THE
KETTO GANRYU JIMA • 1955 • Inagaki Hiroshi • JPN • SAMURAI (PART III) (USA) ○ DUEL AT GANRYU ISLAND ○ MUSASHI AND KOJIRO
KETTO HANNYA-ZAKA • 1943 • Ito Daisuke • JPN • DUEL AT HANNYA-ZAKA
KETTO KACHIDOKIBASHI • 1958 • Namiki Kyotaro • JPN
KETTO KAGIYA NO TSUJI • 1951 • Mori Issei • JPN • DUEL AT THE KEYMAKER'S CORNER ○ DUEL AT KAGIYA CORNER, THE
KETTU JA KARHU • 1973 • Partanen Heikki, Rautoma Riitta • FNL • FOX AND BEAR
KEUSCHE GELIEBTE, DIE • 1940 • Tourjansky Victor • FRG
KEUSCHE JOSEF, DER • 1930 • Jacoby Georg • FRG
KEUSCHE JOSEF, DER • 1953 • Boese Carl • FRG
KEUSCHE KOKOTTE, DIE • 1929 • Seitz Franz • FRG
KEUSCHE LEBEMANN, DER • 1952 • Boese Carl • FRG
KEUSCHE SUNDERIN, DIE • 1943 • Stockel Joe • FRG
KEUSCHE SUSANNE, DIE • 1926 • Eichberg Richard • FRG • CHASTE SUSANNE ○ VIRTUOUS SUSANNAH, THE
KEVIN ALEC • 1977 • Shaffer Beverly • DOC • CND
KEVIN AND CHERYL • 1972 • Thornhill Michael • DOC • ASL
KEW GARDENS • 1937 • Leacock Philip • DCS • UKN
KEWI • 1949 • Bose Debaki • IND • POET, THE
KEY see **KAGI** • 1974
KEY, THE • Shuval Menakhein • ISR
KEY, THE • 1913 • *Francis Alec B.* • USA
KEY, THE • 1916 • Hollingsworth Alfred • SHT • USA
KEY, THE • 1934 • Curtiz Michael • USA • HIGH PERIL
KEY, THE • 1958 • Reed Carol • UKN
KEY, THE • 1968 • Atamanov Lev • ANM • USS
KEY, THE • 1977 • Godfrey Bob • ANS • UKN
KEY, THE • 1987 • Fourouzesh Ibrahim • IRN
KEY, THE see **SLEUTEL, DE** • 1963
KEY, THE see **KLJUC** • 1965
KEY, THE see **KLIC** • 1971
KEY, THE see **CHIAVE, LA** • 1984
KEY, THE (USA) see **KAGI** • 1959
KEY AND THE RING, THE see **NYCKELN OCH RINGEN** • 1947
KEY CLUB WIVES • 1968 • Clay Adam? • USA • WIVES, THE
KEY EXCHANGE • 1985 • Kellman Barnet • USA
KEY LARGO • 1948 • Huston John • USA
KEY MAN • 1955 • Guilfoyle Paul • USA • LIFE AT STAKE, A (UKN)
KEY MAN, THE • 1957 • Tully Montgomery • UKN
KEY OF FATE, THE see **TROOPER O'BRIEN** • 1928
KEY OF LIFE, THE • 1910 • *Morin Pilar* • USA
KEY OF THE WORLD, THE • 1918 • Leigh J. L. V. • UKN
KEY TO A FORTUNE, THE • 1915 • *Kalem* • USA
KEY TO HARMONY • 1935 • Walker Norman • UKN • CHANCE AT HEAVEN
KEY TO MURDER, THE • 1956 • *Dollar Lynn* • USA
KEY TO PARADISE see **NOGLEN TIL PARADIS** • 1970
KEY TO POSSESSION, THE • 1915 • *Ellis Robert* • USA
KEY TO POWER, THE • 1918 • Parke William • USA
KEY TO REBECCA, THE • 1985 • Hemmings David • TVM • USA
KEY TO SCOTLAND, THE • 1935 • Grierson Marion • DOC • UKN
KEY TO THE CITY • 1949 • Sidney George • USA
KEY TO THE FUTURE • 1966 • Short Anthony • UKN
KEY TO THE MYSTERY, THE • 1915 • *Picture Playhouse Film* • USA
KEY TO THE PAST, THE • 1915 • Bartlett Charles • USA
KEY TO YESTERDAY, THE • 1914 • *Blackwell Carlyle* • USA
KEY UNDER THE MAT, THE • 1908 • *Lubin* • USA
KEY WEST • 1972 • Leacock Philip • TVM • USA
KEY WITNESS • 1947 • Lederman D. Ross • USA
KEY WITNESS • 1960 • Karlson Phil • USA
KEYBOARD STRATEGY, A • 1915 • Van Deusen Courtlandt • USA
KEYHOLE, THE • 1933 • Curtiz Michael • USA
KEYHOLE, THE see **NOGLEHULLET** • 1974
KEYHOLE KATIE • 1933 • Lamont Charles • SHT • USA
KEYS, THE • 1917 • *Essanay* • USA
KEYS, THE see **SCHLUSSEL, DIE** • 1974
KEYS OF HEAVEN, THE • 1908 • Gilbert Arthur • UKN
KEYS OF HEAVEN, THE • 1928 • Freund Karl • UKN
KEYS OF THE KINGDOM, THE • 1944 • Stahl John M. • USA
KEYS OF THE RIGHTEOUS, THE • 1918 • Storm Jerome • USA
KEYS TO FREEDOM • 1989 • Feke Steve • USA
KEYS TO HAPPINESS see **KLYUCHI SHCHASTYA** • 1913
KEYSTONE HOTEL • 1935 • Staub Ralph • USA
KEZBAN • 1968 • Aksoy Orhan • TRK
KEZENFOGVA • 1963 • Hersko Anna • HNG • HAND IN HAND
KEZUNKBE VETTUK A BEKE UGYET • 1951 • Jancso Miklos (c/d) • SHT • HNG • WE TOOK OVER THE CAUSE OF PEACE
KGB -THE SECRET WAR see **LETHAL** • 1984
KGOD • 1980 • Friedberg Rick • USA • PRAY TV
KH4 • 1970 • Schoerstein John • DCS • UKN
KHAAN DOST • 1976 • *Kapoor Raj* • IND
KHABARDA! • 1931 • Chiaureli Mikhail • USS • OUT OF THE WAY!
KHADRA AND SINDBAD THE SOUTHERNER see **KHADRA WA SINDIBAD EL KHEBLI** • 1952
KHADRA WA SINDIBAD EL KHEBLI • 1952 • Ziada El Sayad • EGY • KHADRA AND SINDBAD THE SOUTHERNER
KHAINA, AL- • 1965 • el Sheikh Kamal • EGY • INFIDELE, L'
KHAIR WA ASH-SHARR, AL- • 1946 • Hilmy Ibrahim Hassan • EGY • BIEN ET LE MAL, LE
KHAIT' AR-RAFI, AL- • 1971 • Barakat Henry • EGY • FIL FIN, LE
KHAJURAHO ETERNAL • Chaudhri Amin • USA
KHAK • 1973 • Kimiyaei Massoud • IRN • EARTH, THE
KHAMOSH • 1985 • Vinod Vidhu • IND
KHAMSIN • 1982 • Waxman Daniel • ISR • HAMSIN ○ HOT WIND ○ EASTERN WIND
KHAN • 1975 • Haller Daniel • TVM • USA
KHAN AL-KHALILI • 1967 • Salem Atef • EGY
KHAN ASPAROUKH • 1981 • Staikov Lyudmil • BUL
KHANDAR • 1983 • Sen Mrinal • IND • RUINS, THE
KHANDOBACHI AAN • 1968 • Nayak Prabhakar • IND
KHANE-KHARAB • 1975 • Karimi Nosrattolah • IRN • RUINED
KHANEH-E-KHODA • 1967 • Moghadam Jalal • DOC • IRN • GOD'S MANSION
KHANEH SIAH AST • 1962 • Farrohzad Forough • IRN • HOUSE IS BLACK, THE
KHAN'S COMMAND see **FARMAN-E-KHAN** • 1967
KHARIJ • 1983 • Sen Mrinal • IND • CASE IS CLOSED, THE ○ KHARJI
KHARJI see **KHARIJ** • 1983
KHARTOUM • 1966 • Dearden Basil • UKN
KHASAN-ARBAKESH • 1967 • Kimyagarov Boris • USS
KHATABALA • 1971 • Yerzinkyan Yuri • USS • COMMOTION
KHAT'AWAT NAHWA AS-SALAM • 1975 • Nahhass Hashim An- • SHT • EGY • PAS VERS LA PAIX
KHATEM SULEIMAN • 1947 • Ramzi Hassan • EGY • SOLOMON'S RING
KHATIB MAMA • 1971 • Wahab Fatin Abdel • EGY • FIANCE DE MA MERE, LE
KHAVAH • 1919 • Davenport Charles E. • USA
KHAVAL GATHA see **KHAYAL GATHA** • 1989
KHAWF, AL- • 1972 • Marzouk Said • EGY • PEUR, LA
KHAYAL GATHA • 1989 • Shahani Kumar • DOC • IND • KHAYAL SAGA, THE (UKN) ○ KHAVAL GATHA
KHAYAL SAGA, THE (UKN) see **KHAYAL GATHA** • 1989
KHAYYAT' AS-SAYYIDAT • 1970 • Salem Atef • SYR • COUTURIER DES DAMES, LE
KHAZ-PUSH see **HAZ-PUSH** • 1928
KHAZAKKI see **KASAKI** • 1961
KHAZDENI ZA TRI MORYA (USS) see **PARDESI** • 1957
KHEMAIS TARNAN • 1964 • Khalifa Omar • DCS • TNS
KHEVSUR BALLAD see **KHEVSURSKAYA BALLADA** • 1965
KHEVSURSKAYA BALLADA • 1965 • Managadze Shota • USS • KHEVSUR BALLAD ○ BALLAD OF KHEVSUR ○ HEVSUR BALLAD, THE ○ HEVSURSKAIA BALLADA ○ LAST VENGEANCE, THE ○ LAST VENDETTA, THE
KHEYA • 1967 • Gosthi Rupak • IND • FERRY
KHILYADA ZHERAVI • 1968 • Kovachev Hristo • DOC • BUL • THOUSAND CRANES, A
KHLEB • 1918 • Boleslawski Richard, Sushkevich Boris • USS • BREAD
KHLEB I ROZI • 1960 • Filippov Fyodor • USS • BREAD AND ROSES
KHLIFA AL-AGRAA • 1968 • Ben Halima Hamouda • TNS • KHLIFA LA TEIGNE
KHLIFA LA TEIGNE see **KHLIFA AL-AGRAA** • 1968
KHMUROE UTRO • 1959 • Roshal Grigori, Andjaparidze Marija • USS • GLOOMY MORNING, A ○ BLEAK MORNING ○ GREY DAWN
KHO CHUE SUTHEE SAM SEE CHAT • 1990 • Supakanj J. D., Amatyakul Kriangkrai, Kicharoen Kiat, Pun-lom Vachara • THL
KHODAHAFEZ TEHRAN • 1967 • Khachikian Samouel • IRN • GOODBYE TEHRAN
KHOMSAN • 1990 • Siam Jazz • THL • HOLY SPIRITS
KHON PHUU KAOW • 1979 • Kounavudhi Vichit • THL • MOUNTAIN PEOPLE, THE ○ KHON POO KHAO
KHON POO KHAO see **KHON PHUU KAOW** • 1979
KHON SONG CHAO • 1989 • Siam Jazz • THL
KHOON-E-NAHAG • 1953 • Sahu Kishore • IND • HAMLET (USA)
KHOON-KA-KHOON • 1935 • Modi Sohrab • IND • HAMLET (USA) ○ KHUN KAKHUN ○ BLOOD FOR BLOOD
KHORDA see **DEATHMASTER, THE** • 1972
KHOROOS • 1973 • Gharib Shapoor • IRN • CLOCK, THE
KHOSHGELE GHAHRAMAN • 1967 • Jourak Fereydoun • IRN • BEAUTIFUL HERO, THE
KHOUROUG MIN EL GUANA, EL • 1967 • Mulficar Mahmoud • EGY • DRIVEN OUT OF PARADISE
KHOUROUJ 67, AL- • 1968 • Siam Ali • JRD • EXODUS
KHOVANSCHINA see **KHOVANSHCHINA** • 1959
KHOVANSHCHINA • 1959 • Stroyeva Vera • USS • KHOVANSCHINA
KHOZHDENIYE ZA TRI MORYA see **PARDESI** • 1957
KHRISHNA ARJUN • 1935 • IND
KHRONIKA ODNOGO DNIA • 1963 • Zalakevicius Vitautus • USS • CHRONICLE OF A SINGLE DAY ○ CHRONICLE OF ONE DAY
KHRONIKA PIKIRUYUSHCHEVO BOMBARDIROVSHCHIKA • 1968 • Birman Naum • USS • STORY OF A DIVE BOMBER, THE

KHRUSTALNYY BASHMACHOK • 1961 • Rou Aleksandr, Zakharov Rostislav • USS • CINDERELLA (USA) ○ GLASS SLIPPER, THE ○ GRUSTAINI BASHMACHOK
KHUBSURAT BALA • 1934 • Madhok D. N. • IND • BEAUTIFUL GIRL
KHULUD • 1948 • Zulficar Izzeddine • EGY • IMMORTALITY
KHUN-E-NAHAK • 1928 • *Excelsior* • IND • HAMLET (USA)
KHUN KAKHUN see **KHOON-KA-KHOON** • 1935
KHUN-SA THE OPIUM EMPEROR • 1983 • Srichue Siwat • THL • OPIUM LORD, THE
KHVESKA • 1920 • Ivanovsky Alexander • USS
KHWAB-E-HASTI • 1934 • Masteri Homi • IND • MAGIC FLUTE (USA)
KHYBER PATROL • 1954 • Friedman Seymour • USA
KI BESZEL ITT SZERELEMROL?! • 1980 • Bacso Peter • HNG • LET'S TALK ABOUT LOVE
KI NO KAWA • 1966 • Nakamura Noboru • JPN • KII RIVER, THE ○ KI RIVER
KI RIVER see **KI NO KAWA** • 1966
KIA see **EYE OF THE EAGLE II** • 1989
KIALLITAS KEPEI, EGY • 1954 • Jancso Miklos • SHT • HNG • PICTURES AT AN EXHIBITION
KIALTAS ES KIALTAS • 1988 • Kezdi-Kovacs Zsolt • HNG • CRY AND CRY AGAIN
KIALTO • 1964 • Meszaros Marta • DCS • HNG • PROCLAMATION
KIBA OKAMINOSUKE JIGOKUGIRI • 1967 • Gosha Hideo • JPN • KIBA OKAMINOSUKE'S SWORD OF HELL
KIBA OKAMINOSUKE'S SWORD OF HELL see **KIBA OKAMINOSUKE JIGOKUGIRI** • 1967
KIBITZER, THE • 1930 • Sloman Edward • USA • BUSYBODY (UKN)
KIBO NO AOZORA • 1960 • Kurata Fumindo • JPN • HOPE OF BLUE SKY
KIBO NO SEISHUN • 1942 • Yamamoto Kajiro • JPN • HOPE OF YOUTH, THE
KICHIGAI BURAKU • 1957 • Shibuya Minoru • JPN • UNBALANCED WHEEL, THE
KICHIKU • 1978 • Nomura Yoshitaro • JPN • POSSESSED
KICK, THE • 1983 • van Elst Gerrit • DOC • NTH
KICK BACK, THE • 1922 • Paul Val • USA
KICK-BOXER see **GOROTSUKI** • 1968
KICK BOXER see **KICKBOXER** • 1989
KICK IN • 1917 • Fitzmaurice George • USA
KICK IN • 1922 • Fitzmaurice George • USA
KICK IN • 1931 • Wallace Richard • USA
KICK IN HIGH LIFE, THE • 1920 • Ray Albert, Herman Al • SHT • USA
KICK IN THE BACK see **TADYAK SA LIKOD** • 1968
KICK IN TIME, A • 1940 • Fleischer Dave • ANS • USA
KICK ME • 1975 • Swarthe Robert • USA
KICK ME I'M BILL BAILEY • 1905 • Redfern Jasper • UKN
KICK OFF, THE • 1926 • Ruggles Wesley • USA
KICK-OFF!, THE see **KICKOFF, THE** • 1931
KICK-OFF, THE see **GRIDIRON FLASH** • 1934
KICK-OUT, THE • 1915 • Thornby George T. • USA
KICK START • 1987 • Sandford Charles • SHT • ASL
KICK START see **AFRAID TO DANCE** • 1988
KICKAPOO JUICE • 1944 • Swift Howard • ANS • USA
KICKBOXER • 1989 • Worth David • USA • KICK BOXER
KICKED IN THE KITCHEN • 1917 • Hutchinson Craig • SHT • USA
KICKED OUT • 1917 • De Haven Carter • SHT • USA
KICKED OUT • 1918 • Roach Hal • SHT • USA
KICKIN' THE CONGA 'ROUND • 1942 • Fleischer Dave • ANS • USA
KICKIN' THE CROWN AROUND • 1933 • White Sam • USA
KICKING THE GERM OUT OF GERMANY • 1918 • Roach Hal • SHT • USA
KICKING THE MOON AROUND • 1938 • Forde Walter • UKN • PLAYBOY, THE (USA) ○ MILLIONAIRE MERRY-GO-ROUND
KICKOFF, THE • 1931 • Stevens George • SHT • USA • KICK-OFF!, THE
KICKS • 1985 • Wiard William • TVM • USA
KICMA • 1976 • Gilic Vlatko • YGS • BACKBONE ○ GASP ○ ASPHYXIA
KICO • 1951-52 • Vukotic Dusan • ASS • YGS
KICSI, DE NAGYON EROS • 1989 • Grunwalsky Ferenc • HNG • LITTLE, BUT VERY STRONG ○ LITTLE BUT TOUGH
KICSODA ON? • 1985 • Bokor Pierre • MTV • HNG
KID, THE • 1910 • Powell Frank • USA
KID, THE • 1913 • *Fisher Kate* • USA
KID, THE • 1916 • North Wilfred • USA
KID, THE • 1921 • Chaplin Charles • USA
KID, THE see **PUSTIUL** • 1962
KID AND THE COWBOY, THE • 1919 • Eason B. Reeves • SHT • USA
KID AND THE SLEUTH, THE • 1912 • *Baggot King* • USA
KID AUTO RACES AT VENICE • 1914 • Lehrman Henry • USA
KID BLUE • 1973 • Frawley James • USA
KID BOOTS • 1926 • Tuttle Frank • USA
KID BROTHER • 1956 • Hammid Alexander • USA
KID BROTHER • 1968 • Buenaventura Augusto • PHL
KID BROTHER, THE • 1927 • Wilde Ted • USA
KID BROTHER, THE • 1988 • Gagnon Claude • CND
KID CAME BACK, THE • 1919 • *Klever Pictures* • SHT • USA
KID CANFIELD THE REFORM GAMBLER • 1922 • *Canfield Kid* • USA
KID CANFIELD: THE REFORMED GAMBLER • 1912 • Davis Ulysses • USA
KID COLOSSUS, THE (UKN) see **ROOGIE'S BUMP** • 1954
KID COLTER • 1985 • O'Malley David • USA
KID COMES BACK, THE • 1938 • Eason B. Reeves • USA • DON'T PULL YOUR PUNCHES (UKN)
KID COURAGEOUS • 1935 • Bradbury Robert North • USA
KID CREOLE AND THE COCONUTS: LIVE IN CONCERT "AT THE RITZ" NEW YORK • 1982 • Dubin Jay • USA
KID DYNAMITE • 1943 • Fox Wallace • USA • QUEEN OF BROADWAY
KID FOR TWO FARTHINGS, A • 1955 • Reed Carol • UKN
KID FROM AMARILLO, THE • 1951 • Nazarro Ray • USA • SILVER CHAINS (UKN)
KID FROM ARIZONA, THE • 1931 • Horner Robert J. • USA
KID FROM BORNEO • 1933 • McGowan Robert • SHT • USA
KID FROM BROKEN GUN, THE • 1952 • Sears Fred F. • USA
KID FROM BROOKLYN, THE • 1946 • McLeod Norman Z. • USA
KID FROM CANADA, THE • 1957 • Mander Kay • UKN
KID FROM CLEVELAND, THE • 1949 • Kline Herbert • USA
KID FROM COLLEGE see **BAND PLAYS ON, THE** • 1934
KID FROM GOWER GULCH, THE • 1950 • Drake Oliver • USA
KID FROM KANSAS, THE • 1941 • Nigh William • USA
KID FROM KOKOMO, THE • 1939 • Seiler Lewis • USA • ORPHAN OF THE RING, THE (UKN)
KID FROM LEFT FIELD, THE • 1953 • Jones Harmon • USA
KID FROM LEFT FIELD, THE • 1979 • Aldrich Robert • TVM • USA
KID FROM MARS, THE • 1961 • Kneitel Seymour • ANS • USA
KID FROM NOT-SO-BIG, THE • 1978 • Crain William • TVM • USA
KID FROM NOWHERE, THE • 1982 • Bridges Beau • TVM • USA
KID FROM SANTA FE, THE • 1940 • Johnston Raymond K. • USA
KID FROM SPAIN, THE • 1932 • McCarey Leo • USA
KID FROM TEXAS, THE • 1939 • Simon S. Sylvan • USA
KID FROM TEXAS, THE • 1950 • Neumann Kurt • USA • TEXAS KID, OUTLAW (UKN)
KID FROM THE KLONDYKE • 1911 • Shaw Harold • USA
KID GALAHAD • 1937 • Curtiz Michael • USA • BATTLING BELLHOP
KID GALAHAD • 1962 • Karlson Phil • USA
KID GLOVE KILLER • 1942 • Zinnemann Fred • USA • ALONG CAME MURDER
KID GLOVE KISSES • 1932 • Edwards Harry J. • SHT • USA
KID GLOVES • 1929 • Enright Ray • USA
KID GLOVES see **SPLIT DECISIONS** • 1988
KID HAYSEED • 1928 • Lamont Charles • SHT • USA
KID, HUWAG KANG SUSUKO • 1988 • Gallaga Peque • PHL • DON'T GIVE UP
KID IL MONELLO DEL WEST • 1973 • Amoroso Roberto • ITL
KID-ING THE LANDLORD • 1920 • Davey Horace • SHT • USA
KID IS CLEVER, THE • 1918 • Powell Paul • USA
KID MAGICIANS, THE • 1915 • Franklin Sidney A., Franklin Chester M. • USA
KID MILLIONS • 1934 • Del Ruth Roy • USA
KID MONK BARONI • 1952 • Schuster Harold • USA • YOUNG PAUL BARONI (UKN)
KID 'N HOLLYWOOD • 1933 • Lamont Charles • SHT • USA • KID'N' HOLLYWOOD
KID NIGHTINGALE • 1939 • Amy George • USA
KID OF ROARING CAMP, THE • 1911 • *Champion* • USA
KID ORY AND HIS CREOLE JAZZ BAND see **SARAH VAUGHN AND HERB JEFFRIES** • 1950
KID PINK AND THE MAHARAJAH • 1914 • *Oliver Guy* • USA
KID POLITICS • 1918 • *Boy City Film* • SHT • USA
KID RANGER, THE • 1936 • Bradbury Robert North • USA
KID REGAN'S HANDS • 1914 • Turner Otis • USA
KID RIDES AGAIN, THE • 1943 • Newfield Sam • USA
KID RODELO • 1966 • Carlson Richard • USA, SPN
KID SENTIMENT • 1968 • Godbout Jacques • CND
KID SHERIFF, THE • 1913 • *Church Fred* • USA
KID SISTER, THE • 1927 • Graves Ralph • USA • HER SISTER'S HONOUR
KID SISTER, THE • 1945 • Newfield Sam • USA
KID SNATCHERS • 1917 • Mayo Archie • SHT • USA
KID STAKES, THE • 1927 • Ordell Tal • ASL
KID STUFF • 1976 • Carnimeo Giuliano • ITL, SPN
KID TABACO • 1954 • Gomez Urquiza Zacarias • MXC
KID THE KIDDER • 1930 • McCarey Ray • USA
KID TRICKS • 1927 • Lamont Charles • SHT • USA
KID VENGEANCE • 1977 • Manduke Joe • USA
KID WHO COULDN'T MISS, THE • 1983 • Cowan Paul • DOC • CND
KID WITH THE 200 I.Q., THE • 1982 • Martinson Leslie H. • TVM • USA
KID WITH THE BROKEN HALO, THE • 1982 • Martinson Leslie H. • TVM • USA
KIDCO • 1984 • Maxwell Ronald F. • USA
KIDDER & KO • 1918 • *Washburn Bryant* • USA
KIDDIE • 1911 • Haldane Bert • UKN
KIDDIE CURE • 1940 • Cahn Edward L. • SHT • USA
KIDDIE KONCERT • 1948 • Lundy Dick • ANS • USA
KIDDIE LEAGUE • 1959 • Smith Paul J. • ANS • USA
KIDDIE REVUE • 1936 • *Lantz Walter (P)* • ANS • USA
KIDDIES' CAKEWALK, THE • 1903 • *Paul R. W.* • UKN
KIDDIES' CHRISTMAS, THE • 1911 • *Lubin* • USA
KIDDIES IN THE RUINS, THE • 1918 • Pearson George • UKN
KIDDIE'S KAPTAIN KIDD, THE • 1916 • *Chamberlain Riley* • USA
KIDDIE'S KITTY, A • 1955 • Freleng Friz • ANS • USA
KIDDIES ON PARADE • 1935 • Moss Stewart B. • UKN
KIDDIN' THE KITTEN • 1952 • McKimson Robert • ANS • USA
KIDDING SISTER • 1917 • Davey Horace • USA
KIDDING THE BOSS • 1914 • Davis Ulysses • USA
KIDDING THE GOATS • 1915 • *Mina* • USA
KIDD'S TREASURE • 1910 • *Lubin* • USA
KIDDUS, KIDS AND KIDDO • 1915 • Dillon John Francis • USA
KIDLAT MEETS GRINGO • 1967 • Garces Armando • PHL
KIDLAT SA KARATE • 1968 • Feleo Ben • PHL • LIKE LIGHTNING IN KARATE
KID'N' HOLLYWOOD see **KID 'N HOLLYWOOD** • 1933
KIDNAP, THE see **UNOS** • 1952
KIDNAP BLUES • 1983 • Asai Shimpei • JPN
KIDNAP NEWS see **YUKAI HODO** • 1983
KIDNAP OF MARY LOU, THE see **MILANO ODIA: LA POLIZIA NO PUO SPARARE** • 1974
KIDNAP SYNDICATE • 1975 • Di Leo Fernando • ITL
KIDNAPPED • 1907 • Fitzhamon Lewin • UKN
KIDNAPPED • 1915 • Golden Joseph A.? • USA
KIDNAPPED • 1916 • *Emerald* • SHT • USA
KIDNAPPED • 1917 • Crosland Alan • *Forum Films* • USA
KIDNAPPED • 1917 • Terwilliger George W. • *Niagara* • SHT • USA
KIDNAPPED • 1935 • *Holger-Madsen* • DNM
KIDNAPPED • 1938 • Werker Alfred L., Preminger Otto (U/c) • USA
KIDNAPPED • 1948 • Beaudine William • USA
KIDNAPPED • 1960 • Stevenson Robert • UKN
KIDNAPPED • 1971 • Mann Delbert • USA, UKN • DAVID AND CATRIONA
KIDNAPPED • 1985 • SAF
KIDNAPPED • 1987 • Avedis Howard • USA
KIDNAPPED see **DIZZY LIMIT, THE** • 1930
KIDNAPPED see **UNOS** • 1952
KIDNAPPED BRIDE, THE • 1914 • *Lubin* • USA
KIDNAPPED BRIDE, THE • 1917 • McRae Henry • SHT • USA
KIDNAPPED BY INDIANS • 1914 • Montgomery Frank E. • USA
KIDNAPPED BY REDSKINS • 1914 • *Belmont Film* • USA
KIDNAPPED CHILD, THE • 1904 • Barker Will • UKN
KIDNAPPED CO-ED see **HITCH-HIKE TO HELL** • 1978
KIDNAPPED CONDUCTOR, THE • 1912 • *Kalem* • USA
KIDNAPPED FOR HATE • 1908 • *Kalem* • USA
KIDNAPPED FOR REVENGE • 1913 • *All-British Films* • UKN
KIDNAPPED HEIRESS, THE • 1915 • *Courtot Marguerite* • USA
KIDNAPPED KING, THE • 1909 • *Carlile C. Douglas* • UKN
KIDNAPPED KING, THE • 1915 • Evans Joe • UKN
KIDNAPPED LOVER, THE • 1915 • MacGregor Norval • USA
KIDNAPPED MEN see **UOMINI RAPITI** • 1965
KIDNAPPED PUGILIST, THE • 1914 • *Rex* • USA • PUGILIST'S ROMANCE, A
KIDNAPPED SERVANT, THE • 1910 • Rains Fred • UKN
KIDNAPPED STOCKBROKER, THE • 1915 • Humphrey William • USA
KIDNAPPED TRAIN, THE • 1913 • *Kirkwood James* • USA
KIDNAPPED (UKN) see **MISS FANE'S BABY IS STOLEN** • 1934
KIDNAPPED (UKN) see **SOCIAL ERROR** • 1935
KIDNAPPER • 1903 • *Bitzer Billy (Ph)* • USA
KIDNAPPER, THE see **SEQUESTRADOR, EL** • 1958
KIDNAPPER AND THE CHILD, THE • 1906 • Fitzhamon Lewin • UKN
KIDNAPPERS, THE • 1953 • Leacock Philip • UKN • LITTLE KIDNAPPERS, THE (USA)
KIDNAPPERS, THE • 1964 • Romero Eddie • USA, PHL • MAN ON THE RUN
KIDNAPPERS, THE see **RAPTORES, OS** • 1969
KIDNAPPET • 1982 • Methling Sven • DNM • KIDNAPPING
KIDNAPPING see **KIDNAPPET** • 1982
KIDNAPPING BY INDIANS • 1899 • *Mitchell & Kenyon* • UKN
KIDNAPPING CAROLINE • 1920 • *Christie* • SHT • USA
KIDNAPPING -CAUCASIAN STYLE see **KAKAZSKAYA PLENNITZA** • 1967
KIDNAPPING FATHER • 1913 • *Carewe Edwin* • USA
KIDNAPPING IN THE STARS see **RAPTO EN LAS ESTRELLAS** • 1971
KIDNAPPING OF BABY JOHN, THE see **BABY JOHN DOE** • 1986
KIDNAPPING OF BABY JOHN DOE, THE see **BABY JOHN DOE** • 1986
KIDNAPPING OF BANKER FUX, THE see **UNOS BANKERE FUXE** • 1923
KIDNAPPING OF DOLLY, THE • 1912 • *Imp* • USA
KIDNAPPING OF THE PRESIDENT, THE • 1980 • Mendeluk George • CND
KIDNAPPING OF THE SUN AND MOON, THE (USA) see **NAP ES A HOLD EL RABLASA, A** • 1969
KIDNAPPING (PAGA O UCCIDIAMO TUO FIGLIO) see **20,000 DOLLARI SPORCHI DI SANGUE** • 1969
KIDNAPPING THE KID • 1914 • Murphy J. A. • USA
KIDS • 1914 • Thornby Robert T. • USA
KIDS • 1918 • *Christie* • USA
KIDS • 1920 • *Moranti Milburn* • USA
KIDS see **PATSANI** • 1983
KIDS AND CORSETS • 1915 • Davey Horace • USA
KIDS AND KIDLETS • 1920 • *Harrison James* • SHT • USA
KIDS AND KIDS • 1915 • *Zenith Films* • USA
KIDS ARE ALRIGHT, THE • 1979 • Stein Jeff • UKN
KIDS ARE UNITED, THE • 1980 • Barron Steve • DOC • UKN
KID'S CLEVER, THE • 1929 • Craft William James • USA
KIDS DON'T TELL • 1985 • O'Steen Sam • TVM • USA
KID'S GAMES • 1976 • Saab Jocelyne • SHT • LBN
KIDS IN THE SHOP, THE • 1935 • Fleischer Dave • ANS • USA
KIDS IS KIDS • 1920 • Parrott Charles • SHT • USA
KID'S KITE, THE • 1910 • Martinek H. O. • UKN
KID'S LAST FIGHT, THE • 1933 • Lamont Charles • SHT • USA
KID'S LAST FIGHT, THE • 1941 • Luby S. Roy • USA
KID'S LAST FIGHT, THE (UKN) see **LIFE OF JIMMY NOLAN, THE** • 1933
KIDS LIKE THESE • 1987 • Brown George Stanford • TVM • USA
KID'S NAP, THE • 1914 • *Lubin* • USA
KIDS ON A BELFRY • 1965 • Hartwig Jania • ANM • PLN
KIDS TOGETHER • 1919 • Scott Will • UKN
KIDS WHO KNEW TOO MUCH, THE • 1980 • Clouse Robert • USA
KIE A MUVESZET • 1975 • Kovacs Andras • DOC • HNG • PEOPLE AND ART
KIEDY MILOSC BYLA ZBRODNIA (RASSENSCHANDE) • 1968 • Rybkowski Jan • PLN • WHEN LOVE WAS A CRIME (RASSENSCHANDE) ○ RASSENSCHANDE
KIEDY SNIEG PADA TAK • 1961 • Laskowski Jan • ANS • PLN • WHEN THE SNOW FALLS THIS WAY
KIEDY TY SPISZ • 1950 • Wajda Andrzej • PLN • WHEN YOU ARE ASLEEP ○ WHILE YOU'RE ASLEEP ○ WHILE YOU SLEEP
KIENHOLZ 2 ON EXHIBIT • 1968 • Steel June • USA
KIEPIE EN KANDAS • 1980 • SAF
KIERION • 1974 • Theos Dimosthenis • GRC
KIEROWCA DOSKONALY • 1971 • Giersz Witold • ANS • PLN • PERFECT DRIVER, THE
KIERUNEK BERLIN • 1968 • Passendorfer Jerzy • PLN • DIRECTION BERLIN
KIERUNEK NOWA HUTA • 1951 • Munk Andrzej • DCS • PLN • DIRECTION: NOWA HUTA
KIERUNEK SOCJALIZM • 1959 • Ziarnik Jerzy • DOC • PLN • DIRECTION SOCIALISM

KIERUNEK WENEZUELA • 1958 • Wionczek Roman • DOC • PLN • DIRECTION VENEZUELA

KIESELSTEINE • 1983 • Stepanik Lukas • AUS • PEBBLES

KIETA NIKKOSEN • 1960 • Murayama Shinji • JPN • SECRET PASSAGE

KIEV COMEDY, A see **ZA DVUMYA ZAYTSAMI** • 1961

KIEV COMEDY: OR, CHASING TWO HARES see **ZA DVUMYA ZAYTSAMI** • 1961

KIEV DIRECTION, THE see **NA KIYEVSKOM NAPRAVYENII** • 1968

KIEV'S FRESCOES • 1971 • Paradjanov Sergei • USS

KIFAYA YA IN • 1955 • Mustafa Hassam Eddin • EGY • ASSEZ DE TRISTESSE

KIFF TEBBI • 1927 • Camerini Mario • ITL

KIFFER'S HIGH FINANCE • 1919 • Miller Frank • SHT • UKN

KIGA KAIGYO • 1965 • Uchida Tomu • JPN • FUGITIVE FROM THE PAST, A ○ FUGITIVE FROM NOWHERE, A ○ HUNGER STRAITS ○ STRAITS OF HUNGER

KIGANJO NO BOKEN • 1965 • Taniguchi Senkichi • JPN • ADVENTURES OF TAKLA MAKAN ○ ADVENTURE IN TAKLAMAKAN ○ ADVENTURE IN THE STRANGE STONE CASTLE

KIGEKI DAI SHOGEKI see **ONSEN GERIRA DAI SHOGEKI** • 1968

KIGEKI DANTAI RESSHA • 1967 • Segawa Shoji • JPN • LOCAL LINE LOVE

KIGEKI: DOROBO GAKKO • 1968 • Yuge Taro • JPN • PROFESSOR THIEF

KIGEKI EKIMAE GAKUEN • 1967 • Inoue Kazuo • JPN • CAMPUS IN FRONT OF A STATION

KIGEKI EKIMAE KAIDAN • 1964 • Saeki Kozo • JPN • GHOST STORY OF FUNNY ACT IN FRONT OF TRAIN STATION

KIGEKI EKIMAE KAZAN • 1968 • Yamada Tatsuo • JPN • VOLCANO OF STATION FRONT PLAZA

KIGEKI EKIMAE TANKEN • 1967 • Inoue Kazuo • JPN • EXPLORATION IN FRONT OF THE STATION

KIGEKI HACHURUI • 1968 • Watanabe Yusuke • JPN • SEXPLOITERS, THE

KIGEKI: HANAYOUN SENSO • 1971 • Saito Koichi • JPN

KIGEKI HATSUMOUDE RESHA • 1968 • Segawa Masaharu • JPN • COMEDY TRAIN SERIES: NEW YEAR TRIP

KIGEKI: IPPATSU SHOBU • 1967 • Yamada Yoji • JPN • GREATEST CHALLENGE OF ALL

KIGEKI KAKUEKITEISHA • 1965 • Inoue Kazuo • JPN • RETIREMENT OF MR. NAPOLEON, THE

KIGEKI KEIBA HISHO-HO IPPATSU SHOBU • 1968 • Segawa Masaharu • JPN • COMEDY, HORSE RACE, SHOT GAMBLING

KIGEKI-KEIBA HISSHOHO • 1967 • Segawa Shoji • JPN • HORSE MANIAC, THE

KIGEKI KYUKO RESSHA • 1967 • Segawa Masaharu • JPN • EXPRESS TRAIN

KIGEKI-OBUROSHIKI • 1967 • Nakahira Ko • JPN • FREE ISLAND, THE ○ OBUROSHIKI

KIGEKI: ONNAWA DOKYO • 1970 • Morisaki Azuma • JPN • WOMEN CAN'T BE BEATEN

KIGEKI, OTTO URIMASU • 1968 • Segawa Masaharu • JPN • HUSBAND FOR SALE

KIGEKI TOKYO NO INAKAPPE • 1967 • Senno Koji • JPN • BUMPKIN OF TOKYO, A

KIHAJOLNI VESZELYES • 1978 • Zsombolyai Janos • HNG • DON'T LEAN OUT OF THE WINDOW ○ DO NOT LEAN OUT OF THE WINDOW

KIHLAUS • 1955 • Blomberg Erik • FNL • BETROTHAL, THE

KII RIVER, THE see **KI NO KAWA** • 1966

KIIROI KARASU • 1957 • Gosho Heinosuke • JPN • BEHOLD THY SON ○ YELLOW CROW

KIIROI TAIYO • 1967 • *Aoi Eiga* • JPN • YELLOW SUN

KIISKIMARKKINAT • 1959 • Heino Niilo • FNL

KIKANSHA C-57 • 1940 • Imaizumi • JPN • STEAM LOCOMOTIVE C-57

KIKE WADATSUMI NO KOE • 1950 • Sekigawa Hideo • JPN • LISTEN TO THE ROAR OF THE OCEAN

KIKEN NA NENREI • 1957 • Horiiki Kiyoshi • JPN

KIKEN RYOKO • 1959 • Nakamura Noboru • JPN • VAGABOND LOVERS ○ DANGEROUS VOYAGE ○ KIYEN RYOKO

KIKI • 1926 • Brown Clarence • USA

KIKI • 1931 • Taylor Sam • USA

KIKI • 1932 • Billon Pierre • FRN

KIKI • 1932 • Lamac Carl • FRG

KIKI • 1934 • Matarazzo Raffaello • ITL

KIKI'S DELIVERY SERVICE see **MAJO NO TAKKYUBIN** • 1989

KIKLOP • 1983 • Vrdoljak Antun • YGS • CYCLOPS, THE

KIKO AND KIKAY see **KIKO EN KIKAY** • 1968

KIKO AND THE HONEY BEARS • 1936 • Davis Mannie, Gordon George • ANS • USA

KIKO EN KIKAY • 1968 • Feleo Ben • PHL • KIKO AND KIKAY

KIKO FOILS A FOX • 1936 • Davis Mannie, Gordon George • ANS • USA

KIKO THE KANGAROO • 1936-37 • *Terry Paul (P)* • ASS • USA

KIKOS • Saakyants Robert • ANM • USS

KIKO'S CLEANING DAY • 1937 • Gordon George • ANS • USA

KIKU AND ISAMU see **KIKU TO ISAMU** • 1959

KIKU TO ISAMU • 1959 • Imai Tadashi • JPN • KIKU AND ISAMU

KIKYO • 1950 • Ohba Hideo • JPN • RETURN TO THE CAPITAL

KIKYO • 1964 • Nishikawa Katsumi • JPN • HOMECOMING

KIL 1 • 1964 • Miller Arnold Louis • UKN • SKIN GAME, THE ○ SKIN GAMES

KILAS, O MAU DA FITA see **QUILAS, O MAU DA FITA** • 1980

KILAT SENJA • 1977 • Sudarmadji S. • MLY • LIGHTNING AT DUSK

KILDARE OF STORM • 1918 • Franklin Harry L. • USA

KILENC HONAP • 1976 • Meszaros Marta • HNG • NINE MONTHS

KILENCES KORTEREM, A see **9-ES KORTEREM** • 1955

KILENCVEN KILENC see **KILENCVENKILENC** • 1918

KILENCVENKILENC • 1918 • Curtiz Michael • HNG • NINETY NINE ○ KILENCVEN KILENC

KILI WATCH • 1974 • Lagrange Yvan • FRN

KILJOYS, THE • 1921 • Roach Hal • SHT • USA

KILJUNEN FAMILY, THE see **KILJUSEN HERRASVAKI** • 1982

KILJUSEN HERRASVAKI • 1982 • Kuortti Matti • FNL • THAT KILJUNEN FAMILY ○ KILJUNEN FAMILY, THE

KILKENNY PRIMARY SCHOOL • 1973 • Crombie Donald • DOC • ASL

KILL • 1970 • Ewing Iain • CND

KILL! • 1971 • Gary Romain • FRN, ITL, FRG • KILL, KILL, KILL

KILL! see **KIRU** • 1968

KILL see **DEATHDREAM** • 1972

KILL, THE • 1968 • Graver Gary • USA

KILL A DRAGON • 1967 • Moore Michael • USA

KILL, ALEX, KILL • 1983 • Zarindast Tony • USA

KILL AND GO HIDE see **CHILD, THE** • 1977

KILL AND KILL AGAIN • 1980 • Hall Ivan • SAF

KILL AT THE END see **ZABIC NA KONCU** • 1990

KILL BABY KILL (USA) see **OPERAZIONE PAURA** • 1966

KILL-BOTS see **CHOPPING MALL** • 1986

KILL CASTRO • 1978 • Barton Peter • USA

KILL CASTRO see **CUBA CROSSING** • 1980

KILL CHINTO see **MATEN A CHINTO** • 1990

KILL CRAZY • 1989 • Heavener David • USA

KILL FACTOR, THE see **DEATH DIMENSION** • 1978

KILL FOR LOVE • 1979 • Pakdivijit Vinit • THL

KILL HER GENTLY • 1957 • Saunders Charles • UKN

KILL HIM FOR ME see **EN LA PALMA DE TU MANO** • 1950

KILL-JOY, THE • 1917 • Wright Fred E. • USA

KILL, KILL, KILL see **KILL!** • 1971

KILL ME, COP see **ZABIJ MNIE, GLINO** • 1988

KILL ME GENTLY see **UBIJ ME NEZNO** • 1981

KILL ME IF YOU CAN (UKN) see **CARYL CHESSMAN STORY, THE** • 1977

KILL ME, PIG see **ZABIJ MNIE, GLINO** • 1988

KILL ME QUICK, I'M COLD see **FAI IN FRETTA AD UCCIDERMI.. HO FREDDO** • 1967

KILL ME TOMORROW • 1957 • Fisher Terence • UKN

KILL ME WITH KISSES see **STRAZIAMI MA DI BACI SAZIAMI** • 1968

KILL-OFF, THE • 1989 • Greenwald Maggie • USA

KILL OR BE KILLED • 1943 • Lye Len • SHT • UKN

KILL OR BE KILLED • 1950 • Nosseck Max • USA

KILL OR BE KILLED • 1967 • *Darren James* • MTV • USA

KILL OR BE KILLED • 1980 • Hall Ivan • USA • KARATE KILL

KILL OR BE KILLED (USA) see **UCCIDI O MUORI** • 1967

KILL OR CURE • 1914 • Lambart Harry • USA

KILL OR CURE • 1923 • Roach Hal • SHT • USA

KILL OR CURE • 1962 • Pollock George • UKN

KILL OR CURE see **BONNE TISANE, LA** • 1957

KILL PATRICE, UN SHERIF PAS COMME LES AUTRES • 1969 • Reichenbach Francois • SHT • FRN

KILL POINT • 1984 • Harris Frank • USA • KILLPOINT

KILL SQUAD • 1981 • Donahue Patrick G. • HKG • CODE OF HONOUR

KILL THAT FLY • 1914 • Birch Cecil • UKN

KILL THAT LOVE see **TRZEBA ZABIC TE MILOSC** • 1972

KILL THAT RAT • 1941 • Bishop Terry • DOC • UKN

KILL THE BLACK SHEEP see **ZABIJCIE CZARNA OWCE** • 1972

KILL THE GOLDEN GOOSE • 1979 • Hong Elliot • USA

KILL THE KILLER see **KOROSHIYA O BARASE** • 1969

KILL THE KILLERS see **KOROSHIYA O BARASE** • 1969

KILL THE LION see **MATEN AL LEON** • 1975

KILL THE NERVE • 1922 • Roach Hal • SHT • USA

KILL THE NIGHT ROSE see **YORU NO BARA O KESE** • 1966

KILL THE SHOGUN • 1981 • Lee D. Young • HKG

KILL THE UMPIRE • 1916 • Lyons Eddie, Moran Lee • SHT • USA

KILL THE UMPIRE • 1950 • Bacon Lloyd • USA

KILL THE YOUNG BOSS see **WAKAOYABUN O KESE** • 1967

KILL THEM ALL AND COME BACK ALONE (USA) see **AMMAZZALI TUTTI E TORNA SOLO** • 1969

KILL TO LOVE • 1981 • Tam Kav Ming • HKG

KILL ZONE • 1985 • Prior David A. • USA

KILLDOZER • 1974 • London Jerry • TVM • USA

KILLE OCH EN TJEJ, EN • 1974 • Hallstrom Lasse • SWD • BOY MEETS GIRL ○ LOVER AND HIS LASS, THE

KILLED AGAINST ORDERS • 1915 • West Langdon • USA

KILLED AT WAR • 1962 • Panfilov Gleb • SHT • USS

KILLED BY WHOM? • 1916 • Le Viness Carl M. • SHT • USA

KILLED SUNDAY see **ZABITA NEDELE** • 1970

KILLEMANN HAT'N KLAPS • 1919 • Bolten-Baeckers Heinrich • FRG

KILLER 77 ALIVE OR DEAD see **SICARIO 77 VIVO O MORTO** • 1966

KILLER, THE • 1921 • Hickman Howard • USA

KILLER, THE see **MYSTERY RANCH** • 1932

KILLER, THE see **KURBANLIK KATIL** • 1967

KILLER, THE see **MANGLILIGPIT, ANG** • 1968

KILLER, THE see **MATADOR, O** • 1968

KILLER, THE see **DADDY'S DEADLY DARLING** • 1972

KILLER, THE see **DIPHUT YINGHUNG** • 1989

KILLER, THE (UKN) see **SACRED WIVES OF VENGEANCE, THE** • 1973

KILLER ADIOS • 1968 • Zeglio Primo • ITL, SPN

KILLER APE • 1953 • Bennet Spencer Gordon • USA

KILLER AT LARGE • 1936 • Selman David • USA

KILLER AT LARGE • 1947 • Beaudine William • USA

KILLER BAT see **DEVIL BAT** • 1941

KILLER BEES • 1974 • Harrington Curtis • TVM • USA

KILLER BEHIND THE MASK see **SAVAGE WEEKEND** • 1976

KILLER BY NIGHT • 1971 • McEveety Bernard • TVM • USA • CITY BY NIGHT, THE

KILLER CALIBRE 32 see **KILLER CALIBRO 32** • 1967

KILLER CALIBRO 32 • 1967 • Brescia Alfonso • ITL • KILLER CALIBRE 32

KILLER CLANS see **LIU-HSING, HU-TIEH, CHIEN** • 1977

KILLER COMES BACK, THE see **ARAPPOINOWA GOMENDAZE** • 1967

KILLER CONSTABLE see **WAN-JEN-CHAN** • 1980

KILLER CONTRACTED • 1984 • Ormerod James • MTV • UKN

KILLER COP see **POLIZIA HA LE MANI LEGATE, LA** • 1975

KILLER DILL • 1947 • Collins Lewis D. • USA

KILLER DILLER • 1948 • Binney Josh • USA

KILLER DINO (UKN) see **DINO** • 1957

KILLER DOG • 1936 • Tourneur Jacques • SHT • USA

KILLER ELITE, THE • 1975 • Peckinpah Sam • USA

KILLER EXPOSED • 1983 • Ormerod James • MTV • UKN

KILLER FISH • 1979 • Margheriti Antonio • ITL, BRZ • KILLER FISH AGGUATO SUL FUNDO ○ DEADLY TREASURE OF THE PIRANHA ○ KILLERFISH

KILLER FISH AGGUATO SUL FUNDO see **KILLER FISH** • 1979

KILLER FORCE see **DIAMOND MERCENARIES, THE** • 1975

KILLER GORO see **BURAI HITOKIRI GORO** • 1968

KILLER GRIZZLY see **GRIZZLY** • 1976

KILLER IN EVERY CORNER • 1974 • *Magee Patrick* • MTV • UKN

KILLER IN THE FAMILY, A • 1983 • Heffron Richard T. • TVM • USA

KILLER IN THE FOG see **KIRI NI MUSEBU YORU** • 1968

KILLER IN THE MIRROR • 1986 • De Felitta Frank • TVM • USA

KILLER IN WAITING • 1982 • Ferguson Michael • MTV • UKN

KILLER INSIDE ME, THE • 1976 • Kennedy Burt • USA

KILLER INSTINCT • 1985 • Fruet William • CND

KILLER INSTINCT • 1989 • Lister David • SAF

KILLER INSTINCT see **BEHIND ENEMY LINES** • 1988

KILLER INSTINCT, THE see **BAKER COUNTY U.S.A.** • 1981

KILLER IS LOOSE, THE • 1956 • Boetticher Budd • USA

KILLER KID • 1967 • Savona Leopoldo • ITL

KILLER KLOWNS FROM OUTER SPACE • 1988 • Chiodo Stephen • USA

KILLER LACKS A NAME, THE (USA) see **NUESTRO AGENTE EN CASABLANCA** • 1966

KILLER LEOPARD • 1954 • Beebe Ford • USA

KILLER LIKES CANDY, THE (USA) see **KILLER PER SUA MAESTA, UN** • 1968

KILLER MAN (USA) see **SCOUMOUNE, LA** • 1973

KILLER MCCOY • 1947 • Rowland Roy • USA

KILLER METEORS, THE • 1984 • Lo Wei • HKG • JACKIE CHAN VERSUS JIMMY WANG YU

KILLER NUN (UKN) see **SUOR OMICIDI** • 1979

KILLER OF HIS MAJESTY, A see **KILLER PER SUA MAESTA, UN** • 1968

KILLER OF KILLERS, THE see **MECHANIC, THE** • 1972

KILLER OF ONE HUNDRED MEN AT ICHINJI TEMPLE • 1925 • *Tanaka Kinuyo* • JPN

KILLER OF SEVEN MEN see **NANIWA KYOKAKU: DOKYO SHICHININ GIRI** • 1967

KILLER OF SHEEP • 1978 • Burnett Charles • USA

KILLER OF SNAKE, FOX OF SHAOLIN • San Pao • HKG

KILLER OF YOUTH, A see **SEISHUN NO SATSUJIN-SHA** • 1976

KILLER ON A HORSE (UKN) see **WELCOME TO HARD TIMES** • 1967

KILLER ON BOARD • 1977 • Leacock Philip • TVM • USA

KILLER PANTHER, THE see **SCHWARZE PANTHER VON RATANA, DER** • 1963

KILLER PARTY • 1986 • Fruet William • USA • APRIL FOOL ○ FOOL'S NIGHT

KILLER PATROL • 1968 • Buenaventura Augusto • PHL

KILLER PER SUA MAESTA, UN • 1968 • Chentrens Federico, Cloche Maurice • ITL, FRN, FRG • TUEUR AIME LES BONBONS, LE (FRN) ○ ZUCKER FUR DEN MORDER (FRG) ○ KILLER LIKES CANDY, THE (USA) ○ KILLER OF HIS MAJESTY, A

KILLER SECONDS • 1986 • Hurme Juhani • FNL

KILLER SHARK • 1950 • Boetticher Budd • USA

KILLER SHREWS, THE • 1959 • Kellogg Ray • USA

KILLER SPORES see **MAN FROM ATLANTIS: THE KILLER SPORES, THE** • 1977

KILLER SPY (USA) see **PLEINS FEUX SUR STANISLAS** • 1965

KILLER THAT STALKED NEW YORK, THE • 1950 • McEvoy Earl • USA • FRIGHTENED CITY, THE (UKN)

KILLER! (UKN) see **QUE LA BETE MEURE** • 1969

KILLER VOLCANO see **ST. HELENS** • 1981

KILLER WALKS, A • 1952 • Drake Ronald • UKN

KILLER WHALE see **KUJIRA GAMI** • 1962

KILLER WHO WOULDN'T DIE, THE • 1976 • Hale William • TVM • USA • OHANIAN

KILLER WITH A LABEL (UKN) see **ONE TOO MANY** • 1950

KILLER WITH THE THIRD EYE, THE see **TERZO OCCHIO, IL** • 1966

KILLER WITH TWO FACES • 1974 • Scholz-Conway John • TVM • UKN

KILLER YOUTH, THE see **SEISHUN NO SATSUJIN-SHA** • 1976

KILLERFISH see **KILLER FISH** • 1979

KILLERS see **BOYS NEXT DOOR, THE** • 1985

KILLERS, THE • 1946 • Siodmak Robert • USA • MAN AFRAID, A

KILLERS, THE • 1964 • Siegel Don • TVM • USA • ERNEST HEMINGWAY'S THE KILLERS ○ JOHNNY NORTH

KILLERS ARE AMONG US, THE see **CARRASCOS ESTAO ENTRE NOS** • 1968

KILLERS ARE CHALLENGED see **SPIE UCCIDONO A BEIRUT, LE** • 1965

KILLER'S CAGE • 1960 • von Theumer Ernst Ritter • USA, MXC • CODE OF SILENCE

KILLER'S CANYON (UKN) see **JIM IL PRIMO** • 1964

KILLER'S CARNIVAL (USA) see **GERN HAB' ICH DIE FRAUEN GEKILLT** • 1966

KILLER'S DELIGHT • 1980 • Hoenak Jeremy • USA

KILLERS FROM SPACE • 1954 • Wilder W. Lee • USA

KILLER'S KEY, A see **ARU KOROSHIYA NO KAGI** • 1967

KILLER'S KISS • 1955 • Kubrick Stanley • USA

KILLER'S LOVE see **SHASHOU QING** • 1988

KILLER'S MOON • 1978 • Birkinshaw Alan • UKN

KILLERS OF KILIMANJARO • 1959 • Thorpe Richard • UKN

KILLERS OF THE CASTLE OF BLOOD see **IVANNA** • 1970

KILLERS OF THE EAST (USA) see **VENDETTA DEI TUGHS, LA** • 1955

KILLERS OF THE PRAIRIE (UKN) see **KING OF THE SIERRAS** • 1938

KILLERS OF THE WILD • 1940 • Hutchison Charles, Moore Vin • USA

KILLERS OF THE WILD • 1976 • Ryan Robert J. • USA

KILLERS ON PARADE see **YUHI NI AKAI NO KAO** • 1961

KILLERS ON THE PHONE, THE (UKN) see **ASSASSINO E AL TELEFONO, L'** • 1972

KILLERS THREE • 1968 • Kessler Bruce • USA

KILLERS WHO WORE COLLARS see **PACK, THE** • 1977

KILLING, THE • 1956 • Kubrick Stanley • USA • CLEAN BREAK
KILLING A SUNDAY see **ZABITA NEDELE** • 1970
KILLING AFFAIR, A • 1977 • Sarafian Richard C. • TVM • USA • BEHIND THE BADGE
KILLING AFFAIR, A • 1988 • Saperstein David • USA
KILLING AT HELL'S GATE • 1981 • Jameson Jerry • TVM • USA • HELL AND HIGH WATER
KILLING AT MONTE CARLO (UKN) see **CRIMEN** • 1960
KILLING BOTTLE, THE see **KOKUSAI HIMITSU KEISATSU: ZETTAI ZETSUMEI** • 1967
KILLING CANILER KRALI • 1967 • Inanc Cetin • TRK • KILLING, KING OF CRIMINALS
KILLING CARS • 1986 • Verhoeven Michael • FRG
KILLING CORPSES DO NOT TALK see **KILLING OLULER KONUSMAZ** • 1967
KILLING DAD • 1989 • Austin Michael • UKN
KILLING 'EM SOFTLY • 1985 • Fischer Max • CND
KILLING FIELDS, THE • 1983 • Joffe Roland • UKN
KILLING FRANKESTAYNA KARSI • 1967 • Akinci Nuri • TRK • KILLING VS. FRANKENSTEIN
KILLING GAME, THE • 1987 • Merhi Joseph • USA
KILLING GAME, THE (USA) see **JEU DE MASSACRE** • 1967
KILLING HEAT (USA) see **GRASS IS SINGING, THE** • 1981
KILLING HOUR, THE • 1984 • Mastroianni Armand • USA • CLAIRVOYANT, THE
KILLING IN ISTANBUL see **KILLING ISTANBULDA** • 1967
KILLING IN MONTE CARLO see **CRIMEN** • 1960
KILLING IS EASY see **ZABIJET JE SNADNE** • 1972
KILLING ISTANBULDA • 1967 • Atadeniz Yilmaz • TRK • KILLING IN ISTANBUL
KILLING JOKE • 1980 • Deruddere Dominique • SHT • BLG
KILLING KIND, THE • 1973 • Harrington Curtis • USA • PSYCHOPATH, THE
KILLING, KING OF CRIMINALS see **CANILER KRALI KILLING** • 1967
KILLING, KING OF CRIMINALS see **KILLING CANILER KRALI** • 1967
KILLING MACHINE • 1983 • de la Loma Jose Antonio • SPN, MXC
KILLING ME SOFTLY see **MITGIFT** • 1975
KILLING OF A CHINESE BOOKIE, THE • 1976 • Cassavetes John • USA
KILLING OF AMERICA, THE • 1982 • Renan Sheldon • DOC • USA
KILLING OF AN EGG, THE see **EI OM ZEEP** • 1977
KILLING OF ANGEL STREET, THE • 1981 • Crombie Donald • ASL
KILLING OF HORACE • 1914 • *Keystone* • USA
KILLING OF RANDY WEBSTER, THE • 1981 • Wanamaker Sam • TVM • USA
KILLING OF SANTA CLAUS, THE (UKN) see **ASSASSINAT DU PERE NOEL, L'** • 1941
KILLING OF SATAN, THE • 1983 • Pinon Efren C. • PHL
KILLING OF SISTER GEORGE, THE • 1968 • Aldrich Robert • USA
KILLING OLULER KONUSMAZ • 1967 • Figenli Yavuz • TRK • KILLING CORPSES DO NOT TALK
KILLING STONE • 1978 • Landon Michael • TVM • USA
KILLING THE DEVIL see **VRAZDA INZENYRA CERTA** • 1968
KILLING TIME see **MACON COUNTY LINE** • 1974
KILLING TIME, THE • 1987 • King Rick • USA
KILLING TO LIVE • 1931 • Korolevitch Vladimir
KILLING TOUCH, THE see **FATAL GAMES** • 1984
KILLING URGE see **JET STORM** • 1959
KILLING VS. FRANKENSTEIN see **KILLING FRANKESTAYNA KARSI** • 1967
KILLING WITH KINDNESS see **VLASTNE SE NIC NESTALO** • 1988
KILLINGS AT OUTPOST ZETA • 1980 • Sandler Allan, Emenegger Robert • USA
KILLJOY • 1981 • Moxey John Llewellyn • TVM • USA
KILLMAN • De Grasse Herbert Jean • SHT • USA
KILLPOINT see **KILL POINT** • 1984
KILLZONE: TOUR OF DUTY, THE see **NAM: TOUR OF DUTY** • 1987
KILMA, REINA DE LAS AMAZONAS • 1975 • Iglesias Miguel • SPN
KILME MIESTA • 1984 • Lehtinen Virke • FNL • THREE MEN
KILMENY • 1915 • Apfel Oscar • USA
KILOMETRO 12 • 1961 • Pamplona Clemente • SPN
KILOMETRO II • 1938 • Soffici Mario • ARG
KILOS ARE COMING, THE • 1974 • Arioli Don, Nelson Barrie* • ANS • CND
KILROY ON DECK (UKN) see **FRENCH LEAVE** • 1948
KILROY, THE LONELY REVENGER • 1973 • Einarson Oddvar • SHT • NRW
KILROY WAS HERE • 1947 • Karlson Phil • USA
KILTIES • 1927 • Taurog Norman • SHT • USA
KILTIES ARE COMING, THE • 1951 • Hill Robert Jordan • UKN • LADS AND LASSIES ON PARADE
KILTIES THREE • 1918 • Sandground Maurice • UKN
KIM • 1950 • Saville Victor • USA
KIM • 1984 • Davies John • TVM • USA
KIM OI! • 1975 • Pham-Lai • BLG
KIMBERLEY DIAMOND ROBBERY, THE • 1910 • SAF
KIMBERLEY JIM • 1963 • Nofal Emil • SAF
KIMBO, THE WHITE LION see **JUNGLE TATEI**
KIMEN • 1973 • Solbakken Erik • NRW • SEED, THE
KIMG OF NEW YORK, THE • 1990 • Ferrara Abel • USA
KIMI GA KAGAYAKU TOKI • 1985 • Morikawa Tokihisa • JPN • GLITTERING YOU
KIMI GA SEISHUN NO TOKI • 1967 • Saito Buichi • JPN • CAUGHT IN HER OWN PLOT
KIMI GA WAKAMONO • 1970 • Fukasaku Kinji • JPN • OUR DEAR BUDDIES
KIMI MATEDOMO • 1949 • Nakamura Noboru • JPN
KIMI NI SHIAWASE O: SENTIMENTAL BOY • 1967 • Maruyama Seiji • JPN • HAPPINESS FOR YOU: SENTIMENTAL BOY
KIMI NO NAWA • 1954 • Ohba Hideo • JPN • WHAT IS YOUR NAME ○ WHAT'S YOUR NAME ○ ALWAYS IN MY HEART
KIMI SHINITAMAU KOTO NAKARE • 1954 • Maruyama Seiji • JPN • FOREVER BE MINE ○ YOU SHOULDN'T DIE
KIMI TO BOKU • 1941 • Tasaka Tomotaka • JPN • YOU AND I
KIMI TO IKU MICHI see **KIMI TO YUKU MICHI** • 1936
KIMI TO WAKARETE • 1932 • Naruse Mikio • JPN • APART FROM YOU
KIMI TO YUKU MICHI • 1936 • Naruse Mikio • JPN • ROAD I TRAVEL WITH YOU, THE ○ KIMI TO IKU MICHI
KIMI URUWASHIKU • 1956 • Nakamura Noboru • JPN • BEAUTIFUL FEELING
KIMI WA HADASHI NO KAMI O MITAKA • 1985 • Soo-Gil Kim • JPN • HAVE YOU SEEN THE BAREFOOT GOD?
KIMI WA KOIBITO • 1967 • Saito Buichi • JPN • MY LOVER
KIMI YO FUNDO NO KAWA A WATARE • 1975 • Sato Junya • JPN • YOU, ACROSS THE RIVER OF WRATH ○ ACROSS THE RIVER OF WRATH
KIMIKO see **TSUMA YO BARA NO YONI** • 1935
KIMIMO SHUSSEGA DEKIRU • 1964 • Sugawa Eizo • JPN • YOU CAN SUCCEED TOO (USA)
KIMONA TRAGEDY, A • 1913 • *Mack H. S.* • USA
KIMPEI FROM KOINA see **KOINA NO KIMPEI** • 1954
KIMSESIZIM • 1967 • Pecen Nevzat • TRK • I AM LONELY
KIMSOBO PODROZNIK • 1953 • Nehrebecki Wladyslaw • ANS • PLN • KIMSOBO THE TRAVELLER
KIMSOBO THE TRAVELLER see **KIMSOBO PODROZNIK** • 1953
KIMURA NAGATONOKAMI • 1918 • Ishiyama M. • JPN • NAGATONOKAMI KIMURA
KIN see **KANE** • 1926
KIN see **RODNIA** • 1983
KIN FOLK see **ALL THE LOVIN' KINFOLK** • 1970
KINA VENDEGEI VOLTUNK • 1957 • Jancso Miklos • SHT • HNG • WE HAVE BEEN THE GUESTS OF CHINA ○ OUR VISIT TO CHINA
KINCSKERESO KIS KODMON • 1973 • Szemes Mihaly • HNG • MAGIC JACKET, THE
KIND DEEDS see **WISE KID, THE** • 1922
KIND DER DONAU, DAS • 1950 • Jacoby Georg • AUS
KIND DER STRASSE 1, DAS • 1921 • Neff Wolfgang • FRG
KIND DER STRASSE 2, DAS • 1921 • Neff Wolfgang • FRG
KIND DES ANDERN, DAS • 1923 • *Diegelmann Wilhelm* • FRG
KIND –EIN HUND, EIN • 1923 • Boese Carl • FRG • SPIEL VON KLEINEN SEELEN, EIN
KIND–HEARTED ANT, THE (USA) see **MRAV DOBRA SRCA** • 1965
KIND–HEARTED BOOTBLACK OR GENEROSITY REWARDED, A • 1908 • *Vitagraph* • USA
KIND HEARTED PERCIVAL • 1911 • Wilson Frank? • UKN
KIND HEARTS AND CORONETS • 1949 • Hamer Robert • UKN
KIND HEARTS ARE MORE THAN CORONETS • 1913 • Stow Percy • UKN
KIND, ICH FREU' MICH AUF DEIN KOMMEN • 1933 • Gerron Kurt • FRG • AMOR AN DER LEINE
KIND LADY • 1935 • Seitz George B. • USA • HOUSE OF MENACE
KIND LADY • 1951 • Sturges John • USA
KIND MEN MARRY, THE see **IN NAME ONLY** • 1939
KIND MILLIONAIRE, THE see **PYTLAKOVA SCHOVANKA** • 1949
KIND OF ENGLISH, A • 1987 • Amin Ruhul • UKN
KIND OF LOVE, A see **LIKE MOTHER, LIKE DAUGHTER** • 1969
KIND OF LOVING, A • 1962 • Schlesinger John • UKN
KIND OLD LADY, THE • 1908 • *Tyler Walter* • UKN
KIND OLD MAN, THE • 1912 • *Eclair* • USA
KIND RUFT, DAS • 1914 • Gad Urban • FRG
KIND UND DIE WELT, DAS • 1931 • Frowein Eberhard • FRG
KIND VAN DE ZON • 1975 • van Nie Rene • NTH • ANNA, CHILD OF THE DAFFODILS ○ CHILD OF THE DAFFODILS
KINDAN NO JOJI • 1967 • Ogawa Kinya • JPN • FORBIDDEN AFFAIR
KINDAN NO KAJITSU • 1968 • Kaji Noboru • JPN • FORBIDDEN FRUIT, THE
KINDAN NO SUNA • 1957 • Horiuchi Manao • JPN • UNDERWATER ROMANCE ○ BLACK NETS
KINDAR L'INVULNERABILE • 1965 • Civirani Osvaldo • ITL • KINDAR THE INVULNERABLE (USA)
KINDAR THE INVULNERABLE (USA) see **KINDAR L'INVULNERABILE** • 1965
KINDER AUS NR.67, DIE see **KINDER AUS NR.67 ODER HEIL HITLER, ICH HATT GERN 'N PAAR PFERDEAPPEL..** • 1980
KINDER AUS NR.67 ODER HEIL HITLER, ICH HATT GERN 'N PAAR PFERDEAPPEL.. • 1980 • Bartelmess-Weller Usch, Meyer Werner • FRG • CHILDREN FROM NUMBER 67, THE ○ KINDER AUS NR.67, DIE
KINDER DER FINSTERNIS 1 • 1921 • Dupont E. A. • FRG • MANN AUS NEAPEL, DER ○ CHILDREN OF DARKNESS ○ MAN FROM NAPLES, THE ○ CHILDREN OF THE DARKNESS
KINDER DER FINSTERNIS 2 • 1921 • Dupont E. A. • FRG • KAMPFENDE WELTEN ○ WORLDS IN STRUGGLE
KINDER DER LANDSTRASSE • 1919 • Eichberg Richard • FRG
KINDER DER LIEBE • 1919 • Dessauer Siegfried, Enger Mogens • FRG
KINDER DER REVOLUTION • 1923 • Theyer Hans • AUS
KINDER DER STRASSE • 1928 • Boese Carl • FRG • RAZZIA
KINDER DER ZEIT • 1922 • Licho Adolf Edgar • FRG
KINDER DES GENERALS, DIE • 1912 • Gad Urban • FRG, DNM • GENERALENS BORN (DNM)
KINDER IM FRAGEALTER • 1965 • Lemmel Dieter H. • FRG
KINDER IM KRIEG • 1986 • Mohammadi Babak • AUS • CHILDREN IN THE WAR
KINDER, MUTTER UND EIN GENERAL • 1955 • Benedek Laslo • FRG • CHILDREN, MOTHERS AND A GENERAL
KINDER VON FURNA, DIE • 1975 • Schocher Christian • DOC • SWT
KINDER VON GERICHT • 1931 • Klaren Georg C. • FRG • SACHE AUGUST SCHULZE, DIE
KINDER VON HEUTE • 1923 • Gunsburg Arthur • FRG
KINDERARZT, DER • 1910 • Stark Kurt • FRG
KINDERARZT DR. ENGEL • 1936 • Riemann Johannes • FRG • DR. ENGEL, CHILD SPECIALIST (USA)
KINDERGARTEN • 1962 • Cote Guy-L. • DCS • CND
KINDERGARTEN • 1989 • Polaco Jorge • ARG
KINDERGARTEN COP • 1990 • Reitman Ivan • USA
KINDERMADCHEN FUR PAPA GESUCHT • 1957 • Quest Hans • FRG
KINDERSEELEN KLAGEN EUCH AN • 1927 • Bernhardt Curtis • FRG
KINDERTRAGODIE • 1927 • Jutzi Phil • FRG
KINDEST MAN I KNOW, THE • 1973 • Sharlandgiev Ljobomir • BUL
KINDLED COURAGE • 1923 • Worthington William • USA
KINDLING • 1915 • De Mille Cecil B. • USA
KINDLY REMOVE YOUR HAT: OR, SHE DIDN'T MIND • 1913 • Stow Percy • UKN
KINDLY SCRAM • 1943 • Geiss Alec • ANS • USA
KINDRED, THE • 1986 • Obrow Jeffrey, Carpenter Stephen • USA
KINDRED OF THE DUST • 1922 • Walsh Raoul • USA
KINEGRAFFITI • 1964 • Cantrill Arthur, Cantrill Corinne • SHT • ASL
KINEK A TORVENYE? • 1979 • Szonyi Sandor S. • HNG • WHOSE LAW IS IT?
KINEKATURE COMEDIES • 1918 • Rains Fred • SER • UKN
KINEMA GIRL, THE • 1914 • Stow Percy • UKN
KINEMA NO TENCHI • 1987 • Yamada Yoji • JPN • WHEN CINEMA WAS YOUNG
KINEMACOLOR SONGS • 1911 • Bouwmeester Theo • UKN
KINEMACOLOUR PUZZLE • 1909 • Smith G. A. • UKN
KINEMAPOEMS • 1914 • Cornwallis Donald • SER • UKN
KINEMATOGRAPH FIEND, THE • 1911 • *Gaumont* • UKN
KINEQUIPS • 1914 • Wilson Rex? • SER • UKN
KINESISKE VASE, DEN see **VASENS HEMMELIGHED** • 1913
KINETIC ART: SERIES ONE, PROGRAMME 1, THE • 1968 • *Universal Education & Visual Arts* • ANT • USA
KINETIC ART: SERIES ONE, PROGRAMME 2, THE • 1968 • *Universal Education & Visual Arts* • ANT • USA
KINETIC ART: SERIES ONE, PROGRAMME 3, THE • 1968 • *Universal Education & Visual Arts* • ANT • USA
KINETIC ART: SERIES TWO, PROGRAMME 1, THE • 1970 • *Universal Education & Visual Arts* • ANT • USA
KINETIC ART: SERIES TWO, PROGRAMME 2, THE • 1970 • *Universal Education & Visual Arts* • ANT • USA
KINETIC ART: SERIES TWO, PROGRAMME 3, THE • 1970 • *Universal Education & Visual Arts* • ANT • USA
KINETIC ART SHOW –STOCKHOLM • 1961 • Breer Robert • USA
KINETIC CATALOG • 1965-69 • Mideke Michael • SHT • USA
KINETO'S SIDESPLITTERS NO.1 • 1915 • Booth W. R. • UKN
KINFOLK see **ALL THE LOVIN' KINFOLK** • 1970
KING • 1978 • Mann Abby • TVM • USA
KING, THE • 1902 • Moss Hugh • UKN
KING, THE • 1930 • Horne James W. • SHT • USA
KING, THE • 1968 • Bear Looney • USA
KING, THE see **O' RE** • 1988
KING: A FILMED RECORD.. MONTGOMERY TO MEMPHIS • 1970 • Mankiewicz Joseph L., Lumet Sidney • DOC • USA
KING AND COUNTRY • 1964 • Losey Joseph • UKN
KING AND FOUR QUEENS, THE • 1956 • Walsh Raoul • USA
KING AND I, THE • 1956 • Lang Walter • USA
KING AND MISTER BIRD, THE see **ROI ET L'OISEAU, LE** • 1979
KING AND QUEEN, THE • 1985 • Paramo Jose Antonio • MTV • SPN
KING AND THE BIRD, THE see **ROI ET L'OISEAU, LE** • 1979
KING AND THE CHORUS GIRL, THE • 1937 • LeRoy Mervyn • USA • ROMANCE IS SACRED (UKN) ○ ROMANCE IN PARIS
KING AND THE COPPER, THE • 1913 • O'Sullivan Tony • USA
KING AND THE GENERAL, THE see **TSAR I GENERAL** • 1966
KING AND THE JESTER, THE • 1901 • *Warwick Trading Co* • UKN
KING AND THE JESTER, THE (USA) see **FRANCOIS 1er ET TRIBOULET** • 1908
KING AND THE LION, THE • *Puppet Films* • ANS • USA
KING AND THE MAN, THE • 1914 • *Kerrigan J. Warren* • USA
KING AND THE WOMAN, THE see **KRAL A ZENA** • 1967
KING APE see **KING KONG** • 1933
KING ARTHUR • Sutherland Hal • ANM • USA
KING ARTHUR • 1980 • Akehi Masayuki • ANM • JPN
KING ARTHUR, THE YOUNG WARLORD • 1975 • Hayers Sidney, Jackson Pat, Sasdy Peter • UKN • KING ARTHUR, THE YOUNG WARRIOR
KING ARTHUR, THE YOUNG WARRIOR see **KING ARTHUR, THE YOUNG WARLORD** • 1975
KING ARTHUR WAS A GENTLEMAN • 1942 • Varnel Marcel • UKN
KING BABY'S BIRTHDAY • 1914 • MacGregor Norval • USA
KING BOLESLAUS THE BOLD see **BOLESLAW SMIALY** • 1970
KING BOXER • 1971 • Cheng Chang Ho, Liu Chia-Liang • HKG • FIVE FINGERS OF DEATH ○ INVINCIBLE BOXER
KING BOXER 2 • Kong Joseph • HKG
KING BY FORCE, A • 1914 • *Melies* • USA
KING CAN DO NO WRONG, THE • 1913 • *Weber Lois* • USA
KING CASIMIR THE GREAT see **KAZIMIERZ WIELKI** • 1975
KING CHARLES • 1913 • Noy Wilfred • UKN
KING CHARLIE see **HIS PREHISTORIC PAST** • 1914
KING CHRONICLE, THE • 1988 • Brittain Don • CND
KING COBRA see **JAWS OF SATAN** • 1981
KING COLE AND HIS TRIO • 1950 • Cowan Will • SHT • USA
KING COWBOY • 1928 • De Lacy Robert • USA • COWBOY KING (UKN)
KING CRAB • 1980 • Chomsky Marvin • TVM • USA
KING CREOLE • 1958 • Curtiz Michael • USA
KING DANFORTH RETIRES • 1913 • *Baggot King* • USA
KING DAVID • 1985 • Beresford Bruce • UKN, USA • STORY OF DAVID, THE
KING–DEER see **DEER KING, THE** • 1970
KING DICK see **NANO E LA STREGA, IL** • 1975
KING DINOSAUR • 1955 • Gordon Bert I. • USA
KING ELEPHANT see **AFRICAN ELEPHANT, THE** • 1971
KING FOR A DAY • 1940 • Fleischer Dave • ANS • USA
KING FOR A DAY • 1983 • Volev Nikolai • BUL
KING FOR A NIGHT • 1933 • Neumann Kurt • USA
KING FRAT • 1979 • Wiederhorn Ken • USA
KING GAME, THE see **HRA NA KRALE** • 1967
KING GOES FORTH TO FRANCE, THE • 1986 • Manttari Anssi • FNL
KING GUN see **GATLING GUN, THE** • 1972
KING HARISHCHANDRA see **HARISHCHANDRA** • 1912
KING HENDRIK • 1965 • SAF
KING HENRY V see **HENRY V** • 1945
KING IN NEW YORK, A • 1957 • Chaplin Charles • UKN

KING IN SHADOW see **HERRSCHER OHNE KRONE** • 1957
KING IS COMING, THE see **KUNGEN KOMMER** • 1936
KING JOHN • 1899 • *Tree Beerbohm* • UKN
KING KELLY OF THE U.S.A. • 1934 • Fields Leonard • USA • IRISH AND PROUD OF IT (UKN)
KING KLUNK • 1933 • Lantz Walter, Nolan William • ANS • USA
KING KODA'S WEDDING see **BAGUE DU ROI KODA, LA** • 1962
KING KONG • 1932 • de Limur Jean • FRN
KING KONG • 1933 • Schoedsack Ernest B., Cooper Merian C. • USA • EIGHTH WONDER OF THE WORLD, THE ○ KING APE ○ KONG
KING KONG • 1962 • Mistry Babhubhai • IND
KING KONG • 1976 • Guillermin John • USA
KING KONG ESCAPES (USA) see **KINGO KONGO NO GYAKUSHU** • 1967
KING KONG LIVES • 1986 • Guillermin John • USA
KING KONG TAI GODZILLA see **KINGO KONGO TAI GOJIRA** • 1962
KING KONG VS. GODZILLA (USA) see **KINGO KONGO TAI GOJIRA** • 1962
KING KONG'S COUNTERATTACK see **KINGO KONGO NO GYAKUSHU** • 1967
KING KONG'S REVENGE see **KINGO KONGO NO GYAKUSHU** • 1967
KING LAVRA see **KRAL LAVRA** • 1950
KING LEAR • 1909 • Ranous William V. • USA
KING LEAR • 1916 • Warde Ernest C. • USA
KING LEAR • 1970 • Brook Peter • UKN, DNM
KING LEAR • 1976 • Rumbelow Steven • UKN
KING LEAR • 1983 • Elliott Michael • MTV • UKN
KING LEAR • 1987 • Godard Jean-Luc • FRN
KING LEAR see **KAROL LIR** • 1969
KING LOG • 1932 • *Grierson John (P)* • DOC • UKN
KING LOONEY XIV • 1935 • *Terry Paul/ Moser Frank (P)* • ANS • USA
KING MATHIAS I see **KROL MACIUS I** • 1957
KING MATT I see **KROL MACIUS I** • 1957
KING MATTHEW I see **KROL MACIUS I** • 1957
KING MIDAS • Sturlis Edward • ANM • PLN
KING MIDAS AND THE GOLDEN TOUCH • 1949 • *Coronet* • SHT • USA
KING MIDAS JUNIOR • 1942 • Sommer Paul, Hubley John • ANS • USA
KING MURDER, THE • 1932 • Thorpe Richard • USA
KING, MURRAY • 1969 • Hoffman David, Gordon Jonathan • USA
KING NEPTUNE • 1932 • Gillett Burt • ANS • USA
KING O' MAKE-BELIEVE, THE • 1916 • Broadwell Robert B. • SHT • USA
KING OF '49ERS • 1942 • *O'Brien Joseph/ Mead Thomas (P)* • SHT • USA
KING OF A PENNY see **DOKA O** • 1926
KING OF AFRICA • 1968 • SAF
KING OF AFRICA see **ONE STEP TO HELL** • 1968
KING OF ALCATRAZ • 1938 • Florey Robert • USA • KING OF THE ALCATRAZ (UKN)
KING OF AMERICA • 1982 • Magyar Dezso • TVM • USA
KING OF AYODHYA, THE see **AYODHYECHA RAJA** • 1932
KING OF BEGGARS, THE • 1910 • *Atlas* • USA
KING OF BERLENG, THE see **REI DAS BERLENGAS, O** • 1977
KING OF BOASTFULNESS see **HARI NG YABANG** • 1968
KING OF BODA see **BODAKUNGEN** • 1920
KING OF BULLIES, THE see **KULHANBEYLER KRALI** • 1967
KING OF BURLESQUE • 1935 • Lanfield Sidney • USA
KING OF CHANCE, THE • 1914 • *Sais Marin* • USA
KING OF CHESS see **OOSHO** • 1948
KING OF CHINATOWN • 1939 • Grinde Nick • USA
KING OF CLOVES, THE see **MILLIONS** • 1936
KING OF CLUBS, THE • 1905 • Martin J. H.? • UKN
KING OF COINERS • 1912 • *Australian Photo Play Co* • ASL
KING OF COINS • 1903 • Collins Alf? • UKN
KING OF COMEDY, THE • 1982 • Scorsese Martin • USA
KING OF COOKS, THE • 1917 • *Bickel George* • SHT • USA
KING OF CRIME, THE • 1914 • Northcote Sidney • UKN
KING OF CRIMINALS, THE see **SUPERARGO EL GIGANTE** • 1967
KING OF DALARNA see **KUNGEN AV DALARNA** • 1953
KING OF DIAMONDS, THE • 1918 • Scardon Paul • USA
KING OF DODGE CITY • 1941 • Hillyer Lambert • USA
KING OF FRIDAY NIGHT, THE • 1985 • Gray John • CND
KING OF GAMBLERS • 1937 • Florey Robert • USA • CZAR OF THE SLOT MACHINES
KING OF HEARTS (USA) see **ROI DE COEUR, LE** • 1966
KING OF HOCKEY • 1936 • Smith Noel • USA • KING OF THE ICE RINK (UKN)
KING OF ILLUSIONISTS, THE • 1911 • *Gaumont* • UKN
KING OF INDIGO, THE • 1911 • Bouwmeester Theo • UKN
KING OF JAZZ, THE • 1930 • Anderson John Murray, Fejos Paul (U/c) • USA
KING OF JAZZ, THE • 1930 • Neumann Kurt • USA
KING OF KAZAM, THE • 1911 • *Wills Nat* • USA
KING OF KINGS • 1961 • Ray Nicholas • USA • JESUS
KING OF KINGS see **KRAL KRALU** • 1963
KING OF KINGS see **KIRALLAR KIRALI** • 1965
KING OF KINGS, THE • 1927 • De Mille Cecil B. • USA
KING OF KONG ISLAND • 1978 • Mauri Roberto • SPN • KONG ISLAND ○ EVE OF THE WILD WOMAN
KING OF KUNG FU • 1973 • Chiang I Hsing • HKG • HE WALKS LIKE A TIGER
KING OF KUNG FU see **YUNG-CH'UN TA-HSIUNG** • 1978
KING OF LOVE, THE • 1987 • Wilkinson Anthony • TVM • USA
KING OF MARVIN GARDENS • 1972 • Rafelson Bob • USA
KING OF PARIS, THE • 1934 • Raymond Jack • UKN
KING OF PARIS, THE see **KOROL PARIZHA** • 1917
KING OF POETS AND THE BIRD OF PASSAGE, THE see **RUNON KUNINGAS JA MUUTTOLINTU** • 1940
KING OF SEVEN DIALS, THE • 1914 • Weston Charles • UKN
KING OF SOHO see **STREET OF SIN, THE** • 1928
KING OF SPAIN'S REVIEW, THE • 1905 • Hepworth Cecil M. • UKN
KING OF SWORDSMEN (USA) see **I-TAI CHIEN-WANG** • 1969
KING OF THE ALCATRAZ (UKN) see **KING OF ALCATRAZ** • 1938
KING OF THE ALDERS, THE see **ROI DES AULNES, LE** • 1908
KING OF THE ANIMALS see **KING OF THE BEASTS** • 1960
KING OF THE ARENA • 1933 • James Alan • USA
KING OF THE BANDITS • 1947 • Cabanne W. Christy • USA
KING OF THE BEASTS • 1960 • Ratz Gunter • ANM • GDR • KING OF THE ANIMALS
KING OF THE BUGS • 1930 • Foster John, Bailey Harry • ANS • USA
KING OF THE BULLWHIP • 1951 • Ormond Ron • USA
KING OF THE CANDLE see **REI DA VELA, O** • 1984
KING OF THE CANNIBAL ISLANDS • 1908 • *Bitzer Billy (Ph)* • USA
KING OF THE CARNIVAL • 1955 • Adreon Franklin • SRL • USA
KING OF THE CASTLE • 1925 • Edwards Henry • UKN
KING OF THE CASTLE • 1936 • Davis Redd • UKN
KING OF THE CHILDREN see **HAI ZI WANG** • 1987
KING OF THE CIRCUS • 1921 • McGowan J. P. • SRL • USA
KING OF THE CIRCUS see **ZIRKUSKONIG, DER** • 1924
KING OF THE CITY see **CLUB LIFE** • 1987
KING OF THE COINERS • 1911 • Rolfe Alfred • ASL
KING OF THE CONGO see **KING OF THE KONGO** • 1952
KING OF THE CORAL SEA • 1954 • Robinson Lee • ASL
KING OF THE COWBOYS • 1943 • Kane Joseph • USA
KING OF THE DAMNED • 1936 • Forde Walter • UKN
KING OF THE FOREST RANGERS • 1946 • Bennet Spencer Gordon, Brannon Fred C. • SRL • USA
KING OF THE GAMBLERS • 1948 • Blair George • USA
KING OF THE GRIZZLIES • 1970 • Kelly Ron • USA, CND
KING OF THE GYPSIES • 1978 • Pierson Frank R. • USA
KING OF THE GYPSIES see **REY DE LOS GITANOS, EL** • 1933
KING OF THE HERD • 1927 • Mattison Frank S. • USA
KING OF THE HILL • 1974 • Brittain Don, Canell Marrin • CND
KING OF THE ICE RINK (UKN) see **KING OF HOCKEY** • 1936
KING OF THE JOROPO-DANCE see **ALIAS EL REY DE JOROPO** • 1978
KING OF THE JUNGLE • 1927 • Cullison Webster • SRL • USA
KING OF THE JUNGLE • 1933 • Humberstone H. Bruce, Marcin Max • USA
KING OF THE JUNGLELAND see **DARKEST AFRICA** • 1936
KING OF THE KEYBOARD • 1943 • Shepherd Horace • UKN
KING OF THE KHYBER RIFLES • 1953 • King Henry • USA
KING OF THE KHYBER RIFLES (UKN) see **BLACK WATCH, THE** • 1929
KING OF THE KITCHEN • 1918 • *Gribbon Harry* • SHT • USA
KING OF THE KNIGHTS, THE see **GECELERIN KRALI** • 1967
KING OF THE KONGO • 1929 • Thorpe Richard • SRL • USA
KING OF THE KONGO • 1952 • Bennet Spencer Gordon, Grissell Wallace A. • SRL • USA • MIGHTY THUNDA, THE ○ KING OF THE CONGO
KING OF THE LUMBERJACKS • 1940 • Clemens William • USA
KING OF THE MACKEREL FISHERS, THE see **ROI DU MAQUILLAGE, LE** • 1904
KING OF THE MARDI GRAS • 1935 • Fleischer Dave • ANS • USA
KING OF THE MONGOLS • 1960 • Kato Tai • JPN • GENGHIS KHAN AND HIS MONGOLS
KING OF THE MOUNTAIN • 1981 • Nosseck Noel • USA
KING OF THE MOUNTAIN see **BEDTIME STORY** • 1964
KING OF THE MOUNTAINS see **ETERNAL LOVE** • 1929
KING OF THE MOUNTIES • 1942 • Witney William • SRL • USA
KING OF THE NEIGHBORHOOD, THE see **REY DEL BARRIO, EL** • 1949
KING OF THE NEWSBOYS • 1938 • Vorhaus Bernard • USA
KING OF THE NIGHT • 1975 • Babenco Hector • BRZ
KING OF THE OLYMPICS see **KING OF THE OLYMPICS: THE LIVES AND LOVES OF AVERY BRUNDAGE** • 1988
KING OF THE OLYMPICS: THE LIVES AND LOVES OF AVERY BRUNDAGE • 1988 • Philips Lee • TVM • USA • KING OF THE OLYMPICS
KING OF THE PACK • 1926 • Richardson Frank • USA
KING OF THE PECOS • 1936 • Kane Joseph • USA
KING OF THE PEOPLE, A • 1917 • Nash Percy • UKN
KING OF THE RING • 1909 • *Selig* • USA
KING OF THE RING see **KOROL MANEZHA** • 1970
KING OF THE RITZ • 1932 • Gallone Carmine • UKN
KING OF THE ROAD (USA) see **IM LAUF DER ZEIT** • 1976
KING OF THE ROARING TWENTIES -THE STORY OF ARNOLD ROTHSTEIN • 1961 • Newman Joseph M. • USA • BIG BANKROLL, THE (UKN)
KING OF THE ROCKET MEN • 1949 • Brannon Fred C. • SRL • USA
KING OF THE RODEO • 1929 • McRae Henry • USA
KING OF THE ROYAL MOUNTED • 1936 • Bretherton Howard • USA
KING OF THE ROYAL MOUNTED • 1940 • Witney William, English John • SRL • USA • YUKON PATROL, THE
KING OF THE SADDLE • 1926 • Craft William James • USA
KING OF THE SHARPSHOOTERS, THE (USA) see **ROI DES TIREURS, LE** • 1905
KING OF THE SIERRAS • 1938 • *Gn* • USA • KILLERS OF THE PRAIRIE (UKN)
KING OF THE SLUMS see **HARI NG SLUMS** • 1968
KING OF THE STALLIONS • 1942 • Finney Edward • USA
KING OF THE STREET, THE see **KRAL ULICE** • 1935
KING OF THE STREETS see **ALIEN WARRIOR** • 1985
KING OF THE SUMAVA, THE see **KRAL SUMAVY** • 1959
KING OF THE SWORDSMEN KINGS • 1970 • Kwok Nan-Hung • HKG
KING OF THE TEXAS RANGERS • 1941 • Witney William, English John • SRL • USA
KING OF THE TURF, THE • 1926 • Hogan James P. • USA • AGES OF LOVE, THE
KING OF THE TURF, THE • 1939 • Green Alfred E. • USA
KING OF THE TWO DAY WONDER • 1979 • Anderson Kevin • ASL
KING OF THE UNDERWORLD • 1939 • Seiler Lewis • USA • UNLAWFUL
KING OF THE UNDERWORLD • 1952 • Gover Victor M. • UKN
KING OF THE VIKINGS • 1960 • Lucia Luis • SPN
KING OF THE WHITE ELEPHANT, THE • 1941 • Vasudhara Sunh • USA
KING OF THE WILD • 1931 • Thorpe Richard, Eason B. Reeves • SRL • USA
KING OF THE WILD HORSES • 1933 • Haley Earl • USA • KING OF THE WILD (UKN)
KING OF THE WILD HORSES • 1947 • Archainbaud George • USA
KING OF THE WILD STALLIONS • 1959 • Springsteen R. G. • USA
KING OF THE WILD (UKN) see **KING OF THE WILD HORSES** • 1933
KING OF THE WIRE, THE • 1915 • Miller Ashley • USA
KING OF THE ZOMBIES • 1941 • Yarbrough Jean • USA
KING OF THIEVES, THE see **DOLANDIRICILAR SAHI** • 1961
KING OF TRAMPS see **SERSERILER KRALI** • 1967
KING OF TROLLEBO, THE see **TROLLEBOKUNGEN** • 1924
KING OF TROUBLE, THE see **REI DA PILANTRAGEM, O** • 1969
KING OF TROUBLE, THE see **ALIAS EL REY DE JOROPO** • 1978
KING OF WHALES, THE • 1934 • Sanderson Challis • UKN
KING OF WILD HORSES, THE • 1924 • Jackman Fred • USA
KING ON HORSEBACK (USA) see **TOUR, PRENDS GARDE!, LA** • 1958
KING ON MAIN STREET, THE • 1925 • Bell Monta • USA
KING, QUEEN, JOKER • 1921 • Chaplin Sydney • USA • JOKER, THE
KING, QUEEN, KNAVE (USA) see **HERZBUBE** • 1972
KING RALPH I • 1990 • Ward David S. • USA
KING RAT • 1965 • Forbes Bryan • USA
KING RENE'S DAUGHTER • 1913 • *Fealy Maude* • USA
KING RICHARD AND THE CRUSADERS • 1954 • Butler David • USA
KING ROBERT OF SICILY • 1912 • Plumb Hay • UKN
KING ROBERT OF SICILY • 1913 • *Essanay* • USA
KING ROBOT see **MOTHER RILEY MEETS THE VAMPIRE** • 1952
KING ROUNDER • 1964 • Rasinski Connie • ANS • USA
KING SCATTERBRAIN'S TROUBLES • 1908 • *Pathe* • FRN
KING SINGER • 1978 • Olivier Richard • BLG
KING SIZE • 1969 • Pindal Kaj • SHT • CND
KING SIZE see **KINGSAJZ** • 1988
KING-SIZE CANARY • 1947 • Avery Tex • ANS • USA
KING SIZE WOMAN • 1966 • Beresford Bruce • DCS • UKN
KING SOLOMON • 1918 • Gillstrom Arvid E. • SHT • USA
KING SOLOMON OF BROADWAY • 1935 • Crosland Alan • USA
KING SOLOMON'S JUDGMENT see **SALOMOS DOM** • 1914
KING SOLOMON'S MINES • 1918 • Lucoque H. Lisle • SAF
KING SOLOMON'S MINES • 1937 • Stevenson Robert • UKN
KING SOLOMON'S MINES • 1950 • Bennett Compton, Marton Andrew • USA
KING SOLOMON'S MINES • 1984 • Thompson J. Lee • USA
KING SOLOMON'S TREASURE • 1976 • Rakoff Alvin • SAF
KING SPRUCE • 1920 • Clements Roy • USA
KING STEPS OUT, THE • 1936 • von Sternberg Josef • USA
KING, THE DETECTIVE • 1911 • *Rea Isabella* • USA
KING, THE DETECTIVE, AND THE SMUGGLERS • 1912 • *Baggot King* • USA
KING THE DETECTIVE IN FORMULA 879 • 1914 • *Baggot King* • USA
KING THE DETECTIVE IN THE JARVIS CASE • 1913 • Baggot King • USA
KING THE DETECTIVE IN THE MARINE MYSTERY • 1914 • Baggot King • USA
KING THRUSHBEARD • 1967 • Beck Walter • GDR
KING TUT-ANKH-AMEN'S EIGHTH WIFE • 1923 • Remo Andrew • USA • MYSTERY OF TUT-ANKH-AMEN'S EIGHTH WIFE, THE
KING TUT'S TOMB • 1950 • Davis Mannie • ANS • USA
KING UBU see **UBU ROI** • 1977
KING WHO HAD NO HEART, THE see **KUNINGAS JOLLA EI OLLUT SYNDANTA** • 1983
KING WITH THE ELASTIC HEAD, THE see **REY DE LA CABEZA ELASTICA, EL**
KING WITHOUT A CROWN, THE • 1937 • Tourneur Jacques • SHT • USA
KING ZILCH • 1933 • *Terry Paul/ Moser Frank (P)* • ANS • USA
KINGDOM AND THE BEAUTY, THE see **CH'IEN LUNG HUANG YU KU-NIANG** • 1980
KINGDOM AND THE BEAUTY, THE (USA) see **CHIANG SHAN MEI JEN** • 1959
KINGDOM COME • 1919 • Holt George • SHT • USA
KINGDOM FOR A HORSE • 1935 • Sparling Gordon • DCS • CND • AU ROYAUME DU CHEVAL
KINGDOM FOR A HOUSE, A see **KONINKRIJK VOOR EEN HUIS, EEN** • 1949
KINGDOM IN THE CLOUDS (USA) see **TINERETE FARA BATRINETE** • 1968
KINGDOM IN THE WILDS see **VILDMARKSRIKE, ETT** • 1964
KINGDOM OF DIAMONDS, THE see **HIRAK RAJARDESHE** • 1978
KINGDOM OF DOVES, THE • 1988 • Korras Giorgos • GRC
KINGDOM OF EROTICISM, THE see **EMANUELLE GIALLA** • 1971
KINGDOM OF HOPE, THE • 1917 • Windom Lawrence C. • SHT • USA
KINGDOM OF HUMAN HEARTS, THE • 1921 • Cosper Wilbert Leroy • USA
KINGDOM OF ISLANDS, A • 1956 • Carlsen Henning • SHT • DNM
KINGDOM OF LOVE, THE • 1918 • Lloyd Frank • USA
KINGDOM OF NEK CHAND, THE • 1981 • Cox Paul • DOC • ASL
KINGDOM OF NOSEY LAND, THE • 1915 • Matthews H. C. • USA
KINGDOM OF RAM, THE see **RAM RAJYA** • 1967
KINGDOM OF THE FAIRIES, THE see **ROYAUME DES FEES, LE** • 1903
KINGDOM OF THE POISON MOTH see **DOKUGA OKOKU** • 1959
KINGDOM OF THE SAND (UKN) see **CONQUISTATORE DELL'ATLANTIDA, IL** • 1965
KINGDOM OF THE SPIDERS • 1977 • Cardos John Bud • USA
KINGDOM OF TWILIGHT, THE • 1929 • MacDonald Alexander • UKN

KINGDOM OF WOMEN, THE see **BABYE TSARSTVO** • 1968
KINGDOM OF YOUTH, THE • 1918 • Badger Clarence • USA
KINGDOM ON THE WATERS, A see **VADVIZORSZAG** • 1952
KINGDOM WITHIN, THE • 1922 • Schertzinger Victor • USA
KINGFISHER CAPER, THE • 1975 • De Villiers Dirk • SAF
KINGFISHER'S ROOST, THE • 1922 • Chaudet Louis W., Hurst Paul C. • USA
KINGMAKER CONNECTION, THE see **MANNETJESMAKER, DE** • 1983
KINGO KONGO NO GYAKUSHU • 1967 • Honda Inoshiro, Rankin Arthur Jr.(Usa Version) • JPN • KING KONG ESCAPES (USA) ○ KING KONG'S COUNTERATTACK ○ REVENGE OF KING KONG, THE ○ KING KONG'S REVENGE
KINGO KONGO TAI GOJIRA • 1962 • Honda Inoshiro, Montgomery Thomas (Usa Vers) • JPN • KING KONG VS. GODZILLA (USA) ○ KING KONG TAI GODZILLA
KINGORO NO KAIGUN TAISHO • 1960 • Magatani Morehei • JPN
KINGORO NO NARIKIN WO • 1958 • Magatani Morehei • JPN
KINGPIN • 1985 • Walker Mike • NZL
KINGPIN, THE • 1967 • Saez Nilo • PHL
KINGS AND DESPERATE MEN • 1981 • Kanner Alexis • CND • KINGS AND DESPERATE MEN: A HOSTAGE INCIDENT
KINGS AND DESPERATE MEN: A HOSTAGE INCIDENT see **KINGS AND DESPERATE MEN** • 1981
KINGS AND QUEENS • 1956 • Czinner Paul • SHT • UKN
KING'S BLUNDER, THE see **KRALOVSKY OMYL** • 1968
KING'S BOOK, THE see **SIAVASH IN PERSEPOLIS** • 1966
KING'S BREAKFAST, THE • 1928 • Miller Frank • UKN
KING'S BREAKFAST, THE • 1937 • Reiniger Lotte • ANS • UKN
KING'S BREAKFAST, THE • 1963 • Toye Wendy • SHT • UKN
KING'S CREEK LAW • 1923 • Maloney Leo, Williamson Bob • USA
KING'S CUP, THE • 1933 • Wilcox Herbert, Cullen Robert J. • UKN
KING'S DAUGHTER, THE • 1916 • Elvey Maurice • UKN
KING'S DAUGHTER, THE • 1934 • *Terry Paul/ Moser Frank (P)* • ANS • USA
KING'S DIAMOND, THE • 1908 • *Lubin* • USA
KINGS DO NO DIE see **KRALLAR OLMEZ** • 1967
KING'S ENGLISH, THE • 1932 • Field Mary • DOC • UKN
KING'S FILM, THE see **PELICULA DEL REY, LA** • 1986
KING'S GAME, THE • 1915 • *Gold Rooster* • USA
KING'S GAME, THE • 1916 • Miller Ashley • USA
KINGS GO FORTH • 1958 • Daves Delmer • USA
KING'S HIGHWAY, THE • 1927 • Hill Sinclair • UKN
KINGS IN EXILE • 1937 • Field Mary • UKN
KING'S JESTER, THE • 1935 • *Mintz Charles (P)* • ANS • USA
KING'S JESTER, THE (USA) see **RE SI DIVERTE, IL** • 1941
KING'S KNIGHT, THE see **CAPITAN, LE** • 1945
KING'S MAN, THE • 1913 • Bowman William J. • USA
KING'S MEADOW GARDENS see **KONGENS ENGHAVE** • 1967
KING'S MESSENGER • 1908 • *Bitzer Billy (Ph)* • USA
KING'S MESSENGER, THE • 1913 • *Solax* • USA
KING'S MINISTER, THE • 1914 • Shaw Harold • UKN
KING'S MOVE IN THE CITY, THE • 1914 • Brabin Charles J. • USA
KINGS OF ENDINGS see **KRALJEVA ZAVRSNICA** • 1987
KINGS OF PETROL see **PETROL KRALLARI** • 1979
KINGS OF THE FOREST • 1912 • Campbell Colin • USA
KINGS OF THE OLYMPICS • 1948 • *Lerner Geraldine (Ed)* • DOC • FRG
KINGS OF THE ROAD see **IM LAUF DER ZEIT** • 1976
KINGS OF THE SUN • 1963 • Thompson J. Lee • USA • INCA
KINGS OR BETTER • 1931 • Buzzell Edward • SHT • USA
KING'S ORDERS see **ARASA KATTALAI** • 1967
KING'S OUTCAST, THE • 1915 • Dewsbury Ralph • UKN • HIS VINDICATION (USA)
KING'S PARDON, THE • 1908 • Porter Edwin S. • USA
KING'S PARDON, THE • 1911 • Aylott Dave • UKN
KING'S PEOPLE, THE • 1937 • Stumar John S.
KING'S PERIL, THE • 1911 • Martinek H. O. • UKN
KING'S PIRATE, THE • 1967 • Weis Don • USA
KING'S RHAPSODY • 1955 • Wilcox Herbert • UKN
KING'S ROMANCE, THE • 1914 • Batley Ernest G. • UKN • REVOLUTIONIST, THE (USA) ○ REVOLUTION
KING'S ROW • 1942 • Wood Sam • USA
KING'S SENTENCE, THE • 1962 • Latallo Katarzyna • ANM • PLN
KING'S SERVICE, THE • 1905 • *Gale & Polden* • SER • UKN
KING'S STORY, A • 1967 • Booth Harry • DOC • UKN
KING'S STREET see **KUNGSGATAN** • 1943
KING'S THIEF, THE • 1955 • Leonard Robert Z. • USA
KINGS UP • 1934 • Lantz Walter, Nolan William • ANS • USA
KING'S VACATION, THE • 1933 • Adolfi John G. • USA
KING'S VENGEANCE, THE • 1916 • *Puritan* • USA
KING'S WHORE, THE • 1990 • Corti Axel • AUS, FRN, UKN
KINGSAJZ • 1988 • Machulski Juliusz • PLN • KING SIZE ○ KINGSIZE
KINGSGATE • 1990 • Darcus Jack • CND
KINGSIZE see **KINGSAJZ** • 1988
KINGSTON see **KINGSTON: THE POWER PLAY** • 1976
KINGSTON PENITENTIARY • 1958 • Watson Patrick • DOC • CND
KINGSTON: THE POWER PLAY • 1976 • Day Robert • TVM • USA • NEWSPAPER GAME, THE ○ KINGSTON
KINIGI, I • 1976 • Angelopoulos Theo • GRC • HUNTERS, THE ○ KYNIGHI, I ○ HUNTSMEN, THE
KINJIRARETA KUCHIBIRU • 1957 • Horiiki Kiyoshi • JPN • FORBIDDEN LIPS
KINJITE • 1989 • Thompson J. Lee • USA • FORBIDDEN SUBJECTS ○ KINJITE: FORBIDDEN SUBJECTS
KINJITE: FORBIDDEN SUBJECTS see **KINJITE** • 1989
KINK IN THE PICASSO, A • 1990 • Gracie Marc • ASL
KINKAID, GAMBLER • 1916 • Wells Raymond • USA
KINKAKU-JI • 1975 • Takabayashi Yoichi • JPN • KINKAKU-JI TEMPLE, THE
KINKAKU-JI TEMPLE, THE see **KINKAKU-JI** • 1975
KINKAN-SHOKU • 1975 • Yamamoto Satsuo • JPN • ANNULAR ECLIPSE ○ ANNUAL ECLIPSE
KINKISHA, THE • 1978 • McArdle Tom • IRL
KINKY COACHES AND THE POM-POM PUSSYCATS, THE see **CRUNCH** • 1980
KINKY DARLINGS, THE (UKN) see **PER UNA VALIGIA PIENA DI DONNE** • 1964
KINMON-TO NI KAKERU HASHI • 1962 • Matsuo Akinori • JPN • RAINBOW OVER THE KINMEN
KINNHAKEN, DER • 1962 • Thiel Heinz • GDR
KINNO JIDAI • 1927 • Kinugasa Teinosuke • JPN • EPOCH OF LOYALTY
KINO-CONCERT 1941 • 1941 • Rappaport Herbert (c/d) • USS • LENINGRAD MUSIC HALL
KINO EYE see **KINO-GLAZ** • 1924
KINO-GLAZ • 1924 • Vertov Dziga • USS • CINEMA EYE ○ LIFE UNAWARES ○ CAMERA EYE ○ KINO EYE
KINO KIETA OTOKO • 1941 • Makino Masahiro • JPN • MAN WHO DISAPPEARED YESTERDAY, THE
KINO PRAVDA • 1922-25 • Vertov Dziga • SER • USS • FILM TRUTH ○ CINEMA-TRUTH
KINO, THE PADRE ON HORSEBACK • 1977 • Kennedy Ken • USA
KINO V DEREVNE • 1930 • Ptushko Alexander • ANS • USS • CINEMA IN THE COUNTRY
KINO ZA DVADTSAT LET • 1940 • Shub Esther, Pudovkin V. I. • USS • TWENTY YEARS OF SOVIET CINEMA ○ 20 LET SOVETSKOGO KINO ○ TWENTY YEARS OF CINEMA
KINOATOMAT • 1967 • Cincera Raduz • CZC
KINODNEVIK GLUMOVA • 1923 • Eisenstein Sergei • SHT • USS • GLUMOV'S DIARY ○ GLURUMOV'S FILM DIARY
KINOKONCERT K25 LETIJU KRASNOJ ARMII • 1943 • Gerasimov Sergei, Dzigan Yefim, Kalatozov Mikhail • USS • FILM CONCERT FOR THE RED ARMY'S 25TH ANNIVERSARY ○ MOSCOW MUSIC HALL
KINONIA MAS ADIKISE, I • 1967 • Santas Thanos • GRC • SOCIETY WRONGED US ○ WRONGED, THE
KINPEIBEI see **CHIN-P'ING-MEI** • 1969
KINSHIP OF COURAGE, THE • 1915 • *Majestic* • USA
KINSMAN, THE • 1919 • Edwards Henry • UKN
KINUYO MONOGATARI • 1930 • Gosho Heinosuke • JPN • STORY OF KINUYO ○ KINUYO STORY, THE
KINUYO STORY, THE see **KINUYO MONOGATARI** • 1930
KIP AND DAVID • 1963 • Cantrill Arthur, Cantrill Corinne • ASL
KIP NOLL SUPERSTAR • Higgins William • USA
KIPAS AKAR WANGI • 1981 • Karya Teguh • INN • FAN, THE
KIPPERBANG see **P'TANG YANG KIPPERBANG** • 1982
KIPPS • 1921 • Shaw Harold • UKN
KIPPS • 1941 • Reed Carol • UKN, USA • REMARKABLE MR. KIPPS, THE
KIRAF AL-LUBNANYA, AL- • 1972 • Nasser George • SHT • LBN
KIRALIK KADIN • 1967 • Erakalin Ulku • TRK • WOMAN FOR HIRE, A
KIRALLAR KIRALI • 1965 • Olgac Bilge • TRK • KING OF KINGS
KIRALYGILKOSSAG -EGY MERENYLET ANATOMIAJA • 1984 • Bokor Pierre • HNG • REGICIDE -ANATOMY OF AN ASSASSINATION
KIRARE YOSABURO • 1960 • Ito Daisuke • JPN • SLASHED YOSABURO
KIRBAC ALTINDA • 1967 • Saydam Nejat • TRK • UNDER THE WHIP
KIRETSU • 1968 • Kimata Akihiro • JPN • CREVICE
KIRI ARU JOJI • 1959 • Shibuya Minoru • JPN • AFFAIR IN THE MIST
KIRI NI MUSEBU YORU • 1968 • Umezu Meijiro • JPN • HARBOR LIGHT YOKOHAMA (USA) ○ KILLER IN THE FOG
KIRI NO AME • 1924 • Kinugasa Teinosuke • JPN • FOG AND RAIN
KIRI NO MINATO • 1923 • Mizoguchi Kenji • JPN • FOGGY HARBOR (USA) ○ ANNA CHRISTIE ○ HARBOUR IN THE FOG
KIRI NO MINATO NO AKAI HANA • 1962 • Murayama Shinji • JPN • LOVE AT THE FOGGY HARBOUR
KIRI NO NAKA NO OTOKO • 1958 • Kurahara Koreyoshi • JPN • MAN IN THE FOG, A
KIRI THE CLOWN • 1966-69 • Image Jean • ASS • FRN
KIRIGAKURE SAIZO • 1964 • Tanaka Tokuzo • JPN • TWILIGHT FOG
KIRIK BIR ASK HIKAYESI • 1982 • Kavur Omer • TRK • BROKEN HEARTED LOVE STORY, A
KIRINJI • 1926 • Kinugasa Teinosuke • JPN
KIRJE • 1978 • Hyytiainen Pekka • FNL • LETTER, THE
KIRK DOUGLAS • 1967 • Piwowski Marek • PLN
KIRKE OG ORGEL • 1930 • Schneevoigt George • DNM
KIRKWOOD HAUNTING, THE • 1978 • McDougall Don • MTV • USA
KIRLIAN WITNESS, THE • 1981 • Sarno Jonathan • USA • PLANTS ARE WATCHING, THE
KIRMES • 1960 • Staudte Wolfgang • FRG • KERMES
KIRMIZI FENER SOKAGI • 1968 • Baytan Natuk • TRK • RED LIGHT STREET
KIROKUNAKI SEISHUN • 1967 • Abe Takao • JPN • YOUTH WITHOUT DOCUMENTS
KIRPITCHIKI • 1925 • Obolenski, Doller Mikhail • USS • LITTLE BRICKS
KIRPLANGIC FIRTINASI • 1985 • Candemir Atilla • TRK • SWALLOW STORM, THE
KIRSCHEN IN NACHBARS GARTEN • 1956 • Engels Erich • FRG
KIRSCHEN IN NACHBARS GARTEN, DIE • 1927 • Neufeld Max • FRG
KIRSCHEN IN NACHBARS GERTEN • 1935 • Engels Erich • FRG
KIRU • 1962 • Misumi Kenji • JPN • DESTINY'S SON
KIRU • 1968 • Okamoto Kihachi • JPN • KILL!
KIRYUIN HANAKO NO SHOGAI • 1983 • Gosha Hideo • JPN • LIFE OF HANAKO KIRYUIN, A
KIS EMBER, NAGY VAROS • 1967 • Macskassy Gyula, Varnai Gyorgy • ANS • HNG • LITTLE MAN, BIG CITY
KIS KATALIN HAZASSAGA • 1949 • Mariassy Felix • HNG • CATHERINE'S MARRIAGE
KIS VALENTINO, A • 1979 • Jeles Andras • HNG • LITTLE VALENTINO, THE
KISA • 1973 • Djordjevic Purisa • YGS • RAIN
KISAH YANTI see **TANDES** • 1984
KISAN KANYA • 1937 • Gidwani Moti B. • IND
KISAPMATA • 1981 • De Leon Mike • PHL • IN THE WINKING OF AN EYE
KISEKI • 1963 • Kuri Yoji • ANS • JPN • LOCUST
KISENGA MAN OF AFRICA see **MEN OF TWO WORLDS** • 1946
KISERTET LUBLON • 1977 • Ban Robert • HNG • PHANTOM ON HORSEBACK, THE ○ HAUNTED CITY, THE
KISETSU-FU • 1977 • Saito Koichi • JPN • SEASONAL WIND, THE
KISETSUFU NO KANATANI • 1958 • Sekigawa Hideo • JPN • BEYOND THE SEASONAL WIND
KISHIN YURI KEIJI • 1924 • Kinugasa Teinosuke • JPN
KISKAKAS GYEMANT FELKRAJCARJA, A • 1950 • Macskassy Gyula • ANS • HNG • DIAMOND OF THE LITTLE COCKEREL, THE ○ LITTLE COCK'S HALFPENNY, THE
KISKRACAR • 1954 • Keleti Marton • HNG • PENNY
KISLALAR DOLDU BUGUN • 1968 • Figenli Yavuz • TRK • BARRACKS ARE FULL TODAY, THE
KISMAMA see **KLEINE MUTTI** • 1934
KISMAT • 1943 • *Biswas Anil (M)* • IND
KISMAT-KI-BHUL-SUDHA see **KALKOOT** • 1935
KISMET • 1914 • Bantock Leedham • UKN
KISMET • 1916 • *California Motion P.c.* • USA
KISMET • 1916 • Berger Martin • FRG
KISMET • 1920 • Gasnier Louis J. • USA
KISMET • 1930 • Dillon John Francis • USA
KISMET • 1931 • Dieterle William • FRG
KISMET • 1944 • Dieterle William • USA • ORIENTAL DREAMS
KISMET • 1955 • Minnelli Vincente, Donen Stanley (U/c) • USA
KISMET KA DHANI • 1946 • *Gulab* • IND
KISPUS • 1956 • Balling Erik • DNM
KISS • 1970 • Levitte Jean • FRN
KISS see **KISS, THE** • 1964
KISS 23480/72 see **BEIJO 23480/72** • 1989
KISS, THE • 1899 • Hepworth Cecil M. • UKN
KISS, THE • 1900 • Porter Edwin S. • USA
KISS, THE • 1913 • Reid Wallace • USA
KISS, THE • 1914 • Davis Ulysses • USA
KISS, THE • 1915 • *Sweeney Peggy* • USA
KISS, THE • 1916 • Henderson Dell • USA
KISS, THE • 1921 • Conway Jack • USA
KISS, THE • 1929 • Feyder Jacques • USA
KISS, THE • 1964 • Warhol Andy • USA • KISS
KISS, THE • 1969 • Popescu-Gopo Ion • ANM • RMN
KISS, THE • 1988 • Densham Pen • CND, USA
KISS, THE see **BAISER, LE** • 1929
KISS, THE see **SARUTUL** • 1965
KISS, THE see **SUUDELMA** • 1969
KISS, THE see **POLJUBAC** • 1970
KISS AND A TUMBLE, A (USA) see **BROKEN BROOM, THE** • 1904
KISS AND MAKE UP • 1921 • Christie Al • USA
KISS AND MAKE UP • 1934 • Thompson Harlan • USA
KISS AND TELL • 1945 • Wallace Richard • USA
KISS AND THE SWORD, THE see **IRON GLOVE, THE** • 1954
KISS BARRIER, THE • 1925 • Neill R. William • USA
KISS BEFORE DYING, A • 1956 • Oswald Gerd • USA
KISS BEFORE DYING, A • 1990 • Dearden James • USA
KISS BEFORE THE MIRROR • 1933 • Whale James • USA
KISS DADDY GOODBYE • 1981 • Regan Patrick • USA
KISS FOR CINDERELLA, A • 1926 • Brenon Herbert • USA
KISS FOR CORLISS, A • 1949 • Wallace Richard • USA • ALMOST A BRIDE
KISS FOR ME, A • 1957 • Li Han-Hsiang • HKG
KISS FOR SUSIE, A • 1917 • Thornby Robert T. • USA
KISS FROM BEYOND THE GRAVE, THE see **BESO DE ULTRATUMBA, EL** • 1962
KISS FROM EDDIE, A see **AROUSERS, THE** • 1971
KISS FROM THE STADIUM, A see **POLIBEK ZE STADIONU** • 1948
KISS HER see **KYSS HENNE!** • 1940
KISS HER GOODBYE • 1959 • Lipton Albert • USA
KISS IN A TAXI, A • 1927 • Badger Clarence • USA
KISS IN AUSTRALIA • 1980 • Weis Bob • DOC • ASL
KISS IN THE DARK, A • 1909 • *Essanay* • USA
KISS IN THE DARK, A • 1925 • Tuttle Frank • USA
KISS IN THE DARK, A • 1949 • Daves Delmer • USA
KISS IN THE DARK, A see **DO AND DARE** • 1922
KISS IN THE TUNNEL, THE • 1899 • *Riley Brothers* • UKN
KISS IN THE TUNNEL, THE • 1899 • Smith G. A. • UKN
KISS IN TIME, A • 1921 • Heffron Thomas N. • USA
KISS & KILL (USA) see **TODESKUSS DES DR. FU MAN CHU, DER** • 1968
KISS KISS.. BANG BANG • 1966 • Tessari Duccio • ITL, SPN
KISS KISS BANG BANG see **BANG BANG GANG, THE** • 1970
KISS KISS, KILL KILL (UKN) see **KOMMISSAR X: JAGD AUF UNBEKANNT** • 1965
KISS KISS, KILL KILL (USA) see **SOMEONE AT THE TOP OF THE STAIRS** • 1974
KISS ME! • 1904 • *Biograph* • USA
KISS ME • 1918 • Reardon James • UKN
KISS ME AGAIN • 1925 • Lubitsch Ernst • USA
KISS ME AGAIN • 1931 • Seiter William A. • USA • TOAST OF THE LEGION (UKN) ○ MADEMOISELLE MODISTE
KISS ME AND DIE see **LADY IN RED, THE** • 1979
KISS ME, BABY • 1961 • Hunt Lillian • USA
KISS ME, CAROLINE • 1920 • Christie Al • SHT • USA • KISS ME, KAROLINE
KISS ME CAT • 1953 • Jones Charles M. • ANS • USA
KISS ME DEADLY • 1955 • Aldrich Robert • USA
KISS ME GENERAL (UKN) see **MARTIN SOLDAT** • 1966
KISS ME GOOD NIGHT • 1914 • *Johnson Arthur* • USA
KISS ME GOODBYE • 1982 • Mulligan Robert • USA
KISS ME GOODBYE (USA) see **GOING GAY** • 1933
KISS ME, KAROLINE see **KISS ME, CAROLINE** • 1920
KISS ME KATE • 1953 • Sidney George • USA
KISS ME, KILL ME • 1976 • O'Herlihy Michael • TVM • USA
KISS ME, KILL ME see **T.A.G., THE ASSASSINATION GAME** • 1982
KISS ME KILLER • Maceignac Roland • FRN
KISS ME, KISS ME, KISS ME! • 1967 • Milligan Andy • USA
KISS ME, MARISA see **PHILISE ME, MARITSA** • 1931
KISS ME MATE • 1969 • *Streeter Maria* • USA
KISS ME MONSTER (USA) see **BESAME, MONSTRUO** • 1968

KISS ME QUICK! • 1920 • Blystone John G. • SHT • USA
KISS ME QUICK! • 1964 • Meyer Russ • USA • DR. BREEDLOVE ○ DR. BREEDLOVE OR HOW I LEARNED TO STOP WORRYING AND LOVE
KISS ME QUICK see **SARUTALI** • 1968
KISS ME SERGEANT • 1930 • Banks Monty • UKN
KISS ME SOFT RUBBER • 1984 • Coh Zvank • ANM • YGS
KISS ME STUPID • 1964 • Wilder Billy • USA
KISS ME (UKN) see **LOVE KISS, THE** • 1930
KISS ME WITH LUST • Pallardy Jean-Marie? • FRN
KISS MEETS THE PHANTOM • 1978 • Hessler Gordon • TVM • USA • KISS MEETS THE PHANTOM OF THE PARK ○ ATTACK OF THE PHANTOMS ○ PHANTOM OF THE PARK, THE ○ KISS: THE PHANTOM OF THE PARK
KISS MEETS THE PHANTOM OF THE PARK see **KISS MEETS THE PHANTOM** • 1978
KISS MY GRITS see **SUMMER HEAT** • 1983
KISS MY HAND see **FERRENTE** • 1973
KISS, NEARLY, A • 1914 • Collins Edwin J.? • UKN
KISS OF CLAY, THE • 1914 • Kinder Stuart • UKN
KISS OF DEATH • 1947 • Hathaway Henry • USA
KISS OF DEATH, THE see **DODSKYSSEN** • 1917
KISS OF DISHONOR, THE • 1915 • MacGregor Norval • USA
KISS OF EVIL (USA) see **KISS OF THE VAMPIRE, THE** • 1962
KISS OF FIRE • 1955 • Newman Joseph M. • USA
KISS OF FIRE see **GOUBBIAH MON AMOUR** • 1956
KISS OF HATE, THE • 1916 • Nigh William • USA
KISS OF HER FLESH, THE • 1968 • Findlay Michael • USA
KISS OF JUDAS, THE • 1913 • *Solax* • USA
KISS OF LIFE see **BEIJO DE VIDA, O** • 1976
KISS OF MARY JANE, THE • 1911 • Melies Gaston • USA
KISS OF MARY PICKFORD, THE see **POTSELUI MERI PIKFORD** • 1927
KISS OF RETRIBUTION, THE • 1913 • Brooke Van Dyke • USA
KISS OF SALVATION, THE • 1913 • *Melies* • USA
KISS OF THE SPIDER WOMAN • 1984 • Babenco Hector • BRZ
KISS OF THE TARANTULA, THE • 1972 • Munger Chris • USA • SHUDDERS
KISS OF THE TIGER, THE • 1989 • Haffter Peter • FRG
KISS OF THE VAMPIRE, THE • 1962 • Sharp Don • UKN • KISS OF EVIL (USA)
KISS-OFF • 1968 • *D-J Productions* • USA
KISS ON THE CRUISE, THE see **KYSSEN PA KRYSSEN** • 1950
KISS OR KILL • 1918 • Clifton Elmer • USA
KISS PAPA • 1926 • Roberts Stephen • SHT • USA
KISS, PART III: WOMEN'S WAYS, THE see **KUCHIZUKE III: ONNA DOSHI** • 1955
KISS THE BLOOD OFF MY HANDS • 1948 • Foster Norman • USA • BLOOD ON MY HANDS (UKN) ○ UNAFRAID, THE
KISS THE BOYS GOODBYE • 1941 • Schertzinger Victor • USA
KISS THE BRIDE • 1919 • Sidney Scott • USA
KISS THE BRIDE GOODBYE • 1944 • Stein Paul L. • UKN
KISS THE DEAD (USA) see **KUSSE, DIE TOTEN** • 1958
KISS THE GIRLS AND MAKE THEM DIE • 1966 • Levin Henry, Maiuri Dino • USA, ITL • SE TUTTE LE DONNE DEL MONDO (ITL) ○ OPERAZIONE PARADISO ○ OPERATION PARADISE ○ IF ALL THE WOMEN IN THE WORLD
KISS THE GIRLS AND MAKE THEM DIE! see **KISS THE GIRLS AND SEE THEM DIE!** • 1968
KISS THE GIRLS AND SEE THEM DIE! • 1968 • *Inter-American Film Dist.* • USA • KISS THE GIRLS AND MAKE THEM DIE!
KISS THE NIGHT see **CANDY REGENTAG** • 1987
KISS THE OTHER SHEIK see **OGGI DOMANI DOPODOMANI** • 1965
KISS: THE PHANTOM OF THE PARK see **KISS MEETS THE PHANTOM** • 1978
KISS THEM FOR ME • 1957 • Donen Stanley • USA
KISS TOMORROW GOODBYE • 1950 • Douglas Gordon • USA
KISSED • 1922 • Baggot King • USA
KISSED IN A HAREM • 1920 • *Bletcher Billy* • USA
KISSER PLANT • 1964 • Rasinski Connie • ANS • USA
KISSES • 1922 • Karger Maxwell • USA
KISSES see **KUCHIZUKE** • 1957
KISSES AND KURSES • 1930 • Lantz Walter, Nolan William • ANS • USA
KISSES BY COMMAND see **GAY DIPLOMAT** • 1931
KISSES FOR AUNTIE see **TANDES** • 1984
KISSES FOR BREAKFAST • 1941 • Seiler Lewis • USA • SHE STAYED KISSED
KISSES FOR MY PRESIDENT • 1964 • Bernhardt Curtis • USA • KISSES FOR THE PRESIDENT
KISSES FOR THE PRESIDENT see **KISSES FOR MY PRESIDENT** • 1964
KISSES RIGHT AND LEFT see **KYS TIL HOJRE OG VENSTRE** • 1969
KISSIN' COUSINS • 1964 • Nelson Gene • USA
KISSING BANDIT, THE • 1948 • Benedek Laslo • USA
KISSING BUTTERFLY, THE • 1917 • *La Salle* • USA
KISSING COUPLE, THE • 1896 • UKN
KISSING CUP see **GIFT, THE** • 1913
KISSING CUP'S RACE • 1920 • West Walter • UKN
KISSING CUP'S RACE • 1930 • Knight Castleton • UKN
KISSING DUET, THE • 1899 • *Haydon & Urry* • UKN
KISSING DUET FROM "THE GEISHA" • 1909 • *Warwick Trading Co* • UKN
KISSING GERM • 1914 • *Columbus* • USA
KISSING KATE • 1913 • Henderson Dell • USA
KISSING PILLS • 1912 • *Lubin* • USA
KISSOGRAM GIRLS see **SEXY SECRETS OF THE KISSOGRAM GIRLS, THE**
KISUKA • 1965 • *Tsuburaya Eiji* • JPN
KISZTIHAND BUDAPEST • 1975 • Lisziak Elek • HNG • HELLO BUDAPEST
KIT CARSON • 1910 • *Bison* • USA
KIT CARSON • 1928 • Werker Alfred L., Ingraham Lloyd • USA
KIT CARSON • 1940 • Seitz George B. • USA
KIT CARSON OVER THE GREAT DIVIDE • 1925 • Mattison Frank S. • USA • WITH KIT CARSON OVER THE GREAT DIVIDE
KIT CARSON'S WOOING • 1911 • Boggs Frank • USA
KIT FOR KAT • 1948 • Freleng Friz • ANS • USA
KIT, THE ARKANSAW TRAVELER • 1914 • Buel Kenean • USA
KIT THE WHALE AND KOT THE CAT • 1970 • Gurvich Irina • ANS • USS
KITA NO MISAKI • 1975 • Kumai Kei • JPN • CAPE OF THE NORTH
KITA NO SANNIN • 1945 • Saeki • JPN • THREE MEN OF THE NORTH, THE
KITAGUNI NO RYOJO • 1967 • Nishikawa Katsumi • JPN • JOURNEY TO THE NORTH
KITAHODAKA ZESSHO • 1968 • Sawashima Tadashi • JPN • CRY OF THE MOUNTAIN (USA) ○ CALL OF THE MOUNTAIN
KITAKITSUNE MONGATARI • 1978 • Kurahara Koreyoshi, Taketazu Minoru • JPN • GLACIER FOX, THE ○ FOX STORY
KITCHEN • 1966 • Warhol Andy • USA • KITCHENETTE
KITCHEN • 1969 • Zwartjes Frans • SHT • NTH
KITCHEN, THE • 1961 • Hill James • UKN
KITCHEN, THE • 1977 • Rakoff Alvin • MTV • UKN
KITCHEN CHILD, THE • 1989 • Perino • SHT • UKN
KITCHEN COUNTESS, THE • 1914 • Dewsbury Ralph • UKN
KITCHEN CYNIC, THE • 1944 • Yates Hal • SHT • USA
KITCHEN DISCOURSES WITH REBEL WOMEN see **KUCHENGESPRACHE MIT REBELLINEN** • 1985
KITCHEN HERO, A • 1918 • Curtis Allen • SHT • USA
KITCHEN LADY, THE • 1918 • Cline Eddie • SHT • USA
KITCHEN MAID'S DREAM, THE • 1907 • Blackton J. Stuart • USA
KITCHEN MECHANIC, THE • 1913 • *White Pearl* • USA
KITCHEN OF THE RICH, THE see **ZENGIN MUTFAGI** • 1988
KITCHEN PEACE see **DAIDOKORO TAIHEIKI** • 1963
KITCHEN POLICE • 1919 • Lyons Eddie, Moran Lee • SHT • USA
KITCHEN ROMANCE, A • 1917 • Moss Howard S. • ANM • USA
KITCHEN SINK • 1989 • McLean Alison • NZL • KITCHEN SINK -A NIGHTMARE COME TRUE
KITCHEN SINK -A NIGHTMARE COME TRUE see **KITCHEN SINK** • 1989
KITCHEN TALENT • 1928 • Roberts Stephen • SHT • USA
KITCHEN THINK • 1974 • Mishkin Lee, Halas John • ANS • UKN
KITCHEN TOTO, THE • 1987 • Hook Harry • UKN
KITCHENELLA • 1917 • Curtis Allen • SHT • USA
KITCHENETTE see **KITCHEN** • 1966
KITE see **TAKO** • 1987
KITE, THE • 1915 • *Kb* • USA
KITE, THE see **GHUDDI** • 1979
KITE FROM ACROSS THE WORLD, THE see **CERFVOLANT DU BOUT DU MONDE, LE** • 1957
KITE FROM THE END OF THE WORLD, THE see **CERFVOLANT DU BOUT DU MONDE, LE** • 1957
KITE MOB, THE • 1938 • Delamar Mickey, Kavanagh Denis • UKN
KITES see **LETUN** • 1931
KITES DON'T SPARE THEIR PREY see **KORSHUNY DOBYCHEI NE DELYATSYA** • 1989
KITH AND KIN • 1913 • *Ammex* • USA
KITNOU • 1924 • Peguy Robert • FRN
KITORES • 1971 • Bacso Peter • HNG • OUTBREAK
KITOSCH, L'UOMO CHE VENIVA DAL LORD • 1967 • Merino Jose Luis • ITL, SPN • KITOSCH, THE MAN WHO CAME FROM THE NORTH
KITOSCH, THE MAN WHO CAME FROM THE NORTH see **KITOSCH, L'UOMO CHE VENIVA DAL LORD** • 1967
KITRO see **GE-GE-GE NO KITARO** • 1968
KITSCH • 1919 • Pick Lupu • FRG • TRAGODIE EINER INTRIGANTIN, DIE
KITSOS AND HIS BROTHERS see **KITSOS KE T'ADHELFIA TOU, O** • 1968
KITSOS KE T'ADHELFIA TOU, O • 1968 • Paraskhakis Pavlos • GRC • KITSOS AND HIS BROTHERS
KITSOS, MINI KE SOUVLAKIA • 1968 • Santas Thanos • GRC • KITSOS, MINI-SKIRTS AND SOUVLAKIA
KITSOS, MINI-SKIRTS AND SOUVLAKIA see **KITSOS, MINI KE SOUVLAKIA** • 1968
KITSUNE • 1939 • Shibuya Minoru • JPN • FOX, THE
KITTE-NO GENSO • 1959 • Kuri Yoji • ANS • JPN • FANTASIA OF STAMPS ○ STAMP FANTASIA
KITTEN IN THE CAGE • 1968 • MacLeod Richard • USA
KITTEN NURSERY, THE • 1901 • Smith G. A. • UKN
KITTEN ON THE KEYS see **DO YOU LOVE ME?** • 1946
KITTEN SITTER, THE • 1949 • Donnelly Eddie • ANS • USA
KITTEN WITH A WHIP • 1964 • Heyes Douglas • USA
KITTENS' MITTENS • 1940 • Lovy Alex • ANS • USA
KITTENS NOT CARRIED • 1967 • Pinkava Josef • CZC
KITTY • 1929 • Saville Victor • UKN
KITTY • 1945 • Leisen Mitchell • USA
KITTY see **KATKA** • 1949
KITTY AND THE BAGMAN • 1982 • Crombie Donald • ASL
KITTY AND THE BANDITS • 1912 • *Payne Edna* • USA
KITTY AND THE COWBOYS • 1911 • Thompson Frederick A. • USA
KITTY AND THE MARRIAGE BROKER see **MODEL AND THE MARRIAGE BROKER, THE** • 1951
KITTY AND THE WORLD CONFERENCE see **KITTY UND DIE WELTKONFERENZ** • 1939
KITTY AT BOARDING SCHOOL • 1912 • *Edison* • USA
KITTY CADDY • 1947 • Marcus Sid • ANS • USA
KITTY CAN'T HELP IT see **CARHOPS** • 1980
KITTY CARSTAIRS (UKN) see **BEYOND LONDON LIGHTS** • 1928
KITTY CORNERED • 1955 • Tendlar Dave • ANS • USA
KITTY FOILED • 1948 • Hanna William, Barbera Joseph • ANS • USA
KITTY FOYLE • 1940 • Wood Sam • USA
KITTY FROM KANSAS CITY • 1931 • Fleischer Dave • ANS • USA
KITTY FROM KILLARNEY • 1926 • Bacon Lloyd • SHT • USA
KITTY FROM THE CITY • 1916 • Wulze Harry • SHT • USA
KITTY FROM THE CITY • 1971 • Smith Paul J. • ANS • USA
KITTY GETS THE BIRD • 1941 • *Mintz Charles (P)* • ANS • USA
KITTY IN DREAMLAND • 1911 • Booth W. R.? • UKN
KITTY IN DREAMLAND • 1912 • *Eclipse* • FRN
KITTY KELLY, M.D. • 1919 • Hickman Howard • USA
KITTY KORNERED • 1946 • Clampett Robert • ANS • USA
KITTY MACKAY • 1917 • North Wilfred • USA
KITTY MAHONE • 1900 • Gibbons Walter • UKN
KITTY: RETURN TO AUSCHWITZ • 1979 • Morley Peter • DOC • UKN
KITTY SCHWINDELT SICH INS GLUCK • 1932 • Juttke Herbert • FRG • AUSGERECHNET 13
KITTY TAILLEUR • 1921 • Richardson Frank • UKN
KITTY THE DRESSMAKER • 1911 • Bouwmeester Theo • UKN
KITTY UND DIE GROSSE WELT • 1956 • Weidenmann Alfred • FRG
KITTY UND DIE WELTKONFERENZ • 1939 • Kautner Helmut • FRG • KITTY AND THE WORLD CONFERENCE
KITTY'S HOLD-UP • 1912 • *Mccoy Gertrude* • USA
KITTY'S KNIGHT • 1913 • *Essanay* • USA
KIULEANDRA • 1985 • Nicolaescu Sergiu • RMN
KIVALINA OF THE ICE LANDS • 1925 • Rossman Earl • USA
KIVANCSISAG • 1970 • Macskassy Gyula, Varnai Gyorgy • ANS • HNG • CURIOSITY
KIVENPYORITTAJAN KULA • 1979 • Mollberg Rauni • FNL • STONEROLLER'S VILLAGE, THE
KIYEN RYOKO see **KIKEN RYOKO** • 1959
KIZ KOLUNDA DAMGA VAR • 1967 • Refig Halit • TRK • BRANDED GIRL, THE
KIZGIN ADAM • 1968 • Figenli Yavuz • TRK • ANGRY MAN, THE
KIZGIN TOPRAK • 1974 • Tuna Feyzi • TRK • GRAVE, THE
KIZIL MASKE • 1968 • Inanc Cetin • *Atasoy Irfan* • TRK • RED MASK
KIZIL MASKE • 1968 • Ziyal Tolgay • *Cehre Nebahat* • TRK • RED MASK
KIZIL TEHLIKE • 1967 • Saydam Nejat • TRK • RED PERIL
KIZIL VAZO • 1961 • Yilmaz Atif • TRK • RED VASE, THE
KIZILCIKLAR OLDU MU? • 1967 • Saner Hulki • TRK • ARE THE BLACKBERRIES RIPE?
KIZILIRMAK -KARAKOYOUN • 1967 • Akat Lutfu • TRK • RED RIVER -BLACK SHEEP
KIZIM DUYMASIN • 1967 • Evin Semih • TRK • DON'T TELL MY DAUGHTER
KIZOKU NO KAIDAN • 1959 • Yoshimura Kozaburo • JPN • ARISTOCRAT'S STAIRS
KIZU DARAKE NO SANGA • 1964 • Yamamoto Satsuo • JPN • PUBLIC BENEFACTOR, A ○ TYCOON ○ MOUNTAINS AND RIVERS WITH SCARS ○ POWER OF GOLD, THE
KIZUSENRYO • 1960 • Tanaka Tokuzo • JPN
KJAERE LILLE NORGE • 1973 • Bohwim Knut • NRW • LULLABY OF NORWAY
KJAERE MAREN • 1976 • During Jan Erik • NRW
KJAERLEIKENS FERJEREISER • 1979 • Nicolayssen Hans Otto • NRW • COMMUTER KIND OF LOVE, A ○ ACROSS THE FJORD
KLABAUTERMANDEN • 1969 • Carlsen Henning • DNM, SWD, NRW • WE ARE ALL DEAD DEMONS ○ KLABAUTERMANDEN ○ WE ARE ALL DEMONS
KLABAUTERMANDEN see **KLABAUTERMANDEN** • 1969
KLABAUTERMANN, DER • 1919 • Brenken Arthur • FRG
KLABAUTERMANN, DER • 1924 • Merzbach Paul • FRG • HOBGOBLIN, THE
KLABRIASPARTIE, DIE • 1915 • Danuky Nunek • FRG
KLABZUBA'S ELEVEN see **KLAPZUBOVA JEDENACTKA** • 1938
KLACKARNA I TAKET • 1952 • *Redig Rune (Ed)* • SWD
KLADD UND DATSCH, DIE PECHVOGEL • 1926 • Jutzi Phil • FRG
KLADIVO NA CARODEJNICE • 1969 • Vavra Otakar • CZC • HAMMER AGAINST WITCHES, A ○ HAMMER FOR THE WITCHES ○ WITCHHAMMER
KLAKSON • 1965 • Rakonjac Kokan • YGS • KLAXON
KLAMMER AUF, KLAMMER ZU • 1966 • Costard Hellmuth • FRG • QUOTE, UNQUOTE
KLANN • 1970 • Ledoux Patrick • BLG
KLANNINGEN • 1964 • Sjoman Vilgot • SWD • DRESS, THE (UKN)
KLANSMAN, THE • 1974 • Young Terence • USA • BURNING CROSS, THE
KLAPPERSTORCHVERBAND, DER • 1919 • Froelich Carl • FRG
KLAPPERSTORCHVERBAND, DER see **NACHT MIT HINDERNISSEN, EINE** • 1937
KLAPZUBOVA JEDENACTKA • 1938 • Brom Ladislav • CZC • KLABZUBA'S ELEVEN
KLARA LUST • 1972 • Grede Kjell • SWD
KLARAR BANANEN BIFFEN? • 1958 • Frisk Ragnar • SWD
KLAREM HIMMEL UND LACHENDEM HERRN IS NICHT ZU TRAUEN • 1980 • Mainka Maximilliane • FRG
KLART TILL DRABBNING • 1937 • Adolphson Edvin • SWD • CLEARED FOR ACTION (USA) ○ CLEAR THE DECKS FOR ACTION
KLASSENKEILE • 1968 • Gottlieb Franz J. • FRG • SPANKING AT SCHOOL
KLASSENVERHALTNISSE • 1984 • Straub Jean-Marie, Huillet Daniele • FRG, FRN • CLASS CONDITIONS ○ CLASS RELATIONS
KLASSEZAMMEKUNFT see **D'KLASSEZAMMEKUNFT** • 1988
KLASSKAMRATER • 1952 • Bauman Schamyl • SWD • CLASS MATES
KLATKI • 1967 • Kijowicz Miroslaw • SHT • PLN • CAGES
KLATSCH • 1920 • Stein Josef • FRG
KLATSCHE, DIE • 1939 • Ulmer Edgar G. • USA • LIGHT AHEAD, THE ○ FISHE DA KRIN
KLAUN FERDINAND A RAKETA • 1962 • Polak Jindrich • CZC • CLOWN FERDINAND AND THE ROCKET ○ ROCKET TO NOWHERE
KLAVIERKONZERT NR.4 IN G -DUR LUDWIG VAN BEETHOVEN • 1967 • Seggelke Herbert • FRG • BEETHOVEN PIANO CONCERTO NO.4 (UKN)
KLAXON • 1975 • Thomas Gayle • ANM • CND
KLAXON see **KLAKSON** • 1965
KLEBOLIN KLEBT ALLES • 1909 • Bolten-Baeckers Heinrich • FRG
KLEC PRO DVA • 1967 • Mach Jaroslav • CZC • CAGE FOR TWO, A
KLEE WYCK see **KLEE WYCK: THE STORY OF EMILY CARR** • 1946

KLEE WYCK: THE STORY OF EMILY CARR • 1946 • Crabtree Grant • DCS • CND • KLEE WYCK
KLEIDER DER ANGELIKA, DIE • 1915 • *Ebert & Co* • FRG
KLEIDER MACHEN LEUTE • 1922 • Steinhoff Hans • AUS
KLEIDER MACHEN LEUTE • 1940 • Kautner Helmut • FRG • CLOTHES MAKE THE MAN ○ CLOTHES MAKE PEOPLE
KLEIN BESTEL • 1972 • Smit Boud • NTH
KLEIN DOORTJE • 1917 • Zelnik Friedrich • FRG
KLEIN DORRIT • 1934 • Lamac Carl • FRG
KLEINE AUS AMERIKA, DIE • 1925 • *Boheme-Film* • FRG
KLEINE AUS DER KONFEKTION, DIE • 1925 • Neff Wolfgang • FRG • GROSSTADTKAVALIERE ○ WARENHAUSMADCHEN
KLEINE CHAOS, DAS • 1967 • Fassbinder R. W. • FRG • LITTLE CHAOS, THE
KLEINE DAGMAR, DIE • 1921 • Halm Alfred • FRG
KLEINE FREUNDIN BRAUCHT EIN JEDER MANN, EINE • 1927 • Heidemann Paul • FRG
KLEINE FRIEREN AUCH IN SOMMER • 1977 • von Gunten Peter • SWT
KLEINE FURSTIN, DIE • 1916 • Larsen Viggo • FRG
KLEINE GRENZVERKEHR • 1943 • Deppe Hans • FRG
KLEINE HELDIN, DIE • 1915 • Halm Alfred • FRG
KLEINE HERZOG, DER • 1924 • Walther-Fein Rudolf • FRG • UM THRON UND LIEBE
KLEINE HOFKONZERT, DAS • 1945 • Verhoeven Paul • FRG
KLEINE INGE UND IHRE DREI VATER, DIE • 1926 • Osten Franz • FRG
KLEINE KUNO, DER • 1959 • Jung-Alsen Kurt • GDR
KLEINE LEUTE-MAL GANZ GROSS • 1958 • Fredersdorf Herbert B. • FRG
KLEINE MADCHEN-GROSSE SORGEN • 1941 • Barlog Boleslav • FRG
KLEINE MELODIE AUS WIEN • 1948 • Emo E. W. • AUS
KLEINE MIDINETTE, DIE • 1921 • Neff Wolfgang • FRG
KLEINE MIT DEM SUSSEN PO, DIE • 1975 • Fritsch Willi • AUS
KLEINE MUCK, DER • 1921 • Prager Wilhelm • FRG
KLEINE MUTTI • 1934 • Koster Henry • FRG • LITTLE MOTHER ○ KISMAMA
KLEINE NACHTMUSIK, EINE • 1939 • Hainisch Leopold • FRG
KLEINE NAPOLEON, DER see **SO SIND DIE MANNER** • 1922
KLEINE PRINZ, DER • 1966 • Wolf Konrad • GDR • LITTLE PRINCE, THE
KLEINE RESIDENZ • 1942 • Zerlett Hans H. • FRG
KLEINE SCHORNSTEINFEGER, DAS • 1935 • Reiniger Lotte • ANS • FRG • LITTLE CHIMNEY SWEEP, THE ○ CHIMNEY SWEEP
KLEINE SCHWINDLERIN, DIE • 1933 • Meyer Johannes • FRG
KLEINE SEITENSPRUNG, DER • 1931 • Schunzel Reinhold • FRG
KLEINE SKLAVIN, DIE • 1928 • Fleck Jacob, Fleck Luise • FRG
KLEINE SOMMERMELODIE, EINE • 1944 • von Collande Volker • FRG
KLEINE STAATSANWALT, DER • Bohm Hark • FRG
KLEINE STADT WILL SCHLAFEN GEHEN, DIE • 1954 • Konig Hans H. • FRG
KLEINE SUNDERIN, DIE see **SCHWARZFAHRT INS GLUCK** • 1938
KLEINE UND DAS GROSSE GLUCK, DAS • 1953 • Hellberg Martin • GDR • LITTLE AND THE BIG HAPPINESS, THE
KLEINE UND DIE GROSSE LIEBE, DIE • 1938 • von Baky Josef • FRG • MINOR LOVE AND THE REAL THING, THE
KLEINE UND IHR KAVALIER, DIE • 1926 • Lowenbein Richard • FRG
KLEINE VAMPIR, DER see **BUBCHEN** • 1968
KLEINE VOM BUMMEL, DIE • 1925 • Eichberg Richard • FRG
KLEINE VOM FILM, DIE • 1922 • Werckmeister Hans • FRG
KLEINE VOM VARIETE, DIE • 1926 • Schwarz Hanns • FRG
KLEINE WELT IM DUNKELEM, EINE • 1938 • Richter Hans • SWT • SMALL WORLD IN THE DARK, A
KLEINE WERELD, DIE • 1973 • van der Linden Charles Huguenot • DOC • NTH • THIS TINY WORLD
KLEINE ZAUBERER UND DIE GROSSE FUNF, DER • 1977 • Stranka Erwin • GDR • LITTLE MAGICIAN AND THE BAD MARK, THE
KLEINER EMMENTALFILM • 1971 • Luginbuhl Bernhard • SWT
KLEINER FILM EINER GROSSEN STADT: DIE STADT DUSSELDORF AM RHEIN • 1935 • Ruttmann Walter • DOC • FRG • KLEINER FILM EINER GROSSEN STADT: DUSSELDORF
KLEINER FILM EINER GROSSEN STADT: DUSSELDORF see **KLEINER FILM EINER GROSSEN STADT: DIE STADT DUSSELDORF AM RHEIN** • 1935
KLEINER GOLDENER BERG, EIN • 1936 • Elling Alwin • FRG • HUMMEL-HUMMEL ○ EHEKRACH
KLEINER MANN, GANZ GROSS • 1938 • Stemmle R. A. • FRG
KLEINER MANN, GANZ GROSS • 1957 • Grimm Hans • FRG
KLEINER MANN -WAS NUN? • 1933 • Wendhausen Fritz • FRG
KLEINER SCHWINDEL AM WOLFGANGSEE • 1949 • Antel Franz • AUS
KLEINER VORSCHUSS AUF DIE SELIGKEIT, EIN • 1929 • Speyer Jaap • FRG
KLEINER WAGEN -GROSSE LIEBE • 1949 • Kayser Ulrich • FRG
KLEINES BEZIRKSGERICHT • 1938 • Elling Alwin • FRG
KLEINES BIEST MIT LANGEN HAAREN • 1958 • Martin Paul • FRG
KLEINES MADEL -GROSSES GLUCK • 1953 • Emo E. W. • FRG
KLEINES ZELT UND GROSSE LIEBE • 1956 • Geis Rainer • FRG • TWO IN A SLEEPING BAG (USA)
KLEINHOFF HOTEL • 1977 • Lizzani Carlo • ITL • PASSIONATE STRANGERS, THE
KLEINSTADTPOET, DER • 1940 • von Baky Josef • FRG
KLEINSTADTSUNDER • 1927 • Rahn Bruno • FRG • SMALL TOWN SINNERS (USA)
KLEPTOMANIA TABLETS • 1912 • Batley Ernest G. • UKN
KLEPTOMANIAC, THE • 1905 • Porter Edwin S. • USA
KLEPTOMANIAC, THE • 1914 • Buckland Warwick? • UKN
KLEPTOMANIACS • 1917 • *Rhodes Billie* • SHT • USA
KLEPTOMANIACS see **LOVE HAPPY** • 1949
KLEPTOMANIN, DIE • 1918 • Gad Urban, Arno • FRG
KLETTERMAXE • 1927 • Reiber Willy • FRG
KLETTERMAXE • 1952 • Hoffmann Kurt • FRG
KLEVER KIDDIES • 1919 • *Barry Eddie* • SHT • USA
KLIATVA MOLODYCH • 1944 • Vertov Dziga, Svilova Elizaveta • USS • OATH OF YOUTH, THE ○ YOUTH'S OATH
KLIBBERKLEESCHEN • 1987 • Scheuer Paul, Hausemer Maisy, Fautsch Georges • DOC • LXM
KLIC • 1971 • Cech Vladimir • CZC • KEY, THE
KLIMA VON VANCOUNT, DAS • 1918 • May Joe • FRG
KLINCZ • 1980 • Andrejew Piotr • PLN • CLINCH
KLINKAART • 1958 • Meyer Paul • BLG
KLIOU THE KILLER see **KLIOU THE TIGER** • 1936
KLIOU THE TIGER • 1936 • de La Falanie Marquis • USA • KLIOU THE KILLER
KLIPPEN DER EHE • 1929 • Rudensky Dyk • FRG
KLIPPET • 1982 • Halldoff Jan • SWD • SHAM, THE
KLISTO PARATHIRO • 1976 • Vellopoulos Ermis • GRC • CLOSED WINDOW
KLIZI-PUZI • 1968 • Grgic Zlatko • ANS • YGS, FRG • TWIDDLE-TWADDLE
KLJUC • 1965 • Papic Krsto • YGS • KEY, THE
KLOCKAN PA RONNEBERGA • 1944 • Skoglund Gunnar • SWD • CLOCK AT RONNEBERGA, THE
KLOCKORNA I GAMLA STAN • 1946 • Hylten-Cavallius Ragnar • SWD • BELLS OF THE OLD TOWN
KLODEN ROKKER • 1978 • Menzer John • DNM
KLOGE MAND, DEN • 1956 • Iversen Jon • DNM
KLOKA GUBBEN • 1938 • Wallen Sigurd • SWD • NATURE HEALER, THE
KLOKSLAG TWAALF • 1936 • Joannon Leo • NTH
KLONDIKE • 1932 • Rosen Phil • USA • DOCTOR'S SACRIFICE, THE (UKN)
KLONDIKE ANNIE • 1936 • Walsh Raoul • USA • KLONDIKE LOU
KLONDIKE CASANOVA • 1946 • Sparber I. • ANS • USA
KLONDIKE FEVER see **JACK LONDON'S KLONDIKE FEVER** • 1980
KLONDIKE FURY • 1942 • Howard William K. • USA
KLONDIKE KATE • 1943 • Castle William • USA
KLONDIKE KID, THE • 1932 • Jackson Wilfred • ANS • USA
KLONDIKE LOU see **KLONDIKE ANNIE** • 1936
KLONDIKE STRIKE OUT • 1961 • Tendlar Dave • ANS • USA
KLONDYKE BUBBLE, THE • 1914 • *Hawley Ormi* • USA
KLONDYKE STEAL, A • 1911 • *Vitagraph* • USA
KLOPKA ZA GENERALA • 1971 • Stamenkovic Miomir • YGS • TRIP FOR THE GENERAL, A
KLOPOTLIWY GOSC • 1971 • Ziarnik Jerzy • PLN • DIFFICULT GUEST, THE
KLOPOTY Z CIEPLEM • 1965 • Giersz Witold • ANS • PLN • TROUBLES WITH HEAT
KLOSTER VON SENDOMIR, DAS • 1919 • Meinert Rudolf • FRG
KLOSTER WENDHUSEN • 1920 • *Meller Edith* • FRG
KLOSTERFRIEDE • 1917 • Gad Urban • FRG
KLOSTERJAGER, DER • 1920 • Osten Franz? • FRG
KLOSTERJAGER, DER • 1935 • Obal Max • FRG
KLOSTERJAGER, DER • 1953 • Reinl Harald • FRG
KLOSTERSCHULERINNEN, DIE • 1971 • Schroeder Eberhard • FRG • SEX LIFE IN A CONVENT (UKN)
KLOSTRET I SENDOMIR • 1920 • Sjostrom Victor • SWD • MONASTERY OF SENDOMIR, THE (USA) ○ SECRET OF THE MONASTERY (UKN)
KLOTZ AM BEIN • 1958 • Vogel Frank • GDR
KLOVNEN • 1926 • Sandberg Anders W. • SWD • HEART OF A CLOWN ○ CLOWN
KLUB DER ENTGLEISTEN • 1921 • Petersen Rolf • FRG
KLUB DER NEUN, DER • 1917 • Neuss Alwin • FRG
KLUB DER SCHWARZEN 13 DAMEN, DER • 1915 • *Saturn-Film* • FRG
KLUB SZACHISTOW • 1967 • Lesiewicz Witold • PLN • CHESS CLUB
KLUBBEN • 1978 • Skolmen Roar • NRW • YOUTH CLUB, THE
KLUBVENNEN see **NATTENS MYSTERIUM** • 1916
KLUGE MARIANNE, DIE • 1943 • Thimig Hans • FRG
KLUGE SCHWIEGERMUTTER, DIE • 1939 • Deppe Hans • FRG
KLUGEN FRAUEN, DIE • 1935 • Feyder Jacques • FRG
KLUPKO • 1972 • Grgic Zlatko • ANS • YGS • BALL, THE
KLUTE • 1971 • Pakula Alan J. • USA
KLUTZ, THE see **DEUX PIEDS DANS LA MEME BOTTINE, LES** • 1974
KLUVEN VARLD, EN • 1948 • Sucksdorff Arne • DCS • SWD • DIVIDED WORLD, A
KLYATVA • 1946 • Chiaureli Mikhail • USS • VOW, THE (USA)
KLYATVA TIMURA • 1942 • Kuleshov Lev • USS • OATH OF TIMUR, THE ○ TIMUR'S OATH
KLYUCH BYEZ PRAVA PEREDACHI • 1977 • Asanova Dinara • USS • PRIVATE KEY
KLYUCHI SHCHASTYA • 1913 • Protazanov Yakov, Gardin Vladimir • USS • KEYS TO HAPPINESS
KNABE EROS, DER • 1920 • Legband Paul • FRG
KNABE IN BLAU, DER • 1919 • Murnau F. W. • FRG • EMERALD OF DEATH (USA) ○ TODESSMARAGD, DER ○ BOY IN BLUE, THE
KNACK, THE see **KNACK.. AND HOW TO GET IT, THE** • 1965
KNACK.. AND HOW TO GET IT, THE • 1965 • Lester Richard • UKN • KNACK, THE
KNALL UND FALL ALS HOCHSTAPLER • 1952 • Marischka Hubert • AUS, FRG
KNALLHARDA FIGHTEN, DEN • 1961 • *Hellqvist Carl-Axel (Edt)* • SWD
KNAVE OF CLUBS, THE • 1914 • *Lubin* • USA
KNAVE OF DIAMONDS, THE • 1921 • Plaissetty Rene • UKN
KNAVE OF HEARTS • 1954 • Clement Rene • UKN, FRN • LOVERS, HAPPY LOVERS (USA) ○ MONSIEUR RIPOIS ○ LOVER BOY
KNAVE OF HEARTS, THE • 1919 • Thornton F. Martin • UKN
KNAVE OF SPADES see **WALET PIKOWY** • 1960
KNAVE OF SPADES see **KAPETAN FANTIS BASTOUNIS, O** • 1968
KNAVES AND THE KNIGHT, THE • 1915 • *Miller Rube* • USA
KNEE ACTION • 1937 • Lamont Charles • SHT • USA
KNEE DEEP IN DAISIES • 1926 • Mander Miles • UKN
KNEEL OR FIGHT see **LUMUHOD KA O LUMABAN** • 1968
KNELL FOR THE BAREFOOTED see **ZVONY PRE BOSYCH** • 1965
KNEUSS • 1978 • Meili Gaudenz • SWT, FRG
KNICKERBACKER KNIGHTS • 1934 • Schwarzwald Milton • SHT • USA
KNICKERBOCKER BUCKAROO, THE • 1919 • Parker Albert • USA
KNICKERBOCKER HOLIDAY • 1944 • Brown Harry J. • USA
KNICKERS AHOY • 1975 • Antel Franz • FRG
KNIEDIEP • 1975 • SAF
KNIFE, THE • 1918 • Vignola Robert G. • USA
KNIFE, THE see **BLACK HAND** • 1949
KNIFE, THE see **MES, HET** • 1960
KNIFE, THE see **NOZ** • 1967
KNIFE, THE see **SIKKIN, AS-** • 1970
KNIFE FIGHTERS see **NAVAJEROS, LOS** • 1980
KNIFE FOR THE LADIES, A • 1973 • Spangler Larry • USA • SILENT SENTENCE
KNIFE GRINDER see **SKARSLIPAREN** • 1913
KNIFE IN THE HEAD see **MESSER IM KOPF** • 1978
KNIFE IN THE HEART see **KNIVEN I HJERTET** • 1981
KNIFE IN THE WATER (UKN) see **NOZ W WODZIE** • 1961
KNIFE NUMBER SIX • 1934 • *Sound City* • SHT • UKN
KNIFE OF THE PARTY, THE • 1934 • Jason Leigh • SHT • USA
KNIFE THROWER, THE • 1951 • Weinberg Maxwell • USA
KNIFE TO GRIND, A • 1913 • Kellino W. P. • UKN
KNIFERS, THE see **NAVAJEROS, LOS** • 1980
KNIGA V DEREVNE • 1929 • Ptushko Alexander • ANS • USS • BOOK IN THE COUNTRY
KNIGHT, THE • 1980 • Majewski Janusz • PLN
KNIGHT AND THE FRIAR, THE • 1912 • *Majestic* • USA
KNIGHT AND THE GIRL, THE see **ENAS IPPOTIS YIA TI VASOULA** • 1968
KNIGHT AND WARRIOR see **NINJA OPERATION: KNIGHT AND WARRIOR** • 1987
KNIGHT BEFORE CHRISTMAS, THE • 1914 • Johnson Tefft • USA
KNIGHT DUTY • 1933 • Gillstrom Arvid E. • USA
KNIGHT ERRANT, A • 1907 • Martin J. H. • UKN
KNIGHT ERRANT, A • 1913 • *Reliance* • USA
KNIGHT ERRANT, THE • 1911 • *Bosworth Hobart* • USA
KNIGHT ERRANT, THE • 1922 • Ridgwell George • UKN
KNIGHT FOR A DAY, A • 1946 • Hannah Jack • ANS • USA
KNIGHT FOR A NIGHT, A • 1920 • *Hines Johnny* • USA
KNIGHT FOR VASOULA, A see **ENAS IPPOTIS YIA TI VASOULA** • 1968
KNIGHT IN ARMOR, THE • 1912 • *Solax* • USA
KNIGHT IN ARMOUR, A • 1914 • Cooper Toby • UKN
KNIGHT IN GHOST TOWN, A see **TROUBLE IN SUNDOWN** • 1939
KNIGHT IN LONDON, A • 1929 • Pick Lupu • UKN
KNIGHT IN SANDALS, A see **ENAS IPPOTIS ME TSAROUHIA** • 1968
KNIGHT-MARE HARE • 1955 • Jones Charles M. • ANS • USA
KNIGHT MYSTERY, THE see **CHEVALIER MYSTERE, LE** • 1907
KNIGHT OF BLACK ART, THE see **TAMBOURIN FANTASTIQUE ILLUSION FANTASTIQUE** • 1908
KNIGHT OF CYCLONE GULCH, THE • 1913 • *Kalem* • USA
KNIGHT OF HER DREAMS, THE • 1913 • *Nestor* • USA
KNIGHT OF LOVE, A • 1987 • Derek John • USA
KNIGHT OF THE CURSED CASTLE see **CAVALIERE DEL CASTELLO MALEDETTO, IL** • 1959
KNIGHT OF THE DRAGON, THE • 1986 • Colomo Fernando • SPN • STAR KNIGHT ○ KNIGHTS OF THE DRAGON, THE
KNIGHT OF THE DREAM, THE see **RYTSAR MECHTY** • 1964
KNIGHT OF THE EUCHARIST • 1922 • *Flanagan James* • USA
KNIGHT OF THE GOLD STAR, THE see **KAVALER ZOLOTOI ZVEZDY** • 1950
KNIGHT OF THE NIGHT, A • 1916 • Hill Robert F. • SHT • USA
KNIGHT OF THE NIGHT, THE see **CHEVALIER DE LA NUIT, LE** • 1954
KNIGHT OF THE PLAINS • 1938 • Newfield Sam • USA
KNIGHT OF THE RANGE, A • 1916 • Jaccard Jacques • USA
KNIGHT OF THE ROAD, A • 1911 • Griffith D. W. • USA
KNIGHT OF THE ROAD, A • 1914 • Buckland Warwick • UKN
KNIGHT OF THE SNOWS, THE (USA) see **CHEVALIER DES NEIGES, LE** • 1912
KNIGHT OF THE STREET see **GAITO NO KISHI** • 1928
KNIGHT OF THE SWORD, THE see **SANTO DE LA ESPADA, EL** • 1970
KNIGHT OF THE TRAIL, A • 1911 • *Bison* • USA
KNIGHT OF THE TRAIL, A • 1917 • *W.h. Productions* • USA
KNIGHT OF THE TRAILS, A • 1915 • Hart William S. • USA • PROWLERS OF THE PLAINS
KNIGHT OF THE TV SCREEN see **GYULA VITEZ TELEN NYARON** • 1971
KNIGHT OF THE WEST, A • 1921 • McKenzie Robert • USA
KNIGHT OF TROUBLE, A • 1914 • Jackson Harry • USA
KNIGHT OF WESTERN LAND, A • 1918 • *Hart Neal* • SHT • USA
KNIGHT RIDER • 1981 • Haller Daniel • TVM • USA • KNIGHT RIDER: THE ORIGINAL TV MOVIE
KNIGHT RIDER: THE ORIGINAL TV MOVIE see **KNIGHT RIDER** • 1981
KNIGHT RUNNING WILD, A see **ENAS IPPOTIS ME TSAROUHIA** • 1968
KNIGHT WITHOUT ARMOUR • 1937 • Feyder Jacques • UKN, FRN • CHEVALIER SANS ARMURE, LE (FRN)
KNIGHT WITHOUT ARMOUR see **RITSAR BEZ BRONYA** • 1966
KNIGHTRIDER 2: NIGHT OF THE JUGGERNAUT • 1985 • Fenady George • TVM • USA
KNIGHTRIDERS • 1981 • Romero George A. • USA
KNIGHTS see **EXCALIBUR** • 1981
KNIGHTS, THE see **DWAJ RYCERZE** • 1964
KNIGHTS AND EMERALDS • 1986 • Emes Ian • UKN
KNIGHTS AND KNIGHTIES • 1920 • Pratt Gilbert • SHT • USA
KNIGHTS AND LADIES • 1913 • Smalley Phillips • USA
KNIGHTS AND LADIES • 1928 • Miller Frank • UKN
KNIGHTS BEFORE CHRISTMAS • 1930 • Foster Lewis R. • SHT • USA
KNIGHTS FOR A DAY • 1936 • Lantz Walter • ANS • USA
KNIGHTS FOR A DAY • 1937 • Lee Norman, Ginever Aveling • UKN
KNIGHT'S MOVE • 1963 • Lukashevich Tatyana • USS

KNIGHTS MUST FALL • 1949 • Freleng Friz • ANS • USA

KNIGHTS OF FREEDOM • 1947 • Dimmock F. Hayden • UKN

KNIGHTS OF GOLDEN GLOVE, THE see **ARANYKESZTYU LOVAGJAI, AZ** • 1968

KNIGHTS OF TERROR (USA) see **TERRORE DEI MANTELLI ROSSI, IL** • 1963

KNIGHTS OF THE BATHTUB • 1916 • Chaudet Louis W. • SHT • USA

KNIGHTS OF THE BLACK CROSS see **KRZYZACY** • 1960

KNIGHTS OF THE BLACK EAGLE see **CONDOTTIERI** • 1937

KNIGHTS OF THE CITY • 1985 • Orlando Dominic • USA

KNIGHTS OF THE DRAGON, THE see **KNIGHT OF THE DRAGON, THE** • 1986

KNIGHTS OF THE RANGE • 1940 • Selander Lesley • USA

KNIGHTS OF THE ROUND TABLE • 1953 • Thorpe Richard • USA, UKN

KNIGHTS OF THE SADDLE • 1917 • *Selig* • SHT • USA

KNIGHTS OF THE SQUARE TABLE • 1917 • Crosland Alan • USA

KNIGHTS OF THE TEUTONIC ORDER, THE see **KRZYZACY** • 1960

KNIGHTS OUT • 1929 • Taurog Norman • SHT • USA

KNIGHTY-KNIGHT BUGS • 1958 • Freleng Friz • ANS • USA

KNIPLINGER see **GREVINDENS AERE** • 1918

KNITTING PRETTY see **TETKE PLETKE** • 1969

KNIVE • 1954 • Carlsen Henning • SHT • DNM

KNIVEN I HJERTET • 1981 • Thomsen Christian Braad • DNM • KNIFE IN THE HEART

KNIVES OF THE AVENGERS (USA) see **COLTELLI DEL VENDICATORE, I** • 1967

KNIVSTIKKEREN see **FARLIG FORBRYDER, EN** • 1913

KNOCK • 1950 • Lefranc Guy • FRN • DR. KNOCK (USA)

KNOCK see **KNOCK, OU LE TRIOMPHE DE LA MEDECINE** • 1925

KNOCK AT ANY DOOR • 1958 • Fyodorova Marina • USS

KNOCK AT THE WRONG DOOR, A see **DO YOU TAKE THIS STRANGER?** • 1970

KNOCK DOWN • 1960 • Matsuo Akinori • JPN

KNOCK KNOCK! • 1940 • Lantz Walter • ANS • USA

KNOCK ME • 1908 • *Tyler Walter* • UKN

KNOCK ON ANY DOOR • 1949 • Ray Nicholas • USA

KNOCK ON THE DOOR, THE • 1923 • Curran William Hughes • USA

KNOCK ON WOOD • 1954 • Panama Norman, Frank Melvin • USA

KNOCK, OU LE TRIOMPHE DE LA MEDECINE • 1925 • Hervil Rene • FRN • KNOCK

KNOCK, OU LE TRIOMPHE DE LA MEDECINE • 1933 • Jouvet Louis, Goupillieres Roger • FRN

KNOCK-OUT • 1922 • du Plessis Armand • AUS

KNOCK OUT • 1935 • Zerlett Hans H., Lamac Carl • FRG • JUNGES MADCHEN -EINE JUNGER MANN, EIN

KNOCK OUT • 1987 • Tassios Pavlos • GRC

KNOCK-OUT see **K.O.** • 1968

KNOCK OUT, THE • 1914 • Sennett Mack • USA • COUNTED OUT ○ PUGILIST, THE ○ KNOCKOUT, THE

KNOCK OUT BLOW, THE • 1917 • West Walter • UKN

KNOCK-OUT BLOW, THE see **EGG CRATE WALLOP, THE** • 1919

KNOCK OUT COP, THE (USA) see **PIEDONE LO SBIRRO** • 1973

KNOCK-OUT DUGAN'S FIND • 1915 • *Selig* • USA

KNOCKABOUT KELLY, MAGICIAN • 1914 • *Melies Gaston(P)* • FRN

KNOCKER, THE see **DOUBLE DEALING** • 1923

KNOCKER AND THE NAUGHTY BOYS, THE • 1903 • Stow Percy? • UKN

KNOCKERS UP • 1963 • Gaylord A. J. • USA

KNOCKING AT HEAVEN'S DOOR • 1980 • Seiden Joseph • USA

KNOCKING 'EM COLD • 1920 • Edwards Harry J. • SHT • USA

KNOCKING 'EM OVER see **WARMING UP** • 1928

KNOCKING ON THE DOOR, THE • 1923 • Coleby A. E. • SHT • UKN

KNOCKING OUT KNOCKOUT KELLY • 1916 • Dillon John Francis • USA

KNOCKNAGOW • 1918 • O'Donovan Fred • IRL

KNOCKOUT • 1941 • Clemens William • USA

KNOCKOUT • 1965 • Cayton William • CMP • USA

KNOCKOUT • 1970 • Barretto Vic • SAF

KNOCKOUT • 1977 • Jacobs Jim • CMP • USA

KNOCKOUT see **NOKAUT** • 1971

KNOCKOUT see **NOCAUT** • 1983

KNOCKOUT #2 • 1966 • Cayton William • CMP • USA

KNOCKOUT, A • 1920 • *Mann Hank* • SHT • USA

KNOCKOUT, THE • 1915 • *Ovey George* • USA

KNOCKOUT, THE • 1918 • Lyons Eddie, Moran Lee • SHT • USA

KNOCKOUT, THE • 1923 • Butler Alexander • UKN

KNOCKOUT, THE • 1923 • Roach Hal • SHT • USA

KNOCKOUT, THE • 1925 • Hillyer Lambert • USA

KNOCKOUT, THE • 1932 • Mack Anthony, French Lloyd • SHT • USA

KNOCKOUT, THE see **KNOCK OUT, THE** • 1914

KNOCKOUT AT THE "BREAKFAST CLUB" see **STJARNSMALL I FRUKOSTKLUBBEN** • 1950

KNOCKOUT BLOW, THE • 1912 • Thornton F. Martin? • UKN

KNOCKOUT CLERGYMAN, THE see **PRASTEN SOM SLOG KNOCKOUT** • 1943

KNOCKOUT DROPS • 1935 • Lamont Charles • SHT • USA

KNOCKOUT DROPS see **TOKYO NO TEKISASU-JIN** • 1957

KNOCKOUT KID, THE • 1925 • Rogell Albert S. • USA

KNOCKOUT KISSES • 1933 • Marshall George • SHT • USA

KNOCKOUT REILLY • 1927 • St. Clair Malcolm • USA • KNOCKOUT RILEY

KNOCKOUT RILEY see **KNOCKOUT REILLY** • 1927

KNOCKOUT WALLOP, THE • 1915 • *Sterling* • USA

KNOCKS AND OPPORTUNITIES • 1916 • *Morris Reggie* • SHT • USA

KNOCTURNE • 1972 • Kuchar George, Kuchar Mike • USA

KNOKKEN VOOR TWEE • 1982 • van der Meulen Karst • NTH • THREE'S A CROWD

KNOPPCHEN UND SEINE SCHWIEGERMUTTER • 1922 • Bolten-Baeckers Heinrich • FRG

KNOT, THE see **WEZEL** • 1961

KNOT, THE see **JAZOL** • 1985

KNOT IN THE HANDKERCHIEF, THE see **UZEL NA KAPESNIKU** • 1958

KNOT IN THE PLOT, A • 1910 • Griffith D. W.? • USA

KNOTS • 1975 • Munro David • UKN

KNOTTED CORD, THE • 1916 • Parke William • SHT • USA

KNOTTY KNOT, A • 1913 • *Champion* • USA

KNOW HOW TO SAY NO see **UMYEI SKAZAT -NYET** • 1976

KNOW OF A FLAT? see **NEVITE O BYTE?** • 1947

KNOW THY CHILD • 1921 • Barrett Franklyn • ASL

KNOW THY WIFE • 1918 • *Rodney Earl* • USA

KNOW YOUR ALLY: BRITAIN • 1944 • *Capra Frank (P)* • DOC • USA

KNOW YOUR BABY • 1947 • Crawley Judith • DOC • CND

KNOW YOUR ENEMY: GERMANY • 1945 • *Capra Frank (P)* • DOC • USA

KNOW YOUR ENEMY: JAPAN • 1945 • Ivens Joris, Capra Frank • DOC • USA

KNOW YOUR MEN • 1921 • Giblyn Charles • USA

KNOW YOUR MONEY • 1940 • Newman Joseph M. • SHT • USA

KNOW YOUR NEIGHBOR • 1918 • *Lynne Ethel* • SHT • USA

KNOW YOUR OWN COUNTRY • 1925 • *Commonwealth Government* • SER • ASL

KNOWHUTIMEAN? • 1983 • Cherry John • USA

KNOWING MEN • 1930 • Glyn Elinor • UKN

KNOWING TO LEARN see **COMMENT SAVOIR** • 1966

KNOWLEDGE, THE • 1979 • Brooks Bob • MTV • UKN

KNOWN ONLY BY SIGHT see **IKH ZNALI TOLKO V LITSO** • 1967

KNOWPLACE • 1967 • Rimmer David, Spring Sylvia, Herbison Bob • CND

KNOX UND DIE LUSTIGEN VAGABUNDEN • 1935 • Emo E. W. • AUS • ZIRKUS SARAN

KNUCKLE-MEN see **TERMINAL ISLAND** • 1973

KNUD • 1966 • Roos Jorgen • DOC • DNM

KNUD RAMUSSEN'S MEMORIAL EXPEDITION TO CAPE SEDDON see **KNUD RAMUSSENS MINDEEKSPEDITION TIL KAP SEDDON** • 1983

KNUD RAMUSSENS MINDEEKSPEDITION TIL KAP SEDDON • 1983 • Roos Jorgen • DOC • DNM • KNUD RAMUSSEN'S MEMORIAL EXPEDITION TO CAPE SEDDON

KNUDEPROBLEM, ET • 1959 • Carlsen Henning • SHT • DNM

KNUT AND THE KERNEL, THE • 1915 • Haldane Bert • UKN

KNUT FORMO'S LAST HUNTING TRIP see **KNUT FORMOS SISTE JAKT** • 1973

KNUT FORMOS SISTE JAKT • 1973 • During Jan Erik • NRW • KNUT FORMO'S LAST HUNTING TRIP ○ REINDEER ○ REIN

KNUT LOSER KNUTEN • 1938 • *Valfilm* • SWD

KNUTE ENTFLOHEN, DER • 1917 • Stein Josef • FRG

KNUTE ROCKNE -ALL AMERICAN • 1940 • Bacon Lloyd, Howard William K. (U/c) • USA • MODERN HERO, A (UKN)

KNUTSEN OG LUDVIGSEN • 1974 • Winger Ola • NRW

KNUTZY KNIGHTS • 1954 • White Jules • SHT • USA

KNYAZ IGOR • 1970 • Tikhomirov Roman • USS • PRINCE IGOR

KO-KO AT THE CIRCUS • 1927 • Fleischer Dave • ANS • USA

KO-KO BACK TRACKS • 1927 • Fleischer Dave • ANS • USA

KO-KO BAFFLES THE BULLS • 1926 • Fleischer Dave • ANS • USA

KO-KO BEATS TIME • 1929 • Fleischer Dave • ANS • USA

KO-KO CELEBRATES THE FOURTH • 1925 • Fleischer Dave • ANS • USA

KO-KO CHOPS SUEY • 1927 • Fleischer Dave • ANS • USA

KO-KO CLEANS UP • 1928 • Fleischer Dave • ANS • USA

KO-KO EATS • 1925 • Fleischer Dave • ANS • USA

KO-KO EXPLORES • 1927 • Fleischer Dave • ANS • USA

KO-KO GETS EGG-CITED • 1927 • Fleischer Dave • ANS • USA

KO-KO GOES OVER • 1928 • Fleischer Dave • ANS • USA

KO-KO HEAVE HO • 1928 • Fleischer Dave • ANS • USA

KO-KO HOPS OFF • 1927 • Fleischer Dave • ANS • USA

KO-KO HOT AFTER IT • 1927 • Fleischer Dave • ANS • USA

KO-KO IN 1999 • 1924 • Fleischer Dave • ANS • USA

KO-KO IN THE FADE-AWAY • 1927 • Fleischer Dave • ANS • USA

KO-KO IN THE ROUGH • 1928 • Fleischer Dave • ANS • USA

KO-KO IN TOYLAND • 1925 • Fleischer Dave • ANS • USA

KO-KO KICKS • 1927 • Fleischer Dave • ANS • USA

KO-KO KIDNAPPED • 1927 • Fleischer Dave • ANS • USA

KO-KO LAMPS ALADDIN • 1928 • Fleischer Dave • ANS • USA

KO-KO MAKES 'EM LAUGH • 1927 • Fleischer Dave • ANS • USA

KO-KO NEEDLES THE BOSS • 1927 • Fleischer Dave • ANS • USA

KO-KO NUTS • 1925 • Fleischer Dave • ANS • USA

KO-KO ON THE RUN • 1925 • Fleischer Dave • ANS • USA

KO-KO ON THE TRACK • 1928 • Fleischer Dave • ANS • USA

KO-KO PACKS UP • 1925 • Fleischer Dave • ANS • USA

KO-KO PLAYS POOL • 1927 • Fleischer Dave • ANS • USA

KO-KO SEES SPOOKS • 1925 • Fleischer Dave • ANS • USA

KO-KO SMOKES • 1928 • Fleischer Dave • ANS • USA

KO-KO SQUEALS • 1928 • Fleischer Dave • ANS • USA

KO-KO STEPS OUT • 1926 • Fleischer Dave • ANS • USA

KO-KO THE BARBER • 1925 • Fleischer Dave • ANS • USA

KO-KO THE CLOWN • 1922-29 • Fleischer Dave • ASS • USA

KO-KO THE CONVICT • 1927 • Fleischer Dave • ANS • USA

KO-KO THE HOT SHOT • 1924 • Fleischer Dave • ANS • USA

KO-KO THE KID • 1927 • Fleischer Dave • ANS • USA

KO-KO THE KNIGHT • 1927 • Fleischer Dave • ANS • USA

KO-KO THE KOP • 1927 • Fleischer Dave • ANS • USA

KO-KO TRAINS 'EM • 1925 • Fleischer Dave • ANS • USA

KO KOO KIDS • 1922 • Santell Alfred • SHT • USA

KO-KO'S ACT • 1928 • Fleischer Dave • ANS • USA

KO-KO'S BAWTH • 1928 • Fleischer Dave • ANS • USA

KO-KO'S BIG PULL • 1928 • Fleischer Dave • ANS • USA

KO-KO'S BIG SALE • 1929 • Fleischer Dave • ANS • USA

KO-KO'S CATCH • 1928 • Fleischer Dave • ANS • USA

KO-KO'S CHASE • 1928 • Fleischer Dave • ANS • USA

KO-KO'S CLOCK • 1927 • Fleischer Dave • ANS • USA

KO-KO'S CONQUEST • 1929 • Fleischer Dave • ANS • USA

KO-KO'S COURTSHIP • 1928 • Fleischer Dave • ANS • USA

KO-KO'S CRIB • 1929 • Fleischer Dave • ANS • USA

KO-KO'S DOG GONE • 1928 • Fleischer Dave • ANS • USA

KO-KO'S EARTH CONTROL • 1928 • Fleischer Dave • ANS • USA

KO-KO'S FIELD DAZE • 1928 • Fleischer Dave • ANS • USA

KO-KO'S FOCUS • 1929 • Fleischer Dave • ANS • USA

KO-KO'S GERM JAM • 1928 • Fleischer Dave • ANS • USA

KO-KO'S HAREM SCAREM • 1929 • Fleischer Dave • ANS • USA

KO-KO'S HAUNTED HOUSE • 1928 • Fleischer Dave • ANS • USA

KO-KO'S HOT DOG • 1928 • Fleischer Dave • ANS • USA

KO-KO'S HOT INK • 1929 • Fleischer Dave • ANS • USA

KO-KO'S HYPNOTISM • 1929 • Fleischer Dave • ANS • USA

KO-KO'S KANE • 1927 • Fleischer Dave • ANS • USA

KO-KO'S KINK • 1928 • Fleischer Dave • ANS • USA

KO-KO'S KNOCK-DOWN • 1929 • Fleischer Dave • ANS • USA

KO-KO'S KOSY KORNER • 1928 • Fleischer Dave • ANS • USA

KO-KO'S MAGIC • 1928 • Fleischer Dave • ANS • USA

KO-KO'S PARADE • 1928 • Fleischer Dave • ANS • USA

KO-KO'S PARADISE • 1926 • Fleischer Dave • ANS • USA

KO-KO'S QUEEN • 1927 • Fleischer Dave • ANS • USA

KO-KO'S QUEST • 1927 • Fleischer Dave • ANS • USA

KO-KO'S REWARD • 1929 • Fleischer Dave • ANS • USA

KO-KO'S SAXAPHONIES • 1929 • Fleischer Dave • ANS • USA

KO-KO'S SIGNALS • 1929 • Fleischer Dave • ANS • USA

KO-KO'S TATTOO • 1928 • Fleischer Dave • ANS • USA

KO-KO'S THANKSGIVING • 1925 • Fleischer Dave • ANS • USA

KO-KO'S WAR DOGS • 1928 • Fleischer Dave • ANS • USA

KO-NO-PIEL-KA • 1981 • Leszczynski Witold • PLN • KONOPIELKA

KO-ON • 1927 • Mizoguchi Kenji • JPN • IMPERIAL GRACE, THE (USA) ○ GRATITUDE TO THE EMPEROR

KO PRIDE LEV see **KAD DODJE LAV** • 1973

KO PRIDE LJUBEZEN see **QUAND VIENT L'AMOUR** • 1955

KO TO TAMO PEVA? • 1981 • Sijan Slobodan • YGS • WHO'S THAT SINGING OVER THERE? ○ KDO NEKI TAM POJE ○ WHO'S SINGING THERE

KO ZORIJO JAGODE • 1979 • Ranfl Rajko • YGS • WHEN STRAWBERRIES RIPEN ○ KAD ZRIJU JAGODE ○ STRAWBERRY TIME

KOBANZAME • 1949 • Kinugasa Teinosuke • JPN

KOBAYASHI TAKIJI see **TAKIJI KOBAYASHI** • 1974

KOBBERBRYLLUP • 1933 • Schneevoigt George • DNM

KOBENHAVN 43 see **OKTOBER-DAGE** • 1970

KOBENHAVN, KALUNDBORG OG-? • 1934 • Holger-Madsen, Brandstrup Ludvig • DNM

KOBI AND MALI • Yeshurun Isaac • MTV • ISR

KOBIETA W KAPELUSZU • 1984 • Rozewicz Stanislaw • PLN • WOMAN IN THE HAT

KOBITO TO AOMUSHI • 1950 • *Toei Doga* • ANS • JPN • DWARF AND THE CATERPILLAR, THE

KOBNI TELEFON see **USODNI TELEFON** • 1987

KOBO SHINSENGUMI • 1930 • Ito Daisuke • JPN • RISE AND FALL OF SHINSENGUMI, THE

KOBUTORI • 1958 • ANS • JPN • OLD MAN AND HIS HEN, THE

KOCAOGLAN • 1964 • Demirel • TRK

KOCAR DO VIDNE • 1966 • Kachyna Karel • CZC • COACH TO VIENNA, THE ○ UNWILLING SAMARITAN, THE ○ CARRIAGE TO VIENNA

KOCERO, MOUNTAIN WOLF see **DAGLARIN KURDU KOCERO** • 1964

KOCHA, LUBI, SZANUJE • 1934 • Waszynski Michael • PLN

KOCHAJ ALBO RZUC • 1977 • Checinski Sylwester • PLN • BIG DEAL

KOCHAJMY MASZYNY • 1973 • Sturlis Edward • PLN • LET'S LOVE THE MACHINES

KOCHAJMY SIE • 1975 • Wojciechowski Krzysztof • PLN • LET'S LOVE ONE ANOTHER ○ LOVE THY NEIGHBOUR ○ LET US LOVE

KOCHAJMY SYRENKI • 1967 • Rutkiewicz Jan • PLN • LET'S LOVE THE "SIRENS" ○ LET'S LOVE SIRENS ○ LOVE YOUR CAR

KOCHANKOWIE MOE MAMY • 1985 • Piwowarski Radoslaw • PLN • MY MOTHER'S LOVERS

KOCHUBEI • 1958 • Ozerov Yury • USS

KOCICI SLOVO • 1960 • Pojar Bretislav • SHT • CZC • ETWAS VERSPRICHT ○ CAT'S WORD OF HONOR, A ○ WORD OF A CAT, THE

KOCICI SKOLA • 1960 • Pojar Bretislav • ANM • CZC • SCHOOL FOR CATS

KOCKA • 1972 • Grgic Zlatko • ANS • YGS • DICE, THE

KOCKIJN, EEN KERMISKRONIEK • 1966 • Bloem Rein • NTH

KOCKSGATAN 48 • 1940 • 1972 • Bergenstrahle Johan • SWD • FOREIGNERS ○ JAG HETER STELIOS

KOD FOTOGRAFA • 1959 • Mimica Vatroslav • ANS • YGS • AT THE PHOTOGRAPHER'S ○ IN THE PHOTOGRAPH

KODACHI O TSUKAU ONNA • 1944 • Marune Santaro • JPN • WOMAN USING A SHORT SWORD

KODACHI O TSUKAU ONNA • 1961 • Ikehiro Kazuo • JPN • WOMAN USING A SHORT SWORD

KODAK GHOST POEMS -PART 1: THE ADVENTURES OF THE EXQUISITE CORPSE • 1968 • Noren Andrew • USA

KODAMA WA YONDEIRU • 1959 • Honda Inoshiro • JPN

KODEKS PULTUSKI • 1958 • Jaworski Tadeusz • DOC • PLN • PULTUSK CODE, THE

KODIVETTAM • 1977 • Gopalakrishnan Adoor • IND • ASCENT

KODO • 1984 • Holender Jacques • DCS • CND

KODO NIPON • 1940 • *Tsuburaya Eiji* • JPN

KODOKAN HAMONJO • 1968 • Inoue Akira • JPN • VIOLENT JUDOIST, THE ○ JUDO SCHOOL EXPULSION LETTER

KODOMO NO ME • 1955 • *Takamine Hideko* • JPN • CHILDREN'S EYES

KODOMO NO SHIKI • 1939 • Shimizu Hiroshi • JPN • FOUR SEASONS OF CHILDREN

KODOU see **CODOU** • 1972

KODRAT • 1986 • Rahardjo Slamet • INN

KOEN • 1944 • Melson Soren • DNM • COW, THE

KOENIGSMARK • 1924 • Perret Leonce • FRN

KOENIGSMARK • 1935 • Tourneur Maurice • FRN • CRIMSON DYNASTY, THE

KOENIGSMARK • 1935 • Tourneur Maurice • UKN

KOENIGSMARK • 1953 • Bussi Solange • FRN, ITL

KOEPUTKIAIKUINEN JA SIMON ENKELIT • 1979 • Pasanen Spede • FNL • TEST-TUBE ADULT AND SIMO'S ANGELS, THE

KOFFER DES HERRN O.F., DIE • 1931 • Granowsky Alexis • FRG • LUGGAGE OF MR. O.F., THE ○ MR. O.F.'S 13 CASES

KOFFER MIT DYNAMIT • 1964 • *Hoffmann Jutta* • GDR, CZC • SUITCASE WITH DYNAMITE

KOFU KUGO NE SHUSSAN • 1972 • Saito Koichi • JPN

KOFUKU • 1982 • Ichikawa Kon • JPN • LONELY HEARTS (USA) ○ HAPPINESS

KOFUKU ENO SHOTAI • 1947 • *Takamine Hideko* • JPN • INVITATION TO HAPPINESS

KOFUKU-GO SHUPPAN • 1981 • Saito Koichi • JPN • SAILING OF THE SHIP KOFUKU-GO, THE

KOFUKU NO KIROI HANKACHI • 1977 • Yamada Yoji • JPN • YELLOW HANDKERCHIEF OF HAPPINESS, A

KOFUKU O HAITATSU SURU MUSUME • 1954 • *Wakao Ayako* • JPN • GIRL WHO DISTRIBUTED HAPPINESS, THE

KOFUKU SEZU • 1959 • *Tsuburaya Eiji* • JPN

KOFUN • 1968 • Okuwaki Toshio • JPN • EXCITEMENT

KOGA MANSION see **KOGA YASHIKI** • 1949

KOGA YASHIKI • 1949 • Kinugasa Teinosuke • JPN • KOGA MANSION

KOGAN NO MISSHI • 1959 • Kato Tai • JPN • MISSION TO HELL

KOGDA DEREVYA BYLI BOLSHIMI • 1962 • Kulidjanov Lev • USS • WHEN THE TREES WERE TALL (USA) ○ WHEN THE TREES GREW TALL

KOGDA DOZHD I VYETER STUCHAT V OKNO • 1968 • Brench Alois • USS • WHEN WIND AND RAIN BEATS ON THE WINDOW

KOGDA NASTUPAYET SENTYABR.. • 1977 • Keosayan Edmond • USS • WHEN SEPTEMBER COMES

KOGDA TSVETUT ROZY • 1959 • Yarmatov Kamil • USS • WHEN ROSES BLOOM

KOGE • 1964 • Kinoshita Keisuke • JPN • SCENT OF INCENSE, THE

KOGUMA NO KOROCHAN • 1958 • *Kyohai-T.c.j.* • ANS • JPN • KOROCHAN THE LITTLE BEAR

KOHANA see **YOSHIWARA** • 1937

KOHARU KYOGEN • 1942 • Aoyagi Nobuo • JPN • KOHARU'S PERFORMANCE

KOHARU'S PERFORMANCE see **KOHARU KYOGEN** • 1942

KOHAYAGAWA-KE NO AKI • 1961 • Ozu Yasujiro • JPN • AUTUMN OF THE KOHAYAGAWA FAMILY, THE ○ EARLY AUTUMN ○ LAST OF SUMMER, THE ○ END OF SUMMER, THE

KOHLHEISEL'S DAUGHTERS see **KOHLHIESELS TOCHTER** • 1920

KOHLHIESEL'S DAUGHTERS see **KOHLHIESELS TOCHTER** • 1930

KOHLHIESEL'S DAUGHTERS see **KOHLHIESELS TOCHTER** • 1943

KOHLHIESEL'S DAUGHTERS see **KOHLHIESELS TOCHTER** • 1962

KOHLHIESELS TOCHTER • 1920 • Lubitsch Ernst • FRG • KOHLHEISEL'S DAUGHTERS ○ HIS TWO DAUGHTERS

KOHLHIESELS TOCHTER • 1930 • Behrendt Hans • FRG • KOHLHIESEL'S DAUGHTERS

KOHLHIESELS TOCHTER • 1943 • Hoffmann Kurt • FRG • KOHLHIESEL'S DAUGHTERS

KOHLHIESELS TOCHTER • 1962 • von Ambesser Axel • FRG • KOHLHIESEL'S DAUGHTERS

KOHO JSEM VCERA LIBAL • 1935 • Svoboda • CZC • WHO I KISSED YESTERDAY

KOHOUT PLASI SMRT • 1961 • Cech Vladimir • CZC • COCK OF THE DAWN ○ COCK THAT SCARES DEATH

KOHRAA • 1964 • Naug Biren • IND

KOI • 1924 • Kinugasa Teinosuke • JPN • LOVE

KOI A SUTTA ONNA • 1958 • Harada Hasuo • JPN

KOI GESHO • 1955 • Honda Inoshiro • JPN • LOVE TIDE

KOI NO DAIBOKEN • 1970 • Hani Susumu • JPN • GREAT ADVENTURE OF LOVE

KOI NO FUUNJI • 1945 • Yamamoto Kajiro • JPN • MISFORTUNES OF LOVE

KOI NO HIGHWAY • 1967 • Saito Buichi • JPN • HIGHWAY OF LOVE, THE

KOI NO INOCHIO • 1961 • Masumura Yasuzo • JPN • LOVE AND LIFE

KOI NO KATAMICHI-KIPPU • 1960 • Shinoda Masahiro • JPN • ONE-WAY TICKET FOR LOVE ○ ONE WAY TICKET TO LOVE

KOI NO MEXICAN ROCK: KOI TO YUME TO BOKEN • 1967 • Sakurai Hideo • JPN • LOVE'S GREAT ADVENTURE

KOI NO TOKYO • 1932 • Gosho Heinosuke • JPN • LOVE IN TOKYO

KOI NO UKISHIMA (JPN) see **ILHA DOS AMORES, A** • 1978

KOI O SHIPOYO: KIRINU NO HANA • 1967 • Miyazaki Mamoru • JPN • LET US LOVE

KOI TO BUSHI • 1925 • Kinugasa Teinosuke • JPN • LOVE AND A WARRIOR

KOI TO TAIYO TO GANG • 1962 • Ishii Teruo • JPN • ALL RASCALS

KOI TOWA NARINA • 1924 • Kinugasa Teinosuke • JPN

KOI WA INAMONO AJINAMONO • 1958 • Mizuko Harumi • JPN

KOI YAMABIKO • 1959 • Makino Masahiro • JPN

KOIBITO • 1951 • Ichikawa Kon • JPN • SWEETHEART, THE ○ LOVER

KOIBITO • 1960 • Nakamura Noboru • JPN • MY LOVE

KOIBITO O SAGASO • 1967 • Morinaga Kenjiro • JPN • FIVE BRIDGES, THE

KOIBITO TO YONDE MITAI • 1968 • Morinaga Kenjiro • JPN • PUPPY-LOVE SINGERS, THE

KOIBUMI • 1953 • Tanaka Kinuyo • JPN • LOVE LETTER

KOIBUMI • 1985 • Kumashiro Tatsumi • JPN • LOVE LETTER

KOIBUMI SAIBAN • 1951 • Nakamura Noboru • JPN • LOVE LETTER TRIAL

KOICHI TANBEI • 1936 • Inagaki Hiroshi • JPN

KOIKAZE DOCHU • 1957 • Matsuda Sadatsugu • JPN • BREEZE OF LOVE

KOINA NO GINPEI • 1933 • Kinugasa Teinosuke • JPN • GIMPEI FROM KOINA

KOINA NO GINPEI • 1961 • Tanaka Tokuzo • JPN • SILVER MEDAL OF LOVE

KOINA NO KIMPEI • 1954 • *Otowa Nobuko* • JPN • KIMPEI FROM KOINA

KOISURU • 1975 • Saito Koichi • JPN • TO LOVE

KOISURU ONNA TACHI • 1987 • Omori Kazuki • JPN • LOVING GIRLS

KOISURU TSUMA • 1947 • Hagiwara Ryo • JPN • WIFE IN LOVE, A

KOIYA KOI NASUNA KOI • 1962 • Uchida Tomu • JPN • LOVE, THY NAME BE SORROW ○ LOVE NOT AGAIN ○ MAD FOX, THE ○ CUNNING FOX, THE

KOJAK AND THE MARCUS-NELSON MURDERS see **MARCUS-NELSON MURDERS, THE** • 1973

KOJAK: THE BELARUS FILE • 1985 • Markowitz Robert • TVM • USA • BELARUS FILE, THE

KOJAK: THE CHINATOWN MURDERS • 1974 • Szwarc Jeannot • TVM • USA

KOJAK: THE PRICE OF JUSTICE • 1987 • Metzger Alan • TVM • USA

KOJIMA NO HARU • 1940 • Toyoda Shiro • JPN • SPRING ON LEPER'S ISLAND

KOJIN KOJITSU • 1961 • Shibuya Minoru • JPN • THIEF AND CULTURE ORDER, A

KOJIRO see **SASAKI KOJIRO** • 1967

KOJIRO SASAKI see **SASAKI KOJIRO** • 1951

KOKA KOLA EN LA SANGRE see **FORMULA SECRETA, LA** • 1965

KOKA KOLA IN THE BLOOD see **FORMULA SECRETA, LA** • 1965

KOKAB'S SECRET • 1990 • Massoumi Kazem • IRN

KOKASHI MUSO • 1932 • Itami Mansaku • JPN • PEERLESS PATRIOT

KOKEIMU • 1964 • Takechi Tetsuji • JPN

KOKETSU NO KYOJIN • 1956-59 • SER • JPN • SUPER GIANT ○ SUPERGIANT

KOKEZARU NO TSUBO • 1954 • Misumi Kenji • JPN • BASKET WITH LICHEN

KOKHONO MEGH • 1968 • Agradoot • IND • SUDDEN CLOUDS

KOKILA • 1937 • *Biswas Anil (M)* • IND

KOKILA • 1977 • Mahendra Balu • IND

KOKKINA PHANARIA • 1962 • Georgiadis Vassilis • GRC • RED LANTERNS (USA)

KOKO, A TALKING GORILLA see **KOKO, LE GORILLE QUI PARLE** • 1977

KOKO FLANEL • 1989 • Coninx Stijn • BLG

KOKO KANSAN MIES • 1973 • Laihanen Veikko • DOC • FNL • MAN FOR THE WHOLE NATION, A

KOKO, LE GORILLE QUI PARLE • 1977 • Schroeder Barbet • DOC • FRN • KOKO, A TALKING GORILLA ○ KOKO THE GORILLA

KOKO LEMON MUSUME • 1967 • Ichimura Hirokazu • JPN • LEMON GIRLS ON THE GO

KOKO NI IZUMI ARI • 1955 • Imai Tadashi • JPN • HERE IS A SPRING ○ HERE IS A FOUNTAIN

KOKO POPS • 1981 • Starkiewicz Antoinette • ANS • ASL

KOKO THE GORILLA see **KOKO, LE GORILLE QUI PARLE** • 1977

KOKODA CRESCENT • 1988 • Robinson Ted • ASL

KOKOKARA HAJIMARU • 1965 • Tsuboshima Takashi • JPN • BEAST CALLED MAN, THE

KOKON • 1964 • Oonk Jan • SHT • NTH

KOKORO • 1955 • Ichikawa Kon • JPN • HEART, THE

KOKORO • 1973 • Shindo Kaneto • JPN • HEART

KOKORO NO JITSUGETSU • 1931 • Tasaka Tomotaka • JPN • HEART OF REALITY

KOKORO NO SANMYAKU • 1966 • Yoshimura Kozaburo • JPN • HEART OF THE MOUNTAINS, THE

KOKORO OGORERU ONNA • 1930 • Toyoda Shiro • JPN • HEART OF A PROUD WOMAN, THE

KOKORO TSUKI NO GOTOKU • 1947 • Inagaki Hiroshi • JPN

KOKOSEI BANCHO • 1970 • Obimori Michihiko • JPN • WAYOUT, WAY IN (USA)

KOKOSEI GEISHA • 1968 • Yuge Taro • JPN • STUDENT GEISHA

KOKOTSU NO HITO • 1973 • Toyoda Shiro • JPN

KOKOTSU NO IZUMI • 1967 • Yamamoto Shinya • JPN • SPRING OF ECSTASY

KOKOVIOS AND SPAROS IN THE SPIDER'S WEB see **KOKOVIOS KE SPAROS STA DIATIA TIS ARAHNIS** • 1967

KOKOVIOS KE SPAROS STA DIATIA TIS ARAHNIS • 1967 • Grigoriou Grigoris • GRC • KOKOVIOS AND SPAROS IN THE SPIDER'S WEB ○ TWO SMALL FISH IN THE SPIDER'S WEB

KOKS I KULISSEN • 1983 • Thomsen Christian Braad • DNM • WILD IN THE WINGS ○ LADIES ON THE ROCKS

KOKUHAKU • 1968 • Ohnuma Hiroshi • JPN • CONFESSION, A

KOKUHAKUTEKI JOYU-RON • 1971 • Yoshida Yoshishige • JPN • CONFESSIONS, THEORIES, ACTRESSES ○ ACTRESSES

KOKUSAI HIMITSU KEISATSU: ZETTAI ZETSUMEI • 1967 • Taniguchi Senkichi • JPN • KILLING BOTTLE, THE ○ ZETTAI ZETSUMEI

KOKUSAI MITSUYUDAN • 1944 • Ito Daisuke • JPN • INTERNATIONAL SMUGGLING GANG

KOKYO • 1923 • Mizoguchi Kenji • JPN • NATIVE COUNTRY ○ FURUSATO

KOKYO • 1972 • Yamada Yoji • JPN • HOME FROM THE SEA

KOL MAMZER MELECH • 1968 • Zohar Uri • ISR • EVERY BASTARD A KING (USA) ○ EVERY MAN A KING

KOLBERG • 1944 • Harlan Veit • FRG

KOLCHAK TAPES, THE see **NIGHT STALKER** • 1971

KOLCSONKERT CSECSEMOK, A • 1914 • Curtiz Michael • HNG • BORROWED BABIES

KOLCSONKERT KASTELY, A • 1935 • Vajda Ladislao • HNG • BORROWED CASTLE, THE

KOLEDZY • 1956 • Nasfeter Janusz • SHT • PLN • FRIENDS, THE

KOLEJ 56 • 1989 • Fauzee Ahmad • MLY

KOLEJARSKI SLOWO • 1953 • Munk Andrzej • DCS • PLN • RAILWAYMAN'S PLEDGE, A ○ RAILWAYMAN'S WORD, A

KOLEKCIONAR • 1971 • Blazekovic Milan • ANM • YGS • COLLECTOR

KOLESKABE • 1954 • Carlsen Henning • SHT • DNM

KOLIBELNAYA • 1937 • Vertov Dziga • USS • LULLABY

KOLIBRI see **COLIBRI** • 1924

KOLIK SLOV STACI LASCE • 1961 • Sequens Jiri • CZC • LOVE WITHOUT WORDS

KOLINGENS GALOSCHER • 1912 • Magnusson Charles, Jaenzon Julius • SWD • VAGABOND'S GALOSHES, THE

KOLIVCHTCHINA • 1933 • Kavaleridze Ivan • USS

KOLKA see **DRUG MOI, KOLKA** • 1961

KOLLEGE KAPERS • 1929 • Harman Bobby • UKN

KOLLEGE KOMMT GLEICH • 1943 • Anton Karl • FRG

KOLLEGI • 1963 • Sakharov Alexei • USS • COLLEAGUES

KOLLEJSKII REGISTRATOR • 1925 • Jeliabujski Yuri • USS • POSTMASTER, THE

KOLOKOL SAYATA • 1967 • Agzamov Yuldash • USS • BELL OF SAYAT

KOLOLYEVSKAYA REGATA • 1967 • Chulyukin Yuri • USS • ROYAL REGATTA

KOLONAKI BEHAVIOUR ZERO see **KOLONAKI DIAGOGI MIDEN** • 1967

KOLONAKI DIAGOGI MIDEN • 1967 • Zografakis Stelios • GRC • KOLONAKI BEHAVIOUR ZERO

KOLONIALSKANDAL see **COLONIALSKANDAL** • 1927

KOLONIE LANFIERI • 1969 • Schmidt Jan • CZC, USS • LANFIERI COLONY, THE ○ LANFIERE

KOLONNE X • 1929 • Schunzel Reinhold • FRG

KOLORATUREN • 1931 • Fischinger Oskar • ANS • FRG • COLORATURA

KOLOROWA KRONIKA • 1962 • Lomnicki Jan • DOC • PLN • COLOURFUL CHRONICLE

KOLOROWE PONCZOCHY • 1960 • Nasfeter Janusz • PLN • COLOURED STOCKINGS

KOLOROWY SWIAT • 1961 • Lomnicki Jan • DOC • PLN • COLOURFUL WORLD

KOLORY ZYCIA • 1975 • Szpakowicz Piotr • PLN • COLOURS OF LIFE

KOLT 15 GAP • 1971 • Milosevic Mica, Jovanovic Jovan • SHT • YGS

KOLUMBOWIE • 1970 • Morgenstern Janusz • SER • PLN • COLUMBUSES, THE

KOLYBELNAYA • 1960 • Kalik Mikhail • USS • LULLABY (USA) ○ CRADLE SONG

KOLYOK • 1959 • Szemes Mihaly • HNG • OUR KID

KOM I MIN SANG • 1968 • Sarno Joe • SWD • TO INGRID MY LOVE, LISA (USA) ○ COME INTO MY BED ○ "YES!" (COUNT THE POSSIBILITIES) ○ "YES!"

KOM SAAM VANAAND • 1949 • SAF

KOM TILLBAKA, DE • 1962 • Troell Jan • DOC • SWD • RETURN, THE

KOM TOT RUS • 1977 • SAF

KOMAL GANDHAR • 1961 • Ghatak Ritwik • IND • E-FLAT

KOMANDA S NASIEJ ULICY • 1953 • Maslyukov Alexei • USS • TEAM FROM OUR STREET

KOMANDIRAT NA OTRIADA • 1959 • Mundrov Dutcho • BUL • COMMANDER OF THE DETACHMENT, THE

KOMANDOLAR GELIYOR • 1968 • Okcugil Nejat • TRK • COMMANDOS ARE COMING, THE

KOMANTZCHE, DER • 1979 • Achternbusch Herbert • FRG

KOMBRIG IVANOV • 1923 • Rasumny Alexander • USS • BEAUTY AND THE BOLSHEVIK

KOME • 1957 • Imai Tadashi • JPN • MEN OF THE RICE FIELDS ○ PEOPLE OF THE RICE-FIELD ○ RICE

KOMEDI I HAGERSKOG • 1968 • Anderberg Torgny • SWD • COMEDY AT HAGERSKOG ○ ODD LOVERS

KOMEDIA POMYLEK • 1968 • Rozewicz Stanislaw, Zarzycki Jerzy • PLN • COMEDY OF ERRORS

KOMEDIANT, DE • 1986 • de Jonge Freek • NTH • PERFORMER, THE

KOMEDIANTER see **KOMODIANTEN** • 1912

KOMEDIANTI • 1954 • Vicek Vladimir • CZC

KOMEDIANTY • 1961 • Kaniewska Maria • PLN • COMEDIANS, THE ○ ON THE THRESHOLD OF ART

KOMEDIE OM GELD • 1936 • Ophuls Max • NTH • TROUBLE WITH MONEY, THE ○ COMEDY ABOUT MONEY, A ○ COMEDY ON MONEY

KOMEDIE S KLIKOU • 1964 • Krska Vaclav • CZC • COMEDY AROUND A DOOR HANDLE

KOMICK ZASSHI NANKA IRANAI • 1987 • Takita Yojiro • JPN • NO MORE COMIC MAGAZINES

KOMINIARCZYK • 1960 • Nehrebecki Wladyslaw • ANS • PLN • LITTLE CHIMNEY BOY, THE ○ CHIMNEY-SWEEPER, THE

KOMISARI I DRITES • 1966 • Anagosti Dhimiter, Gjika Viktor • ALB • COMMISSAR OF LIGHT, THE

KOMISARIO PALMU • 1960-69 • Kassila Matti • SRL • FNL • POLICE INSPECTOR PALMU

KOMITET DEVYATNADTSATI • 1972 • Kulish Savva • USS • COMMITTEE OF THE NINETEEN ○ COMMITTEE OF NINETEEN

KOMM, LIEBE MALD UND MACHE see **TOLLDREISTEN GESCHICHTEN DES HONORE DE BALZAC** • 1969

KOMM NACH WIEN -ICH ZEIG DIR WAS • 1969 • Thiele Rolf • FRG, AUS

KOMM NUR, MEIN LIEBSTES VOGELEIN • 1968 • Thiele Rolf • FRG, ITL • COME NOW, MY DEAR LITTLE BIRD

KOMM' ZU MIR ZUM RENDEZVOUS • 1930 • Boese Carl • FRG

KOMM ZU MIR ZURUCK • 1944 • Paul Heinz • FRG

KOMM ZURUCK • 1953 • Braun Alfred • FRG

KOMMANDANT VOM KONIGSTEIN, DER • 1915 • *Rensie-Film* • FRG

KOMMANDANT VON MOLINETTE, DER • 1967 • Erler Rainer • FRG, YGS • COMMANDER OF MOLINETTE, THE ○ FAST EIN HELD

KOMMANDO LEOPARD • 1985 • Margheriti Antonio • ITL, FRG • COMMANDO LEOPARD

KOMMEN SIE AM ERSTEN.. see **KOMMEN SIE ERST AM ERSTEN** • 1951

KOMMEN SIE ERST AM ERSTEN • 1951 • Engel Erich • FRG • KOMMEN SIE AM ERSTEN..

KOMMISSAR X -DREI BLAUE PANTHER • 1968 • Parolini Gianfranco • FRG, ITL • COMMISSIONER X -THREE BLUE PANTHERS

KOMMISSAR X -DREI GRUNE HUNDE • 1967 • Zehetgruber Rudolf, Parolini Gianfranco • FRG, ITL, FRN • COMMISSAIRE X TRAQUE LES CHIENS VERTS (FRN) ○ COMMISSIONER X -THREE GREEN DOGS

KOMMISSAR X -HUNTER OF THE UNKNOWN see **KOMMISSAR X: JAGD AUF UNBEKANNT** • 1965

KOMMISSAR X: JAGD AUF UNBEKANNT • 1965 • Zehetgruber Rudolf, Parolini Gianfranco • FRG, ITL, YGS • DODICI DONNE D'ORO (ITL) ○ KISS KISS, KILL KILL (UKN) ○ KOMMISSAR X -HUNTER OF THE UNKNOWN

KOMMISSAR X: JAGT DIE ROTEN TIGER • 1971 • Reinl Harald, Romitelli Giancarlo • FRG, ITL, PKS • F.B.I. OPERAZIONE PAKISTAN ○ TIGER GANG

KOMMT VON DER LIEBE, DAS • 1921 • Bolten-Baeckers Heinrich? • FRG

KOMMT VON SEKT, DAS • 1922 • Bolten-Baeckers Heinrich • FRG

KOMMUNIST • 1957 • Raizman Yuli • USS • COMMUNIST, THE

KOMMUNISTI • 1975 • Ozerov Yury • USS, BUL • COMMUNISTS

KOMODIANTEN • 1912 • Gad Urban • FRG, DNM • KOMEDIANTER

KOMODIANTEN • 1915 • *Lund Grete* • FRG

KOMODIANTEN • 1924 • Grune Karl • FRG

KOMODIANTEN • 1941 • Pabst G. W. • FRG • PLAYERS, THE ○ ACTORS, THE

KOMODIANTEN DES LEBENS • 1924 • Jacoby Georg • FRG

KOMODIANTENKIND, DAS • 1923 • Sauer Fred • FRG

KOMODIE DER LEIDENSCHAFTEN • 1921 • Leni Paul • FRG

KOMODIE DES HERZENS • 1924 • Gliese Rochus • FRG

KOMODIE DES LEBENS • 1920 • Illes Eugen • FRG

KOMOIUTA BUSHUOROSHI • 1935 • Miyata Mitsuzo • JPN

KOMORI-ZOSHI • 1927 • Yamazaki • JPN

KOMORNI HARMONIE • 1963 • Schorm Evald • MTV • CZC • CHAMBER HARMONY

KOMOSOL, LEADER OF ELECTRIFICATION see **K.SH.E.** • 1932

KOMOSOL, PATRON OF ELECTRIFICATION see **K.SH.E.** • 1932

KOMP, A • 1963 • Ventilla Istvan • HNG

KOMPLETT AUF ERLENHOF • 1950 • Froelich Carl • FRG

KOMPLIZE VON CINCINNATI, DER • 1920 • Eichgrun Bruno • FRG

KOMPLOTT IM BANKVIERTEL, DAS • 1921 • Sauer Fred • FRG

KOMPOSITION IN BLAU • 1935 • Fischinger Oskar • ANM • FRG • COMPOSITION IN BLUE

KOMPOZITOR GLINKA • 1952 • Alexandrov Grigori • USS • MAN OF MUSIC (USA) ○ GLINKA, MAN OF MUSIC ○ GLINKA

KOMPOZITOR SERGEY PROKOFYEV • 1961 • Stepanova Lidiya • USS • PROKOFIEFF -HIS LIFE AND MUSIC

KOMPROMIS • 1972 • Ryszka Henryk • PLN • COMPROMISE

KOMPUTERY • 1967 • Zanussi Krzysztof • DOC • PLN • COMPUTERS

KOMSOMOL • 1932 • Ivens Joris • USS • PESN O GEROJACH ○ SONG OF HEROES (UKN) ○ YOUTH SPEAKS

KOMSOMOL CELEBRATION • 1958 • Makhnach Leonid • DOC • USS

KOMSOMOLSK • 1938 • Gerasimov Sergei • USS • FROZEN NORTH, THE (UKN) ○ CITY OF YOUTH

KOMST VAN JOACHIM STILLER, DE • 1976 • Kumel Harry • BLG • RETURN OF JOACHIM STILLER, THE

KOMTESSE HELLA • 1916 • Rippert Otto? • FRG

KON • 1968 • Giersz Witold • ANS • PLN • PORTRAIT OF A HORSE, THE ○ HORSE, THE

KON A SPRAWA POLSKA • 1967 • Trzos-Rastawiecki Andrzej • ANM • PLN • HORSE AND POLISH AFFAIRS, THE

KON-TIKI • 1951 • Nordemar Olle • DOC • SWD

KONA • 1982 • Skulason Helgi • ICL • WOMAN

KONA COAST • 1968 • Johnson Lamont • USA

KONCERT • 1954 • Belan Branko • YGS

KONCERT • 1961 • Szabo Istvan • SHT • HNG • CONCERT

KONCERT • 1962 • Perski Ludwik • DOC • PLN • CONCERT, THE

KONCERT, A • 1982 • Koltay Gabor • HNG • CONCERT, THE

KONCERT NA EKRENIE SLASK • 1956 • Lesiewicz Witold • PLN • SILESIA IN BLACK AND GREEN ○ SONG OF SILESIA

KONCERT NA KONCI LETA • 1978 • Vlacil Frantisek • CZC • CONCERT AT THE END OF SUMMER

KONCERT PRO STUDENTY • 1970 • Schorm Evald • MTV • CZC • CONCERT FOR STUDENTS

KONCERT WAWEL • 1960 • Lomnicki Jan • DOC • PLN • WAWEL CONCERT, THE

KONCERT ZA MASINSKU PUSKU • 1959 • Vukotic Dusan • ANS • YGS • CONCERTO FOR SUB-MACHINE GUN (USA) ○ CONCERTO FOR MACHINE GUN

KONCHU DAISENSO • 1968 • Nihonmatsu Kazui • JPN • WAR OF INSECTS ○ GENOCIDE (USA)

KONDELIK -FATHER-IN-LAW, VEJVARA -SON-IN-LAW see **TCHAN KONDELIK A ZET VEJVARA** • 1929

KONDELIK -FATHER, VEJVARA -BRIDEGROOM see **OTEC KONDELIK A ZENICH VEJVARA** • 1926

KONDURA • 1977 • Benegal Shyam • IND • SAGE FROM THE SEA, THE ○ ANUGHARAM ○ BOON, THE

KONEC AGENTA W4C PROSTREDNICTVIM PSA PANA FOUSTKY • 1967 • Vorlicek Vaclav • CZC • END OF AGENT W4C THROUGH MR. FOUSTKA'S DOG, THE

KONEC JASNOVIDCE • 1958 • *Chytilova Vera* • CZC

KONEC KRYCHLE • 1979 • Smetana Zdenek • ANS • CZC • END OF THE CUBE, THE

KONEC MILOVANI • 1913 • Stafl Otakar, Urban Max • CZC • END OF LOVEMAKING

KONEC SRPNA V HOTELU OZON • 1966 • Schmidt Jan • CZC • END OF AUGUST AT THE HOTEL OZONE, THE (USA) ○ END OF AUGUST IN HOTEL OZONE

KONEC VELKE EPOCHY • 1966 • Moskalyk Antonin • CZC • END OF A GREAT ERA, THE

KONEK-GORBUNOK • 1947 • Ivanov-Vano Ivan • ANS • USS • LITTLE HUMPBACKED HORSE, THE ○ HUNCHBACK PONY, THE ○ MAGIC HORSE, THE

KONEKO MONOGATARI • 1987 • Hata Masanori • JPN • ADVENTURES OF A KITTY

KONEKO NO RAKUGAKI • 1957 • *Toei Poga* • ANS • JPN • SCRIBBLING KITTEN, THE

KONETS STAROY BERYOZOVSKI • 1961 • Eisimont Viktor • USS • APARTMENT IN MOSCOW (USA)

KONFERENZ-DALMETSCHER • 1964 • Houwer Rob • FRG

KONFETTI • 1936 • Marischka Hubert • AUS • CONFETTI

KONFLIKT • 1937 • Branner Per-Axel • SWD • CONFLICT

KONFLIKTY • 1960 • Szczechura Daniel • ANS • PLN • CONFLICTS ○ CONFLICT

KONFRONTATION • 1975 • Lyssy Rolf • SWT • ASSASSINATION IN DAVOS (UKN)

KONG see **KING KONG** • 1933

KONG HAAKON V • 1951 • Carlsen Henning • DNM

KONG ISLAND see **KING OF KONG ISLAND** • 1978

KONGA • 1961 • Lemont John • UKN • I WAS A TEENAGE GORILLA

KONGA ROJA • 1943 • Galindo Alejandro • MXC

KONGA, THE WILD STALLION • 1940 • Nelson Sam • USA • KONGA (UKN)

KONGA (UKN) see **KONGA, THE WILD STALLION** • 1940

KONGA YO see **TERREUR SUR LA SAVANE** • 1962

KONGBUFENZI see **K'UNG-PU FEN-TZU** • 1986

KONGEN BOD • 1938 • *Henning-Jensen Bjarne* • DNM

KONGENS ENGHAVE • 1967 • Orsted Claus, Brydesen Lars • SWT • DNM • KING'S MEADOW GARDENS

KONGI'S HARVEST • 1971 • Davis Ossie • USA, NGR, SWD

KONGO • 1932 • Cowen William J. • USA

KONGO-EXPRESS • 1939 • von Borsody Eduard • FRG

KONGO-ROO • 1946 • Swift Howard • ANS • USA

KONGRESS AMUSIERT SICH, DER • 1966 • von Radvanyi Geza • AUS, FRG, FRN • CONGRESS OF LOVE, THE ○ WIENER KONGRESS

KONGRESS TANZT, DER • 1931 • Charell Erik • FRG

KONGRESS TANZT, DER • 1955 • Antel Franz • AUS

KONIEC CZY POCZATEK? • 1956 • Perski Ludwik • DOC • PLN • BEGINNING OR THE END?, THE

KONIEC NASZEGO SWIATA • 1964 • Jakubowska Wanda • PLN • END OF OUR WORLD, THE

KONIEC NOCY • 1957 • Dziedzina Julian, Komorowski Pawel, Uszycka Walentyna • PLN • END OF THE NIGHT, THE ○ END OF NIGHT

KONIG, DER • 1913 • Mack Max • FRG

KONIG AMUSIERT SICH, DER • 1918 • Fleck Luise, Fleck Jacob • AUS • RIGOLETTO

KONIG DER BERGE, DER • 1915 • *Saturn-Film* • FRG

KONIG DER HOCHSTAPLER, DER see **MANOLESCU** • 1929

KONIG DER MANEGE • 1954 • Marischka Ernst • AUS

KONIG DER MANEGE, DER • 1921 • Delmont Joseph • FRG

KONIG DER MITTELSTURMER, DER • 1927 • Freisler Fritz • FRG

KONIG DER NACHT, DER • 1917 • Dessauer Siegfried • FRG

KONIG DES MONT-BLANC, DER see **EWIGE TRAUM, DER** • 1934

KONIG FUR EINE NACHT • 1956 • May Paul • FRG

KONIG IHRES HERZEN, DER • 1918 • *Trautmann Ludwig* • FRG

KONIG KRAUSE • 1919 • Bolten-Baeckers Heinrich • FRG

KONIG LACHELT -PARIS LACHT, DER see **POSTILLON VON LONJUMEAU, DER** • 1936

KONIG MAKOMBE see **HERRIN DER WELT 4, DIE** • 1919

KONIG MOTOR • 1915 • Jacoby Georg • FRG

KONIG NICOLO see **KONIG NICOLO ODER SO IST DAS LEBEN** • 1919

KONIG NICOLO ODER SO IST DAS LEBEN • 1919 • Legband Paul • FRG • KONIG NICOLO

KONIG RICHARD III • 1922 • Oswald Richard? • FRG

KONIG UND DIE KLEINEN MADCHEN, DER • 1925 • Malasomma Nunzio • FRG

KONIG VON GOLCONDA 1, DER • 1921 • Maschke Max • FRG

KONIG VON GOLCONDA 2, DER • 1921 • Maschke Max • FRG • STURZENDE BERG, DER

KONIG VON GOLCONDA 3, DER • 1921 • Maschke Max • FRG • UM EIN KONIGREICH

KONIG VON PARIS, DER • 1920 • Lund Erik • FRG

KONIG VON PARIS, DER • 1930 • Mittler Leo • FRG

KONIGIN DER ALTSTADT, DIE • 1925 • *Gold-Film* • FRG

KONIGIN DER ARENA • 1952 • Meyer Rolf • FRG

KONIGIN DER LANDSTRASSE • 1948 • von Cziffra Geza • AUS

KONIGIN DER LIEBE • 1936 • Buch Fritz Peter • FRG

KONIGIN DES VARIETES, DIE • 1927 • Guter Johannes • FRG

KONIGIN DES WELTBALDES, DIE • 1926 • FRG

KONIGIN EINER NACHT • 1951 • Hoffmann Kurt • FRG

KONIGIN EINER NACHT, DIE • 1930 • Wendhausen Fritz • FRG

KONIGIN ELISABETHS DOCHTER • 1915 • Gildemeijer Johan • DNM • QUEEN ELIZABETH'S DAUGHTER

KONIGIN KAROLINE VON ENGLAND • 1923 • Raffe Rolf • FRG

KONIGIN LUISE • 1911 • Porten Franz • FRG • QUEEN LUISE

KONIGIN LUISE • 1957 • Liebeneiner Wolfgang • FRG

KONIGIN LUISE 1 • 1927 • Grune Karl • FRG • JUGEND DER KONIGIN LUISE, DIE ○ QUEEN LUISE

KONIGIN LUISE 2 • 1928 • Grune Karl • FRG

KONIGIN SEINES HERZENS, DIE • 1928 • Janson Victor • FRG • WIEN, DU STADT MEINER TRAUME ○ QUEEN OF MY HEART

KONIGIN VOM MOULIN-ROUGE, DIE • 1926 • Wiene Robert • AUS • DUCHESS OF THE FOLIES BERGERES, THE

KONIGLICHE BETTLER • 1917 • Oswald Richard • FRG

KONIGLICHE HOHEIT • 1953 • Braun Harald • FRG

KONIGS PAUSOLE see **ABENTEUER DES KONIGS PAUSOLE, DIE** • 1933

KONIGSGRENADIERE, DIE • 1925 • von Bolvary Geza • FRG

KONIGSKINDER • 1950 • Kautner Helmut • FRG

KONIGSKINDER • 1962 • Beyer Frank • GDR • INVINCIBLE LOVE ○ ROYAL CHILDREN

KONIGSLIEBCHEN • 1924 • Schall Heinz • FRG

KONIGSLOGE, DIE • 1929 • Foy Bryan • FRG, USA • QUEEN OF THE NIGHT CLUBS

KONIGSTIGER • 1935 • Randolf Rolf • FRG

KONIGSTOCHTER VON TRAVANKORE, DIE • 1917 • Rippert Otto • FRG

KONIGSWALZER • 1935 • Maisch Herbert • FRG • ROYAL WALTZ, THE (USA)

KONIGSWALZER • 1955 • Tourjansky Victor • FRG

KONIKAPINA • 1976 • Niskanen Mikko, Suominen Tapio • FNL • HACK REBELLION, THE

KONINKRIJK VOOR EEN HUIS, EEN • 1949 • Speyer Jaap • NTH • KINGDOM FOR A HOUSE, A

KONIOK GORBUNOK see **SKAZKA O KONKE-GORBUNKE** • 1961

KONJ • 1972 • Stalter Pavao • YGS • HORSE, THE

KONJIKI YASHA • 1923 • Kinugasa Teinosuke • JPN • GOLDEN DEMON, THE

KONJIKI YASHA • 1954 • Shima Koji • JPN • GOLDEN DEMON (USA) ○ DEMON OF GOLD

KONJUH PLANINOM • 1966 • Hadzic Fadil • YGS • SONG FOR THE DEAD MINERS, A

KONJUNKTURRITTER • 1934 • Kampers Fritz • FRG

KONKETSUJI • 1952 • Sekigawa Hideo • JPN • MIXED-BLOOD CHILDREN

KONKETSUJI RIKA • 1973 • Yoshimura Kozaburo • JPN • RIKA, THE MIXED-BLOOD GIRL

KONKI • 1961 • Yoshimura Kozaburo • JPN • MARRIAGEABLE AGE ○ MARRIAGE TIME

KONKURRENZ PLATZT ,DIE • 1929 • Obal Max • FRG

KONKURS • 1963 • Forman Milos • CZC • TALENT COMPETITION ○ AUDITION, THE ○ COMPETITION

KONNA ONNA NI DARE GA SHITA • 1949 • Yamamoto Satsuo • JPN

KONNEN GEDANKEN TOTEN? • 1920 • Tostary Alfred • FRG

KONNEN TIERE DENKEN? • 1938 • FRG

KONNEN TOTE LEBEN - - ? see **GESPENSTER** • 1922

KONNYU TESTI SERTES • 1984 • Szomjas Gyorgy • HNG • LIGHT PHYSICAL INJURIES

KONNYUVER • 1989 • Szomjas Gyorgy • HNG • FAST & LOOSE

KONO HAHA O MIYO • 1930 • Tasaka Tomotaka • JPN • BEHOLD THIS MOTHER

KONO HIROI SORA NO DOTOKA NI • 1954 • Kobayashi Masaki • JPN • SOMEWHERE BENEATH THE WIDE SKY ○ SOMEWHERE UNDER THE BROAD SKY

KONO KO O NOKOSHITE • 1984 • Kinoshita Keisuke • JPN • LEAVING THOSE CHILDREN ○ LEAVING THIS CHILD

KONO KOE NAKI SAKEBI • 1965 • Ichimura Hirokazu • JPN • SOUNDLESS CRY

KONO KUBI ICHIMAN-GOKU • 1963 • Ito Daisuke • JPN

KONO NEDELYA • 1919 • Vertov Dziga • SER • USS • CINE WEEKLY ○ WEEKLY REELS

KONO TEN NO NIJI • 1958 • Kinoshita Keisuke • JPN • ETERNAL RAINBOW, THE ○ RAINBOW OF THIS SKY, THE

KONO WAKASA ARU KAGIRI • 1961 • Kurahara Koreyoshi • JPN • THAT YOUTH MAY BE ETERNAL

KONOPIELKA see **KO-NO-PIEL-KA** • 1981

KONPEKI NO SORA TOKU • 1960 • Inoue Kazuo • JPN • GOODBYE TO GLORY

KONRAD ALBERT POCCI, DER FUSSBALL GRAF VOM AMMERLAND -DAS VORLAUFIG LETZTE KAPITEL EINER CHRONIK.. • 1967 • Syberberg Hans-Jurgen • DOC • FRG • KONRAD ALBERT POCCI, THE FOOTBALL COUNT OF THE AMMERLAND -PROVISIONALLY THE LAST CHAPTER OF A C...

KONRAD ALBERT POCCI, THE FOOTBALL COUNT OF THE AMMERLAND -PROVISIONALLY THE LAST CHAPTER OF A C... see **KONRAD ALBERT POCCI, DER FUSSBALL GRAF VOM AMMERLAND -DAS VORLAUFIG LETZTE KAPITEL EINER CHRONIK..** • 1967

KONSEQUENZ, DIE • 1977 • Petersen Wolfgang • FRG • CONSEQUENCE, THE

KONSERT-VALS • 1940 • Trauberg Ilya, Dubson M. • USS • CONCERT VALSE ○ CONCERT WALTZ

KONSERTO YIA POLIVOLA • 1967 • Dimopoulos Dinos • GRC • CONCERTO FOR MACHINE-GUNS ○ CASE OF HIGH TREASON, A

KONSERTTI • 1963 • Makinen Aito • DOC • FNL • CONCERT, A

KONSERVENBRAUT, DIE • 1915 • Wiene Robert • FRG

KONSKA OPERA see **LIMONADOVY JOE** • 1964

KONSTANTINOPEL - PARIS see **FRAU MIT DEN MILLIONEN 3, DIE** • 1923

KONSTEN ATT ALSKA • 1947 • Skoglund Gunnar • SWD • ART OF LOVE

KONSTGJORDA SVENSSON • 1929 • Edgren Gustaf • SWD • FALSE SVENSSON

KONSUL I INNI • 1971 • Gradowski Bohdan • DOC • PLN • CONSUL AND OTHERS

KONSUL STROTTHOFF • 1954 • Engel Erich • FRG

KONTAKT! • 1956 • Muller Nils R. • NRW

KONTE PILLA • 1967 • Ramanna T. R. • IND • FLYING SAUCER

KONTESA DORA • 1990 • Berkovic Zvonimir • YGS • COUNTESS DORA

KONTI-SKAN • 1965 • Barfod Bent • ANS • DNM

KONTRAKT • 1980 • Zanussi Krzysztof • PLN • CONTRACT ○ CONTRAKT

KONTROVERSIAL • 1981 • Brocka Lino • PHL • CONTROVERSY!

KONTRYBUCJA • 1967 • Lomnicki Jan • PLN • CONTRIBUTION

KONTSERT MASTEROV UKRAINSKOVO ISKUSSTVA • 1952 • Barnet Boris • USS • CONCERT OF THE MASTERS OF UKRAINIAN ART

KONVEYER SMERTI • 1933 • Pyriev Ivan • USS • CONVEYOR OF DEATH, THE

KONYA WA ODORO • 1967 • Yuge Taro • JPN • LET'S DANCE TONIGHT

KONYAKCI • 1965 • Basaran Tunc • TRK • DRUNKARD, THE

KONYAKU SAMBA GARASU • 1956 • Sugie Toshio • JPN • THREE YOUNG MEN AND A DREAM GIRL

KONYAKU YUBIWA • 1950 • Kinoshita Keisuke • JPN • ENGAGEMENT RING ○ ENGEIJI RINGU

KONYETS SANKT-PETERBURGA • 1927 • Pudovkin V. I. • USS • END OF ST. PETERSBURG, THE

KONYETS "SATURNA" • 1968 • Azarov Vilen • USS • END OF "SATURN", THE
KONZEN KOJYOKI • 1968 • Yamamoto Shinya • JPN • RELATIONSHIP BEFORE MARRIAGE
KONZERT, DAS • 1931 • Mittler Leo • FRG
KONZERT, DAS • 1944 • Verhoeven Paul • FRG
KONZERT IN TIROL • 1938 • Martin Karl Heinz • FRG
KOOKY LOOPY • 1961 • Hanna William, Barbera Joseph • ANS • USA
KOOTJIE EMMER • 1977 • SAF
KOPASZKUTYA • 1981 • Szomjas Gyorgy • HNG • BALD DOG
...KOPCHEN IN DAS WASSER, SCHWANZCHEN IN DIE HOH • 1969 • Fornbacher Helmut • FRG
KOPERNIKUS • 1972 • Petelska Ewa, Petelski Czeslaw • GDR
KOPF DES GONZALEZ, DER • 1920 • Osten Franz • FRG
KOPF HOCH, CHARLY! • 1926 • Wolff Willi • FRG
KOPF HOCH, JOHANNES • 1941 • de Kowa Viktor • FRG
KOPFJAGER VON BORNEO, DIE • 1936 • von Plessen Victor • FRG, NTH
KOPFSTAND • 1981 • Lauscher Ernst Josef • AUS • HEADSTAND
KOPFSTAND, MADAM! • 1967 • Rischert Christian • FRG • HEADSTAND, MADAM!
KOPFUBER INS GLUCK • 1930 • Steinhoff Hans • FRG
KOPORTOS • 1980 • Gyarmathy Livia • HNG
KOPPANYI AGA TESTAMENTUMA, A • 1967 • Zsurzs Eva • HNG • TESTAMENT OF KOPPANY'S AGHA, THE
KOPRIVSHTITSA • Topaldgikov Stefan • BUL
KOPRU • 1976 • Goren Serif • TRK • BRIDGE, THE
KOPYTEM SEM, KOPYTEM TAM • 1988 • Chytilova Vera • CZC • TAINTED HORSEPLAY
KORA TERRY • 1940 • Jacoby Georg • FRG
KORABLI SHTURMUYUT BASTIONY • 1953 • Romm Mikhail • USS • SHIPS STORM THE BASTIONS, THE ○ SHIPS ATTACKING FORTS ○ ADMIRAL USHAKOV, THE SHIPS ARE STORMING THE BASTIONS
KORACI KROZ MAGLE • 1967 • Skrigin Zorz • YGS • STEPS IN THE FOG
KORAL • 1974 • Czurko Edward • SHT • PLN
KORAL LIR see **KAROL LIR** • 1969
KORALLENPRINZESSEN, DIE • 1937 • Janson Victor • FRG, YGS • AN DER BLAUEN ADRIA
KORBUDA • 1965 • Khintibdze A. • ANS • USS
KORCZAK see **DR. KURCZAK** • 1989
KORD KAMPHUES, DER RICHTER VON COESFELD • 1919 • Kirsch Richard • FRG
KOREA • 1959 • Ford John • DOC • USA
KOREA AFTER THE WAR • 1953-54 • Devlin Bernard • DCS • CND
KOREA PATROL • 1951 • Nosseck Max • USA
KOREAN ALPHABET • 1968 • Tae Kim In • ANS • CND
KOREGA BETONAMU SENSODA • 1968 • Oya Soichi • DOC • JPN • REPORT FROM THE VIETNAM WAR
KORHINTA • 1955 • Fabri Zoltan • HNG • MERRY GO ROUND ○ KARUSSELL
KORI MOU I PSEFTRA, I • 1967 • Tatasopoulos Stelios • GRC • MY DAUGHTER IS A LIAR
KORI TIS PENTAYIOTISSAS, I • 1967 • Tempos Antonis • GRC • PENTAYIOTISSA'S DAUGHTER
KORITSI ME TA PARAMYTHIA • 1957 • Lambrinos Andreas • GRC • JEUNE FILLE AUX CONTES, LA
KORITSI ME TA XANTHA MALLIA, TO • 1969 • Dimopoulos Dinos • GRC • TEACHER WITH THE GOLDEN HAIR, THE
KORITSI META MAVRA, TO • 1956 • Cacoyannis Michael • GRC • GIRL IN BLACK, THE (USA) ○ FILLE EN NOIR, LA
KORITSI TIS ORGIS, TO • 1967 • Laskos Orestis • GRC • ANGRY GIRL, THE
KORITSI TOU 17, TO • 1969 • Likas Petros • GRC • GIRL FROM WARD 17, THE
KORITSI TOU STRATIOTI, TO • 1970 • Damianos Alexis • GRC • I SEE A SOLDIER
KORITSIA STON ILIO • 1969 • Georgiadis Vassilis • GRC • GIRLS IN THE SUN
KORKARLEN • 1921 • Sjostrom Victor • SWD • STROKE OF MIDNIGHT, THE (USA) ○ THY SOUL SHALL BEAR WITNESS ○ GREY CART, THE ○ PHANTOM CARRIAGE, THE ○ PHANTOM CHARIOT, THE ○ PHANTOM HORSE, THE ○ CLAY
KORKOCIAG • 1970 • Piwowski Marek • DOC • PLN • CORKSCREW
KORKUNC MUCADELE • 1967 • Aykanat Orhan • TRK • FRIGHTENING CONFLICT, THE
KORKUNC YUMRUK • 1967 • Okcugil Cevat • TRK • FRIGHTENING FIST, THE
KORKUSUZ YABANCI • 1968 • Duru Ugur • TRK • FEARLESS STRANGER, THE
KORKUSZLAR • 1965 • Evin Semih • TRK
KORLALEN • 1958 • Mattsson Arne • SWD • PHANTOM CARRIAGE, THE ○ PHANTOM CHARIOT, THE
KORLEVA EKRANA • 1916 • Bauer Yevgeni • USS • QUEEN OF THE SCREEN
KORN • 1943 • Henning-Jensen Bjarne • DNM • CORN
KORNBLUMENBLAU • 1939 • Pfeiffer Hermann • FRG
KORNSPEKULANTENDATTER • 1915 • Holger-Madsen • DNM
KOROCHAN THE LITTLE BEAR see **KOGUMA NO KOROCHAN** • 1958
KOROGLU • 1968 • Yilmaz Atif • TRK
KOROGO • 1964 • Keita Georges • IVC
KOROIDARA, I • 1967 • Karayannis Kostas • GRC • LAUGHING-STOCK, THE
KOROL' ARENY • 1973 • Chulyukin Yuri • USS
KOROL MANEZHA • 1970 • Chulyukin Yuri • USS • KING OF THE RING
KOROL PARIZHA • 1917 • Bauer Yevgeni • USS • KING OF PARIS, THE
KORONA RUSSKOI IMPERII • 1971 • Keosayan Edmond • USS • RETURN OF THE ELUSIVE AVENGERS, THE ○ CROWN OF THE RUSSIAN EMPIRE, THE
KOROSHI • 1967 • Yates Peter, Truman Michael • TVM • UKN
KOROSHI NO RAKUIN • 1967 • Suzuki Seijun • JPN • BRANDED TO KILL
KOROSHITA HITA • 1929 • Inagaki Hiroshi • JPN
KOROSHITANO WA DAREDA • 1957 • Nakahira Ko • JPN • WHO IS THE MURDERER
KOROSHIYA O BARASE • 1969 • Ikehiro Kazuo • JPN • KILL THE KILLER ○ KILL THE KILLERS
KOROTKIYE VSTRYECHI • 1968 • Muratova Kira • USS • SHORT ENCOUNTERS, LONG FAREWELLS ○ BRIEF ENCOUNTERS ○ SHORT ENCOUNTERS ○ SHORT MEETINGS ○ SHORT MEETINGS AND LONG FAREWELLS
KOROWOD • 1967 • Trzos-Rastawiecki Andrzej • DOC • PLN • PAGEANT
KORPINPOLSKA • 1979 • Lehmuskallio Markku • FNL • RAVEN'S DANCE, THE
KORPS MARINIERS, HET • 1966 • Verhoeven Paul* • DCS • NTH
KORRIDA • 1983 • Neuland Olev • USS • CORRIDA, LA
KORRIDOREN • 1968 • Halldoff Jan • SWD • CORRIDOR, THE
KORSEL MED GRONLANDSKE HUNDE • 1896 • Elfelt Peter • DNM
KORSHUNY DOBYCHEI NE DELYATSYA • 1989 • Gazhiu Valeri • USS • KITES DON'T SPARE THEIR PREY
KORT AR SOMMAREN • 1962 • Henning-Jensen Bjarne • SWD • SHORT IS THE SUMMER (USA) ○ PAN
KORT FRA DANMARK • 1972 • DOC • DNM • DENMARK BETWEEN DANES
KORTE SOMMER, DEN • 1975 • Fleming Edward • DNM • BRIEF SUMMER ○ THAT BRIEF SUMMER
KORTIK • 1954 • Vengerov Vladimir • USS • DIRK ○ DAGGER
KORTNER SPRICHT SHYLOCK see **FRITZ KORTNER SPRICHT SHYLOCK** • 1966
KORTNERGESCHICHTE • 1980 • Ophuls Marcel • MTV • FRG
KORVETTENKAPITAN, DER • 1930 • Walther-Fein Rudolf • FRG • BLAUE JUNGS VON DER MARINE
KORZEN • 1965 • Giersz Witold • ANS • PLN • ROOT, THE
KOSAK UND DIE NACHTIGALL, DER • 1935 • Jutzi Phil • AUS
KOSAKEN-ENDE see **TARAS BULBA 2** • 1924
KOSATSU • 1978 • Shindo Kaneto • JPN • STRANGULATION
KOSAVA • 1975 • Lazic Dragoslav • YGS • THEY CALL THE WIND KOSAVA
KOSCIUSZKI • 1938 • Lejtes Joseph • PLN
KOSEI • 1927 • Tasaka Tomotaka • JPN
KOSHAI • 1980 • Hossain Amjad • BNG • BUTCHER, THE
KOSHELI • 1990 • Ghimiray Tulshi • NPL
KOSHER KITTY KELLY • 1926 • Horne James W. • USA
KOSHIBEN GANBARE • 1931 • Naruse Mikio • JPN • HARDWORKING CLERK, THE ○ FLUNKY, WORK HARD!
KOSHIKEI • 1968 • Oshima Nagisa • JPN • DEATH BY HANGING (UKN)
KOSHISH • 1972 • IND • EFFORT
KOSHITSU NO TECHNIQUE • 1967 • Mukoi Kan • JPN • TECHNIQUE IN A PRIVATE ROOM
KOSHOKU GO-NIN ONNA • 1948 • Nobuchi Akira • JPN • SAIKAKU'S FIVE WOMEN
KOSHOKU ICHIDAI ONNA see **SAIKAKU ICHIDAI ONNA** • 1952
KOSHOKU ICHIDAI OTOKO • 1961 • Masumura Yasuzo • JPN • ALL FOR LOVE
KOSHOKU MANSION-SHITSU • 1968 • Ogawa Kinya • JPN • LUSTFUL ROOM IN AN APARTMENT
KOSHOKUMA • 1968 • Kimata Akitaka • JPN • EROTIC DEVIL
KOSICE • 1963 • Vignati Alejandro • SHT • ARG
KOSKENLASKIJAN MORSIAN • 1922 • Karu Erkki • FNL • LOG-ROLLER'S BRIDE, THE
KOSKENLASKIJAN MORSIAN • 1937 • Vaala Valentin • FNL
KOSMETIKKREVOLUSJONEN • 1977 • Einarson Eldar • NRW • COSMETIC REVOLUTION, THE
KOSMITCHESKY REIS • 1935 • Zhuravlev Vasili • USS • COSMIC VOYAGE, THE ○ SPACE SHIP, THE ○ COSMIC VESSEL ○ COSMICAL PASSAGE
KOSMOS TRELLATHIKE, O • 1967 • Thalassinos Errikos • GRC • MAD WORLD, THE
KOSODATE GOKKO • 1978 • Imai Tadashi • JPN • BRINGING UP THE CHILDREN
KOSTAS • 1979 • Cox Paul • ASL
KOSTER WALTZ see **KOSTERVALSEN** • 1958
KOSTERVALSEN • 1958 • Husberg Rolf • SWD • KOSTER WALTZ
KOSTIMIRANI RENDEZ-VOUS • 1965 • Dovnikovic Borivoj • ANM • YGS • MEETING OF THE FASHION SHOW, THE ○ MEETING AT THE FASHION SHOW ○ HISTORY OF COSTUME, A ○ COSTUME MEETING
KOSTNICE • 1970 • Svankmajer Jan • ANM • CZC • OSSUARY, THE
KOSTUR POSTAVLJA ZAMKU • 1962 • Vrbanic Ivo • YGS • SKELETON SETS THE TRAP ○ TRAPPED BY A SKELETON
KOSURE OOKAMI see **SHOGUN ASSASSIN** • 1980
KOSURE OOKAMI N.2 see **SHOGUN ASSASSIN** • 1980
KOSZALIN REGION, THE see **ZIEMIA KOSZALINSKA** • 1961
KOSZIVU EMBER FIAI, A • 1965 • Varkonyi Zoltan • HNG • MEN AND BANNERS
KOSZONOM, MEGVAGYUNK.. • 1981 • Lugossy Laszlo • HNG • WE'RE GETTING ALONG..
KOT I MYSZ (PLN) see **KATZ UND MAUS** • 1967
KOTA 905 • 1960 • Relja Mate • YGS
KOTAN NO KUCHIBUE • 1959 • Naruse Mikio • JPN • WHISTLE IN MY HEART, A ○ WHISTLING IN KOTAN
KOTCH • 1971 • Lemmon Jack • USA
KOTEI NO INAI HACHIGATSU • 1978 • Yamamoto Satsuo • JPN • AUGUST WITHOUT THE EMPEROR ○ AUGUST WITHOUT EMPEROR
KOTELEK • 1968 • Mariassy Felix • HNG • BONDAGE
KOTETSU NO KYOJIN -CHIKYU METZUBO SUNZEN • 1957 • Ishii Teruo • JPN • SUPER GIANT 4 (USA)
KOTETSU NO KYOJIN -KAISEIJIN NO MAJYO • 1957 • Ishii Teruo, Mitsuwa Akira, Akasaka Koreyoshi • JPN • INVADERS FROM THE PLANETS ○ DEVILS FROM THE PLANETS ○ SUPER GIANT 3
KOTI VALIGAYA • 1986 • Fonseka Gamini • SLN
KOTIA PAIN • 1989 • Jarvi-Laturi Ilkka • FNL • HOMEBOUND ESCAPE FROM THE PAST ○ HOMEBOUND
KOTIMAANI OMPI SUOMI • Kaarresalo-Kasari Eila • SHT • FNL • FINLAND, MY SWEET HOME
KOTO • 1963 • Nakamura Noboru • JPN • TWIN SISTERS OF KYOTO ○ OLD CAPITAL, THE
KOTO • 1980 • Ichikawa Kon • JPN • ANCIENT CITY ○ ANCIENT CITY OF KOTO, THE
KOTO NO TAIYO • 1968 • Yoshida Kenji • JPN • NO GREATER LOVE THAN THIS (USA)
KOTO NO TSUME • 1957 • Horikawa Hiromichi • JPN
KOTO -THE LAKE OF TEARS see **UMI NO KOTO** • 1966
KOTO YUSHU: ANE IMOUTO • 1967 • Misumi Kenji • JPN • SISTERS AND I, THE ○ ANE IMOUTI
KOTOFEI KOTOFEITCH • 1937 • Ivanov-Vano Ivan • ANS • USS
KOTORO TO NIKUTAI NO TABI • 1958 • Masuda Toshio • JPN
KOTOSHI NO KOI • 1962 • Kinoshita Keisuke • JPN • NEW YEAR'S LOVE ○ THIS YEAR'S LOVE
KOTOU NO UMEKI • 1968 • Seki Koji • JPN • GROAN FROM A SOLITARY ISLAND
KOTOVSKY • 1943 • Fainzimmer Alexander • USS
KOTSUMA NANKIN • 1960 • Sakai Tatsuo • JPN • SOME PUMPKIN
KOU-HUN CHIANG T'OU • 1976 • Ho Meng-Hua • HKG • SOUL CATCHING BLACK MAGIC, THE
KOUBLA AL ALHIRA, AL • 1967 • Mulficar Mahmoud • EGY • LAST KISS, THE
KOUBLA FIL SAHARA'A • 1927 • Lama Ibrahim • EGY
KOUCHIBOUGUAC • 1978 • Borremans Guy (c/d) • CND
KOUHZAD • 1967 • Bagheri Ebrahim • IRN
KOUKARACHA • 1983 • Dolidze Siko, Dolidze Keti • USS • COUCARACHA
KOUKLOS, O • 1968 • Jackson Stelios, Ikonomou Nikos • GRC • OUR AUNT FROM AFRICA ○ MALE DOLL, THE
KOUKOUSEI TO ONNA KYOUSHI: HIJOU NO SEI SHUN • 1962 • Onchi Hideo • JPN • HIGH SCHOOL STUDENT AND WOMAN TEACHER: MERCILESS YOUTH
KOUMIKO MYSTERY, THE (USA) see **MYSTERE KOUMIKO, LE** • 1964
KOUNIA POU SE KOUNAGE • 1967 • Galani Rena • GRC • IMPOSSIBLE TASK, AN
KOUNTY FAIR • 1929 • Lantz Walter, Nolan William • ANS • USA
KOUSAGI MONOGATARI • 1954 • *Toei Doga* • ANS • JPN • BABY BUNNY, THE
KOUTAREKI • 1936 • *Tsuburaya Eiji* • JPN
KOUZELNA PRAHA RUDOLFA II • 1982 • Jires Jaromil • DOC • CZC • ENCHANTING PRAGUE OF RUDOLF II, THE ○ MAGIC PRAGUE OF RUDOLF II, THE
KOUZELNE DOBRODRUZSTVI • 1983 • Kachlik Antonin • CZC • ENCHANTING ADVENTURE, AN ○ EXCITING ADVENTURE, AN
KOUZELNIKUV NAVRAT • 1985 • Kachlik Antonin • CZC • CONJURER'S RETURN
KOUZELNY CIRKUS • 1977 • Schorm Evald (c/d) • CZC • MAGIC CIRCUS, THE
KOUZELNY DUM • 1939 • Vavra Otakar • CZC • ENCHANTED HOUSE, THE ○ MAGIC HOUSE, THE ○ ENCHANTING HOUSE, THE
KOUZELNY SVET KARLA ZEMANA • 1963 • Rozkopal Zdenek • SHT • CZC • MAGIC WORLD OF KAREL ZEMAN, THE
KOUZMA KRIOUTCHKOV • 1914 • Gardin Vladimir • USS • GHOSTS
KOVACEV SEGRT • 1961 • Bourek Zlatko • ANS • YGS • BLACKSMITH'S APPRENTICE, THE
KOVBOY ALI • 1966 • Atadeniz Yilmaz • TRK
KOVCEG • 1968 • Grgic Zlatko (c/d) • ANS • YGS • SUITCASE, THE
KOWASHIYA JINROKU • 1968 • Ichimura Yasukazu • JPN • REALTIONSHIP WRECKER
KOYA NO DUTCHWIVES • 1967 • Yamatoya Jiku • JPN • DUTCH WIVES OF THE WILD, THE
KOYA NO TAMASHII • 1937 • Inagaki Hiroshi • JPN • SPIRIT OF WILDERNESS
KOYA NO TOSEININ • 1968 • Sato Junya • JPN • DRIFTING AVENGER, THE
KOYAANISQATSI • 1977-83 • Reggio Godfrey • USA
KOYDEN INDIM SEHIRE • 1975 • Egilmez Ertem • TRK • FROM THE VILLAGE TO THE TOWN
KOZANOGLU • 1967 • Yilmaz Atif • TRK
KOZARA • 1962 • Bulajic Velko • YGS • HILL OF DEATH
KOZELKEP • 1983 • Kovacs Andras • HNG
KOZELROL: A VER • 1966 • Jancso Miklos • SHT • HNG • CLOSE UP: THE BLOOD
KOZIAJT ROG see **KOZUU POS** • 1972
KOZIAT ROG see **KOZUU POS** • 1972
KOZIOTOECZEK • 1953 • Marszalek Lechoslaw • ANS • PLN • STUBBORN LITTLE GOAT ○ LITTLE GOAT, THE
KOZLONOH • 1918 • Rautenkranzova Olga • CZC
KOZMO GOES TO SCHOOL • 1961 • Kneitel Seymour • ANS • USA
KOZOS UTON • 1953 • Jancso Miklos (c/d) • SHT • HNG • ON A COMMON PATH ○ ORDINARY WAYS
KOZOU MONOGATARI • 1987 • Kinoshita Ryo • JPN • BABY ELEPHANT STORY
KOZURE OHKAMI • 1972 • Saito • JPN • WOLF WITH CHILD
KOZURE OHKAMI • 1973 • Misumi Kenji • JPN • LIGHTNING SWORDS OF DEATH (USA) ○ LIGHTNING SWORD OF DEATH (UKN) ○ SWORD OF VENGEANCE III ○ BABY CART IN HELL ○ BABY CART AT THE RIVER STYX
KOZUU POS • 1972 • Andonov Metodi • BUL • GOAT HORN, THE (USA) ○ KOZIAJT ROG ○ KOZIAT ROG
KRAASNOYE I CHYORNOYE • 1976 • Gerasimov Sergei • USS • ROUGE ET LE NOIR, LE ○ RED AND BLACK
KRABAT CARODEJUV UCEN see **CARODEJUV UCEN** • 1977
KRACH IM FORSTHAUS • 1943 • Dammann Gerhard • FRG
KRACH IM HINTERHAUS • 1935 • Harlan Veit • FRG • TROUBLE BACK STAIRS (USA)
KRACH IM HINTERHAUS • 1949 • Kobler Erich • FRG
KRACH IM VORDERHAUS • 1941 • Heidemann Paul • FRG
KRACH UM JOLANTHE • 1934 • Froelich Carl • FRG
KRACH UM JOLANTHE see **FROHLICHE DORF, DAS** • 1955
KRACH UND GLUCK UM KUNNEMANN • 1937 • Wegener Paul • FRG • ROW AND JOY ABOUT KUNNEMANN (USA)
KRACT AFFAIR, A • 1916 • SAF
KRADETSAT NA PRASKOVI • 1964 • Radev Vulo • BUL • PEACH THIEF, THE
KRADJA DRAGULJA • 1959 • Feman Mladen • ANS • YGS • GREAT JEWEL ROBBERY, THE (USA)
KRADZIEZ • 1976 • Andrejew Piotr • PLN
KRAFT DER LIEBE see **JAHR DES HERRN, DAS** • 1950
KRAFT DES MICHAEL ARGOBAST, DIE • 1917 • Neuss Alwin • FRG

KRAFT–MAYR, DER see **WENN DIE MUSIK NICHT WAR'** • 1935
KRAFTLEISTUNGEN DER PFLANZEN • 1938 • FRG
KRAFTMEIER, DER • 1916 • Lubitsch Ernst • FRG
KRAHEN FLIEGEN UM DEN TURM • 1917 • May Joe • FRG
KRAIAT NA LYATOTO see **KRAYAT NA LYATOTO** • 1967
KRAJ RATA • 1985 • Kresoja Dragan • YGS • END OF THE WAR, THE
KRAJCAR TORTENETE, EGY • 1917 • Curtiz Michael • HNG • STORY OF A PENNY, THE
KRAJINA S NABYTKEM • 1985 • Smyczek Karel • CZC • LANDSCAPE WITH FURNITURE
KRAJOBRAZ PO BITWIE • 1970 • Wajda Andrzej • PLN • LANDSCAPE AFTER THE BATTLE ○ LANDSCAPE AFTER BATTLE
KRAJOWA RADA NARODOWA 1943 • 1945 • Bossak Jerzy • DOC • PLN • HOME NATIONAL COUNCIL 1943
KRAKATIT • 1948 • Vavra Otakar • CZC
KRAKATOA, EAST OF JAVA • 1969 • Kowalski Bernard • USA • VOLCANO
KRAKGULDET • 1969 • Krantz Leif • MTV • SWD • FOOL'S GOLD
KRAKONOS A LYZNICI • 1981 • Plivova-Simkova Vera • CZC • KRAKONOS AND THE SKIS ○ KRAKONOS AND SKIERS
KRAKONOS AND SKIERS see **KRAKONOS A LYZNICI** • 1981
KRAKONOS AND THE SKIS see **KRAKONOS A LYZNICI** • 1981
KRAL A ZENA • 1967 • Schorm Evald • MTV • CZC • KING AND THE WOMAN, THE
KRAL KIM? • 1968 • Inanc Cetin • TRK • WHO IS THE KING?
KRAL KRALU • 1963 • Fric Martin • CZC • KING OF KINGS
KRAL LAVRA • 1950 • Zeman Karel • ANS • CZC • KING LAVRA
KRAL SUMAVY • 1959 • Kachyna Karel • CZC • SMUGGLERS OF DEATH ○ KING OF THE SUMAVA, THE
KRAL ULICE • 1935 • Cikan Miroslav • CZC • KING OF THE STREET, THE
KRALICI VE VYSOKE TRAVE • 1961 • Gajer Vaclav • CZC • RABBITS IN THE TALL GRASS
KRALJ PETROLEJA (YGS) see **OELPRINZ, DER** • 1965
KRALJEVA ZAVRSNICA • 1987 • Tomic Zivorad • YGS • KINGS OF ENDINGS
KRALJEVSKI VOZ • 1983 • Djordjevic Aleksandar • YGS • TRAIN TO KRALJEVO, THE
KRALLAR OLMEZ • 1967 • Gorec Ertem • TRK • KINGS DO NO DIE
KRALLE, DIE • 1919 • Muller-Hagen Carl • FRG
KRALOVSKA POLOVACKA (CZC) see **CHASSE ROYALE, LA** • 1969
KRALOVSKY OMYL • 1968 • Danek Oldrich • CZC • ROYAL MISTAKE, THE ○ KING'S BLUNDER, THE
KRAMARZ • 1990 • Baranski Andrzej • PLN • PEDDLER
KRAMBAMBULI • 1940 • Kostlin Karl • FRG • GESCHICHTE EINES HUNDES, DIE
KRAMER VS. KRAMER • 1979 • Benton Robert • USA
KRANE'S BAKERY SHOP see **KRANES KONDITORI** • 1950
KRANES KONDITORI • 1950 • Henning-Jensen Astrid • NRW • KRANE'S BAKERY SHOP
KRANKENSCHWESTERN–REPORT, DER • 1973 • Boos Walter • FRG
KRANKHEITSBILD DES SCHLACHTENER–PROBLEM UNTEROFFIZIERS IN DER ENDSELACHT, DAS* • 1971 • Zemann E., Kluge Alexander, Zemann O. Mai • FRG
KRANT, DE • 1968 • Noman Theo Van Haren • SHT • NTH
KRAPULA see **HELLYYS** • 1972
KRASAVICE KATA • 1919 • Binovec Vaclav • CZC • KATIA THE BEAUTY
KRASNAYA DEREVNYA • 1935 • Brodyansky Boris, Korsh-Sablin Vladimir • USS
KRASNAYA PALATKA • 1969 • Kalatozov Mikhail • USS, ITL • TENDA ROSSA, LA (ITL) ○ RED TENT, THE
KRASNAYA PLOSHAD • 1971 • Ordynsky Vassily • USS • RED SQUARE ○ KRASNAYA PLOSHCHAD
KRASNAYA PLOSHCHAD see **KRASNAYA PLOSHAD** • 1971
KRASNAYA PRESNYA • 1926 • Room Abram, Sheffer • USS • RED PRESNYA
KRASNOYE YABLOKO • 1975 • Okeyev Tolomush • USS • RED APPLE, THE
KRASNYE DIAVOLIATA • 1923 • Perestiani Ivan • USS • LITTLE RED DEVILS, THE ○ TSITELI ESHMAKUNEBI
KRASNYE KOLOKOLA • 1981 • Bondarchuk Sergei • USS, ITL, MXC • TEN DAYS THAT SHOOK THE WORLD ○ RED BELLS: MEXICO IN FLAMES ○ MEXICO IN FLAMES ○ LIFE OF JOHN REED, THE ○ RED BELLS ○ INSURGENT MEXICO ○ CAMPANAS ROJAS
KRASNYE PARTIZANY • 1924 • Viskovski Vyacheslav • USS • RED PARTISANS
KRASSE FUCHS, DER • 1926 • Wiene Conrad • FRG
KRASSIMIRA POPOVA • 1971 • Haitov Nikolai • BUL • END OF A SONG, THE
KRAVA NA GRANICI • 1964 • Vunak Dragutin • ANS • YGS • COW ON THE FRONTIER (USA)
KRAVA NA MJESECU • 1959 • Vukotic Dusan • YGS • COW AND THE MOON, THE ○ COW ON THE MOON, THE
KRAVATA, KOIATO.. • 1966 • Donev Donyo, Topouzanov Christo • BUL • COW THAT.., THE ○ COW WHO.., THE ○ COW WHICH.., THE
KRAWATTEN FUR OLYMPIA • 1976 • Lukschy Stefan, Schmige Hartmann • FRG • TIES FOR THE OLYMPICS
KRAWATTENMACHER • 1922 • Justitz Emil • FRG • WUCHERER VON BERLIN, DER
KRAYAT NA LYATOTO • 1967 • Mundrov Dutcho • BUL • END OF THE SUMMER, THE ○ KRAIAT NA LYATOTO ○ END OF SUMMER
KRAYS, THE • 1990 • Medak Peter • UKN
KRAZY KAT • 1916-17 • *Hearst International* • ASS • USA
KRAZY KAT • 1926-27 • Nolan William • ASS • USA
KRAZY KAT • 1927-29 • *Mintz Charles B. (P)* • ASS • USA
KRAZY KAT • 1929-39 • *Mintz Charles B.(P)* • ASS • USA
KRAZY KAT AND IGNATZ MOUSE • 1916 • Herriman George • ANS • USA
KRAZY KAT BUGOLOGIST • 1916 • Herriman George • ANS • USA
KRAZY MUSIC • 1938 • *Mintz Charles (P)* • ANS • USA
KRAZY SPOOKS • 1933 • *Mintz Charles (P)* • ANS • USA
KRAZY'S BEAR TALE • 1939 • *Mintz Charles (P)* • ANS • USA
KRAZY'S MAGIC • 1938 • *Mintz Charles (P)* • ANS • USA
KRAZY'S NEWSREEL • 1936 • *Mintz Charles (P)* • ANS • USA
KRAZY'S RACE OF TIME • 1937 • *Mintz Charles (P)* • ANS • USA
KRAZY'S SHOE SHOP • 1939 • *Mintz Charles (P)* • ANS • USA
KRAZY'S TRAVEL SQUAWKS • 1938 • *Mintz Charles (P)* • ANS • USA
KRAZY'S WATERLOO • 1934 • *Mintz Charles (P)* • ANS • USA
KRC • 1979 • Sprajc Bozo • YGS • CRAMP
KREBSFISCHERIN, DIE see **TRUBE WASSER** • 1960
KRECEK • 1946 • Zeman Karel • ANS • CZC • SLUGGARD, THE ○ HAMSTER, THE
KREISE • 1933 • Fischinger Oskar • ANS • FRG • CIRCLE
KREIVI • 1970 • von Bagh Peter • FNL • COUNT, THE
KREJCOVSKA POVIDKA • 1954 • *Stallich Jan (Ph)* • CZC • TAILOR'S STORY, THE
KREK • 1967 • Dovnikovic Borivoj • ANS • YGS • SERGEANT, THE
KREMLIEVSKIE KURANTY • 1970 • Georgiev Viktor • USS • KREMLIN CHIMES, THE
KREMLIN CHIMES, THE see **KREMLIEVSKIE KURANTY** • 1970
KREMLIN LETTER, THE • 1970 • Huston John • USA
KREPI OBORONU • 1930 • Ptushko Alexander • ANS • USS
KRESSIN UND DIE TOTE TAUBE IN DER BEETHOVENSTRASSE • 1972 • Fuller Samuel • FRG • DEAD PIGEON ON BEETHOVENSTRASSE ○ DEAD PIGEON ON BEETHOVEN STREET
KRESTYANIYE • 1935 • Ermler Friedrich • USS • PEASANTS
KRESTYANYE • 1972 • Galin I. • DOC • USS • PEASANTS
KREUTZER SONATA see **KREUTZEROVA SONATA** • 1926
KREUTZER SONATA 1 • 1915 • Brenon Herbert • USA
KREUTZER SONATA, THE • 1911 • Chardynin Pyotr • USS
KREUTZER SONATA, THE • 1914 • Gardin Vladimir • USS
KREUTZER SONATA, THE • Schweitzer Mikhail • USS
KREUTZER SONATA, THE see **SONATE A KREUTZER, LA** • 1956
KREUTZER SONATA, THE (USA) see **KREUTZERSONATE, DIE** • 1937
KREUTZEROVA SONATA • 1926 • Machaty Gustav • CZC • KREUTZER SONATA
KREUTZERSONATE, DIE • 1922 • Petersen Rolf • FRG
KREUTZERSONATE, DIE • 1937 • Harlan Veit • FRG • KREUTZER SONATA, THE (USA)
KREUZ AM JAGERSTEIG, DAS • 1954 • Kugelstadt Hermann • FRG
KREUZ AM TEUFELSGRAT, DAS • 1924 • *Heimhuber J.* • FRG
KREUZELSCHREIBER, DER • 1945 • von Borsody Eduard • FRG
KREUZER EMDEN • 1932 • Ralph Louis • FRG • CRUISER EMDEN ○ EMDEN, THE
KREUZIGET SIE! • 1919 • Jacoby Georg • FRG • FRAU AM SCHEIDEWEGE, DIE
KREUZZUG DES WEIBES • 1926 • Berger Martin • FRG • UNWELCOME CHILDREN
KRI–KRI, DIE HERZOGIN VON TARABAC • 1920 • Zelnik Friedrich • FRG
KRI–KRI MANGIA I GAMBERI • 1913 • Gambardella Giuseppe • ITL • BLOOMER AND THE EGG POWDER
KRIBBEBIJTER, DE • 1936 • Koster Henry, Winar Ernest • NTH • CROSS–PATCH, THE
KRIEG BRACHTE FRIEDEN, DER • 1915 • *Paul Albert* • FRG
KRIEG IM FRIEDEN • 1925 • Boese Carl • FRG
KRIEG ODER FRIEDEN see **DU UND MANCHER KAMARAD..** • 1956
KRIEG UND FRIEDEN • 1983 • Kluge Alexander • FRG
KRIEG VERSOHNT, DER • 1915 • Trautmann Ludwig • FRG
KRIEGHOFF • 1981 • Sullivan Kevin • MTV • CND
KRIEGSDAMON • 1915 • *Trautmann Ludwig* • FRG
KRIEGSGERICHT • 1959 • Meisel Kurt • FRG • COURT MARTIAL (USA)
KRIEGSGESETZ (FRG) see **LEGGE DI GUERRA** • 1961
KRIEMHILDE'S REVENGE see **NIBELUNGEN 2, DIE** • 1924
KRIEMHILD'S DREAM OF HAWKS • 1923 • Lang Fritz • FRG
KRIEMHILDS RACHE see **NIBELUNGEN 2, DIE** • 1924
KRIGENS FJENDE • 1915 • Holger-Madsen • DNM • ACOSTATES FOSTE OFFER ○ MUNITION CONSPIRACY, THE
KRIGERNES BORN • 1979 • Johansen Ernst • DNM • WARRIOR CHILDREN
KRIGET AR SLUT (SWD) see **GUERRE EST FINIE, LA** • 1966
KRIGETS ANSIKTE see **KRIGETS VANVETT** • 1963
KRIGETS VANVETT • 1963 • Sjoberg Tore • DOC • SWD, JPN • FACE OF WAR, THE (USA) ○ KRIGETS ANSIKTE
KRIGSFORBRYTARE • 1962 • Sjoberg Tore • SWD • SECRETS OF THE NAZI CRIMINALS (USA) ○ MEIN KAMPF II ○ SECRETS OF THE NAZI WAR CRIMINALS
KRIGSKORRESPONDENTEN • 1913 • Gluckstadt Wilhelm • DNM • WAR CORRESPONDENT, THE
KRIGSMANS ERINRAN • 1947 • Faustman Erik • SWD • SOLDIER'S DUTIES, A
KRIK • 1963 • Jires Jaromil • CZC • CRY, THE (UKN) ○ FIRST CRY, THE
KRIK? KRAK! TALES OF A NIGHTMARE • 1988 • Gee, Avila • USA, CND, CUB
KRIMINAL • 1966 • Lenzi Umberto • ITL
KRIMINALGAADEN I KINGOSGADE • 1916 • Davidsen Hjalmar • DNM
KRIMINALKOMMISSAR EYCK • 1940 • Harbich Milo • FRG
KRIMINALPOLIZEI, ABTEILUNG "MORD" • 1920 • Dessauer Siegfried • FRG
KRIMINALPOLIZEI –ABTEILUNG MORD see **GEHEIMPOLIZISTEN** • 1929
KRIMINALREPORTER HOLM • 1932 • Engels Erich • FRG
KRIMINALTANGO • 1960 • von Cziffra Geza • FRG
KRINJABO • 1956 • Regnier Michel • DCS • IVC
KRIS • 1946 • Bergman Ingmar • SWD • CRISIS
KRISCHNA • 1941 • Stuart Henry • FRG • ABENTEUER IM INDISCHER DSCHUNGEL
KRISHNA see **KRISHNARJUN YUDDHA** • 1945
KRISHNA see **GOKUL CHA RAJA** • 1950
KRISHNA ARJUN YUDDHA • 1922 • IND
KRISHNA JANMA see **SHRI KRISHNA JANMA** • 1918
KRISHNA KUMAR • 1924 • *Patel Manecklal (P)* • IND • MASTER KRISHNA
KRISHNA LEELA • 1935 • Rao Ch. Narasimba • IND • DRAMA OF KRISHNA
KRISHNA LEELA • 1945 • Bose Debaki • IND • DRAMA OF KRISHNA
KRISHNA MAYA • 1920 • *Kohinoor* • IND
KRISHNA MAYA see **MADARI MOHAN** • 1940
KRISHNA NARADI • 1926 • *Krishna* • IND
KRISHNA NARADI • 1936 • *Sunadaram Talkies* • IND
KRISHNA SAKHA • 1925 • *Aurora* • IND
KRISHNA SAMBHAV • 1926 • *United Pictures Syndicate* • IND • EIGHTH INCARNATION, THE
KRISHNA SATYABHAMA • 1921 • IND
KRISHNA SATYABHAMA • 1951 • *Manik* • IND
KRISHNA SUDAMA • 1936 • Barma Phani • IND
KRISHNA TULA • 1922 • *Bharat* • IND
KRISHNA TULABARAM • 1937 • *Saradambal T. M.* • IND • KRISHNA WEIGHED
KRISHNA UNDER CHARGE OF THEFT • 1925 • IND
KRISHNA VIVAH see **GANESH MAHIMA** • 1950
KRISHNA WEIGHED see **KRISHNA TULABARAM** • 1937
KRISHNABHAKTA BODANA • 1944 • Wadia J. B. H. • IND • TEACHER OF KRISHNA'S DEVOTEE
KRISHNARJUN YUDDHA • 1945 • Sinha Mohan • IND • KRISHNA ○ ARJUN FIGHT
KRISHNA'S MARRIAGE see **GANESH MAHIMA** • 1950
KRISHNA'S VICTORY see **KRISHNAVIJAYAM** • 1949
KRISHNAVATAR • 1932 • *Santukumari* • IND • INCARNATION OF KRISHNA
KRISHNAVIJAYAM • 1949 • Nadkarni Sundarao • IND • KRISHNA'S VICTORY
KRISS ROMANI • 1962 • Schmidt Jean • FRN
KRISTALLEN • 1930 • Moll J. C. • NTH • CRYSTALS
KRISTALLEN DEN FINA • 1954 • Melander Carl-Olov • SWD
KRISTIAN • 1939 • Fric Martin • CZC • CHRISTIAN (USA)
KRISTIINA • 1966 • Tolonen Asko • SHT • FNL
KRISTIN KOMMENDERAR • 1946 • Edgren Gustaf • SWD • KRISTIN TAKES COMMAND
KRISTIN TAKES COMMAND see **KRISTIN KOMMENDERAR** • 1946
KRISTINA TALKING PICTURES • 1976 • Rainer Yvonne • USA
KRISTINUS BERGMANN • 1948 • Henning-Jensen Astrid, Henning-Jensen Bjarne • DNM
KRISTOFFERS HUS • 1979 • Forsberg Lars Lennart • SWD • CHRISTOPHER'S HOUSE
KRISTOPHER KOLUMBUS, JR. • 1939 • Clampett Robert • ANS • USA
KRISTOVE ROKY • 1967 • Jakubisko Juraj • CZC • CRUCIAL YEARS ○ INDECISIVE YEARS
KRITSI TOU LOUNA PARK, TO • 1968 • Karayannis Kostas • GRC • GIRL AT LUNA PARK, THE ○ GIRL AT THE FAIR, THE
KRIVE ZRCADLO • 1956 • Kachyna Karel • CZC • CROOKED MIRROR
KRIVI PUT (YGS) see **CROOKED ROAD, THE** • 1965
KRIZ U POTOKA • 1921 • Kolar J. S. • CZC • CROSS AT THE BROOK, THE
KRIZNO OBDOBJE • 1981 • Slak Franci • YGS • KRIZNO RAZDOBLJE ○ TIME OF CRISIS ○ YEAR OF CRISIS
KRIZNO RAZDOBLJE see **KRIZNO OBDOBJE** • 1981
KRIZOVA TROJKA • 1948 • Gajer Vaclav • CZC • THREE CROSSES
KROK DO TMY • 1938 • Fric Martin • CZC • MADMAN IN THE DARK
KROKODILLEN IN AMSTERDAM • 1990 • Apon Annette • NTH • CROCODILES IN AMSTERDAM
KROL MACIUS I • 1957 • Jakubowska Wanda • PLN • KING MATHIAS I ○ KING MATTHEW I ○ KING MATT I
KROLEWNA I OSIOLEK • 1959 • Badzian Teresa • PLN • PRINCESS AND THE LITTLE DONKEY, THE
KROLOWA PRZEDMIESCIA • 1937 • Bodo Eugene • QUEEN OF THE MARKET PLACE (USA)
KROLOWA PSZCZOL • 1977 • Nasfeter Janusz • PLN • QUEEN BEE, THE
KRONANS GLADA GOSSAR • 1952 • *Redig Rune (Ed)* • SWD
KRONANS KACKA GOSSAR • 1940 • Wallen Sigurd • SWD • BRAVE BOYS IN UNIFORM
KRONANS KAVALJERER • 1930 • Edgren Gustaf • SWD • CROWN'S CAVALIERS, THE ○ GENTLEMEN IN UNIFORM
KRONANS RALLARE • 1932 • Hildebrand Weyler • SWD
KRONBLOM • 1947 • Bolander Hugo • SWD
KRONBLOM KOMMER TILL STAN • 1949 • Bolander Hugo • SWD
KRONE DES LEBENS, DIE • 1918 • Rippert Otto? • FRG
KRONE VON KERKURA, DIE • 1917 • Zelnik Friedrich • FRG
KRONIKA • 1968 • Gaal Istvan • SHT • HNG • CHRONICLE
KRONIKA CZTERECH LAT • 1965 • Wionczek Roman • DOC • PLN • CHRONICLE OF FOUR YEARS
KRONIKA JEDNOG ZLOCINA • 1974 • Zafranovic Lordan • YGS • CHRONICLE OF A CRIME
KRONIKA JUBILEUSZOWA • 1959 • Munk Andrzej • DOC • PLN • POLSKA KRONIKA FILMOVA NR 52 A–B ○ JUBILEE STORY ○ JUBILEE CHRONICLE
KRONIKA KOSZALINA • 1960 • Wionczek Roman • DOC • PLN • CHRONICLE OF KOSZALIN
KRONIKA POD PSEM • 1959 • Makarczynski Tadeusz • DOC • PLN • DOG'S NEWSREEL, THE ○ DIARY OF A DOG
KRONIKA WIELKIEJ BUDOWY • 1961 • Wionczek Roman • DOC • PLN • CHRONICLE OF A GREAT CONSTRUCTION, THE
KRONIKA WYPADKOW MILOSNYCH • 1985 • Wajda Andrzej • PLN • CHRONICLE OF AMOROUS INCIDENTS, A ○ CHRONICLE OF A LOVE AFFAIR
KRONIKA ZHAVEHO LETA • 1972 • Sequens Jiri • CZC • CHRONICLE OF A HOT SUMMER
KRONISKE USKYLD, DEN • 1985 • Fleming Edward • DNM • CHRONICLE INNOCENCE, THE
KRONJUWELEN • 1950 • Cap Frantisek • FRG
KRONOS • 1957 • Neumann Kurt • USA
KRONOS (USA) see **CAPTAIN KRONOS –VAMPIRE HUNTER** • 1972
KRONPRINSEN • 1979 • Bang-Hansen Pal • NRW • CROWN PRINCE, THE
KRONPRINZ RUDOLF ODER: DAS GEHEIMNIS VON MAYERLING • 1919 • Randolf Rolf • FRG

KRONPRINZ RUDOLF UND DIE TRAGODIE VON MAYERLING • 1924 • *Eiko-Film* • FRG
KRONPRINZ RUDOLFS LETZTE LIEBE • 1956 • Jugert Rudolf • AUS
KRONVITTNET • 1989 • Lindstrom Jon • SWD • EXPERIMENT IN MURDER
KRONZEUGIN, DIE • 1937 • Jacoby Georg • FRG
KROTITELJ • 1961 • Gospodnetic Darko • ANS • YGS • LION TAMER, THE
KROTITELJ DIVLJIH KONJA • 1966 • Dragic Nedeljko • ANS • YGS • TAMER OF WILD HORSES (USA)
KROTKI DZIEN PRACI • 1982 • Kieslowski Krzysztof • PLN • SHORT DAY'S WORK, A
KROTKI FILM O MILOSCI • 1988 • Kieslowski Krzysztof • PLN • SHORT FILM ABOUT LOVE, A (UKN)
KROTKI FILM O ZABIJANIU • 1988 • Kieslowski Krzysztof • PLN • SHORT FILM ABOUT KILLING, A (UKN) ○ THOU SHALT NOT KILL
KROV LYUDSKAYA NE VODITSA • 1960 • Makarenko Nikolai • USS • MAN'S BLOOD IS THICKER THAN WATER ○ LET THE BLOOD OF MAN NOT FLOW
KROV ZA KROV, SMERT ZA SMERT • 1941 • Vertov Dziga, Svilova Elizaveta • USS • BLOOD FOR BLOOD, DEATH FOR DEATH
KROZ GRANJE NEBO • 1958 • Jankovic Stole • YGS • SKY THROUGH THE LEAVES, THE ○ SKY THROUGH THE TREES, THE
KRTEK A MEDICINA • Miler Zdenek • ANM • CZC, FRG • MOLE AND MEDICINE
KRTEK A ZELENA HVEZDA • 1969 • Miler Zdenek • ANS • CZC • MOLE AND THE GREEN STAR, THE (USA)
KRTEK VE MESTE • Miler Zdenek • ANM • CZC, FRG • MOLE IN THE CITY
KRTEK VE SNU • Miler Zdenek • ANM • CZC, FRG • MOLE IN DREAMLAND
KRTINY • 1981 • Podskalsky Zdenek • CZC • CHRISTENING PARTY, THE
KRUDT MED KNALD • 1943 • *Holger-Madsen* • DNM
KRUDT OG KLUNKER • 1959 • Hovmand Annelise • DNM • POWDER AND SHOT
KRUGER-MILJOENE, DIE see **KRUGER MILLIONS, THE** • 1967
KRUGER MILLIONS, THE • 1967 • Hall Ivan • SAF • KRUGER-MILJOENE, DIE
KRUGER'S DREAM OF EMPIRE • 1900 • Booth W. R. • UKN
KRUH • 1959 • Rychman Ladislav • CZC • CIRCLE, THE
KRULL • 1982 • Yates Peter • UKN
KRUSENDULLER • 1969 • Steinaa Ib • ANS • DNM • SPIRALS
KRUSH GROOVE • 1985 • Schultz Michael • USA • RAP ATTACK
KRUSTYO RAKOVSKI • 1990 • Tosheva Nevena • BUL
KRUT OCH KARLEK • 1957 • Blomgren Bengt • SWD • GUNPOWDER AND LOVE
KRUTYE GORKI • 1956 • Rozantsev Nikolai • USS • STEEP HILLS
KRUZHEVA • 1928 • Yutkevich Sergei • USS • LACE
KRVAVA BAJKA • 1971 • Jankovic Branimir Tori • YGS • FAIRY TALE OF BLOOD ○ BLOODY TALE
KRVAVA KOSULJA • 1957 • Skrigin Zorz • YGS • BLOODY SHIRT, THE
KRVAVA PANI • Kubal Viktor • ANM • CZC • BLOOD-STAINED LADY, THE
KRVAVI JASTREBOVI ALJASKE see **BLUTIGEN GEIER VON ALASKA, DIE** • 1973
KRVAVI PUT • 1955 • Novakovic Rados, Bergstrom Kare • YGS, NRW • BLOODY ROAD, THE ○ BLODVEIEN
KRVOPIJCI • 1989 • Sorak Dejan • YGS • BLOODSIPPERS
KRYEPKI ORYESHEK • 1968 • Vulfovich Teodor • USS • HARD NUT TO CRACK, A ○ HARD LITTLE NUT, A
KRYLIA KHOLOPA • 1926 • Tarich Yuri • USS • WINGS OF THE SERF
KRYLYA • 1966 • Shepitko Larissa • USS • CAPTAIN OF THE GUARDS ○ WINGS
KRYLYA KHOLOPAL • 1926 • Pyriev Ivan • USS • IVAN THE TERRIBLE ○ WINGS OF A SERF
KRYLYA PESNI • 1966 • Aimanov Shaken • USS • WINGS OF SONG
KRYLYA PYESNI • 1967 • Mambetov A. • USS • WINGS OF SONG
KRYPSKYTERRE • 1981 • Nicolayssen Hans Otto • NRW • POACHERS
KRYPTONIM "OKTAN" • 1959 • Hoffman Jerzy, Skorzewski Edward • DCS • PLN • CRYPTONYM "OKTAN"
KRYSS MED ALBERTINA, PAA • 1940 • Branner Per-Axel • SWD • CRUISE IN THE ALBERTINA, A (USA)
KRYSTYNA ET SA NUIT • 1977 • Conrad Charles • BLG • CHRISTINE ET SA NUIT
KRZYK • 1983 • Sass Barbara • PLN • SCREAM, THE
KRZYSZTOF PENDERECKI • 1967 • Zanussi Krzysztof • MTV • PLN
KRZYZ I TOPOR • 1972 • Dziworski Bogdan • PLN • CROSS AND AXE
KRZYZ WALECZNYCH • 1959 • Kutz Kazimierz • PLN • CROSS OF VALOUR, THE
KRZYZACY • 1960 • Ford Aleksander • PLN • KNIGHTS OF THE TEUTONIC ORDER, THE ○ KNIGHTS OF THE BLACK CROSS ○ BLACK CROSS (USA)
KSAFNIKOS EROTAS • 1984 • Tsemberopoulos Yorgos • GRC • SUDDEN LOVE
KSIAZATKO • 1937 • Tom Konrad, Szwbego Stanislaw • LOTTERY PRINCE, THE (USA)
KTO ODZHDZA V DAZDI • 1977 • Holly Martin • CZC • HE WHO LEAVES IN THE RAIN
KTO PRIDUMAL KOLESO? • 1967 • Shredel Vladimir • USS • WHO INVENTED THE WHEEL?
KTO VERNYOTSYA, DOLYUBIT • 1968 • Osyka Leonid • USS • LOVE COMES TO THOSE WHO RETURN
KTO WIERZY W BOCIANY • 1971 • Stawinski Jerzy Stefan, Amiradzibi Helena • PLN • WHO BELIEVES IN THE STORK
KTOKOLWIEK WIE.. • 1966 • Kutz Kazimierz • PLN • WHOEVER MAY KNOW..
KU-FU? DALLA SICILIA CON FURORE • 1973 • Cicero Nando • ITL
KU KLUX KLAN -THE INVISIBLE EMPIRE • 1965 • Leacock Richard • DOC • USA
KU-KUNUTS • 1945 • Wickersham Bob • ANS • USA
K'U LIEN • 1983 • Wang T'Ung • TWN • PORTRAIT OF A FANATIC
KUAI KO • 1981 • Yeo Ban Yee • HKG • STRANGER FROM CANTON
KUAN-JEN! WO YAO.. see **YUAN WANG A! TA JEN!** • 1976
KUANG-YIN-TE KUSHIH • 1983 • T'Ao Te-Ch'En, Yang Te-Ch'Ang, K'O Yi-Cheng, Chang Yi • TWN • IN OUR TIME
KUARUP • 1988 • Guerra Ruy • BRZ
KUBAN COSSACKS, THE see **KUBANSKIE KAZAKI** • 1949
KUBANSKIE KAZAKI • 1949 • Pyriev Ivan • USS • COSSACKS OF THE KUBAN ○ KUBAN COSSACKS, THE
KUBBI AND IYALA see **KUBBI MATTU IYALA** • 1989
KUBBI MATTU IYALA • 1989 • Suvarna Sadanand • IND • KUBBI AND IYALA
KUBI • 1968 • Moritani Shiro • JPN • JUDGE AND JEOPARDY
KUBI NO ZA • 1929 • Makino Masahiro • JPN • BEHEADING PLACE
KUBINKE, DER BARBIER, UND DIE DREI DIENSTMADCHEN • 1926 • Boese Carl • FRG
KUCA • 1976 • Zizic Bogdan • YGS • HOUSE, THE
KUCA NA OBALI • 1954 • Kosanovic Bosko • YGS, FRG, AUS
KUCANGDE LIANQING • 1988 • Wu Jiaxin, Nie Xinru • CHN • LOVE HURTS
KUCHELA, DEVOTEE TO THE GOD see **BHAKTHA KUCHELA** • 1935
KUCHELA, DEVOTEE TO THE GOD see **BHAKTHA KUCHELA** • 1963
KUCHENGESPRACHE MIT REBELLINEN • 1985 • Berger Karin, Trallori Lisbeth N., Holzinger Elizbeth, Podgornik Charlotte • AUS • KITCHEN DISCOURSES WITH REBEL WOMEN
KUCHIBUE O FUKU WATARIDORI • 1958 • Tasaka Katsuhiko • JPN • WHISTLES OF MIGRATORY BIRDS
KUCHIKUKAN YUKIKAZE • 1964 • Yamada Tatsuo • JPN • DESTROYER YUKIKAZE
KUCHIZUKE • 1957 • Masumura Yasuzo • JPN • KISSES
KUCHIZUKE III: ONNA DOSHI • 1955 • Naruse Mikio • JPN • KISS, PART III: WOMEN'S WAYS, THE ○ FIRST KISS, THE
KUCHNIA POLSKA • 1990 • Bromski Yacek • PLN • POLISH CUISINE
KUCKELIKAKA • 1949 • Rosencrantz Margareta • SWD
KUCKUCKS, DIE • 1949 • Deppe Hans • GDR
KUCKUCKSEI, DAS • 1949 • Firner Walter • AUS
KUCKUCKSEI IM GANGSTERNEST • 1970 • Spieker Franz-Josef • FRG
KUCKUCKSJAHRE • 1967 • Moorse Georg • SWT, FRG • YEARS OF THE CUCKOO
KUCUK BALIKAR • 1989 • Pirhasan Baris • TRK
KUCUK KOVBOY • 1974 • Zurli Guido • TRK, ITL • LITTLE COWBOY, THE
KUD PUKLO DA PUKLO • 1975 • Grlic Rajko • YGS • WHICHEVER WAY THE BALL BOUNCES
KUDA POSLE KISE? • 1967 • Slijepcevic Vladan • YGS • WHERE AFTER THE RAIN? ○ KADE PO DOZDOT ○ WHERE TO, AFTER THE RAIN?
KUDRAT • 1970 • Kadarisman S. • MLY • POWER OF GOD, THE
KUDREMOTTE • 1977 • Iyer G. V. • IND • HORSE'S EGG
KUDUMBAM • 1967 • Nair M. Krishnan • IND • FAMILY
KUDUZ • 1988 • Kenovic Ademir • YGS
KUDUZ RECEP • 1967 • Sagiroglu Duygu • TRK • ASLAN ARKADASIM ○ RECEP THE ENRAGED ○ MY BRAVE FRIEND
KUDY KAM • 1956 • Borsky Vladimir • CZC • WHENCE AND WHERE TO
KUEI-HUA HSIANG • 1987 • Ch'En K'Un-Hou • TWN • OSMANTHUS ALLEY
KUEI-MA CHIH-TO HSING • 1981 • Hsu K'O • HKG • FOR THE RIGHT SOLUTION ○ ALL THE WRONG CLUES
KUEI MAH SUENG SING • 1975 • Hui Michael • HKG • GAMES GAMBLERS PLAY
KUEI-MEI, A WOMAN see **WO CHE-YANG KUO-LE YI-SHENG** • 1985
KUEI-WU LI-JEN • 1969 • BEAUTIFUL GHOST (USA)
KUESTET-SHESKAMIT • 1971-77 • Lamothe Arthur • DOC • CND • AUTRE MONDE, L'
KUHLE WAMPE • 1932 • Dudow Slatan • FRG • WHITHER GERMANY? (UKN) ○ WEM GEHORT DIE WELT ○ KUHLE WAMPE OR WHO OWNS THE WORLD?
KUHLE WAMPE OR WHO OWNS THE WORLD? see **KUHLE WAMPE** • 1932
KUHNE SCHWIMMER, DER • 1934 • Jacoby Georg • FRG
KUHNE SCHWIMMER, DER • 1957 • Anton Karl • FRG
KUIN UNI JA VARJO • 1937 • Saakka Toivo • FNL • LIKE A DREAM AND A SHADOW
KUJANJUOKSU • 1971 • Kurkvaara Maunu • FNL • GAUNTLET, THE
KUJIRA GAMI • 1962 • Tanaka Tokuzo • JPN • KILLER WHALE
KUKACKA V TEMNEM LESE • 1985 • Korner Vladimir • CZC, PLN • CUCKOO IN A DARK WOOD, A
KUKAN, THE BATTLE CRY OF CHINA • 1941 • Scott Rey • DOC • USA
KUKLA S MILLIONAMI • 1928 • Komarov Sergei • USS • DOLL WITH MILLIONS, THE
KUKSI see **VALAHOL EUROPABAN** • 1947
KUKULI • 1961 • Figueroa Luis, Nisiyama Eulogio, Villanueva • PRU
KUKURYDZA • 1955 • Lomnicki Jan • DOC • PLN • MAIZE
KULASHS, PEUPLE INFIDELE, LES • 1971-74 • Bertolino Daniel • DOC • CND
KULAY ROSAS ANG PAG-IBIG • 1968 • de Guzman Armando • PHL • LOVE IS PINK
KULDETES • 1979 • Kosa Ferenc • HNG • PORTRAIT OF A CHAMPION
KULDIPAK see **PAHADI HEERA** • 1938
KULHANBEYLER KRALI • 1967 • Alpaslan Mumtaz • TRK • KING OF BULLIES, THE
KULHAVY DABEL • 1968 • Herz Juraj • CZC • LIMPING DEVIL, THE ○ LAME DEVIL, THE
KULICKA • 1963 • Tyrlova Hermina • ANS • CZC • LITTLE BALL, THE
KULISSEN-ZAUBER • 1915 • Bolten-Baeckers Heinrich?, Peukert Leo? • FRG
KULISSER I HOLLYWOOD • 1974 • Sjoman Vilgot • SHT • SWD
KULKURIN VALSSI • 1941 • Saakka Toivo • FNL • VAGABOND'S WALTZ, THE
KULLA-GULLA • 1956 • Bergstrom Hakan • SWD
KULONOS HAZASSAG • 1951 • Keleti Marton • HNG • STRANGE MARRIAGE
KULONOS ISMERTELOJEL • 1955 • Varkonyi Zoltan • HNG • STRONG MARK OF IDENTITY, A
KULTUR • 1918 • Le Saint Edward J. • USA
KULVAROSI LEGENDA • 1957 • Mariassy Felix • HNG • SUBURBAN LEGEND
KUMA • 1975 • Yilmaz Atif • TRK
KUMAK THE SLEEPY HUNTER • 1953 • Duncan Alma • ANM • CND
KUMANDER DIMAS • 1968 • Avellana Lamberto V. • PHL • COMMANDER DIMAS
KUMAR SAMBHABER ASHTAM SWARGA • 1969 • *Ghatak Ritwik* • IND
KUMARI • *Rnfc* • NPL • VIRGIN, THE
KUMARI MON • 1962 • *Ghatak Ritwik* • IND
KUMBHA MELA -SAME AS IT EVER WAS • 1983 • Falzon Albert • DOC • ASL
KUMMATY • 1978 • Aravindan G. • IND • BOGEY MAN, THE
KUMO GA CHIGIRERU TOKI • 1961 • Gosho Heinosuke • JPN • AS THE CLOUDS SCATTER
KUMO NAGARURU HATENI • 1953 • Ieki Miyoji • JPN • BEYOND THE FLOATING CLOUD
KUMO NI MUKATTE TATSU • 1962 • Takizawa Eisuke • JPN • FACING THE CLOUDS
KUMO NO OZU • 1929 • Tasaka Tomotaka • JPN • THRONE OF CLOUDS
KUMOEMON TOCHUKEN see **TOCHUKEN KUMOEMON** • 1936
KUMONOSU-JO • 1957 • Kurosawa Akira • JPN • CASTLE OF THE SPIDER'S WEB, THE ○ THRONE OF BLOOD ○ COBWEB CASTLE
KUMONOSU YASHIKI • 1959 • Sawashima Chu • JPN • ACTOR DETECTIVE
KUN EN TIGGER • 1912 • Holger-Madsen • DNM
KUN ISALLA ON HAMMASSARKY • 1923 • Karu Erkki • SHT • FNL • WHEN FATHER HAS TOOTHACHE
KUN-KUN HUNG-CH'EN • 1990 • Yim Ho • TWN
KUN ON TUNTEET • 1953 • Blomberg Erik • FNL • WHEN THERE ARE FEELINGS
KUN ONNI PETTAA • 1913 • Tallroth Konrad • FNL
KUN SANDHEDEN • 1975 • Ornbak Henning • DNM • NOTHING BUT THE TRUTH
KUN TAIVAS PUTOAA • 1972 • Jarva Risto • FNL • WHEN THE SKIES FALL ○ WHEN THE HEAVENS FALL
KUNDAN • 1987 • Fazil Javed • PKS • GOLD
KUNDELEK • 1969 • Hornicka Lidia • ANS • PLN • BASTARD, THE (USA)
KUNDSKABENS TRAE • 1981 • Malmros Nils • DNM • TREE OF KNOWLEDGE, THE
KUNG AKO'Y IIWAN MO • 1981 • Guillen Laurice • PHL
KUNG FU • 1971 • Thorpe Jerry • TVM • USA
KUNG-FU • 1979 • Kijowski Janusz • PLN
KUNG FU EMPEROR • Pao Shiue-Li • HKG
KUNG FU EXECUTIONER • 1981 • Lin Chan Wai • HKG
KUNG FU EXORCIST • 1976 • *Leen Kathy* • HKG
KUNG FU FIGHTING • 1974 • Doo Kwang Gee • HKG
KUNG FU FROM BEYOND THE GRAVE • 1982 • *Sing Sonny* • HKG
KUNG FU GANGBUSTERS see **NA-TZU HAN**
KUNG FU GIRL, THE • 1975 • Lo Wei • HKG • NONE BUT THE BRAVE
KUNG FU-GIRL FIGHTER • 1971 • Hou Chin • HKG
KUNG FU HALLOWEEN • 1981 • Lam Chi Kam, Lui Sun • HKG
KUNG FU HERO • Wan Hung Lo • HKG
KUNG FU KILLERS, THE • 1974 • Trenchard-Smith Brian • MTV • ASL
KUNG FU MASTER • 1979 • *Chang Wu Lang* • HKG • KUNG FU MASTER NAMED DRUNK CAT
KUNG-FU-MASTER • 1988 • Varda Agnes • FRN • DON'T SAY IT!
KUNG FU MASTER NAMED DRUNK CAT see **KUNG FU MASTER** • 1979
KUNG FU -THE HEADCRUSHER • 1973 • Chiang Hung • HKG
KUNG FU -THE HEADCRUSHER see **CHUEH-TOU LAO-HU CHUANG** • 1973
KUNG FU -THE MOVIE • 1986 • Lang Richard • TVM • USA
KUNG FU WARRIOR • *Chang Lei* • HKG
KUNG-FU WU-SU • 1977 • Magneron Jean-Luc • DOC • FRN
KUNG FU ZOMBIE • 1981 • Hwa I Hung • HKG
KUNG MANGARAP KA'T MAGISING • 1977 • De Leon Mike • PHL • IF YOU DREAM AND WAKE UP
K'UNG-PU FEN-TZU • 1986 • Yang Te-Ch'Ang • TWN • TERRORISER, THE ○ KONGBUFENZI
K'UNG-PU-TE CH'ING-JEN • 1982 • Chiang Lang • TWN • THIRD FACE, THE
KUNG SHAN LING YU • 1978 • Hu King • HKG • RAINING IN THE MOUNTAINS ○ RAINING ON THE MOUNTAIN
KUNG-TZU CHIAO • 1981 • Yen Hao • HKG
KUNGAJAKT • 1944 • Sjoberg Alf • SWD • ROYAL HUNT, THE
KUNGEN AV DALARNA • 1953 • Bernhard Gosta • SWD • KING OF DALARNA
KUNGEN KOMMER • 1936 • Hylten-Cavallius Ragnar • SWD • KING IS COMING, THE
KUNGFU HARAKIRI • 1973 • Masumura Yasuzo • JPN
KUNGLIGA JOHANSSON • 1934 • Cederstrand Solve • SWD • 83:AN I LUMPEN ○ ROYAL JOHANSSON
KUNGLIGA PATRASKET • 1945 • Ekman Hasse • SWD • ROYAL BABBLE, THE
KUNGLIGT AVENTYR, ETT • 1956 • Birt Daniel • SWD, UKN • LAUGHING IN THE SUNSHINE
KUNGSGATAN • 1943 • Cederlund Gosta • SWD • KING'S STREET
KUNGSLEDEN • 1964 • Hoglund Gunnar • SWD • OBSESSION (USA) ○ MY LOVE AND I (UKN) ○ ROYAL TRACK, THE
KUNI LEMEL IN TEL-AVIV • 1977 • Silberg Joel • ISR
KUNIN NO SHIKEISHU • 1957 • Furukawa Takumi • JPN • CONDEMNED

KUNINGAS JOLLA EI OLLUT SYNDANTA • 1983 • Hartzell Paivi, Helminen Liisa • FNL • SATU KUNINKAASTA JOLLA EI OLLUT SYNDANTA ○ KING WHO HAD NO HEART, THE

KUNISADA CHUJI • 1960 • Taniguchi Senkichi • JPN • GAMBLING SAMURAI

KUNISADA CHUJI see **CHUJI KUNISADA** • 1933

KUNKUMA BHARANI • 1968 • Ragaviah Vedhantham • IND • VERMILION BOX

KUNLUN COLUMN, THE • 1989 • CHN

KUNO HANABIRA • 1960 • Mizuko Harumi • JPN

KUNSHO • 1954 • Shibuya Minoru • JPN • MEDALS ○ MEDAL, A

KUNST DES EMAILS, DIE • 1958 • Turck Walter C. • FRG

KUNST EN VLIEGWERK see **KUNST & VLIEGWERK** • 1989

KUNST & VLIEGWERK • 1989 • van der Meulen Karst • NTH • KUNST EN VLIEGWERK ○ AT STALLING SPEED

KUNST ZU HEIRATEN, DIE • 1917 • Larsen Viggo • FRG

KUNSTLERLAUNEN • 1920 • *Veidt Conrad* • FRG • MALER, DIE LIEBE UND DAS FRAULEIN, DER

KUNSTLERLIEBE • 1925 • Krause Karl Otto • FRG

KUNSTLERLIEBE • 1935 • Wendhausen Fritz • FRG

KUNSTLERSPESEN • 1919 • Ostermayr Peter • FRG

KUNSTNERS GENNEMBRUD, EN • 1915 • Holger-Madsen • DNM • SOUND OF THE VIOLIN, THE ○ DODES SJAEL, DEN

KUNSTSEIDENE MADCHEN, DAS • 1960 • Duvivier Julien • FRG, FRN • GRANDE VIE, LA (FRN)

KUNTE KINTE'S GIFT see **ROOTS: KUNTA KINTE'S GIFT** • 1988

KUNTILANAK • 1974 • Timoer Ratno • INN • VAMPIRE, THE

KUNWARI • 1937 • Sudarshan Pandit, Roy Prafulla • IND • WIDHWA ○ UNMARRIED GIRL ○ WIDOW

KUO-CHUNG NU-SHENG • 1989 • Ch'En Kuo-Fu • TWN • HIGHSCHOOL GIRLS

KUOPIO • 1963 • Mollberg Rauni • DCS • FNL

KUPFERNE HOCHZEIT, DIE • 1948 • Ruhmann Heinz • FRG

KUPPLERIN, DIE • 1924 • *Neutral-Film* • FRG

KUR PRANVERA VONOHET • 1980 • Kreyeziu Ekrem • YGS • WHEN SPRING IS LATE ○ KAD PROJECE KASNI

KURA NO NAKA • 1982 • Takabayashi Yoichi • JPN • IN A WAREHOUSE

KURAGEJIMA see **KAMIGAMI NO FUKAKI YOKUBO** • 1968

KURAGEJIMA -LEGENDS FROM A SOUTHERN ISLAND see **KAMIGAMI NO FUKAKI YOKUBO** • 1968

KURAGEJIMA: TALES FROM A SOUTHERN ISLAND see **KAMIGAMI NO FUKAKI YOKUBO** • 1968

KURAMA TENGU APPEARS IN YOKOHAMA see **KURAMA TENGU YOKOHAMA NI ARAWARU** • 1942

KURAMA TENGU: KAKUBEI-JISHI NO MAKI • 1938 • Makino Masahiro, Masuda Teiji • JPN • KURAMA TENGU: THE BOOK OF KAKUBEI'S LION CUB

KURAMA TENGU: SATSUMA NO MISSHI • 1941 • Suganuma Kanji • JPN • KURAMA TENGU: SECRET AGENT FROM SATSUMA ○ SATSUMA NO MISSHI

KURAMA TENGU: SECRET AGENT FROM SATSUMA see **KURAMA TENGU: SATSUMA NO MISSHI** • 1941

KURAMA TENGU: THE BOOK OF KAKUBEI'S LION CUB see **KURAMA TENGU: KAKUBEI-JISHI NO MAKI** • 1938

KURAMA TENGU YOKOHAMA NI ARAWARU • 1942 • Ito Daisuke • JPN • KURAMA TENGU APPEARS IN YOKOHAMA

KURAYAMI NO USHIMATSU • 1935 • Kinugasa Teinosuke • JPN

KURBAGALAR • 1985 • Goren Serif • TRK • FROGS

KURBANLIK KATIL • 1967 • Akat Lutfu • TRK • SACRIFICED KILLER, THE ○ KILLER, THE

KUREIZI OGON SAKUSEN • 1967 • Tsuboshima Takashi • JPN • LAS VEGAS FREE-FOR-ALL (USA) ○ CRAZY OGON SAKUSEN

KURENAI NO NAGAREBOSHI • 1967 • Masuda Toshio • JPN • WHISTLING KILLER, THE

KURENAI NO TSUBASA • 1958 • Nakahira Ko • JPN • CRIMSON WINGS

KURFURSTENDAMM • 1920 • Oswald Richard • FRG • HOLLENSPUK IN 6 AKTEN, EIN

KURIER DES ZAREN, DER • 1935 • Eichberg Richard • FRG • TSAR'S COURIER, THE

KURIER VON LISSABON, DER • 1920 • Stern? • FRG

KURITON SUKUPOLVI • 1937 • Ilmari Wilho • FNL

KURITON SUKUPOLVI • 1957 • Kassila Matti • FNL • UNRULY GENERATION, THE

KURKSHETRA • 1946 • Sharma Rameshwar • IND

KURNELL STORY, THE • 1957 • Hall Ken G. • DOC • ASL

KURNICH AN-NIL • 1956 • Saleh Tewfik • SHT • EGY • CORNICHE DU NIL

KURO HIME DRAGON, THE • ANM • JPN

KURO NO CHOTOKKYU • 1964 • Masumura Yasuzo • JPN • SUPER-EXPRESS

KURO NO HOKOKUSHU • 1963 • Masumura Yasuzo • JPN • BLACK REPORT

KURO NO SHISOSHA • 1962 • Masumura Yasuzo • JPN • BLACK TEST CAR, THE

KURO TOKAGE • 1962 • *Kyo Machiko* • JPN • BLACK LIZARD

KUROBARA NO YAKATA • 1969 • Fukasaku Kinji • JPN • BLACK ROSE ○ BLACK ROSE INN, THE

KUROBE NO TAIYO • 1968 • Kumai Kei • JPN • TUNNEL TO THE SUN (USA) ○ SUN OVER THE KUROBE GORGE ○ SAND OF KUROBE, THE

KURODA SEICHUROKU • 1938 • Kinugasa Teinosuke • JPN

KURODA SODO • 1956 • Uchida Tomu • JPN • DISORDER OF THE KURODA CLAN

KUROHYO • 1953 • Tanaka Shigeo • JPN • SPIES

KUROI AME • 1989 • Imamura Shohei • JPN • BLACK RAIN

KUROI GASHU see **KUROI GOSHO** • 1960

KUROI GOSHO • 1960 • Horikawa Hiromichi • JPN • LOST ALIBI, THE ○ BLACK BOOK, THE ○ KUROI GASHU

KUROI JUNIN NO ONNA • 1961 • Ichikawa Kon • JPN • TEN BLACK WOMEN ○ TEN DARK WOMEN

KUROI KAFUN • 1958 • Ohba Hideo • JPN • TRUE LOVE

KUROI KAIKYO • 1964 • Ezaki Jissei • JPN • BLACK CHANNEL

KUROI KAWA • 1957 • Kobayashi Masaki • JPN • BLACK RIVER

KUROI KIKORI TO SHIROI KIKORI • 1959 • *Toei* • ANS • JPN • GOOD AND BAD WOODCUTTERS, THE

KUROI TAIYO • 1964 • Kurahara Koreyoshi • JPN • BLACK SUN, THE

KUROI TOBAKUSHI • 1965 • Nakahira Ko • JPN • BLACK GAMBLER, THE

KUROI USHIO • 1954 • Yamamura So • JPN • BLACK TIDE

KUROKI TARO NO BOKEN • 1977 • Morisaki Azuma • JPN • ADVENTURE OF KUROKI TARO

KURONEKO see **YABU NO NAKA NO KURONEKO** • 1968

KUROOBI SANGOKUSHI • 1956 • Taniguchi Senkichi • JPN • BLACK BELT HISTORY OF THREE COUNTRIES ○ RAINY NIGHT DUEL

KUROTAKA-MARU • 1927 • Tasaka Tomotaka • JPN • BLACK HAWK

KUROTOKAGE • 1968 • Fukasaku Kinji • JPN • BLACK LIZARD (USA)

KUROUMA NO DANSHICHI • 1948 • Inagaki Hiroshi • JPN • BOY WITH THE BLACK HORSE, THE

KUROUN KAIDOU • 1948 • Matsuda, Mori Kazuo • JPN • LINE OF BLACK CLOUDS, A

KURRAGOMMA • 1963 • Lindgren Lars-Magnus • SWD • HIDE AND SEEK

KURS AUF DIE EHE see **WELLEN DER LEIDENSCHAFT** • 1930

KURSUN ATA ATA BITER • 1985 • Elci Umit • TRK • HERO'S WAY

KURSUN YOLU • 1968 • Ucanoglu Yucel • TRK • BULLET ROAD

KURSUNLARIN KANUNU • 1969 • Ergun Nuri • TRK

KURSUNLARIN YAGMURU see **SON VURGUN** • 1968

KURT AND VALDE see **KURT OG VALDE** • 1983

KURT OG VALDE • 1983 • Kristensen Hans • DNM • KURT AND VALDE

KURTISANE VON VENEDIG, DIE • 1921 • Neufeld Max • AUS

KURTISANE VON VENEDIG, DIE • 1924 • Feher Friedrich • AUS • NACKTE WEIB, DAS

KURUTTA IPPEIJI • 1927 • Kinugasa Teinosuke • JPN • PAGE OF MADNESS, A (UKN) ○ PAGE OUT OF ORDER, A ○ CRAZY PAGE, A

KURUTTA ITONAMI • 1967 • Sasaki Moto • JPN • MAD CONDUCT OF LOVE

KURUTTA KAJITSU • 1956 • Nakahira Ko • JPN • THIS SCORCHING SEA ○ AFFAIR AT KAMAKURA ○ CRAZED FRUIT ○ JUVENILE PASSION

KURUZSLO, A • 1917 • Curtiz Michael • HNG • CHARLATAN, THE

KURZER PROZESS • 1967 • Kehlmann Michael • FRG • SHORT WORK

KUSAMEIKYU • 1983 • Terayama Shuji • JPN • LABYRINTH OF GRASS

KUSHA LAILA • 1940 • Bose Debaki • IND

KUSHIRO NO YORU • 1968 • Inoue Umeji • JPN • SHADOW IN THE MIST

KUSHU • 1938 • Tasaka Tomotaka • JPN • AIR RAID

KUSHUME RUMAL • 1985 • Ghimiray Tulshi • NPL • COLOURED HANDKERCHIEF, A ○ KUSUME RUMAL

KUSO TENGOKU • 1968 • Matsumori Takashi • JPN • IMAGINARY PARADISE

KUSS DES FURSTEN, DER • 1912 • Stark Kurt • FRG

KUSS IN DER SOMMERNACHT, EIN • 1933 • Seitz Franz • FRG

KUSS' MICH CASANOVA see **MARCHEN VOM GLUCK** • 1949

KUSS MICH NOCH EINMAL • 1956 • Weiss Helmut • FRG

KUSS NACH LADENSCHLUSS, EIN see **ANNETTE IM PARADIES** • 1934

KUSSE DER IRA TOSCARI, DIE • 1922 • Erdmann-Jesnitzer • FRG

KUSSE, DIE MAN IM DUNKELN STIEHLT • 1918 • Matull Kurt? • FRG • KUSSE, DIE MAN STIEHLT IM DUNKELN

KUSSE, DIE MAN NICHT VERGISST • 1928 • Jacoby Georg • FRG

KUSSE, DIE MAN STIEHLT IM DUNKELN see **KUSSE, DIE MAN IM DUNKELN STIEHLT** • 1918

KUSSE, DIE TOTEN • 1915 • *Deutsche Bioscop* • FRG

KUSSE, DIE TOTEN • 1958 • Jacob Peter • FRG • KISS THE DEAD (USA)

KUSSEN IST KEINE SUND' • 1926 • Walther-Fein Rudolf • FRG • LETZTE EINQUARTIERUNG, DIE

KUSSEN IST KEINE SUND' • 1950 • Marischka Hubert • AUS

KUSSVERBOT, DAS • 1920 • Czerny Ludwig • FRG

KUSTENS GLADA KAVALJERER • 1938 • Arvedson Ragnar • SWD • COAST'S HAPPY CAVALIERS, THE (USA) ○ MERRY BOYS OF THE COAST ARTILLERY

KUSTER BEATON • 1930 • *A.s.f.i.* • SHT • UKN

KUSTOM KAR KOMMANDOS • 1965 • Anger Kenneth • SHT • USA

KUSUME RUMAL see **KUSHUME RUMAL** • 1985

KUSZA • 1963 • Nehrebecki Wladyslaw • ANS • PLN • CROSSBOW, THE

KUTABARE GURENTAI • 1960 • Suzuki Seijun • JPN

KUTABARE YARODOMO • 1953 • Suzuki Kiyonori • JPN

KUTASEK A KUTILKA JAK RANO VASTAVALI • 1952 • Trnka Jiri • ANS • CZC • HOW KUTASEK AND KUTILKA GOT UP IN THE MORNING ○ KUTASEK AND KUTILKA

KUTASEK AND KUTILKA see **KUTASEK A KUTILKA JAK RANO VASTAVALI** • 1952

KUTE KIDS VS. KUPID • 1918 • Holbrook John K. • USA

KUTIJE • 1967 • Stalter Pavao • ANS • YGS • BOXES

KUTSU • 1927 • Uchida Tomu • JPN • PAIN

KUTSUKATE TOKIJIRO • 1934 • Kinugasa Teinosuke • JPN • TOJIJIRO OF KUTSUKATE

KUTTEL • 1961 • Menzel Siegfried • GDR

KUTUZOV • 1944 • Petrov Vladimir • USS • 1812

KUTYA EJI DALA • 1983 • Body Gabor • HNG • DOG'S NIGHT SONG, THE

KUU ON VAARALLINEN • 1961 • Sarkka Toivo • FNL • PRELUDE TO ECSTASY (USA)

KUUMA KISSA? • 1968 • Kivikoski Erkko • FNL • HOT CAT?

KUUMAT KUNDIT • 1976 • Itkonen Jussi • FNL • HOT WHEELS

KUUTAMOSONAATTI • 1987 • Soinio Olli • FNL • MOONLIGHT SONATA

KUYU • 1968 • Erksan Metin • TRK • WELL, THE

KUYUCAKLI YUSUF • 1985 • Tuna Feyzi • TRK • YUSUF FROM KUYUCAK

KUZDOK • 1977 • Jankovics Marcell • ANS • HNG • FIGHT, THE

KUZHANTHAIKKAGA • 1968 • Madhavan P. • IND • FOR THE CHILD'S SAKE

KUZIS STARI MOJ • 1974 • Kljakovic Vanca • YGS • GET IT MAN

KUZMICH • 1959 • Talankin Igor • USS

KUZNECHIK • 1980 • Grigoryev Boris • USS • GRASSHOPPER, THE

KUZURETA KANNO • 1968 • Aki Keizo • JPN • BROKEN ECSTASY

KVAR • 1977 • Radivojevic Milos • YGS • BREAKDOWN

KVARNEN • 1921 • Brunius John W. • SWD • MILL, THE

KVARTERET KORPEN • 1963 • Widerberg Bo • SWD • RAVEN'S END

KVARTERETS BUSUNGAR see **SEXTETTEN KARLSSON** • 1945

KVARTERETS OLYCKSFAGEL • 1948 • Holmgren Per Gosta • SWD • UNLUCKY FELLOW OF THE BLOCK

KVARTETTEN SOM SPRANGDES • 1936 • Bornebusch Arne • SWD

KVARTETTEN SOM SPRANGDES • 1950 • Molander Gustaf • SWD • QUARTET THAT SPLIT UP, THE

KVICK SOM BLIXTEN • 1927 • Jahr Adolf • SWD • QUICK AS LIGHTNING

KVINDE AF FOLKET, EN • 1909 • *Blom August* • DNM • WOMAN OF THE PEOPLE, A

KVINDE ER OVERFLODIG, EN • 1956 • Axel Gabriel • DNM

KVINDELIGE DAEMON, DEN • 1913 • Dinesen Robert • DNM

KVINDEN HAN MODTE • 1914 • Davidsen Hjalmar • DNM

KVINDESAND • 1979 • Bjorkman Stig • DNM • THROUGH THE MIRROR

KVINNA I LEOPARD • 1958 • Molander Jan • SWD • WOMAN IN A LEOPARD-SKIN

KVINNA I VITT • 1949 • Mattsson Arne • SWD • WOMAN IN WHITE

KVINNA OMBORD, EN • 1941 • Skoglund Gunnar • SWD • WOMAN ON BOARD, A

KVINNA UTAN ANSIKTE • 1947 • Molander Gustaf • SWD • WOMAN WITHOUT A FACE

KVINNAN BAKOM ALLT • 1951 • Faustman Erik, Jacobsen Johan • SWD • NELJA RAKKAUTTA -FYRA GANGER KARLEK ○ ALT DETTE -OG ISLAND MED ○ ALT DETTE -OG ISLAND OGSA ○ WOMAN BEHIND EVERYTHING

KVINNAN GOR MEJ GALEN • 1949 • Larsson Borje • SWD • THAT WOMAN DRIVES ME CRAZY

KVINNAN SOM FORSVANN • 1949 • Angstrom Anders • SWD • WOMAN WHO DISAPPEARED, THE

KVINNAN TAR BEFELAT • 1942 • Olsson Gunnar • SWD • WOMAN TAKES COMMAND

KVINNAS ANSIKTE, EN • 1938 • Molander Gustaf • SWD • WOMAN'S FACE, A

KVINNAS MORGONDAG, EN • 1930 • Bergman Gustaf • SWD • TOMORROW FOR A WOMAN

KVINNENE • 1979 • Blom Per • NRW • WOMEN, THE

KVINNLIG SPION 503 • 1959 • Jeppesen • DNM • FEMALE SPY 503

KVINNODROM • 1955 • Bergman Ingmar • SWD • JOURNEY INTO AUTUMN (UKN) ○ DREAMS (USA) ○ WOMEN'S DREAMS

KVINNOHUSET • 1953 • Faustman Erik • SWD • HOUSE OF WOMEN

KVINNOR I FANGENSKAP • 1943 • Molander Olof • SWD • WOMEN IN PRISON

KVINNOR I VANTRUM • 1946 • Folke Gosta • SWD • WOMEN IN A WAITING ROOM

KVINNORNA KRING LARSSON • 1934 • Bauman Schamyl • SWD • WOMEN AROUND LARSSON, THE

KVINNORNA PA TAKET • 1989 • Nykvist Carl-Gustaf • SWD • WOMAN ON THE ROOF, THE (UKN)

KVINNORS VANTAN • 1952 • Bergman Ingmar • SWD • SECRETS OF WOMEN (USA) ○ WAITING WOMEN (UKN)

KVISH LELO MOTZA • 1983 • Yosha Yaki • ISR • DEAD END STREET

KW+ • 1970 • Danis Aime • DCS • CND

KWAHERI • 1964 • *Chudnow David* • DOC • USA • WITCH DOCTOR AND THE VIRGIN, THE ○ VANISHING AFRICA

KWAIDAN • 1964 • Kobayashi Masaki • JPN • WEIRD TALES ○ KAIDAN ○ GHOST STORIES

KWAIDAN YANAGI ZOSHI • 1932 • *Tsuburaya Eiji (Ph)* • JPN

KWANNON VON OKADERA, DIE • 1920 • Froelich Carl • FRG

KWARTECIK • 1966 • Sturlis Edward • ANM • PLN • LITTLE QUARTET, THE ○ QUARTET, THE

KWATANG • 1967 • Cayado Tony • PHL

KWEER KUSS, A • 1915 • Aylott Dave? • UKN

KWESTIA SUMIENIA • 1967 • Petelska Ewa, Petelski Czeslaw • MTV • PLN • MATTER OF CONSCIENCE, A

KWIATY SOFII • 1967 • Gradowski Bohdan • DOC • PLN • FLOWERS OF SOFIA

KWIECIEN • 1961 • Lesiewicz Witold • PLN • LAST BATTLE, THE

KWIKSTERTJIE, DIE • 1974 • SAF

KWINANA OIL REFINERY, THE • 1956 • Riley Ronald H. • DOC • UKN

KWOK SU YUEH BEARS A CHILD IN THE COFFIN • Hu Chieh • TWN

KYATSU O NIGASUNE • 1956 • Suzuki Hideo • JPN • I SAW THE KILLER

KYBERNETICKA BABICKA • 1962 • Trnka Jiri • CZC • CYBERNETIC GRANDMOTHER, THE ○ CYBERNETIC GRANDMA ○ CYBERNETIC GRANNY

KYBERNETICKY DEDECEK • 1964 • Hofman Eduard • ANS • PLN

KYI PYAR • 1980 • U Kyee Myint • BRM • BLUE STAR

KYK NA DIE STERRE • 1960 • SAF

KYM SA SKONCI TATO NOC • 1965 • Solan Peter • CZC • BEFORE THIS NIGHT IS OVER ○ BEFORE TONIGHT IS OVER

KYNIGHI, I see **KINIGI, I** • 1976

KYO • 1968 • Ichikawa Kon • JPN • KYOTO

KYO MO MATA KAKUTE ARINAN • 1959 • Kinoshita Keisuke • JPN • THUS ANOTHER DAY

KYO NI IKIRU • 1959 • Masuda Toshio • JPN • WE LIVE TODAY

KYO NO INOCHI • 1957 • Tasaka Tomotaka • JPN • PLEASURES FOR LIFE
KYODAI • 1955 • Ieki Miyoji • JPN • SISTERS
KYODAI JINGI GYAKUEN NO SAKAZUKI • 1968 • Suzuki Noribumi • JPN • BROTHERS' CODE -THE BACK RELATION
KYODAI JINGI: KANTO ANIKIBUN • 1967 • Nakajima Sadao • JPN • DUTY OF BROTHERHOOD: KANTO AFFAIR
KYODAI JINGI: KANTO INOCHISHIRAZU • 1967 • Yamashita Kosaku • JPN • DUTY OF BROTHERHOOD: A DAREDEVIL OF KANTO
KYODAI JINGI: ZOKU KANTO SANKYODAI • 1967 • Yamashita Kosaku • JPN • DUTY OF BROTHERHOOD: THREE BROTHERS OF KANTO
KYOEN • 1929 • Tasaka Tomotaka • JPN • BANQUET
KYOEN • 1954 • Sekigawa Hideo • JPN • ORGY
KYOFU NIKEI NINGEN • 1969 • Ishii Teruo • JPN • HORROR OF A DEFORMED MAN ○ HORROR OF MALFORMED MEN
KYOJIN TO GANGU • 1958 • Masumura Yasuzo • JPN • BUILD-UP, THE
KYOKAKU HARUSAME-GASA • 1960 • Watanabe Kunio • JPN • SPRING RAIN UMBRELLA
KYOKAKU NO OKITE • 1967 • Torii Motohiro • JPN • CODE OF CHIVALRY
KYOKAKU RETSUDEN • 1968 • Makino Masahiro • JPN • HISTORIES OF THE CHIVALROUS
KYOKAKUDO • 1967 • Suzuki Noribumi • JPN • GAMBLER'S LAW, THE
KYOKANOKO MUSUME DOJOJI • 1956 • *Nakamura Utaemon* • JPN • DOJOJI TEMPLE
KYOKATSU KOSO WAGA JINSEI • 1968 • Fukasaku Kinji • JPN • BLACKMAIL IS MY LIFE
KYOKO TO SHIZUKO • 1926 • Ito Daisuke • JPN • PANIC AND CALM
KYOKOTSU ICHIDAI • 1967 • Makino Masahiro • JPN • CHIVALROUS LIFE, THE
KYOKUBADAN NO JOO • 1925 • Mizoguchi Kenji • JPN • QUEEN OF THE CIRCUS (USA) ○ QUEEN OF CIRCUS
KYOMO WARE OZORANI ARI • 1964 • Furusawa Kengo • JPN • TIGER FLIGHT (USA)
KYONETSU NO KISETSU • 1960 • Kurahara Koreyoshi • JPN • WEIRD LOVE MAKERS, THE (USA) ○ WILD LOVE-MAKERS, THE ○ WARPED ONES, THE
KYOREN NO BUTO • 1924 • Kinugasa Teinosuke • JPN • DANCE TRAINING
KYOREN NO ONNA SHISHO • 1926 • Mizoguchi Kenji • JPN • PASSION OF A WOMAN TEACHER, THE (USA) ○ LOVE-MAD TUTORESS, THE
KYORETSU NO JYOJI • 1968 • Ogawa Kinya • JPN • DAZZLING AFFAIRS
KYOSHITSU NO KODOMOTACHI • 1954 • Hani Susumu • DOC • JPN • CHILDREN IN THE CLASSROOM
KYOSHU • 1988 • Nakajima Takehiro • JPN • HOMESICKNESS
KYOSO JOSHIKO • 1970 • Wakamatsu Koji • JPN • RUNNING IN MADNESS, DYING IN LOVE
KYOSO MIKKA-KAN • 1927 • Uchida Tomu • JPN
KYOTO see **KYO** • 1968
KYOYA COLLAR SHOP, THE see **KYOYA RAIYA** • 1922
KYOYA RAIYA • 1922 • Tanaka Eizo • JPN • KYOYA COLLAR SHOP, THE
KYPROS • 1976 • Kittou Thekla, Papadimitrakis Lambros • DOC • GRC • CYPRUS
KYRIAKATIKO XYPNIMA • 1953 • Cacoyannis Michael • GRC • WINDFALL IN ATHENS (USA) ○ REVEIL DU DIMANCHE
KYRITZ - PYRITZ • 1931 • Wolff Carl Heinz • FRG
KYRKOHERDEN • 1970 • Wickman Torgny • SWD • LUSTFUL VICAR, THE (UKN) ○ VICAR, THE
KYS OG KAERLIGHED • 1914 • Holger-Madsen • DNM • LOVE AND WAR
KYS TIL HOJRE OG VENSTRE • 1969 • Roos Ole • DNM • LOVE AND KISSES ○ KISSES RIGHT AND LEFT
KYSKE LEVEMAND, DEN • 1974 • Hedman Werner, Hedman Trine • DNM
KYSS HENNE! • 1940 • Hildebrand Weyler • SWD • KISS HER
KYSSEN PA KRYSSEN • 1950 • Mattsson Arne • SWD • KISS ON THE CRUISE, THE
KYUBI NO KITSUNE TO TOBIMARU • 1969 • Yagi Shinichi • ANM • JPN • FOX WITH NINE TAILS, THE (USA)
KYUCHAN NO DEKKAI YUME • 1967 • Yamada Yoji • JPN • LET'S HAVE A DREAM
KYUJIN RYOKO • 1962 • Nakamura Noboru • JPN
KYUJU KYUHOMME NO KIMOSUME • 1959 • Magatani Morehei • JPN
KYUKETSU DOKURO SEN • 1968 • Matsuno Hiroki • JPN • LIVING SKELETON
KYUKETSU GA • 1956 • *Ikebe Ryo* • JPN
KYUKETSUKI GOKEMIDORO • 1968 • Sato Hajime • JPN • GOKE, BODY SNATCHER FROM HELL ○ GOKE THE VAMPIRE
KYUPORA NO ARU MACHI • 1962 • Urayama Kirio • JPN • CUPOLA, WHERE THE FURNACES GLOW ○ FOUNDRY TOWN, THE ○ STREET WITH THE CUPOLA, THE
KYUSHO ZEME • 1968 • Mukoi Hiroshi • JPN • TOUCHED ON THE RAW
KYVADLO, JAMA A MADEJE • 1983 • Svankmajer Jan • ANM • CZC • PIT, THE PENDULUM AND HOPE, THE ○ PIT AND THE PENDULUM, THE
KZ 9 LAGER DI STERMINIO • 1978 • Mattei Bruno • ITL

L

L.A. 2017 see **LA 2017** • 1970
L.A.B.C. • 1988 • Kerrigan George • USA
L.A. BOUNTY • 1988 • Keeter Worth • USA
L.A. CRACKDOWN • 1988 • Merhi Joseph • USA
L.A. CRACKDOWN II • 1988 • Merhi Joseph • USA
L.A. HEAT • 1988 • Merhi Joseph • USA
L.A. LAW • 1986 • Holbit Gregory • TVM • USA
L.A., MY HOME TOWN • 1977 • Haydon Geoff • UKN
L.A. STREETFIGHTERS see **NINJA TURF** • 1986
L.A. THRILLER see **SUNSET STRIP** • 1984
L.A.X. • 1980 • Ziolkowski Fabrice
L.B.J. • 1968 • Alvarez Santiago • DOC • CUB
L' OU 'L • 1974 • Gagne Jean, Gagne Serge • DOC • CND
L.S. LOWRY 'THE INDUSTRIAL ARTIST' • 1973 • Thompson Philip • DOC • UKN
L-SHAPED ROOM, THE • 1962 • Forbes Bryan • UKN
L.X. CLUE, THE • 1917 • King Burton L. • USA
LA 2017 • 1970 • Spielberg Steven • MTV • USA • L.A. 2017
LA ANAM • 1957 • Abu Saif Salah • EGY • NO TOMORROW
LA BAMBA • 1987 • Valdez Luis • USA • BAMBA, LA
LA BRUYERE • 1964-69 • Rohmer Eric • MTV • FRN
LA BUNICI • 1988 • Dragoi Sorin • RMN • AT GRANDPARENTS'
LA CONGA NIGHTS • 1940 • Landers Lew • USA
LA DE LOS OJOS COLOR DEL TIEMPO • 1952 • Amadori Luis Cesar • ARG • PASOS PELIGROSOS
LA DOVE NON BATTE IL SOLE • 1975 • Margheriti Antonio • ITL, HKG, SPN • STRANGER AND THE GUNFIGHTER, THE (USA) ○ BLOOD MONEY (UKN)
LA DOVE SCENDE IL SOLE (ITL) see **UNTER GEIERN** • 1964
LA ELVE LEVE! • 1981 • Greve Bredo • NRW • ALTE 79
LA FAYETTE • 1963 • Dreville Jean • FRN, ITL • SPADA PER DUE BANDIERE, UNA (ITL)
LA GALE • 1989 • Jallili Abolfazl • IRN • SCABIES
LA-HAUT SUR CES MONTAGNES • 1946 • McLaren Norman • ANS • CND
LA-HAUT SUR CES MONTAGNES • 1946 • Palardy Jean • DCS • CND • UP THERE ON THOSE MOUNTAINS
LA KAM LOK • 1983 • Pakdivijit Chalong • THL • CHASER, THE
LA LA LUCILLE • 1920 • Lyons Eddie, Moran Lee • USA
LA MILO • 1906 • *Urban Trading Co* • UKN
LA' OS VAERE • 1974 • Nielsen Lasse, Johansen Ernst • DNM • LEAVE US ALONE
LA OU AILLEURS • 1969 • Leduc Jacques, Bernier Pierre • SHT • CND
LA PALOMA • 1930 • Fleischer Dave • ANS • USA
LA PALOMA • 1934 • Martin Karl Heinz • FRG
LA PALOMA • 1954 • Martin Paul • FRG
LA PATRU PASI DE INFINIT • 1964 • Munteanu Francisc • RMN • FOUR STEPS TO THE INFINITE
LA PORTILE PAMINTULUI • 1966 • Saizescu Geo • RMN • AT THE GATES OF THE EARTH
LA POUPEE see **POUPEE, LA** • 1920
LA REVANCHE • 1916 • Lincoln W. J. • ASL
LA TUT'FI' ASH-SHAMS see **LA TUTFI EL SHEMS** • 1961
LA TUTFI EL SHEMS • 1961 • Abu Saif Salah • EGY • SUN WILL NEVER SET, THE ○ LA TUT'FI' ASH-SHAMS
LA VIRSTA DRAGOSTEI • 1963 • Munteanu Francisc • RMN • AT THE AGE OF LOVE
LA WAKT LEB HOB • 1963 • Abu Saif Salah • EGY • LA WAQTA LI AL-HUBB ○ PAS DE TEMPS POUR L'AMOUR
LA WAQTA LI AL-HUBB see **LA WAKT LEB HOB** • 1963
LAAASKA • 1978 • Brdecka Jiri • ANM • CZC • AAAMOUR
LAAMBAYE • 1972 • Traore Mahama Johnson • SNL • LAMBAYE
LAATSTE ORDEEL, HET • 1970 • Henderickx Guido • BLG • LAST JUDGMENT, THE
LAATSTE REIS, DE • 1987 • Hin Kees • NTH • LAST JOURNEY, THE
LAATSTE SCOT, HET • 1945 • Ferno John • DOC • NTH • LAST SHOT, THE
LAATSTE TREIN, DE • 1975 • van Zuylen Erik • NTH • LAST TRAIN, THE
LAB KUSH • 1967 • Chatterjee Ashoke • IND
LABAKAN • 1956 • Krska Vaclav • CZC
LABAN PETTERQVIST TRAINING FOR THE OLYMPIC GAMES see **LABAN PETTERQVIST TRAVAR FOR OLYMPISKA SPELEN** • 1912
LABAN PETTERQVIST TRAVAR FOR OLYMPISKA SPELEN • 1912 • Bjorck Lars • SWD • LABAN PETTERQVIST TRAINING FOR THE OLYMPIC GAMES
LABBRA DI LURIDO BLU • 1975 • Petroni Giulio • ITL
LABBRA PROIBITE (ITL) see **QUAND TU LIRAS CETTE LETTRE** • 1953
LABBRA ROSSE • 1960 • Bennati Giuseppe • ITL, FRN • FAUSSES INGENUES (FRN) ○ RED LIPS (USA) ○ YOUNG LIPS
LABBRA SERRATE • 1942 • Mattoli Mario • ITL
LABDA VARASZA, A • 1962 • Meszaros Marta • DCS • HNG • SPELL OF THE BALL, THE
LABEDZI SPIEW • 1962 • Antczak Jerzy • SHT • PLN • SWAN SONG
LABERINT • 1979 • Villaronga Agustin • SPN • LABYRINTH
LABERINTO • 1983 • Alea Tomas Gutierrez • CUB • LABYRINTH
LABERINTO DE PASIONES • 1970 • *Enriquez Ernesto* • MXC
LABERINTO DE PASIONES • 1982 • Almodovar Pedro • SPN • LABYRINTH OF PASSIONS
LABIOS ROJOS • 1960 • Franco Jesus • SPN
LABIOS SELLADOS see **CREO EN DIOS** • 1940
LABIOS SEM BEIJOS • 1930 • Mauro-Humberto • BRZ • LIPS WITHOUT KISSES
LABIRINTO, O • 1953 • Mendes Joao • SHT • PRT
LABIRINTUS • 1976 • Kovacs Andras • HNG • LABYRINTH
LABORATORY • 1980 • Emenegger Robert, Sandler Allan • USA
LABORATORY OF MEPHISTOPHELES (USA) see **CABINET DE MEPHISTOPHELE, LE** • 1897
LABOREMUS see **AM WEBSTUHL DER ZEIT** • 1921
LABOUR COLLEGE • 1966 • Rubbo Michael • DOC • CND
LABOUR LEADER, THE • 1917 • Bentley Thomas • UKN
LABOUR RICHARD, LE • 1939 • Proulx Maurice • DCS • CND
LABRADOR: LAND OUT OF TIME • 1977 • Macartney-Filgate Terence • CND
LABURNUM GROVE • 1936 • Reed Carol • UKN
LABYRINT • 1963 • Lenica Jan • ANS • PLN • LABYRINTH
LABYRINT • 1990 • Jires Jaromil • FRG
LABYRINT SRDCE • 1961 • Krejcik Jiri • CZC • LABYRINTH OF THE HEART, THE
LABYRINTH • 1959 • Thiele Rolf • FRG
LABYRINTH • 1986 • Henson Jim • UKN
LABYRINTH see **LABYRINT** • 1963
LABYRINTH see **LABYRINTHE** • 1967
LABYRINTH see **REFLECTION OF FEAR, A** • 1973
LABYRINTH see **LABIRINTUS** • 1976
LABYRINTH see **HOMME EN COLERE, L'** • 1978
LABYRINTH see **LABERINT** • 1979
LABYRINTH see **LABERINTO** • 1983
LABYRINTH, THE • 1913 • *Rex* • USA
LABYRINTH, THE • 1915 • Hopper E. Mason • USA
LABYRINTH DER LIEBE, DAS • 1920 • Halden Karl • FRG
LABYRINTH DES GRAUENS • 1921 • Curtiz Michael • AUS • WEGE DES SCHRECKENS
LABYRINTH OF GRASS see **KUSAMEIKYU** • 1983
LABYRINTH OF PASSIONS see **LABERINTO DE PASIONES** • 1982
LABYRINTH OF SEX, A see **JOSHIGAKUSEI SEI NO MEIRO** • 1968
LABYRINTH OF SEX, THE (UKN) see **NEL LABIRINTO DEL SESSO** • 1969
LABYRINTH OF THE HEART, THE see **LABYRINT SRDCE** • 1961
LABYRINTHE • 1967 • Kroitor Roman, Low Colin • CND • LABYRINTH
LABYRINTHE • 1981 • Jaulmes Philippe • FRN
LABYRINTHE, LE • 1972 • Regnier Michel • DCS • CND
LABYRINTHE, LE • 1977 • Barouh Pierre • FRN
LABYRINTHS • 1986 • Koulev Henri • DOC • BUL
LAC AUX DAMES • 1934 • Allegret Marc • FRN
LAC AUX DESIRS, LE see **LIMNI TON POTHON, I** • 1958
LAC CLAIR, LE • 1941 • Tessier Albert • DCS • CND
LAC D'ARGENT, LE • 1923 • Roudes Gaston • FRN
LAC DES MORTS-VIVANTS, LE • 1980 • Rollin Jean • FRN, SPN • LAGO DEL MUERTOS VIVIENTES, EL (SPN) ○ LAKE OF THE LIVING DEAD, THE ○ ZOMBIES' LAKE ○ ZOMBIE LAKE
LAC ENCHANTE, LE see **FEE LIBELLULE, LA** • 1908
LACE • 1984 • Hale William • TVM • USA, UKN
LACE see **GREVINDENS AERE** • 1918
LACE see **KRUZHEVA** • 1928
LACE II • 1985 • Hale William • TVM • USA
LACEMAKER, THE (USA) see **DENTELLIERE, LA** • 1977
LACEMAKER'S DREAM, THE • 1910 • *Lux* • FRN
LACEY RITUALS, THE • 1973 • Lacey Bruce • UKN
LACHDOKTOR, DER • 1937 • Sauer Fred • FRG • LAUGH DOCTOR, THE (USA)
LACHE BAJAZZO! • 1919 • Oswald Richard • FRG • LAUGH BAJAZZO!
LACHE BAJAZZO • 1943 • Hainisch Leopold • FRG
LACHELN DER KLEINEN BEATE, DAS • 1919 • Schubert Georg • FRG
LACHENDE DRITTE, DER • 1936 • Zoch Georg • FRG
LACHENDE EHEMANN, DER • 1926 • Walther-Fein Rudolf • FRG
LACHENDE ERBEN • 1933 • Ophuls Max • FRG
LACHENDE GRAUEN, DAS • 1920 • Pick Lupu • FRG
LACHENDE GRILLE, DIE • 1926 • Zelnik Friedrich • FRG
LACHENDE HERZEN • 1919 • *Werckmeister Lotte* • FRG
LACHENDE MASKE, DIE • 1918 • Zeyn Willy • FRG
LACHENDE SEELE, DIE • 1918 • Alexander Georg • FRG
LACHENDE TOD, DER • 1918 • Kahn William • FRG
LACHENDE VAGABUND, DER • 1958 • Engel Thomas • FRG
LACHENDEN MANN, DER • 1966 • Heynowski Walter, Scheumann Gerhard • GDR • LAUGHING MAN, THE
LACHENDES WEINEN • 1923 • *Boheme-Film* • FRG
LACHENITE OBOUKVI NA NEZNAINYA VOIN • 1979 • Vulchanov Rangel • BUL • UNKNOWN SOLDIER'S PATENT LEATHER SHOES, THE
LACHES VIVENT D'ESPOIR, LES • 1961 • Bernard-Aubert Claude • FRN • MY BABY IS BLACK! (USA) ○ COLOURS OF LOVE, THE
LACHEZ LES CHIENNES • 1972 • Launois Bernard • FRN
LACHKABINETT • 1953 • Holsboer Willem • FRG
LACK OF EVIDENCE see **I BRIST PA BEVIS** • 1943
LACK OF PROOF • 1987 • Fahmy Ashraf • EGY
LACKEY, THE • 1914 • *Johnstone Lamar* • USA
LACKEY AND THE LADY, THE • 1919 • Bentley Thomas • UKN
LACKEY AND THE LADY TIGER see **SHE-MAO-HO HUN-HSING CH'UAN** • 1980
LACKRA SKALDJUREN, DE • 1920 • Brunius Pauline • SHT • SWD
LACOMBE LUCIEN • 1973 • Malle Louis • FRN, FRG, ITL • NOME E COGNOME: LACOMBE LUCIEN (ITL)
LACONDONNES, THE • 1958 • Kelly Ron • CND
LACRIMA DE FATA, O • 1980 • Demian Iosif • RMN • GIRL'S TEARS, A
LACRIMA D'ORO, LA • 1912 • Lolli Alberto Carlo • ITL
LACRIMA SUL VISO, UNA • 1964 • Fizzarotti Ettore Maria • ITL
LACRIME D'AMORE • 1956 • Mercanti Pino • ITL
LACRIME D'AMORE • 1970 • Amendola Mario • ITL
LACRIME DE SANGUE • 1944 • Brignone Guido • ITL • TEARS OF BLOOD (USA) ○ VIE DEL PECCATO, LE ○ NOTTURNO ○ DONNA SOLA, UNA
LACRIME DI SPOSA • 1955 • Chimirri Sante • ITL
LACRIME E SORRISI • 1936 • Matarazzo Raffaello • ITL
LACRIME NAPULITANE • 1984 • Ippolito Ciro • ITL • NEAPOLITAN TEARS
LACROSSE see **LEARNING LACROSSE** • 1965
LACTICINIOS DA MADIERA • 1960 • Queiroga Perdigao • SHT • PRT
LACY AND THE MISSISSIPPI QUEEN • 1978 • Butler Robert • TVM • USA
LAD, THE • 1935 • Edwards Henry • UKN
LAD: A DOG • 1962 • Avakian Aram, Martinson Leslie H. • USA
LAD AN' A LAMP, A • 1932 • McGowan Robert • SHT • USA
LAD AND THE FIRE, THE • 1962 • Stiopul Savel • RMN
LAD AND THE LION, THE • 1917 • Green Alfred E. • USA
LAD FROM OLD IRELAND, THE • 1910 • Olcott Sidney • USA
LAD FROM OUR TOWN (USA) see **PAREN IZ NASHEGO GORODA** • 1942
LAD IN BAGDAD, A • 1938 • Hardaway Ben, Dalton Cal • ANS • USA
LAD IN BAGDAD, A • 1968 • Smith Paul J. • ANS • USA
LAD IN HIS LAMP, A • 1948 • McKimson Robert • ANS • USA

LAD IN SHORTS see **AMORE PIU BELLO, L'** • 1959

LAD ISBJORNENE DANSE • 1989 • Larsen Birger • DNM • LET THE POLAR BEARS DANCE

LADALI • 1949 • *Biswas Anil (M)* • IND

LADAN • 1968 • Alfredson Hans, Danielsson Tage • SWD • BOX, THE

LADDER, THE • 1966 • Dunning George • ANS • UKN

LADDER, THE see **SCHODY** • 1964

LADDER IMP, THE see **LADDER JINX, THE** • 1922

LADDER INTO THE SKY see **LYESTNITSA V NYEBO** • 1967

LADDER JINX, THE • 1922 • Robbins Jess • USA • LADDER IMP, THE

LADDER OF FAME, THE • 1917 • *Watson Harry Jr.* • USA

LADDER OF FORTUNE, THE • 1915 • Easton Clem • USA

LADDER OF LIES, THE • 1920 • Forman Tom • USA

LADDER OF LIFE, THE • 1912 • *Benham Harry* • USA

LADDER OF LOVE, THE • 1915 • *Balboa* • USA

LADDER OF SUCCESS, THE see **YORU NO SUGAO** • 1958

LADDER OF SWORDS • 1989 • Hull Norman • UKN

LADDIE • 1909 • *Edison* • USA

LADDIE • 1914 • Lessey George A. • USA

LADDIE • 1920 • Merwin Bannister • UKN

LADDIE • 1926 • Meehan James Leo • USA

LADDIE • 1934 • Stevens George • USA

LADDIE • 1940 • Hively Jack • USA

LADDIE see **BUBCHEN** • 1968

LADDIE BE GOOD • 1928 • Cohn Bennett • USA

LADDY AND HIS LAMP • 1964 • Kneitel Seymour • ANS • USA

LADENPRINZ, DER • 1928 • Schonfelder Erich • FRG

LADIES • 1955 • Kolijamov L.

LADIES see **DAMY** • 1954

LADIES AND GENTLEMEN • 1964 • Giersz Witold • ANS • PLN

LADIES AND GENTLEMEN see **SIGNORE E SIGNORI** • 1966

LADIES AND GENTLEMEN: MR. LEONARD COHEN • 1965 • Brittain Don, Owen Don • CND

LADIES AND GENTLEMEN, THE FABULOUS STAINS • 1982 • Adler Lou • USA

LADIES AND GENTLEMEN, THE ROLLING STONES • 1974 • Binzer Rollin • DOC • USA

LADIES AND LADIES see **DOLCI SIGNORE, LE** • 1967

LADIES AT EASE • 1927 • Storm Jerome • USA

LADIES AT PLAY • 1926 • Green Alfred E. • USA • DESPERATE WOMAN, A

LADIES, BE CAREFUL OF YOUR SLEEVES see **ONNA WA TOMOTO O GYOJIN** • 1931

LADIES BEWARE • 1927 • Giblyn Charles • USA

LADIES CHOICE • 1929 • Burns Neal • USA

LADIES CLUB, THE • 1986 • Greek Janet • USA • VIOLATED ○ SISTERHOOD, THE

LADIES COURAGEOUS • 1944 • Rawlins John • USA • WHEN LADIES FLY

LADIES CRAVE EXCITEMENT • 1935 • Grinde Nick • USA

LADIES' DAY • 1943 • Goodwins Leslie • USA

LADIES' DOCTOR see **GINECOLOGO DELLA MUTUA, IL** • 1977

LADIES FIRST • 1918 • Grainger Ray, Fishback Fred C. • SHT • USA

LADIES FIRST • 1930 • Stevens George • SHT • USA

LADIES FIRST see **HOLD THAT LION** • 1926

LADIES FIRST see **ELMER AND ELSIE** • 1934

LADIES FIRST (USA) see **FEMMES D'ABORD, LES** • 1962

LADIES IN DISTRESS • 1938 • Meins Gus • USA

LADIES IN LOVE • 1930 • Lewis Edgar • USA • WINGS OF SONG (UKN)

LADIES IN LOVE • 1936 • Griffith Edward H. • USA

LADIES IN RETIREMENT • 1941 • Vidor Charles • USA

LADIES IN THE GREEN HATS, THE (USA) see **CES DAMES AUX CHAPEAUX VERTS** • 1937

LADIES' JOURNAL, THE see **DAMERNES BLAD** • 1911

LADIES LOVE BRUTES • 1930 • Lee Rowland V. • USA

LADIES LOVE DANGER • 1935 • Humberstone H. Bruce • USA

LADIES' MAN • 1931 • Mendes Lothar • USA

LADIES' MAN • 1947 • Russell William D. • USA

LADIES' MAN see **LEMMY POUR LES DAMES** • 1961

LADIES' MAN, A • 1922 • Stromberg Hunt • USA

LADIES' MAN, THE • 1961 • Lewis Jerry • USA

LADIES MUST DANCE • 1920 • Clemens James • USA

LADIES MUST DRESS • 1927 • Heerman Victor • USA

LADIES MUST EAT • 1929 • *Sennett Mack (P)* • SHT • USA

LADIES MUST LIVE • 1921 • Tucker George Loane • USA

LADIES MUST LIVE • 1940 • Smith Noel • USA

LADIES MUST LOVE • 1933 • Dupont E. A. • USA • FOUR WISE GIRLS

LADIES MUST PLAY • 1930 • Cannon Raymond • USA

LADIES' NIGHT • 1980 • Lewis Harry • USA • PASSIONS NOCTURNES

LADIES' NIGHT IN A TURKISH BATH • 1928 • Cline Eddie • USA • LADIES' NIGHT (UKN)

LADIES' NIGHT (UKN) see **LADIES' NIGHT IN A TURKISH BATH** • 1928

LADIES NOT ALLOWED • 1932 • Santley Joseph • SHT • USA

LADIES OF LEISURE • 1926 • Buckingham Thomas • USA

LADIES OF LEISURE • 1930 • Capra Frank • USA

LADIES OF THE 80s • 1985 • Richards Mark • USA

LADIES OF THE BIG HOUSE • 1932 • Gering Marion • USA

LADIES OF THE BOIS DE BOULOGNE, THE see **DAMES DU BOIS DE BOULOGNE, LES** • 1945

LADIES OF THE CHORUS • 1948 • Karlson Phil • USA

LADIES OF THE JURY • 1932 • Sherman Lowell • USA

LADIES OF THE LOTUS • 1986 • Simandl Lloyd A., Nicolle Douglas • CND

LADIES OF THE MOB • 1928 • Wellman William A. • USA

LADIES OF THE MOB see **HOUSE OF WOMEN** • 1962

LADIES OF THE NIGHT CLUB • 1928 • Archainbaud George • USA

LADIES OF THE PARK (USA) see **DAMES DU BOIS DE BOULOGNE, LES** • 1945

LADIES OF WASHINGTON • 1944 • King Louis • USA

LADIES ON THE ROCKS see **KOKS I KULISSEN** • 1983

LADIES ONLY see **COMPARTIMENT DE DAMES SEULES** • 1934

LADIES PREFERRED • 1928 • Lamont Charles • SHT • USA

LADIES SHOULD LISTEN • 1934 • Tuttle Frank • USA

LADIES' TAILOR, THE see **MODOSTROS, O** • 1967

LADIES THEY TALK ABOUT • 1933 • Keighley William, Bretherton Howard • USA

LADIES TO BOARD • 1924 • Blystone John G. • USA

LADIES' WAR, THE • 1914 • North Wilfred • USA

LADIES WHO DO • 1963 • Pennington-Richards C. M. • UKN

LADRA, LA • 1955 • Bonnard Mario • ITL, FRN • ANGES AUX MAINS NOIRES, LES (FRN)

LADRAO DE QUEM SE FALA, O • 1969 • Campos Henrique • PRT

LADRAO, PRECISA-SE • 1946 • do Canto Jorge Brum • PRT

LADRI DI BICICLETTE • 1948 • De Sica Vittorio • ITL • BICYCLE THIEVES (UKN) ○ BICYCLE THIEF, THE

LADRI DI SAPONETTE • 1989 • Nichetti Maurizio • ITL • ICICLE THIEF (UKN)

LADRI, I • 1959 • Fulci Lucio • ITL

LADRIDO, EL • 1977 • Lazaga Pedro • SPN

LADRO, IL • 1940 • Rossi Antonio G. • ITL

LADRO DELLA GIOCONDA, IL (ITL) see **ON A VOLE LA JOCONDE** • 1965

LADRO DI BAGDAD, IL • 1961 • Lubin Arthur, Vailati Bruno • ITL, FRN • VOLEUR DE BAGDAD, LE (FRN) ○ THIEF OF BAGDAD, THE (USA)

LADRO DI CRIMINI, IL (ITL) see **VOLEUR DE CRIMES, LES** • 1969

LADRO DI DAMASCO, IL • 1963 • Amendola Mario • ITL • SWORD OF DAMASCUS (USA)

LADRO DI DONNE (ITL) see **VOLEUR DE FEMMES, LE** • 1936

LADRO DI STELLE see **INCANTO DI MEZZANOTTE** • 1940

LADRO DI VENEZIA, IL • 1950 • Brahm John • ITL • THIEF OF VENICE, THE (USA)

LADRO IN PARADISO, UN • 1952 • Paolella Domenico, Amato Giuseppe • ITL

LADRO LUI, LADRO LEI • 1958 • Zampa Luigi • ITL

LADRO SONO IO! • 1940 • Calzavara Flavio • ITL

LADRON • 1971 • Roche Luis Armando • VNZ • THIEF

LADRON, EL • 1947 • Bracho Julio • MXC

LADRON CANTA BOLEROS, EL • 1950 • Cahen Enrique • ARG

LADRON DE AMOR • 1930 • Howard David, Scully William J. • USA

LADRON DE CADAVERES • 1956 • Mendez Fernando • MXC • THIEF OF CORPSES ○ BODY SNATCHERS ○ GRAVE ROBBERS

LADRON DE GUANTE BLANCO, UN • 1945 • Gascon Jose • SPN

LADRON EN SEDA see **THIEF IN SILK** • 1952

LADRON QUE ROBA A LADRON • 1959 • Salvador Jaime • MXC

LADRONA, LA • 1953 • Gomez Muriel Emilio • MXC

LADRONA PARA UN ESPIA • 1966 • Balcazar Jaime Jesus • SPN

LADRONE, IL • 1979 • Festa Campanile Pasquale • ITL • BAD THIEF, THE

LADRONES DE NINOS • 1957 • Alazraki Benito • MXC

LADRONES SOMOS GENTE HONRADA • 1956 • Ramirez Pedro L. • SPN

LADRONES SOMOS GENTE HONRADA, LOS • 1942 • Iquino Ignacio F. • SPN

LADRONZUELA • 1949 • Delgado Agustin P. • MXC

LADS AND LASSIES ON PARADE see **KILTIES ARE COMING, THE** • 1951

LADS OF THE VILLAGE, THE • 1919 • Lorraine Harry • UKN

LADS OF THE YELLOW FLAG, THE see **RAGAZZI DI BANDIERA GIALLA, I** • 1967

LADY see **LADY, THE** • 1925

LADY, DIE • 1964 • Albin Hans, Berneis Peter • FRG, FRN • GAMES OF DESIRE (USA)

LADY L • 1965 • Ustinov Peter • USA, ITL, FRN

LADY, THE • 1925 • Borzage Frank • USA • LADY

LADY, THE • 1989 • TRK

LADY, THE see **SECRET OF MADAME BLANCHE, THE** • 1933

LADY, THE see **XUNAN** • 1983

LADY, THE see **SENYORA, LA** • 1987

LADY AND DEATH, THE see **DAMA DE LA MUERTE, LA** • 1946

LADY AND GENT • 1932 • Roberts Stephen • USA • CHALLENGER, THE

LADY AND HER FAVOURITES, THE see **SHUKUJO TO HIJE** • 1931

LADY AND HER LUGGAGE, THE see **VEZLA DAMA ZAVAZADLA** • 1965

LADY AND HER MAID, THE • 1913 • Angeles Bert • USA

LADY AND THE BANDIT, THE • 1951 • Murphy Ralph • USA • DICK TURPIN'S RIDE (UKN)

LADY AND THE BEARD, THE see **SHUKUJO TO HIJE** • 1931

LADY AND THE BURGLAR, THE • 1910 • Merwin Bannister • USA

LADY AND THE BURGLAR, THE • 1915 • Blache Herbert • USA • BURGLAR AND THE LADY, THE

LADY AND THE CHAUFFEUR, THE see **DAME UND IHR CHAUFFEUR, DIE** • 1928

LADY AND THE COWBOY, THE • 1970 • Papadopoulos Costas • SHT • GRC

LADY AND THE DOCTOR, THE (UKN) see **LADY AND THE MONSTER, THE** • 1944

LADY AND THE DRAGON, THE see **BIJO TO KAIRYU** • 1955

LADY AND THE GLOVE, THE • 1913 • Thompson Frederick A. • USA

LADY AND THE GYPSY, THE see **FEKETE SZEM EJSZAKAJA** • 1958

LADY AND THE HIGHWAYMAN, THE • 1988 • Hough John • TVM • UKN

LADY AND THE MOB, THE • 1939 • Stoloff Ben • USA • MRS. LEONARD MISBEHAVES

LADY AND THE MONSTER, THE • 1944 • Sherman George • USA • LADY AND THE DOCTOR, THE (UKN) ○ MONSTER AND THE LADY, THE ○ TIGER MAN ○ MONSTER, THE

LADY AND THE MOUSE, THE • 1913 • Griffith D. W. • USA

LADY AND THE OUTLAW, THE see **BILLY TWO HATS** • 1974

LADY AND THE PAUPER, THE see **ARHONTISA KE O ALITIS, I** • 1968

LADY AND THE TRAMP • 1955 • Luske Hamilton, Geronimi Clyde, Jackson Wilfred • ANM • USA

LADY AND THE WATCHDOG, THE • 1912 • Urban Max • CZC

LADY ANGELA AND THE BOY • 1912 • Buckland Warwick? • UKN

LADY AT HER MORNING TOILET • 1900 • *Warwick Trading Co* • UKN

LADY AT MIDNIGHT • 1948 • Newfield Sam • USA

LADY AUDLEY'S JEWELS • 1913 • *Steppling John* • USA

LADY AUDLEY'S SECRET • 1906 • *Walturdaw* • UKN

LADY AUDLEY'S SECRET • 1908 • *Kalem* • USA

LADY AUDLEY'S SECRET • 1912 • Turner Otis • USA

LADY AUDLEY'S SECRET • 1915 • Farnum Marshall • USA • SECRETS OF SOCIETY, THE

LADY AUDLEY'S SECRET • 1920 • Denton Jack • UKN

LADY AVENGER • 1987 • Decoteau David • USA

LADY BABBIE • 1913 • *Tennant Barbara* • USA

LADY BAFFLES AND DETECTIVE DUCK • 1915 • *Powers* • SHS • USA

LADY BAFFLES AND DETECTIVE DUCK IN KIDNAPPING THE KING'S KIDS • 1915 • Curtis Allen • USA

LADY BAFFLES AND DETECTIVE DUCK IN SAVED BY A SCENT • 1915 • Curtis Allen • USA

LADY BAFFLES AND DETECTIVE DUCK IN THE DREAD SOCIETY OF SACRED SAUSAGES • 1915 • Curtis Allen • USA

LADY BAFFLES AND DETECTIVE DUCK IN " THE GREAT EGG ROBBERY" • 1915 • Curtis Allen • USA

LADY BAFFLES AND DETECTIVE DUCK IN THE LOST ROLL • 1915 • Curtis Allen • USA

LADY BAFFLES AND DETECTIVE DUCK IN THE ORE MYSTERY • 1915 • Curtis Allen • USA

LADY BAFFLES AND DETECTIVE DUCK IN THE 18-CARROT MYSTERY • 1915 • Curtis Allen • USA

LADY BAFFLES AND DETECTIVE DUCK IN WHEN THE WETS WENT DRY • 1915 • Curtis Allen • USA

LADY BARBARA • 1970 • Amendola Mario • ITL

LADY BARBER, THE • 1898 • Smith G. A. • UKN

LADY BARBER, THE • 1905 • *Cricks & Sharp* • UKN

LADY BARBER, THE • 1924 • *Sennett Mack (P)* • SHT • USA

LADY BARBER OF ROARING GULCH, THE • 1912 • *Nestor* • USA

LADY BARBERS, THE • 1910 • *Selig* • USA

LADY BARNACLE • 1917 • Collins John H. • USA

LADY BE CAREFUL • 1936 • Reed Theodore • USA

LADY BE GAY (UKN) see **LAUGH IT OFF** • 1939

LADY BE GOOD • 1928 • Wallace Richard • USA

LADY BE GOOD • 1941 • McLeod Norman Z. • USA

LADY BE KIND • 1941 • Ackland Rodney • UKN

LADY BEAULAY'S NECKLACE • 1911 • Bouwmeester Theo • UKN

LADY BECOMES A MAID see **FROKEN BLIR PIGA** • 1936

LADY BEHAVE! • 1938 • Corrigan Lloyd • USA • LADY MISBEHAVES, THE

LADY BELLHOPS SECRET, A • 1919 • *Sunshine* • SHT • USA

LADY BETTY'S STRATEGY • 1910 • *Gibson Frances* • USA

LADY BEWARE • 1987 • Arthur Karen • USA

LADY BEWARE see **THIRTEENTH GUEST, THE** • 1932

LADY BEWARE see **GUARD THE GIRL!** • 1935

LADY BLUE • 1985 • Nelson Gary • TVM • USA

LADY BODYGUARD • 1943 • Clemens William • USA

LADY BOLERO see **SENORA BOLERO** • 1989

LADY BY CHOICE • 1934 • Burton David • USA

LADY CALLED ANDREW, A see **SENORA LLAMADA ANDRES, UNA** • 1970

LADY CANDALE'S DIAMONDS • 1910 • Wormald S.? • UKN

LADY CAROLINE LAMB • 1972 • Bolt Robert • UKN, ITL • PECCATO D'AMORE (ITL)

LADY CHAPLIN STORY, THE see **MISSIONE SPECIALE LADY CHAPLIN** • 1966

LADY CHARLIE see **BUSY DAY, A** • 1914

LADY CHASER see **LADY CHASERS** • 1946

LADY CHASERS • 1946 • Newfield Sam • USA • LADY CHASER

LADY CHATTERLEY'S LOVER • 1981 • Jaeckin Just • UKN, FRN • AMANT DE LADY CHATTERLEY, L' (FRN)

LADY CHATTERLEY'S LOVER see **AMANT DE CHATTERLEY, L'** • 1955

LADY CLARE • 1911 • *Thanhouser* • USA

LADY CLARE, THE • 1912 • Miller Ashley • UKN, USA

LADY CLARE, THE • 1919 • *Odette Mary* • UKN

LADY COCOA • 1975 • Cimber Matt • USA

LADY COMMANDO • 1989 • Ara Shamim • PKS

LADY CONFESSES, THE • 1945 • Newfield Sam • USA

LADY CONSENTS, THE • 1936 • Roberts Stephen • USA • INDESTRUCTIBLE MRS. TALBOT, THE

LADY CRAVED EXCITEMENT, THE • 1950 • Searle Francis • UKN

LADY DANCES, THE see **MERRY WIDOW, THE** • 1934

LADY DESIRE • 1968 • Newman Harry • ITL, FRG

LADY DETECTIVE, THE • 1915 • Evans Joe • UKN

LADY DETECTIVE, THE • 1917 • *Ovey George* • USA

LADY DOCTOR • 1980 • Michaels Richard • TVM • USA

LADY DOCTOR, THE • 1910 • *Powers* • USA

LADY DOCTOR, THE • 1913 • *Cornwall Blanche* • USA

LADY DOCTOR, THE • 1914 • Smalley Phillips • USA

LADY DOCTOR, THE (USA) see **TOTO, VITTORIO E LA DOTTORESSA** • 1957

LADY DOCTOR OF GRIZZLY GULCH, THE • 1915 • Curtis Allen • USA

LADY DOCTORS see **ARZTRINNEN** • 1983

LADY DOCTOR'S SURGERY see **FUJINKAI NO HIMITSU** • 1959

LADY DRACULA • 1976 • Gottlieb Franz J. • FRG

LADY DRACULA see **CEREMONIA SANGRIETA** • 1972

LADY DRACULA see **LEGENDARY CURSE OF LEMORA, THE** • 1974

LADY DRUMMER, THE • 1916 • *Tincher Fay* • SHT • USA

LADY ESCAPES, THE • 1937 • Forde Eugene J. • USA

LADY EVE, THE • 1941 • Sturges Preston • USA

LADY EVE, THE see **BIRDS AND THE BEES, THE** • 1956

LADY FIGHTS BACK, A • 1944 • *Nesbitt John* • SHT • USA

LADY FIGHTS BACK, THE • 1939 • Carruth Milton • USA

LADY FISHBOURNE'S COMPLETE GUIDE TO BETTER TABLE MANNERS • 1976 • Perlman Janet • CND

LADY FOR A DAY • 1933 • Capra Frank • USA

LADY FOR A NIGHT • 1941 • Jason Leigh • USA

LADY FRANKENSTEIN (USA) see **FIGLIA DI FRANKENSTEIN, LA** • 1971

LADY FREDERICK see **DIVORCEE, THE** • 1919

LADY FROM BOSTON, THE (UKN) see **PARDON MY FRENCH** • 1951
LADY FROM CHEYENNE • 1941 • Lloyd Frank • USA
LADY FROM CHUNGKING • 1942 • Nigh William • USA
LADY FROM CONSTANTINOPLE, THE (UKN) see **SZIGET A SZARAZFOLDON** • 1968
LADY FROM HELL see **JIGOKU NO KIFUJIN** • 1949
LADY FROM HELL, THE • 1926 • Paton Stuart • USA • INTERRUPTED WEDDING, THE
LADY FROM LISBON • 1942 • Hiscott Leslie • UKN
LADY FROM LONGACRE, THE • 1921 • Marshall George • USA
LADY FROM LOUISIANA • 1941 • Vorhaus Bernard • USA
LADY FROM MUSAHINO, THE (UKN) see **MUSASHINO FUJIN** • 1951
LADY FROM NOWHERE, THE • 1931 • Thorpe Richard • USA
LADY FROM NOWHERE, THE • 1936 • Wiles Gordon • USA
LADY FROM PARIS, THE • Noa Manfred • FRG
LADY FROM SHANGHAI see **SHANHAI NO ONNA** • 1952
LADY FROM SHANGHAI, THE • 1948 • Welles Orson • USA
LADY FROM TEXAS, THE • 1951 • Pevney Joseph • USA
LADY FROM THE MOVIE, THE see **DAMA DO CINE SHANGHAI!, A** • 1987
LADY FROM THE SEA, THE • 1911 • Marston Theodore • USA
LADY FROM THE SEA, THE • 1916 • Wells Raymond • SHT • USA
LADY FROM THE SEA, THE • 1929 • Knight Castleton • UKN • GOODWIN SANDS, THE
LADY FROM THE SHANGHAI CINEMA, THE (UKN) see **DAMA DO CINE SHANGHAI!, A** • 1987
LADY FROM YESTERDAY, THE • 1985 • Day Robert • TVM • USA
LADY GAMBLES, THE • 1949 • Gordon Michael • USA
LADY GANGSTER • 1942 • Florey Robert • USA
LADY GENERAL, THE (USA) see **HUA MU-LAN** • 1965
LADY GODIVA • 1911 • Blackton J. Stuart • USA
LADY GODIVA • 1920 • Moest Hubert • FRG
LADY GODIVA • 1928 • Banfield George J., Eveleigh Leslie • UKN
LADY GODIVA • 1955 • Lubin Arthur • USA • LADY GODIVA OF COVENTRY (UKN)
LADY GODIVA see **LADY GODIVA RIDES** • 1969
LADY GODIVA (LOVES ON TWO CONTINENTS) see **LADY GODIVA RIDES** • 1969
LADY GODIVA MEETS TOM JONES see **LADY GODIVA RIDES** • 1969
LADY GODIVA OF COVENTRY (UKN) see **LADY GODIVA** • 1955
LADY GODIVA REIGNS see **LADY GODIVA RIDES** • 1969
LADY GODIVA RIDES • 1969 • Stephen A. C. • USA • LADY GODIVA (LOVES ON TWO CONTINENTS) ○ LADY GODIVA REIGNS ○ LADY GODIVA ○ LADY GODIVA RIDES AGAIN ○ LADY GODIVA MEETS TOM JONES
LADY GODIVA RIDES AGAIN • 1951 • Launder Frank • UKN • BEAUTY QUEEN
LADY GODIVA RIDES AGAIN see **LADY GODIVA RIDES** • 1969
LADY GREY • 1980 • Keeter Worth • USA
LADY HAMILTON • 1921 • Oswald Richard • FRG
LADY HAMILTON see **LADY HAMILTON ZWISCHEN SCHMACH UND LIEBE** • 1968
LADY HAMILTON (UKN) see **THAT HAMILTON WOMAN** • 1941
LADY HAMILTON ZWISCHEN SCHMACH UND LIEBE • 1968 • Christian-Jaque • FRN, ITL, FRG • CALDE NOTTI DI LADY HAMILTON, LE (ITL) ○ EMMA HAMILTON ○ AMOURS DE LADY HAMILTON, LES (FRN) ○ LADY HAMILTON ○ MAKING OF A LADY, THE
LADY HAS NO ALIBI, THE see **ANA** • 1957
LADY HAS PLANS, THE • 1942 • Lanfield Sidney • USA • GIRL HAS PLANS, THE
LADY HELEN'S ESCAPADE • 1909 • Griffith D. W. • USA
LADY ICE • 1973 • Gries Tom • USA • MASTERS, THE
LADY IN A CAGE • 1964 • Grauman Walter • USA
LADY IN A JAM • 1942 • La Cava Gregory • USA • SHELTERED LADY, THE
LADY IN A SYRTAKI DANCE, A see **MIA KIRIA STA BOUZOUKIA** • 1968
LADY IN A TRAP • 1981 • Soebarjo Ismail • INN
LADY IN BLACK, THE • 1913 • *Gish Dorothy* • USA
LADY IN BLACK, THE • 1921 • Gordon Edward R. • UKN
LADY IN BLACK, THE see **DAMEN I SVART** • 1958
LADY IN CEMENT • 1968 • Douglas Gordon • USA
LADY IN DANGER • 1934 • Walls Tom • UKN • MAN SAVES THE QUEEN
LADY IN DANGER see **LAST SONG, THE** • 1980
LADY IN DISTRESS, A • 1915 • Smalley Phillips • USA
LADY IN DISTRESS (USA) see **WINDOW IN LONDON, A** • 1939
LADY IN ERMINE, THE • 1927 • Flood James • USA
LADY IN FURS, THE • 1925 • Greenwood Edwin • UKN • SABLES OF DEATH
LADY IN HIGH HEELS, THE • 1925 • Greenwood Edwin • UKN • HEEL TAPS
LADY IN JEWELS, THE • 1925 • Greenwood Edwin • UKN • HEARTS TRUMP DIAMONDS
LADY IN LACE, THE • 1925 • Greenwood Edwin • UKN • CAUGHT IN THE WEB
LADY IN LOVE, A • 1920 • Edwards Walter • USA
LADY IN MOTION • 1982 • White Helene B. • MTV • CND
LADY IN QUESTION, THE • 1940 • Vidor Charles • USA • IT HAPPENED IN PARIS
LADY IN RED, THE • 1935 • Freleng Friz • ANS • USA
LADY IN RED, THE • 1979 • Teague Lewis • USA • GUNS, SIN AND BATHTUB GIN ○ KISS ME AND DIE
LADY IN SCARLET, THE • 1935 • Lamont Charles • USA
LADY IN SILK STOCKINGS, THE • 1925 • Greenwood Edwin • UKN • WEAKNESS OF MEN, THE
LADY IN THE CAR WITH GLASSES AND A GUN, THE (UKN) see **DAME DANS L'AUTO AVEC DES LUNETTES ET UN FUSIL, LA** • 1970
LADY IN THE DARK • 1944 • Leisen Mitchell • USA
LADY IN THE DEATH HOUSE • 1944 • Sekely Steve • USA
LADY IN THE FOG • 1952 • Newfield Sam • UKN • SCOTLAND YARD INSPECTOR (USA)
LADY IN THE IRON MASK • 1952 • Murphy Ralph • USA
LADY IN THE LAKE • 1946 • Montgomery Robert • USA
LADY IN THE LIBRARY, A • 1916 • Drew Sidney • SHT • USA
LADY IN THE LIBRARY, THE • 1917 • Jones Edgar • USA
LADY IN THE MORGUE • 1938 • Garrett Otis • USA • CASE OF THE MISSING BLONDE, THE (UKN)
LADY IN THE SHADOWS see **TERROR, THE** • 1963
LADY IN THE TRAIN, THE see **SAYIDAT EL KITAR** • 1951
LADY IN WHITE • 1988 • La Loggia Frank • USA
LADY IN WHITE see **VITA FRUN** • 1962
LADY IN WHITE, THE (USA) see **DAMA BIANCA, LA** • 1938
LADY INGER OF OSTRAT see **FRU INGER TOL OSTRAT** • 1975
LADY IS A SQUARE, THE • 1959 • Wilcox Herbert • UKN
LADY IS A TRAMP, THE see **THAT GIRL IS A TRAMP**
LADY IS A WHORE, THE • 1972 • Efstratiadis Omiris • GRC • TWO FACES OF LOVE, THE ○ NAUGHTY NIGHTS
LADY IS FICKLE, THE (USA) see **DONNA E MOBILE, LA** • 1942
LADY IS THE BOSS, THE see **CHANG-JEN MEN** • 1983
LADY IS WAITING, THE, THE see **FULL OF LIFE** • 1956
LADY IS WILLING, THE • 1934 • Miller Gilbert • UKN
LADY IS WILLING, THE • 1942 • Leisen Mitchell • USA
LADY JANE • 1985 • Nunn Trevor • UKN
LADY JANE GREY see **TUDOR ROSE** • 1936
LADY JANE GREY: OR, THE COURT OF INTRIGUE • 1923 • Greenwood Edwin • UKN
LADY JANE'S FLIGHT • 1908 • Blackton J. Stuart • USA
LADY JENNIFER • 1915 • Vickers James W. • UKN
LADY JULIA see **FRAULEIN JULIE** • 1921
LADY KILLER • 1933 • Del Ruth Roy • USA • FINGERMAN
LADY KILLER • 1989 • Schenkel Carl • USA
LADY KILLER, THE • 1913 • *Garwood Billy* • USA
LADY KILLER, THE • 1915 • MacGregor Norval • USA
LADY KILLER, THE • 1916 • Quirk William • SHT • USA
LADY-KILLER IN TROUBLE see **OZVEGY MENYASSZONYOK** • 1964
LADY KILLER OF ROME, THE (USA) see **ASSASSINO, L'** • 1961
LADY KILLERS • 1916 • *Heinie & Louie* • USA
LADY KILLER'S DOOM, A • 1918 • Raymaker Herman C. • SHT • USA
LADY KUNG FU • 1971 • Huang Feng • HKG
LADY LEONE, THE • 1912 • Salter Harry • USA
LADY LETMERE'S JEWELLERY • 1908 • Sims George R. • UKN
LADY, LET'S DANCE • 1944 • Woodruff Frank • USA
LADY LIBERTINE • 1983 • Kikoine Gerard • FRN, CND, USA • FRANK AND I
LADY LIBERTY (USA) see **MORTADELLA, LA** • 1971
LADY LIES, THE • 1929 • Henley Hobart • USA
LADY LION, A • 1928 • Sandrich Mark • SHT • USA
LADY LUCK • 1936 • Lamont Charles • USA
LADY LUCK • 1940 • Beaudine William • USA
LADY LUCK • 1946 • Marin Edwin L. • USA
LADY LUCK see **LUCKY LADY, THE** • 1926
LADY LUCK see **SIGNORA FORTUNA** • 1937
LADY LUCY RUNS AWAY • 1911 • Noy Wilfred • UKN
LADY LUNA(TIC)'S HAT, THE • 1908 • Smith Jack ? • UKN
LADY MACBETH • 1918 • Guazzoni Enrico • ITL
LADY MACBETH OF MTSENSK (UKN) see **KATERINA ISMAYLOVA** • 1966
LADY MARIONS SOMMARFLIRT • 1913 • Sjostrom Victor • SWD • LADY MARION'S SUMMER FLIRTATION ○ LADY MARION'S SUMMER FLIRT
LADY MARION'S SUMMER FLIRT see **LADY MARIONS SOMMARFLIRT** • 1913
LADY MARION'S SUMMER FLIRTATION see **LADY MARIONS SOMMARFLIRT** • 1913
LADY MARY'S LOVE see **NAADIGE FROKEN, DEN** • 1911
LADY MISBEHAVES, THE see **LADY BEHAVE!** • 1938
LADY MISLAID, A • 1958 • MacDonald David • UKN
LADY MORGAN'S REVENGE see **VENDETTA DI LADY MORGAN, LA** • 1966
LADY MUSASHINO (USA) see **MUSASHINO FUJIN** • 1951
LADY NOGGS -PEERESS • 1920 • Morgan Sidney • UKN
LADY OBJECTS, THE • 1938 • Kenton Erle C. • USA
LADY OF BURLESQUE • 1943 • Wellman William A. • USA • STRIPTEASE LADY (UKN) ○ G-STRING MURDERS, THE
LADY OF CAYENAS, THE • 1913 • Zimmerman E. • VNZ
LADY OF CHANCE, A • 1928 • Leonard Robert Z. • USA • LITTLE ANGEL, THE
LADY OF DECEIT (UKN) see **BORN TO KILL** • 1947
LADY OF DREAMS, A • 1915 • Morrisey Edward • USA
LADY OF LEBANON see **CHATELAINE DU LIBAN, LA** • 1956
LADY OF LYONS, THE • 1913 • Bary Leon • UKN
LADY OF MONZA, THE (USA) see **MONACA DI MONZA, LA** • 1969
LADY OF MUSASHINO, THE see **MUSASHINO FUJIN** • 1951
LADY OF MYSTERY (UKN) see **CLOSE CALL FOR BOSTON BLACKIE, A** • 1946
LADY OF QUALITY, A • 1913 • Dawley J. Searle • USA
LADY OF QUALITY, A • 1924 • Henley Hobart • USA
LADY OF RED BUTTE, THE • 1919 • Schertzinger Victor • USA
LADY OF SCANDAL, THE • 1930 • Franklin Sidney A. • USA • HIGH ROAD, THE (UKN)
LADY OF SECRETS • 1936 • Gering Marion • USA
LADY OF SHALLOT, THE • 1912 • Neame Elwin • UKN
LADY OF SHALOTT, THE • 1915 • Williams C. Jay • USA
LADY OF SPIRITS, A • 1914 • Williams C. Jay • USA
LADY OF THE BOULEVARDS (UKN) see **NANA** • 1934
LADY OF THE CAMELIAS, THE • 1922 • Collins Edwin J. • UKN
LADY OF THE CAMELIAS, THE see **DAMEN MED KAMELIORNA** • 1925
LADY OF THE CAMELIAS, THE see **DAME AUX CAMELIAS, LA** • 1981
LADY OF THE CAMELLIAS, THE see **SIGNORA DALLE CAMELIE, LA** • 1915
LADY OF THE CYCLAMEN, THE • 1915 • Le Saint Edward J. • USA
LADY OF THE DUGOUT • 1918 • Van Dyke W. S. • USA
LADY OF THE EVENING see **PUPA DEL GANGSTER, LA** • 1975
LADY OF THE HAREM, THE • 1926 • Walsh Raoul • USA
LADY OF THE HOUSE • 1978 • Nelson Ralph, Sherman Vincent • TVM • USA
LADY OF THE ISLAND, THE • 1914 • Crane Frank H. • USA
LADY OF THE LAKE, THE • 1912 • Blackton J. Stuart • USA
LADY OF THE LAKE, THE • 1928 • Fitzpatrick James A. • UKN
LADY OF THE LAKE, THE see **DONNA DEL LAGO, LA** • 1965
LADY OF THE LIGHTHOUSE, THE • 1915 • Lambart Harry, Ridgwell George • USA
LADY OF THE LINES, THE see **DAMA NA KOLEJICH** • 1965
LADY OF THE NIGHT • 1924 • Bell Monta • USA
LADY OF THE NIGHT • 1933 • Wellman William A. • USA • MIDNIGHT MARY
LADY OF THE NIGHT see **SIGNORA DELLA NOTTE, LA** • 1985
LADY OF THE NIGHT (UKN) see **LADY OF THE PAVEMENTS** • 1929
LADY OF THE PAVEMENTS • 1929 • Griffith D. W. • USA • LADY OF THE NIGHT (UKN)
LADY OF THE PHOTOGRAPH, THE • 1917 • Turbett Ben • USA
LADY OF THE ROSE (UKN) see **BRIDE OF THE REGIMENT** • 1930
LADY OF THE SEVEN MOONS • Khoury Samir • LBN
LADY OF THE SNOWS, THE • 1915 • *Travers Richard C.* • USA
LADY OF THE TRAIN, THE see **SAYIDAT EL KITAR** • 1951
LADY OF THE TRAM LINES see **DAMA NA KOLEJICH** • 1965
LADY OF THE TROPICS • 1939 • Conway Jack • USA
LADY OF THE TROPICS (UKN) see **HIS BROTHER'S WIFE** • 1936
LADY OF VENGEANCE • 1957 • Balaban Burt • UKN
LADY OF VICTORIES, THE • 1928 • Neill R. William • SHT • USA
LADY OGIN see **OGIN SAMA** • 1977
LADY ON A TRAIN • 1945 • David Charles • USA
LADY ON THE BUS • 1978 • d'Almeida Neville • BRZ
LADY ON THE COUCH • 1974 • Tribe Oscar • USA
LADY ON THE FENCE, THE see **NAAKT OVER DE SCHUTTING** • 1973
LADY ON THE RUN • 1974 • *Universal* • MXC
LADY ON THE TRACKS, THE (USA) see **DAMA NA KOLEJICH** • 1965
LADY OR THE LIONS, THE • 1908 • Wormald S. • UKN
LADY OR THE TIGER, THE • 1908 • *Edison* • USA
LADY OR THE TIGER?, THE • 1941 • Zinnemann Fred • SHT • USA
LADY OR THE TIGERS, THE • 1914 • Parsons Thomas • USA
LADY OSCAR see **BERUSAIYU NO BARA** • 1978
LADY OUTLAW • 1911 • Rolfe Alfred • ASL
LADY OWNER, THE • 1923 • West Walter • UKN
LADY PANAME • 1949 • Jeanson Henri • FRN
LADY PAYS OFF, THE • 1951 • Sirk Douglas • USA
LADY PEGGY'S ESCAPE • 1913 • Olcott Sidney • USA
LADY PLAY YOUR MANDOLIN • 1931-32 • Ising Rudolf • ANS • USA
LADY! PLEASE! • 1932 • *Sennett Mack (P)* • SHT • USA
LADY PLUMPTON'S MOTOR • 1904 • Fitzhamon Lewin • UKN
LADY POLICE, THE • 1912 • *Lubin* • USA
LADY POSSESSED • 1952 • Spier William, Kellino Roy • USA
LADY PRESIDENT, THE see **PRESIDENTESSA, LA** • 1952
LADY RAFFLES • 1928 • Neill R. William • USA
LADY RAFFLES RETURNS • 1916 • Cunard Grace, Ford Francis • SHT • USA • MASTER CROOKS, THE
LADY REFUSES, THE • 1931 • Archainbaud George • USA
LADY REPORTER (UKN) see **BULLDOG EDITION** • 1936
LADY ROBINHOOD • 1925 • Ince Ralph • USA
LADY ROSE'S DAUGHTER • 1920 • Ford Hugh • USA
LADY SAYS NO, THE • 1951 • Ross Frank • USA
LADY SCARFACE • 1941 • Woodruff Frank • USA
LADY SEEKS ROOM (USA) see **URILANY SZOBAT KERES** • 1938
LADY SINGS THE BLUES • 1972 • Furie Sidney J. • USA
LADY SLAVEY, THE • 1916 • Haldane Bert • UKN • SLAVEY'S LEGACY, THE
LADY STAY DEAD • 1982 • Bourke Terry • ASL
LADY SURRENDERS, A • 1930 • Stahl John M. • USA • BLIND WIVES (UKN)
LADY SURRENDERS, A (USA) see **LOVE STORY** • 1944
LADY TAKES A CHANCE, THE • 1943 • Seiter William A., Hathaway Henry (U/c) • USA • COWBOY AND THE GIRL, THE
LADY TAKES A FLYER, THE • 1958 • Arnold Jack • USA • GAME CALLED LOVE, A
LADY TAKES A SAILOR, THE • 1949 • Curtiz Michael • USA
LADY TEACHER see **TEACHARAMMA** • 1968
LADY TETLEY'S DECREE • 1920 • Paul Fred • UKN
LADY, THE DEVIL AND THE FASHION MODEL, THE see **DAME, DER TEUFEL UND DIE PROBIERMAMSELL, DIE** • 1918
LADY THE TIGER • 1908 • Porter Edwin S. • USA
LADY THIEF AND THE BAFFLED BOBBIES, THE • 1903 • Stow Percy? • UKN
LADY TO LOVE, A • 1929 • Sjostrom Victor • USA • SUNKISSED
LADY TRUCKERS see **FLATBED ANNIE & SWEETIEPIE: LADY TRUCKERS** • 1979
LADY TUBBS • 1935 • Crosland Alan • USA • GAY LADY, THE (UKN)
LADY TUNDRA • Miroshnichenko S. • DOC • USS
LADY TYPIST, THE • 1904 • *Warwick Trading Co* • UKN
LADY UNTOUCHABLE • 1968 • Balilla Bert, Ocampo Anthony • PHL
LADY VAMPIRE see **LEGENDARY CURSE OF LEMORA, THE** • 1974
LADY VANISHES, THE • 1938 • Hitchcock Alfred • UKN • LOST LADY
LADY VANISHES, THE • 1979 • Page Anthony • UKN
LADY VIOLETTA • 1922 • *Lukas Paul*
LADY WANTS MINK, THE • 1953 • Seiter William A. • USA
LADY WAS A GHOST, THE see **KAIDAN DOCHU** • 1958
LADY WAS TO DIE, A see **FORBIDDEN** • 1949
LADY WHIRLWIND • 1971 • *Mao Angela* • HKG
LADY WHO DARED, THE • 1931 • Beaudine William • USA • DEVIL'S PLAYGROUND
LADY WHO EARNS, THE see **UDYOGHASTHA** • 1967
LADY WHO LIED, THE • 1925 • Carewe Edwin • USA
LADY WINDERMERES FACHER • 1935 • Hilpert Heinz • FRG
LADY WINDERMERE'S FAN • 1916 • Paul Fred • UKN
LADY WINDERMERE'S FAN • 1925 • Lubitsch Ernst • USA
LADY WINDERMERE'S FAN see **HISTORIA DI UNA MALA MUJER** • 1948
LADY WINDERMERE'S FAN (UKN) see **FAN, THE** • 1949
LADY WITH A BADGE see **INCIDENT AT CRESTRIDGE** • 1981

LADY WITH A LITTLE DOG see **DAMA S SOBACHKOI** • 1960
LADY WITH A PAST • 1932 • Griffith Edward H. • USA • REPUTATION (UKN)
LADY WITH A RIBBON, A see **RIBON O MUSUBU FUJIN** • 1939
LADY WITH RED HAIR • 1940 • Bernhardt Curtis • USA
LADY WITH SEVEN FACES see **NANATSU NO KAO NO ONNA** • 1969
LADY WITH SHORT LEGS, THE see **DAMA S MALOU NOZKOU** • 1919
LADY WITH SUNFLOWERS, THE see **NAPRAFORGOS HOLGY, A** • 1918
LADY WITH THE BLACK GLOVE, THE see **DAME MIT DEM SCHWARZEN HANDSCHUH, DIE** • 1919
LADY WITH THE COLOURED GLOVES, THE see **DAMEN MED DE LYSER HANDSKER** • 1942
LADY WITH THE DOG, THE (USA) see **DAMA S SOBACHKOI** • 1960
LADY WITH THE LAMP, THE • 1951 • Wilcox Herbert • UKN
LADY WITH THE LIGHT GLOVES, THE (USA) see **DAMEN MED DE LYSER HANDSKER** • 1942
LADY WITH THE LITTLE DOG, THE see **DAMA S SOBACHKOI** • 1960
LADY WITH THE MASK, THE see **DAME MIT DER MASKE, DIE** • 1928
LADY WITH THE SMALL FOOT, THE see **DAMA S MALOU NOZKOU** • 1919
LADY WITHOUT CAMELIAS, THE (UKN) see **SIGNORA SENZA CAMILIE, LA** • 1953
LADY WITHOUT PASSPORT, A • 1950 • Lewis Joseph H. • USA • VISA
LADYBIRD, THE • 1927 • Lang Walter • USA
LADYBUG, THE see **BIEDRONKA** • 1964
LADYBUG, LADYBUG • 1963 • Perry Frank • USA
LADYFINGERS see **ALIAS LADYFINGERS** • 1921
LADYHAWKE • 1984 • Donner Richard • USA
LADYKILLERS • 1988 • Lewis Robert • USA
LADYKILLERS, THE • 1955 • Mackendrick Alexander • UKN
LADY'O see **BERUSAIYU NO BARA** • 1978
LADY'S FIRST LESSON ON THE BICYCLE, A • 1902 • Williamson James • UKN
LADY'S FROM KENTUCKY, THE • 1939 • Hall Alexander • USA
LADY'S MORALS, A • 1930 • Franklin Sidney A. • USA • JENNY LIND (UKN)
LADY'S NAME, A • 1918 • Edwards Walter • USA
LADY'S PROFESSION, A • 1933 • McLeod Norman Z. • USA • GOOD COMPANY
LADY'S PURSE, A • 1909 • *Essanay* • USA
LADY'S TAILOR, A • 1919 • Kenton Erle C., Grey Ray • SHT • USA
LAEGENS HUSTRU see **MENS PESTEN RASER** • 1913
LAEREAAR, ET • 1914 • Blom August • DNM • REFORMATION, THE
LAF U SRCU • 1982 • Milosevic Mica • YGS • GREAT GUY AT HEART, A
LAFAYETTE • 1962 • Dreville Jean • FRN, ITL • LAFAYETTE (UNA SPADA PER DUE BANDIERE) (ITL)
LAFAYETTE ESCADRILLE • 1958 • Wellman William A. • USA • HELL BENT FOR GLORY (UKN)
LAFAYETTE (UNA SPADA PER DUE BANDIERE) (ITL) see **LAFAYETTE** • 1962
LAFAYETTE, WE COME! • 1918 • Perret Leonce • USA
LAFFIN' FOOL, THE • 1927 • Cohn Bennett • USA
LAFFTIME • 1948 • Guiol Fred • USA
LAG MET WENA • 1977 • SAF
LAGAN • 1940 • *Sircar B. N. (P)* • IND
LAGARDERE • 1968 • Decourt Jean-Pierre • FRN • AVENTURES DE LAGARDERE, LES
LAGARITA CON PIEL DE MUJER, UNA (SPN) see **LUCERTOLA CON LA PELLE DI DONNA, UNA** • 1971
LAGARTA DO SOBREIRO, A • 1947 • Coelho Jose Adolfo • SHT • PRT
LAGE LANDEN, DE • 1961 • Sluizer George • DCS • NTH • HOLD BACK THE SEA
LAGER NIS • 1987 • Stamenkovic Miomir • YGS • CONCENTRATION CAMP NIS
LAGER SSADIS KASTRAT KOMMANDATUR • 1976 • Garrone Sergio • ITL • SSADIS LAGER KASTRAT KOMMANDATUR
LAGO DE LOS CISNES, EL • 1953 • Rovira Beleta Francisco • SPN
LAGO DEL MUERTOS VIVIENTES, EL (SPN) see **LAC DES MORTS-VIVANTS, LE** • 1980
LAGO DI SATANA, IL see **REVENGE OF THE BLOOD BEAST, THE** • 1966
LAGO SAGRADO, EL • 1982 • Boero Hugo • BLV
LAGOONS, THE • 1986 • Nicolle Douglas • DOC • CND
LAGOR I DUNKLET • 1942 • Ekman Hasse • SWD • FLAMES IN THE DARK
LAGOURDETTE, GENTLEMAN CAMBRIOLEUR • 1916 • Feuillade Louis • FRN
LAGRIMAS DE AMOR • 1958 • Blake Alfonso Corona • MXC
LAGRIMAS DE MI BARRIO • 1972 • *Estudios America* • MXC
LAGRIMAS DE SANGRE • 1946 • Pardave Joaquin • MXC
LAGRIMAS ROBADAS • 1953 • Soler Julian • MXC
LAGRIME E SORRISI • 1912 • Negroni Baldassare • ITL
LAGUNA DE DOS TIEMPOS • 1982 • Maldonado Eduardo • DOC • MXC • LAKE IN TWO TEMPOS
LAGUNA HEAT • 1987 • Langton Simon • TVM • USA
LAGUNA NEGRA, LA • 1952 • Ruiz-Castillo Arturo • SPN
LAGUNILLA, MI BARRIO • 1980 • Araiza Raul • MXC • LAGUNILLA, MY NEIGHBOUR
LAGUNILLA, MY NEIGHBOUR see **LAGUNILLA, MI BARRIO** • 1980
LAH NAL-KHULUD • 1952 • Barakat Henry • EGY • CHANT IMMORTEL
LAHEV A SVET • 1963 • Smetana Zdenek • CZC • WORLD IN A BOTTLE, THE
LAHIRE OU LE VALET DE COEUR • 1922 • Feuillade Louis • FRN
LAHN, AL- • 1957 • Salman Mohammed • LBN • PREMIERE MELODIE, LA
LAHOMA • 1920 • Lewis Edgar • USA
LAHUREY • 1989 • Ghimiray Tulshi • NPL
LAIA • 1970 • Lluch Vicente • SPN
LAIDE, LA • 1909 • Carre Michel • FRN
LAIERMANN, DER • 1920 • Fleck Jacob, Fleck Luise • AUS
LAILA • 1937 • Schneevoigt George • SWD, DNM • JAGAD AV VARGARNA
LAILA • 1958 • Husberg Rolf • SWD, FRG • LAILA -LIEBE UNTER DER MITTERNACHTSSONNE (FRG) ○ MAKE WAY FOR LILA (USA) ○ LILA
LAILA • 1990 • Islam Nazaral • PKS • LOVE
LAILA see **CALL OF GOD, THE** • 1927
LAILA, BENT AL SAHRA • 1937 • *Hafez Bahija* • EGY • LAILA, DAUGHTER OF THE DESERT
LAILA, DAUGHTER OF THE DESERT see **LAILA, BENT AL SAHRA** • 1937
LAILA -LIEBE UNTER DER MITTERNACHTSSONNE (FRG) see **LAILA** • 1958
LAILA MAJNU • 1979 • Mizan Ibne • BNG
LAILAT EL JUMAA • 1945 • Salim Kamel • EGY • FRIDAY EVENING
LAILAT EL KADR • 1952 • Sidky Hussein • EGY • NIGHT OF MIRACLES, THE
LAILAT ZAFAF • 1966 • Barakat Henry • EGY • NUIT DE NOCES
LAILATUN MIN UMRI • 1954 • Salem Atef • EGY • NUIT DE MA VIE, UNE
LAILATUN WAHIDA • 1968 • Arafa Saad • EGY • RIEN QU'UNE NUIT
LAILU YAKHAF ASH-SHAMS, AL- • 1966 • Badie Mustapha • ALG • NIGHT FEARS SUN ○ NUIT A PEUR DU SOLEIL, LA
LAILUN WA QIDHBAN • 1972 • Fahmy Ashraf • EGY • NUITS ET BARREAUX
LAIN ULKOPUOLELLA • 1988 • Makela Ville • FNL • BEYOND THE LAW
LAIR OF THE WHITE WORM, THE • 1989 • Russell Ken • UKN
LAIR OF THE WOLF, THE • 1912 • *Kalem* • USA
LAIR OF THE WOLF, THE • 1917 • Swickard Charles • USA
LAIRD OF MCGILLICUDDY, THE • 1913 • *Carney Augustus* • USA
LAIRD O'KNEES, THE • 1916 • Humphrey Orral • SHT • USA
LAIRD'S DAUGHTER, THE • 1912 • *Selig* • USA
LAISSE ALLER, C'EST UNE VALSE • 1970 • Lautner Georges • FRN • TAKE IT EASY, IT'S A WALTZ (USA) ○ TROUBLESHOOTERS (UKN)
LAISSE BETON • 1983 • Le Peron Serge • FRN
LAISSE-MOI REVER • 1978 • Menegoz Robert • DOC • FRN • DROLE DE DIAM'S
LAISSEZ-LES VIVRE! • 1969 • Zuber Christian • DOC • FRN
LAISSEZ-PASSER • 1976-77 • Bertolino Daniel, Floquet Francois • DSS • CND
LAISSEZ TIRER LES TIREURS • 1964 • Lefranc Guy • FRN, ITL • LASCIATE SPARARE.. CHI CI SA FARE (ITL)
LAJAWAB • 1950 • *Biswas Anil (M)* • IND
LAJKONIK • 1960 • Kruger M. • ANM • PLN
LAJLA • 1929 • Schneevoigt George • NRW
LAJWANTI • 1958 • Suri Narendra • IND
LAK YUM YA D'ALIM see **LAKA YOM YA ZALEM** • 1951
LAKA YOM YA ZALEM • 1951 • Abu Saif Salah • EGY • YOUR DAY WILL COME ○ LAK YUM YA D'ALIM
LAKE, THE see **ONNA NO MISUMI** • 1966
LAKE, THE see **GOL** • 1982
LAKE CONSTANCE • Zaorski Janusz • PLN
LAKE IN TWO TEMPOS see **LAGUNA DE DOS TIEMPOS** • 1982
LAKE MAN, THE see **HOMME DU LAC, L'** • 1962
LAKE OF DRACULA (USA) see **CHIOSU ME** • 1971
LAKE OF DREAMS, THE • 1912 • *Gordon Phyllis* • USA
LAKE OF FAIRIES, THE • 1963 • Sibianu Gheorghe • ANM • RMN • LAKE OF THE FAIRIES
LAKE OF ILLUSION see **MABOROSHI NO MIZUUMI** • 1982
LAKE OF SHARKS, THE see **TINTIN ET LE LAC AUX REQUINS** • 1972
LAKE OF TEARS see **UMI NO KOTO** • 1966
LAKE OF THE FAIRIES see **LAKE OF FAIRIES, THE** • 1963
LAKE OF THE LIVING DEAD, THE see **LAC DES MORTS-VIVANTS, LE** • 1980
LAKE PIPELINE • 1958 • Nadler Henry • UKN
LAKE PLACID SERENADE • 1944 • Sekely Steve • USA
LAKELAND STORY • 1950 • Barber Leslie • UKN
LAKHARANI • 1935 • Bedekar Vishram • IND
LAKHON MEIN EIK • 1967 • Mir Raza • PKS • ONE IN A MILLION
LAKI-LAKI PILIHAN • 1973 • Prijono Ami • INN
LAKME: LES STANCES • 1906 • Gilbert Arthur • UKN
LAKOTA • 1989 • Sholder Jack • USA
LAKSEMANA DO RE MI see **LAXMANA DO-RE-ME** • 1971
LAKSHMI OF THE HOME see **GRIHA LAKSHMI** • 1967
LAL AGHNIHAT ELMOUTAKASRA • 1964 • Malouf Yusuf • LBN • BROKEN WINGS, THE
LAL-E-YAMAN • 1934 • Wadia Homi • IND
LAL KUNWAR • 1952 • *Burman S. D. (M)* • IND
LALAI DREAMTIME • 1976 • Edols Michael • DOC • ASL
LALAPALOOSA • 1936 • Yarbrough Jean • SHT • USA
LALKA • 1968 • Has Wojciech J. • PLN • DOLL, THE
LALKA 594 • 1967 • Sanchez-Ariza Jose • PLN
LALKAR • 1969 • Sagar Ramanand • IND
LALLA E IL FUNGHETTO • 1948 • Pagot Nino, Pagot Tony • ITL
LALLA VINDER • 1932 • Schneevoigt George • DNM
LAM AH CHUN • *Fong-Fong Josephine Siu* • HKG
LAM AH CHUN BLUNDERS AGAIN see **LIN YA-CHEN LAO-HU YU HSIEH HSIA** • 1980
LAMA AVENGER, THE • *Li Bruce* • HKG
LAMA NEL CORPO, LA • 1966 • Scardamaglia Elio, De Felice Domenico • ITL, FRN • NUITS DE L'EPOUVANTE, LES (FRN) ○ MURDER CLINIC, THE (USA) ○ MURDER SOCIETY, THE ○ REVENGE OF THE LIVING DEAD ○ NIGHT OF TERRORS, THE ○ BLADE IN THE BODY, THE
LAMADEL GIUSTIZIERE, LA see **DON CESARE DI BAZAN** • 1942
LAMB • 1986 • Gregg Colin • UKN
LAMB, THE • 1915 • Cabanne W. Christy • USA
LAMB, THE • 1918 • Roach Hal • SHT • USA
LAMB, THE see **LAMM, DAS** • 1964
LAMB AND THE LION, THE • 1919 • Grandon Francis J. • USA
LAMB IN A JAM, A • 1945 • Sparber I. • ANS • USA
LAMB, THE WOMAN, THE WOLF, THE • 1914 • Dwan Allan • USA
LAMBADA • 1990 • Curi Giandomenico • ITL
LAMBAYE see **LAAMBAYE** • 1972
LAMBERT & CO. • 1964 • Pennebaker D. A. • SHT • USA
LAMBERT FUHLT SICH BEDROHT • 1949 • von Cziffra Geza • AUS
LAMBERT THE SHEEPISH LION • 1952 • Hannah Jack • ANS • USA
LAMBERTVILLE STORY, THE • 1949 • *Kaufman Boris (Ph)* • SHT • USA
LAMBETH WALK, THE • 1900 • Gibbons Walter • UKN
LAMBETH WALK, THE • 1939 • De Courville Albert • UKN
LAMBIRIS AGAINST THE OUTLAWS see **LAMBIRIS ENANTION TON PARANOMON, O** • 1967
LAMBIRIS ENANTION TON PARANOMON, O • 1967 • Yazis John • GRC • LAMBIRIS AGAINST THE OUTLAWS
LAMBS' ALLSTAR GAMBLER NO.3 • 1932 • Santley Joseph • SHT • USA
LAMBS OF DOVE COURT, THE • 1920 • Sandground Maurice • UKN
LAMBS WILL GAMBLE • 1930 • *Mintz Charles (P)* • ANS • USA
LAME BRAINS AND LUNATICS • 1918 • Howe J. A. • SHT • USA
LAME DEVIL, THE see **KULHAVY DABEL** • 1968
LAME DEVIL, THE see **DIABLO COJUELO, EL** • 1970
LAME DOGS TREACHERY • 1914 • *Kalem* • USA
LAME DUCK, THE • 1931 • Mainwaring Bernerd • UKN
LAME LENA AND CROSS-EYED PER see **HALTA LENA OCH VINDOGDE PER** • 1924
LAME LENA AND CROSS-EYED PER see **HALTA LENA OCH VINDOGDE PER** • 1933
LAME MAN, THE • 1913 • *Solax* • USA
LAMEGO • 1954 • Queiroga Perdigao • SHT • PRT
LAMENT FOR A BANDIT see **LLANTO POR UN BANDIDO** • 1964
LAMENT FOR ART O LAOGHAIRE, THE • 1975 • Quinn Bob • IRL
LAMENT OF A WHITE LILY see **SHIRAYURI WA NAGEKU** • 1925
LAMENT OF THE PATH, THE see **PATHER PANCHALI** • 1955
LAMENTATIONS see **DUNG-AW** • 1981
LAMENTATIONS: A MONUMENT TO THE DEAD WORLD • 1985 • Elder Bruce • CND
LAMENTATIONS SANS MUR see **MABKA BILA HA'IT** • 1974
LAMENTO • 1977 • Vallois Philippe • FRN
LAMES ET CUIVRES see **BLADES AND BRASS** • 1967
LAMIEL • 1967 • Aurel Jean • FRN, ITL
LAMJATA • 1974 • Dinov Todor • BUL
LAMM, DAS • 1964 • Staudte Wolfgang • FRG • LAMB, THE
LAMORE • 1980 • Mavrikios Dimitris • GRC
L'AMOUR THE MERRIER • 1957 • Kneitel Seymour • ANS • USA
LAMP, THE • 1987 • Chaney Warren • USA
LAMP, THE see **LAMPA** • 1959
LAMP, THE see **OUTING, THE** • 1987
LAMP IN ASSASSIN MEWS, THE • 1962 • Grayson Godfrey • UKN
LAMP IN THE DESERT • 1922 • Thornton F. Martin • UKN
LAMP OF DESTINY, THE • 1919 • Butler Alexander • UKN
LAMP OF HASHEM, THE see **KANDIL OM HASHEM** • 1968
LAMP POST FAVORITES • 1948 • Moore Harold James • SHT • USA
LAMP STILL BURNS, THE • 1943 • Elvey Maurice • UKN
LAMP THAT LIGHTS THE HOME, THE see **GHAR KA CHIRAG** • 1967
LAMP THAT SMOKES, THE see **LAMPE QUI FILE, LA** • 1909
LAMPA • 1959 • Polanski Roman • PLN • LAMP, THE
LAMPAANSYOJAT • 1972 • Huunonen Seppo • FNL • MUTTON EATERS, THE ○ SHEEP EATERS, THE
LAMPADA ALLA FINESTRA, UNA • 1940 • Talamo Gino • ITL
LAMPADA DELLA NONNA, LA • 1913 • Maggi Luigi • ITL
LAMPE QUI FILE, LA • 1909 • Cohl Emile • ANS • FRN • LAMP THAT SMOKES, THE ○ SMOKING LAMP, THE
LAMPENFIEBER • 1960 • Hoffmann Kurt • FRG
LAMPES MAZDA, LES • 1940 • Grimault Paul • ANS • FRN • MAZDA LAMPS, THE
LAMPLIGHTER, THE • 1921 • Mitchell Howard M. • USA
LAMPLIGHTER, THE • 1937 • *Lantz Walter (P)* • ANS • USA
LAMURU • 1933 • Gosho Heinosuke • JPN • AMOUR, L'
LAN ATARIF • 1961 • el Sheikh Kamal • EGY • JE N'AVOUERAI PAS ○ CHANTAGE
LANA • 1985 • SAF
LANA TURNER see **MORE MILK, EVETTE** • 1965
LANCASHIRE AT WORK AND PLAY • 1934 • Taylor Donald • DOC • UKN
LANCASHIRE LASS, A • 1915 • Wilson Frank • UKN
LANCASHIRE LUCK • 1937 • Cass Henry • UKN
LANCASTER MILLER AFFAIR, THE see **VICTIMS OF PASSION** • 1986
LANCE ET COMPTE • 1987 • Lord Jean-Claude • SER • CND • HE SHOOTS, HE SCORES
LANCE MAIOR • 1968 • Back Silvio • BRZ • BIGGER PLAY
LANCELOT AND GUINEVERE • 1962 • Wilde Cornel • UKN • SWORD OF LANCELOT
LANCELOT DU LAC • 1974 • Bresson Robert • FRN, ITL • LANCELOT OF THE LAKE (USA) ○ GRAAL, LE ○ GRAIL, THE
LANCELOT OF THE LAKE (USA) see **LANCELOT DU LAC** • 1974
LANCEMENT D'UN NAVIRE A LA CIOTAT • 1895 • Lumiere Louis • FRN
LANCER SPY • 1937 • Ratoff Gregory • USA
LANCIERI NERI, I • 1963 • Gentilomo Giacomo • ITL, FRN • CHARGE OF THE BLACK LANCERS (USA) ○ LANCIERS NOIRS, LES (FRN)
LANCIERS NOIRS, LES (FRN) see **LANCIERI NERI, I** • 1963
LAND see **ZEMYA** • 1957
LAND, THE • 1942 • Flaherty Robert • DOC • USA
LAND, THE • 1955 • Shvachko A., Buchma A.
LAND, THE see **ZEME ZEMI** • 1962
LAND, THE see **ARD, EL** • 1969
LAND ACROSS SEA, THE see **TANAH SABRANG** • 1938
LAND AM NIL • 1950 • Oertel Curt • FRG
LAND AND PEOPLE see **ZEMLYA I LYUDI** • 1955

LAND AND SEA • 1913 • Collins Edwin J. • UKN
LAND AND SONS see **LAND OG SYNIR** • 1978
LAND AND THE LAW (UKN) see **BLACK MARKET RUSTLERS** • 1943
LAND APART • 1974 • SAF
LAND AT LOW TIDE • 1896 • Acres Birt • UKN
LAND BARON OF SAN TEE, THE • 1912 • Dwan Allan • USA
LAND BEFORE TIME, THE • 1989 • Bluth Don • ANM • USA
LAND BEYOND THE LAW • 1937 • Eason B. Reeves • USA
LAND BEYOND THE LAW, THE • 1927 • Brown Harry J. • USA
LAND BEYOND THE SUNSET, THE • 1912 • Dawley J. Searle • USA
LAND DER FINSTERNIS, DAS • 1921 • *Sannom Emilie* • FRG
LAND DER LIEBE • 1937 • Schunzel Reinhold • FRG
LAND DES LACHELNS, DAS • 1930 • Reichmann Max • FRG
LAND DES LACHELNS, DAS • 1952 • Deppe Hans • FRG • LAND OF SMILES (USA)
LAND DES SCHWEIGENS UND DER DUNKELKEIT • 1971 • Herzog Werner • FRG • LAND OF SILENCE AND DARKNESS
LAND FOR MEN • 1945 • Cherry Evelyn Spice, Cherry Lawrence W. • DOC • CND
LAND FOR ROSE see **TERRA PARA ROSE** • 1988
LAND GIRL • 1942 • Page John • UKN
LAND IN A TRANCE see **TERRA EM TRANSE** • 1967
LAND IN ANGUISH see **TERRA EM TRANSE** • 1967
LAND IN TRUST • 1948 • Garceau Raymond • DCS • CND • SAUVONS NOS SOLS
LAND IS A SINFUL SONG, THE see **MAA ON SYNTINEN LAULAU** • 1973
LAND IS BRIGHT, THE • 1943 • Wood Sam • DOC • USA
LAND IS FOREVER LAND see **TERRA E SEMPRE TERRA** • 1951
LAND JUST OVER YONDER, THE • 1916 • *Chesebro George N.* • USA
LAND LUBBERS, THE • 1916 • *Pokes & Jabbs* • USA
LAND MUST PROVIDE, THE • 1968 • Owtram Philip • UKN
LAND O' LIZARDS • 1916 • Borzage Frank • USA
LAND OF ADVENTURE, THE • 1915 • Beaumont Harry • USA
LAND OF ANGELS, THE see **ANGYALOK FOLDJE** • 1962
LAND OF BEAUTIFUL FLOWERS, THE see **PAIS DE BELLA FLOR, EL** • 1975
LAND OF BUDDHA, THE • Chaudhri Amin • USA
LAND OF DEAD THINGS, THE • 1913 • Morty Frank • USA
LAND OF DEATH, THE • 1912 • Dwan Allan • USA
LAND OF DESIRE, THE see **SKEPP TILL INDIALAND** • 1947
LAND OF DOOM • 1984 • Maris Peter • USA
LAND OF DREAMS, THE see **SAGOLANDET** • 1988
LAND OF ENCHANTMENT: SOUTHWEST U.S.A. see **SOUTHWEST, THE** • 1945
LAND OF FATE, THE see **PRAESTEN I VEJLBY** • 1920
LAND OF FIGHTING MEN • 1938 • James Alan • USA
LAND OF FIRE see **TIERRA DE FUEGO** • 1965
LAND OF FIVE CONTINENTS, THE • 1960 • Hadzic Fadil • YGS
LAND OF FUN, THE • 1941 • Marcus Sid • ANS • USA
LAND OF FURY (USA) see **SEEKERS, THE** • 1954
LAND OF GIANTS, THE see **MATERIK GIGANTOV** • 1975
LAND OF GRACE see **TIERRA DE GRACIA** • 1988
LAND OF HEART'S DESIRE see **ARCADIANS, THE** • 1927
LAND OF HOPE, THE • 1921 • Griffith Edward H. • USA
LAND OF HOPE AND GLORY • 1909 • Yates Frank D. • UKN
LAND OF HOPE AND GLORY • 1927 • Knoles Harley • UKN
LAND OF HUNTED MEN • 1943 • Luby S. Roy • USA
LAND OF JAZZ, THE • 1920 • Furthman Jules G. • USA
LAND OF LIARS see **ARD EL NEFAK** • 1968
LAND OF LIBERTY • 1958 • Werner Gosta • SHT • SWD
LAND OF LONG SHADOWS, THE • 1917 • Van Dyke W. S. • USA
LAND OF LOST WATCHES • 1951 • Kneitel Seymour • ANS • USA
LAND OF LOVE'S DREAMS, THE see **ENCHANTED CITY, THE** • 1921
LAND OF MIGHT, THE • 1912 • Fahrney Milton • USA
LAND OF MIRACLES • 1945 • Vinnitsky Andrei • USS
LAND OF MIRAGES, THE see **DELIBABOK ORSZAGA** • 1984
LAND OF MISSING MEN, THE • 1930 • McCarthy John P. • USA
LAND OF MY FATHERS • 1921 • Rains Fred • UKN
LAND OF MY FATHERS • 1951 • Fancey E. J. • UKN
LAND OF MYSTERY, THE • 1920 • Shaw Harold • UKN
LAND OF NO RETURN, THE • 1975 • Bateman Kent • USA • CHALLENGE TO SURVIVE ○ SURVIVAL ELEMENT ○ SNOWMAN
LAND OF NOWHERE, THE • 1917 • *Miller Rube* • SHT • USA
LAND OF OPPORTUNITY, THE • 1920 • Ince Ralph • SHT • USA
LAND OF OUR FATHERS see **ZEMLYA OTTSOV** • 1968
LAND OF OURS, A see **NASHA ZEMYA** • 1953
LAND OF OZ, THE • 1910 • *Selig* • USA
LAND OF PLENTY see **ER ET YNDIGT LAND, DER** • 1983
LAND OF PLENTY, THE see **CUCCAGNA, LA** • 1962
LAND OF PROMISE • 1946 • Rotha Paul • DOC • UKN
LAND OF PROMISE, THE • 1912 • *Imp* • USA
LAND OF PROMISE, THE • 1917 • Kaufman Joseph • USA
LAND OF PROMISE, THE • 1935 • Leman Juda
LAND OF PROMISE, THE (UKN) see **HITCHIN' POSTS** • 1920
LAND OF PROMISE (UKN) see **ZIEMIA OBIECANA** • 1974
LAND OF RYE see **RAGENS RIKE** • 1929
LAND OF RYE see **RAGENS RIKE** • 1951
LAND OF SILENCE AND DARKNESS see **LAND DES SCHWEIGENS UND DER DUNKELKEIT** • 1971
LAND OF SMILES (USA) see **LAND DES LACHELNS, DAS** • 1952
LAND OF THE ALVARGONZALEZ see **TIERRA DE LOS ALVARGONZALEZ, LA** • 1969
LAND OF THE BLUE DAUGHTERS, THE • 1930 • Foster Lewis R. • SHT • USA
LAND OF THE BLUE MOUNTAINS, THE see **SINEGORIYA** • 1945
LAND OF THE CANNIBALS, THE see **CHEZ LES MANGEURS D'HOMMES** • 1928
LAND OF THE FATHERS • Sluizer George • LBN
LAND OF THE FATHERS, LAND OF THE SONS • 1989 • Hoffmann Nico • FRG
LAND OF THE FREE, THE see **ONE MORE AMERICAN** • 1918
LAND OF THE GIANTS: GULLIVER'S TRAVELS PART 2 see **GULLIVER'S TRAVELS: PART 2** • 1983
LAND OF THE INCAS • 1937 • Fitzpatrick James • SHT • USA
LAND OF THE LAWLESS • 1927 • Buckingham Thomas • USA
LAND OF THE LAWLESS • 1947 • Hillyer Lambert • USA
LAND OF THE LOST, THE • 1914 • Sheldon Roy • USA
LAND OF THE LOST, THE • 1948 • Sparber I. • ANS • USA
LAND OF THE LOST JEWELS • 1950 • Sparber I. • ANS • USA
LAND OF THE MIDNIGHT FUN • 1939 • Avery Tex • ANS • USA
LAND OF THE MINOTAUR • 1976 • Carayannis Costa • USA, UKN • DEVIL'S MEN, THE ○ MINOTAUR ○ DEVIL'S PEOPLE, THE
LAND OF THE MONSTERS • 1975 • Malatesta Guido • ITL
LAND OF THE NURSERY RHYMES, THE • 1912 • Melford Mark • UKN
LAND OF THE OPEN RANGE • 1942 • Killy Edward • USA
LAND OF THE OUTLAWS • 1944 • Hillyer Lambert • USA
LAND OF THE PHARAOHS • 1955 • Hawks Howard • USA
LAND OF THE SILVER FOX • 1928 • Enright Ray • USA
LAND OF THE SIX GUNS • 1940 • Johnston Raymond K. • USA
LAND OF THE SOVIETS see **STRANA SOVIETOV** • 1937
LAND OF THE SUN • 1932 • Stern Seymour • USA
LAND OF THE UNDAUNTED see **WU T'U WU MIN** • 1975
LAND OF THE WATTLE see **SQUATTER'S DAUGHTER, THE** • 1910
LAND OF TOMORROW • 1950 • Coffey Frank • DOC • ASL
LAND OF TOYS • 1940 • Obratsov • SHT • USS
LAND OF WANTED MEN • 1932 • Fraser Harry L. • USA
LAND OF WATER • 1940 • Pearson George • DCS • UKN
LAND OF WHITE ALICE • 1959 • Van Dyke Willard • DOC • USA
LAND OG SYNIR • 1978 • Gudmundsson Agust • ICL • LAND AND SONS
LAND OHNE FRAUEN, DAS (FRG) see **TERRA SENZA DONNE** • 1929
LAND RAIDERS • 1970 • Juran Nathan • USA • DAY OF THE LAND GRABBER
LAND SALESMAN, THE • 1913 • Lehrman Henry, Sennett Mack (Spv) • USA
LAND SHARKS VS. SEA DOGS • 1912 • *Bosworth Hobart* • USA
LAND SHORT OF PEOPLE • 1947 • DOC • UKN • THIS MODERN AGE NO.15
LAND THAT TIME FORGOT, THE • 1974 • Connor Kevin • UKN, USA
LAND THIEVES, THE • 1911 • Dwan Allan • USA
LAND UNKNOWN, THE • 1957 • Vogel Virgil W. • USA • HIDDEN VALLEY, THE
LAND VAN MIJN OUDERS, HET • 1983 • Bloem Marion • DOC • NTH
LAND WE LIVE IN, THE see **MY COUNTRY** • 1922
LAND WE LOVE, THE see **HERO'S ISLAND** • 1962
LAND WITHOUT BREAD see **HURDES, LAS** • 1932
LAND WITHOUT MUSIC • 1936 • Forde Walter • UKN • FORBIDDEN MUSIC (USA)
LANDAMANN STAUFFACHER • 1941 • Lindtberg Leopold • SWT
LANDARZTIN, DIE • 1958 • May Paul • FRG
LANDFALL • 1949 • Annakin Ken • UKN
LANDFALL • 1975 • Maunder Paul • NZL
LANDFALL ASIA • 1964 • Sparling Gordon • CND
LANDING • 1974 • Kiisk Kaliu • USS
LANDING AT LOW TIDE • 1899 • *Haydon & Urry* • UKN
LANDING OF THE HOSE REEL, THE • 1915 • Neilan Marshall • USA
LANDING OF THE PILGRIMS • 1940 • Rasinski Connie • ANS • USA
LANDING OF THE PILGRIMS, THE • 1915 • West Langdon • USA
LANDING STRIPLING • 1962 • Deitch Gene • ANS • USA
LANDLADIES BEWARE • 1913 • Aylott Dave? • UKN
LANDLADY, THE • 1920 • *Franey William* • USA
LANDLADY, THE • 1938 • Boulting Roy • UKN
LANDLADY'S PORTRAIT, THE • 1909 • *Edison* • USA
LANDLESS WOLVES, THE see **MEKANSIZ KURTLAR** • 1968
LANDLOPER, THE • 1918 • Irving George • USA
LANDLORD, THE • 1922 • Kenton Erle C. • SHT • USA
LANDLORD, THE • 1970 • Ashby Hal • USA
LANDLORD, THE see **LUSTY LANDLORD, THE** • 1970
LANDLORDING IT • 1953 • Barclay David • SHT • USA
LANDLORD'S TROUBLES, A • 1913 • Nicholls George, Sennett Mack (Spv) • USA
LANDLUBBER, THE • 1912 • *Roland Ruth* • USA
LANDLUBBER, THE • 1922 • Roach Hal • SHT • USA
LANDON'S LEGACY • 1916 • Turner Otis • USA
LANDPOMMERANZE, DIE • 1919 • Schmelter Franz • FRG
LANDRU • 1923 • AUS
LANDRU • 1962 • Chabrol Claude • FRN, ITL • BLUEBEARD
LANDRUSH • 1946 • Keays Vernon • USA • CLAW STRIKES, THE (UKN)
LANDSBYKIRKEN see **DANSKE LANDSBYKIRKE, DEN** • 1947
LANDSCAPE • 1969 • Rimmer David • CND
LANDSCAPE • 1972 • Engel Jules • ANS • USA
LANDSCAPE • 1974 • Lenica Jan • ANS • USA
LANDSCAPE AFTER BATTLE see **KRAJOBRAZ PO BITWIE** • 1970
LANDSCAPE AFTER THE BATTLE see **KRAJOBRAZ PO BITWIE** • 1970
LANDSCAPE IN THE MIST see **TOPIO STIN OMIHLI** • 1988
LANDSCAPE IN WHITE see **HVITT LANDSKAP** • 1984
LANDSCAPE OF GEOMETRY, THE • 1982 • Lavut Martin • SER • CND
LANDSCAPE WITH A HERO, THE see **PEJZAZ Z BOHATEREM** • 1970
LANDSCAPE WITH FURNITURE see **KRAJINA S NABYTKEM** • 1985
LANDSCAPE WITH HERO see **PEJZAZ Z BOHATEREM** • 1970
LANDSCAPES OF KEWLIN, THE • 1959 • Yu Ch'L • CHN
LANDSCAPES OF SOUTHERN CHINA, THE see **DEL-KINA TAJAIN** • 1957
LANDSCHAFTSGARTNER, DIE • 1969 • Gloor Kurt • SWT
LANDSFLYKTIGE, DE • 1921 • Stiller Mauritz • SWD • IN SELF DEFENSE (USA) ○ EXILES, THE (UKN) ○ EMIGRANTS, THE ○ GUARDED LIPS
LANDSHOVDINGENS DOTTRAR • 1915 • Sjostrom Victor • SWD • GOVERNOR'S DAUGHTERS, THE
LANDSKAMP • 1932 • Skoglund Gunnar • SWD
LANDSLIDE • 1937 • Pedelty Donovan • UKN
LANDSLIDE • 1960 • Sarkisov G. • USS
LANDSTORMENS LILLA ARGBIGGA • 1941 • Jerring Nils • SWD • LITTLE SHREW OF THE VETERAN RESERVES
LANDSTORMENS LILLA LOTTA • 1939 • Hildebrand Weyler • SWD • LITTLE WRAC OF THE VETERAN RESERVES
LANDSTRASSE UND GROSSTADT • 1921 • Wilhelm Carl • FRG
LANDSTREICHER, DIE • 1916 • Fleck Jacob, Fleck Luise • AUS
LANDSTREICHER, DIE • 1937 • Lamac Carl • FRG • HOBOES, THE
LANDSTRYKERE • 1988 • Solum Ola • NRW • WAYFARERS ○ WANDERERS
LANDVOGT VON GREIFENSEE, DER • 1979 • Bolliger Wilfried • SWT
LANE IN PARADISE, A see **ULICKA V RAJI** • 1936
LANE THAT HAD NO TURNING, THE • 1922 • Fleming Victor • USA
LANFIERE see **KOLONIE LANFIERI** • 1969
LANFIERI COLONY, THE see **KOLONIE LANFIERI** • 1969
LANG-HUA • 1976 • Li Hsing • HKG • WAVES, THE
LANG IST DER WEG • 1948 • Fredersdorf Herbert B., Goldstein Marek • FRG • LONG IS THE ROAD
LANG-LASSE I DELSBO • 1949 • Johansson Ivar • SWD • TALL LASSE FROM DELSBO
LANG-TZU YI CHAO • 1979 • HKG • LEGENDARY STRIKE, THE
LANGA VAGEN, DEN • 1947 • Bergstrom Torsten • SWD • LONG ROAD
LANGAGE DE L'ECRAN • 1947 • Rozier Jacques • SHT • FRN
LANGAGE DU SOURIRE, LE see **QUATRE SOURIRES, LES** • 1958
LANGE BEINE, LANGE FINGER • 1966 • Vohrer Alfred • FRG
LANGE RITT ZUR SCHOLE, DER • GDR • LONG RIDE TO SCHOOL, THE
LANGER SAMSTAG • 1989 • Muller Hans Christian • FRG • LONG SATURDAY
LANGFORD REED'S LIMERICKS • 1935 • Barrington A. F. C. • UKN
LANGIT AT LUPA • 1967 • D'Lanor • PHL • HEAVEN AND EARTH
LANGIT AY PARA SA AKIN, ANG • 1968 • de Guzman Armando • PHL • HEAVEN IS FOR ME
LANGIT PETANG • 1982 • Mohd Shahrom • MLY
LANGIT SA LUPA, ANG • 1968 • Nepomuceno Luis • PHL • HEAVEN ON EARTH
LANGIT TIDAK SELALU CERAH • 1979 • Sudarmadji S. • MLY • TEARS AND SORROW
LANGKAH SUMBANG • 1978 • Lokman Z. • MLY
LANGKHA DEANG • 1987 • Mukdasanit Euthana • THL • RED ROOF, THE
LANGLOIS • 1972 • Hershon Eila, Guerra Roberto • FRN
LANGOK • 1941 • Kalmar Laszlo • HNG
LANGOUSTE AU PETIT DEJEUNER, UNE (FRN) see **ARAGOSTE A COLAZIONE** • 1979
LANGS ONGEBAENDE KLINGEN • 1948 • van der Horst Herman • NTH • ALONG UNTRODDEN DUNES
LANGSAME TOD, DER • 1920 • Wilhelm Carl • FRG • NACH LIEBE SCHMACHTEN, DIE ○ VERLEUGNETEN JAHRE, DIE
LANGSAMER SOMMER • 1976 • Cook John • AUS • SLOW SUMMER
LANGT BORTA OCH NARA • 1977 • Ahrne Marianne • SWD • NEAR AND FAR AWAY
LANGTA EFTER KARLEK • 1968 • Broberg Robban • SWD • LONGING FOR LOVE
LANGTAN see **NATTLEK** • 1966
LANGTAN TILL HAVET • 1931 • Brunius John W. • SWD • LONGING FOR THE SEA
LANGTURSCHAUFFOR • 1981 • Ringaard Peter D. • DNM • TRUCK DRIVER
LANGUAGE ALL MY OWN, A • 1935 • Fleischer Dave • ANS • USA
LANGUAGE OF FACES • 1963 • Korty John • DCS • USA
LANGUAGE OF LOVE 2 see **KARLEKENS SPRAK 2** • 1974
LANGUAGE OF LOVE (UKN) see **KARLEKENS SPRAK** • 1969
LANGUAGE OF THE DUMB, THE • 1915 • Hansel Howell? • USA
LANGUE DE LA HONTE, LA • 1979 • Durand Philippe • FRN • YEZH AR VEZH
LANGUE DE VELOURS • 1973 • Roy Jean-Claude • FRN
LANGUE DOCIENNE, LA • 1976 • Leenhardt Roger • DCS • FRN
LANGUE DU QUEBEC, LA • 1972 • Lamothe Arthur • DCS • CND
LANGUE PARLEE ET LANGUE ECRITE • 1972 • Lamothe Arthur • DCS • CND
LANGUES CHAUDES • 1977 • Desvilles Jean • FRN
LANGUES DE PETITES FILLES • Love John • FRN
LANGUES DE VELOURS • 1975 • Roy Jean-Claude • FRN
LANGUES PROFONDES • Blanc Michel • FRN
LANGUES SALOPES • Renier Gerard • FRN
LANGUIDI BACI.. PERFIDE CAREZZE • 1977 • Angeli Alfredo • ITL
LANIGAN'S RABBI • 1976 • Antonio Lou • TVM • USA • FRIDAY THE RABBI SLEPT LATE
LANK FLOWER HAS ALREADY FLOWN, THE see **DEJA S'ENVOLE LA FLEUR MAIGRE** • 1960
LANKA DAHAN • 1918 • Phalke Dada • IND • BURNING OF LANKA, THE ○ BURNING OF DAHAN, THE
LANKA DAHAN • 1935 • Rau Sadasiva • IND • BURNING OF DAHAN ○ BURNING OF CEYLON
LANKA LAXMI • 1927 • *Kanhere Prod.* • IND
LANKADAHAN • 1933 • *Shree Krishna* • IND • BURNING OF DAHAN, THE ○ BURNING OF CEYLON, THE

LANKAKI LADI • 1925 • *Navinchandra* • IND • FAIRY OF CEYLON (USA)
LANNEKEN WEDDING, THE see **HOCHZEIT VON LANNECKEN, DIE** • 1964
LANTERN, THE see **LUCERNA** • 1925
LANTERN, THE see **UTA ANDON** • 1960
LANTERN HILL • 1990 • Sullivan Kevin • CND
LANTERN MYSTERY, THE • 1938 • Tyrlova Hermina, Dodel Karel • ANM • CZC
LANTERN OF DIOGENES, THE see **LINTERNA DE DIOGENES, LA** • 1925
LANTERN STREET, THE see **TENG-LUNG CHIEH** • 1977
LANTERN UNDER A FULL MOON see **MEIGATSU SOMATO** • 1951
LANTERNA DEL DIAVOLO, LA • 1931 • Campogalliani Carlo • ITL
LANTERNE DES MORTS, LA • 1949 • de Casembroot Jacques • FRN
LANTERNE MAGIQUE, LA • 1903 • Melies Georges • FRN • MAGIC LANTERN, THE (USA)
LANY ELINDUL, EGY • 1937 • Sekely Steve • HNG • GIRL'S START, A
LANYARCOK TUKORBEN • 1973 • Ban Robert • HNG • PARALLEL FACES
LANZA TUS PENAS AL VIENTO • 1966 • Soler Julian • MXC
LANZAS COLORADAS, LAS • 1972 • Briz Jose • VNZ, SPN, FRN • COLOURED LANCES, THE
LAO • 1968 • Bedel Jean-Pierre • CND
LAO JING • 1985 • Wu Tianming • CHN • OLD WELL, THE
LAO-SHIH SZU-KA-YEH-TA • 1983 • Sung Ts'Un-Shou • TWN • LILY IN THE VALLEY, A
LAO-SHIH, SZU-TI-YEH-K'A • 1982 • Sung Ts'Un-Shou • TWN • GOODBYE, MY TEACHER
LAOKOON • 1970 • Mergl Vaclav • ANS • CZC
LAONIANG GOUSAO • 1985 • Ye Jianxing • CHN • SHOW
LAONIANG GOUSAO • 1987 • Shu Kei • HKG • SOUL
LAOS, THE FORGOTTEN WAR see **GUERRA OLVIDADA, LA** • 1967
LAPIN 360 • 1972 • Lewis Robert Michael • USA
LAPIN A DEUX TETES, JOURNAL FILME NO.6, LE • 1981 • Morder Joseph • FRN
LAPINS VERSUS POISSONS • 1970 • Moreau Michel • DCS • CND
LAPIQUE • 1965 • Reichenbach Francois • SHT • FRN
LAPIS • 1963-66 • Whitney James • ANS • USA
LAPIZ MAGICO, EL • 1981 • Darino Eduardo • URG
LAPLANDERS, THE see **SAME-JAKKI** • 1957
LAPP BLOOD see **LAPPBLOD** • 1948
LAPPBLOD • 1948 • Frisk Ragnar • SWD • LAPP BLOOD
LAPPLANDER'S LIFE, THE see **SAME AELLIN** • 1972
LAPSUUTENI • 1967 • Mollberg Rauni • MTV • FNL • MY CHILDHOOD
LAPUALAISMORSIAN • 1967 • Niskanen Mikko • FNL • GIRL OF FINLAND
LAPUTA • 1986 • Sanders Helma • FRG
LAR DE CATASSOL, O • 1959 • Ribeiro Antonio Lopes • SHT • PRT
LARAMIE • 1949 • Nazarro Ray • USA
LARAMIE KID, THE • 1935 • Webb Harry S. • USA
LARAMIE MOUNTAINS • 1952 • Nazarro Ray • USA • MOUNTAIN DESPERADOES (UKN)
LARAMIE TRAIL, THE • 1944 • English John • USA
LARARINNA PA VIFT • 1941 • Larsson Borje • SWD • SCHOOLMISTRESS ON THE SPREE
LARCENY • 1948 • Sherman George • USA
LARCENY IN HER HEART • 1946 • Newfield Sam • USA
LARCENY INC. • 1942 • Bacon Lloyd • USA
LARCENY LANE (UKN) see **BLONDE CRAZY** • 1931
LARCENY OF THE AIR • 1937 • Pichel Irving • USA
LARCENY STREET (USA) see **SMASH AND GRAB** • 1937
LARCENY WITH MUSIC • 1943 • Lilley Edward • USA
LARGA AGONIA DE LOS PECES FUERA DEL AGUA ,LA • 1970 • Rovira Beleta Francisco • SPN
LARGA NOCHE DE JULIO, LA • 1974 • Comeron Luis Jose • SPN
LARGA NOCHE DEL AMOR, LA • 1968 • Madrid Jose Luis • SPN
LARGAS VACACIONES DEL 36, LAS • 1975 • Camino Jaime • SPN • LONG HOLIDAYS OF 36, THE
LARGE NIGHT, A • 1913 • *Eclair* • USA
LARGE ROPE, THE • 1953 • Rilla Wolf • UKN • LONG ROPE, THE
LARGER THAN LIFE see **HE COULDN'T SAY NO** • 1938
LARGEST BOAT EVER LAUNCHED SIDEWAYS, THE • 1913 • Sennett Mack • USA
LARGHETTO • 1967 • Kondek Waclaw • PLN
LARGO • 1970 • Blazekovic Milan, Ilic Bronko • ANS • YGS
LARGO DIA DEL AGUILA, EL (SPN) see **BATTAGLIA D'INGHILTERRA, LA** • 1969
LARGO RETORNO, UN • 1974 • Lazaga Pedro • SPN • LONG RETURNING, A ○ FOR THE LOVE OF ANNA
LARGO VIAJE • 1967 • Kaulen Patricio • CHL • LONG JOURNEY
LARGO VIAJE HACIA LA MUERTE, UN • 1968 • Fernandez Unsain Jose Maria • MXC • LONG VOYAGE TOWARDS DEATH, A
LARGUEZ LES VOILES see **SECRET DU FLORIDA, LE** • 1946
LARIAT KID, THE • 1929 • Eason B. Reeves • USA
LARIAT THROWER, THE (?) see **CROSS ROADS** • 1922
LARIATS AND SIX SHOOTERS • 1931 • Neitz Alvin J. • USA • FEARLESS DEPUTY, THE (UKN)
LARK, THE see **RUN FOR YOUR MONEY, A** • 1949
LARK, THE see **PACSIRTA** • 1964
LARK IN CAMP, A • 1900 • *Paul R. W.* • UKN
LARK STILL SINGS, THE • 1954 • Wedderburn Hugh • UKN
LARKS IN TOYLAND • 1913 • Cooper Arthur • UKN
LARKS ON A STRING see **SKRIVANCI NA NITICH** • 1969
LARKS ON A THREAD see **SKRIVANCI NA NITICH** • 1969
LARK'S SONG, THE see **SKRIVANCI PISEN** • 1933
LARM UM WEIDEMANN • 1935 • Hubler-Kahla J. A. • FRG
LARME DANS L'OCEAN, UNE • 1971 • Glaeser Henri • FRN
LARMES DE COLETTE, LES • 1926 • Barberis Rene • FRN
LARMES DE CROCODILE, LES • 1965 • Delpire Robert • SHT • FRN
LARMES DE PAIX • 1970 • Marzouk Said • SHT • EGY • TEARS OF PEACE
LARMES DE SANG • 1979 • Akika Ali, Autissier Anne-Marie • DOC • FRN, ALG
LAROUSSI AND THE FANTASIA • 1981 • Shatalow Peter • MTV • CND
LARRIMORE CASE, THE • 1916 • *Sisson Vera* • SHT • USA
LARRY • 1974 • Graham William A. • TVM • USA
LARRY AND 'ERB GET A JOB • 1915 • *A.a.a.* • UKN
LARRY JOHNSON • 1970 • Hammond John Jr. • SHT • USA
LARRY O'NEILL, GENTLEMAN • 1915 • Easton H. C. • USA
LARRY'S RECENT BEHAVIOR • 1963 • Wieland Joyce • SHT • USA
LARRY'S REVENGE • 1913 • Calvert Charles? • UKN
LARS HARD • 1948 • Faustman Erik • SWD
LARS I PORTEN • 1984 • Erlsbo Leif • NRW • LARS IN THE DOORWAY ○ ON THE THRESHOLD
LARS IN THE DOORWAY see **LARS I PORTEN** • 1984
LARS-OLE 5.C • 1973 • Malmros Nils • DNM • LARS OLE 5C
LARS OLE 5C see **LARS-OLE 5.C** • 1973
LARSSON I ANDRA GIFTET • 1935 • Bauman Schamyl • SWD • LARSSON IN HIS SECOND MARRIAGE
LARSSON IN HIS SECOND MARRIAGE see **LARSSON I ANDRA GIFTET** • 1935
LARZAC • 1973 • Bloch Dominique, Haudiquet Philippe, Levy Isabelle • DOC • FRN • GARDAREM LOU LARZAC
LARZAC 75-77 see **BATISSEURS, LES** • 1977
LAS DE MENDEZ • 1927 • Delgado Fernando • SPN
LAS PALMAS • Lorente German
LAS QUE TIENEN QUE SERVIR • 1967 • Forque Jose Maria • SPN • THOSE WHO HAVE TO SERVE
LAS VEGAS, 500 MILLONES • 1968 • Isasi Antonio • SPN, FRN, FRG • AN EINEM FREITAG IN LAS VEGAS (FRG) ○ HOMMES DE LAS VEGAS, LES (FRN) ○ RADIOGRAFIA D'UN COLPO D'ORO (ITL) ○ THEY CAME TO ROB LAS VEGAS (USA)
LAS VEGAS A-GO-GO • 1967 • Carlos Luciano B. • PHL
LAS VEGAS BY NIGHT see **SPREE** • 1967
LAS VEGAS FREE-FOR-ALL (USA) see **KUREIZI OGON SAKUSEN** • 1967
LAS VEGAS GIRLS • 1981 • Tobalina Carlos • USA
LAS VEGAS HILLBILLYS • 1966 • Pierce Arthur C. • USA
LAS VEGAS LADY • 1976 • Nosseck Noel • USA • RAID ON CAESARS
LAS VEGAS NIGHTS • 1941 • Murphy Ralph • USA • GAY CITY, THE (UKN)
LAS VEGAS SHAKEDOWN • 1955 • Salkow Sidney • USA
LAS VEGAS STORY, THE • 1952 • Stevenson Robert • USA
LAS VEGAS WEEKEND • 1986 • Trevillion Dale • USA
LASCA • 1913 • *Grant Harry* • USA
LASCA • 1919 • Dawn Norman • USA
LASCA OF THE RIO GRANDE • 1931 • Laemmle Edward • USA
LASCIA CANTARE IL CUORE • 1943 • Savarese Roberto • ITL
LASCIAPASSARE PER IL MORTO • 1962 • Gariazzo Mario • ITL • PASSPORT FOR A CORPSE (USA)
LASCIATE OGNI SPERANZA • 1937 • Righelli Gennaro • ITL • ABANDON ALL HOPE ○ LEAVE ALL HOPE
LASCIATE SPARARE.. CHI CI SA FARE (ITL) see **LAISSEZ TIRER LES TIREURS** • 1964
LASCIATECI IN PACE • 1954 • Girolami Marino • ITL
LASCIATEMI CANTARE! see **CANTATE CON ME!** • 1940
LASCIVIOUSNESS OF THE VIPER, THE see **JASEI NO IN** • 1920
LASERBLAST • 1978 • Raye Michael • USA
LASERBLAST II • 1985 • *Band Charles (P)* • USA
LASERMAN, THE • 1988 • Wang Cheng-Fang • USA
LASH, THE • 1916 • Young James • USA
LASH, THE • 1930 • Lloyd Frank • USA • ADIOS (UKN)
LASH, THE • 1934 • Edwards Henry • UKN
LASH OF DESTINY, THE • 1916 • Terwilliger George W. • USA
LASH OF FATE, THE • 1912 • *Rex* • USA
LASH OF JEALOUSY, THE see **MODERN OTHELLO, A** • 1917
LASH OF PINTO PETE, THE • 1924 • Ford Francis • USA
LASH OF POWER, THE • 1917 • Salter Harry • USA
LASH OF THE CZAR, THE see **BYELI OREL** • 1928
LASH OF THE LAW • 1926 • *Bailey Bill* • USA
LASH OF THE PENITENTES, THE • 1936 • Carroll Zelma • USA
LASH OF THE WHIP • 1924 • Ford Francis • USA
LASHEEN • 1938 • Kamp Fritz • EGY
LASKA • 1972 • Kachyna Karel • CZC • LOVE
LASKA A LIDE • 1937 • Kubasek Vaclav, Vancura Vladislav • CZC • LOVE AND PEOPLE
LASKA MEZI KAPKAMI DESTE • 1978 • Kachyna Karel • CZC • LOVE BETWEEN THE RAINDROPS ○ LOVE AMONG RAINDROPS
LASKA NELASKAVA • 1969 • Plichta Dimitrij • CZC • UNKIND LOVE
LASKA V BARVACH KARNEVALU • 1974 • Schorm Evald (c/d) • CZC • LOVE IN MARDI GRAS COLORS
LASKY ALEXANDRA DUMASE ST. • 1970 • Kachyna Karel • MTV • CZC • LOVES OF ALEXANDER DUMAS SR., THE
LASKY HRY SALIVE • 1972 • Krejcik Jiri • CZC • TRICKS OF DECEPTIVE LOVE
LASKY JEDNE PLAVOVLASKY • 1965 • Forman Milos • CZC • LOVES OF A BLONDE (USA) ○ BLONDE IN LOVE, A (UKN)
LASS DIE SONNE WIEDER SCHEINEN • 1955 • Marischka Hubert • FRG
LASS FROM THE STORMY CROFT, THE see **TOSEN FRAN STORMYRTORPET** • 1917
LASS JUCKEN, KUMPEL • 1972 • Marischka Franz • FRG
LASS MICH AM SONNTAG NICHT ALLEIN • 1959 • Rabenalt Arthur M. • FRG
LASS O' THE LIGHT • 1912 • Brenon Herbert • USA
LASS O' THE LOOMS, A • 1919 • Denton Jack • UKN
LASS OF GLOUSTER, THE • 1912 • *Pathe* • USA
LASS OF THE LUMBERLANDS, A • 1916 • Hurst Paul C., McGowan J. P. • SRL • USA
LASS O'KILLIKRANKIE, THE • 1914 • *Albert Elsie* • USA
LASS WHO COULDN'T FORGET, THE • 1911 • *Kalem* • USA
LASS WHO LOVED A SAILOR, THE • 1910 • *Essanay* • USA
LASS WHO LOVES A SAILOR, THE • 1909 • *Urban Trading Co* • UKN
LASSANDA • 1974 • Perera K. A. W. • SLN
LASSATOK FELEIM! • 1968 • Fazekas Lajos • HNG • SIGNAL
LASSE-MAJA • 1941 • Olsson Gunnar • SWD
LASSE MANSSON FRA SKANE • 1921 • Sandberg Anders W. • DNM
LASSE OG GEIR see **HISTORIEN OM LASSE OG GEIR** • 1975
LASSET DIE KLEINEN ZU MIR KOMMEN • 1920 • Neufeld Max • AUS
LASSIE, THE see **MALKATA** • 1959
LASSIE AND HER DOG, THE • 1901 • *Warwick Trading Co* • UKN
LASSIE COME HOME • 1943 • Wilcox Fred M. • USA
LASSIE FROM LANCASHIRE • 1938 • Carstairs John Paddy • UKN
LASSIE: THE NEW BEGINNING • 1979 • Chaffey Don • TVM • USA
LASSIE, THE VOYAGER • 1966 • Moder Dick, Hively Jack • USA
LASSIE'S BIRTHDAY, THE • 1910 • *Edison* • USA
LASSIE'S GREAT ADVENTURE • 1963 • Beaudine William • MTV • USA • LASSIE'S GREATEST ADVENTURE (UKN) ○ JOURNEY, THE
LASSIE'S GREATEST ADVENTURE (UKN) see **LASSIE'S GREAT ADVENTURE** • 1963
LASSITER • 1984 • Young Roger • USA
LASSOED BY MOTOR • 1905 • *Urban Trading Co* • UKN
LASSOING A LION • 1915 • Santschi Thomas • USA
LASST UNS TOTEN, COMPANEROS see **VAMOS A MATAR COMPANEROS!** • 1970
LAST, DIE • 1916 • *Servaes Dagny* • FRG
LAST, THE see **ULTIMI, GLI** • 1963
LAST ABDICATION see **SAIGO NO JOITO** • 1945
LAST ACT • 1990 • Masihi Varuzh Karim • IRN
LAST ACT, THE • 1915 • Wilson Ben • USA
LAST ACT, THE • 1916 • *Barriscale Bessie* • USA
LAST ACT, THE see **LETZTE AKT, DER** • 1955
LAST ACT, THE see **POSLEDNI DEJSTVI** • 1970
LAST ACT OF MARTIN WESTON, THE • 1971 • Jacot Michael • CND
LAST ADVENTURE, THE • 1916 • Calvert E. H. • SHT • USA
LAST ADVENTURE, THE see **SISTA AVENTYRET, DEN** • 1975
LAST ADVENTURE, THE (UKN) see **AVENTURIERS, LES** • 1966
LAST ADVENTURE OF ARSEN LUPIN, THE see **ARSEN LUPIN UTOLSO KALANDJA** • 1921
LAST ADVENTURE OF THE SKELETON'S HAND, THE see **JUVELERERNES SKROEK** • 1915
LAST ADVENTURERS, THE • 1937 • Kellino Roy • UKN • DOWN TO THE SEA IN SHIPS
LAST ADVENTURES OF SHERLOCK HOLMES, THE • 1923 • Ridgwell George • SER • UKN
LAST AFTER GOD, THE see **OSTATNI PO BOGU** • 1968
LAST ALARM • 1900 • *Bitzer Billy (Ph)* • USA
LAST ALARM, THE • 1926 • Apfel Oscar • USA
LAST ALARM, THE • 1940 • West William • USA
LAST AMERICAN HERO, THE • 1973 • Johnson Lamont • USA • HARD DRIVER ○ I GOT A NAME
LAST AMERICAN PREPPY, THE see **MAKING THE GRADE** • 1984
LAST AMERICAN VIRGIN, THE • 1982 • Davidson Boaz • USA
LAST AND FIRST DAY, THE see **DEN POSLEDNII, DEN PERVYI** • 1960
LAST ANGRY MAN, THE • 1959 • Mann Daniel • USA
LAST ANGRY MAN, THE • 1974 • Freedman Jerrold • TVM • USA
LAST APPEAL, THE • 1911 • *Imp* • USA
LAST APPEAL, THE • 1921 • Paul Fred • UKN
LAST ARISTOCRATS, THE see **ZUIHOUDE GUIZU** • 1988
LAST ASSAULT, THE • 1971 • Ozerov Yury • USS
LAST ASSAULT, THE • 1985 • Nicolaescu Sergiu • RMN
LAST ASSIGNMENT, THE • 1914 • Edwin Walter • USA
LAST ATTRACTION, THE see **POSLEDNII ATTRAKZION** • 1929
LAST BACHELOR, THE • 1974 • Yanchev Vladimir • BUL
LAST BALL IN NOVEMBER, THE see **NOIEMBRIE, ULTIMUL BAL** • 1989
LAST BANDIT, THE • 1949 • Kane Joseph • USA
LAST BARRICADE, THE • 1938 • Bryce Alex • UKN
LAST BATTALION, THE see **LETZTE KOMPANIE, DIE** • 1967
LAST BATTLE, THE • 1976 • Heskiya Zako • BUL
LAST BATTLE, THE see **KWIECIEN** • 1961
LAST BATTLE, THE see **DERNIER COMBAT, LE** • 1982
LAST BEND, THE see **DERNIER TOURNANT, LE** • 1939
LAST BET, THE see **TELEFTAIO STICHIME** • 1989
LAST BETRAYAL, THE see **SANNIN NO KAOYAKU** • 1960
LAST BETROTHAL, THE see **DERNIERES FIANCAILLES, LES** • 1973
LAST BINGE, THE see **POSLEDNI MEJDAN** • 1983
LAST BLITZKRIEG, THE • 1959 • Dreifuss Arthur • USA
LAST BLOCKHOUSE, THE • 1913 • Melford George • USA
LAST BLOOD see **MURDER IN COWETA COUNTY** • 1982
LAST BOHEMIAN, THE see **UTOLSO BOHEM, AZ** • 1912
LAST BOHEMIAN, THE see **POSLEDNI BOHEM** • 1931
LAST BOOTY, THE see **POSLEDNI LUP**
LAST BOTTLE, THE • 1919 • Harrison Saul • SHT • USA
LAST BOTTLE AT THE CLUB, THE see **LAST GLASS OF THE TWO OLD SPORTS, THE** • 1901
LAST BREAKFAST IN PARADISE • 1982 • Stewart Meg • ASL
LAST BRIDE OF SALEM, THE • 1974 • Donovan Tom • TVM • USA
LAST BRIDGE, THE see **LETZTE BRUCKE, DIE** • 1954
LAST BULLET, THE see **CROOKED RIVER** • 1951
LAST BULLET, THE see **TEK KURSUN** • 1968
LAST BULLET, THE see **ULTIMUL CARTUS** • 1973
LAST BUT ONE, THE see **UTOLSO ELOTTI EMBER, AZ** • 1963
LAST CABIN BOY, THE see **ULTIMO GRUMETE, EL** • 1983
LAST CALL • 1985 • Oross Emerich • HNG
LAST CALL, THE • 1909 • *Lubin* • USA
LAST CALL, THE (UKN) see **LAST PERFORMANCE, THE** • 1927
LAST CANNIBALS, THE see **BLANDT MENNESKEAEDERE PA NY GUINEA** • 1954
LAST CARD see **HULING BARAHA** • 1968
LAST CARD, THE • 1915 • Ingraham Lloyd • USA
LAST CARD, THE • 1917 • *W.h. Productions* • USA
LAST CARD, THE • 1921 • Veiller Bayard • USA • WOMAN NEXT DOOR, THE
LAST CARTOON MAN, THE • 1974 • Hale Jeffrey, Lamb Derek • USA

LAST CARTRIDGES, THE see **DERNIERES CARTOUCHES, LES** • 1897
LAST CASTLE, THE see **ECHOES OF A SUMMER** • 1975
LAST CHALLENGE, THE • 1916 • Shaw Harold • UKN
LAST CHALLENGE, THE • 1967 • Thorpe Richard • USA • PISTOLERO OF RED RIVER ○ PISTOLERO
LAST CHANCE • 1986 • Brown Alastair • CND, ASL
LAST CHANCE, THE • 1921 • Cullison Webster • USA
LAST CHANCE, THE • 1926 • Carpenter Horace B. • USA
LAST CHANCE, THE • 1937 • Bentley Thomas • UKN
LAST CHANCE, THE see **SCACCO INTERNAZIONALE** • 1968
LAST CHANCE, THE see **HARMADIK NEKIFUTAS** • 1973
LAST CHANCE, THE see **ULTIMA CHANCE, L'** • 1973
LAST CHANCE, THE (USA) see **LETZTE CHANCE, DIE** • 1945
LAST CHANTS FOR A SLOW DANCE • 1980 • Jost Jon • USA
LAST CHAPTER, THE • 1915 • Taylor William D. • USA
LAST CHAPTER, THE • 1966 • Rothman Benjamin, Rothman Lawrence • DOC • USA
LAST CHAPTER, THE • 1974 • Tringham David • SHT • UKN
LAST CHARGE, THE (USA) see **LEGGENDA DI FRA' DIAVOLO, LA** • 1962
LAST CHASE, THE • 1980 • Burke Martyn • CND
LAST CHECKOUT, THE see **INTRUDER** • 1988
LAST CHIEFTAIN, THE see **POSLEDNIAT VOYVODA** • 1968
LAST CHILD, THE • 1971 • Moxey John Llewellyn • TVM • USA
LAST CHORUS • Jeremy John • UKN
LAST CIGARETTE, THE • 1917 • Howard George Bronson • SHT • USA
LAST CIRCLE, THE see **UTOLSO KOR, AZ** • 1968
LAST CIRCLE IN MONZA see **POSLEDNJI KRUG U MONCI** • 1990
LAST CIRCUS SHOW, THE (USA) see **VENDITORE DI PALLONCINI, IL** • 1974
LAST COASTLINE, THE • 1974 • Davidson Ian • DOC • ASL
LAST COMBAT, THE (UKN) see **DERNIER COMBAT, LE** • 1982
LAST COMMAND, THE • 1928 • von Sternberg Josef • USA • GENERAL, THE
LAST COMMAND, THE • 1955 • Lloyd Frank • USA
LAST COMMAND, THE (UKN) see **PRISONER OF JAPAN** • 1942
LAST COMPANY, THE see **LETZTE KOMPANIE, DIE** • 1930
LAST CONCERT, THE • 1915 • *Glickman Ellis F.* • USA
LAST CONFLICT, THE see **PRISONER IN THE MIDDLE** • 1975
LAST COUPLE OUT see **SISTA PARET UT** • 1956
LAST COUPON, THE • 1932 • Bentley Thomas • UKN
LAST COURT MARTIAL, THE see **A-TEAM: THE COURT MARTIAL, THE** • 1985
LAST CROOKED MILE, THE • 1946 • Ford Philip • USA
LAST CRUSADE, THE • 1922 • Ridgwell George • UKN
LAST CRUSADE, THE see **MIHAI VITEAZUL** • 1971
LAST CRUSADER, THE see **UKANASKNELI JVAROSNEBI** • 1934
LAST CRY FOR HELP, A • 1979 • Sitowitz Hal • TVM • USA
LAST CURTAIN, THE • 1937 • MacDonald David • UKN
LAST CZAR, THE see **NUITS DE RASPOUTINE, LES** • 1960
LAST DANCE, THE • 1912 • *Greenwood Winnifred* • USA
LAST DANCE, THE • 1930 • Pembroke Scott • USA
LAST DANCE, THE • 1931 • *Van Beuren* • ANS • USA
LAST DAWN, THE see **UTOLSO HAJNAL, AZ** • 1917
LAST DAY, THE • 1975 • McEveety Bernard • TVM • USA
LAST DAY, THE see **POSLEDNJI DAN** • 1952
LAST DAY AND THE FIRST DAY, THE see **DEN POSLEDNII, DEN PERVYI** • 1960
LAST DAY, FIRST DAY see **DEN POSLEDNII, DEN PERVYI** • 1960
LAST DAY OF SAMURAI • 1962 • *Nakamura Senjaku* • JPN
LAST DAY OF SUMMER, THE see **OSTATNI DZIEN LATA** • 1958
LAST DAY OF THE COMMANDER GUANIPA, THE see **ULTIMO DIA DEL COMANDANTE GUANIPA, EL** • 1971
LAST DAY OF THE SCHOOL HOLIDAY, THE • 1964 • Zhebrunas Arunas • USS
LAST DAY OF THE WAR, THE (USA) see **ULTIMO DIA DE LA GUERRA, EL** • 1969
LAST DAY OF WINTER, THE see **ZUIHOU YIGE DONGRI** • 1987
LAST DAYS, THE see **OSTATNI DNI** • 1968
LAST DAYS OF BOOT HILL • 1947 • Nazarro Ray • USA • ON BOOT HILL (UKN)
LAST DAYS OF CONTRITION, THE • 1990 • Kerr Richard • DOC • CND
LAST DAYS OF DOLWYN, THE • 1949 • Williams Emlyn • UKN • WOMAN OF DOLWYN (USA) ○ DOLWYN
LAST DAYS OF EDO, THE see **EDO SAIGO NO HI** • 1941
LAST DAYS OF FRANK AND JESSE JAMES, THE • 1986 • Graham William A. • TVM • USA
LAST DAYS OF GOMORRHA, THE see **LETZTEN TAGE VON GOMORRA, DIE** • 1974
LAST DAYS OF MAN ON EARTH see **FINAL PROGRAMME, THE** • 1973
LAST DAYS OF MUSSOLINI see **MUSSOLINI ULTIMO ATTO** • 1974
LAST DAYS OF PATTON, THE • 1986 • Mann Delbert • TVM • USA
LAST DAYS OF PLANET EARTH, THE see **NOSTRADAMUS NO DAIYOGEN** • 1974
LAST DAYS OF POMPEII, THE • 1900 • Booth W. R. • UKN
LAST DAYS OF POMPEII, THE • 1935 • Schoedsack Ernest B. • USA
LAST DAYS OF POMPEII, THE • 1984 • Hunt Peter • USA
LAST DAYS OF POMPEII, THE see **ULTIMI GIORNI DI POMPEI, GLI** • 1926
LAST DAYS OF POMPEII, THE (USA) see **ULTIMI GIORNI DI POMPEI, GLI** • 1913
LAST DAYS OF POMPEII, THE(UKN) see **LETZTEN TAGE VON POMPEI, DIE** • 1959
LAST DAYS OF POMPEII, THE(USA) see **DERNIERS JOURS DE POMPEI, LES** • 1948
LAST DAYS OF THE VICTIM see **ULTIMOS DIAS DE LA VICTIMA** • 1982
LAST DEAL, THE • 1910 • Griffith D. W. • USA
LAST DEATH OF THE DEVIL, THE see **GEKKO KAMEN** • 1959
LAST DETAIL, THE • 1973 • Ashby Hal • USA
LAST DEWDROP, THE • 1979 • Vuthivichai Suchart • THL
LAST DINOSAUR, THE • 1977 • Grasshoff Alex, Kotani Tom • USA, JPN
LAST DITCH GLORY see **GONIN NO TOTSUGEKITAI** • 1961
LAST DOOR, THE • 1921 • Earle William P. S. • USA
LAST DOOR, THE • 1921 • Ince Ralph • USA
LAST DRAGON, THR • 1985 • Schultz Michael • USA • BERRY GORDY'S THE LAST DRAGON ○ LAST DRAGONS, THE
LAST DRAGONS, THE see **LAST DRAGON, THR** • 1985
LAST DRINK OF WHISKEY, THE • 1914 • Dillon Eddie • USA
LAST DROP OF WATER, THE • 1911 • Griffith D. W. • USA
LAST DUEL, THE see **MIYAMOTO MUSASHI V** • 1965
LAST EDITION, THE • 1925 • Johnson Emory • USA
LAST EGYPTIAN, THE • 1914 • *Macdonald J. Farrell* • USA
LAST ELECTRIC KNIGHT, THE • 1986 • Fargo James • MTV • USA
LAST EMBRACE • 1979 • Demme Jonathan • USA
LAST EMBRACE see **HOYO** • 1954
LAST EMPEROR, THE • 1987 • Bertolucci Bernardo • UKN
LAST EMPEROR, THE see **HUO LONG** • 1985
LAST ENCAMPMENT, THE • 1914 • Haldane Bert? • UKN
LAST ENCOUNTER • 1918 • Rasumny Alexander • USS
LAST ENCOUNTER see **ULTIMO ENCUENTRO** • 1967
LAST ENEMY, THE (USA) see **ULTIMA NEMICA, L'** • 1938
LAST ESCAPE see **TOBO RESSHA** • 1966
LAST ESCAPE, THE • 1970 • Grauman Walter • USA • OSS
LAST EVENINGS WITH TERESA see **ULTIMATAS TARDES CON TERESA** • 1984
LAST EXIT BEFORE ROISSY (USA) see **DERNIERE SORTIE AVANT ROISSY** • 1976
LAST EXIT TO BROOKLYN • 1989 • Edel Ulrich • USA, FRG
LAST EXPRESS, THE • 1938 • Garrett Otis • USA
LAST EYEWITNESS, THE • Lee Doo-Yong • SKR
LAST FAREWELL, THE • 1911 • Bouwmeester Theo? • UKN
LAST FAREWELL, THE see **LITTLE HOUSE; THE LAST FAREWELL** • 1984
LAST FARM IN THE VALLEY, THE see **SIDASTI BOERINN I DALNUM** • 1949
LAST FEELINGS (UKN) see **ULTIMO SAPORE DELL'ARIA, L'** • 1978
LAST FERRY, THE • 1989 • Krzystek Waldemar • PLN
LAST FIGHT, THE • 1983 • Williamson Fred • USA
LAST FLIGHT, THE • 1931 • Dieterle William • USA • SPENT BULLETS
LAST FLIGHT, THE (USA) see **EQUIPAGE, L'** • 1927
LAST FLIGHT OF NOAH'S ARK, THE • 1980 • Jarrott Charles • USA
LAST FLING, THE • 1987 • Allen Corey • TVM • USA
LAST FORM see **SISTA RINGEN** • 1955
LAST FOUR DAYS, THE see **CETIRI DANA DO SMRTI** • 1977
LAST FOUR DAYS, THE (USA) see **MUSSOLINI ULTIMO ATTO** • 1974
LAST FROM SABUDARA, THE see **POSLEDNY IZ SABUDARA** • 1957
LAST FRONTIER, THE • 1926 • Seitz George B. • USA
LAST FRONTIER, THE • 1932 • Bennet Spencer Gordon, Storey Thomas L. • SRL • USA • BLACK GHOST
LAST FRONTIER, THE • 1934 • Finnie Richard S. • DOC • CND
LAST FRONTIER, THE • 1979 • Stoneman John • MTV • CND
LAST FRONTIER, THE • 1986 • Wincer Simon • TVM • USA
LAST FRONTIER, THE see **LAST FRONTIER UPRISING, THE** • 1947
LAST FRONTIER, THE see **SPACE RAGE** • 1985
LAST FRONTIER, THE (UKN) see **SAVAGE WILDERNESS** • 1955
LAST FRONTIER UPRISING, THE • 1947 • Selander Lesley • USA • LAST FRONTIER, THE
LAST GALLANTRY, THE see **ZANKYO NO SAKAZUKI** • 1967
LAST GAME see **SISTA LEKEN, DEN** • 1983
LAST GAME, THE • 1980 • Beck Martin* • USA
LAST GAME, THE (USA) see **TRETIU TAYM** • 1963
LAST GANGSTER, THE • 1937 • Ludwig Edward • USA
LAST GANGSTER, THE (UKN) see **ROGER TOUHY, GANGSTER** • 1944
LAST GENERATION, THE • 1966 • Graham William A. • TVM • USA
LAST GENTLEMAN, THE • 1934 • Lanfield Sidney • USA
LAST GIANTS: A QUEST FOR SURVIVAL, THE • 1983 • Stoneman John • MTV • CND
LAST GIRAFFE, THE • 1979 • Couffer Jack • TVM • USA
LAST GLASS OF THE TWO OLD SPORTS, THE • 1901 • Smith G. A. • UKN • LAST BOTTLE AT THE CLUB, THE
LAST GLEAMING see **JA, VI ELSKER** • 1983
LAST GLORY OF TROY, THE see **LEGGENDA DI ENEA, LA** • 1962
LAST GOAL, THE (UKN) see **KET FELIDO A POKOLBAN** • 1961
LAST GRAVE AT DIMBAZA • 1975 • Mahomo Nana • SAF
LAST GREAT TREASURE, THE see **MOTHER LODE** • 1980
LAST GRENADE, THE • 1970 • Flemyng Gordon • UKN • GRIGSBY
LAST GUEST, THE • 1912 • *Powers* • USA
LAST GUN, THE see **JIM IL PRIMO** • 1964
LAST GUNFIGHT see **ANKOKUGAI NO TAIKETSU** • 1960
LAST GUNFIGHTER, THE • 1959 • Shonteff Lindsay • CND • DEVIL'S SPAWN, THE ○ HIRED GUN
LAST GYPSY TENT, THE • 1958 • Hadzic Fadil • YGS
LAST HARD MEN, THE • 1976 • McLaglen Andrew V. • USA
LAST HAUL, THE see **HIS LAST HAUL** • 1928
LAST HILL, THE see **MALACHEV KIRGAN** • 1944
LAST HOLDUP, THE see **SON VURGUN** • 1968
LAST HOLIDAY • 1950 • Cass Henry • UKN
LAST HOLIDAYS, THE • 1970 • Kremnev V. • USS
LAST HOME LACE-MAKERS, THE see **LETZTEN HEIMPOSAMENTER, DIE** • 1936
LAST HOPE, THE see **BIRMINGHAM GIRL'S LAST HOPE, A** • 1917
LAST HORROR FILM, THE • 1982 • Winters David • UKN • FANATIC
LAST HORSEMAN, THE • 1944 • Berke William • USA
LAST HOUR, THE • 1921 • Chiaureli Mikhail • USS
LAST HOUR, THE • 1923 • Sloman Edward • USA • BLIND JUSTICE
LAST HOUR, THE • 1929 • Chiaureli Mikhail • USS
LAST HOUR, THE • 1930 • Forde Walter • UKN
LAST HOURS BEFORE MORNING • 1975 • Hardy Joseph • TVM • USA
LAST HOUSE ON DEAD END STREET • 1981 • Juno Victor • USA • FUN HOUSE, THE
LAST HOUSE ON THE LEFT, THE • 1972 • Craven Wes • USA
LAST HUNDRED DAYS OF NAPOLEON, THE see **WATERLOO** • 1970
LAST HUNDRED YARDS, THE • 1922 • Sanderson Challis • UKN
LAST HUNGRY CAT, THE • 1961 • Freleng Friz • ANS • USA
LAST HUNT, THE • 1955 • Brooks Richard • USA
LAST HUNTER see **APOCALISSE DOMANI** • 1980
LAST HUNTER, THE see **CACCIATORE 2** • 1981
LAST HURRAH, THE • 1958 • Ford John • USA
LAST HURRAH, THE • 1978 • Sherman Vincent • TVM • USA
LAST ILLUSION, THE see **RUF, DER** • 1949
LAST IMAGES OF THE SHIPWRECK see **ULTIMAS IMAGENES DEL NAUFRAGIO** • 1989
LAST INCH, THE • 1959 • Vulfovich Teodor, Kurikhin Nikita • USS
LAST INDIAN, THE • 1938 • Rasinski Connie • ANS • USA
LAST INNOCENT MAN, THE • 1987 • Spottiswoode Roger • TVM • USA
LAST INSTALLMENT, THE • 1945 • Hart Walter • USA
LAST ISLAND, THE • 1988 • Kaczender George • CND
LAST ISLAND, THE • 1989 • Gorris Marleen • NTH
LAST ITALIAN TANGO, THE (UKN) see **ULTIMO TANGO A ZAGAROL** • 1973
LAST JAPANESE SOLDIER, THE see **SAIGO NO NIHONHEI** • 1960
LAST JOURNEY, THE • 1935 • Vorhaus Bernard • UKN
LAST JOURNEY, THE • 1936 • Brahm John • USA
LAST JOURNEY, THE see **LAATSTE REIS, DE** • 1987
LAST JOY, THE see **POSLEDNI RADOST** • 1921
LAST JUDGEMENT see **SAIGO NO SHINPAN** • 1965
LAST JUDGEMENT BUT ONE, THE see **UTOLSO ELOTTI ITELET, AZ** • 1980
LAST JUDGMENT, THE see **LAATSTE ORDEEL, HET** • 1970
LAST JUDGMENT, THE (USA) see **GIUDIZIO UNIVERSALE, IL** • 1961
LAST KILLER, THE see **ULTIMO KILLER, L'** • 1967
LAST KING, THE • Chung Jin-Woo • SKR
LAST KING OF THE INCAS, THE see **ULTIMO REY DE LOS INCAS, EL** • 1967
LAST KING OF WALES, THE • 1922 • Ridgwell George • UKN
LAST KISS, THE see **KOUBLA AL ALHIRA, AL** • 1967
LAST LADY, THE • 1968 • *Aratama Michiyo* • JPN
LAST LAP • 1928 • Mitchell Bruce • USA
LAST LAUGH see **GARGALHADA FINAL** • 1980
LAST LAUGH, THE • 1911 • *Leonard Marion* • USA
LAST LAUGH, THE • 1913 • *Essanay* • USA
LAST LAUGH, THE • 1928 • Roberts Stephen • SHT • USA
LAST LAUGH, THE (USA) see **LETZTE MANN, DER** • 1924
LAST LEAF, THE • 1917 • Miller Ashley • SHT • USA
LAST LESSON, THE • 1962 • Klopcic Matjaz • SHT • YGS
LAST LETTER, A see **O SCRISOARE PIERDUTA** • 1956
LAST LETTER, THE see **AAKHRI KHAT** • 1967
LAST LION, THE • 1973 • De Witt Elmo • SAF
LAST LOAD, THE • 1948 • Baxter John • UKN
LAST LOOK, THE • 1909 • *Pathe* • FRN
LAST LOVE IN TIERRA DEL FUEGO see **ULTIMO AMOR EN TIERRA A DEL FUEGO, EL** • 1979
LAST LOVE OF LAURA ADLER, THE • 1989 • Heffner Avram • ISR
LAST LOVE (USA) see **LETZTE LIEBE** • 1938
LAST LUMBER CAMP, THE see **VIIMEINEN SAVOTTA** • 1977
LAST MAIL, THE • 1933 • Davis Mannie • ANS • USA
LAST MAN, THE • 1916 • Wolbert William • USA
LAST MAN, THE • 1924 • Bracken Bertram • USA
LAST MAN, THE • 1924 • Reel Frederick Jr. • USA
LAST MAN, THE • 1932 • Higgin Howard • USA
LAST MAN, THE • 1958 • Frankenheimer John • MTV • USA
LAST MAN, THE see **LETZTE MANN, DER** • 1924
LAST MAN, THE see **POSLEDNI MUZ** • 1934
LAST MAN, THE see **DERNIER HOMME, LE** • 1969
LAST MAN IN THE WORLD, THE • 1966 • Kelly Ron • CND
LAST MAN ON EARTH, THE • 1924 • Blystone John G. • USA
LAST MAN ON EARTH, THE see **ULTIMO VARON SOBRE LA TIERRA, EL** • 1933
LAST MAN ON EARTH, THE (USA) see **ULTIMO UOMO DELLA TERRA, L'** • 1964
LAST MAN TO HANG, THE • 1956 • Fisher Terence • UKN
LAST MAN'S CLUB, THE • 1914 • *Selig* • USA
LAST MANUSCRIPT, THE see **UTOLSO KEZIRAT, AZ** • 1986
LAST MARRIED COUPLE IN AMERICA, THE • 1980 • Cates Gilbert • USA
LAST MASQUERADE, THE see **POSLEDNI MASKARAD** • 1934
LAST MEETING, THE (USA) see **ULTIMO ENCUENTRO, EL** • 1939
LAST MELODRAMA, THE see **DERNIER MELODRAME, LE** • 1978
LAST MELODY, THE (USA) see **ULTIMA MELODIA, LA** • 1938
LAST MEMORIES see **SON HATIRA** • 1968
LAST MERCENARY, THE • 1984 • Siciliano Mario • ITL
LAST MERCENARY, THE (USA) see **MERCENARIO, EL** • 1968
LAST MESSAGE, THE see **TIEN CHYE EE PIE CHU** • 1975
LAST MESSAGE FROM SAIGON see **OPERATION C.I.A.** • 1965
LAST METRO, THE (USA) see **DERNIER METRO, LE** • 1980
LAST MILE, THE • 1932 • Bischoff Sam • USA
LAST MILE, THE • 1959 • Koch Howard W. • USA
LAST MILLIONAIRE, THE see **DERNIER MILLIARDAIRE, LE** • 1934
LAST MISSION OF THE SABOTEUR "CLOUD", THE see **POSLEDNJI PODVIG DIVERZANTA OBLAKA** • 1979
LAST MOHICAN, THE • 1966 • Leaf Paul • USA
LAST MOMENT, THE • 1923 • Reed J. Parker Jr. • USA
LAST MOMENT, THE • 1928 • Fejos Paul • USA • DERNIER MOMENT, LE
LAST MOMENT, THE • 1966 • Yasin Al • USA
LAST MOMENTS OF ANNE BOLEYN see **TOUR DE LONDRES: OU, LES DERNIER MOMENTS D'ANNE DE BOLEYN, LA** • 1905
LAST MONTH OF AUTUMN, THE see **POSLEDNII MESYATS OSENI** • 1965
LAST MOUST OF HAMLIN • 1955 • Rasinski Connie • ANS • USA

LAST MOVIE, THE • 1971 • Hopper Dennis • USA • CHINCHERO
LAST MUSKETEER, THE • 1952 • Witney William • USA
LAST MUSKETEER, THE (USA) see **VICOMTE DE BRAGELONNE, LE** • 1954
LAST NEWSREEL: 1999, THE • 1972 • Craig Ray • USA
LAST NIGHT see **SISTA NATTEN** • 1957
LAST NIGHT, THE • 1929 • Sandberg Anders W. • DNM
LAST NIGHT, THE see **POSLEDNAYA NOCH** • 1937
LAST NIGHT, THE see **LETZTE NACHT, DIE** • 1961
LAST NIGHT, THE see **LEILA EL AKHIRA, EL** • 1963
LAST NIGHT, THE see **SON GECE** • 1967
LAST NIGHT AT THE ALAMO • 1983 • Pennell Eagle • USA
LAST NIGHT OF CHILDHOOD, THE see **ULTIMA NOAPTE A COPILARIEI** • 1966
LAST NIGHT'S LIGHT see **TSO-YEH-CHIH TENG** • 1983
LAST NINJA, THE • 1983 • Graham William A. • TVM • USA
LAST NIP, THE • 1920 • Hohenvest John • SHT • USA
LAST NO, THE • 1979 • Dovnikovic Borivoj • ANM • YGS
LAST NOTCH, THE • 1911 • Dwan Allan • USA
LAST OF ENGLAND, THE • 1987 • Jarman Derek • UKN
LAST OF HER CLAN, THE • 1917 • King Burton L. • SHT • USA
LAST OF HER TRIBE, THE • 1912 • *Santschi Thomas* • USA
LAST OF HIS PEOPLE, THE • 1919 • Bradbury Robert North • USA
LAST OF MRS. CHEYNEY, THE • 1929 • Franklin Sidney A., Arzner Dorothy (U/c) • USA
LAST OF MRS. CHEYNEY, THE • 1937 • Boleslawski Richard, Fitzmaurice George • USA
LAST OF PHILIP BANTER, THE • 1986 • Hachuel Herve • USA
LAST OF SHEILA, THE • 1973 • Ross Herbert • USA
LAST OF SUMMER, THE see **KOHAYAGAWA-KE NO AKI** • 1961
LAST OF THE AMERICAN HOBOES, THE • 1974 • Moody Titus • USA
LAST OF THE BADMEN • 1957 • Landres Paul • USA
LAST OF THE BADMEN see **TEMPO DEGLI AVVOLTI, IL** • 1967
LAST OF THE BIG GUNS see **PAPERBACK HERO** • 1972
LAST OF THE BLACK HAND GANG, THE • 1912 • Plumb Hay? • UKN
LAST OF THE BLUE DEVILS, THE • 1979 • Ricker Bruce • USA
LAST OF THE BUCCANEERS • 1950 • Landers Lew • USA
LAST OF THE CARNABYS, THE • 1917 • Parke William • USA
LAST OF THE CLINTONS • 1935 • Fraser Harry L. • USA
LAST OF THE COMANCHEROS, THE • 1971 • Adamson Al • USA
LAST OF THE COMANCHES • 1952 • De Toth Andre • USA • SABRE AND THE ARROW, THE (UKN)
LAST OF THE COWBOYS, THE see **GREAT SMOKEY ROADBLOCK, THE** • 1976
LAST OF THE DANDY, THE • 1910 • Aylott Dave • UKN
LAST OF THE DESPERADOES see **LAST OF THE DESPERADOS** • 1955
LAST OF THE DESPERADOS • 1955 • Newfield Sam • USA • LAST OF THE DESPERADOES
LAST OF THE DUANES, THE • 1919 • Edwards J. Gordon • USA
LAST OF THE DUANES, THE • 1924 • Reynolds Lynn • USA
LAST OF THE DUANES, THE • 1930 • Werker Alfred L. • USA
LAST OF THE DUANES, THE • 1941 • Tinling James • USA
LAST OF THE FAST GUNS, THE • 1958 • Sherman George • USA
LAST OF THE FEW • 1960 • Millin David • SAF
LAST OF THE GHOSTBUSTERS, THE see **GHOSTBUSTERS II** • 1989
LAST OF THE GOOD GUYS, THE • 1978 • Flicker Theodore J. • TVM • USA
LAST OF THE GREAT SURVIVORS, THE • 1983 • Jameson Jerry • TVM • USA
LAST OF THE HARGROVES, THE • 1914 • Collins John H. • USA
LAST OF THE IMPERIAL ARMY, THE see **SAIGO NO NIHONHEI** • 1960
LAST OF THE INGRAHAMS, THE • 1917 • Edwards Walter • USA
LAST OF THE KNUCKLEMEN, THE • 1979 • Burstall Tim • ASL
LAST OF THE LINE, THE • 1915 • Hunt Jay, Ince Thomas H. (Spv) • USA
LAST OF THE LONE WOLF, THE • 1930 • Boleslawski Richard • USA
LAST OF THE LONG HAIRED BOYS, THE • 1968 • Everett Peter • UKN
LAST OF THE MADISONS, THE • 1913 • Brenon Herbert • USA
LAST OF THE MAFFIA, THE • 1915 • Goldin Sidney M. • USA
LAST OF THE MOBILE HOT-SHOTS, THE • 1970 • Lumet Sidney • USA • BLOOD KIN
LAST OF THE MOE HIGGINS, THE • 1931 • Buzzell Edward • SHT • USA
LAST OF THE MOHICANS • 1932 • Beebe Ford, Eason B. Reeves • SRL • USA
LAST OF THE MOHICANS • Mathew Cano
LAST OF THE MOHICANS, THE • 1911 • *Powers* • USA
LAST OF THE MOHICANS, THE • 1911 • Marston Theodore • *Thanhouser* • USA
LAST OF THE MOHICANS, THE • 1920 • Tourneur Maurice, Brown Clarence • USA
LAST OF THE MOHICANS, THE • 1936 • Seitz George B., Fox Wallace • USA
LAST OF THE MOHICANS, THE • 1977 • Conway James L. • TVM • USA
LAST OF THE MORGANS, THE • 1916 • Mong William V. • SHT • USA
LAST OF THE NABOBS, THE see **MAGYAR NABOB -KARPATHY ZOLTAN, EGY** • 1966
LAST OF THE NIGHT RIDERS, THE • 1917 • McRae Henry • SHT • USA
LAST OF THE NOMADS see **SAME-JAKKI** • 1957
LAST OF THE OPEN RANGE, THE • 1920 • *Arrow* • USA
LAST OF THE PAGANS • 1935 • Thorpe Richard • USA • MALA
LAST OF THE PONY RIDERS • 1953 • Archainbaud George • USA
LAST OF THE RED HOT LOVERS • 1972 • Saks Gene • USA
LAST OF THE REDMEN • 1947 • Sherman George • USA • LAST OF THE REDSKINS (UKN)
LAST OF THE REDSKINS (UKN) see **LAST OF THE REDMEN** • 1947
LAST OF THE RENEGADES (USA) see **WINNETOU II** • 1964
LAST OF THE SAMURAI see **SHINSENGUMI ONITAICHO** • 1954
LAST OF THE SAXONS, THE • 1910 • Blackton J. Stuart • USA
LAST OF THE SECRET AGENTS?, THE • 1966 • Abbott Norman • USA
LAST OF THE SHCUNUE • 1971 • Griffiths Mark • SHT • USA
LAST OF THE SKI BUMS, THE • 1969 • Barrymore Dick • USA
LAST OF THE SMUGGLERS, THE • 1914 • *Kineto* • UKN
LAST OF THE STILLS • 1915 • King Burton L. • USA
LAST OF THE SUMMER WINE: GETTING SAM HOME • 1983 • Bell Alan J. W. • TVM • UKN • GETTING SAM HOME
LAST OF THE SUMMER WINE: UNCLE OF THE BRIDE • 1985 • Bell Alan J. W. • TVM • UKN • UNCLE OF THE BRIDE
LAST OF THE TROUBADOURS, THE • 1917 • Smith David • SHT • USA
LAST OF THE TWO DOLLAR — • 1970 • *Chancellor Films* • USA
LAST OF THE VIKINGS (USA) see **ULTIMO DEI VICHINGHI, L'** • 1961
LAST OF THE WARRENS • 1936 • Bradbury Robert North • USA
LAST OF THE WERKELMANNS, THE see **LETZTE WERKELMANN, DER** • 1972
LAST OF THE WILD HORSES • 1948 • Lippert Robert L • USA
LAST OF THEIR RACE, THE • 1914 • *Madison Cleo* • USA
LAST OLD LADY, THE • 1913 • *Ramo* • USA
LAST ORIGINAL B-MOVIE, THE see **BODY FEVER** • 1972
LAST OUTLAW, THE • 1919 • Ford John • USA
LAST OUTLAW, THE • 1927 • Rosson Arthur • USA
LAST OUTLAW, THE • 1936 • Cabanne W. Christy • USA
LAST OUTPOST, THE • 1935 • Barton Charles T., Gasnier Louis J. • USA
LAST OUTPOST, THE • 1951 • Foster Lewis R. • USA • CAVALRY CHARGE
LAST PAGE, THE • 1952 • Fisher Terence • UKN • MANBAIT (USA)
LAST PAIR OUT see **SISTA PARET UT** • 1956
LAST PARADE, THE • 1931 • Kenton Erle C. • USA
LAST PARADISE, THE see **ULTIMO PARADISO, L'** • 1956
LAST PARADISES, THE see **LETZTEN PARADIESE, DIE** • 1968
LAST PARTEITAG IN NUREMBERG, THE see **OSTATNI PARTEITAG W NORYMBERDZE** • 1946
LAST PARTY OF CHAUVINISTS, THE see **SAIGO NO JOITO** • 1945
LAST PAYMENT (USA) see **KARUSSEL DES LEBENS** • 1919
LAST PEDESTRIAN, THE • Bevc Joze • DOC • YGS
LAST PERFORMANCE, THE • 1912 • *Pathe* • USA
LAST PERFORMANCE, THE • 1927 • Fejos Paul • USA • ERIC THE GREAT ILLUSIONIST ○ LAST CALL, THE (UKN) ○ ERIC THE GREAT
LAST PICTURE SHOW, THE • 1971 • Bogdanovich Peter • USA
LAST PLANE FROM CORAMAYA, THE • 1989 • Roberts Randy • TVM • USA
LAST PLANE OUT • 1983 • Nelson David • USA
LAST PLANTATION, THE see **FOGO MORTO** • 1976
LAST PLATOON • 1988 • Robinson Paul D. • USA
LAST POLKA, THE • 1984 • Blanchard John • USA
LAST PORNO FLICK, THE see **MAD, MAD MOVIE MAKERS, THE** • 1974
LAST POSSE, THE • 1953 • Werker Alfred L. • USA
LAST POST, THE • 1929 • Shurey Dinah • UKN
LAST PRECINCT, THE • 1986 • Averback Hy • TVM • USA
LAST PREY OF THE VAMPIRE, THE see **ULTIMA PREDA DEL VAMPIRO, L'** • 1960
LAST QUEST, THE • 1912 • *Powers* • USA
LAST RACE, THE see **POSLEDNJA TRKA** • 1979
LAST RAMPAGE, THE see **REKVIJEM** • 1971
LAST REBEL, THE • 1915 • Terwilliger George W. • USA
LAST REBEL, THE • 1918 • Hamilton G. P. • USA
LAST REBEL, THE • 1971 • McCoy Denys • USA, ITL
LAST REBEL, THE (USA) see **ULTIMO REBELDE, EL** • 1956
LAST REFLECTIONS ON A WAR: BERNARD FALL • 1968 • Fox Beryl • DOC • CND
LAST REHEARSAL, THE • 1973 • Koutelidakis Nikos • SHT • GRC
LAST RELIC, THE see **POSLEDNAYA RELIKVIYA** • 1971
LAST RELICS see **POSLEDNAYA RELIKVIYA** • 1971
LAST REMAKE OF BEAU GESTE, THE • 1977 • Feldman Marty • USA
LAST RESORT, THE • 1985 • Buzby Zane • USA • CLUB SANDWICH
LAST REUNION, THE • 1978 • Wertz Jay • USA
LAST RHINO, THE • 1961 • Geddes Henry • UKN
LAST RIDE, THE • 1932 • Worne Duke • USA
LAST RIDE, THE • 1944 • Lederman D. Ross • USA
LAST RIDE OF THE DALTON GANG, THE • 1979 • Curtis Dan • TVM • USA
LAST RIDE TO SANTA CRUZ, THE (USA) see **LETZTE RITT NACH SANTA CRUZ, DER** • 1964
LAST RIGHT, THE • 1983 • Fortier Bob • MTV • CND
LAST RITES • 1980 • Paris Domonic • USA • DRACULA'S LAST RITES
LAST RITES • 1988 • Bellisario Donald P. • USA • SANCTUARY
LAST RITES see **ANTARJALLI YATRA** • 1988
LAST ROAD, THE • 1963 • Agakhanov Kh. • USS
LAST ROGUE, THE • 1964 • Mirsky Lev • USS
LAST ROLL-CALL, THE (USA) see **GRANDE APPELLO, IL** • 1936
LAST ROMAN, THE • 1968 • Siodmak Robert • FRG, RMN
LAST ROMANTIC LOVER, THE see **DERNIER AMANT ROMANTIQUE, LE** • 1978
LAST ROMANTICS, THE see **ULTIMOS ROMANTICOS, LOS** • 1979
LAST ROSE, THE • 1911 • *Powers* • USA
LAST ROSE, THE • 1915 • Johnson Arthur • USA
LAST ROSE FROM CASANOVA, THE see **POSLEDNI RUZE OD CASANOVY** • 1966
LAST ROSE OF SUMMER, THE • 1912 • *Clayton Ethel* • USA
LAST ROSE OF SUMMER, THE • 1920 • Ward Albert • UKN
LAST ROSE OF SUMMER, THE • 1937 • Fitzpatrick James A. • UKN
LAST ROUND, THE • 1914 • Haldane Bert? • UKN
LAST ROUND, THE • 1915 • *Apex* • USA
LAST ROUND-UP, THE • 1934 • Hathaway Henry • USA • BORDER LEGION, THE
LAST ROUND-UP, THE • 1943 • Davis Mannie • ANS • USA
LAST ROUND-UP, THE • 1947 • English John • USA
LAST ROUNDUP, THE • 1929 • McGowan J. P. • USA
LAST RUN, THE • 1971 • Fleischer Richard • USA
LAST RUN, THE • 1985 • SAF
LAST RUN, THE see **THOMPSON'S LAST RUN** • 1986
LAST RUN OF THE OLD SANTA FE COACH, THE • 1913 • *Frontier* • USA
LAST SACRIFICE, THE • 1975 • Todorovsky Petr • USS
LAST SAFARI, THE • 1967 • Hathaway Henry • UKN
LAST SALARY, THE see **DESEBAGATO** • 1987
LAST SAMURAI • 1989 • Mayersberg Paul • USA
LAST SATURDAY, THE see **ULTIMO SABADO, EL** • 1968
LAST SCENE OF ALL, THE • 1914 • Miller Ashley • USA
LAST SCENT, THE • 1917 • Beaudine William • SHT • USA
LAST SCHOOLBELL, THE • 1989 • Lazarkiewicz Magdalena • PLN
LAST SEASON, THE • 1987 • Zahr Raja • USA
LAST SENTENCE, THE • 1917 • Turbett Ben • USA
LAST SHOT, THE • 1913 • *Essanay* • USA
LAST SHOT, THE • 1914 • *Reliance* • USA
LAST SHOT, THE • 1916 • Terwilliger George W. • SHT • USA
LAST SHOT, THE • 1920 • *Coburn Wallace* • SHT • USA
LAST SHOT, THE • 1926 • Barnett Charles • UKN
LAST SHOT, THE see **LAATSTE SCOT, HET** • 1945
LAST SHOT, THE see **POSLEDNI VYSTREL** • 1950
LAST SHOT, THE see **OSTATNI STRZAL** • 1958
LAST SHOT, THE see **TEMPS DES LOUPS -TEMPO DI VIOLENZA, LE** • 1970
LAST SHOT YOU HEAR, THE • 1969 • Hessler Gordon • UKN
LAST SNOWS OF SPRING, THE (UKN) see **ULTIMA NEVE DI PRIMAVERA** • 1973
LAST SOLDIER, THE see **ULTIMO SOLDADO, O** • 1980
LAST SONG • Berry Dennis • SWT
LAST SONG, THE • 1980 • Levi Alan J. • TVM • USA • LADY IN DANGER
LAST SONG, THE see **CANTICO FINAL** • 1976
LAST STAGE, THE (UKN) see **OSTATNI ETAP** • 1948
LAST STAGECOACH WEST • 1957 • Kane Joseph • USA
LAST STAKE, THE • 1923 • Bentley Thomas • UKN
LAST STAND, THE • 1930 • Nelson Jack • SHT • USA
LAST STAND, THE • 1938 • Lewis Joseph H. • USA
LAST STAND OF THE DALTON BOYS, THE • 1912 • Kenyon Jack • SHT • USA
LAST STARFIGHTER, THE • 1984 • Castle Nick • USA
LAST STEP DOWN, THE • 1970 • Ramport Lawrence • USA
LAST STOP, THE • 1956 • Gries Tom • USA
LAST STOP, THE see **POSLEDNJA POSTAJA** • 1972
LAST STOP, THE (USA) see **OSTATNI ETAP** • 1948
LAST STRAW, THE • 1910 • *Defender* • USA
LAST STRAW, THE • 1920 • Clift Denison, Swickard Charles • USA
LAST STRAW, THE • 1934 • *Terry Paul/ Moser Frank (P)* • ANS • USA
LAST STRAW, THE • 1988 • Walker Giles • CND
LAST STREET BOY, THE (USA) see **ULTIMO SCIUSCIA, L'** • 1946
LAST STRONGHOLD, THE • 1963 • Joseph Stanley • DCS • UKN
LAST SUMMER • 1969 • Perry Frank • USA
LAST SUMMER, THE see **POSLEDNI LETO** • 1937
LAST SUMMER, THE see **POSLEDNO LYATO** • 1974
LAST SUMMER, THE see **SISTA LEKEN, DEN** • 1983
LAST SUMMER WON'T HAPPEN • 1969 • Gessner Peter • DOC • USA
LAST SUNSET, THE • 1961 • Aldrich Robert • USA
LAST SUPPER, THE • 1914 • Johnston Lorimer • USA
LAST SUPPER, THE see **ULTIMA CENA, LA** • 1977
LAST SURVIVOR, THE • 1975 • Katzin Lee H. • TVM • USA
LAST SURVIVOR, THE see **ULTIMO MONDO CANNIBALE** • 1977
LAST SURVIVOR, THE (USA) see **PAESE DEL SESSO SELVAGGIO, IL** • 1972
LAST SWINDLER, THE see **POSLYEDNI ZHULIK** • 1967
LAST TANGO IN MADRID, THE see **ULTIMO TANGO EN MADRID, EL** • 1975
LAST TANGO IN PARIS (UKN) see **ULTIMO TANGO A PARIGI, L'** • 1972
LAST TASMANIAN, THE • 1978 • Haydon Tom • ASL
LAST TEMPEST, THE see **YING T'AI CH'I HSUEH** • 1976
LAST TEMPTATION see **SUOR LETIZIA** • 1956
LAST TEMPTATION OF CHRIST, THE • 1988 • Scorsese Martin • USA, CND
LAST TEN DAYS, THE (USA) see **LETZTE AKT, DER** • 1955
LAST TEN DAYS OF ADOLF HITLER, THE see **LETZTE AKT, DER** • 1955
LAST TEN DAYS OF HITLER, THE see **LETZTE AKT, DER** • 1955
LAST TENANT, THE • 1978 • Taylor Jud • TVM • USA
LAST THREE DAYS • Chakraborty Prafulla • IND
LAST THREE DAYS, THE see **ULTIMI TRE GIORNI, GLI** • 1978
LAST THRUST, THE • 1916 • *Humphrey Orral* • USA
LAST TIDE, THE • 1931 • Argyle John F. • UKN
LAST TIME I SAW ARCHIE, THE • 1961 • Webb Jack • USA
LAST TIME I SAW PARIS, THE • 1954 • Brooks Richard • USA
LAST TIME WITH YOU, THE see **SENINLE SONDEFA** • 1980
LAST TO GO • 1971 • Potterton Gerald • ANS • CND
LAST TOMAHAWK, THE see **LETZTE MOHIKANER, DER** • 1965
LAST TOMB OF LIGEIA see **TOMB OF LIGEIA, THE** • 1964
LAST TOUCH OF LOVE, THE • 1978 • Ottini Philip • USA
LAST TRACK see **POSLEDNJI KOLOSEK** • 1956
LAST TRAIL, THE • 1921 • Flynn Emmett J. • USA
LAST TRAIL, THE • 1927 • Seiler Lewis • USA
LAST TRAIL, THE • 1933 • Tinling James • USA
LAST TRAIN, THE • 1960 • Muller Geoffrey • UKN
LAST TRAIN, THE see **TRAIN, LE** • 1973
LAST TRAIN, THE see **LAATSTE TREIN, DE** • 1975
LAST TRAIN, THE see **POSLEDNI VIAK** • 1982

LAST TRAIN FROM BOMBAY • 1952 • Sears Fred F. • USA
LAST TRAIN FROM GUN HILL • 1959 • Sturges John • USA
LAST TRAIN FROM MADRID, THE • 1937 • Hogan James P. • USA
LAST TRAIN TO BERLIN see **REKVIJEM** • 1971
LAST TRAP, THE • 1935 • Lamont Charles • USA
LAST TRICK, THE see **POSLEDNI TRIK PANA SCHWARZWALLDEA A PANA EDGARA** • 1964
LAST TRICK OF MR. SCHWARZWALD AND MR. EDGAR, THE see **POSLEDNI TRIK PANA SCHWARZWALLDEA A PANA EDGARA** • 1964
LAST TWO MINUTES, THE • 1989 • PHL
LAST TYCOON, THE • 1957 • Frankenheimer John • MTV • USA
LAST TYCOON, THE • 1976 • Kazan Elia • USA
LAST UNICORN, THE • 1982 • Rankin Arthur Jr., Bass Jules • ANM • USA
LAST VACATION, THE (USA) see **DERNIERES VACANCES, LES** • 1947
LAST VALLEY, THE • 1970 • Clavell James • UKN
LAST VENDETTA, THE see **KHEVSURSKAYA BALLADA** • 1965
LAST VENGEANCE, THE see **KHEVSURSKAYA BALLADA** • 1965
LAST VICTIM, THE • 1975 • Sotos Jim • USA • FORCED ENTRY
LAST VICTIM, THE see **SON KURBAN** • 1967
LAST VIDEO AND TESTAMENT • 1984 • Sasdy Peter • TVM • UKN
LAST VOLUNTEER, THE • 1914 • Apfel Oscar • USA
LAST VOYAGE, THE • 1959 • Stone Andrew L. • USA
LAST WAGER, THE see **TELEFTAIO STICHIME** • 1989
LAST WAGON, THE • 1956 • Daves Delmer • USA
LAST WALTZ, THE • 1936 • Barry Gerald, Mittler Leo • UKN
LAST WALTZ, THE • 1978 • Scorsese Martin • USA
LAST WALTZ, THE see **LETZTE WALZER, DER** • 1934
LAST WALTZ, THE (USA) see **LETZTE WALZER, DER** • 1927
LAST WALTZ, THE (USA) see **LETZTE WALZER, DER** • 1953
LAST WAR, THE (USA) see **SEKAI DAI SENSO** • 1961
LAST WARNING, THE • 1929 • Leni Paul • USA
LAST WARNING, THE • 1938 • Rogell Albert S. • USA
LAST WARRIOR, THE • 1989 • Wragge Martin • SAF
LAST WARRIOR, THE see **FINAL EXECUTIONER, THE** • 1983
LAST WARRIOR, THE (UKN) see **FLAP** • 1969
LAST WAVE, THE • 1977 • Weir Peter • ASL
LAST WHITE MAN, THE • 1924 • Mattison Frank S. • USA
LAST WILL, THE • 1914 • Davis Ulysses • USA
LAST WILL OF DR. MABUSE, THE see **TESTAMENT DES DR. MABUSE, DAS** • 1932
LAST WILL OF DR. MABUSE, THE see **TESTAMENT DES DR. MABUSE, DAS** • 1962
LAST WINTER, THE • 1990 • Johnston Aaron Kim • CND
LAST WINTER, THE see **HAKHOREFF HA'AKHARON** • 1983
LAST WISH, THE • 1949 • Lee Sam • UKN
LAST WISH, THE see **PERMINTAAN TERAKHIR** • 1974
LAST WISHES • 1983 • Vulchanov Rangel • BUL
LAST WITCH, THE • 1957 • Bahna Vladimir • CZC
LAST WITNESS • 1985 • Weiss E. Bruce • USA
LAST WITNESS, THE • 1925 • Paul Fred • UKN
LAST WITNESS, THE see **LETZTE ZEUGE, DER** • 1960
LAST WOMAN, THE (USA) see **ULTIMA DONNA, L'** • 1976
LAST WOMAN OF SHANG, THE (USA) see **TA CHI** • 1962
LAST WOMAN ON EARTH, THE • 1961 • Corman Roger • USA • WORLD WITHOUT WOMEN
LAST WORD, THE • 1915 • *Manley Charles "daddy"* • USA
LAST WORD, THE • 1979 • Boulting Roy • UKN
LAST WORD, THE see **POSLEDNATA DOUMA** • 1973
LAST WORD IS MINE, THE see **SON SOZ BENIM** • 1967
LAST WORDS see **LETZTE WORTE** • 1967
LAST YEAR AT MARIENBAD (USA) see **ANNEE DERNIERE A MARIENBAD, L'** • 1961
LAST YEAR IN MARIENBAD (UKN) see **ANNEE DERNIERE A MARIENBAD, L'** • 1961
LAST YEARS OF CHILDHOOD, THE see **LETZTEN JAHRE DER KINDHEIT, DIE** • 1980
LAST YEARS TIMETABLE • 1909 • Fitzhamon Lewin • UKN
LASTBILEN • 1977 • Mattsson Arne • SWD • LORRY, THE
LASTEN ELOKUVAMUSIKAALI • 1973 • Talaskivi Jaakko • FNL • SCREEN MUSICAL FOR CHILDREN, A
LASTER see **LASTER DER MENSCHHEIT** • 1927
LASTER, DAS • 1915 • Oswald Richard • FRG
LASTER DER MENSCHHEIT • 1927 • Meinert Rudolf • FRG • LUSTS OF MANKIND ○ LASTER
LASTER DES SPIELS, DAS • 1923 • *Buchowetzki Dimitri* • FRG
LASTIMA DE ROPA • 1961 • Gomez Landero Humberto • MXC
LASTING LESSON, A • 1915 • Coyle Walter • USA
LAT DIOR • 1975 • Senghor Blaise • SNL
LATA LENA OCH BLAOGDE PER • 1947 • Wallen Lennart • SWD • HALTA LENA OCH VINDOGDE PER ○ LAZY LENA AND BLUE-EYED PER
LATCHKEY, THE • 1910 • *Thanhouser* • USA
LATE AFTERNOON see **POZNE POPOLUDNIE** • 1964
LATE AFTERNOON OF A FAUN, THE see **FAUNOVO VELMI POZDNI ODPOLEDNE** • 1984
LATE AT NIGHT • 1946 • Chorlton Michael • UKN
LATE AUTUMN see **AKIBIYORI** • 1960
LATE AUTUMN -ONCE UPON A DAY IN SWEDEN • 1987 • von Strauss Ulf • DOC • SWD
LATE CHRISTOPHER BEAN, THE see **CHRISTOPHER BEAN** • 1933
LATE CHRYSANTHEMUMS see **BANGIKU** • 1954
LATE EDWINA BLACK, THE • 1951 • Elvey Maurice • UKN • OBSESSED (USA)
LATE EXTRA • 1935 • Parker Albert • UKN
LATE FOR DINNER • 1990 • Richter W. D. • USA
LATE FOR WORK • 1904 • Mottershaw Frank • UKN
LATE GEORGE APLEY, THE • 1947 • Mankiewicz Joseph L. • USA
LATE GREAT PLANET EARTH, THE • 1978 • Amram Robert • DOC • USA
LATE HOURS • 1921 • Roach Hal • SHT • USA
LATE LAMENTED, THE • 1917 • *Thurman Mary* • SHT • USA
LATE LAMENTED, THE • 1922 • Roach Hal • SHT • USA
LATE LIZ, THE • 1971 • Ross Dick • USA
LATE LODGERS • 1921 • Roach Hal • SHT • USA
LATE MAN, THE • 1972 • Lynch Paul • CND
LATE MATHIAS PASCAL, THE (USA) see **HOMME DE NULLE PART, L'** • 1936
LATE MATTHEW PASCAL, THE see **FEU MATTHIAS PASCAL** • 1925
LATE MR. JONES, THE • 1913 • Young James • USA
LATE MRS. EARLY, THE • 1911 • Crane Frank H. • USA
LATE NANCY IRVING, THE • 1984 • Sasdy Peter • TVM • UKN
LATE NIGHT FINAL • 1954 • Tully Montgomery • UKN
LATE PERFORMANCE see **FUNCION DE NOCHE** • 1982
LATE SEASON see **UTOSZEZON** • 1967
LATE SHOW, THE • 1969 • Wakely Michael • UKN
LATE SHOW, THE • 1977 • Benton Robert • USA
LATE SPRING see **BANSHUN** • 1949
LATE SUMMER BLUES see **BLUES HAHOFESH HAGADOL** • 1987
LATE SUPERIMPOSITIONS see **NUMBER 14** • 1964-65
LATE WINTER AND EARLY SPRING • 1957 • Brealey Gil • SHT • ASL
LATELLE -AERIAL HIGH ROPE CYCLISTS • 1903 • *Urban Trading Co.* • UKN
LATELY • Wurst Charles • SHT • USA
LATENT IMAGE • 1988 • Perelman Pablo • CHL
LATENT SPARK, THE • 1911 • *Phillips Edward* • USA
LATENT SPARK, THE • 1913 • *American* • USA
LATENT SPARK, THE • 1914 • Edwards Walter? • USA
LATERNA FTOHIA KE FILOTIMO • 1956 • Sakellarios Alekos • GRC • LATERNA, PAUVRETE ET GENEROSITE
LATERNA MAGICA • 1967 • Kijowicz Miroslaw • ANS • PLN
LATERNA MAGIKA • 1958 • Radok Alfred, Forman Milos • SHT • CZC
LATERNA MAGIKA II • 1960 • Forman Milos (c/d) • CZC
LATERNA, PAUVRETE ET GENEROSITE see **LATERNA FTOHIA KE FILOTIMO** • 1956
LATEST FASHIONS IN SKIRTS, THE • 1910 • *Pathe* • USA
LATEST FROM PARIS, THE • 1927 • Wood Sam • USA • PULLMAN PARTNERS
LATEST IN GARTERS, THE • 1910 • *Essanay* • USA
LATEST IN PANTS, THE • 1920 • Lyons Eddie, Moran Lee • SHT • USA
LATEST IN VAMPIRES, THE • 1916 • Myers Harry • SHT • USA
LATEST NEWS, THE • 1904 • *Warwick Trading Co* • UKN
LATEST STYLE AIRSHIP • 1908 • Zecca Ferdinand • FRN
LATHE OF HEAVEN, THE • 1980 • Loxton David, Barzyk Fred • TVM • USA
LATHERED TRUTH • 1916 • Myers Harry • SHT • USA
LATIGO see **SUPPORT YOUR LOCAL GUNFIGHTER** • 1971
LATIGO, EL • 1939 • Bohr Jose • WHIP, THE (USA)
LATIGO NEGRO, EL • 1957 • Orona Vicente • MXC
LATIGO NEGRO CONTRA EL ANIMA DEL AHORCADO, EL • 1957 • Orona Vicente • MXC
LATIGO NEGRO CONTRA LOS FARSANTES, EL • 1959 • Curiel Federico • MXC
LATIN BLOOD • 1914 • *Lubin* • USA
LATIN HI-HATTIN • 1938 • Schwarzwald Milton • SHT • USA
LATIN LOVE (USA) see **GREEK STREET** • 1930
LATIN LOVER EN ACAPULCO, UN • 1968 • Cortes Fernando • MXC • LATIN LOVER IN ACAPULCO, A
LATIN LOVER IN ACAPULCO, A see **LATIN LOVER EN ACAPULCO, UN** • 1968
LATIN LOVERS • 1953 • LeRoy Mervyn • USA
LATIN LOVERS (USA) see **ITALIANE E L'AMORE, LE** • 1961
LATIN LOVERS (USA) see **AMANTI LATINI, GLI** • 1965
LATIN QUARTER • 1945 • Sewell Vernon • UKN • FRENZY (USA)
LATIN QUARTER see **QUARTIER LATIN** • 1928
LATINO • 1985 • Wexler Haskell • USA
LATITUDE 55 • 1981 • Juliani John • CND
LATITUDE AND LONGITUDE • 1947 • Simpson Margaret, Hardy Ken • UKN
LATITUDE ZERO see **IDO ZERO DAISAKUSEN** • 1969
LATO NAD BALTYKIEM • 1964 • Slesicki Wladyslaw • DOC • PLN • SUMMER BY THE BALTIC ○ SUMMER ON THE BALTIC
LATT SAHEB • 1967 • Valia Hari • IND • GOVERNOR
LATTJO MED BOCCACCIO • 1949 • Bernhard Gosta • SWD • LATTJO MED SVEND ASMUSSEN ○ FUN WITH BOCCACCIO
LATTJO MED SVEND ASMUSSEN see **LATTJO MED BOCCACCIO** • 1949
LATUDE • 1911 • Bourgeois Gerard • FRN
LAUBENKOLONIE see **LUSTIGEN MUSIKANTEN, DIE** • 1930
LAUCHA'S WEDDING see **CASAMIENTO DE LAUCHA, EL** • 1977
LAUDE DELLA VITA E LA LAUDE DELLA MORTE, LA • 1916 • Falena Ugo • ITL
LAUERNDER TOD see **EISENBAHNKONIG 2, DER** • 1921
LAUF, HASE, LAUF • 1979 • Ninaus Alfred • AUS • RUN, RABBIT, RUN
LAUFEN LERNEN • 1980 • Bruckner Jutta • FRG
LAUFENDE BERG, DER • 1941 • Deppe Hans • FRG
LAUFER VON MARATHON, DER • 1933 • Dupont E. A. • FRG • MARATHON RUNNER, THE
LAUGH AND GET RICH • 1931 • La Cava Gregory • USA • BOARD AND ROOM
LAUGH AND THE WORLD LAUGHS see **HABIT OF HAPPINESS, THE** • 1916
LAUGH AND THE WORLD LAUGHS WITH YOU • 1925 • Butler Alexander • UKN
LAUGH BACK, THE • 1930 • Roberts Stephen • SHT • USA
LAUGH BAJAZZO! see **LACHE BAJAZZO!** • 1919
LAUGH, CLOWN, LAUGH • 1928 • Brenon Herbert • USA
LAUGH DOCTOR, THE (USA) see **LACHDOKTOR, DER** • 1937
LAUGH IT OFF • 1939 • Rogell Albert S. • USA • LADY BE GAY (UKN)
LAUGH IT OFF • 1940 • Baxter John • UKN
LAUGH LITTLE CLOWN see **ONCE IN A BLUE MOON** • 1935
LAUGH-O-GRAMS • 1922-23 • *Disney Walt (P)* • ASS • USA
LAUGH OF SCORN, THE • 1916 • Wilson Ben • SHT • USA
LAUGH ON DAD, THE • 1912 • *Bison* • USA
LAUGH ON DAD, THE • 1919 • Tinsdale A. C. • ASL
LAUGH THAT DIED, THE • 1915 • *Fuller Mary* • USA
LAUGH THAT OFF • 1924 • Roach Hal • SHT • USA
LAUGH WITH MAX LINDER (UKN) see **EN COMPAGNIE DE MAX LINDER** • 1964
LAUGH YOUR BLUES AWAY • 1943 • Barton Charles T. • USA • HOW DO YOU DO
LAUGHING • 1977 • Purdum Richard • UKN
LAUGHING AND CRYING see **PLAC A SMICH** • 1898
LAUGHING ANNE • 1953 • Wilcox Herbert • UKN
LAUGHING AT DANGER • 1924 • Horne James W. • USA
LAUGHING AT DANGER • 1940 • Bretherton Howard • USA
LAUGHING AT DEATH • 1929 • Fox Wallace • USA
LAUGHING AT LIFE • 1933 • Beebe Ford • USA
LAUGHING AT TROUBLE • 1937 • Strayer Frank • USA
LAUGHING BILL HYDE • 1918 • Henley Hobart • USA
LAUGHING BOY • 1934 • Van Dyke W. S. • USA
LAUGHING CAVALIER, THE • 1917 • Bramble A. V., Stannard Eliot • UKN
LAUGHING GAS • 1907 • Blackton J. Stuart • SHT • USA
LAUGHING GAS • 1907 • Porter Edwin S. • USA
LAUGHING GAS • 1914 • Chaplin Charles • USA • TUNING HIS IVORIES ○ DENTIST, THE ○ DOWN AND OUT
LAUGHING GAS • 1915 • *Starlight* • USA
LAUGHING GAS • 1920 • Buckingham Thomas • SHT • USA
LAUGHING GAS • 1921 • Kenton Erle C. • SHT • USA
LAUGHING GAS • 1931 • *Iwerks Ub (P)* • ANS • USA
LAUGHING GRAVY • 1931 • Horne James W. • SHT • USA
LAUGHING IN THE SUNSHINE see **KUNGLIGT AVENTYR, ETT** • 1956
LAUGHING IRISH EYES • 1936 • Santley Joseph • USA
LAUGHING LADIES • 1925 • Roach Hal • SHT • USA
LAUGHING LADY, THE • 1929 • Schertzinger Victor • USA
LAUGHING LADY, THE • 1946 • Stein Paul L. • UKN
LAUGHING MAN, THE see **LACHENDEN MANN, DER** • 1966
LAUGHING MASK, THE see **IRON CLAW, THE** • 1916
LAUGHING NIGGER, THE • 1907 • Gilbert Arthur • UKN
LAUGHING POLICEMAN, THE • 1973 • Rosenberg Stuart • USA • INVESTIGATION OF MURDER, AN (UKN)
LAUGHING POWDER • 1911 • *Aquila* • ITL
LAUGHING SASKIA, THE see **NEVETO SZASZKIA, A** • 1916
LAUGHING SINNERS • 1931 • Beaumont Harry • USA • TORCH SONG, THE
LAUGHING SONG • 1907 • *Walturdaw* • UKN
LAUGHING SONG, THE • 1909 • *Warwick Trading Co* • UKN
LAUGHING-STOCK, THE see **KOROIDARA, I** • 1967
LAUGHING WOMAN, THE (USA) see **FEMINA RIDENS** • 1969
LAUGHTER • 1930 • D'Arrast Harry D'Abbadie • USA
LAUGHTER AND TEARS • 1921 • Doxat-Pratt B. E. • UKN
LAUGHTER AND TEARS • 1928 • Parkinson H. B. • UKN
LAUGHTER IN HELL • 1933 • Cahn Edward L. • USA
LAUGHTER IN PARADISE • 1951 • Zampi Mario • UKN
LAUGHTER IN THE AIR (UKN) see **MYRT AND MARGE** • 1933
LAUGHTER IN THE DARK • 1969 • Richardson Tony • UKN, FRN, ITL • CHAMBRE OBSCURE, LA (FRN)
LAUGHTER OF FOOLS, THE • 1933 • Brunel Adrian • UKN
LAUGHTERHOUSE • 1984 • Eyre Richard • UKN • SINGLETON'S PLUCK
LAUKAUS TEEHTAALLA • 1972 • Kivikoski Erkko • FNL • SHOT IN THE FACTORY, THE ○ GUNSHOT IN THE FACTORY
LAULU TULIPUNAISESTA KUKASTA • 1938 • Tulio Teuvo • FNL • SONG OF THE SCARLET FLOWER, THE
LAULU TULIPUNAISESTA KUKASTA • 1971 • Niskanen Mikko • FNL • SONG OF THE SCARLET FLOWER, THE ○ SONG OF THE BLOOD-RED FLOWER
LAUNCELOT AND ELAINE • 1909 • *Vitagraph* • USA
LAUNCHING, THE • 1963 • Birkett Michael • UKN
LAUNDRESS, THE • 1914 • *Beery Wallace* • USA
LAUNDRESS AND THE LADY, THE • 1913 • *Brennan John E.* • USA
LAUNDRY • 1923 • Fleischer Dave • ANS • USA
LAUNDRY, THE • 1919 • Reisner Charles F. • SHT • USA
LAUNDRY, THE • 1946 • Hughes Harry • UKN • LOST IN THE WASH
LAUNDRY BLUES • 1930 • Foster John, Davis Mannie • ANS • USA
LAUNDRY CLEAN-UP, A • 1917 • *Triangle* • USA
LAUNDRY GIRL, THE • 1919 • Frenguelli Albert G., Mellor Edith • UKN • BECAUSE
LAUNDRY LADY'S LUCK • 1911 • *Essanay* • USA
LAUNDRY LIZ • 1916 • *Tincher Fay* • USA
LAUNDRY MIX-UP, A • 1917 • Ray John • USA
LAUNDRYMAN'S MISTAKE, THE • 1910 • Wilson Frank? • UKN
LAUNE EINES LEBEMANNES, DIE • 1920 • Hacker Gottfried? • FRG
LAUNEN DES GLUCKS, DIE • 1918 • *Reicher Ernst* • FRG
LAUNEN DES SCHICKSALS • Mack Max • FRG
LAUNEN EINER WELTDAME • 1914 • *Durieux Tilla* • FRG
LAUNEN EINES MILLIARDARS, DIE • 1919 • Wellin Arthur • FRG
LAURA • 1944 • Preminger Otto • USA
LAURA • 1955 • Brahm John • MTV • USA
LAURA • 1968 • Avrameas Nikos • GRC
LAURA • 1968 • Moxey John Llewellyn • TVM • USA
LAURA • 1970 • *Jo-Jo Dist.* • USA
LAURA • 1986 • Boszormenyi Geza • HNG
LAURA • 1987 • Herralde Gonzalo • SPN
LAURA see **CORBEAU, LE** • 1943
LAURA see **CORPO, IL** • 1974
LAURA see **LAURA, LES OMBRES DE L'ETE** • 1979
LAURA IN LOVE • 1970 • *Stacey Dist.* • USA
LAURA LANSING SLEPT HERE • 1988 • Schaefer George • TVM • USA • PENTHOUSE PARADISE
LAURA LAUR • 1988 • Sauriol Brigitte • CND
LAURA, LES OMBRES DE L'ETE • 1979 • Hamilton David • FRN • LAURA, SHADOWS OF A SUMMER ○ LAURA
LAURA LEY • 1989 • Sipman Jenne • NTH
LAURA NUDA • 1961 • Ferrari Nicolo • ITL, FRN
LAURA, SHADOWS OF A SUMMER see **LAURA, LES OMBRES DE L'ETE** • 1979
LAUREATE • 1932 • Etting Emlen • SHT • USA
LAUREL AND HARDY IN TOYLAND see **BABES IN TOYLAND** • 1934
LAUREL AND HARDY MURDER CASE, THE see **LAUREL-HARDY MURDER CASE, THE** • 1930

LAUREL AND HARDY'S LAUGHING 20'S • 1965 • Youngson Robert • CMP • USA
LAUREL-HARDY MURDER CASE, THE • 1930 • Parrott James • SHT • USA • LAUREL AND HARDY MURDER CASE, THE
LAUREL OF TEARS, THE • 1915 • MacDonald J. Farrell • USA
LAUREL-WREATH OF FAME, THE • 1912 • *Bushman Francis X.* • USA
LAURELES, LOS • 1959 • Salvador Jaime • MXC
LAURELS see **COURONNES** • 1909
LAURENCE • 1962 • Saguez Guy • SHT • FRN
LAURETTE • 1969 • Lasry Pierre • CND
LAURETTE OU LE CACHET ROUGE • 1931 • de Casembroot Jacques • FRN
LAURO PUNALES • 1966 • Cardona Rene • MXC
LAUSBUBENGESCHICHTEN • 1964 • Kautner Helmut • FRG
LAUT UND LIESE IST DER LIEBE • 1972 • Dziuba Helmut • GDR
LAUTA MANCIA • 1956 • De Agostini Fabio • ITL
LAUTARY see **LEUTARY, THE** • 1971
LAUTER LIEBE • 1940 • Ruhmann Heinz • FRG
LAUTER LUGEN • 1938 • Ruhmann Heinz • FRG
LAUTLOSE WAFFEN (FRG) see **ESPION, L'** • 1966
LAUTREAMONT • 1971 • Kupissonoff Jacques • SHT • BLG
LAUTREC 85 • 1985 • Prefontaine Michel • MTV • CND
LAV KUSH • 1951 • Bhatt Nanabhai • IND
LAVA see **LAWA** • 1989
LAVA-KUSA • 1963 • *Varalaxmi S.* • IND
LAVA OR A TALE OF ADAM MICKIEWICZ'S FOREFATHERS see **LAWA** • 1989
LAVAL KEEPS UP WITH THE TIMES • 1952 • Blais Roger • DCS • CND
LAVANDERAS DE PORTUGAL • 1957 • Torrado Ramon, Gaspard-Huit Pierre • SPN, FRN • LAVANDIERES DU PORTUGAL, LES (FRN)
LAVANDIERES DU PORTUGAL, LES (FRN) see **LAVANDERAS DE PORTUGAL** • 1957
LAVATORI DELLA PIETRA • 1955-59 • Taviani Paolo, Taviani Vittorio • DCS • ITL
LAVATORY MODERNE • 1900-01 • Blache Alice • FRN
LAVENDEL • 1953 • Rabenalt Arthur M. • FRG, AUS
LAVENDER AND LACE • 1932 • Hanna Pat • SHT • ASL
LAVENDER AND OLD LACE • 1921 • Ingraham Lloyd • USA
LAVENDER BATH LADY, THE • 1922 • Baggot King • USA
LAVENDER HILL MOB, THE • 1951 • Crichton Charles • UKN
LAVERNA • 1978 • Klimovsky Leon • SPN
LAVETE THESSIS • 1973 • Marangos Thodoros • GRC • GET ON YOUR MARKS ○ TA FILIATRA
LAVEUSES • 1896-97 • Lumiere Louis • FRN
LAVINA • 1946 • Cikan Miroslav • CZC
LAVINIA COMES HOME • 1916 • Dowlan William C. • SHT • USA
LAVIRINT SMRTI (YGS) see **OLD SUREHAND I** • 1965
LAVISH INVITATION, A see **HANAYAHANARU SHOTAI** • 1968
LAW, THE • 1974 • Badham John • TVM • USA
LAW, THE see **LAW AND ORDER** • 1940
LAW, THE see **LOI, LA** • 1958
LAW, THE see **ZAKON** • 1989
LAW-ABIDING CITIZEN, A see **ENAS NOMOTAGIS POLITIS** • 1973
LAW AGAINST LAW see **RENO** • 1923
LAW AND AUDREY • 1952 • Sparber I. • ANS • USA
LAW AND DISORDER • 1940 • MacDonald David • UKN
LAW AND DISORDER • 1958 • Crichton Charles, Cornelius Henry • UKN
LAW AND DISORDER • 1974 • Passer Ivan • USA
LAW AND HIS SON, THE • 1913 • O'Sullivan Tony • USA
LAW AND JAKE WADE, THE • 1958 • Sturges John • USA
LAW AND JUSTICE • 1917 • *Big U* • SHT • USA
LAW AND LADY LOVERLY, THE see **LAW AND THE LADY, THE** • 1951
LAW AND LAWLESS see **LAW AND THE LAWLESS** • 1932
LAW AND LEAD • 1936 • Hill Robert F. • USA
LAW AND ORDER • 1917 • Smith David • SHT • USA
LAW AND ORDER • 1921 • Roach Hal • SHT • USA
LAW AND ORDER • 1932 • Cahn Edward L. • USA • GUNS A'BLAZING ○ SAINT JOHNSON
LAW AND ORDER • 1940 • Taylor Ray • USA • LUCKY RALSTON (UKN) ○ LAW, THE
LAW AND ORDER • 1942 • Newfield Sam • USA • BILLY THE KID'S LAW AND ORDER ○ DOUBLE ALIBI, THE
LAW AND ORDER • 1950 • Donnelly Eddie • ANS • USA
LAW AND ORDER • 1953 • Juran Nathan • USA
LAW AND ORDER • 1970 • Wiseman Frederick • DOC • USA
LAW AND ORDER • 1976 • Chomsky Marvin • TVM • USA
LAW AND ORDER see **AFTER DARK** • 1923
LAW AND ORDER ON THE BAR L RANCH • 1911 • Dwan Allan • USA
LAW AND ORDER (UKN) see **FAST BULLETS** • 1936
LAW AND ORDER (UKN) see **FUGITIVE SHERIFF, THE** • 1936
LAW AND THE FIST, THE see **PRAWO I PIESC** • 1964
LAW AND THE LADY, THE • 1916 • Wells Raymond • USA
LAW AND THE LADY, THE • 1924 • McCutcheon John L. • USA
LAW AND THE LADY, THE • 1951 • Knopf Edwin H. • USA • LAW AND LADY LOVERLY, THE
LAW AND THE LAWLESS • 1932 • Schaefer Armand • USA • LAW AND LAWLESS
LAW AND THE MAN • 1928 • Pembroke Scott • USA
LAW AND THE MAN, THE • 1910 • *Nestor* • USA
LAW AND THE MAN, THE • 1910 • *Vitagraph* • USA
LAW AND THE OUTLAW • 1925 • *Mix Tom* • USA
LAW AND THE OUTLAW, THE • 1913 • Duncan William • USA
LAW AND THE WOMAN, THE • 1922 • Stanlaws Penrhyn • USA
LAW AND TOMBSTONE, THE see **HOUR OF THE GUN** • 1967
LAW AT SILVER CAMP, THE • 1915 • *Rodgers Walter L.* • USA
LAW BEYOND THE RANGE • 1935 • Beebe Ford • USA
LAW BRINGERS, THE • 1920 • Ince Ralph • USA
LAW COMES TO GUNSIGHT, THE • 1947 • Hillyer Lambert • USA • BACKFIRE (UKN)
LAW COMES TO TEXAS, THE • 1939 • Levering Joseph • USA
LAW COMMANDS, THE • 1937 • Nigh William • USA
LAW DECIDES, THE • 1916 • Earle William P. S. • USA
LAW DEMANDS, THE • 1924 • Hoyt Harry O. • USA
LAW DEMANDS, THE (UKN) see **RECKLESS RIDER, THE** • 1931
LAW DIVINE, THE • 1920 • Sanderson Challis, Parkinson H. B. • UKN
LAW ENFORCERS, THE (UKN) see **POLIZIA RINGRAZIA, LA** • 1972
LAW FOR TOMBSTONE • 1937 • Jones Buck • USA
LAW FORBIDS, THE • 1924 • Robbins Jess • USA
LAW HUSTLERS, THE see **LAW RUSTLERS, THE** • 1923
LAW IN HER HANDS, THE • 1936 • Clemens William • USA
LAW IN THE SADDLE • 1930 • Levigard Josef • SHT • USA
LAW IN THEIR OWN HANDS, THE • 1913 • Wilson Frank? • UKN
LAW IS THE LAW, THE (USA) see **LOI C'EST LA LOI, LA** • 1958
LAW KUNTU GHANI • 1942 • Barakat Henry • EGY • SI J'ETAIS RICHE
LAW MEN • 1944 • Hillyer Lambert • USA
LAW NORTH OF 65, THE • 1917 • Campbell Colin • SHT • USA
LAW OF COMPENSATION, THE • 1913 • *August Edwin* • USA
LAW OF COMPENSATION, THE • 1917 • Steger Julius, Golden Joseph A. • USA
LAW OF DESIRE, THE see **LEY DEL DESEO, LA** • 1986
LAW OF DUTY, THE • 1915 • Powers Francis • USA
LAW OF FEAR • 1928 • Storm Jerome • USA
LAW OF GOD, THE • 1912 • Dwan Allan • USA
LAW OF HIS KIND, THE • 1914 • *Rex* • USA
LAW OF HUMANITY, THE • 1913 • *Ostriche Muriel* • USA
LAW OF LIFE, THE • 1916 • Webster Harry Mcrae • SHT • USA
LAW OF LIFE, THE • 1940 • Stolper Alexander, Ivanov B. • USS
LAW OF LIFE, THE see **NOMOS TIS ZOIS, O** • 1967
LAW OF LOVE, THE • 1915 • MacDonald J. Farrell • USA
LAW OF LOVE, THE • 1915 • Myers Harry • USA
LAW OF MEN, THE • 1919 • Niblo Fred • USA
LAW OF NATURE, THE • 1916 • August Edwin • SHT • USA
LAW OF NATURE, THE • 1919 • Fischer David G. • USA
LAW OF SMUGGLING, THE see **HUDUTLARIN KANUNU** • 1966
LAW OF SUCCESS, THE • 1916 • *Lowery William* • SHT • USA
LAW OF THE 45'S • 1935 • McCarthy John P. • USA • MYSTERIOUS MR. SHEFFIELD (UKN)
LAW OF THE BADLANDS • 1945 • Scholl Jack • SHT • USA
LAW OF THE BADLANDS • 1950 • Selander Lesley • USA
LAW OF THE BARBARY COAST • 1949 • Landers Lew • USA
LAW OF THE BORDER, THE • 1920 • Ridgwell George • SHT • USA
LAW OF THE CANYON • 1947 • Nazarro Ray • USA • PRICE OF CRIME, THE (UKN)
LAW OF THE DOG, THE see **LEI DO CAO, A** • 1967
LAW OF THE GOLDEN WEST • 1949 • Ford Philip • USA
LAW OF THE GREAT LOVE, THE see **ZAKON VELIKOI LYUBVI** • 1945
LAW OF THE GREAT NORTHWEST, THE • 1918 • Wells Raymond • USA
LAW OF THE GUNHAMMER, THE see **LEI DO CAO, A** • 1967
LAW OF THE JUNGLE • 1942 • Yarbrough Jean • USA
LAW OF THE JUNGLE see **LEY DEL MONTE, LA** • 1989
LAW OF THE LAND • 1976 • Vogel Virgil W. • TVM • USA
LAW OF THE LAND, THE • 1917 • Tourneur Maurice • USA
LAW OF THE LASH • 1947 • Taylor Ray • USA
LAW OF THE LAWLESS • 1964 • Claxton William F. • USA
LAW OF THE LAWLESS, THE • 1923 • Fleming Victor • USA
LAW OF THE LUMBERJACK, THE • 1914 • *Clifford William* • USA
LAW OF THE MACHETE, THE see **LEY DE MACHETE, LA** • 1971
LAW OF THE MOUNTAINS, THE • 1909 • Olcott Sidney • USA
LAW OF THE MOUNTED • 1928 • McGowan J. P. • USA
LAW OF THE NORTH • 1932 • Fraser Harry L. • USA
LAW OF THE NORTH, THE • 1912 • Cox George L. • USA
LAW OF THE NORTH, THE • 1917 • George Burton • USA
LAW OF THE NORTH, THE • 1918 • Willat Irvin V. • USA
LAW OF THE NORTHWEST • 1943 • Berke William • USA
LAW OF THE OPEN, THE • 1915 • *Powers* • USA
LAW OF THE PAMPAS • 1939 • Watt Nate • USA • ARGENTINA
LAW OF THE PANHANDLE • 1950 • Collins Lewis D. • USA
LAW OF THE PLAINS • 1929 • *Tyler Tom* • USA
LAW OF THE PLAINS • 1938 • Nelson Sam • USA
LAW OF THE RANGE • 1941 • Taylor Ray • USA
LAW OF THE RANGE, THE • 1911 • Fahrney Milton • USA
LAW OF THE RANGE, THE • 1914 • McRae Henry • USA
LAW OF THE RANGE, THE • 1927 • Nigh William • USA • TEXAS RANGER, THE
LAW OF THE RANGER, THE • 1937 • Bennet Spencer Gordon • USA
LAW OF THE RIO GRANDE • 1931 • Cohn Bennett, Sheldon Forrest • USA • WANTED MEN (UKN)
LAW OF THE RIO (UKN) see **RIDERS OF THE RIO** • 1931
LAW OF THE SADDLE • 1943 • De Lay Melville • USA
LAW OF THE SEA • 1932 • Brower Otto • USA • LURE OF THE SEA
LAW OF THE SIBERIAN TAIGA • 1930 • Bolshintsov M. • USS
LAW OF THE SIERRAS, THE see **SALOMY JANE** • 1923
LAW OF THE SIX GUN • 1955 • Landers Lew • USA
LAW OF THE SNOW COUNTRY • 1926 • Hurst Paul C. • USA
LAW OF THE STREETS (USA) see **LOI DES RUES, LA** • 1956
LAW OF THE TEXAN • 1938 • Clifton Elmer • USA
LAW OF THE TIMBER • 1941 • Ray Bernard B. • USA
LAW OF THE TONG • 1931 • Collins Lewis D. • USA
LAW OF THE TROPICS • 1941 • Enright Ray • USA
LAW OF THE UNDERWORLD • 1938 • Landers Lew • USA
LAW OF THE VALLEY • 1944 • Bretherton Howard • USA
LAW OF THE WEST • 1932 • Bradbury Robert North • USA
LAW OF THE WEST • 1949 • Taylor Ray • USA
LAW OF THE WEST, THE • 1910 • *Selig* • USA
LAW OF THE WEST, THE • 1912 • Ince Thomas H. • USA
LAW OF THE WILD • 1934 • Schaefer Armand, Eason B. Reeves • SRL • USA
LAW OF THE WILD, THE • 1913 • *Tennant Barbara* • USA
LAW OF THE WILDS, THE • 1915 • *Rich Vivian* • USA
LAW OF THE WOLF • 1941 • Johnston Raymond K. • USA
LAW OF THE YUKON, THE • 1920 • Miller Charles • USA
LAW OF VENGEANCE see **TO THE LAST MAN** • 1933
LAW OF VENGEANCE, THE see **FADDIJA** • 1950
LAW OF VIOLENCE, THE • *Greenwood George* • ITL
LAW OR LOYALTY • 1926 • Harris Lawson • USA
LAW OR THE LADY • 1911 • *Champion* • USA
LAW OR THE LADY, THE • 1912 • *Costello Maurice* • USA
LAW RIDES, THE • 1936 • Bradbury Robert North • USA
LAW RIDES AGAIN, THE • 1943 • James Alan • USA
LAW RIDES WEST, THE (UKN) see **SANTA FE TRAIL, THE** • 1930
LAW RUSTLERS, THE • 1923 • King Louis • USA • BEYOND THE LAW (UKN) ○ LAW HUSTLERS, THE
LAW THAT DIVIDES, THE • 1919 • Mitchell Howard M. • USA
LAW THAT FAILED, THE • 1917 • *Hanlon Alma* • USA
LAW THEY FORGOT, THE (USA) see **LEY QUE OLVIDARON, LA** • 1938
LAW UNTO HERSELF, A • 1914 • *Rex* • USA
LAW UNTO HERSELF, A • 1918 • Worsley Wallace • USA
LAW UNTO HIMSELF, A • 1914 • *Leonard Robert* • USA
LAW UNTO HIMSELF, A • 1916 • Brockwell Robert • USA
LAW VS. BILLY THE KID, THE • 1954 • Castle William • USA
LAW WEST OF TOMBSTONE, THE • 1938 • Tryon Glenn • USA
LAWA • 1989 • Konwicki Tadeusz • PLN • LAVA OR A TALE OF ADAM MICKIEWICZ'S FOREFATHERS ○ LAVA
LAWAT AL-HUBB see **LAWET EL HUB** • 1959
LAWBREAKERS, THE • 1913 • *Bison* • USA
LAWBREAKERS, THE • 1915 • *Reliance* • USA
LAWBREAKERS, THE • 1961 • Newman Joseph M. • USA
LAWET EL HUB • 1959 • Abu Saif Salah • EGY • AGONY OF LOVE ○ LAWAT AL-HUBB
LAWFUL CHEATERS • 1925 • O'Connor Frank • USA
LAWFUL HOLDUP, THE • 1911 • Dwan Allan • USA
LAWFUL LARCENY • 1923 • Dwan Allan • USA
LAWFUL LARCENY • 1930 • Sherman Lowell • USA
LAWINE, DIE • 1923 • Curtiz Michael • AUS • AVALANCHE
LAWLESS, THE • 1949 • Losey Joseph • USA • DIVIDING LINE, THE (UKN)
LAWLESS, THE see **PARANOMI, I** • 1958
LAWLESS, THE see **HORS-LA-LOI, LES** • 1969
LAWLESS BORDERS • 1935 • McCarthy John P. • USA • BORDER PATROL, THE (UKN)
LAWLESS BREED • 1946 • Fox Wallace • USA • LAWLESS CLAN
LAWLESS BREED, THE • 1952 • Walsh Raoul • USA
LAWLESS CLAN see **LAWLESS BREED** • 1946
LAWLESS CODE • 1949 • Drake Oliver • USA
LAWLESS COWBOYS • 1951 • Collins Lewis D. • USA
LAWLESS EIGHTIES, THE • 1957 • Kane Joseph • USA
LAWLESS EMPIRE • 1945 • Keays Vernon • USA • POWER OF POSSESSION (UKN)
LAWLESS FRONTIER, THE • 1935 • Bradbury Robert North • USA
LAWLESS LAND • 1936 • Ray Albert • USA
LAWLESS LAND see **KANUNSUZ TOPRAK** • 1967
LAWLESS LAND, THE • 1988 • Hess Jon • CND
LAWLESS LEGION, THE • 1929 • Brown Harry J. • USA
LAWLESS LOVE • 1918 • Thornby Robert T. • USA
LAWLESS MEN • 1924 • Hart Neal • USA
LAWLESS NINETIES, THE • 1936 • Kane Joseph • USA
LAWLESS PLAINSMEN • 1942 • Berke William • USA • ROLL ON (UKN)
LAWLESS RANGE, THE • 1936 • Bradbury Robert North • USA
LAWLESS RIDER, THE • 1954 • Canutt Yakima • USA
LAWLESS RIDERS • 1935 • Bennet Spencer Gordon • USA
LAWLESS STREET, A • 1955 • Lewis Joseph H. • USA
LAWLESS TRAILS • 1926 • Sheldon Forrest • USA
LAWLESS VALLEY • 1932 • McGowan J. P. • USA
LAWLESS VALLEY • 1938 • Howard David • USA
LAWLESS WOMAN, THE • 1931 • Thorpe Richard • USA
LAWMAN • 1970 • Winner Michael • USA
LAWMAN IS BORN, A • 1937 • Newfield Sam • USA
LAWMAN WITHOUT A GUN • 1977 • Freedman Jerrold • TVM • USA
LAWRENCE DURRELL • 1968 • Bonniere Rene • DCS • CND
LAWRENCE OF ARABIA • 1935 • Haines Ronald • UKN
LAWRENCE OF ARABIA • 1962 • Lean David • UKN, USA
LAWRENCE OF ARABIA -THE MASTER ILLUSIONIST see **MASTER ILLUSIONIST, THE** • 1984
LAWRENCE'S ORCHARD • 1952 • Haupe Wlodzimierz, Bielinska Halina • ANM • PLN • ORCHARD OF PERE LAURENT, THE
LAWS AND OUTLAWS • 1918 • Howe J. A. • SHT • USA
LAW'S DECREE, THE • 1914 • Salter Harry • USA
LAW'S DECREE, THE • 1915 • *Craig Nell* • USA
LAW'S INJUSTICE, THE • 1916 • Sloman Edward • SHT • USA
LAW'S LASH, THE • 1928 • Smith Noel • USA
LAWS OF DISORDER: PART 3 -MOLECULES AT WORK, THE • 1969 • Griffiths Peter • DOC • UKN • MOLECULES AT WORK
LAW'S OUTLAW, THE • 1918 • Smith Cliff • USA
LAW'S THE LAW, THE see **CHEATING CHEATERS** • 1927
LAWYER, THE • 1970 • Furie Sidney J. • USA
LAWYER, DOG AND BABY • 1913 • *Thanhouser Twins* • USA
LAWYER MAN • 1932 • Dieterle William • USA
LAWYER OF THE POOR, THE see **ADVOKAT CHUDYCH** • 1941
LAWYER QUINCE • 1914 • Shaw Harold • UKN
LAWYER QUINCE • 1924 • Haynes Manning • UKN
LAWYER'S MESSAGE, THE • 1911 • Fitzhamon Lewin? • UKN
LAWYER'S SECRET, THE • 1916 • Cochrane George • SHT • USA
LAWYER'S SECRET, THE • 1931 • Gasnier Louis J., Marcin Max • USA
LAXDALE HALL • 1952 • Eldridge John • UKN • SCOTCH ON THE ROCKS (USA)
LAXMANA DO-RE-ME • 1971 • Ramlee P. • MLY • THEIR LORDSHIPS DO-RE-ME ○ LAKSEMANA DO RE MI
LAXMI NARAYAN • 1951 • Bhatt Nanabhai • IND • LAXMI THE GUARD
LAXMI POOJA • 1957 • Desai Jayant • IND
LAXMI THE GUARD see **LAXMI NARAYAN** • 1951
LAY DOWN YOUR ARMS see **NED MED VAABNENE** • 1914
LAY OFF! • 1919 • Lyons Eddie, Moran Lee • SHT • USA
LAY OFF • 1988 • Colosimo Rosa
LAY THAT RIFLE DOWN • 1955 • Lamont Charles • USA

LAYALY EL TAWILA, EL • 1967 • Diaeddin Ahmed • EGY • LONG NIGHTS, THE
LAYLA AK AKHIRA, AL- see LEILA EL AKHIRA, EL • 1963
LAYOUT • 1968 • Piper Hans-Albert • FRG
LAYOUT, THE • 1969 • Sarno Joe • USA
LAYOUT FOR 5 MODELS • 1973 • Gaudioz John • UKN
LAYTON.. BAMBOLE E KARATE (ITL) see CARRE DE DAMES POUR UN AS • 1966
LAZ • 1957 • Gertler Viktor • HNG • FEVER
LAZAM LAZAM • 1971 • Ben Salah Mohamed • SHT • ALG • IL FAUT, IL FAUT
LAZARILLO DE TORMES, EL • 1925 • Rey Florian • SPN
LAZARILLO DE TORMES, EL • 1959 • Ardavin Cesar • SPN • LAZARILLO (USA)
LAZARILLO (USA) see LAZARILLO DE TORMES, EL • 1959
LAZARO see WHERE THE RIVER RUNS BLACK • 1986
LAZARUS SYNDROME, THE • 1979 • Thorpe Jerry • TVM • USA
LAZIENKI PARK IN WARSAW, THE see WARSZAWSKIE LAZIENKI • 1960
LAZIEST MAN, THE • 1914 • *Lubin* • USA
LAZINESS • 1980 • Radanowicz Georg • MTV • SWT
LAZOS DE FUEGO • 1948 • Cardona Rene • MXC
LAZY BILL HUDSON • 1912 • *Washburn Alice* • USA
LAZY BONES • 1934 • Fleischer Dave • ANS • USA
LAZY BONES see HALLELUJAH, I'M A BUM • 1933
LAZY BOY, THE • 1909 • Fitzhamon Lewin • UKN
LAZY DAYS • 1929 • McGowan Robert • SHT • USA
LAZY FARMER BROWN • 1910 • *Edison* • USA
LAZY JIM'S LUCK • 1908 • Raymond Charles? • UKN
LAZY LENA AND BLUE-EYED PER see LATA LENA OCH BLAOGDE PER • 1947
LAZY LIGHTNING • 1926 • Wyler William • USA
LAZY LITTLE BEAVER • 1947 • Donnelly Eddie • ANS • USA
LAZY LOUIS • 1913 • *Joker* • USA
LAZY MARTIN • 1957 • Tyrlova Hermina • ANM • CZC
LAZY MEN OF THE FERTILE VALLEY, THE see TEMBELIDES TIS EFORIS KILADAS, I • 1976
LAZY RIVER • 1934 • Seitz George B. • USA • LOUISIANA
LAZY RIVER • 1968 • Dunning George • ANM • UKN
LAZY SA POHLI • 1952 • Bielik Palo • CZC • MOUNTAINS ARE STIRRING, THE
LAZY WORKMEN • 1905 • Mottershaw Frank • UKN
LAZYBONES • 1925 • Borzage Frank • USA
LAZYBONES • 1935 • Powell Michael • UKN
LAZYBONES see LENORA • 1949
LAZZARELLA • 1957 • Bragaglia Carlo Ludovico • ITL
LBJ: THE EARLY YEARS • 1987 • Werner Peter • TVM • USA
LE GRECO see EL GRECO • 1966
LE HAVRE • 1959 • Kyrou Ado • SHT • FRN
LE MANS • Civirani Osvaldo • ITL
LE MANS • 1971 • Katzin Lee H. • USA
LE MANS, 1952 • 1952 • Mason Bill • DOC • UKN
LE MANS SCORCIATOIA PER L'INFERNO • 1970 • Civirani Osvaldo • ITL
LEA, L'HIVER • 1970 • Monnet Marc • FRN
LEA LYON see LYON LEA • 1915
LEAD, THE • 1989 • Kimiyaei Massoud • IRN
LEAD DRESS, THE • 1985 • Murray Virginia • ASL
LEAD, KINDLY LIGHT • 1912 • *Learn Bessie* • USA
LEAD KINDLY LIGHT • 1916 • Page J. Hamilton • UKN • PRODIGAL DAUGHTER, THE
LEAD KINDLY LIGHT • 1918 • Wilson Rex • UKN
LEAD KINDLY LIGHT • 1928 • Parkinson H. B., Edwards J. Steven • SHT • UKN
LEAD LAW (UKN) see CROOKED TRAIL, THE • 1936
LEAD SHOES, THE • 1950 • Peterson Sidney • SHT • USA
LEADBELLY • 1976 • Parks Gordon • USA
LEADEN TIME see BLEIERNE ZEIT, DIE • 1981
LEADER • 1964 • Conner Bruce • SHT • USA
LEADER see CAUDILLO • 1976
LEADER, THE see CAUDILLO, EL • 1968
LEADER OF HIS FLOCK, THE • 1913 • *Baggot King* • USA
LEADER OF MEN, A • 1913 • *Johnson Arthur* • USA
LEADER OF THE BAND • 1987 • Hyams Nessa • USA
LEADER OF THE BAND, THE • 1912 • *Leonard Marion* • USA
LEADER OF THE PACK, THE see HELL'S ANGELS ON WHEELS • 1967
LEADER SALADIN, THE see NASSER SALAH-EL-DINE, EL • 1963
LEADING EDGE, THE • 1985 • Reusch Peter • MTV • CND
LEADING EDGE, THE • 1988 • Firth Michael • NZL
LEADING LADY, THE • 1911 • Finley Ned • USA
LEADING LADY, THE • 1913 • Finley Ned • USA
LEADING LADY'S BABY, THE • 1912 • *Pathe* • USA
LEADING LIZZIE ASTRAY • 1914 • Arbuckle Roscoe, Dillon Eddie • USA
LEADING MAN, THE • 1912 • Sennett Mack • USA
LEADING MAN, THE see ONLY MAN, THE • 1925
LEADING MAN, THE see HAUPTDARSTELLER, DER • 1978
LEADVILLE GUNSLINGER • 1952 • Keller Harry • USA
LEAF • 1962 • Hudson Fred • SHT • USA
LEAF FROM NATURE'S BOOK, A • 1920 • Parrott James • SHT • USA
LEAF FROM THE PAST, A • 1914 • Carleton Lloyd B. • USA
LEAF IN THE STORM, A • 1913 • Taylor Stanner E. V. • USA
LEAGUE OF FRIGHTENED MEN, THE • 1937 • Green Alfred E. • USA
LEAGUE OF GANGSTERS see GANG DOMES • 1963
LEAGUE OF GENTLEMEN, THE • 1960 • Dearden Basil • UKN
LEAGUE OF MERCY • 1911 • *Vitagraph* • USA
LEAGUE OF NATIONS • 1924 • Fleischer Dave • ANS • USA
LEAH • 1987 • Morry Susan • DCS • CND
LEAH KLESCHNA • 1913 • Dawley J. Searle • USA
LEAH THE FORSAKEN • 1908 • Brooke Van Dyke • USA
LEAH THE FORSAKEN • 1912 • Brenon Herbert • USA
LEAK, THE • 1917 • Beaudine William • SHT • USA
LEAK IN THE DYKE, A • 1965 • Mendelsohn Jack • ANS • USA
LEAK IN THE FOREIGN OFFICE, A • 1914 • *Cruze James* • USA
LEAKY FAUCET, THE • 1959 • Taras Martin B. • ANS • USA
LE'AM NE'ELAN DANIEL WAKS • 1972 • Heffner Avram • ISR • BUT WHERE IS DANIEL VAX? (USA)
LEAN ON ME • 1988 • Avildsen John G. • USA
LEAN ON ME • 1989 • Moyle Allan • USA
LEAN WOLF'S END • 1911 • *Kalem* • USA
LEANDER CLICKS see HOT TIP • 1935
LEANDRAS, LAS • 1960 • Martinez Solares Gilberto • MXC
LEANDRAS, LAS • 1969 • Martin Eugenio • SPN
LEANYPORTRE • 1971 • Szabo Istvan • DCS • HNG • PORTRAIT OF A GIRL, A
LEAO DA ESTRELA, O • 1947 • Duarte Arthur • PRT
LEAP, THE • 1916 • McRae Henry • SHT • USA
LEAP, THE see SKOK • 1968
LEAP AND LOOK THEREAFTER • 1916 • Curtis Allen • SHT • USA
LEAP FOR A LIFE, A • 1910 • *Kalem* • USA
LEAP FOR LIFE, A • 1914 • *Kalem* • USA
LEAP FOR LIFE, A • 1915 • *Blevins Malcolm* • USA
LEAP FOR LOVE, A • 1912 • *Imp* • USA
LEAP FROG RAILWAY • 1905 • *Bitzer Billy (Ph)* • USA
LEAP IN THE DARK, A (USA) see SALTO NEL VUOTO • 1979
LEAP INTO THE VOID (UKN) see SALTO NEL VUOTO • 1979
LEAP TO FAME • 1918 • Blackwell Carlyle • USA
LEAP YEAR • 1912 • *Prior Herbert* • USA
LEAP YEAR • 1920 • Goldberg Rube • ANS • USA
LEAP YEAR • 1921 • Cruze James • USA • SKIRT SHY
LEAP YEAR • 1932 • Walls Tom • UKN
LEAP YEAR • 1962 • Efros Anatoli • USS
LEAP YEAR COMEDY, A • 1912 • Dwan Allan • USA • LEAP YEAR COWBOY, THE ○ FEBRUARY 29
LEAP YEAR COWBOY, THE see LEAP YEAR COMEDY, A • 1912
LEAP YEAR DELUSION, A • 1912 • *Powers* • USA
LEAP YEAR ELOPEMENT, A • 1912 • *Savoyard Eugene* • USA
LEAP YEAR LOTTERY PRIZE, A • 1912 • *Johnson Arthur* • USA
LEAP-YEAR PROPOSAL • 1912 • Baker George D.? • USA
LEAP YEAR PROPOSALS • 1912 • *Bunny John* • USA
LEAP YEAR PROPOSALS OF AN OLD MAID • 1908 • *Vitagraph* • USA
LEAP YEAR TANGLE, A • 1916 • Christie Al • SHT • USA
LEAP YEAR WOOING, A • 1916 • Ellis Robert • SHT • USA
LEAPFROG • 1900 • *Riley Brothers* • UKN
LEAPFROG AS SEEN BY THE FROG • 1900 • Hepworth Cecil M. • UKN
LEAPING see SPRINGEN • 1986
LEAPING LOVE • 1929 • Doane Warren • SHT • USA
LEAPING LUCK • 1928 • Roberts Stephen • SHT • USA
LEARN, BABY, LEARN see LEARNING TREE, THE • 1969
LEARN FROM EXPERIENCE see KAFUKU • 1937
LEARN POLIKNESS • 1938 • Fleischer Dave • ANS • USA
LEARNIN' OF JIM BENTON, THE • 1917 • Smith Cliff • USA
LEARNING • 1969 • Anderson Robert • DSS • CND
LEARNING FAST • 1982 • Preston Gaylene • DOC • NZL
LEARNING LACROSSE • 1965 • Jackson Douglas • DOC • CND • LACROSSE
LEARNING MODULES FOR RURAL CHILDREN • 1975 • Benegal Shyam • DCS • IND
LEARNING RINGETTE • 1982 • Ianzelo Tony, Graziades Bill • DOC • CND
LEARNING TO BE A FATHER • 1915 • Jaccard Jacques • USA
LEARNING TO FLY see NAUKA LATANIA • 1978
LEARNING TO LOVE • 1925 • Franklin Sidney A. • USA
LEARNING TO WALK • 1978 • Dovnikovic Borivoj • ANM • YGS
LEARNING TREE, THE • 1969 • Parks Gordon • USA • LEARN, BABY, LEARN
LEASE OF LIFE • 1954 • Frend Charles • UKN
LEATHER AND NYLON see SOLEIL DES VOYOUS, LE • 1967
LEATHER BOYS, THE • 1963 • Furie Sidney J. • UKN
LEATHER BURNERS, THE • 1943 • Henabery Joseph • USA
LEATHER GIRLS, THE see FASTER, PUSSYCAT! KILL! KILL! • 1965
LEATHER GLOVES • 1948 • Quine Richard, Asher William • USA • LOSER TAKE ALL (UKN)
LEATHER GOODS LADY, THE • 1915 • *Bayne Beverly* • USA
LEATHER NECKER, THE • 1935 • Ripley Arthur • SHT • USA
LEATHER PUSHERS, THE • 1922 • Kenton Erle C. • USA
LEATHER PUSHERS, THE • 1930 • Kelley Albert • SRL • USA
LEATHER SAINT, THE • 1956 • Ganzer Alvin • USA
LEATHER STOCKING • 1909 • Griffith D. W. • USA
LEATHERLIP • 1972 • SAF
LEATHERNECK, THE • 1929 • Higgin Howard • USA
LEATHERNECKING • 1930 • Cline Eddie • USA • PRESENT ARMS (UKN)
LEATHERNECKS HAVE LANDED, THE • 1936 • Bretherton Howard • USA • MARINES HAVE LANDED, THE (UKN)
LEATHERPUSHERS, THE • 1940 • Rawlins John • USA
LEATHERSTOCKING • 1924 • Seitz George B. • SRL • USA
LEAVE see IZIN • 1975
LEAVE ALL FAIR • 1985 • Walker Mike • NZL
LEAVE ALL HOPE see LASCIATE OGNI SPERANZA • 1937
LEAVE 'EM LAUGHING • 1928 • Bruckman Clyde • USA
LEAVE 'EM LAUGHING • 1981 • Cooper Jackie • TVM • USA
LEAVE HER TO HEAVEN • 1945 • Stahl John M. • USA
LEAVE IT TO BLANCHE • 1934 • Young Harold • UKN
LEAVE IT TO BLONDIE • 1945 • Berlin Abby • USA
LEAVE IT TO GERRY • 1924 • Gillstrom Arvid E. • USA
LEAVE IT TO HENRY • 1949 • Yarbrough Jean • USA
LEAVE IT TO LESTER • 1930 • Cambria Frank, Cozine Ray • USA • HONEYMOON HARMONY (UKN)
LEAVE IT TO ME • 1920 • Flynn Emmett J. • USA
LEAVE IT TO ME • 1922 • Roach Hal • SHT • USA
LEAVE IT TO ME • 1930 • King George • UKN
LEAVE IT TO ME • 1933 • Banks Monty • UKN • HELP
LEAVE IT TO ME • 1937 • Smith Herbert • UKN
LEAVE IT TO ME see SOCIAL HIGHWAYMAN, THE • 1926
LEAVE IT TO ME see NECHTE TO NA MNE! • 1955
LEAVE IT TO SMILEY • 1914 • *Komic* • USA
LEAVE IT TO SUSAN • 1919 • Badger Clarence • USA
LEAVE IT TO THE IRISH • 1944 • Beaudine William • USA
LEAVE IT TO THE IRISH see LUCK OF THE IRISH, THE • 1948
LEAVE IT TO THE MARINES • 1951 • Newfield Sam • USA
LEAVE ME ALONE • 1971 • Theuring Gerhard • FRG
LEAVE ME ALONE see EMAK BAKIA • 1926
LEAVE ROBINSON ALONE! see HAGYJATOK ROBINSONT • 1989
LEAVE TO REMAIN • 1989 • Blair Les • UKN
LEAVE US ALONE see LA' OS VAERE • 1974
LEAVE US CHASE IT • 1947 • Swift Howard • ANS • USA
LEAVE WELL ENOUGH ALONE • 1939 • Fleischer Dave • ANS • USA
LEAVE YESTERDAY BEHIND • 1978 • Michaels Richard • TVM • USA
LEAVEN OF GOOD, THE • 1914 • *Hall Mayre* • USA
LEAVENWORTH CASE, THE • 1923 • Giblyn Charles • USA
LEAVENWORTH CASE, THE • 1936 • Collins Lewis D. • USA
LEAVES see HOJAS • 1970
LEAVES ARE WIDE, THE see SIROKO JE LISCE • 1981
LEAVES FROM A MOTHER'S ALBUM • 1916 • Stow Percy • UKN
LEAVES FROM MY LIFE • 1921 • Gordon Edward R. • SER • UKN
LEAVES FROM SATAN'S BOOK see BLADE AF SATANS BOG • 1919
LEAVES FROM THE BOOKS OF CHARLES DICKENS • 1912 • Bentley Thomas • UKN
LEAVES IN THE STORM • 1912 • *Rex* • USA
LEAVES OF A ROMANCE • 1911 • Porter Edwin S. • USA
LEAVES OF MEMORY • 1914 • Mackenzie Donald • USA
LEAVING • 1970 • Channell David • UKN
LEAVING HOME • 1986 • Bartlett Hall • USA
LEAVING HOME see MILES TO GO • 1986
LEAVING IT TO CISSY • 1916 • Middleton Edwin • USA
LEAVING IT TO THE EXPERTS • 1955 • Parker Gudrun • CND
LEAVING OF LAWRENCE, THE • 1915 • Warren Giles R. • USA
LEAVING THE ARMY • 1900 • *Paul R. W.* • UKN
LEAVING THE FACTORY • 1896 • dos Reis Aurelio Da Paz • PRT
LEAVING THIS CHILD see KONO KO O NOKOSHITE • 1984
LEAVING THOSE CHILDREN see KONO KO O NOKOSHITE • 1984
LEB' WOHL CHRISTINA • 1945 • Frohlich Gustav • FRG • UMARMT DAS LEBEN
LEBANESE MISSION, THE (USA) see CHATELAINE DU LIBAN, LA • 1956
LEBANON IN THE HEART • 1976 • Hajjar Rafik • LBN
LEBANON IN THE OLD DAYS see LUBNAN AYYAM ZAMAN • 1983
LEBANON WHY • 1976 • Chamchoum George • DOC • LBN
LEBBRA BIANCA • 1951 • Trapani Enzo • ITL • BRIEF RAPTURE (USA)
LEBEDINOYE OZERO • 1957 • Tulubyeva Zoya • USS • SWAN LAKE (USA)
LEBEDINOYE OZERO • 1968 • Dudko Apollinari, Sergeyev Konstantin • USS • SWAN LAKE (UKN)
LEBEMANN see VERKANNTE LEBEMANN, DER • 1936
LEBEN AM SEIDEN FADEN • 1973 • Stern Horst • FRG • LIFE ON A SILKEN THREAD
LEBEN ANTON BRUCKNERS, DAS • 1974 • Fischer Hans Conrad • DOC • AUS • LIFE OF ANTON BRUCKNERS, THE
LEBEN BEGINNT, DAS • 1959 • Carow Heiner • GDR • LIFE BEGINS
LEBEN BEGINNT UM ACHT, DAS • 1962 • Kehlmann Michael • FRG
LEBEN DER FRAUEN, DAS see WINDROSE, DIE • 1956
LEBEN DER HEILIGEN ELISABETH, DAS • 1917 • Frey Karl • FRG
LEBEN DIE TOTEN? • 1919 • Mack Max • FRG
LEBEN, EIN • 1973 • Schramm Herbert • FRG • LIFE, A
LEBEN EIN FILM, DAS • 1923 • *Western Film Co.* • FRG
LEBEN EIN TRAUM, DAS • 1917 • Wiene Robert • FRG
LEBEN EINES TITANEN, DAS see MICHELANGELO • 1940
LEBEN FUR DO, EIN • 1954 • Ucicky Gustav • FRG
LEBEN GEHT WEITER, DAS • 1945 • Liebeneiner Wolfgang • FRG
LEBEN IN CHANDIGARH, DAS see VIE A CHANDIGARH, LA • 1966
LEBEN KANN SO SCHON SEIN, DAS • 1938 • Hansen Rolf • FRG • ULTIMO ○ LIFE CAN BE SO BEAUTIFUL
LEBEN LANG, EIN • 1940 • Ucicky Gustav • FRG
LEBEN MIT UWE • 1974 • Warneke Lothar • GDR
LEBEN MOZARTS, DAS • 1967 • Fischer Hans Conrad • DOC • FRG, AUS • LIFE OF MOZART, THE (USA) ○ LEBENS MOZART, DAS
LEBEN RUFT, DAS • 1944 • Rabenalt Arthur M. • FRG
LEBEN UM LEBEN • 1916 • Eichberg Richard • FRG
LEBEN UM LEBEN • 1918 • *Desmond Olga* • FRG
LEBEN UND HOLLENFAHRT EINES WOLLUSTLINGS see PRINZ KUCKUCK • 1919
LEBEN UND LUGE • 1919 • Illes Eugen • FRG
LEBEN UNSERER PRASIDENTEN, DAS • 1950 • Thorndike Andrew • DOC • GDR • WILHELM PIECK, THE LIFE OF OUR PRESIDENT ○ LEBEN WILHELM PIECK
LEBEN VON ADOLF HITLER, DAS • 1961 • Rotha Paul • DOC • FRG • LIFE OF ADOLF HITLER, THE
LEBEN WIE IM PARADIES, EIN see AM SONNTAG WILL MEIN SUSSER MIT MIR SEGELN GEHN • 1961
LEBEN WILHELM PIECK see LEBEN UNSERER PRASIDENTEN, DAS • 1950
LEBEN ZU ZWEIT • 1968 • Zschoche Hermann • GDR • LIFE TOGETHER
LEBENDE BUDDHAS • 1924 • Wegener Paul • FRG • LIVING BUDDHAS (USA) ○ GOTTER VON TIBET
LEBENDE FACKEL, DIE • 1920 • Delmont Joseph • FRG
LEBENDE LEICHHAM, DER (FRG) see ZHIVOI TRUP • 1929
LEBENDE LEICHNAM, DER • 1918 • Oswald Richard • FRG • LIVING CORPSE, THE ○ LIVING DEAD, THE
LEBENDE PROPELLER, DER • 1921 • Eichberg Richard • FRG
LEBENDE RATSEL, DAS • 1916 • Piel Harry • FRG
LEBENDE TOTE, DER see HERR DER WELT 2, DER • 1918
LEBENDE TOTE, DIE • 1919 • Biebrach Rudolf • FRG
LEBENDE WARE • 1966 • Luderer Wolfgang • GDR
LEBENDE WARE see GEHETZTE FRAUEN • 1927
LEBENDER SCHATTEN, DER see SCHATTEN, DER • 1918
LEBENDES DES MENSCHEN, DAS • 1921 • Oswald Richard • FRG
LEBENS MOZART, DAS see LEBEN MOZARTS, DAS • 1967
LEBENS WURFELSPIEL, DAS • 1925 • Paul Heinz • FRG
LEBENSBILD, EIN see SCHLEMIHL • 1915

LEBENSBORN • 1961 • Klinger Werner • FRG • ORDERED TO LOVE (USA)
LEBENSHUNGER • 1922 • Guter Johannes • FRG
LEBENSKUNSTLER, EIN • 1925 • Holger-Madsen • FRG
LEBENSLAUFE • Junge Winifried? • DOC • GDR
LEBENSLIED, DAS • 1926 • Bergen Arthur • FRG
LEBENSROULETTE, DAS • 1922 • Dessauer Siegfried • FRG
LEBENSSTURME • 1923 • Berger Friedrich • FRG
LEBENSWOGEN • 1917 • Fleck Jacob, Fleck Luise • AUS
LEBENSZEICHEN • 1967 • Herzog Werner • FRG • SIGNS OF LIFE (USA) ○ FEUERZEICHEN
LECCION DE AMOR, UNA • 1955 • Ortega Juan J. • MXC
LECCIONES DE BUEN AMOR • 1943 • Gil Rafael • SPN
LECHE-MOI PARTOUT • 1977 • Leroi Francis • FRN
LECHER see **LETCHER** • 1974
LECHERO, EL • 1951 • Aguirre Javier • SHT • SPN
LECLERC • 1948 • Regnier Jean • DOC • FRN
LECON DE BICYCLETTE • 1896-97 • Lumiere Louis • FRN
LECON DE CONDUITE • 1945 • Grangier Gilles • FRN • CAPRICES DE MICHELINE, LES
LECON DE DANSE • 1897 • Blache Alice • FRN
LECON DE DANSE • 1900 • Blache Alice • FRN
LECON DE DESSIN, LA see **STATUE ANIMEE, LA** • 1903
LECON DES MONGOLIENS, LA • 1973 • Moreau Michel • DOC • CND
LECON DU PASSE, LA • 1976 • Dansereau Fernand, Rossignol Yolande • DCS • CND
LECON PARTICULIERE, LA • 1968 • Boisrond Michel • FRN • TENDER MOMENT, THE (USA) ○ PRIVATE LESSON, THE
LECONS DE BOXE • 1897-98 • Blache Alice • FRN
LECONS DE SLAVA, LES • 1978 • Reichenbach Francois • SER • FRN
LECTRICE, LA • 1988 • Deville Michel • FRN
LECTURE ON MAN, A • 1962 • Williams Richard • ANS • UKN
LECTURE QUOTIDIENNE • 1900-01 • Blache Alice • FRN
LECTURER, A see **BASUDEV** • 1984
LECUMBERRI • 1976 • Ripstein Arturo • MXC
LED ASTRAY • 1909 • Brooke Van Dyke • USA
LED BY LITTLE HANDS • 1910 • *Selig* • USA
LEDA AND THE ELEPHANT • 1946 • Frez Ilya • SHT • USS
LEDA, GIUSEPPE E AMEDEO • 1984 • Avati Pupi • ITL
LEDA SENZA SIGNO • 1917 • Gallone Carmine • ITL
LEDA (USA) see **A DOUBLE TOUR** • 1959
LEDER VAN ONS • 1971 • Buyens Frans • BLG
LEDERSTRUMPF 1 • 1920 • Wellin Arthur • FRG • WILDTOTER, DER
LEDERSTRUMPF 2 • 1920 • Wellin Arthur • FRG • LETZTE DER MOHIKANER, DER
LEDIGE FRAU, DIE • 1915 • Del Zopp Rudolf • FRG
LEDIGE MUTTER • 1928 • Sauer Fred • FRG • SPINSTER MOTHERS
LEDIGE TOCHTER • 1926 • Boese Carl • FRG
LEDOLOM • 1931 • Barnet Boris • USS • THAW (UKN) ○ LYODOLOM
LEE BLOUNT GOES HOME • 1916 • Worthington William • SHT • USA
LEECH, THE • 1915 • Buel Kenean • USA
LEECH, THE • 1921 • Hancock Herbert • USA
LEECH OF INDUSTRY, A • 1914 • *Cummings Irving* • USA
LEECH WOMAN, THE • 1960 • Dein Edward • USA
LEEDVERMAAK • 1989 • Weisz Frans • NTH • WEDDING PARTY, THE
LEESPLANKJE, HET • 1973 • van der Keuken Johan • DOC • NTH • READING LESSON, THE
LEEU VAN PUNDA MARIA, DIE • 1954 • SAF
LEEUW VAN VLAANDEREN, DE • 1984 • Claus Hugo • BLG, NTH • LION OF FLANDERS, THE
LEFT ALONE see **UNDER MINDERNES TRAE** • 1913
LEFT FOR DEAD see **I MISS YOU, HUGS AND KISSES** • 1978
LEFT HAND BRAND, THE • 1924 • Hart Neal • USA
LEFT HAND OF GOD, THE • 1955 • Dmytryk Edward • USA
LEFT HAND OF JIRO see **AKAI HATOBA** • 1958
LEFT HAND OF THE LAW, THE see **POLIZIA INTERVIENE: ORDINE DI UCCIDERE!, LA** • 1975
LEFT-HANDED FAN see **HIDARE UCHIWA** • 1935
LEFT-HANDED FATE (USA) see **FATA MORGANA** • 1966
LEFT-HANDED GUN, THE • 1958 • Penn Arthur • USA
LEFT HANDED LAW • 1937 • Selander Lesley • USA
LEFT-HANDED MAN, THE • 1913 • Griffith D. W. • USA
LEFT-HANDED SMITH, THE • 1964 • Ivanov-Vano Ivan • ANM • USS • LEFT HANDER, THE
LEFT-HANDED WOMAN, THE see **LINKSHANDIGE FRAU, DIE** • 1978
LEFT HANDER, THE see **LEFT-HANDED SMITH, THE** • 1964
LEFT HOOK, A • 1911 • *Reliance* • USA
LEFT IN THE LURCH • 1915 • Collins Edwin J.? • UKN
LEFT IN THE SOUP • 1917 • Beaudine William • SHT • USA
LEFT IN THE TRAIN • 1914 • *Thanhouser* • USA
LEFT IN TRUST • 1911 • Coleby A. E. • UKN • SAVED BY A CHILD (USA)
LEFT OF THE LINE • 1941-45 • MacDonald David • DOC • UKN
LEFT OUT • 1909 • *Edison* • USA
LEFT, RIGHT AND CENTRE • 1959 • Gilliat Sidney • UKN
LEFT TURN ON THE LANE, THE • VTN
LEFT WITH FIVE GIRLS see **PET HOLEK NA KRKU** • 1967
LEFTIST NIGHT'S DREAM, THE • 1988 • Katsouridis Dinos • GRC
LEFTOVER LADIES • 1931 • Kenton Erle C. • USA • BROKEN LINKS (UKN)
LEFTOVERS, THE • 1986 • Schneider Paul • TVM • USA
LEFTOVERS FROM THE NORTH • 1969 • Pasanen Spede • FNL
LEFTY FARRELL see **TWO OF A KIND** • 1951
LEG AND A LEGACY, A • 1912 • *Powers* • USA
LEG FIGHTERS, THE • 1980 • Lee Tso Nam • HKG • INVINCIBLE KUNG FU LEGS, THE
LEGACY • 1963 • Snodgrass Richard • USA
LEGACY • 1975 • Arthur Karen • USA
LEGACY • 1979 • Vinton Will • ANS • USA
LEGACY see **ADAM HAD FOUR SONS** • 1941
LEGACY, THE • 1899 • Smith G. A. • UKN
LEGACY, THE • 1910 • *Vitagraph* • USA
LEGACY, THE • 1979 • Marquand Richard • USA, UKN • LEGACY OF MAGGIE WALSH
LEGACY OF BLOOD see **BLOOD LEGACY** • 1971
LEGACY OF BLOOD see **LEGACY OF HORROR** • 1978
LEGACY OF FOLLY, THE • 1915 • *Meredith Lois* • USA
LEGACY OF HAPPINESS • 1912 • *Mead Dwight* • USA
LEGACY OF HORROR • 1978 • Milligan Andy • USA • LEGACY OF BLOOD
LEGACY OF MAGGIE WALSH see **LEGACY, THE** • 1979
LEGACY OF SATAN • 1973 • Damiano Gerard • USA
LEGACY OF THE FIVE HUNDRED THOUSAND, THE see **GOJUMAN-NIN NO ISAN** • 1963
LEGAL ADVICE • 1916 • Mix Tom • SHT • USA
LEGAL EAGLES • 1986 • Reitman Ivan • USA
LEGAL LARCENY (UKN) see **SILVER CITY RAIDERS** • 1943
LEGAL LIGHT, THE • 1915 • Mix Tom • USA
LEGALLY DEAD • 1910 • *Powers* • USA
LEGALLY DEAD • 1923 • Parke William • USA
LEGALLY RIGHT • 1913 • *Garwood Billy* • USA
LEGATIONENS GIDSEL see **MYSTISKE SELSKABSDAME** • 1916
LEGATO • 1950 • Bendtsen Henning • ANS • DNM
LEGATO • 1978 • Gaal Istvan • HNG • TIES
LEGE HUIS, HET • 1975 • van der Heyde Nikolai • BLG • EMPTY HOUSE, THE
LEGEND • 1970 • *Nfb* • SHT • CND
LEGEND • 1985 • Scott Ridley • USA
LEGEND see **LEGENDA** • 1968
LEGEND ABOUT AN ICY HEART see **LEGENDA O LEDYANOM SERDTSE** • 1957
LEGEND ABOUT THE DEATH AND RESURRECTION OF TWO YOUNG MEN see **MEZTELEN VAGY** • 1972
LEGEND ABOUT THE ICE HEART see **LEGENDA O LEDYANOM SERDTSE** • 1957
LEGEND ABOUT THE STEWED HARE see **LEGENDA A NYULPAPRIKASROL** • 1975
LEGEND BEAUTIFUL, THE • 1915 • *Garwood William* • USA
LEGEND IN LEOTARDS see **RETURN OF CAPTAIN INVINCIBLE** • 1982
LEGEND OF 7 GOLDEN VAMPIRES, THE • 1974 • Baker Roy Ward • UKN, HKG • LEGEND OF THE SEVEN GOLDEN VAMPIRES, THE ○ 7 BROTHERS MEET DRACULA, THE ○ DRACULA AND THE SEVEN GOLDEN VAMPIRES
LEGEND OF A CRUEL GIANT • 1968 • Ivanov-Vano Ivan • ANM • USS
LEGEND OF A DUEL TO THE DEATH see **SHITO NO DENSETSU** • 1963
LEGEND OF A GHOST (USA) see **LEGENDE DU FANTOME, LA** • 1907
LEGEND OF A MERMAID • 1984 • Ikeda Toshiharu • JPN
LEGEND OF ALFRED PACKER, THE • 1980 • Dray Jim Robertson • USA
LEGEND OF BHASMASUR, THE see **BHASMASUR MOHINI** • 1913
LEGEND OF BIG JOHN, THE see **ELECTRA GLIDE IN BLUE** • 1973
LEGEND OF BIGFOOT, THE • 1976 • Marx Ivan • USA
LEGEND OF BILLIE JEAN, THE • 1985 • Robbins Matthew • USA • FAIR IS FAIR ○ LEGEND OF BILLY JEAN, THE
LEGEND OF BILLY JEAN, THE see **LEGEND OF BILLIE JEAN, THE** • 1985
LEGEND OF BLACK CHARLEY, THE see **LEGEND OF NIGGER CHARLEY, THE** • 1972
LEGEND OF BLACK ROCK, THE • 1914 • Hamilton G. P.? • USA
LEGEND OF BLACK THUNDER MOUNTAIN, THE • 1979 • Breemer Tom • USA
LEGEND OF BLOOD CASTLE see **CEREMONIA SANGRIETA** • 1972
LEGEND OF BLOOD MOUNTAIN, THE • 1965 • Cramer Massey • USA
LEGEND OF BOGGY CREEK, THE • 1973 • Pierce Charles B. • USA
LEGEND OF BRUCE LEE, THE see **GOODBYE, BRUCE LEE** • 1975
LEGEND OF BYAMEE, THE • 1963 • Burstall Tim • SHT • ASL
LEGEND OF CAGLIOSTRO, THE • 1912 • *Gaumont* • FRN
LEGEND OF COYOTE ROCK, THE • 1945 • Nichols Charles • ANS • USA
LEGEND OF CUSTER, THE • 1968 • Graham William A., Foster Norman • TVM • USA
LEGEND OF DAMIEN PARER, THE • 1963 • Brealey Gil • DOC • ASL
LEGEND OF DOOM HOUSE, THE see **MALPERTIUS** • 1972
LEGEND OF EARL DURAND, THE • 1974 • Patterson John • USA
LEGEND OF FRANK WOODS, THE • 1977 • Smith Hagen, Robinson Richard • USA
LEGEND OF FRENCHIE KING, THE (UKN) see **PETROLEUSES, LES** • 1971
LEGEND OF GOSTA BERLING, THE see **GOSTA BERLINGS SAGA** • 1924
LEGEND OF GRIZZLY ADAMS, THE • 1987 • Shanks Don • USA
LEGEND OF HELL HOUSE, THE • 1973 • Hough John • UKN, USA
LEGEND OF HILLBILLY JOHN, THE • 1972 • Newland John • USA • WHO FEARS THE DEVIL? ○ BALLAD OF HILLBILLY JOHN, THE
LEGEND OF HOLLYWOOD, THE • 1924 • Hoffman Renaud • USA
LEGEND OF HORROR • 1972 • Davies Bill • USA
LEGEND OF JIMMY BLUE EYES, THE • 1964 • Clouse Robert • SHT • USA
LEGEND OF JOHN HENRY, THE • 1973 • Weiss Sam • SHT • USA
LEGEND OF JUDO, THE see **SUGATA SANSHIRO** • 1945
LEGEND OF KASPER HAUSER, THE see **JEDER FUR SICH UND GOTT GEGEN ALLE** • 1974
LEGEND OF KING ARTHUR, THE • 1985 • Bennett Rodney • MTV • UKN, ASL
LEGEND OF KING COPHETUA, THE • 1912 • Neame Elwin • UKN
LEGEND OF LADY BLUE, THE • 1978 • Fabritzi A. • USA
LEGEND OF LAKE DESOLATION • 1911 • *Pathe* • USA
LEGEND OF LASSITER • 1979 • Robinson Lee • MTV • ASL
LEGEND OF LIZZIE BORDEN, THE • 1975 • Wendkos Paul • TVM • USA
LEGEND OF LOBO, THE • 1962 • Algar James • USA
LEGEND OF LOCH NESS • 1976 • Martin Richard • USA
LEGEND OF LOS TAOS, THE • Gormley Charles • DOC • UKN
LEGEND OF LOVE see **LEGENDA O LASCE** • 1957
LEGEND OF LOVE see **SHIRIN FARHAD** • 1980
LEGEND OF LOVERS LEAP, THE • 1913 • *Lubin* • USA
LEGEND OF LYLAH CLARE, THE • 1968 • Aldrich Robert • USA
LEGEND OF MACHINE GUN KELLY, THE (UKN) see **MELVIN PURVIS, G-MAN** • 1974
LEGEND OF MOUNT ARARAT, THE see **AGRI DAGIN EFSANESI** • 1976
LEGEND OF MUSASHI, THE see **MIYAMOTO MUSASHI** • 1954
LEGEND OF NELLIE BLY see **ADVENTURES OF NELLIE BLY, THE** • 1981
LEGEND OF NIGGER CHARLEY, THE • 1972 • Goldman Martin • USA • LEGEND OF BLACK CHARLEY, THE
LEGEND OF ORPHEUS, THE • 1909 • *Pathe* • FRN
LEGEND OF PAUL AND PAULA, THE see **LEGENDE VON PAUL UND PAULA, DIE** • 1973
LEGEND OF POLICHINELLE, THE see **LEGENDE DE POLICHINELLE, LA** • 1907
LEGEND OF PRAGUE, THE (UKN) see **GOLEM, LE** • 1935
LEGEND OF PRINCESS MOON see **TAKETORI MONOGATARI** • 1988
LEGEND OF PROVENCE, THE • 1913 • *Cruze James* • USA
LEGEND OF ROBIN HOOD, THE • 1972 • ANM • ASL
LEGEND OF ROCKABYE POINT, THE • 1955 • Avery Tex • ANS • USA • ROCKABYE LEGEND
LEGEND OF RUDOLPH VALENTINO, THE • 1963 • Ferguson Graeme • USA
LEGEND OF ST. NICHOLAS, THE see **LEGENDE DE SAINT-NICOLAS, LA** • 1904
LEGEND OF ST. NICHOLAS, THE see **LEGGENDA DI S. NICOLA, LA** • 1908
LEGEND OF SAINT URSULA, THE see **LEGGENDA DI SANT'ORSA, LA** • 1948
LEGEND OF SCAR FACE, THE • 1910 • *Lanning Frank* • USA
LEGEND OF SIRIUS, A see **SIRIUS NO DENSETSU** • 1982
LEGEND OF SLEEPY HOLLOW • 1908 • *Kalem* • USA
LEGEND OF SLEEPY HOLLOW • 1972 • *Bosustow Stephen (P)* • ANS • USA
LEGEND OF SLEEPY HOLLOW, THE • 1912 • *Eclair* • USA
LEGEND OF SLEEPY HOLLOW, THE • 1949 • Geronimi Clyde • ANM • USA
LEGEND OF SLEEPY HOLLOW, THE • 1980 • Schellerup Henning • TVM • USA
LEGEND OF SPIDER FOREST (USA) see **VENOM** • 1974
LEGEND OF STIRLING KEEP, THE • 1909 • Dawley J. Searle • USA
LEGEND OF THE AMAZON RIVER, THE see **LEYENDA DEL AMAZONAS, LA** • 1977
LEGEND OF THE AMULET, THE • 1914 • *Darkfeather Mona* • USA
LEGEND OF THE BALANCED ROCK, THE • 1912 • *Solax* • USA
LEGEND OF THE BAYOU see **EATEN ALIVE** • 1976
LEGEND OF THE BEAR'S WEDDING see **LOKIS** • 1926
LEGEND OF THE BOY AND THE EAGLE, THE • 1967 • Couffer Jack • TVM • USA
LEGEND OF THE CHRYSANTHEMUM • 1912 • *Ambrosio* • ITL
LEGEND OF THE CROSS, THE see **LEGGENDA DELLA CROCE, LA** • 1909
LEGEND OF THE DOGS OF SATOMI see **SATOMI HAKKEN DEN** • 1984
LEGEND OF THE DRUM, THE see **NINO DEL TAMBOR, EL** • 1981
LEGEND OF THE EIGHT SAMURAI • 1984 • Kaduwara Haruki • JPN
LEGEND OF THE FOOL KILLER, THE see **FOOL KILLER, THE** • 1963
LEGEND OF THE FOREST, THE • 1969 • Laius Leida • USS
LEGEND OF THE FORGET-ME-NOTS • 1909 • *Pathe* • FRN
LEGEND OF THE FORTRESS OF SURAM see **LEGENDA SURAMSKOI KREPOSTI** • 1986
LEGEND OF THE FOX see **FEI-HU-WAI CHUAN** • 1981
LEGEND OF THE GOLDEN GODDESS, THE see **TRADER HORNEE** • 1970
LEGEND OF THE GOLDEN GUN • 1979 • Levi Alan J. • TVM • USA
LEGEND OF THE GOLDEN PEARL, THE • 1987 • Kwan Teddy Robin • HKG
LEGEND OF THE HOLY DRINKER, THE (UKN) see **LEGGENDA DEL SANTO BEVITORE, LA** • 1988
LEGEND OF THE ICY HEART see **LEGENDA O LEDYANOM SERDTSE** • 1957
LEGEND OF THE LAKE, THE • 1911 • *Cines* • ITL
LEGEND OF THE LAWMAN (UKN) see **PART 2 WALKING TALL** • 1975
LEGEND OF THE LIGHTHOUSE, THE • 1909 • *Gaumont* • FRN
LEGEND OF THE LILACS, THE • 1914 • *Eclair* • FRN
LEGEND OF THE LONE RANGER, THE • 1981 • Fraker William A. • USA
LEGEND OF THE LONE TREE, THE • 1914 • Davis Ulysses • USA
LEGEND OF THE LOST • 1957 • Hathaway Henry • USA, ITL • TIMBUCTU (ITL)
LEGEND OF THE LOST ARROW, THE • 1912 • *Bosworth Hobart* • USA
LEGEND OF THE MOUNTAIN (USA) see **SHAN-CHUNG CH'UAN-CHI** • 1978
LEGEND OF THE NARAYAMA see **NARAYAMA BUSHI-KO** • 1958
LEGEND OF THE NORTHWEST see **BEARHEART OF THE GREAT NORTHWEST** • 1964
LEGEND OF THE PHANTOM TRIBE, THE • 1914 • *Bison* • USA
LEGEND OF THE PIED PIPER, THE • 1949 • *Coronet* • SHT • USA
LEGEND OF THE POISONED POOL, THE • 1915 • Sloman Edward • USA
LEGEND OF THE SEA WOLF see **LUPO DEI MARI, IL** • 1975

LEGEND OF THE SEVEN GOLDEN VAMPIRES, THE see **LEGEND OF 7 GOLDEN VAMPIRES, THE** • 1974
LEGEND OF THE SILENT NIGHT, THE • 1969 • Rasky Harry (c/d) • MTV • USA
LEGEND OF THE SKYLARK, THE • 1967 • Miheles Aurel • SHT • RMN
LEGEND OF THE SNOW CHILD, THE • 1914 • *Chamberlin Riley* • USA
LEGEND OF THE SURAM FORTRESS see **LEGENDA SURAMSKOI KREPOSTI** • 1986
LEGEND OF THE TERROR see **ALAMAT NG KILABOT** • 1967
LEGEND OF THE THREE AXES • 1910 • *Pathe Freres* • FRN
LEGEND OF THE TREE OF LIFE, THE see **IGOROTA, THE LEGEND OF THE TREE OF LIFE** • 1967
LEGEND OF THE TRUE CROSS see **INVENZIONE DELLA CROCE, L'** • 1949
LEGEND OF THE UNDINES, THE see **LEGENDE DES ONDINES, LA** • 1910
LEGEND OF THE WEREWOLF • 1974 • Francis Freddie • UKN
LEGEND OF THE WHITE SNAKE see **HAKUJA-SHO** • 1984
LEGEND OF THE WILD • 1981 • *Haggerty Don* • USA
LEGEND OF THE WITCHES • 1969 • Leigh Malcolm • UKN
LEGEND OF THE WOLF WOMAN (USA) see **LUPA MANNARA, LA** • 1976
LEGEND OF THYL UYLENSPIEGEL, THE see **LEGYENDA O TILYE ULENSHPIGELYE** • 1975
LEGEND OF TIANYUAN MOUNTAIN, THE • 1981 • Xie Jin • CHN
LEGEND OF TICHBORNE DOLE, THE • 1926 • Croise Hugh • UKN
LEGEND OF TILL EULENSPIEGEL, THE see **LEGYENDA O TILYE ULENSHPIGELYE** • 1975
LEGEND OF TOHNO see **TOHNO MONOGATARI** • 1983
LEGEND OF TOM DOOLEY, THE • 1959 • Post Ted • USA
LEGEND OF VALENTINO, THE • 1975 • Shavelson Melville • TVM • USA
LEGEND OF WALKS FAR WOMAN, THE • 1982 • Damski Mel • TVM • USA
LEGEND OF WILLIAM TELL, THE (USA) see **WILHELM TELL** • 1934
LEGEND OF WOLF LODGE, THE • 1988 • Campbell Graeme • CND • INTO THE FIRE
LEGEND OF YOUNG DICK TURPIN, THE • 1965 • Neilson James • UKN
LEGEND OR WAS IT?, A see **SHITO NO DENSETSU** • 1963
LEGENDA • 1968 • Blaier Andrei • RMN • THEN CAME THE LEGEND ○ LEGEND
LEGENDA A NYULPAPRIKASROL • 1975 • Kabay Barna • HNG • LEGEND ABOUT THE STEWED HARE ○ RABBIT STEW, THE
LEGENDA A VONATON • 1962 • Renyi Tamas • HNG • TALES OF A LONG JOURNEY
LEGENDA O LASCE • 1957 • Krska Vaclav • CZC • LEGEND OF LOVE
LEGENDA O LEDYANOM SERDTSE • 1957 • Shengelaya Eldar • USS • LEGEND ABOUT THE ICE HEART ○ LEGEND ABOUT AN ICY HEART ○ LEGEND OF THE ICY HEART
LEGENDA SINFONICA • 1947 • Bava Mario, Melani M. • ITL
LEGENDA SURAMSKOI KREPOSTI • 1986 • Paradjanov Sergei, Abachidze Dodo • USS • LEGEND OF THE FORTRESS OF SURAM ○ LEGEND OF THE SURAM FORTRESS
LEGENDARY CHAMPIONS • 1968 • Chapin Harry • DOC • USA
LEGENDARY CURSE OF LEMORA, THE • 1974 • Blackburn Richard • USA • LEMORA, THE LADY DRACULA ○ LADY DRACULA ○ LADY VAMPIRE ○ LEMORA
LEGENDARY HEROES OF CHEN CHOW, THE see **CHOU YEN LI CHUAN** • 1977
LEGENDARY JUDGE, THE • 1958 • Wilder Donald A. • CND
LEGENDARY OUTLAW, THE see **KANNESHWARA RAMA** • 1976
LEGENDARY STRIKE, THE see **LANG-TZU YI CHAO** • 1979
LEGENDARY WEAPONS OF CHINA see **SHIH-BA PAN WU-YI** • 1981
LEGENDARY WEAPONS OF KUNG FU see **SHIH-BA PAN WU-YI** • 1981
LEGENDE D'AIGLE, LA • 1911 • Chautard Emile • FRN
LEGENDE DE LA FILEUSE, LA • 1907 • Feuillade Louis • FRN
LEGENDE DE L'ARC-EN-CIEL, LA • 1909 • *Gance Abel* • FRN
LEGENDE DE POLICHINELLE, LA • 1907 • Zecca Ferdinand • FRN • LEGEND OF POLICHINELLE, THE
LEGENDE DE RIP VAN WINCKLE, LA • 1905 • Melies Georges • FRN • RIP VAN WINKLE (USA) ○ RIP'S DREAM ○ REVE DE RIP, LE
LEGENDE DE SAINT-NICOLAS, LA • 1904 • Blache Alice • FRN • LEGEND OF ST. NICHOLAS, THE
LEGENDE DE SAINTE URSULE, LA see **LEGGENDA DI SANT'ORSA, LA** • 1948
LEGENDE DE SOEUR BEATRIX, LA • 1923 • de Baroncelli Jacques • FRN
LEGENDE DE TERRE BLANCHE, LA • 1947-51 • Verneuil Henri • SHT • FRN
LEGENDE DES ONDINES, LA • 1910 • *Pathe* • FRN • LEGEND OF THE UNDINES, THE
LEGENDE DES PHARES, LA • 1909 • Feuillade Louis • FRN
LEGENDE DU BON CHEVALIER, LA • 1919 • Burguet Charles • FRN
LEGENDE DU FANTOME, LA • 1907 • de Chomon Segundo • FRN • LEGEND OF A GHOST (USA)
LEGENDE DU JUIF ERRANT, LA • 1909 • Jasset Victorin • FRN
LEGENDE D'UN SIECLE, LA see **JOHN MOVIE** • 1983
LEGENDE VON DER HEILIGEN SIMPLICIA, DIE • 1920 • May Joe • FRG • HEILIGE SIMPLICIA, DIE
LEGENDE VON PAUL UND PAULA, DIE • 1973 • Carow Heiner • GDR • LEGEND OF PAUL AND PAULA, THE
LEGENDE VON SUNDE UND STRAFE, DIE see **SODOM UND GOMORRA** • 1922
LEGENDES ET CHATEAUX • 1971 • Hella Patrick • BLG
LEGENDES ET REALITES INUIT • 1978 • Hoedeman Co, Leaf Caroline • CMP • CND • LEGENDS AND LIFE OF THE INUIT
LEGENDS ABOUT ANIKA see **ANIKINA VREMENA** • 1954
LEGENDS AND LIFE OF THE INUIT see **LEGENDES ET REALITES INUIT** • 1978
LEGENDS OF THE BAT see **PIEN-FU CH'UAN-CHI** • 1978
LEGENDS OF THE EVERGLADES, THE • 1913 • *Excelsior* • USA
LEGENDS OF THE WILDERNESS • 1920 • *Henry Gale* • SHT • USA
LEGENYANA • 1989 • Garas Dezso • HNG • PREGNANT PAPA, THE
LEGER VAN GEHOUWEN STEEN, EEN • 1957 • Noman Theo Van Haren • DOC • NTH • ARMY OF HEWN STONE, AN
LEGERE ET COURT VETUE • 1952 • Laviron Jean • FRN
LEGGE, LA (ITL) see **LOI, LA** • 1958
LEGGE DEI GANGSTERS, LA • 1969 • Marcellini Siro • ITL • GANGSTERS' LAW
LEGGE DEL MITRA, LA see **VITE PERDUTE** • 1958
LEGGE DEL VIZIO, LA (ITL) see **FILLES DE NUIT** • 1958
LEGGE DELLA TROMBA, LA • 1963 • Tretti Augusto • ITL
LEGGE DELLA VENDETTA, LA see **FADDIJA** • 1950
LEGGE DELLA VIOLENZA, LA • 1969 • Crea Gianni • ITL • TUTTI O NESSUNO
LEGGE DI GUERRA • 1961 • Paolinelli Bruno • ITL, FRN, FRG • KRIEGSGESETZ (FRG) ○ LIEBE FREIHEIT UND VERRAT
LEGGE DI SANGUE • 1948 • Capuano Luigi • ITL
LEGGE E LA LEGGE, LA (ITL) see **LOI C'EST LA LOI, LA** • 1958
LEGGE VIOLENTA DELLA SQUADRA ANTICRIMINE, LA • 1976 • Massi Stelvio • ITL • CROSS SHOT (USA)
LEGGENDA AZZURRA • 1941 • Guarino Joseph • ITL
LEGGENDA DEI NIBELUNGHI, LA see **SIGFRIDO** • 1959
LEGGENDA DEL RUBINO, LA • 1985 • Margheriti Antonio • ITL
LEGGENDA DEL SANTO BEVITORE, LA • 1988 • Olmi Ermanno • ITL, FRN • LEGEND OF THE HOLY DRINKER, THE (UKN)
LEGGENDA DELLA CROCE, LA • 1909 • *Ambrosio* • ITL • LEGEND OF THE CROSS, THE
LEGGENDA DELLA PRIMAVERA, LA • 1941 • Chili Giorgio W. • ITL
LEGGENDA DI ENEA, LA • 1962 • Rivalta Giorgio • ITL, FRN • CONQUERANTS HEROIQUES (FRN) ○ LAST GLORY OF TROY, THE ○ AVENGER, THE (USA) ○ WAR OF THE TROJANS, THE
LEGGENDA DI FAUST, LA • 1949 • Gallone Carmine • ITL • FAUST AND THE DEVIL
LEGGENDA DI FRA' DIAVOLO, LA • 1962 • Savona Leopoldo • ITL • LAST CHARGE, THE (USA) ○ FRA DIAVOLO
LEGGENDA DI GENOVEFFA, LA (ITL) see **GENOVEVA** • 1951
LEGGENDA DI S. NICOLA, LA • 1908 • *Itala* • ITL • LEGEND OF ST. NICHOLAS, THE
LEGGENDA DI SANT'ORSA, LA • 1948 • Emmer Luciano, Gras Enrico • ITL • LEGEND OF SAINT URSULA, THE ○ LEGENDE DE SAINTE URSULE, LA
LEGGENDA DI UNA VOCE see **ENRICO CARUSO** • 1951
LEGGENDA DL PIAVE, LA • 1952 • Freda Riccardo • ITL
LEGGENDARIO CONQUISTATORE, IL (ITL) see **CONQUISTADORES DEL PACIFICO, LOS** • 1963
LEGHORN BLOWS AT MIDNIGHT, THE • 1950 • McKimson Robert • ANS • USA
LEGHORN HAT, THE (USA) see **FLORENTINER HUT, DER** • 1939
LEGHORN SWOGGLED • 1951 • McKimson Robert • ANS • USA
LEGHOSSZABB NAP, A • 1988 • Peterffy Andras • HNG • LONGEST DAY, THE
LEGION CONDOR • 1939 • Ritter Karl • FRG
LEGION DE HEROES • 1941 • Fortuny Juan, Seville Armando • SPN
LEGION DEL SILENCIO, LA • 1955 • Forque Jose Maria, Nieves Conde Jose Antonio • SPN
LEGION OF DEATH, THE • 1918 • Browning Tod • USA
LEGION OF HONOR, THE • 1928 • Ryder Alexandre • FRN
LEGION OF LOST FLYERS • 1939 • Cabanne W. Christy • USA
LEGION OF MISSING MEN • 1937 • MacFadden Hamilton • USA
LEGION OF NO RETURN, THE see **LEGIONE DEI DANNATI, LA** • 1969
LEGION OF NO RETURN, THE (UKN) see **QUEL MALEDETTO PONTE SULL'ELBA** • 1968
LEGION OF TERROR • 1937 • Coleman C. C. Jr. • USA
LEGION OF THE CONDEMNED • 1928 • Wellman William A. • USA
LEGION OF THE DAMNED see **LEGIONE DEI DANNATI, LA** • 1969
LEGION OF THE DOOMED • 1958 • Brooks Thor L. • USA
LEGION OF THE LAWLESS • 1940 • Howard David • USA
LEGION OF THE LOST see **SERGEANT X** • 1931
LEGION OF THE PHANTOM TRIBE • 1914 • *Bison* • USA
LEGION OF THE STREETS see **LEGION ULICY** • 1932
LEGION OF VALOR, THE see **LET 'EM HAVE IT** • 1935
LEGION SAUTE SUR KOLWEZI, LA • 1979 • Coutard Raoul • FRN
LEGION ULICY • 1932 • Ford Aleksander • PLN • LEGION OF THE STREETS ○ STREET LEGION, THE
LEGIONARIOS, LOS • 1957 • Delgado Agustin P. • MXC
LEGIONE DEI DANNATI, LA • 1969 • Lenzi Umberto • ITL • BATTLE OF THE COMMANDOS (USA) ○ LEGION OF THE DAMNED ○ LEGION OF NO RETURN, THE
LEGIONE STRANIERA • 1953 • Franchina Basilio • ITL • TROUBLE FOR THE LEGION
LEGIONI DI CLEOPATRA, LE • 1960 • Cottafavi Vittorio • ITL, FRN, SPN • LEGIONS DE CLEOPATRE, LES (FRN) ○ LEGIONS OF THE NILE (UKN)
LEGIONNAIRE, LE • 1914 • Pouctal Henri • FRN
LEGIONNAIRES IN PARIS • 1927 • Gillstrom Arvid E. • USA • FRENCH LEAVE (UKN)
LEGIONS DE CLEOPATRE, LES (FRN) see **LEGIONI DI CLEOPATRA, LE** • 1960
LEGIONS D'HONNEUR • 1938 • Gleize Maurice • FRN
LEGION'S LAST PATROL, THE (UKN) see **MARSCHIER UND KREPIER** • 1962
LEGIONS OF THE NILE (UKN) see **LEGIONI DI CLEOPATRA, LE** • 1960
LEGITIMA DEFENSA • 1953 • Gomez Urquiza Zacarias • MXC
LEGITIME DEFENSE • Grimbert C. • FRN
LEGITIME VIOLENCE • 1982 • Leroy Serge • FRN
LEGRANDE'S REVENGE • 1915 • *Lewis Sheldon* • USA
LEGS • 1970 • Lennon John, Ono Yoko • USA • UP YOUR LEGS FOREVER
LEGS • 1982 • Freedman Jerrold • TVM • USA • ROCKETTES
LEGS AMERINDIEN, LE • 1976 • Dansereau Fernand, Rossignol Yolande • DCS • CND
LEGS OF THE LAME • 1985 • Pittman Bruce • MTV • CND
LEGSZEBB FERFIKOR • 1972 • Simo Sandor • HNG • IN THE PRIME OF LIFE
LEGUIGNON, GERISSEUR see **MONSIEUR LEGUIGNON, GUERISSEUR** • 1953
LEGUMES VIVANTS, LES • 1910 • Cohl Emile • ANS • FRN • LIVING VEGETABLES, THE
LEGY JO MINDHALALIG • 1936 • Sekely Steve • HNG • BE TRUE UNTIL DEATH
LEGY JO MINDHALALIG • 1960 • Ranody Laszlo • HNG • BE GOOD UNTIL DEATH ○ BE GOOD FOREVER
LEGYENDA O TILYE ULENSHPIGELYE • 1975 • Alov Alexander, Naumov Vladimir • USS • LEGEND OF THYL UYLENSPIEGEL, THE ○ LEGEND OF TILL EULENSPIEGEL, THE
LEHI • 1963 • Baker De Vere • USA • VOYAGE OF THE LEHI IV
LEHMANNS BRAUTFAHRT • 1916 • *Rieck Arnold* • FRG
LEHRER HEIDER • 1950 • Pohl Arthur • GDR
LEHRER HOFER • 1975 • Lilienthal Peter • FRG • TEACHER HOFER
LEHRER IM WANDEL • 1963 • Kluge Alexander • SHT • FRG • TEACHERS IN TRANSFORMATION
LEHRER MATTHIESEN • 1917 • Larsen Viggo • FRG
LEHRMADCHEN-SEX • 1972 • Hofbauer Ernst • FRG
LEI DA TERRA -ALENTEJO 76, A • 1976 • Grupo Zero • PRT
LEI DO CAO, A • 1967 • Valadao Jece • BRZ • LAW OF THE GUNHAMMER, THE ○ LAW OF THE DOG, THE
LEIBEIGENE, DIE • 1919 • Matull Kurt? • FRG
LEIBEIGENEN, DIE • 1927 • Eichberg Richard • FRG • BONDAGE
LEIBEIGENSCHAFT see **SEINES BRUDERS LEIBEIGENER** • 1921
LEIBESSPIELE IM SCHNEE (AUS) see **SKI FEVER** • 1967
LEIBHAFTIGE UNSCHULD, DIE see **GANZ GROSSES KIND, EIN** • 1952
LEIBHUSAREN UND IHRE GESCHICHTE, DIE see **TOTENKOPFREITER** • 1917
LEICHENSACHE ZERNIK • 1972 • Nitzschke Helmut • GDR
LEICHTE ISABELL, DIE • 1927 • Busch Eddy, Wellin Arthur • FRG
LEICHTE KAVALLERIE • 1927 • Randolf Rolf • FRG
LEICHTE KAVALLERIE • 1935 • Hochbaum Werner • FRG
LEICHTE MADCHEN, DAS • 1940 • Buch Fritz Peter • FRG
LEICHTE MUSE • 1941 • Rabenalt Arthur M. • FRG • WAS EINE FRAU IM FRUHLING TRAUMT
LEICHTES BLUT • 1943 • Boese Carl • FRG
LEICHTSINN UND LEBEWELT • 1919 • Zelnik Friedrich • FRG
LEICHTSINN UND LIEBE • 1925 • *Hauschild-Film* • FRG
LEICHTSINN UND PFLICHT • 1916 • Wellin Arthur • FRG
LEICHTSINNIGE JUGEND • 1931 • Mittler Leo • FRG
LEID, DAS • 1916 • Sauer Fred • FRG
LEID DER LIEBE, DAS • 1916 • Biebrach Rudolf • FRG
LEID GEHT UM DIE WELT, EIN • 1958 • von Bolvary Geza • FRG
LEIDEN DES JUNGEN WERTHER, DIE • 1976 • Gunther Egon • GDR • SORROWS OF YOUNG WERTHER, THE
LEIDENDES LAND • 1922 • Lampadius Hanns • FRG
LEIDENSCHAFT • 1940 • Janssen Walter • FRG • PASSION (USA)
LEIDENSCHAFT, DIE LIEBSCHAFTEN DER HELLA VON GILSA • 1925 • Eichberg Richard • FRG
LEIDENSCHAFTEN see **INTERNO BERLINESE** • 1985
LEIDENSCHAFTLICHE BLUMCHEN • 1978 • Farwagi Andre • FRG • PASSION FLOWER HOTEL (USA) ○ BOARDING SCHOOL ○ VIRGIN CAMPUS
LEIDENSWEG DER EVA GRUNWALD, DER • 1922 • Eichberg Richard • FRG
LEIDENSWEG DER INGE KRAFFT, DER • 1921 • Dinesen Robert • FRG
LEIDENSWEG DER KLEINEN LI-LO, DER • 1925 • Hermann Otto • FRG
LEIDENSWEG EINES ACHTZEHNJAHRIGEN, DER • 1920 • Frowein Eberhard • FRG • IN KETTEN DER LEIDENSCHAFT
LEIDVOLLE LIEBE • 1918 • Schonfeld Carl • FRG
LEIL WA KHAWANA • 1989 • Fahmy Ashraf • EGY • NIGHT AND TRAITORS
LEILA AL-AMIRA • 1947 • Mustafa Niazi • SYR
LEILA AND THE WOLVES see **LEILA WAL DHIAB** • 1984
LEILA EL AKHIRA, EL • 1963 • el Sheikh Kamal • EGY • LAST NIGHT, THE ○ LAYLA AK AKHIRA, AL- ○ DERNIERE NUIT, LA
LEILA ET LES AUTRES • 1977 • Mazif Sid-Ali • ALG
LEILA IN IRAQ • 1949 • IRQ
LEILA WAL DHIAB • 1984 • Srour Heini • LBN • LEILA AND THE WOLVES
LEILAT GHARAM • 1951 • Badrakhan Ahmed • EGY
LEILI I MEDJNUN • 1959 • Berezantseva Tatyana, Valamt-Zade G. • USS
LEINEN AUS IRLAND • 1939 • Helbig Heinz • FRG
LEIRIA 61 • 1961 • Campos Antonio • SHT • PRT
LEISE FLEHEN MEINE LIEDER • 1933 • Forst Willi, Asquith Anthony • FRG, UKN • SCHUBERTS UNVOLLENDETE SYMPHONIE ○ UNFINISHED SYMPHONY (USA) ○ LOVER DIVINE (USA)
LEISURE • 1966 • Kuchar George • USA
LEISURE • 1977 • Petty Bruce • SHT • ASL
LEISURE HAS COME TO STAY see **FRITIDEN ER ALLEREDE BEGYNDT** • 1962
LEITE, O • 1972 • de Macedo Antonio • SHT • PRT
LEITENANT BASIL • 1970 • Lysenko Yuri • USS • LIEUTENANT BASIL
LEITZACH • 1961 • *Houwer Rob (P)* • FRG
LEIYU • 1983 • Sun Daolin • CHN • THUNDERSTORM
LEJANIA • 1985 • Diaz Jesus • CUB • PARTING OF THE WAYS
LEJON PA STAN • 1959 • Folke Gosta • SWD • LION IN TOWN

LEJONET OCH JUNGFRUN • 1974 • Lindgren Lars-Magnus • SWD • LION AND THE VIRGIN, THE
LEJONSOMMAR • 1968 • Axelman Torbjorn • SWD • SUMMER OF THE LION ○ VIBRATION
LEJOS DE LOS ARBOLES • 1970 • Esteva Jacinto • SPN
LEJOS DEL CIELO • 1950 • Catrani Catrano • ARG
LEK PA REGNBAGEN • 1958 • Kjellgren Lars-Eric • SWD • PLAYING ON THE RAINBOW ○ RAINBOW GAME, THE
LEKAA EL TANI, EL • 1967 • el Saifi Hassan • EGY • THEY WILL MEET AGAIN
LEKARSTWO NA MILOSC • 1965 • Batory Jan • PLN • CURE OF LOVE, A
LEKCJA ANATOMII see **ANATOMIE STUNDE** • 1977
LEKCJA LATANIA • 1978 • Idziak Slawomir • PLN • FLYING LESSONS
LEKKAMRATERNA • 1915 • Stiller Mauritz • SWD • PLAYMATES, THE
LEKKO see **VIEREN MARR** • 1954
LEKTION, EN see **FLYVEREN OG JOURNALISTE ENS HUSTRU** • 1911
LEKTION I KARLEK, EN • 1954 • Bergman Ingmar • SWD • LESSON IN LOVE, A
LEKTRO • 1927 • Timoshenko S. • USS • ELECTRA
LELEJSKA GORA • 1968 • Velimirovic Zdravko • YGS • MOUNTAIN OF LAMENT ○ MOUNTAIN OF HORROR
LELEKLATO SUGAR • 1918 • Desy Alfred • HNG • MIND-DETECTING RAY, THE
LELICEK VE SLUZBACH SHERLOCKA HOLMESA • 1932 • Lamac Carl • CZC • LELICHEK IN SHERLOCK HOLMES'S SERVICE
LELICHEK IN SHERLOCK HOLMES'S SERVICE see **LELICEK VE SLUZBACH SHERLOCKA HOLMESA** • 1932
LELIK IS MY OFFER • 1975 • SAF
LELKA • 1967 • Arsenov Pavel • SHT • USS
LEM MIEN KUEL see **GHOSTLY FACE, THE**
LEMKES SEL. WITWE • 1928 • Boese Carl • FRG
LEMKES SEL. WITWE • 1957 • Weiss Helmut • FRG
LEMMY FOR THE WOMEN (USA) see **LEMMY POUR LES DAMES** • 1961
LEMMY POUR LES DAMES • 1961 • Borderie Bernard • FRN • LEMMY FOR THE WOMEN (USA) ○ LADIES' MAN
LEMON, THE • 1912 • MacMackin Archer • USA
LEMON DROP KID, THE • 1934 • Neilan Marshall • USA
LEMON DROP KID, THE • 1951 • Lanfield Sidney, Tashlin Frank (U/c) • USA
LEMON (FOR ROBERT HUOT) • 1969 • Frampton Hollis • USA
LEMON GIRLS ON THE GO see **KOKO LEMON MUSUME** • 1967
LEMON GROVE KIDS MEET THE GREEN GRASSHOPPER AND THE VAMPIRE LADY FROM OUTER SPACE, THE • Rotter Ted • SHT • USA
LEMON GROVE KIDS MEET THE MONSTERS, THE • 1966 • Steckler Ray Dennis • SHT • USA
LEMON HEARTS • 1960 • Zimmerman Vernon • SHT • USA
LEMON IN THEIR GARDEN OF LOVE, THE • 1916 • *Myers Harry* • SHT • USA
LEMON MERINGUE • 1931 • Sweet Harry • SHT • USA
LEMON POPSICLE 4: SAPICHES see **PRIVATE POPSICLE: LEMON POPSICLE IV** • 1982
LEMON POPSICLE 5 see **BABY LOVE -LEMON POPSICLE V** • 1983
LEMON POPSICLE (USA) see **ESKIMO LIMON** • 1978
LEMON SISTERS, THE • 1989 • Chopra Joyce • USA
LEMON SKY • 1987 • Egleson Jan • TVM • USA
LEMONADE AIDS CUPID • 1915 • Curtis Allen • USA
LEMONADE JOE • 1940 • Brdecka Jiri • ANS • CZC
LEMONADE JOE (USA) see **LIMONADOVY JOE** • 1964
LEMORA see **LEGENDARY CURSE OF LEMORA, THE** • 1974
LEMORA, THE LADY DRACULA see **LEGENDARY CURSE OF LEMORA, THE** • 1974
LEMPAD OF BALI • 1980 • Blair Lorne, Darling John • DOC • INN
LEM'S COLLEGE CAREER • 1916 • Christie Al • SHT • USA
LEM'S HOT CHOCOLATE • 1912 • *Imp* • USA
LEN HAWKIN'S CONFESSION • 1935 • Micheaux Oscar • USA
LENA • 1915 • Seay Charles M. • USA
LENA • 1981 • Green Eytan • ISR
LENA • 1984 • Bykov Rolan • USS
LENA AND THE GEESE • 1912 • Griffith D. W. • USA
LENA AND THE GRAPES • 1936 • Kudryavtseva A. • USS
LENA: MY 100 CHILDREN see **LENA: MY HUNDRED CHILDREN** • 1988
LENA: MY HUNDRED CHILDREN • 1988 • Sherin Edwin • TVM • USA • LENA: MY 100 CHILDREN
LENA RIVERS • 1910 • *Thanhouser* • USA
LENA RIVERS • 1914 • *Garrison Film* • USA
LENA RIVERS • 1914 • *Whitman Features* • USA
LENA RIVERS • 1925 • Bennett Whitman • USA
LENA RIVERS • 1932 • Rosen Phil • USA
LENA WARNSTETTEN • 1925 • Eriksen Erich • FRG
LENA'S FLIRTATION • 1913 • *Champion* • USA
LENBENDIGE TOTE, DER • 1918 • Bauer Leopold? • FRG
LEND A PAW • 1941 • Geronimi Clyde • ANS • USA
LEND ME A MORNING • 1989 • Bernal Ishmael • PHL
LEND ME YOUR EAR (UKN) see **LIVING GHOST, THE** • 1942
LEND ME YOUR HEART • 1978 • Khin Soe • BRM
LEND ME YOUR HUSBAND • 1924 • Cabanne W. Christy • USA
LEND ME YOUR HUSBAND • 1935 • Hayward Frederick • UKN
LEND ME YOUR HUSBAND see **PRESTAME TU MARIDO** • 1973
LEND ME YOUR NAME • 1918 • Balshofer Fred J. • USA
LEND ME YOUR STABLE • 1962 • Brennan Richard • ASL
LEND ME YOUR WIFE • 1912 • *Quirk Billy* • USA
LEND ME YOUR WIFE • 1916 • *Perez Tweedledum* • SHT • USA
LEND ME YOUR WIFE • 1935 • Kellino W. P. • UKN
LEND ME YOUR WIFE • 1988 • Revach Zeev • ISR
LEND ME YOUR WIFE see **CHICKEN IN THE CASE, THE** • 1921
LENDA DAS AMENDOEIRAS, A • 1950 • Rosa Americo Leite • SHT • PRT
LENDA DE UBIRAJARA, A • 1975 • de Oliveira Andre Luiz • BRZ
LENDEMAIN COMME HIER, UN • 1970 • Bulbulian Maurice • DOC • CND
LENGYELVER • 1920 • von Bolvary Geza • HNG
LENI RIEFENSTAHL (HITLER'S CAMERA) • 1965 • Lavut Martin • DOC • CND
LENIN • 1948 • Romm Mikhail • USS • VLADIMIR ILYITCH LENIN
LENIN • 1950 • Beleyev Vassili • USS
LENIN, DIN GAVJYV! • 1972 • Stenbaek Kirsten • DNM • LENIN, YOU RASCAL!
LENIN GANG, THE • 1971 • Stenbaek Kirsten • DNM
LENIN IN 1918 see **LENIN V 1918 GODU** • 1939
LENIN IN OCTOBER see **LENIN V OKTYABRE** • 1937
LENIN IN PARIS see **LENIN V PARIDZHE** • 1981
LENIN IN POLAND see **LENIN V POLSHE** • 1966
LENIN IN SWITZERLAND see **LENIN V SHVEITZARII** • 1966
LENIN SUOMESSA see **LUOTTAMUS, ELI LENIN JA SUOMI** • 1975
LENIN V 1918 GODU • 1939 • Romm Mikhail • USS • LENIN IN 1918
LENIN V OKTYABRE • 1937 • Romm Mikhail • USS • LENIN IN OCTOBER
LENIN V PARIDZHE • 1981 • Yutkevich Sergei • USS • LENIN IN PARIS
LENIN V POLSHE • 1966 • Yutkevich Sergei • USS, PLN • PORTRAIT OF LENIN (USA) ○ LENIN IN POLAND ○ LENIN W POLSCE
LENIN V SHVEITZARII • 1966 • Alexandrov Grigori • USS • LENIN IN SWITZERLAND
LENIN W POLSCE see **LENIN V POLSHE** • 1966
LENIN, YOU RASCAL! see **LENIN, DIN GAVJYV!** • 1972
LENINE V POLSKE • 1961 • Alexandrov Grigori • USS
LENINGRAD COWBOYS GO AMERICA • 1988 • Kaurismaki Aki • FNL, SWD
LENINGRAD FIGHTS! see **LENINGRAD V BORBYE** • 1942
LENINGRAD IN COMBAT see **LENINGRAD V BORBYE** • 1942
LENINGRAD - KYOTO see **BYAKU-YA NO SHIRABE** • 1975
LENINGRAD MUSIC HALL • 1943 • Shapiro Mikhail, Menaker Leonid, Tsekhanovsky M. M., Timoshenko S., Minkin Adolph • USS
LENINGRAD MUSIC HALL see **KINO-CONCERT 1941** • 1941
LENINGRAD SEGODNYA • 1927 • Trauberg Ilya • DOC • USS • LENINGRAD TODAY
LENINGRAD SYMPHONY • 1958 • Agranenko Zakhar • USS
LENINGRAD TODAY see **LENINGRAD SEGODNYA** • 1927
LENINGRAD V BORBYE • 1942 • Karmen Roman, Uchitel Y., Komarevtsev N., Solovtsev Valeri • USS • DAYS AND NIGHTS IN LENINGRAD ○ DEFENCE OF LENINGRAD, THE ○ LENINGRAD IN COMBAT ○ LENINGRAD FIGHTS!
LENINIST FILM-TRUTH see **LENINSKAYA KINO-PRAVDA** • 1925
LENIN'S ADDRESS see **ADRES LENINA** • 1929
LENINSKAYA KINO-PRAVDA • 1925 • Vertov Dziga • USS • LENINIST FILM-TRUTH
LENKA AND PRIM see **TRAPENI** • 1961
LENNY • 1974 • Fosse Bob • USA
LENNY BRUCE • 1967 • *Magnuson John (P)* • USA • LENNY BRUCE CONCERT ○ LENNY BRUCE PERFORMANCE FILM
LENNY BRUCE CONCERT see **LENNY BRUCE** • 1967
LENNY BRUCE PERFORMANCE FILM see **LENNY BRUCE** • 1967
LENNY BRUCE STORY, THE • 1969 • Rosenberg Stuart • USA
LENNY BRUCE WITHOUT TEARS • 1972 • Baker Fred • USA
LENNY LIVE AND UNLEASHED • 1989 • Harries Andy • UKN
LENORA • 1949 • Hofman Eduard • ANS • CZC • LAZYBONES
LENTAVAT LUUPAAT • 1984 • Pasanen Spede • FNL • FLYING BONEHEADS ○ FLYING DIMWITS
LENZ • Rockwell Alexander
LENZ • 1971 • Moorse Georg • FRG
LENZ • 1987 • Szirtes Andras • HNG
LEO AND LOREE • 1980 • Paris Jerry • USA
LEO CORRIVEAU, MARECHAL-FERRANT • 1977 • Gosselin Bernard, Plamondon Leo • DCS • CND
LEO, KING OF THE JUNGLE • Bisney Al • ANM • USA
LEO MAKES GOOD • 1913 • *Imp* • USA
LEO REISMAN AND HIS ORCHESTRA • 1942 • Negulesco Jean • SHT • USA
LEO SONNYBOY • 1989 • Lyssy Rolf • SWT
LEO THE LAST • 1970 • Boorman John • UKN
LEO UND SEINE ZWEI BRAUTE • 1921 • Peukert Leo • FRG
LEOFOROS TOU MISOUS, I • 1968 • Foskolos Nikos • GRC • HIGHWAY OF HATE, THE
LEON, EL • 1971 • Carretero Amaro • ANS • SPN • LION, THE
LEON GARROS IS LOOKING FOR HIS FRIENDS see **VINGT MILLE LIEUES SUR LA TERRE** • 1960
LEON GUERRERO AGAINST THE DEADLY 7 see **LEON GUERRERO LABAN SA 7 KILABOT** • 1968
LEON GUERRERO LABAN SA 7 KILABOT • 1968 • Gallardo Cesar Chat • PHL • LEON GUERRERO AGAINST THE DEADLY 7
LEON KRUCZKOVSKI • 1970 • Czurko Edward • SHT • PLN
LEON KRUCZKOWSKI • 1964 • Morgenstern Janusz • DCS • PLN
LEON LA LUNE • 1957 • Jessua Alain • SHT • FRN
LEON MORIN, PRETRE • 1961 • Melville Jean-Pierre • FRN, ITL • FORGIVEN SINNER, THE (USA) ○ LEON MORIN, PRIEST
LEON MORIN, PRIEST see **LEON MORIN, PRETRE** • 1961
LEON OF THE TABLE D'HOTE • 1910 • *Thanhouser* • USA
LEON.. TOUT COURT • 1932 • Francis Joe • FRN
LEONA DE CASTILLA, LA • 1951 • de Orduna Juan • SPN
LEONA GOES A-HUNTING see **HELP WANTED -MALE!** • 1920
LEONARD DE VINCI • 1952 • Arcady • SHT • FRN
LEONARD FRENCH'S STAINED GLASS SCREENS • 1969 • Thornhill Michael • DOC • ASL
LEONARD PART 6 • 1987 • Weiland Paul • USA
LEONARD - TENDLER BOXING EXHIBITION • 1923 • *Britton Leon D. (P)* • USA
LEONARDO DA VINCI • 1952 • Emmer Luciano • ITL
LEONARDO DA VINCI • 1972 • Castellani Renato • MTV • ITL
LEONARDO DA VINCI: THE TRAGIC PURSUIT OF PERFECTION • 1953 • Fulchignoni Enrico • UKN, FRN • TRAGIC PURSUIT OF PERFECTION, THE
LEONARDO PROCEEDINGS, THE see **EXPEDIENTE LEONARDO** • 1977
LEONARDO'S DIARY see **LEONARDUV DENIK** • 1974
LEONARDO'S LAST SUPPER • 1976 • Barnes Peter • UKN
LEONARDUV DENIK • 1974 • Svankmajer Jan • ANS • CZC • LEONARDO'S DIARY
LEONCE • 1909 • Perret Leonce • SER • FRN
LEONCE AIME LES BELGES • 1915 • Perret Leonce • FRN
LEONE A SETTE TESTE, IL • 1971 • Rocha Glauber • ITL, FRN, BRZ • LEONE HAVE SEPT CABEZAS, DER ○ LION HAS SEVEN HEADS, THE
LEONE DI AMALFI, IL1 • 1951 • Francisci Pietro • ITL • RIBELLE DI AMALFI, IL
LEONE DI DAMASCO, IL • 1942 • D'Errico Corrado • ITL
LEONE DI SAN MARCO, IL • 1964 • Capuano Luigi • ITL • LION OF ST. MARK, THE (USA)
LEONE DI TEBE, IL • 1964 • Ferroni Giorgio • ITL, FRN • LION DE THEBES, LE (FRN) ○ LION OF THEBES, THE (USA) ○ HELEN OF TROY ○ HELENE, REINE DE TROIE
LEONE HAVE SEPT CABEZAS, DER see **LEONE A SETTE TESTE, IL** • 1971
LEONES DEL RING, LOS • 1972 • *Estudios America* • MXC
LEONESSE, LE • 1970 • Righini Oscar • ITL
LEONI AL SOLE • 1961 • Caprioli Vittorio • ITL
LEONI DI PIETROBURGO, I • 1972 • Siciliano Mario • ITL
LEONI SCATTERRATI, I (ITL) see **LIONS SONT LACHES, LES** • 1961
LEONIE • 1913 • Merwin Bannister • USA
LEONOR • 1975 • Bunuel Juan • FRN, ITL, SPN
LEONORA • 1986 • Strahan Derek • ASL
LEONORA DOS SETE MARES • 1955 • Christensen Carlos Hugo • ARG
LEONSKI see **DEATH OF A SOLDIER** • 1986
LEONTINE (UKN) see **FAUT PAS PRENDRE LES ENFANTS DU BON DIEU POUR DES CANARDS SAUVAGES** • 1968
LEONTINES EHEMANNER • 1928 • Wiene Robert • FRG
LEOPARD, LE • 1984 • Sussfeld Jean-Claude • FRN
LEOPARD, LE see **FAHD, AL-** • 1972
LEOPARD, THE • 1917 • *Lugosi Bela* • HNG
LEOPARD, THE (USA) see **GATTOPARDO, IL** • 1963
LEOPARD AVENGER, THE • 1913 • *Lux* • FRN
LEOPARD IN THE SNOW • 1977 • O'Hara Gerry • UKN, CND
LEOPARD LADY, THE • 1928 • Julian Rupert • USA
LEOPARD MAN, THE • 1943 • Tourneur Jacques • USA
LEOPARD QUEEN, THE • 1909 • Boggs Frank • USA
LEOPARD SKIN, THE • 1964-65 • Landow George • USA
LEOPARD TAMER, THE • 1913 • Parker Lem B. • USA
LEOPARD WOMAN, THE • 1920 • Ruggles Wesley • USA
LEOPARDESS, THE • 1923 • Kolker Henry • USA
LEOPARDI DI CHURCHILL, I • 1970 • Pradeaux Maurizio • ITL, SPN • LEOPARDOS DE CHURCHILL, LOS (SPN) ○ CHURCHILL'S LEOPARDS
LEOPARDOS DE CHURCHILL, LOS (SPN) see **LEOPARDI DI CHURCHILL, I** • 1970
LEOPARD'S BRIDE, THE • 1916 • *Gibson Margaret* • USA
LEOPARD'S FOUNDLING, THE • 1914 • Grandon Francis J. • USA
LEOPARD'S LAIR, THE • 1915 • Martin E. A. • USA
LEOPARD'S SPOTS, THE • 1918 • Hepworth Cecil M. • UKN
LEOPOLD FIST NINJA, THE • Ho Godfrey • HKG
LEOPOLD LE BIEN-AIME • 1933 • Brun Arno-Charles • FRN
LEOPOLD THE SEE-THROUGH CRUMBPICKER • 1970 • *Firebird Films* • ANS • USA
LEOS EHEROMAN • 1922 • Peukert Leo • FRG
LEO'S GREAT CURE • 1913 • *Imp* • USA
LEOS JANACEK • 1974 • Jires Jaromil • DOC • CZC
LEO'S LOVE LETTER • 1913 • *Imp* • USA
LEO'S VACATION • 1913 • *Imp* • USA
LEPA PARADA • 1970 • Milosevic Branko • YGS • QUITE A SHOW
LEPAIN 5 • 1920 • Ralph Louis • FRG
LEPAIN 6 • 1920 • Ralph Louis • FRG
LEPAIN, DER KONIG DER VERBRECHER 3 • 1920 • Ralph Louis • FRG
LEPAIN, DER KONIG DER VERBRECHER 4 • 1920 • Ralph Louis • FRG
LEPER • 1976 • Hoffman Jerzy • PLN
LEPER, THE • 1913 • *Champion* • USA
LEPER'S COAT, THE • 1914 • *Weber Lois* • USA
LEPKE • 1974 • Golan Menahem • USA
LEPO JE ZIVETI NA DEZELI • 1974 • Bevc Joze • SHT • YGS • BEAUTY OF COUNTRY LIFE, THE
LEPRECHAUN, THE • 1908 • Porter Edwin S. • USA
LEPRECHAUN'S GOLD • 1949 • Tytla Bill • ANS • USA
LEPREUSE, LA • 1926 • Puchalski Eduard • PLN
LEPROSY see **TRAD** • 1971
LEPSI PAN • 1971 • Schorm Evald • MTV • CZC • WELL-TO-DO GENTLEMAN, A
LEPTIROV OBLAK • 1977 • Randic Zdravko • YGS • BUTTERFLY CLOUD
LEPURI ME PESE KEMBE • 1983 • Ymeri Ismail • YGS • FIVE-LEGGED HARE, THE ○ ZEC S PET NOGU
LERHJERTET see **GULDETS GIFT** • 1916
LERMONTOV • 1943 • Gendelstein Albert • USS
LERPAR • 1977 • Couto Luis • PRT
LES • 1953 • Vengerov Vladimir • USS • FOREST, THE
LES BOYS • 1965 • Post Howard • ANS • USA
LES BROWN • 1948 • Scholl Jack • SHT • USA
LES BROWN AND HIS BAND OF RENOWN • 1949 • Cowan Will • SHT • USA • LES BROWN AND THE BAND OF RENOWN
LES BROWN AND THE BAND OF RENOWN see **LES BROWN AND HIS BAND OF RENOWN** • 1949
LES BROWN GOES TO TOWN • 1965 • *Universal* • SHT • USA
LES DARCY BEATS GEORGE CHIP • 1916 • ASL
LES GIRLS • 1957 • Cukor George • USA
LES MCCANN LTD. • 1962 • Binder Steve • SHT • USA
LES MISERABLES • 1909 • *Vitagraph* • USA
LES MISERABLES • 1909 • *Edison* • USA
LES MISERABLES • 1909 • Blackton J. Stuart • USA
LES MISERABLES • 1918 • Lloyd Frank • USA
LES MISERABLES • 1922 • *Parkinson H. B.* • UKN
LES MISERABLES • 1935 • Boleslawski Richard • USA • MISERABLES, LES
LES MISERABLES • 1952 • Milestone Lewis • USA
LES MISERABLES • 1978 • Jordan Glenn • TVM • USA
LES MISERABLES see **BOUASSA, EL** • 1944

LES MISERABLES see **RE MIZERABURU** • 1950
LES MISERABLES (USA) see **MISERABILI, I** • 1947
LES PATTERSON SAVES THE WORLD • 1986 • Miller George* • ASL
LESBIAN TWINS see **VIRGIN WITCH** • 1970
LESBIAN VAMPIRES -THE HEIRESS OF DRACULA see **VAMPYROS LESBOS -DIE ERBIN DES DRACULA** • 1971
LESBO • 1969 • Mulargia Edoardo, Andrews Eric • ITL
LESLIE JEFFRIES AND HIS ORCHESTRA • 1936 • Shepherd Horace • UKN
LESNAYA PESNYA • 1961 • Ivchenko Viktor • USS • SONG OF THE FOREST (USA)
LESS THAN DUST see **LESS THAN THE DUST** • 1916
LESS THAN KIN • 1918 • Crisp Donald • USA
LESS THAN THE DUST • 1916 • Emerson John • USA • LESS THAN DUST
LESS THAN ZERO • 1987 • Kanievska Marek • USA
LESS WAL KELAB, AL- see **LISSU WA AL-KILAB, AL-** • 1962
LESSER EVIL, THE • 1912 • Griffith D. W. • USA
LESSON, A • 1960 • Tyrlova Hermina • ANM • CZC
LESSON, THE • 1910 • Griffith D. W. • USA
LESSON, THE • 1912 • *Melies* • USA
LESSON, THE • 1913 • *Powers* • USA
LESSON, THE • 1913 • *American* • USA
LESSON, THE • 1913 • Buckland Warwick? • UKN
LESSON, THE • 1913 • Eagle Oscar • *Selig* • USA
LESSON, THE • 1916 • *Essanay* • SHT • USA
LESSON, THE • 1917 • Giblyn Charles • USA
LESSON, THE see **TSENA CHELOVEKA** • 1928
LESSON BY THE SEA, THE • 1910 • *Vitagraph* • USA
LESSON FOR SOMEBODY, A • 1916 • Smith David • SHT • USA
LESSON FOR WIDOWS see **ONNA NO URAMADO** • 1960
LESSON FROM LIFE, A • 1916 • *Empress Marie* • SHT • USA
LESSON FROM THE FAR EAST, A • 1915 • Easton Clem • USA
LESSON IN A DEAD LANGUAGE • 1980 • Majewski Janusz • PLN
LESSON IN BRIDGE, A • 1914 • *Reliance* • USA
LESSON IN DOMESTIC ECONOMY, A • 1909 • *Vitagraph* • USA
LESSON IN ELECTRICITY, A • 1909 • Stow Percy • UKN
LESSON IN GOLF, A • 1932 • Murphy Dudley • USA • FORE
LESSON IN HISTORY, A see **UROK ISTORIJI** • 1957
LESSON IN HUSBANDS, A • 1911 • *Baggot King* • USA
LESSON IN JEALOUSY, A • 1913 • Lambart Harry • USA
LESSON IN LABOR, A • 1916 • Powell Paul • SHT • USA
LESSON IN LIFE, A see **UROK ZHIZNI** • 1955
LESSON IN LOVE see **LOVER COME BACK** • 1946
LESSON IN LOVE see **LICAO DE AMOR** • 1975
LESSON IN LOVE, A see **LEKTION I KARLEK, EN** • 1954
LESSON IN MECHANICS, A • 1914 • Cabanne W. Christy • USA
LESSON IN PALMISTRY, A • 1909 • *Lubin* • USA
LESSON IN ROMANCE, A • 1915 • Calvert E. H. • USA
LESSON IN VISUAL LANGUAGE • 1978-83 • Thompson Peter • DSS • ASL
LESSON LEARNED, A • 1911 • *Edison* • USA
LESSON NO.1 • 1929 • Parrott James • SHT • USA
LESSON OF LIFE see **UROK ZHIZNI** • 1955
LESSON OF THE FLAMES, THE • 1914 • Ridgely Richard • USA
LESSON OF THE NARROW STREET, THE • 1915 • Drew Sidney • USA
LESSON THE CHILDREN TAUGHT, THE • 1913 • *Powers* • USA
LESSON TO MASHERS, A • 1913 • Henderson Dell • USA
LESSON TO THE INFINITE, A • Nicolaescu Sergiu • RMN
LESSONS FOR WIVES (UKN) see **FRENCH DRESSING** • 1927
LESSONS FROM THE GARBAGE see **NYAMANTON** • 1986
LESSONS IN COURTSHIP • 1912 • *Vitagraph* • USA
LESSONS IN LOVE • 1915 • *Forde Hal* • USA
LESSONS IN LOVE • 1921 • Withey Chet • USA
LESSONS IN LOVE (UKN) see **EDUCATION SENTIMENTALE, L'** • 1961
LESSONS OF HISTORY (WILL AND ARIEL DURRANT), THE • 1978 • Rasky Harry • CND
LEST WE FORGET • 1909 • Salter Harry • USA
LEST WE FORGET • 1914 • Elvey Maurice • UKN
LEST WE FORGET • 1914 • O'Brien Jack • USA
LEST WE FORGET • 1917 • Drew Sidney, Drew Sidney Mrs. • SHT • USA
LEST WE FORGET • 1918 • Perret Leonce • USA
LEST WE FORGET • 1934 • Baxter John • UKN
LEST WE FORGET • 1935 • Badgley Frank C. • CMP • CND
LEST WE FORGET see **HANGMEN ALSO DIE** • 1943
LEST WE FORGET see **OB ETOM ZABY VAT NELZYA** • 1954
LESTER PERSKY STORY, THE see **SOAP OPERA** • 1964
LESTER PERSKY STORY -A SOAP OPERA, THE see **SOAP OPERA** • 1964
LESTNITSA V NEBO see **LYESTNITSA V NYEBO** • 1967
LET ALL YOUR LOVES KNOW see **OZNAMUJE SE RASKAM VASUIM** • 1988
LET BYGONES BE BYGONES • 1909 • *Lubin* • USA
LET CHARLIE DO IT • 1972 • Smith Paul J. • ANS • USA
LET 'EM ALL COME • 1899 • *Warwick Trading Co.* • UKN
LET 'EM HAVE IT • 1935 • Wood Sam • USA • FALSE FACES (UKN) ○ LEGION OF VALOR, THE
LET 'EM QUARREL • 1913 • Trimble Larry • USA
LET 'ER BUCK • 1925 • Sedgwick Edward • USA
LET 'ER GO • 1920 • Davis James • SHT • USA
LET 'ER GO GALLEGHER • 1928 • Clifton Elmer • USA • GALLEGHER (UKN)
LET FIDO DO IT • 1919 • Smith Noel • SHT • USA
LET FREEDOM RING • 1939 • Conway Jack • USA • SONG OF THE WEST
LET FREEDOM RING see **IT'S IN THE AIR** • 1935
LET GEORGE DO IT • 1938 • Hall Ken G. • ASL • IN THE NICK OF TIME
LET GEORGE DO IT • 1940 • Varnel Marcel • UKN
LET GO OF MY BEARD see **ERESZD EL A SZAKALLAMAT!** • 1975
LET HIM BUCK • 1924 • Morrow Frank • USA
LET HUEY DO IT • 1943 • *O'Brien Joseph/ Mead Thomas (P)* • SHT • USA
LET IT ALL HANG OUT (USA) see **MANN MIT DEM GOLDENEN PINSEL, DER** • 1971
LET IT BE • 1970 • Lindsay-Hogg Michael • DOC • UKN
LET IT BE ME • 1936 • Freleng Friz • ANS • USA
LET IT BLEED • 1971 • *Halas John (P)* • ANS • UKN
LET IT RAIN • 1927 • Cline Eddie • USA
LET IT RIDE • 1989 • Pytka Joe • USA
LET IT ROCK • 1988 • Klick Roland • USA • WHITE STAR
LET IT SHINE • 1962 • Karelov Yevgyeni • USS
LET JOY REIGN SUPREME.. (USA) see **QUE LA FETE COMMENCE..** • 1975
LET JUSTICE BE DONE (UKN) see **JUSTICE EST FAITE** • 1951
LET KATHY DO IT • 1916 • Franklin Chester M., Franklin Sidney A. • USA
LET ME CALL YOU SWEETHEART • 1932 • Fleischer Dave • ANS • USA
LET ME DREAM AGAIN • 1900 • Smith G. A. • UKN
LET ME EXPLAIN • 1930 • Pearce A. Leslie • USA
LET ME EXPLAIN DEAR • 1932 • Gerrard Gene, Miller Frank • UKN
LET ME LIKE A SOLDIER FALL • 1906 • Gilbert Arthur • UKN
LET ME LIVE see **JEEVIKAN ANUVADHIKKU** • 1967
LET ME MAKE A COMPLAINT • 1964 • Ryazanov Eldar • USS • GIVE ME A COMPLAINT BOOK, PLEASE
LET ME REST IN PEACE see **NYUGODJAK BEKEDEN** • 1983
LET ME REVENGE • 1979 • Kamel Mahida, Abaza Rouchdy • EGY
LET MRTVE PTICE • 1974 • Pavlovic Zivojin • YGS • DEAD BIRD'S FLIGHT
LET MUSIC BE THE MESSAGE • 1983 • Jubenvill Ken • SHT • CND
LET MY GRAVE BE OF MARBLE see **MEARIM MERMERDEN OLSUN** • 1968
LET MY PEOPLE GO • 1961 • Krish John • SHT • UKN
LET MY PEOPLE LIVE • 1942 • Ulmer Edgar G. • DCS • USA
LET NO MAN ESCAPE • 1914 • *Stonehouse Ruth* • USA
LET NO MAN PUT ASUNDER • 1912 • *Baggot King* • USA
LET NO MAN PUT ASUNDER • 1913 • *Bushman Francis X.* • USA
LET NO MAN PUT ASUNDER • 1924 • Blackton J. Stuart • USA
LET NO MAN WRITE MY EPITAPH • 1960 • Leacock Philip • USA • REACH FOR TOMORROW
LET NOT MAN PUT ASUNDER • 1911 • *Solax* • USA
LET NOT ONE DEVIL CROSS THE BRIDGE see **AL' YLI PAASTA PERHANAA** • 1968
LET NOT THE SUN BE PUT OUT see **PARA QUE EL SOL NO SE APAGUE** • 1979
LET SLEEPING DOGS LIE • 1910 • Fitzhamon Lewin? • UKN
LET THE BALLOON GO • 1976 • Howes Oliver • ASL
LET THE BALLOON GO SUPPORT PROGRAMME • 1976 • Noyce Phil • SHT • ASL
LET THE BLOOD OF MAN NOT FLOW see **KROV LYUDSKAYA NE VODITSA** • 1960
LET THE GOOD TIMES ROLL • 1973 • Levin Sidney, Abel Bob • DOC • USA
LET THE MUSIC BE • 1989 • Nel Frans • SAF
LET THE PEOPLE LAUGH see **SING AS YOU SWING** • 1937
LET THE PEOPLE SING • 1942 • Baxter John • UKN
LET THE POLAR BEARS DANCE see **LAD ISBJORNENE DANSE** • 1989
LET THE PRISONERS GO -FOR IT'S SPRING see **SLAPP FANGARNE LOSS -DET AR VAR!** • 1976
LET THEM BE MARRIED • 1981 • Diamandopoulos Jiannis • GRC
LET THEM LIVE! • 1937 • Young Harold • USA • STONES CRY OUT, THE
LET THEM REST see **REQUIESCANT** • 1967
LET THERE BE BOYS • 1969 • Pierce Jack • ANT • USA
LET THERE BE LIGHT • 1915 • Bertram William • USA
LET THERE BE LIGHT • 1945 • Huston John • DOC • USA
LET THERE BE LIGHT • 1981 • Huston John • DOC • USA
LET THERE BE LIGHT see **ES WERDE LICHT! 1** • 1918
LET THERE BE NO DAWN see **SAFAK SOKMESIN** • 1968
LET US BE GAY • 1930 • Leonard Robert Z. • USA
LET US DESTROY THIS WALL see **SONO KABE O KUDARE** • 1959
LET US FIGHT WITHOUT ARMS see **SILAHSIZ DOGUSELIM** • 1967
LET US GIVE THANKS • 1910 • *Champion* • USA
LET US HAVE PEACE • 1914 • *Wilson Ben* • USA
LET US LIVE • 1939 • Brahm John • USA
LET US LIVE see **BIRAKIN YASIYALIM** • 1967
LET US LIVE THROUGH IT ONCE MORE see **PRZEZYJMY TO JESZCZE RAZ** • 1964
LET US LOVE see **KOI O SHIPOYO: KARIBU NO HANA** • 1967
LET US LOVE see **KOCHAJMY SIE** • 1975
LET US MAKE MUSIC • 1966 • Langestraat Bob • NTH
LET US PLAY SEX see **INKRAKTARNA** • 1974
LET US REJOICE see **GAUDEAMUS** • 1912
LET US SMOOTH THE WAY • 1911 • *Nestor* • USA
LET WILLIE DO IT • 1912 • *Compson John* • USA
LET WOMEN ALONE • 1925 • Powell Paul • USA • ON THE DOTTED LINE ○ ON THE SHELF ○ DOTTED LINE, THE
LET WOMEN JUDGE ME see **AS ME KRINOUN I YINEKES** • 1968
LET YOURSELF GO see **SO'S YOUR UNCLE** • 1943
LETACI VELIKOG NEBA • 1978 • Arhanic Marijan • YGS • FLYERS IN THE GREAT SKY ○ FLYERS OF THE OPEN SKY, THE
LETCHER • 1974 • Vincent Chuck • USA • LECHER
LETECI FABIJAN • 1968 • Grgic Zlatko, Kolar Boris, Zaninovic Ante • ANS • YGS • FLYING FABIAN
LETHAL • 1984 • Little Dwight H. • USA • KGB -THE SECRET WAR
LETHAL ATTRACTION see **HEATHERS** • 1989
LETHAL FILM see **LIVSFARLIG FILM** • 1988
LETHAL OBSESSION see **JOKER, THE** • 1987
LETHAL PURSUIT • 1988 • Jones Don • USA
LETHAL WEAPON • 1987 • Donner Richard • USA
LETHAL WEAPON 2 • 1989 • Donner Richard • USA
LETIAT JOURAVLY see **LETYAT ZHURAVLI** • 1957
LETITIA • 1916 • Davenport Harry • SHT • USA
LETIZIA • 1964 • Bjorkman Stig • SWD
LETO • 1949 • Wallo K. M. • CZC • SUMMER
LETO S KOVBOJEM • 1977 • Novak Ivo • CZC • SUMMER WITH A COWBOY
LETOKRUHY • 1972 • Filan Ludovit • CZC • YEARS OF LIFE, THE
LETRA ESCARLATA, LA (SPN) see **SCHARLACHROTE BUCHSTABE, DER** • 1972
LET'S ALL SING LIKE THE BIRDIE'S SING • 1934 • Fleischer Dave • ANS • USA
LET'S ALL SING TOGETHER see **SQUARE DANCE** • 1944
LET'S BE FAMOUS • 1939 • Forde Walter • UKN
LET'S BE FASHIONABLE • 1920 • Ingraham Lloyd • USA
LET'S BE HAPPY • 1957 • Levin Henry • UKN
LET'S BE RITZY • 1934 • Ludwig Edward • USA • MILLIONAIRE FOR A DAY (UKN)
LET'S BUILD • 1923 • Roach Hal • SHT • USA
LET'S CELEBRAKE • 1938 • Fleischer Dave • ANS • USA
LET'S COGITATE • 1948 • Barclay David • SHT • USA
LET'S CRY • 1961 • Mekas Adolfas • USA
LET'S DANCE • 1933 • Scotto Aubrey • USA
LET'S DANCE • 1936 • Miller David • SHT • USA
LET'S DANCE • 1950 • McLeod Norman Z. • USA
LET'S DANCE THE SIRTAKI see **SIKO HOREPSE SITAKI** • 1967
LET'S DANCE THE SOUL • 1967 • de Villa Jose • PHL
LET'S DANCE TONIGHT see **KONYA WA ODORO** • 1967
LET'S DO IT see **JUDY'S LITTLE NO-NO** • 1969
LET'S DO IT see **MASKE KU'VI** • 1976
LET'S DO IT see **DOING IT** • 1984
LET'S DO IT AGAIN • 1953 • Hall Alexander • USA • LOVE SONG
LET'S DO IT AGAIN • 1976 • Poitier Sidney • USA
LET'S DO THE PSYCHEDELLIC '68 • 1967 • Mia Rosa • PHL
LET'S DO THINGS • 1931 • Roach Hal • SHT • USA
LET'S EAT • 1932 • Lantz Walter, Nolan William • ANS • USA
LET'S ELOPE • 1919 • Robertson John S. • USA • NAUGHTY WIFE, THE
LET'S FACE IT • 1943 • Lanfield Sidney • USA
LET'S FALL IN LOVE • 1934 • Burton David • USA
LET'S FIGHT • 1918 • Wilson Ben • SHT • USA
LET'S FINISH THE JOB • 1928 • *Better Films* • USA
LET'S GET A DIVORCE • 1918 • Giblyn Charles • USA
LET'S GET HARRY • 1986 • Rosenberg Stuart (Smithee Alan) • USA
LET'S GET LAID • 1977 • Clarke James Kenelm • UKN • FIONA
LET'S GET LOST • 1989 • Weber Bruce • USA
LET'S GET MARRIED • 1926 • La Cava Gregory • USA
LET'S GET MARRIED • 1937 • Green Alfred E. • USA
LET'S GET MARRIED • 1960 • Scott Peter Graham • UKN
LET'S GET MOVIN' • 1936 • Fleischer Dave • ANS • USA
LET'S GET THOSE ENGLISH GIRLS see **A NOUS LES PETITES ANGLAISES** • 1975
LET'S GET TOUGH! • 1942 • Fox Wallace • USA
LET'S GO • 1918 • Roach Hal • SHT • USA
LET'S GO • 1923 • Howard William K. • USA
LET'S GO • 1937 • *Mintz Charles (P)* • ANS • USA
LET'S GO see **ACTION** • 1921
LET'S GO see **FAST LIFE** • 1932
LET'S GO, BARBARA see **VAMONOS, BARBARA** • 1977
LET'S GO BUST see **PANIC BUTTON.. OPERAZIONE FISCO** • 1962
LET'S GO COLLEGIATE • 1941 • Yarbrough Jean • USA • FAREWELL TO FAME (UKN)
LET'S GO CRAZY • 1951 • Cullimore Alan J. • UKN
LET'S GO GALLAGHER • 1925 • De Lacy Robert, Gruen James • USA
LET'S GO HIPPIE see **LETSGO HIPPIE** • 1968
LET'S GO HUNTING IN THE WOODS see **DO LESICKA NA CEKANOU** • 1966
LET'S GO LATIN • 1948 • Moore Harold James • SHT • USA
LET'S GO MERRY GO ROUND • 1967 • Feleo Ben • PHL
LET'S GO NAKED see **STRIP, STRIP, HOORAY!** • 1932
LET'S GO NATIVE • 1930 • McCarey Leo • USA
LET'S GO NATIVE see **HAVE BIKINI WILL TRAVEL** • 1962
LET'S GO NAVY • 1951 • Beaudine William • USA
LET'S GO ON see **IDEMO DALJE** • 1983
LET'S GO PLACES • 1930 • Strayer Frank • USA • MIRTH AND MELODY (UKN)
LET'S GO SKIING • 1933 • Sparling Gordon • DCS • CND
LET'S GO STEADY • 1945 • Lord Del • USA
LET'S GO STEPPING • 1945 • Yates Hal • SHT • USA
LET'S GO TO PARIS see **NOUS IRONS A PARIS** • 1949
LET'S GO TO THE MOVIES see **VAMOS AL CINE** • 1970
LET'S GO TO THE PARTY, GIRLS see **AMICHE ANDIAMO ALLA FESTA** • 1975
LET'S GO! WAKADAISHO • 1967 • Iwauchi Katsumi • JPN • LET'S GO, YOUNG GUY! (USA)
LET'S GO WITH PANCHO VILLA (USA) see **VAMONOS CON PANCHO VILLA** • 1935
LET'S GO, YOUNG GUY! (USA) see **LET'S GO! WAKADAISHO** • 1967
LET'S HANG ON • 1967 • Santiago Pablo • PHL • DISCOTHEQUE
LET'S HAVE A DREAM see **KYUCHAN NO DEKKAI YUME** • 1967
LET'S HAVE A MURDER • 1950 • Blakeley John E. • UKN
LET'S HAVE A PARTY see **FEEST, HET** • 1963
LET'S HAVE A SONG ABOUT THE BOYS • 1909 • *Warwick Trading Co.* • UKN
LET'S HAVE FUN • 1943 • Barton Charles T. • USA
LET'S HAVE SUCCESS see **FRAM FOR FRAMGANG** • 1938
LET'S HAVE THE WAR IN PEACE see **TENGAMOS LA GUERRA EN PAZ** • 1977
LET'S HOPE IT WILL BE A GIRL see **SPERIAMO CHE SIA FEMMINA** • 1985
LET'S HOPE IT'S A GIRL (USA) see **SPERIAMO CHE SIA FEMMINA** • 1985
LET'S JUST GO TO THE MOVIES • 1978 • Burns Tim • DOC • ASL
LET'S KEEP A DOG see **TARTSUNK KUTYAT** • 1975
LET'S KILL UNCLE • 1966 • Castle William • USA
LET'S LIVE A LITTLE • 1948 • Wallace Richard • USA
LET'S LIVE AGAIN • 1948 • Leeds Herbert I. • USA
LET'S LIVE TONIGHT • 1935 • Schertzinger Victor • USA • ONCE A GENTLEMAN

LET'S LIVE UNTIL MONDAY see **DOZHIVYOM DO PONEDYELNIKA** • 1968
LET'S LOVE AND LAUGH • 1931 • Eichberg Richard • UKN • BRIDEGROOM FOR TWO (USA) ○ BRIDEGROOM'S WIDOW, THE
LET'S LOVE ONE ANOTHER see **KOCHAJMY SIE** • 1975
LET'S LOVE SIRENS see **KOCHAJMY SYRENKI** • 1967
LET'S LOVE THE MACHINES see **KOCHAJMY MASZYNY** • 1973
LET'S LOVE THE "SIRENS" see **KOCHAJMY SYRENKI** • 1967
LET'S MAKE A DIRTY MOVIE see **ATTENTION LES YEUX** • 1975
LET'S MAKE A MILLION • 1937 • McCarey Ray • USA • ONE MAN'S BONUS
LET'S MAKE A NIGHT OF IT • 1937 • Cutts Graham • UKN • RADIO REVUE OF 1937
LET'S MAKE IT LEGAL • 1951 • Sale Richard • USA • DON'T CALL ME MOTHER
LET'S MAKE LAUGH see **PIAO-TS'O CH'I-JIH CH'ING** • 1984
LET'S MAKE LOVE • 1960 • Cukor George • USA
LET'S MAKE LOVE ONCE AGAIN see **HAJDE DA SE VOLIMO. JOS JEDAMPUT** • 1989
LET'S MAKE MUSIC • 1940 • Goodwins Leslie • USA
LET'S MAKE RHYTHM • 1947 • Grissell Wallace A. • SHT • USA
LET'S MAKE UP (USA) see **LILACS IN THE SPRING** • 1954
LET'S MAKE WHOOPEE see **RED WINE** • 1928
LET'S MAKE WHOOPEE TOMORROW, DARLING..! see **ZITRA TO ROZTOCIME, DRAHOUSKU** • 1977
LET'S NOT LOSE OUR HEADS see **NON PERDIAMO LA TESTA** • 1959
LET'S NOT MUDDLE THE WATER • 1989 • Bahrani Shahriar • IRN • DO NOT MUDDY THE WATER
LET'S PAINT • 1924 • Quiribet Gaston • UKN
LET'S PLAY • 1931 • Roberts Stephen • SHT • USA
LET'S PLAY see **HRAJEME SI** • 1957
LET'S PLAY DOCTOR • 1964 • Hais Jai • USA
LET'S PLAY IN THE WORLD see **JUGUEMOS EN EL MUNDO** • 1972
LET'S PLAY KING see **NEWLY RICH** • 1931
LET'S PRETEND • 1920 • Reardon James • UKN
LET'S PRETEND • 1922 • Paul Fred • UKN • CASTLES IN THE AIR
LET'S PRETEND WE'RE SWEETHEARTS (UKN) see **IN PARIS A. W.O.L.** • 1936
LET'S RING DOORBELLS • 1935 • *Mintz Charles (P)* • ANS • USA
LET'S ROCK • 1958 • Foster Harry • USA • KEEP IT COOL (UKN)
LET'S SAY ONE NIGHT FOR DINNER see **METTI, UNA SERA A CENA** • 1969
LET'S SCARE JESSICA TO DEATH • 1971 • Hancock John • USA
LET'S SEE IT CLEARLY see **VEDIAMOCI CHIARO** • 1984
LET'S SHAKE HANDS • 1963 • Klopcic Matjaz • SHT • YGS • I REACH FOR YOUR HAND
LET'S SHAKE ON IT see **QUA LA MANO** • 1980
LET'S SING A COLLEGE SONG • 1947 • Moore Harold James • SHT • USA
LET'S SING A LOVE SONG • 1949 • Parker Benjamin R. • SHT • USA
LET'S SING A WESTERN SONG • 1947 • Moore Harold James • SHT • USA
LET'S SING AGAIN • 1936 • Neumann Kurt • USA
LET'S SPEND THE NIGHT TOGETHER • 1983 • Ashby Hal • DOC • USA
LET'S STEP ON IT TOMORROW, DARLING see **ZITRA TO ROZTOCIME, DRAHOUSKU** • 1977
LET'S STICK TOGETHER • 1952 • Hannah Jack • ANS • USA
LET'S SWITCH! • 1975 • Rafkin Alan • TVM • USA
LET'S TALK ABOUT COMPUTERS • 1975 • Czurko Edward • SHT • PLN
LET'S TALK ABOUT LOVE see **KI BESZEL ITT SZERELEMROL?!** • 1980
LET'S TALK ABOUT MEN (USA) see **QUESTA VOLTA PARLIAMO DI UOMINI** • 1965
LET'S TALK ABOUT WOMEN (USA) see **SE PERMETTETE, PARLIAMO DI DONNE** • 1964
LET'S TALK IT OVER • 1934 • Neumann Kurt • USA
LET'S TALK SPINACH • 1951 • Kneitel Seymour • ANS • USA
LET'S TALK TONIGHT see **HABLAMAS ESTA NOCHE** • 1981
LET'S TALK TURKEY • 1939 • Feist Felix E. • SHT • USA
LET'S TRY AGAIN • 1934 • Miner Worthington • USA • MARRIAGE SYMPHONY, THE (UKN) ○ SOUR GRAPES
LET'S WAIT TILL MONDAY see **DOZHIVYOM DO PONEDYELNIKA** • 1968
LET'S YOU AND HIM FIGHT • 1934 • Fleischer Dave • ANS • USA
LETSGO HIPPIE • 1968 • Santiago Pablo • PHL • LET'S GO HIPPIE
LETTER, THE • 1912 • *Branscombe Lily* • USA
LETTER, THE • 1929 • Bell Monta, de Limur Jean • USA
LETTER, THE • 1940 • Wyler William • USA
LETTER, THE • 1969 • Ne'Eman Yehuda • SHT • ISR
LETTER, THE • 1982 • Erman John • TVM • USA
LETTER, THE see **LITERA** • 1962
LETTER, THE see **KIRJE** • 1978
LETTER BOX THIEF, THE • 1909 • Williamson James? • UKN
LETTER FOR EVIE, A • 1945 • Dassin Jules • USA • ALL THE THINGS YOU ARE
LETTER FROM A KUCI DOCTOR • Keko Endri • DOC • ALB
LETTER FROM A NOVICE see **LETTERE DI UNA NOVIZIA** • 1960
LETTER FROM AN UNKNOWN WOMAN • 1948 • Ophuls Max • USA
LETTER FROM AN UNKNOWN WOMAN see **RESSALAH MIN EMRAA MAGHOOLA** • 1962
LETTER FROM CAPRI see **CAPRICCIO** • 1987
LETTER FROM CARACAS, A see **CARTA DE CARACAS** • 1973
LETTER FROM EAST ANGLIA, A • 1953 • Whitby Cynthia • UKN
LETTER FROM HOME, A • 1914 • *Travers Richard C.* • USA
LETTER FROM HOME, A • 1941 • Reed Carol • DCS • UKN
LETTER FROM KOREA (UKN) see **YANK IN KOREA, A** • 1951
LETTER FROM SIBERIA (USA) see **LETTRE DE SIBERIE** • 1958
LETTER FROM THE ISLE OF WIGHT, A • 1954 • Salt Brian • UKN
LETTER FROM THE WIFE see **STIR PATRA** • 1970
LETTER FROM ULSTER, A • 1942 • Hurst Brian Desmond • DOC • UKN
LETTER FROM WALES, A • 1953 • Lloyd George • UKN
LETTER IN THE SAND, A • 1907 • Fitzhamon Lewin • UKN
LETTER M see **SLOWCE M** • 1964
LETTER OF INTRODUCTION • 1938 • Stahl John M. • USA
LETTER OF WARNING, A • 1932 • Daumery John • UKN • UNDISCLOSED
LETTER THAT NEVER CAME OUT, THE • 1914 • Brabin Charles J. • USA
LETTER THAT WAS NEVER SENT, THE (USA) see **NEOTPRAVLENNOE PISMO** • 1960
LETTER THAT WASN'T SENT, THE see **NEOTPRAVLENNOE PISMO** • 1960
LETTER TO A FRIEND • 1977 • Hoffman Sonia • SHT • ASL
LETTER TO BREZHNEV • 1985 • Bernard Chris • UKN
LETTER TO DADDY, A • 1915 • Morrisey Edward • USA
LETTER TO FATHER CHRISTMAS • 1910 • *Eclair* • FRN
LETTER TO JANE: INVESTIGATION OF A STILL • 1972 • Godard Jean-Luc, Gorin Jean-Pierre • FRN • LETTRE A JANE
LETTER TO MOTHER, A • 1913 • *Victor* • USA
LETTER TO PARADISE see **BREV TILL PARADISET** • 1990
LETTER TO THE NEXT GENERATION • 1990 • Klein James • DOC • USA
LETTER TO THE PRINCESS, A • 1912 • Miller Ashley • UKN
LETTER TO THE STORK, A • 1911 • *Atlas* • USA
LETTER TO THREE HUSBANDS, A see **THREE HUSBANDS** • 1950
LETTER TO THREE WIVES, A • 1948 • Mankiewicz Joseph L. • USA • THREE WIVES
LETTER TO THREE WIVES, A • 1985 • Elikann Larry • TVM • USA
LETTER TO UNCLE SAM, A • 1913 • *Mccoy Gertrude* • USA
LETTER WITH THE BLACK SEALS, THE • 1912 • *Troyano John* • USA
LETTER WITH THE FEATHERS • 1953 • Shih Hui • CHN
LETTERA ALL'ALBA • 1949 • Bianchi Giorgio • ITL
LETTERA APERTA A UN GIORNALE DELLA SERA • 1970 • Maselli Francesco • ITL • OPEN LETTER TO AN EVENING PAPER
LETTERA DAL VENEZUELA • 1961 • Russo Renzo • DOC • ITL
LETTERA DALL'AFRICA, UNA • 1951 • Bonzi Leonardo • DOC • ITL
LETTERA NAPOLETANA • 1954 • Pastina Giorgio • ITL
LETTERE AL SOTTOTENENTE • 1943 • Alessandrini Goffredo • ITL
LETTERE DAL FRONTE • 1975 • Schiraldi Vittorio • ITL
LETTERE D'AMORE DI SUA ECCELLENZA see **CENTO LETTERE D'AMORE** • 1940
LETTERE DI UNA NOVIZIA • 1960 • Lattuada Alberto • ITL, FRN • NOVICE, LA (FRN) ○ LETTER FROM A NOVICE ○ RITA (USA) ○ NOVICE, THE
LETTERS • 1972 • Sluizer George • DOC • BRZ, NTH
LETTERS see **STANLEY AND IRIS** • 1989
LETTERS, THE • 1922 • Cooper George A. • UKN
LETTERS, THE • 1973 • Nelson Gene, Krasny Paul • USA
LETTERS ENTANGLED • 1915 • *King Henry* • USA
LETTERS FROM A DEAD MAN see **PISMA MYORTVOVO CHELOVYEKA** • 1986
LETTERS FROM CHINA see **BEFORE SPRING** • 1958
LETTERS FROM FRANK • 1979 • Parone Edward • TVM • USA
LETTERS FROM JAPAN see **CARTAS DEL JAPON** • 1972
LETTERS FROM MARUSIA see **ACTAS DE MARUSIA** • 1974
LETTERS FROM MY WINDMILL see **LETTRES DE MON MOULIN, LES** • 1954
LETTERS FROM POLAND • 1978 • Turkiewicz Sophia • SHT • ASL
LETTERS FROM THE ISLE OF ECCENTRICS see **PISMA S OSTROVA CHUDAKOV** • 1967
LETTERS FROM THE PARK • 1988 • Alea Tomas Gutierrez • CUB, SPN
LETTERS FROM THREE LOVERS • 1973 • Erman John • TVM • USA
LETTERS FROM TWO PRISONS • 1975 • Ben Ammar Abdul Latif • TNS
LETTER'S MISSION, THE • 1915 • *Essanay* • USA
LETTERS OF A LIFETIME • 1912 • *Thanhouser* • USA
LETTERS OF CREDIT • 1921 • Paul Fred • UKN
LETTERS OF FIRE • 1919 • *Guinan Texas* • SHT • USA
LETTERS TO AN UNKNOWN LOVER • 1985 • Duffell Peter • UKN, FRN • LOUVES, LES (FRN)
LETTERS TO JULIA • Kardos Ferenc • SHT • HNG
LETTERS TO THE LIVING • 1964 • Vinogradov Valentin • USS
LETTI SBAGLIATI • 1965 • Steno • ITL
LETTI SELVAGGI • 1979 • Zampa Luigi • ITL • TIGERS IN LIPSTICK (USA) ○ WILD BEDS
LETTIE LIMELIGHT IN HER LAIR • 1903 • Smith G. A. • UKN
LETTING GO • 1970 • Hart Harvey • CND
LETTING GO • 1985 • Bender Jack • TVM • USA
LETTING IN THE SUNSHINE • 1933 • Lane Lupino • UKN
LETTO, IL (ITL) see **SECRETS D'ALCOVE** • 1954
LETTO A TRE PIAZZE • 1960 • Steno • ITL
LETTO DI SABBIA • 1964 • Principe Albino • ITL
LETTO IN PIAZZA, IL • 1976 • Gaburro Bruno Alberto • ITL • SEX DIARY
LETTOMANIA • 1976 • Rigo Vincenzo • ITL
LETTRE, LA • 1930 • Mercanton Louis • FRN
LETTRE, UNE see **RISALA** • 1966
LETTRE A FREDDY BUACHE • 1982 • Godard Jean-Luc • DOC • SWT
LETTRE A JANE see **LETTER TO JANE: INVESTIGATION OF A STILL** • 1972
LETTRE BRULANTE, UNE see **PATTES DE MOUCHE, LES** • 1936
LETTRE DE PARIS • 1945 • Leenhardt Roger • DCS • FRN
LETTRE DE PARIS ET D'AILLEURS • 1975 • Reichenbach Francois • SER • FRN
LETTRE DE SIBERIE • 1958 • Marker Chris • DOC • FRN • LETTER FROM SIBERIA (USA)
LETTRE OUVERTE see **LETTRE OUVERTE A UN MARI** • 1953
LETTRE OUVERTE A UN MARI • 1953 • Joffe Alex • FRN • LETTRE OUVERTE
LETTRES, LES • 1914 • Feuillade Louis • FRN
LETTRES A MICHEL PETRUCCIANI • 1984 • Cassenti Frank • FRN
LETTRES A UN FUNAMBULE • 1964 • Gagne Jacques • SHT • CND
LETTRES D'AMOUR • 1942 • Autant-Lara Claude • FRN
LETTRES D'AMOUR EN SOMALIE • 1981 • Mitterand Frederic • DOC • FRN
LETTRES D'AMOURS PERDUES • 1983 • Salis Robert • FRN
LETTRES DE MON MOULIN, LES • 1954 • Pagnol Marcel • FRN • LETTERS FROM MY WINDMILL
LETTRES DE STALINGRAD • 1969 • Katz Gilles • FRN
LETTY LYNTON • 1932 • Brown Clarence • USA
LETTY'S LOST LEGACY • 1920 • *Supreme Comedies* • USA
LETUN • 1931 • Trauberg Ilya • SHT • USS • KITES
LETYAT ZHURAVLI • 1957 • Kalatozov Mikhail • USS • CRANES ARE FLYING, THE ○ LETIAT JOURAVLY
LETZTE AKT, DER • 1955 • Pabst G. W. • AUS • LAST TEN DAYS, THE (USA) ○ LAST TEN DAYS OF HITLER, THE ○ TEN DAYS TO DIE ○ LAST TEN DAYS OF ADOLF HITLER, THE ○ LAST ACT, THE
LETZTE ANZUG, DER • 1917 • Lubitsch Ernst • FRG
LETZTE ATEMZUG, DER see **FORTUNATO 3** • 1921
LETZTE AUGENBLICK, DER • 1918 • *Ziener Bruno* • FRG
LETZTE BRUCKE, DIE • 1954 • Kautner Helmut • AUS • LAST BRIDGE, THE
LETZTE CHANCE, DIE • 1945 • Lindtberg Leopold • SWT • LAST CHANCE, THE (USA)
LETZTE DER MOHIKANER, DER see **LEDERSTRUMPF 2** • 1920
LETZTE DERER VON SKAGEN, DIE • 1916 • Obal Max • FRG
LETZTE DROSCHKE VON BERLIN, DIE • 1926 • Boese Carl • FRG
LETZTE EINES ALTEN GESCHLECHTES, DER • 1916 • Justitz Emil • FRG
LETZTE EINQUARTIERUNG, DIE see **KUSSEN IST KEINE SUND'** • 1926
LETZTE FHRT DER SANTA MARGARETA, DIE • 1935 • Zoch Georg • FRG
LETZTE FLUG, DER • 1915 • Jacoby Georg • FRG
LETZTE FORT, DAS • 1928 • Bernhardt Curtis • FRG
LETZTE FUSSGANGER, DER • 1960 • Thiele Wilhelm • FRG
LETZTE GAVALORSTELLUNG DES ZIRKUS WOLFSOHN, DIE • 1928 • Gambino Domenico M. • FRG
LETZTE GEHEIMNIS, DAS see **ARZT OHNE GEWISSEN** • 1959
LETZTE HEUER, DER • 1951 • Fiedler E. F. • GDR
LETZTE HOHENHAUS, DER • 1915 • *Bb-Film-Fabrikation* • FRG
LETZTE KAMPF, DER • 1923 • Piel Harry • FRG
LETZTE KAPITEL, DAS • 1961 • Liebeneiner Wolfgang • FRG
LETZTE KOMPANIE, DIE • 1930 • Bernhardt Curtis • FRG • THIRTEEN MEN AND A GIRL ○ LAST COMPANY, THE
LETZTE KOMPANIE, DIE • 1967 • Umgelter Fritz • FRG, ITL • LAST BATTALION, THE ○ HANDVOLL HELDEN, EINE
LETZTE LIEBE • 1919 • *Hoffmann Ernst* • FRG
LETZTE LIEBE • 1938 • Schulz Fritz • AUS • LAST LOVE (USA)
LETZTE LIEBE, DIE see **VERBOTENE LIEBE** • 1927
LETZTE LIEBESDIENST, DER • 1918 • Hanus Emerich • FRG
LETZTE LIEBESNACHT DER INGE TOLMEIN, DIE • 1918 • Eichberg Richard • FRG
LETZTE MANN, DER • 1924 • Murnau F. W. • FRG • LAST LAUGH, THE (USA) ○ LAST MAN, THE
LETZTE MANN, DER • 1955 • Braun Harald • FRG
LETZTE MASKE, DIE • 1922 • Hanus Emerich • FRG
LETZTE MOHIKANER, DER • 1965 • Reinl Harald • FRG, ITL, SPN • VALLE DELLE OMBRE ROSSE, LA (ITL) ○ LAST TOMAHAWK, THE
LETZTE NACHT, DIE • 1927 • Cutts Graham • FRG
LETZTE NACHT, DIE • 1949 • York Eugen • FRG
LETZTE NACHT, DIE • 1961 • Kunert Joachim • GDR • LAST NIGHT, THE
LETZTE PARTIE, DIE • 1915 • *Platen Karl* • FRG
LETZTE RECHNUNG ZAHLST DU SELBST, DIE • 1969 • FRG
LETZTE REZEPT, DAS • 1952 • Hansen Rolf • FRG • DESIRES (USA)
LETZTE RITT NACH SANTA CRUZ, DER • 1964 • Olsen Rolf • FRG, AUS • LAST RIDE TO SANTA CRUZ, THE (USA)
LETZTE ROSE see **MARTHA** • 1935
LETZTE RUNDE, DIE • 1940 • Klinger Werner • FRG
LETZTE SCHLOSS, DER • 1920 • Seitz Franz • FRG
LETZTE SCHREI, DER • 1975 • van Ackeren Robert • FRG
LETZTE SCHUSS, DER • 1951 • Seitz Franz* • FRG
LETZTE SENSATION DES ZIRKUS FARINI, DIE • 1923 • Krafft Uwe Jens • FRG • TIGER DES ZIRKUS FARINI, DER
LETZTE SOMMER, DER • 1954 • Braun Harald • FRG
LETZTE SONNENSOHN, DER • 1919 • Lund Erik • FRG
LETZTE SOUPER, DAS • 1928 • Bonnard Mario • FRG
LETZTE SPIEL, DAS • 1916 • Heymann Robert • FRG
LETZTE STUNDE, DIE • 1920 • Buchowetzki Dimitri • FRG
LETZTE TAG, DER • 1913 • Mack Max • FRG
LETZTE UNTERTAN, DER • 1919 • Walther-Fein Rudolf • FRG
LETZTE VOM BARENHOF, DER • 1921 • *Beck-Gaden Hanns* • FRG
LETZTE WALZER, DER • 1927 • Robison Arthur • FRG • LAST WALTZ, THE (USA)
LETZTE WALZER, DER • 1934 • Jacoby Georg • FRG • LAST WALTZ, THE
LETZTE WALZER, DER • 1953 • Rabenalt Arthur M. • FRG • LAST WALTZ, THE (USA)
LETZTE WERKELMANN, DER • 1972 • Eggers Jorg A. • AUS • LAST OF THE WERKELMANNS, THE
LETZTE WORTE • 1967 • Herzog Werner • SHT • FRG • LAST WORDS
LETZTE ZEUGE, DER • 1919 • Gartner Adolf • FRG
LETZTE ZEUGE, DER • 1960 • Staudte Wolfgang • FRG • LAST WITNESS, THE
LETZTEN DREI DER ALBATROS, DIE • 1965 • Becker Wolfgang • FRG, ITL, FRN • MORTE VIENE DA MANILA, LA (ITL) ○ MUTINY IN THE SOUTH SEAS

LETZTEN HEIMPOSAMENTER, DIE • 1936 • Yersin Yves • SWT • LAST HOME LACE-MAKERS, THE
LETZTEN JAHRE DER KINDHEIT, DIE • 1980 • Kuckelmann Norbert • FRG • LAST YEARS OF CHILDHOOD, THE
LETZTEN KOLCZAKS, DIE • 1920 • Halm Alfred • FRG • POLENBLUT
LETZTEN MENSCHEN, DIE • 1919 • Oswald Richard • FRG
LETZTEN NACHTE DER MRS. ORCHARD, DIE see **ANWALT DES HERZENS, DER** • 1927
LETZTEN PARADIESE, DIE • 1968 • Schuhmacher Eugen • DOC • FRG • LAST PARADISES, THE
LETZTEN TAGE VON GOMORRA, DIE • 1974 • Sanders Helma • FRG • LAST DAYS OF GOMORRHA, THE
LETZTEN TAGE VON POMPEI, DIE • 1959 • Bonnard Mario • FRG, ITL, SPN • ULTIMI GIORNI DI POMPEII, GLI (ITL) ○ LAST DAYS OF POMPEII, THE(UKN)
LETZTEN VIER VON SANTA CRUZ, DIE • 1936 • Klinger Werner • FRG
LETZTEN WERDEN DIE ERSTEN SEIN, DIE • 1957 • Hansen Rolf • FRG
LETZTEN ZWEI VOM RIO BRAVO, DIE • 1964 • Rieger Manfred • FRG, ITL, SPN
LETZTES FACH UNTEN • 1955 • Jung-Alsen Kurt • GDR
LEUCHTE ASIENS, DIE • 1925 • Osten Franz • FRG
LEUCHTENDE SCHATTEN • 1945 • von Cziffra Geza • FRG
LEUCHTER DES KAISERS, DIE • 1924 • Neufeld Max • AUS
LEUCHTER DES KAISERS, DIE • 1936 • Hartl Karl • AUS • EMPEROR'S CANDLESTICKS, THE
LEUCHTFEHER • 1954 • Staudte Wolfgang • GDR • BEACON
LEUR DERNIERE NUIT • 1953 • Lacombe Georges • FRN • THEIR LAST NIGHT (USA)
LEUTARY, THE • 1971 • Lotyanu Emil • USS • LAUTARY
LEUTE MIT DEM SONNENSTICH, DIE • 1936 • Hoffmann Carl • FRG
LEUTE MIT FLUGELN • 1960 • Wolf Konrad • GDR • MEN WITH WINGS ○ PEOPLE WITH WINGS
LEUTNANT AUF BEFEHL • 1916 • Lubitsch Ernst • FRG
LEUTNANT IHRER MAJESTAT, DER • 1929 • Fleck Jacob, Fleck Luise • FRG
LEUTNANT WARST DU EINST BEI DEN HUSAREN • 1930 • Noa Manfred • FRG
LEV A KROTITEL • 1953 • *Stallich Jan (Ph)* • SHT • CZC
LEV A PISNICKA • 1959 • Pojar Bretislav • ANS • CZC • LION AND THE SONG, THE ○ LION AND THE DITTY, THE
LEV FARLIGT • 1944 • Falk Lauritz • SWD • LIVE DANGEROUSLY
LEV I ZAYATS • 1949 • Dezkhin V., Filippov G. • USS • LION AND THE HARE, THE
LEV LIVET LEENDE • 1936 • Brunius Pauline • SWD
LEV S BILOU HRIVOU • 1987 • Jires Jaromil • CZC • LION WITH THE WHITE MANE
LEVA LO DIAVOLO TUO DAL CONVENTO • 1973 • Antel Franz • ITL
LEVA PA "HOPPET" • 1951 • Gentele Goran • SWD • LIVING AT THE "HOPE"
LEVANDE MUMIEN, DEN • 1917 • Magnussen Fritz • SWD • LIVING MUMMY, THE
LEVANDE SKOGEN, DEN • 1966 • Wesslen Stig • DOC • SWD
LEVANTE • 1989 • Muller Beni • DOC • SWT
LEVANTE DAS SAIAS, O • 1968 • Porto Ismar • BRZ • RAISING OF SKIRTS, THE
LEVE SITT LIV • 1982 • Wam Svend, Vennerod Petter • NRW • VICTORIA L.
LEVEL 4350 • 1966 • Spry Robin • DOC • CND
LEVEL, THE • 1914 • Davis Ulysses • USA
LEVEL, THE • 1915 • Sloman Edward • USA
LEVEN DAT WE DROOMDEN, HET • 1984 • de Hert Robbe • BLG • LIFE OF OUR DREAMS, THE
LEVENDE LADDER, DE • 1913 • Binger Maurits H. • NTH
LEVENSSCHADUWEN • 1916 • Frenkel Theo Sr. • NTH • LIFE'S SHADOWS
LEVER, THE • 1966 • Lambart Evelyn • ANS • CND
LEVI AND FAMILY AT CONEY ISLAND • 1910 • *Atlas* • USA
LEVI AND MCGINNIS RUNNING FOR OFFICE • 1913 • *Imp* • USA
LEVI STRAUSS STORY, THE • 1976 • Elfick David • SHT • ASL
LEVIATHAN • 1966 • Keigel Leonard • FRN • FOOTBRIDGE, THE
LEVIATHAN • 1988 • Palat Marek • ANS • PLN
LEVIATHAN • 1989 • Cosmatos George Pan • USA
LEVIN'S MILL • 1980 • Seemann Horst • GDR
LEVINSKY'S HOLIDAY • 1913 • *Majestic* • USA
LEVI'S DILEMMA • 1910 • *Essanay* • USA
LEVI'S LUCK • 1914 • *Komic* • USA
LEVITY AND LAITY • 1922 • Drury William • UKN
LEVRES CLOSES • 1906 • Blache Alice • FRN • SEALED LIPS
LEVRES DE SANG • 1974 • Rollin Jean • FRN • JENNIFER
LEVRES ENTROUVERTES • Rollin Jean • FRN
LEVRES GLOUTONNES • Bonnot Paul • FRN
LEVRES ROUGES, LES see **ROUGE AUX LEVRES, LE** • 1970
LEVY AND GOLIATH (USA) see **LEVY ET GOLIATH** • 1987
LEVY ET CIE • 1930 • Hugon Andre • FRN
LEVY ET GOLIATH • 1987 • Oury Gerard • FRN • LEVY AND GOLIATH (USA)
LEVY'S SEVEN DAUGHTERS • 1915 • Van Wally • USA
LEW DOCKSTADER IN MINSTREL MISHAPS OR LATE FOR REHEARSAL • 1908 • *Dockstader Lew* • USA
LEW TREMBLY • 1916 • *Vogue* • USA
LEW TYLER'S WIFE • 1926 • Knoles Harley • USA
LEWD ONES, THE see **INRAN** • 1968
LEWE SONDER JOU, DIE • 1971 • SAF
LEWIS HARDCASTLE'S DUSKY SYNCOPATERS • 1930 • *Balcon Michael (P)* • SHT • UKN
LEY DE LAS PISTOLAS, LA • 1959 • Alazraki Benito • MXC
LEY DE MACHETE, LA • 1971 • Torres Miguel • VNZ • LAW OF THE MACHETE, THE
LEY DE UNA RAZA, LA • 1967 • Gonzalvo Jose Luis • SPN • JUAN PEDRO EL DALLADOR
LEY DEL DESEO, LA • 1986 • Almodovar Pedro • SPN • LAW OF DESIRE, THE
LEY DEL FORESTERO, LA (SPN) see **SIE NANNTEN IHN GRINGO** • 1966
LEY DEL GAVILAN, LA • 1966 • Salvador Jaime • MXC
LEY DEL HAREN, LA • 1933 • Seiler Lewis • USA
LEY DEL KARATE EN EL OESTE, LA • 1973 • Balcazar Alfonso • SPN
LEY DEL MAR, LA • 1950 • Iglesias Miguel • SPN
LEY DEL MAS RAPIDO, LA • 1958 • Cardona Rene • MXC
LEY DEL MONTE, LA • 1974 • *Cima* • MXC
LEY DEL MONTE, LA • 1989 • Castano Patricia, Trujillo Adelaida • DOC • CLM • LAW OF THE JUNGLE
LEY FUGA • 1952 • Gomez Muriel Emilio • MXC
LEY QUE OLVIDARON, LA • 1938 • Ferreyra Jose • ARG • LAW THEY FORGOT, THE (USA)
LEYCHA • 1964 • Ivanov-Vano Ivan • ANM • USS
LEYENDA DE AMOR, UNA • 1978 • Salazar Abel • MXC
LEYENDA DE FERIA • 1945 • de Orduna Juan • SPN
LEYENDA DE RODRIGO, LA • 1977 • Pablo Julian • MXC
LEYENDA DEL ALCALDE DE ZALAMEA, LA • 1972 • Camus Mario • SPN
LEYENDA DEL AMAZONAS, LA • 1977 • Darino Eduardo • ANM • URG • LEGEND OF THE AMAZON RIVER, THE
LEYENDA DEL ANGEEL ENMASCARADO, LA • 1990 • Buil Jose • MXC
LEYENDA DEL BANDIDO, LA • 1942 • Mendez Fernando • MXC
LEYENDA DEL BANDIDO, LA • 1965 • de Anda Raul Jr. • MXC
LEYENDA DEL TAMBOR, LA see **NINO DEL TAMBOR, EL** • 1981
LEYENDA ROTA • 1939 • Fernandez Cuenca Carlos • SPN
LEYLAKLAR ALTINDA • 1968 • Utku Umit • TRK • UNDER THE GLYCINS
LEZIONI DI VIOLONCELLO CON TOCCATA E FUGA • 1976 • Montemurri Davide • ITL • DOPO L'ADOLESCENZA
LEZIONI PRIVATE • 1975 • De Sisti Vittorio • ITL • PRIVATE LESSON, THE
LI CHIAMAVANO I TRE MOSCHETTIERI, INVECE ERANO QUATTRO • 1973 • Amadio Silvio • ITL
LI HSIAO-LUNG CH'UAN-CHI see **BRUCE LEE: THE MAN - THE MYTH** • 1976
LI SHIZHEN, THE GREAT PHARMACOLOGIST • 1956 • Shen Fu • CHN
LI SHUANGSHUANG • 1962 • Lu Ren • CHN
LI TING LANG • 1920 • Swickard Charles • USA
LIAISONS AMOUREUSES, LES see **MORTE-SAISON DES AMOURS, LA** • 1961
LIAISONS DANGEREUSES 1960, LES see **LIAISONS DANGEREUSES, LES** • 1959
LIAISONS DANGEREUSES, LES • 1959 • Vadim Roger • FRN, ITL • RELAZIONI PERICOLOSE (ITL) ○ DANGEROUS LOVE AFFAIRS ○ LIAISONS DANGEREUSES 1960, LES
LIAISONS DANGEREUSES, LES see **DANGEROUS LIAISONS** • 1988
LIAISONS PARTICULIERES, LES • 1974 • Pecas Max • FRN • ANY TIME ANYWHERE (UKN)
LIAISONS PARTICULIERES, LES see **CLAUDE ET GRETA** • 1970
LIAISONS PERVERSES, LES • 1975 • Sullivan Edgar P. • FRN
LIANA see **LYANA** • 1955
LIANA, LA SCHIVA BIANCA (ITL) see **LIANE, DIE WEISSE SKLAVIN** • 1957
LIAN'AI MIYU • 1987 • Chen Anqi • HKG • CHAOS BY DESIGN
LIANBRON • 1965 • Nykvist Sven • SWD • VINE BRIDGE, THE
LIANE • 1987 • Stranka Erwin • GDR
LIANE, DAS MADCHEN AUS DEM URWALD • 1956 • von Borsody Eduard • FRG • LIANE, JUNGLE GODDESS (USA) ○ LIANE -WHITE SLAVE
LIANE, DIE WEISSE SKLAVIN • 1957 • Leitner Hermann, Talamo Gino • FRG, ITL • LIANA, LA SCHIVA BIANCA (ITL) ○ JUNGLE GIRL AND THE SLAVER
LIANE, JUNGLE GODDESS (USA) see **LIANE, DAS MADCHEN AUS DEM URWALD** • 1956
LIANE -WHITE SLAVE see **LIANE, DAS MADCHEN AUS DEM URWALD** • 1956
LIANG HSAIO-WU-CHIH • 1981 • Ye Jianxing • HKG • SEALED WITH A KISS
LIANG SHAN-PO AND CHU YING-TAI • 1953 • Huang Sha, Sang Hu • CHN • LIANG SHANBO AND ZHU YINGTAI
LIANG SHAN-PO YU CHU YING-T'AI • 1963 • Hu King, Li Han-Hsiang • HKG • ETERNAL LOVE ○ LOVE ETERNE, THE
LIANG SHANBO AND ZHU YINGTAI see **LIANG SHAN-PO AND CHU YING-TAI** • 1953
LIANGJIA FUNU • 1985 • Huang Jianzhong • CHN • GIRL OF A GOOD FAMILY ○ WOMANKIND, THE ○ GOOD WOMAN, A
LIANNA • 1983 • Sayles John • USA
LIAO ZHONGHAI • 1983 • Tang Xiaodan • CHN
LIAR, THE • 1912 • Dwan Allan • USA
LIAR, THE • 1918 • *Purkall* • USA
LIAR, THE • 1918 • Lawrence Edmund • *Fox* • USA
LIAR, THE see **PSEFTIS, O** • 1968
LIAR, THE see **LOGNEREN** • 1970
LIAR, THE see **KADHDHAB, AL-** • 1975
LIAR, THE see **VALEHTELIJA** • 1980
LIAR, THE see **MENTIROSO, O** • 1988
LIAR AND THE NUN, THE see **LUGNER UND DIE NONNE, DER** • 1967
LIAR AND THE THIEF, THE • 1910 • *Thanhouser* • USA
LIARS, THE (USA) see **MENTEURS, LES** • 1961
LIAR'S MOON • 1981 • Fisher David • USA
LIAR'S NIGHT, THE see **NOCHE DEL EMBUSTERO, LA** • 1972
LIBAN DANS LA TOURMENTE, LE • 1975 • Saab Jocelyne, Stocklin Jorg • LBY, FRN
LIBEL • 1959 • Asquith Anthony • UKN
LIBELED LADY • 1936 • Conway Jack • USA
LIBELLEN • 1938 • FRG
LIBELLULE, LA • 1901 • Melies Georges • FRN • DRAGON FLY, THE (USA)
LIBELULA PARA CADA MUERTO, UNA • 1973 • Klimovsky Leon • SPN
LIBERA AMORE MIO • 1975 • Bolognini Mauro • ITL
LIBERA USCITA • 1951 • Coletti Duilio • ITL
LIBERACE: BEHIND THE MUSIC see **LIBERACE: THE UNTOLD STORY** • 1987
LIBERACE: THE UNTOLD STORY • 1987 • Greene David • TVM • USA • LIBERACE: BEHIND THE MUSIC
LIBERAL PARTY IN ONTARIO, THE • 1968 • Sheppard Gordon H. • DOC • CND
LIBERATED CHINA see **OSVOBOZHDYONNY KITAI** • 1950
LIBERATED FRANCE see **OSVOBOZHDENNAYA FRANTSYA** • 1946
LIBERATED LAND see **FELSZABADULT FOLD** • 1950
LIBERATION • 1975 • Bouchouchi Mourad, Beloufa Farouq • ALG
LIBERATION • 1980 • Muller John • MTV • CND
"LIBERATION" • 1981 • Guegan Gerard • FRN • TOUTES LES HISTOIRES DE DRAGON ONT UN FOND DE VERITE
LIBERATION see **MUKTI** • 1937
LIBERATION see **OSVOBOZHDENIYE** • 1940
LIBERATION see **STUDIE IV** • 1954
LIBERATION see **OSVOBOZHDENIE** • 1970
LIBERATION DES TERRITORIAUX • 1896 • Melies Georges • FRN • BREAKING UP OF THE TERRITORIAL ARMY
LIBERATION OF AUSCHWITZ, THE • 1986 • von Zur Muhlen Irmgard • DOC • USA
LIBERATION OF L.B. JONES, THE • 1970 • Wyler William • USA
LIBERATION OF PRAGUE see **OSVOBOZENI PRAHY** • 1976
LIBERATION OF THE MANNIQUE MECHANIQUE, THE • 1967 • Arnold Steven • SHT • USA
LIBERATOR see **OSLOBODILAC** • 1971
LIBERATOR, THE • 1918 • *Pagano Ernest* • SRL • ITL • MACISTE IN THE LIBERATOR
LIBERATORS, THE • 1967 • Zaninovic Stejpan • DOC • YGS
LIBERATORS, THE • 1987 • Johnson Kenneth • TVM • USA
LIBERDADE PARA JOSE DIOGO • 1975 • Teles Luis Galvao • PRT
LIBERER LE CINEMA AFRICAIN • 1975 • Boughedir Ferid • TNS
LIBERI ARMATI PERICOLOSI • 1976 • Guerrieri Romolo • ITL
LIBERTAD PROVISIONAL • 1976 • Bodegas Roberto • SPN • PROVISIONAL FREEDOM
LIBERTE • 1937 • Kemm Jean • FRN • GRANDE PASSION, LA
LIBERTE see **LIBERTE 1** • 1962
LIBERTE 1 • 1962 • Ciampi Yves • FRN, SNL • LIBERTE
LIBERTE CHERIE see **A NOUS LA LIBERTE** • 1931
LIBERTE, EGALITE, CHOUCROUTE • 1984 • Yanne Jean • FRN
LIBERTE, EGALITE, SEXUALITE see **SEXOLOGOS** • 1969
LIBERTE EN CROUPE, LA • 1970 • Molinaro Edouard • FRN
LIBERTE, LA NUIT • 1983 • Garrel Philippe • FRN
LIBERTE, LIBERTE CHERIE • 1933 • Bernard Raymond • FRN
LIBERTE SURVEILLEE • 1957 • Aisner Henri, Voltchek Vladimir • FRN, CZC
LIBERTINE, THE • 1916 • Steger Julius, Golden Joseph A. • USA
LIBERTINE, THE see **MATIARCA, LA** • 1968
LIBERTINES, LES • 1970 • Chenal Pierre • FRN
LIBERTY • 1929 • McCarey Leo • SHT • USA
LIBERTY • 1986 • Sarafian Richard C. • TVM • USA
LIBERTY see **LIBERTY, A DAUGHTER OF THE U.S.A.** • 1916
LIBERTY see **BRONTE: CRONACA DI UN MASSACRO CHE I LIBRI DI STORIA NON HANNO RACCONTATO** • 1972
LIBERTY, A DAUGHTER OF THE U.S.A. • 1916 • Jaccard Jacques, McRae Henry • SRL • USA • LIBERTY
LIBERTY BELLE • 1982 • Kane Pascal • FRN
LIBERTY BELLES • 1914 • Kirkwood James?, Henderson Dell? • USA
LIBERTY BELLES • 1916 • Henderson Dell • SHT • USA
LIBERTY BOND JIMMY • 1918 • Carewe Edwin • SHT • USA
LIBERTY BOND SHORT see **LIBERTY LOAN BOND SHORT** • 1918
LIBERTY CROWN • 1970 • Conner Bruce • USA
LIBERTY FOR US (USA) see **A NOUS LA LIBERTE** • 1931
LIBERTY HALL • 1914 • Shaw Harold • UKN
LIBERTY LOAN BOND SHORT • 1918 • Griffith D. W. • SHT • USA • BUY LIBERTY BONDS ○ LIBERTY BOND SHORT
LIBERTY OR DEATH • Korabov Nicolai • BUL
LIBERTY PARTY, THE • 1915 • *Hamilton Lloyd V.* • USA
LIBERTY ROAD see **HELL'S HIGHWAY** • 1932
LIBERTY STREET BLUES • 1988 • Gladu Andre • DOC • CND
LIBERXINA 90 • 1971 • Duran Carlos • SPN
LIBIDO • 1965 • Gastaldi Ernesto, Salerno Vittorio • ITL
LIBIDO • 1971 • Bergonzelli Sergio • ITL
LIBIDO • 1973 • Murray John B., Burstall Tim, Schepisi Fred, Baker David, Moreau Roland, Perdriaud Georges, Talansier Jean • ASL
LIBIDO • 1988 • Kazakov Varna Velislav • ANM • BUL
LIBIDO see **SEI NO KIGEN** • 1967
LIBRARIAN, THE • 1912 • *Edison* • USA
LIBRARY IS OPEN, THE see **BIBLIOTEKET ER ABENT** • 1948
LIBRARY OF CONGRESS • 1945 • Hammid Alexander • DOC • USA
LIBRE COMME DES LOUPS EN CAGE see **WOLFPEN PRINCIPLE** • 1974
LIBRE SERVICE • 1978 • Payer Roch Christophe • SER • CND
LIBRO DE BUEN AMOR I, EL • 1974 • Aznar Tomas • SPN • BOOK OF GOOD LOVE, THE
LIBRO DE BUEN AMOR II, EL • 1976 • Bayarri Jaime • SPN
LIBYA • 1942 • Cornelius Henry • SHT • UKN
LIBYE, DESERT VIVANT • 1973-74 • Valcour Pierre • DOC • CND
LICAO DE AMOR • 1975 • Escorel Eduardo • BRZ • LESSON IN LOVE
LICEALE, LA • 1975 • Tarantini Michele Massimo • ITL • UNDERGRADUATE GIRLS
LICEALE AL MARE CON L'AMICA DE PAPA, LA • 1980 • Girolami Marino • ITL
LICEALE NELLA CLASSE DEI REPETENTI, LA • 1978 • Laurenti Mariano • ITL
LICEALE SEDUCE I PROFESSORI, LA • 1979 • Laurenti Mariano • ITL
LICEENII • 1987 • Corjos Nicolae • RMN • GRADUATES, THE
LICEM U LICE • 1963 • Bauer Branko • YGS • FACE TO FACE
LICENCE TO THINK see **PERMISO PARA PENSAR** • 1988
LICENSE TO DRIVE • 1988 • Beeman Greg • USA
LICENSE TO KILL • 1984 • Taylor Jud • TVM • USA
LICENSE TO KILL • 1989 • Glen John • UKN
LICENSE TO KILL (USA) see **NICK CARTER VA TOUT CASSER** • 1964

LICENSED TO KILL • 1965 • Shonteff Lindsay • UKN • SECOND BEST SECRET AGENT IN THE WHOLE WIDE WORLD, THE (USA)
LICENSED TO LOVE AND KILL • 1979 • Shonteff Lindsay • UKN • NO.1 LICENSED TO LOVE AND KILL
LICENSED TO TERMINATE see **NINJA OPERATION 3: LICENSED TO TERMINATE** • 1987
LICENZA PREMIO • 1951 • Neufeld Max • ITL
LICHAAM EN ZIEL • 1968 • Daalder Renee • SHT • NTH
LICHNAYA ZHIZN KUZYAEVA VALENTINA • 1968 • Maslennikov Igor • USS • VALENTIN KUZYAEV'S PRIVATE LIFE
LICHNOYE DELO • 1932 • Vasiliev Sergei, Vasiliev Georgi • USS • PERSONAL AFFAIR, A ○ PERSONAL MATTER, A ○ AFFAIRE PERSONNELLE, UNE
LICHNOYE DELO ANNY AKHMATOVOY • 1989 • Aranovitch Semyon • USS • STORY OF ANN AKHMATOVA, THE
LICHT DER LIEBE, DAS see **WENN DU NOCH EINE MUTTER HAST..** • 1954
LICHT DES LEBENS, DAS • 1918 • Stein Josef • FRG
LICHT IM DUNKELN, DAS • 1916 • Neuss Alwin • FRG
LICHT IN DER FINSTERNIS see **ROSEN FUR BETTINA** • 1956
LICHT IN DER NACHT, DAS • 1918 • Albes Emil • FRG
LICHT SPIEL NUR 1 • Stiegler Robert • SHT • USA
LICHT UM MITTERNACHT, DAS • 1922 • von Wolzogen Hans • FRG
LICHT UND FINSTERNIS • 1920 • Forsten Hans • FRG
LICHT VON JENSIETS DER STRASSE • 1959 • Liebeneiner Wolfgang • FRG
LICHTENSTEIN IN LONDON • 1968 • Beresford Bruce • DCS • UKN
LICHTKONZERT NO.2 • 1935 • Fischinger Oskar • ANS • FRG
LICHTSTRAHL IM DUNKEL, EIN • 1917 • May Joe • FRG
LICKERISH QUARTET, THE • 1970 • Metzger Radley H. • USA, FRG, ITL • HIDE AND SEEK
LICKETY SPLAT • 1961 • Jones Charles M. • ANS • USA
LICNE STVARI • 1980 • Mandic Aleksandar • YGS • PERSONAL AFFAIRS
LICZE NA WASZE GRZECHY • 1963 • Zarzycki Jerzy • PLN • EXPECTED SINS, THE ○ YOUR SINS COUNT
LIDE BDETE • 1961 • Hofman Eduard • ANS • PLN • PEOPLE, WATCH OUT!
LIDE JAKO TY • 1960 • Blumenfeld Pavel • CZC • MEN OF KLADNO, THE ○ PEOPLE LIKE YOU
LIDE JEDNOHO SRDCE • 1953 • Jasny Vojtech, Kachyna Karel • DOC • CZC • PEOPLE OF ONE HEART
LIDE NA KOLEKACH • 1966 • Fric Martin • CZC • PEOPLE ON WHEELS ○ LIDE Z MARINGOTEK ○ LIFE ON WHEELS
LIDE NA KRE • 1937 • Fric Martin • CZC • PEOPLE ON THE ICEBERG ○ LOST ON THE ICE ○ PEOPLE ON A GLACIER ○ PEOPLE ON AN ICEBERG
LIDE Z MARINGOTEK see **LIDE NA KOLEKACH** • 1966
LIDE Z METRA • 1974 • Jires Jaromil • CZC • PEOPLE OF THE METRO ○ PEOPLE FROM THE METRO ○ PEOPLE IN THE SUBWAY ○ PEOPLE FROM THE UNDERGROUND
LIDELSE • 1945 • Cederlund Gosta • SWD • PASSION
LIDERCNYOMAS • 1920 • Fejos Paul • HNG • MARK OF THE PHANTOM, THE ○ LORD ARTHUR SAVILLE'S CRIME ○ NIGHTMARE ○ HALLUCINATION
LIDO MYSTERY, THE (UKN) see **ENEMY AGENTS MEET ELLERY QUEEN** • 1942
LIDOIRE • 1932 • Tourneur Maurice • FRN
LIDUSKA OF THE STAGE see **MUSIKANTSKA LIDUSKA** • 1940
LIE, THE • 1909 • *Edison* • USA
LIE, THE • 1911 • *Thanhouser* • USA
LIE, THE • 1912 • *Imp* • USA
LIE, THE • 1913 • *Moore Owen* • USA
LIE, THE • 1914 • *Lubin* • USA
LIE, THE • 1914 • Dwan Allan • *Goldseal* • USA
LIE, THE • 1914 • Wilson Frank • UKN
LIE, THE • 1915 • *Reliance* • USA
LIE, THE • 1918 • Dawley J. Searle • USA
LIE, THE • 1970 • Bridges Alan • TVM • UKN
LIE, THE see **NO MAN OF HER OWN** • 1950
LIE CHAIR, THE • 1975 • Cronenberg David • CND
LIE DETECTOR, THE (UKN) see **TRUTH ABOUT MURDER, THE** • 1946
LIE HUOZHONG YONGSHENG • 1965 • Shui Hua • CHN • RED CRAG
LIE NOT TO YOUR WIFE • 1912 • *Mace Fred* • USA
LIE OF NINA PETROVNA, THE (USA) see **MENSONGE DE NINA PETROVNA, LA** • 1937
LIE SUBLIME, THE • 1916 • Otto Henry • SHT • USA
LIE THAT BECAME THE TRUTH, THE • 1915 • Batley Ethyle • UKN
LIE THAT FAILED, THE • 1913 • *Thanhouser* • USA
LIE THAT FAILED, THE • 1918 • Berthelet Arthur • SHT • USA
LIEB, EIN DIEB, EIN WARENHAUS, EIN • 1928 • Wagner Karl Theodor • FRG
LIEB HEIMATLAND • 1926 • Claudius Erich • FRG
LIEB UND SEELE see **ROTHENBURGER, DIE** • 1918
LIEB VATERLAND MAGST RUHIG SEIN • 1976 • Klick Roland • FRG
LIEBE • 1919 • Noa Manfred • FRG
LIEBE • 1927 • Czinner Paul • FRG • HERZOGIN VON LANGEAIS, DIE ○ HISTOIRE DES TREIZE
LIEBE • 1956 • Haechler Horst • FRG
LIEBE 47 • 1949 • Liebeneiner Wolfgang • FRG
LIEBE, EINE • 1969 • Strobel Hans Rolf, Tichawsky Heinz • FRG
LIEBE ALS KODER see **SCHREI NACH LUST** • 1968
LIEBE AM SCHEIDEWEG see **GEHEIMNIS EINER AERZTIN, DAS** • 1955
LIEBE AUF BEFEHL • 1931 • Riemann Johannes, Franck Ernst L. • FRG
LIEBE AUF DEN ERSTEN BLICK • 1918 • *Weisse Hanni* • FRG
LIEBE AUF DEN ERSTEN TON • 1932 • Froelich Carl • FRG
LIEBE AUF EIS • 1950 • Meisel Kurt • FRG
LIEBE AUF KRUMMEN BEINEN • 1959 • Engel Thomas • FRG • EVERY DOG HAS HIS DAY
LIEBE AUGUSTIN, DER • 1940 • Emo E. W. • FRG
LIEBE AUGUSTIN, DER • 1960 • Thiele Rolf • FRG
LIEBE BEI HOF see **MEIN LIEBSTER IST EIN JAGERSMANN** • 1933
LIEBE DER ASRA, DIE • 1922 • Berger Josef • FRG
LIEBE DER BAJADERE, DIE • 1918 • Gade Svend • FRG
LIEBE DER BAJADERE, DIE see **GOTTER, MENSCHEN UND TIERE** • 1925
LIEBE DER BRUDER ROTT, DIE • 1929 • Waschneck Erich • FRG • IRRLICHTER ○ WILL O' THE WISP
LIEBE DER HETTY RAYMOND, DIE • 1917 • May Joe • FRG
LIEBE DER JEANNE NEY, DIE • 1927 • Pabst G. W. • FRG • LOVE OF JEANNE NEY, THE (USA) ○ LUSTS OF THE FLESH (UKN) ○ LOVES OF JEANNE NEY, THE
LIEBE DER MARIA BONDE, DIE • 1918 • Hanus Emerich • FRG
LIEBE DER MARION BACH, DIE • 1919 • Bolten-Baeckers Heinrich • FRG
LIEBE DER MITSU, DIE see **TOCHTER DES SAMURAI, DIE** • 1937
LIEBE DER SKLAVIN, DIE • 1920 • Illes Eugen • FRG
LIEBE DES MAHARADSCHA, DIE • 1936 • Rabenalt Arthur M., Alessandrini Goffredo • FRG, ITL • DONNA TRA DUE MONDI, UNA (ITL) ○ BETWEEN TWO WORLDS (USA) ○ MAHARAJA'S LOVE, THE ○ WEISSE FRAU DES MAHARADSCHA, DIE
LIEBE DES VANROYK, DIE • 1918 • Pick Lupu • FRG
LIEBE, DIE DEN KOPF VERLIERT • 1956 • Engel Thomas • AUS
LIEBE DUMME MAMA • 1934 • Boese Carl • FRG
LIEBE DURCH DIE AUTOTURE • 1972 • Saller Eddy • AUS • LOVE THROUGH THE CAR DOOR
LIEBE DURCH DIE HINTERTUR • 1969 • Antel Franz • FRG, AUS • WILD, WILLING AND SEXY (UKN)
LIEBE EINER KONIGIN, DIE • 1923 • Wolff Ludwig • FRG
LIEBE FAMILIE, DIE • 1957 • Weiss Helmut • AUS
LIEBE FREIHEIT UND VERRAT see **LEGGE DI GUERRA** • 1961
LIEBE FREUNDIN • 1949 • Steinbock Rudolf • AUS • ZWEIMAL VERLIEBT
LIEBE GEHT SELTSAME WEGE • 1927 • Kaufmann Fritz • FRG
LIEBE GEHT SELTSAME WEGE • 1937 • Zerlett Hans H. • FRG
LIEBE, HASS UND GELD • 1919 • Eriksen Erich • FRG
LIEBE IM DREIVIERTELTAKT • 1937 • Marischka Hubert • AUS, CZC • WIENER FIAKERLIED
LIEBE IM FINANZAMT • 1952 • Hoffmann Kurt • FRG • WOCHENEND IM PARADIES
LIEBE IM GLEITFLUG • 1938 • Grundgens Gustaf • FRG • LOVE IN STUNT FLYING (USA)
LIEBE IM KUHSTALL • 1928 • Froelich Carl • FRG
LIEBE IM MAI • 1928 • Wohlmuth Robert • AUS
LIEBE IM RAUSCH see **COLONIALSKANDAL** • 1927
LIEBE IM RING • 1930 • Schunzel Reinhold • FRG
LIEBE IM SCHNEE • 1928 • Obal Max • FRG
LIEBE IN DEUTSCHLAND, EINE (FRG) see **AMOUR EN ALLEMAGNE, UN** • 1983
LIEBE IN UNIFORM • 1932 • Jacoby Georg • FRG
LIEBE IST DER FRAUEN MACHT, DIE • 1924 • Bluen Georg • FRG • KABALE UND LIEBE IM ZIRKUS
LIEBE IST JA NUR EIN MARCHEN • 1955 • Rabenalt Arthur M. • FRG
LIEBE IST KALTER ALS DER TOD • 1969 • Fassbinder R. W. • FRG • LOVE IS COLDER THAN DEATH (UKN)
LIEBE IST LIEBE • 1932 • Martin Paul • FRG • LOVE IS LOVE
LIEBE IST NUR EIN WORT • 1971 • Vohrer Alfred • FRG • LOVE IS ONLY A WORD (UKN)
LIEBE IST ZOLLFREI • 1941 • Emo E. W. • FRG
LIEBE, JAZZ UND UEBERMUT • 1957 • Ode Erik • FRG
LIEBE KANN LUGEN • 1937 • Helbig Heinz • FRG
LIEBE KANN WIE GIFT SEIN • 1958 • Harlan Veit • FRG • GIRL OF SHAME
LIEBE KENNT KEIN GEBOT • 1925 • *Basch Siegmund (P)* • FRG
LIEBE LASST SICH NICHT ERZWINGEN see **ZWISCHEN HIMMEL UND HOLLE** • 1934
LIEBE, LIEBE • 1928 • Berger Ludwig • FRG
LIEBE LIED, DER • 1925 • van Treek Fred • FRG
LIEBE, LIED UND SPORT see **MOTORBRAUT, DIE** • 1924
LIEBE, LUFT UND LAUTER LUGEN • 1959 • Beauvais Peter • FRG • LOVE, AIR AND A LOT OF LIES
LIEBE LUST UND LEID, DER • 1926 • Gerron Kurt • FRG
LIEBE MACHT BLIND • 1923 • Mendes Lothar • FRG • LOVE MAKES ONE BLIND ○ LOVE MAKES US BLIND ○ LOVE BLINDS US
LIEBE MIT 16 • 1975 • Zschoche Hermann • GDR
LIEBE MIT ZWANZIG (FRG) see **AMOUR A VINGT ANS, L'** • 1962
LIEBE MUSS VERSTANDEN SEIN! • 1933 • Steinhoff Hans • FRG • LOVE HAS ITS REASONS!
LIEBE MUTTER, MIR GEHT ES GUT • 1971 • Ziewer Christian • FRG • DEAR MOTHER, I'M DOING WELL
LIEBE NACH NOTEN • 1945 • von Cziffra Geza • FRG
LIEBE OHNE ILLUSION • 1955 • Engel Erich • FRG
LIEBE PILGERFAHRT, DER • 1922 • Protazanov Yakov • FRG
LIEBE, SCHERZ UND ERNST • 1932 • Wenzler Franz • FRG • BUNBURY
LIEBE, SIE WAR NUR EIN TRAUM, DIE • 1917 • Alexander Georg • FRG
LIEBE SIEGT, DIE • 1934 • Zoch Georg • FRG
LIEBE SO SCHON WIE LIEBE • 1971 • Lemke Klaus • FRG
LIEBE SOMMER UND MUSIK • 1956 • Marischka Hubert • FRG
LIEBE, TANZ UND 1000 SCHLAGER • 1955 • Martin Paul • FRG
LIEBE, TOD UND TEUFEL • 1922 • Wenter Adolf • FRG
LIEBE, TOD UND TEUFEL • 1934 • Hilpert Heinz, Steinbicker Reinhart • FRG • DEVIL IN A BOTTLE, THE ○ IMP IN THE BOTTLE, THE ○ LOVE, DEATH AND THE DEVIL
LIEBE UND ALLTAG • 1930 • Gunther Herbert E. • FRG
LIEBE UND CHAMPAGNER • 1930 • Land Robert • FRG
LIEBE UND DAS TELEPHON, DIE • 1925 • Schwarz Hanns • FRG
LIEBE UND DER CO-PILOT, DIE • 1961 • Groschopp Richard • GDR
LIEBE UND DIE ERSTE EISENBAHN, DIE • 1934 • Preis Hasso • FRG • LOVE AND THE FIRST RAILROAD (USA)
LIEBE UND DIEBE • 1928 • Froelich Carl • FRG • HOTELRATTE, DIE ○ LOVE AND THIEVES
LIEBE UND EHE • 1923 • *Nivo-Film* • FRG
LIEBE UND LEBEN 1 • 1918 • Schmidthassler Walter • FRG • SEELE DES KINDES, DIE
LIEBE UND LEBEN 2 • 1918 • Schmidthassler Walter • FRG • TOCHTER DES SENATORS, DIE
LIEBE UND LEBEN 3 • 1918 • Boese Carl • FRG • ZWEI WELTEN
LIEBE UND LIST • 1915 • Del Zopp Rudolf • FRG
LIEBE UND SO WEITER • 1968 • Moorse Georg • FRG
LIEBE UND TELEPHON see **FRAULEIN VOM AMT, DAS** • 1925
LIEBE UND TROMPETENBLASEN • 1925 • Eichberg Richard • FRG
LIEBE UND TROMPETENBLASEN • 1954 • Weiss Helmut • FRG
LIEBE UND TROMPETENKLANG see **ABENTEUER EINES JUNGEN HERRN IN POLEN** • 1934
LIEBE UNTER 17 • 1970 • Winston R. B. • FRG • LOVE UNDER 17 (UKN)
LIEBE VERBOTEN -HEIRATEN ERLAUBT • 1959 • Meisel Kurt • FRG
LIEBE VOM ZIGEUNER STAMMT.., DIE • 1920 • Staufen Hans • FRG
LIEBE -WIE DIE FRAU SIE WUNSCHT • 1957 • Becker Wolfgang • FRG
LIEBE WILL GELERNT SEIN • 1963 • Hoffmann Kurt • FRG
LIEBE ZU EINER TOTEN, DIE • 1915 • Zangenberg Einar • FRG
LIEBELEI • 1927 • Fleck Jacob, Fleck Luise • FRG • PASSION'S FOOL
LIEBELEI • 1932 • Ophuls Max • FRG • LIGHT LOVE (USA)
LIEBELEI • 1933 • Ophuls Max • FRN • HISTOIRE D'AMOUR, UNE ○ YOUNG LOVE
LIEBELEI see **ELSKOVSLEG** • 1913
LIEBELEI UND LIEBE • 1938 • Rabenalt Arthur M. • FRG
LIEBENSTRAUM • 1928 • Stone Andrew L. • USA
LIEBER KARL • 1985 • Knilli Maria • AUS, FRG • DEAR CHARLES
LIEBERSCHULER, DER see **ES WAR NICHT DIE NACHTIGALL** • 1974
LIEBERSWACHEN • 1953 • Hinrich Hans • FRG
LIEBES-ABC, DAS • 1916 • Stifter Magnus • FRG • ABC OF LOVE, THE
LIEBES DER BARONIN VON S., DIE • 1924 • Galeen Henrik • FRG • LOVE LETTERS OF BARONESS S. ○ GESCHICHTE EINER EHE, DIE
LIEBES -HINTERTREPPEN • 1921 • Werner Karl • FRG
LIEBES-KORRIDOR, DER • 1920 • Gad Urban • FRG
LIEBES LAGER • 1977 • Gicca Enzo • ITL
LIEBESABENTEUER DER SCHONEN EVELYNE ODER DIE MORDMUHLE AUF EVANSHILL • 1921 • Eichberg Richard • FRG
LIEBESARZT, DER • 1931 • Schonfelder Erich • FRG
LIEBESATHLET, DER see **TICKY-TACKY I** • 1918
LIEBESBORSE, DIE see **CAFE ELECTRIC** • 1927
LIEBESBRIEF DER KONIGIN, DER • 1916 • Wiene Robert • FRG • EMPRESS'S LOVE LETTER, THE
LIEBESBRIEFE • 1943 • Zerlett Hans H. • FRG
LIEBESBRIEFE AUS DEM ENGADIN • 1938 • Trenker Luis • FRG • LOVE LETTERS FROM THE ENGADINE (USA)
LIEBESBRIEFE AUS MITTENWALD see **GELIEBTES FRAULEIN DOKTOR** • 1954
LIEBESBRIEFE EINER PORTUGIESISCHEN NONNE • 1977 • Franco Jesus • SWT
LIEBESBRIEFE EINER VERLASSENEN, DIE • 1924 • Hanus Emerich • FRG
LIEBESBRUCKE, DIE • 1916 • Karfiol William • FRG
LIEBESCHULE BLUTJUNGER MADCHEN • 1973 • von Jess Gabriel • FRG
LIEBESERKLARUNG • 1988 • Hubschmid Edi, Bischof Ursula • CMP • SWT • EXPLANATION OF LOVE, AN
LIEBESERWACHEN • 1936 • Maisch Herbert • FRG • HERBST MELODIE
LIEBESEXPRESS, DER • 1930 • Wiene Robert • FRG • ACHT TAGE GLUCK
LIEBESFEUER • 1925 • Stein Paul L. • FRG • FIRES OF LOVE
LIEBESFILIALE, DIE • 1931 • Wolff Carl Heinz • FRG
LIEBESGABE, EINE • 1915 • Del Zopp Rudolf • FRG
LIEBESGESCHICHTE, EINE • 1954 • Jugert Rudolf • FRG
LIEBESGESCHICHTEN • 1943 • Tourjansky Victor • FRG
LIEBESGESCHICHTEN see **MADELS VON HEUTE** • 1925
LIEBESGLUCK EINER BLINDEN, DAS • 1909 • Biebrach Rudolf • FRG
LIEBESGRUSSE AUS DER LEDERHOSE • 1973 • Marischka Franz • FRG
LIEBESGRUSSE AUS DER LEDERHOSE • 1978 • Otto Gunter • FRG
LIEBESHANDEL • 1926 • Speyer Jaap • FRG • AGENTUR UBERSEE
LIEBESHEIRAT • 1945 • Lingen Theo • FRG
LIEBESHOLLE • 1928 • Gallone Carmine • FRG, PLN, ITL • INFERNO DELL'AMORE, L' (ITL) ○ PAWNS OF PASSION
LIEBESKAFIG, DER • 1925 • Schonfelder Erich • FRG
LIEBESKARNEVAL • 1928 • Genina Augusto • FRG
LIEBESKARUSSELL, DAS • 1965 • Strobel Hans Rolf, Thiele Rolf, Weidenmann Alfred, von Ambesser Axel • FRG • WHO WANTS TO SLEEP
LIEBESKLEEBLATT • 1930 • Nosseck Max • FRG
LIEBESKOMMANDO • 1931 • von Bolvary Geza • FRG • LOVE'S COMMAND
LIEBESKOMODIE • 1942 • Lingen Theo • FRG
LIEBESKRIEG NACH NOTEN • 1953 • Hartl Karl • FRG
LIEBESLAUBE, DIE • 1922 • Neff Wolfgang • FRG
LIEBESLEBEN DES SCHONEN FRANZ, DAS • 1956 • Nosseck Max • AUS
LIEBESLEGENDE see **PREUSSICHE LIEBESGESCHICHTE** • 1938
LIEBESLEUTE • 1935 • Waschneck Erich • FRG • HERMANN UND DOROTHEA VON HEUTE
LIEBESLIED • 1931 • David Constantin J. • FRG, ITL
LIEBESLIED • 1935 • Buch Fritz Peter, Fredersdorf Herbert B. • FRG
LIEBESMARKT, DER • 1930 • Paul Heinz • FRG
LIEBESMELODIE see **GANZE WELT DREHT SICH UM LIEBE, DIE** • 1935
LIEBESNACHT, EINE • 1933 • May Joe • FRG

LIEBESNACHTE • 1929 • Sauer Fred • FRG • GEFAHREN DER BRAUTZEIT
LIEBESNACHTE IN DER TAIGA • 1967 • Philipp Harald • FRG • LOVE-NIGHTS IN THE TAIGA ○ CODE NAME IS KILL
LIEBESNEST 1, DAS • 1922 • Walther-Fein Rudolf • FRG
LIEBESNEST 2, DAS • 1922 • Walther-Fein Rudolf • FRG
LIEBESOPFER • 1918 • Schmidthassler Walter • FRG
LIEBESPREMIERE • 1943 • Rabenalt Arthur M. • FRG
LIEBESPROBE, DIE • 1915 • *Oliver-Film* • FRG
LIEBESQUELLE, DIE • 1965 • Hofbauer Ernst • AUS • FOUNTAIN OF LOVE, THE (USA) ○ SEX IN THE GRASS (UKN)
LIEBESREGEN • 1927 • Walther-Fein Rudolf • FRG
LIEBESROMAN DES CESARE UBALDI, DER • 1922 • Schall Heinz • FRG
LIEBESROMAN IM HAUSE HABSBURG, EIN see **GEHEIMNIS UM JOHANN ORT, DAS** • 1932
LIEBESSCHULE • 1940 • Kulb Karl G. • FRG
LIEBESSPIEL • 1931 • Fischinger Oskar • ANS • FRG • LOVE-GAMES
LIEBESSPIELE JUNGER MADCHEN • 1972 • Gottlieb Franz J. • FRG • HUNGRY FOR SEX (UKN) ○ LOVE GAMES FOR YOUNG GIRLS ○ LOVE GAMES OF YOUNG GIRLS
LIEBESTAUMEL • 1920 • Hartwig Martin • FRG
LIEBESTOLLEN APOTHEKER TOCHTER, DIE • 1972 • Antel Franz • FRG
LIEBESTRAGODIE DES HOMUNCULUS, DIE see **HOMUNCULUS 3** • 1916
LIEBESTRAUM • 1932 • Newman Widgey R. • UKN
LIEBESTRAUM • 1951 • Martin Paul • FRG • DREAMS OF DEATH (USA) ○ TODLICHEN TRAUME, DIE ○ DEADLY DREAMS
LIEBESTRAUME • 1935 • Hille Heinz • FRG, AUS, HNG
LIEBESURLAUB see **SIEBENTE JUNGE, DER** • 1941
LIEBESVOGEL (FRG) see **LOVE BIRDS** • 1969
LIEBESWALZER • 1930 • Thiele Wilhelm • FRG • LOVE WALTZ, THE
LIEBESWIRBEL see **DREIMAL KOMODIE** • 1945
LIEBET DAS LEBEN • 1924 • Asagaroff Georg • FRG
LIEBET DIE MANNER • 1915 • Schmelter Franz • FRG
LIEBFRAUMILCH • 1928 • Froelich Carl • FRG
LIEBGARDIST, DIE see **GARDEOFFIZIER, DER** • 1926
LIEBLING DER FRAUEN, DER • 1911 • *Freund Karl (Ph)* • FRG
LIEBLING DER FRAUEN, DER • 1921 • Wilhelm Carl • FRG
LIEBLING DER GOTTER • 1930 • Schwarz Hanns • FRG • DARLING OF THE GODS (USA)
LIEBLING DER GOTTER • 1960 • Reinhardt Gottfried • FRG • SWEETHEART OF THE GODS (USA) ○ FAVOURITE OF THE GODS
LIEBLING DER MATROSEN • 1937 • Sirk Douglas, Hinrich Hans • AUS
LIEBLING DER WELT • 1949 • Neufeld Max • AUS, FRN • HOHEIT DARF NICHT KUSSEN ○ ROSEN DER LIEBE
LIEBLING, ICH MUSS DICH ERSCHIESSEN • 1962 • Goslar Jurgen • FRG
LIEBLING SCHONER FRAUEN, DER see **BEL AMI** • 1939
LIEBLINGSFRAU DES MAHARADSCHA 3, DIE • 1920 • Mack Max • FRG
LIEBSCHAFTEN DER KATE KELLER, DIE • 1919 • Froelich Carl • FRG
LIEBSCHAFTEN DES HEKTOR DALMORE, DIE • 1921 • Oswald Richard • FRG
LIEBSJAGD DURCH 7 BETTEN • 1974 • *Robert Leichtman Productions* • FRG
LIECHANG ZHASA • 1985 • Tian Zhuangzhuang • CHN • ON THE HUNTING GROUND
LIED, DAS MEINE MUTTER SANG, DAS • 1928 • Eriksen Erich • FRG
LIED DER COLOMBINE, DAS • 1918 • *Toelle Carola* • FRG
LIED DER HEIMAT, DAS see **ZWISCHEN UNS DIE BERGE** • 1956
LIED DER HOHEN TAUERN, DAS see **LIED VON KAPRUN, DAS** • 1955
LIED DER LIEBE, DAS see **WENN DIE MUSIK NICHT WAR'** • 1935
LIED DER MATROSEN, DAS • 1958 • Maetzig Kurt, Reisch Gunter • GDR • SAILOR'S SONG ○ SONG OF THE SAILORS, THE
LIED DER MUTTER, DAS • 1918 • Neuss Alwin • FRG
LIED DER NACHTIGALL, DAS • 1943 • Lingen Theo • FRG
LIED DER NATIONEN, DAS • 1931 • Meinert Rudolf • FRG
LIED DER PUSZTA, DAS • 1920 • Boese Carl • FRG
LIED DER SONNE, DAS • 1933 • Neufeld Max • FRG
LIED DER STROME, DAS • 1954 • Ivens Joris • FRG • SONG OF THE RIVERS, THE
LIED DER WUSTE, DAS • 1939 • Martin Paul • FRG • DESERT SONG (USA)
LIED DES LEBENS, DAS • 1916 • Neuss Alwin • FRG
LIED DES NARREN, DAS • 1919 • *Peterhans Josef* • FRG
LIED, EIN KUSS, EIN MADEL, EIN • 1932 • von Bolvary Geza • FRG
LIED EINER NACHT, DAS • 1932 • Litvak Anatole • FRG
LIED FUR DICH, EIN • 1933 • May Joe • FRG
LIED GEHT UM DIE WELT, EIN • 1933 • Oswald Richard • FRG, UKN • MY SONG GOES ROUND THE WORLD (UKN) ○ JOSEPH SCHMIDT STORY, THE
LIED IN MY HART • 1970 • SAF
LIED IST AUS, DAS • 1930 • von Bolvary Geza • FRG
LIED KLAGT AN, EIN • 1936 • Zoch Georg • FRG
LIED VOM GLUCK, DAS • 1933 • Boese Carl • FRG • SONG OF HAPPINESS, THE (USA) ○ ES GIBT NUR EINE MELODIE
LIED VOM LEBEN, DAS • 1931 • Granowsky Alexis • FRG • SONG OF LIFE
LIED VOM TROMPETER, DAS • 1964 • Petzold Konrad • GDR
LIED VON DER GLOCKE, DAS • 1907 • *Freund Karl (Ph)* • FRG
LIED VON KAPRUN, DAS • 1955 • Kutter Anton • FRG, AUS • LIED DER HOHEN TAUERN, DAS
LIED VON NEAPEL, DAS (FRG) see **ASCOLTAMI** • 1957
LIEFDE VIR LELIK • 1972 • SAF
LIEFDESBEKENTENISSEN • 1967 • Verstappen Wim • NTH • CONFESSIONS OF LOVING COUPLES
LIEFSTE MADELEIN • 1976 • SAF
LIEFSTE VEERTJIE • 1975 • SAF
LIEH-HUO CH'ING-CH'UN • 1983 • T'An Chia-Ming • HKG • NOMAD
LIEH SHIH CHI HUA • 1975 • Ting Shan-Hsi • HKG • OPERATION REGINA ○ QUEEN'S RANSOM, A
LIEN-CH'ENG CHUEH • 1979 • Mou Tun-Fei • HKG • MYSTERY OF CONSECUTIVE CONNECTIONS, THE
LIEN DE PARENTE • 1985 • Rameau Willy • FRN
LIEN-K'AO TA-MENG • 1988 • Chang Yi-Ch'En • TWN
LIENS DE SANG, LES • 1978 • Chabrol Claude • FRN, CND • BLOOD RELATIVES (USA)
LIES • 1983 • Wheat Ken, Wheat Jim • USA
LIES see **USO** • 1963
LIES MY FATHER TOLD ME • 1960 • Chaffey Don • UKN
LIES MY FATHER TOLD ME • 1975 • Kadar Jan • CND • MENSONGES QUE MON PERE ME CONTAIT, LES
LIETO FINE • 1983 • Arbore Renzo • ITL • HAPPY END
LIEU DU CRIME, LE • 1985 • Techine Andre • FRN • SCENE OF THE CRIME (USA)
LIEUT. DANNY, U.S.A. • 1916 • Edwards Walter • USA
LIEUT. DARING R.N. SAVES H.M.S. MEDINA see **LIEUTENANT DARING R.N. AND THE SECRET SERVICE AGENTS** • 1911
LIEUTENANT BASIL see **LEITENANT BASIL** • 1970
LIEUTENANT CARIBINIER, THE see **TENENTE DEI CARABINIERI, IL** • 1985
LIEUTENANT CRAIG -MISSING see **TI RITROVERO** • 1949
LIEUTENANT DARING, AERIAL SCOUT • 1914 • Batley Ernest G.? • UKN
LIEUTENANT DARING AND THE DANCING GIRL • 1913 • Raymond Charles • UKN
LIEUTENANT DARING AND THE INTERNATIONAL JEWEL THIEVES see **LIEUTENANT DARING AND THE MYSTERY OF ROOM 41** • 1913
LIEUTENANT DARING AND THE LABOUR RIOTS • 1913 • Raymond Charles • UKN
LIEUTENANT DARING AND THE MYSTERY OF ROOM 41 • 1913 • Weston Charles • UKN • LIEUTENANT DARING AND THE INTERNATIONAL JEWEL THIEVES
LIEUTENANT DARING AND THE PHOTOGRAPHING PIGEON • 1912 • Raymond Charles • UKN
LIEUTENANT DARING AND THE PLANS OF THE MINEFIELDS • 1912 • Martinek H. O. • UKN • INTERNATIONAL SPIES, THE (USA)
LIEUTENANT DARING AND THE SHIP'S MASCOT • 1912 • Aylott Dave • UKN
LIEUTENANT DARING AND THE STOLEN INVENTION • 1914 • Batley Ernest G. • UKN
LIEUTENANT DARING AVENGES THE INSULT TO THE UNION JACK • 1912 • Aylott Dave • UKN
LIEUTENANT DARING DEFEATS THE MIDDLEWEIGHT CHAMPION • 1912 • Raymond Charles • UKN
LIEUTENANT DARING QUELLS A REBELLION • 1912 • Raymond Charles? • UKN
LIEUTENANT DARING R.N. • 1935 • Denham Reginald • UKN
LIEUTENANT DARING R.N. AND THE SECRET SERVICE AGENTS • 1911 • Aylott Dave • UKN • LIEUT. DARING R.N. SAVES H.M.S. MEDINA
LIEUTENANT DARING R.N. AND THE WATER RATS • 1924 • Gordon Edward R., Youngdeer James, Moran Percy • UKN
LIEUTENANT GERANIUM AND THE STEALED ORDERS • 1914 • Aylott Dave • UKN
LIEUTENANT GOVERNOR, THE • 1915 • Totten Joseph Byron • USA
LIEUTENANT GREY OF THE CONFEDERACY • 1911 • *Selig* • USA
LIEUTENANT JONES • 1913 • Parker Lem B. • USA
LIEUTENANT KITE see **PORUCHIK KIZHE** • 1934
LIEUTENANT LILLY AND THE PLANS OF THE DIVIDED SKIRT • 1912 • Plumb Hay • UKN
LIEUTENANT LILLY AND THE SPLODGE OF OPIUM • 1913 • Plumb Hay • UKN
LIEUTENANT MADCAP see **LOJNANT GALENPENNA** • 1917
LIEUTENANT NATASSA • 1971 • Foskolos Nikos • GRC
LIEUTENANT PIE'S LOVE STORY • 1913 • Plumb Hay • UKN
LIEUTENANT PIMPLE AND THE STOLEN INVENTION • 1914 • Evans Fred, Evans Joe • UKN
LIEUTENANT PIMPLE AND THE STOLEN SUBMARINE • 1914 • Evans Fred, Evans Joe • UKN
LIEUTENANT PIMPLE GOES TO MEXICO • 1914 • Evans Fred, Evans Joe • UKN
LIEUTENANT PIMPLE, GUN RUNNER • 1914 • Evans Fred, Evans Joe • UKN
LIEUTENANT PIMPLE, KING OF THE CANNIBAL ISLANDS • 1914 • Evans Fred, Evans Joe • UKN
LIEUTENANT PIMPLE ON SECRET SERVICE • 1913 • Evans Fred, Evans Joe • UKN
LIEUTENANT PIMPLE'S DASH FOR THE POLE • 1914 • Evans Fred, Evans Joe • UKN
LIEUTENANT PIMPLE'S SEALED ORDERS • 1914 • Evans Fred, Evans Joe • UKN
LIEUTENANT ROBIN CRUSOE U.S.N. see **LT. ROBIN CRUSOE U. S.N.** • 1966
LIEUTENANT ROSE AND THE BOXERS • 1911 • Stow Percy • UKN
LIEUTENANT ROSE AND THE CHINESE PIRATES • 1910 • Stow Percy • UKN
LIEUTENANT ROSE AND THE FOREIGN SPY • 1910 • Stow Percy • UKN
LIEUTENANT ROSE AND THE GUN-RUNNERS • 1910 • Stow Percy • UKN
LIEUTENANT ROSE AND THE HIDDEN TREASURE • 1912 • Stow Percy • UKN
LIEUTENANT ROSE AND THE MOORISH RAIDERS • 1912 • Stow Percy • UKN
LIEUTENANT ROSE AND THE PATENT AEROPLANE • 1912 • Stow Percy • UKN
LIEUTENANT ROSE AND THE ROBBERS OF FINGALL'S CREEK • 1910 • Stow Percy • UKN
LIEUTENANT ROSE AND THE ROYAL VISIT • 1911 • Stow Percy • UKN
LIEUTENANT ROSE AND THE SEALED ORDERS • 1914 • Stow Percy • UKN
LIEUTENANT ROSE AND THE STOLEN BULLION • 1913 • Stow Percy • UKN
LIEUTENANT ROSE AND THE STOLEN CODE • 1911 • Stow Percy • UKN
LIEUTENANT ROSE AND THE STOLEN SHIP • 1912 • Stow Percy • UKN
LIEUTENANT ROSE AND THE STOLEN SUBMARINE • 1910 • Stow Percy • UKN
LIEUTENANT ROSE AND THE TRAIN WRECKERS • 1912 • Stow Percy • UKN
LIEUTENANT ROSE IN CHINA SEAS • 1912 • Stow Percy • UKN
LIEUTENANT SCHUSTER'S WIFE • 1972 • Rich David Lowell • TVM • USA
LIEUTENANT SMITH • 1943 • Vorkapich Slavko • SHT • USA
LIEUTENANT WORE SKIRTS, THE • 1955 • Tashlin Frank • USA
LIEUTENANT'S BRIDE, THE • 1912 • Haldane Bert? • UKN
LIEUTENANT'S COUNTRY see **PAIS DOS TENENTES, O** • 1988
LIEUTENANT'S LAST FIGHT • 1912 • Ince Thomas H. • USA • CUSTER'S LAST FIGHT
LIEUX GEOMETRIQUES • Cantagrel Marc • DOC • FRN
LIEVE JONGENS • 1979 • de Lussanets Paul • NTH • DEAR BOYS
LIEVRE ER LES GRENOUILLES, LA • 1969 • Antonescu Victor • ANS • FRN • HARES AND THE FROGS, THE (USA)
LIEVRE ET LA TORTUE, LE • *Tadie Cinema* • SHT • FRN • TORTOISE AND THE HARE, THE (USA)
LIFE • 1920 • Vale Travers • USA
LIFE • 1928 • Millar Adelqui • UKN • JUAN JOSE
LIFE see **ZHIZN** • 1927
LIFE see **ZENDEGUI** • 1969
LIFE see **RENSHENG** • 1985
LIFE, A • 1988 • Cole Frank • DOC • CND
LIFE, A see **LEBEN, EIN** • 1973
LIFE, THE (UKN) see **DEROBADE, LA** • 1979
LIFE AFTER DARK (UKN) see **GIRLS IN THE NIGHT** • 1953
LIFE AFTER DEATH • 1983 • Chang Il-Ho • SKR
LIFE AFTER LIFE see **CHANCES ARE** • 1988
LIFE AFTER NINETY MINUTES • 1965 • Nemec Jan, Schmidt Jan • CZC
LIFE AND ADVENTURES OF JOHN VANE, THE AUSTRALIAN BUSHRANGER • 1910 • Fitzgerald S. • ASL
LIFE AND ADVENTURES OF NICHOLAS NICKLEBY, THE see **NICHOLAS NICKLEBY** • 1948
LIFE AND ADVENTURES OF SANTA CLAUS • 1986 • Rankin Arthur Jr., Bass Saul • ANM • USA
LIFE AND AMAZING ADVENTURES OF ROBINSON CRUSOE, THE • 1973 • Govorukhin S. • USS
LIFE AND ASSASSINATION OF THE KINGFISH, THE • 1977 • Collins Robert • TVM • USA
LIFE AND BATTLES OF DANIEL BOONE see **LIFE OF DANIEL BOONE** • 1912
LIFE AND DEATH see **LIV OG DOD** • 1980
LIFE AND DEATH (A STRUGGLE) see **SHENGSI XIAN** • 1985
LIFE AND DEATH OF 9413, A HOLLYWOOD EXTRA, THE • 1928 • Florey Robert, Vorkapich Slavko • SHT • USA • SUICIDE OF A HOLLYWOOD EXTRA ○ HOLLYWOOD RHAPSODY ○ HOLLYWOOD EXTRA, A
LIFE AND DEATH OF A SPHERE • 1948 • Anderson Dorsey • SHT • USA
LIFE AND DEATH OF COLONEL BLIMP, THE • 1943 • Powell Michael, Pressburger Emeric • UKN • COLONEL BLIMP (USA)
LIFE AND DEATH OF FERDINAND LYUS, THE see **ZHIZN I SMYERT FERDINANDA LYUSA** • 1977
LIFE AND DEATH OF LIEUTENANT SCHMIDT, THE • 1917 • Rasumny Alexander (c/d) • USS
LIFE AND DEATH OF PUSHKIN, THE see **JIZN I SMERT Q.S. POUCHKINA** • 1910
LIFE AND FLIGHT OF THE REV. BUCK SHOTTE, THE • 1968 • Weir Peter • SHT • ASL • LIFE AND TIMES OF THE REV. BUCK SHOTTE, THE
LIFE AND INCREDIBLE ADVENTURES OF ROBINSON CRUSOE, THE SAILOR FROM YORK, THE see **DOBRODRUZSTVI ROBINSONA CRUSOE, NAMORNIKA Z YORKU** • 1982
LIFE AND LEGEND OF BUFFALO JONES, THE • 1976 • *Guinn Rick* • USA
LIFE AND LOVES OF A SHE-DEVIL, THE see **SHE DEVIL** • 1989
LIFE AND LOVES OF BEETHOVEN, THE (USA) see **GRAND AMOUR DE BEETHOVEN, UN** • 1936
LIFE AND LOVES OF DR. PAUL JOSEPH GOEBBELS, THE see **ENEMY OF WOMEN** • 1944
LIFE AND LOVES OF MOZART, THE (USA) see **REICH MIR DIE HAND, MEIN LEBEN** • 1955
LIFE AND MESSAGE OF SWAMI VIVEKANANDA • 1964 • *Roy Bhimal (P)* • IND
LIFE AND MIRACLES OF BLESSED MOTHER CABRINI, THE • 1946 • Battistoni Aurelio • ITL
LIFE AND MOVING PICTURES • 1915 • *Gribbon Harry* • USA
LIFE AND MUSIC OF GIUSEPPE VERDI, THE see **GIUSEPPE VERDI** • 1938
LIFE AND MUSIC OF GIUSEPPE VERDI, THE (USA) see **GIUSEPPE VERDI** • 1953
LIFE AND OPINION OF MASSEUR ICHI, THE see **ZATO ICHI MONOGATARI** • 1962
LIFE AND PASSION OF CHRIST • 1908 • *Pathe* • FRN
LIFE AND PASSION OF CHRIST see **PASSION DE NOTRE-SEIGNEUR JESUS-CHRIST, LA** • 1905
LIFE AND SAND see **V PESKAKH SREDNEI AZII** • 1943
LIFE AND TIMES OF A CRIMINAL, THE see **FORBRYDERS LIV OG LEVNED, EN** • 1916
LIFE AND TIMES OF A HAPPY HOOKER, THE see **LIFE AND TIMES OF XAVIER HOLLANDER, THE** • 1974
LIFE AND TIMES OF EDWIN ALONZO BOYD, THE • 1983 • Rose Les • CND
LIFE AND TIMES OF GRIZZLY ADAMS, THE • 1975 • Friedenberg Richard • USA
LIFE AND TIMES OF JUDGE ROY BEAN, THE • 1972 • Huston John • USA • HANGING JUDGE, THE
LIFE AND TIMES OF ROSIE THE RIVETER, THE see **ROSIE THE RIVETER** • 1980
LIFE AND TIMES OF THE CHOCOLATE KILLER, THE see **CHOCOLATE KILLER, THE** • 1986
LIFE AND TIMES OF THE REV. BUCK SHOTTE, THE see **LIFE AND FLIGHT OF THE REV. BUCK SHOTTE, THE** • 1968

LIFE AND TIMES OF XAVIER HOLLANDER, THE • 1974 • Spangler Larry • USA • LIFE AND TIMES OF A HAPPY HOOKER, THE
LIFE AND WORK OF PAUL STRAND, THE • 1984 • Walker John • CND
LIFE AND WORKS OF RICHARD WAGNER, THE • 1913 • Klaw Dr.
LIFE AT FORSBYHOLM see **LIVET PA FORSBYHOLM** • 1948
LIFE AT STAKE see **HRA O ZIVOT** • 1956
LIFE AT STAKE, A • 1915 • Jaccard Jacques • USA
LIFE AT STAKE, A (UKN) see **KEY MAN** • 1955
LIFE AT STAKE OR THE ARMSTRONG MYSTERY, A • 1915 • *Apex* • USA
LIFE AT THE TOP • 1965 • Kotcheff Ted • UKN
LIFE –BE IN IT • 1976 • Stitt Alexander • SHT • ASL
LIFE BEGINS • 1932 • Flood James, Nugent Elliott • USA • DAWN OF LIFE, THE (UKN)
LIFE BEGINS see **LEBEN BEGINNT, DAS** • 1959
LIFE BEGINS AGAIN • 1943 • Alexander Donald • DOC • UKN
LIFE BEGINS ANEW (USA) see **ZU NEUEN UFERN** • 1937
LIFE BEGINS ANEW (USA) see **VITA RICOMINCIA, LA** • 1945
LIFE BEGINS AT 8.30 • 1942 • Pichel Irving • USA • LIGHT OF HEART, THE (UKN)
LIFE BEGINS AT 17 • 1958 • Dreifuss Arthur • USA
LIFE BEGINS AT COLLEGE see **LIFE BEGINS IN COLLEGE** • 1937
LIFE BEGINS AT FORTY • 1935 • Marshall George • USA
LIFE BEGINS EARLY see **ZYCIE ZACZYNA SIE WCZESNIE** • 1961
LIFE BEGINS FOR ANDY HARDY • 1941 • Seitz George B. • USA
LIFE BEGINS FOR ANDY PANDA • 1939 • Lovy Alex • ANS • USA
LIFE BEGINS IN COLLEGE • 1937 • Seiter William A. • USA • JOY PARADE, THE (UKN) ○ LIFE BEGINS AT COLLEGE
LIFE BEGINS NOW see **NU BORGAR LIVET** • 1948
LIFE BEGINS TODAY see **I DAG BORJAR LIVET** • 1939
LIFE BEGINS TOMORROW see **MORGEN BEGINNT DAS LEBEN** • 1933
LIFE BEGINS TOMORROW see **VIE COMMENCE DEMAIN, LA** • 1950
LIFE BEGINS WITH LOVE • 1937 • McCarey Ray • USA
LIFE BOAT, THE • 1911 • *Morrison James* • USA
LIFE-BRINGING WATER see **ELTETO TISZA-VIZ** • 1954
LIFE CAN BE SO BEAUTIFUL see **LEBEN KANN SO SCHON SEIN, DAS** • 1938
LIFE CHASE, A • 1916 • Vale Travers • USA
LIFE CLASSES • 1986 • MacGillivray William D. • MTV • CND
LIFE CONTINUES see **A ZIVOT JDE DAL..** • 1935
LIFE DANCES ON (USA) see **CARNET DE BAL, UN** • 1937
LIFE DOESN'T SPARE see **VIATA NU IARTA** • 1957
LIFE DRAMA OF NAPOLEON BONAPARTE AND EMPRESS JOSEPHINE OF FRANCE • 1909 • *Vitagraph* • USA
LIFE FOR A KISS, A • 1912 • Dwan Allan • USA
LIFE FOR A LIFE, A • 1906 • Raymond Charles? • UKN
LIFE FOR A LIFE, A • 1909 • *Lubin* • USA
LIFE FOR A LIFE, A • 1910 • *Vitagraph* • USA
LIFE FOR A LIFE, A • 1913 • Calvert Charles? • UKN
LIFE FOR A LIFE, A see **ZHIZN ZA ZHIZN** • 1916
LIFE FOR A LIFE, A see **NECROMANCY** • 1972
LIFE FOR A WOMAN • 1979 • Kreps Bonnie • CND
LIFE FOR CHRISTINE • 1980 • Goldschmidt John • MTV • UKN
LIFE FOR JAN KASPAR • 1959 • Sis Vladimir • CZC
LIFE FOR LIFE • 1913 • *Selig* • USA
LIFE FOR LIFE see **ZYCIE ZA ZYCIE** • 1990
LIFE FOR RUTH • 1962 • Dearden Basil • UKN • WALK IN THE SHADOW (USA) ○ CONDEMNED TO LIFE
LIFE FOR THE CZAR • 1911 • Goncharov Vasili M. • USS
LIFE FORCE • 1974 • Mellen Peter • DOC • CND
LIFE GAME, THE • 1970 • Lavut Martin • CND
LIFE GOES ON • 1983 • Nolte William • USA
LIFE GOES ON see **SORRY YOU'VE BEEN TROUBLED** • 1932
LIFE GOES ON see **A ZIVOT JDE DAL..** • 1935
LIFE GOES ON see **LIVET GAR VIDARE** • 1941
LIFE GOES ON see **ELET MEGY TOVABB, AZ** • 1959
LIFE GOES ON see **VIE CONTINUE, LA** • 1981
LIFE GUARD, THE • 1915 • Hotaling Arthur D. • USA
LIFE HAS BECOME A SIN see **YASAMAK HARAM OLDU** • 1968
LIFE HESITATES AT 40 • 1936 • Parrott Charles, Law Harold • SHT • USA
LIFE HISTORY OF A MOSQUITO • 1922 • Monkman Noel • SHT • ASL
LIFE IN A CITADEL see **ZHIZN V TSITADEL** • 1947
LIFE IN A TIN see **VITA IN SCATOLA, UNA** • 1967
LIFE IN BLOOM see **MICHURIN** • 1947
LIFE IN BLOSSOM see **MICHURIN** • 1947
LIFE IN DANGER • 1959 • Bishop Terry • UKN
LIFE IN DEATH see **ZHIZN V SMERTI** • 1914
LIFE IN DENMARK see **LIVET I DANMARK** • 1971
LIFE IN EMERGENCY WARD 10 • 1959 • Day Robert • UKN • EMERGENCY WARD 10
LIFE IN GERMANY • 1965 • Thorndike Andrew, Thorndike Annelie • DOC • GDR
LIFE IN HALVES • 1966 • Lazarchuk I. • ANS • USS
LIFE IN HELL see **VIE A L'ENVERS, LA** • 1964
LIFE IN HER HANDS • 1951 • Leacock Philip • UKN
LIFE IN PINK see **VIATA IN ROZ** • 1969
LIFE IN SEVILLA see **VIVIR EN SEVILLA** • 1979
LIFE IN SLOW MOTION see **ZPOMALENY ZIVOT** • 1962
LIFE IN SOMETOWN U.S.A. • 1938 • Keaton Buster • SHT • USA
LIFE IN THE ANTARCTIC see **DR. MAWSON IN THE ANTARCTIC** • 1913
LIFE IN THE ARCTIC • 1953 • Zguridi Alexander • USS
LIFE IN THE BALANCE • 1929 • Smith Percy • UKN
LIFE IN THE BALANCE • 1935 • Field Mary • UKN
LIFE IN THE BALANCE, A • 1913 • *Kalem* • USA
LIFE IN THE BALANCE, A • 1913 • Sennett Mack • *Keystone* • USA
LIFE IN THE BALANCE, A • 1915 • *Baggot King* • USA
LIFE IN THE BALANCE, A • 1955 • Horner Harry • USA • MATTER OF LIVE AND DEATH, A
LIFE IN THE CITADEL see **ZHIZN V TSITADEL** • 1947
LIFE IN THE COUNTRY see **LIVET PA LANDET** • 1924
LIFE IN THE COUNTRY see **LIVET PA LANDET** • 1943
LIFE IN THE DEPTHS OF THE FOREST see **LIVET I FINNSKOGARNA** • 1947
LIFE IN THE MOUNTAINS, A • 1959 • Hani Susumu • DOC • JPN
LIFE IN THE NEXT CENTURY • 1909 • Bourgeois Gerard • FRN
LIFE IN THE PINK see **OPERATION PETTICOAT** • 1977
LIFE IN THE RAW • 1933 • King Louis • USA
LIFE IN THE WEST • 1915 • *Alhambra* • USA
LIFE INSURANCE TRAINING FILM • 1975 • *Halas John (P)* • UKN
LIFE IS A BED OF ROSES (USA) see **VIE EST UN ROMAN, LA** • 1983
LIFE IS A CIRCUS • 1958 • Guest Val • UKN
LIFE IS A DREAM see **LIVET ER EN DROM** • 1971
LIFE IS A MASS PHENOMENON see **ZIVOT JE MASOVNA POJAVA** • 1971
LIFE IS A MOMENT • 1978 • Radi Mohamed • EGY
LIFE IS A TANGO (USA) see **VIDA ES UN TANGO** • 1939
LIFE IS BEAUTIFUL see **PROSTOI SLUCHAI** • 1932
LIFE IS BEAUTIFUL see **ZYCIE JEST PIEKNE** • 1959
LIFE IS BEAUTIFUL see **ZIVOT JE LEP** • 1985
LIFE IS FOR LIVING see **ADMI** • 1939
LIFE IS LIKE A SOMERSAULT see **JINSEI TOMBOGAERI** • 1946
LIFE IS LIKE THAT see **VIDA QUIS ASSIM, A** • 1968
LIFE IS LOST MY SON • 1978 • Salem Atef • EGY
LIFE IS MARVELOUS see **ZYCIE JEST PIEKNE** • 1959
LIFE IS NOT A SIN • 1956 • Hladnik Bostjan • SHT • YGS
LIFE IS REAL • 1934 • *Mckinney Nina Mae* • USA
LIFE IS RISING FROM THE RUINS • 1945 • Kadar Jan • CZC
LIFE IS STRANGE see **STRANA LA VITA** • 1988
LIFE IS THERE TO BE LIVED see **LIVET MASTE LEVAS** • 1943
LIFE IS VERY GOOD see **PROSTOI SLUCHAI** • 1932
LIFE IS WONDERFUL see **VITA E BELLA, LA** • 1980
LIFE, LIBERTY AND PURSUIT ON THE PLANET OF THE APES • 1974 • *Mcdowell Roddy* • MTV • USA
LIFE LINE, THE • 1915 • Johnson Arthur • USA
LIFE LINE, THE • 1919 • Tourneur Maurice • USA • ROMANY RYE
LIFE LINE IN SPACE • Pederson Con, Jackson Ben • ANS • USA
LIFE LINES see **LIFELINES** • 1960
LIFE, LOVE AND LIBERTY • 1913 • *Fielding Romaine* • USA
LIFE, LOVE, DEATH (UKN) see **VIE, L'AMOUR, LA MORT, LA** • 1968
LIFE MASK, THE • 1918 • Crane Frank H. • USA
LIFE OF A CHESS-PLAYER, THE see **OOSHO ICHIDAI** • 1955
LIFE OF A COMMUNIST WRITER, THE see **TAKIJI KOBAYASHI** • 1974
LIFE OF A COUNTRY DOCTOR see **FUNDOSHI ISHA** • 1960
LIFE OF A COWBOY, THE • 1906 • Porter Edwin S. • USA
LIFE OF A FILM DIRECTOR:RECORD OF KENJI MIZOGUCHI see **ARU EIGAKANTOKU NO SHOGAI: MIZOGUCHI KENJI NO KIROKU** • 1974
LIFE OF A HIRED BIKE, THE • 1910 • *Warwick Trading Co* • UKN
LIFE OF A HORSE DEALER see **BAKURO ICHIDAI** • 1951
LIFE OF A HORSE TRADER see **BAKURO ICHIDAI** • 1951
LIFE OF A JACKEROO, THE • 1913 • Barrett Franklyn • ASL
LIFE OF A LONDON ACTRESS, THE • 1919 • Butler Alexander • UKN
LIFE OF A LONDON SHOPGIRL, THE • 1914 • Raymond Charles • UKN
LIFE OF A MAN see **HITO NO ISSHO, PARTS I, II & III** • 1928
LIFE OF A MAN, THE see **ZOI ENOS ANTHROPOU, I** • 1968
LIFE OF A MINER, THE see **BARABAS** • 1971
LIFE OF A MOTHER, THE see **HISTORIEN OM EN MODER** • 1912
LIFE OF A PLANT, THE • 1926 • Smith Percy • UKN
LIFE OF A RAILWAY WORKER see **TETSURO NO IKIRU** • 1951
LIFE OF A RICKSHAW MAN, THE see **MUHOMATSU NO ISSHO** • 1963
LIFE OF A ROSE, THE • 1912 • *Solax* • USA
LIFE OF A WOMAN see **ONNA NO ISSHO** • 1962
LIFE OF A WOMAN, A see **ONNA NO ISSHO** • 1953
LIFE OF A WOMAN BY SAIKAKU see **SAIKAKU ICHIDAI ONNA** • 1952
LIFE OF A WOMAN IN THE MEIJI ERA, THE see **MEIJI ICHIDAI ONNA** • 1935
LIFE OF A WOMAN IN THE MEIJI ERA, THE see **MEIJI ICHIDAI ONNA** • 1955
LIFE OF ABRAHAM LINCOLN • 1908 • *Essanay* • USA
LIFE OF ABRAHAM LINCOLN, THE • 1915 • West Langdon • USA
LIFE OF ADAM LINDSAY GORDON, THE • 1916 • Lincoln W. J., Barnes G. H. • ASL • LIFE'S ROMANCE OF ADAM LINDSAY GORDON
LIFE OF ADOLF HITLER, THE see **LEBEN VON ADOLF HITLER, DAS** • 1961
LIFE OF AN ACTOR, THE see **GEIDO ICHIDAI OTOKO** • 1940
LIFE OF AN ACTRESS • 1927 • Nelson Jack • USA • ROMANCE OF AN ACTRESS
LIFE OF AN ACTRESS, THE • 1915 • Weston Charles • UKN
LIFE OF AN AMERICAN COWBOY, THE • 1905 • Porter Edwin S. • USA
LIFE OF AN AMERICAN FIREMAN, THE • 1903 • Porter Edwin S. • USA
LIFE OF AN AMERICAN POLICEMAN • 1905 • Porter Edwin S. • USA
LIFE OF AN ARTIST see **BUHAY ARTISTA** • 1967
LIFE OF AN ARTIST, THE (USA) see **GEIDO ICHIDAI OTOKO** • 1940
LIFE OF AN ENGLISH FIREMAN, THE (USA) see **GREAT CITY FIRE, THE** • 1903
LIFE OF AN OFFICE WORKER see **KAISHAIN SEIKATSU** • 1930
LIFE OF ANTON BRUCKNERS, THE see **LEBEN ANTON BRUCKNERS, DAS** • 1974
LIFE OF BANGOKU see **BANGOKU NO ISSHO** • 1932
LIFE OF BEETHOVEN, THE • 1929 • Otto Hans • FRG
LIFE OF "BIG TIM" SULLIVAN, THE • 1914 • *Gotham Film* • USA
LIFE OF BRIAN • 1979 • Jones Terry • UKN • MONTY PYTHON'S LIFE OF BRIAN
LIFE OF BUDDHA, THE see **SHAKA** • 1962
LIFE OF BUFFALO BILL, THE • 1911 • Panzer Paul • USA
LIFE OF CHARLES PEACE, THE • 1905 • Mottershaw Frank • UKN
LIFE OF CHARLES PEACE, THE see **CHARLES PEACE** • 1905
LIFE OF CHIKUZAN, THE see **CHIKUZAN HITORI TABI** • 1976
LIFE OF CHIKUZAN, TSUGARU GAMISEN PLAYER see **CHIKUZAN HITORI TABI** • 1976
LIFE OF CHOPIN, THE • 1938 • Fitzpatrick James A. • UKN
LIFE OF CHRIST • 1907 • *Biograph* • USA
LIFE OF CHRIST, THE • 1912 • *Kalem* • USA
LIFE OF CHRIST, THE see **VIE DU CHRIST, LA** • 1906
LIFE OF CHRIST, THE see **PASSION, LA** • 1914
LIFE OF DANIEL BOONE • 1912 • *Republic* • USA • LIFE AND BATTLES OF DANIEL BOONE
LIFE OF DONIZETTI, THE (USA) see **CAVALIERE DEL SOGNO, IL** • 1946
LIFE OF EMILE ZOLA, THE • 1937 • Dieterle William • USA • I ACCUSE (UKN)
LIFE OF GENERAL RAFAEL URIBEM, THE • 1914 • Di Domenico Vicente • CLM
LIFE OF GENERAL VILLA, THE • 1914 • Walsh Raoul, Cabanne W. Christy • USA • OUTLAW'S REVENGE, THE ○ LIFE OF VILLA, THE
LIFE OF GENEVIEVE, THE • 1922 • *Korwin Lydia* • USA
LIFE OF GRIEF, A see **STI ZOI MAZI SOU PONESA** • 1968
LIFE OF HANAKO KIRYUIN, A see **KIRYUIN HANAKO NO SHOGAI** • 1983
LIFE OF HER OWN, A • 1950 • Cukor George • USA
LIFE OF JESUS, THE see **JESUS OF NAZARETH** • 1977
LIFE OF JIMMY NOLAN, THE • 1933 • Mayo Archie • USA • KID'S LAST FIGHT, THE (UKN) ○ SUCKER
LIFE OF JOHN BUNYAN –PILRIM'S PROGRESS • 1912 • *Oland Warner* • USA
LIFE OF JOHN REED, THE see **KRASNYE KOLOKOLA** • 1981
LIFE OF JUANITA CASTRO, THE • 1965 • Warhol Andy • USA
LIFE OF LORD BUDDHA • 1922 • IND
LIFE OF LORD KITCHENER, THE • 1917 • Wilson Rex, Stanton W. Dane • UKN
LIFE OF LORD ROBERTS V.C., THE • 1914 • Pearson George • UKN
LIFE OF LUXURY, A see **HIDARE UCHIWA** • 1935
LIFE OF MAN, THE (USA) see **HITO NO ISSHO, PARTS I, II & III** • 1928
LIFE OF MATSU THE UNTAMED, THE see **MUHOMATSU NO ISSHO** • 1943
LIFE OF MATTHEW, THE see **ZYWOT MATEUSZA** • 1968
LIFE OF MOSES, THE • 1910 • Blackton J. Stuart • USA
LIFE OF MOZART, THE (USA) see **LEBEN MOZARTS, DAS** • 1967
LIFE OF OHARU, THE (USA) see **SAIKAKU ICHIDAI ONNA** • 1952
LIFE OF OUR DREAMS, THE see **LEVEN DAT WE DROOMDEN, HET** • 1984
LIFE OF OUR SAVIOUR, THE (USA) see **PASSION, LA** • 1914
LIFE OF PLEASURE, A see **VIDA ALEGRE, LA** • 1987
LIFE OF REILLY, THE • 1923 • La Cava Gregory • SHT • USA
LIFE OF RILEY, THE • 1927 • Beaudine William • USA • RED HOT RILEY (UKN)
LIFE OF RILEY, THE • 1949 • Brecher Irving S. • USA
LIFE OF ROBERT BURNS, THE • 1926 • Sandground Maurice • UKN • IMMORTALS OF BONNIE SCOTLAND
LIFE OF ROBIN BECKETT • 1963 • SHT • ASL • ORDINARY HOUR IN THE EXTRAORDINARY LIFE OF ROBIN BECKETT, AN
LIFE OF RUFUS DAWES • 1911 • Rolfe Alfred • ASL
LIFE OF ST. MARIA GORETTI, THE see **NO, NO, IT'S A SIN** • 1961
LIFE OF SAM DAVIS, THE • 1915 • *Ragsdale James Henry* • USA
LIFE OF SHAKESPEARE, THE • 1914 • McDowell J. B., Growcott Frank R. • UKN • LOVES AND ADVENTURES IN THE LIFE OF SHAKESPEARE ○ LOVES, ADVENTURES AND LIFE OF WILLIAM SHAKESPEARE ○ LIFE OF SHAKESPEARE: HIS INTRIGUES AND ROMANCES
LIFE OF SHAKESPEARE: HIS INTRIGUES AND ROMANCES see **LIFE OF SHAKESPEARE, THE** • 1914
LIFE OF SHREE KRISHNA BHAGWAN see **SHREE KRISHNA BHAGWAN** • 1935
LIFE OF SIMON BOLIVAR, THE (USA) see **SIMON BOLIVAR** • 1941
LIFE OF SIR WALTER SCOTT, THE • 1926 • Sandground Maurice • UKN • IMMORTALS OF BONNIE SCOTLAND
LIFE OF THE BEES see **HAYAT AL NAHEL** • 1985
LIFE OF THE COUNTRY DOCTOR see **FUNDOSHI ISHA** • 1960
LIFE OF THE FILM DIRECTOR, A see **ARU EIGAKANTOKU NO SHOGAI: MIZOGUCHI KENJI NO KIROKU** • 1974
LIFE OF THE LAND, THE • McLean Grahame • NZL
LIFE OF THE LAY PREACHER, THE see **EVANGELIEMANDENS LIV** • 1914
LIFE OF THE MOLDS • 1955 • Van Dyke Willard • DOC • USA
LIFE OF THE PARTY, THE • 1920 • Henabery Joseph • USA
LIFE OF THE PARTY, THE • 1930 • Del Ruth Roy • USA
LIFE OF THE PARTY, THE • 1934 • Dawson Ralph • UKN
LIFE OF THE PARTY, THE • 1937 • Seiter William A. • USA
LIFE OF THE PARTY: THE STORY OF BEATRICE • 1982 • Johnson Lamont • TVM • USA
LIFE OF TIGER FLOWERS, THE see **FIGHTING DEACON, THE** • 1926
LIFE OF TOLSTOY, THE see **UKHOD VELIKOVO STARTZA** • 1912
LIFE OF TROUBLE, A see **BELALI HAYAT** • 1968
LIFE OF VERGIE WINTERS, THE • 1934 • Santell Alfred • USA
LIFE OF VILLA, THE see **LIFE OF GENERAL VILLA, THE** • 1914
LIFE OF WASHINGTON, THE see **WASHINGTON UNDER THE AMERICAN FLAG** • 1909
LIFE ON A PERCH see **LIVET PA EN PINNE** • 1942
LIFE ON A SILKEN THREAD see **LEBEN AM SEIDEN FADEN** • 1973
LIFE ON AN ENGLISH REFORMATORY SHIP • 1907 • *Cricks & Sharp* • UKN
LIFE ON THE BORDER • 1911 • *Selig* • USA
LIFE ON THE EDGE • 1989 • Burman Tom • USA

LIFE ON THE HEGN FARM (USA) see **LIVET PAA HEGNSGAARD** • 1939
LIFE ON THE MISSISSIPPI • 1980 • Hunt Peter • MTV • USA
LIFE ON WHEELS see **LIDE NA KOLEKACH** • 1966
LIFE ONCE AGAIN see **ZYCIE RAL JESZCZE** • 1964
LIFE ONCE MORE see **ZYCIE RAL JESZCZE** • 1964
LIFE OR DEATH see **HAYAT OU MAUT** • 1955
LIFE OR DEATH –A TECHNOLOGICAL CHOICE see **LIV ELLER DOD –ET TEKNOLOGISK VALG** • 1987
LIFE OR GOLD • 1912 • *Republic* • USA
LIFE OR HONOR? • 1918 • Lawrence Edmund • USA
LIFE OR REPUTATION? see **UYIRA MANAMA** • 1968
LIFE PASSED BY see **ZIVOT SEL KOLEM** • 1913
LIFE POD • 1980 • *Penny Joe* • USA
LIFE RETURNS • 1934 • Frenke Eugene • USA
LIFE ROADS see **DOROGA U MIR** • 1929
LIFE SAVER, THE • 1911 • Salter Harry • USA
LIFE SAVER, THE • 1913 • North Wilfred • USA
LIFE SAVERS • 1916 • *Plump & Runt* • SHT • USA
LIFE SAVERS, THE • 1913 • *Gem* • USA
LIFE SAVERS, THE • 1914 • *Crystal* • USA
LIFE SAVING UP-TO-DATE (USA) see **SYSTEME DU DOCTEUR SOUFLAMORT, LE** • 1905
LIFE SIGNS see **ELETJEL** • 1954
LIFE SIZE • 1973 • Berlanga Luis Garcia • SPN, ITL, FRN • GRANDEUR NATURE (FRN) ○ TAMANO NATURAL ○ LOVE DOLL
LIFE-STORY see **ZYCIORYS** • 1974
LIFE STORY OF A CERTAIN SWORDSMAN, THE see **ARU KENGO NO SHOGAI** • 1959
LIFE STORY OF BAAL ,THE • 1978 • Bennett Edward • UKN
LIFE STORY OF CHARLES CHAPLIN, THE • 1926 • Parkinson H. B. • UKN
LIFE STORY OF DAVID LLOYD GEORGE, THE • 1918 • Elvey Maurice • UKN
LIFE STORY OF JOHN LEE –THE MAN THEY COULD NOT HANG, THE • 1917 • *Sterry & Haldane* • ASL
LIFE STORY OF JOHN LEE –THE MAN THEY COULD NOT HANG, THE • 1921 • Sterry Arthur • ASL
LIFE STORY OF TASUKE SHIOBARA, THE • 1912 • JPN
LIFE STORY OF THE TAWNY OWL, THE • 1936 • Field Mary • UKN • TAWNY OWL, THE
LIFE STUDY • 1973 • *Miro Bartholomew Jr.* • USA
LIFE TO BE LIVED • Howard Godfrey • UKN
LIFE TOGETHER see **VIE A DEUX, LA** • 1958
LIFE TOGETHER see **LEBEN ZU ZWEIT** • 1968
LIFE TRIUMPHS • 1979 • Malyan Ghenrikh • USS
LIFE TRIUMPHS see **VIATA INVINGE** • 1951
LIFE UNAWARES see **KINO-GLAZ** • 1924
LIFE UNDER THE SOUTHERN CROSS • 1911 • Barrett Franklyn • ASL • JUMPING THE CLAIM ○ ALL FOR GOLD
LIFE UPSIDE-DOWN (USA) see **VIE A L'ENVERS, LA** • 1964
LIFE WAS AT STAKE see **HRA O ZIVOT** • 1956
LIFE WAS THE STAKE (UKN) see **HRA O ZIVOT** • 1956
LIFE WE LIVE, THE • 1913 • *Mackley Arthur* • USA
LIFE WITH ALKIS • 1988 • Kollatos Dimitris • GRC
LIFE WITH BLONDIE • 1945 • Berlin Abby • USA
LIFE WITH DADDY see **FAR LAVER SOVSEN** • 1967
LIFE WITH FATHER • 1947 • Curtiz Michael • USA
LIFE WITH FEATHERS • 1945 • Freleng Friz • ANS • USA
LIFE WITH FIDO • 1942 • Rasinski Connie • ANS • USA
LIFE WITH HENRY • 1941 • Reed Theodore • USA
LIFE WITH LOOPY • 1960 • Hanna William, Barbera Joseph • ANS • USA
LIFE WITH SENILITY see **HANA ICHIMOMME** • 1985
LIFE WITH THE LYONS • 1954 • Guest Val • UKN • FAMILY AFFAIR (USA)
LIFE WITH TOM • 1953 • Hanna William, Barbera Joseph • ANS • USA
LIFE WITHOUT A GUITAR • 1962 • Hanibal Jiri • CZC
LIFE WITHOUT SOUL • 1916 • Smiley Joseph • USA
LIFE WORTH WHILE • 1915 • *Thanhouser* • USA
LIFEBOAT • 1944 • Hitchcock Alfred • USA
LIFEBOAT, THE • 1914 • *Williams Eric* • UKN
LIFEFORCE • 1985 • Hooper Tobe • UKN • SPACE VAMPIRES
LIFEGUARD • 1975 • Petrie Daniel • USA
LIFEGUARDS • 1956 • Carlsen Henning • SHT • DNM
LIFEGUARDSMAN, THE • 1916 • Bayley Frank G. • UKN
LIFELINE see **BEAUTIFUL STRANGER, THE** • 1954
LIFELINE TO CATHY • 1977 • Gudmundsson Agust • SHT • UKN
LIFELINES • 1960 • Emshwiller Ed • SHT • USA • LIFE LINES
LIFER AND THE LADY, THE • 1986 • Kastner John • DOC • CND
LIFERITIS • 1914 • *Crystal* • USA
LIFE'S A FINE THING, BROTHER! see **ZHIZN KHOROSHAYA SHTUKA, BRAT!** • 1967
LIFE'S A FUNNY PROPOSITION • 1919 • Heffron Thomas N. • USA
LIFE'S A GAME OF CARDS • 1908 • Porter Edwin S. • USA
LIFE'S A STAGE • 1929 • Phillips Arthur • UKN
LIFE'S BIG LITTLE MAN • 1990 • Srichuae Thoranong • THL • SEVEN LADIES
LIFE'S BLIND ALLEY • 1916 • Ricketts Thomas • USA
LIFE'S CHANGING TIDE • 1915 • Reehm George E. • USA
LIFE'S CONFLICTS see **LIVETS KONFLIKTER** • 1913
LIFE'S CROSSROADS • 1928 • Lewis Edgar • USA • SILKEN LADY, THE (UKN)
LIFE'S CRUCIBLE • 1914 • Santschi Thomas • USA
LIFE'S CRUCIBLE • 1915 • Bernstein Isadore • USA
LIFE'S DARK ROAD • 1914 • Wilson Frank? • UKN
LIFE'S DARN FUNNY • 1921 • Fitzgerald Dallas M. • USA
LIFE'S FURROW • 1915 • Lloyd Frank • USA
LIFE'S GAME • 1915 • *Gonzales Myrtle* • USA
LIFE'S GREATEST GAME • 1924 • Johnson Emory • USA
LIFE'S GREATEST PROBLEM • 1919 • Blackton J. Stuart, Clifton Elmer • USA • SAFE FOR DEMOCRACY
LIFE'S GREATEST QUESTION • 1921 • Revier Harry • USA
LIFE'S HARDY MEN • 1987 • Niskanen Mikko • FNL
LIFE'S HARMONY • 1916 • Borzage Frank, Johnston Lorimer • SHT • USA
LIFE'S HIGHWAY see **SHAHRAHE ZENDEGI** • 1968
LIFE'S JUST GREAT see **LIVET AR STENKUL** • 1967
LIFE'S LESSON • 1912 • *Powers* • USA
LIFE'S LIKE THAT • 1929 • Cannon Raymond • USA
LIFE'S LOTTERY • 1914 • O'Brien John B. • USA
LIFE'S LOTTERY • 1916 • *Sunset* • USA
LIFE'S MAELSTROM • 1916 • Hunt Jay • SHT • USA
LIFE'S MIRROR (USA) see **SPIEGEL DES LEBENS** • 1938
LIFE'S MOCKERY • 1928 • Hill Robert F. • USA • REFORM
LIFE'S MYSTERIES • 1915 • Fahrney Milton • USA
LIFE'S PATHWAY • 1913 • *La Badie Florence* • USA
LIFE'S PENDULUM • 1917 • Leonard Robert Z. • SHT • USA
LIFE'S PITFALLS • 1915 • Ridgwell George • USA
LIFE'S ROMANCE OF ADAM LINDSAY GORDON see **LIFE OF ADAM LINDSAY GORDON, THE** • 1916
LIFE'S SHADOWS • 1916 • Nigh William, Thompson David • USA
LIFE'S SHADOWS see **LEVENSSCHADUWEN** • 1916
LIFE'S SHADOWS see **ROSA DIAMANT, DER** • 1925
LIFE'S SHOP WINDOW • 1914 • Brenon Herbert, Belmar Henry • USA
LIFE'S STAIRCASE • 1915 • Cooley Frank • USA
LIFE'S STREAM • 1914 • Reehm George E. • USA
LIFE'S SUPREME TREASURE • 1911 • *Powers* • USA
LIFE'S TEMPTATIONS • 1914 • *Imperator Films* • USA
LIFE'S TWIST • 1920 • Cabanne W. Christy • USA
LIFE'S WEAVING • 1913 • *Calvert E. H.* • USA
LIFE'S WHIRLPOOL • 1916 • O'Neil Barry • USA
LIFE'S WHIRLPOOL • 1917 • Barrymore Lionel • USA
LIFE'S WORTH LIVING see **DOCTOR BULL** • 1933
LIFE'S YESTERDAYS • 1915 • Johnston Lorimer • USA
LIFESPAN • 1975 • Whitelaw Alexander • NTH, BLG, USA
LIFETAKER, THE • 1975 • Papas Michael • UKN
LIFETIME PENANCE, A • 1911 • *Yankee* • USA
LIFETIMER, THE • 1913 • Duncan William • USA
LIFT, DE • 1983 • Maas Dick • NTH • LIFT, THE ○ GOING UP
LIFT, THE • 1965 • Krancer Bert • UKN
LIFT, THE • 1974 • Kucia Jerzy • ANS • PLN
LIFT, THE see **LIFT, DE** • 1983
LIFT TO THE SCAFFOLD (UKN) see **ASCENSEUR POUR L'ECHAFAUD, L'** • 1957
LIFT YOUR HEAD, COMRADE • 1942 • Hankinson Michael • UKN
LIFTED VEIL, THE • 1913 • *White Pearl* • USA
LIFTED VEIL, THE • 1917 • Baker George D. • USA
LIFTING SHADOWS • 1920 • Perret Leonce • USA
LIFTING THE BAN OF COVENTRY • 1915 • North Wilfred • USA
LIFTING THE LID • 1905 • *Bitzer Billy (P)* • USA
LIG VAN 'N EEU • 1942 • SAF
LIGA DE LAS CANCIONES, LA • 1941 • Urueta Chano • MXC
LIGA DE LAS MUCHACHAS, LA • 1949 • Cortes Fernando • MXC
LIGA NO ES COSA DE HOMBRES, LA • 1972 • Iquino Ignacio F. • SPN
LIGABUE • 1978 • Nocita Salvatore • ITL
LIGEIA • Ronet Maurice • FRN
LIGEIA see **TOMB OF LIGEIA, THE** • 1964
LIGERAMENTE VIUDAS • 1975 • Aguirre Javier • SPN
LIGEUD AD LUFTVEJEN • 1958 • Carlsen Henning • SHT • DNM
LIGHT • 1915 • Morgan Sidney • UKN
LIGHT • 1962 • Kosa Ferenc • HNG
LIGHT • 1971 • Hoving Hattum • NTH
LIGHT see **BREATH** • 1975
LIGHT see **LYS** • 1987
LIGHT, THE • 1916 • Dowlan William C. • USA
LIGHT, THE • 1919 • Edwards J. Gordon • USA
LIGHT, THE • 1938 • Newman Widgey R. • UKN
LIGHT, THE see **LUZ, LA** • 1917
LIGHT, THE see **YEELEN** • 1987
LIGHT ACROSS THE STREET, THE (USA) see **LUMIERE D'EN FACE, LA** • 1955
LIGHT AFTER DARKNESS • 1912 • Coleby A. E. • UKN
LIGHT AHEAD, THE see **KLATSCHE, DIE** • 1939
LIGHT AND SHADOW • 1990 • Gharib Shapoor • IRN
LIGHT AND SHADOW see **HIKARITOKAGE** • 1946
LIGHT AND STONE • 1960 • Iliesu Mirel • DOC • RMN
LIGHT AT DUSK, THE • 1916 • Lewis Edgar • USA
LIGHT AT THE EDGE OF THE WORLD, THE • 1971 • Billington Kevin • SPN, USA, LCH
LIGHT BEYOND, THE • 1911 • *Nestor* • USA
LIGHT BLAST see **COLPI DI LUCE** • 1985
LIGHT BRIGADE, THE • 1990 • Labonte Francois • SHT • CND
LIGHT ETERNAL, THE see **DEVIL'S CIRCUS, THE** • 1925
LIGHT FANTASTIC • 1962 • McCarty Robert • USA
LIGHT FANTASTIC, THE • 1960 • Russell Ken • MTV • UKN
LIGHT FANTASTIC, THE • 1972 • Bayersdorfer Alan • USA • WATTS UP DOC?
LIGHT FANTASTIC, THE (UKN) see **LOVE IS BETTER THAN EVER** • 1951
LIGHT FANTASTIC PICTURE SHOW, THE • 1974 • Somersaulter J. P., Somersaulter Lillian • ANS • USA
LIGHT FANTASTICK, THE • 1975 • Glover Rupert, Patenaude Michel • CND
LIGHT-FINGERED SYD • 1915 • *Alhambra* • USA
LIGHT FINGERS • 1929 • Henabery Joseph • USA
LIGHT FINGERS • 1957 • Bishop Terry • UKN
LIGHT FOR THE MIND • 1960 • Barclay Robert • SHT • CND
LIGHT FROM DARKNESS • 1973 • Dayan Nissim • ISR • LIGHT OUT OF NOWHERE
LIGHT HEARTS AND LEAKING PIPES • 1920 • Watson William • SHT • USA
LIGHT HOUSEKEEPING • 1926 • Roberts Stephen • SHT • USA
LIGHT IN A WOMAN'S EYES, THE • 1914 • Harvey Harry • USA
LIGHT IN DARKNESS • 1917 • Crosland Alan • USA
LIGHT IN NATURE, A • 1960 • Orrom Michael • SHT • UKN
LIGHT IN OUR WINDOWS see **SINATLE CHVENS PANJREBSHI** • 1969
LIGHT IN THE AFTERNOON, A • 1986 • Williams Paul • USA
LIGHT IN THE CLEARING, THE • 1921 • Hunter T. Hayes • USA
LIGHT IN THE DARK, THE • 1922 • Brown Clarence • USA
LIGHT IN THE DARKNESS see **POKOLENIE** • 1954
LIGHT IN THE FOREST, THE • 1958 • Daugherty Herschel • USA
LIGHT IN THE NIGHT, A • 1968 • ANS • NTH
LIGHT IN THE PIAZZA • 1961 • Green Guy • USA, UKN
LIGHT IN THE WINDOW, A • 1927 • Pembroke Scott • USA
LIGHT IN THE WINDOW, THE • 1908 • *Lubin* • USA
LIGHT IN THE WINDOW, THE • 1910 • *Vitagraph* • USA
LIGHT IN THE WINDOW, THE • 1913 • *Bison* • USA
LIGHT IN THE WINDOW, THE • 1915 • *Lincoln Otto* • USA
LIGHT LOVE (USA) see **LIEBELEI** • 1932
LIGHT MACHINE GUN PLATOON • 1941 • Starkey • SHT • USA
LIGHT MODULATOR • 1948 • Dekker Elwood • USA
LIGHT OF A DISTANT STAR, THE see **SVEV DALEKOI ZVESDY** • 1965
LIGHT OF ASAKUSA, THE see **ASAKUSA NO HI** • 1937
LIGHT OF ASIA • 1925 • *Rai Himansu* • IND
LIGHT OF ASIA, THE • 1934 • Osten Franz • IND
LIGHT OF DAY • 1987 • Schrader Paul • USA
LIGHT OF DAY, THE see **TOPKAPI** • 1964
LIGHT OF DISTANT STARS, THE • 1965 • Batalov Alexei • USS
LIGHT OF EYES see **NOYONER ALO** • 1985
LIGHT OF HAPPINESS, THE • 1916 • Collins John H. • USA
LIGHT OF HEART, THE (UKN) see **LIFE BEGINS AT 8.30** • 1942
LIGHT OF LOVE, THE • 1917 • Horning Ben • SHT • USA
LIGHT OF LOVE, THE see **DAWN OF LOVE, THE** • 1916
LIGHT OF OTHER DAYS, THE • Hickey Kieran • IRL
LIGHT OF ST. BERNARD, THE • 1912 • Hale Albert W. • USA
LIGHT OF THOUSANDS OF FAMILIES, THE • 1948 • Sen Fou • CHN
LIGHT OF VICTORY, THE • 1919 • Wolbert William • USA • ISLAND OF ADVENTURE, THE ○ RENEGADE, THE
LIGHT OF WESTERN STARS, THE • 1918 • Swickard Charles • USA
LIGHT OF WESTERN STARS, THE • 1925 • Howard William K. • USA
LIGHT OF WESTERN STARS, THE • 1930 • Brower Otto, Knopf Edwin H. • USA • WINNING THE WEST
LIGHT OF WESTERN STARS, THE • 1940 • Selander Lesley • USA • BORDER RENEGADE
LIGHT O'LOVE • 1915 • *Selig* • USA
LIGHT ON ASAKUSA see **ASAKUSA NO HI** • 1937
LIGHT ON THE HORIZON • 1990 • Sedigh Yusef • IRN
LIGHT ON THE REEF, THE • 1915 • *Foster Morris* • USA
LIGHT ON THE WALL, THE • 1928 • Paul Fred • UKN
LIGHT ON THE WAY, THE • 1912 • Porter Edwin S. • USA
LIGHT ON TROUBLED WATERS, A • 1913 • Edwin Walter • USA
LIGHT OUT OF NOWHERE see **LIGHT FROM DARKNESS** • 1973
LIGHT OVER RUSSIA see **SVET NAD ROSSIEI** • 1947
LIGHT PHYSICAL INJURIES see **KONNYU TESTI SERTES** • 1984
LIGHT PRINCESS, THE • 1985 • Gosling Andrew • MTV • UKN
LIGHT REFLECTIONS • 1948 • Davis James* • USA
LIGHT RHYTHMS • 1930 • Brugiere Francis, Blakeston Oswell • SHT • BLG, UKN
LIGHT SHOWERS • 1922 • Roach Hal • USA
LIGHT, SOUND, DIFFUSE • 1967 • Avildsen John G. • SHT • USA
LIGHT SPECKS see **POLVO DE LUX** • 1988
LIGHT THAT CAME, THE • 1909 • Griffith D. W. • USA
LIGHT THAT FAILED, THE • 1910 • Stow Percy • UKN
LIGHT THAT FAILED, THE • 1912 • *Vitagraph* • USA
LIGHT THAT FAILED, THE • 1912 • *Pathe* • USA
LIGHT THAT FAILED, THE • 1916 • Jose Edward • USA
LIGHT THAT FAILED, THE • 1923 • Melford George • USA
LIGHT THAT FAILED, THE • 1939 • Wellman William A. • USA
LIGHT THAT FAILED, THE • 1980 • Hsu V. V. • IND, USA
LIGHT THAT KILLS, THE • 1913 • *Gaumont* • USA
LIGHT TO LEEWARD, THE see **HOMEWARD BOUND** • 1923
LIGHT TOUCH, THE • 1951 • Brooks Richard • USA
LIGHT TOUCH, THE (USA) see **TOUCH AND GO** • 1955
LIGHT UP THE SKY • 1960 • Gilbert Lewis* • UKN • SKYWATCH (USA)
LIGHT WAY, THE see **SVETYLI PUT** • 1940
LIGHT WITHIN, THE • 1918 • Trimble Larry • USA
LIGHT WOMAN, A • 1920 • Cox George L. • USA
LIGHT WOMAN, A • 1928 • Brunel Adrian • UKN • DOLORES
LIGHT WOMAN, THE • 1913 • *Smalley Phillips* • USA
LIGHT YEAR • 1968 • Markson Morley • CND
LIGHT YEARS AWAY • 1981 • Tanner Alain • IRL, FRN, UKN • ANNEES LUMIERE, LES (FRN)
LIGHTBEARER, THE • 1916 • *Travers Richard C.* • SHT • USA
LIGHTED CANDLE, THE • 1912 • *Majestic* • USA
LIGHTED LAMP, THE • 1917 • Berthelet Arthur • SHT • USA
LIGHTER BURDEN, A • 1913 • Pearson George • UKN
LIGHTER THAN HARE • 1960 • Freleng Friz • ANS • USA
LIGHTER THAT FAILED, THE • 1927 • Parrott James • SHT • USA
LIGHTFOOTED DARKEY, THE • 1899 • *Warwick Trading Co* • UKN
LIGHTHORSEMEN, THE • 1987 • Wincer Simon • ASL
LIGHTHOUSE • 1906 • *Bitzer Billy (Ph)* • USA
LIGHTHOUSE, THE • 1946 • Wisbar Frank • USA
LIGHTHOUSE, THE see **MAYAK** • 1942
LIGHTHOUSE, THE see **YOROKOBI MO KANASHIMI MO IKUTOSHITSUKI** • 1957
LIGHTHOUSE BY THE SEA, THE • 1911 • Porter Edwin S. • USA
LIGHTHOUSE BY THE SEA, THE • 1915 • Totten Joseph Byron • USA
LIGHTHOUSE BY THE SEA, THE • 1924 • St. Clair Malcolm • USA
LIGHTHOUSE IN THE FOG see **FARI NELLA NEBBIA** • 1942
LIGHTHOUSE KEEPER, THE • 1909 • *Walturdaw* • UKN
LIGHTHOUSE KEEPER, THE • 1911 • *Pickford Mary* • USA
LIGHTHOUSE KEEPER'S DAUGHTER, THE • 1908 • *Lubin* • USA
LIGHTHOUSE KEEPER'S DAUGHTER, THE • 1912 • Dawley J. Searle • USA
LIGHTHOUSE KEEPER'S DAUGHTER, THE (UKN) see **MANINA, LA FILLE SANS VOILE** • 1952

LIGHTHOUSE KEEPER'S FAMILY see **SHIN YOROKOBI MO KANASHIMA MO IKUTOSHITSUKI** • 1985
LIGHTHOUSE KEEPER'S SON, THE • 1915 • *Domino* • USA
LIGHTHOUSE KEEPING • 1932 • *Mintz Charles (P)* • ANS • USA
LIGHTHOUSE KEEPING • 1946 • Hannah Jack • ANS • USA
LIGHTHOUSE KEEPING see **HANIBALOVE ALPE** • 1969
LIGHTHOUSE-KEEPING BLUES • 1964 • Marcus Sid • ANS • USA
LIGHTHOUSE LOVE • 1932 • *Sennett Mack (P)* • SHT • USA
LIGHTHOUSE MOUSE • 1955 • McKimson Robert • ANS • USA
LIGHTHOUSE OF PONENTE, THE • 1989 • Gok Sahin • TRK
LIGHTNIN' • 1925 • Ford John • USA
LIGHTNIN' • 1930 • King Henry • USA
LIGHTNIN' BILL CARSON • 1936 • Newfield Sam • USA
LIGHTNIN' CRANDALL • 1937 • Newfield Sam • USA
LIGHTNIN' IN THE FOREST • 1948 • Blair George • USA
LIGHTNIN' JACK • 1924 • *Perrin Jack* • USA
LIGHTNIN' SHOT • 1928 • McGowan J. P. • USA
LIGHTNIN' SMITH RETURNS • 1931 • Irwin Jack • USA • VALLEY OF THE BADMEN (UKN)
LIGHTNING • 1927 • McKay James C. • USA • DESERT PRINCE, THE
LIGHTNING see **INAZUMA** • 1952
LIGHTNING ADVANCE see **INAZUMA-ZOSHI** • 1952
LIGHTNING ARTIST see **PEINTURE A L'ENVERS** • 1898
LIGHTNING AT DUSK see **KILAT SENJA** • 1977
LIGHTNING BELLHOP, THE • 1916 • Myll Louis • SHT • USA
LIGHTNING BILL • 1926 • Chaudet Louis W. • USA
LIGHTNING BILL • 1931 • Adamson Victor • USA
LIGHTNING BILL POSTER, THE • 1915 • *B & C* • UKN
LIGHTNING BOLT, THE • 1913 • Reid Wallace • USA
LIGHTNING BOLT (USA) see **OPERAZIONE GOLDMAN** • 1966
LIGHTNING BRYCE • 1919 • Hurst Paul C. • SRL • USA
LIGHTNING CARSON RIDES AGAIN • 1938 • Newfield Sam • USA
LIGHTNING CHANGE ARTIST (USA) see **HOMME PROTEE, L'** • 1899
LIGHTNING CONDUCTOR • 1938 • Elvey Maurice • UKN
LIGHTNING CONDUCTOR, THE • 1914 • Hale Walter • USA, ITL
LIGHTNING CONDUCTOR, THE see **GRAMOOTVOD** • 1962
LIGHTNING EXPRESS, THE • 1930 • McRae Henry • SRL • USA
LIGHTNING FLYER • 1931 • Nigh William • USA
LIGHTNING GUNS • 1950 • Sears Fred F. • USA • TAKING SIDES (UKN)
LIGHTNING HUTCH • 1926 • Hutchison Charles • SRL • USA
LIGHTNING LARIATS • 1927 • De Lacy Robert • USA • THRONE FOR A SADDLE, A
LIGHTNING LIVER CURE, THE • 1920 • Kellino W. P. • UKN
LIGHTNING LOVER, THE see **FAST WORKER, THE** • 1924
LIGHTNING OVER WATER • 1980 • Wenders Wim, Ray Nicholas • USA • NICK'S MOVIE ○ NICK'S FILM
LIGHTNING PAPER HANGER, THE • 1912 • *C.g.p.c.* • USA
LIGHTNING POSTCARD ARTIST, THE • 1908 • Booth W. R. • UKN
LIGHTNING RAIDER, THE • 1919 • Seitz George B. • SRL • USA
LIGHTNING RAIDER, THE • 1924 • Ingraham Lloyd • USA
LIGHTNING RAIDERS • 1945 • Newfield Sam • USA
LIGHTNING RANGE • 1934 • Adamson Victor • USA
LIGHTNING REPORTER • 1926 • Noble Jack • USA
LIGHTNING ROD see **GRAMOOTVOD** • 1962
LIGHTNING-ROD THIEF, THE see **VOLEUR DE PARATONNERRES, LE** • 1946
LIGHTNING ROMANCE • 1924 • Rogell Albert S. • USA
LIGHTNING SKETCH: CHAMBERLAIN, A see **DESSINATEUR CHAMBERLAIN** • 1896
LIGHTNING SKETCH (H.M. QUEEN VICTORIA) see **DESSINATEUR (REINE VICTORIA)** • 1896
LIGHTNING SKETCH (MR. THIERS) see **DESSINATEUR EXPRESS** • 1896
LIGHTNING SKETCH (VON BISMARCK), A see **DESSINATEUR VON BISMARCK** • 1896
LIGHTNING SKETCHES • 1907 • Blackton J. Stuart • USA
LIGHTNING SPEED • 1928 • Bradbury Robert North • USA
LIGHTNING STRIKES TWICE • 1934 • Holmes Ben • USA
LIGHTNING STRIKES TWICE • 1951 • Vidor King • USA
LIGHTNING STRIKES WEST • 1940 • Fraser Harry L. • USA
LIGHTNING SWORD OF DEATH (UKN) see **KOZURE OHKAMI** • 1973
LIGHTNING SWORDS OF DEATH (USA) see **KOZURE OHKAMI** • 1973
LIGHTNING, THE WHITE STALLION • 1986 • Levey William A. • USA
LIGHTNING TRIGGERS • 1935 • Luby S. Roy • USA
LIGHTNING WARRIOR, THE • 1931 • Schaefer Armand, Kline Benjamin • SRL • USA
LIGHTNING WOMAN see **BABAING KIDLAT** • 1964
LIGHTS • 1965 • Menken Marie • USA
LIGHTS AND PEOPLE • 1960 • Kovachev Hristo • DOC • BUL
LIGHTS AND SHADOWS • 1914 • De Grasse Joseph • USA
LIGHTS AND SHADOWS see **LLUMS I OMBRES** • 1988
LIGHTS AND SHADOWS OF CHINATOWN • 1908 • *Selig* • USA
LIGHTS AND SHADOWS OF CHINATOWN • 1912 • *New York Film Co* • USA
LIGHTS AND SHADOWS OF OLD KENTUCKY • 1912 • *Comet* • USA
LIGHTS AND SHADOWS (UKN) see **WOMAN RACKET, THE** • 1929
LIGHTS AT NIGHT see **NATTENS LJUS** • 1957
LIGHTS FANTASTIC, THE • 1942 • Freleng Friz • ANS • USA
LIGHTS FROM CIRCUS LIFE see **STORE HJERTE, DET** • 1924
LIGHTS GO ON IN THE CITY, THE see **GOROD ZAZHIGAET OGNI** • 1958
LIGHTS O' LONDON, THE • 1914 • Haldane Bert? • UKN
LIGHTS O' LONDON, THE • 1922 • Collins Edwin J. • UKN
LIGHTS OF A GREAT CITY • 1906 • *Selig William (P)* • USA
LIGHTS OF ASAKUSA, THE see **ASAKUSA NO HI** • 1937
LIGHTS OF BAKU, THE see **OGNI BAKU** • 1950
LIGHTS OF HOME, THE • 1920 • Paul Fred • UKN
LIGHTS OF LONDON • 1923 • Calvert Charles • UKN
LIGHTS OF NEW YORK • 1928 • Foy Bryan • USA
LIGHTS OF NEW YORK, THE • 1916 • Brooke Van Dyke • USA
LIGHTS OF NEW YORK, THE • 1922 • Brabin Charles J. • USA
LIGHTS OF NIGHT see **NISHI GINZA EKIMAE** • 1958
LIGHTS OF OLD BROADWAY • 1925 • Bell Monta • USA • LITTLE OLD NEW YORK (UKN) ○ MERRY WIVES OF GOTHAM
LIGHTS OF OLD SANTA FE • 1944 • McDonald Frank • USA
LIGHTS OF THE DESERT • 1922 • Beaumont Harry • USA
LIGHTS OF THE MUSIC HALL see **LUCI DEL VARIETA** • 1950
LIGHTS OF VARIETY see **LUCI DEL VARIETA** • 1950
LIGHTS ON THE TOP FLOOR see **LOV U MUTNOM** • 1983
LIGHTS OUT • 1923 • Santell Alfred • USA
LIGHTS OUT • 1932 • Horne James W. • SHT • USA
LIGHTS OUT • 1942 • Donnelly Eddie • ANS • USA
LIGHTS OUT see **CRASHING HOLLYWOOD** • 1938
LIGHTS OUT IN EUROPE • 1940 • Kline Herbert • DOC • USA
LIGHTS OUT (UKN) see **BRIGHT VICTORY** • 1951
LIGHTSHIP, THE • 1985 • Skolimowski Jerzy • USA
LIGHTSHIP, THE see **FEUERSCHIFF, DAS** • 1963
LIGHTWEIGHT LOVER, A • 1920 • Del Ruth Roy • SHT • USA
LIGNE 12, LA see **BOUGNOUL, LE** • 1974
LIGNE 150 • 1969 • Fares Tewfik • SHT • ALG
LIGNE CONTINUE • 1974 • Stampeli Peter, von Gunten Peter • SHT • SWT
LIGNE DE CHALEUR, LA • 1988 • Rose Hubert-Yves • CND • HEAT LINE, THE
LIGNE DE DEMARCATION, LA • 1966 • Chabrol Claude • FRN, ITL • CRIMINAL STORY (ITL) ○ LINE OF DEMARCATION
LIGNE DE MIRE, LA • 1960 • Pollet Jean-Daniel • FRN
LIGNE D'OMBRE, LA • 1971 • Franju Georges • MTV • FRN • SHADOW LINE, THE
LIGNE DROIT, LA • 1961 • Gaillard Jacques • FRN
LIGNER WERKE • 1936 • Alexeieff Alexandre • FRG
LIGNES HORIZONTALES • 1962 • McLaren Norman, Lambart Evelyn • ANS • CND • LINES HORIZONTAL (USA)
LIGNES VERTICALES see **LINES VERTICAL** • 1960
LIGT LAG, EN see **ENLIGT LAG** • 1957
LIGUE STORY • 1972 • Paso Alfonso • SPN
LIIKEMIEHEN MUOTOKUVA • 1970 • von Bagh Peter • SHT • FNL • PORTRAIT OF A BUSINESSMAN
LIJKENSYNODE • 1969 • Zwartjes Frans • SHT • NTH
LIKA, CHEKHOV'S LOVE see **SYUZHET DLYA NEBOLSHOVO RASKAZA** • 1968
LIKA INFOR LAGEN • 1930 • Bergman Gustaf • SWD
LIKA, LYUBOV CHEKHOVA see **SYUZHET DLYA NEBOLSHOVO RASKAZA** • 1968
LIKE A BIRD see **COMO UN PAJARO** • 1969
LIKE A BIRD ON A WIRE see **WIE EIN VOGEL AUF DEM DRAHT** • 1975
LIKE A BOOMERANG see **COMME UN BOOMERANG** • 1976
LIKE A CROW ON A JUNE BUG • 1974 • Dobkin Larry • USA
LIKE A DREAM AND A SHADOW see **KUIN UNI JA VARJO** • 1937
LIKE A DROP IN THE SEA • 1962 • Kollanyi Agoston • HNG
LIKE A FROZEN CHERRY • 1986 • Maslennikov Igor • USS
LIKE A HOUSE ON FIRE see **HORI, MA PANENKO!** • 1967
LIKE A SUMMER STORM • 1972 • Power John • DOC • ASL
LIKE A THIEF IN THE NIGHT see **SOM EN TJUV OM NATTEN** • 1940
LIKE A TURTLE ON ITS BACK see **TORTUE SUR LE DOS, LA** • 1977
LIKE A WIFE, LIKE A WOMAN see **TSUMA TOSHITE ONNA TOSHITE** • 1961
LIKE A WILD BEAST see **YAJU NO YONI MIETE** • 1962
LIKE BABES IN THE WOODS • 1917 • Cochrane George • SHT • USA
LIKE DARBY AND JOAN • 1913 • *Leonard Robert* • USA
LIKE DEAD PEOPLE • 1924 • Di Domenico Vicente • CLM
LIKE FATHER AND SON see **MARVIN AND TIGE** • 1982
LIKE FATHER LIKE DAUGHTER see **DE TAL PEDRO TAL ASTILLA** • 1985
LIKE FATHER, LIKE SON • 1914 • *Melies* • USA
LIKE FATHER, LIKE SON • 1914 • Ricketts Thomas • *American* • USA
LIKE FATHER, LIKE SON • 1916 • *Totten Joseph Byron* • USA
LIKE FATHER, LIKE SON • 1967 • Villaflor Romy • PHL
LIKE FATHER, LIKE SON • 1987 • Daniel Rod • USA
LIKE FATHER, LIKE SON see **PADRI E FIGLI** • 1957
LIKE FATHER, LIKE SON see **YOUNG SINNER, THE** • 1965
LIKE FATHER LIKE SON see **MARVIN AND TIGE** • 1982
LIKE FIRE IS MY LIFE see **WAGA SHOGAI WA HI NO GOTOKU** • 1961
LIKE GRANDFATHER, LIKE GRANDSON see **KAKAV DEDA TAKAV UNUK** • 1984
LIKE HARES see **JAKO ZAJICI** • 1981
LIKE IT IS • 1968 • Rotsler William • USA
LIKE IT IS • 1970 • Schafer Jerry • USA
LIKE KELLY CAN see **LOVE IN THE ROUGH** • 1930
LIKE KNIGHTS OF OLD • 1912 • *Flugarth Edna* • USA
LIKE LIFE ITSELF see **COMO LA VIDA MISMA** • 1985
LIKE LIGHTNING IN KARATE see **KIDLAT SA KARATE** • 1968
LIKE LOVE see **COME L'AMORE** • 1968
LIKE MOM, LIKE ME • 1978 • Pressman Michael • TVM • USA
LIKE MOST PEOPLE see **SOM FOLK AR MEST** • 1944
LIKE MOST WIVES • 1914 • Weber Lois • USA
LIKE MOTHER, LIKE DAUGHTER • 1969 • O'Neil Robert Vincent • USA • KIND OF LOVE, A
LIKE MOTHER MADE • 1918 • *Rhodes Billie* • USA
LIKE NIGHT AND DAY see **SOM NATT OCH DAG** • 1969
LIKE NORMAL PEOPLE • 1979 • Hart Harvey • TVM • USA
LIKE OTHER PEOPLE • 1972 • Morrison Paul • UKN
LIKE POISON see **JAKO GIFT** • 1985
LIKE RABBITS see **JAKO ZAJICI** • 1981
LIKE THE BIG POTS DO • 1929 • Aylott Dave, Symmons E. F. • SHT • UKN
LIKE THE CAT, THEY CAME BACK • 1912 • Sennett Mack • USA
LIKE THE CHANGING HEART OF A BIRD see **JIHI SHINCHO** • 1927
LIKE THE LEAVES (USA) see **COME LE FOGLIE** • 1938
LIKE TWO DROPS OF WATER see **ALS TWEE DRUPPELS WATER** • 1963
LIKE WILDFIRE • 1917 • Paton Stuart • USA
LIKE WOW! see **MR. PEEK-A-BOO'S PLAYMATES** • 1962
LIKEABLE MISTER R., THE • 1969 • Roman Stefan • RMN
LIKELY LADS, THE • 1976 • Tuchner Michael • UKN
LIKELY STORY, A • 1947 • Potter H. C. • USA • FASCINATING NUISANCE, THE
LIKELY STORY, A • 1988 • Grosbard Ulu • USA
LIKENESS OF THE NIGHT, THE • 1921 • Nash Percy • UKN
LIKITY SPLIT • 1974 • Stevens Carter • USA
LIKU-LIKONG LANDAS • 1968 • Borlaza Emmanuel • PHL • CROOKED ROAD
LI'L ABNER • 1940 • Rogell Albert S. • USA • TROUBLE CHASER (UKN)
LI'L ABNER • 1959 • Frank Melvin • USA
LI'L ANJIL • 1936 • *Mintz Charles (P)* • ANS • USA
LIL' EIGHTBALL • 1939 • *Lantz Walter (P)* • ASS • USA
LIL HOB KESSA AKHIRA • 1986 • el Mihi Rafaat • EGY • BROKEN IMAGES
LI'L NOR'WESTER • 1915 • Henderson Lucius • USA
LIL O' LONDON • 1914 • Shaw Harold • UKN
LIL PICARDS • Vehr Bill • USA
LILA • 1964 • Raggett Hugh • SHT • UKN
LILA see **LAILA** • 1958
LILA see **MANTIS IN LACE** • 1969
LILA AKAC • 1934 • Sekely Steve • HNG • WISTERIA
LILA AKAC • 1973 • Sekely Steve • HNG • GIRL WHO LIKED PURPLE FLOWERS, THE
LILAC DOMINO, THE • 1937 • Zelnik Friedrich • UKN
LILAC DREAM • 1987 • Voizard Marc • CND
LILAC SUNBONNET, THE • 1922 • Morgan Sidney • UKN
LILAC TIME • 1928 • Fitzmaurice George • USA • LOVE NEVER DIES (UKN)
LILAC (USA) see **COEUR DE LILAS** • 1931
LILACS IN THE SPRING • 1954 • Wilcox Herbert • UKN • LET'S MAKE UP (USA)
LILAJ • 1967 • Ghaderi Iraj • IRN
LILAS BLANC see **CINQUIEME EMPREINTE, LA** • 1934
LILEIA • 1960 • Lapoknysh Vasil, Vronsky Vakhtong • USS • LILEYA
LILEYA see **LILEIA** • 1960
LILI • 1952 • Walters Charles • USA
LILI • 1990 • Lara Gerardo • MXC • LILY
LILI see **ETERNEL CONFLIT** • 1947
LILI AU LIT • 1966 • Lethem Roland • BLG
LILI MARLEEN • 1981 • Fassbinder R. W. • FRG
LILIES OF THE CITY see **LILIES OF THE STREETS** • 1925
LILIES OF THE FIELD • 1924 • Dillon John Francis • USA
LILIES OF THE FIELD • 1930 • Korda Alexander • USA
LILIES OF THE FIELD • 1934 • Walker Norman • UKN
LILIES OF THE FIELD • 1963 • Nelson Ralph • USA
LILIES OF THE FIELD see **SLNKO, DAZD, LALIE POLNE** • 1972
LILIES OF THE STREETS • 1925 • Levering Joseph • USA • LILIES OF THE CITY
LILIKA • 1971 • Plesa Branko • YGS
LILIOM • 1918 • Curtiz Michael • HNG
LILIOM • 1930 • Borzage Frank • USA
LILIOM • 1934 • Lang Fritz • FRN
LILIOMFI • 1954 • Makk Karoly • HNG
LILITH • 1964 • Rossen Robert • USA
LILITH AND LY (USA) see **LILITH UND LY** • 1919
LILITH UND LY • 1919 • Kober Erich • FRG • LILITH AND LY (USA)
LILJA • 1978 • Gunnlaugsson Hrafn • SHT • ICL • LILY
LILLA HELGONET • 1944 • Hildebrand Weyler • SWD • LITTLE SAINT
LILLA MARTA KOMMER TILLBAKA • 1948 • Ekman Hasse • SWD • LITTLE MARTA RETURNS
LILLE CHAUFFOR, DEN • 1914 • Blom August • DNM • LITTLE CHAUFFEUR, THE
LILLE DANSERINDE, DEN • 1916 • Davidsen Hjalmar • DNM
LILLE ENGELS BRYLLUP, DEN (DNM) see **ENGELEINS HOCKZEIT** • 1913
LILLE ENGELS, DEN (DNM) see **ENGELEIN** • 1912
LILLE FRIDOLF BLIR MORFAR • 1957 • Gunwall Per • SWD • LITTLE FRIDOLF BECOMES A GRANDFATHER
LILLE FRIDOLF OCH JAG • 1956 • Anderberg Torgny • SWD • LITTLE FRIDOLF AND I
LILLE NAPOLEON • 1943 • Edgren Gustaf • SWD • LITTLE NAPOLEON
LILLE SPEJL • 1978 • Fleming Edward • DNM
LILLE TILFAELDIGHED, EN • 1939 • Jacobsen Johan • DNM
LILLE VIRGIL OG ORLA FROSNAPPER • 1979 • Fredholm Gert • DNM • LITTLE VIRGIL AND ORLA FROGSNAPPER
LILLEBROR OCH JAG • 1940 • Hildebrand Weyler • SWD • MY LITTLE BROTHER AND I
LILLI -EIN MADCHEN AUS DER GROSSTADT • 1958 • Leitner Hermann • FRG
LILLI MARLENE • 1950 • Crabtree Arthur • UKN
"LILLI" UND "LILLIS EHE" • 1919 • Speyer Jaap • FRG
LILLIAN GISH IN A LIBERTY LOAN APPEAL • 1918 • *Griffith D. W. (P)* • SHT • USA
LILLIAN ROTH AND HER PIANO BOYS • 1929 • Florey Robert • SHT • USA
LILLIAN RUSSELL • 1940 • Cummings Irving • USA
LILLIAN'S ATONEMENT • 1915 • *Burke David Lewis* • USA
LILLIAN'S DILEMMA • 1914 • North Wilfred • USA
LILLIAN'S HUSBANDS • 1915 • North Wilfred • USA
LILLIE'S NIGHTMARE • 1913 • *Gebhardt George* • USA
LILLIPUT-PUT • 1980 • Bozzetto Bruno • ASS • ITL
LILLIPUTIAN MINUET, THE (USA) see **MENUET LILLIPUTIEN, LE** • 1905
LILLIPUTIAN'S COURTSHIP, THE • 1915 • *Novelty* • USA
LILLO OF THE SULU SEAS • 1916 • Ricketts Thomas • SHT • USA
LILLY HUMBRECHT, DER LEIDENSWEG EINER STIEFTOCHTER • 1922 • Linke Edmund • FRG
LILLY OF THE VALLEY • 1915 • *Premier* • USA
LILLY TURNER • 1933 • Wellman William A. • USA
LILLY'S LOVERS • 1912 • Sennett Mack • USA
LILT OF LOVE, THE • 1915 • Dowlan William C. • USA
LILY • 1982 • Pulido Abraham • VNZ
LILY see **LILJA** • 1978
LILY see **LILI** • 1990
LILY, THE • 1926 • Schertzinger Victor • USA
LILY AIME-MOI • 1975 • Dugowson Maurice • FRN

LILY AND THE ROSE, THE • 1915 • Powell Paul • USA
LILY CHRISTINE • 1932 • Stein Paul L. • UKN
LILY DEN SUFFRAGETTEN see **MODERNA SUFFRAGETTEN, DEN** • 1913
LILY IN BOHEMIA, A • 1915 • North Wilfred • USA
LILY IN LOVE • 1985 • Makk Karoly • HNG, USA • DOUBLE PLAY ○ JATSZANI KELL ○ FITZ AND LILY ○ LOVES OF LILY, THE ○ PLAYERS ○ PLAYING FOR KEEPS
LILY IN THE VALLEY, A see **LAO-SHIH SZU-KA-YEH-TA** • 1983
LILY OF KILLARNEY • 1922 • Sanderson Challis • UKN
LILY OF KILLARNEY • 1927 • Parkinson H. B. • UKN
LILY OF KILLARNEY • 1929 • Ridgwell George • UKN
LILY OF KILLARNEY • 1934 • Elvey Maurice • UKN • BRIDE OF THE LAKE, THE (USA)
LILY OF LAGUNA • 1938 • Mitchell Oswald • UKN
LILY OF LETCHWORTH LOCK • 1912 • Martinek H. O., Moran Percy • UKN
LILY OF LIFE, THE see **LYS DE LA VIE, LE** • 1920
LILY OF POVERTY FLAT, THE • 1915 • *Michelena Beatriz* • USA
LILY OF THE ALLEY • 1923 • Edwards Henry • UKN
LILY OF THE DUST • 1924 • Buchowetzki Dimitri • USA • COMPROMISED
LILY OF THE HARBOR • 1952 • Tzavellas Georges • GRC
LILY OF THE RANCH, THE • 1910 • *Nestor* • USA
LILY OF THE TENEMENTS, THE • 1911 • Griffith D. W. • USA
LILY OF THE VALLEY • 1914 • North Wilfred • *Vitagraph* • USA
LILY OF THE VALLEY, THE • 1914 • Campbell Colin • *Selig* • USA
LILY, TOMBOY • 1915 • Birch Cecil • UKN
LILY TOMLIN • 1986 • Broomfield Nicholas, Churchill Joan • DOC • USA
LILY WAS HERE see **KASSIERE, DE** • 1989
LILY'S BIRTHDAY • 1915 • Birch Cecil • UKN
LILY'S FIRST AID TRAGEDY • 1915 • *Ward Lily* • UKN
LIMANI TON DACRION, TO • 1928 • Gaziadis Dimitrios • GRC • PORT OF TEARS, THE
LIMB OF SATAN, A • 1917 • Stonehouse Ruth • SHT • USA
LIMBO • 1972 • Ricketson James • SHT • ASL
LIMBO • 1972 • Robson Mark • USA • WOMEN IN LIMBO ○ CHAINED TO YESTERDAY
LIMBO see **LIMBO, IL** • 1968
LIMBO, IL • 1968 • Ghione Riccardo • ITL • LIMBO
LIMBO LINE, THE • 1968 • Gallu Samuel • UKN
LIMBURGER AND LOVE • 1910 • *Powers* • USA
LIMBURGER CYCLONE, A • 1917 • Howe J. A. • SHT • USA
LIMBURGER'S VICTORY • 1915 • McKim Edwin • USA
LIME • 1965 • Kovachev Hristo • DOC • BUL
LIME JUICE NIGHTS • 1931 • Foster Lewis R. • SHT • USA
LIMEHOUSE see **LONDON** • 1926
LIMEHOUSE BLUES • 1934 • Hall Alexander • USA • EAST END CHANT ○ LIMEHOUSE NIGHTS
LIMEHOUSE BLUES • 1953 • van Morkerken Emile • SHT • NTH
LIMEHOUSE NIGHTS see **LIMEHOUSE BLUES** • 1934
LIMELIGHT • 1936 • Wilcox Herbert • UKN • BACKSTAGE ○ STREET SINGER'S SERENADE
LIMELIGHT • 1952 • Chaplin Charles • USA
LIMESTONED • 1973 • Bonniere Rene • DCS • CND
LIMEUSE, LES • 1978 • Desvilles Jean • FRN
LIMFJORDEN • 1961 • Carlsen Henning • SHT • DNM
LIMIT, THE • 1972 • Kotto Yaphet • USA • SPEED LIMIT 65 ○ TIME LIMIT
LIMIT, THE • 1979 • Rybkowski Jan • PLN
LIMIT FIRE BRIGADE, THE • 1911 • Aylott Dave? • UKN
LIMIT UP • 1989 • Martini Richard • USA
LIMITE • 1930 • Peixoto Mario • BRZ
LIMITE DEL AMOR, EL • 1976 • Romero-Marchent Rafael • SPN
LIMITED DIVORCE, A • 1912 • Henderson Dell • USA
LIMITED MAIL, THE • 1925 • Hill George W. • USA
LIMITS, THE see **CONFINES, LOS** • 1987
LIMNI TON POTHON, I • 1958 • Zervos Georges • GRC • LAC AUX DESIRS, LE
LIMONADOVY JOE • 1964 • Lipsky Oldrich • CZC • LEMONADE JOE (USA) ○ KONSKA OPERA
LIMOUSINE • 1981 • Bajon Filip • PLN
LIMOUSINE LIFE • 1918 • Dillon John Francis • USA
LIMOUSINE LOVE • 1928 • Guiol Fred • SHT • USA
LIMOUSINE MYSTERY, THE • 1916 • Henderson Lucius • SHT • USA
LIMPAN • 1983 • Roos Staffan • SWD • LOAFY ○ LOAFIE
LIMPING DEVIL, THE see **KULHAVY DABEL** • 1968
LIMPING INTO HAPPINESS • 1914 • Hamilton G. P.? • USA
LIMPING MAN, THE • 1936 • Summers Walter • UKN
LIMPING MAN, THE • 1953 • De La Tour Charles, Endfield Cy • UKN
LIMPING MAN, THE (USA) see **CREEPING SHADOWS** • 1931
LIMPY see **WHEN A FELLER NEEDS A FRIEND** • 1932
LIN DU CANADA, LA • 1947 • Proulx Maurice • DOC • CND
LIN FAMILY SHOP, THE • 1959 • Shui Hua • CHN • LINJIA PUZI
LIN TSE-HSU see **LIN ZEXU** • 1959
LIN YA-CHEN LAO-HU YU HSIEH HSIA • 1980 • Huang Hua-Chi • HKG • LAM AH CHUN BLUNDERS AGAIN
LIN ZEXU • 1959 • Zheng Junli, Chen Fan • CHN • OPIUM WAR, THE ○ LIN TSE-HSU
LINA BRAAKE • 1975 • Sinkel Bernard • FRG • BANK'S INTERESTS CANNOT BE THOSE OF LINA BRAAKE ○ INTERESSEN DER BANK KONNEN NICHT DIE INTERESSEN SEIN, DIE LINA BRAAKE HAT
LINA BROOKE • 1980 • Harrild Anthony • UKN
LINA'S WEDDING see **JENTESPRANGET** • 1973
LINCEUL N'A PAS DE POCHES, UN • 1975 • Mocky Jean-Pierre • FRN
LINCOLN see **GORE VIDAL'S LINCOLN** • 1988
LINCOLN CONSPIRACY, THE • 1977 • Conway James L. • USA
LINCOLN CYCLE, THE • 1917 • Stahl John M. • SER • USA
LINCOLN FOR THE DEFENCE • 1913 • *Pilot* • USA
LINCOLN HIGHWAYMAN, THE • 1920 • Flynn Emmett J. • USA
LINCOLN IN THE WHITE HOUSE • 1939 • McGann William • USA
LINCOLN, THE LOVER • 1914 • Ince Ralph • USA
LINCOLN'S GETTYSBURG ADDRESS • 1912 • Blackton J. Stuart, Young James • USA
LINCOLNSHIRE POACHER, THE • 1947 • UKN
LINDA • 1929 • Reid Dorothy • USA
LINDA • 1960 • Sharp Don • UKN
LINDA • 1973 • Smight Jack • USA
LINDA AND ABILENE • 1969 • Hansen Mark • USA
LINDA BE GOOD • 1947 • McDonald Frank • USA
LINDA JOY • 1985 • MacGillivray William D. • CND
LINDA LOVELACE FOR PRESIDENT • 1975 • Guzman Claudio • USA • HOT NEON
LINDA LOVELACE MEETS MISS JONES • 1977 • Spaveni Angelo • USA
LINDBERGH KIDNAPPING CASE, THE • 1976 • Kulik Buzz • TVM • USA
LINDENWIRTIN, DIE • 1930 • Jacoby Georg • FRG
LINDENWIRTIN AM RHEIN, DIE • 1927 • Randolf Rolf • FRG
LINDENWIRTIN VOM DONAUSTRAND, DIE • 1957 • Quest Hans • AUS
LINDIE • 1971 • SAF
LINDSAY KEMBLE'S ADELAIDE ESCAPADES • 1915 • *Krischock H.(P)* • ASL
LINDSAY KEMP CIRCUS, THE • 1973 • Marzaroli Oscar, Coronado Celestino • DOC • UKN
LINE • 1961 • Christensen Nils Reinhardt • NRW • PASSIONATE DEMONS, THE (USA)
LINE • 1969 • Rainer Yvonne • SHT • USA
LINE, THE • 1970 • McGill Chris • DOC • ASL
LINE, THE • 1977 • Godfrey Bob • ANS • UKN
LINE, THE • 1980 • Siegel Robert • USA
LINE, THE see **LINEA, LA** • 1971
LINE AT HOGAN'S, THE • 1912 • Dillon Eddie • USA
LINE CRUISING SOUTH • 1933 • *Grierson John (P)* • DOC • UKN
LINE DESCRIBING A CONE • 1975 • Maccoll Anthony • USA
LINE ENGAGED • 1935 • Mainwaring Bernerd • UKN
LINE IS BUSY, THE • 1970 • *Cosmos Films* • USA
LINE OF APOGEE • 1968 • Williams Lloyd Michael • USA
LINE OF BLACK CLOUDS, A see **KUROUN KAIDOU** • 1948
LINE OF DEMARCATION see **LIGNE DE DEMARCATION, LA** • 1966
LINE OF DESTINY see **REKAVA** • 1957
LINE OF DUTY see **U.S. MARSHALS: WACO & RHINEHART** • 1987
LINE OF FIRE • 1988 • Cook Bruce • USA
LINE OF LIFE, THE see **JEEVAN REKHA**
LINE OF LIFE, THE see **REKAVA** • 1957
LINE OF SCREAMMAGE • 1956 • Kneitel Seymour • ANS • USA
LINE RIDER, THE • 1914 • *Eclair* • USA
LINE RIDER'S SISTER, THE • 1913 • *Frontier* • USA
LINE RUNNERS, THE • 1920 • Dawn Norman • SHT • USA
LINE SEX see **LINJE SEX** • 1958
LINE TO SKYE, THE • 1974 • McConnell Edward • DCS • UKN
LINE TO TCHERVA HUT, THE • 1937 • Cavalcanti Alberto • DOC • UKN • LINE TO THE TSCHIERVA-HUT, THE ○ LINE TO TSCHIERA, THE
LINE TO THE TSCHIERVA-HUT, THE see **LINE TO TCHERVA HUT, THE** • 1937
LINE TO TSCHIERA, THE see **LINE TO TCHERVA HUT, THE** • 1937
LINE-UP, THE • 1913 • Humphrey William • USA
LINE-UP, THE • 1934 • Higgin Howard • USA • IDENTITY PARADE (UKN)
LINE-UP, THE see **LINEUP, THE** • 1958
LINE UP AND LAY DOWN see **PRENEZ LA QUEUE COMME TOUT LE MONDE** • 1972
LINEA, LA • 1971 • Cavandoli Osvaldo • SHT • ITL • LINE, THE
LINEA DEL CIELO, LA • 1984 • Colomo Fernando • SPN • SKYLINE
LINEA DEL DESTINO, LA • 1972 • *Estudio America* • MXC
LINEA DEL FIUME, LA • 1976 • Scavarda Aldo • ITL
LINEAGE • 1980 • Fraser Chris • DOC • ASL
LINEAR ACCELERATOR • 1952 • Halas John • ANS • UKN
LINEAR PROGRAMMING • 1966 • *Halas John (P)* • ANS • UKN
LINEMAN, THE • 1911 • *Imp* • USA
LINEMAN AND THE GIRL, THE • 1911 • *Powers* • USA
LINER CRUISING SOUTH • 1934 • Wright Basil • DOC • UKN
LINES HORIZONTAL (USA) see **LIGNES HORIZONTALES** • 1962
LINES OF WHITE ON A SULLEN SEA • 1909 • Griffith D. W. • USA
LINES VERTICAL • 1960 • McLaren Norman, Lambart Evelyn • ANS • CND • LIGNES VERTICALES ○ VERTICAL LINES
LINESMAN, THE • 1965 • Griffiths Peter • DCS • UKN
LINEUP, THE • 1958 • Siegel Don • USA • LINE-UP, THE
LINGE TURBULENT, LE • 1909 • Cohl Emile (c/d) • ANS • FRN • TURBULENT LINEN, THE
LINGERIE • 1928 • Melford George • USA
LINGERIES INTIMES • Roy Jean-Claude • FRN
LINGUA D'ARGENTO see **ECCO LINGUA D'ARGENTO** • 1976
LINIE 1 • Hauff Reinhard • FRG
LINJE SEX • 1958 • Blomgren Bengt • SWD • KARLEKSBARN ○ LINE SEX
LINJIA PUZI see **LIN FAMILY SHOP, THE** • 1959
LINK • 1986 • Franklin Richard • UKN
LINK, THE see **BLOOD LINK** • 1983
LINK IN THE CHAIN, THE • 1914 • Lund O. A. C. • USA
LINK OF FATE, THE see **KADER BAGI** • 1967
LINK-SPAN • 1956 • Clark Michael • UKN
LINK THAT BINDS, THE • 1914 • Lloyd Frank • USA
LINK THAT HELD, THE • 1911 • *Edison* • USA
LINKED BY FATE • 1912 • *Melies* • USA
LINKED BY FATE • 1919 • Ward Albert • UKN
LINKED TOGETHER • 1912 • *Mcleod Elsie* • USA
LINKS DER ISAR -RECHTS DER SPREE • 1929 • Seitz Franz • FRG
LINKS DER ISAR -RECHTS DER SPREE • 1940 • May Paul • FRG
LINKS OF JUSTICE • 1958 • Varnel Max • UKN
LINKS OF LOVE see **PAIR OF HANDCUFFS, A** • 1912
LINKSHANDIGE FRAU, DIE • 1978 • Handke Peter • FRG • LEFT-HANDED WOMAN, THE
LINTERNA DE DIOGENES, LA • 1925 • Stahl Carlos • MXC • LANTERN OF DIOGENES, THE
LINTUMIES • 1977 • Putkinen Seppo • ANM • FNL • BIRD MAN, THE
LINUS • 1979 • Sjoman Vilgot • SWD • LINUS AND THE MYSTERIOUS RED BRICK HOUSE
LINUS AND THE MYSTERIOUS RED BRICK HOUSE see **LINUS** • 1979
LIO EN EL LABORATORIO • 1967 • Torrado Ramon • SPN
LIOLA • 1964 • Blasetti Alessandro • ITL, FRN • VERY HANDY MAN, A (USA)
LION, THE • 1914 • *Kerrigan J. Warren* • USA
LION, THE • 1948 • Felstead Bert • UKN
LION, THE • 1962 • Cardiff Jack • UKN, USA
LION, THE see **LEON, EL** • 1971
LION AND THE CROSS, THE • 1961 • Rasky Harry • MTV • USA
LION AND THE DITTY, THE see **LEV A PISNICKA** • 1959
LION AND THE GIRL, THE • 1916 • Cavender Glen • SHT • USA
LION AND THE GNAT, THE (USA) see **LION ET LE MOUCHERON, LE** • 1932
LION AND THE GOAT, THE • ANS • CZC
LION AND THE HARE, THE see **LEV I ZAYATS** • 1949
LION AND THE HAWK, THE see **MEMED** • 1983
LION AND THE HORSE, THE • 1952 • King Louis • USA
LION AND THE HOUSE, THE • 1932 • *Sennett Mack (P)* • SHT • USA
LION AND THE LAMB, THE • 1931 • Seitz George B. • USA
LION AND THE MOUSE • 1943 • Davis Mannie • ANS • USA
LION AND THE MOUSE, THE • 1914 • O'Neil Barry • USA
LION AND THE MOUSE, THE • 1919 • Terriss Tom • USA
LION AND THE MOUSE, THE • 1928 • Bacon Lloyd • USA
LION AND THE MOUSE, THE • 1976 • Lambart Evelyn • ANS • CND
LION AND THE SONG, THE see **LEV A PISNICKA** • 1959
LION AND THE SOUSE, THE • 1924 • *Sennett Mack (P)* • SHT • USA
LION AND THE VIRGIN, THE see **LEJONET OCH JUNGFRUN** • 1974
LION AROUND • 1950 • Hannah Jack • ANS • USA
LION AT WORLD'S END, THE • 1971 • Hill James, Travers Bill • UKN
LION DE THEBES, LE (FRN) see **LEONE DI TEBE, IL** • 1964
LION DES MOGOLS, LE • 1924 • Epstein Jean • FRN
LION DEVENU VIEUX, LE • 1929 • Starevitch Ladislas • ANS • FRN • OLD LION, THE
LION DOWN • 1951 • Kinney Jack • ANS • USA
LION EN CAGE, LE • 1983 • Noel Jean-Guy • SER • CND
LION ET LE MOUCHERON, LE • 1932 • Starevitch Ladislas • ANS • FRN • LION AND THE GNAT, THE (USA)
LION HAS SEVEN HEADS, THE see **LEONE A SETTE TESTE, IL** • 1971
LION HAS WINGS, THE • 1939 • Powell Michael, Hurst Brian Desmond, Brunel Adrian • UKN
LION-HEARTED BRAVE, THE see **ASLAN YUREKLI KABADAYI** • 1967
LION-HEARTED RESAT see **ASLAN YUREKLI RESAT** • 1967
LION HUNT • 1949 • Donnelly Eddie • ANS • USA
LION HUNT • 1955 • Whitney John • ANS • USA
LION HUNT, THE • 1938 • Davis Mannie • ANS • USA
LION HUNTER, THE • 1914 • Martin E. A. • USA
LION HUNTERS, THE • 1913 • *Gaumont* • USA
LION HUNTERS, THE • 1951 • Beebe Ford • USA • BOMBA AND THE LION HUNTERS (UKN)
LION HUNTERS, THE see **CHASSE AU LION A L'ARC, LA** • 1967
LION IN THE HOUSE, A • 1919 • *Century* • SHT • USA
LION IN THE ROAR • 1956 • Kneitel Seymour • ANS • USA
LION IN TOWN see **LEJON PA STAN** • 1959
LION IN WINTER, THE • 1968 • Harvey Anthony • UKN
LION IS IN THE STREETS, A • 1953 • Walsh Raoul • USA
LION MAN see **CURSE OF THE VOODOO** • 1965
LION MAN, THE • 1920 • Wells Jack, Russell Albert • SRL • USA
LION MAN, THE • 1936 • McCarthy John P. • USA
LION OF AFRICA, THE • 1987 • Connor Kevin • TVM • USA
LION OF FLANDERS, THE see **LEEUW VAN VLAANDEREN, DE** • 1984
LION OF ST. MARK, THE (USA) see **LEONE DI SAN MARCO, IL** • 1964
LION OF SPARTA see **300 SPARTANS, THE** • 1962
LION OF THE DESERT • 1979 • Akkad Moustapha • UKN, LBY • OMAR MUKHTAR: LION OF THE DESERT
LION OF THE MOUNTAINS, THE see **DAGLAR ASLANI** • 1967
LION OF THEBES, THE (USA) see **LEONE DI TEBE, IL** • 1964
LION PAWS AND LADY FINGERS • 1920 • Fishback Fred C. • SHT • USA
LION SAVANT, LE • 1902 • Blache Alice • FRN
LION SPEAKS, THE • 1963 • SAF
LION SPECIAL, A • 1919 • Davis James • SHT • USA
LION TAMER, THE • 1909 • *Selig* • USA
LION TAMER, THE • 1915 • *Horseshoe* • UKN
LION TAMER, THE • 1934 • Stallings George • ANS • USA
LION TAMER, THE • 1960 • Halas John • ANS • UKN
LION TAMER, THE • 1961 • Vukotic Dusan • ANS • YGS
LION TAMER, THE see **HOUP-LA!** • 1928
LION TAMER, THE see **KROTITELJ** • 1961
LION, THE GRIFFIN AND THE KANGAROO, THE • 1951 • Tait Margaret, Hollander Peter • UKN
LION, THE LAMB, THE MAN, THE • 1914 • De Grasse Joseph • USA
LION, THE WITCH AND THE WARDROBE, THE • 1972 • *Lonsdale Patricia (P)* • SRL • UKN
LION, THE WITCH AND THE WARDROBE, THE • 1978 • Melendez Bill • ANM • USA, UKN
LION TONIC, THE • 1912 • *Cines* • ITL
LION WITH THE WHITE MANE see **LEV S BILOU HRIVOU** • 1987
LIONCEAUX, LES • 1959 • Bourdon Jacques • FRN • PLAYFUL KIND, THE
LIONEL FORGET • 1968 • Dansereau Fernand • DCS • CND
LIONEL HAMPTON AND HERB JEFFRIES • 1955 • Cowan Will • SHT • USA

LIONEL HAMPTON AND HIS ORCHESTRA • 1949 • Cowan Will • SHT • USA
LIONEL LION • 1944 • Sommer Paul • ANS • USA
LIONHEART • 1968 • Forlong Michael • UKN
LIONHEART • 1987 • Schaffner Franklin J. • USA
LIONHEART CHIEF, THE • 1916 • Dillon John Francis • USA
LIONMAN • 1980 • Baitan Natuch • TRK
LION'S ALLIANCE, THE • 1920 • Fishback Fred C. • SHT • USA
LIONS AND LADIES • 1919 • Griffin Frank C. • SHT • USA
LIONS ARE FREE, THE • 1967 • Hill James • MTV • USA
LIONS ARE LOOSE, THE (USA) see **LIONS SONT LACHES, LES** • 1961
LION'S BREATH, THE • 1916 • Davey Horace • SHT • USA
LION'S BRIDE, THE • 1908 • *Selig* • USA
LION'S BRIDE, THE • 1913 • *Vitagraph* • USA
LION'S BRIDE, THE • 1914 • Mackenzie Donald • USA
LION'S BUSY, THE • 1950 • Freleng Friz • ANS • USA
LION'S BUSY, THE • 1961 • Kneitel Seymour • ANS • USA
LION'S CLAWS, THE • 1918 • Jaccard Jacques, Harvey Harry • SRL • USA
LION'S CUBS, THE • 1915 • Dewsbury Ralph • UKN
LION'S DANCE see **SHISHI NO ZA** • 1953
LIONS DANS LA NUIT, LES • 1913-18 • Durand Jean • FRN
LION'S DEN, THE • 1919 • Baker George D. • USA
LION'S DEN, THE • 1936 • Newfield Sam • USA • SINGLE SHOT BARTON (UKN)
LION'S DEN, THE • 1989 • Holland Agnieszka • FRG
LION'S DEN, THE see **BOCA DEL LOBO, LA** • 1988
LIONS FOR BREAKFAST • 1974 • Davidson William • CND
LION'S FRIEND, THE • 1934 • *Terry Paul/ Moser Frank (P)* • ANS • USA
LION'S HOLIDAY, THE • 1966 • Hitruck Fedor • ANS • USS
LION'S JAWS AND KITTEN'S PAWS • 1920 • Watson William • SHT • USA
LION'S LAIR, THE • 1917 • Pearson W. B. • SHT • USA
LIONS LOVE • 1969 • Varda Agnes • USA
LION'S MATE, THE • 1915 • Santschi Thomas • USA
LION'S MOUSE, THE • 1922 • Apfel Oscar • UKN
LION'S NEMESIS, THE • 1916 • *Gibson Margaret* • SHT • USA
LIONS ON THE LOOSE • 1941 • Freeman Marjorie • SHT • USA
LION'S ROAR, THE • 1928 • Sennett Mack • SHT • USA
LION'S SHARE, THE • 1978 • Eggleston Colin • MTV • ASL
LION'S SHARE, THE • 1985 • SAF
LION'S SHARE, THE see **PARTE DEL LEON, LA** • 1978
LIONS SONT LACHES, LES • 1961 • Verneuil Henri • FRN, ITL • LEONI SCATTERRATI, I (ITL) ○ LIONS ARE LOOSE, THE (USA)
LION'S TALE, A • Ungerer Walter • SHT • USA
LION'S WARD, THE • 1915 • MacGregor Norval • USA
LION'S WHISKERS, THE • 1925 • *Sennett Mack (P)* • SHT • USA
LIOS DE BARBA AZUL, LOS • 1954 • Martinez Solares Gilberto • MXC
LIP 73-74: LE GOUT DU COLLECTIF • 1973 • Dubosc Dominique, Lessing Hans • DOC • FRN
LIP SERVICE • 1970 • *Kirt Films Int.* • USA
LIP SERVICE • 1985 • Macy W. H. • USA
LIP SMACKERS • 1978 • USA
LIPPS AND MCCAINE • 1978 • Chinn Robert C. • USA • SEXY ADVENTURES OF LIPPS AND MCCAINE, THE ○ HOT COWGIRLS
LIPS • 1964 • Warhol Andy • USA
LIPS FORBIDDEN TO TALK see **WATASHI WA KAI NI NARITAI** • 1959
LIPS OF BLOOD (UKN) see **CHEMINS DE LA VIOLENCE, LES** • 1972
LIPS WITHOUT KISSES see **LABIOS SEM BEIJOS** • 1930
LIPSKY'S CHRISTMAS DINNER • 1934 • Samuelson G. B. • UKN
LIPSTICK • 1976 • Johnson Lamont • USA
LIPSTICK (USA) see **ROSSETTO, IL** • 1960
LIPTON CUP, THE • 1913 • Parker Lem B. • USA
LIQA' FI AL-GHURUB • 1959 • Arafa Saad • EGY • RENDEZ-VOUS AU CRESPUSCULE
LIQUEFACTION DES CORPS DURS • 1909 • de Chomon Segundo • FRN • LIQUEFACTION OF SOLID BODIES
LIQUEFACTION OF SOLID BODIES see **LIQUEFACTION DES CORPS DURS** • 1909
LIQUEUR DU COUVERT, LA • 1903 • Blache Alice • FRN
LIQUID AIR, THE • 1909 • *Gaumont* • FRN
LIQUID DYNAMITE • 1915 • Madison Cleo • USA
LIQUID ELECTRICITY • 1907 • Blackton J. Stuart • USA • INVENTOR'S GALVANIC FLUID, THE ○ LIQUID ELECTRICITY OR THE INVENTOR'S GALVANIC FLUID
LIQUID ELECTRICITY OR THE INVENTOR'S GALVANIC FLUID see **LIQUID ELECTRICITY** • 1907
LIQUID GOLD • 1919 • Kennedy Aubrey M. • USA
LIQUID GOLD • 1920 • Empey Arthur Guy • USA
LIQUID GOLD see **OIL** • 1920
LIQUID JAZZ • 1962 • Kramer Joseph • SHT • USA
LIQUID LOVE • 1913 • *Martin Films* • UKN • LITTLE GRAINS OF LOVE
LIQUID PETROLEUM GASES • 1953 • Segaller Denis • DOC • UKN
LIQUID SKY • 1982 • Tsukerman Slava • USA
LIQUID SUNSHINE • 1919 • Saville Victor • DCS • UKN
LIQUID TREASURE see **WHISKY GALORE** • 1948
LIQUIDATOR, THE • 1966 • Cardiff Jack • USA, UKN
LIQUIRIZIA • 1979 • Samperi Salvatore • ITL • LIQUORICE
LIQUORICE see **LIQUIRIZIA** • 1979
LIRA DO DELIRIO, A • 1979 • Lima Walter Jr. • BRZ • LYRE OF DELIRIUM
LIRE LA TERRE • 1973 • Gagne Jacques • DCS • CND
LIS DE MER, LE • 1970 • Audry Jacqueline • FRN • SEA LILY, THE
LISA see **INSPECTOR, THE** • 1961
LISA AND BALLERS see **BALLERS, THE** • 1969
LISA AND JOEY IN CONNECTICUT • 1965 • Jacobs Ken • USA
LISA AND LOTTIE see **DOPPELTE LOTTCHEN, DAS** • 1950
LISA AND THE DEVIL see **CASA DELL'EXORCISMO, LA** • 1975
LISA BRIGHT AND DARK • 1973 • Szwarc Jeannot • TVM • USA
LISA DAGLI OCCHI BLU • 1969 • Corbucci Bruno • ITL
LISA E IL DIAVOLO see **CASA DELL'EXORCISMO, LA** • 1975
LISA FERENS • 1966 • Bonniere Rene • DCS • CND
LISA FLEURON • 1919 • Roberti Roberto Leone • ITL
LISA, LISA see **CALIFORNIA AXE MASSACRE** • 1974
LISA, THE GREEK TOSCA see **LISA, TOSCA OF ATHENS** • 1961
LISA, TOSCA OF ATHENS • 1961 • Kapsaskis Sokrates • GRC • LISA, THE GREEK TOSCA
LISA'S FOLLY • 1970 • *Chancellor Films* • USA
LISBOA • 1961 • Mendes Joao • SHT • PRT
LISBOA, CRONICA ANEDOTICA • 1930 • de Barros Jose Leitao • PRT • CRONICA ANEDOTICA
LISBOA CULTURAL • 1983 • de Oliveira Manoel • SHT • PRT • CULTURAL LISBON
LISBOA DE ONTEM E DE HOJE • 1948 • Ribeiro Antonio Lopes • SHT • PRT
LISBOA DE ONTEM E DE HOJE • 1956 • Fraga Augusto • SHT • PRT
LISBOA E O PROBLEMA DOS SEUS ACESSOS • 1945 • de Barros Jose Leitao • SHT • PRT
LISBOA MODERNA • 1955 • Garcia Fernando • SHT • PRT
LISBOA, O DIREITO A CIDADE • 1974 • Geada Eduardo • PRT
LISBOA, PEQUENA BIOGRAFIA DE UMA CAPITAL • 1953 • Garcia Fernando • SHT • PRT
LISBON • 1956 • Milland Ray • USA
LISBON STORY • 1946 • Stein Paul L. • UKN
LISELOTTE VON DER PFALZ • 1935 • Froelich Carl • FRG • PRIVATE LIFE OF LOUIS XIV, THE ○ FRAUEN UM DEN SONNENKONIG
LISELOTTE VON DER PFALZ • 1966 • Hoffmann Kurt • FRG
LISETTA (ITL) see **BLUMENMADCHEN VOM GRAND-HOTEL, DAS** • 1934
LISETTE • 1961 • Hugh R. John • USA • CROWD FOR LISETTE, A ○ FALL GIRL
LISI UND DER GENERAL • 1986 • Rissi Mark M. • SWT
LISICE • 1970 • Papic Krsto • YGS • HANDCUFFS
LISKA A DZBAN • 1947 • Latal Stanislav • ANM • CZC • FOX AND THE JUG, THE (USA)
LISKA A VLK • 1956 • Karpas Jan • CZC • FOX AND THE WOLF, THE
LISKA BYSTROUSKA • 1954 • Hofman Eduard • ANS • CZC • CUNNING LITTLE VIXEN, THE ○ FOX, THE
LISLEBANK, A • 1917 • *Mcquire Paddy* • SHT • USA
LISMONIMENA PROSSOPA • 1946 • Tzavellas Georges • GRC • FORGOTTEN FACES
LISSU WA AL-KILAB, AL- • 1962 • el Sheikh Kamal • EGY • VOLEUR ET LES CHIENS, LE ○ EVADE DE L'ENFER ○ LESS WAL KELAB, AL- ○ ESCAPE FROM HELL ○ THIEF AND DOGS
LISSY • 1957 • Wolf Konrad • GDR
LIST OF ADRIAN MESSENGER, THE • 1963 • Huston John • USA
LISTE NOIRE • 1984 • Bonnot Alain • FRN
LISTEN! see **MAN JAIYE** • 1972
LISTEN CHILDREN • 1928 • Taurog Norman • SHT • USA
LISTEN, DARLING • 1938 • Marin Edwin L. • USA
LISTEN, JUDGE • 1952 • Bernds Edward • SHT • USA
LISTEN LESTER • 1924 • Seiter William A. • USA
LISTEN, LET'S MAKE LOVE (USA) see **SCUSI, FACCIAMO L'AMORE?** • 1968
LISTEN LISTEN LISTEN • 1976 • Greene Barbara • DOC • CND
LISTEN TO BRITAIN • 1941 • Jennings Humphrey, McAllister Stewart • DCS • UKN
LISTEN TO HARRY • 1940 • Roush Leslie • SHT • USA
LISTEN TO ME • 1989 • Stewart Douglas Day • USA
LISTEN TO MY MUSIC • 1961 • Henryson Robert • SHT • UKN
LISTEN TO THE BANDS • 1945 • Negulesco Jean • SHT • USA
LISTEN TO THE CITY • 1985 • Mann Ron • CND
LISTEN TO THE LION • 1977 • Safran Henri • SHT • ASL
LISTEN TO THE PRAIRIES • 1945 • Parker Gudrun • DOC • CND • CITY SINGS, A
LISTEN TO THE ROAR OF THE OCEAN see **KIKE WADATSUMI NO KOE** • 1950
LISTEN TO YOUR HEART • 1982 • Taylor Don • TVM • USA
LISTEN UP: THE LIVES OF QUINCY JONES • 1990 • Ross Courtney Sale • DOC • USA
LISTEN WITH YOUR EYES • 1962 • Keatley Philip • CND
LISTENER, THE • 1986 • Jones Kirk • ANS • CND
LISTENER'S LESSON, THE • 1912 • *Missimer Howard* • USA
LISTENING IN • 1926 • Sanderson Challis, Newman Widgey R. • UKN
LISTENING IN • 1932 • *Sennett Mack (P)* • SHT • USA
LISTIA STIN ATHINA • 1969 • Serdaris Vangelis • GRC • ROBBERY, THE
LISTOPAD • 1935 • Vavra Otakar • SHT • CZC • NOVEMBER
LISTOPAD • 1968 • Ioseliani Otar • USS • WHEN LEAVES FALL ○ FALLING LEAVES ○ VENDEMIAIRE ○ GIORGOBISTVE ○ WHEN THE LEAVES FALL
LISZT • 1949 • Micucci • SHT • ITL
LISZT RHAPSODY see **WENN DIE MUSIK NICHT WAR'** • 1935
LISZTOMANIA • 1975 • Russell Ken • UKN
LIT, LE • 1974 • Lemoine Jacques • FRN, CND • PLUMARD EN FOLIE, LE ○ BEDMANIA
LIT, LE • 1981 • Hansel Marion • BLG, SWT • BED, THE
LIT A COLONNES, LE • 1942 • Tual Roland • FRN
LIT A DEUX PLACES, LE • 1965 • Delannoy Jean, Puccini Gianni, Mancori Alvaro, Dupont-Midy Francois • FRN, ITL • RACCONTE A DUE PIAZZE (ITL) ○ DOUBLE BED, THE
LIT A DEUX PLACES, LE see **RENDEZ-VOUS AVEC LA CHANCE** • 1949
LIT CONJUGAL, LE (FRN) see **STORIA MODERNA -L'APE REGINA, UNA** • 1963
LIT DE LA VIERGE, LE • 1969 • Garrel Philippe • FRN
LIT DE MME LEDOUX, LE see **A MOI LE JOUR, A TOI LA NUIT** • 1932
LITA PA MEJ, ALSKLINGI • 1961 • Lindberg Sven • SWD • TRUST ME DARLING
LITAN • 1982 • Mocky Jean-Pierre • FRN • LITAN, LA CITE DES SPECTRES VERT
LITAN, LA CITE DES SPECTRES VERT see **LITAN** • 1982
LITANY OF HAPPY PEOPLE • 1971 • Acimovic Karpo • SHT • YGS
LITEN IDA • 1981 • Mikkelsen Laila • NRW, SWD • GROWING UP ○ LITTLE IDA
LITERA • 1962 • Szczechura Daniel • ANS • PLN • LETTER, THE
LITERATURE AND LOVE • 1913 • Carleton Lloyd B. • USA
LITERATURE LESSON • 1968 • Korenev A. • USS
LITET BO • 1956 • Mattsson Arne • SWD • LITTLE PLACE OF ONE'S OWN, A
LITHOGRAPHS • 1973 • Bonniere Rene • DCS • CND
LITHOPHONIE • 1977 • Dupuis Jean-Paul • FRN
LITIL THUFA • 1979 • Gudmundsson Agust • ICL • MOLEHILL
LITOST • 1970 • Schorm Evald • MTV • CZC • REGRET
LITRI Y SU SOMBRA, EL • 1959 • Gil Rafael • SPN
LITSO FACHIZMA • 1942 • Pudovkin V. I. • USS
LITTERBUG, THE • 1961 • Luske Hamilton • ANS • USA
LITTLE, A LOT, PASSIONATELY, A see **PEU, BEAUCOUP, PASSIONNEMENT.., UN** • 1970
LITTLE ACCIDENT • 1939 • Lamont Charles • USA
LITTLE ACCIDENT, THE • 1930 • Craft William James • USA • UNEXPECTED FATHER
LITTLE ACRES, THE see **PETITS ARPENTS, LES** • 1963
LITTLE ADVENTURERS see **PEQUENOS AVENTUREROS** • 1978
LITTLE ADVENTURES (USA) see **PICCOLI AVVENTURIERI** • 1940
LITTLE ADVENTURESS, THE • 1927 • De Mille William C. • USA • DOVER ROAD, THE
LITTLE ADVENTURESS, THE • 1938 • Lederman D. Ross • USA
LITTLE ALIEN, THE see **ISMERETLEN ISMEROS** • 1988
LITTLE AMERICA see **REAR ADMIRAL RICHARD E. BYRD'S SECOND GREAT ANTARCTIC EXPEDITION INTO LITTLE AMERICA** • 1935
LITTLE AMERICAN, THE • 1917 • De Mille Cecil B. • USA
LITTLE AND BIG (USA) see **MALI I VELIKI** • 1966
LITTLE AND THE BIG HAPPINESS, THE see **KLEINE UND DAS GROSSE GLUCK, DAS** • 1953
LITTLE ANGEL see **ANGELITA** • 1935
LITTLE ANGEL, THE see **LADY OF CHANCE, A** • 1928
LITTLE ANGEL OF CANYON CREEK, THE • 1914 • Sturgeon Rollin S. • USA
LITTLE ANGEL OF ROARING SPRINGS, THE • 1909 • *Kalem* • USA
LITTLE ANGEL -OR THE VIRGIN OF BAMBERG see **ENGELCHEN -ODER DIE JUNGFRAU VON BAMBERG** • 1968
LITTLE ANGEL (USA) see **SONRISA DE LA VIRGEN, LA** • 1957
LITTLE ANGELS OF LUCK • 1910 • Griffith D. W. • USA
LITTLE ANGLERS • 1952 • Rasinski Connie • ANS • USA
LITTLE ANN • 1958 • Dinov Todor • ANM • BUL
LITTLE ANNIE ROONEY • 1925 • Beaudine William • USA
LITTLE ANNIE ROONEY • 1931 • Fleischer Dave • ANS • USA
LITTLE ANYUTA'S DOG see **ANYUTINA DOROGA** • 1968
LITTLE APPLE, THE see **MANZANITA** • 1979
LITTLE ARK, THE • 1972 • Clark James B. • USA
LITTLE ARTIST OF THE MARKET, THE • 1912 • *Tansey Robert* • USA
LITTLE ARTISTS, THE • 1911 • *Cricks & Martin* • UKN
LITTLE AUDRY RIDING HOOD • 1955 • Kneitel Seymour • ANS • USA
LITTLE AURORE'S TRAGEDY see **PETITE AURORE L'ENFANT MARTYRE, LA** • 1951
LITTLE AUTOGOMOBILE, THE • 1914 • *Meredyth Bess* • USA
LITTLE AVENGER, THE • 1911 • *Reliance* • USA
LITTLE BALL, THE see **KULICKA** • 1963
LITTLE BALLERINA, THE • 1947 • Gilbert Lewis* • UKN
LITTLE BAND OF GOLD, THE • 1915 • *Sheerer Will* • USA
LITTLE BANTAMWEIGHT • 1938 • Ising Rudolf • ANS • USA
LITTLE BEAD FISH, THE • 1968 • Tyrlova Hermina • ANM • CZC
LITTLE BEAN OF LA MANCHA see **GARBANCITO DE LA MANCHA** • 1946
LITTLE BEAR AND HE WHO LIVES IN THE WATER, THE • 1969 • ANS • USS
LITTLE BEAR'S JOURNEY • 1966 • Strautman Rasa • ANS • USS
LITTLE BEAU PEPE • 1952 • Jones Charles M. • ANS • USA
LITTLE BEAU PORKY • 1936 • Tashlin Frank • ANS • USA
LITTLE BELL • 1964 • Hsieh Tien • CHN
LITTLE BET, A • 1920 • Mannering Cecil • UKN
LITTLE BIG CHILD see **MISTAWASSIS** • 1977
LITTLE BIG HOCKEY PLAYER see **MALY VELKY HOKEJISTA** • 1982
LITTLE BIG HORN • 1951 • Warren Charles Marquis • USA • FIGHTING SEVENTH, THE (UKN)
LITTLE BIG MAN • 1970 • Penn Arthur • USA
LITTLE BIG SHOT • 1935 • Curtiz Michael • USA
LITTLE BIG SHOT • 1952 • Raymond Jack • UKN
LITTLE BILLIE AND THE BELLOWS • 1913 • Wilson Frank? • UKN
LITTLE BILLY'S CITY COUSIN • 1914 • Thornby Robert T. • USA
LITTLE BILLY'S SCHOOL DAYS • 1916 • *L-Ko* • SHT • USA
LITTLE BILLY'S STRATEGY • 1914 • Thornby Robert T. • USA
LITTLE BILLY'S TRIUMPHS • 1914 • Thornby Robert T. • USA
LITTLE BIRD OF HAPPINESS, THE • 1989 • Derakhshandeh Pooran • IRN
LITTLE BIRD TOLD ME, A • 1934 • Gillett Burt, Tyer James • ANS • USA
LITTLE BIRDIE see **MADARKAK** • 1971
LITTLE BIRDS, ORPHANS AND FOOLS see **VTACKOVIA, SIROTY A BLAZNI** • 1969
LITTLE BIT OF BROADWAY, A see **BRIGHT LIGHTS** • 1925
LITTLE BIT OF FLUFF, A • 1919 • Foss Kenelm • UKN
LITTLE BIT OF FLUFF, A • 1928 • Robbins Jess, Dryden Wheeler • UKN • SKIRTS (USA)
LITTLE BIT OF FLUFF, A • 1935 • Rogers Maclean • UKN
LITTLE BIT OF HEAVEN • 1916 • *Tress Henry* • SHT • UKN
LITTLE BIT OF HEAVEN see **BIT OF HEAVEN, A** • 1928
LITTLE BIT OF HEAVEN, A • 1940 • Marton Andrew • USA
LITTLE BIT OF SUGAR FOR THE BIRDS, A • 1906 • Jeapes Harold • UKN • ADVENTURES OF MAUD, THE

LITTLE BLABBERMOUSE • 1940 • Freleng Friz • ANS • USA
LITTLE BLACK BOX, THE • 1912 • *Essanay* • USA
LITTLE BLACK POM, THE • 1911 • Fitzhamon Lewin? • UKN
LITTLE BLACK SAMBO • 1935 • *Iwerks Ub (P)* • ANS • USA
LITTLE BLACK SAMBO • 1944 • Pal George • ANM • USA
LITTLE BLACK SAMBO, A • 1957-59 • Kawamoto Kihachiro • ANS • JPN
LITTLE BLACK SAMBO HUNTS THE TIGER see **CHIBIKURO SAMBO NO TORA TAIJI** • 1957
LITTLE BLOND LADY, THE • 1914 • *Leonard Robert* • USA • DECISION, THE
LITTLE BLONDE IN BLACK • 1915 • Leonard Robert Z. • USA
LITTLE BLUE AND LITTLE YELLOW • Hilberman David • ANS • USA
LITTLE BLUE BLACKBIRD • 1938 • Lenihan Patrick • ANS • USA
LITTLE BLUE CAP, THE • 1910 • Fitzhamon Lewin • UKN
LITTLE BO BOPPED • 1958 • Hanna William, Barbera Joseph • ANS • USA
LITTLE BO-PEEP • 1917 • Smith Noel, Smith Dick • SHT • USA
LITTLE BOBBY • 1915 • Stevens Will • USA
LITTLE BOBES see **MALY BOBES** • 1961
LITTLE BOO PEEP • 1953 • Kneitel Seymour • ANS • USA
LITTLE BOOTBLACK, A • 1916 • Batley Ethyle • UKN
LITTLE BOSS, THE • 1919 • Smith David • USA
LITTLE BOSS, THE • 1927 • *Mix Ruth* • USA
LITTLE BOY • 1910 • *Selig* • USA
LITTLE BOY AND THE CHARCOAL, THE • Munteanu Stefan • ANM • BUL
LITTLE BOY BLUE • 1912 • *Lubin* • USA
LITTLE BOY BLUE • 1912 • *Powers* • USA
LITTLE BOY BLUE • 1916 • Julian Rupert • USA
LITTLE BOY BLUE • 1933 • *Terry Paul/ Moser Frank (P)* • ANS • USA
LITTLE BOY BLUE • 1936 • *Iwerks Ub (P)* • ANS • USA
LITTLE BOY BLUE • 1963 • *Murray K. Gordon* • MXC
LITTLE BOY BOO • 1954 • McKimson Robert • ANS • USA
LITTLE BOY BOUNTIFUL • 1914 • Buckland Warwick? • UKN
LITTLE BOY CALLED "TAPS", A • 1904 • *Gaumont* • UKN
LITTLE BOY CALLED TAPS, A • 1909 • *Warwick Trading Co* • UKN
LITTLE BOY DOESN'T WASH, THE • 1955 • Sturlis Edward • ANM • PLN
LITTLE BOY LOST • 1953 • Seaton George • USA
LITTLE BOY LOST • 1978 • Bourke Terry • ASL
LITTLE BOY LOST see **BUBCHEN** • 1968
LITTLE BOY SCOUT, THE • 1917 • Grandon Francis J. • USA
LITTLE BOY THAT ONCE WAS HE, THE • 1915 • *West Charles* • USA
LITTLE BOY THAT SANTA CLAUS FORGOT, THE • 1938 • Simpson Harold • UKN
LITTLE BOY WITH A BIG HORN • 1953 • Cannon Robert • ANS • USA
LITTLE BOYS • 1987 • Kokkonen Ere • FNL
LITTLE BOYS NEXT DOOR, THE • 1911 • Stow Percy • UKN
LITTLE BRAVE HEART • 1952 • ANS • USS
LITTLE BREADWINNER, THE • 1916 • Noy Wilfred • UKN
LITTLE BREECHES • 1914 • *Lubin* • USA
LITTLE BRICKS see **KIRPITCHIKI** • 1925
LITTLE BRIDE OF HEAVEN, THE • 1912 • *Fuller Mary* • USA
LITTLE BROADCAST, THE • 1933 • *Paramount* • SHT • USA
LITTLE BROTHER • 1913 • *Russell William* • USA
LITTLE BROTHER see **BRATISHKA** • 1926
LITTLE BROTHER, THE • 1917 • Miller Charles • USA
LITTLE BROTHER OF GOD • 1922 • Thornton F. Martin • UKN
LITTLE BROTHER OF THE RICH, A • 1915 • Bosworth Hobart, Turner Otis • USA
LITTLE BROTHER OF THE RICH, A • 1919 • Reynolds Lynn • USA
LITTLE BROTHER RAT • 1939 • Jones Charles M. • ANS • USA
LITTLE BROWN CALF, THE • 1911 • *Powers* • USA
LITTLE BROWN HEN • 1916 • *Parsons William* • SHT • USA
LITTLE BROWN JUG • 1948 • Kneitel Seymour • ANS • USA
LITTLE BROWN MOLE, THE • 1916 • Ashley Charles E. • SHT • USA
LITTLE BROWNIE'S BRAVERY • 1916 • Elfelt Clifford S. • SHT • USA
LITTLE BUCK CHEEZER • 1937 • Ising Rudolf • ANS • USA
LITTLE BUCKAROO • 1938 • *Mintz Charles (P)* • ANS • USA
LITTLE BUCKAROO, THE • 1928 • King Louis • USA
LITTLE BUGLER, THE • 1914 • Thornby Robert T. • USA
LITTLE BULL, THE see **VAQUILLA, LA** • 1985
LITTLE BUNCH, THE (USA) see **PETITE BANDE, LA** • 1983
LITTLE BURGLAR, THE • 1911 • *Nestor* • USA
LITTLE BURGUNDY • 1968 • Klein Bonnie • CND • PETITE BOURGOGNE, LA
LITTLE BUSTER • 1913 • *Golden Sidney* • USA
LITTLE BUT TOUGH see **KICSI, DE NAGYON EROS** • 1989
LITTLE, BUT VERY STRONG see **KICSI, DE NAGYON EROS** • 1989
LITTLE CAESAR • 1931 • LeRoy Mervyn • USA
LITTLE CAESARIO • 1941 • Allen Robert • ANS • USA
LITTLE CANADIAN, THE • 1954 • Turner Melburn E. • CND
LITTLE CAPTAIN, THE • 1914 • Johnson Tefft • USA
LITTLE CAPTAIN OF THE SCOUTS, THE • 1915 • *De Carlton Grace* • USA
LITTLE CAR, THE see **WIELKA, WIELKA I NAJWIEKSZA** • 1962
LITTLE CATAMOUNT, THE • 1915 • Powell Paul • USA
LITTLE CHAOS, THE see **KLEINE CHAOS, DAS** • 1967
LITTLE CHAPERONE, THE • 1911 • *Powers* • USA
LITTLE CHAUFFEUR, THE see **LILLE CHAUFFOR, DEN** • 1914
LITTLE CHEEZER • 1936 • *Harman Hugh/ Ising Rudolf (P)* • ASS • USA
LITTLE CHEEZER • 1936 • Ising Rudolf • ANS • USA
LITTLE CHEVALIER, THE • 1917 • Crosland Alan • USA
LITTLE CHILD, A • 1911 • *Walthall Henry B.* • USA
LITTLE CHILD SHALL LEAD THEM, A • 1913 • Parker Lem B. • USA
LITTLE CHILD SHALL LEAD THEM, A • 1914 • Batley Ethyle • UKN
LITTLE CHILD SHALL LEAD THEM, A • 1919 • Phillips Bertram • UKN
LITTLE CHILD SHALL LEAD THEM, A see **WHO ARE MY PARENTS?** • 1922
LITTLE CHILD'S LETTER, A • 1910 • *Walturdaw* • UKN
LITTLE CHIMNEY BOY, THE see **KOMINIARCZYK** • 1960
LITTLE CHIMNEY SWEEP, THE see **KLEINE SCHORNSTEINFEGER, DAS** • 1935
LITTLE CHRONICLE, A see **MALA KRONIKA** • 1962
LITTLE CHRYSANTHEMUM • 1915 • *Beauty* • USA
LITTLE CHURCH AROUND THE CORNER • 1923 • Seiter William A. • USA
LITTLE CHURCH AROUND THE CORNER, THE • 1912 • *Princess* • USA
LITTLE CHURCH AROUND THE CORNER, THE • 1916 • Hopper E. Mason? • USA
LITTLE CIGARS • 1973 • Christenberry Chris • USA
LITTLE CIRCUS, THE see **CIRCO MAS PEQUENO DEL MUNDO, EL** • 1963
LITTLE CIRCUS RIDER, THE • 1911 • *Selig* • USA
LITTLE CITY, THE • 1960 • Sremec Rudolf • DOC • YGS
LITTLE CLAYTON FARMFRONT WONDER • 1943 • *O'Brien Joseph/ Mead Thomas (P)* • SHT • USA
LITTLE CLOWN, THE • 1921 • Heffron Thomas N. • USA
LITTLE CLOWN, THE PUP AND THE MOON, THE see **PAJACYK, PIKUS I KSIEZYC** • 1960
LITTLE COCK'S HALFPENNY, THE see **KISKAKAS GYEMANT FELKRAJCARJA, A** • 1950
LITTLE COLONEL, THE • 1935 • Butler David • USA
LITTLE COMRADE • 1919 • Withey Chet • USA
LITTLE CONFEDERATE, A • 1910 • *Powers* • USA
LITTLE CONJURER, THE • 1906 • *Walturdaw* • UKN
LITTLE CONVICT, THE • 1979 • Gross Yoram • ANM • ASL
LITTLE CORPORAL, THE • Negroni Baldassare • ITL
LITTLE CORPORAL, THE see **FIGLIO DI MADAME SANS-GENE, IL** • 1922
LITTLE COUNTRY MOUSE, THE • 1914 • Crisp Donald • USA
LITTLE COWBOY, THE see **KUCUK KOVBOY** • 1974
LITTLE COXSWAIN OF THE VARSITY EIGHT, THE • 1908 • Porter Edwin S. • USA
LITTLE CRIPPLE, THE • 1911 • *Kalem* • USA
LITTLE CUPIDS, THE • 1915 • Franklin Sidney A., Franklin Chester M. • USA
LITTLE CUTUP, THE • 1949 • Sparber I. • ANS • USA
LITTLE DADDY • 1931 • McGowan Robert • SHT • USA
LITTLE DAMOZEL, THE • 1916 • Noy Wilfred • UKN
LITTLE DAMOZEL, THE • 1933 • Wilcox Herbert • UKN
LITTLE DARLING, THE • 1909 • Griffith D. W. • USA
LITTLE DARLINGS • 1980 • Maxwell Ronald F. • USA
LITTLE DARLINGS • 1981 • Clark Jim* • USA
LITTLE DARLINGS, THE • 1914 • Cooper Toby? • UKN
LITTLE DASH, THE • 1972 • *Ouzounov Rashko (P)* • BUL
LITTLE DAUGHTER, THE see **CORECZKA** • 1965
LITTLE DAUGHTER'S LETTER, THE • 1911 • Bouwmeester Theo • UKN
LITTLE DEARS, THE • 1920 • Seiter William A. • SHT • USA
LITTLE DECEIVER, THE • 1915 • *Mayo Edna* • USA
LITTLE DELICATESSEN STORE, THE • 1912 • *Wadsworth William* • USA
LITTLE DETECTIVE, THE • 1908 • *Vitagraph* • USA
LITTLE DETECTIVE, THE • 1915 • *Lubin* • USA
LITTLE DETECTIVE, THE • 1915 • Fahrney Milton • *Cub* • USA
LITTLE DEVIL, A see **PETIT DIABLE, UN** • 1896
LITTLE DEVIL, THE see **PICCOLO DIAVOLO, IL** • 1988
LITTLE DEVIL-MAY-CARE see **DIABLE AU COEUR, LE** • 1927
LITTLE DICK THE MIGHTY MIDGET see **NANO E LA STREGA, IL** • 1975
LITTLE DICK'S FIRST ADVENTURE see **ASH CAN OR LITTLE DICK'S FIRST ADVENTURE** • 1915
LITTLE DICK'S FIRST CASE • 1915 • Franklin Sidney A., Franklin Chester M. • USA
LITTLE DIPLOMAT, THE • 1919 • Paton Stuart • USA
LITTLE DOCTOR, THE see **LITTLE DOCTOR AND THE SICK KITTEN, THE** • 1901
LITTLE DOCTOR AND THE SICK KITTEN, THE • 1901 • Smith G. A. • UKN • LITTLE DOCTOR, THE ○ SICK KITTEN, THE
LITTLE DOCTOR OF THE FOOTHILLS, THE • 1910 • *Essanay* • USA
LITTLE DOG FOR ROGER • 1967 • Le Grice Malcolm • UKN
LITTLE DOGGEREL, A see **CUNNING CANINE, A** • 1913
LITTLE DOLL see **LUTKICA** • 1961
LITTLE DOLL, THE • 1973 • *Cartoon Film* • ANS • USA
LITTLE DOLL'S DRESSMAKER, THE • 1915 • North Wilfred • USA
LITTLE DOLLY DAYDREAM • 1925 • Butler Alexander • UKN
LITTLE DOLLY DAYDREAM • 1978 • Mitchell Oswald • UKN
LITTLE DOOR INTO THE WORLD, THE • 1923 • Dewhurst George • UKN • EVIL THAT MEN DO, THE
LITTLE DOROTHY • 1911 • *Powers* • USA
LITTLE DORRIT • 1913 • Kirkwood James • USA
LITTLE DORRIT • 1920 • Morgan Sidney • UKN
LITTLE DORRIT • 1924 • Sandberg Anders W. • DNM
LITTLE DORRIT • 1987 • Edzard Christine • UKN
LITTLE DOVE'S ROMANCE • 1911 • Ince Thomas H. • USA
LITTLE DRAGONS, THE • 1980 • Hanson Curtis • USA • DRAGONS
LITTLE DRAMAS see **MALE DRAMATY** • 1960
LITTLE DRAMAS OF EVERYDAY LIFE • 1926 • Elliott William J. • SER • UKN
LITTLE DRUDGE, THE • 1911 • *Essanay* • USA
LITTLE DRUMMER GIRL, THE • 1985 • Hill George Roy • USA
LITTLE DUCHESS, THE • 1917 • Knoles Harley • USA • JERRY FOR SHORT
LITTLE DUTCH GIRL, THE • 1915 • Chautard Emile • USA
LITTLE DUTCH MILL • 1934 • Fleischer Dave • ANS • USA
LITTLE DUTCH PLATE • 1935 • Freleng Friz • ANS • USA
LITTLE EASTER FAIRY, THE • 1908 • *Lubin* • SHT • USA
LITTLE EGYPT • 1951 • De Cordova Frederick • USA • CHICAGO MASQUERADE (UKN)
LITTLE EGYPT MALONE • 1915 • Christie Al • USA
LITTLE ELSIE • 1913 • Haldane Bert? • UKN
LITTLE EMILY • 1911 • Powell Frank • UKN
LITTLE ENCHANTRESS, THE • 1913 • *Majestic* • USA
LITTLE ESCAPES see **PETITES FUGUES, LES** • 1978
LITTLE EVA ASCENDS • 1922 • Baker George D. • USA • ON TOUR
LITTLE EVA EGERTON see **LITTLE EVE EDGARTON** • 1916
LITTLE EVE EDGARTON • 1916 • Leonard Robert Z. • USA • LITTLE EVA EGERTON
LITTLE FAMILY AFFAIR, A • 1912 • *Johnson Arthur* • USA
LITTLE FAT RASCAL, THE • 1917 • Moore Vin • SHT • USA
LITTLE FATHER, THE • 1909 • Brooke Van Dyke • USA
LITTLE FAUSS AND BIG HALSY • 1970 • Furie Sidney J. • USA
LITTLE FELLA • 1932 • McGann William • UKN
LITTLE FELLER • 1982 • Eggleston Colin • MTV • ASL
LITTLE FELLOW FROM GAMBO, THE • 1970 • Biggs Julian • CND
LITTLE FIDDLER, THE • 1910 • *August Edwin* • USA
LITTLE FIRE CHIEF, A • 1910 • *Thanhouser* • USA
LITTLE FIREBRAND, THE • 1927 • Hutchison Charles • USA
LITTLE FLOWER see **XIAOHUA** • 1979
LITTLE FLOWER GIRL, THE • 1911 • *Solax* • USA
LITTLE FLOWER GIRL, THE see **FIGHTING CURATE, THE** • 1908
LITTLE FLOWER GIRL AND THE FIGHTING PARSON, THE • 1908 • *Tyler Walter* • UKN
LITTLE FLOWER GIRL'S CHRISTMAS, THE • 1909 • Fitzhamon Lewin • UKN
LITTLE FLYING HORSE, THE see **CABALLITO VOLADOR, EL** • 1982
LITTLE FOX • 1920 • *Lukas Paul* • HNG
LITTLE FOXES, THE • 1941 • Wyler William • USA
LITTLE 'FRAID LADY, THE • 1920 • Adolfi John G. • USA
LITTLE FRAUD, THE • 1916 • Henderson Lucius • SHT • USA
LITTLE FRENCH GIRL, THE • 1925 • Brenon Herbert • USA
LITTLE FRIDOLF AND I see **LILLE FRIDOLF OCH JAG** • 1956
LITTLE FRIDOLF BECOMES A GRANDFATHER see **LILLE FRIDOLF BLIR MORFAR** • 1957
LITTLE FRIEND • 1934 • Viertel Berthold • UKN
LITTLE FRIEND see **DRUZHOK** • 1957
LITTLE FRIKK • Caprino Ivo • ANM • NRW
LITTLE FUGITIVE • 1953 • Ashley Ray, Engel Morris, Orkin Ruth • USA
LITTLE GAME, A • 1971 • Wendkos Paul • TVM • USA
LITTLE GENERAL, THE • 1912 • Evans Fred • UKN
LITTLE GERMAN BAND • 1904 • Porter Edwin S. • USA
LITTLE GIANT, THE • 1926 • Nigh William • USA
LITTLE GIANT, THE • 1933 • Del Ruth Roy • USA
LITTLE GIANT, THE • 1946 • Seiter William A. • USA • ON THE CARPET (UKN)
LITTLE GIRAFFE, THE • 1960 • Badzian Teresa • ANM • PLN
LITTLE GIRL • 1911 • *Powers* • USA
LITTLE GIRL, THE see **O DEVCICU** • 1918
LITTLE GIRL, THE see **MALKATA** • 1959
LITTLE GIRL AND THE OAK, THE see **DJEVOJCICA I HRAST** • 1954
LITTLE GIRL, BIG TEASE • 1975 • Mitrotti Roberto • USA
LITTLE GIRL BY THE LAGOON • 1990 • Zhekan Ali • IRN
LITTLE GIRL, DON'T SAY NO! see **DEVCATKO, NERIKEJ NE!** • 1932
LITTLE GIRL IN A BIG CITY • 1915 • King Burton L. • USA
LITTLE GIRL IN BLUE VELVET, THE see **PETITE FILLE EN VELOURS BLEU, LA** • 1978
LITTLE GIRL IN THE ATTIC, THE • 1915 • Lloyd Frank • USA
LITTLE GIRL LOST • 1988 • Miller Sharron • TVM • USA
LITTLE GIRL NEXT DOOR, THE • 1912 • *Thanhouser* • USA
LITTLE GIRL NEXT DOOR, THE • 1912 • Dawley J. Searle • *Edison* • USA
LITTLE GIRL NEXT DOOR, THE • 1916 • *Greenleaf Charles* • USA
LITTLE GIRL NEXT DOOR, THE • 1923 • Van Dyke W. S. • USA • YOU ARE IN DANGER
LITTLE GIRL SHALL LEAD THEM, A • 1913 • Butler Alexander? • UKN
LITTLE GIRL THAT HE FORGOT, THE • 1914 • *Poynter Beulah* • USA
LITTLE GIRL, THE DOG AND THE SEAL, THE • Hellbom Olle • SWD
LITTLE GIRL WHO DID NOT BELIEVE IN SANTA CLAUS, A • 1949 • *Riddick William Marion* • SHT • USA
LITTLE GIRL WHO DIDN'T BELIEVE IN SANTA CLAUS, THE • 1907 • Porter Edwin S. • USA
LITTLE GIRL WHO LIVES DOWN THE LANE, THE • 1977 • Gessner Nicolas • USA, CND, FRN • PETIT FILLE AU BOUT DU CHEMIN, LA (FRN)
LITTLE GIRLS • 1966 • Wolmark Gilbert • FRN
LITTLE GIRLS BLUE • 1978 • Williams Joanna • USA
LITTLE GIRLS LOST • 1983 • Roter Ted • USA
LITTLE GLORIA.. HAPPY AT LAST • 1982 • Hussein Waris • TVM • USA
LITTLE GOAT, THE see **KOZIOTOECZEK** • 1953
LITTLE GOD, THE • 1914 • Reed Langford • UKN
LITTLE GODFATHER FROM HONGKONG, THE • *Liang Bruce* • HKG
LITTLE GOLD BIRD, THE see **ZLATE PTACE** • 1932
LITTLE GOLD KEY, THE see **ZLATY KLICEK** • 1922
LITTLE GOLD MINE, A • 1912 • Wilson Frank? • UKN
LITTLE GOLDEN KEY, THE see **ZOLOTOI KLYUCHIK** • 1939
LITTLE GOLDFISH, THE • 1939 • Ising Rudolf • ANS • USA
LITTLE GRAINS OF LOVE see **LIQUID LOVE** • 1913
LITTLE GRAINS OF RICE • 1916 • *Gayety* • USA
LITTLE GRANDMA CHARLESTON see **ABUELITA CHARLESTON** • 1961
LITTLE GRAVEL VOICE • 1942 • Ising Rudolf • ANS • USA
LITTLE GRAY HOME, THE • 1914 • *Myers Harry* • USA
LITTLE GRAY LADY, THE • 1914 • Powers Francis • USA
LITTLE GRAY MOUSE, THE • 1916 • Kelley J. Winthrop • SHT • USA
LITTLE GREY HEN, THE see **POULETTE GRISE, LA** • 1947
LITTLE GREY MOUSE, THE • 1920 • Hogan James P. • USA
LITTLE GREY NECK • 1951 • *Sovexport Film* • ANS • USS
LITTLE GREY THING see **SIVOUSHKO** • 1962
LITTLE GUARDIAN ANGEL, THE see **CAREFUL LITTLE ANGEL, THE** • 1956
LITTLE GUY, THE • 1957 • Corman Roger • USA
LITTLE GYPSY, THE • 1915 • Apfel Oscar • USA
LITTLE HAEWELMANN • Schulz Kurt Herbert • ANM • GDR

LITTLE HANDS • 1912 • *Eclair* • USA
LITTLE HARE AND THE WELL, THE • Hempel Johannes, Rarisch Ina • ANM • GDR
LITTLE HE AND SHE • 1914 • *Essanay* • USA
LITTLE HERMAN • 1915 • *Falstaff* • USA
LITTLE HERO, A • 1908 • *Walturdaw* • UKN
LITTLE HERO, A • 1913 • Campbell Colin • *Selig* • USA
LITTLE HERO, A • 1913 • Nicholls George, Sennett Mack (Spv) • *Keystone* • USA
LITTLE HERO, THE • 1913 • *Lubin* • USA
LITTLE HERO, THE • 1915 • Fahrney Milton • USA
LITTLE HERO OF HOLLAND, THE • 1910 • *Thanhouser* • USA
LITTLE HERO OF THE SHAOLIN TEMPLE, THE • *Cheng-Taid Syh* • HKG
LITTLE HEROINE, THE • 1910 • *Powers* • USA
LITTLE HEROINE, THE • 1916 • *Supreme* • USA
LITTLE HIAWATHA • 1937 • Hand David • ANS • USA
LITTLE HOBO, THE • 1914 • Eagle Oscar • USA
LITTLE HOME IN THE WEST, THE • 1915 • Watts Tom • UKN
LITTLE HORSE, THE • Troyanova I. • USS
LITTLE HOUR OF PETER WELLS, THE • 1920 • Doxat-Pratt B. E. • UKN
LITTLE HOUSE, THE • 1952 • Jackson Wilfred • ANS • USA
LITTLE HOUSE: BLESS ALL THE DEAR CHILDREN • 1984 • French Victor • TVM • USA
LITTLE HOUSE IN THE VALLEY, THE • 1914 • Ricketts Thomas • USA
LITTLE HOUSE ON THE PRAIRIE, THE • 1974 • Landon Michael • TVM • USA
LITTLE HOUSE ON THE PRAIRIE: LOOK BACK TO YESTERDAY • 1983 • French Victor • TVM • USA
LITTLE HOUSE; THE LAST FAREWELL • 1984 • Landon Michael • TVM • USA • LAST FAREWELL, THE
LITTLE HOUSEKEEPER, THE • 1910 • Fitzhamon Lewin • UKN
LITTLE HUMPBACKED HORSE, THE • 1939 • Rou Aleksandr • USS
LITTLE HUMPBACKED HORSE, THE see **KONEK-GORBUNOK** • 1947
LITTLE HUMPBACKED HORSE, THE (USA) see **SKAZKA O KONKE-GORBUNKE** • 1961
LITTLE HUNCHBACK, THE • 1913 • Blache Alice • USA
LITTLE HUT, THE • 1957 • Robson Mark • USA
LITTLE IDA see **LITEN IDA** • 1981
LITTLE INCIDENT, THE • 1975 • Gogoberidze Lana • USS
LITTLE INDIAN MARTYR, THE • 1912 • *Selig* • USA
LITTLE "INJIN" • 1911 • *Selig* • USA
LITTLE INTRUDER, THE • 1919 • Apfel Oscar • USA
LITTLE IODINE • 1946 • Le Borg Reginald • USA
LITTLE IRISH GIRL, THE • 1926 • Del Ruth Roy • USA
LITTLE ISLAND • 1969 • Kuri Yoji • ANS • JPN
LITTLE ISLAND, THE • 1958 • Williams Richard • ANM • UKN
LITTLE ITALY • 1921 • Terwilliger George W. • USA
LITTLE JACK • 1914 • *Saunders Jackie* • USA
LITTLE JEWESS, THE • 1914 • *Mackey Edward* • USA
LITTLE JIM • 1909 • Coleby A. E. • UKN
LITTLE JIM: OR, THE COTTAGE WAS A THATCHED ONE • 1902 • Winslow Dicky • UKN
LITTLE JIMMY • 1917 • Moser Frank • ASS • USA
LITTLE JOE AND THE MARVELOUS LAMP see **PEPITO Y LA LAMPARA MARAVILLOSA** • 1971
LITTLE JOE, THE WRANGLER • 1942 • Collins Lewis D. • USA
LITTLE JOE'S DADDY • 1916 • *Puritan* • SHT • USA
LITTLE JOHN RUNNING AMOK • 1976 • Franssen Martin • NTH
LITTLE JOHNNY JET • 1953 • Avery Tex • ANS • USA
LITTLE JOHNNY JONES • 1923 • Rosson Arthur, Hines Johnny • USA
LITTLE JOHNNY JONES • 1929 • LeRoy Mervyn • USA
LITTLE JOURNEY, A • 1926 • Leonard Robert Z. • USA
LITTLE JULES VERNE, THE see **PETIT JULES VERNE, LE** • 1907
LITTLE JUNGLE BOY • 1970 • Brown Mende • ASL
LITTLE KAINTUCK • 1913 • Thornby Robert T. • USA
LITTLE KANGAROO, THE • 1967 • Badzian Teresa • ANM • PLN
LITTLE KATE • 1962 • Tyrlova Hermina • ANM • CZC
LITTLE KATE AND BIG WOLF see **O MALEJ KASI I DUZYM WILKU** • 1963
LITTLE KEEPER OF THE LIGHT, THE • 1912 • *Lawrence Adelaide* • USA
LITTLE KIDDIE MINE, THE • 1911 • *Solax* • USA
LITTLE KIDNAPPERS, THE (USA) see **KIDNAPPERS, THE** • 1953
LITTLE KING, THE • 1933-34 • Stallings George • ASS • USA
LITTLE KNIGHT, THE see **GARBANCITO DE LA MANCHA** • 1946
LITTLE KNIGHT, THE see **PAN WOLODYJOWSKI** • 1969
LITTLE KNOWLEDGE, A • 1913 • Buckland Warwick? • UKN
LITTLE LAD IN DIXIE, A • 1911 • *Vitagraph* • USA
LITTLE LADIES OF THE NIGHT • 1977 • Chomsky Marvin • TVM • USA
LITTLE LADY ACROSS THE WAY, THE • 1915 • Moore Matt • USA
LITTLE LADY EILEEN • 1916 • Dawley J. Searle • USA
LITTLE LADY LAFAYETTE • 1911 • Bouwmeester Theo?, Booth W. R.? • UKN
LITTLE LADY NEXT DOOR, THE • 1915 • Eason B. Reeves • USA
LITTLE LAMBKIN • 1940 • Fleischer Dave • ANS • USA
LITTLE LAMBY • 1937 • Fleischer Dave • ANS • USA
LITTLE LAME SOLDIER, THE • 1927 • Starevitch Ladislas • SHT • FRN
LITTLE LAURA AND BIG JOHN • 1974 • Moberly Luke, Woodburn Bob • USA
LITTLE LEADER, THE • 1911 • *Imp* • USA
LITTLE LEAGUE • 1959 • Regnier Michel • DCS • CND
LITTLE LIAR see **FETITA MINCINOASA** • 1953
LITTLE LIAR, THE • 1916 • Ingraham Lloyd • USA
LITTLE LIAR, THE • 1956 • *Marinescu Violeta* • RMN
LITTLE LIFE GUARD, THE • 1915 • *Radcliff Violet* • USA
LITTLE LILLIAN, TOE DANSEUSE • 1903 • Porter Edwin S. • USA • LITTLE MISS LILLIAN
LITTLE LILLIAN TURNS THE TIDE • 1914 • *Wade Baby Lillian* • USA
LITTLE LION HUNTER • 1939 • Jones Charles M. • ANS • USA
LITTLE LORD FAUNTLEROY • 1914 • Thornton F. Martin • UKN
LITTLE LORD FAUNTLEROY • 1921 • Green Alfred E., Pickford Jack • USA
LITTLE LORD FAUNTLEROY • 1936 • Cromwell John • USA
LITTLE LORD FAUTLEROY • 1980 • Gold Jack • TVM • UKN
LITTLE LOST SHEEP • 1939 • *Mintz Charles (P)* • ANS • USA
LITTLE LOST SISTER • 1917 • Green Alfred E. • USA
LITTLE LOUDER, PLEASE! • 1912 • *Missimer Howard* • USA
LITTLE LUCY LION • 1919 • *Strand* • SHT • USA
LITTLE LULU • 1946-48 • *Paramount* • ASS • USA
LITTLE LUMBERJACK, THE • 1915 • Myers Ray • USA
LITTLE MADCAP, THE • 1908 • *Essanay* • USA
LITTLE MADEMOISELLE, THE • 1915 • Eagle Oscar • USA
LITTLE MADONNA, A • 1914 • Davis Ulysses • USA
LITTLE MAGICIAN, THE • 1908 • *Pathe* • FRN
LITTLE MAGICIAN AND THE BAD MARK, THE see **KLEINE ZAUBERER UND DIE GROSSE FUNF, DER** • 1977
LITTLE MAIL CARRIER, THE • 1914 • Salter Harry • USA
LITTLE MAJOR, THE • 1911 • Porter Edwin S. • USA
LITTLE MALCOLM AND HIS STRUGGLE AGAINST THE EUNUCHS • 1974 • Cooper Stuart • UKN • LITTLE MALCOLM (USA)
LITTLE MALCOLM (USA) see **LITTLE MALCOLM AND HIS STRUGGLE AGAINST THE EUNUCHS** • 1974
LITTLE MAN see **MALI COVEK** • 1957
LITTLE MAN see **SHRAGA KATAN** • 1979
LITTLE MAN, THE (UKN) see **ANNI DIFFICILI** • 1948
LITTLE MAN, BIG CITY see **KIS EMBER, NAGY VAROS** • 1967
LITTLE MAN, WHAT NOW? • 1934 • Borzage Frank • USA
LITTLE MARIANNA'S TRIUMPH • 1917 • Stedman Marshall • SHT • USA
LITTLE MARIE • 1915 • Browning Tod • USA
LITTLE MARJA! see **MARJA PIENI!** • 1972
LITTLE MARTA RETURNS see **LILLA MARTA KOMMER TILLBAKA** • 1948
LITTLE MARY-FIX-IT • 1917 • Conway Jack • USA
LITTLE MARY SUNSHINE • 1916 • King Henry • USA
LITTLE MASCOT, THE • 1916 • *Early Baby* • SHT • USA
LITTLE MASHA AND THE SWANS • 1952 • ANS • USS
LITTLE MATCH GIRL, THE • 1914 • Nash Percy? • UKN
LITTLE MATCH GIRL, THE • 1919 • USS
LITTLE MATCH GIRL, THE • 1937 • *Mintz Charles (P)* • ANS • USA
LITTLE MATCH GIRL, THE • 1953 • *Omnibus Tv* • SHT • DNM
LITTLE MATCH GIRL, THE • 1968 • Watanabe Kuzohiko • ANS • JPN
LITTLE MATCH GIRL, THE • Constance Michael • UKN
LITTLE MATCH GIRL, THE • 1983 • Broodbent Wally, Hoeger Mark • USA
LITTLE MATCH GIRL, THE • 1987 • Lindsay-Hogg Michael • TVM • USA
LITTLE MATCH GIRL, THE see **PETITE MARCHANDE D'ALLUMETTES, LA** • 1928
LITTLE MATCH GIRL, THE (USA) see **LITTLE MATCH SELLER, THE** • 1902
LITTLE MATCH SELLER, THE • 1902 • Williamson James • UKN • LITTLE MATCH GIRL, THE (USA)
LITTLE MATCH SELLER, THE • 1912 • *Selig* • USA
LITTLE MATCHMAKERS, THE • 1915 • *Harris Mildred* • USA
LITTLE MATCHSELLER'S CHRISTMAS, THE • 1910 • *Urban-Eclipse* • FRN
LITTLE MAYORESS, THE • 1916 • Durrant Fred W. • UKN • MILL-OWNER'S DAUGHTER, THE
LITTLE MEENA'S ROMANCE • 1916 • Powell Paul • USA
LITTLE MEG AND I • 1914 • *Kerrigan J. Warren* • USA
LITTLE MEG AND THE WONDERFUL LIFE • 1906 • Fitzhamon Lewin • UKN
LITTLE MEG'S CHILDREN • 1921 • Wynne Bert • UKN
LITTLE MEN • 1934 • Rosen Phil • USA
LITTLE MEN • 1940 • McLeod Norman Z. • USA
LITTLE MERMAID, THE • 1984 • Iscove Robert • TVM • USA
LITTLE MERMAID, THE • 1989 • Musker John, Clements Ron • ANM • USA
LITTLE MERMAID, THE see **NINGYO HIME** • 1974
LITTLE MERMAID, THE see **MAL MORSKA VILA** • 1976
LITTLE MERMAID, THE see **RUSALOCHKA** • 1976
LITTLE MICKEY GROGAN • 1927 • Meehan James Leo • USA • MICKEY GROGAN, CONTRACTOR
LITTLE MICKEY THE MESMERIST • 1913 • Booth W. R.? • UKN
LITTLE MILLINER AND THE THIEF, THE • 1909 • Fitzhamon Lewin • UKN
LITTLE MINISTER, THE • 1913 • Young James • USA
LITTLE MINISTER, THE • 1915 • Nash Percy • UKN
LITTLE MINISTER, THE • 1921 • Stanlaws Penrhyn • USA
LITTLE MINISTER, THE • 1934 • Wallace Richard • USA
LITTLE MISCHIEF • 1914 • *Badgley Helen* • USA
LITTLE MISS BIG • 1946 • Kenton Erle C. • USA • BAXTER MILLIONS, THE (UKN)
LITTLE MISS BOUNTIFUL • 1914 • Bellows Walter Clark • USA
LITTLE MISS BROADWAY • 1938 • Cummings Irving • USA
LITTLE MISS BROADWAY • 1947 • Dreifuss Arthur • USA
LITTLE MISS BROWN • 1915 • Young James • USA
LITTLE MISS DEMURE • 1912 • Rains Fred • UKN
LITTLE MISS DEPUTY • 1919 • *Guinan Texas* • SHT • USA
LITTLE MISS DEVIL • 1952 • Ragaky Mojammed • EGY
LITTLE MISS FIXER • 1917 • *Rhodes Billie* • USA
LITTLE MISS FORTUNE • 1917 • Levering Joseph • USA
LITTLE MISS GROWN-UP • 1918 • MacDonald Sherwood • USA
LITTLE MISS HAPPINESS • 1916 • Adolfi John G. • USA
LITTLE MISS HAWKSHAW • 1921 • Harbaugh Carl • USA
LITTLE MISS HOOVER • 1918 • Robertson John S. • USA • GOLDEN BIRD, THE
LITTLE MISS INNOCENCE see **TEENAGE INNOCENCE**
LITTLE MISS INNOCENT see **TEENAGE INNOCENCE**
LITTLE MISS JAZZ • 1920 • Roach Hal • SHT • USA
LITTLE MISS LILLIAN see **LITTLE LILLIAN, TOE DANSEUSE** • 1903
LITTLE MISS LONDON • 1929 • Hughes Harry • UKN
LITTLE MISS MAKE-BELIEVE • 1914 • *Howley Irene* • USA
LITTLE MISS MARKER • 1934 • Hall Alexander • USA • GIRL IN PAWN, THE (UKN)
LITTLE MISS MARKER • 1980 • Bernstein Walter • USA
LITTLE MISS MOLLY (USA) see **MY IRISH MOLLY** • 1938
LITTLE MISS NO-ACCOUNT • 1918 • Earle William P. S. • USA
LITTLE MISS NOBDOY • 1923 • Noy Wilfred • UKN
LITTLE MISS NOBODY • 1917 • Millarde Harry • USA
LITTLE MISS NOBODY • 1933 • Daumery John • UKN
LITTLE MISS NOBODY • 1936 • Blystone John G. • USA • MATRON'S REPORT, THE
LITTLE MISS NUISANCE • 1915 • *Warner'S Features* • USA
LITTLE MISS OPTIMIST • 1917 • Thornby Robert T. • USA
LITTLE MISS PINKERTON • 1919 • *Strand* • SHT • USA
LITTLE MISS PINKERTON • 1943 • Glazer Herbert • SHT • USA
LITTLE MISS REBELLION • 1920 • Fawcett George • USA
LITTLE MISS ROUGHNECK • 1938 • Scotto Aubrey • USA • WONDER CHILD
LITTLE MISS SMILES • 1922 • Ford John • USA
LITTLE MISS SOMEBODY • 1937 • Tennyson Walter • UKN
LITTLE MISS SOMEBODY see **NOBODY'S KID** • 1921
LITTLE MISS THOROUGHBRED • 1938 • Farrow John • USA
LITTLE MISS TROUBLE AND FRIENDS • 1983 • Bond Trevor, Ward Terry • ANM • USA
LITTLE MISSIONARY, THE • 1917 • Baker Richard Foster • SHT • USA
LITTLE MR. FIXER • 1915 • Lloyd Frank • USA • BILLY'S CUPIDITY
LITTLE MR. JIM • 1946 • Zinnemann Fred • USA • ARMY BRAT
LITTLE MO • 1978 • Haller Daniel • TVM • USA
LITTLE MOCCASINS • 1917 • Wilson Millard K. • SHT • USA
LITTLE MOLE, THE • 1941 • Harman Hugh • ANS • USA
LITTLE MONDAY • 1965 • Kohanyi Julius • SHT • CND
LITTLE MONSTERS • 1989 • Greenberg Richard • USA
LITTLE MONTE CARLO, THE • 1916 • Horne James W. • SHT • USA
LITTLE MOOK see **GESCHICHTE VOM KLEINEN MUCK, DIE** • 1953
LITTLE MOON AND JUD MCGRAW see **GONE WITH THE WEST** • 1969
LITTLE MOONSHINER, THE • 1912 • *Nestor* • USA
LITTLE MORITZ CHASSE LES GRANDS FAUVES • 1912 • Machin Alfred • FRN
LITTLE MORITZ SOLDAT D'AFRIQUE • 1912 • Machin Alfred • FRN
LITTLE MOTHER • 1929 • McGowan Robert • SHT • USA
LITTLE MOTHER • 1972 • Metzger Radley H. • USA, YGS • DON'T CRY FOR ME LITTLE MOTHER ○ BLOOD QUEEN
LITTLE MOTHER see **KLEINE MUTTI** • 1934
LITTLE MOTHER see **BACHELOR MOTHER** • 1939
LITTLE MOTHER, THE • 1908 • Williamson James? • UKN
LITTLE MOTHER, THE • 1910 • *Kalem* • USA
LITTLE MOTHER, THE • 1911 • *Thanhouser* • USA
LITTLE MOTHER, THE • 1912 • Coleby A. E. • UKN
LITTLE MOTHER, THE • 1913 • *Stonehouse Ruth* • USA
LITTLE MOTHER, THE • 1913 • Batley Ethyle • UKN • CHILD MOTHER, THE
LITTLE MOTHER, THE • 1915 • *Wilkey Violet* • USA
LITTLE MOTHER, THE • 1915 • Buckland Warwick? • UKN
LITTLE MOTHER, THE • 1922 • Bramble A. V. • UKN
LITTLE MOTHER AT THE BABY SHOW, THE • 1910 • *Vitagraph* • USA
LITTLE MOTHER OF BLACK PINE TRAIL, THE • 1913 • *Eclair* • USA
LITTLE MOTHER WANTS A MAMMA, A • 1913 • *Imp* • USA
LITTLE MOTHERS (USA) see **MAMELE** • 1938
LITTLE MOTH'S BIG FLAME • 1938 • Marcus Sid • ANS • USA
LITTLE MUCK • 1938 • Hodatyev O. • USS
LITTLE MUCK'S TREASURE see **GESCHICHTE VOM KLEINEN MUCK, DIE** • 1953
LITTLE MURDERS • 1971 • Arkin Alan • USA
LITTLE MURMUR see **CHIISANA SASAYAKI** • 1966
LITTLE MUSIC • 1962 • Badzian Teresa • ANM • PLN
LITTLE MUSIC, A see **MUZYCZKA** • 1961
LITTLE MUSIC TEACHER, THE • 1912 • *Prior Herbert* • USA
LITTLE MUSKETEER, THE see **STING OF VICTORY, THE** • 1916
LITTLE NAPOLEON • 1933 • Brunel Adrian • UKN
LITTLE NAPOLEON see **LILLE NAPOLEON** • 1943
LITTLE NEGRO, THE see **MURZYNEK** • 1960
LITTLE NELL • 1906 • Gilbert Arthur • UKN
LITTLE NELL AND BURGLAR BILL • 1903 • Collins Alf • UKN
LITTLE NELL THE DRUNKARD'S CHILD • 1909 • *Empire Films* • UKN
LITTLE NELLIE KELLY • 1940 • Taurog Norman • USA
LITTLE NELL'S TOBACCO • 1910 • Ince Thomas H. • USA
LITTLE NEMO • 1909 • Blackton J. Stuart • SHT • USA
LITTLE NEMO • 1909 • McCay Winsor • ANS • USA
LITTLE NEZHA FIGHTS GREAT DRAGON KINGS • Elman Louis (Eng. Ver) • ANM • CHN
LITTLE NIGGER BOY, THE see **MURZYNEK** • 1960
LITTLE NIGHT MUSIC, A • 1977 • Prince Harold • USA, AUS, FRG
LITTLE NIKITA • 1988 • Benjamin Richard • USA
LITTLE NOBODY • 1936 • Fleischer Dave • ANS • USA
LITTLE NORSE PRINCE VALIANT see **TAIYO NO OJI: HORUSU NO DAIBOKEN** • 1968
LITTLE NUGGET, THE • 1912 • *Conway Jack* • USA
LITTLE NUNS, THE (USA) see **MONACHINE, LE** • 1963
LITTLE OF WHAT YOU FANCY, A • 1968 • Webb Robert • DOC • UKN
LITTLE OLD-FASHIONED WORLD see **PICCOLO MONDO ANTICO** • 1940
LITTLE OLD LONESOME LITTLE CIRCLE SOUND FILM, THE • ANS • USA
LITTLE OLD MEN OF THE WOODS, THE • 1910 • *Kalem* • USA
LITTLE OLD NEW YORK • 1911 • *Genung Edward* • USA
LITTLE OLD NEW YORK • 1923 • Olcott Sidney • USA
LITTLE OLD NEW YORK • 1940 • King Henry • USA
LITTLE OLD NEW YORK (UKN) see **LIGHTS OF OLD BROADWAY** • 1925
LITTLE ONE see **PUNCHI BABA** • 1968
LITTLE ONE, THE see **U-DELIWE** • 1975

LITTLE ONES, THE • 1965 • O'Connolly Jim • UKN
LITTLE ORBIT THE ASTRODOG • Image Jean • ANM • FRN
LITTLE ORBIT, THE ASTRODOG AND THE SCREECHERS FROM OUTER SPACE • 1977 • ANM • FRN
LITTLE ORGAN PLAYER OF SAN JUAN, THE • 1912 • Campbell Colin • USA
LITTLE ORGANIST, THE • 1912 • *Learn Bessie* • USA
LITTLE ORPHAN, THE • 1910 • Bouwmeester Theo? • UKN
LITTLE ORPHAN, THE • 1916 • Gorman John • USA
LITTLE ORPHAN, THE • 1917 • Conway Jack • USA
LITTLE ORPHAN, THE • 1948 • Hanna William, Barbera Joseph • ANS • USA
LITTLE ORPHAN AIREDALE • 1947 • Jones Charles M. • ANS • USA
LITTLE ORPHAN ANNIE • 1919 • Campbell Colin • USA
LITTLE ORPHAN ANNIE • 1932 • Robertson John S. • USA
LITTLE ORPHAN ANNIE • 1938 • Holmes Ben • USA
LITTLE ORPHAN OR ALL ROADS LEAD TO ROME, THE • 1909 • *Vitagraph* • USA
LITTLE ORPHANS, THE • 1915 • *Wilkey Violet* • USA
LITTLE ORVIE • 1940 • McCarey Ray • USA
LITTLE OUIJA WORK, A • 1918 • Baker Graham • SHT • USA
LITTLE OWL, THE see **UHUKA, A KIS BAGOLY** • 1969
LITTLE PAINTER AND THE MERMAID, THE see **PETIT PEINTRE ET LA SIRENE, LE** • 1958
LITTLE PAL • 1915 • Kirkwood James • USA
LITTLE PAL see **SAY IT WITH SONGS** • 1929
LITTLE PANCHO VANILLA • 1938 • Tashlin Frank • ANS • USA
LITTLE PAPA • 1935 • Meins Gus • SHT • USA
LITTLE PAPER PEOPLE • 1935 • Hoyland Margaret • UKN
LITTLE PARADE, THE (USA) see **PETITE PARADE, LA** • 1930
LITTLE PARTNER • 1916 • Worthington William • SHT • USA
LITTLE PATRIOT, A • 1918 • Bertram William • USA
LITTLE PEACEMAKER, THE • 1909 • *Essanay* • USA
LITTLE PEACEMAKER, THE • 1913 • *Nestor* • USA
LITTLE PEACEMAKER, THE see **TRAIT D'UNION, LE** • 1908
LITTLE PEOPLE • 1935 • Bucquet Harold S. • SHT • USA
LITTLE PEOPLE, THE • 1926 • Pearson George • UKN
LITTLE PEOPLE BURLESQUES • 1930 • Wills J. Elder, Grierson John, Harrison Jack • SER • UKN
LITTLE PEST, THE • 1931 • *Mintz Charles (P)* • ANS • USA
LITTLE PETE AND THE LOOKING GLASS • Wajzer Waclaw • ANS • PLN
LITTLE PETER'S DIARY see **DRUZBA PERE KVRZICE** • 1971
LITTLE PETER'S YARD see **PIKKU PIETARIN PIHA** • 1961
LITTLE PHANTASY, A see **LITTLE PHANTASY ON A 19TH CENTURY PAINTING, A** • 1946
LITTLE PHANTASY ON A 19TH CENTURY PAINTING, A • 1946 • McLaren Norman • ANS • CND • LITTLE PHANTASY, A ○ ISLE OF THE DEAD
LITTLE PICTURE PRODUCER, THE • 1914 • Thornton F. Martin, Rogers Edgar • UKN
LITTLE PIG, THE • 1960 • Wasilewski Zenon • ANM • PLN
LITTLE PIPPIN • 1915 • Huntley G. P. • UKN
LITTLE PIRATE, THE • 1913 • *Reliance* • USA
LITTLE PIRATE, THE • 1917 • Wilson Elsie Jane • USA
LITTLE PLACE OF ONE'S OWN, A see **LITET BO** • 1956
LITTLE POACHER, THE • 1912 • Haldane Bert? • UKN
LITTLE POACHER, THE • 1920 • Sandground Maurice • UKN
LITTLE POET, THE • 1912 • *Essanay* • USA
LITTLE POOL, THE • 1921 • Rosen Phil • USA
LITTLE PRAYER FOR RAIN, A see **VAGABOND LUCK** • 1919
LITTLE PREACHER, THE • 1910 • Melies Gaston • USA
LITTLE PRESENTS see **PIKKU PIETARIN PIHA** • 1961
LITTLE PRINCE, THE • 1973 • Donen Stanley • USA
LITTLE PRINCE, THE • 1979 • Vinton Will • ANS • USA
LITTLE PRINCE, THE see **KLEINE PRINZ, DER** • 1966
LITTLE PRINCE, THE see **MALENKI PRINTS** • 1968
LITTLE PRINCE AND THE EIGHT-HEADED DRAGON, THE (USA) see **WANPAKU OJI NO OROCHITAIJI** • 1963
LITTLE PRINCE: FOR THE LOVE OF ANIMALS, THE • 1983 • ANM
LITTLE PRINCESS, A • 1917 • Neilan Marshall, Hawks Howard (U/c) • USA
LITTLE PRINCESS, THE • 1939 • Lang Walter • USA
LITTLE PRISONER, THE see **HSIAO T'AO-FAN** • 1983
LITTLE PROBLEMS • 1951 • Donnelly Eddie • ANS • USA
LITTLE PROSPECTOR, THE • 1910 • *Essanay* • USA
LITTLE PROSPECTOR, THE • 1915 • *Anderson Broncho Billy* • USA
LITTLE PURITAN, THE • 1915 • *Parsons Smiling Bill* • USA
LITTLE QUACKER • 1950 • Hanna William, Barbera Joseph • ANS • USA
LITTLE QUAKERESS, THE • 1912 • *Majestic* • USA
LITTLE QUARTET, THE see **KWARTECIK** • 1966
LITTLE QUEEN, THE see **PETITE REINE, LA** • 1958
LITTLE RABBIT, THE see **ZAJACZEK** • 1964
LITTLE RAG DOLL, THE • 1909 • *Lubin* • USA
LITTLE RANCHER, THE • 1912 • *Bison* • USA
LITTLE RANGER, THE • 1938 • Douglas Gordon • SHT • USA
LITTLE RASCAL LOVES CRISS-CROSS see **BENGELCHEN LIEBT KREUZ UND QUER** • 1968
LITTLE RAVEN'S SWEETHEART • 1912 • *Pathe* • USA
LITTLE REBEL, THE • 1911 • Salter Harry • USA
LITTLE REBEL, THE • 1915 • Olcott Sidney • USA
LITTLE REBELS, THE (USA) see **CHIENS PERDUS SANS COLLIER** • 1955
LITTLE REBEL'S SACRIFICE, THE • 1917 • Ford Francis • SHT • USA
LITTLE RED DECIDES • 1918 • Conway Jack • USA
LITTLE RED DEVILS, THE see **KRASNYE DIAVOLIATA** • 1923
LITTLE RED DOVE see **PALOMBELLA ROSCA** • 1990
LITTLE RED HEN • 1955 • Rasinski Connie • ANS • USA
LITTLE RED HEN, THE • 1934 • *Iwerks Ub (P)* • ANS • USA
LITTLE RED MONKEY • 1953 • Hughes Ken • UKN • CASE OF THE RED MONKEY, THE (USA)
LITTLE RED RIDING HOOD • 1907 • *Pathe* • FRN
LITTLE RED RIDING HOOD • 1911 • *Essanay* • USA
LITTLE RED RIDING HOOD • 1911 • Coleby A. E. • UKN
LITTLE RED RIDING HOOD • 1911 • Tucker George Loane, Kirkwood James • *Majestic* • USA
LITTLE RED RIDING HOOD • 1917 • *Wholesome Film* • USA
LITTLE RED RIDING HOOD • 1917 • *Edison* • ANS • USA
LITTLE RED RIDING HOOD • 1921 • *Blanton Elma Osborn (P)* • SHT • USA
LITTLE RED RIDING HOOD • 1922 • *Selznick* • USA
LITTLE RED RIDING HOOD • 1922 • Disney Walt • ANS • USA
LITTLE RED RIDING HOOD • 1922 • Dyer Anson • ANS • UKN
LITTLE RED RIDING HOOD • 1925 • Goulding Alf • *Century* • SHT • USA
LITTLE RED RIDING HOOD • 1925 • Lantz Walter • *Standard* • ANS • USA
LITTLE RED RIDING HOOD • 1949 • *Meredith Burgess/ Macarthur Charles (P)* • SHT • USA
LITTLE RED RIDING HOOD • 1949 • *Wahmann Hand Puppets* • ANS • USA
LITTLE RED RIDING HOOD • 1954 • ANS • YGS
LITTLE RED RIDING HOOD • 1967 • Chambers Jack* • CND
LITTLE RED RIDING HOOD • 1983 • Clifford Graeme • MTV • USA
LITTLE RED RIDING HOOD • 1987 • Brooks Adam • USA • CANNON MOVIE TALES: RED RIDING HOOD ○ RED RIDING HOOD
LITTLE RED RIDING HOOD see **PUNAHILKKA** • 1968
LITTLE RED RIDING HOOD AND HER FRIENDS (USA) see **CAPERUCITA Y SUS TRE AMIGOS** • 1960
LITTLE RED RIDING HOOD AND HER THREE FRIENDS see **CAPERUCITA Y SUS TRE AMIGOS** • 1960
LITTLE RED RIDING HOOD AND THE MONSTERS (USA) see **CAPERUCITA Y PULGARCITO CONTRA LOS MONSTRUOS** • 1960
LITTLE RED RIDING HOOD AND THE TIME BOMB • 1968 • Henderickx Guido • SHT • BLG
LITTLE RED RIDING HOOD AND TOM THUMB VS. THE MONSTERS see **CAPERUCITA Y PULGARCITO CONTRA LOS MONSTRUOS** • 1960
LITTLE RED RIDING HOOD IN 2000 see **PIROSKA ES A FARKAS 2000-BEN** • 1987
LITTLE RED RIDING HOOD (USA) see **PETIT CHAPERON ROUGE, LE** • 1928
LITTLE RED RIDING HOOD (USA) see **CAPERUCITA ROJA, LA** • 1960
LITTLE RED RIDING HOOD: YEAR 2000 see **PIROSKA ES A FARKAS 2000-BEN** • 1987
LITTLE RED RIDING RABBIT • 1943 • Freleng Friz • ANS • USA
LITTLE RED RODENT HOOD • 1952 • Freleng Friz • ANS • USA
LITTLE RED SCHOOL MOUSE • 1949 • *Paramount* • ANS • USA
LITTLE RED SCHOOLHOUSE, THE • 1923 • Adolfi John G. • USA • GREATER LAW, THE (UKN)
LITTLE RED SCHOOLHOUSE, THE • 1936 • Lamont Charles • USA • SCHOOLBOY PENITENTIARY (UKN)
LITTLE RED WALKING HOOD • 1937 • Avery Tex • ANS • USA
LITTLE REFORMER • 1917 • Miller Charles • USA
LITTLE RING, THE see **PRSTYNEK** • 1944
LITTLE ROBINSON CORKSCREW • 1924 • Jones F. Richard • SHT • USA
LITTLE ROBINSON CRUSOE • 1924 • Cline Eddie • USA
LITTLE ROCKING CHAIR, THE • 1909 • *Warwick Trading Co* • UKN
LITTLE ROCQUEFORT • 1950-55 • *Terry Paul (P)* • ASS • USA
LITTLE ROMANCE, A • 1979 • Hill George Roy • USA, FRN
LITTLE ROOM, THE • Khodatayeva O. • USS
LITTLE ROVER • 1935 • *Mintz Charles (P)* • ANS • USA
LITTLE ROWDY, THE • 1919 • Beaumont Harry • USA
LITTLE RUBE, THE • 1927 • Taurog Norman • SHT • USA
LITTLE RUNAWAY • 1952 • Hanna William, Barbera Joseph • ANS • USA
LITTLE RUNAWAY, THE • 1918 • Earle William P. S. • USA
LITTLE RUNAWAY, THE see **CHIISANA TOBOSHA** • 1967
LITTLE RUNAWAY, THE see **MALENKI BEGLYETS** • 1967
LITTLE RUNAWAYS, THE • 1915 • Morrisey Edward • USA
LITTLE RURAL RIDING HOOD • 1949 • Avery Tex • ANS • USA
LITTLE SAINT see **LILLA HELGONET** • 1944
LITTLE SALESLADY, THE • 1915 • Taylor Edward C. • USA
LITTLE SAMARITAN, THE • 1916 • Beaumont Harry • SHT • USA
LITTLE SAMARITAN, THE • 1917 • Levering Joseph • USA
LITTLE SAVAGE, THE • 1929 • King Louis • USA
LITTLE SAVAGE, THE • 1959 • Haskin Byron • USA
LITTLE SAW, THE see **EDGAR'S LITTLE SAW** • 1920
LITTLE SCAPEGOAT, THE • 1915 • Morrisey Edward • USA
LITTLE SCHOOL MA'AM, THE • 1916 • Franklin Sidney A., Franklin Chester M. • USA
LITTLE SCHOOL MISTRESS, THE see **MAESTRINA, LA** • 1933
LITTLE SCHOOL MOUSE • 1954 • Hanna William, Barbera Joseph • ANS • USA
LITTLE SCREW, THE • 1927 • Angivstev • ANS • USS
LITTLE SEA NYMPH, THE see **MAL MORSKA VILA** • 1976
LITTLE SENORITA, THE • 1914 • *Ostriche Muriel* • USA
LITTLE SEX, A • 1982 • Paltrow Bruce • USA
LITTLE SHEGO • Babichenko B. • ANS • USS
LITTLE SHEPHERD, THE • 1909 • Porter Edwin S. • USA
LITTLE SHEPHERD OF BARGAIN ROW, THE • 1916 • Wright Fred E. • USA
LITTLE SHEPHERD OF KINGDOM COME, THE • 1920 • Worsley Wallace • USA
LITTLE SHEPHERD OF KINGDOM COME, THE • 1928 • Santell Alfred • USA • KENTUCKY COURAGE
LITTLE SHEPHERD OF KINGDOM COME, THE • 1961 • McLaglen Andrew V. • USA
LITTLE SHEPHERD OF "TUMBLING RUN", THE • 1909 • *Edison* • USA
LITTLE SHEPHERDESS, THE • 1911 • *Selig* • USA
LITTLE SHERIFF, THE • 1912 • *Essanay* • USA
LITTLE SHERIFF, THE • 1914 • Stanley George C. • USA
LITTLE SHOE, THE • 1911 • *Swayne Marian* • USA
LITTLE SHOES, THE • 1917 • Berthelet Arthur • USA
LITTLE SHOP IN FORE STREET, THE • 1926 • Miller Frank • UKN
LITTLE SHOP OF HORRORS • 1986 • Oz Frank • USA
LITTLE SHOP OF HORRORS, THE • 1961 • Corman Roger • USA • PASSIONATE PEOPLE EATER, THE
LITTLE SHREW OF THE VETERAN RESERVES see **LANDSTORMENS LILLA ARGBIGGA** • 1941
LITTLE SHUT IN, THE • 1912 • *Eline Marie* • USA
LITTLE SINGER, THE • 1915 • *Joyce Alice* • USA
LITTLE SINGING TREE, THE see **SINGENDE KLINGENDE BAUMCHEN, DAS** • 1965
LITTLE SINNER • 1935 • Meins Gus • SHT • USA
LITTLE SINNER, THE (USA) see **SCHWARZFAHRT INS GLUCK** • 1938
LITTLE SIREN see **MALA SIRENA** • 1968
LITTLE SISTER • 1909 • *Browning Ethel* • USA
LITTLE SISTER • 1911 • Olcott Sidney • USA
LITTLE SISTER see **FLESH OF MY FLESH** • 1969
LITTLE SISTER, THE • 1914 • *Selig* • USA
LITTLE SISTER, THE • 1914 • *Rex* • USA
LITTLE SISTER, THE • 1984 • Egleson Jan • TVM • USA • TENDER AGE, THE
LITTLE SISTER, THE see **MARLOWE** • 1969
LITTLE SISTER OF EVERYBODY, A • 1918 • Thornby Robert T. • USA
LITTLE SISTER OF THE POOR, THE • 1916 • Mayo Melvin • USA
LITTLE SKEETER • 1969 • Smith Paul J. • ANS • USA
LITTLE SKIPPER, THE • 1913 • *Powers* • USA
LITTLE SLAVEY, THE • 1915 • Morrisey Edward • USA
LITTLE SMARTY • ANS • USS
LITTLE SNOB, THE • 1928 • Adolfi John G. • USA
LITTLE SNOW WAIF, THE • 1913 • Weston Charles • UKN
LITTLE SNOW-WHITE (UKN) see **LITTLE SNOWDROP** • 1910
LITTLE SNOWDROP • 1903 • *Lubin* • USA
LITTLE SNOWDROP • 1910 • *Pathe* • FRN • LITTLE SNOW-WHITE (UKN)
LITTLE SOAP AND WATER, A • 1935 • Fleischer Dave • ANS • USA
LITTLE SOLDIER, THE • 1912 • *Solax* • USA
LITTLE SOLDIER, THE see **PETIT SOLDAT, LE** • 1908
LITTLE SOLDIER, THE see **PETIT SOLDAT, LE** • 1947
LITTLE SOLDIER, THE see **PETIT SOLDAT, LE** • 1961
LITTLE SOLDIER GIRL • 1917 • Grandon Francis J. • USA
LITTLE SOLDIER MAN, THE • 1915 • *Harris Mildred* • USA
LITTLE SOLDIER OF '64, THE • 1911 • Olcott Sidney • USA
LITTLE SOLDIERS see **MALI VOJNICI** • 1968
LITTLE SOMETHING EXTRA, A see **CUBOK** • 1990
LITTLE SPARROW, THE see **MINIK SERCE** • 1979
LITTLE SPECK IN GARNERED FRUIT, A • 1917 • Justice Martin • SHT • USA
LITTLE SPIES • 1986 • Beeman Greg • TVM • USA
LITTLE SPOON, THE (USA) see **PETITE CUILLERE, LA** • 1959
LITTLE SPREEWALD MAIDEN, THE • 1910 • Olcott Sidney • USA
LITTLE SPY, THE • 1911 • *Casey Kenneth* • USA
LITTLE STABS AT HAPPINESS • 1959 • Jacobs Ken • USA
LITTLE STANLEY, LIGHTNING CARTOONIST • 1898 • *Cinematograph Co* • UKN
LITTLE STAR, THE • 1965 • Buchvarova Radka • ANS • BUL • STARLET, THE ○ STAR, THE
LITTLE STATION AGENT, THE • 1910 • *Edison* • USA
LITTLE STOCKING, THE • 1911 • *Imp* • USA
LITTLE STORY, A see **MALA KRONIKA** • 1962
LITTLE STOWAWAY, THE • 1912 • *Selig* • USA
LITTLE STRANGER • 1934 • King George • UKN
LITTLE STRANGER, A • 1908 • Cooper Arthur • UKN
LITTLE STRANGER, THE • 1936 • Fleischer Dave • ANS • USA
LITTLE STRANGER, THE see **GHARIB AL SAGHIR, AL** • 1962
LITTLE STRATEGIST, THE • 1917 • Blackton J. Stuart • SHT • USA
LITTLE STRAW WIFE, THE • 1915 • Totten Joseph Byron • USA
LITTLE STREET SINGER, THE (USA) see **PETITE CHANTEUSE DES RUES, LA** • 1924
LITTLE SUBSTITUTE, THE • 1913 • *Bushman Francis X.* • USA
LITTLE SUGAR HOUSE, THE see **CUKROVA BOUDA** • 1980
LITTLE SUMMER BLUES see **MALE LETNI BLUES** • 1967
LITTLE SUNBEAM • 1914 • *Saunders Jackie* • USA
LITTLE SUNSET • 1915 • *Bosworth Hobart* • USA
LITTLE SWEE' PEA • 1936 • Fleischer Dave • ANS • USA
LITTLE SWEETHEART • 1988 • Simmons Anthony • UKN
LITTLE TEACHER, THE • 1909 • Griffith D. W. • USA
LITTLE TEACHER, THE • 1915 • Sennett Mack • USA
LITTLE TEASE, THE • 1913 • Griffith D. W. • USA
LITTLE TELLEVILLAIN • 1958 • Lovy Alex • ANS • USA
LITTLE TERROR, THE • 1917 • Ingram Rex • USA
LITTLE THEATRE, THE • 1941 • *Mintz Charles (P)* • ANS • USA
LITTLE THEATRE OF JEAN RENOIR, THE (USA) see **PETIT THEATRE DE JEAN RENOIR, LE** • 1969
LITTLE THIEF, THE • 1911 • *Powers* • USA
LITTLE THIEF, THE • 1916 • *Rex* • USA
LITTLE THING AND IDI, THE see **DINGERTJIE EN IDI** • 1978
LITTLE THUMBLET, THE see **PETIT POUCET, LE** • 1900
LITTLE TIGER • 1973 • Evstatieva Marianna • BUL
LITTLE TIME MACHINE, THE • 1967 • Brumberg Valentina, Brumberg Zinaida • ANS • USS
LITTLE TINKER • 1948 • Avery Tex • ANS • USA
LITTLE TOKYO, U.S.A. • 1942 • Brower Otto • USA
LITTLE TOM THUMB • 1903 • *Lubin* • USA
LITTLE TOM'S LETTER • 1911 • Stow Percy • UKN
LITTLE TOOT • 1948 • Geronimi Clyde • ANS • USA
LITTLE TOUGH GUY • 1938 • Young Harold • USA
LITTLE TOUGH GUYS IN SOCIETY • 1938 • Kenton Erle C. • USA
LITTLE TOUGH MICE • 1939 • Lovy Alex • ANS • USA
LITTLE TRAIL, THE • 1930 • *Mintz Charles (P)* • ANS • USA
LITTLE TRAIN, THE • 1959 • Tyrlova Hermina • ANM • CZC
LITTLE TRAIN, THE (USA) see **MALI VLAK** • 1959
LITTLE TRAIN ROBBERY, THE • 1905 • Porter Edwin S. • USA
LITTLE TRAIN (USA) see **PULNOCNI PRIHODA** • 1960
LITTLE TREASURE • 1985 • Sharp Alan • USA
LITTLE TRESPASSER, THE • 1915 • Williams C. Jay • USA
LITTLE TROUBADOUR, THE • 1916 • Le Viness Carl M. • SHT • USA
LITTLE TURNCOAT, THE • 1913 • Balshofer Fred J. • USA
LITTLE UMBRELLA, THE see **PARAPLICKO** • 1956

LITTLE UPSTART, THE • 1915 • Le Saint Edward J. • USA

LITTLE VALENTINO, THE see **KIS VALENTINO, A** • 1979

LITTLE VAMPIRE, THE see **BUBCHEN** • 1968

LITTLE VERA • 1987 • Pichul Valeri • USS

LITTLE VIRGIL AND ORLA FROGSNAPPER see **LILLE VIRGIL OG ORLA FROSNAPPER** • 1979

LITTLE VOLUNTEER, A • 1916 • Windom Lawrence C. • SHT • USA

LITTLE VULGAR BOY, A • 1913 • Noy Wilfred • UKN

LITTLE WAIF AND THE CAPTAIN'S DAUGHTER, THE • 1908 • Stow Percy • UKN

LITTLE WAITRESS • 1932 • Newman Widgey R. • UKN

LITTLE WANDERER, A • 1920 • Mitchell Howard M. • USA

LITTLE WANDERER, THE • 1912 • *Kalem* • USA

LITTLE WARS see **HURUB SAGHIRA** • 1983

LITTLE WELSH GIRL, A • 1920 • Paul Fred • UKN

LITTLE WESTERN see **MALY WESTERN** • 1960

LITTLE WESTERN ROSE, THE • 1911 • *Yankee* • USA

LITTLE WHIRLWIND, THE • 1941 • Thomson Riley • ANS • USA

LITTLE WHITE CRIMES • 1967 • Kaczender George • CND

LITTLE WHITE DOVE see **PALOMITA BLANCA** • 1973

LITTLE WHITE GIRL, THE • 1917 • Baker Richard Foster • SHT • USA

LITTLE WHITE HOUSE, THE • 1929 • Aylott Dave, Symmons E. F. • SHT • UKN

LITTLE WHITE SAVAGE, THE • 1919 • Powell Paul • USA

LITTLE WHITE VIOLET, THE • 1915 • Henderson Lucius • USA

LITTLE WIDOW, THE • 1911 • Boggs Frank • USA

LITTLE WIDOW, THE • 1914 • O'Sullivan Tony • USA

LITTLE WIDOW, THE • 1919 • St. Clair Malcolm, Roach Bert • SHT • USA

LITTLE WIDOW IS A DANGEROUS THING, A • 1913 • Wilson Frank? • UKN

LITTLE WILD GIRL, THE • 1928 • Mattison Frank S. • USA • FLAMING JUSTICE (UKN)

LITTLE WILDCAT • 1922 • Divad David • USA

LITTLE WILDCAT, THE • 1928 • Enright Ray • USA

LITTLE WILLIE AND THE APPLE • 1904 • *Urban Trading Co* • UKN

LITTLE WILLIE AND THE MOUSE see **TOMMY AND THE MOUSE IN THE ART SCHOOL** • 1902

LITTLE WILLIE'S ADVENTURE WITH A TRAMP • 1910 • *Saunders William* • UKN

LITTLE WILLIE'S APPRENTICESHIPS • 1913 • Fitzhamon Lewin • UKN

LITTLE WILLIE'S CORONATION CELEBRATIONS • 1902 • *Paul R. W.* • UKN

LITTLE WILLIE'S WILD WOODBINES • 1909 • *Warwick Trading Co* • UKN

LITTLE WINDOW see **OKENKO** • 1933

LITTLE WIRE-WALKER, THE • 1910 • *Walturdaw* • UKN

LITTLE WISE QUACKER • 1952 • Lundy Dick • ANS • USA

LITTLE WOMEN • 1917 • Samuelson G. B., Butler Alexander • UKN

LITTLE WOMEN • 1919 • Knoles Harley • USA

LITTLE WOMEN • 1933 • Cukor George • USA

LITTLE WOMEN • 1948 • LeRoy Mervyn • USA

LITTLE WOMEN • 1970 • *Stacey Dist.* • USA

LITTLE WOMEN • 1978 • Rich David Lowell • TVM • USA

LITTLE WOMEN • 1983 • ANM • JPN

LITTLE WOODEN HUT • 1909 • *Warwick Trading Co* • UKN

LITTLE WOODEN SOLDIER, THE • 1911 • Bouwmeester Theo • UKN

LITTLE WOODY RIDING HOOD • 1962 • Smith Paul J. • ANS • USA

LITTLE WOOLEN SHOE, THE • 1912 • *Fuller Mary* • USA

LITTLE WORLD OF DON CAMILLO, THE see **PETIT MONDE DE DON CAMILLO, LE** • 1951

LITTLE WRAC OF THE VETERAN RESERVES see **LANDSTORMENS LILLA LOTTA** • 1939

LITTLE YANK, THE • 1917 • Siegmann George • USA

LITTLE YELLOW HOUSE, THE • 1928 • Meehan James Leo • USA

LITTLE YOGHOURT see **STORY OF LITTLE YOGHURT, THE** • 1968

LITTLE ZIZI, THE see **PETIT ZIZI, LE** • 1971

LITTLEST ANGEL, THE • 1950 • *Smart David A. (P)* • ANS • USA

LITTLEST BULLY, THE • 1960 • Taras Martin B. • ANS • USA

LITTLEST HOBO, THE • 1958 • Rondeau Charles R. • USA

LITTLEST HOBO, THE • 1979 • Pearson Peter (c/d) • SER • CND

LITTLEST HORSE THIEVES, THE (USA) see **ESCAPE FROM THE DARK** • 1976

LITTLEST MAGDALENE, THE • 1916 • George Burton • SHT • USA

LITTLEST OUTLAW, THE • 1955 • Gavaldon Roberto • USA

LITTLEST REASON, THE • 1920 • *Stage Women'S War Relief* • USA

LITTLEST REBEL, THE • 1914 • Lewis Edgar • USA

LITTLEST REBEL, THE • 1935 • Butler David • USA

LITTLEST SCOUT • 1919 • Blackton Paula, Blackton J. Stuart (Spv) • USA

LITTLEST WARRIOR, THE • 1975 • ANM • SPN

LITTLEST WARRIOR, THE (USA) see **ANJU TO ZUSHIO-MARU** • 1961

LITTORIA • 1932 • Matarazzo Raffaello • SHT • ITL

LIU-HSING, HU-TIEH, CHIEN • 1977 • Ch'U Yuan • HKG • KILLER CLANS

LIU HSUEH-SHENG • 1977 • Pai Ching-Jui • HKG • FOREIGN STUDENTS

LIU SANJIE • 1961 • Su Li • CHN • THIRD SISTER LIU

LIUBLIU LITEBIA? • 1934 • Gerasimov Sergei • USS • IF I LOVE YOU? ○ DO I LOVE YOU?

LIV • 1967 • Lokkeberg Pal • NRW

LIV ELLER DOD -ET TEKNOLOGISK VALG • 1987 • Tornberg Freddy • SHT • DNM • LIFE OR DEATH -A TECHNOLOGICAL CHOICE

LIV OG DOD • 1980 • Vennerod Petter • NRW • LIFE AND DEATH

LIVAT PA LUCKAN • 1951 • *Redig Rune (Edt)* • SWD

LIVE A LITTLE, LOVE A LITTLE • 1968 • Taurog Norman • USA

LIVE A LITTLE, STEAL A LOT see **MURPH THE SURF** • 1975

LIVE AGAIN • 1936 • Maude Arthur • UKN

LIVE AGAIN, DIE AGAIN • 1974 • Colla Richard A. • TVM • USA

LIVE AND LEARN • 1920 • Parrott Charles, Roach Hal • SHT • USA

LIVE AND LET DIE • 1973 • Hamilton Guy • UKN

LIVE AND LET LIVE • 1921 • Cabanne W. Christy • USA

LIVE AND LET LIVE see **SPY FOR A DAY** • 1940

LIVE AND LET LIVE see **HAPPY FAMILY, THE** • 1952

LIVE BROADCAST see **DIREKTAN PRENOS** • 1983

LIVE CORPSES • 1921 • Svab-Malostransky Josef • CZC

LIVE COWARDS • 1926 • Roberts Stephen • SHT • USA

LIVE DANGEROUSLY see **LEV FARLIGT** • 1944

LIVE FAST, DIE YOUNG • 1958 • Henreid Paul • USA

LIVE FOR LIFE see **VIVRE POUR VIVRE** • 1967

LIVE GHOST, THE • 1934 • Rogers Charles • SHT • USA

LIVE GIRLS see **LIVE GIRLS STRIPPED TO KILL II** • 1989

LIVE GIRLS STRIPPED TO KILL II • 1989 • Ruben Katt Shea • USA • STRIPPED TO KILL 2: LIVE GIRLS ○ LIVE GIRLS

LIVE IN FEAR see **APENA UN DELINCUENTE** • 1947

LIVE IT UP • 1963 • Comfort Lance • UKN • SING AND SWING (USA)

LIVE LIKE A COP, DIE LIKE A MAN see **UOMINI SI NASCE POLIZIOTTI SI MUORE** • 1976

LIVE, LOVE AND BELIEVE • 1911 • *Bushman Francis X.* • USA

LIVE, LOVE AND LEARN • 1937 • Fitzmaurice George • USA

LIVE MUMMY, THE • 1915 • *Britannia* • UKN

LIVE NEWS • 1927 • Lamont Charles • SHT • USA

LIVE NOW -PAY LATER • 1962 • Lewis Jay • UKN

LIVE SPARKS • 1920 • Warde Ernest C. • USA

LIVE TO LOVE see **NAKED GODDESS, THE** • 1959

LIVE TODAY: DIE TOMORROW! see **HADAKA NO JUKYUSAI** • 1970

LIVE TODAY FOR TOMORROW see **ACT OF MURDER, AN** • 1948

LIVE WIRE • 1920 • *Franey William* • SHT • USA

LIVE WIRE, THE • 1912 • *Panzer Paul* • USA

LIVE WIRE, THE • 1914 • Pearson George • UKN

LIVE WIRE, THE • 1916 • *Hippo* • USA

LIVE WIRE, THE • 1925 • Hines Charles • USA

LIVE WIRE, THE • 1937 • Brenon Herbert • UKN

LIVE WIRE HICK, A • 1920 • King Henry • USA

LIVE WIRES • 1921 • Sedgwick Edward • USA

LIVE WIRES • 1923 • Roach Hal • SHT • USA

LIVE WIRES • 1946 • Karlson Phil • USA

LIVE WIRES AND LOVE SPARKS • 1916 • *Ritchie Billie* • SHT • USA

LIVE YOUR OWN WAY (USA) see **WAKAMONO TACHI** • 1967

LIVELY AFFAIR, A • 1912 • Young James • USA

LIVELY ALLEY see **YOKI NO URAMACHI** • 1939

LIVELY CARD PARTY, A • 1898 • *Cinematograph Co* • UKN

LIVELY COCK-FIGHT, A see **COMBAT DE COQS** • 1899

LIVELY DAY, A • 1921 • Granville Harry • UKN

LIVELY DISPUTE, A • 1897 • *Paul R. W.* • UKN

LIVELY LODGINGS • 1904 • *Cricks & Sharp* • UKN

LIVELY POND, THE see **WORLD IN A MARSH** • 1955

LIVELY QUARTER DAY, A • 1906 • Martin J. H.? • UKN

LIVELY SET, THE • 1964 • Arnold Jack • USA

LIVELY SKELETON, A • 1910 • Wormald S.? • UKN

LIVEN • 1929 • Kavaleridze Ivan • USS • DOWNPOUR ○ FLOOD, THE

LIVER EATERS, THE see **SPIDER BABY** • 1964

LIVES see **JEEVITHALU** • 1968

LIVES OF A BENGAL LANCER, THE • 1935 • Hathaway Henry • USA

LIVES OF JENNY DOLAN, THE • 1975 • Jameson Jerry • TVM • USA

LIVES OF PERFORMERS • 1972 • Rainer Yvonne • USA

LIVES OF THE JUNGLE • 1915 • Chaudet Louis W. • USA

LIVES OF THE PUPPETS, THE see **AUS DEM LEBEN DER MARIONETTEN** • 1980

LIVET AR STENKUL • 1967 • Halldoff Jan • SWD • LIFE'S JUST GREAT

LIVET ER EN DROM • 1971 • Frank Ernst • DOC • DNM • LIFE IS A DREAM

LIVET GAR VIDARE • 1941 • Henrikson Anders • SWD • KAMRATHUSTRU ○ LIFE GOES ON

LIVET I DANMARK • 1971 • Leth Jorgen • DNM • LIFE IN DENMARK

LIVET I FINNSKOGARNA • 1947 • Johansson Ivar • SWD • LIFE IN THE DEPTHS OF THE FOREST

LIVET MASTE LEVAS • 1943 • Ahrle Elof • SWD • LIFE IS THERE TO BE LIVED

LIVET PA EN PINNE • 1942 • Hildebrand Weyler • SWD • LIFE ON A PERCH

LIVET PA FORSBYHOLM • 1948 • Ahrle Elof • SWD • LIFE AT FORSBYHOLM

LIVET PA LANDET • 1924 • Hedqvist Ivan • SWD • LIFE IN THE COUNTRY

LIVET PA LANDET • 1943 • Bugler Bror • SWD • LIFE IN THE COUNTRY

LIVET PAA HEGNSGAARD • 1939 • Weel Arne • SWD • LIFE ON THE HEGN FARM (USA)

LIVETS GOGLESPIL • 1916 • Holger-Madsen • DNM • IMPOSSIBLE MARRIAGE, AN

LIVETS KONFLIKTER • 1913 • Sjostrom Victor, Stiller Mauritz (U/c) • SWD • LIFE'S CONFLICTS

LIVETS STORMAGTER • 1918 • Magnussen Fritz • SWD

LIVETS STORME • 1910 • Blom August • DNM • STORMS OF LIFE

LIVETS VAR • 1957 • Mattsson Arne • SWD, ARG • PRIMAVERA DE LA VIDA ○ SPRING OF LIFE

LIVID FLAME, THE • 1914 • Grandon Francis J. • USA

LIVING • 1971 • Zwartjes Frans • SHT • NTH

LIVING see **IKIRU** • 1952

LIVING, THE • 1968 • Wolman Dan • ISR

LIVING, THE see **IKITOSHI IKERUMONO** • 1934

LIVING AND THE DEAD, THE see **ZHIVYE I MERTVYE** • 1964

LIVING APART TOGETHER • 1983 • Gormley Charles • UKN

LIVING AT THE "HOPE" see **LEVA PA "HOPPET"** • 1951

LIVING BETWEEN TWO WORLDS • 1963 • Jackson Horace • USA

LIVING BEYOND YOUR MEANS • 1905 • *Paul R. W.* • UKN

LIVING BLACKBOARD see **CAUCHEMAR DU FANTOCHE, LE** • 1908

LIVING BUDDHAS (USA) see **LEBENDE BUDDHAS** • 1924

LIVING BY THE SWORD see **CHICHIBU SUIKODEN: KAGE O KIRU KEN** • 1967

LIVING BY THEIR WITS • 1918 • Sandground Maurice • UKN

LIVING CAMERA, THE see **NEHRU** • 1962

LIVING CITY, THE • 1955 • Wexler Haskell • SHT • USA

LIVING COFFIN, THE (USA) see **GRITO DE LA MUERTE, EL** • 1958

LIVING COLOR • 1962 • Werner Gosta • SHT • SWD

LIVING CORPSE, THE see **IKERU SHIKABANE** • 1917

LIVING CORPSE, THE see **LEBENDE LEICHNAM, DER** • 1918

LIVING CORPSE, THE see **ZHIVOI TRUP** • 1929

LIVING CORPSE, THE see **ZHIVOI TRUP** • 1953

LIVING CORPSE, THE see **ZHIVOI TRUP** • 1969

LIVING CORPSE, THE (USA) see **NUITS DE FEU** • 1937

LIVING DANGEROUSLY • 1936 • Brenon Herbert • UKN

LIVING DANGEROUSLY • 1988 • Perakis Nikos • GRC

LIVING DAYLIGHTS, THE • 1987 • Glen John • UKN

LIVING DEAD, THE see **LEBENDE LEICHNAM, DER** • 1918

LIVING DEAD, THE see **PSYCHOMANIA** • 1972

LIVING DEAD, THE (USA) see **FUNF UNHEIMLICHE GESCHICHTEN** • 1933

LIVING DEAD, THE (USA) see **SCOTLAND YARD MYSTERY, THE** • 1934

LIVING DEAD AT THE MANCHESTER MORGUE, THE see **FIN DE SEMANA PARA LOS MUERTOS** • 1974

LIVING DEAD MAN, THE see **MORT VIVANT, LE** • 1912

LIVING DEAD MAN, THE see **INHUMAINE, L'** • 1923

LIVING DEAD MAN, THE (USA) see **FEU MATTHIAS PASCAL** • 1925

LIVING DEATH, THE • 1915 • Browning Tod • USA

LIVING DEATH, THE • 1928 • Paul Fred • UKN

LIVING DEATH, THE see **SNAKE PEOPLE** • 1968

LIVING DEITY see **KANKANDA DEIVAM** • 1967

LIVING DESERT, THE • 1953 • Algar James • DOC • USA

LIVING DOLL • 1989 • Litten Peter, Dugdale George • UKN, USA

LIVING DOLL, A see **IKERU NINGYO** • 1929

LIVING DOLL, THE • 1913 • *Gaumont* • USA

LIVING DOLL, THE (USA) see **POUPEE VIVANTE, LA** • 1909

LIVING EARTH, THE • 1978 • Hammid Alexander • USA

LIVING FEAR, THE • 1914 • Smiley Joseph • USA

LIVING FOR LOVE see **MAN TROUBLE** • 1930

LIVING FOREST, THE • 1958 • Kaminsky S., Asmous B. • USS

LIVING FREE • 1972 • Couffer Jack • UKN

LIVING GHOST, THE • 1942 • Beaudine William • USA • LEND ME YOUR EAR (UKN)

LIVING HEAD, THE (USA) see **CABEZA VIVIENTE, LA** • 1961

LIVING HEROES see **ZHIVYE GEROI** • 1959

LIVING IDOL, THE • 1957 • Lewin Albert, Cardona Rene • USA, MXC

LIVING IN A BIG WAY • 1947 • La Cava Gregory • USA

LIVING IN A MOBILE HOME • 1987 • Astley Neville • ANM • UKN

LIVING IS BETTER • 1956 • Kamei Fumio • JPN • IT IS BETTER TO LIVE

LIVING IT UP • 1954 • Taurog Norman • USA

LIVING JAZZ • 1960 • Gold Jack • UKN

LIVING LEGEND • 1980 • Keeter Worth • USA

LIVING LIE, THE • 1916 • Kent Leon D. • SHT • USA

LIVING LIES • 1922 • Chautard Emile • USA

LIVING LIES • 1936 • Field Mary • UKN

LIVING LIKE THE REST OF US • 1982 • Radivojevic Milos • YGS

LIVING MACHINE, THE • 1961 • Koenig Wolf, Kroitor Roman • CND

LIVING MAGOROKU, THE see **IKITEIRU MAGOROKU** • 1943

LIVING MASK, THE • 1928 • *Film Art Guild* • USA

LIVING MELBOURNE • 1910 • ASL

LIVING MEMORY, A • 1912 • *Francis Alec B.* • USA

LIVING MUMMY, THE see **LEVANDE MUMIEN, DEN** • 1917

LIVING NEIGHBOURHOOD, ROOM TO PLAY, THE • 1972 • Vrijman Jan • NTH

LIVING NIGHTMARE see **VOLCA NOC** • 1955

LIVING NIGHTMARE see **ECHOES** • 1983

LIVING ON LOVE • 1937 • Landers Lew • USA • LOVE IN A BASEMENT

LIVING ON TOKYO TIME • 1987 • Okazaki Steven • USA

LIVING ON VELVET • 1935 • Borzage Frank • USA

LIVING ONE'S LIFE see **ZIT SVUJ ZIVOT** • 1963

LIVING PEACH, THE • 1911 • *West William* • USA

LIVING PLAYING CARDS, THE (USA) see **CARTES VIVANTES, LES** • 1905

LIVING PORTRAIT see **IKITEIRU GAZO** • 1948

LIVING PROOF • 1981 • Muller John • DOC • CND

LIVING PROOF see **LIVING PROOF: THE HANK WILLIAMS JR. STORY** • 1982

LIVING PROOF: THE HANK WILLIAMS JR. STORY • 1982 • Lowry Dick • TVM • USA • LIVING PROOF

LIVING RUSSIA OR THE MAN WITH A CAMERA see **CHELOVEK S KINOAPPARATOM** • 1928

LIVING SEA, THE see **UMI WA IKITEIRU** • 1958

LIVING SKELETON see **KYUKETSU DOKURO SEN** • 1968

LIVING SOIL, THE • 1960 • Ram Atma • UKN

LIVING STATUE, THE see **STATUE ANIMEE, LA** • 1903

LIVING STATUES • 1900 • Smith Jack • UKN

LIVING STONES • 1957 • Makarczynski Tadeusz • DOC • PLN

LIVING STREAM, THE see **HORN I NORR, ETT** • 1950

LIVING SWORD, THE • 1971 • Wang Ping • HKG

LIVING SYDNEY • 1914 • *Moulton A. J. (Ph)* • ASL • SYDNEY BY DAY AND NIGHT

LIVING TARGET, THE see **KARUSELLEN** • 1923

LIVING TOYS, THE see **JOUETS VIVANTS, LES** • 1908

LIVING TRADITION • 1960 • Huisken Joop • DOC • GDR

LIVING TRADITION, THE • 1986 • Markson Morley • MTV • CND

LIVING TRAPS • 1961 • Kollanyi Agoston • HNG

LIVING TREE see **HEJ TE ELEVEN FA..** • 1963

LIVING VEGETABLES, THE see **LEGUMES VIVANTS, LES** • 1910

LIVING VENUS • 1961 • Lewis Herschell G. • USA

LIVING WAGE, THE • 1914 • *Selig* • USA

LIVING WAGE, THE • 1915 • *Stanton Richard* • USA
LIVING WATER • 1960 • Shepitko Larissa • SHT • USS
LIVING WITH CRYSTAL FEELING see **NANTONAKU KRYSTAL** • 1981
LIVING WITH STRANGERS • 1935-45 • Sainsbury Frank • DOC • UKN
LIVING WRECK, THE • 1909 • *Urban-Eclipse* • USA
LIVINGSTON CASE, THE • 1910 • Porter Edwin S. • USA
LIVINGSTONE • 1925 • Wetherell M. A. • UKN • STANLEY
LIVRAISON SPECIALE see **SPECIAL DELIVERY** • 1978
LIVRE MAGIQUE, LE • 1900 • Melies Georges • FRN • MAGIC BOOK, THE (USA)
LIVREURS, LES • 1961 • Girault Jean • FRN
LIVRO, O • 1954 • Barreto Victor • BRZ
LIVSFARLIG FILM • 1988 • Osten Suzanne • SWD • LETHAL FILM
LIZ E HELEN • 1972 • Freda Riccardo • ITL
LIZA • 1966 • Masters Quentin • DOC • ASL
LIZA see **CAGNA, LA** • 1972
LIZA AND HER DOUBLE see **LIZA KAI I ALLI, I** • 1961
LIZA KAI I ALLI, I • 1961 • Dimopoulos Dinos • GRC • LIZA AND HER DOUBLE
LIZA ON THE STAGE • 1915 • Evans Joe • UKN
LIZABETH, ADULTERA INNOCENTE (ITL) see **VERLOGENE AKT, DER** • 1969
LIZARD IN A WOMAN'S SKIN, A (UKN) see **LUCERTOLA CON LA PELLE DI DONNA, UNA** • 1971
LIZARD STORIES see **HISTORIA DE LAGARTOS** • 1989
LIZARDS see **BASILISCHI, I** • 1963
LIZA'S LEGACY • 1915 • Evans Joe • UKN
LIZBETH • 1913 • *Mersereau Claire* • USA
LIZ'S CAREER • 1910 • *Lubin* • USA
LIZZIE • 1957 • Haas Hugo • USA
LIZZIE AND THE BEAUTY CONTEST • 1915 • Christie Al • USA
LIZZIE AND THE ICEMAN • 1914 • Smalley Phillips • USA
LIZZIE BREAKS INTO THE HAREM • 1915 • Christie Al • USA
LIZZIE STRATA • 1933 • De Mond Albert • SHT • USA
LIZZIE, THE LIFE SAVER • 1914 • Neilan Marshall • USA
LIZZIE'S FORTUNE • 1914 • *Sterling* • USA
LIZZIE'S LAST LAP • 1924 • Quiribet Gaston • UKN
LIZZIE'S LINGERING LOVE • 1916 • Lehrman Henry • SHT • USA
LIZZIES OF THE FIELD • 1924 • *Sennett Mack (P)* • SHT • USA
LIZZIE'S SHATTERED DREAMS • 1915 • *Howell Alice* • USA
LIZZIE'S WATERLOO • 1919 • Hartigan P. C. • SHT • USA
LIZZIE'S WATERY GRAVE • 1915 • *Jacobs Billy* • USA
LIZZY'S DIRTY CAREER • 1915 • Lyons Eddie • USA
LIZZY'S ESCAPE • 1914 • *Lehrman Henry* • USA
LJEPOTICA 62 • 1962 • Makavejev Dusan • DOC • YGS • MISS YUGOSLAVIA 62
LJETO JE KRIVO ZA SVE • 1962 • Djordjevic Purisa • YGS • SUMMER IS TO BLAME FOR EVERYTHING, THE
LJETO ZA SECANJE • 1990 • Gamulin Bruno • YGS • SUMMER TO REMEMBER, A
LJUBAV see **LJUBEZEN** • 1985
LJUBAV I BIJES • 1979 • Tanovic Bakir • YGS • LOVE AND FURY ○ LOVE AND RAGE
LJUBAV I PO KOJA PSOVKA • 1970 • Vrdoljak Antun • YGS • LOVE AND AN OCCASIONAL SWEARWORD ○ LJUBAV I PONEKA PSOVKA ○ LOVE AND A FEW CURSES
LJUBAV I PONEKA PSOVKA see **LJUBAV I PO KOJA PSOVKA** • 1970
LJUBAV I STRAST • 1932 • Melford Frank
LJUBAV NA BRAZDAMA • 1974 • Duletic Vojko • YGS • LOVE ON THE FURROWS
LJUBAVI BLANKE KOLAK • 1987 • Jurjasevic Boris • YGS • LOVES OF BLANKA KOLAK, THE
LJUBAVNA PISMA S PREDUMISLJAJEM • 1985 • Berkovic Zvonimir • YGS • LOVE LETTERS WITH INTENT
LJUBAVNI SLUCAJ ILI TRAGEDIJA SLUZBENICE P.T.T. • 1967 • Makavejev Dusan • YGS • SWITCHBOARD OPERATOR, THE (UKN) ○ TRAGEDIJA SLUZBENICE P.T.T. ○ LOVE AFFAIR OR THE CASE OF THE MISSING SWITCHBOARD OPERATOR ○ AFFAIR OF THE HEART ○ LOVE DOSSIER
LJUBAVNI ZIVOT BUDIMIRA TRAJKOVICA • 1978 • Karaklajic Dejan • YGS • LOVELY LIFE OF BUDIMIR TRAJKOVIC, THE ○ BELOVED LOVE ○ LOVE-LIFE OF BUDIMIR TRAJKOVIC, THE
LJUBEZEN • 1985 • Ranfl Rajko • YGS • LJUBAV ○ LOVE
LJUBI, LJUBI, AL'GLAVU • 1982 • Calic Zoran • YGS • LOVE, LOVE, BUT DON'T LOSE YOUR HEAD
LJUBICA • 1979 • Golik Kreso • YGS • VIOLET
LJUBITELJ CVECA see **LJUBITELJI CVIJECA** • 1970
LJUBITELJI CVIJECA • 1970 • Dovnikovic Borivoj • ANS • YGS, ITL • FLOWER LOVERS, THE ○ LJUBITELJ CVECA
LJUBLJANA IS BELOVED • 1965 • Klopcic Matjaz • SHT • YGS
LJUBOV I FILM • 1961 • Vrbanic Ivo • ANS • YGS • LOVE AND FILM
LJUBOV' POD MASKOJ • 1915 • Tourjansky Victor • USS
LJUDI SA NERETVE • 1966 • Gluscevic Obrad • YGS • PEOPLE ON THE NERETVA
LJUSET FRAN LUND • 1955 • Lagerkvist Hans • SWD • SHINING LIGHT FROM LUND
LJUSNANDE FRAMTID, DEN • 1941 • Molander Gustaf • SWD • BRIGHT PROSPECTS
LJUTYJ • 1974 • Konchalovsky Andrei • USS
LJUVLIG AR SOMMARNATTEN • 1961 • Mattsson Arne • SWD • SUMMER NIGHT IS SWEET, THE
L'KHAIM • 1911 • Hansen Kai, Maitre Maurice • USS
LLAGA, LA • 1920 • Peredo Luis G. • MXC
LLAGA, LA • 1937 • Peon Ramon • MXC • TORMENT, THE (USA)
LLAMA UN TAL ESTEBAN • 1959 • Ramirez Pedro L. • SPN
LLAMABAN CALAMIDAD, LES • 1972 • Balcazar Alfonso • SPN
LLAMABAN LA MADRINA, LA • 1973 • Ozores Mariano • SPN
LLAMADA, LA • 1965 • Seto Javier • SPN • CALL, THE
LLAMADA DE AFRICA, LA • 1951 • Ardavin Cesar • SPN
LLAMADA DE LA MUERTE, LA • 1959 • Orellana Carlos • NCR, MXC
LLAMADA DEL SEXO, LA • 1976 • Demicheli Tulio • SPN
LLAMADA DEL VAMPIRO, LA • 1973 • Elorrieta Jose Maria • SPN
LLAMADO DE LA HORA, EL • 1970 • Herrera Manuel • CUB • CALL OF THE HOUR, THE
LLAMAN DE JAMAICA, MR. WARD • 1967 • Salvador Julio • SPN, ITL • HALLO WARD! ...E FURONO VACANZE IS SANGUE (ITL)
LLAMAS CONTRA EL VIENTO • 1955 • Gomez Muriel Emilio • MXC
LLAMENME MIKE • 1979 • Gurrola Alfredo • MXC
LLAN KI SHAOKAT • 1954 • *Shantaram V. (P)* • SHT • IND • SYMPHONY OF LIFE
LLANERO, EL • 1963 • Franco Jesus • SPN
LLANO KID, THE • 1939 • Venturini Edward D. • USA
LLANTO DE LA TORTUGA, EL • 1974 • *Conacine* • MXC
LLANTO POR HAMBRE, UN • 1968 • Briz Jose • SPN
LLANTO POR JUAN INDIO • 1965 • Gonzalez Garza Rogelio • MXC
LLANTO POR UN BANDIDO • 1964 • Saura Carlos • SPN, ITL, FRN • WEEPING FOR A BANDIT ○ LAMENT FOR A BANDIT
LLANTO, RISA Y NOCAUT • 1973 • *Matela* • MXC
LLEGADA DE NOCHE • 1949 • Nieves Conde Jose Antonio • SPN
LLEGAR A MAS • 1963 • Fernandez Santos Jesus • SPN
LLEGARON DOS HOMBRES • 1958 • Ardavin Eusebio F., Mattsson Arne • SPN
LLEGARON LOS FRANCESES • 1959 • Klimovsky Leon • SPN
LLEGARON LOS JI-JINS • 1971 • Odreman Mauricio • VNZ • JI-JINS ARRIVED, THE
LLEGARON LOS MARCIANOS (SPN) see **MARZIANI HANNO DODICI MANI, I** • 1964
LLEGARON SIETE MUCHACHAS • 1954 • Viladomat Domingo • SPN
LLEGO LA NINA RAMONA • 1945 • Catrani Catrano • ARG
LLEVAME EN TUS BRAZOS • 1953 • Bracho Julio • MXC
LLORONA, LA • 1933 • Peon Ramon • MXC • CRYING WOMAN, THE
LLORONA, LA • 1959 • Cardona Rene • MXC
LLOVIDO DEL CIELO • 1962 • Ruiz-Castillo Arturo • SPN
LLOVIZNA • 1977 • Olhovich Sergio • MXC • DRIZZLE
LLOYD BROTHERS DOUBLE ROPE ACT • 1901 • *Warwick Trading Co* • UKN
LLOYD GEORGE: THE MENAGE A TROIS SCANDAL see **SECRET LIVES OF THE BRITISH PRIME MINISTERS: LLOYD GEORGE** • 1983
LLOYD OF THE C.I.D. • 1931 • McRae Henry • UKN • DETECTIVE LLOYD (USA)
LLOYDS OF LONDON • 1936 • King Henry • USA
LLUEVE SOBRE SANTIAGO • 1975 • Soto Helvio • FRN, BUL • IL PLEUT SUR SANTIAGO ○ RAIN OVER SANTIAGO
LLUMS I OMBRES • 1988 • Camino Jaime • SPN • LIGHTS AND SHADOWS ○ LUCES Y SOMBRAS
LLUVIA DE ABUELOS • 1949 • Fernandez Bustamente Adolfo • MXC
LLUVIA DE HIJOS • 1948 • Delgado Fernando • SPN
LLUVIA DEL DIABLO, LA • 1975 • *Howard Sandy* • MXC
LLUVIA ROJA • 1949 • Cardona Rene • MXC
LMNO • 1978 • Breer Robert • USA
LO CHIAMAVANO BULLDOZER • 1978 • Lupo Michele • ITL • THEY CALLED HIM BULLDOZER ○ BULLDOZER
LO CHIAMAVANO COSETTA • 1917 • Gallone Carmine • ITL
LO CHIAMAVANO KING • 1971 • Romitelli Giancarlo • ITL • HIS NAME WAS KING (USA)
LO CHIAMAVANO TRESETTE.. GIOCAVA SEMPRE COL MORTO • 1973 • Carnimeo Giuliano • ITL
LO CHIAMAVANO TRINITA • 1970 • Clucher E. B. • ITL • THEY CALL ME TRINITY (UKN) ○ TRINITY IS MY NAME
LO CHIAMAVANO VERITA • 1972 • Perelli Luigi • ITL
LO CHIAMEREMO ANDREA • 1972 • De Sica Vittorio • ITL • WE'LL CALL HIM ANDREA
LO CREDEVANO UNO STINCO DI SANTO • 1972 • Bosch Juan • ITL
LO DEL CESAR • 1987 • Cazals Felipe • MXC, SPN • THAT WHICH IS CAESAR'S
LO IRRITARONO.. E SARTANA FECE PIAZZA PULITA • 1970 • Romero-Marchent Rafael • ITL, SPN
LO-LKP • 1947 • de Haas Max • NTH
LO PAIS • 1974 • Guerin Gerard • FRN • HOMELAND
LO QUE CUESTA VIVIR • 1957 • Nunez Ricardo • SPN
LO QUE EL VIENTO TRAJO • 1941 • Benavides Jose Jr. • MXC
LO QUE IMPORTA ES VIVIR • 1987 • Alcoriza Luis • MXC • IT'S LIVING THAT COUNTS
LO QUE LE PASO A REYNOSO • 1937 • Torres-Rios Leopoldo • ARG
LO QUE LE PASO A SANSON • 1955 • Martinez Solares Gilberto • MXC
LO QUE LE PASO A SANTIAGO • 1988 • Morales Jacobo • PRC • WHAT HAPPENED TO SANTIAGO
LO QUE MAS QUEREMOS • 1970 • *Zacarias* • MXC
LO QUE NO SE PUEDE PERDONAR • 1953 • Rodriguez Roberto • MXC
LO QUE SOLO EL HOMBRE PUEDE SUFRIR • 1942 • Ortega Juan J. • MXC
LO QUE VA DE AYER A HOY • 1945 • Bustillo Oro Juan • MXC
LO SAI CHE I PAPAVERI.. • 1952 • Metz Vittorio, Marchesi Marcello • ITL
LO-SHAN FENG • 1988 • Huang Yu-Shan • TWN • CAVE OF DESIRE, THE
LO, THE POOR BUFFAL • 1948 • Lovy Alex • ANS • USA
LOI THE POOR INDIAN • 1914 • Williams C. Jay • USA
LO VOGLIO MASCHIO • 1971 • Saitta Ugo • ITL
LO VOGLIO MORTO • 1968 • Bianchini Paolo • ITL, SPN • I WANT HIM DEAD
LOADED • 1913 • *Eclair* • USA
LOADED DICE • 1913 • Edwards Walter • USA
LOADED DICE • 1918 • Blache Herbert • USA
LOADED DICE see **CROSS MY HEART** • 1937
LOADED DOOR, THE • 1922 • Pollard Harry • USA
LOADED GUNS (USA) see **COLPO IN CANNA** • 1975
LOADED PISTOLS • 1949 • English John • USA
LOADING LUDWIG • Mattuschka Mara • ANM • AUS
LOAF, THE see **SOUSTO** • 1960
LOAF OF BREAD, A see **SOUSTO** • 1960
LOAFER see **CAICARA** • 1950
LOAFER, THE • 1911 • *Essanay* • USA
LOAFER, THE • 1914 • *Siegmann George* • USA
LOAFERS, THE see **VITELLONI, I** • 1953
LOAFERS AND LOVERS • 1920 • Brown Melville • USA
LOAFER'S LUCKY DAY, THE • 1906 • *Urban Trading Co* • UKN
LOAFER'S MOTHER, THE • 1912 • Anderson G. M. • USA
LOAFIE see **LIMPAN** • 1983
LOAFY see **LIMPAN** • 1983
LOAN SHARK • 1952 • Friedman Seymour • USA
LOAN SHARK, THE • 1912 • *Essanay* • USA
LOAN SHARK, THE • 1912 • *Imp* • USA
LOAN SHARK KING, THE • 1914 • Brooke Van Dyke • USA
LOAN STRANGER, THE • 1942 • Lovy Alex • ANS • USA
LOBA, LA • 1964 • Baledon Rafael • MXC • HORRORES DEL BOSQUE NEGRO, LOS ○ HORRORS OF THE BLACK FOREST ○ SHE-WOLF, THE
LOBA Y LA PALOMA, LA • 1973 • Suarez Gonzalo • SPN • SHE-WOLF AND THE DOVE, THE
LOBAS DEL RING, LAS • 1964 • Cardona Rene • MXC
LOBO, EL • 1971 • Carretero Amaro • ANS • SPN • WOLF, THE
LOBO BLANCO, EL • 1962 • Salvador Jaime • MXC
LOBO SOLITARIO, EL • 1951 • Orona Vicente • MXC
LOBOS DA SERRA • 1942 • do Canto Jorge Brum • PRT
LOBOS DE ADENTRO • 1979 • Sinclair Arturo • VNZ, PRU • WOLVES FROM INSIDE
LOBSTER DRESSING • 1919 • *Lynne Ethel* • USA
LOBSTER NIGHTMARE, THE • 1911 • *Walturdaw* • UKN
LOBSTER SALAD AND MILK • 1913 • *Princess* • USA
LOBSTER STILL PURSUED HIM, THE see **JONES' NIGHTMARE** • 1911
LOBSTERS • 1936 • Mathias John, Moholy-Nagy Laszlo • UKN
LOCA, LA • 1951 • Zacarias Miguel • MXC
LOCA DE LA CASA, LA • 1950 • Bustillo Oro Juan • MXC
LOCA DE LOS MILAGROS, LA • 1973 • *Cima* • MXC
LOCA EXTRAVAGANCIA SEXY, UNA • 1977 • Guevara Enrique • SPN
LOCA JUVENTUD • 1964 • Mur Oti • SPN
LOCA LUZ CARABALLO, LA • 1976 • Sozio Silvia Manrique • VNZ
LOCAL BAD MAN, THE • 1932 • Brower Otto • USA
LOCAL BOY MAKES GOOD • 1931 • LeRoy Mervyn • USA
LOCAL BULLY, THE • 1911 • Melies Gaston • USA
LOCAL COLOR • 1913 • *Kinemacolor* • USA
LOCAL COLOR • 1914 • Finley Ned • USA
LOCAL COLOR • 1917 • *Christie* • SHT • USA
LOCAL COLOR • 1917 • Beaumont Harry • *Essanay* • SHT • USA
LOCAL COLOR • 1977 • Rappaport Mark • USA
LOCAL COLOR ON THE A-1 RANCH • 1916 • Mix Tom • SHT • USA
LOCAL COLOUR • 1932 • Sparling Gordon • DCS • CND
LOCAL HERO • 1983 • Forsyth Bill • UKN
LOCAL LINE LOVE see **KIGEKI DANTAI RESSHA** • 1967
LOCAL ROMANCE, A see **ZIZKOVSKA ROMANCE** • 1958
LOCAL SHOWERS • 1916 • Myll Louis • SHT • USA
LOCAL TRAIN MYSTERY, THE • 1937 • Baerlin Anthony • UKN
LOCANDA DELLE BAMBOLE CRUDELI, LA (ITL) see **RASTHAUS DER GRAUSAMEN PUPPEN, DAS** • 1967
LOCANDIERA, LA • 1944 • Chiarini Luigi • ITL
LOCANDIERA, LA • 1981 • Cavara Paolo • ITL • MISTRESS OF THE INN
LOCAS, LAS • 1977 • Carreras Enrique • ARG • MAD WOMEN, THE
LOCATAIRE DIABOLIQUE, LE • 1909 • Melies Georges • FRN • DIABOLIC TENANT, THE
LOCATAIRE, LE (FRN) see **TENANT, THE** • 1976
LOCATAIRES D'A COTE, LES • 1909 • Cohl Emile • ANS • FRN • TENANTS NEXT DOOR, THE ○ NEXT DOOR NEIGHBORS
LOCATAIRES ET PROPRIETAIRES • 1972 • Regnier Michel • DCS • CND
LOCATIONS see **SCHAUPLATZE** • 1967
LOCENG MAUT • 1976 • Achnas Naz • MLY • BELLS OF DEATH, THE
LOCH LOMOND • 1909 • *Warwick Trading Co* • UKN
LOCH NESS HORROR, THE • 1982 • Buchanan Larry • USA
LOCH NESS MONSTER, THE see **SECRET OF THE LOCH, THE** • 1934
LOCH NESS MYSTERY, THE see **SECRET OF THE LOCH, THE** • 1934
LOCHBUCHHALTER KREMKE • 1930 • Harder M. • FRG
LOCHINVAR • 1909 • Dawley J. Searle • USA
LOCHINVAR • 1915 • Seldon-Truss Leslie • UKN
LOCK OUR DOOR • 1949 • Gilkison Anthony • UKN
LOCK, STOCK AND BARREL • 1970 • Thorpe Jerry • TVM • USA
LOCK UP • 1989 • Flynn John • USA • LOCK-UP
LOCK-UP see **LOCK UP** • 1989
LOCK UP THE SPOONS see **TRUANDS, LES** • 1956
LOCK UP YOUR DAUGHTERS • 1956 • *Katzman Sam (P)* • CMP • USA
LOCK UP YOUR DAUGHTERS! • 1969 • Coe Peter • UKN
LOCK UP YOUR DAUGHTERS see **APE MAN, THE** • 1943
LOCK UP YOUR SPOONS (UKN) see **TRUANDS, LES** • 1956
LOCK YOUR DOORS (UKN) see **APE MAN, THE** • 1943
LOCKE THE SUPERMAN • Fukutomi Hiroshi • ANM • JPN
LOCKED DOOR, THE • 1914 • Johnson Tefft • USA
LOCKED DOOR, THE • 1926 • Coleby A. E. • UKN
LOCKED DOOR, THE • 1929 • Fitzmaurice George • USA
LOCKED DOORS • 1925 • De Mille William C. • USA
LOCKED HEART, THE • 1918 • King Henry • USA
LOCKED HOUSE, THE • 1914 • Baker George D. • USA
LOCKED IN • 1915 • Nicholls George • USA
LOCKED IN see **CAGED** • 1950
LOCKED IN THE VAULTS • 1911 • *Reliance* • USA
LOCKED LIPS • 1920 • Dowlan William C. • USA
LOCKED OUT • 1911 • *Reliance* • USA
LOCKED OUT • 1912 • *Lubin* • USA
LOCKED OUT • 1912 • Golden Joseph A. • *Crystal* • USA
LOCKED OUT • 1915 • Jackson Harry • USA
LOCKED OUT • 1917 • Drew Sidney • SHT • USA
LOCKED OUT see **GIRL IN HIS ROOM, THE** • 1922

LOCKED OUT AT TWELVE • 1913 • Christie Al • USA
LOCKED OUT OF WEDLOCK • 1912 • *Arling Charles* • USA
LOCKED ROOM, THE • 1913 • Bracken Bertram • USA
LOCKENDE GEFAHR • 1950 • York Eugen • FRG
LOCKENDE GEFAHR, DIE • 1924 • Stein Josef • FRG
LOCKENDE STERNE • 1952 • Muller Hans • FRG
LOCKENDE ZIEL, DAS • 1930 • Reichmann Max • FRG • BLICK ZURUCK UND DANN.., EIN ○ HERR KAMMERSANGER, DER
LOCKENDES GIFT • 1928 • Sauer Fred • FRG
LOCKENKOPFCHEN ODER WIE MANIPULIERT MAN DIE WIRKLICHKEIT • 1967 • Schamoni Ulrich • SHT • FRG
LOCKER 69 • 1962 • Harrison Norman • UKN
LOCKER, THE • 1968 • Tomblin Barry • UKN
LOCKET, THE • 1910 • *Capitol* • USA
LOCKET, THE • 1912 • Dwan Allan • USA
LOCKET, THE • 1913 • Thompson Frederick A. • USA
LOCKET, THE • 1915 • Noy Wilfred • UKN
LOCKET, THE • 1946 • Brahm John • USA
LOCKFAGELN • 1972 • Wickman Torgny • SWD • DECOY, THE
LOCKS AND BONDS • 1937 • Goodwins Leslie • SHT • USA
LOCKSMITH AND CHANCELLOR see **SLESAR I KANTZLER** • 1923
LOCKSPITZEL ASEW • 1935 • Jutzi Phil • FRG, AUS
LOCKVOGEL • 1934 • Steinhoff Hans • FRG
LOCKVOGEL DER NACHT • 1969 • Ten Haaf Wilm • FRG
LOCO BOY MAKES GOOD • 1942 • White Jules • SHT • USA
LOCO DE MACUTO, EL • 1978 • de Pedro Manuel • VNZ • MADMAN OF MOCUTO, THE
LOCO LINDO • 1938 • Mom Arturo S. • CRAZY DANDY (USA)
LOCO LOBO • 1947 • Swift Howard • ANS • USA
LOCO LUCK • 1927 • Smith Cliff • USA
LOCO POR ELLAS • 1965 • de la Pedrosa Manuel • MXC, VNZ
LOCO SERENATA, EL • 1940 • Saslavsky Luis • ARG • CRAZY MUSICIAN, THE (USA)
LOCO VENENO • 1988 • Hermoso Miguel • SPN • CRAZY POISON ○ MAD POISON
LOCO Y VAGABUNDO • 1945 • Orellana Carlos • MXC
LOCOMOTIVE NO.B-100 see **PAROVOZ NO.B-100** • 1927
LOCOMOTIVE PF-47 see **PAROWOZ PF-47** • 1949
LOCOMOTIVES • 1934 • Jennings Humphrey • DCS • UKN
LOCOS PELIGROSOS • 1957 • Cortes Fernando • MXC
LOCOS POR LA MUSICA • 1958 • Porter Julio • MXC
LOCOS POR LA TELEVISION • 1956 • Portillo Rafael • MXC
LOCSOLOKOCSI • 1974 • Kezdi-Kovacs Zsolt • HNG • ORANGE WATERING TRUCK, THE
LOCURA DE AMOR • 1911 • de Banos Ricardo • SPN
LOCURA DE AMOR • 1948 • de Orduna Juan • SPN
LOCURA DE DON JUAN, LA • 1939 • Martinez Solares Gilberto • MXC
LOCURA DE DON JUAN, LA • 1948 • Lugones Mario C. • ARG
LOCURA DE TERROR • 1960 • Soler Julian • MXC • MADNESS FROM TERROR ○ TERROR MADNESS
LOCURA DEL ROCK'N ROLL, LA • 1956 • Mendez Fernando • MXC
LOCURA MUSICAL • 1956 • Portillo Rafael • MXC
LOCURA PASIONAL • 1955 • Demicheli Tulio • MXC
LOCURAS DE BARBARA, LAS • 1958 • Demicheli Tulio • MXC, SPN
LOCURAS DE JANE, LAS • 1977 • Coll Joaquin • SPN
LOCURAS DE TIN TAN, LAS • 1951 • Martinez Solares Gilberto • MXC
LOCUST see **KISEKI** • 1963
LOCUST TREE VILLAGE • 1962 • Wang Ping • CHN
LOCUSTS • 1974 • Heffron Richard T. • TVM • USA
LODER, DER • 1915 • Wauer William • FRG
LODEWIJK DE RAET • 1971 • Buyens Frans • BLG
LODGE IN THE WILDERNESS, THE • 1926 • McCarty Henry • USA
LODGE LOONEY LUTHER • 1914 • *Imp* • USA
LODGE NIGHT • 1923 • Roach Hal • SHT • USA
LODGE NIGHT • 1937 • Black Preston • SHT • USA
LODGER, THE • 1898 • *Paul R. W.* • UKN
LODGER, THE • 1932 • Elvey Maurice • UKN • PHANTOM FIEND, THE (USA)
LODGER, THE • 1944 • Brahm John • USA
LODGER, THE see **LODGER: A STORY OF THE LONDON FOG, THE** • 1926
LODGER, THE see **SUBLOKATOR** • 1967
LODGER: A STORY OF THE LONDON FOG, THE • 1926 • Hitchcock Alfred • UKN • CASE OF JONATHAN DREW, THE (USA) ○ LODGER, THE
LODGER HAD THE HADDOCK, THE • 1907 • Cooper Arthur? • UKN
LODGER WHO WASN'T EXACTLY A PAYING GUEST, THE • 1919 • Miller Frank • SHT • UKN
LODGING FOR THE NIGHT • 1914 • Ricketts Thomas • USA
LODGING FOR THE NIGHT, A • 1912 • Griffith D. W. • USA
LODGING HOUSE COMEDY, A • 1906 • Collins Alf? • UKN
LODGINGS FOR TWO • 1915 • Ransom Charles • USA
LODGINGS TO LET • 1905 • Fitzhamon Lewin • UKN
LODO Y ARMINO • 1951 • Ortega Juan J. • MXC
LODZ 1933-1945 • 1945 • Buczkowski Leonard • DOC • PLN
LODZ GHETTO • 1988 • Taverna, Adelson • DOC • USA
LODZ, THE POLISH MANCHESTER see **TETNO POLSKIEGO MANCHESTERU** • 1929
LOED SUPAN • 1980 • Songsri Cherd • THL
LOETOENG KASAROENG • 1927 • Kruger G. • INN
LOFFE AS A VAGABOND see **LOFFE PA LUFFEN** • 1948
LOFFE BECOMES A POLICEMAN see **LOFFE BLIR POLIS** • 1950
LOFFE BLIR POLIS • 1950 • Ahrle Elof • SWD • LOFFE BECOMES A POLICEMAN
LOFFE PA LUFFEN • 1948 • Werner Gosta • SWD • LOFFE AS A VAGABOND ○ LOFFE THE VAGABOND
LOFFE SOM MILJONAR • 1948 • Bernhard Gosta • SWD
LOFFE THE VAGABOND see **LOFFE PA LUFFEN** • 1948
LOFOTEN • 1940 • MacDonald David • DCS • UKN
LOFWOORD, HET • 1970 • Le Bon E. • BLG
LOG CABIN, THE see **SRUB** • 1965
LOG DRIVE, THE see **DRAVE, LA** • 1957
LOG-DRIVER'S BRIDE, THE see **TUKKIPOJAN MORSIAN** • 1931
LOG DRIVER'S WALTZ • 1980 • Weldon John • ANM • CND
LOG HOUSE • 1976 • Rubbo Michael, Poulsson Andreas • CND
LOG JAMMED • 1958 • Smith Paul J. • ANS • USA
LOG OF THE BLACK PEARL, THE • 1974 • McLaglen Andrew V. • TVM • USA
LOG ROLLERS • 1953 • Davis Mannie • ANS • USA
LOG-ROLLER'S BRIDE, THE see **KOSKENLASKIJAN MORSIAN** • 1922
LOGAN see **RAINBOW BOYS, THE** • 1973
LOGAN'S BABIES • 1911 • *O'Connor Edward* • USA
LOGAN'S RUN • 1976 • Anderson Michael • USA
LOGAN'S RUN • 1977 • Day Robert • TVM • USA
LOGE NR.11 see **AUS DEM SCHWARZBUCH EINES POLIZEIKOMMISSARS 1** • 1921
LOGEMENT ET HABITAT • 1969 • Merbah Lamine • DCS • ALG
LOGGER • 1978 • Sens Al • ANS • CND
LOGGING IN THE OTTAWA VALLEY • 1973 • Walton Lloyd A. • DOC • CND
LOGGING INDUSTRY • 1911 • Porter Edwin S. • USA
LOGIS DE L'HORREUR, LE see **UNHEIMLICHE GAST, DER** • 1922
LOGNEREN • 1970 • Thomsen Knud Leif • DNM • LIAR, THE
LOGOS • 1957 • Conger Jane Belson • SHT • USA
LOHA • 1990 • Dar Waheed • PKS • STEEL
LOHENGRIN • 1907 • *Messter Oskar (P)* • FRG
LOHENGRIN • 1915 • *Dahn Felix* • FRG
LOHENGRIN • 1936 • Malasomma Nunzio • ITL
LOHENGRIN • 1947 • Calandri Max • ITL
LOHENGRINS HEIRAT • 1922 • Peukert Leo • FRG
LOHN UND LIEBE • 1973 • Ludcke Marianne, Kratisch Ingo • FRG
LOI, LA • 1958 • Dassin Jules • FRN, ITL • WHERE THE HOT WIND BLOWS (USA) ○ LEGGE, LA (ITL) ○ LAW, THE
LOI C'EST LA LOI, LA • 1958 • Christian-Jaque • FRN, ITL • LEGGE E LA LEGGE, LA (ITL) ○ LAW IS THE LAW, THE (USA)
LOI DE LA VILLE, LA • 1979 • Bouchard Michel • MTV • CND
LOI DES HOMMES, LA • 1961 • Gerard Charles • FRN
LOI DES RUES, LA • 1956 • Habib Ralph • FRN • LAW OF THE STREETS (USA)
LOI DU 21 JUIN 1907, LA • 1942 • Guitry Sacha • SHT • FRN
LOI DU NORD, LA see **PISTE DU NORD, LA** • 1939
LOI DU PARDON, LA • 1906 • Heuze Andre • FRN
LOI DU PRINTEMPS, LA • 1942 • Daniel-Norman Jacques • FRN
LOI DU SURVIVANT, LA • 1966 • Giovanni Jose • FRN • DESESPERADO, LE
LOI SACREE, LA see **JEUNES FILLES EN DETRESSE** • 1939
LOI SAUVAGE, LA • 1988 • Reusser Francis • SWT
LOIN DE LA PATRIE see **BAID AN AL-WATAN** • 1969
LOIN DE MANHATTAN • 1981 • Biette Jean-Claude • FRN
LOIN DES GUITARES see **AU SON DES GUITARES** • 1936
LOIN DU VIETNAM • 1967 • Resnais Alain, Godard Jean-Luc, Varda Agnes, Lelouch Claude, Klein William, Ivens Joris, Marker Chris • FRN • FAR FROM VIETNAM
LOIS GIBBS AND THE LOVE CANAL • 1982 • Jordan Glenn • TVM • USA • CRUSADE FOR LIFE
LOISIRS • 1961 • Patry Pierre, Perron Clement • DCS • CND
LOITERING IS ILLEGAL • 1973 • Tadej Vladimir • YGS
LOJEN OCH TARAR • 1913 • Sjostrom Victor • SWD • SMILES AND TEARS ○ RIDICULE AND TEARS
LOJNANT GALENPENNA • 1917 • Klercker Georg • SWD • LIEUTENANT MADCAP
LOJNANTSHJARTAN • 1942 • Hildebrand Weyler • SWD • HEARTS OF LIEUTENANTS
LOKIS • 1926 • Gardin Vladimir, Eggert Konstantin V. • USS • MARRIAGE OF THE BEAR, THE (USA) ○ LEGEND OF THE BEAR'S WEDDING ○ BEAR'S WEDDING, THE ○ BEAR, THE ○ MEDVEZHYA SVADBA ○ WEDDING OF THE BEAR
LOKIS • 1969 • Majewski Janusz • PLN • BEAR, THE (USA)
LOKVAL IN VENESIE • 1972 • De Witt Elmo • SAF
LOL COXHILL • 1973 • Audsley Mick • DCS • UKN
LOLA • 1914 • *Greenwood Winifred* • USA
LOLA • 1914 • Young James • USA • WITHOUT A SOUL
LOLA • 1961 • Demy Jacques • FRN, ITL • DONNA DI VITA
LOLA • 1981 • Fassbinder R. W. • FRG
LOLA • 1985 • Luna Bigas • SPN
LOLA • 1990 • Novaro Maria • MXC
LOLA '77 see **LULU LA SPOSA EROTICA** • 1977
LOLA CASANOVA • 1948 • Landeta Matilde • MXC
LOLA COLT • 1967 • Marcellini Siro • ITL • LOLA COLT FACCIA A FACCIA CON EL DIABLO ○ FACCIA A FACCIA CON EL DIABLO ○ LOLA COLT FACE TO FACE WITH THE DEVIL
LOLA COLT FACCIA A FACCIA CON EL DIABLO see **LOLA COLT** • 1967
LOLA COLT FACE TO FACE WITH THE DEVIL see **LOLA COLT** • 1967
LOLA DICEN QUE NO VIVE SOLA, LA • 1969 • de Arminan Jaime • SPN
LOLA, DIE APACHENBRAUT 1 • 1921 • Neff Wolfgang • FRG
LOLA, DIE APACHENBRAUT 2 • 1921 • Neff Wolfgang • FRG
LOLA, ESPEJO OSCURO • 1965 • Merino Fernando • SPN
LOLA LA PICONERA • 1951 • Lucia Luis • SPN
LOLA MONTES • 1944 • Roman Antonio • SPN
LOLA MONTES • 1955 • Ophuls Max • FRN, FRG • SINS OF LOLA MONTES, THE (USA) ○ FALL OF LOLA MONTES, THE (UKN) ○ LOLA MONTEZ
LOLA MONTEZ • 1918 • Heymann Robert • FRG
LOLA MONTEZ • 1919 • Walther-Fein Rudolf • FRG
LOLA MONTEZ see **LOLA MONTES** • 1955
LOLA MONTEZ, DIE TANZERIN DES KONIGS • 1922 • Wolff Willi • FRG
LOLA PAZ Y YO • 1974 • Diez Miguel Angel • SHT • SPN
LOLA SE VA A LOS PUERTOS, LA • 1947 • de Orduna Juan • SPN
LOLA THE RAT • 1914 • Costello Maurice, Gaillord Robert • USA
LOLA (UKN) see **GIRL FROM RIO, THE** • 1927
LOLA (UKN) see **YOUNG BLOOD** • 1932
LOLA (USA) see **TWINKY** • 1969
LOLA'S MISTAKE see **THIS REBEL BREED** • 1960
LOLA'S SACRIFICE • 1912 • *Majestic* • USA
LOLA'S SECRET • *Damiani Donatella* • ITL
LOLITA • 1962 • Kubrick Stanley • USA, UKN
LOLITA'S TOCCATO AND FUGUE see **TOCATA Y FUGA DE LOLITA** • 1974
LOLLIPOP AND ROSES • 1917 • Wilson Frank • UKN
LOLLIPOP COVER, THE • 1965 • Chambers Everett • USA
LOLLIPOP (USA) see **ASFALTO SELVAGEM** • 1964
LOLLY MADONNA WAR, THE see **LOLLY MADONNA XXX** • 1973
LOLLY MADONNA XXX • 1973 • Sarafian Richard C. • USA • LOLLY MADONNA WAR, THE
LOLOS DE LOLA, LES • 1974 • Dubois Bernard • FRN
LOMA • 1976 • Jarva Risto • FNL • OLYMPIAN HOLIDAY ○ HOLIDAY, THE
LOMBARDI, LTD. • 1919 • Conway Jack • USA
LOMELIN • 1965 • Reichenbach Francois • SHT • FRN • PORTRAIT D'UN NOVILLERO
LON OF LONE MOUNTAIN • 1915 • De Grasse Joseph • USA
LONA UND IHR KNECHT see **SUNDIGE HOF, DER** • 1933
LONDON • 1926 • Wilcox Herbert • UKN • LIMEHOUSE
LONDON • 1930 • *Holmes Burton* • DOC • USA
LONDON -1942 • 1942 • Annakin Ken • DCS • UKN
LONDON AFTER MIDNIGHT • 1927 • Browning Tod • USA • HYPNOTIST, THE (UKN)
LONDON ASSIGNMENT see **DANGEROUS ASSIGNMENT** • 1950
LONDON ASSURANCE • 1913 • McGill Lawrence • USA
LONDON BELONGS TO ME • 1948 • Gilliat Sidney • UKN • DULCIMER STREET (USA)
LONDON BLACKOUT MURDERS • 1942 • Sherman George • USA • SECRET MOTIVE (UKN)
LONDON BOBBY, A • 1920 • Roach Hal • SHT • USA
LONDON BY DAY AND NIGHT • 1916 • MacMahon Charles • DOC • ASL
LONDON BY NIGHT • 1913 • Butler Alexander? • UKN
LONDON BY NIGHT • 1937 • Thiele Wilhelm • USA • UMBRELLA MAN, THE
LONDON CALLING NAPLES see **DELITTO A POSILLIPO** • 1967
LONDON CAN TAKE IT • 1940 • Jennings Humphrey, Watt Harry • DCS • UKN
LONDON CONNECTION, THE • 1979 • Clouse Robert • UKN • OMEGA CONNECTION, THE (USA)
LONDON CONSPIRACY, THE see **PERSUADERS: LONDON CONSPIRACY, THE** • 1976
LONDON DRAG • 1970 • Benner Richard • USA
LONDON ENTERTAINS • 1951 • Fancey E. J. • UKN
LONDON EXPOSED see **PRIMITIVE LONDON** • 1965
LONDON FANTASY see **FANTASY OF LONDON LIFE, A** • 1950
LONDON FLAT MYSTERY, A see **MYSTERY OF A LONDON FLAT, THE** • 1915
LONDON HAMU • 1968 • Somasekaran C. • SLN • MAN FROM LONDON, THE
LONDON IN A HURRY • 1904 • *Mutoscope & Biograph* • UKN
LONDON IN THE RAW • 1964 • Miller Arnold Louis • UKN
LONDON LOVE • 1926 • Haynes Manning • UKN • WHIRLPOOL, THE
LONDON MELODY • 1930 • Malins Geoffrey H., Stuart Donald • UKN
LONDON MELODY • 1936 • Wilcox Herbert • UKN • GIRLS IN THE STREETS (USA)
LONDON MOODS • 1961 • Russell Ken • MTV • UKN
LONDON MYSTERY, A • 1914 • Calvert Charles • UKN
LONDON NIGHTHAWKS • 1915 • Moran Percy • UKN
LONDON NOBODY KNOWS, THE • 1968 • Cohen Norman • DOC • UKN
LONDON OFF THE TRACK • 1924 • Parkinson H. B., Miller Frank • UKN
LONDON PRIDE • 1920 • Shaw Harold • UKN
LONDON ROCK 'N' ROLL SHOW • 1973 • Clifton Peter • DOC • UKN
LONDON SCENE, THE • 1968 • Green J. S. • DCS • UKN
LONDON -THROUGH MY EYES • 1970 • Crichton Charles • DCS • UKN
LONDON TOWN • 1946 • Ruggles Wesley • UKN • MY HEART GOES CRAZY (USA)
LONDONDERRY AIR, THE • 1938 • Bryce Alex • UKN
LONDONER NEBEL see **WHITECHAPEL** • 1920
LONDONERS, THE • 1940 • Leacock Philip, Taylor John • DOC • UKN
LONDON'S BURNING • 1922 • *Parkinson H. B.(P)* • SHT • UKN
LONDON'S COUNTRY • 1954 • Sharples Syd • UKN
LONDON'S ENEMIES • 1916 • Moran Percy • UKN
LONDON'S UNDERWORLD • 1914 • *Lorraine Harry* • UKN
LONDON'S YELLOW PERIL • 1915 • Elvey Maurice • UKN
LONDRA CHIAMA NAPOLI see **DELITTO A POSILLIPO** • 1967
LONDRA CHIAMA POLO NORD • 1957 • Coletti Duilio • ITL • HOUSE OF INTRIGUE, THE (USA)
LONDRE • 1966 • Meliava Tamaz • USS
LONDRES • 1966 • Fournier Claude • DCS • CND
LONE AVENGER, THE • 1933 • James Alan • USA
LONE BANDIT, THE • 1934 • McGowan J. P. • USA
LONE BILL'S LAST RIDE • 1911 • *Nestor* • USA
LONE CHANCE, THE • 1924 • Mitchell Howard M. • USA • MARK OF CAIN, THE
LONE CHIPMUNKS, THE • 1954 • Kinney Jack • ANS • USA
LONE CLIMBER, THE • 1950 • Hammond William C. • UKN
LONE COWBOY, THE • 1933 • Sloane Paul • USA • HE'S MY PAL ○ PARDNERS
LONE DEFENDER, THE • 1930 • Thorpe Richard • SRL • USA
LONE DOG THE FAITHFUL • 1913 • *Lubin* • USA
LONE EAGLE, THE • 1927 • Johnson Emory • USA • AMERICAN EAGLE, THE ○ WAR EAGLES ○ WAR HAWKS
LONE EAGLE, THE see **EAGLE, THE** • 1925
LONE EAGLE'S TRUST • 1911 • *Powers* • USA
LONE FIGHTER • 1923 • Russell Albert • USA
LONE GAME, THE • 1915 • *Eclair* • USA
LONE GAME, THE • 1915 • Taylor Edward C. • *Edison* • USA
LONE GUN, THE • 1954 • Nazarro Ray • USA
LONE HAND, THE • 1919 • Holt George • SHT • USA
LONE HAND, THE • 1920 • Smith Cliff • USA
LONE HAND, THE • 1922 • Eason B. Reeves, Ross Nat • USA • FALSE PLAY
LONE HAND, THE • 1953 • Sherman George • USA
LONE HAND SAUNDERS • 1926 • Eason B. Reeves • USA
LONE HAND TEXAN, THE • 1947 • Nazarro Ray • USA • CHEAT, THE (UKN)

LONE HAND TEXAS • 1924 • *Cuneo Lester* • USA
LONE HAND WILSON • 1920 • McKee L. S., Moody Harry • USA
LONE HAWK OF THE WATER FRONT see **HATOBA NO TAKA** • 1967
LONE HORSEMAN, THE • 1923 • Caldwell Fred • USA
LONE HORSEMAN, THE • 1929 • McGowan J. P. • USA
LONE JOURNEY, THE see **TABIJI** • 1955
LONE LARRY • 1917 • McRae Henry • SHT • USA
LONE MOUNTIE, THE • 1938 • *Mintz Charles (P)* • ANS • USA
LONE PATROL, THE • 1928 • *Bailey William* • USA
LONE POINT FEUD, THE • 1917 • *Gibson Helen* • SHT • USA
LONE PRAIRIE, THE • 1943 • Berke William • USA • INSIDE INFORMATION (UKN)
LONE RANGER • 1966-67 • Halas John • ASS • UKN
LONE RANGER, THE • 1920 • Wright Mack V. • SHT • USA
LONE RANGER, THE • 1938 • Witney William, English John • SRL • USA
LONE RANGER, THE • 1956 • Heisler Stuart • USA
LONE RANGER AND THE LOST CITY OF GOLD, THE • 1958 • Selander Lesley • USA
LONE RANGER RIDES AGAIN, THE • 1939 • Witney William, English John • SRL • USA
LONE RIDER, THE • 1922 • Dixon Denver, Caldwell Fred • USA
LONE RIDER, THE • 1927 • *Church Fred* • USA
LONE RIDER, THE • 1930 • King Louis • USA
LONE RIDER, THE • 1934 • Tansey Robert • USA
LONE RIDER, THE (UKN) see **LONE RIDER IN TEXAS JUSTICE, THE** • 1941
LONE RIDER AMBUSHED, THE • 1941 • Newfield Sam • USA
LONE RIDER AND THE BANDIT, THE • 1942 • Newfield Sam • USA
LONE RIDER CROSSES THE RIO, THE • 1941 • Newfield Sam • USA
LONE RIDER FIGHTS BACK, THE • 1941 • Newfield Sam • USA
LONE RIDER IN BORDER ROUNDUP • 1943 • Newfield Sam • USA • BORDER ROUNDUP (UKN)
LONE RIDER IN CHEYENNE, THE • 1942 • Newfield Sam • USA
LONE RIDER IN FRONTIER FURY, THE • 1941 • Newfield Sam • USA • FRONTIER FURY (UKN)
LONE RIDER IN GHOST TOWN, THE • 1941 • Newfield Sam • USA
LONE RIDER IN TEXAS JUSTICE, THE • 1941 • Newfield Sam • USA • LONE RIDER, THE (UKN) ○ TEXAS JUSTICE
LONE RIDER RIDES ON, THE • 1941 • Newfield Sam • USA
LONE RUNNER • 1986 • Deodato Ruggero • ITL
LONE SCOUT, THE • 1929 • Cross J. H. Martin • UKN
LONE STALKER, THE see **HITORI OKAMI** • 1968
LONE STAR • 1916 • Sloman Edward • USA
LONE STAR • 1951 • Sherman Vincent • USA
LONE STAR, THE • 1927 • Wyler William • SHT • USA
LONE STAR LAWMAN see **TEXAS LAWMEN** • 1951
LONE STAR LAWMEN • 1941 • Tansey Robert • USA
LONE STAR MOONLIGHT • 1946 • Nazarro Ray • USA • AMONGST THE THIEVES (UKN)
LONE STAR PADRE • 1946 • *Mead Thomas (P)* • SHT • USA
LONE STAR PIONEERS • 1939 • Levering Joseph • USA • UNWELCOME VISITORS (UKN)
LONE STAR RAIDERS • 1940 • Sherman George • USA
LONE STAR RANGER, THE • 1919 • Edwards J. Gordon • USA
LONE STAR RANGER, THE • 1923 • Hillyer Lambert • USA
LONE STAR RANGER, THE • 1930 • Erickson A. F. • USA
LONE STAR RANGER, THE • 1941 • Tinling James • USA
LONE STAR RUSH, THE • 1915 • Mitchell Edmund • USA • GOLD LURE, THE
LONE STAR STATE, THE • 1948 • Sparber I. • ANS • USA
LONE STAR STRANGER, THE • 1931 • Buzzell Edward • SHT • USA
LONE STAR TRAIL, THE • 1943 • Taylor Ray • USA
LONE STAR VIGILANTES, THE • 1942 • Fox Wallace • USA • DEVIL'S PRICE, THE (UKN)
LONE STAR'S RETURN • 1911 • *Bison* • USA
LONE STRANGER AND PORKY, THE • 1939 • Clampett Robert • ANS • USA
LONE TEXAN, THE • 1959 • Landres Paul • USA
LONE TEXAS RANGER • 1945 • Bennet Spencer Gordon • USA
LONE TRAIL, THE • 1932 • Sheldon Forrest, Webb Harry S. • USA
LONE TROUBADOUR, THE (UKN) see **TWO-GUN TROUBADOUR** • 1939
LONE WAGON, THE • 1923 • Mattison Frank S. • USA
LONE WHITE SAIL, THE see **BYELEYET PARUS ODINOKY** • 1937
LONE WOLF • 1987 • Callas John • USA
LONE WOLF, THE • 1917 • Brenon Herbert • USA
LONE WOLF, THE • 1924 • Taylor Stanner E. V. • USA • LONE WOLF'S LAST ADVENTURE
LONE WOLF, THE see **VUK SAMATNJAK** • 1973
LONE WOLF, THE see **BIRYUK** • 1979
LONE WOLF AND HIS LADY, THE • 1949 • Hoffman John • USA
LONE WOLF IN LONDON, THE • 1947 • Goodwins Leslie • USA
LONE WOLF IN MEXICO, THE • 1947 • Lederman D. Ross • USA
LONE WOLF IN PARIS, THE • 1938 • Rogell Albert S. • USA
LONE WOLF KEEPS A DATE, THE • 1941 • Salkow Sidney • USA • ALIAS THE LONE WOLF
LONE WOLF MCQUADE • 1982 • Carver Steve • USA
LONE WOLF MEETS A LADY, THE • 1940 • Salkow Sidney • USA
LONE WOLF RETURNS, THE • 1926 • Ince Ralph • USA • RETURN OF THE LONE WOLF
LONE WOLF RETURNS, THE • 1935 • Neill R. William • USA
LONE WOLF SPY HUNT, THE • 1939 • Godfrey Peter • USA • LONE WOLF'S DAUGHTER, THE (UKN)
LONE WOLF STRIKES, THE • 1940 • Salkow Sidney • USA
LONE WOLF TAKES A CHANCE, THE • 1941 • Salkow Sidney • USA
LONE WOLF'S DAUGHTER, THE • 1919 • Earle William P. S. • USA
LONE WOLF'S DAUGHTER, THE • 1929 • Rogell Albert S. • USA
LONE WOLF'S DAUGHTER, THE (UKN) see **LONE WOLF SPY HUNT, THE** • 1939
LONE WOLF'S LAST ADVENTURE see **LONE WOLF, THE** • 1924
LONE WOLF'S TRUST • 1910 • *Yankee* • USA
LONE WORLD SAIL • 1960 • Halas John • ANS • UKN
LONEDALE OPERATOR, THE • 1911 • Griffith D. W. • USA
LONELIES, THE • 1916 • North Wilfred • SHT • USA
LONELIEST RUNNER, THE • 1977 • Landon Michael • TVM • USA
LONELINESS AND LOVE • 1913 • *Haldeman Edith* • USA
LONELINESS FOR TWO see **SAMOTNOSC WE DWOJE** • 1968
LONELINESS OF NEGLECT • 1912 • Dwan Allan • USA
LONELINESS OF THE HILLS, THE • 1912 • *Kalem* • USA
LONELINESS OF THE LONG DISTANCE RUNNER, THE • 1962 • Richardson Tony • UKN • REBEL WITH A CAUSE
LONELINESS TETE A TETE see **SAMOTNOSC WE DWOJE** • 1968
LONELY ARE THE BRAVE • 1962 • Miller David • USA
LONELY BACHELOR, THE see **NOBLE BACHELOR, THE** • 1921
LONELY BOAT, THE • 1952 • Leacock Richard • DOC • USA
LONELY BOY • 1961 • Koenig Wolf, Kroitor Roman • DCS • CND • PAUL ANKA
LONELY CHILD -THE IMAGINARY WORLD OF CLAUDE VIVIER • 1988 • Silver Jonny • DOC • CND
LONELY CLINT see **CLINT EL SOLITARIO** • 1965
LONELY FISHERMAN, THE • 1915 • Melville Wilbert • USA
LONELY GEISHA, A see **ONNA NO HAISHO** • 1961
LONELY GENTLEMAN • 1908 • *Vitagraph* • USA
LONELY GUY, THE • 1984 • Hiller Arthur • USA
LONELY HEART • 1921 • O'Brien John B. • USA
LONELY HEART see **CORAZON SOLITARIO** • 1972
LONELY HEART, THE • 1913 • Huntley Fred W. • USA
LONELY HEART, THE see **MUSIC LOVERS, THE** • 1970
LONELY HEARTS • 1982 • Cox Paul • ASL
LONELY HEARTS BANDITS • 1950 • Blair George • USA
LONELY HEARTS (USA) see **KOFUKU** • 1982
LONELY HOODLUM see **SABISHIKI RANBOMONO** • 1927
LONELY HORSEMAN, THE see **OSAMELY JEZDEC** • 1966
LONELY HOUSE, THE • 1957 • Tully Montgomery • UKN
LONELY HOUSEWIFE • 1970 • *Janus Ii Productions* • USA • LONELY HOUSEWIVES
LONELY HOUSEWIVES see **LONELY HOUSEWIFE** • 1970
LONELY IN AMERICA • 1990 • *Malik Trilok (P)* • USA
LONELY INN, THE • 1912 • Coleby A. E. • UKN
LONELY JOURNEY OF CHIKUZAN see **CHIKUZAN HITORI TABI** • 1976
LONELY KILLERS see **TUEURS FOUS, LES** • 1972
LONELY KNIGHTS • Less Henry • USA
LONELY LADY, THE • 1983 • Sasdy Peter • USA
LONELY LADY OF GROSVENOR SQUARE, THE • 1922 • Hill Sinclair • UKN
LONELY LANE see **HOROKI** • 1962
LONELY LIFE, THE see **SHAYO NO OMOKAGE** • 1967
LONELY LOVERS • 1915 • Martin E. A. • USA
LONELY MAN see **GUN RIDERS** • 1970
LONELY MAN, THE • 1957 • Levin Henry • USA
LONELY MAN, THE see **SAMAC** • 1958
LONELY NIGHT, THE • 1952 • Jacoby Irving • DOC • USA
LONELY PASSION OF JUDITH HEARNE, THE • 1987 • Clayton Jack • UKN
LONELY PLEASURES see **PLAISIRS SOLITAIRES, LES** • 1976
LONELY PRINCESS, THE • 1913 • Costello Maurice • USA
LONELY PROFESSION, THE • 1969 • Heyes Douglas • TVM • USA • SAVARONA SYNDROME, THE
LONELY RANGE, THE • 1911 • Dwan Allan • USA
LONELY ROAD, A • 1914 • *Fuller Mary* • USA
LONELY ROAD, THE • 1921 • Vanderbosch Alfred • UKN
LONELY ROAD, THE • 1923 • Schertzinger Victor • USA
LONELY ROAD, THE • 1936 • Flood James • UKN • SCOTLAND YARD COMMANDS
LONELY ROUGHNECK, THE see **SABISHIKI RANBOMONO** • 1927
LONELY SALVATION, A • 1914 • *Fuller Mary* • USA
LONELY SHORE • 1964 • Russell Ken • MTV • UKN
LONELY STAGE, THE see **I COULD GO ON SINGING** • 1962
LONELY TRAIL, THE • 1922 • *Beauvais Fred K.* • USA
LONELY TRAIL, THE • 1936 • Kane Joseph • USA
LONELY VILLA, THE • 1909 • Griffith D. W. • USA
LONELY VILLAGE see **SABISHIKI MURA** • 1924
LONELY WHITE SAIL see **BYELEYET PARUS ODINOKY** • 1937
LONELY WIFE, THE (UKN) see **CHARULATA** • 1964
LONELY WIVES • 1931 • Mack Russell • USA
LONELY WOMAN, THE • 1918 • Heffron Thomas N. • USA
LONELY WOMAN, THE see **CHARULATA** • 1964
LONELY WOMAN, THE (UKN) see **VIAGGIO IN ITALIA** • 1953
LONELY WOMAN, THE (USA) see **ROSES ROUGES ET PIMENTS VERTS** • 1973
LONELYHEARTS • 1958 • Donehue Vincent J. • USA • MISS LONELYHEARTS
LONER, THE see **SOLITAIRE, LE** • 1972
LONER, THE see **RUPALI SHAIKATEY** • 1977
LONER, THE see **RUCKUS** • 1980
LONER, THE see **GUDUDE MOUSHAZHE** • 1988
LONERS see **SEULS** • 1981
LONERS, THE • 1972 • Roley Sutton • USA
LONESOME • 1928 • Fejos Paul • USA • SOLITUDE
LONESOME CHAP, THE • 1917 • Le Saint Edward J. • USA
LONESOME CORNERS • 1922 • Jones Edgar • USA
LONESOME COWBOYS • 1968 • Warhol Andy • USA
LONESOME DOVE • 1988 • Wincer Simon • MTV • USA
LONESOME FARM • 1922 • Dewhurst George • UKN
LONESOME GHOSTS • 1937 • Gillett Burt • ANS • USA
LONESOME HEART • 1915 • Pollard Harry • USA
LONESOME HEARTS AND LOOSE LIONS • 1919 • Watson William • SHT • USA
LONESOME HOUSE • 1916 • Cochrane George • SHT • USA
LONESOME JOE • 1913 • *American* • USA
LONESOME JUNCTION • 1908 • *Bitzer Billy (Ph)* • USA
LONESOME LADIES • 1927 • Henabery Joseph • USA
LONESOME LENNY • 1946 • Avery Tex • ANS • USA
LONESOME LUKE • 1915 • Roach Hal • USA
LONESOME LUKE, CIRCUS KING • 1916 • Roach Hal • SHT • USA
LONESOME LUKE FROM LONDON TO LARAMIE • 1917 • Roach Hal • SHT • USA
LONESOME LUKE, LAWYER • 1917 • Roach Hal • SHT • USA
LONESOME LUKE LEANS TO THE LITERARY • 1916 • Roach Hal • SHT • USA • LUKE LEANS TO THE LITERARY
LONESOME LUKE LOLLS IN LUXURY • 1916 • Roach Hal • SHT • USA • LUKE LOLLS IN LUXURY
LONESOME LUKE LOSES PATIENTS • 1917 • Roach Hal • SHT • USA
LONESOME LUKE, MECHANIC • 1917 • Roach Hal • SHT • USA
LONESOME LUKE -MESSENGER • 1917 • Roach Hal • SHT • USA
LONESOME LUKE ON TIN CAN ALLEY • 1917 • Roach Hal • SHT • USA
LONESOME LUKE, PLUMBER • 1917 • Roach Hal • SHT • USA
LONESOME LUKE, SOCIAL GANGSTER • 1915 • MacDonald J. Farrell • SHT • USA • SOCIAL GANGSTER
LONESOME LUKE'S HONEYMOON • 1917 • Roach Hal • SHT • USA
LONESOME LUKE'S LIVELY LIFE • 1917 • Roach Hal • SHT • USA
LONESOME LUKE'S MOVIE MUDDLE • 1916 • Roach Hal • USA
LONESOME LUKE'S WILD WOMEN • 1917 • Roach Hal • SHT • USA
LONESOME MARINER, THE • 1917 • *Coxen Ed* • SHT • USA
LONESOME MISS WIGGS • 1912 • *Cumpson John R.* • USA
LONESOME MOUSE, THE • 1943 • Hanna William, Barbera Joseph • ANS • USA
LONESOME RANGER • 1966 • Marcus Sid • ANS • USA
LONESOME ROAD, THE • 1917 • Smith David • SHT • USA
LONESOME ROBERT • 1912 • *Bushman Francis X.* • USA
LONESOME STRANGER • 1940 • Harman Hugh • ANS • USA
LONESOME TOWN • 1916 • Heffron Thomas N. • USA
LONESOME TRAIL • 1914 • Campbell Colin • USA
LONESOME TRAIL • 1945 • Drake Oliver • USA
LONESOME TRAIL, THE • 1930 • Mitchell Bruce • USA
LONESOME TRAIL, THE • 1955 • Bartlett Richard • USA
LONESOME TRAIL PIONEERS • 1912 • *American* • USA
LONESOME TRAILER, THE • Staub Ralph • SHT • USA
LONESOME WOMEN (USA) see **FRONTEIRAS DO INFERNO** • 1959
LONESOMENESS • 1916 • Reynolds Lynn • SHT • USA
LONG ABSENCE, THE (USA) see **AUSSI LONGUE ABSENCE, UNE** • 1961
LONG AGO TOMORROW (USA) see **RAGING MOON, THE** • 1970
LONG AND HAPPY LIFE, A see **DOLGAYA SCHASTLIVAYA ZHIZN** • 1967
LONG AND SHORT OF IT, THE • 1913 • *Milash Robert* • USA
LONG AND SHORT OF IT, THE see **NAIN ET GEANT** • 1902
LONG AND THE SHORT AND THE TALL, THE • 1960 • Norman Leslie • UKN • JUNGLE FIGHTERS (USA)
LONG ARM, THE • 1956 • Frend Charles • UKN • THIRD KEY, THE (USA)
LONG ARM OF MANNISTER, THE • 1919 • Bracken Bertram • USA
LONG ARM OF THE GODFATHER, THE see **MANO LUNGA DEL PADRINO, LA** • 1972
LONG ARM OF THE LAW • 1984 • Mak Johnny • HKG
LONG ARM OF THE LAW, THE • 1911 • *Kalem* • USA
LONG ARM OF THE LAW, THE • 1914 • *P.i.s.p.* • USA
LONG ARM OF THE SECRET SERVICE, THE • 1915 • *Arey Wayne* • USA
LONG BLUE ROAD, THE see **GRANDE STRADA AZZURRA, LA** • 1957
LONG BODIES, THE • 1947 • Crockwell Douglas • ANS • USA
LONG CHANCE, THE • 1915 • Le Saint Edward J. • USA
LONG CHANCE, THE • 1922 • Conway Jack • USA
LONG COLD NIGHT, THE • 1914 • *Stonehouse Ruth* • USA
LONG CORRIDOR see **SHOCK CORRIDOR** • 1963
LONG DARK HALL, THE • 1951 • Bushell Anthony, Beck Reginald • UKN
LONG DARK NIGHT, A see **BLIND FEAR** • 1989
LONG DARK NIGHT, THE see **PACK, THE** • 1977
LONG DARKNESS, THE see **SHINOBU-GAWA** • 1972
LONG DAY OF THE MASSACRE, THE see **LUNGO GIORNO DEL MASSACRO, IL** • 1968
LONG DAYS, THE • 1973 • Hadzismajlovic Vefik • SHT • YGS
LONG DAYS, THE see **AL-AYYAM AL-TAWILLA** • 1980
LONG DAY'S DYING, THE • 1968 • Collinson Peter • UKN
LONG DAY'S JOURNEY INTO NIGHT • 1962 • Lumet Sidney • USA
LONG DAYS OF SUMMER, THE • 1980 • Curtis Dan • TVM • USA
LONG DEFIANCE, THE see **LUNGA SFIDA, LA** • 1967
LONG DES TROTTOIRS, LE • 1956 • Moguy Leonide • FRN, ITL • DIARY OF A BAD GIRL (USA) ○ WIDTH OF THE PAVEMENT, THE
LONG DISTANCE see **TREASURE OF SAN TERESA, THE** • 1959
LONG DISTANCE WIRELESS PHOTOGRAPHY (USA) see **PHOTOGRAPHIE ELECTRIQUE A DISTANCE, LA** • 1908
LONG DREAM, THE • 1967 • Kelly Ron • CND
LONG DRIVE see **CURSA** • 1975
LONG DUEL, THE • 1967 • Annakin Ken • UKN
LONG EARS • 1961 • Buchvarova Radka • ANS • BUL
LONG-EARS • 1961 • Buchvarova Radka • BUL
LONG FEUD, THE • 1914 • *Broncho* • USA
LONG GONE • 1987 • Davidson Martin • TVM • USA
LONG GOOD FRIDAY, THE • 1980 • Mackenzie John • UKN
LONG GOODBYE, THE • 1973 • Altman Robert • USA
LONG GRAY LINE, THE • 1955 • Ford John • USA
LONG GREEN STOCKING, THE (USA) see **LUNGA CALZA VERDE, LA** • 1961
LONG-GREEN TRAIL, THE • 1917 • Beaumont Harry • SHT • USA
LONG GREY LINE, THE see **BEYOND GLORY** • 1948
LONG HAIR OF DEATH, THE (UKN) see **LUNGHI CAPELLI DELLA MORTE, I** • 1964
LONG-HAIRED HARE • 1949 • Jones Charles M. • ANS • USA

LONG HARD NIGHT, THE (UKN) see **PACK, THE** • 1977
LONG HAUL, THE • 1957 • Hughes Ken • UKN
LONG HAUL MEN, THE • 1966 • Rubbo Michael • DOC • CND
LONG HOLE, THE • 1924 • Wilson Andrew P. • UKN • MOVING HAZARD, HTE
LONG HOLIDAYS OF 36, THE see **LARGAS VACACIONES DEL 36, LAS** • 1975
LONG HOT SUMMER, THE • 1958 • Ritt Martin • USA
LONG HOT SUMMER, THE • 1985 • Cooper Stuart • TVM • USA
LONG IS THE ROAD see **LANG IST DER WEG** • 1948
LONG JOHN SILVER • 1954 • Haskin Byron • ASL • LONG JOHN SILVER RETURNS TO TREASURE ISLAND
LONG JOHN SILVER RETURNS TO TREASURE ISLAND see **LONG JOHN SILVER** • 1954
LONG JOURNEY see **LARGO VIAJE** • 1967
LONG JOURNEY, THE see **DALEKA CESTA** • 1949
LONG JOURNEY BACK • 1978 • Damski Mel • TVM • USA
LONG JOURNEY HOME, THE • 1987 • Holcomb Rod • TVM • USA
LONG JOURNEY INTO A SHORT DAY • 1972 • Levchuk Timofey • USS
LONG JOURNEY OF POPPIE NONGENA • 1989 • Roets Koos • SAF
LONG KNIFE, THE • 1958 • Tully Montgomery • UKN
LONG LANE, A • 1917 • Terwilliger George W. • SHT • USA
LONG LANE, THE • 1914 • Powell Paul • USA
LONG LANE'S TURNING, THE • 1919 • Chaudet Louis W. • USA
LONG LIVE ALL WOMEN!! see **ARRRIBA LAS MUJERES!!** • 1967
LONG LIVE CARRANCHO! see **QUE VIVA CARRANCHO!** • 1967
LONG LIVE GHOSTS! see **AT ZIJI DUCHOVE** • 1976
LONG LIVE KINDNESS see **AT ZIJE NEBOZTIK!** • 1935
LONG LIVE SERVATIUS! see **ELJEN SVERVAC!** • 1987
LONG LIVE THE AIR see **DAYESH VOZDUKH** • 1924
LONG LIVE THE BRIDE AND GROOM (USA) see **VIVAN LOS NOVIOS!** • 1970
LONG LIVE THE DECEASED see **AT ZIJE NEBOZTIK!** • 1935
LONG LIVE THE GHOSTS! see **AT ZIJI DUCHOVE** • 1976
LONG LIVE THE KING • 1923 • Schertzinger Victor • USA
LONG LIVE THE KING • 1926 • McCarey Leo • SHT • USA
LONG LIVE THE KING • 1933 • McGann William • UKN
LONG LIVE THE LADY! see **LUNGA VITA ALLA SIGNORA!** • 1988
LONG LIVE THE LOVED ONE! see **AT ZIJE NEBOZTIK!** • 1935
LONG LIVE THE MIDDLE CLASS see **VIVA LA CLASE MEDIA** • 1980
LONG LIVE THE QUEEN • 1917 • Baker George D. • USA
LONG LIVE THE REPUBLIC! see **AT ZIJE REPUBLIKA!** • 1965
LONG LIVE YOUR DEATH see **VIVA LA MUERTE.. TUA** • 1971
LONG LIVE YOUTH • 1966 • Zafranovic Lordan • DOC • YGS
LONG, LONG TRAIL, THE • 1929 • Rosson Arthur • USA
LONG, LONG TRAIL, THE see **RAMBLIN' KID, THE** • 1923
LONG, LONG TRAIL, THE (UKN) see **TEXAS TO BATAAN** • 1942
LONG, LONG TRAILER, THE • 1953 • Minnelli Vincente • USA
LONG LOOP, THE see **LONG LOOP OF THE PECOS, THE** • 1927
LONG LOOP OF THE PECOS, THE • 1927 • Maloney Leo • USA • LONG LOOP, THE
LONG LOST FATHER • 1934 • Schoedsack Ernest B. • USA
LONG LOST FRIEND, THE see **APPRENTICE TO MURDER** • 1988
LONG MARCH, THE see **LONGUE MARCHE, LA** • 1966
LONG MAY IT WAVE • 1914 • *Lubin* • USA
LONG MEMORY, THE • 1953 • Hamer Robert • UKN
LONG NIGHT, A see **UZUN BIR GECE** • 1987
LONG NIGHT, THE • 1947 • Litvak Anatole • USA
LONG NIGHT, THE • 1976 • King Woodie • USA
LONG NIGHT OF '43, THE see **LUNGA NOTTE DEL '43, LA** • 1960
LONG NIGHT OF VERONICA, THE see **LUNGA NOTTE DI VERONIQUE, LA** • 1966
LONG NIGHTS, THE see **LAYALY EL TAWILA, EL** • 1967
LONG ODDS • 1922 • Coleby A. E. • UKN
LONG PANTS • 1926 • Roach Hal • SHT • USA
LONG PANTS • 1927 • Capra Frank • USA
LONG PATH, THE see **DOLGII PUT** • 1956
LONG PLAY • 1968 • Seto Javier • SPN
LONG PORTAGE, THE • 1913 • Montgomery Frank E., Conway Jack • USA
LONG RED SHADOW, THE • 1968 • Rubens Percival • SAF
LONG RETURNING, A see **LARGO RETORNO, UN** • 1974
LONG RIDE, THE • 1983 • Gabor Pal • USA, HNG • HOSSZU VAGTA (HNG) ○ BRADY'S ESCAPE
LONG RIDE FROM HELL, A (USA) see **VIVO PER LA TUA MORTE** • 1968
LONG RIDE HOME, THE (UKN) see **TIME FOR KILLING, A** • 1967
LONG RIDE TO SCHOOL, THE see **LANGE RITT ZUR SCHOLE, DER**
LONG RIDERS, THE • 1920 • *Jennings Al* • SHT • USA
LONG RIDERS, THE • 1980 • Hill Walter • USA
LONG RIFLE AND THE TOMAHAWK, THE • 1956 • Salkow Sidney, Newfield Sam • MTV • CND
LONG RING, THE • 1916 • *Judy* • SHT • USA
LONG ROAD see **LANGA VAGEN, DEN** • 1947
LONG ROAD, THE • 1911 • Griffith D. W. • USA
LONG ROAD HOME • 1990 • Johnston William • CND
LONG ROAD TO GLORY, THE see **UTRPENIM KE SLAVE** • 1919
LONG ROAD TO TIJUANA see **CAMINO LARGO A TIJUANA** • 1988
LONG ROPE, THE • 1961 • Witney William • USA
LONG ROPE, THE see **LARGE ROPE, THE** • 1953
LONG RUN, THE • 1985 • SAF
LONG SATURDAY see **LANGER SAMSTAG** • 1989
LONG SATURDAY NIGHT, THE (USA) see **VIVEMENT DIMANCHE** • 1983
LONG SEARCH, THE • 1916 • *Big U* • SHT • USA
LONG SEARCH, THE (USA) see **HAN GLOMDE HENNEALDRIG** • 1952
LONG SHADOW, THE • 1961 • Maxwell Peter • UKN
LONG SHADOWS OF THE WIND, THE see **SAYEHAYE BOLANDE BAD** • 1978
LONG SHIFT, THE • 1915 • *Myles Norbert* • USA
LONG SHIPS, THE • 1964 • Cardiff Jack • UKN, YGS • DUGI BRODOVI (YGS)
LONG SHOT • 1978 • Hatton Maurice • UKN
LONG SHOT, THE • 1938 • Lamont Charles • USA
LONG SHOT, THE see **TIGERS DON'T CRY** • 1976
LONG SKIRT, THE • 1911 • *Vitagraph* • USA
LONG SPRINT, THE • 1976 • Alexander Mike • DOC • UKN
LONG STRIKE, THE • 1911 • *Essanay* • USA
LONG STRIKE, THE • 1912 • Brenon Herbert • USA
LONG SUMMER OF GEORGE ADAMS, THE • 1982 • Margolin Stuart • TVM • USA
LONG SUNDAY, THE see **NOZ W WODZIE** • 1961
LONG SWIFT SWORD OF SIEGFRIED, THE (USA) see **SIEGFRIED UND DAS SAGENHAFTE LIEBESLEBEN DER NIBELUNGEN** • 1971
LONG TIME GONE • 1986 • Butler Robert • TVM • USA
LONG TOMORROW, THE see **CRY FOR ME, BILLY** • 1972
LONG TRAIL, THE • 1910 • Boggs Frank • USA
LONG TRAIL, THE • 1917 • Hansel Howell • USA
LONG VOYAGE HOME, THE • 1940 • Ford John • USA
LONG VOYAGE TOWARDS DEATH, A see **LARGO VIAJE HACIA LA MUERTE, UN** • 1968
LONG WAIT, THE • 1954 • Saville Victor • USA
LONG WALK HOME, THE • 1990 • Pearce Richard • USA
LONG WAY, THE • 1914 • Brabin Charles J. • USA
LONG WAY, THE see **DOLGII PUT** • 1956
LONG WAY FOR A MOTOR CAR, A see **HARUKANARU SORO** • 1981
LONG WAY FROM HOME: DADAH IS DEATH, A • 1988 • London Jerry • USA • DADAH IS DEATH
LONG WAY HOME, A • 1981 • Markowitz Robert • TVM • USA
LONG WAY TO OKINAWA • 1963 • *Takarada Akira* • JPN
LONG WAY'S TO GO, A • 1966 • Howe John • CND
LONG WEEKEND • 1978 • Eggleston Colin • ASL
LONG WEEKEND, THE see **PUENTE, EL** • 1977
LONGARM • 1988 • Vogel Virgil W. • TVM • USA
LONGER VOYAGE, THE • 1915 • *Essanay* • USA
LONGEST DAY, THE • 1962 • Marton Andrew, Oswald Gerd, Annakin Ken, Wicki Bernhard • USA
LONGEST DAY, THE see **LEGHOSSZABB NAP, A** • 1988
LONGEST HUNDRED MILES, THE • 1967 • Weis Don • TVM • USA • ESCAPE FROM BATAAN
LONGEST HUNT, THE see **SPARA, GRINGO, SPARA** • 1968
LONGEST JOURNEY, THE see **NAJDUZI PUT** • 1977
LONGEST MOST MEANINGLESS FILM IN THE WORLD, THE • 1970 • Patouillard Vincent • UKN
LONGEST NIGHT, THE • 1936 • Taggart Errol • USA
LONGEST NIGHT, THE • 1972 • Smight Jack • TVM • USA
LONGEST NIGHT, THE see **NAY-DALGATA NOSHT** • 1967
LONGEST ROAD, THE see **NAJDUZI PUT** • 1977
LONGEST SPUR, THE see **HOT SPUR** • 1968
LONGEST YARD, THE • 1975 • Aldrich Robert • USA • MEAN MACHINE, THE (UKN)
LONGHORN, THE • 1951 • Collins Lewis D. • USA
LONGHOUSE PEOPLE, THE • 1951 • Wargon Alan • CND
LONGHU FENGYUN • 1987 • Lam Ringo • HKG • PRISON ON FIRE ○ CITY ON FIRE
LONGING see **AKOGARE** • 1935
LONGING see **KAIPAUS** • 1974
LONGING FOR LOVE see **AI NO KAWAKI** • 1967
LONGING FOR LOVE see **LANGTA EFTER KARLEK** • 1968
LONGING FOR THE SEA see **LANGTAN TILL HAVET** • 1931
LONGITUD DE GUERRA • 1975 • Ortega Gonzalo Martinez • MXC • DURATION OF THE WAR, THE
LONGJA JIAN • 1970 • Wu Ma • HKG • DEAF AND MUTE HEROINE, THE
LONGSHOT • 1981 • Swackhamer E. W. • USA
LONGSHOT, THE • 1986 • Bartel Paul • USA
LONGSTREET • 1970 • Sargent Joseph • TVM • USA
LONGSTREET AT SEVEN PINES • 1911 • *Champion* • USA
LONGTIME COMPANION • 1990 • Rene Norman • USA
LONGUE MARCHE, LA • 1966 • Astruc Alexandre • FRN • LONG MARCH, THE
LONGUE RANDONEE, LA see **JOURNEY FROM ZERO** • 1961
LONGUES ANNEES, LES • 1964 • Tranche Andre • DOC • FRN
LONGXIONG HUDI • 1987 • Chan Jackie • HKG • ARMOUR OF GOD
LONGXU GOU • 1952 • Xian Qun • CHN • DRAGON BEARD DITCH
LONNIE • 1963 • Hale William • USA
LONTANO DA DOVE • 1984 • Casini Stafania, Marciano Francesca • ITL
LOOK see **SE** • 1948
LOOK, THE • 1970 • Wallace Stephen • SHT • ASL
LOOK AFTER AMELIA see **OCCUPE-TOI D'AMELIE** • 1949
LOOK AT LIFE FREIHEIT • Lucas George • SHT • USA
LOOK AT LIV, A • 1977 • Kaplan Richard • DOC • USA
LOOK AT MADNESS see **REGARD SUR LA FOLIE** • 1962
LOOK AT POSTERS, A see **SPOJRZENIE NA PLAKAT** • 1970
LOOK AT SEPTEMBER, A see **SPOJRZENIE NA WRZESIEN** • 1971
LOOK AT THE ROOT • 1929 • Antonovsky B. • ANM • USS
LOOK AT THIS CITY see **SCHAUT AUF DIESE STADT** • 1962
LOOK AT YOUR WORLD • 1954 • Legg Stuart • UKN
LOOK BACK • 1963 • Kiisk Kaliu • USS
LOOK BACK IN ANGER • 1959 • Richardson Tony • UKN
LOOK BEFORE YOU LAUGH see **MAKE MINE A MILLION** • 1959
LOOK BEFORE YOU LEAP see **DAMP DEED, A** • 1913
LOOK BEFORE YOU LEAP see **ALL'S FAIR IN LOVE** • 1921
LOOK BEFORE YOU LOVE • 1948 • Huth Harold • UKN • I KNOW YOU
LOOK DOWN AND DIE see **STEEL** • 1980
LOOK ESARN • 1982 • Kounavudhi Vichit • THL • SON OF THE NORTHEAST
LOOK FOR THE SILVER LINING • 1949 • Butler David • USA • SILVER LINING
LOOK FOR VANDA KOS see **POTRAZI VANDU KOS** • 1957
LOOK FOR YOUR BRIDE see **HANAYOME WA DOKONI IRU** • 1956
LOOK, HE'S FLYING! see **HELE, ON LETI!** • 1985
LOOK IN ANY WINDOW • 1961 • Alland William • USA
LOOK NOT UPON THE WINE • 1913 • Henderson Dell • USA
LOOK OUT! see **POZOR!** • 1959
LOOK OUT BELOW • 1916 • Myll Louis • SHT • USA
LOOK OUT BELOW! • 1919 • Roach Hal • SHT • USA
LOOK OUT BELOW • 1929 • Roberts Stephen • SHT • USA
LOOK OUT FOR GRANNY • 1960 • Kosheverova Nadezhda • USS
LOOK OUT FOR THE CARS see **BEREGIS AVTOMOBILYA!** • 1966
LOOK OUT GIRL, THE • 1928 • Fitzgerald Dallas M. • USA • SHADOWED (UKN)
LOOK OUT, HOOLIGANS! see **UWAGA CHULIGANI!** • 1955
LOOK OUT MR. HAGGIS see **HANDLE WITH CARE** • 1935
LOOK OUT MR. MOTO see **MR. MOTO TAKES A CHANCE** • 1938
LOOK OUT SISTER • 1948 • Pollard Bud • USA
LOOK PLEASANT, PLEASE • 1918 • Roach Hal • SHT • USA
LOOK, SEE WHAT SOKKAR IS DOING • 1977 • Fahmy Ashraf • EGY
LOOK, THE SKY! • Klimov Elem • SHT • USS
LOOK TO THE LAND see **FARMING FOR THE FUTURE** • 1949
LOOK TO THE NORTH • 1944 • Beveridge James • SHT • CND
LOOK UP AND LAUGH • 1935 • Dean Basil • UKN
LOOK! WE HAVE COME THROUGH! • 1978 • Elder Bruce • CND
LOOK WHAT'S HAPPENED TO ROSEMARY'S BABY • 1976 • O'Steen Sam • TVM • USA • ROSEMARY'S BABY II
LOOK WHO'S DRIVING • 1954 • Hurtz William • USA
LOOK WHO'S HERE • 1918 • *Mason Billy* • SHT • USA
LOOK WHO'S LAUGHING • 1941 • Dwan Allan • USA • LOOK WHO'S TALKING
LOOK WHO'S TALKING • 1989 • Heckerling Amy • USA
LOOK WHO'S TALKING see **LOOK WHO'S LAUGHING** • 1941
LOOK YOUR BEST • 1923 • Hughes Rupert • USA • BITTERNESS OF SWEETS, THE
LOOKER • 1981 • Crichton Michael • USA
LOOKIN' FOR SOMEONE (UKN) see **SINGING ON THE TRAIL** • 1946
LOOKIN' GOOD see **CORKY** • 1971
LOOKIN' TO GET OUT • 1980 • Ashby Hal • USA
LOOKING AT MARNIX GIJSEN see **MARNIX GIJSEN ACHTERNA** • 1975
LOOKING AT WILD ANIMALS • 1950 • Dolin Boris • DOC • USS
LOOKING BACK see **OHLEDNUTI** • 1968
LOOKING BACKWARD • 1912 • *Rex* • USA
LOOKING 'EM OVER • 1917 • Clements Roy • SHT • USA
LOOKING FOR A BRIDEGROOM see **BIR DAMAT ARANIYOR** • 1968
LOOKING FOR A FLAT see **NEVITE O BYTE?** • 1947
LOOKING FOR A FORTUNE • 1914 • *Kalem* • USA
LOOKING FOR A HUSBAND see **JOSTOJOEI SHOHAR** • 1968
LOOKING FOR A MOTHER • 1913 • Carleton Lloyd B. • USA
LOOKING FOR A WIFE see **CZLOWIEK Z M-3** • 1968
LOOKING FOR DANGER • 1957 • Jewell Austen • USA
LOOKING FOR ETERNITY see **PORTION D'ETERNITE** • 1990
LOOKING FOR HIS MURDERER see **MANN, DER SEINEN MORDER SUCHT, DER** • 1931
LOOKING FOR JOHN SMITH • 1906 • *Biograph* • USA • SI JONES LOOKING FOR JOHN SMITH
LOOKING FOR LANGSTON • 1990 • Julien Isaac • UKN
LOOKING FOR LODGINGS AT THE SEASIDE • 1910 • Rains Fred • UKN
LOOKING FOR LOVE • 1964 • Weis Don • USA
LOOKING FOR MR. GOODBAR • 1977 • Brooks Richard • USA
LOOKING FOR MUSHROOMS • 1966 • Conner Bruce • SHT • USA
LOOKING FOR SALLY • 1925 • McCarey Leo • SHT • USA
LOOKING FOR THE DERBY RESULT • 1916 • *Urban Trading Co* • SHT • UKN
LOOKING FOR TROUBLE • 1904 • *Paul R. W.* • UKN
LOOKING FOR TROUBLE • 1913 • *Thanhouser* • USA
LOOKING FOR TROUBLE • 1914 • *Beery Wallace* • USA
LOOKING FOR TROUBLE • 1919 • Roach Hal • SHT • USA
LOOKING FOR TROUBLE • 1926 • Bradbury Robert North • USA
LOOKING FOR TROUBLE • 1934 • Wellman William A. • USA
LOOKING FOR TROUBLE • 1951 • Hammond William C. • UKN
LOOKING FOR TROUBLE see **HOLLYWOOD COWBOY** • 1937
LOOKING FOR TROUBLE (UKN) see **TIP-OFF, THE** • 1931
LOOKING FORWARD • 1910 • Marston Theodore • USA
LOOKING FORWARD • 1933 • Brown Clarence • USA • SERVICE (UKN)
LOOKING GLASS, THE see **LOVE IN A FOUR LETTER WORLD** • 1970
LOOKING GLASS WAR, THE • 1969 • Pierson Frank R. • UKN
LOOKING INTO THE NIGHT see **POGLED U NOC** • 1979
LOOKING ON THE BRIGHT SIDE • 1932 • Cutts Graham, Dean Basil • UKN
LOOKING UP • 1977 • Yellen Linda • USA
LOOKS AND SMILES • 1981 • Loach Kenneth • UKN
LOOMING SHADOW, A see **CIEN JUZ NIEDALCKO** • 1984
LOON, THE NORTH AND YOU, THE • 1977 • Walton Lloyd A. • DOC • CND
LOONEY BALLOONISTS • 1936 • *Mintz Charles (P)* • ANS • USA
LOONEY HONEYMOON, A • 1920 • *Christie* • SHT • USA
LOONEY JOE • 1981 • Verstraete Guus Jr. • NTH
LOONEY LION AND MONKEY BUSINESS • 1919 • Moore Vin • SHT • USA
LOONEY LOONEY LOONEY BUGS BUNNY MOVIE, THE • 1981 • Freleng Friz • ANM • USA
LOONEY LOVE AFFAIR, A • 1915 • Davey Horace • USA
LOONIES ON BROADWAY (UKN) see **ZOMBIES ON BROADWAY** • 1945
LOONIZOO • 1953 • *Bentine Michael* • SHT • UKN
LOON'S NECKLACE, THE • 1948 • Crawley Budge • SHT • CND • COLLIER MAGIQUE, LE
LOONY TOM see **LOONY TOM, THE HAPPY LOVER** • 1954
LOONY TOM, THE HAPPY LOVER • 1954 • Broughton James • SHT • USA • LOONY TOM

LOOP • 1977 • Fodorova Anna • UKN
LOOPED FOR LIFE • 1924 • Frame Park • USA
LOOPHOLE • 1954 • Schuster Harold • USA
LOOPHOLE • 1981 • Quested John • UKN
LOOPING • 1975 • Tetzlaff Kurt • GDR
LOOPING THE LOOP • 1928 • Robison Arthur • FRG • TODESCHLEIFE, DIE
LOOPS • 1940 • McLaren Norman • ANS • USA • BOUCLES
LOOPS • 1958 • Clarke Shirley • USA • BRUSSELS LOOPS
LOOPS AND SWOOPS • 1968 • Bartsch Art • ANS • USA
LOOPY DE LOOP • 1959 • Hanna William, Barbera Joseph • ASS • USA
LOOPY'S HARE-DO • 1961 • Hanna William, Barbera Joseph • ANS • USA
LOOPYTONE NEWS • 1935 • *International Productions* • SHT • UKN
LOOS • 1988 • van Gogh Theo • NTH • NO POTATOES
LOOSE ANKLES • 1930 • Wilde Ted • USA
LOOSE CANNONS • 1989 • Clark Bob • USA
LOOSE CHANGE • 1921 • Roach Hal • SHT • USA
LOOSE CHANGE OF CHANCE, THE • 1914 • *Travers Richard C.* • USA
LOOSE CONNECTIONS • 1984 • Eyre Richard • UKN
LOOSE ENDS • 1930 • Walker Norman, Mander Miles • UKN
LOOSE ENDS • 1975 • Morris David Burton • USA
LOOSE ENDS see **SCREWBALL ACADEMY** • 1987
LOOSE IN LONDON • 1953 • Bernds Edward • USA • BOWERY KNIGHTS
LOOSE IN THE CABOOSE • 1947 • Kneitel Seymour • ANS • USA
LOOSE JOINTS see **FLICKS** • 1987
LOOSE LIONS • 1920 • Watson William • SHT • USA
LOOSE LIONS AND FAST LOVERS • 1920 • Fishback Fred C. • SHT • USA
LOOSE LOOT • 1953 • White Jules • SHT • USA
LOOSE NUT, THE • 1945 • Culhane James • ANS • USA
LOOSE PLEASURES see **AMOUR A LA CHAINE, L'** • 1965
LOOSE RELATIONS • 1933 • Edwards Harry J. • SHT • USA
LOOSE SCREWS • 1985 • Zielinski Rafal • CND • SCREWBALLS II: LOOSE SCREWS ○ SUMMER SCHOOL
LOOSE SHOES • 1979 • Miller Ira • USA • COMING ATTRACTIONS
LOOSE TIGHTWAD, A • 1923 • Roach Hal • SHT • USA
LOOSE WOMEN see **MUKIDO JOSEI** • 1967
LOOSENED PLANK, THE • 1914 • Fitzhamon Lewin • UKN
LOOSER THAN LOOSE • 1930 • Horne James W. • SHT • USA
LOOT • 1919 • Dowlan William C. • USA
LOOT • 1970 • Narizzano Silvio • UKN • LOOT.. GIVE ME MONEY, HONEY!
LOOT AND LOVE • 1916 • Semon Larry • SHT • USA • LOVE AND LOOT
LOOT.. GIVE ME MONEY, HONEY! see **LOOT** • 1970
LOOTERS, THE • 1955 • Biberman Abner • USA
LOOTERS, THE (UKN) see **ESTOUFFADE A LA CARAIBE** • 1966
LOOTERS OF LIEGE, THE • 1914 • Thornton F. Martin • UKN
LOPERJENTEN • 1983 • Lokkeberg Vibeke • NRW • BETRAYAL ○ STORY OF CAMILLA, THE
LOPEZ, LE BANDIT • 1930 • Daumery John • FRN
LORANG'S WAY • 1981 • MacDougall Judith, MacDougall David • DOC • USA
LORCA AND THE OUTLAWS • 1985 • Christian Roger • UKN • STARSHIP REDWING ○ 2084 ○ STARSHIP
LORD ALGY • 1914 • *Johnson Arthur* • USA
LORD ALGY'S BEAUTY SHOW • 1908 • Coleby A. E. • UKN
LORD AM ALEXANDERPLATZ, EIN • 1967 • Reisch Gunter • GDR • LORD IN ALEXANDER SQUARE, A ○ LORD AT ALEXANDERPLATZ, A
LORD AND LADY ALGY • 1919 • Beaumont Harry • USA
LORD AND THE GAMBLER, THE see **NUREGAMI SANDO GASA** • 1959
LORD AND THE LADY, THE • 1910 • *Powers* • USA
LORD AND THE PEASANT, THE • 1912 • Dawley J. Searle • USA
LORD ARTHUR SAVILLE'S CRIME see **LIDERCNYOMAS** • 1920
LORD ARTHUR SAVILLE'S CRIME (USA) see **CRIME DE LORD ARTHUR SAVILLE, LE** • 1921
LORD AT ALEXANDERPLATZ, A see **LORD AM ALEXANDERPLATZ, EIN** • 1967
LORD BABS • 1932 • Forde Walter • UKN
LORD BARRINGTON'S ESTATE • 1915 • Dowlan William C. • USA
LORD BARRY'S LOW ACQUAINTANCE • 1913 • *Imp* • USA
LORD BLEND'S LOVE STORY • 1910 • Bouwmeester Theo? • UKN
LORD BROWNING AND CINDERELLA • 1912 • Brooke Van Dyke • USA
LORD BYRON • 1922 • Veidt Conrad • FRG
LORD BYRON OF BROADWAY • 1930 • Nigh William, Beaumont Harry • USA • WHAT PRICE MELODY? (UKN)
LORD CAMBER'S LADIES • 1932 • Levy Benn W. • UKN • CASE OF LADY CAMBER, THE
LORD CHUMLEY • 1914 • Kirkwood James • USA
LORD DURHAM • 1960 • Howe John • CND
LORD EDGWARE DIES • 1934 • Edwards Henry • UKN
LORD ELGIN: VOICE OF THE PEOPLE • 1959 • Biggs Julian • CND
LORD EPPING RETURNS • 1951 • Goodwins Leslie • SHT • USA
LORD FARTHINGAY HOLIDAY • 1970 • *Jo-Jo Dist.* • USA
LORD FEATHERTOP • 1908 • Porter Edwin S. • USA
LORD FOR A DAY, A • 1908 • *Essanay* • USA
LORD FOR A NIGHT see **ARU YO NO TONOSAMA** • 1946
LORD GAVE, THE • 1915 • Morgan Sidney • UKN • WORLD'S DESIRE, THE
LORD HIGH EXECUTIONER, THE • 1906 • Gilbert Arthur • UKN
LORD HIGH EXECUTIONER, THE • 1907 • Morland John • UKN
LORD IN ALEXANDER SQUARE, A see **LORD AM ALEXANDERPLATZ, EIN** • 1967
LORD JEFF • 1938 • Wood Sam • USA • BOY FROM BARNARDO'S, THE
LORD JIM • 1925 • Fleming Victor • USA
LORD JIM • 1965 • Brooks Richard • UKN, USA
LORD JOHN'S JOURNAL • 1916 • Le Saint Edward J. • SRL • USA
LORD LOVE A DUCK • 1966 • Axelrod George • USA
LORD LOVELAND DISCOVERS AMERICA • 1916 • Maude Arthur • USA
LORD LOVES THE IRISH, THE • 1919 • Warde Ernest C. • USA
LORD MAYOR, THE • 1975 • McGill Chris • DOC • ASL
LORD MAYOR STARZYNSKI see **PREZYDENT STARZYNSKI** • 1978
LORD OF THE BORDELLO • 1987 • Imamura Shohei • JPN
LORD OF THE FLIES • 1963 • Brook Peter • UKN
LORD OF THE FLIES • 1989 • Hook Harry • UKN
LORD OF THE JUNGLE • 1935 • *Chandrarao* • IND
LORD OF THE JUNGLE • 1955 • Beebe Ford • USA
LORD OF THE MANOR • 1933 • Edwards Henry • UKN
LORD OF THE RINGS • 1978 • Bakshi Ralph • ANM • USA
LORD OF THE SEA • 1982 • Stoneman John • MTV • CND
LORD OOM PIET • 1962 • SAF
LORD OUVRIER, LE • 1915 • Diamant-Berger Henri • FRN
LORD REGINALDS DERBYRITT • 1924 • Teuber Arthur • FRG
LORD RICHARD IN THE PANTRY • 1930 • Forde Walter • UKN
LORD SHANGO • 1975 • Marsh Raymond • USA • SOULMATES OF SHANGO
LORD SHIVA'S DREAM see **INAUGURATION OF THE PLEASURE DOME** • 1954
LORD TAKES A BRIDE, THE see **OHTORI-JO HANAYOME** • 1957
LORD WINCHELL'S KILLING • 1979 • Heffner Avram • ISR
LORDAGSKVALLAR • 1933 • Bauman Schamyl • SWD • SATURDAY EVENINGS
LORDS AND PIRATES see **TORIMONO DOCHU** • 1959
LORDS OF CREATION • 1967 • Robinson Gerald • ANS • CND
LORDS OF DISCIPLINE, THE • 1983 • Roddam Franc • UKN, USA
LORDS OF FLATBUSH, THE • 1974 • Verona Stephen F., Davidson Martin • USA
LORDS OF HIGH DECISION, THE • 1916 • Harvey John • USA
LORDS OF LITTLE EGYPT • 1961 • Zetterling Mai • DCS • UKN
LORDS OF THE DEEP • 1988 • Fisher Mary Ann • USA
LORDS OF THE FOREST see **SEIGNEURS DE LA FORET, LES** • 1959
LORELEI, DIE • 1927 • Neff Wolfgang • FRG
LORELEI, THE • 1913 • Dawley J. Searle • USA
LORELEI, THE • 1931 • *Terry Paul/ Moser Frank (P)* • ANS • USA
LORELEI MADONNA, THE • 1915 • Sturgeon Rollin S. • USA
LORELEI OF THE SEA, THE see **MODERN LORELEI, A** • 1917
LORELEI'S GRASP, THE (USA) see **GARRAS DE LORELEI, LAS** • 1972
LORENZ V. LORENZ see **EHESACHE LORENZ** • 1959
LORENZACCIO • 1917 • De Liguoro Giuseppe • ITL
LORENZACCIO • 1952 • Pacini Raffaello • ITL
LORENZINO DE' MEDICI • 1935 • Brignone Guido • ITL
LORENZO BURGHARDT • 1918 • Wauer William? • FRG
LORETTE ET LES AUTRES • 1972 • Dante Dominique • FRN
LORGNON ACCUSATEUR, LE • 1905 • Blache Alice • FRN
LORI & CO. • 1917 • *Neumann Lotte* • FRG
LORINCI FONOBAN, A • 1971 • Meszaros Marta • DCS • HNG • AT THE LORINC SPINNERY ○ WOMEN IN THE SPINNERY
LORNA • 1964 • Meyer Russ • USA
LORNA DOONE • 1911 • Marston Theodore • USA
LORNA DOONE • 1912 • Noy Wilfred • UKN
LORNA DOONE • 1915 • MacDonald J. Farrell • USA
LORNA DOONE • 1920 • Lucoque H. Lisle • UKN
LORNA DOONE • 1922 • Tourneur Maurice • USA
LORNA DOONE • 1935 • Dean Basil • UKN
LORNA DOONE • 1951 • Karlson Phil • USA
LORO DE LA SOLEDAD, EL • 1967 • Sernas Juan Antonio, Farias Jorge Enrique • ARG • PARROT OF LONELINESS, THE
LORRAINE, COEUR D'ACIER -UNE RADIO DANS LA VILLE • 1978 • Poirier Alban, Serres Jean • DOC • FRN
LORRAINE OF THE LIONS • 1925 • Sedgwick Edward • USA
LORRKUN, THE • 1964 • Holmes Cecil • DOC • ASL
LORRY, THE see **LASTBILEN** • 1977
LORRY, THE see **KAMIONAT** • 1980
LORRY, THE (UKN) see **CAMION, LE** • 1977
LORSQUE LE DESTIN S'ACHARNE • 1972 • Zarrouk A. • LBY
LORSQUE L'ENFANT PARAIT • 1956 • Boisrond Michel • FRN • BLESSED EVENTS
LORSQU'UNE FEMME VEUT • 1919 • Monca Georges • FRN
LOS ANGELES CONNECTION, THE • *Ireland John* • USA
LOS ANGELES HARBOR • 1913 • Sennett Mack • DOC • USA
LOS DE ABAJO • 1939 • Urueta Chano • MXC • CON LA DIVISION DEL NORTE
LOS DE LA MESA DIEZ • 1960 • Feldman Simon • ARG
LOS NEVADOS • 1986 • Siso Freddy • VNZ
LOS QUE TOCAN EL PIANO • 1968 • Aguirre Javier • SPN • THOSE WHO PLAY THE PIANO
LOS QUE VIVEN DONDE SOPLA EL VIENTO SUAVE • 1973 • Cazals Felipe • MXC • THOSE WHO LIVE WHERE THE SOFT WIND BLOWS
LOS THE SUPERMEN EN LA SELVA (SPN) see **CHE FANNO I NOSTRI SUPERMEN TRA LE VERGINI DELLA GIUNGLA** • 1970
LOS VOM MANN see **MISS HOBBS** • 1921
LOS VOM MANNE! • 1917 • Larsen Viggo • FRG
LOS VOM WEIBE • 1919 • Heidemann Paul, Schubert Georg • FRG
LOSE NO TIME • 1921 • Roach Hal • SHT • USA
LOSER see **CHIEN FOU, LE** • 1966
LOSER SIG, DET • 1977 • Dahl Christer • MTV • SWD • IT'LL WORK OUT
LOSER TAKE ALL (UKN) see **LEATHER GLOVES** • 1948
LOSER TAKES ALL • 1956 • Annakin Ken • UKN
LOSER TAKES ALL • 1989 • Scott James • UKN
LOSER WINS, THE • 1914 • *Princess* • USA
LOSER WINS, THE • 1915 • Batley Ernest G. • UKN
LOSERS, THE • 1970 • Starrett Jack • USA • MEAN COMBAT ○ MISERS, THE
LOSER'S END • 1934 • Ray Bernard B. • USA
LOSER'S END, THE • 1924 • *Maloney Leo* • USA
LOSER'S GAME, THE • 1977-80 • Zaritsky John • MTV • CND
LOSIN' IT • 1982 • Hanson Curtis • USA
LOSING FIGHT, THE • 1914 • Campbell Colin • USA
LOSING GAME, A • 1915 • Plumb Hay? • UKN
LOSING GAME, THE • 1915 • *Karr Darwin* • USA
LOSING GAME, THE (UKN) see **PAY-OFF, THE** • 1930
LOSING GROUND • 1982 • Collins Kathleen • USA
LOSING TO WIN • 1911 • *Kalem* • USA
LOSING WEIGHT • 1916 • Semon Larry • SHT • USA
LOSING WINNER, THE • 1917 • De Haven Carter • SHT • USA
LOSS OF FEELING see **GIBEL SENSATY** • 1935
LOSS OF INNOCENCE (USA) see **GREENGAGE SUMMER, THE** • 1961
LOSS OF SENSATION see **GIBEL SENSATY** • 1935
LOSS OF THE BIRKENHEAD, THE • 1914 • Elvey Maurice • UKN
LOST • 1956 • Green Guy • UKN • TEARS FOR SIMON (USA)
LOST! • 1986 • Rowe Peter • CND • LOST! -A TRUE STORY
LOST see **HIS FORGOTTEN WIFE** • 1924
LOST: A BABY • 1911 • *Essanay* • USA
LOST -A BRIDEGROOM • 1919 • *Vernon Bobby* • SHT • USA
LOST -A COOK • 1917 • *Swain Mack* • SHT • USA
LOST, A HUSBAND • 1912 • *Leonard Marion* • USA
LOST! A LEG OF MUTTON • 1906 • Collins Alf • UKN • LOST LEG OF MUTTON, THE (USA)
LOST, A MONKEY • 1910 • Martinek H. O. • UKN
LOST -A PAIR OF SHOES • 1914 • Kendall Preston • USA
LOST! -A TRUE STORY see **LOST!** • 1986
LOST – A UNION SUIT • 1914 • *Thanhouser* • USA
LOST -A WIFE • 1925 • De Mille William C. • USA
LOST ADDRESS, THE • 1912 • Christie Al • USA
LOST ALIBI, THE see **KUROI GOSHO** • 1960
LOST AND FOUND • 1908. • *Essanay* • USA
LOST AND FOUND • 1916 • Miller Rube • USA
LOST AND FOUND • 1917 • Green Alfred E. • SHT • USA
LOST AND FOUND • Weill Claudia • SHT • USA
LOST AND FOUND • 1979 • Frank Melvin • USA
LOST AND FOUND see **LOST AND FOUND ON A SOUTH SEA ISLAND** • 1923
LOST AND FOUND ON A SOUTH SEA ISLAND • 1923 • Walsh Raoul • USA • LOST AND FOUND ○ PASSION OF THE SEA ○ CAPTAIN BLACKBIRD
LOST AND FOUND -THE STORY OF COOK'S ANCHOR • 1979 • Lean David (c/d) • UKN
LOST AND FOUNDLING • 1944 • Jones Charles M. • ANS • USA
LOST AND FOUNDRY • 1937 • Fleischer Dave • ANS • USA
LOST AND REGAINED • 1910 • *Edison* • USA
LOST AND WON • 1911 • *Selig* • USA
LOST AND WON • 1917 • Young James • USA
LOST AND WON see **ODDS AGAINST** • 1915
LOST AND WON (UKN) see **WHEN DREAMS COME TRUE** • 1929
LOST ANGEL • 1943 • Rowland Roy • USA
LOST ANGELS • 1989 • Hudson Hugh • USA • WALL TIME
LOST APPETITE, THE • 1917 • Chaudet Louis W. • SHT • USA
LOST ARMY, THE see **POPIOLY** • 1966
LOST ARROW, THE • 1914 • *Nestor* • USA
LOST ARTICLES see **IRYUHIN-NASHI** • 1959
LOST AT SEA • 1926 • Gasnier Louis J. • USA
LOST AT THE FRONT • 1927 • Lord Del • USA
LOST ATLANTIS see **ATLANTIDE, L'** • 1921
LOST ATLANTIS see **HERRIN VON ATLANTIS, DIE** • 1932
LOST BAG, THE see **NAAR FRUEN GAAR PAA EVENTYR** • 1913
LOST BATTALION, THE • 1919 • King Burton L. • USA
LOST BATTALION, THE • 1921 • *Glass Gaston* • USA
LOST BATTALION, THE • 1962 • Romero Eddie • USA, PHL
LOST BOUNDARIES • 1949 • Werker Alfred L. • USA
LOST BOYS, THE • 1987 • Schumacher Joel • USA
LOST BRACELET, THE • 1916 • Mayo Melvin • USA
LOST BRIDEGROOM, THE • 1916 • Kirkwood James • USA
LOST BY A HAIR • 1914 • *Rex* • USA
LOST CANNON, THE see **HORKA LASKA** • 1958
LOST CANYON • 1943 • Selander Lesley • USA
LOST CHARTER • 1945 • ANM • USS
LOST CHICK, THE • 1935 • Harman Hugh • ANS • USA
LOST CHILD • 1904 • *Bitzer Billy (Ph)* • USA
LOST CHILD, THE • 1914 • Smiley Joseph • USA
LOST CHILD, THE see **MUNNA** • 1954
LOST CHORD • 1911 • Lincoln W. J. • ASL
LOST CHORD, THE • 1913 • *Travers Richard C.* • USA
LOST CHORD, THE • 1917 • Noy Wilfred • UKN
LOST CHORD, THE • 1925 • Noy Wilfred • USA
LOST CHORD, THE • 1928 • Parkinson H. B., Edwards J. Steven • SHT • UKN
LOST CHORD, THE • 1933 • Elvey Maurice • UKN
LOST CITY, THE • 1920 • Martin E. A. • SRL • USA
LOST CITY, THE • 1935 • Revier Harry • SRL • USA • LOST CITY OF THE LIGURIANS, THE
LOST CITY, THE • 1982 • Dukes Robert • USA
LOST CITY OF ATLANTIS, THE • 1978 • Martin Richard • USA
LOST CITY OF THE JUNGLE • 1946 • Taylor Ray, Collins Lewis D. • SRL • USA
LOST CITY OF THE LIGURIANS, THE see **LOST CITY, THE** • 1935
LOST COLLAR STUD, THE • 1914 • Thornton F. Martin? • UKN
LOST COMBINATION, THE • 1913 • *Cruze James* • USA
LOST COMMAND • 1966 • Robson Mark • USA • NOT FOR HONOR AND GLORY ○ CENTURIONS, THE
LOST CONTINENT, THE • 1951 • Newfield Sam • USA
LOST CONTINENT, THE • 1968 • Carreras Michael, Norman Leslie (U/c) • UKN • PEOPLE OF ABRIMES, THE
LOST CONTINENT, THE see **SESTO CONTINENTE** • 1954
LOST CONTINENT, THE (USA) see **CONTINENTE PERDUTO** • 1955
LOST COPPERHEAD, THE • 1913 • *Victor* • USA
LOST CORD, THE • 1914 • North Wilfred • USA
LOST DAUGHTERS see **VERLORENE TOCHTER 1** • 1918
LOST DAYS OF PEACE, THE see **PAMIETNIK PANI HANKI** • 1963
LOST DEED, THE • 1913 • *Trunnelle Mabel* • USA
LOST DIAMOND, THE • 1913 • *Hollister Alice* • USA
LOST DISPATCH, THE • 1913 • *Buckham Hazel* • USA

LOST DOG, THE • 1912 • *Lubin* • USA
LOST DOG, THE • 1924 • Roach Hal • SHT • USA
LOST DOLL, THE • 1959 • Tyrlova Hermina • ANM • CZC
LOST DREAM, THE • 1949 • Tytla Bill • ANS • USA
LOST EMPIRE, THE • 1924 • *Salisbury Edward A.* • DOC • USA • IN QUEST OF THE GOLDEN PRINCE ○ GOLDEN PRINCE
LOST EMPIRE, THE • 1985 • Wynorski Jim • USA
LOST EXPRESS, THE • 1917 • McGowan J. P. • SRL • USA
LOST EXPRESS, THE • 1926 • McGowan J. P. • USA
LOST EYES see **OJOS PERDIDOS, LOS** • 1967
LOST FACE, THE see **ZTRACENA TVAR** • 1965
LOST FLIGHT • 1969 • Horn Leonard • USA
LOST FOR MANY YEARS • 1910 • *Bison* • USA
LOST FOREST, THE see **PADUREA SPINZURATILOR** • 1965
LOST FREIGHT CAR, THE • 1911 • *Crane Harry Ogden* • USA
LOST GENERATION see **FALAK** • 1968
LOST HANDBAG, THE • 1909 • *Edison* • USA
LOST HANDKERCHIEF, THE • 1908 • *Tyler Walter* • UKN
LOST HAT, THE • 1912 • *Selig* • USA
LOST HAT AND THE PRICE OF ITS RECOVERY, THE • 1902 • *Warwick Trading Co* • UKN
LOST HEART see **KEMANA HATI KAN KU BAWA** • 1979
LOST HEIRESS, THE • 1909 • *Lubin* • USA
LOST HEIRESS, THE (UKN) see **WIFE'S RELATIONS, THE** • 1928
LOST HOMELAND, THE see **IZGUBLJENI ZAVICAJ** • 1981
LOST HONEYMOON • 1947 • Jason Leigh • USA
LOST HONOR OF KATHERINA BLUM, THE (USA) see **VERLORENE EHRE DER KATHERINA BLUM, DIE** • 1975
LOST HONOR OF KATHRYN BECK, THE see **ACT OF PASSION** • 1984
LOST HORIZON • 1937 • Capra Frank • USA • LOST HORIZON OF SHANGRI-LA
LOST HORIZON • 1973 • Jarrott Charles • USA
LOST HORIZON OF SHANGRI-LA see **LOST HORIZON** • 1937
LOST HORSE, THE • 1911 • *Lubin* • USA
LOST HOURS, THE • 1952 • MacDonald David • UKN • BIG FRAME, THE (USA)
LOST HOUSE, THE • 1915 • Cabanne W. Christy • USA
LOST IDOL • 1989 • Pakdivijit Chalong • THL, USA
LOST ILLUSION, THE see **FALLEN IDOL, THE** • 1948
LOST ILLUSIONS • 1911 • Porter Edwin S. • USA
LOST ILLUSIONS see **ELVESZETT ILLUZIOK** • 1983
LOST IN A BIG CITY • 1923 • Irving George • USA
LOST IN A HAREM • 1944 • Reisner Charles F. • USA
LOST IN A HOTEL • 1911 • *Powers* • USA
LOST IN A TURKISH BATH • 1952 • Yates Hal • SHT • USA
LOST IN ALASKA • 1952 • Yarbrough Jean • USA • ABBOTT AND COSTELLO LOST IN ALASKA (UKN) ○ SOURDOUGHS, THE
LOST IN AMERICA • 1985 • Brooks Albert • USA
LOST IN AMSTERDAM • 1988 • de la Parra Pim • NTH
LOST IN BABYLON • 1916 • Wilson Millard K. • SHT • USA
LOST IN CAMBODIA • 1913 • Melies Gaston • USA
LOST IN CHINATOWN • 1909 • *Powhatan* • USA
LOST IN CUDDIHY • 1966 • Schneider Ira
LOST IN LIMEHOUSE: OR, LADY ESMERELDA'S PREDICAMENT • 1933 • Brower Otto • SHT • USA
LOST IN LONDON • 1915 • *Warner'S Features* • USA
LOST IN LONDON • 1985 • Lewis Robert • TVM • USA
LOST IN MID-OCEAN • 1914 • Davis Ulysses • USA
LOST IN PRAGUE see **NAVRAT DOMU** • 1948
LOST IN SIBERIA • 1909 • *Selig* • USA
LOST IN SNOW • 1909 • *Powhatan* • USA
LOST IN SOCIETY • 1920 • *Jennings Al* • SHT • USA
LOST IN THE ALPS • 1907 • Porter Edwin S. • USA
LOST IN THE ARCTIC • 1911 • *Williams Kathlyn* • USA
LOST IN THE ARCTIC see **GREAT WHITE NORTH, THE** • 1928
LOST IN THE BUSH • 1973 • Dodds Peter • ASL
LOST IN THE DARK • Mastrocinque Camillo • ITL
LOST IN THE DARK see **SPERDUTI NEL BUIO** • 1914
LOST IN THE DESERT see **DIRKIE** • 1969
LOST IN THE GARDEN OF THE WORLD • 1975 • Williams Tony • DOC • NZL
LOST IN THE JUNGLE • 1911 • Turner Otis • USA
LOST IN THE LEGION • 1934 • Newmeyer Fred • UKN
LOST IN THE NIGHT • 1913 • *White Pearl* • USA
LOST IN THE SAND see **REVOLUTIONEN I VANDKANTEN** • 1971
LOST IN THE SNOW • 1906 • Mottershaw Frank • UKN
LOST IN THE SOUDAN • 1910 • *Selig* • USA
LOST IN THE STARS • 1974 • Mann Daniel • USA
LOST IN THE STRATOSPHERE • 1934 • Brown Melville • USA • MURDER IN THE STRATOSPHERE
LOST IN THE STREET OF PARIS • 1917 • *Baggot King* • SHT • USA
LOST IN THE STUDIO • 1914 • *Jacobs Billy* • USA
LOST IN THE SUBURBS see **NAVRAT DOMU** • 1948
LOST IN THE SWIM • 1915 • *Mina* • USA
LOST IN THE WASH see **LAUNDRY, THE** • 1946
LOST IN THE WILD • 1976 • Waddington David S. • ASL
LOST IN THE WOODS • 1912 • Wilson Frank • UKN
LOST IN THE WOODS • 1982 • Casson Barry • DOC • CND
LOST IN TRANSIT • 1917 • Crisp Donald • USA
LOST INHERITANCE, THE • 1912 • *Selig* • USA
LOST INVITATION, THE • 1909 • *Edison* • USA
LOST ISLAND see **ISLAND OF THE LOST** • 1967
LOST ISLAND OF KIOGA • 1938 • Witney William, English John • USA
LOST ISLANDS, THE • 1975 • Hughes Bill • ASL
LOST JUNGLE, THE • 1934 • Schaefer Armand, Howard David • SRL • USA
LOST KERCHIEF, THE • 1911 • *Yankee* • USA
LOST KINGDOM, THE see **ANTINEA, L'AMANTE DELLA CITTA SEPOLTA** • 1961
LOST KITTEN, THE • 1912 • *Edison* • USA
LOST LADY see **LADY VANISHES, THE** • 1938
LOST LADY, A • 1924 • Beaumont Harry • USA
LOST LADY, A • 1934 • Green Alfred E. • USA • COURAGEOUS (UKN)
LOST LADY, THE (UKN) see **SAFE IN HELL** • 1931
LOST LAGOON, THE • 1958 • Rawlins John • USA
LOST LEADER, A • 1922 • Ridgwell George • UKN
LOST LEDGE, THE • 1915 • *Clifford William* • USA
LOST LEG OF MUTTON, THE (USA) see **LOST! A LEG OF MUTTON** • 1906
LOST LEGION OF THE BORDER, THE • 1917 • Horne James W. • SHT • USA
LOST LETTER, THE • 1909 • *Centaur* • USA
LOST LETTER, THE • 1911 • *Bison* • USA
LOST LETTERS • 1966 • Romm Mikhail • SHT • USS
LOST LIE, THE • 1918 • Vidor King • SHT • USA
LOST LIFE, A see **VERLORENES LEBEN** • 1975
LOST LIMITED, THE • 1927 • McGowan J. P. • USA
LOST LIVES see **VITE PERDUTE** • 1958
LOST LODE, THE • 1916 • McRae Henry • SHT • USA
LOST, LONELY AND VICIOUS • 1957 • Myers Frank • USA
LOST LORD LOVELL, THE • 1915 • Powell Paul • USA
LOST, LOST, LOST • 1976 • Mekas Jonas • USA
LOST LOVE • Banarji Ashim • IND
LOST LOVE see **YUBUE** • 1967
LOST LOVE JULIANA see **JULIANA DO AMOR PERDIDO** • 1970
LOST LOVE LETTER, THE • 1912 • Stow Percy • UKN
LOST LUCK see **ASHI NI SAWATTA KOUN** • 1930
LOST MAIL SACK, THE • 1914 • *Holmes Helen* • USA
LOST MAN, THE • 1969 • Aurthur Robert Alan • USA • HOW MANY ROADS
LOST MAN, THE see **ANTHROPOS POU HATHIKE, O** • 1976
LOST MARZIPAN CRACKNEL, THE • *Deutscher Fernsehfunk* • ANM • GDR
LOST MELODY, THE • 1914 • Ridgely Richard • USA
LOST MEMORY, THE • 1909 • Fitzhamon Lewin • UKN
LOST MEN (UKN) see **HOMICIDE SQUAD, THE** • 1931
LOST MESSENGER, THE • 1912 • *Prior Herbert* • USA
LOST MESSENGER, THE • 1915 • Nicholls George • USA
LOST MILLIONAIRE, THE • 1913 • Ince Ralph • USA
LOST MISSILE, THE • 1958 • Berke William • USA
LOST MOMENT, THE • 1947 • Gabel Martin • USA
LOST MOMENTS see **VENDITORE DI PALLONCINI, IL** • 1974
LOST MONEY • 1919 • Lawrence Edmund • USA
LOST NECKLACE, THE • 1911 • Golden Joseph A. • USA
LOST NEW YEAR'S DINNER, THE • 1908 • Porter Edwin S. • USA
LOST NOTE, THE • 1913 • Carleton Lloyd B. • USA
LOST ON DRESS PARADE • 1918 • Justice Martin • SHT • USA
LOST ON THE ICE see **LIDE NA KRE** • 1937
LOST ON THE WESTERN FRONT (USA) see **ROMANCE IN FLANDERS, A** • 1937
LOST ONE, THE see **TRAVIATA '53** • 1953
LOST ONE, THE see **PERDIDA** • 1980
LOST ONE, THE (UKN) see **VERLORENE, DER** • 1951
LOST ONE, THE (USA) see **SIGNORA DALLE CAMELIE, LA** • 1948
LOST ONE WIFE see **AS WE LIE** • 1927
LOST ONES, THE see **OLVIDADOS, LOS** • 1950
LOST OVER LONDON • 1934 • Graves Rex • UKN
LOST PALACE, THE see **ISTANA YANG HILANG** • 1961
LOST PARADISE, THE • 1914 • Dawley J. Searle, Apfel Oscar • USA
LOST PARADISE, THE • 1916 • Hansel Howell?, McGill Lawrence? • SHT • USA • BRANDING THE INNOCENT
LOST PARADISE, THE see **ELVESZETT PARADICSOM, AZ** • 1962
LOST PARADISE, THE see **VERLOREN PARADIJS, HET** • 1978
LOST PARADISES, THE see **PARAISOS PERDIDOS, LOS** • 1985
LOST PATROL, THE • 1929 • Summers Walter • UKN
LOST PATROL, THE • 1934 • Ford John • USA
LOST PATROL, THE see **STRACENA VARTA** • 1956
LOST PEOPLE, THE • 1949 • Knowles Bernard, Box Muriel • UKN
LOST PHOTOGRAPH, THE see **POTERYANNAYA FOTOGRAFIYA** • 1959
LOST PILGRIM, THE see **PELERIN PERDU, LE** • 1962
LOST PLANET, THE • 1953 • Bennet Spencer Gordon • SRL • USA • PLANET MEN
LOST PLANET AIRMEN • 1949 • Brannon Fred C. • USA
LOST PLATOON, THE • 1988 • Prior David A. • USA
LOST PLATOON, THE • 1988 • Winters David • USA
LOST PRINCESS, THE • 1919 • Dunlap Scott R. • USA
LOST PROPERTY see **SOUVENIRS PERDUS** • 1950
LOST RANCH • 1937 • Katzman Sam • USA
LOST RECEIPT, THE • 1915 • *Kalem* • USA
LOST RING, THE • 1912 • *Gaumont* • USA
LOST RING: OR, JOHNSON'S HONEYMOON, THE • 1911 • Bouwmeester Theo • UKN
LOST RIVER (UKN) see **TRAIL OF THE RUSTLERS** • 1950
LOST ROMANCE, THE • 1921 • De Mille William C. • USA
LOST SALT: GIFT OF BLOOD, THE • 1990 • Fennell Christian • SHT • CND
LOST SATCHEL, THE • 1915 • *B & C* • UKN
LOST SCOUT ON THE VELDT, THE • 1901 • *Mitchell & Kenyon* • UKN
LOST SECRET, THE • 1915 • *Balboa* • USA
LOST SENTRY, THE see **STRACENA VARTA** • 1956
LOST SERMON, THE • 1914 • *Garwood William* • USA
LOST SEX (UKN) see **HONNO** • 1966
LOST SHADOW, THE (USA) see **VERLORENE SCHATTEN, DER** • 1920
LOST SHEEP, THE • 1909 • Brooke Van Dyke • USA
LOST SHEEP, THE • 1966 • Tumanov Semyon • USS
LOST SHOE, THE see **VERLORENE SCHUH, DER** • 1923
LOST SHUTTLECOCK, THE • 1904 • Collins Alf? • UKN
LOST SON, THE • 1913 • O'Neil Barry • USA
LOST SON, THE • 1974 • Reiniger Lotte • ANS • UKN
LOST SON, THE see **VERLORENE SOHN, DER** • 1934
LOST SOUL see **ANIMA PERSA** • 1976
LOST SOUL, THE • 1926 • Speerger Jan Wenzeslaus • CZC
LOST SOUL, THE see **VERLORENE ICH, DAS** • 1923
LOST SOULS • 1916 • *Roland West Film* • USA
LOST SOULS see **TA SHE** • 1981
LOST SOULS (USA) see **VITE PERDUTE** • 1958
LOST SPECIAL, THE • 1932 • McRae Henry • SRL • USA
LOST SPRING see **MUSHIBAMERU HARU** • 1932
LOST SQUADRON, THE • 1932 • Archainbaud George • USA
LOST STAGE VALLEY (UKN) see **STAGE TO TUCSON** • 1951
LOST, STOLEN OR STRAYED • 1905 • Fitzhamon Lewin • UKN
LOST, STOLEN OR STRAYED • 1921 • Gordon Edward R. • UKN
LOST, STRAYED OR STOLEN • 1914 • *Prescott Vivian* • USA
LOST, STRAYED OR STOLEN • 1915 • *Punchinello* • USA
LOST, STRAYED OR STOLEN • 1916 • *Mcquire Paddy* • SHT • USA
LOST SUMMER, THE see **PROPALO LETO** • 1963
LOST SUNDAY, A see **ZABITA NEDELE** • 1970
LOST SWITCH, THE • 1913 • *Lubin* • USA
LOST - THREE HOURS • 1912 • *Phillips Augustus* • USA
LOST -THREE TEETH • 1915 • Christie Al • USA
LOST TIME • 1989 • Derakhshandeh Pooran • IRN
LOST TRACK, THE see **ZTRACENA STOPA** • 1956
LOST TRAIL, THE • 1910 • *Vitagraph* • USA
LOST TRAIL, THE • 1926 • McGowan J. P. • USA
LOST TRAIL, THE • 1945 • Hillyer Lambert • USA
LOST TRAIL, THE see **ZTRACENA STOPA** • 1956
LOST TREASURE see **THESOURO PERDIDO** • 1927
LOST TREASURE, THE • 1914 • Hamilton G. P.? • USA
LOST TREASURE OF THE AMAZON (UKN) see **JIVARO** • 1954
LOST TREASURE OF THE AZTECS see **SANSONE E IL TESORO DEGLI INCAS** • 1964
LOST TRIBE, THE • 1924 • *Macdonald Kenneth* • USA
LOST TRIBE, THE • 1949 • Berke William • USA
LOST TRIBE, THE • 1983 • Laing John • NZL
LOST, TWENTY-FOUR HOURS • 1916 • Windom Lawrence C. • SHT • USA
LOST VALLEY, THE see **VALLEY OF GWANGI, THE** • 1969
LOST VIRGIN see **B.G. ARU 19 SAI NO NIKKI AGETE YOKKATA** • 1968
LOST VIRGINITY see **VIRGINIDAD PERDIDA** • 1978
LOST VOLCANO, THE • 1950 • Beebe Ford • USA
LOST WATCH, THE see **REFORMATION OF SIERRA SMITH** • 1912
LOST WAY, THE see **CHEMIN PERDU, LE** • 1980
LOST WEEKEND see **LUST WEEKEND** • 1967
LOST WEEKEND, THE • 1945 • Wilder Billy • USA
LOST WILL, THE • 1912 • Fitzhamon Lewin • UKN
LOST WOMEN OF ZARPA see **MESA OF LOST WOMEN** • 1953
LOST WOMEN (UKN) see **MESA OF LOST WOMEN** • 1953
LOST WORLD, A • 1948 • *Encyclopaedia Britannica* • SHT • USA
LOST WORLD, THE • 1925 • Hoyt Harry O. • USA
LOST WORLD, THE • 1960 • Allen Irwin • USA • ORIGIN OF MAN, THE
LOST WORLD OF GLOVES, THE see **ZANIKLY SVET RUKAVIC** • 1982
LOST WORLD OF SINBAD, THE see **DAITOZOKU** • 1963
LOST YEARS • 1912 • *Rex* • USA
LOST YEARS, THE • 1909 • *Centaur* • USA
LOST YEARS, THE • 1911 • *Essanay* • USA
LOST YOUTH see **GIOVENTU PERDUTA** • 1948
LOST ZEPPELIN, THE • 1929 • Sloman Edward • USA
LOSY ZAMKU, LOSY KRAJU.. • 1971 • Perski Ludwik • DOC • PLN • FATE OF THE CASTLE, THE FATE OF THE COUNTRY.., THE
LOT ABOUT A LOTTERY, A • 1920 • *Lane Lupino* • SHT • UKN
LOT IN SODOM • 1933 • Watson James Sibley, Webber Melville • SHT • USA
LOTACAO ESGOTADA • 1972 • Guimaraes Manuel • PRT
LOTELING, DE • 1974 • Verhavert Roland • BLG • CONSCRIT, LE ○ CONSCRIPT, THE
LOTERIE DE LA VIE, LA • 1982 • Gilles Guy • FRN
LOTERIE DU BONHEUR, LA • 1952 • Gehret Jean • FRN
LOTION MIRACULEUSE, LA • 1903 • *Pathe* • FRN • WONDERFUL HAIR RESTORER, A ○ MIRACLE LOTION, THE
LOTION MIRACULEUSE, LA • 1907 • *Pathe* • FRN • HAIR RESTORER, THE
LOTNA • 1959 • Wajda Andrzej • PLN
LOTOMANIA • 1980 • Shandel Thomas • MTV • CND
LOTOSBLUTEN FUR MISS QUON • 1966 • Roland Jurgen • FRG, FRN, ITL • COUP DE GONG A HONG-KONG (FRN) ○ TRAPPOLA PER 4 (ITL) ○ LOTUS FOR MISS QUON, A (USA) ○ LOTUS BLOSSOMS FOR MISS QUON
LOTS OF LUCK • 1985 • Baldwin Peter • TVM • USA
LOTS WEIB • 1965 • Gunther Egon • GDR • LOT'S WIFE
LOT'S WIFE see **LOTS WEIB** • 1965
LOTSA LUCK • 1968 • Smith Paul J. • ANS • USA
LOTTA COIN'S GHOST • 1915 • *Hamilton Lloyd V.* • USA
LOTTA DELL'UOMO PER LA SUA SOPRAVVIVENZA, LA • 1967 • Rossellini Renzo Jr. • ITL
LOTTCHENS HEIRAT • 1920 • Bolten-Baeckers Heinrich? • FRG
LOTTE • 1928 • Froelich Carl • FRG
LOTTE EISNER IN GERMANY • 1980 • Horowitz Mark • USA
LOTTE IN ITALIA • 1969 • Godard Jean-Luc, Gorin Jean-Pierre • FRN, ITL • LUTTES EN ITALIE ○ STRUGGLE IN ITALY
LOTTE IN WEIMAR • 1975 • Gunther Egon • GDR
LOTTE LENYA AND KURT WEILL • 1962 • Russell Ken • MTV • UKN
LOTTE LORE • 1921 • Eckstein Franz • FRG
LOTTE NELL'OMBRA • 1939 • Gambino Domenico M. • ITL • BATTLES IN THE SHADOWS
LOTTEKENS FELDZUG • 1915 • Ziener Bruno • FRG
LOTTERIESCHWEDE, DER • 1958 • Kunert Joachim • GDR • LOTTERY SWEDE, THE
LOTTERISEDDEL NO.22152 • 1915 • Blom August • DNM • BLINDE SKAEBNE, DEN ○ BLIND FATE
LOTTERY • 1983 • Philips Lee • TVM • USA
LOTTERY BRIDE, THE • 1930 • Stein Paul L. • USA • BRIDE SIXTY-SIX
LOTTERY LOVER, THE • 1935 • Thiele Wilhelm • USA
LOTTERY MAN, THE • 1916 • *Bergen Thurlow* • USA
LOTTERY MAN, THE • 1919 • Cruze James • USA
LOTTERY OF LIFE, THE • 1914 • *Film Releases* • USA
LOTTERY PRINCE, THE (USA) see **KSIAZATKO** • 1937
LOTTERY SWEDE, THE see **LOTTERIESCHWEDE, DER** • 1958
LOTTERY TICKET NO.66 • 1911 • Haldane Bert? • UKN
LOTTERY TICKET NUMBER 13 • 1912 • *Forde Victoria* • USA
LOTTERY-WINNER U.K.K. EMPTYBROOK see **LOTTOVOITTAJA UKK TURHAPURO** • 1976

LOTTIE'S PANCAKES • 1907 • Cooper Arthur • UKN • HER FIRST ATTEMPT ○ HER FIRST PANCAKE
LOTTOVOITTAJA UKK TURHAPURO • 1976 • Kokkonen Ere • FNL • LOTTERY-WINNER U.K.K. EMPTYBROOK
LOTU • 1960 • Holmes Cecil • DOC • ASL
LOTUS BLOSSOM • 1921 • Grandon Francis J. • USA
LOTUS BLOSSOMS FOR MISS QUON see **LOTOSBLUTEN FUR MISS QUON** • 1966
LOTUS D'OR, LE • 1916 • Mercanton Louis • FRN
LOTUS EATER, THE • 1921 • Neilan Marshall • USA
LOTUS FLOWER see **PAMPOSH** • 1953
LOTUS FOR MISS QUON, A (USA) see **LOTOSBLUTEN FUR MISS QUON** • 1966
LOTUS HEART see **THAMARAI NENJAM** • 1968
LOTUS LADY • 1930 • Rosen Phil • USA
LOTUS WING • 1967 • Abrams Jerry • SHT • USA
LOTUS WOMAN, THE • 1916 • Millarde Harry • USA
LOU COSTELLO AND HIS 30-FOOT BRIDE see **30-FOOT BRIDE OF CANDY ROCK, THE** • 1959
LOU RAWLS • 1962 • Binder Steve • SHT • USA
LOUBA DANCE • 1907 • *Walturdaw* • UKN
LOUCAS DE BARRO • 1959 • Ribeiro Antonio Lopes • SHT • PRT
LOUCO, O • 1945 • Manuel Vitor • PRT
LOUD SOUP • 1929 • Foster Lewis R. • SHT • USA
LOUD SPEAKER, THE • 1926 • Sanderson Challis, Newman Widgey R. • UKN
LOUDEST WHISPER, THE (UKN) see **CHILDREN'S HOUR, THE** • 1961
LOUDSPEAKER, THE • 1934 • Santley Joseph • USA • RADIO STAR, THE (UKN)
LOUDWATER MYSTERY, THE • 1921 • MacDonald Norman • UKN
LOUFA KAI PARRALAGHI • 1984 • Perakis Nikos • GRC
LOUIE, THE LIFE SAVER • 1913 • *Benham Harry* • USA
LOUIS ARMSTRONG • 1964 • Moore Richard • SHT • USA
LOUIS ARMSTRONG, 1931 see **LOUIS ARMSTRONG -CHICAGO STYLE** • 1976
LOUIS ARMSTRONG -CHICAGO STYLE • 1976 • Philips Lee • TVM • USA • LOUIS ARMSTRONG, 1931
LOUIS CAPET • 1954 • Leenhardt Roger, Vivet Jean-Paul • DCS • FRN • LOUIS XVI
LOUIS CYR, HOMME FORT CANADIEN • 1960 • Benoit Real • DOC • CND
LOUIS DE FUNES E IL NONNO SURGELATO (ITL) see **HIBERNATUS** • 1969
LOUIS-HIPPOLYTE LAFONTAINE • 1962 • Patry Pierre • DCS • CND
LOUIS II DE BAVIERE (FRN) see **LUDWIG II** • 1972
LOUIS-JOSEPH PAPINEAU, LE DEMI-DIEU • 1961 • Carrier Louis-Georges • SHT • CND
LOUIS L'AMOUR'S DOWN THE LONG HILLS see **DOWN THE LONG HILLS** • 1987
LOUIS L'AMOUR'S THE SACKETTS see **SACKETTS, THE** • 1979
LOUIS L'AMOUR'S THE SHADOW RIDERS see **SHADOW RIDERS, THE** • 1982
LOUIS LECOIN • 1966 • Desvilles, Darribehaude • SHT • FRN
LOUIS LUMIERE • 1949 • Lo Duca Joseph-Marie • SHT • FRN
LOUIS LUMIERE • 1964-69 • Rohmer Eric • MTV • FRN
LOUIS MALLE'S INDIA see **INDE FANTOME, L'** • 1969
LOUIS' SICKNESS AT SEA • 1913 • *Keystone* • USA
LOUIS, THERE'S A CROWD DOWNSTAIRS! see **START THE REVOLUTION WITHOUT ME** • 1970
LOUIS XIV SEIZES POWER see **PRISE DE POUVOIR PAR DE LOUIS XIV, LA** • 1966
LOUIS XIX • 1974 • Bokor Pierre • MTV • RMN
LOUIS XVI see **LOUIS CAPET** • 1954
LOUISA • 1950 • Hall Alexander • USA
LOUISA'S BATTLE WITH CUPID • 1915 • *Farley Dot* • USA
LOUISBOURG • 1969 • Kish Albert • DOC • CND
LOUISE • 1939 • Gance Abel • FRN
LOUISE DE LAVALLIERE • 1920 • Burghardt Georg • FRG • AM LIEBESHOF DES SONNENKONIGS
LOUISE (UKN) see **CHERE LOUISE** • 1971
LOUISIANA • 1919 • Vignola Robert G. • USA
LOUISIANA • 1947 • Karlson Phil • USA
LOUISIANA see **LOVE MART, THE** • 1927
LOUISIANA see **LAZY RIVER** • 1934
LOUISIANA see **LOUISIANE** • 1984
LOUISIANA HAYRIDE • 1944 • Barton Charles T. • USA
LOUISIANA LOU • 1900 • Gibbons Walter • UKN
LOUISIANA PURCHASE • 1941 • Cummings Irving • USA
LOUISIANA STORY • 1948 • Flaherty Robert • USA
LOUISIANA TERRITORY • 1953 • Smith Harry W. • USA
LOUISIANE • 1984 • de Broca Philippe • FRN, CND, ITL • LOUISIANA
LOULOU • 1980 • Pialat Maurice • FRN
LOULOUS, LES • 1976 • Cabouat Patrick • FRN • FURIE
LOUP BLANC, LE • 1973 • Sauriol Brigitte • CND
LOUP DES MALVENEURS, LE • 1942 • Radot Guillaume • FRN • WOLF OF THE MALVENEURS, THE
LOUP ET L'AGNEAU, LE • 1955 • Image Jean • ANS • FRN • WOLF AND THE LAMB, THE
LOUP GARON, LE see **GEHETZTE MENSCHEN** • 1932
LOUP-GAROU, LE • 1923 • *Marau Jean* • FRN • WEREWOLF, THE
LOUPE DE GRAND-MERE, LA see **LOUPE DE GRANDMAMAN, LA** • 1901
LOUPE DE GRANDMAMAN, LA • 1901 • Zecca Ferdinand • FRN • LOUPE DE GRAND-MERE, LA ○ GRANDMOTHER'S EYEGLASSES
LOUPEZNICKA POHADKA • 1964 • Hofman Eduard • ANS • PLN • ROBBER'S TALE, THE
LOUPEZNIK • 1931 • Kodicek • CZC • BRIGAND, THE
LOUPIOTE, LA • 1922 • Hatot Georges • FRN
LOUPIOTE, LA • 1923 • Vorins Henri • FRN
LOUPIOTE, LA • 1936 • Kemm Jean, Bouquet Jean-Louis • FRN
LOUPS CHASSENT LA NUIT, LES • 1951 • Borderie Bernard • FRN, ITL • RAGAZZA DI TRIESTE, LA (ITL)
LOUPS DANS LA BERGERIE, LES • 1959 • Bromberger Herve • FRN
LOUPS ENTRE EUX, LES • 1936 • Mathot Leon • FRN
LOUPS ET LES BREBIS, LES • 1945 • Protazanov Yakov • USS
LOURD CHARGEMENT, UN • 1898 • Lumiere Louis • FRN • HEAVY LOAD, A
LOURDES • 1898 • Lumiere Louis • FRN
LOURDES • 1958 • Russell Ken • SHT • UKN
LOURDES AND ITS MIRACLES see **LOURDES ET SES MIRACLES** • 1955
LOURDES ET SES MIRACLES • 1955 • Rouquier Georges • DOC • FRN • LOURDES AND ITS MIRACLES
LOURENCO MARQUES • 1958 • Queiroga Perdigao • SHT • PRT
LOUTCH SMERTI see **LUCH SMERTI** • 1925
LOUTKY JIRIHO TRNKY • 1955 • Sefranka Bruno • SHT • CZC • JIRI TRNKA'S PUPPETS
LOUTYE GHARNE BISTOM • 1968 • Safaei Reza • IRN • TWENTIETH CENTURY ROGUE
LOUVE, LA • 1911 • Carre Michel • FRN
LOUVE, LA • 1948 • Radot Guillaume • FRN • CLAYR FAIT
LOUVE SOLITAIRE, LA • 1968 • Logereau Edouard • FRN, ITL • GATTA DAGLI ARTIGLI D'ORO, LA (ITL)
LOUVES, LES • 1926 • Boudrioz Robert • FRN
LOUVES, LES • 1957 • Saslavsky Luis • FRN • SHE-WOLVES, THE ○ DEMONIAQUE ○ DEMONIAC
LOUVES BRULANTES • 1975 • Desvilles Jean • FRN
LOUVES, LES (FRN) see **LETTERS TO AN UNKNOWN LOVER** • 1985
LOUVRE, LE • Macovet S. • FRN
LOUVRE COME BACK TO ME • 1962 • Jones Charles M. • ANS • USA
LOUVRE MUSEUM, THE see **MUSEE DU LOUVRE, LE** • 1979
LOV NA JELENE • 1972 • Hadzic Fadil • YGS • DEER HUNT, THE
LOV NA MAMUTA • Danek Oldrich • CZC • MAMMOTH HUNT, THE
LOV U MUTNOM • 1983 • Radavanovic Vlasta • YGS • LIGHTS ON THE TOP FLOOR
LOVABLE CHEAT, THE • 1949 • Oswald Richard • USA
LOVABLE TROUBLE • 1941 • Lord Del • SHT • USA
LOVAGIAS UGY • 1937 • Sekely Steve • HNG • AFFAIR OF HONOR, AN
LOVE • 1914 • Protazanov Yakov • USS
LOVE • 1919 • Arbuckle Roscoe • SHT • USA
LOVE • 1920 • Ruggles Wesley • USA
LOVE • 1927 • Goulding Edmund • USA • ANNA KARENINA (UKN)
LOVE • 1967 • Sheppard Gordon H. • CND
LOVE • 1973 • Gilic Vlatko • SHT • YGS
LOVE • 1976 • Umboh Wim • INN
LOVE • 1981 • Zetterling Mai, Ullmann Liv, Dowd Nancy, Cohen Annette • CND
LOVE see **EVE'S DAUGHTER** • 1916
LOVE see **KOI** • 1924
LOVE see **MIRSU** • 1924
LOVE see **KARLEK** • 1952
LOVE see **AI** • 1963
LOVE? see **IGAZ-E?** • 1963
LOVE see **SEVDA** • 1967
LOVE see **SZERELEM** • 1970
LOVE see **LASKA** • 1972
LOVE see **OBICH** • 1973
LOVE see **KARLEKEN** • 1980
LOVE see **LJUBEZEN** • 1985
LOVE see **LAILA** • 1990
LOVE 1-1000 see **KARLEK 1-1000** • 1967
LOVE 65 (UKN) see **KARLEK 65** • 1965
LOVE A LA CARTE (USA) see **ADUA E LE COMPAGNE** • 1960
LOVE A LA MODE • 1930 • Roberts Stephen • SHT • USA
LOVE ADDICT • 1984 • Hebert Pierre (c/d) • CND
LOVE AFFAIR • 1932 • Freeland Thornton • USA
LOVE AFFAIR • 1939 • McCarey Leo • USA
LOVE AFFAIR • 1971 • Evans Roy • UKN
LOVE AFFAIR BROKER, THE see **IRO NO TEHAI-SHI** • 1967
LOVE AFFAIR IN TOYLAND, A see **DRAME CHEZ LES FANTOCHES, UNE** • 1908
LOVE AFFAIR OF A DICTATOR, THE see **DICTATOR, THE** • 1935
LOVE AFFAIR OR THE CASE OF THE MISSING SWITCHBOARD OPERATOR see **LJUBAVNI SLUCAJ ILI TRAGEDIJA SLUZBENICE P.T.T.** • 1967
LOVE AFFAIR: THE ELEANOR & LOU GEHRIG STORY, A • 1977 • Cook Fielder • TVM • USA
LOVE AFLAME • 1917 • Wells Raymond • USA
LOVE AFTER DEATH • 1968 • del Mar Glauco • MXC • UNSATISFIED LOVE
LOVE AHOY see **SEA RACKETEERS** • 1937
LOVE, AIR AND A LOT OF LIES see **LIEBE, LUFT UND LAUTER LUGEN** • 1959
LOVE ALWAYS WINS see **SIEMPRE TRIUNFA EL AMOR** • 1974
LOVE AMONG RAINDROPS see **LASKA MEZI KAPKAMI DESTE** • 1978
LOVE AMONG THE GEYSERS • 1912 • *Wilson Benjamin* • USA
LOVE AMONG THE MILLIONAIRES • 1930 • Tuttle Frank • USA
LOVE AMONG THE ROSES • 1910 • Griffith D. W. • USA
LOVE AMONG THE RUINS • 1975 • Cukor George • TVM • USA
LOVE AMONG THIEVES • 1987 • Young Roger • TVM • USA
LOVE AND A BURGLAR • 1913 • Plumb Hay? • UKN
LOVE AND A FEW CURSES see **LJUBAV I PO KOJA PSOVKA** • 1970
LOVE AND A GOLD BRICK • 1918 • *Vernon Bobby* • USA
LOVE AND A LEGACY • 1915 • Birch Cecil • UKN
LOVE AND A LEMON • 1912 • *Nestor* • USA
LOVE AND A LIAR • 1916 • Chaudet S. • SHT • USA
LOVE AND A LOTTERY TICKET • 1914 • Brenon Herbert • USA
LOVE AND A SAVAGE • 1915 • Christie Al • USA
LOVE AND A SEWING MACHINE • 1911 • Fitzhamon Lewin? • UKN
LOVE AND A TUB • 1914 • Kellino W. P. • UKN
LOVE AND A WARRIOR see **KOI TO BUSHI** • 1925
LOVE AND A WHIRLWIND • 1922 • Macrae Duncan, Shaw Harold • UKN
LOVE AND AMBITION • Warren Edward • USA
LOVE AND AN OCCASIONAL SWEARWORD see **LJUBAV I PO KOJA PSOVKA** • 1970
LOVE AND ANARCHY (USA) see **FILM D'AMORE E D'ANARCHIA: OVVERO STAMATTINA ALLE IO IN VIA DEI FIORI NELLA NOTA CASA DI TOLLERANZA** • 1973
LOVE AND ANGER see **AMORE E RABBIA** • 1969
LOVE AND ANIMALS see **LOVE AND THE ANIMALS** • 1969
LOVE AND ARTILLERY • 1915 • *Novelty* • USA
LOVE AND BASEBALL • 1914 • *Matthewson Christy* • USA
LOVE AND BITTERS • 1915 • *Novelty* • USA
LOVE AND BLAZES • 1917 • Moore Vin • SHT • USA
LOVE AND BLOOD see **AGAPI KE EMA** • 1968
LOVE AND BRASS BUTTONS • 1916 • Davey Horace • SHT • USA
LOVE AND BULLETS • 1914 • Henderson Dell • USA
LOVE AND BULLETS • 1916 • Greene Clay M. • SHT • USA
LOVE AND BULLETS • 1979 • Rosenberg Stuart • USA, UKN
LOVE AND BULLETS see **LOVE, POETRY AND PAINT** • 1914
LOVE AND BUSINESS • 1914 • *Komic* • USA
LOVE AND CAMERAS • 1915 • Birch Cecil • UKN
LOVE AND CARNATIONS • 1916 • *Hippo* • USA
LOVE AND CHARITY • 1911 • *Reliance* • USA
LOVE AND CIRCUMSTANCES • 1913 • *Ammex* • USA
LOVE AND COURAGE • 1913 • Nicholls George, Sennett Mack (Spv) • USA
LOVE AND CURSES • 1938 • Hardaway Ben, Dalton Cal • ANS • USA
LOVE AND DEATH • 1975 • Allen Woody • USA
LOVE AND DEATH • 1990 • Alami M. R. • IRN
LOVE AND DEATH see **AMORE E MORTE** • 1932
LOVE AND DEATH see **SEKAI O KAKERU KOI** • 1959
LOVE AND DEFICIT see **KARLEK OCH KASSABRIST** • 1932
LOVE AND DEVOTION • 1967 • de Guzman Armando • PHL
LOVE AND DOUGH • 1915 • *Brennan John E.* • USA
LOVE AND DOUGHNUTS • 1921 • Del Ruth Roy • SHT • USA • BLOCK HEAD, THE
LOVE AND DOWNHILL SKIING see **KARLEK OCH STORTLOPP** • 1946
LOVE AND DUTY • 1916 • *Plump & Runt* • USA
LOVE AND DYNAMITE • 1914 • Sennett Mack • USA
LOVE AND DYNAMITE see **KARLEK OCH DYNAMIT** • 1933
LOVE AND ELECRICITY • 1914 • *Asher Max* • USA
LOVE AND FAITH (USA) see **OGIN SAMA** • 1977
LOVE AND FASCINATION see **BOJO NO HITO** • 1961
LOVE AND FILM see **LJUBOV I FILM** • 1961
LOVE AND FISH • 1917 • *Triangle* • USA
LOVE AND FLAMES • 1914 • *Lubin* • USA
LOVE AND 'FLUENCE • 1916 • Birch Cecil • UKN
LOVE AND FRIENDSHIP see **ISHQ WA DOSTI** • 1946
LOVE AND FURY see **LJUBAV I BIJES** • 1979
LOVE AND GASOLINE • 1914 • Henderson Dell • USA
LOVE AND GASOLINE • 1920 • Smith Noel • SHT • USA
LOVE AND GLORY • 1924 • Julian Rupert • USA
LOVE AND GOLD • 1913 • *Alden Mary* • USA
LOVE AND GOOD FELLOWSHIP PILLS • 1910 • *Linder Max* • FRN
LOVE AND GRAFT • 1914 • *Asher Max* • USA
LOVE AND GREED see **OTTA GA MITA** • 1964
LOVE AND HANDCUFFS • 1915 • Ayres Sydney • USA
LOVE AND HASH • 1914 • Middleton George E.? • USA
LOVE AND HATE • 1916 • Vincent James • USA
LOVE AND HATE • 1924 • Bentley Thomas • UKN
LOVE AND HATE • 1935 • Gendelstein Albert • USS
LOVE AND HATRED • 1908 • *Urban-Eclipse* • USA
LOVE AND HATRED • 1911 • *Greenwood Reeva* • USA
LOVE AND HISSES • 1934 • White Sam • USA
LOVE AND HISSES • 1937 • Lanfield Sidney • USA
LOVE AND HYPNOTISM • 1912 • *Cattaneo Amelia* • ITL
LOVE AND INSTALLMENTS • 1915 • *Ray Al* • USA
LOVE AND JOURNALISM (UKN) see **KARLEK OCH JOURNALISTIK** • 1916
LOVE AND KISSES • 1925 • Cline Eddie • SHT • USA
LOVE AND KISSES • 1965 • Nelson Ozzie • USA
LOVE AND KISSES see **KYS TIL HOJRE OG VENSTRE** • 1969
LOVE AND KISSES, CAROLINE see **BETWEEN US GIRLS** • 1942
LOVE AND LABOR • 1915 • Steppling John • USA
LOVE AND LARCENY • 1985 • Iscove Ron • CND
LOVE AND LARCENY (USA) see **MATTATORE, IL** • 1960
LOVE AND LATHER • 1916 • *Pokes & Jabbs* • USA
LOVE AND LATHER • 1919 • Pratt Gilbert • SHT • USA
LOVE AND LAUNDRY • 1913 • *Kinemacolor* • USA
LOVE AND LAVALLIERES • 1913 • *Essanay* • USA
LOVE AND LAVALLIERES • 1918 • Howe J. A. • SHT • USA
LOVE AND LAW • 1909 • *Selig* • USA
LOVE AND LAW • 1910 • *Thanhouser* • USA
LOVE AND LAW • 1915 • *Joker* • USA
LOVE AND LAW • 1915 • Sturgeon Rollin S. • *Vitagraph* • USA
LOVE AND LEARN • 1928 • Tuttle Frank • USA
LOVE AND LEARN • 1947 • De Cordova Frederick • USA • WOULD YOU BELIEVE ME
LOVE AND LEMONS • 1912 • Dwan Allan • USA
LOVE AND LET LOVE see **SLEEPING CAR** • 1933
LOVE AND LIFE see **KOI NO INOCHIO** • 1961
LOVE AND LIMBO • 1915 • *Mina* • USA
LOVE AND LIMBURGER • 1913 • *Joker* • USA
LOVE AND LOBSTER • 1918 • Rains Fred • SHT • UKN
LOVE AND LOBSTERS see **HE DID AND HE DIDN'T** • 1916
LOVE AND LOCKSMITHS • 1917 • Christie Al • SHT • USA
LOVE AND LOGS • 1917 • Reed Walter C. • SHT • USA
LOVE AND LONELINESS see **ALLVARSAMMA LEKEN, DEN** • 1977
LOVE AND LOOT see **LOOT AND LOVE** • 1916
LOVE AND LUNCH • 1914 • *Sterling* • USA
LOVE AND LUNCH • 1917 • *International Film Service* • ANS • USA
LOVE AND LUNCH • 1917 • Seiter William A. • *Pyramid* • SHT • USA
LOVE AND LUNCH see **MABEL'S BUSY DAY** • 1914
LOVE AND MAGIC • 1914 • Booth W. R.? • UKN
LOVE AND MARRIAGE • 1970 • Gould Terry • DOC • UKN • SEX, LOVE AND MARRIAGE
LOVE AND MARRIAGE IN POSTER LAND • 1910 • *Edison* • USA
LOVE AND MARRIAGE (USA) see **IDEA FISSA, L'** • 1964

LOVE AND MOLASSES • 1908 • Melies Georges • FRN
LOVE AND MONEY • 1910 • *Bison* • USA
LOVE AND MONEY • 1915 • *Thanhouser* • USA
LOVE AND MONEY • 1982 • Toback James • USA, FRG
LOVE AND MUSIC • 1971 • Pohland Hansjurgen, Sluizer George • FRG • STAMPING GROUND (UKN)
LOVE AND OTHER CRIMES see **ALEX AND THE GYPSY** • 1976
LOVE AND OVERALLS • 1916 • *Gayety* • SHT • USA
LOVE AND PAIN • 1913 • Lehrman Henry, Sennett Mack (Spv) • USA
LOVE AND PAIN (AND THE WHOLE DAMN THING) • 1972 • Pakula Alan J. • USA • WIDOWER, THE
LOVE AND PARTING IN SRI LANKA see **SURI-LANKA, NO AI TO WAKARE** • 1976
LOVE AND PEOPLE see **LASKA A LIDE** • 1937
LOVE AND PIES • 1915 • *Starlight* • USA
LOVE AND PLEDGE see **AI TO CHIKAI** • 1945
LOVE AND POLITICS • 1914 • Del Ruth Roy • USA
LOVE AND PROMOTION • 1910 • *Walturdaw* • UKN
LOVE AND RAGE see **LJUBAV I BIJES** • 1979
LOVE AND RUBBISH • 1913 • Lehrman Henry, Sennett Mack (Spv) • USA
LOVE AND SACRIFICE • 1912 • *Eclair* • USA
LOVE AND SACRIFICE (UKN) see **AMERICA** • 1924
LOVE AND SALT WATER • 1914 • Avery Charles • USA
LOVE AND SCIENCE • 1912 • *Eclair* • FRN
LOVE AND SCIENCE • 1912 • *Majestic* • USA
LOVE AND SEPARATION IN SRI LANKA see **SURI-LANKA, NO AI TO WAKARE** • 1976
LOVE AND SKATES • 1915 • *United Film Service* • USA
LOVE AND SODA • 1914 • Hopper E. Mason • USA
LOVE AND SONGS see **CINTA DAN LAGU** • 1975
LOVE AND SOUR NOTES • 1915 • *Ritchie Billy* • USA
LOVE AND SPANISH ONIONS • 1915 • Collins Edwin J.? • UKN
LOVE AND SPIRITS • 1914 • *Shields Ernest* • USA
LOVE AND STATISTICS see **KARLEK OCH STATISTIK**
LOVE AND SURGERY • 1914 • *Ritchie Billy* • USA
LOVE AND SWORDS • 1915 • McKim Edwin • USA
LOVE AND TEARS • 1912 • *Lubin* • USA
LOVE AND THE ANIMALS • 1969 • *Milne Lorus J.* • USA • SEX AND THE ANIMALS ○ LOVE AND ANIMALS
LOVE AND THE BOXING GLOVES • 1914 • Birch Cecil • UKN
LOVE AND THE DEVIL • 1929 • Korda Alexander • USA
LOVE AND THE FIRST RAILROAD (USA) see **LIEBE UND DIE ERSTE EISENBAHN, DIE** • 1934
LOVE AND THE FRENCHWOMAN (USA) see **FRANCAISE ET L'AMOUR, LA** • 1960
LOVE AND THE ICEMAN • 1917 • Christie Al • USA
LOVE AND THE JOURNALIST see **KARLEK OCH JOURNALISTIK** • 1916
LOVE AND THE LAW • 1910 • Porter Edwin S. • USA
LOVE AND THE LAW • 1912 • Reid Wallace • USA
LOVE AND THE LAW • 1913 • *Clayton Marguerite* • USA
LOVE AND THE LAW • 1919 • Lewis Edgar • USA • TROOP TRAIN, THE
LOVE AND THE LEOPARD • 1915 • Martin E. A. • USA
LOVE AND THE MIDNIGHT AUTO SUPPLY • 1978 • Polakoff James • USA • MIDNIGHT AUTO SUPPLY, THE ○ RIP OFF
LOVE AND THE SINGLE SAILOR see **HOW TO PICK UP A GIRL** • 1967
LOVE AND THE STOCK MARKET • 1911 • *Edison* • USA
LOVE AND THE TELEPHONE • 1913 • *Majestic* • USA
LOVE AND THE VARSITY • 1913 • Stow Percy • UKN
LOVE AND THE WOMAN • 1919 • Johnson Tefft • USA
LOVE AND THE WORKMAN • 1913 • *Victor* • USA
LOVE AND THE ZEPPELIN see **VZDUCHOLOD A LASKA** • 1947
LOVE AND THIEVES see **LIEBE UND DIEBE** • 1928
LOVE AND TIGERS see **SEVODNYA -NOVYI ATTRAKSION** • 1964
LOVE AND TITLE • 1914 • Lewis Will • USA
LOVE AND TREACHERY • 1912 • *Reehm George E.* • USA
LOVE AND TREASON see **HOB WA KHYANA** • 1968
LOVE AND TROUBLE • 1913 • *Lubin* • USA
LOVE AND TROUBLE • 1915 • *Beery Wallace* • USA
LOVE AND TROUT • 1916 • Robertson John S. • SHT • USA
LOVE AND VACCINATION • 1916 • Christie Al • SHT • USA
LOVE AND VENGEANCE • 1914 • Lehrman Henry • USA
LOVE AND VETERAN RESERVES see **KARLEK OCH LANDSTORM** • 1931
LOVE AND WAR • 1909 • *Edison* • USA
LOVE AND WAR • 1911 • Coleby A. E. • UKN
LOVE AND WAR • 1912 • *Majestic* • USA
LOVE AND WAR see **KYS OG KAERLIGHED** • 1914
LOVE AND WAR see **WAR AND LOVE** • 1985
LOVE AND WAR see **IN LOVE AND WAR** • 1987
LOVE AND WAR IN MEXICO • 1913 • *Lubin* • USA
LOVE AND WAR IN TOYLAND • 1913 • Thornton F. Martin, Rogers Edgar • UKN
LOVE AND WATER • 1915 • *Sterling* • USA
LOVE AND WOODEN SHOES • 1914 • Brabec Josef • CZC
LOVE AROUND THE CORNER see **AMOR A LA VUELTA DE LA ESQUINA** • 1985
LOVE AS BAIT see **SCHREI NACH LUST** • 1968
LOVE AS DISORDER see **AFFAIR OF THE SKIN, AN** • 1963
LOVE AT ARMS • 1912 • Rains Fred • UKN
LOVE AT FIRST BITE • 1950 • White Jules • SHT • USA
LOVE AT FIRST BITE • 1979 • Dragoti Stan • USA
LOVE AT FIRST FIGHT see **FIGHTING COLLEEN, A** • 1919
LOVE AT FIRST FLIGHT • 1928 • Cline Eddie • SHT • USA
LOVE AT FIRST FRIGHT • *Brendel El* • SHT • USA
LOVE AT FIRST GULP • 1980 • Evans Warren • USA • DRACULA EXOTICA
LOVE AT FIRST SIGHT • 1910 • *Essanay* • USA
LOVE AT FIRST SIGHT • 1928 • *Sennett Mack (P)* • SHT • USA
LOVE AT FIRST SIGHT • 1930 • Lewis Edgar • USA
LOVE AT FIRST SIGHT • 1973 • Noonan Chris • SHT • ASL
LOVE AT FIRST SIGHT • 1976 • Bromfield Rex • CND
LOVE AT FIRST SIGHT see **COLPO DI FULMINE** • 1985
LOVE AT FREEZING POINT see **DRAGOSTE LA 0** • 1964
LOVE AT GLOUCESTER PORT • 1911 • *Tapley Rose* • USA
LOVE AT LARGE • 1989 • Rudolph Alan • USA
LOVE AT NIGHT (USA) see **IMPASSE DES VERTUS** • 1955
LOVE AT SEA • 1936 • Brunel Adrian • UKN
LOVE AT SECOND BITE • 1990 • Dragoti Stan • USA
LOVE AT SECOND SIGHT • 1934 • Merzbach Paul • UKN • GIRL THIEF, THE (USA)
LOVE AT STAKE • 1988 • Moffitt John • USA • BURNIN' LOVE
LOVE AT THE CIRCUS • 1914 • Batley Ethyle • UKN
LOVE AT THE FOGGY HARBOUR see **KIRI NO MINATO NO AKAI HANA** • 1962
LOVE AT THE TOP (USA) see **MOUTON ENRAGE, LE** • 1974
LOVE AT THE WHEEL • 1921 • Merwin Bannister • UKN
LOVE AT TWENTY (USA) see **AMOUR A VINGT ANS, L'** • 1962
LOVE AUCTION, THE • 1919 • Lawrence Edmund • USA
LOVE BAN, THE see **IT'S A 2'6" ABOVE THE GROUND WORLD** • 1972
LOVE BANDIT, THE • 1924 • Henderson Dell • USA
LOVE BEACH see **PLAYA DEL AMOR, LA** • 1980
LOVE BEFORE BREAKFAST • 1936 • Lang Walter • USA
LOVE BEFORE TEN • 1913 • Parker Lem B. • USA
LOVE BEGINS AT 20 • 1936 • McDonald Frank • USA • ALL ONE NIGHT (UKN)
LOVE BEGINS ON FRIDAY • 1972 • Calotescu Virgil • RMN
LOVE BETWEEN THE RAINDROPS see **LASKA MEZI KAPKAMI DESTE** • 1978
LOVE BEWITCHED, A see **AMOR BRUJO, EL** • 1985
LOVE BIRD see **KATHAL PARAVAI** • 1967
LOVE BIRDS • 1934 • Seiter William A. • USA • NIAGARA FALLS ○ TWO GLUCKS
LOVE BIRDS • 1969 • Caiano Mario • ITL, FRG • STRANA VOGLIA D'AMARE, UNA ○ LIEBESVOGEL (FRG)
LOVE BIRDS, THE see **MEOTO ZENZAI** • 1968
LOVE BLACKMAILER, THE see **ADULTEROUS AFFAIR** • 1966
LOVE BLINDS US see **LIEBE MACHT BLIND** • 1923
LOVE BLOSSOMS FOR THE FIRST TIME • 1980 • Umboh Wim • INN
LOVE BOAT, THE • 1976 • Kinon Richard • TVM • USA
LOVE BOAT II • 1977 • Averback Hy • TVM • USA
LOVE BOUND • 1932 • Hill Robert F. • USA
LOVE BOX, THE • 1972 • White Billy, White Teddy • UKN • LOVE CAMP ○ SEX BOX, THE
LOVE BRAND, THE • 1923 • Paton Stuart • USA
LOVE BROKERS, THE • 1918 • Hopper E. Mason • USA
LOVE BUG, THE • 1925 • Roach Hal • SHT • USA
LOVE BUG, THE • 1969 • Stevenson Robert • USA
LOVE BUG RIDES AGAIN, THE • 1972 • Stevenson Robert • USA • HERBIE RIDES AGAIN (UKN)
LOVE BUGS, THE • 1917 • *Price Kate* • USA
LOVE BURGLAR, THE • 1919 • Cruze James • USA
LOVE BURGLARS AND A BULLDOG • 1916 • Miller Rube • USA
LOVE BUS • 1975 • *Hawks George* • USA
LOVE BUSINESS • 1931 • McGowan Robert • SHT • USA
LOVE BUTCHER, THE • 1983 • Angel Mikel, Jones Don • USA
LOVE BY APPOINTMENT see **NATALE IN CASA D'APPUNTAMENTO** • 1976
LOVE BY CORRESPONDENCE see **POCHTOVY ROMAN** • 1969
LOVE BY REQUEST see **VLUBIEN PO SOBSTVENNOMU ZHELANIJU** • 1983
LOVE BY THE LIGHT OF THE MOON • 1901 • Porter Edwin S. • USA
LOVE BY THE POUND • 1914 • Williams C. Jay • USA
LOVE CAGE, THE (UKN) see **FELINS, LES** • 1964
LOVE CALL, THE • 1919 • Chaudet Louis W. • USA
LOVE CAME DOWN BY PARACHUTE see **AMOR DESCEU EM PARAQUEDAS, O** • 1968
LOVE CAMP see **LOVE BOX, THE** • 1972
LOVE CAMP see **TODESGOTTIN DES LIEBESCAMPS, DIE** • 1981
LOVE CAMP 7 • 1968 • Frost R. L. • USA • LOVE CAMP SEVEN
LOVE CAMP SEVEN see **LOVE CAMP 7** • 1968
LOVE CAPTIVE, THE • 1934 • Marcin Max • USA • HUMBUG, THE
LOVE CHARM • 1914 • *Columbus* • USA
LOVE CHARM, THE • 1921 • Heffron Thomas N. • USA
LOVE CHASE, A • 1917 • *Depp Harry* • USA
LOVE CHASE, THE • 1911 • *Nestor* • USA
LOVE CHASE, THE • 1913 • *Tennant Barbara* • USA
LOVE CHASE, THE see **MOUTARADA GHARAMIA** • 1968
LOVE CHASTISED see **SA TUKTAS KARLEKEN** • 1955
LOVE CHEAT, THE • 1919 • Archainbaud George • USA
LOVE CHILD • 1982 • Peerce Larry • USA
LOVE CHILD, THE • 1987 • Smith Robert • UKN
LOVE CHILD, THE see **LOVE ME.. PLEASE** • 1969
LOVE CHILD (UKN) see **CHILD UNDER A LEAF** • 1974
LOVE CHILDREN • 1970 • *Mj Productions* • USA
LOVE CHILDREN, THE see **PSYCH-OUT** • 1968
LOVE CIRCLE, THE (UKN) see **METTI, UNA SERA A CENA** • 1969
LOVE CIRCLES • 1984 • Kikoine Gerard • UKN
LOVE CLAIM, THE • 1917 • Clifton Elmer • USA
LOVE CLINIC, THE • 1968 • Sebastian Ferdinand • USA
LOVE COMES ALONG • 1930 • Julian Rupert • USA
LOVE COMES QUIETLY • 1973 • van der Heyde Nikolai • BLG • ANGELA
LOVE COMES TO MAGOO • 1958 • McDonald Tom • ANS • USA
LOVE COMES TO MOONEYVILLE • 1936 • Black Preston • SHT • USA
LOVE COMES TO THOSE WHO RETURN see **KTO VERNYOTSYA, DOLYUBIT** • 1968
LOVE COMET, THE • 1916 • Wright Walter • SHT • USA
LOVE COMMANDMENT, THE (USA) see **DU SOLLST NICHT STEHLEN** • 1928
LOVE COMMANDS (USA) see **AMOR MANDA, EL** • 1940
LOVE COMPLEX, THE see **SLEEPWALKER, THE** • 1922
LOVE CONQUERS • 1911 • Bouwmeester Theo • UKN
LOVE CONQUERS CRIME • 1912 • Rains Fred • UKN
LOVE CONTRACT, THE • 1932 • Selpin Herbert • UKN
LOVE CRAZE, THE • 1918 • Kelley J. Winthrop • SHT • USA
LOVE CRAZY • 1941 • Conway Jack • USA
LOVE CRAZY see **ASKINLA DIVANEYIM** • 1967
LOVE CRAZY WOMEN see **PREMIER ETE, LE** • 1975
LOVE CRISIS see **RENAI HIJOJI** • 1933
LOVE CULT, THE • 1966 • Dee T. A. • USA
LOVE CYCLES (USA) see **DAMA SPATHI** • 1966
LOVE, DAGGER AND TREASON • 1969 • Shengelaya Eldar • USS
LOVE DARES ALL • 1913 • *Anderson* • UKN • SAILOR'S SWEETHEART, A
LOVE, DEATH • 1973 • Gershuny Theodore • USA • LOVE ME MY WAY (UKN)
LOVE, DEATH AND THE DEVIL see **LIEBE, TOD UND TEUFEL** • 1934
LOVE DECIDES • 1911 • *Lubin* • USA
LOVE DEFENDER, THE • 1919 • Johnson Tefft • USA
LOVE DISCO see **DISCOTECA DEL AMOR, LA** • 1980
LOVE DISGUISED • 1914 • *Joker* • USA
LOVE DOCTOR, THE • 1916 • *Gayety* • USA
LOVE DOCTOR, THE • 1917 • Scardon Paul • USA
LOVE DOCTOR, THE • 1929 • Brown Melville • USA
LOVE DOCTOR, THE see **BOOMERANG, THE** • 1925
LOVE DOCTORS, THE • 1969 • Ross Bon • USA
LOVE DOES STRANGE THINGS TO PEOPLE see **TULIPANI DI HAARLEM, I** • 1970
LOVE DOLL see **LIFE SIZE** • 1973
LOVE DOLL, THE • 1970 • Feder L. • USA
LOVE DOPE, THE • 1917 • *Herz Ralph* • SHT • USA
LOVE DOSSIER see **LJUBAVNI SLUCAJ ILI TRAGEDIJA SLUZBENICE P.T.T.** • 1967
LOVE DREAM • 1988 • Finch Charles • ITL
LOVE DREAMS • 1981 • Vydra Alan • USA
LOVE DROPS • 1910 • *Edison* • USA
LOVE DUET, THE see **BRAND IN DER OPER** • 1930
LOVE DUTY AND CRIME • 1924 • Garzon Pedro Moreno • CLM
LOVE, DYNAMITE AND BASEBALL • 1916 • Dillon John Francis • USA
LOVE 'EM AND BEAT 'EM see **PASS THE GRAVY** • 1928
LOVE 'EM AND FEED 'EM • 1927 • Bruckman Clyde • SHT • USA
LOVE 'EM AND LEAVE 'EM • 1926 • Tuttle Frank • USA
LOVE 'EM AND WEEP • 1927 • Guiol Fred • SHT • USA
LOVE EMILIA! see **SZERESSETEK ODOR EMILIAT** • 1970
LOVE EPIDEMIC, THE • 1975 • Trenchard-Smith Brian • ASL
LOVE ETERNAL (UKN) see **ETERNEL RETOUR, L'** • 1943
LOVE ETERNE, THE see **LIANG SHAN-PO YU CHU YING-T'AI** • 1963
LOVE EXORCIST see **DADDY'S DEADLY DARLING** • 1972
LOVE EXPERT, THE • 1920 • Kirkland David, Emerson John (Spv) • USA
LOVE EXPERTS, THE see **SEXPERTS -TOUCHED BY TEMPTATION** • 1965
LOVE EXPRESS see **RENAI TOKKYU** • 1954
LOVE EXPRESS, THE see **KARLEKSEXPRESSEN** • 1932
LOVE FACTORY (USA) see **BIANCO, ROSSO, GIALLO, ROSA** • 1965
LOVE + FEAR + TORMENT see **PEUR ET L'AMOUR, LA** • 1967
LOVE FEAST, THE (USA) see **IMMER WENN ES NACHT WIRD** • 1961
LOVE FEROZ, EL • 1972 • Garcia Sanchez Jose Luis • SPN • CRUEL LOVE
LOVE FEVER • 1931 • McGowan Robert • SHT • USA
LOVE FIELD • 1990 • Kaplan Jonathan • USA
LOVE FIGHTERS see **TUFF TURF** • 1984
LOVE FILM see **SZERELMESFILM** • 1970
LOVE FINDS A WAY • 1909 • Griffith D. W. • USA
LOVE FINDS A WAY • 1912 • *Eclair* • USA
LOVE FINDS A WAY • 1912 • *Vitagraph* • USA
LOVE FINDS A WAY • 1914 • *Simon Louis* • USA
LOVE FINDS A WAY • 1915 • Santschi Thomas • USA
LOVE FINDS A WAY (UKN) see **ALIAS FRENCH GERTIE** • 1930
LOVE FINDS ANDY HARDY • 1938 • Seitz George B. • USA
LOVE, FIREWORKS AND THE JANITOR • 1915 • MacMackin Archer • USA
LOVE FLOWER, THE • 1920 • Griffith D. W. • USA • BLACK BEACH
LOVE FOOLERY CASE OF A FRESH SEVERED HEAD see **NAMAKUBI JOCHI JIKEN** • 1967
LOVE FOR EVER • 1969 • Georgiadis Vassilis • GRC
LOVE FOR LOVE (USA) see **AMOR CON AMOR SE PAGA** • 1940
LOVE FOR RANSOM see **ROGER & HARRY: THE MITERA TARGET** • 1977
LOVE FOR RENT • 1979 • Miller David • TVM • USA • LOVE FOR SALE
LOVE FOR SALE see **LOVE FOR RENT** • 1979
LOVE FOR THREE ORANGES see **LYUBOV K TREM APELSINAM** • 1970
LOVE-FORSAKEN CORNER, A see **BEI AIQING YIWANGDE JIAOLUO** • 1981
LOVE FROM A STRANGER • 1937 • Lee Rowland V. • UKN
LOVE FROM A STRANGER • 1947 • Whorf Richard • USA • STRANGER WALKED IN, A (UKN)
LOVE FROM MUSIC see **KARLEK EFTER NOTER** • 1935
LOVE FROM OUT OF THE GRAVE • 1913 • *Film D'Art* • FRN
LOVE FROM PARIS • 1970 • *Stacey Dist.* • USA
LOVE FROM PARIS see **MONTPI** • 1957
LOVE GAMBLE, THE • 1925 • Le Saint Edward J. • USA
LOVE GAMBLER, THE • 1922 • Franz Joseph J. • USA
LOVE GAME, THE • 1980 • Vazov Yanoush • BUL
LOVE GAME, THE see **KARA LEKEN, DEN** • 1959
LOVE GAME, THE (USA) see **JEUX DE L'AMOUR, LES** • 1960
LOVE-GAMES see **LIEBESSPIEL** • 1931
LOVE GAMES FOR YOUNG GIRLS see **LIEBESSPIELE JUNGER MADCHEN** • 1972
LOVE GAMES OF YOUNG GIRLS see **LIEBESSPIELE JUNGER MADCHEN** • 1972
LOVE GENERATION, THE • 1967 • *Chaudhri Amin* • USA
LOVE GERMS • 1909 • *Lubin* • USA
LOVE GIRL, THE • 1916 • Leonard Robert Z. • USA
LOVE GOD?, THE • 1969 • Hiken Nat • USA
LOVE GODDESSES, THE • 1965 • Ferguson Graeme, Turell Saul J. • USA
LOVE HABIT, THE • 1930 • Lachman Harry • UKN
LOVE HAPPY • 1949 • Miller David • USA • KLEPTOMANIACS
LOVE HAS ITS REASONS! see **LIEBE MUSS VERSTANDEN SEIN!** • 1933
LOVE HAS MANY FACES • 1965 • Singer Alexander • USA

LOVE HATE see **ALBATROS, L'** • 1971
LOVE, HATE AND A WOMAN • 1921 • Horan Charles • USA
LOVE, HATE AND DEATH see **MONTOYAS Y TARANTOS** • 1988
LOVE HATE LOVE • 1970 • McCowan George • TVM • USA
LOVE HATH WROUGHT A MIRACLE • 1912 • Young James • USA
LOVE HEEDS NOT SHOWERS • 1911 • Moore Owen • USA
LOVE HERMIT, THE • 1916 • *Russell William* • USA
LOVE, HOLLYWOOD STYLE see **SHANNON'S WOMEN** • 1969
LOVE, HONOR AND ? • 1919 • Miller Charles • USA
LOVE HONOR AND BEHAVE • 1919 • *Sennett* • SHT • USA
LOVE, HONOR AND BEHAVE • 1920 • Jones F. Richard, Kenton Erle C. • USA
LOVE, HONOR AND BEHAVE • 1938 • Logan Stanley • USA • EVERYBODY WAS VERY NICE
LOVE, HONOR AND GOODBYE • 1945 • Rogell Albert S. • USA
LOVE, HONOR AND HE PAYS • 1932 • Buzzell Edward • SHT • USA
LOVE, HONOR AND OBEY • 1920 • De Cordova Leander • USA
LOVE, HONOR AND OBEY see **INDEPENDENCE DAY** • 1983
LOVE, HONOR AND OH, BABY! • 1933 • Buzzell Edward • SHT • USA
LOVE, HONOR AND OH-BABY! • 1940 • Lamont Charles • USA
LOVE-HOTEL IN TIROL • 1978 • Antel Franz • AUS, FRG
LOVE HOUR, THE • 1925 • Raymaker Herman C. • USA
LOVE HOURS, THE see **LUSTING HOURS, THE** • 1967
LOVE HUNGER, THE • 1919 • Earle William P. S. • USA
LOVE HUNGER (USA) see **FLOR DEL IRUPE, LA** • 1964
LOVE HUNGRY • 1928 • Heerman Victor • USA
LOVE-HUNGRY GIRLS (UKN) see **GARCES, LES** • 1973
LOVE HUNTER, THE • 1909 • *Phoenix* • USA
LOVE HURTS • 1982 • Demme Jonathan • USA
LOVE HURTS • 1989 • Yorkin Bud • USA
LOVE HURTS see **KUCANGDE LIANQING** • 1988
LOVE IMAGE, THE (UKN) see **FACE ON THE BARROOM FLOOR, THE** • 1923
LOVE IN 4 DIMENSIONS (USA) see **AMORE IN 4 DIMENSIONI** • 1963
LOVE-IN '72 • 1971 • *Southern Linda* • USA
LOVE IN A BASEMENT see **LIVING ON LOVE** • 1937
LOVE IN A BOARDING HOUSE • 1913 • Fitzhamon Lewin • UKN
LOVE IN A BUNGALOW • 1937 • McCarey Ray • USA
LOVE IN A COTTAGE • 1940 • White Volney • ANS • USA
LOVE IN A FALLEN CITY • 1984 • Hsu An-Hua • HKG
LOVE IN A FIX • 1912 • *Irish Films* • UKN
LOVE IN A FOUR LETTER WORLD • 1970 • Sone John • CND • LOVE IS A FOUR LETTER WORD • SEX ISN'T SIN (UKN) ○ VIENS, MON AMOUR ○ LOOKING GLASS, THE
LOVE IN A GOLDFISH BOWL • 1961 • Sher Jack • USA
LOVE IN A HAMMOCK • 1901 • Porter Edwin S. • USA
LOVE IN A HOT CLIMATE (USA) see **SANG ET LUMIERES** • 1954
LOVE -IN A HURRY • 1919 • *Christie* • USA
LOVE IN A HURRY • 1919 • Henderson Dell • *World* • USA • ALLIES
LOVE IN A LAUNDRY • 1912 • Wilson Frank? • UKN
LOVE IN A MIRROR see **AMOR EN UN ESPEJO** • 1968
LOVE IN A MIST • 1916 • Hepworth Cecil M. • UKN
LOVE IN A POLICE STATION • 1927 • *Sennett Mack (P)* • SHT • USA
LOVE IN A POND • 1931 • Foster John, Davis Mannie • ANS • USA
LOVE IN A TAXI • 1980 • Sickinger Robert • USA
LOVE IN A TEASHOP • 1913 • von Herkomer Hubert • UKN
LOVE IN A TEPEE • 1911 • *Imp* • USA
LOVE IN A WOMEN'S PRISON see **DIARIO SEGRETO DI UN CARCERE FEMMINILE** • 1973
LOVE IN A WOOD • 1915 • Elvey Maurice • UKN
LOVE IN AN APARTMENT HOTEL • 1913 • Griffith D. W. • USA
LOVE IN AN ATTIC • 1923 • Greenwood Edwin • UKN
LOVE IN ARMOR • 1915 • Cogley Nick • USA
LOVE-IN ARRANGEMENT, THE • 1980 • Larkin Charles • USA
LOVE-IN ARRANGEMENTS see **SLIP UP** • 1974
LOVE IN BAGHDAD see **HUBB FI BAGHDAD** • 1986
LOVE IN BLOOM • 1935 • Nugent Elliott • USA • WIN OR LOSE
LOVE IN CHAINS • 1970 • *Kingslie Productions* • USA
LOVE IN COLD BLOOD see **ICE HOUSE, THE** • 1969
LOVE IN DANGER see **KALAU BERPAUT DI-DAHAN RAPOH** • 1970
LOVE IN EXILE • 1936 • Werker Alfred L. • UKN
LOVE IN FOUR EASY LESSONS (UKN) see **SPOGLIAMOCI COSI SENZA PUDOR..** • 1977
LOVE IN GERMANY, A (USA) see **AMOUR EN ALLEMAGNE, UN** • 1983
LOVE IN GINZA see **GINZA NO KOI NO MONOGATARI** • 1962
LOVE IN HIGH GEAR • 1932 • Strayer Frank • USA
LOVE IN JAMAICA (USA) see **A LA JAMAIQUE** • 1956
LOVE IN JERUSALEM see **MARGO SHELI** • 1971
LOVE IN LAS VEGAS (UKN) see **VIVA LAS VEGAS** • 1963
LOVE IN MARDI GRAS COLORS see **LASKA V BARVACH KARNEVALU** • 1974
LOVE IN MEXICO • 1910 • *Bison* • USA
LOVE IN MOROCCO (USA) see **BAROUD** • 1931
LOVE IN NEPAL • 1987 • *Shabnam* • NPL, BNG, PKS
LOVE IN OUR TIME • 1968 • Allan Elkan • DOC • UKN
LOVE IN PAWN • 1953 • Saunders Charles • UKN
LOVE IN QUARANTINE • 1910 • Powell Frank • USA
LOVE IN QUARANTINE (USA) see **AMORE IN QUARANTENA** • 1938
LOVE IN ROME see **AMORE A ROMA, UN** • 1960
LOVE IN SEPTEMBER • 1936 • Cline Eddie • SHT • USA
LOVE IN STUNT FLYING (USA) see **LIEBE IM GLEITFLUG** • 1938
LOVE IN SUSPENSE • 1917 • Beaudine William • SHT • USA
LOVE IN THE AFTERNOON • 1957 • Wilder Billy • USA • FASCINATION
LOVE IN THE AFTERNOON (UKN) see **AMOUR L'APRES-MIDI, L'** • 1972
LOVE IN THE AIR see **AMOR EN EL AIRE** • 1967
LOVE IN THE ARMY see **SLUBY ULANSKIE** • 1935
LOVE IN THE CITY see **AMORE IN 4 DIMENSIONI** • 1963
LOVE IN THE CLOUDS see **AMOR EN LAS NUBES** • 1968
LOVE IN THE DARK • 1913 • *Kinemacolor* • USA
LOVE IN THE DARK • 1922 • Beaumont Harry • USA • PAGE TIM O'BRIEN
LOVE IN THE DESERT • 1929 • Melford George • USA
LOVE IN THE GHETTO • 1912 • Reid Hal • USA
LOVE IN THE GHETTO • 1913 • Eagle Oscar • USA
LOVE IN THE HILLS • 1911 • *Essanay* • USA
LOVE IN THE HILLS • 1911 • Griffith D. W. • *Ab* • USA
LOVE IN THE KARNAK see **GHARAM FIL KARNAK** • 1967
LOVE IN THE PACIFIC • 1970 • Sulistrowski Zygmunt • DOC • USA
LOVE IN THE RAIN see **HUBBUN TAHTA AL-MAT'AR** • 1975
LOVE IN THE ROUGH • 1930 • Reisner Charles F. • USA • LIKE KELLY CAN
LOVE IN THE SNOW see **YUKIGUNI** • 1965
LOVE IN THE SUBURB see **KERTES HAZAK UTCAJA** • 1962
LOVE IN THE SUBURBS • 1900 • *Bitzer Billy (Ph)* • USA
LOVE IN THE TROPICS see **TROPISK KAERLIGHED** • 1911
LOVE IN THE VINEYARD see **ILS SONT DANS LES VIGNES** • 1951
LOVE IN THE WELSH HILLS • 1921 • Dudley Bernard • UKN
LOVE IN THE WEST see **"HELL TO PAY" AUSTIN** • 1916
LOVE IN THE WILDERNESS • 1920 • Butler Alexander • UKN
LOVE IN TOKYO see **KOI NO TOKYO** • 1932
LOVE IN WAITING • 1948 • Pierce Douglas • UKN • AT YOUR SERVICE
LOVE INCOGNITO • 1913 • *Watson Minor* • USA
LOVE-INS, THE • 1967 • Dreifuss Arthur • USA
LOVE INSURANCE • 1920 • Crisp Donald • USA
LOVE IS A BALL • 1962 • Swift David • USA • ALL THIS AND MONEY TOO (UKN) ○ GRAND DUKE AND MR. PIMM, THE
LOVE IS A CAROUSEL • 1970 • Cheverton Roy P. • USA
LOVE IS A DAY'S WORK see **GIORNATA BALORDA, LA** • 1960
LOVE IS A DOG FROM HELL (USA) see **CRAZY LOVE** • 1987
LOVE IS A FAT WOMAN see **AMOR ES UNA MUJER CORDA, EL** • 1987
LOVE IS A FOUR-LETTER WORD • 1964 • Frost R. L. • USA • LOVE IS AN EXCITING WORD
LOVE IS A FOUR LETTER WORD see **LOVE IN A FOUR LETTER WORLD** • 1970
LOVE IS A FUNNY THING (USA) see **HOMME QUI ME PLAIT, L'** • 1969
LOVE IS A HEADACHE • 1937 • Thorpe Richard • USA
LOVE IS A MANY-SPLENDORED THING • 1955 • King Henry • USA • MANY-SPLENDORED THING, A
LOVE IS A RACKET • 1932 • Wellman William A. • USA
LOVE IS A RACKET see **ATHLETE INCOMPLET, L'** • 1932
LOVE IS A SCANDAL see **HUB BAHDALA, EL** • 1951
LOVE IS A SPLENDID ILLUSION • 1970 • Clegg Tom • UKN • SWEDISH DREAM
LOVE IS A WEAPON see **HELL'S ISLAND** • 1955
LOVE IS A WILFUL BIRD see **LYUBOVTA E NEMIRNA PTITSA** • 1990
LOVE IS A WOMAN (USA) see **DEATH IS A WOMAN** • 1966
LOVE IS AN AWFUL THING • 1922 • Heerman Victor • USA
LOVE IS AN EXCITING WORD see **LOVE IS A FOUR-LETTER WORD** • 1964
LOVE IS BEST • 1911 • *Imp* • USA
LOVE IS BETTER THAN EVER • 1951 • Donen Stanley • USA • LIGHT FANTASTIC, THE (UKN)
LOVE IS BLIND • 1909 • Porter Edwin S. • USA
LOVE IS BLIND • 1912 • *Walthall Henry B.* • USA
LOVE IS BLIND • 1913 • Dwan Allan • USA
LOVE IS BLIND • 1957 • Davis Mannie • ANS • USA
LOVE IS BLIND see **KAERLIGHED GOR BLIND** • 1912
LOVE IS BLONDE • 1928 • Sandrich Mark (c/d) • SHT • USA
LOVE IS CALLING YOU • 1934 • Neilan Marshall • USA
LOVE IS COLDER THAN DEATH (UKN) see **LIEBE IST KALTER ALS DER TOD** • 1969
LOVE IS CRUEL see **MALUPIT ANG PAG-IBIG** • 1967
LOVE IS DANGEROUS • 1933 • Thorpe Richard • USA • WOMEN ARE DANGEROUS (UKN) ○ LOVE IS LIKE THAT
LOVE IS FOREVER • 1982 • Bartlett Hall • TVM • USA • COMEBACK, THE
LOVE IS LAW see **LOVE'S LAW** • 1916
LOVE IS LIKE THAT see **LOVE IS DANGEROUS** • 1933
LOVE IS LIKE THAT (UKN) see **JAZZ CINDERELLA** • 1930
LOVE IS LIKE THE SUN see **AMORE E COME IL SOLE, L'** • 1968
LOVE IS LOVE • 1919 • Dunlap Scott R. • USA
LOVE IS LOVE see **LIEBE IST LIEBE** • 1932
LOVE IS MONEY see **LOVE OR MONEY** • 1920
LOVE IS MY PROFESSION (USA) see **EN CAS DE MALHEUR** • 1958
LOVE IS MY UNDOING see **E L'AMOR CHE MI ROVINA** • 1951
LOVE IS NEVER SILENT • 1985 • Sargent Joseph • TVM • USA • SHATTERED SILENCE
LOVE IS NEWS • 1937 • Garnett Tay • USA
LOVE IS NOT ENOUGH • 1978 • Dixon Ivan • TVM • USA
LOVE IS ON THE AIR • 1937 • Grinde Nick • USA • RADIO MURDER MYSTERY, THE (UKN)
LOVE IS ONLY A WORD (UKN) see **LIEBE IST NUR EIN WORT** • 1971
LOVE IS PINK see **KULAY ROSAS ANG PAG-IBIG** • 1968
LOVE IS SHARED LIKE SWEETS see **MEOTO ZENZAI** • 1955
LOVE IS STRANGE see **AMOR ES ESTRANY, EL** • 1988
LOVE IS STRENGTH see **AI WA CHIKARA DA** • 1930
LOVE IS WAR • 1969 • Henriksen R. Lasse • NRW
LOVE IS WHEN YOU MAKE IT see **BEL AGE, LE** • 1958
LOVE IS WHERE IT'S AT • 1968 • Knight Sidney • USA
LOVE ITALIAN STYLE see **FEMMINE DI LUSSO** • 1960
LOVE ITALIAN STYLE see **AMORE ALL'ITALIANA** • 1966
LOVE KEYS, THE • 1974 • Thiele Rolf • FRG
LOVE KISS, THE • 1930 • Snody Robert R. • USA • KISS ME (UKN)
LOVE KNOWS NO LAWS • 1912 • *Reliance* • USA
LOVE KNOWS NO LAWS • 1915 • *Beauty* • USA
LOVE KNOWS NO PITY see **ASKIN MERHAMETI YOKTUR** • 1967
LOVE KRAZY • 1932 • *Mintz Charles (P)* • ANS • USA
LOVE LAND • 1974 • USA
LOVE, LAUGHS AND LATHER • 1917 • Roach Hal • SHT • USA
LOVE LAUGHS AT ANDY HARDY • 1946 • Goldbeck Willis • USA • UNCLE ANDY HARDY
LOVE LAUGHS AT DYSPEPSIA • 1916 • Clements Roy • SHT • USA
LOVE LAUGHS AT LOCKSMITHS • 1904 • *Paul R. W.* • UKN
LOVE LAUGHS AT LOCKSMITHS • 1908 • *Vitagraph* • USA
LOVE LAUGHS AT LOCKSMITHS • 1913 • Ince Ralph • USA
LOVE LAUGHS AT THE LAW • 1916 • Curtis Allen • SHT • USA
LOVE LEAD THEM THROUGH LIFE see **ZIVOTEM VEDLA JE LASKA** • 1928
LOVE LEADS THE WAY • 1984 • Mann Delbert • TVM • USA
LOVE LESSON, THE • 1921 • Roach Hal • SHT • USA
LOVE LETTER • 1982 • Higashi Yoichi • JPN
LOVE LETTER see **KOIBUMI** • 1953
LOVE LETTER see **KOIBUMI** • 1985
LOVE LETTER, THE • 1923 • Baggot King • USA
LOVE LETTER FROM A MURDERER see **CARTA DE AMOR DE UN ASESINO** • 1972
LOVE LETTER TRIAL see **KOIBUMI SAIBAN** • 1951
LOVE LETTERS • 1917 • Neill R. William • USA
LOVE LETTERS • 1924 • Soloman David • USA
LOVE LETTERS • 1945 • Dieterle William • USA
LOVE LETTERS • 1966 • Heynowski Walter • DOC • GDR
LOVE LETTERS see **ITAZURA** • 1959
LOVE LETTERS see **MY LOVE LETTERS** • 1983
LOVE LETTERS, THE • 1905 • Stow Percy • UKN
LOVE LETTERS FROM TERALBA ROAD • 1977 • Wallace Stephen • ASL
LOVE LETTERS FROM THE ENGADINE (USA) see **LIEBESBRIEFE AUS DEM ENGADIN** • 1938
LOVE LETTERS OF A STAR • 1936 • Foster Lewis R., Carruth Milton • USA • CASE OF THE CONSTANT GOD
LOVE LETTERS OF BARONESS S. see **LIEBES DER BARONIN VON S., DIE** • 1924
LOVE LETTERS WITH INTENT see **LJUBAVNA PISMA S PREDUMISLJAJEM** • 1985
LOVE LIAR, THE • 1916 • Wilbur Crane • USA
LOVE LIER, THE • 1915 • Harvey Harry • USA
LOVE LIES • 1931 • Lane Lupino • UKN
LOVE, LIFE AND LAUGHTER • 1923 • Pearson George • UKN
LOVE, LIFE AND LAUGHTER • 1934 • Elvey Maurice • UKN
LOVE LIFE AND LAUGHTER AT SWAYTHLING COURT • 1926 • Brunel Adrian • UKN
LOVE, LIFE AND LIBERTY • 1913 • *Bison* • USA
LOVE LIFE OF A GORILLA, THE • 1937 • USA
LOVE-LIFE OF BUDIMIR TRAJKOVIC, THE see **LJUBAVNI ZIVOT BUDIMIRA TRAJKOVICA** • 1978
LOVE LIGHT, THE • 1921 • Marion Frances • USA
LOVE LIKE THAT, A see **BREAKFAST FOR TWO** • 1937
LOVE, LIVE AND LAUGH • 1929 • Howard William K. • USA
LOVE, LIVE WITH THE STARS see **AI YO HOSHI TO TOMONI** • 1947
LOVE LIVES ON • 1985 • Peerce Larry • TVM • USA
LOVE LOOPS THE LOOP • 1918 • Wright Walter, Del Ruth Hampton • SHT • USA
LOVE, LOOT AND CRASH • 1915 • Cogley Nick • USA
LOVE, LOOT AND LIQUOR • 1914 • Henderson Dell • USA
LOVE LOTTERY, THE • 1954 • Crichton Charles • UKN
LOVE, LOVE, BUT DON'T LOSE YOUR HEAD see **LJUBI, LJUBI, AL'GLAVU** • 1982
LOVE, LUCK AND A DONKEY • 1915 • *Federal* • USA
LOVE, LUCK AND A PAINT BRUSH • 1913 • *Lyons Eddie* • USA
LOVE, LUCK AND CANDY • 1914 • *Sterling* • USA
LOVE, LUCK AND GASOLINE • 1910 • *Vitagraph* • USA
LOVE, LUCK AND GASOLINE • 1914 • North Wilfred • USA
LOVE, LUCK AND LOOT • 1917 • Hunter T. Hayes • SHT • USA
LOVE, LUST AND ECSTASY • 1983 • Milonakos Ilias • GRC
LOVE, LUST AND VIOLENCE • 1975 • Meisel Norbert • USA
LOVE LUTY OF ROMANY, THE • 1913 • *Bayne Beverly* • USA
LOVE MACHINE see **PLEASURE MACHINES, THE** • 1969
LOVE MACHINE, THE • 1971 • Haley Jack Jr. • USA
LOVE MACHINES, THE see **PLEASURE MACHINES, THE** • 1969
LOVE-MAD TUTORESS, THE see **KYOREN NO ONNA SHISHO** • 1926
LOVE MADNESS • 1920 • Henabery Joseph • USA
LOVE MADNESS see **BURNING QUESTION, THE** • 1940
LOVE MAGGY • 1921 • Granville Fred Leroy • UKN
LOVE MAGIC see **YOU NEVER KNOW WOMEN** • 1926
LOVE MAGNET, THE • 1916 • Santell Alfred • SHT • USA
LOVE MAKERS, THE see **VIACCIA, LA** • 1961
LOVE MAKERS, THE see **LOVEMAKERS.. CARNAL STYLE, THE** • 1970
LOVE MAKES 'EM WILD • 1927 • Ray Albert • USA
LOVE MAKES ONE BLIND see **LIEBE MACHT BLIND** • 1923
LOVE MAKES US BLIND see **LIEBE MACHT BLIND** • 1923
LOVE-MAKING HOT STYLE see **FLASH LOVE** • 1971
LOVE MANIA • 1924 • St. John Al • SHT • USA
LOVE MANIAC, THE see **BLOOD OF GHASTLY HORROR** • 1972
LOVE MART, THE • 1927 • Fitzmaurice George • USA • LOUISIANA
LOVE, MARY • 1985 • Day Robert • TVM • USA
LOVE MASK, THE • 1916 • Reicher Frank • USA
LOVE MASSACRE see **AI SHA** • 1981
LOVE MASTER, THE • 1924 • Trimble Larry, Murfin Jane • USA
LOVE MATCH see **PARTIE DE PLAISIR, UNE** • 1974
LOVE MATCH, THE • 1955 • Paltenghi David • UKN
LOVE MATES (USA) see **ANGLAR, FINNS DOM?** • 1961
LOVE ME • 1918 • Neill R. William • USA
LOVE ME! see **ALSKA MEJ!** • 1986
LOVE ME AND THE WORLD IS MINE • 1908 • *Warwick Trading Co* • UKN
LOVE ME AND THE WORLD IS MINE • 1928 • Dupont E. A. • USA • IMPLACABLE DESTINY
LOVE ME, BABY, LOVE ME (UKN) see **STORIA D'AMORE, UNA** • 1969
LOVE ME BEFORE DARK see **NICHIBOTSUMAE NI AISHITE** • 1967
LOVE ME DARLING (UKN) see **MED KAERLIG HILSEN** • 1971
LOVE ME DEADLY • 1972 • Lacerte Jacques • USA • SECRETS OF THE DEATH ROOM

LOVE ME FOR MYSELF ALONE see **SQUARE DECEIVER, THE** • 1917
LOVE ME FOREVER • 1935 • Schertzinger Victor • USA • ON WINGS OF SONG (UKN)
LOVE ME GENTLY • 1974 • van Ackeren Robert • FRG
LOVE ME LIKE I DO • 1970 • Hearn J. Van • USA
LOVE ME LITTLE, LOVE ME LONG • 1915 • Wilson Frank? • UKN
LOVE ME, LOVE ME, LOVE ME • 1962 • Williams Richard • ANS • UKN
LOVE ME -LOVE ME NOT • 1962 • *Stevens Craig* • MTV • USA
LOVE ME, LOVE MY BISCUITS • 1917 • Beaudine William • SHT • USA
LOVE ME, LOVE MY DOG • 1909 • *Lubin* • USA
LOVE ME LOVE MY DOG • 1910 • Fitzhamon Lewin • UKN
LOVE ME, LOVE MY DOG • 1912 • *Robinson Gertrude* • USA
LOVE ME, LOVE MY DOG • 1913 • *Apollo* • USA
LOVE ME, LOVE MY DOG • 1916 • Figman Max • SHT • USA
LOVE ME, LOVE MY DOG • 1932 • *Carr Jane* • SHT • UKN
LOVE ME, LOVE MY MOUSE • 1966 • Jones Charles M. • ANS • USA
LOVE ME, LOVE MY WIFE (UKN) see **ADDIO ALEXANDRA!** • 1969
LOVE ME MY WAY (UKN) see **LOVE, DEATH** • 1973
LOVE ME NOT? • 1988 • Panoussopoulos George • GRC
LOVE ME OR LEAVE ME • 1955 • Vidor Charles • USA
LOVE ME OR LEAVE ME • 1970 • *Cosmos Films* • USA
LOVE ME.. PLEASE • 1969 • Peters Victor • USA • LOVE CHILD, THE
LOVE ME TENDER • 1956 • Webb Robert D. • USA
LOVE ME THE WAY I AM see **NOVIA PARA DAVID, UNA** • 1985
LOVE ME TONIGHT • 1932 • Mamoulian Rouben • USA
LOVE, MELODY see **MELODY** • 1971
LOVE MERCHANT, THE • 1966 • Sarno Joe • USA • ANOTHER WOMAN, ANOTHER DAY ○ LOVE MERCHANTS
LOVE MERCHANTS see **LOVE MERCHANT, THE** • 1966
LOVE MICROBE • 1907 • McCutcheon Wallace • USA
LOVE – MIRTH – MELODY • 1934 • Tracy Bert • UKN
LOVE MODELS • 1970 • *Stacey Dist.* • USA
LOVE, MOTHER see **CSOK, ANYU** • 1986
LOVE MOULDS LABOR • 1911 • Golden Joseph A. • USA
LOVE, MUMPS AND BUMPS • 1915 • MacMackin Archer • USA
LOVE, MUSIC AND CANNONBALLS • 1916 • Miller Rube • USA
LOVE MY DOG • 1927 • Roach Hal • SHT • USA
LOVE -MY WAY • 1966 • Hudson Arch • USA
LOVE NEST • 1951 • Newman Joseph M. • USA
LOVE NEST see **LOVE NET, THE** • 1918
LOVE NEST, THE • 1922 • Physioc Wray • USA
LOVE NEST, THE • 1923 • Cline Eddie, Keaton Buster • SHT • USA
LOVE NEST, THE • 1933 • Bentley Thomas • UKN
LOVE NEST, THE see **MODERN MATRIMONY** • 1923
LOVE NEST ON WHEELS • 1937 • Lamont Charles • SHT • USA
LOVE NET, THE • 1918 • Johnson Tefft • USA • LOVE NEST
LOVE NEVER DIES • 1916 • Worthington William • USA
LOVE NEVER DIES • 1921 • Vidor King • USA
LOVE NEVER DIES (UKN) see **LILAC TIME** • 1928
LOVE NEVER FAILS see **MUGIBUE** • 1955
LOVE NEW AND OLD see **SHAMISEN TO OTOBAI** • 1961
LOVE–NIGHTS IN THE TAIGA see **LIEBESNACHTE IN DER TAIGA** • 1967
LOVE NO MORE see **ASKA TOVBE** • 1968
LOVE NOT AGAIN see **KOIYA KOI NASUNA KOI** • 1962
LOVE NOW.. PAY LATER • 1966 • Rolos Don • USA • SIN NOW.. PAY LATER ○ NUDES ON CREDIT
LOVE NOW, PAY LATER see **WAHRHEIT UBER ROSEMARIE, DIE** • 1959
LOVE NOW.. PAY LATER (USA) see **INFERNO ADDOSSO, L'** • 1959
LOVE O' THE PARENT • 1915 • Ayres Sydney • USA
LOVE OBJECT, THE • 1967 • Schain Don • USA
LOVE OF '64, THE • 1913 • *Lubin* • USA
LOVE OF A CLOWN (PAGLIACCI) (USA) see **PAGLIACCI** • 1949
LOVE OF A GYPSY, THE • 1908 • Raymond Charles? • UKN
LOVE OF A HUNCHBACK, THE • 1909 • *Empire Films* • UKN
LOVE OF A KINGDOM • 1936 • Lejtes Joseph • PLN
LOVE OF A NAUTCH GIRL • 1909 • Stow Percy • UKN
LOVE OF A PATRIOT see **BARBARA FRIETCHIE** • 1924
LOVE OF A ROMANY LASS, THE • 1909 • Rosenthal Joe • UKN
LOVE OF A SAVAGE, THE • 1909 • *Bison* • USA
LOVE OF A SIREN, THE • 1911 • *Cines* • ITL
LOVE OF AN ACTRESS, THE • 1914 • Noy Wilfred • UKN
LOVE OF AN ISLAND MAID, THE • 1912 • *Bosworth Hobart* • USA
LOVE OF BEAUTY, THE • 1913 • *Lubin* • USA
LOVE OF BOB • 1918 • *Boy City Film* • USA
LOVE OF CHRYSANTHEMUM • 1910 • Brooke Van Dyke • USA
LOVE OF CONCHITA, THE • 1913 • *Majestic* • USA
LOVE OF GHAROON, THE see **ESHGHE GHAROON** • 1968
LOVE OF JEANNE NEY, THE (USA) see **LIEBE DER JEANNE NEY, DIE** • 1927
LOVE OF JOHN RUSKIN, THE • 1912 • *Gardner Helen* • USA
LOVE OF LADY IRMA, THE • 1910 • Powell Frank, Griffith D. W. • USA
LOVE OF LIFE see **JINSEI NO AI** • 1923
LOVE OF LIFE (UKN) see **ARTUR RUBINSTEIN: L'AMOUR DE LA VIE** • 1970
LOVE OF LONG AGO, A • 1912 • *La Badie Florence* • USA
LOVE OF LOTI SAN, THE • 1915 • Carleton Lloyd B. • USA
LOVE OF MADAME SAND, THE see **SONG TO REMEMBER, A** • 1945
LOVE OF MADGE O'HARA, THE • 1917 • Campbell Colin • SHT • USA
LOVE OF MARY WEST, THE • 1915 • King Burton L. • USA
LOVE OF MEN, THE • 1913 • *Darkfeather Mona* • USA
LOVE OF ORO SAN, THE • 1914 • Stanley George C. • USA
LOVE OF PENELOPE, THE • 1913 • Grandon Francis J. • USA
LOVE OF PERDITION see **AMOR DE PERDICAO** • 1977
LOVE OF PIERRE LAROSSE, THE • 1914 • Marston Theodore • USA
LOVE OF PRINCESS OLGA, THE • 1917 • Thayer Otis B. • SHT • USA
LOVE OF PRINCESS YOLANDE, THE • 1914 • *Albert Elsie* • USA
LOVE OF SERAFIM FROLOV, THE • 1969 • Tumanov Semyon • USS
LOVE OF SPORT (USA) see **SPORTSZERELEM** • 1938
LOVE OF SUMAKO THE ACTRESS, THE see **JOYU SUMAKO NO KOI** • 1947
LOVE OF SUMMER MORN, THE • 1911 • *Joyce Alice* • USA
LOVE OF SUNYA, THE • 1927 • Parker Albert • USA
LOVE OF THE FLAG, THE • 1912 • *Karr Darwin* • USA
LOVE OF THE PASHA'S SON, THE • 1909 • Blackton J. Stuart (Spv) • USA
LOVE OF THE POINTED BEARD MAN, THE see **MILOSC AZPICBRODKI** • 1978
LOVE OF THE PRINCESS see **SUJAKO MON** • 1957
LOVE OF THE WEST, THE • 1911 • Dwan Allan • USA • WESTERN LOVE
LOVE OF THEIR LIVES, THE • 1915 • Nash Percy? • UKN
LOVE OF TOKIWA, THE • 1914 • Davis Ulysses • USA
LOVE OF WOMEN see **SINGED** • 1927
LOVE OF WOMEN, THE • 1915 • Smiley Joseph • USA
LOVE OF WOMEN, THE • 1924 • Bennett Whitman • USA
LOVE, OIL AND GREASE • 1914 • Neilan Marshall • USA
LOVE OLD AND NEW see **SHAMISEN TO OTOBAI** • 1961
LOVE ON A BET • 1936 • Jason Leigh • USA • DON'T BET ON LOVE
LOVE ON A BUDGET • 1938 • Leeds Herbert I. • USA
LOVE ON A DOWNWARD SLOPE • 1973 • Duletic Vojko • YGS
LOVE ON A HORSE see **CONFESSIONS OF A RIDING MISTRESS** • 1977
LOVE ON A LADDER • 1934 • White Sam • SHT • USA
LOVE ON A NON–STOP see **KAERLIGHED UDEN STOP** • 1988
LOVE ON A PILLOW (USA) see **REPOS DU GUERRIER, LE** • 1962
LOVE ON A YACHT • 1915 • *Britannia* • UKN
LOVE ON AN EMPTY STOMACH • 1915 • *Mann Hank* • USA
LOVE ON CREDIT see **KAERLIGHED PA KREDIT** • 1955
LOVE ON CRUTCHES • 1917 • Blystone John G. (Spv) • SHT • USA
LOVE ON ROLLERS • 1920 • Goldaine Mark • SHT • USA
LOVE ON SKATES (UKN) see **DANGER GIRL, THE** • 1916
LOVE ON TAP • 1939 • Sidney George • SHT • USA
LOVE ON THE DOLE • 1941 • Baxter John • UKN
LOVE ON THE FURROWS see **LJUBAV NA BRAZDAMA** • 1974
LOVE ON THE GROUND (USA) see **AMOUR PAR TERRE, L'** • 1984
LOVE ON THE NOSE • 1978 • Bloomfield George • MTV • CND
LOVE ON THE RANGE • 1938 • Pal George • ANS • NTH
LOVE ON THE RIO GRANDE • 1925 • *Cody Bill* • USA
LOVE ON THE RIVIERA • 1924 • Sheppard W. H. • UKN
LOVE ON THE RIVIERA (USA) see **RACCONTI D'ESTATE** • 1958
LOVE ON THE RUN • 1936 • Van Dyke W. S. • USA
LOVE ON THE RUN • 1985 • Trikonis Gus • TVM • USA
LOVE ON THE RUN (USA) see **AMOUR EN FUITE, L'** • 1979
LOVE ON THE SPOT • 1932 • Cutts Graham • UKN
LOVE ON THE WING • 1937 • McLaren Norman • ANS • UKN
LOVE ON TOAST • 1938 • Dupont E. A. • USA
LOVE ON TOUGH LUCK RANCH • 1912 • Anderson G. M. • USA
LOVE ON WHEELS • 1932 • Saville Victor • UKN
LOVE ONE ANOTHER • 1916 • Metcalfe Earl • SHT • USA
LOVE ONE ANOTHER see **GEZEICHNETEN, DIE** • 1921
LOVE ONLY ME • 1935 • Flanz Marta, Krawicz Mecislas • HNG
LOVE OR A THRONE • 1913 • *Baird Leah* • USA
LOVE OR AN EMPIRE • 1916 • Brenon Herbert • SHT • USA
LOVE OR FAME • 1919 • *Hammerstein Elaine* • USA
LOVE OR JUSTICE • 1917 • Edwards Walter • USA
LOVE OR KILL see **YA SEV YA OLDUR** • 1967
LOVE OR LIMELIGHT see **SKYROCKET, THE** • 1926
LOVE OR MONEY • 1920 • King Burton L. • USA • LOVE IS MONEY
LOVE OR MONEY • 1989 • Hallowell Todd • USA
LOVE OR RICHES • 1911 • Bouwmeester Theo • UKN
LOVE OR WEALTH see **PANAMA PASAMA** • 1968
LOVE OVER NIGHT • 1928 • Griffith Edward H. • USA
LOVE PAINS • 1932 • Horne James W. • SHT • USA
LOVE PARADE, THE • 1929 • Lubitsch Ernst • USA • PARADE D'AMOUR
LOVE, PASSION AND PLEASURE see **BEFFE, LICENZE E AMORI DEL DECAMERONE SEGRETO** • 1973
LOVE PAST THIRTY • 1934 • Moore Vin • USA
LOVE PATCHES • 1912 • *Cosmopolitan* • UKN
LOVE, PEPPER AND SWEETS • 1915 • *Pokes & Jabbs* • USA
LOVE PHILTRE OF IKEY SCHOENSTEIN, THE • 1917 • Mills Thomas R. • SHT • USA
LOVE PIKER, THE • 1923 • Hopper E. Mason • USA • LOVE SNOB, THE
LOVE PILL, THE • 1971 • Turner Kenneth • UKN
LOVE PIRATE, THE • 1915 • Dillon Eddie • USA
LOVE PIRATE, THE • 1923 • Thomas Richard • USA • SILENT ACCUSER, THE
LOVE PIRATE, THE • 1970 • Mahon Barry • USA
LOVE PIRATE, THE (UKN) see **VIXEN, THE** • 1916
LOVE PLAY • 1977 • Korber Serge • FRN
LOVE PLAY see **RECREATION, LA** • 1961
LOVE PLOTTERS • 1909 • *Tiger* • USA
LOVE, POETRY AND PAINT • 1914 • Aylott Dave • UKN • LOVE AND BULLETS
LOVE POTION • 1987 • Doyle Julian • USA
LOVE POTION, THE • 1911 • *Powers* • USA
LOVE POTION NUMBER NINE • Safran Fred • SHT • USA
LOVE PROBLEMS (USA) see **ETA DEL MALESSERE, L'** • 1968
LOVE PUNCH, THE • 1930 • Ross Nat • SHT • USA
LOVE QUARANTINED • 1916 • Curtis Allen • SHT • USA
LOVE RACE, THE • 1931 • Lane Lupino, Morton Pat • UKN
LOVE RACE, THE (UKN) see **GIRL O' MY DREAMS** • 1934
LOVE RACKET, THE • 1929 • Seiter William A. • USA • SUCH THINGS HAPPEN (UKN)
LOVE REBELLION, THE • 1967 • Sarno Joe • USA
LOVE REDEEMED (UKN) see **DRAGNET PATROL** • 1931
LOVE REQUITED see **NAGRODZONE UCZUCIA** • 1958
LOVE REWARDED see **NAGRODZONE UCZUCIA** • 1958
LOVE RINGS A BELL • 1980 • Li Hsing • HKG
LOVE RIOT, A • 1916 • Jones F. Richard • SHT • USA
LOVE ROBOTS, THE • 1965 • Wakamatsu Koji • JPN
LOVE ROMANCE OF ADMIRAL SIR FRANCIS DRAKE, THE (USA) see **DRAKE'S LOVE STORY** • 1913
LOVE ROMANCE OF THE GIRL SPY, THE • 1910 • Olcott Sidney • USA
LOVE ROOT, THE see **MANDRAGOLA, LA** • 1965
LOVE, ROSES AND TROUSERS • 1914 • *Fazenda Louise* • USA
LOVE ROUTE, THE • 1915 • Dwan Allan • USA
LOVE ROUTE BY A PITTMAN, THE • 1914 • *Bayne Beverly* • USA
LOVE SCENE see **NUREBA** • 1967
LOVE SCENES • 1984 • Townsend Bud • USA • ECSTASY ○ LOVESCENE
LOVE SEED, A see **YI–K'O HUNG TOU** • 1980
LOVE SHUFFLE, THE see **SEX SHUFFLE, THE** • 1968
LOVE SICK • 1925 • Lamont Charles • SHT • USA
LOVE SICK MAIDENS OF CUDDLETOWN • 1912 • Baker George D. • USA • LOVESICK MAIDENS OF CUDDLETOWN
LOVE SICKNESS AT SEA • 1913 • Sennett Mack • USA
LOVE SLACKER, THE • 1917 • Clements Roy • SHT • USA
LOVE SLAVE OF THE ISLANDS see **CORPO, IL** • 1974
LOVE SLAVES OF THE AMAZON • 1957 • Siodmak Curt • USA
LOVE SNOB, THE see **LOVE PIKER, THE** • 1923
LOVE, SNOW AND ICE • 1915 • Van Wally • USA
LOVE, SOLDIERS AND WOMEN see **DESTINEES** • 1953
LOVE SONG see **LET'S DO IT AGAIN** • 1953
LOVE SONG, THE • 1906 • Gilbert Arthur • UKN
LOVE SONG, THE see **VALENCIA** • 1926
LOVE SONGS (USA) see **PAROLES ET MUSIQUE** • 1985
LOVE SPANISH STYLE see **AMOR A LA ESPANOLA** • 1967
LOVE SPASMS • 1916 • Myers Harry • SHT • USA
LOVE SPECIAL, THE • 1921 • Urson Frank • USA
LOVE SPECIALIST, THE see **RAGAZZA DEL PALIO, LA** • 1957
LOVE, SPEED AND THRILLS • 1915 • Henderson Dell • USA
LOVE SPELL • 1979 • Donavan Tom • UKN
LOVE SPOTS • 1914 • *Planet Films* • UKN
LOVE STARVED see **YOUNG BRIDE** • 1932
LOVE STATUE, THE • 1966 • Durston David E. • USA • STATUE, THE
LOVE STOPPED THE RUNAWAY TRAIN see **SHIOKARI TOGE** • 1973
LOVE STORM, THE see **CAPE FORLORN** • 1930
LOVE STORMS (USA) see **CAPE FORLORN** • 1930
LOVE STORY • 1944 • Arliss Leslie • UKN • LADY SURRENDERS, A (USA)
LOVE STORY • 1970 • Hiller Arthur • USA
LOVE STORY see **DOUCE** • 1943
LOVE STORY 1 • 1971 • Le Grice Malcolm • UKN
LOVE STORY 2 • 1971 • Le Grice Malcolm • UKN
LOVE STORY 3 • 1972 • Le Grice Malcolm • UKN
LOVE STORY, A see **HISTORIA DE AMOR, UNA** • 1968
LOVE STORY FOR YOU, A see **LOVE STORY O KIMI NI** • 1988
LOVE STORY O KIMI NI • 1988 • Sawai Shinichiro • JPN • LOVE STORY FOR YOU, A
LOVE STORY OF ALIETTE BRUNTON, THE • 1924 • Elvey Maurice • UKN
LOVE STORY OF CHARLES II, THE • 1911 • Bouwmeester Theo • UKN
LOVE STORY OF HER YOUTH, THE • 1914 • *Melies* • USA
LOVE STORY OF MR. GILFIL see **MR. GILFIL'S LOVE STORY** • 1920
LOVE STREAMS • 1983 • Cassavetes John • USA
LOVE STRONGER THAN HATE see **KARLEK STARKARE AN HAT** • 1914
LOVE STRONGER THAN HATRED see **KARLEK STARKARE AN HAT** • 1914
LOVE SUBLIME, A • 1917 • Browning Tod, Lucas Wilfred • USA
LOVE SUMMER OF A SCHLEPP, THE • 1990 • Todorov Lyudmil • BUL
LOVE SUNDAE, A • 1926 • Cline Eddie • SHT • USA
LOVE, SUNSHINE AND SONG see **KARLEK, SOLSKEN OCH SANG** • 1948
LOVE SWEDISH STYLE • 1972 • Smith Maurice • USA
LOVE SWEETER THAN LOVE • 1975 • Rafla Hilmy • EGY
LOVE SWINDLE, A • 1918 • Dillon John Francis • USA
LOVE –TAHITI STYLE see **ODISSEA NUDA** • 1961
LOVE TAKES A HOLIDAY see **SHE WROTE THE BOOK** • 1946
LOVE TAKES FLIGHT • 1937 • Nagel Conrad • USA
LOVE TAKES HIS VENGEANCE see **STRASHNAYA MEST** • 1913
LOVE TAPES, THE • 1980 • Reisner Allen • TVM • USA
LOVE TECHNIQUE OF FLOWERS see **HANANO IROMICHI** • 1967
LOVE TEST, THE • 1912 • *Imp* • USA
LOVE TEST, THE • 1912 • Hopper E. Mason • *Essanay* • USA
LOVE TEST, THE • 1913 • *Lubin* • USA
LOVE TEST, THE • 1935 • Powell Michael • UKN
LOVE TEST, THE (UKN) see **TWO CAN PLAY** • 1926
LOVE THAT BRUTE • 1950 • Hall Alexander • USA • TURNED UP TOES
LOVE THAT DARES, THE • 1919 • Millarde Harry • USA
LOVE THAT DOESN'T RETURN (USA) see **AMORE CHE NON TORNA** • 1938
LOVE THAT KNOWS NO BARRIERS, THE • 1961 • Manrok Hossein • SML
LOVE THAT LASTS, THE • 1915 • Ayres Sydney • USA
LOVE THAT LIVES, THE • 1917 • Vignola Robert G. • USA
LOVE THAT LIVES, THE see **STORSTE I VERDEN, DET** • 1919
LOVE THAT NEVER FAILS, THE • 1912 • Davis Ulysses • USA
LOVE, THAT OLD LIE see **ASK ESKI BIR YALAN** • 1968
LOVE THAT PUP • 1949 • Hanna William, Barbera Joseph • ANS • USA
LOVE THAT TURNED, THE • 1913 • *Pathe* • USA
LOVE THAT WHIRLS, THE • 1949 • Anger Kenneth • USA
LOVE, THE CLAIRVOYANT • 1914 • Costello Maurice, Gaillord Robert • USA
LOVE THE FUTURE • 1959 • NKR
LOVE, THE ITALIAN WAY (USA) see **FEMMINE DI LUSSO** • 1960
LOVE THE MAGICIAN see **AMOR BRUJO, EL** • 1985

LOVE THE ONLY LAW (UKN) see **BERG-EJVIND OCH HANS HUSTRU** • 1918
LOVE, THE TYRANT see **LOVE TYRANT, THE** • 1912
LOVE, THE WINNER • 1913 • Johnston Lorimer • USA
LOVE THEFT, THE • 1913 • *Commerford T. J.* • USA
LOVE THERAPY • 1986 • Yossifova Iskra • BUL
LOVE THIEF, THE • 1914 • Parrott Charles • USA
LOVE THIEF, THE • 1916 • Stanton Richard • USA
LOVE THIEF, THE • 1926 • McDermott John • USA
LOVE THIEF, THE see **ROUNDERS, THE** • 1914
LOVE, THIS IS MY SONG • 1967 • de Villa Jose • PHL
LOVE THRILL, THE • 1927 • Webb Millard • USA
LOVE THROUGH A LENS • 1912 • *Steppling John* • USA
LOVE THROUGH THE CAR DOOR see **LIEBE DURCH DIE AUTOTURE** • 1972
LOVE THROUGH THE CENTURIES see **PLUS VIEUX METIER DU MONDE, LE** • 1967
LOVE, THY NAME BE SORROW see **KOIYA KOI NASUNA KOI** • 1962
LOVE THY NEIGHBOR • 1934 • Fleischer Dave • ANS • USA
LOVE THY NEIGHBOR • 1940 • Sandrich Mark • USA
LOVE THY NEIGHBOR • 1970 • *Distripix* • USA
LOVE THY NEIGHBOR • 1984 • Bill Tony • TVM • USA
LOVE THY NEIGHBOR AND HIS WIFE • 1970 • Elliott B. Ron • USA
LOVE THY NEIGHBORS • 1915 • *Lotus* • USA
LOVE THY NEIGHBOUR • 1914 • Cooper Toby? • UKN
LOVE THY NEIGHBOUR • 1973 • Robins John • UKN
LOVE.. THY NEIGHBOUR see **ELSK.. DIN NAESTE** • 1967
LOVE THY NEIGHBOUR see **KOCHAJMY SIE** • 1975
LOVE TIDE see **KOI GESHO** • 1955
LOVE TILL FIRST BLOOD see **SZERELEM ELSO VERIG** • 1985
LOVE TILL SECOND BLOOD see **SZERELEM MASODIK VERIG** • 1988
LOVE TIME • 1934 • Tinling James • USA
LOVE TO ETERNITY (UKN) see **CAGNA, LA** • 1972
LOVE TOKEN, THE • 1908 • Fitzhamon Lewin • UKN
LOVE TOKEN, THE • 1912 • *Jones Edgar* • USA
LOVE TOY, THE • 1926 • Kenton Erle C. • USA
LOVE TRADER, THE • 1930 • Henabery Joseph • USA • ISLAND OF DESIRE (UKN)
LOVE TRAGEDY see **TRAGODIE DER LIEBE** • 1923
LOVE TRAGEDY IN SPAIN, A • 1908 • *Melies* • USA
LOVE TRAIL, THE • 1912 • *Davenport Alice* • USA
LOVE TRAIL, THE • 1913 • *Nestor* • USA
LOVE TRAIL, THE see **DOP DOCTOR, THE** • 1915
LOVE TRANSCENDENT, THE • 1915 • O'Sullivan Tony • USA
LOVE TRAP • 1978 • Clarke James Kenelm • UKN
LOVE TRAP see **CURSE OF THE BLACK WIDOW** • 1977
LOVE TRAP, THE • 1923 • Ince Ralph • USA
LOVE TRAP, THE • 1929 • Wyler William • USA
LOVE TRAP, THE see **PIEGE DE L'AMOUR, LE** • 1919
LOVE TRAP, THE see **HER HUSBAND LIES** • 1937
LOVE TRAP, THE see **COUPLE, UN** • 1960
LOVE TRAVELS BY COACH see **HINTONJARO SZERELEM** • 1954
LOVE TRIO see **RENAI SANBAGARASU** • 1949
LOVE TRIUMPHANT • 1916 • Stafford Harry G. • USA
LOVE TRIUMPHS • 1914 • Myers Harry • USA
LOVE TYRANT, THE • 1911 • *Powers* • SHT • USA
LOVE TYRANT, THE • 1912 • Rolfe Alfred • ASL • LOVE, THE TYRANT
LOVE UNDER 17 (UKN) see **LIEBE UNTER 17** • 1970
LOVE UNDER COVER • 1917 • *Kelly Patrick* • SHT • USA
LOVE UNDER FIRE • 1937 • Marshall George • USA
LOVE UNDER FIRE see **BELOVED ENEMY** • 1936
LOVE UNDER SPANISH SKIES • 1909 • *Selig* • USA
LOVE UNDER THE CRUCIFIX see **OGHIN-SAMA** • 1960
LOVE UNTO WASTE see **DIXIA QING** • 1987
LOVE UP THE POLE • 1936 • Gulliver Clifford • UKN
LOVE VACATION see **AGAZET GHARAM** • 1967
LOVE, VAMPIRE STYLE • 1973 • Baker Anthony • FRG
LOVE VARIATIONS • Grant David • UKN
LOVE VARIATIONS • 1970 • Gould Terry • UKN
LOVE VERSUS CHICKENS • 1915 • *Kalem* • USA
LOVE VERSUS PRIDE • 1913 • Stow Percy • UKN
LOVE VERSUS SCIENCE • 1909 • Smith Jack ? • UKN
LOVE VICTORIOUS, THE • 1914 • *Gold Seal* • USA
LOVE VICTORIOUS, THE • 1914 • Lucas Wilfred • *Powers* • USA
LOVE VICTORY • 1917 • King Burton L. • SHT • USA
LOVE VS. DUTY • 1914 • Edwards Walter • USA
LOVE VS. PRIDE • 1914 • Eagle Oscar • USA
LOVE VS. STRATEGY • 1912 • *Lubin* • USA
LOVE VS. THE LAW • 1913 • *Baggot King* • USA
LOVE WAGER, THE • 1927 • Wheeler Cliff • USA
LOVE WAGER, THE • 1933 • Cyran A. • UKN
LOVE WALTZ, THE see **LIEBESWALZER** • 1930
LOVE WANDERS IN THE NIGHT see **DROMI TIS AGAPIS INE NICHTERIN, I** • 1981
LOVE WANGA • 1941 • *Hoffberg* • USA
LOVE WAR, THE • 1970 • McCowan George • TVM • USA • SIX COLUMN
LOVE, WAR AND A BONNET • 1912 • *Fischer Marguerita* • USA
LOVE WATCHES • 1918 • Houry Henri • USA
LOVE WHIP, THE • 1915 • North Wilfred • USA
LOVE, WHISKERS AND LETTERS • 1911 • *Solax* • USA
LOVE WHISPERS • 1977 • Fahmy Ashraf • EGY
LOVE WILL CONQUER • 1916 • Frazee Edwin • SHT • USA
LOVE WILL CONQUER see **KARLEKEN SEGRAR** • 1916
LOVE WILL CONQUER see **KARLEKEN SEGRAR** • 1949
LOVE WILL FIND A WAY • 1907 • *Warwick Trading Co* • UKN
LOVE WILL FIND A WAY • 1908 • Porter Edwin S. • USA
LOVE WILL FIND A WAY • 1912 • *Powers* • USA
LOVE WILL OUT • 1914 • Davis Ulysses • USA
LOVE WINS • 1909 • *Centaur* • USA
LOVE WINS • 1919 • *Mersereau Violet* • USA
LOVE WINS IN THE END • 1912 • Buckland Warwick • UKN
LOVE WITH A PERFECT STRANGER • 1986 • Davis Desmond • TVM • USA
LOVE WITH A SONG see **TA NASE PISNICKA CESKA** • 1967
LOVE WITH THE PROPER STRANGER • 1963 • Mulligan Robert • USA
LOVE WITH THE PROPER STRANGER see **CUODIAN YUANYANG** • 1965
LOVE WITHOUT END see **KAERLIGHED UDEN STOP** • 1988
LOVE WITHOUT QUESTION • 1920 • Rolfe B. A. • USA
LOVE WITHOUT WORDS see **KOLIK SLOV STACI LASCE** • 1961
LOVE, WOMEN AND FLOWERS see **AMOR, MUJERES Y FLORES** • 1989
LOVE YOU • 1980 • Derek John • USA
LOVE YOU TO DEATH • 1989 • Bergman Robert • USA
LOVE YOU TO DEATH see **DEADLY ILLUSION** • 1987
LOVE YOUR CAR see **KOCHAJMY SYRENKI** • 1967
LOVE YOUR LANDLORD • 1944 • Roberts Charles E. • SHT • USA
LOVE YOUR NEIGHBOR • 1930 • Watson William • USA
LOVE YOUR NEIGHBOR AS YOURSELF, BUT LEAVE HIS WIFE ALONE • 1910 • *Motograff* • USA
LOVEBOUND • 1923 • Otto Henry • USA • END OF THE ROAD, THE
LOVEBOUND • 1932 • *Peerless* • USA • SOULS FOR SABLES (UKN)
LOVEC • Sevcik Igor • ANM • CZC • HUNTER
LOVED AND LOST • 1916 • *Puritan* • USA
LOVED BY A MAORI CHIEF see **LOVED BY A MAORI CHIEFTESS** • 1913
LOVED BY A MAORI CHIEFTESS • 1913 • Melies Gaston • USA • LOVED BY A MAORI CHIEF
LOVED BY TWO see **AKIT KETTEN SZERETNEK** • 1915
LOVED ONE, THE • 1965 • Richardson Tony • UKN
LOVED ONE, THE see **GIRL HE LOVED, THE** • 1940
LOVEJAGTEN • 1907 • Larsen Viggo • DNM
LOVEJOY'S NUCLEAR WAR • 1975 • Keller Dan, Light Chuck • DOC • USA
LOVELAND • 1973 • Franklin Richard • ASL
LOVELESS, THE • 1983 • Bigelow Kathryn, Montgomery Monty • USA • BREAKDOWN
LOVELIER THAN LOVE see **BAKSMALLA** • 1973
LOVELINES • 1984 • Amateau Rod • USA
LOVELORN, THE • 1927 • McCarthy John P. • USA
LOVELORN GEISHA, THE see **YORU NO NAGARE** • 1960
LOVELORN LADY, THE see **PERFECT LADY, THE** • 1931
LOVELORN LEGHORN • 1951 • McKimson Robert • ANS • USA
LOVELY BUT DEADLY • 1983 • Sheldon David • USA • DEADLY AVENGER
LOVELY COLOMBIA • Correa Camilo • CLM
LOVELY FLUTE AND DRUM see **NATSUKASHIKI FUE YA TAIKO** • 1967
LOVELY GIRL see **BINT SHAKIEH** • 1967
LOVELY HUNGARIAN COMEDY see **SZEP MAGYAR KOMEDIA** • 1970
LOVELY LIFE OF BUDIMIR TRAJKOVIC, THE see **LJUBAVNI ZIVOT BUDIMIRA TRAJKOVICA** • 1978
LOVELY MARY • 1916 • Jones Edgar • USA
LOVELY SENORITA, THE • 1914 • Williams C. Jay • USA
LOVELY TO LOOK AT • 1952 • LeRoy Mervyn, Minnelli Vincente (U/c) • USA
LOVELY TO LOOK AT (UKN) see **THIN ICE** • 1937
LOVELY TOUCH, THE see **PSYCHO LOVER, THE** • 1970
LOVELY WAY TO DIE, A • 1968 • Rich David Lowell • USA • LOVELY WAY TO GO, A
LOVELY WAY TO GO, A see **LOVELY WAY TO DIE, A** • 1968
LOVELY YOUNG LADY see **FORTJUSANDE FROKEN, EN** • 1946
LOVEMAKER • 1969 • Liberatore Ugo • ITL • LOVEMAKER (L'UOMO PER FAR L'AMORE)
LOVEMAKER • 1982 • Lee Chang-Ho • SKR
LOVEMAKER, THE (USA) see **CALLE MAYOR** • 1955
LOVEMAKER (L'UOMO PER FAR L'AMORE) see **LOVEMAKER** • 1969
LOVEMAKERS, THE • 1973 • Grimaldi Gianni • ITL
LOVEMAKERS.. CARNAL STYLE, THE • 1970 • Knight Sidney • USA • LOVE MAKERS, THE
LOVEMAKING • 1968 • Brakhage Stan • USA
LOVEMUM see **CSOK, ANYU** • 1986
LOVEPLAY (UKN) see **TAGEBUCH EINER FRUHREIFEN** • 1972
LOVER see **KOIBITO** • 1951
LOVER see **DIWANA** • 1968
LOVER, THE see **AIJIN** • 1953
LOVER, THE see **HAME'AHEV** • 1985
LOVER, THE see **ASHI, AL** • 1986
LOVER AND HIS LASS, THE see **KILLE OCH EN TJEJ, EN** • 1974
LOVER AND THE COUNT, THE • 1911 • Porter Edwin S. • USA
LOVER AND THE MADMAN, THE • 1905 • Paul Robert William • UKN
LOVER BOY • 1988 • Wright Geoffrey • ASL
LOVER BOY see **KNAVE OF HEARTS** • 1954
LOVER BOY (UKN) see **GRAZIE NONNA** • 1975
LOVER BOY (UKN) see **AMANT DE POCHE, L'** • 1977
LOVER COME BACK • 1931 • Kenton Erle C. • USA
LOVER COME BACK • 1946 • Seiter William A. • USA • WHEN LOVERS MEET ○ LESSON IN LOVE
LOVER COME BACK • 1961 • Mann Delbert • USA
LOVER DIVINE (USA) see **LEISE FLEHEN MEINE LIEDER** • 1933
LOVER FOR THE SUMMER, A see **FILLE POUR L'ETE, UNE** • 1960
LOVER OF CAMILLE, THE • 1924 • Beaumont Harry • USA
LOVER OF THE GREAT BEAR, THE see **AMANTE DELL'ORSA MAGGIORE, L'** • 1971
LOVER OF THE MOON see **REVE A LA LUNE** • 1905
LOVER SWORDSMAN, THE see **TO-CH'ING CHIEN-K'O WU-CH'ING CHIEN** • 1978
LOVER WHO TOOK THE CAKE, THE • 1913 • Plumb Hay? • UKN
LOVERBOY • 1984 • Mendeluk George • CND
LOVERBOY • 1989 • Silver Joan Micklin • USA
LOVERS? • 1927 • Stahl John M. • USA • GREAT GALEOTO, THE
LOVERS • 1984 • Tan Han-Chang • TWN
LOVERS see **AIJIN** • 1953
LOVERS see **ADARAWANTHAYO** • 1968
LOVERS see **AMANTI** • 1968
LOVERS see **SCHWARZER KATER: LOVERS** • 1980
LOVERS!, THE • 1972 • Wise Herbert • UKN
LOVERS, THE see **SHOCKPROOF** • 1949
LOVERS, THE see **AMANTS, LES** • 1958
LOVERS, THE see **V LYUBLENNYE** • 1970
LOVERS AND CROWNS see **TANT QU'IL Y AURA DES BETES** • 1956
LOVERS AND LIARS (USA) see **VIAGGIO CON ANITA** • 1979
LOVERS AND LOLLIPOPS • 1956 • Engel Morris, Orkin Ruth • USA
LOVERS AND LUGGERS • 1937 • Hall Ken G. • ASL
LOVERS AND LUNATICS • 1916 • *Compson Betty* • USA
LOVERS AND OTHER RELATIVES see **PECCATO VENIALE** • 1974
LOVERS AND OTHER STRANGERS • 1970 • Howard Cy • USA
LOVERS AND THE MADMAN, THE • 1906 • Paul Robert William • UKN
LOVERS AND THIEVES (USA) see **ASSASSINS ET VOLEURS** • 1957
LOVERS ARRIVE, THE see **ERASTIS ERCHETE, O** • 1956
LOVERS BEHIND TWO WALLS see **ERASTE TOU MESEOU TIHOU, I** • 1968
LOVERS BEYOND THE TOMB see **AMANTI D'OLTRETOMBA** • 1965
LOVERS BY APPOINTMENT • 1970 • *Mor-Rion Films* • USA
LOVER'S CALL see **NEDAA EL OCHAK** • 1960
LOVERS' CHARM, THE • 1907 • Cooper Arthur? • UKN
LOVERS COURAGEOUS • 1932 • Leonard Robert Z. • USA • COURAGE
LOVER'S CRIME, THE • 1904 • Fitzhamon Lewin • UKN
LOVERS' DUET see **JUNJO NIJUSO** • 1967
LOVER'S EXILE, THE • 1981 • Gross Marty • DOC • CND
LOVERS FROM THE FIRST YEAR see **MILENCI V ROCE JEDNA** • 1973
LOVER'S GIFT, THE • 1914 • *Foxe Earle* • USA
LOVER'S GUIDE, THE • 1908 • Porter Edwin S. • USA
LOVERS, HAPPY LOVERS (USA) see **KNAVE OF HEARTS** • 1954
LOVER'S HAZING, A see **MARIAGE DE RAISON ET MARIAGE D'AMOUR** • 1908
LOVERS IN ARABY • 1924 • Brunel Adrian • UKN • BROKEN SAND
LOVERS IN PARIS (USA) see **POT-BOUILLE** • 1957
LOVERS IN QUARANTINE • 1925 • Tuttle Frank • USA
LOVERS IN THE RAIN • 1977 • Chung Jin-Woo • SKR
LOVERS IN THE RAIN • 1978 • Wo Lee-Jin • SKR
LOVERS IN THE SOUTH SEAS • 1938 • Pal George • ANM • UKN
LOVER'S ISLAND • 1925 • Diamant-Berger Henri • USA
LOVERS' KNOT, THE • 1917 • Robertson John S. • SHT • USA
LOVERS' LANE • 1924 • Rosen Phil, Beaudine William (U/c) • USA
LOVERS LIKE US (USA) see **SAUVAGE, LE** • 1975
LOVER'S LOST CONTROL, A • 1915 • Avery Charles • USA
LOVER'S LUCK • 1914 • *Arbuckle Roscoe* • USA
LOVER'S LUCKY PREDICAMENT, THE • 1915 • Curtis Allen • USA
LOVERS' MEETING see **CAPTIVE HEART, THE** • 1946
LOVER'S MIGHT, A • 1916 • Edwards Harry J. • SHT • USA • FIRE CHIEF, THE
LOVERS' MILL, THE • 1910 • *Gaumont* • SHT • FRN
LOVERS MUST LEARN see **ROME ADVENTURE** • 1962
LOVER'S NET (USA) see **AMANTS DU TAGE, LES** • 1955
LOVER'S OATH, A • 1925 • Earle Ferdinand P. • USA
LOVERS OF DEVIL'S ISLAND, THE see **AMANTES DE LA ISLA DEL DIABOLO, LOS** • 1972
LOVERS OF ETERNITY, THE • 1964 • Kuchar George • SHT • USA
LOVERS OF FAITH see **HAK ASIKLARI** • 1967
LOVERS OF GINZA (USA) see **GINZA NO KOIBITOTACHI** • 1961
LOVERS OF LISBON, THE see **AMANTS DU TAGE, LES** • 1955
LOVERS OF MARONA • 1966 • Zarzycki Jerzy • PLN
LOVERS OF MONTPARNASSE, THE (UKN) see **MONTPARNASSE 19** • 1958
LOVERS OF PARIS see **POT-BOUILLE** • 1957
LOVERS OF TERUEL, THE • 1912 • de Banos Ricardo • SPN
LOVERS OF TERUEL, THE (USA) see **AMANTS DE TERUEL, LES** • 1962
LOVERS OF THE DEVIL, THE see **AMANTES DEL DIABLO, LES** • 1971
LOVERS OF THE YEAR ONE see **MILENCI V ROCE JEDNA** • 1973
LOVERS OF TOLEDO, THE (USA) see **AMANTS DE TOLEDE, LES** • 1953
LOVERS OF VERONA, THE (USA) see **AMANTS DE VERONE, LES** • 1948
LOVERS ON A TIGHTROPE (USA) see **CORDE RAIDE, LA** • 1959
LOVERS ON THE SANDS • 1904 • Collins Alf • UKN • STROLL ON THE SANDS, A
LOVERS' ORACLE, THE • 1910 • Melies Gaston • USA
LOVERS' PETTY QUARRELS see **MAY TAMPUHAN, PAMINSAN-MINSAN** • 1968
LOVERS' POST OFFICE • 1914 • Arbuckle Roscoe, Dillon Eddie • USA
LOVER'S PREDICAMENT, THE • 1906 • Martin J. H.? • UKN
LOVERS' QUARREL, A • 1899 • *Warwick Trading Co* • UKN
LOVER'S QUARREL, A • 1907 • Fitzhamon Lewin • UKN
LOVER'S RETURN, A (USA) see **REVENANT, UN** • 1946
LOVERS' ROCK • 1966 • Pan Lei • CHN
LOVERS' ROMANCE, A see **ROMANS O VLYUBLYONNYKH** • 1975
LOVER'S RUSE, A • 1911 • *Solax* • USA
LOVER'S RUSE, THE (USA) see **POISON OR WHISKEY** • 1905
LOVER'S SIGNAL, THE • 1911 • *Imp* • USA
LOVER'S SIGNAL, THE • 1912 • *Lubin* • USA
LOVER'S STRATAGEMS, A • 1908 • Baker George D. • USA
LOVERS' SUICIDE see **NISHIJIN SHINJU** • 1977
LOVERS' SUICIDE IN SONEZAKI see **SONEZAKI SINJU** • 1977
LOVER'S TELEGRAPHIC CODE, THE • 1908 • Porter Edwin S. • USA
LOVERS THREE • 1913 • Smalley Phillips • USA
LOVERS' TRIALS • 1911 • *Powers* • USA
LOVER'S TROUBLES, A • 1903 • Collins Alf? • UKN
LOVERS' WELL, THE • 1910 • *Pathe* • USA

LOVE'S A LUXURY • 1952 • Searle Francis • UKN • CARETAKER'S DAUGHTER, THE (USA)
LOVE'S A-POPPIN • 1953 • White Jules • SHT • USA
LOVE'S ACID TEST • 1914 • *Selig* • USA
LOVES, ADVENTURES AND LIFE OF WILLIAM SHAKESPEARE see **LIFE OF SHAKESPEARE, THE** • 1914
LOVES AND ADVENTURES IN THE LIFE OF SHAKESPEARE see **LIFE OF SHAKESPEARE, THE** • 1914
LOVES AND DEATH OF A SCOUNDREL, THE see **DEATH OF A SCOUNDREL** • 1956
LOVES AND TIMES OF SCARAMOUCHE, THE (USA) see **AVVENTURE E GLI AMORI DI SCARAMOUCHE, LE** • 1976
LOVE'S ARDOUR SUDDENLY COOLED • 1902 • *Paul R. W.* • UKN
LOVE'S AWAKENING • 1910 • *Vitagraph* • USA
LOVE'S AWAKENING • 1910 • *Essanay* • USA
LOVE'S AWAKENING • 1916 • *Sunset* • USA
LOVE'S BATTLE • 1920 • Craft William James • USA
LOVE'S BERRY see **YAGODKI LYUBVI** • 1926
LOVE'S BITTER STRENGTH • 1916 • Hollingsworth Alfred • SHT • USA
LOVE'S BLINDNESS • 1926 • Dillon John Francis • USA
LOVE'S BOOMERANG • 1916 • Hartigan P. C. • USA
LOVE'S BOOMERANG (USA) see **PERPETUA** • 1922
LOVE'S C.Q.D. • 1910 • Melies Gaston • USA
LOVE'S CALL • 1912 • *Majestic* • USA
LOVE'S COMMAND see **LIEBESKOMMANDO** • 1931
LOVE'S CONFUSION see **VERWIRRUNG DER LIEBE** • 1959
LOVE'S CONQUEST • 1918 • Jose Edward • USA • GISMONDA
LOVE'S CONQUEST (UKN) see **RACKETEER, THE** • 1929
LOVE'S CROSS ROADS • 1916 • Golden Joseph A. • USA • BEHIND CLOSED DOORS
LOVE'S CRUCIBLE • 1916 • Chautard Emile • USA
LOVE'S CRUCIBLE (USA) see **VEM DOMER?** • 1922
LOVE'S CRUCIFIXION see **MARTER DER LIEBE** • 1928
LOVE'S CURE FOR GOUT • 1909 • *Empire Films* • UKN
LOVE'S DARK RIDE • 1978 • Mann Delbert • TVM • USA
LOVE'S DECEPTION • 1913 • *Patheplay* • USA
LOVE'S DETOUR • 1924 • Roach Hal • SHT • USA
LOVE'S DEVOTEE see **ELSKOVSLEG** • 1913
LOVE'S DIARY • 1912 • *Pickford Lottie* • USA
LOVE'S EBB AND FLOOD • 1911 • *Yankee* • USA
LOVE'S ENDURING FLAME • 1915 • Coyle Walter • USA
LOVE'S FALSE FACES • 1919 • Jones F. Richard • SHT • USA
LOVE'S FAMILY TREE see **AIJO NO KEIFU** • 1961
LOVE'S FLAME • 1920 • Gregory Carl Louis • USA
LOVE'S FOUR STONE WALLS • 1912 • Porter Edwin S. • USA
LOVE'S FRONTIERS see **FRONTERAS DEL AMOR, LAS** • 1934
LOVE'S GETAWAY • 1916 • *Tincher Fay* • USA
LOVE'S GREAT ADVENTURE see **KOI NO MEXICAN ROCK: KOI TO YUME TO BOKEN** • 1967
LOVE'S GREATEST MISTAKE • 1927 • Sutherland A. Edward • USA
LOVE'S HARVEST • 1920 • Mitchell Howard M. • USA
LOVE'S INFLUENCE • 1922 • Gordon Edward R., Charlton William S. • UKN
LOVE'S INTRIGUE • 1924 • *Sennett Mack (P)* • SHT • USA
LOVE'S JUSTICE • 1913 • Whitman Frank? • USA
LOVE'S LABOR LOST • 1904 • *Warwick Trading Co* • UKN
LOVE'S LABOR LOST • 1911 • *Myers Harry* • USA
LOVE'S LABOR WON • 1933 • Foster John, Davis Mannie • ANS • USA
LOVE'S LABOR WON • 1948 • Davis Mannie • ANS • USA
LOVE'S LANGUID LURE • 1927 • Conley Lige • SHT • USA
LOVE'S LARIAT • 1916 • Marshall George, Carey Harry • USA
LOVE'S LAST LAUGH • 1926 • *Sennett Mack (P)* • SHT • USA
LOVES, LAUGHS AND LATHER • 1917 • *Lloyd Harold* • SHT • USA
LOVE'S LAW • 1916 • Mayo Melvin • SHT • USA • LOVE IS LAW
LOVE'S LAW • 1917 • Johnson Tefft • USA
LOVE'S LAW • 1918 • Grandon Francis J. • USA
LOVE'S LEGACY see **YOKE, THE** • 1915
LOVE'S LONG LANE • 1914 • Jones Edgar • USA
LOVE'S LOTTERY TICKET • 1913 • *Imp* • USA
LOVE'S LUCKY DAY • 1918 • Curtis Allen • SHT • USA
LOVE'S LUNACY • 1915 • *Starlight* • USA
LOVE'S MAGNET • 1914 • *Essanay* • USA
LOVE'S MASQUERADE • 1916 • Henderson Lucius • SHT • USA
LOVE'S MASQUERADE • 1922 • Earle William P. S. • USA
LOVE'S MELODY • 1915 • Morrisey Edward • USA
LOVE'S MESSENGER • 1912 • Henderson Dell • USA
LOVE'S MIRACLE • 1912 • *Snow Marguerite* • USA
LOVE'S MISTAKE (UKN) see **PLAYTHINGS OF HOLLYWOOD** • 1931
LOVE'S MOCKERY see **JANUSKOPF, DER** • 1920
LOVE'S MONOGRAM • 1913 • *Dragon* • USA
LOVES OF A BLONDE, THE see **IUBIRILE UNEI BLONDE** • 1988
LOVES OF A BLONDE (USA) see **LASKY JEDNE PLAVOVLASKY** • 1965
LOVES OF A DICTATOR, THE (USA) see **DICTATOR, THE** • 1935
LOVES OF A FRENCH PUSSYCAT, THE (UKN) see **MADCHEN MIT DER HEISSEN MASCHE, DAS** • 1971
LOVES OF A GREEK PARIS • 1960 • Kyriakopolos C. • GRC
LOVES OF A KABUKI ACTOR, THE see **TOJURO NO KOI** • 1938
LOVES OF A PSYCHIATRIST • 1968 • *Drake Karen* • USA
LOVES OF ACTRESS SUMAKO, THE see **JOYU SUMAKO NO KOI** • 1947
LOVES OF ALEXANDER DUMAS SR., THE see **LASKY ALEXANDRA DUMASE ST.** • 1970
LOVES OF AN ACTRESS • 1928 • Lee Rowland V. • USA
LOVES OF ARIANE, THE • 1931 • Czinner Paul • UKN • ARIANE (USA)
LOVES OF BLANKA KOLAK, THE see **LJUBAVI BLANKE KOLAK** • 1987
LOVES OF CARMEN, THE • 1927 • Walsh Raoul • USA
LOVES OF CARMEN, THE • 1948 • Vidor Charles • USA
LOVES OF CASANOVA, THE see **CASANOVA** • 1927
LOVES OF CASANOVA (USA) see **AVENTURES DE CASANOVA, LES** • 1946
LOVES OF COLETTE see **VIE EN ROSE, LA** • 1947
LOVES OF COLLEEN BAWN, THE see **COLLEEN BAWN, THE** • 1924
LOVES OF COUNT IORGA -VAMPIRE, THE see **COUNT YORGA, VAMPIRE** • 1970
LOVES OF EDGAR ALLAN POE, THE • 1942 • Lachman Harry • USA
LOVES OF FRANISTAN • 1952 • Schwerin Jules • SHT • USA
LOVES OF HERCULES, THE see **AMORI DI ERCOLE, GLI** • 1960
LOVES OF ISADORA, THE see **ISADORA** • 1968
LOVES OF JEANNE NEY, THE see **LIEBE DER JEANNE NEY, DIE** • 1927
LOVES OF JOANNA GODDEN, THE • 1947 • Frend Charles, Hamer Robert (U/c) • UKN
LOVES OF JUAN CHARRASQUEADO, THE see **AMORES DE JUAN CHARRASQUEADO, LOS** • 1968
LOVES OF KAFKA, THE see **AMORES DE KAFKA, LOS** • 1987
LOVES OF LETTY, THE • 1920 • Lloyd Frank • USA
LOVES OF LILY, THE see **LILY IN LOVE** • 1985
LOVES OF LISZT, THE see **SZERELMI ALMOK -LISZT** • 1970
LOVES OF MADAME DUBARRY, THE (USA) see **I GIVE MY HEART** • 1935
LOVES OF MARY, QUEEN OF SCOTS, THE • 1923 • Clift Denison • UKN
LOVES OF OMAR KHAYYAM, THE see **OMAR KHAYYAM** • 1957
LOVES OF ONDINE, THE • 1968 • Warhol Andy • USA
LOVES OF PHARAOH, THE see **WEIB DES PHARAO, DAS** • 1921
LOVES OF RICARDO, THE • 1926 • Beban George • USA
LOVES OF RICARDO, THE • 1928 • Beban George • USA
LOVES OF ROBERT BURNS, THE • 1930 • Wilcox Herbert • UKN
LOVES OF SALAMMBO, THE (USA) see **SALAMBO** • 1961
LOVES OF SUMAKO THE ACTRESS, THE (USA) see **JOYU SUMAKO NO KOI** • 1947
LOVES OF THE MIGHTY see **DANTON** • 1920
LOVES OF THREE QUEENS (USA) see **AMANTE DI PARIDE, L'** • 1955
LOVES OF ULYSSES, THE • 1989 • Vafeas Vassilis • GRC
LOVES OF ZERO, THE • 1928 • Florey Robert • USA • SAD LOVE OF ZERO
LOVE'S OLD DREAM • 1914 • Baker George D. • USA
LOVE'S OLD SWEET SONG • 1909 • *Warwick Trading Co* • UKN
LOVE'S OLD, SWEET SONG • 1910 • *Lubin* • USA
LOVE'S OLD, SWEET SONG • 1913 • France Charles H. • USA
LOVE'S OLD, SWEET SONG • 1915 • *Bondhill Gertrude* • USA
LOVE'S OLD SWEET SONG • 1917 • Thornton F. Martin • UKN
LOVE'S OLD SWEET SONG • 1923 • Lund O. A. C. • USA
LOVE'S OLD SWEET SONG • 1927 • Johnson S. H. • SHT • UKN
LOVE'S OLD SWEET SONG • 1933 • Haynes Manning • UKN • MISSING WITNESS, THE
LOVE'S OPTION • 1928 • Pearson George • UKN • GIRL OF TODAY, A
LOVE'S OUTCAST • 1921 • *Sennett Mack (P)* • SHT • USA
LOVE'S PAY DAY • 1918 • Hopper E. Mason • USA
LOVE'S PENALTY • 1921 • Gilbert John • USA
LOVE'S PILGRIMAGE TO AMERICA • 1916 • Marston Lawrence • USA
LOVE'S POLKA • 1946 • Savchenko Igor • USS • LUCKY BRIDE, THE
LOVE'S PORT see **BANDARGAH-E-ESHGH** • 1967
LOVE'S POTION • 1911 • *Powers* • USA
LOVE'S PRISONER • 1919 • Dillon John Francis • USA
LOVE'S PROBATION • 1915 • *Bondhill Gertrude* • USA
LOVE'S PROTEGE • 1920 • *Carew Ora* • USA
LOVE'S QUARANTINE • 1913 • North Wilfred • USA
LOVE'S RAILROAD • 1912 • *Solax* • USA
LOVE'S REDEMPTION • 1921 • Brewster Eugene V. • *Brewster Publication Co* • USA
LOVE'S REDEMPTION • 1921 • Parker Albert • *Norma Talmadge Film Co* • USA • REGENERATION ISLE ○ PLAYING THE GAME
LOVE'S REFLECTION • 1915 • *Imp* • USA
LOVE'S REFRAIN • 1914 • *Imp* • USA
LOVE'S RENUNCIATION • 1911 • Golden Joseph A. • USA
LOVE'S RESCUE • 1915 • Morgan George • USA
LOVE'S REWARD • 1924 • Roach Hal • SHT • USA
LOVE'S SACRIFICE • 1909 • Porter Edwin S. • USA
LOVE'S SACRIFICE • 1911 • *Thanhouser* • USA
LOVE'S SACRIFICE • 1914 • Ince Thomas H., Clifford William H. • USA
LOVE'S SACRIFICE see **DURCHGANGERIN, DIE** • 1928
LOVE'S SAVAGE FURY • 1979 • Hardy Joseph • TVM • USA
LOVE'S SAVAGE HATE • 1915 • *Lubin* • USA
LOVE'S SORROW • 1910 • *Revier* • USA
LOVE'S STRATAGEM • 1909 • Salter Harry • USA
LOVE'S STRATEGY • 1908 • Coleby A. E. • UKN
LOVE'S STRATEGY • 1910 • Fitzhamon Lewin • UKN
LOVE'S STRATEGY • 1911 • Bouwmeester Theo • UKN
LOVE'S STRATEGY • 1915 • *United Film Service* • USA
LOVE'S STRATEGY • 1915 • *Mutual* • USA
LOVE'S SUNSET • 1913 • Thompson Frederick A. • USA
LOVE'S SUREST PROOF • 1912 • *Gaumont* • USA
LOVE'S SWEET MELODY • 1909 • *Lubin* • USA
LOVE'S SWEET PIFFLE • 1924 • *Sennett Mack (P)* • SHT • USA
LOVE'S TEST • 1911 • *Solax* • USA
LOVE'S TEST (UKN) see **INSPIRATION** • 1928
LOVE'S TOLL • 1916 • Pratt Jack • USA
LOVE'S TRIBUNAL • 1915 • *Wayne Justina* • USA
LOVE'S TRIUMPH (USA) see **TRIONFO DELL'AMORE, IL** • 1938
LOVE'S TRIUMPHS • 1909 • *Kalem* • USA
LOVE'S TURMOIL • 1917 • *Maison Edna* • SHT • USA
LOVE'S VENDETTA • 1915 • *Monty* • USA
LOVE'S VICTORY • 1911 • Fielding Romaine • USA
LOVE'S VICTORY • 1914 • Crane Frank H. • USA
LOVE'S WAY • 1915 • Drew Sidney • USA
LOVE'S WESTERN FLIGHT see **CHILDREN OF FATE** • 1914
LOVE'S WHIRLPOOL • 1924 • Mitchell Bruce • USA
LOVE'S WILDERNESS • 1924 • Leonard Robert Z. • USA • WILDERNESS
LOVE'S YOUNG DREAM • 1914 • France Charles H. • USA
LOVE'S YOUNG SCREAM • 1919 • Roach Hal • SHT • USA
LOVESCENE see **LOVE SCENES** • 1984
LOVESICK • 1937 • *Lantz Walter (P)* • ANS • USA
LOVESICK • 1983 • Brickman Marshall • USA
LOVESICK MAIDENS OF CUDDLETOWN see **LOVE SICK MAIDENS OF CUDDLETOWN** • 1912
LOVESTRUCK see **YOU CAN'T HURRY LOVE** • 1988
LOVETIME • 1921 • Mitchell Howard M. • USA
LOVEY: A CIRCLE OF CHILDREN, PART II • 1978 • Taylor Jud • TVM • USA
LOVEY DOVEY • 1923 • Roach Hal • SHT • USA
LOVEY MARY • 1926 • Baggot King • USA
LOVIISA • 1946 • Vaala Valentin • FNL
LOVIN' FOOL, THE • 1926 • Carpenter Horace B. • USA • LOVING FOOL, THE
LOVIN' MAN • 1972 • Topper Burt • USA
LOVIN' MOLLY • 1973 • Lumet Sidney • USA • MOLLY, GID AND JOHNNY
LOVIN' THE LADIES • 1930 • Brown Melville • USA • ROUGHNECK LOVER
LOVIND O PASARE DE PRADA • 1984 • Demian Iosif • RMN • TO KILL A BIRD OF PREY
LOVING • 1958 • Brakhage Stan • SHT • USA
LOVING • 1970 • Kershner Irvin • USA
LOVING AND LAUGHING • 1971 • Sone John • CND • IMPORTANCE OF BEING SEXY, THE ○ HIPPIE GIRLS, THE
LOVING COUPLES • 1980 • Smight Jack • USA
LOVING COUPLES see **ALSKANDE PAR** • 1964
LOVING COUSINS (USA) see **CUGINI CARNALI** • 1974
LOVING CUP, THE • 1934 • *Sound City* • SHT • UKN
LOVING FEELING • 1969 • Warren Norman J. • UKN
LOVING FOOL, THE see **LOVIN' FOOL, THE** • 1926
LOVING GIRLS see **KOISURU ONNA TACHI** • 1987
LOVING HEARTS • 1910 • *Lubin* • USA
LOVING IN THE RAIN (USA) see **MALE D'AMORE** • 1974
LOVING LIES • 1924 • Van Dyke W. S. • USA
LOVING MEMORY • 1970 • Scott Anthony • UKN
LOVING ONES, THE see **AMOROSAS, AS** • 1968
LOVING TOUCH, THE see **PSYCHO LOVER, THE** • 1970
LOVING WALTER (USA) see **WALTER** • 1982
LOVING YOU • 1957 • Kanter Hal • USA
LOVTSI GUBOK • 1960 • Zakharias Manos • USS • SPONGE DIVERS
LOW BLOW • 1986 • Harris Frank • USA • SAVAGE SUNDAY
LOW BLOW, THE • 1970 • *Kent John* • USA
LOW FINANCE • 1960 • *Halas John (P)* • ANS • UKN
LOW FINANCIER, A • 1914 • MacGregor Norval • USA
LOW MIDNIGHT see **TACNO U PONOC** • 1960
LOW OF THE SEA, THE see **MER MERE** • 1975
LOW-RANK SOLDIERS see **ZOUHEI MONOGATARI** • 1963
LOW SOCIETY see **HSIA-LIU SHE-HUI** • 1977
LOW-TIDE see **OSEKA** • 1968
LOW VISIBILITY • 1985 • Gruben Patricia • CND
LOW WATER • 1968 • Robinson Tom Scott • UKN
LOWCY BIZONOW • 1970 • Nehrebecki Wladyslaw • ANS • PLN • BISON HUNTERS, THE
LOWE VON BABYLON, DER (FRG) see **RUINAS DE BABILONIA, LAS** • 1959
LOWE VON VENEDIG, DER • 1923 • Stein Paul L. • FRG
LOWENBRAUT, DIE • *Salmonova Lyda* • FRG
LOWER DEPTHS, THE • Yurenev Vladimir
LOWER DEPTHS, THE see **BAS-FONDS, LES** • 1936
LOWER DEPTHS, THE see **DONZOKO** • 1957
LOWER RHINE FOLKS (USA) see **VOM NIEDERRHEIN, DIE** • 1933
LOWER THE BOOM • 1950 • Cowan Will • ANS • USA
LOWEST CRIME, THE see **CHANTAGE** • 1955
LOWEST MAN, THE see **FUTEKI NA OTOKO** • 1958
LOWICZ MERRY-GO-ROUND, THE see **KARUZELA LOWICKA** • 1958
LOWLAND • 1974 • Uher Stefan • CZC
LOWLAND see **TIEFLAND** • 1954
LOWLAND CINDERELLA, A • 1921 • Morgan Sidney • UKN
LOWLAND VILLAGE • Catling Darrell • DCS • UKN
LOYAL 47, THE (USA) see **GENROKU CHUSHINGURA PART I** • 1941
LOYAL 47 OF THE GENROKU ERA, THE (UKN) see **GENROKU CHUSHINGURA PART I** • 1941
LOYAL DESERTER, A • 1912 • *Selig* • USA
LOYAL FORTY-SEVEN RONIN, THE see **CHUSHINGURA** • 1932
LOYAL FORTY-SEVEN RONIN, THE see **CHUSHINGURA** • 1934
LOYAL FORTY-SEVEN RONIN, THE see **CHUSHINGURA** • 1939
LOYAL FORTY-SEVEN RONIN, THE see **CHUSHINGURA** • 1954
LOYAL FORTY-SEVEN RONIN, THE see **CHUSHINGURA** • 1958
LOYAL FORTY-SEVEN RONIN, THE see **CHUSHINGURA** • 1962
LOYAL FRIENDS see **VERNYE DRUZYA** • 1954
LOYAL HEART • 1946 • Mitchell Oswald • UKN
LOYAL HEARTS • 1913 • *Pilot* • USA
LOYAL INDIAN, THE • 1909 • *Tiger* • USA
LOYAL LIVES • 1923 • Giblyn Charles • USA
LOYAL REBEL, THE • 1915 • Rolfe Alfred • ASL • EUREKA STOCKADE
LOYAL ROYALTY • 1962 • Kuwahara Bob • ANS • USA
LOYAL SOLDIER OF PANCHO VILLA, A see **DORADO DE PANCHO VILLA, UN** • 1966
LOYAL SONS OF THE PEOPLE see **NARODA VYERNYYE SYNY** • 1968
LOYALTIES • 1933 • Dean Basil • UKN
LOYALTIES • 1986 • Wheeler Anne • CND
LOYALTY • 1918 • Pratt Jack • USA
LOYALTY FOR LOYALTY • 1976 • Korabov Nicolai • USS, BUL
LOYALTY OF A SAVAGE, THE • 1914 • *Warner'S Features* • USA
LOYALTY OF DON LUIS VERDUGO • 1911 • *Joyce Alice* • USA
LOYALTY OF JUMBO, THE • 1914 • Martin E. A. • USA
LOYALTY OF LOVE • Brignone Guido • ITL
LOYALTY OF SYLVIA, THE • 1912 • *Vitagraph* • USA
LOYOLA, THE SOLDIER SAINT see **CAPITAN DE LOYOLA, EL** • 1948
LOZANA ANDALUZA, LA • 1976 • Escriva Vicente • SPN
LSD, A TRIP TO TERROR see **LSD, VIAJE AL TERROR**

LSD -INFERNO PER POCHI DOLLARI • 1967 • Mida Massimo • ITL • LSD UN'ATOMICA NEL CERVELLO
LSD UN'ATOMICA NEL CERVELLO see **LSD -INFERNO PER POCHI DOLLARI** • 1967
LSD, VIAJE AL TERROR • *Hispaner* • SPN, ARG • LSD, A TRIP TO TERROR
LSD WALL • 1965 • Hawkins John H. • SHT • USA
LT. ROBIN CRUSOE U.S.N. • 1966 • Paul Byron • USA • LIEUTENANT ROBIN CRUSOE U.S.N.
LU, A KOKOTT • 1918 • Curtiz Michael • HNG • LU, THE COQUETTE ○ LU, THE COCOTTE
LU BAN DE CHUANSHUO • 1958 • Sun Yu • CHN • FOLK TALES OF LU BAN
LU-PING HUA • 1989 • Yang Li-Kuo • TWN • ROUGH ICE FLOWER
LU TEMPU DI LI PISCI SPATA • 1954 • De Seta Vittorio • ITL
LU, THE COCOTTE see **LU, A KOKOTT** • 1918
LU, THE COQUETTE see **LU, A KOKOTT** • 1918
LU TING CHI • 1979 • Li Han-Hsiang • HKG • HISTORY OF LU TING, THE
LU (UKN) see **TOTE VON BEVERLY HILLS, DIE** • 1964
LUANA, DAUGHTER OF THE VIRGIN FOREST see **LUANA, LA FIGLIA DELLA FORESTA VERGINE** • 1968
LUANA, LA FIGLIA DELLA FORESTA VERGINE • 1968 • Infascelli Roberto • ITL • LUANA, DAUGHTER OF THE VIRGIN FOREST ○ JUNGLE GODDESS (USA) ○ LUANA, VIRGIN OF THE JUNGLE
LUANA, VIRGIN OF THE JUNGLE see **LUANA, LA FIGLIA DELLA FORESTA VERGINE** • 1968
LUANDA • 1957 • Spiguel Miguel • SHT • PRT
LUANDA DIA A DIA • 1961 • Queiroga Perdigao • SHT • PRT
LUANDA YA NO ES DE SAN BABLO • 1976 • Alvarez Santiago • DOC • CUB
LUANG TA • 1980 • Cheyaroon Permpol • THL • TEMPLE BELLS
LUBATU KULLI YUM • 1971 • Shawqi Khalil • EGY • JEU DE CHAQUE JOUR, LE ○ NAFAR WAHID
LUBNAN AYYAM ZAMAN • 1983 • Shahal Randa • LBN • LEBANON IN THE OLD DAYS
LUBOV YAROVAYA • 1970 • Fetin Vladimir • USS
LUBUSHKA • 1961 • Kaplunovsky Vladimir • USS
LUC ET DENISE FRADETTE CLARINETTISTE ET PIANISTE • 1972-73 • Brault Francois • DCS • CND
LUC PEIRE'S ENVIRONMENT • 1972 • Mil J. • BLG
LUCA, BAMBINO MIO • 1971 • Fernandez Ramon • ITL
LUCAN • 1977 • Greene David • TVM • USA
LUCAS • 1986 • Seltzer David • USA
LUCAS TANNER • 1974 • Donner Richard • USA
LUCCIOLA • 1917 • Genina Augusto • ITL
LUCE DEL MONDO, LA • 1935 • Righelli Gennaro • ITL • PADRONE DEL MONDO, IL
LUCE DEMERS SHEFFERVILLE • 1981 • Lesaunier Daniel • MTV • CND
LUCE NELLE TENEBRE • 1941 • Mattoli Mario • ITL
LUCE SUL MONTE • 1959 • Dal Fabbro Rinaldo, Costa Mario • DOC • ITL
LUCEBERT, DICTER-SCHILDER • 1962 • van der Keuken Johan • SHT • NTH
LUCECITA • 1976 • Madrid Jose Luis • SPN
LUCERNA • 1925 • Lamac Carl • CZC • LANTERN, THE
LUCERTOLA CON LA PELLE DI DONNA, UNA • 1971 • Fulci Lucio • ITL, SPN • LAGARITA CON PIEL DE MUJER, UNA (SPN) ○ VENIN DE LA PEUR, LA (FRN) ○ LIZARD IN A WOMAN'S SKIN, A (UKN) ○ SCHIZOID (USA)
LUCES DE BARRIADA • 1940 • O'Quigley Roberto • MXC • NEIGHBORHOOD LIGHTS (USA)
LUCES DE BOHEMIA • 1985 • Diez Miguel Angel • SPN • BOHEMIAN LIGHTS
LUCES DE MIS ZAPATOS • 1973 • Puenzo Luis • ARG • SHINE ON MY SHOES
LUCES Y SOMBRAS see **LLUMS I OMBRES** • 1988
LUCETTE • 1924 • Feuillade Louis • FRN
LUCH SMERTI • 1925 • Kuleshov Lev • USS • DEATH RAY, THE ○ LOUTCH SMERTI
LUCHA CON LA PANTERA, LA • 1974 • Bojorquez Alberto • MXC • FIGHT WITH THE PANTHER, THE
LUCHA LIBRE see **FURIA DEL RING, LA** • 1961
LUCHA POR LA HERENCIA • 1911 • Mulhauser Otto • SPN
LUCHADOR FENOMENA, EL • 1952 • Cortes Fernando • MXC • PHENOMENAL WRESTLER, THE
LUCHADORAS CONTRA EL MEDICO ASESINO, LAS • 1962 • Cardona Rene • MXC • WRESTLING WOMEN VS. THE MURDERING DOCTOR, THE ○ DOCTOR OF DOOM (USA)
LUCHADORAS CONTRA EL ROBOT ASESINO, LAS • 1969 • Cardona Rene • MXC • WRESTLING WOMEN VS. THE MURDERING ROBOT, THE ○ ASESINO LOCO Y EL SEXO, EL ○ SEX MONSTER ○ MAD MURDERER AND SEX, THE
LUCHADORAS CONTRA LA MOMIA, LAS • 1964 • Cardona Rene • MXC • WRESTLING WOMEN VS. THE AZTEC MUMMY, THE (USA)
LUCI DEL VARIETA • 1950 • Lattuada Alberto, Fellini Federico • ITL • VARIETY LIGHTS (USA) ○ LIGHTS OF THE MUSIC HALL ○ LIGHTS OF VARIETY ○ FOOTLIGHTS
LUCI SOMMERSE • 1934 • Millar Adelqui • ITL • DON PABLO IL BANDITO
LUCIA • 1969 • Solas Humberto • CUB
LUCIA DI LAMMERMOOR • 1910 • Pastrone Giovanni • ITL
LUCIA DI LAMMERMOOR • 1948 • Ballerini Piero • ITL
LUCIA MCCARTNEY • 1970 • Neves David • BRZ
LUCIANA • 1955 • Gambino Domenico M. • ITL
LUCIANO • 1962 • Baldi Gian Vittorio • ITL • VITA BRUCIATA, UNA ○ MADRE IGNOTA
LUCIANO • 1964 • Guerin Claudio • SPN
LUCIANO ROMERO • 1959 • Urueta Chano • MXC • VENGANZA FATAL
LUCIANO SERRA PILOTA • 1938 • Rossellini Roberto, Alessandrini Goffredo • ITL
LUCIANO TAJOLI see **ROMANZO DELLA MIA VITA, IL** • 1953
LUCIANO, UNA VITA BRUCIATA see **LUCIANO (VIA DEI CAPELLARI)** • 1960
LUCIANO (VIA DEI CAPELLARI) • 1960 • Baldi Gian Vittorio • ITL • LUCIANO, UNA VITA BRUCIATA ○ VIA DEI CAPELLARI
LUCIE • 1963 • Stekly Karel • CZC • LUCY
LUCIE • 1979 • During Jan Erik • NRW
LUCIE DE TRECOEUR • 1922 • Genina Augusto • ITL
LUCIEN BROUILLARD • 1982 • Carriere Bruno • CND
LUCIEN GUITRY see **COMEDIEN, LE** • 1947
LUCIEN LEUWEN • 1973 • Autant-Lara Claude • MTV • FRN
LUCIFER • 1987 • Eyres John • UKN • GOODNIGHT, GOD BLESS
LUCIFER COMPLEX, THE • 1978 • Hewitt David L., Flocker James T. • USA
LUCIFER PROJECT, THE see **BARRACUDA** • 1978
LUCIFER RISING (2ND VERSION) • 1980 • Anger Kenneth • USA
LUCIFER RISING, CHAPTER ONE • 1971 • Anger Kenneth • USA
LUCILE • 1912 • Marston Theodore • USA
LUCILE • 1924 • Monca Georges • FRN
LUCILLE • 1970 • Moreau Michel • DCS • CND
LUCILLE LOVE, THE GIRL OF MYSTERY • 1914 • Ford Francis • SRL • USA
LUCILLE THE WAITRESS • 1914 • Ford John? • USA
LUCILLE, THE WAITRESS • 1916 • Bailey William • SHT • USA
LUCINDA LEARNS TO SELL • 1961 • Spencer John • UKN
LUCIO FLAVIO, O PASSAGEIRO DA AGONIA • 1978 • Babenco Hector • BRZ • LUCIO FLAVIO (UKN)
LUCIO FLAVIO (UKN) see **LUCIO FLAVIO, O PASSAGEIRO DA AGONIA** • 1978
LUCIO VAQUEZ • 1966 • Cardona Rene • MXC
LUCK • 1923 • Burr C. C. • USA
LUCK AND PLUCK • 1919 • Dillon Eddie • USA
LUCK AND SAND • 1925 • Maloney Leo • USA
LUCK ARRIVES see **LYCKAN KOMMER** • 1942
LUCK CHARM, THE • 1916 • Smith David • SHT • USA
LUCK COMES OUT OF THE CLOUDS see **AMPHITRYON** • 1935
LUCK IN ODD NUMBERS • 1914 • *Essanay* • USA
LUCK IN OLD CLOTHES • 1918 • *Ebony* • SHT • USA
LUCK IN PAWN • 1919 • Edwards Walter • USA
LUCK OF A DIVER • 1908 • Codman John • UKN
LUCK OF A SAILOR, THE • 1934 • Milton Robert • UKN • CONTRABAND
LUCK OF BARRY LYNDON, THE see **BARRY LYNDON** • 1975
LUCK OF GERALDINE LAIRD, THE • 1920 • Sloman Edward • USA
LUCK OF GINGER COFFEY, THE • 1959 • Hart Harvey • MTV • CND
LUCK OF GINGER COFFEY, THE • 1964 • Kershner Irvin • CND, USA
LUCK OF HOG WALLON GULCH, THE • 1914 • *Joker* • USA
LUCK OF JANE, THE • 1916 • Smith David • SHT • USA
LUCK OF LIFE, THE • 1907 • Cooper Arthur • UKN
LUCK OF RECKLESS REDDY, THE • 1911 • *Kalem* • USA
LUCK OF ROARING CAMP • 1911 • Lincoln W. J. • ASL
LUCK OF ROARING CAMP, THE • 1910 • Porter Edwin S. • USA
LUCK OF ROARING CAMP, THE • 1917 • France Floyd • SHT • USA
LUCK OF ROARING CAMP, THE • 1937 • Willat Irvin V. • USA
LUCK OF STATION FRONT PLAZA, THE see **EKIMAE KAIUN** • 1968
LUCK OF THE CARDS, THE • 1909 • Bouwmeester Theo? • UKN
LUCK OF THE DRAW, THE • 1980 • Copping Robin • ASL
LUCK OF THE FOOLISH, THE • 1924 • *Sennett Mack (P)* • SHT • USA
LUCK OF THE GAME, THE see **ZUCKERBROT UND PEITSCHE** • 1968
LUCK OF THE GAME (UKN) see **GRIDIRON FLASH** • 1934
LUCK OF THE IRISH, THE • 1920 • Dwan Allan • USA
LUCK OF THE IRISH, THE • 1935 • Pedelty Donovan • UKN
LUCK OF THE IRISH, THE • 1948 • Koster Henry • USA • THAT SHAMROCK TOUCH ○ SHAMROCK TOUCH, THE ○ FEAR OF LITTLE MEN, THE ○ LEAVE IT TO THE IRISH
LUCK OF THE NAVY • 1938 • Lee Norman • UKN • NORTH SEA PATROL (USA)
LUCK OF THE NAVY, THE • 1927 • Paul Fred • UKN
LUCK OF THE RED LION, THE • 1912 • Plumb Hay? • UKN
LUCK OF THE TURF • 1936 • Faye Randall • UKN
LUCK THAT JEALOUSY BROUGHT, THE • 1917 • Mix Tom • SHT • USA
LUCK TOUCHED MY LEGS see **ASHI NI SAWATTA KOUN** • 1930
LUCKIEST GIRL IN THE WORLD, THE • 1936 • Buzzell Edward • USA
LUCKIEST GUY IN THE WORLD • 1947 • Newman Joseph M. • SHT • USA
LUCKIEST MAN IN THE WORLD, THE • 1989 • Gilroy Frank D. • USA
LUCKY • 1985 • SAF
LUCKY 13 see **UNA SU TREDICI** • 1969
LUCKY BANG BANG'S SEX CLUB INTERNATIONAL see **SEX CLUB INTERNATIONAL** • 1967
LUCKY BEGINNERS • 1935 • Douglas Gordon • SHT • USA
LUCKY BLAZE • 1933 • Newman Widgey R. • UKN
LUCKY BLOWOUT, A • 1915 • *Sherry J. Barney* • USA
LUCKY BOB • 1911 • *Bison* • USA
LUCKY BOOTS see **GUN PLAY** • 1935
LUCKY BOY • 1929 • Taurog Norman, Wilson Charles C. • USA
LUCKY BRIDE, THE see **LOVE'S POLKA** • 1946
LUCKY BROOCH, THE see **LYCKONALEN** • 1916
LUCKY CARD, THE • 1911 • *Anderson Broncho Billy* • USA
LUCKY CARSON • 1921 • North Wilfred • USA
LUCKY CHANCE, A • 1913 • *Lubin* • USA
LUCKY CISCO KID • 1940 • Humberstone H. Bruce • USA • ROGUE OF THE RIO GRANDE
LUCKY COHEN • 1913 • Hotaling Arthur D. • USA
LUCKY CORNER, THE • 1936 • Meins Gus • SHT • USA
LUCKY CORRIGAN • 1936 • Lamont Charles • USA
LUCKY DAN • 1922 • Howard William K. • USA
LUCKY DAYS • 1935 • Denham Reginald • UKN
LUCKY DAYS (UKN) see **SING A JINGLE** • 1944
LUCKY DEAL, A • 1915 • Mix Tom • USA
LUCKY DECEPTION, A • 1914 • Christie Al • USA
LUCKY DEVIL • 1925 • Tuttle Frank • USA
LUCKY DEVILS • 1933 • Ince Ralph • USA
LUCKY DEVILS • 1941 • Landers Lew • USA
LUCKY DIE TWICE, THE see **SRETNI UMIRU DVAPUT** • 1967
LUCKY DISAPPOINTMENT, A • 1914 • Mackley Arthur • USA
LUCKY DOG • 1912 • *Wadsworth William* • USA
LUCKY DOG • 1933 • Myers Zion • SHT • USA
LUCKY DOG • 1956 • Rasinski Connie • ANS • USA
LUCKY DOG, A • 1917 • Robbins Jess • SHT • USA
LUCKY DOG'S DAY, A • 1920 • Watson William • SHT • USA
LUCKY DRAGON NO.5, THE see **DAIGO FUKURYU MARU** • 1959
LUCKY DUCK, THE • 1940 • Rasinski Connie • ANS • USA
LUCKY DUCKY • 1948 • Avery Tex • ANS • USA
LUCKY EL INTREPIDO • 1967 • Franco Jesus • SPN
LUCKY ELOPEMENT, THE • 1914 • Ince Ralph • USA
LUCKY ESCAPE FOR DAD, A • 1913 • Haldane Bert? • UKN
LUCKY FALL, A • 1912 • *Lubin* • USA
LUCKY FIVE, THE • Mattoli Mario • ITL
LUCKY FLIGHT • 1949 • Nemolyaev V. • USS
LUCKY FOOL • 1927 • *West Billy* • USA
LUCKY FUGITIVES • 1936 • Grinde Nick • CND
LUCKY GALOSHES see **KALOSZE SZCZESCIA** • 1958
LUCKY GHOST • 1941 • Buell Jed • USA
LUCKY GIRL • 1932 • Gerrard Gene, Miller Frank • UKN
LUCKY GIRLS (USA) see **QUI COMINCIA L'AVVENTURA** • 1975
LUCKY GOLD PIECE, A • 1916 • Wilson Ben • SHT • USA
LUCKY HOLD UP, A • 1912 • *Eclair* • USA
LUCKY HORSESHOE, THE • 1906 • Mottershaw Frank • UKN
LUCKY HORSESHOE, THE • 1911 • Sennett Mack, Henderson Dell • USA
LUCKY HORSESHOE, THE • 1925 • Blystone John G. • USA
LUCKY IN LOVE • 1929 • Webb Kenneth • USA
LUCKY JADE • 1937 • Summers Walter • UKN
LUCKY JIM • 1909 • Griffith D. W. • USA
LUCKY JIM • 1912 • *Champion* • USA
LUCKY JIM • 1914 • Wilson Frank? • UKN
LUCKY JIM • 1957 • Boulting John • UKN
LUCKY JO • 1964 • Deville Michel • FRN
LUCKY JORDAN • 1942 • Tuttle Frank • USA
LUCKY KENT • 1931 • Shmidthoff V. • USS
LUCKY LADIES • 1932 • Rawlins John* • UKN
LUCKY LADY • 1975 • Donen Stanley • USA
LUCKY LADY, THE • 1926 • Walsh Raoul • USA • LADY LUCK
LUCKY LARKIN • 1930 • Brown Harry J. • USA
LUCKY LARRIGAN • 1932 • McCarthy John P. • USA
LUCKY LARRY'S LADY LOVE • 1916 • *Marshall Boyd* • SHT • USA
LUCKY LEAP, A • 1915 • Frazee Edwin • USA
LUCKY LEAP, A • 1916 • Clements Roy • SHT • USA
LUCKY LEGS • 1942 • Barton Charles T. • USA
LUCKY LOSER • 1934 • Denham Reginald • UKN
LUCKY LOSER, A • 1915 • Louis Will • USA
LUCKY LOSER, THE • 1912 • *Eclair* • USA
LUCKY LOSERS • 1950 • Beaudine William • USA
LUCKY LUCIANO • 1973 • Rosi Francesco • ITL, FRN • RE: LUCKY LUCIANO (USA) ○ A PROPOSITO LUCKY LUCIANO
LUCKY LUKE • 1971 • Goscinny Rene, Morris • ANM • FRN, BLG • LUCKY LUKE: DAISY TOWN
LUCKY LUKE AND THE DALTON GANG see **BALLADE DES DALTON, LA** • 1978
LUCKY LUKE: BALLAD OF THE DALTONS see **BALLADE DES DALTON, LA** • 1978
LUCKY LUKE: DAISY TOWN see **LUCKY LUKE** • 1971
LUCKY LUKE, LES DALTONS EN CAVALE • 1983 • Hanna William, Barbera Joseph, Morris • ANM • USA, FRN • DALTONS EN CAVALE, LES
LUCKY LULU • 1944 • Kneitel Seymour • ANS • USA
LUCKY MAN • 1912 • *Majestic* • USA
LUCKY MASCOT see **BRASS MONKEY, THE** • 1948
LUCKY ME • 1954 • Donohue Jack • USA
LUCKY MISTAKE, A • 1913 • Johnston Lorimer • USA
LUCKY MISTAKE, A • 1916 • Ellis Robert • SHT • USA
LUCKY MIX-UP, A • 1912 • *Essanay* • USA
LUCKY NECKLACE, THE • 1906 • Fitzhamon Lewin • UKN
LUCKY NICK CAIN • 1951 • Newman Joseph M. • USA • I'LL GET YOU FOR THIS (UKN)
LUCKY NIGHT • 1939 • Taurog Norman • USA
LUCKY NUGGET, THE • 1913 • *Ammex* • USA
LUCKY NUMBER • 1951 • Hannah Jack • ANS • USA
LUCKY NUMBER • 1961 • *Biswas Anil (M)* • IND
LUCKY NUMBER, THE • 1921 • Roach Hal • SHT • USA
LUCKY NUMBER, THE • 1933 • Asquith Anthony • UKN • FIVE AND SIX
LUCKY ONE, THE • 1917 • *Mason Billy* • SHT • USA
LUCKY ONE, THE see **TIHERAKIAS, O** • 1968
LUCKY PARTNERS • 1940 • Milestone Lewis • USA
LUCKY PIE, THE • 1908 • Fitzhamon Lewin? • UKN
LUCKY PIERRE • 1961 • Lewis Herschell G. • USA • ADVENTURES OF LUCKY PIERRE, THE
LUCKY PIERRE see **MOUTARDE ME MONTE AU NEZ, LA** • 1974
LUCKY PIG, A • 1906 • Raymond Charles? • UKN
LUCKY PIGS • 1939 • Harrison Ben • ANS • USA
LUCKY PIGS • 1970 • Le Grice Malcolm • UKN
LUCKY RALSTON (UKN) see **LAW AND ORDER** • 1940
LUCKY RUBE, THE • 1914 • *Lubin* • USA
LUCKY SAN see **RAKKI-SAN** • 1952
LUCKY SHOT, THE • 1910 • *Thanhouser* • USA
LUCKY SHOT, THE • 1914 • *Reliance* • USA
LUCKY SLIP, A • 1917 • *Gibson Margaret* • USA
LUCKY SPURS • 1926 • Carpenter Horace B.?, Clegg V. V.? • USA
LUCKY STAR • 1929 • Borzage Frank • USA
LUCKY STAR, THE • 1980 • Fischer Max • CND, NTH • BELLE ETOILE, LA
LUCKY STARS • 1925 • Edwards Harry J. • SHT • USA
LUCKY STIFF • 1988 • Perkins Anthony • USA • MR. CHRISTMAS DINNER
LUCKY STIFF, THE • 1949 • Foster Lewis R. • USA
LUCKY STONE, THE • 1913 • Trimble Larry • UKN
LUCKY STREET • 1960 • *Halas John (P)* • ANS • UKN
LUCKY STRIKE • 1988 • Taylor Roderick • USA
LUCKY STRIKE, A • 1915 • Hotaling Arthur D. • USA
LUCKY STRIKE, THE see **GROSSE GLUCK, DAS** • 1967
LUCKY SWEEP, A • 1932 • Bramble A. V. • UKN

LUCKY TERROR • 1936 • James Alan • USA
LUCKY TEXAN, THE • 1934 • Bradbury Robert North • USA
LUCKY TO BE A WOMAN (USA) see **FORTUNA DI ESSERE DONNA, LA** • 1956
LUCKY TO ME • 1939 • Bentley Thomas • UKN
LUCKY TONY see **SZCZESCIARZ ANTONI** • 1961
LUCKY TOOTHACHE, A • 1910 • Sennett Mack • USA
LUCKY TRAMP, A • 1916 • *Perez Tweedledum* • SHT • USA
LUCKY TRANSFER, THE • 1915 • Browning Tod • USA
LUCKY TUMBLE, A • 1916 • Currier Frank • SHT • USA
LUCKY (UKN) see **BOY, A GIRL AND A DOG, A** • 1946
LUCKY VEST, THE • 1914 • France Charles H. • USA
LUCKY WISHBONE, THE • 1905 • *Paley & Steiner* • USA
LUCKY WORKER, THE see **TALIHLI AMELE** • 1981
LUCRECE • 1943 • Joannon Leo • FRN
LUCRECE BORGIA • 1935 • Gance Abel • FRN • LUCRETIA BORGIA
LUCRECE BORGIA • 1953 • Christian-Jaque • FRN, ITL • LUCREZIA BORGIA (ITL) ○ SINS OF THE BORGIAS (USA)
LUCRETIA • 1987 • Blomkvist Heidi • ANS • CND
LUCRETIA BORGIA see **ETERNAL SIN, THE** • 1917
LUCRETIA BORGIA see **LUCRECE BORGIA** • 1935
LUCRETIA LOMBARD • 1923 • Conway Jack • USA • FLAMING PASSION
LUCREZIA see **LUCREZIA BORGIA, L'AMANTE DEL DIAVOLO** • 1968
LUCREZIA BORGIA • 1910 • Caserini Mario • ITL
LUCREZIA BORGIA • 1910 • Falena Ugo • ITL
LUCREZIA BORGIA • 1919 • Genina Augusto • ITL
LUCREZIA BORGIA • 1922 • Oswald Richard • FRG • LUKREZIA BORGIA
LUCREZIA BORGIA • 1940 • Hinrich Hans • ITL
LUCREZIA BORGIA (ITL) see **LUCRECE BORGIA** • 1953
LUCREZIA BORGIA, L'AMANTE DEL DIAVOLO • 1968 • Civirani Osvaldo • ITL, AUS • LUCREZIA BORGIA, THE DEVIL'S LOVER ○ LUCREZIA
LUCREZIA BORGIA: OR, PLAYTHING OF POWER • 1923 • Greenwood Edwin • UKN
LUCREZIA BORGIA, THE DEVIL'S LOVER see **LUCREZIA BORGIA, L'AMANTE DEL DIAVOLO** • 1968
LUCREZIA GIOVANE • 1974 • Ercoli Luciano • ITL
LUCY see **LUCIE** • 1963
LUCY GALLANT • 1955 • Parrish Robert • USA • OIL TOWN
LUCY MAUD MONTGOMERY: THE ROAD TO GREEN GABLES • 1975 • Macartney-Filgate Terence • DOC • CND
LUCY'S ELOPEMENT • 1915 • *Barnes Justus D.* • USA
LUCY'S LOVER • 1911 • *American* • USA
LUDA KUCA • 1981 • Ristic Ljubisa • YGS • HOUSE IN A MESS, A
LUDA NOGA • 1965 • Ranitovic Branko • ANS • YGS • CRAZY LEG
LUDAS MATYI • 1949 • Nadasdy Kalman • HNG • MATTIE, THE GOOSEBOY
LUDAS MATYI • 1977 • Dargay Attila • ANM • HNG • MATTIE THE GOOSEBOY ○ MATTIG THE GOOSEBOY ○ MATT THE GOOSEBOY
LUDE GODINE • 1979 • Calic Zoran • YGS • CRAZY YEARS
LUDI DANI • 1978 • Babic Nikola • YGS • CRAZY DAYS
LUDIONS, LES • 1965 • Poirier Anne-Claire • DCS • CND
LUDLOW'S AEROPLANE • 1905 • *Bitzer Billy (Ph)* • USA
LUDO see **MESSIEURS LUDOVIC** • 1945
LUDO SRCE • 1959 • Kostelac Nikola • ANS • YGS • CRAZY HEART, A
LUDOT-VORNIMAC see **CUDOTVORNI MAC** • 1949
LUDWIG • 1964 • Klick Roland • FRG
LUDWIG • 1987 • Gisler Marcel • SWT
LUDWIG see **LUDWIG II** • 1972
LUDWIG AUF FREIERSFUSZEN • 1969 • Seitz Franz* • FRG
LUDWIG DER ZWEITE, KONIG VON BAYERN • 1929 • Dieterle William • FRG • LUDWIG II, KING OF BAVARIA
LUDWIG FROM GERMANY • 1911 • *Benner Yale* • USA
LUDWIG II • 1955 • Kautner Helmut • FRG • GLANZ UND ENDE EINES KONIGS
LUDWIG II • 1972 • Visconti Luchino • ITL, FRN, FRG • LOUIS II DE BAVIERE (FRN) ○ LUDWIG
LUDWIG II, KING OF BAVARIA see **LUDWIG DER ZWEITE, KONIG VON BAYERN** • 1929
LUDWIG II, KONIG VON BAYERN • 1919 • Raffe Rolf • FRG • SCHWEIGEN AM STARNBERGER SEE, DAS
LUDWIG II -REQUIEM FRU EINEN JUNGFRAULICHEN KONIG • 1972 • Syberberg Hans-Jurgen • FRG • LUDWIG: REQUIEM FOR A VIRGIN KING
LUDWIG: REQUIEM FOR A VIRGIN KING see **LUDWIG II -REQUIEM FRU EINEN JUNGFRAULICHEN KONIG** • 1972
LUDWIG VAN BEETHOVEN • 1954 • Jaap Max • GDR
LUDWIG VAN BEETHOVEN • 1970 • Fischer Hans Conrad • DOC • FRG, AUS
LUDWIG VON BEETHOVEN • 1926 • Fitzpatrick James A. • UKN
LUDWIG'S COOK see **THEODOR HIERNEIS ODER: WIE MAN EHEM. HOFKOCH WIRD** • 1972
LUDWIK WARYNSKI • 1978 • Jakubowska Wanda • PLN
LUDZIE I PTAKI • 1972 • Zeman Bronislaw • PLN • PEOPLE AND BIRDS
LUDZIE I RYBY • 1962 • Slesicki Wladyslaw • DOC • PLN • PEOPLE AND FISH
LUDZIE W DRODZE • 1960 • Karabasz Kazimierz • DCS • PLN • PEOPLE ON THE ROAD ○ PEOPLE ON THE MOVE
LUDZIE WISLY • 1937 • Ford Aleksander • PLN • PEOPLE OF THE VISTULA ○ VISTULA PEOPLE, THE
LUDZIE Z BAZY • 1962 • Wionczek Roman • DOC • PLN • PEOPLE FROM THE BASE
LUDZIE Z DROGI • 1961 • Karabasz Kazimierz • PLN
LUDZIE Z POCIAGU • 1961 • Kutz Kazimierz • PLN • PEOPLE ON A TRAIN ○ PANIC ON A TRAIN
LUDZIE Z PUSTEGO OBSZARU • 1957 • Karabasz Kazimierz, Slesicki Wladyslaw • DCS • PLN • PEOPLE FROM THE EMPTY AREA ○ PEOPLE FROM EMPTY PLACES
LUELLA'S LOVE STORY • 1913 • Lytton L. Rogers, Young James • USA
LUFAREN OCH RASMUS • 1955 • Husberg Rolf • SWD • RASMUS AND THE TRAMP
LUFFAR-PETTER • 1922 • Petschler Eric A. • SWD • PETER THE TRAMP (USA)
LUFT-TORPEDO, DAS • 1913 • *Gero Louis* • FRG • AIR TORPEDO, THE (USA)
LUFTBUREN • 1973 • Forslund Bengt • SWD • AIR CAGE, THE
LUFTENS VAGABOND • 1933 • Hildebrand Weyler • SWD
LUFTFAHRT UBER DEN OZEAN, DIE • 1924 • Neff Wolfgang • FRG • HARALDS KUHNSTE ABENTEUER
LUFTPIRATEN, DIE • 1920 • Piel Harry • FRG
LUFTSCHIFF, DAS • 1983 • Simon Rainer • GDR • AIRSHIP
LUGAR DEL HUMO, EL • 1980 • Landeck Eva • URG
LUGAR DO MORTO, O • 1984 • Vasconcelos Antonio-Pedro • PRT
LUGAR EN EL SOL, UN • 1990 • Velazco Arturo • MXC • PLACE IN THE SUN, A
LUGAR LLAMADA "GLORY", UN (SPN) see **HOLLE VON MANITOBA, DIE** • 1965
LUGAR SIN LIMITES • 1977 • Estrada Jose • MXC
LUGAR SIN LIMITES, EL • 1976 • Ripstein Arturo • MXC • PLACE WITHOUT LIMITS, THE
LUGE, DIE • 1950 • Frohlich Gustav • FRG
LUGE, DIE see **ENDE VOM LIEDE, DAS** • 1919
LUGE DER PIA MAHREN, DIE • 1919 • von Woringen Paul • FRG
LUGE EINES SOMMERS, DIE • 1922 • Lund Erik • FRG
LUGE UND WAHRHEIT see **AUS DEN ERINNERUNGEN EINES FRAUENARZTES 2** • 1921
LUGEN AUF RUGEN • 1931 • Janson Victor • FRG
LUGEN HABEN HUBSCHE BEINE • 1956 • Ode Erik • AUS
LUGGAGE IN ADVANCE • 1913 • Haldane Bert? • UKN
LUGGAGE OF MR. O.F., THE see **KOFFER DES HERRN O.F., DIE** • 1931
LUGGAGE OF THE GODS! • 1983 • Kendall David • USA
LUGHER • 1981 • van Gogh Theo • NTH
LUGNER, DER • 1961 • Vajda Ladislao • FRG
LUGNER UND DIE NONNE, DER • 1967 • Thiele Rolf, Czech J. • AUS • LIAR AND THE NUN, THE
LUHA SA KARIMLAN • 1968 • de Jesus Ding M. • PHL • TEARS IN THE DARK
LUI • 1904 • Blache Alice • FRN
LUI ET MOI see **CLOCHARD MILLIARDAIRE, LE** • 1950
LUI, LEI E IL NONNO • 1961 • Majano Anton Giulio • ITL
LUI PER LEI • 1970 • Rispoli Claudio • ITL
LUIGI XI RE DI FRANCIA • 1909 • Maggi Luigi • ITL
LUIGI'S LADIES • 1988 • Morris Judy • ASL
LUIS ESPINAL EN EL PUEBLO • 1980 • Dagron Alfonso Gumucio • BLV
LUIS PARDO • 1927 • Villanueva Enrique Cornejo • PRU
LUISA SANFELICE • 1942 • Menardi Leo • ITL
LUISE, KONIGIN VON PREUSSEN • 1931 • Froelich Carl • FRG • LUISE, QUEEN OF PRUSSIA
LUISE MILLERIN • 1922 • Froelich Carl • FRG • KABALE UND LIEBE
LUISE, QUEEN OF PRUSSIA see **LUISE, KONIGIN VON PREUSSEN** • 1931
LUISITO • 1943 • Amadori Luis Cesar • ARG • MUJER CON PANTALONES, UNA
LUITENANT KERKHOFBLOMMEN ,DE • 1964 • Verhavert Roland • SHT • BLG
LUJO A SU ALCANCE, UN • 1975 • Fernandez Ramon • SPN
LUK EROSA • 1988 • Domaradzki Jerzy • PLN • CUPID'S BOW
LUK KRALOVNY DOROTKY • 1970 • Schmidt Jan • CZC • BOW OF QUEEN DOROTHY, THE
LUKAS KAPITEL 15 see **VERLORENE SOHN, DER** • 1918
LUKAS LASST GRUSSEN • 1988 • Kuert Beat • SWT • LUKAS SENDS HIS REGARDS
LUKAS SENDS HIS REGARDS see **LUKAS LASST GRUSSEN** • 1988
LUKE AND THE BANG-TAILS • 1916 • Roach Hal • SHT • USA
LUKE AND THE BOMB THROWERS • 1916 • Roach Hal • SHT • USA
LUKE AND THE MERMAIDS • 1916 • Roach Hal • SHT • USA
LUKE AND THE RURAL ROUGHNECKS • 1916 • Roach Hal • SHT • USA
LUKE, CRYSTAL GAZER • 1916 • Roach Hal • SHT • USA
LUKE DOES THE MIDWAY • 1916 • Roach Hal • SHT • USA
LUKE FOILS THE VILLAIN • 1916 • Roach Hal • SHT • USA
LUKE, GLADIATOR • 1916 • Roach Hal • SHT • USA
LUKE JOINS THE NAVY • 1916 • Roach Hal • SHT • USA
LUKE LAUGHS LAST • 1916 • Roach Hal • SHT • USA
LUKE LEANS TO THE LITERARY see **LONESOME LUKE LEANS TO THE LITERARY** • 1916
LUKE LOCATES THE LOOT • 1916 • Roach Hal • SHT • USA
LUKE LOLLS IN LUXURY see **LONESOME LUKE LOLLS IN LUXURY** • 1916
LUKE LUGS LUGGAGE • 1916 • Roach Hal • SHT • USA
LUKE, PATIENT PROVIDER • 1916 • Roach Hal • SHT • USA
LUKE PIPS THE PIPPINS • 1916 • Roach Hal • SHT • USA
LUKE, RANK IMPERSONATOR • 1916 • *Lloyd Harold* • SHT • USA
LUKE RIDES ROUGH-SHOD • 1916 • Roach Hal • SHT • USA
LUKE, THE CANDY CUT-UP • 1916 • Roach Hal • SHT • USA
LUKE THE CHAUFFEUR • 1916 • Roach Hal • SHT • USA
LUKE, THE RURAL ROUGHNECK see **RURAL ROUGHNECKS** • 1916
LUKE WINS YE LADYE FAIRE • 1917 • Roach Hal • SHT • USA
LUKE'S BUSY DAY • 1917 • Roach Hal • SHT • USA • LUKE'S BUSY DAYS
LUKE'S BUSY DAYS see **LUKE'S BUSY DAY** • 1917
LUKE'S DOUBLE • 1916 • Roach Hal • SHT • USA
LUKE'S FATAL FLIVVER • 1916 • Roach Hal • SHT • USA
LUKE'S FIREWORKS FIZZLE • 1916 • Roach Hal • SHT • USA
LUKE'S LAST LIBERTY see **LUKE'S LOST LIBERTY** • 1917
LUKE'S LATE LUNCHERS • 1916 • Roach Hal • SHT • USA • LUKE'S LATE LUNCHES
LUKE'S LATE LUNCHES see **LUKE'S LATE LUNCHERS** • 1916
LUKE'S LIVELY LIFE • 1916 • *Lloyd Harold* • SHT • USA
LUKE'S LOST LAMB • 1916 • Roach Hal • SHT • USA
LUKE'S LOST LIBERTY • 1917 • Roach Hal • SHT • USA • LUKE'S LAST LIBERTY
LUKE'S MOVIE MUDDLE • 1916 • Roach Hal • SHT • USA
LUKE'S NEWSIE KNOCKOUT • 1916 • *Lloyd Harold* • SHT • USA
LUKE'S PLUMBING BLUNDERS • 1917 • *Lloyd Harold?* • SHT • USA
LUKE'S PREPAREDNESS PREPARATION • 1916 • Roach Hal • SHT • USA
LUKE'S SHATTERED SLEEP • 1917 • Roach Hal • SHT • USA
LUKE'S SOCIETY MIXUP • 1916 • Roach Hal • SHT • USA
LUKE'S SPEEDY CLUB LIFE • 1916 • Roach Hal • SHT • USA
LUKE'S TROLLEY TROUBLES • 1917 • Roach Hal • SHT • USA
LUKE'S WASHFUL WAITING • 1916 • Roach Hal • SHT • USA
LUKI • 1978 • SAF
LUKKET AVDELING • 1972 • Berg Arnljot • NRW • CLOSED WARD
LUKREZIA BORGIA see **LUCREZIA BORGIA** • 1922
LUKSUSCHAUOREN • 1915 • Dinesen Robert • DNM
LUL • 1988 • Zohar Uri • ISR • CHICKEN COOP
LULA MIRA • 1962 • Grgic Zlatko • ANS • YGS • CALUMET, THE ○ LULU MIRA
LULLABY • 1937 • Newman Widgey R. • UKN
LULLABY see **FORGET-ME-NOT** • 1936
LULLABY see **KOLIBELNAYA** • 1937
LULLABY see **UKOLEBAVKA** • 1948
LULLABY, THE • 1924 • Bennett Chester • USA
LULLABY, THE (UKN) see **SIN OF MADELON CLAUDET, THE** • 1931
LULLABY FOR MY SON see **SHUSSE KOMORIUTA** • 1967
LULLABY LAND • 1933 • Jackson Wilfred • ANS • USA
LULLABY OF BARELAND • 1964 • Conde Manuel S. • USA
LULLABY OF BROADWAY, THE • 1951 • Butler David • USA
LULLABY OF HAMAGURE see **HAMAGURE NO KOMORIUTA** • 1973
LULLABY OF NORWAY see **KJAERE LILLE NORGE** • 1973
LULLABY (USA) see **KOLYBELNAYA** • 1960
LULLI OU LE VIOLON BRISE • 1908 • Melies Georges • FRN • BROKEN VIOLIN, THE ○ LULLY OU LE VIOLON BRISE
LULLY OU LE VIOLON BRISE see **LULLI OU LE VIOLON BRISE** • 1908
LULU • 1915 • Genina Augusto • ITL
LULU • 1917 • von Antalffy Alexander • FRG
LULU • 1918 • Curtiz Michael • HNG
LULU • 1953 • Cerchio Fernando • ITL
LULU • 1962 • Seto Javier • SPN
LULU • 1962 • Thiele Rolf • AUS • NO ORCHIDS FOR LULU (UKN)
LULU • 1967 • Leacock Richard • DOC • USA
LULU • 1977 • Chase Ronald • USA
LULU • 1980 • Borowczyk Walerian • ITL
LULU see **BUCHSE DER PANDORA, DIE** • 1929
LULU AT THE ZOO • 1944 • Sparber I. • ANS • USA
LULU BELLE • 1948 • Fenton Leslie • USA
LULU BY NIGHT see **LULU DE NOCHE** • 1985
LULU DE NOCHE • 1985 • Martinez Lazaro Emilio • SPN • LULU BY NIGHT
LULU GETS THE BIRDIE • 1944 • Sparber I. • ANS • USA
LULU IN HOLLYWOOD • 1944 • Sparber I. • ANS • USA
LULU LA SPOSA EROTICA • 1977 • Moffa Paolo, Brescia Alfonso • ITL • LOLA '77
LULU MIRA see **LULA MIRA** • 1962
LULU THE TOOL (USA) see **CLASSE OPERAIA VA IN PARADISO, LA** • 1971
LULUAI'S DREAM, THE • 1966 • Dimond Peter • DOC • ASL
LULU'S ANARCHIST • 1912 • *Neason Hazel* • USA
LULU'S DOCTOR • 1912 • Young James • USA
LULU'S LOST LOTHARIO • 1915 • *Cunningham Arthur* • USA
LUMAAQ -AN ESKIMO LEGEND see **LUMAAQ -UNE LEGENDE ESQUIMO** • 1975
LUMAAQ -UNE LEGENDE ESQUIMO • 1975 • Hoedeman Co • ANS • CND • LUMAAQ -AN ESKIMO LEGEND
LUMACONE, IL • 1974 • Cavara Paolo • ITL
LUMBER CAMP, THE • 1937 • *Lantz Walter (P)* • ANS • USA
LUMBER CHAMP, THE • 1933 • Lantz Walter • ANS • USA
LUMBER JACK AND JILL • 1949 • Kneitel Seymour • ANS • USA
LUMBER JACK-RABBIT • 1954 • Jones Charles M. • ANS • USA
LUMBER JERKS • 1955 • Freleng Friz • ANS • USA
LUMBER TOWN see **PUEBLO DE MADERA** • 1989
LUMBER YARD GANG, THE • 1916 • Ford Francis • USA
LUMBERCAMP TALES see **NUORUUTENI SAVOTAT** • 1988
LUMBERJACK • 1944 • Selander Lesley • USA
LUMBERJACK, THE • 1925 • Barkas Geoffrey • UKN
LUMIEI • 1947 • Pasinetti Francesco • ITL
LUMIERE • 1953 • Paviot Paul • SHT • FRN
LUMIERE • 1966 • Allegret Marc • SHT • FRN
LUMIERE, LA • 1976 • Moreau Jeanne • FRN • LUMIERE (USA)
LUMIERE A KOORDI • 1951 • Rappaport Herbert • USS
LUMIERE D'EN FACE, LA • 1955 • Lacombe Georges • FRN • LIGHT ACROSS THE STREET, THE (USA) ○ FEMALE AND THE FLESH
LUMIERE D'ETE • 1942 • Gremillon Jean • FRN • SUMMER LIGHT (USA)
LUMIERE DOUCE see **DHAW AL-KHAFIT, ADH-** • 1961
LUMIERE ET L'AMOUR, LA • 1911 • Perret Leonce • FRN
LUMIERE POUR TOUS • 1963 • Hamina Mohamed Lakhdar • DCS • ALG
LUMIERE QUI TUE, LA • 1912 • Fescourt Henri • FRN
LUMIERE (USA) see **LUMIERE, LA** • 1976
LUMIERE VERTE, LA • 1968 • Shawqi Khalil • SHT • EGY
LUMIERES DE LA VILLE, LES see **ADHWA' AL-MADINA** • 1972
LUMIERES DE MA VILLE, LES • 1950 • Bigras Jean-Yves • CND
LUMIERES DE PARIS • 1938 • Pottier Richard • FRN
LUMIERES DU SOIR, LES • 1956 • Vernay Robert • FRN
LUMIGRAPH 1 • 1955-69 • Fischinger Oskar, Fischinger Elfriede • SHT • USA
LUMIKUNINGATAR • 1987 • Hartzell Paivi • FNL • SNOW QUEEN, THE
LUMINA PALIDA A DURERII • 1980 • Mihu Iulian • RMN • PALE LIGHT OF SORROW, THE
LUMINIS-2 • 1970 • Carretero Amaro • ANS • SPN
LUMINOUS PROCURESS • 1971 • Arnold Steven • USA

LUMMEL VON DER ERSTEN BANK I. ZUR HOLLE MIT DEN PAUKERN, DIE • 1968 • Jacobs Werner • FRG • RASCALS OF THE FRONT BENCH I. TO HELL WITH TEACHERS, THE
LUMMEL VON DER ERSTEN BANK II: ZUM TEUFEL MIT PER PENNE, DIE • 1968 • Jacobs Werner • FRG • ZUM TEUFEL MIT PER PENNE, DIE ○ RASCALS OF THE FRONT BENCH II: TO THE DEVIL WITH SCHOOL, THE
LUMMEL VON DER ERSTEN BANK III, DIE • 1969 • Reinl Harald • FRG • PEPE, DER PAUKERSCHRECK ○ PEPE – HIS TEACHER'S FRIGHT
LUMMOX • 1930 • Brenon Herbert • USA
LUMPACI THE VAGABOND see **BOSE GEIST LUMPACI VAGABUNDUS, DER** • 1922
LUMPACI THE VAGABOND see **LUMPAZIVAGABUNDUS** • 1937
LUMPACI VAGABUNDUS see **BOSE GEIST LUMPACI VAGABUNDUS, DER** • 1922
LUMPACI VAGABUNDUS see **LUMPAZIVAGABUNDUS** • 1937
LUMPAZIVAGABUNDUS • 1937 • von Bolvary Geza • AUS • LUMPACI VAGABUNDUS ○ LUMPACI THE VAGABOND
LUMPAZIVAGABUNDUS • 1956 • Antel Franz • AUS
LUMPAZIVAGABUNDUS • 1965 • Zbonek Edwin • AUS
LUMPEN UND SEIDE • 1924 • Oswald Richard • FRG
LUMPENBALL • 1930 • Wolff Carl Heinz • FRG
LUMPENGRETE • 1918 • *Kuhnberg Leontine* • FRG
LUMPENKAVALIERE • 1932 • Boese Carl • AUS • WIENER LUMPENKAVALIERE
LUMPENLIESEL • 1915 • Oberlander Hans • FRG
LUMPENMULLERS LIESCHEN • 1918 • Mendel Georg Victor • FRG
LUMSDEN • 1975 • Raymont Peter • DOC • CND
LUMUHA PATI MGA ANGEL • 1972 • Brocka Lino • PHL
LUMUHOD KA O LUMABAN • 1968 • Gallardo Cesar Chat • PHL • KNEEL OR FIGHT
LUNA, LA • 1979 • Bertolucci Bernardo • ITL, USA
LUNA CRIOLLA • 1938 • Sevilla Raphael J. • MXC • CREOLE MOON (USA)
LUNA DE MIEL see **HONEYMOON** • 1959
LUNA DE MIEL EN CONDOMINIO • 1966 • Cortes Fernando • MXC, PRC
LUNA DE MIEL PARA NUEVE • 1963 • Delgado Agustin P. • MXC
LUNA DE SANGRE • 1950 • Rovira Beleta Francisco • SPN
LUNA DE TOBALITO, LA • 1968 • Gijon Salvador • ANS • SPN • MOON OF TOBALITO, THE
LUNA DE VERANO • 1958 • Lazaga Pedro • SPN
LUNA DI MIELE • 1941 • Gentilomo Giacomo • ITL
LUNA DU MIELE IN TRE • 1976 • Vanzina Carlo • ITL
LUNA EN LA SERRANIA • 1965 • Almedros Gregorio • SPN
LUNA ENAMORADA, LA • 1945 • Diaz Morales Jose • MXC • AMORES DE UN TORERO, LOS
LUNA NUOVA • 1955 • Capuano Luigi • ITL
LUNA–PARK see **WESOLE MIASTECZKO** • 1958
LUNA ROSSA • 1951 • Zorri Armando • ITL
LUNA VALE UN MILLON, LA • 1945 • Rey Florian • SPN
LUNACHEIA • 1988 • Fresnot Alain • BRZ • FULL MOON
LUNAR DE LA FAMIGLIA, EL • 1952 • Mendez Fernando • MXC
LUNATIC see **NIGHT VISITOR, THE** • 1970
LUNATIC AND THE BOMB, THE • 1912 • Wilson Frank? • UKN
LUNATIC ASYLUM • 1925 • *Lane Lupino* • UKN
LUNATIC AT LARGE, A • 1910 • *Vitagraph* • USA
LUNATIC AT LARGE, A • 1912 • Edwards Henry • UKN
LUNATIC AT LARGE, THE • 1927 • Newmeyer Fred • USA
LUNATIC AT LIBERTY, THE • 1911 • Wilson Frank? • UKN
LUNATIC EXPECTED, A • 1910 • Wilson Frank? • UKN
LUNATICS, THE (USA) see **SYSTEME DU DOCTEUR GOUDRON ET DU PROFESSEUR PLUME, LE** • 1909
LUNATICS, THE (USA) see **SYSTEME DU DOCTEUR GOUDRON ET DU PROFESSEUR PLUME, LE** • 1912
LUNATICS IN POLITICS • 1920 • Smith Dick • SHT • USA
LUNATICS IN POWER • 1909 • Dawley J. Searle? • USA
LUNATYCY • 1959 • Poreba Bohdan • PLN • SLEEPWALKERS
LUNCH • 1917 • Hotaling Arthur D. • SHT • USA
LUNCH • 1973 • McDowell Curt • USA
LUNCH, THE see **RUCAK** • 1972
LUNCH, UN • 1899-00 • Blache Alice • FRN
LUNCH HOUND • 1927 • Lantz Walter • ANS • USA
LUNCH HOUR • 1962 • Hill James • UKN
LUNCH ON THE GRASS (UKN) see **DEJEUNER SUR L'HERBE, LE** • 1959
LUNCH ROOM LEGACY, A • 1916 • Ellis Robert • USA
LUNCH WAGON • 1981 • Pintoff Ernest • USA • LUNCH WAGON GIRLS ○ COME 'N' GET IT
LUNCH WAGON GIRLS see **LUNCH WAGON** • 1981
LUNCH WITH A PUNCH • 1952 • Sparber I. • ANS • USA
LUNCHBREAK CAFE, THE see **CAFE LUNCHRASTEN** • 1954
LUNCHEON AT TWELVE • 1933 • Parrott Charles • SHT • USA
LUNCHEON FOR THREE • 1914 • Dewsbury Ralph • UKN
LUNDI PERDU see **VERLOREN MAANDAG** • 1973
LUNDI –UNE CHAUMIERE, UN COEUR • 1978 • Leduc Jacques • DOC • CND
LUNDUN • 1971 • Dewdney Alexander Keewatin • CND
LUNE A UN METRE, LA see **HOMME DANS LA LUNE, L'** • 1898
LUNE AVEC LES DENTS, LA • 1967 • Soutter Michel • SWT • MOON WITH HIS TEETH, THE
LUNE DANS LE CANIVEAU, LA • 1983 • Beineix Jean-Jacques • FRN, ITL • MOON IN THE GUTTER (UKN)
LUNE DANS SON TABLIER, LA • 1909 • Cohl Emile • ANS • FRN • MOON IN HIS APRON, THE ○ MOON FOR YOUR LOVE
LUNE DE MIEL • 1935 • Ducis Pierre-Jean • FRN
LUNE DE MIEL • 1986 • Jamain Patrick • CND, FRN • HONEYMOON
LUNE DES LAPINS, LA • 1971 • Anger Kenneth • FRN • RABBITS MOON
LUNEGARDE • 1944 • Allegret Marc • FRN
LUNES • 1960 • Artero Antonio • SHT • SPN
LUNES EN EL ZOOLOGICO, UN • 1971 • Villafuerte Santiago • DOC • CUB
LUNES, MARTE, MYERKOLES.. • 1976 • Brocka Lino • PHL
LUNES PRIMEIRO, DOMINGO SIETE • 1968 • Soto Helvio • CHL • MONDAY 1ST, SUNDAY 7TH ○ MONDAY – SUNDAY
LUNETTES FEERIQUES, LES • 1909 • Cohl Emile • ANS • FRN • FAIRY SPECTACLES, THE ○ X-RAY GLASSES, THE
LUNETTES NOIRES, LES see **NADHDHARA AS–SAWDA', AN–** • 1962
LUNG–CH'ANG SHIH–JIH • 1969 • Tu Larry C. H. • TWN • CITY CALLED DRAGON, A (USA) ○ TEN DAYS IN DRAGON CITY ○ DRAGON CITY
LUNG–CHENG–HU TOU • 1973 • Clouse Robert • HKG, USA • ENTER THE DRAGON (USA)
LUNG HU TOU • 1969 • Chang Ch'Eh • HKG • CHINESE BOXER, THE
LUNG–MEN K'E–CHEN • 1966 • Hu King • HKG • DRAGON GATE INN (USA) ○ LUNG–MEN K'O–CHAN ○ DRAGON INN
LUNG–MEN K'O–CHAN see **LUNG–MEN K'E–CHEN** • 1966
LUNG SHAO–YEH • 1981 • Chan Jackie • HKG • DRAGON'S LORD, THE ○ DRAGON LORD
LUNGA CALZA VERDE, LA • 1961 • Gavioli Roberto, Gavioli Gino • ITL • LONG GREEN STOCKING, THE (USA)
LUNGA CAVALCATA DELLA VENDETTA, LA • 1972 • Boccia Tanio • ITL
LUNGA FILA DI CROCI, UNA • 1969 • Garrone Sergio • ITL • NO ROOM TO DIE (UKN)
LUNGA MANICA, LA • 1947 • Mantici • SHT • ITL
LUNGA MARCIA, LA • 1971 • Scavolini Romano • MTV • ITL
LUNGA MARCIA PER PECHINO • 1962 • Di Giammatteo Fernaldo • DOC • ITL • LUNGA STRADA PER PECHINO, LA
LUNGA NOTTE DEI DISERTORI, LA • 1970 • Siciliano Mario • ITL • SETTE DI MARSA MATRUH, I
LUNGA NOTTE DEL '43, LA • 1960 • Vancini Florestano • ITL • LONG NIGHT OF '43, THE
LUNGA NOTTE DEL TERRORE, LA see **DANZA MACABRA** • 1964
LUNGA NOTTE DI LOUISE, LA (ITL) see **CHERE LOUISE** • 1971
LUNGA NOTTE DI TOMBSTONE, LA • 1968 • Balcazar Jaime Jesus • ITL
LUNGA NOTTE DI VERONIQUE, LA • 1966 • Vernuccio Gianni • ITL • LONG NIGHT OF VERONICA, THE ○ BUT YOU WERE DEAD (UKN)
LUNGA OMBRA DEL LUPO, LA • 1971 • Manera Gianni • ITL
LUNGA SFIDA, LA • 1967 • Zanchin Nino • ITL, FRG • LONG DEFIANCE, THE
LUNGA SPIAGGIA FREDDA, LA • 1971 • Gastaldi Ernesto • ITL
LUNGA STRADA AZZURRA, LA see **GRANDE STRADA AZZURRA, LA** • 1957
LUNGA STRADA PER PECHINO, LA see **LUNGA MARCIA PER PECHINO** • 1962
LUNGA STRADA SENZA POLVERE, LA • 1978 • Tau Sergio • ITL
LUNGA VITA ALLA SIGNORA! • 1988 • Olmi Ermanno • ITL • LONG LIVE THE LADY!
LUNGHE NOTTI DELLA GESTAPO, LE • 1977 • De Agostini Fabio • ITL • RED NIGHTS OF THE GESTAPO, THE
LUNGHI CAPELLI DELLA MORTE, I • 1964 • Margheriti Antonio • ITL • LONG HAIR OF DEATH, THE (UKN)
LUNGHI GIORNI DELLA VENDETTA, I • 1967 • Vancini Florestano • ITL, SPN • FACCIA D'ANGELO
LUNGHI GIORNI DELL'ODIO, I • 1968 • Baldanello Gianfranco • ITL • THIS MAN CAN'T DIE (USA) ○ LUSTY BRAWLERS
LUNGHING FUDAI TSUKTSAP • 1990 • Chan Frankie • HKG • ARMOUR OF GOD 2: OPERATION EAGLE, THE
LUNGO GIORNO DEL MASSACRO, IL • 1968 • Cardone Alberto • ITL • LONG DAY OF THE MASSACRE, THE
LUNGO GIORNO DELLA VIOLENZA, IL • 1971 • Scotese Giuseppe Maria • ITL
LUNGO, IL CORTO, IL GATTO, IL • 1967 • Fulci Lucio • ITL • TALL, THE SHORT, THE CAT, THE
LUNGO VIAGGIO, IL • 1975 • Giraldi Franco • MTV • ITL
LUNHUI • 1988 • Huang Jianxin • CHN • SAMSARA
LUNKHEAD, THE • 1929 • Sennett Mack • SHT • USA
LUNNYYE NOCHI • 1967 • Reshotnikov Yuri • USS
LUNYLAND PICTURES • 1914 • Budd Leighton • ASS • USA
LUOGHI VERDIANI • 1948 • Emmer Luciano, Gras Enrico • ITL • SULLE ROME DI VERDI
LUOTTAMUS see **LUOTTAMUS, ELI LENIN JA SUOMI** • 1975
LUOTTAMUS, ELI LENIN JA SUOMI • 1975 • Laine Edvin, Tregubovich Viktor • FNL, USS • CONFIDENCE, OR LENIN IN FINLAND ○ LENIN SUOMESSA ○ TRUST ○ LUOTTAMUS
LUPA, LA • 1953 • Lattuada Alberto • ITL • SHE–WOLF, THE ○ VIXEN, THE ○ DEVIL IS A WOMAN, THE
LUPA, LA • 1955 • Lucia Luis • SPN
LUPA MANNARA, LA • 1976 • Di Silvestro Rino • ITL • LEGEND OF THE WOLF WOMAN (USA) ○ DAUGHTER OF A WEREWOLF ○ WOLFWOMAN ○ WEREWOLF WOMAN
LUPE • 1966 • Warhol Andy • USA
LUPE • 1967 • Rodriguez-Soltero Jose • USA
LUPE BALAZOS • 1963 • Urueta Chano • MXC
LUPENI '29 • Dragan Mircea • RMN
LUPI ATTACCANO IN BRANCO, I • 1970 • Cirino Franco • ITL
LUPI NELL'ABISSO • 1959 • Amadio Silvio • ITL, FRN • WOLVES OF THE DEEP (USA)
LUPINEK CASE, THE see **PRIPAD LUPINEK** • 1960
LUPINS • 1936 • Field Mary • UKN
LUPITA • Rodriguez-Soltero Jose • USA
LUPO • 1970 • Golan Menahem • ISR
LUPO DEI MARI, IL • 1975 • Vari Giuseppe • ITL • WOLF LARSEN (USA) ○ LEGEND OF THE SEA WOLF ○ WOLF OF THE SEVEN SEAS
LUPO DELLA FRONTIERA, IL • 1952 • Anton Edoardo, Scanziani Piero • ITL
LUPO DELLA SILA, IL • 1949 • Coletti Duilio • ITL • WOLF OF THE SILA, THE (UKN) ○ LURE OF THE SILA (USA) ○ WOLF OF SILA, THE
LUPO E L'AGNELLO, IL • 1980 • Massaro Francesco • ITL, FRN • COUCOU, LE (FRN)
LUPO GOES TO NEW YORK • 1977 • Davidson Boaz • ISR
LUPONINI DE CHICAGO • 1935 • Bohr Jose • MXC
LUPUS • 1982 • Farmanara Bahman • CND
LURDHA MAGDANI see **LURDZHA MAGDANY** • 1956
LURDJA MAGDANI see **LURDZHA MAGDANY** • 1956
LURDZHA MAGDANY • 1956 • Abuladze Tengiz, Chkheidze Revaz • USS • MAGDANA'S DONKEY (USA) ○ LURDJA MAGDANI ○ LURDHA MAGDANI ○ MAGDANAS LURJA
LURE, THE • 1914 • Blache Alice • USA
LURE, THE • 1933 • Maude Arthur • UKN
LURE O' THE WINDIGO, THE • 1914 • Grandon Francis J. • USA
LURE OF A WIDOW, THE • 1915 • Van Wally • USA
LURE OF A WOMAN, THE • 1921 • Simms J. M. • USA
LURE OF AMBITION • 1919 • Lawrence Edmund • USA
LURE OF BROADWAY, THE see **BRIGHT LIGHTS, THE** • 1916
LURE OF CROONING WATERS, THE • 1920 • Rooke Arthur • UKN
LURE OF DRINK, THE • 1915 • Coleby A. E. • UKN
LURE OF EGYPT, THE • 1921 • Hickman Howard • USA
LURE OF GOLD • 1922 • Hart Neal • USA
LURE OF GOLD, THE • 1910 • *Bison* • USA
LURE OF GOLD, THE • 1916 • *Puritan* • SHT • USA
LURE OF HEART'S DESIRE, THE • 1916 • Grandon Francis J. • USA
LURE OF HOLLYWOOD, THE • 1931 • Arbuckle Roscoe • USA
LURE OF JADE, THE • 1921 • Campbell Colin • USA
LURE OF LABRADOR, THE • 1925 • Frissell Varick • DOC • CND
LURE OF LONDON, THE • 1911 • Noy Wilfred • UKN
LURE OF LONDON, THE • 1914 • Haldane Bert? • UKN
LURE OF LOVE, THE • 1924 • Dadmun Leon E. • USA
LURE OF LUXURY, THE • 1918 • Wilson Elsie Jane • USA
LURE OF MAMMON, THE • 1915 • *Marinoff Fania* • USA
LURE OF MILLIONS • 1914 • *Prometheus Films* • DNM
LURE OF NEW YORK, THE • 1913 • Rolands George K. • USA
LURE OF THE ATLANTIC • 1929 • Lee Norman • UKN
LURE OF THE BUSH • 1918 • Flemming Claude • ASL
LURE OF THE CAR WHEELS, THE • 1914 • *Shumway L. C.* • USA
LURE OF THE CIRCUS, THE • 1917 • Pearson W. B. • SHT • USA
LURE OF THE CIRCUS, THE • 1919 • McGowan J. P. • SRL • USA
LURE OF THE CITY, THE • 1910 • *American* • USA
LURE OF THE CITY, THE • 1911 • Porter Edwin S. • USA
LURE OF THE CITY, THE • 1913 • Apfel Oscar • USA
LURE OF THE CITY, THE • 1916 • *Gayety* • USA
LURE OF THE FOOTLIGHTS • 1912 • Buckland Warwick? • UKN
LURE OF THE FOOTLIGHTS, THE • 1912 • *Panzer Paul* • USA
LURE OF THE GEISHA, THE • 1914 • *Clifford William* • USA
LURE OF THE GOWN, THE • 1909 • Griffith D. W. • USA
LURE OF THE GREEN TABLE • 1914 • *Parsons William E.* • USA
LURE OF THE ISLANDS • 1942 • Yarbrough Jean • USA
LURE OF THE JUNGLE, THE see **PAW** • 1959
LURE OF THE LADIES, THE • 1914 • Eagle Oscar • USA
LURE OF THE MASK, THE • 1915 • Ricketts Thomas • USA
LURE OF THE MINE • 1929 • *Bill Montana* • USA
LURE OF THE NIGHT CLUB, THE • 1927 • Buckingham Thomas • USA
LURE OF THE ORIENT • 1920 • Conway Jack • USA
LURE OF THE PICTURE, THE • 1912 • *Daly W. R.* • USA
LURE OF THE PIT, THE • 1914 • *Lubin* • USA
LURE OF THE ROAD, THE • 1913 • *Selig* • USA
LURE OF THE SACRED PEARL, THE • 1913 • Melies Gaston • USA
LURE OF THE SAWDUST, THE • 1914 • Ricketts Thomas • USA
LURE OF THE SEA see **LAW OF THE SEA** • 1932
LURE OF THE SILA (USA) see **LUPO DELLA SILA, IL** • 1949
LURE OF THE STAGE, THE • 1913 • *White Pearl* • USA
LURE OF THE SWAMP, THE • 1957 • Cornfield Hubert • USA
LURE OF THE TRACK • 1925 • *Lewis Sheldon* • USA
LURE OF THE VIOLIN, THE • 1913 • Miller Charles? • USA
LURE OF THE WEST • 1926 • Neitz Alvin J. • USA
LURE OF THE WEST, THE • 1915 • *Eclair* • USA
LURE OF THE WILD, THE • 1925 • Strayer Frank • USA
LURE OF THE WILDERNESS • 1952 • Negulesco Jean • USA • CRY OF THE SWAMP
LURE OF THE WORLD, THE • 1915 • Calvert Charles? • UKN
LURE OF THE YUKON • 1924 • Dawn Norman • USA
LURE OF THE YUKON, THE • 1914 • *Wier Edward S.* • USA
LURE OF VANITY, THE • 1911 • *Vitagraph* • USA
LURE OF WOMEN, THE • 1915 • Vale Travers • USA
LURE OF YOUTH, THE • 1921 • Rosen Phil • USA • WHITE ASHES
LURED • 1919 • Parrott Charles • SHT • USA
LURED • 1947 • Sirk Douglas • USA • PERSONAL COLUMN (UKN)
LURED AND CURED • 1917 • Davis James • SHT • USA
LURED BUT CURED • 1916 • *Russell Dan* • SHT • USA
LURED BY A PHANTOM OR THE KING OF THULE (USA) see **ROI DE THULE, LE** • 1910
LURED FROM HOME • 1904 • *Mutoscope & Biograph* • UKN
LURED FROM SQUASH CENTER • 1914 • *Powers* • USA
LURING LIGHTS, THE • 1915 • Vignola Robert G. • USA
LURING LIPS • 1921 • Baggot King • USA
LURING SHADOWS • 1920 • Levering Joseph • USA
LURK • 1965 • Burckhardt Rudy • USA
LURKERS • 1988 • Findlay Roberta • USA
LURKING PERIL, THE • 1916 • Ellis Robert • USA
LURKING PERIL, THE • 1920 • King Burton L.?, Morgan George? • SRL • USA
LURKING VAMPIRE, THE see **VAMPIRO ACECHA, EL**
LUSCIOUS • 1982 • Slobodian Bill • USA
LUSSURIA • 1985 • D'Amato Joe • ITL • LUST
LUST • 1980 • Kovach June • MTV • SWT
LUST see **LUSSURIA** • 1985
LUST AND THE FLESH • 1965 • Orlando Tony • USA
LUST AT FIRST BITE see **DRACULA SUCKS** • 1978
LUST FOR A VAMPIRE • 1970 • Sangster Jimmy • UKN • TO LOVE A VAMPIRE
LUST FOR ECSTASY • 1964 • Kuchar George, Kuchar Mike • USA
LUST FOR EVIL see **PLEIN SOLEIL** • 1960
LUST FOR FREEDOM • 1987 • Louzil Eric • USA • GEORGIA COUNTY LOCKUP

LUST FOR GOLD • 1910 • Haldane Bert? • UKN
LUST FOR GOLD • 1922 • Darling Roy • ASL
LUST FOR GOLD • 1949 • Simon S. Sylvan • USA • GREED
LUST FOR GOLD • 1957 • Pravov Ivan • USS
LUST FOR GOLD see **DUHUL AURULUI** • 1974
LUST FOR LIFE • 1956 • Minnelli Vincente • USA
LUST FOR LOVE (UKN) see **MAHLZEITEN** • 1967
LUST FOR LOVING: BLACK HOODS see **SEDE DE AMAR: CAPUZES NEGROS** • 1980
LUST FOR REVENGE • 1975 • Kalia Andreas • GRC
LUST FOR THE SUN • 1958 • Kunz Werner • SWT • AROUND THE WORLD WITH NOTHING ON
LUST IN SPACE • Kidder Miles • USA • LUST IN SPACE: CONTACT IS MADE
LUST IN SPACE: CONTACT IS MADE see **LUST IN SPACE**
LUST IN THE DUST • 1985 • Bartel Paul • USA
LUST IN THE SUN (UKN) see **DANS LA POUSSIERE DU SOLEIL** • 1971
LUST IN THE SWAMPS (UKN) see **POTHI STON KATARAMENO VALTO** • 1967
LUST OF DRACULA, THE • USA
LUST OF THE AGES, THE • 1917 • Revier Harry • USA
LUST OF THE RED MAN, THE • 1914 • Hamilton G. P. • USA
LUST OF THE VAMPIRE see **VAMPIRI, I** • 1956
LUST ON THE ORIENT XPRESS • 1986 • McDonald Tim • USA
LUST SEEKERS, THE see **GOOD MORNING AND GOODBYE!** • 1967
LUST TO KILL, A • 1957 • Drake Oliver • USA
LUST WEEKEND • 1967 • Sullivan Ron • USA • LOST WEEKEND
LUSTFUL AMAZONS, THE (UKN) see **MACISTE CONTRE LA REINE DES AMAZONS** • 1974
LUSTFUL BRUTE see **IROGOKUDOH** • 1968
LUSTFUL DESIRES see **FUR TRAP, THE** • 1978
LUSTFUL ROOM IN AN APARTMENT see **KOSHOKU MANSION-SHITSU** • 1968
LUSTFUL TURK, THE • 1968 • Elliott B. Ron • USA
LUSTFUL VICAR, THE (UKN) see **KYRKOHERDEN** • 1970
LUSTGARDEN • 1961 • Kjellin Alf • SWD • PLEASURE GARDEN
LUSTIGE EHEMANN, DER • 1919 • Lasko Leo • FRG
LUSTIGE KLEEBLATT, DAS • 1933 • Engels Erich • FRG • GASTHAUS ZUR TREUEN LIEBE
LUSTIGE KRIEG DES HAUPTMANN PEDRO, DER • 1959 • Becker Wolfgang • FRG
LUSTIGE WITWE, DIE • 1962 • Jacobs Werner • AUS, FRN
LUSTIGE WITWENBALL, DER • 1936 • Elling Alwin • FRG
LUSTIGE WITWER, DER • 1920 • Bolten-Baeckers Heinrich • FRG
LUSTIGE WITWER, DER • 1929 • Land Robert • FRG
LUSTIGEN MUSIKANTEN, DIE • 1930 • Obal Max • FRG • LAUBENKOLONIE
LUSTIGEN VAGABUNDEN, DIE • 1912 • Valentin Karl • FRG
LUSTIGEN VAGABUNDEN, DIE • 1928 • Fleck Jacob, Fleck Luise • FRG
LUSTIGEN VAGABUNDEN, DIE • 1940 • von Alten Jurgen • FRG
LUSTIGEN VAGABUNDEN, DIE • 1963 • Nachmann Kurt • AUS • DAS HABEN DIE MADCHEN GERN
LUSTIGEN VIER VON DER TANKSTELLE, DIE • 1972 • Antel Franz • AUS, FRG • MERRY QUARTET FROM THE PETROL STATION, THE
LUSTIGEN WEIBER, DIE • 1935 • Hoffmann Carl • FRG
LUSTIGEN WEIBER VON TIROL, DIE • 1964 • Billian Hans • FRG
LUSTIGEN WEIBER VON WIEN, DIE • 1931 • von Bolvary Geza • FRG
LUSTIGEN WEIBER VON WINDSOR, DIE • 1950 • Wildhagen Georg • GDR • MERRY WIVES OF WINDSOR, THE
LUSTIGEN WEIBER VON WINDSOR, DIE • 1965 • Tressler Georg • AUS, UKN • MERRY WIVES OF WINDSOR, THE
LUSTING HOURS, THE • 1967 • *Riva Anna* • USA • LOVE HOURS, THE ○ WANTING HOUR
LUSTRO I JA • 1963 • Zukowska Jadwiga • PLN • MIRROR AND I, THE
LUSTS OF MANKIND see **LASTER DER MENSCHHEIT** • 1927
LUSTS OF THE FLESH (UKN) see **LIEBE DER JEANNE NEY, DIE** • 1927
LUSTY BRAWLERS see **LUNGHI GIORNI DELL'ODIO, I** • 1968
LUSTY BUSTY BROWN see **ADVENTURES OF BUSTY BROWN, THE** • 1964
LUSTY LANDLORD, THE • 1970 • *Impressive Art Productions* • USA • LANDLORD, THE
LUSTY MEN, THE • 1952 • Ray Nicholas, Parrish Robert (U/c) • USA • THIS MAN IS MINE
LUSTY NEIGHBORS • 1970 • *Stacey Dist.* • USA
LUSTY WIVES OF CANTERBURY, THE (UKN) see **RACCONTI DI CANTERBURY N.2., I** • 1974
LUTA CONTINUA, LA • 1971 • van Lieropl Robert • PRT • STRUGGLE CONTINUES, THE ○ FIGHT GOES ON, THE
LUTE, EL • 1987 • Aranda Vicente • SPN • LUTE CAMINA O REVIENTE, EL ○ RUN FOR YOUR LIFE
LUTE CAMINA O REVIENTE, EL see **LUTE, EL** • 1987
LUTE II, EL see **MANANA SERE LIBRE** • 1988
LUTHER • 1927 • Kyser Hans • FRG
LUTHER • 1974 • Green Guy • UKN, USA, CND
LUTKA SNOVA see **DREAM DOLL** • 1979
LUTKICA • 1961 • Dovnikovic Borivoj • ANS • YGS • DOLL, A ○ LITTLE DOLL
LUTO RIGUROSO • 1977 • Larraz Jose R. • SPN
LUTRING see **SVEGLIATI E UCCIDI (LUTRING)** • 1966
LUTRING.. REVEILLE-TOI ET MEURS (FRN) see **SVEGLIATI E UCCIDI (LUTRING)** • 1966
LUTT MATTEN UND DIE WEISSE MUSCHEL • 1964 • Zschoche Hermann • GDR
LUTTE • 1895 • Skladanowsky Max, Skladanowsky Emil • FRG
LUTTE, LA • 1961 • Jutra Claude, Brault Michel, Fournier Claude, Carriere Marcel • DCS • CND • WRESTLING
LUTTE CONTRE LE GASPILLAGE, LA • 1951 • Sevestre • SHT • FRN
LUTTE DE GENERATIONS • 1972 • Hashim Anwar • EGY
LUTTE DE KARAGEUZ, LA • 1957 • Tilmissani Abdel-Qadir At- • SHT • EGY
LUTTE DES TRAVAILLEURS D'HOPITAUX, LA • 1976 • Bulbulian Maurice, Arcand Denys • DOC • CND
LUTTE POUR LA VIE, LA • 1905-10 • Heuze Andre • FRN
LUTTE POUR LA VIE, LA • 1914 • Protazanov Yakov • USS
LUTTES DES HEROS see **SIRA AL-ABT'AL** • 1961
LUTTES EN ITALIE see **LOTTE IN ITALIA** • 1969
LUTTES EXTRAVAGANTES • 1899 • Melies Georges • FRN • EXTRAORDINARY WRESTLING MATCH, AN (USA)
LUTTEURS, LES • 1982 • Tchissoukou Jean-Michel • CNG • WRESTLERS, THE
LUTTEURS AMERICAINS • 1903 • Blache Alice • FRN
LUTTIE'S LOVERS • 1914 • *Joker* • USA
LUTZOWER • 1972 • GDR
LUTZOWS WILDE VERWEGENE JAGD • 1927 • Oswald Richard • FRG
LUV • 1967 • Donner Clive • USA
LUX, DER KONIG DER VERBRECHER • 1929 • Heuberger Edmund • FRG
LUX, DER SPURHUND VON STRATFORD • 1916 • Becker Ernst • FRG
LUX MUNDI -LICHT DER WELT • 1968 • Reissner Rudolf • DOC • FRG • LUX MUNDI -LIGHT OF THE WORLD
LUX MUNDI -LIGHT OF THE WORLD see **LUX MUNDI -LICHT DER WELT** • 1968
LUXURE, LA • 1976 • Pecas Max • FRN
LUXURIOUS LOU • 1915 • Physioc Wray • USA
LUXURY • 1921 • Perez Marcel • USA • UNMARRIED BRIDE, THE
LUXURY GIRLS (USA) see **FANCIULLE DI LUSSO** • 1953
LUXURY LINER • 1933 • Mendes Lothar • USA
LUXURY LINER • 1948 • Whorf Richard • USA
LUXUSBAD, DAS • 1917 • Hofer Franz • FRG
LUXUSWEIBCHEN • 1925 • Schonfelder Erich • FRG
LUZ, LA • 1917 • de la Bandera Manuel • MXC • LIGHT, THE
LUZ DE UN FOSFORO, LA • 1940 • Torres-Rios Leopoldo • ARG
LUZ EN MI CAMINO, UNA • 1938 • Bohr Jose • MXC
LUZ VEM DO ALTO, A • 1959 • Campos Henrique • PRT
LUZIA see **LUZIA HOMEM** • 1988
LUZIA HOMEM • 1988 • Barreto Fabio • BRZ • LUZIA
LUZ'S REASONS see **MOTIVOS DE LUZ, LOS** • 1985
LYANA • 1955 • Barnet Boris • USS • LIANA
LYAS FLIRT MIT DEM HEILIGEN • 1919 • Reicher Ernst • FRG
LYAUTEY, BATISSEUR D'EMPIRE • 1947 • Lucot Rene • SHT • FRN
LYCANTHROPUS • 1962 • Heusch Paolo • ITL, AUS • WEREWOLF IN A GIRLS' DORMITORY (USA) ○ BEI VOLLMOND MORD (AUS) ○ I MARRIED A WEREWOLF (UKN) ○ GHOUL IN SCHOOL, THE
LYCANTHROPUS • 1979 • Pirri Massimo • ITL
LYCEE DE JEUNES FILLES, UN • 1896 • Melies Georges • FRN • ACADEMY FOR YOUNG LADIES
LYCEE SUR LA COLLINE, LE • 1953 • Rouquier Georges • SHT • FRN
LYCEENNES PERVERSES • 1978 • Raphael Peter • FRN
LYCEENNES REDOUBLENT, LES • 1979 • Laurenti Mariano • FRN, ITL
LYCKAN KOMMER • 1942 • Ekman Hasse • SWD • LUCK ARRIVES
LYCKANS GULLGOSSAR • 1932 • Johansson Ivar, Wallen Sigurd • SWD • DARLINGS OF FORTUNE
LYCKLIGA INGENJORERNA • 1988 • Svenstedt Stefania Lopez • DOC • SWD • APPROACHING ZERO, 000
LYCKLIGA SKITAR • 1970 • Sjoman Vilgot • SWD • BLUSHING CHARLIE (UKN) ○ HAPPY SHITS
LYCKLIGA VESTKOPING • 1937 • Arvedson Ragnar • SWD • HAPPY VESTKOPING
LYCKODROMMEN • 1963 • Abramson Hans • SWD • DREAM OF HAPPINESS
LYCKONALEN • 1916 • Stiller Mauritz • SWD • LUCKY BROOCH, THE ○ MOTORCAR APACHES, THE
LYCKORIDDARE, EN • 1921 • Brunius John W. • SWD • FORTUNE HUNTER, A
LYDA SSANIN • 1922 • Zelnik Friedrich • FRG
LYDIA • 1918 • Holger-Madsen • DNM • MUSIC HALL STAR, THE
LYDIA • 1941 • Duvivier Julien • USA
LYDIA ATE THE APPLE see **POZEGNANIA** • 1958
LYDIA BAILEY • 1952 • Negulesco Jean • USA
LYDIA GILMORE • 1916 • Porter Edwin S., Ford Hugh • USA
LYESNAYA BYL • 1927 • Tarich Yuri • USS • FOREST STORY
LYESTNITSA V NYEBO • 1967 • Vabalas Raimondas • USS • LADDER INTO THE SKY ○ STAIRCASE TO THE SKY ○ LESTNITSA V NEBO ○ STAIRS TO THE SKY
LYETO 43-VO GODA • 1968 • Kasymova Margarita • USS • SUMMER OF '43, THE
LYFTET • 1977 • Dahl Christer • SWD • SCORE, THE
LYGERI, I • 1968 • Katsimitsoulias Andreas • GRC
LYIN' HUNTER, THE • 1937 • *Mintz Charles (P)* • ANS • USA
LYIN' LION, THE • 1949 • Rasinski Connie • ANS • USA
LYIN' MOUSE, THE • 1937 • Freleng Friz • ANS • USA
LYIN' TAMER • 1925 • Lantz Walter • ANS • USA
LYIN' TAMER, A • 1920 • Reisner Charles F. • SHT • USA
LYING JIM • 1914 • Barker Reginald • USA
LYING LIPS • 1916 • Sloman Edward • USA
LYING LIPS • 1921 • Wray John Griffith • USA • MAGIC LIFE, THE
LYING LIPS • 1939 • Micheaux Oscar • USA
LYING TRUTH, THE • 1922 • Fairfax Marion • USA
LYING WIVES • 1925 • Abramson Ivan • USA
LYKKEDROMME • 1915 • Davidsen Hjalmar • DNM
LYKKEHJULET • 1926 • Gad Urban • DNM • GAY HUSKIES, THE
LYKKELIG SKILSMISSE, EN • 1974 • Carlsen Henning • DNM, FRN • DIVORCE HEUREUX, UN (FRN) ○ HAPPY DIVORCE, A
LYKKEN • 1916 • Holger-Madsen • DNM • ROAD TO HAPPINESS, THE ○ GUIDING CONSCIENCE
LYKKEN ER EN UNDERLIG FISK • 1989 • Wendel Linda • DNM • HAPPINESS IS A CURIOUS CATCH
LYNBROOK TRAGEDY, THE • 1914 • Buel Kenean • USA
LYNCH AND ROPE see **LYNCH TO SHIBARI** • 1967
LYNCH TO SHIBARI • 1967 • Kishi Shintaro • JPN • LYNCH AND ROPE
LYNET • 1933 • *Holger-Madsen* • DNM
LYNMOUTH • 1913 • Pearson George • DCS • UKN
LYNN SEYMOUR • 1964 • King Allan • CND
LYNX • 1989 • Reichle Franz • DOC • SWT
LYNX, THE • 1914 • Bernard-Deschamps • FRN
LYNXEYE ON THE PROWL • 1915 • Read James • UKN
LYNXEYE TRAPPED • 1915 • Read James • UKN
LYNXEYE'S NIGHT OUT • 1915 • Read James • UKN
LYODOLOM see **LEDOLOM** • 1931
LYOGKAYA RUKA • 1967 • Kasper Veljo • USS • HE BRINGS LUCK ○ HAND OF LUCK
LYON LEA • 1915 • Korda Alexander, Pasztory Miklos M. • HNG • LEA LYON
LYON, PLACE BELLECOUR • 1895 • Lumiere Louis • FRN
LYON, PLACE DES CORDELIERS • 1895 • Lumiere Louis • FRN
LYON'S DEN • 1980 • Parker Graham • MTV • CND
LYONS IN PARIS, THE • 1955 • Guest Val • UKN
LYON'S MAIL • 1919 • *Irving Henry B.* • USA
LYONS MAIL, THE • 1916 • Paul Fred • UKN
LYONS MAIL, THE • 1931 • Maude Arthur • UKN
LYOTCHIKI • 1935 • Raizman Yuli • USS • MEN ON WINGS ○ PILOTS, THE ○ FLYERS
LYRE OF DELIRIUM see **LIRA DO DELIRIO, A** • 1979
LYS • 1987 • Thorsen Jens Jorgen • DNM • LIGHT
LYS CASSE, LE • 1988 • Melancon Andre • DOC • CND • DEATH OF A SILENCE
LYS DE LA VIE, LE • 1920 • Fuller Loie • FRN • LILY OF LIFE, THE
LYS D'OR, LE • 1910 • Perret Leonce • FRN
LYS ROUGE, LE • 1920 • Maudru Charles • FRN
LYSET I NATTEN • 1953 • Roos Jorgen • DOC • DNM
LYSIS • 1948 • Markopoulos Gregory J. • SHT • USA
LYSISTRATA • 1948 • Stoger Alfred • AUS
LYSISTRATA • 1968 • Matt Jon • USA
LYSTENSTYRET see **HUSKORS, ET** • 1914
LYUBIMETZ 13 • 1958 • Yanchev Vladimir • BUL • FAVOURITE NO.13
LYUBIT CHELOVYEKA • 1972 • Gerasimov Sergei • USS • TO LOVE A PERSON ○ GRADOSTROYITELI ○ CITY-BUILDERS, THE ○ FOR THE LOVE OF MAN ○ TO LOVE A MAN
LYUBOV K TREM APELSINAM • 1970 • Titov Victor • USS, BUL • LOVE FOR THREE ORANGES
LYUBOV YAROVAYA • 1970 • Frid Ya. • USS
LYUBOVTA E NEMIRNA PTITSA • 1990 • Vulchanov Rangel • BUL • LOVE IS A WILFUL BIRD
LYUDI • 1966 • Chukhrai Grigori • USS • PEOPLE
LYUDI GREKHA I KROVI • 1917 • Chargonin Alexander • USS • PEOPLE OF SIN AND BLOOD
LYUDI I ZVERI • 1962 • Gerasimov Sergei, Kohlert Lutz • USS, GDR • MENSCHEN UND TIERE (GDR) ○ MEN AND BEASTS ○ PEOPLE AND BEASTS
LYUDI NA MOSTU • 1960 • Zarkhi Alexander • USS • PEOPLE ON THE BRIDGE ○ MEN ON THE BRIDGE
LYULSKI DOZHD • 1967 • Khutsiev Marlen • USS • JULY SHOWER, A ○ YULSKII DOZHD ○ JULY RAIN ○ RAIN IN JULY
LYUTY • 1974 • Okeyev Tolomush • USS • GREY FIERCE ONE, THE ○ FIERCE ONE, THE ○ FEROCIOUS ONE, THE

M

M • 1931 • Lang Fritz • FRG • MORDER UNTER UNS
M • 1951 • Losey Joseph • USA
M-88 • 1970 • Bral Jacques • FRN
M.A.S. • 1942 • Marcellini Romolo • ITL
M.A.D.D. -MOTHERS AGAINST DRUNK DRIVERS • 1982 • Graham William A. • TVM • USA
M.A.R.S. see **RADIO-MANIA** • 1923
M COMME MATHIEU • 1970 • Adam Jean-Francois • FRN
M. ERICH ZANN • 1975 • Venisse Alain, Cazassus Bernard • FRN • MONSIEUR ERICH ZANN
M FOR MOTORIZATION see **M JAK MOTORYZACJA** • 1972
M. HERMAN SMITH-JOHANNSEN DIT JACK RABBIT • 1975 • Brault Francois • DCS • CND
M JAK MOTORYZACJA • 1972 • Trzos-Rastawiecki Andrzej • SHT • PLN • M FOR MOTORIZATION
M. LE MAIRE • 1953 • Garceau Raymond • DCS • CND • MR. MAYOR
M. LEBIDOIS PROPRIETAIRE • 1922 • Colombier Piere • FRN
M. LECOQ • 1915 • *La Badie Florence* • USA
M.M.M.83 -MISSIONE MORTALE MOLO 83 • 1966 • Bergonzelli Sergio • ITL, FRN, SPN • OBJECTIF HAMBOURG MISSION 083 (FRN) ○ M.M.M.83 (USA) ○ M.M.M.83 -OPERATION, DEATH ON WHARF 83
M.M.M.83 -OPERATION, DEATH ON WHARF 83 see **M.M.M.83 -MISSIONE MORTALE MOLO 83** • 1966
M.M.M.83 (USA) see **M.M.M.83 -MISSIONE MORTALE MOLO 83** • 1966
M (METROPOLIS) • 1988 • O'Neill Maria De Mater • SHT • PRC
M.P. CASE, THE see **ZAAK M.P., DE** • 1960
M. PINSON, POLICIER • 1915 • Feyder Jacques, Ravel Gaston • FRN
M STATION: HAWAII • 1970 • Lord Jack • TVM • USA
M.T.B. see **HELL BOATS** • 1969
M.T. DOME'S AWFUL NIGHT • 1916 • *Armstrong Billy* • USA
M TUTTI W TOI • 1975 • Mangini Gino • ITL
M3: THE GEMINI STRAIN see **PLAGUE** • 1978
MA A ADH-DHIKRAYAT • 1960 • Arafa Saad • EGY • SOUVENIRS D'AMOUR
MA AND DAD • 1912 • *Thanhouser* • USA
MA AND PA • 1922 • Del Ruth Roy • SHT • USA
MA AND PA KETTLE • 1949 • Lamont Charles • USA
MA AND PA KETTLE AT HOME • 1954 • Lamont Charles • USA

MA AND PA KETTLE AT THE FAIR • 1952 • Barton Charles T. • USA
MA AND PA KETTLE AT WAIKIKI • 1955 • Sholem Lee • USA
MA AND PA KETTLE BACK ON THE FARM • 1951 • Sedgwick Edward • USA
MA AND PA KETTLE GO TO PARIS (UKN) see **MA AND PA KETTLE ON VACATION** • 1953
MA AND PA KETTLE GO TO TOWN • 1950 • Lamont Charles • USA • GOING TO TOWN (UKN)
MA AND PA KETTLE ON VACATION • 1953 • Lamont Charles • USA • MA AND PA KETTLE GO TO PARIS (UKN)
MA AND PA PLAY POKER • 1914 • *Joker* • USA
MA AND THE BOYS • 1913 • *Crystal* • USA
MA BARKER'S KILLER BROOD • 1960 • Karn Bill • USA
MA BELLE • 1983 • Tammer Peter • DOC • ASL
MA BELLE MARSEILLE see **JUSTIN DE MARSEILLE** • 1934
MA BLONDE, ENTENDS-TU DANS LA VILLE? • 1979 • Gilson Rene • FRN
MA CHE MUSICA MAESTRO • 1971 • Laurenti Mariano • ITL
MA CHERE TERRE • 1976-77 • Brault Michel, Gladu Andre • DCS • CND
MA CHERIE • 1980 • Dubreuil Charlotte • BLG, FRN
MA CHERIE see **HABIBATI** • 1973
MA CHI TE LO FARE? • 1948 • Ferronetti Ignazio • ITL • SIRENA DEL GOLFO, LA
MA CHI TI HA DATO LA PATENTE? • 1970 • Cicero Nando • ITL
MA COME FANNO A FARLI COSI BELLI? • 1980 • Bozzetto Bruno • ASS • ITL
MA COUSINE DE VARSOVIE • 1931 • Gallone Carmine • FRN
MA ES HOLNAP • 1912 • Curtiz Michael • HNG • TODAY AND TOMORROW
MA FAMILLE • 1928-38 • Tessier Albert • DCS • CND
MA FEMME EST FORMIDABLE • 1951 • Hunebelle Andre • FRN
MA FEMME EST PDG see **MERATI MOUDIR AME** • 1966
MA FEMME EST UNE HIPPIE see **ZAWGATI MINA AL-HIBBI** • 1972
MA FEMME EST UNE PANTHERE • 1961 • Bailly Raymond • FRN • MY WIFE IS A PANTHER (USA)
MA FEMME EST UNE SORCIERE (FRN) see **I MARRIED A WITCH** • 1942
MA FEMME ET LE CHIEN see **ZAWGATI WA AL-KALB** • 1970
MA FEMME.. HOMME D'AFFAIRES • 1932 • de Vaucorbeil Max • FRN
MA FEMME, MA GOSSE ET MOI see **AMOUR EST UN JEU, L'** • 1957
MA FEMME, MA VACHE ET MOI • 1951 • Devaivre Jean • FRN
MA FEMME S'APPELLE REVIENS • 1982 • Leconte Patrice • FRN
MA FEMME VOUS PLAIT, J'ADORE LA VOTRE see **FEMMES VICIEUSES** • 1974
MA FILLE • 1911 • Carre Michel • FRN
MA HERMANO FIDEL • 1977 • Alvarez Santiago • DOC • CUB
MA, HE'S MAKING EYES AT ME • 1940 • Schuster Harold • USA
MA HOGAN'S NEW BOARDER • 1915 • Longford Raymond • ASL
MA JEANNETTE ET MES COPAINS • 1953 • Menegoz Robert • SHT • FRN
MA-K'O P'O-LO • 1975 • Chang Ch'Eh • HKG • MARCO POLO
MA L'AMOR • 1913 • Caserini Mario • ITL
MA LASKA S JAKUBEM • 1982 • Matejka Vaclav • CZC • MY LOVE WITH JAMES
MA LIHHYA ZAHR • 1948 • Barakat Henry • EGY • C'EST BIEN MA VEINE
MA-MA • 1976 • Bostan Elisabeta • RMN, USS, FRN
MA-NIM, THE see **JANYEONMON** • 1985
MA NO IKE • 1923 • Kinugasa Teinosuke • JPN • SPIRIT OF THE POND, THE
MA NON C'E BISOGNO DI DENARO see **NON C'E BISOGNO DI DENARO** • 1933
MA NON E UNA COSA SERIA • 1936 • Camerini Mario • ITL, FRG • MANN DER NICHT NEIN SAGEN KANN, DER (FRG) ○ BUT IT'S NOTHING SERIOUS (USA)
MA NUIT CHEZ MAUD • 1969 • Rohmer Eric • FRN • MY NIGHT WITH MAUD (UKN) ○ MY NIGHT AT MAUD'S (USA)
MA PETITE FOLIE • 1953 • Labro Maurice • FRN
MA PETITE MARQUISE • 1937 • Peguy Robert • FRN
MA POMME • 1950 • Sauvajon Marc-Gilbert • FRN
MA SKRYF MATRIEK • 1975 • SAF
MA SOEUR see **UKHTI** • 1970
MA SOEUR ANNE see **BARON FANTOME, LE** • 1942
MA SOEUR DE LAIT • 1938 • Boyer Jean • FRN
MA TANTE • 1903 • Zecca Ferdinand • FRN
MA TANTE D'HONFLEUR • 1923 • Saidreau Robert • FRN
MA TANTE D'HONFLEUR • 1931 • Maurice D. B. • FRN
MA TANTE D'HONFLEUR • 1948 • Jayet Rene • FRN
MA TANTE DICTATEUR • 1939 • Pujol Rene • FRN • MONSIEUR NICOLAS, NOURRICE
MA TAQULSHI-LI AH'AD • 1951 • Barakat Henry • EGY • NE LE DIS A PERSONNE
MA VAGY HOLNAP • 1965 • Kovacs Andras • DCS • HNG • TODAY OR TOMORROW
MA VART HUS FORSKONASFRAN TIGRAR • 1973 • Axelman Torbjorn • SWD • HOUSE SAFE FOR TIGERS, A
MA VIE see **HAYATI** • 1970
MA VIE C'EST A MOI • 1986 • Macina Michael • MTV • CND
MAA • 1951 • Roy Bimal • IND
MAA BHOOMI • 1979 • Ghose Goutam • IND • OUR LAND
MAA ON SYNTINEN LAULAU • 1973 • Mollberg Rauni • FNL • EARTH IS A SINFUL SONG, THE (USA) ○ EARTH IS OUR SINFUL SONG ○ LAND IS A SINFUL SONG, THE
MAA VANDINA • 1967 • Pratyagathma K. • IND • OUR SISTER-IN-LAW
MAADI VEETU MAAPILLAI • 1967 • Chary S. K. A. • IND • SON-IN-LAW WHO STAYS ON THE TOP FLOOR, THE
MA'AGALIM • 1980 • Schehori Idith • ISR • CIRCLES
MAAN • 1954 • *Biswas Anil (M)* • IND
MAANEPRINSESSEN • 1916 • Holger-Madsen • DNM • MYSTERIOUS LADY, THE ○ KAMAELEONEN ○ MAY FLY, THE
MAANGALYA BHAAGYAM • 1958 • Raghunath T. R. • IND
MAARAKAT ALGER see **BATTAGLIA DI ALGERI, LA** • 1965
MAARAKAT MADINAT AL JAZAER see **BATTAGLIA DI ALGERI, LA** • 1965
MAARAKE • 1985 • Assaf Roger • LBN
MAARETA MARUNA see **MARJA PIENI!** • 1972
MAASEUDUN TELEVAISUUS? • 1970 • Jarva Risto • SHT • FNL • WHAT IS THE FUTURE OF RURAL SETTLEMENTS?
MABABANGONG BANGUNGOT • 1977 • Tahimik Kidlat • PHL • PERFUMED NIGHTMARE, THE
MABAD AL-HUBB • 1961 • Salem Atef • EGY • TEMPLE DE L'AMOUR, LE
MABEL AND FATTY'S SIMPLE LIFE see **MABEL'S AND FATTY'S SIMPLE LIFE** • 1915
MABEL AT THE WHEEL • 1914 • Normand Mabel, Sennett Mack • USA • HIS DAREDEVIL QUEEN ○ HOT FINISH
MABEL, FATTY AND THE LAW • 1915 • Normand Mabel, Dillon Eddie • USA
MABEL LOST AND WON • 1915 • Normand Mabel • USA
MABEL'S ADVENTURES • 1912 • Sennett Mack • USA
MABEL'S AND FATTY'S MARRIED LIFE • 1915 • Normand Mabel, Dillon Eddie • USA
MABEL'S AND FATTY'S SIMPLE LIFE • 1915 • Normand Mabel, Dillon Eddie • USA • FATTY AND MABEL'S SIMPLE LIFE ○ MABEL AND FATTY'S SIMPLE LIFE
MABEL'S AND FATTY'S WASH DAY • 1915 • Normand Mabel, Dillon Eddie • USA
MABEL'S AWFUL MISTAKE • 1913 • Sennett Mack • USA
MABEL'S BARE ESCAPE see **MABEL'S BEAR ESCAPE** • 1914
MABEL'S BEAR ESCAPE • 1914 • Nicholls George • USA • MABEL'S BARE ESCAPE
MABEL'S BEAU • 1912 • *Trunnelle Mabel* • USA
MABEL'S BLUNDER • 1914 • *Normand Mabel* • USA
MABEL'S BUSY DAY • 1914 • Chaplin Charles, Normand Mabel • USA • CHARLIE AND THE SAUSAGES ○ LOVE AND LUNCH ○ HOT DOGS
MABEL'S DRAMATIC CAREER • 1913 • Sennett Mack, Nicholls George • USA
MABEL'S FLIRTATION see **HER FRIEND THE BANDIT** • 1914
MABEL'S HEROES • 1913 • Nicholls George, Sennett Mack (Spv) • USA
MABEL'S LATEST PRANK • 1914 • Sennett Mack • USA
MABEL'S LOVERS • 1912 • Sennett Mack • USA
MABEL'S MARRIED LIFE • 1914 • Chaplin Charles, Normand Mabel • USA • WHEN YOU'RE MARRIED ○ SQUAREHEAD, THE
MABEL'S NERVE • 1914 • Nicholls George • USA
MABEL'S NEW HERO • 1913 • Sennett Mack • USA
MABEL'S NEW JOB • 1914 • Normand Mabel, Nicholls George • USA
MABEL'S STORMY LOVE AFFAIR • 1914 • Nicholls George • USA
MABEL'S STRANGE PREDICAMENT • 1914 • Lehrman Henry, Sennett Mack • USA • HOTEL MIXUP
MABEL'S STRATAGEM • 1912 • Nicholls George • USA
MABEL'S WILFUL WAY • 1915 • Arbuckle Roscoe, Normand Mabel • USA
MABKA BILA HA'IT • 1974 • Nahhass Hashim An- • SHT • EGY • LAMENTATIONS SANS MUR
MABODET EL GAMAHIR • 1967 • Rafla Hilmy • EGY • PUBLIC IDEAL, THE
MABOROSHI GISTANE • 1958 • Mori Masaki • JPN
MABOROSHI KUROZUKIN: YAMI NI TOBU KAGE • 1967 • Kurata Junji • JPN • BLACK NINJA
MABOROSHI NO UMA • 1955 • Shima Koji • JPN • PHANTOM HORSE, THE
MABOROSHI NO MIZUUMI • 1982 • Hashimoto S. • JPN • LAKE OF ILLUSION
MABOULE • 1969 • Hoedeman Co • ANS • CND • ODDBALL
MABRUK ALIK • 1974 • Jabara Jad-Allah • SDN
MABUL • 1927 • Ivanov-Barkov Yevgeni • USS • FLOOD
MABUTA NO HAHA • 1931 • Inagaki Hiroshi • JPN • IMAGE OF A MOTHER, THE
MAC AND ME • 1989 • Raffill Stewart • USA
MACABRA see **DEMONOID, MESSENGER OF DEATH** • 1981
MACABRE • 1958 • Castle William • USA
MACABRE see **MACABRO** • 1980
MACABRE CONCERT see **CONCIERTO MACABRO**
MACABRE DR. SCIVANO, THE see **MACABRO DR. SCIVANO, O** • 1971
MACABRE LEGACY, A (USA) see **HERENCIA MACABRA** • 1940
MACABRE MARK, THE see **HUELLA MACABRA, LA** • 1962
MACABRE SERENADE see **HOUSE OF EVIL, THE** • 1968
MACABRE TRUNK, THE (USA) see **BAUL MACABRO, EL** • 1936
MACABRO • 1980 • Bava Lamberto • ITL • FROZEN TERROR ○ MACABRE
MACABRO DR. SCIVANO, O • 1971 • Calhado R., Cacador Rosalvo • BRZ • MACABRE DR. SCIVANO, THE
MACABRO (USA) see **TABU N.2** • 1965
MACADAM • 1946 • Blistene Marcel, Feyder Jacques (U/c) • FRN • BACK STREETS OF PARIS (USA)
MACADAM FLOWERS, THE (USA) see **FLEURS DE MACADAM, LES** • 1969
MACAHANS, THE • 1976 • McEveety Bernard • TVM • USA
MACAO • 1952 • von Sternberg Josef, Ray Nicholas (U/c) • USA
MACAO • 1988 • Klopfenstein Clemens • SWT
MACAO, L'ENFER DU JEU • 1939 • Delannoy Jean • FRN • MASK OF KOREA (USA) ○ GAMBLING HELL (UKN) ○ ENFER DU JEU, L'
MACAQUE, LE • 1972 • Suter Daniel • SWT
MACARIO • 1959 • Gavaldon Roberto • MXC
MACARIO CONTRO FANTOMAS see **MACARIO CONTRO ZAGOMAR** • 1944
MACARIO CONTRO ZAGOMAR • 1944 • Ferroni Giorgio • ITL • MACARIO CONTRO FANTOMAS
MACARONI see **MACCHERONI** • 1986
MACARONI BLUES see **MAKARONI BLUES** • 1985
MACARONI EATING COMPETITION • 1899 • Hepworth Cecil M. • UKN
MACARONI FEAST, A • 1905 • Collins Alf? • UKN
MACARONI SLEUTH, A • 1917 • Chaudet Louis W. • SHT • USA
MACARTHUR • 1977 • Sargent Joseph • USA • MACARTHUR: THE REBEL GENERAL (UKN)
MACARTHUR: THE REBEL GENERAL (UKN) see **MACARTHUR** • 1977
MACARTHUR'S CHILDREN see **SETOUCHI SHONEN YAKYUDAN** • 1984
MACAU • 1960 • Spiguel Miguel • SHT • PRT
MACAU, JOIA DO ORIENTE • 1957 • Spiguel Miguel • SHT • PRT
MACBETH • 1898 • *Robertson J. Forbes* • USA
MACBETH • 1908 • Blackton J. Stuart • USA
MACBETH • 1909 • Calmettes Andre • FRN
MACBETH • 1910 • Caserini Mario • ITL
MACBETH • 1911 • *Benson Frank* • UKN
MACBETH • 1913 • *Bourchier Arthur* • UKN, FRG
MACBETH • 1916 • FRN
MACBETH • 1916 • Emerson John • USA
MACBETH • 1921 • Oswald Richard • FRG
MACBETH • 1922 • Parkinson H. B. • UKN
MACBETH • 1922 • Schall Heinz • FRG
MACBETH • 1945 • Cass Henry • UKN
MACBETH • 1946 • Bradley David • USA
MACBETH • 1948 • Welles Orson • USA
MACBETH • 1950 • Stenholm Katherine • USA
MACBETH • 1953 • Deane Charles • UKN
MACBETH • 1961 • Schaefer George • UKN
MACBETH • 1970 • Gorrie John • MTV • UKN
MACBETH • 1971 • Polanski Roman • UKN
MACBETH • 1987 • d'Anna Claude • FRN
MACBETH • 1987 • Pentti Pauli • FNL
MACBETH see **MAGBET** • 1969
MACCABEI, I • 1910 • Guazzoni Enrico • ITL
MACCHERONI • 1986 • Scola Ettore • ITL • MACARONI
MACCHIA ROSA, UNA • 1970 • Muzii Enzo • ITL
MACCHIE SOLARI • 1975 • Crispino Armando • ITL
MACCHINA AMMAZZACATTIVI, LA • 1948 • Rossellini Roberto • ITL • ONE MACHINE TO KILL BAD PEOPLE ○ INFERNAL MACHINE, THE
MACCHINA CINEMA, LA • 1978 • Petraglia Sandro, Bellocchio Marco, Rulli Stefano, Agosti Silvano • ITL • CINEMA MACHINE, THE (USA)
MACDONALD see **SECRET LIVES OF THE BRITISH PRIME MINISTERS: MACDONALD, THE** • 1983
MACDONALD OF THE CANADIAN MOUNTIES (UKN) see **PONY SOLDIER** • 1952
MACDONALD'S FARM • 1951 • Cowan Will • SHT • USA
MACDOUGAL'S AEROPLANE • 1915 • Read James • UKN
MACE • 1988 • Simpson Michael A. • USA
MACE see **SOFIA CONSPIRACY, THE** • 1988
MACEDOINE see **OPERATION MACEDOINE** • 1970
MACEDONIA'S PART OF HELL see **MAKEDONSKI DEO PAKLA** • 1972
MACH 78 see **DAREDEVIL DRIVERS** • 1978
MACH' MICH GLUCKLICH • 1935 • Robison Arthur • FRG
MACH MIR DIE WELT ZUM PARADIES (FRG) see **FOR HENNES SKULL** • 1930
MACHE ALLES • 1971 • Nachmann Kurt • FRG • BED PARTNERS
MACHEKHA • 1973 • Bondarev Oleg • USS
MACHETE • 1958 • Neumann Kurt • USA
MACHI • 1939 • Yamamoto Satsuo • JPN • STREET
MACHI • 1961 • Yagi Miyoji • JPN • OUR TOWN
MACHI-BUSE • 1970 • Inagaki Hiroshi • JPN • AMBUSH, THE
MACHI KARA MACHI E TSUMUJI-KAGE • 1961 • Matsuo Akinori • JPN • FOR THIS WE FIGHT
MACHI NI IZUMI GA ATTA • 1968 • Asano Masao • JPN • WHERE LOVE SPRINGS
MACHI NO HITOBITO • 1926 • Gosho Heinosuke • JPN • TOWN PEOPLE ○ PEOPLE IN THE TOWN
MACHI NO MONOGATARI • 1924 • Hosoyama K. • JPN • STORY OF THE STREETS, A
MACHI NO TEJINASHI • 1925 • Murata Minoru • JPN • STREET JUGGLER
MACHI NO UWASA MO SANJU GO NICHI • 1960 • Murayama Mitsuo • JPN
MACHI TO GESUI • 1953 • Hani Susumu • DOC • JPN • DRAINS IN THE CITY ○ TOWN AND ITS DRAINS, THE
MACHIBOKE NO ONNA • 1946 • Makino Masahiro • JPN • WOMAN WHO IS WAITING
MACHINE see **MASZYNA** • 1961
MACHINE, DIE • 1973 • Sanders Helma • FRG
MACHINE, LA • 1977 • Vecchiali Paul • FRN
MACHINE A PARLER D'AMOUR, LA • 1963 • Rossi Jean-Baptiste • SHT • FRN
MACHINE A REFAIRE LA VIE, LA • 1924 • Duvivier Julien, Lepage Henri • FRN • MACHINE FOR RECREATING LIFE, A (USA)
MACHINE A REFAIRE LA VIE, LA • 1933 • Duvivier Julien, Lepage Henri • FRN
MACHINE A RETROUVER LE TEMPS, LA • 1956 • Image Jean • ANS • FRN • MISTER WISTER THE TIME TWISTER (USA)
MACHINE A VAPEUR, PHYSIQUE ET RATIONALITE, LA • 1970 • Lamothe Arthur • DCS • CND
MACHINE AGE, THE see **KALYUG** • 1980
MACHINE ET L'HOMME, LA • 1962 • Mitry Jean • SHT • FRN
MACHINE FOR RECREATING LIFE, A (USA) see **MACHINE A REFAIRE LA VIE, LA** • 1924
MACHINE GUN, THE • 1971 • Thornhill Michael • SHT • ASL
MACHINE GUN KELLY • 1958 • Corman Roger • USA
MACHINE GUN MAMA • 1944 • Young Harold • USA
MACHINE GUN MCCAIN (USA) see **INTOCCABILI, GLI** • 1969
MACHINE HUMAINE, LA • 1956 • Mitry Jean • SHT • FRN
MACHINE MON AMIE • 1960 • Daquin Louis • SHT • FRN
MACHINE OF EDEN, THE • 1970 • Brakhage Stan • USA
MACHINE STOPS, THE • 1964 • Saville Philip • UKN
MACHINE THAT THINKS, A • 1924 • *Bray John R. (P)* • ANS • USA
MACHINE VOLANTE, LA • 1902 • Zecca Ferdinand • FRN
MACHINERIE, LA see **MACHINES** • 1946
MACHINES • 1946 • Mulholland Donald • SHT • CND • MACHINERIE, LA
MACHINES A SOUS, LES • 1976 • Launois Bernard • FRN
MACHINES (USA) see **MASCHINE, DIE** • 1966
MACHINING OF METALS, THE • 1952 • Cole Lionel • DOC • UKN

MACHISMO see **MACHISMO -40 GRAVES FOR 40 GUNS** • 1970
MACHISMO -40 GRAVES FOR 40 GUNS • 1970 • Hunt Paul • USA • FORTY GRAVES FOR FORTY GUNS ○ GREAT GUNDOWN, THE ○ EL SALVEJO ○ MACHISMO ○ SAVAGE, THE
MACHNOWER SCHLEUSEN, DIE • 1927 • Jutzi Phil • FRG
MACHO, EL • 1977 • Andrei Marcello • ITL • EL MACHO
MACHO CALLAHAN • 1970 • Kowalski Bernard • USA
MACHOES, OS • 1972 • Farias Reginaldo • BRZ
MACHORKA-MUFF • 1962 • Straub Jean-Marie • SHT • FRG
MACHT DER BERGE, DIE • 1938 • Ucicky Gustav • FRG • POWER OF THE MOUNTAINS, THE (USA)
MACHT DER FINSTERNIS, DIE • 1923 • Wiene Conrad • FRG • POWER OF DARKNESS, THE
MACHT DER GEFUHLE, DIE • 1983 • Kluge Alexander • FRG
MACHT DER LIEBE, DIE see **SOHNE DER NACHT 2** • 1921
MACHT DER MANNER IST DIE GEDULD DER FRAUEN, DIE • 1978 • Perincioli Cristina • FRG • POWER OF MEN IS THE PATIENCE OF WOMEN, THE
MACHT DER MARY MURTON, DIE • 1921 • Porges Friedrich • AUS
MACHT DER VERSCHWORENEN see **GEHEIMBUNDSKLAVEN 2** • 1922
MACHT DER VERSUCHUNG • 1922 • Stein Paul L. • FRG
MACHT DES BLUTES 1 • 1921 • Eichberg Richard? • FRG • TOD IN VENEDIG, DER
MACHT DES BLUTES 2 • 1921 • Eichberg Richard? • FRG • IN DER SCHLINGE DES INDERS
MACHT DES GOLDES, DIE • 1912 • Gad Urban • FRG, DNM • GULDEN MAGT ○ GOLDEN MAGT
MACHT DES SCHICKSALS, DIE • 1915 • *Oliver-Film* • FRG
MACHT IN DUNKELN • 1947 • Wallbruck Hermann • AUS
MACHUCHAL AGENTE "O" EN NEW YORK • 1966 • Cortes Fernando • MXC, PRC
MACISTE • 1915 • Pastrone Giovanni • ITL
MACISTE AGAINST HERCULES IN THE VALE OF WOE see **MACISTE CONTRO ERCOLE NELLA VALLE DEI GUAI** • 1962
MACISTE ALLA CORTE DEL GRAN KHAN • 1961 • Freda Riccardo • FRN, ITL • GEANT A LA COUR DE KUBLAI KHAN, LE (FRN) ○ GOLIATH AND THE GOLDEN CITY ○ SAMSON AND THE SEVEN MIRACLES OF THE WORLD (USA) ○ MACISTE AT THE COURT OF THE GREAT KHAN
MACISTE ALLA CORTE DELLO ZAR • 1964 • Boccia Tanio • ITL • SAMSON VS. THE GIANT KING (USA) ○ GIANT OF THE LOST TOMB (UKN) ○ ATLAS AGAINST THE CZAR ○ MACISTE AT THE COURT OF THE CZAR
MACISTE ALL'INFERNO • 1926 • Brignone Guido • ITL • MACISTE IN HELL (USA)
MACISTE ALL'INFERNO • 1962 • Freda Riccardo • ITL • WITCH'S CURSE, THE (USA) ○ WITCHES CURSE, THE ○ MACISTE IN HELL
MACISTE ALPINO • 1916 • Pastrone Giovanni (c/d) • ITL
MACISTE AND THE NIGHT QUEEN see **MACISTE L'UOMO PIU FORTE DEL MONDO** • 1961
MACISTE AT THE COURT OF THE CZAR see **MACISTE ALLA CORTE DELLO ZAR** • 1964
MACISTE AT THE COURT OF THE GREAT KHAN see **MACISTE ALLA CORTE DEL GRAN KHAN** • 1961
MACISTE BROTHERS, THE see **INVINCIBILI FRATELLI MACISTE, GLI** • 1965
MACISTE CONTRE LA REINE DES AMAZONS • 1974 • de Nesle Robert • FRN • LUSTFUL AMAZONS, THE (UKN)
MACISTE CONTRE LES HOMMES DE PIERRE (FRN) see **MACISTE E LA REGINA DI SAMAR** • 1964
MACISTE CONTRO ERCOLE NELLA VALLE DEI GUAI • 1962 • Mattoli Mario • ITL • HERCULES IN THE VALE OF WOE (USA) ○ MACISTE AGAINST HERCULES IN THE VALE OF WOE
MACISTE CONTRO GLI UOMINI DELLA LUNA see **MACISTE E LA REGINA DI SAMAR** • 1964
MACISTE CONTRO I CACCIATORI DI TESTE • 1962 • Malatesta Guido • ITL • COLOSSUS AND THE HEADHUNTERS (UKN) ○ MACISTE CONTRO I TAGLIATORI DI TESTE
MACISTE CONTRO I MONGOLI • 1964 • Paolella Domenico • ITL • HERCULES AGAINST THE MONGOLS (USA)
MACISTE CONTRO I MOSTRI • 1962 • Malatesta Guido • ITL • FIRE MONSTERS AGAINST THE SON OF HERCULES (USA) ○ COLOSSUS OF THE STONE AGE(UKN) ○ MACISTE VS. THE MONSTERS
MACISTE CONTRO I TAGLIATORI DI TESTE see **MACISTE CONTRO I CACCIATORI DI TESTE** • 1962
MACISTE CONTRO IL VAMPIRO • 1961 • Gentilomo Giacomo, Corbucci Sergio • ITL • GOLIATH AND THE VAMPIRES (USA) ○ VAMPIRES, THE ○ MACISTE VS. THE VAMPIRE
MACISTE CONTRO LA MORTE • 1919 • Campogalliani Carlo • ITL
MACISTE CONTRO LO SCEICCO • 1925 • Camerini Mario • ITL
MACISTE CONTRO LO SCEICCO • 1962 • Paolella Domenico • ITL • SAMSON AGAINST THE SHEIK (USA)
MACISTE E LA REGINA DI SAMAR • 1964 • Gentilomo Giacomo • ITL, FRN • MACISTE CONTRE LES HOMMES DE PIERRE (FRN) ○ MACISTE ET LA REINE DE SAMAR ○ HERCULES AGAINST THE MOON MEN (USA) ○ MACISTE CONTRO GLI UOMINI DELLA LUNA ○ MACISTE VS. THE MOON MEN
MACISTE ET LA REINE DE SAMAR see **MACISTE E LA REGINA DI SAMAR** • 1964
MACISTE, GLADIATEUR DE SPARTE (FRN) see **MACISTE IL GLADIATORE DI SPARTA** • 1964
MACISTE, GLADIATOR OF SPARTA see **MACISTE IL GLADIATORE DI SPARTA** • 1964
MACISTE I • 1919 • Campogalliani Carlo • ITL
MACISTE IL GLADIATORE DI SPARTA • 1964 • Caiano Mario • ITL, FRN • TERROR OF ROME AGAINST THE SON OF HERCULES (USA) ○ MACISTE, SPARTAN GLADIATOR ○ MACISTE, GLADIATEUR DE SPARTE (FRN) ○ MACISTE, GLADIATOR OF SPARTA
MACISTE IL GLADIATORE PIU FORTE DEL MONDO • 1962 • Lupo Michele • ITL • DEATH IN THE ARENA (USA) ○ COLOSSUS OF THE ARENA ○ MACISTE, THE STRONGEST GLADIATOR IN THE WORLD
MACISTE IN GENGIS KHAN'S HELL see **MACISTE NELL'INFERNO DII GENGHIS KHAN** • 1964
MACISTE IN HELL see **MACISTE ALL'INFERNO** • 1962
MACISTE IN HELL (USA) see **MACISTE ALL'INFERNO** • 1926
MACISTE IN KING SOLOMON'S MINES see **MACISTE NELLE MINIERE DI RE SALOMONE** • 1964
MACISTE IN THE LIBERATOR see **LIBERATOR, THE** • 1918
MACISTE IN THE VALLEY OF KINGS see **MACISTE NELLA VALLE DEI RE** • 1960
MACISTE, L'EROE PIU GRANDE DEL MONDO • 1963 • Lupo Michele • ITL • GOLIATH AND THE SINS OF BABYLON (USA) ○ SINS OF BABYLON, THE ○ MACISTE, THE WORLD'S GREATEST HERO
MACISTE L'UOMO PIU FORTE DEL MONDO • 1961 • Leonviola Antonio • ITL • MOLE MEN VS. THE SON OF HERCULES (USA) ○ MACISTE AND THE NIGHT QUEEN ○ STRONGEST MAN IN THE WORLD, THE (UKN) ○ MACISTE, THE STRONGEST MAN IN THE WORLD
MACISTE MAGNIFICENT see **MARVELOUS MACISTE, THE** • 1915
MACISTE NELLA TERRA DEI CICLOPI • 1961 • Leonviola Antonio • ITL • ATLAS AGAINST THE CYCLOPS (USA) ○ MONSTER FROM THE UNKNOWN WORLD ○ ATLAS IN THE LAND OF THE CYCLOPS ○ ATLAS VS. THE CYCLOPS
MACISTE NELLA VALLE DEI RE • 1960 • Campogalliani Carlo • ITL, FRN, YGS • GEANT DE LA VALLEE DES ROIS, LE (FRN) ○ MACISTE THE MIGHTY (UKN) ○ SON OF SAMSON (USA) ○ GIANT OF THE VALLEY OF KINGS ○ MACISTE IN THE VALLEY OF KINGS
MACISTE NELLE MINIERE DI RE SALOMONE • 1964 • Regnoli Piero • ITL • SAMSON IN KING SOLOMON'S MINES (USA) ○ MACISTE IN KING SOLOMON'S MINES
MACISTE NELL'INFERNO DII GENGHIS KHAN • 1964 • Paolella Domenico • ITL • HERCULES AGAINST THE BARBARIANS (USA) ○ MACISTE IN GENGIS KHAN'S HELL
MACISTE POLIZIOTTO • 1918 • Roberti Roberto Leone • ITL
MACISTE, SPARTAN GLADIATOR see **MACISTE IL GLADIATORE DI SPARTA** • 1964
MACISTE THE MIGHTY (UKN) see **MACISTE NELLA VALLE DEI RE** • 1960
MACISTE, THE STRONGEST GLADIATOR IN THE WORLD see **MACISTE IL GLADIATORE PIU FORTE DEL MONDO** • 1962
MACISTE, THE STRONGEST MAN IN THE WORLD see **MACISTE L'UOMO PIU FORTE DEL MONDO** • 1961
MACISTE, THE WORLD'S GREATEST HERO see **MACISTE, L'EROE PIU GRANDE DEL MONDO** • 1963
MACISTE TURISTA • 1917 • Sierra Chano • MXC
MACISTE UND DER STRAFLING NR.51 • 1922 • *Pagano Bartolomeo* • FRG
MACISTE UND DIE CHINESISCHE TRUHE • 1923 • Boese Carl • FRG
MACISTE UND DIE TOCHTER DES SILBERKONIGS • 1922 • Borgnotto Romano Luigi • FRG
MACISTE VS. THE MONSTERS see **MACISTE CONTRO I MOSTRI** • 1962
MACISTE VS. THE MOON MEN see **MACISTE E LA REGINA DI SAMAR** • 1964
MACISTE VS. THE VAMPIRE see **MACISTE CONTRO IL VAMPIRO** • 1961
MACK, THE • 1973 • Campus Michael • USA • MACK AND HIS PACK, THE
MACK AND HIS PACK, THE see **MACK, THE** • 1973
MACK AT IT AGAIN • 1914 • Sennett Mack • USA
MACK THE KNIFE • 1989 • Golan Menahem • UKN • THREE-PENNY OPERA, THE
MACK THE KNIFE • 1989 • Tatoulis John, Smith Colin • ASL • IN TOO DEEP
MACKA • 1971 • Bourek Zlatko • YGS • CAT, THE
MACKAN • 1977 • Svensson Birgitta • SWD
MACKENNA'S GOLD • 1968 • Thompson J. Lee • USA
MACKEREL MOOCHER • 1962 • Hannah Jack • ANS • USA
MACKINTOSH • 1969 • Grigor Murray • DOC • UKN
MACKINTOSH AND T.J. • 1976 • Chomsky Marvin • USA
MACKINTOSH MAN, THE • 1973 • Huston John • USA, UKN
MACLOVIA • 1948 • Fernandez Emilio • MXC
MACOCHA • 1919 • Fencl Antonin • CZC
MACOMBER AFFAIR, THE • 1947 • Korda Zoltan • USA • WITHOUT HONOR
MACON COUNTY LINE • 1974 • Compton Richard • USA • KILLING TIME
MACON MALADROIT, LE • 1898 • Melies Georges • FRN • CLUMSY MASON, A
MACONS, LES • 1905 • Blache Alice • FRN
MACOUN THE TRAMP see **TULAK MACOUN** • 1939
MACRO (GUIDA UCCIDE IL VENERDI) • 1976 • Massi Stelvio • ITL
MACSKAJATEK • 1974 • Makk Karoly • HNG • CATSPLAY (USA) ○ CAT'S GAME
MACU, LA MUJER DEL POLICIA • 1986 • Hoogensteijn Solveig • VNZ • MACU, THE POLICEMAN'S WIFE
MACU, THE POLICEMAN'S WIFE see **MACU, LA MUJER DEL POLICIA** • 1986
MACUMBA see **DRAPEAU BLANC D'OXALA, LE** • 1969
MACUMBA LOVE • 1960 • Fowley Douglas • USA
MACUNAIMA • 1970 • de Andrade Joaquim Pedro • BRZ
MACUSHLA • 1937 • Bryce Alex • UKN • UNAUTHORISED ROAD
MAD ABOUT MEN • 1954 • Thomas Ralph • UKN
MAD ABOUT MONEY (USA) see **STARDUST** • 1937
MAD ABOUT MOONSHINE • 1941 • D'Arcy Harry • SHT • USA
MAD ABOUT MUSIC • 1938 • Taurog Norman • USA
MAD ABOUT OPERA (USA) see **FOLLIE PER L'OPERA** • 1948
MAD ADVENTURES OF RABBI JACOB, THE (USA) see **AVENTURES DE RABBI JACOB, LES** • 1973
MAD AS A MARS HARE • 1963 • Jones Charles M. • ANS • USA
MAD AT THE WORLD • 1955 • Essex Harry • USA
MAD ATLANTIC see **DOTO ICHIMAN-KAIRI** • 1966
MAD BAKER, THE • 1972 • *Maxwell Len/ Petok Ted (P)* • ANS • USA
MAD BOMBER, THE • 1973 • Gordon Bert I. • USA
MAD BOY, THE see **SHA HSIAO-TZU** • 1976
MAD BULL • 1977 • Doniger Walter, Steckler Len • TVM • USA • AGGRESSOR, THE
MAD BUTCHER, THE see **WURGER KOMMT AUF LEISEN SOCKEN, DER** • 1971
MAD BUTCHER OF VIENNA, THE see **WURGER KOMMT AUF LEISEN SOCKEN, DER** • 1971
MAD CANADIAN, THE • 1976 • Fortier Bob • CND
MAD CHECKMATE see **SEI SIMPATICHE CAROGNE** • 1968
MAD CLOUDS, THE see **NUAGES FOUS, LES** • 1962
MAD CONDUCT OF LOVE see **KURUTTA ITONAMI** • 1967
MAD, CRAZY AND VENGOS see **TRELLOS, PALAVOS KE VENGOS** • 1967
MAD DANCER, THE • 1925 • King Burton L. • USA
MAD DANE, THE see **GALE DANSKER, DEN** • 1970
MAD DOCTOR, THE • 1933 • Hand David • ANS • USA
MAD DOCTOR, THE • 1941 • Whelan Tim • USA • DATE WITH DESTINY, A (UKN)
MAD DOCTOR, THE • 1970 • *Stacey Dist.* • USA
MAD DOCTOR OF BLOOD ISLAND • 1969 • Romero Eddie, De Leon Gerardo • USA, PHL • TOMB OF THE LIVING DEAD ○ BLOOD DOCTOR
MAD DOCTOR OF MARKET STREET, THE • 1942 • Lewis Joseph H. • USA • TERROR OF THE ISLANDS
MAD DOG • 1976 • Mora Philippe • ASL • MAD DOG MORGAN
MAD DOG, THE • 1906 • Aylott Dave • UKN
MAD DOG, THE • 1932 • Gillett Burt • ANS • USA
MAD DOG, THE see **CHIEN FOU, LE** • 1966
MAD DOG COLL • 1961 • Balaban Burt • USA
MAD DOG GANG, THE • 1983 • Jennings Ross • TVM • UKN
MAD DOG MORGAN see **MAD DOG** • 1976
MAD DOG SCARE, A • 1910 • *Selig* • USA
MAD DOGS AND ENGLISHMEN • 1971 • Adidge Pierre • USA • JOE COCKER -MAD DOGS AND ENGLISHMEN
MAD EMPEROR, THE (USA) see **PATRIOTE, LE** • 1938
MAD EMPRESS, THE • 1939 • Contreras Torres Miguel • MXC, USA • CARLOTTA, THE MAD EMPRESS (UKN) ○ HOMBRE O DEMONIO (MXC)
MAD ESCAPADE OF A PLAYBOY, A see **MR. PEEK-A-BOO'S PLAYMATES** • 1962
MAD EXECUTIONERS, THE (USA) see **HENKER VON LONDON, DER** • 1963
MAD FOX, THE see **KOIYA KOI NASUNA KOI** • 1962
MAD FOXES, THE • Gray Paul • USA
MAD GAME, THE • 1933 • Cummings Irving • USA
MAD GARDENER'S SONG, THE see **CHANSON DU JARDINIER FOU, LA** • 1960
MAD GENIUS, THE • 1931 • Curtiz Michael • USA
MAD GHOUL, THE • 1943 • Hogan James P. • USA
MAD HATTER, THE • 1940 • Marcus Sid • ANS • USA
MAD HATTER, THE • 1948 • Lundy Dick • ANS • USA
MAD HATTER, THE see **BREAKFAST IN HOLLYWOOD** • 1946
MAD HATTERS, THE • 1935 • Campbell Ivar • UKN
MAD HEART see **RIDERA** • 1967
MAD HERMIT, THE • 1910 • *Thanhouser* • USA
MAD HERMIT, THE • 1914 • *Bison* • USA
MAD HERMIT, THE • 1917 • Ford Francis • SHT • USA
MAD HOLIDAY • 1936 • Seitz George B. • USA • COCKEYED CRUISE
MAD HOUR • 1928 • Boyle Joseph C. • USA
MAD HOUSE, A • 1934 • *Terry Paul/ Moser Frank (P)* • ANS • USA
MAD HOUSE, THE • 1934 • *Educational* • SHT • USA
MAD INFATUATION, A • 1910 • Bouwmeester Theo • UKN
MAD KING • 1933 • Farrow John • USA
MAD KING, THE • 1932 • *Terry Paul/ Moser Frank (P)* • ANS • USA
MAD LITTLE ISLAND (USA) see **ROCKETS GALORE** • 1958
MAD LOVE • 1935 • Freund Karl • USA • HANDS OF ORLAC (UKN)
MAD LOVE see **SAPPHO** • 1921
MAD LOVE OF A HOT VAMPIRE, THE • 1971 • *Parker Jim* • USA
MAD LOVER see **ENEMY OF WOMEN** • 1944
MAD LOVER, THE see **MODERN OTHELLO, A** • 1917
MAD, MAD HEART.. see **CUORE MATTO.. MATTO DA LEGARE** • 1967
MAD, MAD MONSTERS • 1972 • ANM • USA
MAD, MAD MOVIE MAKERS, THE • 1974 • Marsh Raymond • USA • LAST PORNO FLICK, THE
MAD MAD (UKN) see **NO PLACE TO LAND** • 1958
MAD.. MAD.. YOUTHS see **SHABAB MAGNOUN GEDDAN** • 1967
MAD MAESTRO, THE • 1939 • Harman Hugh • ANS • USA
MAD MAGAZINE PRESENTS UP THE ACADEMY see **UP THE ACADEMY** • 1980
MAD MAGICIAN, THE • 1954 • Brahm John • USA
MAD MAID OF THE FOREST, THE • 1915 • Clark Jack J. • USA
MAD MAJOR, THE see **SZALONY MAJOR** • 1972
MAD MAN'S WARD, THE • 1914 • Salter Harry • USA
MAD MARATHON, A • 1913 • *Selig* • USA
MAD MARRIAGE, THE • 1921 • Sturgeon Rollin S. • USA
MAD MARRIAGE, THE • 1925 • Donovan Frank P. • USA • SOULS ADRIFT
MAD MARTINDALES, THE • 1942 • Werker Alfred L. • USA • NOT FOR CHILDREN
MAD MASQUERADE (UKN) see **WASHINGTON MASQUERADE** • 1932
MAD MAX • 1979 • Miller George • ASL
MAD MAX 2 • 1981 • Miller George • ASL • ROAD WARRIOR, THE (USA)
MAD MAX: BEYOND THUNDERDOME • 1985 • Miller George, Ogilvie George • ASL
MAD MELODY • 1931 • Foster John, Davis Mannie • ANS • USA
MAD MEN OF EUROPE see **ENGLISHMAN'S HOME, AN** • 1939
MAD MESH • 1968 • Perry Dave • ASL
MAD MINER, THE • 1909 • *Selig* • USA
MAD MISS MANTON, THE • 1938 • Jason Leigh • USA
MAD MISSION • 1981 • Tseng Chih-Wei • HKG
MAD MISSION 2 see **TSUI-CHIA P'AI-TANG** • 1982
MAD MISSION 2: ACES GO PLACES see **TSUI-CHIA P'AI-TANG** • 1982
MAD MISSION 3 see **MAD MISSION 3: OUR MAN IN BOND STREET** • 1984

MAD MISSION 3: OUR MAN IN BOND STREET • 1984 • Xu Ke • HKG • OUR MAN FROM BOND STREET ○ ACES GO PLACES 3 ○ MAD MISSION 3
MAD MISSION 4 • 1986 • Lam Ringo • HKG
MAD MISSION PART 2: ACES GO PLACES see **TSUI-CHIA P'AI-TANG** • 1982
MAD MOKES AND MOTORS • 1915 • Collins Edwin J.? • UKN
MAD MONKEY, THE see **MONO LOCO, EL** • 1989
MAD MONKEY, THE (USA) see **BAG OF MONKEY NUTS, A** • 1911
MAD MONSTER • 1942 • Newfield Sam • USA
MAD MONSTER PARTY • 1967 • Bass Jules • ANM • USA
MAD MOUNTAINEER, THE • 1914 • Moore Tom • USA
MAD MURDERER AND SEX, THE see **LUCHADORAS CONTRA EL ROBOT ASESINO, LAS** • 1969
MAD MUSICIAN, THE • 1909 • Mottershaw Frank • UKN
MAD NEST • Hirsch Hy • SHT • USA
MAD NIGHT, A see **ZWARIOWANA NOC** • 1967
MAD PARADE, THE • 1931 • Beaudine William • USA • FORGOTTEN WOMEN (UKN)
MAD POISON see **LOCO VENENO** • 1988
MAD ROOM, THE • 1969 • Girard Bernard • USA
MAD SAINT see **PAGLA THAKUR** • 1967
MAD SCULPTOR, THE • 1913 • *Handworth Octavia* • USA
MAD SEA see **MARE MATTO** • 1963
MAD SEX see **SESSO MATTO** • 1973
MAD SHADOWS • 1979 • Till Eric • CND
MAD STAMPEDE, THE • 1917 • MacDonald J. Farrell • SHT • USA
MAD TALON, THE • 1919 • *Hansen Juanita* • USA
MAD TRAPPER, THE • 1979 • Hart Harvey • USA
MAD TRAPPER, THE see **CHALLENGE TO BE FREE** • 1972
MAD TRAPPER OF THE YUKON see **CHALLENGE TO BE FREE** • 1972
MAD WEDNESDAY (UKN) see **SIN OF HAROLD DIDDLEBOCK, THE** • 1946
MAD WHIRL, THE • 1925 • Seiter William A. • USA • JAZZ PARENTS
MAD WOMAN, THE • 1920 • Terwilliger George W. • SHT • USA
MAD WOMEN, THE see **LOCAS, LAS** • 1977
MAD WORLD, THE see **KOSMOS TRELLATHIKE, O** • 1967
MAD YOUTH • 1940 • Kent Willis • USA
MADAGASCAR • 1954 • Rouy • SHT • FRN
MADALENA • 1960 • Dimopoulos Dinos • GRC • MADDALENA
MADALJON SA TRI SRCA • 1962 • Slijepcevic Vladan • YGS • MEDALLION WITH THREE HEARTS
MADAM, THE • 1969 • *Stacey Dist.* • USA
MADAM BAVRI • 1989 • Islam Nazaral • PKS • MADAME BAVRI
MADAM BO' PEEP • 1917 • Withey Chet • USA
MADAM FLIRT AND HER ADOPTED UNCLE • 1908 • *Lubin* • USA
MADAM KITTY (USA) see **SALON KITTY** • 1976
MADAM SANS GIN • 1925 • Ruggles Wesley • SHT • USA
MADAM SATAN • 1930 • De Mille Cecil B. • USA
MADAM WHO? • 1917 • Barker Reginald • USA
MADAMA, LA • 1976 • Tessari Duccio • ITL
MADAMA ARLECCHINO see **SIGNORA ARLECCHINO, LA** • 1918
MADAMA BUTTERFLY • 1955 • Gallone Carmine • ITL, JPN • MADAME BUTTERFLY (UKN)
MADAMA MUSASHINO see **MUSASHINO FUJIN** • 1951
MADAME DE.. • 1953 • Ophuls Max • FRN, ITL • GIOIELLI DI MADAME DE.., I (ITL) ○ DIAMOND EARRINGS, THE ○ EARRINGS OF MADAME DE.., THE (USA)
MADAME O • 1970 • Fukuda Seiichi • JPN
MADAME AE MA • 1983 • Chong In-Yap • SKR
MADAME AKI see **YUSHU HEIYA** • 1963
MADAME AND WIFE see **MADAMU TO NYOBO** • 1931
MADAME BABYLAS AIME LES ANIMAUX • 1911 • Machin Alfred • FRN
MADAME BAVRI see **MADAM BAVRI** • 1989
MADAME BEHAVE • 1925 • Sidney Scott • USA • AL CHRISTIE'S "MADAME BEHAVE" ○ MADAME LUCY
MADAME BLAUBERT see **SCHICKSAL EINER SCHONEN FRAU, DAS** • 1932
MADAME BOVARY • 1933 • Renoir Jean • FRN
MADAME BOVARY • 1937 • Lamprecht Gerhard • FRG
MADAME BOVARY • 1949 • Minnelli Vincente • USA
MADAME BOVARY, IT'S ME see **PANI BOVARY TO JA** • 1977
MADAME BOVARY THAT'S ME see **PANI BOVARY TO JA** • 1977
MADAME BUTTERFLY • 1915 • Olcott Sidney • USA
MADAME BUTTERFLY • 1932 • Gering Marion • USA
MADAME BUTTERFLY (UKN) see **MADAMA BUTTERFLY** • 1955
MADAME CLAIRO • 1910 • *Powers* • USA
MADAME CLAUDE • 1978 • Jaeckin Just • FRN • FRENCH WOMAN, THE (USA)
MADAME CLAUDE 2 • 1981 • Mimet Francois • FRN • INTIMATE MOMENTS
MADAME COQUETTE • 1914 • *Theby Rosemary* • USA
MADAME CUBIST • 1916 • Henderson Lucius • SHT • USA
MADAME CURIE • 1943 • LeRoy Mervyn • USA
MADAME CYCLONE • 1916 • Ghione Emilio • ITL
MADAME DE MODE • 1912 • *Edison* • USA
MADAME DE THEBES • 1915 • Stiller Mauritz • SWD • SON OF DESTINY (UKN)
MADAME DEATH see **SENORA MUERTE, LA** • 1968
MADAME D'ORA • 1918 • von Cserepy Arzen • FRG
MADAME DOUBLE X • 1914 • *Beery Wallace* • USA
MADAME DU BARRY • 1910 • de Morlhon Camille • FRN
MADAME DU BARRY • 1934 • Dieterle William • USA
MADAME DU BARRY • 1954 • Christian-Jaque • FRN, ITL • DU BARRY, LA ○ MISTRESS DU BARRY
MADAME DUBARRY • 1919 • Lubitsch Ernst • FRG • PASSION (USA)
MADAME DUBARRY • 1928 • Neill R. William • SHT • USA
MADAME DUBARRY see **DU BARRY** • 1918
MADAME ET LE MORT • 1942 • Daquin Louis • FRN
MADAME ET SON AUTO • 1958 • Vernay Robert • FRN
MADAME ET SON FILLEUL • 1919 • Monca Georges • FRN
MADAME ET SON FLIRT • 1945 • de Marguenat Jean • FRN
MADAME FAIRUZ see **FAIRUZ HANIN** • 1951
MADAME FLIRT • 1918 • Negroni Baldassare • ITL
MADAME FRANKENSTEIN see **FIGLIA DI FRANKENSTEIN, LA** • 1971
MADAME G • 1952 • Miesch Jean-Luc • FRN
MADAME GUILLOTINE • 1931 • Fogwell Reginald • UKN
MADAME HAT AUSGANG • 1931 • Thiele Wilhelm • FRG
MADAME IM STRANDBAD • 1929 • *Bird Betty* • FRG
MADAME JEALOUSY • 1918 • Vignola Robert G. • USA
MADAME JULIE see **FILS DE L'AUTRE, LE** • 1931
MADAME JULIE (UKN) see **WOMAN BETWEEN, THE** • 1931
MADAME LA PRESIDENTE • 1916 • Lloyd Frank • USA • MADAME PRESIDENTE
MADAME LOUISE • 1951 • Rogers Maclean • UKN
MADAME LUCY see **MADAME BEHAVE** • 1925
MADAME MACHT EINEN SEITENSPRUNG • 1927 • Otto Hans • FRG
MADAME MYSTERY • 1926 • Laurel Stan, Wallace • SHT • USA
MADAME NE VEUT PAS D'ENFANTS • 1932 • Landau Constantin, Steinhoff Hans • FRN
MADAME NICOTINE • 1908 • *Gaudio Antonio (Ph)* • USA
MADAME OLGA'S PUPILS see **SEX ACADEMY**
MADAME PEACOCK • 1920 • Smallwood Ray C. • USA
MADAME PIMPERNEL (UKN) see **PARIS UNDERGROUND** • 1945
MADAME POMPADOUR • 1927 • Wilcox Herbert • UKN
MADAME PRESIDENTE see **MADAME LA PRESIDENTE** • 1916
MADAME PUTIPHAR see **FRU POTIFAR** • 1911
MADAME Q • 1929 • McCarey Leo • SHT • USA
MADAME RACKETEER • 1932 • Hall Alexander, Gribble Harry Wagstaff • USA • SPORTING WIDOW, THE (UKN)
MADAME RECAMIER • 1920 • Delmont Joseph • FRG
MADAME RECAMIER • 1928 • Ravel Gaston (c/d) • FRN
MADAME RECAMIER: OR, THE PRICE OF VIRTUE • 1923 • Greenwood Edwin • UKN
MADAME REX • 1911 • Griffith D. W. • USA
MADAME ROSA (USA) see **VIE DEVANT SOI, LA** • 1977
MADAME ROSE • Bernard Jean Laurent • FRN
MADAME SANS-GENE • 1909 • Larsen Viggo • DNM
MADAME SANS-GENE • 1911 • Calmettes Andre • FRN
MADAME SANS-GENE • 1911 • Pouctal Henri • FRN
MADAME SANS-GENE • 1921 • Negroni Baldassare • ITL
MADAME SANS-GENE • 1925 • Perret Leonce • USA
MADAME SANS-GENE • 1941 • Richebe Roger • FRN
MADAME SANS-GENE • 1945 • Amadori Luis Cesar • ARG • EN LA CORTE DE NAPOLEON
MADAME SANS-GENE • 1961 • Christian-Jaque • FRN, ITL, SPN • MADAME (UKN)
MADAME SANS JANE • 1925 • Roach Hal • SHT • USA
MADAME SE MUERT • 1961 • Cayrol Jean, Durand Claude • FRN
MADAME SHALL NOT KNOW see **OKUSAMA NI SHIRASU BEKARAZU** • 1937
MADAME SHERRY • 1917 • Dean Ralph • USA
MADAME SIN • 1971 • Greene David • UKN, USA
MADAME SOPRANI • 1963 • Giersz Witold • ANS • PLN
MADAME SOUSATZKA • 1989 • Schlesinger John • UKN
MADAME SPHINX • 1918 • Heffron Thomas N. • USA
MADAME SPY • 1918 • Gerrard Douglas • USA
MADAME SPY • 1934 • Freund Karl • USA
MADAME SPY • 1942 • Neill R. William • USA
MADAME TALLIEN • 1911 • de Morlhon Camille • FRN
MADAME TALLIEN • 1916 • Guazzoni Enrico • ITL
MADAME (UKN) see **MADAME SANS-GENE** • 1961
MADAME UND IHRE NICHTE • 1969 • Schroeder Eberhard • FRG
MADAME WAGT EINEN SEITENSPRUNG see **IM HOTEL "ZUR SUSSEN NACHTIGALL"** • 1928
MADAME WANTS NO CHILDREN see **MADAME WUNSCHT KEINE KINDER** • 1926
MADAME WHITE SNAKE see **BYAKU FUJIN NO YUREN** • 1956
MADAME WHITE SNAKE see **PAI-SHE CHUAN** • 1963
MADAME WHO? • 1918 • Barker Reginald • USA
MADAME WUNSCHT KEINE KINDER • 1926 • Korda Alexander • FRG • MADAME WANTS NO CHILDREN
MADAME WUNSCHT KEINE KINDER • 1932 • Steinhoff Hans • FRG, AUS
MADAME X • 1916 • Marion George F. • USA
MADAME X • 1920 • Lloyd Frank • USA
MADAME X • 1929 • Barrymore Lionel • USA • ABSINTHE
MADAME X • 1937 • Wood Sam, Machaty Gustav (U/c) • USA
MADAME X • 1960 • Laskos Orestis • GRC
MADAME X • 1966 • Rich David Lowell • USA
MADAME X • 1981 • Miller Robert Ellis • TVM • USA
MADAME X, DIE FRAU FUR DISKRETE BERATUNG • 1929 • Hofer Franz • FRG
MADAME X EINE ABSOLUTE HERRSCHERIN • 1978 • Ottinger Ulrike • FRG
MADAME X UND DIE "SCHWARZE HAND" • 1920 • Sauer Fred • FRG
MADAME ZENOBIA • 1973 • Cemano Eduardo • USA • ZENOBIA
MADAMIGELLA DI MAUPIN • 1966 • Bolognini Mauro • ITL, FRN • CHEVALIER DE MAUPIN, LE (FRN)
MADAM'S TANTRUMS • 1906 • *Walturdaw* • UKN
MADAMU TO NYOBO • 1931 • Gosho Heinosuke • JPN • NEIGHBOUR'S WIFE AND MINE, THE ○ MADAME AND WIFE ○ NEXT DOOR MADAME AND MY WIFE
MADAN MAJARI • 1934 • Prem Dhani Ram • IND
MADARA • 1972 • Jissoji Akio • JPN
MADARI MOHAN • 1940 • *Satyarani* • IND • KRISHNA MAYA
MADARKAK • 1971 • Boszormenyei Geza • HNG • BIRDIES ○ LITTLE BIRDIE
MADCAP, THE • 1913 • Conway Jack? • USA
MADCAP, THE • 1916 • Dowlan William C. • USA
MADCAP ADVENTURE, A • 1915 • Marston Theodore • USA
MADCAP ADVENTURES OF MR. TOAD, THE • 1949 • Algar James, Kinney Jack • ANM • USA
MADCAP AMBROSE • 1916 • Fishback Fred C. • SHT • USA
MADCAP AMBROSE • 1920 • *Hallmark* • USA
MADCAP ISLAND, THE see **HYOKKORI HYOTAN JIMA** • 1967
MADCAP MADGE • 1917 • West Raymond B. • USA
MADCAP MAGOO • 1955 • Burness Pete • ANS • USA
MADCAP MARY • 1914 • *Eagle Films* • UKN
MADCAP MODELS • 1941-43 • *Pal George (P)* • ASS • USA
MADCAP OF THE HILLS, THE • 1913 • *Cummings Irving* • USA
MADCAP OF THE VELD • 1920 • SAF
MADCAP QUEEN OF CRONA, THE • 1916 • Ford Francis • SHT • USA
MADCAP QUEEN OF GREDSHOFFEN, THE • 1915 • *Ford Francis* • USA
MADCAP (UKN) see **TAMING THE WILD** • 1936
MADCHEN AM KREUZ • 1929 • Fleck Jacob, Fleck Luise • FRG • SCHAM
MADCHEN AUF DEM BRETT, DAS • 1967 • Maetzig Kurt • GDR • GIRL ON THE DIVING BOARD, THE ○ GIRL ON THE BOARD, THE
MADCHEN AUS DEM GOLDENEN WESTEN, DAS • 1922 • Werckmeister Hans • FRG
MADCHEN AUS DEM KAUFHAUS X, DAS • 1918 • *Kuhnberg Leontine* • FRG
MADCHEN AUS DEM SUMPF, DAS • 1921 • Eichgrun Bruno • FRG
MADCHEN AUS DEM WARENHAUS, DAS see **MADEL AUS DEM WARENHAUS, DAS** • 1923
MADCHEN AUS DEM WILDEN WESTEN, DAS • 1919 • Schonfelder Erich • FRG
MADCHEN AUS DER ACKERSTRASSE 1, DAS • 1919 • Schunzel Reinhold • FRG
MADCHEN AUS DER ACKERSTRASSE 2, DAS • 1920 • Funck Werner • FRG
MADCHEN AUS DER ACKERSTRASSE 3, DAS see **WIE DAS MADCHEN AUS DER ACKERSTRASSE DIE HEIMAT FAND 3** • 1923
MADCHEN AUS DER FREMDE, DAS • 1921 • Jacoby Georg • FRG
MADCHEN AUS DER FREMDE, DAS • 1927 • Eckstein Franz • FRG
MADCHEN AUS DER FREMDE, DAS see **SEINE EXZELLENZ VON MADAGASKAR 1** • 1921
MADCHEN AUS DER KONFEKTION, DAS • 1951 • Boese Carl • FRG • UNSCHULD IN NOTEN
MADCHEN AUS DER OPIUMHOHLE, DAS • 1920 • *Andersen Iven* • FRG
MADCHEN AUS DER SUDSEE, DAS • 1950 • Muller Hans • FRG
MADCHEN AUS FLANDERN, EIN • 1956 • Kautner Helmut • FRG • GIRL FROM FLANDERS, THE (USA)
MADCHEN AUS FRISCO, DAS • 1927 • Neff Wolfgang • FRG
MADCHEN AUS PARIS, EIN • 1954 • Seitz Franz* • FRG
MADCHEN AUS ZWEITER HAND, EIN • 1976 • Ziebell Alexander • FRG • SECONDHAND GIRL
MADCHEN BEIM FRAUENARTZ • 1971 • Hofbauer Ernst • FRG
MADCHEN CHRISTINE, DAS • 1949 • Rabenalt Arthur M. • FRG • CHRISTINA (USA)
MADCHEN, DAS WARTETE, DAS • 1921 • Larsen Frederik • FRG
MADCHEN DER STRASSE, DAS • 1928 • Genina Augusto • FRG • SCAMPOLO ○ MADCHEN VON DER STRASS, DAS
MADCHEN, DIE MAN NICHT HEIRATET • 1924 • von Bolvary Geza • FRG
MADCHEN DIE NACH LIEBE SCHREIEN • 1973 • Dietrich Erwin C. • FRG • GIRLS WHO CRY OUT FOR LOVE (UKN)
MADCHEN, DIE SPURLOS VERSCHWINDEN see **KAMPF UM BLOND** • 1932
MADCHEN FUR ALLES • 1937 • Boese Carl • FRG
MADCHEN FUR DIE MAMBO-BAR • 1959 • Gluck Wolfgang • FRG • GIRLS FOR THE MAMBO BAR, THE (UKN) ○ $100 A NIGHT (USA)
MADCHEN GEHT AN LAND, EIN • 1938 • Hochbaum Werner • FRG • GIRL GOES ON SHORE, A
MADCHEN HINTER GITTERN • 1949 • Braun Alfred • FRG • GIRLS BEHIND BARS
MADCHEN HINTER GITTERN • 1965 • Zehetgruber Rudolf • FRG
MADCHEN, HUTET EUCH! • 1928 • Arnheim Valy • FRG
MADCHEN IM TIGERFELL, DAS see **GELIEBTE BESTIE** • 1959
MADCHEN IM VORZIMMER • 1940 • Lamprecht Gerhard • FRG
MADCHEN IN GEFAHR see **ENGEL IM SEPAREE -MADCHEN IN GEFAHR** • 1929
MADCHEN IN UNIFORM • 1931 • Sagan Leontine • FRG • MAIDENS IN UNIFORM ○ GIRLS IN UNIFORM
MADCHEN IN UNIFORM • 1958 • von Radvanyi Geza • FRG, FRN • JEUNE FILLES EN UNIFORME (FRN) ○ CHILDREN IN UNIFORM
MADCHEN IN WEISS • 1936 • Janson Victor • FRG • ICH BIN AUF DER WELT, UM GLUCKLICH ZU SEIN
MADCHEN IN WITTSTOCK • 1976 • Koepp Volker • GDR
MADCHEN IRENE, DAS • 1936 • Schunzel Reinhold • FRG
MADCHEN JOHANNA, DAS • 1935 • Ucicky Gustav • FRG • JOAN OF ARC
MADCHEN, MADCHEN • 1967 • Fritz Roger • FRG • GIRLS, GIRLS (UKN)
MADCHEN MARION, DAS • 1956 • Schleif Wolfgang • FRG • PREIS DER NATIONEN
MADCHEN MIT BEZIEHUNGEN • 1950 • von Rathony Akos • FRG
MADCHEN MIT DEM GOLDHELM, DAS • 1919 • Janson Victor • FRG
MADCHEN MIT DEM GUTEN RUF, DAS • 1938 • Schweikart Hans • FRG
MADCHEN MIT DEM MINI, DAS • 1965 • Milan Paul • AUS
MADCHEN MIT DEN FUNF NULLEN, DAS • 1927 • Bernhardt Curtis • FRG • GROSSE LOS, DAS
MADCHEN MIT DEN KATZENAUGEN, DAS • 1958 • York Eugen • FRG
MADCHEN MIT DEN SCHWEFELHOLZCHEN, DAS see **ARMES KLEINES MADCHEN** • 1924
MADCHEN MIT DEN SCHWEFELHOLZERN, DAS • 1925 • Bagier Guido • FRG
MADCHEN MIT DER HEISSEN MASCHE, DAS • 1971 • Billian Hans • FRG • LOVES OF A FRENCH PUSSYCAT, THE (UKN)
MADCHEN MIT POKURA, EIN • 1934 • von Cserepy Arzen • FRG
MADCHEN MIT SCHWACHEM GEDACHTNIS • 1956 • von Cziffra Geza • FRG
MADCHEN MIT SER PROTEKTION, DAS • 1925 • Mack Max • FRG

MADCHEN MIT ZUKUNFT • 1954 • Engel Thomas • FRG
MADCHEN OHNE GEWISSEN, DAS • 1922 • Kahn William • FRG
MADCHEN OHNE GRENZEN • 1955 • von Radvanyi Geza • FRG
MADCHEN OHNE HEIMAT, DAS • 1926 • David Constantin J. • FRG, AUS • VOM FREUDENHAUS IN DIE EHE
MADCHEN OHNE PYJAMA, DAS • 1957 • Quest Hans • FRG
MADCHEN OHNE VATERLAND, DAS • 1912 • Gad Urban • FRG, DNM • PIGEN UNDEN FAEDRELAND
MADCHEN ROSEMARIE, DAS • 1958 • Thiele Rolf • FRG • ROSEMARY (USA) ○ GIRL ROSEMARIE, THE
MADCHEN SCAMPOLO, DAS see **SCAMPOLO** • 1958
MADCHEN UND DER STAATSANWALT, DAS • 1962 • Goslar Jurgen • FRG
MADCHEN UND DIE MANNER, DAS • 1919 • Noa Manfred • FRG • GIRL AND THE MEN, THE
MADCHEN UND MANNER see **HARTE MANNER -HEISSE LIEBE** • 1956
MADCHEN VOM MOORHOF, DAS • 1935 • Sirk Douglas • FRG
MADCHEN VOM MOORHOF, DAS • 1958 • Ucicky Gustav • FRG • GIRL OF THE MOORS, THE (USA)
MADCHEN VOM PFARRHOF, DAS • 1955 • Lehner Alfred • AUS
MADCHEN VOM VARIETE, DAS see **WAHRE JAKOB, DER** • 1931
MADCHEN VON 16½, EIN • 1958 • Balhaus Carl • GDR
MADCHEN VON DER HEILSARMEE, DAS • 1927 • Kahn William • FRG
MADCHEN VON DER STRASS, DAS see **MADCHEN DER STRASSE, DAS** • 1928
MADCHEN VON FANO, DAS • 1940 • Schweikart Hans • FRG
MADCHEN VON GESTERN NACHT, DAS • 1938 • Brauer Peter P. • FRG • GIRL OF LAST NIGHT, THE (USA)
MADCHEN VON VALENCIA, DAS see **SCHMUGGLERBRAUT VON MALORCA, DIE** • 1929
MADCHEN WIE DAS MEER, EIN (FRG) see **GRANDE SAUTERELLE, LA** • 1967
MADCHEN ZUM HEIRATEN • 1932 • Thiele Wilhelm • FRG
MADCHENHANDEL • 1926 • Speyer Jaap • FRG
MADCHENHANDLER VON KAIRO, DER • *Wernicke Otto* • FRG
MADCHENHIRT, DER • 1919 • Grune Karl • FRG
MADCHENJAHRE EINER KONIGIN • 1936 • Engel Erich • FRG
MADCHENJAHRE EINER KONIGIN • 1954 • Marischka Ernst • AUS • PURSUIT AND LOVES OF QUEEN VICTORIA, THE ○ STORY OF VICKIE, THE (USA)
MADCHENKRIEG • 1977 • Sinkel Bernard • FRG • GIRL'S WAR
MADCHENPENSIONAT • 1936 • von Bolvary Geza • AUS • PRINZESSIN DAGMAR
MADCHENRAUBER • 1936 • Sauer Fred • FRG
MADCHENSCHICKSALE • 1928 • Lowenbein Richard • FRG
MADDALENA • 1954 • Genina Augusto • ITL
MADDALENA • 1972 • Kawalerowicz Jerzy • ITL, YGS • MAGDALENA
MADDALENA see **MADALENA** • 1960
MADDALENA FERAT • 1921 • Roberti Roberto Leone • ITL
MADDALENA ZERO IN CONDOTTA • 1936 • Vajda Ladislao • HNG
MADDALENA ZERO IN CONDOTTA • 1940 • De Sica Vittorio • ITL
MADDENING BLOW, THE see **CILDIRTAN DARBE** • 1967
MADDENING DESIRE see **ADEM ILE HAVVA** • 1967
MADDENING LIPS see **CILDIRTAN DUDAKLAR** • 1967
MADDEST CAR IN THE WORLD, THE see **VERRUCKTESTE AUTO DER WELT, DAS** • 1974
MADDINGLEY • 1954 • Bilcock David Sr. • DOC • ASL
MADE • 1972 • Mackenzie John • UKN
MADE A COWARD • 1913 • Duncan William • USA
MADE FOR EACH OTHER • 1939 • Cromwell John • USA
MADE FOR EACH OTHER • 1972 • Bean Robert B. • USA
MADE FOR LAUGHS • 1952 • Anderson James M. • UKN
MADE FOR LOVE • 1926 • Sloane Paul • USA
MADE IN AFRICA • 1919 • Miller Ashley • SHS • USA
MADE IN ARGENTINA • 1987 • Jusid Juan Jose • ARG
MADE IN AUSTRALIA • 1962 • Rafferty Chips • DOC • ASL
MADE IN AUSTRALIA • 1975 • Friedrichs Zbigniew • ASL
MADE IN COLOMBIA • 1974 • Emiliani Manuel Bousquets • SHT • CLM
MADE IN GERMANY • 1914 • Batley Ernest G.? • UKN
MADE IN GERMANY • 1957 • Schleif Wolfgang • FRG
MADE IN GERMANY UND U.S.A. • 1974 • Thome Rudolf • FRG
MADE IN GREECE • 1988 • Angelopoulos Panos • GRC
MADE IN HAWAII see **HANAUMA BAY** • 1985
MADE IN HEAVEN • 1921 • Schertzinger Victor • USA
MADE IN HEAVEN • 1952 • Carstairs John Paddy • UKN
MADE IN HEAVEN • 1987 • Rudolph Alan • USA
MADE IN IRAN see **SAKHTE IRAN** • 1978
MADE IN ITALY • 1965 • Loy Nanni • ITL, FRN • A L'ITALIENNE (FRN)
MADE IN JAPAN • 1972 • Kinoshita Ren-Zo • ANS • JPN
MADE IN PARADISE • 1969 • Weisz Frans • SHT • NTH
MADE IN PARIS • 1965 • Sagal Boris • USA
MADE IN QUEBEC • 1986 • Prefontaine Michel • MTV • CND
MADE IN SWEDEN • 1969 • Bergenstrahle Johan • SWD
MADE IN THE KITCHEN • 1921 • *Sennett Mack (P)* • SHT • USA
MADE IN U.S.A. • 1966 • Godard Jean-Luc • FRN
MADE IN USA • 1988 • Friedman Ken • USA • USA TODAY
MADE MANIFEST • 1980 • Brakhage Stan • SHT • USA
MADE ON BROADWAY • 1933 • Beaumont Harry • USA • GIRL I MADE, THE (UKN)
MADE-TO-ORDER HERO, A • 1928 • Lewis Edgar • USA
MADEIRA • 1957 • Garcia Fernando • SHT • PRT
MADEIRA DE CABINDA • 1973 • Mendes Joao • SHT • PRT
MADEIRA, UMA CANCAO • 1957 • Garcia Fernando • SHT • PRT
MADEJA DE LANA AZUL CELESTE, UNA • 1964 • Madrid Jose Luis • SPN
MADEL AUF DER SCHAUKEL, DAS • 1926 • Basch Felix • FRG
MADEL AUS DEM VOLKE, EIN • 1927 • Fleck Jacob, Fleck Luise • FRG
MADEL AUS DEM WARENHAUS, DAS • 1923 • *Hofer-Film* • FRG • MADCHEN AUS DEM WARENHAUS, DAS
MADEL AUS DER HOLLE, DAS • 1922 • Zelnik Friedrich • FRG
MADEL AUS DER PROVINZ, DAS • 1929 • Bauer James • FRG
MADEL AUS GUTER FAMILIE, EIN • 1935 • Muller-Hagen Carl • FRG
MADEL AUS NEM BOHMERWALD • 1965 • Rieger August • FRG
MADEL AUS U.S.A., DAS • 1930 • Lamac Carl • FRG
MADEL DER STRASSE, EIN • 1933 • Steinhoff Hans • FRG
MADEL MIT DER MASKE, DAS • 1922 • Janson Victor • FRG
MADEL MIT DER PEITSCHE, DAS • 1929 • Lamac Carl • FRG
MADEL MIT TEMPERAMENT, EIN • 1928 • Janson Victor • FRG
MADEL MIT TEMPO, EIN see **ES TUT SICH WAS UM MITTERNACHT** • 1934
MADEL VOM BALLETT, DAS • 1918 • Lubitsch Ernst • FRG
MADEL VOM BALLETT, EIN • 1936 • Lamac Carl • FRG
MADEL VOM BUCHNERHOF, DAS • 1925 • *Arnold & Richter* • FRG
MADEL VOM MONTPARNASSE, DAS • 1932 • Schwarz Hanns • FRG
MADEL VON CAPRI, DAS see **WAISE VON CAPRI, DIE** • 1924
MADEL VON DER OPERETTE, DAS see **RUHIGES HEIM MIT KUCHENBENUTZUNG** • 1929
MADEL VON DER REEPERBAHN, EIN • 1930 • Anton Karl • FRG, CZC • MENSCHEN IM STURM
MADEL VON NEBENAN, DAS • 1917 • Otto Paul • FRG
MADEL VON PICCADILLY 1, DAS • 1921 • Zelnik Friedrich • FRG • GIRL OF PICCADILLY, A
MADEL VON PICCADILLY 2, DAS • 1921 • Zelnik Friedrich • FRG
MADEL VON PONTECUCULI, DAS • 1924 • Czerny Ludwig • FRG
MADEL WIRBELT DURCH DIE WELT, EIN • 1934 • Jacoby Georg • FRG
MADELAINE, ANATOMIA DI UN INCUBO • 1974 • Mauri Roberto • ITL
MADELAINE MOREL • 1916 • *Gray Betty* • SHT • USA
MADELEINE • 1921 • Philippi Siegfried • FRG
MADELEINE • 1928 • Freund Karl • UKN
MADELEINE • 1950 • Lean David • UKN • STRANGE CASE OF MADELEINE, THE
MADELEINE • 1969 • Spring Sylvia • CND
MADELEINE DE VERCHERES • 1913 • CND
MADELEINE IS.. • 1970 • Spring Sylvia • CND
MADELEINE -MADELEINE • 1963 • Kristl Vlado • FRG
MADELEINE MERCIER VIOLINISTE • 1972-73 • Brault Francois • DCS • CND
MADELEINE, MON AMOUR • 1971 • Zizic Bogdan • SHT • YGS
MADELEINE -TEL. 13 62 11 • 1958 • Meisel Kurt • FRG • MADELEINE (USA)
MADELEINE UND DER LEGIONAR • 1958 • Staudte Wolfgang • FRG • ESCAPE FROM SAHARA (USA) ○ VERKAUFTES LEBEN
MADELEINE (USA) see **MADELEINE -TEL. 13 62 11** • 1958
MADELEINE'S CHRISTMAS • 1912 • Smiley Joseph • USA
MADELINE • 1952 • Cannon Robert • ANS • USA
MADELINE'S REBELLION • 1911 • Porter Edwin S. • USA
MADELON see **MELODY OF LOVE, THE** • 1928
MADELON see **PORT OF SEVEN SEAS** • 1938
MADELON, LE • 1955 • Boyer Jean • FRN
MADELON DU BATAILLON, LA see **MARGOTON DU BATAILLON, LA** • 1933
MADELON OF THE REDWOODS see **FALSE EVIDENCE** • 1919
MADELS IM ARREST • 1915 • *Perry Ida* • FRG
MADELS RAN AN DIE FRONT! • 1915 • Rippert Otto • FRG
MADELS VON HEUTE • 1925 • Freisler Fritz • FRG • LIEBESGESCHICHTEN
MADELS VON HEUTE • 1933 • Selpin Herbert • FRG
MADELS VON IMMENHOF, DIE • 1955 • Schleif Wolfgang • FRG
MADEMOISELLE • 1966 • Richardson Tony • UKN, FRN
MADEMOISELLE 100 MILLIONS • 1913 • Tourneur Maurice • FRN
MADEMOISELLE -AGE 39 • 1956 • Sakellarios Alekos • GRC
MADEMOISELLE ANGE (FRN) see **ENGEL AUF ERDEN, EIN** • 1959
MADEMOISELLE BEATRICE • 1942 • de Vaucorbeil Max • FRN
MADEMOISELLE DE LA FERTE • 1949 • Dallier Roger • FRN
MADEMOISELLE DE LA SEIGLIERE • 1920 • Antoine Andre, Denola Georges • FRN
MADEMOISELLE DE PARIS • 1955 • Kapps Walter • FRN • MADEMOISELLE FROM PARIS (USA)
MADEMOISELLE DE SADE E I SOUI VIZI see **JULIETTE DE SADE** • 1969
MADEMOISELLE DOCTEUR • 1936 • Pabst G. W. • FRN • SALONIQUE, NID D'ESPIONS ○ SPIES FROM SALONIKA
MADEMOISELLE DOCTEUR • 1937 • Greville Edmond T. • UKN • STREET OF SHADOWS (USA)
MADEMOISELLE ET SON GANG • 1956 • Boyer Jean • FRN
MADEMOISELLE FIFI • 1944 • Wise Robert • USA • SILENT BELL, THE
MADEMOISELLE FRANCE (UKN) see **REUNION IN FRANCE** • 1942
MADEMOISELLE FROM ARMENTIERES • 1926 • Elvey Maurice • UKN
MADEMOISELLE FROM PARIS (USA) see **MADEMOISELLE DE PARIS** • 1955
MADEMOISELLE GOBETTE see **PRESIDENTESSA, LA** • 1952
MADEMOISELLE JOSETTE, MA FEMME • 1932 • Berthomieu Andre • FRN
MADEMOISELLE JOSETTE, MA FEMME • 1950 • Berthomieu Andre • FRN
MADEMOISELLE JOSETTE, MA FEMME see **FRAULEIN JOSETTE, MEINE FRAU** • 1926
MADEMOISELLE MA MERE • 1937 • Decoin Henri • FRN
MADEMOISELLE MIDNIGHT • 1924 • Leonard Robert Z. • USA
MADEMOISELLE MODISTE • 1926 • Leonard Robert Z. • USA
MADEMOISELLE MODISTE • 1952 • Reinert Emile Edwin • FRN • NAUGHTY MARTINE (USA)
MADEMOISELLE MODISTE see **KISS ME AGAIN** • 1931
MADEMOISELLE MOZART • 1935 • Noe Yvan • FRN • MEET MISS MOZART (USA)
MADEMOISELLE PARLEY VOO • 1928 • Elvey Maurice • UKN
MADEMOISELLE PIGALLE see **CETTE SACREE GAMINE** • 1955
MADEMOISELLE PIMPLE • 1915 • Evans Fred, Evans Joe • UKN
MADEMOISELLE ROSIE AQUINALDO • 1901 • *Warwick Trading Co* • UKN
MADEMOISELLE S'AMUSE • 1947 • Boyer Jean • FRN
MADEMOISELLE STRIP-TEASE • 1957 • Foucaud Pierre • FRN
MADEMOISELLE SWING • 1941 • Pottier Richard • FRN
MADEMOISELLE TIPTOES • 1918 • King Henry • USA
MADEMOISELLE X • 1944 • Billon Pierre • FRN
MADEN • 1978 • Ozkan Yavuz • TRK • MINE, THE
MADERO OF MEXICO • 1942 • Lee Sammy • USA
MADEROS DE SAN JUAN, LOS • 1946 • Bustillo Oro Juan • MXC
MADGE OF THE MOUNTAINS • 1911 • Kent Charles • USA
MADH BHARE NAIN • 1955 • *Burman S. D. (M)* • IND
MADHATTAN ISLAND • 1947 • Kneitel Seymour • ANS • USA
MADHOUSE • 1974 • Clark Jim • UKN, USA • REVENGE OF DR. DEATH, THE
MADHOUSE • 1983 • Hellman Oliver • ITL
MADHOUSE, THE • 1929 • Roberts Stephen • SHT • USA
MADHOUSE MANSION (USA) see **GHOST STORY** • 1974
MADHUCHANDRA • 1967 • Datta Raj • IND
MADHUMATI • 1958 • Roy Bimal • IND
MADICKEN • 1979 • Graffman Goran • SWD • MISCHIEVOUS MEG
MADIGAN • 1968 • Siegel Don • USA
MADIGAN: PARK AVENUE BEAT • 1973 • March Alex • TVM • USA
MADIGAN: THE LISBON BEAT • 1973 • Sagal Boris • TVM • USA
MADIGAN: THE LONDON BEAT • 1971 • Smight Jack • TVM • USA
MADIGAN: THE MIDTOWN BEAT • 1972 • Smight Jack • TVM • USA
MADIGAN: THE NAPLES BEAT • 1973 • Sagal Boris • TVM • USA
MADIGAN'S MILLIONS see **MILLIPILLERI** • 1966
MADINA, AL- • 1971 • Salamuni Samy • EGY • VILLE, UNE ○ CITY, A
MADINA BOE • 1968 • Massip Jose • DOC • CUB • GUERRA OLVIDADO, LA
MADININA • 1973 • Bertolino Daniel • DCS • CND
MADININA, VINGT-CINQ ANS D'ANTILLES • 1973 • Valcour Pierre • DOC • CND
MADISON AVENUE • 1962 • Humberstone H. Bruce • USA
MADISON SQUARE ARABIAN NIGHT, A • 1918 • Miller Ashley • SHT • USA
MADISON SQUARE GARDEN • 1932 • Brown Harry J. • USA
MADLA FROM THE BRICK-KILN see **MADLA Z CIHELNY** • 1933
MADLA Z CIHELNY • 1933 • Slavinsky Vladimir • CZC • MADLA FROM THE BRICK-KILN
MADLY • 1971 • Kahane Roger • FRN, ITL • MADLY, IL PIACERE DELL'UOMO (ITL)
MADLY see **DELICESINE** • 1976
MADLY, IL PIACERE DELL'UOMO (ITL) see **MADLY** • 1971
MADLY SAD PRINCESS, THE see **SILENE SMUTNA PRINCEZNA** • 1968
MADMAN • 1982 • Giannone Joe • USA • MADMAN MARZ
MADMAN see **CAMP 708** • 1977
MADMAN, THE • 1911 • *Essanay* • USA
MADMAN, THE see **FOU, LE** • 1970
MADMAN IN THE DARK see **KROK DO TMY** • 1938
MADMAN MARZ see **MADMAN** • 1982
MADMAN OF LAB 4, THE see **FOU DU LABO 4, LE** • 1967
MADMAN OF MOCUTO, THE see **LOCO DE MACUTO, EL** • 1978
MADMAN'S BRIDE, THE • 1907 • Fitzhamon Lewin? • UKN
MADMAN'S DEFENCE, A • 1977 • Grede Kjell • MTV • SWD
MADMAN'S FATE, THE • 1906 • Martin J. H.? • UKN
MADMEN OF EUROPE (USA) see **ENGLISHMAN'S HOME, AN** • 1939
MADMEN OF MANDORAS, THE • 1964 • Bradley David • USA • THEY SAVED HITLER'S BRAIN ○ RETURN OF MR. H., THE
MADMEN'S TRIAL see **SUD SUMASSHEDSHICH** • 1962
MADNESS • 1971 • Rau Cesare • ITL
MADNESS FROM TERROR see **LOCURA DE TERROR** • 1960
MADNESS OF DR. TUBE, THE see **FOLIE DU DOCTEUR TUBE, LA** • 1916
MADNESS OF HELEN, THE • 1916 • Vale Travers • USA
MADNESS OF LOVE, THE • 1922 • Physioc Wray • USA
MADNESS OF THE HEART • 1949 • Bennett Charles • UKN
MADNESS OF THE VALIANT, THE see **FOLIE DES VAILLANTS, LA** • 1926
MADNESS OF YOUTH • 1923 • Storm Jerome • USA
MADO • 1965 • Kuri Yoji • ANS • JPN • WINDOW, THE
MADO • 1976 • Sautet Claude • FRN, ITL, FRG
MADO MAVROGENOUS • 1970 • Carayannis Costa • GRC
MADO POSTE RESTANTE • 1989 • Adabakhian Alexander • FRN
MADOL DUWA • 1975 • Peries Lester James • SLN • ENCHANTED ISLAND
MADONA DE CEDRO, A • 1968 • Coimbra Carlos • BRZ • CEDAR MADONNA, THE ○ VIRGIN OF CEDAR, THE
MADONA DE LA ROSAS, LA • 1913 • Perojo Benito • SHT • SPN
MADONE DE L'ATLANTIQUE, LA • 1936 • Weill Pierre • FRN
MADONE DES SLEEPINGS, LA • 1928 • Gleize Maurice • FRN
MADONE DES SLEEPINGS, LA • 1955 • Diamant-Berger Henri • FRN
MADONNA • 1967 • Kuchar Mike • SHT • USA
MADONNA, THE • 1915 • Cooley Frank • USA
MADONNA AM PORTAL, DIE • 1923 • Durec Monsieur • FRG
MADONNA CHE SILENZIO C'E STASERA • 1983 • Ponzi Maurizio • ITL
MADONNA DELLE ROSE • 1954 • Di Gianni Enzo • ITL
MADONNA DI CARAVAGGIO, LA • 1932 • D'Isernia Gian • ITL
MADONNA GRAZIA • 1917 • Gallone Carmine • ITL
MADONNA IM FEGEFEUER • 1929 • Reichmann Max • FRG • MEIN HERZ GEHORT DIR..
MADONNA IN KETTEN • 1949 • Lamprecht Gerhard • FRG

MADONNA IN SCHNEE see **WANDERNDE BILD, DAS** • 1920
MADONNA IN THE SNOW see **WANDERNDE BILD, DAS** • 1920
MADONNA MIT DEN LILIEN, DIE • 1919 • *Zelnik Friedrich* • FRG
MADONNA OF AVENUE A, THE • 1929 • Curtiz Michael • USA
MADONNA OF NEDERMUNSTER, THE see **MADONNA VAN NEDERMUNSTER, DE** • 1973
MADONNA OF THE CELLS, A • 1925 • Paul Fred • UKN
MADONNA OF THE DESERT • 1948 • Blair George • USA
MADONNA OF THE NIGHT, THE • 1916 • Bertram William • SHT • USA
MADONNA OF THE POOR, A • 1914 • *Ostriche Muriel* • USA
MADONNA OF THE SEVEN MOONS • 1944 • Crabtree Arthur • UKN
MADONNA OF THE SLEEPING CARS, THE • 1978 • *Kristel Sylvia*
MADONNA OF THE SLUMS, THE • 1913 • Ford Francis • USA
MADONNA OF THE SLUMS, THE • 1920 • Terwilliger George W. • SHT • USA
MADONNA OF THE STORM, THE • 1913 • Griffith D. W. • USA
MADONNA OF THE STREETS • 1924 • Carewe Edwin • USA
MADONNA OF THE STREETS • 1930 • Robertson John S. • USA
MADONNA VAN NEDERMUNSTER, DE • 1973 • Jacobs Jos • BLG • MADONNA OF NEDERMUNSTER, THE
MADONNA, WO BIST DU? • Jacoby Georg • FRG
MADONNAS AND MEN • 1920 • Rolfe B. A. • USA
MADONNA'S SECRET, THE • 1946 • Thiele Wilhelm • USA
MADONNINA DELLA SEGGIOLA, LA • 1920 • Lolli Alberto Carlo • DOC • ITL
MADONNINA D'ORO, LA • 1950 • Carpentieri Luigi • ITL
MADRAGOA • 1950 • Queiroga Perdigao • PRT
MADRE • 1916 • Palermi Amleto • ITL
MADRE A LA FUERZA • 1939 • O'Quigley Roberto • MXC
MADRE ADORADA • 1948 • Cardona Rene • MXC
MADRE ALEGRIA • 1935 • Buchs Jose • SPN
MADRE ALEGRIA • 1950 • Nunez Ricardo • ARG
MADRE FOLLE, LA • 1922 • Gallone Carmine • ITL
MADRE IGNOTA see **LUCIANO** • 1962
MADRE ITALIANA • 1927 • Rosa Silvio Laurenti • ITL
MADRE MARIA, LA • 1974 • Demare Lucas • ARG • MOTHER MARY
MADRE QUERIDA • 1935 • Orol Juan • MXC
MADRE QUERIDA • 1950 • Orol Juan • MXC
MADRE RITORNO, UNA • 1953 • Montero Roberto Bianchi • ITL
MADRE SELVA • 1944 • Amadori Luis Cesar • ARG
MADRE TIERRA • 1976 • Arenas Roberto Triana • DOC • CLM
MADRECITA, LA • 1973 • *Diana* • MXC
MADRECITA, LA see **MI MADRECITA** • 1940
MADRES DEL MUNDO • 1936 • Aguilar Rolando • MXC
MADRES SOLTERAS • 1974 • del Amo Antonio • SPN
MADRESELVA • 1939 • Amadori Luis Cesar • ARG • HONEYSUCKLE (USA)
MADRI PERICOLOSE • 1960 • Paolella Domenico • ITL
MADRID • 1986 • Patino Basilio Martin • SPN
MADRID 36 see **ESPANA LEAL EN ARMAS** • 1937
MADRID DE MIS SUENOS • 1942 • Neufeld Max, Cominetti Gian M. • SPN, ITL • BUONGIORNO, MADRID! (ITL)
MADRID EN EL ANO 2000 • 1925 • Noriega Manuel • SPN • MADRID IN THE YEAR 2000
MADRID IN THE YEAR 2000 see **MADRID EN EL ANO 2000** • 1925
MADRID, LA PUERTA MAS CORDIAL • 1967 • Aguirre Javier • SHT • SPN
MADRIGUERA, LA • 1969 • Saura Carlos • SPN • HONEYCOMB (USA) ○ DEN, THE
MADRINA DEL DIABLO, LA • 1937 • Peon Ramon • MXC • DEVIL'S GODMOTHER, THE (USA)
MADRON • 1970 • Hopper Jerry • USA, ISR • HIS NAME WAS MADRON (UKN)
MADRUGADA • 1957 • Roman Antonio • SPN
MADUNNELLA • 1948 • Grassi Ernesto • ITL
MADWOMAN OF CHAILLOT, THE • 1969 • Forbes Bryan, Huston John • UKN, USA
MAE WEST • 1982 • Philips Lee • TVM • USA
MAELKEHYGEIJNE • 1954 • Carlsen Henning • SHT • DNM
MAELSTROM • 1972 • Bock Larry • SHT • USA
MAELSTROM, THE • 1910 • Salter Harry • USA
MAELSTROM, THE • 1913 • Morty Frank • USA
MAELSTROM, THE • 1917 • Scardon Paul • USA
MAERKELIG KAERLIGHED, EN • 1968 • Malmros Nils • DNM • ODD KIND OF LOVE, AN ○ STRANGE LOVE, A
MAE'S SUITORS • 1911 • *Mcleod Elsie* • USA
MAESTRINA, LA • 1933 • Brignone Guido • ITL • LITTLE SCHOOL MISTRESS, THE
MAESTRINA, LA • 1942 • Bianchi Giorgio • ITL
MAESTRO see **IL MAESTRO** • 1989
MAESTRO, IL • 1957 • Fabrizi Aldo, Manzanos Eduardo • ITL, SPN • MAESTRO, EL (SPN) ○ TEACHER AND THE MIRACLE, THE ○ TEACHER, THE
MAESTRO, LE • 1977 • Vital Claude • FRN
MAESTRO, THE • 1964 • Halas John • ANS • UKN
MAESTRO, UN • 1978 • del Real Cayetano • SPN
MAESTRO DI DON GIOVANNI, IL • 1952 • Krims Milton, Vassarotti Vittorio • ITL • CROSSED SWORDS (USA)
MAESTRO DI VIGEVANO, IL • 1963 • Petri Elio • ITL • SCHOOL TEACHER FROM VIGEVANO, THE
MAESTRO DI VIOLINO, IL • 1976 • Fago Giovanni • ITL
MAESTRO DO-MI-SOL-DO, IL • 1906 • Melies Georges • FRN • PROFESSOR DO-MI-SOL-DO
MAESTRO E MARGHERITA, IL (ITL) see **MAJSTOR I MARGARITA** • 1973
MAESTRO, EL (SPN) see **MAESTRO, IL** • 1957
MAESTRO KOKO • 1969 • Grgic Zlatko, Kolar Boris, Zaninovic Ante • ANS • YGS, FRG • NESTANAK MAESTRA KOKO
MAESTRO LANDI • 1935 • Forzano Giovacchino • ITL
MAESTRO LEUITA, EL • 1940 • Amadori Luis Cesar • ARG
MAESTRO OF THE COMICS • 1945 • Clancy Carl C. • SHT • USA
MAEVA • 1961 • Bonsignori Umberto • USA • MAEVA, PORTRAIT OF A TAHITIAN GIRL ○ TRUE DIARY OF A WAHINE ○ PAGAN HELLCAT ○ WAHINE ○ TRUE STORY OF A WAHINE ○ CONFESSIONS OF A WAHINE ○ TRUE DIARY OF A VAHINE
MAEVA, PORTRAIT OF A TAHITIAN GIRL see **MAEVA** • 1961
MAEVE • 1982 • Murphy Pat, Davies John • UKN
MAFFIA, LA • 1972 • Torre-Nilsson Leopoldo • ARG • MAFIA (UKN)
MAFFIA DU PLAISIR, LA • 1970 • Roy Jean-Claude • FRN
MAFFIA FAIT LA LOI, LA (FRN) see **GIORNO DELLA CIVETTA, IL** • 1967
MAFIA see **IN NOME DELLA LEGGE** • 1949
MAFIA ALLA SBARRA • 1963 • Palella Oreste • ITL
MAFIA BOSS: SIE TOTEN WIE SCHAKALE, DER (FRG) see **MALA ORDINA, LA** • 1972
MAFIA DEL CRIMEN, LA • 1957 • Bracho Julio • MXC
MAFIA FAIT LA LOI, LA see **GIORNO DELLA CIVETTA, IL** • 1967
MAFIA GIRLS, THE • 1969 • Ross Ed • USA
MAFIA KID • 1988 • Morrissey Paul • USA • THROWBACK ○ SPIKE OF BENSONHURST
MAFIA KINGPIN • 1983 • Anderson Michael • USA
MAFIA MI FA UN BAFFO, LA • 1975 • Garrone Riccardo • ITL
MAFIA MOB (UKN) see **VIVA AMERICA!** • 1969
MAFIA OLUM SACIYOR • 1968 • Aslan Mehmet • TRK • MAFIA SPREADS DEATH
MAFIA PRINCESS • 1986 • Collins Robert • TVM • USA
MAFIA SPREADS DEATH see **MAFIA OLUM SACIYOR** • 1968
MAFIA (UKN) see **MAFFIA, LA** • 1972
MAFIA (USA) see **GIORNO DELLA CIVETTA, IL** • 1967
MAFIA VERSUS NINJA • 1985 • *Lou Alexander* • HKG
MAFIA WARFARE see **SCOUMOUNE, LA** • 1973
MAFIAEN -DET ER OSSE MIG • 1974 • Ornbak Henning • DNM
MAFIOSI, I • 1961 • Mauri Roberto • ITL
MAFIOSO • 1962 • Lattuada Alberto • ITL
MAFISH TAFAHUM • 1962 • Salem Atef • EGY • IMPOSSIBILITE DE S'ENTENDRE
MAFRA E OS SEUS CELEBRES CARRILHOES • 1934 • Vieira Manuel Luis • SHT • PRT
MAFROOR • 1988 • Askari Hassan • PKS
MAFU CAGE, THE • 1978 • Arthur Karen • USA • MY SISTER, MY LOVE (USA) ○ DEVIATION ○ CAGE, THE
MAG • 1987 • Vlacil Frantisek • CZC • MAGICIAN, THE
MAGA LESZ A FERJEM • 1938 • Gaal Bela • HNG • YOU WILL BE MY HUSBAND (USA)
MAGARAZ • 1915 • Tourjansky Victor • USS
MAGASH HAKESSEF • 1983 • Ne'Eman Yehuda • ISR • ON A GOLDEN PLATTER
MAGASINS DU XIXe SIECLE see **STROBOSCOPES, LES** • 1963
MAGASISKOLA • 1970 • Gaal Istvan • HNG • FALCONS, THE
MAGAZINE COOKING • 1914 • Murphy J. A. • USA
MAGBET • 1969 • Wajda Andrzej • PLN • MACBETH ○ MAKBET
MAGD, DIE • 1911 • Stark Kurt • FRG
MAGD, DIE • 1976 • Jent Louis • MTV • SWT • MAID, THE
MAGD VON HEILIGENBLUT, DIE • 1956 • Lehner Alfred • AUS
MAGDA • 1912 • de Banos Ricardo • SPN
MAGDA • 1917 • Chautard Emile • USA
MAGDA • 1946 • Elias Francisco • MXC
MAGDA see **HEIMAT** • 1938
MAGDA IS EXPELLED see **MAGDAT KICSAPJAK** • 1935
MAGDALENA • 1920 • Majer Vladimir • CZC
MAGDALENA • 1954 • Pardave Joaquin • MXC
MAGDALENA see **MADDALENA** • 1972
MAGDALENA'S TRUE VOCATION see **VERDADERA VOCACION DE MAGDALENA, LA** • 1971
MAGDALENE • 1908 • *Holger-Madsen* • DNM
MAGDALENE • 1989 • Teuber Monica • SILENT NIGHT
MAGDALENE OF THE HILLS, A • 1917 • Noble John W. • USA
MAGDANA'S DONKEY (USA) see **LURDZHA MAGDANY** • 1956
MAGDANAS LURJA see **LURDZHA MAGDANY** • 1956
MAGDAT KICSAPJAK • 1935 • Vajda Ladislao • HNG • DISMISSED FROM SCHOOL ○ MAGDA IS EXPELLED
MAGEE see **MAGEE AND THE LADY** • 1977
MAGEE AND THE LADY • 1977 • Levitt Gene • TVM • ASL, USA • SHE'LL BE SWEET ○ MAGEE
MAGELLAN • Frampton Hollis • USA
MAGELLAN'S RETURN see **RETURN OF MAGELLAN, THE** • 1974
MAGGIE • 1978 • Svensson Birgitta • SWD
MAGGIE • 1981 • Healey Barry • MTV • CND
MAGGIE • 1988 • Donev Peter • BUL
MAGGIE, THE • 1953 • Mackendrick Alexander • UKN • HIGH AND DRY (USA)
MAGGIE AND PIERRE • 1983 • Lavut Martin • CND
MAGGIE PEPPER • 1919 • Withey Chet • USA
MAGGIE, THE DOCK RAT • 1908 • *Kalem* • USA
MAGGIE THE MILL GIRL • 1916 • *Pyramid* • SHT • USA
MAGGIE TRIES SOCIETY LIFE • 1913 • *Panzer Paul* • USA
MAGGIE'S FIRST FALSE STEP • 1917 • Griffin Frank C. • SHT • USA
MAGGIE'S HONEST LOVER • 1914 • *Nestor* • USA
MAGGIORATO FISICO, IL (ITL) see **VOUS PIGEZ?** • 1955
MAGGOT, THE • 1972 • Dunning George • ANS • UKN
MAGIA • 1917 • Korda Alexander • HNG • MAGIC
MAGIA A PREZZI MODICI • 1950 • Freda Riccardo • SHT • ITL
MAGIA NEGRA see **MISTERIOS DE LA MAGIA NEGRA** • 1957
MAGIA NUDA • 1975 • Castiglioni Alfredo, Castiglioni Angelo, Guerrasio Guido • ITL
MAGIA VERDE • 1953 • Napolitano Gian Gaspare • ITL • GREEN MAGIC (USA)
MAGIC • 1908 • *Pathe* • FRN
MAGIC • 1978 • Attenborough Richard • USA
MAGIC see **MAGIA** • 1917
MAGIC ADVENTURE see **MAGICA AVENTURA** • 1968
MAGIC ALBUM, THE • 1908 • Zecca Ferdinand • FRN
MAGIC ALPHABET, THE • 1942 • Tourneur Jacques • SHT • USA
MAGIC ART • 1932 • Foster John, Bailey Harry • ANS • USA
MAGIC ARTS, THE • 1976 • Petty Bruce • ANS • ASL
MAGIC ASTER • 1964 • CHN
MAGIC ATLAS, THE see **ATLAS MAGIQUE, L'** • 1935
MAGIC BAG, THE see **PLASTIKKPOSEN** • 1985
MAGIC BEANS, THE • 1939 • Kline Lester • ANS • USA
MAGIC BICYCLE, THE see **ZACZAROWANY ROWER** • 1955
MAGIC BIRD, THE (USA) see **PUTIFERIO VA ALLA GUERRA** • 1968
MAGIC BLADE, THE see **T'IEN-YA, MING YUEH, TAO** • 1977
MAGIC BON-BONS, THE • 1915 • *Macmillan Violet* • SHT • USA
MAGIC BOOK • 1960 • Halas John • ANS • UKN
MAGIC BOOK, THE (USA) see **LIVRE MAGIQUE, LE** • 1900
MAGIC BOTTLE, THE • 1906 • Booth W. R.? • UKN
MAGIC BOTTLE, THE • 1915 • *Wise Thomas A.* • USA
MAGIC BOTTLES • 1905 • *Pathe* • FRN
MAGIC BOW, THE • Schulz Kurt Herbert • ANM • GDR
MAGIC BOW, THE • 1946 • Knowles Bernard • UKN
MAGIC BOX, THE • 1908 • Smith Jack ? • UKN
MAGIC BOX, THE • 1951 • Boulting John • UKN
MAGIC BOX, THE • 1958 • Topaldgikov Stefan • BUL
MAGIC BOX, THE see **GIRL WITH THE MAGIC BOX, THE** • 1965
MAGIC BOY • Yamamoto Sanze • JPN
MAGIC BOY (USA) see **SHONEN SARUTOBI SASUKE** • 1960
MAGIC BRICKS • 1905 • *Pathe* • FRN
MAGIC BRUSH, THE • Wan Tchao-Tchen • ANM • CHN
MAGIC BRUSH, THE • 1970 • *Popov* • USS
MAGIC BULLET, THE see **DR. EHRLICH'S MAGIC BULLET** • 1940
MAGIC CANVAS, THE • 1948 • Halas John • ANS • UKN
MAGIC CARPET • 1925 • Lantz Walter • ANS • USA
MAGIC CARPET • 1971 • Graham William A. • TVM • USA
MAGIC CARPET, THE • 1909 • Booth W. R. • UKN
MAGIC CARPET, THE • 1913 • *Lux* • SHT • USA
MAGIC CARPET, THE • 1948 • Atamanov A. L. • ANS • USS
MAGIC CARPET, THE • 1951 • Landers Lew • USA
MAGIC CARTOONS see **JOYEUX MICROBES, LES** • 1909
MAGIC CASK, THE • Schulz Kurt Herbert • ANM • GDR
MAGIC CAT • 1969 • *Chan Poo Choo* • HKG
MAGIC CATALOGUE, THE • 1956 • Vukotic Dusan • ANS • YGS
MAGIC CHAIR, THE see **BUVOS SZEK** • 1952
MAGIC CHALKS, THE • 1950 • *Gb Instructional* • SHT • UKN
MAGIC CHRISTIAN, THE • 1969 • McGrath Joseph • UKN
MAGIC CHRISTMAS TREE, THE • 1964 • Parish Richard C. • USA
MAGIC CIRCUS, THE see **CIRCO MAGICO, EL** • 1977
MAGIC CIRCUS, THE see **KOUZELNY CIRKUS** • 1977
MAGIC CITY see **MAYIKI POLIS, I** • 1955
MAGIC CITY, THE (USA) see **MAYAVI NAGARI** • 1928
MAGIC CLOAK OF OZ, THE • 1914 • MacDonald J. Farrell • USA
MAGIC CLOCK, THE (USA) see **WUNDERUHR, DIE** • 1928
MAGIC COIFFEUR • 1961 • Cuny Louis • SHT • FRN
MAGIC CUP, THE • 1921 • Robertson John S. • USA
MAGIC CURSE, THE • 1978 • Lu Chun, To Man Po • HKG
MAGIC DICE • 1908 • *Pathe* • FRN
MAGIC DICE • 1908 • *Gaumont* • FRN
MAGIC DOLL see **JADUI-E-PUTLI** • 1946
MAGIC DONKEY, THE (UKN) see **PEAU D'ANE** • 1970
MAGIC DRAM, A • 1957-59 • Kawamoto Kihachiro • ANS • JPN
MAGIC EGGS see **OMELETTE FANTASTIQUE, L'** • 1909
MAGIC ELIXIR, THE • 1912 • *Cines* • ITL
MAGIC ELK see **TROLLALGEN** • 1927
MAGIC EXTINGUISHER, THE • 1901 • Williamson James • UKN
MAGIC EYE, THE • 1918 • Berger Rea • USA
MAGIC FACE, THE • 1951 • Tuttle Frank • USA
MAGIC FAN see **EVENTAIL ANIME, L'** • 1909
MAGIC FAN, THE see **FAKIR'S FAN, THE** • 1911
MAGIC FEATURE, THE see **NUMBER 12** • 1943-58
MAGIC FIDDLE, THE • 1957 • Forlong Michael • SHT • NRW
MAGIC FIRE • 1956 • Dieterle William • USA
MAGIC FISH, THE • 1934 • *Terry Paul/ Moser Frank (P)* • ANS • USA
MAGIC FISH, THE • 1938 • Rou Aleksandr • USS
MAGIC FLAME, THE • 1927 • King Henry • USA
MAGIC FLOWER, THE • 1910 • *Kalem* • USA
MAGIC FLUKE, THE • 1949 • Hubley John • ANS • USA
MAGIC FLUTE see **JADUI BANSARI** • 1948
MAGIC FLUTE, THE • 1910 • *Pathe* • FRN
MAGIC FLUTE, THE • 1927 • *Imperial* • IND
MAGIC FLUTE, THE • 1962 • SHT • UAR
MAGIC FLUTE, THE • 1977 • Thomas Gayle • ANM • CND • FLUTE MAGIQUE, LA
MAGIC FLUTE, THE see **FLUTE MAGIQUE, LA** • 1906
MAGIC FLUTE, THE see **PAPAGENO** • 1935
MAGIC FLUTE, THE see **FLUTE MAGIQUE, LA** • 1946
MAGIC FLUTE, THE see **ZAUBERFLOTE, DIE** • 1976
MAGIC FLUTE, THE (USA) see **TROLLFLOJTEN** • 1975
MAGIC FLUTE (USA) see **KHWAB-E-HASTI** • 1934
MAGIC FOUNTAIN, THE • 1961 • David Allan • USA
MAGIC FOUNTAIN, THE • 1962 • Lamas Fernando • USA, SPN • FUENTE MAGICA, LA (SPN)
MAGIC FOUNTAIN PEN, THE • 1907 • Blackton J. Stuart • USA • BIRTH AND ADVENTURES OF A FOUNTAIN PEN
MAGIC GAME, THE • 1927 • Bray John R. • ANS • USA
MAGIC GAME, THE see **TAIKAPELI** • 1984
MAGIC GARDEN, THE • 1908 • *Paul R. W.* • UKN
MAGIC GARDEN, THE • 1927 • Meehan James Leo • USA
MAGIC GARDEN, THE (USA) see **PENNYWHISTLE BLUES** • 1951
MAGIC GARDEN OF STANLEY SWEETHEART, THE • 1970 • Horn Leonard • USA
MAGIC GIFT, THE • 1956 • Wasilewski Zenon • ANM • PLN
MAGIC GLASS, THE • 1914 • Plumb Hay • UKN
MAGIC GLASS, THE • 1988 • Gavala Maria • GRC
MAGIC GUITAR • 1968 • Torres Mar S. • PHL
MAGIC HANDKERCHIEF, THE • 1908 • *Pathe* • FRN
MAGIC HAT, THE see **RABIHA -TAKIET EL EKHFAA** • 1944
MAGIC HAT, THE (USA) see **CHAPEAU MAGIQUE, LE** • 1903
MAGIC HOE, THE • 1960 • Topaldgikov Stefan • ANM • BUL
MAGIC HOOD, THE (USA) see **FUSHIGINA ZUKIN** • 1958
MAGIC HOOP, THE see **CERCEAU MAGIQUE, LA** • 1908
MAGIC HORSE • 1935 • Shukla Kanubhai, Yagnik Raja • IND
MAGIC HORSE, THE • 1954 • Reiniger Lotte • ANS • UKN
MAGIC HORSE, THE see **KONEK-GORBUNOK** • 1947

MAGIC HORSE (USA) see **MAYAKUDARAI** • 1949
MAGIC HOUR, THE • 1925 • *Cranfield & Clark* • SHT • USA
MAGIC HOUSE, THE see **KOUZELNY DUM** • 1939
MAGIC IMAGE see **MAGIQUE IMAGE, LA** • 1951
MAGIC IN MUSIC see **HARDBOILED CANARY, THE** • 1941
MAGIC IN THE SKY • 1981 • Raymont Peter • DOC • CND
MAGIC IS ALIVE, MY FRIENDS • 1985 • SAF
MAGIC JACKET, THE see **KINCSKERESO KIS KODMON** • 1973
MAGIC JAZZ BO, THE • 1917 • Sautell Albert A. • SHT • USA
MAGIC KINGS see **REYES MAGOS** • 1974
MAGIC LABORATORY, THE • 1962 • Gagliardo Elio • ITL
MAGIC LAMP, THE • 1924 • Lantz Walter • ANS • USA
MAGIC LAMP, THE see **FANOUS EL SEHRI, EL** • 1959
MAGIC LAND OF MOTHER GOOSE, THE • 1966 • Lewis Herschell G. • USA • SANTA CLAUS VISITS THE LAND OF MOTHER GOOSE ○ SANTA VISITS THE MAGIC LAND OF MOTHER GOOSE
MAGIC LANTERN, THE (USA) see **LANTERNE MAGIQUE, LA** • 1903
MAGIC LANTERN II • 1960 • Kadar Jan, Klos Elmar • CZC
MAGIC LIFE, THE see **LYING LIPS** • 1921
MAGIC LIGHTER (USA) see **FYRTOJET** • 1946
MAGIC LOTUS LANTERN • 1959 • CHN
MAGIC MAID, THE • 1917 • *Christie* • USA
MAGIC MAKINILYA • 1970 • de Guzman Armando • PHL • MAGIC TYPEWRITER
MAGIC MAKO see **MAHO NO MAKOCHAN** • 1971
MAGIC MARBLE, THE • 1951 • Catling Darrell • SHT • UKN
MAGIC MARK see **JADUI-SINDOOR** • 1948
MAGIC MELODY • 1913 • *Lubin* • USA
MAGIC MELODY, THE • 1909 • *Essanay* • USA
MAGIC MILL, THE • ANS • USS
MAGIC MINERAL • 1959 • Blais Roger • DCS • CND • FIBRES DE PIERRE
MAGIC MIRROR • 1908 • Zecca Ferdinand • FRN
MAGIC MIRROR • 1970 • *Stacey Dist.* • USA
MAGIC MIRROR, THE • 1915 • *Shields Ernest* • SHT • USA
MAGIC MIRROR, THE • 1917 • Calvert E. H. • SHT • USA
MAGIC MOLECULE, THE • 1964 • Chapman Christopher, O'Connor Hugh • DOC • CND
MAGIC MOUNTAIN, THE see **ZAUBERBERG, DER** • 1982
MAGIC MUMMY, THE • 1933 • Foster John, Stallings George • ANS • USA
MAGIC MUSIC • 1911 • *Eclair* • FRN
MAGIC NICKEL, THE • 1913 • *Pollard Harry (P)* • USA
MAGIC NIGHT (USA) see **GOODNIGHT VIENNA** • 1932
MAGIC OF CATCHY SONGS • 1908 • Melies Georges • FRN
MAGIC OF LASSIE, THE • 1978 • Chaffey Don • USA
MAGIC OF LOVE • 1910 • Stow Percy • UKN
MAGIC OF MELIES • CMP • FRN
MAGIC OF MUSIC, THE • 1955 • Shepherd Horace • SHT • UKN
MAGIC OF SPRING, THE • 1917 • *Edison* • SHT • USA
MAGIC OF THE DIAMOND see **MAGIE DU DIAMANT** • 1958
MAGIC OF THE KITE, THE (USA) see **CERFVOLANT DU BOUT DU MONDE, LE** • 1957
MAGIC OF THE RIVER see **REKA CARUJE** • 1945
MAGIC OF WALT DISNEY WORLD, THE • 1972 • Leetch Tom • DCS • USA
MAGIC OF WHEELS, THE see **CZAR KOLEK** • 1967
MAGIC ON A STICK • 1946 • Endfield Cy • SHT • USA
MAGIC ON BROADWAY • 1937 • Fleischer Dave • ANS • USA
MAGIC ON LOVE ISLAND see **VALENTINE MAGIC ON LOVE ISLAND** • 1980
MAGIC ORCHESTRA see **JADUI-SHEHANAI** • 1948
MAGIC OXEN see **KET BORS OKROCSKE** • 1955
MAGIC PAINTBRUSH, THE • 1954 • Tsin Si • ANS • CHN
MAGIC PEAR TREE, THE • 1968 • Murakami Jimmy T. • ANS • USA
MAGIC PENCIL, THE • 1940 • White Volney • ANS • USA
MAGIC PENCIL, THE • 1954 • Tsin Si • ANM • CHN
MAGIC PICTURE see **JADUI-CHITRA** • 1948
MAGIC PIG, THE • 1917 • Moss Howard S. • ANM • USA
MAGIC PIPES, THE • 1910 • *Gaumont* • UKN
MAGIC PLUS FOURS, THE • 1924 • Wilson Andrew P. • UKN
MAGIC POT, THE • 1955 • Gavioli Roberto, Gavioli Gino • ANM • ITL
MAGIC PRAGUE OF RUDOLF II, THE see **KOUZELNA PRAHA RUDOLFA II** • 1982
MAGIC -QUEEN IN HUNGARY • 1987 • Zsombolyai Janos • HNG
MAGIC RING • 1985 • SAF
MAGIC RING see **JADUI-ANGOOTHI** • 1948
MAGIC RING, THE • 1906 • Fitzhamon Lewin • UKN
MAGIC RING, THE • 1911 • Bouwmeester Theo • UKN
MAGIC RING, THE • 1956 • Negus Olive • UKN
MAGIC ROSES • 1906 • *Pathe* • FRN
MAGIC SALESMAN, THE • 1914 • *Gaumont* • USA
MAGIC SAMURAI, THE • 1969 • Diaz Leody M. • PHL
MAGIC SCREEN • 1912 • *Pathe* • FRN
MAGIC SEED, THE see **VOLSHEBNOYE ZERNO** • 1942
MAGIC SERPENT (USA) see **KAIRYU DAIKESSEN** • 1966
MAGIC SHAVING POWDER • 1909 • *Walturdaw* • UKN
MAGIC SHELL, THE • 1941 • Davis Mannie • ANS • USA
MAGIC SHOES • 1935 • Flemming Claude • SHT • ASL
MAGIC SHOES, THE • 1913 • *Elmer Clarence* • USA
MAGIC SHOW, THE • 1981 • Campbell Norman • DOC • CND
MAGIC SKIN, THE • 1913 • *Kerrigan J. Warren* • SHT • USA
MAGIC SKIN, THE • 1915 • Ridgely Richard • USA
MAGIC SKIN, THE see **DESIRE** • 1920
MAGIC SKIN, THE see **SLAVE OF DESIRE** • 1923
MAGIC SKIS • 1960 • ANS • CZC
MAGIC SLIPPER • 1948 • Davis Mannie • ANS • USA
MAGIC SLIPPERS, THE see **CENDRILLON** • 1912
MAGIC SOUNDS, THE see **CAROBNI ZVUCI** • 1957
MAGIC SPECTACLES • 1961 • Wehling Bob • USA • TICKLED PINK ○ MAGICAL SPECTACLE
MAGIC SQUARES • 1914 • Nikola Louis • ANM • UKN
MAGIC STATUE see **MAZO** • 1939
MAGIC STICKS • 1987 • Keglevic Peter • FRG
MAGIC STRENGTH • 1944 • Wickersham Bob • ANS • USA
MAGIC STRINGS • 1955 • Stewart John R. F. • SHT • UKN
MAGIC SWORD, THE • 1902 • Paul Robert William • UKN
MAGIC SWORD, THE • 1962 • Gordon Bert I. • USA • ST. GEORGE AND THE 7 CURSES (UKN) ○ ST. GEORGE AND THE DRAGON ○ SORCERER'S CURSE, THE
MAGIC SWORD, THE • 1970 • HKG
MAGIC SWORD, THE (USA) see **CUDOTVORNI MAC** • 1949
MAGIC SWORD: OR, A MEDIAEVAL MYSTERY, THE • 1901 • Booth W. R. • UKN
MAGIC TABLE, THE • SHT • HNG
MAGIC TABLE, THE see **TABLE MAGIQUE, LA** • 1908
MAGIC THIEF, THE • 1969 • *Choa Chun* • HKG
MAGIC TOUCH, THE • Catling Darrell • DCS • UKN
MAGIC TOUCH, THE • 1958 • Li Han-Hsiang • HKG
MAGIC TOWN • 1947 • Wellman William A. • USA
MAGIC TOYSHOP, THE • 1986 • Wheatley David • TVM • UKN
MAGIC TREASURE, THE • ANS • USS
MAGIC TREE, THE • 1970 • McDermott Gerald • ANS • USA
MAGIC TWIG, THE • 1955 • Aksenchuk Ivan • ANS • USS
MAGIC TYPEWRITER see **MAGIC MAKINILYA** • 1970
MAGIC UMBRELLA, THE • *Pathe* • USA
MAGIC VALLEY see **MAYA MAHAL** • 1928
MAGIC VEST, THE • 1917 • Walsh James O., Taylor Rex, Richmond J. A. • USA
MAGIC VILLAGE, THE see **VILLAGE MAGIQUE, LE** • 1955
MAGIC VIOLIN, THE see **UKARE BAIORIN** • 1955
MAGIC VOYAGE OF SINBAD, THE (USA) see **SADKO** • 1953
MAGIC WALTZ see **VARAZSKERINGO** • 1918
MAGIC WAND, THE • 1912 • Wharton Theodore • USA
MAGIC WAND, THE • 1922 • Wynn George • UKN
MAGIC WAND, THE • 1935 • Khosla Dwarka • IND
MAGIC WEAVER, THE (USA) see **MARYA-ISKUSNITSA** • 1960
MAGIC WHITE SERPENT, THE see **HAKUJA DEN** • 1958
MAGIC WHITE SERPENT, THE see **PAI-SHE CHUAN** • 1963
MAGIC WORLD OF KAREL ZEMAN, THE see **KOUZELNY SVET KARLA ZEMANA** • 1963
MAGIC WORLD OF TOPO GIGIO (THE ITALIAN MOUSE), THE see **AVVENTURE DI TOPO GIGIO, LE** • 1961
MAGIC WORLD OF WATARI, THE • 1970 • *Yoshinobu Keneko* • JPN
MAGICA AVENTURA • 1968 • Delgado Cruz • SPN • MAGIC ADVENTURE
MAGICAL HAT, THE see **DIVOTVORNY KLOBOUK** • 1952
MAGICAL MAESTRO • 1952 • Avery Tex • ANS • USA
MAGICAL MATCHES • 1912 • *Urban Charles (P)* • UKN
MAGICAL MYSTERIES • 1914 • Booth W. R.? • UKN
MAGICAL MYSTERY TOUR • 1967 • *Beatles, The* • MTV • UKN
MAGICAL PRESS, THE • 1907 • Booth W. R. • UKN
MAGICAL SPECTACLE see **MAGIC SPECTACLES** • 1961
MAGICALULU • 1945 • Kneitel Seymour • ANS • USA
MAGICIAN, THE • 1900 • Porter Edwin S. • USA
MAGICIAN, THE • 1926 • Ingram Rex • USA
MAGICIAN, THE • Renc Ivan, Hobl Pavel • ANS • CZC
MAGICIAN, THE • 1960 • *Halas John (P)* • ANS • UKN
MAGICIAN, THE • 1972 • Krausne Charles • SHT • USA
MAGICIAN, THE • 1973 • Peranne Antti • ANS • FNL
MAGICIAN, THE • 1976 • Bonniere Rene • SHT • CND
MAGICIAN, THE see **MAGICIEN, LE** • 1932
MAGICIAN, THE see **CZARODZIEJ** • 1962
MAGICIAN, THE see **CZARNOKSIEZNIK** • 1964
MAGICIAN, THE see **HEXER, DER** • 1964
MAGICIAN, THE see **MAG** • 1987
MAGICIAN, THE (USA) see **MAGICIEN, LE** • 1898
MAGICIAN, THE (USA) see **ANSIKTET** • 1958
MAGICIAN FISHERMAN, THE • 1913 • France Charles H. • USA
MAGICIAN MICKEY • 1937 • Hand David • ANS • USA
MAGICIAN OF BENGAL, THE • 1925 • *Royal Art Studio* • IND
MAGICIAN OF DREAMS, THE see **MAGO DE LOS SUENOS, EL** • 1966
MAGICIAN OF LUBLIN, THE • 1978 • Golan Menahem • ISR, FRG • MAGIER, DER
MAGICIANS, THE see **MAGICIENNES, LES** • 1960
MAGICIAN'S APPRENTICE, THE see **CARODEJUV UCEN** • 1977
MAGICIAN'S CAVERN, THE (USA) see **ANTRE DES ESPRITS, L'** • 1901
MAGICIAN'S DAUGHTER, THE • 1938 • Feist Felix E. • SHT • USA
MAGICIAN'S LOVE TEST • 1909 • *Cines* • ITL
MAGICIANS OF THE SILVER SCREEN see **BAJECNI MUZI S KLIKOU** • 1979
MAGICIEN, LE • 1898 • Melies Georges • FRN • MAGICIAN, THE (USA) ○ BLACK MAGIC
MAGICIEN, LE • 1932 • *Gemier Firmin* • FRN • MAGICIAN, THE
MAGICIEN, LE • 1959 • Borowczyk Walerian • SHT • FRN
MAGICIENNES, LES • 1960 • Friedman Serge • FRN • DOUBLE DECEPTION (USA) ○ FRANTIC ○ MAGICIANS, THE
MAGICIENS, LES • 1975 • Chabrol Claude • FRN, FRG, ITL • PROFEZIA DI UN DELITTO (ITL) ○ INITIATION A LA MORT
MAGICIENS DE WANZERBE, LES see **MAGICIENS NOIRS, LES** • 1949
MAGICIENS NOIRS, LES • 1949 • Rouch Jean, Griaule • DCS • FRN • OUANZERBE, CAPITALE DE LA MAGIE ○ MAGICIENS DE WANZERBE, LES
MAGIE A TRAVERS LES AGES, LA • 1906 • Melies Georges • FRN • OLDEN AND NEW STYLE CONJURING (USA)
MAGIE BLANCHE • 1958 • Deroisy Lucien • BLG
MAGIE DIABOLIQUE • 1898 • Melies Georges • FRN • BLACK ART (USA) ○ DIABOLICAL MAGIC ○ DEVILISH MAGIC
MAGIE DU DIAMANT • 1958 • Roos Jorgen • DOC • BLG • MAGIC OF THE DIAMOND
MAGIE DU FER BLANC, LA • 1934 • Tedesco Jean • SHT • FRN
MAGIE MODERNE • 1931 • Buchowetzki Dimitri • FRN • TELEVISION
MAGIE MODERNE • 1959 • Image Jean • ANS • FRN
MAGIE NOIRE • 1904 • Blache Alice • FRN
MAGIER, DER see **MAGICIAN OF LUBLIN, THE** • 1978
MAGIKI POLIS, I see **MAYIKI POLIS, I** • 1955
MAGING AKIN KA LAMANG • 1988 • Brocka Lino • PHL • BE MINE ALONE
MAGIQUE IMAGE, LA • 1951 • Musidora • FRN • MAGIC IMAGE
MAGIRAMA • 1956 • Gance Abel, Kaplan Nelly • FRN
MAGISKA CIRKELN, DEN • 1971 • Berglund Per • SWD • BEYOND THE LINE OF DUTY
MAGISTRARNA PA SOMMARLOV • 1941 • Bauman Schamyl • SWD • TEACHERS ON A SUMMER HOLIDAY
MAGISTRATE, THE • 1921 • Merwin Bannister • UKN
MAGISTRATE, THE see **THOSE WERE THE DAYS** • 1934
MAGISTRATE, THE see **MAGISTRATO, IL** • 1959
MAGISTRATE'S DAUGHTER, THE • 1918 • Sandground Maurice • UKN
MAGISTRATE'S STORY, THE • 1915 • West Langdon • USA
MAGISTRATO, IL • 1959 • Zampa Luigi • ITL, SPN • MAGISTRATE, THE
MAGLIARI, I • 1959 • Rosi Francesco • ITL • HAWKERS, THE
MAGLUP EDILEMEYENLER • 1976 • Yilmaz Atif • TRK • INVINCIBLE ONES, THE
MAGNA GRECIA • 1949 • Tomei Giuliano • ITL
MAGNACCIO, IL • 1968 • De Rosis Franco • ITL • PIMP, THE
MAGNAS MISKA • 1916 • Korda Alexander • HNG • MISKA THE MAGNATE ○ MISKA THE GREAT
MAGNAS MISKA • 1949 • Keleti Marton • HNG • MICKEY MAGNATE
MAGNATE • 1988 • Bajon Filip • PLN
MAGNATE, THE • 1973 • Grimaldi Gianni • ITL
MAGNATE OF PARADISE, THE • 1915 • Brabin Charles J. • USA
MAGNET, THE • 1950 • Frend Charles • UKN
MAGNET LABORATORY • 1959 • Leacock Richard • DOC • USA
MAGNET OF DESTRUCTION, THE • 1915 • *Thanhouser* • USA
MAGNET OF DOOM see **AINE DES FERCHAUX, L'** • 1963
MAGNETIC EYE, THE • 1908 • *Lubin* • USA
MAGNETIC FLUID, THE • 1912 • *Pathe* • FRN
MAGNETIC FLUTE, THE • 1912 • *Pathe* • FRN
MAGNETIC INFLUENCE, A • 1912 • UKN
MAGNETIC KITCHEN (USA) see **CUISINE MAGNETIQUE** • 1908
MAGNETIC MAID, THE • 1913 • *Imp* • USA
MAGNETIC MONSTER, THE • 1953 • Siodmak Curt • USA
MAGNETIC MOON, THE • 1954 • *Reed Roland (P)* • USA
MAGNETIC PERSONALITY, A • 1912 • *Lux* • FRN
MAGNETIC REMOVAL • 1908 • *Pathe*
MAGNETIC SQUIRT, THE • 1909 • Halot Georges • FRN
MAGNETIC TELESCOPE, THE • 1942 • Fleischer Dave • ANS • USA
MAGNETIC TRACK see **SLAD MAGNETYCZNY** • 1978
MAGNETIC UMBRELLA, THE • 1911 • *Pathe* • FRN
MAGNETIC VAPOUR • 1908 • *Lubin* • FRN
MAGNETISEUR, LE • 1897 • Melies Georges • FRN • WHILE UNDER A HYPNOTIST'S INFLUENCE (UKN) ○ HYPNOTIST AT WORK, A
MAGNETISM • 1951 • Durst John • UKN
MAGNETS, THE • 1914 • *Joker* • USA
MAGNIFICENCE OF BRAVERY, THE see **SHOKOH-E-JAVANMARDI** • 1968
MAGNIFICENT, THE • 1981 • Chen Shao Peng • HKG
MAGNIFICENT ADVENTURE see **PASSPORT TO DESTINY** • 1943
MAGNIFICENT ADVENTURER see **MAGNIFICO AVVENTURIERO, IL** • 1964
MAGNIFICENT AMBERSONS, THE • 1942 • Welles Orson • USA
MAGNIFICENT AMBERSONS, THE see **PAMPERED YOUTH** • 1925
MAGNIFICENT BAKYA • 1965 • Silos Octavio • PHL
MAGNIFICENT BANDIDAS • 1968 • Marquez Artemio • PHL • MAGNIFICENT BANDITS
MAGNIFICENT BANDIT • 1967 • Diaz Leody M. • PHL
MAGNIFICENT BANDITS see **MAGNIFICENT BANDIDAS** • 1968
MAGNIFICENT BODYGUARDS • 1984 • Lo Wei • HKG
MAGNIFICENT BROTHERS • 1967 • Gaudite Solano • PHL
MAGNIFICENT BRUTE, THE • 1921 • Thornby Robert T. • USA • BLOOD BROTHER TO THE PINES
MAGNIFICENT BRUTE, THE • 1936 • Blystone John G. • USA • FOOL FOR BLONDES, A
MAGNIFICENT CHIVALRY, THE • 1973 • Lee So • HKG
MAGNIFICENT CONCUBINE, THE (USA) see **YANG KWEI FEI** • 1962
MAGNIFICENT CUCKOLD, THE see **MAGNIFICO CORNUTO, IL** • 1964
MAGNIFICENT DOLL, THE • 1946 • Borzage Frank • USA
MAGNIFICENT DOPE, THE • 1942 • Lang Walter • USA • MAGNIFICENT JERK, THE
MAGNIFICENT FLIRT, THE • 1928 • D'Arrast Harry D'Abbadie • USA
MAGNIFICENT FRAUD, THE • 1939 • Florey Robert • USA
MAGNIFICENT ISLANDS • 1965 • Zguridi Alexander • DOC • USS
MAGNIFICENT JERK, THE see **MAGNIFICENT DOPE, THE** • 1942
MAGNIFICENT LIE, THE • 1931 • Viertel Berthold • USA
MAGNIFICENT MAGICAL MAGNET OF SANTA MESA see **ADVENTURES OF FREDDIE** • 1977
MAGNIFICENT MALES • 1969 • Elfick David • SHT • ASL
MAGNIFICENT MARCH, THE see **WSPANIALY MARSZ** • 1970
MAGNIFICENT MATADOR, THE • 1955 • Boetticher Budd • USA • BRAVE AND THE BEAUTIFUL, THE (UKN)
MAGNIFICENT MEDDLER, THE • 1917 • Wolbert William • USA
MAGNIFICENT MS • 1979 • Christian Damon • USA
MAGNIFICENT NATURAL FIST • Ho Godfrey • HKG
MAGNIFICENT OBSESSION • 1935 • Stahl John M. • USA
MAGNIFICENT OBSESSION • 1954 • Sirk Douglas • USA
MAGNIFICENT OUTCAST (UKN) see **ALMOST A GENTLEMAN** • 1939
MAGNIFICENT REBEL, THE • 1960 • Tressler Georg • USA, FRG
MAGNIFICENT ROGUE, THE • 1947 • Rogell Albert S. • USA
MAGNIFICENT ROUGHNECKS • 1956 • Rose Sherman A. • USA
MAGNIFICENT SEVEN, THE • 1960 • Sturges John • USA
MAGNIFICENT SEVEN, THE see **SHICHININ NO SAMURAI** • 1954
MAGNIFICENT SEVEN DEADLY SINS, THE • 1971 • Stark Graham • UKN

MAGNIFICENT SEVEN RIDE, THE • 1972 • McCowan George • USA
MAGNIFICENT SHOWMAN, THE (UKN) see **CIRCUS WORLD** • 1963
MAGNIFICENT SINNER see **KATJA** • 1959
MAGNIFICENT SIX AND ½, THE • 1968 • Booth Harry • SRL • UKN
MAGNIFICENT TEXAN, THE see **MAGNIFICO TEXANO, IL** • 1967
MAGNIFICENT TOMORROW see **FARDAYE BA SHOKOH** • 1968
MAGNIFICENT TONY CARRERA, THE see **MAGNIFICO TONY CARRERAS, EL** • 1968
MAGNIFICENT TRAMP, THE (USA) see **ARCHIMEDE, LE CLOCHARD** • 1959
MAGNIFICENT TWO, THE • 1967 • Owen Cliff • UKN • WHAT HAPPENED AT CAMPO GRANDE? (USA)
MAGNIFICENT WARRIORS • 1987 • Chung Chi-Man Davi • HKG
MAGNIFICENT YANKEE, THE • 1950 • Sturges John • USA • MAN WITH THIRTY SONS, THE (UKN)
MAGNIFICENT ZORRO, THE • 1968 • Marquez Artemio • PHL
MAGNIFICHE SETTE, LE • 1961 • Girolami Marino • ITL
MAGNIFICHE TRE, LE see **ADORABILI E BUGIARDE** • 1959
MAGNIFICI BRUTOS DEL WEST, I • 1965 • Girolami Marino • ITL, FRN, SPN
MAGNIFICI TRE, I • 1961 • Simonelli Giorgio C. • ITL
MAGNIFICO AVVENTURIERO, IL • 1964 • Freda Riccardo • ITL, FRN, SPN • MAGNIFICENT ADVENTURER
MAGNIFICO CEFFO DA GALERA, UN • 1973 • Calic Zoran • ITL
MAGNIFICO CORNUTO, IL • 1964 • Pietrangeli Antonio • ITL, FRN • COCU MAGNIFIQUE, LE (FRN) ○ MAGNIFICENT CUCKOLD, THE
MAGNIFICO GLADIATORE, IL • 1964 • Brescia Alfonso • ITL
MAGNIFICO ROBIN HOOD, IL • 1970 • Montero Roberto Bianchi • ITL, SPN • NUEVAS AVENTURAS DE ROBIN DE LOS BOSQUES, LAS (SPN)
MAGNIFICO TEXANO, IL • 1967 • Capuano Luigi • ITL, SPN • MAGNIFICENT TEXAN, THE ○ COLT CONTRO TUTTI, UNA
MAGNIFICO TONY CARRERA, IL see **MAGNIFICO TONY CARRERAS, EL** • 1968
MAGNIFICO TONY CARRERAS, EL • 1968 • de la Loma Jose Antonio • SPN, FRG, ITL • CARRERA –DAS GEHEIMNIS DER BLONDEN KATZE (FRG) ○ MAGNIFICO TONY CARRERA, IL ○ CARRERA –THE SECRET OF THE BLONDE CAT ○ MAGNIFICENT TONY CARRERA, THE
MAGNIFICO WEST, IL • 1972 • Crea Gianni • ITL
MAGNIFIQUE, LE see **COMMENT DETRUIRE LA REPUTATION DU PLUS CELEBRE AGENT SECRET DU MONDE** • 1973
MAGNOLIA see **RIVER OF ROMANCE** • 1929
MAGNUM • 1982 • Austin Ray • TVM • USA
MAGNUM BARRACUDA • 1968 • Diaz Leody M. • PHL
MAGNUM FORCE • 1973 • Post Ted • USA
MAGNUM SPECIAL PER TONY SAITTA, UNA (ITL) see **BLAZING MAGNUM** • 1977
MAGNUM THRUST • 1981 • Bellamy Earl • USA
MAGNUS • 1989 • Bertelsson Thrainn • ICL
MAGO, EL • 1948 • Delgado Miguel M. • MXC
MAGO DE LOS SUENOS, EL • 1966 • Macian Francisco • SPN • DREAM MAKER, THE ○ MAGICIAN OF DREAMS, THE
MAGO PER FORZA • 1952 • Metz Vittorio, Marchesi Marcello, Girolami Marino • ITL • COMPELLED TO BE A MAGICIAN
MAGOICHI SAGA, THE see **SHIRIKURAE MAGOICHI** • 1969
MAGOKORO • 1939 • Naruse Mikio • JPN • SINCERITY
MAGOKORO • 1953 • Kobayashi Masaki • JPN • SINCERE HEART ○ SINCERITY
MAGOO AT SEA • 1964 • *Upa* • ANM • USA
MAGOO BEATS THE HEAT • 1956 • Burness Pete • ANS • USA
MAGOO BREAKS PAR • 1957 • Burness Pete • ANS • USA
MAGOO GOES OVERBOARD • 1957 • Burness Pete • ANS • USA
MAGOO GOES SKIING • 1954 • Burness Pete • ANS • USA
MAGOO GOES WEST • 1953 • Burness Pete • ANS • USA
MAGOO IN THE KING'S SERVICE • 1964 • *Upa* • ANM • USA
MAGOO MAKES NEWS • 1955 • Burness Pete • ANS • USA
MAGOO MEETS FRANKENSTEIN • 1961 • *Upa* • ANS • USA
MAGOO SAVES THE BANK • 1957 • Burness Pete • ANS • USA
MAGOO SLEPT HERE • 1953 • Burness Pete • ANS • USA
MAGOO'S CANINE CAPER see **MAGOO'S CANINE MUTINY** • 1956
MAGOO'S CANINE MUTINY • 1956 • Burness Pete • ANS • USA • MAGOO'S CANINE CAPER
MAGOO'S CHECK-UP • 1955 • Burness Pete • ANS • USA
MAGOO'S CRUISE • 1958 • Larriva Rudy • ANS • USA
MAGOO'S EXPRESS • 1955 • Burness Pete • ANS • USA
MAGOO'S GLORIOUS FOURTH • 1957 • Burness Pete • ANS • USA
MAGOO'S HOMECOMING • 1959 • Turner Gil • ANS • USA
MAGOO'S LODGE BROTHER • 1959 • Larriva Rudy • ANS • USA
MAGOO'S MASQUERADE • 1957 • Larriva Rudy • ANS • USA
MAGOO'S MASTERPIECE • 1953 • Burness Pete • ANS • USA
MAGOO'S MOOSE HUNT • 1957 • Cannon Robert • ANS • USA
MAGOO'S PRIVATE WAR • 1957 • Larriva Rudy • ANS • USA
MAGOO'S PROBLEM CHILD • 1956 • Burness Pete • ANS • USA
MAGOO'S PUDDLE JUMPER • 1956 • Burness Pete • ANS • USA
MAGOO'S THREE-POINT LANDING • 1958 • Burness Pete • ANS • USA
MAGOO'S YOUNG MANHOOD • 1958 • Burness Pete • ANS • USA • YOUNG MANHOOD OF MR. MAGOO, THE
MAGOROKU IS STILL ALIVE see **IKITEIRU MAGOROKU** • 1943
MAGOT DE JOSEFA, LE • 1963 • Autant-Lara Claude • FRN, ITL • PILA DELLA PEPPA, LA (ITL)
MAGPAKAILAN MAN • 1968 • Garces Armando • PHL • FOREVER
MAGPIE, THE • 1917 • Stevens Edwin • SHT • USA
MAGPIE MADNESS • 1948 • Donnelly Eddie • ANS • USA
MAGPIE STRATEGY, THE see **STRATEGIJA SVRAKE** • 1987
MAGRITTE • Maben D'Adriann • FRN
MAGRITTE: THE FALSE MIRROR • 1970 • Sylvester David • DCS • UKN
MAGUAR • 1960 • Sturlis Edward • ANM • PLN
MAGUL PORUWA • 1967 • Jayamanne B. A. W., Ramanathan S. • SLN • WEDDING, THE
MAGUS, THE • 1968 • Green Guy • UKN • GOD GAME, THE
MAGY GENERACIO, A • 1985 • Andras Ferenc • HNG • GREAT GENERATION, THE
MAGYAR FOLD EREJE, A • 1917 • Curtiz Michael • HNG • STRENGTH OF THE HUNGARIAN SOIL, THE
MAGYAR NABOB –KARPATHY ZOLTAN, EGY • 1966 • Varkonyi Zoltan • HNG • LAST OF THE NABOBS, THE ○ HUNGARIAN NABOB, A
MAGYAR RAPSZODIA • 1978 • Jancso Miklos • HNG • HUNGARIAN RHAPSODY (USA)
MAGYAR UGARAON, A • 1973 • Kovacs Andras • HNG • FALLOW LAND
MAGYARENFURSTIN, DIE • 1923 • Funck Werner • FRG • ZIRKUS–ROMANZE, EINE
MAGYAROK • 1978 • Fabri Zoltan • HNG • HUNGARIANS (UKN)
MAGYAROK A PRERIN • 1980 • Revesz Gyorgy • HNG • HUNGARIANS ON THE PRAIRIE
MAHA GEET • 1937 • *Biswas Anil (M)* • IND
MAHA MAYA • 1945 • *Jupiter* • IND • GREAT MAGIC
MAHA PRASTHANER PATHEY • 1952 • *Sircar B. N. (P)* • IND
MAHA SATHI • Ranga B. S. • IND
MAHABHARAT • 1919 • *Mandan J. F. (P)* • IND
MAHABHARAT • 1936 • *Tamil Nadu* • IND
MAHABHARATA • 1989 • Brook Peter • FRN
MAHADEV'S VICTORY see **JAI MAHADEV** • 1953
MAHAGEDARA • 1982 • Abeysekera Tissa • SLN
MAHALIA JACKSON see **GOT TO TELL IT: A TRIBUTE TO MAHALIA JACKSON** • 1974
MAHANAGAR • 1963 • Ray Satyajit • IND • BIG CITY, THE (UKN)
MAHANANDA • 1984 • Kavia Mohan • IND
MAHARADSCHA WIDER WILLEN • 1950 • von Rathony Akos • FRG
MAHARAJA, THE see **MAHARAYAS, O** • 1968
MAHARAJAENS YNDLINGSHUSTRU II • 1918 • Blom August • DNM • FAVOURITE WIFE OF THE MAHARAJA II, THE ○ DAUGHTER OF BRAHMA, A
MAHARAJA'S LOVE, THE see **LIEBE DES MAHARADSCHA, DIE** • 1936
MAHARANA PRATAP • 1948 • IND
MAHARATHI KARNA • 1944 • Pendharkar Bhal G. • IND
MAHARAYAS, O • 1968 • Stratzalis Kostas • GRC • MAHARAJA, THE
MAHAREJAENS YNDLINGS HUSTRU • 1916 • Gade Svend • DNM
MAHARISHI • 1984 • Thomas Isaac • CND
MAHASATI • 1944 • Vyas Vishnu • IND
MAHASATI SAVITRI • 1956 • Vaidya Ramnik D. • IND
MAHATIRTHA KALIGHAT • 1967 • Roy Bhupen • IND • KALIGHAT –PLACE OF PILGRIMAGE
MAHATMA • 1936 • Ram Shanta • IND
MAHATMA AND THE MAD BOY • 1972 • Ivory James • IND
MAHATMA KABIR MUNNA • 1954 • *Biswas Anil (M)* • IND
MAHATMA: THE GREAT SOUL • 1962 • Rasky Harry • MTV • USA
MAHIRA • Mack Max
MAHIRU NARI • 1978 • Goto Koichi • JPN • IT'S NOON
MAHIRU NO ANKOKU • 1956 • Imai Tadashi • JPN • DARKNESS AT NOON ○ SHADOWS IN SUNLIGHT
MAHIRU NO ENBUKYOKU • 1949 • Yoshimura Kozaburo • JPN • WALTZ AT NOON
MAHIRU NO HOYO • 1968 • Kataoka Hitoshi • JPN • MIDDAY HUG, A
MAHJONG MADNESS see **EKIMAE MANGAN** • 1967
MAHLER • 1974 • Russell Ken • UKN
MAHLIA LA METISSE • 1942 • Kapps Walter • FRN
MAHLOMOLA • 1976 • SAF
MAHLZEITEN • 1967 • Reitz Edgar • FRG • LUST FOR LOVE (UKN) ○ MEALTIMES
MAHO NO MAKOCHAN • 1971 • Serikawa Yugo • SHT • JPN • MAGIC MAKO
MAHOGANY • 1975 • Gordy Berry • USA
MAHOGANY MUSIC see **SARAH VAUGHN AND HERB JEFFRIES** • 1950
MAHONEY'S ESTATE see **MAHONEY'S LAST STAND** • 1975
MAHONEY'S LAST STAND • 1975 • Hart Harvey • CND • MAHONEY'S ESTATE
MAHOTSUKAI SARI • 1968 • Shitara Hiroshi • ANS • JPN • SALLY, THE WITCH
MAHOVINA NA ASFALTU • 1984 • Rancic Jovan • YGS • MOSS COVERED ASPHALT
MAHUA • 1934 • *Sircar B. N. (P)* • IND
MAHULENA, THE GOLDEN MAIDEN see **MAHULIENA, ZLATA PANNA** • 1987
MAHULIENA, ZLATA PANNA • 1987 • Luther Miroslav • CZC • MAHULENA, THE GOLDEN MAIDEN
MAI 68 • 1975 • Lawaets Gudie • DOC • FRN
MAI EAST • 1968 • Gerstein Cassandra M. • SHT • USA
MAI NAW ZA • Saya Myint • BRM
MAI–SHEN CH'I • 1978 • Hui Michael • HKG • CONTRACT, THE
MAI TI SCORDERO • 1956 • Guarino Joseph • ITL
MAIA IZ TSKHNETI • 1962 • Chkheidze Revaz • USS • MAYA FROM TSKHNETI
MAIBOWLE • 1959 • Reisch Gunter • GDR • MAYBOWL
MAIBRITT • 1964 • Hladnik Bostjan • FRG, SWD
MAICOL • 1990 • Brenta Mario • ITL
MAID, THE see **MAGD, DIE** • 1976
MAID AMONG MAIDS see **PIGA BLAND PIGOR, EN** • 1924
MAID AND A MAN, A • 1915 • Davey Horace • USA
MAID AND A MAN, A • 1918 • *Field Elinor* • USA
MAID AND THE MAN, THE • 1912 • Dwan Allan • USA
MAID AND THE MARTIAN, THE see **PAJAMA PARTY** • 1964
MAID AND THE MILKMAN, THE • 1913 • *Nestor* • USA
MAID AND THE MONEY, THE • 1914 • Plumb Hay? • UKN
MAID AT THE HELM, THE • 1911 • *Bosworth Hobart* • USA
MAID AT WAR, A • 1913 • *Bison* • USA
MAID BY PROXY, A • 1915 • Christie Al • USA
MAID FOR MURDER (USA) see **SHE'LL HAVE TO GO** • 1962
MAID FOR PLEASURE see **FILLES EXPERTES EN JEUX CLANDESTINS** • 1975
MAID FROM HEAVEN, A • 1964 • *Lin Po Ivy* • TWN
MAID FROM JUNGFRUSUND, THE see **JUNGFRU PA JUNGFRUSUND** • 1949
MAID FROM SWEDEN, THE • 1914 • Beggs Lee • USA
MAID HAPPY • 1933 • Markham Mansfield • UKN
MAID IN AMERICA • 1982 • Aaron Paul • TVM • USA
MAID IN CHINA • 1938 • Rasinski Connie • ANS • USA
MAID IN HOLLYWOOD • 1934 • Meins Gus • SHT • USA
MAID IN MOROCCO • 1925 • Lamont Charles • SHT • USA
MAID IN PARIS (USA) see **PARIS COQUIN** • 1955
MAID IN SWEDEN • 1971 • Johnson Floch • SWD, USA
MAID IN THE GARDEN, THE • 1897 • Smith G. A. • UKN
MAID MAD • 1916 • Griffin Frank C. • SHT • USA
MAID MADE MAD, A • 1943 • Lord Del • SHT • USA
MAID O' THE MOUNTAINS, THE • 1915 • Vale Travers • USA
MAID O' THE STORM • 1918 • West Raymond B. • USA
MAID OF BELGIUM, THE • 1917 • Archainbaud George • USA
MAID OF CEFN YDFA, THE • 1908 • Haggar William • UKN
MAID OF CEFN YDFA, THE • 1914 • Haggar William Jr. • UKN
MAID OF HONOR, THE • 1913 • Brabin Charles J. • USA
MAID OF MANDALAY, A • 1913 • Costello Maurice • USA
MAID OF MAORILAND, A see **BETRAYER, THE** • 1921
MAID OF NIAGARA, THE • 1910 • Golden Joseph A. • USA
MAID OF ROMANCE, THE • 1915 • Reehm George E. • USA
MAID OF SALEM • 1937 • Lloyd Frank • USA
MAID OF THE ALPS, A • 1912 • Collins Alf • UKN
MAID OF THE MIST, THE • 1915 • De Grasse Joseph • USA
MAID OF THE MOUNTAINS, A • 1909 • *Essanay* • USA
MAID OF THE MOUNTAINS, THE • 1913 • *Nestor* • USA
MAID OF THE MOUNTAINS, THE • 1932 • Lane Lupino • UKN
MAID OF THE ROCKS, THE • 1912 • *Champion* • USA
MAID OF THE SILVER SEA, A • 1922 • Newall Guy • UKN
MAID OF THE WEST • 1921 • McCullough Philo, Wallace C. R. • USA • WINGS OF LOVE
MAID OF THE WILD, THE • 1915 • *Balboa* • USA
MAID OF WAR, A • 1914 • *Beery Wallace* • USA
MAID OR MAN • 1911 • Ince Thomas H. • USA
MAID STORY, THE • 1964 • *Morishige Hisaya* • JPN
MAID TO ORDER • 1930 • Clifton Elmer • USA
MAID TO ORDER • 1939 • Roberts Charles E. • SHT • USA
MAID TO ORDER • 1987 • Jones Amy • USA
MAID TO ORDER, A • 1916 • *Hardy Babe* • USA
MAID TO ORDER, A • 1917 • *Rhodes Billie* • SHT • USA
MAID TROUBLE • 1946 • Edwards Harry J. • SHT • USA
MAID WANTED • 1918 • Lyons Eddie, Moran Lee • SHT • USA
MAIDANEK see **MAJDANEK –1944** • 1945
MAIDEN, THE (USA) see **MOME PIGALLE, LA** • 1955
MAIDEN AND MEN • 1912 • Dwan Allan • USA
MAIDEN AND THE BEAST, THE see **PANNA A NETVOR** • 1978
MAIDEN CRUISE see **MELODY CRUISE** • 1933
MAIDEN FOR A PRINCE, A see **VERGINE PER IL PRINCIPE, UNA** • 1965
MAIDEN FOR THE PRINCE, A (USA) see **VERGINE PER IL PRINCIPE, UNA** • 1965
MAIDEN IN DISTRESS, A • 1956 • Li Han-Hsiang • HKG
MAIDEN IN THE STORM • 1933 • Shimazu Yasujiro • JPN
MAIDEN OF BEZKYDY, THE see **DEVCICA Z BEZKYD** • 1944
MAIDEN OF THE PIE-FACED INDIANS, THE • 1911 • *Bainbridge Rolinda* • USA
MAIDEN QUEST see **SIEGFRIED UND DAS SAGENHAFTE LIEBESLEBEN DER NIBELUNGEN** • 1971
MAIDEN VOYAGE see **BRIDAL SUITE** • 1939
MAIDENHOOD see **PANENSTVI** • 1937
MAIDENS • 1976 • Thornley Jeni • ASL
MAIDEN'S BRIDGE, THE see **DEVOJACKI MOST** • 1976
MAIDEN'S CHEEK see **XILO VIKE AP TO PARADISO** • 1961
MAIDENS IN UNIFORM see **MADCHEN IN UNIFORM** • 1931
MAIDENS OF FETISH STREET see **GIRLS ON F– STREET, THE** • 1966
MAIDENS OF KASHIMA SEA see **KASHIMANADA NO ONNA** • 1959
MAIDEN'S PARADISE, A (USA) see **CHIMISTE REPOPULATEUR, LE** • 1901
MAIDEN'S TRUST, A • 1917 • Williams Harry • SHT • USA
MAIDS, THE • 1975 • Miles Christopher • UKN, CND
MAIDS A–COURTING • 1920 • Moore Vin • SHT • USA
MAIDS A LA MODE • 1933 • Meins Gus • SHT • USA
MAIDS AND MUSLIN • 1920 • Smith Noel • SHT • USA
MAID'S DOUBLE, THE • 1911 • *Blandick Clara* • USA
MAID'S KID, THE see **JOCHUKKO** • 1955
MAID'S NIGHT OUT • 1938 • Holmes Ben • SHT • USA
MAIDS OF WILKO, THE (USA) see **PANNY Z WILKO** • 1979
MAID'S REVENGE, A • 1911 • *Solax* • USA
MAID'S STRATAGEM, THE • 1912 • *Prescott Vivian* • USA
MAIDSTONE • 1970 • Mailer Norman • USA
MAIDSTONE • 1970 • Pennebaker D. A. • USA
MAIGRET A PIGALLE • 1966 • Landi Mario • ITL, FRN
MAIGRET DIRIGE L'ENQUETE • 1955 • Cordier Stany • FRN
MAIGRET E I GANGSTERS (ITL) see **MAIGRET VOIT ROUGE** • 1963
MAIGRET ER L'AFFAIRE SAINT–FIACRE • 1959 • Delannoy Jean • FRN, ITL
MAIGRET FAIT MOUCHE (FRN) see **MAIGRET UND SEIN GROSSTER FALL** • 1966
MAIGRET SETS A TRAP (UKN) see **MAIGRET TEND UN PIEGE** • 1957
MAIGRET TEND UN PIEGE • 1957 • Delannoy Jean • FRN, ITL • MAIGRET SETS A TRAP (UKN) ○ INSPECTOR MAIGRET (USA) ○ WOMAN BAIT
MAIGRET UND SEIN GROSSTER FALL • 1966 • Weidenmann Alfred • AUS, FRN, ITL • CASO DIFFICILE DEL COMMISSARIO MAIGRET, IL (ITL) ○ MAIGRET FAIT MOUCHE (FRN) ○ ENTER INSPECTOR MAIGRET (USA)
MAIGRET VOIT ROUGE • 1963 • Grangier Gilles • FRN, ITL • MAIGRET E I GANGSTERS (ITL)
MAIHIME • 1951 • Naruse Mikio • JPN • DANCING PRINCESS ○ DANCER, THE ○ DANCING GIRL
MAIL • 1930 • Tsekhanovsky M. M. • USS
MAIL AND FEMALE • 1937 • Newmeyer Fred • SHT • USA
MAIL BAG ROBBERY (USA) see **FLYING SCOT, THE** • 1957
MAIL–BAG ROMANCE, A • 1911 • *Powers* • USA

MAIL BY BOTTLE see **FLASKEPOST** • 1988
MAIL CALL • 1944 • Vorkapich Slavko • SHT • USA
MAIL CLERKS' TEMPTATION, THE • 1912 • *Snow Marguerite* • USA
MAIL DOG • 1947 • Nichols Charles • ANS • USA
MAIL EARLY see **MAIL EARLY FOR CHRISTMAS** • 1941
MAIL EARLY FOR CHRISTMAS • 1941 • McLaren Norman • ANS • CND • MAIL EARLY
MAIL EARLY FOR CHRISTMAS • 1959 • McLaren Norman • ANS • CND
MAIL ORDER BRIDE • 1963 • Kennedy Burt • USA • WEST OF MONTANA (UKN)
MAIL ORDER CONFIDENTIAL • 1968 • *Courtney Michael* • USA
MAIL ORDER HYPNOTIST, A • 1912 • *Selig* • USA
MAIL-ORDER WIFE, THE • 1911 • *Essanay* • USA
MAIL PILOT, THE • 1933 • Hand David • ANS • USA
MAIL ROBBERY, THE • 1925 • *Palmer George (P)* • ASL
MAIL TRAIN (USA) see **INSPECTOR HORNLEIGH GOES TO IT** • 1941
MAIL TROUBLE • 1942 • French Lloyd • SHT • USA
MAIL VAN MURDER, THE • 1957 • Knight John • UKN
MAILLON ET LA CHAINE, LE • 1961 • Ertaud Jacques, Gorsky Bernard • DOC • FRN
MAILMAN, THE • 1923 • Johnson Emory • USA • SENTINELS OF THE SEA
MAIMED IN THE HOSPITAL • 1918 • Hutchinson Craig • SHT • USA
MAIN 1 - 2 - 3 • 1918 • Santell Alfred • SHT • USA
MAIN 4400 • 1916 • Worthington William • SHT • USA
MAIN, LA • 1943 • Tedesco Jean • SHT • FRN
MAIN, LA • 1969 • Glaeser Henri • FRN, ITL • MANO, LA (ITL) ○ HAND, THE
MAIN A COUPER, LA • 1974 • Perier Etienne • FRN, ITL • CADAVERE DI TROPPO, UN (ITL) ○ AND HOPE TO DIE
MAIN A FRAPPE, UNE • 1939 • Roudes Gaston • FRN
MAIN ACTOR, THE (UKN) see **HAUPTDARSTELLER, DER** • 1978
MAIN ATTRACTION, THE • 1962 • Petrie Daniel • UKN
MAIN CHANCE, THE • 1964 • Knight John • UKN
MAIN CHAUDE, LA • 1959 • Oury Gerard • FRN, ITL • MANO CALDA, LA (ITL) ○ ETERNAL ECSTASY
MAIN COUPEE, LA • 1909 • Durand Jean • FRN
MAIN DER FER • 1912 • Perret Leonce • FRN
MAIN DU DIABLE, LA • 1922 • FRN • DEVIL'S HAND, THE
MAIN DU DIABLE, LA • 1942 • Tourneur Maurice • FRN • DEVIL'S HAND, THE (USA) ○ MAIN ENCHANTEE, LA ○ CARNIVAL OF SINNERS
MAIN DU PROFESSEUR HAMILTON, LA • 1903 • Blache Alice • FRN • ROI DES DOLLARS, LE
MAIN DU SQUELETTE, LA • 1915 • Schneevoigt George • FRN • HAND OF THE SKELETON, THE
MAIN ENCHANTEE, LA see **MAIN DU DIABLE, LA** • 1942
MAIN ENEMY, THE see **ENEMIGO PRINCIPAL, EL** • 1973
MAIN EVENT, THE • 1927 • Howard William K. • USA
MAIN EVENT, THE • 1938 • Dare Danny • USA
MAIN EVENT, THE • 1979 • Zieff Howard • USA
MAIN HOON ALLADIN • 1965 • Sippy Ramkishen • IND • I AM ALLADIN
MAIN-MAIN HANTU • 1990 • Lu Chun, Dahalan Junaidi • MLY • GHOST STORY
MAIN MYSTERIEUSE, LA • 1916 • Cohl Emile • ANS • FRN
MAIN NASHE ME HOON • 1959 • *Kapoor Raj* • IND
MAIN NOIRE, LA • 1970 • Pecas Max • FRN, ITL • MANO NERA, LA (ITL)
MAIN PRIZE • 1958 • Novak Ivo • CZC
MAIN QUI A TUE, LA • 1924 • Gleize Maurice • FRN
MAIN QUI ENTREINT, LA • 1915 • Gasnier Louis J. • SHT • FRN • MAX AND THE CLUTCHING HAND (USA) ○ GRASPING HAND, THE
MAIN SECOURABLE, LE • 1908 • Melies Georges • FRN • HELPING HAND
MAIN STREET • 1923 • Beaumont Harry • USA
MAIN STREET see **CALLE MAYOR** • 1955
MAIN STREET AFTER DARK • 1944 • Cahn Edward L. • USA • PADDY ROLLERS
MAIN STREET GIRL (UKN) see **PAROLED FROM THE BIG HOUSE** • 1938
MAIN STREET KID, THE • 1948 • Springsteen R. G. • USA
MAIN STREET LAWYER • 1939 • Murphy Dudley • USA • SMALL TOWN LAWYER (UKN)
MAIN STREET OF PARIS • 1939 • Bernard J.-C. • DCS • FRN
MAIN STREET TO BROADWAY • 1953 • Garnett Tay • USA
MAIN VERTE, LA • 1910 • Desfontaines Henri • FRN
MAIN WOHI HOON • 1967 • Shamshir A. • IND • I AM THE ONE
MAIN ZINDA HOON • 1988 • Mishra Sudhir • IND • I AM LIVING (UKN)
MAINA TADANTA • 1981 • Chakraborty Utpalendu • IND • POST MORTEM
MAINE OCEAN • 1985 • Rozier Jacques • FRN • MAINE-OCEAN
MAINE-OCEAN see **MAINE OCEAN** • 1985
MAINLAND see **BOLSHAYA ZEMLYA** • 1944
MAINLY FOR MEN see **UNSER WUNDERLAND BEI NACHT** • 1959
MAINS ARABES see **AYADI ARABIYYA** • 1975
MAINS BRISEES, LES see **EACH MAN'S SON** • 1953
MAINS D'ORLAC, LES • 1959 • Greville Edmond T. • FRN, UKN • HANDS OF ORLAC, THE (UKN) ○ HANDS OF A STRANGLER
MAINS DOUCES, LES see **AYDI AN-NAIMA, AL-** • 1963
MAINS DU FUTURS, LES • 1969 • Reichenbach Francois • SHT • FRN
MAINS D'YVONNE, LES • 1912 • de Morlhon Camille • FRN
MAINS LIEES, LES • 1955 • Quignon Roland-Jean, Vachet Aloysius, Vandenberghe Paul • FRN
MAINS NEGATIVES, LES • 1978 • Duras Marguerite • SHT • FRN
MAINS NETTES, LES • 1958 • Jutra Claude • CND
MAINS SALES, LES • 1951 • Rivers Fernand • FRN • DIRTY HANDS (USA)
MAINSPRING, THE • 1916 • Conway Jack • USA
MAINSPRING, THE • 1917 • King Henry • USA
MAINTAIN THE RIGHT • 1940 • Newman Joseph M., Veer Willard V. • SHT • USA
MAINTAIN THE RIGHT • 1980 • Rose Les • MTV • CND
MAINTENANT ON L'APPELLE PLATA • 1972 • Colizzi Giuseppe • FRN
MAIORUL SI MOARTEA • 1967 • Boiangiu Alexandru • RMN • MAJOR AND DEATH, THE
MAIRE CHEZ LES LOUPS • 1921 • Durand Jean • FRN
...MAIS LES MONSTRES ETAIENT MUSELES • 1956 • Rigal Andre • SHT • FRN • BUT THE MONSTERS WERE MUZZLED
MAIS NE NOUS DELIVREZ PAS DU MAL • 1970 • Seria Joel • FRN • BUT DO NOT DELIVER US FROM EVIL ○ DON'T DELIVER US FROM EVIL
MAIS NE TE PROMENE DONC PAS TOUTE NUE • 1936 • Joannon Leo • FRN
MAIS OU EST DONC ORNICAR? • 1978 • Van Effenterre Bertrand • FRN
MAIS OU EST DONC PASSE LA 7e COMPAGNIE? • 1973 • Lamoureux Robert • FRN, ITL • DOV'E FINITA LA 7a COMPAGNIA? (ITL)
MAIS OU SONT LES ANGLAIS D'ANTAN • 1967 • Heroux Denis • DCS • CND
MAIS OU SONT LES NEGRES D'ANTAN? • 1962 • Boschet Michel, Martin Andre • ANM • FRN
MAIS QU'EST-CE QUE J'AI FAIT AU BON DIEU POUR AVOIR UNE FEMME QUI BOIT DANS LES CAFES AVEC LES HOMME • 1979 • Saint-Hamon Jan • FRN
MAIS QUEST'CE QU'ELLES VEULENT? • 1977 • Serreau Coline • DOC • FRN • BUT WHAT DO THEY WANT?
MAIS QUI A VU LE VENT see **WHO HAS SEEN THE WIND** • 1977
MAIS QUI DONC A VIOLE LINDA? • 1974 • Franco Jesus • FRN
MAIS QUI DONC M'A FAIT CE BEBE? • 1971 • Gerard Michel • FRN
MAIS TOI TU ES PIERRE • 1971 • Cloche Maurice • FRN
MAISIE • 1939 • Marin Edwin L. • USA
MAISIE GETS HER MAN • 1942 • Del Ruth Roy • USA • SHE GOT HER MAN (UKN)
MAISIE GOES TO RIO • 1944 • Beaumont Harry • USA • YOU CAN'T DO THAT TO ME (UKN)
MAISIE LOU • 1929 • Aylott Dave, Symmons E. F. • SHT • UKN
MAISIE WAS A LADY • 1940 • Marin Edwin L. • USA
MAISIE'S MARRIAGE see **MARRIED LOVE** • 1923
MAISKIE ZVEZDY • 1959 • Rostotsky Stanislav • USS, CZC • STARS IN MAY, THE ○ MAJOVE HVEZDY ○ MAY STARS
MAISON, LA • 1969 • Brach Gerard • FRN
MAISON A L'ENVERS, LA • 1902 • Zecca Ferdinand • FRN
MAISON APPRIVOISEE, UNE • 1980 • Moreau Michel • CND
MAISON AUTOMATIQUE, LA • 1916-24 • Lortac • ANS • FRN
MAISON AUX IMAGES, LA • 1955 • Gremillon Jean • SHT • FRN
MAISON BONNADIEU, LA • 1951 • Carlo-Rim • FRN
MAISON DANS LA DUNE, LA • 1934 • Billon Pierre • FRN • HOUSE ON THE DUNE, THE (USA)
MAISON DANS LA DUNE, LA • 1952 • Lampin Georges • FRN
MAISON D'ARGILE, LA • 1918 • Ravel Gaston • FRN
MAISON DE CAMPAGNE, LA • 1969 • Girault Jean • FRN
MAISON DE JEANNE, LA • 1988 • Clement Magali • FRN
MAISON DE LA CULTURE, LA • 1984 • Beaudry Michel • MTV • CND
MAISON DE LA FLECHE, LA • 1930 • Fescourt Henri • FRN
MAISON DE L'ESPOIR, LA • 1915 • de Baroncelli Jacques • FRN
MAISON DE MOLIERE, LA • 1955 • Touchard Pierre-Aime (c/d) • SHT • FRN
MAISON DE MOLIERE, LA • 1980 • Reichenbach Francois • MTV • FRN
MAISON DE POUPEE • 1972 • Losey Joseph • FRN, UKN • DOLL'S HOUSE, A (UKN)
MAISON DE SABLE, UNE see **BAITAUN MIN RIMAL** • 1972
MAISON D'EN FACE, LA • 1936 • Christian-Jaque • FRN • HOUSE ACROSS THE STREET, THE (USA)
MAISON DES AMANTS, LA • 1972 • Sassy Jean-Paul • CND
MAISON DES BOIS, LA • 1971 • Pialat Maurice • MTV • FRN • HOUSE IN THE WOODS, THE
MAISON DES BORIES, LA • 1969 • Doniol-Valcroze Jacques • FRN
MAISON DES CIGOGNES, LA • BLG • HOUSE OF STORKS, THE
MAISON DES DANSES • 1930 • Tourneur Maurice • FRN
MAISON DES FILLES PERDUES, LA • 1974 • Chevalier Pierre • FRN, ITL • CASA DELLE BAMBOLE CRUDELI, LA (ITL)
MAISON DES LIONS, LA • 1912 • Feuillade Louis • FRN
MAISON DES SEPT JEUNES FILLES, LA • 1941 • Valentin Albert • FRN
MAISON DU CRIME, LA • 1952 • Stengel Christian • FRN
MAISON DU FANTOCHE, LA • 1916 • Cohl Emile • ANS • FRN • FANTOCHE CHERCHE UN LOGEMENT
MAISON DU MALTAIS, LA • 1927 • Fescourt Henri • FRN • KARINA THE DANCER
MAISON DU MALTAIS, LA • 1938 • Chenal Pierre • FRN • SIROCCO (USA)
MAISON DU MYSTERE, LA • 1922 • Volkov Alexander • FRN
MAISON DU MYSTERE, LA • 1933 • Roudes Gaston • FRN
MAISON DU PRINTEMPS, LA • 1949 • Daroy Jacques • FRN
MAISON DU SILENCE, LA see **VOCE DEL SILENZIO, LA** • 1952
MAISON DU SOLEIL, LA • 1929 • Roudes Gaston • FRN
MAISON DU SOUVENIR, LA see **CASA RICORDI** • 1954
MAISON DU VICE, LA • de Nesle Robert • FRN
MAISON EN HANTEE, LA • 1907 • de Chomon Segundo • FRN • HAUNTED HOUSE, THE
MAISON EN ORDRE, LA see **HOUSE IN ORDER** • 1936
MAISON JAUNE DE RIO, LA • 1930 • Peguy Robert, Grune Karl • FRN
MAISON N.13, LA see **MANZIL RAQM THALATHATAASHAR** • 1952
MAISON QUI EMPECHE DE VOIR LA VILLE, LA • 1974 • Audy Michel • FRN
MAISON REINVENTEE: LE MODELE QUEBECOIS, LA • 1976 • Dansereau Fernand, Rossignol Yolande • DCS • CND
MAISON REINVENTEE: L'ESPACE INTERIEUR, LA • 1976 • Dansereau Fernand, Rossignol Yolande • DCS • CND
MAISON SOUS LA MER, LA • 1946 • Calef Henri • FRN
MAISON SOUS LES ARBRES, LA • 1971 • Clement Rene • FRN, ITL • UNICO INDIZIO UNA SCIARPA GIALLA (ITL) ○ DEADLY TRAP, THE (UKN) ○ DEATH SCREAM
MAISON TELLIER, LA • Chevalier Pierre • FRN
MAISON TRANQUILLE, LA • 1901 • Melies Georges • SHT • FRN • WHAT IS HOME WITHOUT THE BOARDER?
MAISON VIDE, LA • 1921 • Bernard Raymond • FRN
MAISONS • 1948 • Dekeukeleire Charles • BLG
MAISONS CLOSES • Hustaix Lucien • FRN
MAISONS DE LA MISERE, LES • 1937 • Storck Henri • DOC • BLG
MAITA • 1919 • Moest Hubert • FRG
MAITIGHAR • 1960 • NPL • HOME OF A MARRIED WOMAN'S PARENTS
MAITRE • Otero Manuel, Leroux Jacques • ANS • FRN • MASTER
MAITRE APRES DIEU • 1950 • Daquin Louis • FRN • SKIPPER NEXT TO GOD
MAITRE BOLBEC ET SON MARI • 1934 • Natanson Jacques • FRN
MAITRE CHEZ SOI • 1932 • Greville Edmond T. • SHT • FRN
MAITRE DE FORGES, LE • 1913 • Pouctal Henri • FRN
MAITRE DE FORGES, LE • 1933 • Rivers Fernand, Gance Abel • FRN
MAITRE DE FORGES, LE • 1947 • Rivers Fernand • FRN
MAITRE DE LA FOUDRE, LE • 1916 • Feuillade Louis • FRN
MAITRE DE MONTPELIER, LE • 1960 • Leenhardt Roger • DCS • FRN
MAITRE DE MUSIQUE, LE • 1988 • Corbiau Gerard • BLG • MUSIC TEACHER, THE (UKN)
MAITRE D'ECOLE, LE • 1981 • Berri Claude • FRN
MAITRE DU PEROU, LE • 1958 • Dansereau Fernand • CND
MAITRE DU TEMPS, LE • 1970 • Pollet Jean-Daniel • FRN, BRZ • MASTER OF TIME, THE
MAITRE EVORA • 1922 • Roudes Gaston • FRN
MAITRE FATMA see **USTADHA FATMA, AL-** • 1952
MAITRE GALIP • 1964 • Pialat Maurice • SHT • FRN
MAITRE NAGEUR, LE • 1978 • Trintignant Jean-Louis • FRN
MAITRES ARTISANS DU CANADA see **CRAFTSMEN OF CANADA** • 1957
MAITRES DU SOLEIL, LES • 1983 • Aublanc Jean-Jacques • FRN
MAITRES DU TEMPS, LES • 1982 • Laloux Rene • ANM • FRN, FRG, SWT
MAITRES FOUS, LES • 1955 • Rouch Jean • DCS • FRN
MAITRES-NAGEURS, LES • 1950 • Lepage Henri • FRN • MAITRES NAGEURS, LES
MAITRES NAGEURS, LES see **MAITRES-NAGEURS, LES** • 1950
MAITRES-SONDEURS, LES see **ROUGHNECKS** • 1960
MAITRESSE • 1976 • Schroeder Barbet • FRN • MISTRESS (USA)
MAITRESSE, LA • 1973 • Van Der Water Anton • CND
MAITRESSES DE VACANCES, LES • 1973 • Unia Pierre • FRN
MAITRESSES POUR COUPLES • 1979 • Roy Jean-Claude • FRN
MAITRESSES TRES PARTICULIERES • 1979 • Bernard-Aubert Claude • FRN
MAIVAISE PLAISANTERIE • 1901 • Melies Georges • FRN • PRACTICAL JOKE IN A BAR ROOM
MAIZE see **KUKURYDZA** • 1955
MAJ FROM MALO see **MAJ PA MALO** • 1947
MAJ PA MALO • 1947 • Bauman Schamyl • SWD • MAJ FROM MALO
MAJA DE LOS CANTARES, LA • 1946 • Perojo Benito • ARG
MAJA DEL CAPOTE, LA • 1944 • Delgado Fernando • SPN
MAJA DESNUDA, LA (ITL) see **NAKED MAJA, THE** • 1959
MAJA ZWISCHEN ZWEI EHEN • 1938 • Kirchhoff Fritz • FRG
MAJD A ZSUZSI • 1938 • Gaal Bela • HNG
MAJD HOLNAP • 1980 • Elek Judit • HNG • HOLNAP MAJD HOLNAP ○ MAYBE TOMORROW
MAJDANEK -1944 • 1945 • Bossak Jerzy, Ford Aleksander • DOC • PLN • MAJDANEK IN 1944 ○ MAJDANEK - CMENTARZYSKO EUROPY ○ MAIDANEK
MAJDANEK -CMENTARZYSKO EUROPY see **MAJDANEK -1944** • 1945
MAJDANEK IN 1944 see **MAJDANEK -1944** • 1945
MAJERAYE SHABE JANVEYE • 1968 • Vahdat Nosratolah • IRN • STORY OF CHRISTMAS NIGHT, THE
MAJESTAT AUF ABWEGEN • 1958 • Stemmle R. A. • FRG
MAJESTAT SCHNEIDET BUBIKOPFE • 1928 • Hylten-Cavallius Ragnar • FRG
MAJESTE BLANCHE, LA see **UN DE LA MONTAGNE** • 1933
MAJESTIC THUNDERBOLT • 1985 • Ho Godfrey • HKG
MAJESTY CAT, THE see **NAN HSIA CHAN CHAO** • 1977
MAJESTY OF THE LAW, THE • 1910 • *Vitagraph* • USA
MAJESTY OF THE LAW, THE • 1915 • Ivers Julia Crawford? • USA
MAJHLI DIDI • 1968 • Mukherjee Hrishikesh • IND • SECOND SISTER
MAJIN NO TSUME see **SATAN NO TSUME** • 1959
MAJIN STRIKES AGAIN (USA) see **DAIMAJIN GUAKUSHU** • 1966
MAJIN, THE HIDEOUS IDOL see **DAIMAJIN** • 1966
MAJIN, THE MONSTER OF TERROR see **DAIMAJIN** • 1966
MAJIN (USA) see **DAIMAJIN** • 1966
MAJNUNAL KAIROUAN • 1937 • Creuzi J. A. • TNS
MAJO NO TAKKYUBIN • 1989 • Miyazaki Hayao • ANM • JPN • KIKI'S DELIVERY SERVICE
MAJOR AND DEATH, THE see **MAIORUL SI MOARTEA** • 1967
MAJOR AND THE JUDGE, THE • 1909 • *Lubin* • USA
MAJOR AND THE MINOR, THE • 1942 • Wilder Billy • USA
MAJOR BARBARA • 1941 • Pascal Gabriel, French Harold, Lean David • UKN
MAJOR BAUK • 1951 • Popovic Nikola • YGS
MAJOR DIFFICULTIES • 1938 • Brock Lou • SHT • USA
MAJOR DUNDEE • 1965 • Peckinpah Sam • USA
MAJOR FROM IRELAND, THE see **MAYOR FROM IRELAND, THE** • 1912
MAJOR GOOGLE • 1936 • *Mintz Charles (P)* • ANS • USA
MAJOR HUBAL see **HUBAL** • 1974

MAJOR KIDSON'S POLICE BLOODHOUNDS • 1908 • *Gaumont* • UKN
MAJOR LEAGUE • 1989 • Ward David S. • USA
MAJOR LIED TILL DAWN, THE • 1938 • Tashlin Frank • ANS • USA
MAJOR THE RED CROSS DOG • 1911 • Bouwmeester Theo • UKN
MAJOR UND DIE STIERE, DER • 1955 • von Borsody Eduard • FRG
MAJOR VIKHR see **MAYOR VIKHR** • 1968
MAJOR WILSON'S LAST STAND • 1899 • *Warwick Trading Co* • UKN
MAJORATSERBE, DER • 1915 • Halm Alfred • FRG
MAJORATSHERR, DER • 1944 • Deppe Hans • FRG
MAJORDOME, LE • 1965 • Delannoy Jean • FRN
MAJORETTES, THE see **ONE BY ONE** • 1986
MAJORITY OF ONE, A • 1961 • LeRoy Mervyn • USA
MAJOR'S DILEMMA, THE • 1917 • SAF
MAJOVE HVEZDY see **MAISKIE ZVEZDY** • 1959
MAJSTER KAT • 1965 • Bielik Palo • CZC • EXECUTIONER, THE ○ HANGMAN, THE
MAJSTOR I MARGARITA • 1973 • Petrovic Aleksandar • YGS, ITL • MAESTRO E MARGHERITA, IL (ITL) ○ MASTER AND MARGARITA, THE
MAJSTOR I SAMPITA • 1987 • Prelic Svetislav Bata • YGS • MASTER AND THE CREAM-PUFF, THE
MAJSTORI • 1981 • Paskaljevic Goran • YGS • MASTERS, THE
MAJSTORI, MAJSTORI • 1982 • Markovic Goran • YGS • WOULD YOU BELIEVE IT?
MAJUBA • 1968 • Millin David • SAF
MAKAI TENSHO • 1981 • Fukasaku Kinji • JPN • SAMURAI REINCARNATION
MAKARONI BLUES • 1985 • Csepcsanyi Bela • NRW • MACARONI BLUES
MAKARRAS CONEXION • 1977 • Calatrava Hermanos • SPN
MAKBET see **MAGBET** • 1969
MAKE A FACE • 1971 • Sperling Karen, Tau Avraham • USA
MAKE A FUNNY FACE • 1972 • Mitta Alexander • USS
MAKE A MILLION • 1935 • Collins Lewis D. • USA
MAKE A WISH • 1937 • Neumann Kurt • USA
MAKE BELIEVE • 1922 • *Parkinson H. B. (P)* • SHT • UKN
MAKE BELIEVE BALLROOM • 1949 • Santley Joseph • USA
MAKE-BELIEVE REVUE, THE • 1935 • *Mintz Charles (P)* • ANS • USA
MAKE-BELIEVE TALES see **PEDARASI PEDDAMMA KATHA** • 1968
MAKE-BELIEVE WIFE, THE • 1918 • Robertson John S. • USA
MAKE FRUITFUL THE LAND • 1945 • Annakin Ken • DOC • UKN
MAKE HASTE TO LIVE • 1954 • Seiter William A. • USA
MAKE IT SNAPPY • 1921 • Roach Hal • SHT • USA
MAKE IT SNAPPY • 1924 • Lamont Charles • SHT • USA
MAKE IT THREE • 1938 • MacDonald David • UKN
MAKE LIKE A THIEF • 1964 • Thompson Palmer, Long Richard • USA, FNL
MAKE LOVE • Kamei Takehiko • ANS • JPN
MAKE LOVE, NOT WAR see **VOLITE SE, A NE RATUJTE** • 1972
MAKE LOVE NOT WAR -DIE LIEBESGESCHICHTE UNSERER ZEIT • 1968 • Klett Werner • FRG • MAKE LOVE NOT WAR -THE LOVE STORY OF OUR TIME
MAKE LOVE NOT WAR -THE LOVE STORY OF OUR TIME see **MAKE LOVE NOT WAR -DIE LIEBESGESCHICHTE UNSERER ZEIT** • 1968
MAKE LOVE, NOT WAR (USA) see **NON FACCIO LA GUERRA, FACCIO L'AMORE** • 1966
MAKE ME A STAR! • 1932 • Beaudine William • USA • GATES OF HOLLYWOOD
MAKE ME A WOMAN see **SISTERS, THE** • 1965
MAKE ME AN OFFER • 1954 • Frankel Cyril • UKN
MAKE ME AN OFFER • 1980 • Paris Jerry • TVM • USA • HOUSE HUNTING
MAKE ME HAPPY • 1977 • FRG
MAKE MINE A DOUBLE (USA) see **NIGHT WE DROPPED A CLANGER, THE** • 1959
MAKE MINE A MILLION • 1959 • Comfort Lance • UKN • LOOK BEFORE YOU LAUGH
MAKE MINE LAUGHS • 1949 • Fleischer Richard • USA
MAKE MINE MINK • 1960 • Asher Robert • UKN
MAKE MINE MUSIC • 1945 • Kinney Jack, Geronimi Clyde, Luske Hamilton, Cormack Robert, Meador Joshua • ANM • USA • SWING STREET
MAKE OUT • 1968 • Clay Adam • USA
MAKE OUT MADAM • 1970 • *Mitam Productions* • USA
MAKE OUT -SUBURBAN STYLE • 1969 • *Mitam Productions* • USA
MAKE THEM DIE SLOWLY see **CANNIBAL FEROX** • 1980
MAKE-UP AND MARRIAGE • 1916 • *Jockey* • USA
MAKE WAY FOR A LADY • 1936 • Burton David • USA
MAKE WAY FOR LILA (USA) see **LAILA** • 1958
MAKE WAY FOR TOMORROW • 1937 • McCarey Leo • USA • YEARS ARE SO LONG, THE ○ WHEN THE WIND BLOWS
MAKE YOUR EYES BEHAVE • 1917 • Hotaling Arthur D. • SHT • USA
MAKE YOUR OWN BED • 1944 • Godfrey Peter • USA
MAKEDONSKA KRVAVA SVADBA • 1968 • Popov Trajce • YGS • BLOODY MACEDONIAN WEDDING, THE ○ BLOODSHED ON THE WEDDING
MAKEDONSKI DEO PAKLA • 1972 • Mimica Vatroslav • YGS • MACEDONIA'S PART OF HELL
MAKEDONSKIOT DEL OD PEKOLOT • 1971 • Mimica Vatroslav • YGS
MAKELAR KODOK • 1990 • INN
MAKENE • Greve Bruno • SHT • NRW • SEAGULLS, THE
MAKER • 1989 • Lokkeberg Vibeke • NRW • SEAGULLS
MAKER OF DIAMONDS, THE see **DIAMOND MAKER, THE** • 1909
MAKER OF DREAMS, THE • 1915 • Vignola Robert G. • USA
MAKER OF GUNS, A • 1915 • *Anderson Mignon* • USA
MAKER OF MEN • 1931 • Sedgwick Edward • USA
MAKERAREMASEN KATSUMADEWA • 1958 • Toyoda Shiro • JPN
MAKERS, MOTIFS AND MATERIALS • 1959 • Hettiarachi P. • DOC • SLN
MAKERS OF MEN • 1925 • Sheldon Forrest • USA
MAKERS OF WINE • 1948 • Monkman Noel • DOC • ASL
MAKEUP • 1937 • Zeisler Alfred • UKN
MAKHDOU OUN, AL- see **MAKHDU UN, AL-** • 1972
MAKHDU UN, AL- • 1972 • Saleh Tewfik • SYR • DECEIVED ONES, THE ○ BETRAYED, THE ○ DUPES, LES ○ MAKHDOU OUN, AL- ○ CHEATED, THE
MAKI ALLAST VALLAL • 1916 • Balazs Bela • HNG
MAKIN' IT • 1970 • Hartog Simon • UKN
MAKIN LAMA, MAKIN ASYIK • 1987 • INN
MAKIN' MOVIES • 1922 • Litson Mason N. • USA
MAKING A BASEBALL BUG • 1913 • *Lubin* • USA
MAKING A CONVERT • 1914 • Collins John H. • USA
MAKING A DIFFERENCE • 1984 • Shekter Louise • DCS • CND
MAKING A LIVING • 1914 • Lehrman Henry • USA • BUSTED JOHNNY, A ○ DOING HIS BEST ○ TROUBLES
MAKING A MAN • 1922 • Henabery Joseph • USA
MAKING A MAN OF HER • 1912 • *Mcdonald Donald* • USA
MAKING A MAN OF HIM • 1910 • *Lubin* • USA
MAKING A MAN OF HIM • 1911 • *Harte Betty* • USA
MAKING A MAN OF HIM • 1912 • Thornton F. Martin? • UKN
MAKING A MAN OF HIM • 1914 • *Captain Kettle* • UKN
MAKING A MAN OF HIS SON • 1911 • *Champion* • USA
MAKING A MAN OF JOHNNY • 1915 • Douglass James • USA
MAKING A WELSH RABBIT • 1903 • *Osterman Kathryn* • USA
MAKING AN AMERICAN CITIZEN • 1912 • *Beggs Lee* • USA
MAKING AN IMPRESSION • 1916 • Currier Frank • SHT • USA
MAKING AUNTIE WELCOME • 1914 • Louis Will • USA
MAKING BISCUIT • 1987 • Laura Sharon • DOC • ASL
MAKING CONTACT • 1986 • Emmerich Roland, Dittrich Klaus • FRG • JOEY
MAKING 'EM MOVE • 1931 • Foster John, Bailey Harry • ANS • USA • IN A CARTOON STUDIO
MAKING FRIENDS • 1936 • Fleischer Dave • ANS • USA
MAKING GOOD • 1912 • *Imp* • USA
MAKING GOOD • 1912 • Melies Gaston • USA
MAKING GOOD • 1913 • *Lubin* • USA
MAKING GOOD • 1913 • *Essanay* • USA
MAKING GOOD • 1916 • Mix Tom • SHT • USA
MAKING GOOD • 1923 • *Morrison Pete* • USA
MAKING GOOD • 1932 • Lantz Walter, Nolan William • ANS • USA
MAKING GOOD see **RIGHT WAY, THE** • 1921
MAKING GOOD RESOLUTIONS • 1922 • Dudley Bernard • UKN
MAKING GOOD WITH HER FAMILY • 1914 • Jackson Harry • USA
MAKING GOOD WITH MOTHER • 1919 • *Grossmith Laurence* • SHT • USA
MAKING HEROES • 1912 • Porter Edwin S. • USA
MAKING HIM OVER -FOR MINNIE • 1914 • *Essanay* • USA
MAKING HIMSELF A HERO • 1913 • *Komic* • USA
MAKING IT • 1971 • Erman John • USA
MAKING IT • 1984 • Allen Tom C. • MTV • CND
MAKING IT see **FIGLIO DELLE STELLE, IL** • 1979
MAKING IT HAPPEN • 1985 • Casson Barry • DOC • CND
MAKING IT MOVE • 1977 • Halas John • ANS • UKN
MAKING IT (UKN) see **VALSEUSES, LES** • 1974
MAKING LOVE • 1982 • Hiller Arthur • USA
MAKING MATTERS WORSE • 1915 • *Ovey George* • USA
MAKING MICHAEL JACKSON'S THRILLER • 1984 • DOC • USA
MAKING MR. RIGHT • 1987 • Seidelman Susan • USA
MAKING MONKEY BUSINESS • 1917 • Curtis Allen • SHT • USA
MAKING MOTHER OVER • 1911 • *Kalem* • USA
MAKING MOUNTIES • 1936 • Sparling Gordon • DCS • CND
MAKING MOUNTIES • 1950 • Sparling Gordon • DCS • CND
MAKING MOVING PICTURES • 1908 • *Vitagraph* • USA
MAKING MUSIC • 1960 • Henryson Robert • SHT • UKN
MAKING MUSIC TOGETHER • 1973 • *Halas John (P)* • ANS • UKN
MAKING OF A BALLET, THE • 1973 • Vrijman Jan • NTH
MAKING OF A GALLERY, THE • 1965 • Burstall Tim • DOC • ASL
MAKING OF A LADY, THE see **LADY HAMILTON ZWISCHEN SCHMACH UND LIEBE** • 1968
MAKING OF A LEGEND -GONE WITH THE WIND • 1989 • Hinton David • DOC • USA
MAKING OF A MALE MODEL • 1983 • Moore Irving J. • TVM • USA
MAKING OF A MAN, THE • 1911 • Griffith D. W. • USA
MAKING OF A MARTYR, THE • 1976 • Zaritsky John • MTV • CND
MAKING OF A PRESIDENT, 1960, THE • 1981 • Stuart Mel • MTV • USA
MAKING OF A WOMAN, THE • 1913 • Ricketts Thomas • USA
MAKING OF AGNES OF GOD, THE • 1985 • Dale Holly, Cole Janis • DOC • CND • QUIET ON THE SET FILMING AGNES OF GOD
MAKING OF AN AUTOMOBILE TYRE, THE • 1913 • Sennett Mack • DOC • USA
MAKING OF ART PAPER, THE see **MANUFACTURE OF ART PAPER, THE** • 1921
MAKING OF BOB MASON'S WIFE, THE • 1917 • King Burton L. • SHT • USA
MAKING OF BOBBY BURNIT, THE • 1914 • Apfel Oscar • USA
MAKING OF BRONCHO BILLY, THE • 1913 • Anderson G. M. • USA
MAKING OF CASTAWAY, THE • 1986 • Berman Brigitte • DOC • CND
MAKING OF CROOKS, THE • 1916 • Daly William Robert • SHT • USA
MAKING OF FULTON, THE • 1916 • *American Bioscpoe* • SHT • USA
MAKING OF HIM, THE • 1914 • Terwilliger George W. • USA
MAKING OF JUDY CHICAGO'S DINNER PARTY, THE see **RIGHT OUT OF HISTORY: THE MAKING OF JUDY CHICAGO'S DINNER PARTY** • 1980
MAKING OF LA CAGE, THE • 1985 • Shatalow Peter • CND
MAKING OF MADDALENA, THE • 1916 • Lloyd Frank • USA
MAKING OF O'MALLEY see **GREAT O'MALLEY, THE** • 1937
MAKING OF O'MALLEY, THE • 1925 • Hillyer Lambert • USA
MAKING OF STAR WARS / EMPIRE STRIKES BACK, THE • 1980 • *Kurtz Gary (P)* • DOC • USA
MAKING OF THE GORDONS, THE • 1922 • Sanderson Challis • UKN
MAKING OF THE WORLD, THE • 1970 • Vitandis Gheorghe • RMN
MAKING OF WEDGWOOD, THE • Catling Darrell • DCS • UKN
MAKING OPERA • 1988 • Azzopardi Anthony • DOC • CND
MAKING OVER FATHER • 1915 • MacMackin Archer • USA
MAKING OVER GRANDPA • 1915 • *Royal* • USA
MAKING OVER OF GEOFFREY MANNING, THE • 1915 • Davenport Harry • USA
MAKING OVER OF MOTHER, THE • 1916 • Davey Horace • SHT • USA
MAKING OVERTURES • 1984 • Walker John • CND
MAKING OVERTURES -THE STORY OF A COMMUNITY ORCHESTRA • 1986 • Weinstein Larry • DCS • CND
MAKING PAPER MONEY • 1922 • Dudley Bernard • UKN
MAKING PHOTOPLAYS IN EGYPT • 1912 • Olcott Sidney • DOC • USA
MAKING SAUSAGES • 1897 • Smith G. A. • UKN • END OF ALL THINGS, THE
MAKING SHERRY WINES AT XERES • 1910-12 • Melies Gaston • USA
MAKING STARS • 1935 • Fleischer Dave • ANS • USA
MAKING THE DIRT FLY • 1907 • Porter Edwin S. • USA
MAKING THE GRADE • 1921 • Butler Fred J. • USA • SOPHIE SEMENOFF
MAKING THE GRADE • 1929 • Green Alfred E. • USA
MAKING THE GRADE • 1947 • Shepherd Horace • UKN
MAKING THE GRADE • 1984 • Walker Dorian • USA • LAST AMERICAN PREPPY, THE ○ PREPPIES
MAKING THE HEADLINES • 1938 • Collins Lewis D. • USA
MAKING THE VARSITY • 1928 • Wheeler Cliff • USA
MAKING THEM COUGH UP • 1914 • Henderson Dell • USA
MAKING THINGS HUM • 1916 • Fahrney Milton • USA
MAKING TRANSITIONS • 1986 • Ianzelo Tony • MTV • CND
MAKING UNCLE JEALOUS • 1912 • *Francis Alec B.* • USA
MAKING UTU • 1983 • Preston Gaylene • NZL
MAKING WAVES see **WINDRIDER** • 1986
MAKING WHOOPEE • 1928 • Lamont Charles • SHT • USA
MAKIOKA SISTERS, THE • 1983 • Ichikawa Kon • JPN
MAKIOKA SISTERS, THE see **SASAMEYUKI** • 1950
MAKIOKA SISTERS, THE see **SASAMEYUKI** • 1959
MAKKA NA UBUGE • 1968 • Watanabe Mamoru • JPN • SCARLET HAIR
MAKKERS STAAKT UW WILD GERAAS • 1960 • Rademakers Fons • NTH • THAT JOYOUS EVE
MAKKHETES • 1916 • Curtiz Michael • HNG • SEVEN OF CLUBS
MAKO: THE JAWS OF DEATH see **JAWS OF DEATH, THE** • 1976
MAKSIMENKO BRIGAD, A • 1950 • Koza • HNG • MAXIMENKO BRIGADE, THE
MAKTUB see **MEKTOUB?** • 1970
MAKULU • 1972 • SAF • ROGUE LION
MAL, EL • 1965 • Gazcon Gilberto • MXC, USA • RAGE, THE
MAL AIRE • 1951 • Perla Alejandro • SPN, FRN • MALAIRE
MAL AMADO, O • 1974 • Silva Fernando Matos • PRT • BAD LOVE
MAL D'AFRICA • 1967 • Nievo Stanis • DOC • ITL • AFRICAN SICKNESS
MAL DE ESPANA • 1918 • de Barros Jose Leitao • PRT
MAL DE MER, LE • 1912 • Linder Max • FRN
MAL DE PARLER, LE • 1972 • Moreau Michel • DCS • CND
MAL DES AUTRES, LE • 1959 • Logereau Edouard • SHT • FRN
MAL DES SIECLES, LE see **CAS DU DOCTEUR GALLOY, LE** • 1949
MAL DRUNTER, MAL DRUBER • 1960 • Weiss Helmut • FRG • DRUNTER UND DRUBER
MAL DU SIECLE, LE • 1950 • Lelouch Claude • DCS • FRN
MAL MORSKA VILA • 1976 • Kachyna Karel • CZC • LITTLE MERMAID, THE ○ LITTLE SEA NYMPH, THE
MAL PARTIS, LES • 1975 • Rossi Jean-Baptiste • FRN
MAL WALDRON • 1971 • Hillgruber Hans-Gert • SHT • FRG
MALA see **LAST OF THE PAGANS** • 1935
MALA-FEMMINA • 1919 • Palermi Amleto • ITL
MALA HEMBRA • 1950 • Delgado Miguel M. • MXC
MALA KRONIKA • 1962 • Mimica Vatroslav • ANS • YGS • EVERYDAY CHRONICLE (USA) ○ LITTLE CHRONICLE, A ○ LITTLE STORY, A
MALA NOCHE • Van Sant Gus • USA
MALA ORDINA, LA • 1972 • Di Leo Fernando • ITL, FRG • MAFIA BOSS: SIE TOTEN WIE SCHAKALE, DER (FRG) ○ MANHUNT IN MILAN (UKN) ○ ITALIAN CONNECTION, THE (USA) ○ MAN ON THE RUN ○ MANHUNT
MALA PIANTA, LA • 1911 • Caserini Mario • ITL
MALA SIRENA • 1968 • Marks Aleksandar, Jutrisa Vladimir • ANS • YGS • LITTLE SIREN ○ SMALL MERMAID, A
MALA THE MAGNIFICENT (UKN) see **ESKIMO** • 1933
MALA VIDA, LA • 1973 • Fregonese Hugo • ARG • WRONG SIDE OF THE TRACKS, THE
MALA YERBA • 1940 • Soria Gabriel • MXC
MALABARS SONT AU PARFUM, LES • 1965 • Lefranc Guy • FRN
MALABESTIA • 1978 • Leoncini Leonida • ITL
MALACA • 1960 • Spiguel Miguel • SHT • PRT
MALACARNE • 1947 • Mercanti Pino, Zucca Giuseppe • ITL
MALACCA • 1986 • Sjoman Vilgot • SWD
MALACHEV KIRGAN • 1944 • Heifitz Josif, Zarkhi Alexander • USS • MALAKHOV BURIAL-MOUND, THE ○ LAST HILL, THE
MALACHIAS see **WUNDER DES MALACHIAS, DAS** • 1961
MALACHI'S COVE • 1974 • Herbert Henry • UKN • SEAWEED CHILDREN, THE
MALADE HYDROPHOPE, LE • 1900 • Melies Georges • FRN • MAN WITH WHEELS IN HIS HEAD, THE (USA) ○ GOUTY PATIENT, THE
MALADE IMAGINAIRE, LE • 1897 • Melies Georges • FRN • IMAGINARY PATIENT, AN
MALADE IMAGINAIRE, LE • 1934 • Jaquelux, Merenda Marc • FRN
MALADIE CONTAGIEUSE see **CORBEAU, LE** • 1943

MALADIE DE HAMBOURG, LA (FRN) see **HAMBURGER KRANKEIT, DIE** • 1980
MALADIES CONTAGIEUSES, LES • Tessier Albert • DCS • CND
MALADOLESCENZA • 1977 • Murgia Piergiuseppe • ITL
MALAFEMMINA • 1957 • Fizzarotti Armando • ITL
MALAGA • 1954 • Sale Richard • UKN • FIRE OVER AFRICA (USA)
MALAGA (USA) see **MOMENT OF DANGER** • 1960
MALAGACHE ADVENTURE, THE see **AVENTURE MALGACHE** • 1944
MALAGUENA • 1956 • Nunez Ricardo • SPN
MALAGUENA, LA • 1947 • Delgado Agustin P. • MXC
MALAIRE see **MAL AIRE** • 1951
MALAJLUCKAN see **SAMVETSOMMA ADOLF** • 1936
MALAK AS-SAGHIR, AL- • 1958 • el Sheikh Kamal • EGY • PETIT ANGE, LE
MALAK EL RAHMA • 1947 • Wahby Youssef • EGY • ANGEL OF MERCY, THE
MALAKHOV BURIAL-MOUND, THE see **MALACHEV KIRGAN** • 1944
MALAKOOT • 1975 • Haritash Khosrow • IRN • DIVINE ONE, THE
MALAKUN WA SHAITAN • 1960 • el Sheikh Kamal • EGY • ANGE ET DEMON
MALAMONDO • 1964 • Lewis Jack • USA
MALAMONDO, I • 1964 • Cavara Paolo • DOC • ITL
MALANDRO (USA) see **OPERA DO MALANDRO** • 1985
MALANGA • 1967 • Dewdney Alexander Keewatin • CND
MALAREK: A STREET KID WHO MADE IT • 1988 • Cardinal Roger • CND
MALAREN • 1981 • Du Rees Goran, Olofsson Christina • SWD • PAINTER, THE
MALARIA • 1919 • Gliese Rochus • FRG
MALARIA • 1942 • Gourguet Jean • FRN
MALARIA • 1982 • List Niki • AUS
MALARPIRATER • 1923 • *Molander Gustaf (Sc)* • SWD • PIRATES ON LAKE MALAR
MALARPIRATER • 1959 • Holmgren Per Gosta • SWD • PIRATES ON LAKE MALAR
MALASPINA • 1947 • Fizzarotti Armando • ITL
MALATESTA • 1970 • Lilienthal Peter • FRG
MALATESTA'S CARNIVAL • 1972 • Speeth Christopher • USA • MALATESTA'S CARNIVAL OF BLOOD
MALATESTA'S CARNIVAL OF BLOOD see **MALATESTA'S CARNIVAL** • 1972
MALATO IMMAGINARIO, IL • 1979 • Cervi Tonino • ITL
MALAVENTURA • 1988 • Gutierrez Aragon Manuel • SPN • MISFORTUNE ○ MISADVENTURE
MALAVITA • 1951 • Furlan Rate • ITL
MALAVITA • 1976 • Pettinari Daniele • ITL
MALAVITA ATTACCA.. LA POLIZIA RISPONDE, LA • 1977 • Caiano Mario • ITL
MALAY NIGHTS • 1932 • Hopper E. Mason • USA • SHADOWS OF SINGAPORE (UKN)
MALAYA • 1949 • Thorpe Richard • USA • EAST OF THE RISING SUN (UKN)
MALAYA see **BEYOND THE BLUE HORIZON** • 1942
MALAYISCHE DSCHONKE, DIE • 1924 • Obal Max • FRG
MALAYSIA 5 • 1974 • Aristorenas Jun • MLY
MALAZGIRT KAHRAMANI ALPASLAN • 1967 • Gurses Muharrem • TRK • ALPASLAN, THE HERO OF MALAZGIRT
MALCASADA, LA • 1950 • Diaz Morales Jose • MXC
MALCHALIVITE PATEKI • 1967 • Ikonomov Vladislav • BUL • SILENT PATHS, THE
MALCHIK I GOLUB • 1958 • Konchalovsky Andrei, Ostashenko E. • USS • BOY AND A PIGEON, A ○ BOY AND THE PIGEON, THE
MALCOLM • 1986 • Tass Nadia • ASL
MALCOLM STRAUSS' SALOME see **SALOME** • 1923
MALCOLM X • 1972 • *Worth Marvin (P)* • DOC • USA
MALDENIYE SIMION • 1986 • Nihalsingha D. B. • SLN
MALDICAO DE MARIALVA, A • de Macedo Antonio • PRT
MALDICION DE FRANKENSTEIN, LA • 1972 • Franco Jesus • SPN
MALDICION DE LA BESTIA, LA • 1975 • Iglesias Miguel, de Ossorio Amando • SPN • WEREWOLF AND THE YETI, THE ○ NIGHT OF THE HOWLING BEAST
MALDICION DE LA LLORONA, LA • 1961 • Baledon Rafael • MXC • CURSE OF THE CRYING WOMAN, THE (USA) ○ CASA EMBRUJADA, LA ○ WITCH HOUSE, THE
MALDICION DE LA MOMIA AZTECA, LA • 1957 • Portillo Rafael • MXC • CURSE OF THE AZTEC MUMMY, THE (USA)
MALDICION DE LOS KARNSTEIN, LA (SPN) see **CRIPTA E L'INCUBO, LA** • 1964
MALDICION DE MI RAZA, LA • 1964 • Orol Juan • MXC, PRC • CURSE OF MY RACE, THE
MALDICION DE NOSTRADAMUS, LA • 1959 • Curiel Federico, Segar Stig (Usa Vers) • MXC • CURSE OF NOSTRADAMUS, THE (USA)
MALDICION DEL ORO, LA • 1964 • Salvador Jaime • MXC • CURSE OF GOLD, THE
MALDICION GITANA • 1953 • Mihura Jeronimo • SPN
MALDITA CIUDAD • 1954 • Rodriguez Ismael • MXC
MALDITAS PISTOLAS DE DALLAS, LAS • 1965 • Zabalza Jose Maria • SPN
MALDITAS SEAN LAS MUJERES • 1919 • Stahl Carlos • MXC
MALDITAS SEAN LAS MUJERES • 1936 • Bustillo Oro Juan • MXC
MALDITOS, LOS • 1965 • Salvador Jaime • MXC
MALDITOS SEAN LOS HOMBRES see **ESOS HOMBRES!** • 1936
MALDONNE • 1927 • Gremillon Jean • FRN • MISDEAL
MALDONNE • 1947-51 • Verneuil Henri • SHT • FRN
MALDONNE • 1968 • Gobbi Sergio • ITL, FRN
MALE AND FEMALE • 1919 • De Mille Cecil B. • USA • ADMIRABLE CRICHTON, THE (UKN)
MALE AND FEMALE see **MALE AND FEMALE SINCE ADAM AND EVE** • 1961
MALE AND FEMALE SINCE ADAM AND EVE • 1961 • Rinaldi Carlos • ARG • MALE AND FEMALE ○ SOULS OF SIN
MALE ANIMAL, THE • 1942 • Nugent Elliott • USA
MALE COMPANION (USA) see **MONSIEUR DE COMPAGNIE, UN** • 1964
MALE D'AMORE • 1974 • Brialy Jean-Claude • ITL, FRN • AMOUR DE PLUIE, UN (FRN) ○ LOVING IN THE RAIN (USA)
MALE DOLL, THE see **KOUKLOS, O** • 1968
MALE DRAMATY • 1960 • Nasfeter Janusz • PLN • LITTLE DRAMAS
MALE DU SIECLE, LE • 1975 • Berri Claude • FRN • MALE OF THE CENTURY (USA)
MALE FARM, THE see **STUD FARM, THE** • 1969
MALE & FEMALE SEXUALIS see **GUTTER TRASH** • 1969
MALE GOVERNESS, THE • 1917 • Dillon John Francis • SHT • USA
MALE HUNT (USA) see **CHASSE A L'HOMME, LA** • 1964
MALE LETNI BLUES • 1967 • Hanibal Jiri • CZC • LITTLE SUMMER BLUES
MALE MAN, THE • 1931 • Fleischer Dave • ANS • USA
MALE OF THE CENTURY (USA) see **MALE DU SIECLE, LE** • 1975
MALE OF THE SPECIES • 1968 • Jarrott Charles • MTV • UKN
MALE OSCURO, IL • 1990 • Monicelli Mario • ITL • DARK ILLNESS, THE
MALE SERVICE • 1966 • Hudson Arch • USA
MALE SHREW WHO BECAME A LAMB, THE see **STRINGLOS POV EYINE ARNAKI, O** • 1968
MALE STESTI see **VCERA NEDELE BYLA** • 1938
MALE TECHNIQUES • 1970 • USA
MALE WANTED • 1923 • *Gordon Huntley* • USA
MALEDETTI, I see **BEATRICE CENCI** • 1956
MALEDETTI VI AMERO • 1980 • Giordana Mario Tullio • ITL
MALEDETTO IMBROGLIO, UN • 1959 • Germi Pietro • ITL • FACTS OF MURDER, THE ○ CURSED TANGLE, A ○ SORDID AFFAIR, A
MALEDICTION see **NEFREEN** • 1973
MALEDICTION DE BELPHEGOR, LA • 1967 • Combret Georges, Maley Jean • FRN, ITL • S2S BASE MORTE CHIAMA SUNIPER (ITL) ○ CURSE OF BELPHEGOR, THE
MALEFICE, LE • 1912 • Feuillade Louis • FRN
MALEFICES • 1962 • Decoin Henri • FRN • WHERE THE TRUTH LIES (USA) ○ EVIL SPELL ○ SORCERY ○ EVIL SPIRITS
MALEFICIO • 1950 • Perla Alejandro • SPN
MALEFICIO • 1954 • Klimovsky Leon, de Fuentes Fernando, Rey Florian • ARG, SPN, MXC • TRES CITAS CON EL DESTINO (SPN) ○ WITCHCRAFT ○ THREE DATES WITH DESTINY
MALEFICIO ANELLO, IL • 1916 • Falena Ugo • ITL
MALEMORT DU CANARD, LA • 1929 • Silka • FRN
MALENCONTRE • 1920 • Dulac Germaine • FRN
MALENKA see **MALENKA, LA SOBRINA DEL VAMPIRO** • 1968
MALENKA, LA NIPOTE DEL VAMPIRO (ITL) see **MALENKA, LA SOBRINA DEL VAMPIRO** • 1968
MALENKA, LA SOBRINA DEL VAMPIRO • 1968 • de Ossorio Amando • SPN, ITL • MALENKA, LA NIPOTE DEL VAMPIRO (ITL) ○ MALENKA THE VAMPIRE ○ FANGS OF THE LIVING DEAD (USA) ○ NIECE OF THE VAMPIRE, THE ○ VAMPIRE'S NIECE, THE ○ MALENKA
MALENKA THE VAMPIRE see **MALENKA, LA SOBRINA DEL VAMPIRO** • 1968
MALENKI BEGLYETS • 1967 • Bocharov Edvard, Kinugasa Teinosuke • USS, JPN • CHISAI TOBASHA (JPN) ○ LITTLE RUNAWAY, THE
MALENKI PRINTS • 1968 • Zhebrunas Arunas • USS • LITTLE PRINCE, THE
MALER, DIE LIEBE UND DAS FRAULEIN, DER see **KUNSTLERLAUNEN** • 1920
MALER UND SEIN MODELL, DER • 1925 • Manoussi Jean • FRG
MALES, LES • 1970 • Carle Gilles • CND
MALESIA MAGICA • 1962 • Fabbri Lionetto • DOC • ITL
MALETA, LA • 1960 • Ruiz Raul • SHT • CHL
MALEVIL • 1981 • de Chalonge Christian • FRN, FRG
MALFALDA • 1981 • Marques Carlos, Venegas Jose Luis • ANM • ARG
MALFRAY • 1949 • Resnais Alain, Hessens Robert • DCS • FRN
MALHEUR DES AUTRES, LE • 1969 • Doniol-Valcroze Jacques • FRN
MALHEUR N'ARRIVE JAMAIS SEUL, UN • 1903 • Melies Georges • FRN • MISFORTUNE NEVER COMES ALONE (USA) ○ ACCIDENTS NEVER HAPPEN SINGLY
MALHEUR QUI PASSE, LE • 1916 • Feuillade Louis • FRN
MALHEURS D'ALFRED, LES • 1972 • Richard Pierre • FRN • MALHEURS D'ALFRED OU APRES LA PLUIE LE MAUVAIS TEMPS, LES
MALHEURS D'ALFRED OU APRES LA PLUIE LE MAUVAIS TEMPS, LES see **MALHEURS D'ALFRED, LES** • 1972
MALHEURS DE LA GUERRE, LA • 1962 • Storck Henri • DOC • BLG • SORROWS OF THE WAR, THE
MALHEURS DE SOPHIE, LES • 1945 • Audry Jacqueline • FRN
MALHEURS DE SOPHIE, LES • 1979 • Brialy Jean-Claude • FRN
MALHEURS D'OCTAVIE, LES • 1979 • Hurban Roland • FRN
MALI COVEK • 1957 • Cukulic Zivan • YGS • LITTLE MAN
MALI I VELIKI • 1966 • Grgic Zlatko • ANS • YGS • LITTLE AND BIG (USA)
MALI-MALI MEETS BATANGUENO • 1968 • Feleo Ben • PHL
MALI: PORTRAIT D'UN PAYS PAUVRE • 1977 • Floquet Francois • DOC • CND
MALI TODAY • 1978 • Kouyate Djibril, Segovic Branco • DCS • MLI
MALI VLAK • 1959 • Vunak Dragutin • ANS • YGS • LITTLE TRAIN, THE (USA) ○ SMALL TRAIN, A
MALI VOJNICI • 1968 • Cengic Bato • YGS • PLAYING AT SOLDIERS ○ LITTLE SOLDIERS
MALIA • 1946 • Amato Giuseppe • ITL
MALIA • 1976 • Nasca Sergio • ITL • VERGINE E DI NOME MARIA
MALIBRAN, LA • 1943 • Guitry Sacha • FRN
MALIBU • 1982 • Swackhamer E. W. • TVM • USA
MALIBU BEACH • 1978 • Rosenthal Robert J. • USA • SUNSET COVE (UKN)
MALIBU BEACH PARTY • 1940 • Freleng Friz • ANS • USA
MALIBU BIKINI SHOP, THE see **BIKINI SHOP, THE** • 1986
MALIBU EXPRESS • 1986 • Sidaris Andy • USA
MALIBU HIGH • 1979 • Berwick Irvin?, Foldes Lawrence D.? • USA
MALIBU HOT SUMMER see **SIZZLE BEACH USA** • 1986
MALICE IN SLUMBERLAND • 1942 • Geiss Alec • ANS • USA
MALICE IN THE PALACE • 1949 • White George • SHT • USA
MALICE IN WONDERLAND • 1985 • Trikonis Gus • TVM • USA
MALICIEUSE CHRISTINA • Sanders Bob W. • FRN
MALICIOUS ADOLESCENT, THE see **ADOLESCENTUL RAUTACIOS** • 1968
MALICIOUS (USA) see **MALIZIA** • 1973
MALICIOUSNESS OF THE SNAKE'S EVIL, THE see **JASEI NO IN** • 1920
MALIKA FI GEHENNAM • 1947 • Ramzi Hassan • EGY • ANGELS IN HELL
MALIKAT AL-LAYL • 1971 • Ramzi Hassan • EGY • REINE DE LA NUIT, LA
MALIKI SALOMI • 1953 • Hussein Mohamed • IND
MALIKMATA • 1967 • Abelardo Richard • PHL
MALIN PLAISIR, LE • 1974 • Toublanc-Michel Bernard • FRN
MALINA • 1990 • Schroeter Werner • FRG
MALINCONICO AUTUNNO • 1958 • Matarazzo Raffaello • SPN, ITL
MALINOVY KOKTEJL • 1982 • Sieberova Ladislava • CZC • RASPBERRY COCKTAIL
MALIOTENAM • 1963-64 • Fournier Claude • DCS • CND
MALISH GHIRAK • 1958 • Barakat Henry • EGY • JE N'AI QUE TOI
MALIZIA • 1973 • Samperi Salvatore • ITL • MALICIOUS (USA)
MALIZIE DI VENERE, LE • 1969 • Dallamano Massimo • ITL • VENERE NUDA
MALKACOGLU -KARA KORSAN • 1968 • Duru Sureyya • TRK • MALKOCOGLU, THE BLACK PIRATE
MALKAT HAKVISH • 1972 • Golan Menahem • ISR • HIGHWAY QUEEN, THE (UKN) ○ QUEEN OF THE ROAD
MALKATA • 1959 • Korabov Nicolai • BUL • LITTLE GIRL, THE ○ LASSIE, THE
MALKATA ROUSSALKA see **RUSALOCHKA** • 1976
MALKOCOGLU KRALLARA KARSI • 1967 • Duru Sureyya, Conturk Remzi • TRK • MALKOCOGLU VS. THE KINGS
MALKOCOGLU, THE BLACK PIRATE see **MALKACOGLU -KARA KORSAN** • 1968
MALKOCOGLU VS. THE KINGS see **MALKOCOGLU KRALLARA KARSI** • 1967
MALLACOOTA STAMPEDE • 1981 • Tammer Peter • ASL
MALLARME • 1964-69 • Rohmer Eric • MTV • FRN
MALLE DE MARIAGE, LA • 1912 • Linder Max • FRN
MALLENS, THE • 1978-80 • Roberts Roy • MTV • UKN
MALLORY • 1976 • Sagal Boris • TVM • USA • MALLORY: CIRCUMSTANTIAL EVIDENCE
MALLORY: CIRCUMSTANTIAL EVIDENCE see **MALLORY** • 1976
MALMAISON • 1922 • Stein Paul L. • FRG
MALMEQUER • 1918 • de Barros Jose Leitao • PRT
MALOCCHIO • 1975 • Siciliano Mario • ITL
MALOM A POKOLBAN • 1987 • Maar Gyula • HNG • MILLS OF HELL
MALOMBRA • 1916 • Gallone Carmine • ITL
MALOMBRA • 1916 • Guazzoni Enrico • ITL
MALOMBRA • 1942 • Soldati Mario • ITL
MALOMBRA see **MALOMBRA: LE PERVERSIONI SESSUALI DI UNA ADOLESCENTE** • 1983
MALOMBRA: LE PERVERSIONI SESSUALI DI UNA ADOLESCENTE • 1983 • Gaburro Bruno Alberto • ITL • MALOMBRA, THE SEXUAL PERVERSIONS OF AN ADOLESCENT ○ MALOMBRA
MALOMBRA, THE SEXUAL PERVERSIONS OF AN ADOLESCENT see **MALOMBRA: LE PERVERSIONI SESSUALI DI UNA ADOLESCENTE** • 1983
MALONE • 1987 • Cokliss Harley • USA
MALOOLA FROM PALOONA • 1915 • Aylott Dave? • UKN
MALOSTRANSTI MUSKETYRI • 1932 • Innemann Svatopluk • CZC • MUSKETEERS OF LITTLE SIDE, THE
MALOU • 1980 • Meerapfel Jeanine • FRG
MALOU DE MONTMARTRE see **DUPONT-BARBES** • 1951
MALOVANI PRO KOCKU • 1960 • Pojar Bretislav • ANM • CZC • DRAWING FOR CATS ○ PAINTING FOR THE CAT
MALPAS MYSTERY, THE • 1960 • Hayers Sidney • UKN
MALPERTIUS • 1972 • Kumel Harry • FRN, BLG, FRG • MALPERTIUS: HISTOIRE D'UNE MAISON MAUDITE ○ LEGEND OF DOOM HOUSE, THE ○ MAUDITE: LEGEND OF DOOM HOUSE
MALPERTIUS: HISTOIRE D'UNE MAISON MAUDITE see **MALPERTIUS** • 1972
MALPRACTICE • 1988 • Bennett Bill • ASL
MALQUERIDA, LA • 1949 • Fernandez Emilio • MXC
MALRIF AIGLE ROYAL • 1959 • Hessens Robert • FRN
MALSCHIFF, DER • 1965 • Spieker Franz-Josef • FRG
MALSTROMMEN see **STORE FALD, DET** • 1911
MALTA STORY • 1953 • Hurst Brian Desmond • UKN
MALTAMOUR • 1973 • Grigor Murray • DOC • UKN
MALTESE BIPPY, THE • 1969 • Panama Norman • USA • INCREDIBLE WEREWOLF MURDERS, THE ○ STRANGE CASE OF ..!#*%?, THE ○ WHO KILLED COCK RUBIN?
MALTESE CONNECTION, THE see **FINAL JUSTICE** • 1984
MALTESE CROSS MOVEMENT, THE • 1968 • Dewdney Alexander Keewatin • CND
MALTESE FALCON, THE • 1931 • Del Ruth Roy • USA • DANGEROUS FEMALE
MALTESE FALCON, THE • 1941 • Huston John • USA
MALTESE PROJECT, THE see **FINAL JUSTICE** • 1984
MALTESES ,BURGUESES E AS VEZES.. • 1973 • Semedo Artur • PRT
MALU TIANSHI • 1937 • Yuan Muzhi • CHN
MALUALA • 1979 • Giral Sergio • CUB
MALUN WA NISA' • 1960 • Al Imam Hassan • EGY • ARGENT ET LES FEMMES, L'
MALUPIT ANG PAG-IBIG • 1967 • de Villa Jose • PHL • LOVE IS CRUEL
MALUQUINHA DE ARROIOS, A • 1970 • Campos Henrique • PRT
MALVA • 1924 • Dinesen Robert • FRG • SPANISH PASSION
MALVA • 1957 • Braun Vladimir • USS
MALVADO CARABEL, EL • 1934 • Neville Edgar • SPN
MALVADO CARABEL, EL • 1955 • Fernan-Gomez Fernando • SPN

MALVADO CARABEL, EL • 1960 • Baledon Rafael • MXC
MALVADOS, LOS • 1965 • Blake Alfonso Corona • MXC
MALVALOCA • 1926 • Perojo Benito • SPN
MALVALOCA • 1942 • Marquina Luis • SPN
MALVALOCA • 1954 • Torrado Ramon • SPN
MALVILLE: ETAT DE SIEGE • 1977 • Poljinsky Serge • DOC • FRN
MALY • 1970 • Dziedzina Julian • PLN • SMALL ONE, THE
MALY BOBES • 1961 • Valasek Jan • CZC • LITTLE BOBES
MALY VELKY HOKEJISTA • 1982 • Pinkava Josef, Cvrcek Radim • CZC • LITTLE BIG HOCKEY PLAYER
MALY WESTERN • 1960 • Giersz Witold • ANS • PLN • LITTLE WESTERN ○ SMALL WESTERN
MALZENSTWO Z ROZSADKU • 1967 • Bareja Stanislaw • PLN • MARRIAGE OF CONVENIENCE
MAMA • 1973 • Prijono Ami • INN
MAMA • 1988 • Berger • SHT • SPN
MAMA BEHAVE • 1926 • McCarey Leo • SHT • USA
MAMA CUMPLE CIEN ANOS • 1979 • Saura Carlos • SPN • MUMMY'S A HUNDRED TODAY ○ MAMA TURNS 100 ○ MAMA TURNS A HUNDRED
MAMA DE LA NOVA, LA • 1978 • Carreras Enrique • ARG • MOTHER OF THE BRIDE
MAMA DE NIEBLA • 1980 • Ayala Fernando • ARG • MOTHER MIST
MAMA DRACULA see **MAMMA DRACULA** • 1980
MAMA GLORIA • 1941 • Harlan Richard • ARG
MAMA GOT MARRIED • 1969 • Melnikov Vitali • USS
MAMA I NEED YOU see **KAASAN NAGAIKI SHITENE** • 1962
MAMA, ICH LEBE • 1977 • Wolf Konrad • GDR • MUM –I'M ALIVE ○ MAMA, I'M ALIVE
MAMA, I'M ALIVE see **MAMA, ICH LEBE** • 1977
MAMA INES • 1945 • Soler Fernando • MXC
MAMA IS MAD • 1985 • van Hemert Ruud • NTH
MAMA LOVE PAPA • 1933 • McLeod Norman Z. • USA • MAMA LOVES PAPA
MAMA LOVES PAPA • 1931 • Stevens George • SHT • USA
MAMA LOVES PAPA • 1945 • Strayer Frank • USA
MAMA LOVES PAPA see **MAMA LOVE PAPA** • 1933
MAMA NO ENDAN • 1937 • Shibuya Minoru • JPN • MOTHER'S MARRIAGE PROPOSAL
MAMA NOS QUITA LOS NOVIOS • 1951 • Rodriguez Roberto • MXC
MAMA OH MAMA • 1980 • Mahmud Ahmad • MLY
MAMA.. PAPA.. • 1982 • De Geer-Bergenstrahle Marie-Louise • SHT • SWD
MAMA RUNS WILD • 1937 • Staub Ralph • USA
MAMA SANTISSIMA see **COMPLICATO INTRIGO DI DONNE, VICOLI E DELITTI, UN** • 1985
MAMA STEPS OUT • 1937 • Seitz George B. • USA
MAMA TURNS 100 see **MAMA CUMPLE CIEN ANOS** • 1979
MAMA TURNS A HUNDRED see **MAMA CUMPLE CIEN ANOS** • 1979
MAMA (USA) see **AMA, EL** • 1930
MAMAGAY • 1979 • Gaitan Jorge • VNZ, CLM
MAMAIA • 1967 • Varela Jose • FRN
MAMALIK, AL- • 1965 • Salem Atef • EGY • REVOLT OF THE MAMELUKES ○ MAMELUKES, THE
MAMAN • 1990 • Goupil Romain • FRN
MAMAN COLIBRI • 1929 • Duvivier Julien • FRN
MAMAN COLIBRI • 1937 • Dreville Jean • FRN
MAMAN ET LA PUTAIN, LA • 1973 • Eustache Jean • FRN • MOTHER AND THE WHORE, THE (USA)
MAMAN JONES • 1974 • Senechal Georges • FRN
MAMAN N'IRA PLUS A LA FETE • 1908 • Feuillade Louis • FRN
MAMAN POPEE see **MAMAN POUPEE** • 1919
MAMAN POUPEE • 1919 • Gallone Carmine • ITL • MAMAN POPEE
MAMA'S AFFAIRS • 1921 • Fleming Victor • USA
MAMA'S BABY BOY • 1923 • Mayo Archie • SHT • USA
MAMA'S BIRTHDAY PRESENT • 1910 • *Kalem* • USA
MAMA'S D-E-A-R • 1915 • Birch Cecil • UKN
MAMA'S DIRTY GIRLS • 1974 • Hayes John • USA
MAMA'S GONE A-HUNTING • 1977 • Maxwell Peter • MTV • ASL
MAMA'S LITTLE PIRATES • 1934 • Meins Gus • SHT • USA
MAMA'S NEW HAT • 1939 • Freleng Friz • ANS • USA
MAMATHE • 1968 • Swamy Y. R. • IND • AFFECTION
MAMBA • 1930 • Rogell Albert S. • USA
MAMBA • 1988 • Orfini Mario • ITL
MAMBO • 1952 • Belson Jordan • ANS • USA
MAMBO • 1954 • Rossen Robert • ITL, USA
MAMBRU SE FUE A LA GUERRA • 1985 • Fernan-Gomez Fernando • SPN • MARLBOROUGH WENT TO WAR ○ MAMBRU WENT TO WAR
MAMBRU WENT TO WAR see **MAMBRU SE FUE A LA GUERRA** • 1985
MAME • 1974 • Saks Gene • USA
MAMELE • 1938 • Tom Konrad, Green Joseph • PLN • LITTLE MOTHERS (USA) ○ MATECIKA
MAMELUKES, THE see **MAMALIK, AL-** • 1965
MAMI • Vaszary Janos
MAMIE BOLTON • 1912 • *Eclair* • USA
MAMIE ROSE see **MORKE PUNKT, DET** • 1911
MAMITO • 1980 • Lara Christian • FRN
MAMITSCHKA • 1955 • Thiele Rolf • FRG
MAMMA • 1941 • Brignone Guido • ITL, FRG • MUTTER (FRG)
MAMMA • 1982 • Osten Suzanne • SWD • OUR LIFE IS NOW
MAMMA DRACULA • 1980 • Szulzinger Boris • FRN, BLG • MAMA DRACULA
MAMMA EBE • 1985 • Lizzani Carlo • ITL
MAMMA GIFTER SAG • 1937 • Johansson Ivar • SWD • MOTHER MARRIES
MAMMA MIA CHE IMPRESSIONE! • 1951 • Savarese Roberto • ITL
MAMMA MIA E ARRIVATO COSI SIA • 1973 • Caltabiano Alfio • ITL
MAMMA, PERDONAMI! • 1955 • Vari Giuseppe • ITL
MAMMA ROMA • 1962 • Pasolini Pier Paolo • ITL
MAMMA SCONOSCIUTA • 1957 • Campogalliani Carlo • ITL
MAMMA TAR SEMESTER • 1957 • Bauman Schamyl • SWD • MOTHER TAKES A HOLIDAY
MAMMA WANTED, A • 1912 • *Pathe* • USA
MAMMALS see **SSAKI** • 1962
MAMMAME • 1985 • Ruiz Raul • FRN
MAMMA'S ANGEL CHILD • 1910 • *Lubin* • USA
MAMMA'S BOY • 1912 • *Baggot King* • USA
MAMMA'S BOY • 1920 • Roach Hal • SHT • USA
MAMMA'S BOY, THE see **PSYCHO FROM TEXAS** • 1982
MAMMA'S BOYS • 1916 • *Plump & Runt* • USA
MAMMASANTISSIMA, IL • 1979 • Brescia Alfonso • ITL
MAMMO KENKOKU NO REIMEI • 1932 • Mizoguchi Kenji • JPN • DAWN OF THE FOUNDATION OF MANCHUKUO AND MONGOLIA ○ DAWN OF MONGOLIA, THE (USA) ○ MANMO KENGOKU NO REIMEI ○ DAWN IN MANCHURIA ○ DAWN OF MANCHUKUO AND MONGOLIA, THE
MAMMON AND THE ARCHER • 1918 • Webb Kenneth • SHT • USA
MAMMOTH HUNT, THE see **LOV NA MAMUTA**
MAMMY • 1930 • Curtiz Michael • USA
MAMMY • 1950 • Stelli Jean • FRN
MAMMY'S CHILD • 1913 • *Powers* • USA
MAMMY'S GHOST • 1911 • *Vitagraph* • USA
MAMMY'S ROSE • 1916 • Douglass James • SHT • USA
MAMNU FI LEILET EL DOKHLA • 1976 • el Saifi Hassan • EGY • FORBIDDEN ON WEDDING-NIGHT
MAMOUR-E-0008 • 1967 • Bagheri Ebrahim • IRN • OFFICIAL 0008
MAMOUR-E-114 • 1967 • Poorsaeid Esmaeil • IRN • OFFICIAL 114
MAMOURET see **BRISEUR DE CHAINES, LE** • 1941
MAMPOU HATTENSHI: UMI NO GOZUKU • 1942 • Arai Ryohei • JPN • POWERFUL SEA CLAN ○ UMI NO GOZUKU ○ DEVELOPMENT HISTORY OF THE SOUTHERN SEA: TRIBES OF THE OCEAN
MAMSELL JOSABETH • 1963 • Fischer Gunnar • SHT • SWD • MISS JOSABETH
MAMSELL NITOUCHE • 1931 • Lamac Carl • FRG
MAMSELL UNNUTZ • 1918 • Mendel Georg Victor • FRG
MA'MSELLE JO see **SILENT YEARS** • 1921
MAM'SELLE STRIPTEASE see **EN EFFEUILLANT LA MARGUERITE** • 1956
MAMTA • 1967 • Sen Asit • IND • AFFECTION
MAMY WATER • 1955 • Rouch Jean • FRN • PECHE ET LE CULTE DE LA MER
MAMY WATTA • 1962 • Darene Robert • FRN, GBN • CAGE, LA ○ CAGE, THE
MAMZA • 1985 • SAF
MAM'ZELLE BONAPARTE • 1941 • Tourneur Maurice • FRN
MAM'ZELLE NITOUCHE • 1931 • Allegret Marc • FRN
MAM'ZELLE NITOUCHE • 1954 • Allegret Yves • FRN, ITL • SANTARELLINA (ITL) ○ OH NO, MAM'ZELLE
MAM'ZELLE PIGALLE see **CETTE SACREE GAMINE** • 1955
MAM'ZELLE SOURIS • 1958 • Paviot Paul • SHS • FRN
MAM'ZELLE SPAHI • 1934 • de Vaucorbeil Max • FRN
MAN • 1911 • *Yankee* • USA
MAN • 1967 • Duga Don • ANS • USA
MAN see **AADMI** • 1968
MAN see **HOMBRE** • 1970
MAN, A • 1912 • *Macpherson Jeanie* • USA
MAN, THE • 1910 • Griffith D. W. • USA
MAN, THE • 1972 • Sargent Joseph • USA
MAN, THE • 1985 • SAF
MAN, THE see **AADMI** • 1958
MAN, THE see **NINGEN** • 1962
MAN, THE (USA) see **NINGEN** • 1925
MAN.. A CITY, A see **HOMBRE.. UNA CIUDAD, UN** • 1980
MAN, A GIRL AND A LION, A • 1917 • Grandon Francis J. • SHT • USA
MAN, A GIRL AND ANOTHER MAN, A • 1914 • *Rex* • USA
MAN, A HORSE, A PISTOL, A see **UOMO, UN CAVALLO, UNA PISTOLA, UN** • 1968
MAN, A WOMAN AND A BANK, A see **VERY BIG WITHDRAWAL, A** • 1979
MAN, A WOMAN AND A CHILD, A see **MAN, WOMAN AND CHILD** • 1983
MAN, A WOMAN AND A KILLER, A • 1975 • Richardson Richard A., Schmidt Richard R., Wang Wayne • USA
MAN ABOUT THE HOUSE • 1974 • Robins John • UKN
MAN ABOUT THE HOUSE, A • 1947 • Arliss Leslie • UKN
MAN ABOUT TOWN • *Randall Bob* • SHT • USA
MAN ABOUT TOWN • 1931 • Elliot Grace • SHT • USA
MAN ABOUT TOWN • 1932 • Dillon John Francis • USA
MAN ABOUT TOWN • 1939 • Sandrich Mark • USA
MAN ABOUT TOWN, A • 1923 • Roach Hal • SHT • USA
MAN ABOUT TOWN (USA) see **SILENCE EST D'OR, LE** • 1946
MAN ABOVE THE LAW • 1918 • Wells Raymond • USA
MAN ACCUSED • 1959 • Tully Montgomery • UKN
MAN ACROSS THE STREET, THE • 1916 • Otto Henry • SHT • USA
MAN AFRAID • 1957 • Keller Harry • USA
MAN AFRAID, A • 1915 • *Travers Richard C.* • USA
MAN AFRAID, A see **KILLERS, THE** • 1946
MAN AFRAID OF HIS WARDROBE • 1915 • Bertram William • USA
MAN AGAINST MAN see **OTOKO TAI OTOKO** • 1960
MAN AGAINST THE MOB • 1988 • Stern Steven Hilliard • TVM • USA • CROSSING THE MOB ○ TROUBLE IN THE CITY OF ANGELS
MAN AGAINST WOMAN • 1932 • Cummings Irving • USA
MAN ALIVE • 1945 • Enright Ray • USA • AMOROUS GHOST, THE
MAN ALIVE see **REVOLVER AUX CHEVEUX ROUGES, LE** • 1974
MAN ALONE, A • 1955 • Milland Ray • USA
MAN ALONE, THE • 1923 • Clifford William H. • USA
MAN ALTHOUGH A THIEF, A • 1905 • Mottershaw Frank • UKN
MAN AMONG MEN, A • 1912 • *Selig* • USA
MAN AMONG MEN, A • 1912 • *Reliance* • USA
MAN AMONG MEN, A see **DANSEI NO.1** • 1955
MAN AMPLIFIERS • 1970 • *University Of California* • USA
MAN AND 8 GIRLS, A see **MAN -EIGHT GIRLS, A** • 1968
MAN AND A GIRL, A • 1910 • *Powers* • USA
MAN AND A SERVING MAID, A • 1912 • Plumb Hay? • UKN
MAN AND A WOMAN: 20 YEARS LATER, A (USA) see **HOMME ET UNE FEMME: VINGT ANS DEJA, UN** • 1985
MAN AND A WOMAN, A • 1913 • *Hunt Irene* • USA
MAN AND A WOMAN, A • 1916 • Lyndhurst F. L. • UKN
MAN AND A WOMAN, A see **MAN AND THE WOMAN, A** • 1917
MAN AND A WOMAN, A see **JOHN MEADE'S WOMAN** • 1937
MAN AND A WOMAN, A (UKN) see **HOMME ET UNE FEMME, UN** • 1966
MAN AND BEAST • 1917 • McRae Henry • USA
MAN AND BOY • 1972 • Swackhamer E. W. • USA
MAN AND CHILD see **HOMME ET L'ENFANT, L'** • 1956
MAN AND COLOUR -KALEIDOSCOPE see **KALEIDOSCOPE** • 1967
MAN AND FIRE see **HOMBRE Y EL FUEGO, EL** • 1970
MAN AND HIS ANGEL • 1916 • King Burton L. • USA
MAN AND HIS BEES, A • 1909 • Fitzhamon Lewin? • UKN
MAN AND HIS BOTTLE, THE • 1908 • Fitzhamon Lewin • UKN
MAN AND HIS BROTHER • 1914 • *Kerrigan J. Warren* • USA
MAN AND HIS DOG, A • 1952 • Murphy Mervyn • ASL
MAN AND HIS DOG OUT FOR AIR, A • 1957 • Breer Robert • ANS • USA
MAN AND HIS KINGDOM • 1928 • Elvey Maurice • UKN
MAN AND HIS MASTER • 1915 • Vale Travers • USA
MAN AND HIS MATE, A • 1915 • Adolfi John G. • USA
MAN AND HIS MATE (UKN) see **ONE MILLION B.C.** • 1940
MAN AND HIS MONEY, A • 1915 • De Grasse Joseph • USA
MAN AND HIS MONEY, A • 1919 • Beaumont Harry • USA
MAN AND HIS OTHER SELF • 1913 • Parker Lem B. • USA
MAN AND HIS PRISON, A see **HOMEM E SUA JAULA, UM** • 1969
MAN AND HIS SHADOW, THE (USA) see **COVJEK I SJENA** • 1960
MAN AND HIS SIN, A see **HOMME ET SON PECHE, UN** • 1948
MAN AND HIS SOUL • 1916 • Noble John W. • USA
MAN AND HIS TOOLS • 1962 • Hubley John • ANS • USA
MAN AND HIS WOMAN • 1920 • Blackton J. Stuart • USA
MAN AND HIS WOMAN, A see **FREUDUS SEXUALIS** • 1965
MAN AND HIS WOMAN, A (USA) see **HOMME EN OR, UN** • 1934
MAN AND HIS WORK, A • 1915 • Nicholls George • USA
MAN AND HIS WORLD • 1966 • Thoms Albie • SHT • ASL
MAN AND HIS WORLD, A • 1967 • Vukotic Dusan, Dovnikovic Borivoj • ANS • YGS
MAN AND MACHINE • 1966 • Sens Al • ANS • CND • MAN AND THE MACHINE
MAN AND MAID • 1925 • Schertzinger Victor • USA
MAN AND MAN • 1970 • *Signature Films* • DOC • USA
MAN AND MORALITY • 1916 • Myers Harry • SHT • USA
MAN AND THE BEAST, THE see **EXTRANO CASO DEL HOMBRE Y LA BESTIA, EL** • 1951
MAN AND THE BEAST, THE see **HOMBRE Y LA BESTIA, EL** • 1962
MAN AND THE BEAST, THE see **HOMBRE Y LA BESTIA, EL** • 1972
MAN AND THE DEVIL see **PHANTOM KILLER, THE** • 1942
MAN AND THE DOLL, THE see **HOMME ET LA POUPEE, L'** • 1922
MAN AND THE GIANT -AN ESKIMO LEGEND, THE see **HOMME ET LE GEANT -UNE LEGENDE ESQUIMO, L'** • 1975
MAN AND THE GIRL, THE • 1909 • Olcott Sidney • USA
MAN AND THE LATCHKEY, THE • 1908 • Fitzhamon Lewin • UKN
MAN AND THE LAW • 1915 • Beal Frank • USA
MAN AND THE LAW, THE • 1909 • *Phoenix* • USA
MAN AND THE MACHINE see **MAN AND MACHINE** • 1966
MAN AND THE MASTER, THE • 1914 • O'Sullivan Tony • USA
MAN AND THE MOMENT, THE • 1918 • Bocchi Arrigo • UKN
MAN AND THE MOMENT, THE • 1929 • Fitzmaurice George • USA
MAN AND THE MONSTER, THE (USA) see **HOMBRE Y EL MONSTRUO, EL** • 1958
MAN AND THE MOON • 1955 • Kimball Ward • SHT • USA
MAN AND THE SNAKE, THE • 1972 • Rydman Sture • SHT • UKN
MAN AND THE TANK, THE see **ANTHROPOS KAI TO TANK, O** • 1978
MAN AND THE WOMAN, A • 1917 • Blache Alice • USA • MAN AND A WOMAN, A
MAN AND THE WOMAN, THE • 1908 • Griffith D. W. • USA
MAN AND WIFE • 1923 • McCutcheon John L. • USA
MAN AND WIFE • 1969 • *Cimber Matt* • USA
MAN AND WIFE see **NO OTHER WOMAN** • 1933
MAN AND WIFE see **HE AND SHE** • 1970
MAN AND WOMAN • 1913 • Davis Will S. • USA
MAN AND WOMAN • 1920 • Logue Charles A. • USA
MAN AROUND THE HOUSE, THE • 1955 • Barclay David • SHT • USA
MAN AT LARGE • 1941 • Forde Eugene J. • USA
MAN AT SIX, THE • 1931 • Hughes Harry • UKN • GABLES MYSTERY, THE (USA)
MAN AT THE BULLFIGHT see **TOGYU NI KAKERU OTOKO** • 1960
MAN AT THE CARLTON TOWER • 1961 • Tronson Robert • UKN
MAN AT THE GATE, THE • 1941 • Walker Norman • UKN • MEN OF THE SEA
MAN AT THE KEY, THE • 1915 • *Stanton Richard* • USA
MAN AT THE TOP • 1973 • Vardy Mike • UKN
MAN AT THE WHEEL, THE • 1916 • Wilson Frank • UKN
MAN BAIT • 1926 • Crisp Donald • USA
MAN BEAST • 1955 • Warren Jerry • USA
MAN, BEAST AND VIRTUE see **UOMO, LA BESTIA E LA VIRTU, L'** • 1953
MAN BEHIND THE CURTAIN, THE • 1910 • *Powers* • USA
MAN BEHIND THE CURTAIN, THE • 1916 • Van Deusen Courtlandt • USA
MAN BEHIND THE DOOR, THE • 1914 • Van Wally • USA
MAN BEHIND THE GUN, THE • 1952 • Feist Felix E. • USA
MAN BEHIND THE MASK, THE • 1914 • Buckland Warwick? • UKN
MAN BEHIND THE MASK, THE • 1936 • Powell Michael • UKN
MAN BEHIND THE SUN see **HAK TAIYEUNG 731** • 1988
MAN BEHIND "THE TIMES", THE • 1917 • Wilson Frank • UKN
MAN BELONGS TO THE EARTH • 1974 • Ferguson Graeme • DOC • USA
MAN BENEATH, THE • 1919 • Worthington William • USA

MAN BETRAYED, A • 1937 • Auer John H. • USA • CITADEL OF CRIME (UKN) ○ WHEEL OF FORTUNE

MAN BETWEEN, THE • 1914 • *Kerrigan J. Warren* • USA

MAN BETWEEN, THE • 1923 • Fox Finis • USA

MAN BETWEEN, THE • 1953 • Reed Carol • UKN

MAN BITES LOVEBUG • 1937 • Lord Del • SHT • USA

MAN BRAUCHT KEIN GELD • 1931 • Boese Carl • FRG

MAN BY THE ROADSIDE, THE see **MENSCH AM WEGE, DER** • 1923

MAN CALLED ADAM, A • 1966 • Penn Leo • USA

MAN CALLED BACK • 1932 • Florey Robert • USA

MAN CALLED BLADE, A see **MANNAJA** • 1977

MAN CALLED DAGGER, A • 1966 • Rush Richard • USA • WHY SPY?

MAN CALLED FLINTSTONE, A • 1966 • Hanna William, Barbera Joseph • ANM • USA

MAN CALLED GANNON, A • 1969 • Goldstone James • USA

MAN CALLED GRINGO, A (UKN) see **SIE NANNTEN IHN GRINGO** • 1966

MAN CALLED HORSE, A • 1970 • Silverstein Elliot • USA

MAN CALLED INTREPID, A • 1979 • Carter Peter • TVM • UKN, CND

MAN CALLED NOON, THE • 1973 • Collinson Peter • UKN, SPN, ITL • CHIAMAVANO MEZZOGIORNO, LO (ITL)

MAN CALLED PETER, A • 1955 • Koster Henry • USA

MAN CALLED SARGE, A • 1988 • Gillard Stuart • USA

MAN CALLED SLEDGE, A (UKN) see **SLEDGE** • 1970

MAN CALLED SULLIVAN, A (UKN) see **GREAT JOHN L., THE** • 1944

MAN CALLED TIGER, A • 1981 • Lo Wei • HKG

MAN CAME TO KILL, A see **HOMBRE VINO A MATAR, UN** • 1968

MAN CANNOT BE RAPED see **MANRAPE** • 1978

MAN CASTS ANCHOR, A see **CHELOVYEK BROSAYET YAKOR** • 1968

MAN CHU • 1983 • Kim Soo-Yong • SKR • AFFAIR IN LATE AUTUMN, AN ○ END OF AUTUMN, THE

MAN CLOSE TO YOU, A see **MUZHCHINA OKOLO VAS** • 1979

MAN COULD GET KILLED, A • 1966 • Neame Ronald, Owen Cliff • USA • WELCOME, MR. BEDDOES

MAN CRAZY • 1927 • Dillon John Francis • USA

MAN CRAZY • 1954 • Lerner Irving • USA

MAN CRAZY see **NAUGHTY FLIRT, THE** • 1931

MAN DETAINED • 1961 • Tronson Robert • UKN

MAN DETAINED see **DARK MAN, THE** • 1951

MAN DIE ZIJN HAAR KORT LIET KNIPPEN • 1966 • Delvaux Andre • BLG • MAN WHO HAD HIS HAIR CUT SHORT, THE (UKN) ○ MAN WITH A SHAVEN HEAD, THE ○ HOMME AU CRANE RASE, L'

MAN DOWNSTAIRS, THE • 1934 • Greenwood Edwin • UKN

MAN DRINKING see **COMIC FACE** • 1897

MAN EATER see **ANTHROPOPHAGOUS** • 1980

MAN EATER OF HYDRA see **GEHEIMNIS DER TODESINSEL, DAS** • 1967

MAN-EATING SHARKS • 1932 • *Sennett Mack (P)* • SHT • USA

MAN EATING TIGER see **SPRING TONIC** • 1935

MAN -EIGHT GIRLS, A • 1968 • *Castelmagne Andrea* • USA • MAN AND 8 GIRLS, A ○ GUY, EIGHT GIRLS, A

MAN ELSKER, DEN • Thomsen Christian Braad • DNM • ONE YOU LOVE, THE

MAN EN PAARD • 1966 • Hidding H. • NTH

MAN ESCAPED, A (USA) see **CONDAMNE A MORT S'EST ECHAPPE, UN** • 1956

MAN ESCAPED, OR THE WIND BLOWETH WHERE IT LISTETH, A see **CONDAMNE A MORT S'EST ECHAPPE, UN** • 1956

MAN EVERYBODY WANTS TO MURDER, THE see **MANNEN SOM ALL VILLE MORDA** • 1940

MAN FACING SOUTHEAST (USA) see **HOMBRE MIRANDO AL SUDESTE** • 1986

MAN FOLLOWING THE SUN see **CHELOVEK IDYOT ZA SOLNTSEM** • 1962

MAN FOND OF FUNERALS, THE see **COVJEK KOJI JE VOLIO SPROVODE** • 1989

MAN FOR A' THAT, A • 1914 • *Bushman Francis X.* • USA

MAN FOR A' THAT, A • 1915 • Walsh Raoul • USA • MAN FOR ALL THAT, A

MAN FOR ALL SEASONS, A • 1966 • Zinnemann Fred • UKN

MAN FOR ALL SEASONS, A • 1988 • Heston Charlton • USA

MAN FOR ALL THAT, A • 1911 • *Chagnon Jack* • USA

MAN FOR ALL THAT, A see **MAN FOR A' THAT, A** • 1915

MAN FOR BURNING, A see **UOMO DA BRUCIARE, UN** • 1962

MAN FOR EMMANUELLE, A (UKN) see **IO, EMMANUELLE** • 1969

MAN FOR FIVE SEASONS, THE see **TREFLE A CINQ FEUILLES, LE** • 1971

MAN FOR HANGING, A • 1973 • Lightfield William?, Mazzuca Joseph A.? • USA

MAN FOR MAN, A • 1966 • Tosheva Nevena • DOC • BUL

MAN FOR THE WHOLE NATION, A see **KOKO KANSAN MIES** • 1973

MAN FOUR-SQUARE, A • 1926 • Neill R. William • USA

MAN FRIDAY • 1975 • Gold Jack • UKN, MXC

MAN FROM 1997 • 1957 • *Garner James* • MTV • USA

MAN FROM A FAR COUNTRY, A see **FROM A FAR COUNTRY: POPE JOHN PAUL II** • 1981

MAN FROM ABASHIRI STRIKES AGAIN, THE see **SHIN ABASHIRI BANGAICHI** • 1968

MAN FROM ANOTHER STAR, THE see **HERR VOM ANDERN STERN, DER** • 1948

MAN FROM ARGENTINE, THE • 1915 • Ayres Sydney?, Reynolds Lynn? • USA

MAN FROM ARIZONA, THE • 1932 • Fraser Harry L. • USA

MAN FROM ATLANTIS, THE • 1977 • Katzin Lee H. • TVM • USA

MAN FROM ATLANTIS: THE DEATH SCOUTS, THE • 1977 • Daniels Marc • TVM • USA • DEATH SCOUTS

MAN FROM ATLANTIS: THE DISAPPEARANCES, THE • 1977 • Dubin Charles S. • TVM • USA • DISAPPEARANCES, THE

MAN FROM ATLANTIS: THE KILLER SPORES, THE • 1977 • Badiyi Reza • TVM • USA • KILLER SPORES

MAN FROM BEYOND, THE • 1922 • King Burton L. • USA

MAN FROM BITTER RIDGE, THE • 1955 • Arnold Jack • USA

MAN FROM BITTER ROOTS, THE • 1916 • Apfel Oscar • USA

MAN FROM BLANKLEYS, THE • 1930 • Green Alfred E. • USA

MAN FROM BLANKLEYS, THE see **FOURTEENTH MAN, THE** • 1920

MAN FROM BROADWAY • 1924 • *Sunset Productions* • USA

MAN FROM BRODNEY'S, THE • 1923 • Smith David • USA

MAN FROM BUTTON WILLOW, THE • 1965 • Detiege David • ANM • USA

MAN FROM C.O.T.T.O.N., THE see **GONE ARE THE DAYS!** • 1963

MAN FROM C.O.T.T.O.N. OR HOW I STOPPED WORRYING AND LEARNED TO LOVE THE BOLL WEEVIL, THE see **GONE ARE THE DAYS!** • 1963

MAN FROM CAIRO, THE • 1953 • Enright Ray, Anton Edoardo • USA, ITL • DRAMMA NELLA KASBAH (ITL) ○ CRIME SQUAD (UKN) ○ AVVENTURA AD ALGERI

MAN FROM CANYON CITY, THE see **QUE VIVA CARRANCHO!** • 1967

MAN FROM CHEYENNE • 1942 • Kane Joseph • USA

MAN FROM CHICAGO, THE • 1930 • Summers Walter • UKN

MAN FROM CLOVER GROVE, THE • 1977 • Hillman William • USA

MAN FROM COCODY (USA) see **GENTLEMAN DE COCODY, LE** • 1965

MAN FROM COLORADO, THE • 1949 • Levin Henry • USA

MAN FROM DAKOTA, THE • 1940 • Fenton Leslie • USA • AROUSE AND BEWARE (UKN)

MAN FROM DEATH VALLEY, THE • 1931 • Nosler Lloyd • USA

MAN FROM DEEP RIVER, THE see **PAESE DEL SESSO SELVAGGIO, IL** • 1972

MAN FROM DEL RIO, THE • 1956 • Horner Harry • USA

MAN FROM DOWN UNDER, THE • 1943 • Leonard Robert Z. • USA

MAN FROM DOWNING STREET, THE • 1922 • Jose Edward • USA

MAN FROM DRAGON LAND, THE • 1912 • *Clark Frank* • USA

MAN FROM EGYPT, THE • 1916 • Semon Larry • SHT • USA

MAN FROM ESFEHAN, A see **MARDI AZ ESFEHAN** • 1967

MAN FROM FRISCO • 1944 • Florey Robert • USA

MAN FROM FUNERAL RANGE, THE • 1918 • Edwards Walter • USA

MAN FROM GALVESTON, THE • 1964 • Conrad William • USA

MAN FROM GLENGARRY, THE • 1922 • McRae Henry • CND

MAN FROM GOD'S COUNTRY • 1924 • Neitz Alvin J. • USA

MAN FROM GOD'S COUNTRY • 1958 • Landres Paul • USA

MAN FROM GUNTOWN, THE • 1935 • Beebe Ford • USA

MAN FROM HARDPAN, THE • 1927 • Maloney Leo • USA

MAN FROM HEADQUARTERS • 1942 • Yarbrough Jean • USA

MAN FROM HEADQUARTERS, THE • 1928 • Worne Duke • USA

MAN FROM HELL, THE • 1934 • Collins Lewis D. • USA

MAN FROM HELL'S EDGES • 1932 • Bradbury Robert North • USA

MAN FROM HELL'S RIVER, THE • 1922 • Cummings Irving • USA • HELL'S RIVER

MAN FROM HOME, THE • 1914 • De Mille Cecil B., Apfel Oscar • USA

MAN FROM HOME, THE • 1922 • Fitzmaurice George • UKN

MAN FROM HONGKONG, THE see **CHIH TAO HUANG LUNG** • 1975

MAN FROM INDIA, THE • 1914 • Wilson Frank • UKN

MAN FROM ISTANBUL, THE see **COLPO GROSSO A GALATA BRIDGE** • 1965

MAN FROM KANGAROO, THE • 1920 • Lucas Wilfred, Meredyth Bess • ASL

MAN FROM LARAMIE, THE • 1955 • Mann Anthony • USA

MAN FROM LONDON, THE see **LONDON HAMU** • 1968

MAN FROM LONE MOUNTAIN, THE • 1925 • Wilson Ben • USA

MAN FROM LOST RIVER, THE • 1921 • Lloyd Frank • USA

MAN FROM MAISINICU, THE see **HOMBRE DE MAISINICU, EL** • 1973

MAN FROM MAJORCA, THE see **MANNEN FRAN MALLORCA** • 1984

MAN FROM MALLORCA, THE see **MANNEN FRAN MALLORCA** • 1984

MAN FROM MANHATTAN, THE • 1916 • Halloway Jack • USA

MAN FROM MARS, THE see **RADIO-MANIA** • 1923

MAN FROM MEDICINE HAT, THE see **MANAGER OF THE B. & A., THE** • 1916

MAN FROM MEXICO, THE • 1914 • Heffron Thomas N. • USA

MAN FROM MONTANA, THE • 1917 • Marshall George • USA

MAN FROM MONTANA, THE • 1941 • Taylor Ray • USA • MONTANA JUSTICE (UKN)

MAN FROM MONTEREY, THE • 1933 • Wright Mack V. • USA

MAN FROM MONTREAL, THE • 1939 • Cabanne W. Christy • USA

MAN FROM MOROCCO, THE • 1945 • Greene Max • UKN

MAN FROM MUSIC MOUNTAIN • 1938 • Kane Joseph • *Autry Gene* • USA

MAN FROM MUSIC MOUNTAIN • 1943 • Kane Joseph • *Rogers Roy* • USA

MAN FROM NAPLES, THE see **KINDER DER FINSTERNIS 1** • 1921

MAN FROM NEVADA, THE • 1929 • McGowan J. P. • USA

MAN FROM NEVADA, THE (UKN) see **NEVADAN, THE** • 1950

MAN FROM NEW MEXICO, THE • 1932 • McCarthy John P. • USA

MAN FROM NEW YORK, THE • 1923 • *Church Fred* • USA

MAN FROM NOWHERE see **CHELOVEK NIOTKUDA** • 1961

MAN FROM NOWHERE, A • 1920 • Ford Francis • USA

MAN FROM NOWHERE, THE • Wolf Michael

MAN FROM NOWHERE, THE • 1914 • *Kerrigan J. Warren* • USA

MAN FROM NOWHERE, THE • 1915 • Storm Jerome • USA

MAN FROM NOWHERE, THE • 1916 • Otto Henry • USA

MAN FROM NOWHERE, THE • 1918 • *Finley Ned* • SHT • USA

MAN FROM NOWHERE, THE • 1930 • McGowan J. P. • USA • WESTERN HONOR

MAN FROM NOWHERE, THE • 1975 • Hill James • UKN

MAN FROM NOWHERE, THE see **HOMME DE NULLE PART, L'** • 1936

MAN FROM NOWHERE, THE (USA) see **ARIZONA COLT** • 1966

MAN FROM O.R.G.Y., THE • 1970 • Hill James A. • USA • REAL GONE GIRLS, THE

MAN FROM OKLAHOMA, THE • 1926 • Webb Harry S.?, Sheldon Forrest? • USA

MAN FROM OKLAHOMA, THE • 1945 • McDonald Frank • USA

MAN FROM OKLAHOMA, THE (USA) see **RANCH DEGLI SPIETATI, IL** • 1965

MAN FROM OREGON, THE • 1915 • Edwards Walter? • USA

MAN FROM OUTSIDE, THE • 1913 • Apfel Oscar • USA

MAN FROM PAINTED POST, THE • 1917 • Henabery Joseph • USA

MAN FROM PLANET ALPHA, THE • 1967 • *Toho* • JPN

MAN FROM PLANET EARTH see **CHELOVEK S PLANETA ZEMLYA** • 1959

MAN FROM PLANET X, THE • 1951 • Ulmer Edgar G. • USA

MAN FROM RAINBOW VALLEY • 1946 • Springsteen R. G. • USA

MAN FROM RED GULCH, THE • 1925 • Mortimer Edmund • USA

MAN FROM RIO, THE see **HOMME DE RIO, L'** • 1963

MAN FROM S.E.X., THE (USA) see **NO.1 OF THE SECRET SERVICE** • 1978

MAN FROM SCOTLAND YARD, THE • 1944 • Haines Ronald • UKN

MAN FROM SNOWY RIVER, THE • 1920 • Smith Beaumont, Wells John • ASL

MAN FROM SNOWY RIVER, THE • 1982 • Miller George* • ASL

MAN FROM SNOWY RIVER II, THE • 1987 • Burrowes Geoff • ASL • RETURN TO SNOWY RIVER PART II (USA) ○ UNTAMED, THE

MAN FROM SONORA • 1951 • Collins Lewis D. • USA

MAN FROM SPACE, A • 1967 • ANM • GRC

MAN FROM SUNDOWN, THE • 1939 • Nelson Sam • USA • WOMAN'S VENGEANCE, A (UKN)

MAN FROM TANGIER • 1957 • Comfort Lance • UKN • THUNDER OVER TANGIER

MAN FROM TASCOSA, THE • 1940 • Wright Mack V. • USA

MAN FROM TEHRAN, A see **MARDI AZ TEHRAN** • 1967

MAN FROM TEN STRIKE, THE see **GOLD MADNESS** • 1923

MAN FROM TEXAS • 1939 • Herman Al • USA

MAN FROM TEXAS, THE • 1910 • *Bison* • USA

MAN FROM TEXAS, THE • 1915 • Mix Tom • USA

MAN FROM TEXAS, THE • 1921 • Wilson Ben • USA

MAN FROM TEXAS, THE • 1948 • Jason Leigh • USA

MAN FROM THE ALAMO, THE • 1953 • Boetticher Budd • USA

MAN FROM THE BIG CITY, THE (UKN) see **IT HAPPENED OUT WEST** • 1937

MAN FROM THE BLACK HILLS • 1952 • Carr Thomas • USA

MAN FROM THE CITY, THE • 1913 • *Excelsior* • USA

MAN FROM THE COMET, THE see **MANN AUF DEM KOMETEN, DER** • 1925

MAN FROM THE DESERT, THE • 1915 • Davis Ulysses • USA

MAN FROM THE DINER'S CLUB, THE • 1963 • Tashlin Frank • USA

MAN FROM THE EAST, A see **...E POI LO CHIAMARONO IL MAGNIFICO** • 1972

MAN FROM THE EAST, THE • 1911 • *Selig* • USA

MAN FROM THE EAST, THE • 1912 • Dwan Allan • USA

MAN FROM THE EAST, THE • 1914 • Mix Tom • USA

MAN FROM THE EAST, THE (USA) see **HIGASHI KARA KITA OTOKO** • 1961

MAN FROM THE FIRST CENTURY see **MUZ Z PRVNIHO STOLETI** • 1961

MAN FROM THE FOLIES BERGERE, THE (UKN) see **FOLIES-BERGERE** • 1935

MAN FROM THE FOOTHILLS, THE • 1912 • *Briscoe Jesse* • USA

MAN FROM THE GOLDEN WEST, THE • 1913 • *Corbett James J.* • USA

MAN FROM THE GRAVE, A • 1963 • Lee Yong-Min • SKR

MAN FROM THE HIGH COUNTRY, THE see **HIGH COUNTRY** • 1984

MAN FROM THE METEOR, THE • 1954 • Romero George A. • SHT • USA

MAN FROM THE MIRROR, A • 1967 • Wasilewski Zenon • ANM • PLN

MAN FROM THE NORTH POLE, THE • 1912 • Golden Joseph A. • USA

MAN FROM THE OTHER SIDE, THE see **MANNEN FRAN ANDRA SIDEN** • 1971

MAN FROM THE PAST, THE • 1924 • Vale Travers • USA

MAN FROM THE PAST, THE see **MUZ Z PRVNIHO STOLETI** • 1961

MAN FROM THE PHOTOGRAPHY DEPARTMENT, THE see **COVEK SA FOTOGRAFIJE** • 1963

MAN FROM THE QUIET STREETS, THE see **COVJEK 12 MIRNE ULICE** • 1957

MAN FROM THE RESTAURANT, THE see **CHELOVEK IZ RESTARANA** • 1927

MAN FROM THE RIO GRANDE, THE • 1926 • *Kesterson George* • USA

MAN FROM THE RIO GRANDE, THE • 1943 • Bretherton Howard • USA

MAN FROM THE SEA, THE • 1914 • Ince John • USA

MAN FROM THE WEST, THE • 1912 • *Baggot King* • USA

MAN FROM THE WEST, THE • 1913 • *Phillips Augustus* • USA

MAN FROM THE WEST, THE • 1914 • *Ryan Mary* • USA

MAN FROM THE WEST, THE • 1926 • Rogell Albert S. • USA

MAN FROM THIS PLANET, THE see **MIES TALTA TAHDELTA** • 1958

MAN FROM THIS STAR, THE see **MIES TALTA TAHDELTA** • 1958

MAN FROM THUNDER RIVER, THE • 1943 • English John • USA

MAN FROM TIAJUANA, THE • 1917 • Horne James W. • SHT • USA

MAN FROM TOMORROW (UKN) see **CYBORG 2087** • 1966

MAN FROM TORONTO, THE • 1933 • Hill Sinclair • UKN

MAN FROM TOWN, THE • 1915 • Morgan George • USA

MAN FROM TUMBLEWEEDS, THE • 1940 • Lewis Joseph H. • USA

MAN FROM UTAH, THE • 1934 • Bradbury Robert North • USA

MAN FROM WYOMING, A • 1930 • Lee Rowland V. • USA

MAN FROM WYOMING, THE • 1924 • Bradbury Robert North • USA

MAN FROM YESTERDAY, THE • 1932 • Viertel Berthold • USA
MAN FROM YESTERDAY, THE • 1949 • Mitchell Oswald • UKN
MAN FROM YUKON, THE • 1916 • Ellis Robert • SHT • USA
MAN-GETTER, THE • 1919 • *Hart Neal* • SHT • USA
MAN GETTER, THE • 1923 • *Farnum Franklyn* • USA • TRAIL'S END, THE?
MAN GETTER, THE see **TRAIL'S END** • 1922
MAN GLOMMER INGENTING • 1942 • Ohberg Ake • SWD • NOTHING WILL BE FORGOTTEN
MAN GOES THROUGH THE WALL, A see **MANN GEHT DURCH DIE WAND, EIN** • 1959
MAN GOOD FOR NOTHING • 1916 • *Flugrath Edna* • USA
MAN HAM GERYE KARDAM • 1968 • Khachikian Samouel • IRN • I CRIED TOO
MAN HATER, THE • 1914 • Martin E. A. • USA
MAN HATER, THE • 1917 • Parker Albert • USA
MAN HATER, THE • 1920 • *Cunard Grace* • SHT • USA
MAN HATERS, THE • 1922 • Roach Hal • SHT • USA
MAN HE FOUND, THE see **WHIP HAND, THE** • 1951
MAN HE MIGHT HAVE BEEN, THE • 1913 • Miller Ashley • USA
MAN HE MIGHT HAVE BEEN, THE • 1916 • King Burton L. • SHT • USA
MAN HE USED TO BE, THE • 1916 • Mullin Eugene • SHT • USA
MAN HIGHER UP, THE • 1913 • *Powers* • USA
MAN HIGHER UP, THE • 1913 • Thompson Frederick A. • *Vitagraph* • USA
MAN HOUSEMAID, THE • 1909 • Coleby A. E. • UKN
MAN HUNT • 1908 • *Kalem* • USA
MAN HUNT • 1933 • Cummings Irving • USA • DIAMOND CUT DIAMOND
MAN HUNT • 1936 • Clemens William • USA
MAN HUNT • 1938 • *Lantz William (P)* • ANS • USA
MAN HUNT • 1941 • Lang Fritz • USA
MAN HUNT, THE • 1911 • Dwan Allan • USA
MAN HUNT, THE • 1912 • *Pathe* • USA
MAN HUNT, THE • 1916 • Scardon Paul • SHT • USA
MAN HUNT, THE • 1918 • Vale Travers • USA
MAN HUNT AT SAN REMO, THE • 1917 • Horne James W. • SHT • USA
MAN HUNTER, THE • 1919 • Lloyd Frank • USA • MAN WHO REPAID, THE
MAN HUNTER, THE • 1930 • Lederman D. Ross • USA
MAN HUNTER, THE • 1969 • Taylor Don • TVM • USA
MAN HUNTERS • 1923 • *Rialto Productions* • USA
MAN HUNTERS, THE • 1914 • Henderson Dell • USA
MAN HUNTERS, THE • 1916 • *Stull Walter* • SHT • USA
MAN HUNTERS OF THE CARIBBEAN • 1938 • SHT • USA
MAN I ABANDONED, THE • 1982 • Kim Soo-Yong • SKR
MAN I CURED • 1941 • D'Arcy Harry • SHT • USA
MAN I KILLED, THE (UKN) see **BROKEN LULLABY** • 1932
MAN I LIKE, A (UKN) see **HOMME QUI ME PLAIT, L'** • 1969
MAN I LOVE, A see **HOMME QUI ME PLAIT, L'** • 1969
MAN I LOVE, THE • 1929 • Wellman William A. • USA
MAN I LOVE, THE • 1947 • Walsh Raoul • USA
MAN I LOVE, THE see **CHELOVEK KOTOROGO YA LYUBLYU** • 1966
MAN I MARRIED, THE • 1940 • Pichel Irving • USA • I MARRIED A NAZI
MAN I MARRY, THE • 1936 • Murphy Ralph • USA
MAN I WANT, THE • 1934 • Hiscott Leslie • UKN • DIGGING DEEP
MAN IN 5A, THE • 1982 • Fischer Max • CND • MAN NEXT DOOR, THE ○ NEIGHBOUR, THE
MAN IN 23, THE • 1911 • *Nestor* • USA
MAN IN A BUBBLE • 1980-82 • Peterson Sidney • USA
MAN IN A COCKED HAT (USA) see **CARLTON-BROWNE OF THE F.O.** • 1958
MAN IN A FRAME, A • 1966 • Hitruck Fedor • ANM • USS
MAN IN A HURRY see **KATAKU NO HITO** • 1985
MAN IN A HURRY (USA) see **HOMME PRESSE, L'** • 1976
MAN IN BLACK, THE • 1914 • Le Saint Edward J. • USA
MAN IN BLACK, THE • 1950 • Searle Francis • UKN
MAN IN BLUE, THE • 1925 • Laemmle Edward • USA
MAN IN BLUE, THE • 1937 • Carruth Milton • USA
MAN IN DEMAND, THE • 1955 • MacDonald David • UKN • PRICE OF VANITY, THE
MAN IN DIE DONKER • 1962 • SAF
MAN IN FLIGHT • 1957 • *Disney Walt* • USA
MAN IN GRAY, A • 1960 • Zac Pino • ANS • ITL
MAN IN GREY, THE • 1943 • Arliss Leslie • UKN
MAN IN HALF MOON STREET, THE • 1944 • Murphy Ralph • USA
MAN IN HIDING, THE • 1915 • *Millarde Harry* • USA
MAN IN HIDING, THE see **HOMBRE OCULTO, EL** • 1970
MAN IN HIDING (USA) see **MANTRAP** • 1953
MAN IN HIM, THE • 1915 • *Alhambra* • USA
MAN IN HIM, THE • 1916 • *Anderson G. M.* • SHT • USA
MAN IN HIS PLACE, THE • 1916 • Batley Ernest G. • UKN
MAN IN HOBBLES, THE • 1928 • Archainbaud George • USA
MAN IN IRONS, THE • 1915 • Horne James W. • USA
MAN IN LOVE, A see **HOMME AMOUREUX, UN** • 1986
MAN IN MOTLEY • 1915 • Calvert E. H. • USA
MAN IN MOTLEY, THE • 1916 • Dewsbury Ralph • UKN
MAN IN MY LIFE, THE see **RAJUL FI HAYATI** • 1961
MAN IN OUTER SPACE (USA) see **MUZ Z PRVNIHO STOLETI** • 1961
MAN IN POLAR REGIONS • 1967 • Clarke Shirley • USA
MAN IN POSSESSION, THE • 1915 • Birch Cecil • *Bamforth* • UKN
MAN IN POSSESSION, THE • 1915 • Kellino W. P. • *Homeland* • UKN
MAN IN POSSESSION, THE • 1931 • Wood Sam • USA
MAN IN POSSESSION, THE (UKN) see **PERSONAL PROPERTY** • 1937
MAN IN RUE NOIR, THE see **MAN WHO COULD CHEAT DEATH, THE** • 1959
MAN IN SEARCH OF MAN • 1974 • Vaidya Prem • IND
MAN IN SILENCE • 1959 • Halas John • ANS • UKN
MAN IN SKIRTS, THE • 1914 • *De Forrest Charles* • USA
MAN IN SPACE • 1955 • Kimball Ward • USA
MAN IN THE ATTIC • 1914 • *Frontier* • USA
MAN IN THE ATTIC • 1954 • Fregonese Hugo • USA
MAN IN THE ATTIC, THE • 1915 • Dewsbury Ralph • UKN
MAN IN THE BACK SEAT, THE • 1961 • Sewell Vernon • UKN
MAN IN THE BARN, THE • 1937 • Tourneur Jacques • SHT • USA
MAN IN THE BLACK CAPE, THE see **HOMEM DA CAPA PRETA, O** • 1986
MAN IN THE BOX, THE • 1908 • *Griffith D. W.* • USA
MAN IN THE BROWN SUIT, THE • 1988 • Grint Alan • USA
MAN IN THE CABIN, THE • 1913 • *Anderson Broncho Billy* • USA
MAN IN THE CHAIR, THE • 1915 • Kent Leon D. • USA
MAN IN THE CLOUDS • 1967 • Beaver Patrick, Spragg Reg • UKN
MAN IN THE COUCH, THE • 1914 • *Komic* • USA
MAN IN THE DARK • 1953 • Landers Lew • USA • MAN WHO LIVED TWICE, THE
MAN IN THE DARK, THE • 1914 • Collins John H. • USA
MAN IN THE DARK (USA) see **BLIND CORNER** • 1963
MAN IN THE DINGHY (USA) see **INTO THE BLUE** • 1951
MAN IN THE FOG, A see **KIRI NO NAKA NO OTOKO** • 1958
MAN IN THE GLASS BOOTH, THE • 1975 • Hiller Arthur • USA
MAN IN THE GOLDEN MASK VS. THE INVISIBLE ASSASSIN see **ASESINO INVISIBLE, EL** • 1964
MAN IN THE GRAY FLANNEL SUIT, THE • 1956 • Johnson Nunnally • USA
MAN IN THE HAMPER, THE • 1913 • *Lubin* • USA
MAN IN THE HISPANO-SUIZA, THE see **HOMME A L'HISPANO, L'** • 1932
MAN IN THE HOUSE, THE • 1914 • *Ab* • USA
MAN IN THE IRON MASK, THE • 1928 • Banfield George J., Eveleigh Leslie • UKN
MAN IN THE IRON MASK, THE • 1939 • Whale James • USA
MAN IN THE IRON MASK, THE • 1977 • Newell Mike • TVM • USA, UKN
MAN IN THE KITCHEN, A see **KARL I KOKET, EN** • 1954
MAN IN THE MAKING, A • 1912 • *Edison* • USA
MAN IN THE MIDDLE • 1963 • Hamilton Guy • UKN, USA • WINSTONE AFFAIR, THE
MAN IN THE MIDDLE (UKN) see **MED FARA FOR LIVET** • 1959
MAN IN THE MIRROR, THE • 1936 • Elvey Maurice • UKN
MAN IN THE MOON • 1960 • Dearden Basil • UKN
MAN IN THE MOON, THE see **HOMME DANS LA LUNE, L'** • 1898
MAN IN THE MOON, THE see **CLAIRE DE LUNE ESPAGNOL** • 1909
MAN IN THE MOON, THE see **MANDEN I MANEN** • 1986
MAN IN THE MOONLIGHT, THE • 1919 • Powell Paul • USA
MAN IN THE MOONLIGHT MASK, THE see **GEKKO KAMEN** • 1958
MAN IN THE NET, THE • 1959 • Curtiz Michael • USA
MAN IN THE OPEN, A • 1919 • Warde Ernest C. • USA
MAN IN THE OVERCOAT, THE see **OMUL IN LODEN** • 1979
MAN IN THE PEACE TOWER, THE • 1951 • Blais Roger • DCS • CND • HOMME DANS LA TOUR, L'
MAN IN THE RAINCOAT, THE (UKN) see **HOMME A L'IMPERMEABLE, L'** • 1957
MAN IN THE RIGHT PLACE, A • 1973 • Sakharov Alexei • USS
MAN IN THE ROAD, THE • 1956 • Comfort Lance • UKN
MAN IN THE ROUGH • 1928 • Fox Wallace • USA
MAN IN THE SADDLE • 1951 • De Toth Andre • USA • OUTCAST, THE (UKN)
MAN IN THE SADDLE, THE • 1926 • Reynolds Lynn?, Smith Cliff? • USA
MAN IN THE SADDLE, THE • 1928 • Newman Widgey R. • USA • RECKLESS COURAGE, A
MAN IN THE SANTA CLAUS SUIT, THE • 1979 • Allen Corey • TVM • USA
MAN IN THE SHADE, THE see **CHOVEKAT V SYANKA** • 1967
MAN IN THE SHADOW • 1956 • Arnold Jack • USA • PAY THE DEVIL (UKN)
MAN IN THE SHADOW • 1957 • Tully Montgomery • UKN
MAN IN THE SHADOW, THE • 1926 • Hartford David M. • USA
MAN IN THE SHADOWS, THE • 1915 • McEvoy Charles • UKN
MAN IN THE SICK ROOM, THE • 1913 • *Solax* • USA
MAN IN THE SKY • 1957 • Crichton Charles • UKN • DECISION AGAINST TIME (USA)
MAN IN THE SOMBRERO, THE • 1916 • Ricketts Thomas • SHT • USA
MAN IN THE STEEL MASK, THE see **WHO?** • 1974
MAN IN THE STORM see **ARASHI NO NAKA NO OTOKO** • 1957
MAN IN THE STORM see **ARASHI NI TATSU** • 1968
MAN IN THE STREET, THE • 1913 • Eagle Oscar • USA
MAN IN THE STREET, THE • 1914 • Brabin Charles J. • USA
MAN IN THE STREET, THE • 1926 • Bentley Thomas • UKN • MAN OF MYSTERY
MAN IN THE TAXI, THE • 1911 • *Lubin* • USA
MAN IN THE TRUNK, THE • 1917 • Howard George Bronson • SHT • USA
MAN IN THE TRUNK, THE • 1942 • St. Clair Malcolm • USA
MAN IN THE TRUNK, THE see **VALISE, LA** • 1973
MAN IN THE VAULT • 1956 • McLaglen Andrew V. • USA
MAN IN THE VAULT, THE • 1914 • *Coombs Guy* • USA
MAN IN THE WATER, THE • 1963 • Stevens Mark • USA • ESCAPE FROM HELL ISLAND
MAN IN THE WHITE CLOAK, THE • 1913 • *Great Northern* • SHT • DNM
MAN IN THE WHITE SUIT, THE • 1951 • Mackendrick Alexander • UKN
MAN IN THE WILDERNESS • 1971 • Sarafian Richard C. • USA, SPN
MAN IN THE WORLD OF MEN, A • 1913 • *August Edwin* • USA
MAN IN VOGUE, THE see **HOMBRA DE MODA, EL** • 1980
MAN IN WHITE, THE see **D'HOMME A HOMMES** • 1948
MAN, INC. • 1970 • Languirand Jacques • CND
MAN INSIDE, THE • 1912 • Melies Gaston • USA
MAN INSIDE, THE • 1916 • Adolfi John G. • USA
MAN INSIDE, THE • 1958 • Gilling John • UKN
MAN INSIDE, THE • 1989 • Roth Bobby • USA, FRN
MAN INTO SUPERMAN • 1974 • Fox Beryl • DOC • CND
MAN INTO WOMAN • 1982 • Ruane John • DOC • ASL
MAN IS A SOCIAL BEING see **CLOVEK JE TVOR SPOLECENSKY** • 1960
MAN IS ARMED, THE • 1956 • Adreon Franklin • USA
MAN IS BORN, A • 1956 • Ordynsky Vassily • USS
MAN IS IN PAIN • 1955 • Jordan Larry • SHT • USA
MAN IS NOT A BIRD, A see **COVJEK NIJE TICA** • 1965
MAN IS SATISFIED, THE see **HOMME EST SATISFAIT, L'** • 1906
MAN IS TEN FEET TALL, A (UKN) see **EDGE OF THE CITY** • 1956
MAN IST NUR ZWEIMAL JUNG • 1958 • Weiss Helmut • AUS
MAN JAIYE • 1972 • Ishara B. R. • IND • LISTEN!
MAN JUDGING WOMAN see **OTOKO O SABAKU ONNA** • 1948
MAN KAN INTE VALDTAS (SWD) see **MANRAPE** • 1978
MAN KILLER see **PRIVATE DETECTIVE 62** • 1933
MAN LEBT NUR EINMAL • 1952 • Neubach Ernst • FRG
MAN LIFE PASSED BY, THE • 1923 • Schertzinger Victor • USA
MAN LIKE EVA, A see **MANN WIE EVA, EIN** • 1983
MAN LIKE US, A • 1975 • Kirkov Lyudmil • BUL
MAN LOOKING SOUTHEAST see **HOMBRE MIRANDO AL SUDESTE** • 1986
MAN MADE • Young Robert • DOC • UKN
MAN MADE MONSTER • 1941 • Waggner George • USA • ELECTRIC MAN, THE (UKN) ○ ATOMIC MONSTER, THE ○ MYSTERIOUS DR. R.
MAN-MADE WOMEN • 1928 • Stein Paul L. • USA
MAN MAKER, THE (UKN) see **TWENTY DOLLARS A WEEK** • 1924
MAN-MAN, THE • 1917 • Tucker George Loane • USA
MAN MANQUE UN RICHE MARIAGE • 1911 • Linder Max • FRN
MAN MASTE JU LEVA • 1978 • Vinterheden Margareta • SWD • I'VE GOT TO LIVE
MAN MISSING see **YOU HAVE TO RUN FAST** • 1961
MAN MONKEY, THE • 1907 • *Walturdaw* • UKN
MAN MONKEY, THE • 1909 • *Pathe* • FRN
MAN, MONSTERS AND MYSTERIES • 1975 • Clarke Les • SHT • USA
MAN MUSSTE NOCHMAL ZWANZIG SEIN • 1958 • Quest Hans • AUS
MAN MUST LIVE, A • 1925 • Sloane Paul • USA
MAN NAHN U • 1960 • Saleh Tewfik • EGY • QUI SOMMES-NOUS? ○ WHO ARE WE?
MAN NAMED JOHN, A (UKN) see **E VENNE UN UOMO** • 1964
MAN NAMED ROCCA, A (USA) see **NOMME LA ROCCA, UN** • 1962
MAN NENNT ES AMORE • 1961 • Thiele Rolf • FRG
MAN NENNT ES LIEBE • 1953 • Reinhardt John • FRG
MAN NEXT DOOR, THE • 1913 • Sennett Mack • USA
MAN NEXT DOOR, THE • 1923 • Schertzinger Victor?, Smith David? • USA
MAN NEXT DOOR, THE see **TONARI-NO YARO** • 1965
MAN NEXT DOOR, THE see **MAN IN 5A, THE** • 1982
MAN NOBODY KNOWS, THE • 1925 • Kenepp Errett Leroy • USA
MAN O' WARS MAN, THE • 1914 • *Shea Thomas E.* • USA
MAN OCH KVINNA • 1939 • Fejos Paul, Skoglund Gunnar • SWD, THL • JUNGLE OF CHANG (USA) ○ HANDFUL OF RICE, A ○ HANDVOLL RIS, EN ○ POIGNEE DE RIZ, UNE ○ HOMME ET FEMME
MAN OF A STORMY ERA see **SHOWA NO INOCHI** • 1968
MAN OF A THOUSAND FACES • 1957 • Pevney Joseph • USA
MAN OF ACTION • 1933 • Melford George • USA
MAN OF ACTION, A • 1923 • Horne James W. • USA
MAN OF AFFAIRES see **HIS LORDSHIP** • 1936
MAN OF AFFAIRS (USA) see **HIS LORDSHIP** • 1936
MAN OF AFRICA • 1953 • Frankel Cyril • DOC • UKN
MAN OF ARAN • 1934 • Flaherty Robert • DOC • UKN
MAN OF ASHES see **RIH AL SADD** • 1986
MAN OF BRONZE, THE • 1918 • Hartford David M. • USA
MAN OF BRONZE (UKN) see **JIM THORPE -ALL AMERICAN** • 1951
MAN OF CERTAIN GLORY, A • 1960 • Hawkins Robert • UKN
MAN OF CONFLICT • 1953 • Makelim Hal • USA
MAN OF CONQUEST • 1939 • Nicholls George Jr., Eason B. Reeves (U/c) • USA
MAN OF COURAGE • 1922 • *Lincoln E. K.* • USA
MAN OF COURAGE • 1943 • Thurn-Taxis Alexis • USA
MAN OF DESIRE, THE see **HOMME DE DESIR, L'** • 1970
MAN OF DESTINY see **ODETS** • 1924
MAN OF DESTINY, THE • 1914 • Edwin Walter • USA
MAN OF EARTH see **NJERIU PREJ DHEU** • 1985
MAN OF EVIL (USA) see **FANNY BY GASLIGHT** • 1944
MAN OF FLOWERS • 1983 • Cox Paul • ASL
MAN OF GOD, THE • 1915 • Terwilliger George W. • USA
MAN OF HER CHOICE, THE • 1914 • *Powers* • USA
MAN OF HIM, THE • 1913 • Jones Edgar • USA
MAN OF HIS WORD, A • 1917 • Tucker George Loane • USA
MAN OF HIS WORD, A (USA) see **JELF'S** • 1915
MAN OF HONOR, A • 1911 • *Bison* • USA
MAN OF HONOR, A • 1916 • *Marlo George* • SHT • USA
MAN OF HONOR, A • 1919 • Balshofer Fred J. • USA
MAN OF IMMORTALITY, A see **TA-HU YING-LIEH** • 1982
MAN OF IRON • 1935 • McGann William • USA
MAN OF IRON • 1973 • Chang Ch'Eh, Pao Houeh-Li • HKG
MAN OF IRON see **CZLOWIEK Z ZELAZA** • 1980
MAN OF IRON, A • 1915 • *Farrington Frank* • USA
MAN OF IRON, A • 1925 • Bennett Whitman • USA
MAN OF IRON, THE • 1914 • Vignola Robert G. • USA
MAN OF IRON (UKN) see **FERROVIERE, IL** • 1956
MAN OF IT, THE • 1915 • *Hunt Irene* • USA
MAN OF KINTAIL • 1959 • Barclay Robert • MTV • CND
MAN OF LA MANCHA • 1972 • Hiller Arthur • USA, ITL • UOMO DELLA MANCHA, L' (ITL)
MAN OF LEGEND (USA) see **SERGENTE KLEMS, IL** • 1971
MAN OF LETTERS • 1927 • Newfield Sam • SHT • USA
MAN OF MARBLE see **CZLOWIEK Z MARMARU** • 1978
MAN OF MAYFAIR • 1931 • Mercanton Louis • UKN
MAN OF MIGHT, THE • 1919 • Duncan William, Smith Cliff? • SRL • USA
MAN OF MUSIC • 1959 • Blais Roger • DCS • CND
MAN OF MUSIC (USA) see **KOMPOZITOR GLINKA** • 1952
MAN OF MYSTERY see **MAN IN THE STREET, THE** • 1926
MAN OF MYSTERY, A • 1912 • Wilson Frank? • UKN
MAN OF MYSTERY, THE • 1917 • *Imp* • SHT • USA
MAN OF MYSTERY, THE • 1917 • Thompson Frederick A. • *Vitagraph* • USA
MAN OF MYSTERY, THE • 1920 • *Coburn Wallace* • SHT • USA

MAN OF NERVE, A • 1925 • Chaudet Louis W. • USA
MAN OF PARTS, A • 1915 • Van Wally • USA
MAN OF PASSION, A see **PASION DE HOMBRE** • 1988
MAN OF POSITION, A • 1923 • Mayo Archie • SHT • USA
MAN OF PRINCIPLE, A see **CONDORES NO ENTIERRAN TODOS LOS DIAS** • 1985
MAN OF QUALITY, A • 1926 • Ruggles Wesley • USA
MAN OF SENTIMENT • 1933 • Thorpe Richard • USA
MAN OF SHAME, THE • 1915 • Myers Harry • USA
MAN OF SORROW, A • 1916 • Apfel Oscar • USA • HOODMAN BLIND
MAN OF STONE, A • 1921 • Archainbaud George • USA
MAN OF STONE, THE see **GOLEM, LE** • 1935
MAN OF STRAW see **UOMO DI PAGLIA, L'** • 1957
MAN OF THE ACCURSED VALLEY see **UOMO DELLA VALLE MALEDETTA, L'** • 1964
MAN OF THE BRAZIL-TREE, THE see **HOMEM DO PAU BRASIL, O** • 1981
MAN OF THE BRAZILIAN LOG, THE see **HOMEM DO PAU BRASIL, O** • 1981
MAN OF THE CENTURY see **ROVESNIK VEKA** • 1960
MAN OF THE EARTH, A • 1915 • *Lukas Paul* • HNG
MAN OF THE EAST (UKN) see **...E POI LO CHIAMARONO IL MAGNIFICO** • 1972
MAN OF THE FAMILY (UKN) see **TOP MAN** • 1943
MAN OF THE FOREST • 1926 • Waters John • USA
MAN OF THE FOREST • 1933 • Hathaway Henry • USA • CHALLENGE OF THE FRONTIER
MAN OF THE FOREST, THE • 1921 • Hampton Benjamin B. • USA
MAN OF THE FUTURE, THE see **RAJUL EL MOSTAKBUL** • 1947
MAN OF THE HILLS • 1914 • *Powers* • USA
MAN OF THE HILLS, A • 1915 • Franz Joseph J. • USA
MAN OF THE HOUR, THE • 1914 • Tourneur Maurice • USA
MAN OF THE HOUR (UKN) see **COLONEL EFFINGHAM'S RAID** • 1945
MAN OF THE HOUR (USA) see **HOMME DU JOUR, L'** • 1935
MAN OF THE MOMENT • 1935 • Banks Monty • UKN • WATER NYMPH
MAN OF THE MOMENT • 1955 • Carstairs John Paddy • UKN
MAN OF THE MOMENT (USA) see **TOKI NO UJIGAMI** • 1932
MAN OF THE NORTH see **TOHOKU NO ZUNMUTACHI** • 1957
MAN OF THE OPEN SEAS see **HOMME DU LARGE, L'** • 1920
MAN OF THE PEOPLE • 1937 • Marin Edwin L. • USA • TO THE VICTOR
MAN OF THE PEOPLE, A • 1913 • *Nestor* • USA
MAN OF THE RIGHT MOMENT, THE see **TOKI NO UJIGAMI** • 1932
MAN OF THE SAHARA see **MARDE-SAHRA** • 1968
MAN OF THE SEA • 1948 • Randone Belisario L.
MAN OF THE SOIL see **MATIRA MANISHA** • 1967
MAN OF THE SOIL, THE see **FOLD EMBRE, A** • 1917
MAN OF THE STREET see **SMESNY PAN** • 1969
MAN OF THE WEST • 1958 • Mann Anthony • USA
MAN OF THE WIDE-OPEN SPACES, THE see **HOMME DU LARGE, L'** • 1920
MAN OF THE WILDERNESS, A • 1913 • *Majestic* • USA
MAN OF THE WOODS • 1913 • *Selig* • USA
MAN OF THE WORLD • 1931 • Wallace Richard • USA • GENTLEMAN OF THE STREETS
MAN OF THE WORLD, A see **MIROVOY PAREN** • 1972
MAN OF THE YEAR (USA) see **HOMO EROTICUS** • 1971
MAN OF TIN • 1940 • *Mintz Charles (P)* • ANS • USA
MAN OF TODAY, THE see **MARD-E-ROUZ** • 1968
MAN OF TWO WORLDS • 1934 • Ruben J. Walter • USA
MAN OF TWO WORLDS see **HOUSE IN THE SQUARE, THE** • 1951
MAN OF VICTORY, THE see **HOSHIYO NAGEKUNA: SHORI NO OTOKO** • 1967
MAN OF VIOLENCE • 1970 • Walker Pete • UKN • SEX RACKETEERS, THE
MAN ON A MISSION • 1965 • Gardner Robert • USA
MAN ON A STAIRCASE • 1970 • Cannon Roy • SHT • UKN
MAN ON A STRING • 1960 • De Toth Andre • USA • CONFESSIONS OF A COUNTERSPY (UKN)
MAN ON A STRING • 1971 • Sargent Joseph • TVM • USA
MAN ON A SWING • 1974 • Perry Frank • USA
MAN ON A TIGHTROPE • 1953 • Kazan Elia • USA
MAN ON AMERICA'S CONSCIENCE, THE (UKN) see **TENNESSEE JOHNSON** • 1942
MAN ON EDGE • 1971 • Dayan Nissim • SHT • ISR
MAN ON FIRE • 1957 • MacDougall Ranald • USA
MAN ON FIRE • 1987 • Chouraqui Elie • FRN, ITL
MAN ON FIRE, A • 1967 • Pehlman Carl • USA
MAN ON OTHER PEOPLE'S CARE, THE see **HRANJENIK** • 1970
MAN ON THE BEACH, A • 1956 • Losey Joseph • UKN
MAN ON THE BOX, THE • 1914 • De Mille Cecil B., Apfel Oscar, Buckland Wilfred • USA
MAN ON THE BOX, THE • 1925 • Reisner Charles F. • USA
MAN ON THE BRINK see **PIEN-YUAN JEN** • 1981
MAN ON THE CASE, THE • 1914 • Dwan Allan • USA
MAN ON THE CLIFF • 1955 • Hartford-Davis Robert • DCS • UKN
MAN ON THE CRIB, THE • 1915 • *Crossette Films* • USA
MAN ON THE EIFFEL TOWER, THE • 1949 • Meredith Burgess • USA, FRN • HOMME DE LA TOUR EIFFEL, L'
MAN ON THE FLYING TRAPEZE, THE • 1934 • Fleischer Dave • ANS • USA
MAN ON THE FLYING TRAPEZE, THE • 1935 • Bruckman Clyde • USA • MEMORY EXPERT, THE (UKN)
MAN ON THE FLYING TRAPEZE, THE • 1947 • Hughes Ken • SHT • UKN
MAN ON THE FLYING TRAPEZE, THE • 1954 • Parmelee Ted • ANS • USA
MAN ON THE LEDGE • 1955 • Allen Lewis • MTV • USA
MAN ON THE LINE, THE see **MUZ NA DRATE** • 1985
MAN ON THE MOVE see **JIGSAW** • 1971
MAN ON THE OUTSIDE • 1973 • Sagal Boris • TVM • USA
MAN ON THE PROWL • 1957 • Napoleon Art • USA
MAN ON THE ROOF, THE see **MANNEN PA TAKET** • 1977
MAN ON THE RUN • 1949 • Huntington Lawrence • UKN
MAN ON THE RUN see **KIDNAPPERS, THE** • 1964
MAN ON THE RUN see **MALA ORDINA, LA** • 1972
MAN ON THE RUN, A see **MUZ NA UTEKU** • 1968
MAN ON THE RUN, A see **HOMME EN FUITE, L'** • 1981
MAN ON THE TRACK see **CZLOWIEK NA TORZE** • 1956
MAN ON THE TRAIL • 1950 • Dolin Boris • DOC • USS
MAN ON THE WALL, THE see **MANN AUF DER MAUER, DER** • 1983
MAN ON WATCH, THE • 1915 • Horne James W. • USA
MAN, ONE FAMILY • 1947 • Montagu Ivor • DOC • UKN
MAN ONLY CRIES FOR LOVE see **DONNE.. BOTTE E BERSAGLIERI** • 1968
MAN OP DEN ACHTERGROND, DE • 1923 • Winar Ernest • NTH
MAN OR GUN • 1958 • Gannaway Albert C. • USA
MAN OR HIS MONEY, THE • 1913 • Buckland Warwick? • UKN
MAN OR MONEY? • 1915 • Webster Harry Mcrae • USA
MAN OR MOUSE • 1964 • Grooms Red • SHT • USA
MAN OR MOUSE see **THERE'S ONE BORN EVERY MINUTE** • 1942
MAN OUTSIDE • 1965 • Marzano Joseph • USA
MAN OUTSIDE • 1986 • Stouffer Mark • USA • HIDDEN FEAR
MAN OUTSIDE, THE • 1913 • *Imp* • USA
MAN OUTSIDE, THE • 1913 • *Essanay* • USA
MAN OUTSIDE, THE • 1933 • Cooper George A. • UKN
MAN OUTSIDE, THE • 1967 • Gallu Samuel • UKN
MAN OVERBOARD • 1899 • *Mutoscope & Biograph* • UKN
MAN OVERBOARD • 1899 • *Warwick Trading Co* • UKN
MAN OVERBOARD • 1915 • MacGregor Norval • USA
MAN OVERBOARD • 1972 • Narliev Khodzhakuli • USS
MAN OVERBOARD see **MUZ PRES PALUBU** • 1981
MAN PASAND • 1979 • Chatterjee Basu • IND
MAN PAYS, THE • 1924 • Roach Hal • SHT • USA
MAN POWER see **MANPOWER** • 1927
MAN, PRIDE AND VENGEANCE see **UOMO, L'ORGOGLIO, LA VENDETTA, L'** • 1967
MAN, PRIDE, REVENGE see **UOMO, L'ORGOGLIO, LA VENDETTA, L'** • 1967
MAN-PROOF • 1937 • Thorpe Richard • USA • FOUR MARYS, THE
MAN PROPOSES • 1917 • *Otto Jean* • USA
MAN PROPOSES see **DARING YOUNG MAN, THE** • 1935
MAN PROPOSES GOD DISPOSES • 1925 • Butler Alexander • UKN
MAN REDE MIR NICHT VON LIEBE • 1943 • Engel Erich • FRG
MAN RUSTLIN' • 1926 • Andrews Del • USA
MAN SAVES THE QUEEN see **LADY IN DANGER** • 1934
MAN SCHENKT SICH ROSEN, WENN MAN VERLIEBT IST • 1929 • Dessauer Siegfried • FRG
MAN SERVANT, THE • 1915 • *Henderson Jack* • USA
MAN SHE BROUGHT BACK, THE • 1922 • Miller Charles • USA
MAN SHOHAR MIKHAM • 1968 • Ghaem-Maghami Savad • IRN • I WANT A HUSBAND
MAN SKU VAERE NOGET VED MUSIKKEN • 1969 • Carlsen Henning • DNM • OH, TO BE ON THE BANDWAGON
MAN-SLASHING HORSE-PIERCING SWORD see **ZANJIN ZANBA KEN** • 1929
MAN SOLL ES NICHT FUR MOGLICH HALTEN ODER MACISTE UND DIE JAVANERIN • 1922 • Krafft Uwe Jens • FRG
MAN, SOME WOMEN, A see **SEY SEYETI** • 1980
MAN SOMETIMES ERRS see **EMBER NEHA TEVED, AZ** • 1938
MAN SPIED ON, A see **NERAWARETA OTOKO** • 1956
MAN SPIELT NICHT MIR DER LIEBE • 1949 • Deppe Hans • FRG
MAN SPIELT NICHT MIT DER LIEBE! • 1926 • Pabst G. W. • FRG • DON'T PLAY WITH LOVE ○ ONE DOES NOT PLAY WITH LOVE
MAN SPRICHT DEUTSCH • 1988 • Muller Hans Christian • FRG
MAN SPRICHT UBER JACQUELINE • 1937 • Hochbaum Werner • FRG
MAN STEIGT NACH • 1928 • Metzner Erno • FRG
MAN TAKING OFF HIS GLOVES, THE see **TEBUKURO O NUGASU OTOKO** • 1946
MAN TAMER, THE • 1921 • Harris Harry B. • USA
MAN THAT CORRUPTED HADLEYBURG, THE • 1980 • Rosenblum Ralph • USA
MAN, THAT DUAL PERSONALITY see **HOMME, CETTE DUALITE, L'** • 1958
MAN THAT MIGHT HAVE BEEN, THE • 1914 • Humphrey William • USA
MAN THE ARMY MADE, A • 1917 • Phillips Bertram • UKN
MAN THE CREATOR • 1962 • Sukhdev S. • IND
MAN THE LIFEBOAT • 1904 • Hough Harold? • UKN
MAN THE MAKER • 1978 • Darino Eduardo • ANM • URG
MAN, THE MISSION AND THE MAID, THE • 1915 • Marston Theodore • USA
MAN THE POLLUTER • 1973 • Pindal Kaj, Arioli Don, Mills Michael • ANS • CND
MAN, THE WOMAN AND THE MONEY, THE see **MOGLIE BIONDA, LA** • 1965
MAN THERE WAS, A see **TERJE VIGEN** • 1917
MAN THEY COULD NOT ARREST, THE • 1931 • Hunter T. Hayes • UKN • MAN THEY COULDN'T ARREST, THE (USA)
MAN THEY COULD NOT HANG, THE • 1934 • Longford Raymond • ASL
MAN THEY COULD NOT HANG, THE • 1939 • Grinde Nick • USA
MAN THEY COULDN'T ARREST, THE (USA) see **MAN THEY COULD NOT ARREST, THE** • 1931
MAN THEY SCORNED, THE • 1912 • Barker Reginald • USA
MAN THOU GAVEST ME, THE see **ETERNAL STRUGGLE, THE** • 1923
MAN TO BEAT JACK JOHNSON, THE • 1910 • *Tyler Films* • UKN
MAN TO BURN, A see **UOMO DA BRUCIARE, UN** • 1962
MAN TO DESTROY, THE see **COVJEK KOGA TREBA UBITI** • 1979
MAN TO KILL, A see **HOMME A ABATTRE, UN** • 1967
MAN TO KILL, THE see **COVJEK KOGA TREBA UBITI** • 1979
MAN TO MAN • 1911 • Trimble Larry • USA
MAN TO MAN • 1914 • *Frontier* • USA
MAN TO MAN • 1915 • *Balboa* • USA
MAN TO MAN • 1915 • MacDonald Donald • *Mustang* • USA
MAN TO MAN • 1921 • Dwan Allan • USA • BARBER JOHN'S BOY
MAN TO MAN • 1922 • Paton Stuart • USA
MAN TO MAN • 1931 • Dwan Allan • USA • BARBER JOHN'S BOY
MAN TO MAN • 1988 • Baxley Craig R. • USA
MAN TO MAN TALK (USA) see **PREMIER MAI** • 1958
MAN TO MEN (USA) see **D'HOMME A HOMMES** • 1948
MAN TO REMEMBER, A • 1938 • Kanin Garson • USA
MAN TO RESPECT, A (UKN) see **UOMO DA RISPETTARE, UN** • 1972
MAN TRACKERS, THE • 1921 • Kull Edward • USA
MAN TRAIL, THE • 1915 • Calvert E. H. • USA
MAN TRAILER, THE • 1934 • Hillyer Lambert • USA
MAN-TRAP • 1961 • O'Brien Edmond • USA • DEADLOCK ○ RESTLESS
MAN TRAP, THE • 1917 • Clifton Elmer • USA
MAN TROUBLE • 1930 • Viertel Berthold • USA • LIVING FOR LOVE
MAN UNCONQUERABLE, THE • 1922 • Henabery Joseph • USA
MAN UNDER COVER, THE • 1922 • Browning Tod • USA
MAN UNDER SUSPICION • 1984 • Kuckelmann Norbert • FRG
MAN UNDER THE BED, THE • 1912 • *Vitagraph* • USA
MAN UNDER THE BED, THE • 1912 • *Reliance* • USA
MAN UNDER THE BRIDGE, THE see **EMBER A HID ALLATT** • 1934
MAN UNDER THE SEA see **CLOVEK POD VODOU** • 1961
MAN UNDER WATER see **CLOVEK POD VODOU** • 1961
MAN UNDERNEATH, THE • 1911 • *Yankee* • USA
MAN UPSTAIRS, THE • 1926 • Del Ruth Roy • USA
MAN UPSTAIRS, THE • 1958 • Chaffey Don • UKN
MAN VAN BUITE • 1972 • SAF
MAN VANISHES, A see **NINGEN JOHATSU** • 1967
MAN VERSUS MAN • 1983 • Anand Shashi • DCS • IND
MAN VS. MAN see **OTOKO TAI OTOKO** • 1960
MAN WANTED • 1912 • *Crystal* • USA
MAN WANTED • 1912 • *Lubin* • USA
MAN WANTED • 1922 • Dillon John Francis • USA
MAN WANTED • 1932 • Dieterle William • USA • DANGEROUS BRUNETTE
MAN WANTS TO LIVE! see **HOMMES VEULENT VIVRE!, LES** • 1961
MAN WHEN HE'S A MAN, A see **HOMBRE CUANDO ES HOMBRE, EL** • 1982
MAN WHO, THE • 1921 • Karger Maxwell • USA
MAN WHO BEAT DAN DOLAN, THE • 1915 • *Ritchie Willie* • USA
MAN WHO BENEFITS BY BEING INVISIBLE, THE see **HOMBRE QUE LOGRO SER INVISIBLE, EL** • 1957
MAN WHO BOUGHT LONDON, THE • 1916 • Thornton F. Martin • UKN
MAN WHO BROKE 1,000 CHAINS, THE • 1987 • Mann Daniel • TVM • USA • UNCHAINED
MAN WHO BROKE HIS HEART, THE see **WHARF ANGEL** • 1934
MAN WHO BROKE THE BANK AT MONTE CARLO, THE • 1935 • Roberts Stephen • USA
MAN WHO BUYS THE WORLD, THE see **HONEM QUE COMPROU O MUNDO, O** • 1968
MAN WHO CALLED AFTER DARK, THE • 1916 • Coyle Walter • SHT • USA
MAN WHO CAME AT DINNER, THE • 1969 • *Fleetan Films* • USA
MAN WHO CAME BACK, THE • 1911 • *Yankee* • USA
MAN WHO CAME BACK, THE • 1914 • *Eclair* • USA
MAN WHO CAME BACK, THE • 1914 • *Beauty* • USA
MAN WHO CAME BACK, THE • 1916 • *Rancho* • USA
MAN WHO CAME BACK, THE • 1921 • Parkinson H. B. • UKN
MAN WHO CAME BACK, THE • 1924 • Flynn Emmett J. • USA
MAN WHO CAME BACK, THE • 1931 • Walsh Raoul • USA
MAN WHO CAME BACK, THE (UKN) see **SWAMP WATER** • 1941
MAN WHO CAME FROM UMMO, THE see **HOMBRE QUE VINO DEL UMMO, EL** • 1970
MAN WHO CAME TO DINNER, THE • 1941 • Keighley William • USA
MAN WHO CAME TO KILL A RAT, THE see **DIAL RAT FOR TERROR** • 1972
MAN WHO CAN'T STOP, THE • 1973 • Rubbo Michael • ASL, CND
MAN WHO CHANGED HIS MIND, THE • 1928 • Gow Ronald, Mee Captain • UKN
MAN WHO CHANGED HIS MIND, THE • 1936 • Stevenson Robert • UKN • MAN WHO LIVED AGAIN, THE (USA) ○ BRAINSNATCHER(S), THE ○ DR. MANIAC
MAN WHO CHANGED HIS NAME, THE • 1928 • Bramble A. V. • UKN
MAN WHO CHANGED HIS NAME, THE • 1934 • Edwards Henry • UKN
MAN WHO CHEATED HIMSELF, THE • 1951 • Feist Felix E. • USA
MAN WHO CHEATED LIFE, THE (USA) see **STUDENT VON PRAG, DER** • 1926
MAN WHO COULD CHEAT DEATH, THE • 1959 • Fisher Terence • UKN • MAN IN RUE NOIR, THE
MAN WHO COULD NOT COMMIT SUICIDE, THE • 1907 • Fitzhamon Lewin • UKN
MAN WHO COULD NOT FORGET, THE see **DEBT OF HONOUR** • 1936
MAN WHO COULD NOT LAUGH, THE see **MANNEN SOM IKKE KUNNE LE** • 1968
MAN WHO COULD NOT LOSE • 1914 • Blackwell Carlyle • USA
MAN WHO COULD NOT SLEEP, THE • 1915 • Collins John H. • USA
MAN WHO COULD TALK TO KIDS, THE • 1973 • Wrye Donald • USA
MAN WHO COULD WALK THROUGH WALLS, THE see **MANN GEHT DURCH DIE WAND, EIN** • 1959
MAN WHO COULD WORK MIRACLES, THE • 1936 • Mendes Lothar • UKN
MAN WHO COULDN'T BEAT GOD, THE • 1915 • Costello Maurice, Gaillord Robert • USA
MAN WHO COULDN'T GET ENOUGH, THE see **CONFESSIONS OF A SEX MANIAC** • 1975
MAN WHO COULDN'T LAUGH, THE • 1910 • Stow Percy • UKN

MAN WHO COULDN'T SAY NO, A see **MIES JOKA EI OSANNUT SANOA EI** • 1975
MAN WHO COULDN'T SAY NO, THE see **GIANT OF NORWAY, THE** • 1939
MAN WHO COULDN'T WALK, THE • 1960 • Cass Henry • UKN
MAN WHO CREATED A MIRACLE, THE see **HOMBRE QUE HIZO EL MILAGRO, EL** • 1958
MAN WHO CRIED WOLF, THE • 1937 • Foster Lewis R. • USA • TOO CLEVER TO LIVE
MAN WHO DARED, THE • 1913 • *Tennant Barbara* • USA
MAN WHO DARED, THE • 1920 • Flynn Emmett J. • USA
MAN WHO DARED, THE • 1933 • MacFadden Hamilton • USA
MAN WHO DARED, THE • 1939 • Wilbur Crane • USA • CITY IN TERROR
MAN WHO DARED, THE • 1946 • Sturges John • USA
MAN WHO DARED GOD, THE • 1917 • Weber Lois • USA
MAN WHO DID NOT RETURN, THE see **MUZ, KTORY SA NEVRATIL** • 1959
MAN WHO DIED, THE • 1910 • *Lubin* • USA
MAN WHO DIED, THE • 1915 • *Kb* • USA
MAN WHO DIED TWICE, THE • 1958 • Kane Joseph • USA
MAN WHO DIED TWICE, THE • 1970 • Sargent Joseph • TVM • USA
MAN WHO DIED TWICE, THE see **SILENCIEUX, LE** • 1972
MAN WHO DIGS FOR FISH, THE • 1979 • Long Jack • CND
MAN WHO DISAPPEARED, THE • 1914 • Brabin Charles J. • SRL • USA
MAN WHO DISAPPEARED YESTERDAY, THE see **KINO KIETA OTOKO** • 1941
MAN WHO FAILED • 1913 • *Solax* • USA
MAN WHO FELL TO EARTH, THE • 1976 • Roeg Nicolas • UKN
MAN WHO FELL TO EARTH, THE • 1987 • Roth Robert J. • TVM • USA
MAN WHO FIGHTS ALONE, THE • 1924 • Worsley Wallace • USA
MAN WHO FINALLY DIED, THE • 1962 • Lawrence Quentin • UKN
MAN WHO FORGOT, THE • 1916 • Batley Ernest G. • UKN
MAN WHO FORGOT, THE • 1917 • Chautard Emile • USA
MAN WHO FORGOT, THE • 1919 • Thornton F. Martin • UKN
MAN WHO FORGOT, THE • 1927 • Harwood A. R. • ASL
MAN WHO FOUND HIMSELF, THE • 1915 • Crane Frank H. • USA
MAN WHO FOUND HIMSELF, THE • 1925 • Green Alfred E. • USA • UP THE RIVER
MAN WHO FOUND HIMSELF, THE • 1937 • Landers Lew • USA
MAN WHO FOUND OUT, THE • 1915 • *Ainsworth Sidney* • USA
MAN WHO GAVE UP SMOKING, THE see **MANNEN SOM SLUTADE ROKA** • 1972
MAN WHO GUARDS THE GREENHOUSE, THE see **ROSE CAFE, THE** • 1987
MAN WHO HAD EVERYTHING, THE • 1920 • Green Alfred E. • USA
MAN WHO HAD HIS HAIR CUT SHORT, THE (UKN) see **MAN DIE ZIJN HAAR KORT LIET KNIPPEN** • 1966
MAN WHO HAD POWER OVER WOMEN, THE • 1970 • Krish John • UKN
MAN WHO HAD TO SING, THE (USA) see **COVJEK KOJI JE MORAO PJEVATI** • 1970
MAN WHO HAUNTED HIMSELF, THE • 1970 • Dearden Basil • UKN
MAN WHO HID ANNE FRANK, THE • 1981 • Rasky Harry • CND
MAN WHO INVENTED GOLD, THE • MacLaine Christopher • SHT • USA
MAN WHO KEPT SILENCE, THE • 1911 • Haldane Bert? • UKN
MAN WHO KILLED BILLY THE KID, THE see **...E DIVENNE IL PIU SPIETATO BANDITO DEL SUD** • 1967
MAN WHO KNEW, THE • 1914 • Humphrey William • USA
MAN WHO KNEW MORE, THE • 1985 • Samadi Yadollah • IRN
MAN WHO KNEW TOO MUCH, THE • 1934 • Hitchcock Alfred • UKN
MAN WHO KNEW TOO MUCH, THE • 1956 • Hitchcock Alfred • USA
MAN WHO LAUGHS, THE • 1927 • Leni Paul • USA
MAN WHO LAUGHS, THE see **HOMME QUI RIT, L'** • 1909
MAN WHO LAUGHS, THE (USA) see **GRINSENDE GESICHT, DAS** • 1921
MAN WHO LAUGHS, THE (USA) see **UOMO CHE RIDE, L'** • 1966
MAN WHO LEARNED, THE • 1910 • Porter Edwin S. • USA
MAN WHO LEARNED TO FLY, THE • 1908 • Fitzhamon Lewin • UKN
MAN WHO LEFT HIS WILL ON FILM, THE (UKN) see **TOKYO SENSO SENGO HIWA** • 1970
MAN WHO LIED, THE • 1914 • *Kerrigan J. Warren* • USA
MAN WHO LIES, THE see **MUZ KTORY LUZE** • 1968
MAN WHO LIKED FUNERALS, THE • 1959 • Eady David • UKN
MAN WHO LIKED LEMONS, THE • 1923 • Cooper George A. • UKN
MAN WHO LIVED AGAIN, THE (USA) see **MAN WHO CHANGED HIS MIND, THE** • 1936
MAN WHO LIVED TWICE, THE • 1936 • Lachman Harry • USA
MAN WHO LIVED TWICE, THE see **MAN IN THE DARK** • 1953
MAN WHO LIVED TWICE, THE see **CRYSTALBRAIN L'UOMO DAL CERVELLO DI CRISTALLO** • 1970
MAN WHO LOST, THE • 1910 • *Kalem* • USA
MAN WHO LOST, BUT WON, THE • 1914 • *Gaden Alexander* • USA
MAN WHO LOST HIMSELF, THE • 1920 • Baker George D. • USA
MAN WHO LOST HIMSELF, THE • 1941 • Ludwig Edward • USA
MAN WHO LOST HIS MEMORY, THE see **MANN OHNE GEDACHTNIS** • 1983
MAN WHO LOST HIS SHADOW, THE see **RAGOL EL LAZI FAKAD ZILLOH, EL** • 1968
MAN WHO LOVED BEARS, THE • 1980 • Stouffer Marty • DOC • USA
MAN WHO LOVED CAT DANCING, THE • 1973 • Sarafian Richard C. • USA
MAN WHO LOVED LOVE, THE (USA) see **HOMME QUI AIMANT LES FEMMES, L'** • 1977
MAN WHO LOVED MACHINES, THE • 1983 • Goldsmith Sidney • CND
MAN WHO LOVED REDHEADS, THE • 1955 • French Harold • UKN
MAN WHO LOVED WOMEN, THE • 1983 • Edwards Blake • USA
MAN WHO LOVED WOMEN, THE (UKN) see **HOMME QUI AIMANT LES FEMMES, L'** • 1977
MAN WHO MADE BYZANTIUM TREMBLE, THE see **BIZANSI TITRETEN ADAM** • 1967
MAN WHO MADE DIAMONDS, THE • 1937 • Ince Ralph • UKN
MAN WHO MADE GOOD, THE • 1912 • Dawley J. Searle • USA
MAN WHO MADE GOOD, THE • 1917 • Aylott Dave • UKN
MAN WHO MADE GOOD, THE • 1917 • Rosson Arthur • USA
MAN WHO MADE THE ARMY, THE • 1917 • Pearson George • DCS • UKN
MAN WHO MARRIED HIS OWN WIFE, THE • 1922 • Paton Stuart • USA
MAN WHO MIGHT HAVE BEEN, THE • 1913 • *Selig* • USA
MAN WHO MISUNDERSTOOD, THE • 1914 • *Imp* • USA
MAN WHO MURDERED, THE see **MANN, DER DEN MORD BEGING, DER** • 1930
MAN WHO NEVER WAS, THE • 1956 • Neame Ronald • UKN
MAN WHO PAID, THE • 1914 • O'Sullivan Tony • USA • MAN WHO PAYED, THE
MAN WHO PAID, THE • 1922 • Apfel Oscar • USA
MAN WHO PAWNED HIS SOUL, THE (UKN) see **UNKNOWN BLONDE** • 1934
MAN WHO PAYED, THE see **MAN WHO PAID, THE** • 1914
MAN WHO PLANTED TREES, THE • 1987 • Back Frederic • ANM • CND • CRAC
MAN WHO PLAYED GOD, THE • 1922 • Weight F. Harmon • USA • SILENT VOICE, THE
MAN WHO PLAYED GOD, THE • 1932 • Adolfi John G. • USA • SILENT VOICE, THE (UKN)
MAN WHO PLAYED SQUARE, THE • 1924 • Santell Alfred • USA
MAN WHO RECLAIMED HIS HEAD, THE • 1934 • Ludwig Edward • USA
MAN WHO REPAID, THE see **MAN HUNTER, THE** • 1919
MAN WHO RETURNED FROM AFAR, THE see **HOMME QUI REVIENT DE LOIN, L'** • 1949
MAN WHO RETURNED TO LIFE, THE • 1942 • Landers Lew • USA
MAN WHO RODE THE TYPHOON, THE see **FUSOKU YONJU METORU** • 1958
MAN WHO SAVED THE DAY, THE • 1917 • *Reid Wallace* • SHT • USA
MAN WHO SAW TOMORROW, THE • 1922 • Green Alfred E. • USA
MAN WHO SAW TOMORROW, THE • 1981 • Guenette Robert • USA
MAN WHO SEEKS HIS OWN MURDERER, THE see **MANN, DER SEINEN MORDER SUCHT, DER** • 1931
MAN WHO SHOT LIBERTY VALANCE, THE • 1962 • Ford John • USA
MAN WHO SKIED DOWN EVEREST, THE • 1974 • Nyznik Bruce, Zeniya Isao • CND, JPN • SKIEUR DE L'EVEREST, LE
MAN WHO SLEEPS, A see **HOMME QUI DORT, UN** • 1973
MAN WHO SLEPT, THE • 1914 • *Lyons Eddie* • USA
MAN WHO SOLD HIMSELF, THE see **MANN, DER SICH VERKAUFT, DER** • 1925
MAN WHO SOLD HIS SOUL, THE see **HOMME QUI VENDAIT SON AME, L'** • 1943
MAN WHO SOLD HIS SOUL TO THE DEVIL, THE see **HOMME QUI VENDIT SON AME AU DIABLE, L'** • 1920
MAN WHO STAKES HIS LIFE, A see **INOCHI O KAKERU OTOKO** • 1958
MAN WHO STAYED AT HOME • 1915 • Hepworth Cecil M. • UKN
MAN WHO STAYED AT HOME, THE • 1919 • Blache Herbert • USA
MAN WHO STOLE THE EARTH, THE see **SKY RANGER, THE** • 1921
MAN WHO STOLE THE MOON, THE see **SKY RANGER, THE** • 1921
MAN WHO STOLE THE SUN, THE see **TAIYO O NUSUNDA OTOKO** • 1979
MAN WHO STOOD STILL, THE • 1916 • Crane Frank H. • USA
MAN WHO TALKED TOO MUCH, THE • 1940 • Sherman Vincent • USA • SENTENCE, THE
MAN WHO TAMED THE VICTORS, THE see **MANDEN, DER SEJREDE** • 1917
MAN WHO THOUGHT HE WAS POISONED, THE • 1910 • Fitzhamon Lewin? • UKN
MAN WHO THOUGHT LIFE, THE see **MANDEN DER TAENKTE TING** • 1969
MAN WHO THOUGHT THINGS, THE see **MANDEN DER TAENKTE TING** • 1969
MAN WHO TOOK A CHANCE, THE • 1917 • Worthington William • USA
MAN WHO TRIED TO FORGET, THE • 1913 • *Nestor* • USA
MAN WHO TURNED TO STONE, THE • 1957 • Kardos Leslie • USA • PETRIFIED MAN, THE
MAN WHO TURNED UP JUICE, THE see **HOMEM QUE VIROU SUCO, O** • 1981
MAN WHO TURNED WHITE, THE • 1919 • Frame Park • USA • SHEIK OF ARABY, THE
MAN WHO UNDERSTOOD WOMEN, THE • 1959 • Johnson Nunnally • USA
MAN WHO VANISHED, THE • 1913 • *Kalem* • USA
MAN WHO VANISHED, THE • 1914 • West Langdon • USA
MAN WHO VANISHED, THE • 1915 • *Apex* • USA
MAN WHO WAGGED HIS TAIL, THE (UKN) see **ANGELO E SCESO A BROOKLYN, UN** • 1957
MAN WHO WAITED, THE • 1910 • *Powers* • USA
MAN WHO WAITED, THE • 1922 • Luddy Edward I. • USA
MAN WHO WALKED ALONE, THE • 1945 • Cabanne W. Christy • USA
MAN WHO WALKED THROUGH THE WALL, THE (USA) see **MANN GEHT DURCH DIE WAND, EIN** • 1959
MAN WHO WANTED TO LIVE FOREVER, THE • 1970 • Trent John • CND • ONLY WAY OUT IS DEAD, THE (UKN) ○ HEART FARM, THE ○ HEARTFARM
MAN WHO WAS AFRAID, THE • 1917 • Wright Fred E. • USA
MAN WHO WAS AFRAID, THE • 1920 • SAF
MAN WHO WAS MISUNDERSTOOD, THE • 1914 • *Baggot King* • USA
MAN WHO WAS NEVER CAUGHT, THE • 1915 • Physioc Wray • USA
MAN WHO WAS NEVER KISSED, THE • 1914 • *Moore Matt* • USA • WOMAN WHO WON, THE
MAN WHO WAS NOBODY, THE • 1960 • Tully Montgomery • UKN
MAN WHO WASN'T, THE • 1915 • Plumb Hay? • UKN
MAN WHO WASN'T THERE, THE • 1983 • Malmuth Bruce • USA
MAN WHO WATCHED THE TRAINS GO BY, THE • 1952 • French Harold • UKN • PARIS EXPRESS (USA)
MAN WHO WENT, THE • 1915 • Batley Ethyle • UKN
MAN WHO WENT OUT, THE • 1915 • *Mayall Herschal* • USA
MAN WHO WENT OUT OF FASHION, THE see **NEMODLENIC** • 1927
MAN WHO WENT SANE, THE • 1916 • Mills Thomas R. • SHT • USA
MAN WHO WENT UP IN SMOKE, THE see **SVED AKINEK NYOMA VESZETT, A** • 1980
MAN WHO WOKE UP, THE • 1918 • McLaughlin J .w. • USA
MAN WHO WON, THE • 1918 • Wilson Rex • UKN
MAN WHO WON, THE • 1919 • Scardon Paul • USA
MAN WHO WON, THE • 1923 • Wellman William A. • USA
MAN WHO WON, THE (USA) see **MR. BILL THE CONQUEROR** • 1932
MAN WHO WOULD BE GUILTY, THE • 1990 • Roos Ole • DNM
MAN WHO WOULD BE KING, THE • 1975 • Huston John • USA
MAN WHO WOULD NOT DIE, THE • 1916 • Russell William • USA
MAN WHO WOULD NOT DIE, THE • 1975 • Arkless Robert • USA
MAN WHO WOULDN'T DIE, THE • 1942 • Leeds Herbert I. • USA • MILLION DOLLAR GHOST
MAN WHO WOULDN'T MARRY, THE • 1913 • Edwin Walter • USA
MAN WHO WOULDN'T TALK, THE • 1940 • Burton David • USA
MAN WHO WOULDN'T TALK, THE • 1958 • Wilcox Herbert • UKN
MAN WHO WOULDN'T TELL, THE • 1918 • Young James • USA
MAN WHOSE PRICE WENT UP, THE see **MUZ, KTERY STOUPL V CENE** • 1967
MAN WITH 100 FACES see **CRACKERJACK** • 1938
MAN WITH A CLOAK, THE • 1951 • Markle Fletcher • USA
MAN WITH A CONSCIENCE, THE (UKN) see **TOMORROW WE LIVE** • 1942
MAN WITH A DOG • 1958 • Arliss Leslie • UKN
MAN WITH A DOG, A see **MUZ SE PSEM** • 1968
MAN WITH A DRAGON TATTOO see **HANA TO RYU** • 1962
MAN WITH A GUN • 1958 • Tully Montgomery • UKN
MAN WITH A GUN, THE see **CHELOVEK S RUZHYOM** • 1938
MAN WITH A HAT • 1973 • Wadhawan Jamie, Alex Kosta • UKN
MAN WITH A HUNDRED FACES, THE (USA) see **CRACKERJACK** • 1938
MAN WITH A MARRIED WOMAN'S HAIRDO, A see **BOKU NO MARUMAGE** • 1933
MAN WITH A MILLION (USA) see **MILLION POUND NOTE, THE** • 1953
MAN WITH A MOVIE CAMERA, THE see **CHELOVEK S KINOAPPARATOM** • 1928
MAN WITH A PACKAGE, THE • 1917 • Beaudine William • USA
MAN WITH A RAZOR, THE • 1913 • *Komic* • USA
MAN WITH A RECORD, THE • 1915 • Siegmann George • USA
MAN WITH A RIFLE, THE see **CHELOVEK S RUZHYOM** • 1938
MAN WITH A SCAR, THE • 1914 • *Captain Kettle* • UKN
MAN WITH A SHAVEN HEAD, THE see **MAN DIE ZIJN HAAR KORT LIET KNIPPEN** • 1966
MAN WITH A TATTOO see **TATTOO ARI** • 1982
MAN WITH A THOUSAND INVENTIONS, THE see **HOMME AUX MILLE INVENTIONS, L'** • 1910
MAN WITH AN UMBRELLA (UKN) see **DET REGNAR PA VAR KARLEK** • 1946
MAN WITH BOGART'S FACE, THE • 1980 • Day Robert • USA • SAM MARLOWE, PRIVATE EYE
MAN WITH CONNECTIONS, THE (USA) see **PISTONNE, LE** • 1970
MAN WITH FIVE HEADS see **MELOMANE, LE** • 1903
MAN WITH MY FACE, THE • 1951 • Montagne Edward J. • USA
MAN WITH NINE FINGERS, THE • 1916 • Sandberg Anders W. • SRL • DNM
MAN WITH NINE LIVES • Saito • JPN
MAN WITH NINE LIVES, THE • 1940 • Grinde Nick • USA • BEHIND THE DOOR (UKN)
MAN WITH ONE RED SHOE, THE • 1985 • Dragoti Stan • USA • TALL BLOND MAN WITH ONE BLACK SHOE, THE ○ MISCHIEF
MAN WITH ONLY ONE NOTE, THE see **HOMBRE DE UNA SOLA NOTE, UN** • 1988
MAN WITH THE AXE, THE see **PARASHURAM** • 1978
MAN WITH THE BALLOONS, THE (USA) see **UOMO DAI PALLONCINI, L'** • 1964
MAN WITH THE BRAIN GRAFT, THE see **HOMME AU CERVEAU GREFFE, L'** • 1971
MAN WITH THE CAMERA see **CHELOVEK S KINOAPPARATOM** • 1928
MAN WITH THE CAMERA, THE • 1911 • *Comet* • USA
MAN WITH THE CARNATION, THE • 1981 • Tzimas Nikos • GRC
MAN WITH THE DEADLY LENS, THE (UKN) see **WRONG IS RIGHT** • 1982
MAN WITH THE ELECTRIC VOICE, THE (UKN) see **FIFTEEN WIVES** • 1934
MAN WITH THE FUTURE, THE • 1914 • *Lubin* • USA
MAN WITH THE GADGET, THE see **MANN MIT DEM OBJEKTIV, DER** • 1963

MAN WITH THE GLASS EYE, THE • 1916 • *Lonsdale Henry* • UKN
MAN WITH THE GLOVE, THE • 1914 • *Coombs Guy* • USA
MAN WITH THE GOLDEN ARM, THE • 1955 • Preminger Otto • USA
MAN WITH THE GOLDEN FIST, THE see **HOMBRE DEL PUNO DE ORO, EL** • 1966
MAN WITH THE GOLDEN GUN, THE • 1974 • Hamilton Guy • UKN
MAN WITH THE GOLDEN KEYS (USA) see **HOMME AUX CLEFS D'OR, L'** • 1956
MAN WITH THE GOLDEN MASK, THE see **UOMO CHE RIDE, L'** • 1966
MAN WITH THE GOLDEN TOUCH, THE see **ARANYEMBER, AZ** • 1917
MAN WITH THE GOLDEN TOUCH, THE see **ARANYEMBER, AZ** • 1962
MAN WITH THE GREEN CARNATION, THE (USA) see **TRIALS OF OSCAR WILDE, THE** • 1960
MAN WITH THE GREY GLOVE, THE (USA) see **UOMO DAL GUANTO GRIGIO, L'** • 1949
MAN WITH THE GUN, THE • 1955 • Wilson Richard • USA • TROUBLE SHOOTER, THE (UKN)
MAN WITH THE GUN, THE see **CHELOVEK S RUZHYOM** • 1938
MAN WITH THE HOD, THE • 1916 • Miller Rube • USA
MAN WITH THE HOE, THE • 1914 • *Thanhouser* • USA
MAN WITH THE IRON HEAD, THE • 1912 • *Cricks & Martin* • UKN
MAN WITH THE IRON HEART, THE • 1915 • Nicholls George • USA
MAN WITH THE LIMP, THE • 1917 • *Larkin George* • USA
MAN WITH THE LIMP, THE • 1923 • Coleby A. E. • UKN
MAN WITH THE MAGNETIC EYES, THE • 1945 • Haines Ronald • UKN
MAN WITH THE MANDOLIN, THE see **HOMBRE DE LA MANDOLINA, EL** • 1983
MAN WITH THE PACKAGE, THE • 1917 • Beaudine William • SHT • USA
MAN WITH THE PERFECT SHOT, THE see **UOMO DAL COLPO PERFETTO, L'** • 1967
MAN WITH THE POWER, THE • 1977 • Sgarro Nicholas • TVM • USA
MAN WITH THE PUNCH, THE • 1920 • Laemmle Edward • SHT • USA
MAN WITH THE PUPPETS, THE • 1912 • *Nordisk* • SHT • DNM
MAN WITH THE RUBBER HEAD, THE (USA) see **HOMME A LA TETE EN CAOUTCHOUC, L'** • 1902
MAN WITH THE SCAR, THE • 1915 • Wilson Frank • UKN
MAN WITH THE STEEL WHIP • 1954 • Adreon Franklin • SRL • USA
MAN WITH THE SYNTHETIC BRAIN, THE see **BLOOD OF GHASTLY HORROR** • 1972
MAN WITH THE TRANSPLANTED BRAIN, THE see **HOMME AU CERVEAU GREFFE, L'** • 1971
MAN WITH THE TWISTED LIP, THE • 1921 • Elvey Maurice • UKN
MAN WITH THE TWISTED LIP, THE • 1951 • Grey Richard M. • UKN
MAN WITH THE WEIRD BEARD, THE • 1946 • Gould Dave • SHT • USA
MAN WITH THE WHISTLING NOSE, THE see **FISCHIO AL NASO, IL** • 1967
MAN WITH THE WHITE GLOVES, THE see **HOMME AU GANTS BLANCS, L'** • 1908
MAN WITH THE X-RAY EYES, THE (UKN) see **X -THE MAN WITH THE X-RAY EYES** • 1963
MAN WITH THE YELLOW EYES see **PIANETI CONTRO DI NOI, I** • 1961
MAN WITH THIRTY SONS, THE (UKN) see **MAGNIFICENT YANKEE, THE** • 1950
MAN WITH THREE COFFINS, THE • 1988 • I Jang-Ho • SKR
MAN WITH THREE WIVES, A • 1909 • *Sweet Blanche* • USA
MAN WITH TWO BRAINS, THE • 1983 • Reiner Carl • USA
MAN WITH TWO FACES, A see **MARDE DO CHEHRE** • 1968
MAN WITH TWO FACES, THE • 1934 • Mayo Archie • USA • MYSTERIOUS MR. CHAUTARD, THE ○ DARK TOWER
MAN WITH TWO FACES, THE see **ZOUL WIJHAIN** • 1949
MAN WITH TWO FACES (USA) see **TROUBLED WATERS** • 1964
MAN WITH TWO HEADS • 1982 • Williams Scott • USA
MAN WITH TWO HEADS see **THING WITH TWO HEADS, THE** • 1972
MAN WITH TWO HEADS, THE • 1971 • Milligan Andy • UKN, USA • DR. JEKYLL AND MR. BLOOD
MAN WITH TWO HEARTS, THE see **KETSZIVU FERFI, A** • 1916
MAN WITH TWO LIVES, THE • 1942 • Rosen Phil • USA
MAN WITH TWO MOTHERS, THE • 1922 • Bern Paul • USA
MAN WITH TWO NAMES, THE see **CZLOWIEK O DWU NAZWISKACH** • 1971
MAN WITH WAX FACES, THE see **FIGURES DE CIRE** • 1912
MAN WITH WHEELS IN HIS HEAD, THE (USA) see **MALADE HYDROPHOPE, LE** • 1900
MAN WITH YOUR VOICE, A see **TALK OF THE DEVIL** • 1936
MAN WITHIN, THE • 1912 • *Nestor* • USA
MAN WITHIN, THE • 1914 • Reid Wallace • USA
MAN WITHIN, THE • 1916 • Mix Tom • SHT • USA
MAN WITHIN, THE • 1947 • Knowles Bernard • UKN • SMUGGLERS, THE (USA)
MAN WITHIN, THE (USA) see **ANDERE, DER** • 1930
MAN WITHOUT A BODY, THE • 1957 • Wilder W. Lee, Saunders Charles • UKN
MAN WITHOUT A CASE, THE • 1932 • Stroyeva Vera • USS
MAN WITHOUT A CONSCIENCE, THE • 1925 • Flood James • USA
MAN WITHOUT A COUNTRY • 1973 • Mann Delbert • TVM • USA
MAN WITHOUT A COUNTRY see **MUKOKUSEKI-MONO** • 1951
MAN WITHOUT A COUNTRY, THE • 1909 • Merwin Bannister • USA
MAN WITHOUT A COUNTRY, THE • 1917 • Warde Ernest C. • USA
MAN WITHOUT A COUNTRY, THE • 1925 • Lee Rowland V. • USA • AS NO MAN HAS LOVED
MAN WITHOUT A COUNTRY, THE see **HOMBRE SIN PATRIA, EL** • 1922
MAN WITHOUT A FACE see **WHO?** • 1974
MAN WITHOUT A FACE, THE • 1928 • Bennet Spencer Gordon • SRL • USA
MAN WITHOUT A FACE, THE • 1935 • King George • UKN
MAN WITHOUT A FACE, THE see **HOMBRE SIN ROSTRO, EL** • 1950
MAN WITHOUT A FACE, THE see **HOMME SANS VISAGE, L'** • 1974
MAN WITHOUT A FUTURE, THE see **MANDEN UDEN FREMTID** • 1915
MAN WITHOUT A HEART, THE • 1924 • King Burton L. • USA
MAN WITHOUT A MAP, THE see **MOETSUKITA CHIZU** • 1968
MAN WITHOUT A NAME see **MANN OHNE NAMEN 1, DER** • 1920-21
MAN WITHOUT A NAME see **MENSCH OHNE NAMEN** • 1932
MAN WITHOUT A NAME see **AZONOSITAS** • 1976
MAN WITHOUT A NAME, THE see **CLOUDED NAME, THE** • 1919
MAN WITHOUT A PASSPORT see **CHELOVEK BEZ PASPORTA** • 1966
MAN WITHOUT A SOUL, THE • 1916 • Tucker George Loane • UKN • I BELIEVE
MAN WITHOUT A STAR • 1955 • Vidor King • USA
MAN WITHOUT A STAR see **MARD-E-BESETARE** • 1968
MAN WITHOUT A WIFE see **AKATON MIES** • 1983
MAN WITHOUT DESIRE, THE • 1923 • Brunel Adrian • UKN
MAN WITHOUT FEAR, THE • 1914 • *Bauer Arthur* • USA
MAN WITHOUT MERCY see **GONE WITH THE WEST** • 1969
MAN WITHOUT NATIONALITY, THE see **MUKOKUSEKI-MONO** • 1951
MAN WITHOUT SKIRTS • 1930 • Foster Lewis R. • SHT • USA
MAN, WOMAN AND CHILD • 1983 • Richards Dick • USA • MAN, A WOMAN AND A CHILD, A
MAN, WOMAN AND DOG see **OTOKO TO ONNA TO INU** • 1964
MAN, WOMAN AND SIN • 1927 • Bell Monta • USA • FIRES OF YOUTH
MAN, WOMAN AND WIFE • 1929 • Laemmle Edward • USA • FALLEN ANGELS
MAN -WOMAN -MARRIAGE • 1921 • Holubar Allen • USA
MAN WORTH WHILE, A • 1912 • Melies Gaston • USA
MAN WORTH WHILE, THE • 1921 • Fielding Romaine • USA
MAN WOUNDED • 1943 • Bull Donald • UKN
MAN ZONDER HART, DE • 1937 • Joannon Leo • NTH
MANA • 1944 • Rappaport Herbert • USS
MANAGED MONEY • 1934 • Lamont Charles • SHT • USA
MANAGER OF THE B. & A., THE • 1916 • McGowan J. P. • USA • MAN FROM MEDICINE HAT, THE
MANAGERESS, THE • 1989 • King Christopher • USA
MANAMALAYO • 1967 • Bawanandan T. • SLN • PLAYBOYS
MANANA • 1957 • Nunes Jose Maria • SPN
MANANA CUANDO AMANEZCA • 1954 • Seto Javier • SPN
MANANA DE COBRE • 1985 • Mora Miguel • MXC • BITTER TASTE IN THE MORNING
MANANA DE DOMINGO • 1966 • Gimenez-Rico Antonio • SPN
MANANA LLEGA EL PRESIDENTE • 1972 • Colomo Fernando • SPN
MANANA SERAN HOMBRES • 1960 • Galindo Alejandro • MXC
MANANA SERE LIBRE • 1988 • Aranda Vicente • SPN • TOMORROW I'LL BE FREE ○ LUTE II, EL
MANANA SERS OTRO DIA • 1967 • Camino Jaime • SPN • TOMORROW WILL BE ANOTHER DAY ○ TOMORROW IS ANOTHER DAY
MANANAYAN • 1978 • Brocka Lino • PHL
MANANITAS, LAS • 1948 • Bustillo Oro Juan • MXC
MANAOS • 1980 • Castellari Enzo G., Figueroa Alberto Vazquez • ITL, SPN, VNZ
MANASADEEKA see **MNASIDIKA** • 1969
MANASAKHI • 1968 • Chary S. K. A. • IND
MANASCHI • 1965 • Shamshiev Bolotbek • DOC • USS
MANASSA DEVI • 1937 • Pillai Jayagopal • IND
MANBAIT (USA) see **LAST PAGE, THE** • 1952
MANBEAST! MYTH OR MONSTER • 1978 • Webster Nicholas • USA
MANCHA DE SANGRE, LA • 1937 • Maugard Adolfo Best • MXC • BLOOD STAIN, THE
MANCHA QUE LIMPIA • 1924 • Buchs Jose • SPN
MANCHAS DE SANGRE EN LA LUNA • 1951 • Marquina Luis, Dein Edward • SPN
MANCHAS DE SANGRE EN UN COCHE NUEVO • 1974 • Mercero Antonio • SPN
MANCHE ET LA BELLE, UNE • 1957 • Verneuil Henri • FRN • WHAT PRICE MURDER (USA) ○ EVIL THAT IS EVE, THE
MANCHESTER MAN, THE • 1920 • Wynne Bert • UKN
MANCHU EAGLE MURDER CAPER MYSTERY, THE • 1975 • Hargrove Dean • USA
MANCHURIAN CANDIDATE, THE • 1962 • Frankenheimer John • USA
MANCORNADORA, LA • 1948 • Cortazar Ernesto • MXC
MANDA, LA see **TALPA** • 1955
MANDABI (USA) see **MANDAT, LE** • 1968
MANDACARU VERMELHO • 1961 • dos Santos Nelson Pereira • BRZ
MANDAGARNA MED FANNY • 1977 • Forsberg Lars Lennart • SWD • ROBERT AND FANNY
MANDALA • 1953 • Belson Jordan • ANS • USA
MANDALA • 1968 • *Bym Productions* • ANS • USA
MANDALA • 1981 • Lim Kwon-Taek • SKR • TWO MONKS
MANDALAY • 1934 • Curtiz Michael • USA
MANDARA -ZAUBER DER SCHWARZEN WILDNIS • 1960 • Gardi Rene, Zbinden Charles • SWT
MANDARIN, DER • 1915 • Wiene Conrad • AUS
MANDARIN MYSTERY, THE • 1936 • Staub Ralph • USA
MANDARINA, LA (ITL) see **MANDARINE, LA** • 1971
MANDARINE, LA • 1971 • Molinaro Edouard • FRN, ITL • MANDARINA, LA (ITL)
MANDARINO PER TEO, UN • 1960 • Mattoli Mario • ITL
MANDARIN'S GOLD • 1919 • Apfel Oscar • USA
MANDAT, LE • 1968 • Sembene Ousmane • SNL, FRN • MONEY ORDER, THE (UKN) ○ MANDABI (USA)
MANDAT D'AMENER • 1953 • Pierre-Louis • FRN
MANDELA • 1987 • Saville Philip • TVM • UKN
MANDEN, DER SEJREDE • 1917 • Holger-Madsen • DNM • MAN WHO TAMED THE VICTORS, THE ○ FIGHTING INSTINCT
MANDEN DER TAENKTE TING • 1969 • Ravn Jens • DNM • MAN WHO THOUGHT LIFE, THE ○ MAN WHO THOUGHT THINGS, THE
MANDEN I MANEN • 1986 • Clausen Erik • DNM • MAN IN THE MOON, THE ○ DARK SIDE OF THE MOON, THE
MANDEN PA SVANEGARDEN • 1972 • Mossin Ib • DNM
MANDEN UDEN FREMTID • 1915 • Holger-Madsen • DNM • MAN WITHOUT A FUTURE, THE
MANDEN UDEN SMIL • 1916 • Holger-Madsen • DNM
MANDHKAI • 1989 • MNG
MANDI • 1983 • Benegal Shyam • IND • MARKETPLACE
MANDINGA • 1977 • Pinzauti Mario • ITL
MANDINGA EN LA SIERRA • 1939 • Navarro Isidoro • ARG
MANDINGO • 1975 • Fleischer Richard • USA
MANDIR • 1937 • Kardar A. R. • IND
MANDLIGE HUSASSISTENT • 1938 • Lauritzen Lau Jr. • DNM
MANDOLIN, THE • 1973 • Velchev Ilya • BUL
MANDRAGOLA, LA • 1965 • Lattuada Alberto • ITL, FRN • MANDRAGORE, LA (FRN) ○ MANDRAGOLA -THE LOVE ROOT ○ MANDRAKE, THE ○ LOVE ROOT, THE
MANDRAGOLA -THE LOVE ROOT see **MANDRAGOLA, LA** • 1965
MANDRAGORA see **GALGMANNEN** • 1945
MANDRAGORE see **ALRAUNE** • 1927
MANDRAGORE see **ALRAUNE** • 1952
MANDRAGORE, LA (FRN) see **MANDRAGOLA, LA** • 1965
MANDRAKE • 1979 • Falk Harry • TVM • USA
MANDRAKE see **ALRAUNE** • 1918
MANDRAKE see **ALRAUNE** • 1918
MANDRAKE see **ALRAUNE** • 1927
MANDRAKE see **ALRAUNE** • 1952
MANDRAKE, THE see **MANDRAGOLA, LA** • 1965
MANDRAKE KILLINGE KARSI • 1967 • Pekmezoglu Oksal • TRK • MANDRAKE VS. KILLING
MANDRAKE THE MAGICIAN • 1939 • Nelson Sam, Deming Norman • SRL • USA
MANDRAKE VS. KILLING see **MANDRAKE KILLINGE KARSI** • 1967
MANDRIN • 1923 • Fescourt Henri • FRN
MANDRIN • 1947 • Jayet Rene • FRN
MANDRIN • 1963 • Le Chanois Jean-Paul • FRN, ITL • MANDRIN, BANDIT GENTILHOMME
MANDRIN, BANDIT GENTILHOMME see **MANDRIN** • 1963
MANDY • 1952 • Mackendrick Alexander • UKN • CRASH OF SILENCE (USA) ○ STORY OF MANDY, THE
MANDY'S CHICKEN DINNER • 1914 • *Lubin* • USA
MANDY'S SOCIAL WHIRL • 1911 • *Lubin* • USA
MANEATER • 1973 • Edwards Vince • TVM • USA • EVASION
MANEATER • 1981 • Pearse John • SHT • UKN
MANEATER see **SHARK!** • 1969
MANEATER OF KUMAON • 1948 • Haskin Byron • USA
MANEATERS ARE LOOSE! • 1978 • Galfas Timothy • TVM • USA
MANEGE • 1927 • Reichmann Max • FRG
MANEGE • 1937 • Gallone Carmine • FRG • DRAMMA AL CIRCO, UN
MANEGENS BORN • 1914 • Davidsen Hjalmar • DNM
MANEGERAUSCH • 1920 • Illes Eugen • FRG
MANEGES • 1949 • Allegret Yves • FRN • WANTON, THE (UKN) ○ CHEAT, THE (USA) ○ RIDING FOR A FALL
MANEGES DE L'IMAGINAIRE, LES • 1981 • Danan Joseph • FRN
MANET OU LE NOVATEUR MALGRE LUI • 1980 • Leenhardt Roger • FRN
MANETTE see **MANETTE OU LES DIEUX DE CARTON** • 1965
MANETTE OU LES DIEUX DE CARTON • 1965 • Adam Camil • CND • MANETTE
MANEWRY MILOSNE • 1936 • Nowina-Przybylski Jan • PLN
MANFISH • 1955 • Wilder W. Lee • USA • CALYPSO (UKN)
MANGA • 1977 • Kuri Yoji • ANS • JPN • MONGA
MANGALA • 1950 • Vasan S. S. • IND
MANGALA • 1974 • Thotawatte Titus • SLN
MANGALSUTRA • 1968 • Tate Ashok • IND
MANGANINNIE • 1980 • Honey John • ASL
MANGAYARAKARASI • 1949 • Banerji Jiten • IND
MANGER • 1961 • Carle Gilles, Portugais Louis • DCS • CND
MANGIA see **EAT AND RUN** • 1986
MANGIATI VIVI see **MANGIATI VIVI DAI CANNIBALI** • 1980
MANGIATI VIVI DAI CANNIBALI • 1980 • Lenzi Umberto • ITL • EATEN ALIVE BY THE CANNIBALS ○ DEFY TO THE LAST PARADISE ○ CANNIBALS ○ EATEN ALIVE ○ DOOMED TO DIE ○ MANGIATI VIVI
MANGLILIGPIT, ANG • 1968 • Santiago Pablo • PHL • KILLER, THE
MANGO TREE, THE • 1977 • Dobson Kevin • ASL
MANGU • 1955 • Ansari N. A. • IND
MANHA CINZENTA • 1969 • Sao Paulo Olney • BRZ • GREY MORNING
MANHA DE SOL EM DAMAO • 1959 • Spiguel Miguel • SHT • PRT
MANHA NA ROCA • 1945-56 • Mauro-Humberto • SHT • BRZ
MANHA SUBMERSA • 1980 • Antonio Lauro • PRT • MORNING UNDERSEA
MANHANDLED • 1924 • Dwan Allan • USA
MANHANDLED • 1949 • Foster Lewis R. • USA
MANHANDLERS, THE • 1973 • Madden Lee • USA
MANHATTA see **MANNAHATTA** • 1921
MANHATTAN • 1924 • Burnside R. H. • USA
MANHATTAN • 1979 • Allen Woody • USA
MANHATTAN ANGEL • 1948 • Dreifuss Arthur • USA
MANHATTAN BABY see **OCCHIO DEL MALE, L'** • 1982
MANHATTAN BUTTERFLY • 1935 • Collins Lewis D. • USA • MIDNIGHT BUTTERFLY (UKN)
MANHATTAN COCKTAIL • 1928 • Arzner Dorothy • USA
MANHATTAN COCKTAIL • 1928 • Schertzinger Victor • USA
MANHATTAN COWBOY • 1928 • McGowan J. P. • USA
MANHATTAN HEARTBEAT • 1940 • Burton David • USA
MANHATTAN KNIGHT, A • 1920 • Beranger George A. • USA
MANHATTAN KNIGHTS • 1928 • King Burton L. • USA
MANHATTAN LOVE SONG • 1934 • Fields Leonard • USA
MANHATTAN MADNESS • 1916 • Dwan Allan • USA

MANHATTAN MADNESS • 1925 • McDermott John • USA
MANHATTAN MADNESS see **WOMAN WANTED** • 1935
MANHATTAN MADNESS (UKN) see **ADVENTURE IN MANHATTAN** • 1936
MANHATTAN MARY see **FOLLOW THE LEADER** • 1930
MANHATTAN MELODRAMA • 1934 • Van Dyke W. S. • USA
MANHATTAN MEMORIES • 1948 • Moore Harold James • SHT • USA
MANHATTAN MERRY-GO-ROUND • 1937 • Reisner Charles F. • USA • MANHATTAN MUSIC BOX (UKN)
MANHATTAN MONKEY BUSINESS • 1935 • Parrott Charles, Law Harold • SHT • USA
MANHATTAN MOON • 1935 • Walker Stuart • USA • SING ME A LOVE SONG (UKN)
MANHATTAN MUSIC BOX (UKN) see **MANHATTAN MERRY-GO-ROUND** • 1937
MANHATTAN PARADE • 1931 • Bacon Lloyd • USA
MANHATTAN PROJECT, THE see **DEADLY GAME** • 1986
MANHATTAN PROJECT: THE DEADLY GAME, THE see **DEADLY GAME** • 1986
MANHATTAN SHAKEDOWN • 1939 • Barsha Leon • USA
MANHATTAN TOWER • 1932 • Strayer Frank • USA
MANHOLE COVERS • 1954 • Peterson Sidney • USA
MANHOOD • 1941 • Barnet Boris • USS
MANHOOD see **MUT** • 1939
MANHOOD'S REWARD • 1909 • *Powers* • USA
MANHUNT see **MALA ORDINA, LA** • 1972
MANHUNT, THE • 1986 • De Angelis Fabrizio • ITL
MANHUNT, THE see **HAJKA** • 1978
MANHUNT FOR CLAUDE DALLAS • 1986 • London Jerry • TVM • USA
MANHUNT FOR MURDER (USA) see **SAIGNEE, LA** • 1971
MANHUNT IN MILAN (UKN) see **MALA ORDINA, LA** • 1972
MANHUNT IN SPACE • 1954 • *Reed Roland* • MTV • USA
MANHUNT IN THE AFRICAN JUNGLE see **SECRET SERVICE IN DARKEST AFRICA** • 1943
MANHUNT IN THE JUNGLE • 1958 • McGowan Tom • USA
MANHUNT OF MYSTERY ISLAND • 1945 • Bennet Spencer Gordon, Grissell Wallace A., Canutt Yakima • SRL • USA
MANHUNT (UKN) see **FROM HELL TO TEXAS** • 1958
MANHUNTER • 1974 • Grauman Walter • TVM • USA
MANHUNTER • 1986 • Mann Michael • USA • RED DRAGON
MANI • 1975 • Maniatis Sakis • GRC
MANI DI FATA • 1984 • Steno • ITL • FAIRY HANDS
MANI DI UNA DONNA SOLA, LE • 1979 • Rossati Nello • ITL
MANI IN ALTO • 1961 • Bianchi Giorgio • ITL, FRN • EN PLEINE BAGARRE (FRN) ○ DESTINATION FURY (USA) ○ INTERPOL STRIPTEASE
MANI SPORCHE, LE • 1978 • Petri Elio • MTV • ITL
MANI SULLA CITTA, LE • 1963 • Rosi Francesco • ITL • HANDS OVER THE CITY (USA) ○ HANDS ON THE TOWN ○ HANDS ON THE CITY
MANIA • 1918 • Illes Eugen • FRG
MANIA • 1974 • Polselli Renato • ITL
MANIA • 1985 • Panoussopoulos George • GRC
MANIA • 1987 • Sheppard John, Lynch Paul, Robertson David M. • CND
MANIA see **EAT AND RUN** • 1986
MANIA DI GRANDEZZA (ITL) see **FOLIE DES GRANDEURS, LA** • 1971
MANIA (USA) see **FLESH AND THE FIENDS, THE** • 1960
MANIAC • 1934 • Esper Dwain • USA
MANIAC • 1962 • Carreras Michael • UKN
MANIAC • 1977 • Compton Richard • USA • TOWN THAT CRIED TERROR, THE ○ ASSAULT ON PARADISE ○ RANSOM
MANIAC • 1980 • Lustig William • USA
MANIAC, THE • 1911 • Salter Harry • USA
MANIAC AT LARGE see **PASSI DI DANZA SU UNA LAMA SI RASOIO** • 1973
MANIAC BARBER, THE • 1902 • *Biograph* • USA
MANIAC CHASE • 1904 • Porter Edwin S. • USA
MANIAC COOK, THE • 1909 • Griffith D. W. • USA
MANIAC COP • 1988 • Lustig William • USA
MANIAC MANSION see **AMUCK** • 1978
MANIACI, I • 1964 • Fulci Lucio • ITL
MANIACS ARE LOOSE, THE see **THRILL KILLERS, THE** • 1965
MANIAC'S GUILLOTINE, THE • 1902 • Haggar William • UKN
MANIACS ON WHEELS (USA) see **ONCE A JOLLY SWAGMAN** • 1948
MANIACS THREE • 1914 • Dillon Eddie • USA
MANIC 5 • 1965 • Rivard Fernand • DCS • CND
MANIC 5 • 1967 • Belanger Fernand • MTV • CND
MANICOMIO • 1952 • Delgado Luis Maria, Fernan-Gomez Fernando • SPN
MANICOMIO • 1957 • Diaz Morales Jose • MXC
MANICURE, THE • 1913 • *Grandin Ethel* • USA
MANICURE GIRL, THE • 1913 • Williams C. Jay • USA
MANICURE GIRL, THE • 1914 • *Ritchie Billie* • USA
MANICURE GIRL, THE • 1916 • King Burton L. • SHT • USA
MANICURE GIRL, THE • 1925 • Tuttle Frank • USA
MANICURE LADY, THE • 1911 • Sennett Mack • USA
MANICURIST, THE • 1912 • *Champion* • USA
MANICURIST, THE • 1916 • Sterling Ford • SHT • USA
MANICURIST AND THE MUTT, THE • 1913 • *Roland Ruth* • USA
MANIFEST, DAS • 1974 • Lepeniotis Antonis • AUS • MANIFEST, THE
MANIFEST, THE see **MANIFEST, DAS** • 1974
MANIFESTO • Preston Richard • USA
MANIFESTO • 1989 • Makavejev Dusan • USA, YGS
MANIGUA SIN DIOS, LA • 1948 • Ruiz-Castillo Arturo • SPN
MANIKA: THE GIRL WHO LIVED TWICE • 1989 • Villiers Francois • FRN
MANILA BY NIGHT see **CITY AFTER DARK** • 1981
MANILA CALLING • 1942 • Leeds Herbert I. • USA
MANILA, HONGKONG, SINGAPORE • 1967 • *De Villa Nestor* • PHL
MANILA: IN THE CLAWS OF DARKNESS see **MAYNILA, SA MGA KUKO NG LIWANAG** • 1975
MANILA IN THE CLAWS OF LIGHT see **MAYNILA, SA MGA KUKO NG LIWANAG** • 1975
MANILA: IN THE CLAWS OF NEON see **MAYNILA, SA MGA KUKO NG LIWANAG** • 1975
MANILA, OPEN CITY • 1968 • Romero Eddie • PHL
MANILA (UKN) see **MAYNILA, SA MGA KUKO NG LIWANAG** • 1975
MANILY KEY JANBAZ • 1989 • Mohammad Jan • PKS
MANIN DENSHA • 1957 • Ichikawa Kon • JPN • CROWDED TRAIN, THE ○ CROWDED STREETCAR, THE
MANINA, LA FILLE SANS VOILE • 1952 • Rozier Willy • FRN • LIGHTHOUSE KEEPER'S DAUGHTER, THE (UKN) ○ GIRL IN THE BIKINI, THE (USA)
MANIOBRAS • 1970 • Torres Miguel • CUB • MANOEUVRES
MANIONS, THE • 1981 • Dubin Charles S., Sargent Joseph • MTV • USA
MANIPULATION DE LA FERMETURE A GLISSIERE • 1971 • Moreau Michel • SHT • CND
MANIPULATOR, THE • 1972 • SAF
MANIPULATOR, THE • 1980 • Nelson Dusty • USA
MANIPULATOR, THE see **B.J. PRESENTS** • 1971
MANIPULATOR, THE see **INTERNECINE PROJECT, THE** • 1974
MANIPULE ET LES JEUX VIDEO • 1986 • Beaudry Michel • MTV • CND
MANITAS DE PLATA • 1966 • Reichenbach Francois • SHT • FRN
MANITOBA -FESTIVAL COUNTRY • 1970 • Barclay Robert • SHT • CND
MANITOU, THE • 1978 • Girdler William • USA
MANITOU TRAIL, THE • 1925 • Barkas Geoffrey • UKN
MANIZALES CITY • 1925 • CLM
MANJA • 1982 • Nair M. T. Vasudevan • IND • MIST, THE
MANJA VALEWSKA • 1936 • Rovensky Josef • AUS
MANJI • 1964 • Masumura Yasuzo • JPN • PASSION (UKN) ○ ALL MIXED UP
MANJI • 1964 • Shindo Kaneto • JPN • PASSION
MANJIL • 1936 • Kapoor Prithviraj • IND
MANJUDHAR • 1947 • *Biswas Anil (M)* • IND
MANK DINNE • 1968 • Udayashankar Chi • IND • WITLESS
MANKILLERS • 1987 • Prior David A. • USA • TWELVE WILD WOMEN
MANKILLERS, THE see **FASTER, PUSSYCAT! KILL! KILL!** • 1965
MANKIND see **AI-YE** • 1950
MANKINDA • 1957 • Vanderbeek Stan • SHT • USA
MANKO BANDH • *Rnfc* • NPL • DAM OF ONE'S MIND, THE
MANLY MAN, A • 1911 • Ince Thomas H. • USA
MANLY TIMES • 1977 • Zahariev Edward • BUL
MANMO KENGOKU NO REIMEI see **MAMMO KENKOKU NO REIMEI** • 1932
MANN AN DER KETTE, DER • 1920 • Attenberger Toni • FRG
MANN AUF ABWEGEN, EIN • 1940 • Selpin Herbert • FRG
MANN AUF DEM KOMETEN, DER • 1925 • Halm Alfred • FRG • MAN FROM THE COMET, THE
MANN AUF DEN SCHIENEN, DER see **CZLOWIEK NA TORZE** • 1956
MANN AUF DER FLASCHE, DER • 1920 • Ostermayr Ottmar • FRG
MANN AUF DER MAUER, DER • 1983 • Hauff Reinhard • FRG • MAN ON THE WALL, THE
MANN AUS DEM JENSEITS, DER • 1925 • Noa Manfred • FRG
MANN AUS NEAPEL, DER see **KINDER DER FINSTERNIS 1** • 1921
MANN AUS STAHL, DER • 1922 • Delmont Joseph • FRG
MANN AUS ZELLE 19, DER • 1922 • Seitz Franz • FRG
MANN, DEM MAN DEN NAMEN STAHL, DER • 1945 • Staudte Wolfgang • FRG
MANN, DEN DAS SCHICKSAL SANDTE, DER • 1924 • *Deutsche Mutoscop* • FRG
MANN, DEN NIEMAND SAH, DER • 1921 • *Kay-Film* • FRG
MANN, DER DEN MORD BEGING, DER • 1930 • Bernhardt Curtis • FRG • NACHTE AM BOSPORUS ○ MAN WHO MURDERED, THE
MANN, DER NACH DER OMA KAM, DER • 1972 • Oehme Roland • GDR
MANN, DER NICHT LIEBEN DARF, DER see **GEHEIMNIS DES ABBE X, DAS** • 1927
MANN, DER NICHT LIEBT, DER • 1929 • Brignone Guido • FRG
MANN DER NICHT NEIN SAGEN KANN, DER (FRG) see **MA NON E UNA COSA SERIA** • 1936
MANN, DER SEINEN MORDER SUCHT, DER • 1931 • Siodmak Robert • FRG • LOOKING FOR HIS MURDERER ○ JIM, DER MANN MIT DER NARBE ○ JIM, THE MAN WITH THE SCAR ○ MAN WHO SEEKS HIS OWN MURDERER, THE
MANN, DER SHERLOCK HOLMES, DER • 1937 • Hartl Karl • FRG
MANN, DER SICH SELBER SUCHT, DER • 1950 • von Cziffra Geza • FRG
MANN, DER SICH VERKAUFT, DER • 1925 • Steinhoff Hans • FRG • MAN WHO SOLD HIMSELF, THE
MANN DER SICH VERKAUFT, DER • 1959 • von Baky Josef • FRG
MANN DER TAT, DER • 1919 • Janson Victor • FRG
MANN DER TAT, DER see **SILBERKONIG 2, DER** • 1921
MANN, DER ZWEIMAL LEBEN WOLLTE, DER • 1950 • Tourjansky Victor • FRG
MANN FALLT VOM HIMMEL, EIN see **GEHEIMAGENT, DER** • 1932
MANN FUR MANN • 1939 • Stemmle R. A. • FRG
MANN FUR MEINE FRAU, EIN • 1943 • Marischka Hubert • FRG
MANN GEGEN MANN • 1928 • Piel Harry • FRG
MANN GEHORT INS HAUS, EIN • 1945 • Marischka Hubert • FRG • BANKERL UNTERM BIRNBAUM
MANN GEHT DURCH DIE WAND, EIN • 1959 • Vajda Ladislao • FRG • MAN WHO WALKED THROUGH THE WALL, THE (USA) ○ MAN GOES THROUGH THE WALL, A ○ MAN WHO COULD WALK THROUGH WALLS, THE
MANN IM DUNKEL, DER • 1930 • Heuberger Edmund • FRG
MANN IM DUNKEL, DER see **JAGD NACH DEM TODE 3, DIE** • 1921
MANN IM EIS, DER • 1916 • Sauer Fred • FRG
MANN IM FEUER, DER • 1926 • Waschneck Erich • FRG • FIREMAN, THE
MANN IM HINTERGRUND, DER • 1923 • Winar Ernest • FRG
MANN IM KELLAR, DER • 1914 • May Joe • FRG
MANN IM MONDE, DER • 1918 • Leffler Robert • FRG
MANN IM NEBEL, DER • 1919 • Greenbaum Mutz • FRG
MANN IM SALZ, DER • 1921 • *Munchener Lichtspielkunst* • FRG
MANN IM SATTEL, DER • 1925 • Noa Manfred • FRG
MANN IM SATTEL, DER • 1945 • Piel Harry • FRG
MANN IM SCHATTEN • 1961 • Rabenalt Arthur M. • AUS
MANN IM SCHRANK, DER • 1921 • Bock-Stieber Gernot • FRG
MANN IM SPIEGEL, DER • 1917 • Wiene Robert • FRG
MANN IM STEINBRUCH, DER • 1916 • Zangenberg Einar • FRG
MANN IM STROM, DER • 1958 • York Eugen • FRG
MANN IN DER FALLE, DER • 1920 • Neff Wolfgang • FRG
MANN IN DER WANNE, DER • 1952 • Antel Franz • AUS
MANN IN FESSELN, DER see **PHANTOME DES GLUCKS** • 1929
MANN MEINES LEBENS, DER • 1954 • Engel Erich • FRG
MANN MIT DEM GLASAUGE, DER • 1968 • Vohrer Alfred • FRG • TERROR ON HALF MOON STREET (USA)
MANN MIT DEM GOLDENEN PINSEL, DER • 1971 • Marischka Franz • FRG, ITL • UOMO DAL PENNELLO D'ORO, L' (ITL) ○ LET IT ALL HANG OUT (USA)
MANN MIT DEM LAUBFROSCH, DER • 1928 • Lamprecht Gerhard • FRG
MANN MIT DEM OBJEKTIV, DER • 1963 • Vogel Frank • GDR • MAN WITH THE GADGET, THE
MANN MIT DEM SPLITTER, DER see **WELT WILL BELOGEN SEIN, DIE** • 1926
MANN MIT DEN 1000 MASKEN, DER see **UPPERSEVEN L'UOMO DA UCCIDERE** • 1966
MANN MIT DEN DREI FRAUEN, DER • 1920 • Sauer Fred • FRG
MANN MIT DEN EISERNENNERVEN, DER see **MANN OHNE NAMEN 5, DER** • 1920-21
MANN MIT DEN SIEBEN MASKEN, DER • 1918 • Larsen Viggo • FRG
MANN MIT DER EISERNEN MASKE, DER • 1922 • Glass Max • FRG
MANN MIT DER FALSCHEN BANKNOTE, DER • 1927 • Mengon Romano • FRG
MANN MIT DER LEUCHTENDEN STIRN, DER • 1915 • Sauer Fred • FRG
MANN MIT DER PRANKE, DER • 1935 • van der Noss Rudolf • FRG
MANN MIT DER TODESMASKE, DER • 1920 • Dengel Edy • FRG
MANN MIT GRUNDSATZEN, EIN • 1943 • von Bolvary Geza • FRG
MANN MIT HERZ, EIN • 1932 • von Bolvary Geza • FRG
MANN MUSS NICHT IMMER SCHON SEIN, EIN • 1956 • Quest Hans • FRG
MANN OHNE BERUF, DER • 1922 • Firmans Josef • FRG
MANN OHNE GEDACHTNIS • 1983 • Gloor Kurt • SWT • MAN WHO LOST HIS MEMORY, THE
MANN OHNE GEDACHTNIS, DER • 1915 • *Projektions-Ag* • FRG
MANN OHNE GENACHTNIS, DER • 1919 • Bolten-Baeckers Heinrich • FRG
MANN OHNE HERZ, DER • 1924 • Koebner Franz W. • FRG
MANN OHNE KOPF, DER • 1916 • Neher Louis • FRG
MANN OHNE KOPF, DER • 1927 • Malasomma Nunzio • FRG
MANN OHNE NAMEN 1, DER • 1920-21 • Jacoby Georg • FRG • MILLIONENDIEB, DER ○ MAN WITHOUT A NAME
MANN OHNE NAMEN 2, DER • 1920-21 • Jacoby Georg • FRG • KAISER DER SAHARA, DER
MANN OHNE NAMEN 3, DER • 1920-21 • Jacoby Georg • FRG • GELBE BESTIEN
MANN OHNE NAMEN 4, DER • 1920-21 • Jacoby Georg • FRG • GOLDENE FLUT, DIE
MANN OHNE NAMEN 5, DER • 1920-21 • Jacoby Georg • FRG • MANN MIT DEN EISERNENNERVEN, DER
MANN OHNE NAMEN 6, DER • 1920-21 • Jacoby Georg • FRG • SPRUNG UBER DEN SCHATTEN, DER
MANN OHNE NERVEN, DER • 1924 • Piel Harry • FRG
MANN OHNE SCHLAF, DER • 1926 • Boese Carl • FRG
MANN SEINER FRAU, DER • 1925 • Basch Felix • FRG • HER HUSBAND'S WIFE
MANN UBER BORD • 1921 • Grune Karl • FRG
MANN UM MITTERNACHT, DER • 1924 • Holger-Madsen • FRG
MANN VERGISST DIE LIEBE, EIN • 1955 • von Collande Volker • FRG
MANN, VON DEM MAN SPRICHT, DER • 1937 • Emo E. W. • AUS
MANN VON OBERZALBERG – ADOLF UND MARLENE, DER see **ADOLF UND MARLENE** • 1977
MANN WIE EVA, EIN • 1983 • Gabrea Radu • FRG • MAN LIKE EVA, A
MANN WIE MAXIMILIAN, EIN • 1944 • Deppe Hans • FRG
MANN WILL NACH DEUTSCHLAND, EIN • 1934 • Wegener Paul • FRG
MANN WITH A FLUTE • 1960 • Craven Thomas • SHT • USA
MANNA • 1915 • Otto Henry • USA
MANNAHATTA • 1921 • Sheeler Charles, Strand Paul • SHT • USA • MANHATTA
MANNAJA • 1977 • Martino Sergio • ITL • MAN CALLED BLADE, A
MANNE BLEUE, LA • 1945 • Blais Roger • DCS • CND
MANNEKANG I ROTT • 1958 • Mattsson Arne • SWD • MODEL IN RED
MANNEKANGEN • 1913 • Stiller Mauritz • SWD • FASHION MODEL, THE ○ MODEL, THE
MANNEKEN PIS CASE, THE see **ZAAK M.P., DE** • 1960
MANNEN FRAN ANDRA SIDEN • 1971 • Yegorov Yuri • SWD, USS • CHELOVEK S DRUGOI STORONI (USS) ○ MAN FROM THE OTHER SIDE, THE
MANNEN FRAN MALLORCA • 1984 • Widerberg Bo • SWD, DNM • MAN FROM MALLORCA, THE ○ MAN FROM MAJORCA, THE
MANNEN I MORKER • 1955 • Mattsson Arne • SWD • MEN IN DARKNESS
MANNEN PA TAKET • 1977 • Widerberg Bo • SWD • MAN ON THE ROOF, THE ○ ABOMINABLE MAN, THE
MANNEN SOM ALL VILLE MORDA • 1940 • Bornebusch Arne • SWD • MAN EVERYBODY WANTS TO MURDER, THE
MANNEN SOM BLEV MILJONAR • 1980 • Arehn Mats • SWD • TO BE A MILLIONAIRE

MANNEN SOM GICK UPP I ROK (SWD) see **SVED AKINEK NYOMA VESZETT, A** • 1980

MANNEN SOM IKKE KUNNE LE • 1968 • Hermansson Bo • NRW • MAN WHO COULD NOT LAUGH, THE

MANNEN SOM SLUTADE ROKA • 1972 • Danielsson Tage • SWD • MAN WHO GAVE UP SMOKING, THE

MANNEN UTAN ANSIKTE • 1959 • Band Albert • SWD, USA • FACE OF FIRE (USA)

MANNEQUIN • 1926 • Cruze James • USA

MANNEQUIN • 1933 • Cooper George A. • UKN

MANNEQUIN • 1937 • Borzage Frank • USA

MANNEQUIN • 1976 • Pessis Claude • FRN

MANNEQUIN • 1986 • Gottlieb Michael • USA • PERFECT TIMING

MANNEQUIN, DAS • 1960 • Dorries Bernhard • FRG

MANNEQUIN, LE • 1977 • Ben Aicha Sadok • TNS

MANNEQUIN ASSASSINE, LE • 1947 • de Herain Pierre • FRN

MANNEQUIN VIVANT, LE • 1914 • Protazanov Yakov • USS

MANNEQUINS • 1933 • Hervil Rene • FRN

MANNEQUINS DE PARIS • 1956 • Hunebelle Andre • FRN

MANNEQUINS FUR RIO • 1954 • Neumann Kurt • FRG

MANNER • 1986 • Dorrie Doris • FRG • MEN

MANNER AND JUSTICE OF SEX see **SHIKIDO JINGI** • 1968

MANNER DER FRAU CLARISSA, DIE • 1922 • Wassermann Walter • FRG

MANNER DER SYBIL, DIE • 1922 • Zelnik Friedrich • FRG

MANNER IM GEFAHRLICHEN ALTER • 1954 • Schroth Carl-Heinz • FRG

MANNER IN DEN BESTEN JAHREN ERZAHLEN SEXGESCHICHTEN • 1967 • Fronz Fritz • AUS • MEN IN THEIR PRIME TELL SEX STORIES

MANNER MUSSEN ES SEIN • 1939 • Rabenalt Arthur M. • FRG • MEN ARE THAT WAY (USA)

MANNER MUSSEN SO SEIN see **GELIEBTE BESTIE** • 1959

MANNER OHNE BERUF • 1929 • Piel Harry • FRG

MANNER SIND ZUM LIEBEN DA • 1969 • Schmidt Eckhardt • FRG • GIRLS FROM ATLANTIS, THE

MANNER UM LUCIE, DIE • 1931 • Korda Alexander • FRG

MANNER VOM BLAUEN KREUZ, DIE see **BLEKITNY KRZYZ** • 1956

MANNER VOR DER EHE • 1927 • David Constantin J. • FRG

MANNER VOR DER EHE • 1936 • Boese Carl • FRG

MANNERHEIM –MARSHAL OF FINLAND see **MANNERHEIM –SUOMEN MARSALKKA** • 1968

MANNERHEIM –SUOMEN MARSALKKA • 1968 • Uusitalo Kari • DOC • FNL • MANNERHEIM –MARSHAL OF FINLAND

MANNERS AND THE MAN • 1915 • *Totten Joseph Byron* • USA

MANNERWIRTSCHAFT • 1941 • Meyer Johannes • FRG

MANNES WERDEGANG • 1927 • Randolf Rolf • FRG

MANNES WORT, EINES • 1919 • Lund Erik • FRG

MANNESMANN • 1937 • Ruttmann Walter • FRG

MANNETJESMAKER, DE • 1983 • Hylkema Hans • NTH • KINGMAKER CONNECTION, THE

MANNISKAN LANDSCAP • 1964 • Werner Gosta • SHT • SWD • HUMAN LANDSCAPE

MANNISKAN OCH JORDEN • 1983 • von Strauss Ulf • SWD

MANNISKOR I STAD • 1946 • Sucksdorff Arne • DCS • SWD • RHYTHM OF A CITY ○ SYMPHONY OF A CITY ○ PEOPLE IN THE CITY ○ STOCKHOLM STORY

MANNISKOR MOTS OCH LJUV MUSIC UPPSTAR I HJARTET (SWD) see **MENNESKER MODES OG SOD MUSIK OPSTAR I HJERTET** • 1968

MANNISKORS RIKE • 1949 • Folke Gosta • SWD • REALM OF MAN

MANNY'S ORPHANS see **HERE COME THE TIGERS** • 1978

MANO 1 • 1953 • Sechan Edmond • SHT • FRN

MANO, LA (ITL) see **MAIN, LA** • 1969

MANO A MANO • 1932 • Boytler Arcady • MXC • MANO IN MANO ○ HAND TO HAND

MANO CALDA, LA (ITL) see **MAIN CHAUDE, LA** • 1959

MANO CHE NUTRE LA MORTE, LA • 1975 • Garrone Sergio • ITL

MANO DE DIOS, LA • 1965 • Salvador Jaime • MXC

MANO DE UN HOMBRE MUERTO, EL • 1963 • Franco Jesus • SPN • HAND OF A DEAD MAN, THE

MANO DELLA MORTA, LA • 1949 • Campogalliani Carlo • ITL

MANO DELLA STRANIERO, LA • 1954 • Soldati Mario • ITL, FRN • STRANGER'S HAND, THE (USA)

MANO DENGONBAN • 1958 • Murayama Shinji • JPN • TOKYO PATROL –TAXI–DRIVER MURDERS

MANO DI VELLUTO • 1967 • Fecchi Ettore • ITL

MANO DI VELLUTO • 1979 • Castellano, Pipolo • ITL • VELVET HANDS

MANO EN LA TRAMPA, LA • 1961 • Torre-Nilsson Leopoldo • ARG • HAND IN THE TRAP, THE

MANO IN MANO see **MANO A MANO** • 1932

MANO LUNGA DEL PADRINO, LA • 1972 • Bonomi Nardo • ITL • LONG ARM OF THE GODFATHER, THE

MANO NEGRA, LA • 1980 • Colomo Fernando • SPN • BLACK HAND, THE

MANO NERA, LA • 1973 • Racioppi Antonio • ITL, SPN • BLACK HAND, THE

MANO NERA, LA (ITL) see **MAIN NOIRE, LA** • 1970

MANO QUE APRIETA, LA • 1964 • Crevenna Alfredo B. • MXC

MANO ROSSO, LA (ITL) see **ROTE HAND, DIE** • 1960

MANO SPIETATO DELLE LEGGE, LA • 1973 • Gariazzo Mario • ITL • BLOODY HANDS OF THE LAW

MANO SUL FUCILE, LA • 1963 • Turolla Luigi • ITL

MANOBRAS DE TANCOS • 1919 • de Albuquerque Ernesto • SHT • PRT

MANOEUVRE • 1979 • Wiseman Frederick • DOC • USA

MANOEUVRES • 1968 • Dovnikovic Borivoj • ANM • YGS

MANOEUVRES • 1989 • Sanders Helma • FRG

MANOEUVRES see **MANIOBRAS** • 1970

MANOEUVRES OF THE FRENCH ARMY see **GRANDES MANOEUVRES** • 1896

MANOIR DE LA PEUR, LE • 1927 • Machin Alfred • FRN • HOUSE OF FEAR, THE

MANOIR DE LA PEUR, LE • 1927 • Wulschleger Henry • FRN

MANOIR DU DIABLE, LE • 1896 • Melies Georges • FRN • HAUNTED CASTLE, THE (USA) ○ MANOR OF THE DEVIL, THE ○ DEVIL'S MANOR, THE ○ DEVIL'S CASTLE, THE

MANOLAKIS O TEDDYBOYS • 1967 • Melissinos Vangelis • GRC • MANOLAKIS THE TEDDYBOY

MANOLAKIS THE TEDDYBOY see **MANOLAKIS O TEDDYBOYS** • 1967

MANOLESCU • 1929 • Tourjansky Victor • FRG • KONIG DER HOCHSTAPLER, DER

MANOLESCU, DER FURST DER DIEBE • 1933 • Wolff Willi • FRG

MANOLESCUS MEMOIREN • 1920 • Oswald Richard • FRG • FURST LAHORY, DER KONIG DER DIEBE

MANOLESTA • 1981 • Festa Campanile Pasquale • ITL

MANOLETE • 1944 • Gance Abel • FRN

MANOLIS • 1962 • Crosfield Paul H. • UKN

MANOLO, GUARDIA URBANO • 1956 • Salvia Rafael J. • SPN

MANOLO, LA NUIT • 1973 • Ozores Mariano • SPN

MANOMETRE • 1930-32 • Room Abram • USS

MANON • 1948 • Clouzot Henri-Georges • FRN

MANON • 1986 • Chalbaud Roman • VNZ

MANON 70 • 1968 • Aurel Jean • FRN, FRG, ITL • HEMMUNGSLOSE MANON (FRG)

MANON 326 see **ROUTE DU BAGNE, LA** • 1945

MANON DE MONTMARTRE • 1914 • Feuillade Louis • FRN

MANON DE MONTMARTRE • 1919 • Feyder Jacques • FRN

MANON DES SOURCES • 1952 • Pagnol Marcel • FRN • MANON OF THE SPRINGS

MANON DES SOURCES • 1985 • Berri Claude • FRN • JEAN DE FLORETTE 2e PARTIE ○ MANON OF THE SPRING

MANON LECOMTE HARPISTE • 1972-73 • Brault Francois • DCS • CND

MANON LESCAUT • 1910 • Pastrone Giovanni • ITL

MANON LESCAUT • 1914 • *Cavalieri Lina* • USA

MANON LESCAUT • 1919 • Zelnik Friedrich • FRG • HOHE LIED DER LIEBE, DAS

MANON LESCAUT • 1926 • Robison Arthur • FRG

MANON LESCAUT • 1940 • Gallone Carmine • ITL

MANON OF THE SPRING see **MANON DES SOURCES** • 1985

MANON OF THE SPRINGS see **MANON DES SOURCES** • 1952

MANONE IL LADRONE • 1974 • Margheriti Antonio • ITL

MANOR OF THE DEVIL, THE see **MANOIR DU DIABLE, LE** • 1896

MANORS AROUND THE LAKE see **GARDARNA RUNT SJON** • 1957

MANOS A LA OBRA • Barrios Jaime • DOC • USA • HANDS TO WORK

MANOS ARRIBA • 1957 • Galindo Alejandro • MXC

MANOS ARRIBA, CADAVER, ESTAS DETENIDO • 1972 • Klimovsky Leon • SPN

MANOS DE SEDA • 1951 • Urueta Chano • MXC

MANOS, HANDS OF FATE see **MANOS, THE HANDS OF FATE** • 1966

MANOS SUCIAS • 1957 • de la Loma Jose Antonio • SPN

MANOS, THE HANDS OF FATE • 1966 • Warren Hal • USA • MANOS, HANDS OF FATE

MANOS TORPES • 1969 • Romero-Marchent Rafael • SPN

MANOUANE RIVER LUMBERJACKS see **BUCHERONS DE LA MANOUANE** • 1962

MANOUCHE • 1989 • Begazo Luis Carlos • BRZ

MANOVERBALL • 1956 • Kulb Karl G. • FRG

MANOVERZWILLING see **WENN POLDI INS MANOVER ZIEHT** • 1956

MANOVRE D'AMORE • 1941 • Righelli Gennaro • ITL • GUERRA IN TEMPO DI PACE

MANPOWER • Reeve Leonard • DOC • UKN

MANPOWER • 1927 • Badger Clarence • USA • MAN POWER ○ DYNAMITE

MANPOWER • 1941 • Walsh Raoul • USA

MANQUE, LE • 1941 • Dianoux Robert, Heinic Christian, Sejaud Jean • DOC • FRN

MANRAPE • 1978 • Donner Jorn • SWD, FNL • MAN KAN INTE VALDTAS (SWD) ○ MIESTA EI VOI RAISKATA ○ MAN CANNOT BE RAPED ○ MEN CAN'T BE RAPED

MAN'S A MAN, A • 1912 • *Solax* • USA

MAN'S A MAN, A • 1913 • *Reliance* • USA

MAN'S ADAPTABILITY TO COLD • 1960 • Anderson Robert • DOC • CND

MAN'S AFFAIR, A • 1949 • Lewis Jay • UKN

MAN'S ANGLE, THE • 1942 • Roush Leslie • SHT • USA

MAN'S AWAKENING, A • 1913 • *Majestic* • USA

MAN'S BEST FRIEND • 1912 • *Eclair* • USA

MAN'S BEST FRIEND • 1914 • *Frontier* • USA

MAN'S BEST FRIEND • 1935 • Kull Edward • USA

MAN'S BEST FRIEND • 1941 • Lantz Walter • ANS • USA

MAN'S BEST FRIEND • 1952 • Kinney Jack • ANS • USA

MAN'S BLOOD IS THICKER THAN WATER see **KROV LYUDSKAYA NE VODITSA** • 1960

MAN'S CALLING • 1912 • Dwan Allan • USA

MAN'S CASTLE, A • 1933 • Borzage Frank • USA

MAN'S COUNTRY • 1938 • Hill Robert F. • USA

MAN'S COUNTRY, A • 1919 • Kolker Henry • USA

MAN'S CROSSROADS, A • 1914 • *Heron Andrew (P)* • UKN

MAN'S DESIRE • 1919 • Ingraham Lloyd • USA

MAN'S DUTY • 1913 • Dwan Allan • USA

MAN'S DUTY, A • 1912 • Reid Hal • USA

MAN'S ENEMY • 1914 • Powell Frank? • USA

MAN'S FAITH, A • 1914 • *Johnson Arthur* • USA

MAN'S FATE • 1917 • *Tower Halsey S.* • USA

MAN'S FAVORITE SPORT? • 1964 • Hawks Howard • USA

MAN'S FIGHT, A • 1919 • Heffron Thomas N. • USA

MAN'S FIGHT, A • 1927 • *Independent Pictures* • USA

MAN'S FRIEND, A • 1916 • Bertram William • SHT • USA

MAN'S GAME, A • 1934 • Lederman D. Ross • USA • FIRE PATROL

MAN'S GENESIS • 1912 • Griffith D. W. • USA

MAN'S GIRLHOOD see **AUS EINES MANNES MADCHENJAHREN** • 1919

MAN'S GREAT ADVERSARY see **ELSKOVS MAGT** • 1912

MAN'S GREATEST FRIEND • 1938 • Newman Joseph M. • SHT • USA

MAN'S GREED FOR GOLD • 1913 • *Kalem* • USA

MAN'S HARDEST FIGHT, A • 1916 • Hunt Jay • SHT • USA

MAN'S HEAD • 1958 • Heyer John • DCS • ASL

MAN'S HEART see **OTOKO GOKORO** • 1925

MAN'S HERITAGE (UKN) see **SPIRIT OF CULVER, THE** • 1939

MAN'S HOME, A • 1921 • Ince Ralph • USA

MAN'S HOPE (UKN) see **ESPOIR** • 1939

MANS KVINNA • 1945 • Skoglund Gunnar • SWD • WOMAN FOR MEN

MAN'S LAND, A • 1932 • Rosen Phil • USA

MAN'S LAW • 1915 • Campbell Colin • USA

MAN'S LAW, A • 1917 • Davenport Harry • USA

MAN'S LAW AND GOD'S • 1922 • Fox Finis • USA

MAN'S LAW (UKN) see **NO MAN'S LAW** • 1927

MAN'S LIFE, A see **HITO NO ISSHO, PARTS I, II & III** • 1928

MAN'S LONELY VOICE • Sokurov Alexander • USS

MAN'S LUST FOR GOLD • 1912 • Griffith D. W. • USA

MAN'S MAKING, THE • 1915 • Pratt Jack • USA

MAN'S MAN, A • 1917 • Apfel Oscar • USA

MAN'S MAN, A • 1923 • Apfel Oscar • USA

MAN'S MAN, A • 1929 • Cruze James • USA

MAN'S MATE, A • 1924 • Mortimer Edmund • USA • APACHE, THE

MAN'S PAST, A • 1927 • Melford George • USA

MAN'S PEST FRIEND • 1945 • Kneitel Seymour • ANS • USA

MAN'S PLAYTHING • 1920 • Horan Charles • USA

MAN'S PREROGATIVE • 1915 • Nicholls George • USA

MAN'S SACRIFICE, A • 1915 • Baker George D. • USA

MAN'S SHADOW, A • 1912 • Collins Edwin J. • UKN

MAN'S SHADOW, A • 1915 • Terriss Tom • USA

MAN'S SHADOW, A • 1920 • Morgan Sidney • UKN

MAN'S SIN, THE • 1916 • *De Carlton Grace* • SHT • USA

MAN'S SIZE • 1923 • Mitchell Howard M. • USA

MAN'S SOUL, A • 1914 • *Mcgowan J. P.* • USA

MAN'S TEMPTATION, A • 1915 • *Wilson Ben* • USA

MAN'S VALUE see **TSENA CHELOVEKA** • 1928

MAN'S WAY, A • 1910 • *Powers* • USA

MAN'S WAY, A • 1914 • *American* • USA

MAN'S WOMAN • 1917 • Vale Travers • USA • HOUSE CAT, THE

MAN'S WOMAN, A • 1913 • *Mecca* • USA

MAN'S WORD, A see **JACK'S WORLD** • 1912

MAN'S WORD, A see **ERKEK ADAM SOZUNDE DURUR** • 1967

MAN'S WORK, A • 1916 • *Junior John* • SHT • USA

MAN'S WORLD, A • 1918 • Blache Herbert • USA

MAN'S WORLD, A • 1942 • Barton Charles T. • USA

MAN'S WORLD, A see **DADDY'S GONE A'HUNTING** • 1925

MAN'S WORLDLY APPEARANCE see **HITO NO YO NO SUGATA** • 1928

MANSARD MYSTERY, THE • 1916 • Paton Stuart • USA

MANSFIELD PARK • 1986 • Giles David • MTV • UKN

MANSION DE ARAUCAIMA, LA • 1985 • Mayolo Carlos • CLM

MANSION DE LA LOCURA, LA • 1971 • Moctezuma Juan Lopez • MXC • MANSION OF MADNESS, THE ○ HOUSE OF MADNESS

MANSION DE LA NIEBLA, LLA • 1972 • Lara Polop Francisco • SPN, ITL • QUANDO MARTA URLO DALLA TOMBA (ITL) ○ MURDER MANSION, THE (USA)

MANSION OF ACHING HEARTS, THE • 1925 • Hogan James P. • USA

MANSION OF MADNESS, THE see **MANSION DE LA LOCURA, LA** • 1971

MANSION OF MYSTERY • 1927 • Horner Robert J. • SRL • USA

MANSION OF MYSTERY, A • 1913 • Parker Lem B. • USA

MANSION OF SOBS, THE • 1914 • Ince John • USA

MANSION OF THE DOOMED • 1975 • Pataki Michael • USA • TERROR OF DR. CHANEY, THE (UKN) ○ MASSACRE MANSION

MANSION OF TRAGEDY, A • 1915 • Totten Joseph Byron • USA

MANSLAUGHTER • 1922 • De Mille Cecil B. • USA

MANSLAUGHTER • 1930 • Abbott George • USA

MANSON • 1972 • Hendrickson Robert • DOC • USA • MANSON FAMILY, THE

MANSON FAMILY, THE see **MANSON** • 1972

MANSTER, THE • 1962 • Breakston George, Crane Kenneth L. • USA, JPN • MANSTER –HALF MAN HALF MONSTER, THE ○ SPLIT, THE (UKN)

MANSTER –HALF MAN HALF MONSTER, THE see **MANSTER, THE** • 1962

MANTAN MESSES UP • 1946 • Newfield Sam • SHT • USA

MANTEAU ROUGE, LE (FRN) see **MANTELLO ROSSO, IL** • 1955

MANTEGNA • 1971 • Ashton Dudley Shaw • DOC • UKN

MANTEL, DER • 1955 • Schleif Wolfgang • FRG • OVERCOAT, THE (USA)

MANTEL DER LIEFTE, DER • 1978 • Ditvoorst Adriaan • NTH • CLOAK OF CHARITY, THE

MANTELLI E SPADE INSANGUINATE • 1960 • McDonald Frank, Juran Nathan • ITL

MANTELLO ROSSO, IL • 1955 • Scotese Giuseppe Maria • ITL, FRN • MANTEAU ROUGE, LE (FRN) ○ RED CLOAK, THE (USA) ○ REVOLTES, LES

MANTENUTO, IL • 1961 • Tognazzi Ugo • ITL

MANTHAN • 1976 • Benegal Shyam • IND • CHURNING, THE

MANTILHA DE BEATRIZ, A • 1946 • Maroto Eduardo G. • PRT, SPN • MANTILLA DE BEATRIZ, LA

MANTILLA DE BEATRIZ, LA see **MANTILHA DE BEATRIZ, A** • 1946

MANTIS see **MODLISZKA** • 1960

MANTIS FIST FIGHTER see **THUNDERING MANTIS, THE** • 1980

MANTIS IN LACE • 1969 • Rotsler William • USA • LILA

MANTIS UNDER FALCON CLAWS • Wong Mitch • HKG • MANTIS VERSUS FALCON CLAWS

MANTIS VERSUS FALCON CLAWS see **MANTIS UNDER FALCON CLAWS**

MANTLE OF CHARITY, THE • 1918 • Sloman Edward • USA

MANTLE OF DECEIT, THE • 1916 • Hill Robert F. • SHT • USA

MANTLE OF RED EVANS, THE • 1912 • *Stedman Myrtle* • USA

MANTRA–MUGHDHA see **MONTRA MUGHDO** • 1949

MANTRAP • 1926 • Fleming Victor • USA

MANTRAP • 1953 • Fisher Terence • UKN • MAN IN HIDING (USA) ○ WOMAN IN HIDING

MANTRAP, THE • 1943 • Sherman George • USA

MANU, IL CONTRABBANDIERE • 1948 • De Caro Lucio • ITL

MANUAL OF ARMS • 1966 • Frampton Hollis • USA

MANUEL • 1979 • Anzola Alfredo J. • VNZ

MANUEL • 1984 • Vargas Rafael

MANUEL • 1990 • Labonte Francois • CND • MANUEL LE FILS EMPRUNTE

MANUEL AND CLEMENTE see **MANUEL Y CLEMENTE** • 1986

MANUEL GARCIA • 1913 • Quesada Enrique Diaz • CUB
MANUEL LE FILS EMPRUNTE see **MANUEL** • 1990
MANUEL RODRIGUEZ • 1972 • Guzman Patricio • CHL
MANUEL Y CLEMENTE • 1986 • Palmero Javier • SPN • MANUEL AND CLEMENTE
MANUELA • Francel Hubert • FRN
MANUELA • 1957 • Hamilton Guy • UKN • STOWAWAY GIRL (USA)
MANUELA • 1966 • Solas Humberto • CUB
MANUELA • 1975 • Garcia Pelayo Gonzalo • SPN
MANUFACTURE OF ART PAPER, THE • 1921 • Hepworth Cecil M. • DOC • UKN • MAKING OF ART PAPER, THE
MANUFACTURE OF STEEL IN AUSTRALIA • 1915 • ASL
MANUFACTURES • 1967 • Jaworski Tadeusz • DOC • PLN
MANUGANG NI DRAKULA, MGA • 1964 • PHL • SECRETS OF DRACULA, THE
MANUS IMMACULATA • 1920 • Walther-Fein Rudolf • FRG • UNBEFLECKTE HAND, DIE
MANUSCRIPT FOUND IN SARAGOSSA see **REKOPIS ZNALEZIONY W SARAGOSSIE** • 1965
MANUSCRIPTS • 1987 • Minoui Mehrzad • IRN
MANUSCRITTO NELLA BOTTIGLIA see **PAZZO D'AMORE** • 1943
MANUTARA see **VULTURE, THE** • 1967
MANXMAN, THE • 1916 • Tucker George Loane • UKN
MANXMAN, THE • 1929 • Hitchcock Alfred • UKN
MANY A SIP • 1931 • Sandrich Mark • SHT • USA
MANY A SLIP • 1911 • Fitzhamon Lewin? • UKN
MANY A SLIP • 1917 • Terwilliger George W. • SHT • USA
MANY A SLIP • 1918 • Christie Al • SHT • USA
MANY A SLIP • 1920 • Harrison Eric • UKN
MANY A SLIP • 1931 • Moore Vin • USA
MANY DAYS HAVE PASSED see **BAHUT DIN HUWE** • 1954
MANY GHOST-CATS see **KAIBYO RANBU** • 1956
MANY HAPPY RETURNS • 1913 • Plumb Hay? • UKN
MANY HAPPY RETURNS • 1916 • Collins Edwin J.? • UKN
MANY HAPPY RETURNS • 1918 • Edwards Harry J. • SHT • USA
MANY HAPPY RETURNS • 1922 • Roach Hal • SHT • USA
MANY HAPPY RETURNS • 1934 • McLeod Norman Z. • USA
MANY HAPPY RETURNS • 1986 • Stern Steven Hilliard • TVM • USA
MANY-HEADED MAN see **HOMME DE TETES, UN** • 1898
MANY IS THE TIME • 1908 • Gilbert Arthur • UKN
MANY LOVES OF HILDA CRANE, THE see **HILDA CRANE** • 1956
MANY PEOPLE see **SOBO** • 1937
MANY PHASES OF LIFE, THE see **KAHAN KAHAN SE GUZAR GAVA** • 1981
MANY RIVERS TO CROSS • 1954 • Rowland Roy • USA
MANY SAPPY RETURNS • 1938 • Lord Del • SHT • USA
MANY SCRAPPY RETURNS • 1926 • Roach Hal • SHT • USA
MANY-SPLENDORED THING, A see **LOVE IS A MANY-SPLENDORED THING** • 1955
MANY TANKS • 1942 • Fleischer Dave • ANS • USA
MANY TANKS MR. ATKINS • 1938 • Neill R. William • UKN
MANY WARS AGO see **UOMINI CONTRO** • 1970
MANY WATERS • 1931 • Rosmer Milton • UKN
MANYA, DIE TURKIN • 1915 • Piel Harry • FRG
MANZANA DE LA DISCORDIA, LA • 1968 • Cazals Felipe • MXC • BONE OF CONTENTION, THE
MANZANAS DE DOROTEA, LAS • 1956 • de Anda Raul • MXC
MANZANEDA • 1964 • Artero Antonio • SHT • SPN
MANZANITA • 1979 • Arce A. • ANS • VNZ • LITTLE APPLE, THE
MANZIL • 1936 • *Roy Bimal (Ph)* • IND
MANZIL • 1960 • *Burman S. D. (M)* • IND
MANZIL MAYA • 1936 • *Sircar B. N. (P)* • IND
MANZIL RAQM THALATHATAASHAR • 1952 • el Sheikh Kamal • EGY • MAISON N.13, LA
MANZOOR • 1949 • *Sircar B. N. (P)* • IND
MAO LE VEUT • 1965 • *Lassally Walter (Ph)* • SHT • UKN
MAORI MAID'S LOVE • 1916 • Longford Raymond • NZL
MAOS SANGRENTAS • 1954 • Christensen Carlos Hugo • BRZ • VIOLENT AND THE DAMNED, THE (USA) ○ ASSASSINS IN THE SUN ○ ASSASSINOS
MAP FOR 19 YEARS OLD, A see **JUKYUSAI NO CHIZU** • 1979
MAP OF THE OCEAN see **UMI NO CHIZU** • 1959
MAPANTSULA • 1988 • Schmitz Oliver • SAF • ONE LOOK SHOOK THE WORLD
MAPANTSULA II • 1985 • SAF
MAPLE VIEWING see **MOMIJIGARI** • 1897
MAPLEVILLE STORY, THE • 1946 • Sparling Gordon • CND
MAPPIRA SHAIN YUKYODEN • 1968 • Hasebe Toshiaki • JPN • STATUS SEEKERS
MAPS IN ACTION • 1945 • Lambart Evelyn • ANS • CND
MAPULE • 1977 • SAF
MAPUTO: MERIDIANO NOVO • 1976 • Alvarez Santiago • DOC • CUB
MAQUILLAGE • 1932 • Anton Karl • FRN • JE T'ATTENDRAI
MAQUILLAGE see **SANS LENDEMAIN** • 1939
MAQUINAS E MAQUINISTAS • 1938 • Telmo Cottinelli • SHT • PRT
MAR, EL • 1976 • *Conacine* • MXC
MAR ABIERTO • 1946 • Torrado Ramon • SPN
MAR BRAVO • 1981 • MXC, SPN • ROUGH SEA
MAR CORRENTE • 1967 • dos Santos Luiz Paulino • BRZ • FLOWING SEA
MAR DE ROSAS • 1979 • Soares Ana Carolina Texeira • BRZ • SEA OF ROSES, A
MAR PORTUGUES • 1952 • Mendes Joao • SHT • PRT
MAR SANGRIENTO • 1964 • Portillo Rafael • MXC • GAVIOTA ROJA, LA
MAR Y TU, EL • 1951 • Fernandez Emilio • MXC • TU Y EL MAR
MARA • 1958 • Herrero Miguel • SPN
MARA • 1985 • Linders Angella • SHT • NTH
MARA MARU • 1952 • Douglas Gordon • USA
MARA OF THE WILDERNESS • 1965 • McDonald Frank • USA
MARACAIBO • 1958 • Wilde Cornel • USA
MARACAIBO PETROLEUM COMPANY • 1974 • Oropeza Daniel • VNZ
MARACEK, PASS ME A PEN see **MARECKU, PODEJTE MI PERO!** • 1976
MARAH THE PYTHONESS • 1914 • Smiley Joseph • USA
MARAJO, BARREIRA DO MAR • 1967 • Luxardo Libero • BRZ • MARAJO, BARRIER OF THE SEA
MARAJO, BARRIER OF THE SEA see **MARAJO, BARREIRA DO MAR** • 1967
MARAKATUMBA, MA NON E UNA RUMBA • 1951 • Trapani Enzo • ITL
MARANHAO • 1966 • Rocha Glauber • SHT • BRZ
MARAPURANI KATHA • 1967 • Ramachandra Rao V. • IND • UNFORGETTABLE STORY
MARASCHINO CHERRY • 1977 • Metzger Radley H. • USA
MARASTOON • 1979 • Cote Guy-L. • CND
MARAT/DE SADE see **PERSECUTION AND ASSASSINATION OF JEAN-PAUL MARAT AS PERFORMED BY THE INMATES OF THE ASYLUM..** • 1966
MARATHON • 1973 • Bugajski Ryszard • MTV • PLN
MARATHON • 1980 • Cooper Jackie • USA
MARATHON, THE • 1919 • Roach Hal • SHT • USA
MARATHON, THE see **MARATON** • 1968
MARATHON CRAZE, THE • 1909 • *Vitagraph* • USA
MARATHON FAMILY, THE see **MARATONCI TRCE POCASNI KRUG** • 1983
MARATHON GIRL see **GADIS MARATHON** • 1981
MARATHON MAN • 1976 • Schlesinger John • USA
MARATHON MANIACS • 1917 • Hutchinson Craig • SHT • USA
MARATHON POLONAIS • 1927 • Bieganski Victor • PLN
MARATHON RACE, THE • 1909 • *Vitagraph* • USA
MARATHON RUNNER, THE see **LAUFER VON MARATHON, DER** • 1933
MARATON • 1968 • Novak Ivo • CZC • MARATHON, THE
MARATON DE BAILE • 1957 • Cardona Rene • MXC
MARATONCI TRCE POCASNI KRUG • 1983 • Sijan Slobodan • YGS • MARATHON FAMILY, THE
MARATRE, LA • 1906 • Blache Alice • FRN
MARATTOM • 1989 • Aravindan G. • IND • MASQUERADE (UKN)
MARAUDERS see **MARODORER** • 1934
MARAUDERS, THE • 1912 • Dwan Allan • USA
MARAUDERS, THE • 1947 • Archainbaud George • USA
MARAUDERS, THE • 1955 • Mayer Gerald • USA
MARAUDERS, THE see **MERRILL'S MARAUDERS** • 1962
MARAUDERS OF THE SEA • 1962 • *Morgan Terence* • MTV • UKN
MARAVILLA • 1957 • Seto Javier • SPN
MARAVILLA DEL TOREO • 1942 • Sevilla Raphael J. • MXC • MARVELS OF THE BULL RING (USA)
MARAVILLAS • 1980 • Gutierrez Aragon Manuel • SPN • MIRACLES
MARAVILLAS DE VENEZUELA • 1973 • Roman A. • DOC • VNZ • MARVELS OF VENEZUELA
MARBLE, THE • 1963 • Tyrlova Hermina • ANM • CZC
MARBLE, THE • 1966 • Primm John • SHT • USA
MARBLE, THE see **STUITER, DE** • 1971
MARBLE HEADS • 1917 • Curtis Allen • SHT • USA
MARBLE HEART, THE • 1909 • *Vitagraph* • USA • SCULPTOR'S DREAM, THE
MARBLE HEART, THE • 1913 • *Cruze James* • USA
MARBLE HEART, THE • 1915 • *Baggot King* • USA
MARBLE HEART, THE • 1916 • Buel Kenean, Brenon Herbert (Spv) • USA
MARBLE RETURNS, THE • 1951 • Catling Darrell • UKN
MARBLES see **GULOCKY** • 1983
MARC DURAND PIANISTE • 1972-73 • Brault Francois • DCS • CND
MARC MATO, AGENTE S.077 (SPN) see **S 077 SPIONAGGIO A TANGERI** • 1965
MARCA DE SATANAS, LA • 1956 • Urueta Chano • MXC • MARK OF SATAN, THE
MARCA DEL CUERVO, LA • 1957 • Cardona Rene • MXC
MARCA DEL GAVILAN, LA • 1959 • Curiel Federico • MXC
MARCA DEL HOMBRE LOBO, LA • 1968 • Equiluz Enrique L. • SPN • FRANKENSTEIN'S BLOODY TERROR (USA) ○ WOLFMAN OF COUNT DRACULA, THE ○ HELL'S CREATURES ○ VAMPIRE OF DR. DRACULA ○ MARK OF THE WOLF MAN, THE
MARCA DEL MUERTO, LA • 1960 • Cortes Fernando • MXC • MARK OF DEATH, THE
MARCA DEL ZORRILLO, LA • 1950 • Martinez Solares Gilberto • MXC
MARCADA POR LOS HOMBRES • 1977 • Merino Jose Luis • SPN
MARCADOS, LOS • 1975 • Mariscal Alberto • MXC • THEY CALL HIM MARCADO (UKN)
MARCADOS PARA VIVER • 1976 • do Rosario Maria • BRZ • BRANDED FOR LIFE
MARCANTONIO E CLEOPATRA • 1913 • Guazzoni Enrico • ITL
MARCANTONIO E CLEOPATRA • 1918 • Guazzoni Enrico • ITL
MARCCO, DER BEZWINGER DES TODES • 1925 • Stockel Joe • FRG
MARCCO, DER RINGER DES MIKADO • 1922 • Stockel Joe • FRG
MARCCO, DER SCHREI IN DER WUSTE see **SCHREI IN DER WUSTE, DER** • 1924
MARCCO, DER TODESKANDIDAT • 1922 • Stockel Joe • FRG
MARCCO KENNT KEINE FURCHT • 1922 • Stockel Joe? • FRG
MARCCO UNTER GAUKLERN UND BESTIEN 1 • 1923 • Delmont Joseph • FRG
MARCCO UNTER GAUKLERN UND BESTIEN 2 • 1923 • Delmont Joseph • FRG
MARCCOS ERSTE LIEBE • 1925 • Stockel Joe • FRG
MARCCOS SCHWERER SIEG • 1922 • Stockel Joe • FRG
MARCCOS TOLISTE WETTE • 1926 • Seitz Franz • FRG
MARCEL • 1969 • Cox Paul • SHT • ASL
MARCEL ALLAIN • 1966 • Franju Georges • FRN
MARCEL, TA MERE T'APPELLE • 1962 • Colombat Jacques • ANM • FRN
MARCELINO BREAD AND WINE see **MARCELINO PAN Y VINO** • 1954
MARCELINO PAN Y VINO • 1954 • Vajda Ladislao • SPN • MARCELINO (USA) ○ MIRACLE OF MARCELINO, THE ○ MARCELINO BREAD AND WINE
MARCELINO (USA) see **MARCELINO PAN Y VINO** • 1954
MARCELLA • 1922 • Gallone Carmine • ITL
MARCELLA • 1937 • Brignone Guido • ITL
MARCELLINI MILLIONS, THE • 1917 • Crisp Donald • USA
MARCELLO, I'M SO BORED • 1966 • Strawbridge John, Milius John • ANS • USA
MARCELO Y MARIA • 1964 • Martinez Solares Gilberto • MXC
MARCELO ZONA SUL • 1970 • de Oliveira Xavier • BRZ
MARCH, THE • 1963 • Blue James • USA • MARCH TO WASHINGTON, THE
MARCH ALMONDS • 1989 • Piwowarski Radoslaw • PLN
MARCH HARE, THE • 1919 • Miller Frank • UKN
MARCH HARE, THE • 1921 • Campbell Maurice • USA
MARCH HARE, THE • 1956 • O'Ferrall George M. • UKN
MARCH, MARCH, BOOM-BOOM-BOOM! • 1964 • Vabalas Raimondas • USS • MARCH, MARCH! TRA-TA-TA!
MARCH, MARCH! TRA-TA-TA! see **MARCH, MARCH, BOOM-BOOM-BOOM!** • 1964
MARCH OF CRIME see **SECRET SEVEN, THE** • 1940
MARCH OF FREEDOM, THE • 1939 • *O'Brien Joseph/ Mead Thomas (P)* • SHT • USA
MARCH OF THE AMAZONS, THE • 1902 • Smith G. A. • UKN
MARCH OF THE LIGHT CAVALRY • 1907 • Gilbert Arthur • UKN
MARCH OF THE MACHINES, THE (USA) see **MARCHE DES MACHINES, LA** • 1928
MARCH OF THE MONSTERS, THE see **KAIJU SOSHINGEKI** • 1968
MARCH OF THE MOVIES • 1938 • Gaye Howard • UKN
MARCH OF THE MOVIES see **FILM PARADE, THE** • 1933
MARCH OF THE MOVIES, THE • 1965 • Fancey E. J. • UKN
MARCH OF THE SPRING HARE • 1969 • Baran Jack • USA • ROOMMATES
MARCH OF THE TOYS see **BABES IN TOYLAND** • 1934
MARCH OF THE WOODEN SOLDIERS see **BABES IN TOYLAND** • 1934
MARCH OF TIME, THE • 1936 • Anstey Edgar • DOC • UKN
MARCH OF TIME, THE see **BROADWAY TO HOLLYWOOD** • 1933
MARCH ON MARINES • 1940 • Eason B. Reeves • SHT • USA
MARCH ON PARIS 1914 (OF GENERAL ALEXANDER VON KLUCK) -AND HIS MEMORY OF JESSEE HOLLADAY, THE • 1977 • Gutman Walter • USA
MARCH OR DIE • 1977 • Richards Dick • UKN
MARCH TO ALDERMASTON • 1959 • *Anderson Lindsay* • DCS • UKN
MARCH TO ROME, THE see **MARCIA SU ROMA, LA** • 1962
MARCH TO THE DRINA see **MARS NA DRINU** • 1964
MARCH TO THE GALLOWS see **STRAFBATAILLON 999** • 1960
MARCH TO WASHINGTON, THE see **MARCH, THE** • 1963
MARCH TOWARDS THE SUN see **IDE KU SLONCU** • 1955
MARCH WINDS • 1908 • Coleby A. E. • UKN
MARCHA AL NORTE • 1977 • Ruiz Jorge • SHT • BLV • TOWARDS THE NORTH
MARCHAND D'AMOUR • 1935 • Greville Edmond T. • FRN
MARCHAND DE BALLONS, LE • 1902 • Blache Alice • FRN
MARCHAND DE BONHEUR, LE • 1927 • Guarino Joseph • FRN
MARCHAND DE COCO, LE • 1899-00 • Blache Alice • FRN
MARCHAND DE PLAISIR, LE • 1923 • Catelain Jacques • FRN
MARCHAND DE REVES, LES • 1976 • Ifticene Mohamed • ALG
MARCHAND DE SABLE, LE • 1931 • Hugon Andre • FRN • EL GUELMOUNA, MARCHAND DE SABLE
MARCHAND DE VENISE, LE • 1952 • Billon Pierre • FRN, ITL • MERCANTE DI VENEZIA, IL (ITL)
MARCHAND DES NOTES, LE • 1942 • Grimault Paul • ANS • FRN
MARCHAND D'IMAGES, LE • 1910 • Velle Gaston • FRN • FAIRY BOOKSELLER, THE (USA)
MARCHANDES D'ILLUSIONS • 1954 • Andre Raoul • FRN • NIGHTS OF SHAME (USA) ○ VENDORS OF DREAMS ○ WOMEN WITHOUT HOPE
MARCHANDS DE FILLES • 1957 • Cloche Maurice • FRN • SELLERS OF GIRLS (USA) ○ GIRL SELLERS, THE ○ GIRL MERCHANTS ○ MARKET IN WOMEN, THE
MARCHANDS DE LA MORT, LA see **TUGGAR AL-MAWT** • 1957
MARCHANDS D'ESCLAVES (FRN) see **ANTHAR L'INVINCIBILE** • 1965
MARCHE • 1896-97 • Lumiere Louis • FRN
MARCHE, LA • 1951 • Audiard Michel • FRN
MARCHE A LA VOLAILLE • 1899-00 • Blache Alice • FRN
MARCHE A L'OMBRE • 1984 • Blanc Michel • FRN
MARCHE AUX POISSONS DE BRUXELLES • 1897 • Alexandre M. • BLG
MARCHE DES MACHINES, LA • 1928 • Deslaw Eugene • SHT • FRN • MARCH OF THE MACHINES, THE (USA)
MARCHE DES ROIS, LA • 1913 • Feuillade Louis • FRN
MARCHE DES SPECTRE, LA • 1975 • Franju Georges • MTV • FRN
MARCHE FRANCAISE • 1956 • Fabiani Henri, Vogel Raymond • SHT • FRN
MARCHE FUNEBRE DE CHOPIN, LA • 1907 • Melies Georges • FRN • CHOPIN'S FUNERAL MARCH BURLESQUED (USA)
MARCHE NUPTIALE, LA • 1928 • Hugon Andre • FRN
MARCHE NUPTIALE, LA • 1934 • Bonnard Mario • FRN
MARCHE OU CREVE • 1960 • Lautner Georges • FRN, BLG
MARCHE PAS SUR MES LACETS • 1977 • Pecas Max • FRN
MARCHE SUR ROME, LA (FRN) see **MARCIA SU ROMA, LA** • 1962
MARCHEN AUS ALT-WIEN • 1923 • Thiele Wilhelm • AUS • CARL MICHAEL ZIEHRERS MARCHEN AUS ALT-WIEN
MARCHEN VOM GLUCK • 1949 • de Glahs Arthur • AUS • KUSS' MICH CASANOVA
MARCHEN VOM STERNENPRINZEN, DAS • 1925 • *Glombeck Robert* • FRG
MARCHENSCHLOSS, DAS • 1961 • Zschoche Hermann • GDR • FAIRY TALE CASTLE
MARCHESA D'ARMINIANI, DIE • 1920 • Halm Alfred • FRG
MARCHESE DEL GRILLO, IL • 1981 • Monicelli Mario • ITL, FRN • MARQUIS S'AMUSE, LE (FRN) ○ MARQUIS DEL GRILLO, THE
MARCHESE DI RUVOLITO, IL • 1939 • Matarazzo Raffaello • ITL
MARCHEURS D'ENTRE SAMBRE ET MEUSE, LES • 1975 • Storck Henri • SHT • BLG
MARCHI ROSSO, IL • 1918 • Campogalliani Carlo • ITL
MARCHING ALONG • 1933 • Tyer James • ANS • USA
MARCHING ALONG (UKN) see **STARS AND STRIPES FOREVER** • 1952

MARCHING THE COLORS • 1942 • Glover Guy • ANS • CND
MARCHING TO GEORGIE • 1929 • Watson William • USA
MARCHIO DI KRIMINAL, IL • 1967 • Cerchio Fernando • ITL, SPN • MARK OF KRIMINAL, THE
MARCH'S CHILD see **NATA DI MARZO** • 1958
MARCIA NUZIALE • 1916 • Gallone Carmine • ITL
MARCIA NUZIALE • 1934 • Bonnard Mario • ITL
MARCIA NUZIALE • 1966 • Ferreri Marco • ITL • WEDDING MARCH
MARCIA O CREPA (ITL) see **MARSCHIER UND KREPIER** • 1962
MARCIA O MUERE (SPN) see **MARSCHIER UND KREPIER** • 1962
MARCIA RESNICK'S BAD BOYS • 1985 • Mann Ron • CND
MARCIA SU ROMA, LA • 1962 • Risi Dino • ITL, FRN • MARCHE SUR ROME, LA (FRN) ○ MARCH TO ROME, THE
MARCIA TRIONFALE • 1976 • Bellocchio Marco • ITL • VICTORY MARCH (USA) ○ TRIUMPHAL MARCH
MARCIANO • 1979 • Kowalski Bernard • TVM • USA
MARCO • 1973 • Robbie Seymour • USA
MARCO, DER CLOWN (FRG) see **CAMP VOLANT** • 1932
MARCO OF RIO • 1969 • Rocco Pat • USA
MARCO POLO • 1962 • Fregonese Hugo, Pierotti Piero, Freda Riccardo (U/c) • FRN, ITL • AVVENTURA DI UN ITALIANO IN CINA, L' (ITL)
MARCO POLO • 1984 • Montaldo Giuliano • MTV • ITL, USA
MARCO POLO see **MA-K'O P'O-LO** • 1975
MARCO POLO JUNIOR VERSUS THE RED DRAGON • 1972 • Porter Eric • ASL
MARCO THE MAGNIFICENT (USA) see **FABULEUSE AVENTURE DE MARCO POLO, LA** • 1965
MARCO VISCONTI • 1908 • Caserini Mario • ITL
MARCO VISCONTI • 1913 • Falena Ugo • ITL
MARCO VISCONTI • 1941 • Bonnard Mario • ITL
MARCO'S THEME see **TEMA DI MARCO, IL** • 1972
MARCO'S THESIS see **TEMA DI MARCO, IL** • 1972
MARCUS GARLAND • 1925 • Micheaux Oscar • USA
MARCUS-NELSON MURDERS, THE • 1973 • Sargent Joseph • TVM • USA • KOJAK AND THE MARCUS-NELSON MURDERS
MARCUS WELBY, M.D. • 1968 • Rich David Lowell • TVM • USA • MATTER OF HUMANITIES
MARCUSIANA, LA see **DONNA AD UNA DIMENSIONE** • 1969
MARCY • 1969 • Sarno Joe • USA
MARD • 1985 • Manmohan • IND
MARD, AL- see **MARED, EL** • 1964
MARD-E-BESETARE • 1968 • Bahadori Azizolah • IRN • MAN WITHOUT A STAR
MARD-E-HANJARE-TALAEI • 1968 • Misaghye Mehdi • IRN • SWEET-VOICED MAN, A
MARD-E-ROUZ • 1968 • Afshar Mousa • IRN • MAN OF TODAY, THE
MARD-E-SARGARDAN • 1967 • Vaeziyan Jozeph • IRN • WONDERING MAN, THE
MARDE DO CHEHRE • 1968 • Byc-Imanverdi Resa • IRN • MAN WITH TWO FACES, A
MARDE-NAMAREI • 1967 • Koushan Mahmoud • IRN • INVISIBLE MAN
MARDE-SAHRA • 1968 • Jarahzade Sirous • IRN • MAN OF THE SAHARA
MARDI AND THE MONKEY • 1953 • Mander Kay • UKN
MARDI AZ ESFEHAN • 1967 • Shervan Amir • IRN • MAN FROM ESFEHAN, A
MARDI AZ TEHRAN • 1967 • Ajrame Farough • IRN • MAN FROM TEHRAN, A
MARDI GRAS • Grand'Ry Genevieve • BLG
MARDI GRAS • 1931 • Weill Pierre • FRN
MARDI GRAS • 1958 • Goulding Edmund • USA
MARDI GRAS MASSACRE • 1982 • Weis Jack • USA • CRYPT OF DARK SECRETS
MARDI GRAS MIX-UP, A • 1912 • *Kalem* • USA
MARDI GRAS PROCESSION, THE see **CORTEGE DU BOEUF GRAS PASSANT PLACE DE LA CONCORDE** • 1897
MARDI -UN JOUR ANONYME • 1978 • Leduc Jacques • DCS • CND
MARDOLA CONTEST, THE see **KAMPEN OM MARDOLA** • 1972
MARE • 1940 • Baffico Mario • ITL
MARE, IL • 1962 • Patroni Griffi Giuseppe • ITL • SEA, THE
MARE, THE • 1985 • Jekan Ali • IRN
MARE ALTA • 1968 • Coutin Carlos Eugenio • BRZ • HIGH TIDE
MARE AU DIABLE, LA • 1923 • Caron Pierre • FRN
MARE AUX GARCONS, LA • 1963 • Pappe Julien • FRN
MARE DI GUAI, UN • 1940 • Bragaglia Carlo Ludovico • ITL
MARE DI NAPOLI, IL • 1919 • Gallone Carmine • ITL
MARE MATTO • 1963 • Castellani Renato • ITL, FRN • MER A BOIRE, LA (FRN) ○ MAD SEA
MARE NOSTRUM • 1925 • Ingram Rex • USA • OUR SEA
MARE NOSTRUM • 1948 • Gil Rafael • SPN
MARECHAL-FERRANT, LE • 1895 • Lumiere Louis • FRN
MARECHIARO • 1949 • Ferroni Giorgio • ITL
MARECKU, PODEJTE MI PERO! • 1976 • Lipsky Oldrich • CZC • MARACEK, PASS ME A PEN
MARED, EL • 1964 • Issa Sayyed • EGY • GIANT, THE ○ MARD, AL-
MAREE, LA • 1967 • Audy Michel • CND
MAREE MONTANTE see **RISING TIDE, THE** • 1949
MAREE MONTANTE SUR BRISE-LAMES • 1896 • Melies Georges • FRN • TIDE RISING OVER THE BREAKWATER
MAREEA, THE FOSTER MOTHER • 1914 • Davis Ulysses • USA
MAREEA, THE HALF-BREED • 1914 • Davis Ulysses • USA
MAREJADA • 1952 • Toussaint Carlos • MXC
MARE'S TAIL • 1969 • Larcher David • UKN
MARESI • 1948 • Thimig Hans • AUS • ANGEKLAGTE HAT DAS WORT, DER
MARGARET • 1965 • Csoke Jozsef • DOC • HNG
MARGARET BOURKE-WHITE: THE TRUE STORY • 1989 • Schillman Lawrence • TVM • USA
MARGARET LAURENCE • 1985 • Caulfield Paul • DOC • CND
MARGARET MORRIS • 1973 • Grigor Murray • DOC • UKN
MARGARET OF CORTONA see **MARGHERITA DA CORTONA** • 1950
MARGARETE • 1918 • Zelnik Friedrich • FRG • GESCHICHTE EINER GEFALLENEN, DIE
MARGARETHE UND DER CHAUFFEUR • 1927 • Palermi Amleto • FRG
MARGARET'S AWAKENING • 1912 • *Essanay* • USA
MARGARET'S PAINTING • 1913 • Carleton Lloyd B. • USA
MARGARIT AND MARGARITA • 1990 • Volev Nikolai • BUL
MARGARITA AND THE MISSION FUNDS • 1913 • Parker Lem B. • USA
MARGARITA AZUL • 1974 • de Pedro Manuel • DCS • VNZ • BLUE MARGARITA
MARGARITA, PERO ES QUE NO VAS A CAMBIAR? • 1978 • Chumez Chumy • SPN
MARGARITA SE LLAMA MI AMOR • 1961 • Fernandez Ramon • SPN
MARGARITA Y LA LOBO • 1970 • Bartolome Cecilia • SHT • SPN
MARGARITKA • 1965 • Dinov Todor • ANS • BUL • DAISY, THE
MARGARITOS, LOS • 1954 • Cardona Rene • MXC
MARGE, LA • 1976 • Borowczyk Walerian • FRN • STREETWALKER, THE (UKN)
MARGEM, A • 1967 • Candeias Ozvaldo R. • BRZ • MARGIN, THE (USA) ○ BORDER, THE ○ BANK, THE
MARGHERITA DA CORTONA • 1950 • Bonnard Mario • ITL • MIRACLES OF ST. MARGARET (USA) ○ MARGARET OF CORTONA
MARGHERITA DELLA NOTTE (ITL) see **MARGUERITE DE LA NUIT** • 1955
MARGHERITA FRA I TRE • 1942 • Perilli Ivo • ITL
MARGIE • 1924-26 • Fleischer Dave • ANS • USA
MARGIE • 1940 • Smith Paul Gerard, Garrett Otis • USA
MARGIE • 1946 • King Henry • USA
MARGIE OF THE UNDERWORLD • 1915 • Melville Wilbert • USA
MARGIN, THE see **MARGINAIS, OS** • 1968
MARGIN, THE (USA) see **MARGEM, A** • 1967
MARGIN FOR ERROR • 1943 • Preminger Otto • USA
MARGIN FOR MURDER (UKN) see **MICKEY SPILLANE'S MARGIN FOR MURDER** • 1981
MARGINADAS, LAS • 1974 • Iquino Ignacio F. • SPN
MARGINAIS, OS • 1968 • Soares Paulo Leite, Kondler Moises, Correa Carlos Alberto Prates • BRZ • DELINQUENTS, THE ○ MARGIN, THE
MARGINAL, LE • 1983 • Deray Jacques • FRN
MARGINAL LAND, THE see **FUMO-CHITAI** • 1975
MARGO SHELI • 1971 • Golan Menahem • ISR • MARGO (USA) ○ MY LOVE IN JERUSALEM ○ LOVE IN JERUSALEM
MARGO (USA) see **MARGO SHELI** • 1971
MARGOT DE PLAISANCE • 1919 • Delmont Joseph? • FRG
MARGOTON DU BATAILLON, LA • 1933 • Darmont Jacques • FRN • MADELON DU BATAILLON, LA
MARGUERITE • 1971 • Chen Betty Yao-Jung • ANS • USA
MARGUERITE: 3 • 1939 • Lingen Theo • FRG • FRAU FUR DREI, EINE
MARGUERITE BOURGEOIS • 1954 • Proulx Maurice • DCS • CND
MARGUERITE DE LA NUIT • 1955 • Autant-Lara Claude • FRN, ITL • MARGHERITA DELLA NOTTE (ITL) ○ MARGUERITE OF THE NIGHT
MARGUERITE OF THE NIGHT see **MARGUERITE DE LA NUIT** • 1955
MARGY OF THE FOOTHILLS • 1916 • Bertram William?, Chatterton Thomas? • SHT • USA
MARHABAN AIUHA AL-HUBB • 1962 • Salman Mohammed • LBN • BIENVENUE A L'AMOUR
MARI A L'ESSAI, UN • 1912 • Fescourt Henri • FRN
MARI A PRIX FIXE, UN • 1963 • de Givray Claude • FRN
MARI ACHETE, UN • 1913 • Protazanov Yakov • USS
MARI, C'EST UN MARI, UN • 1976 • Friedman Serge • FRN
MARI DE LA FEMME A BARBE, LE (FRN) see **DONNA SCIMMIA, LA** • 1964
MARI DE LA REINE, LA see **ECHEC AU ROI** • 1931
MARI DE LA REINE, LE see **PLUS BEAU GOSSE DE FRANCE, LE** • 1937
MARI DES QUATRE, LE see **JAWS AL-ARBARA** • 1949
MARI GARCON, LE • 1933 • Cavalcanti Alberto • FRN • GARCON DIVORCE, LE
MARI GENANT, UN • 1911 • Desfontaines Henri • FRN
MARI REVE, LE • 1936 • Capellani Roger • FRN • VIE DE CHIEN, UNE ○ ACHILLE
MARIA • 1916 • Otto Paul? • FRG
MARIA • 1918 • Zatarain Rafael Bermudez • MXC
MARIA • 1919 • Ziener Bruno • FRG
MARIA • 1938 • Urueta Chano • MXC
MARIA • 1947 • Folke Gosta • SWD
MARIA • 1971 • *Clasa* • MXC
MARIA • 1975 • Arehn Mats • SWD
MARIA • 1977 • King Allan • MTV • CND
MARIA • 1989 • Espindola Luisa Fernanda • SHT • RMN
MARIA see **SALIUT, MARIA!** • 1970
MARIA, LA • 1922 • del Diestro Alfredo • CLM
MARIA AND NAPOLEON see **MARYSIA I NAPOLEON** • 1966
MARIA ANTONIA LA CARAMBA • 1950 • Ruiz-Castillo Arturo • SPN
MARIA ANTONIETTA, REGINA DI FRANCIA (ITL) see **MARIE-ANTOINETTE** • 1955
MARIA BONITA, QUEEN OF CANGACO see **MARIA BONITA, RAINHA DO CANGACO** • 1968
MARIA BONITA, RAINHA DO CANGACO • 1968 • Borges Miguel • BRZ • MARIA BONITA, QUEEN OF CANGACO
MARIA CANDELARIA • 1943 • Fernandez Emilio • MXC • PORTRAIT OF MARIA ○ XOCHIMILCO
MARIA CARMEN'S SPAIN • 1985 • Chbib Bachar • CND
MARIA CHAPDELAINE • 1934 • Duvivier Julien • FRN
MARIA CHAPDELAINE • 1983 • Carle Gilles • CND
MARIA CHAPDELAINE see **NAKED HEART, THE** • 1950
MARIA CRISTINA • 1951 • Pereda Ramon • MXC
MARIA DABROWSKA • 1967 • Zanussi Krzysztof • MTV • PLN
MARIA DE LA O • 1936 • Elias Francisco • SPN
MARIA DE LA O • 1957 • Torrado Ramon • SPN
MARIA DE LA NUIT • 1936 • Rozier Willy • FRN • NUIT D'ESPAGNE
MARIA DE MI CORAZON • 1980 • Hermosillo Jaime Humberto • MXC • MY DEAREST MARIA
MARIA DEL MAR • 1952 • Soler Fernando • MXC
MARIA DI MAGDALA • 1918 • Gallone Carmine • ITL
MARIA, DIE GESCHICHTE EINES HERZENS • 1926 • Feher Friedrich • FRG • GRAUE HAUS, DAS
MARIA, DIE MAGD • 1936 • Harlan Veit • FRG
MARIA DO MAR • 1930 • de Barros Jose Leitao • PRT
MARIA DOLORES • 1952 • Elorrieta Jose Maria • SPN
MARIA D'ORO UND BELLO BLUE • 1976 • Kauka Rolf • ANM • FRG, ITL • ONCE UPON A TIME (USA)
MARIA DU BOUT DU MONDE • 1950 • Stelli Jean • FRN
MARIA ELENA • 1935 • Sevilla Raphael J. • MXC
MARIA EUGENIA • 1942 • Gregorio Castillo Felipe • MXC
MARIA EVERE • 1919 • Zelnik Friedrich • FRG
MARIA ILONA • 1939 • von Bolvary Geza • FRG
MARIA ISABEL • 1968 • Curiel Federico • MXC
MARIA LA O • 1947 • Fernandez Bustamente Adolfo • MXC, CUB
MARIA, LA SANTA • 1977 • Fandino Roberto • SPN
MARIA LA VOZ • 1954 • Bracho Julio • MXC
MARIA MADDELENA see **SPADA E LA CROCE, LA** • 1959
MARIA MAGDALENA • 1918 • Rist Preben • FRG
MARIA MAGDALENA • 1919 • Schunzel Reinhold • FRG
MARIA MAGDALENA • 1945 • Contreras Torres Miguel • MXC
MARIA MALIBRAN • 1943 • Brignone Guido • ITL
MARIA MARTEN • 1928 • West Walter • UKN
MARIA MARTEN see **MARIA MARTEN: OR, THE MURDER IN THE RED BARN** • 1935
MARIA MARTEN: OR, THE MURDER AT THE RED BARN • 1902 • Winslow Dicky • UKN
MARIA MARTEN: OR, THE MURDER AT THE RED BARN • 1913 • Elvey Maurice • UKN
MARIA MARTEN: OR, THE MURDER IN THE RED BARN • 1935 • Rosmer Milton • UKN • MURDER IN THE OLD RED BARN (USA) ○ MARIA MARTEN
MARIA MARTINEZ LOPEZ • 1971 • Glasmacher Dieter, Rosenthal Kurt • ANS • FRG
MARIA MARUSJKA • 1973 • Tuhus Oddvar Bull • NRW
MARIA, MATRICULA DE BILBAO • 1960 • Vajda Ladislao • SPN
MARIA MIRABELA • Popescu-Gopo Ion • RMN
MARIA MONTECRISTO • 1950 • Amadori Luis Cesar • MXC
MARIA MORENA • 1951 • Forque Jose Maria, Lazaga Pedro • SPN • VENDETTA
MARIA NAP • 1984 • Elek Judit • HNG • MARIA'S DAY
MARIA NIEMAND UND IHRE ZWOLF VATER • 1915 • Moest Hubert • FRG
MARIA NO OYUKI • 1935 • Mizoguchi Kenji • JPN • OYUKI THE MADONNA (USA) ○ OYUKI THE VIRGIN (UKN) ○ VIRGIN FROM OYUKI, THE
MARIA OF THE ANT VILLAGE see **ARI NO MACHI NO MARIA** • 1958
MARIA OF THE STARS • 1989 • Mauch Thomas • FRG
MARIA OF THE STREET OF ANTS see **ARI NO MACHI NO MARIA** • 1958
MARIA PA KVARNGARDEN • 1945 • Mattsson Arne • SWD • MARIE IN THE WINDMILL
MARIA PAPOILA • 1937 • de Barros Jose Leitao • PRT
MARIA PAWLOWNA • 1919 • Justitz Emil • FRG
MARIA PISTOLAS • 1962 • Cardona Rene • MXC
MARIA R. E GLI ANGELI DI TRASTEVERE • 1975 • Elfride • ITL
MARIA RICCHEZZA • 1969 • Glori Vittorio Musy • ITL
MARIA ROMA • 1913 • McGill Lawrence • USA
MARIA ROSA • 1916 • De Mille Cecil B. • USA
MARIA ROSA • 1946 • Barth-Moglia Luis • ARG
MARIA ROSA • 1964 • Moreno Armando • SPN
MARIA SI MIRABELLA IN TRANZISTORIA • 1989 • Popescu-Gopo Ion • RMN
MARIA STUART • 1959 • Stoger Alfred • AUS
MARIA STUART 1 • 1927 • Feher Friedrich • FRG
MARIA STUART 2 • 1927 • Feher Friedrich • FRG
MARIA, THE MAGIC WEAVER see **MARYA-ISKUSNITSA** • 1960
MARIA THE WONDERFUL WEAVER see **MARYA-ISKUSNITSA** • 1960
MARIA THERESIA • 1951 • Reinert Emile Edwin • AUS
MARIA TUDOR • 1920 • Gartner Adolf • FRG
MARIA VICTORIA CARRASCO • 1974 • Blanco Javier • DOC • VNZ
MARIA ZEF • 1981 • Cottafavi Vittorio • ITL
MARIA ZEF see **CONDANNATA SENZA COLPA** • 1954
MARIACHI CANTA, EL • 1962 • Ortiz Ramos Jose • MXC
MARIACHI DESCONOCIDO, EL • 1953 • Martinez Solares Gilberto • MXC
MARIACHIS • 1949 • Fernandez Bustamente Adolfo • MXC
MARIAGE • 1975 • Lelouch Claude • FRN • MARRIAGE
MARIAGE A LA MODE, LE • 1973 • Mardore Michel • FRN
MARIAGE A L'ITALIENNE (FRN) see **MATRIMONIO ALL'ITALIANA** • 1964
MARIAGE A RESPONSABILITE LIMITEE • 1933 • de Limur Jean • FRN
MARIAGE AMERICAIN, UN • 1909 • Linder Max • FRN
MARIAGE AU TELEPHONE • 1912 • Linder Max • FRN
MARIAGE BLANC • 1989 • Brisseau Jean-Claude • FRN
MARIAGE D'AMOUR • 1918 • Hugon Andre • FRN
MARIAGE D'AMOUR • 1942 • Decoin Henri • FRN
MARIAGE DE BABYLAS, LE • 1921 • Starevitch Ladislas • FRN • MARRIAGE OF BABYLAS, THE (USA)
MARIAGE DE CHIFFON, LE • 1918 • Lolli Alberto Carlo • ITL
MARIAGE DE CHIFFON, LE • 1941 • Autant-Lara Claude • FRN
MARIAGE DE FIGARO • 1989 • Coggio Roger • FRN
MARIAGE DE FIGARO, LE • 1959 • Meyer Jean • FRN • MARRIAGE OF FIGARO, THE (USA)
MARIAGE DE L'AIMEE, LE • 1911 • Feuillade Louis • FRN • MARIAGE DE L'AINEE, LE
MARIAGE DE L'AINEE, LE see **MARIAGE DE L'AIMEE, LE** • 1911
MARIAGE DE L'AMOUR • 1914 • *Pathe* • FRN • MARRIAGE OF PSYCHE AND CUPID, THE ○ MARRIAGE OF CUPID, THE (USA)
MARIAGE DE MADEMOISELLE BEULEMANS, LE • 1950 • Cerf Andre • FRN, BLG
MARIAGE DE MINUIT • 1923 • du Plessis Armand • FRN
MARIAGE DE MISS NELLY, LE • 1913 • Feuillade Louis • FRN
MARIAGE DE MLLE BEULEMANS, LE • 1926 • Duvivier Julien • FRN

MARIAGE DE MLLE BEULEMANS, LE • 1932 • Choux Jean • FRN
MARIAGE DE MONACO, LE • 1956 • Masson Jean • SHT • FRN
MARIAGE DE RAISON, LE • 1916 • Feuillade Louis • FRN
MARIAGE DE RAISON ET MARIAGE D'AMOUR • 1908 • Melies Georges • FRN • LOVER'S HAZING, A
MARIAGE DE RAMUNTCHO, LE • 1946 • de Vaucorbeil Max • FRN
MARIAGE DE ROSINE, LE • 1932 • Colombier Piere • FRN
MARIAGE DE SARAH, LE • 1931 • Greville Edmond T. • SHT • FRN
MARIAGE DE THOMAS POIVROT • 1908 • Melies Georges • FRN • FUN WITH THE BRIDAL PARTY
MARIAGE DE VERENA, LE • 1938 • Daroy Jacques • FRN, SWT • BATARDE, LA
MARIAGE DE VICTOIRE, LE see **MARIAGE DE VICTORINE, LE** • 1907
MARIAGE DE VICTORINE, LE • 1907 • Melies Georges • FRN • HOW BRIDGET'S LOVER ESCAPED (USA) ○ MARIAGE DE VICTOIRE, LE
MARIAGE DU HIBOU, LE see **OWL WHO MARRIED A GOOSE, THE** • 1974
MARIAGE EN BLANC see **WEDDING IN WHITE** • 1972
MARIAGE IMPREVU • 1913 • Linder Max • FRN
MARIAGE PAR CORRESPONDANCE • 1904 • Melies Georges • FRN • WEDDING BY CORRESPONDENCE, A
MARIAGE PAR PROCURATION see **VINGT-QUATRE HEURES DE PERM'** • 1940
MARIAGE PAR SUGGESTION • 1916 • Cohl Emile • ANS • FRN
MARIAGE ROYAL, UN • 1983 • Jean Jacques • MTV • CND
MARIAGES DE MLLE LEVY, LES • 1936 • Hugon Andre • FRN
MARIAN • 1977 • Cortes Luis • SPN
MARIAN ROSE WHITE • 1982 • Day Robert • TVM • USA
MARIAN, THE HOLY TERROR • 1914 • Duncan William • USA
MARIANA • 1968 • Guerrero Juan • MXC
MARIANA, MARIANA • 1987 • Isaac Alberto • MXC
MARIANDL see **HOFRAT GEIGER, DER** • 1947
MARIANELA • 1940 • Perojo Benito • SPN
MARIANELA • 1972 • Fons Angelino • SPN
MARIANNA • 1915 • Stafford Harry G. • USA
MARIANNA • 1967 • Paskaru Vasili • USS
MARIANNA SIRCA see **AMORE ROSSO** • 1953
MARIANNE • 1929 • Leonard Robert Z. • USA
MARIANNE • 1953 • Holmsen Egil • SWD
MARIANNE • 1978 • Black Noel • USA • MIRRORS
MARIANNE AND JULIANNE see **BLEIERNE ZEIT, DIE** • 1981
MARIANNE DE MA JEUNESSE • 1954 • Duvivier Julien • FRN, FRG • MARIANNE OF MY YOUTH (USA) ○ MARIANNE (FRG)
MARIANNE, EIN WEIB AUS DEM VOLKE • 1915 • *Sandrock Adele* • AUS
MARIANNE -FLOTTANS LILLA FASTMO see **FLOTTANS LILLA FASTMO** • 1930
MARIANNE (FRG) see **MARIANNE DE MA JEUNESSE** • 1954
MARIANNE OF MY YOUTH (USA) see **MARIANNE DE MA JEUNESSE** • 1954
MARIAROSA LA GUARDONA • 1973 • Girolami Marino • ITL
MARIA'S DAY see **MARIA NAP** • 1984
MARIA'S HOURS see **HORAS DE MARIA, AS** • 1977
MARIA'S LOVERS • 1984 • Konchalovsky Andrei • USA
MARIA'S SACRIFICE • 1914 • Humphrey William • USA
MARIBEL Y LA EXTRANA FAMILIA • 1960 • Forque Jose Maria • SPN
MARIDO A PRECIO FIJO, UN • 1942 • Delgras Gonzalo • SPN
MARIDO DE IDA Y VUELTA • 1957 • Lucia Luis • SPN
MARIDO, EL (SPN) see **MARITO, IL** • 1958
MARIDO SOLTEIRO, UM • 1952 • Garcia Fernando • PRT
MARIDO Y MUJER • 1932 • Howard David • USA
MARIDOS ENGANAN DE 7 A 9, LOS • 1946 • Cortes Fernando • MXC
MARIDOS NO CENAN EN CASA, LOS • 1956 • Mihura Jeronimo • SPN
MARIE • 1921-22 • Durand Jean • SER • FRN
MARIE • 1964 • Vorlicek Vaclav • CZC
MARIE • 1972 • Geissendorfer Hans W. • FRG
MARIE • 1986 • Donaldson Roger • USA • MARIE: A TRUE STORY
MARIE see **TAVASZI ZAPOR** • 1932
MARIE see **CASQUE D'OR** • 1952
MARIE see **TETE EN FLEURS** • 1969
MARIE -A HUNGARIAN LEGEND see **TAVASZI ZAPOR** • 1932
MARIE A MAL AUX DENTS, LE • 1912 • Cohl Emile • ANS • FRN
MARIE: A TRUE STORY see **MARIE** • 1986
MARIE-ANNE • 1980 • Walters Martin • TVM • CND
MARIE ANTOINETTE • 1922 • Meinert Rudolf • FRG
MARIE ANTOINETTE • 1938 • Van Dyke W. S., Duvivier Julien (U/c) • USA
MARIE-ANTOINETTE • 1955 • Delannoy Jean • FRN, ITL • MARIA ANTONIETTA, REGINA DI FRANCIA (ITL) ○ SHADOW OF THE GUILLOTINE (USA) ○ MARIE ANTOINETTE
MARIE-ANTOINETTE • 1956 • Sassy Jean-Paul • SHT • FRN
MARIE ANTOINETTE see **MARIE-ANTOINETTE** • 1955
MARIE BASCHKIRTZEFF see **TAGEBUCH DER GELIEBTEN, DAS** • 1936
MARIE-CHANTAL CONTRE LE DOCTEUR KHA • 1965 • Chabrol Claude • FRN, ITL, SPN • MARIE CHANTAL CONTRO DR. KHA (ITL)
MARIE CHANTAL CONTRO DR. KHA (ITL) see **MARIE-CHANTAL CONTRE LE DOCTEUR KHA** • 1965
MARIE-CHRISTINE • 1970 • Jutra Claude • SHT • CND
MARIE D'AMOUR UND IHRE LIEBHABER • 1924 • Brenken Kurt • FRG
MARIE DE LA COIFFEUSE, LE • 1990 • Leconte Patrice • FRN
MARIE DES ANGOISSES • 1935 • Bernheim Michel • FRN
MARIE DES ISLES • 1959 • Combret Georges • FRN, ITL • FLIBUSTIERI DELLA MARTINICA, I (ITL) ○ MARIE OF THE ISLES (USA) ○ WILD AND THE WANTON, THE
MARIE DU PORT, LA • 1949 • Carne Marcel • FRN
MARIE ET LE CURE • 1969 • Medveczky Diourka • SHT • FRN
MARIE GALANTE • 1934 • King Henry • USA
MARIE GREEN AND HER MERRIE MEN • 1941 • Negulesco Jean • SHT • USA
MARIE -HUNGARIAN LEGEND • 1932 • Fejos Paul • UKN
MARIE IN THE CITY see **MARIE S'EN VA-T-EN VILLE** • 1988
MARIE IN THE WINDMILL see **MARIA PA KVARNGARDEN** • 1945
MARIE-JOSE BEDARD ORGANISTE • 1972-73 • Brault Francois • DCS • CND
MARIE LA BOHEMIENNE • 1922 • Durand Jean • FRN
MARIE LA FEMME AU SINGE • 1922 • Durand Jean • FRN
MARIE LA GAIETE • 1921 • Durand Jean • FRN
MARIE LA MISERE • 1945 • de Baroncelli Jacques • FRN
MARIE, LEGENDE HONGROISE • 1932 • Fejos Paul • FRN • HISTOIRE D'AMOUR, UNE
MARIE LLOYD AT HOME AND BUNKERED • 1913 • *Magnet Producing Co* • UKN
MARIE LLOYD, JR. • 1926 • *Deforest Phonofilm* • SHT • UKN
MARIE LLOYD'S LITTLE JOKE • 1909 • Booth W. R.? • UKN
MARIE-LOUISE • 1944 • Lindtberg Leopold • SWT
MARIE, LTD. • 1919 • Webb Kenneth • USA
MARIE LUMIERE • 1958 • Bourguignon Serge • FRN
MARIE MADELEINE • 1965 • De Marchi Luigi • ITL
MARIE MADELEINE • 1976 • Payet Alain • FRN
MARIE-MARTINE • 1942 • Valentin Albert • FRN • D'OU VIENT MARIE-MARTINE? ○ MARIE MARTINE
MARIE MARTINE see **MARIE-MARTINE** • 1942
MARIE-OCTOBRE • 1958 • Duvivier Julien • FRN • SECRET MEETING (USA) ○ MARIE OCTOBRE
MARIE OCTOBRE see **MARIE-OCTOBRE** • 1958
MARIE OF THE ISLES (USA) see **MARIE DES ISLES** • 1959
MARIE-POUPEE • 1976 • Seria Joel • FRN • MARIE POUPEE ○ MARIE THE DOLL
MARIE POUPEE see **MARIE-POUPEE** • 1976
MARIE POUR MEMOIRE • 1968 • Garrel Philippe • FRN
MARIE-QUOEUR • 1971 • Fortune Sam • CND
MARIE RAMBERT REMEMBERS • 1960 • Russell Ken • MTV • UKN
MARIE SALOPE • Love John • FRN
MARIE S'EN VA-T-EN VILLE • 1988 • Lepage Marquise • CND • MARIE IN THE CITY
MARIE SOLEIL • 1964 • Bourseiller Antoine • FRN
MARIE THE DOLL see **MARIE-POUPEE** • 1976
MARIE TUDOR • 1965 • Gance Abel • MTV • FRN
MARIE UGUAY • 1982 • Labrecque Jean-Claude • CND
MARIE-VICTORIN • 1963 • Perron Clement • DCS • CND
MARIE WALEWSKA (UKN) see **CONQUEST** • 1937
MARIEE DU REGIMENT, LA • 1935 • Cammage Maurice • FRN
MARIEE EST TROP BELLE, LA • 1956 • Gaspard-Huit Pierre • FRN • BRIDE IS MUCH TOO BEAUTIFUL, THE (USA) ○ BRIDE IS TOO BEAUTIFUL, THE (UKN)
MARIEE ETAIT EN NOIR, LA • 1968 • Truffaut Francois • FRN, ITL • SPOSA IN NERO, LA (ITL) ○ BRIDE WORE BLACK, THE (UKN)
MARIENSTADT ADVENTURE, THE see **PRZYGODA NA MARIENSZTACIE** • 1954
MARIES DE L'AN DEUX, LES see **MARIES DE L'AN II, LES** • 1970
MARIES DE L'AN II, LES • 1970 • Rappeneau Jean-Paul • FRN, ITL, RMN • SPOSI DELL'ANNO SECONDO, GLI (ITL) ○ SWASHBUCKLER, THE (USA) ○ SCOUNDREL, THE ○ MARIES DE L'AN DEUX, LES
MARIES D'UN JOUR, LES • 1916 • Feuillade Louis • FRN
MARIE'S JOKE WITH THE FLYPAPERS • 1910 • Martinek H. O. • UKN
MARIE'S MILLIONS see **TILLIE'S PUNCTURED ROMANCE** • 1914
MARIE'S MILLIONS (UKN) see **TILLIE'S PUNCTURED ROMANCE** • 1928
MARIGOLD • 1938 • Bentley Thomas • UKN
MARIGOLD MAN • 1970 • Leder Paul • USA
MARIGOLDS IN AUGUST • 1980 • Devenish Ross • SAF
MARIGUANA • 1936 • Bohr Jose • MXC • MONSTRUO VERDE, EL
MARIHUANA • 1936 • Esper Dwain • USA • MARIHUANA: DEVIL'S WEED WITH ROOTS IN HELL ○ MARIJUANA: THE DEVIL'S WEED ○ MARIHUANA: THE DEVIL'S WEED
MARIHUANA • 1950 • Klimovsky Leon • SPN
MARIHUANA: DEVIL'S WEED WITH ROOTS IN HELL see **MARIHUANA** • 1936
MARIHUANA, MARIHUANA • 1973 • Wadhawan Jamie • UKN
MARIHUANA SMOKE see **HUMO DE MARIHUANA** • 1968
MARIHUANA: THE DEVIL'S WEED see **MARIHUANA** • 1936
MARIJKA NEVERNICE • 1934 • Vancura Vladislav • CZC • UNFAITHFUL MARIJKA, THE ○ MARIJKA THE ADULTERESS
MARIJKA THE ADULTERESS see **MARIJKA NEVERNICE** • 1934
MARIJUANA see **ASSASSIN OF YOUTH** • 1936
MARIJUANA HELL • 1970 • Jacopetti Roland • USA
MARIJUANA: THE DEVIL'S WEED see **MARIHUANA** • 1936
MARIKA see **DEUX FAVORIS, LES** • 1936
MARIKA see **MASKE IN BLAU** • 1953
MARIKEN VAN NIEUMEGHEN • 1974 • Stelling Jos • NTH
MARIKENS BRYLLUP • 1972 • Andersen Knut • NRW • MARIKEN'S WEDDING DAY
MARIKEN'S WEDDING DAY see **MARIKENS BRYLLUP** • 1972
MARILI • 1959 • von Baky Josef • FRG
MARILYN • 1953 • Rilla Wolf • UKN • ROADHOUSE GIRL ○ MARION
MARILYN • 1963 • *Twentieth Century Fox* • DOC • USA
MARILYN see **MARILYN: THE UNTOLD STORY** • 1980
MARILYN, MON AMOUR • 1985 • Lemoine Michel • SWT • MARILYN, MY LOVE
MARILYN, MY LOVE see **MARILYN, MON AMOUR** • 1985
MARILYN OF TOKYO, A see **MONRO NO YONA ONNA** • 1964
MARILYN: THE UNTOLD STORY • 1980 • Flynn John, Arnold Jack, Schiller Lawrence • TVM • USA • MARILYN
MARILYN TIMES FIVE • 1969-73 • Conner Bruce • SHT • USA
MARILYNE • White Jack* • FRN
MARIMBA • 1981 • Craven Wes • USA
MARIN CHANTANT, LE see **ANGE GARDIEN, L'** • 1933
MARIN FALIERO • 1909 • De Liguoro Giuseppe • ITL
MARINA • 1944 • Salvador Jaime • MXC
MARINA • 1960 • Martin Paul • FRG
MARINA THE SAVAGE • 1919 • Slavinsky Vladimir • CZC
MARINAI, DONNE E GUAI • 1958 • Simonelli Giorgio C. • ITL, SPN
MARINAI IN COPERTA • 1967 • Corbucci Bruno • ITL • SAILORS ON DECK
MARINAI SENZA STELLE • 1943 • De Robertis Francesco • ITL • MARINARETTI
MARINARETTI see **MARINAI SENZA STELLE** • 1943
MARINATED MARINER • 1950 • McCollum Hugh • SHT • USA
MARINE BATTLEGROUND • 1966 • Lee Manli • USA, SKR
MARINE CIRCUS • 1939 • Fitzpatrick James • SHT • USA
MARINE FLUVIALE • 1947 • Tedesco Jean • SHT • FRN
MARINE FOLLIES • 1936 • Schwarzwald Milton • SHT • USA
MARINE HIGHWAY • 1968 • Perry Margaret • DOC • CND
MARINE ISSUE • 1986 • Amar Denis • GIB • INSTANT JUSTICE
MARINE LAW • 1913 • Dwan Allan • USA
MARINE MARCHANDE see **NAVIGATION MARCHANDE** • 1954
MARINE RAIDERS • 1944 • Schuster Harold • USA
MARINELEUTNANT VON BRINKEN • 1918 • *Enger Mogens* • FRG • SCHUDSCHEIN DES PANDOLA, DER
MARINELLA • 1936 • Caron Pierre • FRN
MARINERS OF THE SKY see **NAVY BORN** • 1936
MARINES • 1928 • Gance Abel • SHT • FRN
MARINES, LES • 1957 • Reichenbach Francois • SHT • FRN
MARINES ARE COMING, THE • 1935 • Howard David • USA
MARINES ARE HERE, THE • 1938 • Rosen Phil • USA
MARINES COME THROUGH, THE • 1943 • Gasnier Louis J. • USA • FIGHT ON, MARINES
MARINE'S FATE • 1953 • Shmaruk I., Ivchenko Viktor • USS
MARINES FLY HIGH, THE • 1940 • Nicholls George Jr., Stoloff Ben • USA
MARINES HAVE A WORD FOR IT, THE see **SOUTH SEA WOMAN** • 1953
MARINES HAVE LANDED, THE (UKN) see **LEATHERNECKS HAVE LANDED, THE** • 1936
MARINES IN THE MAKING • 1942 • Polesie Herbert • SHT • USA
MARINES, LET'S GO • 1961 • Walsh Raoul • USA
MARINETTI • 1968 • Thoms Albie • ASL
MARINHAS • 1929 • Coelho Jose Adolfo • SHT • PRT
MARINICA • 1953 • Popescu-Gopo Ion • SHT • RMN
MARINICA'S BODKIN see **SURUBUL LUI MARINICA** • 1955
MARINO DE LOS PUNOS DE ORO, EL • 1968 • Gil Rafael • SPN • SAILOR WITH THE GOLDEN FISTS, THE
MARINOS KONTARAS • 1947 • Tzavellas Georges • GRC
MARIO • 1914 • Edwards Walter? • USA
MARIO • 1984 • Beaudin Jean • CND
MARIO BANANA • 1964 • Warhol Andy • SHT • USA
MARIO CANO • 1989 • Loboguerrero Camila • CLM
MARIO-CARTOONS • 1914 • *Bamforth & Co* • SER • UKN
MARIO DE PIETRO AND HIS ESTUDIANTINA • 1936 • Shepherd Horace • UKN
MARIO PUZO'S SEVEN GRAVES FOR ROGAN see **SEVEN GRAVES FOR ROGAN** • 1981
MARIO PUZO'S "THE FORTUNATE PILGRIM" • 1988 • Cooper Stuart • TVM • USA • FORTUNATE PILGRIM, THE
MARION • 1921 • Roberti Roberto Leone • ITL
MARION see **MARILYN** • 1953
MARION BROWN • 1970 • Kotulla Theodor • SHT • FRG • SEE THE MUSIC
MARION, DAS GEHORT SICH NICHT • 1932 • Emo E. W. • FRG
MARION DELORME • 1918 • Krauss Henry • FRN
MARIONA REBULL • 1947 • Saenz De Heredia Jose Luis • SPN
MARIONETKI • 1934 • Protazanov Yakov • USS • MARIONETTES
MARIONETTE • 1939 • Gallone Carmine • ITL
MARIONETTE • 1963 • Dovnikovic Borivoj • ANS • `YGS
MARIONETTE PERFORMANCE • 1903 • *Paul R. W.* • UKN
MARIONETTEN • 1915 • Lowenbein Richard • FRG
MARIONETTEN • 1918 • Lubitsch Ernst • FRG
MARIONETTEN • 1958 • Lemmel Dieter H. • SHT • FRG • MARIONETTES
MARIONETTEN DER FURSTIN, DIE • 1923 • Zelnik Friedrich • FRG
MARIONETTEN DER LEIDENSCHAFT • 1919 • Pick Lupu • FRG
MARIONETTEN DES TEUFELS 1 • 1920 • Brandt Johannes • FRG
MARIONETTEN DES TEUFELS 2 • 1920 • Brandt Johannes • FRG • SUCHENDE SEELE, EINE
MARIONETTES • 1898 • *Cinematograph Co* • UKN
MARIONETTES • 1939-48 • Carleton Ben • UKN
MARIONETTES see **MARIONETKI** • 1934
MARIONETTES see **MARIONETTEN** • 1958
MARIONETTES, THE • 1917 • Mills Thomas R. • SHT • USA
MARIONETTES, THE • 1918 • Chautard Emile • USA
MARIONNETTES, LES see **ARA IS, AL-** • 1959
MARIONNETTISTE, LE • 1963 • Languepin Jean-Jacques • SHT • FRN
MARIONS-NOUS • 1931 • Mercanton Louis • FRN • SA NUIT DE NOCES
MARIPOSA EN LA NOCHE, UNE • 1976 • Bo Armando • ARG • BUTTERFLY IN THE NIGHT, A
MARIPOSA QUE VOLO SOBRE EL MAR • 1951 • Obregon Antonio • SPN
MARIPOSAS DISECADAS, LAS • 1977 • Vejar Sergio • MXC
MARIPOSAS NEGRAS • 1953 • Christensen Carlos Hugo • MXC • BLACK BUTTERFLIES ○ DARK BUTTERFLIES
MARIQUITA, LA • 1913 • Fescourt Henri • FRN
MARIS DE LEONTINE, LES • 1947 • Le Henaff Rene • FRN • T'EN SOUVIENS-TU MON AMOUR?
MARIS DE MA FEMME, LES • 1936 • Cammage Maurice • FRN
MARIS, LES FEMMES, LES AMANTS, LES • 1988 • Thomas Pascal • FRN
MARISA LA CIVETTA • 1957 • Bolognini Mauro • ITL, SPN
MARISA'S PRESENCE see **PRESENCA DE MARISA** • 1988
MARISCAL DEL INFIERNO, EL • 1974 • Klimovsky Leon • SPN
MARISOL, RUMBO A RIO • 1963 • Palacios Fernando • SPN
MARISOL'S FOUR WEDDINGS see **CUATRO BODAS DE MARISOL, LAS** • 1967
MARITAL CRISIS OF NUMBSKULL EMPTYBROOK, THE • 1981 • Kokkonen Ere • FNL

MARITAL FULFILLMENT • 1970 • Sebastian Ferdinand • DOC • USA
MARITAL JOKES • 1988 • Grubcheva Ivanka • ANT • BUL
MARITAL MIRAGE, A • 1912 • *Republic* • USA
MARITAL RELATIONS see **MEOTO ZENZAI** • 1955
MARITANA • 1922 • Wynn George • UKN
MARITANA • 1927 • Parkinson H. B. • UKN
MARITE • 1947 • Stroyeva Vera • USS
MARITI A CONGRESO • 1961 • D'Amico Luigi Filippo • ITL
MARITI IN CITTA • 1957 • Comencini Luigi • ITL • HUSBANDS IN TOWN
MARITI IN PERICOLO • 1961 • Morassi Mauro • ITL
MARITI -TEMPESTA D'AMORE, I • 1941 • Mastrocinque Camillo • ITL • PARABOLA DEI MARITI, LA
MARITIMERS see **GOIN' DOWN THE ROAD** • 1970
MARITO, IL • 1958 • Loy Nanni, Puccini Gianni, Palacios Fernando • ITL, SPN • MARIDO, EL (SPN)
MARITO E MIO E L'AMMAZZO QUANDO MI PARE, IL • 1967 • Festa Campanile Pasquale • ITL • HE'S MY HUSBAND AND I'LL KILL HIM WHEN I LIKE ○ DROP DEAD, MY LOVE
MARITO E MOGLIE • 1952 • De Filippo Eduardo • ITL • HUSBAND AND WIFE
MARITO IN COLLEGIO, IL • 1977 • Lucidi Maurizio • ITL
MARITO IN CONDOMINIO, UN • 1963 • Dorigo Angelo • ITL
MARITO PER ANNA ZACCHEO, UN • 1953 • De Santis Giuseppe • ITL • HUSBAND FOR ANNA, A
MARITO PER IL MESE DI APRILE, UN • 1941 • Simonelli Giorgio C. • ITL
MARITO POVERO, IL • 1947 • Amata Gaetano • ITL
MARITZA CAPRILES • 1974 • Cosmi Carlo • VNZ
MARIUS • 1931 • Korda Alexander, Pagnol Marcel • FRN
MARIUS A PARIS • 1930 • Lion Roger • FRN • PETITE FEMME DU FLORIDA, LA
MARIUS, AMATEUR DE CIDRE • 1931 • Greville Edmond T. • SHT • FRN
MARIUS BARBEAU ET L'ART TOTEMIQUE • 1959 • Benoit Real • DOC • CND
MARIUS BARBEAU ET LE FOLKLORE CANADIEN-FRANCAIS • 1959 • Benoit Real • DOC • CND
MARIUS ET OLIVE A PARIS • 1935 • Epstein Jean (U/c) • FRN
MARIUS' SWAN SONG • 1910 • *Vitagraph* • USA
MARIUTCH • 1930 • Fleischer Dave • ANS • USA
MARIZINIA • 1962 • Sulistrowski Zygmunt • USA, BRZ • MARIZINIA, THE WITCH BENEATH THE SEA ○ WITCH BENEATH THE SEA, THE
MARIZINIA, THE WITCH BENEATH THE SEA see **MARIZINIA** • 1962
MARIZZA, CALLED THE SMUGGLER'S MADONNA see **MARIZZA, GENANNT DIE SCHMUGGLERMADONNA** • 1920
MARIZZA, GENANNT DIE SCHMUGGLERMADONNA • 1920 • Murnau F. W. • FRG • SCHONE TIER, DAS ○ SCHMUGGLERMADONNA, DIE ○ MARIZZA, CALLED THE SMUGGLER'S MADONNA
MARJA PIENI! • 1972 • Bergholm Eija-Elina • FNL • MAARETA MARUNA ○ POOR MARIA ○ POOR MARJA! ○ LITTLE MARJA!
MARJOE • 1972 • Smith Howard, Kernochan Sarah • DOC • USA
MARJOLIN OU LA FILLE MANQUE • 1921 • Feuillade Louis • FRN
MARJORIE MORNINGSTAR • 1958 • Rapper Irving • USA
MARJORIE'S DIAMOND RING • 1912 • *Mcleod Elsie* • USA
MARJORY'S GOLDFISH • 1914 • Kinder Stuart • UKN
MARJUCA ILI SMRT • 1987 • Kljakovic Vanca • YGS • MARJUCA OR DEATH
MARJUCA OR DEATH see **MARJUCA ILI SMRT** • 1987
MARK • 1962 • Johnston George F. • SHT • USA
MARK, THE • 1961 • Green Guy • UKN
MARK CARLETON see **FORGOTTEN VICTORY** • 1939
MARK COLPISCE ANCORA • 1977 • Massi Stelvio • ITL
MARK DONEN AGENTE 27 see **MARK DONEN AGENTE Z 7** • 1966
MARK DONEN AGENTE Z 7 • 1966 • Romitelli Giancarlo • ITL, SPN, FRG • Z.7. OPERATION REMBRANDT (SPN) ○ Z7 OPERATION REMBRANDT (USA) ○ KARATE IN TANGIERS FOR AGENT Z-7 ○ MARK DONEN AGENTE 27
MARK DOUBLE CROSS see **TATAK DOUBLE CROSS** • 1968
MARK I LOVE YOU • 1980 • Hellstrom Gunnar • TVM • USA
MARK IL POLIZIOTTO • 1975 • Massi Stelvio • ITL • BLOOD, SWEAT AND FEAR (USA)
MARK IL POLIZIOTTO SPARA PER PRIMO • 1975 • Massi Stelvio • ITL
MARK MURPHY • 1962 • Binder Steve • SHT • USA
MARK OF A CHAMPION, THE • 1968 • Brault Francois • DCS • CND
MARK OF A GENTLEMAN, THE • 1916 • Worthington William • SHT • USA
MARK OF BLOOD see **RAKTA REKHA** • 1968
MARK OF CAIN • 1985 • Pittman Bruce • CND
MARK OF CAIN, THE • 1916 • De Grasse Joseph • USA
MARK OF CAIN, THE • 1917 • Fitzmaurice George • USA
MARK OF CAIN, THE • 1948 • Hurst Brian Desmond • UKN
MARK OF CAIN, THE see **LONE CHANCE, THE** • 1924
MARK OF CANCER, THE see **ZNAMENI RAKA** • 1967
MARK OF DEATH, THE see **MARCA DEL MUERTO, LA** • 1960
MARK OF EVIL, THE see **AKU NO MONSHO** • 1964
MARK OF KARDO, THE • 1967 • Villar Felix • PHL
MARK OF KRIMINAL, THE see **MARCHIO DI KRIMINAL, IL** • 1967
MARK OF SATAN, THE see **MARCA DE SATANAS, LA** • 1956
MARK OF STINGAREE, THE • 1917 • *Boardman True* • SHT • USA
MARK OF TERROR see **DRUMS OF JEOPARDY** • 1931
MARK OF THE APACHE (UKN) see **TOMAHAWK TRAIL** • 1957
MARK OF THE AVENGER see **MYSTERIOUS RIDER, THE** • 1938
MARK OF THE BEAST • 1923 • Dixon Thomas • USA
MARK OF THE BEAST, THE • 1981 • Verhoeff Pierre • NTH
MARK OF THE CLAW, THE see **GIANT CLAW, THE** • 1957
MARK OF THE CLAW (UKN) see **DICK TRACY'S DILEMMA** • 1947
MARK OF THE DEVIL • 1984 • Guest Val • UKN
MARK OF THE DEVIL, PART II see **HEXEN: GESCHANDET UND ZU TODE GEQUALT** • 1972
MARK OF THE DEVIL (USA) see **BRENN, HEXE, BRENN** • 1969
MARK OF THE FROG • 1928 • Heath Arch B. • SRL • USA
MARK OF THE GORILLA • 1950 • Berke William • USA
MARK OF THE GUN • 1969 • Compo • USA
MARK OF THE HAWK (USA) see **ACCUSED** • 1957
MARK OF THE LASH • 1911 • Gavin John F. • ASL
MARK OF THE LASH • 1948 • Taylor Ray • USA
MARK OF THE PHANTOM, THE see **LIDERCNYOMAS** • 1920
MARK OF THE PHOENIX • 1958 • Rogers Maclean • UKN
MARK OF THE RENEGADE • 1951 • Fregonese Hugo • USA • DON RENEGADE
MARK OF THE SPUR • 1932 • McGowan J. P. • USA
MARK OF THE VAMPIRE • 1935 • Browning Tod • USA
MARK OF THE VAMPIRE • 1957 • Landres Paul • USA • VAMPIRE, THE
MARK OF THE VAMPIRE, THE see **SENAL DEL VAMPIRO, LA** • 1943
MARK OF THE WEST see **CURSE OF THE UNDEAD** • 1959
MARK OF THE WHISTLER • 1944 • Castle William • USA • MARKED MAN, THE (UKN)
MARK OF THE WITCH • 1970 • Moore Tom* • USA
MARK OF THE WITCH see **BRENN, HEXE, BRENN** • 1969
MARK OF THE WOLF MAN, THE see **MARCA DEL HOMBRE LOBO, LA** • 1968
MARK OF ZORRO, THE • 1920 • Niblo Fred • USA
MARK OF ZORRO, THE • 1940 • Mamoulian Rouben • USA
MARK OF ZORRO, THE • 1974 • McDougall Don • TVM • USA
MARK TWAIN, AMERICAN • 1976 • Wilbor Robert • USA
MARKED BULLET, THE (UKN) see **PRAIRIE STRANGER** • 1941
MARKED BY DARKNESS • 1959 • Uher Stefan • CZC
MARKED CARD, THE • 1913 • *Champion* • USA
MARKED CARDS • 1918 • D'Elba Henri • USA
MARKED FOR DEATH • 1990 • Little Dwight H. • USA
MARKED FOR LIFE • 1911 • *Solax* • USA
MARKED FOR LOVE • 1967 • Clay Adam • USA • MARKED X FOR LOVE
MARKED FOR MURDER • 1945 • Clifton Elmer • USA
MARKED GUN, THE • 1912 • *American* • USA
MARKED MAN, A • 1916 • Miller Frank • UKN
MARKED MAN, A • 1917 • Ford John • USA
MARKED MAN, THE see **HOMME A ABATTRE, L'** • 1936
MARKED MAN, THE see **ZENKA MONO** • 1968
MARKED MAN, THE (UKN) see **MARK OF THE WHISTLER** • 1944
MARKED MEN • 1920 • Ford John • USA
MARKED MEN • 1940 • Newfield Sam • USA
MARKED MEN see **TEXAS BAD MAN, THE** • 1932
MARKED MONEY • 1928 • Bennet Spencer Gordon • SRL • USA
MARKED "NO FUNDS" • 1916 • *Myers Harry* • SHT • USA
MARKED ONE, THE • 1963 • Searle Francis • UKN
MARKED: SACRAMENTADOS see **TATAK: SACRAMENTADOS** • 1968
MARKED TIME-TABLE, THE • 1910 • Griffith D. W. • USA
MARKED TRAIL, THE • 1910 • *Anderson Broncho Billy* • USA
MARKED TRAILS • 1944 • McCarthy John P. • USA
MARKED WOMAN • 1937 • Bacon Lloyd • USA
MARKED WOMAN, THE • 1914 • Lund O. A. C. • USA
MARKED X FOR LOVE see **MARKED FOR LOVE** • 1967
MARKENS GRODE • 1921 • Schneevoigt George • SWD, NRW
MARKET see **BAZAR-E-HUSN** • 1988
MARKET DAY (TROUVILLE) see **JOUR DE MARCHE A TROUVILLE** • 1896
MARKET IN WOMEN, THE see **MARCHANDS DE FILLES** • 1957
MARKET OF HUMAN FLESH • 1923 • Shimazu Yasujiro • JPN
MARKET OF MIRACLES see **JARMAK CUDOW** • 1966
MARKET OF SOULS, THE • 1919 • De Grasse Joseph • USA
MARKET OF VAIN DESIRE, THE • 1916 • Barker Reginald • USA
MARKET PLACE see **TORI** • 1962
MARKET PRICE OF LOVE, THE • 1915 • *Kirk Ann* • USA
MARKET SQUARE, THE • 1928 • Miller Frank • UKN
MARKET WOMAN'S MISHAP, THE • 1904 • Mottershaw Frank • UKN
MARKETA LAZAROVA • 1967 • Vlacil Frantisek • CZC
MARKETPLACE see **MANDI** • 1983
MARKNADSAFTON • 1948 • Johansson Ivar • SWD • EVENING OF THE FAIR
MARKO ASINTADO • 1967 • Santiago Cirio H. • PHL • SHARPSHOOTER
MARKO PASA • 1967 • Saner Hulki • TRK • MARKO PASHA
MARKO PASHA see **MARKO PASA** • 1967
MARKO POLO (YGS) see **FABULEUSE AVENTURE DE MARCO POLO, LA** • 1965
MARKO THE HERO see **YUNAK MARKO** • 1953
MARKSMAN, THE • 1953 • Collins Lewis D. • USA
MARKSMAN, THE see **FREISCHUTZ, DER** • 1968
MARKSMEN see **STRELTZI** • 1967
MARKSWOMAN, THE • 1915 • King Burton L. • USA
MARKURELLS I WADKOPING • 1930 • Sjostrom Victor • SWD, FRG • VATER UND SOHN (FRG) ○ FATHER AND SON (USA)
MARLBOROUGH WENT TO WAR see **MAMBRU SE FUE A LA GUERRA** • 1985
MARLENE • 1948 • de Herain Pierre • FRN • PORTE D'OR, LA
MARLENE • 1983 • Schell Maximilian • DOC • FRG
MARLENE -DER AMERIKANISCHE TRAUM • 1987 • Kratz Kathe • AUS • MARLENE -THE AMERICAN DREAM
MARLENE -THE AMERICAN DREAM see **MARLENE -DER AMERIKANISCHE TRAUM** • 1987
MARLIE THE KILLER • 1928 • Smith Noel • USA
MARLOWE • 1969 • Bogart Paul • USA • LITTLE SISTER, THE
MARMA YOGI • 1951 • Ramnoth K. • IND
MARMADUKE AND HIS ANGEL • 1915 • Wilson Frank? • UKN
MARMAILLE, LA • 1935 • Bernard-Deschamps • FRN
MARMALADE REVOLUTION (USA) see **MARMELADUPPRORET** • 1980
MARMARA HASAN • 1968 • Aslan Mehmet • TRK
MARMELADUPPRORET • 1980 • Josephson Erland • SWD • MARMALADE REVOLUTION (USA)
MARMERPOEL, DIE • 1972 • SAF
MARMITE DIABOLIQUE, LA • 1903 • Velle Gaston • FRN • DIABOLICAL POT, THE
MARNIE • 1964 • Hitchcock Alfred • USA
MARNIX GIJSEN ACHTERNA • 1975 • Claes J. • BLG • LOOKING AT MARNIX GIJSEN
MAROC 7 • 1966 • O'Hara Gerry • UKN
MARODEURE DER LIEBE • 1924 • *Tobolski Tadeus* • FRG
MARODORER • 1934 • von Hau Herbert • SWD • MARAUDERS
MAROKKANISCHE NACHTE see **ABENTEUERIN VON MONTE CARLO 2, DIE** • 1921
MAROONED • 1913 • Kirkwood James • USA
MAROONED • 1916 • Calvert E. H. • SHT • USA
MAROONED • 1918 • *Jaxon* • USA
MAROONED • 1933 • Hiscott Leslie • UKN
MAROONED • 1969 • Sturges John • USA
MAROONED HEARTS • 1920 • Archainbaud George • USA
MARQUE DES PLAISIRS PASSES, LA • 1913 • Protazanov Yakov • USS
MARQUES DE SALAMANCA, EL • 1948 • Neville Edgar • SPN
MARQUES, LA MENOR Y EL TRAVESTI, EL • 1982 • Balcazar Alfonso • SPN • INSATIABLE ALICIA AND THE MARQUIS
MARQUESA DEL BARRIO, LA • 1950 • Zacarias Miguel • MXC
MARQUESONA, LA • 1939 • Ardavin Eusebio F. • SPN
MARQUIS • 1897 • *Paul R. W.* • UKN
MARQUIS • 1989 • Xhonneux Henri • FRN
MARQUIS AND MISS SALLY, THE • 1918 • Watt Allen • SHT • USA
MARQUIS DE SADE, DER (FRG) see **DE SADE** • 1969
MARQUIS DE SADE: JUSTINE • 1968 • Franco Jesus • FRG, ITL, FRN • JUSTINE OVVERO LE DISAVVENTURE DELLA VERTU (ITL) ○ JUSTINE AND JULIET ○ INFORTUNES DE LA VERTU, LES(FRN) ○ JUSTINE
MARQUIS DE SADE'S JUSTINE see **CRUEL PASSION** • 1977
MARQUIS DEL GRILLO, THE see **MARCHESE DEL GRILLO, IL** • 1981
MARQUIS D'EON, DER SPION DER POMPADOUR • 1928 • Grune Karl • FRG
MARQUIS D'OR, DER • 1920 • Schunzel Reinhold • FRG
MARQUIS PREFERRED • 1929 • Tuttle Frank • USA
MARQUIS S'AMUSE, LE (FRN) see **MARCHESE DEL GRILLO, IL** • 1981
MARQUIS VON BOLIBAR, DER • 1922 • Porges Friedrich • AUS
MARQUISE DE TREVENEC, LA • 1913 • Fescourt Henri • FRN
MARQUISE D'O, LA • 1976 • Rohmer Eric • FRN, FRG • MARQUISE VON O., DIE (FRG) ○ MARQUISE OF O.., THE (USA)
MARQUISE OF O.., THE (USA) see **MARQUISE D'O, LA** • 1976
MARQUISE VON O., DIE • 1920 • Legband Paul • FRG
MARQUISE VON O., DIE (FRG) see **MARQUISE D'O, LA** • 1976
MARQUISE VON POMPADOUR, DIE • 1922 • Halm Alfred • FRG
MARQUISE VON POMPADOUR, DIE • 1930 • Wolff Willi • FRG
MARQUISE VON PORNO, LA • 1977 • Pierson Claude • FRN
MARQUITTA • 1928 • Renoir Jean • FRN
MARRAINE DE CHARLEY, LA • 1935 • Colombier Piere • FRN
MARRAINE DE CHARLEY, LA • 1959 • Chevalier Pierre • FRN
MARRAINE DU REGIMENT, LA • 1938 • Rosca Gabriel • FRN
MARRAKECH, CAPITAL DU SUD • 1948 • Mineur Jean • SHT • FRN
MARRIAGE • 1911 • *Reliance* • USA
MARRIAGE • 1918 • Kirkwood James • USA
MARRIAGE • 1927 • Neill R. William • USA
MARRIAGE • 1930-40 • Bose Nitin • IND
MARRIAGE • 1945 • Annensky Isider • USS
MARRIAGE • 1973 • Umboh Wim • INN
MARRIAGE see **KEKKON** • 1947
MARRIAGE see **MARIAGE** • 1975
MARRIAGE, A see **BROKEN PROMISE** • 1983
MARRIAGE, THE • 1967 • Sheppard Gordon H. • CND
MARRIAGE, THE • 1968 • Campani Paul • ANS • ITL
MARRIAGE, THE • 1973 • Li Hsing • HKG
MARRIAGE, THE see **DUGUN** • 1974
MARRIAGE A LA CARTE • 1912 • *Crystal* • USA
MARRIAGE A LA CARTE • 1931 • Elliot Grace • USA
MARRIAGE A LA CARTE see **MARRYING MONEY** • 1915
MARRIAGE A LA MODE • 1918 • Townley Robin H. • USA
MARRIAGE AGENCY, THE see **AKTENSKAPSBYRAN** • 1913
MARRIAGE AND OTHER FOUR LETTER WORDS • 1975 • Rick Jr. • USA
MARRIAGE ARGENTINIAN STYLE see **MATRIMONIO A LA ARGENTINA** • 1968
MARRIAGE BARGAIN, THE • 1935 • Ray Albert • USA • WOMAN OF DESTINY (UKN)
MARRIAGE BED, THE • 1986 • Lavut Martin • MTV • CND
MARRIAGE BOND, THE • 1916 • Marston Lawrence • USA
MARRIAGE BOND, THE • 1932 • Elvey Maurice • UKN
MARRIAGE BROKER, THE see **ASCHENBROEDEL** • 1916
MARRIAGE BROKER, THE see **AMERICANER SCHADCHEN** • 1939
MARRIAGE BUBBLE, THE • 1918 • Edwards Walter • SHT • USA
MARRIAGE BUREAU, THE see **AKTENSKAPSBYRAN** • 1913
MARRIAGE BY CONTRACT • 1928 • Flood James • USA
MARRIAGE BY MOTOR see **RUNAWAY MATCH, THE** • 1903
MARRIAGE BY PROXY • 1918 • *Vernon Bobby* • USA
MARRIAGE CAME TUMBLING DOWN, THE (USA) see **CE SACRE GRAND-PERE** • 1968
MARRIAGE CEREMONY see **KEKKON SHIKI KEKKON SHIKI** • 1963
MARRIAGE CHANCE, THE • 1922 • Del Ruth Hampton • USA
MARRIAGE CHEAT, THE • 1924 • Wray John Griffith • USA
MARRIAGE CIRCLE, THE • 1924 • Lubitsch Ernst • USA
MARRIAGE CIRCUS, THE • 1925 • Kennedy Edgar, Morris Reggie • SHT • USA
MARRIAGE CLAUSE, THE • 1926 • Weber Lois • USA • STAR MAKER, THE
MARRIAGE CONSULTATION see **KEKKON SODAN** • 1965
MARRIAGE DROPOUTS • 1969 • Goetz Tommy • USA
MARRIAGE FOR CONVENIENCE • 1919 • Olcott Sidney • USA
MARRIAGE FOR MODERNS • 1949 • Hammid Alexander • USA
MARRIAGE FOR MONEY, A • 1914 • *Eclair* • USA
MARRIAGE FOR REVENGE, A • 1916 • Curtis Allen • SHT • USA
MARRIAGE FORBIDDEN • 1936 • Goldstone Phil • USA • DAMAGED GOODS

MARRIAGE GAME, THE • 1912 • *Majestic* • USA
MARRIAGE GAME, THE see **AKTENSKAPSLEKEN** • 1935
MARRIAGE-GO-ROUND • 1961 • Lang Walter • USA
MARRIAGE GREEK STYLE • 1965 • Georgiadis Vassilis • GRC
MARRIAGE HOTEL, THE see **GASTHAUS ZUR EHE, DAS** • 1926
MARRIAGE HUMOR • 1933 • Edwards Harry J. • SHT • USA
MARRIAGE IN HASTE • 1910 • *Lubin* • USA
MARRIAGE IN THE MODERN MANNER see **ZAWAG ALLA TARIKA EL HADISSA** • 1968
MARRIAGE IN THE MOON, A see **MATRIMONIO INTERPLANETARIO, UN** • 1910
MARRIAGE IN THE SHADOW see **EHE IM SCHATTEN** • 1947
MARRIAGE IN TRANSIT • 1925 • Neill R. William • USA
MARRIAGE IS A PRIVATE AFFAIR • 1944 • Leonard Robert Z. • USA
MARRIAGE IS ALIVE AND WELL • 1980 • Mayberry Russ • TVM • USA
MARRIAGE JAPANESE STYLE see **KEKKON SHIMASU** • 1969
"MARRIAGE LICENSE?" • 1926 • Borzage Frank • USA • PELICAN, THE
MARRIAGE LIE, THE • 1918 • Paton Stuart • USA
MARRIAGE LINES, THE • 1921 • Noy Wilfred • UKN
MARRIAGE LOTTERY, THE • 1913 • *Imp* • USA
MARRIAGE MAKER, THE • 1923 • De Mille William C. • USA • FAUN, THE ○ SPRING MAGIC
MARRIAGE MANUAL, THE • 1970 • *Screenpix* • DOC • USA
MARRIAGE MARKET, THE • 1917 • Ashley Arthur • USA
MARRIAGE MARKET, THE • 1923 • Le Saint Edward J. • USA
MARRIAGE MORALS • 1923 • Nigh William • USA
MARRIAGE NOT, A • 1918 • *Triangle* • USA
MARRIAGE OF A YOUNG STOCKBROKER, THE • 1971 • Turman Lawrence • USA
MARRIAGE OF ARTHUR, THE • 1916 • Julian Rupert • USA
MARRIAGE OF BABYLAS, THE (USA) see **MARIAGE DE BABYLAS, LE** • 1921
MARRIAGE OF BALZAMINOV, THE (USA) see **ZHENITBA BALZAMINOVA** • 1965
MARRIAGE OF CONVENIENCE • 1960 • Donner Clive • UKN
MARRIAGE OF CONVENIENCE see **MALZENSTWO Z ROZSADKU** • 1967
MARRIAGE OF CONVENIENCE, A • 1910 • *Warwick Trading Co* • UKN
MARRIAGE OF CONVENIENCE, A • 1912 • Young James • USA
MARRIAGE OF CONVENIENCE, A see **BORNEVENNERNE** • 1914
MARRIAGE OF CONVENIENCE, THE see **FRAULEIN JOSETTE, MEINE FRAU** • 1926
MARRIAGE OF CONVENIENCE (UKN) see **HIRED WIFE** • 1934
MARRIAGE OF CORBAL, THE • 1936 • Grune Karl • UKN • PRISONER OF CORBAL (USA)
MARRIAGE OF CUPID, THE (USA) see **MARIAGE DE L'AMOUR** • 1914
MARRIAGE OF FIGARO, THE see **FIGAROS HOCHZEIT** • 1920
MARRIAGE OF FIGARO, THE see **FIGAROS HOCHZEIT** • 1949
MARRIAGE OF FIGARO, THE (USA) see **MARIAGE DE FIGARO, LE** • 1959
MARRIAGE OF FIGARO, THE (USA) see **HOCHZEIT DES FIGARO, DIE** • 1968
MARRIAGE OF KITTY, THE • 1915 • Melford George • USA
MARRIAGE OF MARCIA, THE see **TENDER HOUR, THE** • 1927
MARRIAGE OF MARIA BRAUN, THE (UKN) see **EHE DER MARIA BRAUN, DIE** • 1979
MARRIAGE OF MOLLY-O, THE • 1916 • Powell Paul • USA
MARRIAGE OF MUGGINS V.C. AND A FURTHER EXPLOIT, THE • 1910 • Aylott Dave • UKN
MARRIAGE OF NIATANA, THE • 1913 • *Majestic* • USA
MARRIAGE OF PSYCHE AND CUPID, THE see **MARIAGE DE L'AMOUR** • 1914
MARRIAGE OF THE BEAR, THE (USA) see **LOKIS** • 1926
MARRIAGE OF THE BLESSED • 1989 • Makhmalbaf Mohsen • IRN
MARRIAGE OF THE PENS see **NOCES DE PLUMES** • 1968
MARRIAGE OF THE SWALLOW, THE see **NOCES D'HIRONDELLE, LES** • 1968
MARRIAGE OF WILLIAM ASHE, THE • 1916 • Hepworth Cecil M. • UKN
MARRIAGE OF WILLIAM ASHE, THE • 1921 • Sloman Edward, Veiller Bayard (Spv) • USA
MARRIAGE ON APPROVAL • 1933 • Higgin Howard • USA • MARRIED IN HASTE (UKN)
MARRIAGE ON THE AIR see **GAWAZ ALAL HAWAA** • 1976
MARRIAGE ON THE ROCKS • 1965 • Donohue Jack • USA
MARRIAGE OR DEATH • 1912 • *Pathe* • USA
MARRIAGE PIT, THE • 1920 • Thompson Frederick A. • USA
MARRIAGE PLAYGROUND, THE • 1929 • Mendes Lothar • USA • CHILDREN, THE
MARRIAGE PRICE, THE • 1919 • Chautard Emile • USA
MARRIAGE RING, THE • 1918 • Niblo Fred • USA
MARRIAGE ROWS • 1931 • Arbuckle Roscoe • USA
MARRIAGE SPECULATION, THE • 1917 • Miller Ashley • USA
MARRIAGE SYMPHONY, THE (UKN) see **LET'S TRY AGAIN** • 1934
MARRIAGE, TEL AVIV STYLE • 1979 • Silberg Joel • ISR
MARRIAGE TIME see **KONKI** • 1961
MARRIAGE TRAP, THE see **YAGODKI LYUBVI** • 1926
MARRIAGE UNDER TERROR see **REVOLUTIONSBRYLLUP** • 1927
MARRIAGE VOW, THE • 1932 • Lamont Charles • SHT • USA
MARRIAGE VOWS • 1949 • Sparber I. • ANS • USA
MARRIAGE WAGER, THE • 1914 • *Ince John* • USA
MARRIAGE WAR, THE • 1932 • Lamont Charles • SHT • USA
MARRIAGE WHIRL, THE • 1925 • Santell Alfred • USA • MODERN MADNESS (UKN)
MARRIAGE WOWS • 1930 • Fleischer Dave • ANS • USA
MARRIAGE WRESTLER, THE see **AKTENSKAPSBROTTAREN** • 1964
MARRIAGE: YEAR ONE • 1971 • Graham William A. • TVM • USA • YEAR 1
MARRIAGEABLE AGE see **KONKI** • 1961
MARRIAGEABLE DAUGHTERS see **GIFTAS VUXNAR DOTTRAR** • 1933
MARRIAGES see **SPOSI** • 1988
MARRIAGES ARE MADE • 1918 • Harbaugh Carl • USA
MARRIED? • 1925 • Terwilliger George W. • USA
MARRIED A YEAR • 1916 • McDermott John • SHT • USA
MARRIED ALIVE • 1927 • Flynn Emmett J. • USA
MARRIED AND IN LOVE • 1940 • Farrow John • USA • DISTANT FIELDS
MARRIED AT LAST • 1913 • *B & C* • UKN
MARRIED BACHELOR • 1941 • Buzzell Edward • USA
MARRIED BEFORE BREAKFAST • 1937 • Marin Edwin L. • USA • YOU'LL BE MARRIED BY NOON
MARRIED BLISS • 1905 • Collins Alf • UKN
MARRIED BLISS see **TILL OUR SHIP COMES IN** • 1919
MARRIED BUT SINGLE • 1917 • Quirk William • SHT • USA
MARRIED BUT SINGLE (UKN) see **THIS THING CALLED LOVE** • 1940
MARRIED BY ACCIDENT • 1917 • Clements Roy • SHT • USA
MARRIED BY INSTALLMENT • 1915 • *Royal* • USA
MARRIED COUPLE see **ZUG NASSOUI** • 1983
MARRIED COUPLE, A • 1970 • King Allan • CND • COUPLE MARIE, UN
MARRIED FLAPPER, THE • 1922 • Paton Stuart • USA • NEVER MIND TOMORROW ○ THEY'RE OFF
MARRIED FLIRTS • 1924 • Vignola Robert G. • USA
MARRIED FOR LOVE • 1910 • Coleby A. E. • UKN
MARRIED FOR MILLIONS • 1906 • *Bitzer Billy (Ph)* • USA
MARRIED FOR MONEY • 1915 • Bary Leon • UKN
MARRIED IN DISGUISE • 1915 • *Farley Dot* • USA
MARRIED IN HASTE • 1910 • Fitzhamon Lewin • UKN
MARRIED IN HASTE • 1912 • Rains Fred • UKN
MARRIED IN HASTE • 1913 • *Eclair* • USA
MARRIED IN HASTE • 1919 • Rosson Arthur • USA
MARRIED IN HASTE see **JITNEY ELOPEMENT, A** • 1915
MARRIED IN HASTE (UKN) see **CONSOLATION MARRIAGE** • 1931
MARRIED IN HASTE (UKN) see **MARRIAGE ON APPROVAL** • 1933
MARRIED IN HOLLYWOOD • 1929 • Silver Marcel • USA
MARRIED IN NAME ONLY • 1917 • Lawrence Edmund • USA
MARRIED LADY BORROWS MONEY, A see **OKUSAMA SHAKUYOSHO** • 1936
MARRIED LIFE • 1920 • Kenton Erle C. • USA
MARRIED LIFE • 1921 • Treville Georges • UKN
MARRIED LIFE see **GIFTAS** • 1926
MARRIED LIFE see **KEKKON NO SEITAI** • 1941
MARRIED LIFE see **GIFTAS** • 1957
MARRIED LIFE, A see **MESHI** • 1951
MARRIED LIFE, THE SECOND YEAR • 1914 • Weston Charles • UKN
MARRIED LOVE • 1923 • Butler Alexander • UKN • MAISIE'S MARRIAGE
MARRIED MAN, A • 1982 • Jarrott Charles • MTV • UKN
MARRIED MEN • 1914 • *Lubin* • USA
MARRIED NEIGHBORS • 1925 • Lamont Charles • SHT • USA
MARRIED ON CREDIT • 1915 • *Ritchie Billie* • USA
MARRIED ON HORSEBACK • 1910 • *Bison* • USA
MARRIED ON THE WING • 1916 • Shields Ernest • SHT • USA
MARRIED ONES, THE • 1913 • Hertz Aleksander • PLN
MARRIED OR SINGLE • 1933 • Brice Monte • SHT • USA
MARRIED PEOPLE • 1922 • Ballin Hugo • USA
MARRIED TO A MORMON • 1922 • Parkinson H. B. • UKN
MARRIED TO THE MOB • 1988 • Demme Jonathan • USA
MARRIED TOO YOUNG • 1962 • Moskov George • USA • I MARRIED TOO YOUNG
MARRIED VIRGIN, THE • 1918 • Flynn Emmett J. • USA
MARRIED WOMAN, A see **FEMME MARIEE, UNE** • 1964
MARRIED WOMAN, THE see **FEMME MARIEE, UNE** • 1964
MARRIED WOMAN NEEDS A HUSBAND, A see **SENORA CASADA NECEISITA MARIDO** • 1935
MARRRIAGE ITALIAN STYLE (USA) see **MATRIMONIO ALL'ITALIANA** • 1964
MARRY A MILLIONAIRE see **ASU ENO SEISO** • 1959
MARRY-GO-ROUND • 1943 • Kneitel Seymour • ANS • USA
MARRY IN HASTE • 1924 • Worne Duke • USA
MARRY ME • 1925 • Cruze James • USA
MARRY ME • 1932 • Thiele Wilhelm • UKN, FRG
MARRY ME • 1949 • Fisher Terence • UKN • I WANT TO GET MARRIED
MARRY ME AGAIN • 1953 • Tashlin Frank • USA
MARRY ME! MARRY ME! (USA) see **MAZEL TOV OU LE MARIAGE** • 1968
MARRY MY WIFE • 1919 • Lyons Eddie, Moran Lee • SHT • USA
MARRY THE BOSS'S DAUGHTER • 1941 • Freeland Thornton • USA
MARRY THE GIRL • 1928 • Rosen Phil • USA • HOUSE OF DECEIT, THE (UKN)
MARRY THE GIRL • 1935 • Rogers Maclean • UKN
MARRY THE GIRL • 1937 • McGann William • USA
MARRY THE POOR GIRL • 1921 • Ingraham Lloyd • USA
MARRYIN' • 1920 • *Gibson Hoot* • SHT • USA
MARRYIN' MARION • 1920 • Russell Albert • SHT • USA
MARRYING GRETCHEN • 1914 • Duncan William • USA
MARRYING KIND, THE • 1952 • Cukor George • USA
MARRYING MAN, THE • 1990 • Rees Jerry • USA
MARRYING MARY (UKN) see **GETTING MARY MARRIED** • 1919
MARRYING MOLLY • 1919 • *Vernon Bobby* • USA
MARRYING MONEY • 1915 • Young James • USA • MARRIAGE A LA CARTE
MARRYING OFF DAD • 1918 • *Hampton Ruth* • SHT • USA
MARRYING SUE • 1914 • Johnson Tefft • USA
MARRYING UNDER DIFFICULTIES • 1908 • Fitzhamon Lewin? • UKN
MARRYING WIDOWS • 1934 • Newfield Sam • USA
MARS • 1908 • de Chomon Segundo • FRN
MARS • 1931 • Lantz Walter, Nolan William • ANS • USA
MARS AND BEYOND • 1967 • *Cbs/union Carbide* • USA
MARS AT EASTER see **NE JOUEZ PAS AVEC LES MARTIANS** • 1967
MARS ATTACKS THE WORLD • 1938 • Hill Robert F., Beebe Ford • USA • ROCKET SHIP (UKN) ○ DEADLY RAY FROM MARS, THE
MARS-AVRIL • 1944 • Pronin Vassily • USS
MARS CALLING see **RADIO-MANIA** • 1923
MARS EN CAREME see **NE JOUEZ PAS AVEC LES MARTIANS** • 1967
MARS, GOD OF WAR see **MARTE, DIO DELLA GUERRA** • 1962
MARS INVADES PUERTO RICO see **FRANKENSTEIN MEETS THE SPACE MONSTER** • 1965
MARS NA DRINU • 1964 • Mitrovic Zika • YGS • MARCH TO THE DRINA
MARS NEEDS WOMEN • 1968 • Buchanan Larry • USA
MARSCHALL VORWARTS • 1932 • Paul Heinz • FRG
MARSCHIER UND KREPIER • 1962 • Wisbar Frank • FRG, SPN, ITL • MARCIA O CREPA (ITL) ○ MARCIA O MUERE (SPN) ○ LEGION'S LAST PATROL, THE (UKN) ○ COMMANDO (USA) ○ SPRUNG IN DIE HOLLE ○ HEROS SANS RETOUR (FRN)
MARSE COVINGTON • 1915 • Carewe Edwin • USA
MARSEILLAISE, LA • 1912 • Cohl Emile • ANS • FRN
MARSEILLAISE, LA • 1937 • Renoir Jean • FRN • MARSEILLAISE, THE
MARSEILLAISE, LA see **CAPTAIN OF THE GUARD** • 1930
MARSEILLAISE, THE see **MARSEILLAISE, LA** • 1937
MARSEILLE CONTRACT, THE • 1974 • Parrish Robert • UKN, USA, FRN • MARSEILLE CONTRAT (FRN) ○ DESTRUCTORS, THE (USA) ○ THAT'S WHAT FRIENDS ARE FOR ○ WHAT ARE FRIENDS FOR?
MARSEILLE CONTRAT (FRN) see **MARSEILLE CONTRACT, THE** • 1974
MARSEILLE MES AMOURS • 1939 • Daniel-Norman Jacques • FRN
MARSEILLE, PREMIER PORT DE FRANCE • 1945 • Mineur Jean • SHT • FRN
MARSEILLES CONNECTION, THE • 1984 • Castellari Enzo G. • ITL
MARSHA see **MARSHA, THE EROTIC HOUSEWIFE** • 1970
MARSHA, THE EROTIC HOUSEWIFE • 1970 • Davis Don • USA • MARSHA
MARSHAL BRAVESTARR see **BRAVESTARR: THE LEGEND** • 1986
MARSHAL OF AMARILLO • 1948 • Ford Philip • USA
MARSHAL OF CEDAR ROCK • 1953 • Keller Harry • USA
MARSHAL OF CRIPPLE CREEK • 1947 • Springsteen R. G. • USA
MARSHAL OF GUNSMOKE • 1944 • Keays Vernon • USA
MARSHAL OF HELDORADO • 1950 • Carr Thomas • USA • BLAZING GUNS
MARSHAL OF LAREDO • 1945 • Springsteen R. G. • USA
MARSHAL OF MESA CITY, THE • 1939 • Howard David • USA
MARSHAL OF MONEYMINT, THE • 1922 • Clements Roy • USA
MARSHAL OF RENO • 1944 • Grissell Wallace A. • USA
MARSHAL TITO IN POLAND see **MARSZALEK TITO W POLSCE** • 1946
MARSHALL MCLUHAN • 1965 • Lavut Martin • CND
MARSHALL MCLUHAN • 1967 • Macartney-Filgate Terence • DOC • CND
MARSHALL'S CAPTURE, THE • 1913 • Duncan William • USA
MARSHALL'S DAUGHTER, THE • 1953 • Berke William • USA • MARSHAL'S DAUGHTER, THE
MARSHALL'S HONEYMOON, THE • 1912 • *Eclair* • USA
MARSHAL'S DAUGHTER, THE see **MARSHALL'S DAUGHTER, THE** • 1953
MARSHALS IN DISGUISE • 1954 • McDonald Frank • MTV • USA
MARSHMALLOW MOON (UKN) see **AARON SLICK FROM PUNKIN CRICK** • 1951
MARSIEN, LE • 1970 • Sauve Alain • CND
MARSUPIALS: THE HOWLING 3, THE see **HOWLING III, THE** • 1987
MARSYAS • 1962 • Gassan Arnold • SHT • USA
MARSZALEK TITO W POLSCE • 1946 • Bossak Jerzy • DOC • PLN • MARSHAL TITO IN POLAND
MARTA • 1913 • Curtiz Michael • HNG
MARTA • 1954 • Elias Francisco • SPN
MARTA • 1971 • Nieves Conde Jose Antonio • SPN, ITL • BLOODBATH
MARTA OF THE JUNGLE • 1916 • Davis Ulysses • SHT • USA
MARTA OF THE LOWLANDS • 1914 • Dawley J. Searle • USA
MARTE, DIO DELLA GUERRA • 1962 • Baldi Marcello • ITL • VENUS AGAINST THE SON OF HERCULES (USA) ○ MARS, GOD OF WAR
MARTE INVADE A PUERTO RICO see **FRANKENSTEIN MEETS THE SPACE MONSTER** • 1965
MARTEAU-PIQUEUR, LE • 1981 • Bitsch Charles L. • FRN
MARTER DER LIEBE • 1928 • Gallone Carmine • FRG • LOVE'S CRUCIFIXION
MARTES 13 • 1952 • Diaz Morales Jose • MXC
MARTES Y TRECE • 1961 • Lazaga Pedro • SPN
MARTHA • 1916 • Schonwald Gustav • FRG
MARTHA • 1922 • Wynn George • UKN
MARTHA • 1923 • Disney Walt • ANS • USA
MARTHA • 1927 • Parkinson H. B. • UKN
MARTHA • 1935 • Anton Karl • FRG • LETZTE ROSE
MARTHA • 1935 • Anton Karl • FRN • DERNIERES ROSES, LES
MARTHA • 1967 • Balling Erik • DNM
MARTHA • 1974 • Fassbinder R. W. • FRG
MARTHA DUBRONSKY • 1984 • Kuert Beat • SWT
MARTHA JELLNECK • 1989 • Wessel Kai • FRG
MARTHA, RUTH AND EDIE • 1988 • Bailey Norma, Suissa Daniele J., Saltzman Deepa Mehta • CND
MARTHA'S DECISION • 1913 • *American* • USA
MARTHA'S REBELLION • 1912 • Trimble Larry • USA
MARTHA'S REBELLION • 1914 • Miller Ashley • USA
MARTHA'S ROMANCE see **MARTHA'S ROMEO** • 1915
MARTHA'S ROMEO • 1915 • Ransom Charles • USA • MARTHA'S ROMANCE
MARTHA'S VINDICATION • 1916 • Franklin Sidney A., Franklin Chester M. • USA • SILENCE OF MARTHA, THE
MARTHE RICHARD AU SERVICE DE LA FRANCE • 1937 • Bernard Raymond • FRN • MARTHE RICHARD ESPIONNE AU SERVICE DE LA FRANCE
MARTHE RICHARD ESPIONNE AU SERVICE DE LA FRANCE see **MARTHE RICHARD AU SERVICE DE LA FRANCE** • 1937
MARTHYRER SEINES HERZENS • 1918 • Justitz Emil • AUS • BEETHOVENS LEBENSROMAN
MARTIAL DANCES OF MALABAR • 1957 • Zils Paul • IND
MARTIAL HERO, THE • Le Cho Kwan • HKG

MARTIAL MONKS OF SHAOLIN • 1983 • Ho Godfrey • HKG • MARTIAL MONKS OF SHAOLIN TEMPLE
MARTIAL MONKS OF SHAOLIN TEMPLE see **MARTIAL MONKS OF SHAOLIN** • 1983
MARTIAN ARRIVES ON AN AUTUMN NIGHT, A see **PRILETEL MARSIANIN V OSENNUYU NOCH** • 1980
MARTIAN CHRONICLES, THE • 1979 • Anderson Michael • TVM • USA
MARTIAN IN MOSCOW • 1964 • Halas John • ASS • UKN
MARTIAN IN PARIS, A see **MARTIEN A PARIS, UN** • 1960
MARTIAN MAGOO • 1960 • *Upa* • ANS • USA
MARTIAN SPACE PARTY • 1972 • *Ossman David* • SHT • USA
MARTIAN THRU GEORGIA • 1962 • Jones Charles M. • ANS • USA
MARTIANS • 1989 • Johnson Patrick Read • USA
MARTIANS, THE see **DISCO VOLANTE, IL** • 1964
MARTIANS ARRIVED, THE see **MARZIANI HANNO DODICI MANI, I** • 1964
MARTIANS COME BACK • 1956 • Pintoff Ernest • ANS • USA
MARTIANS GO HOME • 1988 • Odell David • USA
MARTIANS HAVE TWELVE HANDS see **MARZIANI HANNO DODICI MANI, I** • 1964
MARTIEN A PARIS, UN • 1960 • Daninos Jean-Daniel • FRN • MARTIAN IN PARIS, A
MARTIEN DE NOEL, LE • 1970 • Gosselin Bernard • CND • CHRISTMAS MARTIAN, THE (USA)
MARTIN • 1978 • Romero George A. • USA
MARTIN • 1980 • Risan Leidulv • NRW • HENRETTELSEN ○ EXECUTION, THE
MARTIN • 1989 • Axel Gabriel • DNM
MARTIN AGRIPPA • 1969 • Beresford Bruce • DCS • UKN
MARTIN AND GASTON see **MARTIN ET GASTON** • 1950
MARTIN ANDERSEN NEXOS SIDSTE REJSE • 1954 • Roos Jorgen • DOC • DNM
MARTIN CHUZZLEWIT • 1912 • Apfel Oscar, Dawley J. Searle • USA
MARTIN CHUZZLEWIT • 1914 • Vale Travers • USA
MARTIN CUCKOO see **KAKUK MARCI** • 1973
MARTIN, DER FINDLING see **MEMOIREN EINES KAMMERDIENERS 1** • 1921
MARTIN EDEN • 1914 • Bosworth Hobart • USA
MARTIN EDEN see **ADVENTURES OF MARTIN EDEN, THE** • 1942
MARTIN ET GASTON • 1950 • Gruel Henri • SHT • FRN • MARTIN AND GASTON
MARTIN ET LEA • 1978 • Cavalier Alain • FRN
MARTIN FIERRO • 1968 • Torre-Nilsson Leopoldo • ARG
MARTIN FIERRO • 1989 • Laverde Fernando • CLM, ARG, CUB
MARTIN GARATUZA • 1935 • Soria Gabriel • MXC
MARTIN IN THE CLOUDS see **MARTIN U OBLACIMA** • 1960
MARTIN JOHNSON'S JUNGLE ADVENTURES see **JUNGLE ADVENTURES** • 1921
MARTIN JONAS • 1974 • Slivka Martin • CZC
MARTIN –KVA BETYR "HINRICHTEN"? • 1980 • Risan Leidulv • NRW • MARTIN –WHAT DOES "HINRICHTEN" MEAN?
MARTIN LOWE, FINANCIER • 1915 • Lloyd Frank • USA
MARTIN LOWE, FIXER • 1915 • Lloyd Frank • USA
MARTIN LUTHER • 1923 • Wustenhagen Karl • FRG
MARTIN LUTHER • 1953 • Pichel Irving • USA
MARTIN LUTHER, HIS LIFE AND TIME • 1924 • *Lutheran Film Division* • USA
MARTIN MAKES IT TO THE TOP see **MARTIN NA VRHU** • 1969
MARTIN NA VRHU • 1969 • Grgic Zlatko • ANS • YGS • MARTIN MAKES IT TO THE TOP
MARTIN OF THE MOUNTED • 1926 • Wyler William • SHT • USA
MARTIN ROME see **CRY OF THE CITY** • 1948
MARTIN ROMERO EL RAPIDO see **RAPIDO, EL** • 1964
MARTIN ROUMAGNAC • 1946 • Lacombe Georges • FRN • ROOM UPSTAIRS, THE (USA)
MARTIN SANTOS, EL LLANERO • 1960 • de la Serna Mauricio • MXC
MARTIN SOLDAT • 1966 • Deville Michel • FRN • KISS ME GENERAL (UKN)
MARTIN SPEAKING see **RING UP MARTIN 224466** • 1966
MARTIN THE COBBLER • 1976 • Vinton Will • ANS • USA
MARTIN TOCCAFERRO • 1954 • De Mitri Leonardo • ITL
MARTIN U OBLACIMA • 1960 • Bauer Branko • YGS • MARTIN IN THE CLOUDS
MARTIN –WHAT DOES "HINRICHTEN" MEAN? see **MARTIN –KVA BETYR "HINRICHTEN"?** • 1980
MARTINA • 1949 • Rabenalt Arthur M. • FRG
MARTINA, LA • 1971 • *Peliculas Rodriguez* • MXC
MARTINACHE MARRIAGE, THE • 1917 • Bracken Bertram • USA
MARTINE ET LE CID • 1977 • Koleva Maria • DCS • FRN
MARTINI AND HIS BAND NO.1 • 1930 • *Balcon Michael (P)* • SHT • UKN
MARTINI AND HIS BAND NO.2 • 1930 • *Balcon Michael (P)* • SHT • UKN
MARTINS AND THE COYS, THE • 1946 • Kinney Jack • ANS • USA
MARTIN'S DAY • 1984 • Gibson Alan • CND
MARTINSKLAUSE • 1951 • Haussler Richard • FRG
MARTIR DEL CALVARIO, EL • 1952 • Morayta Miguel • MXC
MARTIRI D'ITALIA, I • 1927 • Rosa Silvio Laurenti • ITL
MARTIRIO DI S. STEFANO • 1912 • *Latium* • ITL • MARTYR OF ST. STEFANO, THE
MARTY • 1955 • Mann Delbert • USA
MARTYR, THE • 1911 • Porter Edwin S. • USA
MARTYR, THE • 1963 • Tomita Kasuhiro • SHT • JPN
MARTYR, THE see **MARTYRER –DR. KORCZAK UND SEINE KINDER, DER** • 1974
MARTYR DE BOUGIVAL, LE • 1949 • Loubignac Jean • FRN
MARTYR OF ST. STEFANO, THE see **MARTIRIO DI S. STEFANO** • 1912
MARTYR OF THE PRESENT, A • 1915 • Ayres Sydney • USA
MARTYR OR CRANK? • 1909 • *Lubin* • USA
MARTYR SEX, THE • 1924 • Worne Duke • USA
MARTYRDOM OF ADOLF BECK, THE • 1909 • Sims George R. • UKN
MARTYRDOM OF NURSE CAVELL, THE • 1916 • Mason C. Post, Gavin John F. • ASL
MARTYRDOM OF PHILIP STRONG, THE see **MARTYRDOM OF PHILLIP STRONG, THE** • 1916
MARTYRDOM OF PHILLIP STRONG, THE • 1916 • Ridgely Richard • USA • MARTYRDOM OF PHILIP STRONG, THE
MARTYRDOM OF THOMAS A BECKET, THE • 1908 • Stow Percy • UKN
MARTYRE • 1926 • Burguet Charles • FRN
MARTYRE DE L'OBESE, LE • 1932 • Chenal Pierre • FRN
MARTYRE DE SAINT ETIENNE, LE • 1912 • Andreani Henri • FRN
MARTYRED PRESIDENTS • 1901 • Porter Edwin S. • USA
MARTYRER –DR. KORCZAK UND SEINE KINDER, DER • 1974 • Ford Aleksander • FRG, ISR • MARTYRS –DR. KORCZAK AND HIS CHILDREN ○ MARTYR, THE ○ SIE SIND FREI, DR. KORCZAK
MARTYRERIN DER LIEBE • 1915 • Biebrach Rudolf • FRG
MARTYRIUM, DAS • 1920 • Stein Paul L. • FRG
MARTYRS –DR. KORCZAK AND HIS CHILDREN see **MARTYRER –DR. KORCZAK UND SEINE KINDER, DER** • 1974
MARTYRS OF LOVE see **MUCEDNICI LASKY** • 1966
MARTYRS OF THE ALAMO, THE • 1915 • Cabanne W. Christy • USA
MARTYRS OF YESTERDAY see **IN THE LAND OF THE SETTING SUN** • 1919
MARUHI TORUKO BURO • 1968 • Murayama Shinji • JPN • SECRET TURKISH BATH
MARUJA • 1967 • de Guzman Armando • PHL
MARUJA see **GRAY WOLF'S GHOST, THE** • 1919
MARUJA EN EL INFIERNO • 1983 • Lombardi Francisco • PRU
MARUSA NO ONNA • 1987 • Itami Juzo • JPN • WOMAN PROSECUTED FOR TAX EVASION, A ○ TAXING WOMAN, A
MARUSA NO ONNA 2 • 1988 • Itami Juzo • JPN • TAXING WOMAN PART II, A
MARUSIA • 1938 • Bulgakov Leo • USA
MARUTHANAD ELAVARSEE • 1950 • Kashilingam G. • IND
MARUZZELLA • 1956 • Capuano Luigi • ITL
MARVA COLLINS STORY, THE • 1981 • Levin Peter • TVM • USA
MARVADA CARNE • 1986 • Klotzel Andre • BRZ • STRONG MEAT
MARVELLLOUS CURE, A see **VIDUNDERLIGE HAARELIXIR, DEN** • 1909
MARVELLOUS CAPILLARY ELIXER • 1901 • Williamson James • UKN
MARVELLOUS EGG PRODUCING WITH SURPRISING DEVELOPMENTS see **DANSEUSE MICROSCOPIQUE, LA** • 1902
MARVELLOUS FLUID • 1909 • *Lobel Leopold* • FRN
MARVELLOUS HAIR RESTORER, THE • 1901 • Williamson James • UKN
MARVELLOUS HARTLEY BARREL JUMPERS, THE • 1903 • *Urban Trading Co* • UKN
MARVELLOUS HOOP, THE see **GUIRLANDE MERVEILLEUSE, LA** • 1903
MARVELLOUS INVENTION, A • 1911 • *Gaumont* • FRN
MARVELLOUS KARLSSON see **ALLA TIDERS KARLSSON** • 1936
MARVELLOUS KUNG FU • Chin Sheng-En • HKG • MARVELLOUS STUNTS OF KUNG FU
MARVELLOUS LAND OF OZ, THE • 1982 • *Children'S Theatre Od Minneapolis* • USA
MARVELLOUS MELBOURNE • 1910 • *Spencer C. (P)* • ASL
MARVELLOUS SNAKE-MAN, THE • 1988 • Loon Ti • KMP
MARVELLOUS STUNTS OF KUNG FU see **MARVELLOUS KUNG FU**
MARVELLOUS SYRINGE, THE • 1903 • Collins Alf? • UKN
MARVELLOUS WREATH, THE (USA) see **GUIRLANDE MERVEILLEUSE, LA** • 1903
MARVELOUS COW, THE • 1911 • *Solax* • USA
MARVELOUS CURE, A • *Nordisk* • DNM
MARVELOUS FOUNTAIN, THE see **FONTAINE MERVEILLEUSE, LA** • 1908
MARVELOUS HIND LEG, THE see **GIGUE MERVEILLEUSE, LA** • 1909
MARVELOUS HIVE, THE see **RUCHE MERVEILLEUSE, LA** • 1905
MARVELOUS INVENTION, A • 1911 • *Gaumont* • FRN
MARVELOUS JOURNEY OF NILS HOLGERSSON, THE see **NILS HOLGERSSONS UNDERBARA RESA** • 1962
MARVELOUS MACISTE, THE • 1915 • *Pagano Ernesto* • ITL • MACISTE MAGNIFICENT
MARVELOUS MARATHONER, A • 1915 • *Marshall Boyd* • USA
MARVELOUS PEARL, THE • 1909 • *Cines* • ITL
MARVELOUS SUSPENSION AND EVOLUTION (USA) see **FEMME VOLANTE, LA** • 1902
MARVELOUS TRANSFORMATIONS • 1911 • *Pathe* • FRN
MARVELOUS VISION OF JOAN OF ARC, THE (USA) see **MERVEILLEUSE VUE DE JEAN D'ARC, LA**
MARVELS OF SKI see **WUNDER DES SCHNEESCHUHS 1, DIE** • 1920
MARVELS OF THE BULL RING (USA) see **MARAVILLA DEL TOREO** • 1942
MARVELS OF VENEZUELA see **MARAVILLAS DE VENEZUELA** • 1973
MARVIN AND TIGE • 1982 • Weston Eric • USA • LIKE FATHER AND SON ○ LIKE FATHER LIKE SON
MARVIN DIGS • 1967 • Bakshi Ralph • ANS • USA
MARVO MOVIE • 1968 • Keen Jeff • USA
MARX BROTHERS AT THE CIRCUS see **AT THE CIRCUS** • 1939
MARX BROTHERS GO WEST, THE (UKN) see **GO WEST** • 1940
MARX FOR BEGINNERS • 1978 • Godfrey Bob (c/d) • ANS • UKN
MARXISM • 1969 • Kaczender George • DOC • CND
MARY • 1909 • *Warwick Trading Co* • UKN
MARY • 1915 • West Langdon • USA
MARY • 1931 • Hitchcock Alfred • FRG • SIR JOHN GREIFT EIN!
MARY see **MURDER** • 1930
MARY, LA • 1974 • Tinayre Daniel • ARG
MARY AND JOSEPH see **MARY AND JOSEPH: A STORY OF FAITH** • 1979
MARY AND JOSEPH: A STORY OF FAITH • 1979 • Till Eric • TVM • USA • MARY AND JOSEPH
MARY AND JULIE see **OK KETTEN** • 1977
MARY AND NAPOLEON see **MARYSIA I NAPOLEON** • 1966
MARY ANN • 1918 • Korda Alexander • HNG
MARY ANN IN SOCIETY • 1917 • Stonehouse Ruth • SHT • USA
MARY BLOODY MARY • 1973 • Moctezuma Juan Lopez • MXC • MARY, MARY, BLOODY MARY
MARY BURNS, FUGITIVE • 1935 • Howard William K. • USA
MARY CARY see **NOBODY'S KID** • 1921
MARY ELLEN COMES TO TOWN • 1920 • Clifton Elmer • USA
MARY-FIND-THE-GOLD • 1921 • Pearson George • UKN • MARY FIND THE GOLD
MARY FIND THE GOLD see **MARY-FIND-THE-GOLD** • 1921
MARY FROM AMERICA • 1917 • Gerrard Douglas • SHT • USA
MARY GIRL • 1917 • Elvey Maurice • UKN
MARY GREEN'S HUSBAND • 1914 • *Universal* • USA
MARY 'GUSTA see **PETTICOAT PILOT, A** • 1918
MARY HAD A LITTLE.. • 1961 • Buzzell Edward • UKN
MARY HAD A LOVELY VOICE • 1910 • Stow Percy • UKN
MARY HAS HER WAY • 1912 • Plumb Hay? • UKN
MARY IS DRY • 1905 • Haggar William • UKN
MARY JANE ENTERTAINS • 1914 • Baker George D. • USA
MARY JANE HARPER CRIED LAST NIGHT • 1977 • Reisner Allen • TVM • USA
MARY JANE'S LOVERS • 1909 • Porter Edwin S. • USA
MARY JANE'S LOVES • 1909 • Fitzhamon Lewin? • UKN
MARY JANE'S MISHAP: OR, DON'T FOOL WITH THE PARAFFIN • 1903 • Smith G. A. • UKN
MARY JANE'S PA • 1917 • Earle William P. S. • USA
MARY JANE'S PA • 1935 • Keighley William • USA • WANDERLUST (UKN)
MARY, KEEP YOUR FEET STILL • 1916 • Conway Jack • USA
MARY LATIMER, NUN • 1920 • Haldane Bert • UKN
MARY LAWSON'S SECRET • 1917 • O'Brien John B. • USA
MARY LOU • 1928 • Zelnik Friedrich • FRG
MARY LOU • 1948 • Dreifuss Arthur • USA
MARY MAGDALENE • 1914 • *Kennedy Features* • USA
MARY MAGDALENE see **SPADA E LA CROCE, LA** • 1959
MARY MAKE BELIEVE • 1916 • *Unicorn* • USA
MARY, MARY • 1963 • LeRoy Mervyn • USA
MARY, MARY • 1976 • Morris Bernhard • USA
MARY, MARY, BLOODY MARY see **MARY BLOODY MARY** • 1973
MARY MORELAND • 1917 • Powell Frank • USA
MARY MOVES IN • 1919 • Christie Al • SHT • USA
MARY NAMES THE DAY (UKN) see **DR. KILDARE'S WEDDING DAY** • 1941
MARY OF BRIARWOOD DELL • 1913 • Haldane Bert? • UKN
MARY OF SCOTLAND • 1936 • Ford John • USA
MARY OF THE MINES • 1912 • Morty Frank, Balshofer Fred J. • USA
MARY OF THE MOVIES • 1923 • McDermott John • USA
MARY O'ROURKE see **BACHELOR'S WIFE, A** • 1919
MARY PICKFORD'S KISS see **POTSELUI MERI PIKFORD** • 1927
MARY POPPINS • 1964 • Stevenson Robert • USA
MARY QUEEN OF SCOTS • 1922 • Greenwood Edwin • UKN
MARY, QUEEN OF SCOTS • 1971 • Jarrott Charles • UKN, USA
MARY, QUEEN OF TOTS • 1925 • Roach Hal • SHT • USA
MARY REGAN • 1919 • Weber Lois • USA
MARY RYAN, DETECTIVE • 1949 • Berlin Abby • USA
MARY SAVES THE SCULPTOR • 1913 • *Gaumont* • USA
MARY STEVENS, M.D. • 1933 • Bacon Lloyd • USA
MARY STUART • 1913 • Dawley J. Searle • USA
MARY THE COSTER • 1910 • Fitzhamon Lewin • UKN
MARY THE FISHERGIRL • 1914 • Northcote Sidney • UKN
MARY THE FLOWER GIRL • 1913 • Coleby A. E.? • UKN
MARY WAS A HOUSEMAID • 1910 • Stow Percy • UKN
MARY WAS LOVE see **THOSE WHO LOVE** • 1929
MARY WHITE • 1977 • Taylor Jud • TVM • USA
MARY WOOD, DIE TOCHTER DES STRAFLINGS • 1919 • Molter Ernst • FRG
MARYA-ISKUSNITSA • 1960 • Rou Aleksandr • USS • MARIA THE WONDERFUL WEAVER ○ MAGIC WEAVER, THE (USA) ○ MARIA, THE MAGIC WEAVER
MARYA SKLODOWSKA-CURIE. EIN MADCHEN, DAS DIE WELT VERANDERT • 1972 • Staudte Wolfgang • MTV • FRG
MARYJANE • 1968 • Dexter Maury • USA
MARYJKA • 1934 • Nowina-Przybylski Jan • PLN
MARYLAND • 1940 • King Henry • USA
MARYLAND 1777 • 1909 • *Centaur Film* • USA
MARYLEE MIXES IN • 1918 • Ensminger Robert • USA
MARY'S ANKLE • 1920 • Ingraham Lloyd • USA
MARY'S BIRTHDAY • 1949 • Reiniger Lotte • ANS • UKN
MARY'S BOOMERANG • 1917 • *Rhodes Billie* • SHT • USA
MARY'S CHAUFFEUR • 1912 • *Trunnelle Mabel* • USA
MARY'S CONVERT • 1914 • *Imp* • USA
MARY'S DUKE • 1915 • Henderson Lucius • USA
MARY'S FRAME-UP • 1918 • *Rhodes Billie* • USA
MARY'S GOAT • 1912 • *Thanhouser* • USA
MARYS GROSSES GEHEIMNIS • 1928 • Brignone Guido • FRG • MRS. BROWN FROM CHICAGO
MARY'S LAMB • 1915 • Mackenzie Donald • USA
MARY'S LITTLE LAMB • 1935 • *Iwerks Ub (P)* • ANS • USA
MARY'S LITTLE LOBSTER • 1920 • Cline Eddie • SHT • USA
MARY'S MAMMY • 1929 • Aylott Dave, Symmons E. F. • SHT • UKN
MARY'S MASQUERADE • 1911 • Merwin Bannister • USA
MARY'S MERRY MIXUP • 1917 • *Rhodes Billie* • SHT • USA
MARY'S MISTAKE • 1916 • *Gayety* • USA
MARY'S NEW BLOUSE • 1914 • Batley Ethyle? • UKN
MARY'S NEW HAT • 1913 • France Charles H. • USA
MARY'S NIGHTMARE • 1920 • *Christie* • SHT • USA
MARY'S PATIENTS • 1914 • *Imp* • USA
MARY'S POLICEMAN • 1912 • Wilson Frank? • UKN
MARY'S ROMANCE • 1913 • Smalley Phillips • USA
MARYS START IN DIE EHE see **ICH BLEIB' BEI DIR** • 1931
MARY'S STRATAGEM • 1911 • Melies Gaston • USA
MARY'S TEMPTATION • 1913 • O'Neil Barry • USA
MARY'S WORK • 1921 • Paul Fred, Raymond Jack • UKN
MARYSA • 1935 • Rovensky Josef • CZC
MARYSE • 1917 • de Morlhon Camille • FRN
MARYSIA I KRASNOLUDKI • 1961 • Szeski Jerzy, Paradowski Konrad • PLN • ORPHAN MARY AND THE DWARFS

MARYSIA I NAPOLEON • 1966 • Buczkowski Leonard • PLN • MARIA AND NAPOLEON ○ MARY AND NAPOLEON
MARYSKA AND THE WOLF'S CASTLE see **O MARYSCE A VLCIM HRADKU** • 1980
MARZIANI HANNO DODICI MANI, I • 1964 • Castellano, Pipolo • ITL, SPN • LLEGARON LOS MARCIANOS (SPN) ○ SIAMO QUATTRO MARZIANI ○ TWELVE HANDED MEN OF MARS, THE ○ MARTIANS ARRIVED, THE ○ MARTIANS HAVE TWELVE HANDS
MARZIANO A ROMA • 1979 • Pingitore Pier Francesco • ITL
MARZIPAN OF THE SHAPES • 1920 • Hunter A. C. • UKN
MAS ALLA DE LA AVENTURA • 1980 • Finn Oscar Barney • ARG • BEYOND ADVENTURE
MAS ALLA DE LA MUERTE • 1935 • Peon Ramon • MXC
MAS ALLA DE LAS MONTANAS • 1967 • Ramati Alexander • SPN, USA • DESPERATE ONES, THE (USA) ○ BEYOND THE MOUNTAINS
MAS ALLA DE ORINOCO see **HOMBRE DE LA FURIA, EL** • 1965
MAS ALLA DEL AMOR • 1944 • Fernandez Bustamente Adolfo • MXC
MAS ALLA DEL CUYUNI • 1977 • Odreman Mauricio • VNZ • ON THE OTHER SIDE OF CUYUNI
MAS ALLA DEL DESEO • 1976 • Nieves Conde Jose Antonio • SPN
MAS ALLA DEL OLVIDO • 1956 • del Carril Hugo • ARG
MAS ALLA DEL RIO MINO • 1969 • Torrado Ramon • SPN
MAS ALLA DEL SEXO • 1967 • Plasencia Arturo • VNZ • BEYOND SEX
MAS ALLA DEL SILENCIO • Bolivar Cesar • VNZ • BEYOND SILENCE
MAS ALLA DEL SOL • 1975 • Fregonese Hugo • ARG • BEYOND THE SUN
MA'S APRON STRINGS • 1913 • Thompson Frederick A. • USA
MAS BONITA QUE NINGUNA • 1964 • Amadori Luis Cesar • SPN
MAS CERCA DE TI see **CUBA NO KOIBITO** • 1970
MAS FABULOSO GOLPE DE FAR-WEST, EL • 1971 • de la Loma Jose Antonio • SPN, ITL, FRN • BOLDEST JOB IN THE WEST, THE
MAS FINA QUE LAS GALLINAS • 1976 • Yague Jesus • SPN
MAS FUERTE QUE EL AMOR • 1953 • Demicheli Tulio • MXC, CUB
MAS FUERTE QUE EL DEBER • 1930 • Sevilla Raphael J. • MXC
MA'S GIRLS • 1915 • Mix Tom • USA
MAS MERAH • Ghosh Dhiresh • MLY
MAS NEGRO QUE LA NOCHE • 1974 • *Conacine* • MXC
MASACRE • 1972 • *Churubusco Azteca* • MXC
MASACRE • 1978 • Lugo Alfredo • VNZ, ITL • MASSACRE
MASADA • 1980 • Sagal Boris • TVM • USA • ANTAGONISTS, THE (UKN)
MASAJISTA DE SENORAS • 1971 • *Prod. Film Re-Al* • MXC
MAS'ALA AL KUBRA, AL • 1983 • Jamil Mohammed Shoukry • IRQ • CLASHING LOYALTIES
MASAMOD • 1920 • *Lukas Paul* • HNG
MASCAGNI see **MELODIE IMMORTALI** • 1953
MASCAMOR • 1918 • Marodon Pierre • FRN
MASCAMOR • 1923 • Raulet Georges • ITL
MASCARA • 1987 • Conrad Patrick • BLG
MASCARA, LA • 1977 • Iquino Ignacio F. • SPN
MASCARA DE CARNE, LA • 1956 • de Anda Raul • MXC
MASCARA DE HIERRO, LA • 1959 • Rodriguez Joselito • MXC
MASCARA DE JADE, LA • 1962 • Martinez Arturo • MXC
MASCARA DE LA MUERTE, LA • 1960 • Gomez Urquiza Zacarias • MXC • MASK OF DEATH, THE
MASCARA DE SCARAMOUCHE, LA (SPN) see **SCARAMOUCHE** • 1963
MASCARA ROJO, LA • 1960 • Peon Ramon • MXC
MASCARADE • 1980-84 • Hoedeman Co • ANS • CND • MASQUERADE
MASCARAS DEL ENEMIGO, LAS • 1975 • Sanjines Jorge • BLV
MASCHENKA • 1987 • Goldschmidt John • UKN
MASCHERA, LA • 1988 • Infascelli Fiorella • ITL • MASK, THE
MASCHERA DEL DEMONIO, LA • 1960 • Bava Mario • ITL, FRG • STUNDE WENN DRAKULA KOMMT, DIE (FRG) ○ REVENGE OF THE VAMPIRE (UKN) ○ BLACK SUNDAY (USA) ○ MASK OF THE DEMON ○ HOUSE OF FRIGHT ○ DEMON'S MASK, THE
MASCHERA DI CESARE BORGIA, LA • 1941 • Coletti Duilio • ITL • AI TEMPI DI CESARE BORGIA
MASCHERA DI MISTERO • 1916 • Caserini Mario • ITL • MASK OF MYSTERY
MASCHERA E IL VOLTO, LA • 1919 • Genina Augusto • ITL
MASCHERA E IL VOLTO, LA • 1942 • Mastrocinque Camillo • ITL
MASCHERA NERA • 1952 • Ratti Filippo M. • ITL
MASCHERA SUL CUORE, LA (ITL) see **CAPITAINE FRACASSE, LE** • 1942
MASCHERE BIANCHE • 1921 • Ghione Emilio • ITL
MASCHERE E LA VITA, LE • 1950 • Gattinara Carlo Castelli • ITL
MASCHERO DI FERRO, LA • 1909 • Pastrone Giovanni • ITL
MASCHI E FEMMINE • 1972 • Caminito Augusto, Scardamaglia Francesco • ITL
MASCHIACCIO • 1917 • Genina Augusto • ITL
MASCHINE, DIE • 1966 • Urchs Wolfgang • ANS • FRG • MACHINES (USA)
MASCHINO, FEMMINA, FIORE, FRUTTO • 1979 • Mitti Ruggero • ITL
MASCHIO LATINO.. CERCASI • 1977 • Narzisi Gianni • ITL
MASCHIO RUSPANTE, IL • 1972 • Racioppi Antonio • ITL
MASCOT see **KABALA** • 1982
MASCOT, THE • 1934 • Starevitch Ladislas • ANS • FRN
MASCOT, THE see **MASCOTTE** • 1930
MASCOT OF COMPANY D, THE • 1910 • *Bison* • USA
MASCOT OF TROOP C, THE • 1911 • Blache Alice • USA
MASCOTS, THE • 1898 • *Chard'S Vitagraph* • UKN
MASCOTTCHEN • 1929 • Basch Felix • FRG
MASCOTTE • 1920 • Basch Felix • FRG
MASCOTTE • 1930 • Ford Aleksander • PLN • MASCOT, THE
MASCOTTE, LA • 1935 • Mathot Leon • FRN
MASCOTTE, UNE • 1917 • de Baroncelli Jacques • FRN
MASCOTTE DEI DIAVOLI BLU, LA • 1948 • Baltieri C. A. • ITL
MASCULIN-FEMININ • 1966 • Godard Jean-Luc • FRN, SWD • MASKULINUM-FEMININUM (SWD) ○ MASCULINE-FEMININE ○ MASCULIN-FEMININ 15 FAITS PRECIS
MASCULIN-FEMININ 15 FAITS PRECIS see **MASCULIN-FEMININ** • 1966
MASCULINE-FEMININE see **MASCULIN-FEMININ** • 1966
MASCULINE MYSTIQUE, THE • 1984 • Walker Giles • CND
MASELLA, LES see **VIVRE EN MUSIQUE** • 1965
M*A*S*H • 1970 • Altman Robert • USA
M*A*S*H: GOODBYE, FAREWELL, AMEN • 1983 • Alda Alan • TVM • USA
MASHAL • 1950 • *Burman S. D. (M)* • IND
MASH'D • 1977 • Smith Emton • USA
MASHENKA • 1942 • Raizman Yuli • USS
MASHER, THE • 1910 • Sennett Mack • USA
MASHER AND THE NURSEMAID, THE • 1905 • Mottershaw Frank • UKN
MASHER COP, THE • 1913 • Henderson Dell • USA
MASHERS, THE • 1914 • Smalley Phillips • USA
MASHERS AND SPLASHERS • 1915 • Burstein Louis • USA
MASHER'S DILEMMA, THE • 1904 • Collins Alf? • UKN
MASHER'S MISHAP, THE • 1914 • *Eclectic* • USA
MASHO NO HADA see **NEMURI KYOSHIRO BURAIHIKAE: MASHO NO HADA** • 1967
MASHO NO NATSU • 1981 • Ninagawa Yukio • JPN • DEVIL'S SUMMER
MASHO NO ONNA • 1968 • Yanase Kan • JPN • WOMAN OF ILL REPUTE, A
MASIRAH AL-QHADRAA, AL- • 1975 • Ben Baraka Sohail • SHT • MRC
MASK • 1981 • Rimoch Ernesto • UKN
MASK • 1984 • Bogdanovich Peter • USA
MASK, THE • 1913 • *Rex* • USA
MASK, THE • 1918 • Heffron Thomas N. • USA • MASK OF RICHES
MASK, THE • 1921 • Bracken Bertram • USA
MASK, THE • 1953 • Chaffey Don • UKN
MASK, THE • 1961 • Roffman Julian • USA, CND • EYES OF HELL, THE (UKN) ○ SPOOKY MOVIE SHOW, THE
MASK, THE see **MASCHERA, LA** • 1988
MASK-A-RAID • 1931 • Fleischer Dave • ANS • USA
MASK, A RING, A PAIR OF HANDCUFFS, A • 1915 • French Charles K. • USA
MASK AND DESTINY, THE see **SHUZENJI MONOGATARI** • 1955
MASK AND DRUM • 1974 • Nichol Robert L. • MTV • CND
MASK AND THE SWORD, THE see **SINGOALLA** • 1949
MASK K' POPS • 1967 • Wenceslao Jose Pepe • PHL
MASK OF COMEDY, THE see **UPSTAGE** • 1926
MASK OF DEATH, THE see **MASCARA DE LA MUERTE, LA** • 1960
MASK OF DESTINY, THE (USA) see **SHUZENJI MONOGATARI** • 1955
MASK OF DIJON, THE • 1946 • Landers Lew • USA
MASK OF DIMITRIOS, THE • 1944 • Negulesco Jean • USA
MASK OF DUST • 1954 • Fisher Terence • UKN • RACE FOR LIFE (USA)
MASK OF FORTUNE, THE • 1916 • Cochrane George • SHT • USA
MASK OF FU MANCHU, THE • 1932 • Brabin Charles J., Vidor Charles (U/c) • USA
MASK OF FU MANCHU, THE see **FACE OF FU MANCHU, THE** • 1965
MASK OF FURY (USA) see **FIRST YANK INTO TOKYO** • 1945
MASK OF HORROR, THE (USA) see **MASQUE D'HORREUR, LE** • 1912
MASK OF KOREA (USA) see **MACAO, L'ENFER DU JEU** • 1939
MASK OF LOPEZ, THE • 1924 • Rogell Albert S. • USA
MASK OF LOVE, THE • 1917 • De Grasse Joseph • SHT • USA
MASK OF LOVE, THE see **SUCH MEN ARE DANGEROUS** • 1930
MASK OF MARCELLA see **COOL MILLION** • 1972
MASK OF MURDER • 1986 • Mattsson Arne • SWD
MASK OF MYSTERY see **MASCHERA DI MISTERO** • 1916
MASK OF PHARAOH see **SOUTH OF ALGIERS** • 1952
MASK OF RICHES see **MASK, THE** • 1918
MASK OF SHEBA, THE • 1969 • Rich David Lowell • TVM • USA
MASK OF THE AVENGER • 1951 • Karlson Phil • USA
MASK OF THE DEATH see **MASKA CRVENE SMRTI** • 1969
MASK OF THE DEMON see **MASCHERA DEL DEMONIO, LA** • 1960
MASK OF THE DRAGON • 1951 • Newfield Sam • USA
MASK OF THE GOLEM see **GOLEM, LE** • 1966
MASK OF THE HIMALAYAS see **STORM OVER TIBET** • 1952
MASK OF THE KLU KLUX KLAN, THE • 1923 • *Coigne Frank B. (P)* • USA
MASK OF THE MUSKETEERS • 1960 • *Scott Gordon* • ITL
MASK OF THE RED DEATH see **MASKA CRVENE SMRTI** • 1969
MASK OF THE RED DEATH, THE • 1911 • *Ambrosio* • ITL
MASKA CRVENE SMRTI • 1969 • Stalter Pavao, Ranitovic Branko • ANS • YGS, USA • MASQUE OF THE RED DEATH, THE (USA) ○ MASK OF THE RED DEATH ○ MASK OF THE DEATH
MASKARAD • 1941 • Gerasimov Sergei • USS • MASQUERADE
MASKARADA • 1971 • Hladnik Bostjan • YGS • MASQUERADE
MASKARADA • 1984 • Hladnik Bostjan • YGS • MASQUERADE
MASKE 74 • 1919 • Arnheim Valy • FRG
MASKE, DIE • 1919 • Dupont E. A. • FRG
MASKE, DIE • 1922 • Steinhoff Hans • FRG
MASKE DES TODES, DIE • 1920 • Bauer James • FRG
MASKE FALLT, DIE • 1930 • Dieterle William • FRG
MASKE IN BLAU • 1953 • Jacoby Georg • FRG • MARIKA
MASKE KU'VI • 1976 • Nielsen Lasse, Arnfred Morten, Bruus Morten • DNM • LET'S DO IT
MASKED • 1920 • Wright Mack V. • SHT • USA
MASKED ANGEL • 1928 • O'Connor Frank • USA • HER LOVE COTTAGE (UKN)
MASKED AVENGER, THE • 1922 • Fanning Frank • USA
MASKED BRIDE, THE • 1925 • Cabanne W. Christy, von Sternberg Josef • USA
MASKED CONQUEROR, THE (USA) see **ZORRO ALLA CORTE DI SPAGNA** • 1962
MASKED CUPID, THE • 1917 • *Walker Johnnie* • SHT • USA
MASKED DANCER, THE • 1914 • King Burton L. • USA
MASKED DANCER, THE • 1915 • Sargent George L. • USA
MASKED DANCER, THE • 1924 • King Burton L. • USA
MASKED DOCTOR, THE see **ZOKU SEX DOCTOR NO KIROKU** • 1968
MASKED EMOTIONS • 1929 • Butler David, Hawks Kenneth • USA
MASKED FACE, THE see **TVAR POD MASKOU** • 1970
MASKED FATE • 1915 • Morgan George • USA
MASKED HEART, THE • 1917 • Sloman Edward • USA
MASKED LOVER, THE • 1928 • *Hollyday Jack* • USA
MASKED LOVER, THE see **MASKOVANA MILENKA** • 1940
MASKED MAMAS • 1926 • *Sennett Mack (P)* • SHT • USA
MASKED MARVEL, THE • 1924 • Del Ruth Roy • SHT • USA
MASKED MARVEL, THE • 1943 • Bennet Spencer Gordon • SRL • USA
MASKED MARVELS, THE • 1917 • Curtis Allen • SHT • USA
MASKED MENACE, THE • 1927 • Heath Arch B. • SRL • USA
MASKED MIRTH • 1917 • Williamson Robin E. • SHT • USA
MASKED MIX-UP, A • 1913 • Hotaling Arthur D. • USA
MASKED PIRATE, THE (UKN) see **PIRATI DI CAPRI, I** • 1949
MASKED RAIDERS • 1949 • Selander Lesley • USA
MASKED RIDER, THE • 1914 • *Maison Edna* • USA
MASKED RIDER, THE • 1916 • Balshofer Fred J. • USA
MASKED RIDER, THE • 1919 • Kennedy Aubrey M. • SRL • USA
MASKED RIDER, THE • 1922 • Sanderson Challis • UKN
MASKED RIDER, THE • 1941 • Beebe Ford • USA
MASKED SMUGGLER, THE • 1912 • Collins Edwin J. • UKN
MASKED STRANGER, THE (UKN) see **DURANGO KID, THE** • 1940
MASKED SUBSTITUTE, THE • 1915 • Dowlan William C. • USA
MASKED TERROR see **DOKURO KYOJO** • 1957
MASKED WOMAN, THE • 1916 • Worthington William • SHT • USA
MASKED WOMAN, THE • 1927 • Balboni Silvano • USA
MASKED WRESTLER, THE • 1914 • *Essanay* • USA
MASKELI BESLER • 1968 • Atadeniz Yilmaz • TRK • FIVE MASKED MEN
MASKELI BESLERIN DONUSU • 1968 • Atadeniz Yilmaz • TRK • RETURN OF THE FIVE MASKED MEN, THE
MASKELYNE THE MAGICIAN • *Paul R. W. (P)* • UKN
MASKEN • 1920 • Wauer William • FRG
MASKEN • 1929 • Meinert Rudolf • FRG
MASKENFEST DES LEBENS, DAS • 1918 • Biebrach Rudolf • FRG
MASKERADA • 1986 • Kijowski Janusz • PLN • MASQUERADE
MASKERADE • 1934 • Forst Willi • AUS • MASQUERADE IN VIENNA
MASKERADE see **MASQUERADE** • 1965
MASKERAGE • 1952 • de Haas Max • DOC • NTH
MASKIERTE LIEBE • 1912 • Stark Kurt • FRG
MASKIERTE SCHRECKEN, DER • 1919 • Jutzi Phil • FRG
MASKOVANA MILENKA • 1940 • Vavra Otakar • CZC • MASKED LOVER, THE ○ SWEETHEART IN MASK
MASKS • 1968 • Godfrey Bob • ANS • UKN
MASKS see **PERSONA** • 1966
MASKS AND FACES • 1914 • Marston Lawrence • USA
MASKS AND FACES • 1917 • Paul Fred • UKN
MASKS AND MEMORIES • 1934 • Mack Roy • SHT • USA
MASKS AND MISHAPS • 1917 • Semon Larry • SHT • USA
MASKS OF DEATH • 1984 • Baker Roy Ward • UKN
MASKS OF THE DEVIL, THE • 1928 • Sjostrom Victor • USA
MASKULINUM-FEMININUM (SWD) see **MASCULIN-FEMININ** • 1966
MASNADIERI, I • 1962 • Bonnard Mario • ITL • ROME 1585 (USA)
MASOCH • 1979 • Taviani Franco B. • ITL • CONFESSIONI DI WANDA SACHER VON MASOCH, LE
MASON OF THE MOUNTED • 1932 • Fraser Harry L. • USA
MASON'S NEW ASSISTANT, A • 1914 • *Melies* • USA
MASQUE BALL, THE • 1916 • Fahrney Milton • USA
MASQUE DE FER, LE • 1954 • Pottier Richard • FRN
MASQUE DE FER, LE • 1962 • Decoin Henri • FRN, ITL • UOMO DALLA MASCHERA DI FERRO, L' (ITL)
MASQUE DE PLOMB, LE • 1974 • Franju Georges • MTV • FRN
MASQUE DE TOUT ANKH AMON, LE see **TRESOR DES PHARAONS, LE** • 1954
MASQUE D'HOLLYWOOD, LE • 1931 • Daumery John, Badger Clarence • FRN
MASQUE D'HORREUR, LE • 1912 • Gance Abel • FRN • MASK OF HORROR, THE (USA)
MASQUE DIABOLIQUE G. MELIES • 1898 • Melies Georges • FRN
MASQUE DU DIABLE, LE • 1976 • Laguionie Jean-Francois • ANS • FRN
MASQUE OF THE RED DEATH, THE • 1964 • Corman Roger • UKN, USA
MASQUE OF THE RED DEATH, THE • 1989 • Brand Larry • USA
MASQUE OF THE RED DEATH, THE (USA) see **MASKA CRVENE SMRTI** • 1969
MASQUE QUI TOMBE, LE • 1933 • Bonnard Mario • FRN
MASQUE RAID, THE • 1937 • *Mintz Charles (P)* • ANS • USA
MASQUERADE • 1929 • Birdwell Russell J. • USA
MASQUERADE • 1964 • Dearden Basil • UKN • OPERATION MASQUERADE ○ SHABBY TIGER, THE
MASQUERADE • 1965 • Topouzanov Christo • ANS • BUL • MASKERADE
MASQUERADE • 1967 • Dlz • PHL
MASQUERADE • 1987 • Swaim Bob • USA • DYING FOR LOVE
MASQUERADE see **PLEASURE CRAZED** • 1929
MASQUERADE see **ESCAPADE** • 1935
MASQUERADE see **MASKARAD** • 1941
MASQUERADE see **MASKARADA** • 1971
MASQUERADE see **MASCARADE** • 1980-84
MASQUERADE see **MASKARADA** • 1984
MASQUERADE see **MASKERADA** • 1986
MASQUERADE, THE • 1924 • Fleischer Dave • ANS • USA

MASQUERADE BANDIT, THE • 1926 • De Lacy Robert • USA • TABLES TURNED, THE
MASQUERADE COP, THE • 1910 • *Essanay* • USA
MASQUERADE HERO, THE • 1915 • *Mina* • USA
MASQUERADE IN MEXICO • 1945 • Leisen Mitchell • USA
MASQUERADE IN VIENNA see **MASKERADE** • 1934
MASQUERADE PARTY, THE • 1934 • *Mintz Charles (P)* • ANS • USA
MASQUERADE (UKN) see **MARATTOM** • 1989
MASQUERADER, THE • 1914 • *Kalem* • USA
MASQUERADER, THE • 1914 • Chaplin Charles • *Keystone* • USA • FEMALE IMPERSONATOR, THE ○ PUTTING ONE OVER
MASQUERADER, THE • 1922 • Young James • USA • JOHN CHILCOTE, M.P. ○ MONTE CARLO, JR.
MASQUERADER, THE • 1933 • Wallace Richard • USA
MASQUERADERS • 1906 • *Bitzer Billy (Ph)* • USA
MASQUERADERS, THE • 1908 • *Lubin* • USA
MASQUERADERS, THE • 1911 • *Powers* • USA
MASQUERADERS, THE • 1913 • *Reliance* • USA
MASQUERADERS, THE • 1915 • *Superba* • USA
MASQUERADERS, THE • 1915 • Kirkwood James • *Famous Players* • USA
MASQUERADING IN BEAR CANYON • 1913 • *Frontier* • USA
MASQUES • 1953 • Alexeieff Alexandre, Violet George • ANS • FRN
MASQUES • 1987 • Chabrol Claude • FRN
MASQUES ET VISAGES DE JAMES ENSOR • 1950 • Haesaerts Paul • BLG
MASS • 1964 • Baillie Bruce • SHT • USA • MASS (FOR THE DAKOTA SIOUX)
MASS • 1976 • Sjostrom Asa • UKN
MASS APPEAL • 1984 • Jordan Glenn • USA
MASS (FOR THE DAKOTA SIOUX) see **MASS** • 1964
MASS IS OVER, THE see **MESSA E' FINITA, LA** • 1985
MASS MIRACLE • 1980 • Pavlov Ivan • BUL
MASS MOUSE MEETING • 1943 • Geiss Alec • ANS • USA
MASS MURDERER see **MURDERLUST** • 1988
MASS PRODUCTION OF EGGS see **NAGYUZEMI TOJASTERMELES** • 1962
MASS STRUGGLE • Kavaleridze Ivan • USS
MASS VIOLATION, THE see **SENGO ZANKOKU MONOGATARI** • 1968
MASSA ALUNKOT see **MASSA HA'ALUNKOT** • 1977
MASSA HA'ALUNKOT • 1977 • Ne'Eman Yehuda • ISR • JOURNEY OF STRETCHERS ○ MASSA ALUNKOT ○ PARATROOPERS
MASSACRE • 1934 • Crosland Alan • USA
MASSACRE • 1956 • King Louis • USA
MASSACRE see **MASACRE** • 1978
MASSACRE, LE • 1969 • Reichenbach Francois • FRN
MASSACRE, THE • 1914 • Griffith D. W. • USA
MASSACRE AT CENTRAL HIGH • 1976 • Daalder Renee • USA • BLACKBOARD MASSACRE (UKN)
MASSACRE AT FORT HOLMAN (USA) see **RAGIONE PER VIVERE E UNA PER MOURIRE, UNA** • 1972
MASSACRE AT FORT PERDITION (USA) see **FUERTE PERDIDO** • 1965
MASSACRE AT MARBLE CITY (UKN) see **GOLDSUCHER VON ARKANSAS, DIE** • 1964
MASSACRE AT SAND CREEK • 1956 • Hiller Arthur • MTV • USA
MASSACRE AT THE GRAND CANYON see **MASSACRO AL GRANDE CANYON** • 1964
MASSACRE AT THE ROSEBUD see **GREAT SIOUX MASSACRE, THE** • 1965
MASSACRE CANYON • 1954 • Sears Fred F. • USA
MASSACRE DE PLAISIR see **MASSACRE POUR UNE ORGIE** • 1966
MASSACRE EN DENTELLES • 1951 • Hunebelle Andre • FRN
MASSACRE FOR AN ORGY (USA) see **MASSACRE POUR UNE ORGIE** • 1966
MASSACRE GUN, THE see **MINAGOROSHI NO KENJU** • 1967
MASSACRE HARBOUR • 1968 • Peyser John • USA
MASSACRE HILL (USA) see **EUREKA STOCKADE** • 1948
MASSACRE HOSPITAL see **X-RAY** • 1981
MASSACRE IN A SUPERMARKET see **MASSACRE NON SUPERMERCADO** • 1968
MASSACRE IN CRETE see **MASSACRES DE CRETE** • 1897
MASSACRE IN ROME (UKN) see **RAPPRESAGLIA** • 1973
MASSACRE MANIA (USA) see **HIPNOS FOLLIA DI UN MASSACRO** • 1967
MASSACRE MANSION see **MANSION OF THE DOOMED** • 1975
MASSACRE NON SUPERMERCADO • 1968 • Tanko J. B. • BRZ • MASSACRE IN A SUPERMARKET
MASSACRE OF PLEASURE (UKN) see **MASSACRE POUR UNE ORGIE** • 1966
MASSACRE OF SANTA FE TRAIL, THE • 1912 • Montgomery Frank E. • USA
MASSACRE OF THE FOURTH CAVALRY, THE • 1912 • *Darkfeather Mona* • USA
MASSACRE ON CONDOR PASS see **POTATO FRITZ** • 1975
MASSACRE PLAY see **GIOCO AL MASSACRO** • 1990
MASSACRE POUR UNE ORGIE • 1966 • Grosdard Jean-Loup • LXM • MASSACRE FOR AN ORGY (USA) ○ MASSACRE OF PLEASURE (UKN) ○ MASSACRE DE PLAISIR
MASSACRE RIVER • 1949 • Rawlins John • USA
MASSACRES DE CRETE • 1897 • Melies Georges • FRN • MASSACRE IN CRETE
MASSACRO AL GRANDE CANYON • 1964 • Antonini Alfredo, Corbucci Sergio • ITL • MASSACRE AT THE GRAND CANYON
MASSACRO DELLA FORESTA NERA, IL • 1966 • Baldi Ferdinando • ITL, FRG • ARMINIUS THE TERRIBLE ○ HERMANN DER CHERUSKER: DIE SCHACHT IM TEUTOBURGER WALD
MASSAGE GIRLS see **MASSAGE GIRLS IN BANGKOK**
MASSAGE GIRLS IN BANGKOK • Morn J. A. • HKG • MASSAGE GIRLS
MASSAGE PARLOUR (UKN) see **MASSAGESALON -DER BLUTJUNGEN MADCHEN** • 1972
MASSAGE PARLOUR WIFE • Spinello Barry • USA
MASSAGESALON -DER BLUTJUNGEN MADCHEN • 1972 • Schroeder Eberhard • FRG • MASSAGE PARLOUR (UKN)
MASSAGGIATRICI, LE • 1962 • Fulci Lucio • ITL, FRN
MASSAGUIN EL THALATHA, EL • 1968 • Mustafa Hassam Eddin • EGY • THREE PRISONERS, THE
MASSAI • 1976 • Levaton Jean-Noel, Luyat Jean-Claude • DOC • FRN
MASSARATI AND THE BRAIN • 1982 • Hart Harvey • TVM • USA
MASSAY SAHIB • 1983 • Krishen Pradip • IND • MASSEY SAHIB
MASSEBA • 1988 • Zabransky Milos • CZC
MASSES' MUSIC, THE (USA) see **DAHANA-ARANJA** • 1976
MASSEUR ICHI THE FUGITIVE see **ZATO ICHI KYOJOTABI** • 1963
MASSEUR'S CURSE see **KAIDAN KASANEGAFUCHI** • 1970
MASSEUSES DE HONG KONG, LES • Baudricourt Michel • FRN
MASSEY SAHIB see **MASSAY SAHIB** • 1983
MASSIVE MOVIE MERMAID, A • 1915 • *Cunningham Arthur* • USA
MASSIVE RETALIATION • 1984 • Cohen Thomas A. • USA
MASSNAHMEN GEGEN FANATIKER • 1968 • Herzog Werner • DCS • FRG • MEASURES AGAINST FANATICS
MASTARNAS MATCH • 1959 • Gunwall Per • SWD • INGO VS. FLOYD
MASTER see **MAITRE**
MASTER, THE • 1984 • Hillman William Byron • USA
MASTER, THE see **RODA TORNET, DET** • 1914
MASTER, THE see **MISTAZ** • 1966
MASTER AND HIS SERVANTS, THE see **HERREN OZ HANS TJENERE** • 1959
MASTER AND MAN • 1913 • Dawley J. Searle • USA
MASTER AND MAN • 1915 • Nash Percy • UKN
MASTER AND MAN • 1929 • Cooper George A. • UKN
MASTER AND MAN • 1934 • Harlow John • UKN
MASTER AND MARGARITA, THE see **MAJSTOR I MARGARITA** • 1973
MASTER AND PUPIL • 1912 • Dawley J. Searle • USA
MASTER AND THE CREAM-PUFF, THE see **MAJSTOR I SAMPITA** • 1987
MASTER AND THE MAN, THE • 1911 • *Pickford Mary* • USA
MASTER BEATER, THE • 1969 • Carmello Charles • USA • DIRTY HAWK, THE ○ HOT SEX TRAMP
MASTER BOB'S LAST RACE • 1914 • *Warner'S Features* • USA
MASTER CRACKSMAN, THE • 1913 • Apfel Oscar • USA
MASTER CROOK, THE • 1913 • Weston Charles • UKN
MASTER CROOK, THE • 1918 • *Breese Edmund* • USA
MASTER CROOK OUTWITTED BY A CHILD, THE • 1914 • Batley Ernest G. • UKN
MASTER CROOK TURNS DETECTIVE, THE • 1914 • Batley Ernest G. • UKN
MASTER CROOKS, THE see **LADY RAFFLES RETURNS** • 1916
MASTER CUPID, DETECTIVE • 1911 • *Essanay* • USA
MASTER DETECTIVE AND RASMUS see **MASTERDETEKTIVEN OCH RASMUS** • 1953
MASTER DETECTIVE LEADS A DANGEROUS LIFE, THE see **MASTERDETEKTIVEN LEVER FARLIGT** • 1957
MASTER EAGLE see **KARTAL EFE** • 1967
MASTER FIGHTER • 1967 • Gaudite Solano • PHL
MASTER FIXIT • 1913 • Ince Ralph • USA
MASTER GOE • Calinescu Bob • ANM • RMN
MASTER GUNFIGHTER, THE • 1975 • Laughlin Tom • USA
MASTER HAND, THE • 1914 • *Princess* • USA
MASTER HAND, THE • 1915 • Knoles Harley • USA
MASTER HAND (USA) see **OSHO** • 1973
MASTER IDEAL see **KANTOR IDEAL** • 1932
MASTER ILLUSIONIST, THE • 1984 • Caulfield Michael, Burton Geoff • DOC • ASL • LAWRENCE OF ARABIA -THE MASTER ILLUSIONIST
MASTER KEY, THE • 1915 • Leonard Robert Z. • SRL • USA
MASTER KEY, THE • 1945 • Taylor Ray, Collins Lewis D. • SRL • USA
MASTER KILLER see **SHAO-LIN SAN-SHIH-LIU FANG** • 1977
MASTER KRISHNA see **KRISHNA KUMAR** • 1924
MASTER LOVE • 1945 • Peguy Robert • FRN
MASTER MAGICIAN ALCOFRISBAS see **ENCHANTEUR ALCOFRISBAS, L'** • 1903
MASTER MAN, THE • 1919 • Warde Ernest C. • USA
MASTER MECHANIC, THE • 1910 • *Lubin* • USA
MASTER MIND, THE • 1914 • Apfel Oscar, De Mille Cecil B. • USA
MASTER MIND, THE see **MASTERMIND, THE** • 1920
MASTER MINDS • 1949 • Yarbrough Jean • USA
MASTER MINDS see **GENIUS AT WORK** • 1946
MASTER MUMMER, THE • 1915 • Edwin Walter • USA
MASTER MUSICIAN, THE • 1986 • Dehlavi Jamil • PKS
MASTER MYSTERY, THE • 1919 • King Burton L., Bingham E. Douglas • SRL • USA • HOUDINI
MASTER NIKIFOR see **MISTRZ NIKIFOR** • 1956
MASTER NINJA 2, THE • 1984 • *Van Cleef Lee* • MTV • USA • NINJA MASTER 2
MASTER NINJA, THE • 1984 • *Van Cleef Lee* • MTV • USA • NINJA MASTER
MASTER OF ALL TRADES see **SPETSIALIST PO VISICHKO** • 1962
MASTER OF BALLANTRAE, THE • 1953 • Keighley William • UKN
MASTER OF BALLANTRAE, THE • 1984 • Hickox Douglas • TVM • USA
MASTER OF BANKDAM, THE • 1947 • Forde Walter • UKN
MASTER OF BEASTS, THE • 1922 • *Vogt Charles* • USA
MASTER OF BOYANA, THE • 1980 • Zhandov Zahari • BUL
MASTER OF BRAVERY, A • 1975 • *Universal* • MXC
MASTER OF CRAFT, A • 1922 • Bentley Thomas • UKN
MASTER OF DEATH, THE see **HERR DES TODES, DER** • 1914
MASTER OF DRAGONARD HILL see **DRAGONARD** • 1987
MASTER OF EXISTENCE • 1932 • Ptushko Alexander • ANS • USS
MASTER OF GRAY, THE • 1918 • Watts Tom • UKN
MASTER OF GYMNASTICS • 1967 • Csoke Jozsef • DOC • HNG
MASTER OF HER SOUL • 1916 • *Adair Robyn* • SHT • USA
MASTER OF HIMSELF • 1913 • *Kerrigan J. Warren* • USA
MASTER OF HIS HOME • 1917 • Edwards Walter • USA
MASTER OF HIS HOUSE, THE • 1915 • Beggs Lee • USA
MASTER OF HORROR (USA) see **OBRAS MAESTRAS DEL TERROR** • 1960
MASTER OF KUNG FU, THE see **DEATH KICK** • 1974
MASTER OF LASSIE see **HILLS OF HOME** • 1948
MASTER OF LAUGHTER • 1953 • *Cornelis Marcel* • UKN
MASTER OF LOVE see **RACCONTI PROIBITI.. DI NIENTE VESTITI** • 1972
MASTER OF LOVE, THE see **HERR DER LIEBE, DER** • 1919
MASTER OF MAN, THE see **NAME THE MAN** • 1924
MASTER OF MEN • 1933 • Hillyer Lambert • USA
MASTER OF MEN, A • 1913 • Coleby A. E.? • UKN
MASTER OF MEN, A • 1917 • Noy Wilfred • UKN
MASTER OF MERRIPIT, THE • 1915 • Noy Wilfred • UKN
MASTER OF MILLIONS, A • 1911 • *Thanhouser* • USA
MASTER OF MUSIC, A • 1919 • *Parsons William* • SHT • USA
MASTER OF NUREMBURG, THE see **MEISTER VON NURNBERG, DER** • 1926
MASTER OF TERROR see **4D MAN, THE** • 1959
MASTER OF THE BENGALS, THE • 1915 • Chaudet Louis W. • USA
MASTER OF THE FLYING GUILLOTINE • 1975 • Wang Yu • HKG • ONE-ARMED BOXER VERSUS THE FLYING GUILLOTINE
MASTER OF THE GAME • 1984 • Hart Harvey, Connor Kevin • MTV • USA
MASTER OF THE GARDEN, THE • 1913 • *Selig* • USA
MASTER OF THE HOUSE see **DU SKAL AERE DIN HUSTRU** • 1925
MASTER OF THE HOUSE, THE • 1914 • *Stanton Richard* • USA
MASTER OF THE HOUSE, THE • 1915 • *Steger Julius* • USA
MASTER OF THE ISLANDS (UKN) see **HAWAIIANS, THE** • 1970
MASTER OF THE MINE • 1914 • Bowman William J. • USA
MASTER OF THE RANGE • 1928 • *Lyons Cliff (Tex)* • USA
MASTER OF THE STRONG, THE • 1914 • Vale Travers • USA
MASTER OF THE SWORD, THE • 1915 • *Anderson Augusta* • USA
MASTER OF THE VINEYARD, THE • 1911 • Dwan Allan • USA
MASTER OF THE WORLD • 1961 • Witney William • USA
MASTER OF THE WORLD see **HERR DER WELT, DER** • 1934
MASTER OF THE WORLD see **PADRONE DEL MONDO, IL** • 1982
MASTER OF THE WORLD, THE • 1914 • *Werner Karl* • SHT • USA
MASTER OF TIME, THE see **MAITRE DU TEMPS, LE** • 1970
MASTER OF WINTER SPORTS see **MISTVI ZIMNICH SPORTI** • 1955
MASTER OF WOMAN, THE see **ETERNAL STRUGGLE, THE** • 1923
MASTER OVER LIFE AND DEATH see **HERR UBER LEBEN UND TOD** • 1955
MASTER PAINTER, THE • 1913 • Lytton L. Rogers • USA
MASTER PAINTER NIKIFOR see **MISTRZ NIKIFOR** • 1956
MASTER PASSION, THE • 1917 • Ridgely Richard • USA
MASTER PHYSICIAN, THE • 1915 • *Tolnaes Gunner* • DNM
MASTER PIECE, THE • 1970 • Van Horn Lee • USA
MASTER PLAN, THE • 1954 • Endfield Cy • UKN
MASTER RACE, THE • 1944 • Biberman Herbert J. • USA
MASTER ROGUE, THE • 1914 • *Melford George* • USA
MASTER ROGUES OF EUROPE, THE • 1915 • *Big U* • USA
MASTER SAMUEL see **MASTERMAN** • 1920
MASTER SHAKESPEARE, STROLLING PLAYER • 1916 • Sullivan Frederick • USA
MASTER SMILES, THE • 1916 • *Wehlen Emmy* • SHT • USA
MASTER SONG SCENAS • 1922 • Parkinson H. B. • UKN • CAPITOL SONG CYCLE
MASTER SPY • 1963 • Tully Montgomery • UKN
MASTER SPY, THE • 1914 • Weston Charles • UKN
MASTER SPY, THE • 1917 • Wells Jack, Benedict Kingsley • SHT • USA
MASTER STROKE • 1987 • el Tayeb Atif • EGY
MASTER STROKE, A • 1920 • Bennett Chester • USA
MASTER-STROKE IN THE SERVICE OF SIFAR see **COLPO SENSAZIONALE AL SERVIZIO DEL SIFAR** • 1968
MASTER SWINDLERS, THE • 1916 • Horne James W. • SHT • USA
MASTER THIEF, THE see **MASTERTJUVEN** • 1915
MASTER-THIEF, THE see **STORTJUVEN** • 1979
MASTER TOUCH, THE (USA) see **UOMO DA RISPETTARE, UN** • 1972
MASTER WILL SHAKESPEARE • 1936 • Tourneur Jacques • SHT • USA
MASTER WITH CRACKED FINGERS, THE • *Chan Jackie* • HKG
MASTER ZOARD see **ZOARD MESTER** • 1917
MASTERBLASTER • 1986 • Wilder Glen R. • USA
MASTERDETEKTIVEN BLOMKVIST • 1947 • Husberg Rolf • SWD • BLOMKVIST THE MASTER DETECTIVE
MASTERDETEKTIVEN LEVER FARLIGT • 1957 • Hellbom Olle • SWD • MASTER DETECTIVE LEADS A DANGEROUS LIFE, THE
MASTERDETEKTIVEN OCH RASMUS • 1953 • Husberg Rolf • SWD • MASTER DETECTIVE AND RASMUS
MASTERFUL HIRELING, THE • 1915 • *Christy Ivan* • USA
MASTERKATTEN I STOVLAR • 1918 • Brunius John W. • SWD • PUSS IN BOOTS
MASTERLESS FORTY-SEVEN, THE see **SALARY-MAN CHUSHINGURA** • 1960
MASTERMAN • 1920 • Sjostrom Victor • SWD • MASTER SAMUEL ○ EXECUTIONER, THE
MASTERMIND • 1969 • March Alex • USA, JPN
MASTERMIND, THE • 1920 • Webb Kenneth • USA • MASTER MIND, THE
MASTERPIECE, THE • 1915 • *Liberty* • USA
MASTERPIECE OF MURDER, A • 1986 • Dubin Charles S. • TVM • USA
MASTERS, THE see **LADY ICE** • 1973
MASTERS, THE see **MAJSTORI** • 1981
MASTERS AND SLAVES • 1978 • Reda Aly • EGY
MASTER'S MODEL, THE • 1915 • *Gane Nolan* • USA
MASTERS OF KARATE • 1968 • Garces Armando • PHL
MASTERS OF MEN • 1923 • Smith David • USA
MASTERS OF THE LAND see **SENHORES DA TERRA, OS** • 1971
MASTERS OF THE SEA see **HERREN DER MEERE** • 1922

MASTERS OF THE UNIVERSE • 1987 • Goddard Gary • USA • MASTERS OF THE UNIVERSE: THE MOTION PICTURE

MASTERS OF THE UNIVERSE II • 1989 • Pyun Albert • USA

MASTERS OF THE UNIVERSE: THE MOTION PICTURE see **MASTERS OF THE UNIVERSE** • 1987

MASTERS OF VENUS • 1962 • Morris Ernest • SRL • UKN

MASTER'S RAZOR, THE • 1906 • Green Tom? • UKN

MASTERSHIP • 1934 • Ginever Aveling • UKN

MASTERSON OF KANSAS • 1954 • Castle William • USA

MASTERTJUVEN • 1915 • Stiller Mauritz • SWD • MASTER THIEF, THE ○ ACE OF THIEVES ○ SON OF FATE, THE

MASTERWORKS OF TERROR see **OBRAS MAESTRAS DEL TERROR** • 1960

MASTERY OF THE SEA • 1941 • Cavalcanti Alberto • DCS • UKN

MASTROIANNI • 1965 • Pearson Peter • DOC • CND

MASTURA • 1974 • Achnas Naz • MLY

MASUCCIO SALERNITANO • 1972 • Amadio Silvio • ITL

MASUREN, DIE • 1915 • Danuky Nunek • FRG

MASZYNA • 1961 • Szczechura Daniel • ANS • PLN • MACHINE

MAT • 1926 • Pudovkin V. I. • USS • MOTHER

MAT • 1956 • Donskoi Mark • USS • MOTHER ○ 1905

MAT • 1989 • Panfilov Gleb • USS • MOTHER

MAT AND THE FLY • 1930 • ANS • FRN

MAT GELAP • 1990 • Al-Bakri Zarul Shahrin • MLY • ZANY CARTOONIST, THE

MAT' MARIJA • 1983 • Kolosov Sergei • USS • MOTHER MARIA

MAT RAJA KAPOR • Amin M., Sentul Mat

MAT THAT MATTERED, THE • 1914 • Aylott Dave • UKN

MATA AU HI MADE • 1932 • Ozu Yasujiro • JPN • UNTIL THE DAY WE MEET AGAIN ○ TILL WE MEET AGAIN

MATA AU HI MADE • 1950 • Imai Tadashi • JPN • UNTIL THE DAY WE MEET AGAIN ○ UNTIL WE MEET AGAIN

MATA AU HIMADE: KOIBITO NO IZUMI • 1967 • Miyazaki Mamoru • JPN • FOUNTAIN OF LOVE

MATA HARI • 1927 • Feher Friedrich • FRG

MATA HARI • 1931 • Fitzmaurice George • USA

MATA-HARI • 1984 • Harrington Curtis • USA • MATA HARI

MATA HARI see **SPIONIN, DIE** • 1921

MATA HARI see **MATA-HARI** • 1984

MATA-HARI AGENT H-21 • 1965 • Richard Jean-Louis • FRN, ITL • MATA HARI, AGENTE SEGRETO H21 (ITL) ○ MATA HARI AGENT H-21 (USA)

MATA HARI AGENT H-21 (USA) see **MATA-HARI AGENT H-21** • 1965

MATA HARI, AGENTE SEGRETO H21 (ITL) see **MATA-HARI AGENT H-21** • 1965

MATA HARI'S DAUGHTER (USA) see **FIGLIA DI MATA HARI, LA** • 1955

MATA MAHAKALI • 1968 • Desai Dhirubhai • IND • GODDESS KALI

MATADOR • 1985 • Almodovar Pedro • SPN • BULLFIGHTER

MATADOR, O • 1968 • Cezar Amaro, Eccio Egyido • BRZ • KILLER, THE

MATADOR MAGOO • 1957 • Burness Pete • ANS • USA

MATAF, LE • 1972 • Leroy Serge • FRN, ITL

MATAGI • 1983 • Goto Toshio • JPN • MATAGI, BEAR HUNTER ○ TRADITIONAL HUNTER, A

MATAGI, BEAR HUNTER see **MATAGI** • 1983

MATAIX AND JOSEPH'S COAT • 1973 • Le Grice Malcolm • UKN

MATALO • 1970 • Canevari Cesare • ITL

MATALOS Y VUELVE (SPN) see **AMMAZZALI TUTTI E TORNA SOLO** • 1969

MATANGO • 1963 • Honda Inoshiro, Tsuburaya Eiji • JPN • ATTACK OF THE MUSHROOM PEOPLE (USA) ○ MATANGO -FUNGUS OF TERROR

MATANGO -FUNGUS OF TERROR see **MATANGO** • 1963

MATAR AL NANI • 1988 • Bodegas Roberto • SPN • TO KILL "EL NANI"

MATAR ES MORIR UN POCO • 1987 • Olivera Hector • ARG, USA • TWO TO TANGO

MATAR NO ES FACIL • 1966 • Vejar Sergio • MXC

MATAR O MORIR • 1960 • Peon Ramon • MXC

MATAR POR MATAR • 1977 • Sbert Toni • MXC

MATARON A VENANCIO FLOREZ • 1981 • Rodriguez • URG

MATATABI • 1973 • Ichikawa Kon • JPN • WANDERERS, THE ○ TRAMPS, THE

MATATABI SEN ICHIYA • 1936 • Inagaki Hiroshi • JPN • JOURNEY OF A THOUSAND AND ONE NIGHTS

MATCH, THE see **MERKOZES, A** • 1981

MATCH, THE see **PARTITA, LA** • 1988

MATCH-BREAKER, THE • 1921 • Fitzgerald Dallas M. • USA

MATCH CONTRE LA MORT • 1959 • Bernard-Aubert Claude • FRN, ITL • MATCH CONTRO LA MORTE (ITL)

MATCH CONTRO LA MORTE (ITL) see **MATCH CONTRE LA MORT** • 1959

MATCH DE BOXE (ECOLE DE JOINVILLE) • 1897 • Melies Georges • FRN • BOXING MATCH

MATCH DE PRESTIDIGITATION • 1904 • Melies Georges • FRN • WAGER BETWEEN TWO MAGICIANS: OR, JEALOUS OF MYSELF, A (USA)

MATCH GIRL • 1966 • Meyer Andrew • SHT • USA

MATCH GIRL • 1968 • Miheles Aurel • SHT • RMN

MATCH IN QUARANTINE, A • 1917 • De La Parelle M. • USA

MATCH KID, THE • 1933 • *Mintz Charles (P)* • ANS • USA

MATCH KING, THE • 1932 • Bretherton Howard, Keighley William • USA

MATCH MAKERS, THE • 1917 • Drew Sidney, Drew Sidney Mrs. • SHT • USA

MATCH-MAKING DADS • 1914 • *Lubin* • USA

MATCH-MAKING MARSHAL, THE • 1955 • McDonald Frank • MTV • USA

MATCH MASTER, THE see **STREICHHOLZKUNSTLER, DER** • 1913

MATCH OF DRAGON AND TIGER • 1973 • Yu Kuan Jen • HKG

MATCH OF MEN: TATTOO OF DEVA KING, THE see **OTOKO NO SHOBU: NIO NO IREZUMI** • 1967

MATCH PLAY • 1930 • Sennett Mack • SHT • USA

MATCHE DE BOXE ENTRE PATINEURS A ROULETTES • 1912 • Linder Max • FRN

MATCHES • 1913 • Dwan Allan • USA

MATCHES see **ZUNDHOLZER** • 1960

MATCHES see **ALLUMETTES** • 1963

MATCHES (MADE IN ENGLAND) • 1910 • UKN

MATCHIN' JIM • 1916 • Borzage Frank • SHT • USA

MATCHING BILLY • 1918 • *Parsons William* • SHT • USA

MATCHING DREAMS • 1916 • Eason B. Reeves • SHT • USA

MATCHING OF ANNA, THE see **PROXENIO TIS ANNAS, TO** • 1971

MATCHLESS • 1967 • Lattuada Alberto • ITL

MATCHLESS • 1974 • Papadopoulos John • ASL

MATCHLESS CONQUEROR, THE • 1972 • Chang Ping-Han • HKG

MATCHLESS SWORD see **HIRYU NO KEN** • 1937

MATCHMAKER, THE • 1911 • Salter Harry • USA

MATCHMAKER, THE • 1958 • Anthony Joseph • USA

MATCHMAKER, THE (USA) see **PARANINFO, IL** • 1934

MATCHMAKERS, THE • 1916 • Ridgwell George • SHT • USA

MATCHMAKING MAMAS • 1929 • Edwards Harry J. • SHT • USA

MATCHSELLER, THE • 1967 • Lewis Laurie • SHT • USA

MATCHSTICK PALS, THE see **PRATELE NA SIRKACH** • 1960

MATE DOMA IVA? • 1964 • Hobl Pavel • CZC • DO YOU KEEP A LION AT HOME?

MATE OF THE JOHN M., THE • 1911 • *Keefe Zena* • USA

MATE OF THE SALLY ANN, THE • 1917 • King Henry • USA • PEGGY REBELS

MATE OF THE SCHOONER "SADIE", THE • 1913 • *King Henry* • USA

MATE OR THE ALDEN BESSE, THE • 1911 • *Bosworth Hobart* • USA

MATECIKA see **MAMELE** • 1938

MATED IN THE WILDS • 1921 • Ramster P. J. • ASL

MATELAS ALCOOLIQUE, LE • 1906 • Blache Alice • FRN

MATELOT 512, LE • 1984 • Allio Rene • FRN

MATEMATICA ZERO AMOR DEZ • 1958 • Christensen Carlos Hugo • ARG

MATEN A BRANDT • 1973 • *Warner* • USA

MATEN A CHINTO • 1990 • Isaac Alberto • MXC • KILL CHINTO

MATEN AL LEON • 1975 • Estrada Jose • MXC • KILL THE LION

MATENME PORQUE ME MUERO!!! • 1951 • Rodriguez Ismael • MXC

MATER AMATISIMA • 1980 • Salgot Jose Antonio • SPN • BELOVED MOTHER ○ MOTHER, DEARLY LOVED

MATER DEI • 1951 • Cordero Emilio • ITL

MATER DOLOROSA • 1909 • de Morlhon Camille • FRN

MATER DOLOROSA • 1909 • Feuillade Louis • FRN

MATER DOLOROSA • 1911 • Chautard Emile • FRN

MATER DOLOROSA • 1912 • Caserini Mario • ITL

MATER DOLOROSA • 1917 • Gance Abel • FRN

MATER DOLOROSA • 1922 • von Bolvary Geza • FRG

MATER DOLOROSA • 1924 • Delmont Joseph • FRG

MATER DOLOROSA • 1932 • Gance Abel • FRN

MATER DOLOROSA • 1943 • Gentilomo Giacomo • ITL

MATER NOSTRA • 1936 • Soria Gabriel • MXC

MATERASSI SISTERS, THE see **SORELLE MATERASSI** • 1943

MATERIA • 1962 • Urbanski Kazimierz • PLN • MATTER, THE

MATERIA -DER CLUB DER TOTEN • 1920 • Schildau Max • FRG

MATERIAUX NOUVEAU, DEMEURES NOUVELLES • 1956 • Colpi Henri • SHT • FRN

MATERIELS ARMEES DE SURVIE • 1960 • Herman Jean • FRN

MATERIK GIGANTOV • 1975 • Konchalovsky Andrei • USS • LAND OF GIANTS, THE

MATERINSKOYE POLYE • 1968 • Bazarov Gennadi • USS • MOTHER'S FIELD, THE

MATERNAL SPARK, THE • 1917 • Hamilton G. P. • USA

MATERNALE, LA • 1978 • Gagliardo Giovanna • ITL • MOTHER AND DAUGHTER

MATERNELLE, LA • 1925 • Roudes Gaston • FRN

MATERNELLE, LA • 1933 • Benoit-Levy Jean, Epstein Marie • FRN • NURSERY SCHOOL

MATERNELLE, LA • 1948 • Diamant-Berger Henri • FRN

MATERNELLE D'ACCUEIL • 1976 • Lamothe Arthur • DCS • CND

MATERNELLE ESQUIMAUDE DE FORT-CHIMO, LA • 1965 • Lavoie Richard • DCS • CND

MATERNIDAD IMPOSIBLE • 1954 • Gomez Muriel Emilio • MXC

MATERNIDAD SIN HOMBRES • 1968 • Rinaldi Carlos • ARG • MOTHERHOOD WITHOUT MEN

MATERNITE • 1929 • Benoit-Levy Jean • FRN • MATERNITY

MATERNITE • 1934 • Choux Jean • FRN • TOUT POUR TOI, MON ENFANT ○ POUR TOI, MON ENFANT

MATERNITE CLANDESTINE • 1953 • Gourguet Jean • FRN

MATERNITY • 1917 • O'Brien John B. • USA

MATERNITY see **MATERNITE** • 1929

MATERNITY HOSPITAL • 1971 • Vukotic Dusan • ANS • YGS

MATES see **COLEGAS** • 1983

MATES, THE • 1960 • Pavlovsky V. • USS

MATES AND MISMATES • 1912 • *Powers* • USA

MATES AND MODELS • 1919 • Smith Noel • SHT • USA

MATES OF THE MURRUMBIDGEE • 1911 • Rolfe Alfred • ASL

MATEWAN • 1988 • Sayles John • USA

MATHATA • 1984 • SAF

MATHE PEDI MOU GRAMATA • 1981 • Marangos Thodoros • GRC • GO TO SCHOOL, SON

MATHEMATICIAN, THE • 1976 • Hayward Stan • UKN

MATHEMATICS • 1966-67 • Goldsmith Sidney • SER • CND

MATHEMATICS AT YOUR FINGERTIPS • 1961 • Howe John • DOC • CND

MATHEMATIQUES • 1967 • Beaudin Jean • SER • CND

MATHIAS KNEISSL • 1971 • Hauff Reinhard • FRG

MATHIAS SANDORF see **MATHIAS SANDORFF** • 1962

MATHIAS SANDORFF • 1920 • Fescourt Henri • FRN

MATHIAS SANDORFF • 1962 • Lampin Georges • FRN, ITL, SPN • GRANDE RIBELLE, IL (ITL) ○ MATHIAS SANDORF

MATHILDE • 1985 • Poppe Emil • SHT • NTH

MATHILDE MOHRING see **ICH GLAUBE AN DICH** • 1945

MATHILUKAL • 1990 • Gopalakrishnan Adoor • IND • WALLS, THE

MATHRU BHUMI • 1968 • Dissanayake Wimalanath • SLN • MOTHERLAND

MATI see **BEYOND REASON** • 1977

MATIARCA, LA • 1968 • Festa Campanile Pasquale • ITL • MATRIARCH, THE ○ LIBERTINE, THE

MATIELAND • 1955 • SAF

MATIERES NOUVELLES • 1964 • Storck Henri • DOC • BLG

MATILDA • 1978 • Mann Daniel • USA

MATILDA'S FLING • 1915 • Louis Will • USA

MATILDA'S LEGACY • 1915 • Hotaling Arthur D. • USA

MATILDA'S WINNING WAYS • 1910 • *Lubin* • USA

MATIMBANG ANG DUGO SA TUBIG • 1967 • D'Lanor • PHL • BLOOD IS THICKER THAN WATER

MATIN • 1950 • Brault Michel • SHT • CND

MATIN COMME LES AUTRES, UN • 1954 • Bellon Yannick • FRN

MATIN, MIDI ET SOIR AU ZOUTE • 1935 • Gopax Robert • BLG

MATIN ROUGE, UN • 1982 • Aublanc Jean-Jacques • FRN

MATINEE • 1976 • Hermosillo Jaime Humberto • MXC

MATINEE • 1990 • Martin Richard • CND

MATINEE COWBOY see **SIDEWALK COWBOY, THE** • 1968

MATINEE IDOL • 1933 • King George • UKN

MATINEE IDOL • 1955 • *Halas John (P)* • ANS • UKN

MATINEE IDOL • 1986 • Pachard Henri • USA

MATINEE IDOL, THE • 1907 • *Walturdaw* • UKN

MATINEE IDOL, THE • 1910 • *Powers* • USA

MATINEE IDOL, THE • 1917 • Quirk William • SHT • USA

MATINEE IDOL, THE • 1928 • Capra Frank • USA

MATINEE LADIES • 1927 • Haskin Byron • USA

MATINEE MIX-UP, A • 1912 • Christie Al • USA

MATINEE MOUSE • 1966 • Ray Tom • ANS • USA

MATINEE WIVES • 1970 • Stewart Ken • USA

MATING • 1913 • *Moore Matt* • USA

MATING, THE • 1915 • Sidney Scott? • USA

MATING, THE • 1918 • Thompson Frederick A. • USA

MATING CALL, THE • 1928 • Cruze James • USA

MATING GAME, THE • 1958 • Marshall George • USA

MATING MODERN STYLE see **FORTUNA DI ESSERE DONNA, LA** • 1956

MATING OF MARCELLA, THE • 1918 • Neill R. William • USA

MATING OF MARCUS, THE • 1924 • Kellino W. P. • UKN

MATING OF MILLIE, THE • 1948 • Levin Henry • USA

MATING OF THE SABINE WOMEN, THE see **RAPTO DE LAS SABINAS, EL** • 1958

MATING SEASON, THE • 1951 • Leisen Mitchell • USA

MATING SEASON, THE • 1980 • Moxey John Llewellyn • TVM • USA

MATING URGE, THE • 1958 • *Brown Howard C. (P)* • DOC • USA

MATINS INFIDELES, LES • 1988 • Beaudry Jean, Bouvier Francois • CND

MATIOUETTE, LA • 1982 • Techine Andre • FRN

MATIRA MANISHA • 1967 • Sen Mrinal • IND • MAN OF THE SOIL ○ TWO BROTHERS

MATISSE OR THE TALENT FOR HAPPINESS see **MATISSE OU LE TALENT DU BONHEUR** • 1960

MATISSE OU LE TALENT DU BONHEUR • 1960 • Ophuls Marcel • SHT • FRN • MATISSE OR THE TALENT FOR HAPPINESS

MATKA JOANNA OD ANIOLOW • 1961 • Kawalerowicz Jerzy • PLN • DEVIL AND THE NUN, THE (UKN) ○ JOAN OF THE ANGELS (USA) ○ MOTHER JOAN OF THE ANGELS ○ MOTHER JOAN AND ANGELS

MATKA KRACMERKA • 1934 • Slavinsky Vladimir • CZC • MOTHER KRACMERKA

MATKA KROLOW • 1983 • Zaorski Janusz • PLN • MOTHER OF KROLS ○ MOTHER OF KINGS, THE

MATKALLA SEIKKAILUUN (FNL) see **BOTTE I FARTEN** • 1945

MATLOSA • 1982 • Herman Villi • SWT

MATLUB RAJULUN WAHID • 1974 • Nasser George • LBN, SYR • ON DEMANDE UN HOMME ○ ONE MAN WANTED

MATO ELES? • 1982 • Bianchi Sergio • DOC • BRZ • DO I KILL THEM?

MATOMENA CHRISTOUYENNA • 1951 • Zervos Georges • GRC • NOEL SANGLANT

MATOMENA HELIOVASILEMA • 1959 • Lambrinos Andreas • GRC • BLOODY TWILIGHT

MATOMENI YI • 1967 • Efstratiadis Omiris • GRC • BLEEDING EARTH

MATOU, LE • 1985 • Beaudin Jean • CND • ALLEY CAT, THE

MATOU A FAMILIA E FOI AO CINEMA • 1970 • Bressane Julio • BRZ

MATOU A FAMILIA E FOI AO CINEMA • 1989 • d'Almeida Neville • BRZ • HE KILLED HIS FAMILY AND WENT TO THE MOVIES

MATOUS SONT ROMANTIQUES, LES • 1981 • Sotha • FRN

MATOUS THE SHOEMAKER see **O SEVCI MATOUSOVI** • 1948

MATRATZEN TANGO • 1972 • Schroeder Eberhard • FRG • SECRETS OF NAKED GIRLS ○ WHEN GIRLS UNDRESS

MATRI-PHONY • 1942 • Edwards Harry J. • SHT • USA

MATRIARCH, THE see **MATIARCA, LA** • 1968

MATRIARCHATE • 1977 • Kirkov Lyudmil • BUL

MATRICES • 1966 • *Halas John (P)* • ANS • UKN

MATRICULE 20.007 • 1969 • Revol Robert • SHT • FRN

MATRICULE 33 • 1933 • Anton Karl • FRN

MATRIMANIAC, THE • 1916 • Powell Paul • USA

MATRIMONIACS, THE • 1920 • Goldaine Mark • SHT • USA

MATRIMONIAL ACCIDENT, A • 1917 • *Triangle* • USA

MATRIMONIAL ADVERTISEMENT, A • 1914 • *Melies* • USA

MATRIMONIAL ADVICE COLUMN see **PORADNIK MATRYMONIALNY** • 1968

MATRIMONIAL AGENCY OF ROARING GULCH, THE • 1912 • *Nestor* • USA

MATRIMONIAL ANNOUNCEMENT see **FRIARANNONSEN** • 1955

MATRIMONIAL BED, THE • 1930 • Curtiz Michael • USA • MATRIMONIAL PROBLEM, A (UKN)

MATRIMONIAL BLISS • 1915 • *Starlight* • USA

MATRIMONIAL BLISS • 1916 • Storrie Kelly • UKN

MATRIMONIAL BOOMERANG, A • 1915 • Mix Tom • USA

MATRIMONIAL BREAKER • 1918 • *Triangle* • USA

MATRIMONIAL DELUGE, A • 1913 • Duncan William • USA

MATRIMONIAL HOLIDAYS see **EHEFERIEN** • 1927

MATRIMONIAL IDOL, A • 1911 • *Powers* • USA

MATRIMONIAL MANOEUVRES • 1913 • North Wilfred, Costello Maurice • USA

MATRIMONIAL MARTYR, A • 1916 • *Roland Ruth* • USA
MATRIMONIAL MIX-UP, A • 1916 • *Heinie & Louie* • USA
MATRIMONIAL MUDDLE, A • 1912 • Stow Percy • UKN
MATRIMONIAL PROBLEM, A (UKN) see **MATRIMONIAL BED, THE** • 1930
MATRIMONIAL RAFFLE, A • 1913 • *Gaumont* • USA
MATRIMONIAL REVOLUTION, THE see **REVOLUCION MATRIMONIAL, LA** • 1975
MATRIMONIAL SHOCK, A • 1917 • Davis James • SHT • USA
MATRIMONIAL STAGES • 1908 • *Urban-Eclipse* • USA
MATRIMONIAL SUBSTITUTE, THE • 1912 • *Majestic* • USA
MATRIMONIAL SURPRISE, A • 1911 • *Powers* • USA
MATRIMONIAL VENTURE OF THE BAR X HANDS, THE • 1913 • *Kalem* • USA
MATRIMONIAL WARFARE see **GUERRA CONJUGAL** • 1974
MATRIMONIAL WEB, THE • 1921 • Jose Edward • USA
MATRIMONIO, IL • 1954 • Petrucci Antonio • ITL
MATRIMONIO A LA ARGENTINA • 1968 • Carreras Enrique • ARG • MARRIAGE ARGENTINIAN STYLE
MATRIMONIO AL DESNUDO • 1974 • Fernandez Ramon • SPN
MATRIMONIO ALLA FRANCESE (ITL) see **TONNERRE DE DIEU, LE** • 1965
MATRIMONIO ALLA MODO • 1951 • Emmer Luciano • ITL
MATRIMONIO ALL'ITALIANA • 1964 • De Sica Vittorio • ITL, FRN • MARIAGE A L'ITALIENNE (FRN) ○ MARRRIAGE ITALIAN STYLE (USA)
MATRIMONIO DI CATERINA, IL • 1982 • Comencini Luigi • MTV • ITL • HUSBAND FOR CATERINA, A
MATRIMONIO DI FIGARO, IL • 1913 • Maggi Luigi • ITL
MATRIMONIO IDEALE, UN • 1939 • Mastrocinque Camillo • ITL
MATRIMONIO INTERPLANETARIO, UN • 1910 • Novelli Enrico • ITL • MARRIAGE IN THE MOON, A ○ INTERPLANETARY WEDDING, AN
MATRIMONIO SEGRETO, IL • 1943 • Mastrocinque Camillo • ITL
MATRIMONIO SINTETICO • 1947 • Soler Julian • MXC
MATRIMONIO Y MORTAJA • 1949 • Mendez Fernando • MXC
MATRIMONIOS JUVENILES • 1958 • Diaz Morales Jose • MXC
MATRIMONIOS SEPERADOS • 1969 • Ozores Mariano • SPN
MATRIMONY • 1915 • Sidney Scott • USA
MATRIMONY, THE • Ch'En K'Un-Hou • TWN
MATRIMONY IN THE SHADOWS see **EHE IM SCHATTEN** • 1947
MATRIMONY'S SPEED LIMIT • 1913 • *Solax* • USA
MATRIOSKA • 1970 • Hoedeman Co • ANS • CND
MATRIX • 1970 • Whitney John • ANS • USA
MATRON'S REPORT, THE see **LITTLE MISS NOBODY** • 1936
MATROSE PERUGINO, DER • 1923 • Zelnik Friedrich • FRG
MATROSOWCY • 1951 • Banach • SHT • PLN
MATSI KHVITIA see **MATSY KHVITIYA** • 1969
MATSUKAWA DERAILMENT INCIDENT see **MATSUKAWA JIKEN** • 1960
MATSUKAWA JIKEN • 1960 • Yamamoto Satsuo • JPN • MATSUKAWA DERAILMENT INCIDENT
MATSURI NO JUNBI • 1975 • Kuroki Kazuo • JPN • PREPARE FOR THE FAIR
MATSY KHVITIYA • 1969 • Shengelaya Georgi • USS • MATSI KHVITIA ○ MATZI HVITIA
MATSYA GANDHA OR BHISHMA PRATIGNYA • 1934 • Mehta Dakubhai • IND
MATT • 1918 • Coleby A. E. • UKN
MATT HELM • 1975 • Kulik Buzz • TVM • USA
MATT HOUSTON • 1982 • Lang Richard • TVM • USA
MATT RYKER: MUTANT HUNT see **MUTANT HUNT** • 1986
MATT THE GOOSEBOY see **LUDAS MATYI** • 1977
MATTA MATTA MATTA CORSA IN RUSSIA, UNA • 1974 • Prosperi Franco, Ryazanov Eldar • ITL
MATTANZA -EIN LIEBESTRAUM • 1969 • FRG
MATTATORE, IL • 1960 • Risi Dino • ITL, FRN • HOMME AUX CENT VISAGES, L' (FRN) ○ LOVE AND LARCENY (USA)
MATTAWIN, RIVIERE SAUVAGE, LA • 1958 • Brault Michel, Sylvestre Claude • SHT • CND
MATTEI AFFAIR, THE (UKN) see **CASO MATTEI, IL** • 1972
MATTER, THE see **MATERIA** • 1962
MATTER OF BUSINESS, A • 1912 • *Johnson Arthur* • USA
MATTER OF CARE, A • 1969 • Holmes Cecil • DOC • ASL
MATTER OF CHOICE, A • 1963 • Sewell Vernon • UKN
MATTER OF CHOICE, A • 1978 • Mankiewicz Francis • MTV • CND
MATTER OF CONSCIENCE, A see **KWESTIA SUMIENIA** • 1967
MATTER OF CONSCIENCE, A see **THEMA SINIDHISEOS** • 1972
MATTER OF CONVICTION, A see **YOUNG SAVAGES, THE** • 1961
MATTER OF COURT, A • 1914 • Henderson Dell • USA
MATTER OF DAYS, A (USA) see **A QUELQUES JOURS PRES** • 1968
MATTER OF DIGNITY, A see **TELEFTEO PSEMMA, TO** • 1957
MATTER OF DISCIPLINE, A • 1973 • *King Tim (P)* • UKN
MATTER OF DRESS, A • 1913 • *Travers Richard* • USA
MATTER OF FACTS, A see **PRAVO STANJE STVARI** • 1964
MATTER OF FAT, A • 1969 • Weintraub William • DOC • CND
MATTER OF HIGH EXPLOSIVES, A • 1914 • Ransom Charles • USA
MATTER OF HONOUR, A (UKN) see **TECNICAS DE DUELO** • 1988
MATTER OF HUMANITIES see **MARCUS WELBY, M.D.** • 1968
MATTER OF INNOCENCE, A see **PRETTY POLLY** • 1967
MATTER OF LIFE AND DEATH, A • 1946 • Powell Michael, Pressburger Emeric • UKN • STAIRWAY TO HEAVEN (USA) ○ TALE OF TWO WORLDS, A
MATTER OF LIFE AND DEATH, A • 1981 • Mayberry Russ • TVM • USA
MATTER OF LIFE AND DEATH, A see **PA LIV OCH DOD** • 1943
MATTER OF LIFE AND DEATH, A see **JIBAN MRITYU** • 1967
MATTER OF LIFE AND DEATH, A see **PA LIV OCH DOD** • 1986
MATTER OF LIVE AND DEATH, A see **LIFE IN THE BALANCE, A** • 1955
MATTER OF LOVE, A • 1979 • Vincent Chuck • USA
MATTER OF MATRIMONY, A • 1913 • *Bennett Charles* • USA
MATTER OF MORALS, A • 1960 • Cromwell John • USA, SWD • SISTA STEGEN, DE (SWD)
MATTER OF MURDER, A • 1949 • Gilling John • UKN
MATTER OF PARENTAGE, A • 1915 • *Powers* • USA
MATTER OF PRIDE, A • 1961 • King Allan • CND
MATTER OF PRIDE, A see **BEG, BORROW OR STEAL** • 1937
MATTER OF RECORD, A • 1914 • Myers Harry • USA
MATTER OF RESISTANCE, A (USA) see **VIE DE CHATEAU, LA** • 1966
MATTER OF SEX, A • 1984 • Grant Lee • TVM • USA • WOMEN OF WILLMAR, THE
MATTER OF SOIL, A • 1985 • Dodd Thomas • DOC • CND
MATTER OF SURVIVAL, A • 1969 • Devlin Bernard • SHT • CND • DECISION CAPITALE, UNE
MATTER OF TIME, A • 1976 • Minnelli Vincente • USA, UKN, ITL • NINA
MATTER OF VALOUR, A see **DAI CHUSHINGUSA** • 1957
MATTER OF WHO, A • 1961 • Chaffey Don • UKN
MATTER OF WIFE.. AND DEATH, A • 1975 • Chomsky Marvin • TVM • USA
MATTER TO SETTLE, A see **SPRAWA DO ZALATWIENIA** • 1953
MATTHAUS-PASSION • 1949 • Marischka Ernst • AUS, ITL • PASSIONE SECONDO SAN MATTEO, LA (ITL) ○ ST. MATTHEW PASSION (USA)
MATTHEW THE SHOEMAKER see **O SEVCI MATOUSOVI** • 1948
MATTHEW'S PASSION see **MUKE PO MATI** • 1976
MATTHIAS THE JUST see **MATYAS, AZ IGAZSAGOS** • 1986
MATTI DA SLEGARE • 1976 • Agosti Silvano, Bellocchio Marco, Rulli Stefano, Petraglia Sandro • ITL • FIT TO BE UNTIED (USA)
MATTIE, THE GOOSEBOY see **LUDAS MATYI** • 1949
MATTIE THE GOOSEBOY see **LUDAS MATYI** • 1977
MATTIG THE GOOSEBOY see **LUDAS MATYI** • 1977
MATTINO see **RAGAZZO CHE SORRIDE, IL** • 1969
MATTINO DI PRIMAVERA • 1957 • Solito Giacinto • ITL, FRN
MATTO, IL • 1979 • Giornelli Franco • ITL
MATTO REGIERT • 1946 • Lindtberg Leopold • SWT
MATTSCHICHE DANCE • 1907 • *Walturdaw* • UKN
MATTY see **VILDMARKSSOMMAR** • 1957
MATTY JOINS THE JUVENILE POLICE FORCE • 1914 • *Imp* • USA
MATTY'S DECISION • 1915 • *Matthewson Christy* • USA
MATTY'S LOVE AFFAIR • 1916 • *Juvenile Film* • USA
MATURA • 1964 • Rybczynski Boguslaw • DCS • PLN
MATURA • 1965 • Konwicki Tadeusz • PLN • ENTRANCE EXAMINATION
MATURAREISE • 1943 • Steiner • FRN • JEUNE FILLES AUJOURD'HUI
MATURE WINE see **ZRALE VINO** • 1981
MATURZYSCI • 1972 • Halladin Danuta • DOC • PLN • SCHOOL LEAVERS, THE
MATUSHKA • 1973 • Lind John • UKN
MATUSHKA see **VIADUKT** • 1983
MATUTA • 1965 • Cox Paul • SHT • ASL
MATYAS, AZ IGAZSAGOS • 1986 • Ujvary Laszlo Jr. • ANM • HNG • MATTHIAS THE JUST
MATYSIAK'S HOUSE, THE see **DOM MATYSIAKOW** • 1966
MATZI HVITIA see **MATSY KHVITIYA** • 1969
MAU MAU • 1955 • Price Elwood G.
MAUD • 1911 • Noy Wilfred • UKN
MAUD, DIE GROSSE SENSATION • 1923 • *Allianz-Film-Vertriebsges* • FRG
MAUD LEWIS, A WORLD WITHOUT SHADOWS • 1975 • Beaudry Diane • CND
MAUD MULLER • 1911 • *Williams Kathlyn* • USA
MAUD MULLER • 1912 • Ricketts Thomas • USA
MAUD ROCKEFELLERS WETTE • 1924 • Eriksen Erich • FRG
MAUD (UKN) see **NAKED HEARTS** • 1916
MAUDE MULLER • 1909 • *Essanay* • USA
MAUDE MULLER MODERNIZED • 1916 • *Bates Louise Emerald* • SHT • USA
MAUDE'S NAUGHTY LITTLE BROTHER • 1900 • Porter Edwin S. • USA
MAUDIE'S ADVENTURE • 1913 • Stow Percy • UKN
MAUDITE, LA • 1949 • de Meyst E. G. • FRN
MAUDITE GALETTE, LA • 1972 • Arcand Denys • CND
MAUDITE: LEGEND OF DOOM HOUSE see **MALPERTIUS** • 1972
MAUDITE SOIT LA GUERRE • 1910 • Feuillade Louis • FRN
MAUDITE SOIT LA GUERRE • 1913 • Machin Alfred • BLG, FRN • MOULIN MAUDIT, LE ○ CURSED BE WAR
MAUDITS, LES • 1946 • Clement Rene • FRN • SOUS-MARIN BLESSE, LE ○ DAMNED, THE (USA)
MAUDITS SAUVAGE, LES • 1971 • Lefebvre Jean-Pierre • CND • THOSE DAMNED SAVAGES
MAUD'S GLOVE • 1914 • *Melies* • USA
MAUERBLUME IN BALLHAUS PARADOX • 1968 • Lorenzen Rudolf • FRG
MAULA BUX • 1988 • Malik Yonus • PKS • ROD, THE
MAULA SAIN • 1988 • PKS • SAINT
MAULE, EL • 1983 • Bustamente Patricio, Bustamente Juan Carlos • DOC • CHL
MAULKORB, DER • 1938 • Engel Erich • FRG
MAULKORB, DER • 1958 • Staudte Wolfgang • FRG
MAULWURFE • 1920 • Holz Artur • FRG
MAUNG MAUNG NAI PATHAMA ACHIT • 1983 • U Kyee Myint • BRM • MG MG AND HIS FIRST LOVE
MAUPRAT • 1926 • Epstein Jean • FRN
MAURI • 1987 • Mita Merata • NZL
MAURICE • 1987 • Ivory James • UKN
MAURICIO, MON AMOUR • 1976 • Bosch Juan • SPN
MAURIE • 1973 • Mann Daniel • USA • BIG MO
MAURIN DES MAURES • 1932 • Hugon Andre • FRN
MAURITZ STILLER • Werner Gosta • DOC • SWD
MAURIZIO, PEPPINO E LE INDOSSATRICI • 1962 • Ratti Filippo M. • ITL
MAURIZIUS CASE, THE (USA) see **AFFAIRE MAURIZIUS, L'** • 1953
MAURO THE GYPSY • 1972 • Henson Laurence • UKN
MAUSEFALLE, DIE • 1922 • Kobe Hanns • FRG
MAUSOLEUM • 1982 • Dugan Michael • USA
MAUSOLEUM • 1983 • Franzese Michael, Zimmerman Jerry • USA
MAUVAIS COEUR PUNI • 1904 • Blache Alice • FRN
MAUVAIS COUPS, LES • 1961 • Leterrier Francois • FRN • NAKED AUTUMN (USA)
MAUVAIS FILS, UN • 1981 • Sautet Claude • FRN • BAD SON, A
MAUVAIS GARCON, LE • 1921 • Diamant-Berger Henri • FRN
MAUVAIS GARCON, UN • 1936 • Boyer Jean • FRN • MON PRISONNIER
MAUVAIS OEIL, LE • 1938 • Dekeukeleire Charles • BLG
MAUVAIS SANG • 1986 • Carax Leos • FRN • NIGHT IS YOUNG, THE
MAUVAISE CONDUITE • 1984 • Almendros Nestor, Jiminez-Leal Orlando • FRN • IMPROPER CONDUCT (USA)
MAUVAISE GRAINE • 1934 • Wilder Billy, Esway Alexander • FRN
MAUVAISE RICHE, LE • 1902 • Zecca Ferdinand • FRN
MAUVAISE SOUPE, LA • 1899-00 • Blache Alice • FRN
MAUVAISES FREQUENTATIONS, LES • 1967 • Eustache Jean, Godard Jean-Luc • CMP • FRN • BAD COMPANY (USA)
MAUVAISES HERBES • 1896 • Lumiere Louis • FRN • BRULURES D'HERBE, LES
MAUVAISES HERBES, LES • 1938-40 • Tessier Albert • DCS • CND
MAUVAISES MANIERES, LES see **VILAINES MANIERES, LES** • 1973
MAUVAISES RECONTRES, LES • 1955 • Astruc Alexandre • FRN
MAUVENTS, LES see **TEMPETE SUR LES MAUVENTS** • 1952
MAVERICK, THE • 1912 • *Solax* • USA
MAVERICK, THE • 1952 • Carr Thomas • USA
MAVERICK QUEEN, THE • 1956 • Kane Joseph • USA
MAVI • 1978 • Mordente Tony • USA
MAVILKA • 1915 • Phalke Dada • IND
MAVIS OF THE GLEN • 1915 • Leonard Robert Z. • USA
MAVRO STAHI, TO • 1968 • Mihailidis Kostas • GRC • BLACK EAR OF CORN, THE
MAW AND PAW • 1953 • Smith Paul J. • ANS • USA
MAWAR MERAH • 1987 • MLY • RED ROSE
MAWAS • 1985 • Osman Aziz M. • MTV • MLY
MAWED MAA EL RAIS • 1989 • Rahi Mohamed • EGY • APPOINTMENT WITH THE PRESIDENT
MAWID MA'A AL-MAGHUL • 1959 • Salem Atef • EGY • RENDEZ-VOUS AVEC L'INCONNU
MAWLID YA DUNIA • 1975 • Kamal Hussein • EGY • MONDE EST UNE FETE, LE
MAX see **MAX ET LES FERRAILLEURS** • 1970
MAX A MONACO • 1913 • Linder Max • FRN
MAX A UN DUEL • 1911 • Linder Max • FRN
MAX AERONAUTE • 1908 • Linder Max • FRN
MAX AMOUREUX DE LA TEINTURIERE • 1912 • Linder Max • FRN
MAX AND HIS DONKEY see **MAX ET SON ANE** • 1911
MAX AND MAURICE • 1912 • *Boss Yale* • USA
MAX AND MORITZ • 1978 • Halas John • ANS • UKN
MAX AND THE CLUTCHING HAND (USA) see **MAIN QUI ENTREINT, LA** • 1915
MAX AND THE GHOSTS see **PEHAVY MAX A STRASIDLA** • 1987
MAX AND THE LADY DOCTOR see **MAX ET LA DOCTORESSE** • 1914
MAX ASSASSINE see **QUI A TUE MAX?** • 1913
MAX ASTHMATIQUE • 1913 • Linder Max • FRN
MAX AU CONVENT • 1913 • Linder Max • FRN
MAX BECKMANN • 1961 • Angella • SHT • ITL
MAX BOXEUR PAR AMOUR • 1912 • Linder Max • FRN • BOXEUR PAR AMOUR
MAX CHAMPION DE BOXE • 1910 • Linder Max • FRN
MAX CHERCHE UNE FIANCEE • 1910 • Linder Max • FRN
MAX COCHER DE FIACRE • 1912 • Linder Max • FRN
MAX COLLECTIONNEUR DE CHAUSSURES • 1913 • Linder Max • FRN
MAX COMES ACROSS • 1917 • Linder Max • SHT • USA • MAX GOES TO AMERICA (UKN)
MAX CUISINIER PAR AMOUR • 1911 • Linder Max • FRN • MAX ET JANE FONT DES CREPES
MAX DANS LES AIRES • 1914 • Linder Max • FRN
MAX DANS SA FAMILLE • 1911 • Linder Max • FRN
MAX DECORE see **MEDAILLE DE SAUVETAGE, LA** • 1914
MAX, DER TASCHENDIEB • 1962 • Moszkowicz Imo • FRG
MAX, DER VIELGEPRUFTE • 1920 • Grunwald Willy • FRG
MAX DEVRAIT PORTER DES BRETELLES • 1915 • Linder Max • FRN
MAX DIAMOND • 1967 • Feleo Ben • PHL
MAX DOMINO • 1979 • Pardo Gerardo • MXC
MAX DUGAN RETURNS • 1983 • Ross Herbert • USA
MAX EMULE DE TARTARIN • 1912 • Linder Max • FRN • EMULE DE TARTARIN
MAX EN CONVALESCENCE • 1911 • Linder Max • FRN
MAX EN VACANCES see **MAX PART EN VACANCES** • 1913
MAX ENTRE DEUX FEMMES see **MAX ENTRE DEUX FEUX** • 1915
MAX ENTRE DEUX FEUX • 1915 • Linder Max • FRN • MAX ENTRE DEUX FEMMES
MAX ERNST -ENTDECKUNGSFAHRTEN INS UNBEWUSSTE • 1962 • Schamoni Peter, Lamb Carl • SHT • FRG • MAX ERNST -JOURNEYS OF DISCOVERY INTO THE UNCONSCIOUS
MAX ERNST -JOURNEYS OF DISCOVERY INTO THE UNCONSCIOUS see **MAX ERNST -ENTDECKUNGSFAHRTEN INS UNBEWUSSTE** • 1962
MAX ESCAMOTEUR see **SUCCES DE LA PRESTIDIGITATION, LE** • 1912
MAX EST CHARITABLE • 1911 • Linder Max • FRN
MAX EST DISTRAIT • 1911 • Linder Max • FRN
MAX ET JANE EN VOYAGE DE NOCES • 1911 • Linder Max • FRN • VOYAGE DE NOCES, LE
MAX ET JANE FONT DES CREPES see **MAX CUISINIER PAR AMOUR** • 1911
MAX ET JANE VEULENT FAIRE DU THEATRE • 1912 • Linder Max • FRN
MAX ET LA BONNE A TOUT FAIRE • 1912 • Linder Max • FRN
MAX ET LA DOCTORESSE • 1914 • Linder Max • FRN • MAX AND THE LADY DOCTOR
MAX ET LA MAIN QUI ETREINT • 1915 • Linder Max • FRN
MAX ET LE BATON DE ROUGE • 1914 • Linder Max • FRN
MAX ET LE BILLET DOUX • 1913 • Linder Max • FRN • BILLET DOUX, LE
MAX ET LE COMMISSAIRE • 1913 • Linder Max • FRN
MAX ET LE MARI JALOUX • 1914 • Linder Max • FRN
MAX ET LE QUINQUINA • 1911 • Linder Max • FRN • MAX VICTIME DU QUINQUINA
MAX ET LE RENDEZ-VOUS • 1913 • Linder Max • FRN

MAX ET LE SAXE • 1915 • Linder Max • FRN
MAX ET L'ENTENTE CORDIALE • 1912 • Linder Max • FRN • ENTENTE CORDIALE
MAX ET LES CREPES • 1913 • Linder Max • FRN
MAX ET LES FEMMES • 1912 • Linder Max • FRN • OH! LES FEMMES!
MAX ET LES FERRAILLEURS • 1970 • Sautet Claude • FRN, ITL • COMMISSARIO PELLISSIER, IL (ITL) ○ MAX
MAX ET L'ESPION • 1915 • Linder Max • FRN
MAX ET L'INAUGURATION DE LA STATUE see **INAUGURATION DE LA STATUE, L'** • 1913
MAX ET SA BELLE-MERE • 1911 • Linder Max • FRN
MAX ET SON ANE • 1911 • Linder Max • FRN • MAX AND HIS DONKEY
MAX ET SON CHIEN DICK • 1912 • Linder Max • FRN
MAX FAIT DE LA PHOTO • 1913 • Linder Max • FRN
MAX FAIT DES CONQUETES • 1913 • Linder Max • FRN
MAX FAIT DU SKI • 1910 • Gasnier Louis J. • FRN
MAX GOES TO AMERICA (UKN) see **MAX COMES ACROSS** • 1917
MAX HAS A BIRTHDAY • 1915 • Batley Ernest G.? • UKN
MAX HAUFLER, DER STUMME • 1983 • Dindo Richard • SWT • MAX HAUFLER THE MUTE
MAX HAUFLER THE MUTE see **MAX HAUFLER, DER STUMME** • 1983
MAX HAVELAAR • 1976 • Rademakers Fons • NTH, INN
MAX HEADROOM • 1985 • Morton Rocky, Jankel Annabel • UKN • MAX HEADROOM: THE ORIGINAL STORY ○ MAX HEADROOM FILM, THE ○ MAX HEADROOM STORY, THE
MAX HEADROOM FILM, THE see **MAX HEADROOM** • 1985
MAX HEADROOM STORY, THE see **MAX HEADROOM** • 1985
MAX HEADROOM: THE ORIGINAL STORY see **MAX HEADROOM** • 1985
MAX HYPNOTISE • 1911 • Linder Max • FRN • MAX HYPNOTISED
MAX HYPNOTISED see **MAX HYPNOTISE** • 1911
MAX ILLUSIONISTE • 1914 • Linder Max • FRN
MAX IN A TAXI • 1917 • Linder Max • SHT • USA
MAX IN THE MORNING • 1965 • Bairstow David • DOC • CND
MAX JALOUX • 1914 • Linder Max • FRN
MAX JOCKEY PAR AMOUR • 1912 • Linder Max • FRN • JOCKEY PAR AMOUR
MAX LANCE LA MODE • 1912 • Linder Max • FRN
MAX & LAURA & HENK & WILLIE • 1989 • Ruven Paul • NTH
MAX LINDER CONTRE NICK WINTER • 1912 • Linder Max • FRN
MAX MAITRE D'HOTEL • 1914 • Linder Max • FRN
MAX MEDECIN MALGRE LUI • 1914 • Linder Max • FRN
MAX MON AMOUR • 1986 • Oshima Nagisa • FRN • MAX MY LOVE
MAX MY LOVE see **MAX MON AMOUR** • 1986
MAX N'AIME PAS LES CHATS • 1913 • Linder Max • FRN
MAX-OUT • 1970 • Kaylor Robert • USA
MAX PART EN VACANCES • 1913 • Linder Max • FRN • VACANCES DE MAX, LES ○ MAX EN VACANCES
MAX PEDICURE • 1914 • Linder Max • FRN • PEDICURE, THE
MAX PEINTRE PAR AMOUR • 1912 • Linder Max • FRN • PEINTRE PAR AMOUR
MAX PRATIQUE TOUS LES SPORTS • 1913 • Linder Max • FRN
MAX PREND UN BAIN • 1910 • Linder Max • FRN
MAX, PROFESSEUR DE TANGO • 1912 • Linder Max • FRN • MAX, TANGO TEACHER ○ TOO MUCH MUSTARD
MAX REPREND SA LIBERTE • 1912 • Linder Max • FRN
MAX ROACH • 1967 • Leduc Francois • SHT • FRN • CINE JAZZ
MAX SAUVETEUR • 1914 • Linder Max • FRN
MAX SE MARIE • 1911 • Linder Max • FRN
MAX SE TROMPE D'ETAGE • 1910 • Linder Max • FRN
MAX, TANGO TEACHER see **MAX, PROFESSEUR DE TANGO** • 1912
MAX TOREADOR • 1913 • Linder Max • FRN
MAX TROUVE UNE FIANCEE • 1911 • Linder Max • FRN
MAX UND SEINE ZWEI FRAUEN • 1915 • Bolten-Baeckers Heinrich • FRG
MAX VEUT GRANDIR • 1912 • Linder Max • FRN
MAX VICTIME DU QUINQUINA see **MAX ET LE QUINQUINA** • 1911
MAX VIRTUOSE • 1913 • Linder Max • FRN
MAX WALL -FUNNY MAN • 1975 • Scoffield John • UKN
MAX WANTS A DIVORCE • 1917 • Linder Max • SHT • USA
MAXANITO • 1989 • Straub Rudolph • SWT
MAXHOSA • 1975 • Stephenson Lynton • SAF
MAXI CAT • 1970 • Grgic Zlatko • ANS • YGS
MAXIE • 1954 • von Borsody Eduard • AUS
MAXIE • 1985 • Aaron Paul • USA • I'LL MEET YOU IN HEAVEN ○ FREE SPIRIT
MAXIM MAXIMYCH TAMAN • 1967 • Rostotsky Stanislav • USS
MAXIM TRILOGY, THE see **TRILOGIYA O MAXIME** • 1932-38
MAXIME • 1958 • Verneuil Henri • FRN
MAXIMENKO BRIGADE, THE see **MAKSIMENKO BRIGAD, A** • 1950
MAXIMIZING PRODUCTION • 1984 • Gordon Lee • DOC • CND, USA
MAXIMKA • 1953 • Braun Vladimir • USS
MAXIMUM • 1918 • Halm Alfred • FRG
MAXIMUM • 1962 • Gunwall Per • SWD
MAXIMUM OVERDRIVE • 1986 • King Stephen • USA
MAXIMUM SECURITY • 1987 • Duke Bill • USA
MAXIMUM SECURITY • 1989 • Thomas John G. • USA
MAXIMUM THRUST • 1987 • Kincaid Tim • USA
MAXIXE BRASILIENNE, THE • 1913 • *Selsior Films* • UKN
MAX'S ICE SCREAM see **DEBUTS D'UN PATINEUR, LES** • 1906
MAX'S MONEY • 1914 • *Royal* • USA
MAXWELL ARCHER, DETECTIVE (USA) see **MEET MAXWELL ARCHER** • 1939
MAXWELL STREET BLUES • 1980 • Williams Linda, Zaritsky Raul • USA
MAXWELL'S DEMON • 1968 • Frampton Hollis • SHT • USA
MAY see **MIAS** • 1975
MAY 1ST see **1 MAJA** • 1938
MAY 17 see **17TH MAY, A FILM ABOUT RITUALS**
MAY AND DECEMBER • 1907 • Coleby A. E.? • UKN
MAY AND DECEMBER • 1910 • Griffith D. W. • USA
MAY AND DECEMBER • 1913 • *Broncho* • USA
MAY AND FRANK • 1975 • Bonniere Rene • CND
MAY BLOSSOM • 1915 • Dwan Allan • USA
MAY BLOSSOM see **MAYBLOSSOM** • 1917
MAY DAYS • 1920 • Fitzpatrick James A.* • USA
MAY EVENTS see **BYLO TO V MAJI** • 1951
MAY FAIRY TALE see **POHADKA MAJE** • 1940
MAY FLY, THE see **MAANEPRINSESSEN** • 1916
MAY GOD FORGIVE YOU.. I CAN'T see **DIO PERDONA.. IO NO!** • 1967
MAY I BORROW YOUR WIFE? see **FAR JAG LANA DIN FRU?** • 1959
MAY I CALL YOU PETRUSHKA? • 1980 • Heymann Karl-Heinz • GDR
MAY I GO OUT? • 1968 • Wenceslao Jose Pepe • PHL
MAY I HAVE THE FLOOR? see **JA PRASU SLOVA** • 1975
MAY I SIR? see **FAR JAG LOV, MAGISTERN!** • 1947
MAY I TAKE THE FLOOR? see **JA PRASU SLOVA** • 1975
MAY MORNING IN OXFORD see **DELITTO A OXFORD** • 1970
MAY NIGHT • 1952 • Rou Aleksandr • USS
MAY QUEEN, THE • 1914 • *Favourite Films* • UKN
MAY RAIN AND SILK PAPER see **SAMIDARE ZOSHI** • 1924
MAY STARS see **MAISKIE ZVEZDY** • 1959
MAY STORY, THE see **POHADKA MAJE** • 1926
MAY STORY, THE see **POHADKA MAJE** • 1940
MAY TAMPUHAN, PAMINSAN-MINSAN • 1968 • Torres Mar S. • PHL • LOVERS' PETTY QUARRELS
MAY THE BEST MAN WIN • 1989 • McCarthy Mike* • USA
MAY.. THE PALESTINIANS • 1974 • Hajjar Rafik • SHT • LBN
MAY WAY FOR THE JAGUARS see **SUSUME JAGUARS TEKIZEN JORIKU** • 1968
MAYA • 1936 • Barua Pramathesh Chandra • IND • ILLUSION
MAYA • 1949 • Bernard Raymond • FRN
MAYA • 1957 • Schombs Franz, Schneider Wolf, Opferman H. C., Koch Walter, Senft Haro, Vesely Herbert • FRG
MAYA • 1966 • Berry John • USA
MAYA • 1979 • Hernandez Theo • FRN
MAYA • 1982 • Peries Sumitra • SLN • ILLUSION
MAYA AND BREUDA see **MEDEA** • 1976
MAYA BAZAR • 1939 • Powar G. P. • IND • FANTASY BAZAAR
MAYA BAZAR • 1949 • Dharamadhikari Datta • IND • FANTASY BAZAAR
MAYA BAZAR • 1959 • Mistry Babhubhai • IND • FANTASY BAZAAR
MAYA DARPAN • 1972 • Shahani Kumar • IND • MIRROR OF ILLUSION
MAYA FROM TSKHNETI see **MAIA IZ TSKHNETI** • 1962
MAYA -JUST AN INDIAN • 1913 • *Frontier* • USA
MAYA KAJAL • 1937 • Lahiri Tulsi • IND
MAYA MACHINDRA see **GORAKHNATH** • 1951
MAYA MAHAL • 1928 • *Sharada* • IND • MAGIC VALLEY
MAYA MANIDHAN • 1958 • *Sriram* • IND
MAYA MARIGA • 1984 • Mohapatra Nirad M. • IND • MIRAGE, THE
MAYA MOHINI • 1928 • IND
MAYA PLISETSKAYA • 1964 • Katanyan Vasili • DOC • USS • PLISTSKAYA DANCES (USA) ○ MAYYA PLISETSKAYA
MAYA PLISETSKAYA • 1983 • Szintai Istvan • DOC • FNL
MAYAK • 1942 • Donskoi Mark • USS • LIGHTHOUSE, THE ○ BEACON, THE ○ SIGNAL, THE
MAYAKOVSKY LAUGHS see **MAYAKOVSKY SMEYOTSYA** • 1976
MAYAKOVSKY NACHINALSYA TAK • 1959 • Pipinashvili Konstantin • USS • THIS IS HOW MAYAKOVSKY BEGAN
MAYAKOVSKY SMEYOTSYA • 1976 • Yutkevich Sergei, Karanovich Anatoli • USS • MAYAKOVSKY LAUGHS
MAYAKUDARAI • 1949 • *Sobhanachala* • IND • MAGIC HORSE (USA)
MAYAPRITI • 1989 • Thapa B. S. • NPL • BELOVED
MAYAVATHI • 1949 • Sundaram T. R. • IND
MAYAVI NAGARI • 1928 • *Young India Pictures* • IND • MAGIC CITY, THE (USA)
MAYBE see **CHAI** • 1924
MAYBE BABY see **FOR KEEPS** • 1988
MAYBE DARWIN WAS RIGHT • 1942 • Eason B. Reeves • SHT • USA
MAYBE I'LL COME HOME IN THE SPRING • 1970 • Sargent Joseph • TVM • USA
MAYBE IT'S LOVE • 1930 • Wellman William A. • USA
MAYBE IT'S LOVE • 1935 • McGann William • USA • HALFWAY TO HEAVEN
MAYBE MOONSHINE • 1916 • Beaudine William • SHT • USA
MAYBE SOME OTHER TIME • 1988 • Beyzai Bahram • IRN
MAYBE THIS TIME • 1980 • McGill Chris • ASL
MAYBE TOMORROW • 1973 • McGill Chris • SHT • ASL
MAYBE TOMORROW see **MAJD HOLNAP** • 1980
MAYBLOSSOM • 1917 • Jose Edward • USA • MAY BLOSSOM
MAYBOWL see **MAIBOWLE** • 1959
MAYDAY AT 40,000 FEET • 1976 • Butler Robert • TVM • USA
MAYDAY IN PARIS see **PREMIER MAI** • 1958
MAYERLING • 1936 • Litvak Anatole • FRN
MAYERLING • 1957 • Litvak Anatole • MTV • USA
MAYERLING • 1968 • Young Terence • UKN, FRN
MAYERLING TO SARAJEVO (USA) see **DE MAYERLING A SARAJEVO** • 1940
MAYERLING (USA) see **TRAGODIE IM HAUSE HABSBURG** • 1924
MAYFAIR GIRL • 1933 • King George • UKN • SOCIETY GIRL
MAYFAIR MELODY • 1937 • Woods Arthur • UKN
MAYFLOWER, THE • 1935 • *Terry Paul/ Moser Frank (P)* • ANS • USA
MAYFLOWER MADAM • 1987 • Antonio Lou • TVM • USA
MAYFLOWER: THE PILGRIM'S ADVENTURE • 1979 • Schaefer George • TVM • USA
MAYHEM • 1986 • Merhi Joseph • USA
MAYIKI POLIS, I • 1955 • Koundouros Nikos • GRC • MAGIC CITY ○ CITE MAGIQUE, LA ○ MAGIKI POLIS, I
MAYNILA, SA MGA KUKO NG LIWANAG • 1975 • Brocka Lino • PHL • NAIL OF BRIGHTNESS, THE (USA) ○ MANILA (UKN) ○ MANILA IN THE CLAWS OF LIGHT ○ MANILA: IN THE CLAWS OF NEON ○ MANILA: IN THE CLAWS OF DARKNESS
MAYOL • 1900-07 • Blache Alice • SER • FRN
MAYONAKA NO HANAZONO • 1967 • Takagi Takeo • JPN • MIDNIGHT FLOWER BED
MAYONAKA NO KAO • 1958 • Uno Jukichi • JPN • FACE AT MIDNIGHT
MAYONAKA NO SHOJO • 1959 • Hozumi Toshimasa • JPN
MAYOR FROM IRELAND, THE • 1912 • Olcott Sidney • USA • MAJOR FROM IRELAND, THE
MAYOR, MAYOR • 1989 • Maslarov Plamen • BUL
MAYOR OBJECTS, THE see **AYAW NI MAYOR** • 1967
MAYOR OF 44TH STREET • 1942 • Green Alfred E. • USA
MAYOR OF CASTERBRIDGE, THE • 1921 • Morgan Sidney • UKN
MAYOR OF FILBERT, THE • 1919 • Cabanne W. Christy • USA
MAYOR OF HELL, THE • 1933 • Mayo Archie • USA
MAYOR VIKHR • 1968 • Tashkov Yevgyeni • USS • MAJOR VIKHR
MAYORDOMO, EL see **ANIMAS TRUJANO, EL HOMBRE IMPORTANTE** • 1961
MAYORDOMO PARA TODO • 1975 • Ozores Mariano • SPN
MAYORES CON REPAROS • 1967 • Fernan-Gomez Fernando • SPN • ADULTS WITH OBJECTIONS
MAYOR'S CRUSADE, THE • 1912 • *West William H.* • USA
MAYOR'S DECISION, THE • 1915 • Dowlan William C. • USA
MAYOR'S DILEMMA, THE (USA) see **OTAGES, LES** • 1939
MAYOR'S FALL FROM GRACE, THE • 1916 • Smith David • SHT • USA
MAYOR'S MANICURE, THE • 1914 • *Maison Edna* • USA
MAYOR'S NEST, THE • 1932 • Rogers Maclean • UKN
MAYOR'S NEST, THE (UKN) see **RETURN OF DANIEL BOONE, THE** • 1941
MAYOR'S SECRET, THE see **HORETA TSUYOMI** • 1968
MAYOR'S SECRETARY, THE • 1914 • Buel Kenean • USA
MAYOR'S WATERLOO, THE • 1913 • *Lang Pete* • USA
MAYPOLE CARVING • 1981 • Paakspuu Kalli • DOC • CND
MAYPOLE DANCE • 1903 • Porter Edwin S. • USA
MAYTIME • 1923 • Gasnier Louis J. • USA
MAYTIME • 1937 • Leonard Robert Z. • USA
MAYTIME IN MAYFAIR • 1949 • Wilcox Herbert • UKN
MAYTIME TALE, A see **POHADKA MAJE** • 1926
MAYULA • 1986 • Pradhan Shambhu • NPL • BELOVED
MAYYA PLISETSKAYA see **MAYA PLISETSKAYA** • 1964
MAZ POD LOZKIEM • 1967 • Rozewicz Stanislaw • MTV • PLN • HUSBAND UNDER THE BED
MAZ SWOJEJ ZONY • 1961 • Bareja Stanislaw • PLN • HIS WIFE'S HUSBAND
MAZAHER, EL • 1945 • Salim Kamel • EGY • APPEARANCES
MAZARIN STONE, THE see **STONE OF MAZARIN, THE** • 1923
MAZDA LAMPS, THE see **LAMPES MAZDA, LES** • 1940
MAZE, THE • 1953 • Menzies William Cameron • USA
MAZE, THE • 1960 • Preston Richard • USA
MAZE OF FATE, THE • 1911 • *Imp* • USA
MAZEL TOV • 1924 • *Picon Molly* • USA
MAZEL TOV OU LE MARIAGE • 1968 • Berri Claude • FRN • MARRY ME! MARRY ME! (USA)
MAZEPA • 1968 • Borowczyk Walerian • FRN
MAZEPA • 1975 • Holoubek Gustaw • PLN • MAZEPPA
MAZEPPA • 1908 • Dudley Frank • UKN
MAZEPPA • 1909 • Goncharov Vasili M. • USS
MAZEPPA • 1910 • Boggs Frank • USA
MAZEPPA • 1914 • Puchalski Eduard • PLN
MAZEPPA • 1919 • Berger Martin • FRG
MAZEPPA see **MAZEPA** • 1975
MAZES AND MONSTERS see **RONA JAFFE'S MAZES & MONSTERS** • 1982
MAZIE PUTS ONE OVER • 1915 • Smiley Joseph? • USA
MAZLICEK • 1934 • Fric Martin • CZC • EFFEMINATE ONE, THE ○ DARLING
MAZO • 1939 • Inagaki Hiroshi • JPN • MAGIC STATUE ○ MAZOU
MAZOU see **MAZO** • 1939
MAZOVIA see **MAZOWSZE** • 1955
MAZOWSZE • 1955 • Makarczynski Tadeusz • DOC • PLN • MAZOVIA
MAZOWSZE ENSEMBLE, THE • 1952 • Makarczynski Tadeusz • DOC • PLN
MAZUR FILE, THE see **PEAU ET LES OS, LA** • 1960
MAZURKA • 1935 • Forst Willi • FRG
MAZURKA • 1970 • Hilbard John • DNM
MAZURKA DEL BARONE, DELLA SANTA E DEL FICO FIORONE • 1975 • Avati Pupi • ITL
MAZURKA DER LIEBE • 1957 • Muller Hans • GDR • BETTELSTUDENT, DER
MAZURKA DI PAPA, LA • 1938 • Biancoli Oreste • ITL • DAME E I CAVALIERI, LE ○ TEMPI FELICI ○ DURA MINGA
MAZURKA PA SENGEKANTEN • 1970 • Hilbard John • DNM • BEDROOM MAZURKA (UKN)
MAZZABUBU.. QUANTE CORNA STANNO QUAGGIU • 1971 • Laurenti Mariano • ITL
MAZZETTA, LA • 1978 • Corbucci Sergio • ITL • PAYOFF, THE
MBKS • 1973 • Le Grice Malcolm • UKN
M'BLIMEY • 1931 • Wills J. Elder • UKN
M'BOLO GABON • 1967 • GBN
MCBRIDE'S BRIDE • 1914 • *Roland Ruth* • USA
MCBUS • 1969 • May Derek • CND
MCCABE AND MRS. MILLER • 1971 • Altman Robert • USA • PRESBYTERIAN CHURCH WAGER, THE
MCCANN • 1973 • Sharad John S. • SHT • UKN
MCCARN PLAYS FATE • 1914 • *Kelsey F. A.* • USA
MCCLOUD: A LITTLE PLOT IN TRANQUIL VALLEY • 1971 • Smight Jack • TVM • USA
MCCLOUD: FIFTH MAN IN A STRING QUARTET • 1972 • Mayberry Russ • TVM • USA
MCCLOUD: GIVE MY REGRETS TO BROADWAY • 1972 • Antonio Lou • TVM • USA
MCCLOUD: SOMEBODY'S OUT TO GET JENNY • 1971 • Smight Jack • TVM • USA
MCCLOUD: THE DISPOSAL MAN • 1971 • Sagal Boris • TVM • USA
MCCLOUD: TOP OF THE WORLD, MA! • 1971 • March Alex • TVM • USA
MCCLOUD: WHO KILLED MISS U.S.A.? • 1969 • Colla Richard A. • USA • PORTRAIT OF A DEAD GIRL
MCCONNELL STORY, THE • 1955 • Douglas Gordon • USA • TIGER IN THE SKY (UKN)

MCCOY: DOUBLE TAKE • 1975 • Quine Richard • TVM • USA
MCCULLOCHS, THE • 1975 • Baer Max • USA • WILD MCCULLOCHS, THE
MCDOUGAL'S REST FARM • 1947 • Davis Mannie • ANS • USA
MCFADDEN'S FLATS • 1927 • Wallace Richard • USA
MCFADDEN'S FLATS • 1935 • Murphy Ralph • USA
MCGANN AND HIS OCTETTE • 1913 • Dillon Eddie • USA
MCGINTY AND THE COUNT • 1915 • *Edison* • USA
MCGLUSKY THE SEA ROVER • 1935 • Summers Walter • UKN • HELL'S CARGO (USA)
MCGUERINS FROM BROOKLYN, THE • 1942 • Neumann Kurt • USA
MCGUFFIN, THE • 1985 • Bucksey Colin • UKN
MCGUIRE GO HOME (USA) see **HIGH BRIGHT SUN, THE** • 1964
MCGUIRE OF THE BIG SNOWS see **MCGUIRE OF THE MOUNTED** • 1923
MCGUIRE OF THE MOUNTED • 1923 • Stanton Richard • USA • MCGUIRE OF THE BIG SNOWS
MCGUIRK, THE SLEUTH • 1912 • *Crystal* • USA
MCHALE'S NAVY • 1964 • Montagne Edward J. • USA
MCHALE'S NAVY JOINS THE AIR FORCE • 1965 • Montagne Edward J. • USA
MCIVOR • 1972 • Bonniere Rene • SHT • CND
MCKEE RANKIN'S "49" • 1911 • *Bosworth Hobart* • USA
MCKENNA OF THE MOUNTED • 1932 • Lederman D. Ross • USA
MCKENZIE BREAK, THE • 1970 • Johnson Lamont • UKN
MCLINTOCK! • 1963 • McLaglen Andrew V. • USA
MCMASTERS, THE • 1970 • Kjellin Alf • USA • MCMASTERS.. TOUGHER THAN THE WEST ITSELF!, THE ○ BLOOD CROWD, THE
MCMASTERS.. TOUGHER THAN THE WEST ITSELF!, THE see **MCMASTERS, THE** • 1970
MCMILLAN AND WIFE: COP OF THE YEAR • 1972 • Lewis Robert Michael • TVM • USA
MCMILLAN AND WIFE: THE DEVIL, YOU SAY • 1973 • March Alex • TVM • USA
MCNAB VISITS THE COMET • 1910 • FRN
MCNAB'S VISIT TO LONDON • 1905 • Cooper Arthur • UKN
MCNAUGHTON'S DAUGHTER • 1976 • London Jerry • TVM • USA
MCQ • 1974 • Sturges John • USA
MCQUADE OF THE TRAFFIC SQUAD • 1915 • Nowland Eugene • USA
MCQUEEN • 1969 • Bonniere Rene • SHS • CND
MCSWEENEY'S MASTERPIECE • 1914 • *White Pearl* • USA
MCVEAGH OF THE SOUTH SEAS • 1915 • *Carey Harry* • USA
MCVICAR • 1980 • Clegg Tom • UKN
ME • 1976 • Palmer John • CND
ME, A GROUPIE see **ICH -EIN GROUPIE** • 1970
ME ALONE see **JA SAM** • 1959
ME AN' BILL • 1914 • Campbell Colin • USA
ME AND BILL • 1912 • Campbell Colin • USA
ME AND CAPTAIN KIDD • 1919 • Apfel Oscar • USA
ME AND CHARLEY see **MIG OG CHARLY** • 1978
ME AND GOTT see **ME UND GOTT** • 1918
ME AND HIM • 1988 • Dorrie Doris • USA
ME AND M' PAL (USA) see **ME AND ME MOKE** • 1916
ME AND MARLBOROUGH • 1935 • Saville Victor • UKN
ME AND ME MOKE • 1916 • Shaw Harold • UKN • ME AND M' PAL (USA)
ME AND MY BROTHER • 1968 • Frank Robert • USA
ME AND MY GAL • 1932 • Walsh Raoul • USA • PIER 13 (UKN)
ME AND MY GAL see **UNMARRIED** • 1939
ME AND MY GIRL (USA) see **MORD EM'LY** • 1922
ME AND MY GRANDFATHER see **EN ES A NAGYAPAM** • 1954
ME AND MY KID BROTHER see **MIG OG MIN LILLEBROR** • 1967
ME AND MY KID BROTHER AND THE SMUGGLERS see **MIG OG MIN LILLEBROR -OG STORSMUGLERNE** • 1968
ME AND MY PAL • 1933 • Rogers Charles, French Lloyd • USA
ME AND MY PAL • 1939 • Bentley Thomas • UKN
ME AND MY SISTER see **IO E MIA SORELLA** • 1988
ME AND MY TWO PALS • 1906 • Raymond Charles? • UKN
ME AND MYSELF • 1930 • Stoll Lincoln • UKN
ME AND THE BOYS • 1929 • Saville Victor • SHT • UKN
ME AND THE COLONEL • 1958 • Glenville Peter • USA
ME AND THE GIRLS • 1985 • Gold Jack • MTV • UKN
ME AND THE MAN IN THE MOON • 1929 • Aylott Dave, Symmons E. F. • SHT • UKN
ME AND YOU see **MIG OG DIG** • 1969
ME, BEBIA, ILIKO DA ILARIONI see **YA BABUSHKA, ILIKO I ILLARION** • 1963
ME CAI DE LA NUBE • 1974 • *Filmicas Agrasanchez* • MXC
ME CANSE DE ROGARLE • 1964 • Gomez Muriel Emilio • MXC
ME CASE CON UN CURA • 1968 • Cortes Fernando • MXC • I MARRIED A PRIEST
ME CASE CON UNA ESTRELLA • 1951 • Amadori Luis Cesar • ARG
ME, CHIARA AND LO SCURO see **IO, CHIARA E LO SCURO** • 1983
ME DEBES UN MUERTO • 1971 • Saenz De Heredia Jose Luis • SPN
ME DICEN EL CONSENTIDO • 1961 • Toussaint Carlos • MXC
ME FAIRE CA A MOI.. • 1961 • Grimblat Pierre • FRN • IT MEANS THAT TO ME (USA)
ME FALTAS TU • 1970 • Martin Eugenio • SPN
ME FEELIN'S IS HURT • 1940 • Fleischer Dave • ANS • USA
ME FOVO KE PATHOS • 1972 • Foskolos Nikos • GRC • WITH FEAR AND PASSION
ME, GANGSTER • 1928 • Walsh Raoul • USA
ME, GRANDMOTHER, ILIKO AND HILLARION see **YA BABUSHKA, ILIKO I ILLARION** • 1963
ME GUSTAN VALENTONES • 1958 • Soler Julian • MXC
ME GUSTATODAS • 1953 • Ortega Juan J. • MXC, CUB
ME HA BESADO UN HOMBRE • 1944 • Soler Julian • MXC
ME HA GUSTADO UN HOMBRE • 1964 • Martinez Solares Gilberto • MXC, USA
ME HAS HECHO PERDER EL JUICIO • 1973 • de Orduna Juan • SPN
ME HE DE COMER ESA TUNA • 1944 • Zacarias Miguel • MXC
ME, HIM AND I • 1914 • *Universal* • USA
ME IMPORTA POCO • 1959 • Morayta Miguel • MXC
ME LI MANGIO VIVI! (ITL) see **BOULANGER DE VALORGUE, LE** • 1952
ME LLAMAN EL CANTACLARO • 1964 • Salvador Jaime • MXC
ME LLAMAN LA CHATA AGUAYO • 1988 • MXC • I'M CALLED CHATA AGUAYO
ME LO DIJO ADELA see **NECESITA UN MARIDO** • 1954
ME + ME + ME see **EU + EU + EU** • 1969
ME, ME, ME.. AND NO OTHERS see **IO, IO, IO.. E GLI ALTRI** • 1966
ME, MOTHER AND YOU see **IO, MAMMETA E TU** • 1958
ME MUSICAL NEPHEWS • 1942 • Kneitel Seymour • ANS • USA
ME, MYSELF AND I • 1969 • Dwoskin Stephen • USA, UKN
ME, NATALIE • 1969 • Coe Fred • USA
ME NO KABE • 1958 • Ohba Hideo • JPN • INVISIBLE WALL
ME NO SAVEY • 1971-74 • Bertolino Daniel • DOC • CND
ME PERDERE CONTIGO • 1953 • Gomez Urquiza Zacarias • MXC
ME PERSIGUE UNA MUJER • 1946 • Soler Fernando • MXC
ME QUIERO CASAR • 1966 • Soler Julian • MXC
ME QUIERO CASAR CONTIGO • 1951 • Mihura Jeronimo • SPN
ME SIENTO EXTRANA • 1977 • Marti Maqueda Enrique • SPN
ME TRAES DE UN ALA • 1952 • Martinez Solares Gilberto • MXC
ME UND GOTT • 1918 • Gittens Wyndham • USA • ME AND GOTT
ME (USA) see **ENFANCE NUE, L'** • 1968
ME WITHOUT YOU see **ONE HOUR LATE** • 1935
MEA CULPA see **KAPLAN VON SAN LORENZO, DER** • 1953
ME'ACHOREI HA'SORAGIM • 1984 • Barbash Uri • ISR • BEYOND THE WALLS ○ BEYOND THESE WALLS
MEADOW, THE (USA) see **PRATO, IL** • 1979
MEADOW LARK, THE • 1913 • *Edison* • USA
MEAL, THE • 1975 • Hugh R. John • USA
ME'AL HEKHORAVOT • 1936 • Axelrod Nathan • ISR
MEAL TICKET see **THIS IS THE LIFE** • 1935
MEAL TICKET, THE • 1914 • Vale Travers • USA
MEALIE KIDS, THE • 1917 • SAF
MEALS BY WEIGHT • 1912 • *Majestic* • USA
MEALTIME MAGIC • 1952 • Jason Will • SHT • USA
MEALTIMES see **MAHLZEITEN** • 1967
MEAN BLOW see **PODFUK** • 1985
MEAN BUSINESS • Suarez Bobby A. • HKG • DEVIL'S THREE
MEAN COMBAT see **LOSERS, THE** • 1970
MEAN DOG BLUES • 1978 • Stuart Mel • USA
MEAN FRANK AND CRAZY TONY see **SUO NOME FACEVA TREMARE.. INTERPOL IN ALLARME, IL** • 1973
MEAN JOHNNY BURROWS • 1976 • Williamson Fred • USA • STREET WARRIOR ○ HIT MAN, THE
MEAN MACHINE, THE (UKN) see **LONGEST YARD, THE** • 1975
MEAN SEASON, THE • 1985 • Borsos Philip • USA
MEAN STREETS • 1973 • Scorsese Martin • USA
MEAN STREETS OF KUNG FU • 1983 • Yang Teo • HKG
MEANDERS see **MEANDRE** • 1966
MEANDRE • 1966 • Saucan Mircea • RMN • MEANDERS
MEANEST GAL IN TOWN, THE • 1934 • Mack Russell • USA • ONCE OVER LIGHTLY
MEANEST MAN IN THE WORLD, THE • 1923 • Cline Eddie • USA
MEANEST MAN IN THE WORLD, THE • 1943 • Lanfield Sidney • USA
MEANEST MAN ON EARTH, THE • 1909 • Fitzhamon Lewin • UKN
MEANEST MEN IN THE WEST, THE • 1967 • Fuller Samuel, Dubin Charles S. • MTV • USA
MEANING, THE see **ARTH** • 1983
MEANS AND ENDS • 1985 • Michenaud Gerald • USA
MEANS AND MORALS • 1915 • Calvert E. H. • USA
MEANS AND THE END, THE • 1914 • *Holmes Rapley* • USA
MEANTIME • 1983 • Leigh Mike • UKN
MEANWHILE, FAR FROM THE FRONT see **SECRET WAR OF HARRY FRIGG, THE** • 1968
MEANY, MINY, MOE • 1936-37 • *Lantz Walter (P)* • ASS • USA
MEARIM MERMERDEN OLSUN • 1968 • Karamanbey Cetin • TRK • LET MY GRAVE BE OF MARBLE
MEASURE FOR MEASURE • 1909 • *Lubin* • USA
MEASURE FOR MEASURE • 1963 • Ratz Gunter • ANM • GDR
MEASURE FOR MEASURE • 1978 • Davis Desmond • TVM • UKN
MEASURE FOR MEASURE • 1980 • Dyulgerov Georgi • BUL
MEASURE OF A MAN, THE • 1911 • Porter Edwin S. • USA
MEASURE OF A MAN, THE • 1914 • Powell Frank • USA
MEASURE OF A MAN, THE • 1915 • De Grasse Joseph • USA
MEASURE OF A MAN, THE • 1916 • Conway Jack • USA
MEASURE OF A MAN, THE • 1924 • Rosson Arthur • USA
MEASURE OF LEON DUBRAY, THE • 1915 • Otto Henry • USA
MEASURE OF MAN • 1969 • *Halas John (P)* • ANS • UKN
MEASURE OF MAN, THE • 1916 • *Buffalo* • SHT • USA
MEASURES AGAINST FANATICS see **MASSNAHMEN GEGEN FANATIKER** • 1968
MEAT • 1976 • Wiseman Frederick • DOC • USA
MEAT-GRINDER see **FLEISCHWOLF** • 1990
MEAT IS MEAT see **WURGER KOMMT AUF LEISEN SOCKEN, DER** • 1971
MEAT THE CLEAVER • 1980 • Sutherland Joseph • DOC • CND
MEATBALL • 1974 • Damiano Gerard • USA
MEATBALLS • 1979 • Reitman Ivan • CND • ARRETE DE RAMER, T'ES SUR LE SABLE ○ SUMMER CAMP
MEATBALLS III • 1987 • Mendeluk George • USA • MEATBALLS III: SUMMER JOB
MEATBALLS III: SUMMER JOB see **MEATBALLS III** • 1987
MEATBALLS PART II • 1984 • Wiederhorn Ken • USA • SPACE KID
MEATCLEAVER MASSACRE • 1977 • Lee Evan • USA • HOLLYWOOD MEATCLEAVER MASSACRE
MEATDAZE • 1968 • Keen Jeff • UKN
MEATEATER, THE • 1979 • Savage Derek • USA
MEATLESS DAYS AND SLEEPLESS NIGHTS • 1918 • De Vonde Chester M. • SHT • USA
MEATLESS FLYDAY • 1944 • Freleng Friz • ANS • USA
MEATLESS TUESDAY • 1943 • Culhane James • ANS • USA
MEAT/RACK • 1970 • Thomas Michael* • USA • STREET/RACK
MECANICA NACIONAL • 1972 • Alcoriza Luis • MXC • NATIONAL MECHANICS
MECANICIEN, LE • 1910 • Del Colle Ubaldo Maria • ITL
MECANICIENS DE L'ARMEE DE L'AIR, LES • 1959 • Lelouch Claude • DOC • FRN
MECANIQUE • 1956 • Bail Rene • CND
MECANISMO INTERIOR • 1971 • Barco Ramon • SPN • INTERIOR MECHANISM
MECANO'S VACUUM CLEANER • Lortac • FRN
MECAVA • 1978 • Vrdoljak Antun • YGS • STORM, THE
MECHA ORTIZ GERMAN KRAUSS see **CASA DE LAS SOMBRAS, LA** • 1976
MECHANIC, THE • 1972 • Winner Michael • USA • KILLER OF KILLERS, THE
MECHANICAL BALLET, THE see **BALLET MECANIQUE, LE** • 1924
MECHANICAL BANANAS (UKN) see **BANANES MECANIQUES** • 1973
MECHANICAL BIRD • 1952 • Donnelly Eddie • ANS • USA
MECHANICAL BUTCHER, THE see **CHARCUTERIE MECANIQUE** • 1895
MECHANICAL COW • 1932 • Lantz Walter, Nolan William • ANS • USA
MECHANICAL COW, THE • 1927 • Disney Walt • ANS • USA
MECHANICAL COW, THE • 1937 • Zander Jack • ANS • USA
MECHANICAL FIRING OF COAL • 1961 • Ellitt Jack • DOC • UKN
MECHANICAL FLEA, THE • 1964 • Ivanov-Vano Ivan • ANM • USS
MECHANICAL HANDY-MAN, THE • 1937 • *Lantz Walter (P)* • ANS • USA
MECHANICAL HUSBAND, A • 1910 • Wormald S.? • UKN
MECHANICAL LEGS, THE • 1908 • Collins Alf? • UKN
MECHANICAL MAN see **AJAANTRIK** • 1958
MECHANICAL MAN, THE • 1915 • Curtis Allen • SHT • USA
MECHANICAL MAN, THE • 1932 • Lantz Walter, Nolan William • ANS • USA
MECHANICAL MARY ANNE, THE • 1910 • Fitzhamon Lewin? • UKN
MECHANICAL MONSTERS, THE • 1941 • Fleischer Dave • ANS • USA
MECHANICAL PIANO, THE see **NEOKONTCHENNIA PIESSA DLIA MEKANITCHESKOVO PIANINA** • 1977
MECHANICAL PRINCIPLES • 1930 • Steiner Ralph • SHT • USA
MECHANICAL SAW, THE see **UNDER SAVKLINGENS TAENDER** • 1913
MECHANICAL STATUE AND THE INGENIOUS SERVANT, THE • 1907 • Blackton J. Stuart • USA
MECHANICS OF LOVE, THE • 1955 • Maas Willard, Moore Bob • SHT • USA
MECHANICS OF THE BRAIN, THE see **MEKHANIKHA GOLOVNOVO MOZGA** • 1926
MECHANIZACJA ROBOT ZIEMNYCH • 1951 • Has Wojciech J. • DCS • PLN • MECHANIZATION OF FIELD WORK
MECHANIZATION OF FIELD WORK see **MECHANIZACJA ROBOT ZIEMNYCH** • 1951
MECHTA • 1943 • Romm Mikhail • USS • DREAM ○ METSHTA
MECQUE 1964, LA • 1964 • Essid Hamadi • SHT • TNS
MECS.., LES FLICS.., ET LES PUTAINS, LES see **TRINGLEUSES, LES** • 1974
MED DEJ I MIN ARMAR • 1940 • Ekman Hasse • SWD • WITH YOU IN MY ARMS
MED FARA FOR LIVET • 1959 • Bjornefeldt Peter B. • SWD, UKN • MAN IN THE MIDDLE (UKN) ○ 48 HOURS TO LIVE (USA)
MED FOLKET FOR FOSTERLANDET • 1938 • Wallen Sigurd • SWD • WITH THE PEOPLE FOR THE COUNTRY
MED FOLKET FOR FOSTERLANDET • 1950 • Lingheim Emil A. • SWD
MED GLORIAN PA SNED • 1957 • Ekman Hasse • SWD • WITH THE HALO ASKEW
MED KAERLIG HILSEN • 1971 • Axel Gabriel • DNM • LOVE ME DARLING (UKN) ○ WITH LOVE AND KISSES
MED KARLEK, SOLSKEN OCH SANG see **KARLEK, SOLSKEN OCH SANG** • 1948
MED LIVET SOM INSATS • 1940 • Sjoberg Alf • SWD • THEY STAKED THEIR LIVES
MED MORD I BAGAGET • 1963 • Younger Tom • SWD, FRG, UKN • NO TIME TO KILL
MED SVIGA LOEVI • 1967 • Knudsen Osvaldur • DOC • ICL
MED VAPEN I HAND • 1913 • Klercker Georg • SWD • ARMS IN YOUR HANDS
MEDAGLIONE INSANGUINATO, IL see **PERCHE?** • 1975
MEDAILLE DE SAUVETAGE, LA • 1914 • Linder Max • FRN • MAX DECORE
MEDAILLES, LES • 1973 • Merbah Lamine • ALG
MEDAILLON DER LADY SINGTON, DAS • 1920 • Kohne Friedel • FRG
MEDAL, A see **KUNSHO** • 1954
MEDAL FOR BENNY, A • 1945 • Pichel Irving • USA
MEDAL FOR THE GENERAL • 1944 • Elvey Maurice • UKN • GAY INTRUDERS, THE (USA)
MEDAL FROM THE DEVIL see **AKUMA KARA NO KUNSHO** • 1967
MEDAL FROM THE GENERAL see **AKUMA KARA NO KUNSHO** • 1967
MEDAL OF HONOR, THE • 1912 • *Gem* • USA
MEDAL OF HONOR, THE • 1913 • *Lubin* • USA
MEDALLA DEL TORERO, LA • 1924 • Buchs Jose • SPN
MEDALLION, THE • 1911 • *Selig* • USA
MEDALLION WITH THREE HEARTS see **MADALJON SA TRI SRCA** • 1962
MEDALLON DEL CRIMEN, EL • 1955 • Bustillo Oro Juan • MXC
MEDALS see **KUNSHO** • 1954
MEDALS (UKN) see **SEVEN DAYS LEAVE** • 1930
MEDAN PORTEN VAR STANGD • 1946 • Ekman Hasse • SWD • WHEN THE DOOR WAS CLOSED
MEDAN STADEN SOVER • 1950 • Kjellgren Lars-Eric • SWD • WHILE THE CITY SLEEPS
MEDBEJLERENS HAEVN • 1910 • *Blom August* • DNM • CAUGHT IN HIS OWN TRAP

MEDDIG EL AZ EMBER? • 1967 • Elek Judit • SHT • HNG • HOW LONG DOES MAN MATTER?
MEDDLER, THE • 1915 • Shaw Brinsley • USA
MEDDLER, THE • 1925 • Rosson Arthur • USA
MEDDLER, THE see **ANAKATOSOURAS, O** • 1967
MEDDLERS, THE • 1912 • Dwan Allan • USA
MEDDLERS AND MOONSHINERS • 1918 • Basil Joseph • SHT • USA
MEDDLESOME DARLING, THE • 1915 • Smiley Joseph • USA
MEDDLESOME MIKE • 1914 • Collins Edwin J.? • UKN
MEDDLIN' STRANGER, THE • 1927 • Thorpe Richard • USA
MEDDLING PARSON, THE • 1911 • *Nestor* • USA
MEDDLING POLICEMAN, THE • 1904 • Haggar William • UKN
MEDDLING WITH MARRIAGE • 1917 • Calvert E. H. • SHT • USA
MEDDLING WOMEN • 1924 • Abramson Ivan • USA
MEDEA • 1920 • Lubitsch Ernst • FRG
MEDEA • 1970 • Pasolini Pier Paolo • ITL, FRG, FRN • MEDEE (FRN)
MEDEA • 1976 • Dassin Jules • GRC • MAYA AND BREUDA
MEDEA • 1980 • Stockl Ula • FRG
MEDEA'S RETURN see **EPISTROFI TIS MIDIAS, I** • 1968
MEDECIN DE GAFIRE, LE • Diop Mustapha • NGR • DOCTOR OF GAFIRE, THE
MEDECIN DES NEIGES, LE • 1942 • Ichac Marcel • DCS • FRN
MEDECIN DES PAUVRES, LE • 1914 • Desfontaines Henri • FRN
MEDECIN DES SOLS • 1953 • Bourguignon Serge • FRN
MEDECIN DU NORD, LE • 1954 • Palardy Jean • DCS • CND
MEDECIN MALGRE LUI, LE • 1910 • Chautard Emile • FRN
MEDECIN MALGRE LUI, LE • 1955 • Henry-Jacques • FRN, EGY, MRC
MEDECIN VETERINAIRE, LE • 1962 • Bigras Jean-Yves • DCS • CND
MEDECINE D'AUJOUD'HUI, LA • 1959 • Proulx Maurice • DCS • CND
MEDEE (FRN) see **MEDEA** • 1970
MEDENA VEZA • 1970 • Holly Martin • CZC • COPPER TOWER, THE
MEDENI MESEC • 1989 • Radovic Milos • YGS • HONEYMOON
MEDENI MJESEC • 1984 • Babic Nikola • YGS • HONEYMOON
MEDES, LES see **POW WOW TE MORT BEN J'JOUE PU** • 1980
MEDEVEDEFF'S BALALAIKA ORCHESTRA • 1929 • *Bsfp* • SHT • UKN • CAMERA COCKTALES NO.1
MEDIAEVAL CASTLES • 1950 • Kinross Felicity • UKN
MEDIAEVAL VILLAGE • 1936 • Holmes J. B. • DOC • UKN
MEDIANOCHE • 1948 • Davison Tito • MXC
MEDIAS DE SEDA, LA • 1955 • Morayta Miguel • MXC
MEDIAS Y CALCETINES • 1969 • Ribas Antoni • SPN
MEDIATOR, THE • 1916 • Turner Otis • USA
MEDIC, THE see **TOUBIB, LE** • 1979
MEDICAL CARE • 1953 • Makarczynski Tadeusz • DOC • PLN
MEDICAL DEVIATE see **REGINA DEI CANNIBALI, LA** • 1979
MEDICAL MYSTERY, A • 1925 • Templeman Harcourt • UKN
MEDICAL STORY • 1975 • Nelson Gary • TVM • USA
MEDICINE BAG, THE • 1914 • *Miller'S 101 Ranch* • USA
MEDICINE BALL CARAVAN • 1971 • Reichenbach Francois • USA, FRN • WE HAVE COME FOR YOUR DAUGHTERS (UKN) ○ CARAVANE D'AMOUR, LA (FRN)
MEDICINE BEND • 1916 • McGowan J. P. • USA
MEDICINE BOTTLE, THE • 1909 • Griffith D. W. • USA
MEDICINE MAN, THE • 1910 • *Powers* • USA
MEDICINE MAN, THE • 1917 • Smith Cliff • USA
MEDICINE MAN, THE • 1930 • Pembroke Scott • USA
MEDICINE MAN, THE • 1933 • Davis Redd • UKN
MEDICINE MAN, THE see **DOCTOR'S ORDERS** • 1934
MEDICINE MAN (UKN) see **THAT TEXAS JAMBOREE** • 1946
MEDICINE MAN'S VENGEANCE, THE • 1914 • *Darkfeather Mona* • USA
MEDICINE MEN, THE • 1929 • Taurog Norman • SHT • USA
MEDICINE OF THE FUTURE, THE • 1912 • *Lux* • FRN
MEDICINE SHOW, THE • 1933 • *Mintz Charles (P)* • ANS • USA
MEDICINE SHOW, THE see **PARADE OF THE WEST** • 1930
MEDICINE SHOW AT STONE GULCH, THE • 1914 • *Brennan John E.* • USA
MEDICO CONDOTTO see **RIVALITA** • 1953
MEDICO DE GUARDIA • 1950 • Fernandez Bustamente Adolfo • MXC
MEDICO DE LAS LOCAS, EL • 1943 • Patino Gomez Alfonso • MXC
MEDICO DE LAS LOCAS, EL • 1955 • Morayta Miguel • MXC
MEDICO DEI PAZZI, IL • 1954 • Mattoli Mario • ITL
MEDICO DELLA MUTUA, IL • 1968 • Zampa Luigi • ITL • BE SICK.. IT'S FREE ○ PANEL DOCTOR, THE
MEDICO DELLE DONNE, IL • 1962 • Girolami Marino • ITL
MEDICO E LO STREGONE, IL • 1957 • Monicelli Mario • ITL, FRN • DOCTOR AND THE WIZARD, THE ○ DOCTOR AND THE QUACK
MEDICO.. LA STUDENTESSA, IL • 1976 • Amadio Silvio • ITL
MEDICO OF PAINTED SPRINGS, THE • 1941 • Hillyer Lambert • USA • DOCTOR'S ALIBI, THE (UKN)
MEDICO PER FORZA, IL • 1931 • Campogalliani Carlo • ITL
MEDICOS, LOS • 1978 • Ayala Fernando • ARG • DOCTORS, THE
MEDIEVAL • Munteanu Stefan • ANM • RMN
MEDIEVAL CHURCH SCULPTURE see **NEDERLANDSE BEELDHOUWKUNST TIJDENS DE LATE MIDDELEEUWEN** • 1951
MEDIEVAL VILLAGE, THE • 1940 • Field Mary • DOC • UKN
MEDIKUS, A • 1916 • Curtiz Michael • HNG • APOTHECARY, THE
MEDIOCRES, LOS • 1962 • Gonzalez Servando • MXC
MEDITATION • 1968 • Spoecker Peter D. • SHT • USA
MEDITATION ON VIOLENCE • 1948 • Deren Maya • SHT • USA
MEDITERRANEAN CRUISE • 1930 • *Holmes Burton* • DOC • USA
MEDITERRANEAN HOLIDAY (USA) see **FLYING CLIPPER – TRAUMREISE UNTER WEISSEN SEGELN** • 1962
MEDITERRANEE • 1963 • Pollet Jean-Daniel • SHT • FRN
MEDIUM, DAS • 1921 • Rosenfeld Herman • FRG
MEDIUM, IL • 1979 • Amadio Silvio • ITL
MEDIUM, THE • 1934 • Sewell Vernon • UKN
MEDIUM, THE • 1951 • Hammid Alexander • USA
MEDIUM, THE • 1951 • Menotti Gian-Carlo • ITL
MEDIUM, THE • 1985 • Koprowicz Jacek • PLN
MEDIUM BLUES • 1985 • Prefontaine Michel • CND
MEDIUM COOL • 1969 • Wexler Haskell • USA • CONCRETE WILDERNESS
MEDIUM EXPOSED, THE • 1906 • Martin J. H.? • UKN
MEDIUM RARE • 1989 • Madden Paul • USA
MEDIUM SPIRITS • 1921 • Morris Reggie • SHT • USA
MEDIUM'S NEMESIS, THE • 1913 • *Thanhouser Kid* • USA
MEDJU JASTREBOVIMA (YGS) see **UNTER GEIERN** • 1964
MEDUSA • 1973 • Hessler Gordon • USA
MEDUSA AGAINST THE SON OF HERCULES (USA) see **PERSEO L'INVINCIBILE** • 1962
MEDUSA RAFT, THE see **SPLAV MEDUZE** • 1981
MEDUSA TOUCH, THE • 1977 • Gold Jack • UKN
MEDUSA VS. THE SON OF HERCULES see **PERSEO L'INVINCIBILE** • 1962
MEDUSAN PAA • 1974 • Bergholm Eija-Elina • FNL • HEAD OF MEDUSA, THE
MEDVED • 1961 • Fric Martin • MTV • CZC • BEAR, THE
MEDVEZHYA SVADBA see **LOKIS** • 1926
MEENAKSHI • 1942 • *Sircar B. N. (P)* • IND
MEER, DAS • 1927 • Felner Peter Paul • FRG
MEER RUFT, DAS • 1933 • Hinrich Hans • FRG
MEERABAI • 1933 • *Sircar B. N. (P)* • IND
MEERABAI • 1935-47 • Bose Debaki • IND
MEERABAI • 1946 • Ahmed W. Z. • IND • MIRABAI
MEERMIN, DE • 1971 • Diddens G. • BLG
MEET A MIRACLE • 1980 • Mason Richard • DOC • ASL
MEET BOSTON BLACKIE • 1941 • Florey Robert • USA
MEET DANNY WILSON • 1952 • Pevney Joseph • USA
MEET DR. CHRISTIAN • 1939 • Vorhaus Bernard • USA
MEET GISELE • 1950 • Blais Roger • DCS • CND
MEET JOHN DOE • 1941 • Capra Frank • USA • JOHN DOE, DYNAMITE (UKN)
MEET JOHN DOUGHBOY • 1941 • Clampett Robert • ANS • USA
MEET LEONID ENGIBAROV • 1966 • Lisakovitch Viktor • DOC • USS
MEET MARKET see **CRUISING BAR** • 1990
MEET MARLON BRANDO • 1966 • Maysles Albert, Maysles David • DOC • USA
MEET MAXWELL ARCHER • 1939 • Carstairs John Paddy • UKN • MAXWELL ARCHER, DETECTIVE (USA)
MEET ME AFTER THE SHOW • 1951 • Sale Richard • USA
MEET ME AT DAWN • 1947 • Freeland Thornton • UKN • GAY DUELLIST, THE (USA)
MEET ME AT THE FAIR • 1952 • Sirk Douglas • USA
MEET ME IN LAS VEGAS • 1956 • Rowland Roy • USA • VIVA LAS VEGAS! (UKN)
MEET ME IN MOSCOW (USA) see **YA SHAGAYU PO MOSKVE** • 1964
MEET ME IN ST. LOUIS • 1944 • Minnelli Vincente • USA
MEET ME, JESUS • Ungerer Walter • SHT • USA
MEET ME ON BROADWAY • 1946 • Jason Leigh • USA
MEET ME TONIGHT • 1952 • Pelissier Anthony • UKN • TONIGHT AT 8.30 (USA)
MEET MISS BOBBY SOCKS see **MEET MISS BOBBY SOX** • 1944
MEET MISS BOBBY SOX • 1944 • Tryon Glenn • USA • MEET MISS BOBBY SOCKS
MEET MISS MARPLE see **MURDER SHE SAID** • 1961
MEET MISS MOZART (USA) see **MADEMOISELLE MOZART** • 1935
MEET MISTER BEAT • 1961 • Barnett Ivan • UKN
MEET MISTER CALLAGHAN • 1954 • Saunders Charles • UKN
MEET MR. KRINGLE • 1956 • Stevenson Robert • MTV • USA • MIRACLE ON 34TH STREET (UKN)
MEET MR. LUCIFER • 1953 • Pelissier Anthony • UKN
MEET MR. MALCOLM • 1954 • Birt Daniel • UKN
MEET MR. PENNY • 1938 • MacDonald David • UKN
MEET MOTHER MAGOO • 1956 • Burness Pete • ANS • USA
MEET MY GIRL • 1926 • Bacon Lloyd • SHT • USA
MEET MY SISTER • 1933 • Daumery John • UKN
MEET MY WIFE • 1917 • Marshall George • SHT • USA
MEET NERO WOLFE • 1936 • Biberman Herbert J. • USA
MEET PETER VOSS (USA) see **PETER VOSS, DER HELD DES TAGES** • 1959
MEET ROY ROGERS • 1941 • Parsons Harriet • SHT • USA
MEET SEXTON BLAKE • 1944 • Harlow John • UKN
MEET SIMON CHERRY • 1949 • Grayson Godfrey • UKN
MEET THE APPLEGATES • 1989 • Lehmann Michael • USA
MEET THE BARON • 1933 • Lang Walter • USA
MEET THE BOYFRIEND • 1930 • Taurog Norman • SHT • USA
MEET THE BOYFRIEND • 1937 • Staub Ralph • USA
MEET THE CHUMP • 1941 • Cline Eddie • USA
MEET THE DANES see **HURRA FOR OS** • 1963
MEET THE DUCHESS see **IRISH FOR LUCK** • 1936
MEET THE DUKE • 1949 • Corbett James • UKN
MEET THE FEEBLES • 1989 • Jackson Peter • ANM • NZL
MEET THE FLEET • 1940 • Eason B. Reeves • SHT • USA
MEET THE FOLKS • 1927 • Christie Al • USA
MEET THE GHOSTS see **ABBOTT AND COSTELLO MEET FRANKENSTEIN** • 1948
MEET THE GIRLS • 1938 • Forde Eugene J. • USA
MEET THE MAJOR • 1938 • Ceder Ralph • USA
MEET THE MISSUS • 1924 • Roach Hal • SHT • USA
MEET THE MISSUS • 1937 • Santley Joseph • USA • MISSUS AMERICA
MEET THE MISSUS • 1940 • St. Clair Malcolm • USA • HIGGINS FAMILY, THE
MEET THE MOB see **SO'S YOUR AUNT EMMA!** • 1942
MEET THE NAVY • 1946 • Travers Alfred • UKN
MEET THE NELSONS see **HERE COME THE NELSONS** • 1952
MEET THE PEOPLE • 1944 • Reisner Charles F. • USA
MEET THE PIONEERS • 1948 • Anderson Lindsay • DCS • UKN
MEET THE PRINCE • 1926 • Henabery Joseph • USA
MEET THE PRINCE • 1932 • Edwards Harry J. • SHT • USA
MEET THE PRINCE see **HOW TO HANDLE WOMEN** • 1928
MEET THE PRINCE (UKN) see **COWBOY PRINCE, THE** • 1924
MEET THE PROFESSOR • 1935 • Schwarzwald Milton • SHT • USA
MEET THE QUADS • 1951 • Stafford Roland • DOC • UKN
MEET THE SET see **MEET THE SEX** • 1969
MEET THE SEX • 1969 • *American Film Dist. Corp* • USA • MEET THE SET
MEET THE STEWARTS • 1942 • Green Alfred E. • USA
MEET THE WIFE • 1919 • *Strand* • SHT • USA
MEET THE WIFE • 1931 • Pearce A. Leslie • USA
MEET THE WILDCAT • 1940 • Lubin Arthur • USA
MEET WHIPLASH WILLIE (UKN) see **FORTUNE COOKIE, THE** • 1966
MEETING, THE • 1917 • Robertson John S. • *Broadway Star* • SHT • USA
MEETING, THE • 1917 • Terwilliger George W. • *Niagara Film Studios* • SHT • USA
MEETING, THE • 1964 • Hassan Mamoun • UKN
MEETING, THE • *Martin Gary* • USA
MEETING, THE • 1970 • Olexova Jana • ANM • CZC
MEETING, THE see **MEGURI-AI** • 1968
MEETING, THE see **ENCUENTRO, EL** • 1972
MEETING A MILESTONE • 1989 • Ghose Goutam • DOC • IND
MEETING AGAIN see **SAIKAI** • 1953
MEETING AGAIN see **SAIKAI** • 1974
MEETING AT DUSK see **SPOTKANIE W MROKU** • 1960
MEETING AT MIDNIGHT see **CHARLIE CHAN IN BLACK MAGIC** • 1944
MEETING AT THE FASHION SHOW see **KOSTIMIRANI RENDEZ-VOUS** • 1965
MEETING AT THE ZOO, A see **SPOTKANIE W ZOO** • 1962
MEETING FOR A CHEATING, A • 1916 • *Ritchie Billie* • SHT • USA
MEETING GYORGY LUKACS see **TALALKOZAS LUKACS GYORGGYEL** • 1972
MEETING HEARTS see **HJARTAN SOM MOTAS** • 1914
MEETING HIS MATCH • 1912 • *Powers* • USA
MEETING IN A DREAM see **DREAM ENCOUNTER** • 1957
MEETING IN A MEADOW see **NA LIVADI** • 1957
MEETING IN BUCHAREST, THE see **SETKANI V BUKURESTI** • 1954
MEETING IN JULY see **SETKANI V CERVENI** • 1977
MEETING IN THE FOREST, THE see **RENDEZ-VOUS EN FORET, LE** • 1972
MEETING IN WARSAW, A see **SPOTKANIE W WARSZAWIE** • 1955
MEETING IS OPEN, THE • 1987 • Rossenov Ivan • DOC • BUL
MEETING LIFE see **MOTE MED LIVET** • 1952
MEETING MAMIE'S MOTHER • 1912 • *Lubin* • USA
MEETING MAZIE • 1933 • Horne James W. • SHT • USA
MEETING MR. JONES • 1914 • Henderson Dell • USA
MEETING OF FRIENDSHIP • 1965 • Stoyanov Yuli • DOC • BUL
MEETING OF THE FASHION SHOW, THE see **KOSTIMIRANI RENDEZ-VOUS** • 1965
MEETING OF THE WAYS, THE • 1912 • *Costello Maurice* • USA
MEETING OF TWO HEARTS see **DO DILON KI DASTAN** • 1967
MEETING ON 69TH STREET • 1969 • Peacock Kemper • USA
MEETING ON THE ATLANTIC see **SPOTKANIE NA ATLANTYKU** • 1980
MEETING ON THE ELBE see **VSTRECHA NA ELBE** • 1949
MEETING ON THE FERRY • 1964 • Egiazarov G. • USS
MEETING ONE'S CONSCIENCE see **NAVSTRYECHU SOVESTI** • 1967
MEETING SHIPS see **SKEPP SOM MOTAS** • 1916
MEETING WITH FRANCE see **VSTRETCHA S FRANTZIEI** • 1960
MEETING WITH FREDDY REYNA, A see **ENCUENTRO CON FREDDY REYNA** • 1979
MEETING WITH SHADOWS, A see **SCHUZKA SE STINY** • 1982
MEETING WITH THE PAMIR MOUNTAINS • 1960 • Makhnach Leonid • DOC • USS
MEETINGS AND PARTINGS • 1974 • Ishmukhamedov Elyor • USS
MEETINGS IN WARSAW see **SPOTKANIA W WARSZAWIE** • 1965
MEETINGS OF ANNA, THE see **RENDEZ-VOUS D'ANNA, LES** • 1978
MEETINGS WITH REMARKABLE MEN • 1979 • Brook Peter • UKN
MEETINGS WITH WARSAW see **SPOTKANIA W WARSZAWIE** • 1965
MEEUW, DE • 1972 • van der Vennet H. • BLG
MEEUWEN STERVEN IN DE HAVEN • 1955 • Verhavert Roland • BLG • SEAGULLS DIE IN THE HARBOUR
MEFIEZ-VOUS DES BLONDES • 1950 • Hunebelle Andre • FRN
MEFIEZ-VOUS, FILLETTES • 1957 • Allegret Yves • FRN • YOUNG GIRLS BEWARE (USA)
MEFIEZ-VOUS, MESDAMES! • 1963 • Hunebelle Andre • FRN, ITL • CHI VUOL DORMIRE NEL MIO LETTO? (ITL)
MEFISTOFELES! see **EXTRANO CASO DEL DR. FAUSTO, EL** • 1969
MEG • 1926 • Shaw Walter • UKN
MEG KER A NEP • 1971 • Jancso Miklos • HNG • RED PSALM (UKN) ○ AND THE PEOPLE STILL ASK ○ PEOPLE STILL ASK ○ RED SONG
MEG O' THE MOUNTAINS • 1914 • Ridgely Richard • USA
MEG O' THE WOODS • 1918 • Phillips Bertram • UKN
MEG OF THE CLIFFS • 1915 • Mayo Melvin • USA
MEG OF THE MINES • 1914 • *Marsh Mae* • USA
MEG OF THE SLUMS • 1916 • *Millais Helena* • UKN
MEG THE LADY • 1916 • Elvey Maurice • UKN
MEGAFORCE • 1982 • Needham Hal • USA
MEGAFORCE 7.9 see **JISHIN RETTO** • 1980
MEGALES AGAPES • 1968 • Konstantinou Panayotis • GRC • GREAT LOVES
MEGALEXANDROS, O • 1980 • Angelopoulos Theo • GRC • ALEXANDER THE GREAT
MEGALI APOFASI • 1977 • Dadiras Dimis • GRC • BIG DECISION
MEGALL AZ IDO • 1981 • Gothar Peter • HNG • TIME STANDS STILL ○ IDO VAN ○ TIME
MEGALOMEDIA • 1980 • Petty Bruce • ANS • ASL
MEGALOS DHIHASMOS • 1968 • Grigoriou Grigoris • GRC • BIG SPLIT ○ REVENGE

MEGALOS EROTIKOS, O • 1972 • Voulgaris Pantelis • GRC • GREAT LOVE SONGS, THE
MEGAN CARIE • 1980 • Sullivan Kevin • SHT • CND
MEGANO, EL • 1955 • Espinosa Julio Garcia, Alea Tomas Gutierrez • CUB
MEGANTIC OUTLAW • 1970 • Kelly Ron • CND
MEGARA • 1975 • Tsemberopoulos Yorgos, Maniatis Sakis • GRC
MEGATON YE-YE • 1965 • Yague Jesus • SPN
MEGAWATTS • 1973 • Gagne Jacques • DCS • CND
MEGERE APPRIVOISEE, LA • 1911 • Desfontaines Henri • FRN
MEGERE RECALCITRANTE, LE • 1900 • Zecca Ferdinand • FRN
MEGFAGYOTTGYERMEK, A • 1921 • Balazs Bela • HNG
MEGFELELO EMBER, A • 1959 • Revesz Gyorgy • HNG • RIGHT MAN, THE
MEGH • 1961 • Dutt U. • IND
MEGH O ROUDRA • 1969 • Devi Arundhuti • IND
MEGHALLGATAS • 1969 • Jeles Andras • SHT • HNG
MEGHE DHAKA TARA see **MEGHEY DHAAKA TAARA** • 1959
MEGHER ANEK RANG • 1977 • Rashid Harunar • BNG • CLOUD HAS MANY COLOURS, THE
MEGHEY DHAAKA TAARA • 1959 • Ghatak Ritwik • IND • RED STAR HIDDEN BY THE MOON, THE ○ CLOUD-CAPPED STAR, THE ○ MEGHE DHAKA TARA ○ STAR UNDER THE COVER OF CLOUD
MEGHNA, MEGHNA see **DHIREY BAHE MEGHNA** • 1973
MEGLIO VEDOVA • 1967 • Tessari Duccio • ITL, FRN • BETTER A WIDOW (USA)
MEGSZALLOTTAK • 1961 • Makk Karoly • HNG • FANATICS, THE ○ POSSESSED, THE
MEGURI-AI • 1968 • Onchi Hideo • JPN • TWO HEARTS IN THE RAIN ○ MEETING, THE
MEHERJAN • 1977 • Islam Baby • BNG
MEHMAAN • 1953 • *Biswas Anil (M)* • IND
MEHMED MY HAWK see **MEMED** • 1983
MEHMET, THE DECEIVER see **YOLSUZ MEHMET** • 1967
MEHRBAN • 1967 • Singh A. Bhim • IND • MERCIFUL, THE
MEHRI TO PLIO • 1968 • Damianos Alexis • GRC • TO THE SHIP ○ JUSQU'AU BATEAU
MEHRMALS TAGLICH • 1969 • FRG
MEI HUA • 1976 • Liu Chia-Ch'Ang • HKG • VICTORY
MEIDAN POIKAMME • 1929 • Karu Erkki • FNL • OUR BOYS
MEIDAN POIKAMME MERELLA • 1933 • Karu Erkki • FNL • OUR BOYS AT SEA
MEIDEKEN • 1937 • Deppe Hans • FRG • GELEGENHEIT MACHT DIEBE
MEIDO NO KAOYAKU • 1957 • Murayama Mitsuo • JPN • UNDERWORLD BOSS ○ HELL'S BOSS
MEIER • 1986 • Timm Peter • FRG
MEIER UND CO. see **MORITZ MACHT SEIN GLUCK** • 1930
MEIGATSU SOMATO • 1951 • Kinugasa Teinosuke • JPN • LANTERN UNDER A FULL MOON
MEIGUO XIN • 1987 • Fong Yuk-Ping • HKG • JUST LIKE WEATHER
MEIJI GANNEN • 1932 • Ito Daisuke • JPN • FIRST YEAR OF THE MEIJI ERA, THE
MEIJI HARU AKI • 1968 • Gosho Heinosuke • JPN • GIRL OF THE MEIJI PERIOD, A ○ SEASONS OF MEIJI
MEIJI ICHIDAI ONNA • 1935 • Tasaka Tomotaka • JPN • LIFE OF A WOMAN IN THE MEIJI ERA, THE
MEIJI ICHIDAI ONNA • 1955 • Ito Daisuke • JPN • LIFE OF A WOMAN IN THE MEIJI ERA, THE
MEIJI SAMURAI see **KAMIKAZE REN** • 1933
MEIJI-TENNO TO MICHIRO-SENSO • 1957 • Watanabe Kunio • JPN • EMPEROR MEIJI AND THE RUSSO-JAPANESE WAR, THE
MEIKEN KOTETSU TO KONDO ISAMU • 1959 • Ikeda Tomiyasu • JPN
MEILLEURE BOBONNE, LA • 1930 • Allegret Marc • FRN
MEILLEURE FACON DE MARCHER, LA • 1976 • Miller Claude • FRN • BEST WAY TO WALK, THE ○ BEST WAY, THE
MEILLEURE MAITRESSE, LA • 1929 • Hervil Rene • FRN
MEILLEURE PART, LA • 1956 • Allegret Yves • FRN, ITL • ANNI CHE NON RITORNANO, GLI (ITL)
MEILTAHAN TAMA KAY • 1974 • Kassila Matti • FNL • YES, THAT WE CAN ○ EASY DOES IT
MEIN BRUDER JOSUA see **BAUER VON BRUCKNERHOF, DER** • 1956
MEIN FREUND, DER CHAUFFEUR • 1925 • Waschneck Erich • FRG
MEIN FREUND, DER DIEB • 1951 • Weiss Helmut • FRG
MEIN FREUND, DER MILLIONAR • 1931 • Behrendt Hans • FRG
MEIN FREUND HARRY • 1928 • Obal Max • FRG
MEIN FREUND SCHNEIDER • 1915 • MacQuarrie Murdock • USA
MEIN FREUND SHORTY see **HEISS WEHT DER WIND** • 1964
MEIN GANZES HERZ IST VOLL MUSIK • 1959 • Weiss Helmut • FRG
MEIN HEIDELBERG, ICH KANN DICH NICHT VERGESSEN • 1927 • Bauer James • FRG
MEIN HERZ DARFST DU NICHT FRAGEN • 1952 • Martin Paul • FRG
MEIN HERZ GEHORT DIR.. see **MADONNA IM FEGEFEUER** • 1929
MEIN HERZ IST EINE JAZZBAND • 1928 • Zelnik Friedrich • FRG
MEIN HERZ RUFT NACH DIR • 1934 • Gallone Carmine • FRG
MEIN HERZ SEHNT SICH NACH LIEBE • 1931 • Thiele Eugen • FRG • HELLSEHER, DER ○ CLAIRVOYANT, THE
MEIN IN FRIGHT • 1938 • Sidney George • SHT • USA • MEN IN FRIGHT
MEIN IST DER RACHE see **FLUCH, DER** • 1925
MEIN IST DIE RACHE • 1917 • Meinert Rudolf • FRG
MEIN IST DIE WELT see **UNSICHTBARER GEHT DURCH DIE STADT, EIN** • 1933
MEIN KAMPF II see **KRIGSFORBRYTARE** • 1962
MEIN KAMPF, MY CRIMES • 1940 • Lee Norman • UKN
MEIN KAMPF (USA) see **BLODIGA TIDEN, DEN** • 1960
MEIN KIND • 1956 • Pozner, Machalz • FRG • MY CHILD
MEIN LEBEN • 1920 • *Middendorf Kurt* • FRG
MEIN LEBEN FUR DAS DEINES • 1927 • Luitz-Morat • FRG
MEIN LEBEN FUR IRLAND • 1941 • Kimmich Max W. • FRG • IRISCHE TRAGODIE
MEIN LEBEN FUR MARIA ISABELL • 1935 • Waschneck Erich • FRG • MY LIFE FOR MARIA ISABELL (USA)
MEIN LEOPOLD • 1919 • Bolten-Baeckers Heinrich • FRG
MEIN LEOPOLD • 1924 • Bolten-Baeckers Heinrich • FRG
MEIN LEOPOLD • 1931 • Steinhoff Hans • FRG
MEIN LEOPOLD see **HERZ BLEIBT ALLEIN, EIN** • 1955
MEIN LIEBER KATRINA • 1914 • *Field George* • USA
MEIN LIEBER KATRINA CATCHES A CONVICT • 1914 • Ricketts Thomas • USA
MEIN LIEBER ROBINSON • 1972 • Graf Roland • GDR
MEIN LIEBSTER IST EIN JAGERSMANN • 1933 • Kolm Walter • AUS • LIEBE BEI HOF
MEIN MANN DARF ES NICHT WISSEN • 1944 • Heidemann Paul • FRG • SABINE UND DER ZUFALL
MEIN MANN, DAS WIRTSCHAFTSWUNDER • 1961 • Erfurth Ulrich • FRG
MEIN MANN -DER NACHTREDAKTEUR • 1919 • Gad Urban • FRG
MEIN ONKEL, DER GANGSTER (ITL) see **TONTONS FLINGEURS, LES** • 1963
MEIN SCHATZ IST AUS TIROL • 1958 • Quest Hans • FRG
MEIN SCHATZ, KOMM MIT ANS BLAUE MEER • 1959 • Schundler Rudolf • FRG
MEIN SCHULFREUND see **SCHULFREUND, DER** • 1960
MEIN SOHN, DER HERR MINISTER • 1937 • Harlan Veit • FRG
MEIN VATER, DER AFFE UND ICH • 1972 • Antel Franz • AUS
MEIN VATER, DER SCHAUSPIELER • 1956 • Siodmak Robert • FRG
MEIN VATERHAUS STEHT IN DEN BERGEN • 1960 • Leitner Hermann • AUS
MEIN WILLE IST GESETZ • 1919 • Pick Lupu • FRG
MEINE 16 SOHNE • 1956 • Domnick Hans • FRG
MEINE 99 BRAUTE • 1958 • Vohrer Alfred • FRG
MEINE 365 LIEBHABER see **JOSEFINE MUTZENBACHER 2 TEIL: MEINE 365 LIEBHABER** • 1971
MEINE COUSINE AUS WARSCHAU • 1931 • Boese Carl • FRG
MEINE FRAU DAS CALL GIRL see **IMMER ARGER MIT DEM BETT** • 1961
MEINE FRAU, DIE FILMSCHAUSPIELERIN • 1918 • Lubitsch Ernst • FRN
MEINE FRAU, DIE HOCHSTAPLERIN • 1931 • Gerron Kurt • FRG
MEINE FRAU, DIE PERLE • 1937 • Elling Alwin • FRG
MEINE FRAU, DIE SCHUTZENKONIGIN • 1934 • Boese Carl • FRG
MEINE FRAU MACHT MUSIK • 1958 • Hinrich Hans • FRG • MY WIFE MAKES MUSIC ○ SOLO ZU VIERT
MEINE FRAU TERESA • 1942 • Rabenalt Arthur M. • FRG • MY WIFE TERESA
MEINE FREUNDIN BARBARA • 1937 • Kirchhoff Fritz • FRG • MY FRIEND BARBARA
MEINE FREUNDIN JOSEFINE • 1942 • Zerlett Hans H. • FRG
MEINE FREUNDIN SYBILLE • 1967 • Luderer Wolfgang • GDR • MY GIRL-FRIEND SYBILLE ○ MY FRIEND SYBILLE
MEINE HEIMAT IST TAGLICH WOANDERS see **GELIEBTE BESTIE** • 1959
MEINE HERREN SOHNE • 1945 • Stemmle R. A. • FRG
MEINE KINDER UND ICH • 1955 • Schleif Wolfgang • FRG
MEINE NICHTE SUSANNE • 1950 • Liebeneiner Wolfgang • FRG
MEINE SCHONE MAMA • 1958 • Martin Paul • FRG, AUS
MEINE SCHWESTER UND ICH • 1929 • Noa Manfred • FRG
MEINE SCHWESTER UND ICH • 1954 • Martin Paul • FRG
MEINE STUNDE NULL • 1969 • Hasler Joachim, Becker Jurek • GDR • MY ZERO HOUR
MEINE TANTE -DEINE TANTE • 1927 • Froelich Carl • FRG
MEINE TANTE -DEINE TANTE • 1939 • Boese Carl • FRG
MEINE TANTE, DEINE TANTE • 1956 • Boese Carl • FRG
MEINE TOCHTER LEBT IN WIEN • 1940 • Emo E. W. • FRG
MEINE TOCHTER PATRICIA • 1959 • Liebeneiner Wolfgang • AUS
MEINE TOCHTER TUT DAS NICHT • 1940 • Zerlett Hans H. • FRG
MEINE TOCHTER UND ICH • 1963 • Engel Thomas • FRG
MEINE VIER JUNGEN • 1944 • Rittau Gunther • FRG
MEINEID • 1929 • Jacoby Georg • FRG
MEINEIDBAUER, DER • 1926 • Fleck Jacob, Fleck Luise • FRG
MEINEIDBAUER, DER • 1941 • Hainisch Leopold • FRG
MEINEIDBAUER, DER • 1956 • Jugert Rudolf • FRG
MEINES VATERS PFERDE • 1954 • Lamprecht Gerhard • FRG
MEIR EZOFEWICZ • 1914 • Hertz Aleksander • PLN
MEIRAN • 1929 • *Tsuburaya Eiji (Ph)* • JPN • BRIGHTNESS AND DARKNESS
MEISJE MET HET RODE HAAT, HET • 1981 • Verbong Ben • NTH • GIRL WITH THE RED HAIR, THE (USA)
MEISJES • 1966 • Houwer Rob • NTH
MEISSNER PORZELLAN • 1907 • Porten Friedrich • FRG
MEISTER, DER • 1920 • *Reicher Ernst* • FRG
MEISTER DER WELT, DER • 1927 • Righelli Gennaro • FRG
MEISTER IM BOSEN, DER • 1920 • *Clou-Filmges* • FRG
MEISTER VON NURNBERG, DER • 1926 • Berger Ludwig • FRG • MASTER OF NUREMBURG, THE
MEISTERBOXER, DER • 1934 • Sauer Fred • FRG • PANTOFFELHELDEN
MEISTERDETEKTIV, DER • 1933 • Seitz Franz • FRG
MEISTERDETEKTIV, DER • 1944 • Marischka Hubert • FRG, AUS • REIZENDE FAMILIE, EINE
MEISTERDIEB, DER see **BARON BUNNYS ERLEBNISSE 1** • 1921
MEISTERSCHUSS, DER • 1920 • Brunner Rolf • FRG
MEISTERSINGER, DER • 1929 • Berger Ludwig • FRG
MEISTERSINGER VON NURNBERG, DIE • 1970 • Lindtberg Leopold • MTV • FRG
MEISTERSPRINGER VON KURNBERG, DIE • 1923 • Fekete Alfred, Zurn Walther • FRG
MEITO BIJOMARU • 1945 • Mizoguchi Kenji • JPN • FAMOUS SWORD BIJOMARU, THE (USA) ○ BIJOMARU, THE NOTED SWORD ○ SWORD, THE (UKN) ○ NOTED SWORD, THE ○ BIJOMARU SWORD, THE
MEIYOUHANGBIAODE HELIU • 1985 • Wu Tianming • CHN • UNCHARTED RIVER ○ RIVER WITHOUT BUOYS, THE
MEJ OCH DEJ see **MIG OG DIG** • 1969
MEJOR ALCALDE, EL REY, EL • 1973 • Gil Rafael • SPN
MEJOR DEL MUNDO, EL • 1968 • Coll Julio • SPN
MEJOR EDUCACION, YA • 1974 • Handler Mario • DOC • VNZ • BETTER EDUCATION, JUST NOW
MEJOR ES REIR, LO • 1931 • Emo E. W. • SPN
MEJOR REGALO, EL • 1973 • Aguirre Javier • SPN
MEJOR TESORO, EL • 1966 • Almedros Gregorio • SPN
MEJU • 1960 • Magatani Morehei • JPN
MEKAGOJIRA NO GYAKUSHU • 1975 • Honda Inoshiro • JPN • MONSTERS FROM AN UNKNOWN PLANET ○ TERROR OF MECHAGODZILLA ○ ESCAPE OF MEGAGODZILLA, THE ○ TERROR OF GODZILLA, THE
MEKANIK-PIGEN • 1918 • Lauritzen Lau • DNM
MEKANSIZ KURTLAR • 1968 • Duru Yilmaz • TRK • LANDLESS WOLVES, THE
MEKHANIKHA GOLOVNOVO MOZGA • 1926 • Pudovkin V. I. • USS • MECHANICS OF THE BRAIN, THE ○ CONDITIONED REFLEXES
MEKISHIKO MUSHUKU • 1962 • Kurahara Koreyoshi • JPN • CALL OF MEXICO, THE
MEKSIKANETS • 1957 • Kaplunovsky Vladimir • USS • MEXICAN, THE (USA)
MEKSYK • 1958 • Wionczek Roman • DOC • PLN • MEXICO
MEKTOUB? • 1970 • Ghalem Ali • ALG, FRN • MAKTUB
MEKURA-GUMO • 1929 • Inagaki Hiroshi • JPN
MEL, UM ALIMENTO NATURAL, O • 1931 • Coelho Jose Adolfo • SHT • PRT
MELA • 1949 • Sunny S. U. • IND
MELA CARNIVAL • 1986 • PKS
MELAMPO see **CAGNA, LA** • 1972
MELANCHOLIA • 1989 • Engel Andi • UKN
MELANCHOLY BABY • 1979 • Gabus Clarisse • FRN, BLG, SWT
MELANCHOLY DAME, THE • 1929 • Gillstrom Arvid E. • SHT • USA
MELANCHOLY FIRESIDE TALES see **ZWAAR MOEDIGE VERHALEN VOOR BIJ DE CENTRALE VERWARMING** • 1975
MELANCHOLY TALES see **ZWAAR MOEDIGE VERHALEN VOOR BIJ DE CENTRALE VERWARMING** • 1975
MELANCOLICAS, LAS • 1973 • Moreno Alba Rafael • SPN
MELANIE • 1981 • Bromfield Rex • CND
MELANIE AND ME • 1975 • Fitchett Christopher • ASL
MELANIE ROSE • 1988 • Kollek Amos • USA
MELBA • 1953 • Milestone Lewis • UKN
MELBA • 1987 • Fisher Rodney • MTV • ASL
MELBOURNE CUP • 1896 • Sestier Marius • ASL
MELBOURNE CUP • 1897 • ASL
MELBOURNE CUP • 1925 • ASL
MELBOURNE CUP -1914 • 1914 • *Krischock H. (Ph)* • ASL
MELBOURNE IN NATURAL COLOUR • 1913 • ASL
MELBOURNE MYSTERY, THE • 1913 • ASL
MELBOURNE RENDEZVOUS (USA) see **RENDEZ-VOUS A MELBOURNE** • 1956
MELBOURNE TIMETABLE • 1963 • Burstall Tim • SHT • ASL
MELBOURNE'S AGRICULTURAL SHOW • 1906 • *Best & Baker* • ASL
MELBURN CONFESSION, THE • 1913 • *Calvert E. H.* • USA
MELCHIOR DAS MEDIUM • 1919 • AUS
MELGAR see **MELGAR, EL POETA INSURGENTA INSURGENTE** • 1982
MELGAR, EL POETA INSURGENTA INSURGENTE • 1982 • Garcia Federico • CUB, PRU • MELGAR
MELGAREJO • 1937 • Barth-Moglia Luis • ARG
MELHOR DA RUA • 1966 • Correia Artur • ANS • PRT
'MELIA NO GOOD • 1917 • Dwan Allan (Spv) • USA
MELIMOT BEYERUSHALAIM see **SELLOUT, THE** • 1975
MELINDA • 1972 • Robertson Hugh A. • USA
MELISMAS • 1963 • Briz Jose' • SHT • SPN
MELISSA • Korber Serge • FRN
MELISSA OF THE HILLS • 1917 • Kirkwood James • USA
MELISSA: THE TOTAL FEMALE • 1970 • Penton Arthur • USA
MELISSOKOMOS, O • 1986 • Angelopoulos Theo • GRC, FRN • APICULTEUR, L' (FRN) ○ BEEKEEPER, THE
MELITA'S RUSE • 1912 • Melies Gaston • USA
MELITA'S SACRIFICE • 1913 • Melville Wilbert • USA
MELLA • Pineda Enrique • CUB
MELLAH DE MARRAKECH, LE • 1948 • Mineur Jean • SHT • FRN
MELLAN LIV OCH DOD • 1917 • Klercker Georg • SWD • BETWEEN LIFE AND DEATH
MELLEM MUNTRE MUSIKANTER • 1925 • Lauritzen Lau • DNM
MELLEM VENNER • 1963 • Nyrup Poul • DNM • DAYS OF SIN AND NIGHTS OF NYMPHOMANIA (USA) ○ DAYS OF SIN, NIGHTS OF NYMPH.. ○ DAYS OF SHAME AND NIGHTS OF EXCESS ○ DAYS OF SIN AND NIGHTS OF MADNESS
MELLER DRAMMER • 1914 • Martin E. A. • USA
MELO • 1932 • Czinner Paul • FRN
MELO • 1986 • Resnais Alain • FRN
MELOCOTON EN ALMIBAR • 1960 • del Amo Antonio • SPN
MELODI OM VAREN, EN • 1933 • Lindlof John • SWD • SPRINGTIME TUNE
MELODI OM VAREN, EN • 1943 • Hildebrand Weyler • SWD • HANDLAR OM KARLEK, DET ○ SWING I HJARTER
MELODIA DE ARRABAL • 1933 • Gasnier Louis J., Rey Florian • SPN, FRN
MELODIA MISTERIOSA, LA • 1955 • Fortuny Juan • SPN
MELODIA PERDIDA, LA • 1952 • Demicheli Tulio • ARG
MELODIA PROHIBIDA • 1934 • Strayer Frank • USA • FORBIDDEN MELODY
MELODIAS DE ANTANO see **EN TIEMPOS DE DON PORFIRIO** • 1939
MELODIAS DE HOY • 1960 • Elorrieta Jose Maria • SPN
MELODIAS INOLVIDABLES • 1958 • Salvador Jaime • MXC
MELODIAS PORTENAS • 1937 • Barth-Moglia Luis • ARG
MELODIC INVERSION • 1958 • Hugo Ian • SHT • USA
MELODIE DER LIEBE • 1932 • Jacoby Georg • FRG • RIGHT TO HAPPINESS
MELODIE DER WELT • 1929 • Ruttmann Walter • FRG • MELODY OF THE WORLD ○ WORLD MELODY
MELODIE DES HERZENS • 1929 • Schwarz Hanns • FRG • MELODY OF THE HEART ○ HEART'S MELODY

MELODIE DES HERZENS • 1950 • Liebeneiner Wolfgang • FRG • MELODY OF THE HEART
MELODIE DES SCHICKSALS • 1950 • Schweikart Hans • FRG
MELODIE DI SOGNO see **RITORNO** • 1940
MELODIE EN SOUS-SOL • 1962 • Verneuil Henri • FRN, ITL • COLPO GROSSO AL CASINO (ITL) ○ ANY NUMBER CAN WIN (USA) ○ BIG SNATCH, THE ○ BIG GRAB, THE
MELODIE ETERNE • 1940 • Gallone Carmine • ITL • ETERNAL MELODIES
MELODIE IMMORTALI • 1953 • Gentilomo Giacomo • ITL • MASCAGNI
MELODIE, MA GRAND-MERE • 1983 • Goulet Stella • MTV • CND
MELODIE POUR TOI • 1941 • Rozier Willy • FRN
MELODIE UND RHYTHMUS • 1959 • Olden John • FRG
MELODIEN FRAN GAMLA STA'N • 1939 • Frisk Ragnar • SWD • MELODY FROM THE OLD TOWN
MELODIES • 1926 • Ford Francis • USA
MELODIES BY MARTIN • 1955 • *Martin Freddie* • SHT • USA
MELODIES OF THE MOMENT • 1938 • Shepherd Horace • UKN
MELODIES OF THE VERA QUARTER see **MELODII VERIYSKOVO KVARTALA** • 1973
MELODIES OF THE VERI SUBURB see **MELODII VERIYSKOVO KVARTALA** • 1973
MELODIES OF THE VERIYSKI NEIGHBOURHOOD see **MELODII VERIYSKOVO KVARTALA** • 1973
MELODIES OLD AND NEW • 1942 • Cahn Edward L. • SHT • USA
MELODII VERIYSKOVO KVARTALA • 1973 • Shengelaya Georgi • USS • MELODIES OF THE VERIYSKI NEIGHBOURHOOD ○ MELODIES OF THE VERI SUBURB ○ MELODIES OF THE VERA QUARTER
MELODIOUS MIX-UP, A • 1915 • Ward Chance E. • USA
MELODRAMA? • 1981 • Panayotopoulos Nikos • GRC
MELODRAMA OF YESTERDAY • 1912 • *Fischer Margarita* • USA
MELODRAME • 1976 • Jorge Jean-Louis • FRN
MELODRAMMA • 1934 • Land Robert, Simonelli Giorgio C. • ITL
MELODRAMMORE • 1978 • Costanzo Maurizio • ITL
MELODY • 1911 • *Daly William F.* • USA
MELODY • 1953 • Nichols Charles, Kimball Ward • ANS • USA
MELODY • 1971 • Hussein Waris • UKN • S.W.A.L.K. ○ LOVE, MELODY ○ TO LOVE SOMEBODY
MELODY AND ART • 1914 • Vale Travers • USA
MELODY AND MOONLIGHT • 1940 • Santley Joseph • USA
MELODY AND ROMANCE • 1937 • Elvey Maurice • UKN
MELODY CLUB • 1949 • Berman Monty • UKN
MELODY CRUISE • 1933 • Sandrich Mark • USA • MAIDEN CRUISE
MELODY FOR THREE • 1941 • Kenton Erle C. • USA
MELODY FOR TWO • 1937 • King Louis • USA
MELODY FROM HEAVEN see **PAI HUA P'IAO, HSUEH HUA P'IAO** • 1977
MELODY FROM THE OLD TOWN see **MELODIEN FRAN GAMLA STA'N** • 1939
MELODY GARDEN • 1944 • Keays Vernon • SHT • USA
MELODY GIRL (UKN) see **SING, DANCE, PLENTY HOT** • 1940
MELODY HAUNTS MY MEMORY, THE (USA) see **SAMO JEDNOM SE LJUBI** • 1981
MELODY HAUNTS MY REVERIE, THE see **SAMO JEDNOM SE LJUBI** • 1981
MELODY IN F • 1932 • Newman Widgey R. • UKN
MELODY IN GRAY see **HANARE GOZE, ORIN** • 1978
MELODY IN LOVE • 1978 • Frank Hubert • FRG
MELODY IN SPRING • 1934 • McLeod Norman Z. • USA
MELODY IN THE DARK • 1949 • Hill Robert Jordan • UKN
MELODY INN (UKN) see **RIDING HIGH** • 1943
MELODY LANE • 1929 • Hill Robert F. • USA
MELODY LANE • 1941 • Lamont Charles • USA
MELODY LINGERS ON, THE • 1935 • Burton David • USA
MELODY MAESTRO • 1946 • Cowan Will • SHT • USA
MELODY MAKER, THE • 1933 • Hiscott Leslie • UKN
MELODY MAKER (UKN) see **DING DONG WILLIAMS** • 1945
MELODY MAN, THE • 1930 • Neill R. William • USA
MELODY MOODS • 1950 • *Universal* • SHT • USA
MELODY OF DEATH • 1922 • Thornton F. Martin • UKN
MELODY OF DEATH, THE • 1917 • Gerrard Douglas • SHT • USA
MELODY OF DOOM, THE • 1915 • Beal Frank • USA
MELODY OF FATE, THE • 1911 • *Powers* • USA
MELODY OF LIFE (UKN) see **SYMPHONY OF SIX MILLION** • 1932
MELODY OF LOVE, THE • 1912 • *Bushman Francis X.* • USA
MELODY OF LOVE, THE • 1916 • Kerrigan J. Warren • SHT • USA
MELODY OF LOVE, THE • 1928 • Heath Arch B. • USA • MADELON
MELODY OF MY HEART • 1936 • Noy Wilfred • UKN
MELODY OF THE HEART see **MELODIE DES HERZENS** • 1929
MELODY OF THE HEART see **MELODIE DES HERZENS** • 1950
MELODY OF THE PLAINS • 1937 • Newfield Sam • USA
MELODY OF THE SEA see **HAVETS MELODI** • 1934
MELODY OF THE WORLD see **MELODIE DER WELT** • 1929
MELODY OF YOUTH (UKN) see **THEY SHALL HAVE MUSIC** • 1939
MELODY PARADE • 1943 • Dreifuss Arthur • USA
MELODY PARADE • 1944 • Collins Lewis D. • SHT • USA
MELODY RANCH • 1940 • Santley Joseph • USA
MELODY STAMPEDE • 1945 • Cowan Will • SHT • USA
MELODY TIME • 1946 • Scholl Jack • SHT • USA
MELODY TIME • 1948 • Sharpsteen Ben, Luske Hamilton, Kinney Jack, Jackson Wilfred, Geronimi Clyde • ANM • USA
MELODY TRAIL • 1935 • Kane Joseph • USA
MELOMANE, LE • 1903 • Melies Georges • FRN • MELOMANIAC, THE (USA) ○ MAN WITH FIVE HEADS
MELOMANIAC, THE • 1966 • Stefanescu Horia • ANS • RMN
MELOMANIAC, THE (USA) see **MELOMANE, LE** • 1903
MELON AFFAIR, THE • 1979 • Lieberman Art • USA
MELON-DRAMA, A • 1931 • Sandrich Mark • SHT • USA
MELONS BALADEURS, LES • 1911 • Cohl Emile • ANS • FRN
MELONY • 1974 • Lavut Martin • DOC • CND
MELTING MILLIONS • 1917 • Turner Otis • USA
MELTING MILLIONS • 1927 • Bennet Spencer Gordon • SRL • USA
MELTING POT, THE • 1915 • Fitzmaurice George?, Olcott Sidney? • USA
MELTING POT, THE • 1976 • Miles Dekes • CND
MELTING POT, THE (UKN) see **BETTY CO-ED** • 1946
MELUKA, DIE ROSE VON MARAKESCH • 1930 • Schwarz Werner, Ben Rahi Mohamed, Waly Ahmed • FRG
MELUSINE • 1944 • Steinhoff Hans • FRG
MELVIN AND HOWARD • 1980 • Demme Jonathan • USA
MELVIN PURVIS see **MELVIN PURVIS, G-MAN** • 1974
MELVIN PURVIS, G-MAN • 1974 • Curtis Dan • TVM • USA • LEGEND OF MACHINE GUN KELLY, THE (UKN) ○ MELVIN PURVIS ○ G-MAN
MELVIN: SON OF ALVIN see **SON OF ALVIN** • 1984
MELVIN'S REVENGE • 1949 • Lewis Jerry • SHT • USA
MELZER • 1983 • Butler Heinz • SWT
MEMBER OF PARLIAMENT • 1920 • Protazanov Yakov • USS
MEMBER OF TATTERSALLS, A • 1919 • Ward Albert • UKN
MEMBER OF THE GOVERNMENT see **CHLEN PRAVITELSTVA** • 1940
MEMBER OF THE JURY • 1937 • Mainwaring Bernerd • UKN
MEMBER OF THE WEDDING, THE • 1952 • Zinnemann Fred • USA
MEMBRES DE LA FAMILLE, LES see **BIJOUX DE FAMILLE, LES** • 1974
MEMBURU MAKELAR MAYAT • 1986 • INN
MEME LE SOLEIL A DES TACHES • 1976 • Sokolowski Claude • DOC • FRN
MEME LES MOMES ONT DU VAGUE A L'AME • 1979 • Daniel Jean-Louis • FRN
MEME LES MOULES ONT DU VAGUE A L'AME see **BLUFF** • 1982
MEMED • 1983 • Ustinov Peter • UKN, YGS • MEHMED MY HAWK ○ LION AND THE HAWK, THE
MEMENTO • 1968 • Osmanli Dimitri • YGS
MEMENTO MEI • 1963 • Charlot Martin • USA
MEMENTOS see **DOEA TANDA MATA** • 1985
MEMO FOR JOE • 1944 • Fleischer Richard • SHT • USA
MEMO MELBOURNE • 1979 • Bilcock David Jr. • DOC • ASL
MEMO OF A TWENTY-ONE-YEAR-OLD • 1983 • Kim Hyo-Chon • SKR
MEMO TO MARS • 1954 • *U.s. Rubber & Wilding* • SHT • USA
MEMOIRE, LA see **HADDUTA MISRIYA** • 1982
MEMOIRE BATTANTE • 1983 • Lamothe Arthur • DOC • CND
MEMOIRE COMMUNE • 1977 • Poidevin Patrick • FRN
MEMOIRE COURTE, LA • 1961 • Torrent Henri, Premysler Francine • FRN
MEMOIRE COURTE, LA • 1979 • de Gregorio Eduardo • FRN, BLG • SHORT MEMORY
MEMOIRE EN FETE • 1964 • Forest Leonard • DCS • CND
MEMOIRE FERTILE, LA • 1981 • Khleifi Michel • BLG, FRG, NTH
MEMOIRE INDIENNE • 1967 • Regnier Michel • DCS • CND
MEMOIREN DER TRAGODIN THAMAR, DIE • 1917 • Reinert Robert • FRG
MEMOIREN DES SATANS, DIE • 1917 • Heymann Robert • FRG • MEMOIRS OF SATAN, THE
MEMOIREN EINER FILMDIVA • 1924 • Zelnik Friedrich • FRG
MEMOIREN EINES KAMMERDIENERS 1 • 1921 • Teuber Arthur • FRG • MARTIN, DER FINDLING
MEMOIREN EINES KAMMERDIENERS 2 • 1921 • Teuber Arthur • FRG • BASQUINES VERGELTUNG
MEMOIREN EINES MONCHS, DIE • 1924 • Feher Friedrich • FRG
MEMOIRES DE LA VACHE YOLANDE, LES • 1950 • Neubach Ernst • FRN
MEMOIRES D'UN FLIC • 1955 • Foucaud Pierre • FRN
MEMOIRES D'UN TRICHEUR, LES see **ROMAN D'UN TRICHEUR, LE** • 1936
MEMOIRES D'UNE ENFANT DES ANDES • 1985 • Mallet Marilu • CND • ANDAHAYLILLAS
MEMOIRS • 1985 • Chbib Bachar • CND
MEMOIRS OF A CRIMINAL, THE see **FORBRYDERS LIV OG LEVNED, EN** • 1916
MEMOIRS OF A FRENCH WHORE (USA) see **DEROBADE, LA** • 1979
MEMOIRS OF A MEXICAN see **MEMORIAS DE UN MEXICANO** • 1950
MEMOIRS OF A RIVER see **TUTAJOSOK** • 1988
MEMOIRS OF A SURVIVOR • 1981 • Gladwell David • UKN
MEMOIRS OF SATAN, THE see **MEMOIREN DES SATANS, DIE** • 1917
MEMORABLE DAY, THE • 1975 • Donev Peter • BUL
MEMORABLE PILGRIMAGE OF THE EMPEROR KANGA MUSSA FROM MALI TO MECCA see **DENKWURDIGE WALLFAHRT DES KAISERS KANGA MUSSA VON MALI NACH MEKKA** • 1977
MEMORANDUM • 1967 • Brittain Don, Spotton John • DOC • CND • POUR MEMOIRE
MEMORANDUM FOR A SPY • 1965 • Rosenberg Stuart • TVM • USA • ASYLUM FOR A SPY
MEMORANDUM ON ANA see **APUNTE SOBRE ANA** • 1971
MEMORIA • 1976 • Macian Francisco • SPN
MEMORIA DE HELENA, LA • 1970 • Neves David • BRZ • MEMORIES OF HELENE
MEMORIA E GLI ANNI, LA see **ANNI DURI** • 1979
MEMORIAL DAY • 1983 • Sargent Joseph • TVM • USA
MEMORIAL DE SAINT-HELENE, LE • 1911 • Carre Michel, Barbier • FRN
MEMORIAL TO MARTIN LUTHER KING • 1969 • Fox Beryl • DOC • USA
MEMORIALE DALLE ROVINE • 1973 • Frezza Andrea • MTV • ITL
MEMORIAS AND CONFISSOES • 1982 • de Oliveira Manoel • PRT • MEMORIES AND CONFESSIONS
MEMORIAS DE LETICIA VALLE • 1978 • Rivas Miguel Angel • SPN • MEMORIES OF LETICIA VALLE
MEMORIAS DE MI GENERAL, LAS • 1960 • de la Serna Mauricio • MXC
MEMORIAS DE UN MEXICANO • 1950 • Toscano Carmen • DOC • MXC • MEMOIRS OF A MEXICAN
MEMORIAS DE UN PAJARO • 1971 • Ardavin Cesar • SHT • SPN
MEMORIAS DE UNA VAMPIRESA • 1945 • Peon Ramon • MXC
MEMORIAS DEL DESARROLLO see **MEMORIAS DEL SUBDESARROLLO** • 1968
MEMORIAS DEL SUBDESARROLLO • 1968 • Alea Tomas Gutierrez • CUB • MEMORIES OF UNDERDEVELOPMENT ○ MEMORIAS DEL DESARROLLO
MEMORIAS DEL SUBSUELO • 1981 • Sarquis Nicolas • ARG • MEMORIES FROM THE UNDERGROUND
MEMORIAS DO CARCERE • 1984 • dos Santos Nelson Pereira • BRZ • MEMORIES OF IMPRISONMENT ○ MEMORIES OF PRISON
MEMORIAS Y OLVIDOS • 1987 • Feldman Simon • ARG • MEMORIES AND OBLIVION
MEMORIES • 1912 • *Arling Charles* • USA
MEMORIES • 1913 • *Weber Lois* • USA
MEMORIES • 1914 • Le Saint Edward J. • USA
MEMORIES • 1919 • *Lancaster Theodore P.* • USA
MEMORIES • 1925 • Backner Arthur • UKN
MEMORIES • 1929 • Jeffrey R. E. • UKN
MEMORIES • 1971 • Noyce Phil • SHT • ASL
MEMORIES • 1973 • Locker Kenneth • UKN
MEMORIES • 1986 • Dalen Zale R. • CND
MEMORIES see **ZWISCHENGLEIS** • 1978
MEMORIES AND CONFESSIONS see **MEMORIAS AND CONFISSOES** • 1982
MEMORIES AND OBLIVION see **MEMORIAS Y OLVIDOS** • 1987
MEMORIES AT CHKALOV • 1967 • Lisakovitch Viktor • DOC • USS
MEMORIES FROM THE BOSTON CLUB see **MINNEN FRAN BOSTONKLUBBEN** • 1909
MEMORIES FROM THE UNDERGROUND see **MEMORIAS DEL SUBSUELO** • 1981
MEMORIES IN MEN'S SOULS • 1914 • Brooke Van Dyke • USA
MEMORIES NEVER DIE • 1982 • Stern Sandor • TVM • USA
MEMORIES OF '49 • 1912 • *Solax* • USA
MEMORIES OF A RIVER see **TUTAJOSOK** • 1988
MEMORIES OF A ROSE, THE • 1962 • Nicolaescu Sergiu • RMN • ROSE'S MEMORY, THE
MEMORIES OF A STRANGE NIGHT see **UTOLSO VACSORA** • 1961
MEMORIES OF A SUMMER IN BERLIN see **ERINNERUNG AN EINEN SOMMER IN BERLIN** • 1972
MEMORIES OF AN ACTRESS, THE • 1957 • Stiopul Savel • RMN
MEMORIES OF DUKE • 1980 • Keys Gary • DOC • USA
MEMORIES OF EUROPE • 1941 • Fitzpatrick James • CMP • USA
MEMORIES OF FAMOUS HOLLYWOOD COMEDIANS • 1951 • Staub Ralph • USA
MEMORIES OF HELENE see **MEMORIA DE HELENA, LA** • 1970
MEMORIES OF HIS YOUTH • 1913 • O'Neil Barry • USA
MEMORIES OF IMPRISONMENT see **MEMORIAS DO CARCERE** • 1984
MEMORIES OF LETICIA VALLE see **MEMORIAS DE LETICIA VALLE** • 1978
MEMORIES OF LONG AGO • 1913 • *Dragon* • USA
MEMORIES OF LONG AGO • 1913 • *Ryno* • USA
MEMORIES OF ME • 1988 • Winkler Henry • USA
MEMORIES OF PARIS see **SOUVENIRS DE PARIS**
MEMORIES OF PATIO DAYS OR ROAD OF YESTERDAY • 1912 • *Vitagraph* • USA
MEMORIES OF PRISON see **MEMORIAS DO CARCERE** • 1984
MEMORIES OF THE FUTURE see **RECUERDOS DEL PORVENIR, LOS** • 1968
MEMORIES OF THE FUTURE see **ERINNERUNGEN AUS DER ZUKUNFT** • 1969
MEMORIES OF THE STARS see **WYCIECZKA W KOSMOS** • 1961
MEMORIES OF UNDERDEVELOPMENT see **MEMORIAS DEL SUBDESARROLLO** • 1968
MEMORIES OF YEARS AGO • 1914 • *Frontier* • USA
MEMORIES OF YOUNG DAYS see **WAKAKI HI NO KANGEKI** • 1931
MEMORIES -PSALM 46 • 1927 • Barnett Charles • UKN
MEMORIES THAT HAUNT • 1914 • Lambart Harry • USA
MEMORIES WITHIN MISS AGGIE • 1974 • Damiano Gerard • USA
MEMORY • 1914 • Buckland Warwick? • UKN
MEMORY • 1974 • Nichev Ivan • BUL
MEMORY see **PAMYAT** • 1972
MEMORY, THE • 1978 • Malass Mohammed • MTV • SYR
MEMORY EPISODES see **SMRITICHITRE** • 1983
MEMORY EXPERT, THE (UKN) see **MAN ON THE FLYING TRAPEZE, THE** • 1935
MEMORY FOR TWO (UKN) see **I LOVE A BAND LEADER** • 1945
MEMORY FRAGMENTS see **GUERRE OUBLIEE, LA** • 1988
MEMORY LANE • 1926 • Stahl John M. • USA
MEMORY MILL, THE • 1916 • *Lewis Grace* • SHT • USA
MEMORY OF A ROSE see **TSUIOKU NO BARA** • 1936
MEMORY OF EVA RYKER, THE • 1980 • Grauman Walter • TVM • USA
MEMORY OF HIS MOTHER, THE • 1908 • Stow Percy • UKN
MEMORY OF JUSTICE, THE • 1976 • Ophuls Marcel • USA, FRG
MEMORY OF LOVE see **IN NAME ONLY** • 1939
MEMORY OF LOVE see **HAN GLOMDE HENNEALDRIG** • 1952
MEMORY OF OUR DAY see **PAMET NASEHO DNE** • 1963
MEMORY OF THE HEART see **PAMYAT SERDTSA** • 1958
MEMORY OF THE PEOPLE • 1964 • Lisakovitch Viktor • DOC • USS
MEMORY OF THE TWIN GIRL • 1976 • Sharlandgiev Ljobomir • BUL
MEMORY OF US • 1974 • Dyal H. Kaye • USA
MEMORY ROOM see **JOBBE-KHANEH** • 1975
MEMORY SONG BOOK • 1951 • Cowan Will • SHT • USA
MEMORY TREE, THE • 1915 • Johnston Lorimer • USA
MEMORY TRICKS • 1941 • Jason Will • SHT • USA
MEMORY'S TRAGIC LEAP • 1912 • *Republic* • USA
MEMPHIS BELLE • 1989 • Caton-Jones Michael • UKN
MEMPHIS BELLE, THE • 1943 • Wyler William • DOC • USA
MEMPHIS SLIM • 1960 • Bruynoghe Yannick • DOC • BLG
MEN • 1918 • Vekroff Perry N. • USA
MEN • 1924 • Buchowetzki Dimitri • USA
MEN • 1973 • Keosayan Edmond • USS
MEN see **MANNER** • 1986

MEN, THE • 1950 • Zinnemann Fred • USA • BATTLE STRIPE
MEN, THE see **MUSKARCI** • 1962
MEN ABOUT TOWN see **SVETACI** • 1969
MEN AGAINST SPEED • 1958 • Rogell Albert S. • USA
MEN AGAINST THE ARCTIC • 1956 • Hibler Winston • DOC • USA
MEN AGAINST THE ICE • 1960 • Bairstow David • DOC • CND
MEN AGAINST THE SEA • 1935 • Sewell Vernon • DCS • UKN
MEN AGAINST THE SKY • 1940 • Goodwins Leslie • USA
MEN AGAINST THE SUN • 1953 • Stafford Brendan J. • KNY
MEN ALLT A HREINU • 1983 • Gudmundsson Agust • ICL • ON TOP
MEN AND AUTOMATION • 1958 • Fraser Donald • DOC • CND
MEN AND BANNERS see **KOSZIVU EMBER FIAI, A** • 1965
MEN AND BEASTS see **LYUDI I ZVERI** • 1962
MEN AND JOBS see **DELA Y LYUDI** • 1932
MEN AND MICROBES • 1951 • de Haas Max • NTH
MEN AND MOBS • 1947 • Heyer John • DOC • ASL
MEN AND MUSLIN • 1913 • *Solax* • USA
MEN AND NATURE see **MORG ERU DAGS AUGU** • 1980
MEN AND OIL • 1948-51 • Harris Roy • DOC • UKN
MEN AND WAR see **SENSO TO NINGEN** • 1970
MEN AND WOLVES (USA) see **UOMINI E LUPI** • 1956
MEN AND WOMEN • 1914 • Kirkwood James • USA
MEN AND WOMEN • 1925 • De Mille William C. • USA
MEN AND WOMEN (UKN) see **NOITE VAZIA** • 1965
MEN ARE CHILDREN TWICE (USA) see **VALLEY OF SONG** • 1953
MEN ARE LIKE THAT • 1930 • Tuttle Frank • USA • SHOW-OFF, THE ○ VIRTUOUS WIFE, THE
MEN ARE LIKE THAT see **ARIZONA** • 1931
MEN ARE NOT GODS • 1936 • Reisch Walter • UKN
MEN ARE SUCH FOOLS • 1932 • Nigh William • USA • SECOND FIDDLE
MEN ARE SUCH FOOLS • 1938 • Berkeley Busby • USA
MEN ARE SUCH LIARS see **TRUTH ABOUT MURDER, THE** • 1946
MEN ARE SUCH RASCALS see **UOMINI, CHE MASCALZONI.., GLI** • 1932
MEN ARE THAT WAY (USA) see **MANNER MUSSEN ES SEIN** • 1939
MEN AT THEIR BEST • 1915 • Myers Harry • USA
MEN AT WORK • 1990 • Estevez Emilio • USA
MEN BEHIND BARS (UKN) see **DUFFY OF SAN QUENTIN** • 1954
MEN BEHIND THE METERS • 1940 • Elton Arthur • UKN
MEN CALL IT LOVE • 1931 • Selwyn Edgar • USA • AMONG THE MARRIED
MEN CAN'T BE RAPED see **MANRAPE** • 1978
MEN DON'T LEAVE • 1989 • Brickman Paul • USA
MEN FROM THE MINISTRY, THE • 1971 • SAF
MEN FROM THE MONASTERY see **SHAOLIN TZU-TI** • 1975
MEN FROM THE SEA • 1946 • Gunn Gilbert • DOC • UKN
MEN FROM ZIMBABOUE • 1982 • Kent Larry • MTV • CND
MEN HATERS' CLUB, THE • 1910 • *Vitagraph* • USA
MEN-HUNTERS • 1963 • Petelska Ewa, Petelski Czeslaw • PLN
MEN IN BLACK • 1934 • McCarey Ray • SHT • USA
MEN IN DANGER • 1938 • Jackson Pat • DCS • UKN
MEN IN DARKNESS see **MANNEN I MORKER** • 1955
MEN IN EXILE • 1937 • Farrow John • USA
MEN IN FRIGHT see **MEIN IN FRIGHT** • 1938
MEN IN HER DIARY • 1945 • Barton Charles T. • USA
MEN IN HER LIFE • 1931 • Beaudine William • USA
MEN IN HER LIFE, THE • 1941 • Ratoff Gregory • USA • TONIGHT BELONGS TO US ○ WOMAN OF DESIRE
MEN IN MASKS see **AFTER DARK** • 1923
MEN IN OFFSIDE, THE see **MUZI V OFFSIDU** • 1931
MEN IN THE MOUNTAINS see **EMBEREK A HAVASON** • 1942
MEN IN THE OFFSIDE see **MUZI V OFFSIDU** • 1931
MEN IN THE PARK, THE • 1972 • Geertsen George • ANS • CND
MEN IN THE RAW • 1923 • Marshall George • USA
MEN IN THEIR PRIME TELL SEX STORIES see **MANNER IN DEN BESTEN JAHREN ERZAHLEN SEXGESCHICHTEN** • 1967
MEN IN WAR • 1957 • Mann Anthony • USA
MEN IN WHITE • 1934 • Boleslawski Richard • USA
MEN IN WHITE see **HOMMES EN BLANC, L'** • 1955
MEN LIKE THESE • 1931 • Summers Walter • UKN • TRAPPED IN A SUBMARINE (USA)
MEN MUST FIGHT • 1932 • Selwyn Edgar • USA • WHAT WOMEN GIVE
MEN NEVER BEND see **ANDRES DHEN LIYIZOUN POTE, I** • 1968
MEN NEVER CRY see **CHLAPI PRECE NEPLACOU** • 1980
MEN OF ACTION • 1935 • James Alan • USA
MEN OF ACTION MEET WOMEN OF DRAKULA • 1969 • Marquez Artemio • PHL
MEN OF AFRICA • 1940 • Shaw Alexander • UKN
MEN OF AMERICA • 1932 • Ince Ralph • USA • GREAT DECISION (UKN)
MEN OF ARNHEIM • 1945 • Hurst Brian Desmond, Young Terence • DOC • UKN
MEN OF BAKU see **BAKINTSY** • 1938
MEN OF BOYS TOWN • 1941 • Taurog Norman • USA
MEN OF BRAZIL • 1960 • de Carvalho Nelson Marcellino • BRZ
MEN OF CHANCE • 1932 • Archainbaud George • USA
MEN OF DARING • 1927 • Rogell Albert S. • USA
MEN OF DESTINY (UKN) see **MEN OF TEXAS** • 1942
MEN OF DIMITROVGRAD see **DIMITROVGRADTSI** • 1956
MEN OF IRELAND (USA) see **WEST OF KERRY** • 1938
MEN OF KLADNO, THE see **LIDE JAKO TY** • 1960
MEN OF PURPOSE • 1925 • *Chester R. B.* • DOC • USA
MEN OF ROCHDALE • 1944 • Bennett Compton • DOC • UKN
MEN OF SAN QUENTIN • 1942 • Beaudine William • USA
MEN OF SHERWOOD FOREST • 1954 • Guest Val • UKN
MEN OF SOULS, THE see **SOULIOTES** • 1970
MEN OF STEEL • 1926 • Archainbaud George • USA
MEN OF STEEL • 1932 • King George • UKN
MEN OF STEEL see **STEEL** • 1980
MEN OF STEEL (UKN) see **BILL CRACKS DOWN** • 1937
MEN OF TEXAS • 1942 • Enright Ray • USA • MEN OF DESTINY (UKN) ○ DEEP IN THE HEART OF TEXAS
MEN OF THE ALPS • 1939 • Cavalcanti Alberto • DOC • UKN
MEN OF THE BLUE CROSS see **BLEKITNY KRZYZ** • 1956
MEN OF THE BLUE FLAME • 1976 • BUL, USS
MEN OF THE CASPIAN see **KAPISKIE LIUDI** • 1944
MEN OF THE CITY see **I'LL WAIT FOR YOU** • 1941
MEN OF THE DAWN see **SILENT LOVER, THE** • 1926
MEN OF THE DEEP (UKN) see **ROUGH, TOUGH AND READY** • 1945
MEN OF THE DESERT • 1917 • Van Dyke W. S. • USA
MEN OF THE DRAGON • 1974 • Falk Harry • TVM • USA
MEN OF THE FIGHTING LADY • 1954 • Marton Andrew • USA
MEN OF THE FLEET • 1973 • Leiterman Richard • DOC • CND
MEN OF THE HOUR • 1935 • Hillyer Lambert • USA
MEN OF THE LIGHTSHIP • 1940 • MacDonald David • DOC • UKN
MEN OF THE MINES • 1945 • MacKane David • UKN
MEN OF THE MOMENT • 1914 • *Goff Charles* • UKN
MEN OF THE MOUNTAINS • 1915 • Jones Edgar • USA
MEN OF THE NIGHT • 1926 • Rogell Albert S. • USA
MEN OF THE NIGHT • 1934 • Hillyer Lambert • USA • STAKE OUT, THE
MEN OF THE NORTH • 1930 • Roach Hal • USA
MEN OF THE PLAINS • 1936 • Hill Robert F. • USA
MEN OF THE RICE FIELDS see **KOME** • 1957
MEN OF THE SEA see **MAN AT THE GATE, THE** • 1941
MEN OF THE SEA (USA) see **MIDSHIPMAN EASY** • 1935
MEN OF THE SEA (USA) see **HOMBRES DEL MAR** • 1938
MEN OF THE SKY • 1931 • Green Alfred E. • USA
MEN OF THE SKY • 1942 • Eason B. Reeves • SHT • USA
MEN OF THE SOIL • 1944-45 • Ladouceur Jean-Paul • ANS • CND
MEN OF THE TIMBERLAND • 1941 • Rawlins John • USA
MEN OF THE WEST • 1911 • *Champion* • USA
MEN OF TOHOKU, THE see **TOHOKU NO ZUNMUTACHI** • 1957
MEN OF TOMORROW • 1932 • Korda Zoltan, Sagan Leontine • UKN • YOUNG APOLLO
MEN OF TOMORROW • 1959 • Travers Alfred • UKN
MEN OF TWO WORLDS • 1946 • Dickinson Thorold • UKN • KISENGA MAN OF AFRICA ○ WITCH DOCTOR
MEN-OF-WAR see **ORLOGSMAN** • 1943
MEN OF YESTERDAY • 1936 • Baxter John • UKN
MEN OF ZANZIBAR, THE • 1922 • Lee Rowland V. • USA
MEN OFF-SIDE see **MUZI V OFFSIDU** • 1931
MEN ON AN ISLAND see **MEZCZYZNI NA WYSPIE** • 1962
MEN ON CALL • 1931 • Blystone John G. • USA
MEN ON HER MIND • 1944 • Fox Wallace • USA
MEN ON HER MIND (UKN) see **GIRL FROM TENTH AVENUE, THE** • 1935
MEN ON THE BRIDGE see **LYUDI NA MOSTU** • 1960
MEN ON THE MOUNTAIN see **EMBEREK A HAVASON** • 1942
MEN ON WHEELS see **PEOPLE ON WHEELS** • 1963
MEN ON WINGS see **LYOTCHIKI** • 1935
MEN ONLY MEAN TROUBLE see **NIJE LAKO S MUSKARCIMA** • 1985
MEN O'WAR • 1929 • Foster Lewis R. • SHT • USA
M'EN REVENANT PAR LES EPINETTES • 1975 • Brault Francois • CND
MEN SHE MARRIED, THE • 1916 • Vale Travers • USA
MEN TAMERS, THE • 1927 • *Herschell C. R. (Ph)* • ASL
MEN THINK ONLY ABOUT THAT see **HOMBRES PIENSAN SOLO EN ESO, LOS** • 1977
MEN WANT TO LIVE see **HOMMES VEULENT VIVRE!, LES** • 1961
MEN WERE DECEIVERS EVER • 1911 • Aylott Dave? • UKN
MEN WERE DECEIVERS EVER • 1917 • Haldane Bert • UKN
MEN WHO DARE • 1912 • *Robinson Gertrude* • USA
MEN WHO DID NOT FEAR DEATH, THE see **AZ-JANGOZASHTEGAN** • 1968
MEN WHO FORGET • 1923 • Gillmer Reuben • USA
MEN WHO HAVE MADE LOVE TO ME • 1918 • Berthelet Arthur • USA
MEN WHO TREAD ON THE TIGER'S TAIL, THE see **TORA NO OO FUMA OTOKOTACHI** • 1945
MEN WILL DECEIVE • 1914 • Fitzhamon Lewin? • UKN
MEN WITH STEEL FACES • 1940 • Eason B. Reeves, Brower Otto • USA • COULDN'T POSSIBLY HAPPEN (UKN)
MEN WITH WHIPS see **RANGLE RIVER** • 1937
MEN WITH WINGS • 1938 • Wellman William A. • USA
MEN WITH WINGS see **LEUTE MIT FLUGELN** • 1960
MEN WITHIN, THE • 1912 • *Nestor* • USA
MEN WITHOUT FEAR (UKN) see **ACTION GALORE** • 1925
MEN WITHOUT HONOUR • 1939 • Newman Widgey R. • UKN
MEN WITHOUT LAW • 1930 • King Louis • USA
MEN WITHOUT LAW • 1937 • Seiler Lewis • USA
MEN WITHOUT NAMES • 1935 • Murphy Ralph • USA
MEN WITHOUT SOULS • 1940 • Grinde Nick • USA
MEN WITHOUT WINGS see **MUZI BEZ KRIDEL** • 1946
MEN WITHOUT WOMEN • 1930 • Ford John • USA
MEN WITHOUT WORK • 1968 • Zilnik Zelimir • SHT • YGS
MEN, WOMEN AND MONEY • 1919 • Melford George • USA
MEN, WOMEN AND MONEY • 1924 • *Miller Walter* • USA
MEN, WOMEN AND MOTION • 1948 • Parker Benjamin R. • SHT • USA
MEN WOMEN LOVE • 1926 • *Macfadden True Story Pictures* • USA
MEN WOMEN LOVE (UKN) see **SALVATION NELL** • 1931
MENACE • 1934 • Brunel Adrian • UKN • WHEN LONDON SLEEPS (USA) ○ SABOTAGE
MENACE • 1934 • Murphy Ralph • USA
MENACE, LA • 1915 • Fescourt Henri • FRN
MENACE, LA • 1960 • Oury Gerard • FRN, ITL • MENACE, THE (USA)
MENACE, LA • 1977 • Corneau Alain • FRN, CND
MENACE, THE • 1913 • Dwan Allan • USA
MENACE, THE • 1916 • Ellis Robert • SHT • USA
MENACE, THE • 1918 • Robertson John S. • USA
MENACE, THE • 1928 • *Ainsworth Virginia* • ASL
MENACE, THE • 1932 • Neill R. William • USA
MENACE, THE (USA) see **MENACE, LA** • 1960
MENACE DE MORT • 1949 • Leboursier Raymond • FRN • AVENTURE A PIGALLE
MENACE FROM OUTER SPACE • 1954 • *Reed Roland (P)* • MTV • USA
MENACE IN THE NIGHT (USA) see **FACE IN THE NIGHT** • 1957
MENACE OF CARLOTTA, THE see **CARLOTTA THE BEAN STRINGER** • 1914
MENACE OF FATE, THE • 1914 • *Hollister Alice* • USA
MENACE OF THE MOUNTAIN • 1972 • McEveety Vincent • USA • MENACE ON THE MOUNTAIN
MENACE OF THE MUTE, THE • 1915 • Miller Ashley • USA
MENACE OF THE RISING SUN, THE • 1942 • *O'Brien Joseph/ Mead Thomas (P)* • SHT • USA
MENACE ON THE MOUNTAIN see **MENACE OF THE MOUNTAIN** • 1972
MENACE (UKN) see **INTRUS, LES** • 1971
MENACES • 1939 • Greville Edmond T. • FRN • CINQ JOURS D'ANGOISSE ○ GRANDE ALERTE, LA ○ ANGOISSE
MENACING PAST, THE • 1915 • *Anderson Mignon* • USA
MENACING PAST, THE • 1922 • *Cheseboro George* • USA
MENACING SHADOWS (UKN) see **FRONTIER GUNLAW** • 1946
MENAGE • 1986 • Blier Bertrand • FRN
MENAGE A QUATTRO see **COMPROMESSO EROTICO, IL** • 1977
MENAGE A TROIS • 1982 • Forbes Bryan • UKN
MENAGE A TROIS see **JUVENTUD, DIVINO TESORO** • 1977
MENAGE ALL'ITALIANA • 1965 • Indovina Franco • ITL
MENAGERE, LA see **HOUSEWIFE, THE** • 1974
MENAGERIE, THE see **STAR TREK: THE MENAGERIE** • 1967
MENAGERIE MIXUP, A • 1917 • *Hamilton Lloyd V.* • SHT • USA
MENANTI HARI ESOK • 1976 • Shamsuddin Jins • MLY • WAITING FOR TOMORROW
MENDED LUTE, THE • 1909 • Griffith D. W. • USA
MENDELISM • 1971 • Hebert Pierre • ANS • CND
MENDELSOHN'S SPRING SONG • 1910 • *Imp* • USA
MENDELSSOHN • 1926 • Fitzpatrick James A. • USA
MENDER, THE • 1915 • Bertram William • USA
MENDER OF NETS, THE • 1912 • Griffith D. W. • USA
MENDER OF WAYS, A • 1914 • *Premier* • USA
MENDERES BRIDGE, THE see **MENDERES KOPRUSU** • 1968
MENDERES KOPRUSU • 1968 • Gultekin Sirri • TRK • MENDERES BRIDGE, THE
MENDIANTE DE SAINT-SUPLICE, LA • 1923 • Burguet Charles • FRN
MENDIANTS, LES • 1986 • Jacquot Benoit • FRN
MENDIANTS ET ORGUEILLEUX • 1971 • Poitrenaud Jacques • FRN, TNS
MENE • 1973 • VNZ, FRN, ITL
MENEER KLOMP • 1978 • Jongerius Otto • NTH • MR. KLOMP
MENESGAZDA • 1978 • Kovacs Andras • HNG • CHIEF OF THE HORSE FARM, THE ○ STUD-FARM, THE
MENESTREL DE LA REINE ANNE, LE • 1913 • Feuillade Louis • FRN
MENESTYKSENMAKU • 1983 • Kurkvaara Maunu • FNL • TASTE OF SUCCESS, A
MENEUR DE JOIES, LE • 1929 • Burguet Charles • FRG
MENG • 1984 • Mai Ling-Cheh, Shen Yueh-Ming, Ch'En Chu-Chao • HKG • I DO!
MENG LUNG KUO CHIANG • 1972 • Lee Bruce • HKG • RETURN OF THE DRAGON (USA) ○ WAY OF THE DRAGON
MENG LUNG SHA • 1961 • Wang Ping • CHN
MENGZHONG REN • 1985 • Ou Dingping • HKG • DREAM LOVERS
MENILMONTANT • 1926 • Kirsanoff Dimitri • FRN
MENILMONTANT • 1936 • Guissart Rene • FRN
MENINA DA RADIO, A • 1944 • Duarte Arthur • PRT
MENINA DO LADO, A • 1988 • Salva Alberto • BRZ • GIRL NEXT DOOR, THE
MENINO DE ENGENHO • 1966 • Lima Walter Jr. • BRZ • BOY FROM THE PLANTATIONS, THE
MENINO E O VENTO, O • 1967 • Christensen Carlos Hugo • BRZ • BOY AND THE WIND, THE
MENNESKER MODES OG SOD MUSIK OPSTAR I HJERTET • 1968 • Carlsen Henning • DNM, SWD • MANNISKOR MOTS OCH LJUV MUSIC UPPSTAR I HJARTET (SWD) ○ PEOPLE MEET (UKN) ○ PEOPLE MEET AND SWEET MUSIC FILLS THE HEART (USA)
MENNYEI SEREGEK • 1984 • Kardos Ferenc • HNG • HEAVENLY HOSTS
MENOPAUSE STORY, THE • 1982 • Belec Marilyn A. • CND
MENOR, LA • 1976 • Maso Pedro • SPN
MENORES DE EDAD • 1950 • Delgado Miguel M. • MXC
MEN'S CLUB, THE • 1986 • Medak Peter • USA
MEN'S FIGHTING -KANTO ARASHI see **OTOKO NO SHOBU - KANTO ARASHI** • 1967
MEN'S OUTING see **HERRENPARTIE** • 1964
MENS PESTEN RASER • 1913 • Holger-Madsen • DNM • DURING THE PLAGUE ○ LAEGENS HUSTRU ○ UNDER PESTEN
MEN'S SUMMER, THE see **SUMMER OF MEN, THE** • 1970
MEN'S TALK • 1969 • Shatrov Igor • USS
MENSAJE, EL • 1953 • Fernan-Gomez Fernando • SPN
MENSAJE DE LA MUERTE, EL • 1952 • Gomez Urquiza Zacarias • MXC
MENSAJEROS DE PAZ • 1957 • Elorrieta Jose Maria • SPN
MENSCH AM WEGE, DER • 1923 • Dieterle William • FRG • MAN BY THE ROADSIDE, THE
MENSCH GEGEN MENSCH • 1924 • Steinhoff Hans • FRG
MENSCH MIT DEN MODERNEN NERVEN, DER • 1988 • Minck Bady, Stratil Stefan • AUS
MENSCH ODER AFFE see **DARWIN** • 1919
MENSCH OHNE NAMEN • 1932 • Ucicky Gustav • FRG • MAN WITHOUT A NAME
MENSCH UND BESTIE • 1963 • Zbonek Edwin • FRG, YGS • COVEK I ZVER
MENSCH UND MAMMON see **EISENBAHNKONIG 1, DER** • 1921
MENSCHEN • 1919 • Berger Martin • FRG
MENSCHEN see **DUDU, EIN MENSCHENSCHICKSAL** • 1924
MENSCHEN AM MEER • 1925 • Lasko Leo • FRG
MENSCHEN AM SONNTAG • 1929 • Siodmak Robert, Ulmer Edgar G. • DOC • FRG • PEOPLE ON SUNDAY
MENSCHEN, DIE DAS STAUFERJAHR VORBEREITEN, DIE • 1978 • Kluge Alexander • DOC • FRG • PEOPLE PREPARING THE STAUFER ANNIVERSARY, THE ○ MENSCHEN, DIE STAUFER-AUSSTELLUNG VORBEREITEN, DIE
MENSCHEN, DIE DURCHS LEBEN IRREN • 1918 • Wauer William • FRG

MENSCHEN, DIE STAUFER-AUSSTELLUNG VORBEREITEN, DIE see **MENSCHEN, DIE DAS STAUFERJAHR VORBEREITEN, DIE** • 1978
MENSCHEN DIE VORUBERZIEHN • 1941 • Haufler Max • SWT
MENSCHEN HINTER GETTERN • 1930 • Fejos Paul • FRG
MENSCHEN IM BUSCH • 1930 • Dalsheim Friedrich • FRG
MENSCHEN IM FEUER • 1930 • Piel Harry • FRG
MENSCHEN IM HOTEL • 1959 • Reinhardt Gottfried • FRG, FRN • GRAND HOTEL (FRN)
MENSCHEN IM KAFIG • 1930 • Dupont E. A. • FRG
MENSCHEN IM NEBEL • 1924 • Bock-Stieber Gernot • FRG
MENSCHEN IM NETZ • 1959 • Wirth Franz Peter • FRG • UNWILLING AGENT (USA) ○ PEOPLE IN THE NET
MENSCHEN IM RAUSCH • 1921 • Geisendorfer Julius • FRG
MENSCHEN IM STURM • 1934 • Fejos Paul • AUS
MENSCHEN IM STURM • 1935 • Hochbaum Werner • FRG
MENSCHEN IM STURM • 1941 • Buch Fritz Peter • FRG
MENSCHEN IM STURM see **MADEL VON DER REEPERBAHN, EIN** • 1930
MENSCHEN IM WERK • 1958 • Lamprecht Gerhard • SHT • FRG
MENSCHEN IN GOTTES HAND • 1948 • Meyer Rolf • FRG
MENSCHEN IN KETTEN • 1919 • Grune Karl • FRG
MENSCHEN NENNEN ES LIEBE, DIE see **VERLORENE TOCHTER 3** • 1919
MENSCHEN OHNE VATERLAND • 1937 • Maisch Herbert • FRG
MENSCHEN, TIERE, SENSATION • 1938 • Piel Harry • FRG
MENSCHEN UND MASKEN • 1913 • Piel Harry • FRG
MENSCHEN UND MASKEN 1 • 1923 • Piel Harry • FRG • FALSCHE EMIR, DER
MENSCHEN UND MASKEN 2 • 1923 • Piel Harry • FRG • GEFAHRLICHES SPIEL, EIN
MENSCHEN UND TIERE (GDR) see **LYUDI I ZVERI** • 1962
MENSCHEN UNTER HAIEN • 1945 • Hass Hans • FRG
MENSCHEN UNTEREINANDER • 1926 • Lamprecht Gerhard • FRG
MENSCHEN VOM VARIETE • 1939 • von Baky Josef • FRG, HNG
MENSCHEN VON HEUTE • 1920 • Basch Felix • FRG
MENSCHEN ZWEITER GUTE • 1930 • Wangel Hedwig, Meery Julius • FRG
MENSCHENFEIND, DER • 1923 • Walther-Fein Rudolf • FRG
MENSCHENFRAUEN • 1980 • Export Valie • AUS • HUMAN WOMAN ○ HUMANWOMEN
MENSCHENLEBEN IN GEFAHR • 1926 • Gerhardt Karl • FRG
MENSCHENOPFER • 1922 • Wilhelm Carl • FRG
MENSCHHEIT ANWALT 1, DER • 1920 • Rippert Otto • FRG • WUNDER DER ZEITEN, DAS
MENSEN EN STAAL • 1966 • Dupont Frans • NTH
MENSEN VAN MORGEN • 1965 • Brusse Kees • NTH • PEOPLE OF TOMORROW
MENSONGE, LE • 1911 • Carre Michel • FRN
MENSONGE, LE • 1974 • Andrien Jean-Jacques • BLG, FRN, TNS • FILS D'AMR EST MORT, LE ○ SON OF AMR IS DEAD!, THE
MENSONGE DE NINA PETROVNA, LA • 1937 • Tourjansky Victor • FRN • LIE OF NINA PETROVNA, THE (USA) ○ NINA PETROVNA
MENSONGES • 1945 • Stelli Jean • FRN • HISTOIRES DE FEMMES
MENSONGES • 1958 • Granier-Deferre Pierre • FRN
MENSONGES, LES • 1927 • Marodon Pierre • FRN
MENSONGES D'EVE, LES see **AKAZIB HAWA** • 1969
MENSONGES QUE MON PERE ME CONTAIT, LES see **LIES MY FATHER TOLD ME** • 1975
MENTAL MECHANISMS • 1947-49 • Anderson Robert, Jackson Stanley R. • DSS • CND
MENTAL POISE • 1938 • Rowland Roy • SHT • USA
MENTAL SCIENCE • 1910 • *Powers* • USA
MENTAL SUICIDE • 1913 • Dwan Allan • USA
MENTAL SYMPTOMS • 1951 • Anderson Robert • DSS • CND
MENTEURS, LES • 1961 • Greville Edmond T. • FRN • HOUSE OF SIN (UKN) ○ LIARS, THE (USA) ○ TWISTED LIVES
MENTEURS, LES • 1979 • Chabrol Claude • FRN
MENTEUSE, LA see **ADORABLE MENTEUSE** • 1961
MENTEUSES, LES see **GRANDS MOYENS, LES** • 1976
MENTIONED IN CONFIDENCE • 1917 • Jones Edgar • USA
MENTIR DE LOS DEMAS, EL • 1919 • Guidi Roberto • ARG
MENTIRA, LA • 1952 • Ortega Juan J. • MXC
MENTIRA TIENE CABELLOS ROJOS, LA • 1960 • Isasi Antonio • SPN
MENTIRAS PIADOSAS • 1988 • Ripstein Arturo • MXC • WHITE LIES (UKN)
MENTIROSA • 1961 • Cahen Enrique • SPN
MENTIROSA, LA • 1942 • Amadori Luis Cesar • ARG
MENTIROSA, LA (SPN) see **BUGIARDA, LA** • 1965
MENTIROSO, O • 1988 • Schumemann Werner • BRZ • LIAR, THE
MENU • 1933 • Grinde Nick • SHT • USA
MENUET • 1982 • Rademakers Lili • NTH, BLG
MENUET LILLIPUTIEN, LE • 1905 • Melies Georges • FRN • LILLIPUTIAN MINUET, THE (USA)
MENUETT, DAS • 1919 • Czerny Ludwig • FRG
MENUISIERS • 1896-97 • Lumiere Louis • FRN
MENYASSZONY GYONYORU, A • 1987 • Gabor Pal • HNG, ITL • SPOSA ERA BELLISSIMA, LA (ITL) ○ BRIDE WAS RADIANT, THE
MENZI AND MENZIWA • 1985 • SAF
MENZOGNA • 1952 • Del Colle Ubaldo Maria • ITL
MENZOGNA, LA • 1916 • Genina Augusto • ITL
MENZOGNA, LA • 1916 • Ghione Emilio • ITL
MEO PATACCA • 1972 • Ciorciolini Marcello • ITL
MEOTO BOSHI • 1927 • Kinugasa Teinosuke • JPN • STAR OF MARRIED COUPLES
MEOTO ZENSHU • 1927 • Tasaka Tomotaka • JPN
MEOTO ZENZAI • 1955 • Toyoda Shiro • JPN • LOVE IS SHARED LIKE SWEETS ○ MARITAL RELATIONS
MEOTO ZENZAI • 1968 • Doi Michiyoshi • JPN • LOVE BIRDS, THE
MEPHISTO • 1912 • De Manby Alfred, Thornton F. Martin • UKN
MEPHISTO • 1930 • Debain Henri, Winter Nick • FRN
MEPHISTO • 1980 • Mnouchkine Ariane • FRN
MEPHISTO • 1982 • Szabo Istvan • AUS, HNG, FRG
MEPHISTO AND THE MAIDEN • 1909 • *Selig* • USA
MEPHISTO-VALSE • 1951 • Ventura Ray • FRN
MEPHISTO WALTZ, THE • 1971 • Wendkos Paul • USA
MEPHISTO'S AFFINITY • 1908 • *Lubin* • USA
MEPHISTO'S PLIGHT • 1911 • Coleby A. E. • UKN • DIPPY'S PLIGHT (USA)
MEPHISTO'S SON • 1906 • *Pathe* • FRN • DEVIL'S SON MAKES A NIGHT OF IT IN PARIS, THE
MEPRIS, LE • 1963 • Godard Jean-Luc • FRN, ITL • DISPREZZO, IL (ITL) ○ CONTEMPT (USA)
MEPRIS N'AURA QU'UN TEMPS, LE • 1970 • Lamothe Arthur • DOC • CND • HELL NO LONGER
MEPRISE, LA see **CRUELLE MEPRISE** • 1962
MER, LA • 1968 • Bendeddouche Ghaouti • SHT • ALG
MER A BOIRE, LA (FRN) see **MARE MATTO** • 1963
MER CARAIBE • 1955 • de Hubsch • SHT • FRN
MER COULEUR DE LARMES, LA • 1980 • de Sienne Serge • FRN
MER CRUELLE, LA see **BAS YA BAHR** • 1971
MER DES CORBEAUX, LA see **MOR' VRAN** • 1930
MER EN FLAMMES, LA see **DOCUMENTS SECRETS** • 1940
MER ET LES JOURS, LA • 1959 • Vogel Raymond, Kaminker Alain • SHT • FRN • SEA AND THE DAYS, THE
MER MERE • 1975 • Grgic Zlatko • ANS • YGS • LOW OF THE SEA, THE ○ DEEP THREAT
MER OM OSS BARN I BULLERBYN • 1988 • Hallstrom Lasse • SWD • MORE ABOUT THE CHILDREN OF BULLERBY VILLLAGE
MER PAR GROS TEMPS, LA • 1895 • Lumiere Louis • FRN
MER ROUGE, LA • 1952 • Cousteau Jacques • FRN
MER SERA HAUTE A 16 HEURES, LA • 1954 • Drach Michel • SHT • FRN
MERA MUNNA • 1967 • Madhusudan • IND • MY CHILD
MERA NAAM JOKER • 1972 • Kapoor Raj • IND • MY NAME IS JOKER
MERA NAM JOHAR • 1968 • Sarankant • IND • MY NAME IS JOHAR
MERA, THE MEDIUM • 1914 • *Luna Film Industrie* • FRN
MERATI MAGNOUNA.. MAGNOUNA.. • 1968 • Halim Hilmy • EGY • MY WIFE IS MAD.. MAD.. MAD ○ IMRAATY MAJNUNA
MERATI MOUDIR AME • 1966 • Wahab Fatin Abdel • EGY • IMRA'ATI MUDIR AM ○ MA FEMME EST PDG
MERAVIGLIA DELLE ALPI, LA see **EUROPA DALL'ALTO** • 1960
MERAVIGLIA DI DAMASCO, LA see **ACCADDE A DAMASCO E FEBBRE** • 1943
MERAVIGLIE DI ALADINO, LE • 1962 • Levin Henry, Bava Mario • ITL, FRN • WONDERS OF ALADDIN, THE (USA) ○ MILLE ET UNE NUITS, LES (FRN)
MERAVIGLIOSA • 1958 • Marcellini Siro, Arevalo Carlos • ITL, SPN • DOS RIVALES, LOS (SPN)
MERAVIGLIOSE AVVENTURE DI GUERRIN MESCHINO, LE • 1952 • Francisci Pietro • ITL
MERAVIGLIOSE AVVENTURE DI MARCO POLO, LE (ITL) see **FABULEUSE AVENTURE DE MARCO POLO, LA** • 1965
MERAVIGLIOSE AVVENTURE DI ZORRO, LE • 1978 • Valenzano Luigi • ITL
MERBABIES • 1938 • Stallings George • ANS • USA
MERCADO DE ABASTO • 1954 • Demare Lucas • ARG
MERCADO NEGRO • 1953 • Land Kurt • ARG
MERCADO PROHIBIDO • 1952 • Seto Javier • SPN
MERCANTE DI SCHIAVE, IL • 1942 • Coletti Duilio • ITL • MERCHANT OF SLAVES (USA)
MERCANTE DI SCHIAVE, IL see **ANTHAR L'INVINCIBILE** • 1965
MERCANTE DI VENEZIA, IL • 1911 • Falena Ugo • ITL • MERCHANT OF VENICE, THE (USA)
MERCANTE DI VENEZIA, IL (ITL) see **MARCHAND DE VENISE, LE** • 1952
MERCANTI DI VERGINI • 1969 • Dall'Ara Renato • ITL
MERCATO DELLE FACCE, IL • 1952 • Zurlini Valerio • DCS • ITL
MERCATOR see **TROIS-MATS "MERCATOR"** • 1935
MERCENAIRE, LE • 1962 • Perier Etienne, Bandini Baccio • FRN, ITL • SPADACCINO DI SIENA, LO (ITL) ○ SWORDSMAN OF SIENA (USA) ○ MERCENARIO, IL
MERCENAIRES, LES see **DIAMOND MERCENARIES, THE** • 1975
MERCENAIRES EN QUETE D'AUTEURS • 1983 • D'Aix Alain (c/d) • MTV • CND
MERCENARI MUOIONO ALL'ALBA, I (ITL) see **CAPITAINE SINGRID** • 1967
MERCENARIES, THE • 1967 • Cardiff Jack • UKN, SAF • DARK OF THE SUN (USA)
MERCENARIES, THE • 1970 • Carter Peter • CND
MERCENARIES, THE see **SENGOKU BURAI** • 1952
MERCENARIES: SWEET VIOLENT TONY, THE see **CUBA CROSSING** • 1980
MERCENARIO, EL • 1968 • Muller Dieter • SPN, FRG, ITL • GROSSE TREIBJAGD, DIE (FRG) ○ ULTIMO MERCENARIO, L' (ITL) ○ LAST MERCENARY, THE (USA) ○ ULTIMO MERCENARIO, EL ○ BIG HUNT, THE
MERCENARIO, IL • 1968 • Corbucci Sergio • ITL, SPN, FRN • SALARIO PARA MATAR (SPN) ○ PROFESSION GUN, A (UKN) ○ MERCENARY, THE (USA)
MERCENARIO, IL see **MERCENAIRE, LE** • 1962
MERCENARIO, IL (SPN) see **DJANGO** • 1966
MERCENARIOS, LOS (SPN) see **RIVOLTA DEI MERCENARI, LA** • 1962
MERCENARY, THE see **DJANGO** • 1966
MERCENARY, THE (USA) see **MERCENARIO, IL** • 1968
MERCENARY FIGHTERS see **FREEDOM FIGHTERS** • 1987
MERCENARY MOTIVE, A • 1925 • Templeman Harcourt • UKN
MERCHANT CONVOY see **MERCHANT SEAMAN** • 1941
MERCHANT FATHER (USA) see **PADRE MERCADER** • 1939
MERCHANT MAYOR OF INDIANAPOLIS, THE • 1912 • Davis Ulysses • USA
MERCHANT OF FOUR SEASONS, THE see **HANDLER DER VIER JAHRESZEITEN, DER** • 1971
MERCHANT OF MENACE, THE • 1933 • Sweet Harry • SHT • USA
MERCHANT OF SLAVES (USA) see **MERCANTE DI SCHIAVE, IL** • 1942
MERCHANT OF THE FOUR SEASONS, THE see **HANDLER DER VIER JAHRESZEITEN, DER** • 1971
MERCHANT OF VENICE, THE • 1908 • Ranous William V.?, Blackton J. Stuart (Spv) • USA
MERCHANT OF VENICE, THE • 1912 • Marston Theodore • USA
MERCHANT OF VENICE, THE • 1914 • Smalley Phillips, Weber Lois • USA
MERCHANT OF VENICE, THE • 1916 • West Walter • UKN
MERCHANT OF VENICE, THE • 1919 • Dyer Anson • ANS • UKN
MERCHANT OF VENICE, THE • 1922 • Sanderson Challis • UKN
MERCHANT OF VENICE, THE • 1927 • Newman Widgey R. • UKN
MERCHANT OF VENICE, THE see **KAUFMANN VON VENEDIG, DER** • 1923
MERCHANT OF VENICE, THE (USA) see **MERCANTE DI VENEZIA, IL** • 1911
MERCHANT SEAMAN • 1941 • Holmes J. B. • DOC • UKN • MERCHANT CONVOY
MERCHANTS OF WAR • 1989 • Mackenzie Peter • USA
MERCI MONSIEUR GROCK see **AU REVOIR, MONSIEUR GROCK** • 1949
MERCI NATERCIA • 1960 • Kast Pierre • FRN • NATERCIA
MERCIA THE FLOWER GIRL • 1913 • Charrington Arthur • UKN
MERCIFUL, THE see **MEHRBAN** • 1967
MERCILESS CHASE see **AMANSIZ TAKIP** • 1967
MERCILESS TRAP, THE • 1964 • *Sato Makoto* • JPN
MERCREDI -PETITS SOULIERS, PETITS PAINS • 1978 • Leduc Jacques • DOC • CND
MERCY ISLAND • 1941 • Morgan William • USA
MERCY MERRICK • 1913 • Edwin Walter • USA
MERCY ON A CRUTCH • 1915 • *Thanhouser* • USA
MERCY ON YOUR PARENTS see **BIL WALIDAIN IHSANAN** • 1976
MERCY OR MURDER • 1987 • Gethers Steve • TVM • USA
MERCY PLANE • 1940 • Harlan Richard • USA • WONDER PLANE (UKN)
MERCY, THE MUMMY MUMBLED • 1918 • *Ebony* • SHT • USA
MERE, LA • 1953 • Marcus Manole, Mihu Iulian • RMN • PINCHING APPLES
MERE COUPABLE, LA • 1913 • Pouctal Henri • FRN
MERE DE LA MARIEE, LA see **UM AL-ARUSSA** • 1963
MERE DE NANA, LA • 1909 • Jasset Victorin • FRN
MERE DE TANT D'ENFANTS see **MOTHER OF MANY CHILDREN** • 1976
MERE DU MOINE, LA • 1909 • Feuillade Louis • FRN
MERE ET L'ENFANT, LA • 1959 • Demy Jacques, Masson Jean • SHT • FRN
MERE HUMDUM MERE DOST • 1968 • Kumar Amar • IND • MY DEAREST FRIEND
MERE HUZOOR • 1968 • Kumar Vinod • IND • MY LORD
MERE ROSII • 1976 • Tatos Alexandru • RMN • RED APPLES
MERE, UNE FILLE, UNE (FRN) see **ANYA ES LEANYA** • 1981
MERELY A MAID • 1920 • Roach Hal • SHT • USA
MERELY A MARRIED MAN • 1915 • Avery Charles • USA
MERELY A MILLIONAIRE • 1912 • *Bosworth Hobart* • USA
MERELY MARRYING MARY • 1919 • *Strand* • SHT • USA
MERELY MARY ANN • 1916 • Adolfi John G. • USA
MERELY MARY ANN • 1920 • Le Saint Edward J. • USA
MERELY MARY ANN • 1931 • King Henry • USA
MERELY MR. HAWKINS • 1938 • Rogers Maclean • UKN
MERELY MOTHER • 1914 • Vale Travers • USA
MERELY MRS. STUBBS • 1917 • Edwards Henry • UKN
MERELY PLAYERS • 1915 • *West Billie* • USA
MERELY PLAYERS • 1918 • Apfel Oscar • USA
MEREN JUHLAT • 1963 • Kurkvaara Maunu • FNL • FESTIVALS OF THE SEA ○ FEAST OUT AT SEA, THE ○ FEAST AT SEA ○ FEAST BY THE SEA
MERENYLET • 1958 • Varkonyi Zoltan • HNG • CRIME AT DAWN
MERES FRANCAISES • 1917 • Mercanton Louis, Hervil Rene • FRN
MERES TOU 1936 see **IMERES TOU '36** • 1972
MERETTE • 1982 • Lagrange Jean-Jacques • MTV • SWT
MERHAMET • 1967 • Seden Osman • TRK • PITY
MERI KAHANI • 1983 • Dutta Asha • IND • MY STORY
MERI SOORAT • 1963 • *Burman S. D. (M)* • IND
MERIDIAN 7-1212 see **TIME OUT FOR MURDER** • 1938
MERIDIAN 100 see **MERIDIANO 100** • 1974
MERIDIAN ZERO see **POLUDNIK ZERO** • 1970
MERIDIANO 100 • 1974 • Joscowicz Alfredo • MXC • MERIDIAN 100
MERIDIENNE, LA • 1988 • Amiguets Jean-Francois • SWT
MERIJNTJE GIJZEN'S JEUGD • 1936 • Gerron Kurt • NTH
MERKEN SIESICH DIESES GESICHT • 1985 • Meseck Gerhard • AUS • REMEMBER THAT FACE!
MERKOZES, A • 1981 • Kosa Ferenc • HNG • MATCH, THE
MERLE, LE • 1958 • McLaren Norman, Lambart Evelyn • ANS • CND • BLACKBIRD, THE
MERLE BLANC, LE • 1944 • Houssin Jacques • FRN
MERLIN AND THE KNIGHTS OF KING ARTHUR see **EXCALIBUR** • 1981
MERLIN AND THE SWORD see **ARTHUR THE KING** • 1983
MERLIN THE MAGIC MOUSE • 1967 • Lovy Alex • ANS • USA
MERLO MASCHINO, IL • 1971 • Festa Campanile Pasquale • ITL
MERLUSSE • 1935 • Pagnol Marcel • FRN
MERMAID see **DENIZ KIZI** • 1987
MERMAID, THE • 1910 • *Thanhouser* • USA
MERMAID, THE • 1912 • Fitzhamon Lewin • UKN
MERMAID, THE • 1913 • *Boyle Irene* • USA
MERMAID, THE • 1966 • Kao Li • HKG
MERMAID, THE • 1973 • *Freeway Films* • USA
MERMAID, THE see **AROUSSET EL BAHR** • 1947
MERMAID, THE (USA) see **SIRENE, LA** • 1904
MERMAID ON LAND, A see **RIKU NO NINGYO** • 1926
MERMAIDS • 1990 • Benjamin Richard • USA
MERMAIDS AND SEA ROBBERS see **NINGYO SHOTEN** • 1959
MERMAIDS AND WITCHES see **GORGONES KE MANGES** • 1968
MERMAIDS FOR LOVE see **GORGONES KE MANGES** • 1968
MERMAID'S LOVE, A • 1971 • *Che Fu* • TWN
MERMAIDS OF THE THAMES • 1914 • Storrie Kelly • UKN

MERMAIDS OF TIBERON, THE • 1962 • Lamb John • USA • AQUA SEX, THE ○ VIRGIN AQUA SEX, THE
MERMOZ • 1942 • Cuny Louis • FRN
MEROBEK ANGAN–ANGAN see **SECANGKIR KOPI PAHIT** • 1985
MERRILL MURDER MYSTERY, THE • 1913 • *Patheplay* • USA
MERRILL'S MARAUDERS • 1962 • Fuller Samuel • USA • MARAUDERS, THE
MERRILY WE GO TO HELL • 1932 • Arzner Dorothy • USA • MERRILY WE GO TO .... (UKN)
MERRILY WE GO TO .... (UKN) see **MERRILY WE GO TO HELL** • 1932
MERRILY WE LIVE • 1938 • McLeod Norman Z. • USA
MERRILY WE SING • 1946 • Moore Harold James • SHT • USA
MERRILY YOURS • 1933 • Lamont Charles • SHT • USA
MERRY ANDREW • 1958 • Kidd Michael • USA
MERRY ANDREW see **HANDY ANDY** • 1934
MERRY ANDREWS • Chaudet Louis W. • USA
MERRY BEGGARS, THE • 1910 • Fitzhamon Lewin? • UKN
MERRY BOYS OF THE COAST ARTILLERY see **KUSTENS GLADA KAVALJERER** • 1938
MERRY BOYS OF THE FLEET see **FLOTTANS MUNTERGOKAR** • 1955
MERRY BOYS OF THE NAVY see **FLOTTANS GLADA GOSSAR** • 1954
MERRY CAFE • 1936 • *Mintz Charles (P)* • ANS • USA
MERRY CAVALIER, THE • 1926 • Smith Noel • USA
MERRY CHASE • 1950 • Davis Mannie • ANS • USA
MERRY CHASE, A • 1915 • *Aubrey & Kendig* • USA
MERRY CHASE, THE • 1948 • Bianchi Giorgio • ITL
MERRY CHRISTMAS AND A HAPPY NEW YEAR, A • 1909 • *Vitagraph* • USA
MERRY CHRISTMAS, HAPPY NEW YEAR see **BUON NATALE, BUON ANNO** • 1989
MERRY CHRISTMAS INDEED! see **ACH, DU FROHLICHE..** • 1962
MERRY CHRISTMAS, MR. LAWRENCE • 1982 • Oshima Nagisa • JPN, UKN
MERRY CHRISTMAS OR KARLIK'S WINTER ADVENTURE see **VESELE VANOCE ANEB KARLIKOVO ZIMNI DOBRODRUZSTVI**
MERRY CHRISTMAS TO ALL OUR FRIENDS, A • 1911 • Kinder Stuart? • UKN
MERRY CIRCUS, THE see **VESELY CIRKUS** • 1951
MERRY COMES TO TOWN • 1937 • King George • UKN
MERRY DOG • 1933 • Lantz Walter, Nolan William • ANS • USA
MERRY DWARFS, THE • 1928 • Disney Walt • ANS • USA
MERRY FRINKS, THE • 1934 • Green Alfred E. • USA • HAPPY FAMILY, THE (UKN)
MERRY FROLICS OF SATAN, THE (USA) see **400 FARCES DU DIABLE, LES** • 1906
MERRY–GO–ROUND • 1919 • Lawrence Edmund • USA
MERRY–GO–ROUND • 1923 • Julian Rupert, von Stroheim Erich • USA
MERRY–GO–ROUND • 1948 • Binney Josh • UKN
MERRY–GO–ROUND • 1978 • Rivette Jacques • FRN
MERRY–GO–ROUND see **KARUSELLEN** • 1923
MERRY–GO–ROUND see **ONCE IN A LIFETIME** • 1932
MERRY–GO–ROUND see **MORE THE MERRIER, THE** • 1943
MERRY GO ROUND see **KORHINTA** • 1955
MERRY–GO–ROUND, A see **CHEVAUX DE BOIS, LES** • 1896
MERRY–GO–ROUND, THE • Zykmund V., Vesela A. • ANM • CZC
MERRY–GO–ROUND, THE • 1962 • Kobakhidze Mikhail • SHT • USS
MERRY–GO–ROUND, THE • 1966 • Ballantyne Tanya • SHT • CND
MERRY–GO–ROUND, THE see **ATLI KARINCA DONUYOR** • 1968
MERRY–GO–ROUND, THE see **KARUSEL** • 1971
MERRY–GO–ROUND IN FULL SWING, THE see **KARUSELLEN GAR** • 1940
MERRY GO ROUND IN THE JUNGLE • 1957 • *Upa* • ANS • USA
MERRY–GO–ROUND IN THE MOUNTAINS see **KARUSELLEN I FJALLEN** • 1955
MERRY–GO–ROUND OF 1938 • 1937 • Cummings Irving • USA
MERRY–GO–ROUND OF FATE, THE see **KARUSSEL DES TODES, DAS** • 1928
MERRY JAIL–BIRDS • 1919 • Fishback Fred C. • SHT • USA
MERRY JESTER, THE see **JESTER'S JOKE, THE** • 1912
MERRY KITTENS, THE • 1935 • Gillett Burt, Culhane James • ANS • USA
MERRY LIFE, THE see **VIDA ALEGRE, LA** • 1987
MERRY MADCAPS, THE • 1942 • Le Borg Reginald • SHT • USA
MERRY–MAKING IN ISTANBUL see **ISTANBULDA CUMB US VAR** • 1968
MERRY MANNEQUINS • 1937 • Iwerks Ub • ANS • USA
MERRY MARY • 1916 • *Drumier Jack* • SHT • USA
MERRY MARY'S MARRIAGE • 1915 • *L-Ko* • USA
MERRY MAVERICKS • 1951 • Bernds Edward • SHT • USA
MERRY MEN OF SHERWOOD, THE • 1932 • Newman Widgey R. • UKN
MERRY MERMAIDS • 1918 • Davis James • SHT • USA
MERRY MICROBES, THE see **JOYEUX MICROBES, LES** • 1909
MERRY MINSTREL MAGOO • 1959 • Larriva Rudy • ANS • USA
MERRY MIX–UP, A • 1916 • Fahrney Milton • USA
MERRY MIX–UP, A • 1957 • White Jules • SHT • USA
MERRY MODELS, THE • 1915 • *Turpin Ben* • USA
MERRY MONAHANS, THE • 1944 • Lamont Charles • USA
MERRY MONARCH, THE • 1933 • Granowsky Alexis • UKN
MERRY MOTOR–MENDERS, THE • 1916 • *Hamilton Lloyd V.* • SHT • USA
MERRY MOUSE CAFE, THE • 1941 • *Mintz Charles (P)* • ANS • USA
MERRY MOVING MEN, THE • 1915 • *Hamilton Lloyd V.* • USA
MERRY MUTINEERS • 1936 • *Mintz Charles (P)* • ANS • USA
MERRY NIGHT, A • 1914 • Aylott Dave • UKN • SOME EVENING
MERRY OLD SOUL • 1935 • Freleng Friz • ANS • USA
MERRY OLD SOUL, THE • 1933 • Lantz Walter, Nolan William • ANS • USA
MERRY QUARTET FROM THE PETROL STATION, THE see **LUSTIGEN VIER VON DER TANKSTELLE, DIE** • 1972
MERRY RASPLYUYEV DAYS see **VESYOLYYE RASPLYUYEVSKIYE DNI** • 1966
MERRY SCHOOLDAYS • 1900 • *Warwick Trading Co* • UKN
MERRY SHOEMAKER, THE see **GLADE SKOMAKAREN, DEN** • 1955
MERRY TOWN, THE see **WESOLE MIASTECZKO** • 1958
MERRY WIDOW, THE • 1913 • *Solax* • USA
MERRY WIDOW, THE • 1925 • von Stroheim Erich • USA
MERRY WIDOW, THE • 1934 • Lubitsch Ernst • USA • LADY DANCES, THE
MERRY WIDOW, THE • 1952 • Bernhardt Curtis • USA
MERRY WIDOW, THE see **VIG OZVEGY, A** • 1918
MERRY WIDOW HAT, THE • 1908 • *Vitagraph* • USA
MERRY WIDOW TAKES ANOTHER PARTNER, THE • 1910 • *Vitagraph* • USA
MERRY WIDOW WALTZ, THE • 1908 • Zecca Ferdinand • SHT • FRN
MERRY WIDOW WALTZ CRAZE, THE • 1908 • Porter Edwin S. • USA
MERRY WIDOWER • 1926 • Roach Hal • SHT • USA
MERRY WIVES, THE see **CECH PANEN KUTNOHORSKYCH** • 1938
MERRY WIVES OF GOTHAM see **LIGHTS OF OLD BROADWAY** • 1925
MERRY WIVES OF PIMPLE, THE see **PIMPLE'S MERRY WIVES** • 1916
MERRY WIVES OF RENO • 1934 • Humberstone H. Bruce • USA
MERRY WIVES OF WINDSOR, THE • 1910 • Boggs Frank? • USA
MERRY WIVES OF WINDSOR, THE see **LUSTIGEN WEIBER VON WINDSOR, DIE** • 1950
MERRY WIVES OF WINDSOR, THE see **LUSTIGEN WEIBER VON WINDSOR, DIE** • 1965
MERRY WORLD OF LEOPOLD Z., THE see **VIE HEUREUSE DE LEOPOLD Z., LA** • 1965
MERRYMAKERS • 1925 • Bacon Lloyd • SHT • USA
MERSEKELT EGOV • 1970 • Kezdi-Kovacs Zsolt • HNG • TEMPERATE ZONE
MERTON OF THE GOOFIES • 1925 • Ruggles Wesley • SHT • USA
MERTON OF THE MOVIES • 1924 • Cruze James • USA
MERTON OF THE MOVIES • 1947 • Alton Robert • USA
MERTVIYE DUSHI • 1960 • Trauberg Leonid • USS • DEAD SOULS
MERVEILLEUSE ANGELIQUE • 1964 • Borderie Bernard • FRN, ITL, FRG • ANGELIQUE –THE ROAD TO VERSAILLES (UKN)
MERVEILLEUSE JOURNEE, LA • 1928 • Barberis Rene • FRN
MERVEILLEUSE JOURNEE, LA • 1932 • Wyler Robert, Mirande Yves • FRN
MERVEILLEUSE JOURNEE, UNE • 1980 • Vital Claude • FRN
MERVEILLEUSE TRAGODIEDE LOURDES, LA • 1933 • Fabert Henri • FRN
MERVEILLEUSE VIE DE JEANNE D'ARC, LA • 1928 • de Gastyne Marco • FRN • SAINT JOAN THE MAID
MERVEILLEUSE VISITE, LA • 1973 • Carne Marcel • FRN, ITL
MERVEILLEUSE VUE DE JEAN D'ARC, LA • FRN • MARVELOUS VISION OF JOAN OF ARC, THE (USA)
MERVEILLEUX AUTOMNE, UN see **BELLISSIMO NOVEMBRE, UN** • 1968
MERVEILLEUX EVENTAIL VIVANT, LE • 1904 • Melies Georges • SHT • FRN • WONDERFUL LIVING FAN, THE (USA) ○ EVENTAIL MAGIQUE, L'
MERVEILLEUX PARFUM D'OSEILLE, UN • 1969 • Bassi Rinaldo • FRN
MERY FOR EVER see **MERY PER SEMPRE** • 1988
MERY PER SEMPRE • 1988 • Risi Marco • ITL • MERY FOR EVER
MES, HET • 1960 • Rademakers Fons • NTH • KNIFE, THE
MES ENFANTS see **AWLADI** • 1951
MES ESPERENCES EN 1908 • 1908 • Ouimet Leo • CND
MES–ESTIMATIONS • 1929 • Greville Edmond T. • SHT • FRN
MES EVASIONS • 1962 • Rebillard Georges • FRN
MES FEMMES AMERICAINES • 1966 • Polidoro Gian Luigi • FRN, ITL • MOGLIE AMERICANA, UNA (ITL) ○ RUN FOR YOUR WIFE (USA)
MES MEILLEURS COPAINS • 1989 • Poire Jean Marie • FRN
MES NUITS AVEC.. ALICE, PENELOPE, ARNOLD, MAUD ET RICHARD • 1976 • Mulot Claude • FRN • GRANDE BAISE, LA ○ WHAT A PERFORMER
MES NUITS SONT PLUS BELLES QUE VOS JOURS • 1988 • Zulawski Andrzej • FRN
MES PETITES AMOUREUSES • 1975 • Eustache Jean • FRN • MY LITTLE LOVES
MES TANTES ET MOI • 1936 • Noe Yvan • FRN
MESA OF LOST WOMEN • 1953 • Ormond Ron, Trevos Herbert • USA • LOST WOMEN (UKN) ○ LOST WOMEN OF ZARPA
MESAVENTURE DE SHYLOCK, UNE see **MIROIR DE VENISE, UNE MESAVENTURE DE SHYLOCK, LE** • 1905
MESAVENTURE VAN EEN FRANSCH HEERTJE ZONDER PANTALON OP HET STRAND TE ZANDVOORT • 1905 • Mullens Willy • NTH • ADVENTURE OF A FRENCH GENTLEMAN WITHOUT TROUSERS ○ ADVENTURES OF A FRENCH GENTLEMAN WITHOUT HIS TROUSERS
MESAVENTURES DE JOBARD, LES • 1911 • Cohl Emile • ANS • FRN
MESAVENTURES DE M. BOIT–SANS–SAIF, LES • 1904 • Melies Georges • FRN • MISCHANCES OF A DRUNKARD, THE
MESAVENTURES D'UN AERONAUTE • 1901 • Melies Georges • FRN • BALLOONIST'S MISHAP, THE (USA)
MESAVENTURES D'UN CHARBONNIER • 1899-00 • Blache Alice • FRN
MESAVENTURES D'UN EXPLORATEUR see **INFORTUNES D'UN EXPLORATEUR, LES** • 1900
MESAVENTURES D'UNE TETE DE VEAU • 1898 • Zecca Ferdinand • FRN • MISADVENTURES OF A CALF'S HEAD, THE
MESAVENTURES D'UNE TETE DE VEAU, LES • 1899 • Blache Alice • FRN
MESDAMES ET MESSIEURS see **SIGNORE E SIGNORI** • 1966
MESDAMES ET MONSIEURS, LA FETE! • 1976 • Beaudry Michel, Danis Aime • DOC • CND
MESDAMES, MESSIEURS • 1960 • McLaren Norman • ANS • CND • DISCOURSE DE BIENVENUE DE NORMAN MCLAREN ○ OPENING SPEECH (USA) ○ NORMAN MCLAREN'S OPENING SPEECH
MESDEMOISELLE, LES see **OJOSAN** • 1961
MESE • 1963 • Karpati Gyorgy • HNG • FAIRY TALE
MESE A TIZENKET TALALATROL • 1956 • Makk Karoly • HNG • TALE ON THE TWELVE POINTS ○ TALE OF 12 POINTS
MESE DI ONESTA, UN • 1950 • Gambino Domenico M. • ITL
MESE MARIANO • 1928 • Roberti Roberto Leone • ITL
MESEAUTO • 1936 • Gaal Bela • HNG
MESEK AZ IROGEPROL • 1916 • Korda Alexander • HNG • TYPEWRITER'S TALE, A ○ TYPEWRITER TALES ○ TALES OF THE TYPEWRITER
MESERA DEL CAFE DEL PUERTO, LA • 1954 • Orol Juan • MXC
MESES Y LOS DIAS, LOS • 1971 • Bojorquez Alberto • MXC • MONTHS AND DAYS
MESHES OF FATE • 1915 • *Federal* • USA
MESHES OF THE AFTERNOON • 1943 • Deren Maya, Hammid Alexander • SHT • USA
MESHI • 1951 • Naruse Mikio • JPN • MARRIED LIFE, A ○ REPAST ○ RICE, THE
MESHTE NASTRESHU • 1963 • Karyukov Mikhail • USS • DREAM COME TRUE, A
MESHWAR OMAR • 1986 • Khan Mohamed • EGY • OMAR'S JOURNEY
MESIC NAD REKOU • 1953 • Krska Vaclav • CZC • MOON OVER THE RIVER
MESKAL LE CONTREBANDIER • 1909 • Jasset Victorin • FRN
MESMERIAN EXPERIMENT, A (USA) see **BAQUET DE MESMER, LE** • 1905
MESMERISED see **MESMERIZED** • 1984
MESMERIST, THE • 1898 • Smith G. A. • UKN
MESMERIST, THE • 1908 • *Pathe* • FRN
MESMERIST, THE • 1915 • Nash Percy? • UKN
MESMERIST AND COUNTRY PEOPLE • 1899 • *Edison* • USA
MESMERIZED • 1984 • Laughlin Michael • NZL, ASL, UKN • MESMERISED
MESMERIZED MAIDENS • 1970 • *Able Film Co* • USA
MESMERIZING MOE • 1911 • *Yankee* • USA
MESONERA DEL TORMES, LA • 1919 • Buchs Jose, Roesset Julio • SPN
MESQUITE BUCKAROO • 1940 • Webb Harry S. • USA
MESQUITE'S GRATITUDE, THE • 1911 • *Kalem* • USA
MESRINE • 1983 • Genoves Andre • FRN
MESS PRODUCTION • 1945 • Kneitel Seymour • ANS • USA
MESSA DE REQUIEM • 1969 • Clouzot Henri-Georges • FRN
MESSA E' FINITA, LA • 1985 • Moretti Nanni • ITL • MASS IS OVER, THE
MESSAGE see **UZENET** • 1967
MESSAGE, THE • 1909 • Griffith D. W. • USA
MESSAGE, THE • 1915 • *Reliance* • USA
MESSAGE, THE • 1918 • Edwards Henry • UKN
MESSAGE, THE • 1930 • Collins Sewell • UKN
MESSAGE, THE • 1956 • Pratt Enrico • UKN
MESSAGE, THE • 1966 • Desjardins Arnaud • DOC • FRN
MESSAGE, THE see **SANDESAYA** • 1960
MESSAGE, THE (UKN) see **RISALAH, AL–** • 1976
MESSAGE D'AMOUR see **RISALAT GAHRAM** • 1953
MESSAGE FOR HELP, A • 1915 • *Bison* • USA
MESSAGE FROM ACROSS THE SEA, A • 1914 • *Lockwood Harold* • USA
MESSAGE FROM BEYOND, A • 1911 • *Morrison James* • USA
MESSAGE FROM BEYOND, A • 1912 • *Blache Alice (P)* • USA
MESSAGE FROM CANTERBURY • 1944 • Hoellering George • UKN
MESSAGE FROM GENEVA • 1936 • Cavalcanti Alberto • DOC • UKN
MESSAGE FROM HOME, A • 1913 • *Selig* • USA
MESSAGE FROM MARS, A • 1903 • Barrett Franklyn • NZL
MESSAGE FROM MARS, A • 1913 • Waller Wallett • UKN
MESSAGE FROM MARS, A • 1921 • Karger Maxwell • USA
MESSAGE FROM NIAGARA, A • 1912 • *Thanhouser* • USA
MESSAGE FROM SPACE, THE see **UCHU KARANO MESSAGE** • 1977
MESSAGE FROM THE EAST, A • 1910 • *Electrograff* • USA
MESSAGE FROM THE HILLS, A • 1916 • *Buffalo* • SHT • USA
MESSAGE FROM THE MOON, A • 1912 • Sennett Mack, Henderson Dell • USA
MESSAGE FROM THE SEA, A • 1905 • Haggar William • UKN
MESSAGE FROM THE SKY, A see **0 – 18** • 1915
MESSAGE FROM THE WEST, A • 1911 • *Nestor* • USA
MESSAGE IN THE BOTTLE, A • 1911 • Ince Thomas H. • USA
MESSAGE IN THE COCOANUT, THE • 1913 • *Majestic* • USA
MESSAGE IN THE ROSE, THE • 1914 • Merwin Bannister • USA
MESSAGE OF AN ARROW, THE • 1909 • *Bison* • USA
MESSAGE OF EMILE COUE, THE • 1923 • McCutcheon John L. • USA
MESSAGE OF HOPE, THE • 1923 • *Murphy Genevieve M.* • USA
MESSAGE OF THE ARROW, THE • 1911 • Golden Joseph A. • USA
MESSAGE OF THE FLOWERS, THE • 1913 • *Billington Francelia* • USA
MESSAGE OF THE LILIES • 1918 • Edwards J. Gordon • USA
MESSAGE OF THE MIND • 1914 • *Balboa* • USA
MESSAGE OF THE MOUSE, THE • 1917 • Blackton J. Stuart • USA
MESSAGE OF THE PALMS, THE • 1913 • *Kalem* • USA
MESSAGE OF THE ROSE, THE • 1913 • Melville Wilbert • USA
MESSAGE OF THE SEA, A • 1910 • *Bison* • USA
MESSAGE OF THE SEA, THE • 1913 • *Gaumont* • USA
MESSAGE OF THE SPEAR see **MOORA NEYA** • 1911
MESSAGE OF THE SUN DIAL, THE • 1914 • Ridgely Richard • USA
MESSAGE OF THE VIOLIN, THE • 1910 • Griffith D. W. • USA

MESSAGE THROUGH FLAMES, A • 1915 • *Anderson Mignon* • USA
MESSAGE TO GARCIA, A • 1916 • Ridgely Richard • USA
MESSAGE TO GARCIA, A • 1936 • Marshall George • USA
MESSAGE TO GRACIAS, A • 1964 • McKimson Robert • ANS • USA
MESSAGE TO HEADQUARTERS, THE • 1913 • *Cruze James* • USA
MESSAGE TO HEAVEN, THE • 1913 • *Solax* • USA
MESSAGE TO KELLY, A • 1947 • Southwell Harry • ASL
MESSAGE TO MY DAUGHTER, A • 1973 • Lewis Robert Michael • TVM • USA
MESSAGE TO NAPOLEON, A see **BUDSKAB TIL NAPOLEON PAA ELBA, ET** • 1909
MESSAGE TO SANDRA see **SKILABOD TIL SONDRU** • 1983
MESSAGE TO THE FUTURE • 1970 • Nepp Jozsef • SRL • HNG
MESSAGE TO THE TWENTY-FIRST CENTURY, A • 1970 • Brittain Don • CND
MESSAGER, LE • 1937 • Rouleau Raymond • FRN
MESSAGER DE LA LUMIERE, LE • 1938 • Grimault Paul • ANS • FRN
MESSAGER DE LA PRESSE • 1959 • Masson Jean • SHT • FRN
MESSAGES • 1961 • Zaninovic Stejpan • DOC • YGS
MESSAGES, MESSAGES • Arnold Steven • USA
MESSALINA • 1910 • Caserini Mario • ITL
MESSALINA • 1910 • Guazzoni Enrico • ITL
MESSALINA • 1910 • Zecca Ferdinand • FRN
MESSALINA • 1923 • Guazzoni Enrico • ITL
MESSALINA • 1951 • Gallone Carmine • ITL • AFFAIRS OF MESSALINA, THE (USA)
MESSALINA see **MESSALINA VENERE IMPERATRICE** • 1960
MESSALINA AGAINST THE SON OF HERCULES (USA) see **ULTIMO GLADIATORE, L'** • 1965
MESSALINA, MESSALINA • 1977 • Corbucci Bruno • ITL
MESSALINA VENERE IMPERATRICE • 1960 • Cottafavi Vittorio • ITL • MESSALINA
MESSALINE • 1910 • Andreani Henri • FRN
MESSE DE MINUIT, LA • 1906 • Blache Alice • FRN
MESSE DOREE, LA • 1975 • Montresor Beni • FRN, ITL • NELLA PROFONDA LUCE DEI SENSI (ITL)
MESSE EN SI MINEUR, LA • 1990 • Guillermin Jean-Louis • FRN
MESSE NERE DELLA CONTESSA DRACULA, LE see **NACHT DER VAMPIRE** • 1970
MESSE SUR LE MONDE DE TEILHARD DE CHARDIN, LA • 1963 • Delouche Dominique • SHT • FRN
MESSED UP MOVIE MAKERS • 1966 • Bakes George, Chiarito Al • ANS • USA
MESSENGER, THE • 1918 • Gillstrom Arvid E. • SHT • USA
MESSENGER, THE • 1921 • Aubrey Jimmy • USA
MESSENGER, THE • 1987 • Williamson Fred • USA • MESSENGER OF DEATH
MESSENGER AT DAWN see **POSEL USVITU** • 1949
MESSENGER BOY, THE • 1931 • Luddy Edward I. • SHT • USA
MESSENGER BOY MAGICIAN, THE • 1910 • *Lubin* • USA
MESSENGER BOY'S MISTAKE, THE • 1903 • Porter Edwin S. • USA
MESSENGER BOY'S SWEETHEART, THE • 1910 • *Capitol* • USA
MESSENGER FROM THE MOON see **TSUKIYORI NO SHISHA** • 1954
MESSENGER NO.845 • 1914 • *Reliance* • USA
MESSENGER OF DAWN see **POSEL USVITU** • 1949
MESSENGER OF DEATH • 1914 • *Mather Charles* • USA
MESSENGER OF DEATH • 1988 • Thompson J. Lee • USA • AVENGING ANGELS
MESSENGER OF DEATH see **MESSENGER, THE** • 1987
MESSENGER OF GLADNESS, A • 1914 • *Badgely Helen* • USA
MESSENGER OF PEACE • 1950 • Strayer Frank • USA
MESSENGER OF THE BLESSED VIRGIN • 1930 • *Mission Film Society* • USA
MESSENGER TO KEARNEY, A • 1912 • Huntley Fred W. • USA
MESSENGER TO SATSUMA see **SATSUMA HIKYAKU-TOKAI HEN** • 1932
MESSER IM KOPF • 1978 • Hauff Reinhard • FRG • KNIFE IN THE HEAD
MESSIA, IL • 1975 • Rossellini Roberto • ITL, USA • MESSIAH (USA)
MESSIAH OF EVIL • 1975 • Huyck Willard, Katz Gloria • USA • REVENGE OF THE SCREAMING DEAD ○ RETURN OF THE LIVING DEAD ○ DEAD PEOPLE ○ SECOND COMING, THE
MESSIAH (USA) see **MESSIA, IL** • 1975
MESSIDOR • 1979 • Tanner Alain • SWT, FRN • CONTRE COEUR
MESSIEURS LES RONDS DE CUIR • 1936 • Mirande Yves • FRN
MESSIEURS LES RONDS-DE-CUIR • 1959 • Diamant-Berger Henri • FRN
MESSIEURS LUDOVIC • 1945 • Le Chanois Jean Paul • FRN • LUDO
MESSING AROUND • 1988 • Nivelli Mickey • USA
MESSIRE TWARDOWSKI • 1920 • Bieganski Victor • PLN
MESSRS. SCHWARZWALD AND EDGAR'S LAST TRICK see **POSLEDNI TRIK PANA SCHWARZWALLDEA A PANA EDGARA** • 1964
MEST' KINEMATOGRAFICESKOGO OPERATORA • 1912 • Starevitch Ladislas • USS • REVENGE OF THE KINEMATOGRAPH CAMERAMAN ○ CAMERAMAN'S REVENGE, THE
MESTA TUT TIKHIYE • 1967 • Shchukin Georgi • USS • IT'S CALM HERE ○ PEACE AND QUIET
MESTECKO NA DLANI • 1942 • Binovec Vaclav • CZC • VILLAGE IN YOUR PALM, THE ○ OUR LITTLE TOWN
MESTERDETEKTIVERNE • 1918 • Lauritzen Lau • DNM
MESTIZA, LA • 1955 • Ochoa Jose • SPN
MESTIZO • 1965 • Buchs Julio • SPN
MESTO ME NADEJE • 1978 • *Schorm Evald* • CZC • TOWN OF MY HOPE, THE
MESTO V NOCI • 1960 • Sefranka Bruno • CZC • CITY AT NIGHT
MESTO ZIVE VODY • 1934 • Hammid Alexander • DCS • CZC • CITY OF LIVE WATER
MESTOMA SVOU TVAR • 1958 • Kachyna Karel • CZC • CITY HAS YOUR FACE, THE
MESU GA OSU KUIKOROSO: KAMAKIRI • 1967 • Inoue Umeji • JPN • TENDER LUST
MESU GA OSU O KUIKOROSU: SANBIKI NO KAMAKIRI • 1967 • Inoue Umeji • JPN • STRONGER SEX, THE
MESU INU • 1951 • Kimura Keigo • JPN • ENCHANTRESS
MESU OOKAMI • 1967 • Tatsugami Noboru • JPN • FEMALE WOLF
MESU-OSU NO HONNO • 1967 • Ogawa Kinya • JPN • INSTINCT OF MALE AND FEMALE
MESURE POUR RIEN, UNE see **WINTER WEEKEND** • 1952
MESZAROS LASZLO EMLEKERE • 1968 • Meszaros Marta • DCS • HNG • IN MEMORIAM LASZLO MESZAROS
MET LIEFDE VAN ADELE • 1974 • SAF
MET MAN EN MACHT • 1966 • Moonen Jan • NTH
MET SCHERM EN SCHILD • 1966 • Moonen Jan • NTH
META • 1947 • Howard Robert • SHT • USA
METADATA • 1971 • Foldes Peter • ANS • CND
METAFISICA DO CHOCOLATE, A • 1966 • Costa Jose Fonseca • SHT • PRT
METAL FORCE see **NIGHTSTICK** • 1987
METAL HURLANT see **HEAVY METAL** • 1981
METAL MESSIAH • 1977 • Takacs Tibor • CND
METAL WORKERS - ARTISANS DES METAUX • 1976 • Fortier Bob • DOC • CND
METALFORCE see **NIGHTSTICK** • 1987
METALL • 1931-33 • Richter Hans • USS
METALL DES HIMMELS • 1934 • Ruttmann Walter • FRG • HEAVENLY METAL
METALLO BLUES • 1985 • Macina Michael • CND
METALSTORM see **METALSTORM: THE DESTRUCTION OF JARED-SYN** • 1983
METALSTORM: THE DESTRUCTION OF JARED-SYN • 1983 • Band Charles • USA • METALSTORM
METAMOFOSIS DEL JEFE DE LA POLICIA POLITICA see **TRANSFORMACION DE UN AGENTE DE POLICIA** • 1973
METAMORFEUS • 1969 • Brdecka Jiri • ANS • CZC • METAMORPHOSIS
METAMORFOSIS • 1971 • Esteva Jacinto • SPN
METAMORFOZA • 1964 • Marks Aleksandar, Jutrisa Vladimir • ANS • YGS • METAMORPHOSIS (USA)
METAMORPHOSE • 1945 • van der Horst Herman • SHT • NTH • METAMORPHOSIS
METAMORPHOSE • 1975 • Leclerq Christian, Sossah Francis • DOC • FRN
METAMORPHOSE DES CLOPORTES • 1965 • Granier-Deferre Pierre • FRN, ITL • SOTTO IL TALLONE (ITL) ○ CLOPORTES (USA)
METAMORPHOSE DU VIOLINCELLE, LA • 1961 • Delouche Dominique • SHT • FRN
METAMORPHOSES • 1912 • *C.g.p.c.* • FRN
METAMORPHOSES • 1968 • Coderre Laurent • ANS • CND
METAMORPHOSES • 1978 • Takashi • ANM • JPN, USA • WINDS OF CHANGE
METAMORPHOSES COMIQUES, LES • 1912 • Cohl Emile • ANS • FRN
METAMORPHOSES DU PAPILLON, LES • 1906 • Velle Gaston • FRN • METAMORPHOSIS OF THE BUTTERFLY, THE
METAMORPHOSES DU PAYSAGE INDUSTRIEL, LES • 1964-69 • Rohmer Eric • MTV • FRN
METAMORPHOSES DU ROI DE PIQUE, LES • 1903 • Velle Gaston • FRN • METAMORPHOSIS OF THE KING OF SPADES, THE
METAMORPHOSIS • Calinescu Bob • ANM • RMN
METAMORPHOSIS • 1914 • *Ayres Sydney* • USA
METAMORPHOSIS • 1951 • Hampton William J. • USA
METAMORPHOSIS • 1953 • Mazzetti Lorenza • SHT • UKN
METAMORPHOSIS • 1962 • Hurtado Angel • VNZ
METAMORPHOSIS • 1968 • Mesaros Titus • DOC • RMN
METAMORPHOSIS • 1971 • *Film Images* • ANS • USA
METAMORPHOSIS • 1975 • Greenwald Barry • SHT • CND
METAMORPHOSIS • 1975 • Nemec Jan • SHT • FRG
METAMORPHOSIS see **FANTASMAGORIE** • 1908
METAMORPHOSIS see **METAMORPHOSE** • 1945
METAMORPHOSIS see **METAMORFEUS** • 1969
METAMORPHOSIS see **EVIL SPAWN** • 1987
METAMORPHOSIS OF MR. SAMSA • 1977 • Leaf Caroline • ANS • CND
METAMORPHOSIS OF THE BUTTERFLY, THE see **METAMORPHOSES DU PAPILLON, LES** • 1906
METAMORPHOSIS OF THE CHIEF OF THE POLITICAL POLICE see **TRANSFORMACION DE UN AGENTE DE POLICIA** • 1973
METAMORPHOSIS OF THE KING OF SPADES, THE see **METAMORPHOSES DU ROI DE PIQUE, LES** • 1903
METAMORPHOSIS U.S.A. OR THE SOUL OF WHITE FOLK: A RACIAL FANTASY • Kelly Dexter • SHT • USA
METAMORPHOSIS (USA) see **METAMORFOZA** • 1964
METAMORPHOSIS (USA) see **FORVANDLINGEN** • 1975
METANASTES, I • 1976 • Antonopoulos Giorgos • GRC • IMMIGRANTS, THE
METANOIA • Bolotowsky Ilya • SHT • USA
METANOMEN • 1966 • Bartlett Scott • SHT • USA
METAYER, LE • 1975 • Louhichi Taieb • SHT • TNS
METELLO • 1970 • Bolognini Mauro • ITL
METEMPSICOSI • 1913 • *Hesperia* • ITL
METEMPSYCHOSE • 1908 • Zecca Ferdinand • FRN
METEMPSYCHOSIS II • Betts Larry • SHT • USA
METEMPSYCO • 1963 • Boccacci Antonio • ITL, FRG • TOMB OF TORTURE (USA) ○ METEMPSYCOSE
METEMPSYCOSE see **METEMPSYCO** • 1963
METEO • 1989 • Monory Andras M. • HNG
METEOR • 1979 • Neame Ronald • USA
METEOR see **DHOOMA KETHU** • 1968
METEOR, THE • 1902 • *Biograph* • USA
METEOR AND SHADOW • 1985 • Spetsiotis Takis • GRC
METEOR MONSTER • 1958 • Marquette Jacques • USA • TEENAGE MONSTER
METEORANGO KID -HEROI INTERGALATICO • 1969 • Oliveira Andre Luiz • BRZ • METEORANGO KID -INTERGALACTIC HERO
METEORANGO KID -INTERGALACTIC HERO see **METEORANGO KID -HEROI INTERGALATICO** • 1969
METER IN THE KITCHEN • 1916 • Ellis Robert • SHT • USA
METHISTAKAS TOU LIMANIOU, O • 1967 • Kiriakopoulos Hristos • GRC • DRUNK OF THE PORT, THE
METHOD, THE • 1987 • Destein Joseph • USA
METHOD AND MADNESS • 1950 • Marshall Herbert • UKN • MR. PASTRY DOES THE LAUNDRY
METHOD AND MAW, THE • 1962 • Kneitel Seymour • ANS • USA
METHOD IN HIS ILLNESS • 1913 • *Komic* • USA
METHODE DU PROFESSEUR NEURA, LA • 1912 • Fescourt Henri • FRN
METHODS see **MODSZEREK** • 1968
METHODS OF MARGARET, THE • 1914 • North Wilfred • USA
METHYSTAKOS, O • 1950 • Tzavellas Georges • GRC • DRUNKARD, THE ○ IVROGNE, L'
METIER DE DANSEUR • 1953 • Baratier Jacques • FRN
METIER DE FOUS • 1948 • Hunebelle Andre • FRN
METIER DES AUTRES, LE • 1960 • Enrico Robert • FRN
METIERS D'ART • 1935 • Storck Henri • DOC • BLG
METLA • 1972 • Grgic Zlatko • ANS • YGS • BROOM, THE
METRALLETA STEIN • 1974 • de la Loma Jose Antonio • SPN
METRIPOLITANO DE LISBOA • 1961 • Duarte Arthur • SHT • PRT
METRO • 1950 • Leenhardt Roger • DCS • FRN
METRO, LE • 1934 • Franju Georges, Langlois Henri • DCS • FRN
METRO AT NIGHT, THE see **MOSKVA STROYIT METRO** • 1934
METRO E LUNGO, UN • 1961 • Olmi Ermanno • DCS • ITL • METRO LUNGO CINQUE, UN
METRO LUNGO CINQUE, UN see **METRO E LUNGO, UN** • 1961
METRO PEOPLE see **GENTE DEL METRO** • 1976
METROCOM • 1967 • Santiago Pablo • PHL
METROGRAPHIC • 1960 • Speich Vittorio • SHT • USA
METROPOLE • 1947 • Palardy Jean • DCS • CND
METROPOLE see **TRAIN DES SUICIDES, LE** • 1931
METROPOLES see **MITROPOLIS** • 1975
METROPOLIS • 1926 • Lang Fritz • FRG
METROPOLIS • 1984 • Moroder Giorgio, Lang Fritz • FRG
METROPOLIS see **GIGANTE DI METROPOLIS, IL** • 1961
METROPOLIS see **MITROPOLIS** • 1975
METROPOLIS II • 1969 • Hasse Paul • SHT • USA
METROPOLIS ORGANISM, THE • 1971 • Vitale Frank • CND
METROPOLITAIN see **ILLUMINATIONS, LES** • 1958
METROPOLITAN • 1935 • Boleslawski Richard • USA
METROPOLITAN • 1938 • Cam Maurice • FRN
METROPOLITAN • 1990 • Stillman Whit • USA
METROPOLITAN NOCTURNE • 1935 • Jason Leigh • SHT • USA
METROPOLITAN SYMPHONY (USA) see **TOKAI KOKYOGAKU** • 1929
METROSCOPIX • 1953 • *Mgm* • SHT • USA
METROSHIMA • 1947 • Drahos Tom • FRN
METSHTA see **MECHTA** • 1943
METTE FALK -SAKEN • 1981 • Risan Leidulv • NRW
METTI CHE TI ROMPO IL MUSO • 1973 • Vari Giuseppe • ITL
METTI LO DIAVOLO TUO NE LO MIO INFERNO • 1972 • Albertini Bitto • ITL • PUT YOUR DEVIL INTO MY HELL (UKN)
METTI, UNA SERA A CENA • 1969 • Patroni Griffi Giuseppe • ITL • ONE NIGHT AT DINNER (USA) ○ LOVE CIRCLE, THE (UKN) ○ LET'S SAY ONE NIGHT FOR DINNER ○ IMAGINE ONE EVENING FOR DINNER
METTLE OF A MAN, THE • 1914 • *Benham Harry* • USA
METTLE OF JERRY MCGUIRE, THE • 1915 • McGowan J. P. • USA
METTRE AU MONDE • 1974 • Dansereau Fernand, Rossignol Yolande • SHT • CND
MEU AMOR • 1980 • Couto Luis • PRT • MY LOVE
MEU NOM E.. TONHO • 1970 • Candeias Ozvaldo R. • BRZ
MEU NOME E LAMPIAO • 1970 • Silveira Mozael • BRZ
MEU PE DE LARANJA LIMA, O • 1970 • Teixeira Aurelio • BRZ
MEULE, LA • 1962 • Allio Rene • FRN • HAYSTACK, THE
MEUNIER TU DORS • 1944 • MacKay Jim • ANS • CND
MEUNIERE DEBAUCHEE, LA • 1935 • D'Arrast Harry D'Abbadie • FRN • TRICORNE, LE
MEURTRE • 1964 • Kamler Piotr • SHT • FRN • MURDER
MEURTRE A ETE COMMIS, UN • 1937 • Orval Claude • FRN
MEURTRE A IBIZA • Monnet Marc • FRN
MEURTRE EN 45 TOURS • 1960 • Perier Etienne • FRN • MURDER AT 45 RPM
MEURTRE EST UN MEURTRE, UN • 1972 • Perier Etienne • FRN, ITL • SEDIA A ROTELLE, LA (ITL) ○ MURDER IS A MURDER, A (UKN) ○ MURDER IS A MURDER.. IS A MURDER, A
MEURTRES • 1950 • Pottier Richard • FRN • THREE SINNERS (USA)
MEURTRES A DOMICILE • 1981 • Lobet Marc • BLG, FRN
MEURTRES A ROME • 1976 • Lorente German • FRN
MEURTRES AU SOLEIL (FRN) see **VERANO PARA MATAR, UN** • 1973
MEURTRIER, LE • 1962 • Autant-Lara Claude • FRN, ITL, FRG • OMICIDA, L' (ITL) ○ MORDER, DER (FRG) ○ ENOUGH ROPE (USA) ○ MURDERER, THE
MEURTRIERE, LA see **DEMUTIGE UND DIE SANGERIN, DER** • 1925
MEURTRIERS, LES see **QATALA, AL-** • 1971
MEUS AMIGOS • 1973 • Teles Antonio Da Cunha • PRT
MEUS OITO ANOS • 1945-56 • Mauro-Humberto • SHT • BRZ
MEVAZAR PORTRAIT see **TRIPTYCH** • 1978
MEWS EN MEIJN • 1965 • Fischer Max • NTH
MEXICALI KID, THE • 1938 • Fox Wallace • USA
MEXICALI ROSE • 1929 • Kenton Erle C. • USA • GIRL FROM MEXICO, THE (UKN)
MEXICALI ROSE • 1939 • Sherman George • USA
MEXICALI SHMOES • 1959 • Freleng Friz • ANS • USA
MEXICAN, THE • 1911 • *Lubin* • USA
MEXICAN, THE • 1911 • Dwan Allan • *American* • USA
MEXICAN, THE • 1914 • Mix Tom • USA
MEXICAN, THE • Schefer Mandy • USA
MEXICAN, THE (UKN) see **HURRICANE HORSEMAN** • 1931
MEXICAN, THE (USA) see **MEKSIKANETS** • 1957
MEXICAN AFFAIR, A see **FLOR DE MAYO** • 1957

MEXICAN AS IT IS SPOKEN • 1911 • Melies Gaston • USA
MEXICAN BASEBALL • 1947 • Davis Mannie • ANS • USA
MEXICAN BILL • 1909 • *Lubin* • USA
MEXICAN BOARDERS • 1962 • Freleng Friz • ANS • USA
MEXICAN BUS RIDE (USA) see **SUBIDA AL CIELO** • 1951
MEXICAN CAT DANCE • 1963 • Freleng Friz • ANS • USA
MEXICAN CONSPIRACY OUTGENERALED • 1913 • *Russell Martha* • USA
MEXICAN COURTSHIP, A • 1912 • Melville Wilbert • USA
MEXICAN DIPLOMATS, THE • 1932 • Martirosyan Amasi, Kalantar L. • USS
MEXICAN ELOPEMENT, A • 1912 • *Pathe* • USA
MEXICAN FILIBUSTERERS • 1911 • *Kalem* • USA
MEXICAN FREE-FOR-ALL see **CRAZY MEXICAN DAISAKUSEN** • 1968
MEXICAN GAMBLER, THE • 1913 • *Patheplay* • USA
MEXICAN HAYRIDE • 1948 • Barton Charles T. • USA
MEXICAN INSURRECTOS, THE • 1916 • *Sunset* • SHT • USA
MEXICAN JOAN OF ARC, THE • 1911 • *Kalem* • USA
MEXICAN JOYRIDE • 1947 • Davis Arthur • ANS • USA
MEXICAN LOTHARIO, A • 1910 • *Bison* • USA
MEXICAN LOVE AFFAIR, A • 1910 • *Bison* • USA
MEXICAN MANHUNT • 1953 • Bailey Rex • USA
MEXICAN MIX-UP, A • 1912 • *Nestor* • USA
MEXICAN MIX-UP, A • 1919 • *Jester* • SHT • USA
MEXICAN MOUSEPIECE • 1966 • McKimson Robert • ANS • USA
MEXICAN PEARL SMUGGLERS • 1913 • *Gaumont* • USA
MEXICAN QUARTER see **BORDER CAFE** • 1937
MEXICAN REBELLION, THE • 1914 • *Ammex* • USA
MEXICAN RENEGADE, A • 1913 • *Frontier* • USA
MEXICAN REVOLUTIONIST, THE • 1912 • *Kalem* • USA
MEXICAN ROMANCE, A • 1912 • *Lubin* • USA
MEXICAN ROSE GARDEN, A • 1911 • *Kalem* • USA
MEXICAN SLEEP PRODUCER, THE • 1913 • *Mace Fred* • USA
MEXICAN SPITFIRE • 1939 • Goodwins Leslie • USA
MEXICAN SPITFIRE AT SEA • 1942 • Goodwins Leslie • USA
MEXICAN SPITFIRE OUT WEST • 1940 • Goodwins Leslie • USA
MEXICAN SPITFIRE SEES A GHOST • 1942 • Goodwins Leslie • USA
MEXICAN SPITFIRE'S BABY • 1941 • Goodwins Leslie • USA
MEXICAN SPITFIRE'S BLESSED EVENT • 1943 • Goodwins Leslie • USA
MEXICAN SPITFIRE'S ELEPHANT • 1942 • Goodwins Leslie • USA
MEXICAN SPY, THE • 1913 • Melville Wilbert • USA
MEXICAN SPY IN AMERICA, A • 1914 • McRae Henry • USA
MEXICAN SUITE • 1972 • Keys Gary • DOC • USA
MEXICAN SWEETHEARTS • 1909 • Griffith D. W. • USA
MEXICAN TRAGEDY, A • 1913 • *Whitman Velma* • USA
MEXICAN WARRIOR, A • 1914 • *Baggot King* • USA
MEXICAN WOMAN, THE (USA) see **MUJER MEXICANA** • 1937
MEXICANA • 1945 • Santell Alfred • USA
MEXICANO, EL • 1944 • Delgado Agustin P. • MXC
MEXICANO, EL • 1965 • Cardona Rene • MXC
MEXICANO, EL • 1976 • Hernandez Mario • MXC
MEXICANO FEO, EL • 1983 • Crevenna Alfredo B. • MXC • UGLY AMERICAN, THE
MEXICANO TU PUEDES • 1985 • Estrada Jose • MXC • YOU CAN DO IT MEXICAN
MEXICANOS AL GRITO DE GUERRA • 1943 • Galvez Alvaro, Fuentes • MXC • HISTORIA DEL HIMNO NACIONAL
MEXICAN'S CHICKENS, THE • 1915 • *Kalem* • USA
MEXICAN'S CRIME • 1909 • *Bison* • USA
MEXICAN'S DEFEAT, THE • 1913 • *Gebhardt George* • USA
MEXICAN'S FAITH, THE • 1910 • *Anderson Broncho Billy* • USA
MEXICAN'S GRATITUDE, A • 1909 • Anderson G. M. • USA
MEXICAN'S GRATITUDE, THE • 1914 • Ridgely Richard • USA
MEXICAN'S JEALOUSY, THE • 1910 • *Bison* • USA
MEXICAN'S LAST RAID, THE • 1914 • *Nestor* • USA
MEXICAN'S LOVE AFFAIR, THE • 1912 • Rains Fred • UKN
MEXICAN'S REVENGE, THE • 1909 • *Vitagraph* • USA
MEXICAN'S WARD, A • 1910 • *Bison* • USA
MEXICO • 1919 • Stahl Carlos • MXC
MEXICO • 1930 • Lantz Walter, Nolan William • ANS • USA
MEXICO • 1938 • FRG
MEXICO • 1970 • Kracht Fritz Andre • FRG
MEXICO see **MEKSYK** • 1958
MEXICO see **SOY MEXICO** • 1970
MEXICO 2000 • 1981 • Gonzalez Rogelio A. • MXC
MEXICO CANTA see **CANTO A MI TIERRA** • 1938
MEXICO DE MI CORAZON • 1963 • Delgado Miguel M. • MXC • DOS MEXICANAS EN MEXICO
MEXICO DE MIS RECUERDOS • 1943 • Bustillo Oro Juan • MXC • MEXICO OF MY MEMORIES
MEXICO DE MIS RECUERDOS • 1963 • Bustillo Oro Juan • MXC
MEXICO DE NOCHE • 1974 • *Filmicas Agrasanchez* • MXC
MEXICO IN FLAMES see **KRASNYE KOLOKOLA** • 1981
MEXICO, LA REVOLUCION CONGELADA see **MEXICO: THE FROZEN REVOLUTION** • 1970
MEXICO LINDO • 1938 • Pereda Ramon • MXC
MEXICO LINDO Y QUERIDO • 1958 • Bracho Julio • MXC
MEXICO MAGICO • 1980 • Tavera, Zermeno, Mandoki Luis • MXC
MEXICO - MEXICO • 1968 • Reichenbach Francois • DOC • FRN, MXC
MEXICO, MEXICO, RA, RA, RA • 1974 • Alatriste Gustavo • MXC
MEXICO MIX, A • 1914 • *Joker* • USA
MEXICO NUEVO • 1963 • Reichenbach Francois • SHT • FRN
MEXICO NUNCA DUERME • 1958 • Galindo Alejandro • MXC
MEXICO OF MY MEMORIES see **MEXICO DE MIS RECUERDOS** • 1943
MEXICO, SOON see **JUTRO MEKSYK** • 1965
MEXICO: THE FROZEN REVOLUTION • 1970 • Gleyzer Raymundo • USA, ARG • MEXICO, LA REVOLUCION CONGELADA
MEXICO TODAY • 1916 • Gobbett D. W. • MXC
MEXICO TOMORROW see **JUTRO MEKSYK** • 1965
MEXIKANERIN, DIE • 1919 • Wolff Carl Heinz • FRG
MEYER ALS SOLDAT • 1914 • *Lubitsch Ernst* • FRG
MEYER AUF DER ALM • 1913 • *Lubitsch Ernst* • FRG
MEYER AUS BERLIN • 1918 • Lubitsch Ernst • FRG
MEYER UND MEIER ODR DIE KUNSTSTOPFERIN • 1915 • Del Zopp Rudolf • FRG
MEZCZYZNI NA WYSPIE • 1962 • Laskowski Jan • PLN • MEN ON AN ISLAND
MEZEI PROFETA • 1947 • Ban Frigyes • HNG • PROPHET OF THE FIELD, THE
MEZEK • 1985 • Drha Vladimir • CZC
MEZES TANCOS • 1975 • Jankovics Marcell • ANM • HNG
MEZHPLANETNAYA REVOLUTSIYA • 1924 • *Alexeyev V. (Ph)* • ANM • USS • INTERPLANETARY REVOLUTION
MEZTELEN VAGY • 1972 • Gyongyossy Imre • HNG • YOU'RE NUDE ○ LEGEND ABOUT THE DEATH AND RESURRECTION OF TWO YOUNG MEN
MEZTIZO, EL • 1989 • Handler Mario • VNZ, CUB • MIXED BLOOD, THE ○ MIXED-BLOOD, THE
MEZZANOTTE • 1915 • Genina Augusto • ITL
MEZZANOTTE D'AMORE • 1970 • Fizzarotti Ettore Maria • ITL
MEZZANOTTE TRISTE see **MIDNIGHT BLUE** • 1979
MEZZOGIORNO DE FUCCO PER AN HAO see **MIO NOME E SHANGHAI JOE, IL** • 1973
MG MG AND HIS FIRST LOVE see **MAUNG MAUNG NAI PATHAMA ACHIT** • 1983
MGA ALABOK SA LUPA • 1967 • Herrera Armando A. • PHL • DUSTS OF THE EARTH
MGA TIGRE SA LOOBAN • 1968 • Saez Nilo • PHL • TIGERS IN THE SLUMS
MGHANNAWATI, AL- • 1978 • Issa Sayyed • EGY
MGM STORY, THE • 1951 • Hoffman Herman • USA
MGM'S BIG PARADE OF COMEDY see **BIG PARADE OF COMEDY** • 1964
MI ADORABLE ESCLAVA • 1961 • Elorrieta Jose Maria • SPN • MY ADORABLE SLAVE
MI ADORADA CLEMENTINA • 1953 • Baledon Rafael • MXC • MY ADORED CLEMENTINE
MI ADORADO JUAN • 1949 • Mihura Jeronimo • SPN
MI ADORADO SALVAJE • 1951 • Salvador Jaime • MXC
MI ALMA POR UN AMOR • 1963 • Baledon Rafael • MXC
MI AMORCITO DE SUECIA • 1972 • *Prods. Leo* • MXC
MI CABALLO EL CANTADOR • 1977 • Hernandez Mario • MXC
MI CABALLO PRIETO REBELDE • 1966 • Martinez Arturo • MXC
MI CALLE • 1960 • Neville Edgar • SPN
MI CAMPEON • 1951 • Urueta Chano • MXC
MI CANCION ERES TU • 1955 • Rodriguez Roberto • MXC
MI CANCION ES PARA TI • 1965 • Torrado Ramon • SPN
MI CANDIDATO • 1937 • Urueta Chano • MXC • MY CANDIDATE (USA)
MI-CAREME A PARIS, LA • 1897 • Melies Georges • FRN
MI CHUANG JIN SANJIAO • 1988 • Zheng Dongtian • CHN • ADVENTURE IN THE GOLDEN TRIANGLE
MI DESCONOCIDA ESPOSA • 1955 • Gout Alberto • MXC
MI -DVOE MUZHCHIN • 1963 • Lysenko Yuri • USS • WE, TWO MEN ○ WE ARE TWO
MI ENEMIGO EL DOCTOR • 1944 • de Orduna Juan • SPN
MI ESPOSA BUSCA NOVIA • 1947 • Orellana Carlos • MXC
MI ESPOSA ME COMPRENDE • 1957 • Soler Julian • MXC
MI ESPOSA Y LA OTRA • 1951 • Crevenna Alfredo B. • MXC
MI FANTASTICA ESPOSA • 1943 • Maroto Eduardo G. • SPN
MI GENERAL • 1987 • *Fernan Gomez Fernando* • SPN • EDUCATING THE GENERALS
MI HEROE • 1964 • Martinez Solares Gilberto • MXC
MI HIJA HILDEGART • 1977 • Fernan-Gomez Fernando • SPN • MY DAUGHTER HIDEGART
MI HIJA VERONICA • 1950 • Gomez Bascuas Enrique • SPN
MI HIJO NO ES LO QUE PARECE • 1974 • Fons Angelino • SPN • MY SON ISN'T WHAT HE SEEMS
MI INFLUYENTE MUJER • 1955 • Gonzalez Rogelio A. • MXC
MI KIS UGYEINK, A • 1988 • Magyar Jozsef • DOC • HNG • OUR LITTLE AFFAIRS
MI LESZ? • 1966 • Kern Andras, Edelenyi Janos • HNG • WHAT NOW?
MI LESZ VELED ESZTERKE? • 1968 • Ban Robert • HNG • WHAT WILL BECOME OF YOU, ESTHER? ○ ESTHER AND THE MEN ○ ESZTERKE
MI LUPE Y MI CABALLO • 1942 • Toussaint Carlos, Duquesa Olga • MXC
MI MADRE ES CULPABLE • 1959 • Soler Julian • MXC
MI MADRECITA • 1940 • Elias Francisco • MXC • MADRECITA, LA
MI MANDA PICONE • 1984 • Loy Nanni • ITL • PICONE SENT ME
MI MARIDO • 1950 • Salvador Jaime • MXC
MI MARIDO Y SUS COMPLEJOS • 1969 • Delgado Luis Maria • SPN
MI MUJER ES DOCTOR (SPN) see **TOTO, VITTORIO E LA DOTTORESSA** • 1957
MI MUJER ES MUY DECENTE DENTRO DE LO QUE CABE • 1974 • Drove Antonio • SPN
MI MUJER ESTA LOCA • 1952 • Cahen Enrique • ARG
MI MUJER, LA SUECA Y YO • 1967 • Buhr Arturo Garcia • ARG • MY WIFE, THE SWEDE AND I
MI MUJER ME GUSTA MAS • 1960 • Roman Antonio • SPN
MI MUJER NECESITA MARIDO • 1958 • Aguilar Rolando • MXC
MI MUJER NO ES MIA • 1950 • Soler Fernando • MXC
MI NINO, MI CABALLO Y YO • 1958 • Delgado Miguel M. • MXC
MI NINO TIZOC • 1971 • *Peliculas Rodriguez* • MXC
MI NOCHE DE BODAS • 1953 • Diaz Morales Jose • MXC
MI NOCHE DE BODAS • 1961 • Demicheli Tulio • SPN, MXC • GALLO GIRO EN ESPANA, EL
MI NOVIA ES UNA FANTASMA • 1944 • Mujica Francisco • ARG • MY BRIDE IS A GHOST
MI NOVIO ES UN SALVAJE • 1953 • Vejar Carlos • MXC
MI PAPA TUVO LA CULPA • 1952 • Diaz Morales Jose • MXC
MI PERMETTE, BABBO! • 1956 • Bonnard Mario • ITL
MI PREFERIDA • 1950 • Urueta Chano • MXC
MI PRIMER ACTOR ES UN POETA • 1971 • Foucher Bernard • VNZ • MY FIRST ACTOR IS A POET
MI PRIMER AMOR • 1972 • *Estudios America* • MXC
MI PRIMER PECADO • 1976 • Summers Manuel • SPN
MI PRIMO AMOR • 1971 • *Filmadora Chapultepec* • MXC
MI PROFESORA PARTICULAR • 1973 • Camino Jaime • SPN • MY PRIVATE TEACHER
MI QUERIDA SENORITA • 1971 • de Arminan Jaime • SPN • MY DEAREST SENORITA
MI QUERIDO CAPITAN • 1950 • Martinez Solares Gilberto • MXC
MI REINO POR UN TORERO • 1943 • Rivero Fernando A. • MXC
MI REVOLVER ES LA LEY • 1963 • Gomez Urquiza Zacarias • MXC
MI, RUSSKI NAROD • 1964 • Stroyeva Vera • USS • WE, THE RUSSIAN PEOPLE ○ WE ARE THE RUSSIANS
MI SECRETARIA ESTA LOCA, LOCA, LOCA • 1967 • Dubois Albert • ARG • MY SECRETARY IS MAD, MAD, MAD
MI SOCIO • 1982 • Agazzi Paolo • BLV
MI TI LAMPSI STA MATIA • 1966 • Glykofridis Panos • GRC • ECLAT DE GLOIRE
MI TIO JACINTO • 1956 • Vajda Ladislao • SPN, ITL • PEPOTE
MI ULTIMO CANTO • 1924 • Ferreyra Jose • ARG
MI ULTIMO TANGO • 1960 • Amadori Luis Cesar • SPN
MI VEDRAI TORNARE • 1966 • Fizzarotti Ettore Maria • ITL
MI VIDA EN TUS MANOS • 1934 • Obregon Antonio • SPN
MI VIDA ES UNA CANCION • 1962 • Delgado Miguel M. • MXC
MI VIDA POR LA TUYA • 1950 • Gavaldon Roberto • MXC
MI VIUDA ALEGRE • 1941 • Delgado Miguel M. • MXC
MI VIUDA Y YO • 1954 • Cahen Enrique • ARG
MI WA JUKUSHITARI • 1959 • Tanaka Shigeo • JPN • RIPE AND MARRIAGEABLE
MIA CANZONE AL VENTO, LA • 1939 • Brignone Guido • ITL
MIA DROGA SI CHIAMA JULIE, LA (ITL) see **SIRENE DU MISSISSIPPI, LA** • 1969
MIA ITALIDHA AP' TI KIPSELI • 1968 • Dimopoulos Dinos • GRC • ITALIAN GIRL FROM KIPSELA, AN
MIA KIRIA STA BOUZOUKIA • 1968 • Dalianidis Ioannis • GRC • LADY IN A SYRTAKI DANCE, A
MIA LEGGE, LA (ITL) see **GRANGES BRULEES, LES** • 1973
MIA LUANG • 1986 • Kounavudhi Vichit • THL • PRINCIPAL WIFE
MIA MERA, O PATERAS MOU • 1968 • Wakeman Frederic • GRC • ONE DAY, MY FATHER
MIA MOGLIE NON SI TOCCA (ITL) see **PRINTEMPS, L'AUTOMNE ET L'AMOUR ,LE** • 1955
MIA MOGLIE SI DIVERTE (ITL) see **UNSERE KLEINE FRAU** • 1938
MIA MOGLIE UN CORPO PER L'AMORE • 1972 • Imperoli Mario • ITL • SIMONA UN CORPO PER TUTTI
MIA NONNA POLIZIOTTO • 1958 • Steno • ITL
MIA SIGNORA, LA • 1964 • Brass Tinto, Comencini Luigi, Bolognini Mauro • ITL
MIA VALLE, LA • 1955 • Olmi Ermanno • DOC • ITL
MIA VITA E TUA, LA • 1953 • Masini Giuseppe • ITL
MIA VITA SEI TU, LA • 1934 • Francisci Pietro • ITL
MIA ZOI TIN ECHOME • 1958 • Tzavellas Georges • GRC • WE HAVE ONLY ONE LIFE ○ WE ONLY LIVE ONCE
MIAD, AL- • 1955 • Kamel Morsi Ahmad • EGY • RENDEZ-VOUS, LE
MIAMI • 1924 • Crosland Alan • USA
MIAMI see **MOON OVER MIAMI** • 1941
MIAMI BEACH BUG POLICE • 1986 • Tropia Marc C., Tropia Tano • USA
MIAMI BLUES • 1989 • Armitage George • USA
MIAMI CONNECTION • 1987 • Park Richard • USA
MIAMI EXPOSE • 1956 • Sears Fred F. • USA
MIAMI HORROR • 1985 • De Martino Alberto • ITL
MIAMI MANIACS • 1956 • Rasinski Connie • ANS • USA
MIAMI RENDEZVOUS see **PASSION HOLIDAY** • 1963
MIAMI STORY, THE • 1954 • Sears Fred F. • USA
MIAMI SUPER COPS • 1985 • Corbucci Bruno • ITL • MIAMI SUPERCOPS
MIAMI SUPERCOPS see **MIAMI SUPER COPS** • 1985
MIAMI VICE • 1984 • Carter Thomas • TVM • USA
MIAMI VICE: DOWN FOR THE COUNT • 1987 • Compton Richard • TVM • USA
MIAMI VICE: GOLDEN TRIANGLE • 1985 • Anspaugh David, Brown George Stanford • TVM • USA
MIAMI VICE: THE PRODIGAL SON • 1985 • Glaser Paul Michael • TVM • USA
MIARKA, DAUGHTER OF THE BEAR (USA) see **MIARKA, LA FILLE A L'OURSE** • 1920
MIARKA, LA FILLE A L'OURSE • 1920 • Mercanton Louis • FRN • MIARKA, DAUGHTER OF THE BEAR (USA) ○ GYPSY PASSION
MIARKA, LA FILLE A L'OURSE • 1937 • Choux Jean • FRN
MIAS • 1975 • Psarras Tasos • GRC • MAY
MIAS PENTARAS NIATA • 1967 • Dadiras Dimis • GRC • PENNILESS YOUTH
MIASTECZKO • 1956 • Ziarnik Jerzy • DOC • PLN • SMALL TOWN, THE
MIASTO • 1963 • Kijowicz Miroslaw • ANS • PLN • TOWN, THE
MIASTO NIEUJARZMIONE • 1950 • PLN • UNDEFEATED CITY
MIBOJIN ZEME • 1968 • Yamashita Osamu • JPN • WIDOW TORTURE
MICE AND MEN • 1916 • Dawley J. Searle • USA
MICE-CAPADES • 1952 • Kneitel Seymour • ANS • USA
MICE FOLLIES • 1954 • Hanna William, Barbera Joseph • ANS • USA
MICE FOLLIES • 1960 • McKimson Robert • ANS • USA
MICE, FOXES AND GALLOWSHILL • 1970 • Plivova-Simkova Vera • USS
MICE IN COUNCIL • 1934 • *Terry Paul/ Moser Frank (P)* • ANS • USA
MICE PARADISE • 1951 • Sparber I. • ANS • USA
MICE WILL PLAY • 1938 • Avery Tex • ANS • USA
MICENIKS • 1960 • Kneitel Seymour • ANS • USA
MICHAEL • 1924 • Dreyer Carl T. • FRG • HEART'S DESIRE (UKN) ○ CHAINED (USA) ○ MIKAEL
MICHAEL see **MICHAL** • 1968
MICHAEL, A MONGOL BOY • 1961 • Sutton Heather • UKN
MICHAEL AND HELGA (USA) see **HELGA UND MICHAEL** • 1968
MICHAEL AND KITTY • 1985 • Alianak Hrant • MTV • CND
MICHAEL AND MARY • 1931 • Saville Victor • UKN
MICHAEL ARNOLD AND DR. LYNN • 1914 • *Leonard Robert* • USA
MICHAEL BRYAN • 1961 • Rothberg Lee • SHT • USA

MICHAEL DAVITT'S HOME MOVIE ABOUT THE LAND OF THE SCOTS • 1973 • Eadie Douglas • UKN
MICHAEL DWYER • 1912 • *Irish Film* • UKN
MICHAEL KOHLHAAS -DER REBELL • 1969 • Schlondorff Volker • FRG • MICHAEL KOHLHAAS (USA) ○ MICHAEL KOHLHAAS -THE REBEL
MICHAEL KOHLHAAS -THE REBEL see **MICHAEL KOHLHAAS -DER REBELL** • 1969
MICHAEL KOHLHAAS (USA) see **MICHAEL KOHLHAAS -DER REBELL** • 1969
MICHAEL MCSHANE, MATCHMAKER • 1912 • Trimble Larry • USA, UKN
MICHAEL O'HALLORAN • 1923 • Meehan James Leo • USA
MICHAEL O'HALLORAN • 1937 • Brown Karl • USA • ANY MAN'S WIFE
MICHAEL O'HALLORAN • 1948 • Rawlins John • USA
MICHAEL SHAYNE, PRIVATE DETECTIVE • 1940 • Forde Eugene J. • USA
MICHAEL STROGOFF • 1910 • Dawley J. Searle • USA
MICHAEL STROGOFF • 1914 • Blache Alice • USA • COURIER TO THE CZAR, THE
MICHAEL STROGOFF • 1914 • Carleton Lloyd B. • USA
MICHAEL STROGOFF see **MIGUEL STROGOFF** • 1943
MICHAEL STROGOFF see **MICHELE STROGOFF** • 1956
MICHAEL STROGOFF (UKN) see **SOLDIER AND THE LADY, THE** • 1937
MICHAEL STROGOFF (USA) see **MICHEL STROGOFF** • 1926
MICHAEL THE BRAVE see **MIHAI VITEAZUL** • 1971
MICHAELA'S MORNING • 1967 • Calinescu Bob • ANS • RMN • MIHAELA'S MORNING
MICHAELLA • 1968 • Cavens Andre • BLG
MICHAELS OF AFRICA, THE • 1958 • SAF
MICHAL • 1968 • Trzos-Rastawiecki Andrzej • DOC • PLN • MICHAEL
MICHE • 1931 • de Marguenat Jean • FRN
MICHEL PELLUS • 1979 • Zielinski Rafal • CND
MICHEL SIMON • 1964 • Roos Ole • SHT • DNM
MICHEL SIMON SOUS LE PLATRE • 1940 • Pichonnier Paul, Pichonnier Jean • FRN
MICHEL STROGOFF • 1926 • Tourjansky Victor • FRN • MICHAEL STROGOFF (USA)
MICHEL STROGOFF • 1935 • de Baroncelli Jacques, Eichberg Richard • FRN
MICHEL STROGOFF • 1956 • Natan Emile • FRN, FRG
MICHEL STROGOFF • 1968 • Lautner Georges • FRN
MICHEL STROGOFF see **TRIOMPHE DE MICHEL STROGOFF, LE** • 1961
MICHEL STROGOFF (FRN) see **MICHELE STROGOFF** • 1956
MICHELANGELO • 1940 • Oertel Curt, Lyford Richard (Usa Version) • FRG, SWT • TITAN: THE STORY OF MICHELANGELO, THE ○ LEBEN EINES TITANEN, DAS ○ TITAN, THE (USA)
MICHELE STROGOFF • 1956 • Gallone Carmine • ITL, FRN, FRG • MICHEL STROGOFF (FRN) ○ REVOLT OF THE TARTARS ○ MICHAEL STROGOFF
MICHELE STROGOFF see **STROGOFF** • 1970
MICHELENE see **MICHELENE AND THE DEVICE** • 1968
MICHELENE AND THE DEVICE • 1968 • Roberts R. Jack • USA • MICHELENE
MICHELINE • 1921 • Kemm Jean • FRN
MICHELINO CUCCHIARELLA • 1964 • Longo Tiziano • ITL
MICHELINO LA B • 1956 • Olmi Ermanno • DOC • ITL
MICHELLE (USA) see **SEXY GANG** • 1967
MICHEL'S MIXED UP MUSICAL BIRD • 1978 • Legrand Michel • USA
MICHETONNEUSE, LA • 1971 • Leroi Francis • FRN
MICHI • 1956 • Fujiwara Sugio • JPN • ROAD, THE
MICHIGAN KID, THE • 1928 • Willat Irvin V. • USA • GAMBLER, THE
MICHIGAN KID, THE • 1947 • Taylor Ray • USA
MICHMAN PANIN • 1960 • Schweitzer Mikhail • USS • WARRANT-OFFICER PANIN ○ MIDSHIPMAN PANIN
MICHURIN • 1947 • Dovzhenko Alexander, Solntseva Yulia • USS • LIFE IN BLOSSOM ○ LIFE IN BLOOM
MICHWAR • 1973 • Sayf Samir • SHT • EGY • PARCOURS, LE
MICK • 1976 • Noyce Phil • DCS • ASL
MICK REVISITED • 1978 • Noyce Phil • DCS • ASL
MICKEY • 1919 • Jones F. Richard, Young James • USA
MICKEY • 1948 • Murphy Ralph • USA
MICKEY AND HIS GOAT • 1917 • O'Brien Willis • USA
MICKEY AND THE SEAL • 1948 • Nichols Charles • ANS • USA
MICKEY CUTS UP • 1931 • Gillett Burt • ANS • USA
MICKEY DOWN UNDER • 1948 • Nichols Charles • ANS • USA
MICKEY GROGAN, CONTRACTOR see **LITTLE MICKEY GROGAN** • 1927
MICKEY IN ARABIA • 1932 • Jackson Wilfred • ANS • USA
MICKEY MAGNATE see **MAGNAS MISKA** • 1949
MICKEY MOUSE ANNIVERSARY SHOW, THE • 1968 • Stevenson Robert, Kimball Ward • USA
MICKEY ONE • 1965 • Penn Arthur • USA
MICKEY PLAYS PAPA • 1934 • Gillett Burt • ANS • USA
MICKEY SPILLANE'S MARGIN FOR MURDER • 1981 • Haller Daniel • TVM • USA • MARGIN FOR MURDER (UKN)
MICKEY SPILLANE'S "MURDER ME, MURDER YOU" • 1982 • Nelson Gary • TVM • USA
MICKEY STEPS OUT • 1931 • Gillett Burt • ANS • USA
MICKEY THE KID • 1939 • Lubin Arthur • USA
MICKEY'S AMATEURS • 1937 • Colvig Pinto, Pfeiffer Walt, Penner Ed • ANS • USA
MICKEY'S APE MAN • 1933 • Duffy J. A. • USA
MICKEY'S BIRTHDAY PARTY • 1942 • Thomson Riley • ANS • USA
MICKEY'S CHOO-CHOO • 1928 • Disney Walt, Iwerks Ub • ANS • USA
MICKEY'S CHRISTMAS CAROL • 1984 • Mattinson Burney • ANS • USA
MICKEY'S CIRCUS • 1936 • Sharpsteen Ben • ANS • USA
MICKEY'S DELAYED DATE • 1947 • Nichols Charles • ANS • USA
MICKEY'S ELEPHANT • 1936 • Luske Hamilton • ANS • USA
MICKEY'S FIRE BRIGADE • 1935 • Sharpsteen Ben • ANS • USA
MICKEY'S FOLLIES • 1928 • Jackson Wilfred • ANS • USA
MICKEY'S GALA PREMIERE • 1933 • Gillett Burt • ANS • USA
MICKEY'S GARDEN • 1935 • Jackson Wilfred • ANS • USA
MICKEY'S GOOD DEED • 1932 • Gillett Burt • ANS • USA
MICKEY'S GRAND OPERA • 1936 • Jackson Wilfred • ANS • USA
MICKEY'S KANGAROO • 1935 • Hand David • ANS • USA
MICKEY'S MAN FRIDAY • 1935 • Hand David • ANS • USA
MICKEY'S MECHANICAL MAN • 1933 • Jackson Wilfred • ANS • USA
MICKEY'S MELLERDRAMMER • 1933 • Jackson Wilfred • ANS • USA
MICKEY'S NAUGHTY NIGHTMARES • 1917 • O'Brien Willis • USA
MICKEY'S NIGHTMARE • 1932 • Gillett Burt • ANS • USA
MICKEY'S ORPHANS • 1931 • Gillett Burt • ANS • USA
MICKEY'S PAL PLUTO • 1933 • Gillett Burt • ANS • USA
MICKEY'S PARROT • 1938 • Roberts Bill • ANS • USA
MICKEY'S POLO TEAM • 1936 • Hand David • ANS • USA
MICKEY'S REVIVAL • 1976 • Jackson Wilfred • ANS • USA
MICKEY'S REVUE • 1932 • Jackson Wilfred • ANS • USA
MICKEY'S SERVICE STATION • 1935 • Sharpsteen Ben • ANS • USA
MICKEY'S STEAMROLLER • 1934 • Hand David • ANS • USA
MICKEY'S TRAILER • 1938 • Sharpsteen Ben • ANS • USA
MICKI AND MAUDE • 1983 • Edwards Blake • USA
MICKY FLYNN'S ESCAPADE • 1914 • *Kalem* • USA
MICKY THE MOOCHER • 1912 • *Art Films* • UKN
MICKY'S PAL • 1912 • Blache Alice, Warren Edward • USA
MICRO MOVIES • 1953-54 • Devlin Bernard • DCS • CND
MICRO-PHONIES • 1945 • Bernds Edward • SHT • USA
MICROBE, THE • 1919 • Otto Henry • USA
MICROBES • 1916 • *Rolma* • SHT • USA
MICROCOSMOS • 1976 • Delgado Cruz • SHT • SPN
MICROELECTROLYSE DE L'ARGENT • 1958 • Painleve Jean • SHT • FRN
MICROFONO E VOSTRO, IL • 1952 • Bennati Giuseppe • ITL
MICROPHONE TEST see **PROBA DE MICROFON** • 1980
MICROPHONE TESTING see **PROBA DE MICROFON** • 1980
MICROSCOPE, THE see **MIKROSKOP, DAS** • 1988
MICROSCOPE MYSTERY, THE • 1916 • Powell Paul • USA
MICROSCOPIA see **FANTASTIC VOYAGE** • 1966
MICROSCOPIA ELECTRONICA • 1974 • Cordido Ivork • DOC • VNZ
MICROSCOPIC MYSTERIES • 1932 • Lund Hugo • SHT • USA
MICROSCOPIE A BORD D'UN BATEAU DE PECHE • 1936 • Painleve Jean • SHT • FRN
MICROSCOPIE MODERNE • 1960 • Tavano Fred • SHT • FRN
MICROSECOND • 1969 • McLaughlin Dan • ANS • USA
MICROSPOOK • 1949 • Bernds Edward • SHT • USA
MICROWAVE MASSACRE • 1979 • Berwick Wayne • USA
MICSODA EJSZAKA • 1958 • Revesz Gyorgy • HNG • WHAT A NIGHT!
MICTLAND • 1970 • Kamffer Raul • MXC
MID-DAY MISS see **MID-DAY MISTRESS** • 1968
MID-DAY MISTRESS • 1968 • Emyl Rolf • USA • BUSINESS MAN'S LUNCH, THE ○ MID-DAY MISS
MID EAST • 1945 • Hurley Frank • DOC • ASL
'MID KENTUCKY HILLS • 1913 • Finley Ned • USA
MID-KNIGHT RIDER • 1984 • Wurth David • USA
MID-LENT PROCESSION IN PARIS see **CORTEGE DE LA MI-CAREME** • 1897
MID-NIGHTLY WEDDING, THE • 1914 • Cooper Toby? • UKN
MID-SUMMER LOVE TANGLE, A • 1914 • *Fischer Margarita* • USA
'MID THE CANNON'S ROAR • 1910 • *Edison* • USA
MIDARAZUMA • 1968 • Mukoi Hiroshi • JPN • OBSCENE WIFE
MIDARE-GAMI • 1961 • Kinugasa Teinosuke • JPN • DISHEVELLED HAIR
MIDARE-GUMO • 1967 • Naruse Mikio • JPN • TWO IN THE SHADOW ○ SCATTERED CLOUDS
MIDAREGAMI • 1967 • Kobayashi Satoru • JPN • DISHEVELLED HAIR
MIDARERU • 1964 • Naruse Mikio • JPN • YEARNING ○ DESIRE
MIDARETA KANKEI • 1967 • Nishihara Giichi • JPN • IMMORAL RELATIONSHIP
MIDAS OF THE DESERT, THE • 1915 • *Edwards Walter* • USA
MIDAS RUN • 1969 • Kjellin Alf • USA • RUN ON GOLD, A (UKN)
MIDAS TOUCH, THE • 1939 • MacDonald David • UKN
MIDAS TOUCH, THE see **ELDORADO** • 1988
MIDAS VALLEY • 1985 • Trikonis Gus • TVM • USA
MIDCHANNEL • 1920 • Garson Harry • USA
MIDDAY see **POLDIEN** • 1931
MIDDAY HUG, A see **MAHIRU NO HOYO** • 1968
MIDDAY OR MIDNIGHT? • 1914 • *Melies* • USA
MIDDAY SUN • 1990 • Keating Lulu • CND
MIDDIES SHORTENING SAIL • 1901 • *Bitzer Billy (Ph)* • USA
MIDDLE AGE CRAZY • 1980 • Trent John • CND • GOING ON 40
MIDDLE-AGE SPREAD • 1979 • Reid John • NZL
MIDDLE COURSE, THE • 1961 • Tully Montgomery • UKN
MIDDLE EAST IS BURNING, THE see **ORTASARK YANIYOR** • 1967
MIDDLE GAME • 1974 • Lavut Martin • DOC • CND
MIDDLE MAN, THE see **DAHANA-ARANJA** • 1976
MIDDLE OF NOWHERE see **WEBSTER BOY, THE** • 1962
MIDDLE OF THE NIGHT • 1959 • Mann Delbert • USA
MIDDLE OF THE WORLD, THE see **MILIEU DU MONDE, LE** • 1975
MIDDLE PASSAGE, THE • 1978 • Fielding Tom • USA
MIDDLE WATCH, THE • 1930 • Walker Norman • UKN
MIDDLE WATCH, THE • 1939 • Bentley Thomas • UKN
MIDDLEMAN, THE • 1915 • Tucker George Loane • UKN
MIDDLEMAN, THE (UKN) see **DAHANA-ARANJA** • 1976
MIDGET SHERLOCK HOLMES, A • 1912 • *Pathe* • USA
MIDGET'S REVENGE • 1913 • Angeles Bert • USA
MIDGET'S ROMANCE, THE • 1913 • *Vitagraph* • USA
MIDI A QUATORZE HEURES • 1972 • Foldes Peter • ANM • FRN
MIDI-MINUIT • 1970 • Philippe Pierre • FRN • NOON TO MIDNIGHT
MIDINETTE • 1955 • Forest Leonard, Blais Roger • DCS • CND
MIDLANDERS, THE • 1920 • Park Ida May, De Grasse Joseph • USA
MIDMORNING SCHEDULE see **GOZENCHO NO JIKANWARI** • 1972
MIDNATGAESTEN • 1924 • Holger-Madsen • DNM • MIDNIGHT HOSTS
MIDNATTSSOLENS SON • 1939 • Brooks Thor L., Husberg Rolf • SWD
MIDNIGHT • 1917 • Holubar Allen • SHT • USA
MIDNIGHT • 1922 • Campbell Maurice • USA
MIDNIGHT • 1930 • Foster John, Davis Mannie • ANS • USA
MIDNIGHT • 1931 • King George • UKN
MIDNIGHT • 1932 • Pal George • ANM • HNG
MIDNIGHT • 1934 • Erskine Chester • USA • CALL IT MURDER
MIDNIGHT • 1939 • Leisen Mitchell • USA
MIDNIGHT • 1981 • Russo John • USA • BACKWOODS MASSACRE
MIDNIGHT • 1989 • Vane Norman Thaddeus • USA
MIDNIGHT ACE, THE • 1928 • *Kelly Mabel* • USA
MIDNIGHT ADVENTURE see **PULNOCNI PRIHODA** • 1960
MIDNIGHT ADVENTURE see **PRIKLYUCHENI V POLUNOSHT** • 1964
MIDNIGHT ADVENTURE, A • 1909 • Griffith D. W. • USA
MIDNIGHT ADVENTURE, A • 1911 • *Nestor* • USA
MIDNIGHT ADVENTURE, A • 1913 • *Wilson Frank?* • UKN
MIDNIGHT ADVENTURE, A • 1928 • Worne Duke • USA
MIDNIGHT ALARM, THE • 1914 • *Joker* • USA
MIDNIGHT ALARM, THE • 1919 • *Parsons "smiling" Bill* • SHT • USA
MIDNIGHT ALARM, THE • 1923 • Smith David • USA
MIDNIGHT ALIBI • 1934 • Crosland Alan • USA • OLD DOLL'S HOUSE
MIDNIGHT ANGEL see **PACIFIC BLACKOUT** • 1942
MIDNIGHT AT MADAME TUSSAUD'S • 1936 • Pearson George • UKN • MIDNIGHT AT THE WAX MUSEUM (USA)
MIDNIGHT AT MAXIM'S • 1915 • Sargent George L. • USA
MIDNIGHT AT THE OLD MILL • 1916 • *Hamilton Lloyd V.* • USA
MIDNIGHT AT THE WAX MUSEUM (USA) see **MIDNIGHT AT MADAME TUSSAUD'S** • 1936
MIDNIGHT AUTO SUPPLY, THE see **LOVE AND THE MIDNIGHT AUTO SUPPLY** • 1978
MIDNIGHT BELL, A • 1913 • France Charles H. • USA
MIDNIGHT BELL, A • 1917 • Richmond J. A. • SHT • USA
MIDNIGHT BELL, A • 1921 • Ray Charles • USA
MIDNIGHT BLUE • 1979 • Del Balzo Raimondo • ITL • MEZZANOTTE TRISTE
MIDNIGHT BREAKS • 1988 • Postma Laurens C. • UKN
MIDNIGHT BRIDE, THE • 1920 • Humphrey William J. • USA
MIDNIGHT BURGLAR, A • 1918 • Ensminger Robert • USA
MIDNIGHT BUTTERFLY (UKN) see **MANHATTAN BUTTERFLY** • 1935
MIDNIGHT CABARET • 1923 • Semon Larry • SHT • USA
MIDNIGHT CAFE, THE • Martin Frederic • SHT • USA
MIDNIGHT CALL see **IN THE NAME OF THE LAW** • 1922
MIDNIGHT CALL, A • 1913 • *Balboa* • USA
MIDNIGHT CALL, THE • 1914 • Huntley Fred W. • USA
MIDNIGHT CALLER, THE • 1984 • SAF
MIDNIGHT CHILD, THE see **ENFANT DE MINUIT, L'** • 1930
MIDNIGHT CLUB • 1933 • Hall Alexander, Somnes George • USA
MIDNIGHT COP • 1988 • Patzak Peter • USA
MIDNIGHT COP • 1989 • Mann Farhad • USA
MIDNIGHT COURT • 1937 • McDonald Frank • USA
MIDNIGHT COWBOY • 1969 • Schlesinger John • USA
MIDNIGHT COWGIRL • 1970 • Fizz Gene • USA • THEY CAME TOGETHER
MIDNIGHT CROSSING • 1988 • Holzberg Roger • USA
MIDNIGHT CUPID, A • 1910 • Griffith D. W. • USA
MIDNIGHT DADDIES • 1930 • Sennett Mack • USA
MIDNIGHT DANCER (USA) see **BELINDA** • 1987
MIDNIGHT DISTURBANCE, A • 1909 • *Essanay* • USA
MIDNIGHT DOLLS see **MUNECAS DE MEDIA NOCHE** • 1979
MIDNIGHT ELOPEMENT, A • 1912 • Nicholls George, Sennett Mack (Spv) • USA
MIDNIGHT EPISODE • 1950 • Parry Gordon • UKN
MIDNIGHT EPISODE, A (USA) see **BON LIT, UN** • 1899
MIDNIGHT ESCAPADE, A • 1916 • *Jockey* • USA
MIDNIGHT EVENT, THE see **PULNOCNI PRIHODA** • 1960
MIDNIGHT EXPRESS • 1978 • Parker Alan • USA
MIDNIGHT EXPRESS, THE • 1908 • *Lubin* • USA
MIDNIGHT EXPRESS, THE • 1924 • Hill George W. • USA
MIDNIGHT FACES • 1926 • Cohn Bennett • USA • MIDNIGHT FIRES
MIDNIGHT FIRES see **MIDNIGHT FACES** • 1926
MIDNIGHT FLOWER, THE • 1923 • Peacocke Leslie T. • USA
MIDNIGHT FLOWER BED see **MAYONAKA NO HANAZONO** • 1967
MIDNIGHT FLYER, THE • 1918 • *Gibson Helen* • SHT • USA
MIDNIGHT FLYER, THE • 1925 • Forman Tom • USA
MIDNIGHT FROLIC • 1917 • Moss Howard S. • ANM • USA
MIDNIGHT FROLICS • 1938 • Iwerks Ub • ANS • USA
MIDNIGHT GAMBOLS (USA) see **SINLESS SINNER, A** • 1919
MIDNIGHT GHOST, THE see **GHABA NUS EL LAIL** • 1947
MIDNIGHT GIRL, THE • 1919 • *Philipp Adolf* • USA
MIDNIGHT GIRL, THE • 1925 • Noy Wilfred • USA
MIDNIGHT GRADUATE, THE • 1970 • Brown Don • USA
MIDNIGHT GUEST, THE • 1923 • Archainbaud George • USA • ONE DARK NIGHT ○ FLESH
MIDNIGHT HEAT • 1983 • Mahler Richard • USA
MIDNIGHT HOSTS see **MIDNATGAESTEN** • 1924
MIDNIGHT HOUR, THE • 1985 • Bender Jack • TVM • USA • IN THE MIDNIGHT HOUR
MIDNIGHT IN A TOY SHOP see **MIDNITE IN A TOY SHOP** • 1930
MIDNIGHT IN PARIS (USA) see **MONSIEUR LA SOURIS** • 1942
MIDNIGHT IN THE GRAVEYARD see **V POLNOCH NA KLADBISCHE** • 1909
MIDNIGHT INCIDENT, A see **PULNOCNI PRIHODA** • 1960
MIDNIGHT INTERRUPTIONS • 1902 • *Warwick Trading Co* • UKN
MIDNIGHT INTRUDER • 1904 • Porter Edwin S. • USA
MIDNIGHT INTRUDER • 1937 • Lubin Arthur • USA
MIDNIGHT JOGGER, THE • 1970 • *Fleetan Films* • USA

MIDNIGHT KISS, THE • 1926 • Cummings Irving • USA • PIGS

MIDNIGHT LACE • 1960 • Miller David • USA

MIDNIGHT LACE • 1981 • Nagy Ivan • TVM • USA

MIDNIGHT LADY • 1932 • Thorpe Richard • USA • DREAM MOTHER (UKN)

MIDNIGHT LIFE • 1928 • Dunlap Scott R. • USA • MIDNIGHT (UKN)

MIDNIGHT LIMITED • 1926 • Apfel Oscar • USA

MIDNIGHT LIMITED, THE • 1940 • Bretherton Howard • USA

MIDNIGHT LOVERS • 1926 • Dillon John Francis • USA

MIDNIGHT MADNESS • 1918 • Julian Rupert • USA

MIDNIGHT MADNESS • 1928 • Weight F. Harmon • USA

MIDNIGHT MADNESS • 1980 • Nankin Michael, Wechter David • USA

MIDNIGHT MADNESS see **MR. PATMAN** • 1980

MIDNIGHT MADONNA • 1937 • Flood James • USA

MIDNIGHT MAIL, THE • 1915 • Buckland Warwick? • UKN

MIDNIGHT MAN, THE • 1917 • Clifton Elmer • USA

MIDNIGHT MAN, THE • 1920 • Horne James W. • SRL • USA

MIDNIGHT MAN, THE • 1974 • Lancaster Burt, Kibbee Roland • USA

MIDNIGHT MANHUNT see **ONE EXCITING NIGHT** • 1945

MIDNIGHT MARAUDER, THE • 1911 • Powell Frank • USA

MIDNIGHT MARAUDERS • 1912 • Stow Percy • UKN

MIDNIGHT MARY • 1932 • Hubbard Lucien • USA

MIDNIGHT MARY see **LADY OF THE NIGHT** • 1933

MIDNIGHT MASS see **POLNOCNA OMSA** • 1962

MIDNIGHT MATINEE • 1989 • Martin Richard • USA

MIDNIGHT MELODIES • 1944 • Collins Lewis D. • SHT • USA

MIDNIGHT MELODY see **MURDER IN THE MUSIC HALL** • 1946

MIDNIGHT MENACE • 1937 • Hill Sinclair • UKN • BOMBS OVER LONDON (USA) ○ MIDNIGHT SPECIAL

MIDNIGHT MESSAGE, A • 1913 • *Joyce Alice* • USA

MIDNIGHT MESSAGE, THE • 1926 • Hurst Paul C. • USA • FOILED

MIDNIGHT MOLLY • 1925 • Ingraham Lloyd • USA

MIDNIGHT MORALS • 1932 • Hopper E. Mason • USA

MIDNIGHT MYSTERY • 1930 • Seitz George B. • USA • HAWK ISLAND

MIDNIGHT MYSTERY, A • 1917 • Mong William V. • SHT • USA

MIDNIGHT OFFERINGS • 1981 • Holcomb Rod • TVM • USA

MIDNIGHT ON THE BARBARY COAST • 1929 • Horner Robert J. • USA

MIDNIGHT PARASITES, THE • 1972 • Kuri Yoji • ANS • JPN

MIDNIGHT PATROL • 1932 • Cabanne W. Christy • USA

MIDNIGHT PATROL, THE • 1918 • Willat Irvin V., Ince Thomas H. (Spv) • USA

MIDNIGHT PATROL, THE • 1933 • French Lloyd • SHT • USA

MIDNIGHT PHANTASY, A • 1903 • *Biograph* • USA

MIDNIGHT PHANTOM • 1935 • Ray Bernard B. • USA

MIDNIGHT PHANTOM see **FANTASMA DELLA MEZZANOTTE** • 1911

MIDNIGHT PLEASURES (UKN) see **QUI COMINCIA L'AVVENTURA** • 1975

MIDNIGHT PLEASURES (USA) see **A MEZZANOTTE VA LA RONDA DEL PIACERE** • 1975

MIDNIGHT PLOWBOY see **SUNSET GIRLS**

MIDNIGHT PROWLERS, THE • 1915 • *Pokes & Jabbs* • USA

MIDNIGHT RAIDERS, THE • 1920 • Neitz Alvin J. • USA

MIDNIGHT RAIDERS (UKN) see **OKLAHOMA RAIDERS** • 1943

MIDNIGHT REHEARSAL see **HATASVADADASZOK** • 1983

MIDNIGHT RIDE OF PAUL REVERE • 1907 • Porter Edwin S. • USA

MIDNIGHT RIDE OF PAUL REVERE, THE • 1914 • Brabin Charles J. • USA

MIDNIGHT ROMANCE, A • 1919 • Weber Lois • USA

MIDNIGHT ROSE • 1928 • Young James • USA

MIDNIGHT RUN • 1988 • Brest Martin • USA

MIDNIGHT SCARE, A • 1914 • *Crystal* • USA

MIDNIGHT SECRETS • 1924 • Nelson Jack • USA

MIDNIGHT SERENADE • 1947 • Ganzer Alvin • SHT • USA

MIDNIGHT SHADOWS • 1924 • Ford Francis • USA

MIDNIGHT SNACK, THE • 1941 • Hanna William, Barbera Joseph • ANS • USA

MIDNIGHT SON, THE • 1900 • Gibbons Walter • UKN

MIDNIGHT SONG see **PAATHIRA PAATTU** • 1967

MIDNIGHT SPECIAL see **MIDNIGHT MENACE** • 1937

MIDNIGHT SPECIAL, THE • 1930 • Worne Duke • USA

MIDNIGHT SPECTER, THE see **SPETTRO DI MEZZANOTTE, LO** • 1915

MIDNIGHT STAGE, THE • 1919 • Warde Ernest C. • USA

MIDNIGHT STORY, THE • 1956 • Pevney Joseph • USA • APPOINTMENT WITH A SHADOW (UKN)

MIDNIGHT SUMMONS, THE • 1924 • Paul Fred • UKN

MIDNIGHT SUN, THE • 1926 • Buchowetzki Dimitri • USA

MIDNIGHT SUN, THE • 1958 • Vogel Virgil W. • USA

MIDNIGHT SUN AT SCARO, THE see **SUN, THE** • 1903

MIDNIGHT SUPPER, A • 1909 • Porter Edwin S. • USA

MIDNIGHT SUPPER, A • 1914 • *De Forrest Charlie* • USA

MIDNIGHT TAXI • 1937 • Forde Eugene J. • USA

MIDNIGHT TAXI, THE • 1928 • Adolfi John G. • USA

MIDNIGHT THIEVES • 1926 • *Rawlinson Herbert* • USA

MIDNIGHT TOLL, THE • 1916 • *Laemmle* • USA

MIDNIGHT TRAGEDY, A • 1914 • *Kalem* • USA

MIDNIGHT TRAIL, THE • 1918 • Sloman Edward • USA

MIDNIGHT TRAIN see **PULNOCNI KOLONA** • 1972

MIDNIGHT (UKN) see **MIDNIGHT LIFE** • 1928

MIDNIGHT VISITOR see **SHU TO MIDORI** • 1956

MIDNIGHT VISITOR, A • 1911 • *Solax* • USA

MIDNIGHT VISITOR, THE • 1914 • *Rex* • USA

MIDNIGHT WARNING, THE • 1933 • Bennet Spencer Gordon • USA

MIDNIGHT WARRIOR • 1989 • Merhi Joseph • USA

MIDNIGHT WATCH, THE • 1924 • Lamont Charles • SHT • USA

MIDNIGHT WATCH, THE • 1927 • Hunt Charles J. • USA

MIDNIGHT WEDDING • 1912 • Longford Raymond • ASL

MIDNIGHT WEDDING, THE • 1912 • *Gaumont* • USA

MIDNIGHT WEDDING, THE • 1914 • Batley Ernest G. • UKN

MIDNITE IN A TOY SHOP • 1930 • Jackson Wilfred • ANS • USA • MIDNIGHT IN A TOY SHOP

MIDNITE SPARES • 1982 • Masters Quentin • ASL

MIDORI NO DAICHI • 1942 • Shimazu Yasujiro • JPN • GREEN EARTH, THE

MIDORI NO FURUSATO • 1946 • *Hara Setsuko* • JPN • GREEN NATIVE COUNTRY

MIDSHIPMAID, THE • 1932 • De Courville Albert • UKN • MIDSHIPMAID GOB (USA)

MIDSHIPMAID GOB (USA) see **MIDSHIPMAID, THE** • 1932

MIDSHIPMAN, THE • 1925 • Cabanne W. Christy • USA

MIDSHIPMAN EASY • 1915 • Elvey Maurice • UKN

MIDSHIPMAN EASY • 1935 • Reed Carol • UKN • MEN OF THE SEA (USA)

MIDSHIPMAN JACK • 1933 • Cabanne W. Christy • USA • GLORY COMMAND

MIDSHIPMAN PANIN see **MICHMAN PANIN** • 1960

MIDSOMMER see **GAMLE KOBMANDSHUS, DET** • 1911

'MIDST WOODLAND SHADOWS • 1914 • Ince Ralph • USA

MIDSTREAM • 1929 • Flood James • USA

MIDSUMMER DAY'S SMILE, A see **UN SURIS IN PLINA VARA** • 1963

MIDSUMMER DAY'S WORK • 1939 • Cavalcanti Alberto • DOC • UKN

MIDSUMMER MADNESS • 1920 • De Mille William C. • USA

MIDSUMMER MADNESS • 1964 • Halas John, Batchelor Joy • ANS • UKN

MIDSUMMER MUSH • 1933 • Parrott Charles • SHT • USA

MIDSUMMER MUSIC • 1960 • Swift • SHT • UKN

MIDSUMMER NIGHT see **MITTSOMMERNACHT** • 1967

MIDSUMMER NIGHTMARE • 1957 • Halas John • ANS • UKN

MIDSUMMER NIGHT'S DREAM see **SOGNO DI UNA NOTTE ESTATE** • 1984

MIDSUMMER NIGHT'S DREAM, A • 1909 • *Footit* • FRN

MIDSUMMER NIGHT'S DREAM, A • 1909 • Kent Charles?, Blackton J. Stuart (Spv) • USA

MIDSUMMER NIGHT'S DREAM, A • 1913 • *Tommasi Socrate* • ITL

MIDSUMMER NIGHT'S DREAM, A • 1935 • Reinhardt Max, Dieterle William • USA

MIDSUMMER NIGHT'S DREAM, A • 1953 • Deane Charles • UKN

MIDSUMMER NIGHT'S DREAM, A • 1958 • Cartier Rudolph • MTV • UKN

MIDSUMMER NIGHT'S DREAM, A • 1961 • Sackler Howard

MIDSUMMER NIGHT'S DREAM, A • 1966 • Eriksen Dan, Balachine George • USA

MIDSUMMER NIGHT'S DREAM, A • 1968 • Hall Peter • UKN

MIDSUMMER NIGHT'S DREAM, A • 1968 • Kemp-Welch Joan • MTV • UKN

MIDSUMMER NIGHT'S DREAM, A • 1969 • *Apache Mike* • USA

MIDSUMMER NIGHT'S DREAM, A • 1984 • Coronado Celestino • SPN, UKN

MIDSUMMER NIGHT'S DREAM, A see **SOMMERNACHTSTRAUM, EIN** • 1913

MIDSUMMER NIGHT'S DREAM, A see **SEN NOCI SVATOJANSKE** • 1959

MIDSUMMER NIGHT'S DREAM, A (USA) see **ELFENSZENE AUS DEM SOMMERNACHTSTRAUM** • 1917

MIDSUMMER NIGHT'S DREAM, A (USA) see **SOMMERNACHTSTRAUM, EIN** • 1925

MIDSUMMER NIGHT'S SEX COMEDY, A • 1982 • Allen Woody • USA

MIDSUMMER NIGHT'S STEAM, A • 1927 • Sandrich Mark • SHT • USA

MIDSUMMER SEX • 1971 • Stivell Arne • SWD

MIDSUMMER–TIME see **GAMLE KOBMANDSHUS, DET** • 1911

MIDSUMMER'S NIGHT IN SWEDEN • 1967 • Kunz Werner • SHT

MIDT I EN JAZZTID • 1969 • Thomsen Knud Leif • DNM • JAZZ ALL AROUND

MIDT OM NATTEN • 1984 • Balling Erik • DNM • IN THE MIDDLE OF THE NIGHT

MIDVINTERBLOT • 1945 • Werner Gosta • SHT • SWD • MIDWINTER SACRIFICE ○ MIDWINTER BLOOD

MIDWAY • 1976 • Smight Jack • USA • BATTLE OF MIDWAY (UKN)

MIDWESTERN FLOODS • 1962 • Fournier Claude • DOC • USA

MIDWIFE, THE • 1961 • Sakellarios Alekos • GRC

MIDWINTER BLOOD see **MIDVINTERBLOT** • 1945

MIDWINTER MADNESS • 1916 • Kelley J. Winthrop • SHT • USA

MIDWINTER NIGHT'S DREAM, A • 1912 • *Lubin* • USA

MIDWINTER NIGHT'S DREAM OR LITTLE JOE'S LUCK, A • 1906 • Blackton J. Stuart • USA

MIDWINTER SACRIFICE see **MIDVINTERBLOT** • 1945

MIDWINTER TRIP TO LOS ANGELES, A • 1912 • Dwan Allan • DOC • USA

MIEDA LLEGO A JALISCO, EL • 1949 • Sevilla Raphael J. • MXC

MIEDO • 1956 • Klimovsky Leon • SPN

MIEDOS, LOS • 1980 • Doria Alejandro • ARG • FEARS

MIEDZY BRZEGAMI • 1962 • Lesiewicz Witold • PLN • BETWEEN TWO SHORES

MIEDZY WRZESNIEM A MAJEM • 1969 • Wionczek Roman • PLN • BETWEEN SEPTEMBER AND MAY

MIEHEN TIE • 1940 • Tapiovaara Nyrki, Blomberg Erik, Hytonen Hugy • FNL • WAY OF A MAN, THE ○ ONE MAN'S FATE

MIEI PRIMI QUARANT'ANNI, I • 1988 • Vanzina Carlo • ITL • MY FIRST FORTY YEARS

MIEJSCE • 1965 • Sturlis Edward • PLN • FUNCTION, THE ○ POSITION, THE

MIEJSCE DLA JEDNEGO • 1965 • Lesiewicz Witold • PLN • ROOM FOR ONE

MIEJSCE NA ZIEMI • 1960 • Rozewicz Stanislaw • PLN • NO PLACE ON EARTH ○ PLACE ON EARTH, A ○ PLACE IN THE WORLD, A

MIEJSLE DLA CZLOWIEKA • 1972 • Wionczek Roman • PLN • ROOM FOR MEN

MIEL NECTAR, LA • 1942 • Proulx Maurice • DCS • CND

MIEL SE FUE DE LA LUNA, LA • 1951 • Soler Julian • MXC

MIELE DEL DIAVOLO, IL • 1987 • Fulci Lucio • ITL • DEVIL'S HONEY, THE

MIELOTT BEFEJEZI ROPTET A DENEVER • 1988 • Timar Peter • HNG • BEFORE THE END OF THE BAT'S FLIGHT ○ BEFORE THE BAT'S FLIGHT IS DONE ○ DENEVER MIELOTT BEFEJEZI ROPT

MIENTE Y SERAS FELIZ • 1939 • Sevilla Raphael J. • MXC

MIENTRAS EL CUERPO AGUANTE • 1958 • Martinez Solares Gilberto • MXC

MIENTRAS ME DURE LA VIDA • 1981 • Otaduy Carlos • ARG • AS LONG AS I LIVE

MIENTRAS MEXICO DUERME • 1938 • Galindo Alejandro • MXC • WHILE MEXICO SLEEPS (USA)

MIENTRE BUENOS AIRES DUERME • 1921 • Ferreyra Jose • ARG

MIERCOLES DE CENIZA • 1958 • Gavaldon Roberto • MXC

MIERCOLES EN LA MANANA • 1972 • *Ratjac Inc* • MXC

MIERT? • 1966 • Hersko Anna • HNG • WHY?

MIERTVY SEZON • 1969 • Kulish Savva • USS • DEAD SEASON

MIES ES MUCHA, LA • 1949 • Saenz De Heredia Jose Luis • SPN

MIES JOKA EI OSANNUT SANOA EI • 1975 • Jarva Risto • FNL • MAN WHO COULDN'T SAY NO, A

MIES TALTA TAHDELTA • 1958 • Witikka Jack • FNL • MAN FROM THIS PLANET, THE ○ MAN FROM THIS STAR, THE

MIESTA EI VOI RAISKATA see **MANRAPE** • 1978

MIETER SCHULZE GEGEN ALLE • 1932 • Froelich Carl • FRG

MIEUX VAUT ETRE RICHE ET BIEN PORTANT QUE FAUCHE ET MAL FOUTU • 1980 • Pecas Max • FRN, SPN, FRG

MIEUX VAUT FAIRE L'AMOUR • 1968 • Antel Franz • FRN, ITL

MIEZE STREMPELS WERDEGANG • 1915 • Hecker Waldemar • FRG • STREMPELS MIEZE

MIEZE VON BOLLE, DIE • 1915 • *Weixler Dorrit* • FRG

MIFANWY –A TRAGEDY • 1913 • Neame Elwin • UKN

MIFFY • 1921 • Buxton Dudley • ASS • UKN

MIG OG CHARLY • 1978 • Arnfred Morten, Kristiansen Henning • DNM • ME AND CHARLEY

MIG OG DIG • 1969 • Henning-Jensen Astrid • DNM, SWD • MEJ OCH DEJ ○ ME AND YOU

MIG OG MAFIAEN • 1973 • Ornbak Henning • DNM

MIG OG MIN LILLEBROR • 1967 • Lauritzen Lau Jr. • DNM • ME AND MY KID BROTHER

MIG OG MIN LILLEBROR OG BOLLE • 1969 • Lauritzen Lau Jr., Lauritzen Lisbeth • DNM

MIG OG MIN LILLEBROR –OG STORSMUGLERNE • 1968 • Lauritzen Lau Jr. • DNM • ME AND MY KID BROTHER AND THE SMUGGLERS

MIGGLE'S MAID • 1916 • Wilson Frank • UKN

MIGHT AND THE MAN • 1917 • Dillon Eddie • USA

MIGHT OF THE HAND see **BIGAT NG KAMAY** • 1968

MIGHTIER HAND, A • 1910 • *Powers* • USA

MIGHTIER THAN THE SWORD (UKN) see **GIRL WITH IDEAS, THE** • 1937

MIGHTY, THE • 1929 • Cromwell John • USA

MIGHTY ATOM, THE • 1911 • Coleby A. E. • UKN

MIGHTY ATOM, THE • 1913 • *Wright Mabel* • USA

MIGHTY ATOMS • 1930 • Smith Percy • UKN • MITEY ATOMS

MIGHTY BARNUM, THE • 1934 • Lang Walter • USA

MIGHTY CRUSADERS, THE (UKN) see **GERUSALEMME LIBERATA** • 1957

MIGHTY DEBRAU, THE • 1923 • *Delman Film Corp* • USA

MIGHTY DWARF, THE see **ISSUN BOSHI** • 1959

MIGHTY GORGA, THE • 1969 • Hewitt David L. • USA

MIGHTY HOLD, THE • 1915 • Bertram William • USA

MIGHTY HUNTER, THE • 1912 • *Majestic* • USA

MIGHTY HUNTER, THE • 1913 • *Majestic* • USA

MIGHTY HUNTERS • 1940 • Jones Charles M. • ANS • USA

MIGHTY INVADERS, THE (USA) see **GERUSALEMME LIBERATA** • 1957

MIGHTY JACK • Mitsoti Kazuho • JPN

MIGHTY JOE YOUNG • 1949 • Schoedsack Ernest B. • USA • MR. JOSEPH YOUNG OF AFRICA

MIGHTY JUNGLE, THE • 1964 • Belgard Arnold, Dalie Dave • USA

MIGHTY JUNGLE, THE • 1964 • Rodriguez Ismael • USA, MXC

MIGHTY KHAN, THE see **PREDONI DELLA STEPPA, I** • 1964

MIGHTY LAK A GOAT • 1942 • Glazer Herbert • SHT • USA

MIGHTY LAK' A ROSE • 1923 • Carewe Edwin • USA

MIGHTY LAK' A ROSE • 1929 • Aylott Dave, Symmons E. F. • SHT • UKN

MIGHTY LIKE A MOOSE • 1926 • McCarey Leo • SHT • USA

MIGHTY MARKO, THE see **YUNAK MARKO** • 1953

MIGHTY MCGURK, THE • 1946 • Waters John • USA

MIGHTY MOUSE AND THE KILKENNY CATS • 1945 • Davis Mannie • ANS • USA

MIGHTY MOUSE AND THE MAGICIAN • 1948 • Donnelly Eddie • ANS • USA

MIGHTY MOUSE AND THE PIRATES • 1945 • Rasinski Connie • ANS • USA

MIGHTY MOUSE AND THE WOLF • 1945 • Donnelly Eddie • ANS • USA

MIGHTY MOUSE IN ALADDIN'S LAMP • 1947 • Donnelly Eddie • ANS • USA • ALADDIN'S LAMP

MIGHTY MOUSE IN GOONS FROM THE MOON • 1951 • Rasinski Connie • ANS • USA • GOONS FROM THE MOON

MIGHTY MOUSE IN GYPSY LIFE • 1945 • Rasinski Connie • ANS • USA • GYPSY LIFE

MIGHTY MOUSE IN HANSEL AND GRETEL • 1952 • Rasinski Connie • ANS • USA • HANSEL AND GRETEL

MIGHTY MOUSE IN KRAKATOA • 1945 • Rasinski Connie • ANS • USA

MIGHTY MOUSE IN MOTHER GOOSE'S BIRTHDAY PARTY • 1950 • Rasinski Connie • ANS • USA • MOTHER GOOSE'S BIRTHDAY PARTY

MIGHTY MOUSE IN PREHISTORIC PERILS • 1952 • Rasinski Connie • ANS • USA • PREHISTORIC PERILS

MIGHTY MOUSE IN SVENGALI'S CAT • 1946 • Donnelly Eddie • ANS • USA • SVENGALI'S CAT

MIGHTY MOUSE IN THE GREAT SPACE RACE see **MIGHTY MOUSE: THE GREAT SPACE CHASE** • 1983

MIGHTY MOUSE IN THE WITCH'S CAT • 1948 • Davis Mannie • ANS • USA • WITCH'S CAT, THE

MIGHTY MOUSE MEETS BAD BILL BUNION • 1945 • Davis Mannie • ANS • USA

MIGHTY MOUSE MEETS DEADEYE DICK • 1947 • Rasinski Connie • ANS • USA
MIGHTY MOUSE MEETS JEKYLL AND HYDE CAT • 1944 • Davis Mannie • ANS • USA
MIGHTY MOUSE RIDES AGAIN see **SUPER MOUSE RIDES AGAIN** • 1943
MIGHTY MOUSE: THE GREAT SPACE CHASE • 1983 • Friedman Ed, Kachivas Lou • ANM • USA • MIGHTY MOUSE IN THE GREAT SPACE RACE
MIGHTY NAVY, THE • 1941 • Fleischer Dave • ANS • USA
MIGHTY PEKING MAN, THE • 1977 • Ho Meng-Hua • HKG
MIGHTY QUINN, THE • 1989 • Schenkel Carl • USA • FINDING MAUBEE
MIGHTY ROCK • 1970 • Saez Nilo • PHL
MIGHTY SAMSON, THE see **SAMSUN EL KABIR** • 1948
MIGHTY STEAM CALLIOPE, THE • 1978 • Ianzelo Tony • DOC • CND
MIGHTY STREAM • 1940 • Eisenstein Sergei • USS
MIGHTY THERMITE, THE • 1961 • Kneitel Seymour • ANS • USA
MIGHTY THUNDA, THE see **KING OF THE KONGO** • 1952
MIGHTY TIMBER • 1948 • Parker Benjamin R. • SHT • USA
MIGHTY TREVE, THE • 1937 • Collins Lewis D. • USA • TREVE
MIGHTY TUNDRA, THE (UKN) see **TUNDRA** • 1936
MIGHTY URSUS (USA) see **URSUS** • 1961
MIGHTY WARRIOR, THE see **VENDETTA DI URSUS, LA** • 1961
MIGHTYMAN I • 1979 • SAF
MIGHTYMAN II • 1979 • SAF
MIGNON • 1900-07 • Blache Alice • FRN
MIGNON • 1909 • *Lubin* • USA
MIGNON • 1912 • Blache Alice • USA • CHILD OF FATE, THE
MIGNON • 1915 • Beyfuss Alex E. • USA
MIGNON • 1922 • Rist Preben • FRG
MIGNON E PARTITA • 1988 • Archibugi Francesca • ITL, FRN • MIGNON HAS LEFT
MIGNON HAS LEFT see **MIGNON E PARTITA** • 1988
MIGNONETTE • 1916 • Kelley J. Winthrop • SHT • USA
MIGOVE V KIBRITENA KOUTIYA • 1979 • Evstatieva Marianna • BUL • MOMENTS IN A MATCHBOX
MIGRANT FISHERMEN • Hettiarachi P. • DOC • SLN
MIGRANTS, THE • 1974 • Gries Tom • TVM • USA
MIGRATION • 1969 • Rimmer David • CND
MIGRATIONS see **SEOBE** • 1989
MIGRATORY BIRDS OF SNOW see **YUKI NO WATARIDORI** • 1957
MIGRATORY BIRDS UNDER THE MOON see **TSUKI NO WATARIDORI** • 1951
MIGUEL PRO (SPN) see **RAIN FOR A DUSTY SUMMER** • 1971
MIGUEL STROGOFF • 1943 • Delgado Miguel M. • MXC • CORREO DEL ZAR, EL ○ MICHAEL STROGOFF
MIGUELIN • 1964 • Valcarcel Horacio • SPN
MIGUEL'S NAVIDAD • 1977 • Mendeluk George • MTV • MXC
MIGUITAS EN LA CAMA • 1949 • Lugones Mario C. • ARG
MIGUITAS Y EL CARBONERO • 1957 • Grinan Jorge • SPN
MIHAELA'S MORNING see **MICHAELA'S MORNING** • 1967
MIHAI VITEAZUL • 1971 • Nicolaescu Sergiu • RMN, FRN, ITL • LAST CRUSADE, THE ○ MICHAEL THE BRAVE
MIHEZTARTAS VEGETT • 1971 • Darday Istvan • SHT • HNG • FOR YOUR EDIFICATION
MIJN NACHTEN MET SUSAN, OLGA, ALBERT, JULIE, PIET & SANDRA • 1974 • de la Parra Pim • NTH • MY NIGHTS WITH SUSAN, SANDRA, OLGA AND JULIE ○ MY NIGHTS WITH SUSAN, OLGA, ALBERT, JULIE, BILL AND SANDRA ○ SECRETS OF NAUGHTY SUSAN
MIJN VADER WOONT IN RIO • 1989 • Sombogaart Ben • NTH • MY FATHER LIVES IN RIO
MIJN VRIEND • 1980 • Rademakers Fons • NTH, BLG • JUDGE'S FRIEND, THE (UKN) ○ MY FRIEND ○ MIJN VRIEND OF HET VERGORGEN LEVEN VAN JULES DEPRAETER ○ MON AMI
MIJN VRIEND OF HET VERGORGEN LEVEN VAN JULES DEPRAETER see **MIJN VRIEND** • 1980
MIKADO, THE • 1926 • UKN
MIKADO, THE • 1939 • Schertzinger Victor • UKN
MIKADO, THE • 1967 • Burge Stuart • UKN
MIKADO, THE see **FAN FAN** • 1918
MIKAEL see **MICHAEL** • 1924
MIKAN NO TAIKYOKU • 1982 • Sato Junya, Ji-Shun Duan • JPN, CHN • UNFINISHED CHESS MATCH ○ GO MASTERS, THE
MIKAZUKI SASAHO-GIRI • 1931 • Inagaki Hiroshi • JPN
MIKE • 1926 • Neilan Marshall • USA
MIKE • 1990 • Duggan M. B. • SHT • CND
MIKE ALONE IN THE JUNGLE • 1915 • Aylott Dave • UKN
MIKE AND JAKE AMONG THE CANNIBALS • 1913 • *Joker* • USA
MIKE AND JAKE AS HEROES • 1913 • *Joker* • USA
MIKE AND JAKE AS PUGILISTS • 1913 • *Asher Max* • USA
MIKE AND JAKE AT COLLEGE • 1913 • *Asher Max* • USA
MIKE AND JAKE AT THE BEACH • 1913 • *Asher Max* • USA
MIKE AND JAKE GO FISHING • 1913 • *Joker* • USA
MIKE AND JAKE GO IN FOR MATRIMONY • 1914 • *Joker* • USA
MIKE AND JAKE IN MEXICO • 1913 • *Joker* • USA
MIKE AND JAKE IN SOCIETY • 1913 • *Joker* • USA
MIKE AND JAKE IN THE CLUTCH OF CIRCUMSTANCES • 1914 • *Asher Max* • USA
MIKE AND JAKE IN THE WILD WEST • 1913 • *Joker* • USA
MIKE AND JAKE JOIN THE ARMY • 1914 • *Joker* • USA
MIKE AND JAKE LIVE CLOSE TO NATURE • 1914 • *Joker* • USA
MIKE AND MEYER GO FISHING • 1915 • *World* • USA
MIKE AND STEFANI • 1952 • Williams R. Maslyn • DOC • ASL
MIKE AND THE MERMAID • 1964 • *Brodie Kevin* • USA
MIKE AND THE MISER • 1916 • Aylott Dave • UKN
MIKE AND THE ZEPPELIN RAID • 1915 • Aylott Dave • UKN
MIKE BACKS THE WINNER • 1916 • Aylott Dave • UKN
MIKE DONEGAL'S ESCAPE • 1915 • *Ridgely Cleo* • USA
MIKE FRIGHT • 1934 • Meins Gus • SHT • USA
MIKE JOINS THE FORCE • 1914 • *Royal* • USA
MIKE JOINS THE FORCE • 1914 • Aylott Dave • UKN
MIKE MURPHY AS A PICTURE ACTOR • 1914 • Aylott Dave • UKN
MIKE MURPHY, BROKER'S MAN • 1914 • Aylott Dave • UKN
MIKE MURPHY, MOUNTAINEER • 1914 • Aylott Dave • UKN
MIKE MURPHY V.C. • 1914 • Aylott Dave • UKN
MIKE MURPHY'S DREAM OF LOVE AND RICHES • 1914 • Aylott Dave • UKN • MURPHY'S MILLIONS
MIKE MURPHY'S DREAM OF THE WILD WEST • 1914 • Aylott Dave • UKN
MIKE MURPHY'S MARATHON • 1915 • Aylott Dave • UKN
MIKE SEARCHES FOR HIS LONG LOST BROTHER • 1914 • *Asher Max* • USA
MIKE THE AVENGER • 1914 • *Selig* • USA
MIKE THE HOUSEMAID • 1910 • *Lubin* • USA
MIKE THE MASQUERADER • 1960 • Kneitel Seymour • ANS • USA
MIKE, THE MISER • 1911 • Merwin Bannister • USA
MIKE, THE TIMID COP • 1913 • *Kalem* • USA
MIKE WINS THE CHAMPIONSHIP • 1914 • Aylott Dave • UKN
MIKELA • 1964 • Shengelaya Eldar • SHT • USS
MIKE'S BRAINSTORM • 1912 • *Santschi Thomas* • USA
MIKE'S ELOPEMENT • 1915 • *Gordon Harold* • USA
MIKE'S GOLD MINE • 1915 • Aylott Dave • UKN
MIKE'S HERO • 1911 • *Plumer Lincoln* • USA
MIKE'S MARRIAGE see **MIKES PANTREVETE, O** • 1968
MIKE'S MURDER • 1982 • Bridges James • USA
MIKES PANTREVETE, O • 1968 • Dalianidis Ioannis • GRC • MIKE'S MARRIAGE
MIKEY AND NICKY • 1976 • May Elaine • USA
MIKHAILO LOMONOSSOV • 1955 • Ivanov Alexander • USS
MIKHALI • 1960 • Ingram John • UKN
MIKI THE SWORDSMAN see **HIRATE MIKI** • 1951
MIKIS THEODORAKIS • 1982 • Trintignant Nadine • DOC • FRN
MIKKAI • 1960 • Nakahira Ko • JPN • SECRET RENDEZVOUS, A ○ ASSIGNATION, THE
MIKKEL • 1948 • Roos Jorgen, Weismann Carl • DOC • DNM
MIKLAT, HA • 1989 • Mashrawi • ISR • SHELTER, THE (UKN)
MIKLOS AKLI see **AKLI MIKLOS** • 1986
MIKLOS BORSOS see **BORSOS MIKLOS** • 1966
MIKOLAJ KOPERNIK • 1954 • Nasfeter Janusz • SHT • PLN • NICOLAUS COPERNICUS
MIKOLAS ALES • 1951 • Krska Vaclav • CZC
MIKOSCH RUCKT EIN • 1928 • Randolf Rolf • FRG • VATER RUCKT EIN
MIKREH ISHA • 1969 • Katmor Jacques Morry • ISR • WOMAN'S CASE, A
MIKRES APHRODITES • 1962 • Koundouros Nikos • GRC • YOUNG APHRODITES (USA) ○ PETITES APHRODITES
MIKROKOSMOS • 1966 • Takacs Gabor • DOC • HNG
MIKROSKOP, DAS • 1988 • Thome Rudolf • FRG • MICROSCOPE, THE
MIKULECKE POLE • 1981 • Jires Jaromil • CZC • MIKULEK MEADOW
MIKULEK MEADOW see **MIKULECKE POLE** • 1981
MIL AMORES, EL • 1954 • Gonzalez Rogelio A. • MXC
MIL CAMINOS TIENE LA MUERTE • 1976 • Cruz Javier • MXC • THOUSAND ROADS -THOUSAND DEATHS
MIL ESTUDIANTES Y UNA MUCHACHA • 1941 • Bustillo Oro Juan • MXC
MIL GRITOS TIENE LA NOCHE • 1982 • Simon Piquer • SPN, USA, ITL • 100 CRIES HAS THE NIGHT ○ PIECES
MIL HUIT CENT QUATORZE • 1910 • Feuillade Louis • FRN
MIL MASCARAS • 1966 • Salvador Jaime • MXC
MIL MILLONES PARA UNA RUBIA • 1972 • Lazaga Pedro • SPN
MIL OJOS DEL ASESINO, LOS • 1972 • Bosch Juan • SPN
MIL Y UNA NOCHES, LAS • 1957 • Cortes Fernando • MXC
MILACEK PLUKU • 1931 • Longen • CZC • FAVORITE OF THE REGIMENT, THE
MILADY • 1922 • Diamant-Berger Henri • FRN
MILADY • 1932 • Diamant-Berger Henri • FRN
MILADY • 1975 • Leterrier Francois • FRN
MILADY AND THE MUSKETEERS (USA) see **BOIA DI LILLA, IL** • 1953
MILADY O' THE BEAN STALK • 1918 • Bertram William • USA
MILADY'S BOUDOIR • 1915 • *Rea Isabel* • USA
MILAGRO A LOS COBARDES • 1961 • Mur Oti • SPN • MIRACLE FOR THE COWARDS ○ MIRACLE OF THE COWARDS
MILAGRO BEANFIELD WAR, THE • 1987 • Redford Robert • USA
MILAGRO DE AMOR, UN • 1949 • Cortazar Ernesto • MXC
MILAGRO DE CRISTO, EL • 1940 • Elias Francisco • MXC
MILAGRO DEL CANTE, EL • 1967 • Zabalza Jose Maria • SPN • CANTE-MIRACLE
MILAGRO DEL SACRISTAN, EL • 1953 • Elorrieta Jose Maria • SPN
MILAGRO EN LA CIUDAD? • 1953 • Xiol Juan • SPN
MILAGRO EN ROMA • 1988 • Naranjo Lisandro Duque • CLM, SPN • MIRACLE IN ROME
MILAGROS DE SAN MARTIN DE PORRES • 1963 • Baledon Rafael • MXC
MILAK, DER GRONLANDJAGER • 1927 • Asagaroff Georg, Villinger Dr. • FRG
MILAN • 1946 • *Biswas Anil (M)* • IND
MILAN • 1967 • Subba Rao B. A. • IND • REUNION
MILAN NOIR • 1989 • Chammah Ronald • FRN
MILANESE STORY, A see **STORIA MILANESE, UNA** • 1962
MILANESI A NAPOLI • 1954 • Di Gianni Enzo • ITL
MILANO CALIBRO 9 • 1972 • Di Leo Fernando • ITL • CONTRACT, THE (UKN) ○ CALIBRE 9
MILANO DIFENDERSI O MORIRE • 1977 • Martucci Gianni Antonio • ITL
MILANO: IL CLAN DEI CALABRSEI • 1974 • Stegani Giorgio • ITL
MILANO MILIARDARIA • 1951 • Girolami Marino, Marchesi Marcello, Metz Vittorio • ITL
MILANO ODIA: LA POLIZIA NO PUO SPARARE • 1974 • Lenzi Umberto • ITL • ALMOST HUMAN (USA) ○ KIDNAP OF MARY LOU, THE
MILANO ROVENTE • 1973 • Lenzi Umberto • ITL
MILANO TREMA: LA POLIZIA VUOLE GIUSTIZIA • 1973 • Martino Sergio • ITL • VIOLENT PROFESSIONALS, THE (UKN) ○ POLIZIA VUOLE GIUSTIZIA, LA
MILANO VIOLENTA • 1976 • Caiano Mario • ITL
MILAREPA • 1974 • Cavani Liliana • ITL
MILCZACA GWIAZDA (PLN) see **SCHWEIGENDE STERN, DER** • 1960
MILCZACE SLADY • 1961 • Kuzminski Zbigniew • PLN • SILENT CLUES
MILCZENIE • 1963 • Kutz Kazimierz • PLN • SILENCE, THE (UKN)
MILD CARGO • 1934 • Stallings George • ANS • USA • BROWNIE BUCKS THE JUNGLE
MILD WEST, THE • 1947 • Kneitel Seymour • ANS • USA
MILDRED • 1960 • Hanna Nancy, Linnecar Vera • UKN
MILDRED PIERCE • 1945 • Curtiz Michael • USA
MILDRED'S DOLL • 1914 • *Domino* • USA
MILE, LE see **MILE DE JULES LADOUMEGUE, LE** • 1932
MILE A MINUTE • 1924 • Mattison Frank S.?, Carpenter Horace B.? • USA
MILE-A-MINUTE KENDALL • 1918 • Taylor William D. • USA
MILE A MINUTE LOVE • 1937 • Clifton Elmer • USA
MILE-A-MINUTE MAN, THE • 1926 • Nelson Jack • USA
MILE-A-MINUTE MONTY • 1915 • *Lubin* • USA
MILE-A-MINUTE MONTY • 1915 • *Essanay* • USA
MILE-A-MINUTE ROMEO • 1923 • Hillyer Lambert • USA
MILE A MINUTE (UKN) see **RIDERS OF SANTA FE** • 1944
MILE DE JULES LADOUMEGUE, LE • 1932 • Lods Jean • DCS • FRN • MILE, LE
MILENCI V ROCE JEDNA • 1973 • Balik Jaroslav • CZC • LOVERS FROM THE FIRST YEAR ○ LOVERS OF THE YEAR ONE
MILES AGAINST MINUTES • 1924 • Morrison Lee • UKN
MILES FROM HOME • 1988 • Sinise Gary • USA • FARM OF THE YEAR
MILES OF FIRE see **OGNENNYE VERSTY** • 1957
MILES TO GO • 1986 • Greene David • TVM • USA • LEAVING HOME
MILES TO GO BEFORE I SLEEP • 1973 • Cook Fielder • TVM • USA
MILESTONE MELODIES • 1925 • Butler Alexander • SER • UKN
MILESTONES • 1916 • Bentley Thomas • UKN
MILESTONES • 1920 • Scardon Paul • USA
MILESTONES • 1975 • Kramer Robert, Douglas John* • USA
MILESTONES OF LIFE • 1915 • *Anderson Mignon* • USA
MILESTONES OF THE MOVIES • 1966 • Clarke Charles G. (c/d) • USA
MILI • 1975 • Mukherjee Hrishikesh • IND
MILIAN • 1969 • Gale David, Watson Albert • UKN
MILIARDARI, I • 1957 • Malatesta Guido • ITL
MILIARDI, CHE FOLLIA! • 1942 • Brignone Guido • ITL
MILIEU, LE • 1965-66 • Garceau Raymond • DCS • CND
MILIEU DU MONDE, LE • 1975 • Tanner Alain • SWT, FRN • MIDDLE OF THE WORLD, THE
MILION ZA LAURE • 1970 • Przybyla Hieronim • PLN • ONE MILLION FOR LAURA
MILIONAIR, AL- • 1950 • Rafla Hilmy • EGY • MILLIONNAIRE, LE
MILIONARIO, O • 1962 • Queiroga Perdigao • PRT
MILIONARIO POR ILUSION • 1973 • Lugo Alfredo • VNZ • ILLUSION OF BEING A MILLIONAIRE, THE
MILIONE DI DOLLARI PER SETTE ASSASSINI, UN • 1966 • Lenzi Umberto • ITL
MILIONER • 1977 • Szyszko Sylwester • PLN • MILLIONAIRE
MILIONI NA OTAKU • 1954 • Bauer Branko • YGS • MILLIONS ON AN ISLAND
MILITAIRE ET NOURRICE • 1904 • Blache Alice • FRN
MILITANT, THE • 1914 • Daly William Robert • USA
MILITANT DES AURES, LE • 1967 • Bendeddouche Ghaouti • DCS • ALG
MILITANT SCHOOLMA'AM, A • 1915 • Mix Tom • USA
MILITANT SUFFRAGETTE see **BUSY DAY, A** • 1914
MILITANT SUFFRAGETTE, A • 1912 • *Snow Marguerite* • USA
MILITARE E MEZZO, UN • 1960 • Steno • ITL
MILITARY ACADEMY • 1950 • Lederman D. Ross • USA
MILITARY ACADEMY WITH THAT 10TH AVENUE GANG • 1950 • Lederman D. Ross • USA • SENTENCE SUSPENDED (UKN)
MILITARY AIR-SCOUT, THE • 1911 • Humphrey William • USA
MILITARY APPRENTICES see **APPRENTIS MILITAIRES, LES** • 1897
MILITARY HONOR see **HONOR MILITAR** • 1919
MILITARY JUDAS, A • 1913 • Hunt Jay • USA
MILITARY LIFE, PLEASANT LIFE see **ZIVOT VOJENSKY, ZIVOT VESELY** • 1934
MILITARY MADNESS • 1917 • *Pokes & Jabbs* • SHT • USA
MILITARY MAIDS (UKN) see **CORPORAL KATE** • 1926
MILITARY POLICEMEN (UKN) see **OFF LIMITS** • 1952
MILITARY SECRET • 1945 • Legoshin Vladimir
MILITARY TACTICS • 1904 • Collins Alf? • UKN
MILIZIA TERRITORIALE • 1935 • Bonnard Mario • ITL
MILJONAR FOR EN DAG • 1926 • Persson Edvard • SWD • MILLIONAIRE FOR A DAY
MILJONARVET • 1917 • Tallroth Konrad • SWD • MILLION INHERITANCE
MILJOONALIIGA • 1968 • Kurkvaara Maunu • FNL • MILLION GANG
MILK AND HONEY • 1988 • Yates Rebecca, Salzman Glen • CND
MILK AND MONEY • 1936 • Avery Tex • ANS • USA
MILK AND YEGGS • 1921 • Reisner Charles F. • SHT • USA
MILK FED HERO, A • 1918 • Phillips R. W. • SHT • USA
MILK-FED VAMP, A • 1917 • Kirkland David • SHT • USA
MILK FOR BABY • 1938 • Davis Mannie • ANS • USA
MILK FROM GRANGE HILL FARM • 1945-52 • Napier-Bell J. B. • DOC • UKN
MILK MAID, THE • 1905 • Collins Alf? • UKN
MILK WE DRINK, THE • 1913 • Sennett Mack • DOC • USA
MILK WHITE FLAG, A • 1916 • Heffron Thomas N. • SHT • USA
MILKA -A FILM ABOUT TABOOS see **MILKA -ELOKUVA TABUISTA** • 1980
MILKA -ELOKUVA TABUISTA • 1980 • Mollberg Rauni • FNL • MILKA -A FILM ABOUT TABOOS ○ TABU
MILKFED BOY, THE • 1914 • *Willis Paul* • USA
MILKMAID, THE • 1955 • Sarkka Toivo • FNL
MILKMAN, THE • 1932 • *Iwerks Ub (P)* • ANS • USA

MILKMAN, THE • 1950 • Barton Charles T. • USA
MILKMAN FROM MAEKULA • 1966 • Laius Leida • USS
MILKMAN'S REVENGE, THE • 1913 • *Chamberlain Riley* • USA
MILKMAN'S WEDDING, THE • 1907 • Fitzhamon Lewin • UKN
MILKO! see **TRIALS OF A MILKMAN, THE** • 1916
MILKY WAIF, THE • 1946 • Hanna William, Barbera Joseph • ANS • USA
MILKY WAY, THE • 1917 • *Barry Eddie* • USA
MILKY WAY, THE • 1922 • Van Dyke W. S. • USA
MILKY WAY, THE • 1936 • McCarey Leo • USA
MILKY WAY, THE • 1940 • Ising Rudolf • ANS • USA
MILKY WAY, THE see **INNOCENTS OF CHICAGO, THE** • 1932
MILKY WAY, THE see **SAMANYOLU** • 1967
MILKY WAY, THE see **VOIE LACTEE, LA** • 1968
MILL, THE see **KVARNEN** • 1921
MILL, THE see **MLYN** • 1971
MILL, THE see **TAHUNA AL AMM FABRE** • 1987
MILL BUYERS, THE • 1912 • Salter Harry • USA
MILL BY THE ZUYDER ZEE, THE • 1915 • *Borzage Frank* • USA
MILL GIRL, THE • 1913 • Buckland Warwick? • UKN
MILL OF LIFE, THE • 1914 • *Costello Maurice* • USA
MILL OF LUCK AND PLENTY, THE see **MOARA CU NOROC** • 1956
MILL OF THE GODS, THE • 1911 • *Solax* • USA
MILL OF THE STONE MAIDENS see **MULINO DELLE DONNE DI PIETRA, IL** • 1960
MILL OF THE STONE WOMEN (USA) see **MULINO DELLE DONNE DI PIETRA, IL** • 1960
MILL ON THE FLOSS, THE • 1915 • Moore W. Eugene • USA
MILL ON THE FLOSS, THE • 1937 • Whelan Tim • UKN
MILL ON THE HEATH, THE • 1913 • Calvert Charles? • UKN
MILL ON THE PO, THE see **MULINO DEL PO, IL** • 1949
MILL ON THE RIVER see **MULINO DEL PO, IL** • 1949
MILL-OWNER'S DAUGHTER, THE see **LITTLE MAYORESS, THE** • 1916
MILL PILL see **MILLIPILLERI** • 1966
MILL POND • 1929 • Foster John • ANS • USA
MILL STREAM, THE • 1914 • *Baggot King* • USA
MILLARIO A GO GO • 1965 • Cortes Fernando • MXC, PRC
MILLBROOK REPORT, THE see **REPORT FROM MILLBROOK** • 1966
MILLE AL MINUTO see **1000 CHILOMETRI AL MINUTO** • 1940
MILLE BAISERS DE FLORENCE • 1970 • Gilles Guy • FRN
MILLE CHILOMETRI PER UNA LETTERA • 1910 • Novelli Enrico • ITL
MILLE DI GARIBALDI, I • 1933 • Blasetti Alessandro • ITL • GESUZZA, LA SPOSA GARIBALDINA ◦ 1860
MILLE DOLLARI SUL NERO • 1966 • Cardone Alberto • ITL
MILLE E UNA DONNA • 1964 • Loy Mino • DOC • ITL • THOUSAND AND ONE WOMEN, A
MILLE E UNA NOTTE ALL'ITALIANA • 1972 • Infascelli Carlo, Racioppi Antonio • ITL
MILLE E UNA NOTTE.. E UN'ALTRA ANCORA • 1972 • Bomba Enrico • ITL
MILLE ET DEUXIEME NUIT, LA • 1933 • Volkov Alexander • FRN
MILLE ET UNE MAINS, LES see **ALF YAD WA YAD** • 1972
MILLE ET UNE NUITS, LES (FRN) see **MERAVIGLIE DI ALADINO, LE** • 1962
MILLE ET UNE PERVERSIONS DE FELICIA, LES • 1975 • Pecas Max • FRN
MILLE, I • 1912 • Caserini Mario • ITL
MILLE LIRE AL MESE • 1939 • Neufeld Max • ITL
MILLE MIGLIA • 1953 • Mason Bill • DOC • UKN
MILLE MILLIARDS DE DOLLARS • 1981 • Verneuil Henri • FRN
MILLE MOTS • 1973 • Mingrone Massimo • ITL, CND • THOUSAND WORDS, A
MILLE-PATTES FAIT DES CLAQUETTES, LE • 1977 • Girault Jean • FRN
MILLE PECCATI.. NESSUNA VIRTU • 1969 • Martino Sergio • ITL • MONDO SEX (UKN)
MILLE VILLAGES • 1960 • Vilardebo Carlos ◦ SHT • FRN
MILLENIUM • 1989 • Anderson Michael • CND
MILLENIUM JUMP • 1946 • Crouch William Forest • SHT • USA
MILLER AND HIS SON, THE • Molas Zet • CZC
MILLER AND THE SWEEP, THE • 1897 • Paul Robert William? • UKN
MILLER AND THE SWEEP, THE • 1897 • Smith G. A. • UKN
MILLER AND THE SWEEP, THE (NO.2) • 1897 • Smith G. A. • UKN
MILLER KARAFIAT, THE see **PAN OTEC KARAFIAT** • 1935
MILLER OF BURGUNDY, THE • 1912 • Eagle Oscar • USA
MILLER ON THE BLACK RIVER, THE see **MOLNAR A CSERNA REKAN** • 1974
MILLER'S BEAUTIFUL WIFE, THE (USA) see **BELLA MUGNAIA, LA** • 1955
MILLER'S CROSSING • 1989 • Coen Joel • USA
MILLER'S DAUGHTER • 1905 • Porter Edwin S. • USA
MILLER'S DAUGHTER, THE • 1934 • Freleng Friz • ANS • USA
MILLER'S DOCUMENT, THE see **MILLERS DOKUMENT** • 1916
MILLERS DOKUMENT • 1916 • Tallroth Konrad • SWD • MILLER'S DOCUMENT, THE
MILLER'S WIFE, THE see **BELLA MUGNAIA, LA** • 1955
MILLERSON CASE, THE • 1947 • Archainbaud George • USA • CRIME DOCTOR'S VACATION, THE
MILLES ET UN MILLIONS, LES see **TOUTE LA VILLE ACCUSE** • 1955
MILLHOUSE -A WHITE COMEDY • 1971 • De Antonio Emile • USA
MILLI FJALLS OG FJORU • 1948 • Gudmundsson Loftur • ICL • FROM MOUNTAIN TO SEASHORE ◦ BETWEEN MOUNTAIN AND SHORE
MILLIARD DANS UN BILLIARD, UN • 1965 • Gessner Nicolas • FRN, ITL, FRG • ALLARME IN CINQUE BANCHE (ITL) ◦ DIAMANTEN-BILLARD (FRG) ◦ DIAMONDS ARE BRITTLE (UKN)
MILLIARDAIRE! see **EXTRAVAGANTE MISSION, L'** • 1945
MILLIARDAIRE, LA • Geral Hubert • FRN
MILLIARDENSOUPER, DAS • 1923 • Janson Victor • FRG
MILLIARDENTESTAMENT, DAS • 1920 • Seitz Franz • FRG
MILLIE • 1931 • Dillon John Francis • USA
MILLIEME FENETRE, LA • 1960 • Menegoz Robert • DOC • FRN
MILLIE'S DAUGHTER • 1947 • Salkow Sidney • USA
MILLINER, THE • 1920 • *Lukas Paul* • HNG
MILLINERY BOMB, A • 1913 • North Wilfred • USA
MILLINERY MAN, THE • 1915 • *Clayton Ethel* • USA
MILLINERY MIX-UP, A • 1914 • Seay Charles M. • USA
MILLING THE MILITANT • 1914 • *Royal* • USA
MILLING THE MILITANTS • 1913 • Stow Percy • UKN
MILLION, LE • 1931 • Clair Rene • FRN
MILLION, THE • 1915 • *Abeles Edward* • USA
MILLION A MINUTE, A • 1916 • Noble John W. • USA
MILLION BID, A • 1914 • Ince Ralph • USA
MILLION BID, A • 1927 • Curtiz Michael • USA
MILLION DOLLAR BABY • 1935 • Santley Joseph • USA
MILLION DOLLAR BABY • 1941 • Bernhardt Curtis • USA • MISS WHEELWRIGHT DISCOVERS AMERICA
MILLION DOLLAR BABY • 1974 • Beresford Bruce • MTV • ASL
MILLION DOLLAR BRIDE, THE • 1914 • *Komic* • USA
MILLION DOLLAR CAT • 1944 • Hanna William, Barbera Joseph • ANS • USA
MILLION DOLLAR CHASE see **IPPATSU DAIBOKEN** • 1968
MILLION DOLLAR COLLAR, THE • 1929 • Lederman D. Ross • USA
MILLION DOLLAR COLLAR, THE • 1963 • McEveety Vincent • USA
MILLION DOLLAR DIAMOND see **DIAMOND, THE** • 1954
MILLION DOLLAR DIXIE DELIVERANCE, THE • 1978 • Mayberry Russ • TVM • USA
MILLION DOLLAR DOLLIES, THE • 1918 • Perret Leonce • USA
MILLION DOLLAR DUCK, THE • 1971 • McEveety Vincent • USA
MILLION DOLLAR FACE • 1981 • O'Herlihy Michael • TVM • USA
MILLION DOLLAR GHOST see **MAN WHO WOULDN'T DIE, THE** • 1942
MILLION DOLLAR HANDICAP, THE • 1925 • Sidney Scott • USA • PRIDE OF THE PADDOCK, THE
MILLION DOLLAR INFIELD • 1982 • Cooper Hal • TVM • USA
MILLION DOLLAR JOB see **FILM JOHNNIE, A** • 1914
MILLION DOLLAR KID • 1944 • Fox Wallace • USA
MILLION DOLLAR LEGS • 1932 • Cline Eddie • USA
MILLION DOLLAR LEGS • 1939 • Grinde Nick, Dmytryk Edward (U/c) • USA
MILLION DOLLAR MADNESS • 1985 • Goldwasser Yankul • ISR
MILLION DOLLAR MAN (UKN) see **HOMME QUI VALAIT DES MILLIARDS, L'** • 1967
MILLION DOLLAR MANHUNT (USA) see **ASSIGNMENT REDHEAD** • 1956
MILLION DOLLAR MERMAID • 1953 • LeRoy Mervyn • USA • ONE-PIECE BATHING SUIT, THE (UKN)
MILLION DOLLAR MIX-UP, THE • 1909 • *Selig* • USA
MILLION DOLLAR MYSTERY • 1927 • Hunt Charles J. • USA
MILLION DOLLAR MYSTERY • 1987 • Fleischer Richard • USA • MONEY MANIA
MILLION DOLLAR MYSTERY, THE • 1914 • Hansel Howell • SRL • USA
MILLION DOLLAR NOTES • 1935 • Waller Fred • SHT • USA
MILLION DOLLAR PROFILE see **SMARTEST GIRL IN TOWN, THE** • 1936
MILLION DOLLAR PURSUIT • 1951 • Springsteen R. G. • USA
MILLION DOLLAR RACKET • 1937 • Hill Robert F. • USA
MILLION DOLLAR RANSOM • 1934 • Roth Murray • USA
MILLION DOLLAR RIP-OFF, THE • 1976 • Singer Alexander • TVM • USA • MONEY TO BURN
MILLION DOLLAR ROBBERY, THE • 1914 • Blache Alice • USA
MILLION DOLLAR SMASH, A • 1916 • *Hutton Lucille* • SHT • USA
MILLION DOLLAR SWINDLE, THE see **PUBLIC DEFENDER, THE** • 1931
MILLION DOLLAR TATTOO see **TATOUE, LE** • 1968
MILLION DOLLAR TRIO • 1952 • Dassin Jules • SHT • USA
MILLION DOLLAR WEEKEND • 1948 • Raymond Gene • USA
MILLION DOLLARS, A • 1913 • *Karr Darwin* • USA
MILLION DOLLARS, A see **DOLLARMILJONEN** • 1926
MILLION DOLLARS SNATCH see **CH'I-PAI-WAN TA CHIEH-AN** • 1976
MILLION FOR A BABY, A • 1916 • Beaumont Harry • SHT • USA
MILLION FOR LOVE, A • 1928 • Hill Robert F. • USA
MILLION FOR MARY, A • 1916 • Berger Rea • USA
MILLION GANG see **MILJOONALIIGA** • 1968
MILLION GIRLS, A see **HYAKUMAN-NIN NO MUSUMETACHI** • 1963
MILLION-HARE, THE • 1963 • McKimson Robert • ANS • USA
MILLION HID, A • 1915 • *Superba* • USA
MILLION IN JEWELS, A • 1914 • *Holmes Helen* • USA
MILLION IN PEARLS, A • 1914 • *Victor* • USA
MILLION IN SIGHT, A • 1917 • Chaudet Louis W. • SHT • USA
MILLION INHERITANCE see **MILJONARVET** • 1917
MILLION POUND NOTE, THE • 1953 • Neame Ronald • UKN • MAN WITH A MILLION (USA)
MILLION POUND NOTE, THE see **EGYMILLIO FONTOS BANKO, AS** • 1916
MILLION RYO MONEY POT, THE see **HYAKUMAN-RYO NO TSUBO** • 1935
MILLION TO BURN, A • 1923 • Parke William • USA
MILLION TO ONE, A • 1937 • Shores Lynn • USA
MILLION TOUT-PUISSANT, LE • 1985 • Moreau Michel • CND
MILLIONAERDRENGEN see **NED MED MILLIONAERDRENGEN** • 1913
MILLIONAIRE see **MILIONER** • 1977
MILLIONAIRE, THE • 1917 • Gillstrom Arvid E. • SHT • USA
MILLIONAIRE, THE • 1921 • Conway Jack • USA
MILLIONAIRE, THE • 1927 • Micheaux Oscar • USA
MILLIONAIRE, THE • 1931 • Adolfi John G. • USA
MILLIONAIRE, THE • 1978 • Weis Don • TVM • USA
MILLIONAIRE AL MOUZAYYAF, AL • 1968 • el Saifi Hassan • EGY • PHONEY MILLIONAIRE, THE
MILLIONAIRE AND THE GOOSE, THE • 1913 • *Brennan John E.* • USA
MILLIONAIRE AND THE RANCH GIRL, THE • 1910 • *Anderson Broncho Billy* • USA
MILLIONAIRE AND THE SQUATTER, THE • 1911 • *Essanay* • USA
MILLIONAIRE BABY, THE • 1915 • Marston Lawrence • USA
MILLIONAIRE BARBER, THE • 1911 • *Essanay* • USA
MILLIONAIRE BILLIE • 1916 • Greene Clay M. • SHT • USA
MILLIONAIRE CABBY, THE • 1915 • Martin E. A. • USA
MILLIONAIRE CAT, THE • 1932 • Sandrich Mark • SHT • USA
MILLIONAIRE COP, THE • 1912 • *Baggot King* • USA
MILLIONAIRE COWBOY • 1915 • Sandberg Anders W. • DNM
MILLIONAIRE COWBOY, THE • 1913 • *Winterhoff Carl* • USA • COWBOY MILLIONAIRE, THE
MILLIONAIRE COWBOY, THE • 1924 • Garson Harry • USA
MILLIONAIRE DROOPY • 1956 • Avery Tex • ANS • USA
MILLIONAIRE ENGINEER, THE • 1915 • Lessey George A. • USA
MILLIONAIRE FOR A DAY • 1920 • Empey Arthur Guy • USA
MILLIONAIRE FOR A DAY see **MILJONAR FOR EN DAG** • 1926
MILLIONAIRE FOR A DAY, A • 1912 • *Cumpson John* • USA
MILLIONAIRE FOR A DAY, A • 1921 • North Wilfred • USA
MILLIONAIRE FOR A DAY (UKN) see **LET'S BE RITZY** • 1934
MILLIONAIRE FOR A MINUTE, A • 1915 • Curtis Allen • USA
MILLIONAIRE FOR CHRISTY, A • 1951 • Marshall George • USA • NO ROOM FOR THE GROOM
MILLIONAIRE HOBO • 1939 • *Mintz Charles (P)* • ANS • USA
MILLIONAIRE IN TROUBLE • 1978 • Silberg Joel • ISR
MILLIONAIRE KID • 1936 • Ray Bernard B. • USA
MILLIONAIRE MERRY-GO-ROUND see **KICKING THE MOON AROUND** • 1938
MILLIONAIRE MILKMAN, THE • 1910 • *Thanhouser* • USA
MILLIONAIRE ORPHAN, THE • 1926 • Horner Robert J. • USA
MILLIONAIRE PAUPERS, THE • 1915 • De Grasse Joseph • USA
MILLIONAIRE PAUPERS, THE • 1919 • *National Film Corp. Of America* • SHT • USA
MILLIONAIRE PIRATE, THE • 1919 • Julian Rupert • USA
MILLIONAIRE PLAYBOY, THE • 1940 • Goodwins Leslie • USA • GLAMOUR BOY (UKN)
MILLIONAIRE PLAYBOY (UKN) see **PARK AVENUE LOGGER** • 1937
MILLIONAIRE PLUNGER, THE • 1916 • Horne James W. • SHT • USA
MILLIONAIRE POLICEMAN, THE • 1926 • Le Saint Edward J. • USA
MILLIONAIRE TRAMP, A • 1910 • *Motograph* • USA
MILLIONAIRE VAGABONDS, THE • 1912 • Parker Lem B. • USA
MILLIONAIRE VAGRANT, THE • 1917 • Schertzinger Victor • USA
MILLIONAIRE WHO STOLE THE SUN, THE see **O MILIONARI, KTERY UKRADL SLUNCE** • 1948
MILLIONAIRE WOMEN see **MILLIONAIRE'S WOMEN** • 1969
MILLIONAIRES • 1926 • Raymaker Herman C. • USA
MILLIONAIRE'S ADVENTURE, THE • 1910 • *Lubin* • USA
MILLIONAIRES BY MISTAKE • 1916 • *Hamilton Lloyd V.* • USA
MILLIONAIRE'S DOUBLE, THE • 1917 • Davenport Harry • USA
MILLIONAIRES FOR A DAY see **MILLIONNAIRES D'UN JOUR** • 1949
MILLIONAIRE'S HUNDRED DOLLAR BILL, THE • 1915 • Humphrey William • USA
MILLIONAIRES IN PRISON • 1940 • McCarey Ray • USA
MILLIONAIRE'S NEPHEW, THE • 1911 • Bouwmeester Theo • UKN
MILLIONAIRE'S SON, THE • 1916 • Horkheimer H. M., Horkheimer E. D. • SHT • USA
MILLIONAIRE'S WARD, THE • 1913 • *Standing Jack* • USA
MILLIONAIRE'S WOMEN • 1969 • USA • MILLIONAIRE WOMEN
MILLIONAIRESS, THE • 1960 • Asquith Anthony • UKN
MILLIONAIRHA-YE-GORESNE • 1967 • Riyahi Esmaeil • IRN • POOR MILLIONAIRES
MILLIONAR, DER see **GELD INS HAUS** • 1945
MILLIONAR FUR 3 TAGE • 1963 • Sedlmayer • MTV • FRG
MILLIONARE see **ICH MOCHT' SO GERN MIR DIR ALLEIN SEIN** • 1937
MILLIONEN AUF DER STRASSE see **MILLIONENRAUB 1** • 1921
MILLIONEN DER YVETTE, DIE • 1956 • Hellberg Martin • GDR • YVETTE'S MILLIONS
MILLIONEN-MINE, THE • 1914 • Piel Harry • FRG
MILLIONENDIEB, DER see **MANN OHNE NAMEN 1, DER** • 1920-21
MILLIONENERBSCHAFT • 1937 • Rabenalt Arthur M. • AUS
MILLIONENERBSCHAFT, DIE • 1920 • Halm Alfred • FRG
MILLIONENKOMPAGNIE, DIE • 1925 • Sauer Fred • FRG
MILLIONENMADEL, DAS • 1919 • Halm Alfred • FRG
MILLIONENRAUB 1 • 1921 • Wellin Arthur • FRG • MILLIONEN AUF DER STRASSE
MILLIONENRAUB IM RIVIERAEXPRESS • 1927 • Delmont Joseph • FRG
MILLIONENSCHIEBER • 1922 • Walther-Fein Rudolf • FRG
MILLIONENSCHUSTER, DER • 1916 • Schmelter Franz • FRG
MILLIONENTESTAMENT, DAS • 1932 • Engels Erich • FRG • QUERKOPF, DER
MILLIONNAIRE, LE see **MILIONAIR, AL-** • 1950
MILLIONNAIRES D'UN JOUR • 1949 • Hunebelle Andre • FRN • SIMPLE CASE OF MONEY, A (USA) ◦ MILLIONAIRES FOR A DAY
MILLIONS • 1936 • Hiscott Leslie • UKN • KING OF CLOVES, THE
MILLIONS DE LA BONNE, LES • 1913 • Feuillade Louis • FRN
MILLIONS DE MA TANTE, LES • 1933 • de Limur Jean • FRN
MILLIONS EN FUITE, LES see **FLUGTEN FRA MILLIONERNE** • 1934
MILLIONS FOR DEFENCE • 1914 • Davis Ulysses • USA
MILLIONS IN BUSINESS AS USUAL • 1959 • Burckhardt Rudy • SHT • USA
MILLIONS IN FLIGHT (USA) see **FLUGTEN FRA MILLIONERNE** • 1934
MILLIONS IN STORE see **DEVIL AND MISS JONES, THE** • 1941
MILLIONS IN THE AIR • 1935 • McCarey Ray • USA

MILLIONS LIKE US • 1943 • Launder Frank, Gilliat Sidney • UKN • WOMEN WITHOUT UNIFORM
MILLIONS ON AN ISLAND see **MILIONI NA OTAKU** • 1954
MILLIPILL, THE see **MILLIPILLERI** • 1966
MILLIPILLERI • 1966 • Kokkonen Ere, Virtanen Jukka, Pasanen Spede, Praeger Stanley, Gentili Giorgio, Gentili Giorgio • FNL • MILLIPILL, THE ◦ MILL PILL ◦ DOLLARO PER 7 VIGLIACCHI, UN ◦ TESTAMENTO DE MADIGAN, EL ◦ MADIGAN'S MILLIONS
MILLON EN LA BASURA, UN • 1967 • Forque Jose Maria • SPN
MILLONARIA, LA • 1937 • Momplet Antonio • ARG
MILLONARIO POR UN DIA • 1963 • Cahen Enrique • SPN
MILLONES DE CHAFLAN LOS • 1938 • Aguilar Rolando • MXC
MILLONES DE POLICHINELA, LOS • 1941 • Delgras Gonzalo • SPN
MILLS BLUE RHYTHM BAND • 1933 • Mack Roy • SHT • USA
MILLS BROTHERS ON PARADE, THE • 1956 • *Mills Brothers* • SHT • USA
MILLS OF HELL see **MALOM A POKOLBAN** • 1987
MILLS OF POWER, THE see **TISSERANDS DU POUVOIR, LES** • 1988
MILLS OF THE GODS • 1935 • Neill R. William • USA
MILLS OF THE GODS, THE • 1909 • Griffith D. W. • USA
MILLS OF THE GODS, THE • 1912 • *Nestor* • USA
MILLS OF THE GODS, THE • 1912 • Ince Ralph • *Vitagraph* • USA
MILLS OF THE GODS, THE • 1914 • Hunt Jay • USA
MILLS OF THE GODS, THE see **GOTTES MUHLEN MAHLEN LANGSAM** • 1939
MILLS OF THE GODS: VIET NAM, THE • 1965 • Fox Beryl • DOC • CND
MILLSTONE, THE • 1917 • *Erbograph* • USA
MILLSTONE, THE see **TOUCH OF LOVE, A** • 1969
MILLSTONES • 1916 • *Karr Darwin* • SHT • USA
MILLY, MARIA AND I see **MILLY, MARIA OCH JAG** • 1938
MILLY, MARIA OCH JAG • 1938 • Gregers Emanuel • DNM • MILLY, MARIA AND I
MILO BARUS, DER STARKSTE MANN DER WELT • 1983 • Stegmuller Henning • FRG
MILORD L'ARSOVILLE • 1955 • Haguet Andre • FRN
MILOSC AZPICBRODKI • 1978 • Rzeszewski Janusz, Jahoda Mieczyslaw • PLN • LOVE OF THE POINTED BEARD
MILOSC DWUDZIESTOLATKOW see **AMOUR A VINGT ANS, L'** • 1962
MILOSC WSZYSTKO ZWYCIEZA • 1936 • Krawicz Mecislas • PLN
MILOU EN MAI • 1989 • Malle Louis • FRN, ITL • MILOU IN MAY (UKN)
MILOU IN MAY (UKN) see **MILOU EN MAI** • 1989
MILPITAS MONSTER, THE • 1975 • Burrill Robert L. • USA
MILTON • 1912 • Desfontaines Henri • FRN
MILTON • 1965 • Wolman Dan • ISR
MILTON MYSTERY, THE see **RECEIVED PAYMENT** • 1922
MIME MARCEAU, LE • 1965 • Delouche Dominique • SHT • FRN
MIMESIS • 1966 • Sibianu Gheorghe • ANM • RMN
MIMETISM • 1964 • *Bucharesti* • ANS • RMN
MIMI • 1935 • Stein Paul L. • UKN • BOHEME, LA
MIMI BLUETTE FIORE DEL MIO GIARDINO • 1976 • Di Palma Carlo • ITL
MIMI FIORE DI PORTO • 1919 • D'Ambra Lucio • ITL
MIMI LA DOUCE • 1968 • *Fearless Productions* • USA
MIMI METALLURGICO FERITO NELL'ONORE • 1972 • Wertmuller Lina • ITL • SEDUCTION OF MIMI, THE (USA) ◦ MIMI THE METALWORKER ◦ WOUNDED IN HONOUR
MIMI PINSON • 1923 • Bergerat Theo • FRN
MIMI PINSON • 1958 • Darene Robert • FRN
MIMI THE METALWORKER see **MIMI METALLURGICO FERITO NELL'ONORE** • 1972
MIMI THE PROPHET see **PROFETA MIMI, EL** • 1972
MIMI-TROTTIN • 1921 • Andreani Henri • FRN
MIMINASHI HACCHI • 1970 • *Toho* • ANS • JPN
MIMINO • 1977 • Daneliya Georgi • USS
MIMIZUKO SEPPO • 1958 • Hisamatsu Seiji • JPN • OWL LECTURE
MIMOSA • 1910 • Perret Leonce • FRN
MIMOSA'S SWEETHEART • 1913 • *Mace Fred* • USA
MIMOZA • 1974 • Szpakowicz Piotr • PLN
MIN AGL IMRA'A • 1959 • el Sheikh Kamal • EGY • POUR UNE FEMME
MIN AGLI HUBBI • 1959 • el Sheikh Kamal • EGY • POUR MON AMOUR
MIN ALSKANDE • 1979 • Grede Kjell • SWD • MY BELOVED ◦ MY LOVE
MIN AND BILL • 1930 • Hill George W. • USA • DARK STAR
MIN BEDSTEFAR ER EN STOK • 1967 • Henning-Jensen Astrid • DNM • MY GRANDFATHER IS A STICK
MIN FARMORS HUS • 1984 • Pedersen Frode • DNM • GRANDMA'S HOUSE
MIN FORSTE MONOCLE • 1911 • Blom August • DNM • HERR STORMS FORSTE MONOCLE ◦ HIS FIRST MONOCLE
MIN FRU HAR EN FASTMAN • 1926 • Berthels Theodor • SWD
MIN KARA AR EN ROS • 1963 • Ekman Hasse • SWD • MY LOVE IS A ROSE ◦ MY LOVE IS LIKE A ROSE
MIN KONES FERIE • 1967 • Hilbard John • DNM • MY WIFE'S HOLIDAY
MIN MARION • 1975 • Muller Nils R. • NRW
MIN QURB AS-SAFSAF • 1972 • Haddad Moussa • ALG • AUPRES DU PEUPLIER ◦ SOUS LE PEUPLIER
MIN SOSTERS BORN NAR DE ER VAERST • 1971 • Reenberg Annelise • DNM
MIN SOSTERS BORN PA BRYLLUPSREJSE • 1967 • Reenberg Annelise • DNM • MY SISTER'S CHILDREN ON HONEYMOON
MIN SOSTERS BORN VAELTER BYEN • 1968 • Reenberg Annelise • DNM • MY SISTER'S CHILDREN ARE PAINTING THE TOWN RED
MIN SVARMOR DANSOSEN • 1936 • Brooks Thor L. • SWD • MY MOTHER-IN-LAW THE DANCER
MIN SYSTER OCH JAG • 1950 • Bauman Schamyl • SWD • MY SISTER AND I
MIN VAN BALTHAZAR (SWD) see **AU HASARD BALTHAZAR** • 1966
MIN VAN OSCAR (SWD) see **MON PHOQUE ET ELLES** • 1951
MIN VEN LEVY • 1914 • Holger-Madsen • DNM • MY FRIEND LEVY
MINA, LA • 1958 • Bennati Giuseppe • ITL
MINA AL-QALB LI AL-QALB • 1951 • Barakat Henry • EGY • DE COEUR DE COEUR
MINA CYCLE see **DAYEREH MINA** • 1974
MINA DE ORO • 1974 • Cosmi Carlo, Hohermuth Harold • DOC • VNZ • GOLDMINE
MINA DE VANGHEL see **CRIMES DE L'AMOUR, LES** • 1951
MINA DROMMARS STAD • 1976 • Skogsberg Ingvar • SWD • CITY OF MY DREAMS ◦ MY DREAM CITY
MINA.. FUORI LA GUARDIA • 1961 • Tamburella Armando W. • ITL
MINA, THE WIND OF LIBERTY see **MINA: VIENTO DE LIBERTAD** • 1976
MINA: VIENTO DE LIBERTAD • 1976 • Eceiza Antonio • MXC, CUB • MINA, THE WIND OF LIBERTY
MINAGOROSHI NO KENJU • 1967 • Hasebe Yasuharu • JPN • MASSACRE GUN, THE
MINAGOROSHI NO REIKA • 1968 • Kato Yasushi • JPN • I, THE EXECUTIONER
MINAMATA FOR MEDICAL SCIENCE • 1974 • Tsuchimoto Noriaki • DOC • JPN
MINAMATA IKKI • 1972 • Tsuchimoto Noriaki • JPN • REVOLT OF THE MINAMATA VICTIMS
MINAMATA, ITS 30 YEARS see **MINAMATA, SONO 30 NEN** • 1988
MINAMATA -KANJASAN TO SONO SEKAI • 1971 • Tsuchimoto Noriaki • DOC • JPN • MINAMATA (USA)
MINAMATA, SONO 30 NEN • 1988 • Tsuchimoto Noriaki • DOC • JPN • MINAMATA, ITS 30 YEARS
MINAMATA (USA) see **MINAMATA -KANJASAN TO SONO SEKAI** • 1971
MINAMI KAZE • 1939 • Shibuya Minoru • JPN • SOUTH WIND
MINAMI NO KAZE • 1942 • Yoshimura Kozaburo • JPN • SOUTH WIND
MINAMI NO KAZE TO NAMI • 1961 • Hashimoto S. • JPN • SOUTH WIND AND WAVES
MINAMI NO SHIMA NI YUKI GA FURA • 1961 • Hisamatsu Seiji • JPN • SNOW IN THE SOUTH SEAS (USA)
MINAMI-TAIHEIYO NAMI TAKASHI • 1962 • Watanabe Kunio • JPN • KAMIKAZE -SUICIDE SOLDIER, THE
MINAMI TAIHEIYO NO WAKADAISHO • 1967 • Furusawa Kengo • JPN • JUDO CHAMPION
MINAMOTO NO YOSHITSUNE • 1955 • Hagiwara Ryo • JPN • FUGITIVE HERO
MINAS BLOOD see **SANGUE MINEIRO** • 1929
MINAS DE PENACOVA • 1915 • de Albuquerque Ernesto • SHT • PRT
MINASHIGO HACCHI OTSUKISAMANO MAMA • 1971 • *Toho* • ANS • JPN
MINATO NO UWAKIKAZE • 1936 • Toyoda Shiro • JPN • HARBOUR OF FICKLE WINDS
MINCE MEET • 1968 • Douglas James* • ANS • USA
MIND BENDERS, THE • 1962 • Dearden Basil • UKN • PIT, THE
MIND BLOWER see **MIND BLOWERS** • 1970
MIND BLOWERS • 1970 • *Janus Ii Productions* • USA • MINDBLOWERS ◦ MIND BLOWER
MIND BLOWERS, THE • 1968 • Renvok Harlan • USA
MIND CURE, THE • 1912 • Smalley Phillips • USA
MIND-DETECTING RAY, THE see **LELEKLATO SUGAR** • 1918
MIND GAMES • 1989 • Yari Bob • USA
MIND KILLER • 1987 • Krueger Michael • USA • BRAIN CREATURE ◦ MINDKILLER
MIND MACHINE see **BRAIN MACHINE, THE** • 1972
MIND NEEDER, THE • 1938 • Lord Del • SHT • USA
MIND OF MR. REEDER, THE • 1939 • Raymond Jack • UKN • MYSTERIOUS MR. REEDER, THE (USA)
MIND OF MR. SOAMES, THE • 1969 • Cooke Alan • UKN
MIND OF NICOLAS POUSSIN -THE SEVEN SACRAMENTS, THE • 1968 • Ashton Dudley Shaw • DOC • UKN • POUSSIN -THE SEVEN SACRAMENTS
MIND OVER MOTOR • 1915 • Calvert E. H. • USA
MIND OVER MOTOR • 1923 • Lascelle Ward • USA
MIND OVER MOUSE • 1947 • Yates Hal • SHT • USA
MIND OVER MURDER • 1979 • Nagy Ivan • TVM • USA • ARE YOU ALONE TONIGHT?
MIND READER, THE • 1908 • *Pathe* • FRN
MIND READER, THE • 1933 • Del Ruth Roy • USA
MIND SHADOWS • 1988 • Honigmann Hedy • CND, NTH • HORSENSCHIMMEN ◦ HERSENSCHIMMEN ◦ OUT OF MIND
MIND SNATCHERS, THE • 1972 • Girard Bernard • USA • HAPPINESS CAGE, THE
MIND-SWEEPERS • Hunt Paul • USA
MIND THE BABY • 1912 • *Cosmopolitan Films* • UKN
MIND THE PAINT • 1912 • Stow Percy • UKN
MIND-THE-PAINT-GIRL • 1916 • *Famous Players* • USA
MIND THE PAINT GIRL see **MIND-THE-PAINT GIRL, THE** • 1919
MIND-THE-PAINT GIRL, THE • 1919 • North Wilfred • USA • MIND THE PAINT GIRL
MIND THE WET PAINT • 1903 • Collins Alf? • UKN
MIND WARP see **BRAIN MACHINE, THE** • 1972
MIND YOUR OWN BUSINESS • 1907 • Smith Jack ? • UKN
MIND YOUR OWN BUSINESS • 1936 • McLeod Norman Z. • USA
MINDANAO • 1968 • Borlaza Emmanuel • PHL
MINDBLOWERS see **MIND BLOWERS** • 1970
MINDEN KEZDET NEHEZ • 1966 • Revesz Gyorgy • HNG • EVERY BEGINNING IS HARD ◦ ALL BEGINNINGS ARE HARD
MINDEN SZERDAN • 1980 • Gyarmathy Livia • HNG • EVERY WEDNESDAY
MINDENNAP ELUNK • 1963 • Renyi Tamas • HNG • TWO DAYS -LIKE THE OTHERS
MINDENNAPI TORTENETEK • 1955 • Meszaros Marta • DCS • HNG • EVERYDAY STORIES
MINDER: AN OFFICER AND A CAR SALESMAN • 1988 • Baker Roy Ward • TVM • UKN
MINDER GELUKKIGE TERUGKEER VAN JOSZEF KATUS NAAR HET LAND VAN REMBRANDT, DE see **JOSZEF KATUS** • 1966
MINDERJAHRIGE, DIE • 1921 • Tostary Alfred • FRG
MINDFIELD • 1990 • Lord Jean-Claude • CND
MINDING THE BABY • 1917 • *Cub* • USA
MINDING THE BABY • 1917 • Clements Roy • *Nestor* • SHT • USA
MINDING THE BABY • 1931 • *Mintz Charles (P)* • ANS • USA
MINDING THE BABY • 1931 • Fleischer Dave • ANS • USA
MINDKILLER see **MIND KILLER** • 1987
MIND'S AWAKENING, THE • 1914 • *Larkin Dolly* • USA
MINDSCAPE see **PAYSAGISTE, LE** • 1976
MINDWARP: AN INFINITY OF TERROR see **GALAXY OF TERROR** • 1981
MINE • 1928 • *B.s.f.p.* • SHT • UKN
MINE • 1982 • Yilmaz Atif • TRK
MINE, THE • 1936 • Holmes J. B. • DOC • UKN • COAL
MINE, THE see **MADEN** • 1978
MINE ALL MINE • 1929 • Aylott Dave, Symmons E. F. • SHT • UKN
MINE ALL MINE • 1969 • Phillips Derek • ANS • UKN
MINE AND A MARATHON, A • 1913 • *Nestor* • USA
MINE AT LAST • 1909 • Brooke Van Dyke • USA
MINE HUNTER • 1968 • Santiago Pablo • PHL
MINE IN VISTA • 1940 • De Robertis Francesco • ITL
MINE KONTA MOU, AGAPIMENE • 1968 • Avrameas Nikos • GRC • WE MUST NOT PART, MY DARLING ◦ STAY NEAR ME DARLING
MINE OF BURIED IDEALS see **SACHTA POHRBENYCH IDEI** • 1921
MINE ON THE YUKON, THE • 1912 • *Edison* • USA
MINE OWN EXECUTIONER • 1947 • Kimmins Anthony • UKN
MINE-PILOT, THE see **MINLOTSEN** • 1916
MINE SWINDLER, THE • 1912 • *Kalem* • USA
MINE TO KEEP • 1923 • Wilson Ben • USA
MINE WITH THE IRON DOOR, THE • 1924 • Wood Sam • USA
MINE WITH THE IRON DOOR, THE • 1936 • Howard David • USA
MINED AND COUNTER-MINED • 1926 • Miller Frank • UKN
MINEFIELD! • 1944 • Boulting Roy • DCS • UKN
MINEIRINHO DEAD OR ALIVE see **MINEIRINHO VIVO OU MORTO** • 1967
MINEIRINHO VIVO OU MORTO • 1967 • Teixeira Aurelio • BRZ • MINEIRINHO DEAD OR ALIVE
MINER, THE • 1966 • Spry Robin • DOC • CND
MINER AFFAIR, A • 1945 • White Jules • SHT • USA
MINER AND CAMILLE, THE • 1910 • *Edison* • USA
MINERS see **CHAKHTIERY** • 1936
MINER'S BABY, THE • 1914 • *Reliance* • USA
MINER'S CLAIM, THE • 1912 • *Lux* • USA
MINER'S CURSE, THE • 1911 • Rolfe Alfred • ASL
MINER'S DAUGHTER, THE • 1905 • Codman John • UKN
MINER'S DAUGHTER, THE • 1906 • Williamson James • UKN
MINER'S DAUGHTER, THE • 1908 • *Lubin* • USA
MINER'S DAUGHTER, THE • 1908 • *Vitagraph* • USA
MINER'S DAUGHTER, THE • 1911 • ASL
MINER'S DAUGHTER, THE • 1927 • ASL
MINER'S DAUGHTER, THE • 1950 • Cannon Robert • ANS • USA
MINER'S DESTINY, THE • 1913 • *Patheplay* • USA
MINERS' DETACHMENT, THE see **CRVENI UDAR** • 1975
MINERS' FILM, THE • 1975 • Cinema Action • UKN
MINERS FORTY-NINERS • 1951 • Sparber I. • ANS • USA
MINER'S MASCOT, THE • 1912 • Aylott Dave • UKN
MINERS OF DONETSK, THE see **DONETSKY SHAKTERY** • 1950
MINERS OF THE DON see **DONETSKY SHAKTERY** • 1950
MINER'S PERIL, THE • 1914 • Mackley Arthur • USA
MINERS' PICNIC, THE • 1960 • Russell Ken • MTV • UKN
MINER'S REQUEST, THE • 1912 • *Essanay* • USA
MINER'S ROMANCE, A • 1914 • *Mcquarrie Murdock* • USA
MINER'S SACRIFICE, THE • 1910 • *Kalem* • USA
MINER'S SWEETHEART, A • 1910 • *Bison* • USA
MINER'S SWEETHEART, THE • 1910 • *Lubin* • USA
MINER'S WIDOW, THE • 1912 • *Nestor* • USA
MINER'S WIFE, THE • 1911 • Dwan Allan • USA
MINERVA LOOKS OUT INTO THE ZODIAC • 1960 • Jordan Larry • SHT • USA
MINERVA TRADUCE EL MAR • 1962 • Solas Humberto, Veitia Hector • CUB
MINERVA'S MISSION • 1915 • Powell Paul • USA
MINES AND MATRIMONY • 1916 • Beaudine William • SHT • USA
MINES OF KILIMANJARO, THE • 1986 • Guerrini Mino • ITL
MINESTRONE, IL • 1980 • Citti Sergio • ITL • HUNGER
MINESWEEPER • 1943 • Berke William • USA
MING CHIEN • 1980 • T'An Chia-Ming • HKG • SWORD, THE
MING GREEN • 1966 • Markopoulos Gregory J. • SHT • USA
MING RAGAZZI • 1973 • Margheriti Antonio • ITL
MING-T'IEN CHIH YU WO • 1982 • Li Li-An • TWN • SAILING FOR TOMORROW
MING-YUEH CHI-SHIH YUAN • 1990 • Ch'En Yao-Ch'I • TWN
MING-YUEH TAO HSUEH-YEH CHIEN-CHOU • 1978 • Ch'U Yuan • HKG • PURSUIT OF VENGEANCE
MINGALOO • 1958 • Zichy Theodore • UKN
MINGLING SPIRITS • 1916 • Christie Al • SHT • USA
MINGUS • 1968 • Reichman Thomas • DOC • USA
MINHA NOITE DE NUPCIAS, A • 1931 • Emo E. W. • PRT
MINHO • 1957 • Mendes Joao • SHT • PRT
MINI-AFFAIR, THE • 1968 • Amram Robert • UKN
MINI FOUSTA KE KARATE • 1967 • Silinos Vangelis • GRC • MINI-SKIRT AND KARATE
MINI-MIDI • 1968 • Freeman Robert • SHT • FRN • WORLD OF FASHION (USA) ◦ HIER, AUJOURD'HUI, DEMAIN
MINI MINI TOTSUGEKI TAI • 1968 • Umezu Meijiro • JPN • MINI-SKIRT CORPS
MINI-MOVIE • 1971 • Zetterling Mai • SHT • UKN
MINI-SKIRT AND KARATE see **MINI FOUSTA KE KARATE** • 1967
MINI-SKIRT CORPS see **MINI MINI TOTSUGEKI TAI** • 1968
MINI-SKIRT LOVE • 1967 • Campa Lou • USA
MINI-SQUIRTS, THE • 1967 • Bakshi Ralph • ANS • USA
MINI WEEKEND • 1967 • Robin Georges • UKN • TOMCAT, THE (USA)

MINIA • 1978 • Veroiu Mircea • RMN • CHRONICLE OF THE BAREFOOT EMPERORS
MINIATURE, LA • 1909 • Carre Michel • FRN
MINIATURE, THE • 1910 • *Edison* • USA
MINIATURE BROADCAST, A • 1934 • *Harrison Harry B.* • SHT • UKN
MINIATURE CIRCUS, THE • 1908 • *Pathe* • FRN
MINIATURE PORTRAIT, THE • 1914 • O'Brien John B. • USA
MINIATURES see **MINIATURY** • 1968
MINIATURES TURQUES see **MUNAMNAMAT TURKIYYA** • 1969
MINIATURY • 1968 • Kijowicz Miroslaw • ANS • PLN • MINIATURES
MINIATURY KODEKSU BEHEMA • 1953 • Lenartowicz Stanislaw • PLN • CRACOW IN THE YEAR 1500
MINIHOLIDAY • 1968 • Moore Lawrence • SHT • UKN
MINIK SERCE • 1979 • Yilmaz Atif • TRK • LITTLE SPARROW, THE
MINIMUM CHARGE NO COVER • 1976 • Dale Holly, Cole Janis • DOC • CND
MININ AND POZHARSKY see **MININ I POZHARSKY** • 1939
MININ I POZHARSKY • 1939 • Pudovkin V. I., Doller Mikhail • USS • MININ AND POZHARSKY
MINING COAL • 1968 • Junarkar R. S. • IND
MINING EXPERT'S ORDEAL, THE • 1913 • *Nestor* • USA
MINIONS • Heinz John • SHT • USA
MINISKIRT MOB, THE • 1968 • Dexter Maury • USA
MINISTER, THE • 1915 • Lessey George A. • USA
MINISTER AND THE OUTLAW, THE • 1912 • *Jones Edgar* • USA
MINISTER OF INTELLIGENCE, THE • 1984 • Keenan Haydn • DOC • ASL
MINISTERE DE L'EDUCATION • 1980-84 • Pool Lea • DSS • CND
MINISTERIAL PRESIDENT, THE see **MINISTERPRESIDENTEN** • 1916
MINISTERN • 1971 • Kulle Jarl • SWD • HOME SECRETARY, THE
MINISTERPRESIDENTEN • 1916 • Klercker Georg • SWD • MINISTERIAL PRESIDENT, THE
MINISTER'S DAUGHTER, THE • 1909 • *Edison* • USA
MINISTER'S NEW SUIT, THE • 1910 • *Powers* • USA
MINISTER'S SON, THE • 1911 • *Yankee* • USA
MINISTER'S TEMPTATION, THE • 1913 • Brabin Charles J. • USA
MINISTER'S WIFE, THE see **MUJER DEL MINISTO, LA** • 1981
MINISTRATEN, DIE • 1990 • Paulus Wolfram • AUS, FRG • ALTAR BOYS, THE
MINISTRO Y YO, EL • 1975 • *Cantinflas* • MXC
MINISTRY, THE see **DEPARTEMENTET** • 1981
MINISTRY OF FEAR • 1944 • Lang Fritz • USA
MINITA, LA • 1967 • Iquino Ignacio F. • SPN
MINITRIP • 1983 • Joassin Pierre • BLG
MINIVER STORY, THE • 1950 • Potter H. C. • UKN, USA
MINLOTSEN • 1916 • Stiller Mauritz • SWD • MINE-PILOT, THE
MINNA VON BARNHELM • 1962 • Hellberg Martin • GDR
MINNE L'INGENUE LIBERTINE • 1950 • Audry Jacqueline • FRN • MINNE (USA) ○ INGENUE LIBERTINE, L'
MINNE (USA) see **MINNE L'INGENUE LIBERTINE** • 1950
MINNEN FRAN BOSTONKLUBBEN • 1909 • Magnusson Charles • SWD • MEMORIES FROM THE BOSTON CLUB
MINNESOTA CLAY • 1965 • Corbucci Sergio • ITL, FRN, SPN • HOMME DU MINNESOTA, L' (FRN)
MINNIE • 1922 • Neilan Marshall, Urson Frank • USA
MINNIE AND MOSKOWITZ • 1971 • Cassavetes John • USA
MINNIE, THE MEAN MANICURIST • 1915 • *Cooper Claude* • USA
MINNIE THE MERMAID • 1942 • *Soundies* • SHT • USA
MINNIE THE MOOCHER • 1932 • Fleischer Dave • ANS • USA
MINNIE THE MOOCHER'S WEDDING DAY see **SWING WEDDING** • 1937
MINNIE THE TIGER • 1915 • Beaudine William • USA
MINNIE, THE WIDOW • 1913 • Hotaling Arthur D. • USA
MINOR CHORD, THE • 1911 • *Imp* • USA
MINOR LOVE AND THE REAL THING, THE see **KLEINE UND DIE GROSSE LIEBE, DIE** • 1938
MINOR MIRACLE, A • 1983 • Lomas Raoul • USA
MINOR MIRACLE, A see **YOUNG GIANTS** • 1983
MINORENNE, LA • 1974 • Amadio Silvio • ITL
MINOR'S JUSTICE, THE • 1913 • McRae Henry • USA
MINOTAUR see **LAND OF THE MINOTAUR** • 1976
MINOTAUR, THE • 1910 • *Vitagraph* • USA • THESEUS AND THE MINOTAUR
MINOTAUR, THE (USA) see **TESEO CONTRO IL MINOTAURO** • 1961
MINOTAUR -THE WILD BEAST OF CRETE, THE see **TESEO CONTRO IL MINOTAURO** • 1961
MINOUCHE, FILLETTE INSATIABLE • 1980 • de Castellanne Henri • FRN
MINSA'Y ISANG GAMU-GAMO • 1977 • Concio Lupita • PHL • ONCE A MOTH
MINSHU NO TEKI • 1946 • Imai Tadashi • JPN • ENEMY OF THE PEOPLE, AN ○ PEOPLE'S ENEMY, THE
MINSTREL BOY, THE • 1937 • Morgan Sidney • UKN
MINSTREL CARNIVAL see **HARMONY LANE** • 1935
MINSTREL MAN • 1944 • Lewis Joseph H. • USA
MINSTREL MAN • 1977 • Graham William A. • TVM • USA
MINSTREL MANIA • 1949 • Cowan Will • SHT • USA
MINSTREL MISHAP • 1908 • Porter Edwin S. • USA
MINSTREL SHOW, THE • 1932 • *Mintz Charles (P)* • ANS • USA
MINSTREL'S SONG see **SLOWCE M** • 1964
MINT CONDITION see **MONEY TO BURN** • 1973
MINT MEN • 1960 • Tendlar Dave • ANS • USA
MINTS OF HELL, THE • 1919 • Frame Park • USA
MINUET BY MOZART • 1931 • Fischinger Oskar • ANS • FRG
MINUIT CHAMPS-ELYSEES • 1953 • Blanc Roger • FRN
MINUIT, PLACE PIGALLE • 1928 • Hervil Rene • FRN
MINUIT, PLACE PIGALLE • 1934 • Richebe Roger • FRN
MINUIT QUAI DE BERCY • 1952 • Stengel Christian • FRN
MINUIT TRENTE-CINQ • 1912 • Fescourt Henri • FRN
MINUS FRAME • 1976 • Papadakis Leonidas • SHT • GRC
MINUTA ZA UMOR • 1962 • Kavcic Jane • YGS • MINUTE FOR MURDER, A
MINUTE AND A ½ MAN, THE • 1959 • Tendlar Dave • ANS • USA
MINUTE AND THE MAID, THE • 1911 • *Reliance* • USA
MINUTE DE VERITE, LA • 1952 • Delannoy Jean • FRN, ITL • ORA DELLA VERITA, L' (ITL) ○ MOMENT OF TRUTH, THE
MINUTE FOR MURDER, A see **MINUTA ZA UMOR** • 1962
MINUTE HANDS, THE see **MINUTEROS, LOS** • 1973
MINUTE MAN, THE • 1911 • *Ogle Charles* • USA
MINUTE PAPILLON • 1959 • Lefevre Jean • FRN
MINUTE TO PRAY, A SECOND TO DIE, A (USA) see **MINUTO PER PREGARE, UN ISTANTE PER MORIRE, UN** • 1967
MINUTE ZERO • 1968 • Tropa Alfredo • SHT • PRT
MINUTEROS, LOS • 1973 • Ruiz Raul • SHT • CHL • STREET PHOTOGRAPHER, THE ○ MINUTE HANDS, THE
MINUTO DE BONDAD, UN • 1953 • Gomez Muriel Emilio • MXC
MINUTO PER PREGARE, UN ISTANTE PER MORIRE, UN • 1967 • Giraldi Franco • ITL, USA • MINUTE TO PRAY, A SECOND TO DIE, A (USA) ○ DEAD OR ALIVE ○ ESCONDIDO
MINUTOS ANTES • 1956 • Gamboa Jose Luis • SPN
MINX, THE • 1969 • Jacobs Raymond • USA
MIO • 1970 • Hani Susumu • JPN, FRN, ITL
MIO AMICO BENITO, IL • 1962 • Bianchi Giorgio • ITL
MIO AMICO JEKYLL, IL • 1960 • Girolami Marino • ITL • MY FRIEND, DR. JEKYLL (USA)
MIO CARO ASSASSINO • 1972 • Valerii Tonino • ITL
MIO CARO DOTTOR GRASLER • 1990 • Faenza Roberto • ITL, HNG • MY DEAR DOCTOR GRASLER
MIO CORPO CON RABBIA, IL • 1972 • Natale Roberto • ITL
MIO CORPO PER UN POKER, IL see **BELLE STARR STORY, THE** • 1968
MIO DIO, COME SONO CADUTA IN BASSO! • 1974 • Comencini Luigi • ITL • TILL MARRIAGE DO US PART (USA)
MIO FIGIO (ITL) see **RUE DES PRAIRIES** • 1959
MIO FIGLIO NERONE • 1956 • Steno • ITL, FRN • WEEK-ENDS DE NERON, LES (FRN) ○ NERO'S MISTRESS (USA) ○ NERO'S WEEKEND ○ NERO'S BIG WEEKEND
MIO FIGLIO PROFESSORE • 1946 • Castellani Renato • ITL • MY SON, THE PROFESSOR ○ PROFESSOR, MY SON (USA)
MIO IN THE LAND OF FARAWAY see **MIO, MIN MIO!** • 1987
MIO MAO • 1970 • Ferrari Nicolo • ITL
MIO, MIN MIO! • 1987 • Grammatikov Vladimir • SWD, USS, NRW • MIO IN THE LAND OF FARAWAY
MIO NOME E MALLORY: "M" COME MORTE, IL • 1971 • Moroni Mario • ITL
MIO NOME E NESSUNO, IL • 1974 • Valerii Tonino • ITL, FRN, FRG • MY NAME IS NOBODY
MIO NOME E PECOS, IL see **DUE ONCE DI PIOMBO** • 1966
MIO NOME E SHANGAY JOE, IL see **MIO NOME E SHANGHAI JOE, IL** • 1973
MIO NOME E SHANGHAI JOE, IL • 1973 • Caiano Mario • ITL • MEZZOGIORNO DE FUCCO PER AN HAO ○ MIO NOME E SHANGAY JOE, IL ○ FIGHTING FISTS OF SHANGHAI JOE, THE ○ TO KILL OR TO DIE ○ SHANGHAI JOE
MIO NON MUORE • 1913 • Caserini Mario • ITL
MIO PADRE AMORE MIO • 1979 • Maraini Dacia • ITL
MIO PADRE MONSIGNORE • 1971 • Racioppi Antonio • ITL
MIO ZIO BENIAMINO (ITL) see **MON ONCLE BENJAMIN** • 1969
MIOCHE, LE • 1936 • Moguy Leonide • FRN • PAPA PROSPER
MIONESHEIOI • 1988 • ICL
MIQUETTE • 1940 • Boyer Jean • FRN • DEMOISELLE DU TABAC, LA ○ MIQUETTE ET SA MERE
MIQUETTE ET SA MERE • 1914 • Pouctal Henri • FRN
MIQUETTE ET SA MERE • 1933 • Diamant-Berger Henri, Maurice D. B., Rollan Henry • FRN
MIQUETTE ET SA MERE • 1949 • Clouzot Henri-Georges • FRN • MIQUETTE (USA)
MIQUETTE ET SA MERE see **MIQUETTE** • 1940
MIQUETTE (USA) see **MIQUETTE ET SA MERE** • 1949
MIR DIR DURCH DICK UND DUNN • 1934 • Seitz Franz • FRG
MIR KOMMT KEINER AUS • 1917 • Fleck Luise, Fleck Jacob • AUS • SCHWARZE HAND, DIE
MIR LON NID LUGG • 1940 • Haller Hermann • SWT
MIR NACH. CANAILLEN! • 1964 • Kirsten Ralf • GDR
MIR VKHODYASHCHEMU • 1961 • Alov Alexander, Naumov Vladimir • USS • PEACE TO HIM WHO ENTERS (USA) ○ PEACE TO THE NEWCOMER ○ PEACE TO HIM
MIRA • 1971 • Rademakers Fons • BLG, NTH • TELEURGANG VAN DE WATERHOEK, DE
MIRA • 1977 • Gulzar • IND
MIRA KA CHITRA • 1960 • *Biswas Anil (M)* • IND
MIRA MIAS YINEKAS, I • 1968 • Galani Rena • GRC • WOMAN'S FATE, A
MIRABAI see **MEERABAI** • 1946
MIRACLE see **WOMAN'S FAITH, A** • 1925
MIRACLE see **AMORE, L'** • 1948
MIRACLE see **KEITSIK** • 1989
MIRACLE, A • 1954 • Breer Robert, Hulten Pontus • SHT • USA • MIRACLE, UN
MIRACLE, LE • 1912 • Carre Michel • FRN
MIRACLE, THE • 1912 • Ranous William V. • USA
MIRACLE, THE • 1913 • Bentley Thomas • UKN
MIRACLE, THE • 1914 • *Truesdell Fred* • USA
MIRACLE, THE • 1915 • *Spaulding Eleanor* • USA
MIRACLE, THE • 1923 • Coleby A. E. • UKN
MIRACLE, THE • 1959 • Rapper Irving • USA
MIRACLE, THE • 1990 • Jordan Neil • UKN, IRL
MIRACLE, THE see **MIRAKLET** • 1914
MIRACLE, THE see **MUAGEZA, EL** • 1963
MIRACLE, THE see **MOJEZE** • 1968
MIRACLE, THE see **NESS BA'AYARA** • 1968
MIRACLE, THE see **MIRACOLUL** • 1988
MIRACLE, UN see **TRESOR DE CANTENAC, LE** • 1949
MIRACLE, UN see **MIRACLE, A** • 1954
MIRACLE AT BEAUHARNOIS • 1931 • Sparling Gordon • CND
MIRACLE AT VIGGIU see **MIRACOLO A VIGGIU** • 1951
MIRACLE BABY, THE • 1923 • Paul Val • USA
MIRACLE CAN HAPPEN, A • 1948 • Vidor King, Fenton Leslie • USA • ON OUR MERRY WAY (UKN)
MIRACLE CHILD (HE GIVETH AND TAKETH), THE see **MOONSHINE VALLEY** • 1922
MIRACLE DE L'EAU • Des Vallieres Jean • SHT • FRN
MIRACLE DE SAINT HUBERT, THE see **BERNARD LE BUCHERON** • 1907
MIRACLE DES AILES, LE • 1956 • Mitry Jean • SHT • FRN
MIRACLE DES LOUPS, LE • 1924 • Bernard Raymond • FRN • MIRACLE OF THE WOLVES, THE (USA)
MIRACLE DES LOUPS, LE • 1930 • Bernard Raymond • FRN • MIRACLE OF THE WOLVES, THE
MIRACLE DES LOUPS, LE • 1961 • Hunebelle Andre • FRN, ITL • BLOOD ON HIS SWORD (USA) ○ MIRACLE OF THE WOLVES, THE
MIRACLE DES ROSES, LE • 1908 • Cohl Emile • ANS • FRN • MIRACLE OF THE ROSES, THE
MIRACLE DU BRAHMIN, LE see **MIRACLES DE BRAHMANE, LES** • 1900
MIRACLE DU CIEL see **MOGEZAT EL SAMAA** • 1956
MIRACLE DU CURE CHAMBERLAND, LE • 1952 • Tessier Albert • DCS • CND
MIRACLE FOR THE COWARDS see **MILAGRO A LOS COBARDES** • 1961
MIRACLE FROM HEAVEN, A see **MOGEZAT EL SAMAA** • 1956
MIRACLE FROM MARS see **RED PLANET MARS** • 1952
MIRACLE GIRL, THE see **TCHOUDESNITSA** • 1936
MIRACLE IN A CORNFIELD • 1947 • *Nesbitt John* • USA
MIRACLE IN A MANGER see **TIME TO REMEMBER, A** • 1988
MIRACLE IN HARLEM • 1937 • Micheaux Oscar • USA
MIRACLE IN HARLEM • 1949 • Kemp Jack • USA
MIRACLE IN MILAN see **MIRACOLO A MILANO** • 1951
MIRACLE IN MINNESOTA • 1964 • Jamieson Richard N. • USA
MIRACLE IN ROME see **MILAGRO EN ROMA** • 1988
MIRACLE IN SOHO • 1957 • Amyes Julian • UKN
MIRACLE IN THE RAIN • 1956 • Mate Rudolph • USA
MIRACLE IN THE SAND see **THREE GODFATHERS** • 1936
MIRACLE IN THE TOWN, A see **NESS BA'AYARA** • 1968
MIRACLE IN VALBY see **MIRAKLET I VALBY** • 1989
MIRACLE KID, THE • 1942 • Beaudine William • USA
MIRACLE LOTION, THE see **LOTION MIRACULEUSE, LA** • 1903
MIRACLE MAKERS, THE • 1923 • Van Dyke W. S. • USA
MIRACLE MAN, THE • 1919 • Tucker George Loane • USA
MIRACLE MAN, THE • 1932 • McLeod Norman Z. • USA
MIRACLE MAN, THE see **DAY THE LORD GOT BUSTED, THE** • 1976
MIRACLE MAN, THE see **IHMEMIES** • 1979
MIRACLE MAN, THE (USA) see **ZNACHOR** • 1938
MIRACLE MARY • 1913 • Daly William Robert • USA
MIRACLE MILE • 1989 • De Jarnatt Steve • USA
MIRACLE MONEY • 1938 • Fenton Leslie • SHT • USA
MIRACLE OF FATHER MALACHIAS, THE see **WUNDER DES MALACHIAS, DAS** • 1961
MIRACLE OF FATIMA (UKN) see **MIRACLE OF OUR LADY OF FATIMA, THE** • 1952
MIRACLE OF KATHY MILLER, THE • 1981 • Lewis Robert • TVM • USA
MIRACLE OF LIFE, THE • 1915 • Pollard Harry • USA
MIRACLE OF LIFE, THE • 1926 • Taylor Stanner E. V. • USA
MIRACLE OF LIFE, THE (UKN) see **OUR DAILY BREAD** • 1934
MIRACLE OF LOVE see **SON RISE: A MIRACLE OF LOVE** • 1979
MIRACLE OF LOVE, A • 1913 • *Carewe Edwin* • USA
MIRACLE OF LOVE, A • 1916 • Carleton Lloyd B. • USA
MIRACLE OF LOVE, THE • 1920 • Leonard Robert Z. • USA
MIRACLE OF LOVE, THE (USA) see **OSWALT KOLLE: DAS WUNDER DER LIEBE -SEXUALITAT IN DER EHE** • 1968
MIRACLE OF MALACHIAS, THE see **WUNDER DES MALACHIAS, DAS** • 1961
MIRACLE OF MANHATTAN, THE • 1921 • Archainbaud George • USA
MIRACLE OF MARCELINO, THE see **MARCELINO PAN Y VINO** • 1954
MIRACLE OF MILAN, THE see **WUNDER VON MAILAND, DAS** • 1967
MIRACLE OF MONEY, THE • 1920 • Henley Hobart • USA
MIRACLE OF MORGAN'S CREEK • 1944 • Sturges Preston • USA
MIRACLE OF OUR LADY OF FATIMA, THE • 1952 • Brahm John • USA • MIRACLE OF FATIMA (UKN)
MIRACLE OF ST. ANTHONY see **MIRACOLO DI SANT'ANTONIO, IL** • 1931
MIRACLE OF SAINT THERESE • 1959 • Bernier George
MIRACLE OF SANTA'S WHITE REINDEER, THE • 1963 • *Winniger Charles* • USA • MIRACLE OF THE WHITE REINDEER, THE
MIRACLE OF SISTER BEATRICE, THE • 1939 • Dixon Harry T. • USA
MIRACLE OF TEREZIN, THE • 1966 • Woods Grahame • CND
MIRACLE OF THE BELLS, THE • 1948 • Pichel Irving • USA
MIRACLE OF THE BLIND BEGGAR • *Loyola Film* • SHT • USA
MIRACLE OF THE COWARDS see **MILAGRO A LOS COBARDES** • 1961
MIRACLE OF THE HEART: A BOYS TOWN STORY • 1986 • Brown George Stanford • TVM • USA
MIRACLE OF THE HILLS, THE • 1959 • Landres Paul • USA
MIRACLE OF THE NECKLACE • 1909 • *Lux* • FRN
MIRACLE OF THE ROSES, THE • 1913 • *Patheplay* • USA
MIRACLE OF THE ROSES, THE see **MIRACLE DES ROSES, LE** • 1908
MIRACLE OF THE ROSES, THE see **ROSAS DEL MILAGRO, LAS** • 1959
MIRACLE OF THE VISTULA, THE see **CUD NAD WISLA** • 1920
MIRACLE OF THE WHITE REINDEER, THE see **MIRACLE OF SANTA'S WHITE REINDEER, THE** • 1963
MIRACLE OF THE WHITE STALLIONS, THE • 1962 • Hiller Arthur • USA • FLIGHT OF THE WHITE STALLIONS, THE (UKN)
MIRACLE OF THE WOLVES, THE see **MIRACLE DES LOUPS, LE** • 1930
MIRACLE OF THE WOLVES, THE see **MIRACLE DES LOUPS, LE** • 1961
MIRACLE OF THE WOLVES, THE (USA) see **MIRACLE DES LOUPS, LE** • 1924
MIRACLE OF TOMORROW, THE • 1923 • Piel Harry • FRG
MIRACLE ON 34TH STREET • 1973 • Cook Fielder • TVM • USA
MIRACLE ON 34TH STREET, THE • 1947 • Seaton George • USA • BIG HEART, THE (UKN)

MIRACLE ON 34TH STREET (UKN) see **MEET MR. KRINGLE** • 1956
MIRACLE ON 49TH STREET see **SCOUNDREL, THE** • 1935
MIRACLE ON ICE • 1981 • Stern Steven Hilliard • TVM • USA
MIRACLE ON MAIN STREET, A • 1940 • Sekely Steve • USA
MIRACLE ON THE BMT • 1963 • Burckhardt Rudy • SHT • USA
MIRACLE RACKET see **TARNISHED ANGEL** • 1938
MIRACLE RIDER, THE • 1935 • Schaefer Armand, Eason B. Reeves • SRL • USA
MIRACLE SONG, THE (USA) see **CANCION DEL MILAGRO, LA** • 1940
MIRACLE SOUS L'INQUISITION, UN • 1904 • Melies Georges • FRN • MIRACLE UNDER THE INQUISITION, A (USA)
MIRACLE UNDER THE INQUISITION, A (USA) see **MIRACLE SOUS L'INQUISITION, UN** • 1904
MIRACLE WEAVER, THE see **TEJEDOR DE MILAGROS, EL** • 1961
MIRACLE WINDOW, THE (USA) see **WUNDERFENSTER, DAS** • 1952
MIRACLE WOMAN • 1931 • Capra Frank • USA
MIRACLE WORKER, THE • 1962 • Penn Arthur • USA
MIRACLE WORKER, THE • 1979 • Aaron Paul • TVM • USA
MIRACLE WORKER, THE see **CHUDOTVORETS** • 1960
MIRACLES • 1934 • Petrov-Bytov P. • USS
MIRACLES • 1986 • Kouf Jim • USA
MIRACLES see **PRO CHUDESA CHELOVYECHSKIYE** • 1968
MIRACLES see **MARAVILLAS** • 1980
MIRACLES DE BRAHMANE, LES • 1900 • Melies Georges • FRN • MIRACLES OF BRAHMIN, THE (USA) ○ MIRACLE DU BRAHMIN, LE
MIRACLES DO HAPPEN • 1938 • Rogers Maclean • UKN
MIRACLES FOR SALE • 1939 • Browning Tod • USA
MIRACLES IN MUD • Hopkins Willie • ANS • USA
MIRACLES N'ONT LIEU QU'UNE FOIS, LES • 1950 • Allegret Yves • FRN, ITL • MIRACOLI NON SI RIPETONI, I (ITL)
MIRACLES OF BRAHMIN, THE (USA) see **MIRACLES DE BRAHMANE, LES** • 1900
MIRACLES OF CREATION see **WUNDER DER SCHOPFUNG** • 1925
MIRACLES OF ST. MARGARET (USA) see **MARGHERITA DA CORTONA** • 1950
MIRACLES OF THE JUNGLE • 1921 • Martin E. A., Conway James • SRL • USA
MIRACLES STILL HAPPEN see **ES GESCHEHEN NOCH WUNDER** • 1951
MIRACLES STILL HAPPEN (USA) see **MIRACOLI ACCADONO ANCORA, I** • 1974
MIRACOLI ACCADONO ANCORA, I • 1974 • Scotese Giuseppe Maria • ITL, USA • MIRACLES STILL HAPPEN (USA) ○ STORY OF JULIANE KOEPCKE, THE
MIRACOLI NON SI RIPETONI, I (ITL) see **MIRACLES N'ONT LIEU QU'UNE FOIS, LES** • 1950
MIRACOLO, IL • 1919 • Caserini Mario • ITL
MIRACOLO A MILANO • 1951 • De Sica Vittorio • ITL • MIRACLE IN MILAN
MIRACOLO A VIGGIU • 1951 • Giachino Luigi Maria • ITL • MIRACLE AT VIGGIU
MIRACOLO DI SANT'ANTONIO, IL • 1931 • Neroni Nicola Fausto • ITL • MIRACLE OF ST. ANTHONY
MIRACOLUL • 1988 • Marascu Todur • RMN • MIRACLE, THE
MIRACULE, LE • 1986 • Mocky Jean-Pierre • FRN
MIRACULOUS BRAIN TEASER, THE see **ZAZRACNY HLAVOLAM** • 1967
MIRACULOUS BROTHERS, THE see **FRATELLI MIRACOLOSI, I** • 1949
MIRACULOUS EGGS • 1907 • *Lubin* • USA
MIRACULOUS HAPPENINGS see **O VECECH NADPRIROZENYCH** • 1958
MIRACULOUS JOURNEY • 1948 • Newfield Sam • USA
MIRACULOUS MAIDEN, THE see **PANNA ZAZRACNICA** • 1966
MIRACULOUS MANDARIN, THE • 1975 • Szinetar Miklos • HNG
MIRACULOUS MANDARIN, THE see **CSODALATOS MANDARIN, A** • 1965
MIRACULOUS PUZZLE see **ZAZRACNY HLAVOLAM** • 1967
MIRACULOUS RECOVERY, A • 1911 • Noy Wilfred • UKN
MIRACULOUS ROSES, THE see **ROSAS DEL MILAGRO, LAS** • 1959
MIRACULOUS SPRING, THE • 1967 • Sturlis Edward • ANM • PLN
MIRACULOUS SWORD, THE see **CUDOTVORNI MAC** • 1949
MIRACULOUS VIRGIN, THE see **PANNA ZAZRACNICA** • 1966
MIRADAD QUE MATAN • 1953 • Cortes Fernando • MXC
MIRAGE • 1965 • Dmytryk Edward • USA
MIRAGE • 1981 • Gehr Ernie • USA
MIRAGE see **HAGRINGEN** • 1959
MIRAGE see **ESPEJISMO** • 1973
MIRAGE, LE see **SARAB, AS-** • 1970
MIRAGE, THE • 1912 • *Eclair* • FRN • DEATH OF A DREAM, THE
MIRAGE, THE • 1920 • Rooke Arthur • UKN
MIRAGE, THE • 1924 • Archainbaud George • USA
MIRAGE, THE see **MAYA MARIGA** • 1984
MIRAGE ESKADER • 1975 • SAF
MIRAGE IN THE NORTH see **SEVERNOE SIIANIE** • 1926
MIRAGES • 1937 • Ryder Alexandre • FRN • SI TU M'AIMES
MIRAGES • 1975 • Aubier Pascal • FRN
MIRAGES see **PRELUDY POUSTE** • 1982
MIRAGES DE PARIS • 1932 • Ozep Fedor • FRN • NUITS DE PARIS
MIRAGGIO, IL • 1920 • D'Ambra Lucio • ITL
MIRAI NO SHUSSE • 1927 • Uchida Tomu • JPN • RISING IN THE WORLD
MIRAKEL, DAS • 1912 • Reinhardt Max • FRG
MIRAKEL DER LIEBE • 1926 • von Cardowa Lauda • FRG
MIRAKLET • 1914 • Sjostrom Victor • SWD • MIRACLE, THE
MIRAKLET I VALBY • 1989 • Sandgren Ake • DNM, SWD • MIRACLE IN VALBY
MIRAMAR • 1969 • el Sheikh Kamal • EGY
MIRAMAR PRAIA DE ROSAS • 1938 • de Oliveira Manoel • SHT • PRT
MIRANDA • 1948 • Annakin Ken • UKN
MIRANDA • 1985 • Brass Tinto • ITL
MIRANDA, ANG LAGALAG NO SIRENA • 1966 • Abelardo Richard • PHL • MIRANDA, THE WANDERING MERMAID
MIRANDA OF THE BALCONY see **SLAVES OF DESTINY** • 1924
MIRANDA, THE WANDERING MERMAID see **MIRANDA, ANG LAGALAG NO SIRENA** • 1966
MIRANDY SMILES • 1918 • De Mille William C. • USA
MIRCEA • 1989 • Nicolaescu Sergiu • RMN • PROUD HERITAGE
MIRCH MASALA • 1985 • Mehta Ketan • IND • CHILLI BOUQUET
MIRCO THE INVISIBLE • 1958 • Topaldgikov Stefan • ANM • BUL • MIRKO THE INVISIBLE
MIRE, THE see **NETEPICHNAYA ISTORIA** • 1978
MIREASA DIN TREN • 1980 • Bratu Lucian • RMN • BRIDE FROM THE TRAIN, THE
MIREILLE • 1906 • Feuillade Louis, Blache Alice • FRN
MIREILLE • 1922 • Servaes Ernest • FRN
MIREILLE • 1933 • Gaveau Rene, Servaes Ernest • FRN
MIREILLE DANS LA VIE DES AUTRES • 1979 • Buchet Jean-Marie • FRN, BLG
MIREILLE MATHIEU • 1966 • Reichenbach Francois • SHT • FRN
MIRELE EFROS • 1939 • Berne Josef
MIREN • 1963 • Chiba • JPN • REGRETS
MIRI • 1983 • Trope Zippi • ISR
MIRIAM • 1957 • Markus William • FNL
MIRIAM MAKEBA • 1973 • Tabio Juan Carlos • CUB
MIRIAM ROZELLA • 1924 • Morgan Sidney • UKN
MIRIS POLJSKOG CVECA • 1977 • Karanovic Srdjan • YGS • FRAGRANCE OF WILD FLOWERS, THE ○ SCENT OF WILD FLOWERS, THE ○ FIELD-FLOWERS SMELL
MIRIS, TAMJAN I ZLATO • 1971 • Babaja Ante • YGS • MYRRH, GOLD AND FRANKENCENSE ○ MIRIS ZLATO I TAMJAN ○ ODEUR, GOLD AND INCENSE
MIRIS ZEMLJE • 1979 • Jovanovic Dragovan • YGS, PLN • SCENT OF THE EARTH, THE
MIRIS ZLATO I TAMJAN see **MIRIS, TAMJAN I ZLATO** • 1971
MIRJA • 1977 • USA
MIRKA • 1970 • Cox Paul • SHT • ASL
MIRKO AND SLAVKO see **MIRKO I SLAVKO** • 1974
MIRKO I SLAVKO • 1974 • Jankovic Branimir Tori • YGS • MIRKO AND SLAVKO
MIRKO THE INVISIBLE see **MIRCO THE INVISIBLE** • 1958
MIRLITON • 1977 • van Eyck Robert • BLG
MIROIR • 1946 • Lamy Raymond • FRN
MIROIR A DEUX FACES, LE • 1958 • Cayatte Andre • FRN, ITL • MIRROR HAS TWO FACES, THE (USA)
MIROIR AUX ALOUETTES, LE • 1934 • Le Bon Roger, Steinhoff Hans • FRN
MIROIR DE CAGLIOSTRO, LE • 1899 • Melies Georges • FRN • CAGLIOSTRO'S MIRROR (USA) ○ MIRROR OF CAGLIOSTRO, THE
MIROIR DE LA VIE, LE see **ASTROLOGIE** • 1952
MIROIR DE VENISE, UNE MESAVENTURE DE SHYLOCK, LE • 1905 • Melies Georges • FRN • VENETIAN LOOKING-GLASS, THE (USA) ○ MESAVENTURE DE SHYLOCK, UNE
MIROIR MAGIQUE, LE • 1908 • Perret Leonce • FRN
MIROIRS ET PLIAGES • 1970 • Moreau Michel • DCS • CND
MIRON, EL • 1977 • Larraz Jose R. • SPN
MIRONOV TRIAL, THE see **PROZESS MIRONOVA** • 1920
MIROVOY PAREN • 1972 • Dubrovin Yu. • USS • MAN OF THE WORLD, A
MIRROR • 1970 • Schorstein Jon • UKN
MIRROR, A see **TUKOR, EGY** • 1971
MIRROR, THE • Schoerstein John • UKN
MIRROR, THE • 1911 • *Pickford Mary* • USA
MIRROR, THE • 1913 • O'Sullivan Tony • USA
MIRROR, THE • 1914 • *Greenwood Winnifred* • USA
MIRROR, THE • 1915 • Kaufman Joseph • USA
MIRROR, THE • 1917 • Powell Frank • USA
MIRROR, THE • 1957 • Babaja Ante • SHT • YGS
MIRROR, THE see **SPIEGEL DES LEBENS** • 1938
MIRROR, THE see **OGLEDALO** • 1971
MIRROR, THE see **AYNA**
MIRROR AND I, THE see **LUSTRO I JA** • 1963
MIRROR AND MARKHEIM, THE • 1954 • Lemont John • SHT • UKN
MIRROR ANIMATIONS see **NUMBER 11** • 1956
MIRROR CRACK'D, THE • 1980 • Hamilton Guy • UKN, USA
MIRROR DEATH RAY OF DR. MABUSE, THE see **TODESSTRAHLEN DES DR. MABUSE, DIE** • 1964
MIRROR HAS TWO FACES, THE (USA) see **MIROIR A DEUX FACES, LE** • 1958
MIRROR, MIRROR • 1978 • Fleming Edward • DNM
MIRROR, MIRROR • 1979 • Lee Joanna • TVM • USA
MIRROR OF CAGLIOSTRO, THE see **MIROIR DE CAGLIOSTRO, LE** • 1899
MIRROR OF DEATH • 1987 • Warren Deryn • USA
MIRROR OF FEAR, THE • 1917 • Ellis Robert • SHT • USA
MIRROR OF FLESH, THE see **ESPELHO DE CARNE, O** • 1984
MIRROR OF HOLLAND see **SPIEGEL VAN HOLLAND** • 1950
MIRROR OF ILLUSION see **MAYA DARPAN** • 1972
MIRROR OF JUSTICE, THE • 1915 • Reynolds Lynn • USA
MIRROR OF LIFE, THE • 1909 • *Pathe* • FRN
MIRROR OF LIFE, THE • 1916 • *Piedmont Films* • USA
MIRROR OF THE FUTURE • 1910 • *Pathe* • FRN
MIRROR OF THE WITCH, THE see **ESPEJO DE LA BRUJA, EL** • 1960
MIRROR (UKN) see **ZERKALO** • 1974
MIRROR WITH THREE FACES see **GLACE A TROIS FACES, LA** • 1927
MIRRORED REASON • 1980 • Vanderbeek Stan • USA
MIRRORMAN, THE see **SPIEGELMENSCH, DER** • 1923
MIRRORS • 1985 • Winer Harry • TVM • USA
MIRRORS see **MARIANNE** • 1978
MIRRORS OF SILENCE, THE see **ESPEJOS DEL SILENCIO, LOS** • 1989
MIRRORS' STREET see **VIA DEGLI SPECCHI** • 1983
MIRSU • 1924 • Kinugasa Teinosuke • JPN • LOVE
MIRT SOST SHI AMIT • 1972 • Gerima Haile • ETH • HARVEST: 3000 YEARS
MIRTH AND MAGIC • 1928 • *De Forest Phonofilms* • SHT • UKN
MIRTH AND MELODY • 1951 • Shepherd Horace • UKN
MIRTH AND MELODY (UKN) see **LET'S GO PLACES** • 1930
MIRTH AND MYSTERY • 1912 • Kinder Stuart • UKN
MIRTHFUL MARY, A CASE FOR THE BLACK LIST • 1903 • Haggar William • UKN
MIRTHFUL MARY IN THE DOCK • 1904 • Haggar William • UKN
MIRZA NOROOZ' SHOES • 1985 • Motevaselani Mohamad • IRN
MIS ABUELITAS.. NOMAS! • 1959 • de la Serna Mauricio • MXC
MIS DIAS CON VERONICA • 1980 • Lescovich Nestor • ARG • MY DAYS WITH VERONICA
MIS HIJOS • 1944 • Cardona Rene • MXC
MIS MANOS • 1965 • Cahero Julio • MXC
MIS PADRESS DIVORCIAN • 1957 • Soler Julian • MXC
MIS SECRETARIAS PRIVADAS • 1958 • Rodriguez Roberto • MXC
MIS-SENT LETTER, THE • 1912 • *Essanay* • USA
MIS STON • 1958 • Mitrovic Zika • YGS • MISS STONE
MIS-TAKES • 1972 • Schwartz Lillian, Knowlton Kenneth • ANS • USA
MIS TRES VIUDAS ALEGRES • 1953 • Cortes Fernando • MXC
MISADVENTURE see **MALAVENTURA** • 1988
MISADVENTURES OF A CALF'S HEAD, THE see **MESAVENTURES D'UNE TETE DE VEAU** • 1898
MISADVENTURES OF A CLAIM AGENT, THE see **CLAIM AGENT'S MIS-ADVENTURE, THE** • 1911
MISADVENTURES OF A CYCLE THIEF, THE • 1909 • Wormald S.? • UKN
MISADVENTURES OF A MIGHTY MONARCH, THE • 1913 • Baker George D. • USA
MISADVENTURES OF BILL THE PLUMBER, THE • 1911 • Martinek H. O. • UKN
MISADVENTURES OF BUSTER KEATON, THE • 1955 • Hilton Arthur • USA
MISADVENTURES OF DON QUIXOTE AND SANCHO PANZA, THE see **TRAPALHADAS DE DOM QUIXOTE & SANCHO PANCA, AS** • 1980
MISADVENTURES OF MERLIN JONES, THE • 1964 • Stevenson Robert • USA
MISADVENTURES OF MIKE MURPHY, THE • 1913 • Aylott Dave • UKN • MURPHY AND THE MAGIC CAP
MISANTHROPE, LE • 1964 • Carrier Louis-Georges • CND
MISAPPROPRIATED TURKEY, A • 1913 • *Ab* • USA
MISBEHAVIN' • 1981 • Vincent Chuck • USA
MISBEHAVING HUSBANDS • 1940 • Beaudine William • USA
MISBEHAVING LADIES • 1931 • Beaudine William • USA • ONCE THERE WAS A PRINCESS (UKN) ○ QUEEN OF MAIN STREET
MISC. HAPPENINGS • 1961-62 • Vanderbeek Stan • USA
MISCELLANEOUS BRIGADE, THE • 1969 • Dragan Mircea • RMN
MISCHA THE BEAR • 1947 • Trnka Jiri • ANS • CZC
MISCHANCES OF A DRUNKARD, THE see **MESAVENTURES DE M. BOIT-SANS-SAIF, LES** • 1904
MISCHANCES OF A PHOTOGRAPHER • 1908 • Melies Georges • FRN
MISCHEVIOUS BUTTERFLY see **DUSHTU PARJAPATI** • 1967
MISCHEVIOUS ROBBER, THE • 1956 • Dolin Boris • DOC • USS
MISCHEVIOUS SKETCH, A (USA) see **CARTON FANTASTIQUE, LE** • 1907
MISCHIEF • 1931 • Raymond Jack • UKN
MISCHIEF • 1969 • Shand Ian • UKN
MISCHIEF • 1985 • Damski Mel • USA • HEART AND SOUL
MISCHIEF see **ITAZURA** • 1967
MISCHIEF see **MAN WITH ONE RED SHOE, THE** • 1985
MISCHIEF AND A MIRROR • 1916 • MacMackin Archer • USA
MISCHIEF MAKER, THE • 1914 • Thompson Frederick A. • USA
MISCHIEF MAKER, THE • 1916 • Adolfi John G. • USA
MISCHIEF-MAKERS, THE (UKN) see **MISTONS, LES** • 1958
MISCHIEF MAN, THE • 1920 • *Lew Cody Films* • USA
MISCHIEVOUS BACHELOR, THE see **NEZBEDNY BAKALAR** • 1946
MISCHIEVOUS ELF, THE • 1909 • *Edison* • USA
MISCHIEVOUS GIRLS • 1907 • Fitzhamon Lewin • UKN
MISCHIEVOUS HEDGEHOG, THE • 1952 • Popescu-Gopo Ion • ANM • RMN
MISCHIEVOUS MARGERY • 1912 • Kinder Stuart • UKN
MISCHIEVOUS MEG see **MADICKEN** • 1979
MISCHIEVOUS PUCK • 1911 • Bouwmeester Theo, Booth W. R.? • UKN
MISCHIEVOUS TUTOR, THE see **NEZBEDNY BAKALAR** • 1946
MISCONDUCT • 1966 • *Higgins Shad* • USA
MISCREANTS OF THE MOTOR WORLD • 1926 • Engholm F. W. • UKN
MISDEAL • 1981 • Trent John • CND • BEST REVENGE (USA)
MISDEAL see **MALDONNE** • 1927
MISE A NU • 1965 • Lapoujade Robert • SHT • FRN
MISE A SAC • 1967 • Cavalier Alain • FRN, ITL • NOTTE PER 5 RAPINE, UNA (ITL) ○ TORN TO BITS
MISE AUX FERS DE DREYFUS • 1899 • Melies Georges • FRN
MISE EIRE • 1958 • Morrison George • IRL
MISE EN COMMUN • 1965-66 • Garceau Raymond • DCS • CND
MISER, THE • 1913 • *Lubin* • USA
MISER, THE • 1913 • Barker Reginald? • *Kb* • USA
MISER, THE see **SPANGORAMENOS, O** • 1967
MISER, THE see **AVARO, L'** • 1990
MISER, THE (USA) see **AVARE, L'** • 1908
MISER AND HIS DAUGHTER, THE • 1904 • *Mitchell & Kenyon* • UKN
MISER AND THE CHILD, THE • 1909 • Fitzhamon Lewin • UKN
MISER AND THE MAID, THE • 1912 • Buckland Warwick • UKN
MISER MINER, THE • 1911 • Melies Gaston • USA
MISER MURRAY'S WEDDING PRESENT • 1914 • Brooke Van Dyke • USA
MISER OF MONTEREY, THE • 1915 • Montgomery Frank E.? • USA
MISER OR THE GOLD COUNTRY, THE see **SONGE D'OR DE L'AVARE, LE** • 1900
MISERABILI, I • 1947 • Freda Riccardo • ITL • LES MISERABLES (USA)
MISERABLE, LES • 1918 • Lloyd Frank • USA

MISERABLE ONES, THE see **SEFILLER** • 1967
MISERABLE ONES, THE see **ZAVALLILAR** • 1975
MISERABLES, LES • 1911 • Capellani Albert • FRN
MISERABLES, LES • 1925 • Fescourt Henri • FRN
MISERABLES, LES • 1933 • Bernard Raymond • FRN
MISERABLES, LES • 1957 • Le Chanois Jean-Paul • FRN, FRG, ITL
MISERABLES, LES • 1982 • Hossein Robert • FRN
MISERABLES, LES see **LES MISERABLES** • 1935
MISERABLES, LOS • 1943 • Rivero Fernando A. • MXC
MISERE AU BORINAGE see **BORINAGE** • 1933
MISERE DES AUTRES, LA • 1960 • Devlin Bernard • CND
MISERERE see **POQUIANCHIS, LAS** • 1976
MISERERE (IL TROVATORE) • 1906 • Gilbert Arthur • UKN
MISERIA • 1974 • Cordido Ivork • DOC • VNZ • MISERY
MISERIA E NOBILITA • 1941 • D'Errico Corrado • ITL
MISERIA E NOBILITA • 1954 • Mattoli Mario • ITL • POVERTY AND NOBILITY (USA)
MISERICORDE • 1917 • de Morlhon Camille • FRN
MISERICORDIA • 1919 • Pick Lupu • FRG
MISERICORDIA • 1952 • Gomez Urquiza Zacarias • MXC
MISERICORDIA see **TOTET NICHT MEHR!** • 1919
MISERIE DEL SIGNOR TRAVET, LE • 1946 • Soldati Mario • ITL • HIS YOUNG WIFE (USA)
MISERS, THE see **LOSERS, THE** • 1970
MISER'S AVARICE, THE • 1901 • *Warwick Trading Co* • UKN
MISER'S CHILD, THE • 1910 • Olcott Sidney • USA
MISER'S DAUGHTER, THE • 1910 • Salter Harry • USA
MISER'S DAUGHTER, THE • 1912 • *Walthall Henry B.* • USA
MISER'S DOOM, THE • 1899 • Booth W. R. • UKN
MISER'S DREAM OF GOLD, THE (USA) see **SONGE D'OR DE L'AVARE, LE** • 1900
MISER'S FATE, THE • 1909 • *Anglo-American Films* • UKN
MISER'S GIFT, THE • 1916 • Kerrigan J. M. • IRL
MISER'S HEART, THE • 1911 • Griffith D. W. • USA
MISER'S LEGACY, THE • 1915 • O'Sullivan Tony • USA
MISER'S LESSON, THE • 1910 • Haldane Bert? • UKN
MISER'S POLICY, THE • 1913 • *American* • USA
MISER'S REVERSION, THE • 1914 • *Bracy Sidney* • USA
MISER'S SON, THE • 1913 • *Shay William* • USA
MISERY • 1990 • Reiner Rob • USA
MISERY see **MISERIA** • 1974
MISERY see **JAD** • 1976
MISERY FARM • 1929 • Aylott Dave, Symmons E. F. • SHT • UKN
MISFIRE see **BOMSALVA** • 1977
MISFIT, THE see **NEPOVODENY PANACEK** • 1951
MISFIT BARON, A • 1916 • *Parsons Bill* • SHT • USA
MISFIT BECOMES CHAPERON see **GALLOPING KID, THE** • 1922
MISFIT BRIGADE, THE see **WHEELS OF TERROR** • 1987
MISFIT EARL, A • 1919 • Lowry Ira M. • USA
MISFIT FIGURE, THE see **NEPOVODENY PANACEK** • 1951
MISFIT MILLIONAIRE, A • 1917 • Santell Alfred • SHT • USA
MISFIT WIFE, THE • 1920 • Mortimer Edmund • USA
MISFITS • 1988 • Inch Kevin • USA
MISFITS, THE • 1961 • Huston John • USA
MISFITS, THE see **SURPRISING ENCOUNTER, A** • 1913
MISFITS AND MATRIMONY • 1918 • Howe J. A. • SHT • USA
MISFITS OF SCIENCE • 1985 • Parriott James • USA
MISFORTUNE see **MALAVENTURA** • 1988
MISFORTUNE, A • 1973 • Loach Kenneth • MTV • UKN
MISFORTUNE HUNTERS • 1920 • *Fay Hugh* • USA
MISFORTUNE NEVER COMES ALONE (USA) see **MALHEUR N'ARRIVE JAMAIS SEUL, UN** • 1903
MISFORTUNES OF AN EXPLORER see **INFORTUNES D'UN EXPLORATEUR, LES** • 1900
MISFORTUNES OF LOVE see **KOI NO FUUNJI** • 1945
MISFORTUNES OF MR. AND MRS. MOTT ON THEIR TRIP TO TAHITI, THE • 1913 • Melies Gaston • USA
MISGUIDED BOBBY, THE • 1905 • Martin J. H.? • UKN
MISGUIDED MISSILE • 1958 • Smith Paul J. • ANS • USA
MISGUIDED TOUR, A • 1960 • *Halas John (P)* • ANS • UKN
MISHA THE BALL • 1956 • Tyrlova Hermina • ANM • CZC
MISHAP, THE • 1915 • *Atla* • USA
MISHAPS OF BONEHEAD IN SEARCH OF AN HEIRESS, THE • 1910 • *Centaur* • USA
MISHAPS OF MARCELINE, THE • 1915 • *Thanhouser* • USA
MISHAPS OF MUSTY SUFFER, THE • 1916-17 • SER • USA
MISHAPS OF THE NEW YORK – PARIS RACE (USA) see **RAID PARIS NEW YORK EN AUTOMOBILE, LE** • 1908
MISHIMA see **MISHIMA: A LIFE IN FOUR CHAPTERS** • 1985
MISHIMA: A LIFE IN FOUR CHAPTERS • 1985 • Schrader Paul • USA • MISHIMA
MISHKA AGAINST YUDENICH see **MISHKI PROTIV YUDENICHA** • 1925
MISHKA AND MASHKA • 1964 • Lazarchuk A. • ANS • USS
MISHKI PROTIV YUDENICHA • 1925 • Kozintsev Grigori, Trauberg Leonid • USS • MISHKA AGAINST YUDENICH ○ MISKA VERSUS YUDENICH ○ BEARS VERSUS YUDENICH, THE
MISHPACHAT SIMCHON • 1964 • Silberg Joel • ISR • SIMCHON FAMILY, THE (USA)
MISION BLANCA • 1945 • de Orduna Juan • SPN
MISION CUMPLIDA • 1968 • Martinez Solares Gilberto • MXC • MISSION ACCOMPLISHED
MISION EN GINEBRA • 1967 • de la Loma Jose Antonio • SPN
MISION EN MARRUECOS • 1959 • Arevalo Carlos • SPN
MISION EXTRAVAGANTE • 1953 • Gascon Jose • SPN
MISION LISBOA • 1965 • Demicheli Tulio • SPN, ITL • 077, INTRIGO A LISBONA (ITL) ○ DA 077: INTRIGO A LISBONA ○ ESPIONAGE IN LISBON
MISION SECRETA EN EL CARIBE • 1971 • Eguiluz Enrique L. • SPN • SECRET MISSION IN THE CARIBBEAN
MISION SUICIDA • 1971 • Curiel Federico • MXC • SUICIDE MISSION (USA)
MISJUDGED • 1915 • Worthington William • USA
MISJUDGED • 1917 • Terwilliger George W. • SHT • USA
MISJUDGED MR. HARTLEY, THE • 1915 • *Washburn Bryant* • USA
MISJUDGING OF MR. HUBBY, THE • 1913 • *Carney Augustus* • USA
MISKA THE GREAT see **MAGNAS MISKA** • 1916
MISKA THE MAGNATE see **MAGNAS MISKA** • 1916
MISKA VERSUS YUDENICH see **MISHKI PROTIV YUDENICHA** • 1925
MISKENDT see **GLAEDENS DAG** • 1918
MISLAYED GENIE, THE • 1972 • Haims Eric Jeffrey • USA
MISLEADING CLUE, THE • 1915 • *Santa Barbara* • USA
MISLEADING EVIDENCE • 1912 • *Gebhardt George* • USA
MISLEADING LADY, THE • 1916 • Berthelet Arthur • USA
MISLEADING LADY, THE • 1920 • Irving George • USA
MISLEADING LADY, THE • 1932 • Walker Stuart • USA • SENSATION
MISLEADING MISS, A • 1914 • Plumb Hay? • UKN
MISLEADING WIDOW, THE • 1919 • Robertson John S. • USA • BILLETED
MISLUKKING, DE • 1987 • de Ridder Hans • NTH • FAILURE, THE
MISMATCH • 1979 • Hannam Ken • MTV • ASL
MISMATCH see **CHARLIE'S KIDS** • 1989
MISMATED • 1915 • Lessey George A. • USA
MISMATED • 1916 • *Valdez Reina* • SHT • USA
MISMATES • 1916 • Bracken Bertram • SHT • USA
MISMATES • 1926 • Brabin Charles J. • USA
MISOLOVKA • 1972 • Grgic Zlatko • ANS • YGS • MOUSETRAP, THE
MISPLACED • 1989 • Yansen • USA
MISPLACED FOOT, A • 1914 • Nicholls George • USA
MISPLACED HUSBANDS • 1928 • Lamont Charles • SHT • USA
MISPLACED JEALOUSY • 1911 • Sennett Mack • USA
MISPLACED LOVE • 1913 • *White Pearl* • USA
MISPLACED TWINS, THE • 1915 • *Farley Dot* • USA
MISS A RAOUL, LA • 1963 • Goretta Claude • SHT • SWT
MISS ADVENTURE • 1916 • Wolbert William • SHT • USA
MISS ADVENTURE • 1919 • Reynolds Lynn • USA
MISS-ADVENTURES AT MEGABOOB MANOR • *Wynn Pat D. D.* • UKN
MISS ALL-AMERICAN BEAUTY • 1982 • Trikonis Gus • TVM • USA
MISS ALLAHRAKHI • 1988 • PKS
MISS AMBITION • 1918 • Houry Henri • USA
MISS AND MRS. SWEDEN see **MISS OCH MRS. SWEDEN** • 1970
MISS ANNIE ROONEY • 1942 • Marin Edwin L. • USA
MISS APRIL see **FROKEN APRIL** • 1958
MISS ARABELLA SNAITH • 1912 • *Cruze James* • USA
MISS ARABIAN NIGHTS • 1913 • Eagle Oscar • USA
MISS ARIZONA • 1919 • Thayer Otis B. • USA
MISS ARIZONA • 1987 • Sandor Pal • HNG, ITL
MISS AUBEPINE • 1978 • Benazeraf Jose • FRN
MISS AUBRY'S LOVE AFFAIR • 1912 • *Hayward Lillian* • USA
MISS AUSTEN'S ADVENTURE • 1913 • Calvert Charles? • UKN
MISS AUSTRALIA • 1926 • *Union Theatres* • ASL
MISS AUSTRALIA QUEST • 1926 • *Fox Films* • ASL
MISS BANGALORE • 1967 • Murthy P. S. • IND
MISS BERYLL.. DIE LAUNE EINES MILLIONARS • 1920 • Zelnik Friedrich • FRG
MISS BILLIE BUTTONS • 1916 • Christie Al • USA
MISS BLOSSOM • 1916 • Reynolds Lynn • USA
MISS BLUEBEARD • 1925 • Tuttle Frank • USA
MISS BRACEGIRDLE DOES HER DUTY • 1926 • Greenwood Edwin • UKN
MISS BRACEGIRDLE DOES HER DUTY • 1936 • Garmes Lee • UKN
MISS BREWSTER'S MILLIONS • 1926 • Badger Clarence • USA
MISS CAPTAIN KIDDO • 1917 • *Lasalida Film* • USA
MISS CARIBBEAN see **MISS CARIBE** • 1988
MISS CARIBE • 1988 • Colomo Fernando • SPN • MISS CARIBBEAN
MISS CATASTROPHE • 1956 • Kirsanoff Dimitri • FRN
MISS CHARITY • 1921 • Collins Edwin J. • UKN
MISS CHATTERER'S EXPERIENCE • 1911 • *Essanay* • USA
MISS CHAUFFEUR see **FRAULEIN CHAUFFEUR** • 1928
MISS CHIC see **FROKEN CHIC** • 1959
MISS CHURCH MOUSE see **FROKEN KYRKRATTA** • 1941
MISS CINDERELLA • 1914 • *Eclectic* • USA
MISS CINDERELLA • 1917 • *Rhodes Billie* • USA
MISS COW-BOY see **VENDETTA EN CAMARGUE** • 1949
MISS CRUSOE • 1919 • Crane Frank H. • USA
MISS CUPLE • 1959 • Lazaga Pedro • SPN
MISS DE VERE (GIGUE ANGLAISE) • 1896 • Melies Georges • FRN • ENGLISH JIG
MISS DEATH see **MISS MUERTE** • 1966
MISS DECEIT • 1915 • Wilson Frank • UKN
MISS DECEPTION • 1917 • Nowland Eugene • USA
MISS DULCIE FROM DIXIE • 1919 • Gleason Joseph • USA
MISS EUROPE see **PRIX DE BEAUTE** • 1930
MISS EVELYNE, DIE BADEFEE • 1929 • Froelich Martin • FRG
MISS FAIRWEATHER OUT WEST • 1913 • *Farley Dot* • USA
MISS FANE'S BABY IS STOLEN • 1934 • Hall Alexander • USA • KIDNAPPED (UKN)
MISS FATTY'S SEASIDE LOVERS • 1915 • Arbuckle Roscoe • USA
MISS FAUST • 1909 • *Pathe* • FRN
MISS FIRECRACKER • 1989 • Schlamme Thomas • USA
MISS FIX-IT (UKN) see **KEEP SMILING** • 1938
MISS FRECKLES • 1915 • Ashley Charles E. • USA
MISS GEORGE WASHINGTON • 1916 • Dawley J. Searle • USA
MISS GINGERSNAP • 1920 • Bertram William • USA
MISS GLADEYE SLIP'S VACATION • 1913 • Stow Percy • UKN
MISS GOLEM see **SLECNA GOLEM** • 1973
MISS GRANT GOES TO THE DOOR • 1940 • Hurst Brian Desmond • UKN
MISS GRANT TAKES RICHMOND • 1949 • Bacon Lloyd • USA • INNOCENCE IS BLISS (UKN)
MISS HELETT • 1926 • Monca Georges, Keroul Maurice • FRN
MISS HELYETT • 1933 • Bourlon Hubert, Kemm Jean • FRN
MISS HOBBS • 1920 • Crisp Donald • USA
MISS HOBBS • 1921 • Kreisler Otto • AUS • TOLLE MISS, DIE ○ LOS VOM MANN
MISS HOLD'S PUPPETS • 1908 • *Pathe* • FRN
MISS INDIA • 1957 • *Burman S. D. (M)* • IND
MISS INFORMED • 1918 • *Rhodes Billie* • USA
MISS INNOCENCE • 1918 • Millarde Harry • USA
MISS ITALIA • 1951 • Coletti Duilio • ITL • MISS ITALY (USA)
MISS ITALY (USA) see **MISS ITALIA** • 1951
MISS JACKIE OF THE ARMY • 1917 • Ingraham Lloyd • USA
MISS JACKIE OF THE NAVY • 1916 • Pollard Harry • USA
MISS JEKYLL AND MADAME HYDE • 1915 • Gaskill Charles L. • SHT • USA
MISS JESSICA IS PREGNANT • 1970 • Anderson Joseph. L. • USA • SPRING NIGHT, SUMMER NIGHT ○ JESSICA
MISS JOSABETH see **MAMSELL JOSABETH** • 1963
MISS JUDE see **TRUTH ABOUT SPRING, THE** • 1964
MISS JULIE • Stenbaek Kirsten • DNM
MISS JULIE • 1972 • Philips Robin, Glenister John • UKN
MISS JULIE see **FROKEN JULIE** • 1912
MISS JULIE see **FROKEN JULIE** • 1951
MISS KEMEKO • 1968 • Kuri Yoji • ANS • JPN
MISS KNOWALL • 1940 • Cutts Graham • UKN • SCAREMONGERS, THE
MISS LESLIE'S DOLLS • 1972 • Prieto Joseph G. • USA
MISS LINA ESBRARD DANSEUSE COSMOPOLITAN ET SERPENTINE • 1902 • Blache Alice • SER • FRN
MISS LOHENGRIN see **MON BEGUIN** • 1929
MISS LONDON LTD. • 1943 • Guest Val • UKN
MISS LONELYHEARTS • 1983 • Dinner Michael • USA
MISS LONELYHEARTS see **LONELYHEARTS** • 1958
MISS LULU BETT • 1921 • De Mille William C. • USA
MISS MACTAGGART WON'T LIE DOWN • 1966 • Searle Francis • UKN
MISS MADCAP MAY • 1915 • Birch Cecil • UKN
MISS MAGNIFICAT • 1970 • *Syntax* • SHT • UKN
MISS MAGNIFICENT see **MS MAGNIFICENT** • 1979
MISS MARPLE: A POCKETFUL OF RYE • 1985 • Slater Guy • TVM • UKN
MISS MARPLE: THE BODY IN THE LIBRARY • 1985 • Narizzano Silvio • TVM • UKN
MISS MARY • 1986 • Bemberg Maria Luisa • ARG
MISS MARY WELTREISE • 1924 • Linke Edmund • FRG
MISS MASQUERADER • 1911 • *Gibson Dorothy* • USA
MISS ME AGAIN • 1925 • Ruggles Wesley • SHT • USA
MISS MEND • 1926 • Barnet Boris, Ozep Fedor • USS
MISS MILLIE'S VALENTINE • 1914 • *Dunbar Helen* • USA
MISS MINK OF 1949 • 1949 • Tryon Glenn • USA
MISS MISCHIEF • 1913 • *Ostriche Muriel* • USA
MISS MISCHIEF • 1919 • Leder Max • UKN
MISS MISCHIEF MAKER • 1918 • MacDonald Sherwood • USA
MISS MISSOURI • 1990 • Chouraqui Elie • FRN
MISS MONA • 1986 • Charef Mehdi • FRN
MISS MORRISON'S GHOSTS • 1981 • Bruce John • TVM • UKN
MISS MUERTE • 1966 • Franco Jesus • SPN, FRN • DAN LES GRIFFES DU MANIAQUE (FRN) ○ DIABOLICAL DR. Z, THE (USA) ○ IN THE GRIP OF THE MANIAC ○ MISS DEATH
MISS NIPPON • 1931 • Uchida Tomu • JPN
MISS NOBODY • 1913 • *Nestor* • USA
MISS NOBODY • 1917 • Parke William • USA
MISS NOBODY • 1920 • Grandon Francis J. • USA
MISS NOBODY • 1926 • Hillyer Lambert • USA
MISS NOBODY FROM NOWHERE • 1914 • Smallwood Ray C. • USA
MISS NUMBER PLEASE see **FOR THE LOVE OF MARY** • 1948
MISS NYMPHET'S ZAP-IN • 1970 • Lewis Herschell G. • USA • ZAP-IN
MISS OCH MRS. SWEDEN • 1970 • Gentele Goran • SWD • MISS AND MRS. SWEDEN
MISS O'GYNIE ET LES HOMMES-FLEURS • 1974 • Pavel Samy • BLG
MISS ONANAHAN see **OHANAHAN** • 1966
MISS OYU (USA) see **OYU-SAMA** • 1951
MISS PACIFIC FLEET • 1935 • Enright Ray • USA
MISS PAUL REVERE • 1922 • *Russell Clark Syndicate* • USA
MISS PEASANT • 1916 • Preobrazhenskaya Olga • USS
MISS PETTICOATS • 1916 • Knoles Harley • USA
MISS PIGALLE • 1957 • Cam Maurice • FRN
MISS PILGRIM'S PROGRESS • 1950 • Guest Val • UKN
MISS PIMPLE, SUFFRAGETTE • 1913 • Evans Fred, Evans Joe • UKN
MISS PINKERTON • 1932 • Bacon Lloyd • USA
MISS POLLY • 1941 • Guiol Fred • USA
MISS PRESIDENT see **MISS PROVIDENT** • 1935
MISS PROVIDENT • 1935 • Marton Andrew • HNG • MISS PRESIDENT
MISS RAFFLES • 1914 • Marston Theodore • USA
MISS RIGHT • 1981 • Williams Paul • USA
MISS ROBIN CRUSOE • 1954 • Frenke Eugene, Dupont E. A. (U/c) • USA
MISS ROBIN HOOD • 1952 • Guillermin John • UKN
MISS ROBINSON CRUSOE • 1912 • *La Badie Florence* • USA
MISS ROBINSON CRUSOE • 1917 • Cabanne W. Christy • USA
MISS SADIE THOMPSON • 1953 • Bernhardt Curtis • USA
MISS SARAH SAMPSON • 1919 • Abter Adolf • FRG
MISS SEX see **ALSKLING PA VIFT** • 1964
MISS SEXY see **MISS WA WAW** • 1967
MISS SHERLOCK HOLMES • 1908 • Porter Edwin S. • USA
MISS SHUMWAY CASTS A SPELL see **MISS SHUMWAY JETTE UN SORT** • 1962
MISS SHUMWAY JETTE UN SORT • 1962 • Jabely Jean • FRN, ARG • BLONDE COMME CA!, UNE ○ MISS SHUMWAY CASTS A SPELL
MISS SIMKIN'S SUMMER BOARDER • 1912 • *Blanchard Eleanor* • USA
MISS SIMPKIN'S BOARDERS • 1910 • Stow Percy • UKN
MISS SNAKE PRINCESS see **HEBI HIME-SAMA** • 1940
MISS STICKY-MOUFIE-KISS • 1915 • Drew Sidney • USA
MISS STONE see **MIS STON** • 1958
MISS SUNBEAM see **FROKEN SOLKATT** • 1948
MISS SUSIE SLAGLE'S • 1945 • Berry John • USA
MISS SUWAN • 1922 • McRay Henry • THL
MISS TAQU OF TOKIO • 1912 • Hale Albert W. • USA
MISS TATLOCK'S MILLIONS • 1948 • Haydn Richard • USA
MISS TATTY'S DIARY see **TI-TI JIH-CHI** • 1977
MISS TELEVISION see **SUSIE STEPS OUT** • 1946
MISS TERRY TAKES A LIBERTY • 1974 • Worthy John Robert • USA
MISS TOMBOY AND FRECKLES • 1914 • North Wilfred • USA
MISS TRILLIE'S BIG FEET • 1915 • *Burke Joe* • USA
MISS TRIXIE OF THE FOLLIES • 1917 • *Strand* • USA
MISS TULIP STAYS THE NIGHT • 1955 • Arliss Leslie • UKN

MISS TUTTI FRUTTI • 1920 • Curtiz Michael • ITL
MISS U.S.A. • 1917 • Millarde Harry • USA
MISS UNIVERSO EN EL PERU • *Chaski* • PRU
MISS V FROM MOSCOW • 1943 • Herman Al • USA • INTRIGUE IN PARIS
MISS VENUS • 1921 • Czerny Ludwig • FRG
MISS WA WAW • 1967 • Reyes Efren • PHL • MISS SEXY
MISS WARREN'S BROTHER • 1916 • Marston Theodore • USA
MISS WHEELWRIGHT DISCOVERS AMERICA see **MILLION DOLLAR BABY** • 1941
MISS WILDCAT see **FROKEN VILDKATT** • 1941
MISS WINDBAG • 1963 • Kalmar Laszlo • HNG
MISS YUGOSLAVIA 62 see **LJEPOTICA 62** • 1962
MISSAO DE CACA ANTI-SUBMARINA • 1957 • Simoes Quirino • SHT • PRT
MISSBRAUCHT • 1959 • Schamoni Peter • SHT • FRG
MISSBRAUCHTEN LIEBESBRIEFE, DIE • 1940 • Lindtberg Leopold • SWT
MISSED FORTUNE, A • 1952 • White Jules • SHT • USA
MISSES FINCH AND THEIR NEPHEW BILLY, THE • 1911 • *Finch Flora* • USA
MISSES STOOGE, THE • 1935 • Parrott James • SHT • USA
MISSHANDLINGEN • 1970 • Forsberg Lasse • SWD • ASSAULT, THE
MISSHITSU NO HOYO • 1967 • Takeda Ario • JPN • HUG IN A SECRET ROOM
MISSILE BASE AT TANIAK • 1953 • Adreon Franklin • USA
MISSILE MONSTERS • 1958 • Brannon Fred C. • USA
MISSILE TO THE MOON • 1959 • Cunha Richard E. • USA
MISSILE TO THE MOON see **CAT WOMEN OF THE MOON** • 1953
MISSILE X • 1978 • Martinson Leslie H. • USA, FRG, IRN • MISSILE X: GEHEIMAUFTRAG NEUTRONENBOMBE (FRG) ○ CRUISE MISSILE ○ MISSILE X: THE NEUTRON BOMB INCIDENT
MISSILE X: GEHEIMAUFTRAG NEUTRONENBOMBE (FRG) see **MISSILE X** • 1978
MISSILE X: THE NEUTRON BOMB INCIDENT see **MISSILE X** • 1978
MISSILES FROM HELL see **BATTLE OF THE V 1** • 1958
MISSING • 1917 • Shaw Brinsley • SHT • USA
MISSING • 1918 • Young James, Blackton J. Stuart (Spv) • USA
MISSING • 1982 • Costa-Gavras • USA
MISSING ADMIRALTY PLANS, THE see **STJAALNE ANSIGT, DET** • 1914
MISSING ARE DEADLY, THE • 1975 • McDougall Don • TVM • USA
MISSING BANK NOTE, THE see **MISSING LINKS, THE** • 1915
MISSING, BELIEVED MARRIED • 1937 • Carstairs John Paddy • UKN
MISSING BONDS, THE • 1913 • *Greeson Elsie* • USA
MISSING BRACELET, THE • 1916 • *Sunset* • USA
MISSING BRIDE, A • 1914 • Lehrman Henry • USA
MISSING BRIDEGROOM, THE • 1910 • *Powers* • USA
MISSING BRIDEGROOM, THE • 1910 • *Yankee* • USA
MISSING BULLET, THE • 1919 • McGowan J. P. • SHT • USA
MISSING CHILDREN: A MOTHER'S STORY • 1982 • Lowry Dick • TVM • USA
MISSING CLUE, THE • 1915 • Beggs Lee • USA
MISSING CORPSE, THE • 1945 • Herman Al • USA
MISSING DAUGHTERS • 1924 • Clifford William H. • USA
MISSING DAUGHTERS • 1939 • Coleman C. C. Jr. • USA
MISSING DIAMOND, THE • 1913 • *Lubin* • USA
MISSING EVIDENCE • 1939 • Rosen Phil • USA
MISSING EVIDENCE see **GREAT SWINDLE, THE** • 1941
MISSING FINANCIER, THE • 1917 • Ellis Robert • SHT • USA
MISSING FINGER, THE • 1912 • *Lubin* • USA
MISSING GENIE, THE • 1963 • Rasinski Connie • ANS • USA
MISSING GIRLS • 1936 • Rosen Phil • USA • WHEN GIRLS LEAVE HOME (UKN)
MISSING GUEST, THE • 1938 • Rawlins John • USA
MISSING HEAD, THE see **STRANGE CONFESSION** • 1945
MISSING HEIR, THE • 1911 • *Thanhouser* • USA
MISSING HEIRESS, THE • 1916 • Ellis Robert • SHT • USA
MISSING HUSBAND • 1919 • Lyons Eddie, Moran Lee • SHT • USA
MISSING HUSBANDS see **ATLANTIDE, L'** • 1921
MISSING IN ACTION • 1984 • Zito Joseph • USA
MISSING IN ACTION 2: THE BEGINNING • 1985 • Hool Lance • USA • BATTLE RAGE
MISSING IN ACTION 3 see **BRADDOCK: MISSING IN ACTION III** • 1988
MISSING JEWELS, THE • 1913 • Hotaling Arthur D. • USA
MISSING JEWELS, THE • 1914 • *Lawrence Adelaide* • USA
MISSING JUROR, THE • 1945 • Boetticher Budd • USA
MISSING LADY, THE • 1946 • Karlson Phil • USA
MISSING LEGACY: OR, THE STORY OF A BROWN HAT, THE • 1906 • Collins Alf? • UKN
MISSING LINK • 1988 • Hughes David, Hughes Carol • USA
MISSING LINK, THE • 1917 • Kellino W. P. • UKN
MISSING LINK, THE • 1927 • Reisner Charles F. • USA
MISSING LINK, THE see **HALAKA EL SAFKUDA, EL** • 1949
MISSING LINK, THE see **CHAINON MANQUANT, LE** • 1981
MISSING LINKS, THE • 1915 • Ingraham Lloyd • USA • MISSING BANK NOTE, THE
MISSING LOCKET, THE • 1916 • *Early Baby* • SHT • USA
MISSING MAN, THE • 1915 • *Baird Elizabeth* • USA
MISSING MAN, THE • 1953 • Hughes Ken • UKN
MISSING MILLION, THE • 1942 • Brandon Phil • UKN
MISSING MILLIONAIRE, THE • 1916 • Horne James W. • SHT • USA
MISSING MILLIONS • 1922 • Henabery Joseph • USA
MISSING MOUSE, THE • 1953 • Hanna William, Barbera Joseph • ANS • USA
MISSING MUMMY, THE • 1915 • *Duncan Bud* • USA
MISSING NECKLACE, THE • 1916 • *Puritan* • USA
MISSING NOTE, THE • 1961 • Brandt Michael • UKN
MISSING PAGE, THE • 1914 • Martin E. A. • USA
MISSING PENCIL, THE see **IZGUBLJENA OLOVKA** • 1960
MISSING PEOPLE, THE • 1939 • Raymond Jack • UKN
MISSING PERSONS • 1953 • Falconer Alun • UKN
MISSING PIECES • 1983 • Hodges Mike • TVM • USA • PRIVATE INVESTIGATION, A
MISSING PRINCESS, THE • 1954 • Scobie Alastair, Leslie Desmond • UKN
MISSING PRINCIPAL, THE see **FORSVUNDNE FULDMAEGTIG, DEN** • 1972
MISSING REMBRANDT, THE • 1932 • Hiscott Leslie • UKN • SHERLOCK HOLMES AND THE MISSING REMBRANDT (USA) ○ STRANGE CASE OF THE MISSING REMBRANDT, THE
MISSING RING, THE • 1913 • *Cummings Irving* • USA
MISSING RUBY, THE • 1915 • Santschi Thomas • USA
MISSING SCIENTISTS • 1955 • Sekely Steve • USA
MISSING TEN DAYS (USA) see **TEN DAYS IN PARIS** • 1939
MISSING THE TIDE • 1918 • West Walter • UKN
MISSING THREE QUARTER, THE • 1923 • Ridgwell George • UKN
MISSING TIARA, THE • 1912 • Calvert Charles? • UKN
MISSING TWENTY-FIVE DOLLARS, THE • 1914 • Seay Charles M. • USA
MISSING WALLET, THE • 1917 • *August Edwin* • SHT • USA
MISSING WILL, THE • 1911 • *Bunny John* • USA
MISSING WITNESS • 1937 • Clemens William • USA • MISSING WITNESSES
MISSING WITNESS, THE • 1913 • Heffron Thomas N. • USA
MISSING WITNESS, THE • 1916 • Brenon Herbert • SHT • USA
MISSING WITNESS, THE see **LOVE'S OLD SWEET SONG** • 1933
MISSING WITNESSES see **MISSING WITNESS** • 1937
MISSING WOMAN • 1951 • Ford Philip • USA
MISSING YOU ATOO see **TAAN TA YA DAI ATOO YE** • 1983
MISSION, LA • 1971 • Merbah Lamine • ALG
MISSION, THE • 1984 • Sayyad Parviz • USA, FRG • FERESTADEH
MISSION, THE • 1986 • Joffe Roland • UKN
MISSION A TANGER see **MISSION A TANGIER** • 1949
MISSION A TANGIER • 1949 • Hunebelle Andre • FRN • JE TIRE MA REVERENCE ○ MISSION A TANGER
MISSION ACCOMPLISHED see **MISION CUMPLIDA** • 1968
MISSION BATANGAS • 1967 • Larsen Keith • USA • ...EXCEPT PEOPLE GET KILLED ○ OPERATION PACIFIC ○ BATANGAS
MISSION BELLS • 1913 • *American* • USA
MISSION BELLS • 1913 • *Kinemacolor* • USA
MISSION BLOODY MARY (USA) see **AGENTE 077 -MISSIONE BLOODY MARY** • 1965
MISSION CARRIER, THE • 1911 • *Kalem* • USA
MISSION CASABLANCA see **A 077, SFIDA AI KILLERS** • 1965
MISSION DIABOLIQUE see **FUCHS DE PARIS, DER** • 1957
MISSION FATHER, THE • 1911 • Melies Gaston • USA
MISSION FOR A KILLER see **FURIA A BAHIA POUR OSS 117** • 1965
MISSION FROM MARS • 1968 • Lopez John • ANS • USA
MISSION GALACTICA; THE CYCLON ATTACK • 1979 • Edwards Vince, Nyby Christian Ii • TVM • USA
MISSION HILL • 1982 • Jones Robert • USA • NEIGHBOURHOOD: MISSION HILL, THE ○ NEIGHBOURHOOD, THE
MISSION IMPOSSIBLE (USA) see **CHIEN-NU YU-HU** • 1970
MISSION IMPOSSIBLE VS. THE MOB • 1969 • Geller Bruce, Stanley Paul • MTV • USA
MISSION IN MOROCCO • 1959 • Squire Anthony • USA • MISSION TO MOROCCO
MISSION IN THE DESERT, THE • 1911 • *American* • USA
MISSION KILL • 1984 • Winters David • USA
MISSION MANILA • 1988 • Mackenzie Peter • USA • WEB
MISSION MARS • 1968 • Webster Nicholas • USA • RED PLANET MARS ○ DESTINATION MARS
MISSION MONTE CARLO see **PERSUADERS: MISSION MONTE CARLO, THE** • 1975
MISSION OF A BULLET, THE • 1912 • *Roland Ruth* • USA
MISSION OF A FLOWER, THE • 1908 • Coleby A. E. • UKN
MISSION OF DANGER • 1959 • Tourneur Jacques, Waggner George • MTV • USA
MISSION OF DEATH see **APOSTOLI THANATOU** • 1968
MISSION OF MR. FOO, THE • 1915 • Collins John H. • USA
MISSION OF MORRISON, THE • 1915 • *Reliance* • USA
MISSION OF PATIENCE, THE • 1916 • Vignola Robert G. • USA
MISSION OF STATE, A • 1916 • Ellis Robert • USA
MISSION OF THE SEA HAWK • 1962 • *Morgan Terence* • MTV • UKN
MISSION OVER KOREA • 1953 • Sears Fred F. • USA • EYES OF THE SKIES (UKN)
MISSION SECRETE: LA CASTIGLIONE see **CASTIGLIONE, LA** • 1953
MISSION SHIP • 1953 • Anderson Robert • DOC • CND
MISSION SPECIALE • 1945 • de Canonge Maurice • FRN
MISSION SPECIALE A CARACAS • 1965 • Andre Raoul • FRN, ITL, SPN • SPECIAL MISSION TO CARACAS
MISSION SPELLBOUND • 1984 • SAF
MISSION STARDUST (USA) see **PERRY RHODAN -SOS AUS DEM WELTALL** • 1967
MISSION TERMINATE • 1987 • Maharaj Anthony • USA • COOPER ○ MISSION: TERMINATE
MISSION: TERMINATE see **MISSION TERMINATE** • 1987
MISSION TIRAN see **HA'MATARAH TIRAN** • 1968
MISSION TO GLORY • 1979 • Kennedy Ken • USA
MISSION TO HELL see **KOGAN NO MISSHI** • 1959
MISSION TO HELL see **SAVAGE!** • 1962
MISSION TO HELL (USA) see **SFIDA VIENE DA BANGKOK, LA** • 1965
MISSION TO HONG KONG see **GEHEIMNIS DER DREI DSCHUNKEN, DAS** • 1965
MISSION TO KABUL • 1971 • Kvinikhidze Leonid • USS
MISSION TO MOROCCO see **MISSION IN MOROCCO** • 1959
MISSION TO MOSCOW • 1943 • Curtiz Michael • USA
MISSION TO PARADISE see **BIKINI PARADISE** • 1964
MISSION TO TOKYO (UKN) see **ATOUT COEUR A TOKYO POUR OSS 117** • 1966
MISSION TRAIL, THE • 1919 • *Hart Neal* • SHT • USA
MISSION WAIF, THE • 1911 • Melies Gaston • USA
MISSION WANDERING PLANET see **MISSIONE PIANETA ERRANTE** • 1965
MISSION WORKER, THE • 1911 • *Selig* • USA
MISSIONAIRE, LE see **MISSIONAIRE, UN** • 1955
MISSIONAIRE, UN • 1955 • Cloche Maurice • FRN • MISSIONAIRE, LE
MISSIONARIES IN DARKEST AFRICA • 1912 • Olcott Sidney • DOC • USA
MISSIONARY, THE • 1918 • Wharton Theodore • USA
MISSIONARY, THE • 1982 • Loncraine Richard • UKN
MISSIONARY AND THE ACTRESS, THE • 1913 • Parker Lem B. • USA
MISSIONARY AND THE MAID, THE • 1909 • *Edison* • USA
MISSIONARY BOX, THE • 1913 • *Rex* • USA
MISSIONARY'S DAUGHTER, THE • 1908 • Stow Percy • UKN
MISSIONARY'S GRATITUDE, THE • 1911 • *Bison* • USA
MISSIONARY'S TRIUMPH, THE • 1913 • *Patheplay* • USA
MISSIONE APOCALISSE • 1966 • Malatesta Guido • ITL, SPN • 087 MISION APOCALIPSIS (SPN) ○ 087 MISSION APOCALISSE ○ 087 MISSION APOCALYPSE
MISSIONE DEL MANDRILLO, LA • 1977 • Zurli Guido • ITL
MISSIONE EROICA -I POMPIERI 2 • 1987 • Capitani Giorgio • ITL • HEROIC MISSION -THE FIREMEN 2
MISSIONE PIANETA ERRANTE • 1965 • Margheriti Antonio • ITL • WAR BETWEEN THE PLANETS (USA) ○ PLANET ON THE PROWL ○ MISSION WANDERING PLANET
MISSIONE SABBIE ROVENTI • 1966 • Brescia Alfonso • ITL
MISSIONE SPAZIO TEMPO ZERO • 1969 • Gavioli Roberto, Bernardi Marcello • ITL
MISSIONE SPECIALE LADY CHAPLIN • 1966 • De Martino Alberto • ITL, SPN, FRN • OPERACION LADY CHAPLIN (SPN) ○ OPERATION LADY CHAPLIN ○ 077: SPECIAL MISSION LADY CHAPLIN ○ LADY CHAPLIN STORY, THE ○ OPERAZIONE LADY CHAPLIN
MISSIONER, THE • 1922 • Ridgwell George • UKN
MISSIONER'S PLIGHT, THE • 1913 • Wilson Frank? • UKN
MISSIONS DE FRANCE • 1939 • Ichac Marcel • DCS • FRN
MISSIONS SECRETES see **DOCUMENTS SECRETS** • 1940
MISSISSIPPI • 1931 • Mack Russell • USA
MISSISSIPPI • 1935 • Sutherland A. Edward • USA
MISSISSIPPI BLUES • 1983 • Tavernier Bertrand, Parrish Robert • FRN, USA
MISSISSIPPI BURNING • 1988 • Parker Alan • USA
MISSISSIPPI GAMBLER • 1942 • Rawlins John • USA • DANGER ON THE RIVER
MISSISSIPPI GAMBLER • 1953 • Mate Rudolph • USA
MISSISSIPPI GAMBLER, THE • 1929 • Barker Reginald • USA
MISSISSIPPI HARE • 1948 • Jones Charles M. • ANS • USA
MISSISSIPPI-ILLUSION • 1961 • Schamoni Peter, Houwer Rob • FRG
MISSISSIPPI MERMAID (USA) see **SIRENE DU MISSISSIPPI, LA** • 1969
MISSISSIPPI MOODS • 1937 • Goodwins Leslie • SHT • USA
MISSISSIPPI RHYTHM • 1949 • Abrahams Derwin • USA
MISSISSIPPI SLOW BOAT • 1961 • Smith Paul J. • ANS • USA
MISSISSIPPI SUMMER • 1968 • Poayer William • USA
MISSISSIPPI SWING • 1941 • Rasinski Connie • ANS • USA
MISSISSIPPI TRAGEDY, A • 1913 • *Nilsson Anna Q.* • USA
MISS/MRS. • 1972 • Dove Linda • UKN
MISSOURI BREAKS, THE • 1976 • Penn Arthur • USA
MISSOURI OUTLAW, A • 1941 • Sherman George • USA
MISSOURI STORY, THE see **ROMANCE OF ROSY RIDGE, THE** • 1947
MISSOURI TRAVELER, THE • 1958 • Hopper Jerry • USA
MISSOURIANS, THE • 1950 • Blair George • USA
MISSUS AMERICA see **MEET THE MISSUS** • 1937
MISSY • 1916 • Reynolds Lynn • SHT • USA
MIST, THE see **MANJA** • 1982
MIST IN THE VALLEY • 1923 • Hepworth Cecil M. • UKN
MIST OF ERRORS, A • 1913 • Buckland Warwick? • UKN
MIST (UKN) see **SIS** • 1989
MISTACHIPU • 1971 • Lamothe Arthur • DOC • CND • GRANDE RIVIERE, LA
MISTAKE, THE • 1910 • Salter Harry • USA
MISTAKE, THE • 1913 • Griffith D. W. • USA
MISTAKE, THE see **ENGANO, O** • 1968
MISTAKE IN JUDGMENT, A • 1913 • Seay Charles M. • USA
MISTAKE IN RUSTLERS, A • 1916 • Mix Tom • SHT • USA
MISTAKE IN TYPESETTING, A • 1915 • Beggs Lee • USA
MISTAKE OF MAMMY LOU, THE • 1915 • *Arey Wayne* • USA
MISTAKEN ACCUSATION, A • 1913 • *Bushman Francis X.* • USA
MISTAKEN BANDIT, THE • 1910 • *Anderson Broncho Billy* • USA
MISTAKEN BATH HOUSE, THE • 1914 • *Sterling* • USA
MISTAKEN CALLING, A • 1912 • *Blanchard Eleanor* • USA
MISTAKEN FOR A BURGLAR IN HIS OWN HOUSE • 1905 • Green Tom? • UKN
MISTAKEN IDENTITY • 1906 • Martin J. H.? • UKN
MISTAKEN IDENTITY • 1909 • Bouwmeester Theo? • UKN
MISTAKEN IDENTITY • 1910 • *Kalem* • USA
MISTAKEN IDENTITY • 1910 • Aylott Dave? • UKN
MISTAKEN IDENTITY • 1912 • *Selig* • USA
MISTAKEN IDENTITY • 1919 • *King Anita* • USA
MISTAKEN IDENTITY • 1939 • Tennyson Walter • UKN
MISTAKEN IDENTITY, A (USA) see **QUIPROQUO** • 1908
MISTAKEN INTENTION • 1910 • *Gaumont* • UKN
MISTAKEN INTENTIONS • 1913 • *Quirk Billy* • USA
MISTAKEN MASHER, THE • 1913 • Sennett Mack • USA
MISTAKEN ORDERS • 1926 • McGowan J. P. • USA • GREAT RAILWAY ROBBERY, THE
MISTAKEN WATCH, A • 1914 • *Royal* • USA
MISTAKES WILL HAPPEN • 1911 • *Edison* • USA
MISTAKES WILL HAPPEN • 1914 • *Royal* • USA
MISTAKES WILL HAPPEN • 1915 • *Federal* • USA
MISTAKES WILL HAPPEN • 1916 • Mix Tom • SHT • USA
MISTAKING IN SPELLING, A • 1912 • Young James • USA
MISTASSINI • 1971 • Cardinal Roger • DCS • CND
MISTAWASSIS • 1977 • Borris Clay • CND • LITTLE BIG CHILD
MISTAZ • 1966 • Antczak Jerzy • PLN • MASTER, THE
MR. 8 BALL • 1967 • To-Chi-Qui • PHL
MISTER 44 • 1916 • Otto Henry • USA
MISTER 420 see **SHRI 420** • 1955
MISTER 880 • 1950 • Goulding Edmund • USA
MR. A. JONAH • 1910 • *Selig* • USA
MR. ACE • 1946 • Marin Edwin L. • USA
MR. ADAM • 1933 • Christie Al • USA

MR. ALDRICH'S BOY see **HENRY AND DIZZY** • 1942
MR. ANATOL SEEKS A MILLION see **PAN ANATOL SZUKA MILIONA** • 1959
MR. ANATOL'S HAT see **KAPELUSZ PANA ANATOLA** • 1958
MR. ANATOL'S INSPECTION see **INSPEKCJA PANA ANATOLA** • 1959
MR. AND MISERABLE JONES see **DANGEROUS CURVE AHEAD** • 1921
MISTER AND MISTLETOE • 1955 • Sparber I. • ANS • USA
MR. AND MRS. 55 • 1955 • Dutt Guru • IND
MR. AND MRS. ANONYMOUS see **SOMETHING TO LIVE FOR** • 1952
MR. AND MRS. BO JO JONES • 1971 • Day Robert • TVM • USA
MR. AND MRS. CUGAT see **ARE HUSBANDS NECESSARY?** • 1942
MR. AND MRS. DUFF • 1909 • Melies Georges • FRN
MISTER AND MRS. EDGEHILL • 1985 • Millar Gavin • MTV • UKN
MR. AND MRS. HONEYSUCKLE AND THE BEE • 1902 • *Warwick Trading Co* • UKN
MR. AND MRS. INNOCENCE ABROAD • 1913 • *Baird Leah* • USA
MR. AND MRS. IS THE NAME • 1935 • Freleng Friz • ANS • USA
MR. AND MRS. NORTH • 1941 • Sinclair Robert B. • USA
MR. AND MRS. PIECAN –THE GIDDY HUSBAND • 1915 • Evans Joe • UKN
MR. AND MRS. POORLUCK SEPARATE • 1911 • Fitzhamon Lewin • UKN
MR. AND MRS. SMITH • 1941 • Hitchcock Alfred • USA
MR. AND MRS. SUSPICIOUS • 1911 • *Lubin* • USA
MR. AND MRS. SWORDPLAY see **CHANBARA FUFU** • 1930
MISTER ANTONIO • 1929 • Flood James, Reicher Frank • USA
MR. ARKADIN see **CONFIDENTIAL REPORT** • 1955
MR. ARTIST see **PAN PLASTYK** • 1964
MR. ASHTON WAS INDISCREET (UKN) see **SENATOR WAS INDISCREET, THE** • 1947
MR. BARNES OF NEW YORK • 1914 • Costello Maurice, Gaillord Robert • USA
MR. BARNES OF NEW YORK • 1922 • Schertzinger Victor • USA
MR. BEAMISH GOES SOUTH • 1953 • Wall John, Burn Oscar • UKN
MR. BELVEDERE GOES TO COLLEGE • 1949 • Nugent Elliott • USA
MR. BELVEDERE RINGS THE BELL • 1951 • Koster Henry • USA
MR. BIDDLE'S CRIME WAVE • 1959 • *Mcdowall Roddy* • MTV • USA
MR. BIG • 1943 • Lamont Charles • USA • SCHOOL FOR JIVE
MR. BIGMAN see **NAGYEMBER, A** • 1968
MR. BILL LOOKS BACK • 1980 • Williams Walter • ANS • USA
MR. BILL THE CONQUEROR • 1932 • Walker Norman • UKN • MAN WHO WON, THE (USA) ○ BILL THE CONQUEROR
MR. BILLINGS PUTS THINGS RIGHT see **MR. BILLINGS SPENDS HIS DIME** • 1923
MR. BILLINGS SPENDS HIS DIME • 1923 • Ruggles Wesley • USA • MR. BILLINGS PUTS THINGS RIGHT
MR. BILLION • 1977 • Kaplan Jonathan • USA • SCRAMBLE
MR. BILL'S REAL LIFE ADVENTURES • 1986 • Drake Jim • USA
MR. BINGLE • 1922 • Wharton Leopold • USA
MR. BINGLES' MELODRAMA • 1914 • Baker George D. • USA
MISTER BINGO, THE BACHELOR • 1917 • MacGregor Norval • SHT • USA
MR. BIXBIE'S DILEMMA • 1915 • *Shea William* • USA
MR. BLANDING BUILDS HIS DREAM HOUSE • 1948 • Potter H. C. • USA
MR. BLINK OF BOHEMIA • 1915 • Drew Sidney • USA
MISTER BLOT IN OUTER SPACE • 1988 • PLN
MR. BOGGS STEPS OUT • 1938 • Wiles Gordon • USA
MR. BOLTER'S INFATUATION • 1912 • Baker George D. • USA
MR. BOLTER'S NIECE • 1912 • Thompson Frederick A. • USA
MR. BORLAND THINKS AGAIN • 1940 • Rotha Paul • UKN
MR. BOROKA'S ANGUISH see **BOROKA UR SZORONGASAI** • 1972
MR. BRAGG, A FUGITIVE • 1911 • Sennett Mack, Henderson Dell • USA
MR. BREAKNECK'S INVENTION • 1910 • Stow Percy • UKN
MR. BRIDE • 1932 • Parrott Charles • SHT • USA
MR. BRIGGS CLOSES THE HOUSE • 1918 • Beaudine William • SHT • USA
MISTER BROADWAY • 1933 • Ulmer Edgar G. • USA
MR. BROADWAY • 1933 • Walker Johnnie • USA
MISTER BROWN • 1972 • Andrieux Roger • FRN, USA
MR. BROWN COMES DOWN THE HILL • 1966 • Cass Henry • UKN
MR. BROWN'S BATHING TENT • 1905 • Stow Percy • UKN
MISTER BUDDWING • 1965 • Mann Delbert • USA • WOMAN WITHOUT A FACE (UKN)
MR. BUDDY BRIGGS, BURGLAR • 1916 • *Morris Dave* • SHT • USA
MR. BUG GOES TO TOWN • 1941 • Fleischer Dave, Fleischer Max • ANM • USA • HOPPITY GOES TO TOWN (UKN)
MR. BUMBLE see **IF YOU KNOW WHAT I MEAN** • 1982
MR. BUMBLE THE BEADLE • 1898 • *Paul R. W.* • UKN
MR. BUMPS, COMMUTOR • 1916 • *Novelty* • USA
MR. BUMPTIOUS, DETECTIVE • 1911 • Merwin Bannister • USA
MR. BUNNYHUG BUYS A HAT FOR HIS BRIDE • 1914 • Baker George D. • USA
MR. BUTT-IN • 1906 • *Bitzer Billy (Ph)* • USA
MR. BUTTLES • 1915 • Totten Joseph Byron • USA
MR. CANTON AND LADY ROSE see **KEITSIK** • 1989
MR. CARLSON OF ARIZONA • 1915 • Fielding Romaine • USA
MR. CELEBRITY • 1941 • Beaudine William • USA
MR. CHEDWORTH STEPS OUT • 1939 • Hall Ken G. • ASL
MR. CHESHER'S TRACTION ENGINES • 1962 • Russell Ken • MTV • UKN
MR. CHRISTMAS DINNER see **LUCKY STIFF** • 1988
MR. CHUMP • 1938 • Clemens William • USA
MR. CINDERELLA • 1914 • *Gane Nolan* • USA
MR. CINDERELLA • 1926 • Taurog Norman • SHT • USA
MR. CINDERELLA • 1936 • Sedgwick Edward • USA
MISTER CINDERS • 1934 • Zelnik Friedrich • UKN
MISTER CLOWN AMONG THE LILLIPUTIANS see **MONSIEUR CLOWN CHEZ LES LILLIPUTIENS** • 1909
MR. CLYDE GOES TO BROADWAY • 1940 • Lord Del • SHT • USA
MR. CO-ED see **BATHING BEAUTY** • 1944
MR. COCONUT • 1989 • Gao Zhizen • HKG
MR. COHEN TAKES A WALK • 1935 • Beaudine William • UKN
MR. COLLINS' ADVENTURES see **HERR COLLINS AVENTYR** • 1943
MR. CONGRESSMAN see **WASHINGTON STORY** • 1952
MR. CORBETT'S GHOST • 1987 • Huston Danny • UKN
MISTER CORY • 1957 • Edwards Blake • USA
MR. DALY'S WEDDING DAY • 1914 • West Langdon • USA
MR. DAUBER AND THE MYSTIFYING PICTURES (USA) see **PEINTRE BARBOUILLARD ET TABLEAU DIABOLIQUE, LE** • 1905
MISTER DEATHMAN • 1983 • Moore Michael • USA
MR. DEEDS GOES TO TOWN • 1936 • Capra Frank • USA
MR. DENNING DRIVES NORTH • 1951 • Kimmins Anthony • UKN
MISTER DESIGNER see **PAN PLASTYK** • 1964
MR. DESTINY • 1990 • Orr James • USA
MR. DIDDLEM'S WILL • 1912 • Stow Percy • UKN
MR. DIPPY DIPPED • 1913 • *Stine Charlie* • USA
MR. DIRT see **SCHMUTZ** • 1986
MR. DISTRICT ATTORNEY • 1941 • Morgan William • USA
MR. DISTRICT ATTORNEY • 1947 • Sinclair Robert B. • USA
MR. DISTRICT ATTORNEY IN THE CARTER CASE • 1941 • Vorhaus Bernard • USA • CARTER CASE, THE (UKN)
MR. DODD TAKES THE AIR • 1937 • Green Alfred E. • USA
MISTER DODEK see **PAN DODEK** • 1969
MR. DOLAN OF NEW YORK • 1917 • Wells Raymond • USA
MR. DOODLES KICKS OFF • 1938 • Goodwins Leslie • USA
MR. DRAKE'S DUCK • 1951 • Guest Val • UKN
MR. DUCK STEPS OUT • 1940 • King Jack • ANS • USA
MISTER DYNAMIT –MORGEN KUSST EUCH DER TOD • 1967 • Gottlieb Franz J. • AUS, FRG, ITL • MUORI LENTAMENTE.. TA LA GODI DI PIU (ITL) ○ DIE SLOWLY, YOU'LL ENJOY IT MORE ○ MR. DYNAMITE –DEATH WILL KISS YOU TOMORROW
MR. DYNAMITE • 1935 • Crosland Alan • USA
MR. DYNAMITE • 1941 • Rawlins John • USA
MR. DYNAMITE –DEATH WILL KISS YOU TOMORROW see **MISTER DYNAMIT –MORGEN KUSST EUCH DER TOD** • 1967
MR. EDITOR IS CRAZY (USA) see **PAN REDAKTOR SZALEJE** • 1938
MR. ELEPHANT see **PAN SLON** • 1960
MR. ELEPHANT GOES TO TOWN • 1940 • Davis Arthur • ANS • USA
MR. EMMANUEL • 1944 • French Harold • UKN
MR. FAINTHEART (UKN) see **$10 RAISE** • 1935
MR. FATIMA • 1920 • *Barry Eddie* • SHT • USA
MR. FIX see **RIFFRAFF** • 1947
MR. FIX-IT • 1918 • Dwan Allan • USA
MR. FIXER see **MR. FIXIT** • 1912
MR. FIXIT • 1912 • *Lubin* • USA
MR. FIXIT • 1912 • Sennett Mack • *Keystone* • USA • MR. FIXER
MISTER FIXIT MY DAD • 1971 • Thornhill Michael • DOC • ASL
MR. FLIP • 1909 • *Essanay* • USA
MR. FLIRT IN WRONG • 1915 • *L-Ko* • USA
MISTER FLOW • 1936 • Siodmak Robert • FRN • AMANTS TRAQUES, LES ○ COMPLIMENTS OF MR. FLOW
MR. FORBUSH AND THE PENGUINS • 1972 • Viola Albert T., Sucksdorff Arne • UKN • CRY OF THE PENGUINS (USA)
MR. FORD'S TEMPER • 1913 • Thompson Frederick A. • USA
MR. FORE BY FORE • 1944 • Swift Howard • ANS • USA
MR. FOUR FLUSH • 1910 • *Selig* • USA
MISTER FREEDOM • 1969 • Klein William • FRN
MR. FRENHOFER AND THE MINOTAUR • 1949 • Peterson Sidney • SHT • USA
MR. FROG WENT A-COURTING • 1974 • Lambart Evelyn • ANS • CND
MR. FROST • 1990 • Setbon Philippe • USA
MR. FULLER PEP • 1916-17 • *Powers P. A. (P)* • ASS • USA
MR. FUZZ • 1908 • *Pathe* • FRN
MR. GALLAGHER AND MR. SHEAN • 1931 • Fleischer Dave • ANS • USA
MR. GILBERT AND MR. SULLIVAN see **STORY OF GILBERT AND SULLIVAN, THE** • 1953
MR. GILFIL'S LOVE STORY • 1920 • Bramble A. V. • UKN • LOVE STORY OF MR. GILFIL
MISTER GIMMICK • 1968 • To-Chi-Qui • PHL
MR. GOODE, THE SAMARITAN • 1916 • Dillon Eddie • USA
MR. GOOSE GOES HUNTING see **APO LAHTARA SE LAHTARA** • 1967
MR. GREEN'S BET • 1971 • Sremec Rudolf • DOC • YGS
MR. GREX OF MONTE CARLO • 1915 • Reicher Frank • USA
MR. GRIGGS RETURNS (UKN) see **COCKEYED MIRACLE, THE** • 1946
MR. GROUCH AT THE SEASHORE • 1912 • Henderson Dell, Sennett Mack (Spv) • USA
MR. H.C. ANDERSEN • 1950 • Haines Ronald • UKN • HAN CHRISTIAN ANDERSEN (USA)
MR. HABETIN DEPARTS see **PAN HABETIN OCHAZI** • 1949
MR. HADLEY'S UNCLE • 1914 • *Komic* • USA
MR. HALPERN AND MR. JOHNSON • 1983 • Rakoff Alvin • USA
MR. HARE AND MR. HEDGEHOG • 1963 • Rauer Albert • ANS • USA
MISTER HAWARDEN see **MONSIEUR HAWARDEN** • 1968
MR. HAYASHI • 1961 • Baillie Bruce • SHT • USA
MISTER HEAD see **MONSIEUR TETE** • 1959
MR. HENPECK'S ADVENTURE WITH A BURGLAR • 1908 • *Tyler Walter* • UKN
MR. HENPECK'S DILEMMA • 1913 • Pearson George • UKN
MR. HENPECK'S QUIET BANK HOLIDAY • 1906 • Raymond Charles? • UKN
MR. HENPECK'S REVOLT • 1909 • *Anglo-American Films* • UKN
MR. HERCULES AGAINST KARATE see **SCHIAFFONI E KARATI** • 1974
MR. HEX • 1946 • Beaudine William • USA • PRIDE OF THE BOWERY, THE (UKN)
MR. HOBBS TAKES A VACATION • 1962 • Koster Henry • USA
MR. HOBO (USA) see **GUV'NOR, THE** • 1935
MR. HOOPS, THE DETECTIVE • 1912 • *Comet* • USA
MR. HOOVER AND I • 1990 • De Antonio Emile • DOC • USA, UKN
MR. HORATIO KNIBBLES • 1971 • Hird Robert • UKN
MR. HORN • 1979 • Starrett Jack • TVM • USA
MR. HOUSEKEEPER • 1916 • Metcalfe Earl • SHT • USA
MR. HOUSEKEEPER see **HERR HUSASSISTENEN** • 1939
MR. HUBBY'S WIFE • 1912 • *Carney Augustus* • USA
MR. HUGHES AND HIS CHRISTMAS TURKEY • 1904 • Codman John • UKN
MR. HULOT'S HOLIDAY (USA) see **VACANCES DE M. HULOT** • 1952
MR. HURRY-UP OF NEW YORK • 1907 • *Bitzer Billy (Ph)* • USA
MR. HYPPO • 1923 • Roach Hal • SHT • USA
MR. IKL'S JUBILEE see **JUBILEJ GOSPODINA IKLA** • 1955
MR. IMPERIUM • 1951 • Hartman Don • USA • YOU BELONG TO MY HEART ○ ALWAYS IN MY HEART
MR. INDIA • 1988 • Kapoor Shekhar • IND
MR. INQUISITIVE • 1911 • *Lubin* • USA
MR. INSIDE / MR. OUTSIDE • 1973 • Graham William A. • TVM • USA
MR. INVISIBLE see **INAFFERRABILE E INVINCIBILE MR. INVISIBILE, L'** • 1970
MR. JACK, A DOCTOR BY PROXY • 1916 • Williams C. Jay • SHT • USA
MR. JACK A HALLROOM HERO • 1916 • Williams C. Jay • SHT • USA
MR. JACK DUCKS THE ALIMONY • 1916 • Williams C. Jay • SHT • USA
MR. JACK GOES INTO BUSINESS • 1916 • Williams C. Jay • SHT • USA
MR. JACK HIRES A STENOGRAPHER • 1916 • Williams C. Jay • SHT • USA
MR. JACK INSPECTS PARIS • 1916 • Williams C. Jay • SHT • USA
MR. JACK, THE HASH MAGNET • 1916 • Williams C. Jay • SHT • USA
MR. JACK TRIFLES • 1916 • Williams C. Jay • SHT • USA
MR. JACK WINS A DOUBLE-CROSS • 1916 • Williams C. Jay • SHT • USA
MR. JACK'S ARTISTIC SENSE • 1916 • Williams C. Jay • SHT • USA
MR. JACK'S HAT AND THE CAT • 1916 • Williams C. Jay • SHT • USA
MR. JARR AND CIRCUMSTANTIAL EVIDENCE • 1915 • Davenport Harry • USA
MR. JARR AND GERTRUDE'S BEAUX • 1915 • Davenport Harry • USA
MR. JARR AND LOVE'S YOUNG DREAM • 1915 • Davenport Harry • USA
MR. JARR AND THE CAPTIVE MAIDEN • 1915 • Davenport Harry • USA
MR. JARR AND THE DACHSHUND • 1915 • Davenport Harry • USA
MR. JARR AND THE LADIES' CUP • 1915 • Davenport Harry • USA
MR. JARR AND THE LADY REFORMER • 1915 • Davenport Harry • USA
MR. JARR AND THE VISITING FIREMAN • 1915 • Davenport Harry • USA
MR. JARR BRINGS HOME A TURKEY • 1915 • Davenport Harry • USA
MR. JARR TAKES A NIGHT OFF • 1915 • Davenport Harry • USA
MR. JARR VISITS HIS HOME TOWN • 1915 • Davenport Harry • USA
MR. JARR'S BIG VACATION • 1915 • Davenport Harry • USA
MR. JARR'S MAGNETIC FRIEND • 1915 • Davenport Harry • USA
MISTER JEFFERSON GREEN • 1913 • Henderson Dell • USA
MISTER JERICO • 1969 • Hayers Sidney • MTV • UKN
MR. JIM –AMERICAN, SOLDIER AND GENTLEMAN see **DOLINA MIRU** • 1956
MR. JINKS BUYS A DRESS • 1913 • *Hevener Jerold T.* • USA
MISTER JOHNSON • 1990 • Beresford Bruce • USA
MISTER JOLLY LIVES NEXT DOOR see **COMIC STRIP PRESENTS: MISTER JOLLY LIVES NEXT DOOR** • 1987
MR. JONES AT A BALL • 1908 • Griffith D. W. • USA
MR. JONES' COMICAL EXPERIENCE WITH A GHOST see **REVENANT, LE** • 1903
MR. JONES HAS A CARD PARTY • 1909 • Griffith D. W. • USA
MR. JONES HAS A TILE LOOSE • 1908 • Stow Percy • UKN
MR. JORDAN COMES TO TOWN see **HERE COMES MR. JORDAN** • 1941
MR. JOSEPH YOUNG OF AFRICA see **MIGHTY JOE YOUNG** • 1949
MR. JUSTICE GOES HUNTING see **STRANGER IN TOWN, A** • 1943
MR. JUSTICE RAFFLES • 1921 • Ames Gerald, Quiribet Gaston • UKN
MR. K. –GREEN STREET • 1960 • Chytilova Vera • SHT • CZC
MR. KARLSSON MATE AND HIS SWEETHEARTS see **STYRMAN KARLSSONS FLAMMOR** • 1925
MR. KARLSSON MATE AND HIS SWEETHEARTS see **STYRMAN KARLSSONS FLAMMOR** • 1938
MR. KENNEDY, MR. REAGAN AND THE BIG, BEAUTIFUL, BELEAGUERED AMERICAN DREAM • 1967 • Solway Clifford • DOC • CND
MR. KING PAA EVENTYR see **AEGTESKAB OG PIGESJOV** • 1914
MR. KINGSTREET'S WAR • 1971 • Rubens Percival • SAF
MR. KINKY (UKN) see **PROFETA, IL** • 1967
MR. KLEIN see **MONSIEUR KLEIN** • 1976
MR. KLOMP see **MENEER KLOMP** • 1978
MR. KNOW-HOW IN HOT WATER • 1961 • Dunning George • ANS • UKN
MR. KOREK • 1958 • ANM • PLN

MR. KOUMAL CARRIES THE TORCH • 1968 • Deitch Gene • ANS • CZC
MR. KRANE • 1957 • *Hardwicke Cedric* • MTV • USA
MR. LAHTINEN TAKES FRENCH LEAVE see **HERRA LAHTINEN LAHTEE LIPETTIIN** • 1939
MR. LEGUIGNON, HEALER see **MONSIEUR LEGUIGNON, GUERISSEUR** • 1953
MR. LEMON OF ORANGE • 1931 • Blystone John G. • USA
MR. LENS AND THE WILDERNESS • 1960 • Kotowski Jerzy • ANM • PLN
MISTER LEWIS • 1965 • Craddock Malcolm • UKN
MR. LIMPET see **INCREDIBLE MR. LIMPET, THE** • 1964
MR. LOGAN see **FAME AND FORTUNE** • 1918
MR. LOGAN, U.S.A. • 1918 • Reynolds Lynn • USA
MR. LORD SAYS NO (USA) see **HAPPY FAMILY, THE** • 1952
MR. LOVE • 1985 • Battersby Roy • TVM • UKN • MISTER LOVE
MISTER LOVE see **MR. LOVE** • 1985
MR. LUCKY • 1943 • Potter H. C. • USA
MR. LUCKY see **RAKKI-SAN** • 1952
MR. LYNDON AT LIBERTY • 1915 • Shaw Harold • UKN
MISTER MAGOO • 1949 • Hubley John • ANS • USA
MISTER MAGOO IN SHERWOOD FOREST • 1964 • Levitow Abe • ANM • USA
MISTER MAGOO IN THE KING'S SERVICE • 1964 • Levitow Abe • ANM • USA
MISTER MAGOO –MAN OF MYSTERY • 1964 • Levitow Abe • ANM • USA
MISTER MAGOO'S CHRISTMAS CAROL • 1964 • Levitow Abe • ANM • USA
MISTER MAGOO'S FAVORITE HEROES • 1964 • Levitow Abe • ANM • USA
MISTER MAGOO'S HOLIDAY FESTIVAL • 1970 • Levitow Abe • ANM • USA
MISTER MAGOO'S LITTLE SNOW WHITE • 1964 • Levitow Abe • ANM • USA
MISTER MAGOO'S STORY BOOK • 1964 • Levitow Abe • ANM • USA
MISTER MAGROOTER'S MARVELOUS MACHINE • *Modern Film Rentals* • ANS • USA
MR. MAJESTYK • 1974 • Fleischer Richard • USA
MR. MARI'S GIRLS • 1967 • Hennigar William K. • USA
MR. MARSH COMES TO SCHOOL • 1961 • Krish John • UKN
MR. MARZIPAN'S MARRIAGE see **ZENIDBA GOSPODINA MARCIPANA** • 1963
MR. MASKELEYNE SPINNING PLATES AND BASINS • 1896 • *Paul R. W.* • UKN
MR. MAX (USA) see **SIGNOR MAX, IL** • 1937
MR. MAYOR see **M. LE MAIRE** • 1953
MR. MCIDIOT'S ASSASSINATION • 1916 • *Griffith Ray* • SHT • USA
MR. MEAN (USA) see **DESTINAZIONE ROMA** • 1977
MR. MEEK'S MISSUS • 1914 • Plumb Hay? • UKN
MR. MEEK'S NIGHTMARE • 1914 • Plumb Hay? • UKN
MR. MEESON'S WILL • 1915 • Sullivan Frederick • USA
MR. MEESON'S WILL (UKN) see **GRASP OF GREED, THE** • 1916
MR. MIKE'S MONDO VIDEO • 1979 • O'Donoghue Michael • USA
MR. MILLER MUDDLES THROUGH • 1918 • *Keystone* • SHT • USA
MR. MILLER'S ECONOMIES • 1918 • Beaudine William • SHT • USA
MR. MINTERN'S MISADVENTURES • 1913 • Ranous William V. • USA
MR. MIX AT THE MARDI GRAS • 1910 • *Selig* • USA
MR. MOM • 1983 • Dragoti Stan • USA • MR. MUM
MR. MONEY GAGS • 1957 • Sparber I. • ANS • USA
MR. MONSTER • 1969 • Mesghali Farshid • ANS • IRN
MR. MOOCHER • 1944 • Wickersham Bob • ANS • USA
MR. MOONLIGHT • 1984 • SAF
MR. MOSENSTEIN • 1904 • Collins Alf? • UKN
MISTER MOSES • 1964 • Neame Ronald • UKN
MR. MOTO AND THE PERSIAN OIL CASE see **RETURN OF MR. MOTO, THE** • 1965
MR. MOTO IN DANGER ISLAND • 1939 • Leeds Herbert I. • USA • MR. MOTO ON DANGER ISLAND (UKN) ○ DANGER ISLAND
MR. MOTO ON DANGER ISLAND (UKN) see **MR. MOTO IN DANGER ISLAND** • 1939
MR. MOTO TAKES A CHANCE • 1938 • Foster Norman • USA • LOOK OUT MR. MOTO
MR. MOTO TAKES A VACATION • 1939 • Foster Norman • USA
MR. MOTORBOAT'S LAST STAND • 1933 • Florey John, Huff Theodore • USA
MR. MOTO'S GAMBLE • 1938 • Tinling James • USA
MR. MOTO'S LAST WARNING • 1939 • Foster Norman • USA
MR. MOUSE see **MONSIEUR LA SOURIS** • 1942
MR. MOUSE TAKES A TRIP • 1940 • Geronimi Clyde • ANS • USA
MR., MRS. AND MISS LONELY • 1981 • Kumashiro Tatsumi • JPN
MR. & MRS. BRIDGE • 1990 • Ivory James • USA
MISTER MUGG • 1933 • Horne James W. • SHT • USA
MR. MUGGS RIDES AGAIN • 1945 • Fox Wallace • USA
MR. MUGGS STEPS OUT • 1943 • Beaudine William • USA
MR. MUGWUMP AND THE BABY • 1910 • Wilson Frank? • UKN
MR. MUGWUMP TAKES HOME THE WASHING • 1910 • Wilson Frank? • UKN
MR. MUGWUMP'S BANKNOTES • 1910 • Wilson Frank? • UKN
MR. MUGWUMP'S CLOCK • 1911 • Wilson Frank? • UKN
MR. MUGWUMP'S HIRED SUIT • 1910 • Wilson Frank? • UKN
MR. MUGWUMP'S JEALOUSY • 1910 • Wilson Frank? • UKN
MR. MUM see **MR. MOM** • 1983
MR. MUSIC • 1950 • Haydn Richard • USA
MR. NICE GUY • 1987 • Wolfond Henry • USA
MISTER NO LEGS see **AMAZING MISTER NO LEGS, THE** • 1981
MR. NOAD'S ADLESS DAY • 1914 • *Joker* • USA
MR. NOBODY • 1927 • Miller Frank • UKN
MR. NOBODY see **MONSIEUR PERSONNE** • 1936
MR. NORTH • 1988 • Huston Danny • USA
MR. NOVAK • 1949 • Zeman Borivoj • CZC
MR. O.F.'S 13 CASES see **KOFFER DES HERRN O.F., DIE** • 1931
MR. OPP • 1917 • Reynolds Lynn • USA
MR. ORCHID (USA) see **PERE TRANQUILLE, LE** • 1948
MISTER PAGANINI • 1915 • Physioc Wray • USA
MR. PALLET GOES OUT LANDSCAPING • 1909 • *Urban-Eclipse* • USA
MR. PARKER –HERO • 1917 • Drew Sidney, Drew Sidney Mrs. • SHT • USA
MR. PASTRY DOES THE LAUNDRY see **METHOD AND MADNESS** • 1950
MR. PATMAN • 1980 • Guillermin John • CND • MIDNIGHT MADNESS ○ CROSSOVER ○ PATMAN ○ SHADOWS OF DARKNESS
MR. PEABODY AND THE MERMAID • 1948 • Pichel Irving • USA
MR. PEARSON • 1963 • Pennebaker D. A. • CND
MR. PECK GOES CALLING • 1911 • Sennett Mack, Henderson Dell • USA
MR. PECKSNIFF FETCHES THE DOCTOR • 1904 • *Paul R. W.* • UKN • OH, WHAT A SURPRISE!
MR. PEEK-A-BOO (USA) see **GAROU-GAROU LE PASSE-MURAILLE** • 1950
MR. PEEK-A-BOO'S PLAYMATES • 1962 • Ashcroft Ronnie • USA • MAD ESCAPADE OF A PLAYBOY, A ○ NAKED LIKE WOW! ○ LIKE WOW! ○ WOW!
MR. PENICKA AND MISS BROLLY • 1970 • Sequens Jiri • CZC
MR. PEPPERIE TEMPER • 1915 • *Kalem* • USA
MR. PERRIN AND MR. TRAILL • 1948 • Huntington Lawrence • UKN
MR. PETERS' PETS • 1962 • *Sonney Amusement* • USA • PETEY'S SWEETIES
MR. PHARAOH AND HIS CLEOPATRA • 1959 • Weis Don • USA
MR. PHYSICAL CULTURE'S SURPRISE PARTY • 1909 • *Vitagraph* • USA
MR. PICKWICK IN A DOUBLE BEDDED ROOM • 1913 • Noy Wilfred • UKN
MR. PICKWICK'S CHRISTMAS AT WARDLE'S • 1901 • Booth W. R.? • UKN
MR. PICKWICK'S PREDICAMENT • 1912 • Dawley J. Searle • USA
MR. PIDDIE REBELS • 1912 • *Champion* • USA
MR. PIM PASSES BY • 1921 • Ward Albert • UKN
MR. PLUME HAS A DREAM • 1947-50 • Wasilewski Zenon • ANM • PLN
MR. POO see **PUSAN** • 1953
MR. POORLUCK AS AN AMATEUR DETECTIVE • 1912 • Wilson Frank? • UKN
MR. POORLUCK BUYS SOME CHINA • 1911 • Fitzhamon Lewin? • UKN
MR. POORLUCK BUYS SOME FURNITURE • 1910 • Fitzhamon Lewin? • UKN
MR. POORLUCK GETS MARRIED • 1909 • Fitzhamon Lewin • UKN
MR. POORLUCK, JOURNALIST • 1913 • Wilson Frank? • UKN
MR. POORLUCK REPAIRS HIS HOUSE • 1913 • Wilson Frank? • UKN
MR. POORLUCK'S DREAM • 1910 • Fitzhamon Lewin • UKN
MR. POORLUCK'S I.O.U.'S • 1913 • Wilson Frank? • UKN
MR. POORLUCK'S LUCKY HORSESHOE • 1910 • Fitzhamon Lewin • UKN
MR. POORLUCK'S RIVER SUIT • 1912 • Plumb Hay? • UKN
MR. POTTER OF TEXAS • 1922 • Wharton Leopold • USA
MR. POTTS GOES TO MOSCOW (USA) see **TOP SECRET** • 1952
MR. PREEDY AND THE COUNTESS • 1925 • Pearson George • UKN
MR. PRINGLE AND SUCCESS • 1917 • Beaumont Harry • SHT • USA
MR. PROHACK see **DEAR MR. PROHACK** • 1949
MR. PROKOUK ACROBAT see **PAN PROKOUK AKROBATEM** • 1959
MR. PROKOUK AND THE RED TAPE see **PAN PROKOUK URADUJE** • 1947
MR. PROKOUK BUREAUCRAT see **PAN PROKOUK URADUJE** • 1947
MR. PROKOUK, DETECTIVE see **PAN PROKOUK DETEKTIVEN** • 1958
MR. PROKOUK, FRIEND OF LITTLE ANIMALS see **PAN PROKOUK, PRITEL ZVIRATEK** • 1955
MR. PROKOUK IN TEMPTATION see **PAN PROKOUK V POKUSENI** • 1947
MR. PROKOUK IN THE OFFICE see **PAN PROKOUK URADUJE** • 1947
MR. PROKOUK IS FILMING see **PAN PROKOUK FILMUJE** • 1948
MR. PROKOUK LEAVES FOR VOLUNTEER WORK see **PAN PROKOUK JEDE NA BRIGADU** • 1947
MR. PROKOUK MAKES A FILM see **PAN PROKOUK FILMUJE** • 1948
MR. PROKOUK ON A BRIGADE see **PAN PROKOUK JEDE NA BRIGADU** • 1947
MR. PROKOUK THE ANIMAL FANCIER see **PAN PROKOUK, PRITEL ZVIRATEK** • 1955
MR. PROKOUK, THE ANIMAL LOVER see **PAN PROKOUK, PRITEL ZVIRATEK** • 1955
MR. PROKOUK, THE DETECTIVE see **PAN PROKOUK DETEKTIVEN** • 1958
MR. PROKOUK THE INVENTOR see **PAN PROKOUK VYNALEZCEM** • 1949
MR. PROKOUK, THE WATCHMAKER see **PAN PROKOUK HODINAREM** • 1972
MR. PROKOUK'S TEMPTATION see **PAN PROKOUK V POKUSENI** • 1947
MR. PROUDFOOT SHOWS A LIGHT • 1941 • Mason Herbert • UKN
MR. PU see **PUSAN** • 1953
MR. PUNTILA AND HIS SERVANT MATTI see **HERRA PUNTILA JA HANEN RENKINSA MATTI** • 1979
MR. PUNTILA AND HIS VALET MATTI see **HERR PUNTILA UND SEIN KNECHT MATTI** • 1955
MISTER QUILP • 1974 • Tuchner Michael • UKN • OLD CURIOSITY SHOP, THE ○ QUILP
MR. QUINCEY OF MONTE CARLO • 1933 • Daumery John • UKN
MISTER RADIO • 1924 • Malasomma Nunzio • FRG
MR. RADISH AND MR. CARROT see **DAIKON TO NINJIN** • 1964
MR. RECKLESS • 1948 • McDonald Frank • USA
MR. REEDER IN ROOM 13 • 1938 • Lee Norman • UKN • MYSTERY OF ROOM 13 (USA)
MR. RICCO • 1974 • Bogart Paul • USA
MISTER ROBERTS • 1955 • Ford John, Leroy Mervyn • USA
MR. ROBIDA, PROPHET AND EXPLORER OF TIME see **MONSIEUR ROBIDA, PROPHETE ET EXPLORATEUR DU TEMPS** • 1963
MR. ROBINSON CRUSOE • 1932 • Sutherland A. Edward • USA
MR. ROCK AND ROLL • 1957 • Dubin Charles S. • USA
MR. ROSSI see **SIGNOR ROSSI**
MR. ROSSI BUYS A CAR (USA) see **SIGNOR ROSSI COMPERA L'AUTOMOBILA, IL** • 1966
MISTER ROSSI LOOKS FOR HAPPINESS see **SIGNOR ROSSI CERCA LA FELICITA, IL** • 1976
MR. RUBBER STAMP AND EDISONS see **PAN RAZITKO A EDISONI** • 1980
MR. RYHE REFORMS • 1913 • *Mason Billy* • USA
MR. RZEPKA AND HIS SHADOW see **PAN RZEPKA I JEGO CIEN** • 1957
MR. SANTA CLAUS • 1914 • Ridgwell George • USA
MR. SARDONICUS • 1961 • Castle William • USA • SARDONICUS
MR. SATAN • 1938 • Woods Arthur • UKN
MISTER SAVAGE see **AMERICAN COMMANDOS** • 1985
MISTER SCARFACE see **PADRONI DELLA CITTA, I** • 1977
MISTER SCOUTMASTER • 1953 • Levin Henry • USA • MR. SCOUTMASTER
MR. SCOUTMASTER see **MISTER SCOUTMASTER** • 1953
MISTER SEBASTIAN see **SEBASTIAN** • 1967
MR. SELKIE • 1979 • Squire Anthony • UKN
MR. SERVADAC'S ARK see **NA KOMETE** • 1970
MISTER SHATTER see **CALL HIM MR. SHATTER** • 1975
MR. SHOESTRING IN THE HOLE see **UP THE FLUE** • 1917
MR. SHOME see **BHUVAN SHOME** • 1969
MR. SILENT HASKINS • 1915 • Hart William S., Smith Cliff • USA
MISTER SKEETER • 1985 • Finbow Colin • UKN
MR. SKEFFINGTON • 1944 • Sherman Vincent • USA
MR. SKITCH • 1933 • Cruze James • USA
MR. SLOTTER'S JUBILEE (UKN) see **EEN PAK SLAAG** • 1979
MISTER SMARTY • 1936 • Black Preston • SHT • USA
MR. SMITH, BARBER • 1912 • *Cumpson John* • USA
MR. SMITH CARRIES ON • 1937 • Laurance Lister • UKN
MR. SMITH GOES GHOST • 1950 • *Markham Pigmeat* • USA
MR. SMITH GOES TO WASHINGTON • 1939 • Capra Frank • USA
MR. SMITH WAKES UP • 1929 • Hill Sinclair • UKN
MR. SMUG • 1943 • Castle William • SHT • USA
MR. SNELL IN THE COUNTRY • 1910 • *Centaur* • USA
MR. SNIFFKIN'S WIDOW • 1914 • Seay Charles M. • USA
MR. SOFT TOUCH • 1949 • Levin Henry, Douglas Gordon • USA • HOUSE OF SETTLEMENT (UKN)
MR. SPRIGGS BUYS A DOG • 1913 • Henderson Dell • USA
MR. STEVE (USA) see **ETRANGE MONSIEUR STEVE, L'** • 1957
MR. STOP see **MONSIEUR STOP** • 1910
MR. STRAUSS TAKES A WALK • 1944 • Pal George • ANS • USA
MR. STRINGFELLOW SAYS NO • 1937 • Faye Randall • UKN • ACCIDENTAL SPY
MR. STUBBS' PEN • 1915 • *Lubin* • USA
MR. SUPER INVISIBLE see **INAFFERRABILE E INVINCIBILE MR. INVISIBILE, L'** • 1970
MR. SURUJ see **SURUJ MIA** • 1985
MR. SWANKER GOES SHOOTING • 1912 • *Heron Andrew (P)* • UKN
MR. SYCAMORE • 1975 • Kohner Pancho • USA
MR. TAU AND CLAUDIA • 1971 • Polak Jindrich • CZC, FRG
MR. TAU (USA) see **PAN TAU**
MR. TEASE AND HIS PLAYTHINGS see **STEAM HEAT** • 1963
MISTER TEN PERCENT • 1967 • Scott Peter Graham • UKN
MR. TIBBS' CINDERELLA • 1912 • *Steppling John* • USA
MR. TNT • 1985 • SAF
MR. TOOTS' TOOTH • 1913 • *Edison* • USA
MR. TOPAZE • 1961 • Sellers Peter • UKN • I LIKE MONEY (USA)
MR. TREATER'S TREAT • 1913 • *Essanay* • USA
MR. TROUBLESOME • 1909 • Codman John • UKN
MR. TRULL FINDS OUT • 1940 • Rodakiewicz Henwar • USA
MR. TRUMPET see **PAN TRABA** • 1960
MR. TUBBY'S TRIUMPH • 1910 • Aylott Dave • UKN
MR. TVARDOVSKI (USA) see **PAN TVARDOVSKI** • 1916
MR. UNIVERSE • 1951 • Lerner Joseph • USA
MR. UNIVERSE • 1988 • Szomjas Gyorgy • HNG
MISTER UNSICHTBAR see **INAFFERRABILE E INVINCIBILE MR. INVISIBILE, L'** • 1970
MR. UP'S TRIP TRIPPED UP • 1912 • *Missimer Howard* • USA
MR. V see **PIMPERNEL SMITH** • 1941
MISTER V see **PIMPERNEL SMITH** • 1941
MR. VALIANT see **BOTCHAN SHAIN** • 1954
MR. VALIANT RIDES AGAIN see **ZOKU BOTCHAN SHAIN** • 1954
MR. VAMARE • 1916 • Ford Francis • SHT • USA
MR. VICTOR see **MONSIEUR VICTOR OU LA MACHINE A RETROUVER LE TEMPS** • 1957
MR. WALLACK'S WALLET • 1915 • *Tincher Fay* • USA
MISTER WASHINGTON GOES TO TOWN • 1940 • Buell Jed, Beaudine William (U/c) • USA
MR. WHAT'S-HIS-NAME • 1935 • Ince Ralph • UKN
MR. WHITNEY HAD A NOTION • 1949 • Mayer Gerald • USA
MR. WILLIAMS WAKES UP • 1947 • Weisenborn Gordon • USA
MR. WIN LUCKY • 1967 • Bakshi Ralph • ANS • USA
MR. WINKLE GOES TO WAR • 1944 • Green Alfred E. • USA • ARMS AND THE WOMAN (UKN)
MR. WISE GUY • 1942 • Nigh William • USA
MR. WISE, INVESTIGATOR • 1911 • Hopper E. Mason • USA
MISTER WISTER THE TIME TWISTER (USA) see **MACHINE A RETROUVER LE TEMPS, LA** • 1956
MR. WONDERBIRD see **BERGERE ET LE RAMONEUR, LA** • 1953

MR. WONG AT HEADQUARTERS (UKN) see **FATAL HOUR, THE** • 1940
MR. WONG, DETECTIVE • 1938 • Nigh William • USA
MR. WONG IN CHINATOWN • 1939 • Nigh William • USA
MR. WRIGHT IS WRONG • 1917 • *Essanay* • USA
MR. WRONG • 1986 • Preston Gaylene • NZL • DARK OF THE NIGHT (USA)
MR. WU • 1918 • Pick Lupu • FRG
MR. WU • 1919 • Elvey Maurice • UKN
MR. WU • 1927 • Nigh William • USA
MISTER X • 1967 • Vivarelli Piero • ITL, SPN
MISTER X • 1970 • van der Linden Rupert • ANS • NTH
MISTER, YOU ARE A WIDOWER see **PANE, VY JSTE VDOVA** • 1971
MISTER ZEHN PROZENT –NIEZEN UND MONETEN • 1967 • Zurli Guido • FRG, ITL • SIGNPRESS CONTRO SCOTLAND YARD (ITL)
MISTERI DEL MATO GRASSO, I • 1953 • Curti Alfredo, Ceccon Hidalgo, Calamara Aldo • DOC • ITL
MISTERI DELLA GIUNGLA NERA, I • 1954 • Callegari Gian Paolo, Murphy Ralph • ITL • MYSTERY OF THE BLACK JUNGLE (USA) ○ BLACK DEVILS OF KALI, THE
MISTERI DELLA GIUNGLA NERA, I • 1964 • Capuano Luigi • ITL, FRG • GEHEIMNIS DER LEDERSCHLINGE, DAS (FRG) ○ MYSTERY OF THUG ISLAND, THE (USA)
MISTERI DI PARIGI, I • 1958 • Cerchio Fernando, Rivalta Giorgio • ITL, FRN • MYSTERES DE PARIS, LES (FRN)
MISTERI DI ROMA, I • 1963 • Zavattini Cesare, Bisiach Gianni, Bizzarri Libero, Carbone Mario, D'Alessandro Angelo, Del Fra Lino, Di Gianni Luigi, Ferrara Giuseppe, Giannarelli Ansano, Macchi Giulio, Mazzetti Lorenza, Mida Massimo, Muzii Enzo, Nelli Piero, Nuzzi Paolo, Partesano Dino, Vento Giovanni • DOC • ITL • MYSTERIES OF ROME, THE ○ WONDERS OF ROME, THE
MISTERI DI VENEZIA, I • 1951 • Ferronetti Ignazio • ITL • FARO ABBANDONATO, IL
MISTERIO • 1981 • Violante Marcela Fernandez • MXC
MISTERIO DE HURACAN RAMIREZ, EL • 1962 • Rodriguez Joselito • MXC
MISTERIO DE LA COBRA, EL • 1958 • Gomez Urquiza Zacarias • MXC • MYSTERY OF THE COBRA, THE
MISTERIO DE LA DAMA DE GRIS, EL • 1939 • Bauer James • ARG
MISTERIO DE LA NARANJAS AZULES, EL (SPN) see **TINTIN ET LES ORANGES BLEUES** • 1965
MISTERIO DE LA PUERTA DEL SOL, EL • 1928 • Elias Francisco • SPN
MISTERIO DE LA VIDA, EL • 1971 • Balcazar Jaime Jesus • SPN • MYSTERY OF LIFE, THE
MISTERIO DE LOS HONGOS ALUCINANTES, EL • 1968 • Martinez Solares Gilberto • MXC • MYSTERY OF THE HALLUCINATING MUSHROOMS, THE
MISTERIO DEL CARRO EXPRESS, EL • 1952 • Gomez Urquiza Zacarias • MXC
MISTERIO DEL CASTILLO ROJO, EL • 1972 • Franco Jesus • SPN
MISTERIO DEL CUARTO AMARILLO, EL • 1947 • ARG • MYSTERY OF THE YELLOW ROOM, THE
MISTERIO DEL LATIGO NEGRO, EL • 1957 • Orona Vicente • MXC
MISTERIO DEL ROSTRO PALIDO, EL • 1935 • Bustillo Oro Juan • MXC • MYSTERY OF THE GHASTLY FACE, THE ○ MYSTERY OF THE PALLID FACE,THE
MISTERIOS DE LA IMPERIAL TOLEDO, LOS • 1928 • Buchs Jose • SPN
MISTERIOS DE LA MAGIA NEGRA • 1957 • Delgado Miguel M. • MXC • RETURN FROM THE BEYOND (USA) ○ MYSTERIES OF BLACK MAGIC ○ MAGIA NEGRA
MISTERIOS DE TANGER, LOS • 1942 • Fernandez Cuenca Carlos • SPN
MISTERIOS DE TANGER, LOS see **AGUILAS DE ACERO** • 1927
MISTERIOS DE ULTRATUMBA • 1958 • Mendez Fernando • MXC • BLACK PIT OF DR. M., THE (USA) ○ MYSTERIES FROM BEYOND THE TOMB
MISTERIOS DEL HAMPA, LOS • 1944 • Orol Juan • MXC
MISTERIOS DEL ROSARIO, LOS • 1959 • Breen Joseph • SPN, USA • REDEEMER, THE (USA)
MISTERIOSO SENOR MARQUINA, EL • 1942 • Urueta Chano • MXC
MISTERIOSO SENOR VAN EYCK, EL • 1964 • Navarro Agustin • SPN, ITL • MISTERIOSO SIGNOR VAN EYCK, IL (ITL)
MISTERIOSO SIGNOR VAN EYCK, IL (ITL) see **MISTERIOSO SENOR VAN EYCK, EL** • 1964
MISTERIOSO TIO SYLAS, EL • 1947 • Schliepper Carlos • ARG • MYSTERIOUS UNCLE SILAS, THE
MISTERIOSO VIAJERO DEL CLIPPER, EL • 1944 • Delgras Gonzalo • SPN
MISTERO DEI BAULI NERI, IL • 1918 • Maggi Luigi • ITL
MISTERO DEI TREI CONTINENTI, IL • 1959 • Dieterle William • ITL, FRG, FRN • MYSTERES D'ANGKOR, LES (FRN) ○ HERRIN DER WELT (FRG) ○ MISTRESS OF THE WORLD (USA) ○ MYSTERY OF THREE CONTINENTS, THE ○ MYSTERIES OF ANGKOR, THE ○ FRN ○ APOCALISSE SULL FIUME GIALLO
MISTERO DEL TIEMPO INDIANO, IL • 1964 • Camerini Mario • ITL, FRN, FRG • MYSTERE DU TEMPLE HINDOU, LE (FRN) ○ MYSTERY OF THE INDIAN TEMPLE
MISTERO DELL'ISOLA MALATESTA, IL • 1965 • Pierotti Piero • ITL • GIANT OF THE EVIL ISLAND (USA)
MISTERO DI BELLAVISTA, IL • 1985 • De Crescenzo Luciano • ITL • MYSTERY OF BELLAVISTA, THE
MISTERO DI OBERWALD, IL • 1979 • Antonioni Michelangelo • MTV • ITL • OBERWALD MYSTERY, THE
MISTERO DI OSIRIS, IL • 1921 • *Talisman* • USA • MYSTERY OF THE JEWELS, THE
MISTERO DI QUELLA NOTTE, IL • 1917 • Serena Gustavo • ITL
MISTIGRI • 1931 • Lachman Harry • FRN
MISTINGUETT DETECTIVE • 1917 • Hugon Andre • FRN
MISTLETOE, A see **JEMIOLA** • 1974
MISTLETOE BOUGH, THE • 1904 • Stow Percy • UKN
MISTLETOE BOUGH, THE • 1923 • Collins Edwin J. • UKN
MISTLETOE BOUGH, THE • 1926 • Calvert Charles • UKN
MISTLETOE BOUGH, THE • 1938 • Newman Widgey R. • SHT • UKN
MISTLETOES see **FAGYONGYOK** • 1979
MISTO V HOUFU • 1964 • Brynych Zbynek, Krska Vaclav • CZC • PLACE IN THE CROWD, A
MISTONS, LES • 1958 • Truffaut Francois • SHT • FRN • MISCHIEF-MAKERS, THE (UKN)
MISTR TREBONSKY • 1950 • Kudlac Frantisek • CZC • CZECH GOTHIC PAINTING ○ CZECHOSLOVAK GOTHIC
MISTRAL, LE • 1942 • Houssin Jacques • FRN
MISTRAL'S DAUGHTER • 1984 • Hickox Douglas • MTV • USA
MISTRESS • 1987 • Tuchner Michael • TVM • USA
MISTRESS see **MOGLIE AMANTE** • 1978
MISTRESS, THE • 1982 • Remy Jack • USA
MISTRESS, THE see **VASSA ZHELEZNOVA** • 1953
MISTRESS, THE see **ALSKARINNAN** • 1962
MISTRESS, THE see **PADRONA E SERVITA, LA** • 1976
MISTRESS, THE (USA) see **GAN** • 1953
MISTRESS AND MAID • 1910 • *Thanhouser* • USA
MISTRESS DU BARRY see **MADAME DU BARRY** • 1954
MISTRESS FOR THE SUMMER, A (USA) see **FILLE POUR L'ETE, UNE** • 1960
MISTRESS HOLLE • Hempel Johannes • ANM • GDR
MISTRESS HOLLE • 1965 • Kolditz Gottfried • GDR
MISTRESS NELL • 1915 • Kirkwood James • USA
MISTRESS OF A FOREIGNER (USA) see **TOJIN OKICHI** • 1930
MISTRESS OF ATLANTIS, THE see **HERRIN VON ATLANTIS, DIE** • 1932
MISTRESS OF DEADWOOD BASIN, THE • 1914 • *Leonard Robert* • USA
MISTRESS OF HACIENDA DEL CERRO, THE • 1911 • *Kalem* • USA
MISTRESS OF HIS HOUSE, THE • 1914 • *Razeto Stella* • USA
MISTRESS OF PARADISE • 1981 • Medak Peter • TVM • USA
MISTRESS OF SHENSTONE, THE • 1921 • King Henry • USA
MISTRESS OF THE AIR, THE • 1914 • *Seidell Florence* • USA
MISTRESS OF THE APES • 1979 • Buchanan Larry • USA
MISTRESS OF THE INN see **LOCANDIERA, LA** • 1981
MISTRESS OF THE MOUNTAINS (USA) see **GENTE COSI** • 1950
MISTRESS OF THE WORLD see **HERRIN DER WELT, DIE** • 1919
MISTRESS OF THE WORLD (USA) see **MISTERO DEI TREI CONTINENTI, IL** • 1959
MISTRESS PAMELA • 1973 • O'Connolly Jim • UKN
MISTRESS (USA) see **MAITRESSE** • 1976
MISTRESSES OF DR. JEKYLL see **SECRETO DEL DR. ORLOFF, EL** • 1964
MISTROVSTVI SVETA LETECKYCH MODELARU • 1957 • Kachyna Karel • DOC • CZC • WORLD CHAMPIONSHIP OF AIR MODELS
MISTRZ NIKIFOR • 1956 • Lomnicki Jan • DOC • PLN • MASTER PAINTER NIKIFOR ○ MASTER NIKIFOR
MISTRZ TANCA • 1969 • Gruza Jerzy • SHT • PLN
MISTS OF AUTUMN see **BRUMES D'AUTOMNE** • 1929
MISTS OF TIME • 1969 • Carey Patrick • DOC • IRL
MISTVI ZIMNICH SPORTI • 1955 • Fric Martin • CZC • MASTER OF WINTER SPORTS
MISTY • 1961 • Clark James B. • USA
MISTY see **SEXPERT** • 1976
MISTY BEETHOVEN see **OPENING OF MISTY BEETHOVEN, THE** • 1976
MISTY VILLAGE see **ANGEMAEUL** • 1983
MISUNDERSTANDING • 1958 • Babaja Ante • SHT • YGS
MISUNDERSTANDING see **PAREXIYISSI** • 1983
MISUNDERSTANDING, THE • 1912 • Southwell Gilbert • UKN
MISUNDERSTOOD • 1971 • Mesghali Farshid • ANS • IRN
MISUNDERSTOOD • 1983 • Schatzberg Jerry • USA
MISUNDERSTOOD see **AERESOPREJSNING, EN** • 1914
MISUNDERSTOOD see **INCOMPRESO** • 1966
MISUNDERSTOOD BOY, A • 1913 • Griffith D. W. • USA
MISUNDERSTOOD GIANT, THE • 1960 • Rasinski Connie • ANS • USA
MIT 17 WEINT MAN NICHT • 1960 • Vohrer Alfred • FRG
MIT 300 PS VOLLGAS • 1919 • Arnheim Valy • FRG
MIT BESTEN EMPFEHLUNGEN • 1963 • Nachmann Kurt • AUS
MIT CSINALT FELSEGED 3 – 5 – 19? • 1964 • Makk Karoly • HNG • HIS MAJESTY'S DATES
MIT DEM KURBELKASTEN UM DEN ERDBALL see **COLIN ROSS MIT DEM KURBELKASTEN UM DIE ERDE** • 1924
MIT DEN AUGEN EINER FRAU • 1942 • Kulb Karl G. • FRG
MIT DJANGO KAM DER TOD (FRG) see **UOMO, L'ORGOGLIO, LA VENDETTA, L'** • 1967
MIT EICHENLAUB UND FEIGENBLATT • 1968 • Spieker Franz-Josef • FRG • WITH LAURELS AND FIGLEAF
MIT EVA FING DIE SUNDE AN • 1958 • Umgelter Fritz, Coppola Francis Ford • FRG • PLAYGIRLS AND THE BELLBOY, THE ○ BELLBOY AND THE PLAYGIRLS, THE
MIT GOTT FUR KAISER UND REICH • 1916 • Fleck Jacob, Fleck Luise • AUS
MIT HERZ UN HAND FURS VATERLAND • 1915 • Fleck Jacob, Fleck Luise • AUS
MIT HIMBEERGEIST GEHT ALLES BESSER • 1960 • Marischka Georg • AUS
MIT LIVS EVENTYR • 1955 • Roos Jorgen • DOC • DNM • MY LIFE STORY ○ STORY OF MY LIFE, THE
MIT MEINEN AUGEN • 1944 • Zerlett Hans H. • FRG • IM TEMPEL DER VENUS
MIT MIR NICHT, MADAM! • 1969 • Oehme Roland, Warneke Lothar • GDR
MIT MIR WILL KEINER SPIELEN • 1976 • Herzog Werner • SHT • FRG • NO ONE WILL PLAY WITH ME
MIT MUSIK DURCHS LEBEN OU SINGENDE JUGEND • 1938 • Neufeld Max • AUS, NTH • SINGENDE JUGEND
MIT ROSEN FANGT DIE LIEBE AN • 1957 • Hamel Peter • AUS
MIT SIEBZEHN BEGINNT DAS LEBEN • 1953 • Martin Paul • FRG
MIT STARREM BLICK AUFS GELD • 1983 • Reidemeister Helga • FRG
MIT TEUFLISCHEN GRUSSEN (FRG) see **DIABOLIQUEMENT VOTRE** • 1967
MIT UNS DAS VOLK • 1927 • Fuhrmann H. • FRG
MIT VERSIEGELTER ORDER • 1938 • Anton Karl • FRG • UNDER SEALED ORDERS (USA)
MIT VORZUGLICHER HOCHACHTUNG • 1967 • Heynowski Walter, Scheumann Gerhard • DOC • GDR • WITH SPECIAL PRAISE
MIT ZUCKERBROT UND PEITSCHE see **ZUCKERBROT UND PEITSCHE** • 1968
MITAD DEL CIELO, LA • 1985 • Gutierrez Aragon Manuel • SPN • HALF OF HEAVEN
MITAD Y MITAD • 1921 • Vallejo Enrique J. • MXC
MITAKHAT LA'AF • 1983 • Goldwasser Ya'Akov • ISR
MITAS ME SANKARIT • 1980 • Makinen Visa • FNL • WE, THE HEROES
MITASARETA SEIKATSU • 1962 • Hani Susumu • JPN • FULL LIFE, A (USA)
MITCHELL • 1975 • McLaglen Andrew V. • USA
MITE MAKES RIGHT, THE • 1948 • Tytla Bill • ANS • USA
MITE OF LOVE, THE • 1920 • Terwilliger George W. • SHT • USA
MITEY ATOMS see **MIGHTY ATOMS** • 1930
MITGIFT • 1975 • Verhoeven Michael • FRG • POISONOUS DOWRY ○ KILLING ME SOFTLY
MITGIFTJAGER • 1927 • Ravel Gaston • FRG
MITHILA • 1974 • Luneau Georges, Segarra Ludovic • DOC • FRN
MITO, IL • 1963 • Sala Adimaro • ITL • VIOLENZA E L'AMORE, LA ○ MYTH, THE (USA) ○ PUSHOVER, THE
MITO KOMON • 1960 • Matsuda Sadatsugu • JPN
MITO KOMON MANYUKI • 1958 • Misumi Kenji • JPN
MITO KOMONUMI O WATARU • 1961 • Watanabe Kunio • JPN • ACROSS THE LOCK GATE TO THE SEA
MITO KROMON TO ABARE HIME • 1958 • Mori Masaki • JPN
MITREA COCOR • 1952 • Iliu Victor • RMN
MITROPOLIS • 1975 • Sfikas Kostas • DOC • GRC • METROPOLIS ○ METROPOLES
MITSOU • 1956 • Audry Jacqueline • FRN • MITSOU OU COMMENT L'ESPRIT VIENT AUX FILLES
MITSOU OU COMMENT L'ESPRIT VIENT AUX FILLES see **MITSOU** • 1956
MITSUGETSU • 1984 • Hashiura Masato • JPN • HONEYMOON
MITSUME NO CHOJIN • 1958 • Mori Issei • JPN
MITSUYUSEN • 1954 • Sugie Toshio • JPN • BLACK FURY ○ SMUGGLING SHIP
MITT FOLK AR ICKE DITT • 1944 • Hildebrand Weyler • SWD • MY PEOPLE ARE NOT YOURS
MITT HEM AR COPACABANA • 1966 • Sucksdorff Arne • DOC • SWD • MY HOME IS COPACABANA
MITT LIV SOM HUND • 1986 • Hallstrom Lasse • SWD • MY LIFE AS A DOG (UKN)
MITT ME TONIGHT • *Columbia* • SHT • USA
MITTEN, THE • 1968 • ANS • USS
MITTEN IN DEUTSCHLAND • 1978 • Schnabel Pavel • DCS • FRG
MITTEN INS HERZ • 1984 • Dorrie Doris • FRG • STRAIGHT TO THE HEART (USA) ○ RIGHT TO THE HEART
MITTERNACHT • 1918 • Dupont E. A. • FRG
MITTERNACHTS-TAXE, DIE • 1929 • Piel Harry • FRG
MITTERNACHTSBESUCH • 1920 • Gartner Adolf • FRG
MITTERNACHTSGOTTIN, DIE • 1920 • Henning Hanna • FRG
MITTERNACHTSLIEBE • 1931 • Genina Augusto, Froelich Carl • FRG
MITTERNACHTSSCHIFF, DAS • 1915 • Gartner Adolf • FRG
MITTERNACHTSVENUS, DIE • 1951 • Dorfler Ferdinand • FRG
MITTERNACHTSZUG, DER • 1923 • Bauer James • FRG
MITTSOMMERNACHT • 1967 • May Paul • FRG • MIDSUMMER NIGHT
MITTSU NO AI • 1954 • Kobayashi Masaki • JPN • THREE LOVES
MITYA • 1927 • Okhlopkov Nikolai • USS
MIUDO DA BICA, O • 1963 • Esteves Constantino • PRT
MIUGAI WONGHAU • 1990 • Liu Guochang • HKG • QUEEN OF TEMPLE STREET
MIVTZA KAHIR • 1966 • Golan Menahem • ISR, FRG • EINER SPIELT FALSCH (FRG) ○ TRUNK TO CAIRO (USA)
MIX IN MASKS, A • 1911 • *Lubin* • USA
MIX ME A PERSON • 1962 • Norman Leslie • UKN
MIX-UP • 1913 • *Rice Herbert* • USA
MIX-UP, A • 1915 • *Grandin* • USA
MIX-UP AT MAXIMS, THE • 1915 • Lyons Eddie • USA
MIX-UP AT MURPHY'S, A • 1914 • Dillon Eddie? • USA
MIX-UP FOR MAISIE • 1915 • Roach Hal • USA
MIX-UP IN ART, A • 1916 • Millarde Harry • USA
MIX-UP IN BANDITS, A • 1913 • *Nestor* • USA
MIX-UP IN BLACK, A • 1916 • Louis Will • SHT • USA
MIX-UP IN DRESS SUIT CASES, A • 1915 • Beggs Lee • USA
MIX-UP IN HEARTS, A • 1917 • Gillstrom Arvid E. • SHT • USA
MIX-UP IN MALES, A • 1915 • Fahrney Milton • USA
MIX-UP IN MOVIES, A • 1916 • Mix Tom • SHT • USA
MIX-UP IN PEDIGREES, A • 1913 • *Majestic* • USA
MIX-UP IN PHOTOS, A • 1916 • Dillon John Francis • USA
MIX-UP IN RAIN COATS, A • 1911 • Sennett Mack • USA
MIX-UP IN SUIT CASES, A • 1911 • *Reliance* • USA
MIX-UP IN THE GALLERY, A see **CHUTE DE CINQ ETAGES, UNE** • 1906
MIX-UP ON THE PLAINS, A • 1914 • *Selig* • USA
MIXED AFFAIR, A • 1912 • Henderson Dell • USA
MIXED AND FIXED • 1915 • *Pokes & Jabbs* • USA
MIXED BABIES • 1905 • Mottershaw Frank • UKN
MIXED BABIES • 1908 • McCutcheon Wallace • USA
MIXED BATHING • 1904 • Collins Alf • UKN
MIXED BATHING • 1935 • Field Mary • UKN
MIXED BATHING AT HOME • 1905 • Collins Alf? • UKN
MIXED BLOOD • 1916 • Swickard Charles • USA
MIXED BLOOD • 1984 • Morrissey Paul • USA, FRN • NEW YORK, AVENUE O ○ COCAINE ○ DOWN TOWN ○ AVENUE O
MIXED BLOOD, THE see **MEZTIZO, EL** • 1989
MIXED-BLOOD, THE see **MEZTIZO, EL** • 1989
MIXED-BLOOD CHILDREN see **KONKETSUJI** • 1952
MIXED BOTTLES • 1912 • *Crystal* • USA
MIXED BRIDES AND PALE-FACED INJUNS • 1916 • *Unicorn* • USA
MIXED COLOR SCHEME, A • 1917 • Hunter T. Hayes • SHT • USA
MIXED COLORS • 1913 • *Pathe* • USA

MIXED COMPANY • 1974 • Shavelson Melville • USA
MIXED COUPLE SEX see **FUFU KOKAN** • 1968
MIXED DOUBLE • 1970 • Barfod Bent • DNM
MIXED DOUBLES • 1933 • Morgan Sidney • UKN
MIXED DOUBLES see **EX-FLAME** • 1930
MIXED DRINKS • 1919 • *Depp Harry* • SHT • USA
MIXED FACES • 1922 • Lee Rowland V. • USA
MIXED FAMILY see **ZAKKYO KAZOKU** • 1956
MIXED FLATS • 1915 • Louis Will • USA
MIXED FRUIT • 1970 • USA
MIXED FRUIT see **FAIRY TALE FOR ADULTS: OR, THE HALF-FAST LOVER, THE** • 1970
MIXED IDENTITIES • 1912 • *Reliance* • USA
MIXED IDENTITIES • 1913 • Humphrey William • USA
MIXED JUSTICE (UKN) see **TWO-FISTED JUSTICE** • 1942
MIXED KIDS • 1916 • Davey Horace • SHT • USA
MIXED MAGIC • 1936 • *Keaton Buster* • SHT • USA
MIXED MAILS • 1914 • *Ab* • USA
MIXED MALES • 1915 • Douglass James • USA
MIXED MARRIAGES see **WICKEDNESS PREFERRED** • 1927
MIXED MASTER • 1956 • McKimson Robert • ANS • USA
MIXED MATRIMONY • 1917 • Chaudet Louis W. • SHT • USA
MIXED NUTS • 1913 • Dillon Eddie • USA
MIXED NUTS • 1917 • *Svenson Alfred* • SHT • USA
MIXED NUTS • 1919 • Clements Roy • SHT • USA
MIXED NUTS • 1934 • Parrott James • SHT • USA
MIXED PETS • 1911 • *Solax* • USA
MIXED PICKLES • 1913 • *Ramo* • USA
MIXED RELATIONS • 1916 • Tucker George Loane • UKN
MIXED SAMPLE TRUNKS, THE • 1912 • *Missimer Howard* • USA
MIXED SIGNALS • 1913 • *Kinemacolor* • USA
MIXED TALES • 1919 • Lyons Eddie, Moran Lee • SHT • USA
MIXED UP ELOPEMENT, A • 1915 • Christie Al • USA
MIXED-UP HONEYMOON, A • 1914 • *Joker* • USA
MIXED VALUES • 1915 • Dillon Eddie • USA
MIXED WIRES • 1915 • Otto Henry • USA
MIXED WIVES • 1919 • Beaudine William • SHT • USA
MIXING CARDS • 1915 • *Superba* • USA
MIXING IT UP • 1915 • *Kalem* • USA
MIXTEC see **DEADLY STRANGER** • 1988
MIXUMMERDAYDREAM • 1968 • Hoving Hattum • NTH
MIXUP, THE • 1911 • *Imp* • USA
MIXUP AT RANDOLPHS, A • 1916 • Dillon John Francis • USA
MIYA BIBI RAJI • 1960 • *Burman S. D. (M)* • IND
MIYA SAMA • 1907 • Morland John • UKN
MIYAMA NO OTOME • 1919 • Kayeriyama Norimasa • JPN
MIYAMOTO MUSASHI • 1940 • Inagaki Hiroshi • JPN • MUSASHI MIYAMOTO
MIYAMOTO MUSASHI • 1944 • Mizoguchi Kenji • JPN • SWORDSMAN, THE (UKN) ○ MUSASHI MIYAMOTO
MIYAMOTO MUSASHI • 1954 • Inagaki Hiroshi • JPN • LEGEND OF MUSASHI, THE ○ SAMURAI
MIYAMOTO MUSASHI I • 1961 • Uchida Tomu • JPN • UNTAMED FURY
MIYAMOTO MUSASHI II • 1962 • Uchida Tomu • JPN • DUEL WITHOUT END
MIYAMOTO MUSASHI III • 1963 • Uchida Tomu • JPN • WORTHLESS DUEL, THE
MIYAMOTO MUSASHI IV • 1964 • Uchida Tomu • JPN • DUEL AT ICHIJOJI TEMPLE, THE
MIYAMOTO MUSASHI V • 1965 • Uchida Tomu • JPN • LAST DUEL, THE
MIZAR • 1953 • De Robertis Francesco • ITL • FROGMAN SPY (UKN) ○ SABOTAGGIO IN MARE
MIZEJICI SVET • 1932 • Ulehla Vladimir, Wasserbauer Milos • CZC • DISAPPEARING WORLD ○ MIZICI SVET
MIZICI SVET see **MIZEJICI SVET** • 1932
MIZPAH: OR, LOVE'S SACRIFICE • 1915 • Kinder Stuart • UKN
MIZU DE KAKARETA MONOGATARI • 1965 • Yoshida Yoshishige • JPN • FORBIDDEN LOVE
MIZUGI NO HANAYOME • 1954 • Sugie Toshio • JPN • BRIDE IN A BATHING SUIT
MLAD I ZVRAV KAO RUZA • 1972 • Jovanovic Jovan • YGS • YOUNG AND HEALTHY AS A ROSE
MLADA LETA • 1952 • Krska Vaclav • CZC • EARLY YEARS, THE ○ YOUTHFUL YEARS
MLADE DNY • 1956 • *Stallich Jan (Ph)* • CZC • YOUNG DAYS, THE
MLADI • 1960 • Kadar Jan, Klos Elmar • DOC • CZC • TIME OF YOUTH ○ YOUTH
MLADY MUZ A BILA VELRYBA • 1978 • Jires Jaromil • CZC • YOUNG MAN AND THE WHITE WHALE, THE ○ YOUNG MAN AND MOBY DICK, THE
M'LISS • 1915 • Lund O. A. C. • USA
M'LISS • 1918 • Neilan Marshall • USA
M'LISS • 1936 • Nicholls George Jr. • USA
MLLE AIDA AND HER TROUPE OF PERFORMING DOGS • 1902 • *Warwick Trading Co* • UKN
MLLE. DESIREE see **DESTIN FABULEUX DE DESIREE CLARY, LE** • 1941
MLLE HANAFI see **ANISSA HANAFI, AL-** • 1954
MLLE IRENE THE GREAT • 1931 • Cline Eddie • SHT • USA
MLLE LA MODE • 1914 • Pollard Harry • USA
MLLE PAULETTE • 1918 • Wells Raymond • USA
MLODOSC CHOPINA • 1952 • Ford Aleksander • PLN • YOUTH OF CHOPIN, THE ○ CHOPIN'S YOUTH ○ YOUNG CHOPIN
MLODY LAS • 1935 • Lejtes Joseph • PLN
MLODZI Z BRZOZY • 1970 • Halladin Danuta • DOC • PLN • YOUNG PEOPLE FROM BRZOZA
M'LORD OF THE WHITE ROAD • 1923 • Rooke Arthur • UKN
MLYN • 1971 • Kijowicz Miroslaw • ANS • PLN • MILL, THE
MLYNAR A JEHO DITE • 1928 • Molas Zet • CZC
MMAMPODI • 1983 • SAF
MME. BLANCHE, BEAUTY DOCTOR • 1915 • *Chamberlain Riley* • USA
MME OLGA'S MASSAGE PARLOR • 1965 • Mawra Joseph P. • USA • OLGA'S MASSAGE PARLOR ○ OLGA'S PARLOR
MME PAULETTE • 1918 • Wells Raymond • USA
MMILA WE BAKWEDITI • 1985 • SAF
MNASIDIKA • 1969 • *Weste Robert* • USA • MANASADEEKA
MNE DVADTSAT LET • 1961-63 • Khutsiev Marlen • USS • I AM TWENTY YEARS OLD ○ I AM TWENTY ○ ILYITCH SQUARE ○ ILYICH ZASTAVA
MNISTIRES TIS PINELOPIS, I • 1968 • Kiriakopoulos Hristos • GRC • PENELOPE'S LOVERS
MO' BETTER BLUES • 1990 • Lee Spike • USA
MO HOHOZUE WA TSUKANAI • 1979 • Higashi Yoichi • JPN • NO MORE EASY GOING
MO TAKU-TO BUNKADAIKA-KUMEI • 1969 • Oshima Nagisa • JPN
MO-TENG PAO-PIAO • 1981 • Hui Michael • HKG • SECURITY UNLIMITED
MO-TOY COMEDIES • 1917 • *Toyland Films Corp* • ASS • USA
MOA • 1987 • Wahlgren Anders • SWD
MOABIT NOTEBOOK, THE see **MOABITSKAYA TETRAD** • 1968
MOABITSKAYA TETRAD • 1968 • Kvinikhidze Leonid • USS • MOABIT NOTEBOOK, THE
MOAN AND GROAN INC. • 1929 • McGowan Robert • SHT • USA
MOANA see **MOANA -A ROMANCE OF THE GOLDEN AGE** • 1926
MOANA -A ROMANCE OF THE GOLDEN AGE • 1926 • Flaherty Robert, Flaherty Frances Hubbard • DOC • USA • MOANA: THE LOVE LIFE OF A SOUTH SEA SIREN ○ MOANA
MOANA: THE LOVE LIFE OF A SOUTH SEA SIREN see **MOANA -A ROMANCE OF THE GOLDEN AGE** • 1926
MOANS AND GROANS • 1935 • *Terry Paul / Moser Frank (P)* • ANS • USA
MOARA CU NOROC • 1956 • Iliu Victor • RMN • MILL OF LUCK AND PLENTY, THE
MOARTEA LUI IPU • 1972 • Nicolaescu Sergiu • RMN • IPU'S DEATH
MOARTEA LUI JOE INDIANUL • 1968 • Iacob Mihai • RMN • DEATH OF JOE THE INDIAN, THE
MOASKAR EL BANAT • 1967 • Shawqi Khalil • EGY • CAMP DE JEUNES FILLES, LE ○ MUASKARI AL-BANAT ○ GIRLS' CAMP
MOB, THE • 1951 • Parrish Robert • USA • REMEMBER THAT FACE (UKN)
MOB, THE • 1971 • Grubcheva Ivanka • BUL
MOB, THE see **CROWD, THE** • 1927
MOB RULE see **FURY** • 1936
MOB STORY • 1990 • Markiw Jancarlo, Markiw Gabriel • CND
MOB TOWN • 1941 • Nigh William • USA
MOB WAR • 1978 • Davis Bobby • USA
MOB WAR • 1988 • Ingvordsen J. Christian • USA
MOBBY JACKSON • 1961 • Dall'Ara Renato • ITL
MOBILE COMPOSITION • 1930 • Jacobs Lewis, Gercon Jo, Louis Hershell • USA
MOBILE-HOME GIRLS see **JOUISSANCES A DOMICILE** • 1985
MOBILE TWO • 1975 • Moessinger David • TVM • USA
MOBILIER, LE • 1976 • Dansereau Fernand, Rossignol Yolande • DCS • CND
MOBILIER FIDELE, LE • 1910 • Cohl Emile • ANS • FRN • AUTOMATIC MOVING COMPANY, THE
MOBILIZING MASS. STATE TROOPS • 1905 • *Bitzer Billy (Ph)* • USA
MOBILMACHUNG IN DER KUCHE • 1914 • Schmelter Franz • FRG
MOBILMACHUNG IN DER KUCHE 2 • 1915 • Schmelter Franz • FRG • IHR GEBURTSTAG
MOBILMACHUNG IN DER KUCHE 3 • 1915 • Schmelter Franz • FRG
MOBLIERTE HERR, DER • 1915 • Edel Edmund • FRG
MOBLIERTE ZIMMER • 1929 • Sauer Fred • FRG
MOBS, INC. • 1955 • *Onyx* • USA • MOBS INCORPORATED (UKN)
MOBS INCORPORATED (UKN) see **MOBS, INC.** • 1955
MOBSTER, THE (UKN) see **I, MOBSTER** • 1958
MOBY DICK • 1930 • Bacon Lloyd • USA
MOBY DICK • 1956 • Huston John • USA, UKN
MOBY DICK • 1977 • *Pertwee Jon* • ANM • UKN
MOBY DICK see **DAMON DES MEERES** • 1931
MOBY DUCK • 1965 • McKimson Robert • ANS • USA
MOC OSUDU • 1969 • Brdecka Jiri • ANS • CZC • POWER OF DESTINY ○ FORCE OF DESTINY, THE
MOCAMBIQUE • 1966 • SAF
MOCAMBIQUE • 1968 • Simoes Quirino • SHT • PRT
MOCAMBIQUE 65 • 1965 • de Almeida Manuel Faria • SHT • PRT
MOCCASIN PRINT, THE • 1914 • *Frontier* • USA
MOCCASINS • 1925 • Bradbury Robert North • USA
MOCCESSEN THE HUMAN SNAKE • 1898 • *Cinematograph Co* • UKN
MOCDERTJIE see **MOEDERTJIE** • 1931
MOCHUELO, EL • 1905 • de Banos Ricardo • SPN
MOCK AUCTIONEER, THE • 1926 • Engholm F. W. • UKN
MOCK BARONETS, THE • 1908 • *Urban-Elipse* • USA
MOCK MARRIAGE, A • 1913 • Nicholls George • USA
MOCK TRIAL see **HANDLE WITH CARE** • 1958
MOCK WAR see **GIYERA PATANI** • 1968
MOCKERY • 1912 • *Wilder Marshall P.* • USA
MOCKERY • 1927 • Christensen Benjamin • USA • TERROR
MOCKING BIRD, THE see **BLACK BIRD, THE** • 1925
MOCNE UDERZENIE • 1967 • Passendorfer Jerzy • PLN • BIG BEAT ○ HARD BLOW
MOCNE UDERZENIE -OPUS 2 • 1967 • Trzos-Rastawiecki Andrzej • DOC • PLN • HARD BLOW -OPUS 2
MOCO DE 74 ANOS, UM • 1963 • dos Santos Nelson Pereira • SHT • BRZ
MOD • 1964 • De Palma Brian • SHT • USA
MOD ATT LEVA • 1982 • Romare Ingela, Andersson Marit • SWD • COURAGE TO LIVE
MOD LYSET • 1919 • Holger-Madsen • DNM • TOWARDS THE LIGHT
MOD STJERNERNE see **HANS GODE GENIUS** • 1920
MODAE • 1964 • Inoue Umeji • JPN • NIGHT OF THE HONEYMOON
MODARNA FRUAR • 1932 • Adolphson Edvin • SWD • MODERN WIVES
MODE REVEE, LA • 1939 • L'Herbier Marcel • SHT • FRN
MODEL • 1974 • Sfikas Kostas • GRC
MODEL • 1980 • Wiseman Frederick • DOC • USA
MODEL 46 • 1916 • Chaudet Louis W. • SHT • USA
MODEL, THE • 1915 • USA
MODEL, THE • 1916 • Buss Harry • UKN
MODEL, THE see **MANNEKANGEN** • 1913
MODEL AND THE MARRIAGE BROKER, THE • 1951 • Cukor George • USA • KITTY AND THE MARRIAGE BROKER
MODEL BEHAVIOUR • 1984 • Gardner Bud • USA
MODEL COOK, THE • 1916 • *Drew Sidney* • SHT • USA
MODEL COURTSHIP • 1903 • *Bitzer Billy (Ph)* • USA
MODEL DAIRY, THE • 1922 • *Terry Paul* • ANS • USA
MODEL FOR MURDER • 1959 • Bishop Terry • UKN
MODEL FOR ST. JOHN, THE • 1912 • Young James • USA
MODEL FRAME-UP, A • 1915 • Coigne Frank B. • USA
MODEL FROM MONTMARTRE, THE (USA) see **FEMME NUE, LA** • 1926
MODEL FROM PARIS see **THAT MODEL FROM PARIS** • 1926
MODEL GIRL • 1954 • De Lane Lea William • UKN
MODEL HUNTERS, THE • 1970 • *Mj Productions* • USA
MODEL HUSBAND, A • 1916 • Myers Harry • SHT • USA
MODEL HUSBAND, A • 1919 • Lyons Eddie, Moran Lee • SHT • USA
MODEL HUSBAND, A • 1920 • De Haven Carter • SHT • USA
MODEL HUSBAND (USA) see **MUSTERGATTE, DER** • 1937
MODEL IN RED see **MANNEKANG I ROTT** • 1958
MODEL JANITOR, THE • 1917 • *Ham & Bud* • SHT • USA
MODEL LOVE see **RAGAZZA DI NOME GIULIO, LA** • 1970
MODEL MARAUDER, A • 1917 • *Boardman True* • SHT • USA
MODEL MUDDLE • 1955 • *Halas John (P)* • ANS • UKN
MODEL MURDER CASE, THE (USA) see **GIRL IN THE HEADLINES** • 1963
MODEL SHOP • 1969 • Demy Jacques • USA
MODEL WIFE • 1941 • Jason Leigh • USA
MODEL WIFE, A • 1915 • *Kalem* • USA
"MODEL" WIFE, A • 1915 • North Wilfred • *Vitagraph* • USA
MODEL YOUNG MAN, A • 1914 • Young James • USA
MODELAGE EXPRESS • 1903 • Blache Alice • FRN
MODELE, UN see **MUDIL** • 1974
MODELE IRASCIBLE, UN • 1897 • Melies Georges • FRN • IRRITABLE MODEL, AN
MODELING • 1921 • Fleischer Dave • SHT • USA
MODELING FOR MONEY • 1938 • Miller David • SHT • USA
MODELL BIANKA • 1951 • Groschopp Richard • GDR
MODELL VON MONTPARNASSE, DIE see **ADIEU MASCOTTE** • 1929
MODELLA, LA • 1920 • Caserini Mario • ITL
MODELLE DI VIA MARGUTTA, LE • 1946 • Scotese Giuseppe Maria • ITL
MODELLHAUS CREVETTE • 1930 • Neufeld Max • FRG • SOLD
MODELLING EXTRAORDINARY • 1912 • Booth W. R. • UKN
MODELO DE LA CALLE FLORIDA, LA • 1939 • Irigoyen Julio • ARG
MODEL'S ADVENTURE, THE see **WOMAN'S VILES, A** • 1915
MODELS AND WIVES • 1931 • Lamont Charles • SHT • USA
MODEL'S CONFESSION, THE • 1918 • Park Ida May • USA
MODELS IN CHARCOAL see **NUDE IN CHARCOAL** • 1963
MODELS INC. • 1952 • Le Borg Reginald • USA • THAT KIND OF GIRL (UKN) ○ CALL GIRL
MODEL'S MA • 1907 • *Bitzer Billy (Ph)* • USA
MODEL'S REDEMPTION, THE • 1910 • *Imp* • USA
MODENA, CITTA DEL EMILIA ROSSA • 1950 • Lizzani Carlo • DOC • ITL
MODERATO CANTABILE • 1960 • Brook Peter • FRN, ITL • SEVEN DAYS.. SEVEN NIGHTS (UKN)
MODERN ANANIAS, A • 1912 • *Selig* • USA
MODERN ATLANTA, A • 1912 • *Vitagraph* • USA
MODERN BLUEBEARD, A see **MODERNO BARBA AZUL, EL** • 1946
MODERN BRIGANDAGE see **BRIGANDAGE MODERNE** • 1905
MODERN CAIN, A • 1925 • *Ward Norman* • USA
MODERN CARACAS • 1974 • Hohermuth Harold • DOC • VNZ
MODERN CINDERELLA, A • 1908 • Stow Percy • UKN
MODERN CINDERELLA, A • 1910 • Blackton J. Stuart • USA
MODERN CINDERELLA, A • 1911 • Dawley J. Searle • USA
MODERN CINDERELLA, A • 1917 • Adolfi John G. • USA
MODERN CINDERELLA, THE see **WHEN TOMORROW COMES** • 1939
MODERN COURTSHIP, A • 1910 • *Vitagraph* • USA
MODERN DAUGHTERS • 1927 • Hunt Charles J. • USA
MODERN DAY FAGIN, A • 1905 • *Walturdaw* • UKN
MODERN DIANAS, THE • 1911 • *Fuller Mary* • USA
MODERN DICK WHITTINGTON, A • 1913 • Stow Percy • UKN
MODERN DR. JEKYLL, A • 1909 • *Selig* • USA
MODERN DR. JEKYLL, THE see **DR. JEKYLL AND MR. HYDE** • 1908
MODERN DON JUAN, A • 1907 • Fitzhamon Lewin? • UKN
MODERN DON JUAN, A • 1914 • Somers Dalton • UKN
MODERN DUBARRY, A see **DUBARRY VON HEUTE, EINE** • 1926
MODERN ENOCH ARDEN, A • 1915 • King Burton L. • USA
MODERN ENOCH EDEN, A • 1916 • Badger Clarence, Avery Charles • SHT • USA
MODERN FABLE, A see **MODERNA BASNA** • 1965
MODERN FACTORY TALE, A • 1914 • *Smalley Phillips* • USA
MODERN FREE LANCE, A • 1914 • Pollard Harry • USA
MODERN GALATEA, A • 1907 • Booth W. R.? • UKN
MODERN GARRICK, A • 1913 • *Patheplay* • USA
MODERN GEORGE WASHINGTON, A • 1910 • Aylott Dave? • UKN
MODERN GIRLS • 1986 • Kramer Jerry • USA
MODERN GRACE DARLING, A • 1908 • Gobbett T. J.? • UKN
MODERN GUIDE TO HEALTH • 1946 • Halas John, Batchelor Joy • ANS • UKN
MODERN HERCULES, A • 1916 • *Rolma* • SHT • USA
MODERN HERCULES, A • 1916 • *Hippo* • USA
MODERN HERO, A • 1911 • Bouwmeester Theo • UKN
MODERN HERO, A • 1934 • Pabst G. W. • USA
MODERN HERO, A (UKN) see **KNUTE ROCKNE -ALL AMERICAN** • 1940
MODERN HIGHWAYMAN, A • 1912 • *Imp* • USA
MODERN HIGHWAYMAN, A • 1914 • Somers Dalton • UKN
MODERN HUSBANDS • 1919 • Grandon Francis J. • USA
MODERN INVENTIONS • 1937 • King Jack • ANS • USA

MODERN JACK THE RIPPER, A see **FARLIG FORBRYDER, EN** • 1913
MODERN JEAN VAL JEAN: OR, A FRAME UP, A • 1930 • *Hagen Al* • USA • FRAME UP, A
MODERN JEKYLL AND HYDE, A • 1913 • *Broderick Robert* • USA
MODERN KNIGHT, A • 1916 • Bertram William • SHT • USA
MODERN KNIGHT, A (UKN) see **THUNDERING THROUGH** • 1925
MODERN KNIGHT ERRANT, A • 1910 • *Vitagraph* • USA
MODERN LOCHINVAR, A • 1913 • *Thanhouser* • USA
MODERN LORELEI, A • 1917 • Otto Henry • USA • LORELEI OF THE SEA, THE
MODERN LOVE • 1918 • Leonard Robert Z. • USA
MODERN LOVE • 1929 • Heath Arch B. • USA
MODERN LOVE POTION, A • 1910 • Fitzhamon Lewin? • UKN
MODERN MADNESS see **BIG NOISE, THE** • 1936
MODERN MADNESS (UKN) see **MARRIAGE WHIRL, THE** • 1925
MODERN MAGDALEN, A • 1915 • Davis Will S. • USA
MODERN MAGIC • 1908 • *Pathe* • FRN
MODERN MAN • 1990 • Benson Robby • USA
MODERN MARRIAGE • 1923 • Windom Lawrence C. • USA
MODERN MARRIAGE see **MODERN MATRIMONY** • 1923
MODERN MARRIAGE, A • 1950 • Landres Paul • USA • FRIGID WIFE
MODERN MASTERS • 1976 • Salvat Keith • DOC • ASL
MODERN MATRIMONY • 1923 • Heerman Victor • USA • MODERN MARRIAGE ○ LOVE NEST, THE
MODERN MELNOTTE, A • 1914 • *Maison Edna* • USA
MODERN MESSENGER BOY, THE • 1910 • *Essanay* • USA
MODERN MIRACLE, THE (UKN) see **STORY OF ALEXANDER GRAHAM BELL, THE** • 1939
MODERN MONTE CRISTO, A • 1917 • Moore W. Eugene • USA
MODERN MONTE CRISTO, A see **STEPPING FAST** • 1923
MODERN MONTE CRISTO, A see **DIAMOND FRONTIER** • 1940
MODERN MOTHER GOOSE • 1917 • *Fort Dearborn Photoplays* • USA
MODERN MOTHERS • 1928 • Rosen Phil • USA
MODERN MUSKETEER, A • 1917 • Dwan Allan • USA
MODERN MYSTERY, A • 1912 • Booth W. R. • UKN
MODERN NOBLE, A • 1915 • *Chatterton Thomas* • USA
MODERN OIL REFINERY, A • 1954 • Crosfield Michael • DOC • UKN
MODERN OLIVER TWIST, A • 1906 • Blackton J. Stuart • USA
MODERN OTHELLO, A • 1914 • Pollard Harry • USA
MODERN OTHELLO, A • 1917 • Perret Leonce • USA • SHADOW OF NIGHT, THE ○ LASH OF JEALOUSY, THE ○ MAD LOVER, THE
MODERN PAUL, A • 1916 • Mayo Melvin • SHT • USA
MODERN PAUL PRY, A • 1910 • Coleby A. E. • UKN
MODERN PIRATES, THE • 1906 • Cooper Arthur • UKN • RAID OF THE ARMOURED MOTOR, THE
MODERN POLISH JAZZ GROUPS see **JAZZ W POLSCE** • 1964
MODERN PORTIA, A • 1912 • *Lubin* • USA
MODERN PROBLEMS • 1981 • Shapiro Ken • USA
MODERN PRODIGAL, THE • 1910 • Griffith D. W. • USA
MODERN PRODIGAL, THE • 1913 • *Brooke Van Dyke* • USA
MODERN PROSPECTOR, THE • 1958 • Bigras Jean-Yves • DCS • CND
MODERN PROSPECTOR, THE • 1958 • Fraser Donald • DOC • CND
MODERN PSYCHE, A • 1913 • Brooke Van Dyke • USA
MODERN PYGMALION AND GALATEA, A • 1911 • Bouwmeester Theo, Booth W. R.? • UKN
MODERN RED RIDING HOOD, A • 1935 • *Terry Paul/ Moser Frank (P)* • ANS • USA
MODERN RHYTHM • 1963 • Henryson Robert • SHT • UKN
MODERN RIP, A • 1911 • *Selig* • USA
MODERN RIP VAN WINKLE, A • 1914 • Pollard Harry? • USA
MODERN ROBINSON, A (USA) see **ROBINSON I SKARGARDEN** • 1920
MODERN ROMANCE • 1917 • *Figman Max* • SHT • USA
MODERN ROMANCE • 1981 • Brooks Albert • USA
MODERN ROMANCE, A • 1913 • *Imp* • USA
MODERN SALOME, A • 1920 • Perret Leonce • USA
MODERN SAMSON, A • 1907 • *Cines* • ITL
MODERN SAMSON, A • 1914 • Kendall Preston • USA
MODERN SCHOOL see **MODERNE ECOLE** • 1909
MODERN SCULPTORS • 1908 • *Pathe* • SHT • FRN
MODERN SHERLOCK, A • 1917 • *Triangle* • USA
MODERN SLAVES • 1912 • *Rex* • USA
MODERN SNARE, THE • 1913 • Reid Wallace • USA
MODERN SPHINX, A • 1916 • Bartlett Charles • SHT • USA
MODERN SPORTS COACHING • 1970 • Ternovszky Bela • HNG • SPORTS COACHING
MODERN STAGE DANCES • 1904 • *Paul R. W.* • UKN
MODERN STEELCRAFT • Catling Darrell • DCS • UKN
MODERN SUFFRAGETTE, THE see **MODERNA SUFFRAGETTEN, DEN** • 1913
MODERN THELMA, A • 1916 • Adolfi John G. • USA
MODERN TIMES • 1936 • Chaplin Charles • USA
MODERN VENDETTA, A • 1914 • Eagle Oscar • USA
MODERN WIFE, THE see **FREE LOVE** • 1930
MODERN WITNESS, A • 1913 • *Kirkwood James* • USA
MODERN WIVES see **MODARNA FRUAR** • 1932
MODERN WOMAN, A see **DAGENS DONNA** • 1989
MODERN YARN, A • 1911 • *Pathe* • FRN
MODERN YOUTH • 1926 • Nelson Jack • USA
MODERNA BASNA • 1965 • Marks Aleksandar, Jutrisa Vladimir • ANS • USA • MODERN FABLE, A
MODERNA SUFFRAGETTEN, DEN • 1913 • Stiller Mauritz • SWD • IN MRS. PANKHURST'S FOOTSTEPS ○ MODERN SUFFRAGETTE, THE ○ LILY DEN SUFFRAGETTEN ○ SUFFRAGETTEN, DEN ○ SUFFRAGETTE, THE
MODERNE CASANOVA, DER • 1928 • Obal Max • FRG
MODERNE ECOLE • 1909 • Cohl Emile (c/d) • ANS • FRN • MODERN SCHOOL
MODERNE EHEN • 1924 • Otto Hans • FRG
MODERNE MITGIFT • 1932 • Emo E. W. • FRG
MODERNE PARIS ODER DER HERR APOTHEKER HEIRATET, DER • 1915 • Bolten-Baeckers Heinrich • FRG
MODERNE PIRATEN • 1928 • Noa Manfred • FRG
MODERNE SKLAVEN • 1920 • *Ideal-Film* • FRG
MODERNE TOCHTER • 1919 • Noa Manfred • FRG • DEMI-VIERGES
MODERNER DON JUAN, EIN • 1927 • Zelnik Friedrich • FRG
MODERNO BARBA AZUL, EL • 1946 • Salvador Jaime • MXC • BOOM IN THE MOON (USA) ○ MODERN BLUEBEARD, A
MODERNS, THE • 1988 • Rudolph Alan • USA
MODERNS, THE see **GENDAIJIN** • 1952
MODERS KAERLIGHED, EN see **HISTORIEN OM EN MODER** • 1912
MODERS KAERLIGHED, EN see **STORSTE KAERLIGHED, DEN** • 1914
MODERSKAPETS KVAL OCH LYCKA • 1945 • Johansson Ivar • SWD • SUFFERING AND HAPPINESS OF MOTHERHOOD
MODEST HERO, A • 1913 • Henderson Dell • USA
MODEST YOUNG MAN, A • 1909 • Porter Edwin S. • USA
MODESTA • 1956 • Doniger Benji • PRC
MODESTY BLAISE • 1966 • Losey Joseph • UKN
MODIFICATION, LA • 1970 • Worms Michel • FRN, ITL • MOGLIE NUOVA, LA (ITL)
MODIGA MINDRE MAN • 1968 • Krantz Leif • SWD • BRAVE LITTLE MAN
MODIGLIANI OF MONTPARNASSE (USA) see **MONTPARNASSE 19** • 1958
MODISE • 1984 • SAF
MODISTE, THE • 1917 • Gillstrom Arvid E. • SHT • USA
MODLISZKA • 1960 • Marczak Karol • PLN • MANTIS
MODO DI ESSERE DONNA, UN • 1973 • Pavoni Pier Ludovico • ITL
MODOSTROS, O • 1967 • Laskos Orestis • GRC • LADIES' TAILOR, THE
MODRE I FREMMED FAEDRELAND • 1986 • Jensen Ingrid Oustrup • DOC • DNM • MOTHERS IN A FOREIGN MOTHERLAND
MODRE Z NEBE • 1962 • Hofman Eduard • ANS • PLN • BLUE FROM HEAVEN
MODRE Z NEBE • 1983 • Koval Ota • CZC • BLUE FROM HEAVEN
MODREHJAELPEN • 1942 • Dreyer Carl T. • DCS • DNM • HELP FOR MOTHERS ○ GOOD MOTHERS
MODS AND ROCKERS • 1964 • Hume Kenneth • UKN • GO GO BIG BEAT (USA)
MODSZEREK • 1968 • Vas Judit • HNG • METHODS
MODULATIONS • 1972 • Klein Judith • ANS • CND
MODULO see **MODULO: VARIATIONS SUR UN DESIGN** • 1974
MODULO: VARIATIONS SUR UN DESIGN • 1974 • Moretti Pierre • CND • MODULO
MODUS OPERANDI • 1967 • Garcia Eddie • PHL
MOEBIUS FLIP • 1969 • *Summit* • SHT • USA
MOEDERTJIE • 1931 • Albrecht Joseph • SAF • MOCDERTJIE
MOEMOEA • 1980 • Arnaud Dominique • FRN
MOERO SEISHUN • 1968 • Matsumori Takashi • JPN • FLAME OF YOUTH, THE
MOERO TAIYO • 1967 • Matsumori Takashi • JPN • BURNING SUN, THE
MOERU AKI • 1978 • Kobayashi Masaki • JPN • GLOWING AUTUMN ○ BURNING AUTUMN
MOERU KUMO • 1967 • Nomura Takeshi • JPN • BURNING CLOUDS
MOERU OZORA • 1940 • Abe Yutaka • JPN • BURNING SKY, THE ○ MOYURU OZORA ○ FLAMING SKY
MOERU TAIRIKU • 1968 • Nishimura Shogoro • JPN • BLAZING CONTINENT
MOETSUKITA CHIZU • 1968 • Teshigahara Hiroshi • JPN • RUINED MAP, THE (USA) ○ MAN WITHOUT A MAP, THE ○ BURNED MAP, THE
MOGAMBO • 1953 • Ford John • USA
MOGEN SIE IN FRIEDEN RUH'EN (FRG) see **REQUIESCANT** • 1967
MOGEZAT EL SAMAA • 1956 • Salem Atef • EGY • MIRACLE FROM HEAVEN, A ○ MUJIZAT AS-SAMA ○ MIRACLE DU CIEL
MOGG MEGONE • 1909 • Blackton J. Stuart (Spv) • USA
MOGHO DAKAN • 1976 • Coulibaly Sega • MLI • DESTIN
MOGHOLHA • 1974 • Kimiavi Parviz • IRN • MONGOLS, THE
MOGHREB see **BOURRASQUE** • 1935
MOGHTASIBOUN, EL • 1989 • Marzouk Said • EGY • RAPISTS, THE
MOGLI DEGLI ALTRI, LE (ITL) see **RAVISSANTE** • 1961
MOGLI PERICOLOSE • 1958 • Comencini Luigi • ITL
MOGLIAMANTE see **MOGLIE AMANTE** • 1978
MOGLIE AMANTE • 1978 • Vicario Marco • ITL • WIFEMISTRESS (USA) ○ MOGLIAMANTE ○ WIFE ○ MISTRESS
MOGLIE AMERICANA, UNA (ITL) see **MES FEMMES AMERICAINES** • 1966
MOGLIE BELLA, LA • 1924 • Genina Augusto • ITL
MOGLIE BIONDA, LA • 1965 • Salce Luciano • ITL, FRN • MAN, THE WOMAN AND THE MONEY, THE
MOGLIE CHE SI GETTO DALLA FINESTA, LA • 1919 • D'Ambra Lucio • ITL
MOGLIE DEL PRETE, LA • 1970 • Risi Dino • ITL, FRN • PRIEST'S WIFE, THE (UKN) ○ FEMME DU PRETRE, LA (FRN)
MOGLIE DI MIO PADRE, LA • 1976 • Bianchi Andrea • ITL • CONFESSIONS OF A FRUSTRATED HOUSEWIFE (UKN) ○ MY FATHER'S WIFE ○ CONFESSIONS OF A FRUSTRATED WIFE
MOGLIE DI SUA ECCELLENZA, LA • 1913 • Genina Augusto • ITL
MOGLIE E BUOI.. • 1956 • De Mitri Leonardo • ITL • BRIDE FOR FRANK, A (USA)
MOGLIE E LE ARANCE, LA • 1917 • D'Ambra Lucio • ITL
MOGLIE E UGUALE PER TUTTI, LA • 1955 • Simonelli Giorgio C. • ITL
MOGLIE GIAPPONESE, LA • 1968 • Polidoro Gian Luigi • ITL • JAPANESE WIFE, THE
MOGLIE GIOVANE, LA • 1975 • D'Eramo Giovanni • ITL
MOGLIE IN BIANCO.. L'AMANTE AL PEPE, LA • 1981 • Tarantini Michele Massimo • ITL
MOGLIE IN CASTIGO, LA • 1943 • Menardi Leo • ITL
MOGLIE IN PERICOLO, UNA • 1939 • Neufeld Max • ITL • WIFE IN DANGER, A (USA)
MOGLIE IN VACANZA, L'AMANTE IN CITTA, LA • 1980 • Martino Sergio • ITL • WIFE ON HOLIDAY.. THE MISTRESS IN TOWN, THE
MOGLIE, MARITO E.. • 1920 • Genina Augusto • ITL
MOGLIE NUDA E SICILIANA • 1978 • Bianchi Andrea • ITL
MOGLIE NUOVA, LA (ITL) see **MODIFICATION, LA** • 1970
MOGLIE PER UNA NOTTE • 1950 • Camerini Mario • ITL • WIFE FOR A NIGHT (USA)
MOGLIE PIU BELLA, LA • 1970 • Damiani Damiano • ITL
MOGLIE VERGINE, LA • 1976 • Girolami Marino • ITL • VALENTINA -THE VIRGIN WIFE ○ VIRGIN WIFE
MOGLIETTINA, LA • 1975 • Solari Alberto • ITL • INSIDE AMY
MOGREM TAHT EL EKHTEBAR • 1968 • Shukry Abdel Moneim • EGY • CRIMINAL ON PROBATION, A
MOHABBAT KE ANSU • 1932 • *Sircar B. N. (P)* • IND
MOHAMED ALI • 1971 • Haines Fred, Krebbes Seemore, Bertschi Ernst • SWT • BADDEST DADDY IN THE WHOLE WORLD, THE
MOHAMMAD, MESSENGER OF GOD (USA) see **RISALAH, AL-** • 1976
MOHAMMEDANISCHE BAUKUNST • 1958 • Kirschner Klaus • FRG
MOHAN JOSHI HAZIR HO • 1984 • Mirza Saeed • IND • COURT SUMMONS JOSHI, THE
MOHAWK • 1956 • Neumann Kurt • USA
MOHAWK'S TREASURE, THE • 1916 • *Hiawatha* • USA
MOHAWK'S WAY, A • 1910 • Griffith D. W. • USA
MOHICAN'S DAUGHTER, THE • 1922 • Taylor Stanner E. V. • USA
MOHINI AVATAR • 1925 • IND • MOHINI INCARNATION OF GOD
MOHINI INCARNATION OF GOD see **MOHINI AVATAR** • 1925
MOHLALIFI • 1985 • SAF
MOHNA • 1980 • Kabir Alamgir • BNG • CONFLUENCE
MOHOMONO GINPEI • 1937 • Inagaki Hiroshi • JPN • MUHOUMONO GINPEI ○ GINPEI THE OUTLAW
MOHR UND DIE RABEN VON LONDON • 1969 • Dziuba Helmut • GDR
MOI AUSSI, J'ACCUSE • 1923 • Machin Alfred • FRN
MOI DRUG IVAN LAPSHIN • 1986 • Gherman Alexei • USS • MY FRIEND IVAN LAPSHIN
MOI ET LA JUSTICE see **DA'IRAT AL-INTIQAM** • 1975
MOI ET LES HOMMES DE QUARANTE ANS • 1964 • Pinoteau Jack • FRN, FRG, ITL • CAROLINE UND DIE MANNER UBER VIERZIG (FRG)
MOI ET L'IMPERATRICE • 1932 • Martin Paul, Hollander Friedrich • FRN • IMPERATRICE ET MOI, L'
MOI, FLEUR BLEUE • 1977 • Le Hung Eric • FRN • STOP CALLING ME BABY!
MOI, J'AIME TOUT • 1973 • Gagne Jacques • DCS • CND
MOI J'DIS QU'C'EST BIEN • 1973 • Zarifian Christian • FRN
MOI JE • 1973 • Godard Jean-Luc • FRN
MOI, LUI, ET ELLE see **ANA WA HUWWA WA HIYYA** • 1963
MOI MLADSHII BRAT • 1962 • Zarkhi Alexander • USS • MY YOUNGER BROTHER
MOI, PIERRE RIVIERE see **MOI, PIERRE RIVIERE, AYANT EGORGE MA MERE, MA SOEUR ET MA FRERE** • 1977
MOI, PIERRE RIVIERE, AYANT EGORGE MA MERE, MA SOEUR ET MA FRERE • 1977 • Allio Rene • FRN • MOI, PIERRE RIVIERE ○ I, PIERRE RIVIERE
MOI RODINA • 1932 • Heifitz Josif, Zarkhi Alexander • USS • MY FATHERLAND ○ MY HOMELAND ○ MY COUNTRY
MOI SIN • 1928 • Chervyakov Yevgeni • USS • MY SON
MOI, TINTIN • 1975 • Roanne Henri, Valet Gerard • DOC • FRN
MOI, UN JOUR.. • 1967 • Dansereau Mireille • SHT • CND
MOI, UN NOIR • 1957 • Rouch Jean • FRN • I, A NEGRO (UKN) ○ TREICHVILLE
MOI UNIVERSITETI • 1940 • Donskoi Mark • USS • UNIVERSITY OF LIFE ○ MY UNIVERSITIES
MOI Y'EN A VOULOIR DES SOUS! • 1973 • Yanne Jean • FRN
MOIDODYR • 1927 • ANM • USS
MOINDRE GESTE, LE • 1970 • Daniel Jean-Pierre, Deligny Ferdinand • FRN
MOINE, LE • 1972 • Kyrou Ado • FRN, ITL, FRG • MONACA, IL (ITL) ○ MONK, THE
MOINEAU, LE see **ASFOUR, EL** • 1973
MOINEAUX DE PARIS • 1952 • Cloche Maurice • FRN
MOINES DE SAINT-BENOIT, LES • 1951 • Blais Roger • DCS • CND
MOINHOS DE PORTUGAL • 1965 • Spiguel Miguel • SHT • PRT
MOIRA • 1912 • Rolfe Alfred • ASL • MYSTERY OF THE BUSH, THE
MOIRA see **WOMEN WOMEN WOMEN MOIRA** • 1970
MOIRE • Munari Bruno, Piccardo Marcello • SHT • ITL
MOIRES: DALI/OSTER NEWSREEL • 1954 • Kirsanoff Dimitri • SHT • FRN
MOIS A WOUKANG, UN • 1980 • Regnier Michel • DOC • CND
MOIS D'AVRIL SONT MEURTRIERS, LES • 1986 • Heynemann Laurent • FRN
MOIS LE PLUS BEAU, LE • 1968 • Blanc Guy • FRN
MOISE • 1978 • Demare Lucas • VNZ, ARG
MOISE ET L'AMOUR see **ROI DU VILLAGE, LE** • 1962
MOISE ET SALOMON PARFUMEURS • 1935 • Hugon Andre • FRN
MOISE SAUVE DES EAUX • 1910 • Andreani Henri • FRN
MOISES PADILLA STORY • 1961 • De Leon Gerardo • PHL
MOISSON, LA • 1966 • Lamothe Arthur • DCS • CND
MOISSON DE LA GLAISE, LA • 1945 • Palardy Jean • DCS • CND
MOISSON DE LA MER, LA • 1944 • Palardy Jean • DCS • CND
MOISSON DE L'ESPOIR, LES • 1969 • Reichenbach Francois • SHT • FRN • ISRAEL
MOISSON D'UNE VIE, LA • 1949 • Lavoie Hermenegilde • DOC • CND
MOISSON SERA BELLE, LA • 1954 • Villet • SHT • FRN
MOISSONS D'AUJOURD'HUI • 1951 • Dupont Jacques • DOC • FRN • NEW FARMING IN FRANCE
MOIST EYES see **NEMLI GOZLER** • 1967
MOIST LIPS see **NEMLI DUDAKLAR** • 1967
MOITI DE POLKA • 1908 • Melies Georges • FRN
MOITIE DE L'AMOUR, LA • 1985 • Jimenez Mary • BLG, FRN
MOJ • 1920 • Biebrach Rudolf • FRG

MOJ DRUGI OZENEK • 1964 • Kuzminski Zbigniew • PLN • MY SECOND MARRIAGE
MOJ STARY • 1962 • Nasfeter Janusz • PLN • MY OLD MAN ○ MY DAD
MOJ TATA NA ODREDJENO VREME • 1984 • Jelic Milan • YGS • MY TEMPORARY FATHER
MOJ TEATR • 1960 • Perski Ludwik • DOC • PLN • MY THEATRE
MOJA DRAGA IZA • 1979 • Duletic Vojko • YGS • MY DARLING IZA ○ MY PRECIOUS IZA
MOJA ULICA • 1965 • Halladin Danuta • DOC • PLN • MY STREET
MOJA WOJNA, MOJA MILOSC • 1975 • Nasfeter Janusz • PLN • MY WAR -MY LOVE
MOJADO POWER • 1981 • Arau Alfonso • MXC • WETBACK POWER
MOJAVE FIREBRAND • 1944 • Bennet Spencer Gordon • USA
MOJAVE KID, THE • 1927 • Bradbury Robert North • USA
MOJAZAT • 1974 • Sadeghpoor Iraj • IRN • PUNISHMENT
MOJDODYR • 1939 • Ivanov-Vano Ivan • ANS • USS
MOJE LASKA • 1964 • Hofman Eduard • ANS • PLN
MOJE MIASTO • 1947 • Has Wojciech J. • DCS • PLN • MY TOWN
MOJE, NIE DAM • 1964 • Zukowska Jadwiga • PLN • IT'S MINE
MOJE ZENA PENELOPA • 1955 • Hofman Eduard • ANS • PLN
MOJEZE • 1968 • Mirsamadzadeh • IRN • MIRACLE, THE
MOJU • 1969 • Masumura Yasuzo • JPN • BLIND BEAST, THE (USA)
MOKEY • 1942 • Root Wells • USA • MOKEY DELANO
MOKEY DELANO see **MOKEY** • 1942
MOKHTAR • 1968 • Ben Aicha Sadok • TNS
MOKUSEKI • 1940 • Gosho Heinosuke • JPN • WOODEN HEAD ○ WOOD AND STONE
MOKUZHONGDE HUANXIANG • 1988 • Wang Jixing • CHN • VISIONS FROM A JAIL CELL
MOLANNA Z PIASKOWEGO DOMKU • 1959 • Jaskolska Aleksandra • PLN
MOLAR MIX-UP, A • 1916 • Beaudine William • SHT • USA
MOLBA • 1969 • Abuladze Tengiz • USS • PRAYER, THE ○ ENTREATY, THE ○ SUPPLICATION ○ APPEAL, THE
MOLCHANIYE DOKTORA IVENSA • 1973 • Metalnikov Budimir • USS • SILENCE OF DOCTOR IVENS, THE ○ SILENCE OF DR. EVANS, THE ○ DR. EVANS' SILENCE
MOLDAVIAN FAIRY TALE see **MOLDAVSKAIA SKAZKA** • 1951
MOLDAVSKAIA SKAZKA • 1951 • Paradjanov Sergei • SHT • USS • MOLDAVIAN FAIRY TALE
MOLE, THE • 1955 • Miler Zdenek • ASS • CZC
MOLE, THE see **TOPO, EL** • 1971
MOLE AND MEDICINE see **KRTEK A MEDICINA**
MOLE AND THE GREEN STAR, THE (USA) see **KRTEK A ZELENA HVEZDA** • 1969
MOLE AND THE MOTOR CAR, THE • 1963 • Miler Zdenek • ANS • CZC
MOLE IN DREAMLAND see **KRTEK VE SNU**
MOLE IN THE CITY see **KRTEK VE MESTE**
MOLE MEN VS. THE SON OF HERCULES (USA) see **MACISTE L'UOMO PIU FORTE DEL MONDO** • 1961
MOLE PEOPLE, THE • 1956 • Vogel Virgil W. • USA
MOLECULA • 1965 • Delgado Cruz • SHT • SPN
MOLECULA EN ORBITA • 1970 • Delgado Cruz • ANM • SPN • MOLECULE IN ORBIT
MOLECULAR MIXUP • 1964 • Tendlar Dave • ANS • USA
MOLECULE IN ORBIT see **MOLECULA EN ORBITA** • 1970
MOLECULES • 1966 • Bonniere Rene • DCS • CND • IMPERIAL OIL
MOLECULES AT WORK see **LAWS OF DISORDER: PART 3 - MOLECULES AT WORK, THE** • 1969
MOLEHILL see **LITIL THUFA** • 1979
MOLESTER, THE see **NEVER TAKE SWEETS FROM A STRANGER** • 1960
MOLESTERS, THE (USA) see **SITTLICHKEITSVERBRECHER, DER** • 1963
MOLIERE • 1910 • Perret Leonce • FRN
MOLIERE • 1913 • Perret Leonce • FRN
MOLIERE • 1955 • Tildian, de Chessin • SHT • FRN
MOLIERE • 1975 • Mnouchkine Ariane • FRN, ITL
MOLIERE • 1978 • *Lelouch Claude (P)* • MTV • FRN
MOLINOS DE VIENTO • 1940 • Sanchez Arthur • WINDMILLS
MOLITVA • Gvozdanovic Radivoj • ANS • YGS • PRAYER, THE
MOLLENARD • 1937 • Siodmak Robert • FRN • CAPITAINE CORSAIRE ○ CAPITAINE MOLLENARD ○ HATRED
MOLLIE AND THE OIL KING • 1914 • *Billington Francelia* • USA
MOLLIE'S MILLIONS • 1920 • *Malone Molly* • USA
MOLLIE'S MUMPS • 1920 • *Malone Molly* • USA
MOLLY • 1950 • Hart Walter • USA • GOLDBERGS, THE
MOLLY • 1983 • Lander Ned • ASL
MOLLY see **SEX IN SWEDEN** • 1977
MOLLY O' • 1921 • Jones F. Richard • USA
MOLLY AND I • 1920 • Mitchell Howard M. • USA
MOLLY AND I see **MY UNMARRIED WIFE** • 1918
MOLLY AND LAWLESS JOHN • 1972 • Nelson Gary • USA
MOLLY AND ME • 1929 • Ray Albert • USA
MOLLY AND ME • 1945 • Seiler Lewis • USA • MOLLY, BLESS HER
MOLLY BAWN • 1916 • Hepworth Cecil M. • UKN
MOLLY, BLESS HER see **MOLLY AND ME** • 1945
MOLLY CURES A COWBOY • 1940 • Yarbrough Jean • SHT • USA
MOLLY ENTANGLED • 1917 • Thornby Robert T. • USA
MOLLY, GID AND JOHNNY see **LOVIN' MOLLY** • 1973
MOLLY, GO GET 'EM • 1918 • Ingraham Lloyd • USA
MOLLY LEARNS TO MOTE • 1912 • Stow Percy • UKN
MOLLY MAGUIRES, THE • 1970 • Ritt Martin • USA
MOLLY MAGUIRES, OR LABOR WARS IN THE COAL MINES, THE • 1908 • *Kalem* • USA
MOLLY MAKE-BELIEVE • 1916 • Dawley J. Searle • USA
MOLLY MOO-COW • 1935-36 • Gillett Burt, Palmer Tom • ASS • USA
MOLLY MOO-COW AND RIP VAN WINKLE • 1935 • Gillett Burt, Palmer Tom • ANS • USA
MOLLY MOO-COW AND ROBINSON CRUSOE • 1936 • Gillett Burt, Palmer Tom • ANS • USA
MOLLY MOO-COW AND THE BUTTERFLIES • 1935 • Gillett Burt, Palmer Tom • ANS • USA
MOLLY MOO-COW AND THE INDIANS • 1935 • Gillett Burt, Palmer Tom • ANS • USA
MOLLY OF THE FOLLIES • 1919 • Sloman Edward • USA
MOLLY OF THE MOUNTAINS • 1915 • *Mitchell Rhea* • USA
MOLLY PITCHER • 1911 • Davis Ulysses • *Champion* • USA
MOLLY PITCHER • 1911 • Olcott Sidney • *Kalem* • USA
MOLLY, THE DRUMMER BOY • 1914 • Lessey George A. • USA
MOLLYCODDLE, THE • 1915 • Cooley Frank • USA
MOLLYCODDLE, THE • 1920 • Fleming Victor • USA
MOLLY'S BURGLAR • 1913 • Haldane Bert? • UKN
MOLLY'S MALADY • 1915 • Davey Horace • USA
MOLLY'S MISTAKE • 1913 • *Melies* • USA
MOLN OVER HELLESTA • 1956 • Husberg Rolf • SWD • CLOUDS OVER HELLESTA
MOLNAR A CSERNA REKAN • 1974 • Lakatos Vince, Lakatos Ivan • SHT • HNG • MILLER ON THE BLACK RIVER, THE
MOLO • 1969 • Solarz Wojciech • PLN • PIER, THE
MOLOCH • 1978 • Barberena Eduardo • SHT • VNZ
MOLODAYA GVARDIYA • 1948 • Gerasimov Sergei • USS • YOUNG GUARD, THE
MOLODOST NASHEI STRANY • 1946 • Yutkevich Sergei • DOC • USS • YOUTH OF OUR COUNTRY, THE ○ YOUNG YEARS OF OUR COUNTRY ○ OUR COUNTRY'S YOUTH
MOLODYYE • 1972 • Moskalenko N. • USS • YOUNG PEOPLE
MOLOKAI • 1959 • Lucia Luis • SPN
MOLOYI • 1978 • SAF
MOLOYI • 1983 • SAF
MOLTI SOGNI PER LE STRADE • 1948 • Camerini Mario • ITL • STREET HAS MANY DREAMS, THE (UKN) ○ WOMAN TROUBLE (USA)
MOM AND DAD • 1944 • Beaudine William • USA • FAMILY STORY, A (UKN)
MOM, THE WOLFMAN AND ME • 1980 • Levy Edmond • TVM • USA
MOME, LE • 1986 • Corneau Alain • FRN
MOME AUX BOUTONS, LA • 1958 • Lautner Georges • FRN
MOME PIGALLE, LA • 1955 • Rode Alfred • FRN • MAIDEN, THE (USA) ○ SCANDAL IN MONTMARTRE
MOME VERT-DE-GRIS, LA • 1952 • Borderie Bernard • FRN • POISON IVY (USA) ○ GUN MOLL
MOMENT 403, LE • 1974 • Bokor Pierre • MTV • RMN
MOMENT, A • 1978 • Jankovic Stole • YGS
MOMENT, THE see **OYEBLIKKET** • 1977
MOMENT, THE see **CLIPA** • 1979
MOMENT, THE see **OJEBLIKKET** • 1981
MOMENT BEFORE, THE • 1916 • Vignola Robert G. • USA
MOMENT BEFORE DEATH, THE • 1915 • Melville Wilbert • USA
MOMENT BY MOMENT • 1978 • Wagner Jane • USA
MOMENT D'EGAREMENT, UN • 1978 • Berri Claude • FRN • IN A WILD MOMENT (USA) ○ ONE WILD MOMENT ○ SUMMER AFFAIR, A
MOMENT FOR MUSIC see **SWEET AND LOWDOWN** • 1944
MOMENT IN LOVE, A • 1956 • Clarke Shirley • SHT • USA
MOMENT IN THE STARS, THE • 1975 • Kulidjanov Lev • USS
MOMENT IN TIME, A • 1953 • McNaughton Richard Q. • UKN
MOMENT OF DANGER • 1960 • Benedek Laslo • UKN • MALAGA (USA) ○ TAKERS, THE
MOMENT OF DARKNESS, A • 1915 • Hepworth Cecil M. • UKN
MOMENT OF DECISION • 1962 • Knight John • UKN
MOMENT OF DECISION see **TRENUTKI ODLOCITVE** • 1955
MOMENT OF INDISCRETION • 1958 • Varnel Max • UKN
MOMENT OF KILLING, THE see **MOMENTO DI UCCIDERE, IL** • 1968
MOMENT OF MADNESS, A • 1914 • West Langdon • USA
MOMENT OF PASSION • 1960 • Plyta Mary
MOMENT OF PEACE, A see **CHWILA POKOJU** • 1965
MOMENT OF QUIET, A see **CHWILA CISZY** • 1965
MOMENT OF REMINISCENCE: 1944/45, A see **CHWILA WSPOMNIEN: ROK 1944/45** • 1964
MOMENT OF REMINISCENCE 1947, A see **CHWILA WSPOMNIEN: ROK 1947** • 1964
MOMENT OF REMINISCENCE 1956/57, A see **CHWILA WSPOMNIEN: ROK 1956/57** • 1964
MOMENT OF REMINISCENCE 1958-1964, A see **CHWILA WSPOMNIEN 1958-64** • 1965
MOMENT OF REMINISCENCE: THE YEAR 1945/46 see **CHWILA WSPOMNIEN: ROK 1945/46** • 1964
MOMENT OF SACRIFICE, THE • 1915 • *Thanhouser* • USA
MOMENT OF TERROR see **HIKINIGE** • 1966
MOMENT OF TRUTH see **NEVER LET GO** • 1960
MOMENT OF TRUTH see **3.15** • 1985
MOMENT OF TRUTH, THE • 1985 • SAF
MOMENT OF TRUTH, THE see **MINUTE DE VERITE, LA** • 1952
MOMENT OF TRUTH, THE (USA) see **MOMENTO DELLA VERITA, IL** • 1965
MOMENT OF VICTORY, THE • 1918 • Smith David • SHT • USA
MOMENT TO KILL, THE see **MOMENTO DI UCCIDERE, IL** • 1968
MOMENT TO MOMENT • 1966 • LeRoy Mervyn • USA
MOMENTO DE LA VERDAD, EL see **MOMENTO DELLA VERITA, IL** • 1965
MOMENTO DELLA VERITA, IL • 1965 • Rosi Francesco • ITL, SPN • MOMENT OF TRUTH, THE (USA) ○ MOMENTO DE LA VERDAD, EL ○ VIVIR DESVIVIENDOSE
MOMENTO DI UCCIDERE, IL • 1968 • Carnimeo Giuliano • ITL, FRG • MOMENT OF KILLING, THE ○ MOMENT TO KILL, THE
MOMENTO PIU BELLO, IL • 1957 • Emmer Luciano • ITL • MOST WONDERFUL MOMENT, THE
MOMENTOS • 1981 • Bemberg Maria Luisa • ARG • MOMENTS
MOMENTOS DE LA VIDA DI MARTI see **ROSA BLANCA, LA** • 1953
MOMENTOUS DECISION, A • 1913 • *Lubin* • USA
MOMENTS • 1974 • Crane Peter • UKN
MOMENTS see **MOMENTS DE LA VIE D'UNE FEMME** • 1979
MOMENTS see **MOMENTOS** • 1981
MOMENT'S CARESS, A • 1971 • *Ott Angelika* • FRG
MOMENTS DE LA VIE D'UNE FEMME • 1979 • Bat-Adam Michal • FRN, ISR • EACH OTHER ○ MOMENTS
MOMENTS IN A MATCHBOX see **MIGOVE V KIBRITENA KOUTIYA** • 1979
MOMENTS IN THE FOREST • Homoki-Nagy Istvan • DOC • HNG
MOMENT'S MADNESS, A • 1920 • *Namara Margarite* • USA
MOMENTS OF LOVE • 1975 • Hershey B. • USA
MOMENTS OF PLAY • 1987 • Leth Jorgen • DOC • DNM
MOMENTS THAT MADE HISTORY see **SEESAW AND THE SHOES, THE** • 1945
MOMENTUM • 1969 • Belson Jordan • SHT • USA
MOMIA AZTECA, LA • 1957 • Portillo Rafael • MXC • AZTEC MUMMY, THE (USA)
MOMIA AZTECA CONTRA EL ROBOT HUMANO, LA see **ROBOT HUMANO, EL** • 1959
MOMIE, LA • 1913 • Feuillade Louis • FRN • MUMMY, THE
MOMIE, LA see **MUMIA, AL-** • 1969
MOMIE DU ROI, LA • 1909 • Bourgeois Gerard • FRN • MUMMY OF THE KING RAMESES, THE (USA)
MOMIJIGARI • 1897 • Shibata Tsunekichi • JPN • MAPLE VIEWING
MOMMA DON'T ALLOW • 1955 • Reisz Karel, Richardson Tony • SHT • UKN
MOMMA THE DETECTIVE see **SEE CHINA AND DIE** • 1982
MOMMIE DEAREST • 1981 • Perry Frank • USA
MOMMILA 1917, MURHAT see **MOMMILAN VERITEOT 1917** • 1973
MOMMILA BLOODBATH, THE see **MOMMILAN VERITEOT 1917** • 1973
MOMMILA MURDERS, THE see **MOMMILAN VERITEOT 1917** • 1973
MOMMILAN VERITEOT 1917 • 1973 • Pennanen Jotaarkka • FNL • MOMMILA BLOODBATH, THE ○ MURDERS AT MOMMILA, 1917 ○ MOMMILA 1917, MURHAT ○ MOMMILA MURDERS, THE
MOMMY LOVES PUPPY • 1940 • Fleischer Dave • ANS • USA
MOMOIRO DENWA • 1967 • Nishihara Giichi • JPN • PINK TELEPHONE
MOMOIRO NO MUSUME • 1933 • Yamamoto Kajiro • JPN
MOMOTARO SAMURAI • 1957 • Misumi Kenji • JPN • FREELANCE SAMURAI
MOMTSETO SI OTIVA • 1972 • Staikov Lyudmil • BUL
MON AMANT L'ASSASSIN • 1931 • Bussi Solange • FRN • MY LOVER, THE MURDERER ○ EXCENTRIQUE, L'
MON AME • 1975 • Sobel Mark • MTV • CND
MON AMI see **MIJN VRIEND** • 1980
MON AMI LE CAMBRIOLEUR • 1950 • Lepage Henri • FRN
MON AMI PIERROT • 1960 • Grospierre Louis • SHT • FRN
MON AMI SAINFOIN • 1949 • Sauvajon Marc-Gilbert • FRN
MON AMI SYLVIE • 1972 • Reichenbach Francois • DOC • FRN
MON AMI TIM • 1932 • Forrester Jack • FRN • FORCATS DER LA MER, LES ○ BOURRASQUES ○ RAFALES
MON AMI VICTOR! • 1930 • Berthomieu Andre • FRN
MON AMIE PIERRETTE • 1967 • Lefebvre Jean-Pierre • CND
MON AMOUR see **GOUBBIAH MON AMOUR** • 1956
MON AMOUR EST PRES DE TOI • 1943 • Pottier Richard • FRN
MON AMOUR, MON AMOUR • 1967 • Trintignant Nadine • FRN • MY LOVE, MY LOVE ○ MY LIFE, MY LIFE
MON AND INO see **ANI IMOTO** • 1977
MON BEGUIN • 1929 • Behrendt Hans • FRN • MISS LOHENGRIN
MON CHAPEAU • 1932 • Guissart Rene • FRN
MON CHER SUJET • 1986 • Mieville Anne-Marie • SWT, FRN
MON CHIEN • 1956 • Franju Georges • DCS • FRN
MON COEUR AU RALENTI • 1927 • de Gastyne Marco • FRN
MON COEUR BALANCE • 1932 • Guissart Rene • FRN
MON COEUR EST ROUGE • 1976 • Rosier Michele • FRN
MON COEUR ET SES MILLIONS • 1931 • Berthomieu Andre • FRN • JEUX DE L'HUMOUR ET DU HASARD, LES ○ FRIPOUILLES ET CIE
MON COEUR INCOGNITO • 1930 • Antoine Andre-Paul, Noa Manfred • FRN
MON COEUR T'APPELLE • 1934 • Veber Serge, Gallone Carmine • FRN
MON COQUIN DE PERE • 1958 • Lacombe Georges • FRN, ITL
MON CORPS EST A MOI • 1967 • Varda Agnes • FRN • MY BODY BELONGS TO ME
MON COUSIN ALBERT see **DOUCEUR D'AIMER, LA** • 1930
MON CURE, CHAMPION DU REGIMENT • 1955 • Couzinet Emile • FRN • MON CURE CHEZ LES PARACHUTISTS
MON CURE CHEZ LES NUDISTES • 1983 • Thomas Robert • FRN
MON CURE CHEZ LES PARACHUTISTS see **MON CURE, CHAMPION DU REGIMENT** • 1955
MON CURE CHEZ LES RICHES • 1926 • Donatien E. B. • FRN
MON CURE CHEZ LES RICHES • 1932 • Donatien E. B. • FRN
MON CURE CHEZ LES RICHES • 1938 • Boyer Jean • FRN
MON CURE CHEZ LES RICHES • 1952 • Diamant-Berger Henri • FRN
MON CURE CHEZ LES THAILANDAISES • 1983 • Thomas Robert • FRN
MON DEPUTE see **EUSEBE, DEPUTE** • 1938
MON DEPUTE ET SA FEMME • 1937 • Cammage Maurice • FRN
MON DOMAINE see **FARM HOMES BEAUTIFUL** • 1947
MON ENFANCE A MONTREAL • 1970 • Chabot Jean • CND
MON FRANGIN DU SENEGAL • 1953 • Lacourt Guy • FRN
MON GANT ME FAIT MOURIR • 1976 • Dussault Louis • CND
MON GOSSE DE PERE • 1930 • de Limur Jean • FRN
MON GOSSE DE PERE • 1952 • Mathot Leon • FRN
MON JOURNAL see **JOURNAL ANIME, LE** • 1908
MON MARI EST MERVEILLEUX • 1952 • Hunebelle Andre • FRN
MON OEIL • 1966 • Lefebvre Jean-Pierre • CND • MY EYE
MON ONCLE • 1917 • Feuillade Louis • FRN
MON ONCLE • 1957 • Tati Jacques • FRN • MY UNCLE (USA) ○ MY UNCLE, MR. HULOT
MON ONCLE ANTOINE • 1971 • Jutra Claude • CND • MY UNCLE ANTOINE (USA)
MON ONCLE BENJAMIN • 1924 • Leprince Rene • FRN
MON ONCLE BENJAMIN • 1969 • Molinaro Edouard • FRN, ITL • AMOROUS ADVENTURES OF UNCLE BENJAMIN, THE (UKN) ○ MIO ZIO BENIAMINO (ITL)

MON ONCLE D'AMERIQUE • 1980 • Resnais Alain • FRN • MY AMERICAN UNCLE (UKN)
MON ONCLE D'ARLES see **COUP DE MISTRAL, UN** • 1933
MON ONCLE DU TEXAS • 1962 • Guez Robert • FRN
MON ONCLE ET MON CURE • 1938 • Caron Pierre • FRN
MON PARIS • 1928 • Guyot Albert • FRN • MY PARIS
MON PARRAIN, MON AMOUR • Geral Hubert • FRN
MON PERE AVAIT RAISON • 1936 • Guitry Sacha • FRN
MON PERE LA-HAUT SUR L'ARBRE see **ABI FAWQA ASH-SHAGARA** • 1969
MON PETIT see **MONTPI** • 1957
MON PHOQUE ET ELLES • 1951 • Billon Pierre • FRN, SWD • MIN VAN OSCAR (SWD) ○ AKES LILLA FELSTEG
MON POTE LE GITAN • 1959 • Gir Francois • FRN
MON PREMIER AMOUR • 1978 • Chouraqui Elie • FRN
MON PRISONNIER see **MAUVAIS GARCON, UN** • 1936
MON ROYAUME POUR EN CHEVAL • 1978 • Bourguignon Serge • DOC • FRN
MON SANG, MES LARMES ET MON SOURIRE see **DAMI, WA DUMUI WA-BTISAMATI** • 1973
MON SEUL AMOUR see **HUBBI AL-WAHID** • 1960
MON TRESOR see **KENZI** • 1947
MON VILLAGE see **QARIATY** • 1972
MON VILLAGE, UN VILLAGE PARMI TANT D'AUTRES see **QARIATY** • 1972
MONA • 1909 • *Warwick Trading Co* • UKN
MONA • 1913 • *Nestor* • USA
MONA • 1970 • Osco Bill • USA • MONA THE VIRGIN NYMPH
MONA see **MONA JA PALAVAN RAKKAUDEN AIKA** • 1983
MONA AND THE TIME OF BURNING LOVE see **MONA JA PALAVAN RAKKAUDEN AIKA** • 1983
MONA JA PALAVAN RAKKAUDEN AIKA • 1983 • Niskanen Mikko • FNL • MONA AND THE TIME OF BURNING LOVE ○ MONA
MONA KENT see **SIN OF MONA KENT, THE** • 1961
MONA, L'ETOILE SANS NOM • 1966 • Colpi Henri • FRN, RMN • POUR UNE ETOILE SANS NOM ○ FOR A NAMELESS STAR
MONA LISA • 1986 • Jordan Neil • UKN
MONA LISA, THE • 1926 • Maude Arthur • USA
MONA LISA TAILS • 1969 • USA
MONA OF THE MODOCS • 1913 • *Bison* • USA
MONA THE VIRGIN NYMPH see **MONA** • 1970
MONA Y TEMBA • 1976 • Luna Bigas • SHT • SPN
MONACA, IL (ITL) see **MOINE, LE** • 1972
MONACA DI MONZA, LA • 1947 • Pacini Raffaello • ITL
MONACA DI MONZA, LA • 1962 • Gallone Carmine • ITL, FRN
MONACA DI MONZA, LA • 1969 • Visconti Eriprando • ITL • AWFUL STORY OF THE NUN OF MONZA, THE (UKN) ○ LADY OF MONZA, THE (USA) ○ STORIA LOMBARDA, UNA ○ NUN OF MONZA, THE
MONACA SANTA • 1948 • Brignone Guido • ITL
MONACHE DI SANT'ARCANGELO, LE • 1973 • Paolella Domenico • ITL, FRN • NUN AND THE DEVIL, THE (UKN)
MONACHINE, LE • 1963 • Salce Luciano • ITL • LITTLE NUNS, THE (USA)
MONACO DI MONZA, IL • 1963 • Corbucci Sergio • ITL • MONK OF MONZA, THE
MONANGAMBEEE • 1969 • Maldoror Sarah • SHT • ANG
MONARCH • 1980 • Flutsch Johannes, Stelzer Manfred • FRG
MONARKI OG DEMOKRATI • 1977 • Roos Jorgen • DOC • DNM
MONASTERIO DE LOS BUITRES, EL • 1972 • *Churubusco Azteca* • MXC
MONASTERO DI SANTA CHIARA • 1951 • Sequi Mario • ITL • NAPOLI HA FATTO UN SOGNO
MONASTERY OF SENDOMIR, THE (USA) see **KLOSTRET I SENDOMIR** • 1920
MONASTIRAKI • 1978 • Angheli Gay • DOC • GRC
MONCH CON SANTAREM, DER • 1924 • Mendes Lothar • FRG
MONCH MIT DER PEITSCHE, DER • 1967 • Vohrer Alfred • FRG • MONK WITH THE WHIP, THE
MONCH VON ST. BARTHOLOMA, DER • 1930 • Beck-Gaden Hanns • FRG • GEHEIMNIS VOM KONIGSSEE, DAS
MONCHE, MADCHEN UND PANDUREN • 1952 • Dorfler Ferdinand • FRG
MOND IS NUR A NACKERTE KUGEL, DER • 1980 • Graser Jorg • FRG • MOON IS BUT A NAKED GLOBE, THE
MONDAY 1ST, SUNDAY 7TH see **LUNES PRIMEIRO, DOMINGO SIETE** • 1968
MONDAY HOLIDAY • 1989 • Perez Maria Regina, Escobar Juan • SHT • CLM
MONDAY MORNING • 1965 • Piskov Hristo, Aktasheva Irina • BUL
MONDAY MORNING • 1989 • BUL
MONDAY MORNING IN A CONEY ISLAND POLICE COURT • 1908 • McCutcheon Wallace?, Griffith D. W.? • USA
MONDAY OR TUESDAY see **PONEDELJAK ILI UTORAK** • 1966
MONDAY – SUNDAY see **LUNES PRIMEIRO, DOMINGO SIETE** • 1968
MONDAY, TUESDAY, WEDNESDAY • 1987 • Saperstein David • USA • MY SISTER'S KEEPER
MONDAY'S CHILD (USA) see **CHICA DEL LUNES, LA** • 1967
MONDE A L'ETALAGE, LE see **WORLD ON SHOW, THE** • 1958
MONDE A RAPROCHER, UN • 1977 • Lesaunier Daniel • MTV • CND
MONDE DE L'ENFANCE, LE • 1970 • Lamothe Arthur • DCS • CND
MONDE DE PAUL DELVAUX, LE • 1946 • Storck Henri • DOC • BLG • WORLD OF PAUL DELVAUX, THE
MONDE DES FEMMES, LE • 1956 • Forest Leonard • SHT • CND
MONDE DES MARAIS, LE • 1963 • Dhuit • SHT • FRN
MONDE DU SILENCE, LE • 1956 • Cousteau Jacques, Malle Louis • FRN • SILENT WORLD, THE
MONDE EN ARMES, LE • 1939 • Oser Jean • FRN
MONDE EN FEU, LE • 1958 • Ronzon Alexandre • DOC • FRN
MONDE EN PARADE, LA • 1931 • Deslaw Eugene • FRN
MONDE EN RACCOURCI, LE see **FAIM DU MONDE, LA** • 1958
MONDE EST A NOUS, LE • 1930 • Champreux Maurice • FRN
MONDE EST UNE FETE, LE see **MAWLID YA DUNIA** • 1975
MONDE ETAIT PLEIN DE COULEURS, LE • 1972 • Perisson Alain • FRN
MONDE INSTANTANE, LE • 1960 • Rossif Frederic • SHT • FRN
MONDE OU L'ON S'ENNUIE, LE • 1934 • de Marguenat Jean • FRN
MONDE SANS SOLEIL, LE • 1964 • Cousteau Jacques, Cousteau Simone, Falco Albert • DOC • FRN, ITL • MONDO SENZA SOLEIL,IL (ITL) ○ JACQUES-YVES COUSTEAU'S WORLD WITHOUT SUN ○ WORLD WITHOUT SUN (USA)
MONDE TREMBLERA, LE • 1939 • Pottier Richard • FRN • REVOLTE DES VIVANTS, LES ○ DEATH PREDICTER, THE ○ REVOLT OF THE LIVING, THE ○ WORLD WILL SHAKE, THE
MONDE TROUBLANT, UN • 1953 • de Gastyne Marco • SHT • FRN
MONDE VA NOUS PRENDRE POUR DE SAUVAGES, LE • 1964 • Godbout Jacques, Bujold Francoise • DCS • CND • PEOPLE MIGHT LAUGH AT US
MONDEA ROTA, LA • 1960 • Ortega Juan J. • MXC
MONDENO • 1965 • Briz Jose • SHT • SPN
MONDES EN BOITES, LES • 1934 • Bohdziewicz Antoni • SHT • FRN
MONDO BALORDO • 1964 • Montero Roberto Bianchi • DOC • ITL • FOOLISH WORLD
MONDO BIZARRO • 1966 • Frost R. L. • USA
MONDO CALDO DI NOTTE • 1962 • Russo Renzo • DOC • ITL
MONDO CANDIDA • 1975 • Jacopetti Gualtiero, Prosperi Franco* • ITL
MONDO CANE • 1962 • Jacopetti Gualtiero • DOC • ITL • DOG'S LIFE, A
MONDO CANE N.2 • 1963 • Jacopetti Gualtiero, Prosperi Franco* • ITL • MONDO PAZZO (USA) ○ CRAZY WORLD, INSANE WORLD ○ MONDO INSANITY
MONDO CANNIBALE see **PAESE DEL SESSO SELVAGGIO, IL** • 1972
MONDO DAYTONA • 1968 • Willard Frank • DOC • USA
MONDO DEI MIRACOLI, IL • 1959 • Capuano Luigi • ITL • WORLD OF MIRACLES, THE
MONDO DEI SENSI DI EMY WONG, IL • 1978 • Albertini Bitto • ITL
MONDO DEPRAVADOS see **MUNDO DEPRAVADOS** • 1967
MONDO DI NOTTE, IL • 1960 • Vanzi Luigi • DOC • ITL • WORLD BY NIGHT (USA)
MONDO DI NOTTE N.2, IL see **MONDO DI NOTTE NUMERO DUE, IL** • 1961
MONDO DI NOTTE N.3 • 1963 • Proia Gianni • ITL • ECCO (USA)
MONDO DI NOTTE NUMERO DUE, IL • 1961 • Proia Gianni, Russo Mario L. F. • DOC • ITL • MONDO DI NOTTE N.2, IL ○ WORLD BY NIGHT NO.2
MONDO DI NOTTE OGGI • 1976 • Proia Gianni • ITL
MONDO EROTICO • 1973 • Ratti Filippo M. • ITL
MONDO EXOTICA see **NAUGHTY DALLAS** • 1964
MONDO FREUDO • 1966 • Frost R. L. • DOC • USA • WORLD OF FREUD, THE
MONDO HOLLYWOOD • 1967 • Cohen Robert Carl • USA • HIPPIE HOLLYWOOD: THE ACID-BLASTING FREAKS ○ IMAGE
MONDO HOMO • Terry Norbert • USA
MONDO I • 1979 • Kramreither Anthony • CND
MONDO II • 1979 • Kramreither Anthony • CND
MONDO INFAME • 1963 • Montero Roberto Bianchi • DOC • ITL
MONDO INSANITY see **MONDO CANE N.2** • 1963
MONDO KEY see **WORST CRIME OF ALL!, THE** • 1966
MONDO KEYHOLE see **WORST CRIME OF ALL!, THE** • 1966
MONDO LE CONDANNA, IL • 1953 • Franciolini Gianni • ITL • WORLD CONDEMNS THEM, THE
MONDO MACABRO see **TABU N.2** • 1965
MONDO MATTO AL NEON • 1963 • Veo Carlo • DOC • ITL
MONDO MIOVO, IL • 1982 • Scola Ettore • ITL, FRN • NUIT DE VARENNES, LA (FRN)
MONDO MOD • 1967 • Perry Peter • DOC • USA
MONDO NELLA MIA TASCA, IL (ITL) see **AN EINEM FREITAG UM HALB ZWOLF** • 1961
MONDO NEW YORK • 1988 • Keith Harvey • USA
MONDO NOUVEAU, UN (FRN) see **MONDO NUOVO, UN** • 1965
MONDO NUDE • 1979 • Kay Anthony • DOC • CND
MONDO NUDO • 1963 • De Feo Francesco, Viola Albert T. • DOC • ITL • NAKED WORLD (USA)
MONDO NUOVO, IL • 1982 • Scola Ettore • ITL • NEW WORLD, THE
MONDO NUOVO, UN • 1965 • De Sica Vittorio • ITL, FRN • MONDO NOUVEAU, UN (FRN) ○ YOUNG WORLD, A (USA) ○ NEW WORLD, A
MONDO OSCENITA • 1966 • Mawra Joseph P. • USA • WORLD OF OBSCENITY
MONDO PAZZO GENTE MATTA • 1966 • Polselli Renato • ITL
MONDO PAZZO (USA) see **MONDO CANE N.2** • 1963
MONDO PORNO DI DUE SORELLE, IL • 1979 • Gardner Fred • ITL
MONDO PORNO OGGI • 1976 • Mariuzzo Giorgio • ITL
MONDO ROCCO • 1970 • Rocco Pat • ANT • USA
MONDO SARA NOSTRO, IL • 1957 • Rovira Beleta Francisco • ITL
MONDO SENZA SOLEIL,IL (ITL) see **MONDE SANS SOLEIL, LE** • 1964
MONDO SEX (UKN) see **MILLE PECCATI.. NESSUNA VIRTU** • 1969
MONDO SEXO • 1967 • Berrystein Dale • USA
MONDO SEXY DI NOTTE • 1962 • Loy Mino • DOC • ITL
MONDO SI RIVELA, UN see **CITTA PROIBITE, LE** • 1963
MONDO SI SPOGLIA E SI TRAVESTE, IL • 1970 • Antonelli Lamberto • ITL
MONDO STRIP • 1980 • Kay Anthony, Daux Robert Diez • CND
MONDO SULLE PIAGE, IL • 1962 • Rossellini Renzo Jr. • DOC • ITL
MONDO TEENO • 1967 • Visconti Eriprando, Herman Norman • DOC • USA, ITL, UKN • REVOLTA DEI TEENAGERS, LA (ITL) ○ TEENAGE REBELLION
MONDO TEETH • 1970 • USA
MONDO TOPLESS • 1966 • Meyer Russ • USA
MONDO TRASHO • 1970 • Waters John* • USA
MONDO VUOLE COSI, IL • 1946 • Bianchi Giorgio • ITL
MONDO WEIRDO see **THRILL KILLER, THE** • 1965
MONDRIAAN • 1972 • Crama Nico • NTH
MONE CURE CHEZ LES PAUVRES • 1956 • Diamant-Berger Henri • FRN
MONEDA EN EL AIRE, UNA • 1990 • Zuniga Ariel • MXC • TO SPIN A COIN
MONEGROS • 1969 • Artero Antonio • SHT • SPN
MONELLE (USA) see **AMOUREUX SONT SEULS AU MONDE, LES** • 1947
MONELLO DELLA STRADA, IL • 1951 • Borghesio Carlo • ITL • STREET ARAB
MONEMVASIA • 1964 • Saris George • GRC
MONET • Delouche Dominique • SHT • FRN
MONETA • 1963 • Alov Alexander, Naumov Vladimir • MTV • USS • COIN, THE
MONEY • 1915 • Keane James • *Keanograph* • USA
MONEY • 1915 • Marston A. C.?, Marston Lawrence? • *Ab* • USA
MONEY • 1917 • *Keanograph* • USA
MONEY • 1921 • Macrae Duncan • UKN
MONEY • 1968 • Burckhardt Rudy • USA
MONEY • 1989 • Dorrie Doris • FRG
MONEY see **PENGE** • 1916
MONEY see **ARGENT, L'** • 1928
MONEY see **PENGAR** • 1946
MONEY see **ARGENT, L'** • 1983
MONEY?, A • 1912 • *Steppling John* • USA
MONEY, THE • 1977 • Workman Chuck • USA • DIRTY MONEY
MONEY A PICKLE • 1938 • McLaren Norman • ANS • UKN • MONY A PICKLE
MONEY AND LOVE see **DENARA E D'AMORE** • 1936
MONEY AND MYSTERY • 1917 • McRae Henry • SHT • USA
MONEY AND THE WOMAN • 1940 • Howard William K. • USA
MONEY AND THREE BAD MEN see **GENNAMA TO BIJO TO SAN-AKUNIN** • 1958
MONEY BALL • 1979 • *A-I* • USA
MONEY-BOX PIG, A • 1964 • Milchin L. • ANS • USS
MONEY CHANGERS, THE • 1920 • Conway Jack • USA • WHAT SHALL IT PROFIT A MAN
MONEY CHASERS see **FA CH'IEN HAN** • 1978
MONEY CORPORAL, THE see **MONEY CORRAL, THE** • 1919
MONEY CORRAL, THE • 1919 • Hart William S., Hillyer Lambert • USA • MONEY CORPORAL, THE
MONEY DANCE, THE see **DOKONJO MONOGATARI -ZENI NO ODORI** • 1964
MONEY FOR JAM see **YIA MIA TRIPIA DRAHMI** • 1968
MONEY FOR JAM (UKN) see **IT AIN'T HAY** • 1943
MONEY FOR NOTHING • 1913 • Collins Edwin J. • UKN
MONEY FOR NOTHING • 1914 • *Sphinx Films* • UKN
MONEY FOR NOTHING • 1916 • Elvey Maurice • UKN
MONEY FOR NOTHING • 1926 • Brunel Adrian • SHT • UKN
MONEY FOR NOTHING • 1932 • Banks Monty • UKN
MONEY FOR SPEED • 1933 • Vorhaus Bernard • UKN
MONEY FROM HOME • 1953 • Marshall George • USA
MONEY FROM THE SKY see **PENGAR FRAN SKYN** • 1939
MONEY GAME, THE • 1972 • Petty Bruce • ANS • ASL
MONEY-GO-ROUND • 1966 • Rakoff Alvin • UKN
MONEY GOD, OR DO RICHES BRING HAPPINESS, THE • 1914 • *Metropolitan Film* • USA
MONEY GULF, THE • 1915 • *Millarde Harry* • USA
MONEY HABIT, THE • 1924 • Niebuhr Walter • UKN
MONEY IN MY POCKET • 1962 • Jourdan Erven • USA
MONEY IN THE BANK • 1911 • *Kalem* • USA
MONEY ISN'T EVERYTHING • 1918 • Sloman Edward • USA
MONEY ISN'T EVERYTHING • 1925 • Bentley Thomas • UKN
MONEY ISN'T EVERYTHING (UKN) see **JEEPERS CREEPERS** • 1939
MONEY JUNGLE, THE • 1968 • Lyon Francis D. • USA • BILLION DOLLAR CAPER, THE
MONEY KINGS, THE • 1912 • Brooke Van Dyke • USA
MONEY LEECHES, THE • 1915 • *Sais Marin* • USA
MONEY LENDER, THE • 1914 • *Eclectic* • USA
MONEY LENDERS, THE • 1916 • McRae Henry • SHT • USA
MONEY MAD • 1908 • Griffith D. W. • USA
MONEY MAD • 1918 • Henley Hobart • USA
MONEY MAD • 1934 • Richardson Frank • UKN
MONEY MAD see **PAYING THE PIPER** • 1921
MONEY MADNESS • 1917 • McRae Henry • USA
MONEY MADNESS • 1948 • Newfield Sam • USA
MONEY MADNESS • 1977 • Mason Michael • DOC • USA
MONEY MAGIC • 1917 • Wolbert William • USA
MONEY MAID MEN • 1916 • *Stull Walter* • SHT • USA
MONEY-MAKER • 1970 • *Stacey Dist.* • USA
MONEY-MAKER, THE see **PENZCSINALO** • 1963
MONEY-MAKING COATS • 1913 • Kellino W. P. • UKN
MONEY MANIA see **MILLION DOLLAR MYSTERY** • 1987
MONEY MANIAC, THE • 1921 • Perret Leonce • USA • RACE FOR MILLIONS, A
MONEY, MARBLES AND CHALK • 1973 • Nagy Ivan • USA
MONEY MASTER, THE • 1915 • Fitzmaurice George • USA
MONEY MASTER, THE see **WISE FOOL, A** • 1921
MONEY MEANS NOTHING • 1932 • Templeman Harcourt, Wilcox Herbert • UKN • BUTLER'S MILLIONS, THE
MONEY MEANS NOTHING • 1934 • Cabanne W. Christy • USA
MONEY MILL, THE • 1917 • Robertson John S. • USA
MONEY MIX-UP, A • 1920 • Goldaine Mark • USA
MONEY, MONEY • 1968 • Varela Jose • FRN
MONEY! MONEY! MONEY! • 1915 • Kaufman Joseph • USA
MONEY! MONEY! MONEY! • 1923 • Forman Tom • USA
MONEY, MONEY, MONEY see **CAVE SE REBIFFE, LE** • 1961
MONEY, MONEY, MONEY (USA) see **PRESIDENT, LE** • 1960
MONEY, MONEY, MONEY (USA) see **AVENTURE C'EST L'AVENTURE, L'** • 1972
MONEY MOON, THE • 1920 • Paul Fred • UKN
MONEY MOVERS, THE • 1979 • Beresford Bruce • ASL
MONEY ON THE SIDE • 1982 • Collins Robert • TVM • USA
MONEY OR YOUR LIFE see **PENIZE NEBO ZIVOT** • 1932
MONEY OR YOUR LIFE see **BOURSE ET LA VIE, LA** • 1965
MONEY ORDER, THE (UKN) see **MANDAT, LE** • 1968
MONEY PIT, THE • 1986 • Benjamin Richard • USA
MONEY SQUAWKS • 1940 • White Jules • SHT • USA
MONEY TALKS • 1914 • *Essanay* • USA
MONEY TALKS • 1919 • Fishback Fred C. • SHT • USA

MONEY TALKS • 1926 • Mayo Archie • USA
MONEY TALKS • 1932 • Lee Norman • UKN
MONEY TALKS • 1972 • Funt Allen • DOC • USA
MONEY TALKS see **DOKONJO MONOGATARI –ZENI NO ODORI** • 1964
MONEY TALKS IN DARKTOWN • 1915 • *Historical Feature Film* • USA
MONEY TO BURN • 1911 • Porter Edwin S. • USA
MONEY TO BURN • 1916 • Calvert E. H. • SHT • USA
MONEY TO BURN • 1920 • Newmeyer Fred, Roach Hal • SHT • USA
MONEY TO BURN • 1922 • Lee Rowland V. • USA
MONEY TO BURN • 1926 • Lang Walter • USA
MONEY TO BURN • 1939 • Meins Gus • USA
MONEY TO BURN • 1956 • Uys Jamie • SAF
MONEY TO BURN • 1964 • Potterton Gerald • CND
MONEY TO BURN • 1973 • Lewis Robert Michael • TVM • USA • MINT CONDITION
MONEY TO BURN • 1976 • Stone Virginia Lively • USA
MONEY TO BURN see **THA TA KAPSO TA LEFTA MOU** • 1968
MONEY TO BURN see **MILLION DOLLAR RIP–OFF, THE** • 1976
MONEY TO LOAN • 1939 • Newman Joseph M. • SHT • USA
MONEY TRAP, THE • 1965 • Kennedy Burt • USA
MONEY (USA) see **KANE** • 1926
MONEY WAS DIRTY, THE see **HRIMA ITAN VROMIKO, TO** • 1967
MONEY, WOMEN AND GUNS • 1958 • Bartlett Richard • USA
MONEY WORKS WONDERS • 1914 • Batley Ernest G.? • UKN
MONEYBALL see **HOW TO BEAT THE HIGH COST OF LIVING** • 1980
MONEYCHANGERS, THE • 1976 • Sagal Boris • TVM • USA • ARTHUR HAILEY'S THE MONEYCHANGERS
MONEYLENDER'S MISTAKE, THE • 1910 • Fitzhamon Lewin? • UKN
MONEY'S MOCKERY • 1917 • Gerrard Douglas • SHT • USA
MONEY'S TIGHT • 1988 • Richards Dick • USA • GOIN' TO THE CHAPEL
MONGA see **MANGA** • 1977
MONGANGA • 1957 • Cauvin Andre • BLG
MONGKOK KAMUN • 1988 • Wong Ka-Wai • HKG • AS TEARS GO BY
MONGOLI, I • 1961 • De Toth Andre, Savona Leopoldo, Freda Riccardo • ITL, FRN • MONGOLS, LES (FRN) ○ MONGOLS, THE
MONGOLIAN CONSPIRACY, THE see **COMPLOT MONGOL, EL** • 1976
MONGOLOID • 1978 • Conner Bruce • SHT • USA
MONGOLS, THE see **MONGOLI, I** • 1961
MONGOLS, THE see **MOGHOLHA** • 1974
MONGOLS, LES (FRN) see **MONGOLI, I** • 1961
MONGO'S BACK IN TOWN • 1971 • Chomsky Marvin • TVM • USA • STEEL WREATH
MONGREL • 1983 • Burns Robert • USA
MONGREL AND MASTER • 1914 • *Essanay* • USA
MONGRELS • 1918 • White Jack • SHT • USA
MONGUZOK SZIGETEN, A • 1959 • Kollanyi Agoston, Szigethy Kalman • HNG, YGS • OSTRVO MUNGOSA ○ ISLAND OF THE MONGOOSES, THE ○ ISLAND OF MONGOOSES, THE
MONICA see **MONIKA: DIE SECHZEHNJAEHRIGEN** • 1975
MONICA, CORAZON DORMIDO • 1977 • Nieves Conde Jose Antonio • SPN
MONICA STOP • 1967 • Delgado Luis Maria • SPN
MONICA: THE GIRL WHO LIVED TWICE • 1989 • Villiersvila Francois • FRN
MONICA VOGELSANG • 1919 • Biebrach Rudolf • FRG
MONICA'S THING • 1969 • Brand Rex • USA
MONIHARA • 1968 • SHT • IND
MONIKA • 1937 • Helbig Heinz • FRG • MUTTER KAMPFT UM IHR KIND, EINE
MONIKA: DIE SECHZEHNJAEHRIGEN • 1975 • Steinberger Charles • FRG • SWEET SIXTEEN ○ MONICA
MONIKA (USA) see **SOMMAREN MED MONIKA** • 1953
MONIQUE • 1970 • Bown John • UKN
MONIQUE see **NEW YORK AFTER MIDNIGHT** • 1983
MONIQUE LEYRAC IN CONCERT • 1965 • Owen Don • CND
MONIQUE –MEIN HEISSER SCHOSS • 1978 • Saller Eddy • AUS • MONIQUE –MY HOT LAP
MONIQUE –MY HOT LAP see **MONIQUE –MEIN HEISSER SCHOSS** • 1978
MONIQUE MY LOVE • 1969 • Woodcock Peter • USA • SHE'S MONIQUE MY LOVE
MONISMANIA 1995 see **MONISMANIEN 1995** • 1975
MONISMANIEN 1995 • 1975 • Fant Kenne • SWD • MONISMANIA 1995
MONITORS, THE • 1969 • Shea Jack • USA
MONJA ALFEREZ, LA • 1944 • Gomez Muriel Emilio • MXC • ENSIGN NUN, THE
MONJA, CASADA, VIRGEN Y MARTIR • 1935 • Bustillo Oro Juan • MXC • NUN, MARRIED WOMAN, VIRGIN AND MARTYR
MONJA Y UN DON JUAN, UNA • 1972 • Ozores Mariano • SPN
MONJE, EL • 1984 • Casillas Jaime • MXC
MONJE BLANCO, EL • 1945 • Bracho Julio • MXC
MONJE LOCO, EL • 1940 • Galindo Alejandro • MXC
MONK, THE • 1969 • McCowan George • TVM • USA
MONK, THE • 1990 • Lara Paco • UKN
MONK, THE see **MOINE, LE** • 1972
MONK AND THE WOMAN, THE • 1917 • Barrett Franklyn • ASL
MONK IN THE MONASTERY WINE CELLARS, THE • 1902 • Smith G. A. • UKN
MONK IN THE STUDIO, THE • 1902 • Smith G. A. • UKN
MONK OF MONZA, THE see **MONACO DI MONZA, IL** • 1963
MONK WITH THE WHIP, THE see **MONCH MIT DER PEITSCHE, DER** • 1967
MONKEY see **HSI-YU CHI** • 1960
MONKEY, THE • 1959 • Yang Tei • ANS • CHN • APE, THE
MONKEY, THE • 1961 • Jordan Larry • ANS • USA
MONKEY ACCOMPLICE, THE • 1913 • *Solax* • USA
MONKEY AND THE ICE CREAM, THE • 1904 • Redfern Jasper • UKN
MONKEY BITE, A • 1911 • *Pathe* • USA
MONKEY BUSINESS • 1915 • *Clayton Ethel* • USA
MONKEY BUSINESS • 1920 • *Universal* • SHT • USA
MONKEY BUSINESS • 1920 • Cline Eddie • *Sunshine* • SHT • USA
MONKEY BUSINESS • 1926 • McGowan Robert • SHT • USA
MONKEY BUSINESS • 1931 • McLeod Norman Z. • USA
MONKEY BUSINESS • 1952 • Hawks Howard • USA • BE YOUR AGE
MONKEY BUSINESS see **CIRCUS ROOKIES** • 1928
MONKEY BUSINESS see **TADAIMA ZEROHIKI** • 1957
MONKEY BUSINESS IN AFRICA • 1931 • Sennett Mack • SHT • USA
MONKEY BUSINESSMEN • 1946 • Bernds Edward • SHT • USA
MONKEY COMES AGAIN, THE • 1970 • *Tieng Ching* • HKG
MONKEY DOODLES • 1960 • Kneitel Seymour • ANS • USA
MONKEY FARM, THE • 1923 • Seiler Lewis, Stoloff Ben • SHT • USA
MONKEY GOD, THE • 1960 • *Shaw* • HKG
MONKEY GRIP • 1982 • Cameron Ken • ASL
MONKEY HUSTLE • 1976 • Marks Arthur • USA
MONKEY IN WINTER, A (USA) see **SINGE EN HIVER, UN** • 1962
MONKEY INTO MAN • 1940 • Alexander Donald, Hawes Stanley, Cherry Evelyn Spice • USA
MONKEY LAND, A JUNGLE ROMANCE • 1908 • *Vitagraph* • USA
MONKEY LOVE • 1935 • *Mintz Charles (P)* • ANS • USA
MONKEY, MAID, MAN • 1917 • *Price Kate* • SHT • USA
MONKEY MAN, THE • 1908 • *Pathe* • SHT • FRN
MONKEY MEAT • 1930 • *Terry Paul/ Moser Frank (P)* • ANS • USA
MONKEY MELODIES • 1930 • Gillett Burt • ANS • USA
MONKEY MISSION, THE • 1981 • Brinckerhoff Burt?, Mayberry Russ? • TVM • USA
MONKEY MIX–UP, A • 1923 • Seiler Lewis, Stoloff Ben • SHT • USA
MONKEY MONEY (UKN) see **MONNAIE DE SINGE** • 1965
MONKEY, MONKEY see **MONNAIE DE SINGE** • 1965
MONKEY ON MY BACK • 1957 • De Toth Andre • USA • BARNEY ROSS STORY, THE
MONKEY ON THE BACK • 1956 • Biggs Julian • CND
MONKEY SHINES • 1915 • *Aubrey James* • USA
MONKEY SHINES • 1920 • *Barry Eddie* • USA
MONKEY SHINES • 1932 • Whitman Phil • SHT • USA
MONKEY SHINES see **MONKEY SHINES: AN EXPERIMENT IN FEAR** • 1988
MONKEY SHINES: AN EXPERIMENT IN FEAR • 1988 • Romero George A. • USA • MONKEY SHINES
MONKEY STUFF • 1919 • Campbell William • SHT • USA
MONKEY TALKS, THE • 1927 • Walsh Raoul • USA
MONKEY WOMAN see **DONNA SCIMMIA, LA** • 1964
MONKEY WRETCHES • 1935 • Lantz Walter • ANS • USA
MONKEYKING, THE see **DA NO TIEN GU** • 1961
MONKEYNUTS see **CROQUETTE** • 1927
MONKEY'S CABARET, THE • 1914 • *Joker* • USA
MONKEYS, GO HOME • 1967 • McLaglen Andrew V. • USA
MONKEYS IN THE ATTIC: A FILM OF EXPLODING DREAMS • 1974 • Markson Morley • CND • DES SINGES DANS LE GRENIER
MONKEY'S MOON • Macpherson Kenneth • USA
MONKEY'S PAW, THE • 1915 • Northcote Sidney • UKN
MONKEY'S PAW, THE • 1923 • Haynes Manning • UKN
MONKEY'S PAW, THE • 1933 • Ruggles Wesley • USA
MONKEY'S PAW, THE • 1948 • Lee Norman • UKN
MONKEY'S REVENGE, THE • 1899 • *Warwick Trading Co* • UKN
MONKEY'S TEETH, THE see **DENTS DU SINGE, LES** • 1960
MONKEY'S UNCLE, THE • 1965 • Stevenson Robert • USA
MONKEYSHINES • 1910 • *Atlas* • USA
MONKS, THE • 1898 • *Paul R. W.* • UKN
MONKS A LA MODE • 1923 • Seiler Lewis, Stoloff Ben • SHT • USA
MONK'S MACARONI FEAST, THE • 1902 • Smith G. A. • UKN
MONK'S RUSE FOR LUNCH, THE • 1902 • Smith G. A. • UKN
MONK'S SACRIFICE, A • 1914 • *Melies* • USA
MONMOUTH REBELLION see **ASHRIDGE CASTLE –THE MONMOUTH REBELLION** • 1926
MONNA VANNA • 1917 • Illes Eugen • FRG
MONNA VANNA • 1922 • Eichberg Richard • FRG
MONNAIE DE 1.000F, LA • 1908 • Cohl Emile • ANS • FRN
MONNAIE DE LAPIN, LA • 1899 • Blache Alice • FRN • RABBIT'S MONEY, THE
MONNAIE DE SINGE • 1965 • Robert Yves • FRN, ITL, SPN • SETTE FALSARI, I (ITL) ○ MONKEY MONEY (UKN) ○ MONKEY, MONKEY
MONO LISO? see **PROC SE USMIVAS, MONO LISO?** • 1966
MONO LOCO, EL • 1989 • Trueba Fernando • SPN, USA • MAD MONKEY, THE ○ SUENO DEL MONO LOCO, EL
MONOCHROME PAINTER YVES KLINE see **MONOKUROHMU NO GAKA: YVES KLINE** • 1966
MONOCLE, THE (USA) see **MONOCLE RIT JAUNE, LE** • 1964
MONOCLE GIVES A SICKLY SMILE, THE see **MONOCLE RIT JAUNE, LE** • 1964
MONOCLE –ME AND JOE CHAMBERLAIN, THE • 1901 • Smith G. A. • UKN
MONOCLE NOIR, LE • 1961 • Lautner Georges • FRN • BLACK MONOCLE, THE (USA)
MONOCLE RIT JAUNE, LE • 1964 • Lautner Georges • FRN, ITL • ISPETTORE SPARA A VISITA, L' (ITL) ○ MONOCLE, THE (USA) ○ MONOCLE GIVES A SICKLY SMILE, THE
MONOGRAM J.O., THE • 1911 • Porter Edwin S. • USA
MONOGRAMMED CIGARETTE, THE • 1910 • *Yankee* • USA
MONOGRAMMED CIGARETTE, THE • 1913 • *Williams G. A.* • USA
MONOKUROHMU NO GAKA: YVES KLINE • 1966 • Noda • JPN • MONOCHROME PAINTER YVES KLINE
MONOLITH! see **MONOLITH MONSTERS, THE** • 1957
MONOLITH MONSTERS, THE • 1957 • Sherwood John • USA • MONOLITH!
MONOLOG • 1972 • Averbach Ilya • USS • MONOLOGUE
MONOLOGUE • 1985 • Humaloja Timo • MTV • FNL
MONOLOGUE see **MONOLOG** • 1972
MONOLOGUE see **ANANTARAM** • 1986
MONOLOGUE NORD–SUD, UN • 1982 • Godbout Jacques • CND
MONOLUTTEUR, LE • 1904 • Blache Alice • FRN
MONOMANIA • 1917 • *Rolma* • SHT • USA
MONOPOLIST, THE • 1915 • *Pathe* • USA
MONOPOLIZED, THE • 1915 • *Victory* • USA
MONRO NO YONA ONNA • 1964 • Shibuya Minoru • JPN • MARILYN OF TOKYO, A
MONS • 1926 • Summers Walter • DOC • UKN • BATTLE OF MONS, THE
MONSEIGNEUR • 1949 • Richebe Roger • FRN
MONSIEUR • 1911 • *Edison* • USA
MONSIEUR • 1964 • Le Chanois Jean-Paul • FRN, ITL, FRG • INTRIGO A PARIGI (ITL)
MONSIEUR • 1989 • Toussaint Jean-Philippe • BLG, FRN
MONSIEUR ALBERT • 1932 • Anton Karl • FRN
MONSIEUR ALBERT • 1975 • Renard Jacques • FRN • ENFANTS DE GAYAN, LES
MONSIEUR ALBERT PROPHETE • 1963 • Rouch Jean • DOC • FRN
MONSIEUR ALIBI see **COPIE CONFORME** • 1946
MONSIEUR ARKADIN see **CONFIDENTIAL REPORT** • 1955
MONSIEUR BADIN • 1977 • Ceccaldi Daniel • MTV • FRN
MONSIEUR BALBOSS • 1976 • Marboeuf Jean • FRN
MONSIEUR BEAUCAIRE • 1905 • Blackton J. Stuart • USA
MONSIEUR BEAUCAIRE • 1924 • Olcott Sidney • USA
MONSIEUR BEAUCAIRE • 1946 • Marshall George • USA
MONSIEUR BEGONIA • 1937 • Hugon Andre • FRN
MONSIEUR BENOIT PERD LA TETE see **FLORENCE EST FOLLE** • 1944
MONSIEUR BEULEMANS GARDE CIVIQUE • 1913 • Machin Alfred • NTH
MONSIEUR BIBI see **FAUT CE QU'IL FAUT** • 1940
MONSIEUR BLUEBEARD • 1914 • *Mcquarrie Murdock* • USA
MONSIEUR BRELOQUE A DISPARU • 1937 • Peguy Robert • FRN
MONSIEUR BRETONNEAU • 1939 • Esway Alexander • FRN
MONSIEUR CHARLEMAGNE • 1913 • Poirier Leon • FRN
MONSIEUR CHASSE • 1914 • Pouctal Henri • FRN
MONSIEUR CHASSE • 1946 • Rozier Willy • FRN
MONSIEUR CLOWN CHEZ LES LILLIPUTIENS • 1909 • Cohl Emile • ANS • FRN • MISTER CLOWN AMONG THE LILLIPUTIANS
MONSIEUR COCCINELLE • 1938 • Bernard-Deschamps • FRN • COCCINELLE ALFRED
MONSIEUR COGNAC see **WILD AND WONDERFUL** • 1964
MONSIEUR CORDON • 1933 • Prevert Pierre • SHT • FRN
MONSIEUR DE 5 HEURES, LE • 1938 • Caron Pierre • FRN
MONSIEUR DE COMPAGNIE, UN • 1964 • de Broca Philippe • FRN, ITL • POI TI SPOSERO (ITL) ○ MALE COMPANION (USA) ○ I WAS A MALE SEX BOMB
MONSIEUR DE CRAC see **AVENTURES DE BARON DE CRAC, LES** • 1913
MONSIEUR DE FALINDOR • 1946 • Le Henaff Rene • FRN
MONSIEUR DE MINUIT, LE • 1931 • Lachman Harry • FRN
MONSIEUR DE POUCEAUGNAC • 1932 • Ravel Gaston, Lekain Tony • FRN
MONSIEUR DE VOLTAIRE • 1963 • Leenhardt Roger • DCS • FRN
MONSIEUR DES LOURDINES • 1942 • de Herain Pierre • FRN
MONSIEUR DUPONT HOMME BLANC see **JUNGLE EN FOLIE, LA** • 1952
MONSIEUR DURAND SENATEUR • 1932 • Peguy Robert • FRN
MONSIEUR ERICH ZANN see **M. ERICH ZANN** • 1975
MONSIEUR ET MADAME CURIE • 1953 • Franju Georges • DCS • FRN
MONSIEUR ET MADAME SONT PRESSES • 1901 • Zecca Ferdinand • FRN
MONSIEUR FABRE • 1951 • Diamant-Berger Henri • FRN • AMAZING MONSIEUR FABRE, THE
MONSIEUR FANTOMAS • 1937 • Moerman Ernst • SHT • BLG
MONSIEUR GANGSTER (USA) see **TONTONS FLINGEURS, LES** • 1963
MONSIEUR GAZON • 1929 • Diamant-Berger Henri • FRN
MONSIEUR GREGOIRE S'EVADE • 1945 • Daniel-Norman Jacques • FRN
MONSIEUR GRIERSON see **GRIERSON** • 1973
MONSIEUR GUILLAUME TREMBLAY • 1976-77 • Brault Michel, Gladu Andre • DCS • CND
MONSIEUR HAWARDEN • 1968 • Kumel Harry • NTH, BLG • MISTER HAWARDEN
MONSIEUR HECTOR • 1940 • Cammage Maurice • FRN • NEGRE DU NEGRESCO, LE
MONSIEUR HIRE • 1988 • Leconte Patrice • FRN
MONSIEUR HIRE'S ENGAGEMENT • 1989 • Leconte Patrice • FRN
MONSIEUR HULOT NEL CAOS DEL TRAFFICO (ITL) see **TRAFIC** • 1971
MONSIEUR HULOT'S HOLIDAY see **VACANCES DE M. HULOT** • 1952
MONSIEUR INGRES • 1967 • Leenhardt Roger • DCS • FRN
MONSIEUR JOURNAULT • 1976 • Cote Guy-L. • DOC • CND
MONSIEUR KLEIN • 1976 • Losey Joseph • FRN, ITL • CHI E MR. KLEIN? (ITL) ○ MR. KLEIN
MONSIEUR LA CAILLE see **M'SIEUR LA CAILLE** • 1955
MONSIEUR LA SOURIS • 1942 • Lacombe Georges • FRN • MIDNIGHT IN PARIS (USA) ○ MR. MOUSE
MONSIEUR LE BUREAU • 1920 • Luitz-Morat • FRN
MONSIEUR LE DIRECTEUR • 1924 • Saidreau Robert • FRN
MONSIEUR LE DUC • 1930 • de Limur Jean • FRN
MONSIEUR LE DUC • 1933 • Autant-Lara Claude • FRN
MONSIEUR LE FOX • 1930 • Guzman Roberto • SPN
MONSIEUR LE FOX • 1930 • Roach Hal • FRN
MONSIEUR LE MAIRE • 1939 • Severac Jacques • FRN • D'R HERR MAIRE
MONSIEUR LE MARECHAL • 1931 • Lamac Carl • FRN • FELD MARECHAL
MONSIEUR LE MARQUIS see **TAMBOUR BATTANT** • 1933
MONSIEUR LE PRESIDENT–DIRECTEUR GENERAL • 1966 • Girault Jean • FRN • APPELEZ–MOI MAITRE
MONSIEUR LE PROGRESSISTE see **SAYYID AT–TAQADDUMI, AS–** • 1973
MONSIEUR LE VAGABOND • 1933 • Vandal Marion • FRN
MONSIEUR LECOQ • 1914 • Tourneur Maurice • FRN
MONSIEUR LECOQ • 1968 • Holt Seth

MONSIEUR LEGUIGNON, GUERISSEUR • 1953 • Labro Maurice • FRN • LEGUIGNON, GERISSEUR ○ MR. LEGUIGNON, HEALER

MONSIEUR LEGUIGNON LAMPISTE • 1951 • Labro Maurice • FRN

MONSIEUR, MADAME ET BIBI • 1932 • Boyer Jean, Neufeld Max • FRN

MONSIEUR MURDERER see **IDENTITE JUDICAIRE** • 1950

MONSIEUR NICKOLA DUPREE • 1915 • *Ward Ernest* • USA

MONSIEUR NICOLAS, NOURRICE see **MA TANTE DICTATEUR** • 1939

MONSIEUR PAPA • 1977 • Monnier Philippe • FRN

MONSIEUR PERSONNE • 1936 • Christian-Jaque • FRN • MR. NOBODY

MONSIEUR PIPELET see **IMPOSSIBLE MONSIEUR PIPELET, L'** • 1955

MONSIEUR POINTU • 1975 • Longpre Bernard, Leduc Andre • ANS • CND

MONSIEUR PROSPER • 1936 • Peguy Robert • FRN

MONSIEUR PUC AUX ENFERS see **ARMOIRE VOLANTE, L'** • 1948

MONSIEUR RAMEAU • Guillon Madelaine • FRN

MONSIEUR RIPOIS see **KNAVE OF HEARTS** • 1954

MONSIEUR ROBIDA, PROPHETE ET EXPLORATEUR DU TEMPS • 1963 • Kast Pierre • SHT • FRN • MR. ROBIDA, PROPHET AND EXPLORER OF TIME

MONSIEUR ROBINSON CRUSOE (USA) see **ROBINSON ET LE TRIPORTEUR** • 1959

MONSIEUR SANS-GENE • 1935 • Anton Karl • FRN • SATYRE, LE

MONSIEUR SCRUPULE, GANGSTER • 1953 • Daroy Jacques • FRN

MONSIEUR STOP • 1910 • Cohl Emile • ANS • FRN • MR. STOP

MONSIEUR SUZUKI • 1959 • Vernay Robert • FRN • VERSAILLES AFFAIR, THE

MONSIEUR TAXI • 1952 • Hunebelle Andre • FRN

MONSIEUR TETE • 1959 • Lenica Jan, Gruel Henri • ANS • FRN • MISTER HEAD

MONSIEUR VAUTOUR • 1914 • Desfontaines Henri • FRN

MONSIEUR VERDOUX • 1947 • Chaplin Charles, Florey Robert • USA

MONSIEUR VICTOR see **MONSIEUR VICTOR OU LA MACHINE A RETROUVER LE TEMPS** • 1957

MONSIEUR VICTOR OU LA MACHINE A RETROUVER LE TEMPS • 1957 • Image Jean • ANS • FRN • MONSIEUR VICTOR ○ MR. VICTOR

MONSIEUR VIEUX-BOIS • 1916-24 • Lortac • ANS • FRN

MONSIEUR VINCENT • 1947 • Cloche Maurice • FRN

MONSIEUR ZIVACO see **KAITO ZIVACO** • 1967

MONSIGNOR • 1983 • Perry Frank • USA

MONSOON • 1953 • Amateau Rod • USA

MONSOON see **ISLE OF FORGOTTEN SINS** • 1943

MONSTER • 1979 • Strock Herbert L., Hartford Ken? • USA • IT CAME FROM THE LAKE ○ MONSTROID

MONSTER see **HUMANOIDS FROM THE DEEP** • 1980

MONSTER, THE • 1925 • West Roland • USA

MONSTER, THE • 1927 • Tan To Yu • CHN

MONSTER, THE • 1985 • Ayyari Kianoush • IRN

MONSTER, THE see **LADY AND THE MONSTER, THE** • 1944

MONSTER, THE see **WAHSH, EL** • 1954

MONSTER, THE see **MONSTRUO, EL** • 1971

MONSTER, THE see **I DON'T WANT TO BE BORN** • 1975

MONSTER, THE (USA) see **MONSTRE, LE** • 1903

MONSTER A GO-GO! • 1965 • Lewis Herschell G., Rebane Bill • USA • TERROR AT HALFDAY

MONSTER AND A HALF, A see **MOSTRO E MEZZO, UN** • 1964

MONSTER AND I, THE (USA) see **NEMAN I VI** • 1964

MONSTER AND THE APE, THE • 1945 • Bretherton Howard • SRL • USA

MONSTER AND THE GIRL • 1941 • Heisler Stuart • USA • D.O.A.

MONSTER AND THE GIRL, THE • 1914 • Blache Alice • USA

MONSTER AND THE LADY, THE see **LADY AND THE MONSTER, THE** • 1944

MONSTER AND THE STRIPPER, THE • 1973 • USA

MONSTER AND YOU, THE see **NEMAN I VI** • 1964

MONSTER BARAN, THE see **DAIKAIJU BARAN** • 1958

MONSTER CLUB, THE • 1980 • Baker Roy Ward • UKN

MONSTER DEMOLISHER (USA) see **NOSTRADAMUS Y EL DESTRUCTOR DE MONSTRUOS** • 1960

MONSTER DOG • 1986 • Anderson Clyde • USA

MONSTER DOG, THE see **PET, THE** • 1917

MONSTER FROM A PREHISTORIC PLANET (USA) see **DAIKYAJU GAPPA** • 1967

MONSTER FROM GALAXY 27, THE see **NIGHT OF THE BLOOD BEAST** • 1958

MONSTER FROM GREEN HELL see **MONSTER FROM THE GREEN HELL, THE** • 1958

MONSTER FROM MARS see **ROBOT MONSTER** • 1953

MONSTER FROM THE ARCANUM GALAXY see **MONSTRUM Z GALAXIE ARCANA** • 1981

MONSTER FROM THE GREEN HELL, THE • 1958 • Crane Kenneth L. • USA • MONSTER FROM GREEN HELL

MONSTER FROM THE OCEAN FLOOR • 1954 • Ordung Wyott • USA • IT STALKED THE OCEAN FLOOR ○ MONSTER MAKER

MONSTER FROM THE SURF see **BEACH GIRLS AND THE MONSTER, THE** • 1965

MONSTER FROM THE UNKNOWN WORLD see **MACISTE NELLA TERRA DEI CICLOPI** • 1961

MONSTER GORILLA, THE see **GEKKO KAMEN** • 1959

MONSTER IN THE BASEMENT, THE • 1962 • Kraus Robert • SHT • USA

MONSTER IN THE CLOSET • 1986 • Dahlin Bob • USA • INCREDIBLE CLOSET MONSTER, THE

MONSTER IN THE COAL BIN • 1990 • Schinkel Allen • SHT • CND

MONSTER IN THE NIGHT see **MONSTER ON THE CAMPUS** • 1958

MONSTER ISLAND • 1981 • Simon Piquer • SPN, USA • MYSTERY ON MONSTER ISLAND

MONSTER MAKER see **MONSTER FROM THE OCEAN FLOOR** • 1954

MONSTER MAKER, THE • 1944 • Newfield Sam • USA

MONSTER MAKER, THE • 1966 • Bakshi Ralph • ANS • USA

MONSTER MEETS THE GORILLA, THE (UKN) see **BELA LUGOSI MEETS A BROOKLYN GORILLA** • 1952

MONSTER OF BEYOGLU, THE see **BEYOGLU CANAVARI** • 1968

MONSTER OF CEREMONIES • 1966 • Smith Paul J. • ANS • USA

MONSTER OF FATE, THE see **GOLEM, DER** • 1914

MONSTER OF HIGHGATE PONDS, THE • 1961 • Cavalcanti Alberto • UKN

MONSTER OF LONDON CITY, THE (UKN) see **UNGEHEUER VON LONDON CITY, DAS** • 1964

MONSTER OF MONSTERS GHIDORAH see **SANDAI KAIJU CHIKYU SAIDAI NO KESSEN** • 1965

MONSTER OF PIEDRAS BLANCAS, THE • 1958 • Berwick Irvin • USA

MONSTER OF SANTA TEREZA, THE see **MONSTRO DE SANTA TEREZA, O** • 1980

MONSTER OF TERROR • 1965 • Haller Daniel • UKN • DIE, MONSTER, DIE (USA) ○ HOUSE AT THE END OF THE WORLD

MONSTER OF THE ISLAND, THE see **MOSTRO DELL'ISOLA, IL** • 1954

MONSTER OF THE SHADOW, THE see **MONSTRUO EN LA SOMBRA, EL** • 1954

MONSTER OF THE VOLCANOS, THE see **MONSTRUO DE LOS VOLCANES, EL** • 1962

MONSTER OF THE WAX MUSEUM, THE see **NIGHTMARE IN WAX** • 1969

MONSTER OF VENICE, THE see **MOSTRO DI VENEZIA, IL** • 1965

MONSTER ON PAGE ONE, THE see **SBATTI IL MOSTRO IN PRIMA PAGINA** • 1972

MONSTER ON THE CAMPUS • 1958 • Arnold Jack • USA • MONSTER IN THE NIGHT

MONSTER PRINCE see **KAIJU OJI** • 1968

MONSTER RUMBLE • 1961 • *Glut Don (P)* • SHT • USA

MONSTER SHARK • 1984 • Bava Lamberto • ITL, FRN • DEVOURING WAVES ○ DEVIL FISH

MONSTER SHOW, THE see **FREAKS** • 1932

MONSTER SNOWMAN see **JUJIN YUKI-OTOKO** • 1955

MONSTER SQUAD, THE • 1987 • Dekker Fred • USA

MONSTER STRIKES, THE see **PUSANG ITIM** • 1959

MONSTER THAT CHALLENGED THE WORLD, THE • 1957 • Laven Arnold • USA

MONSTER WALKED, THE (UKN) see **MONSTER WALKS, THE** • 1932

MONSTER WALKS, THE • 1932 • Strayer Frank • USA • MONSTER WALKED, THE (UKN)

MONSTER WANGMAGWI see **WANGMAGWI** • 1967

MONSTER WITH GREEN EYES, THE see **PIANETI CONTRO DI NOI, I** • 1961

MONSTER YONGARY see **DAI KOESU YONGKARI** • 1967

MONSTER ZERO (USA) see **KAIJU DAISENSO** • 1965

MONSTERS, THE see **MOSTRI, I** • 1963

MONSTERS ARE LOOSE, THE see **THRILL KILLERS, THE** • 1965

MONSTERS CRASH THE PAJAMA PARTY • 1965 • Brandon Don • USA

MONSTERS FROM AN UNKNOWN PLANET see **MEKAGOJIRA NO GYAKUSHU** • 1975

MONSTERS FROM THE ARCANE GALAXY see **MONSTRUM Z GALAXIE ARCANA** • 1981

MONSTERS FROM THE MOON see **ROBOT MONSTER** • 1953

MONSTERS INVADE EXPO '70 see **GAMERA TAI DAIMAJU JAIGA** • 1970

MONSTERS OF FRANKENSTEIN see **CASTELLO DELLE DONNE MALEDETTE, IL** • 1973

MONSTERS OF THE DEEP • 1931 • Spitzer Nat

MONSTERS OF THE NIGHT (UKN) see **NAVY VS. THE NIGHT MONSTERS, THE** • 1966

MONSTRE, LE • 1903 • Melies Georges • FRN • MONSTER, THE (USA)

MONSTRE AUX YEUX VERT, LE (FRN) see **PIANETI CONTRO DI NOI, I** • 1961

MONSTRES, LES (FRN) see **MOSTRI, I** • 1963

MONSTRET see **HOPPSAN!** • 1955

MONSTRO DE SANTA TEREZA, O • 1980 • Cobbett William • BRZ • MONSTER OF SANTA TEREZA, THE

MONSTROID see **MONSTER** • 1979

MONSTROSITY • 1964 • Mascelli Joseph • USA • ATOMIC BRAIN, THE

MONSTROUSLY FORBIDDEN DREAMS see **SOGNI MOSTRUOSAMENTE PROIBITI** • 1983

MONSTRUM Z GALAXIE ARCANA • 1981 • Vukotic Dusan • CZC, YGS • MONSTER FROM THE ARCANUM GALAXY ○ MONSTERS FROM THE ARCANE GALAXY

MONSTRUO, EL • 1971 • Carretero Amaro • ANS • SPN • MONSTER, THE

MONSTRUO DE LA MONTANA HUECA, EL (MXC) see **BEAST OF HOLLOW MOUNTAIN, THE** • 1956

MONSTRUO DE LA SOMBRA, EL see **MONSTRUO EN LA SOMBRA, EL** • 1954

MONSTRUO DE LOS VOLCANES, EL • 1962 • Salvador Jaime • MXC • FANTASMA DE LAS NIEVES, EL ○ MONSTER OF THE VOLCANOS, THE ○ PHANTOM OF THE SNOWS, THE

MONSTRUO EN LA SOMBRA, EL • 1954 • Gomez Urquiza Zacarias • MXC, CUB • MONSTRUO DE LA SOMBRA, EL ○ MONSTER OF THE SHADOW, THE

MONSTRUO RESUCITADO, EL • 1953 • Urueta Chano • MXC • DOCTOR CRIMEN ○ RESURRECTED MONSTER, THE

MONSTRUO VERDE, EL see **MARIGUANA** • 1936

MONSTRUOS DEL TERROR, LOS see **HOMBRE QUE VINO DEL UMMO, EL** • 1970

MONT-CARMEL • 1939 • Tessier Albert • DCS • CND

MONT-DRAGON • 1971 • Valere Jean • BLG, FRN

MONT MAUDIT, LE • 1920 • *Cande Adolphe* • FRN • ACCURSED MOUNTAIN, THE

MONT SAINT-MICHEL, MERVEILLE DE L'OCCIDENT, LE • 1934 • Cloche Maurice • FRN

MONTA IN SELLA FIGLIO DI.. • 1972 • Ricci Tonino • ITL

MONTAGNA CHE HA IN VETTA UN LAGO, LA see **KANJUT SAR** • 1961

MONTAGNA DEL DIO CANNIBALE, LA • 1976 • Martino Sergio • ITL • PRISONER OF THE CANNIBAL GOD (UKN) ○ MOUNTAIN IN THE JUNGLE, THE ○ PRIMITIVE DESIRES (USA) ○ SLAVE OF THE CANNIBAL GOD

MONTAGNA DELLA PAURA, LA • 1970 • Ferguson R. • ITL

MONTAGNA DI CRISTALLO, LA (ITL) see **GLASS MOUNTAIN, THE** • 1949

MONTAGNA DI LUCE, LA • 1949 • Risi Dino • SHT • ITL

MONTAGNA DI LUCE, LA • 1965 • Lenzi Umberto • ITL

MONTAGNAIS, LES • 1979 • Labrecque Jean-Claude • CND

MONTAGNE, LA see **GABAL, AL-** • 1965

MONTAGNE D'OR, LA • 1914 • Burguet Charles • FRN

MONTAGNE EST VERTE, LA • 1950 • Leherissey Jean • FRN

MONTAGNE INFIDELE, LA • 1923 • Epstein Jean • FRN

MONTAGNE QUI ACCOUCHE, LA • 1973 • Colombat Jacques • ANM • FRN

MONTAGNE RUSSES NAUTIQUES • 1898 • Melies Georges • FRN • SHOOTING THE CHUTES

MONTAGNE VIVANTE, LA • 1964 • Dhuit • SHT • FRN

MONTAGNES MAGIQUES • 1962 • Enrico Robert • FRN

MONTALVO AND THE CHILD (UKN) see **MONTALVO ET L'ENFANT** • 1989

MONTALVO ET L'ENFANT • 1989 • Mourieras Claude • FRN • MONTALVO AND THE CHILD (UKN)

MONTANA • 1950 • Enright Ray, Walsh Raoul (U/c) • USA

MONTANA see **MONTANA MOON** • 1930

MONTANA ANNA • 1911 • *Selig* • USA

MONTANA BELLE • 1952 • Dwan Allan • USA

MONTANA BILL • 1921 • Goldstone Phil • USA

MONTANA BLOUNT • 1915 • *Ramona* • USA

MONTANA DE ARENA, LA • 1955 • Elorrieta Jose Maria • SPN

MONTANA DESPERADO • 1951 • Fox Wallace • USA

MONTANA INCIDENT • 1952 • Collins Lewis D. • USA

MONTANA JUSTICE (UKN) see **MAN FROM MONTANA, THE** • 1941

MONTANA KID, THE • 1931 • Fraser Harry L. • USA

MONTANA LOVE STORY, A • 1911 • *Powers* • USA

MONTANA MIKE • 1947 • Rogell Albert S. • USA • HEAVEN ONLY KNOWS

MONTANA MIX-UP, A • 1913 • *Mackley Arthur* • USA

MONTANA MOON • 1930 • St. Clair Malcolm • USA • MONTANA

MONTANA REBELDE, LA • 1971 • Torrado Ramon • SPN

MONTANA SAGRADA, LA • 1972 • Jodorowsky Alejandro • MXC, USA • SACRED MOUNTAIN, THE (USA) ○ HOLY MOUNTAIN, THE

MONTANA SCHOOLMARM, THE • 1908 • *Selig* • USA

MONTANA SIN LEY, LA • 1953 • Lluch Miguel • SPN

MONTANA TERRITORY • 1952 • Nazarro Ray • USA

MONTANA TRAP see **POTATO FRITZ** • 1975

MONTANHA DOS SETE ECOS, A • 1953 • Miranda Armando • BRZ

MONTE CARLO • 1920 • Sauer Fred? • FRG

MONTE-CARLO • 1925 • Mercanton Louis • FRN

MONTE CARLO • 1926 • Cabanne W. Christy • USA • DREAMS OF MONTE CARLO

MONTE CARLO • 1930 • Lubitsch Ernst • USA

MONTE-CARLO • 1972 • Reichenbach Francois • DOC • FRN

MONTE CARLO • 1987 • Page Anthony • MTV • USA

MONTE CARLO BABY (USA) see **NOUS IRONS A MONTE CARLO** • 1951

MONTE CARLO, JR. see **MASQUERADER, THE** • 1922

MONTE CARLO MADNESS • 1931 • Schwarz Hanns • UKN

MONTE CARLO NIGHTS • 1934 • Nigh William • USA

MONTE CARLO OR BUST! • 1969 • Annakin Ken • UKN, FRN, ITL • THOSE DARING YOUNG MEN IN THEIR JAUNTY JALOPIES (USA) ○ MONTE CARLO RALLY ○ QUEI TEMERARI SULLE LORO PAZZE, SCATENATE, SCALCINATE CARRIOLE (ITL)

MONTE CARLO RALLY see **MONTE CARLO OR BUST!** • 1969

MONTE CARLO STORY, THE • 1957 • Taylor Sam, Macchi Giulio • USA, ITL • MONTECARLO (ITL)

MONTE-CHARGE, LE • 1962 • Bluwal Marcel • FRN, ITL • MORTE SALE IN ASCENSORE, LA (ITL) ○ PARIS PICK-UP (USA)

MONTE CRIOLLO • 1937 • Mom Arturo S.

MONTE CRISTO • 1911 • *Powers* • USA

MONTE CRISTO • 1912 • Campbell Colin • USA • COUNT OF MONTE CRISTO, THE

MONTE-CRISTO • 1917 • Pouctal Henri • FRN

MONTE CRISTO • 1922 • Flynn Emmett J. • USA

MONTE CRISTO see **COMTE DE MONTE-CRISTO, LE** • 1914

MONTE CRISTO -MASKED AVENGER see **WIFE OF MONTE CRISTO, THE** • 1946

MONTE CRISTO UP-TO-DATE • 1914 • *Melies* • USA

MONTE CRISTO'S REVENGE (UKN) see **RETURN OF MONTE CRISTO, THE** • 1946

MONTE DE LAS BRUJAS, EL • 1970 • Artigot Raul • SPN, MXC • WITCHES' MOUNTAIN

MONTE DE PIEDAD • 1950 • Vejar Carlos Jr. • MXC

MONTE MIRACOLO • 1943 • Trenker Luis • ITL

MONTE WALSH • 1970 • Fraker William A. • USA

MONTECARLO -GRAN CASINO • 1988 • Vanzina Carlo • ITL

MONTECARLO (ITL) see **MONTE CARLO STORY, THE** • 1957

MONTECASSINO • 1947 • Gemmiti Arturo • ITL

MONTECASSINO NEL CERCHIO DI FUOCO • 1961 • Gemmiti Arturo • ITL

MONTECRISTO '70 (ITL) see **SOUS LE SIGNE DE MONTE-CRISTO** • 1968

MONTEE • 1949 • Garceau Raymond • DCS • CND

MONTEE VERS L'ACROPOLE, LA • 1923 • Le Somptier Rene • FRN

MONTENEGRO • 1981 • Makavejev Dusan • SWD, UKN • MONTENEGRO -OR PIGS AND PEARLS

MONTENEGRO -OR PIGS AND PEARLS see **MONTENEGRO** • 1981

MONTEREY JAZZ • 1973 • Abbott Norman • USA

MONTEREY JAZZ FESTIVAL • 1967 • Slate Lane • DOC • USA

MONTEREY POP • 1969 • Leacock Richard, Desmond James, Maysles Albert, Proferes Nick, Feinstein Barry, Murphy Roger, Pennebaker D. A. • USA

MONTEUSES, LES • 1977 • Stephen Richard • FRN

MONTEVERGINE see **GRANDE LUCE, LA** • 1939

MONTEZUMA • 1908 • Gilbert Arthur • UKN
MONTH IN THE COUNTRY, A • 1985 • Lawrence Quentin • UKN
MONTH IN THE COUNTRY, A • 1987 • O'Connor Pat • UKN
MONTHS AND DAYS see **MESES Y LOS DIAS, LOS** • 1971
MONTIEL'S WIDOW see **VIUDA DE MONTIEL, LA** • 1979
MONTMARTRE • 1914 • Leprince Rene • FRN
MONTMARTRE • 1950 • Bernard J.-C. • DCS • FRN
MONTMARTRE see **FLAMME, DIE** • 1922
MONTMARTRE NOCTURNE • 1951 • Bernard J.-C. • DCS • FRN
MONTMARTRE ROSE • 1929 • McEveety Bernard F., Hiatt Frederick • USA
MONTMARTRE-SUR-SEINE • 1941 • Lacombe Georges • FRN
MONTONE INFURIATO, IL (ITL) see **MOUTON ENRAGE, LE** • 1974
MONTOYAS AND TARANTOS see **MONTOYAS Y TARANTOS** • 1988
MONTOYAS Y TARANTOS • 1988 • Escriva Vicente • SPN • LOVE, HATE AND DEATH ○ MONTOYAS AND TARANTOS ○ TARANTOS Y MONTOYAS
MONTPARNASSE • 1929 • Deslaw Eugene • FRN
MONTPARNASSE 19 • 1958 • Becker Jacques • FRN, ITL • MODIGLIANI OF MONTPARNASSE (USA) ○ MONTPARNASSE (ITL) ○ LOVERS OF MONTPARNASSE, THE (UKN)
MONTPARNASSE (ITL) see **MONTPARNASSE 19** • 1958
MONTPI • 1957 • Kautner Helmut • FRG • LOVE FROM PARIS ○ MON PETIT
MONTRA MUGHDO • 1949 • Roy Bimal • IND • MANTRA-MUGHDHA
MONTRE, LA • 1933 • Christian-Jaque • FRN
MONTREAL • 1962 • Kelly Ron • DOC • CND
MONTREAL BLUES • 1972 • Gelinas Pascal • CND
MONTREAL FILM FESTIVAL INTRODUCTORY CLIP • 1980 • Siegel Lois • CND
MONTREAL HISTORIQUE • 1954-55 • Devlin Bernard • DCS • CND
MONTREAL MAIN • 1973 • Vitale Frank, Moyle Allan, McGillivray Maxine • CND • BOULEVARD SAINT-LAURENT MONTREAL
MONTREAL MATIN • 1973 • Shapiro Nesya • DOC • CND
MONTREAL-MODE • 1973 • Cardinal Roger • DCS • CND
MONTREAL, RETOUR AUX QUARTIERS • 1974 • Regnier Michel • DOC • CND
MONTREAL SECOND FRENCH CITY IN THE WORLD • 1965 • Portugais Louis • DCS • CND
MONTREAL UN JOUR D'ETE • 1965 • Arcand Denys • DCS • CND
MONTREALISTES, LES • 1964 • Arcand Denys • SHT • CND
MONTREUR D'OMBRES, LE • 1959 • Bourguignon Serge • FRN
MONTREUR D'OURS, LE • 1984 • Flechet Jean • FRN
MONTREURS DE MARIONNETTE • 1951 • Giraldeau Jacques • DCS • CND
MONTREUX FETE DES NARCISSES • 1901 • Hipleh-Walt Georges • SWT
MONTS EN FLAMMES, LES • 1931 • Hamman Joe, Trenker Luis • FRN • REBELLES, LES
MONTY AND THE MISSIONARY • 1915 • *Lubin* • USA
MONTY BUYS A CAR • 1908 • *Urban Trading Co* • UKN
MONTY LEARNS TO SWIM • 1909 • Booth W. R. • UKN
MONTY OF THE MOUNTIES • 1927 • Lamont Charles • SHT • USA
MONTY PYTHON AND THE HOLY GRAIL • 1974 • Gilliam Terry, Jones Terry • UKN
MONTY PYTHON LIVE AT THE HOLLYWOOD BOWL • 1982 • Hughes Terry, Monty Python • UKN
MONTY PYTHON'S LIFE OF BRIAN see **LIFE OF BRIAN** • 1979
MONTY PYTHON'S THE MEANING OF LIFE • 1983 • Jones Terry • UKN
MONTY WORKS THE WIRES • 1921 • Sanderson Challis, Haynes Manning • UKN
MONTY'S DOUBLE see **I WAS MONTY'S DOUBLE** • 1958
MONTY'S MISTAKE • 1913 • Wilson Frank? • UKN
MONTY'S MONOCLE • 1915 • Birch Cecil • UKN
MONTY'S PROPOSAL • 1913 • Nash Percy • UKN
MONUMENT, THE • 1913 • O'Sullivan Tony • USA
MONUMENT OF MAIDENS LILY see **AH HIMEYURI NO TO** • 1968
MONUMENT OF TOTSUSEKI see **TOTSUSEKI ISEKI** • 1966
MONUMENTO, EL • 1970 • Forque Jose Maria • SPN
MONUMENTOS DE BELEM • 1959 • Ribeiro Antonio Lopes • SHT • PRT
MONY A PICKLE see **MONEY A PICKLE** • 1938
MOOCHER, THE • 1920 • *Franey William* • USA
MOOCHIE OF THE LITTLE LEAGUE • 1959 • Beaudine William • MTV • USA
MOOCHIN' POOCH • 1971 • Smith Paul J. • ANS • USA
MOOCHING THROUGH GEORGIA • 1939 • *Keaton Buster* • SHT • USA
MOOD CONTRAST • 1954 • Bute Mary Ellen, Nemeth Ted J. • ANS • USA
MOOD MAN, THE • 1965 • Gilpin Frank • UKN
MOOD MONDRIAN • 1963 • Menken Marie • SHT • USA
MOODS OF EVIL see **HIDDEN DANGERS** • 1920
MOODS OF LOVE see **FENG HUA HSUEH YUEH** • 1977
MOODS OF LOVE, THE • 1972 • Wickes David • UKN
MOODS OF MEDORA, THE • 1916 • *Balboa* • SHT • USA
MOODS OF THE SEA • 1942 • Vorkapich Slavko (c/d) • SHT • USA
MOOGA JEEVULU • 1968 • Varalakshmi G. • IND • MUTE, THE
MOOIMEISIESFONTEIN • 1978 • De Witt Elmo • SAF • FOUNTAIN OF PRETTY GIRLS
MOOISTE TIJD.., DE • 1963 • Crama Nico • SHT • NTH • HAPPIEST TIME, THE
MOOMBA CONVENTION • 1966 • Murray John B. • SHT • ASL
MOON 44 • 1989 • Emmerich Roland • USA
MOON 69 • 1969 • Bartlett Scott • SHT • USA
MOON AND SIXPENCE, THE • 1942 • Lewin Albert • USA
MOON AND THE SLEDGEHAMMER, THE • 1971 • Trevelyan Philip • DOC • UKN
MOON CHILD see **MOONCHILD** • 1972
MOON CHILD, THE see **NINO DE LA LUNA, EL** • 1988
MOON DIAMOND, THE • 1926 • Coleby A. E. • UKN
MOON-FACED see **OKAME** • 1927
MOON FOR YOUR LOVE see **LUNE DANS SON TABLIER, LA** • 1909
MOON HAS RISEN, THE see **TSUKIWA NOBORINU** • 1955
MOON HUNTING • 1986 • SKR
MOON IN HIS APRON, THE see **LUNE DANS SON TABLIER, LA** • 1909
MOON IN SCORPIO • 1987 • Graver Gary • USA
MOON IN TAURUS • 1980 • Gruber Steff • SWT
MOON IN THE GUTTER (UKN) see **LUNE DANS LE CANIVEAU, LA** • 1983
MOON IS BLUE, THE • 1953 • Preminger Otto • USA
MOON IS BUT A NAKED GLOBE, THE see **MOND IS NUR A NACKERTE KUGEL, DER** • 1980
MOON IS DOWN, THE • 1943 • Pichel Irving • USA
MOON MADNESS • 1920 • Campbell Colin • USA
MOON MADNESS see **SECRET DES SELENITES, LE** • 1981
MOON MAN • 1905 • SHT • UKN
MOON MOUNTAIN • 1984 • SAF
MOON OF ISRAEL see **SKLAVENKONIGIN, DIE** • 1924
MOON OF THE WOLF • 1972 • Petrie Daniel • TVM • USA
MOON OF TOBALITO, THE see **LUNA DE TOBALITO, LA** • 1968
MOON ON THE LEFT • 1929 • Ivanov Alexander (c/d) • USS
MOON OVER BURMA • 1940 • King Louis • USA
MOON OVER HARLEM • 1939 • Ulmer Edgar G. • USA
MOON OVER HER SHOULDER • 1941 • Werker Alfred L. • USA • DANGEROUS BUT PASSABLE
MOON OVER ISRAEL see **SKLAVENKONIGIN, DIE** • 1924
MOON OVER LAS VEGAS • 1944 • Yarbrough Jean • USA
MOON OVER MIAMI • 1941 • Lang Walter • USA • MIAMI
MOON OVER MIAMI • 1990 • Bianchi Edward • USA
MOON OVER MONTANA • 1946 • Drake Oliver • USA
MOON OVER PARADOR • 1988 • Mazursky Paul • USA
MOON OVER SHANGHAI, THE see **SHANGHAI NO TSUKI** • 1941
MOON OVER THE ALLEY • 1975 • Despins Joseph • UKN
MOON OVER THE RIVER see **MESIC NAD REKOU** • 1953
MOON PILOT • 1962 • Neilson James • USA
MOON RIDERS, THE • 1920 • Eason B. Reeves, Russell Albert • SRL • USA
MOON RISES, THE see **TSUKIWA NOBORINU** • 1955
MOON-ROBBERS, THE see **O DWOCH TAKICH CO UKRADLI KSIEZYC** • 1962
MOON ROCK 10 • 1970 • Dunning George • ANS • UKN
MOON STALLION, THE • 1978 • Brooking Dorothea • UKN, FRG
MOON, STARS, SUN see **YITLEUNG, SINGSING, TAIYEUNG** • 1988
MOON-STRUCK MATADOR, THE see **CLAIRE DE LUNE ESPAGNOL** • 1909
MOON THIEVES see **O DWOCH TAKICH CO UKRADLI KSIEZYC** • 1962
MOON VIRILITY • 1976 • Thoms Albie • DOC • ASL
MOON WALK see **TICKLISH AFFAIR, A** • 1963
MOON WITH HIS TEETH, THE see **LUNE AVEC LES DENTS, LA** • 1967
MOON WOLF • 1959 • Nosseck Martin, Freedland Georg • FNL, FRG
MOON ZERO TWO • 1969 • Baker Roy Ward • UKN
MOONAMATHORAL • 1990 • Ramachandran Kallikadu • IND • THIRD ONE, THE
MOONBEAM • 1984 • Downey Robert • USA
MOONBEAM MAGIC • 1924 • Orman Felix • UKN
MOONBEAM MAN, THE see **GEKKO KAMEN** • 1958
MOONBIRD • 1959 • Hubley John • ANS • USA
MOONBIRD • 1960 • Cannon Robert • ANS • USA
MOONCALF, THE • 1986 • Weir Keiran • SHT • ASL
MOONCHILD • 1972 • Gadney Alan • USA • MOON CHILD
MOONCHILD see **NINO DE LA LUNA, EL** • 1988
MOONCUSSERS • 1962 • Neilson James • USA
MOONDYNE • 1913 • Lincoln W. J. • ASL
MOONEY VS. FOWLE see **FOOTBALL** • 1961
MOONFLEET • 1955 • Lang Fritz • USA
MOONFLOWER OF HEAVEN see **TEN NO YUGAO** • 1948
MOONGLOW • 1920 • Bradley William • USA
MOONGLOW • 1955 • Toonder Marten • ANS • NTH
MOONLESS SUNLESS NIGHTS see **NOCHES SIN LUNAS NI SOLES** • 1984
MOONLIGHT • 1914 • *Eclair* • USA
MOONLIGHT • 1982 • Holcomb Rod (Smithee Alan), Cooper Jackie (Smithee Alan) • TVM • USA • MOONLIGHT: MURDER TO GO
MOONLIGHT see **TA-TS'O CHE** • 1983
MOONLIGHT AND CACTUS • 1932 • Arbuckle Roscoe • USA
MOONLIGHT AND CACTUS • 1944 • Cline Eddie • USA
MOONLIGHT AND HONEYSUCKLE • 1921 • Henabery Joseph • USA
MOONLIGHT AND MELODY (UKN) see **MOONLIGHT AND PRETZELS** • 1933
MOONLIGHT AND MONKEY BUSINESS • 1930 • Sandrich Mark • SHT • USA
MOONLIGHT AND NOSES • 1925 • Roach Hal • SHT • USA
MOONLIGHT AND PRETZELS • 1933 • Freund Karl • USA • MOONLIGHT AND MELODY (UKN)
MOONLIGHT FANTASY • 1967 • Shimamura Tatsuo • ANS • JPN
MOONLIGHT FOLLIES • 1921 • Baggot King • USA • BUTTERFLY, THE
MOONLIGHT FOR TWO • 1931-32 • Ising Rudolf • ANS • USA
MOONLIGHT IN HAVANA • 1942 • Mann Anthony • USA
MOONLIGHT IN HAWAII • 1941 • Lamont Charles • USA
MOONLIGHT IN THE RAIN (USA) see **ONNA KAZOKU** • 1961
MOONLIGHT IN THE TROPICS see **ONE NIGHT IN THE TROPICS** • 1940
MOONLIGHT IN VERMONT • 1943 • Lilley Edward • USA
MOONLIGHT MADNESS see **GEKKA NO KYOJIN** • 1927
MOONLIGHT MANIAC • Moberly Luke • USA
MOONLIGHT MASQUERADE • 1942 • Auer John H. • USA
MOONLIGHT MELODIES • 1946 • Cowan Will • SHT • USA
MOONLIGHT MELODIES • 1949 • *Universal* • SHT • USA
MOONLIGHT MELODY see **DALBICH MERRODI** • 1985
MOONLIGHT MURDER • 1936 • Marin Edwin L. • USA
MOONLIGHT: MURDER TO GO see **MOONLIGHT** • 1982
MOONLIGHT ON THE NILE • 1906 • Hepworth Cecil M. • UKN
MOONLIGHT ON THE PRAIRIE • 1936 • Lederman D. Ross • USA
MOONLIGHT ON THE RANGE • 1937 • Newfield Sam • USA
MOONLIGHT RAID (UKN) see **CHALLENGE OF THE RANGE** • 1949
MOONLIGHT SERENADE • Meyer Donald, Collins Frank • ANS • USA
MOONLIGHT SERENADE OR THE MISER PUNISHED, A see **AU CLAIR DE LA LUNE OU PIERROT MALHEUREUX** • 1904
MOONLIGHT SONATA • 1937 • Mendes Lothar • UKN • CHARMER, THE
MOONLIGHT SONATA see **KUUTAMOSONAATTI** • 1987
MOONLIGHT SONATA, THE • 1932 • Newman Widgey R. • UKN
MOONLIGHTER, THE • 1953 • Rowland Roy • USA
MOONLIGHTING • 1982 • Skolimowski Jerzy • UKN
MOONLIGHTING • 1985 • Butler Robert • TVM • USA • MOONLIGHTING: THE ORIGINAL TV MOVIE
MOONLIGHTING MISTRESS • 1971 • *Vendell Veronique* • FRG
MOONLIGHTING SECRETARIES • 1969 • Glick Wizard • USA
MOONLIGHTING: THE ORIGINAL TV MOVIE see **MOONLIGHTING** • 1985
MOONLIGHTING WIVES • 1966 • Sarno Joe • USA
MOONLIT SWORDS see **DAIBOSATSU TOGE** • 1957
MOONLITE -KING OF THE ROAD • 1910 • *Moulton A. J. (Ph)* • ASL • MOONLITE, THE AUSTRALIAN BUSHRANGER ○ CAPTAIN MOONLITE
MOONLITE, THE AUSTRALIAN BUSHRANGER see **MOONLITE -KING OF THE ROAD** • 1910
MOONPLAY • 1962 • Menken Marie • ANS • USA
MOONRAKER • 1979 • Gilbert Lewis* • UKN
MOONRAKER, THE • 1958 • MacDonald David • UKN
MOONREZHUTHU • 1968 • Ramanna T. R. • IND • THREE LETTERS
MOONRISE • 1948 • Borzage Frank • USA
MOONRISE see **TSUKIWA NOBORINU** • 1955
MOONRUNNERS • 1974 • Waldron Cy • USA
MOON'S OUR HOME, THE • 1936 • Seiter William A. • USA
MOON'S STORY, THE see **NIEZWYKLA PODROZ** • 1955
MOON'S TALE, A see **NIEZWYKLA PODROZ** • 1955
MOONSHINE • 1918 • Arbuckle Roscoe • SHT • USA
MOONSHINE see **AU CLAIR DE LA LUNE** • 1982
MOONSHINE BLOOD • 1916 • Dwan Allan • SHT • USA
MOONSHINE COUNTY EXPRESS • 1977 • Trikonis Gus • USA
MOONSHINE MAID AND THE MAN, THE • 1914 • Gaskill Charles L. • USA
MOONSHINE MENACE, THE • 1921 • McGowan J. P. • USA
MOONSHINE MOLLY • 1914 • Cabanne W. Christy • USA
MOONSHINE MOUNTAIN • 1964 • Lewis Herschell G. • USA • WHITE TRASH ON MOONSHINE MOUNTAIN
MOONSHINE TRAIL, THE • 1919 • Blackton J. Stuart • USA
MOONSHINE VALLEY • 1922 • Brenon Herbert • USA • MIRACLE CHILD (HE GIVETH AND TAKETH), THE
MOONSHINE WAR, THE • 1970 • Quine Richard • USA
MOONSHINER • 1920 • Joos Therdo? • SHT • USA
MOONSHINER, THE • 1913 • *Frontier* • USA
MOONSHINERS • 1904 • *Bitzer Billy (Ph)* • USA
MOONSHINERS see **SAMOGONSHCHIKI** • 1961
MOONSHINERS, THE • 1911 • *Walthall William* • USA
MOONSHINERS, THE • 1914 • *Darkfeather Mona* • USA
MOONSHINERS, THE • 1916 • Arbuckle Roscoe • SHT • USA
MOONSHINERS, THE see **SALAVIINANPOLTTAJAT** • 1907
MOONSHINERS, THE see **GONKA ZA SAMOGONKOJ** • 1924
MOONSHINER'S DAUGHTER, THE • 1910 • *Nestor* • USA
MOONSHINER'S DAUGHTER, THE • 1912 • *Payne Edna* • USA
MOONSHINER'S DAUGHTER, THE • 1914 • *Majestic* • USA
MOONSHINER'S DAUGHTER: OR, ABROAD IN OLD KENTUCKY, THE • 1933 • *Rko* • SHT • USA
MOONSHINER'S HEART, A • 1912 • *Anderson Broncho Billy* • USA
MOONSHINER'S LAST STAND, THE • 1913 • *Wilbur Crane* • USA
MOONSHINER'S MISTAKE, THE • 1913 • *Kalem* • USA
MOONSHINER'S TASK, THE • 1912 • *Comet* • USA
MOONSHINER'S TRAIL, THE • 1911 • *Champion* • USA
MOONSHINER'S WIFE, A • 1913 • *Hawley Ormi* • USA
MOONSHINER'S WOMAN • 1968 • Davison D. E. • USA
MOONSHINES • 1915 • *La Pearl Harry* • USA
MOONSHINES AND JAILBIRDS • 1920 • Howe J. A. • SHT • USA
MOONSHOT see **COUNTDOWN** • 1968
MOONSKIN see **RAGAZZA DALLA PELLE DI LUNA, LA** • 1972
MOONSPINNERS, THE • 1964 • Neilson James • UKN
MOONSTONE see **PIERRE DE LUNE**
MOONSTONE, THE • 1909 • *Selig* • USA
MOONSTONE, THE • 1911 • *Urbanora* • UKN
MOONSTONE, THE • 1915 • Crane Frank H. • USA
MOONSTONE, THE • 1934 • Barker Reginald • UKN
MOONSTONE OF FEZ, THE • 1914 • Costello Maurice, Gaillord Robert • USA
MOONSTRUCK • 1909 • *Pathe* • USA
MOONSTRUCK • 1915 • Birch Cecil • UKN
MOONSTRUCK • 1960 • Halas John • ANS • UKN
MOONSTRUCK • 1987 • Jewison Norman • USA
MOONTIDE • 1942 • Mayo Archie, Lang Fritz (U/c) • USA
MOONTRAP • 1988 • Dyke Robert • USA
MOONTRAP, THE (USA) see **POUR LA SUITE DU MONDE** • 1963
MOONTREK see **SECRET DES SELENITES, LE** • 1981
MOONWALK NO.1 see **MOONWALK ONE** • 1972
MOONWALK ONE • 1972 • Kamecke Theo • DOC • USA • MOONWALK NO.1
MOONWALKER • 1988 • Kramer Jerry, Chilvers Colin • USA
MOONWOLF (USA) see **...UND IMMER RUFT DAS HERZ** • 1958
MOORA NEYA • 1911 • Rolfe Alfred • ASL • MESSAGE OF THE SPEAR ○ MOOYA NEEYA
MOORD IN KOMPARTEMENT 1001e • 1961 • SAF
MOORHUND, DER • 1960 • Petzold Konrad • GDR
MOORLAND TRAGEDY, A • 1933 • Wetherell M. A. • UKN
MOORS AND CHRISTIANS see **MOROS Y CRISTIANOS** • 1988
MOORS AND MINARETS • 1923 • Brunel Adrian • SHT • UKN
MOOS AUF DEN STEINEN • 1968 • Lhotzky Georg • AUS • MOSS ON THE STONES

MOOSE HUNT, THE • 1931 • Gillett Burt • ANS • USA

MOOSE HUNT IN CANADA • 1905 • *Bitzer Billy (Ph)* • USA

MOOSE HUNTERS • 1937 • Sharpsteen Ben • ANS • USA

MOOSE ON THE LOOSE • 1952 • Davis Mannie • ANS • USA

MOOYA NEYA see **MOORA NEYA** • 1911

MOP • 1946 • Crouch William Forest • SHT • USA

MOPEY DOPE • 1944 • Lord Del • SHT • USA

MOPPING UP • 1943 • Donnelly Eddie • ANS • USA

MOPS AND HOPS • 1920 • *Universal* • SHT • USA

MOR DEFTER • 1964 • Ergun Nuri • TRK

MOR, JEG HAR PATIENTER • 1972 • Winding Thomas • DNM

MOR OCH DOTTER • 1912 • Stiller Mauritz • SWD • MOTHER AND DAUGHTER

MOR' VRAN • 1930 • Epstein Jean • FRN • MER DES CORBEAUX, LA ○ SEA OF RAVENS, THE

MORA • 1982 • Desclozeaux Leon • FRN

MORAL • 1920 • Illes Eugen • FRG

MORAL • 1928 • Wolff Willi • FRG

MORAL • 1936 • Zerlett Hans H. • FRG

MORAL 63 • 1963 • Thiele Rolf • FRG

MORAL CODE, THE • 1917 • Miller Ashley • USA

MORAL COURAGE • 1917 • Fielding Romaine • USA

MORAL COWARD, A • 1911 • *Powers* • USA

MORAL DEADLINE, THE • 1919 • Vale Travers • USA

MORAL DER GASSE, DIE • 1925 • Speyer Jaap • FRG

MORAL, DER MEISTER DES VERBRECHENS see **GLANZ UND ELEND DER KURTISANEN** • 1920

MORAL DER RUTH HALBFASS, DIE • 1971 • Schlondorff Volker • FRG • MORAL OF RUTH HALBFASS, THE ○ RUTH HALBFASS

MORAL EM CONCORDATA • 1959 • de Barros Fernando • BRZ

MORAL FABRIC, THE • 1916 • West Raymond B.? • USA

MORAL FIBRE • 1921 • Campbell Webster • USA

MORAL LAW, THE • 1918 • Bracken Bertram • USA

MORAL LOVE (UKN) see **SOLO** • 1970

MORAL OF MODERN HOOLIGANS, THE see **GENDAI AKUTO JINGI** • 1965

MORAL OF RUTH HALBFASS, THE see **MORAL DER RUTH HALBFASS, DIE** • 1971

MORAL RIGHT, THE • 1917 • Gerrard Douglas • SHT • USA

MORAL SINNER, THE • 1924 • Ince Ralph • USA

MORAL STORIES ABOUT SEX see **TANMESEK A SZEXROL** • 1988

MORAL SUICIDE • 1918 • Abramson Ivan • USA

MORAL UM MITTERNACHT • 1930 • Sorkin Marc • FRG

MORAL UND LIEBE • 1933 • Jacoby Georg • FRG

MORAL UND SINNLICHKEIT • 1919 • Jacoby Georg • FRG • KEIMENDES LEBEN 3

MORALIST, THE see **MORALISTA, IL** • 1959

MORALISTA, IL • 1959 • Bianchi Giorgio • ITL • MORALIST, THE

MORALITY ABOVE ALL see **MRAVNOST NADRE VSE** • 1937

MORALS • 1921 • Taylor William D. • USA • MORALS OF MARCUS, THE

MORALS FOR MEN • 1925 • Hyman Bernard • USA

MORALS FOR WOMEN • 1931 • Blumenstock Mort • USA • FAREWELL PARTY (UKN)

MORALS OF HILDA, THE • 1916 • Carleton Lloyd B. • USA

MORALS OF MADAME DULSKA, THE • 1930 • Newolyn Boris • PLN

MORALS OF MARCUS, THE • 1915 • Irving Henry George • USA

MORALS OF MARCUS, THE • 1935 • Mander Miles • UKN

MORALS OF MARCUS, THE see **MORALS** • 1921

MORALS OF MEN, THE • 1917 • SER • USA

MORALS OF WEYBURY, THE see **HYPOCRITES, THE** • 1916

MORALSKA PANI DULSKE • 1958 • Krejcik Jiri • CZC • MRS. DULSKA'S MORALS

MORAMBONG • 1958 • Bonnardot Jean-Claude • FRN

MORAN OF THE LADY LETTY • 1922 • Melford George • USA

MORAN OF THE MARINES • 1928 • Strayer Frank • USA

MORAN OF THE MOUNTED • 1926 • Brown Harry J. • USA

MORAST • 1921 • Neff Wolfgang • FRG

MORAVIA • 1955-59 • Taviani Paolo, Taviani Vittorio • DCS • ITL

MORBECTWO see **MORDERSTWO** • 1957

MORBIDONE, IL • 1965 • Franciosa Massimo • ITL, FRN • DREAMER, THE (USA)

MORBO • 1971 • Suarez Gonzalo • SPN

MORBOSITA • 1974 • Russo Luigi • ITL

MORCHID CLOCH IS GANNCHUID CRE • 1988 • MacConghail Muiris • DOC • IRL • ARAN, GREAT ROCK, LITTLE CLAY

MORD AM CANALE GRANDE (FRG) see **VOIR VENISE ET CREVER** • 1966

MORD AM MONTAG • 1968 • Kratzert Hans • GDR • MURDER ON MONDAY

MORD AN DER NEWA ODER UNTER FALSCHEM PASS see **WEIB GEGEN WEIB** • 1918

MORD AUS ERSCHMAHTER LIEBE, DER see **GESCHICHTE DES GRAUEN HAUSES 1, DIE** • 1921

MORD AUS HABSUCHT, DER see **GESCHICHTE DES GRAUEN HAUSES 4, DIE** • 1921

MORD AUS VERWORFENHEIT, DER see **GESCHICHTE DES GRAUEN HAUSES 2, DIE** • 1921

MORD AUS VERZWIEFLUNG, DER see **GESCHICHTE DES GRAUEN HAUSES 3, DIE** • 1921

MORD, DER NIE VERJAHRT, DER • 1968 • Luderer Wolfgang • GDR • MURDER THAT WAS NEVER RECOGNISED, THE

MORD.. DIE TRAGODIE DES HAUSES GARRICK • 1920 • Philippi Siegfried • FRG • ANGST.. DIE TRAGODIE DES HAUSES GARRICK

MORD EM'LY • 1922 • Pearson George • UKN • ME AND MY GIRL (USA)

MORD I MARSTRAND see **SISTA NATTEN** • 1957

MORD I MORKET • 1986 • Lund-Sorensen Sune • DNM • MURDER IN THE DARK

MORD I PARADIS • 1988 • Lund-Sorensen Sune • DNM • MURDER IN PARADISE

MORD IM CAFE CENTRAL see **MORGEN BEGINNT DAS LEBEN** • 1961

MORD IM SAVOY see **SAVOY-HOTEL 217** • 1936

MORD IM BELGESUND see **FUNF UNTER VERDACHT** • 1950

MORD IN DER GREENSTREET, DER • 1921 • Guter Johannes • FRG

MORD LILLA VAN • 1955 • Olin Stig • SWD • MURDER MY LITTLE FRIEND

MORD OHNE SUHNE • 1962 • Balhaus Carl • GDR

MORD OHNE TATER, DER • 1920 • Dupont E. A. • FRG • MURDER WITHOUT CAUSE

MORD UND TOTSCHLAG • 1967 • Schlondorff Volker • FRG • MURDER AND MANSLAUGHTER ○ DEGREE OF MURDER, A

MORDAREN -EN HELT VANLIG PERSON • 1967 • Mattsson Arne • SWD • MURDERER -AN ORDINARY PERSON, THE

MORDAREN UTAN ANSIKTE • 1936 • Sinding Leif • NRW

MORDAZA DEL CANTARO, LA • 1953 • Rey Florian • SPN

MORDBRANNERSKAN • 1926 • Lindlof John • SWD • INCENDIARY

MORDEI HA'OR (ISR) see **SANDS OF BEERSHEBA** • 1965

MORDENDES GELD • 1927 • Greiner Fritz • FRG

MORDER AUF URLAUB • 1965 • Boskovic Bosko • GDR, YGS

MORDER, DER (FRG) see **MEURTRIER, LE** • 1962

MORDER DIMITRI KARAMASOFF, DER • 1931 • Ozep Fedor • FRG • MURDERER DIMITRI KARAMASOFF, THE (USA) ○ KARAMAZOF ○ CRIME OF DIMITRI KARAMAZOV, THE ○ BROTHERS KARAMAZOV, THE

MORDER SIND UNTER UNS, DIE • 1946 • Staudte Wolfgang • FRG • MURDERERS ARE AMONG US, THE (UKN) ○ MURDERERS AMONG US (USA) ○ MURDERERS ARE AMONGST US, THE

MORDER UNTER UNS see **M** • 1931

MORDERCA ZOSTAWIA SLAD • 1967 • Scibor-Rylski Aleksander • PLN • MURDERER LEAVES A CLUE, THE ○ MURDERER LEAVES CLUES, THE ○ MURDERER LEAVES TRACES, THE

MORDERCLUB VON BROOKLYN, DER • 1967 • Jacobs Werner • FRG • MURDER CLUB OF BROOKLYN, THE

MORDERSPIEL • 1961 • Ashley Helmut • FRG, FRN • MURDER PARTY (USA)

MORDERSTWO • 1957 • Polanski Roman • SHT • PLN • MORBECTWO ○ CRIME, THE

MORDI E FUGGI • 1973 • Risi Dino • ITL • BITE AND RUN (USA) ○ DIRTY WEEKEND

MORDNACHT IN MANHATTAN • 1965 • Philipp Harald • FRG

MORDPROZESS DR. JORDAN • 1949 • Engels Erich • FRG

MORDPROZESS MARY DUGAN • 1930 • Robison Arthur • FRG

MORDPROZESS STANLEY, DER see **ABENTEUERIN VON MONTE CARLO 3, DIE** • 1921

MORDS PAS -ON T'AIME • 1976 • Allegret Yves • FRN • FETE DES PERES, LA

MORDSACHE HOLM • 1938 • Engels Erich • FRG

MORDSKAB • 1969 • Christensen Bent • DNM • BUSYBODY

MORDSMADEL, EIN • 1927 • Morgan Sidney • FRG

MORDUS, LES • 1960 • Jolivet Rene • FRN • ONCE BITTEN (USA)

MORDUS DE PARIS, LES • 1964 • Armand Pierre • FRN

MORDVAPEN TILL SALU • 1963 • Holmgren Per Gosta • SWD • MURDER WEAPONS FOR SALE ○ HOKEN

MORDWEIHNACHT 1705 see **TRAGODIE EINES VOLKES 2, DIE** • 1922

MORE • 1969 • Schroeder Barbet • LXM, FRG, FRN

MORE • 1973 • Rose Mitchell • USA

MORE ABOUT NOSTRADAMUS • 1941 • Miller David • SHT • USA

MORE ABOUT THE CHILDREN OF BULLERBY VILLLAGE see **MER OM OSS BARN I BULLERBYN** • 1988

MORE ABOUT THE LANGUAGE OF LOVE see **KARLEKENS SPRAK 2** • 1974

MORE AMAZING THAN A FAIRY-TALE • 1963 • Dolin Boris • DOC • USS

MORE AMERICAN GRAFFITI • 1979 • Norton B. W. L. • USA • PURPLE HAZE (UKN)

MORE AND MORE • 1915 • *Empress* • USA

MORE DEAD THAN ALIVE • 1969 • Sparr Robert • USA

MORE DEADLY THAN THE MALE • 1915 • *Heinie & Louie* • USA

MORE DEADLY THAN THE MALE • 1919 • Vignola Robert G. • USA

MORE DEADLY THAN THE MALE • 1959 • Bucknell Robert • UKN

MORE DESIRES WITHIN YOUNG GIRLS see **SECHS SCHWEDINNEN AUF IBIZA**

MORE EGGS FROM YOUR HENS • 1942 • Bishop Terry • DOC • UKN

MORE EXCELLENT WAY, THE • 1917 • Vekroff Perry N. • USA

MORE FOR PEACE • 1954 • Beaudine William • USA

MORE FUN WITH LIQUID ELECTRICITY see **GALVANIC FLUID** • 1908

MORE HASTE, LESS SPEED • 1917 • *Lynne Ethel* • USA

MORE HASTE, THE LESS SPEED, THE • 1912 • *Imp* • USA

MORE HEAD • 1969 • Glick Wizard • USA

MORE HOT WATER FOR £ESS • 1963 • Sewell George • UKN

MORE HUMAN MIKADO, A • 1907 • Morland John • UKN

MORE I SEE YOU, THE • 1967 • Carlos Luciano B. • PHL

MORE KITTENS • 1936 • Jackson Wilfred • ANS • USA

MORE LIGHT! • Babak M. • DOC • USS

MORE MILK, EVETTE • 1965 • Warhol Andy • USA • MORE MILK YVETTE ○ LANA TURNER

MORE MILK YVETTE see **MORE MILK, EVETTE** • 1965

MORE MONEY THAN MANNERS • 1916 • Semon Larry • SHT • USA

MORE, MORE • 1973 • De Witt Elmo • SAF

MORE PAY -LESS WORK • 1926 • Ray Albert • USA

MORE PEP • 1936 • Fleischer Dave • ANS • USA

MORE, PLEASE • 1929 • Aylott Dave • UKN

MORE PRECIOUS THAN GOLD • 1909 • *Lubin* • USA

MORE PRECIOUS THAN GOLD • 1912 • Dawley J. Searle • USA

MORE SEX PLEASE • 1975 • Damiani Damiano • ITL

MORE SEXY CANTERBURY TALES • 1975 • Gastaldi Romano • ITL

MORE THAN A KISS (UKN) see **DON'T BET ON WOMEN** • 1931

MORE THAN A MIRACLE (USA) see **C'ERA UNA VOLTA** • 1967

MORE THAN A RED COAT • 1973 • Danis Aime • DCS • CND

MORE THAN A SECRETARY • 1936 • Green Alfred E. • USA

MORE THAN FRIENDS • 1915 • Reehm George E. • USA

MORE THAN FRIENDS • 1978 • Burrows James • TVM • USA

MORE THAN HE BARGAINED FOR • 1913 • Wilson Frank • UKN

MORE THAN HE BARGAINED FOR • 1919 • Rooke Arthur • UKN

MORE THAN HIS DUTY • 1910 • Porter Edwin S. • USA

MORE THAN ONE • 1970 • Markowitz Murray • DOC • CND

MORE THAN SISTER • 1979 • Carlson Russ • USA

MORE THAN YOU THINK • 1974 • Singleton Martin • DOC • SAF

MORE THE MERRIER, THE • 1943 • Stevens George • USA • MERRY-GO-ROUND

MORE THINGS CHANGE, THE • 1986 • Nevin Robyn • ASL

MORE TO BE PITIED THAN SCORNED • 1922 • Le Saint Edward J. • USA

MORE TO HIM THAN LIFE • 1916 • Noy Wilfred • UKN

MORE TO THE RIGHT THAN THE LEFT • 1989 • Antonakos Nikos • GRC • FURTHER RIGHT THAN THE RIGHT

MORE TRIFLES OF IMPORTANCE • 1941 • Wrangell Basil • USA

MORE TROUBLE • 1918 • Warde Ernest C. • USA

MORE TRUTH THAN POETRY • 1916 • Dillon John Francis • USA

MORE TRUTH THAN POETRY • 1917 • King Burton L. • USA

MORE WE ARE TOGETHER, THE • 1927 • Edwards J. Steven • UKN

MORE WE ARE TOGETHER, THE • 1944-45 • Jodoin Rene • ANS • CND

MORE WE ARE TOGETHER NO.4, THE • 1947 • Ladouceur Jean-Paul • ANS • CND

MORE WILD WILD WEST • 1980 • Kennedy Burt • TVM • USA

MORECAMBE AND WISE: NIGHT TRAIN TO MURDER • 1984 • McGrath Joseph • TVM • UKN • NIGHT TRAIN TO MURDER

MOREL, DER MEISTER DER KETTE 1 • 1920 • Ralph Louis • FRG • ABSCHNITT: DIE KETTE

MOREL, DER MEISTER DER KETTE 2 • 1920 • Ralph Louis • FRG • ABSCHNITT: GLANZ UND ELEND

MORELOS SIERVO DE LA NACION • 1965 • Bracho Julio • MXC

MORENA • 1986 • Manttari Anssi • FNL

MORENA CLARA • 1936 • Rey Florian • SPN

MORENA CLARA • 1954 • Lucia Luis • SPN

MORENA DE MI COPLA, LA • 1945 • Rivero Fernando A. • MXC

MORENA Y UNA RUBIA, UNA • 1933 • Buchs Jose • SPN

MORENITA CLARA • 1943 • Rodriguez Joselito • MXC

MORESQUE OBIETTIVO ALLUCINANTE • 1967 • Freda Riccardo • ITL, SPN, FRN • COPLAN OUVRE LE FEU A MEXICO (FRN) ○ ENTRE LAS REDES (SPN) ○ BETWEEN THE NETS

MORETO • 1967 • Donev Peter • BUL • SEA, THE

MORFALOUS, LES • 1983 • Verneuil Henri • FRN

MORG ERU DAGS AUGU • 1980 • Olafsson Gudmunder P. • DOC • ICL • MEN AND NATURE

MORGADHINHA DE VALFLOR, A • 1921 • de Albuquerque Ernesto • PRT

MORGAN -A SUITABLE CASE FOR TREATMENT • 1966 • Reisz Karel • UKN • MORGAN! (USA) ○ SUITABLE CASE FOR TREATMENT, A

MORGAN IL PIRATA • 1960 • Zeglio Primo, De Toth Andre • ITL, FRN • CAPITAINE MORGAN (FRN) ○ MORGAN THE PIRATE (USA)

MORGAN KEIBU TO NAZO NO OTOKO • 1961 • Sekigawa Hideo • JPN • DETECTIVE MORGAN AND A MAN OF MYSTERY ○ MYSTERIOUS DETECTIVE MORGAN, THE

MORGAN LE PIRATE • 1909 • Jasset Victorin • FRN

MORGAN STEWART'S COMING HOME • 1987 • Aaron Paul (Smithee Alan), Winsor Terry (Smithee Alan) • USA • HOMEFRONT

MORGAN THE PIRATE (USA) see **MORGAN IL PIRATA** • 1960

MORGAN! (USA) see **MORGAN -A SUITABLE CASE FOR TREATMENT** • 1966

MORGANATIC MARRIAGE, THE • 1909 • Stow Percy • UKN

MORGANE ET SES NYMPHES • 1970 • Gantillon Bruno • FRN

MORGANE, LA SIRENE • 1928 • Perret Leonce • FRN • MORGANE THE ENCHANTRESS

MORGANE THE ENCHANTRESS see **MORGANE, LA SIRENE** • 1928

MORGAN'S LAST RAID • 1929 • Grinde Nick • USA

MORGAN'S RAIDERS • 1918 • Lucas Wilfred • USA

MORGAN'S TREASURE • 1913 • *Powers* • USA

MORGAN'S WALL • 1978 • Goldie Caroline, Orders Ron, Richman Geoff, Richman Marie • UKN

MORGANSON'S FINISH • 1926 • Windermere Fred • USA

MORGARTEN FINDET STATT • 1979 • Muller Beni, Langjahr Erich • DOC • SWT

MORGEN BEGINNT DAS LEBEN • 1933 • Hochbaum Werner • FRG • LIFE BEGINS TOMORROW

MORGEN BEGINNT DAS LEBEN • 1961 • Leitner Hermann • AUS • MORD IM CAFE CENTRAL

MORGEN FALLT DIE SCHULE AUS • 1971 • Jacobs Werner • FRG

MORGEN GATT HET BETER • 1939 • Zelnik Friedrich • NTH

MORGEN IN ALABAMA • 1984 • Kuckelmann Norbert • FRG • TOMORROW IN ALABAMA

MORGEN IST ALLES BESSER • 1948 • Rabenalt Arthur M. • FRG

MORGEN WERDE ICH VERHAFTET • 1939 • Stroux Karl H. • FRG

MORGEN WIRST DU MICH WEINEN • 1959 • Braun Alfred • FRG

MORGENGRAUEN • 1954 • Tourjansky Victor • FRG

MORGENROT • 1933 • Ucicky Gustav • FRG • RED DAWN ○ DAWN

MORGENROTE • 1929 • Neff Wolfgang • FRG

MORGENS UM 7 IST DIE WELT NOCH IN ORDUNG • 1968 • Hoffmann Kurt • FRG • WORLD IS STILL IN ORDER AT SEVEN IN THE MORNING, THE

MORGENSTER, DE • 1957 • van der Linden Charles Huguenot • SHT • NTH • MORNING STAR, THE

MORGIANA • 1972 • Herz Juraj • CZC

MORGONDAGENS MELODI • 1942 • Frisk Ragnar • SWD • TOMORROW'S MELODY

MORGONVAKT • 1945 • Werner Gosta • SHT • SWD • EARLY MORNING

MORI NO ISHIMATSU • 1949 • Yoshimura Kozaburo • JPN • ISHIMATSU OF THE FOREST ○ ISHIMATSU FROM MORI ○ ISHIMATSU OF MORI

MORI NO ISHIMATSU NOIYORI KOWAI • Sawashima Chu • JPN

MORI NO ISHIMATSU YUREI DOCHU • 1959 • Saeki Kozo • JPN • ISHIMATSU TRAVELS WITH GHOSTS

MORI TO MIZUUMI NO MATSURI • 1958 • Uchida Tomu • JPN • OUTSIDERS

MORIANERNA • 1965 • Mattsson Arne • SWD • MORIANNA (I, THE BODY) (USA) ○ MORIANNA ○ I, THE BODY ○ BLACKAMOORS

MORIANNA see **MORIANERNA** • 1965

MORIANNA (I, THE BODY) (USA) see **MORIANERNA** • 1965

MORIARTY see **SHERLOCK HOLMES** • 1922

MORIBUND SPRING see **SAMRTNO PROLJECE** • 1974

MORICZ ZSIGMOND 1879-1942 • 1956 • Jancso Miklos • SHT • HNG • ZSIGMOND MORICZ 1879-1942

MORIR DE PIE • 1955 • Baledon Rafael • MXC

MORIR, DORMIR... TAL VEZ SONAR • 1976 • Mur Oti • SPN

MORIR EN EL GOLFO • 1990 • Pelayo Alejandro • MXC • DYING IN THE GULF

MORIR EN ESPANA • 1965 • Ozores Mariano • SPN

MORIR PARA VIVIR • 1954 • Morayta Miguel • MXC, CUB

MORIR POR LA PATRIA ES VIVIR • 1976 • Alvarez Santiago • DOC • CUB

MORIR UN POCO • 1967 • Covacevich Alvaro • DOC • CHL • TO DIE A LITTLE

MORIRE A ROMA • 1973 • Mingozzi Gianfranco • ITL • VITA IN GIOCO, LA

MORIRE GRATIS • 1968 • Franchina Sandra • ITL • TO DIE FOR NOTHING

MORITA • 1931 • Paul Fred • UKN

MORITURA • 1976 • Pernot Herve • DOC • FRN

MORITURI • 1948 • York Eugen • FRG

MORITURI • 1965 • Wicki Bernhard • USA • SABOTEUR, CODE NAME MORITURI ○ SABOTEUR, THE

MORITURUS • 1920 • *Veidt Conrad* • FRG

MORITZ see **MORITZ, LIEBER MORITZ** • 1978

MORITZ, DEAR MORITZ see **MORITZ, LIEBER MORITZ** • 1978

MORITZ IN DER LITFASSAULE • Losansky Rolf • GDR • MORITZ IN THE ADVERTISING PILLAR

MORITZ IN THE ADVERTISING PILLAR see **MORITZ IN DER LITFASSAULE**

MORITZ, LIEBER MORITZ • 1978 • Bohm Hark • FRG • MORITZ, DEAR MORITZ ○ MORITZ

MORITZ MACHT SEIN GLUCK • 1930 • Speyer Jaap • FRG • MEIER UND CO.

MORKE PUNKT, DET • 1911 • Blom August • DNM • MAMIE ROSE ○ ANNIE BELL

MORKE PUNKT, DET • 1913 • Holger-Madsen • DNM • STEEL KING'S LAST WISH, THE ○ STAALKONGENS VILJE

MORLOVE -EINE ODE FUR HEISENBERG • 1986 • Jamal Samir Aldin • SWT

MORMON, THE • 1912 • Dwan Allan • USA

MORMON CONQUEST • 1938 • Adamson Victor • USA

MORMON MAID, A • 1917 • Leonard Robert Z. • USA

MORMON PERIL, THE see **TRAPPED BY THE MORMONS** • 1922

MORMONENS OFFER • 1911 • Blom August • DNM • VICTIMS OF THE MORMONS, THE

MORMOR OG DE ATTE UNGENE I BYEN • 1976 • Thorstenson Espen • NRW • GRANDMA AND THE EIGHT CHILDREN (USA) ○ GRANDMA AND HER EIGHT GRANDCHILDREN IN THE TOWN

MORMOR OG DE ATTE UNGENE I SKOGEN • 1978 • Thorstenson Espen • NRW • GRANDMA AND HER EIGHT GRANDCHILDREN IN THE FOREST

MORNING • 1968 • Gehr Ernie • USA

MORNING • 1989 • Paz Felipe • SHT • RMN

MORNING see **JUTRO** • 1967

MORNING AFTER, THE • 1915 • *Parsons "smiling" Bill* • USA

MORNING AFTER, THE • 1921 • Roach Hal • SHT • USA

MORNING AFTER, THE • 1970 • Knight Sidney • USA

MORNING AFTER, THE • 1974 • Heffron Richard T. • TVM • USA

MORNING AFTER, THE • 1987 • Lumet Sidney • USA

MORNING AFTER, THE see **NIGHT IN NEW ORLEANS, A** • 1942

MORNING AFTER, THE (USA) see **I SPY** • 1933

MORNING AT BOW STREET, A • 1900 • *Paul R. W.* • UKN

MORNING BEFORE SLEEP, THE • 1969 • Wolman Dan • ISR

MORNING BELLS see **UTRENNIYE KOLOKOLA** • 1968

MORNING CALL • 1957 • Crabtree Arthur • UKN • STRANGE CASE OF DR. MANNING, THE (USA)

MORNING CONFLICTS see **ASA NO HAMON** • 1952

MORNING DAWN see **YOAKE ASAAKE** • 1953

MORNING DEPARTURE • 1949 • Baker Roy Ward • UKN • OPERATION DISASTER (USA)

MORNING FOR JIMMY, A • 1961 • Brown Bobby K. • SHT • UKN

MORNING FOR THE OSONE FAMILY see **OSONE-KE NO ASA** • 1946

MORNING GLORY • 1933 • Sherman Lowell • USA

MORNING HIGHWAY, THE see **UTRENNEYE SHOSSE** • 1989

MORNING IN THE CITY see **AAMUA KAUPUNGISSA** • 1954

MORNING JUDGE • 1926 • Fleischer Dave • ANS • USA

MORNING, JUDGE • 1937 • Goodwins Leslie • SHT • USA

MORNING MAN • 1983 • Purdy Jim • DOC • CND

MORNING MAN, THE • 1986 • Suissa Daniele J. • CND

MORNING NOON AND NIGHT • 1933 • Fleischer Dave • ANS • USA

MORNING, NOON AND NIGHTCLUB • 1937 • Fleischer Dave • ANS • USA

MORNING OF SIX WEEKS, A see **OCHTEND VAN ZES WEKEN, EEN** • 1966

MORNING OF THE 4TH DAY, THE • 1973 • Shirdel K. • IRN

MORNING OF THE BELOVED CITY • 1959 • *Ilyenko Yury (Ph)* • DOC • USS

MORNING OF THE EARTH • 1972 • Falzon Albert • ASL

MORNING ON THE LIEVRE • 1961 • Bairstow David • DOC • CND

MORNING PAPER • Catling Darrell • DCS • UKN

MORNING PAPERS, THE • 1914 • Sennett Mack • DOC • USA

MORNING PATROL • 1988 • Nikolaidis Nikos • GRC

MORNING PREMIERE see **JUTRO PREMIERA** • 1946

MORNING SCHEDULE see **GOZENCHO NO JIKANWARI** • 1972

MORNING STAR, THE see **MORGENSTER, DE** • 1957

MORNING STAR, THE see **SABAH YILDIZI** • 1968

MORNING STAR (USA) see **CHOLPON -UTRENNYAYA ZVEZDA** • 1960

MORNING SUN SHINES, THE (USA) see **ASAHI WA KAGAYAKU** • 1929

MORNING TERROR • 1987 • Neiman L. E. • USA

MORNING TRAINS • 1963 • Dovlatyan Frunze, Mirsky Lev • USS

MORNING UNDERSEA see **MANHA SUBMERSA** • 1980

MORNING WASH, A • 1900 • Smith Jack • UKN

MORNING WITH THE OSONE FAMILY, A see **OSONE-KE NO ASA** • 1946

MORNINGS OF A SENSIBLE YOUTH, THE see **DIMINETILE UNUI BAIAT CUMINTE** • 1966

MORNING'S TREE-LINED STREET see **ASA NO NAMIKI-MICHI** • 1936

MORO AFFAIR, THE see **CASO MORO, IL** • 1987

MORO DE CUMPAS, EL • 1976 • *Aguila* • MXC

MORO NABA • 1957 • Rouch Jean • DCS • FRN

MORO WITCH DOCTOR • 1964 • Romero Eddie • USA, PHL

MOROCCAN MIRAGE see **MOROCCO MIRAGE** • 1935

MOROCCO • 1930 • von Sternberg Josef • USA

MOROCCO • 1958 • King Allan • CND

MOROCCO MIRAGE • 1935 • USA • MOROCCAN MIRAGE

MOROCCO NIGHTS • 1934 • Cline Eddie • SHT • USA

MOROK • 1917 • *Pasquali* • ITL

MOROMETII • 1988 • Gulea Stere • RMN

MORONS FROM OUTER SPACE • 1985 • Hodges Mike • UKN

MOROS Y CRISTIANOS • 1988 • Berlanga Luis Garcia • SPN • MOORS AND CHRISTIANS

MOROZKO • 1924 • Scheljabuschsky Yuri • USS • FATHER FROST

MOROZKO • 1965 • Rou Aleksandr • USS • JACK FROST ○ GRANDFATHER FROST

MORPHEUS IN HELL • 1967 • Chomont Tom S. • SHT • USA

MORPHEUS MIKE • 1917 • O'Brien Willis • ANS • USA

MORPHIA THE DEATH DRUG • 1914 • Hepworth Cecil M. • UKN

MORPHIUM • 1919 • Ziener Bruno • FRG

MORRIS LOVES JACK • 1979 • Hoffman Sonia • SHT • ASL

MORRIS, THE MIDGET MOOSE • 1950 • Hannah Jack • ANS • USA

MORS AUX DENTS, LE • 1979 • Heynemann Laurent • FRN

MORS HUS see **SIN MORS HUS** • 1973

MORSA, LA • 1916 • Negroni Baldassare • ITL

MORSE CODE MELODY • 1963 • Godfrey Bob • SHT • UKN

MORSEL, THE see **SOUSTO** • 1960

MORSIUSSEPPELE • 1954 • Leminen Hannu • FNL • BRIDAL GARLAND, THE

MORSKIYE RASSKAZY • 1967 • Sakharov Alexei, Svetlov Alexandr • USS • SEA STORIES

MORT, LA • 1909 • Feuillade Louis • FRN

MORT A BOIRE, LA see **QUAI DE GRENELLE** • 1950

MORT A PONDU UN OEUF, LA (FRN) see **MORTE HA FATTO L'UOVO, LA** • 1968

MORT AMOUREUSE, LA • Ertaud Jacques • FRN

MORT AU CHAMP D'HONNEUR • 1915 • Perret Leonce • FRN

MORT D'ALEXANDRE, LA see **THANATOS TOU ALEXANDROU, O** • 1967

MORT DE BELLE, LA • 1961 • Molinaro Edouard, Curtis Terry • FRN • PASSION OF SLOW FIRE, THE (USA) ○ END OF BELLE, THE

MORT DE GANDJI, LA • 1965 • Alassane Moustapha • ANS • CND • DEATH OF GANDJI

MORT DE HASSAN TERO, LA • 1974 • Badie Mustapha • ALG

MORT DE L'AVIATEUR, LA • 1919 • Ravel Gaston • FRN

MORT DE LUCRECE, LA • 1913 • Feuillade Louis • FRN

MORT DE L'UTOPIE, LA • 1974 • Amat Jorge • FRN

MORT DE MARIO RICCI, LA • 1983 • Goretta Claude • SWT • DEATH OF MARIO RICCI, THE

MORT DE MOZART, LA • 1909 • Feuillade Louis • FRN

MORT DE ROBERT MACAIRE ET BERTRAND see **ROBERT MACAIRE ET BERTRAND** • 1905

MORT DE SAUL, LA • 1913 • Andreani Henri • FRN

MORT DE VENUS, LA • 1931 • Storck Henri • DOC • BLG

MORT D'HOMME see **CRIME DE CHEMIN ROUGE, LE** • 1932

MORT DU CERF, LA see **CHASSE A COURRE, UNE** • 1951

MORT DU CYNGE, LA • 1937 • Benoit-Levy Jean, Epstein Marie • FRN • BALLERINA (USA) ○ DEATH OF A SWAN, THE

MORT DU DIRECTEUR DE CIRQUE DE PUCES, LA • 1974 • Koerfer Thomas • SWT • OTTOCARO WEISS REFORME SON ENTREPRISE ○ TOD DES FLOHZIRKUSDIREKTORS ○ DEATH OF THE FLEA CIRCUS DIRECTOR, THE

MORT DU DUC D'ENGHIEN, LA • 1912 • Capellani Albert • FRN

MORT DU GRANDPERE, OU LE SOMMEIL DU JUSTE, LA • 1978 • Veuve Jacqueline • SWT, FRN

MORT DU JEUNE POETE, LA • 1973 • Delouche Dominique • SHT • FRN

MORT DU JULIUS CESAR, LA see **REVE DE SHAKESPEARE, LE** • 1907

MORT DU RAT, LA • Aubier Pascal • SHT • FRN

MORT DU SAUL, LA • 1912 • FRN • DEATH OF SAUL, THE

MORT DU SOLEIL, LA • 1921 • Dulac Germaine • FRN • DEATH OF THE SUN, THE

MORT DU SPHINX, LA • 1937 • Carls L. • BLG, UKN • SPHINX, THE

MORT D'UN BUCHERON, LA • 1973 • Carle Gilles • CND • DEATH OF A LUMBERJACK

MORT D'UN CERF see **CHASSE A COURRE, UNE** • 1951

MORT D'UN GUIDE • 1975 • Ertaud Jacques • FRN

MORT D'UN POURRI • 1977 • Lautner Georges • FRN

MORT D'UN TOREADOR, LA • 1907 • Gasnier Louis J. • FRN

MORT D'UN TUEUR, LA • 1963 • Hossein Robert • FRN

MORT EN CE JARDIN, LA • 1956 • Bunuel Luis • FRN, MXC • MUERTE EN ESTE JARDIN, LA (MXC) ○ DEATH IN THE GARDEN ○ GINA (USA) ○ EVIL EDEN ○ EVIL OF EDEN

MORT EN DIRECT, LA (FRN) see **DEATH WATCH** • 1979

MORT EN FRAUDE • 1956 • Camus Marcel • FRN • FUGITIVE IN SAIGON (USA)

MORT EN FUITE, LE • 1936 • Berthomieu Andre • FRN

MORT EN FUITE, LE see **DEUX FONT LA PAIRE, LES** • 1954

MORT INTERDITE • 1941 • Ciampi Yves • FRN

MORT INVISIBLE, LE • 1917 • Cande Adolphe • FRN

MORT NE RECOIT PLUS, LE • 1943 • Tarride Jean • FRN

MORT N'EST PAS A VENDRE, LA • 1960 • Desreumaux Andre • FRN

MORT, OU EST TA VICTOIRE? • 1962 • Bromberger Herve • FRN

MORT OU VIF • 1947 • Tedesco Jean • FRN

MORT OU VIF see **CENT DOLLARS MORT OU VIF** • 1912

MORT QUI FROLE, LA • 1914 • Durand Jean • FRN

MORT QUI RAMPAIT SUR LES TOITS, LE • 1974 • Franju Georges • MTV • FRN

MORT QUI TUE, LA • 1914 • Feuillade Louis • SRL • FRN • DEAD MAN WHO KILLED, THE (USA) ○ MYSTERIOUS FINGERPRINTS, THE ○ FANTOMAS III

MORT SANS IMPORTANCE, UNE • 1947 • Noe Yvan • FRN

MORT SUR PARIS, LA • 1913 • Fescourt Henri • FRN

MORT TROUBLE, LA • 1968 • d'Anna Claude, Boughedir Ferid • TNS, FRN • DEATH TROUBLES

MORT VIVANT, LE • 1912 • Feuillade Louis • FRN • LIVING DEAD MAN, THE

MORTACCI • 1988 • Citti Sergio • ITL • DEAD ONES

MORTADELLA, LA • 1971 • Monicelli Mario • ITL, FRN • LADY LIBERTY (USA)

MORTADELO AND FILOMON IN "THE YETI" see **MORTADELO Y FILOMON EN "EL YETI"** • 1970

MORTADELO Y FILOMON • 1968 • Vara Rafael • ASS • SPN

MORTADELO Y FILOMON EN "EL YETI" • 1970 • Vara Rafael • ANS • SPN • MORTADELO AND FILOMON IN "THE YETI"

MORTAL CLAY (UKN) see **VEM DOMER?** • 1922

MORTAL COILS see **WOMAN'S VENGEANCE, A** • 1947

MORTAL COMBAT • 1981 • Chang Ch'Eh • HKG

MORTAL CRUELTY see **CRUELDADE MORTAL** • 1980

MORTAL ORBIT see **PERRY RHODAN -SOS AUS DEM WELTALL** • 1967

MORTAL PASSIONS • 1990 • Lane Andrew • USA

MORTAL SIN, THE • 1917 • Collins John H. • USA

MORTAL STORM, THE • 1940 • Borzage Frank • USA

MORTAL THOUGHTS • 1990 • Rudolph Alan • USA

MORTALE TRAPPOLA DI BELFAGOR, LA • 1967 • Wilson J. W. • ITL

MORTE A VENEZIA • 1971 • Visconti Luchino • ITL • DEATH IN VENICE (UKN)

MORTE ACCAREZZA A MEZZANOTTE, LA • 1972 • Ercoli Luciano • ITL, SPN • DEATH CHERISHES MIDNIGHT ○ INCUBUS

MORTE AL LAVORO, LA • 1978 • Amelio Gianni • ITL

MORTE BUSSA CUE VOLTE, LA • 1969 • Philipp Harald? • ITL

MORTE CAMMINA CON I TACCI ALTI • 1971 • Ercoli Luciano • ITL

MORTE CHE ASSOLVE • 1917 • Lolli Alberto Carlo • ITL

MORTE CIVILE, LA • 1912 • Falena Ugo • ITL

MORTE CIVILE, LA • 1942 • Poggioli Ferdinando M. • ITL

MORTE CIVILE, LA see **FIGLIA DEL FORZATO, LA** • 1955

MORTE DI UN AMICO • 1959 • Rossi Franco • ITL • DEATH OF A FRIEND

MORTE DI UN BANDITO • 1961 • Amato Giuseppe • ITL

MORTE DI UN OPERATORE • 1979 • Rosati Faliero • MTV • ITL • DEATH OF A CAMERAMAN

MORTE E COME UN RAGNO, LA • 1974 • Cozzi Luigi • ITL

MORTE E NE TUOI OCCHI, LA • 1974 • D'Eramo Giovanni • ITL

MORTE HA FATTO L'UOVO, LA • 1968 • Questi Giulio • ITL, FRN • MORT A PONDU UN OEUF, LA (FRN) ○ CURIOUS WAY TO LOVE, A (UKN) ○ PLUCKED (USA) ○ DEATH HAS LAID AN EGG

MORTE HA VIAGGIATO CON ME, LA • 1957 • de la Loma Jose Antonio, Baldi Marcello • ITL, SPN

MORTE IMPROVVISA, LA see **SCACCO ALLA MAFIA** • 1970

MORTE IN JAGUAR ROSSA, LA (ITL) see **TOD IM ROTEN JAGUAR, DER** • 1968

MORTE IN VATICANO • 1982 • Aliprandi Marcello • ITL, SPN, MXC • DEATH IN THE VATICAN ○ VATICAN CONSPIRACY, THE

MORTE NEGLI OCCHI DEL GATTO, LA • 1973 • Margheriti Antonio • ITL, FRN, FRG • SEVEN DEAD IN THE CAT'S EYES ○ SEVEN DEATHS IN THE CAT'S EYE

MORTE NON CONTA I DOLLARI, LA • 1967 • Freda Riccardo • ITL • DEATH DOES NOT COUNT THE DOLLARS ○ DEATH AT ORWELL ROCK

MORTE NON HA SESSO, LA • 1968 • Dallamano Massimo • ITL, FRG • GEHEIMNIS DER JUNGEN WITWE, DAS (FRG) ○ BLACK VEIL FOR LISA, A (USA) ○ DEATH HAS NO SEX ○ VICOLO CIECO

MORTE PIAGNE, LA • 1920 • Bonnard Mario • ITL

MORTE RISALE A IERI SERA, LA • 1970 • Tessari Duccio • ITL, FRG • DEATH OCCURRED LAST NIGHT (UKN)

MORTE-SAISON DES AMOURS, LA • 1961 • Kast Pierre • FRN • SEASON FOR LOVE, THE (USA) ○ LIAISONS AMOUREUSES, LES ○ SEASON OF LOVE, THE

MORTE SALE IN ASCENSORE, LA (ITL) see **MONTE-CHARGE, LE** • 1962

MORTE SCENDE LEGGERA, LA • 1972 • Savona Leopoldo • ITL

MORTE SCORRE SUL FIUME, LA • 1961 • D'Annibale Aldo • ITL

MORTE SORRIDE ALL'ASSASSINO, LA • 1973 • D'Amato Joe • ITL • DEATH SMILES ON A MURDERER (USA)

MORTE SOSPETTA DI UNA MINORENNE • 1975 • Martino Sergio • ITL

MORTE SULL'ALTA COLLINA, LA • 1969 • Medori Alfredo • ITL

MORTE TRANSPARENTE, A • 1980 • Christensen Carlos Hugo • BRZ • TRANSPARENT DEATH

MORTE VESTITA DI DOLLARI, LA (ITL) see **EINER FRISST DEN ANDEREN** • 1964

MORTE VIENE DA MANILA, LA (ITL) see **LETZTEN DREI DER ALBATROS, DIE** • 1965

MORTE VIENE DAL PIANETA AYTIN, LA • 1967 • Margheriti Antonio • ITL

MORTE VIENE DALLO SPAZIO, LA • 1958 • Heusch Paolo • ITL, FRN • DANGER VIENT DE L'ESPACE, LE ○ DAY THE SKY EXPLODED, THE(USA) ○ DEATH FROM OUTER SPACE ○ DEATH COMES FROM OUTER SPACE

MORTE VIENE DEL BUIO, LA see **COLECCIONISTA DE CADAVERES, EL** • 1967

MORTE-VIVANTE, LA • 1982 • Rollin Jean • FRN

MORTELLE IDYLLE • 1905-10 • Heuze Andre • FRN

MORTELLE RANDONNEE • 1983 • Miller Claude • FRN • DEADLY RUN (UKN)

MORTGAGE, THE • 1912 • Melies Gaston • USA

MORTGAGE ON HIS DAUGHTER, A • 1915 • *Pearce Peggy* • USA

MORTGAGED WIFE, THE • 1918 • Holubar Allen • USA

MORTI NON PAGANO TASSE, I • 1953 • Grieco Sergio • ITL

MORTI NON SI CONTANI, I • 1968 • Romero-Marchent Rafael • ITL, SPN • DEAD ARE COUNTLESS, THE

MORTIMER GRIFFEN, SHALINSKY AND HOW THEY SETTLED THE JEWISH QUESTION • 1971 • King Allan • CND

MORTMAIN • 1915 • Marston Theodore • USA

MORTON DOWNEY IN AMERICA'S GREATEST COMPOSERS • 1932 • Brice Monte • USA

MORTON OF THE MOUNTED (UKN) see **TIMBER TERRORS** • 1935

MORTS EN VITRINE • 1957 • Vogel Raymond • SHT • FRN

MORTS REVIENNENT-ILS?, LES see **DRAME AU CHATEAU D'ACRE, UN** • 1915

MORTU NEGA • 1988 • Gomes • GNB

MORTUARY • 1984 • Avedis Howard • USA • EMBALMED

MORTUARY ACADEMY • 1988 • Schroeder Michael • USA

MORTY • SHT • USA

MOSAIC • 1962 • Timar Istvan • DOC • HNG

MOSAIC • 1966 • Chambers Jack* • DOC • CND

MOSAIC IN CONFIDENCE see **MOSAIK IM VERTRAUEN** • 1955

MOSAIC LAW, THE • 1913 • Ince Thomas H. • USA

MOSAIC (USA) see **MOSAIQUES** • 1964

MOSAICI DI RAVENNA • 1953 • Freda Riccardo • SHT • ITL

MOSAIK IM VERTRAUEN • 1955 • Kubelka Peter • SHT • AUS • MOSAIC IN CONFIDENCE

MOSAIQUES • 1964 • McLaren Norman, Lambart Evelyn • ANS • CND • MOSAIC (USA)

MOSBY'S MARAUDERS • 1967 • O'Herlihy Michael • USA • WILLIE AND THE YANK

MOSCA ADDIO • 1987 • Bolognini Mauro • ITL • MOSCOW, FAREWELL

MOSCA DI GIORNO E DI NOTTE • 1961 • Gandin Michele • DOC • ITL • VIAGGIO A MOSCA

MOSCHETTIERE FANTASMA, IL • 1954 • Calandri Max, French William • ITL

MOSCHETTIERI DEL MARE, I • 1962 • Steno • ITL, FRN • IL ETAIT TROIS FLIBUSTIERS (FRN) ○ MUSKETEERS OF THE SEA (USA) ○ IL ETAIT UN FOIS TROIS FLIBUSTIERS

MOSCONI STORY, THE • 1953 • Barclay David • SHT • USA

MOSCOW see **MOSKVA** • 1927

MOSCOW see **MOSKVA** • 1932

MOSCOW AND MUSCOVITES • 1956 • Grigoriev Roman • DOC • USS

MOSCOW BUILDS THE METRO see **MOSKVA STROYIT METRO** • 1934

MOSCOW – CASSIOPEIA see **MOSKVA – KASSIOPEIA** • 1974

MOSCOW DISTRUSTS TEARS see **MOSKVA SLEZAM NYE VERIT** • 1980

MOSCOW DOES NOT BELIEVE IN TEARS see **MOSKVA SLEZAM NYE VERIT** • 1980

MOSCOW DRAMA • 1909 • Goncharov Vasili M. • USS

MOSCOW, FAREWELL see **MOSCA ADDIO** • 1987

MOSCOW IN OCTOBER see **MOSKVA V OKTYABRE** • 1929

MOSCOW IS BEHIND US see **ZA NAMI MOSKVA** • 1968

MOSCOW – KARA KUM – MOSCOW • 1933 • Karmen Roman • DOC • SHT • USS

MOSCOW LAUGHS (USA) see **VESYOLYE REBYATA** • 1934

MOSCOW MUSIC HALL see **KINOKONCERT K25 LETIJU KRASNOJ ARMII** • 1943

MOSCOW, MY LOVE see **MOSKVA, LYUBOV MOYA** • 1975

MOSCOW NIGHTS • 1935 • Asquith Anthony • UKN • I STAND CONDEMNED (USA) ○ NATACHA

MOSCOW ON THE HUDSON • 1984 • Mazursky Paul • USA

MOSCOW SKY see **NEBO MOSKVY** • 1944

MOSCOW STORY see **GOROD BOLSHOY SUDBY** • 1961

MOSCOW STRIKES BACK (USA) see **RAZGROM NEMETZKIKHY VOISK POD MOSKVOI** • 1942

MOSCOW THAT WEEPS AND LAUGHS (UKN) see **MOSKVA V OKTYABRE** • 1929

MOSCOW TODAY see **CHELOVEK S KINOAPPARATOM** • 1928

MOSE AND FUNNY FACE MAKE ANGEL CAKE • 1924 • Fadman Edwin Miles • ANM • USA

MOSE DI MICHELANGELO, IL • 1920 • Lolli Alberto Carlo • DOC • ITL

MOSE (ITL) see **MOSES** • 1975

MOSELFAHRT AUS LIEBESKUMMER • 1953 • Hoffmann Kurt • FRG

MOSELFAHRT MIT MONIKA • 1944 • von Norman Roger • FRG

MOSES • 1975 • De Bosio Gianfranco • TVM • UKN, ITL • MOSE (ITL) ○ MOSES, THE LAWGIVER

MOSES • 1980 • Davis Charles • MTV • USA

MOSES AND AARON see **MOSES UND ARON** • 1975

MOSES AND THE EXODUS FROM EGYPT • 1907 • *Pathe* • FRN

MOSES IN THE BULLRUSHES • 1903 • *Gaumont* • UKN

MOSES, THE LAWGIVER see **MOSES** • 1975

MOSES UND ARON • 1975 • Straub Jean-Marie, Huillet Daniele • FRG • MOSES AND AARON

MOSHOW HOLIDAY • 1967 • Kuchar George • USA

MOSHUSHI DE QIYU • 1962 • Sang Hu • CHN • STRANGE ADVENTURES OF A MAGICIAN

MOSKAU 1957 • 1957 • Schamoni Peter • SHT • FRG

MOSKAU RUFT • 1959 • Schamoni Peter • SHT • FRG

MOSKAU-SHANGHAI • 1936 • Wegener Paul • FRG • WEG NACH SHANGHAI, DER

MOSKVA • 1927 • Kaufman Mikhail • USS • MOSCOW

MOSKVA • 1932 • Karmen Roman • USS • MOSCOW

MOSKVA – KASSIOPEIA • 1974 • Viktorov Richard • USS • MOSCOW – CASSIOPEIA

MOSKVA, LYUBOV MOYA • 1975 • Mitta Alexander, Ishida Kenji • USS, JPN • MOSKVA, WAGA AI (JPN) ○ MOSCOW, MY LOVE

MOSKVA SLEZAM NYE VERIT • 1980 • Menshov Vladimir • USS • MOSCOW DOES NOT BELIEVE IN TEARS ○ MOSCOW DISTRUSTS TEARS

MOSKVA STROYIT METRO • 1934 • Shub Esther • USS • MOSCOW BUILDS THE METRO ○ METRO AT NIGHT, THE ○ SUBWAY, THE

MOSKVA V OKTYABRE • 1929 • Barnet Boris • USS • MOSCOW THAT WEEPS AND LAUGHS (UKN) ○ MOSCOW IN OCTOBER

MOSKVA, WAGA AI (JPN) see **MOSKVA, LYUBOV MOYA** • 1975

MOSQUITA MUERTA • 1946 • Amadori Luis Cesar • ARG

MOSQUITO • 1922 • Fleischer Dave • ANS • USA

MOSQUITO see **MOSQUITO DER SCHANDER** • 1976

MOSQUITO, THE • Gurney Philip • DOC • UKN

MOSQUITO, THE see **HOW A MOSQUITO OPERATES** • 1910

MOSQUITO COAST, THE • 1986 • Weir Peter • USA

MOSQUITO DER SCHANDER • 1976 • Vajda Marijan • SWT • BLOODLUST ○ MOSQUITO

MOSQUITO, INIMIGO DO HOMEM, O • 1940 • Coelho Jose Adolfo • SHT • PRT

MOSQUITO PETE'S FORTUNE • 1914 • *Eclair* • USA

MOSQUITO SQUADRON • 1969 • Sagal Boris • UKN

MOSS COVERED ASPHALT see **MAHOVINA NA ASFALTU** • 1984

MOSS ON THE STONES see **MOOS AUF DEN STEINEN** • 1968

MOSS ROSE • 1947 • Ratoff Gregory • USA

MOSSAFER • 1975 • Kia-Rostami Abbas • IRN • PASSENGER, THE

MOST • 1946 • Bossak Jerzy • DOC • PLN • BRIDGE, THE

MOST • 1969 • Krvavac Hajrudin • YGS

MOST, THE • 1962 • Sheppard Gordon H. • DCS • CND • ONE TIME AROUND

MOST ATTRACTIVE MAN, A • 1981 • Hartman Rivka • SHT • ASL

MOST BEAUTIFUL, THE see **ICHIBAN UTSUKUSHIKU** • 1944

MOST BEAUTIFUL AGE, THE (USA) see **NEJKRASNEJSI VEK** • 1968

MOST BEAUTIFUL COUPLE IN THE WORLD, THE see **PIU BELLA COPPIA DEL MONDO, LA** • 1968

MOST BEAUTIFUL GIRL IN THE KINGDOM, THE see **PIU BELLA DEL REAME, LA** • 1990

MOST BEAUTIFUL GIRL IN THE WORLD, THE see **DUNYANIN EN GUZEL KADINI** • 1968

MOST BEAUTIFUL NIGHT, THE see **NOCHE MAS HERMOSA, LA** • 1984

MOST BEAUTIFUL THING ON EARTH, THE see **VACKRASTE PA JORDEN, DET** • 1947

MOST BEAUTIFULLY see **ICHIBAN UTSUKUSHIKU** • 1944

MOST DANGEROUS GAME, THE • 1932 • Schoedsack Ernest B., Pichel Irving • USA • HOUNDS OF ZAROFF, THE (UKN) ○ SKULL ISLAND

MOST DANGEROUS GAME, THE see **GAME OF DEATH, A** • 1946

MOST DANGEROUS GAME, THE see **DROLE DE JEU** • 1968

MOST DANGEROUS MAN ALIVE, THE • 1961 • Dwan Allan • USA • STEEL MONSTER, THE

MOST DANGEROUS MAN IN THE WORLD, THE see **AKHTAR RAGOL FIL ALAM** • 1967

MOST DANGEROUS MAN IN THE WORLD, THE (UKN) see **CHAIRMAN, THE** • 1969

MOST DANGEROUS SIN, THE (USA) see **CRIME ET CHATIMENT** • 1956

MOST DANGEROUS SPY, THE • 1981 • Brittain Don • MTV • CND

MOST DANGEROUS WOMAN ALIVE, THE • 1988 • Marnham Christian?, Byers Mark? • USA

MOST FANTASTIC AND MARVELOUS ADVENTURE IN THE JUNGLE see **KARZAN, IL FAVOLOSO UOMO DELLA GIUNGLA** • 1971

MOST GIRLS WILL (UKN) see **HAUSFRAUEN -REPORT II** • 1971

MOST IMMORAL LADY, A • 1929 • Wray John Griffith • USA

MOST IMPORTANT EVENT SINCE MAN EVER SET FOOT ON THE MOON, THE see **EVENEMENT LE PLUS IMPORTANT DEPUIS QUE L'HOMME A MARCHE SUR LA LUNE, L'** • 1973

MOST IMPORTANT THING, THE see **SPRAWA NAJWAZNIEJSWA** • 1946

MOST IMPORTANT THING: LOVE, THE (USA) see **IMPORTANT, C'EST D'AIMER, L'** • 1974

MOST LIVE OF ALL LIVING, THE • 1960 • Makhnach Leonid • DOC • USS

MOST NATURAL THING IN THE WORLD, THE see **NATURLICHSTE SACH DER WELT, DIE** • 1978

MOST PEREYTI NELIEYA • 1960 • Vulfovich Teodor, Kurikhin Nikita • USS • BRIDGE CANNOT BE CROSSED, THE ○ DEATH OF A SALESMAN ○ NO CROSSING THE BRIDGE

MOST PRECIOUS OF ALL • 1957 • Muzykant Yu., Selektor S. • USS

MOST PRECIOUS THING IN LIFE • 1934 • Hillyer Lambert • USA

MOST PROHIBITED SEX, THE see **SEXY PROIBITISSIMO** • 1963

MOST UNLIKELY MILLIONAIRE, THE • 1965 • King Allan • CND

MOST UNUSUAL WOMAN, A see **DONNA SCIMMIA, LA** • 1964

MOST USEFUL TREE IN THE WORLD, THE see **VARLDENS MEST ANVANDBARA TRAD** • 1937

MOST VALUABLE ASSET OF A WOMAN IS HER SILENCE, THE see **HOCHSTE GUT EINER FRAU IST IHR SCHWEIGEN, DAS** • 1981

MOST VALUABLE MADAM, THE see **SAIKO SHUKON FUJIN** • 1959

MOST WANTED • 1976 • Grauman Walter • TVM • USA

MOST WANTED MAN, THE (USA) see **ENNEMI PUBLIC NO.1** • 1953

MOST WANTED MAN IN THE WORLD, THE see **ENNEMI PUBLIC NO.1** • 1953

MOST WONDERFUL MOMENT, THE see **MOMENTO PIU BELLO, IL** • 1957

MOST WONDERFUL MOMENTS OF OUR LIFE, THE see **NAJPIEKNIEJSZE CHWILE NASZEGO ZYCIA** • 1959

MOSTAHIL, AL see **MUSTAHIL, AL-** • 1964

MOSTAKBEL EL MAGHOUL, EL • 1948 • Salem Ahmed • EGY • UNKNOWN FUTURE, THE

MOSTEIROS PORTUGUESES • 1959 • Ribeiro Antonio Lopes • SHT • PRT

MOSTOSTALOWCY • 1960 • Lomnicki Jan • DOC • PLN • STEEL BRIDGE MEN, THE

MOSTRI, I • 1963 • Risi Dino • ITL, FRN • MONSTRES, LES (FRN) ○ OPIATE '67 (USA) ○ MONSTERS, THE ○ 15 FROM ROME

MOSTRO, IL • 1977 • Zampa Luigi • ITL

MOSTRO DELL'ISOLA, IL • 1954 • Montero Roberto Bianchi • ITL • MONSTER OF THE ISLAND, THE

MOSTRO DELL'OPERA, IL see **VAMPIRO DELL'OPERA, IL** • 1961

MOSTRO DI FRANKENSTEIN, IL • 1920 • Testa Eugenio • ITL

MOSTRO DI VENEZIA, IL • 1965 • Tavella Dino • ITL • EMBALMER, THE (USA) ○ MONSTER OF VENICE, THE

MOSTRO E IN TAVOLA.. BARON FRANKENSTEIN see **ANDY WARHOL'S FRANKENSTEIN** • 1974

MOSTRO E MEZZO, UN • 1964 • Steno • ITL • MONSTER AND A HALF, A

MOSURA • 1961 • Honda Inoshiro • JPN • MOTHRA (USA)

MOSURA TAI GOJIRA • 1964 • Honda Inoshiro • JPN • GODZILLA FIGHTS THE GIANT MOTH ○ GODZILLA VS. THE THING (USA) ○ GODZILLA TAI MOTHRA ○ GODZILLA VERSUS THE GIANT MOTH ○ GOJIRA TAI MOSURA ○ GODZILLA VERSUS MOTHRA

MOT D'AMOUR, UN • 1971 • Collet Paul, Drouot Pierre • BLG

MOT DE CAMBRONNE, LE • 1936 • Guitry Sacha • FRN

MOT DE L'ENIGME see **ENIGME, L'** • 1919

MOT HARLIGA TIDEN • 1983 • Terselius Kjell • SWD

MOT NYA TIDER • 1939 • Wallen Sigurd • SWD • TOWARDS NEW TIMES

MOTARDS, LES • 1958 • Laviron Jean • FRN

MOTE AND THE BEAM, THE • 1913 • McGill Lawrence • USA

MOTE I NATTEN • 1946 • Ekman Hasse • SWD • NIGHTLY ENCOUNTER

MOTE MED DJAVULEN • 1973 • Sarno Joe • SWD, SWT

MOTE MED LIVET • 1952 • Werner Gosta • SWD • MEETING LIFE

MOTEL • 1982 • Mandoki Luis • MXC

MOTEL see **PINK MOTEL** • 1983

MOTEL CONFIDENTIAL • 1967 • Stephen A. C. • USA

MOTEL HELL • 1980 • Connor Kevin • USA

MOTEL LIVES see **MOTEL WIVES** • 1968

MOTEL, THE OPERATOR • 1940 • Seiden Joseph • USA

MOTEL WIVES • 1968 • Clay Adam • USA • MOTEL LIVES

MOTEN I SKYMNINGEN • 1957 • Kjellin Alf • SWD • ENCOUNTERS AT DUSK ○ TWILIGHT MEETING

MOTEUR! • 1967 • Lemaitre Maurice • FRN

MOTFORESTILLING • 1973 • Lochen Erik • NRW • REMONSTRANCES

MOTH, THE • 1911 • *Thanhouser* • USA

MOTH, THE • 1914 • *Lubin* • USA

MOTH, THE • 1917 • Jose Edward • USA

MOTH, THE • 1934 • Newmeyer Fred • USA • SEEING IT THROUGH (UKN)

MOTH, THE see **NACHTFALTER** • 1911

MOTH, THE see **CMA** • 1980

MOTH AND RUST • 1921 • Morgan Sidney • UKN

MOTH AND THE FLAME, THE • 1912 • *Melies* • USA

MOTH AND THE FLAME, THE • 1913 • *Macpherson Jeanie* • USA

MOTH AND THE FLAME, THE • 1914 • Olcott Sidney • USA

MOTH AND THE FLAME, THE • 1915 • *Famous Players* • USA

MOTH AND THE FLAME, THE • 1916 • *Pathe* • SHT • USA

MOTH AND THE FLAME, THE • 1938 • Gillett Burt • ANS • USA

MOTH AND THE SPIDER, THE • 1935 • *Terry Paul/ Moser Frank (P)* • ANS • USA

MOTH-ERR • 1964 • Lederberg Dov • SHT • USA

MOTH OF MOONBI • 1926 • Chauvel Charles • ASL

MOTHEATEN SPRING see **MUSHIBAMERU HARU** • 1932

MOTHER • 1910 • *Thanhouser* • USA

MOTHER • 1912 • *Reliance* • USA

MOTHER • 1912 • *Rex* • USA

MOTHER • 1913 • *Powers* • USA

MOTHER • 1913 • *Pathe* • USA

MOTHER • 1914 • *Melies* • USA

MOTHER • 1914 • Tourneur Maurice • *World* • USA

MOTHER • 1916 • *Sunset* • USA

MOTHER • 1920 • Rasumny Alexander • USS

MOTHER • 1927 • Meehan James Leo • USA • WOMAN SEES IT THROUGH, THE

MOTHER • 1948 • Zils Paul • IND

MOTHER • 1989 • Hatami Ali • IRN

MOTHER see **MAT** • 1926

MOTHER see **OKASAN** • 1952

MOTHER see **MAT** • 1956

MOTHER see **AMMA** • 1960

MOTHER see **AMMA** • 1968

MOTHER see **IBUNDA** • 1986

MOTHER see **HAHA** • 1988

MOTHER see **MAT** • 1989

MOTHER, A • 1941 • Lukov Leonid • USS

MOTHER, A see **ANYASAG** • 1974

MOTHER, THE • 1911 • *Selig* • USA

MOTHER, THE • 1918 • Tucker George Loane • USA

MOTHER, THE • 1936 • *Garrick John* • SHT • UKN

MOTHER, THE see **HAHA** • 1929

MOTHER, THE see **HAHA** • 1963

MOTHER, THE see **ANA** • 1967

MOTHER, THE see **EOMI** • 1985

MOTHER AND CHILD • 1910 • *Imp* • USA

MOTHER AND CHILD see **MUTTER UND KIND** • 1924

MOTHER AND CHILD see **MUTTER UND KIND** • 1933

MOTHER AND CHILD see **HAHA TO KO** • 1938

MOTHER-AND-CHILD GRASS see **HAHAKOGUSA** • 1942

MOTHER AND DAUGHTER • 1910 • *Powers* • USA

MOTHER AND DAUGHTER • 1913 • *Solax* • USA

MOTHER AND DAUGHTER see **MOR OCH DOTTER** • 1912

MOTHER AND DAUGHTER see **MATERNALE, LA** • 1978
MOTHER AND DAUGHTER see **ANYA ES LEANYA** • 1981
MOTHER AND DAUGHTER -THE LOVING WAR • 1980 • Brinckerhoff Burt • TVM • USA
MOTHER AND DAUGHTER (USA) see **SREDI DOBRYKH LYUDEY** • 1962
MOTHER AND DAUGHTERS • 1912 • *Nesbitt Miriam* • USA
MOTHER AND ELEVEN CHILDREN see **KAACHAN TO JUICHI-NIN NO KODOMO** • 1966
MOTHER AND GUN see **HAHA TO KENJU** • 1958
MOTHER AND HER CHILD -MATERNITE • 1947 • Paquette Vincent • DOC • CND
MOTHER AND HER CHILDREN, A see **HAHAKOGUSA** • 1959
MOTHER AND SON • 1931 • McCarthy John P. • USA
MOTHER AND SON • 1967 • Nemec Jan • NTH
MOTHER AND SON see **OYEN-SAN** • 1955
MOTHER AND SONS OF 1776, A • 1912 • Fitzhamon Lewin? • UKN
MOTHER AND STEPMOTHER • 1965 • Pcholkin L. • USS
MOTHER AND THE LAW, THE • 1918 • Gorman John • USA
MOTHER AND THE LAW, THE • 1919 • Griffith D. W. • USA
MOTHER AND THE WHORE, THE (USA) see **MAMAN ET LA PUTAIN, LA** • 1973
MOTHER AND WIFE • 1914 • Wilson Ben • USA
MOTHER CALL, THE • 1916 • Reynolds Lynn • SHT • USA
MOTHER CAREY'S CHICKENS • 1938 • Lee Rowland V. • USA
MOTHER COUNTRY see **SANGA-ARI** • 1962
MOTHER COURAGE AND HER CHILDREN see **MUTTER COURAGE UND IHRE KINDER** • 1960
MOTHER DEAR • 1982 • Brocka Lino • PHL
MOTHER, DEARLY LOVED see **MATER AMATISIMA** • 1980
MOTHER DIDN'T TELL ME • 1950 • Binyon Claude • USA
MOTHER, DO NOT SHAME YOUR NAME see **HAHA YO, KIMI NO NA O KEGASU NAKARE** • 1928
MOTHER EARTH • Bose Nitin • IND
MOTHER EARTH see **BOSHUNDHARA** • 1977
MOTHER EARTH RISES see **DAICHI NI TATSU** • 1932
MOTHER ETERNAL • 1921 • Abramson Ivan • USA
MOTHER FOR MAY, A see **FATHER IS A BACHELOR** • 1950
MOTHER, GET MARRIED see **KAACHAN KEKKON SHIROYO** • 1962
MOTHER GETS THE WRONG TONIC • 1913 • Calvert Charles? • UKN
MOTHER GOES SIGHTSEEING see **OKASAN NON TOKYO KENBUTSU** • 1957
MOTHER GOOSE • 1909 • *Edison* • USA
MOTHER GOOSE A GO-GO • 1966 • Harris Jack H. • USA • UNKISSED BRIDE
MOTHER GOOSE GOES HOLLYWOOD • 1938 • Jackson Wilfred • ANS • USA
MOTHER GOOSE IN SWINGTIME • 1939 • Gould Manny • ANS • USA
MOTHER GOOSE LAND • 1925 • Fleischer Dave • ANS • USA
MOTHER GOOSE LAND • 1933 • Fleischer Dave • ANS • USA
MOTHER GOOSE MELODIES • 1931 • Gillett Burt • ANS • USA
MOTHER GOOSE NIGHTMARE • 1945 • Rasinski Connie • ANS • USA
MOTHER GOOSE NURSERY RHYMES • 1902 • Smith G. A. • UKN
MOTHER GOOSE ON THE LOOSE • 1942 • Lantz Walter • ANS • USA
MOTHER GOOSE PRESENTS • 1946 • Harryhausen Ray • ASS • USA • MOTHER GOOSE STORIES
MOTHER GOOSE PRESENTS THE QUEEN OF HEARTS • 1946 • Harryhausen Ray • ANS • USA • QUEEN OF HEARTS, THE
MOTHER GOOSE SERIES, THE • 1911 • *Champion* • USA
MOTHER GOOSE STORIES see **MOTHER GOOSE PRESENTS** • 1946
MOTHER GOOSE'S BIRTHDAY PARTY see **MIGHTY MOUSE IN MOTHER GOOSE'S BIRTHDAY PARTY** • 1950
MOTHER HEART, THE • 1912 • *Rex* • USA
MOTHER HEART, THE • 1914 • Campbell Colin • USA
MOTHER HEART, THE • 1921 • Mitchell Howard M. • USA
MOTHER HEN'S HOLIDAYS • 1937 • *Mintz Charles (P)* • ANS • USA
MOTHER HUBBA-HUBBA HUBBARD • 1947 • Wickersham Bob • ANS • USA
MOTHER HULDA • 1915 • West Raymond B. • USA
MOTHER, I MISS YOU see **HAHA-YO KOISHI** • 1926
MOTHER, I NEED YOU • 1918 • Beal Frank • USA • CURSE OF EVE, THE
MOTHER IN EXILE, A • 1914 • Weston Charles • UKN
MOTHER-IN-LAW, THE • 1916 • *Ritchie Billie* • SHT • USA
MOTHER-IN-LAW HAS ALL THE LUCK • 1909 • Fitzhamon Lewin • UKN
MOTHER-IN-LAW IN LOVE see **ZAMILOVANA TCHYNE** • 1914
MOTHER-IN-LAW IS COMING see **SVARMOR KOMMER** • 1932
MOTHER-IN-LAW ON THE SPREE see **SVARMOR PA VIFT** • 1916
MOTHER-IN-LAW RAISES • 1911 • *Pathe* • USA
MOTHER-IN-LAW WOULD FLY • 1909 • *Walturdaw* • UKN
MOTHER-IN-LAW'S DAY • 1932 • Sweet Harry • SHT • USA
MOTHER-IN-LAW'S DAY • 1945 • Yates Hal • SHT • USA
MOTHER INDIA (UKN) see **BHARAT MATA** • 1957
MOTHER INSTINCT, THE • 1915 • Lucas Wilfred • USA
MOTHER INSTINCT, THE • 1917 • Neill R. William • USA
MOTHER IS A FRESHMAN • 1949 • Bacon Lloyd • USA • MOTHER KNOWS BEST (UKN)
MOTHER JOAN AND ANGELS see **MATKA JOANNA OD ANIOLOW** • 1961
MOTHER JOAN OF THE ANGELS see **MATKA JOANNA OD ANIOLOW** • 1961
MOTHER, JUGS AND SPEED • 1976 • Yates Peter • USA
MOTHER KNOWS BEST • 1928 • Blystone John G. • USA • DOES MOTHER KNOW BEST
MOTHER KNOWS BEST • 1970 • *Kirt Films International* • USA
MOTHER KNOWS BEST (UKN) see **MOTHER IS A FRESHMAN** • 1949
MOTHER KRACMERKA see **MATKA KRACMERKA** • 1934
MOTHER KRAUSEN'S JOURNEY TO HAPPINESS see **MUTTER KRAUSENS FAHRT INS GLUCK** • 1929
MOTHER KUSTERS GOES TO HEAVEN (USA) see **MUTTER KUSTERS FAHRT ZUM HIMMEL** • 1975
MOTHER KUSTER'S TRIP TO HEAVEN (UKN) see **MUTTER KUSTERS FAHRT ZUM HIMMEL** • 1975
MOTHER LODE • 1980 • Heston Charlton • USA • LAST GREAT TREASURE, THE ○ SEARCH FOR THE MOTHER LODE: THE LAST GREAT TREASURE
MOTHER LODE see **YELLOW DUST** • 1936
MOTHER LOVE • 1910 • Salter Harry • USA
MOTHER LOVE • 1912 • *Buckley May* • USA
MOTHER LOVE • 1913 • *Macklin Albert* • USA
MOTHER LOVE • 1914 • *Leonard Marion* • USA
MOTHER LOVE see **AMOR DE MAE** • 1977
MOTHER LOVE AND THE LAW • 1917 • Siegmann George • USA
MOTHER LOVE (UKN) see **MOTHER O' MINE** • 1917
MOTHER LOVE (USA) see **MUTTERLIEBE** • 1929
MOTHER LOVE (USA) see **MUTTERLIEBE** • 1939
MOTHER LOVE VS. GOLD • 1913 • Duncan William • USA
MOTHER MACHREE • 1922 • *Twinkle Amanda* • USA
MOTHER MACHREE • 1928 • Ford John • USA
MOTHER MARIA see **MAT' MARIJA** • 1983
MOTHER MARRIES see **MAMMA GIFTER SAG** • 1937
MOTHER MARY see **MADRE MARIA, LA** • 1974
MOTHER MICHAEL • 1914 • *Eclair* • USA
MOTHER MIST see **MAMA DE NIEBLA** • 1980
MOTHER, MOTHER, MOTHER, PIN A ROSE ON ME • 1924 • Fleischer Dave • ANS • USA
MOTHER NEVER DIES see **HAHA WA SHINAZU** • 1942
MOTHER O' DREAMS • 1914 • *Stonehouse Ruth* • USA
MOTHER O' MINE • 1917 • Julian Rupert • USA • MOTHER LOVE (UKN) ○ MOTHER OF MINE
MOTHER O' MINE • 1921 • Niblo Fred • USA
MOTHER OF DARTMOOR, THE • 1916 • Tucker George Loane • UKN
MOTHER OF HER DREAMS, THE • 1915 • *Thanhouser* • USA
MOTHER OF HIS CHILDREN, THE • 1920 • Le Saint Edward J. • USA
MOTHER OF KINGS, THE see **MATKA KROLOW** • 1983
MOTHER OF KROLS see **MATKA KROLOW** • 1983
MOTHER OF MANY CHILDREN • 1976 • Obomsawin Alanis • CND • MERE DE TANT D'ENFANTS
MOTHER OF MEN • 1938 • Pearson George • UKN
MOTHER OF MEN, A • 1914 • Olcott Sidney • USA
MOTHER OF MINE see **MOTHER O' MINE** • 1917
MOTHER OF MINE see **GRIBICHE** • 1925
MOTHER OF PEARL • 1915 • *Johnson Arthur* • USA
MOTHER OF PEARL see **PARLEMOR** • 1961
MOTHER OF SEVEN, THE • 1914 • MacGregor Norval • USA
MOTHER OF THE BRIDE see **MAMA DE LA NOVA, LA** • 1978
MOTHER OF THE RANCH, THE • 1911 • Dwan Allan • USA
MOTHER OF THE RANCH, THE • 1912 • *Mackley Julia* • USA
MOTHER OF THE SHADOWS • 1914 • *Aoki Tsuru* • USA
MOTHER ON THE QUAY • 1976 • Kenjiro Komuri • JPN
MOTHER OUGHT TO BE LOVED, A see **HAHA O KOWAZUYA** • 1934
MOTHER OUGHT TO MARRY see **SECOND TIME AROUND, THE** • 1961
MOTHER PIN A ROSE ON ME • 1929 • Fleischer Dave • ANS • USA
MOTHER PLUTO • 1936 • Hand David • ANS • USA
MOTHER RILEY IN DRACULA'S DESIRE see **MOTHER RILEY MEETS THE VAMPIRE** • 1952
MOTHER RILEY MEETS THE VAMPIRE • 1952 • Gilling John • UKN • OLD MOTHER RILEY MEETS THE VAMPIRE ○ MY SON THE VAMPIRE (USA) ○ MOTHER RILEY IN DRACULA'S DESIRE ○ KING ROBOT ○ VAMPIRE OVER LONDON ○ MOTHER RILEY RUNS RIOT
MOTHER RILEY RUNS RIOT see **MOTHER RILEY MEETS THE VAMPIRE** • 1952
MOTHER RILEY'S NEW VENTURE see **OLD MOTHER RILEY'S NEW VENTURE** • 1949
MOTHER SHOULD BE LOVED, A see **HAHA O KOWAZUYA** • 1934
MOTHER, SIR! (UKN) see **NAVY WIFE** • 1956
MOTHER STAY AT HOME see **WAGAYA NI HAHA ARE** • 1938
MOTHER SUPERIOR see **TROUBLE WITH ANGELS, THE** • 1966
MOTHER TAKES A HOLIDAY see **MAMMA TAR SEMESTER** • 1957
MOTHER TERESA AND HER WORLD • 1979 • Chiba Shigeki • DOC • JPN
MOTHER-TO-BE • 1971 • Poirier Anne-Claire • CND
MOTHER-TO-BE see **DE MERE EN FILLE** • 1968
MOTHER TONGUE • 1979 • May Derek • CND
MOTHER WANTED see **ANNI TAHTOO AIDIN** • 1988
MOTHER WAS A ROOSTER • 1962 • McKimson Robert • ANS • USA
MOTHER, WIFE, DAUGHTER see **MUSUME TSUMA HAHA** • 1960
MOTHER WORE TIGHTS • 1947 • Lang Walter • USA
MOTHERHOOD • 1914 • *Fischer Margarita* • USA
MOTHERHOOD • 1915 • Carleton Lloyd B. • USA
MOTHERHOOD • 1915 • Weston Harold • UKN • CLIMAX, THE
MOTHERHOOD • 1917 • Nash Percy • UKN
MOTHERHOOD • 1917 • Powell Frank • USA
MOTHERHOOD IS NOT ENOUGH (USA) see **NO BASTA SER MADRE** • 1937
MOTHERHOOD: LIFE'S GREAT MIRACLE • 1928 • *Patton George E.* • USA
MOTHERHOOD OR POLITICS • 1913 • Buckland Warwick • UKN • CASE FOR SOLOMON, A
MOTHERHOOD WITHOUT MEN see **MATERNIDAD SIN HOMBRES** • 1968
MOTHERING HEART, THE • 1913 • Griffith D. W. • USA
MOTHERLAND • 1927 • Samuelson G. B., Davis Rex • UKN
MOTHERLAND see **MATHRU BHUMI** • 1968
MOTHERLAND, THE see **DHARATI-MATA** • 1938
MOTHERLAND FAR FAR AWAY, THE see **HARUKANARI HAHA NO KUNI** • 1950
MOTHERLAND HOTEL see **ANAYURT OTELI** • 1987
MOTHERLAND'S SOLDIER • 1975 • Chulyukin Yuri • USS
MOTHERLESS KIDS, THE • 1914 • *Fischer Margarita* • USA
MOTHERLESS WAIF, A • 1909 • Coleby A. E. • UKN
MOTHERLOVE • 1916 • Elvey Maurice • UKN
MOTHERLY PRAM, THE • 1908 • Fitzhamon Lewin • UKN
MOTHERS, THE see **MUTHERS, THE** • 1968
MOTHER'S ADVICE see **ANDARZI MUDAR** • 1972
MOTHERS AND DAUGHTERS see **DOCHKI MATERI** • 1975
MOTHERS AND FATHERS • 1967 • *Halas John (P)* • ANS • UKN
MOTHERS AND SONS see **POBEDA** • 1938
MOTHER'S ANGEL • 1920 • Lascelle Ward • SHT • USA
MOTHER'S ATONEMENT, A • 1914 • *Boyle Irene* • USA
MOTHER'S ATONEMENT, A • 1915 • De Grasse Joseph • USA
MOTHER'S AWAKENING, A • 1912 • *Rex* • USA
MOTHER'S AWAKENING, A • 1915 • *C.k.* • USA
MOTHER'S BABY BOY • 1914 • *Lubin* • USA
MOTHER'S BANK ROLL • 1912 • *Stuart Julia* • USA
MOTHER'S BIRTHDAY • 1915 • King Burton L. • USA
MOTHER'S BOY • 1911 • Fitzhamon Lewin • UKN
MOTHER'S BOY • 1913 • Lehrman Henry, Sennett Mack (Spv) • USA
MOTHER'S BOY • 1929 • Barker Bradley • USA
MOTHER'S BOY see **HIS MOTHER'S BOY** • 1917
MOTHER'S BOY (UKN) see **PERCY** • 1925
MOTHER'S BUSY WEEK • 1915 • MacMackin Archer • USA
MOTHER'S CARD, A • 1942 • *Mori Masayuki* • JPN
MOTHER'S CARESS see **RYOOK NAM-MAI** • 1960
MOTHER'S CHILD • 1916 • *Hardy Babe* • SHT • USA
MOTHER'S CHOICE, A • 1914 • *Hastings Carey L.* • USA
MOTHER'S CONFESSION, A • 1915 • Abramson Ivan • USA
MOTHERS CRY • 1930 • Henley Hobart • USA
MOTHER'S DARLING • 1921 • Gordon Edward R. • UKN
MOTHER'S DARLING LITTLE BOY • 1914 • *All Films* • USA
MOTHER'S DAY • 1948 • Broughton James • SHT • USA
MOTHER'S DAY • 1980 • Kaufman Charles • USA
MOTHER'S DAY ON WALTON MOUNTAIN • 1982 • Arner Gwen • TVM • USA
MOTHER'S DAY OUT • 1912 • Stow Percy • UKN
MOTHER'S DEVOTION, A see **VYERNOST MATERI** • 1967
MOTHER'S ERROR, A • 1914 • *Melies* • USA
MOTHER'S FAITH, A • 1911 • *Thanhouser* • USA
MOTHER'S FIELD, THE see **MATERINSKOYE POLYE** • 1968
MOTHER'S FIGHT, A see **THORA VAN DEKEN** • 1920
MOTHER'S FIRST LOVE see **HAHA NO HATSUKOI** • 1954
MOTHER'S GRATITUDE, A • 1910 • Wilson Frank? • UKN
MOTHER'S GUIDING HAND • 1916 • *Fearnley Jane* • SHT • USA
MOTHER'S HEART, A • 1910 • *Lubin* • USA
MOTHER'S HEART, A • 1914 • *Vaughn Robert* • USA
MOTHER'S HEART, A see **SERDTSE MATERI** • 1966
MOTHER'S HEART, A see **CUORE DI MAMMA** • 1968
MOTHER'S HOLIDAY • 1932 • Arbuckle Roscoe • USA
MOTHER'S HOUSE see **SIN MORS HUS** • 1973
MOTHER'S IDEAL, A • 1917 • Davis Will S. • USA
MOTHERS IN A FOREIGN MOTHERLAND see **MODRE I FREMMED FAEDRELAND** • 1986
MOTHERS-IN-LAW • 1923 • Gasnier Louis J. • USA
MOTHER'S INFLUENCE, A • 1914 • O'Brien Jack • USA
MOTHER'S INFLUENCE, A • 1916 • Tucker George Loane • UKN
MOTHER'S JOY • 1923 • Roach Hal • SHT • USA
MOTHER'S JUSTICE, A • 1915 • *Mackley Arthur Mrs.* • USA
MOTHER'S LAZY BOY • 1913 • *Wadsworth William* • USA
MOTHER'S LITTLE HELPER • 1962 • Smith Paul J. • ANS • USA
MOTHER'S LOVE, A see **HAHA-YO KOISHI** • 1926
MOTHER'S LOYALTY, A see **VYERNOST MATERI** • 1967
MOTHER'S MAD see **HAHA NO CHIZU** • 1942
MOTHER'S MARRIAGE PROPOSAL see **MAMA NO ENDAN** • 1937
MOTHER'S MEAT & FREUD'S FLESH • 1984 • Demetrios Demetri • CND
MOTHER'S MILLIONS • 1931 • Flood James • USA • SHE-WOLF OF WALL STREET ○ SHE-WOLF
MOTHERS OF LIBERTY • 1918 • Fitzgerald Dallas M., Davis Will S. • USA
MOTHERS OF MEN • 1917 • Robards Willis • USA
MOTHERS OF MEN • 1920 • Jose Edward • USA
MOTHERS OF MEN see **BROADWAY MADONNA, THE** • 1922
MOTHERS OF TODAY • 1939 • Lynn Henry • USA
MOTHER'S OLD ARMCHAIR • 1912 • *Republic* • USA
MOTHER'S REMORSE, A • 1911 • *Pathe* • USA
MOTHER'S ROSES • 1915 • Marston Theodore • USA
MOTHER'S SACRIFICE, A • 1912 • *Trunnelle Mabel* • USA
MOTHER'S SECRET, A • 1918 • Gerrard Douglas • USA
MOTHER'S SIN, A • 1907 • Martin J. H.? • UKN
MOTHER'S SIN, A • 1918 • Mills Thomas R. • USA
MOTHER'S SPIRIT, A • 1913 • *Kinemacolor* • USA
MOTHER'S STRATEGY • 1916 • *Rancho* • USA
MOTHER'S STRATEGY, A • 1912 • *Hawley Ormi* • USA
MOTHER'S WAY, A • 1914 • Morgan George • USA
MOTHLIGHT • 1963 • Brakhage Stan • SHT • USA
MOTHRA (USA) see **MOSURA** • 1961
MOTHS • 1913 • Cabanne W. Christy • USA
MOTHS • 1922 • *Parkinson H. B.* • SHT • UKN
MOTHS AND THE FLAME, THE • 1910 • *Edison* • USA
MOTHWIESE see **SVAERMERE** • 1974
MOTIF • 1956 • D'Avino Carmen • SHT • USA
MOTIFS WITH STONES see **SPIEL MIT STEINEN** • 1965
MOTIG MAUR, EIN • 1979 • Bomann Terje • SHT • NRW • COURAGEOUS ANT, THE
MOTION • 1947 • Hird Henry E. • USA
MOTION • 1967 • Vaitiekunas Vince • SHT • CND
MOTION PAINTING NO.1 • 1949 • Fischinger Oskar • SHT • USA
MOTION PICTURE #1 see **MOTION PICTURES** • 1956
MOTION PICTURE, A • 1973 • Keenan Haydn • SHT • ASL
MOTION PICTURE MAN, THE • 1910 • *Lubin* • USA
MOTION PICTURE TRIP THROUGH DARLINGHURST GAOL, A • 1914 • ASL
MOTION PICTURES • 1956 • Breer Robert • SHT • USA • MOTION PICTURE #1
MOTION TO ADJOURN, A • 1921 • Clements Roy • USA
MOTIVATION • 1984 • Bro Arne, Wivel Anne • DOC • DNM
MOTIVE FOR REVENGE • 1935 • Lynwood Burt • USA
MOTIVO IN MASCHERA • 1956 • Canzio Stefano • ITL
MOTIVOS DE BERTA, LOS • 1985 • Guerin Jose Luis • SPN • BERTA'S MOTIVES ○ BERTA'S REASONS

MOTIVOS DE LUZ, LOS • 1985 • Cazals Felipe • MXC • LUZ'S REASONS
MOTLEY AND MELODY • 1931 • *Nesbitt Max* • SHT • UKN
MOTO-GIRL.. UNE PETITE CHATTE SUR UN ENGIN BRULANT • 1980 • Pirau Reine • FRN
MOTO QUI TUE, LA • Patin Claude • FRN
MOTOCYCLETTE, LA (FRN) see **GIRL ON A MOTORCYCLE** • 1968
MOTOGAZ • 1963 • Urbanski Kazimierz • PLN
MOTOR BANDITS, THE • 1912 • Speer Walter Harold • UKN
MOTOR BIKE ADVENTURE, A • 1905 • Collins Alf? • UKN
MOTOR BOAT BANDITS, THE • 1915 • Kelsey Fred A. • USA
MOTOR BOAT CHAMPIONSHIP IN BRISBANE • 1925 • ASL
MOTOR BOAT MAMAS • 1928 • *Sennett Mack (P)* • SHT • USA
MOTOR BOAT PIRATES ON SYDNEY HARBOUR see **SYDNEY ON THE SPREE** • 1909
MOTOR BUCCANEERS, THE • 1914 • *Bushman Francis X.* • USA
MOTOR BUG, THE • 1913 • *Gem* • USA
MOTOR CAR see **AUTOMOBILE, L'** • 1971
MOTOR CAR OF THE FUTURE • 1910 • *Messter* • FRG
MOTOR CAVALIERS see **MOTORKAVALJERER** • 1951
MOTOR CHAIR, THE • 1911 • *Italia* • ITL
MOTOR COMPETITION, THE • 1905 • Collins Alf? • UKN
MOTOR CYCLES see **PETISTOVKA** • 1949
MOTOR FIEND • 1910 • Golden Joseph A. • USA
MOTOR HIGHWAY, THE • 1975 • Dimitrov Stefan • BUL • HIGHWAY, THE
MOTOR HIGHWAYMAN, THE • 1905 • Cooper Arthur • UKN
MOTOR HOOLIGANS, THE • 1905 • *Paul R. W.* • UKN
MOTOR, LIEBE, LEIDENSCHAFT • 1925 • Paringer Lorenz • FRG
MOTOR MAD • 1906 • *Urban Trading Co* • UKN
MOTOR MAD • 1925 • Taurog Norman • SHT • USA
MOTOR MADNESS • 1937 • Lederman D. Ross • USA • SPEED MAD
MOTOR MAGNATE • 1934 • *Tilley John* • SHT • UKN
MOTOR MANIA • 1950 • Kinney Jack • ANS • USA
MOTOR MANIACS • 1946 • Grissell Wallace A. • SHT • USA
MOTOR MASQUERADE, A • 1905 • Collins Alf? • UKN
MOTOR PATROL • 1950 • Newfield Sam • USA
MOTOR PIRATE, THE • Cooper Arthur
MOTOR PSYCHO! • 1965 • Meyer Russ • USA
MOTOR SCOOTER, THE • 1963 • Pars Heino • ANS • USS
MOTOR-STRUCK see **CZAR KOLEK** • 1967
MOTOR VALET, THE • 1906 • Cooper Arthur • UKN • NEW MOTO VALET, THE
MOTOR VERSUS MOKE • 1906 • *Cricks & Sharp* • UKN
MOTORBOAT PARTY, A • 1913 • *Lubin* • USA
MOTORBOATING • 1917 • De Vonde Chester M. • SHT • USA
MOTORBRAUT, DIE • 1924 • Eichberg Richard • FRG • LIEBE, LIED UND SPORT
MOTORCAR APACHES, THE see **LYCKONALEN** • 1916
MOTORCART, THE see **COCHECITO, EL** • 1960
MOTORCYCLE ADVENTURE, A • 1912 • *Selig* • USA
MOTORCYCLE COSSACKS • 1935 • Samaniego Antonio • SHT • USA
MOTORCYCLE ELOPEMENT, A • 1913 • Henderson Dell • USA
MOTORCYCLE ELOPEMENT, A • 1914 • Bantock Leedham? • UKN
MOTORCYCLE ELOPEMENT, A • 1915 • Williams C. Jay • USA
MOTORCYCLE GANG • 1957 • Cahn Edward L. • USA
MOTORCYCLE MANIA • 1933 • Cummings Jack • SHT • USA
MOTORING • 1911 • *Thanhouser* • USA
MOTORING • 1927 • Dewhurst George • UKN
MOTORING MAMAS • 1929 • *Sennett Mack (P)* • SHT • USA
MOTORING THRU SPAIN • 1927 • *Holmes Burton* • DOC • USA
"?" MOTORIST, THE • 1906 • Booth W. R. • UKN • QUESTIONMARK MOTORIST
MOTORIST'S DREAM, THE • 1915 • Nash Percy? • UKN
MOTORIZZATE, LE • 1963 • Girolami Marino • ITL
MOTORIZZATI, I • 1962 • Mastrocinque Camillo • ITL, SPN
MOTORKAVALJERER • 1951 • Ahrle Elof • SWD • MOTOR CAVALIERS
MOTORVEJ PA SENGEKANTEN • 1972 • Hilbard John • DNM
MOTOTO • 1932 • Kearton Cherry • UKN • FIRE-BABY, THE
MOTOWN 9000 see **DETROIT 9000** • 1973
MOTOWN'S MUSTANG • 1985 • Robinson Mark • USA
MOTS ET LES GESTES, LES see **JOSEPH ET MARIE** • 1979
MOTS ONT UN SENS, LES • 1968 • Marker Chris • FRN
MOTS POUR LE DIRE, LES • 1983 • Pinheiro Jose • FRN
MOTSART I SALYERI • 1962 • Gorikker Vladimir • USS • REQUIEM FOR MOZART (USA) ○ MOZART AND SALIERI
MOTSUMI • 1983 • SAF
MOTTE FLOG ZUM LICHT, EINE • 1915 • Andra Fern? • FRG
MOTTEN IM LICHT • Egger Urs • SWT
MOTYLE • 1973 • Nasfeter Janusz • PLN • BUTTERFLIES
MOTYLI TADY NEZIJI • 1958 • Bernat Miro • CZC • BUTTERFLIES DO NOT LIVE HERE
MOU NGAU • 1989 • Fong Yuk-Ping • HKG • DANCING BULL
MOUCHARDE, LA • 1958 • Lefranc Guy • FRN • WOMEN OF SIN (USA)
MOUCHE, LA • 1903-04 • Blache Alice • FRN
MOUCHETTE • 1966 • Bresson Robert • FRN
MOUETTES, LES • 1916 • Mariaud Maurice • FRN
MOUGGAT DE TINDOUF, LE • 1967 • Kerzabi Ahmed • ALG
MOUKHAREBOUN, AL see **MUKHARRIBUN, AL-** • 1965
MOUL LE YA, MOUL LE YA • 1983 • Lee Doo-Yong • SKR • SPINNING WHEEL, THE ○ WHEEL, THE
MOULAI HAFID ET ALPHONSE XIII • 1912 • Cohl Emile • ANS • FRN
MOULDERS OF MEN • 1927 • Ince Ralph • USA • ENEMIES OF SOCIETY
MOULDERS OF SOULS • 1910 • *Reliance* • USA
MOULDING, THE • 1913 • Ince Ralph • USA
MOULE, LA • 1936 • Delannoy Jean • FRN
MOULED YA DUNIA • 1976 • Kamal Hussein • EGY
MOULIN DANS LE SOLEIL, LE • 1938 • Didier Marc • FRN
MOULIN DES SUPPLICES, LE (FRN) see **MULINO DELLE DONNE DI PIETRA, IL** • 1960
MOULIN DEVELEY SIS A LA QUIELLE, LE • 1971 • Champion Claude • SWT
MOULIN MAUDIT, LE see **MAUDITE SOIT LA GUERRE** • 1913
MOULIN ROUGE • 1928 • Dupont E. A. • UKN
MOULIN ROUGE • 1934 • Lanfield Sidney • USA
MOULIN ROUGE • 1939 • Hugon Andre • FRN
MOULIN ROUGE • 1953 • Huston John • UKN
MOUMOU • 1951 • Jayet Rene • FRN
MOUNA, OR AN ARTIST'S DREAM see **MOUNA, OU LE REVE D'UN ARTISTE** • 1969
MOUNA, OU LE REVE D'UN ARTISTE • 1969 • Duparc Henri • IVC • MOUNA, OR AN ARTIST'S DREAM ○ DREAM OF AN ARTIST
MOUNE ET SON NOTAIRE • 1932 • Bourlon Hubert • FRN
MOUNT CHOPAKA EASTER SUNDAY JACKPOT RODEO • 1979 • Wilson Sandra • MTV • CND
MOUNT DAR TO KALYAR • 1989 • Wah Wah Win Shwe • BRM
MOUNT PINEY • 1968 • Bartsch Art • ANS • USA
MOUNT VERNON • 1949 • Van Dyke Willard • DOC • USA
MOUNTAIN • 1944 • Clement Rene • DCS • FRN
MOUNTAIN, THE • 1935 • Jackson Travis • UKN
MOUNTAIN, THE • 1956 • Dmytryk Edward • USA
MOUNTAIN, THE • 1982 • Verhage Gerrard • DOC • NTH
MOUNTAIN, THE see **GORA** • 1964
MOUNTAIN, THE see **BERG, DER** • 1989
MOUNTAIN AND RIVER OF LOVE see **AI NO SANGA** • 1950
MOUNTAIN BLIZZARD, A • 1910 • *Edison* • USA
MOUNTAIN BLOOD • 1916 • Cochrane George • SHT • USA
MOUNTAIN BRIGAND see **AVVENTURE DI MANDRIN, LE** • 1952
MOUNTAIN CAT, THE see **BERGKATZE, DIE** • 1921
MOUNTAIN CHARLIE • 1982 • Stapleford George • USA
MOUNTAIN DAISY, A • 1916 • *Mutual* • USA
MOUNTAIN DAISY, THE • 1912 • *Nestor* • USA
MOUNTAIN DANCE • 1975 • Kreps Bonnie • CND
MOUNTAIN DESPERADOES (UKN) see **LARAMIE MOUNTAINS** • 1952
MOUNTAIN DEW • 1912 • *Blackwell Carlyle* • USA
MOUNTAIN DEW • 1918 • Heffron Thomas N. • USA
MOUNTAIN EAGLE, THE • 1926 • Hitchcock Alfred • UKN, FRG • BERGADLER, DER (FRG) ○ FEAR O' GOD (USA)
MOUNTAIN EARS • 1939 • Gould Manny • ANS • USA
MOUNTAIN FAMILY ROBINSON • 1979 • Cotter John • USA
MOUNTAIN FESTIVAL IN NEW BRITAIN • 1962 • Marek Dusan • DOC • ASL
MOUNTAIN FEUD, A • 1908 • *Selig* • USA
MOUNTAIN FIGHTERS • 1943 • Eason B. Reeves • SHT • USA
MOUNTAIN FORTRESS • 1956 • Bare Richard L. • MTV • USA
MOUNTAIN FREE • 1973 • Kim Soo-Yong • SKR
MOUNTAIN GIRL, THE • 1915 • Kirkwood James • USA
MOUNTAIN GIRL'S SELF SACRIFICE, THE • 1912 • *Nestor* • USA
MOUNTAIN GOAT, A • 1914 • *Warner'S Features* • USA
MOUNTAIN GOES TO SEA, A • 1943 • Chauvel Charles • DOC • ASL
MOUNTAIN IN THE JUNGLE, THE see **MONTAGNA DEL DIO CANNIBALE, LA** • 1976
MOUNTAIN JUSTICE • 1915 • De Grasse Joseph • USA
MOUNTAIN JUSTICE • 1930 • Brown Harry J. • USA • KETTLE CREEK
MOUNTAIN JUSTICE • 1937 • Curtiz Michael • USA
MOUNTAIN JUSTICE • 1942 • Taylor Ray • USA
MOUNTAIN KATE see **WOOERS OF MOUNTAIN KATE, THE** • 1912
MOUNTAIN KING, THE see **YEDI DAGIN ASLANI** • 1966
MOUNTAIN KING, THE see **SHOOT TO KILL** • 1988
MOUNTAIN LADY • 1918 • Finley Ned • SHT • USA
MOUNTAIN LAW • 1914 • *Rex* • USA
MOUNTAIN LAW • 1914 • *Lubin* • USA
MOUNTAIN LAW, THE • 1911 • *Essanay* • USA
MOUNTAIN MADNESS • 1920 • Carleton Lloyd B. • USA
MOUNTAIN MAID, A • 1910 • *Edison* • USA
MOUNTAIN MAN see **GUARDIAN OF THE WILDERNESS** • 1976
MOUNTAIN MARY • 1915 • Eason B. Reeves • USA
MOUNTAIN MELODY, A • 1915 • De Grasse Joseph • USA
MOUNTAIN MEN, THE • 1980 • Lang Richard • USA
MOUNTAIN MEN, THE • 1984 • Sumner Peter • DOC • ASL
MOUNTAIN MOONLIGHT • 1941 • Grinde Nick • USA • MOVING INTO SOCIETY (UKN)
MOUNTAIN MOTHER, A • 1913 • *Lubin* • USA
MOUNTAIN MUSIC • 1933 • Hackney W. P. • SHT • USA
MOUNTAIN MUSIC • 1937 • Florey Robert • USA
MOUNTAIN MUSIC • 1976 • Vinton Will • ANS • USA
MOUNTAIN NECKLACE • 1969 • Okeyev Tolomush • SHT • USS
MOUNTAIN NYMPH, A • 1916 • Cochrane George • USA
MOUNTAIN OF DAE SAC • Dan Tran The • VTN
MOUNTAIN OF FEAR • 1967 • Gale Joze • UKN, YGS
MOUNTAIN OF FEAR (UKN) see **SRECNO, KEKEC!** • 1964
MOUNTAIN OF HELL • 1985 • SAF
MOUNTAIN OF HORROR see **LELEJSKA GORA** • 1968
MOUNTAIN OF LAMENT see **LELEJSKA GORA** • 1968
MOUNTAIN OF THE GHOSTS, THE • 1974 • Gilling John
MOUNTAIN OF WRATH, THE see **PLANINA NA GNEVOT** • 1968
MOUNTAIN PASS OF LOVE AND HATE, THE see **AIZO TOGE** • 1934
MOUNTAIN PEOPLE, THE see **KHON PHUU KAOW** • 1979
MOUNTAIN RAT, THE • 1914 • Kirkwood James • USA
MOUNTAIN RHYTHM • 1939 • Eason B. Reeves • USA
MOUNTAIN RHYTHM • 1942 • McDonald Frank • USA • HARVEST DAYS (UKN)
MOUNTAIN ROAD, THE • 1960 • Mann Daniel • USA
MOUNTAIN ROMANCE, A • 1938 • Davis Mannie • ANS • USA
MOUNTAIN TRAGEDY, A • 1912 • *Reliance* • USA
MOUNTAIN TRAGEDY, A • 1912 • *Kalem* • USA
MOUNTAIN TRAGEDY, A • 1916 • Cochrane George • SHT • USA
MOUNTAIN TRAITOR, THE • 1914 • *Eclair* • USA
MOUNTAIN VILLAGE, THE see **POHORSKA VESNICE** • 1928
MOUNTAIN VILLAGE SCHOOL • Keko Endri • DOC • ALB
MOUNTAIN WIFE, A • 1910 • Melies Gaston • USA
MOUNTAIN WITCH, THE • 1913 • *Wolfe Jane* • USA
MOUNTAIN WOMAN, THE • 1921 • Giblyn Charles • USA
MOUNTAINEER, THE • 1910 • *Whyte A. G.* • USA
MOUNTAINEER, THE • 1914 • Reid Wallace • USA
MOUNTAINEERS, THE • 1913 • Merwin Bannister • USA
MOUNTAINEER'S HONOR, THE • 1909 • Griffith D. W. • USA
MOUNTAINEER'S REVENGE, THE • 1908 • *Lubin* • USA
MOUNTAINEER'S ROMANCE, THE • 1912 • Raymond Charles • UKN
MOUNTAINOUS • 1897 • *Paul R. W.* • UKN
MOUNTAINS AND RIVERS WITH SCARS see **KIZU DARAKE NO SANGA** • 1964
MOUNTAINS ARE STIRRING, THE see **LAZY SA POHLI** • 1952
MOUNTAINS AT DUSK see **GORY O ZMIERZCHU** • 1970
MOUNTAINS GROW DARK, THE see **YAMA KURURU** • 1921
MOUNTAINS IN FLAME see **DOOMED BATTALION, THE** • 1932
MOUNTAINS O' MOURNE • 1938 • Hughes Harry • UKN
MOUNTAINS OF FIRE see **OGNIOMISTRZ KALEN** • 1961
MOUNTAINS OF MANHATTAN • 1927 • Hogan James P. • USA
MOUNTAINS OF THE MOON • 1958 • Van Dyke Willard • DOC • USA
MOUNTAINS OF THE MOON • 1967 • Jones Harmon • MTV • USA
MOUNTAINS OF THE MOON • 1989 • Rafelson Bob • USA
MOUNTAINS OF THE WEST • 1954 • Fraser Donald • DOC • CND
MOUNTAINS ON FIRE see **OGNIOMISTRZ KALEN** • 1961
MOUNTAINTOP MOTEL see **MOUNTAINTOP MOTEL MASSACRE** • 1986
MOUNTAINTOP MOTEL MASSACRE • 1986 • McCullough Jim • USA • MOUNTAINTOP MOTEL
MOUNTASSAR, AL- • 1969 • Merbah Lamine • ALG
MOUNTBATTEN: THE LAST VICEROY • 1985 • Clegg Tom • MTV • UKN
MOUNTEBANK'S DAUGHTER, THE • 1912 • *Hawley Ormi* • USA
MOUNTED FURY • 1931 • Paton Stuart • USA
MOUNTED OFFICER FLYNN • 1913 • *King Joe* • USA
MOUNTED PATROL, THE see **JIZDNI HLIDKA** • 1936
MOUNTED STRANGER, THE • 1930 • Rosson Arthur • USA
MOUNTIES' CRIME LAB, THE • 1953-54 • Devlin Bernard • DCS • CND
MOUNTING TENSION • 1950 • Burckhardt Rudy • SHT • USA
MOURAMANI MAMADOU TOURE • 1953 • GUN
MOUREZ, NOUS FERONS LE RESTE • 1953 • Stengel Christian • FRN
MOURIR A MADRID • 1962 • Rossif Frederic • DOC • FRN • TO DIE IN MADRID
MOURIR A TRENTE ANS • 1982 • Goupil Romain • DOC • FRN
MOURIR A TUE-TETE • 1979 • Poirier Anne-Claire • CND • SCREAM FROM SILENCE, A ○ SCREAM OF SILENCE, A ○ PRIMAL FEAR
MOURIR D'AIMER • 1970 • Cayatte Andre • FRN, ITL • MOURIRE D'AMORE (ITL) ○ TO DIE OF LOVE (USA)
MOURIR D'AMOUR • 1960 • Fog Dany • FRN
MOURIR POUR VIVRE • 1973 • Liant Francois • CND
MOURIRE D'AMORE (ITL) see **MOURIR D'AIMER** • 1970
MOURNERS, OR A CLEVER UNDERTAKING, THE • 1908 • *Vitagraph* • USA
MOURNING BECOMES ELECTRA • 1947 • Nichols Dudley • USA
MOURNING SUIT, THE • 1975 • Yakir Leonard • CND
MOURSHED, EL • 1989 • el Mougi Ibrahim • EGY • INFORMER, THE
MOUSCHY • 1918 • Moest Hubert • FRG
MOUSE • 1973 • Burstall Tim • SHT • ASL
MOUSE AND CAT (USA) see **MYSZKA I KOTEK** • 1958
MOUSE AND GARDEN • 1950 • Davis Mannie • ANS • USA
MOUSE AND GARDEN • 1960 • Freleng Friz • ANS • USA
MOUSE AND HIS CHILD, THE see **EXTRAORDINARY ADVENTURES OF THE MOUSE AND HIS CHILD, THE** • 1977
MOUSE AND KITTEN see **MYSZKA I KOTEK** • 1958
MOUSE AND THE CAT, THE see **MYSZKA I KOTEK** • 1958
MOUSE AND THE CRAYON, THE see **MOUSE AND THE PENCIL, THE** • 1958
MOUSE AND THE LION, THE • 1913 • Brooke Van Dyke • USA
MOUSE AND THE LION, THE • 1953 • Smith Paul J. • ANS • USA
MOUSE AND THE LION, THE see **EGER ES OROSZLAN** • 1957
MOUSE AND THE PENCIL, THE • 1958 • Buchvarova Radka, Doicheva Zdenka • BUL • MOUSE AND THE CRAYON, THE
MOUSE AND THE WOMAN, THE see **IN THE AFTERNOON OF WAR** • 1981
MOUSE BLANCHE • 1962 • Deitch Gene • ANS • USA
MOUSE CLEANING • 1948 • Hanna William, Barbera Joseph • ANS • USA
MOUSE COMES TO DINNER, THE • 1945 • Hanna William, Barbera Joseph • ANS • USA
MOUSE DIVIDED, A • 1952 • Freleng Friz • ANS • USA
MOUSE EXTERMINATOR, THE • 1940 • *Mintz Charles (P)* • ANS • USA
MOUSE FOR SALE • 1955 • Hanna William, Barbera Joseph • ANS • USA
MOUSE FROM H.U.N.G.E.R., THE • 1967 • Levitow Abe • ANS • USA
MOUSE IN MANHATTAN • 1945 • Hanna William, Barbera Joseph • ANS • USA
MOUSE IN THE HOUSE, A • 1947 • Hanna William, Barbera Joseph • ANS • USA
MOUSE INTO SPACE • 1962 • Deitch Gene • ANS • USA
MOUSE MAZURKA • 1949 • Freleng Friz • ANS • USA
MOUSE MEETS BIRD • 1953 • Rasinski Connie • ANS • USA
MOUSE MEETS LION • 1940 • *Mintz Charles (P)* • ANS • USA
MOUSE MENACE • 1946 • Davis Arthur • ANS • USA
MOUSE MENACE • 1953 • Donnelly Eddie • ANS • USA
MOUSE-MERIZED CAT, THE • 1946 • McKimson Robert • ANS • USA
MOUSE OF TOMORROW, THE • 1942 • Donnelly Eddie • ANS • USA
MOUSE ON 57TH STREET, THE • 1961 • Jones Charles M. • ANS • USA
MOUSE ON THE HOUSE • 1967 • Smith Paul J. • ANS • USA
MOUSE ON THE MOON, THE • 1963 • Lester Richard • UKN • ROCKET FROM FENWICK, A
MOUSE PLACED KITTEN • 1959 • McKimson Robert • ANS • USA
MOUSE TAKEN IDENTITY • 1957 • Freleng Friz • ANS • USA

MOUSE THAT JACK BUILT, THE • 1958 • McKimson Robert • ANS • USA
MOUSE THAT ROARED, THE • 1959 • Arnold Jack • UKN • DAY NEW YORK WAS INVADED, THE
MOUSE TRAP see **ELIPPATHAYAM** • 1981
MOUSE TRAPEZE • 1955 • Sparber I. • ANS • USA
MOUSE TRAPPED • 1959 • Lovy Alex • ANS • USA
MOUSE TRAPPERS • 1941 • Lovy Alex • ANS • USA
MOUSE TREK • 1967 • Bakshi Ralph • ANS • USA
MOUSE TROUBLE • 1944 • Hanna William, Barbera Joseph • ANS • USA
MOUSE WARMING • 1952 • Jones Charles M. • ANS • USA
MOUSE WRECKERS • 1949 • Jones Charles M. • ANS • USA
MOUSETAKEN IDENTITY • 1957 • McKimson Robert • ANS • USA
MOUSETRAP, THE see **MISOLOVKA** • 1972
MOUSETRO HERMAN • 1956 • Sparber I. • ANS • USA
MOUSEUM • 1956 • Kneitel Seymour • ANS • USA
MOUSEY • 1974 • Petrie Daniel • TVM • USA, CND • CAT AND MOUSE (UKN)
MOUSIE COME HOME • 1946 • Culhane James • ANS • USA
MOUSIER HERMAN • 1955 • Tendlar Dave • ANS • USA
MOUSQUETAIRE DE LA REINE, LE • 1909 • Melies Georges • FRN
MOUSQUETAIRES DE LA REINE, LES • 1903 • Melies Georges • FRN • QUEEN'S MUSKETEERS, THE (USA) ○ MUSKETEERS OF THE QUEEN, THE
MOUSSAILLON, LE • 1941 • Gourguet Jean • FRN
MOUSSORGSKI see **MUSSORGSKII** • 1950
MOUSTACHU, LE • 1986 • Chaussois Dominique • FRN
MOUTAHAM AL BARI, AL • 1928 • Badri Ayoub • SYR
MOUTAMARRED, AL • 1968 • Khalifa Omar • TNS • REBELLE, LE ○ MUTAMARRID, AL– ○ REBEL, THE
MOUTAMARRIDOUNE, AL • 1968 • Saleh Tewfik • EGY • REBELS, THE ○ MUTAMARRIDUN, AL–
MOUTARADA GHARAMIA • 1968 • Hafez Magdy • EGY • LOVE CHASE, THE
MOUTARDE ME MONTE AU NEZ, LA • 1974 • Zidi Claude • FRN • FRENCH MUSTARD ○ LUCKY PIERRE
MOUTH AGAPE, THE see **GUEULE OUVERTE, LA** • 1973
MOUTH ORGAN JACK • 1917 • *Kerrigan J. Warren* • USA
MOUTH ORGAN SOLO • 1928 • *British Sound Film Production* • SHT • UKN • MUSICAL MEDLEY NO.6
MOUTH TO MOUTH • 1978 • Duigan John • ASL
MOUTHPIECE, THE • 1932 • Flood James, Nugent Elliott • USA
MOUTHS AND RABBITS • 1977 • Barakat • EGY
MOUTOI TSEMUI • 1990 • Wu Ma • HKG
MOUTON, LE • 1960 • Chevalier Pierre • FRN
MOUTON A CINQ PATTES, LE • 1954 • Verneuil Henri • FRN • SHEEP HAS FIVE LEGS, THE
MOUTON ENRAGE, LE • 1908 • Cohl Emile • ANS • FRN
MOUTON ENRAGE, LE • 1974 • Deville Michel • FRN, ITL • MONTONE INFURIATO, IL (ITL) ○ LOVE AT THE TOP (USA) ○ ENRAGED SHEEP, THE ○ FRENCH WAY, THE ○ SEDUCER, THE
MOUTON NOIR, LE • 1979 • Moscardo Jean-Pierre • FRN
MOUTONNET • 1936 • Sti Rene • FRN • AVENTURE DE M. MOUTONNET, L' ○ MOUTONNET A PARIS
MOUTONNET A PARIS see **MOUTONNET** • 1936
MOUTONS DE PANURGE, LES • 1960 • Girault Jean • FRN
MOUTONS DE PRAXOS, LES see **A L'AUBE DU TROISIEME JOUR** • 1962
MOUVEMENT DESJARDINS EN ACTION, LE • 1963 • Regnier Michel • DCS • CND
MOUVEMENT IMAGE PAR IMAGE, LE see **ANIMATED MOTION** • 1977
MOUVEMENTS INTRAPROTOPLASMIQUES DE L'ELODEE CANADENSIS • 1931 • Painleve Jean • SHT • FRN
MOVE • 1970 • Rosenberg Stuart • USA
MOVE ALONG • 1926 • Taurog Norman • SHT • USA
MOVE OF THE WHITE QUEEN • 1972 • Sadovsky Viktor • USS • WHITE QUEEN TO MOVE
MOVE ON • 1903 • Porter Edwin S. • USA
MOVE ON • 1917 • Roach Hal • SHT • USA
MOVE OVER • 1917 • Clements Roy • SHT • USA
MOVE OVER, DARLING • 1963 • Gordon Michael • USA
MOVED TO TEARS see **NAKASERUZE** • 1965
MOVEITE, A NEW HUSTLING POWDER • 1910 • *Walturdaw* • UKN
MOVEMENT MOVEMENT, THE • 1969 • Parsons Bruce • DCS • UKN, FRN
MOVEMENT PERPETUEL • 1949 • Jutra Claude, Brault Michel • CND
MOVERS AND SHAKERS • 1985 • Asher William • USA
MOVIDA CHUECA, UNA • 1955 • Gonzalez Rogelio A. • MXC
MOVIE, A • 1958 • Conner Bruce • SHT • USA
MOVIE, THE • 1922 • Roach Hal • SHT • USA
MOVIE AND BREAKFAST • 1977 • Steinhardt Alfred • ISR
MOVIE BUG, THE • 1920 • Moore Vin • SHT • USA
MOVIE CLIP see **MOZIKLIP** • 1988
MOVIE CRAZY • 1932 • Bruckman Clyde • USA
MOVIE CRITIC, THE • 1961 • Jordan Larry • USA
MOVIE DUMMY, THE • 1918 • Roach Hal • SHT • USA
MOVIE FANS • 1915 • *Sullivan Billy* • USA
MOVIE FANS • 1920 • Kenton Erle C. • SHT • USA
MOVIE-GO-ROUND • 1949 • Weiss Fred • UKN
MOVIE HERO, A • 1920 • Fishback Fred C. • SHT • USA
MOVIE HOUND, THE • 1927 • Sandrich Mark • SHT • USA
MOVIE HOUSE MASSACRE • 1984 • Raley Alice • USA
MOVIE MAD • 1931 • *Iwerks Ub (P)* • ANS • USA
MOVIE MADNESS • 1920 • *Cohn Productions* • SHT • USA
MOVIE MADNESS • 1952 • Rasinski Connie • ANS • USA
MOVIE MAKER, THE • 1967 • Leytes Joseph • TVM • USA
MOVIE MAKERS, THE see **HOLLYWOOD DREAMING** • 1987
MOVIE MANIACS • 1936 • Lord Del • SHT • USA
MOVIE MEMORIES • 1948 • Shepherd Horace • UKN
MOVIE MONEY • 1916 • Dickson Charles • USA
MOVIE MOVIE • 1978 • Donen Stanley • USA
MOVIE MURDERER, THE • 1970 • Sagal Boris • TVM • USA
MOVIE NIGHT • 1929 • Foster Lewis R. • SHT • USA
MOVIE NUT see **FILM JOHNNIE, A** • 1914
MOVIE NUT, THE • 1915 • *Banner* • USA
MOVIE PESTS • 1944 • Jason Will • SHT • USA
MOVIE PHONY NEWS • 1938 • Lovy Alex • ANS • USA
MOVIE QUEEN, THE • 1914 • *Warner'S Features* • USA
MOVIE QUEEN, THE • 1919 • *Shields Ernie* • SHT • USA
MOVIE RIOT, A • 1919 • Hutchinson Craig • SHT • USA
MOVIE RUSH • 1976 • Fabbri Ottavio • ITL • FEBBRE DEL CINEMA, LA
MOVIE STAR, A • 1916 • Fishback Fred C. • SHT • USA
MOVIE STAR, AMERICAN STYLE OR, LSD, I HATE YOU • 1967 • Zugsmith Albert • USA
MOVIE STRUCK • 1916 • Fahrney Milton • USA
MOVIE STRUCK • 1933 • *Mintz Charles (P)* • ANS • USA
MOVIE STRUCK see **PICK A STAR** • 1937
MOVIE TOWN • 1931 • Sennett Mack • USA
MOVIELAND • 1926 • Taurog Norman • SHT • USA
MOVIEMAKERS • 1971 • Pearse John • USA
MOVIES, THE • 1920 • *Henry Gale* • SHT • USA
MOVIES, THE • 1925 • Arbuckle Roscoe • USA
MOVIES ARE ADVENTURE • 1949 • *Universal* • SHT • USA
MOVIES TAKE A HOLIDAY, THE • 1944 • *Weinberg Herman G./ Richter Hans (P)* • USA
MOVIETONE FOLLIES OF 1929, THE (UKN) see **FOX MOVIETONE FOLLIES OF 1929** • 1929
MOVIN' ON see **IN TANDEM** • 1974
MOVIN' PITCHERS • 1913 • *Selig* • USA
MOVING • 1917 • Jackson Harry • SHT • USA
MOVING • 1988 • Metter Alan • USA
MOVING A PIANO • 1914 • Lyndhurst F. L. • UKN
MOVING AWEIGH • 1944 • *Popeye* • ANS • USA
MOVING DAY • 1907 • Williamson James • UKN
MOVING DAY • 1917 • Chaudet Louis W. • SHT • USA
MOVING DAY • 1919 • *De Haven Carter* • SHT • USA
MOVING DAY • 1936 • Sharpsteen Ben • ANS • USA
MOVING EXPERIENCE, A • 1975 • Dorn Rudi • CND
MOVING FINGER, THE • 1912 • *Branscombe Lily* • USA
MOVING FINGER, THE • 1916 • MacDonald Donald • SHT • USA
MOVING FINGER, THE • 1964 • Moyer Larry • USA
MOVING GUEST, THE • 1927 • *Alt Al* • USA
MOVING HAZARD, HTE see **LONG HOLE, THE** • 1924
MOVING IN • 1908 • Collins Alf? • UKN
MOVING IN see **FIRSTBORN** • 1984
MOVING INTO SOCIETY (UKN) see **MOUNTAIN MOONLIGHT** • 1941
MOVING MELBOURNE • 1906 • *Tait J./ Tait N. (P)* • ASL
MOVING MILLIONS • 1948 • Arthur Noel • UKN
MOVING MOTHER • 1913 • *Ramo* • USA
MOVING MOUNTAINS • 1980 • Sky Laura • DOC • CND
MOVING ON • 1974 • Mason Richard • ASL
MOVING ON see **UPPBROTT** • 1948
MOVING OUT • 1982 • Pattinson Michael • ASL
MOVING PERSPECTIVES • 1968 • Sen Mrinal • DOC • IND
MOVING PICTURE COWBOY, THE • 1914 • Mix Tom • USA
MOVING PICTURE GIRL, THE • 1913 • *Excelsior* • USA
MOVING PICTURE MAN, THE see **CINE SOY YO, EL** • 1977
MOVING PICTURE REHEARSAL, THE • 1910 • Bouwmeester Theo? • UKN
MOVING SAND see **RUCHOME PIASKI** • 1969
MOVING SPIRIT • 1951 • Privett Bob • ANS • UKN
MOVING STATICS • 1969 • Cantrill Arthur, Cantrill Corinne • DOC • UKN
MOVING TARGET • 1988 • Thomson Chris • TVM • USA
MOVING TARGET see **BERSAGLIO MOBILE** • 1967
MOVING TARGET, THE (UKN) see **HARPER** • 1966
MOVING TARGETS • 1983 • Trent John • MTV • CND
MOVING VANITIES • 1939 • Brock Lou • SHT • USA
MOVING VIOLATION • 1970 • *Kirt Films International* • USA
MOVING VIOLATION • 1976 • Dubin Charles S. • USA
MOVING VIOLATIONS • 1985 • Israel Neal • USA
MOVINI'S VENOM see **NIGHT OF THE COBRA WOMAN** • 1972
MOVIOLA BLUES • Ortiz Leon • SHT • USA
MOVITONE FOLLIES OF 1930 (UKN) see **FOX MOVIETONE FOLLIES OF 1930** • 1930
MOW MI ROCKEFELLER • 1990 • Szarak Waldemar • PLN • CALL ME ROCKEFELLER
MOY DOBRY CHELOVYEK • 1974 • Batyrov Ravil • USS • MY GOOD MAN
MOYEN AGE FRANCAIS, LE • 1955 • Vilardebo Carlos • SHT • FRN
MOYORU OZORA • 1940 • *Tsuburaya Eiji* • DOC • JPN
MOYSE ET COHEN, BUSINESSMEN • 1931 • Greville Edmond T. • SHT • FRN
MOYSE, MARCHAND D'HABITS • 1931 • Greville Edmond T. • SHT • FRN
MOYURU OZORA see **MOERU OZORA** • 1940
MOYURU WAKAMONOTACHI see **YAMA NO SANKA: MOYURU WAKAMONO-TACHI** • 1962
MOZAMBIQUE • 1964 • Lynn Robert • UKN
MOZART see **WEN DIE GOTTER LIEBEN** • 1942
MOZART AND SALIERI see **MOTSART I SALYERI** • 1962
MOZART -AUFZEICHNUNGEN EINER JUGEND • 1976 • Kirschner Klaus • FRG
MOZART BROTHERS, THE see **BRODERNA MOZART** • 1986
MOZART IN LOVE • 1975 • Rappaport Mark • USA
MOZART IN PRAG -DON GIOVANNI 67 • 1968 • Esterer Wolfgang • DOC • FRG • MOZART IN PRAGUE -DON GIOVANNI 67
MOZART IN PRAGUE -DON GIOVANNI 67 see **MOZART IN PRAG -DON GIOVANNI 67** • 1968
MOZART RONDO • 1949 • Whitney John • SHT • USA
MOZART STORY, THE • 1948 • Wisbar Frank • USA
MOZART STORY, THE (USA) see **WEN DIE GOTTER LIEBEN** • 1942
MOZART (USA) see **WHOM THE GODS LOVE** • 1936
MOZDA DIOGEN • 1968 • Dragic Nedeljko • ANS • YGS • DIOGENES PERHAPS ○ PERHAPS DIOGENES
MOZGOKEPIPARI • 1936 • HNG • MYSTERIOUS STRANGER, THE (USA)
MOZIKLIP • 1988 • Timar Peter • HNG • MOVIE CLIP
MOZNOSTI DIALOGU • 1982 • Svankmajer Jan • ANS • CZC • DIMENSIONS OF DIALOGUE
MOZO NO.13, EL • 1941 • Torres-Rios Leopoldo • ARG
MOZU • 1961 • Shibuya Minoru • JPN • SHRIKES, THE
MRAV DOBRA SRCA • 1965 • Marks Aleksandar, Jutrisa Vladimir • YGS • KIND-HEARTED ANT, THE (USA) ○ GOOD-HEARTED ANT, THE
MRAVENCI NESOU SMRT • 1985 • Brynych Zbynek • CZC • ANTS BRING DEATH
MRAVNOST NADRE VSE • 1937 • Fric Martin • CZC • MORALITY ABOVE ALL
MRIGAYAA • 1976 • Sen Mrinal • IND • ROYAL HUNT, THE ○ DEER HUNT
MRKACEK CIKO • 1982 • Plivova-Simkova Vera, Kralova Drahomira • CZC • CIKO THE BLINKER ○ BLINKER CIKO
MRLJA NA SAVJESTI • 1968 • Vukotic Dusan • SHT • YGS • STAIN ON THE CONSCIENCE, A
MROWCZE SZLAKI • 1956 • Stanislawski S., Wozniakowski Roman • PLN • ANTS, THE
MRS. AHOU'S HUSBAND see **SHOHAR-E-AHOU RHANOM** • 1968
MRS. ALDEN'S AWAKENING • 1912 • *Francis Evelyn* • USA
MRS. ANDERSSON'S CHARLIE see **ANDERSSONSKANS KALLE** • 1922
MRS. ANDERSSON'S CHARLIE see **ANDERSSONSKANS KALLE** • 1934
MRS. ANDERSSON'S CHARLIE see **ANDERSSONSKANS KALLE** • 1950
MRS. ANDERSSON'S CHARLIE AND HIS NEW PRANKS see **ANDERSSONSKANS KALLE PA NYA UPPTAG** • 1923
MRS. BALFAME • 1917 • Powell Frank • USA
MRS. BARGAINDAY'S BABY • 1910 • Melies Gaston • USA
MRS. BARNACLE BILL • 1934 • French Lloyd • SHT • USA
MRS. BARRINGTON • 1972 • Vincent Chuck • USA
MRS. BARRINGTON'S HOUSE PARTY • 1910 • *Vitagraph* • USA
MRS. BIFFIN'S DEMISE • 1911 • *Yankee* • USA
MRS. BILLINGTON'S FIRST CASE • 1914 • *Essanay* • USA
MRS. BLACK IS BACK • 1914 • Dawley J. Searle • USA
MRS. BROWN FROM CHICAGO see **MARYS GROSSES GEHEIMNIS** • 1928
MRS. BROWN GOES HOME TO HER MOTHER • 1906 • Williamson James • UKN
MRS. BROWN YOU'VE GOT A LOVELY DAUGHTER • 1968 • Swimmer Saul • UKN
MRS. BROWN'S BABY • 1912 • *American* • USA
MRS. BROWN'S BURGLAR • 1913 • *Ward Carrie Clark* • USA
MRS. B'S LAPSE see **FRU BONNETS FELSTEG** • 1917
MRS. CAPPER'S BIRTHDAY • 1985 • Ockrent Mike • MTV • UKN
MRS. CARFAX THE CLEVER see **CLEVER MRS. CARFAX, THE** • 1917
MRS. CARTER'S CAMPAIGN • 1913 • *Burton Charlotte* • USA
MRS. CARTER'S NECKLACE • 1912 • Brooke Van Dyke • USA
MRS. CASE • 1969 • Lasry Pierre • CND
MRS. CASEY'S GORILLA • 1913 • Dillon Eddie • USA
MRS. CASSELL'S PROFESSION see **STRIPED STOCKING GANG, THE** • 1915
MRS. COLUMBO • 1979 • Sagal Boris • TVM • USA
MRS. COOK'S COOKING • 1915 • *Kirtley Virginia* • USA
MRS. CORNEY MAKES TEA • 1913 • Noy Wilfred • UKN
MRS. CRANSTON'S JEWELS • 1912 • *Cornwall Blanche* • USA
MRS. DANE'S DANGER • 1916 • North Wilfred • USA
MRS. DANE'S DEFENCE • 1915 • Taylor Stanner E. V. • USA
MRS. DANE'S DEFENCE • 1933 • Bramble A. V. • UKN
MRS. DANE'S DEFENSE • 1918 • Ford Hugh • USA
MRS. DANVERS' DIVORCE • 1911 • *Yankee* • USA
MRS. DEATH (USA) see **SENORA MUERTE, LA** • 1968
MRS. DELAFIELD WANTS TO MARRY • 1986 • Schaefer George • USA
MRS. DERY see **DERYNE** • 1951
MRS. DERY, WHERE ARE YOU? see **DERYNE, HOL VAN?** • 1975
MRS. DULSKA'S MORALS see **MORALSKA PANI DULSKE** • 1958
MRS. 'ENRI 'AWKINS • 1912 • *Costello Maurice* • USA
MRS. ERRICKER'S REPUTATION • 1920 • Hepworth Cecil M. • UKN
MRS. FITZHERBERT • 1947 • Tully Montgomery • UKN
MRS. GAYLIFE'S VISITORS • 1911 • *American* • USA
MRS. GIBBONS' BOYS • 1962 • Varnel Max • UKN
MRS. GRAY • 1974 • Shebib Donald • CND
MRS. GREEN'S MISTAKE • 1916 • Curtis Allen • SHT • USA
MRS. GUNNESS • 1908 • *Kalem* • USA
MRS. HANKA'S DIARY see **PAMIETNIK PANI HANKI** • 1963
MRS. HILTON'S JEWELS • 1913 • Martin E. A. • USA
MRS. JARR AND THE BEAUTY TREATMENT • 1915 • Davenport Harry • USA
MRS. JARR AND THE SOCIETY CIRCUS • 1915 • Davenport Harry • USA
MRS. JARR'S AUCTION BRIDGE • 1915 • Davenport Harry • USA
MRS. JOHN BULL PREPARED • 1918 • *M.o.i. Cinematograph Dept* • SHT • UKN
MRS. JONES' BIRTHDAY • 1909 • *Arbuckle Roscoe "fatty"* • USA
MRS. JONES ENTERTAINS • 1909 • Griffith D. W. • USA
MRS. JONES' LOVER OR I WANT MY HAT • 1909 • Griffith D. W. • USA
MRS JONES' REST FARM • 1949 • Donnelly Eddie • ANS • USA
MRS. JUGGINS • 1911 • *Walturdaw* • UKN
MRS. LACY'S LEGACY • 1913 • *Powers* • USA
MRS. LADYBUG • 1940 • Ising Rudolf • ANS • USA
MRS. LE TARE LETS APARTMENTS • 1913 • Kellino W. P. • UKN
MRS. LEFFINGWELL'S BOOT see **MRS. LEFFINGWELL'S BOOTS** • 1919
MRS. LEFFINGWELL'S BOOTS • 1919 • Edwards Walter • USA • MRS. LEFFINGWELL'S BOOT
MRS. LEONARD MISBEHAVES see **LADY AND THE MOB, THE** • 1939
MRS. LIRRIPER'S LEGACY • 1912 • *Vitagraph* • USA
MRS. LIRRIPER'S LODGERS • 1912 • Brooke Van Dyke • USA
MRS. LORING'S SECRET (UKN) see **IMPERFECT LADY, THE** • 1947
MRS. LOWELL THOMAS -FUR FARMER • 1944 • *O'Brien Joseph/ Mead Thomas (P)* • SHT • USA
MRS. MADAM MANAGER • 1917 • Curtis Allen • SHT • USA
MRS. MALONEY'S FORTUNE • 1914 • Marston Theodore • USA

MRS. MANLY'S BABY • 1914 • *Beery Wallace* • USA
MRS. MANNING'S WEEKEND see **DEATH GAME** • 1977
MRS. MATTHEWS, DRESSMAKER • 1912 • *Imp* • USA
MRS. MAY COMEDIES • 1925 • Hiscott Leslie • SER • UKN
MRS. MEPHISTOPHELES • 1929 • Croise Hugh • UKN
MRS. MIKE • 1949 • King Louis • USA
MRS. MINIVER • 1942 • Wyler William • USA
MRS. MORTON'S BIRTHDAY • 1913 • *Panzer Paul* • USA
MRS. MURPHY'S COOKS • 1915 • Mix Tom • USA
MRS. O'LEARY'S COW • 1938 • Donnelly Eddie • ANS • USA
MRS. O'MALLEY AND MR. MALONE • 1950 • Taurog Norman • USA
MRS. PARKINGTON • 1944 • Garnett Tay • USA
MRS PEABODY see **NUMBER THIRTEEN** • 1922
MRS. PEYTON'S PEARLS • 1914 • *Kalem* • USA
MRS. PINKHURST'S PROXY • 1914 • *Chamberlin Riley* • USA
MRS. PLUM'S PUDDING • 1915 • Christie Al, Frazee Edwin • USA
MRS. POLLIFAX -SPY • 1971 • Martinson Leslie H. • USA • UNEXPECTED MRS. POLLIFAX, THE
MRS. PRUNE'S BOARDING HOUSE • 1915 • Curtis Allen • USA
MRS. PYM OF SCOTLAND YARD • 1939 • Elles Fred • UKN
MRS. R.: DEATH AMONG FRIENDS see **DEATH AMONG FRIENDS** • 1975
MRS. RABBIT'S HUSBAND TAKES THE SHILLING • 1913 • Stow Percy • UKN
MRS. RAFFLES NEE PIMPLE • 1915 • Evans Fred, Evans Joe • UKN
MRS. RANDOLPH'S NEW SECRETARY • 1915 • Coyle Walter • USA
MRS. REYNOLDS • 1918 • Ashley Arthur • USA
MRS. REYNOLDS NEEDS A NURSE • 1965 • Anderson Robert • DOC • CND
MRS. RICHARD DARE • 1910 • *Solax* • USA
MRS. RIVINGTON'S PRIDE • 1910 • *Lubin* • USA
MRS. ROMANA'S SCENARIO • 1914 • *Edison* • USA
MRS. R'S DAUGHTER • 1979 • Curtis Dan • USA
MRS. RYAN'S DRAMA CLASS • 1969 • Rubbo Michael • CND
MRS. SCRUBB'S DISCOVERY • 1914 • Furniss Harry • UKN
MRS. SHARP AND MISS FLAT • 1913 • *Crystal* • USA
MRS. SIMS SERVES ON THE JURY • 1912 • *Kalem* • USA
MRS. SLACKER • 1918 • Henley Hobart • USA
MRS. SMITHERS' BOARDING SCHOOL • 1907 • *Bitzer Billy (Ph)* • USA
MRS. SOFFEL • 1984 • Armstrong Gillian • USA
MRS. STIGGINS' WASHING PARTY • 1904 • *Cricks & Sharp* • UKN
MRS. STONE'S THING • 1970 • Robertson Joseph F. • USA
MRS. SUNDANCE • 1974 • Chomsky Marvin • TVM • USA
MRS. SUNDANCE RIDES AGAIN see **WANTED: THE SUNDANCE WOMAN** • 1976
MRS. TEMPLE'S TELEGRAM • 1920 • Cruze James • USA
MRS. THOMPSON • 1919 • Wilson Rex • UKN
MRS. TRENWITH COMES HOME • 1914 • *Essanay* • USA
MRS. TWARDOWSKA see **PANI TWARDOWSKA** • 1956
MRS. UPTON'S DEVICE • 1913 • Castle James W. • USA
MRS. USCHYCK • 1973 • Quinn • SHT • FRN
MRS. VAN ALDEN'S JEWEL • 1915 • Vale Travers • USA
MRS. VAN RUYTER'S STRATAGEM • 1914 • *Thanhouser* • USA
MRS. VERSUS MISTRESS • 1986 • Alter Naftali • ISR
MRS. WIGGS OF THE CABBAGE PATCH • 1914 • *Michelena Beatriz* • USA
MRS. WIGGS OF THE CABBAGE PATCH • 1919 • Ford Hugh • USA
MRS. WIGGS OF THE CABBAGE PATCH • 1934 • Taurog Norman • USA
MRS. WIGGS OF THE CABBAGE PATCH • 1942 • Murphy Ralph • USA
MRTVA LADJA • 1972 • Ranfl Rajko • YGS • GHOST SHIP
MRTVI ZIJI • 1922 • Kolar J. S. • CZC • DEAD ARE ALIVE, THE
MRTVY MEZI ZIVYMI • 1947 • Zeman Borivoj • CZC • DEAD AMONG THE LIVING
MS.45 see **ANGEL OF VENGEANCE** • 1980
MS. DON JUAN see **DON JUAN 1973, OU SI DON JUAN ETAIT UNE FEMME** • 1973
MS MAGNIFICENT • 1979 • Sherman Joe • USA • MISS MAGNIFICENT
MS RHYMNEY VALLEY • 1986 • Francis Karl • DOC • IRL
M'SIEUR LA CAILLE • 1955 • Pergament Andre • FRN • JESUS LA CAILLE ○ MONSIEUR LA CAILLE ○ PARASITES, THE
MSTITEL • 1959 • Stekly Karel • CZC • AVENGER, THE
MT. EREBUS DISASTER • Keir John • NZL
MT. GASSAN see **GASSAN** • 1979
MT.HAKKODA see **HAKKODA-SAN** • 1976
MT. PAEKDU • NKR
MTB: MALTA WORLD WAR 2 see **HELL BOATS** • 1969
MUAGEZA, EL • 1963 • el Imam Hassan • EGY • MIRACLE, THE
MUALLIM, AL- • 1974 • Hamada Khalid • SYR • INSTITUTEUR, L'
MUAMARA • 1953 • el Sheikh Kamal • EGY • COMPLOT
MUASKARI AL-BANAT see **MOASKAR EL BANAT** • 1967
MUCEDNICI LASKY • 1966 • Nemec Jan • CZC • MARTYRS OF LOVE
MUCH ADO ABOUT -!! • 1912 • Aylott Dave? • UKN
MUCH ADO ABOUT LITTLE BARBARA see **AWANTURA O BASIE** • 1960
MUCH ADO ABOUT LITTLE BASIA see **AWANTURA O BASIE** • 1960
MUCH ADO ABOUT MOUSING • 1964 • Jones Charles M. • ANS • USA
MUCH ADO ABOUT MURDER see **THEATRE OF BLOOD** • 1973
MUCH ADO ABOUT MUTTON • 1947 • Sparber I. • ANS • USA
MUCH ADO ABOUT NOTHING • 1909 • *Essanay* • USA
MUCH ADO ABOUT NOTHING • 1913 • *White Pearl* • USA
MUCH ADO ABOUT NOTHING • 1940 • Rasinski Connie • ANS • USA
MUCH ADO ABOUT NOTHING see **VIEL LARM UM NICHTS** • 1964
MUCH ADO ABOUT NUTTING • 1953 • Jones Charles M. • ANS • USA
MUCH KISSED BUT NEVER FORGOTTEN see **VIEL GEKUSST UND NICHT VERGESSEN** • 1966
MUCH MYSTERY • 1926 • Roberts Stephen • SHT • USA
MUCH NEEDED LESSON, A • 1915 • *Martin Rea* • USA
MUCH NEEDED REST, A • 1919 • Goldaine Mark • SHT • USA
MUCH OBLIGED • 1917 • Wright Fred E. • SHT • USA
MUCH PLEASURES see **MUITO PRAZER** • 1980
MUCH TOO SHY • 1942 • Varnel Marcel • UKN
MUCH WANTED BABY, A • 1913 • *Frontier* • USA
MUCH WORRY ABOUT A LITTLE BOY see **BOLSHIYE KHLOPOTY IZ-ZA MALENKOVO MALCHIKA** • 1968
MUCHACHA DE LAS BRAGAS DE ORO, LA • 1979 • Aranda Vicente • SPN • GIRL IN THE GOLDEN KNICKERS, THE ○ GIRL IN THE GOLDEN PANTIES, THE
MUCHACHA DE MOSCU, LA • 1940 • Neville Edgar • SPN, ITL
MUCHACHA DEL NILO, LA • 1967 • Elorrieta Jose Maria • SPN, FRG • EMERALD OF ARTATAMA, THE (UKN) ○ GIRL OF THE NILE, THE (USA)
MUCHACHADA DE A BORDO, LA • 1967 • Cahen Enrique • ARG • PRANKS ON BOARD
MUCHACHAS BANADOSE EN EL LAGO • 1897 • Duran Manuel Trujillo • VNZ
MUCHACHAS DE AZUL • 1957 • Lazaga Pedro • SPN
MUCHACHAS DE BAGDAD (SPN) see **BABES IN BAGDAD** • 1952
MUCHACHAS DE UNIFORME • 1950 • Crevenna Alfredo B. • MXC
MUCHACHAS EN VACACIONES • 1957 • Elorrieta Jose Maria • SPN
MUCHACHAS QUE TRABAJAN • 1961 • Cortes Fernando • MXC • CUATRO CURVAS PELIGROSAS
MUCHACHITA DE CHICLANA • 1926 • Ferreyra Jose • ARG
MUCHACHITA DE VALLADOLID, UNA • 1958 • Amadori Luis Cesar • SPN
MUCHACHO ALEGRE, EL • 1947 • Galindo Alejandro • MXC • CHEERFUL LAD, THE
MUCHACHO COMO YO, UN • 1968 • Carreras Enrique • ARG • BOY LIKE ME, A
MUCHACHO DE BUENOS AIRES, UN • 1944 • Irigoyen Julio • ARG
MUCHACHO DE DURANGO, EL • 1961 • Martinez Arturo • MXC
MUCHACHOS DE ANTES NO USABAN ARSENICO, LOS • 1975 • Suarez Jose Martinez • ARG • YESTERDAY'S GUYS USED NO ARSENIC
MUCHACHOS DE LA CIUDAD • 1937 • Ferreyra Jose • ARG
MUCHACHOS IMPACIENTES • 1965 • Saraceni Julio • MXC, ARG
MUCHE • 1924 • Peguy Robert • FRN
MUCHI TO HADA • 1967 • Kishi Shintaro • JPN • WHIP AND SKIN
MUCHLY ENGAGED • 1913 • Smalley Phillips • USA
MUCHLY MARRIED • 1916 • Curtis Allen • SHT • USA
MUCHO LOCOS • 1966 • McKimson Robert • ANS • USA
MUCHO MOUSE • 1957 • Hanna William, Barbera Joseph • ANS • USA
MUCHOTLUK • 1967 • Piwowski Marek • PLN • FLY-KILLER, THE
MUCKE, DIE • 1954 • Reisch Walter • FRG
MUCKER, OS • 1980 • Bodansky Jorge, Gauer Wolf • BRZ • MUCKER, THE
MUCKER, THE see **MUCKER, OS** • 1980
MUD • 1918 • *Griffith Ray* • SHT • USA
MUD • 1963 • Cantrill Arthur, Cantrill Corinne • DOC • ASL
MUD see **STICK UP, THE** • 1978
MUD AND MATRIMONY • 1915 • *Taylor Gladys* • USA
MUD AND SAND • 1923 • Pratt Gilbert • USA
MUD AND SOLDIERS see **TSUCHI TO HEITAI** • 1939
MUD BATH ELOPEMENT, THE • 1914 • *Leonard Robert* • USA
MUD CHRIST see **CRISTO DE LAMA** • 1968
MUD COVERED CITY • 1963 • Taborsky Vaclav • CZC
MUD CURE, THE • 1916 • *Hamilton Lloyd V.* • SHT • USA
MUD HONEY see **ROPE OF FLESH** • 1965
MUD LARK see **PURCHASE PRICE, THE** • 1932
MUD LARKS • 1899 • Hepworth Cecil M. • UKN
MUD MAIDENS • 1970 • *Able Film Co* • USA
MUD RIVER see **DORO NO KAWA** • 1981
MUDANNASSA, AL- • 1974 • Hamada Khalid • SYR
MUDAR DE VIDA • 1967 • Rocha Paulo • PRT • CHANGE IN LIFE, A ○ CHANGING LIFE
MUDDLE IN HORSE THIEVES, A • 1913 • *Mix Tom* • USA
MUDDLED AFFAIR, A • 1915 • *Horseshoe* • UKN
MUDDLED BILL POSTER, THE • 1901 • *Paul R. W.* • UKN
MUDDLED DEAL see **BLONDE CHEAT** • 1938
MUDDLED MILLINERY • 1915 • *Wright Bertie* • UKN
MUDDLED NOTES • 1979 • Dyulgerov Georgi • BUL
MUDDLETON FIRE BRIGADE, THE • 1914 • Birch Cecil • UKN
MUDDY RIVER see **DORO NO KAWA** • 1981
MUDDY ROMANCE • 1913 • Sennett Mack, Nicholls George • USA
MUDDY UNIFORM see **DORODARAKE NO SEIFUKU** • 1967
MUDDY WATER see **NIGORIE** • 1953
MUDDY WATER see **TRUBE WASSER** • 1960
MUDDY WATERS see **NIGORIE** • 1953
MUDDY WATERS RUN DOWN see **AGUAS BAJAN TURBIAS, LAS** • 1951
MUDE THEODOR, DER • 1918 • Peukert Leo • FRG
MUDE THEODOR, DER • 1936 • Harlan Veit • FRG
MUDE THEODOR, DER • 1957 • von Cziffra Geza • FRG
MUDE TOD, DER • 1921 • Lang Fritz • FRG • DESTINY (USA) ○ THREE LIGHTS, THE ○ BEYOND THE WALL ○ WEARY DEATH, THE ○ BETWEEN WORLDS ○ BETWEEN TWO WORLDS
MUDHNIBUN, AL- see **MUZNIBUN, AL** • 1976
MUDHONEY! see **ROPE OF FLESH** • 1965
MUDIL • 1974 • Francis Yussif • MTV • EGY • MODELE, UN
MUDIRU AL-FANNI, AL- • 1964 • Wahab Fatin Abdel • EGY • DIRECTEUR ARTISTIQUE, LE
MUDLARK, THE • 1950 • Negulesco Jean • UKN
MUDUNDU see **ESCLAVE BLANC, L'** • 1936
MUEDA, MEMORIA E MASSACRE • 1980 • Guerra Ruy • BRZ • MUEDA, MEMORY AND MASSACRE
MUEDA, MEMORY AND MASSACRE see **MUEDA, MEMORIA E MASSACRE** • 1980
MUELLE ROJO • 1989 • Urquieta Jose Luis • MXC • RED DOCKERS
MUERA-VIVA DON JUAN! • 1976 • Aznar Tomas • SPN
MUERE UNA MUJER • 1964 • Camus Mario • SPN
MUEROTO FALTA A LA CITA, EL • 1944 • Chenal Pierre • ARG
MUERT-LA-FAIM, LES • 1905-10 • Heuze Andre • FRN
MUERTA BLANCA see **COCAINE WARS** • 1985
MUERTE AL AMANECER • 1959 • Forn Josep Maria • SPN
MUERTE AL AMANECER • 1979 • Lombardi Francisco • VNZ, PRU • DEATH AT DAYBREAK ○ DEATH AT DAWN
MUERTE AL INVASOR • 1961 • Alea Tomas Gutierrez, Alvarez Santiago • DOC • CUB • DEATH TO THE INVADER
MUERTE BUSCA UN HOMBRE, LA • 1971 • Merino Jose Luis • SPN
MUERTE CIVIL • 1910 • Gallo Mario • ARG
MUERTE CIVIL, LA • 1917 • Mezzi Domingo • MXC
MUERTE CRUZO EL RIO BRACO, LA • 1985 • Name Hernando • MXC • DEATH CROSSED THE RIO BRAVO
MUERTE CUMPLE CONDENA • 1965 • Romero-Marchent Joaquin Luis • SPN
MUERTE DE MIKEL, LA • 1984 • Rebolledo Jose Angel, Uribe Imanol • SPN • DEATH OF MIKEL
MUERTE DE PIO BAROJA, LA • 1957 • Bardem Juan Antonio • SPN
MUERTE DE SEBASTIAN ARACHE Y SU POBRE ENTIERRO, LA • 1977 • Sarquis Nicolas • ARG
MUERTE DE UN BUROCRATA, LA • 1966 • Alea Tomas Gutierrez • CUB • DEATH OF A BUREAUCRAT (UKN)
MUERTE DE UN CICLISTA • 1955 • Bardem Juan Antonio • SPN, ITL • AGE OF INFIDELITY (USA) ○ EGOISTI, GLI (ITL) ○ DEATH OF A CYCLIST
MUERTE DE UN GALLERO, LA • 1977 • Hernandez Mario • MXC
MUERTE DE UN PRESIDENTE • 1977 • Madrid Jose Luis • SPN • COMANDO TXIQUIA
MUERTE DE UN PRESIDENTE, LA (SPN) see **PREZZO DEL POTERE, IL** • 1969
MUERTE DE UN QUINQUI, LA • 1975 • Klimovsky Leon • SPN
MUERTE DE VILLA, LA • 1973 • *Aguila* • MXC
MUERTE DEL CHE GUEVARA, LA see **CHE GUEVARA, EL** • 1968
MUERTE DEL ESCORPION, LA • 1975 • Herralde Gonzalo • SPN
MUERTE EN BIKINI, LA • 1966 • Martinez Arturo • MXC
MUERTE EN EL DESFILADERA, LA • 1958 • Urueta Chano • MXC
MUERTE EN EL PARAISO • 1979 • Katz Michel • VNZ • MURDER IN PARADISE
MUERTE EN ESTE JARDIN, LA (MXC) see **MORT EN CE JARDIN, LA** • 1956
MUERTE EN LA FERIA • 1960 • Martinez Arturo • MXC
MUERTE EN PRIMAVERA • 1965 • Iglesias Miguel • SPN
MUERTE ENAMORADA, LA • 1950 • Cortazar Ernesto • MXC • DEATH IN LOVE
MUERTE ES PUNTUAL, LA • 1965 • Vejar Sergio • MXC
MUERTE ESCUCHA, LE • 1970 • Topart Robert • VNZ • DEATH LISTENS
MUERTE ESPERA EN ATENAS, LA see **AGENTE 077 -MISSIONE BLOODY MARY** • 1965
MUERTE INCIERTA, LA • 1972 • Larraz Jose R. • SPN
MUERTE LLAMA A LAS DIEZ, LA • 1973 • Bosch Juan • SPN
MUERTE LLAMA OTRA VEZ, LA • 1964 • Madrid Jose Luis • SPN
MUERTE PASA LISTA, LA • 1959 • Curiel Federico • MXC
MUERTE RONDA A MONICA, LA • 1977 • Fernandez Ramon • SPN
MUERTE SE LLAMA MYRIAM, LA • 1966 • Martin Eugenio • SPN
MUERTE SILBA UN BLUES, LA • 1962 • Franco Jesus • SPN
MUERTE TENIA UN PRECIO, LA (SPN) see **PER QUALCHE DOLLARI IN PIU** • 1965
MUERTE VIAJA DEMASIADO, LA (SPN) see **UMORISMO NERO** • 1965
MUERTE VIVIENTE, LA (MXC) see **SNAKE PEOPLE** • 1968
MUERTE Y EL CRIMEN, LA • 1961 • Galindo Alejandro • MXC
MUERTE Y VIDA EN EL MORRILLO • 1971 • Valdes Oscar • DOC • CUB
MUERTO, EL • 1975 • Olivera Hector • ARG • DEAD ONE, THE
MUERTO ES UN VIVO, EL • 1953 • Blass Yago • ARG
MUERTO HACE LAS MALETAS, EL • 1971 • Franco Jesus • SPN, FRG • TODESRACHER, DER (FRG) ○ DEATH PACKS UP ○ DEATH AVENGER
MUERTO MURIO, EL • 1939 • Galindo Alejandro • MXC • DEAD MAN DIED, THE (USA)
MUERTOS DE MIEDO • 1957 • Salvador Jaime • MXC
MUERTOS DE RISA • 1957 • Fernandez Bustamente Adolfo • MXC • DEAD OF LAUGHTER
MUERTOS HABLAN, LOS • 1935 • Soria Gabriel • MXC • DEAD SPEAK, THE (USA)
MUERTOS, LA CARNE Y EL DIABLO, LOS • 1973 • Oliveira Jose Maria • SPN
MUERTOS NO HABLAN, LOS • 1956 • Salvador Jaime • MXC
MUERTOS NO PERDONAN, LOS • 1963 • Coll Julio • SPN • DEAD DON'T FORGIVE, THE
MUERTOS SI SALEN, LOS • 1976 • Lugo Alfredo • VNZ • WHEN THE DEAD APPEAR
MUET MELOMANE, LE • 1899 • Zecca Ferdinand • FRN
MUFF • 1914 • MacGregor Norval • USA
MUFFLED BELL, THE • 1915 • *Reliance* • USA
MUFID, AL- • 1976 • Laskri Amar • ALG • VENONS-EN AU FAIT
MUFLES, LES • 1928 • Peguy Robert • FRN
MUG TOWN see **MUGTOWN** • 1943
MUGAREM FI IJAZA • 1958 • Abu Saif Salah • EGY • THIEF ON HOLIDAY ○ MUJRIM FI AJAZA
MUGE • 1966 • Mirchev Vassil • BUL • YOUNG MEN, THE
MUGGABLE MARY, STREET COP • 1982 • Stern Sandor • TVM • USA
MUGGER, THE • 1958 • Berke William • USA
MUGGER, THE • 1975 • Lehman Robin • SHT • USA
MUGGINS • 1916 • Elfelt Clifford S. • SHT • USA
MUGGINS V.C. • 1909 • Aylott Dave • UKN

MUGGINS V.C. -THE DEFENCE OF KHUMA HOSPITAL, INDIA • 1912 • Aylott Dave • UKN
MUGGSY • 1919 • MacDonald Sherwood? • USA
MUGGSY BECOMES A HERO • 1910 • Griffith D. W., Powell Frank • USA
MUGGSY IN BAD • 1917 • Ray John • USA
MUGGSY IN SOCIETY • 1917 • Ray John • USA
MUGGSY'S FIRST SWEETHEART • 1910 • Griffith D. W. • USA
MUGGY-DOO BOYCAT • 1963 • Kneitel Seymour • ANS • USA
MUGHAL-E-ATAM • 1960 • Kapoor Prithviraj • IND
MUGHAMARAT SHUSHU • 1966 • Salman Mohammed • LBN • AVENTURES DE CHOUCHOU, LES
MUGHAMMARAT ANTAR WA ALBA • 1948 • Abu Saif Salah • EGY • ADVENTURES OF ANTAR AND ALBA, THE
MUGIBUE • 1955 • Toyoda Shiro • JPN • LOVE NEVER FAILS ○ WHEAT-WHISTLE ○ GRASS-WHISTLE
MUGSY'S GIRLS • 1985 • Brodie Kevin • USA • DELTA PI
MUGTOWN • 1943 • Taylor Ray • USA • MUG TOWN
MUGWUMP'S PAYING GUEST • 1911 • Wilson Frank? • UKN
MUHA • 1967 • Marks Aleksandar, Jutrisa Vladimir • ANS • YGS • FLY, THE (USA)
MUHAIR (USA) see **MUJER DE MI PADRE, LA** • 1967
MUHAMAD ALI THE GREATEST see **MUHAMMED ALI, THE GREATEST** • 1974
MUHAMMED ALI, THE GREATEST • 1974 • Klein William • DOC • FRN • MUHAMAD ALI THE GREATEST
MUHAMMEDAN CONSPIRACY, THE • 1914 • *Cruze James* • USA
MUHARRAJ EL KABIR, EL • 1951 • Shahin Youssef • EGY • GREAT CLOWN, THE ○ MUHARRIG AL-KABIR, AL-
MUHARRIG AL-KABIR, AL- see **MUHARRAJ EL KABIR, EL** • 1951
MUHER DE NADIE, LA • 1948 • Delgras Gonzalo • SPN
MUHLE IM SCHWARZWALD, DIE • 1934 • Berger Josef • FRG • IN EINEM KUHLEN GRUNDE
MUHLE IM SCHWARZWALDERTAL, DIE • 1953 • Kugelstadt Hermann • FRG
MUHLE VON SANSSOUCI, DIE • 1926 • Philippi Siegfried • FRG
MUHOMATSU NO ISSHO • 1943 • Inagaki Hiroshi • JPN • LIFE OF MATSU THE UNTAMED, THE ○ RICKSHAW MAN, THE ○ RICKSHAW MAN, OR THE LIFE OF RECKLESS MATSU
MUHOMATSU NO ISSHO • 1958 • Inagaki Hiroshi • JPN • RIKISHA MAN, THE (USA) ○ RICKSHAW MAN, THE
MUHOMATSU NO ISSHO • 1963 • Murayama Shinji • JPN • LIFE OF A RICKSHAW MAN, THE
MUHOORTHA NAAL • 1967 • Madhavan P. • IND • AUSPICIOUS DAY
MUHOUMONO GINPEI see **MOHOMONO GINPEI** • 1937
MUHSIN BEY • 1987 • Turgul Yavuz • TRK
MUHUDULIHINI • 1983 • Ariyaratna Sunil • SLN
MUHUR GOZLU KADIN • 1967 • Gultekin Sirri • TRK • DARK-EYED WOMAN, THE
MUIDER CIRCLE LIVES AGAIN, THE see **MUIDERKRINGHERLEEFT, DE** • 1949
MUIDERKRINGHERLEEFT, DE • 1949 • Haanstra Bert • SHT • NTH • MUIDER CIRCLE LIVES AGAIN, THE
MUIS HAMEL BIJ DEN CRIFFEUR • 1904 • Mullens Albert, Mullens Willy • NTH
MUITO PRAZER • 1980 • Neves David • BRZ • MUCH PLEASURES
MUJ BRACHA MA PRIMA BRACHU • 1975 • Strnad Stanislav • CZC • MY BROTHER HAS A BROTHER
MUJ PRITEL FABIAN • 1953 • Weiss Jiri • CZC • MY FRIEND THE GYPSY (UKN) ○ MY FRIEND FABIAN
MUJASEMEHA MEKHANDAD • 1976 • Shafaq Toryali • AFG • STATUES ARE LAUGHING, THE
MUJER • 1946 • Urueta Chano • MXC
MUJER, UNA • 1976 • Stagnaro Juan Jose • ARG • WOMAN, A
MUJER AJENA, LA • 1954 • Bustillo Oro Juan • MXC
MUJER AJENA, LA • 1988 • Quiroz Livio • VNZ • OTHER WOMAN, THE
MUJER CELOSA, LA • 1970 • Puig Jaime • SPN
MUJER CON MUJER • 1945 • Rowland William • MXC
MUJER CON PANTALONES, UNA see **LUISITO** • 1943
MUJER CON PASADO, UNA • 1948 • Sevilla Raphael J. • MXC
MUJER CUALQUIERA, UNA • 1949 • Gil Rafael • SPN
MUJER DE A SIES LITROS, LA • 1966 • Gonzalez Rogelio A. • MXC
MUJER DE CABARET, UNA • 1974 • Lazaga Pedro • SPN
MUJER DE DOS CARAS, LA • 1955 • Delgado Miguel M. • MXC
MUJER DE FUEGO • 1988 • Mitrotti Mario • CLM, MXC, VNZ • WOMAN OF FIRE
MUJER DE FUEGO, LA see **SANDRA** • 1952
MUJER DE LA CALLE, UNA • 1939 • Barth-Moglia Luis • ARG
MUJER DE LA TIERRA CALIENTE, LA • 1978 • Forque Jose Maria • SPN
MUJER DE MEDIANOCHE • 1949 • Urruchua Victor • MXC
MUJER DE MI PADRE, LA • 1967 • Bo Armando • ARG, UKN • MUHAIR (USA) ○ MY FATHER'S WIFE
MUJER DE NADIE, LA • 1937 • Sequeyro Adela • MXC • NOBODY'S WOMAN
MUJER DE ORIENTE, UNA • 1946 • Orol Juan • MXC
MUJER DE OTRO, LA • 1967 • Gil Rafael • SPN • ANOTHER MAN'S WOMAN
MUJER DE TODOS, LA • 1946 • Bracho Julio • MXC
MUJER DECENTE, UNA • 1950 • de Anda Raul • MXC
MUJER DEL CARNICERO, LA • 1968 • Rodriguez Ismael, Urueta Chano • MXC • BUTCHER'S WIFE, THE
MUJER DEL GATO, LA • 1970 • Grinella Juan Carlo • SPN, ITL • FEMALE ANIMAL (USA)
MUJER DEL LEON, LA • 1951 • Lugones Mario C. • ARG
MUJER DEL MINISTO, LA • 1981 • de la Iglesia Eloy • SPN, MXC • MINISTER'S WIFE, THE
MUJER DEL OTRO, LA • 1948 • Morayta Miguel • MXC
MUJER DEL PROJIMO, LA • 1974 • *Aguila* • MXC
MUJER DEL PUERTO, LA • 1933 • Boytler Arcady • MXC • HARBOUR WOMAN ○ WOMAN OF THE PORT, THE
MUJER DEL PUERTO, LA • 1949 • Gomez Muriel Emilio • MXC
MUJER DEL ZAPATERO, LA • 1941 • Irigoyen Julio • ARG
MUJER DESNUDA, LA • 1951 • Mendez Fernando • MXC
MUJER DIFERENTE, UNA • 1956 • Blass Yago • ARG
MUJER EN CONDOMINIO • 1956 • Gonzalez Rogelio A. • MXC
MUJER EN LA CALLE, UNA • 1954 • Crevenna Alfredo B. • MXC
MUJER EN UN TAXI, UNA • 1944 • Fogues Juan Jose • SPN
MUJER EN VENTA, UNA • 1934 • Urueta Chano • MXC
MUJER ES COSA DE HOMBRES, LA • 1975 • Yague Jesus • SPN
MUJER ES UN BUEN NEGOCIO, LA • 1976 • Lazarov Valerio • SPN
MUJER ESPERANDO EN UN HOTEL • 1983 • Garcia-Sanz Raul • ANS • SPN
MUJER LEGITIMA, LA • 1945 • Ortega Juan J. • MXC
MUJER MARCADA, LA • 1957 • Morayta Miguel • MXC
MUJER MEXICANA • 1937 • Peon Ramon • MXC • MEXICAN WOMAN, THE (USA)
MUJER MURCIELAGO, LA • 1968 • Cardona Rene • MXC • BATWOMAN (USA) ○ BAT WOMAN, THE
MUJER O FIERA? • 1954 • Delgado Agustin P. • MXC • WOMAN OR BEAST?
MUJER PERDIDA, LA • 1966 • Demicheli Tulio • SPN
MUJER PROHIBIDA, UNA • 1973 • Ruiz Marcos Jose Luis • SPN
MUJER QUE ENGANAMOS, LA • 1944 • Gomez Landero Humberto • MXC
MUJER QUE NO MIENTE, UNA • 1944 • Delgado Miguel M. • MXC
MUJER QUE NO TUVO INFANCIA, LA • 1957 • Davison Tito • MXC
MUJER QUE QUIERE A DOS, LA • 1945 • Urruchua Victor • MXC
MUJER QUE SE VENDIO, LA • 1954 • Delgado Agustin P. • MXC, CUB
MUJER QUE TU QUIERES, LA • 1952 • Gomez Muriel Emilio • MXC
MUJER QUE YO AME, LA • 1950 • Davison Tito • MXC
MUJER QUE YO PERDI, LA • 1949 • Rodriguez Roberto • MXC
MUJER SIN ALMA, LA • 1943 • de Fuentes Fernando • MXC • WOMAN WITHOUT A SOUL
MUJER SIN AMOR, UNA • 1951 • Bunuel Luis • MXC
MUJER SIN CABEZA, LA • 1943 • Cardona Rene • MXC • WOMAN WITHOUT A HEAD, THE
MUJER SIN CABEZA, UNA • 1948 • Amadori Luis Cesar • ARG
MUJER SIN DESTINO, UNA • 1950 • Salvador Jaime • MXC
MUJER SIN LAGRIMAS, LA • 1951 • Crevenna Alfredo B. • MXC
MUJER SIN PRECIO • 1965 • Crevenna Alfredo B. • MXC, PRC
MUJER, UN HOMBRE, UNA CIUDAD, UNA • 1979 • Gomez Manuel Octavio • CUB • WOMAN, A MAN, A CITY, A
MUJER VENEZOLANA DE 30 ANOS, UNA • 1979 • Cordido Enver • VNZ
MUJER X, LA • 1954 • Soler Julian • MXC
MUJER Y LA BESTIA, LA • 1958 • Blake Alfonso Corona • MXC • WOMAN AND THE BEAST, THE
MUJER Y LA SELVA, LA • 1941 • Ferreyra Jose • ARG
MUJER Y UN COBARDE, UNA • 1975 • Balbuena Silvio F. • SPN
MUJERCITAS • 1972 • *Estudios Americas* • MXC
MUJERES AL BORDE DE UN ATAQUE DE NERVIOS • 1988 • Almodovar Pedro • SPN • WOMEN ON THE VERGE OF A NERVOUS BREAKDOWN (UKN)
MUJERES DE DRACULA, LAS see **IMPERIO DE DRACULA, EL** • 1966
MUJERES DE FUEGO • 1958 • Davison Tito • MXC, BRZ
MUJERES DE HOY • 1936 • Peon Ramon • MXC
MUJERES DE LA FRONTERA • 1988 • Arguello Ivan • NCR
MUJERES DE MI GENERAL, LAS • 1950 • Rodriguez Ismael • MXC
MUJERES DE TEATRO • 1951 • Cardona Rene • MXC
MUJERES EN MI VIDA • 1949 • Rivero Fernando A. • MXC
MUJERES EN SOMBRAS • 1951 • Catrani Catrano • ARG
MUJERES ENCANTADORAS • 1957 • Portillo Rafael • MXC
MUJERES ENGANADAS • 1960 • Mendez Fernando • MXC
MUJERES IN ALMA • 1934 • Peon Ramon • MXC • VENGANZA SUPREMA
MUJERES LOS PREFERIEN TONTOS, LAS • 1965 • Saslavsky Luis • ARG
MUJERES MANDAN, LAS • 1936 • de Fuentes Fernando • MXC • WOMEN COMMAND, THE
MUJERES PANTERAS, LAS • 1966 • Cardona Rene • MXC • PANTHER WOMEN, THE
MUJERES QUE TRABAJAN • 1940 • Romero Manuel • WOMEN WHO WORK (USA)
MUJERES QUE TRABAJAN • 1952 • Bracho Julio • MXC
MUJERES SACRIFICADAS • 1951 • Gout Alberto • MXC
MUJERES SIN MANANA • 1951 • Davison Tito • MXC
MUJERES Y TOROS • 1939 • Segura Juan Jose • MXC
MUJERIEGO, EL • 1963 • Perez-Dolc Francesc • SPN
MUJERIEGOS, LOS • 1957 • Salvador Jaime • MXC
MUJIN RETTO • 1970 • Kanai Katsu • JPN • DESERT ARCHIPELAGO, THE
MUJIZAT AS-SAMA see **MOGEZAT EL SAMAA** • 1956
MUJO • 1970 • Jissoji Akio • JPN • ALL IS VANITY ○ THIS PASSING LIFE ○ THIS TRANSIENT LIFE
MUJRIM FI AJAZA see **MUGAREM FI IJAZA** • 1958
MUJRIM KAUN? • 1968 • Vaidya Ramnik D. • IND • WHO IS THE GUILTY ONE?
MUKE PO MATI • 1976 • Zafranovic Lordan • YGS • MATTHEW'S PASSION
MUKH O MUKHOSH • 1956 • Khan Jabbar • BNG
MUKHAMUKHAM • 1984 • Gopalakrishnan Adoor • IND • FACE TO FACE
MUKHARRIBUN, AL- • 1965 • el Sheikh Kamal • EGY • SABOTEURS, LES ○ MOUKHAREBOUN, AL ○ SABOTAGE
MUKIDO JOSEI • 1967 • Matsubara Jiro • JPN • LOOSE WOMEN
MUKOKUSEKI-MONO • 1951 • Ichikawa Kon • JPN • MAN WITHOUT NATIONALITY, THE ○ MAN WITHOUT A COUNTRY
MUKRA • 1988 • Kashmiri Iqbal • PKS • FACE
MUKTI • 1937 • Barua Pramathesh Chandra • IND • LIBERATION
MULATA • 1953 • Martinez Solares Gilberto • MXC
MULATA DE CORDOBA, LA • 1945 • Fernandez Bustamente Adolfo • MXC
MULATSAG • 1989 • Szomjas Gyorgy • DOC • HNG • DAYS OF PEACE AND MUSIC
MULATTO, IL • 1950 • De Robertis Francesco • ITL
MULBERRY LEAVES see **BBONG** • 1985
MULBERRY TREE see **BBONG** • 1985
MULCAHY'S RAID • 1910 • *Essanay* • USA
MULDFLUGTEN • 1979 • Brydesen Lars • DOC • DNM • SOIL DRIFT
MULDOON THE TALKER • 1913 • ASL
MULE DRIVER AND THE GARRULOUS MUTE, THE • 1910 • *Edison* • USA
MULE DRIVERS, THE see **KATIRCILAR** • 1987
MULE MATES • 1917 • Beaudine William • SHT • USA
MULE TRAIN • 1950 • English John • USA
MULEFEATHERS see **WEST IS STILL WILD, THE** • 1977
MULES AND MORTGAGES • 1919 • Howe J. A. • SHT • USA
MULE'S DISPOSITION, THE • 1926 • Lantz Walter • ANS • USA
MULHALL'S GREAT CATCH • 1926 • Garson Harry • USA
MULHER, A SERRA E O MAR, A • 1944 • Miranda Armando • SHT • PRT
MULHER DE TODES, A • 1969 • Sganzerla Rogerio • BRZ • WOMAN OF EVERYONE, THE
MULHER DE VERDADE • 1954 • Cavalcanti Alberto • BRZ • REAL WOMAN, A (USA)
MULHER DO DESEJO, A • 1980 • Christensen Carlos Hugo • BRZ, ARG • WOMAN OF DESIRE
MULHER.. SEMPRE MULHER • 1972 • Schlesinger Hugo • BRZ
MULINO DEL PO, IL • 1949 • Lattuada Alberto • ITL • MILL ON THE PO, THE ○ MILL ON THE RIVER
MULINO DELLE DONNE DI PIETRA, IL • 1960 • Ferroni Giorgio • ITL, FRN • MOULIN DES SUPPLICES, LE (FRN) ○ MILL OF THE STONE WOMEN (USA) ○ DROPS OF BLOOD (UKN) ○ HORRIBLE MILL WOMEN, THE ○ HORROR OF THE STONE WOMEN ○ MILL OF THE STONE MAIDENS
MULL see **MULLAWAY** • 1988
MULLAWAY • 1988 • McLennan Don • ASL • MULL
MULLERS BURO • 1986 • List Niki • AUS • MULLER'S OFFICE
MULLER'S OFFICE see **MULLERS BURO** • 1986
MULLIGAN'S GHOST • 1914 • *Columbus* • USA
MULLIGAN'S STEW • 1977 • Black Noel • TVM • USA
MULLIGAN'S WATERLOO • 1909 • *Edison* • USA
MULLYAYAN • 1989 • Chatterjee Nabyendu • IND
MULOORINA • 1964 • Cobham David • UKN
MULTICULTURALISM • 1985 • Walker John • CND
MULTIPLE AFFAIRS see **TAKUKU KANKEI** • 1968
MULTIPLE CHOICE • 1990 • McGee Debbie • SHT • CND
MULTIPLE MANIACS • 1970 • Waters John* • USA
MULTIPLES, INDETERMINATE NUMBER see **MULTIPLES, NUMERO INDETERMINADO** • 1971
MULTIPLES, NUMERO INDETERMINADO • 1971 • Aguirre Javier • SHT • SPN • MULTIPLES, INDETERMINATE NUMBER
MULTIPLICITY • 1970 • Vaitiekunas Vince • CND
MULTIPLY ONE BY ONE • 1975 • Poloka I. • USS
MULTITUDE see **MULTITYDER** • 1969
MULTITYDER • 1969 • Zieler Mogens • ANS • DNM • MULTITUDE
MUM -I'M ALIVE see **MAMA, ICH LEBE** • 1977
MUMIA, AL- • 1969 • Abdes-Salam Shadi • EGY • NIGHT OF COUNTING THE YEARS, THE ○ MUMIAA, EL ○ MOMIE, LA ○ MUMMIA, LA
MUMIA KOZBESZOL, A • 1967 • Olah Gabor • HNG • MUMMY INTERFERES, THE ○ MUMMY INTERVENES, THE
MUMIAA, EL see **MUMIA, AL-** • 1969
MUMIN • 1971 • *Toho* • ANS • JPN
MUMM, SWEET MUMM • 1989 • Scheuer Paul • LXM
MUMMERS, THE see **MY OLD DUCHESS** • 1933
MUMMER'S DAUGHTER, THE • 1908 • Baker George D. • USA
MUMMIA, LA see **MUMIA, AL-** • 1969
MUMMING BIRDS • 1923 • Brouett Albert • UKN
MUMMY, THE • Blache Alice • FRN
MUMMY, THE • 1911 • *Urban* • UKN
MUMMY, THE • 1911 • *Thanhouser* • USA
MUMMY, THE • 1912 • Coleby A. E.? • UKN
MUMMY, THE • 1914 • *Melies* • USA
MUMMY, THE • 1923 • Taurog Norman • SHT • USA
MUMMY, THE • 1932 • Freund Karl • USA • IM-HO-TEP
MUMMY, THE • 1959 • Fisher Terence • UKN
MUMMY, THE see **MOMIE, LA** • 1913
MUMMY AND THE COWPUNCHERS, THE • 1912 • *Roland Ruth* • USA
MUMMY AND THE HUMMINGBIRD, THE • 1915 • Durkin James • USA
MUMMY INTERFERES, THE see **MUMIA KOZBESZOL, A** • 1967
MUMMY INTERVENES, THE see **MUMIA KOZBESZOL, A** • 1967
MUMMY LOVE • 1926 • Rock Joseph • SHT • USA
MUMMY, MUMMY • Beech J. • SHT • UKN
MUMMY OF THE KING RAMESES, THE (USA) see **MOMIE DU ROI, LA** • 1909
MUMMY STRIKES, THE • 1943 • Sparber I. • ANS • USA
MUMMY'S A HUNDRED TODAY see **MAMA CUMPLE CIEN ANOS** • 1979
MUMMY'S BOYS • 1936 • Guiol Fred • USA
MUMMY'S CURSE, THE • 1944 • Goodwins Leslie • USA
MUMMY'S DARLING see **COCCO DI MAMMA, IL** • 1957
MUMMY'S DUMMIES • 1948 • Bernds Edward • SHT • USA
MUMMY'S FOOT, THE • 1949 • Martin Sobey • SHT • USA
MUMMY'S GHOST, THE • 1944 • Le Borg Reginald • USA
MUMMY'S HAND, THE • 1940 • Cabanne W. Christy • USA
MUMMY'S REVENGE, THE see **VENGANZA DE LA MOMIA, LA** • 1973
MUMMY'S SHROUD, THE • 1967 • Gilling John • UKN
MUMMY'S TOMB, THE • 1942 • Young Harold • USA
MUMPS • 1913 • *Kinemacolor* • USA
MUMPS • 1915 • *Myers Harry* • USA
MUM'S THE WORD • 1913 • *Nestor* • USA
MUM'S THE WORD • 1918 • *Christie* • USA
MUM'S THE WORD • 1918 • *American* • USA
MUM'S THE WORD • 1918 • Lyons Eddie, Moran Lee • *Star* • SHT • USA
MUM'S THE WORD • 1920 • Goldaine Mark • SHT • USA
MUM'S THE WORD • 1926 • McCarey Leo • SHT • USA
MUMSIE • 1927 • Wilcox Herbert • UKN
MUMSY, NANNY, SONNY AND GIRLY • 1969 • Francis Freddie • UKN • GIRLY
MUMU • 1959 • Bobrovsky Anatoli, Teterin Yevgeniy • USS

MUN TET CHEIN NAY WIN THE • 1982 • *Kyaw Hein* • BRM • SUN SETS AT NOON
MUNAKATA SHIMAI • 1950 • Ozu Yasujiro • JPN • MUNAKATA SISTERS, THE ○ MUNEKATA SHIMAI
MUNAKATA SISTERS, THE see **MUNAKATA SHIMAI** • 1950
MUNAMNAMAT TURKIYYA • 1969 • Nahhass Hashim An- • SHT • EGY • MINIATURES TURQUES
MUNCHAUSEN • 1920 • *Felgenauer Richard (Anm)* • ANM • FRG
MUNCHEN–BERLIN WANDERUNG • 1927 • Fischinger Oskar • ANS • FRG
MUNCHEN STRIKE see **SWORD OF GIDEON, THE** • 1986
MUNCHENER BILDERBOGEN • 1924-26 • Fischinger Oskar • ANS • FRG
MUNCHHAUSEN • 1943 • von Baky Josef • FRG • ADVENTURES OF BARON MUNCHAUSEN, THE (USA)
MUNCHHAUSEN IN AFRIKA • 1958 • Jacobs Werner • FRG
MUNCHIES • 1987 • Hirsch Bettina • USA
MUNCHNER G'SCHICHTEN see **BAL PARE** • 1940
MUNCHNERINNEN • 1944 • Mayring Philipp L. • FRG • UBER ALLES DIE LIEBE
MUNDANE ILLUSIONIST, THE see **ILLUSIONNISTE MONDAIN, L'** • 1901
MUNDO ALEGRE DE HELO, O • 1967 • Barros Carlos Alberto De Souza • BRZ • HAPPY WORLD OF HELO, THE
MUNDO DE LAS DROGAS, EL • 1963 • Mariscal Alberto • MXC • WORLD OF DRUGS, THE
MUNDO DE LOS MUERTES, EL see **SANTO Y BLUE DEMON EN EL MUNDO DE LOS MUERTOS** • 1969
MUNDO DE LOS VAMPIROS, EL • 1960 • Blake Alfonso Corona • MXC • WORLD OF THE VAMPIRES, THE (USA)
MUNDO, DEMONIO Y CARMEN • 1978 • Ozores Mariano • SPN
MUNDO, DEMONIO Y CARNE • 1958 • Diaz Morales Jose • MXC • WORLD, THE DEVIL AND THE FLESH, THE
MUNDO DEPRAVADOS • 1967 • Jeffries Herb • USA • WORLD OF THE DEPRAVED ○ MONDO DEPRAVADOS
MUNDO EXTRANO • 1952 • Eichhorn Franz • FRG, BRZ • STRANGE WORLD ○ GOTTIN VOM RIO BENE, DIE
MUNDO LOCO DE LOS JOVENES, EL • 1966 • Fernandez Unsain Jose Maria • MXC
MUNDO NUEVO, UN • 1956 • Cardona Rene • MXC • NEW WORLD, A
MUNDO PARA MI, UN • 1959 • de la Loma Jose Antonio, Duchesne Louis, Metzger Radley H. • SPN, FRN • TENTATIONS (FRN) ○ SOFT SKIN AND BLACK LACE ○ SOFT SKIN ON BLACK SILK
MUNDO QUE SONA MOS, EL • 1962 • Roncal Hugo • BLV
MUNDO SALVAJE DE BARU, EL • 1958 • Orona Vicente • MXC
MUNDO SIGUE, EL • 1963 • Fernan-Gomez Fernando • SPN
MUNECA REINA • 1971 • Olhovich Sergio • MXC • QUEEN DOLL (USA)
MUNECAS DE MEDIA NOCHE • 1979 • *Calderon Stell Guillermo (P)* • MXC • MIDNIGHT DOLLS
MUNECOS INFERNALES • 1960 • Alazraki Benito • MXC • CURSE OF THE DOLL PEOPLE, THE (USA)
MUNEKATA SHIMAI see **MUNAKATA SHIMAI** • 1950
MUNEQUITAS PORTENAS • 1931 • Ferreyra Jose • ARG
MUNICH, OR PEACE IN OUR TIME see **MUNICH, OU LA PAIX POUR CENT ANS** • 1967
MUNICH, OU LA PAIX POUR CENT ANS • 1967 • Ophuls Marcel • DOC • FRG • MUNICH, OR PEACE IN OUR TIME
MUNICIPAL ELECTIONS see **ELECCIONES MUNICIPALES** • 1970
MUNICIPAL REPORT, A see **I WILL REPAY** • 1917
MUNIMJI • 1955 • *Burman S. D. (M)* • IND
MUNITION CONSPIRACY, THE see **KRIGENS FJENDE** • 1915
MUNITION GIRL'S ROMANCE, A • 1917 • Wilson Frank • UKN
MUNITION WORKERS see **CASE OF EXPLOSIVES, A** • 1912
MUNITION WORKER'S CURSE, A • 1917 • *Morris Dave* • SHT • USA
MUNITIONS PLOT, THE • 1917 • Davis James • USA
MUNKA VAGY HIVATAS? • 1963 • Meszaros Marta • DCS • HNG • WORK OR PROFESSION?
MUNKBROGREVEN • 1935 • Adolphson Edvin, Wallen Sigurd • SWD • COUNT FROM MUNKBRO
MUNNA • 1954 • Abbas Khwaya Ahmad • IND • LOST CHILD, THE
MUNRO • 1960 • Deitch Gene • ANS • CZC
MUNSTER, GO HOME! • 1966 • Bellamy Earl • USA
MUNSTER'S REVENGE, THE • 1981 • Weis Don • TVM • USA
MUNTAKEM, EL • 1947 • Abu Saif Salah • EGY • AVENGER, THE ○ MUNTAQIM, AL–
MUNTAQIM, AL– see **MUNTAKEM, EL** • 1947
MUNTRA MUSIKANTER • 1932 • Berthels Theodor, Hildebrand Weyler • SWD • GAY MUSICIANS
MUORI LENTAMENTE.. TA LA GODI DI PIU (ITL) see **MISTER DYNAMIT –MORGEN KUSST EUCH DER TOD** • 1967
MUOTOILIJAN MAAILMA TIMO SARPANEVA • 1976 • Makinen Aito • DOC • FNL • PORTRAIT OF AN INDUSTRIAL DESIGNER
MUPPET MOVIE, THE • 1979 • Frawley James • USA
MUPPETS: HEY CINDERELLA • 1970 • Henson Jim • ANM • USA
MUPPETS TAKE MANHATTAN, THE • 1984 • Oz Frank • USA
MUQABALA • 1972 • Nahhass Hashim An- • SHT • EGY • INTERVIEW
MUR, LE • 1968 • Roullet Serge • FRN
MUR, LE • 1983 • Guney Yilmaz • FRN • GUNEY'S THE WALL ○ WALL, THE ○ DUVAR
MUR, LE see **DEMOLITION D'UN MUR** • 1895
MUR A JERUSALEM, UN • 1968 • Rossif Frederic, Knobler Albert • FRN • WALL IN JERUSALEM, A (USA)
MUR DE BERLIN, LE • 1988 • Butler Yvan • SWT • BERLIN WALL, THE
MUR DE L'ATLANTIQUE, LE • 1970 • Camus Marcel • FRN, ITL • ELMETTO PIENO DI.. FIFA (ITL)
MUR MURS • 1980 • Varda Agnes • DOC • FRN • MURAL MURALS ○ WALL WALLS
MURA DI MALAPAGA, LA (ITL) see **AU–DELA DES GRILLES** • 1948
MURA HACHIBU • 1953 • Imaizumi Yoshiji • JPN • EIGHTY PERCENT OF THE VILLAGE
MURA NI TERU HI • 1928 • Tasaka Tomotaka • JPN • VILLAGE OF THE SHINING SUN
MURA NO HANAYOME • 1927 • Gosho Heinosuke • JPN • VILLAGE BRIDE, THE
MURAGLIA CINESE, LA • 1958 • Lizzani Carlo • DOC • ITL • BEHIND THE GREAT WALL ○ FIUME GIALLO, IL ○ GREAT WALL, THE ○ CHINESE WALL, THE
MURAILLE QUI PLEURE, LA • 1918 • Leprieur Gaston • FRN
MURAILLES DU SILENCE, LES • 1925 • de Carbonnat Louis • FRN
MURAL MURALS see **MUR MURS** • 1980
MURALIWALA see **KALIA MARDAN** • 1934
MURALLA, LA • 1958 • Lucia Luis • SPN
MURALLA VERDE, LA • 1969 • Godoy Armando Robles • PRU • GREEN WALL, THE (USA)
MURALLAS DE PASION • 1943 • Urruchua Victor • MXC
MURALS see **KALKMALERIER** • 1954
MURANGO STORY, THE • 1955 • Landers Lew • MTV • USA
MURAT • 1910 • De Liguoro Giuseppe • ITL
MURATTI GREIFT EIN • 1934 • Fischinger Oskar • ANS • FRG • MURATTI MARCHES ON
MURATTI MARCHES ON see **MURATTI GREIFT EIN** • 1934
MURATTI PRIVAT • 1935 • Fischinger Oskar • ANS • FRG
MURBUR • 1969 • Babic Nikola • YGS
MURCHESON CREEK • 1975 • Bourke Terry • MTV • ASL
MURCIELAGOS, LOS • 1964 • Ortega Juan J. • MXC
MURDER • 1930 • Hitchcock Alfred • UKN • MARY
MURDER see **MEURTRE** • 1964
MURDER see **UBISTVO NA PODMUKAO I SVIREP NACIN I IZ NISKIH POBUDA** • 1970
MURDER, THE see **ASSASSINO, L'** • 1961
MURDER A LA CARTE see **VOICI LE TEMPS DES ASSASSINS** • 1956
MURDER A LA MOD • 1968 • De Palma Brian • USA
MURDER AHOY • 1964 • Pollock George • UKN
MURDER AMONG FRIENDS • 1941 • McCarey Ray • USA
MURDER AND MANSLAUGHTER see **MORD UND TOTSCHLAG** • 1967
MURDER AND THE COMPUTER • 1975 • Stanley Paul • TVM • USA
MURDER ANONYMOUS • 1955 • Hughes Ken • UKN
MURDER AT 3 A.M. • 1953 • Searle Francis • UKN
MURDER AT 45 RPM see **MEURTRE EN 45 TOURS** • 1960
MURDER AT CONVENT GARDEN • 1932 • Hiscott Leslie, Barringer Michael • UKN
MURDER AT DAWN • 1932 • Thorpe Richard • USA • DEATH RAY, THE (UKN)
MURDER AT GLEN ATHOL • 1936 • Strayer Frank • USA
MURDER AT MALIBU BEACH (UKN) see **TRAP, THE** • 1947
MURDER AT MIDNIGHT • 1931 • Strayer Frank • USA
MURDER AT MONTECARLO • 1935 • Ince Ralph • UKN
MURDER AT SCOTLAND YARD • 1952 • Gover Victor M. • UKN
MURDER AT SITE THREE • 1959 • Searle Francis • UKN
MURDER AT TEN • 1935 • Heale Patrick K. • UKN
MURDER AT THE BASKERVILLES (USA) see **SILVER BLAZE** • 1937
MURDER AT THE BURLESQUE (USA) see **MURDER AT THE WINDMILL** • 1949
MURDER AT THE CABARET • 1936 • Fogwell Reginald • UKN
MURDER AT THE GALLOP • 1963 • Pollock George • UKN
MURDER AT THE GRANGE • 1952 • Gover Victor M. • UKN
MURDER AT THE INN • 1934 • King George • UKN
MURDER AT THE MARDI GRAS • 1978 • Annakin Ken • TVM • USA
MURDER AT THE VANITIES • 1934 • Leisen Mitchell • USA
MURDER AT THE WINDMILL • 1949 • Guest Val • UKN • MURDER AT THE BURLESQUE (USA)
MURDER AT THE WORLD SERIES • 1977 • McLaglen Andrew V. • TVM • USA
MURDER BY AGREEMENT see **JOURNEY INTO NOWHERE** • 1963
MURDER BY AN ARISTOCRAT • 1936 • McDonald Frank • USA
MURDER BY CONTRACT • 1958 • Lerner Irving • USA
MURDER BY DEATH • 1976 • Moore Robert • USA
MURDER BY DECREE • 1979 • Clark Bob • CND, UKN • SHERLOCK HOLMES: MURDER BY DECREE (USA)
MURDER BY INVITATION • 1941 • Rosen Phil • USA
MURDER BY NATURAL CAUSES • 1979 • Day Robert • TVM • USA
MURDER BY PHONE see **BELLS** • 1981
MURDER BY PROXY • 1955 • Fisher Terence • UKN • BLACKOUT (USA)
MURDER: BY REASON OF INSANITY • 1985 • Page Anthony • TVM • USA
MURDER BY ROPE • 1936 • Pearson George • UKN
MURDER BY SIGNATURE see **EICHMANN UND DAS DRITTE REICH** • 1961
MURDER BY TELEVISION • 1935 • Sanforth Clifford • USA
MURDER BY THE BOOK • 1987 • Damski Mel • TVM • USA • ALTER EGO
MURDER BY THE CLOCK • 1931 • Sloman Edward • USA
MURDER CAN BE DEADLY (USA) see **PAINTED SMILE, THE** • 1962
MURDER CAN HURT YOU! • 1980 • Duchowny Roger • TVM • USA
MURDER CASE OF HONKIN, THE see **HONKIN SATSUJIN JIKEN** • 1975
MURDER CASE SHIMOYAMA see **BOSATSU, SHIMOYAMA JIKEN** • 1982
MURDER CASES see **FURENZOKU SATSUJIN JIKEN** • 1976
MURDER CHAMBER, THE see **CHARLIE CHAN IN BLACK MAGIC** • 1944
MURDER CLINIC, THE (USA) see **LAMA NEL CORPO, LA** • 1966
MURDER CLUB OF BROOKLYN, THE see **MORDERCLUB VON BROOKLYN, DER** • 1967
MURDER COMMITTED IN A SLY AND CRUEL MANNER AND FROM A LOW MOTIVE see **UBISTVO NA PODMUKAO I SVIREP NACIN I IZ NISKIH POBUBA** • 1970
MURDER CZECH STYLE see **VRAZDA PO CESKU** • 1967
MURDER EAST, MURDER WEST • 1990 • Smith Peter K. • FRG
MURDER ELITE • 1985 • Whatham Claude • UKN
MURDER FOR SALE (USA) see **EINBRECHER** • 1930
MURDER GAME, THE • 1965 • Salkow Sidney • UKN
MURDER GANG, THE see **BLACK HEAT** • 1981
MURDER GO ROUND see **CONDE, UN** • 1970
MURDER GOES TO COLLEGE • 1937 • Reisner Charles F. • USA
MURDER, HE SAYS • 1945 • Marshall George • USA
MURDER IN A CONVOY see **ESCAPE TO DANGER** • 1943
MURDER IN AMSTERDAM see **10.32**
MURDER IN ASPIC • 1978 • Demme Jonathan • TVM • USA
MURDER IN BERMUDA see **BERMUDA MYSTERY** • 1944
MURDER IN COWETA COUNTY • 1982 • Nelson Gary • TVM • USA • LAST BLOOD
MURDER IN DANTE STREET, THE see **UBIISTVO NA UTILITZE DANTE** • 1956
MURDER IN DIAMOND ROW (USA) see **SQUEAKER, THE** • 1937
MURDER IN EDEN • 1961 • Varnel Max • UKN
MURDER IN GREENWICH VILLAGE • 1937 • Rogell Albert S. • USA • PARK AVENUE DAME
MURDER IN ISLAND STREET see **VRAZDA V OSTROVNI ULICI** • 1933
MURDER IN LIMEHOUSE, A • 1919 • Carlton Frank • UKN
MURDER IN LVOV • 1962 • Heynowski Walter • DOC • GDR
MURDER IN MAYFAIR • 1942 • Haines Ronald • UKN
MURDER IN MISSISSIPPI • 1965 • Mawra Joseph P. • USA • MURDER MISSISSIPPI
MURDER IN MUSIC CITY • 1979 • Penn Leo • TVM • USA • COUNTRY MUSIC MURDERS, THE
MURDER IN PARADISE see **MUERTE EN EL PARAISO** • 1979
MURDER IN PARADISE see **MORD I PARADIS** • 1988
MURDER IN PEYTON PLACE • 1977 • Kessler Bruce • TVM • USA
MURDER IN PRIVATE • 1942 • Diamant-Berger Henri
MURDER IN REVERSE • 1945 • Tully Montgomery • UKN • QUERY
MURDER IN SOHO • 1939 • Lee Norman • UKN • MURDER IN THE NIGHT (USA)
MURDER IN SPACE • 1985 • Stern Steven Hilliard • TVM • USA • WHODUNIT? MURDER IN SPACE
MURDER IN SPRING TIME see **WHO KILLED GAIL PRESTON?** • 1938
MURDER IN SWINGTIME • 1937 • Dreifuss Arthur • SHT • USA
MURDER IN TEXAS • 1981 • Hale William • TVM • USA
MURDER IN THE AIR • 1940 • Seiler Lewis • USA
MURDER IN THE AIR (UKN) see **DEATH IN THE AIR** • 1936
MURDER IN THE BIG HOUSE • 1942 • Eason B. Reeves • USA • HUMAN SABOTAGE (UKN) ○ BORN FOR TROUBLE
MURDER IN THE BIG HOUSE (UKN) see **JAILBREAK** • 1936
MURDER IN THE BLUE ROOM • 1944 • Goodwins Leslie • USA
MURDER IN THE CATHEDRAL • 1952 • Hoellering George • UKN
MURDER IN THE CENTRAL COMMITTEE see **ASESINATO EN EL COMITE CENTRAL** • 1982
MURDER IN THE CLOUDS • 1934 • Lederman D. Ross • USA
MURDER IN THE DARK see **MORD I MORKET** • 1986
MURDER IN THE DARK (UKN) see **SENOR JIM** • 1936
MURDER IN THE FAMILY • 1938 • Parker Albert • UKN
MURDER IN THE FAMILY see **CRAZY KNIGHTS** • 1944
MURDER IN THE FAMILY see **CRIME D'OVIDE PLOUFFE, LE** • 1984
MURDER IN THE FLEET • 1935 • Sedgwick Edward • USA
MURDER IN THE FOOTLIGHTS see **TROJAN BROTHERS, THE** • 1946
MURDER IN THE LIBRARY (UKN) see **PLAYTHINGS OF DESIRE** • 1933
MURDER IN THE MUSEUM • 1933 • Shyer Melville • USA
MURDER IN THE MUSIC HALL • 1946 • English John • USA • MIDNIGHT MELODY
MURDER IN THE NIGHT (USA) see **MURDER IN SOHO** • 1939
MURDER IN THE OLD RED BARN (USA) see **MARIA MARTEN: OR, THE MURDER IN THE RED BARN** • 1935
MURDER IN THE ORIENT • 1978 • *Delon Jim* • USA
MURDER IN THE PRIVATE CAR • 1934 • Beaumont Harry • USA • MURDER ON THE RUNAWAY TRAIN (UKN) ○ MURDER ON THE RUNAWAY CAR ○ REAR CAR, THE
MURDER IN THE SENATE see **ASESINATO EN EL SENADO DE LA NACION** • 1984
MURDER IN THE SLAVE TRADE • 1973 • Wendkos Paul • TVM • USA
MURDER IN THE STALLS see **NOT WANTED ON VOYAGE** • 1936
MURDER IN THE STRATOSPHERE see **LOST IN THE STRATOSPHERE** • 1934
MURDER IN THE STUDIO see **CRIME OF HELEN STANLEY, THE** • 1934
MURDER IN THORTON SQUARE, THE (UKN) see **GASLIGHT** • 1944
MURDER IN TIMES SQUARE • 1943 • Landers Lew • USA
MURDER IN TRINIDAD • 1934 • King Louis • USA
MURDER IN YOSHIWARA see **HANA NO YOSHIWARA HYAKUNIN–GIRI** • 1960
MURDER, INC. • 1960 • Balaban Burt, Rosenberg Stuart • USA
MURDER INC. (UKN) see **ENFORCER, THE** • 1951
MURDER INFERNO (UKN) see **BOSS, IL** • 1973
MURDER IS A MURDER, A (UKN) see **MEURTRE EST UN MEURTRE, UN** • 1972
MURDER IS A MURDER.. IS A MURDER, A see **MEURTRE EST UN MEURTRE, UN** • 1972
MURDER IS EASY • 1982 • Whatham Claude • TVM • USA
MURDER IS MY BEAT • 1954 • Ulmer Edgar G. • USA • DYNAMITE ANCHORAGE
MURDER IS MY BUSINESS • 1946 • Newfield Sam • USA
MURDER IS NEWS see **DELAVINE AFFAIR, THE** • 1954
MURDER IS UNPREDICTABLE see **MYSTERIOUS INTRUDER, THE** • 1946
MURDER MAN, THE • 1935 • Whelan Tim • USA
MURDER MANSION, THE (USA) see **MANSION DE LA NIEBLA, LLA** • 1972
MURDER ME, MURDER YOU • 1983 • Nelson Gary • TVM • USA
MURDER MEN, THE see **BLUES FOR A JUNKMAN** • 1962
MURDER MISSISSIPPI see **MURDER IN MISSISSIPPI** • 1965
MURDER MOST FOUL • 1964 • Pollock George • UKN
MURDER MY LITTLE FRIEND see **MORD LILLA VAN** • 1955

MURDER MY SWEET • 1945 • Dmytryk Edward • USA • FAREWELL MY LOVELY (UKN)
MURDER OF A HAM • 1955 • MacDonald David • UKN
MURDER OF A SCHOOLMISTRESS • 1987 • Fahmy Ashraf • EGY
MURDER OF CAPTAIN FRYATT • 1917 • Gavin John F. • ASL
MURDER OF CUENCA, THE see **CRIMEN DE CUENCA, EL** • 1979
MURDER OF DIMITRI KARAMAZOV, THE see **BRATYA KARAMAZOVY** • 1968
MURDER OF DR. HARRIGAN, THE • 1936 • McDonald Frank • USA
MURDER OF ENGINEER DEVIL, THE see **VRAZDA INZENYRA CERTA** • 1968
MURDER OF FATHER CHRISTMAS, THE see **ASSASSINAT DU PERE NOEL, L'** • 1941
MURDER OF FRED HAMPTON, THE • 1971 • Gray Mike • DOC • USA • HAMPTON
MURDER OF MARY PHAGAN, THE • 1988 • Hale William • TVM • USA
MURDER OF MR. DEVIL, THE see **VRAZDA INZENYRA CERTA** • 1968
MURDER OF SQUIRE JEFFREY, THE • 1913 • Aylott Dave • UKN
MURDER OF THE INNOCENTS, THE • 1957 • Bostan Ion • DOC • RMN
MURDER ON A BRIDLE PATH • 1936 • Killy Edward, Hamilton William • USA
MURDER ON A HONEYMOON • 1935 • Corrigan Lloyd • USA • PUZZLE OF THE PEPPER TREE, THE
MURDER ON APPROVAL (USA) see **BARBADOS QUEST** • 1955
MURDER ON FLIGHT 502 • 1975 • McCowan George • TVM • USA
MURDER ON LENOX AVENUE • 1941 • Dreifuss Arthur • USA
MURDER ON MONDAY see **MORD AM MONTAG** • 1968
MURDER ON MONDAY (USA) see **HOME AT SEVEN** • 1952
MURDER ON THE AIR see **TWENTY QUESTIONS MURDER MYSTERY, THE** • 1950
MURDER ON THE BLACKBOARD • 1934 • Archainbaud George • USA
MURDER ON THE BRIDGE see **RICHTER UND SEIN HENKER, DER** • 1976
MURDER ON THE CAMPUS • 1934 • Thorpe Richard • USA • AT THE STROKE OF NINE (UKN) ○ ON THE STROKE OF NINE
MURDER ON THE CAMPUS (USA) see **OUT OF THE SHADOW** • 1961
MURDER ON THE MISSISSIPPI see **MYSTERIOUS CROSSING** • 1936
MURDER ON THE ORIENT EXPRESS • 1974 • Lumet Sidney • UKN
MURDER ON THE ORIENT EXPRESS • 1985 • Megahy Francis • TVM • UKN
MURDER ON THE ROOF • 1930 • Seitz George B. • USA
MURDER ON THE RUE DANTE see **UBIISTVO NA UTILITZE DANTE** • 1956
MURDER ON THE RUNAWAY CAR see **MURDER IN THE PRIVATE CAR** • 1934
MURDER ON THE RUNAWAY TRAIN (UKN) see **MURDER IN THE PRIVATE CAR** • 1934
MURDER ON THE SECOND FLOOR • 1932 • McGann William • UKN
MURDER ON THE SET see **DEATH ON THE SET** • 1935
MURDER ON THE TIBER see **ASSASSINIO SUL TEVERE** • 1979
MURDER ON THE WATERFRONT • 1943 • Eason B. Reeves • USA
MURDER ON THE YUKON • 1940 • Gasnier Louis J. • USA
MURDER ONCE REMOVED • 1971 • Dubin Charles S. • TVM • USA • SECRET KILLING
MURDER ONE see **D.A.: MURDER ONE** • 1969
MURDER ONE DANCER 0 • 1983 • Badiyi Reza • TVM • USA
MURDER OR MERCY • 1974 • Hart Harvey • TVM • USA
MURDER ORDAINED • 1987 • Robe Mike • TVM • USA
MURDER OUR STYLE see **VRAZDA PO CESKU** • 1967
MURDER OVER NEW YORK • 1940 • Lachman Harry • USA • CHARLIE CHAN IN MURDER OVER NEW YORK
MURDER PARTY, THE (USA) see **NIGHT OF THE PARTY, THE** • 1934
MURDER PARTY (USA) see **MORDERSPIEL** • 1961
MURDER PREFERRED • 1951 • Weiss Adrian • USA
MURDER PSALM • 1980 • Brakhage Stan • SHT • USA
MURDER RAP • 1987 • Kuehl Kliff • USA
MURDER REPORTED • 1957 • Saunders Charles • UKN
MURDER RING, THE (UKN) see **ELLERY QUEEN AND THE MURDER RING** • 1941
MURDER SHE SAID • 1961 • Pollock George • UKN, USA • MEET MISS MARPLE
MURDER SHE SINGS • 1986 • Baker Fred • USA
MURDER, SMOKE AND SHADOWS see **COLUMBO: MURDER, SMOKE AND SHADOWS** • 1988
MURDER SOCIETY, THE see **LAMA NEL CORPO, LA** • 1966
MURDER THAT WAS NEVER RECOGNISED, THE see **MORD, DER NIE VERJAHRT, DER** • 1968
MURDER THAT WOULDN'T DIE, THE • 1980 • Satlof Ron • TVM • USA
MURDER TOMORROW • 1938 • Pedelty Donovan • UKN
MURDER: UNTIMATE GROUNDS FOR DIVORCE • 1984 • Barry Morris • UKN
MURDER WEAPONS FOR SALE see **MORDVAPEN TILL SALU** • 1963
MURDER WILL OUT • 1930 • Badger Clarence • USA
MURDER WILL OUT • 1939 • Neill R. William • UKN
MURDER WILL OUT (USA) see **SPECTRE, LE** • 1899
MURDER WILL OUT (USA) see **VOICE OF MERRILL, THE** • 1952
MURDER WITH MIRRORS • 1985 • Lowry Dick • TVM • USA • AGATHA CHRISTIE'S MURDER WITH MIRRORS
MURDER WITH MUSIC • 1941 • Quigley George P. • USA
MURDER WITH NOODLES • 1971 • Foky Otto • ANS • HNG
MURDER WITH PICTURES • 1936 • Barton Charles T. • USA
MURDER WITHOUT CAUSE see **MORD OHNE TATER, DER** • 1920
MURDER WITHOUT CRIME • 1950 • Thompson J. Lee • UKN
MURDER WITHOUT TEARS • 1953 • Beaudine William • USA
MURDERED BY MISTAKE • 1916 • Hutchinson Craig • SHT • USA
MURDERED CONSTABLE, THE • 1938 • Delamar Mickey, Kavanagh Denis • UKN
MURDERED HOUSE, THE • 1989 • Lautner Georges • FRN
MURDERER • 1988 • *Neeli* • PKS
MURDERER, A see **ARU KOROSHIYA** • 1967
MURDERER, THE • 1985 • SAF
MURDERER, THE see **MEURTRIER, LE** • 1962
MURDERER, THE see **FONIAS, O** • 1984
MURDERER –AN ORDINARY PERSON, THE see **MORDAREN – EN HELT VANLIG PERSON** • 1967
MURDERER AND THE GIRL, THE see **ZBRODNIARZ I PANNA** • 1963
MURDERER DIMITRI KARAMASOFF, THE (USA) see **MORDER DIMITRI KARAMASOFF, DER** • 1931
MURDERER FROM ANOTHER WORLD, THE • Lettrich Andrej • CZC • MURDERER FROM BEYOND THE GRAVE
MURDERER FROM BEYOND THE GRAVE see **MURDERER FROM ANOTHER WORLD, THE**
MURDERER HIDES HIS FACE, THE • 1966 • Schulhoff Petr • CZC
MURDERER IS IN THE HOUSE, THE see **GYILKOS A HAZBAN VAN, A** • 1971
MURDERER LEAVES A CLUE, THE see **MORDERCA ZOSTAWIA SLAD** • 1967
MURDERER LEAVES CLUES, THE see **MORDERCA ZOSTAWIA SLAD** • 1967
MURDERER LEAVES TRACES, THE see **MORDERCA ZOSTAWIA SLAD** • 1967
MURDERER LIVES AT NUMBER 21, THE (USA) see **ASSASSIN HABITE AU 21, L'** • 1942
MURDERER MUST DIE, THE see **NANATSU NO DANGAN** • 1959
MURDERER OF PEDRALBES, THE see **ASESINO DE PEDRALBES, EL** • 1978
MURDERER OF YOUTH see **SEISHUN NO SATSUJIN-SHA** • 1976
MURDERERS see **NOUS SOMMES TOUS DES ASSASSINS** • 1952
MURDERERS see **QUATIL HASENNA** • 1988
MURDERERS, THE see **ASESINOS, LOS** • 1968
MURDERERS AMONG US (USA) see **MORDER SIND UNTER UNS, DIE** • 1946
MURDERERS ARE AMONG US, THE (UKN) see **MORDER SIND UNTER UNS, DIE** • 1946
MURDERERS ARE AMONGST US, THE see **MORDER SIND UNTER UNS, DIE** • 1946
MURDERERS ARE COMING, THE see **UBITZI VYKHODYAT NA DOROGU** • 1942
MURDERERS ARE ON THEIR WAY see **UBITZI VYKHODYAT NA DOROGU** • 1942
MURDERER'S COMMAND see **COMANDO DE ASESINOS** • 1968
MURDERERS FROM OTHER WORLDS see **ASESINOS DE OTROS MUNDOS** • 1971
MURDERERS' ROW • 1966 • Levin Henry • USA
MURDERESS, THE see **FONISSA, I** • 1974
MURDERING ANGEL, THE see **ANJO ASSASSINO, O** • 1967
MURDERING MITE, THE see **TOMEI-NINGEN TO HAI-OTOKO** • 1957
MURDERLUST • 1988 • Jones Don • USA • MASS MURDERER
MURDEROCK • 1984 • Fulci Lucio • ITL
MURDEROUS ELOPEMENT, A • 1914 • *Powers* • USA
MURDERS AT MOMMILA, 1917 see **MOMMILAN VERITEOT 1917** • 1973
MURDERS IN THE RUE MORGUE • 1932 • Florey Robert • USA
MURDERS IN THE RUE MORGUE • 1971 • Hessler Gordon • USA
MURDERS IN THE RUE MORGUE, THE • 1914 • *Rosenberg Sol A.* • USA
MURDERS IN THE RUE MORGUE, THE • 1986 • Szwarc Jeannot • TVM • USA
MURDERS IN THE ZOO • 1933 • Sutherland A. Edward • USA
MURDOCK AFFAIR, THE (UKN) see **DEVIL PLAYS, THE** • 1931
MURDOCK TRIAL, THE • 1914 • Trimble Larry • UKN
MURDOCK'S GANG • 1973 • Dubin Charles S. • TVM • USA
MURI SHINJU NIHON NO NATSU • 1967 • Oshima Nagisa • JPN • JAPANESE SUMMER: DOUBLE SUICIDE ○ NIGHT OF THE KILLER
MURIEL, IL TEMPO DI UN RITORNO (ITL) see **MURIEL, OU LE TEMPS D'UN RETOUR** • 1963
MURIEL, OU LE TEMPS D'UN RETOUR • 1963 • Resnais Alain • FRN, ITL • MURIEL, IL TEMPO DI UN RITORNO (ITL) ○ MURIEL (USA)
MURIEL (USA) see **MURIEL, OU LE TEMPS D'UN RETOUR** • 1963
MURIEL'S DOUBLE • 1912 • Haldane Bert? • UKN
MURIEL'S STRATAGEM • 1910 • *Vitagraph* • USA
MURIERON A LA MITAD DEL RIO • 1987 • Nieto Jose Luis • MXC • THEY DIED IN THE MIDDLE OF THE RIVER
MURIETA • 1965 • Sherman George • SPN • JOAQUIN MURRIETA ○ VENDETTA
MURIETTA see **DESPERATE MISSION** • 1971
MURIO HACE QUINCE ANOS • 1954 • Gil Rafael • SPN
MURLIWALA • 1951 • Painter Vasant • IND
MURMUR OF THE HEART (USA) see **SOUFFLE AU COEUR, LE** • 1971
MURO, EL • 1947 • Torre-Nilsson Leopoldo • SHT • ARG • WALL, THE
MURO, IL • 1972 • ANS • ITL • WALL, THE
MURO DEL SILENCIO, EL • 1972 • Alcoriza Luis • MXC • WALL OF SILENCE, THE
MURPH THE SURF • 1975 • Chomsky Marvin • USA • LIVE A LITTLE, STEAL A LOT ○ YOU CAN'T STEAL LOVE
MURPHY AND THE MAGIC CAP see **MISADVENTURES OF MIKE MURPHY, THE** • 1913
MURPHY AND THE MERMAIDS • 1914 • Henderson Dell • USA
MURPHY OF ANZAC • 1916 • Matthews John • ASL
MURPHY'S FAULT • 1988 • Smawley Robert • USA
MURPHY'S I.O.U. • 1913 • Sennett Mack • USA
MURPHY'S LAW • 1986 • Thompson J. Lee • USA
MURPHY'S MILLIONS see **MIKE MURPHY'S DREAM OF LOVE AND RICHES** • 1914
MURPHY'S NEW HIGH HAT • 1913 • *Komic* • USA
MURPHY'S ROMANCE • 1985 • Ritt Martin • USA
MURPHY'S WAKE • 1903 • Collins Alf • UKN
MURPHY'S WAKE • 1906 • *Walturdaw* • UKN
MURPHY'S WAR • 1970 • Yates Peter • UKN
MURRAY THE MASHER • 1912 • *Selig* • USA
MURRI AFFAIR, THE (USA) see **FATTI DI GENTE PER BENE** • 1974
MURROW • 1985 • Gold Jack • TVM • USA
MURS DE MALAPAGA, LES see **AU-DELA DES GRILLES** • 1948
MURS ONT DES OREILLES, LES • 1974 • Girault Jean • FRN
MURUDRUNI • 1962 • SAF
MURZILKA SULLOSPUTNIK • 1959 • Snezhko-Blotskoi A. • ANM • USS
MURZYNEK • 1960 • Kedzierzawska Jadwiga • ANM • PLN • LITTLE NIGGER BOY, THE ○ LITTLE NEGRO, THE
MUSAFIR • 1955 • *Ghatak Ritwik* • IND
MUSAFIRUN'ILA AL-JANUB, MUSAFIRUN' ILA ASH-SHAMAL • 1972 • Awf Samir • SHT • EGY • VOYAGEUR VERS LE NORD, VOYAGEUR VERS LE SUD
MUSASHI AND KOJIRO see **KETTO GANRYU JIMA** • 1955
MUSASHI MIYAMOTO see **MIYAMOTO MUSASHI** • 1940
MUSASHI MIYAMOTO see **MIYAMOTO MUSASHI** • 1944
MUSASHINO FUJIN • 1951 • Mizoguchi Kenji • JPN • LADY FROM MUSAHINO, THE (UKN) ○ LADY MUSASHINO (USA) ○ MADAMA MUSASHINO ○ WOMAN OF MUSASHINO ○ LADY OF MUSASHINO, THE
MUSAWWARAT • 1967 • Oelschlagel Gotz • GDR
MUSCA • 1989 • Reijnders Mark • NTH
MUSCLE • 1984 • Lank Barry • SHT • CND
MUSCLE AND CULTURE • 1968 • Genoves Santiago • ANS • MXC
MUSCLE BEACH • 1948 • Lerner Irving, Strick Joseph • DCS • USA
MUSCLE BEACH PARTY • 1964 • Asher William • USA
MUSCLE BEACH TOM • 1956 • Hanna William, Barbera Joseph • ANS • USA
MUSCLE-BOUND MUSIC • 1926 • *Sennett Mack (P)* • SHT • USA
MUSCLE TUSSLE • 1953 • McKimson Robert • ANS • USA
MUSCLE UP A LITTLE CLOSER • 1957 • White Jules • SHT • USA
MUSCLES AND FLOWERS • 1969 • Gutman Walter • DOC • USA
MUSE ET LA MADONE, LA • 1978 • Companeez Nina • FRN
MUSEE, LE • 1964 • Borowczyk Walerian • ANS • USA
MUSEE DALI • 1981 • Ruiz Raul • DCS • FRN • DALI MUSEUM
MUSEE DANS LA MER, UN • 1953 • Cousteau Jacques • FRN
MUSEE D'ART CONTEMPORAIN, LE • 1973 • Gagne Jacques • DCS • CND
MUSEE DES GROTESQUES, LE • 1911 • Cohl Emile • ANS • FRN
MUSEE DU LOUVRE, LE • 1979 • Uruta Toshio • JPN • LOUVRE MUSEUM, THE
MUSEE GREVIN • 1958 • Demy Jacques, Masson Jean • DCS • FRN
MUSEE VIVANT, LE • 1965 • Storck Henri • DOC • BLG
MUSEN FUSEN • 1924 • Mizoguchi Kenji • JPN • NO MONEY, NO FIGHT (USA) ○ NO FIGHT WITHOUT MONEY
MUSEO CRIOLLO • 1973 • de Pedro Manuel • SHT • VNZ • NATIVE MUSEUM
MUSEO CRIOLLO RAUL SANTANA • 1974 • de Pedro Manuel • VNZ
MUSEO DEI SOGNI, IL • 1949 • Comencini Luigi • ITL
MUSEO DEL CRIMEN, EL • 1944 • Cardona Rene • MXC • MUSEUM OF CRIME, THE
MUSEO DEL HORROR, EL • 1963 • Baledon Rafael • MXC • MUSEUM OF HORROR, THE
MUSEO DELL'AMORE, IL • 1935 • *Lattuada Alberto* • ITL
MUSEUM, THE see **MUZEUM** • 1966
MUSEUM AND THE FURY, THE • 1956 • Hurwitz Leo T. • DOC • USA
MUSEUM MYSTERY • 1937 • Gulliver Clifford • UKN
MUSEUM OF CRIME, THE see **MUSEO DEL CRIMEN, EL** • 1944
MUSEUM OF HORROR, THE see **MUSEO DEL HORROR, EL** • 1963
MUSEUM PIECES see **EMA TON AGALMATON, TO** • 1981
MUSEUM SPOOKS • 1910 • *Walturdaw* • UKN • DREAMS IN A PICTURE GALLERY
MUSEUMSMYSTERIET • 1909 • *Blom August* • DNM • MYSTERY OF THE MUSEUM, THE
MUSGRAVE RITUAL, THE • 1912 • Treville Georges • UKN
MUSGRAVE RITUAL, THE • 1922 • Ridgwell George • UKN
MUSH AND MILK • 1933 • McGowan Robert • SHT • USA
MUSHIBAMERU HARU • 1932 • Naruse Mikio • JPN • LOST SPRING ○ MOTHEATEN SPRING
MUSHROOM BUTTON, THE see **WHOOPS APOCALYPSE** • 1982
MUSHROOM STEW • 1915 • Birch Cecil • UKN
MUSHROOMS • 1984 • Veilleux Pierre • ANS • CND
MUSHUKU NINBETSUCHU • 1963 • Inoue Kazuo • JPN • ESCAPE FROM HELL
MUSHUKUNIN MIKOSHIN NO JOUKICHI • 1972 • Ikehiro Kazuo • JPN • OUTLAW JOUKICHI OF MIKOSHIN
MUSIC • 1949 • Brzozowska Natalia • HNG
MUSIC • 1968 • Tuchner Michael • DOC • UKN
MUSIC see **ONGAKU** • 1972
MUSIC 2 • Young Robert • DOC • UKN
MUSIC A LA KING • 1941 • Le Borg Reginald • SHT • USA
MUSIC ACADEMY, THE • 1964 • Halas John • ANS • UKN
MUSIC AND COMPUTER • 1965 • Somlo Tamas • SHT • HNG
MUSIC AND FLOWERS • 1938 • Schwarzwald Milton • SHT • USA
MUSIC AND MILLIONS see **SUCH IS LIFE** • 1936
MUSIC AND MODELS • 1938 • Schwarzwald Milton • SHT • USA
MUSIC AND MYSTERY see **SINGING COP, THE** • 1938
MUSIC AT NIGHT see **MUZYKA NOCA** • 1959
MUSIC BLASTERS, THE see **YOU'RE DARN TOOTIN'** • 1928
MUSIC BOX, THE • 1932 • Parrott James • SHT • USA
MUSIC BOX, THE • 1989 • Costa-Gavras • USA
MUSIC BOX, THE see **ORGANCHIK** • 1933

MUSIC BOX, THE see **SING AS YOU SWING** • 1937
MUSIC BOX KID, THE • 1960 • Cahn Edward L. • USA
MUSIC CITY, U.S.A. • 1966 • Collins Preston, Dinet James • USA
MUSIC COMPETITION see **MUSIKWETTBEWERB** • 1967
MUSIC FIENDS • 1929 • Sweet Harry • USA
MUSIC FOR EVERYBODY • 1965 • Luske Hamilton • USA
MUSIC FOR MADAME • 1937 • Blystone John G. • USA
MUSIC FOR MILLIONS • 1944 • Koster Henry • USA
MUSIC FOR OLD ANIMALS see **MUSICA PER ANIMALI** • 1990
MUSIC FROM MARS see **HUDBA Z MARSU** • 1954
MUSIC FROM MONTREAL • 1962 • Bairstow David • DOC • CND
MUSIC: FROM POPULAR TO CONCERT STAGE • 1970 • Galanty Sidney • SHT • USA
MUSIC FROM THE STARS • 1938 • Sparling Gordon • DCS • CND
MUSIC GOES ROUND, THE • 1936 • Schertzinger Victor • USA • ROLLING ALONG
MUSIC HALL • 1934 • Baxter John • UKN
MUSIC HALL see **TANGO TANGLES** • 1914
MUSIC HALL MANAGER'S DILEMMA, THE • 1904 • Booth W. R.? • UKN
MUSIC HALL PARADE • 1939 • Mitchell Oswald • UKN
MUSIC-HALL PARADE • 1958 • Gast Michel • SHT • FRN
MUSIC HALL STAR, THE see **LYDIA** • 1918
MUSIC HATH CHARMS • 1910 • *Vitagraph* • USA
MUSIC HATH CHARMS • 1911 • Bouwmeester Theo • UKN
MUSIC HATH CHARMS • 1914 • *Melies* • USA
MUSIC HATH CHARMS • 1915 • *Tincher Fay* • USA
MUSIC HATH CHARMS • 1917 • Drew Sidney, Drew Sidney Mrs. • SHT • USA
MUSIC HATH CHARMS • 1935 • Bentley Thomas, Esway Alexander, Summers Walter, Woods Arthur • UKN
MUSIC HATH CHARMS -NOT • 1914 • Jackson Harry • USA
MUSIC HATH CHARMS (THAT SOOTH THE SAVAGE BREAST) • 1936 • *Lantz Walter (P)* • ANS • USA
MUSIC HATH ITS CHARMS • 1908 • *Pathe* • FRN
MUSIC IN DARKNESS see **MUSIK I MORKER** • 1947
MUSIC IN FLATS • 1915 • Ransom Charles • USA
MUSIC IN MANHATTAN • 1944 • Auer John H. • USA
MUSIC IN MY HEART • 1940 • Santley Joseph • USA
MUSIC IN OUR SCHOOLS • 1953 • Hall Ken G. • DOC • ASL
MUSIC IN PROGRESS: MIKE WESTBROOK -JAZZ COMPOSER • 1978 • Mapleston Charles • DOC • UKN
MUSIC IN THE AIR • 1934 • May Joe • USA
MUSIC IN THE DARK see **MUSIK I MORKER** • 1947
MUSIC IN THE MORGAN MANNER • 1941 • Ceballos Larry • SHT • USA
MUSIC IN THE WIND • 1945 • Palardy Jean • DCS • CND
MUSIC IN YOUR HAIR • 1934 • Parrott Charles • SHT • USA
MUSIC IS MAGIC • 1935 • Marshall George • USA
MUSIC LAND • 1935 • Jackson Wilfred • ANS • USA
MUSIC LESSON, THE • 1932 • *Iwerks Ub (P)* • ANS • USA
MUSIC LOVERS, THE • 1970 • Russell Ken • UKN • LONELY HEART, THE
MUSIC MACHINE, THE • 1978 • Clarke James Kenelm • UKN
MUSIC MACHINE, THE • 1979 • Sharp Ian • UKN
MUSIC MADE SIMPLE • 1938 • Rowland Roy • USA
MUSIC MAKER, THE • 1936 • Shepherd Horace • UKN
MUSIC MAN, THE • 1938 • Halas John • ANS • UKN
MUSIC MAN, THE • 1948 • Jason Will • USA
MUSIC MAN, THE • 1962 • Da Costa Morton • USA
MUSIC MASTER • 1908 • *Bitzer Billy (Ph)* • USA
MUSIC MASTER • 1950 • Blais Roger • DCS • CND
MUSIC MASTER, THE • 1927 • Dwan Allan • USA
MUSIC MASTER, THE see **PERE CHOPIN, LE** • 1943
MUSIC MICE-TRO, THE • 1967 • Larriva Rudy • ANS • USA
MUSIC OF ARCHITECTURE see **NA PRAZSKEM HRADE** • 1932
MUSIC OF GOVIND see **GEET GOVIND** • 1947
MUSIC OF SATYAJIT RAY, THE • 1984 • Chakraborty Utpalendu • DOC • IND
MUSIC OF THE SPHERES • 1983 • Jackson G. Philip • CND
MUSIC ON BOARD see **MUSIK OMBORD** • 1958
MUSIC ON MARS see **HUDBA Z MARSU** • 1954
MUSIC ROOM, THE see **JALSAGHAR** • 1958
MUSIC SWINDLERS, THE • 1916 • Horne James W. • SHT • USA
MUSIC TEACHER, THE • 1910 • *Powers* • USA
MUSIC TEACHER, THE (UKN) see **MAITRE DE MUSIQUE, LE** • 1988
MUSIC THERAPY • 1983 • Armstrong Mary • DOC • CND
MUSIC WILL TELL • 1938 • Yarbrough Jean • SHT • USA
MUSIC WITH MAX JAFFA • 1959 • Searle Francis • UKN
MUSIC WITHOUT WORDS see **HAWAIIAN REVELLERS, THE** • 1928
MUSIC WITHOUT WORDS see **EMILE GRIMSHAW BANJO QUARTETTE** • 1929
MUSICA, LA • 1966 • Seban Paul, Duras Marguerite • FRN
MUSICA DE AYER • 1959 • de Orduna Juan • SPN
MUSICA DE SIEMPRE • 1956 • Davison Tito • MXC
MUSICA EN LA NOCHE • 1955 • Davison Tito • MXC
MUSICA, ESPUELAS Y AMOR • 1954 • Peon Ramon • MXC
MUSICA IN PIAZZA • 1936 • Mattoli Mario • ITL
MUSICA, MUJERES Y AMOR • 1952 • Urueta Chano • MXC
MUSICA NOCTURNA • 1989 • Penzo Jacobo • VNZ • NOCTURNAL MUSIC
MUSICA PER ANIMALI • 1990 • Benni Stefano, Angelucci Umberto • ITL • MUSIC FOR OLD ANIMALS
MUSICA PER TUTTI see **SILENZIO: SI GIRA!** • 1944
MUSICA PROFANA • 1919 • Caserini Mario • ITL
MUSICA PROIBITA • 1943 • Campogalliani Carlo • ITL
MUSICA Y DINERO • 1956 • Portillo Rafael • MXC
MUSICAL AIRWAVES • 1936 • Schwarzwald Milton • SHT • USA
MUSICAL AMBASSADORS • 1972 • Williams Tony • DOC • USA
MUSICAL BANDIT, THE • 1941 • Roberts Charles E. • SHT • USA
MUSICAL BARBER, THE • 1916 • Stratton Edmund F. • SHT • USA
MUSICAL BEAUTY SHOP, THE • 1930 • Banks Monty • UKN
MUSICAL BOX, THE • 1969 • Kotowski Jerzy • ANM • PLN
MUSICAL CHAIRS, THE • 1969 • Collins Warren • SHT • USA
MUSICAL COCKTAIL, A • 1941 • Shepherd Horace • UKN
MUSICAL DECEPTION, A • 1916 • *Unicorn* • USA
MUSICAL ECCENTRIC, THE • 1899 • Evans Will • UKN • WILL EVANS THE LIVING CATHERINE WHEEL
MUSICAL FARMER • 1932 • Jackson Wilfred • ANS • USA
MUSICAL FILM REVUES NOS. 1-10 • 1933 • Smith Herbert • SHS • UKN
MUSICAL MADNESS • 1916 • Beaudine William • SHT • USA
MUSICAL MADNESS • 1951 • Donnelly Eddie • ANS • USA
MUSICAL MARVEL, A • 1917 • Turpin Ben?, Williamson Robin E.? • SHT • USA
MUSICAL MASQUERADE • 1946 • Shepherd Horace • UKN
MUSICAL MEDLEY • 1929 • Jeffrey R. E. • UKN
MUSICAL MEDLEY NO.1 see **VICTORIA GIRLS, THE** • 1928
MUSICAL MEDLEY NO.1 see **JOE THEISS SAXOTETTE** • 1929
MUSICAL MEDLEY NO.2 see **J.H. SQUIRES' CELESTE OCTET** • 1928
MUSICAL MEDLEY NO.2 see **NORAH BLANEY NO.1** • 1929
MUSICAL MEDLEY NO.3 see **WESTMINSTER GLEE SINGERS, THE** • 1927
MUSICAL MEDLEY NO.3 see **HYDE SISTERS, THE** • 1928
MUSICAL MEDLEY NO.3 see **EMILE GRIMSHAW BANJO QUARTETTE** • 1929
MUSICAL MEDLEY NO.4 see **HAWAIIAN REVELLERS, THE** • 1928
MUSICAL MEDLEY NO.4 see **GENTLEMEN THE CHORUS NO.2** • 1929
MUSICAL MEDLEY NO.4 see **JOSEPHINE EARLE** • 1929
MUSICAL MEDLEY NO.5 see **HOUSTON SISTERS, THE** • 1926
MUSICAL MEDLEY NO.5 see **OLLY OAKLEY** • 1927
MUSICAL MEDLEY NO.5 see **CLAPHAM AND DWYER NO.1** • 1929
MUSICAL MEDLEY NO.6 see **MOUTH ORGAN SOLO** • 1928
MUSICAL MEDLEY NO.6 see **VICTORIA GIRLS SKIPPING** • 1928
MUSICAL MEDLEY NO.6 see **NORAH BLANEY NO.2** • 1929
MUSICAL MEDLEYS NOS.1-6 • 1932 • *British Sound Film Productions* • SHS • UKN
MUSICAL MEMORIES • 1932 • Newman Widgey R. • SER • UKN
MUSICAL MEMORIES • 1935 • Fleischer Dave • ANS • USA
MUSICAL MERRYTONE NO.1 • 1936 • Hammer Will • UKN
MUSICAL MIX-UP, A • 1915 • *Boulder Edward* • USA
MUSICAL MOMENTS • 1929 • Jeffrey R. E. • UKN
MUSICAL MOMENTS FROM CHOPIN • 1947 • Lundy Dick • ANS • USA
MUSICAL MOMENTS NOS.1-5 • 1933 • *British Sound Film Productions* • SHS • UKN
MUSICAL MOUNTAINEERS • 1939 • Fleischer Dave • ANS • USA
MUSICAL MUTINY • 1970 • *Mahon Barry (P)* • USA
MUSICAL PIG, THE see **MUZIKALNO PRASE** • 1965
MUSICAL POSTER NUMBER ONE • 1939 • Lye Len • ANS • UKN
MUSICAL RANCH, THE • 1910 • *Lubin* • USA
MUSICAL ROMANCE • 1947 • Shepherd Horace • UKN
MUSICAL STORY, A • 1940 • Rappaport Herbert, Ivanovsky Alexander • USS
MUSICAL TRAMPS see **HIS MUSICAL CAREER** • 1914
MUSICALULU • 1946 • Sparber I. • ANS • USA
MUSICANADA • 1975 • Gillson Malca, Ianzelo Tony • DOC • CND
MUSICI • 1963 • Georgi Katja, Georgi Klaus • ANS • GDR • MUSICIANS
MUSICIAN see **MUZIKANT** • 1947
MUSICIAN IN THE FAMILY, A • 1953 • Parker Gudrun • SHT • CND • MUSICIEN DANS LA FAMILLE, UN
MUSICIANS see **MUSICI** • 1963
MUSICIANS see **MUSICOS** • 1971
MUSICIANS, THE • 1970 • Kobakhidze Mikhail • SHT • USS
MUSICIANS, THE see **MUZYKANCI** • 1960
MUSICIANS, THE see **MUSIKANTER** • 1967
MUSICIAN'S DAUGHTER, THE • 1911 • *Eclair* • USA
MUSICIAN'S DAUGHTER, THE • 1914 • *Fealy Maude* • USA
MUSICIANS FROM THE SAME REGIMENT • 1965 • Kadochnikov A., Kazansky Gennadi • USS
MUSICIAN'S GIRL, THE see **MUSIKANTSKA LIDUSKA** • 1940
MUSICIAN'S LIDUSKA, THE see **MUSIKANTSKA LIDUSKA** • 1940
MUSICIAN'S LOVE STORY, THE • 1909 • *Essanay* • USA
MUSICIAN'S WIFE, THE • 1914 • *Reliance* • USA
MUSICIEN DANS LA FAMILLE, UN see **MUSICIAN IN THE FAMILY, A** • 1953
MUSICIENS DU CIEL, LES • 1939 • Lacombe Georges • FRN
MUSICKERS • 1916 • *Cooper Claude* • USA
MUSICMAKER, THE • 1984 • SAF
MUSICO, POETA Y LOCO • 1947 • Gomez Landero Humberto • MXC
MUSICOMANIE, LA • 1910 • Cohl Emile • ANS • FRN
MUSICOS • 1971 • Nunez Pablo • ANS • SPN • MUSICIANS
MUSIC'S THE THING, THE see **NEM ELHETEK MUZSIKASZO NELKUL** • 1979
MUSIK BEI NACHT • 1953 • Hoffmann Kurt • FRG
MUSIK FUR DICH • 1937 • Emo E. W. • AUS
MUSIK I MORKER • 1947 • Bergman Ingmar • SWD • NIGHT IS MY FUTURE ○ MUSIC IN DARKNESS ○ MUSIC IN THE DARK
MUSIK IM BLUT • 1934 • Waschneck Erich • FRG
MUSIK IM BLUT • 1955 • Ode Erik • FRG
MUSIK IM SALZBURG • 1944 • Maisch Herbert • FRG
MUSIK, MUSIK -UND NUR MUSIK • 1955 • Matray Ernst • FRG
MUSIK OMBORD • 1958 • Lindberg Sven • SWD • MUSIC ON BOARD
MUSIKANTER • 1967 • Skouen Arne • NRW • MUSICIANS, THE
MUSIKANTSKA LIDUSKA • 1940 • Fric Martin • CZC • MUSICIAN'S LIDUSKA, THE ○ MUSICIAN'S GIRL, THE ○ LIDUSKA OF THE STAGE
MUSIKENS MAKT • 1913 • Klercker Georg • SWD • POWER OF MUSIC, THE
MUSIKPARADE • 1956 • von Cziffra Geza • FRG
MUSIKWETTBEWERB • 1967 • Seiler Alexander J. • DOC • SWT • MUSIC COMPETITION
MUSIQUE EN MEDITERRANEE • 1968 • Reichenbach Francois • SHT • FRN
MUSIQUE EN TETE • 1951 • Combret Georges, Orval Claude • FRN
MUSIQUE TROPICALE • 1947-51 • Verneuil Henri • SHT • FRN
MUSIQUIZ • 1952 • Barclay David • SHT • USA
MUSKARCI • 1962 • Djukanovic Milo • YGS • MEN, THE
MUSKETEERS OF LITTLE SIDE, THE see **MALOSTRANSTI MUSKETYRI** • 1932
MUSKETEERS OF PIG ALLEY • 1912 • Griffith D. W. • USA
MUSKETEERS OF THE QUEEN, THE see **MOUSQUETAIRES DE LA REINE, LES** • 1903
MUSKETEERS OF THE SEA (USA) see **MOSCHETTIERI DEL MARE, I** • 1962
MUSKETIER KACZMAREK • 1917 • Froelich Carl • FRG • KACZMAREK
MUSKETIER MEIER II • 1938 • Stockel Joe • FRG
MUSKOKA, A LOOK BACK • 1983 • Kohanyi Julius • CND
MUSODURO • 1954 • Bennati Giuseppe • ITL
MUSS DIE FRAU MUTTER WERDEN? • 1924 • *Projektions-Ag Union* • FRG
MUSS DIE FRAU MUTTER WERDEN? see **PARAGRAPH 144** • 1924
MUSS DIE FRAU MUTTER WERDEN? see **FRAUEN, HUTET EURE MUTTERSCHAFT!** • 1925
MUSS 'EM UP • 1936 • Vidor Charles • USA • HOUSE OF FATE (UKN) ○ GREEN SHADOW, THE ○ SINISTER HOUSE
MUSS I DEN ZUM STADTELE HINAUS • 1962 • Deppe Hans • FRG
MUSS MAN SICH GLEICH SCHEIDEN LASSEN? • 1932 • Behrendt Hans • FRG
MUSS MAN SICH GLEICH SCHEIDEN LASSEN? • 1953 • Schweikart Hans • FRG
MUSSOLINI see **MUSSOLINI ULTIMO ATTO** • 1974
MUSSOLINI AND I • 1985 • Negrin Alberto • TVM • USA • MUSSOLINI: THE DECLINE AND FALL OF IL DUCE
MUSSOLINI SPEAKS • 1933 • *Thomas Lowell* • DOC • USA
MUSSOLINI: THE DECLINE AND FALL OF IL DUCE see **MUSSOLINI AND I** • 1985
MUSSOLINI, THE LAST ACT see **MUSSOLINI ULTIMO ATTO** • 1974
MUSSOLINI: THE LAST FOUR DAYS see **MUSSOLINI ULTIMO ATTO** • 1974
MUSSOLINI ULTIMO ATTO • 1974 • Lizzani Carlo • ITL • MUSSOLINI: THE LAST FOUR DAYS ○ LAST FOUR DAYS, THE (USA) ○ LAST DAYS OF MUSSOLINI ○ MUSSOLINI, THE LAST ACT ○ MUSSOLINI
MUSSOLINIA DI SARDEGNA • 1933 • Matarazzo Raffaello • SHT • ITL
MUSSORGSKII • 1950 • Roshal Grigori • USS • MOUSSORGSKI
MUST WE MARRY? • 1928 • Mattison Frank S. • USA • ONE EMBARRASSING NIGHT (UKN)
MUSTA LUMIKKI • 1971 • Sokka Matti • FNL • BLACK SNOW WHITE
MUSTA RAKKAUS • 1957 • Laine Edvin • FNL • BLACK LOVE
MUSTAA VALKOISELLA • 1968 • Donner Jorn • FNL • BLACK AND WHITE (UKN) ○ BLACK ON WHITE (USA)
MUSTACHES AND BOMBS • 1915 • *Jamison Bud* • USA
MUSTAFA FROM GALATA see **GALATALI MUSTAFA** • 1967
MUSTAFA KAMEL • 1953 • Badrakhan Ahmed • EGY
MUSTAHIL, AL- • 1964 • Kamal Hussein • EGY • IMPOSSIBLE, L' ○ MOSTAHIL, AL
MUSTANG • 1959 • Stephens Peter • USA
MUSTANG • 1975 • Lefebvre Marcel • CND
MUSTANG COUNTRY • 1976 • Champion John • USA
MUSTANG PETE'S LOVE AFFAIR • 1911 • *Todd William* • USA
MUSTANG PETE'S PRESSING ENGAGEMENT • 1915 • *Potel Victor* • USA
MUSTARD PLASTER, THE • 1909 • *Essanay* • USA
MUSTERGATTE, DER • 1937 • Liebeneiner Wolfgang • FRG • MODEL HUSBAND (USA)
MUSTERGATTE, DER • 1956 • Ode Erik • FRG
MUSTERKNABE, DER • 1963 • Jacobs Werner • AUS
MUSTERKNABEN • 1959 • Knittel Johannes • GDR
MUSTY BE YOUNG • 1917 • *Essanay* • USA
MUSTY MUSKETEERS • 1954 • White Jules • SHT • USA
MUSTY'S VACATION • 1917 • *Watson Harry Jr.* • USA
MUSUKO NO KEKKON • 1958 • Shima Koji • JPN • MY SON'S REVOLT
MUSUKO NO SEISHUN • 1952 • Kobayashi Masaki • JPN • MY SON'S YOUTH
MUSULMAN RIGOLO, LE • 1897 • Melies Georges • FRN • FUNNY MAHOMETAN, A
MUSUME • 1926 • Gosho Heinosuke • JPN • DAUGHTER
MUSUME • 1958 • Mori Masaki • JPN
MUSUME DOJIJI • 1945 • Ichikawa Kon • JPN • GIRL AT DOJO TEMPLE, A
MUSUME KAWAIYA • 1928 • Mizoguchi Kenji • JPN • MY LOVING DAUGHTER
MUSUME NO BOKEN • 1958 • Shima Koji • JPN • PERFECT MATE
MUSUME NO GYAKUSHU • 1947 • Nakamura Noboru • JPN • COUNTER-ATTACK OF GIRLS
MUSUME NO KISETSU • 1968 • Higuchi Hiromi • JPN • SEASON FOR GIRLS, A
MUSUME SAMBA GARASU • 1957 • Hozumi Toshimasa • JPN
MUSUME TO WATASHI • 1962 • Horikawa Hiromichi • JPN • MY DAUGHTER AND I
MUSUME TSUMA HAHA • 1960 • Naruse Mikio • JPN • DAUGHTERS, WIVES AND A MOTHER ○ HAHA, TSUMA, MUSUME ○ MOTHER, WIFE, DAUGHTER
MUT • 1939 • Kalatozov Mikhail • USS • MANHOOD ○ COURAGE
MUT ZUM GLUCK, DER • 1917 • von Woringen Paul • FRG
MUT ZUR SUNDE, DER • 1918 • *Albers Hans* • FRG
MUTA DI PORTICI, LA • 1954 • Ansoldi Giorgio • ITL
MUTAMARRID, AL- see **MOUTAMARRED, AL** • 1968
MUTAMARRIDUN, AL- see **MOUTAMARRIDOUNE, AL** • 1968
MUTANT • 1983 • Cardos John Bud • USA • NIGHT SHADOWS
MUTANT see **FORBIDDEN WORLD** • 1982
MUTANT 2 see **ALIEN PREDATORS** • 1987

MUTANT HUNT • 1986 • Kincaid Tim • USA • MATT RYKER: MUTANT HUNT
MUTANT KID, THE • Szarka William • USA • PLUTONIUM BABY
MUTANT ON THE BOUNTY • 1989 • Torrance Robert • USA
MUTANT WAR • 1988 • Piper Brett • USA
MUTATION see **PLAGUE** • 1978
MUTATION, THE • 1967 • Lemaire Jean • ANS • BLG
MUTATION, THE see **MUTATIONS, THE** • 1973
MUTATIONS • 1972 • Schwartz Lillian, Knowlton Kenneth • ANS • USA
MUTATIONS, THE • 1973 • Cardiff Jack • UKN, USA • MUTATION, THE ○ FREAKMAKER, THE
MUTCHAN NO UTA • 1985 • Horikawa Hiromichi • JPN • SONG OF MUTSUKO
MUTE, THE see **MOOGA JEEVULU** • 1968
MUTE APPEAL, A • 1917 • Edwin Walter • USA
MUTE CONNECTION • 1987 • Derakhshandeh Pooran • IRN
MUTE WITNESS, THE • 1913 • Dwan Allan • USA
MUTEKI • 1952 • Taniguchi Senkichi • JPN • FOG HORN
MUTEPPO JIDAI • 1928 • Tasaka Tomotaka • JPN • RECKLESS PERIOD
MUTHERS, THE • 1968 • *Jordan Marsha* • USA • MOTHERS, THE
MUTHERS, THE • 1976 • Santiago Cirio H. • USA
MUTHU CHIPPI • 1968 • Krishnan M. • IND • OYSTER SHELL, THE
MUTIGE SEEFAHRER, THE • 1935 • Deppe Hans • FRG
MUTILATION see **HONENUKI** • 1967
MUTILATOR, THE • 1983 • Cooper Buddy • USA
MUTINEERS, THE • 1949 • Yarbrough Jean • USA • PIRATE SHIP
MUTINES DE L'ELSENEUR, LES • 1936 • Chenal Pierre • FRN
MUTINY • 1916 • Hunt Jay • SHT • USA
MUTINY • 1917 • Reynolds Lynn • USA • MUTINY OF THE AIDEN BESSE, THE (UKN) ○ CRUISE OF THE AIDEN BESSE, THE
MUTINY • 1924 • Thornton F. Martin • UKN • DIANA OF THE ISLANDS
MUTINY • 1952 • Dmytryk Edward • USA
MUTINY, THE see **MUTINY OF THE ELSINORE, THE** • 1920
MUTINY AHEAD • 1934 • Atkins Thomas • USA
MUTINY AIN'T NICE • 1938 • Fleischer Dave • ANS • USA
MUTINY AT FORT SHARP see **PER UN DOLLARO DI GLORIA** • 1966
MUTINY AT FORT SHARP (USA) see **ESCADRON DE LA MUERTE, EL** • 1966
MUTINY IN OUTER SPACE • 1965 • Grimaldi Hugo • USA, ITL • AMMUTINAMENTO NELLO SPAZIO (ITL) ○ INVASION FROM THE MOON ○ SPACE STATION X-14 ○ ATTACK FROM OUTER SPACE
MUTINY IN OUTER SPACE see **SPACE MASTER X-7** • 1958
MUTINY IN SPACE • 1988 • Winters David • USA
MUTINY IN THE ARCTIC • 1941 • Rawlins John • USA
MUTINY IN THE BIG HOUSE • 1939 • Nigh William • USA
MUTINY IN THE COUNTY • 1940 • D'Arcy Harry • SHT • USA
MUTINY IN THE JUNGLE • 1915 • Beal Frank • USA
MUTINY IN THE KITCHEN • 1908 • Coleby A. E. • UKN
MUTINY IN THE SOUTH SEAS see **LETZTEN DREI DER ALBATROS, DIE** • 1965
MUTINY OF MR. HENPECK, THE • 1913 • *Solax* • USA
MUTINY OF THE AIDEN BESSE, THE (UKN) see **MUTINY** • 1917
MUTINY OF THE BODY • 1939 • Parrott Charles • USA
MUTINY OF THE BOUNTY • 1916 • Longford Raymond • ASL
MUTINY OF THE ELSINORE, THE • 1920 • Sloman Edward • USA • MUTINY, THE
MUTINY OF THE ELSINORE, THE • 1937 • Lockwood Roy • UKN
MUTINY ON A RUSSIAN BATTLESHIP • 1905 • Collins Alf • UKN
MUTINY ON THE BLACKHAWK • 1939 • Cabanne W. Christy • USA
MUTINY ON THE BOUNTY • 1935 • Lloyd Frank • USA
MUTINY ON THE BOUNTY • 1962 • Milestone Lewis, Reed Carol • USA
MUTINY ON THE BOUNTY • 1983 • Donaldson Roger • USA, UKN • SAGA OF H.M.S. BOUNTY, THE ○ BOUNTY, THE
MUTINY ON THE BUNNY • 1950 • Freleng Friz • ANS • USA
MUTINY ON THE BUSES • 1972 • Booth Harry • UKN
MUTINY ON THE FOREPOST see **MYATYEZHNAYA ZASTAVA** • 1967
MUTINY ON THE SEAS (UKN) see **OUTSIDE THE THREE MILE LIMIT** • 1940
MUTOSCOPE SHORTS • 1897 • *Bitzer Billy (Ph)* • USA
MUTT AND JEFF • 1916-28 • *Fisher Bud (P)* • ASS • USA
MUTT IN A RUT, A • 1949 • Sparber I. • ANS • USA
MUTT IN A RUT, A • 1959 • McKimson Robert • ANS • USA
MUTTAHIMA, AL- • 1942 • Barakat Henry • EGY • ACCUSEE, L'
MUTTER • 1917 • Henning Hanna • FRG
MUTTER • 1941 • Brignone Guido • FRG
MUTTER AUGEN, DER • Mack Max • FRG
MUTTER COURAGE UND IHRE KINDER • 1955 • Staudte Wolfgang • FRG
MUTTER COURAGE UND IHRE KINDER • 1960 • Palitzsch Peter, Wekwerth Manfred • GDR • MOTHER COURAGE AND HER CHILDREN
MUTTER, DEIN KIND RUFT • 1923 • Gliese Rochus • FRG • BRENNENDE GEHEIMNIS, DAS
MUTTER DER KOMPAGNIE, DIE • 1934 • Seitz Franz • FRG
MUTTER EBENBILD, DER • 1916 • Oberlander Hans • FRG
MUTTER ERDE • 1919 • Burg Eugen • FRG
MUTTER (FRG) see **MAMMA** • 1941
MUTTER HERZBLUT, EINER see **ER IST DEIN BRUDER** • 1923
MUTTER KAMPFT UM IHR KIND, EINE see **MONIKA** • 1937
MUTTER KRAUSENS FAHRT INS GLUCK • 1929 • Jutzi Phil • FRG • MOTHER KRAUSEN'S JOURNEY TO HAPPINESS
MUTTER KUSTERS FAHRT ZUM HIMMEL • 1975 • Fassbinder R. W. • FRG • MOTHER KUSTER'S TRIP TO HEAVEN (UKN) ○ MOTHER KUSTERS GOES TO HEAVEN (USA)
...MUTTER SEIN DAGEGEN SEHR • 1951 • Tourjansky Victor • FRG
MUTTER UND KIND • 1924 • Froelich Carl • FRG • MOTHER AND CHILD
MUTTER UND KIND • 1933 • Steinhoff Hans • FRG • MOTHER AND CHILD
MUTTER UND SOHN • 1915 • *Halden Hans* • FRG
MUTTER UND SOHN • 1924 • Schirokauer Alfred • FRG
MUTTER, VERZAGET NICHT! • 1910 • Gartner Adolf • FRG
MUTTERHERZ • 1923 • von Bolvary Geza • FRG
MUTTERLIEBE • 1929 • Jacoby Georg • FRG • MOTHER LOVE (USA)
MUTTERLIEBE • 1939 • Ucicky Gustav • FRG • MOTHER LOVE (USA)
MUTTERLIED (FRG) see **SOLO PER TE** • 1937
MUTTERSORGEN see **IN DEN KRALLEN DER SCHULD** • 1924
MUTT'N BONES • 1944 • Sommer Paul • ANS • USA
MUTTON EATERS, THE see **LAMPAANSYOJAT** • 1972
MUTTS ABOUT RACING • 1958 • Lah Michael • ANS • USA
MUTTS AND MOTORS • 1918 • Semon Larry • SHT • USA
MUTTS TO YOU • 1938 • Parrott Charles • SHT • USA
MUTTSURI UMON TORIMONO-CHO-KIMEN YASHIKI • 1955 • Yamamoto Kajiro • JPN
MUTUAL MONOGRAPH NO.1: WITH JULIAN STREET AND WALLACE MORGAN • 1915 • *Reliance* • USA
MUTUAL UNDERSTANDING, A • 1913 • Lessey George A. • USA
MUTUALITY • 1984 • Sommers Frank G. • DOC • CND
MUUKALAINEN • 1982 • Lehmuskallio Markku • FNL • STRANGER, A
MUURAHAISPOLKU • 1970 • Makinen Aito, Lehtinen Virke • FNL • SUMMER TRAIL
MUURMANNIN PAKOLAISET • 1926 • Karu Erkki • FNL
MUZ, KTERY STOUPL V CENE • 1967 • Moravec Jan, Podskalsky Zdenek • CZC • MAN WHOSE PRICE WENT UP, THE
MUZ KTORY LUZE • 1968 • Robbe-Grillet Alain • CZC, FRN • HOMME QUI MENT, L' (FRN) ○ MAN WHO LIES, THE ○ SHOCK TROOPS
MUZ, KTORY SA NEVRATIL • 1959 • Solan Peter • CZC • MAN WHO DID NOT RETURN, THE
MUZ NA DRATE • 1985 • Matula Julius • CZC • MAN ON THE LINE, THE
MUZ NA UTEKU • 1968 • Sklenar Vaclav • CZC • MAN ON THE RUN, A
MUZ PRES PALUBU • 1981 • Borek Jaromir • CZC • MAN OVERBOARD
MUZ SE PSEM • 1968 • Krumbachova Ester • CZC • MAN WITH A DOG, A
MUZ Z NEZNAMA • 1939 • Fric Martin • CZC • RELUCTANT MILLIONAIRE
MUZ Z PRVNIHO STOLETI • 1961 • Lipsky Oldrich • CZC • MAN IN OUTER SPACE (USA) ○ MAN FROM THE FIRST CENTURY ○ ZAVINIL TO EINSTEIN ○ MAN FROM THE PAST, THE ○ ALL EINSTEIN'S FAULT
MUZEUM • 1966 • Ziarnik Jerzy • DOC • PLN • MUSEUM, THE
MUZH I DOCH TAMARI ALEXANDROVNY • 1989 • Narutskaya Olga • USS • TAMARA ALEXANDROVNA'S HUSBAND AND DAUGHTER
MUZHCHINA OKOLO VAS • 1979 • Gadzhiu Valeriu • USS • MAN CLOSE TO YOU, A
MUZI BEZ KRIDEL • 1946 • Cap Frantisek • CZC • MEN WITHOUT WINGS
MUZI V OFFSIDU • 1931 • Innemann Svatopluk • CZC • MEN OFF-SIDE ○ MEN IN THE OFFSIDE ○ MEN IN OFFSIDE, THE
MUZIKALNO PRASE • 1965 • Grgic Zlatko • ANS • YGS • MUSICAL PIG, THE
MUZIKANT • 1947 • Cap Frantisek • CZC • MUSICIAN
MUZIO SCEVOLA see **COLOSSO DI ROMA, IL** • 1964
MUZNIBUN, AL • 1976 • Marzouk Said • EGY • CULPRITS, THE ○ MUDHNIBUN, AL-
MUZYCZKA • 1961 • Laskowski Jan • ANS • PLN • LITTLE MUSIC, A
MUZYKA DAWNA • 1964 • Grabowski Stanislaw • PLN • ANCIENT MUSIC
MUZYKA NOCA • 1959 • Stando Robert • PLN • MUSIC AT NIGHT
MUZYKANCI • 1960 • Karabasz Kazimierz • DCS • PLN • MUSICIANS, THE
MUZZLE, THE see **FREEDOM OF THE PRESS** • 1928
MUZZLE, THE see **KANONEN-SERENADE** • 1958
MUZZLE TOUGH • 1954 • Freleng Friz • ANS • USA
MWANA KEBA • Kamba Sebastien • SHT • CNG
MWETT, LE • 1972 • Ze-Lecourt Moise • SHT • CMR
MXC see **SNAKE PEOPLE** • 1968
MY 20TH CENTURY (UKN) see **EN XX. SZAZADOM, A** • 1988
MY ADORABLE SLAVE see **MI ADORABLE ESCLAVA** • 1961
MY ADORED CLEMENTINE see **MI ADORADA CLEMENTINA** • 1953
MY AFRICAN ADVENTURE see **GOING BANANAS** • 1987
MY AIN FOLK • 1944 • Burger Germain • UKN
MY AMERICAN COUSIN • 1985 • Wilson Sandra • CND
MY AMERICAN UNCLE (UKN) see **MON ONCLE D'AMERIQUE** • 1980
MY AMERICAN WIFE • 1922 • Wood Sam • USA • COUNT OF ARIZONA, THE
MY AMERICAN WIFE • 1936 • Young Harold • USA
MY APPRENTICESHIP see **V LYUDKYAKH** • 1939
MY ARTISTICAL TEMPERATURE • 1937 • Fleischer Dave • ANS • USA
MY ASYLUM see **CHIEDO ASILO** • 1979
MY AUNT see **TEYZEM** • 1985
MY AUNTIE see **CHANG-PEI** • 1981
MY AUNT'S MILLIONS see **FASTERS MILLIONER** • 1934
MY AUSTIN SEVEN • 1929 • Aylott Dave, Symmons E. F. • SHT • UKN
MY AYSE see **AYSEM** • 1968
MY BABY • 1912 • Griffith D. W. • USA
MY BABY IS BLACK! (USA) see **LACHES VIVENT D'ESPOIR, LES** • 1961
MY BABY JUST CARES FOR ME • 1931 • Fleischer Dave • ANS • USA
MY BABY LOVES MUSIC see **MY GAL LOVES MUSIC** • 1944
MY BABY'S VOICE • 1912 • *Snow Marguerite* • USA
MY BARE LADY • 1962 • Knight Arthur • UKN • MY SEVEN LITTLE BARES ○ BARE LADY, BARE WORLD ○ IT'S A BARE WORLD
MY BEAUTIFUL LAUNDRETTE • 1985 • Frears Stephen • UKN
MY BED IS NOT FOR SLEEPING (UKN) see **NEGRESCO **** – EINE TODLICHE AFFAIRE** • 1967
MY BELOVED see **DOROGOI MOI CHELOVEK** • 1958
MY BELOVED see **MIN ALSKANDE** • 1979
MY BELOVED BROTHER see **CANIM KARDESIM** • 1973
MY BELOVED CHILD see **ITOSHINO WAGAKO** • 1926
MY BELOVED CHILDREN see **SAYANG ANAKKU SAYANG** • 1975
MY BELOVED MOTHER see **CANIM ANNEM** • 1967
MY BEST FRIEND IS A VAMPIRE • 1988 • Huston Jimmy • USA • I WAS A TEENAGE VAMPIRE
MY BEST FRIEND'S GIRL (USA) see **FEMME DE MON POTE, LA** • 1983
MY BEST GAL • 1944 • Mann Anthony • USA
MY BEST GIRL • 1915 • *Figman Max* • USA
MY BEST GIRL • 1927 • Taylor Sam • USA
MY BILL • 1938 • Farrow John • USA • IN EVERY WOMAN'S LIFE
MY BLOOD RUNS COLD • 1965 • Conrad William • USA
MY BLOODY VALENTINE • 1981 • Mihalka George • CND
MY BLUE HEAVEN • 1929 • Aylott Dave, Symmons E. F. • SHT • UKN
MY BLUE HEAVEN • 1950 • Koster Henry • USA
MY BLUE HEAVEN • 1990 • Beer Ronald • NTH
MY BLUE HEAVEN • 1990 • Ross Herbert • USA
MY BODY BELONGS TO ME see **MON CORPS EST A MOI** • 1967
MY BODY BURNS • 1974 • Pallardy Jean-Marie • FRN
MY BODY HUNGERS • 1967 • Sarno Joe • USA
MY BODY, MY CHILD • 1982 • Chomsky Marvin • TVM • USA
MY BODYGUARD • 1979 • Bill Tony • USA
MY BONNIE • 1925 • Fleischer Dave • ANS • USA
MY BONNIE HIELAND MAGGIE • 1929 • Aylott Dave, Symmons E. F. • SHT • UKN
MY BOTTLE IS DRY • 1946 • Crouch William Forest • SHT • USA
MY BOY • 1919 • Blackton J. Stuart • USA
MY BOY • 1921 • Heerman Victor, Austin Albert • USA
MY BOY JOHNNY • 1944 • Donnelly Eddie • ANS • USA
MY BOYS ARE GOOD BOYS • 1978 • Buckalew Bethel • USA
MY BRAVE FRIEND see **KUDUZ RECEP** • 1967
MY BREAKFAST WITH BLASSIE • 1983 • Legend Johnny, Lautrec Linda • USA
MY BRIDE IS A GHOST see **MI NOVIA ES UNA FANTASMA** • 1944
MY BRIDE IS A GHOST see **KAIDAN BOTAN DORO** • 1968
MY BRILLIANT CAREER • 1979 • Armstrong Gillian • ASL
MY BROER SE BRIL • 1972 • SAF
MY BROTHER • 1929 • Krol G. • USS
MY BROTHER see **KARDESIM BENIM** • 1983
MY BROTHER AGOSTINO • 1911 • *Lubin* • USA
MY BROTHER ANASTASIA • 1973 • *Conte Richard* • ITL
MY BROTHER DOWN THERE see **RUNNING TARGET** • 1956
MY BROTHER HAS A BROTHER see **MUJ BRACHA MA PRIMA BRACHU** • 1975
MY BROTHER HAS COME see **E' ARRIVATO MIO FRATELLO** • 1985
MY BROTHER JONATHAN • 1948 • French Harold • UKN • BROTHER JONATHAN
MY BROTHER, MY LOVE see **ANIKI NO KOIBITO** • 1968
MY BROTHER TALKS TO HORSES • 1946 • Zinnemann Fred • USA
MY BROTHER, THE OUTLAW see **MY OUTLAW BROTHER** • 1951
MY BROTHERS AND I • 1964 • Narliev Khodzhakuli • USS
MY BROTHER'S KEEPER • 1948 • Roome Alfred, Rich Roy • UKN • DOUBLE PURSUIT
MY BROTHER'S WEDDING • 1983 • Burnett Charles • USA
MY BROTHER'S WIFE • 1966 • Wishman Doris • USA
MY BRUDDER SYLVEST • 1913 • *Crystal* • USA
MY BUDDY • 1944 • Sekely Steve • USA
MY BUNNY LIES OVER THE SEA • 1948 • Jones Charles M. • ANS • USA
MY CALLING CARD see **KAYNTIKORTTINI** • 1964
MY CANDIDATE (USA) see **MI CANDIDATO** • 1937
MY CARRIERE FINANCIERE see **MY FINANCIAL CAREER** • 1962
MY CHAMPION • 1981 • Arner Gwen • USA, JPN • RUN, MIKI, RUN
MY CHAUFFEUR • 1985 • Beaird David • USA
MY CHILD see **MEIN KIND** • 1956
MY CHILD see **MERA MUNNA** • 1967
MY CHILDHOOD see **LAPSUUTENI** • 1967
MY CHILDHOOD: JAMES BALDWIN'S HARLEM AND HUBERT HUMPHREY'S SOUTH DAKOTA • 1964 • Horan Don • USA
MY CHILDHOOD/ MY AIN FOLK • 1972-73 • Douglas Bill • UKN
MY CINEMAS • 1989 • TRK
MY CITY see **ORASUL MEU** • 1967
MY CONSCIENCE AND I see **YA I MOYA SOVEST** • 1915
MY COUNTRY • 1918 • *Costello John* • SHT • USA
MY COUNTRY • 1922 • ASL • LAND WE LIVE IN, THE
MY COUNTRY see **MOI RODINA** • 1932
MY COUNTRY FIRST • 1916 • Terriss Tom • USA
MY COUNTRY MY HAT • 1983 • SAF
MY COUNTRY, 'TIS OF THEE • 1916 • Calvert E. H. • SHT • USA
MY COUNTRY'S WINGS (USA) see **ALAS DE MI PATRIA** • 1940
MY COUSIN • 1918 • Jose Edward • USA
MY COUSIN RACHEL • 1952 • Koster Henry • USA
MY CRIME WHILE AT THE FIRST HIGHER SCHOOL see **WAGA ICHIKO JIDAI NO HANZAI** • 1951
MY DAD • 1922 • Smith Cliff • USA
MY DAD see **MOJ STARY** • 1962
MY DADDY THE ASTRONAUT • 1967 • Culhane Shamus • ANS • USA
MY DARK CHANCE see **KARA BAHTIM** • 1968
MY DARK FATE see **ALNIMIN KARA YAZISI** • 1968
MY DARK FATE see **KARA YAZIM** • 1968
MY DARK LADY • 1984 • Keller Frederick King • USA
MY DARLING see **TESORO MIO** • 1979

MY DARLING CLEMENTINE • 1944 • Munro Grant • ANS • CND
MY DARLING CLEMENTINE • 1946 • Ford John • USA
MY DARLING CLEMENTINE see **DRAHOUSEK KLEMENTYNA** • 1959
MY DARLING DAUGHTER'S ANNIVERSARY • 1973 • Pevney Joseph • TVM • USA
MY DARLING IZA see **MOJA DRAGA IZA** • 1979
MY DARLING, MY DARLING • 1986 • Zahariev Edward • BUL
MY DARLING, MY DEAREST see **BELLO MIO BELLEZZA MIA** • 1982
MY DARLING, MY GODDESS see **AI-JEN NU-SHENG** • 1983
MY DARLING SHIKSA see **OVER THE BROOKLYN BRIDGE** • 1983
MY DARLING SLAVE see **SCHIAVA IO CE L'HO E TU NO, LA** • 1973
MY DAUGHTER • 1960 • Zhilin Viktor • USS
MY DAUGHTER AND I see **MUSUME TO WATASHI** • 1962
MY DAUGHTER HILDEGART see **MI HIJA HILDEGART** • 1977
MY DAUGHTER IS A LIAR see **KORI MOU I PSEFTRA, I** • 1967
MY DAUGHTER IS DIFFERENT see **EN LANYON NEM OLYAN, AZ** • 1936
MY DAUGHTER JOY • 1950 • Ratoff Gregory • UKN • OPERATION X (USA)
MY DAUGHTER, SAHAR • 1989 • Gharizadeh Majid • IRN
MY DAYS WITH VERONICA see **MIS DIAS CON VERONICA** • 1980
MY DEAR, BELOVED, ONLY ONE • Asanova Dinara • USS
MY DEAR BODYGUARD see **SEVGILI MUHAFIZIN** • 1970
MY DEAR DOCTOR GRASLER see **MIO CARO DOTTOR GRASLER** • 1990
MY DEAR LOVE • 1911 • Fitzhamon Lewin? • UKN
MY DEAR MAN see **DOROGOI MOI CHELOVEK** • 1958
MY DEAR MISS ALDRICH • 1937 • Seitz George B. • USA
MY DEAR SECRETARY • 1948 • Martin Charles • USA
MY DEAREST FRIEND see **MERE HUMDUM MERE DOST** • 1968
MY DEAREST MARIA see **MARIA DE MI CORAZON** • 1980
MY DEAREST SENORITA see **MI QUERIDA SENORITA** • 1971
MY DEAREST TREASURE see **TESORO MIO** • 1979
MY DEATH IS A MOCKERY • 1952 • Young Tony • UKN
MY DEMON LOVER • 1987 • Loventhal Charles • USA
MY DESTINY see **WAGA TOSO** • 1968
MY DIMITRI, MY DIMITRI see **DIMITRI MOU, DIMITRI MOU** • 1967
MY DINNER WITH ANDRE • 1981 • Malle Louis • USA
MY DOG BUDDY • 1960 • Kellogg Ray • USA
MY DOG PAL • 1920 • Fishback Fred C. • SHT • USA
MY DOG RUSTY • 1948 • Landers Lew • USA
MY DOG SHEP • 1946 • Beebe Ford • USA
MY DOG, THE THIEF • 1969 • Stevenson Robert • USA
MY DOLLY • 1909 • Smith Jack ? • UKN
MY DOUBLE AND HOW HE UNDID ME • 1912 • *Edison* • USA
MY DREAM CITY see **MINA DROMMARS STAD** • 1976
MY DREAM IS YOURS • 1949 • Curtiz Michael • USA
MY DREAMS, MY LOVE AND YOU see **HAYALLERIN, ASKIM VE SEN** • 1987
MY ENEMY THE SEA see **TAIHEIYO HITORIBOTCHI** • 1963
MY ENGLISH GRANDFATHER • 1986 • Dzhordzhadze Nana • USS
MY EYE see **MON OEIL** • 1966
MY FACE RED IN THE SUNSET see **YUHI NI AKAI NO KAO** • 1961
MY FAIR LADY • 1964 • Cukor George • USA
MY FALSE BELOVED see **YALANCI YARIM** • 1974
MY FATHER • Waxman Daniel • SHT • ISR
MY FATHER • 1917 • Chapin Benjamin • *Charter* • SHT • USA
MY FATHER • 1918 • *Chapin* • SHT • USA
MY FATHER see **APA** • 1966
MY FATHER LIVES IN RIO see **MIJN VADER WOONT IN RIO** • 1989
MY FATHER, MY RIVAL • 1986 • Jutra Claude • CND
MY FATHER, MY SON • 1988 • Bleckner Jeff • TVM • USA
MY FATHERLAND see **MOI RODINA** • 1932
MY FATHER'S BURDEN • 1961 • Olusola Segun • NGR
MY FATHER'S HAPPY YEARS see **APAM NEHANY BOLDOG EVE** • 1978
MY FATHER'S HOUSE • 1947 • Kline Herbert • USA
MY FATHER'S HOUSE • 1975 • Segal Alex • TVM • USA
MY FATHER'S MISTRESS see **BAMSE** • 1969
MY FATHER'S WIFE see **MUJER DE MI PADRE, LA** • 1967
MY FATHER'S WIFE see **MOGLIE DI MIO PADRE, LA** • 1976
MY FAULT CONTINUED see **SHIN ONO GA TSUMI** • 1926
MY FAULT NEW VERSION see **SHIN ONO GA TSUMI** • 1926
MY FAULT (USA) see **SHIN ONO GA TSUMI** • 1926
MY FAVORITE BLONDE • 1942 • Lanfield Sidney • USA
MY FAVORITE BRUNETTE • 1947 • Nugent Elliott • USA
MY FAVORITE DUCK • 1942 • Jones Charles M. • ANS • USA
MY FAVORITE GIRL • 1949 • *Universal* • SHT • USA
MY FAVORITE SPY • 1942 • Garnett Tay • USA
MY FAVORITE SPY • 1951 • McLeod Norman Z. • USA
MY FAVORITE WIFE • 1940 • Kanin Garson • USA
MY FAVORITE YEAR • 1983 • Benjamin Richard • USA
MY FIGHT FOR PROSPERITY • 1934 • UKN
MY FIGHTING GENTLEMAN • 1917 • Sloman Edward • USA • FIGHTING GENTLEMAN, THE
MY FINANCIAL CAREER • 1962 • Munro Grant, Potterton Gerald • ANS • CND • MY CARRIERE FINANCIERE
MY FIRST ACTOR IS A POET see **MI PRIMER ACTOR ES UN POETA** • 1971
MY FIRST AND LAST LOVE • 1975 • Rafla Hilmy • EGY
MY FIRST FORTY YEARS see **MIEI PRIMI QUARANT'ANNI, I** • 1988
MY FIRST JURY • 1918 • *Chapin* • SHT • USA
MY FIRST LOVE see **ILK ASKIM** • 1967
MY FIRST LOVE (USA) see **J'AI 17 ANS** • 1945
MY FIRST PRAYER see **NGAYON LAMANG AKO DUMALANGIN** • 1968
MY FIRST SUIT • 1987 • Main Stewart • SHT • NZL
MY FIRST TIME • 1970 • *Able Film Co.* • USA
MY FIRST TWO HUNDRED YEARS see **ELSO KETSZAZ EVEM** • 1985
MY FIRST WIFE • 1985 • Cox Paul • ASL
MY FLAT see **FLAT, THE** • 1963
MY FOOLISH HEART • 1949 • Robson Mark • USA
MY FORBIDDEN PAST • 1951 • Stevenson Robert • USA • CARRIAGE ENTRANCE
MY FOUR YEARS IN GERMANY • 1918 • Nigh William • USA
MY FRENCHMAN WAS VERY TASTY see **COMO ERA GOSTOSO O MEU FRANCES** • 1971
MY FRIEND see **MIJN VRIEND** • 1980
MY FRIEND BARBARA see **MEINE FREUNDIN BARBARA** • 1937
MY FRIEND DEATH see **YUREI HANJO-KI** • 1961
MY FRIEND, DR. JEKYLL (USA) see **MIO AMICO JEKYLL, IL** • 1960
MY FRIEND FABIAN see **MUJ PRITEL FABIAN** • 1953
MY FRIEND FLICKA • 1943 • Schuster Harold • USA
MY FRIEND FROM INDIA • 1914 • Miller Ashley, Beaumont Harry • USA
MY FRIEND FROM INDIA • 1927 • Hopper E. Mason • USA
MY FRIEND IRMA • 1949 • Marshall George • USA
MY FRIEND IRMA GOES WEST • 1950 • Walker Hal • USA
MY FRIEND IVAN LAPSHIN see **MOI DRUG IVAN LAPSHIN** • 1986
MY FRIEND, KOLKA! see **DRUG MOI, KOLKA** • 1961
MY FRIEND LEVY see **MIN VEN LEVY** • 1914
MY FRIEND MENDOZA see **COMPADRE MENDOZA, EL** • 1933
MY FRIEND NICHOLAS • 1961 • Raymond Fernand • UNN
MY FRIEND SYBILLE see **MEINE FREUNDIN SYBILLE** • 1967
MY FRIEND, THE DEVIL • 1922 • Millarde Harry • USA
MY FRIEND THE DEVIL see **ARKADASIM SEYTAN** • 1988
MY FRIEND THE DOCTOR • 1910 • *Selig* • USA
MY FRIEND THE GYPSY (UKN) see **MUJ PRITEL FABIAN** • 1953
MY FRIEND THE KING • 1931 • Powell Michael • UKN
MY FRIEND THE MONKEY • 1939 • Fleischer Dave • ANS • USA
MY FRIEND, THE SAINT see **KAIBIGAN KONG STO. NINO** • 1967
MY FRIENDS see **AMICI MIEI** • 1975
MY FRIENDS 3 see **AMICI MIEI ATTO III** • 1985
MY FRIENDS ACT II see **AMICI MIEI ATTO II** • 1983
MY FRIENDS CALL ME TONY • 1975 • Shaffer Beverly • DOC • CND
MY FRIENDS NEED KILLING • 1977 • Leder Paul • USA
MY GAL LOVES MUSIC • 1944 • Lilley Edward • USA • MY BABY LOVES MUSIC
MY GAL SAL • 1930 • Fleischer Dave • ANS • USA
MY GAL SAL • 1942 • Cummings Irving • USA
MY GEISHA • 1962 • Cardiff Jack • USA
MY GIRL-FRIEND SYBILLE see **MEINE FREUNDIN SYBILLE** • 1967
MY GIRL SALLY • 1935 • Goulding Alf • SHT • USA
MY GIRL SUZANNE • 1919 • *Philipp Adolf* • SHT • USA
MY GIRL TISA • 1948 • Nugent Elliott • USA
MY GIRLFRIEND'S BOYFRIEND(UKN) see **AMI DE MON AMIE, L'** • 1987
MY GIRLFRIEND'S WEDDING • 1969 • McBride Jim • USA
MY GIRL'S A YORKSHIRE GIRL • 1909 • *Warwick Trading Co* • UKN
MY GOOD MAN see **MOY DOBRY CHELOVYEK** • 1974
MY GOODNESS • 1920 • Smith Noel • SHT • USA
MY GRANDFATHER IS A STICK see **MIN BEDSTEFAR ER EN STOK** • 1967
MY GRANDFATHER'S CLOCK • 1934 • Feist Felix E. • SHT • USA
MY GRANDMOTHER see **CHEMI BEBIA** • 1929
MY GRANDPA see **WO-TE YEH-YEH** • 1981
MY GREEN FEDORA • 1935 • Freleng Friz • ANS • USA
MY GUN IS JAMMED see **BARE HUNT; OR MY GUN IS JAMMED** • 1963
MY GUN IS QUICK • 1957 • White George A., Victor Phil • USA
MY GYPSY SWEETHEART • 1933 • Binney Josh • USA
MY HANDS ARE CLAY • 1948 • Tomlinson Lionel • UKN
MY HANDSOME MY BEAUTIFUL see **BELLO MIO BELLEZZA MIA** • 1982
MY HAREM • 1930 • Roberts Stephen • SHT • USA
MY HEART BELONGS TO DADDY • 1942 • Siodmak Robert • USA
MY HEART BELONGS TO THEE see **DIR GEHORT MEIN HERZ** • 1938
MY HEART GOES CRAZY (USA) see **LONDON TOWN** • 1946
MY HEART IS CALLING • 1934 • Gallone Carmine • UKN
MY HEART IS IN THE MOUNTAINS • Khamdamov Rustam • USS
MY HEART IS THAT LAND see **CON EL CORAZON SOBRE LA TIERRA** • 1985
MY HEART SINGS • Mattoli Mario • ITL
MY HEART'S DELIGHT see **HEART'S DESIRE** • 1935
MY HEART'S SECRET see **RAHSIA HATIKU** • 1974
MY HERO • 1912 • Griffith D. W. • USA
MY HERO! (UKN) see **SOUTHERN YANKEE, A** • 1948
MY HOBO see **BURARI BURABURA MONOGATARI** • 1960
MY HOME IS COPACABANA see **MITT HEM AR COPACABANA** • 1966
MY HOME TOWN • 1925 • *Barry Wesley* • USA
MY HOME TOWN • 1928 • Pembroke Scott • USA
MY HOME TOWN • 1953 • Haldane Don • USA
MY HOMELAND • 1976 • Vas Robert • UKN
MY HOMELAND see **MOI RODINA** • 1932
MY HOT DESIRE see **HET AR MIN LANGTAN** • 1956
MY HUSBAND IS GETTING MARRIED TODAY see **I DAG GIFTER SIG MIN MAN** • 1943
MY HUSBAND IS IMPOSSIBLE see **RAGOL DA HAI GANINI, EL** • 1967
MY HUSBAND IS MISSING • 1978 • Michaels Richard • TVM • USA
MY HUSBAND LIES see **HAZASOKIK AZ URAM** • 1913
MY HUSBAND'S FRIEND • 1918 • Farnum Marshall, Ormont James • USA
MY HUSBAND'S FRIEND • 1922 • *Mills Frank* • USA
MY HUSBAND'S OTHER WIFE • 1919 • Blackton J. Stuart • USA
MY HUSBAND'S WIFE • 1918 • Lehrman Henry • USA
MY HUSBAND'S WIVES • 1924 • Elvey Maurice • USA
MY HUSTLER • 1965 • Warhol Andy, Wein Chuck • USA
MY INDIAN ANNA • 1907 • Gilbert Arthur • UKN
MY IRISH MOLLY • 1938 • Bryce Alex • UKN • LITTLE MISS MOLLY (USA)
MY ISLAND HOME • 1961 • Blais Roger • DCS • CND • ESCALE DE VERDURE
MY IZ KRONSTADT • 1936 • Dzigan Yefim • USS • WE ARE FROM KRONSTADT ○ WE FROM KRONSTADT
MY JOURNEYS WITH JACOB see **UTAZAS JAKABBAL** • 1972
MY KID • 1926 • Lamont Charles • SHT • USA
MY KIDNAPPER, MY LOVE • 1980 • Wanamaker Sam • TVM • USA
MY KIND OF TOWN • 1985 • Wilkinson Charles • CND
MY KINGDOM FOR A COOK • 1943 • Wallace Richard • USA
MY KINGDOM FOR A MEAL • 1920 • *Pioneer Film* • SHT • USA
MY LADY FRIENDS • 1921 • Ingraham Lloyd • USA
MY LADY HIGH AND MIGHTY • 1915 • *Fuller Mary* • USA
MY LADY INCOG • 1916 • Olcott Sidney • USA • MY LADY INCOGNITO
MY LADY INCOGNITO see **MY LADY INCOG** • 1916
MY LADY NICOTINE • 1918 • *Rhodes Billie* • USA
MY LADY OF IDLENESS • 1913 • Humphrey William • USA
MY LADY OF WHIMS • 1925 • Fitzgerald Dallas M. • USA
MY LADY PEGGY • 1915 • *Famous Players* • USA
MY LADY ROBIN HOOD • 1919 • *Guinan Texas* • SHT • USA
MY LADY'S ANCLE • 1920 • Anderson Robert* • SHT • USA
MY LADY'S BOOT • 1913 • *Majestic* • USA
MY LADY'S DRESS • 1917 • Butler Alexander • UKN
MY LADY'S DRESS see **BLIND WIVES** • 1920
MY LADY'S GARDEN • 1934 • *Terry Paul/ Moser Frank (P)* • ANS • USA
MY LADY'S GARTER • 1920 • Tourneur Maurice • USA
MY LADY'S LATCH KEY • 1921 • Carewe Edwin • USA
MY LADY'S LIPS • 1925 • Hogan James P. • USA
MY LADY'S MILLIONS see **PARTNERS** • 1916
MY LADY'S PAST • 1929 • Ray Albert • USA
MY LADY'S REVENGE • 1907 • Martin J. H. • UKN
MY LADY'S SLIPPER • 1916 • Ince Ralph • USA • MY LADY'S SLIPPERS
MY LADY'S SLIPPER • 1918 • Richmond J. A. • SHT • USA
MY LADY'S SLIPPERS see **MY LADY'S SLIPPER** • 1916
MY LAND -AND YOURS • 1978 • Roos Lise • DNM
MY LAST DUCHESS see **DROP DEAD, DARLING** • 1966
MY LEARNED FRIEND • 1943 • Hay Will, Dearden Basil • UKN
MY LEFT FOOT • 1989 • Sheridan Jim • UKN, IRL
MY LEGION see **EN LEGIOM, AZ** • 1989
MY LIEDJIE VAN VERLANGE • 1976 • SAF
MY LIFE see **EXTASE** • 1932
MY LIFE AS A DOG (UKN) see **MITT LIV SOM HUND** • 1986
MY LIFE FOR MARIA ISABELL (USA) see **MEIN LEBEN FUR MARIA ISABELL** • 1935
MY LIFE IS LIKE FIRE see **WAGA SHOGAI WA HI NO GOTOKU** • 1961
MY LIFE IS YOURS (UKN) see **PEOPLE VS. DR. KILDARE, THE** • 1941
MY LIFE, MY LIFE see **MON AMOUR, MON AMOUR** • 1967
MY LIFE STORY see **MIT LIVS EVENTYR** • 1955
MY LIFE TO LIVE (USA) see **VIVRE SA VIE** • 1962
MY LIFE WITH CAROLINE • 1941 • Milestone Lewis • USA
MY LIFE WITH MIHALY KAROLYI see **EGYUTT KAROLYI MIHALLYAL -BESZELGETES KAROLYI MIHALYNEVAL** • 1973
MY LIFE WITHOUT STEVE • 1986 • Leahy Gillian, Duncan Digby • SHT • ASL
MY LIFE'S BRIGHT DAY see **WAGA SHOGAI NO KAGAYAKERU HI** • 1948
MY LIPS BETRAY • 1933 • Blystone John G. • USA
MY LITTLE BOY • 1917 • Wilson Elsie Jane • USA
MY LITTLE BROTHER AND I see **LILLEBROR OCH JAG** • 1940
MY LITTLE BUCKAROO • 1938 • Freleng Friz • ANS • USA
MY LITTLE CHICKADEE • 1940 • Cline Eddie • USA
MY LITTLE DEUTSCHER GIRL • 1909 • *Warwick Trading Co* • UKN
MY LITTLE DUCKAROO • 1954 • Jones Charles M. • ANS • USA
MY LITTLE FELLER • 1937 • Lamont Charles • SHT • USA
MY LITTLE GIRL • 1986 • Kaiserman Connie • USA
MY LITTLE LADY BOUNTIFUL • 1908 • Fitzhamon Lewin • UKN
MY LITTLE LOVES see **MES PETITES AMOUREUSES** • 1975
MY LITTLE PONY: THE MOVIE • 1986 • Joens Michael • ANM • USA
MY LITTLE SISTER • 1919 • Buel Kenean • USA
MY LITTLE YIDDISHER BOY • 1909 • *Warwick Trading Co* • UKN
MY LORD see **MERE HUZOOR** • 1968
MY LORD CONCEIT • 1921 • Thornton F. Martin • UKN
MY LORD IN LIVERY • 1909 • *Edison* • USA
MY LORD THE CHAUFFEUR • 1927 • Doxat-Pratt B. E. • UKN
MY LOST ONE • 1915 • Handworth Harry • USA
MY LOVE see **KOIBITO** • 1960
MY LOVE see **WAGA AI** • 1960
MY LOVE see **MIN ALSKANDE** • 1979
MY LOVE see **MEU AMOR** • 1980
MY LOVE AND I (UKN) see **KUNGSLEDEN** • 1964
MY LOVE BURNS see **WAGA KOI WA MOENU** • 1949
MY LOVE CAME BACK • 1940 • Bernhardt Curtis • USA • MY LOVE COMES BACK ○ EPISODE
MY LOVE COMES BACK see **MY LOVE CAME BACK** • 1940
MY LOVE ELECTRA see **SZERELMEM ELEKTRA** • 1974
MY LOVE FOR YOURS see **HONEYMOON IN BALI** • 1939
MY LOVE, FORGIVE ME • 1967 • Rowe George • PHL
MY LOVE HAS BEEN BURNING (UKN) see **WAGA KOI WA MOENU** • 1949
MY LOVE IN JERUSALEM see **MARGO SHELI** • 1971
MY LOVE IS A ROSE see **MIN KARA AR EN ROS** • 1963
MY LOVE IS A SIN see **ASKIM GUNAHIMDIR** • 1968
MY LOVE IS BEYOND THE MOUNTAIN see **WAGA AI WA YAMA NO KANATA NI** • 1948
MY LOVE IS LIKE A ROSE see **MIN KARA AR EN ROS** • 1963
MY LOVE LETTERS • 1983 • Jones Amy • USA • LOVE LETTERS
MY LOVE, MY LOVE see **MON AMOUR, MON AMOUR** • 1967
MY LOVE, MY LOVE see **AMORE, AMORE** • 1968
MY LOVE ON THE OTHER SIDE OF THE MOUNTAIN see **WAGA AI WA YAMA NO KANATA NI** • 1948

MY LOVE TO THE SWALLOWS see **A POZDRAVUJTE VLASTOVKY** • 1972
MY LOVE WITH JAMES see **MA LASKA S JAKUBEM** • 1982
MY LOVER see **KIMI WA KOIBITO** • 1967
MY LOVER, MY SON • 1970 • Newland John • UKN, USA • DON'T YOU CRY ○ HUSH-A-BYE MURDER
MY LOVER, THE MURDERER see **MON AMANT L'ASSASSIN** • 1931
MY LOVING CHILD see **ITOSHINO WAGAKO** • 1926
MY LOVING DAUGHTER see **MUSUME KAWAIYA** • 1928
MY LUCKY STAR • 1933 • Blattner Louis, Harlow John • UKN
MY LUCKY STAR • 1938 • Del Ruth Roy • USA
MY LUCKY STARS see **FUXING GAOZHAO** • 1985
MY MADONNA • 1915 • Blache Alice • USA
MY MAID IS TOO SLOW • 1910 • *Eclair* • FRN
MY MAIN MAN FROM STONY ISLAND • 1980 • Davis Andrew • USA • STONY ISLAND
MY MAN • 1924 • Smith David • USA
MY MAN • 1928 • Mayo Archie • USA
MY MAN ADAM • 1985 • Simon Roger L. • USA
MY MAN AND I • 1952 • Wellman William A. • USA • SHAMELESS
MY MAN GODFREY • 1936 • La Cava Gregory • USA
MY MAN GODFREY • 1957 • Koster Henry • USA
MY MAN JASPER • 1944 • Pal George • ANS • USA
MY MARRIAGE • 1935 • Archainbaud George • USA • BUCCANEER
MY MICHAEL • 1975 • Wolman Dan • ISR
MY MILLINER'S BILL • 1910 • *Edison* • USA
MY MISTAKE • 1927 • Newfield Sam • SHT • USA
MY MOM'S A WEREWOLF • 1989 • Fischa Michael • USA
MY MOTHER • 1917 • Chapin Benjamin • *Charter* • SHT • USA
MY MOTHER • 1918 • Chapin Benjamin • *Chapin* • SHT • USA
MY MOTHER AND THE ROOMER see **SARANG BANK SONNIM KWA OMONI** • 1962
MY MOTHER-IN-LAW • 1904 • Collins Alf? • UKN
MY MOTHER-IN-LAW see **IBU MERTUA KU**
MY MOTHER-IN-LAW IS A GAMBLER see **PETHEROPLIKTOS** • 1968
MY MOTHER-IN-LAW IS AN ATOMIC BOMB see **HAMATI KOMBOLA ZORRIA** • 1952
MY MOTHER-IN-LAW THE DANCER see **MIN SVARMOR DANSOSEN** • 1936
MY MOTHER-IN-LAW'S VISIT • 1907 • *Warwick Trading Co* • UKN
MY MOTHER IS IN SRI LANKA • 1986 • Legnazzi Remo, Neuenschwander Jurg • DOC • SWT
MY MOTHER THE GENERAL see **IMI HAGENERALIT** • 1979
MY MOTHER'S IRISH SHAWLS • 1914 • *August Edwin* • USA
MY MOTHER'S LOVERS see **KOCHANKOWIE MOE MAMY** • 1985
MY MOTHER'S SECRET LIFE • 1984 • Markowitz Robert • TVM • USA
MY MOTHER'S TEAHOUSE see **CH'UN-CH'IU CH'A-SHIH** • 1988
MY MOUNTAIN, SONG 27 • 1969 • Brakhage Stan • USA
MY NAAM IS DINGERTJIE • 1975 • SAF
MY NAME AIN'T SUZIE see **HUAJIE SHIDAI** • 1985
MY NAME IS EBON LUNDIN see **JAG HETER EBON LUNDIN** • 1972
MY NAME IS GUILTY • 1976 • Baldi Ferdinando • ITL
MY NAME IS IVAN (USA) see **IVANOVO DETSTVO** • 1962
MY NAME IS JOHAR see **MERA NAM JOHAR** • 1968
MY NAME IS JOKER see **MERA NAAM JOKER** • 1972
MY NAME IS JULIA ROSS • 1945 • Lewis Joseph H. • USA
MY NAME IS KERIM see **BENIM ADIM KERIM** • 1967
MY NAME IS KOZHA • 1964 • Karsakbaev Abdulla • USS
MY NAME IS LEGEND • 1975 • Kelly Duke • USA
MY NAME IS NOBODY see **MIO NOME E NESSUNO, IL** • 1974
MY NAME IS PECOS see **DUE ONCE DI PIOMBO** • 1966
MY NAME IS PUCK see **PUCK HETEA JAG** • 1951
MY NAME IS ROCCO PAPALEO see **PERMETTE? ROCCO PAPALEO** • 1971
MY NAME IS SUSAN LEE • 1975 • Shaffer Beverly • DOC • CND
MY NAME IS WOMAN • 1970 • *Bahl Ellen* • FRN
MY NAME'S MICK • 1978 • Brown Lou • SHT • ASL
MY NANNY see **TATA MIA** • 1986
MY NATIVE LAND see **YUAN-HSIANG JEN** • 1980
MY NATIVE PLACE • 1949 • NKR
MY NEIGHBOR'S WIFE • 1925 • Geldert Clarence • USA
MY NEPHEW IS A FOREIGNER • 1988 • Evstatieva Marianna • BUL
MY NEW CAR see **IT TAKES TWO** • 1988
MY NEW PARTNER (USA) see **RIPOUX, LES** • 1984
MY NIGHT AT MAUD'S (USA) see **MA NUIT CHEZ MAUD** • 1969
MY NIGHT WITH MAUD (UKN) see **MA NUIT CHEZ MAUD** • 1969
MY NIGHTS WITH MESSALINA see **BACANALES ROMANAS** • 1982
MY NIGHTS WITH SUSAN, OLGA, ALBERT, JULIE, BILL AND SANDRA see **MIJN NACHTEN MET SUSAN, OLGA, ALBERT, JULIE, PIET & SANDRA** • 1974
MY NIGHTS WITH SUSAN, SANDRA, OLGA AND JULIE see **MIJN NACHTEN MET SUSAN, OLGA, ALBERT, JULIE, PIET & SANDRA** • 1974
MY OFFICIAL WIFE • 1914 • Young James • USA
MY OFFICIAL WIFE • 1926 • Stein Paul L. • USA
MY OHIO HOME • 1929 • Aylott Dave, Symmons E. F. • SHT • UKN
MY OLD CHINA • 1931 • Kellino W. P. • UKN
MY OLD DUCHESS • 1933 • Lane Lupino • UKN • OH WHAT A DUCHESS! ○ MUMMERS, THE
MY OLD DUTCH • 1911 • Baker George D. • USA
MY OLD DUTCH • 1915 • Trimble Larry • UKN
MY OLD DUTCH • 1926 • Trimble Larry • USA
MY OLD DUTCH • 1934 • Hill Sinclair • UKN
MY OLD KENTUCKY HOME • 1922 • Smallwood Ray C. • USA
MY OLD KENTUCKY HOME • 1926 • Fleischer Dave • ANS • USA
MY OLD KENTUCKY HOME • 1938 • Hillyer Lambert • USA
MY OLD KENTUCKY HOME • 1946 • Donnelly Eddie • ANS • USA
MY OLD MAN • 1979 • Erman John • TVM • USA
MY OLD MAN see **UNDER MY SKIN** • 1950
MY OLD MAN see **MOJ STARY** • 1962
MY OLD MAN'S A FIREMAN (UKN) see **CHIEF, THE** • 1933
MY OLD MAN'S PLACE (UKN) see **GLORY BOY** • 1973
MY OLD TOWN • 1948 • *Nesbitt John* • SHT • USA
MY ONE AND ONLY • 1929 • Aylott Dave, Symmons E. F. • SHT • UKN
MY OTHER HUSBAND (USA) see **ATTENTION! UNE FEMME PEUT EN CACHER UNE AUTRE** • 1983
MY OUTLAW BROTHER • 1951 • Nugent Elliott • USA • MY BROTHER, THE OUTLAW
MY OWN MASTER see **SVOGA TJELA GOSPODAR** • 1957
MY OWN PAL • 1926 • Blystone John G. • USA
MY OWN TRUE LOVE • 1948 • Bennett Compton • USA
MY OWN UNITED STATES • 1918 • Noble John W. • USA
MY PAL • 1899 • *Warwick Trading Co* • UKN
MY PAL • 1925 • Hayes Ward • USA
MY PAL GUS • 1952 • Parrish Robert • USA • TOP MAN
MY PAL PAUL • 1930 • Lantz Walter, Nolan William • ANS • USA
MY PAL RINGEYE • 1947 • Staub Ralph • SHT • USA
MY PAL THE KING • 1932 • Neumann Kurt • USA
MY PAL THE PRINCE • 1933 • Brice Monte • SHT • USA
MY PAL TRIGGER • 1946 • McDonald Frank • USA
MY PAL WOLF • 1944 • Werker Alfred L. • USA
MY PALIKARI • 1982 • Magyar Dezso?, Dubin Charles S.? • TVM • USA • SILENT REBELLION ○ BIG SHOT
MY PARIS see **MON PARIS** • 1928
MY PART OF THE WORLD • 1969 • Filipovic Vlatko • YGS
MY PARTNER • 1915 • ASL
MY PARTNER • 1916 • *Mcintosh Burr* • USA
MY PARTNER • 1926 • *Higgins Arthur (P)* • ASL
MY PARTNER MR. DAVIS • 1936 • Autant-Lara Claude • UKN • MYSTERIOUS MR. DAVIS, THE
MY PAST • 1931 • Del Ruth Roy • USA • EX-MISTRESS
MY PEOPLE ARE NOT YOURS see **MITT FOLK AR ICKE DITT** • 1944
MY PLEASURE IS MY BUSINESS • 1974 • Waxman Albert • CND
MY PONY BOY • 1929 • Fleischer Dave • ANS • USA
MY POP, MY POP • 1940 • Fleischer Dave • ANS • USA
MY PRAIRIE FLOWER • 1911 • Melies Gaston • USA
MY PRECIOUS IZA see **MOJA DRAGA IZA** • 1979
MY PRINCESS • 1912 • *Johnson Arthur* • USA
MY PRIVATE TEACHER see **MI PROFESORA PARTICULAR** • 1973
MY RAINBOW • 1909 • *Warwick Trading Co* • UKN
MY REPUTATION • 1946 • Bernhardt Curtis • USA
MY REUVEN • 1986 • Rogers Derek • SHT • CND
MY ROLE IS REVENGE see **FUKUSHU SURUWA WARE NI ARI** • 1978
MY S URALA • 1944 • Kuleshov Lev • USS • WE ARE FROM THE URALS ○ WE OF THE URALS
MY SALOMY LIONS • 1920 • Fishback Fred C. • SHT • USA
MY SCIENCE PROJECT • 1985 • Betuel Jonathan R. • USA
MY SCROLLS • 1973 • Singh Hardev • CND
MY SECOND BROTHER see **NIANCHAN** • 1959
MY SECOND MARRIAGE see **MOJ DRUGI OZENEK** • 1964
MY SECRET see **HAMRAAZ** • 1967
MY SECRET LIFE see **COLOMBUS OF SEX** • 1970
MY SECRET LIFE see **SALAINEN ELAMANI** • 1972
MY SECRETARY IS MAD, MAD, MAD see **MI SECRETARIA ESTA LOCA, LOCA, LOCA** • 1967
MY SEVEN LITTLE BARES see **MY BARE LADY** • 1962
MY SEVEN LITTLE SINS (USA) see **J'AVAIS SEPT FILLES** • 1954
MY SEVEN SONS see **SEMERO SINOVEI MOIKH** • 1971
MY SIDE OF THE MOUNTAIN • 1969 • Clark James B. • USA, CND
MY SIN • 1931 • Abbott George • USA
MY SISTER • 1944 • *Sircar B. N. (P)* • IND
MY SISTER see **IMOHTO** • 1974
MY SISTER AND I • 1948 • Huth Harold • UKN • HIGH PAVEMENT
MY SISTER AND I see **MIN SYSTER OCH JAG** • 1950
MY SISTER EILEEN • 1942 • Hall Alexander • USA
MY SISTER EILEEN • 1955 • Quine Richard • USA
MY SISTER, MY LOVE (UKN) see **SYSKONBADD 1782** • 1965
MY SISTER, MY LOVE (USA) see **MAFU CAGE, THE** • 1978
MY SISTER'S BUSINESS • 1970 • Davis Bobby • USA
MY SISTER'S CHILDREN ARE PAINTING THE TOWN RED see **MIN SOSTERS BORN VAELTER BYEN** • 1968
MY SISTER'S CHILDREN ON HONEYMOON see **MIN SOSTERS BORN PA BRYLLUPSREJSE** • 1967
MY SISTER'S KEEPER see **MONDAY, TUESDAY, WEDNESDAY** • 1987
MY SIX CONVICTS • 1952 • Fregonese Hugo • USA
MY SIX LOVES • 1963 • Champion Gower • USA
MY SON • 1925 • Carewe Edwin • USA
MY SON • 1939 • Seiden Joseph • USA
MY SON see **MOI SIN** • 1928
MY SON see **SHODO SATSUJIN, MUSUKO YO** • 1979
MY SON ALONE (UKN) see **AMERICAN EMPIRE** • 1942
MY SON-IN-LAW IS A DOWRY HUNTER see **GAMBROS MOU O PRIKOTHIRAS, O** • 1967
MY SON IS A CRIMINAL • 1939 • Coleman C. C. Jr. • USA
MY SON IS GUILTY • 1940 • Barton Charles T. • USA • CRIME'S END (UKN) ○ COP FROM HELL'S KITCHEN
MY SON ISN'T WHAT HE SEEMS see **MI HIJO NO ES LO QUE PARECE** • 1974
MY SON JOHN • 1952 • McCarey Leo • USA
MY SON, MY LOVER see **ANAK KU SUAMI KU** • 1971
MY SON, MY PRECIOUS see **IMAGI NINGTHEM** • 1982
MY SON, MY SON • 1940 • Vidor Charles • USA
MY SON SAZALI see **ANAK KU SAZALI**
MY SON THE CURATE • 1908 • Aylott Dave • UKN
MY SON, THE HERO • 1943 • Ulmer Edgar G. • USA
MY SON, THE HERO (USA) see **HERMANOS DEL HIERRO, LOS** • 1961
MY SON, THE HERO (USA) see **TITANS, LES** • 1962
MY SON THE KING • 1970 • Kurtz Bob • USA
MY SON, THE PROFESSOR see **MIO FIGLIO PROFESSORE** • 1946
MY SON THE VAMPIRE (USA) see **MOTHER RILEY MEETS THE VAMPIRE** • 1952
MY SONG FOR YOU • 1934 • Elvey Maurice • UKN • SONG FOR YOU, A
MY SONG GOES ROUND THE WORLD (UKN) see **LIED GEHT UM DIE WELT, EIN** • 1933
MY SON'S REVOLT see **MUSUKO NO KEKKON** • 1958
MY SON'S YOUTH see **MUSUKO NO SEISHUN** • 1952
MY SORROWFUL DAYS see **KEDERLI GUNLERIM** • 1967
MY SORROWFUL HEART see **DERTLI GONLUM** • 1968
MY SOUL RUNS NAKED see **RAT FINK** • 1965
MY STARS • 1926 • Arbuckle Roscoe • USA
MY STEPMOTHER WAS AN ALIEN • 1988 • Benjamin Richard • USA
MY STORY see **MERI KAHANI** • 1983
MY STORY WITH TIMES • 1974 • el Imam Hassan • EGY
MY STORY'S YOUR STORY see **CERITAKU CERITAMU** • 1979
MY STREET see **MOJA ULICA** • 1965
MY STUPID BROTHER see **NIISAN NO BAKA** • 1932
MY SURVIVAL AS AN ABORIGINAL • 1979 • Coffey Essie • ASL
MY SWEDISH COUSINS • 1970 • *Kirt Films International* • USA
MY SWEDISH MEATBALL (UKN) see **SPIELST DU MIT SCHRAGEN VOGELN** • 1968
MY SWEET CHARLIE • 1970 • Johnson Lamont • TVM • USA
MY SWEET LADY • 1975 • Haller Daniel, Badham John, Benson Leon, Day Robert, Sargent Joseph • USA
MY SWEET LADY (UKN) see **SUNSHINE PART II** • 1975
MY SWEET LITTLE VILLAGE see **VESNICKO MA STREDISKOVA** • 1985
MY SWEET VILLAGE see **VESNICKO MA STREDISKOVA** • 1985
MY SWEETHEART • 1918 • Milton Meyrick • UKN
MY SYNDICATED LOVE see **VESIKALI YARIM** • 1968
MY TAIL IS MY TICKET see **REP JE ULAZNICA** • 1959
MY TAIL'S MY TICKET see **REP JE ULAZNICA** • 1959
MY TALE IS HOT • 1964 • Tokus Seymour • USA • ALWAYS ON MONDAY ○ MY TALE IS TOLD
MY TALE IS TOLD see **MY TALE IS HOT** • 1964
MY TEARS see **GOZYASLARIM** • 1968
MY TEENAGE DAUGHTER • 1956 • Wilcox Herbert • UKN • TEENAGE BAD GIRL (USA) ○ BAD GIRL
MY TEMPORARY FATHER see **MOJ TATA NA ODREDJENO VREME** • 1984
MY THEATRE see **MOJ TEATR** • 1960
MY THERAPIST • 1983 • Rossi Al • USA
MY THIRD WIFE BY GEORGE see **MY THIRD WIFE GEORGE** • 1968
MY THIRD WIFE GEORGE • 1968 • Kerwin Harry E. • USA • MY THIRD WIFE BY GEORGE
MY TOMATO • 1943 • Jason Will • SHT • USA
MY TOMBOY GIRL • 1915 • Myers Harry • USA
MY TOWN see **MOJE MIASTO** • 1947
MY TOWN see **EN VAROSOM, AZ** • 1959
MY TRUE STORY • 1951 • Rooney Mickey • USA
MY TURN TODAY, YOURS TOMORROW see **OGGI A ME, DOMANI A TE** • 1968
MY TUTOR • 1983 • Bowers George • USA
MY TWELVE PAPAS see **TUCET MYCH TATINKU** • 1960
MY TWO HUSBANDS (UKN) see **TOO MANY HUSBANDS** • 1940
MY TWO LOVES • 1986 • Black Noel • TVM • USA
MY UNCLE ANTOINE (USA) see **MON ONCLE ANTOINE** • 1971
MY UNCLE, MR. HULOT see **MON ONCLE** • 1957
MY UNCLE, THE VAMPIRE see **TEMPI DURI PER I VAMPIRI** • 1959
MY UNCLE (USA) see **MON ONCLE** • 1957
MY UNIVERSITIES see **MOI UNIVERSITETI** • 1940
MY UNMARRIED WIFE • 1918 • Siegmann George • USA • MOLLY AND I
MY USUAL DREAM • 1970 • Triantafillidi Niki • SHT • GRC
MY VALET • 1915 • Sennett Mack • USA
MY VERY BELOVED SON see **FIGLIO MIO INFINITAMENTE CARO** • 1985
MY WACKY, WACKY WORLD see **TA CH'IEN SHIH-CHIEH** • 1975
MY WAR -MY LOVE see **MOJA WOJNA, MOJA MILOSC** • 1975
MY WAY • 1974 • *Stewardson Joe* • SAF
MY WAY see **WINNERS, THE** • 1972
MY WAY see **WAGA MICHI** • 1974
MY WAY HOME • 1977 • Douglas Bill • UKN
MY WAY HOME (UKN) see **IGY JOTTEM** • 1964
MY WEAKNESS • 1933 • Butler David • USA
MY WEAPONS SHOOT FLOWERS, YOURS FIRE RED-HOD LEAD • 1981 • Fafoutis Jiannis • GRC
MY WHITE CITY • 1973 • Lotyanu Emil • DOC • USS
MY WICKED, WICKED WAYS.. THE LEGEND OF ERROL FLYNN, THE • 1985 • Taylor Don • TVM • USA
MY WIDOW AND I (USA) see **SBAGLIO DI ESSERE VIVO, LO** • 1945
MY WIFE • 1918 • Henderson Dell • USA
MY WIFE AND I • 1925 • Webb Millard • USA
MY WIFE AND THE DOG see **ZAWGATI WA AL-KALB** • 1970
MY WIFE IS A PANTHER (USA) see **MA FEMME EST UNE PANTHERE** • 1961
MY WIFE IS AN ACTRESS see **ARTISTA ANG AKING ASAWA** • 1968
MY WIFE IS MAD.. MAD.. MAD see **MERATI MAGNOUNA.. MAGNOUNA..** • 1968
MY WIFE MAKES MUSIC see **MEINE FRAU MACHT MUSIK** • 1958
MY WIFE TERESA see **MEINE FRAU TERESA** • 1942
MY WIFE, THE MISS • 1934 • Sekely Steve • HNG
MY WIFE, THE SWEDE AND I see **MI MUJER, LA SUECA Y YO** • 1967
MY WIFE WON'T LET ME • 1913 • *Tyler* • UKN
MY WIFE'S A TEETOTALER • 1906 • Collins Alf? • UKN
MY WIFE'S AWAY • 1914 • *Komic* • USA
MY WIFE'S AWAY, HURRAH! • 1912 • *Eclair* • USA
MY WIFE'S BEST FRIEND • 1952 • Sale Richard • USA
MY WIFE'S BIRTHDAY • 1912 • *Comet* • USA
MY WIFE'S BONNET • 1912 • Herbert C. D. • USA
MY WIFE'S DOG • 1908 • Williamson James? • UKN
MY WIFE'S ENEMY (USA) see **NEMICO DI MIA MOGLIE, IL** • 1959
MY WIFE'S FAMILY • 1931 • Banks Monty • UKN

MY WIFE'S FAMILY • 1941 • Mycroft Walter C. • UKN
MY WIFE'S FAMILY • 1956 • Gunn Gilbert • UKN
MY WIFE'S FAMILY see **SHADOWS** • 1931
MY WIFE'S GONE TO THE COUNTRY • 1924-26 • Fleischer Dave • ANS • USA
MY WIFE'S GONE TO THE COUNTRY • 1931 • Fleischer Dave • ANS • USA
MY WIFE'S GONE TO THE COUNTRY (HOORAY! HOORAY!) • 1909 • *Essanay* • USA
MY WIFE'S HOLIDAY see **MIN KONES FERIE** • 1967
MY WIFE'S HONOUR see **KARAMET ZAWGATY** • 1967
MY WIFE'S HUSBAND • 1916 • Birch Cecil • UKN
MY WIFE'S HUSBAND see **WEEKEND WIVES** • 1928
MY WIFE'S HUSBAND (USA) see **CUISINE AU BUERRE, LA** • 1963
MY WIFE'S LODGER • 1952 • Elvey Maurice • UKN
MY WIFE'S PET • 1912 • Rains Fred • UKN
MY WIFE'S RELATION • 1922 • Cline Eddie, Keaton Buster • SHT • USA
MY WIFE'S RELATIVES • 1939 • Meins Gus • USA
MY WIFE'S SPIRIT see **AFRIT MERATI** • 1968
MY WILD IRISH ROSE • 1922 • Smith David • USA
MY WILD IRISH ROSE • 1947 • Butler David • USA
MY WOMAN • 1933 • Schertzinger Victor • USA
MY WOMAN see **KADINIM** • 1967
MY WOMAN see **VESIKALI YARIM** • 1968
MY WONDERFUL YELLOW CAR see **FUKEYO HARUKAZE** • 1953
MY WORD, IF I CATCH YOU SMOKING! • 1909 • Coleby A. E. • UKN
MY WORD IF YOU'RE NOT OFF • 1907 • Mottershaw Frank • UKN
MY WORLD DIES SCREAMING see **TERROR IN THE HAUNTED HOUSE** • 1958
MY YIDDISHE MAMA • 1930 • Goldin Sidney M. • USA • YIDDISH MAMA, THE
MY YORKSHIRE LASS • 1916 • *Pyramid* • UKN
MY YOUNG AUNTIE see **CHANG-PEI** • 1981
MY YOUNGER BROTHER see **MOI MLADSHII BRAT** • 1962
MY YOUNGER BROTHER see **ENN THAMBI** • 1968
MY Z DIVIATEJ A • 1961 • Uher Stefan • CZC • FORM 9A
MY ZA MIR • 1951 • Pyriev Ivan, Ivens Joris, Thorndike Andrew, Thorndike Annelie, Huisken Joop • USS, GDR • WORLD FESTIVAL OF SONG AND DANCE ○ FRIENDSHIP TRIUMPHS (USA) ○ FREUNDSCHAFT SIEGT (GDR) ○ NAPROZOD MLOZIEZY SWIATA ○ WE ARE FOR PEACE ○ WE ARE ALL FOR PEACE
MY ZDES ZHIVEM • 1957 • Aimanov Shaken • USS • WE LIVE HERE
MY ZERO HOUR see **MEINE STUNDE NULL** • 1969
MY ZHDOM VAS S POBEDOI • 1941 • Trauberg Ilya, Medvedkin Alexander • USS • WE EXPECT VICTORY THERE ○ COME BACK WITH A VICTORY
MYATYEZHNAYA ZASTAVA • 1967 • Bergunkev Adolf • USS • FACTORY WORKERS IN REVOLT ○ MUTINY ON THE FOREPOST ○ REBELLIOUS BARRIER
MYER'S MISTAKE • 1914 • *Sterling* • USA
MYGLAREN • 1966 • Hassner Rune, Myrdal Jan • SWD
MYITA KYO MYIN • 1986 • *Khin Thida Tun* • BRM
MYITTAR ATHIN-CHE • 1982 • *Khine Kin Oo* • BRM • ETERNAL LOVE
MYLORD ARSOUILLE • 1925 • Leprince Rene • FRN
MYORTVETZ • 1915 • Tairov Alexander • USS • DEAD MAN, THE (USA)
MYRA BRECKENRIDGE • 1970 • Sarne Mike • USA
MYRA MEETS HIS FAMILY see **HUSBAND HUNTER, THE** • 1920
MYRA'S DEN see **MYRA'S BED** • 1967
MYRA'S BED • 1967 • Gaston William • USA • VIOLENT SEX AFFAIR ○ MYRA'S DEN
MYRIAM • 1929 • Guazzoni Enrico • ITL
MYRIAM • 1982 • Williams Lester C. • FRG
MYRNA'S • 1971 • Cayard Bruce • ANS • USA
MYRON see **ID AL-MAIRUN** • 1967
MYRRH, GOLD AND FRANKENCENSE see **MIRIS, TAMJAN I ZLATO** • 1971
MYRSKYLUODON KALASTAJA • 1926 • Karu Erkki • FNL
MYRT AND MARGE • 1933 • Boasberg Al • USA • LAUGHTER IN THE AIR (UKN)
MYRTE OF THE DEMONS (USA) see **MYRTHE EN DE DEMONEN** • 1948
MYRTHE EN DE DEMONEN • 1948 • Schreiber Bruno Paul • NTH, UKN • MYRTE OF THE DEMONS (USA)
MYRTHE UND SCHWERT • 1915 • Schmidthassler Walter • FRG
MYRTLE THE MANICURIST • 1916 • Davenport Harry • USA
MYSELF • 1917 • Chapin Benjamin • SHT • USA
MYSELF WENT YOUNG • 1948 • Beadle Ernest • USA
MYSIA WIEZA • 1974 • Szczechura Daniel • ANS • PLN
MYSL • 1916 • Gardin Vladimir • USS • THOUGHT
MYSORE TONGA • 1968 • Iyer G. V. • IND • HORSE CARRIAGE FROM MYSORE
MYSTERE • 1984 • Vanzina Carlo • ITL
MYSTERE A SHANGAI • 1950 • Blanc Roger • FRN • NUIT DU TREIZE, LA
MYSTERE ALEXINA, LE • 1985 • Feret Rene • FRN • MYSTERY OF ALEXINA, THE (USA)
MYSTERE BARTON, LE • 1948 • Spaak Charles • FRN
MYSTERE DE LA CHAMBRE JAUNE, LE • 1913 • Chautard Emile • FRN • MYSTERY OF THE YELLOW ROOM, THE
MYSTERE DE LA CHAMBRE JAUNE, LE • 1930 • L'Herbier Marcel • FRN • MYSTERY OF THE YELLOW ROOM, THE
MYSTERE DE LA CHAMBRE JAUNE, LE • 1948 • Aisner Henri • FRN • MYSTERY OF THE YELLOW ROOM, THE
MYSTERE DE LA CHAMBRE JAUNE, LE see **ROULETABILLE 1** • 1912
MYSTERE DE LA DAME BLONDE, LE see **JUGEMENT DE MINUIT, LE** • 1932
MYSTERE DE LA JONQUE ROUGE, LE (FRN) see **WEISSE FRACHT FUR HONGKONG** • 1964
MYSTERE DE LA MAISON-BLANCHE, LE • 1935 • Peguy Robert • FRN
MYSTERE DE LA PENSION EDELWEISS, LE see **SURSIS POUR UN VIVANT** • 1958
MYSTERE DE LA TOUR EIFFEL, LE • 1927 • Duvivier Julien • FRN • TRAMEL S'EN FICHE
MYSTERE DE LA VILLA ROSE, LE • 1929 • Greville Edmond T. • SHT • FRN • MYSTERY OF THE VILLA ROSE, THE
MYSTERE DE LA VILLA ROSE, LE • 1929 • Mercanton Louis, Hervil Rene • FRN • MYSTERY OF THE VILLA ROSE, THE
MYSTERE DE L'ATELIER 15, LE • 1957 • Resnais Alain, Heinrich Andre • SHT • FRN
MYSTERE DES ROCHES DE KADOR, LE • 1912 • Perret Leonce • FRN
MYSTERE DU 421, LE • 1937 • Simons Leopold • FRN
MYSTERE DU BOIS BELLEAU, LE see **COLLIER DE CHANVRE, LE** • 1940
MYSTERE DU LIT BLANC, LE • 1911 • Jasset Victorin • FRN
MYSTERE DU QUAI CONTI, LE • 1950 • Lacoste • SHT • FRN
MYSTERE DU TEMPLE HINDOU, LE (FRN) see **MISTERO DEL TIEMPO INDIANO, IL** • 1964
MYSTERE IMBERGER, LE • 1935 • Severac Jacques • FRN • SPECTRE DE M. IMBERGER, LE
MYSTERE KOUMIKO, LE • 1964 • Marker Chris • DOC • FRN • KOUMIKO MYSTERY, THE (USA)
MYSTERE PICASSO, LE • 1956 • Clouzot Henri-Georges • DOC • FRN • MYSTERY OF PICASSO, THE (USA) ○ PICASSO MYSTERY, THE
MYSTERE SAINT-VAL, LE • 1944 • Le Henaff Rene • FRN • SAINT-VAL MYSTERY, THE
MYSTERE SUR MA ROUTE • 1957 • Poitevin Jean-Marie • DOC • CND
MYSTERES D'ANGKOR, LES (FRN) see **MISTERO DEI TREI CONTINENTI, IL** • 1959
MYSTERES DE LA VIE ET DE LA MORT • 1923 • FRN • MYSTERIES OF LIFE AND DEATH
MYSTERES DE L'OMBRE, LES • 1915 • Perret Leonce • FRN
MYSTERES DE PARIS, LES • 1911 • Capellani Albert • FRN • MYSTERIES OF PARIS, THE
MYSTERES DE PARIS, LES • 1912 • Denola Georges • FRN • MYSTERIES OF PARIS, THE
MYSTERES DE PARIS, LES • 1922 • Burguet Charles • FRN • MYSTERIES OF PARIS, THE
MYSTERES DE PARIS, LES • 1935 • Gandera Felix • FRN • MYSTERIES OF PARIS, THE
MYSTERES DE PARIS, LES • 1943 • de Baroncelli Jacques • FRN • MYSTERIES OF PARIS, THE
MYSTERES DE PARIS, LES • 1962 • Hunebelle Andre • FRN, ITL • MYSTERIES OF PARIS
MYSTERES DE PARIS, LES (FRN) see **MISTERI DI PARIGI, I** • 1958
MYSTERES DU CHATEAU DE DES, LES see **MYSTERES DU CHATEAU DU DE, LES** • 1929
MYSTERES DU CHATEAU DU DE, LES • 1929 • Ray Man • SHT • FRN • MYSTERIES OF THE CHATEAU DU DE, THE (USA) ○ MYSTERES DU CHATEAU DE DES, LES
MYSTERES DU CIEL, LES • 1920 • Bourgeois Gerard • FRN
MYSTERIANS, THE (USA) see **CHIKYU BOEIGUN** • 1957
MYSTERIE VAN DE MONDSCHEIN SONATE, HET • 1935 • Gerron Kurt • NTH • MYSTERY OF THE MOONLIGHT SONATA, THE
MYSTERIEN EINES FRISEUR-SALONS • 1922 • Valentin Karl • FRG • MYSTERIES OF A HAIRDRESSER'S SALOON
MYSTERIES • 1968 • Markopoulos Gregory J. • USA
MYSTERIES • 1977 • de Lussanets Paul, Rademakers Fons • NTH
MYSTERIES FROM BEYOND EARTH • 1975 • Gale George • DOC • USA • MYSTERIES FROM BEYOND THE EARTH
MYSTERIES FROM BEYOND THE EARTH see **MYSTERIES FROM BEYOND EARTH** • 1975
MYSTERIES FROM BEYOND THE TOMB see **MISTERIOS DE ULTRATUMBA** • 1958
MYSTERIES FROM BEYOND THE TRIANGLE • 1977 • DOC • USA
MYSTERIES OF A HAIRDRESSER'S SALOON see **MYSTERIEN EINES FRISEUR-SALONS** • 1922
MYSTERIES OF ANGKOR, THE see **MISTERO DEI TREI CONTINENTI, IL** • 1959
MYSTERIES OF BLACK MAGIC see **MISTERIOS DE LA MAGIA NEGRA** • 1957
MYSTERIES OF INDIA, THE (USA) see **INDISCHE GRABMAL I-II, DAS** • 1921
MYSTERIES OF LIFE AND DEATH see **MYSTERES DE LA VIE ET DE LA MORT** • 1923
MYSTERIES OF LONDON, THE • 1915 • Coleby A. E. • UKN
MYSTERIES OF MYRA, THE • 1916 • Wharton Theodore, Wharton Leopold • SRL • USA
MYSTERIES OF NEW YORK (UKN) see **REGGIE MIXES IN** • 1916
MYSTERIES OF PARIS see **MYSTERES DE PARIS, LES** • 1962
MYSTERIES OF PARIS, THE see **MYSTERES DE PARIS, LES** • 1911
MYSTERIES OF PARIS, THE see **MYSTERES DE PARIS, LES** • 1912
MYSTERIES OF PARIS, THE see **MYSTERES DE PARIS, LES** • 1922
MYSTERIES OF PARIS, THE see **MYSTERES DE PARIS, LES** • 1935
MYSTERIES OF PARIS, THE see **MYSTERES DE PARIS, LES** • 1943
MYSTERIES OF ROME, THE see **MISTERI DI ROMA, I** • 1963
MYSTERIES OF THE CHATEAU DU DE, THE (USA) see **MYSTERES DU CHATEAU DU DE, LES** • 1929
MYSTERIES OF THE DEEP • 1960 • Sharpsteen Ben • DOC • USA
MYSTERIES OF THE GODS • 1976 • Reinl Harald • FRG
MYSTERIES OF THE GRAND HOTEL • 1915 • Horne James W. • USA
MYSTERIES OF THE ORIENT see **GEHEIMNISSE DES ORIENTS** • 1928
MYSTERIES OF WARSAW, THE • 1916 • Hertz Aleksander • PLN
MYSTERIET NATTEN TILL DEN 25:E • 1917 • Klercker Georg • SWD • MYSTERY OF THE NIGHT OF THE 25TH, THE
MYSTERIEUSE LADY, LA • 1936 • Peguy Robert • FRN
MYSTERIEUX MONSIEUR SYLVAIN, LE • 1946 • Stelli Jean • FRN • DANGER DE MORT
MYSTERIOUS ACCORDION, THE see **ACCORDEON MYSTERIEUX, L'** • 1906
MYSTERIOUS AIRMAN, THE • 1928 • Revier Harry • SRL • USA
MYSTERIOUS AIRSHIP, THE • 1915 • *Ideal* • USA
MYSTERIOUS ARMOR, THE • 1907 • *Pathe* • FRN
MYSTERIOUS ARMOR, THE • 1910 • *Pantograph* • USA
MYSTERIOUS AVENGER, THE • 1936 • Selman David • USA
MYSTERIOUS BAG, THE • 1901 • *Warwick Trading Co* • UKN
MYSTERIOUS BEAUTY, THE • 1914 • MacGregor Norval • USA
MYSTERIOUS BLACK BOX, THE • 1914 • MacGregor Norval • USA
MYSTERIOUS BOX, THE (USA) see **BOITE A MALICE, LA** • 1903
MYSTERIOUS BRIDE, THE • 1915 • *Knickerbocker Star* • USA
MYSTERIOUS BULLET, THE • 1955 • Gherzo Paul • UKN
MYSTERIOUS CABINET, THE see **ARMOIRE DES FRERES DAVENPORT, L'** • 1902
MYSTERIOUS CAFE, THE • 1901 • Porter Edwin S. • SHT • USA
MYSTERIOUS CARD, THE • 1913 • *Imp* • SHT • USA
MYSTERIOUS CASTLE IN THE CARPATHIANS, THE see **TAJEMNY HRAD V KARPATECH** • 1981
MYSTERIOUS CASTLES OF CLAY • 1978 • *Root Alan (P)* • DOC • USA
MYSTERIOUS CIGARRETTE, THE • 1912 • *Gaumont* • USA
MYSTERIOUS CLIENT, THE • 1918 • Wright Fred E. • USA
MYSTERIOUS COMPANION, THE see **MYSTISKE SELSKABSDAME** • 1916
MYSTERIOUS CONTRAGRAV, THE • 1915 • McRae Henry • USA
MYSTERIOUS COWBOY • 1952 • Davis Mannie • ANS • USA
MYSTERIOUS CREATURE, THE see **CREATURE MYSTERIEUSE, LA** • 1914
MYSTERIOUS CROSSING • 1936 • Lubin Arthur • USA • MURDER ON THE MISSISSIPPI
MYSTERIOUS DESPERADO, THE • 1949 • Selander Lesley • USA
MYSTERIOUS DETECTIVE MORGAN, THE see **MORGAN KEIBU TO NAZO NO OTOKO** • 1961
MYSTERIOUS DOCTOR, THE • 1943 • Stoloff Ben • USA
MYSTERIOUS DR. FU MANCHU, THE • 1929 • Lee Rowland V. • USA
MYSTERIOUS DR. R. see **MAN MADE MONSTER** • 1941
MYSTERIOUS DR. SATAN • 1940 • Witney William, English John • SRL • USA
MYSTERIOUS DOLL, THE • 1913 • *Eclectic* • USA
MYSTERIOUS DOUBLE, THE • 1916 • Ellis Robert • USA
MYSTERIOUS DOUBLE, OR THE TWO GIRLS WHO LOOKED ALIKE, THE • 1909 • *Kalem* • USA
MYSTERIOUS DRUM, A • 1959 • *Puppet & Dentsu Film* • ANS • JPN
MYSTERIOUS EYES • 1913 • *American* • USA
MYSTERIOUS FIND, A • 1954 • Buneyev A. • USS
MYSTERIOUS FINE ARTS, THE see **BEAUX-ARTS MYSTERIEUX, LES** • 1910
MYSTERIOUS FINGERPRINTS, THE see **MORT QUI TUE, LA** • 1914
MYSTERIOUS FLAMES • 1908 • *Pathe* • FRN
MYSTERIOUS FOLDING SCREEN, THE see **PARAVENT MYSTERIEUX, LE** • 1903
MYSTERIOUS FOOTSTEPS • 1917 • Sandberg Anders W. • DNM
MYSTERIOUS GALLANT, A • 1912 • *Selig* • USA
MYSTERIOUS GEORGE see **GEO LE MYSTERIEUX** • 1916
MYSTERIOUS GOODS • 1923 • Seeling Charles R. • USA
MYSTERIOUS HAND, THE • 1913 • *Lubin* • USA
MYSTERIOUS HAND, THE • 1914 • *Ford Francis* • USA
MYSTERIOUS HEADS, THE see **EXTRAORDINARY WAITER, THE** • 1902
MYSTERIOUS HINDU, A see **ENIGMATIC INDIAN, THE** • 1966
MYSTERIOUS HOUSE OF DR. C, THE see **FANTASTICO MUNDO DEL DR. COPPELIUS, EL** • 1966
MYSTERIOUS INTRUDER, THE • 1946 • Castle William • USA • MURDER IS UNPREDICTABLE
MYSTERIOUS INVADER (UKN) see **ASTOUNDING SHE-MONSTER, THE** • 1958
MYSTERIOUS IRON RING, THE • 1917 • Wells Jack • SHT • USA
MYSTERIOUS ISLAND • 1951 • Bennet Spencer Gordon • SRL • USA
MYSTERIOUS ISLAND • 1960 • Endfield Cy • UKN, USA
MYSTERIOUS ISLAND see **TAINSTVENNI OSTROV** • 1941
MYSTERIOUS ISLAND, THE • 1929 • Hubbard Lucien, Tourneur Maurice, Christensen Benjamin • USA
MYSTERIOUS ISLAND, THE see **ILE DE CALYPSO: OU, ULYSSE ET LE GEANT POLYPHEME, L'** • 1905
MYSTERIOUS ISLAND, THE (USA) see **ILE MYSTERIEUSE, L'** • 1973
MYSTERIOUS ISLAND OF BEAUTIFUL WOMEN • 1979 • Pevney Joseph • TVM • USA • ISLAND OF SISTER TERESA, THE
MYSTERIOUS ISLAND OF CAPTAIN NEMO, THE see **ILE MYSTERIEUSE, L'** • 1973
MYSTERIOUS JUG, THE • 1937 • *Lantz Walter (P)* • ANS • USA
MYSTERIOUS KNIGHT see **CHEVALIER MYSTERE, LE** • 1907
MYSTERIOUS KNIGHT, THE (USA) see **CHEVALIER MYSTERE, LE** • 1899
MYSTERIOUS LADY, THE • 1928 • Niblo Fred • USA • WAR IN THE DARK
MYSTERIOUS LADY, THE see **MAANEPRINSESSEN** • 1916
MYSTERIOUS LADY BAFFLES AND DETECTIVE DUCK IN THE SIGNAL OF THE THREE SOCKS, THE • 1915 • Curtis Allen • USA
MYSTERIOUS LADY BAFFLES AND DETECTIVE DUCK IN THE SIGN OF THE SACRED SAFETY PIN, THE • 1915 • Curtis Allen • USA
MYSTERIOUS LADY BAFFLES AND DETECTIVE DUCK IN BAFFLES AIDS CUPID, THE • 1915 • Curtis Allen • USA
MYSTERIOUS LADY'S COMPANION, THE see **MYSTISKE SELSKABSDAME** • 1916
MYSTERIOUS LEOPARD LADY, THE • 1914 • Ford Francis • USA

MYSTERIOUS LODGER, THE • 1914 • Costello Maurice, Gaillord Robert • USA
MYSTERIOUS LOVE OF MRS. WHITE see **HAKUFUJIN NO YOREN** • 1956
MYSTERIOUS MAGICIAN, THE (USA) see **HEXER, DER** • 1964
MYSTERIOUS MECHANICAL TOY, THE • 1903 • Collins Alf • UKN • PHROSO THE MYSTERIOUS MECHANICAL DOLL
MYSTERIOUS MIDGETS, THE • 1904 • *Biograph* • USA
MYSTERIOUS MISS TERRY, THE • 1917 • Dawley J. Searle • USA
MYSTERIOUS MISS X, THE • 1939 • Meins Gus • USA
MYSTERIOUS MR. BROWNING, THE • 1919 • Goldin Sidney M. • USA
MYSTERIOUS MR. CHAUTARD, THE see **MAN WITH TWO FACES, THE** • 1934
MYSTERIOUS MR. DAVEY, THE • 1914 • Drew Sidney • USA
MYSTERIOUS MR. DAVIS, THE see **MY PARTNER MR. DAVIS** • 1936
MYSTERIOUS MR. M., THE • 1946 • Collins Lewis D., Keays Vernon • SRL • USA
MYSTERIOUS MR. MILLER, THE see **MYSTERIOUS MR. TILLER, THE** • 1917
MYSTERIOUS MR. MOTO • 1938 • Foster Norman • USA
MYSTERIOUS MR. NICHOLSON, THE • 1947 • Mitchell Oswald • UKN
MYSTERIOUS MR. REEDER, THE (USA) see **MIND OF MR. REEDER, THE** • 1939
MYSTERIOUS MR. SHEFFIELD (UKN) see **LAW OF THE 45'S** • 1935
MYSTERIOUS MR. TILLER, THE • 1917 • Julian Rupert • USA • MYSTERIOUS MR. MILLER, THE
MYSTERIOUS MR. VALENTINE, THE • 1946 • Ford Philip • USA
MYSTERIOUS MR. WONG, THE • 1935 • Nigh William • USA
MYSTERIOUS MR. WU CHUNG FOO, THE • 1914 • *Feature Photoplay* • USA
MYSTERIOUS MR. X, THE (USA) see **GEHEIMNISVOLLE MISTER X, DER** • 1936
MYSTERIOUS MONK, THE see **TAYINSTVENNY MONAKH** • 1968
MYSTERIOUS MONSTERS, THE see **BIGFOOT, THE MYSTERIOUS MONSTERS** • 1975
MYSTERIOUS MOSE • 1930 • Fleischer Dave • ANS • USA
MYSTERIOUS MRS. M., THE • 1917 • Weber Lois • USA • MYSTERIOUS MRS. MUSSLEWHITE, THE
MYSTERIOUS MRS. MUSSLEWHITE, THE see **MYSTERIOUS MRS. M., THE** • 1917
MYSTERIOUS MYSTERY, A • 1914 • Salter Harry • USA
MYSTERIOUS MYSTERY, THE • 1924 • Roach Hal • SHT • USA
MYSTERIOUS MYSTERY, THE • 1932 • Cline Eddie • SHT • USA
MYSTERIOUS OUTLAW, THE • 1917 • Kelsey Fred A. • SHT • USA
MYSTERIOUS PACKAGE, THE • 1914 • Seay Charles M. • USA
MYSTERIOUS PACKAGE, THE • 1961 • Davis Mannie • ANS • USA
MYSTERIOUS PALANQUIN, THE see **OBORO KAGO** • 1951
MYSTERIOUS PAPER, THE (USA) see **PAPIER PROTEE, LE** • 1896
MYSTERIOUS PEARL, THE • 1921 • Wilson Ben • USA
MYSTERIOUS PHILANTHROPIST, THE • 1913 • Buckland Warwick? • UKN
MYSTERIOUS PILOT, THE • 1937 • Bennet Spencer Gordon • SRL • USA
MYSTERIOUS POACHER, THE • 1950 • Chaffey Don • UKN
MYSTERIOUS PORTRAIT, A (USA) see **PORTRAIT MYSTERIEUX, LE** • 1899
MYSTERIOUS PRINCE • 1934 • Torney R. G. • IND
MYSTERIOUS PRINCESS • 1919 • *Doro Marie* • USA
MYSTERIOUS RABBIT, THE • 1896 • *Paul R. W.* • UKN
MYSTERIOUS RETORT, THE (USA) see **ALCHIMISTE PARAFARAGAMUS OU LA CORNUE INFERNALE, L'** • 1906
MYSTERIOUS RIDER • 1921 • Hampton Benjamin B. • USA
MYSTERIOUS RIDER, THE • 1927 • Waters John • USA
MYSTERIOUS RIDER, THE • 1933 • Allen Fred • USA • FIGHTING PHANTOM
MYSTERIOUS RIDER, THE • 1938 • Selander Lesley • USA • MARK OF THE AVENGER
MYSTERIOUS RIDER, THE • 1942 • Newfield Sam • USA
MYSTERIOUS RIDER, THE (UKN) see **45 CALIBRE ECHO** • 1932
MYSTERIOUS RIDER, THE (USA) see **CAVALIERE MISTERIOSO, IL** • 1948
MYSTERIOUS ROSE, THE • 1914 • Ford Francis • USA
MYSTERIOUS SATELLITE (USA) see **UCHUJIN TOKYO NI ARAWARU** • 1956
MYSTERIOUS SHOT, THE • 1914 • Crisp Donald?, Kirkwood James? • USA
MYSTERIOUS SPANISH LADY, THE • Vehr Bill • USA
MYSTERIOUS STRANGER, THE • 1911 • *Eclipse* • FRN
MYSTERIOUS STRANGER, THE • 1913 • *Calvert E. H.* • USA
MYSTERIOUS STRANGER, THE • 1920 • Robbins Jess • SHT • USA
MYSTERIOUS STRANGER, THE • 1925 • Del Ruth Roy • SHT • USA
MYSTERIOUS STRANGER, THE • 1925 • Nelson Jack • USA
MYSTERIOUS STRANGER, THE • 1948 • Donnelly Eddie • ANS • USA
MYSTERIOUS STRANGER, THE • 1982 • Hunt Peter H. • TVM • USA
MYSTERIOUS STRANGER, THE (UKN) see **WESTERN GOLD** • 1937
MYSTERIOUS STRANGER, THE (UKN) see **CODE OF THE LAWLESS** • 1945
MYSTERIOUS STRANGER, THE (USA) see **MOZGOKEPIPARI** • 1936
MYSTERIOUS TWO see **FOLLOW ME IF YOU DARE** • 1979
MYSTERIOUS UNCLE SILAS, THE see **MISTERIOSO TIO SYLAS, EL** • 1947
MYSTERIOUS VISITOR, THE • 1915 • *Kleine George* • USA
MYSTERIOUS WALL, THE see **TAYINSTVENNAYA STENA** • 1968
MYSTERIOUS WAY, THE • 1913 • *Selig* • USA
MYSTERIOUS WITNESS, THE • 1923 • Zeliff Seymour • USA
MYSTERIOUS WOMAN, THE • 1990 • Wu Ziniu • CHN
MYSTERIOUS WRECK, THE see **GEHEIMNISVOLLE WRACK, DAS** • 1954
MYSTERIOUS X, THE see **HEMMELIGHEDSFULDE X, DET** • 1913
MYSTERIOUS YARN, THE • 1917 • *International Film Services* • ANS • USA
MYSTERIUM • 1921 • Berger Martin • FRG
MYSTERIUM DES KLEINODS ODER DER GEISTERSPUK AUF SCHLOSS DIESTERBERG, DAS • 1918 • Lins-Morstadt Otto • FRG
MYSTERIUM DES LEBENS, DAS • 1938 • Schulz Ulrich K. T., Julich Herta • FRG
MYSTERIUM DES SCHLOSSES CLAUDEN, DAS • 1917 • Meinert Rudolf • FRG
MYSTERIUM VON KOPENHAGEN, DAS see **RAFAELLO, DAS RATSEL VON KOPENHAGEN 1** • 1920
MYSTERY see **RAAZ** • 1967
MYSTERY see **RAHASYAM** • 1967
MYSTERY, THE • 1912 • *Powers* • USA
MYSTERY AND TERROR see **HIWA NG LAGIM** • 1970
MYSTERY AND THE PLEASURE, THE see **OUR INCREDIBLE WORLD** • 1966
MYSTERY AT CATTLE HOUSE • 1982 • Maxwell Peter • ASL
MYSTERY AT MONSTEIN • 1954 • Mendoza Joe • UKN
MYSTERY AT MONTE CARLO (UKN) see **REVENGE AT MONTE CARLO** • 1933
MYSTERY AT SHALLOW CREEK, THE • 1916 • *Sunset* • USA
MYSTERY AT THE VILLA ROSE (USA) see **AT THE VILLA ROSE** • 1929
MYSTERY BRACELET, THE see **COWBOY MUSKETEER, THE** • 1925
MYSTERY BRAND, THE • 1927 • Wilson Ben • USA
MYSTERY BROADCAST • 1943 • Sherman George • USA
MYSTERY CASTLE IN THE CARPATHIANS see **TAJEMNY HRAD V KARPATECH** • 1981
MYSTERY CAVE, THE • 1913 • *Nestor* • USA
MYSTERY CLUB, THE • 1926 • Blache Herbert • USA
MYSTERY FILM, THE • 1924 • *International Cine Corp* • SHT • UKN • WHERE-U-SEER?
MYSTERY GIRL, THE • 1918 • De Mille William C. • USA
MYSTERY HOUSE • 1938 • Smith Noel • USA
MYSTERY IN DRACULA'S CASTLE see **IN DRACULA'S CASTLE** • 1973
MYSTERY IN MEXICO • 1948 • Wise Robert • USA
MYSTERY IN SWING • 1938 • Dreifuss Arthur • USA
MYSTERY IN THE MINE • 1959 • Hill James • SRL • UKN
MYSTERY IN THE MOONLIGHT • 1948 • Donnelly Eddie • ANS • USA
MYSTERY IN THE NORTH CASE, THE • 1917 • Shaw Brinsley • SHT • USA
MYSTERY ISLAND • 1937 • Lipman J. A. • ASL
MYSTERY ISLAND • 1981 • Scott Gene • USA
MYSTERY JUNCTION • 1951 • McCarthy Michael • UKN
MYSTERY LADY, THE • 1914 • *Domino* • USA
MYSTERY LAKE • 1953 • Lansburgh Larry • USA
MYSTERY LINER • 1934 • Nigh William • USA • GHOST OF JOHN HOLLING, THE (UKN)
MYSTERY MAN • 1944 • Archainbaud George • USA
MYSTERY MAN, THE • 1923 • Roach Hal • SHT • USA
MYSTERY MAN, THE • 1935 • McCarey Ray • USA
MYSTERY MANSION • 1983 • Jackson David E. • USA
MYSTERY MIND, THE • 1920 • Sittenham Fred, Davis Will S. • SRL • USA
MYSTERY, MISTER RA • 1984 • Cassenti Frank • FRN
MYSTERY MOUNTAIN • 1934 • Brower Otto, Eason B. Reeves • SRL • USA
MYSTERY OF 13, THE • 1919 • Ford Francis • SRL • USA
MYSTERY OF A HANSOM CAB • 1911 • Lincoln W. J. • ASL
MYSTERY OF A HANSOM CAB • 1925 • Shirley Arthur • ASL
MYSTERY OF A HANSOM CAB, THE • 1915 • Weston Harold • UKN
MYSTERY OF A LONDON FLAT, THE • 1915 • West Walter • UKN • LONDON FLAT MYSTERY, A
MYSTERY OF A TAXI CAB, THE • 1914 • *Asher Max* • USA
MYSTERY OF ALEXINA, THE (USA) see **MYSTERE ALEXINA, LE** • 1985
MYSTERY OF BELLAVISTA, THE see **MISTERO DI BELLAVISTA, IL** • 1985
MYSTERY OF BODY see **W R -MISTERIJE ORGANIZMA** • 1971
MYSTERY OF BOSCOMBE VALE, THE • 1912 • Treville Georges • UKN
MYSTERY OF BRAYTON COURT, THE • 1914 • Costello Maurice, Gaillord Robert • USA
MYSTERY OF BRUDENELL COURT, THE • 1924 • Croise Hugh • UKN
MYSTERY OF BUFFALO GAP, THE • 1914 • *Frontier* • USA
MYSTERY OF CARTER BREENE, THE • 1915 • Broadwell Robert B. • USA
MYSTERY OF CONSECUTIVE CONNECTIONS, THE see **LIEN-CH'ENG CHUEH** • 1979
MYSTERY OF DEAD MAN'S ISLE, THE • 1915 • Warren Giles R. • USA
MYSTERY OF DIAMOND ISLAND, THE (UKN) see **RIP ROARING RILEY** • 1935
MYSTERY OF DR. FU MANCHU, THE • 1923 • Coleby A. E. • SER • UKN
MYSTERY OF DOGSTOOTH CLIFF, THE • 1924 • Croise Hugh • UKN
MYSTERY OF EAGLE'S CLIFF, THE • 1915 • *Arey Wayne* • USA
MYSTERY OF EDWIN DROOD, THE • 1909 • Gilbert Arthur • UKN
MYSTERY OF EDWIN DROOD, THE • 1914 • Terriss Tom • USA
MYSTERY OF EDWIN DROOD, THE • 1935 • Walker Stuart • USA
MYSTERY OF GRANDFATHER'S CLOCK, THE • 1912 • *Joyce Alice* • USA
MYSTERY OF GRAYSON HALL, THE • 1914 • *Hearn Fred J.* • USA
MYSTERY OF GREEN PARK, THE • 1914 • *Urban-Eclipse* • USA
MYSTERY OF HENRI VILLARD, THE • 1915 • Morgan George • USA
MYSTERY OF HENRY MOORE, THE • 1984 • Rasky Harry • MTV • CND
MYSTERY OF HIDDEN HOUSE, THE • 1914 • *Vitagraph* • SHT • USA
MYSTERY OF KASPER HAUSER, THE (USA) see **JEDER FUR SICH UND GOTT GEGEN ALLE** • 1974
MYSTERY OF LAKE LETHE, THE • 1917 • Sturgeon Rollin S. • SHT • USA
MYSTERY OF LIFE • 1931 • Cochrane George • USA
MYSTERY OF LIFE, THE see **MISTERIO DE LA VIDA, EL** • 1971
MYSTERY OF LOST RANCH, THE • 1925 • Webb Harry S., Gibson Tom • USA
MYSTERY OF MANON, THE see **EQUALISER: THE MYSTERY OF MANON, THE** • 1988
MYSTERY OF MARIE ROGET, THE • 1942 • Rosen Phil • USA • PHANTOM OF PARIS
MYSTERY OF MARRIAGE, THE • 1931 • Field Mary • UKN
MYSTERY OF MARY, THE • 1915 • Lambart Harry • USA
MYSTERY OF MR. BERNARD BROWN, THE • 1921 • Hill Sinclair • UKN
MYSTERY OF MR. MARKS, THE • 1914 • Buckland Warwick • UKN • BY WHOSE HAND?
MYSTERY OF MR. WONG, THE • 1939 • Nigh William • USA
MYSTERY OF MR. X, THE • 1934 • Selwyn Edgar • USA • MYSTERY OF THE DEAD POLICE
MYSTERY OF MY LADY'S BOUDOIR, THE • 1917 • Grandon Francis J. • SHT • USA
MYSTERY OF NO.47, THE • 1917 • Thayer Otis B. • USA
MYSTERY OF ORCIVAL, THE • 1916 • MacDonald J. Farrell • SHT • USA
MYSTERY OF PICASSO, THE (USA) see **MYSTERE PICASSO, LE** • 1956
MYSTERY OF PINE CREEK CAMP, THE • 1913 • Olcott Sidney • USA
MYSTERY OF RAJA-DURGADA, THE see **RAJADURGADA RAHASYA** • 1967
MYSTERY OF RICHMOND CASTLE, THE • 1913 • *Midgar Features* • USA
MYSTERY OF ROOM 13, THE • 1915 • Ridgwell George • USA
MYSTERY OF ROOM 13 (USA) see **MR. REEDER IN ROOM 13** • 1938
MYSTERY OF ROOM 29, THE • 1912 • *Selig* • USA
MYSTERY OF ROOM 422 • 1917 • Ellis Robert • SHT • USA
MYSTERY OF ROOM 643, THE • 1914 • *Bushman Francis X.* • USA
MYSTERY OF SEX see **SEX NO SHINPI** • 1968
MYSTERY OF TEMPLE COURT, THE • 1910 • *Vitagraph* • USA
MYSTERY OF THE 13TH GUEST, THE • 1943 • Beaudine William • USA
MYSTERY OF THE £500,000 PEARL NECKLACE, THE • 1913 • Heath Harold • UKN • $1,000,000 PEARL MYSTERY (USA)
MYSTERY OF THE AMSTERDAM DIAMONDS, THE • 1913 • Lessey George A.?, Wilson Ben? • USA
MYSTERY OF THE BLACK JUNGLE (USA) see **MISTERI DELLA GIUNGLA NERA, I** • 1954
MYSTERY OF THE BLACK PEARL, THE • 1912 • *Mackay Cyril* • ASL
MYSTERY OF THE BLOOD, THE see **TAJEMSTVI KRVE** • 1953
MYSTERY OF THE BLUE ORANGES, THE see **TINTIN ET LES ORANGES BLEUES** • 1965
MYSTERY OF THE BLUE ROOM, THE see **ZAHADA MODREHO POKOJE** • 1933
MYSTERY OF THE BRASS BOUND CHEST, THE • 1916 • Horne James W. • SHT • USA
MYSTERY OF THE BRIDE IN WHITE, THE • 1908 • *Kalem* • USA
MYSTERY OF THE BURNING FREIGHT, THE • 1917 • Sidney Scott • SHT • USA
MYSTERY OF THE BUSH, THE see **MOIRA** • 1912
MYSTERY OF THE COBRA, THE see **MISTERIO DE LA COBRA, EL** • 1958
MYSTERY OF THE CRIMSON TRAIL, THE • 1913 • *Risser Marguerite* • USA
MYSTERY OF THE DANCING MEN, THE • 1923 • Ridgwell George • UKN
MYSTERY OF THE DEAD POLICE see **MYSTERY OF MR. X, THE** • 1934
MYSTERY OF THE DIAMOND BELT, THE • 1914 • Raymond Charles • UKN
MYSTERY OF THE DOUBLE CROSS, THE • 1917 • Parke William • SRL • USA
MYSTERY OF THE DOVER EXPRESS, THE • 1913 • Lessey George A. • USA
MYSTERY OF THE EMPTY ROOM, THE • 1915 • Van Deusen Courtlandt • USA
MYSTERY OF THE FADELESS TINTS, THE • 1914 • Lessey George A.?, Wilson Ben? • USA
MYSTERY OF THE FATAL PEARL, THE • 1914 • *American Kineto* • USA
MYSTERY OF THE GANGES RIVER see **GANGA MAIYA** • 1953
MYSTERY OF THE GARRISON, THE • 1908 • Melies Georges • FRN
MYSTERY OF THE GHASTLY FACE, THE see **MISTERIO DEL ROSTRO PALIDO, EL** • 1935
MYSTERY OF THE GLASS COFFIN, THE • 1912 • *Eclair* • FRN
MYSTERY OF THE GLASS TUBES, THE • 1914 • Wilson Ben • USA
MYSTERY OF THE GOLDEN EYE • 1978 • Martin Richard • USA
MYSTERY OF THE GOLDEN EYE, THE • 1948 • Beaudine William • USA • GOLDEN EYE, THE (UKN)
MYSTERY OF THE GRAND HOTEL, THE • 1916 • Horne James W. • USA
MYSTERY OF THE HALLUCINATING MUSHROOMS, THE see **MISTERIO DE LOS HONGOS ALUCINANTES, EL** • 1968
MYSTERY OF THE HAUNTED HOTEL, THE • 1913 • *Thanhouser* • USA
MYSTERY OF THE HIDDEN HOUSE, THE • 1914 • Davis Ulysses • USA
MYSTERY OF THE HINDU IMAGE, THE • 1914 • Walsh Raoul • USA • HINDU IMAGE, THE

MYSTERY OF THE HOODED HORSEMEN, THE • 1937 • Taylor Ray • USA
MYSTERY OF THE INDIAN TEMPLE see **MISTERO DEL TIEMPO INDIANO, IL** • 1964
MYSTERY OF THE JEWEL CASKET • 1905 • *Bitzer Billy (Ph)* • USA
MYSTERY OF THE JEWELS, THE see **MISTERO DI OSIRIS, IL** • 1921
MYSTERY OF THE JUNGLE, THE see **TARZAN Y EL MISTERIO DE LA SELVA** • 1973
MYSTERY OF THE KHAKI TUNIC, THE • 1924 • Croise Hugh • UKN
MYSTERY OF THE LADDER OF LIGHT, THE • 1914 • Lessey George A.?, Wilson Ben? • USA
MYSTERY OF THE LAMA CONVENT, THE see **DR. NICOLA III** • 1909
MYSTERY OF THE LANDLADY'S CAT, THE • 1914 • Kellino W. P. • UKN
MYSTERY OF THE LAUGHING DEATH, THE • 1914 • Miller Ashley • USA
MYSTERY OF THE LEAPING FISH, THE • 1916 • Emerson John • SHT • USA
MYSTERY OF THE LOCKED ROOM, THE • 1915 • Wilson Ben • USA
MYSTERY OF THE LOST CAT, THE • 1913 • *Solax* • USA
MYSTERY OF THE LOST STRADIVARIUS, THE • 1914 • Lessey George A. • USA
MYSTERY OF THE MAN WHO SLEPT, THE • 1915 • *Wilson Ben* • USA
MYSTERY OF THE MARIE CELESTE, THE • 1935 • Clift Denison • UKN • PHANTOM SHIP, THE (USA)
MYSTERY OF THE MILK, THE • 1914 • *Ab* • USA
MYSTERY OF THE MILLION DOLLAR HOCKEY PUCK, THE • 1975 • Lafleur Jean, Svatek Peter • CND
MYSTERY OF THE MOONLIGHT SONATA, THE see **MYSTERIE VAN DE MONDSCHEIN SONATE, HET** • 1935
MYSTERY OF THE MOUNTAINS, A • 1915 • Physioc Wray • USA
MYSTERY OF THE MUSEUM, THE see **MUSEUMSMYSTERIET** • 1909
MYSTERY OF THE NIGHT OF THE 25TH, THE see **MYSTERIET NATTEN TILL DEN 25:E** • 1917
MYSTERY OF THE OCEANS, THE see **TAINA DVUH OKEANOV** • 1955
MYSTERY OF THE OCTAGONAL ROOM, THE • 1914 • Lessey George A. • USA
MYSTERY OF THE OLD CASTLE, THE see **TAGEMNICA STAREGO ZAMKU** • 1956
MYSTERY OF THE OLD MILL, THE • 1914 • Martinek H. O. • UKN
MYSTERY OF THE PALLID FACE,THE see **MISTERIO DEL ROSTRO PALIDO, EL** • 1935
MYSTERY OF THE PINE TREE CAMP, THE • 1913 • *Gaunthier Gene* • USA
MYSTERY OF THE PINE TREE POOL, THE • 1914 • *Gardon James* • USA
MYSTERY OF THE POISON POOL, THE see **MYSTERY OF THE POISONED POOL, THE** • 1914
MYSTERY OF THE POISONED POOL, THE • 1914 • *Rosher Charles (Ph)* • USA • MYSTERY OF THE POISON POOL, THE
MYSTERY OF THE RIVER BOAT • 1944 • Taylor Ray, Collins Lewis D. • SRL • USA
MYSTERY OF THE SEA VIEW HOTEL, THE • 1914 • *Wilson Ben* • USA
MYSTERY OF THE SEALED ART GALLERY, THE • 1914 • Lessey George A.?, Wilson Ben? • USA
MYSTERY OF THE SEVEN CHESTS, THE • 1914 • Martin E. A. • USA
MYSTERY OF THE SILENT DEATH, THE • 1915 • *Cuneo Lester* • USA
MYSTERY OF THE SILENT DEATH, THE • 1928 • Eveleigh Leslie • UKN
MYSTERY OF THE SILVER SKULL, THE • 1913 • North Wilfred, Costello Maurice • USA
MYSTERY OF THE SILVER SNARE, THE • 1914 • Lessey George A.?, Wilson Ben? • USA
MYSTERY OF THE SLEEPER TRUNK, THE • 1909 • Olcott Sidney • USA
MYSTERY OF THE SLEEPING DEATH, THE • 1914 • Buel Kenean • USA
MYSTERY OF THE SNAKESKIN BELT, THE • 1950 • Cadman Frank • UKN
MYSTERY OF THE STOLEN CHILD • 1913 • Costello Maurice, Ranous William V. • USA
MYSTERY OF THE STOLEN JEWELS, THE • 1913 • *Costello Maurice* • USA
MYSTERY OF THE TALKING WIRE, THE • 1914 • Lessey George A. • USA
MYSTERY OF THE TAPESTRY ROOM, THE • 1915 • MacQuarrie Murdock • USA
MYSTERY OF THE TEA DANSANT, THE • 1915 • Horne James W. • USA
MYSTERY OF THE THRONE ROOM, THE • 1915 • *Cunard Grace* • USA
MYSTERY OF THE TORN NOTE, THE • 1910 • *Lubin* • USA
MYSTERY OF THE VILLA ROSE, THE see **MYSTERE DE LA VILLA ROSE, LE** • 1929
MYSTERY OF THE VILLA ROSE, THE see **MYSTERE DE LA VILLA ROSE, LE** • 1929
MYSTERY OF THE WAX MUSEUM, THE • 1933 • Curtiz Michael • USA • WAX MUSEUM
MYSTERY OF THE WENTWORTH CASTLE, THE (UKN) see **DOOMED TO DIE** • 1940
MYSTERY OF THE WHITE CAR, THE • 1914 • *Ford Francis* • USA
MYSTERY OF THE WHITE HANDKERCHIEF, THE • 1947 • Hughes Ken • SHT • UKN
MYSTERY OF THE WHITE ROOM • 1939 • Garrett Otis • USA
MYSTERY OF THE YELLOW ROOM, THE • 1919 • Chautard Emile • USA
MYSTERY OF THE YELLOW ROOM, THE see **MYSTERE DE LA CHAMBRE JAUNE, LE** • 1913
MYSTERY OF THE YELLOW ROOM, THE see **MYSTERE DE LA CHAMBRE JAUNE, LE** • 1930
MYSTERY OF THE YELLOW ROOM, THE see **MISTERIO DEL CUARTO AMARILLO, EL** • 1947
MYSTERY OF THE YELLOW ROOM, THE see **MYSTERE DE LA CHAMBRE JAUNE, LE** • 1948
MYSTERY OF THE YELLOW SUNBONNET, THE • 1914 • *Hollister Alice* • USA
MYSTERY OF THOR BRIDGE, THE • 1923 • Ridgwell George • UKN
MYSTERY OF THREE CONTINENTS, THE see **MISTERO DEI TREI CONTINENTI, IL** • 1959
MYSTERY OF THUG ISLAND, THE (USA) see **MISTERI DELLA GIUNGLA NERA, I** • 1964
MYSTERY OF TUSA, THE • 1913 • *American* • USA
MYSTERY OF TUT-ANKH-AMEN'S EIGHTH WIFE, THE see **KING TUT-ANKH-AMEN'S EIGHTH WIFE** • 1923
MYSTERY OF WALL STREET, A • 1913 • *Anderson Mignon* • USA
MYSTERY OF WASHINGTON SQUARE, THE • 1920 • Rule Beverly C. • USA
MYSTERY OF WEST SEDGWICK, THE • 1913 • *Mccoy Gertrude* • USA
MYSTERY OF WICKHAM HALL, THE • 1914 • *Madison Cleo* • USA
MYSTERY OF YELLOW ASTER MINE, THE • 1913 • Reid Wallace • USA
MYSTERY ON BIRD ISLAND • 1954 • Haggarty John • UKN
MYSTERY ON MONSTER ISLAND see **MONSTER ISLAND** • 1981
MYSTERY PLANE (UKN) see **SKY PIRATE** • 1939
MYSTERY RANCH • 1932 • Howard David • USA • KILLER, THE
MYSTERY RANCH • 1934 • Ray Bernard B. • USA
MYSTERY RANGE • 1937 • Hill Robert F. • USA
MYSTERY RIDER • 1928 • Horner Robert J. • USA
MYSTERY RIDER, THE • 1928 • Nelson Jack • SRL • USA
MYSTERY ROAD, THE • 1921 • Powell Paul • USA, UKN
MYSTERY SEA RAIDER • 1940 • Dmytryk Edward • USA
MYSTERY SHIP • 1941 • Landers Lew • USA
MYSTERY SHIP, THE • 1916 • McRae Henry • USA
MYSTERY SHIP, THE • 1918 • Harvey Harry, Ford Francis • SRL • USA
MYSTERY SHIP, THE (UKN) see **OBEAH** • 1934
MYSTERY SQUADRON • 1933 • Clark Colbert, Howard David • SRL • USA
MYSTERY STREET • 1950 • Sturges John • USA
MYSTERY SUBMARINE • 1950 • Sirk Douglas • USA
MYSTERY SUBMARINE • 1963 • Pennington-Richards C. M. • UKN • DECOY (USA) ○ MYSTERY SUBMARINES
MYSTERY SUBMARINES see **MYSTERY SUBMARINE** • 1963
MYSTERY TRAIN • 1931 • Whitman Phil • USA
MYSTERY TRAIN • 1989 • Jarmusch Jim • USA
MYSTERY TROOPER, THE • 1931 • Paton Stuart • SRL • USA • TRAIL OF THE ROYAL MOUNTED
MYSTERY VALLEY • 1928 • McGowan J. P. • USA
MYSTERY WOMAN • 1935 • Forde Eugene J. • USA
MYSTERY WOMAN, THE • 1915 • *Madison Cleo* • USA
MYSTIC, THE • 1925 • Browning Tod • USA
MYSTIC BALL, THE • 1915 • Daly William Robert • USA
MYSTIC CIRCLE MURDER, THE • 1939 • O'Connor Frank • USA • RELIGIOUS RACKETEERS
MYSTIC FACE • 1919 • Hopper E. Mason • USA • MYSTIC FACES
MYSTIC FACES see **MYSTIC FACE** • 1919
MYSTIC GLOVE, THE • 1914 • *Bamforth* • UKN
MYSTIC HOUR, THE • 1917 • Ridgely Richard • USA
MYSTIC HOUR, THE • 1933 • *Progressive* • USA • AT TWELVE MIDNIGHT (UKN)
MYSTIC JEWEL, THE • 1915 • Conway Jack • USA
MYSTIC MANIPULATIONS • 1911 • Bouwmeester Theo, Booth W. R.? • UKN
MYSTIC MAT, THE • 1913 • Aylott Dave? • UKN
MYSTIC MELODIES • 1909 • *Gaumont* • FRN
MYSTIC MIRROR, THE (USA) see **GEHEIMNISVOLLE SPIEGEL, DER** • 1928
MYSTIC MOONSHINE, THE see **MYSTIC MOONSTONE, THE** • 1913
MYSTIC MOONSTONE, THE • 1913 • Aylott Dave • UKN • MYSTIC MOONSHINE, THE
MYSTIC MOUNTAIN, THE (USA) see **RAPT** • 1934
MYSTIC MOUNTAIN MASSACRE • 1971 • Mabe Byron • USA
MYSTIC PINK • 1976 • McKimson Robert • ANS • USA
MYSTIC PIZZA • 1988 • Petrie Donald • USA
MYSTIC PROPHECIES AND NOSTRADAMUS • 1961 • *Premier Prods* • USA
MYSTIC REINCARNATION • 1902 • *Biograph* • USA
MYSTIC RING, THE • 1912 • Aylott Dave? • UKN
MYSTIC SWING, THE • 1900 • Porter Edwin S. • USA
MYSTIC WARRIOR, THE • 1984 • Heffron Richard T. • TVM • USA
MYSTIC WELL, THE • 1915 • *Orlamond Fritz* • USA
MYSTICAL FLAME, THE (USA) see **FLAMME MERVEILLEUSE, LA** • 1903
MYSTICAL LOVE-MAKING see **DRAME CHEZ LES FANTOCHES, UNE** • 1908
MYSTICAL MAID OF JAMASHA PASS, THE see **MYTH OF JAMASHA PASS, THE** • 1912
MYSTICAL ROSE • 1976 • Lee Michael • ASL
MYSTIFICATION AMUSANTE, LA • 1903 • Velle Gaston • FRN • AMUSING HOAX, THE
MYSTIFIERS, THE see **SYMPHONIE POUR UN MASSACRE** • 1963
MYSTIFIES, LES see **SYMPHONIE POUR UN MASSACRE** • 1963
MYSTIKE FREMMEDE, DEN • 1914 • Holger-Madsen • DNM • DEAL WITH THE DEVIL, A
MYSTIQUE see **BRAINWASH** • 1981
MYSTISKE SELSKABSDAME • 1916 • Blom August • DNM • MYSTERIOUS COMPANION, THE ○ LEGATIONENS GIDSEL ○ MYSTERIOUS LADY'S COMPANION, THE ○ HOSTAGE OF THE EMBASSY, THE
MYSTO FOX • 1946 • Wickersham Bob • ANS • USA
MYSZKA I KOTEK • 1958 • Nehrebecki Wladyslaw • ANS • PLN • MOUSE AND CAT (USA) ○ CAT AND THE MOUSE, THE ○ MOUSE AND KITTEN ○ MOUSE AND THE CAT, THE
MYTEN • 1965 • Halldoff Jan • SWD • MYTH, THE ○ DELIRIUM
MYTH, THE see **MYTEN** • 1965
MYTH, THE (USA) see **MITO, IL** • 1963
MYTH AND REALITY • 1973 • Fortier Bob • MTV • CND
MYTH AND THE REALITY, THE • 1973 • Pindal Kaj • ANS • CND
MYTH-MAKERS, THE see **SEGESVAR** • 1974
MYTH OF JAMASHA PASS, THE • 1912 • Dwan Allan • USA • MYSTICAL MAID OF JAMASHA PASS, THE
MYTHICAL MONSTERS OF THE DEEP • 1982 • Stoneman John • MTV • CND
MZWAKHE MBULI: THE PEOPLE'S POET • 1989 • SHT • SAF

N

'N BEELD VIR JEANNIE • 1976 • SAF
'N DOGTER VAN DIE VELD • 1933 • SAF
N.I.N.I. C'EST FINI • 1908 • Cohl Emile • ANS • FRN
N. N. • 1969 • Domnick Ottomar • FRG
N.N. • 1977 • Dovnikovic Borivoj • ANM • YGS
N.N. A HALAL ANGYALA • 1970 • Hersko Janos • HNG • REQUIEM IN THE HUNGARIAN MANNER
N.O.T.H.I.N.G. see **N:O:T:H:I:N:G** • 1968
N. OR N.W. • 1938 • Lye Len • SHT • UKN • NORTH OR NORTH WEST ○ N OR NW
N OR NW see **N. OR N.W.** • 1938
N.P. IL SEGRETO • 1972 • Agosti Silvano • ITL • N.P. (-THE SECRET) (USA)
N.P. (-THE SECRET) (USA) see **N.P. IL SEGRETO** • 1972
'N PLAN IS 'N BOERDERY • 1954 • SAF
'N SEDER VAL IN WATERKLOOF • 1978 • SAF
N STANDS FOR NELLY • 1911 • Fitzhamon Lewin? • UKN
N.U. • 1948 • Antonioni Michelangelo • DCS • ITL • NETTEZZA URBANA
N.W.T., ONE THIRD OF CANADA, THE • 1975 • Rodgers Bob • MTV • CND
N.Y. CITY FIRE DEPT. • 1903 • *Bitzer Billy (Ph)* • USA
N.Y., N.Y. • 1957 • Thompson Francis • SHT • USA
N-ZONE • 1970 • Lipsett Arthur • CND
NA! • 1973 • Martin Jacques • FRN
NA "BATORYM" DO POLSKI • 1960 • Perski Ludwik • DOC • PLN • ON THE "BATORY" TO POLAND
NA BOCA DA NOITE • 1971 • Lima Walter Jr. • BRZ • IN THE DEPTHS OF THE NIGHT
NA BOCA DO MUNDO • 1980 • Pitanga Antonio • BRZ • IN THE WORLD'S MOUTH
NA CHA see **NA CHA THE GREAT** • 1974
NA CHA THE GREAT • 1974 • Chang Ch'Eh • HKG • NA CHA
NA COMETE see **NA KOMETE** • 1970
NA DE LIEFDE • 1983 • Boon Jaak • BLG • APRES L'AMOUR
NA DE SLOTFASE • 1968 • Le Bon Patrick • SHT • BLG
NA DIKOM BEREGYE • 1967 • Granik Anatoli • USS • ON THE WILD SHORE ○ WILD SHORE, THE
NA DNU • 1969 • Pavlinic Zlatko • ANS • YGS • ON THE BOTTOM
NA DROGACH ARMENII • 1957 • Hoffman Jerzy, Skorzewski Edward • DCS • PLN • ON THE ROADS OF ARMENIA
NA DZIKIM ZACHODZIE • 1970 • Dulz Stanislaw • PLN • IN THE WILD WEST
NA ESTRADA DA VIDA • 1981 • dos Santos Nelson Pereira • BRZ • ON THE HIGHWAY OF LIFE
NA GARGANTA DO DIABLO • 1960 • Khouri Walter Hugo • BRZ • IN THE DEVIL'S THROAT (USA)
NA GRAFSKIKH RAZVALINAKH • 1956 • Skuibin Vladimir • USS • ON THE RUINS OF THE ESTATE
NA IDU I NA VODE • 1959 • Zenyakin Arkadij • USS • ON ICE AND WATER
NA KIYEVSKOM NAPRAVYENII • 1968 • Denisenko Vladimir • USS • IN THE KIEV ZONE ○ KIEV DIRECTION, THE
NA KOHO TO SLOVO PADNE • 1980 • Kachlik Antonin • CZC • WHOSE TURN IS IT
NA KOMETE • 1970 • Zeman Karel • CZC • HECTOR SERVADAC'S ARK ○ MR. SERVADAC'S ARK ○ NA COMETE ○ ON THE COMET ○ ON A COMET ○ ARCHA PANA SERVADACA
NA KRASNOM FRONTE • 1920 • Kuleshov Lev • USS • ON THE RED FRONT
NA KRAY SYVETA.. • 1976 • Nakhapetov Rodion • USS • TO THE EDGE OF THE WORLD.. ○ END OF THE WORLD, THE ○ END OF THE EARTH, THE
NA LANE • 1963 • Novak Ivo • CZC • ON THE TIGHTROPE ○ ON A TIGHTROPE
NA LINII OGNYA -OPERATORY KINOKHRONIKI • 1941 • Vertov Dziga, Svilova Elizaveta • USS • CAMERA REPORTERS ON THE LINE OF FIRE ○ V LINII OGNIA ○ ON THE LINE OF FIRE -FILM REPORTERS ○ IN THE FRONT LINE
NA LIVADI • 1957 • Kostelac Nikola • ANS • YGS • ON A MEADOW ○ MEETING IN A MEADOW
NA MALKIA OSTROV • 1958 • Vulchanov Rangel • BUL • ON THE LITTLE ISLAND ○ ON A SMALL ISLAND
NA MELINE • 1965 • Rozewicz Stanislaw • MTV • PLN • TO THE HANG OUT
NA MIRA DO ASSASSINO • 1968 • Latini Mario • BRZ • IN THE ASSASSIN'S SIGHTS
NA PAPIRNATIH AVIONIH • 1967 • Klopcic Matjaz • YGS • IN PAPER PLANES ○ ON WINGS OF PAPER ○ PAPER PLANES
N'A PAS PRIS LES DES • 1971 • Robbe-Grillet Alain • MTV • FRN
NA PLANIE • 1968 • Ziarnik Jerzy • DOC • PLN • ON THE SET

NA PODHALU • 1967 • Wionczek Roman • DOC • PLN • IN THE PODHALE REGION
NA POKLONY • 1974 • Ilyenko Yury • USS • WITH REGARDS
NA PRAZSKEM HRADE • 1932 • Hammid Alexander • SHT • CZC ○ PRAGUE CASTLE ○ MUSIC OF ARCHITECTURE
NA PRIMAVERA DA VIDA • 1926 • Mauro-Humberto • BRZ • IN THE SPRINGTIME OF LIFE
NA PROGU • 1965 • Karabasz Kazimierz • DCS • PLN • ON THE THRESHOLD
NA PRZELAJ • 1971 • Leski Janusz • PLN • POINT TO POINT ○ HARD TIMES ○ ROUGH LIFE ○ TO WALK ALONE
NA PUTU ZA KATANGU • 1987 • Pavlovic Zivojin • YGS • ON THE ROAD TO KATANGA
NA PYTLACKE STEZCE • 1981 • Gajer Vaclav • CZC • ON THE POACHER'S PATH
NA SAMOTE U LESA • 1976 • Menzel Jiri • CZC • SECLUSION NEAR A FOREST
NA SEMI VETRAKH • 1962 • Rostotsky Stanislav • USS • HOUSE ON THE FRONT LINE, THE (USA) ○ OPEN TO SEVEN WINDS ○ SEVEN WINDS ○ IN THE SEVEN WINDS ○ BETWEEN FOUR WINDS
NA SENDA DO CRIME • 1954 • Bollini Flaminio • BRZ • ROAD TO CRIME
NA SLUNECNI STRANE • 1933 • Vancura Vladislav • CZC • ON THE SUNNY SIDE
NA SREBRNYM GLOBIE • 1977 • Zulawski Andrzej • PLN • AT THE SILVER GLOBE ○ SILVER GLOBE, THE
NA STACJI • 1968 • Wionczek Roman • DOC • PLN • AT THE STATION
NA START • 1937 • Ford Aleksander • DOC • PLN
NA STOKACH KILIMANDZARO • 1970 • Kudla Zdzislaw • PLN • ON THE SLOPES OF KILIMANJARO
NA STRAZY GRANIC • 1960 • Lomnicki Jan • DOC • PLN • ON GUARD AT THE BORDER
NA STRAZY TRWALEGO POKOJU • 1946 • Bossak Jerzy • DOC • PLN • GUARDING PERMANENT PEACE
NA SVOJI ZEMLJI • 1948 • Stiglic France • YGS • ON HIS OWN GROUND
NA TORACH • 1972 • Kosinski Bohdan • DOC • PLN • ON THE TRACK
NA TROSKACH VRASTA ZIVOT • 1946 • Kadar Jan • CZC
NA-TZU HAN • Sun Chia-Wei • HKG • KUNG FU GANGBUSTERS ○ SMUGGLERS
NA VARSHAVSKOM TRAKTE • 1916 • Starevitch Ladislas • USS • ON THE WARSAW HIGHWAY
NA WYLOT • 1973 • Krolikiewicz Grzegorz • PLN • THROUGH AND THROUGH
NA WYSPACH POLINEZJI • 1969 • Nehrebecki Wladyslaw • ANS • PLN • ON THE POLYNESIAN ISLANDS
NA ZIZKOVE VALECNEM VOZE • 1968 • Vosmik Milan • CZC • ON ZIZKA'S FORTIFIED WAGON ○ ON ZIZKA'S WAR WAGON
NAACHI GHAR • 1959 • Tara R. S. • IND
NAADENA PENNU • 1967 • Madhavan Sethu • IND • VILLAGE MAID
NAADIGE FROKEN, DEN • 1911 • Blom August • DNM • LADY MARY'S LOVE
NAAG RANI • 1962 • Bhatt Nanabhai • IND • COBRA GIRL (USA)
NAAKT OVER DE SCHUTTING • 1973 • Weisz Frans • NTH • SAME PLAYER SHOOTS AGAIN ○ NAKED OVER THE FENCE ○ LADY ON THE FENCE, THE
NAAN • 1967 • Ramanna T. R. • IND • SELF
NAAN KANDA SWARGAM • 1960 • Pulliah C. • IND • I DISCOVERED HEAVEN
NAAN YAAR THERIYUMA? • 1967 • Raman V. V. • IND • DO YOU KNOW WHO I AM?
NA'APET • 1977 • Malyan Ghenrikh • USS • NAHAPET
NAAR FRUEN GAAR PAA EVENTYR • 1913 • Blom August • DNM • POMPADOURTASKEN ○ LOST BAG, THE
NAAR FRUEN SKIFTER PIGE see **HUSASSISTENTEN** • 1914
NAAR KJERTENE KALDER • 1915 • Davidsen Hjalmar • DNM
NAAR MAN KEDER SIG PAA LANDET • 1919 • Lauritzen Lau • DNM
NAAR MAN KUN ER UNG • 1943 • Henning-Jensen Bjarne • DNM • TO BE YOUNG
NAAR MASKEN FALDER (DNM) see **WENN DIE MASKE FALLT** • 1912
NAAZ • 1954 • *Biswas Anil (M)* • IND
NABADHATU QALB • 1971 • Francis Yussif • SHT • EGY • BATTEMENTS DE COEUR
NABAT • 1917 • Bauer Yevgeni • USS • ALARM, THE
NABBED • 1915 • *Bison* • USA
NABBED! • 1915 • Collins Edwin J.? • UKN
NABBEM JOINS THE FORCE • 1913 • Collins Edwin J.? • UKN
NABBING A NOBLE • 1917 • Howe J. A. • SHT • USA
NABESHIMA KAIBYODEN • 1949 • Watanabe Kunio • JPN • GHOST-CAT MANSION OF NABESHIMA
NABONGA • 1944 • Newfield Sam • USA • JUNGLE WOMAN, THE ○ GIRL AND THE GORILLA, THE ○ GORILLA
NABUJALA RIJEKA see **PERROI VERSHUES** • 1984
NACALA see **NACHALO** • 1971
NACE UN AMOR • 1938 • Saslavsky Luis • ARG
NACE UN SALTA DE AGUA • 1954 • Castellon Alfredo • SHT • SPN
NACER EN LENINGRADO • 1977 • Solas Humberto • SHT • CUB
NACERADEC, KING OF KIBITZER see **NACERADEC, KRAL KIBICU** • 1932
NACERADEC, KRAL KIBICU • 1932 • Machaty Gustav • CZC • NACERADEC, KING OF KIBITZER
NACH DEM GESETZ • 1919 • Grunwald Willy • FRG
NACH DEM REGEN SCHEINT SONNE • 1949 • Kobler Erich • FRG
NACH DER FINSTERNIS see **AFTER DARKNESS** • 1985
NACH EINEM JAHR • 1963 • Junge Winifried • GDR • AFTER ONE YEAR
NACH GLUCK UND LIEBE SUCHEN, DIE • 1917 • *Andra Fern* • FRG
NACH LIEBE DURSTEN, DIE • 1919 • Moest Hubert • FRG
NACH LIEBE SCHMACHTEN, DIE see **LANGSAME TOD, DER** • 1920
NACH MEINEM LETZTEN UMZUG • 1970 • Syberberg Hans-Jurgen • DOC • FRG • AFTER MY LAST MOVE
NACH REGEN FOLGT SONNE see **VERJUNGUNGSKUR, DIE** • 1950
NACH STOCKHOLM DER LIEBE WEGEN see **SOM HON BADDAR FAR HAN LIGGA** • 1970
NACH WIEN • 1983 • Beyer Friedemann • FRG
NACHA REGULES • 1950 • Amadori Luis Cesar • ARG
NACHALNIK CHUKOTKI • 1967 • Melnikov Vitali • USS • CHIEF OF CHUKOTKA
NACHALO • 1971 • Panfilov Gleb • USS • GIRL FROM THE FACTORY, A ○ BEGINNING, THE ○ DEBUT, THE ○ NACALA
NACHBAR, DER • 1990 • Spielmann Gotz • AUS • NEIGHBOUR, THE
NACHBESUCH IN DER NORTHERNBANK • 1921 • Grune Karl • FRG
NACHE NAGIN BAJE BEEN • 1960 • Harish Tara • IND • DANCE OF COBRA TO PLAYING OF VEENA
NACHENSCHNUR DES TOT • 1919 • *Lugosi Bela* • FRG • NECKLACE OF THE DEAD
NACHI CHEMPIONY see **NASHI CHEMPIONY** • 1950
NACHINGWEA • 1976 • Popovic Dragutin
NACHMITTAG FUR UNS • 1961 • Houwer Rob, Schamoni Peter • FRG
NACHSTE, BITTE, DER • 1930 • Schonfelder Erich • FRG
NACHSTE HERR –DIESELBE DAME, DER • 1968 • von Rathony Akos • FRG • NEXT GENTLEMAN –THE SAME LADY, THE
NACHT, DIE • 1984 • Syberberg Hans-Jurgen • FRG
NACHT AM MONTBLANC see **FEGEFEUER DER LIEBE** • 1951
NACHT AM SEE, DIE • 1963 • Klinger Werner, Thouet Peter M. • FRG
NACHT AN DER DONAU, EINE • 1935 • Boese Carl • FRG • NIGHT ON THE DANUBE, A
NACHT AUF GOLDENHALL, DIE • 1919 • Veidt Conrad • FRG
NACHT DER 12, DIE • 1945 • Schweikart Hans • FRG
NACHT DER EINBRUCHER, DIE • 1921 • Krafft Uwe Jens • FRG • SPLEEN
NACHT DER ENTSCHEIDUNG • 1956 • Harnack Falk • FRG
NACHT DER ENTSCHEIDUNG, DIE • 1919 • Osten Franz • FRG
NACHT DER ENTSCHEIDUNG, DIE • 1931 • Buchowetzki Dimitri • FRG
NACHT DER ENTSCHEIDUNG, DIE • 1938 • Malasomma Nunzio • FRG
NACHT DER GROSSEN LIEBE, DIE • 1933 • von Bolvary Geza • FRG
NACHT DER KONIGIN ISABEAU, DIE • 1920 • Wiene Robert • FRG
NACHT DER MEDICI, DIE • 1922 • Grune Karl • FRG
NACHT DER PRUFUNG, DER • 1920 • Hanus Emerich • FRG
NACHT DER TAUSEND SEELEN, DIE • 1921 • Wenter Adolf • FRG
NACHT DER TOTEN, DIE • 1920 • *Artis-Film* • FRG
NACHT DER VAMPIRE • 1970 • Klimovsky Leon • FRG, SPN • WEREWOLF VS. THE VAMPIRE WOMAN, THE (USA) ○ NOCHE DE WALPURGIS, LA (SPN) ○ SHADOW OF THE WEREWOLF (UKN) ○ WEREWOLF'S SHADOW, THE ○ BLACK HARVEST OF COUNTESS DRACULA, THE ○ SPN ○ MESSE NERE DELLA CONTESSA DRACULA, LE
NACHT DER VERSUCHUNG, DIE • 1932 • Wohlmuth Robert, Lasko Leo • FRG • FREMDENLEGIONAR NR.37
NACHT DER VERWANDLUNG • 1935 • Deppe Hans • FRG • DEMASKIERUNG
NACHT DES GRAUENS • 1916 • Robison Arthur • FRG • NIGHT OF HORROR, A ○ NIGHT OF TERROR, A
NACHT DES GRAUENS, DIE • 1912 • Stark Kurt • FRG
NACHT DES GRAUENS, DIE • 1919 • Sauer Fred • FRG
NACHT DES GRAUENS, EINE see **ZWOLFTE STUNDE, DIE** • 1930
NACHT DES GRAUENS, EINE see **ZWOLFTE STUNDE –EINE NACHTE DES GRAUENS, DIE** • 1930
NACHT DES SCHRECKENS, DIE • 1929 • Righelli Gennaro • FRG • STARKERE MACHT, DIE ○ NIGHT OF FRIGHTS
NACHT FIEL UBER GOTENHAFEN • 1960 • Wisbar Frank • FRG
NACHT GEHORT UNS, DIE • 1929 • Froelich Carl • FRG
NACHT IM FORSTHAUS, DIE • 1933 • Engels Erich • FRG • FALL ROBERTS, DER
NACHT IM GRANDHOTEL, EINE • 1931 • Neufeld Max • FRG
NACHT IM GRENZWALD, DIE • 1968 • Barthel Kurt • GDR • NIGHT IN GRENZWALD, THE
NACHT IM MAI • 1938 • Jacoby Georg • FRG • NIGHT IN MAY, A (USA)
NACHT IM PARADIES, EINE • 1931 • Lamac Carl • FRG
NACHT IM SEPARE, EINE • 1950 • Deppe Hans • FRG
NACHT IN LONDON, EINE • 1928 • Pick Lupu • FRG • NIGHT IN LONDON, A
NACHT IN VENEDIG, DIE • 1942 • Verhoeven Paul • FRG
NACHT IN VENEDIG, EINE • 1934 • Wiene Robert, Gallone Carmine • FRG, ITL • NOTTE A VENEZIA, UNA (ITL)
NACHT IN VENEDIG, EINE • 1953 • Wildhagen Georg • AUS
NACHT IN YOSHIWARA, EINE • 1928 • Hanus Emerich • FRG
NACHT MIT DEM KAISER, DIE • 1936 • Engel Erich • FRG • NIGHT WITH THE EMPEROR
NACHT MIT HINDERNISSEN, EINE • 1937 • Boese Carl • FRG • KLAPPERSTORCHVERBAND, DER ○ STORK SOCIETY, THE (USA)
NACHT OHNE ABSCHIED • 1943 • Waschneck Erich • FRG
NACHT OHNE MORAL, DIE • 1953 • Dorfler Ferdinand • FRG
NACHT OHNE MORGEN, DIE • 1921 • Grune Karl • FRG
NACHT OHNE PAUSE, DIE • 1931 • Marton Andrew, Wenzler Franz • FRG
NACHT OHNE SUNDE, DIE • 1950 • Kulb Karl G. • FRG
NACHT UND DER LEICHNAM, DIE • 1920 • Abter Adolf • FRG
NACHT UND MORGEN • 1916 • von Woringen Paul • FRG
NACHT VAN DE WILDE EZELS, DE • 1989 • de la Parra Pim • NTH • NIGHT OF THE WILD DONKEYS, THE
NACHT VON CORY LANE, DIE • 1916 • Hanus Emerich • FRG
NACHT VON KORNATOWO, DIE • 1915 • *Terwin Johanna* • FRG
NACHT VOR DEM TODE • 1929 • *Artus-Film* • FRG
NACHT VOR DER PREMIERE, DIE • 1959 • Jacoby Georg • FRG • NIGHT BEFORE THE PREMIERE, THE
NACHT ZONDER ZEGEN • 1977 • Dorresteijn Jan • NTH • NIGHT OF DOOM
NACHTASYL • 1919 • Meinert Rudolf • FRG
NACHTDIENST see **WEGE IN DER NACHT** • 1979
NACHTE AM BOSPORUS see **MANN, DER DEN MORD BEGING, DER** • 1930
NACHTE AM NIL • 1949 • Rabenalt Arthur M. • FRG
NACHTE DES CORNELIS BROUWER, DIE • 1921 • Wauer William? • FRG
NACHTFALTER • 1911 • Gad Urban • FRG • MOTH, THE
NACHTGESPENST, DAS • 1953 • Boese Carl • FRG
NACHTGESPRACH, DAS • 1917 • *Kaiser-Titz Erich* • FRG
NACHTGESTALTEN • 1920 • Oswald Richard • FRG • ELEAGABAL KUPERUS
NACHTGESTALTEN • 1929 • Steinhoff Hans • FRG • NUR EIN GASSENMADEL
NACHTKOLONNE • 1931 • Petersen Armin • FRG
NACHTLICHES EREIGNIS, EIN • 1924 • *Deutsche Mutoscop* • FRG
NACHTLOKAL • 1929 • Neufeld Max • AUS
NACHTLOKAL ZUM SILBERMOND, DAS • 1959 • Gluck Wolfgang • FRG • 5 SINNERS (USA) ○ SINNERS, THE ○ CAVERNS OF VICE
NACHTMEERFAHRT, DIE • 1986 • Kino Kitty • AUS • VOYAGE BY NIGHT N
NACHTRATSEL, DAS • 1915 • Larsen Viggo • FRG
NACHTS AUF DEN STRASSEN • 1952 • Jugert Rudolf • FRG • NIGHT ON THE AUTOBAHN, A
NACHTS GING DAS TELEPHON • 1962 • von Cziffra Geza • FRG • PHONE RINGS EVERY NIGHT, THE (USA)
NACHTS IM GRUNEN KAKADU • 1957 • Jacoby Georg • FRG
NACHTS, WENN DER TEUFEL KAM • 1957 • Siodmak Robert • FRG • DEVIL STRIKES AT NIGHT, THE (USA) ○ NAZI TERROR AT NIGHT ○ DEVIL CAME AT NIGHT, THE ○ NIGHTS WHEN THE DEVIL CAME
NACHTSCHATTEN • 1918 • Zelnik Friedrich • FRG
NACHTSCHATTEN • 1972 • Schilling Niklaus • FRG • NIGHTSHADE
NACHTSCHWESTER INGEBORG • 1958 • von Cziffra Geza • FRG
NACHTSTURME • 1923 • Kobe Hanns • FRG
NACHTWACHE • 1949 • Braun Harald • FRG • KEEPERS OF THE NIGHT (USA)
NACIALOTO NA EDNA VACANZIA • 1966 • Heskiya Zako • BUL • HOLIDAY WITH SURPRISES ○ BEGINNING OF A HOLIDAY, THE
NACIDA PARA AMAR • 1958 • Gonzalez Rogelio A. • MXC
NACIDO PARA LA MUSICA • 1959 • Salvia Rafael J. • SPN
NACIDOS PARA CANTAR • 1965 • Gomez Muriel Emilio • MXC, ARG
NACIMIENTO DE SALOME, EL (SPN) see **NASCITA DI SALOME** • 1940
NACION CLANDESTINA, LA • 1989 • Sanjines Jorge • BLV • SECRET NATION, THE ○ HIDDEN NATION, THE
NACIONAL III • 1983 • Berlanga Luis Garcia • SPN • NATIONAL III
NACIONALE PARK, HET • 1968 • Crama Nico • SHT • NTH • NATIONAL PARK, THE
NACIONALNA KLASA DO 785cm3 • 1978 • Markovic Goran • YGS • NATIONAL CLASS UP TO 785cm3 ○ NATIONAL CLASS
NACKT SIND SEINE OPFER see **X + YY –FORMEL DES BOSEN** • 1969
NACKT UND HEISS AUF MYKONOS • 1979 • Tiedemans Claus • FRG • SEXUAL EXTASY ○ HIGH SEASON
NACKT UNTER WOLFEN • 1962 • Beyer Frank • GDR • NAKED AMONG THE WOLVES (USA) ○ NAKED AMONG WOLVES
NACKT WIE GOTT SIE SCHUF • 1958 • Schott-Schobinger Hans, Savona Leopoldo • FRG, ITL, AUS • NUDI COME DIO LI CREO (ITL)
NACKTE BOVARY, DIE • 1969 • Scott John • FRG, ITL • PECCATI DI MADAME BOVARY, I (ITL)
NACKTE MANN AUF DEM SPORTPLATZ, DER • 1974 • Wolf Konrad • GDR • NAKED MAN ON THE ATHLETIC FIELD, THE ○ NAKED MAN ON THE SPORTSGROUND, THE
NACKTE UND DER SATAN, DIE • 1959 • Trivas Victor • FRG • HEAD, THE (USA) ○ HEAD FOR THE DEVIL, A ○ SCREAMING HEAD, THE ○ NAKED AND SATAN, THE
NACKTE WAHRHEIT, DIE • 1931 • Anton Karl • FRG
NACKTE WEIB, DAS see **KURTISANE VON VENEDIG, DIE** • 1924
NACKTEN, DIE • 1919 • Berger Martin • FRG
NAD NAMI SVITA • 1952 • Krejcik Jiri • CZC • DAWN ABOVE US ○ DAWN, THE
NAD NEMANOM RASSVET • 1953 • Fainzimmer Alexander • USS
NAD NIEMNEM • 1939 • Jakubowska Wanda (c/d) • PLN • ON THE NIEMEN RIVER
NAD ODRA • 1965 • Poreba Bohdan • PLN • ON THE ODRA
NAD ORINOKO • 1970 • Nehrebecki Wladyslaw • ANS • PLN • ON THE ORINOCO RIVER
NAD RANEM • 1928 • Ford Aleksander • SHT • PLN • AT DAWN
NADA • 1947 • Neville Edgar • SPN
NADA! • 1973 • Chabrol Claude • FRN, ITL • NADA GANG, THE (USA)
NADA DE NOVO EM OBIDOS • 1933 • do Canto Jorge Brum • SHT • PRT
NADA GANG, THE (USA) see **NADA!** • 1973
NADA MAS QUE UNA MUJER • 1934 • Lachman Harry • USA • ONLY A WOMAN
NADA MENOS QUE TODO UN HOMBRE • 1971 • Gil Rafael • SPN, USA • NOTHING LESS THAN A MAN
NADA MENOS QUE UN ARCANGEL • 1959 • del Amo Antonio • SPN • NOTHING LESS THAN AN ARCHANGEL
NADAHA, EL • 1974 • Kamal Hussein • EGY • NADDAHA, AN– ○ SIRENE, LA
NADARE • 1937 • Naruse Mikio • JPN • AVALANCHE
NADARE • 1952 • Shindo Kaneto • JPN • AVALANCHE
NADARE • 1956 • Yamamoto Satsuo • JPN • AVALANCHE
NADDAHA, AN– see **NADAHA, EL** • 1974
NADEJDA see **NADEZHDA** • 1955
NADEJE • 1963 • Kachyna Karel • CZC • HOPE

NADEZHDA • 1955 • Gerasimov Sergei • USS • NADEJDA
NADEZHDA see **NADYEZHDA** • 1973
NADHDHARA AS-SAWDA', AN- • 1962 • Mustafa Hassam Eddin • EGY • LUNETTES NOIRES, LES
NADHRATU AL-FANNAN • 1970 • Francis Yussif • SHT • EGY • REGARD DE L'ARTISTE, LE
NADI-O-NARI • 1965 • Khan Sadek • BNG • RIVER AND WOMAN
NADIA • 1948 • Wahab Fatin Abdel • EGY
NADIA • 1984 • Cooke Alan • TVM • USA
NADIA, LA FEMME TRAQUEE • 1939 • Orval Claude • FRN • A L'OMBRE DU DEUXIEME BUREAU ○ OMBRE DU DEUXIEME BUREAU, L' ○ NADIA, LA LUTTE SECRETE
NADIA, LA LUTTE SECRETE see **NADIA, LA FEMME TRAQUEE** • 1939
NADIE DIHO NADA see **NADIO DIGO NADA** • 1971
NADIE LO SABRA • 1953 • Torrado Ramon • SPN
NADIE MUERE DOS VECES • 1952 • Spota Luis • MXC
NADIE OYO GRITAR • 1972 • de la Iglesia Eloy • SPN
NADINE • 1987 • Benton Robert • USA
NADINE OF NOWHERE • 1916 • Bourgeois Paul • SHT • USA
NADIO DIGO NADA • 1971 • Ruiz Raul • CHL • NOBODY SAID ANYTHING ○ NOBODY SAID NOTHING ○ NADIE DIHO NADA ○ NO ONE SAID A WORD
NADJA A PARIS • 1964 • Rohmer Eric • SHT • FRN
NADJI THE HINDOO MARVEL • 1903 • *Paul R. W.* • UKN
NADLIDE • 1946 • Wasserman Vaclav • CZC • HERRENVOLK
NADMANTRAPU SIRI • 1968 • Rama Rao T. • IND • UPSTART, THE
NADVEREN • 1970 • de Waal Allan, Christiansen Henning, Nygaard Preben, Davidsen John, Fischer Egon, Thygesen Erik, Lind Peter, Hagens Eric, Norgaard Bjorn, Jensen Peter Louis, Nedergaard Jeffrey, Gernes Poul • DNM
NADYEZHDA • 1973 • Donskoi Mark • USS • NADEZHDA
NADZIEJA I INNE WIERSZE: WLADYSLAW BRONIEWSKI • 1962 • Lomnicki Jan • DOC • PLN • HOPE AND OTHER POEMS: WLADYSAW BRONIEWSKI
NAEB EL AM, EL • 1945 • Kamel Morsi Ahmad • EGY • PUBLIC PROSECUTOR, THE ○ NAIB AL-AM, AN
NAEDE FARGEN, DE • 1948 • Dreyer Carl T. • SHT • DNM • THEY CAUGHT THE FERRY
NAESI • 1986 • I Du-Yong • SKR • EUNUCH
NAESTE STOP, PARADIS • 1981 • Carlsen Jon Bang • DNM • NEST STOP, PARADISE
NAFAR WAHID see **LUBATU KULLI YUM** • 1971
NAFTIS TOU EGEOU, O • 1968 • Stratzalis Kostas • GRC • AEGEAN SAILOR, THE ○ SAILORS, THE
NAG DEVTA • 1962 • Shoni Shantilal • IND
NAG IN THE BAG, A • 1938 • Parrott Charles • SHT • USA
NAGA-NANDA • 1934 • Rao Y. V. • IND
NAGA SALITANG KALANSAY • 1961 • Santiago Pablo • PHL
NAGAAPOY NA DAMBANA • 1967 • Carlos Luciano B. • PHL • FLAMING ALTAR
NAGAGUTSU O HAITA NEKO • 1969 • Yabuki Kimio • ANM • JPN • PUSS IN BOOTS (USA)
NAGANA • 1933 • Frank Ernst L. • USA
NAGANA • 1955 • Bromberger Herve • FRN, ITL
NAGANIACZ • 1963 • Petelska Ewa, Petelski Czeslaw • PLN • BEATER, THE
NAGARDOLA • 1978 • Ahmed Belal • BNG • SWALLOWS ALWAYS COME BACK ○ GIANT WHEEL
NAGARERU • 1956 • Naruse Mikio • JPN • FLOWING
NAGARIK • 1952 • Ghatak Ritwik • IND • CITIZEN, THE
NAGASAKI NO UTA WA WASUREJI • 1952 • Tasaka Tomotaka • JPN • I'LL NEVER FORGET THE SONG OF NAGASAKI
NAGASUGITA HARU • 1957 • Tanaka Shigeo • JPN • BETROTHED
NAGATONOKAMI KIMURA see **KIMURA NAGATONOKAMI** • 1918
NAGAYA SHINSHI-ROKU • 1948 • Ozu Yasujiro • JPN • RECORD OF A TENEMENT GENTLEMAN ○ DIARY OF A TENEMENT GENTLEMAN
NAGBABAGANG LUHA • 1988 • Bernal Ishmael • PHL • FIERY TEARS
NAGEL, DIE • 1971 • Aeschbacher Kurt • ANS • SWT • NAILS
NAGIN • 1955 • IND
NAGIN • 1959 • Qaiser Khalil • PKS • FEMALE COBRA
NAGIN JOGI • 1989 • Butt Mahmood • PKS • COBRA
NAGISA NO SHIROI IE • 1977 • Saito Koichi • JPN • WHITE HOUSE ON THE SHORE, THE
NAGON ATT ALSKA (SWD) see **SEDUCTION OF INGA, THE** • 1973
NAGRA SOMMARKVALLAR PA JORDEN • 1987 • Lindblom Gunnel • SWD • SUMMER NIGHTS ON THE PLANET EARTH
NAGRODY I ODZNACZENIA • 1974 • Lomnicki Jan • PLN • AWARDS AND DECORATIONS ○ PRIZES AND DECORATIONS
NAGRODZONE UCZUCIA • 1958 • Borowczyk Walerian, Lenica Jan • ANS • PLN • REQUITED FEELINGS (UKN) ○ REWARDED FEELINGS ○ NAGRODZONE UCZVTE ○ LOVE REWARDED ○ LOVE REQUITED
NAGRODZONE UCZVTE see **NAGRODZONE UCZUCIA** • 1958
NAGUA • 1983 • Guttman Amos • ISR
NAGURARETA KOCHIYAMA • 1934 • Kinugasa Teinosuke • JPN
NAGURI KOMI KOSHUJI • 1953 • Makino Masahiro • JPN • JIROCHO'S TRAVELS
NAGURIKOMI KANTAI • 1961 • Shimazu Shoichi • JPN • STORMING SQUADRON
NAGUSHACHARITA see **BRAHMARATHAM** • 1949
NAGYEMBER, A • 1968 • Macskassy Gyula, Varnai Gyorgy • ANS • HNG • MR. BIGMAN
NAGYMAMA • 1935 • Gyoergy Istavan • HNG • GRANDMOTHER
NAGYMAMA, A • 1916 • Korda Alexander • HNG • GRANDMOTHER, THE
NAGYUZEMI TOJASTERMELES • 1962 • Meszaros Marta • DCS • HNG • MASS PRODUCTION OF EGGS
NAHANNI • 1962 • Wilder Donald A. • CND
NAHANNI • 1974 • Poirel Jean • DOC • CND
NAHANNI NO.3 • 1971 • Bertolino Daniel • DCS • CND
NAHAPET see **NA'APET** • 1977
NAHARIK SA'ID • 1954 • Wahab Fatin Abdel • EGY • BONJOUR
NAHERIN, DIE • 1915 • *Vallis Lo* • FRG
NAHI ABHI NAHI • Islam Nazaral • PKS
NAHIRA • 1915 • Mack Max • FRG
NAH'NU LA NAZRA ASH-SHUK • 1970 • Kamal Hussein • EGY • NOUS NE FAISONS DE MAL A PERSONNE ○ CHEMIN DE RONCES, UN
NAHOTA • 1969 • Matejka Vaclav • CZC • NAKEDNESS
NAHR, AL • 1977 • Al-Yassiri Fiasal • IRQ • RIVER, THE ○ FLEUVE, LE
NAHWA AL-MAJHUL • 1960 • Saleh Tewfik • SHT • EGY • VERS L'INCONNU
NAI-DALGATA NOSHT see **NAY-DALGATA NOSHT** • 1967
NAI DASIMA • Effendy Basuki • INN
NAI MEN ALLA.. • 1972 • Tassios Pavlos • GRC • EVERYTHING IS IN ORDER, BUT ON THE OTHER HAND.. ○ YES.. BUT..
NAI ROSHANI • 1941 • *Biswas Anil (M)* • IND
NAI ROSHNI • 1967 • Sridhar C. V. • IND • NEW LIGHT
NAIB AL-AM, AN see **NAEB EL AM, EL** • 1945
NAICA AND THE LITTLE FISH • Bostan Elisabeta • SHT • RMN
NAICA AND THE SQUIRRELS • Bostan Elisabeta • SHT • RMN
NAICA AND THE STORK • Bostan Elisabeta • SHT • RMN
NAICA LEAVES FOR BUCHAREST • Bostan Elisabeta • SHT • RMN
NAIDRA, THE DREAM WOMAN • 1914 • *Anderson Mignon* • USA
NAIF AUX QUARANTE ENFANTS, LE • 1958 • Agostini Philippe • FRN
NAIKA SAMBAD • 1967 • Agradoot • IND • HEROINE'S STORY
NAIL, THE • Calinescu Bob • ANM • RMN
NAIL CLIPPERS, THE (UKN) see **PINCE A ONGLES, LA** • 1968
NAIL IN THE BOOT • 1932 • Kalatozov Mikhail • USS
NAIL MARK IN FLESH, A see **NIKU NO TSUMEATO** • 1967
NAIL OF BRIGHTNESS, THE (USA) see **MAYNILA, SA MGA KUKO NG LIWANAG** • 1975
NAILCUTTER, THE see **PINCE A ONGLES, LA** • 1968
NAILED • *Thiemann Paul/ Reinhardt F. (P)* • USS
NAILED AT THE PLATE • 1918 • *Lyons Eddie* • SHT • USA
NAILGUN MASSACRE • 1987 • Lofton Terry, Leslie Bill • USA
NAILING ON THE LID • 1916 • Dillon John Francis • USA
NAILS • 1979 • Borsos Philip • SHT • CND
NAILS see **NAGEL, DIE** • 1971
N'AIMER QUI TOI • 1934 • Berthomieu Andre • FRN
NAIMRNDHU NIL • 1968 • Devan • IND • STAND STRAIGHT
NAIN, LE • 1912 • Feuillade Louis • FRN
NAIN ET GEANT • 1902 • Melies Georges • FRN • DWARF AND THE GIANT, THE (USA) ○ LONG AND SHORT OF IT, THE
NAINA PAIVINA • 1955 • Donner Jorn • SHT • FNL • IN THE DAYS ○ IN THESE DAYS
NAIROBI see **NAIROBI AFFAIR** • 1984
NAIROBI AFFAIR • 1984 • Chomsky Marvin • TVM • USA • NAIROBI
NAIS • 1945 • Leboursier Raymond, Pagnol Marcel • FRN
NAISENKUVIA • 1970 • Donner Jorn • SWD, FNL • PORTRAITS OF WOMEN (UKN)
NAISKOHTALOITA • 1947 • Saakka Toivo • FNL • DESTINIES OF WOMEN
NAISSANCE • 1982 • Kramer Robert • FRN • BIRTH
NAISSANCE APPRIVOISEE, UNE • 1980 • Moreau Michel • CND
NAISSANCE DE LA MARSEILLAISE, LA • 1920 • Desfontaines Henri • FRN
NAISSANCE DE LA PHOTO • 1965 • Leenhardt Roger • DCS • FRN • DAGUERRE OU LA NAISSANCE DE LA PHOTO
NAISSANCE DE L'EMPIRE ROMAIN, LA • 1965 • Kast Pierre • MTV • FRN
NAISSANCE DE SALOME, LA (FRN) see **NASCITA DI SALOME** • 1940
NAISSANCE DES CIGOGNES, LA • 1925 • Gremillon Jean • SHT • FRN
NAISSANCE DES HEURES, LA • 1930 • Greville Edmond T. • SHT • FRN
NAISSANCE DU CINEMA • 1946 • Leenhardt Roger • DOC • FRN
NAISSANCE DU CINEMA, LA • 1960 • Coignon Jean, Degelin Emile • SHT • BLG • BIRTH OF CINEMA, THE
NAISSANCE DU JOUR, LA • 1980 • Demy Jacques • FRN
NAISSANCE DU PLUTONIUM • 1960 • Hulin • SHT • FRN
NAISSANCE D'UN PETROLIER • 1958 • Gaveau Christian • FRN • BIRTH OF A TANKER
NAISSANCE D'UNE CITE • 1964 • Daquin Louis • SHT • FRN
NAISSANCE ET MONT DE PROMETHEE • 1974 • Rivette Jacques • SHT • FRN
NAIVE ONE, THE see **NAIVKO** • 1977
NAIVKO • 1977 • Zivanovic Jovan • YGS • NAIVE ONE, THE
NAJBOLJI • 1989 • Sorak Dejan • YGS • BEST, THE
NAJDOLGIOT PAT see **NAJDUZI PUT** • 1977
NAJDUZI PUT • 1977 • Gapo Branko • YGS • LONGEST ROAD, THE ○ NAJDOLGIOT PAT ○ LONGEST JOURNEY, THE
NAJLEPSZY KOLEGA • 1970 • Trzos-Rastawiecki Andrzej • MTV • PLN • BEST FRIEND
NAJPIEKNIEJSZE CHWILE NASZEGO ZYCIA • 1959 • Ziarnik Jerzy • DOC • PLN • MOST WONDERFUL MOMENTS OF OUR LIFE, THE
N'AJUSTEZ PAS • 1970 • Moretti Pierre • CND
NAJVECI SNJEGOVIC • 1972 • Grgic Zlatko • ANS • YGS • SNOW TIME FOR COMEDY
NAKAKANNIKA • 1949 • Vishwanath G. • IND
NAKANUNYE • 1959 • Petrov Vladimir • USS • ON THE EVE ○ V NAVECHERIETO
NAKASERUZE • 1965 • Matsuo Akinori • JPN • MOVED TO TEARS
NAKE, NIHON KOKUMIN -SAIGO NO SENTOKI • 1956 • Noguchi Hiroshi • JPN • WEEP, PEOPLE OF JAPAN -THE LAST PURSUIT PLANE
NAKED AFRICA • 1957 • Phoenix Ray • DOC • USA
NAKED AFTERNOON, THE • 1976 • Colberg Alan • USA
NAKED ALIBI • 1954 • Hopper Jerry • USA
NAKED AMONG THE WOLVES (USA) see **NACKT UNTER WOLFEN** • 1962
NAKED AMONG WOLVES see **NACKT UNTER WOLFEN** • 1962
NAKED AND SATAN, THE see **NACKTE UND DER SATAN, DIE** • 1959
NAKED AND THE DEAD, THE • 1958 • Walsh Raoul • USA
NAKED AND THE NUDE, THE • 1957 • Kuchar George, Kuchar Mike • USA
NAKED AND VIOLENT see **AMERICA.. COSI NUDA COSI VIOLENTA** • 1970
NAKED AND WILLING see **EROTIC INFERNO** • 1975
NAKED ANGELS • 1969 • Clark Bruce • USA
NAKED APE, THE • 1973 • Driver Donald • USA
NAKED ARE THE CHEATERS (UKN) see **POLITICIANS, THE** • 1970
NAKED AS NATURE INTENDED • 1961 • Marks George Harrison • UKN • AS NATURE INTENDED (USA)
NAKED AS THE WIND FROM THE SEA see **SOM HAVETS NAKNA VIND** • 1968
NAKED AUTUMN (USA) see **MAUVAIS COUPS, LES** • 1961
NAKED BOTTOM see **CON EL CULO AL AIRE** • 1980
NAKED BRIGADE, THE • 1965 • Dexter Maury • USA, GRC • HE GYMNE TAXIARCHIA (GRC)
NAKED BUNYIP, THE • 1970 • Murray John B. • ASL
NAKED CAGE, THE • 1985 • Nicolas Paul • USA
NAKED CAME THE STRANGER • 1975 • Metzger Radley H. • USA
NAKED CELL, THE • 1987 • Crome John • USA
NAKED CHILDHOOD see **ENFANCE NUE, L'** • 1968
NAKED CITIZEN, THE see **CIPLAK VATANDAS** • 1985
NAKED CITY, THE • 1948 • Dassin Jules • USA
NAKED CIVIL SERVANT, THE • 1975 • Gold Jack • TVM • UKN
NAKED COMPLEX, THE • 1964 • Mart Roy • USA
NAKED COUNTESS, THE • 1971 • Nachmann Kurt • FRG
NAKED COUNTRY, THE • 1984 • Burstall Tim • ASL
NAKED "D", THE • 1971 • Nys Guy J. • BLG
NAKED DAWN, THE • 1955 • Ulmer Edgar G. • USA
NAKED EARTH • 1958 • Sherman Vincent • UKN
NAKED EDGE, THE • 1961 • Anderson Michael • UKN
NAKED ENGLAND (UKN) see **INGHILTERRA NUDA** • 1969
NAKED EVIL • 1966 • Goulder Stanley • UKN • EXORCISM AT MIDNIGHT
NAKED EXORCISM (UKN) see **URLO DALLE TENEBRE, UN** • 1975
NAKED EYE, THE • 1957 • Stoumen Louis Clyde • DOC • USA
NAKED FACE, THE • 1984 • Forbes Bryan • USA
NAKED FACE OF NIGHT, THE see **YORU NO SUGAO** • 1958
NAKED FACE OF SHINJUKU, THE see **SHINJUKU NO HADA** • 1968
NAKED FIST • 1918 • *Hart Neal* • SHT • USA
NAKED FIST see **FIRECRACKER** • 1981
NAKED FLAME, THE • 1970 • Matanski Larry • USA
NAKED FOG • 1966 • Sarno Joe • USA • NIGHT FOG
NAKED FURY • 1960 • Saunders Charles • UKN • PLEASURE LOVERS, THE (USA) ○ PLEASURE LOVER
NAKED GENERAL see **HADAKA NO TAISHO** • 1958
NAKED GIRLS OF THE GOLDEN WEST see **IMMORAL WEST - AND HOW IT WAS LOST, THE** • 1962
NAKED GODDESS, THE • 1959 • Hole William Jr. • USA • DEVIL'S HAND, THE ○ WITCHCRAFT ○ DEVIL'S DOLL ○ LIVE TO LOVE
NAKED GOOD EVENING see **HADAKA DE KONBANWA** • 1967
NAKED GUN, THE • 1956 • Dew Edward • USA
NAKED GUN, THE • 1988 • Zucker David • USA • NAKED GUN: FROM THE FILES OF POLICE SQUAD, THE
NAKED GUN: FROM THE FILES OF POLICE SQUAD, THE see **NAKED GUN, THE** • 1988
NAKED HEART, THE • 1950 • Allegret Marc • UKN, CND, FRN • MARIA CHAPDELAINE
NAKED HEARTS • 1916 • Julian Rupert • USA • MAUD (UKN)
NAKED HEARTS see **COEURS VERTS, LES** • 1966
NAKED HILLS, THE • 1956 • Shaftel Josef • USA
NAKED HOURS, THE see **ORE NUDE, LE** • 1964
NAKED HUNT, THE • 1959 • Hale William • USA
NAKED IN THE MIND see **ILE AUX FEMMES NUES, L'** • 1952
NAKED IN THE NIGHT see **ONE NAKED NIGHT** • 1963
NAKED IN THE SUN • 1957 • Hugh R. John • USA
NAKED IN THE WIND (USA) see **ILE AUX FEMMES NUES, L'** • 1952
NAKED ISLAND see **HADAKA NO SHIMA** • 1961
NAKED ISLAND: "THE LAND OF 1001 NUDES" • 1961 • d'Olivier Michel, Tor Gerald • FRN
NAKED JUNGLE, THE • 1954 • Haskin Byron • USA
NAKED KILLING see **RASHOKU SAPPOH NUKIMI** • 1968
NAKED KISS, THE • 1964 • Fuller Samuel • USA
NAKED LIE • 1989 • Colla Richard A. • USA
NAKED LIKE WOW! see **MR. PEEK-A-BOO'S PLAYMATES** • 1962
NAKED LIVES see **VIDAS NUAS** • 1967
NAKED LOVERS • 1977 • Pierson Claude • FRN
NAKED LOVERS, THE see **NAKED ZOO, THE** • 1970
NAKED MAJA, THE • 1959 • Koster Henry, Russo Mario L. F. • USA, ITL, FRN • MAJA DESNUDA, LA (ITL)
NAKED MAN, THE • 1923 • Edwards Henry • UKN
NAKED MAN, THE see **GILO COVIK** • 1968
NAKED MAN, THE see **HOMEM NU, O** • 1968
NAKED MAN ON THE ATHLETIC FIELD, THE see **NACKTE MANN AUF DEM SPORTPLATZ, DER** • 1974
NAKED MAN ON THE SPORTSGROUND, THE see **NACKTE MANN AUF DEM SPORTPLATZ, DER** • 1974
NAKED MIRROR, THE see **SHAKEDOWN, THE** • 1960
NAKED MURDER CASE OF THE ISLAND see **SHIMA TO RATAI JIKEN** • 1931
NAKED NIGHT, THE (USA) see **GYCKLARNAS AFTON** • 1953
NAKED NINETEEN YEAR OLD see **HADAKA NO JUKYUSAI** • 1970
NAKED ODYSSEY see **ODISSEA NUDA** • 1961
NAKED OVER THE FENCE see **NAAKT OVER DE SCHUTTING** • 1973
NAKED PARADISE • 1956 • Corman Roger • USA • THUNDER OVER HAWAII
NAKED PEACOCK, THE • 1974 • Hargrave Denis • USA
NAKED PEOPLE, THE see **WORLD WITHOUT SHAME** • 1962

NAKED PREY, THE • 1966 • Wilde Cornel • USA, SAF
NAKED PURSUIT • 1969 • *Nogami Masayoshi* • JPN
NAKED REVENGE see **CRY FOR ME, BILLY** • 1972
NAKED ROAD, THE see **NAKED SET** • 1962
NAKED RUNNER, THE • 1967 • Furie Sidney J. • UKN
NAKED SEA • 1955 • Miner Allen H. • DOC • USA
NAKED SEARCH, THE see **SHAMELESS, THE** • 1962
NAKED SET • 1962 • *Simar Productions* • USA • NAKED ROAD, THE
NAKED SEX (UKN) see **SEXE NU, LE** • 1974
NAKED SHE DIES see **NUDE.. SI MUORE** • 1968
NAKED SPUR, THE • 1952 • Mann Anthony • USA
NAKED SPUR, THE see **HOT SPUR** • 1968
NAKED STAR, THE see **ESTRELA NULA, A** • 1984
NAKED STREET, THE • 1955 • Shane Maxwell • USA
NAKED STREET GIRLS see **TANZERINNEN FUR TANGER** • 1977
NAKED SUN see **HADAKA NO TAIYO** • 1958
NAKED TEMPTATION see **TENTACION DESNUDA, LA** • 1966
NAKED TEMPTRESS, THE see **NAKED WITCH, THE** • 1964
NAKED TERROR • 1961 • *Joseph Brenner Associates* • DOC • USA
NAKED TOWN, THE see **HADAKA NO MACHI** • 1937
NAKED TRUTH, THE • 1957 • Zampi Mario • UKN • YOUR PAST IS SHOWING (USA)
NAKED TRUTH, THE see **PERFECT LOVER, THE** • 1919
NAKED TRUTH, THE see **T.N.T. (THE NAKED TRUTH)** • 1924
NAKED UNDER LEATHER see **GIRL ON A MOTORCYCLE** • 1968
NAKED VAMPIRE, THE see **VAMPIRE NUE, LA** • 1969
NAKED VENGEANCE • 1986 • Santiago Cirio H. • USA • SATIN VENGEANCE
NAKED VENUS, THE • 1961 • Schested Ove H. • USA
NAKED WEEKEND, THE see **BRAINWASH** • 1981
NAKED WEREWOLF WOMAN • 1983 • Miller Rick • ITL • WEREWOLF WOMAN
NAKED WEST -AND HOW IT WAS LOST, THE see **IMMORAL WEST -AND HOW IT WAS LOST, THE** • 1962
NAKED WINDS OF THE SEA, THE see **SOM HAVETS NAKNA VIND** • 1968
NAKED WITCH, THE • 1964 • Milligan Andy • USA • NAKED TEMPTRESS, THE
NAKED WOMAN, THE (USA) see **FEMME NUE, LA** • 1949
NAKED WORLD OF HARRISON MARKS, THE • 1967 • Marks George Harrison • UKN • DREAM WORLD OF HARRISON MARKS, THE
NAKED WORLD (USA) see **MONDO NUDO** • 1963
NAKED YOUTH see **SEISHUN ZANKOKU MONOGATARI** • 1960
NAKED YOUTH see **WILD YOUTH** • 1961
NAKED ZODIAC • 1969 • Van Meter Ben • USA
NAKED ZOO, THE • 1970 • Grefe William • USA • NAKED LOVERS, THE ○ HALLUCINATORS, THE ○ GROVE, THE
NAKEDNESS see **NAHOTA** • 1969
NAKHLA, AN- • 1976 • Nahhass Hashim An- • SHT • EGY • PALMIER, LE
NAKIA • 1974 • Horn Leonard • TVM • USA
NAKIMUSHI KISHA • 1950 • Sunohara Masahisa • JPN • SENTIMENTAL JOURNALIST
NAKIMUSHI KOZO • 1938 • Toyoda Shiro • JPN • CRYBABY APPRENTICE
NAKINURETA JOJI • 1967 • Nishihara Giichi • JPN • WEEPING AFFAIR
NAKOVAINA ILLI TCHOUK • 1972 • Hristov Hristo • BUL, GDR • ANVIL OR HAMMER ○ NAKOVALNYA ILI CHUK ○ HAMMER OR ANVIL
NAKOVALNYA ILI CHUK see **NAKOVAINA ILLI TCHOUK** • 1972
NAKURAI • 1954 • Roy Bimal • IND • NAUKRI
NAKUSEI DAISENSO • 1977 • Fukuda Jun • JPN • WAR OF THE PLANETS ○ WAKUSEI DAISENSO ○ WAR IN SPACE
NALA DAMYANTI • 1917 • *Madan J. F. (P)* • IND
NALA DAMYANTI • 1945 • IND
NALLA THANGAL • 1935 • *Roy Bimal (Ph)* • IND
NALOUTAI • 1952 • Gaisseau Pierre-Dominique • FRN
NALUM THERINDAVAN • 1968 • Jambu • IND • ONE WHO KNOWS ALL, THE
NAM ANGELS • 1989 • Santiago Cirio H. • USA
NAM: TOUR OF DUTY • 1987 • Norton B. W. L. • USA • KILLZONE: TOUR OF DUTY, THE ○ TOUR OF DUTY
NAMAKEMONO • 1927 • Uchida Tomu • JPN • IDLER
NAMAKUBI JOCHI JIKEN • 1967 • Lgawa Kinya • JPN • LOVE FOOLERY CASE OF A FRESH SEVERED HEAD
NAMASTE • 1976 • SLN, IND
NAMATJIRA THE PAINTER • 1946 • Robinson Lee, Mountford C. P. • DOC • ASL
NAMBEI KORO NO HANAYOME • 1960 • Mizuko Harumi • JPN
NAME, AGE, OCCUPATION • 1942 • Lorentz Pare • SHT • USA
NAME DAY, THE • 1969 • Govorukhin S. • USS
NAME FOR EVIL, A • 1970 • Girard Bernard • USA • THERE IS A NAME FOR EVIL ○ GROVE, THE
NAME FOR HERSELF, A see **IT SHOULD HAPPEN TO YOU** • 1954
NAME OF A GIRL see **JUNI**
NAME OF THE GAME • 1976 • Lehtinen Virke • SHT • FNL
NAME OF THE GAME IS KILL, THE • 1968 • Hellstrom Gunnar • USA • FEMALE TRAP
NAME OF THE GAME IS SEX, THE see **GAME IS SEX, THE** • 1969
NAME OF THE ROSE, THE • 1986 • Annaud Jean-Jacques • ITL, FRG, FRN
NAME THE DAY • 1921 • Roach Hal • SHT • USA
NAME THE MAN • 1924 • Sjostrom Victor • USA • JUDGE AND THE WOMAN, THE ○ MASTER OF MAN, THE
NAME THE WOMAN • 1928 • Kenton Erle C. • USA
NAME THE WOMAN • 1934 • Rogell Albert S. • USA
NAME WAS S.N., THE see **SE LLAMABA S.N.** • 1978
NAMELESS see **FRAULEIN DOKTOR** • 1969
NAMELESS CASTLE • 1920 • *Lukas Paul* • HNG
NAMELESS FEAR, THE • 1915 • *Lubin* • USA
NAMELESS MEN • 1928 • Cabanne W. Christy • USA
NAMENLOS • 1923 • Curtiz Michael • AUS • SCHARLATAN, DER ○ FALSCHE ARZT, DER
NAMENSHEIRAT • 1930 • Paul Heinz • FRG
NAMI • 1952 • Nakamura Noboru • JPN • WAVES, THE
NAMI NO TO • 1960 • Nakamura Noboru • JPN • TRAPPED IN LOVE
NAMI Z LODEJI • 1964 • Cech Vladimir • CZC • PASTURES NEW ○ FALLING AMONG THIEVES
NAMIDA • 1957 • Kawazu Yoshiro • JPN • TEARS ○ BLISS ON EARTH, A
NAMIDA GAWA • 1967 • Misumi Kenji • JPN • HOMELY SISTERS, THE
NAMIDA O SHISHI NO TATEGAMI NI • 1962 • Shinoda Masahiro • JPN • TEARS ON THE LION'S MANE ○ TEARS IN THE LION'S MANE
NAMIKAGE • 1965 • Toyoda Shiro • JPN • SHADOW OF WAVES
NAMING OF CANBERRA, THE • 1913 • Longford Raymond • DOC • ASL
NAMING OF THE RAWHIDE QUEEN • 1913 • *Todd Harry* • USA
NAMLUVY • 1961 • Fric Martin • MTV • CZC • COURTING
NAMMA OORU • 1968 • Shivashankar C. V. • IND • OUR COUNTRY
NAMONAKU MAZUSHIKU UTSUKUSHIKU • 1961 • Matsuyama Zenzo • JPN • HAPPINESS OF US ALONE
NAMRUD, AL- • 1956 • Salem Atef • EGY • INGRAT, L'
NAMU THE KILLER WHALE • 1966 • Benedek Laslo • USA
NAMUKU JOE • 1989 • *Petet Didi* • INN
NAMUS • 1926 • Bek-Nazarov Amo • USS • HONOUR
NAMUS BELASI • 1967 • Kan Kemal • TRK • TROUBLED HONOUR
NAMUS BORCU • 1967 • Inanoglu Turker • TRK • DEBT OF HONOUR
NAMUS VE SILAH • 1971 • Gorec Ertem • TRK
NAN, A COSTER GIRL'S ROMANCE • 1911 • Raymond Charles? • UKN
NAN GOOD-FOR-NOTHING • 1914 • Holmes-Gore Arthur • UKN
NAN HSIA CHAN CHAO • 1977 • Roc T'Ien • HKG • MAJESTY CAT, THE
NAN IN FAIRYLAND • 1912 • Collins Edwin J. • UKN
NAN IN THE SICK ROOM, THE • 1913 • *Solax* • USA
NAN O' THE BACKWOODS • 1915 • Olcott Sidney • USA
NAN OF MUSIC MOUNTAIN • 1917 • Melford George, De Mille Cecil B. (U/c) • USA
NAN OF THE HILLS • 1914 • *Powers* • USA
NAN OF THE NORTH • 1922 • Worne Duke • SRL • USA
NAN OF THE WOODS • 1913 • Huntley Fred W. • USA
NAN PATERSON'S TRIAL • 1905 • *Bitzer Billy (Ph)* • USA
NAN WHO COULDN'T BEAT GOD, THE • 1915 • *Costello Maurice* • USA
NAN WILD • 1927 • Cooper George A. • UKN
NAN YU NU • 1984 • Ts'Ai Chi-Kuang • HKG • HONG KONG, HONG KONG
NANA • 1926 • Renoir Jean • FRN, FRG
NANA • 1934 • Arzner Dorothy • USA • LADY OF THE BOULEVARDS (UKN)
NANA • 1944 • Gorostiza Celestino, Gavaldon Roberto • MXC
NANA • 1955 • Christian-Jaque • FRN, ITL
NANA • 1970 • Ahlberg Mac • SWD, FRN • TAKE ME, LOVE ME (UKN) ○ TAG MEJ -ALSKA MEJ
NANA • 1980 • Cazeneuve Maurice • MTV • FRN
NANA • 1982 • Wolman Dan • FRG, FRN
NANAIRO NO MACHI • 1952 • Yamamoto Kajiro • JPN • RAINBOW-COLOURED STREET
NANAIRO YUBI WA • 1918 • Oguchi • JPN • SEVEN COLORED RING, THE
NANAMI: INFERNO OF FIRST LOVE see **HATSUKOI JIGOKU-HEN** • 1968
NANATSU NO DANGAN • 1959 • Murayama Shinji • JPN • MURDERER MUST DIE, THE
NANATSU NO KAO NO ONNA • 1969 • Maeda Yoichi • JPN • LADY WITH SEVEN FACES
NANATSU NO KAWO NO GUINJI • 1955 • Mori Kazuo • JPN • GUINJI WITH SEVEN FACES
NANBANJI NO SEMUSHI-OTOKO • 1957 • Saito Torajiro • JPN • RETURN TO MANHOOD
NANCE • 1920 • Ward Albert • UKN
NANCY • 1922 • Parkinson H. B. • UKN
NANCY COMES HOME • 1918 • Dillon John Francis • USA
NANCY DREW AND THE HIDDEN STAIRCASE • 1939 • Clemens William • USA
NANCY DREW -DETECTIVE • 1938 • Clemens William • USA
NANCY DREW, REPORTER • 1939 • Clemens William • USA
NANCY DREW -TROUBLE SHOOTER • 1939 • Clemens William • USA
NANCY FROM NAPLES see **OH! SAILOR BEHAVE!** • 1930
NANCY FROM NOWHERE • 1922 • Franklin Chester M. • USA
NANCY GOES TO RIO • 1949 • Leonard Robert Z. • USA
NANCY J. NE PECHERA PAS, LE see **END OF NANCY J., THE** • 1970
NANCY KEITH see **TESTAMENTETS HEMMELIGHED** • 1916
NANCY OF STONY ISLE • 1915 • *Knickerbocker Star* • USA
NANCY: OR, THE BURGLAR'S DAUGHTER • 1908 • Stow Percy • UKN
NANCY STEELE IS MISSING! • 1937 • Marshall George • USA
NANCY WILSON • 1962 • Binder Steve • SHT • USA
NANCY'S BIRTHRIGHT • 1916 • MacQuarrie Murdock • USA
NANCY'S HUSBAND • 1914 • Pollard Harry • USA
NANCY'S PRIVATE AFFAIR see **SMART WOMAN** • 1931
NAND KISHORE • 1951 • Joglekar Vasant • IND
NAND KUMAR • 1937 • Dhaiber Keshavrao • IND
NANE BHAGYAVATHI • 1968 • Iyer G. V. • IND • I AM FORTUNATE
NANETTE • 1939 • Engel Erich • FRG
NANETTE see **NANETTE MACHT ALLES** • 1926
NANETTE MACHT ALLES • 1926 • Boese Carl • FRG • NANETTE
NANETTE OF THE WILDS • 1916 • Kaufman Joseph • USA
NANG MAMATAY NG DAHIL SA IYO • 1968 • Villaflor Romy • PHL • TO DIE FOR YOU
NANGA PARBAT • 1936 • Leberecht Frank • FRG
NANGUILA TOMORROW see **DEMAIN A NANGUILA** • 1960
NANI GA KANOJO O SO SASETA KA? • 1930 • Suzuki Shigeyoshi • JPN • WHAT MADE HER DO IT?
NANIKA OMOROI KOTO NAIKA • 1963 • Kurahara Koreyoshi • JPN • I FLY FOR KICKS
NANIWA ELEGY (UKN) see **NANIWA EREJI** • 1936
NANIWA EREJI • 1936 • Mizoguchi Kenji • JPN • NANIWA ELEGY (UKN) ○ OSAKA ELEGY (USA) ○ NANIWA HIKA
NANIWA HIKA see **NANIWA EREJI** • 1936
NANIWA KYOKAKU: DOKYO SHICHININ GIRI • 1967 • Ozawa Shigehiro • JPN • KILLER OF SEVEN MEN
NANIWA NO KOI NO MONOGATARI • 1959 • Uchida Tomu • JPN • THEIR OWN WORLD ○ DISTRESSED
NANIWA ONNA • 1940 • Mizoguchi Kenji • JPN • WOMAN OF OSAKA, A (USA) ○ WOMAN OF NANIWA
NANIWANAKUTOMO ZEN-IN SHUGO!! • 1967 • Watanabe Yusuke • JPN • EVERYBODY, LET'S GO!
NANKAI NO DAI KETTO • 1966 • Fukuda Jun • JPN • GODZILLA VS. THE SEA MONSTER (USA) ○ EBIRAH, TERROR OF THE DEEP ○ EBIRAH, HORROR OF THE DEEP (UKN) ○ BIG DUEL IN THE NORTH SEA
NANKAI NO DAIKAIJU see **KESSEN NANKAI NO DAIKAIJU** • 1970
NANKAI NO HANATABE • 1942 • Abe Yutaka • JPN • SOUTH SEAS BOUQUET
NANKIN ROAD, SHANGHAI • 1901 • Rosenthal Joe • UKN
NANKING • 1938 • Kamei Fumio • JPN
NANKYOKU MONOGATARI • 1984 • Kurahara Koreyoshi • JPN • ANTARCTICA (USA) ○ ANTARCTIC STORY
NANNINA • 1910 • *Bison* • USA
NANNY • 1931 • Pearson George • SHT • UKN
NANNY, THE • 1965 • Holt Seth • UKN
NANNY DEAR see **TATA MIA** • 1986
NANO E LA STREGA, IL • 1975 • Gibba, Libratti Gioacchino • ITL, FRN • LITTLE DICK THE MIGHTY MIDGET ○ KING DICK
NANON • 1924 • Schwarz Hanns • FRG
NANON • 1938 • Maisch Herbert • FRG
NANOOK OF THE NORTH • 1922 • Flaherty Robert • DOC • USA
NANOU • 1987 • Templeman Connie • UKN
NAN'S DIPLOMACY • 1911 • Salter Harry • USA
NAN'S SACRIFICE • 1908 • *Tyler Walter* • UKN
NAN'S VICTORY • 1914 • Santschi Thomas • USA
NANSHIN JOSEI • 1939 • Ochiai • JPN • SOUTH ADVANCING WOMEN ○ SOUTH ADVANCING GIRLS
NANTO NO HARU • 1925 • Gosho Heinosuke • JPN • SPRING IN SOUTHERN ISLANDS ○ SPRING OF SOUTHERN ISLAND
NANTONAKU KRYSTAL • 1981 • Matsubara Shingo • JPN • LIVING WITH CRYSTAL FEELING
NANU, SIE KENNEN KORFF NOCH NICHT? • 1938 • Holl Fritz • FRG • SO, YOU DON'T KNOW KORFF YET? (USA)
NANYNKA KULICHOVA'S MARRIAGE see **VDAVKY NANYNKY KULICHOVE** • 1925
NAO A RAPAZES MAOS • 1947 • Maroto Eduardo G. • PRT
NAO CAPITANA, LA • 1947 • Rey Florian • SPN
NAO DO EGARAH • 1957 • *Burman S. D. (M)* • IND
NAOHACHI KODOMO TABI • 1934 • Inagaki Hiroshi • JPN • JOURNEY OF EIGHT CHILDREN
NAOMI AND RUFUS KISS • 1964 • Warhol Andy • SHT • USA
NAOMI IS A VISION OF LOVELINESS • 1965 • Jacobs Ken • USA
NAP • 1928 • Croise Hugh • UKN
NAP ES A HOLD EL RABLASA, A • 1969 • Reisenbuchler Sandor • ANS • HNG • KIDNAPPING OF THE SUN AND MOON, THE (USA)
NAPALM • 1970 • Maleh Nabil • SHT • SYR
NAPATIA, THE GREEK SINGER • 1912 • *Cassinelli Dolores* • USA
NAPLES AU BAISER DE FEU • 1925 • Nadejdine Serge • FRN
NAPLES AU BAISER DE FEU • 1937 • Genina Augusto • FRN
NAPLES CONNECTION, THE see **COMPLICATO INTRIGO DI DONNE, VICOLI E DELITTI, UN** • 1985
NAPLES IS A BATTLEFIELD • 1944 • Clayton Jack • SHT • UKN
NAPLES THAT NEVER DIES (USA) see **NAPOLI CHE NON MUORE** • 1930
NAPLO • *Pannonia* • ANS • HNG
NAPLO APAMNAK, ANYAMNAK • 1989 • Meszaros Marta • HNG • DIARY FOR MY FATHER AND MOTHER
NAPLO GYERMEKEIMNEK • 1984 • Meszaros Marta • HNG • DIARY FOR MY CHILDREN
NAPLO SZERELMEIMNEK • 1987 • Meszaros Marta • HNG • DIARY FOR MY LOVES
NAPOLEON • 1926 • Gance Abel, Andreani Henri • FRN • NAPOLEON VU PAR ABEL GANCE
NAPOLEON • 1941 • Amadori Luis Cesar • ARG
NAPOLEON • 1954 • Guitry Sacha • FRN, ITL • NAPOLEONE BONAPARTE (ITL)
NAPOLEON A SAINTE-HELENE • 1954 • Sassy Jean-Paul • SHT • FRN
NAPOLEON A SAINTE-HELENE see **NAPOLEON AUF ST. HELENA** • 1929
NAPOLEON AND JOSEPHINE: A LOVE STORY • 1987 • Heffron Richard T. • MTV • USA
NAPOLEON AND SALLY • 1916 • *E & R Jungle Film* • USA
NAPOLEON AND SAMANTHA • 1972 • McEveety Bernard • USA
NAPOLEON AND THE ENGLISH SAILOR • 1908 • Collins Alf? • UKN
NAPOLEON AT SAINT HELENA • Dawley J. Searle • USA
NAPOLEON AUF ST. HELENA • 1929 • Pick Lupu • FRG • ST. HELENA (DER GEFANGENE KAISER) ○ NAPOLEON A SAINTE-HELENE
NAPOLEON, BEBE ET LES COSAQUES • 1912 • Feuillade Louis • FRN
NAPOLEON BONAPARTE • 1935 • Gance Abel • FRN
NAPOLEON BONAPARTE • 1950 • Tedesco Jean • FRN • NAPOLEON BONAPARTE, EMPEREUR DES FRANCAIS
NAPOLEON BONAPARTE, EMPEREUR DES FRANCAIS see **NAPOLEON BONAPARTE** • 1950
NAPOLEON BUNNY-PART • 1956 • Freleng Friz • ANS • USA
NAPOLEON CLIP • 1963 • Potterton Gerald • CND
NAPOLEON CROSSING THE ALPS • 1903 • *Gaudio Antonio (Ph)* • ITL
NAPOLEON: DU SACRE A SAINTE-HELENE • 1914 • Machin Alfred • NTH

NAPOLEON ET LA SENTINELLE • 1912 • Desfontaines Henri • FRN
NAPOLEON-GAZ • 1925 • Timoshenko S. • USS
NAPOLEON II L'AIGLON • 1961 • Boissol Claude • FRN • AIGLON, L'
NAPOLEON IN RUSSIA • 1910 • Goncharov Vasili M. • USS
NAPOLEON IST AN ALLEM SCHULD • 1938 • Goetz Curt • FRG
NAPOLEON JUNIOR • 1926 • Selander Lesley, Sandrich Mark • SHT • USA
NAPOLEON ON THE ISLAND OF ELBA see **ET BUDSKA TIL NAPOLEON PA ELBA** • 1909
NAPOLEON RACONTE PAR UN VIEUX SOLDAT • 1955 • Jabely Jean • ANM • FRN
NAPOLEON -THE MAN OF DESTINY • 1909 • Blackton J. Stuart • USA
NAPOLEON UND DIE KLEINE WASCHERIN • 1920 • Gartner Adolf • FRG
NAPOLEON VU PAR ABEL GANCE see **NAPOLEON** • 1926
NAPOLEONCITO • 1963 • Martinez Solares Gilberto • MXC
NAPOLEONE • 1951 • Borghesio Carlo • ITL
NAPOLEONE A FIRENZE • 1964 • Pierotti Piero • ITL
NAPOLEONE A SANT'ELENA see **SANT'ELENA PICCOLA ISOLA** • 1943
NAPOLEONE AD AUSTERLITZ (ITL) see **AUSTERLITZ** • 1960
NAPOLEONE BONAPARTE (ITL) see **NAPOLEON** • 1954
NAPOLEON'S BARBER • 1928 • Ford John • SHT • USA
NAPOLEONS KLEINER BRUDER see **SO SIND DIE MANNER** • 1922
NAPOLETANI A MILANO • 1953 • De Filippo Eduardo • ITL
NAPOLI CHE CANTA • 1926 • Roberti Roberto Leone • ITL
NAPOLI CHE CANTA • 1930 • Almirante Mario • ITL, UKN • WHEN NAPLES SINGS
NAPOLI CHE NON MUORE • 1930 • Palermi Amleto • ITL • NAPLES THAT NEVER DIES (USA)
NAPOLI D'ALTRI TEMPI • 1938 • Palermi Amleto • ITL • NAPOLI MIA
NAPOLI E LE TERRE D'OLTREMARE • 1940 • Blasetti Alessandro • DOC • ITL
NAPOLI E MILLE CANZONI see **PERFIDE.. MA BELLE** • 1958
NAPOLI E SEMPRE NAPOLI • 1955 • Fizzarotti Armando • ITL
NAPOLI E TUTTA UNA CANZONE • 1959 • Ferronetti Ignazio • ITL
NAPOLI ESTERNO GIORNO • 1978 • Russo Nino • ITL
NAPOLI, ETERNA CANZONE • 1951 • Siano Silvio • ITL
NAPOLI HA FATTO UN SOGNO see **MONASTERO DI SANTA CHIARA** • 1951
NAPOLI.. I CINQUE DELLA SQUADRA SPECIALE • 1978 • Bianchi Mario • ITL
NAPOLI MIA see **NAPOLI D'ALTRI TEMPI** • 1938
NAPOLI, MILIONARIA • 1950 • De Filippo Eduardo • ITL • SIDE STREET STORY (USA)
NAPOLI PIANGE E RIDE • 1954 • Calzavara Flavio • ITL
NAPOLI SERENATA CALIBRO NOVE • 1978 • Brescia Alfonso • ITL
NAPOLI SI REBELLA • 1977 • Tarantini Michele Massimo • ITL
NAPOLI SOLE MIO! • 1958 • Simonelli Giorgio C. • ITL
NAPOLI SPARA! • 1977 • Caiano Mario • ITL
NAPOLI TERRA D'AMORE • 1956 • Mastrocinque Camillo • ITL
NAPOLI VERDE-BLU • 1935 • Fizzarotti Armando • ITL
NAPOLI VIOLENTA • 1976 • Lenzi Umberto • ITL • DEATH DEALERS (UKN)
NAPONTA KET VONAT • 1977 • Gaal Istvan • MTV • HNG • TWO TRAINS A DAY
NAPPALI SOTETSEG • 1963 • Fabri Zoltan • HNG • DARKNESS BY DAYLIGHT ○ DARKNESS IN DAYTIME ○ DUNKEL BEI TAGESLICHT
NAPRAFORGOS HOLGY, A • 1918 • Curtiz Michael • HNG • LADY WITH SUNFLOWERS, THE
NAPRAWDE WCZORAJ • 1963 • Rybkowski Jan • PLN • YESTERDAY IN FACT
NAPROZOD MLOZIEZY SWIATA see **MY ZA MIR** • 1951
NAPRZOD DO WALKI O POKOJ I SOCJALIZM • 1950 • Bossak Jerzy • DOC • PLN • FORWARD TO THE STRUGGLE FOR FREEDOM AND SOCIALISM
NAPRZOD MLODZIEZY GORNICZA • 1950 • Nasfeter Janusz • SHT • PLN • FORWARD YOUNG MINERS
NAR ANGARNA BLOMMAR • 1946 • Faustman Erik • SWD • WHEN MEADOWS BLOOM
NAR BENGT OCH ANDERS BYTTE HUSTRUR • 1950 • Spjuth Arthur • SWD • WHEN BENGT AND ANDERS SWAPPED WIVES
NAR BLODET SJUDER see **ONDA OGON** • 1947
NAR ENGLE ELSKER • 1985 • Eszterhas Peter • DNM • ANGELS IN LOVE
NAR JAG VAR PRINS UTAV ARKADIEN • 1909 • Magnusson Charles • SWD • WHEN I WAS PRINCE OF ARCADIA
NAR KARLEKEN DODAR • 1913 • Stiller Mauritz • SWD • WHEN LOVE KILLS
NAR KARLEKEN KOM TILL BYN • 1950 • Mattsson Arne • SWD • WHEN LOVE COMES TO THE VILLAGE
NAR KATTEN ER UDE • 1947 • Lauritzen Lau Jr., O'Fredericks Alice • DNM
NAR KONSTNARER ALSKA • 1915 • Stiller Mauritz • SWD • WHEN ARTISTS LOVE
NAR LARMLOCKAN LJUDER • 1913 • Stiller Mauritz • SWD • WHEN THE ALARM BELL RINGS ○ WHEN THE TOCSIN CALLS
NAR MORKRET FALLER • 1960 • Mattsson Arne • SWD • WHEN DARKNESS FALLS
NAR-O-NEY • 1989 • Ebrahimifar Saeed • IRN
NAR ROSORNA SLA UT • 1930 • Adolphson Edvin • SWD • WHEN ROSEBUDS OPEN ○ HALET I MUREN
NAR SEKLET VAR UNGT • 1944 • Olsson Gunnar • SWD • AT THE BEGINNING OF THE CENTURY
NAR SEKLET VAR UNGT • 1961 • *Sahlberg Gardar (Edt)* • SWD
NAR SVARMOR REGERAR • 1914 • Stiller Mauritz • SWD • WHEN MOTHER-IN-LAW DICTATES ○ WHEN MOTHER-IN-LAW REIGNS
NAR SYRENERNA BLOOMAR • 1952 • Johansson Ivar • SWD • WHEN LILACS BLOSSOM
NAR UNGDOMEN VAKNAR • 1943 • Olsson Gunnar • SWD • AWAKENING OF YOUTH, THE
NARA LIVET • 1958 • Bergman Ingmar • SWD • SO CLOSE TO LIFE ○ BRINK OF LIFE (USA)
NARA NARAYAN • 1937 • Rangarao, Ramji • IND
NARA NARAYAN • 1939 • Banerjee Jyotish • IND
NARA TILL HAVET • 1973 • Leijonborg Ingemar • SWD • NEAR THE SEA
NARAD MUNI • 1949 • Desai Raman B. • IND
NARAD-NARADI • 1941 • Torney Dadasaheb • IND
NARAYAMA BUSHI-KO • 1958 • Kinoshita Keisuke • JPN • BALLAD OF NARAYAMA (USA) ○ LEGEND OF THE NARAYAMA ○ BALLAD OF THE NARAYAMA, THE ○ SONG OF THE NARAYAMA
NARAYAMA-BUSHI KO • 1983 • Imamura Shohei • JPN • BALLAD OF NARAYAMA, THE
NARAYANA • 1920 • Poirier Leon • FRN
NARAZUMONO • 1956 • *Mifune Toshio* • JPN • SCOUNDREL
NARBE AM KNIE, DIE • 1917 • Moest Hubert • FRG
NARCISSE • 1939 • d'Aguiar Ayres • FRN
NARCISSUS • 1947 • Richter Hans • USA
NARCISSUS • 1956 • Moore Ben, Maas Willard • USA
NARCISSUS • 1966 • Bakhtadze Vaktang • ANS • USS
NARCISSUS • 1983 • McLaren Norman • CND
NARCISSUS see **NARCISSUS-ECHO** • 1971
NARCISSUS AND PSYCHE see **PSYCHE ES NARCISZ** • 1981
NARCISSUS-ECHO • 1971 • Foldes Peter • ANS • FRN • NARCISSUS
NARCO see **NARKO -EN FILM OM KAERLIGHED** • 1971
NARCO, EL • 1985 • de Alva Alfonso • MXC • PUSHER, THE
NARCO -A FILM ABOUT LOVE see **NARKO -EN FILM OM KAERLIGHED** • 1971
NARCO MEN, THE (USA) see **SAPORE DELLE VENDETTA, IL** • 1968
NARCOSES • 1967 • Graff Philippe • BLG
NARCOSIS see **NARKOSE** • 1929
NARCOSIS see **NARKOS** • 1944
NARCOTIC SPECTRE • 1914 • Sidney Scott • USA
NARCOTIC STORY, THE • 1958 • *Police Science Productions* • USA • DREAD PERSUASION, THE
NARGIS • 1966 • Polkovnikov V. • ANS • USS
NARKINGARNA • 1923 • Edgren Gustaf • SWD • PEOPLE OF NARKE
NARKO see **NARKO -EN FILM OM KAERLIGHED** • 1971
NARKO -EN FILM OM KAERLIGHED • 1971 • Orsted Claus • DNM • NARCO -A FILM ABOUT LOVE ○ NARCO ○ NARKO
NARKOS • 1944 • Larsson Borje • SWD • NARCOSIS
NARKOSE • 1929 • Abel Alfred • FRG • BRIEFE EINER UNBEKANNTEN ○ NARCOSIS
NARKOVER see **BOYS WILL BE BOYS** • 1935
NARODA VYERNYYE SYNY • 1968 • Nebylitski Boris • USS • LOYAL SONS OF THE PEOPLE
NARODNIYE MSTITELI • 1943 • Beleyev Vassili • USS • PARTISANS, THE ○ PEOPLE'S AVENGERS, THE
NARODZINY GAZETY • 1931 • Ford Aleksander • PLN
NARODZINY STATKU • 1961 • Lomnicki Jan • DOC • PLN • BIRTH OF A SHIP, THE ○ SHIP IS BORN, A
NAROZENINY REZISERA Z.K. • 1987 • Balik Jaroslav • CZC • DIRECTOR Z.K.'S BIRTHDAY
NARR DES SCHICKSALS, DER • 1915 • Salten Felix? • FRG
NARR SEINER LIEBE, DER • 1929 • Tschechowa Olga • FRG
NARR UND DIE ANDEREN, DER • 1924 • Bock-Stieber Gernot • FRG • NEUE GENERATION, DIE
NARREN IM SCHNEE • 1938 • Deppe Hans • FRG
NARRENLIEBE • 1924 • *Kroog Gerhard (P)* • FRG
NARRENSCHLOSS, DAS • 1918 • von Woringen Paul • FRG
NARRENTANZ DER LIEBE • 1919 • Wellin Arthur • FRG
NARRIEN ILLAT • 1970 • Suominen Tapio • FNL • NIGHTS OF THE JESTERS
NARRIO DE CAMPEONES • 1983 • Vallejo Fernando • MXC • NEST OF CHAMPIONS
NARRISCHE FABRIK, DIE • 1919 • Piel Harry • FRG
NARRISCHE GLUCK, DAS • 1929 • Guter Johannes • FRG
NARRISCHE WETTE DES LORD ALDINI, DIE • 1923 • Borgnotto Romano Luigi • FRG
NARRITJIN AT DJARRAKPI • 1981 • Dunlop Ian • DOC • ASL
NARROHUT • 1982 • Fink Tone • AUS • FOOLERY
NARROW BRIDGE, THE • Umam Chaerul • INN
NARROW CORNER, THE • 1933 • Green Alfred E. • USA
NARROW CREED, THE • 1916 • Hunt Jay • SHT • USA
NARROW ESCAPE, A • 1911 • *Walthall William* • USA
NARROW ESCAPE, A • 1913 • *Kinemacolor* • USA
NARROW ESCAPE, A • 1914 • *Joker* • USA
NARROW ESCAPE FROM LYNCHING, A • 1909 • Bouwmeester Theo? • UKN
NARROW MARGIN • 1990 • Hyams Peter • USA
NARROW MARGIN, THE • 1952 • Fleischer Richard • USA • TARGET
NARROW PATH, THE • 1916 • Grandon Francis J. • USA • DANGER PATH, THE
NARROW PATH, THE • 1918 • Fitzmaurice George • USA
NARROW ROAD, THE • 1912 • Griffith D. W. • USA
NARROW SQUEAK, A • 1914 • *Joker* • USA
NARROW STREET, THE • 1924 • Beaudine William • USA
NARROW TRAIL, THE • 1917 • Hillyer Lambert, Hart William S. • USA
NARROW VALLEY, THE • 1921 • Hepworth Cecil M. • UKN
NARROWING CIRCLE, THE • 1956 • Saunders Charles • UKN
NARROWS INLET • 1967-80 • Rimmer David • CND
NARSI BHAGAT • 1940 • Bhatt Vijay • IND
NARTAKI • 1940 • *Sircar B. N. (P)* • IND
NARTAKI • 1945 • Bose Debaki • IND
NARTHANASALA • 1963 • Kameswara Rao K. • IND
NARUTO FANTASY see **NARUTO HICHO** • 1957
NARUTO HICHO • 1957 • Kinugasa Teinosuke • JPN • FANTASTIC TALE OF NARUTO, A ○ NARUTO FANTASY
NAS CLOVEK • 1985 • Pogacnik Joze • YGS • OUR MAN ○ NAS COVEK
NAS COVEK see **NAS CLOVEK** • 1985
NAS WAL NIL, EL see **NASSU WA AN-NIL, AN-** • 1968
NASANU NAKA • 1932 • Naruse Mikio • JPN • NOT BLOOD RELATIONS ○ STEPCHILD
NASCE UN CAMPIONE • 1954 • Petri Elio • SHT • ITL
NASCE UNA FAMIGLIA • 1943 • Pasinetti Francesco • ITL
NASCEU UM MENINO • 1946 • Coelho Jose Adolfo • SHT • PRT
NASCITA DI SALOME • 1940 • Choux Jean • ITL, SPN, FRN • NACIMIENTO DE SALOME, EL (SPN) ○ NAISSANCE DE SALOME, LA (FRN)
NASE BLAZNIVA RODINA • 1968 • Valasek Jan • CZC • OUR CRAZY FAMILY ○ OUR FOOLISH FAMILY
NASE KARKULKA • 1960 • Brdecka Jiri • ANS • CZC • OUR LITTLE RED RIDING HOOD ○ OUR RED RIDING HOOD
NASH DOM • 1965 • Pronin Vassily • USS • OUR HOUSE
NASH DVOR • 1956 • Chkheidze Revaz • USS • OUR COURTYARD ○ CHVENI EZO
NASH MILYI DOKTOR • 1958 • Aimanov Shaken • USS • OUR SPLENDID DAUGHTER
NASH OBSHCHII DRUG • 1961 • Pyriev Ivan • USS • OUR MUTUAL FRIEND
NASHA ZEMYA • 1953 • Marinovich Anton • BUL • LAND OF OURS, A
NASHE SERDSTE • 1946 • Stolper Alexander • USS • OUR HEART
NASHESTIVIYE • 1945 • Room Abram, Zhakov Oleg • USS • INVASION
NASHI CHEMPIONY • 1950 • Donskoi Mark • SHT • USS • SPORTING FAME ○ OUR CHAMPIONS ○ SPORTIVNAYA SLAVA ○ NACHI CHEMPIONY
NASHIAT OKTOMVRI • 1967 • Enchev Buryan • DOC • BUL • OUR OCTOBER
NASHORNER, DIE • 1963 • Lenica Jan • ANS • PLN, FRG • RHINOCEROS (USA) ○ RHINOCEROSES
NASHVILLE • 1975 • Altman Robert • USA
NASHVILLE GIRL • 1976 • Trikonis Gus • USA • COUNTRY MUSIC DAUGHTER
NASHVILLE GRAB • 1981 • Conway James L. • TVM • USA
NASHVILLE LADY see **COAL MINER'S DAUGHTER, THE** • 1979
NASHVILLE REBEL • 1966 • Sheridan Jay • USA
NASI FURIANTI • 1937 • Vancura Vladislav, Kubasek Vaclav • CZC • SWAGGERERS, THE ○ OUR DEFIANT ONES
NASI LIPICANCI • 1951 • Badjura Metod, Badjura Milka • YGS • OUR WHITE HORSES FROM LIPICANCI
NASIBANI DEVI • 1927 • IND • GODDESS OF LUCK (USA)
NASILJE NA TRGU • 1961 • Bercovici Leonardo • YGS, ITL • SQUARE OF VIOLENCE (USA)
NASIR SALAH AD-DIN, AN- see **NASSER SALAH-EL-DINE, EL** • 1963
NASLEDJE see **DEDISCINA** • 1985
NASO DI CUOIO (ITL) see **NEZ-DE-CUIR** • 1952
NASREDDIN IN BUKHARA see **NASREDDIN V BUKHARE** • 1943
NASREDDIN V BUKHARE • 1943 • Protazanov Yakov • USS • NASREDDIN IN BUKHARA ○ ADVENTURES IN BOKHARA
NASRUDIN • 1972 • Williams Richard • ANS • UKN
NASSER ASPHALT • 1958 • Wisbar Frank • FRG • WET ASPHALT (USA)
NASSER SALAH-EL-DINE, EL • 1963 • Shahin Youssef • EGY, SWT, FRN • LEADER SALADIN, THE ○ NASIR SALAH AD-DIN, AN- ○ SALADIN AND THE GREAT CRUSADES ○ SALADIN
NASSES ABENTEUER, EIN • 1917 • Karfiol William • FRG
NASSIM-E-AYAR • 1967 • Koushan Esmaeil • IRN
NASSU WA AN-NIL, AN- • 1968 • Shahin Youssef • EGY • CES GENS ET LE NIL ○ NAS WAL NIL, EL ○ PEOPLE AND THE NILE
NASTAN GIFTA see **A VI GIFTA?** • 1936
NASTASIA FILIPOVNA • 1958 • Pyriev Ivan • USS • IDIOT, THE (USA)
NASTOJANJE • 1983 • Filipovic Vlatko • YGS • ENDEAVOUR
NASTUP • 1952 • Vavra Otakar • CZC • FALL IN!
NASTY GIRL, THE see **SCHRECKLICHE MADCHEN, DAS** • 1990
NASTY HABITS • 1976 • Lindsay-Hogg Michael • UKN • ABBESS, THE
NASTY HABITS see **AVENGER, THE** • 1987
NASTY QUACKS • 1945 • Tashlin Frank • ANS • USA
NASTY RABBIT, THE see **SPIES A-GO-GO** • 1963
NASVIDENJE V NASLEDNJI VOJNI • 1981 • Pavlovic Zivojin • YGS • DOVIDJENJA U SLIJEDECEM RATU ○ SEE YOU IN THE NEXT WAR ○ FAREWELL IN THE NEXT WAR
NASZ CZLOWIEK • 1975 • Kieslowski Krzysztof • PLN • OUR MAN
NASZ MARSZALEK • 1947 • Bossak Jerzy • DOC • PLN • OUR MARSHAL
NASZ ZESPOL • 1955 • Has Wojciech J. • PLN • OUR GROUP
NASZDAL, A • 1917 • *Lugosi Bela* • HNG
NASZUT FELARON • 1936 • Sekely Steve • HNG • HALF-PRICE HONEYMOON
NAT GONELLA AND HIS GEORGIANS see **PITY THE POOR RICH** • 1935
NAT "KING" COLE AND JOE ADAMS'S ORCHESTRA • 1951 • Cowan Will • SHT • USA
NAT "KING" COLE AND RUSS MORGAN'S ORCHESTRA • 1953 • Cowan Will • SHT • USA
NAT "KING" COLE MUSICAL STORY, THE • 1955 • Cowan Will • SHT • USA
NAT OVER CILI • 1977 • Alarcon Sebastian, Kosarev Alexandr • USS
NATA DI MARZO • 1958 • Pietrangeli Antonio • ITL, FRN • MARCH'S CHILD ○ BORN IN MARCH
NATACHA see **MOSCOW NIGHTS** • 1935
NATAL DA PORTELA • 1988 • Saraceni Paulo Cesar • DOC • BRZ • ONE-ARMED NATAL
NATAL EM GOA • 1958 • Spiguel Miguel • SHT • PRT
NATAL NA ARTE PORTUGUESA, O • 1954 • Rosa Baptista • SHT • PRT
NATALE AL CAMPO 119 • 1948 • Francisci Pietro • ITL • ESCAPE INTO DREAMS (USA)
NATALE CHE QUASI NON FU, IL • 1965 • Brazzi Rossano • ITL, USA • CHRISTMAS THAT ALMOST WASN'T, THE (USA)
NATALE IN CASA D'APPUNTAMENTO • 1976 • Nannuzzi Armando • ITL • CHRISTMAS TIME IN A BROTHEL ○ CHRISTMAS AT THE BROTHEL ○ LOVE BY APPOINTMENT ○ HOLIDAY HOOKERS
NATALIA • 1979 • Kassila Matti • FNL
NATALIE • 1988 • Cohn Bernard • FRN
NATALIZIO DELLA NANNA • 1923 • Falena Ugo • ITL
NATALKA POLTAVKA • 1936 • Kavaleridze Ivan • USS

NATALKA POLTAVKA • 1937 • Ulmer Edgar G. • USA
NATALYA USHWVI • 1957 • Paradjanov Sergei • DOC • USS
NATAS see **NATAS: A REFLECTION** • 1983
NATAS: A REFLECTION • 1983 • Dunlap Jack • USA • NATAS: THE REFLECTION ○ NATAS
NATAS: THE REFLECTION see **NATAS: A REFLECTION** • 1983
NATASHA see **FRONTOVYYE PODRUGI** • 1942
NATASHA PROSKUROVA • 1915 • Protazanov Yakov • USS
NATASHA ROSTOVA • 1915 • Chardynin Pyotr • USS
NATATION • 1963 • Carle Gilles • DCS • CND
NATATION DE FANTAISIE see **ORNAMENTAL SWIMMING** • 1937
NATE AND HAYES • 1983 • Fairfax Ferdinand • USA, NZL • SAVAGE ISLANDS
NATELLA • 1926 • Bek-Nazarov Amo • USS
NATEN FOR KRISTIANS FODELSDAG • 1908 • *Holger-Madsen* • DNM • NIGHT BEFORE CHRISTIAN'S BIRTHDAY, THE
NATERCIA see **MERCI NATERCIA** • 1960
NATHALIE • 1957 • Christian-Jaque • FRN, ITL • FOXIEST GIRL IN PARIS, THE (USA)
NATHALIE • Milonakos Ilias • GRC
NATHALIE AFTER LOVE (UKN) see **NATHALIE APRES L'AMOUR** • 1970
NATHALIE AGENT SECRET • 1959 • Decoin Henri • FRN, ITL • ATOMIC AGENT (USA)
NATHALIE APRES L'AMOUR • 1970 • Sanders Michael B. • FRN, BLG • NATHALIE AFTER LOVE (UKN)
NATHALIE GRANGER • 1972 • Duras Marguerite • FRN • NATHALIE GRANGIER
NATHALIE GRANGIER see **NATHALIE GRANGER** • 1972
NATHALIE, L'AMOUR S'EVEILLE • 1968 • Chevalier Pierre • FRN
NATHALIE SARRAUTE • 1978 • Benmussa Simone • FRN
NATHAN DER WEISE • 1922 • Noa Manfred • FRG
NATHAN HALE • 1913 • *Bell Gaston* • USA
NATHAN HALE see **HEART OF A HERO, THE** • 1916
NATHANIEL HAWTHORNE'S "TWICE-TOLD TALES" see **TWICE-TOLD TALES** • 1963
NATIKA • 1964 • Solomos G. P. • ITL
NATION AFLAME, A • 1938 • Halperin Victor Hugo • USA
NATION EST NEE, UNE • 1961 • Vieyra Paulin • SNL
NATION EST NEE, UNE • 1972 • CMR
NATION IS BUILT, A • 1937 • Hurley Frank • DOC • ASL
NATION ONCE AGAIN, A • 1946 • Stafford Brendan J. • DOC • UKN
NATION WITH ME, A see **GENTE CONMIGO** • 1967
NATIONAL AQUARIUM PRESENTATION • 1967 • Eames Charles, Eames Ray • SHT • USA
NATIONAL BARN DANCE, THE • 1944 • Bennett Hugh • USA
NATIONAL CHAMPIONSHIP DRAG RACING • 1966 • *Box Office Attractions* • DOC • USA
NATIONAL CLASS see **NACIONALNA KLASA DO 785cm3** • 1978
NATIONAL CLASS UP TO 785cm3 see **NACIONALNA KLASA DO 785cm3** • 1978
NATIONAL CRIME TEST see **CTV'S NATIONAL CRIME TEST** • 1980
NATIONAL DREAM, THE • 1974 • Till Eric, Murray James • SER • CND
NATIONAL FIRE MOBILIZING PROCEDURE • 1942 • Anstey Edgar • DOC • UKN
NATIONAL GAMES, THE see **CHUNGKUO T'I T'AN CH'UN YING HUI** • 1976
NATIONAL HEALTH, THE • 1973 • Gold Jack • UKN • NATIONAL HEALTH, OR NURSE NORTON'S AFFAIR, THE (USA)
NATIONAL HEALTH, OR NURSE NORTON'S AFFAIR, THE (USA) see **NATIONAL HEALTH, THE** • 1973
NATIONAL HERITAGE see **PATRIMONIO NACIONAL** • 1980
NATIONAL III see **NACIONAL III** • 1983
NATIONAL LAMPOON GOES TO THE MOVIES • 1981 • Jaglom Henry, Giraldi Bob • USA • NATIONAL LAMPOON'S MOVIE MADNESS
NATIONAL LAMPOON'S ANIMAL HOUSE • 1978 • Landis John • USA • ANIMAL HOUSE
NATIONAL LAMPOON'S CHRISTMAS VACATION • 1989 • Chechik Jeremiah • USA
NATIONAL LAMPOON'S CLASS REUNION • 1982 • Miller Michael • USA • CLASS REUNION
NATIONAL LAMPOON'S EUROPEAN VACATION • 1985 • Heckerling Amy • USA • EUROPEAN VACATION
NATIONAL LAMPOON'S FAMILY DIES • 1990 • Ashworth Piers • USA
NATIONAL LAMPOON'S MOVIE MADNESS see **NATIONAL LAMPOON GOES TO THE MOVIES** • 1981
NATIONAL LAMPOON'S VACATION • 1983 • Ramis Harold • USA • VACATION
NATIONAL MECHANICS see **MECANICA NACIONAL** • 1972
NATIONAL NUTS • 1916 • Dillon John Francis • USA
NATIONAL PARK, THE see **NACIONALE PARK, HET** • 1968
NATIONAL PARKS.. A NECESSITY see **NATIONALE PARKEN.. NOODZAAK** • 1978
NATIONAL PARKS OF THE NETHERLANDS see **NATIONALE PARKEN.. NOODZAAK** • 1978
NATIONAL REBIRTH DAY: THE OPENING OF THE W-Z ROUTE see **SWIETO ODRODZENIA: TRASA W-Z OTWARTA!** • 1949
NATIONAL RIFLE, THE see **ESCOPETA NACIONAL, LA** • 1978
NATIONAL SHOTGUN, THE see **ESCOPETA NACIONAL, LA** • 1978
NATIONAL VELVET • 1944 • Brown Clarence • USA
NATIONAL YOUTH ORCHESTRA OF GREAT BRITAIN, THE • 1966 • *Anvil* • SHT • UKN
NATIONALE PARKEN.. NOODZAAK • 1978 • Haanstra Bert • DOC • NTH • NATIONAL PARKS OF THE NETHERLANDS ○ NATIONAL PARKS.. A NECESSITY
NATIONALITE: IMMIGRE • 1972 • Sokhona Sidney • DOC • FRN
NATION'S PERIL, A • 1912 • Golden Joseph A. • USA
NATION'S PERIL, A • 1914 • *Clifford William* • USA
NATION'S PERIL, THE • 1914 • Kinder Stuart? • UKN
NATION'S PERIL, THE • 1915 • Terwilliger George W. • USA
NATIR PUJA • 1932 • *Sircar B. N. (P)* • IND
NATIVE COUNTRY see **KOKYO** • 1923
NATIVE COUNTRY, THE see **STRANA RODNAYA** • 1942
NATIVE DOCUMENT • 1978 • Armstrong Mary • DOC • CND
NATIVE DRUMS (USA) see **TAM TAM MAYUMBE** • 1955
NATIVE EARTH • 1945 • Heyer John • DOC • ASL
NATIVE FAUST, A see **FAUSTO CRIOLLO, EL** • 1980
NATIVE FIELDS • 1943 • Babochkin Boris • USS
NATIVE HOUSE, THE see **OTCHII DOM** • 1959
NATIVE INDUSTRIES OF JAVA • 1913 • Melies Gaston • DOC • USA
NATIVE LAND • 1942 • Hurwitz Leo T., Strand Paul • DOC • USA
NATIVE MUSEUM see **MUSEO CRIOLLO** • 1973
NATIVE SON • 1986 • Freedman Jerrold • USA
NATIVE SON (USA) see **SANGRE NEGRA** • 1948
NATIVE STATE • 1918 • *Chapin* • SHT • USA
NATIVE WHO CAUSED ALL THE TROUBLE, THE see **ART OF POLITICS: THE NATIVE WHO CAUSED ALL THE TROUBLE, THE** • 1989
NATIVITE, LA • 1910 • Feuillade Louis • FRN
NATIVITY, THE • 1978 • Kowalski Bernard • TVM • USA
NATIZILI, I • 1967 • Tassios Pavlos • GRC • RIVALS, THE
NATLOGI BETALT • 1957 • Allen Johannes, Anker • DNM • BED WITHOUT BREAKFAST
NATO PER UCCIDERE • 1967 • Mollica Nino • ITL • BORN TO KILL
NATOOSA • 1912 • Sturgeon Rollin S. • USA
NAT'S CONVERSION • 1909 • Coleby A. E. • UKN
NATSEILERE • 1985 • Torstad Tor M. • NRW • NIGHT VOYAGE
NATSU NO ARASHI • 1956 • Nakahira Ko • JPN • SUMMER STORM
NATSU NO IMOTO • 1972 • Oshima Nagisa • JPN • DEAR SUMMER SISTER (USA) ○ SUMMER SISTER
NATSUKASHI NO KAO • 1941 • Naruse Mikio • JPN • DEARLY LOVED FACE, A ○ FACE FROM THE PAST, A
NATSUKASHIKI FUE YA TAIKO • 1967 • Kinoshita Keisuke • JPN • EYES THE SEA AND A BALL, THE ○ LOVELY FLUTE AND DRUM
NATSUKO, HER SEASON see **SHIKI NATSUKO** • 1981
NATSUKO NO BOKEN • 1953 • Nakamura Noboru • JPN • NATSUKO'S VENTURE
NATSUKO'S VENTURE see **NATSUKO NO BOKEN** • 1953
NATT, EN see **EN NATT** • 1931
NATT I HAMN • 1943 • Faustman Erik • SWD • NIGHT IN THE HARBOUR
NATT PA GLIMMINGEHUS, EN • 1954 • Wickman Torgny • SWD • NIGHT AT GLIMMINGE CASTLE
NATT PA SMYGEHOLM, EN • 1933 • Wallen Sigurd • SWD • NIGHT AT SMYGEHOLM, A
NATTBARN • 1956 • Hellstrom Gunnar • SWD • CHILDREN OF THE NIGHT
NATTENS BARN • 1916 • Klercker Georg • SWD • CHILDREN OF THE NIGHT
NATTENS GAADE • 1914 • Davidsen Hjalmar • DNM • IN THE MIST OR THE LOST BRIDE
NATTENS LJUS • 1957 • Kjellgren Lars-Eric • SWD • LIGHTS AT NIGHT
NATTENS MYSTERIUM • 1916 • Holger-Madsen • DNM • WHO KILLED BARNO O'NEAL ○ KLUBVENNEN
NATTENS VAV • 1953 • Mattsson Arne • SWD
NATTEVANDREREN • 1917 • Holger-Madsen • DNM • EDISON MAES DAGBOG ○ OUT OF THE UNDERWORLD
NATTLEK • 1966 • Zetterling Mai • SWD • NIGHT GAMES ○ LANGTAN
NATTLIGA TONER • 1918 • Klercker Georg • SWD • NIGHTLY MUSIC
NATTMARA • 1965 • Mattsson Arne • SWD • NIGHTMARE
NATTMARSCHEN I SANCT ERIKS GRAND • 1909 • Magnusson Charles • SWD • NIGHT MARCH IN ST. ERIK'S LANE, THE
NATTVAKTENS HUSTRU • 1948 • Palm Bengt • SWD • NIGHT WATCHMAN'S WIFE, THE
NATTVARDSGASTERNA • 1963 • Bergman Ingmar • SWD • CUMMUNICANTS, THE (USA) ○ WINTER LIGHT (UKN)
NATTY GANN see **JOURNEY OF NATTY GANN, THE** • 1985
NATUR UND LIEBE • 1928 • *Ufa* • FRG • NATURE AND LOVE
NATUR UND TECHNIK • 1938 • FRG
NATURA E CHIMICA • 1959 • Olmi Ermanno (Spv) • DOC • ITL
NATURAL, THE • 1984 • Levinson Barry • USA
NATURAL BORN GAMBLER, A • 1916 • *Williams Bert* • SHT • USA
NATURAL BORN SALESMAN, A (UKN) see **EARTHWORM TRACTORS** • 1936
NATURAL BOUNDARY, THE see **PRIRODNA GRANICA** • 1971
NATURAL COLOUR PORTRAITURE • 1909 • Smith G. A. • UKN
NATURAL ENEMIES • 1979 • Kanew Jeff • USA • HIDDEN THOUGHTS
NATURAL LAW, THE • 1917 • France Charles H. • USA
NATURAL LAWS REVERSED • 1905 • Green Tom? • UKN
NATURAL MAN, A • 1915 • Davis Ulysses • USA
NATURAL MISTAKE, A • 1914 • Henderson Dell • USA
NATURAL SON, THE • 1912 • *Powers* • USA
NATURAL WONDERS OF THE WEST • 1938 • Smith • SHT • USA
NATURALISEE, LA • 1962 • Cuniot Alain • SHT • FRN
NATURALLY FUNNY MAN, A see **FUNNYMAN** • 1967
NATURALLY, IT'S RUBBER • 1964 • Hopkinson Peter • DCS • UKN
NATURE AND LOVE see **NATUR UND LIEBE** • 1928
NATURE CAMP CONFIDENTIAL • 1961 • Wishman Doris • USA • NATURE CAMP DIARY ○ NUDIST CONFIDENTIAL ○ DIARY OF A NUDIST ○ NUDIST CAMP
NATURE CAMP DIARY see **NATURE CAMP CONFIDENTIAL** • 1961
NATURE FAKIRS • 1907 • *Kalem* • USA
NATURE GIRL, THE • 1919 • Lund O. A. C. • USA
NATURE GIRLS ON THE MOON • 1960 • *Jer & Luna* • USA • NUDES ON THE MOON ○ GIRLS ON THE MOON
NATURE GIRLS UNLIMITED see **BEHIND THE NUDIST CURTAIN** • 1964
NATURE HEALER, THE see **KLOKA GUBBEN** • 1938
NATURE IN THE WRONG • 1933 • Roach Hal • USA • TARZAN IN THE WRONG
NATURE INCORPORATED • 1916 • Worthington William • SHT • USA
NATURE IS QUIETLY BEAUTIFUL see **WU-LI-TE TI-SHENG** • 1983
NATURE MAN, OR A STRUGGLE FOR EXISTENCE, THE • 1915 • *Knowles Joseph* • USA
NATURE MORTE • 1966 • Guillemot Claude • SHT • FRN
NATURE MORTE • 1970 • Lenica Jan • ANS • FRN
NATURE OF HOKKAIDO, THE see **HOKKAIDO NO DAISHIZEN** • 1957
NATURE OF THE BEAST, THE • 1919 • Hepworth Cecil M. • UKN
NATURE OF THE BEAST, THE • 1988 • Rosso Franco • UKN
NATURE OF THINGS, THE • 1969-73 • Bittman Roman • SER • CND
NATURE OF WORK, THE • 1958 • Parker Morten • SER • CND
NATURE RESERVE see **REZERVAT** • 1990
NATURENS HAMND • 1983 • Jarl Stefan • SWD • NATURE'S REVENGE
NATURE'S ATOM BOMB • 1946 • Parker Ben • SHT • USA
NATURE'S BEAUTIFUL PLAYMATES see **NATURE'S SWEETHEARTS** • 1963
NATURE'S CALLING • 1917 • *Kerrigan J. Warren* • SHT • USA
NATURE'S CURE • 1970 • *Stacey Dist.* • USA
NATURE'S GENTLEMAN • 1918 • Thornton F. Martin • UKN
NATURE'S HALF ACRE • 1952 • Algar James • DOC • USA
NATURE'S MISTAKES see **FREAKS** • 1932
NATURE'S NOBLEMAN • 1910 • *Atlas* • USA
NATURE'S NURSERY • 1938 • Alderson John • UKN
NATURE'S PLAYGIRLS INTERNATIONAL see **PALYGIRLS INTERNATIONAL** • 1963
NATURE'S PLAYMATES • 1962 • Lewis Herschell G. • USA
NATURE'S REVENGE see **NATURENS HAMND** • 1983
NATURE'S STRANGEST CREATURES • 1959 • *Disney Walt (P)* • DOC • USA
NATURE'S SWEETHEARTS • 1963 • Wolk Larry • USA • NATURE'S BEAUTIFUL PLAYMATES
NATURE'S TOUCH • 1914 • Ayres Sydney • USA
NATURE'S TRIUMPH see **CURE OF THE MOUNTAINS, THE** • 1915
NATURE'S VENGEANCE • 1913 • *Kirkwood James* • USA
NATURE'S WORK SHOP • 1933 • Lantz Walter, Nolan William • ANS • USA
NATURLICH DIE AUTOFAHRER • 1959 • Engels Erich • FRG
NATURLICHSTE SACH DER WELT, DIE • 1978 • Neukirchen Dorothea • FRG • MOST NATURAL THING IN THE WORLD, THE
NATVRIS KHE see **DREVO ZHELANYA** • 1976
NAU YEUK HAK • 1990 • Law Clara • HKG • FAREWELL CHINA
NAUFRAGE DU PACIFIQUE, LE see **ROBINSON CRUSOE** • 1950
NAUFRAGES DE L'ILE DE LA TORTUE, LES • 1976 • Rozier Jacques • FRN
NAUFRAGES DU QUARTIER, LES • 1980 • Longpre Bernard • ANM • CND • ONE WAY STREET
NAUFRAGEUR, LE see **BLACKOUT** • 1977
NAUFRAGEURS, LES • 1958 • Brabant Charles • FRN
NAUFRAGHI • 1939 • Rosa Silvio Laurenti • ITL
NAUFRAGIO • 1977 • Hermosillo Jaime Humberto • MXC • SHIPWRECK
NAUGHTY • 1927 • Del Ruth Hampton • USA • BAD LITTLE SOW GIRL
NAUGHTY! • 1971 • Long Stanley • DOC • UKN
NAUGHTY ARLETTE (USA) see **ROMANTIC AGE, THE** • 1949
NAUGHTY BABY • 1928 • LeRoy Mervyn • USA • RECKLESS ROSIE (UKN)
NAUGHTY BALL, THE see **FLICEK THE BALL** • 1956
NAUGHTY BIRD, THE • Homoki-Nagy Istvan • HNG
NAUGHTY BLUE KNICKERS see **FOLIES D'ELODIE, LES** • 1981
NAUGHTY BOY • 1927 • Lamont Charles • SHT • USA
NAUGHTY BOY • 1962 • *Burman S. D. (M)* • IND
NAUGHTY BOY, A • 1904 • *Cricks & Sharp* • UKN
NAUGHTY BOYS • 1983 • de Kuyper Eric • NTH
NAUGHTY BUT MICE • 1939 • Jones Charles M. • ANS • USA
NAUGHTY BUT MICE • 1947 • Kneitel Seymour • ANS • USA
NAUGHTY BUT NICE • 1927 • Webb Millard • USA
NAUGHTY BUT NICE • 1939 • Enright Ray • USA • ALWAYS LEAVE THEM LAUGHING
NAUGHTY CARLOTTA see **VENUS OF VENICE** • 1927
NAUGHTY CHICKEN, THE • 1962 • Topaldgikov Stefan • ANM • BUL
NAUGHTY CINDERELLA • 1933 • Daumery John • UKN
NAUGHTY CUTIES see **NAUGHTY DALLAS** • 1964
NAUGHTY DALLAS • 1964 • Buchanan Larry • USA • NAUGHTY CUTIES ○ MONDO EXOTICA
NAUGHTY DR. JEKYLL • USA • DIRTY DR. JEKYLL (?)
NAUGHTY DUCHESS, THE • 1928 • Terriss Tom • USA
NAUGHTY DUCK, THE see **RATOIUL NEASCULTATOR** • 1951
NAUGHTY FLIRT, THE • 1931 • Cline Eddie • USA • MAN CRAZY
NAUGHTY GIRL • 1934 • Shah Chandulal • IND
NAUGHTY GIRL see **CETTE SACREE GAMINE** • 1955
NAUGHTY GIRLS • 1975 • Shillingford Peter • UKN
NAUGHTY HENRIETTA • 1915 • Cooley Frank • USA
NAUGHTY HUSBANDS • 1930 • Benstead Geoffrey • UKN
NAUGHTY KITTEN, THE • 1953 • Paschenko Mstilav • ANS • USS
NAUGHTY LIONS AND WILD MEN • 1920 • Fishback Fred C. • SHT • USA
NAUGHTY LITTLE PRINCESS, THE • 1908 • *Vitagraph* • USA
NAUGHTY MARIETTA • 1912 • *Pathe* • USA
NAUGHTY MARIETTA • 1935 • Van Dyke W. S. • USA
NAUGHTY MARTINE (USA) see **MADEMOISELLE MODISTE** • 1952
NAUGHTY NANETTE • 1927 • Meehan James Leo • USA
NAUGHTY, NAUGHTY! • 1918 • Storm Jerome • USA
NAUGHTY NEIGHBORS • 1939 • Clampett Robert • ANS • USA
NAUGHTY NELLIE • 1914 • *Crystal* • USA
NAUGHTY NETWORK • 1981 • Gator Linus • USA
NAUGHTY NIGHTS see **LADY IS A WHORE, THE** • 1972
NAUGHTY NINETIES, THE • 1940 • Ceballos Larry • USA
NAUGHTY NINETIES, THE • 1945 • Yarbrough Jean • USA • GAY NINETIES, THE

NAUGHTY NUDES • 1965 • Michael James • USA
NAUGHTY NUN (UKN) see **BELLA ANTONIA PRIMA MONICA E POI DIMONIA** • 1972
NAUGHTY NURSES see **TENDER LOVING CARE** • 1974
NAUGHTY ONES, THE see **NEMIRNI** • 1967
NAUGHTY OWL, THE see **UHUKA, A KIS BAGOLY** • 1969
NAUGHTY RABBIT, THE see **NOTTE PAZZA DEL CONIGLIACCIO, LA** • 1967
NAUGHTY ROGUE, THE see **OJO KICHIZA** • 1959
NAUGHTY SCHOOLGIRLS • 1976 • Scardino Jean-Paul • USA
NAUGHTY SHUTTER, THE • 1963 • Helm Sammy • USA
NAUGHTY STEWARDESSES, THE • 1974 • Adamson Al • USA
NAUGHTY STORY, A • 1900 • *Paul R. W.* • UKN
NAUGHTY WIFE, THE see **LET'S ELOPE** • 1919
NAUGHTY WIVES (USA) see **SECRETS OF A DOOR TO DOOR SALESMAN** • 1973
NAUKA BLIZEJ ZYCIA • 1951 • Munk Andrzej • DCS • PLN • SCIENCES CLOSER TO LIFE, THE ○ SCIENCE CLOSER TO LIFE
NAUKA LATANIA • 1978 • Idziak Slawomir • PLN • LEARNING TO FLY
NAUKRI see **NAKURAI** • 1954
NAULAHKA, THE • 1918 • Fitzmaurice George • USA
NAUSICAA • 1970 • Varda Agnes • FRN
NAUTICAL KNIGHTS • 1938 • Schwarzwald Milton • SHT • USA
NAUTICAL NUT • 1967 • Smith Paul J. • ANS • USA
NAV JAWAN • 1937 • Aspi • IND
NAV-JEEVAN • 1939 • Osten Franz • IND
NAVAHO • 1907 • Gilbert Arthur • UKN
NAVAHO RAIN CHANT • 1971 • Dyal Susan • ANS • USA
NAVAJEROS, LOS • 1980 • de la Iglesia Eloy • SPN, MXC • KNIFERS, THE ○ KNIFE FIGHTERS
NAVAJO • 1952 • Foster Norman • USA
NAVAJO BLANKET, THE • 1914 • *Darkfeather Mona* • USA
NAVAJO JOE • 1915 • *Santa Barbara* • USA
NAVAJO JOE • 1966 • Corbucci Sergio • ITL, SPN • JOE, EL IMPLACABLE (SPN) ○ DOLLAR A TESTA, UN
NAVAJO KID • 1945 • Fraser Harry L. • USA
NAVAJO RING, THE • 1915 • Davis Ulysses • USA
NAVAJO RUN • 1966 • Seven Johnny • USA
NAVAJO TRAIL, THE • 1945 • Bretherton Howard • USA
NAVAJO TRAIL RAIDERS • 1949 • Springsteen R. G. • USA
NAVAJO'S BRIDE, THE • 1910 • *Kalem* • USA
NAVAL ACADEMY • 1941 • Kenton Erle C. • USA
NAVAL BOMBER FLEET, THE see **KAIGUN BAKUGEKITAI** • 1940
NAVAL CONTINGENT LEAVING MELBOURNE • 1900 • Perry Joseph H. • DOC • ASL
NAVAL ENGAGEMENT, A • 1906 • Hough Harold • UKN
NAVAL REVIEW AT CHERBOURG, A see **REVUE NAVAL A CHERBOURG** • 1896
NAVAL TREATY, THE • 1922 • Ridgwell George • UKN
NAVE • 1940 • Paolucci Giovanni, Portalupi Piero • ITL • SHIP, THE
NAVE, LA • 1911 • Maggi Luigi • ITL
NAVE, LA • 1919 • D'Annuzio Gabriellino • ITL
NAVE BIANCA, LA • 1941 • Rossellini Roberto • ITL
NAVE DE LOS MONSTRUOS, LA • 1959 • Gonzalez Rogelio A. • MXC • SHIP OF THE MONSTERS, THE
NAVE DELLE DONNE MALEDETTE, LA • 1953 • Matarazzo Raffaello • ITL • SHIP OF CONDEMNED WOMEN, THE (USA)
NAVEL OF THE MOON, THE see **OMBLIGO DE LA LUNA, EL** • 1985
NAVELSTAREN • 1966 • Staugaard Peter • SHT • NTH
NAVIDAD DE LOS POBRES • 1947 • *Lamas Fernando* • ARG
NAVIDADES EN JUNIO • 1960 • Demicheli Tulio • SPN
NAVIGATION BY WIRELESS • 1912 • *Danube* • USA
NAVIGATION MARCHANDE • 1954 • Franju Georges • DOC • FRN • MARINE MARCHANDE
NAVIGATOR, THE • 1924 • Keaton Buster, Crisp Donald • USA
NAVIGATOR, THE • 1934 • Starevitch Ladislas • ANM • FRN
NAVIGATOR, THE • 1988 • Ward Vincent • NZL • NAVIGATOR: A MEDIEVAL ODYSSEY, THE
NAVIGATOR: A MEDIEVAL ODYSSEY, THE see **NAVIGATOR, THE** • 1988
NAVIRE AVEUGLE, LE • 1927 • Guarino Joseph • FRN
NAVIRE DES HOMMES PERDUS, LE see **SCHIFF DER VERLORENEN MENSCHEN, DAS** • 1929
NAVIRE NIGHT, LE • 1979 • Duras Marguerite • FRN
NAVJIVAN • 1935 • *Nangis Miss* • IND
NAVRAT DOMU • 1948 • Fric Martin • CZC • LOST IN THE SUBURBS ○ RETURN HOME ○ PRAGUE ○ LOST IN PRAGUE
NAVRAT JANA PETRU • 1985 • Tapak Martin • CZC • JAN PETRO'S RETURN
NAVRAT ZTRACENEHO SYNA • 1966 • Schorm Evald • CZC • RETURN OF THE PRODIGAL SON, THE
NAVSTEVA Z OBLAK • 1954 • Makovec Milos • CZC
NAVSTRYECHU SOVESTI • 1967 • Khachaturov Albert • USS • TO SATISFY ONE'S CONSCIENCE ○ MEETING ONE'S CONSCIENCE
NAVVIES see **RALLARE** • 1947
NAVVY, THE see **REAL BLOKE, A** • 1935
NAVVY'S FORTUNE, THE • 1910 • Rains Fred • UKN
NAVY see **KAIGUN** • 1943
NAVY, THE • 1930 • Lantz Walter, Nolan William • ANS • USA
NAVY, THE see **KAIGUN** • 1963
NAVY AVIATOR, THE • 1914 • *Ayres Sydney* • USA
NAVY BEANS • 1928 • Lamont Charles • SHT • USA
NAVY, BLUE AND GOLD • 1937 • Wood Sam • USA
NAVY BLUES • 1929 • Brown Clarence • USA
NAVY BLUES • 1937 • Staub Ralph • USA
NAVY BLUES • 1941 • Bacon Lloyd • USA
NAVY BOMBERS see **KAIGUN BAKUGEKITAI** • 1940
NAVY BORN • 1936 • Watt Nate • USA • MARINERS OF THE SKY
NAVY BOUND • 1951 • Landres Paul • USA
NAVY COMES THROUGH, THE • 1942 • Sutherland A. Edward • USA
NAVY HEROES (USA) see **BLUE PETER, THE** • 1954
NAVY IS A SHIP, THE • 1970 • Baylis Peter • DOC • UKN
NAVY LARK, THE • 1959 • Parry Gordon • UKN
NAVY SEALS • 1990 • Teague Lewis • USA
NAVY SECRETS • 1939 • Bretherton Howard • USA
NAVY SPY • 1937 • Lewis Joseph H., Wilbur Crane • USA
NAVY STEPS OUT, THE (UKN) see **GIRL, A GUY AND A GOB, A** • 1941
NAVY VS. THE NIGHT MONSTERS, THE • 1966 • Hoey Michael • USA • MONSTERS OF THE NIGHT (UKN) ○ NIGHT CRAWLERS, THE
NAVY WAY, THE • 1944 • Berke William • USA
NAVY WIFE • 1935 • Dwan Allan • USA • BEAUTY'S DAUGHTER
NAVY WIFE • 1956 • Bernds Edward • USA • MOTHER, SIR! (UKN)
NAVY'S SPECIAL BOY SAILORS see **KAIGUN TOKUBETSU SHONEN HEI** • 1972
NAWA TO CHUBASA • 1967 • Kishi Shintaro • JPN • ROPE AND BREASTS
NAXALITES, THE • 1981 • Abbas Khwaya Ahmad • IND
NAY-DALGATA NOSHT • 1967 • Radev Vulo • BUL • LONGEST NIGHT, THE ○ NAI-DALGATA NOSHT
NAYA ZAMANA • 1971 • *Burman S. D. (M)* • IND
NAYAK • 1966 • Ray Satyajit • IND • HERO, THE
NAYANMONI • 1977 • Hossain Amjad • BNG
NAYDI MENYA • 1968 • Araminas Algirdas • USS • FIND ME
NAYEDINYE S NOCHYU • 1967 • Tretiakov Stanislav, Silayev Boris • USS • ALONE IN THE NIGHT
NAYYA • 1947 • *Biswas Anil (M)* • IND
NAZAR • 1990 • Kaul Mani • IND • EYE
NAZAR SRODOLIA see **NAZAR STODOLYA** • 1954
NAZAR STODOLYA • 1937 • Tasin Georgi • USS
NAZAR STODOLYA • 1954 • Chukhrai Grigori, Ivchenko Viktor • USS • NAZAR SRODOLIA
NAZARE • 1952 • Guimaraes Manuel • PRT
NAZARE see **NAZARE, PRAIA DE PESCADORES** • 1928
NAZARE, PRAIA DE PESCADORES • 1928 • de Barros Jose Leitao, Ribeiro Antonio Lopes • DOC • PRT • NAZARE
NAZARENO CRUZ AND THE WOLF see **NAZARENO CRUZ Y EL LOBO** • 1975
NAZARENO CRUZ Y EL LOBO • 1975 • Favio Leonardo • ARG • NAZARENO CRUZ AND THE WOLF
NAZARIN • 1958 • Bunuel Luis • MXC
NAZDIKIAN • 1986 • PKS • INTIMATE
NAZI AGENT • 1941 • Dassin Jules • USA
NAZI CRIMES AND PUNISHMENT see **NURNBERGER PROZESS, DER** • 1958
NAZI HUNTER: THE BEATE KLARSFELD STORY • 1986 • Lindsay-Hogg Michael • TVM • USA
NAZI SPY RING • 1942 • Herman Al • USA
NAZI TERROR AT NIGHT see **NACHTS, WENN DER TEUFEL KAM** • 1957
NAZIS STRIKE, THE • 1943 • Capra Frank, Litvak Anatole • DOC • USA • WHY WE FIGHT (PART 2): NAZIS STRIKE, THE
NAZO NO YUREISEN • 1958 • Matsuda Sadatsugu • JPN • TRAITORS
NAZRAANA • 1961 • *Kapoor Raj* • IND
NAZTY NUISANCE see **THAT NAZTY NUISANCE** • 1943
NAZYWA SIE BLAZEJ REJDAK, MIESZKA W ROZNICY, W JEDRZEJOWSKIM POWIECIE • 1969 • Gryczelowska Krystyna • DOC • PLN • HIS NAME IS BLAZEJ REJDAK
N'DIANGANE • 1974 • Traore Mahama Johnson • SNL • N'GANGANE ○ STUDENT ○ NJANGAAN
NDINGUWAKABANI • 1983 • SAF
N'DIONGANE • 1965 • Vieyra Paulin • SNL
NE • 1975 • Richard Jacques • FRN
NE BOLIT GOLOVA A DIATLA • 1975 • Asanova Dinara • USS • WOODPECKER NEVER HAS A HEADACHE, THE ○ WOODPECKER HAS NO HEADACHE
NE BOUGEONS PLUS • 1902 • Blache Alice • FRN
NE BOUGEZ PAS • 1941 • Caron Pierre • FRN
NE BOURGEONS PLUS • 1900 • Melies Georges • FRN • DON'T MOVE (USA)
NE COMPROMETTEZ PAS VOS LOISIRS • 1949 • Decae Henri • SHT • FRN
NE DE PERE INCONNU • 1950 • Cloche Maurice • FRN, ITL • BASTARDI, I (ITL)
NE GORIUY! • 1970 • Daneliya Georgi, Gabriadze R. • USS • DON'T GRIEVE! ○ CHEER UP!
NE JOCI, PETRE • 1965 • Stiglic France • YGS • DON'T CRY, PETER ○ NE PLACI, PETRE
NE JOUEZ PAS AVEC LES MARTIANS • 1967 • Lanoe Henri • FRN • COMME MARS EN CAREME ○ REGULAR AS CLOCKWORK ○ MARS EN CAREME ○ MARS AT EASTER ○ DON'T MESS WITH THE MARTIANS ○ DON'T PLAY WITH MARTIANS
NE KOFUN SHICHA IYAYO • 1931 • Naruse Mikio • JPN • NOW DON'T GET EXCITED
NE LE CRIEZ PAS SUR LES TOITS • 1942 • Daniel-Norman Jacques • FRN
NE LE DIS A PERSONNE see **MA TAQULSHI-LI AH'AD** • 1951
NE MIALA BABA KLOPOTU • 1935 • Ford Aleksander • PLN
NE NADO KROVI • 1917 • Protazanov Yakov • USS • BLOOD NEED NOT BE SPILLED
NE NAGINJI SE VAN • 1978 • Zizic Bogdan • YGS • DON'T LEAN OUT THE WINDOW ○ DON'T LEAN OUT
NE NOUS FACHONS PAS • 1965 • Lautner Georges • FRN
NE OKRECI SE, SINE • 1956 • Bauer Branko • YGS • DON'T LOOK BACK, SON
NE PAS STAGNER • 1974 • Lehman Boris • BLG
NE PLACI, PETRE see **NE JOCI, PETRE** • 1965
NE PLEURE PAS • 1977 • Ertaud Jacques • FRN
NE POUR L'ENFER • 1976 • Heroux Denis • FRN, CND, ITL • BORN FOR HELL
NE SE OBRUSHTAI NAZAD • 1971 • Kirkov Lyudmil • BUL • DON'T TURN BACK
NE SIRJ EDESANYAM • 1936 • Pallu Georges
NE SOIS PAS JALOUSIE • 1932 • Genina Augusto • FRN
NE TIREZ PAS DOLLY! • 1937 • Delannoy Jean • FRN
NE UBIJ see **TU NE TUERAS POINT** • 1961
NE ZABUD.. STANTZIYA LUGOVAGA see **NYE ZABUD.. STANTSIYA LUGOVAYA** • 1967
NEA • 1976 • Kaplan Nelly • FRN, FRG • NEA (A YOUNG EMMANUELLE) (USA) ○ YOUNG EMMANUELLE, A
NEA (A YOUNG EMMANUELLE) (USA) see **NEA** • 1976
NEAL OF THE NAVY • 1915 • Harvey William M., Bertram William • SRL • USA
NEAMUL SOIMARESTILOR • 1965 • Dragan Mircea • RMN • HAWKS, THE
NEANDERTHAL MAN, THE • 1953 • Dupont E. A. • USA
NEAPELFRIES, DAS • 1987 • Meili Gaudenz • DOC • SWT
NEAPOLITAN CAROUSEL (USA) see **CAROSELLO NAPOLETANO** • 1954
NEAPOLITAN FANTASY see **CAROSELLO NAPOLETANO** • 1954
NEAPOLITAN HEART (USA) see **CUORE NAPOLETANO** • 1940
NEAPOLITAN TEARS see **LACRIME NAPULITANE** • 1984
NEAPOLITANISCHE GESCHWISTER • 1978 • Schroeter Werner • FRG, ITL • REIGN OF NAPLES, THE ○ NEL REGNO DI NAPOLI ○ REGNO DI NAPOLI
NEAR AND FAR AWAY see **LANGT BORTA OCH NARA** • 1977
NEAR CAPTURE OF JESSE JAMES, THE • 1915 • *Luna* • USA
NEAR DARK • 1987 • Bigelow Kathryn • USA
NEAR DEATH'S DOOR • 1914 • McGowan J. P. • USA
NEAR DUBLIN • 1924 • Ceder Ralph • SHT • USA
NEAR LADY, THE • 1923 • Blache Herbert • USA
NEAR ONES see **APANJAN** • 1968
NEAR RELATIONS see **TJOCKA SLAKTEN** • 1935
NEAR SIGHTED AND FAR OUT • 1964 • Kneitel Seymour • ANS • USA
NEAR-SIGHTED AUTO-PEDIST, THE • 1917 • *Eagle Film* • USA
NEAR-SIGHTED CUPID, A • 1912 • *Selig* • USA
NEAR THE RAINBOW'S END • 1930 • McGowan J. P. • USA
NEAR THE SEA see **NARA TILL HAVET** • 1973
NEAR THE TRAIL'S END • 1931 • Fox Wallace • USA
NEAR TO EARTH • 1913 • Griffith D. W. • USA
NEAR TO US see **PYADOM S NAMI** • 1957
NEAR TRAGEDY, A • 1912 • Sennett Mack • USA
NEAR TRAGEDY, A • 1913 • Weston C. H. • USA
NEARER MY GOD TO THEE • 1917 • Hepworth Cecil M. • UKN
NEAREST AND DEAREST • 1972 • Robins John • UKN
NEARLY A BAKER • 1917 • *U.s.m.p.* • USA
NEARLY A BRIDE • 1915 • *Duncan Bud* • USA
NEARLY A BURGLAR'S BRIDE • 1914 • *Komic* • USA
NEARLY A CHAPERONE • 1918 • *Lyons Eddie* • SHT • USA
NEARLY A DESERTER • 1916 • *U.s.m.p.* • SHT • USA
NEARLY A HEIRESS • 1912 • *Solax* • USA
NEARLY A HERO • 1911 • *Solax* • USA
NEARLY A HERO • 1916 • *Rattenberry Harry* • USA
NEARLY A HUSBAND • 1917 • Hunter T. Hayes • SHT • USA
NEARLY A KING • 1916 • Thompson Frederick A. • USA
NEARLY A LADY • 1915 • Taylor William D. • USA
NEARLY A MAID • 1920 • *Pollard Snub* • SHT • USA
NEARLY A NASTY ACCIDENT • 1961 • Chaffey Don • UKN
NEARLY A PAPA • 1917 • *Belasco Jay* • SHT • USA
NEARLY A PRIZE FIGHTER • 1915 • *Reeves Billy* • USA
NEARLY A QUEEN • 1917 • Curtis Allen • SHT • USA
NEARLY A SCANDAL • 1915 • Ransom Charles • USA
NEARLY A SLACKER • 1918 • Richmond J. A. • SHT • USA
NEARLY A STEPMOTHER • 1914 • *Crystal* • USA
NEARLY A WIDOW • 1914 • Miller Ashley • USA
NEARLY EIGHTEEN • 1943 • Dreifuss Arthur • USA
NEARLY IN MOURNING • 1913 • Smiley Joseph • USA
NEARLY MARRIED • 1914 • *Washburn Bryant* • USA
NEARLY MARRIED • 1916 • *Hippo* • USA
NEARLY MARRIED • 1917 • Withey Chet • USA
NEARLY MARRIED • 1920 • *Banks Monty* • SHT • USA
NEARLY NEWLYWEDS • 1920 • *Harrison Jimmie* • SHT • USA
NEARLY SPLICED • 1916 • *Errol Leon* • SHT • USA
NEARLY WED • 1920 • Moore Vin • SHT • USA
NEARLY WEDS • 1957 • Kneitel Seymour • ANS • USA
NEARLY WIDE AWAKE • 1977 • Hutt David, Turner Martin • UKN
NEARSIGHTED CHAPERONE, THE • 1911 • Hotaling Arthur D. • USA
NEARSIGHTED MARY • 1909 • *Lubin* • USA
NEAT AND TIDY • 1986 • Thompson Marcus • TVM • USA
'NEATH AUSTRAL SKIES • 1913 • Longford Raymond • ASL
NEATH AUSTRALIAN SKIES • 1923 • Longford Raymond • ASL
'NEATH BROOKLYN BRIDGE • 1942 • Fox Wallace • USA • NEATH BROOKLYN BRIDGE ○ NEW YORK MYSTERY
NEATH BROOKLYN BRIDGE see **'NEATH BROOKLYN BRIDGE** • 1942
'NEATH CALVARY'S SHADOW • 1915 • Daly William Robert • USA
'NEATH CANADIAN SKIES • 1946 • Eason B. Reeves • USA
'NEATH THE ARIZONA SKIES • 1934 • Fraser Harry L. • USA
NEATH THE BABABA TREE • 1931 • *Jacoby Irving A. (Anm)* • ANS • USA
'NEATH THE HOMESPUN • 1912 • *Gem* • USA
'NEATH THE LION'S PAW • 1914 • *Melies* • USA
'NEATH THE SOUTHERN CROSS see **BETRAYER, THE** • 1921
'NEATH WESTERN SKIES • 1929 • McGowan J. P. • USA
NEBBIA see **FARI NELLA NEBBIA** • 1942
NEBBIE SUL MARE • 1944 • Pagliero Marcello • ITL
NEBEL • 1963 • Hasler Joachim • GDR
NEBEL UND SOHNE • 1916 • May Joe • FRG
NEBELMORDER • 1964 • York Eugen • FRG • FOG MURDERER, THE
NEBELNACHT • 1969 • Nitzschke Helmut • GDR
NEBENBUHLERIN see **HEILIGE ODER DIRNE** • 1929
NEBESKI ODRED • 1961 • Boskovic Bosko, Nikolic Ilija • YGS • SKY BATTALION, THE
NEBESTI JEZDCI • 1968 • Polak Jindrich • CZC • RIDERS IN THE SKY
...NEBO BYT • 1985 • Holly Martin • CZC • ...OR TO BE KILLED
NEBO MOSKVY • 1944 • Raizman Yuli • USS • MOSCOW SKY
NEBO NASHEGO DETSTVA • 1967 • Okeyev Tolomush • USS • SKY OF OUR CHILDHOOD, THE ○ PASTBISHCHE BAYAKA ○ BAKAI PASTURE ○ NEYEBO BASHEVO DYETSTVA
NEBO ZOVYOT • 1959 • Kozyr Aleksander, Karyukov Mikhail, Colchart Thomas • USS • BATTLE BEYOND THE SUN ○ HEAVENS CALL, THE ○ NIEBO ZOWIET ○ SKY CALLS, THE ○ NEBO ZOWET
NEBO ZOWET see **NEBO ZOVYOT** • 1959
NEBRASKA IL PISTOLERO see **RINGO EN NEBRASKA** • 1965

NEBRASKA UNDER FIRE • 1924 • *Pictorial Sales Bureau* • DOC • USA
NEBRASKAN, THE • 1953 • Sears Fred F. • USA
NEBULA • 1968 • Frerck Robert • SHT • USA
NEBULA 2 • 1969 • Frerck Robert • SHT • USA
NEBULAE • 1964 • Cantrill Arthur, Cantrill Corinne • DOC • ASL
NEBULE • 1973 • Longpre Bernard • ANS • CND
NECESITA UN MARIDO • 1954 • Diaz Morales Jose • MXC • ME LO DIJO ADELA
NECESITO DINERO • 1951 • Zacarias Miguel • MXC
NECESSARY EVIL, THE • 1925 • Archainbaud George • USA
NECESSARY JOURNEY • 1945 • Nieter Hans M. • UKN
NECESSARY MAN, A see **NUZHNY CHELOVYEK** • 1967
NECESSITY • 1988 • Miller Michael • TVM • USA
NECESSITY IS THE MOTHER OF INVENTION • 1909 • Fitzhamon Lewin • UKN
NECHAYEV 1869–1972 see **AUSLIEFERUNG, DIE** • 1974
NECHNI NIC STYSET • 1978 • Koval Ota • CZC • I DON'T WANT TO HEAR ANYTHING
NECHTE TO NA MNE! • 1955 • Fric Martin • CZC • LEAVE IT TO ME
NECK AND NECK • 1920 • *Nat. Film Corp. Of America* • USA
NECK AND NECK • 1931 • Thorpe Richard • USA
NECK AND NECK • 1942 • Davis Mannie • ANS • USA
NECK AND NOOSE • 1919 • Holt George • SHT • USA
NECK 'N NECK • 1927 • Disney Walt • ANS • USA
NECKING • 1967 • Shindo Takae • JPN
NECKLACE, THE • 1909 • Griffith D. W. • USA
NECKLACE, THE • 1985 • Kanakis Nikos • GRC
NECKLACE FOR MY BELOVED, A • 1972 • Abuladze Tengiz • USS
NECKLACE OF CRUSHED ROSE LEAVES, THE • 1912 • *Sawyer Laura* • USA
NECKLACE OF PEARLS, THE • 1915 • *Cooke Ethyle* • USA
NECKLACE OF RAMESES, THE • 1914 • Brabin Charles J. • USA • NECKLET OF RAMESES, THE
NECKLACE OF THE DEAD see **NACHENSCHNUR DES TOT** • 1919
NECKLACE OF THE DEAD, THE see **DODDET HALSBAND, DEN** • 1910
NECKLET OF RAMESES, THE see **NECKLACE OF RAMESES, THE** • 1914
NECO JE VE VZDUCHU • 1981 • Raza Ludvik • CZC • SOMETHING IN THE AIR
NECO NESE VODA see **HRST VODY** • 1971
NECO Z ALENKY • 1987 • Svankmajer Jan • CZC, SWT • SOMETHING FOR ALICE
N'ECRIVEZ JAMAIS see **CAPITAINE BLOMET** • 1947
NECROMANCER • 1988 • Nelson Dusty • USA • NECROMANCER: SATAN'S SERVANT
NECROMANCER, THE • 1903 • *Biograph* • USA
NECROMANCER: SATAN'S SERVANT see **NECROMANCER** • 1988
NECROMANCY • 1972 • Gordon Bert I. • USA • LIFE FOR A LIFE, A ○ TOY FACTORY, THE ○ WITCHING, THE
NECROMANCY see **KAIBYO YONAKI NUMA** • 1957
NECROMICRON (SPN) see **NECRONOMICON –GETRAUMTE SUNDEN** • 1968
NECRONOMICON –DREAMT SIN see **NECRONOMICON –GETRAUMTE SUNDEN** • 1968
NECRONOMICON –GETRAUMTE SUNDEN • 1968 • Franco Jesus • FRG, SPN • NECRONOMICON –DREAMT SIN ○ NECROMICRON (SPN) ○ SUCCUBUS (USA)
NECROPHAGUS (USA) see **DESCUARTIZADOR DE BINBROOK, EL** • 1971
NECROPOLIS • 1970 • Brocani Franco • ITL
NECROPOLIS • 1987 • Hickey Bruce • USA
NED KELLY • 1960 • Burstall Tim • DCS • ASL
NED KELLY • 1970 • Richardson Tony • ASL, UKN • NED KELLY, OUTLAW
NED KELLY, OUTLAW see **NED KELLY** • 1970
NED KELLY THE IRONCLAD BUSHRANGER see **KELLY GANG, THE** • 1910
NED MCCOBB'S DAUGHTER • 1929 • Cowen William J. • USA
NED MED MILLIONAERDRENGEN • 1913 • Holger-Madsen • DNM • ADVENTURES OF A MILLIONAIRE'S SON, THE ○ MILLIONAERDRENGEN
NED MED VAABNENE • 1914 • Holger-Madsen • DNM • DOWN WITH WEAPONS (USA) ○ SURRENDER ARMS ○ LAY DOWN YOUR ARMS
NED WETHERED • 1984 • Whitmore Lee • SHT • ASL
NEDAA EL OCHAK • 1960 • Shahin Youssef • EGY • LOVER'S CALL ○ NIDA' AL-USHSHAQ
NEDELJA • 1968 • Zafranovic Lordan • YGS • SUNDAY
NEDELJNI RUCAK • 1983 • Jelic Milan • YGS • SUNDAY LUNCH
NEDELNITE MATCHOVE • 1975 • Andreikov Todor • BUL • SUNDAY MATCHES ○ SUNDAY GAMES
NEDERLAND • 1983 • Haanstra Bert • SHT • NTH • NETHERLANDS, THE
NEDERLAND –DELTALAND • 1961 • Batchelor Joy • ANS • NTH • DAM THE DELTA
NEDERLANDS AMERICA • 1943 • van Dongen Helen • NTH
NEDERLANDS IN DE WERELD, HET • 1971 • Degelin Emile • BLG
NEDERLANDSE BEELDHOUWKUNST TIJDENS DE LATE MIDDELEEUWEN • 1951 • Haanstra Bert • DOC • NTH • MEDIEVAL CHURCH SCULPTURE ○ DUTCH SCULPTURE
NEDOKONCENY WEEKEND • 1971 • Bedrich Vaclav • ANS • CZC • UNFINISHED WEEKEND
NEDRA • 1915 • Jose Edward • USA
NEDTUR • 1979 • Lindgren Hans • NRW • IF MUSIC BE THE FOOD OF LOVE ○ DOWN TRIP
NEE, NEE, WAS ES NICH' ALLES GIBT see **HERMANNCHEN, DAS** • 1936
NEECHA NAGAR • 1945 • Anand • IND
NEED OF MONEY, THE • 1915 • Morrisey Edward • USA
NEEL AKASHER NEECHEY • 1959 • Sen Mrinal • IND • UNDER THE BLUE SKY
NEEL KAMAL • 1947 • *Kapoor Raj* • IND
NEEL KAMAL • 1968 • Maheshwari Ram • IND • BLUE LOTUS
NEELAKKUYIL • 1954 • Bhaskaran P., Kariatt R. • IND
NEELAMALI THIRUDAN • 1957 • Tirumugam • IND • BANDIT OF THE BLUE MOUNTAIN
NEEM ANAPURNA • 1979 • Dasgupta Buddhadeb • IND • BITTER MORSEL
NE'ER-DO-WELL, THE • 1916 • Campbell Colin • USA
NE'ER DO WELL, THE • 1919 • Sandground Maurice • UKN
NE'ER-DO-WELL, THE • 1923 • Green Alfred E. • USA
NE'ER-DO-WELL AND THE BABY, THE • 1908 • Fitzhamon Lewin? • UKN
NE'ER TO RETURN ROAD, THE • 1913 • *Hayward Lillian* • USA
NEEYUM NAANUM • 1968 • Ramanna • IND • YOU AND I
NEFERTITE REGINA DEL NILO • 1962 • Cerchio Fernando • ITL • QUEEN OF THE NILE (USA)
NEFFE AUS AMERIKA, DER • 1927 • Winar Ernest • FRG
NEFFEN DES HERRN GENERAL, DIE • 1969 • Dietrich Erwin C. • FRG
NEFREEN • 1973 • Taghvai Nasser • IRN • MALEDICTION
NEGATIFS • 1932 • Deslaw Eugene, Darroy Jean • FRN
NEGATIVE CONTACT see **SHINKANSEN DAIBAKUHA** • 1975
NEGATIVES • 1968 • Medak Peter • UKN • SLEEP IS LOVELY
NEGEN EEUWEN SLOTEN • 1966 • Frankfurther P. Hans • NTH
NEGER ERWIN, DER • 1980 • Achternbusch Herbert • FRG
NEGLECTED see **GLAEDENS DAG** • 1918
NEGLECTED BY HIS WIFE see **FORSUMMAD AV SIN FRU** • 1947
NEGLECTED LAND, THE see **PARLOG** • 1975
NEGLECTED LOVER AND THE STILE, THE • 1903 • Stow Percy? • UKN
NEGLECTED MIRACLE, THE • 1984 • Barclay Barry • DOC • NZL
NEGLECTED WIFE, THE • 1914 • *Glaum Louise* • USA
NEGLECTED WIFE, THE • 1917 • Bertram William • SRL • USA
NEGLECTED WIVES • 1920 • King Burton L. • USA
NEGLECTED WOMEN (USA) see **GREAT WELL, THE** • 1924
NEGOCIA AL AGUA • 1913 • Blume Frederico • PRU
NEGRA ANGUSTIAS, LA • 1949 • Landeta Matilde • MXC
NEGRA CONSENTIDA • 1948 • Soler Julian • MXC
NEGRE AMB UN SAXO, UN • 1988 • Bellmunt Francisco • SPN • BLACK MAN WITH A SAX
NEGRE BLANC, LE • 1912 • Gance Abel, Joulot Jean • FRN
NEGRE BLANC, LE • 1925 • Wulschleger Henry, Rimsky Nicolas • FRN
NEGRE DU NEGRESCO, LE see **MONSIEUR HECTOR** • 1940
NEGRES MARRONS DE LA LIBERTE, LES see **WEST INDIES OU LES NEGRES MARRONS DE LA LIBERTE** • 1979
NEGRESCO see **NEGRESCO **** –EINE TODLICHE AFFAIRE** • 1967
NEGRESCO ** –EINE TODLICHE AFFAIRE** • 1967 • Lemke Klaus • FRG • MY BED IS NOT FOR SLEEPING (UKN) ○ NEGRESCO
NEGRITA'S ISLAND • 1957 • Sibianu Gheorghe • ANM • RMN
NEGRO, EL • 1960 • Manet Eduardo • CUB
NEGRO AND THE BLACK, THE see **NEGRO E O PRETO, O** • 1980
NEGRO E O PRETO, O • 1980 • de Oliveira Manoel • PRT • NEGRO AND THE BLACK, THE
NEGRO ES UN BELLO COLOR • 1973 • *Cima* • MXC
NEGRO IN ENTERTAINMENT, THE • 1950 • Trent William Jr. • SHT • USA
NEGRO OF TODAY, THE • 1921 • *C.b. Campbell Studio* • USA
NEGRO QUE TENIA EL ALMA BLANCA, EL • 1927 • Perojo Benito • SPN
NEGRO QUE TENIA EL ALMA BLANCA, EL • 1933 • Perojo Benito • SPN
NEGRO SAILOR, THE • 1945 • Levin Henry • DOC • USA
NEGRO SOLDIER, THE • 1944 • Heisler Stuart, Capra Frank • DOC • USA
NEGYEN AZ ARBAN • 1961 • Revesz Gyorgy • HNG • DANGER ON THE DANUBE (UKN) ○ FOUR CHILDREN IN THE FLOOD
NEHEZ EMBEREK • 1964 • Kovacs Andras • HNG • DIFFICULT PEOPLE
NEHRU • 1962 • Fournier Claude • DOC • USA
NEHRU • 1962 • Leacock Richard, Shuker Gregory • DOC • USA • LIVING CAMERA, THE
NEI-YI-NIEN WO-MEN CH'U KAN HSUEH • 1988 • Li Yu-Ning • TWN • COLD
NEID ODER EIN ANDERER SEIN • 1979 • Pilliod Philippe • SWT
NEIGE • 1981 • Berto Juliet, Roger Jean-Henri • BLG, FRN
NEIGE A FONDU SUR LA MANICOUAGAN • 1965 • Lamothe Arthur • CND
NEIGE A NEIGE, LA • 1951 • Giraldeau Jacques • SHT • CND
NEIGE ETAIT SALE, LA • 1952 • Saslavsky Luis • FRN • SNOW WAS BLACK, THE (USA) ○ STAIN ON THE SNOW, THE
NEIGE SUR LES PAS, LA • 1923 • Etievant Henri • FRN
NEIGE SUR LES PAS, LA • 1941 • Berthomieu Andre • FRN
NEIGES • 1955 • Languepin Jean-Jacques • SHT • FRN
NEIGES DE FRANCE • 1936 • Sussfeld Robert • SHT • FRN
NEIGHBOR PESTS • 1947 • Barclay David • SHT • USA
NEIGHBOR TROUBLE • 1932 • *Sennett Mack (P)* • SHT • USA
NEIGHBORHOOD, THE • 1982 • Katzin Lee H. • TVM • USA
NEIGHBORHOOD HOUSE • 1936 • Parrott Charles, Law Harold • SHT • USA
NEIGHBORHOOD LIGHTS (USA) see **LUCES DE BARRIADA** • 1940
NEIGHBORLY NEIGHBORS • 1914 • *Lubin* • USA
NEIGHBORLY QUARREL, A • 1914 • *Frontier* • USA
NEIGHBORS • 1907 • *Bitzer Billy (Ph)* • USA
NEIGHBORS • 1912 • Sennett Mack • USA
NEIGHBORS • 1913 • *Powers* • USA
NEIGHBORS • 1913 • *Sterling* • USA
NEIGHBORS • 1918 • Crane Frank H. • USA
NEIGHBORS • 1920 • Keaton Buster, Cline Eddie • SHT • USA
NEIGHBORS • 1935 • *Mintz Charles (P)* • ANS • USA
NEIGHBORS • 1981 • Avildsen John G. • USA
NEIGHBORS see **SUJSEDI** • 1970
NEIGHBOR'S KEYHOLE, A • 1918 • Lehrman Henry • SHT • USA
NEIGHBORS' KIDS, THE • 1909 • *Essanay* • USA
NEIGHBOR'S WIVES • 1933 • Eason B. Reeves • USA
NEIGHBOUR see **PADOSAN** • 1968
NEIGHBOUR, THE • 1988 • Peeva Adela • BUL
NEIGHBOUR, THE see **MAN IN 5A, THE** • 1982
NEIGHBOUR, THE see **NACHBAR, DER** • 1990
NEIGHBOURHOOD, THE see **MISSION HILL** • 1982
NEIGHBOURHOOD: MISSION HILL, THE see **MISSION HILL** • 1982
NEIGHBOURING FLATS • 1911 • Wilson Frank? • UKN
NEIGHBOURS • 1912 • Haldane Bert? • UKN
NEIGHBOURS • 1917 • Wilson Frank • UKN
NEIGHBOURS • 1952 • McLaren Norman, Munro Grant • ANS • CND • VOISINS
NEIGHBOURS see **PARDOSI** • 1941
NEIGHBOURS see **AAMNE SAMNE** • 1967
NEIGHBOURS see **VECINOS** • 1981
NEIGHBOURS, THE see **SASIEDZI** • 1969
NEIGHBOURS UNDER FIRE • 1940 • Bond Ralph • UKN
NEIGHBOUR'S WIFE AND MINE, THE see **MADAMU TO NYOBO** • 1931
NEIGUNGSEHE see **FAMILIE BUCHHOLZ** • 1944
NEIL CHOTEM AU CLAVIER see **HANDS IN HARMONY** • 1950
NEIL GOW MAD • 1910 • *Urban Trading Co* • UKN
NEIL GUNN: LIGHT IN THE NORTH • 1973 • Alexander Mike • DOC • UKN
NEIL SIMON'S SEEMS LIKE OLD TIMES see **SEEMS LIKE OLD TIMES** • 1980
NEIT TEVERGEEFS (NTH) see **BUT NOT IN VAIN** • 1948
NEITHER AT HOME OR ABROAD see **SE KI, SE BE** • 1918
NEITHER BLOOD NOR SAND see **NI SANGRE NI ARENA** • 1941
NEITHER BY DAY NOR BY NIGHT • 1974 • Stern Steven Hilliard • USA, ISR
NEITHER IN NOR OUT see **SE KI, SE BE** • 1918
NEITHER THE SEA NOR THE SAND • 1972 • Burnley Fred • UKN
NEJISTA SEZONA • 1987 • Smoljak Ladislav • CZC • UNCERTAIN SEASON
NEJKRASNEJSI VEK • 1968 • Papousek Jaroslav • CZC • MOST BEAUTIFUL AGE, THE (USA) ○ BEST AGE, THE
NEJLEPSI ZENSKA MEHO ZIVOTE • 1967 • Fric Martin • CZC • BEST GIRL IN THE WORLD, THE ○ BEST WOMAN IN MY LIFE, THE ○ BEST GIRL I EVER HAD, THE
NEJVETSI PRANI • 1966 • Spata Jan • CZC • BIGGEST WISH, THE
NEKA DRUGA ZENA • 1981 • Stamenkovic Miodrag-Miki • YGS • SOME OTHER WOMAN
NEKO TO KATSUOBUSHI • 1961 • Horikawa Hiromichi • JPN • CAT AND DRIED BONITO
NEKO TO SHOZO TO FUTARI NO ONNA • 1956 • Toyoda Shiro • JPN • SHOZO, A CAT AND TWO WOMEN ○ CAT, SHOZO AND TWO WOMEN, A ○ CAT AND TWO WOMEN, A
NEKRI POLITIA • 1951 • Iliadis Frixos • GRC • CITE MORTE, LA
NEKSUKE • 1961 • Crama Nico • SHT • NTH
NEL BENE E NEL MALE (ITL) see **VIE CONJUGALE, LA** • 1964
NEL BLU DIPINTO DI BLU • 1959 • Tellini Piero • ITL
NEL BUIO DEL TERRORE • 1972 • Albagnan C. • ITL
NEL CERCHIO • 1977 • Minello Gianni • ITL
NEL GIORNO DEL SIGNORE • 1970 • Corbucci Bruno • ITL
NEL GORGO DEL PECCATO • 1955 • Cottafavi Vittorio • ITL
NEL LABIRINTO DEL SESSO • 1969 • Brescia Alfonso • ITL • LABYRINTH OF SEX, THE (UKN) ○ SEXUAL INADEQUACIES ○ SESSO (USA)
NEL MEZZOGIORNO QUALCOSA E CAMBIATO • 1950 • Lizzani Carlo • DOC • ITL
NEL MIRINO DI BLACK APHRODITE see **BLACK APHRODITE** • 1977
NEL NIDO STRANIERO • 1914 • Negroni Baldassare • ITL
NEL NOME DEL PADRE • 1971 • Bellocchio Marco • ITL • IN THE NAME OF THE FATHER ○ IN NOME DEL PADRE
NEL PAESE DEI SOGNI • 1906 • Velle Gaston • ITL • IN DREAMLAND (USA)
NEL PIU ALTO DEI CIELI • 1976 • Agosti Silvano • ITL
NEL RAGGIO DEL MIO BRACCIO • 1971 • Trentin Giorgio • ITL
NEL REGNO DEI SOGNI • SHT • ITL • IN THE KINGDOM OF DREAMS (USA)
NEL REGNO DI NAPOLI see **NEAPOLITANISCHE GESCHWISTER** • 1978
NEL SEGNO DI ROMA • 1959 • Brignone Guido, Antonioni Michelangelo • ITL, FRN, FRG • SOUS LA SIGNE DE ROME (FRN) ○ SIGN OF THE GLADIATOR (USA) ○ REGINA DEL DESERTO, LA
NEL SILENZIO DELL'URUGUAY • 1988 • Soldini Bruno • SWT
NEL SOLE • 1967 • Grimaldi Aldo • ITL • UNDER THE SUN
NELA –DIE GESCHICHTE EINER MALERIN • 1980 • Fischer Hans Conrad • AUS • NELA –THE STORY OF A PAINTER
NELA –THE STORY OF A PAINTER see **NELA –DIE GESCHICHTE EINER MALERIN** • 1980
NELJA RAKKAUTTA –FYRA GANGER KARLEK see **KVINNAN BAKOM ALLT** • 1951
NELL • 1929 • Aylott Dave, Symmons E. F. • SHT • UKN
NELL DALE'S MEN FOLKS • 1916 • Borzage Frank • SHT • USA
NELL GWYN • 1934 • Wilcox Herbert • UKN
NELL GWYN (USA) see **NELL GWYNNE** • 1926
NELL GWYNN THE ORANGE GIRL • 1911 • Bouwmeester Theo • UKN
NELL GWYNNE • 1914 • *Stuart Nell* • USA
NELL GWYNNE • 1926 • Wilcox Herbert • UKN • NELL GWYN (USA)
NELL OF THE CIRCUS • 1914 • *Spooner Cecil* • USA
NELL OF THE DANCE HALL • 1915 • Melville Wilbert • USA
NELL OF THE PAMPAS • 1912 • Dwan Allan • USA
NELLA CITTA L'INFERNO • 1958 • Castellani Renato • ITL, FRN • AND THE WILD, WILD WOMEN (USA) ○ ENFER DANS LA VILLE, L' (FRN) ○ HELL IN TOWN ○ CAGED
NELLA MISURA IN CUI.. • 1979 • Vivarelli Piero • ITL
NELLA PROFONDA LUCE DEI SENSI (ITL) see **MESSE DOREE, LA** • 1975
NELLA STRETTA MORSA DEL RAGNO • 1971 • Margheriti Antonio • ITL, FRN, FRG • DRACULA IM SCHLOSS DES SCHRECKENS (FRG) ○ WEB OF THE SPIDER (USA) ○ E VENNE L'ALBA.. MA TINTA DIROSSO ○ IN THE GRIP OF THE SPIDER ○ AND COMES THE DAWN.. BUT COLORED RED ○ FRN ○ FANTOMES DE HURLEVENT, LES
NELLA TORMENTA see **TORMENTA** • 1923
NELL'AGRO PONTINO • 1978 • Ferrari Nicolo • ITL
NELL'ANNO DEL SIGNORE • 1969 • Magni Luigi • ITL

NELL'ANNO DELLA CONTESTAZIONE see **DON FRANCO E DON CICCIO NELL'ANNO DELLA CONTESTAZIONE** • 1970
NELL'ANNO DELLA LUNA • 1970 • Marcellini Romolo • ITL
NELLE LUCE DI ROMA • 1938 • *Fusco Giovanni (M)* • SHT • ITL
NELLE PIEGHE DELLA CARNE • 1970 • Bergonzelli Sergio • ITL
NELLIE OF THE CIRCUS • 1939 • Lovy Alex • ANS • USA
NELLIE, THE BEAUTIFUL CLOAK MODEL • 1924 • Flynn Emmett J. • USA
NELLIE, THE FIREMAN'S DAUGHTER • 1917 • *Victor* • USA
NELLIE, THE INDIAN CHIEF'S DAUGHTER • 1938 • *Lantz Walter (P)* • ANS • USA
NELLIE, THE PRIDE OF THE FIRE HOUSE • 1915 • *Moran Lee* • USA
NELLIE, THE SEWING MACHINE GIRL • 1938 • Lovy Alex • ANS • USA
NELLIE'S FARM • 1910 • *Vitagraph* • USA
NELLIE'S NAUGHTY BOARDER • 1919 • Griffin Frank C. • SHT • USA
NELLIE'S NIFTIE NECKLACE • 1917 • *Vim* • USA
NELLIE'S SOLDIER • 1911 • *Solax* • USA
NELL'OCCHIO DELLA VOLPE • 1979 • Drove Antonio • ITL
NELL'S EUGENIC WEDDING • 1914 • *Komic* • USA
NELL'S LAST DEAL • 1911 • *Edison* • USA
NELL'S YELLS • 1939 • Iwerks Ub • ANS • USA
NELLY • 1915 • *Britannia* • UKN
NELLY, DIE BRAUT OHNE MANN • 1923 • Zelnik Friedrich • FRG
NELLY LA GIGOLETTE • 1914 • Ghione Emilio • ITL
NELLY THE PRETTY TYPEWRITER • 1908 • Porter Edwin S. • USA
NELLY'S FOLLY • 1961 • Jones Charles M. • ANS • USA
NELLY'S STRATEGY • 1915 • *Farrington Reenie* • USA
NELLY'S VERSION • 1983 • Hatton Maurice • TVM • UKN
NELSON • 1918 • Elvey Maurice • UKN
NELSON • 1926 • Summers Walter • UKN
NELSON AFFAIR, THE see **BEQUEST TO THE NATION, A** • 1973
NELSON TOUCH, THE see **HIS LORDSHIP** • 1936
NELSON TOUCH, THE (UKN) see **CORVETTE K-225** • 1943
NELSON'S VICTORY • 1907 • Gilbert Arthur • UKN
NELU • 1988 • Doroftei Dorin Mircea • RMN
NEM • 1965 • Revesz Gyorgy • HNG • NO
NEM AMANTES NEM AMIGOS • 1971 • Vitorino Orlando • PRT
NEM ELHETEK MUZSIKASZO NELKUL • 1979 • Sik Ferenc • HNG • MUSIC'S THE THING, THE
NEM TUDO E VERDADE • 1986 • Sganzerla Rogerio • BRZ • IT'S NOT ALL TRUE
NEM VAROK HOLNAPIG • 1967 • Kormos Gyula • HNG • I WON'T WAIT TILL TOMORROW
NEMA BARIKADA • 1949 • Vavra Otakar • CZC • SILENT BARRICADE, THE
NEMA KIALTAS • 1982 • Meszaros Marta • HNG • SILENT CRY
NEMAI • 1971 • Saito Koichi • JPN
NEMAN I VI • 1964 • Kolar Boris • ANS • YGS • MONSTER AND I, THE (USA) ○ MONSTER AND YOU, THE
N'EMBRASSEZ PAS LA BONNE • 1914 • Linder Max • FRN
NEMESIS! • 1912 • *Brooke Van Dyke* • USA
NEMESIS • 1921 • Gallone Carmine • ITL
NEMESIS • 1929 • Eveleigh Leslie • UKN
NEMESIS • 1949 • Bulleid H. A. V. • UKN
NEMESIS • 1989 • Perry Steve • USA
NEMESIS see **FAEDRENES SYND** • 1914
NEMESIS see **JUGENDRAUSCH** • 1927
NEMESIS, THE • 1910 • *Centaur* • USA
NEMESIS, THE • 1915 • King Henry • SHT • USA • BRAND OF MAN, THE
NEMESIS AND THE CANDY MAN • 1918 • Miller Ashley • SHT • USA
NEMESIS THAT PASSED, THE • 1914 • *Victor* • USA
NEMICA, LA • 1952 • Bianchi Giorgio • ITL
NEMICI PER LA PELLE -IL TATUATO (ITL) see **TATOUE, LE** • 1968
NEMICO, IL • 1943 • Giannini Guglielmo • ITL
NEMICO DI MIA MOGLIE, IL • 1959 • Puccini Gianni • ITL • MY WIFE'S ENEMY (USA)
NEMICO PUBBLICO N.1, IL (ITL) see **ENNEMI PUBLIC NO.1** • 1953
NEMIDAREZUMA • 1968 • Yamamoto Shinya • JPN • OBSCENE WIFE
NEMIR • 1983 • Imanovic Ahmet Adi • YGS • UNREST
NEMIRNI • 1967 • Rakonjac Kokan • YGS • RESTLESS ONES, THE ○ NAUGHTY ONES, THE
NEMLI DUDAKLAR • 1967 • Utku Umit • TRK • MOIST LIPS
NEMLI GOZLER • 1967 • Pekmezoglu Oksal • TRK • MOIST EYES
NEMO • 1983 • de Selignac Arnaud • FRN
NEMODLENIC • 1927 • Kubasek Vaclav • CZC • MAN WHO WENT OUT OF FASHION, THE
NEMONOGATARI • 1967 • Kataoka Hitoshi • JPN • BED STORY
NEMU NO KI NO UTA • 1973 • Miyagi Mariko • JPN • BALLAD OF SILK TREE
NEMU NO KI NO UTA GA KIKOERU • 1976 • Miyagi Mariko • JPN • BALLAD OF SILK TREE, PART 2
NEMURERU BIJO • 1968 • Yoshimura Kozaburo • JPN • HOUSE OF THE SLEEPING VIRGINS, THE ○ SLEEPING BEAUTY
NEMURI KYOSHIRO BURAIHIKAE: MASHO NO HADA • 1967 • Ikehiro Kazuo • JPN • TRAIL OF TRAPS, THE ○ MASHO NO HADA
NEMURI KYOSHIRO HITOHADAGUMO • 1968 • Yasuda Kimiyoshi • JPN • HUMAN TARANTULA, THE
NEMURI KYOSHIRO ONNA JIGOKU • 1968 • Tanaka Tokuzo • JPN • RONIN CALLED NEMURI, THE
NEMURITORII • 1974 • Nicolaescu Sergiu • RMN • IMMORTALS, THE
NENANTE NENE • 1968 • Ramachandra Rao V. • IND • I AM INDISPENSABLE
NENAS DEL 7, LAS • 1954 • Rodriguez Roberto • MXC
NENAS DEL MINI-MINI, LAS • 1969 • Lorente German • SPN
NENAVIST • 1978 • Gasparov Samuel • USS • HATRED
NENE • 1923 • de Baroncelli Jacques • FRN
NENE • 1977 • Samperi Salvatore • ITL
NENE BANDACHO • 1970 • Fontana Emilio • BRZ
NENE MONAGANNI • 1968 • Lal S. D. • IND • I AM THE COMPETENT
NENI STALE ZAMRACENO • 1950 • Kachyna Karel, Jasny Vojtech • CZC • CLOUDS WILL ROLL AWAY, THE
NENJIRUKKUM VARAI • 1967 • Sridhar C. V. • IND • TILL THE HEART IS THERE
NENNELLA • 1949 • May Renato • ITL
NEO-IMPRESSIONIST PAINTER, THE (USA) see **PEINTRE NEO-IMPRESSIONISTE, LE** • 1910
NEO-QUEBECOIS, LES • 1967 • Lavoie Richard • DCS • CND
NEOBHODIMIYAT GRESHNIK • 1971 • Shariliev Borislav • BUL • INDISPENSABLE SINNER, THE
NEOBYCEJNA LETA • 1952 • Kachyna Karel, Jasny Vojtech • CZC • EXTRAORDINARY YEARS ○ UNUSUAL YEARS
NEOBYCHAINIYE PRIKLUCHENIYA MISTERA VESTA V STRANYE BOLSHEVIKOV • 1924 • Kuleshov Lev • USS • EXTRAORDINARY ADVENTURES OF MR. WEST IN THE LAND OF THE BOLSHEVIKS
NEOBYKNOVENNAIA VYSTAVKA • 1968 • Shengelaya Eldar • USS • UNUSUAL EXHIBITION, THE ○ ARACHVEULEBRIVI GAMOPENA ○ EXTRAORDINARY EXHIBITION, AN
NEOKONCHENNAYA POVEST • 1955 • Ermler Friedrich • USS • UNFINISHED STORY, AN
NEOKONTCHENNIA PIESSA DLIA MEKANITCHESKOVO PIANINA • 1977 • Mikhalkov Nikita • USS • UNFINISHED WORK FOR MECHANICAL PIANO ○ MECHANICAL PIANO, THE ○ UNFINISHED PIECE FOR PLAYER-PIANO ○ UNFINISHED PIECE FOR MECHANICAL PIANO
NEON • 1980 • Kleindl Gerhard • AUS
NEON, AN ELECRIC MEMOIR • 1986 • Buttignol Rudy • DCS • CND
NEON CEILING, THE • 1970 • Pierson Frank R. • TVM • USA
NEON EPIGRAM, A see **NEONOWA FRASZKA** • 1959
NEON JUNGLE see **NEON TAIHEIKI-KEIEIGAKU NYUMON** • 1967
NEON MAN, THE see **HOME DE NEO, L'** • 1988
NEON MANIACS, THE • 1986 • Mangine Joe • USA
NEON NIGHTS • 1982 • Howard Cecil • USA
NEON PALACE, THE • 1971 • Rowe Peter • CND
NEON TAIHEIKI see **NEON TAIHEIKI-KEIEIGAKU NYUMON** • 1967
NEON TAIHEIKI-KEIEIGAKU NYUMON • 1967 • Isomi Tadahiko • JPN • NEON JUNGLE ○ NEON TAIHEIKI
NEON TRIFLE, THE see **NEONOWA FRASZKA** • 1959
NEONOWA FRASZKA • 1959 • Giersz Witold • ANS • PLN • NEON EPIGRAM, A ○ NEON TRIFLE, THE
NEOPOLITAN BOYS see **SCUGNIZZI** • 1990
NEOPOLITAN MOUSE • 1954 • Hanna William, Barbera Joseph • ANS • USA
NEOTPRAVLENNOE PISMO • 1960 • Kalatozov Mikhail • USS • LETTER THAT WAS NEVER SENT, THE (USA) ○ LETTER THAT WASN'T SENT, THE ○ UNPOSTED LETTER, THE ○ UNSENT LETTER, THE
NEOVY KNOVENNYI MACH • 1955 • Paschenko Mstilav, Dezhkin B. • ANS • USS • UNUSUAL MATCH, AN
NEPHEW'S ARTIFICE, A • 1911 • Haldane Bert? • UKN
NEPHEW'S FROM LABRADOR, THE • 1913 • *Thanhouser* • USA
NEPOBEDIMYIE • 1942 • Kalatozov Mikhail, Gerasimov Sergei • USS • UNCONQUERABLE, THE ○ INVINCIBLE
NEPOKORENNYE • 1945 • Donskoi Mark • USS • UNVANQUISHED, THE ○ TARAS FAMILY, THE ○ UNCONQUERED ○ SEMYA TARASSA
NEPORAZENI • 1956 • Sequens Jiri • CZC • UNVANQUISHED, THE ○ UNCONQUERED, THE
NEPOSYEDY • 1968 • Naroditski Arkadi, Ivanov Viktor • USS • RESTLESS ONES, THE
N'EPOUSE PAS TA FILLE • 1933 • Rozier Willy • FRN
NEPOVODENY PANACEK • 1951 • Tyrlova Hermina, Wallo K. M. • SHT • CZC • MISFIT, THE ○ MISFIT FIGURE, THE ○ BADLY-MADE PUPPET, THE
NEPOVTORIMAYA VESNA • 1957 • Stolper Alexander • USS • UNFORGETTABLE SPRING ○ UNREPEATABLE SPRING
NEPPU • 1934 • Uchida Tomu • JPN • HOT WIND
NEPPU • 1943 • Yamamoto Satsuo • JPN • HOT WIND
NEPRIJATELJ see **SOVRAZNIK** • 1965
NEPRIMIRIMITE • 1964 • Yankov Yanko • BUL • INTRANSIGENTS, THE
NEPROSHENAYA LYUBOV • 1964 • Monakhov Vladimir • USS • UNWILLING LOVE ○ UNINVITED LOVE
NEPTUNE AND AMPHITRITE (USA) see **NEPTUNE ET AMPHITRITE** • 1899
NEPTUNE DISASTER, THE see **NEPTUNE FACTOR, THE** • 1973
NEPTUNE ET AMPHITRITE • 1899 • Melies Georges • FRN • NEPTUNE AND AMPHITRITE (USA)
NEPTUNE FACTOR, THE • 1973 • Petrie Daniel • CND • NEPTUNE FACTOR -AN UNDERSEA ODYSSEY, THE ○ CONQUEST OF THE DEEPS ○ NEPTUNE DISASTER, THE ○ UNDERWATER ODYSSEY, AN
NEPTUNE FACTOR -AN UNDERSEA ODYSSEY, THE see **NEPTUNE FACTOR, THE** • 1973
NEPTUNE NONSENSE • 1936 • Gillett Burt, Palmer Tom • ANS • USA
NEPTUNE'S BRIDE • 1920 • Peacocke Leslie T. • USA
NEPTUNE'S DAUGHTER • 1912 • Cabanne W. Christy • USA
NEPTUNE'S DAUGHTER • 1914 • Brenon Herbert, Turner Otis • USA
NEPTUNE'S DAUGHTER • 1922 • Shipman Nell • USA
NEPTUNE'S DAUGHTER • 1949 • Buzzell Edward • USA
NEPTUNE'S DAUGHTERS • 1903 • *Biograph* • USA
NEPTUNE'S NAUGHTY DAUGHTER • 1917 • Blystone John G. • SHT • USA
NER VAZHI • 1968 • Balu M. G. • IND • STRAIGHT PATH
NERACA KASIH • 1983 • Sulaiman Hengky • INN • SCALES OF LOVE, THE
NERAWARETA OTOKO • 1956 • Nakahira Ko • JPN • MAN SPIED ON, A
NERDS STRIKE BACK, THE see **SURF II** • 1984
NERFS A VIF, LES • Ciampi Yves • FRN
NERIKEJ MI VA SIKU • 1972 • Pojar Bretislav • ANM • CZC • DON'T CALL ME VASICK
NERINA • 1915 • Lolli Alberto Carlo • ITL
NERO • 1922 • Edwards J. Gordon • USA, ITL
NERO see **NERONE** • 1930
NERO AND THE BURNING OF ROME • 1908 • Porter Edwin S. • USA
NERO AND THE BURNING OF ROME (USA) see **NERONE E MESSALINA** • 1953
NERO MUOVE, IL • 1977 • Serra Gianni • MTV • ITL
NERO SU BIANCO • 1969 • Brass Tinto • ITL, UKN • BLACK ON WHITE (USA) ○ ARTFUL PENETRATION, THE ○ SHAMEFUL ○ ATTRACTION (UKN) ○ ARTFUL PENETRATION OF BARBARA, THE ○ NEROSUBIANCO
NERO VENEZIANO • 1978 • Liberatore Ugo • ITL • DAMNED IN VENICE
NERO WOLFE • 1977 • Gilroy Frank D. • TVM • USA
NERONE • 1909 • Maggi Luigi • ITL
NERONE • 1930 • Blasetti Alessandro • ITL • NERO
NERONE • 1977 • Castellacci Mario, Pingitore Pier Francesco • ITL
NERONE '71 • 1962 • Filippi Walter • ITL
NERONE E AGRIPPINA • 1913 • Caserini Mario • ITL
NERONE E MESSALINA • 1953 • Zeglio Primo • ITL • NERO AND THE BURNING OF ROME (USA)
NERO'S BIG WEEKEND see **MIO FIGLIO NERONE** • 1956
NERO'S MISTRESS (USA) see **MIO FIGLIO NERONE** • 1956
NERO'S WEEKEND see **MIO FIGLIO NERONE** • 1956
NEROSUBIANCO see **NERO SU BIANCO** • 1969
NERUA • 1967 • Nishihara Giichi • JPN • TO AIM AT..
NERVE • 1914 • *Balboa* • USA
NERVE AND GASOLINE • 1916 • *Plump & Runt* • USA
NERVEN • 1919 • Reinert Robert • FRG
NERVES AND THE MAN • 1912 • *Mcdermott Marc* • USA
NERVIO, SUPER-SUPER & WAGNER AGAINST THE POWER OF WORLD DARKNESS see **NERVIO, SUPER-SUPER Y WAGNER CONTRA LA NOCHE NEGRA DEL MUNDO** • 1980
NERVIO, SUPER-SUPER Y WAGNER CONTRA LA NOCHE NEGRA DEL MUNDO • 1980 • Bejo Miguel • ARG • NERVIO, SUPER-SUPER & WAGNER AGAINST THE POWER OF WORLD DARKNESS
NERVO AND KNOX • 1926 • Newman Widgey R. • UKN • CAMERA COCKTALES
NERVOUS CURATE, THE • 1910 • Stow Percy • UKN
NERVOUS LEO • 1913 • *Imp* • USA
NERVOUS WRECK, THE • 1926 • Sidney Scott • USA
NERVY NAT KISSES THE BRIDE • 1904 • Porter Edwin S. • USA
NERZE NACHTS AM STRASSENRAND • 1973 • Staudte Wolfgang • MTV • FRG
NESCHOVAVAJTE SE KDYZ PRSI • 1962 • Brynych Zbynek • CZC • DON'T TAKE SHELTER WHEN IT RAINS ○ DON'T TAKE SHELTER FROM THE RAIN
NESHKA ROBEVA AND HER GIRLS • 1985 • Dyulgerov Georgi • BUL • GIRLS AND THEIR NESHKA ROBEVA, THE
NESKOLKO DNEI IZ ZHIZNI I.I. OBLOMOV • 1980 • Mikhalkov Nikita • USS • FEW DAYS IN THE LIFE OF I.I. OBLOMOV, A ○ OBLOMOV
NESKOLKO INTERVYU PO LICHNYM VOPROSAM • 1980 • Gogoberidze Lana • USS • SEVERAL INTERVIEWS ON PERSONAL MATTERS ○ PERSONAL PROBLEMS ○ INTERVIEWS ON PERSONAL PROBLEMS ○ SEVERAL INTERVIEWS ON PRIVATE MATTERS
NESMRTELNA LASKA • 1961 • Hruby Miloslav • CZC • IMMORTAL LOVE
NESPOKOEN PAT • 1955 • Bratanov Ivan, Dakovski Dako • BUL • TROUBLED ROAD
NESS BA'AYARA • 1968 • Filer Leo • ISR • MIRACLE IN THE TOWN, A ○ MIRACLE, THE
NESSA NO BYAKURAN • 1951 • Kimura Keigo • JPN • WHITE ORCHID OF THE HEATING DESERT
NESSA NO CHIKAI • 1941 • Watanabe Kunio • JPN • VOW IN THE DESERT
NESSAA BALA RAJAL • 1952 • Shahin Youssef • EGY • WOMEN WITHOUT MEN ○ NISA' BILA RIJAL
NESSEBUR • Topaldgikov Stefan • BUL
NESSEF EL AKHAR, AL • 1967 • Badrakhan Ahmed • EGY • SECOND HALF, THE
NESSUNO E PERFETTO • 1983 • Festa Campanile Pasquale • ITL
NESSUNO HA TRADITO • 1954 • Montero Roberto Bianchi • ITL
NESSUNO MI PUO GIUDICARE • 1966 • Fizzarotti Ettore Maria • ITL
NESSUNO O TUTTI • 1975 • Agosti Silvano, Petraglia Sandro, Bellocchio Marco, Rulli Stefano • ITL
NESSUNO TORNO INDIETRO • 1943 • Blasetti Alessandro • ITL • ISTITUTO GRIMALDI
NEST, DAS • 1967 • Mayrhofer Friedrich • FRG
NEST, THE • 1927 • Nigh William • USA
NEST, THE • 1943 • Anger Kenneth • USA
NEST, THE • 1988 • Winkless Terence H. • USA
NEST, THE see **NID, LE** • 1926
NEST, THE see **GNIAZDO** • 1974
NEST, THE see **GHARAONDA** • 1977
NEST, THE see **NIDO, EL** • 1980
NEST EGG • 1949 • Harvey Maurice • DOC • UKN
NEST IN THE WIND see **GNEZDO NA VETRU** • 1981
NEST OF CHAMPIONS see **NARRIO DE CAMPEONES** • 1983
NEST OF GENTLEFOLK, A (UKN) see **DVORIANSKOE GNEZDO** • 1969
NEST OF SHADOWS • 1976 • Carter Peter • MTV • CND
NEST OF SPIES see **RAGGIO INFERNALE, IL** • 1967
NEST OF SPIES (USA) see **ALERTE AU DEUXIEME BUREAU** • 1956
NEST OF THE CUCKOO BIRDS, THE • 1965 • Williams Bert • USA
NEST OF THE GENTRY, A see **DVORIANSKOE GNEZDO** • 1969
NEST OF VIPERS see **RITRATTO DI BORGHESIA IN NERO** • 1978
NEST OF VIRGINS, THE see **RINCON DE LAS VIRGENES, EL** • 1972
NEST OF WIND see **GNEZDO NA VETRU** • 1981
NEST ON THE BLACK CLIFF, THE • 1913 • Martinek H. O. • UKN

NEST STOP, PARADISE see **NAESTE STOP, PARADIS** • 1981
NEST UNFEATHERED, A • 1914 • O'Sullivan Tony • USA
NESTANAK MAESTRA KOKO see **MAESTRO KOKO** • 1969
NESTASNI ROBOT • 1956 • Vukotic Dusan • ANS • YGS • DISOBEDIENT ROBOT, THE ○ PLAYFUL ROBOT, THE
NESTBRUCH • 1981 • Kuert Beat • SWT
NESTERKA • 1955 • Zarkhi Alexander • USS
NESTING, THE • 1981 • Weston Armand • USA
NESTO ISMEDJU • 1983 • Karanovic Srdjan • YGS • SOMETHING IN BETWEEN
NESTOR BURMA DETECTIVE DE CHOC • 1981 • Miesch Jean-Luc • FRN • NESTOR BURMA, SCHLOCK DETECTIVE (UKN)
NESTOR BURMA, SCHLOCK DETECTIVE (UKN) see **NESTOR BURMA DETECTIVE DE CHOC** • 1981
NESTS IN THE SUN • 1944 • Monkman Noel • DOC • ASL
NET, THE • 1916 • Platt George Foster • USA
NET, THE • 1923 • Edwards J. Gordon • USA
NET, THE • 1953 • Asquith Anthony • UKN • PROJECT M 7 (USA)
NET, THE see **RED, LA** • 1953
NET OF DECEIT, THE • 1915 • Millarde Harry • USA
NET OF INTRIGUE, THE • 1917 • Ellis Robert • SHT • USA
NETEPICHNAYA ISTORIA • 1978 • Chukhrai Grigori • USS • UNTYPICAL STORY, AN ○ MIRE, THE
NETHERLANDS, THE see **NEDERLAND** • 1983
NETNOU HOOR DIE KINDERS • 1977 • SAF
N'ETRE QUE DEUX • 1938 • Kapps Walter • FRN
NETS see **REDES** • 1934
NETS OF DESTINY • 1924 • Rooke Arthur • UKN
NETSUAISHA • 1960 • Inoue Kazuo • JPN • DEVOTEE
NETSUDEICHI • 1950 • Ichikawa Kon • JPN • HOT MARSHLAND, THE ○ HEAT AND MUD
NETSUJO NO ICHIYA see **JONETSU NO ICHIYA** • 1929
NETTES PFLANZCHEN, EIN • 1916 • Heidemann Paul • FRG
NETTEZZA URBANA see **N.U.** • 1948
NETTIE'S RIDE • 1912 • *Carter Sydney* • UKN
NETTOYAGE PAR LA VIDE • 1908 • Feuillade Louis • FRN
NETTY OR LETTY • 1914 • Marston Theodore • USA
NETWORK • 1976 • Lumet Sidney • USA
NETZ, DAS • 1975 • Purzer Manfred • FRG
NEU AUSTRALISCHE FILM • 1977 • Thoms Albie • DOC • ASL
NEUE DALILA, DIE • 1918 • Gad Urban • FRG
NEUE FIMMEL, DER • 1960 • Beck Walter • GDR • FOOTBALL CRAZY (UKN)
NEUE GENERATION, DIE see **NARR UND DIE ANDEREN, DER** • 1924
NEUE GROSSMACHT, DIE • 1925 • Prager Wilhelm • FRG
NEUE HEISSE REPORT -WAS MANNER NICHT FUR MOGLICH HALTEN, DER • 1971 • Hofbauer Ernst • FRG • SWINGING WIVES (UKN)
NEUE HERR GENERALDIREKTOR, DER • 1919 • Werckmeister Hans • FRG
NEUE LEBEN, DAS • 1918 • Feher Friedrich • FRG
NEUE SCHREIBTISCH, DER • 1915 • Valentin Karl • FRG • NEW DESK, THE
NEUE SCHULMADCHEN-REPORT 2 • 1971 • Hofbauer Ernst • FRG
NEUE WELT • 1954 • Oertel Curt • FRG
NEUER TAG BRICHT AN, EIN see **WO DER ZUG NICHT LANGE HALT** • 1960
NEUES LEBEN • 1930 • Richter Hans • SWT • NEW LIFE
NEUES LEBEN, EIN • 1922 • Frenkel-Bouwmeester Theo • FRG
NEUES VOM HEXER • 1965 • Vohrer Alfred • FRG • AGAIN THE WIZARD
NEUESBERICHT UBER EINE REISE IN EINE STRAHLENDE ZUKUNFT • 1986 • Erler Rainer • FRG, UKN, ASL • NUCLEAR CONSPIRACY, THE
NEUESTE ERLEBNIS, DAS • 1918 • Meinert Rudolf • FRG
NEUF A TROIS, OU LA JOURNEE D'UNE VEDETTE • 1957 • Leduc • SHT • FRN
NEUF DE TREFLE • 1937 • Mayrargue Lucien • FRN
NEUF ETAGES TOUT ACIER • 1960 • Wronecki • SHT • FRN
NEUF GARCONS, UN COEUR • 1947 • Freedland Georg • FRN
NEULAND • 1924 • Grunwald Willy, Behrendt Hans • FRG • GLUCKHAFT SCHIFF, DAS
NEULOVIMYYE MSTITELI • 1967 • Keosayan Edmond • USS • ELUSIVE AVENGERS, THE
NEUN LEBEN HAT DIE KATZ' • 1968 • Stockl Ula • FRG
NEUNSCHWANZIGE KATZE, DIE see **GATTO A NOVE CODE, IL** • 1971
NEUNZIG MINUTEN NACH MITTERNACHT • 1962 • Goslar Jurgen • FRG • TERROR AFTER MIDNIGHT (USA)
NEUNZIG NACHTE UND EIN TAG see **SETTE CONTRO LA MORTE** • 1965
NEUPLNE ZATMENI • 1982 • Jires Jaromil • CZC • PARTIAL ECLIPSE
NEUROSE • 1959 • Thiele Rolf • ITL, FRG
NEUROSIS see **HELENA Y FERNANDA** • 1970
NEUROTICA • 1970 • Pfandler Helmut • AUS
NEUROTICOS, LOS • 1972 • Olivera Hector • ARG • SEXOANALIZADOS, LOS ○ NEUROTICS, THE ○ SEXANALYSED, THE
NEUROTICS, THE see **NEUROTICOS, LOS** • 1972
NEUTRAL PORT • 1940 • Varnel Marcel • UKN
NEUTRAL WATERS • 1969 • Berenshtein V. • USS
NEUTRALIDAD • 1949 • Ardavin Eusebio F. • SPN
NEUTRON AGAINST THE DEATH ROBOTS (USA) see **AUTOMATAS DE LA MUERTE, LOS** • 1961
NEUTRON AND THE BLACK MASK (USA) see **NEUTRON, EL ENMASCARADO NEGRO** • 1960
NEUTRON AND THE COSMIC BOMB (?) see **NEUTRON VS. THE MANIAC** • 1961
NEUTRON BATTLES THE KARATE ASSASSINS (USA) see **NEUTRON CONTRA LOS ASESINOS DEL KARATE** • 1964
NEUTRON CONTRA EL CRIMINAL SADICO • 1964 • Crevenna Alfredo B. • MXC
NEUTRON CONTRA EL DOCTOR CARONTE • 1960 • Curiel Federico • MXC • NEUTRON VS. THE AMAZING DR. CARONTE (USA)
NEUTRON CONTRA LOS ASESINOS DEL KARATE • 1964 • Crevenna Alfredo B. • MXC • NEUTRON BATTLES THE KARATE ASSASSINS (USA)
NEUTRON, EL ENMASCARADO NEGRO • 1960 • Curiel Federico • MXC • NEUTRON AND THE BLACK MASK (USA) ○ BLACK-MASKED NEUTRON
NEUTRON ET LA FISSION, LE • 1965 • Otero Manuel, Leroux Jacques • DCS • FRN
NEUTRON TRAPS THE INVISIBLE KILLERS • 1964 • *Tec* • MXC
NEUTRON VS. THE AMAZING DR. CARONTE (USA) see **NEUTRON CONTRA EL DOCTOR CARONTE** • 1960
NEUTRON VS. THE MANIAC • 1961 • *Ruvinski Wolf* • MXC • NEUTRON AND THE COSMIC BOMB (?)
NEUVA CIGARRA, LA • 1978 • Siro Fernando • VNZ, ARG • NEW CIGARRA, THE
NEUVAINE, LA • 1914 • Feuillade Louis • FRN
NEUVEU DE BEETHOVEN, LE • 1985 • Morrissey Paul • FRN, AUS, FRG • BEETHOVEN'S NEPHEW (USA)
NEVADA • 1910 • *Powers* • USA
NEVADA • 1915 • *Navajo* • USA
NEVADA • 1927 • Waters John • USA
NEVADA • 1936 • Barton Charles T. • USA
NEVADA • 1944 • Killy Edward • USA
NEVADA BADMEN • 1951 • Collins Lewis D. • USA
NEVADA BUCKAROO, THE • 1931 • McCarthy John P. • USA
NEVADA CITY • 1941 • Kane Joseph • USA
NEVADA CYCLONE • 1934 • Ray Bernard B. • SHT • USA
NEVADA GIRL, A • 1909 • *Centaur* • USA
NEVADA KID • 1972 • Mangini Gino • ITL
NEVADA SMITH • 1966 • Hathaway Henry • USA
NEVADA SMITH • 1975 • Douglas Gordon • TVM • USA
NEVADA TRAIL • 1949 • *Universal* • SHT • USA
NEVADAN, THE • 1950 • Douglas Gordon • USA • MAN FROM NEVADA, THE (UKN)
NEVE NA SERRA • 1959 • Mendes Joao • SHT • PRT
NEVER A BACKWARD STEP • 1967 • Brittain Don, Spotton John, Hammond Arthur • CND • PRESSE ET SON EMPIRE, LA
NEVER A DAY WITHOUT ADVENTURES • 1972 • Vetrov V. • USS
NEVER A DULL MOMENT • 1943 • Lilley Edward • USA
NEVER A DULL MOMENT • 1950 • Marshall George • USA • COME SHARE MY LOVE
NEVER A DULL MOMENT • 1968 • Paris Jerry • USA
NEVER AGAIN • 1910 • *Imp* • USA
NEVER AGAIN • 1910 • Griffith D. W. • USA
NEVER AGAIN • 1912 • *Vitagraph* • USA
NEVER AGAIN • 1912 • *Lubin* • USA
NEVER AGAIN • 1913 • *Rex* • USA
NEVER AGAIN • 1914 • Drew Sidney • USA
NEVER AGAIN • 1915 • *Kb* • USA
NEVER AGAIN • 1915 • *Warner'S Features* • USA
NEVER AGAIN • 1915 • Birch Cecil • UKN
NEVER AGAIN • 1915 • Mix Tom • *Selig* • USA
NEVER AGAIN • 1916 • *Vim* • SHT • USA
NEVER AGAIN • 1916 • *Triangle* • USA
NEVER AGAIN • 1920 • *De Haven Carter* • SHT • USA
NEVER AGAIN, EDDIE • 1916 • Christie Al? • SHT • USA
NEVER AGAIN, NEVER! • 1912 • Fitzhamon Lewin? • UKN
NEVER BACK LOSERS • 1961 • Tronson Robert • UKN
NEVER BE HUMBLE BEFORE ANY LIVING PERSON see **DU SOLLST DICH NIE VOR EINEM LEBENDEN MENSCHEN BUCKEN** • 1978
NEVER BOW DOWN BEFORE A LIVING PERSON! see **DU SOLLST DICH NIE VOR EINEM LEBENDEN MENSCHEN BUCKEN** • 1978
NEVER BUG AND ANT • 1969 • Chiniquy Gerry • ANS • USA
NEVER CAN LIVE LIKE THAT • 1956 • NKR
NEVER COME BACK • 1990 • Bolt Ben • TVM • UKN
NEVER COME BACK see **JUST SMITH** • 1933
NEVER COMPLAIN TO YOUR LAUNDRESS • 1907 • Fitzhamon Lewin • UKN
NEVER CRY WOLF • 1983 • Ballard Carroll • USA
NEVER DESPAIR • 1915 • Birch Cecil • UKN
NEVER-ENDING MEMORY see **CHIU-CH'ING MIEN-MIEN** • 1988
NEVER FEAR • 1950 • Lupino Ida • USA
NEVER FORGET THE RING • 1913 • Haldane Bert • UKN
NEVER GIVE A SUCKER AN EVEN BREAK • 1941 • Cline Eddie • USA • WHAT A MAN! (UKN)
NEVER GIVE AN INCH (UKN) see **SOMETIMES A GREAT NOTION** • 1971
NEVER HIT A WOMAN WITH A FLOWER see **ZENU ANI KVETINOU NEUHODIS** • 1966
NEVER IN YOUR LIFE see **ALDRIG I LIVET** • 1957
NEVER KICK A WOMAN • 1936 • Fleischer Dave • ANS • USA
NEVER KILL A SCORPION see **SCHORPIOEN, DE** • 1984
NEVER KNOWN TO SMILE • 1913 • Dillon Eddie • USA
NEVER LATE: OR, THE CONSCIENTIOUS CLERK • 1909 • Stow Percy • UKN
NEVER LET GO • 1960 • Guillermin John • UKN • MOMENT OF TRUTH
NEVER LET ME GO • 1953 • Daves Delmer • UKN, USA
NEVER LIE TO YOUR WIFE • 1916 • Davey Horace • SHT • USA
NEVER LOOK BACK • 1952 • Searle Francis • UKN
NEVER LOVE A HOOKER see **ONE TWO TWO: 122 RUE DE PROVENCE** • 1978
NEVER LOVE A STRANGER • 1958 • Stevens Robert • USA
NEVER MENTION MURDER • 1964 • Burton John N. • UKN
NEVER MIND THE QUALITY FEEL THE WIDTH • 1972 • Baxter Ronnie • UKN
NEVER MIND TOMORROW see **MARRIED FLAPPER, THE** • 1922
NEVER NEVER LAND see **SECOND STAR TO THE RIGHT** • 1980
NEVER NEVER LAND, THE • 1980 • Ohlsson Terry (c/d) • SHT • ASL
NEVER NEVER MURDER, THE • 1961 • Duffell Peter • UKN
NEVER, NOWHERE.. see **SOHA, SEHOL, SENKINEK..** • 1989
NEVER, NOWHERE, TO NO-ONE! (UKN) see **SOHA, SEHOL, SENKINEK..** • 1989
NEVER ON FRIDAY • 1976 • Dixon Ken • USA
NEVER ON SUNDAY (USA) see **POTE TIN KYRIAKI** • 1959
NEVER ON TUESDAY • 1988 • Riskin Adam • USA
NEVER PUT IT IN WRITING • 1963 • Stone Andrew L. • UKN
NEVER PUT OFF TILL TOMORROW • 1925 • Butler Alexander • UKN
NEVER ROB A MAGICIAN • 1984 • SAF
NEVER SAY DIE • 1920 • Forde Walter • UKN
NEVER SAY DIE • 1924 • Crone George J. • USA
NEVER SAY DIE • 1939 • Nugent Elliott • USA
NEVER SAY DIE • 1950 • Milroy Vivian • UKN • DON'T SAY DIE
NEVER SAY DIE • 1988 • Murphy Geoff • NZL • 007 DOWN SHE GOES ○ PARANOID MAN, THE
NEVER SAY DIE see **SHOWA GENROKU HARENCHI BUSHI** • 1968
NEVER SAY GOODBYE • 1946 • Kern James V. • USA
NEVER SAY GOODBYE • 1956 • Hopper Jerry, Sirk Douglas (U/c) • USA
NEVER SAY NEVER AGAIN • 1983 • Kershner Irvin • UKN, USA
NEVER SAY QUIT • 1919 • Dillon Eddie • USA
NEVER SEND A MAN TO MATCH A RIBBON • 1910 • Fitzhamon Lewin? • UKN
NEVER SHALL I RETURN • 1975 • Ramzi Hassan • EGY
NEVER SHALL INVADERS CONQUER see **SA MANLULUPIG DI KA PASISIIL** • 1968
NEVER SHOULD HAVE TOLD YOU • 1937 • Fleischer Dave • ANS • USA
NEVER SHRINK • 1914 • *Ab* • USA
NEVER SO FEW • 1959 • Sturges John • USA • CAMPAIGN BURMA
NEVER SOCK A BABY • 1939 • Fleischer Dave • ANS • USA
NEVER STEAL ANYTHING SMALL • 1959 • Lederer Charles • USA
NEVER STEAL ANYTHING WET see **CATALINA CAPER** • 1967
NEVER STRIKE A WOMAN EVEN WITH A FLOWER see **ZENU ANI KVETINOU NEUHODIS** • 1966
NEVER SURPRISE YOUR WIFE • 1918 • Christie Al • SHT • USA
NEVER TAKE CANDY FROM A STRANGER (USA) see **NEVER TAKE SWEETS FROM A STRANGER** • 1960
NEVER TAKE NO FOR AN ANSWER (UKN) see **PEPPINO E VIOLETTA** • 1951
NEVER TAKE SWEETS FROM A STRANGER • 1960 • Frankel Cyril • UKN • NEVER TAKE CANDY FROM A STRANGER (USA) ○ MOLESTER, THE
NEVER TEASE A LION see **DO NOT ANNOY THE LION** • 1960
NEVER THE DAMES SHALL MEET • 1927 • Parrott James • SHT • USA
NEVER THE TWAIN SHALL MEET • 1925 • Tourneur Maurice • USA
NEVER THE TWAIN SHALL MEET • 1931 • Van Dyke W. S. • USA
NEVER TO LOVE see **BILL OF DIVORCEMENT, A** • 1940
NEVER TOO LATE • 1925 • Sheldon Forrest • USA
NEVER TOO LATE • 1935 • Ray Bernard B. • USA
NEVER TOO LATE • 1965 • Yorkin Bud • USA
NEVER TOO LATE TO MEND • 1911 • *Solax* • USA
NEVER TOO OLD • 1914 • Murphy J. A. • USA
NEVER TOO OLD • 1919 • Jones F. Richard • SHT • USA
NEVER TOO OLD • 1926 • Roach Hal • SHT • USA
NEVER TOO OLD TO WOO • 1917 • Cochrane George • SHT • USA
NEVER TOO YOUNG TO DIE • 1986 • Bettman Gil • USA
NEVER TOO YOUNG TO ROCK • 1975 • Abey Dennis • UKN
NEVER TOUCHED ME • 1919 • Roach Hal • SHT • USA
NEVER TROUBLE TROUBLE • 1931 • Lane Lupino • UKN
NEVER TRUST A GAMBLER • 1951 • Murphy Ralph • USA
NEVER TRUST AN HONEST THIEF see **GOING FOR BROKE** • 1980
NEVER WAVE AT A WAC • 1952 • McLeod Norman Z. • USA • PRIVATE WORE SKIRTS, THE (UKN) ○ NEWEST PROFESSION, THE
NEVER WEAKEN • 1921 • Newmeyer Fred, Taylor Sam • SHT • USA
NEVER WILL YOU BE ALONE see **KAILANMA'Y DI KA MAG-IISA** • 1968
NEVER WITH MY JEMMY see **ALDRIG MED MIN KOFOT** • 1954
NEVERENDING STORY, THE • 1984 • Petersen Wolfgang • UKN, FRG • UNENDLICHE GESCHICHTE, DIE
NEVERENDING STORY II, THE • 1990 • Miller George • FRG
NEVERMORE, FOREVER • 1979 • Doye Jacqueline • FRN
NEVEROYATNA ISTORIA • 1964 • Yanchev Vladimir • BUL • INCREDIBLE STORY, AN
NEVERTHELESS THEY GO ON see **SHIKAMO KARERA WA YUKU PART I & II** • 1931
NEVERWHERE • 1968 • Wadell Michael • SHT • USA
NEVESINJSKA PUSKA • 1963 • Mitrovic Zika • YGS • GUN FROM NEVESINJE
NEVESTA • 1970 • Suchy Jiri • CZC • BRIDE, THE
NEVESTA • 1971 • Sajtinac Borislav • ANS • YGS
NEVESTKA • 1972 • Narliev Khodzhakuli • USS • DAUGHTER-IN-LAW, THE
NEVETO SZASZKIA, A • 1916 • Korda Alexander • HNG • LAUGHING SASKIA, THE
NEVEU DU PEINTRE, LA • 1988 • Dao Moustapha • SHT • BRK • PAINTER'S NEPHEW, THE
NEVEU SILENCIEUX, UN • 1978 • Enrico Robert • FRN
NEVIDNI BATALJON • 1968 • Kavcic Jane • YGS • INVISIBLE BATTALION, THE
NEVINATKA • 1929 • Innemann Svatopluk • CZC • INNOCENTS, THE
NEVINOST BEZ ZASTITE • 1942 • Aleksic D. • YGS
NEVINOST BEZ ZASTITE • 1968 • Makavejev Dusan • YGS • INNOCENCE UNPROTECTED
NEVITE O BYTE? • 1947 • Zeman Borivoj • CZC • LOOKING FOR A FLAT ○ KNOW OF A FLAT?
NEVJERA • 1953 • Pogacic Vladimir • YGS • EQUINOX
NEVTELEN VAR • 1920 • *Lukas Paul* • HNG
NEW ACRES • 1941 • Baxter R. K. Neilson • UKN
NEW ADAM AND EVE, THE • 1915 • Garrick Richard • USA
NEW ADVENTURES OF A CONNECTICUT YANKEE AT KING ARTHUR'S COURT, THE see **NOVYE PRIKLUCHENIA JANKE PRI DVORE KOVOLA ARTURA** • 1989
NEW ADVENTURES OF BARON MUNCHAUSEN • 1915 • Thornton F. Martin • UKN

NEW ADVENTURES OF BATMAN AND ROBIN, THE see **BATMAN AND ROBIN** • 1949
NEW ADVENTURES OF DR. FU MANCHU, THE see **RETURN OF DR. FU MANCHU, THE** • 1930
NEW ADVENTURES OF DON JUAN, THE (UKN) see **ADVENTURES OF DON JUAN, THE** • 1948
NEW ADVENTURES OF GET-RICH-QUICK WALLINGFORD, THE • 1931 • Wood Sam • USA • GET-RICH-QUICK WALLINGFORD ○ NEW WALLINGFORD, THE
NEW ADVENTURES OF HEIDI, THE • 1978 • Senensky Ralph • TVM • USA
NEW ADVENTURES OF J. RUFUS WALLINGFORD, THE • 1916 • Wharton Theodore • SRL • USA
NEW ADVENTURES OF PIPPI LONGSTOCKING, THE • 1988 • Annakin Ken • USA
NEW ADVENTURES OF SCHWEIK, THE see **NOVIYE POKHOZDENIYA SHVEIKA** • 1943
NEW ADVENTURES OF TARZAN, THE • 1935 • Kull Edward, McGaugh Wilbur • SRL • USA • TARZAN AND THE LOST GODDESS ○ TARZAN IN GUATEMALA
NEW ADVENTURES OF TARZAN, THE • 1935 • McGaugh Wilbur, Kull Edward • USA • TARZAN AND THE GREEN GODDESS (UKN)
NEW ADVENTURES OF TERENCE O'ROURKE, THE • 1915 • Turner Otis • SRL • USA
NEW ADVENTURES OF THE BIONIC BOY, THE see **DYNAMITE JOHNSON** • 1978
NEW ADVENTURES OF THE ELUSIVE • 1969 • Keosayan Edmond • USS
NEW ADVENTURES OF WONDER WOMAN, THE • 1977 • Crosland Alan Jr. • TVM • USA
NEW AFFAIRS OF PETTERSSON AND BENDELS see **PETTERSSON & BENDELS NYA AFFARER** • 1945
NEW AGE OF ARCHITECTURE, THE • 1958 • Krumgold Joseph • USA
NEW ALADDIN, A • 1912 • Wilson Frank? • UKN
NEW ALCHEMISTS, THE • 1974 • Henaut Dorothy Todd • DOC • CND • ALCHIMIE NOUVELLE
NEW AMERICANS • 1945 • Vorkapich Slavko • SHT • USA
NEW ANGELS, THE see **NUOVI ANGELI, I** • 1962
NEW APPRENTICE, THE • 1914 • *Columbus* • USA
NEW APPRENTICE: OR, FUN IN A BAKEHOUSE • 1906 • Green Tom • UKN
NEW ARCHITECTURE (USA) see **NIEUWE ARCHITECTUUR** • 1929
NEW ARK, THE • 1963 • Joseph Stanley • DOC • UKN
NEW ART • 1950 • Makarczynski Tadeusz • DOC • PLN
NEW AUDIOSCOPIKS • 1938 • *Smith Pete* • SHT • USA
NEW AUNT, THE • 1929 • *Sennett Mack (P)* • SHT • USA
NEW AVENGERS: THE EAGLE'S NEST, THE • 1976 • Davis Desmond • TVM • UKN
NEW BABY, THE • 1912 • Sennett Mack • *Ab* • USA
NEW BABY, THE • 1913 • Lehrman Henry • *Keystone* • USA
NEW BABYLON see **NOVYI BABILON** • 1929
NEW BANKROLL, THE • 1929 • Sennett Mack • SHT • USA
NEW BARBARIANS, THE see **NUOVI BARBARI, I** • 1983
NEW BEGINNING, A • 1912 • *Hawley Ormi* • USA
NEW BLACK DIAMOND EXPRESS • 1900 • USA
NEW BLACK EMMANUELLE, THE see **EMANUELLE NERA N.2** • 1975
NEW BOARDER, THE • 1912 • *Cosmopolitan* • UKN
NEW BOSS OF BAR X RANCH, THE • 1910 • *Lubin* • USA
NEW BOY, THE • 1914 • Aylott Dave • UKN
NEW BOY STARTED TODAY, A see **DNESKA PRISEL NOVY KLUK** • 1981
NEW BREAKFAST FOOD, THE • 1919 • *Parsons Smiling Bill* • SHT • USA
NEW BROOMS • 1925 • De Mille William C. • USA
NEW BUILDERS • 1944 • Mander Kay • UKN
NEW BUSHWACKERS • 1968 • USA
NEW BUTLER, THE • 1910 • *Imp* • USA
NEW BUTLER, THE • 1912 • *Majestic* • USA
NEW BUTLER, THE • 1914 • *Shields Ernest* • USA
NEW BUTLER, THE • 1915 • Hotaling Arthur D. • USA
NEW BUTLER, THE see **WALL STREET WHIZ, THE** • 1925
NEW CAR, THE • 1931 • *Iwerks Ub (P)* • ANS • USA
NEW CENTURIONS, THE • 1972 • Fleischer Richard • USA • PRECINCT 45 –LOS ANGELES POLICE (UKN)
NEW CHAMPION • 1925 • Eason B. Reeves • USA
NEW CHANNELS FOR SOCKEYE • 1973 • Jones Peter • DOC • CND
NEW CHIEF, THE • 1909 • *Lubin* • USA
NEW CHILEAN SONG see **NUEVA CANCION CHILENA** • 1973
NEW CHINA, THE see **OSVOBOZHDYONNY KITAI** • 1950
NEW CHURCH CARPET, THE • 1911 • *Brower Robert* • USA
NEW CHURCH ORGAN, THE • 1912 • *Bayne Beverly* • USA
NEW CIGARRA, THE see **NEUVA CIGARRA, LA** • 1978
NEW CITIES OF MACARTHUR • 1980 • Robertson Michael • DOC • ASL
NEW CLASS MANAGEMENT see **SHINSENGUMI SHIMATSUKI** • 1963
NEW CLERK, THE • 1912 • *Majestic* • USA
NEW CLERK, THE • 1912 • *Nestor* • USA
NEW CLOTHES see **UBRANIE PRAWIE NOWE** • 1963
NEW CLOWN, THE • 1916 • Paul Fred • UKN
NEW COMMANDMENT, THE • 1925 • Higgin Howard • USA
NEW CONDUCTOR, THE • 1913 • Sennett Mack • USA
NEW CONGRESSMAN, THE • 1911 • *Yankee* • USA
NEW CONSTABLE, THE • 1912 • *Lubin* • USA
NEW COOK, THE • 1911 • *Stanley Frederick* • USA
NEW COOK, THE • 1911 • Fitzhamon Lewin? • UKN
NEW COOK, THE • 1914 • *Shields Ernest* • USA
NEW COP, THE • 1909 • *Essanay* • USA
NEW COWBOY, THE • 1911 • *Bison* • USA
NEW COWPUNCHER, THE • 1912 • Dwan Allan • USA
NEW CREATURE, A see **NUEVA CRIATURA, UNA** • 1971
NEW CROP, THE • 1944 • Annakin Ken • DCS • UKN
NEW CURE FOR DIVORCE, A • 1912 • *Thanhouser* • USA
NEW CZECHOSLOVAKIA see **NOVE CESKOSLOVENSKO** • 1950
NEW DANCE SERIES • 1920 • *Debenham & Co* • SHS • UKN
NEW DAUGHTERS OF JOSHUA MCCABE, THE • 1976 • Bilson Bruce • TVM • USA
NEW DAY AT SUNDOWN • 1957 • Landres Paul • USA
NEW DAY'S DAWN, THE • 1913 • Miller Ashley • USA
NEW DAYS WILL COME see **SHTE DOIDAT NOVI DNI** • 1945
NEW DEAL, A • 1933 • Lantz Walter, Nolan William • ANS • USA
NEW DEAL SHOW, THE • 1937 • Fleischer Dave • ANS • USA
NEW DEATH PENALTY, A (USA) see **NOUVELLE PEINE DE MORT, LA** • 1907
NEW DELHI TIMES • 1985 • Sharma • IND
NEW DENTIST, THE • 1914 • Collins Edwin J.? • UKN
NEW DESK, THE see **NEUE SCHREIBTISCH, DER** • 1915
NEW DEVIL FROM HELL, A • 1965 • Muur Juri • USS
NEW DISCIPLE, THE • 1921 • Sellers Oliver L. • USA
NEW DIVORCE, THE • 1936 • Florey Robert • USA
NEW DIVORCE CURE, A • 1910 • *Selig* • USA
NEW DOMESTIC ANIMAL see **NOVA DOMACA ZIVOTINJA** • 1964
NEW DRESS, THE • 1907 • Fitzhamon Lewin? • UKN
NEW DRESS, THE • 1911 • Griffith D. W. • USA
NEW DRESS, THE • 1915 • *Eclair* • USA
NEW EARTH • 1946 • Popovic Mihailo • YGS
NEW EARTH see **NIEUWE GRONDEN** • 1934
NEW EARTH, THE see **ATARASHIKI TSUCHI** • 1937
NEW EARTH, THE see **PUTHIYA BHOOMI** • 1968
NEW EDISONS, THE see **PANI EDISONI** • 1987
NEW EDITOR, THE • 1911 • *Duncan William* • USA
NEW EDITOR, THE • 1912 • *Wadsworth William* • USA
NEW EDITOR, THE • 1915 • *Lubin* • USA
NEW ENCHANTMENT, THE see **INHUMAINE, L'** • 1923
NEW ENGLAND IDYL, A • 1914 • Edwards Walter • USA
NEW ENGLAND VISIONS PAST AND FUTURE • 1976 • Emshwiller Ed, Thompson William • USA
NEW EVERY DAY see **TAIYO WA HIBI NI ARATANATI** • 1955
NEW EXCUSE, A • 1910 • *Imp* • USA
NEW EXPLOITS OF ELAINE, THE • 1915 • Seitz George B. • SRL • USA
NEW FACE IN HELL (UKN) see **P.J.** • 1967
NEW FACE ON THE RIVER MEUSE • DOC • NTH
NEW FACES • 1954 • Horner Harry • USA
NEW FACES OF 1937 • 1937 • Jason Leigh • USA
NEW FAITH, THE • 1911 • *Selig* • USA
NEW FAMILY, THE see **ATARASHIKI KAZOKU** • 1939
NEW FARMING IN FRANCE see **MOISSONS D'AUJOURD'HUI** • 1951
NEW-FIE • 1968 • Bonniere Rene • DCS • CND
NEW FIGHTERS SHALL ARISE see **VSTANOU NOVI BOJOVNICI** • 1950
NEW FIRE CHIEF, THE • 1912 • *Imp* • USA
NEW FIST OF FURY, THE see **HSIN CHING-WU MEN** • 1976
NEW FOLKS IN TOWN • 1919 • Harvey John Joseph • SHT • USA
NEW FOOTMAN, THE • 1909 • *Urban-Eclipse* • USA
NEW FRANCE, THE see **NUEVA FRANCIA, LA** • 1972
NEW FRONTIER • 1939 • Sherman George • USA • FRONTIER HORIZON
NEW FRONTIER, THE • 1935 • Pierson Carl • USA
NEW FRONTIER, THE • 1950 • *Leacock Richard* • DCS • USA • YEARS OF CHANGE
NEW FRONTIERS • 1940 • Ivens Joris • USA
NEW FRONTIERSMAN, THE • 1937 • Parfitt Eric • UKN
NEW GAME OF DEATH, THE see **GAME OF DEATH 2** • 1981
NEW GENERATION • 1978 • Lowf-Legoff Jean-Pierre • FRN
NEW GENERATION, THE • 1932 • Legg Stuart • DOC • UKN
NEW GENERATION, THE • 1937 • Field Mary • UKN
NEW GENTLEMEN, THE (USA) see **NOUVEAUX MESSIEURS, LES** • 1929
NEW GILGAMES see **UJ GILGAMES** • 1963
NEW GIRL • 1985 • Ison Charles • USA
NEW GIRL, THE • 1916 • Noy Wilfred? • UKN
NEW GIRL, THE • 1969 • Lyubimov Pavel • USS
NEW GIRL IN TOWN • 1977 • Trikonis Gus • USA
NEW GLADIATORS, THE see **ROME 2033: THE FIGHTER CENTURIONS** • 1983
NEW GODFATHERS, THE • 1978 • Brescia Alfonso • ITL
NEW GOVERNESS, THE • 1909 • *Lubin* • USA
NEW GOVERNESS, THE • 1915 • *Horseshoe* • UKN • GOVERNESS'S LOVE AFFAIR, THE
NEW GOWN, THE • 1913 • *Myers Harry* • USA
NEW GRIEF see **NYONIN AISHU** • 1937
NEW GUINEA PATROL • 1958 • Dimond Peter • DOC • ASL
NEW GULLIVER, A see **NOVYI GULLIVER** • 1935
NEW HALFBACK, THE • 1929 • Sennett Mack • SHT • USA
NEW HAT, THE • 1913 • Stow Percy • UKN
NEW HAT FOR NOTHING, A • 1910 • Fitzhamon Lewin • UKN
NEW HEALERS, THE • 1972 • Kowalski Bernard • TVM • USA
NEW HEART, A see **SERDTSYE BETSYA YNOV** • 1956
NEW HERETICS, THE • 1977 • Engelen Philip • SHS • NTH
NEW HEROES WILL ARISE see **VSTANOU NOVI BOJOVNICI** • 1950
NEW HIRED GIRL, THE • 1908 • *Kalem* • USA
NEW HOMESTEAD, THE • 1938 • *Mintz Charles (P)* • ANS • USA
NEW HORIZONS • 1940 • Cherry Evelyn Spice, Cherry Lawrence W. • DOC • CND
NEW HORIZONS see **VYBORGSKAYA STORONA** • 1939
NEW HORIZONS IN STEEL • 1977 • Benegal Shyam • DOC • IND
NEW HOTEL, THE • 1932 • Mainwaring Bernerd • UKN
NEW HOUSE, THE • 1955 • Badzian Teresa • ANM • PLN
NEW HOUSEKEEPER, THE • 1912 • Noy Wilfred • UKN • WANTED A HOUSEKEEPER
NEW HOUSEKEEPER, THE • 1914 • *Royal* • USA
NEW ICE-AGE, THE see **NIEUWE IJSTIJD, DE** • 1974
NEW IMPROVED INSTITUTIONAL QUALITY • 1975 • Landow George • USA
NEW INITIATIVES • 1950 • Grigorov Roumen • DOC • BUL
NEW INTERNS, THE • 1964 • Rich John • USA
NEW INVISIBLE MAN, THE (USA) see **HOMBRE QUE LOGRO SER INVISIBLE, EL** • 1957
NEW JANITOR, THE • 1914 • Chaplin Charles • USA • BLUNDERING BOOB, THE ○ PORTER, THE
NEW JANITOR, THE • 1916 • McKim Edwin • SHT • USA
NEW JANKO THE MUSICIAN see **NOWY JANKO MUZYKANT** • 1960
NEW JAPANESE CINEMA, THE • 1968 • *Filmmaker'S Distribution Centre* • ANT • JPN
NEW JERSEY NIGHTS • 1979 • Soul Veronika • ANS • CND
NEW JITNEY IN TOWN, THE • 1915 • Lessey George A. • USA
NEW JOKE WITH OLD IRON, A see **GLUMA NOVA CU FIER VECHI** • 1965
NEW JOKE WITH SCRAP IRON, A see **GLUMA NOVA CU FIER VECHI** • 1965
NEW JONAH, THE • *Pathe* • FRN
NEW KID IN TOWN see **PARADISE MOTEL** • 1985
NEW KIDS, THE • 1985 • Cunningham Sean S. • USA • STRIKING BACK
NEW KIND OF LOVE, A • 1963 • Shavelson Melville • USA • SAMANTHA
NEW KIND OF WOMAN, A see **SHIN JOSEI KAGAMI** • 1928
NEW KLONDIKE, THE • 1926 • Milestone Lewis • USA
NEW LAND, THE (USA) see **INVANDRARNA** • 1970
NEW LANDLORD, THE see **UJ FOLDESURM, AZ** • 1988
NEW LEAF, A • 1971 • May Elaine • USA
NEW LEASE OF LIFE see **PONNANA VAZHVU** • 1967
NEW LEASE OF LIFE, A • 1912 • *Republic* • USA
NEW LETTER BOX, THE • 1913 • Stow Percy • UKN
NEW LIFE see **NEUES LEBEN** • 1930
NEW LIFE see **NYETT LIF** • 1983
NEW LIFE, A • 1909 • *Edison* • USA
NEW LIFE, A • 1971 • SAF
NEW LIFE, A • 1988 • Alda Alan • USA
NEW LIFE, A see **SUICIDE'S WIFE, THE** • 1979
NEW LIFE FOR GHAZI, A see **FRONTIER INTERLUDE** • 1951
NEW LIFE STYLE, THE (USA) see **HEISSER SAND AUF SYLT** • 1968
NEW LIGHT see **NAI ROSHNI** • 1967
NEW LIVES FOR OLD • 1925 • Badger Clarence • USA
NEW LORD OF THE VILLAGE, THE see **NOUVEAU SEIGNEUR DU VILLAGE, LE** • 1908
NEW LOT, THE • 1942 • Reed Carol • DOC • UKN
NEW LOVE see **REVOLUCION DE LAS FLORES, LA** • 1968
NEW LOVE FOR OLD • 1918 • Wilson Elsie Jane • USA
NEW MAFIA, THE (USA) see **BOSS, IL** • 1973
NEW MAFIA BOSS, THE see **FAMILIARI DELLE VITTIME NON SARANNO AVVERTITI, I** • 1972
NEW MAGDALEN, THE • 1910 • Golden Joseph A. • USA
NEW MAGDALEN, THE • 1912 • Brenon Herbert • USA
NEW MAGDALEN, THE • 1914 • Vale Travers • USA
NEW MAGIC • 1906 • *Pathe* • SHT • FRN
NEW MAID, THE • 1916 • *Jockey* • USA
NEW MAN, THE see **DRUGI CZLOWIEK** • 1961
NEW MAN, THE see **NOWY** • 1969
NEW MANAGER, THE • 1911 • Baker R. E. • USA
NEW MARITAL RELATIONS see **SHIN MEOTO ZENZAI** • 1963
NEW MARSHAL AT GILA CREEK • 1910 • *Lubin* • USA
NEW MASS, THE • Povh Dusan • SHT • YGS
NEW MAVERICK, THE • 1978 • Averback Hy • TVM • USA
NEW MEDICINE MAN, THE • 1914 • *Darkfeather Mona* • USA
NEW MEMBER OF THE LIFE SAVING CREW, THE • 1912 • *Ogle Charles* • USA
NEW METHOD OF RICE PRODUCTION see **ATARASHII KOMEISUKURI** • 1963
NEW MEXICO • 1951 • Reis Irving • USA
NEW MEXICO see **FOUR FACES WEST** • 1948
NEW MICROBE, THE • 1912 • *Cines* • SHT • ITL
NEW MINISTER • 1922 • *Kingston Muriel* • USA
NEW MINISTER OR THE DRUNKARD'S DAUGHTER, THE • 1909 • *Kalem* • USA
NEW MIRROR, THE • 1909 • *Lubin* • USA
NEW MISSION OF JUDEX, THE (USA) see **NOUVELLE MISSION DE JUDEX, LA** • 1917
NEW MONSTERS, THE see **NUOVI MOSTRI, I** • 1977
NEW MOON • 1930 • Conway Jack • USA • PARISIAN BELLE
NEW MOON • 1940 • Leonard Robert Z. • USA
NEW MOON, THE • 1919 • Withey Chet • USA
NEW MOON, THE • 1970 • Lyman Charles • SHT • USA
NEW MORALS FOR OLD • 1932 • Brabin Charles J. • USA • AFTER ALL
NEW MOTO VALET, THE see **MOTOR VALET, THE** • 1906
NEW MOVIETONE FOLLIES OF 1930 see **FOX MOVIETONE FOLLIES OF 1930** • 1930
NEW MUSIC: BOBBY BRADFORD AND JOHN CARTER, THE • 1980 • Bull Peter L. • SHT • USA
NEW NEIGHBOR, THE • 1912 • Nicholls George, Sennett Mack (Spv) • USA
NEW NEIGHBOR, THE • 1953 • Hannah Jack • ANS • USA
NEW NEWS • 1938 • Lamont Charles • SHT • USA
NEW NIAGARA, THE • 1932 • Sparling Gordon • DCS • CND
NEW NOVA SCOTIA • 1962 • Perry Margaret • DOC • CND
NEW NUMBER, THE see **NOVYI ATTRAKTION** • 1957
NEW OFFICER, THE • 1911 • *Lubin* • USA
NEW OLD • 1979 • Clementi Pierre • FRN
NEW ONE-ARMED SWORDSMAN, THE • 1972 • Chang Ch'Eh • HKG • TRIPLE IRONS
NEW OPERATOR, THE • 1911 • *Lubin* • USA
NEW OPERATOR, THE • 1932 • Legg Stuart • DOC • UKN
NEW ORDER AT SJOGARDA see **NYORDNING PA SJOGARDA** • 1944
NEW ORIGINAL WONDER WOMAN, THE • 1975 • Horn Leonard • TVM • USA
NEW ORLEANS • 1929 • Barker Reginald • USA
NEW ORLEANS • 1947 • Lubin Arthur • USA
NEW ORLEANS AFTER DARK • 1958 • Sledge John • USA
NEW ORLEANS BLUES • 1943 • Berne Josef • SHT • USA
NEW ORLEANS BLUES see **BLUES IN THE NIGHT** • 1941
NEW ORLEANS JAZZ • Genns Karl • USA
NEW ORLEANS UNCENSORED • 1955 • Castle William • USA • RIOT ON PIER SIX (UKN)
NEW OWNER OF THE BUSINESS, THE • 1912 • Rains Fred • UKN
NEW PAIN KILLER • 1909 • *Gaumont* • SHT • FRN
NEW PARADISE CINEMA see **NUOVO CINEMA PARADISO** • 1988
NEW PARIS LIDO CLUB BAND, THE • 1928 • *De Forest Phonofilms* • UKN
NEW PARK-KEEPER, THE • 1910 • Rains Fred • UKN
NEW PARTNER, THE • 1910 • *Bison* • USA
NEW PARTNER, THE • 1914 • West Langdon • USA
NEW PASTURES • 1940 • Heyer John • DOC • ASL
NEW PEOPLE, THE • 1969 • Sasdy Peter • MTV • UKN

NEW PEOPLE FOR OLD • 1969 • Kreps Bonnie • CND
NEW PERSONAL HISTORY OF LOVE AFFAIRS see **SHIN JOJI NO RIREKISHO** • 1967
NEW PHOTOGRAPHER, THE • 1915 • *Superba* • USA
NEW PHYSICIAN, THE • 1912 • *Johnson Arthur* • USA
NEW PLANET OF THE APES see **BACK TO THE PLANET OF THE APES** • 1974
NEW POLICEMAN, THE • 1912 • *Majestic* • USA
NEW PORTER, THE • 1916 • Whiting Ralph • SHT • USA
NEW POTOSIS, THE see **NUEROS POTOSIS, LOS**
NEW PROSPECTOR, THE • 1916 • *Hiawatha* • USA
NEW PUPIL, THE • 1913 • Lessey George A. • USA
NEW PUPIL, THE • 1940 • Cahn Edward L. • SHT • USA
NEW RALGIA • 1920 • *Tusun Comedies* • USA
NEW RANCH FOREMAN, THE • 1912 • Grandon Francis J. • USA
NEW RANCH OWNER, THE • 1911 • *Nestor* • USA
NEW RANCH OWNER, THE • 1916 • *Hippo* • USA
NEW RATES • 1934 • Cavalcanti Alberto • UKN
NEW RECRUIT, THE • 1910 • Gobbett T. J.? • UKN
NEW RECRUIT, THE • 1917 • *International Film Service* • ANS • USA
NEW RELATIVE, THE (USA) see **UJ ROKON, AZ** • 1935
NEW REPORTER, THE • 1910 • Fitzhamon Lewin? • UKN
NEW REPORTER, THE • 1914 • O'Sullivan Tony • USA
NEW REPORTER, THE see **CUB REPORTER, THE** • 1922
NEW REPUBLIC, THE • Hettiarachi P. • DCS • SLN
NEW RESIDENCE, THE • 1955 • Bek-Nazarov Amo • USS
NEW ROAD, THE see **SHINDO** • 1936
NEW ROAD MASCOT, THE • 1914 • O'Sullivan Tony • USA • NEW ROAD'S MASCOT, THE
NEW ROAD'S MASCOT, THE see **NEW ROAD MASCOT, THE** • 1914
NEW ROADWAYS • 1939 • Wrangell Basil • SHT • USA
NEW ROCAMBOLE, THE see **NOUVEAU ROCAMBOLE, LE** • 1913
NEW ROMEO AND JULIET, A see **RETABLO PARA ROMEO Y JULIETA, UN** • 1971
NEW SALESMAN, THE • 1916 • *Hamilton Lloyd V.* • USA
NEW SCHOOL, THE • 1944 • Ackland Rodney • UKN • NEW TEACHER, THE
NEW SCHOOL, THE see **NUEVA ESCUELA, LA** • 1973
NEW SCHOOL TEACHER, THE • 1924 • La Cava Gregory • USA
NEW SCHOOLMARM OF GREEN RIVER, THE • 1913 • *Essanay* • USA
NEW SERVANT, THE • 1909 • Bouwmeester Theo? • UKN
NEW SHAMANS, THE see **ARCTIC SPIRITS** • 1982
NEW SHAOLIN BOXERS, THE see **TS'AI-LI-FO HSAIO-TZU** • 1976
NEW SHAWL, THE • 1910 • Salter Harry • USA
NEW SHERIFF, THE • 1913 • Mackley Arthur • USA
NEW SHERIFF, THE • 1915 • *Trump* • USA
NEW SNOW see **SHINSETSU** • 1942
NEW SOUTH WALES HORSE ARTILLERY IN ACTION • 1896 • Sestier Marius • ASL
NEW SPANIARDS, THE see **NUEVOS ESPANOLES, LOS** • 1974
NEW SPARTANS, THE • 1974 • Starrett Jack • UKN
NEW SQUIRE, THE • 1912 • Miller Ashley • USA, UKN
NEW STENOGRAPHER, THE • 1908 • Merwin Bannister • USA
NEW STENOGRAPHER, THE • 1911 • Baker George D. • USA
NEW STRATEGY see **SAIKUN SHIN SENJUTSU** • 1932
NEW SUPERINTENDENT, THE • 1911 • *Rawlinson Herbert* • USA
NEW TALE OF GENJI: SHIZUKA AND YOSHITSUNE see **SHIN HEIKE MONOGATARI: SHIZUKA TO YOSHITSUNE** • 1956
NEW TALES OF THE TAIRA CLAN (UKN) see **SHIN HEIKE MONOGATARI** • 1955
NEW TEACHER, THE • 1915 • *Beery Wallace* • USA
NEW TEACHER, THE • 1922 • Franz Joseph J. • USA
NEW TEACHER, THE see **UCHITEL** • 1939
NEW TEACHER, THE see **NEW SCHOOL, THE** • 1944
NEW TOWN see **CHARLEY IN THE NEW TOWNS** • 1946-47
NEW TOWN, THE see **VILLE NOUVELLE, LA** • 1980
NEW TOWNS FOR OLD • 1943 • Eldridge John • DOC • UKN
NEW TOY see **NOVA IGRACKA** • 1964
NEW TOYS • 1925 • Robertson John S. • USA
NEW TOYS see **NYT LEGETOJ** • 1977
NEW TRICK, A • 1909 • Griffith D. W. • USA
NEW TRIP TO THE MOON (USA) see **VOYAGE DANS LA LUNE** • 1909
NEW TRIUMPH, THE • 1913 • *Summit Films* • UKN
NEW TWINS, THE • 1911 • *Urban Trading Co* • UKN
NEW TYPIST, THE • 1913 • Smalley Phillips • USA
NEW VALET, THE • 1915 • Hotaling Arthur D. • USA
NEW VERSION, A • 1918 • Hepworth Cecil M. • UKN
NEW VICTORIES • Mitrovic Zika • YGS
NEW VILLAGE DOCTOR, THE • 1912 • *Powers* • USA
NEW WAITER, THE • 1930 • Banks Monty • UKN
NEW WALLINGFORD, THE see **NEW ADVENTURES OF GET-RICH-QUICK WALLINGFORD, THE** • 1931
NEW WARRIORS SHALL ARISE see **VSTANOU NOVI BOJOVNICI** • 1950
NEW WAVE see **NOUVELLE VAGUE** • 1989
NEW WAVE FRENCH CONNECTION see **HEXAGONAL'S ROCKERS** • 1978
NEW WAY see **SHINDO** • 1936
NEW WAY OF LIVING, A see **NUEVO MODO DE VIVIR, UN** • 1974
NEW WAY TO WIN, A • 1915 • *Lubin* • USA
NEW WAY TO WIN A GIRL, A • 1913 • *Gem* • USA
NEW WINE • 1941 • Schunzel Reinhold • USA • GREAT AWAKENING, THE (UKN)
NEW WIVES' CONFERENCE see **NIIZUMA KAIGI** • 1949
NEW WIZARD OF OZ, THE see **HIS MAJESTY, THE SCARECROW OF OZ** • 1914
NEW WOMAN, THE • 1905 • Collins Alf? • UKN
NEW WOMAN, THE • 1968 • King Allan • CND
NEW WOMAN AND THE LION, THE • 1912 • *Selig* • USA
NEW WOMAN'S DIALOGUE see **SHIN JOSEI MONDO** • 1955
NEW WOMAN'S GUIDANCE see **SHIN JOSEI KAGAMI** • 1928
NEW WORKER, THE see **NOWY PRACOWNIK** • 1969
NEW WORLD, A • 1958 • Lubin Arthur • MXC
NEW WORLD, A see **MUNDO NUEVO, UN** • 1956
NEW WORLD, A see **MONDO NUOVO, UN** • 1965
NEW WORLD, THE see **MONDO NUOVO, IL** • 1982
NEW WORLDS FOR OLD • 1938 • Sainsbury Frank • DOC • UKN
NEW WRINKLES • 1927 • Taurog Norman • SHT • USA
NEW YEAR, A • 1908 • *Lubin* • USA
NEW YEAR PUNCHBOWL see **SILVESTERPUNSCH** • 1960
NEW YEAR SACRIFICE see **ZHUFU** • 1957
NEW YEAR'S DAY • 1989 • Jaglom Henry • USA
NEW YEAR'S DAY 2000 see **CAPODANNO 2000**
NEW YEAR'S EVE • 1929 • Lehrman Henry • USA
NEW YEAR'S EVE • 1963 • Bottcher Jurgen • DOC • GDR
NEW YEAR'S EVE see **SYLVESTER** • 1923
NEW YEAR'S EVE see **INDISCRETIONS OF EVE** • 1932
NEW YEAR'S EVE see **PRZYGODA NOWOROCZNA** • 1963
NEW YEAR'S EVE see **NOWOROCZNA NOC** • 1965
NEW YEAR'S EVE ON THE SKANE PLAINS see **NYARSAFTON PA SKANSKA SLATTEN** • 1961
NEW YEAR'S EVIL • 1980 • Alston Emmett • USA
NEW YEAR'S LOVE see **KOTOSHI NO KOI** • 1962
NEW YEAR'S NIGHT see **NOWOROCZNA NOC** • 1965
NEW YORK • 1916 • Fitzmaurice George • USA
NEW YORK • 1927 • Reed Luther • USA
NEW YORK • *Leacock Richard (Ph)* • DOC • USA
NEW YORK • 1961 • Torrent Henri • SHT • FRN
NEW YORK see **HALLELUJAH, I'M A BUM** • 1933
NEW YORK, 4 A.M. see **NOWY JORK, CZWARTA RANO** • 1988
NEW YORK 1935 • 1988 • Ferrand-Lafaye • SHT • FRN
NEW YORK AFTER DARK see **NEW YORK AFTER MIDNIGHT** • 1983
NEW YORK AFTER MIDNIGHT • 1983 • Scandelari Jacques • USA, FRN • NEW YORK AFTER DARK ○ AFTER MIDNIGHT ○ FLASHING LIGHTS ○ MONIQUE
NEW YORK APPELLE SUPER DRAGON (FRN) see **NEW YORK CHIAMA SUPERDRAGO** • 1966
NEW YORK, AVENUE O see **MIXED BLOOD** • 1984
NEW YORK BALLADE • 1955 • Reichenbach Francois • SHT • FRN
NEW YORK - BATAVIA • 1987 • Hagen Rien • DOC • NTH
NEW YORK BLACK OUT see **NEW YORK NE REPOND PAS** • 1977
NEW YORK -BY HECK • 1918 • *Nestor* • SHT • USA
NEW YORK CALLING SUPERDRAGON see **NEW YORK CHIAMA SUPERDRAGO** • 1966
NEW YORK CHIAMA SUPERDRAGO • 1966 • Ferroni Giorgio • ITL, FRN, FRG • NEW YORK APPELLE SUPER DRAGON (FRN) ○ SECRET AGENT SUPER DRAGON(USA) ○ HOLLENJAGD AUF HEISSE WARE (FRG) ○ SUPER DRAGON ○ NEW YORK CALLING SUPERDRAGON
NEW YORK CITY -THE MOST • 1968 • Pitt George • DOC • USA
NEW YORK CONFIDENTIAL • 1955 • Rouse Russell • USA
NEW YORK CONNECTION • 1983 • Butler Robert • USA
NEW YORK COWBOY, A • 1911 • *Selig* • USA
NEW YORK EXPERIENCE • 1973 • Russell Rusty • USA
NEW YORK EXPRESZ KABEL • 1921 • *Lukas Paul* • HNG • TELEGRAM FROM NEW YORK, A
NEW YORK EYE AND EAR CONTROL • 1964 • Snow Michael • USA • WALKING WOMAN WORK, A
NEW YORK GAERI NO INAKKAPPE • 1967 • Senno Koji • JPN • GREAT NEW YORK CON GAME, THE
NEW YORK GIRL, A • 1914 • Nicholls George • USA
NEW YORK HAT, THE • 1912 • Griffith D. W. • USA
NEW YORK IDEA, THE • 1920 • Blache Herbert • USA
NEW YORK INFERNAL • Markin Marvin • USA
NEW YORK LADY see **TARNISHED LADY** • 1931
NEW YORK LIGHTBOARD -WELCOME TO CANADA • 1961 • McLaren Norman, Tunis Ron, Pindal Kaj • ANS • CND
NEW YORK LUCK • 1917 • Sloman Edward • USA
NEW YORK MYSTERY see **'NEATH BROOKLYN BRIDGE** • 1942
NEW YORK NE REPOND PAS • 1977 • Matalon Eddy • FRN, CND • ET LA TERREUR COMMENCE ○ NEW YORK BLACK OUT ○ BLACKOUT
NEW YORK, NEW YORK • 1977 • Scorsese Martin • USA
NEW YORK NIGHTS • 1929 • Milestone Lewis • USA • TIN PAN ALLEY
NEW YORK NIGHTS • 1984 • Nuchtern Simon • USA
NEW YORK PARIS EN AUTOMOBILE see **RAID PARIS NEW YORK EN AUTOMOBILE, LE** • 1908
NEW YORK, PAST AND PRESENT • 1916 • *Vitagraph* • SHT • USA
NEW YORK PEACOCK, THE • 1917 • Buel Kenean • USA
NEW YORK RAPID TRANSIT • 1916 • Johnson Tefft • SHT • USA
NEW YORK RIPPER, THE see **SQUARTATORE DI NEW YORK, LO** • 1982
NEW YORK STORIES • 1989 • Allen Woody, Scorsese Martin, Coppola Francis Ford • USA
NEW YORK STORY • 1980 • Raynal Jackie • USA
NEW YORK STORY, THE see **UNHOLY PARTNERS** • 1941
NEW YORK SUR MER see **ONLY ONE NEW YORK** • 1964
NEW-YORK-SUR-MER (FRN) see **ONLY ONE NEW YORK** • 1964
NEW YORK TOWN • 1941 • Vidor Charles • USA
NEW YORK TRIP • 1971 • Furukawa Taku • ANS • JPN
NEW YORK, TWIN PARKS PROJECT -TV CHANNEL 13 • 1974 • Regnier Michel • DOC • CND
NEW YORK UNIVERSITY • 1952 • Van Dyke Willard • DOC • USA
NEW YORKERS, THE see **CHRISTMAS IN JULY** • 1940
NEW YORK'S FINEST • 1988 • Vincent Chuck • USA
NEW YORK'S SOCIETY LIFE AND UNDERWORLD • 1913 • *Exclusive Feature* • USA
NEWAZASHI • 1968 • Sakao Masanao • JPN • SEX EXPERT
NEWBORN, THE see **SPAEDBARNET** • 1953
NEWCASTLE NUT, A • 1922 • *Firth William* • ASL
NEWCOMB'S NECKTIE • 1913 • Williams C. Jay • USA
NEWCOMER, THE • 1938 • Davis Mannie • ANS • USA
NEWCOMER, THE see **NOUVEAU VENU, LE** • 1979
NEWCOMERS: 1740, THE • 1977 • Fournier Claude • CND
NEWCOMERS, THE • 1973 • Kaufman Lloyd • USA
NEWCOMERS, THE • 1976-78 • Till Eric (c/d) • CND
NEWELS OOR MT AUX-SOURCES • 1942 • SAF
NEWER WAY, THE • 1915 • Eason B. Reeves • USA
NEWER WOMAN, THE • 1914 • Crisp Donald • USA
NEWEST PROFESSION, THE see **NEVER WAVE AT A WAC** • 1952
NEWFOUNDLAND SCENE • 1950 • Crawley Budge • DOC • CND
NEWFOUNDLAND SKETCHBOOK • 1983 • Barrie Scott • MTV • CND
NEWLY MARRIED see **NYGIFTA** • 1941
NEWLY RICH • 1922 • Roach Hal • SHT • USA
NEWLY RICH • 1931 • Taurog Norman • USA • FORBIDDEN ADVENTURE (UKN) ○ LET'S PLAY KING
NEWLY RICH, THE • 1915 • Miller Ashley • USA
NEWLY-WEDS • 1960 • Sidelev Sergei • USS
NEWLY-WEDS • 1971 • Moskalenko N. • USS
NEWLYWED SERIES see **SNOOKUMS** • 1912-14
NEWLYWEDS see **GIOVANI MARITI** • 1958
NEWLYWEDS, THE • 1910 • Griffith D. W. • USA
NEWLYWEDS, THE • 1914 • *Lux* • USA
NEWLYWEDS, THE • 1948-52 • Yates Hal • SHS • USA
NEWLYWEDS' DILEMMA, THE • 1914 • *Nestor* • USA
NEWLYWEDS' HOUSE GUEST • Yates Hal • SHT • USA
NEWLYWEDS' MISTAKE, THE • 1917 • *Larkinn George* • SHT • USA
NEWLYWEDS' MIX-UP, THE • 1916 • Lyons Eddie • SHT • USA
NEWLYWEDS' VISIT • 1928 • Newfield Sam • SHT • USA
NEWMAN LAUGH-O-GRAM SERIES • 1920 • Disney Walt • ASS • USA • NEWMAN'S LAUGH-O-GRAMS
NEWMAN SHAME • 1978 • Pringle Julian • MTV • ASL
NEWMAN'S LAUGH-O-GRAMS see **NEWMAN LAUGH-O-GRAM SERIES** • 1920
NEWMAN'S LAW • 1974 • Heffron Richard T. • USA
NEWPORT • 1972 • Le Grice Malcolm • UKN
NEWPORT FESTIVAL see **FESTIVAL** • 1967
NEWPORT JAZZ FESTIVAL 1962 • 1962 • Bregman Buddy • DOC • USA
NEWS #3 • 1962 • Baillie Bruce • SHT • USA
NEWS AT ELEVEN • 1986 • Robe Mike • TVM • USA
NEWS BOY TENOR, THE • 1914 • MacGregor Norval • USA
NEWS FOR THE NAVY • 1937 • McLaren Norman • DCS • UKN
NEWS FROM HOME • 1977 • Akerman Chantal • BLG, FRN
NEWS FROM NOWHERE • 1978 • Hallum Alister • UKN
NEWS FROM THE SOVIET UNION see **FILM NOTITIES UIT DE SOVJET-UNIE** • 1930
NEWS FROM THE VILLAGE see **KADDU BEYKAT** • 1975
NEWS HOUND • 1955 • Sparber I. • ANS • USA
NEWS HOUNDS • 1947 • Beaudine William • USA
NEWS HOUNDS • 1990 • Blair Les • TVM • UKN • NEWSHOUNDS
NEWS IS MADE AT NIGHT • 1939 • Werker Alfred L. • USA
NEWS ITEM, A • 1913 • *White Pearl* • USA
NEWS ITEM ON TAL EL ZAATAR, A • 1976 • Madanat Adnan • SHT • LBN
NEWS ODDITIES • 1940 • *Mintz Charles (P)* • ANS • USA
NEWS PARADE, THE • 1928 • Butler David • USA
NEWS REVIEW NO.2 • 1945 • *Van Dongen Helen (Ed)* • CMP • NTH
NEWSBOY HERO, A • 1911 • *Thanhouser* • USA
NEWSBOY'S CHRISTMAS DREAM, A • 1913 • Collins Edwin J. • UKN
NEWSBOY'S DEBT, THE • 1914 • Cornwallis Donald • UKN
NEWSBOYS' HOME • 1939 • Young Harold • USA
NEWSBOY'S LUCK, A • 1911 • *Lubin* • USA
NEWSFRONT • 1978 • Noyce Phil • ASL
NEWSHOUNDS see **NEWS HOUNDS** • 1990
NEWSIE AND THE LADY, THE (USA) see **CANALLITA Y LA DAMA, EL** • 1939
NEWSPAPER BOYS, THE (USA) see **CHICOS DE LA PRENSA, LOS** • 1936
NEWSPAPER CLIPPINGS • 1918 • *Anderson Claire* • SHT • USA
NEWSPAPER ERROR, A • 1910 • *Powers* • USA
NEWSPAPER GAME, THE see **KINGSTON: THE POWER PLAY** • 1976
NEWSPAPER NEMESIS, A • 1915 • Harvey John • USA
NEWSPAPER STORY see **FRONT PAGE STORY** • 1954
NEWSPAPER TRAIN • 1941 • Lye Len • DCS • UKN
NEWSREEL OF DREAMS NO.1 • 1968 • Vanderbeek Stan • USA
NEWSREEL OF DREAMS NO.2 • 1969 • Vanderbeek Stan • USA
NEWSREEL ON YOUTH IN VILLAGES IN WINTER • 1967 • Zilnik Zelimir • SHT • YGS
NEWSREEL (PORT CHICAGO) • 1966 • Baillie Bruce • USA • PORT CHICAGO
NEWSY AND THE TRAMP, THE • 1911 • *Thanhouser* • USA
NEWTON: THE MIND THAT FOUND THE FUTURE • 1970 • Kaczender George • DOC • CND
NEXT • 1912 • *Trunnelle Mabel* • USA
NEXT • 1918 • Hotaling Arthur D. • SHT • USA
NEXT AISLE OVER • 1919 • Roach Hal • SHT • USA
NEXT AUTUMN see **PROXIMO OTONO, EL** • 1967
NEXT CORNER, THE • 1924 • Wood Sam • USA
NEXT CORNER, THE see **TRANSGRESSION** • 1931
NEXT DOOR see **ZA SCIANA** • 1971
NEXT DOOR MADAME AND MY WIFE see **MADAMU TO NYOBO** • 1931
NEXT DOOR NEIGHBOR, THE see **TALK ABOUT A STRANGER** • 1952
NEXT DOOR NEIGHBORS see **LOCATAIRES D'A COTE, LES** • 1909
NEXT EXIT • 1983 • Lofven Chris • DOC • ASL
NEXT GENERATION, THE • 1913 • Lytton L. Rogers • USA
NEXT GENTLEMAN PLEASE • 1927 • Greenidge John, Messell Rudolf • UKN
NEXT GENTLEMAN -THE SAME LADY, THE see **NACHSTE HERR -DIESELBE DAME, DER** • 1968
NEXT IN COMMAND, THE • 1914 • *Picture Playhouse Film* • USA
NEXT IN LINE (UKN) see **RIDERS OF THE NORTHLAND** • 1942
NEXT MAN, THE • 1976 • Sarafian Richard C. • USA • DOUBLE HIT
NEXT OF KIN • 1982 • Williams Tony • ASL

NEXT OF KIN • 1985 • Egoyan Atom • CND
NEXT OF KIN • 1989 • Irvin John • USA
NEXT OF KIN see **ARVEN** • 1979
NEXT OF KIN, THE • 1908 • Wormald S. • UKN
NEXT OF KIN, THE • 1942 • Dickinson Thorold • UKN
NEXT ONE, THE • 1984 • Mastorakis Nico • USA
NEXT PLEASE • 1915 • *Horseshoe* • UKN
NEXT SEASON, THE see **PROXIMA ESTACION, LA** • 1981
NEXT SPRING • 1961 • Sokolov Viktor • USS
NEXT STOP, GREENWICH VILLAGE • 1976 • Mazursky Paul • USA
NEXT STOP MAKOUVLEI • 1972 • SAF
NEXT SUMMER (USA) see **ETE PROCHAIN, L'** • 1985
NEXT TIME I MARRY, THE • 1938 • Kanin Garson • USA • TRAILER ROMANCE
NEXT TIME WE LIVE (UKN) see **NEXT TIME WE LOVE** • 1936
NEXT TIME WE LOVE • 1936 • Griffith Edward H. • USA • NEXT TIME WE LIVE (UKN)
NEXT TO NO TIME • 1958 • Cornelius Henry • UKN
NEXT! (USA) see **STRANO VIZIO DELLA SIGNORA WARDH, LO** • 1971
NEXT VICTIM!, THE see **STRANO VIZIO DELLA SIGNORA WARDH, LO** • 1971
NEXT VICTIM, THE see **PROXIMA VITIMA, A** • 1984
NEXT VOICE YOU HEAR, THE • 1950 • Wellman William A. • USA
NEXT WEEK-END • 1934 • Dunn Eddie • SHT • USA
NEXT YEAR IN HOLYSLOOT see **VOLGEND JAAR IN HOLYSLOOT** • 1983
NEXT YEAR IN JERUSALEM • 1974 • Rasky Harry • CND
NEYEBO BASHEVO DYETSTVA see **NEBO NASHEGO DETSTVA** • 1967
NEZ, LE • 1963 • Alexeieff Alexandre, Parker Claire • ANS • FRN • SCREEN OF PINS ○ NOSE, THE
NEZ AU VENT • 1957 • Starevitch Ladislas • ANS • FRN • NOSE TO THE WIND
NEZ-DE-CUIR • 1952 • Allegret Yves, Sigurd Jacques • FRN, ITL • NEZ DE CUIR, GENTILHOMME D'AMOUR ○ NASO DI CUOIO (ITL) ○ GENTILUOMO D'AMORE ○ NEZ DE CUIR
NEZ DE CUIR see **NEZ-DE-CUIR** • 1952
NEZ DE CUIR, GENTILHOMME D'AMOUR see **NEZ-DE-CUIR** • 1952
NEZ ET TROIS YEUX, UN see **ANFUN WA THALATH UYUN** • 1972
NEZABIVAEMOE see **NEZABYVAYEMOYE** • 1968
NEZABUVALEMOE see **NEZABYVAYEMOYE** • 1968
NEZABYVAYEMI 1919-1 GOD • 1951 • Chiaureli Mikhail • USS • UNFORGETTABLE YEAR OF 1919, THE (USA)
NEZABYVAYEMOYE • 1968 • Solntseva Yulia • USS • UNFORGETTABLE, THE ○ NEZABUVALEMOE ○ UKRAINE IN FLAMES ○ NEZABIVAEMOE
NEZBEDNY BAKALAR • 1946 • Vavra Otakar • CZC • MISCHIEVOUS BACHELOR, THE ○ MISCHIEVOUS TUTOR, THE
NEZNA • 1968 • Barabas Stanislav • CZC • GENTLE ONE, THE
NEZUMI KOZO TABIMAKURA • 1931 • Ito Daisuke • JPN
N'FUMA • 1960 • Jaworski Tadeusz • DOC • PLN
NGADHNJIM MBI VDEKJEN • Erebara Gesim, Milkani Piro • ALB • VICTORY OVER DEATH
NGAIO • 1989 • *Lanh Than* • VTN • OUR CITY
NGAKA • 1976 • Sabela Simon • SAF
N'GANGANE see **N'DIANGANE** • 1974
NGATI • 1986 • Barclay Barry • NZL
NGAVELE NGASHO • 1983 • SAF
NGAYON LAMANG AKO DUMALANGIN • 1968 • Ravel C. G. • PHL • MY FIRST PRAYER
NGERN NGERN NGERN • 1983 • Mukdasanit Euthana • THL
N'GIRI • 1946 • Deboe Gerard • BLG
NGITNGIT NG PITONG WHISTLE BOMB • 1968 • Osorio Consuelo P. • PHL • SOUND OF 7 WHISTLE BOMBS
NGO TSOI WAKSEWUI DIK YATTSI • 1989 • Wong Taylor • HKG • TRIADS -THE INSIDE STORY
NGWANAKA • 1976 • SAF
NHA QUE • 1989 • Minh Ho Quong • VTN • PEASANT, THE
NI HABLAR DEL PELUQUIN! • 1959 • Galindo Alejandro • MXC
NI LIV • 1957 • Skouen Arne • NRW • WE DIE ALONE ○ NINE LIVES
NI LJUGER • 1969 • Sjoman Vilgot • SWD • PRODUCTION 337 ○ YOU'RE LYING
NI-LO-HO NU-ERH • 1988 • Hou Hsiao-Hsien • TWN • DAUGHTER OF THE NILE ○ NILOUE, NUER ○ NILUOHE NUER
NI POBRE NI RICO, SINO TODO LO CONTRARIO • 1945 • Iquino Ignacio F. • SPN
NI POBRES NI RICOS • 1952 • Cortes Fernando • MXC
NI POBRETONES NI RICACHONES • 1972 • *Oro* • MXC
NI SANGRE NI ARENA • 1941 • Galindo Alejandro • MXC • NEITHER BLOOD NOR SAND
NI SI SCRIVE SUI MURI A MILANO • 1975 • Maiello Raffaele • ITL
NI TU NI YO • 1944 • Delgras Gonzalo • SPN
NI VU, NI CONNU.. • 1958 • Robert Yves • FRN • VIVE MONSIEUR BLAIREAU ○ AFFAIRE BLAIREAU, L'
NI YAKI ZAKANA see **FUTATSO-NO YAKIZAKANA** • 1968
NIAGARA • 1953 • Hathaway Henry • USA
NIAGARA FALLS • 1932 • Arbuckle Roscoe • USA
NIAGARA FALLS • 1941 • Douglas Gordon • USA
NIAGARA FALLS • 1969 • May Derek • SHT • CND
NIAGARA FALLS see **OUT ALL NIGHT** • 1933
NIAGARA FALLS see **LOVE BIRDS** • 1934
NIAGARA FOOLS • 1956 • Smith Paul J. • ANS • USA
NIAGARA HONEYMOON, A • 1912 • *Thanhouser* • USA
NIANCHAN • 1959 • Imamura Shohei • JPN • MY SECOND BROTHER ○ DIARY OF SUEKO
NIANIVIL NINDRAVAL • 1967 • Srinivas V. • IND • BELOVED OF MY SOUL
NIAYE • 1964 • Sembene Ousmane • SHT • SNL
NIBELGUNGHI, I • 1910 • *Milano* • ITL • NIBELUNGEN, THE
NIBELUNG, DIE • 1966 • Reinl Harald • FRG, YGS • WHOM THE GODS WISH TO DESTROY
NIBELUNGEN 1, DIE • 1924 • Lang Fritz, Ruttmann Walter • FRG • SIEGFRIED ○ SIEGFRIEDS TOD ○ DEATH OF SIEGFRIED ○ SIEGFRIED'S DEATH
NIBELUNGEN 2, DIE • 1924 • Lang Fritz • FRG • KRIEMHILDS RACHE ○ KRIEMHILDE'S REVENGE
NIBELUNGEN, THE see **NIBELGUNGHI, I** • 1910
NIBELUNGEN II: KRIEMHILD'S RACHE, DIE • 1967 • Reinl Harald • FRG • NIBELUNGS PART TWO: KRIEMHILD'S REVENGE, THE ○ WHOM THE GODS WISH TO DESTROY
NIBELUNGEN SAGA, THE see **EPOPEA DEI NIBELUNGHI, L'** • 1913
NIBELUNGS PART TWO: KRIEMHILD'S REVENGE, THE see **NIBELUNGEN II: KRIEMHILD'S RACHE, DIE** • 1967
NICARAGUA • 1969 • Schroeter Werner • FRG
NICARAGUA EARTHQUAKE • 1979 • Lasry Pierre • DOC • CND
NICARAGUA: FREE HOMELAND OR DEATH • 1979 • Yglesias Antonio, Vega Victor • DOC
NICARAGUA, SEPTEMBER 1978 • 1979 • Cortes Octavio, Diamand Frank • DOC • NTH
NICARAGUA: THOSE WHO WILL MAKE FREEDOM • 1978 • Navarro Berta • DOC • MXC
NICE AND BIG see **SON ES GROSZ** • 1987
NICE AND FRIENDLY • 1922 • Chaplin Charles • SHT • USA
NICE BRIDE see **CICI GELIN** • 1967
NICE DOGGY • 1952 • Donnelly Eddie • ANS • USA
NICE DREAMS see **CHEECH & CHONG'S NICE DREAMS** • 1981
NICE GIRL? • 1941 • Seiter William A. • USA
NICE GIRL LIKE ME, A • 1969 • Davis Desmond • UKN
NICE GIRLS DON'T EXPLODE • 1987 • Martinez Chuck • USA
NICE GOINGS ON AT HENLEY BEACH • 1914 • ASL
NICE GUYS FINISH LAST see **FOOTSTEPS** • 1972
NICE LITTLE BANK THAT SHOULD BE ROBBED, A • 1958 • Levin Henry • USA • HOW TO ROB A BANK (UKN)
NICE LITTLE GIRL, A • 1915 • *Ward Lily* • USA
NICE MEETING YOU • 1950 • Kneitel Seymour • ANS • USA
NICE NURSEY • 1914 • *Lubin* • USA
NICE PEOPLE • 1922 • De Mille William C. • USA
NICE PLATE OF SPINACH, A see **COZ TAKHLE DAT SI SPENAT?** • 1976
NICE TIME • 1957 • Goretta Claude, Tanner Alain • DCS • UKN
NICE TRY • 1974 • Joyce Michael • UKN
NICE WOMEN • 1932 • Knopf Edwin H. • USA
NICEST MAN IN THE WORLD, THE • 1975 • Rakoff Alvin • MTV • UKN
NICHI-NICHI O HAISHIN • 1958 • Nakamura Noboru • JPN • TRIPLE BETRAYAL
NICHIBOTSUMAE NI AISHITE • 1967 • Hase Kazuo • JPN • LOVE ME BEFORE DARK
NICHIREN • 1978 • Nakamura Noboru • JPN • PRIEST NICHIREN, THE
NICHIREN -A MAN OF MANY MIRACLES see **NICHIREN TO MOKO DAISHURAI** • 1958
NICHIREN TO MOKO DAISHURAI • 1958 • Watanabe Kunio • JPN • NICHIREN -A MAN OF MANY MIRACLES
NICHIRIN • 1925 • Kinugasa Teinosuke • JPN • SUN, THE
NICHIRIN • 1926 • Ito Daisuke • JPN • SUN, THE
NICHIRIN • 1950 • Kinugasa Teinosuke • JPN • SUN, THE
NICHOLAS AND ALEXANDRA • 1971 • Schaffner Franklin J. • UKN
NICHOLAS AND THE OTHERS see **NICOLAS Y LOS DEMAS** • 1986
NICHOLAS NICKLEBY • 1912 • Nicholls George • USA
NICHOLAS NICKLEBY • 1948 • Cavalcanti Alberto • UKN • LIFE AND ADVENTURES OF NICHOLAS NICKLEBY, THE
NICHOLS ON A VACATION, THE • 1910 • Salter Harry • USA
NICHT ALLES WAS FLIEGT ISAT EIN VOGEL • 1978 • Sajtinac Borislav • FRG, YGS • NOT EVERYTHING THAT FLIES IS A BIRD ○ NIJE PRICA SVE STO LETI
NICHT DER HOMOSEXUELLE IST PERVERS.. see **NICHT DER HOMOSEXUELLE IST PERVERS, SONDERN DIE SITUATION, IN DER ER LEBT** • 1971
NICHT DER HOMOSEXUELLE IST PERVERS, SONDERN DIE SITUATION, IN DER ER LEBT • 1971 • von Praunheim Rosa • FRG • NICHT DER HOMOSEXUELLE IST PERVERS..
NICHT HEIRATEN DURFEN, DIE • 1929 • Rudolph Karl Heinz • FRG
NICHT LANGE TAUSCHTE MICH DAS GLUCK? • 1917 • Matull Kurt? • FRG
NICHT LIEBEN DURFEN.., DIE • 1917 • Portegg R. • FRG
NICHT MEHR FLIEHEN • 1955 • Vesely Herbert • FRG • NO MORE FLEEING (USA)
NICHT SCHUMMELN, LIEBLING! • 1973 • Hasler Joachim • GDR
NICHT STERBEN DURFEN, DIE • 1919 • Osten Franz • FRG
NICHT VERSOHNT ODER "ES HILFT NUR GEWALT, WO GEWALT HERRSCHT" • 1965 • Straub Jean-Marie • FRG • ES HILFT NICHT, WO GEWALT HERRSCHT ○ UNRECONCILED ○ NOT RECONCILED, OR "ONLY VIOLENCE HELPS WHERE IT RULES"
NICHTE DES HERZOGS, DIE • 1917 • Mack Max • FRG
NICHTEN DER FRAU OBERST, DIE • 1968 • Dietrich Erwin C. • FRG, ITL • GUESS WHO'S COMING FOR BREAKFAST (UKN) ○ NIECES OF FRAU OBERST, THE
NICHTEN DER FRAU OBERST, PART 2 -MEIN BETT IS MEINE BURG • 1969 • Dietrich Erwin C. • FRG
NICHTS ALS AERGER MIT DER LIEBE • 1956 • Engel Thomas • AUS
NICHTS ALS SUNDE • 1965 • Burger Hanus • GDR
NICHTS ALS ZUFALLE • 1949 • Emo E. W. • FRG
NICK AND NORA • 1975 • Berns Seymour • TVM • USA
NICK CARTER • 1906 • Jasset Victorin • SRL • FRN
NICK CARTER • 1910-11 • Rippert Otto • SER • FRG
NICK CARTER AND THE RED CLUB see **NICK CARTER ET LE TREFLE ROUGE** • 1965
NICK CARTER E IL TRIFOGLIO ROSSO (ITL) see **NICK CARTER ET LE TREFLE ROUGE** • 1965
NICK CARTER ET LE TREFLE ROUGE • 1965 • Savignac Jean-Paul • FRN, ITL • NICK CARTER E IL TRIFOGLIO ROSSO (ITL) ○ NICK CARTER AND THE RED CLUB
NICK CARTER IN PRAGUE see **ADELA JESTE NEVECERELA** • 1977
NICK CARTER, LE ROI DES DETECTIVES • 1908 • Jasset Victorin • SRL • FRN
NICK CARTER, MASTER DETECTIVE • 1939 • Tourneur Jacques • USA
NICK CARTER VA TOUT CASSER • 1964 • Decoin Henri • FRN, ITL • LICENSE TO KILL (USA)
NICK DANGER IN THE CASE OF THE MISSING YOLK • 1983 • Dear William • USA
NICK, DER KONIG DER CHAUFFEURE • 1925 • Wilhelm Carl • FRG
NICK KNATTERTONS ABENTEUER • 1959 • Quest Hans • FRG
NICK OF TIME BABY, THE • 1917 • Badger Clarence • USA • NICK-OF-TIME BABY, THE
NICK-OF-TIME BABY, THE see **NICK OF TIME BABY, THE** • 1917
NICK THE STING see **AMICI DI NICK HEZARD, GLI** • 1976
NICK WINTER AND THE SONAMBULIST THIEF • 1911 • *Pathe* • FRN
NICK WINTER CONTRE NICK WINTER • 1911 • Bourgeois Gerard • FRN
NICKEL HOPPER, THE • 1926 • Jones • SHT • USA
NICKEL MOUNTAIN • 1984 • Denbaum Drew • USA
NICKEL NURSER, THE • 1932 • Doane Warren • SHT • USA
NICKEL QUEEN • 1971 • McCallum John • ASL
NICKEL RIDE, THE • 1975 • Mulligan Robert • USA
NICKELODEON • 1976 • Bogdanovich Peter • UKN, USA
NICKO AND SICKO • 1963 • Gedevanishvili S. • ANS • USS
NICK'S COFFEE POT • 1939 • Rasinski Connie • ANS • USA
NICK'S FILM see **LIGHTNING OVER WATER** • 1980
NICK'S KNICKERS • 1929 • Gannon Wilfred • UKN
NICK'S MOVIE see **LIGHTNING OVER WATER** • 1980
NICKY AND GINO (UKN) see **DOMINICK AND EUGENE** • 1988
NICKY ET KITTY • 1959 • Mercier • SHT • FRN
NICKY'S WORLD • 1974 • Stanley Paul • TVM • USA
NICO see **ABOVE THE LAW** • 1988
NICO: ABOVE THE LAW see **ABOVE THE LAW** • 1988
NICO EL TRACALERO • 1977 • Lugo Alfredo • VNZ • TRACALEROS, LOS ○ TRICKY NICO ○ TRICKY ONES, THE
NICOLAS Y LOS DEMAS • 1986 • Morales Jacobo • PRC • NICHOLAS AND THE OTHERS
NICOLAUS COPERNICUS see **MIKOLAJ KOPERNIK** • 1954
NICOLE ET SA VERTU • 1931 • Hervil Rene • FRN
NICOLE PAS DESSUS PAR DESSOUS • 1978 • Benazeraf Jose • FRN
NICOLENE • 1978 • Du Toit Marie • SAF
NICOLET • 1955 • Rivard Fernand • DSS • CND
NICOTIANA • 1963 • de Macedo Antonio • SHT • PRT
NICOTINE CONSPIRACY, A • 1911 • *Lubin* • USA
NID, LE • 1914 • Poirier Leon • FRN
NID, LE • 1926 • Benoit-Levy Jean • FRN • NEST, THE
NID D'ESPIONS, LE see **TEHERAN '43** • 1979
NIDA' AL-USHSHAQ see **NEDAA EL OCHAK** • 1960
NIDHANAYA • 1971 • Peries Lester James • SLN • TREASURE, THE
NIDO, EL • 1980 • de Arminan Jaime • SPN • NEST, THE
NIDO DE AGUILAS • 1963 • Orona Vicente • MXC
NIDO DE ESPIAS (SPN) see **RAGGIO INFERNALE, IL** • 1967
NIDO DI FALASCO, IL • 1950 • Brignone Guido • ITL
NIE BEDE CIE KOCHAC • 1974 • Nasfeter Janusz • PLN • I WON'T LOVE YOU
NIE ER • 1959 • Zheng Junli • CHN
NIE LUBIE PONIEDZIALKU • 1971 • Chmielewski Tadeusz • PLN • I DON'T LIKE MONDAYS
NIE MA KONCA WIELKIEJ WOJNY • 1959 • Lomnicki Jan • DOC • PLN • NO END TO THE GREAT WAR
NIE MA MOCNYCH • 1975 • Checinski Stanislaw • PLN • NO ONE IS STRONG
NIE MA POWROTU JOHNNY • 1970 • Rahnama Kaveh Pur • PLN • NO RETURN FOR JOHNNY
NIE MAM JUZ ZEBA • 1964 • Laskowski Jan • ANS • PLN • I'VE LOST A TOOTH
NIE POZYLEM DLUGO • 1967 • Bednarczyk Jerzy • DOC • PLN • I DID NOT LIVE LONG
NIE WIEDER LIEBE • 1931 • Litvak Anatole • FRG • NO MORE LOVE (USA)
NIE ZAZNASZ SPOKOJU • 1977 • Waskowski Mieczyslaw • PLN • YOU WILL NOT TASTE PEACE ○ NO PEACE ANY MORE
NIEBEZPIECZENSTWO • 1963 • Kotowski Jerzy • ANS • PLN • DANGER
NIEBEZPIECZNY RAJ • 1930 • Ordynski Ryszard • PLN
NIEBIESKA KULA • 1968 • Kijowicz Miroslaw • ANS • PLN • BLUE BALL, THE
NIEBIESKIE JAK MORZE CZARNE • 1972 • Ziarnik Jerzy • PLN • AS BLUE AS THE BLACK SEA
NIEBLA • 1975 • Jara Jose • SPN • CUATRO NOVIAS DE AUGUSTO PEREZ, LAS
NIEBLA • 1978 • Lopez Diego • MXC • FOG
NIEBLA Y SOL • 1951 • Forque Jose Maria • SPN
NIEBO BEZ SLONCA • 1966 • Rybkowski Jan • DOC • PLN • SKY WITHOUT SUN
NIEBO ZOWIET see **NEBO ZOVYOT** • 1959
NIECE AND THE CHORUS LADY, THE • 1911 • *Edison* • USA
NIECE CAPTIVE, LA • 1969 • Michez Luc • ZRE
NIECE OF THE VAMPIRE, THE see **MALENKA, LA SOBRINA DEL VAMPIRO** • 1968
NIECES OF FRAU OBERST, THE see **NICHTEN DER FRAU OBERST, DIE** • 1968
NIECIEKAWA HISTORIA • 1983 • Jerzy Wojciech • PLN • UNEVENTFUL STORY, AN
NIEDA • 1914 • *Fischer Margarita* • USA
NIEDORAJDA • 1937 • Krawicz Mecislas • PLN • GOOD FOR NOTHING
NIEDZIELA SPRAWIEDLIWOSCI • 1965 • Passendorfer Jerzy • PLN • NO JUSTICE ON SUNDAY ○ SUNDAY OF JUSTICE
NIEDZIELNE DZIECI • 1977 • Holland Agnieszka • PLN • SUNDAY CHILDREN
NIEDZIELNE IGRASZKI • 1988 • Glinski Robert • PLN • SUNDAY PRANKS
NIEDZIELNY PORANEC • 1955 • Munk Andrzej • DCS • PLN • ONE SUNDAY MORNING (UKN) ○ SUNDAY MORNING (USA) ○ ON A SUNDAY MORNING ○ SONNTAGMORGEN IN WARSCHAU, EIN
NIEDZWIEDZ PANA PO EJKO • 1975 • Florkowski Waclaw • PLN
NIEGEKUSSTE MUND, DER • *Abel Alfred* • FRG

NIEJNOSTI • 1968 • Ishmukhamedov Elyor • USS • TENDERNESS ○ NYEZHNOST
NIEKOCHANA • 1966 • Nasfeter Janusz • PLN • NOT LOVED
NIEMAND WEISS ES • 1920 • Pick Lupu • FRG
NIEMANDSLAND • 1931 • Trivas Victor • FRG • HELL ON EARTH (USA) ○ NO MAN'S LAND (UKN) ○ WAR IS HELL
NIEMORALNA HISTORIA • 1990 • Sass Barbara • PLN • IMMORTAL STORY
NIEN HUA JE TS'AO • 1976 • Li Han-Hsiang • HKG • CRAZY SEX
NIENTE DI GRAVE, SUO MARITO E INCINTO (ITL) see **EVENEMENT LE PLUS IMPORTANT DEPUIS QUE L'HOMME A MARCHE SUR LA LUNE, L'** • 1973
NIENTE ROSE PER OSS 117 • 1968 • Desagnat Jean-Pierre, Cerrato Renzo, Hunebelle Andre • FRN, ITL • OSS 117 MURDER FOR SALE (UKN) ○ OSS 117 –DOUBLE AGENT (USA) ○ NO ROSES FOR OSS 117 ○ PAS DE ROSES POUR OSS117
NIEOBECNI • 1963 • Halladin Danuta • DOC • PLN • ABSENT
NIEPOTRZEBNI • 1962 • Lomnicki Jan, Halladin Danuta • DOC • PLN • NOT NEEDED
NIET GENOEG • 1968 • van der Velde • NTH • PAS ASSEZ ○ NOT ENOUGH
NIET INEJ CESTY • 1968 • Zachar Jozef • CZC • THERE'S NO OTHER WAY ○ THERE IS NO OTHER WAY
NIET VOOR DE POEZEN • 1972 • Rademakers Fons • NTH, BLG • BECAUSE OF THE CATS (UKN) ○ RAPE BECAUSE OF THE CATS, THE ○ RAPE, THE
NIET VOOR INGEBEELDE ZIEKEN • 1966 • van der Heyden Jef • NTH
NIETO DEL ZORRO, EL • 1947 • Salvador Jaime • MXC
NIETO SE CONGREVE, EL • 1949 • Torres-Rios Leopoldo • ARG
NIETOS DE DON VENANCIO, LOS • 1945 • Pardave Joaquin • MXC
NIEUWE ARCHITECTUUR • 1929 • Ivens Joris • SHT • NTH • NEW ARCHITECTURE (USA)
NIEUWE GRONDEN • 1934 • Ivens Joris • NTH • NEW EARTH
NIEUWE IJSTIJD, DE • 1974 • van der Keuken Johan • DOC • NTH • NEW ICE-AGE, THE
NIEUWE POLDERS • 1931 • *Van Dongen Helen (Ed)* • NTH
NIEWINNI CZARODZIEJE • 1959 • Wajda Andrzej • PLN • INNOCENT SORCERERS (USA)
NIEZNANY • 1965 • Lesiewicz Witold • PLN • UNKNOWN, THE
NIEZWYKLA PODROZ • 1955 • Haupe Wlodzimierz, Bielinska Halina • ANM • PLN • WHAT THE MOON SAW ○ MOON'S TALE, A ○ MOON'S STORY, THE
NIFTA • 1968 • Mazif Sid-Ali • SHT • ALG
NIFTY NINETIES, THE • 1941 • Thomson Riley • ANS • USA
NIFTY NURSES • 1934 • Jason Leigh • SHT • USA
NIGER '60 see **NIGER –JEUNE REPUBLIQUE, LE** • 1960
NIGER –JEUNE REPUBLIQUE, LE • 1960 • Jutra Claude, Rouch Jean • DOC • CND • NIGER '60
NIGERIA IN FIAMME see **PELLE DEGLI ALTRI, LA** • 1972
NIGGARD, THE • 1914 • Crisp Donald • USA
NIGGER, THE • 1915 • Lewis Edgar • USA
NIGGER BOY'S REVENGE, THE • 1904 • Fitzhamon Lewin • UKN
NIGGER COURTSHIP • 1903 • *Paul R. W.* • UKN
NIGHT • 1930 • Disney Walt • ANS • USA
NIGHT see **NOC** • 1961
NIGHT see **NOC** • 1967
NIGHT see **NISHANT** • 1975
NIGHT, THE see **NOTTE, LA** • 1961
NIGHT, THE (USA) see **YORU** • 1923
NIGHT.. A TRAIN, A see **SOIR, UN TRAIN, UN** • 1968
NIGHT AFFAIR (USA) see **DESORDRE ET LA NUIT, LE** • 1958
NIGHT AFTER DEATH see **NOC POSLIJE SMRTI** • 1984
NIGHT AFTER NIGHT • 1932 • Mayo Archie • USA
NIGHT AFTER NIGHT see **NIGHT AFTER NIGHT AFTER NIGHT** • 1970
NIGHT AFTER NIGHT AFTER NIGHT • 1970 • Force Lewis J. • UKN • HE KILLS NIGHT AFTER NIGHT AFTER NIGHT ○ NIGHT AFTER NIGHT
NIGHT ALARM • 1934 • Bennet Spencer Gordon • USA
NIGHT ALARM, A • 1908 • Raymond Charles? • UKN
NIGHT ALONE • 1938 • Bentley Thomas • UKN
NIGHT AMBUSH (USA) see **ILL MET BY MOONLIGHT** • 1956
NIGHT AND A BLONDE, A • *Herbert Hugh* • SHT • USA
NIGHT AND DAY • 1945 • Weiss Jiri • UKN
NIGHT AND DAY • 1946 • Curtiz Michael • USA
NIGHT AND DAY see **NOCE I DNIE** • 1974
NIGHT AND DAY (USA) see **JACK'S THE BOY** • 1932
NIGHT AND DESIRE • 1977 • el Elmi Yehia • EGY
NIGHT AND FOG IN JAPAN see **NIHON NO YORU TO KIRI** • 1960
NIGHT AND FOG OVER JAPAN see **NIHON NO YORU TO KIRI** • 1960
NIGHT AND FOG (UKN) see **NUIT ET BROUILLARD** • 1955
NIGHT AND MORNING • 1915 • Noy Wilfred • UKN
NIGHT AND THE CITY • 1950 • Dassin Jules • UKN
NIGHT AND THE DAWN, THE see **NOCHE Y EL ALBA, LA** • 1958
NIGHT AND TRAITORS see **LEIL WA KHAWANA** • 1989
NIGHT ANDY CAME HOME, THE see **DEATHDREAM** • 1972
NIGHT ANGEL • 1931 • Goulding Edmund • USA • SCARLET HOURS
NIGHT ANGEL, THE see **ANJO DA NOITE, O** • 1974
NIGHT ANGELS • 1979 • San Andres Luis • USA • NIGHT FLOWERS
NIGHT ANGELS see **ANJOS DA NOITE** • 1988
NIGHT AT EARL CARROLL'S, A • 1940 • Neumann Kurt • USA
NIGHT AT GLIMMINGE CASTLE see **NATT PA GLIMMINGEHUS, EN** • 1954
NIGHT AT SMYGEHOLM, A see **NATT PA SMYGEHOLM, EN** • 1933
NIGHT AT THE BILTMORE BOWL, A • 1935 • USA
NIGHT AT THE CLUB, A • 1913 • *Crystal* • USA
NIGHT AT THE CROSSROADS see **NUIT DU CARREFOUR, LA** • 1932
NIGHT AT THE INN, A • 1914 • Ridgely Richard • USA
NIGHT AT THE MAGIC CASTLE, A • 1988 • Tenenbaum Icek • USA
NIGHT AT THE MOVIES, A • 1937 • Rowland Roy • SHT • USA
NIGHT AT THE OPERA, A • 1935 • Wood Sam • USA
NIGHT AT THE RITZ, A • 1935 • McGann William • USA
NIGHT AT THE SEASHORE see **YO MEREN RANNAULA** • 1980
NIGHT AT THE TROC, A • 1939 • Dreifuss Arthur • SHT • USA
NIGHT ATTACK, A • 1910 • *Empire Films* • UKN
NIGHT BEAST • 1982 • Dohler Don • USA
NIGHT BEAT • 1948 • Huth Harold • UKN
NIGHT BEAT, THE • 1931 • Seitz George B. • USA
NIGHT BEAUTIES (UKN) see **BELLES DE NUITS, LES** • 1952
NIGHT BEFORE, THE • 1921 • St. Clair Malcolm • SHT • USA
NIGHT BEFORE, THE • 1988 • Eberhardt Thom • USA
NIGHT BEFORE CHRISTIAN'S BIRTHDAY, THE see **NATEN FOR KRISTIANS FODELSDAG** • 1908
NIGHT BEFORE CHRISTMAS, A (USA) see **VECHERA NA KHUTORE BLIZ DIKANKI** • 1961
NIGHT BEFORE CHRISTMAS, THE • 1905 • Porter Edwin S. • USA • HANGING STOCKINGS ON A CHRISTMAS TREE
NIGHT BEFORE CHRISTMAS, THE • 1912 • Brooke Van Dyke • USA
NIGHT BEFORE CHRISTMAS, THE • 1933 • Jackson Wilfred • ANS • USA
NIGHT BEFORE CHRISTMAS, THE • 1941 • Hanna William, Barbera Joseph • ANS • USA
NIGHT BEFORE CHRISTMAS, THE • 1951 • Brumberg Valentina, Brumberg L. • ANS • USS
NIGHT BEFORE PEARL HARBOR, THE see **RIKUGUN NAKANO GOKKO KAISEN ZENYA** • 1968
NIGHT BEFORE THE DIVORCE, THE • 1942 • Siodmak Robert • USA
NIGHT BEFORE THE MORNING AFTER, THE • 1979 • Healey Barry • CND
NIGHT BEFORE THE PREMIERE, THE see **NACHT VOR DER PREMIERE, DIE** • 1959
NIGHT BEFORE THE WAR, THE see **KAISEN NO ZENYA** • 1943
NIGHT BELL, THE • 1914 • Wilson Frank? • UKN
NIGHT BIRD • 1935 • Ganguly Dhiren • IND
NIGHT BIRD see **OISEAU DE NUIT** • 1975
NIGHT BIRD, THE • 1928 • Newmeyer Fred • USA
NIGHT BIRDS • 1930 • Eichberg Richard • UKN
NIGHT BIRDS see **GREIFER, DER** • 1930
NIGHT BLOSSOMS • 1966 • Chomont Tom S. • ANS • USA
NIGHT BOAT TO DUBLIN • 1946 • Huntington Lawrence • UKN
NIGHT BREED see **NIGHTBREED** • 1989
NIGHT BRIDE, THE • 1927 • Hopper E. Mason • USA
NIGHT BUTTERFLIES see **YORU NO CHO** • 1957
NIGHT BY THE SEASHORE see **YO MEREN RANNAULA** • 1980
NIGHT CABBIE see **NOCHNOY IZVOZCHIK** • 1929
NIGHT CALL NURSES • 1974 • Kaplan Jonathan • USA
NIGHT CALLER see **DEMON, THE** • 1979
NIGHT CALLER, THE • 1966 • Gilling John • UKN • BLOOD BEAST FROM OUTER SPACE (USA) ○ NIGHT CALLER FROM OUTER SPACE
NIGHT CALLER, THE (UKN) see **PEUR SUR LA VILLE** • 1975
NIGHT CALLER FROM OUTER SPACE see **NIGHT CALLER, THE** • 1966
NIGHT CAP • 1974 • Forcier Andre • SHT • CND
NIGHT CAP, THE see **NIGHTCAP, THE** • 1917
NIGHT CAP, THE see **SECRETS OF THE NIGHT** • 1925
NIGHT CAPER see **THURSDAY'S GAME** • 1974
NIGHT CARGO • 1936 • Hutchison Charles • USA
NIGHT CARGOES • 1962 • Morris Ernest • SRL • UKN
NIGHT CHASE • 1970 • Starrett Jack • TVM • USA
NIGHT CHILD see **NIGHT HAIR CHILD** • 1971
NIGHT CHILD (USA) see **PERCHE?** • 1975
NIGHT CHILDREN • 1953-54 • Devlin Bernard • DCS • CND
NIGHT CLASS • 1931 • Fraser Harry L. • USA
NIGHT CLERK'S NIGHTMARE, THE • 1912 • *Thanhouser* • USA
NIGHT CLUB • 1928 • Florey Robert • USA
NIGHT CLUB • 1929 • Foster John, Davis Mannie • ANS • USA
NIGHT CLUB • 1952 • Harwood A. R. • ASL
NIGHT CLUB • 1988 • Corbucci Sergio • ITL
NIGHT CLUB see **NIGHT CLUB GIRL** • 1944
NIGHT CLUB, THE • 1925 • Urson Frank, Iribe Paul • USA
NIGHT CLUB GIRL • 1944 • Cline Eddie • USA • NIGHT CLUB ○ NIGHT LIFE
NIGHT CLUB GIRL see **GLAMOR GIRL** • 1947
NIGHT CLUB HOSTESS (UKN) see **UNMARRIED** • 1939
NIGHT CLUB LADY, THE • 1932 • Cummings Irving • USA
NIGHT CLUB MURDER see **ROMANCE IN RHYTHM** • 1934
NIGHT CLUB QUEEN • 1934 • Vorhaus Bernard • UKN
NIGHT CLUB SCANDAL • 1937 • Murphy Ralph • USA • CITY HALL SCANDAL
NIGHT CLUB (UKN) see **GIGOLETTE** • 1935
NIGHT COMES TOO SOON • 1948 • Kavanagh Denis • UKN • GHOST OF RASHMON HALL, THE
NIGHT COURT • 1932 • Van Dyke W. S. • USA • JUSTICE FOR SALE (UKN)
NIGHT CRAWLER • 1987 • Little Dwight H. • USA
NIGHT CRAWLERS • 1964 • Goldman Peter Emanuel • SHT • USA
NIGHT CRAWLERS, THE see **NAVY VS. THE NIGHT MONSTERS, THE** • 1966
NIGHT CREATURE • 1978 • Madden Lee • USA • OUT OF THE DARKNESS
NIGHT CREATURES, THE see **ULTIMO UOMO DELLA TERRA, L'** • 1964
NIGHT CREATURES (USA) see **CAPTAIN CLEGG** • 1962
NIGHT CREW see **INTRUDER** • 1988
NIGHT CRIES • 1978 • Lang Richard • TVM • USA
NIGHT CRIES: A RURAL TRAGEDY • 1989 • Moffat Tracey • SHT • ASL
NIGHT CROSSING • 1957 • Tully Montgomery • UKN
NIGHT CROSSING • 1981 • Mann Delbert • UKN
NIGHT CRY, THE • 1926 • Raymaker Herman C. • USA
NIGHT DIGGER, THE • 1971 • Reid Alastair • UKN • ROAD BUILDER, THE
NIGHT DOES STRANGE THINGS, THE (UKN) see **ELENA ET LES HOMMES** • 1956
NIGHT DREAM see **SEN NOCI** • 1985
NIGHT DRIVE see **NIGHT TERROR** • 1976
NIGHT DRIVING • 1956 • Goldscholl Morton, Goldscholl Mildred • ANM • USA
NIGHT DRUM see **YORU NO TSUZUMI** • 1958
NIGHT DUTY • 1904 • Collins Alf? • UKN
NIGHT DUTY: OR, A POLICEMAN'S EXPERIENCES • 1906 • Green Tom? • UKN
NIGHT EATING • 1965 • Vanderbeek Stan • ANS • USA
NIGHT EDITOR • 1946 • Levin Henry • USA • TRESPASSER, THE (UKN)
NIGHT ENCOUNTER • 1954 • McLaren Norman • ANS • CND
NIGHT ENCOUNTER (USA) see **NUIT DES ESPIONS, LA** • 1959
NIGHT EVELYN CAME OUT OF THE GRAVE, THE (USA) see **NOTTE CHE EVELYN USCI DALLA TOMBA, LA** • 1971
NIGHT EXPRESS, THE (UKN) see **WESTERN LIMITED, THE** • 1932
NIGHT EYES • 1990 • Mundhra Jugmohan • USA, IND
NIGHT EYES see **DEADLY EYES** • 1982
NIGHT FEARS SUN see **LAILU YAKHAF ASH-SHAMS, AL-** • 1966
NIGHT FERRY • 1976 • Eady David • UKN
NIGHT FIGHTERS see **NIGHTFORCE** • 1987
NIGHT FIGHTERS, THE (USA) see **TERRIBLE BEAUTY, A** • 1960
NIGHT FLIGHT • 1933 • Brown Clarence • USA
NIGHT FLIGHT • 1979 • Davis Desmond • SHT • UKN
NIGHT FLIGHT see **HIKISAKARETA SEISO** • 1967
NIGHT FLIGHT FROM MOSCOW see **SERPENT, LE** • 1973
NIGHT FLOWER, THE see **PURCHASE PRICE, THE** • 1932
NIGHT FLOWERS see **NIGHT ANGELS** • 1979
NIGHT FLYER, THE • 1928 • Lang Walter • USA
NIGHT FOG see **NAKED FOG** • 1966
NIGHT FREIGHT • 1955 • Yarbrough Jean • USA
NIGHT FRIEND • 1988 • Gerretsen Peter • CND
NIGHT FRIGHT • 1968 • Sullivan James A. • USA • E.T.:THE EXTRA-TERRESTRIAL NASTIE ○ EXTRA-TERRESTRIAL NASTIE ○ NIGHTFRIGHT
NIGHT FULL OF RAIN see **FINE DEL MONDO NEL NOSTRO SOLITO LETTO IN UNA NOTTEPIENA DI PIOGGIA, LA** • 1978
NIGHT FULL OF SURPRISES • 1967 • Hartwig Jania • ANS • PLN • NIGHT OF SURPRISES, A
NIGHT GALLERY • 1969 • Sagal Boris, Spielberg Steven, Shear Barry • TVM • USA
NIGHT GAME • 1989 • Masterson Peter • USA
NIGHT GAMES • 1974 • Taylor Don • TVM • USA
NIGHT GAMES see **NOITE VAZIA** • 1965
NIGHT GAMES see **NATTLEK** • 1966
NIGHT GAMES see **FLASH LOVE** • 1971
NIGHT GAMES (USA) see **JEUX EROTIQUES DE NUIT** • 1979
NIGHT GOD SCREAMED, THE see **NIGHTMARE HOUSE** • 1973
NIGHT GUEST see **NOCNI HOST** • 1961
NIGHT GUY see **YORU NO TEHAISHI** • 1968
NIGHT HAIR CHILD • 1971 • Kelly James • UKN • WHAT THE PEEPER SAW (USA) ○ CHILD OF THE NIGHT ○ NIGHT CHILD
NIGHT HAS A THOUSAND EYES • 1948 • Farrow John • USA
NIGHT HAS EYES, THE • 1942 • Arliss Leslie • UKN • TERROR HOUSE (USA)
NIGHT HAWK, THE • 1921 • Gliddon John • UKN
NIGHT HAWK, THE • 1924 • Paton Stuart • USA
NIGHT HAWK, THE • 1938 • Salkow Sidney • USA
NIGHT HAWKS • 1914 • *Bushman Francis X.* • USA
NIGHT HEAT see **NOTTE BRAVA, LA** • 1959
NIGHT HEAT (UKN) see **CETTE NUIT-LA** • 1958
NIGHT HEAVEN FELL, THE (USA) see **BIJOUTIERS DU CLAIR DE LUNE, LES** • 1958
NIGHT HERDER, THE • 1911 • *Selig* • USA
NIGHT HOLDS A SECRET see **SONO YO NO HIMEGOTO** • 1957
NIGHT HOLDS TERROR, THE • 1955 • Stone Andrew L. • USA
NIGHT HOP • 1950 • Erulkar Sarah • UKN
NIGHT HORROR see **NOCNI DES** • 1914
NIGHT HORSEMEN, THE • 1921 • Reynolds Lynn • USA
NIGHT HUNTER see **IRO** • 1966
NIGHT HUNTER see **AVENGING FORCE** • 1986
NIGHT HUSTLERS, THE • 1968 • O'Donald Bobby • USA
NIGHT IN A HAREM, A see **SON OF SINBAD** • 1955
NIGHT IN ARMOUR, A • 1910 • Fitzhamon Lewin? • UKN
NIGHT IN BANGKOK see **BANGKOK NO YORU** • 1965
NIGHT IN CAIRO, A (UKN) see **BARBARIAN, THE** • 1933
NIGHT IN CASABLANCA, A • 1946 • Mayo Archie • USA
NIGHT IN DREAMLAND, A • 1907 • Blackton J. Stuart • USA
NIGHT IN GRENZWALD, THE see **NACHT IM GRENZWALD, DIE** • 1968
NIGHT IN HAVANA (UKN) see **BIG BOODLE, THE** • 1956
NIGHT IN HEAVEN, A • 1983 • Avildsen John G. • USA • HEAVEN
NIGHT IN HELL, A see **SCHAB NESHINI DOR DJAHANNAM** • 1957
NIGHT IN HONG KONG, A see **HONKON NO YORU** • 1961
NIGHT IN JUNE, A see **JUNINATTEN** • 1940
NIGHT IN KENTUCKY, A • 1915 • *Stonehouse Ruth* • USA
NIGHT IN LONDON • 1968 • Brij • IND
NIGHT IN LONDON, A see **NACHT IN LONDON, EINE** • 1928
NIGHT IN MAY, A • 1910 • Protazanov Yakov • USS
NIGHT IN MAY, A • 1941 • Ekk Nikolai • USS
NIGHT IN MAY, A (USA) see **NACHT IM MAI** • 1938
NIGHT IN MONTMARTRE, A • 1931 • Hiscott Leslie • UKN
NIGHT IN NEW ARABIA, A • 1917 • Mills Thomas R. • USA
NIGHT IN NEW ORLEANS, A • 1942 • Clemens William • USA • MORNING AFTER, THE
NIGHT IN OLD SPAIN, A • 1915 • Melville Wilbert • USA
NIGHT IN PARADISE, A • 1946 • Lubin Arthur • USA
NIGHT IN SEPTEMBER, A see **NOCH V SENTYABRE** • 1939
NIGHT IN THE ARCHIPELAGO, A see **SKARGARDSNATT, EN** • 1953
NIGHT IN THE CHAMBER OF HORRORS, A • 1914 • *Eclair* • FRN
NIGHT IN THE CITY • 1957 • Mitchell Dennis • UKN
NIGHT IN THE HARBOUR see **NATT I HAMN** • 1943
NIGHT IN THE JUNGLE, A • 1915 • Martin E. A. • USA
NIGHT IN THE LIFE OF JIMMY REARDON, A • 1988 • Richert William • USA • JIMMY REARDON
NIGHT IN THE MIRROR, THE see **NOCHE EN EL ESPEJO, LA** • 1962

NIGHT IN THE PICTURE GALLERY • Tovarek A., Zdrubecky J. • ANM • CZC
NIGHT IN THE SHOW, A • 1915 • Chaplin Charles • USA • CHARLIE AT THE SHOW
NIGHT IN TOWN, A • 1913 • Smalley Phillips • USA
NIGHT IN TUNISIA, A • 1980 • Elsom Bryan • SHT • USA
NIGHT INTO MORNING • 1951 • Markle Fletcher • USA
NIGHT INVADER, THE • 1943 • Mason Herbert • UKN
NIGHT IS A SORCERESS, THE see **NUIT EST UNE SORCIERE, LA** • 1959
NIGHT IS ENDING, THE (UKN) see **PARIS AFTER DARK** • 1943
NIGHT IS MADE FOR.. STEALING, THE see **NOTTE E FATTA PER.. RUBARE, LA** • 1967
NIGHT IS MY FUTURE see **MUSIK I MORKER** • 1947
NIGHT IS MY KINGDOM see **NUIT EST MON ROYAUME, LA** • 1951
NIGHT IS NOT FOR SLEEP (UKN) see **TOI LE VENIN** • 1958
NIGHT IS OURS, THE see **NUIT EST A NOUS, LA** • 1929
NIGHT IS THE PHANTOM (UKN) see **FRUSTA E IL CORPO, LA** • 1963
NIGHT IS YOUNG, THE • 1934 • Murphy Dudley • USA
NIGHT IS YOUNG, THE see **MAUVAIS SANG** • 1986
NIGHT JOURNEY • 1938 • Mitchell Oswald • UKN
NIGHT JOURNEY • 1960 • Hammid Alexander • USA
NIGHT JOURNEY see **RESA I NATTEN** • 1954
NIGHT KEY • 1937 • Corrigan Lloyd • USA
NIGHT KILLER see **SILENT MADNESS** • 1984
NIGHT LIFE • 1927 • Archainbaud George • USA
NIGHT LIFE • 1989 • Acomba David • USA
NIGHT LIFE see **NIGHT CLUB GIRL** • 1944
NIGHT LIFE IN HOLLYWOOD • 1922 • Caldwell Fred • USA
NIGHT LIFE IN RENO • 1931 • Cannon Raymond • USA
NIGHT LIFE IN THE ARMY • 1942 • Davis Mannie • ANS • USA
NIGHT LIFE IN TOKYO • 1961 • Davis Mannie • ANS • USA
NIGHT LIFE OF NEW YORK • 1925 • Dwan Allan • USA
NIGHT LIFE OF THE BUGS • 1936 • *Lantz Walter (P)* • ANS • USA
NIGHT LIFE OF THE GODS • 1935 • Sherman Lowell • USA • PRIVATE LIFE OF THE GODS
NIGHT LIGHTS AND DAY HI'S • 1964-65 • Branaman Bob • USA
NIGHT LIKE THIS, A • 1932 • Walls Tom • UKN
NIGHT MAGIC • 1985 • Furey Lewis • CND
NIGHT MAIL • 1935 • Smith Herbert • UKN
NIGHT MAIL • 1936 • Wright Basil, Watt Harry • DOC • UKN
NIGHT MARCH IN ST. ERIK'S LANE, THE see **NATTMARSCHEN I SANCT ERIKS GRAND** • 1909
NIGHT MAYOR, THE • 1932 • Stoloff Ben • USA
NIGHT MESSAGE, THE • 1924 • Sheehan Perley Poore • USA • INNOCENT
NIGHT MONSTER, THE • 1943 • Beebe Ford • USA • HOUSE OF MYSTERY (UKN)
NIGHT MOTH, THE see **NOCNI MOTYL** • 1941
'NIGHT, MOTHER • 1986 • Moore Tom* • USA • NIGHT, MOTHER
NIGHT, MOTHER see **'NIGHT, MOTHER** • 1986
NIGHT MOVES • 1975 • Penn Arthur • USA • DARK TOWER, THE
NIGHT MOVES see **SQUEEZE, THE** • 1980
NIGHT MUSIC, THE see **BARTOK BELA: AZ EJSZAKA ZENEJE** • 1971
NIGHT MUST FALL • 1937 • Thorpe Richard • USA
NIGHT MUST FALL • 1964 • Reisz Karel • UKN
NIGHT MY NUMBER CAME UP, THE • 1955 • Norman Leslie • UKN
NIGHT 'N' GALES • 1937 • Douglas Gordon • SHT • USA
NIGHT NEVER ENDS, THE see **DAR EMTEDADE SHAB** • 1975
NIGHT NURSE • 1931 • Wellman William A. • USA
NIGHT NURSE • 1978 • Auzins Igor • MTV • ASL
NIGHT NURSE, THE • 1988 • Najafi Mohammad-Ali • IRN
NIGHT OF A DEAD WOMAN WHO LIVED, THE see **CASA DE LAS MUERTAS VIVIENTES, LA** • 1972
NIGHT OF A THOUSAND CATS, THE (USA) see **NOCHE DE LOS MIL GATOS, LA** • 1972
NIGHT OF ADVENTURE, A • 1944 • Douglas Gordon • USA • ONE EXCITING NIGHT
NIGHT OF ANGELS, THE see **SHAB-E-FERESHTEGAN** • 1968
NIGHT OF ANGUISH, A • 1913 • *Eclair* • USA
NIGHT OF ANUBIS see **NIGHT OF THE LIVING DEAD** • 1968
NIGHT OF BLOODY HORROR • 1969 • Houck Joy N. Jr. • USA
NIGHT OF COUNTING THE YEARS, THE see **MUMIA, AL-** • 1969
NIGHT OF COURAGE, A • 1987 • Silverstein Elliot • TVM • USA
NIGHT OF CRIME, A • 1942 • Thurn-Taxis Alexis • USA
NIGHT OF DARK SHADOWS • 1971 • Curtis Dan • USA • CURSE OF DARK SHADOWS
NIGHT OF DARKNESS see **REST IN PEACE** • 1982
NIGHT OF DOOM see **NACHT ZONDER ZEGEN** • 1977
NIGHT OF ENCHANTMENT, A • 1917 • *Chaffee Marguerite* • SHT • USA
NIGHT OF EVIL • 1962 • Galbreath Richard • USA
NIGHT OF FAME, A see **AL DIAVOLO LA CELEBRITA** • 1949
NIGHT OF FEAR • 1972 • Bourke Terry • ASL
NIGHT OF FEAR see **EDGE OF FEAR** • 1964
NIGHT OF FEMALE SHAMAN • 1983 • Bae Chang-Ho • SKR
NIGHT OF FRIGHTS see **NACHT DES SCHRECKENS, DIE** • 1929
NIGHT OF HIS LIFE, THE • 1918 • *Archie Willie* • USA
NIGHT OF HORROR, A • Cooper Arthur
NIGHT OF HORROR, A see **NACHT DES GRAUENS** • 1916
NIGHT OF JANUARY 16TH, THE • 1941 • Clemens William • USA
NIGHT OF JUNE 13TH, THE • 1932 • Roberts Stephen • USA
NIGHT OF KARLSTEIN see **NOC NA KARLSTEJNE** • 1973
NIGHT OF LOVE see **TRADITA** • 1954
NIGHT OF LOVE see **DROGUE DU VICE, LA** • 1963
NIGHT OF LOVE, THE • 1927 • Fitzmaurice George • USA
NIGHT OF LUST (USA) see **DROGUE DU VICE, LA** • 1963
NIGHT OF MAGIC, A • 1944 • Wynne Herbert • UKN
NIGHT OF MIRACLES, THE see **LAILAT EL KADR** • 1952
NIGHT OF MYSTERY • 1937 • Dupont E. A. • USA • GREEN MURDER CASE, THE (UKN)
NIGHT OF MYSTERY, A • 1928 • Mendes Lothar • USA • CODE OF HONOUR, THE
NIGHT OF MYSTERY, A see **HIS TIGER LADY** • 1928
NIGHT OF NIGHTS, THE • 1940 • Milestone Lewis • USA • HAPPY ENDING ○ HEAVEN ON A SHOESTRING
NIGHT OF PASSION see **JONETSU NO ICHIYA** • 1929
NIGHT OF PASSION see **DURING ONE NIGHT** • 1961
NIGHT OF PERIL, A • 1912 • Haldane Bert • UKN
NIGHT OF REMEMBRANCE, A see **CELULOZA** • 1953
NIGHT OF RETRIBUTION • 1987 • Bergman Robert • USA • SKULL: A NIGHT OF TERROR
NIGHT OF REVENGE, THE see **HAEVNENS NAT** • 1915
NIGHT OF SAN JUAN, THE (USA) see **NOTTE DI SAN JUAN, LA** • 1971
NIGHT OF SAN LORENZO, THE(UKN) see **NOTTE DI SAN LORENZO, LA** • 1981
NIGHT OF SORROW, THE see **HICRAN GECESI** • 1968
NIGHT OF SOULS, THE • 1915 • *Travers Richard C.* • USA
NIGHT OF SURPRISES, A see **NIGHT FULL OF SURPRISES** • 1967
NIGHT OF TERROR • 1908 • *Bitzer Billy (Ph)* • USA
NIGHT OF TERROR • 1933 • Stoloff Ben • USA
NIGHT OF TERROR • 1972 • Szwarc Jeannot • TVM • USA
NIGHT OF TERROR • 1984 • SAF
NIGHT OF TERROR, A • 1911 • Porter Edwin S. • USA
NIGHT OF TERROR, A • 1913 • *De Lespine Edgena* • USA
NIGHT OF TERROR, A see **NACHT DES GRAUENS** • 1916
NIGHT OF TERRORS, THE see **LAMA NEL CORPO, LA** • 1966
NIGHT OF THE ALIEN see **FUTURE-KILL** • 1984
NIGHT OF THE ASKARI see **WHISPERING DEATH** • 1975
NIGHT OF THE ASSASSIN, THE • 1972 • McNahon Robert • USA
NIGHT OF THE BEAST see **HOUSE OF THE BLACK DEATH** • 1965
NIGHT OF THE BIG HEAT • 1967 • Fisher Terence • UKN • ISLAND OF THE BURNING DAMNED (USA) ○ ISLAND OF THE BURNING DOOMED
NIGHT OF THE BLIND DEAD see **NOCHE DEL TERROR CIEGO, LA** • 1972
NIGHT OF THE BLIND TERROR, THE see **NOCHE DEL TERROR CIEGO, LA** • 1972
NIGHT OF THE BLOOD BEAST • 1958 • Kowalski Bernard • USA • CREATURE FROM GALAXY 27, THE ○ MONSTER FROM GALAXY 27, THE
NIGHT OF THE BLOOD MONSTER (USA) see **PROCESO DE LAS BRUJAS, EL** • 1970
NIGHT OF THE BLOODY APES see **HORRIPLANTE BESTIA HUMANA, LA** • 1970
NIGHT OF THE BRIDE, THE see **NOC NEVESTY** • 1967
NIGHT OF THE CEMETERY, THE see **NUIT DU CIMITIERE, LA** • 1973
NIGHT OF THE CLAW see **ISLAND CLAWS** • 1980
NIGHT OF THE COBRA WOMAN • 1972 • Meyer Andrew • USA, PHL • MOVINI'S VENOM
NIGHT OF THE COMET • 1984 • Eberhardt Thom • USA
NIGHT OF THE CREEPS • 1986 • Dekker Fred • USA • HOMECOMING NIGHT
NIGHT OF THE DAMNED, THE (UKN) see **NOTTE DEI DANNATI, LA** • 1971
NIGHT OF THE DARK FULL MOON see **SILENT NIGHT, BLOODY NIGHT** • 1972
NIGHT OF THE DEATH CULT see **NOCHE DE LAS GAVIOTAS, LA** • 1975
NIGHT OF THE DEMON • 1957 • Tourneur Jacques • UKN • CURSE OF THE DEMON (USA) ○ HAUNTED
NIGHT OF THE DEMON • 1983 • Wasson James C. • USA
NIGHT OF THE DEMON see **CURSE OF MELISSA, THE** • 1971
NIGHT OF THE DEMONS • 1988 • Tenney Kevin S. • USA • HALLOWEEN PARTY
NIGHT OF THE DEVIL • 1974 • *Hallmark* • USA
NIGHT OF THE DEVILS (UKN) see **NOTTE DEI DIAVOLI, LA** • 1972
NIGHT OF THE DOOMED see **AMANTI D'OLTRETOMBA** • 1965
NIGHT OF THE DUB, THE • 1920 • Harvey John Joseph • SHT • USA • NIGHT OF THE PUB, THE
NIGHT OF THE EAGLE • 1962 • Hayers Sidney • UKN • BURN, WITCH, BURN (USA) ○ CONJURE WIFE
NIGHT OF THE EMBASSY BALL, THE • 1915 • *Coombs Guy* • USA
NIGHT OF THE EXORCIST see **SHE WAITS** • 1971
NIGHT OF THE FALCON, THE see **NOCHE DEL HALCON, LA** • 1968
NIGHT OF THE FLESH EATERS see **NIGHT OF THE LIVING DEAD** • 1968
NIGHT OF THE FLOWERS (USA) see **NOTTE DEI FIORI, LA** • 1972
NIGHT OF THE FOLLOWING DAY, THE • 1969 • Cornfield Hubert • USA
NIGHT OF THE FULL MOON see **POONAM KI RAAT** • 1965
NIGHT OF THE FULL MOON see **DONNA DELLA LUNA, LA** • 1988
NIGHT OF THE FULL MOON, THE • 1954 • Taylor Donald • UKN
NIGHT OF THE GARTER • 1933 • Raymond Jack • UKN
NIGHT OF THE GARTER, A • 1913 • *Nestor* • USA
NIGHT OF THE GENERALS, THE • 1966 • Litvak Anatole • UKN, FRN • NUIT DES GENERAUX, LA (FRN)
NIGHT OF THE GHOULS • 1959 • Wood Edward D. Jr. • USA • REVENGE OF THE DEAD
NIGHT OF THE GREAT ATTACK, THE (USA) see **NOTTE DEL GRANDE ASSALTO, LA** • 1960
NIGHT OF THE GRIZZLY, THE • 1966 • Pevney Joseph • USA
NIGHT OF THE HONEYMOON see **MODAE** • 1964
NIGHT OF THE HOWLING BEAST see **MALDICION DE LA BESTIA, LA** • 1975
NIGHT OF THE HUNTER, THE • 1955 • Laughton Charles • USA
NIGHT OF THE IGUANA, THE • 1964 • Huston John • USA
NIGHT OF THE JUGGLER • 1980 • Butler Robert, Furie Sidney J. (U/c) • USA
NIGHT OF THE KILLER see **MURI SHINJU NIHON NO NATSU** • 1967
NIGHT OF THE KNIGHT, THE • 1924 • Quiribet Gaston • UKN
NIGHT OF THE LAUGHING DEAD see **HOUSE IN NIGHTMARE PARK, THE** • 1973
NIGHT OF THE LEPUS • 1972 • Claxton William F. • USA • RABBITS
NIGHT OF THE LIVING DEAD • 1968 • Romero George A. • USA • NIGHT OF THE FLESH EATERS ○ NIGHT OF ANUBIS
NIGHT OF THE LIVING DEAD • 1990 • Romero George A. • USA
NIGHT OF THE LIVING DEAD see **RETURN OF THE LIVING DEAD** • 1985
NIGHT OF THE LOCK-KEEPER, THE see **NUIT DE L'ECLUSIER, LA** • 1988
NIGHT OF THE MAYAS (USA) see **NOCHE DE LOS MAYAS, LA** • 1939
NIGHT OF THE OUTRAGES (UKN) see **NUIT LA PLUS CHAUDE, LA** • 1968
NIGHT OF THE PARTY • 1906 • *Bitzer Billy (Ph)* • USA
NIGHT OF THE PARTY, THE • 1934 • Powell Michael • UKN • MURDER PARTY, THE (USA)
NIGHT OF THE PENCILS, THE • 1987 • Olivera Hector • ARG
NIGHT OF THE PROWLER • 1962 • Searle Francis • UKN
NIGHT OF THE PUB, THE see **NIGHT OF THE DUB, THE** • 1920
NIGHT OF THE PUPPETS • 1980 • SAF
NIGHT OF THE QUARTER MOON, THE • 1959 • Haas Hugo • USA • COLOR OF HER SKIN, THE ○ FLESH AND FLAME
NIGHT OF THE RED WINE see **NOCHE DE VINO TINTO** • 1968
NIGHT OF THE REVOLUTION see **GRAND SOIR, UN** • 1976
NIGHT OF THE SCARECROW see **DARK NIGHT OF THE SCARECROW** • 1981
NIGHT OF THE SCARECROW, THE see **NOITE DO ESPANTALHO, A** • 1974
NIGHT OF THE SEAGULL, THE (USA) see **SUNA NO KAORI** • 1968
NIGHT OF THE SEAGULLS (USA) see **NOCHE DE LAS GAVIOTAS, LA** • 1975
NIGHT OF THE SERPENTS (USA) see **NOTTE DEI SERPENTI, LA** • 1969
NIGHT OF THE SHARKS • 1987 • Ricci Tonino • ITL
NIGHT OF THE SHOOTING STARS (USA) see **NOTTE DI SAN LORENZO, LA** • 1981
NIGHT OF THE SILICATES see **ISLAND OF TERROR** • 1965
NIGHT OF THE SORCERERS • 1970 • *Taylor Jack* • MXC
NIGHT OF THE SORCERESS see **NOCHE DE LOS BRUJOS, LA** • 1973
NIGHT OF THE SPECTERS, THE see **NOTTE DEGLI SPETTRI, LA** • 1913
NIGHT OF THE SPIES, THE see **NUIT DES ESPIONS, LA** • 1959
NIGHT OF THE STORM, THE (UKN) see **WIE DER STURMWIND** • 1957
NIGHT OF THE STRANGLER • 1975 • Houck Joy N. Jr. • USA • VENGEANCE IS MINE
NIGHT OF THE TERROR see **TERROR, THE** • 1963
NIGHT OF THE THREE LOVERS, THE (USA) see **NUIT LA PLUS CHAUDE, LA** • 1968
NIGHT OF THE TIGER, THE see **RIDE BEYOND VENGEANCE** • 1966
NIGHT OF THE VAMPIRE • Mays Peter • SHT • USA
NIGHT OF THE VIBRATOR • 1969 • *Canyon Dist. Co* • USA
NIGHT OF THE WEHRMACHT ZOMBIES see **NIGHT OF THE ZOMBIES** • 1981
NIGHT OF THE WEREWOLF see **CRAVING, THE** • 1985
NIGHT OF THE WILD DONKEYS, THE see **NACHT VAN DE WILDE EZELS, DE** • 1989
NIGHT OF THE WITCHES • 1970 • Larsen Keith • USA • NIGHT OF WITCHES
NIGHT OF THE ZOMBIES • 1981 • Reed Joel M. • USA • NIGHT OF THE WEHRMACHT ZOMBIES ○ CHILLING, THE ○ GAMMA 693
NIGHT OF THE ZOMBIES • 1983 • Mattei Bruno • ITL
NIGHT OF THOUGHT, A • 1966 • Romm Mikhail • USS
NIGHT OF THRILLS, A • 1914 • De Grasse Joseph • USA
NIGHT OF VENGEANCE (USA) see **HAEVNENS NAT** • 1915
NIGHT OF VIOLENCE (USA) see **NOTTI DELLA VIOLENZA, LE** • 1966
NIGHT OF WITCHES see **NIGHT OF THE WITCHES** • 1970
NIGHT ON A BARE MOUNTAIN, A see **NUIT SUR LA MONTE CHAUVE** • 1934
NIGHT ON BALD MOUNTAIN, A (USA) see **NUIT SUR LA MONTE CHAUVE** • 1934
NIGHT ON BARE MOUNTAIN see **HOUSE ON BARE MOUNTAIN, THE** • 1962
NIGHT ON THE AUTOBAHN, A see **NACHTS AUF DEN STRASSEN** • 1952
NIGHT ON THE DANUBE, A see **NACHT AN DER DONAU, EINE** • 1935
NIGHT ON THE ROAD, A • 1914 • *Valdez Rene* • USA
NIGHT ON THE TOWN, A see **FLAM** • 1966
NIGHT ON THE TOWN, A see **ADVENTURES IN BABYSITTING** • 1987
NIGHT OR DAY see **YO VAI PAIVA** • 1962
NIGHT OUT see **SAMEDI SOIR** • 1960
NIGHT OUT, A • 1912 • *Selig* • USA
NIGHT OUT, A • 1914 • France Charles H. • USA
NIGHT OUT, A • 1915 • *Searchlight* • UKN
NIGHT OUT, A • 1915 • Chaplin Charles • USA • CHAMPAGNE CHARLIE
NIGHT OUT, A • 1916 • Baker George D. • USA
NIGHT OUT, THE see **NOTTE BRAVA, LA** • 1959
NIGHT OUT AND A DAY IN, A • 1920 • Sanderson Challis • SHT • UKN
NIGHT OUT, OR HE COULDN'T GO HOME UNTIL MORNING, A • 1908 • *Vitagraph* • USA
NIGHT OWL, THE • 1926 • Brown Harry J. • USA
NIGHT OWLS • 1927 • Sandrich Mark • SHT • USA
NIGHT OWLS • 1929 • Newfield Sam • SHT • USA
NIGHT OWLS • 1930 • Parrott James • SHT • USA
NIGHT PARADE • 1929 • St. Clair Malcolm • USA • SPORTING LIFE (UKN)
NIGHT PARTNERS • 1983 • Nosseck Noel • TVM • USA
NIGHT PASSAGE • 1957 • Neilson James • USA
NIGHT PATHS see **WEGE IN DER NACHT** • 1979
NIGHT PATROL • 1985 • Kong Jackie • USA
NIGHT PATROL, THE • 1926 • Smith Noel • USA

NIGHT PATROL, THE • 1929 • Lee Norman • UKN • CITY OF SHADOWS
NIGHT PEOPLE • 1954 • Johnson Nunnally • USA
NIGHT PLANE FROM CHUNGKING • 1943 • Murphy Ralph • USA
NIGHT PLANE TO AMSTERDAM • 1955 • Hughes Ken • UKN
NIGHT PLEASURE see **YORU NO YOROKOBI** • 1967
NIGHT PORTER, THE • 1930 • Collins Sewell • UKN
NIGHT PORTER, THE (UKN) see **PORTIERE DI NOTTE, IL** • 1974
NIGHT PRAYER see **PREGHIERA DELLA NOTTE**
NIGHT RAIDERS • 1952 • Bretherton Howard • USA
NIGHT REHEARSAL, THE see **NOCNI ZKOUSKA** • 1980
NIGHT RIDE • 1930 • Robertson John S. • USA • DEADLINE AT DAWN
NIGHT RIDE • 1937 • Carstairs John Paddy • UKN
NIGHT RIDER • 1962 • Hinn Michael • SHT • USA
NIGHT RIDER, THE • 1920 • Joos Therdo? • SHT • USA
NIGHT RIDER, THE • 1932 • Nigh William • USA
NIGHT RIDER, THE • 1979 • Averback Hy • TVM • USA
NIGHT RIDERS • 1908 • *Kalem* • USA
NIGHT RIDERS • 1958 • Mendez Fernando • MXC
NIGHT RIDERS see **NOCNI JEZDCI** • 1981
NIGHT RIDERS, THE • 1913 • *Majestic* • USA
NIGHT RIDERS, THE • 1916 • Jaccard Jacques • SHT • USA
NIGHT RIDERS, THE • 1920 • Butler Alexander • UKN
NIGHT RIDERS, THE • 1939 • Sherman George • USA
NIGHT RIDERS OF MONTANA • 1951 • Brannon Fred C. • USA
NIGHT RIDERS OF PETERSHAM, THE • 1914 • Davis Ulysses • USA
NIGHT RIPPER • 1986 • Hatchcock Jeff • USA
NIGHT RIVER see **YORU NO KAWA** • 1956
NIGHT ROADS OF LOVE, THE see **DROMI TIS AGAPIS INE NICHTERIN, I** • 1981
NIGHT ROSE, THE • 1921 • Worsley Wallace • USA • FLOWERS OF DARKNESS ○ VOICES OF THE CITY
NIGHT RUNNER • 1957 • Biberman Abner • USA
NIGHT RUSTLERS, THE • 1910 • *Bison* • USA
NIGHT SCANDAL IN JAPAN see **AKUJO** • 1964
NIGHT SCHOOL see **TERROR EYES** • 1980
NIGHT SCREAMS • 1987 • Plone Allen • USA
NIGHT SHADOWS • 1916 • *Gordon Alfred* • SHT • USA
NIGHT SHADOWS • 1931 • De Courville Albert • UKN
NIGHT SHADOWS see **MUTANT** • 1983
NIGHT SHADOWS OF NEW YORK • 1913 • *Imp* • USA
NIGHT SHE AROSE FROM THE TOMB, THE (UKN) see **NOTTE CHE EVELYN USCI DALLA TOMBA, LA** • 1971
NIGHT SHIFT • 1941 • Kanin Garson • DOC • USA
NIGHT SHIFT • 1942 • Chambers Jack • DOC • UKN
NIGHT SHIFT • 1982 • Howard Ron • USA • NIGHTSHIFT
NIGHT SHIFT see **HARD MAN'S GOOD TO FIND, A** • 1969
NIGHT SHIP, THE • 1925 • McCarty Henry • USA
NIGHT SLAVES • 1970 • Post Ted • TVM • USA
NIGHT SONG • 1947 • Cromwell John • USA
NIGHT SONG see **SWEET LOVE, BITTER** • 1967
NIGHT SPOT • 1938 • Cabanne W. Christy • USA
NIGHT STAGE TO GALVESTON • 1952 • Archainbaud George • USA
NIGHT STALKER • 1971 • Moxey John Llewellyn • TVM • USA • KOLCHACK TAPES, THE
NIGHT STALKER, THE • 1987 • Kleven Max • USA
NIGHT STAR see **AKSAM YILDIZI** • 1967
NIGHT STAR -GODDESS OF ELECTRA see **ROMA CONTRA ROMA** • 1963
NIGHT STRANGLER, THE • 1972 • Curtis Dan • TVM • USA • TIME KILLER, THE
NIGHT STRIPES • 1944 • Kanin Garson • DOC • USA
NIGHT SWIFT • 1945 • Rotha Paul • DOC • UKN
NIGHT TALES OF HOMMOKU see **HOMMOKU YAWA** • 1924
NIGHT TERROR • 1976 • Swackhamer E. W. • TVM • USA • NIGHT DRIVE
NIGHT THAT GOD SCREAMED, THE see **NIGHTMARE HOUSE** • 1973
NIGHT THAT PANICKED AMERICA, THE • 1975 • Sargent Joseph • TVM • USA
NIGHT THAT SOPHIE GRADUATED, THE • 1915 • *Joslin Margaret* • USA
NIGHT THE ANIMALS TALKED, THE • 1970 • Gavioli Roberto • ANS • ITL
NIGHT THE BRIDGE FELL DOWN, THE • 1982 • Fenady George • TVM • USA
NIGHT THE CITY SCREAMED, THE • 1980 • Falk Harry • TVM • USA
NIGHT THE CREATURES CAME see **ISLAND OF TERROR** • 1965
NIGHT THE LIGHTS WENT OUT IN GEORGIA, THE • 1981 • Maxwell Ronald F. • USA
NIGHT THE PROWLER, THE • 1978 • Sharman Jim • ASL
NIGHT THE SILCATES CAME see **ISLAND OF TERROR** • 1965
NIGHT THE SUN CAME OUT, THE see **WATERMELON MAN** • 1970
NIGHT THE SUN CAME OUT ON HAPPY HOLLOW LANE, THE see **WATERMELON MAN** • 1970
NIGHT THE WORLD EXPLODED, THE • 1957 • Sears Fred F. • USA
NIGHT THE WORLD SHOOK, THE see **GORGO** • 1961
NIGHT THEY INVENTED STRIPTEASE, THE see **NIGHT THEY RAIDED MINSKY'S, THE** • 1969
NIGHT THEY KILLED RASPUTIN, THE (USA) see **NUITS DE RASPOUTINE, LES** • 1960
NIGHT THEY RAIDED MINSKY'S, THE • 1969 • Friedkin William • USA • NIGHT THEY INVENTED STRIPTEASE, THE
NIGHT THEY ROBBED BIG BERTHA'S, THE • 1978 • Kares Peter J. • USA
NIGHT THEY SAVED CHRISTMAS, THE • 1984 • Cooper Jackie • TVM • USA
NIGHT THEY TOOK MISS BEAUTIFUL, THE • 1977 • Lewis Robert Michael • TVM • USA
NIGHT TIDE • 1963 • Harrington Curtis • USA
NIGHT TIME IN NEVADA • 1948 • Witney William • USA
NIGHT TO REMEMBER, A • 1943 • Wallace Richard • USA • FRIGHTENED STIFF, A
NIGHT TO REMEMBER, A • 1958 • Baker Roy Ward • UKN
NIGHT TO REMEMBER, A see **SONO YO WA WASURENAI** • 1962
NIGHT TRAIN FOR INVERNESS • 1960 • Morris Ernest • UKN
NIGHT TRAIN FOR THE MILKY WAY, THE see **GINGA-TETSUDO NO YORU** • 1985
NIGHT TRAIN TO KATMANDU • 1988 • Wiemer Robert • USA
NIGHT TRAIN TO MEMPHIS • 1946 • Selander Lesley • USA
NIGHT TRAIN TO MILAN see **CRIMINALE, IL** • 1963
NIGHT TRAIN TO MUNDO FINE • 1966 • Francis Coleman • USA
NIGHT TRAIN TO MUNICH • 1940 • Reed Carol • UKN • NIGHT TRAIN (USA) ○ GESTAPO
NIGHT TRAIN TO MURDER see **MORECAMBE AND WISE: NIGHT TRAIN TO MURDER** • 1984
NIGHT TRAIN TO PARIS • 1964 • Douglas Robert • UKN
NIGHT TRAIN TO TERROR • 1985 • Carr John, Marshak Philip, McGowan Tom, Tallas Gregg R., Schlossberg-Cohen Jay • ANT • USA
NIGHT TRAIN (USA) see **NIGHT TRAIN TO MUNICH** • 1940
NIGHT TRAIN (USA) see **POCIAG** • 1959
NIGHT UNDER MARTIAL LAW, THE see **KAIGENREI NO YORU** • 1981
NIGHT UNTO NIGHT • 1949 • Siegel Don • USA
NIGHT VISION • 1988 • Krueger Michael • USA
NIGHT VISITOR • 1989 • Hitzig Robert • USA
NIGHT VISITOR, THE • 1970 • Benedek Laslo • UKN, DNM • SALEM COMES TO SUPPER ○ LUNATIC ○ SALEM CAME TO SUPPER
NIGHT VISITORS • 1988 • Fulk David • USA
NIGHT VOYAGE see **NATSEILERE** • 1985
NIGHT VOYAGE see **GECE YOLCULUGU** • 1988
NIGHT WAITRESS • 1936 • Landers Lew • USA
NIGHT WALK see **DEATHDREAM** • 1972
NIGHT WALKER, THE • 1964 • Castle William • USA
NIGHT WARNING • 1982 • Asher William • USA • BUTCHER, BAKER, NIGHTMARE MAKER ○ NIGHTMARE MAKER
NIGHT WARS see **NIGHTWARS** • 1987
NIGHT WAS DARK, THE see **RAAT ANDHERI THI** • 1967
NIGHT WAS OUR FRIEND • 1951 • Anderson Michael • UKN
NIGHT WATCH • 1941 • Taylor Donald • UKN
NIGHT WATCH • 1973 • Hutton Brian G. • UKN
NIGHT WATCH see **FIREHOUSE** • 1972
NIGHT WATCH, THE • 1916 • Ellis Robert • USA
NIGHT WATCH, THE • 1926 • Caldwell Fred • USA
NIGHT WATCH, THE • 1928 • Korda Alexander • USA • HIS WIFE'S AFFAIR
NIGHT WATCH, THE (USA) see **TROU, LE** • 1960
NIGHT WATCHER • 1989 • Wheeler David • USA
NIGHT WATCHMAN, THE • 1938 • Jones Charles M. • ANS • USA
NIGHT WATCHMAN'S MISTAKE, THE • 1929 • *Sennett Mack (P)* • SHT • USA
NIGHT WATCHMAN'S WIFE, THE see **NATTVAKTENS HUSTRU** • 1948
NIGHT WE DROPPED A CLANGER, THE • 1959 • Conyers Darcy • UKN • MAKE MINE A DOUBLE (USA)
NIGHT WE GOT THE BIRD, THE • 1960 • Conyers Darcy • UKN
NIGHT WIND • 1948 • Tinling James • USA
NIGHT WITH A CAT, A • 1970 • Hornak Miroslav • CZC
NIGHT WITH A MILLION, A • 1914 • *Bushman Francis X.* • USA
NIGHT WITH MASQUERADERS IN PARIS, A (USA) see **NUIT DE CARNAVAL** • 1908
NIGHT WITH MESSALINA, A see **BACANALES ROMANAS** • 1982
NIGHT WITH SILENA, THE • 1987 • Panayotato Dimitris • GRC
NIGHT WITH THE DEVIL, A • *Toddy* • USA
NIGHT WITH THE EMPEROR see **NACHT MIT DEM KAISER, DIE** • 1936
NIGHT WITH THE GREAT ONE, A • 1969 • *Fields W. C.* • ANT • USA • GREAT ONE, THE ○ W.C. FIELDS
NIGHT WITHOUT PITY • 1962 • Zichy Theodore • UKN
NIGHT WITHOUT SLEEP • 1952 • Baker Roy Ward • USA
NIGHT WITHOUT STARS • 1951 • Pelissier Anthony • UKN
NIGHT WOMEN (USA) see **FEMME SPECTACLE, LA** • 1964
NIGHT WON'T TALK, THE • 1952 • Birt Daniel • UKN
NIGHT WORK • 1930 • Mack Russell • USA
NIGHT WORK • 1939 • Archainbaud George • USA
NIGHT WORKERS, THE • 1917 • Haydon J. Charles • USA
NIGHT WORLD • 1932 • Henley Hobart • USA
NIGHT ZOO see **ZOO LA NUIT, UN** • 1987
NIGHTBIRDS OF LONDON • 1915 • Wilson Frank • UKN
NIGHTBREAKER • 1989 • Markle Peter • USA • ADVANCE TO GROUND ZERO
NIGHTBREED • 1989 • Barker Clive • UKN, USA • NIGHT BREED
NIGHTCAP, THE • 1911 • *Solax* • USA
NIGHTCAP, THE • 1917 • Clements Roy • SHT • USA • SECRETS OF THE NIGHT ○ NIGHT CAP, THE
NIGHTCATS • 1956 • Brakhage Stan • SHT • USA
NIGHTCLEANERS PART 1 • 1975 • Berwick Street Collective • UKN
NIGHTCOMERS, THE • 1972 • Winner Michael • UKN
NIGHTDREAMS • 1981 • Pope F. X. • USA
NIGHTFALL • 1956 • Tourneur Jacques • USA
NIGHTFALL • 1988 • Mayersberg Paul • USA
NIGHTFLYERS • 1987 • Collector Robert • USA
NIGHTFORCE • 1987 • Foldes Lawrence D. • USA • NIGHT FIGHTERS
NIGHTFRIGHT see **NIGHT FRIGHT** • 1968
NIGHTGAMES • 1986 • Arnold Jeffrey • MTV • CND
NIGHTHAWKS • 1978 • Peck Ron, Hallam Paul • UKN
NIGHTHAWKS • 1980 • Malmuth Bruce • USA • HAWKS
NIGHTINGALE see **GRUNYA KORNAKOVA** • 1936
NIGHTINGALE see **UGUISU** • 1938
NIGHTINGALE, THE • 1914 • Thomas Augustus • USA
NIGHTINGALE, THE • 1983 • Passer Ivan • MTV • USA
NIGHTINGALE AND THE ROSE, THE • 1967 • Kabrt Josef • ANS • CZC
NIGHTINGALE, LITTLE NIGHTINGALE see **GRUNYA KORNAKOVA** • 1936
NIGHTINGALE SANG IN BERKELEY SQUARE, A see **BIGGEST BANK ROBBERY, THE** • 1980
NIGHTINGALE'S TAIL, THE • 1959 • Topouzanov Christo • ANM • BUL
NIGHTKILL • 1980 • Post Ted • USA
NIGHTLIFE • 1983 • Lewis Louie • USA
NIGHTLY ENCOUNTER see **MOTE I NATTEN** • 1946
NIGHTLY MUSIC see **NATTLIGA TONER** • 1918
NIGHTMARE • 1914 • Urban Max • CZC
NIGHTMARE • 1942 • Whelan Tim • USA
NIGHTMARE • 1956 • Shane Maxwell • USA
NIGHTMARE • 1963 • Francis Freddie • UKN • HERE'S THE KNIFE, DEAR: NOW USE IT
NIGHTMARE • 1973 • Hale William • TVM • USA
NIGHTMARE • 1981 • Scavolini Romano • USA • NIGHTMARES IN A DAMAGED BRAIN
NIGHTMARE see **LIDERCNYOMAS** • 1920
NIGHTMARE see **NATTMARA** • 1965
NIGHTMARE see **SIMHA SWAPNA** • 1968
NIGHTMARE see **NIGHTMARE IN BADHAM COUNTY** • 1976
NIGHTMARE, A (USA) see **CAUCHEMAR, LE** • 1897
NIGHTMARE ALLEY • 1947 • Goulding Edmund • USA
NIGHTMARE AND SWEET DREAM see **CAUCHEMAR ET DOUX REVE** • 1908
NIGHTMARE AT BITTER CREEK • 1988 • Burstall Tim • TVM • USA
NIGHTMARE AT NOON • 1988 • Mastorakis Nico • USA
NIGHTMARE AT PENDRAGON'S CASTLE (UKN) see **DEADLY PRICE OF PARADISE, THE** • 1978
NIGHTMARE AT SHADOW WOODS • 1987 • Grissmer John • USA • COMPLEX
NIGHTMARE BLOOD BATH • 1971 • *Brady Scott* • USA
NIGHTMARE CASTLE (USA) see **AMANTI D'OLTRETOMBA** • 1965
NIGHTMARE CITY • 1980 • Lenzi Umberto • ITL, SPN • ATAQUE DE LOS ZOMBIES ATOMICOS ○ INCUBO SULLA CITTA CONTAMINATA ○ CITY OF THE WALKING DEAD ○ INVASION OF THE ATOMIC ZOMBIES ○ INVASION DE LOS ZOMBIES ATOMICAS, LA ○ SPN ○ INVASION BY THE ATOMIC ZOMBIES
NIGHTMARE CITY see **CITY OF SHADOWS** • 1986
NIGHTMARE COUNTY • 1977 • MacGregor Sean • USA
NIGHTMARE HONEYMOON • 1972 • Silverstein Elliot • USA • DEADLY HONEYMOON
NIGHTMARE HOTEL • 1970 • Martin Eugenio • SPN
NIGHTMARE HOUSE • 1973 • Madden Lee • USA • NIGHT THAT GOD SCREAMED, THE ○ SCREAM (UKN) ○ NIGHT GOD SCREAMED, THE
NIGHTMARE IN BADHAM COUNTY • 1976 • Moxey John Llewellyn • TVM • USA • NIGHTMARE VACATION ○ NIGHTMARE
NIGHTMARE IN BLOOD • 1976 • Stanley John • USA
NIGHTMARE IN CHICAGO • 1964 • Altman Robert • TVM • USA
NIGHTMARE IN THE SUN • 1965 • Lawrence Marc • USA
NIGHTMARE IN WAX • 1969 • Townsend Bud • USA • MONSTER OF THE WAX MUSEUM, THE ○ CRIMES IN THE WAX MUSEUM
NIGHTMARE MAKER see **NIGHT WARNING** • 1982
NIGHTMARE NEVER ENDS, THE see **CATACLYSM** • 1972
NIGHTMARE OF A MOVIE FAN, THE • 1915 • Giblyn Charles • USA
NIGHTMARE OF TERROR see **DEMONS OF THE MIND** • 1971
NIGHTMARE OF THE GLAD-EYE TWINS, THE • 1913 • Rogers Edgar • UKN • ELSIE'S NIGHTMARE
NIGHTMARE ON ELM STREET 3: DREAM WARRIORS, A • 1987 • Russell Chuck • USA
NIGHTMARE ON ELM STREET 4: THE DREAM MASTER, A • 1989 • Harlin Renny • USA
NIGHTMARE ON ELM STREET, A • 1984 • Craven,Wes • USA
NIGHTMARE ON ELM STREET PART 2: FREDDY'S REVENGE, A • 1985 • Sholder Jack • USA
NIGHTMARE PARK see **HOUSE IN NIGHTMARE PARK, THE** • 1973
NIGHTMARE PASSENGERS see **PASAJEROS DE UNA PESADILLA** • 1984
NIGHTMARE SERIES • 1978 • Brakhage Stan • SHT • USA
NIGHTMARE SISTERS • 1988 • Decoteau David • USA
NIGHTMARE TRACKS see **GREAT RIDE, A** • 1977
NIGHTMARE VACATION see **NIGHTMARE IN BADHAM COUNTY** • 1976
NIGHTMARE VACATION see **SLEEPAWAY CAMP** • 1983
NIGHTMARE VACATION 2 see **UNHAPPY CAMPERS** • 1988
NIGHTMARE VOYAGE see **BLOOD VOYAGE** • 1976
NIGHTMARE WEEKEND • 1986 • Sala Henri • USA, UKN, FRN
NIGHTMARES • 1980 • Lamond John • ASL
NIGHTMARES • 1984 • Sargent Joseph • TVM • USA
NIGHTMARES see **ZMORY** • 1979
NIGHTMARES IN A DAMAGED BRAIN see **NIGHTMARE** • 1981
NIGHTRIDE • 1964 • Mideke Michael • SHT • USA
NIGHTS • 1976 • Katakouzinos George • SHT • GRC
NIGHT'S ADVENTURE, A • 1912 • *Champion* • USA
NIGHT'S ADVENTURE, A • 1915 • *Lubin* • USA
NIGHT'S ADVENTURE, A • 1915 • *Reliance* • USA
NIGHTS AND DAYS see **NOCE I DNIE** • 1974
NIGHTS AND LOVES OF DON JUAN, THE see **CALDE NOTTI DI DON GIOVANNI, LE** • 1971
NIGHT'S END see **RAAT BHORE** • 1956
NIGHT'S END see **NISHANT** • 1975
NIGHTS IN ANDALUSIA (USA) see **ANDALUSISCHE NACHTE** • 1938
NIGHTS IN PRAGUE see **PRAZSKE NOCI** • 1968
NIGHTS IN THE DJURGARD see **DJURGARDSNATTER** • 1933
NIGHTS IN WHITE SATIN • 1987 • Barnard Michael • USA
NIGHT'S LODGING, A • 1915 • Fahrney Milton • USA
NIGHTS OF CABIRIA (USA) see **NOTTI DI CABIRIA, LE** • 1957
NIGHTS OF FIRE see **NUITS DE FEU** • 1937
NIGHTS OF LOVE ON ORESUND see **KARLEKSNATT VID ORESUND, EN** • 1931
NIGHTS OF LUCRETIA BORGIA, THE (USA) see **NOTTI DI LUCREZIA BORGIA, LE** • 1959
NIGHTS OF PRAGUE see **PRAZSKE NOCI** • 1968
NIGHTS OF RASPUTIN (UKN) see **NUITS DE RASPOUTINE, LES** • 1960
NIGHTS OF SHAME (USA) see **MARCHANDES D'ILLUSIONS** • 1954

NIGHTS OF TEMPTATION (UKN) see **NOTTI DI LUCREZIA BORGIA, LE** • 1959

NIGHTS OF TERROR see **TWICE-TOLD TALES** • 1963

NIGHTS OF TERROR, THE see **NOTTI DEL TERRORE, LE** • 1980

NIGHTS OF THE HINTERLAND see **NOITES DO SERTAO** • 1984

NIGHTS OF THE JESTERS see **NARRIEN ILLAT** • 1970

NIGHTS OF THE WEREWOLF, THE see **NOCHES DEL HOMBRE LOBO, LAS** • 1968

NIGHTS OF YASSMIN, THE • 1978 • Barakat • EGY

NIGHTS ON THE CAMPUS see **HOT NIGHTS ON THE CAMPUS** • 1966

NIGHTS WHEN THE DEVIL CAME see **NACHTS, WENN DER TEUFEL KAM** • 1957

NIGHTS WITHOUT LODGING, THE see **NOCHI BYEZ NOCHLYEGA** • 1967

NIGHTS WITHOUT MORNING see **SABAHSIZ GECELER** • 1968

NIGHTS WITHOUT SHELTER see **NOCHI BYEZ NOCHLYEGA** • 1967

NIGHTSCAPES • Preston Richard • ANS • USA

NIGHTSCHOOL • 1987 • Kong Jackie • USA • UNDERACHIEVERS

NIGHTSHADE see **NACHTSCHATTEN** • 1972

NIGHTSHADE FLOWER see **YEI RAI SHAN** • 1951

NIGHTSHIFT • 1982 • Rose Robina • UKN

NIGHTSHIFT see **NIGHT SHIFT** • 1982

NIGHTSHIFT see **STEPHEN KING'S NIGHT SHIFT COLLECTION** • 1986

NIGHTSHIRT BANDIT, THE • 1938 • White Jules • SHT • USA

NIGHTSIDE • 1980 • Kowalski Bernard • TVM • USA

NIGHTSONGS • 1984 • Nabili Marva • TVM • USA

NIGHTSTALK see **NIGHTSTICK** • 1987

NIGHTSTALKER see **DON'T GO NEAR THE PARK** • 1981

NIGHTSTICK • 1987 • Scanlan Joseph L. • CND • NIGHTSTALK ○ CALHOUN ○ METAL FORCE ○ METALFORCE

NIGHTSTICK see **ALIBI** • 1929

NIGHTWARS • 1987 • Prior David A. • USA • NIGHT WARS

NIGHTWATCHMAN, THE • Martinez Gabriel • CLM

NIGHTWATCHMAN, THE • 1928 • *Bard Wilkie* • SHT • UKN

NIGHTWATCHMAN MUST FALL, THE see **ALFRED NOCNI CUVAR** • 1971

NIGHTWING • 1979 • Hiller Arthur • USA, NTH

NIGORIE • 1953 • Imai Tadashi • JPN • MUDDY WATERS ○ MUDDY WATER

NIGURUMA NO UTA • 1959 • Yamamoto Satsuo • JPN • SONG OF THE CART, THE

NIHIKI-NO SAMA • 1959 • Kuri Yoji • ANS • JPN • TWO SAURIES

NIHIKI NO YOJINBO • 1968 • Misumi Kenji • JPN • TWO BODYGUARDS, THE

NIHIKINO SAMNA see **FUTATSO-NO YAKIZAKANA** • 1968

NIHILIST VENGEANCE • 1913 • *Victor* • USA

NIHILISTS, THE • 1914 • *Nestor* • USA

NIHON ANKOKUSHI: CHI NO KOSO • 1967 • Kudo Eiichi • JPN • DARK HISTORY OF JAPAN: STRUGGLE OF BLOOD

NIHON BOKO ANKOKUSHI -IJOSHA NO CHI • 1967 • Wakamatsu Koji • JPN • ABNORMAL BLOOD

NIHON BRIDGE see **NIHONBASHI** • 1929

NIHON CHINBOTSU • 1973 • Moritani Shiro, Meyer Andrew • JPN • TIDAL WAVE (USA) ○ SUBMERSION OF JAPAN, THE ○ NIPPON CHINBOTSU

NIHON DASHUTSU see **NIPPON DASSHUTSU** • 1964

NIHON HANZAISHI HAKUCHU NON BOHKOHKI • 1968 • Sakao Masanao • JPN • JAPANESE CRIMINAL HISTORY - VIOLATION AT NOON

NIHON-ICHI NO OTOKO NO NAKA NO OTOKO • 1967 • Furusawa Kengo • JPN • NO.1 MAN OF JAPAN: THE BEST

NIHON KYOKAKUDEN: SHIRAHA NON SAKAZUKI • 1967 • Makino Masahiro • JPN • CHRONICLE OF JAPANESE OUTLAWS: A TOAST TO SWORDS

NIHON KYOKYAKU DEN ZETSUENJO • 1968 • Makino Masahiro • JPN • CHIVALROUS STORY OF JAPAN

NIHON-MARU • 1976 • Shinoda Masahiro • DOC • JPN • NIHON-MARU SHIP

NIHON-MARU SHIP see **NIHON-MARU** • 1976

NIHON MARUHI FUZOKUSHI CHIBUSA • 1968 • Shindo Takae • JPN • JAPAN'S HISTORY OF SEX CUSTOMS -THE BREASTS

NIHON NO BUYO • 1959 • Hani Susumu • JPN • DANCES IN JAPAN

NIHON NO DON • 1976 • Nakajima Sadao • JPN • BOSS OF JAPAN, A

NIHON NO HIGEKI • 1945 • Kamei Fumio • JPN • JAPANESE TRAGEDY, A

NIHON NO HIGEKI • 1953 • Kinoshita Keisuke • JPN • JAPANESE TRAGEDY, A

NIHON NO ICHIBAN NAGAI HI • 1967 • Okamoto Kihachi • JPN • EMPEROR AND A GENERAL, THE ○ NIPPON NO ICHIBAN NAGAI HI

NIHON NO MON-YO • 1962 • Yoshida Naoya • JPN

NIHON NO SEISHUN • 1968 • Kobayashi Masaki • JPN • DIARY OF A TIRED MAN ○ HYMN TO A TIRED MAN ○ YOUTH OF JAPAN, THE ○ NIPPON NO SEISHUN ○ JAPANESE YOUTH

NIHON NO YORU TO KIRI • 1960 • Oshima Nagisa • JPN • NIGHT AND FOG IN JAPAN ○ FOGGY NIGHT IN JAPAN, A ○ NIGHT AND FOG OVER JAPAN

NIHON SEI FUZOKUSHI MURISHINJA • 1968 • Mukoi Hiroshi • JPN • JAPANESE HISTORY OF SEX CUSTOMS -DOUBLE SUICIDE

NIHON SEIHANZAISHI: TORIMA • 1967 • Yamashita Osamu • JPN • PHANTOM CRIMINAL, A

NIHON SHUNKA KO see **NIHON SHUNKAKU** • 1967

NIHON SHUNKAKU • 1967 • Oshima Nagisa • JPN • TREATISE ON JAPANESE BAWDY SONGS, A ○ SING A SONG OF SEX ○ NIPPON SHUNKA KO ○ NIHON SHUNKA KO

NIHONBASHI • 1929 • Mizoguchi Kenji • JPN • NIHON BRIDGE

NIHONBASHI • 1956 • Ichikawa Kon • JPN • BRIDGE OF JAPAN

NIHONJIN KOKONI-ARI • 1968 • Shimauchi Toshio, Shimizu Susumu • DOC • JPN • JAPANESE ARE HERE, THE

NIHONKAI DAIKAISEN • 1969 • Maruyama Seiji • JPN • BATTLE OF THE JAPAN SEA

NIHONTOU: MIYAIRI KOUHEI NO WAZA • 1976 • Yamauchi • JPN • JAPANESE SWORDS: THE WORK OF KOUHEI MIYAIRI

NIHTA GAMOU • 1967 • Dalianidis Ioannis • GRC • WEDDING NIGHT

NIHYAKUSAN KOCHI • 1981 • Masuda Toshio • JPN • HILL 203

NIILON OPPIVUODET • 1971 • Pakkasvirta Jaakko • FNL • NIILO'S SCHOOL YEARS ○ NIILO'S APPRENTICESHIP

NIILO'S APPRENTICESHIP see **NIILON OPPIVUODET** • 1971

NIILO'S SCHOOL YEARS see **NIILON OPPIVUODET** • 1971

NIINO TSURUCHIYO • 1935 • Ito Daisuke • JPN

NIISAN NO AIJO • 1955 • Maruyama Seiji, Nakagawa Nobuo • JPN • BROTHERLY LOVE

NIISAN NO BAKA • 1932 • Gosho Heinosuke • JPN • MY STUPID BROTHER ○ YOU ARE STUPID, MY BROTHER

NIITAKAYAMA NOBORE • 1968 • Okada Hiroshi • DOC • JPN • SECOND WORLD WAR DOCUMENTARY

NIIZUMA KAIGI • 1949 • Chiba Yasuki • JPN • NEW WIVES' CONFERENCE

NIIZUMA NO SEITEN • 1954 • Ohba Hideo • JPN

NIJE BILO UZALUD • 1957 • Tanhofer Nikola • YGS • IT WAS NOT IN VAIN

NIJE LAKO S MUSKARCIMA • 1985 • Vukobratovic Mihailo • YGS • MEN ONLY MEAN TROUBLE

NIJE NEGO • 1979 • Milosevic Mica • YGS • TIT FOR TAT

NIJE PRICA SVE STO LETI see **NICHT ALLES WAS FLIEGT ISAT EIN VOGEL** • 1978

NIJEMA PROZIVKA • 1974 • Fanelli Mario • YGS • SILENT ROLL CALL, THE

NIJI IKUTABI • 1956 • Shima Koji • JPN

NIJI NO MAKANO LEMMON • 1968 • Saito Koichi • JPN • ROSE BUDS IN THE RAINBOW

NIJI O IDAKU SHOJO • 1948 • Saeki • JPN • VIRGIN WHO EMBRACES A RAINBOW, A

NIJINSKY • 1980 • Ross Herbert • USA, UKN

NIJU-ISSAI NO CHICHI • 1964 • Nakamura Noboru • JPN • OUR HAPPINESS ALONE ○ FATHER AT 21, A

NIJU-SAI ZENGO • 1950 • Yoshimura Kozaburo • JPN • ABOUT TWENTY YEARS OLD

NIJUSHI NO HITOMI • 1954 • Kinoshita Keisuke • JPN • TWENTY-FOUR EYES ○ TWENTY-FOUR HOURS

NIJUSHI NO HITOMI • 1988 • Asama Yoshitaka • JPN • 24 EYES

NIKAI NO HIMAI • 1931 • Naruse Mikio • JPN • SCREAMS FROM THE SECOND FLOOR

NIKDO NIC NEVI • 1947 • Mach Josef • CZC • NOBODY KNOWS ANYTHING ○ NO-ONE KNOWS A THING

NIKDO SE NEBUDE SMAT • 1965 • Bocan Hynek • CZC • NOBODY SHALL BE LAUGHING ○ NO LAUGHING MATTER ○ NOBODY GETS THE LAST LAUGH

NIKITA • 1989 • Besson Luc • FRN

NIKITA IVANOVICH AND SOCIALISM • 1931 • Savchenko Igor • USS

NIKKATSU KOSHINKYOKU -RODO-HEN • 1929 • Tasaka Tomotaka • JPN • NIKKATSU PARADE -LABOUR VOLUME

NIKKATSU KOSHINKYOKU -SUPOTSU-HEN • 1929 • Uchida Tomu • JPN • NIKKATSU PARADE -SPORTS VOLUME

NIKKATSU PARADE -LABOUR VOLUME see **NIKKATSU KOSHINKYOKU -RODO-HEN** • 1929

NIKKATSU PARADE -SPORTS VOLUME see **NIKKATSU KOSHINKYOKU -SUPOTSU-HEN** • 1929

NIKKI, WILD DOG OF THE NORTH • 1961 • Couffer Jack, Haldane Don • USA, CND

NIKKOLINA • 1978 • Yates Rebecca, Salzman Glen • CND

NIKLAS AND HIS PAL see **NIKLAS OCH FIGUREN** • 1972

NIKLAS OCH FIGUREN • 1972 • Andree Ulf • SWD • NIKLAS AND HIS PAL

NIKLASHAUSEN JOURNEY, THE see **NIKLASHAUSER FAHRT** • 1970

NIKLASHAUSER FAHRT • 1970 • Fassbinder R. W., Fengler Michael • FRG • NIKLASHAUSEN JOURNEY, THE

NIKODEM DYZMA • 1957 • Rybkowski Jan • PLN

NIKOLA SUHAJ • 1946 • Krnansky M. J. • CZC

NIKOLA TESLA • 1956 • Pogacic Vladimir • DOC • YGS

NIKOLAI GHIAUROV • 1980 • Korabov Nicolai • BUL

NIKOLAI STAVROGIN • 1915 • Protazanov Yakov • USS

NIKOLAY AMOSOV • 1972 • Zoloyev Timur • DOC • USS

NIKOLAY BAUMAN • 1968 • Tumanov Semyon • USS

NIKON NOKI • 1946 • Kamei Fumio • DOC • JPN

NIKT NIE WOLA • 1960 • Kutz Kazimierz • PLN • NO-ONE CALLING ○ NO ONE CRIES OUT..

NIKTO NE KHOTEL UMIRAT • 1965 • Zalakevicius Vitautus • USS • NO ONE WANTED TO DIE ○ NOBODY WANTED TO DIE

NIKU NO HOKOROBI • 1968 • Komoro Jiro • JPN • RIP OF THE FLESH, A

NIKU NO KYOH-EN • 1968 • Matsubara Jiro • JPN • BEWITCHING OF THE FLESH

NIKU NO SHIIKU • 1968 • Matsubara Jiro, Kishi Shintaro • JPN • BREEDING OF THE FLESH

NIKU NO TSUMEATO • 1967 • Oono Yuji • JPN • NAIL MARK IN FLESH, A

NIKUDAN • 1968 • Okamoto Kihachi • JPN • HUMAN BULLET, A

NIKUI ANCHIKUSHO • 1962 • Kurahara Koreyoshi • JPN • I HATE BUT LOVE

NIKUJIGOKU • 1967 • Matsubara Jiro • JPN • INFERNO OF FLESH

NIKUKEI • 1967 • Komori Haku • JPN • CARNAL PUNISHMENT

NIKUTAI NO GAKKO • 1965 • Kinoshita Ryo • JPN • SCHOOL OF LOVE ○ SCHOOL OF SEX ○ SCHOOL FOR SEX

NIKUTAI NO KEIYAKUSHO • 1968 • Okuwaki Mamoru • JPN • FLESH CONTRACT, THE

NIKUTAI NO MON • 1964 • Suzuki Seijun • JPN • GATE OF FLESH (USA)

NIKUTAI NO SEISO • 1964 • Murayama Shinji • JPN • GORGEOUS GEISHA, THE

NIKUTAI NO YOKKYU • 1968 • Wakamatsu Koji • JPN • CARNAL DESIRE

NIKUTAI NO YUWAKU • 1967 • Nishihara Giichi • JPN • TEMPTATION OF THE FLESH

NIKUTAIBI • 1928 • Ozu Yasujiro • JPN • BODY BEAUTIFUL

NIKUZEME • 1968 • Higashimoto Kaoru • JPN • FLESH TORTURE

NIL ARZAQ, AN- • 1972 • Nahhass Hashim An- • SHT • EGY • RICHESSES DU NIL ○ SUR LE NIL

NILAGIRI EXPRESS • 1968 • Thirumalai • IND

NILE'S SON, THE see **IBN EL NIL** • 1951

NILGUN • 1968 • Egilmez Ertem • TRK

NILLE • 1968 • Henning-Jensen Astrid • DNM

NILO DI PIETRA, IL • 1956 • Rondi Brunello • SHT • ITL

NILOUE, NUER see **NI-LO-HO NU-ERH** • 1988

NILS HOLGERSSONS UNDERBARA RESA • 1962 • Fant Kenne • SWD • WONDERFUL ADVENTURES OF NILS, THE ○ MARVELOUS JOURNEY OF NILS HOLGERSSON, THE

NILSSON • 1965 • Halldoff Jan • SWD

NILUOHE NUER see **NI-LO-HO NU-ERH** • 1988

NIMANTRAN • 1971 • Mazumdar Tarun • IND

NIMFIOS ANIMFEFTOS • 1967 • Laskos Orestis • GRC • BRIDE IN DISTRESS, A ○ UNMARRIED BRIDE

NIMMO STREET • 1962 • Cowan Tom • SHT • ASL

NIMVAJABI • 1967 • Vahdat Nosratolah • IRN • TINY SPAN

NINA • 1956 • Jugert Rudolf • FRG

NINA • 1958 • Boyer Jean • FRN

NINA see **HVIDE SLAVEHANDEL III, DEN** • 1912

NINA see **MATTER OF TIME, A** • 1976

NINA see **T'A** • 1976

NINA B AFFAIR, THE (USA) see **AFFAIRE NINA B** • 1961

NINA DE LA VENTA, LA • 1951 • Torrado Ramon • SPN

NINA DE LUTO, LA • 1964 • Summers Manuel • SPN • GIRL IN MOURNING, THE

NINA DE LUZMELA, LA • 1949 • Gascon Jose • SPN

NINA DE MIS OJOS, LA • 1946 • Sevilla Raphael J. • MXC

NINA DEL GATO, LA • 1953 • Barreto Roman Vinoly • ARG

NINA DEL PATIO, LA • 1967 • de Ossorio Amando • SPN

NINA, IN THE HANDS OF THE IMPOSTORS see **HVIDE SLAVEHANDEL III, DEN** • 1912

NINA MELOVIZINOVA • 1962 • Panfilov Gleb • SHT • USS

NINA, NON FAR LA STUPIDA • 1937 • Malasomma Nunzio • ITL

NINA OF THE THEATRE • 1914 • Melford George • USA

NINA PETROVNA see **MENSONGE DE NINA PETROVNA, LA** • 1937

NINA POPOFF, LA • 1951 • Pereda Ramon • MXC

NINA, THE FLOWER GIRL • 1917 • Ingraham Lloyd • USA

NINA THE GIRL FROM KOSMAJ see **DEVOJKA SA KOSMAJA** • 1972

NINAS.. AL SALON • 1977 • Escriva Vicente • SPN

NINA'S EVENING PRAYER • 1912 • Stow Percy • UKN • NINA'S PRAYER

NINA'S PRAYER see **NINA'S EVENING PRAYER** • 1912

NINCS IDO • 1973 • Kosa Ferenc • HNG • NO TIME ○ BEYOND TIME

NINDU SAMSARAM • 1968 • Rao C. S. • IND • HAPPY FAMILY

NINE AGES OF NAKEDNESS, THE • 1969 • Marks George Harrison • UKN

NINE AND THREE FIFTY SECONDS • 1925 • Carleton Lloyd B. • USA

NINE BACHELORS (USA) see **ILS ETAIENT NEUF CELIBATAIRES** • 1939

NINE CHICKENS, THE see **NINE CHICKS** • 1952

NINE CHICKS • 1952 • Tyrlova Hermina • ANS • CZC • NINE CHICKENS, THE

NINE CIRCLES OF HELL • 1988 • Muchna Milan • CZC, KMP

NINE, DALMUIR WEST • 1962 • Brownlow Kevin • DOC • UKN

NINE DAYS A QUEEN (USA) see **TUDOR ROSE** • 1936

NINE DAYS IN '26 • 1974 • Vas Robert • UKN

NINE DAYS IN ONE YEAR see **DEVYAT DNEI ODNOGO GODA** • 1961

NINE DAYS OF ONE YEAR see **DEVYAT DNEI ODNOGO GODA** • 1961

NINE DAYS' WONDER see **BIG NOISE, THE** • 1928

NINE DEATHS OF THE NINJA • 1985 • Alston Emmett • USA • DEADLY WARRIORS ○ 9 DEATHS OF THE NINJA

NINE EIGHTY FOUR -PRISONER OF THE FUTURE • 1979 • Takacs Tibor • USA • TOMORROW MAN, THE ○ 984: PRISONER OF THE FUTURE ○ PRISONER 984

NINE FORTY-FIVE • 1934 • King George • UKN

NINE GIRLS • 1944 • Jason Leigh • USA

NINE HOURS TO LIVE see **NINE HOURS TO RAMA** • 1963

NINE HOURS TO RAMA • 1963 • Robson Mark • USA, UKN • NINE HOURS TO LIVE

NINE HUNDRED, THE • 1945 • Krimsky Jerrold • UKN

NINE LETTERS TO BERTA see **NUEVE CARTAS A BERTA** • 1967

NINE LIVES see **NI LIV** • 1957

NINE LIVES ARE NOT ENOUGH • 1941 • Sutherland A. Edward • USA

NINE LIVES OF A CAT • 1907 • Porter Edwin S. • USA

NINE LIVES OF ELFEGO BACA, THE • 1959 • Foster Norman • USA

NINE LIVES OF FRITZ THE CAT • 1974 • Taylor Robert • ANM • USA

NINE MEN • 1943 • Watt Harry • UKN

NINE MILLION ANSWER • 1919 • *Miller-Hodkinson* • SHT • USA

NINE MONTHS see **KILENC HONAP** • 1976

NINE MONTHS TO FREEDOM • 1972 • Sukhdev S. • IND

NINE O'CLOCK TOWN, A • 1918 • Schertzinger Victor • USA

NINE OF DIAMONDS, THE • 1910 • *Vitagraph* • USA

NINE POINTS OF THE LAW • 1922 • Mack Wayne • USA • GIRL'S DECISION, A

NINE SECONDS FROM HEAVEN • 1922 • *King Charles* • DNM

NINE SEVEN SIX: EVIL see **976 EVIL** • 1988

NINE-TENTHS OF THE LAW • 1918 • Eason B. Reeves • USA

NINE THIRTY FIFTY-FIVE see **SEPTEMBER 30, 1955** • 1977

NINE TILL SIX • 1932 • Dean Basil • UKN

NINE TO FIVE see **9 TO 5** • 1980

NINE WAYS TO APPROACH HELSINKI see **YHDEKSAN TAPAA LAHESTYA HELSINKIA** • 1983

NINETEEN see **ICH WAR NEUNZEHN** • 1967

NINETEEN AND PHYLLIS • 1920 • De Grasse Joseph • USA

NINETEEN GIRLS AND A SAILOR see **DEVETNAEST DEVOJAKA I MORNA** • 1971
NINETEEN HUNDRED see **NOVECENTO** • 1976
NINETEEN NINETEEN see **1919** • 1984
NINETEEN YEAR OLD MISFIT see **HADAKA NO JUKYUSAI** • 1970
NINETEEN YEAR OLD'S PLAN, A see **JUKYUSAI NO CHIZU** • 1979
NINETEENTH SPRING, THE see **JUKU-SAI NO HARU** • 1933
NINETTE Y UN SENOR DE MURCIA • 1965 • Fernan-Gomez Fernando • SPN
NINETY AND NINE, THE • 1911 • *Kent Charles* • USA
NINETY AND NINE, THE • 1916 • Ince Ralph • USA
NINETY AND NINE, THE • 1922 • Smith David • USA
NINETY BLACK BOXES • 1914 • Giblyn Charles • USA
NINETY DEGREES SOUTH • 1933 • Ponting Herbert • UKN • GREAT WHITE SILENCE, THE ○ STORY OF CAPTAIN SCOTT ○ UNDYING STORY OF CAPTAIN SCOTT, THE ○ WITH CAPTAIN SCOTT TO THE SOUTH POLE
NINETY DEGREES SOUTH see **WITH CAPTAIN SCOTT, R.N., TO THE SOUTH POLE** • 1911
NINETY IN THE SHADE see **TRICET JEONA VE STINU** • 1965
NINETY NINE see **KILENCVENKILENC** • 1918
NINETY NINE PERCENT • 1963 • Mangiamele Giorgio • SHT • ASL
NINETY-TWO IN THE SHADE see **92° IN THE SHADE** • 1975
NINGEN • 1925 • Mizoguchi Kenji • JPN • MAN, THE (USA) ○ HUMAN BEING, THE
NINGEN • 1962 • Shindo Kaneto • JPN • HUMAN BEING, A ○ MAN, THE
NINGEN DOBUTSUEN • 1961 • Kuri Yoji • ANS • JPN • CLAP VOCALISM ○ HUMAN ZOO
NINGEN GYORAI KAITEN • 1955 • Matsubayashi Shue • JPN
NINGEN GYORAI SHUTSUGEKISU • 1955 • Furukawa Takumi • JPN • HUMAN TORPEDOES ATTACK ○ HUMAN TORPEDOES
NINGEN JOHATSU • 1967 • Imamura Shohei • JPN • MAN VANISHES, A
NINGEN KAKUMEI • 1973 • Masuda Toshio • JPN • HUMAN REVOLUTION
NINGEN MOYO • 1949 • Ichikawa Kon • JPN • DESIGN OF A HUMAN BEING ○ HUMAN PATTERNS
NINGEN NO JOKEN I • 1959 • Kobayashi Masaki • JPN • NO GREATER LOVE ○ WAR AND A MAN, THE
NINGEN NO JOKEN II • 1959 • Kobayashi Masaki • JPN • ROAD TO ETERNITY
NINGEN NO JOKEN III • 1961 • Kobayashi Masaki • JPN • SOLDIER'S PRAYER, A
NINGEN NO KABE • 1959 • Yamamoto Satsuo • JPN • HUMAN WALL, THE
NINGEN NO SHOMEI • 1977 • Sato Junya • JPN • WITNESS OF MANKIND
NINGEN NO YAKUSOKU • 1985 • Yoshida Yoshishige • JPN • HUMAN PROMISE ○ HUMAN'S PROMISE
NINGUEM DUAS VEZES • 1984 • Melo Jorge Silva • PRT
NINGUNO DE LOS TRES SE LLAMABA TRINIDAD • 1972 • Ramirez Pedro L. • SPN
NINGYO HIME • 1974 • Katsumada Tomoharu • JPN • PRINCESS MERMAID ○ LITTLE MERMAID, THE
NINGYO SHOTEN • 1959 • Uchikawa Seiichiro • JPN • MERMAIDS AND SEA ROBBERS
NINI FALPALA • 1933 • Palermi Amleto • ITL • FALPALA
NINI TIRABUSCIO, LA DONNA CHE INVENTO LA MOSSA • 1970 • Fondato Marcello • ITL
NINICHE • 1925 • Janson Victor • FRG
NINJA ACADEMY • 1988 • Mastorakis Nico • USA
NINJA AMERICAN WARRIOR • Cheng Tommy • HKG
NINJA AND THE WARRIORS OF FIRE • 1973 • Lambert Bruce
NINJA APOCALYPSE • 1985 • Lee Tommy • HKG
NINJA BUGEICHO • 1967 • Oshima Nagisa • JPN • TALES OF THE NINJA (USA) ○ BAND OF NINJA ○ NINJA BUGELIJO
NINJA BUGELIJO see **NINJA BUGEICHO** • 1967
NINJA CHAMPION • 1986 • Lai Joseph • HKG
NINJA COMMANDMENTS • 1987 • Lai Joseph • HKG
NINJA CONNECTION see **NINJA IN THE KILLING FIELDS**
NINJA DESTROYER • 1986 • Ho Godfrey • HKG
NINJA DRAGON • 1986 • Ho Godfrey • HKG
NINJA FIST OF FIRE • *Chor Yim Yung* • HKG
NINJA HOLOCAUST • 1985 • *Chen Bruce* • HKG
NINJA HUNT • 1986 • Lai Joseph • HKG
NINJA II: REVENGE OF THE NINJA see **REVENGE OF THE NINJA** • 1984
NINJA III: THE DOMINATION • 1984 • Firstenberg Sam • USA
NINJA IN THE KILLING FIELDS • Lam York • HKG • NINJA CONNECTION
NINJA KIDS: KISS OF DEATH • Kuo Joseph • HKG • NINJA KISS OF DEATH KIDS
NINJA KISS OF DEATH KIDS see **NINJA KIDS: KISS OF DEATH**
NINJA MASTER see **MASTER NINJA, THE** • 1984
NINJA MASTER 2 see **MASTER NINJA 2, THE** • 1984
NINJA MISSION, THE • 1984 • Olsson Mats Helge • SWD, UKN
NINJA MURDERS see **DEATH MACHINES** • 1976
NINJA OF THE MAGNIFICENCE see **AMERICAN NINJA THE MAGNIFICENT** • 1988
NINJA OPERATION 2: WAY OF CHALLENGE • 1987 • Lai Joseph • HKG • WAY OF CHALLENGE
NINJA OPERATION 3: LICENSED TO TERMINATE • 1987 • Lai Joseph • HKG • LICENSED TO TERMINATE
NINJA OPERATION 4: THUNDERBOLT ANGELS • 1988 • Lai Joseph • HKG • THUNDERBOLT ANGELS
NINJA OPERATION 5: GODFATHER THE MASTER • 1988 • Lai Joseph • HKG • GODFATHER THE MASTER
NINJA OPERATION 6: CHAMPION ON FIRE • 1988 • Lai Joseph • HKG • CHAMPION ON FIRE
NINJA OPERATION: KNIGHT AND WARRIOR • 1987 • Lai Joseph • HKG • KNIGHT AND WARRIOR
NINJA SHOWDOWN, THE • Lai Joseph • HKG
NINJA SQUAD • 1986 • Wu Kuo-Jen • HKG
NINJA STRIKES BACK, THE • 1983 • *Le Bruce* • HKG
NINJA TERMINATOR • 1985 • Ho Godfrey • HKG
NINJA THE PROTECTOR • 1985 • *Harrison Richard* • HKG
NINJA THUNDERBOLT • 1985 • Ho Godfrey • HKG, TWN, PHL
NINJA TURF • 1986 • Park Richard • USA • L.A. STREETFIGHTERS
NINJA USA • Wu Kuo-Jen
NINJA WARRIORS • 1985 • Lloyd John • USA
NINJA WARS • 1982 • Saito Kosei • JPN
NINJO KAMIFUSEN • 1937 • Yamanaka Sadao • JPN • HUMANITY AND PAPER BALLOONS
NINJUTSU see **YAGYU BUGEICHO -SORYU HIKEN** • 1958
NINJUTSU MUSHA SHUGYO • 1956 • *Tani Tony* • JPN • STUPID SORCERER, THE
NINJUTSU MUSHASHUGYO • 1960 • Fukuda Seiichi • JPN • THREE MAGICIANS, THE
NINKYO KASHI NO ISHIMATSU • 1967 • Suzuki Noribumi • JPN • ISHI OF THE FISH MARKET
NINKYO NAKASENDO • 1960 • Matsuda Sadatsugu • JPN
NINNE PELLADUTHA • 1968 • Srinivas B. V. • IND • I SHALL MARRY ONLY YOU
NINO, EL • 1968 • D'Lanor • PHL • BOY, THE
NINO DE LA LUNA, EL • 1988 • Villaronga Agustin • SPN • MOON CHILD, THE ○ MOONCHILD
NINO DE LAS MONJAS, EL • 1935 • Buchs Jose • SPN
NINO DE LAS MONJAS, EL • 1944 • Villareal Julio • MXC
NINO DE LAS MONJAS, EL • 1958 • Iquino Ignacio F. • SPN
NINO DE ORO, EL • 1973 • *Estudios America* • MXC
NINO DEL TAMBOR, EL • 1981 • Grau Jorge • MXC, SPN • BOY WITH THE DRUM, THE ○ LEYENDA DEL TAMBOR, LA ○ LEGEND OF THE DRUM, THE
NINO ES NUESTRO, EL • 1972 • Summers Manuel • SPN
NINO FIDENCIO, EL • 1981 • Echavarria Nicolas • MXC
NINO PARAMURI, EL • 1980 • Violante Marcela Fernandez • MXC
NINO PERDIDO, EL • 1947 • Gomez Landero Humberto • MXC
NINO Y EL LADRON, EL • 1964 • Demicheli Tulio • MXC, SPN • PRIMERA AVENTURA, LA
NINO Y EL MURO, EL • 1964 • Rodriguez Ismael • MXC, SPN
NINO Y LA ESTRELLA, EL • 1975 • *Gazcon* • MXC
NINO Y LA NIEBLA, EL • 1953 • Gavaldon Roberto • MXC
NINOMIYA SONTOKU NO SHONENJIDAI • 1957 • Murayama Shinji • JPN • BOYHOOD OF AN AGRICULTURAL PIONEER
NINON DE LENCLOS • 1920 • Burg Eugen • FRG
NINOS • 1972 • Roche Luis Armando • VNZ • CHILDREN
NINOS, LOS • 1969 • Villafuerte Santiago • DOC • CUB
NINOS, LOS see **VIENTO DISTANTE** • 1965
NINOTCHKA • 1939 • Lubitsch Ernst • USA
NINSHIN BUNBEN CHUHZETSU • 1968 • Yamamoto Shinya • JPN • PREGNANCY, BIRTH AND ABORTION
NINSHIN TO SEIBYO • 1967 • Ogawa Kinya • JPN • PREGNANCY AND V.D.
NINTH CIRCLE, THE see **DEVETI KRUG** • 1960
NINTH COMMANDMENT, THE • 1913 • *Gem* • USA
NINTH COMPANY, THE see **NIONDE KOMPANIET** • 1988
NINTH CONFIGURATION, THE • 1980 • Blatty William Peter • USA • TWINKLE, TWINKLE, KILLER KANE
NINTH DAY, THE • 1917 • Marshall George • SHT • USA
NINTH DAY, THE • 1956 • Frankenheimer John • MTV • USA
NINTH EXTERNAL WARD see **DOKUZUNCU HARICIYE KOGUSU** • 1967
NINTH GUEST, THE • 1934 • Neill R. William • USA
NINTH HEART, THE see **DEVATE SRDCE** • 1978
NINTH LIFE, THE • 1981 • Ohlsson Terry • SHT • ASL
NINTH OF JANUARY see **DEVIATOE YANVARIA** • 1926
NINTH SUMMER, THE • 1972 • Woods Grahame • CND
NINTH SYMPHONY see **SCHLUSSAKKORD** • 1936
NINTH WINTER OLYMPIC GAMES 1964, THE see **IX OLYMPISCHE WINTERSPIELE 1964 IN INNSBRUCK** • 1964
NINTH WONDER OF THE EAST, THE see **DEVETO CUDO NA ISTOKU** • 1973
NIOBE • 1915 • *Dawn Hazel* • USA
NIOK see **NIOK L'ELEPHANT** • 1957
NIOK L'ELEPHANT • 1957 • Sechan Edmond • SHT • FRN • NIOK
NION IN THE KABARET DE LA VITA • 1987 • Podeswa Jeremy • SHT • CND
NIONDE KOMPANIET • 1988 • Nutley Colin • SWD • NINTH COMPANY, THE
NIP AND TUCK • 1923 • Del Ruth Roy • SHT • USA
NIP OF SCOTCH, A • 1924 • Del Ruth Roy • SHT • USA
NIPA HUT, THOUGH SMALL, A see **BAHAY KUBO KAHIT MUNTI** • 1968
NIPERNAADI • 1983 • Kiisk Kaliu • USS
NIPOTE, LA • 1975 • Rossati Nello • ITL
NIPOTE DEL PRETE, LA • 1977 • Grieco Sergio • ITL
NIPOTE SABELLA, LA • 1959 • Bianchi Giorgio • ITL
NIPOTI DELLA COLONNELLA, LE • 1970 • Mulargia Edoardo • ITL
NIPOTI DI ZORRO, I • 1968 • Ciorciolini Marcello • ITL
NIPOTI MIEI DILETTI • 1974 • Rossetti Franco • ITL
NIPPED • 1914 • *Aoki Tsuru* • USA
NIPPED IN THE BUD • 1918 • Roach Hal • SHT • USA
NIPPER, THE • 1930 • Mercanton Louis • UKN • BRAT, THE
NIPPER AND THE CURATE • 1916 • Crompton Reginald • UKN • CURATE, THE
NIPPER'S BUSY BEE TIME • 1916 • *Lane Lupino* • SHT • UKN
NIPPER'S BUSY HOLIDAY • 1915 • *Lane Lupino* • UKN • HIS BUSY HOLIDAY
NIPPER'S LULLABY, THE • 1912 • *Morey Harry* • USA
NIPPER'S TRANSFORMATIONS, THE • 1912 • *Urban Charles (P)* • ANS • UKN
NIPPON ANKOKUSHI: NASAKE MUYO • 1968 • Kudo Eiichi • JPN • HISTORY OF THE JAPANESE UNDERWORLD, A
NIPPON CHINBOTSU see **NIHON CHINBOTSU** • 1973
NIPPON DASSHUTSU • 1964 • Yoshida Yoshishige • JPN • NIPPON ESCAPE ○ NIHON DASHUTSU ○ ESCAPE FROM JAPAN
NIPPON DOROBO MONOGATARI • 1965 • Yamamoto Satsuo • JPN • BURGLAR STORY, THE
NIPPON ESCAPE see **NIPPON DASSHUTSU** • 1964
NIPPON GERIRA JIDAI • 1968 • Watanabe Yusuke • JPN • FIGHTERS ON FIRE
NIPPON ICHI NO IRO-OTOKO • 1963 • Furusawa Kengo • JPN • BEST PLAYBOY IN JAPAN, THE
NIPPON-ICHI NO URAGIRIOTOKO • 1968 • Sugawa Eizo • JPN • JAPAN FOR SALE
NIPPON ICHINO HORAFUKI OTOKO • 1964 • Furusawa Kengo • JPN • GAY BRAGGART, THE (USA)
NIPPON JOSI DOKUHON • 1937 • Yamamoto Kajiro • JPN
NIPPON KENGO-DEN • 1945 • Takizawa • JPN • GREAT SWORDSMEN OF JAPAN
NIPPON KONCHUKI • 1963 • Imamura Shohei • JPN • INSECT WOMAN, THE (USA) ○ INSECT, THE ○ JAPANESE INSECT STORY
NIPPON KYOKAKUDEN-KIRIKOMI • 1967 • Makino Masahiro • JPN • CHIVALROUS STORY IN JAPAN -THE STORM, A
NIPPON NO ICHIBAN NAGAI HI see **NIHON NO ICHIBAN NAGAI HI** • 1967
NIPPON NO OBACHAN • 1962 • Imai Tadashi • JPN • OLD WOMEN OF JAPAN, THE ○ JAPANESE GRANDMOTHERS
NIPPON NO SEISHUN see **NIHON NO SEISHUN** • 1968
NIPPON OYAFUKO JIDAI • 1968 • Yamamoto Kunihiko • JPN • TIME OF UNDUTIFUL CHILDREN
NIPPON RETTO • 1969 • Kumai Kei • JPN
NIPPON SENGOSHI -MADAMU ONBORO NO SEIKATSU • 1970 • Imamura Shohei • JPN • HISTORY OF POSTWAR JAPAN AS TOLD BY A BAR HOSTESS ○ POSTWAR JAPANESE HISTORY
NIPPON SHUNKA KO see **NIHON SHUNKAKU** • 1967
NIPPON TANJO • 1959 • Inagaki Hiroshi • JPN • THREE TREASURES, THE ○ AGE OF THE GODS ○ BIRTH OF JAPAN
NIPPONTO MONOGATARI • 1957 • Asano Tatsuo • JPN • ART OF SWORDSMITH, THE
NIPPY'S NIGHTMARE • 1917 • O'Brien Willis • USA
NIPUPS • 1934 • Brooks Marty • SHT • USA
NIRALA HINDUSTAN • 1938 • *Biswas Anil (M)* • IND
NIRDOSHI • 1967 • Mirasi Dada • IND • INNOCENT, THE
NIRMALAYAM • 1973 • Nair M. T. Vasudevan • IND • STALE FLOWERS
NIRVANA • 1920 • Bernhardt Fritz • FRG
NIRVANA • 1929 • Aylott Dave, Symmons E. F. • SHT • UKN
NIRVANA • Scott Carlisle • SHT • USA
NIRWANA • 1916 • Wieder Konrad • FRG
NISA' BILA RIJAL see **NESSAA BALA RAJAL** • 1952
NISE DAIGAKUSEI • 1960 • Masumura Yasuzo • JPN • FALSE STUDENT, THE
NISE KEIJI • 1967 • Yamamoto Satsuo • JPN • BOGUS POLICEMAN, THE
NISHANT • 1975 • Benegal Shyam • IND • NIGHT'S END ○ NIGHT
NISHI GINZA EKIMAE • 1958 • Imamura Shohei • JPN • LIGHTS OF NIGHT ○ NISHI GINZA STATION
NISHI GINZA STATION see **NISHI GINZA EKIMAE** • 1958
NISHI YOROPPA NO MAMORI • 1968 • Tanu Tadashi, Ugawa Kiyotaka • DOC • JPN • DEFENCE OF WESTERN EUROPE
NISHIJIN NO SHIMAI • 1952 • Yoshimura Kozaburo • JPN • SISTERS OF NISHIJIN
NISHIJIN SHINJU • 1977 • Takabayashi Yoichi • JPN • LOVERS' SUICIDE
NISHITHEY • 1963 • Agragami • IND
NISHIZUMI SENSHACHO-DEN • 1940 • Yoshimura Kozaburo • JPN • STORY OF TANK COMMANDER NISHIZUMI, THE
NISI TIS APHRODITIS, TO • 1969 • Salenakis George • GRC • VENUS'S ISLAND
NISKAVUOREN HETA • 1952 • Laine Edvin • FNL • HETA OF NISKAVUORI FARM ○ HETA FROM NISKAVUORI
NISKAVUOREN NAISET • 1938 • Vaala Valentin • FNL • WOMEN OF NISKAVUORI
NISKAVUORI • 1984 • Kassila Matti • FNL • FAMILY NISKAVUORI, THE
NISKAVUORI FIGHTS see **NISKAVUORI TAISTELEE** • 1957
NISKAVUORI TAISTELEE • 1957 • Laine Edvin • FNL • NISKAVUORI FIGHTS
NISSAU ARIANA WINDOW • 1969 • Jacobs Ken • USA
NISSA'UN FI HAYATI • 1957 • Wahab Fatin Abdel • EGY • DES FEMMES DANS MA VIE
NISSHOKU NO NATSU • 1956 • Horikawa Hiromichi • JPN • SUMMER THE SUN WAS LOST, THE
NISSO • 1967 • Aripov Marat • USS
NIT • 1983 • Prohmvitake Pakorn • THL
NIT WITTY KITTY • 1951 • Hanna William, Barbera Joseph • ANS • USA
NITCHEVO • 1926 • de Baroncelli Jacques • FRN
NITCHEVO • 1936 • de Baroncelli Jacques • FRN
NITE IN A NITE CLUB, A • 1934 • Schwarzwald Milton • SHT • USA
NITORYU KAIGEN • 1943 • Ito Daisuke • JPN
NITROGEN CYCLE, THE • 1952 • James Thora • UKN
NITTEN RODE ROSER see **19 RODE ROSER** • 1973
NITTI • 1988 • Switzer Michael • TVM • USA • CAPONE'S ENFORCER ○ NITTI: THE ENFORCER
NITTI: THE ENFORCER see **NITTI** • 1988
NITWITS • 1987 • van der Heyde Nikolai • NTH
NITWITS, THE • 1935 • Stevens George • USA
NITWITS ON PARADE, THE • 1949 • Hill Robert Jordan • UKN
NIURKA'S LIFE see **NYURKA'S LIFE** • 1972
NIVEAUX DE LANGUE ET SOCIETE • 1972 • Lamothe Arthur • DCS • CND
NIVENNA GINNA • 1976 • Jayatilaka Amarnath • SLN
NIWA NO KOTORI • 1922 • Kinugasa Teinosuke • JPN • TWO LITTLE BIRDS
NIWATORI WA FUTATABI NAKU • 1954 • Gosho Heinosuke • JPN • COCK CROWS AGAIN, THE ○ HEN WILL SQUAWK AGAIN, A ○ COCK CROWS TWICE, THE
NIX ON DAMES • 1929 • Gallaher Donald • USA
NIX ON HYPNOTRICKS • 1941 • Fleischer Dave • ANS • USA
NIXCHEN • 1919 • Legband Paul • FRG
NIXCHEN • 1926 • Blachnitzky Curt • FRG
NIXENKONIGIN, DIE • 1917 • Neher Louis • FRG
NIXI see **NON MI SPOSO PIU** • 1942
NIYANGALA MAL • 1974 • Sandrasagara Manik • SLN • WILD FLOWER, THE
NIZVODNO OD SUNCA • 1969 • Skubonja Fedor • YGS • DOWNSTREAM FROM THE SUN ○ DOWNSTREAM THE SUN
NJAI DASIMA • 1931 • Soi Lie Tek, Effendi Bakhtiar • INN
NJANGAAN see **N'DIANGANE** • 1974

NJERIU PREJ DHEU • 1985 • Sopi Agim • YGS • COVEK OD ZEMLJE ○ MAN OF EARTH
NJETSCHAJEV 1869–1972 see **AUSLIEFERUNG, DIE** • 1974
NJIH DVOJICA • 1955 • Skrigin Zorz • YGS • TWO PEASANTS
NJU • 1924 • Czinner Paul • FRG • UNVERSTANDENE FRAU, EINE ○ HUSBANDS OR LOVERS?
NKULULEKO • 1985 • SAF
NO • 1979 • Stoneman John • CND
NO see **NEM** • 1965
NO! see **OHI** • 1969
NO.1 • 1974 • Kreck Joachim • DCS • FRG
NO.1 LICENSED TO LOVE AND KILL see **LICENSED TO LOVE AND KILL** • 1979
NO.1 MAN OF JAPAN: THE BEST see **NIHON–ICHI NO OTOKO NO NAKA NO OTOKO** • 1967
NO.1 NEWTON STREET • 1963 • Vulfovich Teodor • USS
NO.1 OF THE SECRET SERVICE • 1978 • Shonteff Lindsay • UKN • MAN FROM S.E.X., THE (USA) ○ ORCHID FOR NO. 1, AN ○ UNDERCOVER LOVER ○ NUMBER ONE OF THE SECRET SERVICE
NO.4 see **YOKO ONO FILM NO.4** • 1967
NO.5 JOHN STREET • 1921 • Foss Kenelm • UKN
NO.7 BRICK ROW • 1922 • Durrant Fred W. • UKN
NO.8 SEILER STREET see **SEILERGASSE 8** • 1960
NO.10 WESTBOUND • 1917 • McRae Henry • SHT • USA
NO.14 see **ONDORT NUMARA** • 1985
NO. 16 MARTIN PLACE • 1916 • Carleton Lloyd B. • SHT • USA
NO.28, DIPLOMAT • 1914 • Botter Harry • USA
NO.93 LOST IN ACTION • SHT • CZC
NO.99 • 1920 • Warde Ernest C. • USA
NO.00173 • 1966 • Habarta Jan • SHT • PLN
NO.329 • 1915 • Giblyn Charles • USA
NO.412–676 • 1969 • Blazekovic Milan • ANM • YGS
NO–ACCOUNT COUNT, THE • 1914 • Hale Albert W. • USA
NO–ACCOUNT SMITH'S BABY • 1914 • *Kb* • USA
NO ACT OF GOD • 1977 • Goldsmith Sidney, Ball Ian • ANM • CND
NO ALIBI • Gurney Philip • DOC • UKN
NO ALLA VIOLENZA • 1978 • Cimarosa Tano • ITL
NO AND YES see **NYET I DA** • 1967
NO ANSWER FROM F.P.1 see **F.P.1 ANTWORTET NICHT** • 1932
NO APPARENT MOTIVE see **BOYS NEXT DOOR, THE** • 1985
NO ARKS • 1969 • Abu • UKN
NO BABIES ALLOWED • 1915 • Curtis Allen • USA
NO BABIES WANTED • 1928 • Harvey John • USA • BABY MOTHER, THE ○ PATSY'S IRISH JOHN
NO BAG LIMIT • 1973 • Vial Andrew • ASL
NO BARKING • 1954 • Jones Charles M. • ANS • USA
NO BASTA SER CHARRO • 1945 • Bustillo Oro Juan • MXC
NO BASTA SER MADRE • 1937 • Peon Ramon • MXC • MOTHERHOOD IS NOT ENOUGH (USA) ○ IT'S NOT ENOUGH TO BE A MOTHER
NO BATHING ALLOWED • 1902 • *Mitchell & Kenyon* • UKN
NO BATHING ALLOWED • 1903 • Williamson James • UKN
NO BEAST SO FIERCE see **STRAIGHT TIME** • 1978
NO BIG DEAL • 1983 • Charlton Robert • USA
NO BIG DEAL see **YU NI MAO NI** • 1980
NO BIZ LIKE SHOE BIZ • 1960 • Hanna William, Barbera Joseph • ANS • USA
NO BLADE OF GRASS • 1970 • Wilde Cornel • UKN
NO BRAKES (UKN) see **OH, YEAH!** • 1929
NO CAUSE FOR ALARM see **FATAL SKY** • 1989
NO C'E AMORE PIU GRANDE • 1955 • Bianchi Giorgio • ITL
NO CENSUS, NO FEELING • 1940 • Lord Del • USA
NO CHEATING • 1927 • Roberts Stephen • SHT • USA
NO CHILDREN • 1921 • Roach Hal • SHT • USA
NO CHILDREN WANTED • 1912 • *Powers* • USA
NO CHILDREN WANTED • 1918 • MacDonald Sherwood • USA
NO CHILD'S LAND see **CHIEDO ASILO** • 1979
NO CLOUDS IN THE SKY see **SORA WA HARETARI** • 1925
NO CLUES see **NYOM NELKUL** • 1983
NO COMPTEU AMBS EL DITS (CARMEN) • 1967 • Portabella Pedro • SPN
NO CONSULTATION TO BE HELD see **HONJITSU KYUSHIN** • 1952
NO CONSULTATION TODAY see **HONJITSU KYUSHIN** • 1952
NO CONTROL • 1927 • Sidney Scott, Babille E. J. • USA
NO COOKING ALLOWED • 1911 • *Tener Marie* • USA
NO CORPSES ALLOWED • 1966 • Carin Vladimir • YGS
NO CREDIT • 1947 • Tregillus Leonard, Luce Ralph • ANS • USA
NO CREDITS see **BES NASLOVA** • 1964
NO CROSSING THE BRIDGE see **MOST PEREYTI NELIEYA** • 1960
NO CUELGUE POR FAVOR! • 1961 • Merenda Victor • SPN
NO CURE LIKE FATHER'S • 1914 • Collins Edwin J.? • UKN
NO DEAD HEROES • 1987 • Miller J. C. • USA
NO DEFENSE • 1921 • Duncan William • USA
NO DEFENSE • 1929 • Bacon Lloyd • USA
NO DEJES LA PUERTA ABIERTA • 1933 • Strayer Frank • USA • DON'T LEAVE THE DOOR OPEN
NO DEPOSIT NO RETURN • 1976 • Tokar Norman • USA
NO DESEARAS AL VECINO DEL QUINTO • 1971 • Fernandez Ramon • SPN • THOU SHALT NOT COVET THY NEIGHBOUR ON THE FIFTH FLOOR
NO DESEARAS LA MUJER DE TU HIJO • 1949 • Rodriguez Ismael • MXC
NO DESEARAS LA MUJER DE TU PROJIMO • 1968 • Lazaga Pedro • SPN • THOU SHALT NOT COVET THY NEIGHBOUR'S WIFE
NO DESEARAS LA MUJER DEL VECINO • 1971 • Merino Fernando • SPN
NO DISPARES CONTRA MI • 1961 • Nunes Jose Maria • SPN
NO DISPONIBLE • 1968 • Herrero Pedro Mario • SPN
NO DOUGH, BOYS • 1944 • White Jules • SHT • USA
NO DOWN PAYMENT • 1957 • Ritt Martin • USA
NO DRUMS, NO BUGLES • 1971 • Ware Clyde • USA • ALTERNATIVE WAR
NO ENCONTRE ROSAS PARA MI MADRE • 1972 • Rovira Beleta Francisco • SPN
NO END see **BEZ KONVA** • 1984
NO END TO THE GREAT WAR see **NIE MA KONCA WIELKIEJ WOJNY** • 1959
NO ENTRY • 1959 • Cowan Tom • SHT • ASL
NO ERAN NADIE • 1982 • Bravo Sergio • CHL • THEY WERE NOBODY
NO ES BUENO QUE EL HOMBRE ESTE SOLO • 1972 • Olea Pedro • SPN • IT IS NOT GOOD THAT MAN SHOULD BE ALONE
NO ES NADA MAMA, SOLO UN JUEGO • 1974 • Forque Jose Maria • VNZ, SPN • IT'S NOTHING MUMMY, JUST A GAME
NO ES PECADO • 1978 • Guevara Enrique • SPN
NO ESCAPE • 1934 • Ince Ralph • UKN
NO ESCAPE • 1936 • Lee Norman • UKN • NO EXIT
NO ESCAPE see **I ESCAPED FROM THE GESTAPO** • 1943
NO ESCAPE see **CITY ON A HUNT** • 1953
NO ESCAPE (UKN) see **OVER THE SANTA FE TRAIL** • 1947
NO ESCAPE (USA) see **PIEGE, LE** • 1958
NO ESTABA EN EL CIELO • 1976 • Velasco Andres • SPN
NO ESTAMOS SOLOS • 1956 • Iglesias Miguel • SPN
NO EVIL EYE! see **CHASME BUDDHOOR** • 1981
NO EXIT • 1930 • Saunders Charles • UKN
NO EXIT • 1962 • Danielewski Tad • USA, ARG • SINNERS GO TO HELL ○ STATELESS ○ HUIS CLOS
NO EXIT see **NO ESCAPE** • 1936
NO EXIT see **HUIS–CLOS** • 1954
NO EXIT (USA) see **SENZA VIA D'USCITA** • 1971
NO EXPERIENCE REQUIRED see **POINTING FINGER, THE** • 1919
NO EXTREMO–ORIENTE PORTUGUES • 1960 • Spiguel Miguel • SHT • PRT
NO EYES TODAY • 1929 • Fleischer Dave • ANS • USA
NO FARE • 1928 • Lamont Charles • SHT • USA
NO FATHER TO GUIDE HIM • 1925 • McCarey Leo • SHT • USA
NO FIGHT WITHOUT MONEY see **MUSEN FUSEN** • 1924
NO FIRMES MAS LETRAS, CIELO • 1972 • Lazaga Pedro • SPN
NO FLIES ON CIS • 1913 • Wilson Frank? • UKN
NO FLIRT ALLOWED • 1915 • *L-Ko* • USA
NO FOOL LIKE AN OLD FOOL • 1914 • *Formby George* • UKN
NO FOOL LIKE AN OLD FOOL • 1915 • Birch Cecil • UKN
NO FORD IN THE FIRE see **V OGNYE BRODA NYET** • 1968
NO FORD THROUGH THE FIRE see **V OGNYE BRODA NYET** • 1968
NO FORGETTING see **NO OLVIDAR** • 1983
NO FORWARDING ADDRESS see **PARTI SAN LAISSER D'ADDRESSE** • 1982
NO FUMADORES • 1940 • Arevalo Carlos • SHT • SPN
NO FUNNY BUSINESS • 1933 • Stafford John, Hanbury Victor • UKN • PROFESSIONAL CO–RESPONDENTS
NO GO! • 1973 • Chase Richard • USA
NO GOING BACK • 1981 • Hicks Scott • DOC • ASL
NO GOLD FOR A DEAD DIVER (UKN) see **TOTER TAUCHER NIMMT KEIN GELD, EIN** • 1975
NO GOOD FOR ANYTHING • 1908 • Rosenthal Joe • UKN
NO–GOOD GUY, THE • 1916 • Edwards Walter • USA
NO GOOD TO DIE FOR THAT see **IL NE FAUT PAS MOURIR** • 1968
NO GRAZIE, IL CAFFE' MI RENDE NERVOSO • 1983 • Gasparini Ludovico • ITL • NO THANKS, COFFEE MAKES ME NERVOUS
NO GREATER GLORY • 1934 • Borzage Frank • USA
NO GREATER GLORY see **QASUM US WAQT KI** • 1976
NO GREATER LOVE • 1912 • *Prescott Vivian* • USA
NO GREATER LOVE • 1932 • Seiler Lewis • USA • DIVINE LOVE (UKN)
NO GREATER LOVE see **ONA ZASHCHISHCHAYET RODINU** • 1943
NO GREATER LOVE see **NINGEN NO JOKEN I** • 1959
NO GREATER LOVE THAN THIS (USA) see **KOTO NO TAIYO** • 1968
NO GREATER LOVE (UKN) see **ALOHA** • 1931
NO GREATER LOVE (UKN) see **EUROPA '51** • 1952
NO GREATER SIN • 1941 • Nigh William • USA • SOCIAL ENEMY NO.1 (UKN)
NO–GUN MAN, THE • 1924 • Garson Harry • USA
NO HABRA MAS PENSAS NI OLVIDO • 1985 • Olivera Hector • ARG • FUNNY DIRTY LITTLE WAR, A
NO HANDS ON THE CLOCK • 1941 • McDonald Frank • USA
NO HARD FEELINGS • 1974 • Parker Alan • MTV • UKN
NO HARD FEELINGS • 1989 • Norton Charles • USA
NO HAUNT FOR A GENTLEMAN • 1952 • Reeve Leonard • UKN
NO HAY CRUCES EN EL MAR • 1968 • Soler Julian • MXC • THERE ARE NO CROSSES IN THE SEA
NO HAY SABADO • 1979 • Herrera Manuel • CUB • NO SUNLESS SEA
NO HIGHWAY • 1951 • Koster Henry • UKN • NO HIGHWAY IN THE SKY (USA)
NO HIGHWAY IN THE SKY (USA) see **NO HIGHWAY** • 1951
NO HOLDS BARRED • 1952 • Beaudine William • USA
NO HOLDS BARRED • 1970 • *Stacey Dist.* • USA
NO HOLIDAY FOR INOCHKIN (UKN) see **DOBRO POZHALOVAT** • 1964
NO HOLIDAY FOR THE GOOD GOD see **PLUS DE VACANCES POUR LE BON DIEU** • 1949
NO HUNTING • 1955 • Hannah Jack • ANS • USA
NO IF'S, AND OR BUTTS • 1954 • Sparber I. • ANS • USA
NO: IL CASO E FELICEMENTE RISOLTO • 1973 • Salerno Vittorio • ITL
NO IMPORTA MORIR • 1969 • Klimovsky Leon • SPN
NO JUSTICE ON SUNDAY see **NIEDZIELA SPRAWIEDLIWOSCI** • 1965
NO KIDDING • 1960 • Thomas Gerald • UKN • BEWARE OF CHILDREN (USA)
NO KNIFE see **FRISCO KID, THE** • 1979
NO LADY • 1931 • Lane Lupino • UKN
NO LAUGHING MATTER see **NIKDO SE NEBUDE SMAT** • 1965
NO LE BUSQUES TRES PIES.. • 1968 • Lazaga Pedro • SPN • DON'T SEARCH FOR THREE FEET..
NO LEAVE, NO LOVE • 1946 • Martin Charles • USA
NO LES DIGAS QUE CAI • 1988 • Aranda Vicente • SPN • DON'T TELL THEM I FELL
NO LES PEDIMOS UN VIAJE A LA LUNA • 1988 • de Lara Maria De Carmen • DOC • MXC • WE DON'T ASK FOR A TRIP TO THE MOON
NO LIMIT • 1931 • Tuttle Frank • USA
NO LIMIT • 1935 • Banks Monty • UKN
NO LIVING WITNESS • 1932 • Hopper E. Mason • USA
NO LONGER ALONE • 1978 • Webster Nicholas • USA
NO LONGER VANISHING • 1955 • McLean Grant • DOC • CND
NO LOVE FOR JOHNNIE • 1961 • Thomas Ralph • UKN
NO LOVE FOR JUDY • 1955 • De Lane Lea Jacques • UKN
NO LOVE PLEASE see **TILOS A SZERELEM** • 1965
NO MAN IS AN ISLAND • 1962 • Goldstone Richard, Monks John Jr. • USA • ISLAND ESCAPE (UKN)
NO MAN OF HER OWN • 1932 • Ruggles Wesley • USA
NO MAN OF HER OWN • 1950 • Leisen Mitchell • USA • LIE, THE
NO MAN WALKS ALONE see **BLACK LIKE ME** • 1964
NO MAN'S DAUGHTER see **ARVACSKA** • 1976
NO MAN'S GOLD • 1926 • Seiler Lewis • USA
NO MAN'S LAND • 1909 • *Selig* • USA
NO MAN'S LAND • 1918 • Davis Will S. • USA
NO MAN'S LAND • 1919 • *Strand* • SHT • USA
NO MAN'S LAND • 1964 • Harvey Russ • USA
NO MAN'S LAND • 1984 • Holcomb Rod • TVM • USA
NO MAN'S LAND • 1985 • Tanner Alain • SWT
NO MAN'S LAND • 1987 • Werner Peter • USA
NO MAN'S LAND see **NO MAN'S LAW** • 1927
NO MAN'S LAND (UKN) see **NIEMANDSLAND** • 1931
NO MAN'S LAW • 1925 • Andrews Del • USA
NO MAN'S LAW • 1927 • Jackman Fred • USA • MAN'S LAW (UKN) ○ NO MAN'S LAND
NO MAN'S RANGE • 1935 • Bradbury Robert North • USA
NO MAN'S WOMAN • 1921 • Mack Wayne, Maloney Leo • USA
NO MAN'S WOMAN • 1955 • Adreon Franklin • USA
NO MAN'S WOMAN see **INGEN MANS KVINNA** • 1953
NO MAPS ON MY TAPS • 1978 • Nierenberg George T. • DOC • USA
NO MARRIAGE TIES • 1933 • Ruben J. Walter • USA • PUBLIC BE SOLD, THE
NO MATARAS • 1943 • Urueta Chano • MXC
NO MATARAS • 1974 • Ardavin Cesar • SPN
NO ME DEFIENDAS COMPADRE • 1949 • Martinez Solares Gilberto • MXC
NO ME DIGAS ADIOS • 1950 • Barth-Moglia Luis • ARG
NO ME OLVIDES NUNCA • 1956 • Ortega Juan J. • MXC, CUB
NO ME PLATIQUE MAS • 1956 • Delgado Miguel M. • MXC
NO ME QUIERAS TANTO • 1949 • Urueta Chano • MXC
NO MEDALS FOR MARTHA see **WEAKER SEX, THE** • 1948
NO MERCY • 1987 • Pearce Richard • USA
NO–MERCY MAN, THE • 1973 • Vance Daniel J. • USA • TRAINED TO KILL
NO MERCY NO FUTURE see **BERUHRTE, DIE** • 1981
NO MIDDLE ROAD see **HRA O ZIVOT** • 1956
NO MINOR VICES • 1948 • Milestone Lewis • USA
NO MIRACLE AT ALL • 1965 • Kamenetsky M., Uphimtsev I. • ANS • USS • HERE ARE SOME MIRACLES
NO MONEY, NO FIGHT (USA) see **MUSEN FUSEN** • 1924
NO MONEY –NO FUN • 1918 • *Pixley Gus* • USA
NO MONKEY BUSINESS • 1935 • Varnel Marcel • UKN
NO MORE BALD HEADS • 1908 • *Pathe* • FRN
NO MORE BETS see **NO VA MAS** • 1982
NO MORE BRIDGE • 1934 • Gillstrom Arvid E. • SHT • USA
NO MORE COMIC MAGAZINES see **KOMICK ZASSHI NANKA IRANAI** • 1987
NO MORE DIVORCES see **ROZWODOW NIE BEDZIE** • 1963
NO MORE EASY GOING see **MO HOHOZUE WA TSUKANAI** • 1979
NO MORE EXCUSES • 1968 • Downey Robert • USA
NO MORE FLEEING (USA) see **NICHT MEHR FLIEHEN** • 1955
NO MORE HATS WANTED • 1909 • Fitzhamon Lewin • UKN
NO MORE HIBAKUSHA • 1983 • Duckworth Martin • DOC • CND
NO MORE HIROSHIMA • 1983 • Duckworth Martin • DCS • CND • PLUS JAMAIS HIROSHIMA
NO MORE LADIES • 1935 • Griffith Edward H., Cukor George (U/c) • USA
NO MORE LOVE (USA) see **NIE WIEDER LIEBE** • 1931
NO MORE, MR. NICE GUY • 1989 • Craven Wes • USA
NO MORE ORCHIDS • 1933 • Lang Walter • USA
NO MORE RELATIVES • 1948 • Yates Hal • SHT • USA
NO MORE TIME see **NON HO TEMPO** • 1973
NO MORE TROUBLES see **EASY GOING GORDON** • 1925
NO MORE WEST • 1934 • Grinde Nick • SHT • USA
NO MORE WOMEN • 1924 • Ingraham Lloyd • USA
NO MORE WOMEN • 1934 • Rogell Albert S. • USA
NO MOTHER TO GUIDE HER • 1923 • Horan Charles • USA
NO MOTHER TO GUIDE HIM • 1919 • St. Clair Malcolm, Kenton Erle C. • SHT • USA
NO MUTTON FOR NUTTIN' • 1943 • *Blackie* • ANS • USA
NO, MY DARLING DAUGHTER! • 1961 • Thomas Ralph • UKN
NO NAME ON THE BULLET • 1959 • Arnold Jack • USA
NO NEED FOR A PASS–WORD • 1967 • Grigoriev Yuri • USS
NO NEWS IS GOOD NEWS • 1943 • Jason Will • SHT • USA
NO NIEGO MI PASADO • 1951 • Gout Alberto • MXC
NO! NO! A THOUSAND TIMES NO!! • 1935 • Fleischer Dave • ANS • USA
NO, NO, IT'S A SIN • 1961 • *National Catholic Film Prod.* • ITL • LIFE OF ST. MARIA GORETTI, THE
NO, NO, LADY • 1931 • Cline Eddie • SHT • USA
NO, NO, NANETTE • 1930 • Badger Clarence • USA
NO, NO, NANETTE • 1940 • Wilcox Herbert • USA
NO NOISE • 1923 • Roach Hal • SHT • USA
NO NUKES • 1980 • Schlossberg Julian, Goldberg Danny, Potenza Anthony • USA
NO ODNOI PLANETE • 1966 • Olshvanger Ilya • USS • ON THE SAME PLANET ○ ONE PLANET
NO OLVIDAR • 1983 • Aguero Ignacio • DCS • CHL • NO FORGETTING
NO–ONE CALLING see **NIKT NIE WOLA** • 1960
NO ONE CAN LOVE YOU see **SEVEMEZ KIMSE SENI** • 1968
NO ONE CRIES FOREVER see **HOLLYWOOD MAN** • 1976
NO ONE CRIES OUT.. see **NIKT NIE WOLA** • 1960

NO ONE IS CRAZIER THAN I AM see **INGEN SA TOKIG SOM JAG** • 1955
NO ONE IS STRONG see **NIE MA MOCNYCH** • 1975
NO ONE IS TO BLAME • 1987 • Petrova Malina • DOC • BUL
NO-ONE KNOWS A THING see **NIKDO NIC NEVI** • 1947
NO ONE MAN • 1932 • Corrigan Lloyd • USA
NO ONE SAID A WORD see **NADIO DIGO NADA** • 1971
NO ONE TO GUIDE HIM • 1916 • *Chaplin Syd* • SHT • USA
NO ONE WANTED TO DIE see **NIKTO NE KHOTEL UMIRAT** • 1965
NO ONE WILL PLAY WITH ME see **MIT MIR WILL KEINER SPIELEN** • 1976
NO ONE WOULD BELIEVE HER see **WELCOME TO ARROW BEACH** • 1973
NO, OR THE VAIN GLORY OF COMMAND • 1990 • de Oliveira Manoel • PRT
NO ORCHIDS FOR LULU (UKN) see **LULU** • 1962
NO ORCHIDS FOR MISS BLANDISH • 1948 • Clowes St. John L. • UKN
NO ORDINARY SUMMER • 1958 • Basov Vladimir • USS
NO OTHER LOVE • 1979 • Pearce Richard • TVM • USA
NO OTHER ONE • 1936 • Fleischer Dave • ANS • USA
NO OTHER WOMAN • 1928 • Tellegen Lou • USA
NO OTHER WOMAN • 1933 • Ruben J. Walter • USA • MAN AND WIFE
NO OYES LADRAR A LOS PERROS? • 1974 • Reichenbach Francois, Howard Noel • MXC, FRN • CAN'T YOU HEAR THE DOGS BARKING? ○ DON'T YOU HEAR THE DOGS BARK? ○ ENTENDS-TU LES CHIENS BOYER? ○ DO YOU HEAR THE DOGS BARKING?
NO PALE GOTHIC SAINTS • 1979 • Mason Richard • DOC • ASL
NO PARAISO DAS SOLTEIRONAS • 1969 • Mazzaropi Amacio • BRZ • IN THE PARADISE OF UNMARRIED WOMEN
NO PARKING • 1921 • Christie Al • USA
NO PARKING • 1938 • Raymond Jack • UKN
NO PARKING HARE • 1954 • McKimson Robert • ANS • USA
NO PEACE AMONG THE OLIVES see **NON C'E PACE TRA GLI ULIVI** • 1950
NO PEACE ANY MORE see **NIE ZAZNASZ SPOKOJU** • 1977
NO PERMANENT RESIDENCE see **BOMZH** • 1989
NO PETS • 1923 • Roach Hal • SHT • USA
NO PHYSICAL CONTACT • 1982 • Desimone Tom • USA
NO PINCHA • 1970 • Engel Tobias • FRN • FORWARD
NO PLACE FOR A LADY • 1943 • Hogan James P. • USA
NO PLACE FOR A MINISTER'S SON • 1912 • Miller Ashley • USA
NO PLACE FOR FATHER • 1913 • *Moreno Antonio* • USA
NO PLACE FOR JENNIFER • 1950 • Cass Henry • UKN
NO PLACE FOR LOVE see **KEIN PLATZ FUR LIEBE** • 1947
NO PLACE IN HELL see **CEHENNEMDE BOS YER YOK** • 1968
NO PLACE LIKE HOME • 1910 • *Selig* • USA
NO PLACE LIKE HOME • 1917 • MacGregor Norval • USA
NO PLACE LIKE HOMICIDE (USA) see **WHAT A CARVE UP** • 1961
NO PLACE LIKE JAIL • 1916 • McKim Edwin • SHT • USA
NO PLACE LIKE JAIL • 1918 • Roach Hal • SHT • USA
NO PLACE LIKE ROME • 1936 • Le Borg Reginald • SHT • USA
NO PLACE LIKE ROME • 1953 • Sparber I. • ANS • USA
NO PLACE ON EARTH see **MIEJSCE NA ZIEMI** • 1960
NO PLACE TO GO • 1927 • LeRoy Mervyn • USA • HER PRIMITIVE MATE (UKN)
NO PLACE TO GO • 1939 • Morse Terry O. • USA
NO PLACE TO HIDE • 1956 • Shaftel Josef • USA, PHL
NO PLACE TO HIDE • 1975 • Schnitzer Robert Allen • USA • REBEL
NO PLACE TO HIDE • 1981 • Moxey John Llewellyn • TVM • USA
NO PLACE TO LAND • 1958 • Gannaway Albert C. • USA • MAD MAD (UKN)
NO PLACE TO RUN • 1972 • Mann Delbert • USA
NO POTATOES see **LOOS** • 1988
NO PRESIDENT • 1967 • Smith Jack** • USA
NO PRIVACY • 1931 • Edwards Harry J. • SHT • USA
NO PROBLEMS IN SUMMER see **NYARON EGYSZERU** • 1963
NO PROFANAR EL SUENO DE LOS MUERTOS see **FIN DE SEMANA PARA LOS MUERTOS** • 1974
NO QUARTER • 1915 • Cooley Frank • USA
NO QUARTER • 1934 • *Hayes George* • SHT • UKN
NO QUESTION ON SATURDAY see **PAS QUESTION LE SAMEDI** • 1965
NO QUESTIONS ASKED • 1951 • Kress Harold F. • USA
NO QUESTIONS ASKED see **HIS MYSTERY GIRL** • 1923
NO QUESTIONS ASKED see **BEWARE OF BACHELORS** • 1928
NO QUIERO, NO QUIERO • 1938 • Elias Francisco • SPN
NO QUIERO PERDER LA HONRA • 1975 • Martin Eugenio • SPN
NO RANSOM • 1934 • Newmeyer Fred • USA • BONDS OF HONOUR (UKN)
NO READ, NO WRITE • 1967 • Camonte Tony • PHL
NO REASON TO STAY • 1966 • Ransen Mort, Pojar Bretislav • SHT • CND
NO REGRETS FOR LOST YOUTH see **WAGA SEISHUN NI KUINASHI** • 1946
NO REGRETS FOR MY YOUTH see **WAGA SEISHUN NI KUINASHI** • 1946
NO REGRETS FOR OUR YOUTH see **WAGA SEISHUN NI KUINASHI** • 1946
NO RELATIONS see **SANS FAMILLE** • 1925
NO RESPONSE FROM CAR 33 see **SANJUSAN-GOSHA OHTOH NASHI** • 1955
NO RESTING PLACE • 1951 • Rotha Paul • UKN
NO RETREAT, NO SURRENDER • 1986 • Yuen Corey • USA
NO RETREAT, NO SURRENDER: RAGING THUNDER • 1989 • Yuen Corey • USA
NO RETURN see **KAERANU SASABUE** • 1926
NO RETURN see **VOZVRATA NYET** • 1975
NO RETURN ADDRESS • 1961 • Grattan Alexander • USA
NO RETURN FOR JOHNNY see **NIE MA POWROTU JOHNNY** • 1970
NO ROAD BACK • 1957 • Tully Montgomery • UKN
NO ROOM AT RAFFLES • 1981 • Barry Ian • SHT • ASL
NO ROOM AT THE INN • 1948 • Birt Daniel • UKN
NO ROOM FOR FATHER • 1904 • Collins Alf? • UKN
NO ROOM FOR THE GROOM • 1952 • Sirk Douglas • USA • ALMOST MARRIED
NO ROOM FOR THE GROOM see **MILLIONAIRE FOR CHRISTY, A** • 1951
NO ROOM FOR WILD ANIMALS see **KEIN PLATZ FUR WILDE TIERE** • 1956
NO ROOM TO DIE (UKN) see **LUNGA FILA DI CROCI, UNA** • 1969
NO ROOM TO RUN • 1978 • Lewis Robert Michael • TVM • ASL
NO ROSES FOR MICHAEL • 1970 • McGill Chris • SHT • ASL
NO ROSES FOR OSS 117 see **NIENTE ROSE PER OSS 117** • 1968
NO SAD SONGS • 1986 • Sheehan Nick • DOC • CND
NO SAD SONGS FOR ME • 1950 • Mate Rudolph • USA
NO SAFE HAVEN • 1987 • Rondell Ronnie • USA
NO SAFETY AHEAD • 1959 • Varnel Max • UKN
NO SAIL • 1945 • Hannah Jack • ANS • USA
NO SCRUPLES see **SENZA SCRUPOLI** • 1985
NO SEX PLEASE -WE'RE BRITISH • 1973 • Owen Cliff • UKN
NO SHOW FOR THE CHAUFFEUR • 1914 • *Eclair* • USA
NO SIR-EE BOB! • 1916 • Smith Sidney • SHT • USA
"NO SIR, ORISON" • 1975 • Landow George • USA
NO SLEEP FOR PERCY • 1955 • Rasinski Connie • ANS • USA
NO SLEEP ON THE DEEP • 1934 • Lamont Charles • SHT • USA
NO SLEEP TILL DAWN (UKN) see **BOMBERS B-52** • 1957
NO SMALL AFFAIR • 1982 • Ritt Martin • USA
NO SMALL AFFAIR • 1984 • Schatzberg Jerry • USA
NO SMOKING • 1915 • Metcalfe Earl • USA
NO SMOKING • 1951 • Kinney Jack • ANS • USA
NO SMOKING • 1955 • Cass Henry • UKN
NO SMOKING • 1967 • Sullivan Mike • USA
NO SOMOS DE PIEDRA • 1968 • Summers Manuel • SPN • WE'RE NOT MADE OF STONE ○ WE ARE NOT OF STONE
NO SOMOS NI ROMEO NI JULIETA • 1969 • Paso Alfonso • SPN
NO, SONO VERGINE! • 1971 • Mancini Cesare • ITL • RELUCTANT VIRGIN, THE
NO SOUP • 1915 • McCray Roy • USA
NO SOY CULPABLE • 1959 • Petrucci Antonio • ITL
NO SOY MONEDITA DE ORO • 1958 • Urueta Chano • MXC
NO SPARKING • 1927 • Beaudine Harold • USA
NO SPEED LIMIT see **HELL BENT FOR LOVE** • 1934
NO STARS IN THE JUNGLE see **EN LA SELVA NO HAY ESTRELLAS** • 1968
NO STEALING see **PROIBITO RUBARE** • 1948
NO STOP-OVER • 1921 • Roach Hal • SHT • USA
NO STORY • 1917 • Mills Thomas R. • SHT • USA
NO SUN IN VENICE (USA) see **SAIT-ON JAMAIS** • 1957
NO SUNLESS SEA see **NO HAY SABADO** • 1979
NO SURRENDER • 1985 • Smith Peter • UKN
NO SURRENDER see **ALYGISTOS, O** • 1967
NO SURVIVORS, PLEASE (USA) see **CHEF WUNSCHT KEINE ZEUGEN, DER** • 1963
NO SWEAT see **ADIOS AMIGO** • 1975
NO SWEETS • 1913 • Brooke Van Dyke • USA
NO TE CASES CON MI MUJER • 1946 • Cortes Fernando • MXC
NO TE DEJARE NUNCA • 1947 • Elias Francisco • MXC
NO TE ENGANES CORAZON • 1936 • Contreras Torres Miguel • MXC • DON'T DECEIVE YOURSELF, MY HEART ○ DON'T FOOL THYSELF -HEART
NO TE METAS • 1989 • Weller Johanan • ISR • DON'T GET INVOLVED (UKN)
NO TE OFENDAS, BEATRIZ • 1952 • Soler Julian • MXC
NO TEARS FOR A KILLER see **TECNICA DI UN OMICIDIO** • 1966
NO TEARS FOR THE DAMNED • 1968 • Collins William • USA
NO THANKS, COFFEE MAKES ME NERVOUS see **NO GRAZIE, IL CAFFE' MI RENDE NERVOSO** • 1983
NO TICKEE -NO WASHEE • 1915 • Stratton Edmund F. • USA
NO TIENE LA CULPA EL INDIO • 1977 • Delgado Miguel M. • MXC
NO TIME see **NINCS IDO** • 1973
NO TIME FOR BREAKFAST (USA) see **DOCTEUR FRANCOISE GAILLAND** • 1975
NO TIME FOR COMEDY • 1940 • Keighley William • USA
NO TIME FOR ECSTASY (USA) see **FETE ESPAGNOLE, LA** • 1961
NO TIME FOR FLOWERS • 1952 • Siegel Don • USA
NO TIME FOR LOVE • 1943 • Leisen Mitchell • USA
NO TIME FOR SERGEANTS • 1958 • LeRoy Mervyn • USA
NO TIME FOR TALK see **TIADA WAKTU BICARA** • 1974
NO TIME FOR TEARS • 1957 • Frankel Cyril • UKN
NO TIME FOR TEARS see **OTOKO ARITE** • 1955
NO TIME FOR TEARS see **KEINE ZEIT FUR TRANEN** • 1984
NO TIME FOR TEARS (UKN) see **PURPLE HEART DIARY** • 1951
NO TIME FOR TENDERNESS see **INGEN TID TIL KOERTERN** • 1957
NO TIME TO DIE • 1958 • Young Terence • UKN • TANK FORCE (USA)
NO TIME TO DIE • 1985 • Ashley Helmut • FRG, INN • HIJACKED TO HELL
NO TIME TO BE YOUNG • 1957 • Rich David Lowell • USA • TEENAGE DELINQUENTS (UKN)
NO TIME TO KILL see **MED MORD I BAGAGET** • 1963
NO TIME TO MARRY • 1938 • Lachman Harry • USA
NO TITLE! • 1916 • Walsh Phil • USA
NO TOMORROW see **SANS LENDEMAIN** • 1939
NO TOMORROW see **INGEN MORGONDAG** • 1957
NO TOMORROW see **LA ANAM** • 1957
NO TOMORROW see **TIADA ESOK BAGIMU** • 1977
NO TOQUEN A LA NEVA • 1976 • Jusid Juan Jose • ARG • DON'T TOUCH THE LITTLE GIRL
NO TOYS FOR CHRISTMAS see **ONCE BEFORE I DIE** • 1965
NO TRACE • 1950 • Gilling John • UKN
NO TREE GROWS • Habeebullah Shyama • DOC • IND
NO TREE IN THE STREET see **NO TREES IN THE STREET** • 1959
NO TREES IN THE STREET • 1959 • Thompson J. Lee • UKN • NO TREE IN THE STREET
NO TRESPASSING • 1912 • *Lubin* • USA
NO TRESPASSING • 1922 • Hollywood Edwin L. • USA • RISE OF ROSCOE PAYNE, THE
NO TRESPASSING see **RED HOUSE, THE** • 1947
NO TRESPASSING see **PRIVATE ROAD** • 1987
NO TRIFLING WITH LOVE see **ON NE BADINE PAS AVEC L'AMOUR** • 1908
NO TRUMPETS, NO DRUMS see **TRACKERS, THE** • 1971
NO TURNING BACK • 1976 • Young Robert • UKN
NO VA MAS • 1982 • Juri Jorge Zuhair • ARG • NO MORE BETS
NO VIETNAMESE EVER CALLED ME NIGGER • 1968 • Loeb David, Weiss Lois • DOC • USA
NO WAY BACK • 1949 • Osiecki Stefan • UKN
NO WAY BACK • 1976 • Williamson Fred • USA
NO WAY BACK • 1988 • Borden Michael • USA
NO WAY BACK see **INGEN VAG TILLBAKA** • 1947
NO WAY BACK (USA) see **WEG OHNE UMKEHR** • 1953
NO WAY OUT • 1950 • Mankiewicz Joseph L. • USA
NO WAY OUT • 1987 • Donaldson Roger • USA • DECEIT
NO WAY OUT see **DHEN EHO DHROMO NA DHIAVO** • 1968
NO WAY OUT see **BRIDE, THE** • 1973
NO WAY OUT (USA) see **TONY ARZENTA** • 1973
NO WAY THEY WANT TO SLOW DOWN • 1975 • Walker Giles • MTV • CND
NO WAY TO TREAT A LADY • 1968 • Smight Jack • USA
NO WEDDING BELLS • 1912 • *Eclair* • USA
NO WEDDING BELLS • 1923 • Semon Larry • USA
NO WEDDING BELLS FOR HER • 1914 • MacGregor Norval • USA
NO WEDDING BELLS FOR JONES • 1913 • *Punch* • USA
NO WOMAN KNOWS • 1921 • Browning Tod • USA
NO, YOU EXAGGERATE see **NON, TU EXAGERES**
NO YUKI, YAMA YUKI, UMIBE YUKI • 1987 • Obayashi Nobuhiko • JPN • ADOLESCENT DAYS
NOA AT 17 • 1982 • Yeshurun Isaac • ISR
NOA NOA • 1974 • Liberatore Ugo • ITL
NOAH see **DELUGE, THE** • 1979
NOAH, THE • 1974 • Boulas Daniel • GRC
NOAH DELTA II • 1986 • Pilz Michael • AUS, FRG, HNG
NOAH KNEW HIS ARK • 1930 • Foster John, Davis Mannie • ANS • USA
NOAH UND DER COWBOY • Tissi Felix • SWT
NOAH'S ARK • 1917 • *Fox* • USA
NOAH'S ARK • 1928 • Curtiz Michael • USA
NOAH'S ARK • 1959 • Justice Bill • ANS • USA
NOAH'S ARK • 1977 • *Halas John (P)* • ANS • UKN
NOAH'S ARK see **TALE OF THE ARK, THE** • 1909
NOAH'S ARK see **ARCHE DE NOE, L'** • 1966
NOAH'S ARK PRINCIPLE, THE • 1984 • Emmerich Roland • USA
NOAH'S ARK (USA) see **ARCHE DE NOE, L'** • 1946
NOAH'S ARKS see **NOE BARKAI** • 1983
NOAH'S LARK • 1929 • Fleischer Dave • ANS • USA
NOAH'S OUTING • 1932 • *Terry Paul/ Moser Frank (P)* • ANS • USA
NOAH'S SHIP see **KESHTYE NOAH** • 1968
NOAH'S STORM see **TOUFAN-E-NOAH** • 1967
NOB HILL • 1945 • Hathaway Henry • USA
NOBBLER'S CARD PARTY • 1905 • Collins Alf? • UKN
NOBBLING THE BRIDGE • 1915 • Collins Edwin J.? • UKN
NOBBY AND THE PEARL MYSTERY • 1913 • Kellino W. P. • UKN
NOBBY THE NEW WAITER • 1913 • Kellino W. P. • UKN
NOBBY THE NUT • 1914 • Kellino W. P. • UKN
NOBBY WINS THE CUP • 1914 • Kellino W. P. • UKN
NOBBY'S JU-JITSU EXPERIMENTS • 1914 • Kellino W. P. • UKN
NOBBY'S STUD • 1914 • Kellino W. P. • UKN
NOBBY'S TANGO TEAS • 1914 • Kellino W. P. • UKN
NOBEL PRIZE, THE • 1964 • Rasky Harry • MTV • USA
NOBEL PRIZE WINNER, THE see **NOBELPRISTAGAREN** • 1917
NOBELPRISTAGAREN • 1917 • Klercker Georg • SWD • NOBEL PRIZE WINNER, THE
NOBI • Ratz Gunter • ANM • GDR
NOBI • 1959 • Ichikawa Kon • JPN • FIRES ON THE PLAIN
NOBLE ART, THE • 1920 • Goodwins Fred • UKN
NOBLE BACHELOR, THE • 1921 • Elvey Maurice • UKN • LONELY BACHELOR, THE
NOBLE CROOK, A see **TWO CROOKS** • 1917
NOBLE DECEPTION, A • 1914 • Buckland Warwick? • UKN
NOBLE ENEMY, A • 1911 • *Fielding Romaine* • USA
NOBLE FRAUD, A • 1917 • *Keystone* • USA
NOBLE HEART, A • 1911 • *Powers* • USA
NOBLE HEART, A • 1911 • Bouwmeester Theo • UKN
NOBLE JESTER, OR FAINT HEART NEVER WON FAIR LADY, A • 1908 • *Vitagraph* • USA
NOBLE LIGNEE, LA see **UNBROKEN LINE, THE** • 1978
NOBLE LOVER, THE • 1916 • *Supreme* • USA
NOBLE OUTCAST, A • 1910 • Coleby A. E. • UKN
NOBLE PROFESSION, A • 1912 • Miller Ashley • USA
NOBLE RED MAN, A • 1911 • *Bison* • USA
NOBLE REVENGE, A • 1911 • Martinek H. O. • UKN
NOBLE SACRIFICE, THE • 1916 • *Supreme* • USA
NOBLE WANDERER, THE see **ROYAL DEMOCRAT, A** • 1919
NOBLES, THE see **DANSAN GWAITSUK** • 1989
NOBLESSE OBLIGE see **DON'T NEGLECT YOUR WIFE** • 1921
NOBLEST OF CALLINGS, THE VILEST OF TRADES, THE • 1971 • Brittain Don, Thomas Ralph L. • CND
NOBLEZA BATURRA • 1935 • Rey Florian • SPN • RUSTIC CHIVALRY (USA)
NOBLEZA BATURRA • 1965 • de Orduna Juan • SPN
NOBLEZA GAUCHA • 1915 • Cairo Humberto • ARG • GAUCHO NOBILITY
NOBLEZA GAUCHA • 1938 • Naon Sebastian M. • GAUCHO CHIVALRY (USA)
NOBLEZA RANCHERA • 1938 • del Diestro Alfredo • MXC
NOBODY • 1921 • West Roland • USA
NOBODY GETS THE LAST LAUGH see **NIKDO SE NEBUDE SMAT** • 1965
NOBODY GUILTY • 1916 • Chaudet Louis W. • SHT • USA
NOBODY HOME • 1916 • Drew Sidney • SHT • USA
NOBODY HOME • 1919 • *Klever Pictures* • SHT • USA
NOBODY HOME see **OUT OF LUCK** • 1919

NOBODY KNOWS see **TOD EINES DOPPELGANGERS, DER** • 1967
NOBODY KNOWS ANYTHING see **NIKDO NIC NEVI** • 1947
NOBODY LIVES FOREVER • 1946 • Negulesco Jean • USA
NOBODY LOVES A DRUNKEN INDIAN see **FLAP** • 1969
NOBODY LOVES A FAT MAN • 1909 • *Phoenix* • USA
NOBODY LOVES A FAT WOMAN • 1911 • *Thanhouser* • USA
NOBODY LOVES FLAPPING EAGLE see **FLAP** • 1969
NOBODY MACHT ALLES • 1921 • Stein Josef • FRG
NOBODY MAKES ME CRY • 1984 • Antonio Lou • CND
NOBODY ORDERED LOVE • 1971 • Hartford-Davis Robert • UKN
NOBODY RUNS FOREVER • 1968 • Thomas Ralph • UKN • HIGH COMMISSIONER, THE (USA)
NOBODY SAID ANYTHING see **NADIO DIGO NADA** • 1971
NOBODY SAID NOTHING see **NADIO DIGO NADA** • 1971
NOBODY SHALL BE LAUGHING see **NIKDO SE NEBUDE SMAT** • 1965
NOBODY WANTED TO DIE see **NIKTO NE KHOTEL UMIRAT** • 1965
NOBODY WAVED GOODBYE • 1964 • Owen Don • CND • DEPART SANS ADIEUX
NOBODY WORKS LIKE A FATHER • 1906 • *Vitagraph* • USA
NOBODY WOULD BELIEVE • 1915 • *Leslie Lilie* • USA
NOBODY'S BABY • 1919 • *Strand* • SHT • USA
NOBODY'S BABY • 1937 • Meins Gus • SHT • USA
NOBODY'S BOY • 1913 • *Kroell Adrienne* • USA
NOBODY'S BOY see **CHIBIKKO REMI TO MEIKEN KAPI** • 1970
NOBODY'S BRIDE • 1923 • Blache Herbert • USA
NOBODY'S BUSINESS • 1926 • Taurog Norman • SHT • USA
NOBODY'S CHILD • 1913 • Heath Harold • UKN
NOBODY'S CHILD • 1915 • Batley Ethyle • UKN
NOBODY'S CHILD • 1919 • Hall George Edwardes • UKN
NOBODY'S CHILD • 1986 • Grant Lee • TVM • USA
NOBODY'S CHILDREN • 1940 • Barton Charles T. • USA
NOBODY'S CHILDREN • 1990 • Clarke Malcolm • USA
NOBODY'S DARLING • 1943 • Mann Anthony • USA
NOBODY'S DAUGHTER see **SYNDENS DATTER** • 1915
NOBODY'S FOOL • 1921 • Baggot King • USA
NOBODY'S FOOL • 1936 • Collins Arthur G. • USA
NOBODY'S FOOL • 1936 • Cummings Irving • USA
NOBODY'S FOOL • 1987 • Purcell Evelyn • USA
NOBODY'S GHOUL • 1962 • Tendlar Dave • ANS • USA
NOBODY'S GIRL • 1920 • Grandon Francis J. • USA
NOBODY'S HOME • 1915 • *Borzage Frank* • USA
NOBODY'S KID • 1921 • Hickman Howard • USA • LITTLE MISS SOMEBODY ○ MARY CARY
NOBODY'S LAND (USA) see **TERRA DI NESSUNO** • 1939
"NOBODY'S" LOVE STORY • 1913 • *Eclair* • USA
NOBODY'S MONEY • 1923 • Worsley Wallace • USA
NOBODY'S PERFECT • 1968 • Rafkin Alan • USA • WINNING POSITION, THE
NOBODY'S PERFECT • 1986 • MacDonald Ramuna • MTV • CND
NOBODY'S PERFECT • 1990 • Kaylor Robert • USA
NOBODY'S PERFEKT • 1981 • Bonerz Peter • USA
NOBODY'S SON see **SENK FILIA, A** • 1917
NOBODY'S THE GREATEST see **GENIO, DUE COMPARI, UN POLLO, UN** • 1976
NOBODY'S WIDOW • 1927 • Crisp Donald • USA
NOBODY'S WIFE • 1918 • Le Saint Edward J. • USA
NOBODY'S WIFE see **SENORA DE NADIE** • 1982
NOBODY'S WOMAN see **MUJER DE NADIE, LA** • 1937
NOBODY'S WOMEN see **FEMMES DE PERSONNE** • 1984
NOBORIRYU TEKKAHADA • 1969 • Ishii Teruo • JPN • FRIENDLY KILLER, THE (USA)
NOC • 1961 • Makarczynski Tadeusz • DOC • PLN • NIGHT
NOC • 1967 • Nasfeter Janusz • PLN • NIGHT
NOC LISTOPADOWA • 1933 • Warnecki J. • PLN
NOC LISTOPADOWA • 1979 • Wajda Andrzej • PLN • NOVEMBER NIGHT
NOC NA KARLSTEJNE • 1973 • Podskalsky Zdenek • CZC • NIGHT OF KARLSTEIN
NOC NEVESTY • 1967 • Kachyna Karel • CZC • NIGHT OF THE BRIDE, THE ○ NUN'S NIGHT, THE
NOC POSLIJE SMRTI • 1984 • Ivanda Branko • YGS • NIGHT AFTER DEATH
NOC POSLUBNA (PLN) see **BROLLOPSNATT, EN** • 1959
NOCAUT • 1983 • Garcia Agraz Jose Luis • MXC • KNOCKOUT
NOCCIOLINE • 1978 • Orfini Mario • ITL
NOCE AU LAC SAINT-FARGEAU, UNE • 1905 • Blache Alice • FRN
NOCE AU VILLAGE, UNE • 1901 • Melies Georges • FRN • FUN IN COURT (USA) ○ CONTEMPT OF COURT
NOCE BLANCHE • 1990 • Brisseau Jean-Claude • FRN • NOCES BLANCHES
NOCE CHEZ LES PETITS BOURGEOIS, LA • 1970 • Allio Rene • FRN
NOCE EN GALILEE • 1988 • Khleifi Michel • BLG • WEDDING IN GALILEE
NOCE EST PAS FINIE, LA • 1971 • Forest Leonard • CND
NOCE I DNIE • 1974 • Antczak Jerzy • PLN • NIGHT AND DAY ○ BOGUMIE I BARBARA ○ NIGHTS AND DAYS ○ WIATR W OCZY
NOCES BARBARES, LES • 1987 • Hansel Marion • BLG
NOCES BLANCHES see **NOCE BLANCHE** • 1990
NOCES D'ARGENT, LES • 1915 • Feuillade Louis • FRN
NOCES DE PAPIER, LES • 1990 • Brault Michel • CND • PAPER WEDDING, A
NOCES DE PLUMES • 1968 • Ledoux Patrick • SHT • BLG • MARRIAGE OF THE PENS
NOCES DE PORCELAINE, LES • 1975 • Coggio Roger • FRN
NOCES DE SABLE • 1948 • Zwobada Andre • FRN, MRC • DAUGHTER OF THE SANDS ○ DESERT WEDDING
NOCES DE SANG (FRN) see **BODAS DE SANGRE** • 1981
NOCES DE SANG OU LE CREATION DE L'OBSTACLE • 1977 • Koleva Maria • DOC • FRN
NOCES DE ZAYN, LES see **URS ZAYN** • 1976
NOCES D'HIRONDELLE, LES • 1968 • Durand Philippe • FRN • MARRIAGE OF THE SWALLOW, THE
NOCES PAYSANNES • 1943 • Storck Henri • BLG
NOCES ROUGES, LES • 1972 • Chabrol Claude • FRN, ITL • AMICO DI FAMIGLIA, L' (ITL) ○ WEDDING IN BLOOD (USA) ○ BLOOD WEDDING (USA) ○ RED WEDDING
NOCES SANGLANTES, LES • 1916 • Feuillade Louis • FRN
NOCES SICILIENNES, LES • 1912 • Feuillade Louis • FRN
NOCES VENITIENNES, LES (FRN) see **PRIMA NOTTE, LA** • 1959
NOCH MINDERJAHRIG • 1957 • Tressler Georg • AUS • UNTER ACHTZEHN ○ UNDER 18
NOCH V SENTYABRE • 1939 • Barnet Boris • USS • NIGHT IN SEPTEMBER, A ○ ONE SEPTEMBER NIGHT
NOCHE AVANZA, LA • 1951 • Gavaldon Roberto • MXC
NOCHE BAJO LA TORMENTA, UNA • 1966 • Elias Moreno Jose • MXC
NOCHE DE CURAS • 1978 • Morales Carlos • SPN • PRIESTS' NIGHT
NOCHE DE ESTRENO • 1950 • Obregon Antonio • SPN
NOCHE DE GARUFA, UNA • 1915 • Ferreyra Jose • ARG
NOCHE DE LA FURIA, LA • 1974 • Aured Carlos • SPN
NOCHE DE LA MUERTA CIEGA, LA see **NOCHE DEL TERROR CIEGO, LA** • 1972
NOCHE DE LAS GAVIOTAS, LA • 1975 • de Ossorio Amando • SPN • NIGHT OF THE SEAGULLS (USA) ○ NIGHT OF THE DEATH CULT ○ BLOOD FEAST OF THE BLIND DEAD
NOCHE DE LOS ASESINOS, LA • 1974 • Franco Jesus • SPN
NOCHE DE LOS BRUJOS, LA • 1973 • de Ossorio Amando • SPN • NIGHT OF THE SORCERESS
NOCHE DE LOS CIEN PAJAROS, LA • 1976 • Romero-Marchent Rafael • SPN
NOCHE DE LOS DIABLOS, LA see **NOTTE DEI DIAVOLI, LA** • 1972
NOCHE DE LOS MAYAS, LA • 1939 • Urueta Chano • MXC • NIGHT OF THE MAYAS (USA)
NOCHE DE LOS MIL GATOS, LA • 1972 • Cardona Rene • MXC • NIGHT OF A THOUSAND CATS, THE (USA)
NOCHE DE LOS MONSTRUOS, LA • 1973 • *America* • MXC
NOCHE DE PERDICION • 1951 • Diaz Morales Jose • MXC
NOCHE DE RECIEN CASADOS • 1941 • Orellana Carlos • MXC
NOCHE DE REYES • 1947 • Lucia Luis • SPN
NOCHE DE RONDA • 1942 • Cortazar Ernesto • MXC
NOCHE DE TERROR see **CASTILLO DE LOS MONSTRUOS, EL** • 1957
NOCHE DE TORMENTA • 1952 • de Mayora Jaime • SPN • ANNETTE
NOCHE DE UNA MUERTO QUE VIVIO, LA see **CASA DE LAS MUERTAS VIVIENTES, LA** • 1972
NOCHE DE VERANO • 1962 • Grau Jorge • SPN
NOCHE DE VINO TINTO • 1968 • Nunes Jose Maria • SPN • NIGHT OF THE RED WINE
NOCHE DE WALPURGIS, LA (SPN) see **NACHT DER VAMPIRE** • 1970
NOCHE DEL DR. VALDES, LA • 1964 • Bartolome Cecilia • SHT • SPN
NOCHE DEL EMBUSTERO, LA • 1972 • Posani Clara • VNZ • LIAR'S NIGHT, THE
NOCHE DEL HALCON, LA • 1968 • Gonzalez Rogelio A. • MXC • NIGHT OF THE FALCON, THE
NOCHE DEL JUEVES, LA • 1960 • Gomez Urquiza Zacarias • MXC
NOCHE DEL MARTES, LA • 1944 • Santillan Antonio • SPN
NOCHE DEL PECADO, LA • 1933 • Contreras Torres Miguel • MXC
NOCHE DEL SABADO, LA • 1950 • Gil Rafael • SPN
NOCHE DEL TERROR CIEGO, LA • 1972 • de Ossorio Amando • SPN, PRT • TOMBS OF THE BLIND DEAD (UKN) ○ NIGHT OF THE BLIND DEAD ○ BLIND DEAD, THE ○ NOCHE DE LA MUERTA CIEGA, LA ○ CRYPT OF THE BLIND DEATH ○ NOITE DO TERROR CEGA, A ○ PRT ○ NIGHT OF THE BLIND TERROR, THE
NOCHE EMBARAZOSA, UNA • 1976 • Cardona Rene?, Cardona Rene Jr.? • MXC • ONCE A NIGHT
NOCHE EN EL ESPEJO, LA • 1962 • Ayala Fernando • ARG • NIGHT IN THE MIRROR, THE
NOCHE EN LA TABARIN, UNA • 1949 • Amadori Luis Cesar • ARG
NOCHE ES NUESTRA, LA • 1951 • Rivero Fernando A. • MXC
NOCHE FANTASTICA • 1943 • Marquina Luis • SPN
NOCHE MAS HERMOSA, LA • 1984 • Gutierrez Aragon Manuel • SPN • MOST BEAUTIFUL NIGHT, THE
NOCHE ORIENTAL, LA • 1986 • Curiel Miguel • VNZ • ORIENTAL NIGHT, THE
NOCHE OSCURA, LA • 1989 • Saura Carlos • SPN • DARK NIGHT, THE
NOCHE TERRIBLE • 1967 • Kuhn Rodolfo • ARG • TERRIBLE NIGHT, THE
NOCHE Y EL ALBA, LA • 1958 • Forque Jose Maria • SPN • NIGHT AND THE DAWN, THE
NOCHE Y TU, LA • 1946 • Urueta Chano • MXC
NOCHES ANDALUZAS (SPN) see **NUITS ANDALOUSES** • 1953
NOCHES DE BUENOS AIRES • 1935 • Barth-Moglia Luis • ARG
NOCHES DE GLORIA • 1937 • Aguilar Rolando • MXC • GLORIOUS NIGHTS
NOCHES DE PALOMA, LAS • 1977 • Isaac Alberto • MXC • PALOMA'S NIGHTS
NOCHES DEL CALIFAS, LAS • 1986 • Garcia Agraz Jose Luis • MXC
NOCHES DEL ESCORPION • 1974 • Balcazar Alfonso • SPN
NOCHES DEL HOMBRE LOBO, LAS • 1968 • Govar Rene • SPN, FRN • NIGHTS OF THE WEREWOLF, THE
NOCHES DEL UNIVERSO • 1963 • Iglesias Miguel, Lorente German • SPN
NOCHES PROHIBIDAS • 1966 • Diaz Morales Jose • MXC, PRC
NOCHES SIN CIELO • 1947 • Iquino Ignacio F. • SPN
NOCHES SIN LUNAS NI SOLES • 1984 • Suarez Jose Martinez • ARG • MOONLESS SUNLESS NIGHTS
NOCHI BYEZ NOCHLYEGA • 1967 • Araminas Algirdas, Karka G. • USS • NIGHTS WITHOUT SHELTER ○ NIGHTS WITHOUT LODGING, THE
NOCHI CHORNI V SOCHI • 1989 • Pichul Vasily • USS
NOCHNOI GOST • 1957 • Shredel Vladimir • USS • GUEST FROM THE DARK, A ○ GUEST IN THE NIGHT
NOCHNOY IZVOZCHIK • 1929 • Tasin Georgi • USS • NIGHT CABBIE
NOCNI DES • 1914 • Palous Jan A. • CZC • NOCTURNAL HORROR (USA) ○ NIGHT HORROR
NOCNI HOST • 1961 • Vavra Otakar • CZC • GUEST IN THE NIGHT, A ○ NIGHT GUEST
NOCNI JEZDCI • 1981 • Holly Martin • CZC • NIGHT RIDERS
NOCNI MOTYL • 1941 • Cap Frantisek • CZC • NIGHT MOTH, THE
NOCNI ZKOUSKA • 1980 • Schorm Evald • CZC • NIGHT REHEARSAL, THE
NOCTURNA • 1979 • Hurwitz Harry • USA • GRANDDAUGHTER OF DRACULA
NOCTURNAL HORROR (USA) see **NOCNI DES** • 1914
NOCTURNAL LOVE YOU'RE LEAVING see **NOCTURNO AMOR QUE TE VAS** • 1986
NOCTURNAL MUSIC see **MUSICA NOCTURNA** • 1989
NOCTURNAL ROMANCE, A • 1949 • Tyrlova Hermina • ANM • CZC
NOCTURNAL SORCERY see **SORCELLERIE NOCTURNE, LA** • 1903
NOCTURNAL SUN • 1989 • Garcia Raul • SHT • BUL
NOCTURNE • 1946 • Marin Edwin L. • USA
NOCTURNE • 1954 • Alexeieff Alexandre, Violet George • ANS • FRN
NOCTURNE, LA • 1919 • Feuillade Louis • FRN
NOCTURNE INDIEN • 1988 • Corneau Alain • FRN
NOCTURNE OF A WOMAN see **ONNA WA YORU KESHOSURU** • 1961
NOCTURNE OF LOVE see **NOCTURNO AMOR QUE TE VAS** • 1986
NOCTURNE (USA) see **NOCTURNO** • 1958
NOCTURNES • 1988 • Aubry Francois • ANS • CND
NOCTURNO • 1915 • Bolten-Baeckers Heinrich • FRG
NOCTURNO • 1935 • Machaty Gustav • AUS • ...UND ALLE DURSTEN NACH LIEBE
NOCTURNO • 1958 • Kostelac Nikola • ANS • YGS • NOCTURNE (USA)
NOCTURNO 29 • 1968 • Portabella Pedro • SPN
NOCTURNO AMOR QUE TE VAS • 1986 • Fernandez Violante Marcela • MXC • NOCTURNAL LOVE YOU'RE LEAVING ○ NOCTURNE OF LOVE
NOCTURNO DE AMOR • 1947 • Gomez Muriel Emilio • MXC
NOCTURNO DER LIEBE • 1918 • Boese Carl • FRG
NOD-O-NODI • 1954 • *Sircar B. N. (P)* • IND
NODDEBO PRAESTEGARD • 1934 • Schneevoigt George • DNM
NODDY IN TOYLAND • 1958 • Rogers Maclean • UKN
NODES • 1981 • Brakhage Stan • USA
NODLANDING • 1952 • Skouen Arne • NRW • BAD LUCK ○ FORCED LANDING
NOE BARKAI • 1983 • Kollanyi Agoston • HNG • NOAH'S ARKS
NOE HELT ANNET • 1985 • Kolstad Morten • NRW • SOMETHING ELSE –ENTIRELY
NOEL 1721 • 1964 • Tropa Alfredo • SHT • PRT
NOEL A L'ILE AUX GRUES • 1964 • Lavoie Richard • SHT • CND
NOEL AU SOLEIL see **VOLEUR DU TIBIDABO, LE** • 1965
NOEL DANS LES TRANCHEES • 1914 • Protazanov Yakov • USS
NOEL D'ARTISTES • 1908 • Perret Leonce • FRN
NOEL DE BEBE, LE • 1911 • Feuillade Louis • FRN
NOEL DE BOUT DE ZAN, LE • 1914 • Feuillade Louis • FRN
NOEL DE FRANCESCA, LE • 1912 • Feuillade Louis • FRN
NOEL DE MADAME BEAUCHAMP, LE • 1980 • Levy Raphael • CND
NOEL DE TOTO, LE • 1916-24 • Lortac • ANS • FRN
NOEL DU POILU, LE • 1916 • Feuillade Louis • FRN
NOEL ET JULIETTE • 1973 • Bouchard Michel • CND
NOEL SANGLANT see **MATOMENA CHRISTOUYENNA** • 1951
NOEMI, DIE BLONDE JUDIN • 1917 • Moest Hubert • FRG
NOGE • 1967 • Zaninovic Ante • ANS • YGS • FEET
NOGENT, ELDORADO DU DIMANCHE • 1929 • Carne Marcel, Sanvoisin Michel • FRN
NOGET OM NORDEM • 1964 • Dreyer Carl T. • SHT • DNM
NOGI SHOGUN TO KUMA-SAN see **NOGI TAISHO TO KUMA-SAN** • 1926
NOGI TAISHO TO KUMA-SAN • 1926 • Mizoguchi Kenji • JPN • GENERAL NOGI AND KUMA-SAN (USA) ○ NOGI SHOGUN TO KUMA-SAN
NOGIKU NO GOTOKI KIMI NARIKI • 1955 • Kinoshita Keisuke • JPN • SHE WAS LIKE A WILD CHRYSANTHEMUM ○ YOU ARE LIKE A DAISY ○ YOU WERE LIKE A WILD CHRYSANTHEMUM
NOGIKU NO HAKA • 1982 • Sawai Shinichiro • JPN • GRAVEYARD OF CHRYSANTHEMUMS
NOGITSUNE SANJI • 1930 • *Tsuburaya Eiji (Ph)* • JPN
NOGLEHULLET • 1974 • Gerber Paul • DNM • KEYHOLE, THE
NOGLEN TIL PARADIS • 1970 • Methling Sven • DNM • KEY TO PARADISE
NOGOMOPHO • 1974 • SAF
NOGUCHI HIDEYO NO SHONEN JIDAI • 1956 • Sekigawa Hideo • JPN • BOYHOOD OF DR. NOGUCHI, THE
NOHOTEI MONOGATARI • 1955 • Fukuda Seiichi • JPN • PRIVATE'S STORY, THE
NOI CANNIBALI • 1954 • Leonviola Antonio • ITL
NOI DELL'OCEANO see **OCEANO CI CHIAMO, L'** • 1958
NOI DOLGOK • 1963 • Nagy Pal • ANS • HNG • ECCENTRICITIES OF WOMEN
NOI DONNE SIAMO FATTE COSI • 1971 • Risi Dino • ITL • WOMEN: SO WE ARE MADE
NOI DUE SENZA DOMANI (ITL) see **TRAIN, LE** • 1973
NOI DUE SOLI • 1953 • Metz Vittorio, Marchesi Marcello, Girolami Marino • ITL
NOI DURI • 1960 • Mastrocinque Camillo • ITL
NOI GANGSTERS (ITL) see **GRAND CHEF, LE** • 1959
NOI INSISTIAMO • 1965 • Amico Gianni • SHT • ITL • WE INSIST
NOI NON SIAMO ANGELI • 1975 • Parolini Gianfranco • ITL
NOI PECCATORI • 1953 • Brignone Guido • ITL
NOI SIAM COME LE LUCCIOLE • 1976 • Berruti Giulio • ITL
NOI SIAMO DUE EVASI • 1959 • Simonelli Giorgio C. • ITL
NOI SIAMO LE COLONNE • 1956 • D'Amico Luigi Filippo • ITL
NOI UOMINI DURI • 1987 • Ponzi Maurizio • ITL • WE THE TOUGH GUYS
NOI VIVI • 1942 • Alessandrini Goffredo • ITL • WE THE LIVING (UKN)

NOIA, LA • 1964 • Damiani Damiano • ITL, FRN • ENNUI ET SA DIVERSION, L'EROTISME, L' (FRN) ○ EMPTY CANVAS, THE (USA)
NOIEMBRIE, ULTIMUL BAL • 1989 • Pita Dan • RMN • LAST BALL IN NOVEMBER, THE
NOIN SEITSEMAN VELJESTA • 1968 • Virtanen Jukka • FNL • ABOUT SEVEN BROTHERS
NOIR ET BLANC • 1961 • Lapoujade Robert • ANS • FRN • BLACK AND WHITE
NOIR ET BLANC • 1987 • Devers Claire • FRN
NOIR PRINTEMPS DES JOURS, LE • 1978 • Poljinsky Serge • FRN
NOIR SUR BLANC see **AMOUREUX SONT SEULS AU MONDE, LES** • 1947
NOIRE DE.., LA • 1967 • Sembene Ousmane • SNL, FRN • BLACK ONE FROM.., THE ○ BLACK GIRL
NOIRS ET BLANCS EN COULEURS • 1976 • Annaud Jean-Jacques • FRN, IVC, SWT • BLACK AND WHITE IN COLOR (USA) ○ VICTOIRE EN CHANTANT, LA ○ BLACK VICTORY
NOIRS JOUENT ET GAGNENT, LES • 1944 • Image Jean • ANS • FRN
NOISE • Stecker Alan • SHT • USA
NOISE • 1965 • Wdowkowna-Oldak Zofia • ANM • PLN
NOISE see **STOY** • 1973
NOISE ANNOYS KO-KO • 1929 • Fleischer Dave • ANS • USA
NOISE FROM THE DEEP, A • 1913 • Sennett Mack • USA
NOISE IN NEWBORO, A • 1923 • Beaumont Harry • USA
NOISE LIKE A FORTUNE, A • 1912 • *Benham Harry* • USA
NOISE OF BOMBS, THE • 1914 • Parrott Charles • USA
NOISY BULLS see **GRAJSKI BIKI** • 1967
NOISY CABARET, THE see **RABAUKENKABARETT, DAS**
NOISY MARTHA • 1986 • *Frankenberg Pia* • FRG
NOISY NAGGERS AND NOSEY NEIGHBORS • 1917 • Semon Larry • SHT • USA
NOISY NEIGHBORS • 1929 • Reisner Charles F. • USA
NOISY NEIGHBORS • 1946 • Yates Hal • SHT • USA
NOISY NOISES • 1929 • McGowan Robert • SHT • USA
NOISY SIX, THE • 1913 • Campbell Colin • USA
NOISY SUITORS, THE • 1913 • Henderson Dell • USA
NOITA PALAA ELAMAAN • 1952 • Hallstrom Roland • FNL • WITCH, THE (USA) ○ WITCH RETURNS TO LIFE, THE
NOITE DO ESPANTALHO, A • 1974 • Ricardo Sergio • BRZ • NIGHT OF THE SCARECROW, THE
NOITE DO TERROR CEGA, A see **NOCHE DEL TERROR CIEGO, LA** • 1972
NOITE E A MADRUGADA, A • 1983 • Ramos Artur • PRT
NOITE VAZIA • 1965 • Khouri Walter Hugo • BRZ • MEN AND WOMEN (UKN) ○ EROS (USA) ○ EROS.. THE BIZARRE ○ NIGHT GAMES
NOITES DO SERTAO • 1984 • Correa Carlos Alberto Prates • BRZ • NIGHTS OF THE HINTERLAND
NOIVA DA CIDADE, A • 1980 • Viany Alex • BRZ • CITY BRIDE, THE
NOIVO DAS CALDAS, O • 1956 • Duarte Arthur • PRT
NOIX DE COCO • 1938 • Boyer Jean • FRN
NOJO AOS CAES • 1970 • de Macedo Antonio • PRT
NOKAUT • 1971 • Draskovic Boro • YGS • KNOCKOUT
NOKF • 1978 • SAF
NOLAN'S WOOING • 1915 • Thayer Otis B. • USA
NOMAD see **LIEH-HUO CH'ING-CH'UN** • 1983
NOMAD RIDERS • 1981 • Roach Frank • USA
NOMADE DE L'OUEST • 1962 • Poirier Anne-Claire • CND
NOMADES • 1959 • Carrier Louis-Georges • SHT • CND
NOMADES, LES see **RUHHAL, AL-** • 1975
NOMADS • 1986 • McTiernan John • USA
NOMADS OF THE DEEP • 1979 • Stoneman John • CND
NOMADS OF THE JUNGLE: MALAYA • 1948 • *De Rochemont Louis (P)* • SHT • USA
NOMADS OF THE NORTH • 1920 • Hartford David M. • USA
NOME E COGNOME: LACOMBE LUCIEN (ITL) see **LACOMBE LUCIEN** • 1973
NOMININGUE DEPUIS QU'IL EXISTE • 1967 • Leduc Jacques • DOC • CND
NOMISUKE KINSHU UNDO • 1928 • Uchida Tomu • JPN
NOMME LA ROCCA, UN • 1962 • Becker Jean • FRN, ITL • MAN NAMED ROCCA, A (USA)
NOMMER ASSEBLIEF • 1981 • Marx Franz • SAF • NUMBER PLEASE
NOMOS TIS ZOIS, O • 1967 • Paraskhakis Pavlos • GRC • LAW OF LIFE, THE
NON ASPETTARE DJANGO, SPARA • 1967 • Mulben Edward • ITL
NON CANTARE, BACIAMI • 1957 • Simonelli Giorgio C. • ITL
NON CANTO PIU • 1943 • Freda Riccardo • ITL
NON C'E BISOGNO DI DENARO • 1933 • Palermi Amleto • ITL • MA NON C'E BISOGNO DI DENARO
NON C'E FUMO SENZA FUOCO (ITL) see **IL N'Y A PAS DE FUMEE SANS FEU** • 1972
NON C'E PACE TRA GLI ULIVI • 1950 • De Santis Giuseppe • ITL • NO PEACE AMONG THE OLIVES ○ BLOOD ON EASTER SUNDAY ○ UNDER THE OLIVE TREE
NON CI CREDO! see **SUPERSTIZIONE** • 1949
NON CI RESTA CHE PIANGERE • 1984 • Benigni Roberto, Troisi Massimo • ITL
NON COMMETTERE ATTI IMPURI • 1971 • Petroni Giulio • ITL
NON-COMMISSIONED OFFICER, THE • 1912 • *Edison* • USA
NON-CONFORMIST PARSON, A • 1919 • Bramble A. V. • UKN • HEART AND SOUL
NON CONTATE SU DI NOI • 1978 • Nuti Sergio • ITL
NON COUPABLE • 1947 • Decoin Henri • FRN • NOT GUILTY (USA)
NON CREDO PIU ALL'AMORE see **PAURA, LA** • 1954
NON DRAMMATIZZIAMO: E SOLO QUESTIONE DI CORNA (ITL) see **DOMICILE CONJUGALE** • 1970
NON E MAI TROPPO TADRI • 1953 • Ratti Filippo M. • ITL
NON E VERO.. MA CI CREDO • 1952 • Grieco Sergio • ITL
NON ESSER GELOSA see **NON SON GELOSA** • 1933
NON-EXISTENT KNIGHT, THE see **CAVALIERE INESISTENTE, IL** • 1970
NON-EXISTENT STORY, A see **ZGODBA KI JE NI** • 1967
NON FACCIO LA GUERRA, FACCIO L'AMORE • 1966 • Rossi Franco • ITL • MAKE LOVE, NOT WAR (USA) ○ DON'T MAKE WAR, MAKE LOVE
NON HO PAURA DI VIVERE • 1952 • Taglioni Fabrizio • ITL
NON HO TEMPO • 1973 • Giannarelli Ansano • ITL • NO MORE TIME ○ SO LITTLE TIME
NON LIEU • 1968 • Stameschkine Michel • SHT • BLG
NON-MATRIMONIAL STORY • 1975 • PLN
NON ME LO DIREI • 1940 • Mattoli Mario • ITL
NON MI DIRE MAI GOOD-BYE • 1967 • Baldanello Gianfranco • ITL
NON MI MUOVO! • 1943 • Simonelli Giorgio C. • ITL
NON MI SPOSO PIU • 1942 • Engel Erich, Amato Giuseppe • ITL, FRG • VIEL LARM UM NIXI (FRG) ○ NIXI
NON PERDIAMO LA TESTA • 1959 • Mattoli Mario • ITL • LET'S NOT LOSE OUR HEADS
NON-PROFESSIONALS, THE • 1986 • Bodrov Sergei • USS
NON SCHERZARE CON LE DONNE • 1957 • Bennati Giuseppe • ITL • GALLI DEL MARE, I
NON SI SEVIZIA UN PAPERINO • 1972 • Fulci Lucio • ITL • DON'T TORTURE THE DUCKLING (USA)
NON SIAMO SPOSATI • 1951 • Pons Gianni • ITL
NON-SKID KID, THE • 1922 • Roach Hal • SHT • USA
NON-SKID LOVE • 1920 • Lyons Eddie, Moran Lee • SHT • USA
NON SON DEGNO DI TE • 1965 • Fizzarotti Ettore Maria • ITL
NON SON GELOSA • 1933 • Bragaglia Carlo Ludovico • ITL • NON ESSER GELOSA
NON SONO PIU GUAGLIONE • 1958 • Paolella Domenico • ITL, FRN
NON SONO SUPERSTIZIOSO.. MA! • 1944 • Bragaglia Carlo Ludovico • ITL
NON SONO UN'ASSASSINO (ITL) see **PIEGE POUR CENDRILLON** • 1965
NON SPARATE SUI BAMBINI • 1978 • Crea Gianni • ITL
NON STA BENE RUBARE IL TESORO • 1967 • Di Nardo Mario • ITL
NON-STOP FLIGHT, THE • 1926 • Johnson Emory • USA
NON STOP KID, THE • 1918 • Roach Hal • SHT • USA • NON-STOP KID, THE
NON-STOP KID, THE see **NON STOP KID, THE** • 1918
NON-STOP NEW YORK • 1937 • Stevenson Robert • UKN
NON STUZZICATE LA ZANZARA • 1967 • Wertmuller Lina • ITL • DON'T STING THE MOSQUITO (USA) ○ DON'T TEASE THE MOSQUITO
NON-SUITED • 1914 • Collins Edwin J.? • UKN
NON TI CONOSCO PIU • 1936 • Malasomma Nunzio • ITL
NON TI PAGO! • 1942 • Bragaglia Carlo Ludovico • ITL
NON TI SCORDAR DI ME • 1935 • Genina Augusto • ITL
NON TI SCORDAR DI ME • 1967 • Battaglia Enzo • ITL
NON TIRATE IL DIAVOLO PER LA CODA (ITL) see **DIABLE PAR LA QUEUE, LE** • 1969
NON TOCCARE LA DONNA BIANCA • 1975 • Ferreri Marco • ITL, FRN • VERA STORIA DEL GENERALE CUSTER, LA ○ TOUCHE PAS LA FEMME BLANC
NON-TRADITIONAL • 1983 • Armstrong Mary • DOC • CND
NON, TU EXAGERES • Bowers Charley • SHT • FRN • NO, YOU EXAGGERATE
NON UCCIDERE (ITL) see **TU NE TUERAS POINT** • 1961
NON VOGLIAMO MORIRE • 1954 • Palella Oreste • ITL
NONA, LA • 1979 • Olivera Hector • ARG • GRANDMA
NONE ARE BORN SOLDIERS see **SOLDATAMI NYE ROZHDAYUTSYA** • 1968
NONE BUT THE BRAVE • 1914 • Weston Charles • UKN
NONE BUT THE BRAVE • 1915 • Kellino W. P. • UKN
NONE BUT THE BRAVE • 1928 • Ray Albert • USA
NONE BUT THE BRAVE • 1963 • Richardson Ken • USA
NONE BUT THE BRAVE • 1965 • Sinatra Frank • USA, JPN • YUSHA NOMI (JPN)
NONE BUT THE BRAVE see **FOR THE LOVE OF MIKE** • 1960
NONE BUT THE BRAVE see **KUNG FU GIRL, THE** • 1975
NONE BUT THE BRAVE DESERVE THE ..? • 1913 • *Moore Matt* • USA
NONE BUT THE BRAVE DESERVE THE FAIR • 1912 • Humphrey William • USA
NONE BUT THE LONELY HEART • 1944 • Odets Clifford • USA
NONE BUT THE LONELY SPY (USA) see **F.B.I. CHIAMA ISTANBUL** • 1964
NONE CAN DO MORE • 1912 • *Rex* • USA
NONE SHALL ESCAPE • 1944 • De Toth Andre • USA
NONE SO BLIND • 1915 • Frank Alexander F. • USA
NONE SO BLIND • 1916 • Mayo Melvin • SHT • USA
NONE SO BLIND • 1923 • King Burton L. • USA • SHYLOCK OF WALL STREET
NONE WITHOUT SIN see **OUDIS ANAMARTITOS** • 1967
NONENTITY, THE • 1922 • Hill Sinclair • UKN
NONGNU • 1964 • Li Tsun • CHN • SERFS
NONKI EKICHO • *Toei* • ANS • JPN • HAPPY-GO-LUCKY STATION-MASTER, A
NONKI YOKOCHO • 1939 • Yamamoto Kajiro • JPN • EASY ALLEY
NONNA FELICITA • 1938 • Mattoli Mario • ITL
NONNA SABELLA, LA • 1957 • Risi Dino • ITL • OH! SABELLA (UKN) ○ GRANDMOTHER SABELLA
NONNE KYSSET • 1968 • Stenbaek Kirsten • DNM • NUN'S KISS, THE
NONNE UND DER HARLEKIN, DIE • 1918 • Halm Alfred • FRG
NONNE UND TANZERIN • 1919 • Eichberg Richard • FRG
NONO NENESSE • 1976 • Rozier Jacques, Thomas Pascal • FRN
NONSENSE • 1920 • White Jack • SHT • USA
NONSENSE NEWSREEL • 1954 • Davis Mannie • ANS • USA
NONSTOP TROUBLE WITH THE SPIES • 1987 • Runze Ottokar • FRG
NOODLE SELLER, A see **RAMENTAISHI** • 1967
NOODLES' RETURN • 1914 • *Sterling* • USA
NOODNIK OF THE NORTH • 1924 • *Turpin Ben* • USA
NOOI VAN MY HART • 1959 • SAF
NOON see **PODNE** • 1968
NOON FERRY, THE see **POLUDENNY PAROM** • 1967
NOON HOUR, THE • 1915 • *West Billie* • USA
NOON IN TUNISIA • 1970 • Lilienthal Peter, Berendt J. E. • DOC • FRG
NOON SUNDAY • 1970 • Bourke Terry • USA, GUM
NOON TO MIDNIGHT see **MIDI-MINUIT** • 1970
NOON (USA) see **POLDIEN** • 1931
NOON WHISTLE, THE • 1923 • Roach Hal • SHT • USA
NOON WINE • 1966 • Peckinpah Sam • TVM • USA
NOON WINE • 1985 • Fields Michael • TVM • USA
NOOR-E-ARAB see **TILASMI TALWAR** • 1935
NOOR-E-YAMAN • 1935 • Wadia J. B. H. • IND
NOOR JEHAN • 1968 • Sadiq M. • IND
NOORD 20-29, DE • 1972 • Bromet Frans • SHT • NTH
NOORI • 1980 • Dutta Subhash • BNG
NOORI • 1988 • Hussain Iltaf • PKS
NOOSE see **I'D GIVE MY LIFE** • 1936
NOOSE, THE • 1928 • Dillon John Francis • USA • GOVERNOR'S WIFE, THE
NOOSE, THE • 1948 • Greville Edmond T. • UKN • SILK NOOSE, THE (USA)
NOOSE, THE • 1988 • Coutsomitis Costas • GRC
NOOSE, THE (USA) see **PETLA** • 1957
NOOSE FOR A GUNMAN • 1960 • Cahn Edward L. • USA
NOOSE FOR A LADY • 1953 • Rilla Wolf • UKN
NOOSE HANGS HIGH, THE • 1948 • Barton Charles T. • USA
NOPEMBER 1828 • 1978 • Karya Teguh • INN • NOVEMBER 1828
NOR THE MOON BY NIGHT • 1958 • Annakin Ken • UKN, SAF • ELEPHANT GUN (USA)
NOR' WEST see **NOROIT** • 1977
NORA • 1923 • Viertel Berthold • FRG
NORA • 1944 • Braun Harald • FRG • DOLL'S HOUSE, A
NORA • 1967 • Zulficar Mahmoud • EGY
NORA DECLARES WAR • 1917 • *Vim* • USA
NORA HELMER • 1974 • Fassbinder R. W. • MTV • FRG • NORA (USA)
NORA IN WONDERLAND • 1970 • Marquez Artemio • PHL
NORA INU • 1949 • Kurosawa Akira • JPN • STRAY DOG
NORA NEKO • 1958 • Kimura Keigo • JPN • STRAY CAT
NORA PRENTISS • 1947 • Sherman Vincent • USA
NORA, THE COOK • 1912 • *Hotely Mae* • USA
NORA (USA) see **NORA HELMER** • 1974
NORAH BLANEY NO.1 • 1929 • *British Sound Film Production* • SHT • UKN • MUSICAL MEDLEY NO.2
NORAH BLANEY NO.2 • 1929 • *British Sound Film Production* • SHT • UKN • MUSICAL MEDLEY NO.6
NORAH MAYER THE QUICK-CHANGE DANCER • 1898 • Williamson James • UKN
NORAH O'NEALE (USA) see **IRISH HEARTS** • 1934
NORAH'S DEBT OF HONOUR • 1912 • Noy Wilfred • UKN
NORA'S BOARDERS • 1913 • *Edison* • USA
NORD 70° 22' • 1929 • Ginet Rene • DOC • FRN
NORD ATLANTIQUE • 1939 • Cloche Maurice • FRN
NORDIC LIVES -SWEDISH CINEMA IN THE EIGHTIES • Sundgren Nils Petter • DOC • SWD
NORDIQUES OU UN PEUPLE SANS ARTIFICE, LES • 1980 • Dansereau Mireille • CND
NORDISK KVADRILLE see **FYRA GANGER FYRA** • 1965
NORDLICHT • 1938 • Fredersdorf Herbert B. • FRG
NORDPOL -AHOI! • 1933 • Marton Andrew • FRG, USA • S.O.S. ICEBERG (UKN)
NORDSEE IST MORDSEE • 1975 • Bohm Hark • FRG • NORTH SEA IS DEAD SEA
NORIKO WA, IMA • 1982 • Matsuyama Zenzo • JPN • NOW, NOT HANDICAPPED NORIKO
NORIS • 1919 • Genina Augusto • ITL
NORLANDROSE • 1914 • Biebrach Rudolf • FRG
NORLISS TAPES, THE • 1973 • Curtis Dan • TVM • USA
NORMA • 1970 • Roter Ted • USA
NORMA FROM NORWAY • 1911 • *Wolff Jane* • USA
NORMA RAE • 1979 • Ritt Martin • USA
NORMA TALMADGE IN A LIBERTY BOND APPEAL • 1918 • *Select* • USA
NORMAL LOVE • 1963 • Smith Jack** • USA • GREAT PATSY TRIUMPH, THE
NORMAL YOUNG MAN, THE see **GIOVANE NORMALE, IL** • 1969
NORMAN ALLEY'S BOMBING OF THE U.S.S. PANAY • 1937 • *Ford Charles E. (P)* • SHT • USA
NORMAN CONQUEST (USA) see **PARK PLAZA 605** • 1953
NORMAN.. IS THAT YOU? • 1976 • Schlatter George • USA
NORMAN JEWISON: FILM MAKER • 1972 • Jackson Douglas • DOC • CND
NORMAN LOVES ROSE • 1982 • Safran Henri • ASL
NORMAN MACCAIG • 1975 • Alexander Mike • DOC • UKN
NORMAN MCLAREN'S OPENING SPEECH see **MESDAMES, MESSIEURS** • 1960
NORMAN NORMAL • 1968 • Lovy Alex • ANS • USA
NORMAN ROCKWELL'S BREAKING HOME TIES • 1987 • Wilder John* • TVM • USA
NORMAN SWORDSMAN (UKN) see **SPADA NORMANNA, LA** • 1971
NORMAN VINCENT PEALE STORY, THE see **ONE MAN'S WAY** • 1964
NORMANDE see **TETE DE NORMANDE ST-ONGE, LA** • 1975
NORMANDIE, LA • 1956 • Leherissey Jean • SHT • FRN
NORMANDIE-NEIMEN • 1959 • Dreville Jean • FRN, USS
NORMANDS, BARBARES ET BATISSEURS • 1980 • Christiani Jean-Noel • SHT • FRN
NORMANDY ROMANCE, A • 1914 • *Pickford Mary* • USA
NORMANNERNE • 1975 • Gernes Poul, Kirkeby Per • DNM
NORMANNI, I • 1962 • Vari Giuseppe • ITL, FRN • ATTACK OF THE NORMANS ○ CONQUEST OF THE NORMANS ○ BLADESTORM
NORME ET USAGE • 1972 • Lamothe Arthur • DCS • CND
NORMETAL • 1959 • Groulx Gilles • DCS • CND
NORMING OF JACK 243, THE • 1975 • Precht Robert • TVM • USA
NOROIT • 1977 • Rivette Jacques • FRN • NORTHWEST WIND (USA) ○ NOR' WEST
NOROSHI WA SHANGHAI NI AGARU • 1944 • Inagaki Hiroshi • JPN • SIGNAL FIRES IN SHANGHAI
NORRLANNINGAR • 1930 • Berthels Theodor • SWD • PEOPLE OF NORRLAND
NORRTULLSLIGAN • 1923 • Lindberg Per • SWD • NORTULL GANG, THE
NORSE ADVENTURE • 1970 • Parker Hjordis Kittel • DOC • USA
NORSEMAN, THE • 1979 • Pierce Charles B. • USA
NORSKE BYGGEKLOSSER • 1972 • Bang-Hansen Pal • NRW • NORWEGIAN BUILDING BLOCKS

NORTE, EL • 1983 • Nava Gregory • USA
NORTE Y SUR • 1934 • Delano Jorge • CHL
NORTENA DE MIS AMORES, LA • 1948 • Urueta Chano • MXC
NORTENO, EL • 1962 • Munoz Manuel • MXC
NORTH • 1969 • Reeve Josef • SHT • CND
NORTH AVENUE IRREGULARS, THE • 1979 • Bilson Bruce • USA • HILL'S ANGELS (UKN)
NORTH BEACH AND RAWHIDE • 1985 • Falk Harry • TVM • USA
NORTH BRIDGE see **PONT DU NORD, LE** • 1982
NORTH BY NORTHWEST • 1959 • Hitchcock Alfred • USA
NORTH CHINA COMMUNE • 1979 • Ianzelo Tony, Richardson Boyce • DOC • CND
NORTH CHINA FACTORY • 1980 • Ianzelo Tony, Richardson Boyce • DOC • CND
NORTH COUNTRY • 1973 • Hayes Ron • DOC • USA
NORTH DALLAS FORTY • 1979 • Kotcheff Ted • USA
NORTH EAST CORNER • 1946 • Eldridge John • DOC • UKN
NORTH FROM THE LONE STAR • 1941 • Hillyer Lambert • USA
NORTH KENSINGTON LAUNDRY BLUES • 1974 • Imray Robin • SHT • UKN
NORTH OF 36 • 1924 • Willat Irvin V. • USA
NORTH OF 49 DEGREES (USA) see **HIS DESTINY** • 1928
NORTH OF 50-50 • 1924 • Roach Hal • SHT • USA
NORTH OF 53 • 1912 • *Robinson Gertrude* • USA
NORTH OF 53 • 1914 • Hamilton G. P.? • USA
NORTH OF 57 • 1924 • *Sennett Mack (P)* • SHT • USA
NORTH OF 60° • 1956 • Howe John • DOC • CND
NORTH OF ALASKA • 1924 • Mattison Frank S. • USA
NORTH OF ARIZONA • 1935 • Webb Harry S. • USA
NORTH OF FIFTY-THREE • 1917 • Stanton Richard?, Taylor William D.? • USA
NORTH OF HUDSON BAY • 1923 • Ford John • USA • NORTH OF THE YUKON (UKN) ○ JOURNEY OF DEATH
NORTH OF NEVADA • 1924 • Rogell Albert S. • USA
NORTH OF NOME • 1925 • Johnston Raymond K. • USA
NORTH OF NOME • 1937 • Nigh William • USA
NORTH OF RIO GRANDE see **NORTH OF THE RIO GRANDE** • 1937
NORTH OF SHANGHAI • 1939 • Lederman D. Ross • USA
NORTH OF SUPERIOR • 1971 • Ferguson Graeme • DCS • CND
NORTH OF THE BORDER • 1946 • Eason B. Reeves • USA
NORTH OF THE GREAT DIVIDE • 1950 • Witney William • USA
NORTH OF THE RIO GRANDE • 1922 • Sturgeon Rollin S.?, Henabery Joseph? • USA
NORTH OF THE RIO GRANDE • 1937 • Watt Nate • USA • NORTH OF RIO GRANDE
NORTH OF THE ROCKIES • 1942 • Hillyer Lambert • USA • FALSE CLUES (UKN)
NORTH OF THE YUKON • 1939 • Nelson Sam • USA
NORTH OF THE YUKON (UKN) see **NORTH OF HUDSON BAY** • 1923
NORTH OR NORTH WEST see **N. OR N.W.** • 1938
NORTH PAL • 1953 • Sparber I. • ANS • USA
NORTH POLE CRAZE, THE • 1909 • *Phoenix* • USA
NORTH SEA • 1938 • Watt Harry • DOC • UKN
NORTH SEA HIJACK • 1980 • McLaglen Andrew V. • UKN • FFOLKES (USA) ○ ASSAULT FORCE ○ ESTHER, RUTH & JENNIFER
NORTH SEA IS DEAD SEA see **NORDSEE IST MORDSEE** • 1975
NORTH SEA PATROL (USA) see **LUCK OF THE NAVY** • 1938
NORTH SHORE • 1987 • Phelps William • USA
NORTH SHORE see **WOMAN IN RED, THE** • 1935
NORTH SOUTH see **POWAQQATSI** • 1988
NORTH SOUTH WEST EAST see **PEI NAN HSI TUNG** • 1984
NORTH STAR • 1925 • Powell Paul • USA
NORTH STAR • 1943 • Milestone Lewis • USA • ARMOURED ATTACK
NORTH TO ALASKA • 1960 • Hathaway Henry • USA
NORTH TO THE KLONDIKE • 1942 • Kenton Erle C. • USA
NORTH WEST FRONTIER • 1959 • Thompson J. Lee • UKN • FLAME OVER INDIA (USA)
NORTH WIND see **VIENTO NORTE** • 1939
NORTH WIND see **VIENTO NORTE** • 1977
NORTH WIND'S MALICE, THE • 1920 • Bern Paul, Harbaugh Carl • USA
NORTH WITH THE SPRING • 1970 • Fox Beryl • DOC • CND
NORTH WOODS • 1931 • Lantz Walter, Nolan William • ANS • USA
NORTHBOUND LIMITED • 1926 • *Palmer George (P)* • ASL
NORTHEAST OF SEOUL • 1972 • Rich David Lowell • USA • NORTHEAST TO SEOUL
NORTHEAST TO SEOUL see **NORTHEAST OF SEOUL** • 1972
NORTHERN BRIDGE, THE see **PONT DU NORD, LE** • 1982
NORTHERN CAMPUS • 1961 • Wilder Donald A. • CND
NORTHERN CODE • 1925 • De La Mothe Leon • USA
NORTHERN COMPOSITION • 1979 • MacKay Bruce • MTV • CND
NORTHERN FISHERMAN • 1963 • Defalco Martin • MTV • CND
NORTHERN FLIGHT see **SKY GIANT** • 1938
NORTHERN FRONTIER • 1935 • Newfield Sam • USA
NORTHERN HARBOUR • 1953 • Makovec Milos • CZC
NORTHERN HEARTS • 1912 • *Republic* • USA
NORTHERN HEARTS • 1913 • *Lockwood Harold* • USA
NORTHERN KNIGHT see **VIKING, THE** • 1931
NORTHERN LIGHTS • 1914 • Lewis Edgar • USA
NORTHERN LIGHTS • 1978 • Hanson John, Nilsson Rob • USA
NORTHERN LIGHTS • 1980 • Lavut Martin • CND
NORTHERN LIGHTS see **HAVLANDET** • 1985
NORTHERN MITES • 1960 • Kneitel Seymour • ANS • USA
NORTHERN MYSTERY, THE • 1924 • Croise Hugh • UKN
NORTHERN PATROL • 1953 • Bailey Rex • USA
NORTHERN PURSUIT • 1943 • Walsh Raoul • USA
NORTHERN RHAPSODY • 1974 • Abalov-Abalyan E. • USS
NORTHERN SPY, THE • 1913 • *Bison* • USA
NORTHERN STAR, THE (USA) see **ETOILE DU NORD, L'** • 1982
NORTHERN SUMMER • 1934 • Shaw Alexander • UKN
NORTHERNERS, THE see **POHJALAISIA** • 1925
NORTHING TRAMP, THE see **STRANGERS ON A HONEYMOON** • 1936
NORTHSTAR • 1985 • Levin Peter • TVM • USA
NORTHVILLE CEMETERY MASSACRE, THE • 1976 • Dear William • USA
NORTHWARDS • 1940 • Cornelius Henry • SHT • UKN
NORTHWEST CONFIDENTIAL • 1969 • *Maya* • SHT • UKN
NORTHWEST HOUNDED POLICE • 1946 • Avery Tex • ANS • USA
NORTHWEST MOUNTED POLICE • 1940 • De Mille Cecil B. • USA
NORTHWEST MOUSIE • 1953 • Kneitel Seymour • ANS • USA
NORTHWEST OUTPOST • 1947 • Dwan Allan • USA • END OF THE RAINBOW (UKN) ○ ONE EXCITING KISS
NORTHWEST PASSAGE • 1939 • Vidor King • USA
NORTHWEST RANGERS • 1942 • Newman Joseph M. • USA
NORTHWEST STAMPEDE • 1948 • Rogell Albert S. • USA
NORTHWEST TERRITORY • 1951 • McDonald Frank • USA
NORTHWEST TRAIL • 1945 • Abrahams Derwin • USA
NORTHWEST WIND (USA) see **NOROIT** • 1977
NORTHWOODS ROMANCE, A • 1913 • *White Glen* • USA
NORTULL GANG, THE see **NORRTULLSLIGAN** • 1923
NORVEGE • 1951 • Bonniere Rene • SHT • FRN
NORWAY REPLIES! • 1944 • Herrick F. Herrick
NORWEGIAN BUILDING BLOCKS see **NORSKE BYGGEKLOSSER** • 1972
NORWOOD • 1970 • Haley Jack Jr. • USA
NORWOOD BUILDER, THE • 1922 • Ridgwell George • UKN
NORWOOD CASE, THE • 1913 • *Crystal* • USA
NORWOOD NECKLACE, THE • 1911 • *Thanhouser* • USA
NOS ANCETRES LES EXPLORATEURS • 1954 • Kast Pierre • SHT • FRN
NOS AVIATEURS OUTRE-MER • 1954-55 • Devlin Bernard • DCS • CND
NOS BEAUX JOURS see **AYYAMINA AL-HILWA** • 1955
NOS BONS ETUDIANTS • 1903-04 • Blache Alice • FRN
NOS DERNIERS JOURS A MOSCOU • 1988 • Duckworth Martin • DOC • CND • OUR LAST DAYS IN MOSCOW
NOS DICEN LAS INTOCABLES • 1963 • Salvador Jaime • MXC
NOS LLEVA LA TRISTEZA • 1964 • Salvador Jaime • MXC
NOS MAITRES, LES DOMESTIQUES • 1931 • Grantham-Hayes H. C. • FRN
NOS MARINS A ANVERS • 1952 • Degelin Emile, de Boe Gerard • BLG
NOS POR CA TODOS BEM • 1977 • Lopes Fernando • PRT • WE ARE ALL GOOD HERE ○ EVERYTHING HERE IS FINE
NOS SOLDATS D'AFRIQUE • 1939 • Cauvin Andre • BLG
NOS TRAICIONARA EL PRESIDENTE? • 1988 • Galvan Fernando Perez • MXC • WILL THE PRESIDENT BETRAY US?
NOS VEREMOS EN EL CIELO • 1955 • Soler Julian • MXC
NOSE, THE • 1966 • Gerstein Mordi • ANS • USA
NOSE, THE see **NEZ, LE** • 1963
NOSE HAS IT, THE • 1942 • Guest Val • UKN
NOSE IN A BOOK, A • 1920 • Eason B. Reeves • SHT • USA
NOSE ON MY FACE, THE see **GIRL IN THE HEADLINES** • 1963
NOSE TO THE WIND see **NEZ AU VENT** • 1957
NOSED OUT • 1934 • Yates Hal • SHT • USA
NOSEY DOBSON • 1976 • Alexander Mike • UKN
NOSEY PARKER • 1906 • Collins Alf? • UKN
NOSEY PARKER • 1913 • Kellino W. P. • UKN
NOSFERAT OU LES EAUX GLACEES DU CALCUL EGOISTE, LE • 1975 • Rabinowicz Maurice • BLG
NOSFERATU see **NOSFERATU -EINE SYMPHONIE DES GRAUENS** • 1921
NOSFERATU, A SYMPHONY OF HORROR see **NOSFERATU - EINE SYMPHONIE DES GRAUENS** • 1921
NOSFERATU A VENEZIA • 1988 • Caminito Augusto • ITL • NOSFERATU IN VENICE ○ VAMPIRE IN VENICE
NOSFERATU -EINE SYMPHONIE DES GRAUENS • 1921 • Murnau F. W. • FRG • NOSFERATU, A SYMPHONY OF HORROR ○ NOSFERATU, THE VAMPIRE (USA) ○ TERROR OF DRACULA, THE ○ NOSFERATU ○ DRACULA ○ SYMPHONIE DES GRAUENS, EINE
NOSFERATU IN VENICE see **NOSFERATU A VENEZIA** • 1988
NOSFERATU -PHANTOM DER NACHT • 1979 • Herzog Werner • FRG, FRN, USA • NOSFERATU, THE VAMPYRE (USA)
NOSFERATU, THE VAMPIRE (USA) see **NOSFERATU -EINE SYMPHONIE DES GRAUENS** • 1921
NOSFERATU, THE VAMPYRE (USA) see **NOSFERATU - PHANTOM DER NACHT** • 1979
NOSHTA SRESHTU 13-I • 1961 • Marinovich Anton • BUL • ON THE EVE OF THE THIRTEENTH
NOSOTRAS LAS SIRVIENTAS • 1951 • Gomez Urquiza Zacarias • MXC
NOSOTRAS LAS TAQUIGRAFAS • 1950 • Gomez Muriel Emilio • MXC
NOSOTROS • 1944 • Rivero Fernando A. • MXC
NOSOTROS AGUERA • 1979 • de la Barra Leonardo • DCS • BLG • WE OUTSIDE
NOSOTROS CUBANOS • 1968 • Bertolino Daniel, Floquet Francois • DOC • CND
NOSOTROS DOS • 1954 • Fernandez Emilio • MXC, SPN • NOSTROS DOS
NOSOTROS LOS DECENTES • 1975 • Ozores Mariano • SPN
NOSOTROS LOS FEOS • 1972 • *Matela* • MXC
NOSOTROS LOS JOVENES • 1965 • Rodriguez Roberto • MXC
NOSOTROS LOS MONOS • 1972 • Valladares Edmund • ARG • WE APES
NOSOTROS LOS MUCHACHOS • 1940 • *Lolito Salvador* • ARG
NOSOTROS LOS POBRES • 1947 • Rodriguez Ismael • MXC • WE THE POOR
NOSOTROS LOS RATEROS • 1949 • Salvador Jaime • MXC
NOSOTROS QUE FUIMOS TAN FELICES • 1976 • Drove Antonio • SPN
NOSSIGNORE (APPUNTI SUL POTERE) • 1976 • Risi Nelo • MTV • ITL
NOSTALGHIA • 1982 • Tarkovsky Andrei • ITL, FRN • NOSTALGIA
NOSTALGIA see **NOSTALGHIA** • 1982
NOSTALGIE • 1937 • Tourjansky Victor • FRN • POSTMASTER'S DAUGHTER, THE
NOSTALGIE see **FRUHLINGSRAUSCHEN** • 1929
NOSTALGIE see **HANIN** • 1971
NOSTALGIE DE LA TERRE see **HANIN AL-ARD** • 1971
NOSTOS -IL RITORNO • 1990 • Piavoli Franco • ITL • NOSTOS -THE HOMECOMING
NOSTOS -THE HOMECOMING see **NOSTOS -IL RITORNO** • 1990
NOSTRA GUERRA, LA • 1943 • Lattuada Alberto • DOC • ITL
NOSTRA PATRIA, LA • 1925 • Ghione Emilio • ITL
NOSTRA PELLE, LA • 1962 • Andreassi Raffaele • ITL
NOSTRA PELLE, LA (ITL) see **CAP DE L'ESPERANCE, LE** • 1951
NOSTRA SIGNORA DEI TURCHI • 1968 • Bene Carmelo • ITL • OUR LADY OF THE TURKS
NOSTRADAMUS • 1936 • Bustillo Oro Juan • MXC
NOSTRADAMUS • 1938-53 • SHS • USA
NOSTRADAMUS AND THE DESTROYER OF MONSTERS see **NOSTRADAMUS Y EL DESTRUCTOR DE MONSTRUOS** • 1960
NOSTRADAMUS, EL GENIO DE LAS TINIEBLAS • 1960 • Curiel Federico, Segar Stig (Usa Vers) • MXC • NOSTRADAMUS, GENIUS FROM THE DARK ○ GENII OF DARKNESS (USA)
NOSTRADAMUS, GENIUS FROM THE DARK see **NOSTRADAMUS, EL GENIO DE LAS TINIEBLAS** • 1960
NOSTRADAMUS IV • 1944 • Endfield Cy • SHT • USA
NOSTRADAMUS NO DAIYOGEN • 1974 • Masuda Toshio • JPN • PROPHECIES OF NOSTRADAMUS: CATASTROPHE 1999 ○ LAST DAYS OF PLANET EARTH, THE ○ CATASTROPHE 1999 ○ NOSTRADAMUS'S GREAT PROPHECY ○ NOSUTORADAMUSU NO DAIYOGEN
NOSTRADAMUS SAYS NO • 1952 • Ballbusch Peter • USA
NOSTRADAMUS Y EL DESTRUCTOR DE MONSTRUOS • 1960 • Curiel Federico, Segar Stig (Usa Vers) • MXC • NOSTRADAMUS AND THE DESTROYER OF MONSTERS ○ MONSTER DEMOLISHER (USA)
NOSTRADAMUS'S GREAT PROPHECY see **NOSTRADAMUS NO DAIYOGEN** • 1974
NOSTRI FIGLI, I see **VINTI, I** • 1952
NOSTRI MARITI, I • 1966 • Risi Dino, Zampa Luigi, D'Amico Luigi Filippo • ITL • OUR HUSBANDS
NOSTRI SOGNI, I • 1943 • Cottafavi Vittorio • ITL
NOSTRO AGENTE A CASABLANCA, IL (ITL) see **NUESTRO AGENTE EN CASABLANCA** • 1966
NOSTRO CAMPIONE, IL • 1955 • Duse Vittorio • ITL
NOSTRO PROSSIMO, IL • 1943 • Gherardi Gherardo, Rossi Antonio G. • ITL
NOSTROMO • 1987 • Lean David • UKN
NOSTROMO see **SILVER TREASURE, THE** • 1926
NOSTROS DOS see **NOSOTROS DOS** • 1954
NOSUTORADAMUSU NO DAIYOGEN see **NOSTRADAMUS NO DAIYOGEN** • 1974
NOSZTY FLU ESTE TOTH MARIVAL, A • 1938 • Sekely Steve • HNG
NOT A CASE OF LATERAL DISPLACEMENT • 1965 • Landow George • USA
NOT A DRUM WAS HEARD • 1924 • Wellman William A. • USA
NOT A GHOST OF A SHOW • 1915 • *Royal* • USA
NOT A HOPE IN HELL • 1960 • Rogers Maclean • UKN
NOT A LADIES' MAN • 1942 • Landers Lew • USA
NOT A LAMB SHALL STRAY • 1915 • *Benton Curtis* • USA
NOT A LOVE STORY see **NOT A LOVE STORY: A FILM ABOUT PORNOGRAPHY** • 1981
NOT A LOVE STORY: A FILM ABOUT PORNOGRAPHY • 1981 • Klein Bonnie • DOC • CND • C'EST SURTOUT PAS DE L'AMOUR ○ NOT A LOVE STORY
NOT A PRETTY PICTURE • 1976 • Coolidge Martha • USA
NOT ANOTHER LOVE STORY • 1978 • Bradshaw John R. • CND
NOT ANOTHER MISTAKE • 1987 • Maharaj Anthony • USA
NOT AS A STRANGER • 1955 • Kramer Stanley • USA
NOT AS REHEARSED • 1913 • Wilson Frank? • UKN
NOT AS WICKED AS THAT see **PAS SI MECHANT QUE CA** • 1975
NOT BLOOD RELATIONS see **NASANU NAKA** • 1932
NOT BUILT FOR RUNNIN' • 1924 • Maloney Leo • USA
NOT BY BREAD ALONE (UKN) see **TYOMIEHEN PAIVAKIRJA** • 1967
NOT BY CHOICE • 1960 • White Douglas • ASL
NOT DAMAGED • 1930 • Sprague Chandler • USA
NOT DETAINED AT THE OFFICE • 1906 • Collins Alf? • UKN
NOT ENOUGH see **NIET GENOEG** • 1968
NOT EVERYTHING THAT FLIES IS A BIRD see **NICHT ALLES WAS FLIEGT ISAT EIN VOGEL** • 1978
NOT EXACTLY GENTLEMEN • 1931 • Stoloff Ben • USA • THREE ROGUES (UKN)
NOT FAR FROM BOLGATANGA • 1982 • Rubbo Michael, Howells Barrie • CND
NOT FAR FROM HOME • 1973 • Owen Don • CND
NOT FAR FROM WARSAW • 1954 • Kaniewska Maria • HNG
NOT FOR CHILDREN see **MAD MARTINDALES, THE** • 1942
NOT FOR EACH OTHER see **BILL OF DIVORCEMENT, A** • 1940
NOT FOR GLORY see **STRANGE CASE OF DR. MEADE** • 1939
NOT FOR HIRE • 1967 • Caguin Mike • PHL
NOT FOR HONOR AND GLORY see **LOST COMMAND** • 1966
NOT FOR MINE • 1913 • *Hodges Little Runa* • USA
NOT FOR MONEY see **IRON PETTICOAT, THE** • 1956
NOT FOR PUBLICATION • 1927 • Ince Ralph • USA
NOT FOR PUBLICATION • 1934 • Greenwood Edwin • SER • UKN
NOT FOR PUBLICATION • 1984 • Bartel Paul • USA, UKN
NOT FOR REAL see **TRICHEURS, LES** • 1958
NOT FOR SALE • 1924 • *Parke William Jr.* • USA
NOT FOR SALE • 1924 • Kellino W. P. • UKN
NOT GHOULTY • 1959 • Kneitel Seymour • ANS • USA
NOT GUILTY • 1908 • Melies Georges • FRN
NOT GUILTY • 1910 • *Thanhouser* • USA
NOT GUILTY • 1911 • Fitzhamon Lewin? • UKN
NOT GUILTY • 1915 • Golden Joseph A. • USA
NOT GUILTY • 1919 • Bocchi Arrigo • UKN
NOT GUILTY • 1921 • Franklin Sidney A. • USA • PARROT AND CO.
NOT GUILTY ENOUGH • 1938 • Lord Del • SHT • USA
NOT GUILTY (USA) see **GENTLEMAN RANKER, THE** • 1913
NOT GUILTY (USA) see **NON COUPABLE** • 1947
NOT IN FRONT OF THE CHILDREN • 1982 • Hardy Joseph • TVM • USA
NOT IN NOTTINGHAM • 1963 • Hanna William, Barbera Joseph • ANS • USA
NOT IN -OR OUT see **SE KI, SE BE** • 1918

NOT IN THE NEWS • 1916 • Ashley Charles E. • SHT • USA
NOT IN THESE • 1912 • *Cosmopolitan* • UKN
NOT JUST ANOTHER AFFAIR • 1982 • Stern Steven Hilliard • TVM • USA • SMUG FIT
NOT LIKE OTHER GIRLS • 1912 • Salter Harry • USA
NOT LIKE OTHER GIRLS • 1913 • *Ramo* • USA
NOT LIKELY! • 1914 • Aylott Dave • UKN
NOT LOVED see **NIEKOCHANA** • 1966
NOT MINE TO LOVE (USA) see **SHLOSHA YAMIN VE YELED** • 1966
NOT MUCH FORCE • 1915 • Louis Will • USA
NOT MY KID • 1985 • Tuchner Michael • TVM • USA
NOT MY SISTER • 1916 • Giblyn Charles • USA
NOT NEEDED see **NIEPOTRZEBNI** • 1962
NOT NEGOTIABLE • 1918 • West Walter • UKN
NOT NOW • 1936 • Fleischer Dave • ANS • USA
NOT NOW, DARLING • 1972 • Cooney Ray, Croft David • UKN
NOT OF THE FLOCK • 1914 • *Ray Charles* • USA
NOT OF THIS EARTH • 1957 • Corman Roger • USA
NOT OF THIS EARTH • 1988 • Wynorski Jim • USA
NOT ON MY ACCOUNT • 1943 • Roberts Charles E. • SHT • USA
NOT ON THE CIRCUS PROGRAM • 1912 • *Calvert Billy* • USA
NOT ON THE PROGRAM • 1912 • *Majestic* • USA
NOT ON YOUR LIFE see **ISLAND OF LOVE** • 1963
NOT ON YOUR LIFE (USA) see **VERDUGO, EL** • 1964
NOT ONE TO SPARE see **WHICH SHALL IT BE?** • 1924
NOT QUITE A LADY • 1928 • Bentley Thomas • UKN
NOT QUITE DECENT • 1929 • Cummings Irving • USA
NOT QUITE HUMAN • 1987 • Stern Steven Hilliard • TVM • USA
NOT QUITE JERUSALEM • 1984 • Gilbert Lewis* • UKN • NOT QUITE PARADISE (USA)
NOT QUITE PARADISE (USA) see **NOT QUITE JERUSALEM** • 1984
NOT RECONCILED, OR "ONLY VIOLENCE HELPS WHERE IT RULES" see **NICHT VERSOHNT ODER "ES HILFT NUR GEWALT, WO GEWALT HERRSCHT"** • 1965
NOT SINCE CASANOVA • 1989 • Thompson Brett • USA
NOT SO BAD AS HE SEEMED • 1910 • Griffith D. W.? • USA
NOT SO DUMB • 1930 • USA • ROSALIE (UKN)
NOT SO DUMB • 1930 • Vidor King • USA • DULCY
NOT SO DUSTY • 1936 • Rogers Maclean • UKN
NOT SO DUSTY • 1956 • Rogers Maclean • UKN
NOT SO LONG AGO • 1925 • Olcott Sidney • USA
NOT SO LOUD • 1931 • Sweet Harry • USA
NOT SO QUIET • 1930 • Lantz Walter, Nolan William • ANS • USA
NOT SO QUIET DAYS see **STILLE DAGE I CLICHY** • 1970
NOT SO QUIET ON THE WESTERN FRONT • 1930 • Banks Monty • UKN
NOT SUCH A FOOL • 1912 • Collins Edwin J. • UKN
NOT SUCH A FOOL AS HE LOOKS • 1907 • Fitzhamon Lewin • UKN
NOT THE BEST OF DAYS see **NYE SAMY UDACHNY DYEN** • 1967
NOT THE MARRYING KIND • 1933 • Hackney W. P. • SHT • USA
NOT THE TYPE • 1927 • Robbins Jess • USA
NOT THE WALKING KIND • 1972 • Wilson Sandra • CND
NOT TONIGHT DARLING! • 1971 • Sloman Anthony • UKN
NOT TONIGHT JOSEPHINE • 1934 • Cline Eddie • SHT • USA
NOT TOO NARROW, NOT TOO DEEP see **STRANGE CARGO** • 1940
NOT TOO THIN TO FIGHT • 1917 • Curtis Allen • SHT • USA
NOT UND VERBRECHEN • 1919 • Sauer Fred • FRG
NOT WANTED • 1913 • Stow Percy • UKN
NOT WANTED • 1915 • West Langdon • USA
NOT WANTED • 1949 • Clifton Elmer • USA • STREETS OF SIN
NOT WANTED ON VOYAGE • 1936 • Reinert Emile Edwin • UKN • TREACHERY ON THE HIGH SEAS (USA) ○ MURDER IN THE STALLS
NOT WANTED ON VOYAGE • 1957 • Rogers Maclean • UKN
NOT WHAT THE DOCTOR ORDERED • 1916 • *Teare Ethel* • SHT • USA
NOT WITH MY WIFE YOU DON'T! • 1966 • Panama Norman • USA
NOT YET, BUT SOON • 1908 • *Selig* • USA
NOT YET DARK • 1974 • Kozantsev N. • USS
NOT YET THE DAY see **HALADEK** • 1981
NOTABLE EVENTS • Darkany Mostafa • MRC
NOTAIRE, LE • 1953 • Devlin Bernard, Garceau Raymond • DCS • CND
NOTATNIK KANADYJSKI • 1961 • Perski Ludwik • DOC • PLN • CANADIAN NOTEBOOK
NOTCH NUMBER ONE • 1916 • *Kalem* • SHT • USA
NOTCH NUMBER ONE • 1924 • *Wilson Ben* • USA • FIRST NOTCH, THE
NOTE FOR SANDRA, A see **SKILABOD TIL SONDRU** • 1983
NOTE IN THE ORANGE, A • 1912 • *Lubin* • USA
NOTE IN THE SHOE, THE • 1909 • Griffith D. W. • USA
NOTE MIT DEM SILBERKREUZ, DIE • 1919 • *Herterich Hilde* • FRG
NOTE SUR UN TRIANGLE • 1966 • Jodoin Rene • ANS • CND • NOTES ON A TRIANGLE (USA)
NOTEBOOK • 1962-63 • Menken Marie • SHT • USA
NOTEBOOK FROM CHINA • 1987 • Leth Jorgen • DOC • DNM
NOTEBOOK OF THINGS GONE see **ZAPISNIK ZMIZELEHO** • 1978
NOTED EEL AND PIE HOUSES • 1975 • Furnham David • UKN
NOTED SWORD, THE see **MEITO BIJOMARU** • 1945
NOTES AND NOTIONS • 1929 • Jeffrey R. E. • UKN
NOTES DE LA VIE, LES • 1973 • Labrecque Jean-Claude • DCS • CND
NOTES FOR A FILM ABOUT DONNA & GAIL • 1966 • Owen Don • CND
NOTES FOR A FILM ON JAZZ see **APPUNTI PER UN FILM SULJAZZ** • 1965
NOTES FOR AN AFRICAN ORESTEIA see **APPUNTI PER UN ORESTIADE AFRICANA** • 1970
NOTES FOR JEROME • 1981 • Mekas Jonas • USA
NOTES FROM PORTUL ROSU • 1957 • Calotescu Virgil • DOC • RMN
NOTES FROM THE GALLOWS see **REPORT** • 1961
NOTES ON A GREEN REVOLUTION • 1972 • Benegal Shyam • DCS • IND
NOTES ON A TRIANGLE (USA) see **NOTE SUR UN TRIANGLE** • 1966
NOTES ON OCTOBER • 1968 • Sremec Rudolf • SHT • YGS
NOTES ON THE CIRCUS • 1966 • Mekas Jonas • USA • CIRCUS NOTEBOOK, THE
NOTES ON THE HISTORY OF A LAKE • 1962 • Kosa Ferenc • SHT • HNG
NOTES ON THE POPULAR ARTS • 1978 • Bass Saul • SHT • USA
NOTES ON THE PORT OF ST. FRANCIS • 1952 • Stauffacher Frank • SHT • USA
NOTES SUR LA CONTESTATION • 1970 • Portugais Louis • DOC • CND
NOTES SUR L'EMIGRATION • 1960 • Esteva Jacinto • SHT • SPN
NOTES TO YOU • 1941 • Freleng Friz • ANS • USA
NOTHEIRAT, DIE • 1920 • von Woringen Paul • FRG
NOTHIN' BUT BLONDES see **BLONDIN I FARA** • 1958
N:O:T:H:I:N:G • 1968 • Sharits Paul J. • USA • N.O.T.H.I.N.G.
NOTHING BARRED • 1961 • Conyers Darcy • UKN
NOTHING BARRED see **TWO WAY STRETCH** • 1960
NOTHING BUT A MAN • 1964 • Roemer Michael • USA
NOTHING BUT A NOTHING • Yuzovsky Mikhail • USA, IND
NOTHING BUT DREAMS see **PUSTI SNOVI** • 1968
NOTHING BUT LIES • 1920 • Windom Lawrence C. • USA
NOTHING BUT LOVE • 1984 • Manttari Anssi • FNL
NOTHING BUT MONEY • 1910 • *American* • USA
NOTHING BUT NERVE • 1918 • Curtis Allen • SHT • USA
NOTHING BUT NERVES • 1942 • Roush Leslie • SHT • USA
NOTHING BUT OLD NOBILITY see **IDEL ADEL ADEL** • 1945
NOTHING BUT PLEASURE • 1940 • *Keaton Buster* • SHT • USA
NOTHING BUT THE BEST • 1963 • Donner Clive • UKN
NOTHING BUT THE NIGHT • 1972 • Sasdy Peter • UKN • RESURRECTION SYNDICATE, THE ○ DEVIL'S UNDEAD, THE (USA)
NOTHING BUT THE TOOTH • 1948 • Davis Arthur • ANS • USA
NOTHING BUT THE TRUTH • 1920 • Kirkland David • USA
NOTHING BUT THE TRUTH • 1929 • Schertzinger Victor • USA
NOTHING BUT THE TRUTH • 1941 • Nugent Elliott • USA
NOTHING BUT THE TRUTH see **ADVENTURES OF BARON MUNCHAUSEN, THE** • 1927
NOTHING BUT THE TRUTH see **RENA RAMA SANNINGEN** • 1939
NOTHING BUT THE TRUTH see **VERITES ET MENSONGES** • 1973
NOTHING BUT THE TRUTH see **KUN SANDHEDEN** • 1975
NOTHING BUT THE TRUTH see **BIG EASY, THE** • 1987
NOTHING BUT TROUBLE • 1918 • Roach Hal • SHT • USA
NOTHING BUT TROUBLE • 1944 • Taylor Sam • USA
NOTHING BUT WIND • 1915 • *Horseshoe* • UKN
NOTHING BY CHANCE • 1975 • Barnett William H. • DOC • USA
NOTHING ELSE MATTERS • 1920 • Pearson George • UKN
NOTHING EVER HAPPENS RIGHT • 1915 • McCray Roy • USA
NOTHING EVER HAPPENS (USA) see **NUNCA PASA NADA** • 1963
NOTHING FLAT • 1927 • Roberts Stephen • SHT • USA
NOTHING HAS HAPPENED HERE see **AQUI NO HA PASADO NADA** • 1974
NOTHING IN COMMON • 1986 • Marshall Garry • USA
NOTHING IS IMPOSSIBLE TO THE MAN see **RIEN N'EST IMPOSSIBLE A L'HOMME** • 1910
NOTHING LASTS FOREVER • 1984 • Schiller Tom • USA
NOTHING LESS THAN A MAN see **NADA MENOS QUE TODO UN HOMBRE** • 1971
NOTHING LESS THAN AN ARCHANGEL see **NADA MENOS QUE UN ARCANGEL** • 1959
NOTHING LIKE EXPERIENCE • 1970 • Carmody Peter • ASL
NOTHING LIKE PUBLICITY • 1936 • Rogers Maclean • UKN
NOTHING MATTERS • 1926 • Taurog Norman • SHT • USA
NOTHING PERSONAL • 1980 • Bloomfield George • CND
NOTHING SACRED • 1937 • Wellman William A. • USA
NOTHING SHALL BE HIDDEN • 1912 • *Imp* • USA
NOTHING TO HIDE • 1981 • Spinelli Anthony • USA
NOTHING TO LOSE see **TIME, GENTLEMEN, PLEASE** • 1952
NOTHING TO WEAR • 1912 • Humphrey William • USA
NOTHING TO WEAR • 1917 • Drew Sidney, Drew Sidney Mrs. • SHT • USA
NOTHING TO WEAR • 1928 • Kenton Erle C. • USA
NOTHING TO WEAR see **SLAVE OF FASHION, A** • 1925
NOTHING UNDER THE DRESS see **SOTTO IL VESTITO NIENTE** • 1985
NOTHING UNDERNEATH (UKN) see **SOTTO IL VESTITO NIENTE** • 1985
NOTHING UNUSUAL see **INGENTING OVANLIGT** • 1957
NOTHING VENTURE • 1948 • Baxter John • UKN
NOTHING WILL BE FORGOTTEN see **MAN GLOMMER INGENTING** • 1942
NOTICE TO QUIT • 1903 • Collins Alf? • UKN
NOTIONS ELEMENTAIRES DE GENETIQUE • 1970 • Hebert Pierre • ANS • CND
NOTORIETY • 1914 • *Baggot King* • USA
NOTORIETY • 1922 • Nigh William • USA
NOTORIETY see **WILD PARTY, THE** • 1923
NOTORIOUS • 1946 • Hitchcock Alfred • USA
NOTORIOUS AFFAIR, A • 1930 • Bacon Lloyd • USA • FAITHFUL
NOTORIOUS BANDIT, THE see **TA E KOU** • 1972
NOTORIOUS BIG SIN CITY see **BIG SIN CITY** • 1970
NOTORIOUS BUT NICE • 1933 • Thorpe Richard • USA
NOTORIOUS CLEOPATRA, THE • 1970 • Stootsberry A. P. • USA
NOTORIOUS CONCUBINES, THE see **CHIN-P'ING-MEI** • 1969
NOTORIOUS DAUGHTER OF FANNY HILL, THE • 1966 • Stootsberry A. P. • USA
NOTORIOUS ELINOR LEE, THE • 1940 • Micheaux Oscar • USA
NOTORIOUS GALLAGHER see **HIS GREAT TRIUMPH** • 1916
NOTORIOUS GENTLEMAN see **SMOOTH AS SILK** • 1946
NOTORIOUS GENTLEMAN, THE • 1935 • Laemmle Edward • USA • I MURDERED A MAN
NOTORIOUS GENTLEMAN, THE (USA) see **RAKE'S PROGRESS, THE** • 1945
NOTORIOUS LADY, THE • 1927 • Baggot King • USA
NOTORIOUS LADY, THE • 1962 • Quine Richard • USA
NOTORIOUS LONE WOLF, THE • 1946 • Lederman D. Ross • USA
NOTORIOUS MAN AND THE ISSEI, THE see **AKUMYO ICHIDAI** • 1967
NOTORIOUS MAN RETURNS, THE see **AKUMYO JU-HACHI BAN** • 1968
NOTORIOUS MISS LISLE, THE • 1920 • Young James • USA
NOTORIOUS MR. MONKS, THE • 1958 • Kane Joseph • USA
NOTORIOUS MRS. CARRICK, THE • 1924 • Ridgwell George • UKN • POOLS OF THE PAST
NOTORIOUS MRS. FAGIN, THE • 1921 • Gordon Edward R. • UKN
NOTORIOUS MRS. SANDS, THE • 1920 • Cabanne W. Christy • USA
NOTORIOUS SOPHIE LANG, THE • 1934 • Murphy Ralph • USA
NOTORIOUS VIRGINS see **FUDATSUKI SHOJO** • 1967
NOTRE, LE • 1955 • Tedesco Jean • SHT • FRN
NOTRE DAME • 1913 • *Patheplay* • USA
NOTRE-DAME, CATHEDRALE DE PARIS • 1957 • Franju Georges • DCS • FRN
NOTRE-DAME D'AMOUR • 1922 • Hugon Andre • FRN
NOTRE-DAME D'AMOUR • 1936 • Caron Pierre • FRN
NOTRE DAME DE LA CROISETTE • 1981 • Schmid Daniel • SWT
NOTRE-DAME DE LA MOUISE • 1941 • Peguy Robert, Delacroix Rene • CND, FRN
NOTRE DAME DE PARIS • 1911 • Capellani Albert • FRN • HUNCHBACK OF NOTRE DAME, THE (USA)
NOTRE-DAME DE PARIS • 1931 • Epstein Jean • FRN
NOTRE DAME DE PARIS • 1957 • Delannoy Jean • FRN, ITL • HUNCHBACK OF NOTRE DAME ○ NOTRE-DAME DE PARIS
NOTRE DAME DE PARIS • 1961 • Gruel Henri • ANS • FRN
NOTRE-DAME DE PARIS see **NOTRE DAME DE PARIS** • 1957
NOTRE DAME OF CRACOW see **SWIATYNIA MARIACKA** • 1961
NOTRE FANFARE CONCOURT • 1907 • *Deed Andre* • FRN
NOTRE HISTOIRE • 1984 • Blier Bertrand • FRN • SEPARATE ROOMS ○ OUR STORY
NOTRE INDUSTRIE see **SINAATUNA** • 1959
NOTRE JEUNESSE EN AUTO SPORT • 1969 • Elnecave Vivianne • CND • OUR SPORTS CAR DAYS
NOTRE MARIAGE • 1984 • Sarmiento Valeria • FRN
NOTRE PAUVRE COEUR • 1916 • Feuillade Louis • FRN
NOTRE PLANETE LA TERRE • 1947 • Painleve Jean • SHT • FRN
NOTRE SANG • 1955 • Leenhardt Roger • DCS • FRN
NOTRE UNIVERS see **UNIVERSE** • 1959
NOTSCHREI HINTER GITTERN • 1927 • Hofer Franz • FRG
NOTTATA, LA • 1974 • Cervi Tonino • ITL
NOTTE, LA • 1961 • Antonioni Michelangelo • ITL, FRN • NUIT, LA (FRN) ○ NIGHT, THE
NOTTE A CALCUTTA, UNA • 1918 • Caserini Mario • ITL
NOTTE A VENEZIA, UNA (ITL) see **NACHT IN VENEDIG, EINE** • 1934
NOTTE A VILLA PARADISO, UNA see **SEGRETO DI VILLA PARADISO, IL** • 1940
NOTTE BRAVA, LA • 1959 • Bolognini Mauro • ITL, FRN • GARCONS, LES (FRN) ○ BAD GIRLS DON'T CRY ○ NIGHT HEAT ○ NIGHT OUT, THE ○ ON ANY STREET
NOTTE CHE EVELYN USCI DALLA TOMBA, LA • 1971 • Miraglia Emilio Paolo • ITL • NIGHT EVELYN CAME OUT OF THE GRAVE, THE (USA) ○ SWEET TO BE KISSED HARD TO DIE ○ NIGHT SHE AROSE FROM THE TOMB, THE (UKN)
NOTTE CON TE, UNA • 1932 • Biancini Ferruccio, Emo E. W. • ITL, FRG
NOTTE DE FORTUNA • 1941 • Matarazzo Raffaello • ITL
NOTTE DEGLI SPETTRI, LA • 1913 • *Volsca* • SHT • ITL • NIGHT OF THE SPECTERS, THE
NOTTE DEI DANNATI, LA • 1971 • Ratti Filippo M. • ITL • NIGHT OF THE DAMNED, THE (UKN)
NOTTE DEI DIAVOLI, LA • 1972 • Ferroni Giorgio • ITL, SPN • NOCHE DE LOS DIABLOS, LA ○ NIGHT OF THE DEVILS (UKN)
NOTTE DEI FIORI, LA • 1972 • Baldi Gian Vittorio • ITL • NIGHT OF THE FLOWERS (USA)
NOTTE DEI SERPENTI, LA • 1969 • Petroni Giulio • ITL • NIGHT OF THE SERPENTS (USA)
NOTTE DEL GRANDE ASSALTO, LA • 1960 • Scotese Giuseppe Maria • ITL, FRN • NIGHT OF THE GREAT ATTACK, THE (USA)
NOTTE DELL'ADDIO, LA • 1966 • Boraccetti Renato • ITL
NOTTE DELL'ALTA MAREA, LA • 1977 • Scattini Luigi • ITL
NOTTE DELLE BEFFE, LA • 1940 • Campogalliani Carlo • ITL
NOTTE DELLE SPIE, LA (ITL) see **NUIT DES ESPIONS, LA** • 1959
NOTTE DELL'INNOMINATO, LA • 1963 • De Marchi Luigi • ITL
NOTTE DELL'ULTIMO GIORNO, LA • 1973 • Sala Adimaro • ITL
NOTTE D'ESTATE CON PROFILO GRECO OCCHI A MANDORLA E ODORE DI BASILICO • 1987 • Wertmuller Lina • ITL • SUMMER NIGHT WITH GREEK PROFILE ALMOND EYES AND THE SCENT OF BASIL
NOTTE DI FIAMMA • 1942 • Kish Ladislao • ITL
NOTTE DI NEBBIA see **UOMINI SENZA DOMANI** • 1947
NOTTE DI SAN JUAN, LA • 1971 • Sanjines Jorge • ITL, BLV • NIGHT OF SAN JUAN, THE (USA) ○ CORAJE DEL PUEBLO, EL ○ COURAGE OF THE PEOPLE, THE
NOTTE DI SAN LORENZO, LA • 1981 • Taviani Paolo, Taviani Vittorio • ITL • NIGHT OF THE SHOOTING STARS (USA) ○ NIGHT OF SAN LORENZO, THE(UKN)
NOTTE DI TEMPESTA • 1946 • Franciolini Gianni • ITL
NOTTE DOPO L'OPERA, UNA • 1942 • Manzari Nicola, Neroni Nicola Fausto • ITL
NOTTE E DONNE PROIBITE • 1963 • Loy Mino • DOC • ITL
NOTTE E FATTA PER.. RUBARE, LA • 1967 • Capitani Giorgio • ITL, SPN • NIGHT IS MADE FOR.. STEALING, THE

NOTTE EROTIQUE see **DROGUE DU VICE, LA** • 1963

NOTTE ITALIANA • 1988 • Mazzacurati Carlo • ITL • ITALIAN NIGHT

NOTTE PAZZA DEL CONIGLIACCIO, LA • 1967 • Angeli Alfredo • ITL • BAD RABBIT'S MAD NIGHT, THE ○ CONIGLIACCIO, LA ○ STRANGE NIGHT, THE ○ NAUGHTY RABBIT, THE

NOTTE PER 5 RAPINE, UNA (ITL) see **MISE A SAC** • 1967

NOTTE PIU LONGA DEL DIAVOLO, LA (ITL) see **PLUS LONGUE NUIT DU DIABLE, LA** • 1971

NOTTE PORTA CONSIGLIO, LA see **ROMA, CITTA LIBERA** • 1948

NOTTE SULLA CITTA (ITL) see **FLIC, UN** • 1972

NOTTI BIANCHE, LE • 1957 • Visconti Luchino • ITL, FRN • NUITS BLANCHES (FRN) ○ WHITE NIGHTS (USA) ○ SLEEPLESS NIGHTS

NOTTI CALDE D'ORIENTE • 1962 • Montero Roberto Bianchi • DOC • ITL • ORIENT BY NIGHT (USA)

NOTTI DEI TEDDY BOYS, LE • 1960 • Schott-Schobinger Leopoldo • ITL, FRG

NOTTI DEL TERRORE, LE • 1980 • Bianchi Andrea • ITL • NIGHTS OF TERROR, THE ○ ZOMBIE HORROR ○ ZOMBIE 3

NOTTI DELLA VIOLENZA, LE • 1966 • Mauri Roberto • ITL • NIGHT OF VIOLENCE (USA)

NOTTI DI CABIRIA, LE • 1957 • Fellini Federico • ITL, FRN • NUITS DE CABIRIA, LES (FRN) ○ NIGHTS OF CABIRIA (USA) ○ CABIRIA (UKN)

NOTTI DI LUCREZIA BORGIA, LE • 1959 • Grieco Sergio • ITL, FRN • NUITS DE LUCRECE BORGIA, LES (FRN) ○ NIGHTS OF TEMPTATION (UKN) ○ NIGHTS OF LUCRETIA BORGIA, THE (USA)

NOTTI NUDE • 1963 • Fecchi Ettore • ITL

NOTTI PECCAMINOSE DE PIETRO L'ARETINO • 1972 • Scarpelli Manilo • ITL

NOTTI PORNO NEL MONDO, LE • 1977 • Mattei Bruno • ITL

NOTTI PORNO NEL MONDO N.2, LE • 1978 • D'Amato Joe • ITL

NOTTRAUUNG, DIE • 1916 • Albes Emil • FRG

NOTTURNO • 1951 • Sala Vittorio • DOC • ITL

NOTTURNO see **LACRIME DE SANGUE** • 1944

NOTTURNO DI CHOPIN • 1913 • Maggi Luigi • ITL

NOUA • 1972 • Tolbi Abdelaziz • ALG

N'OUBLIE PAS TON PERE AU VESTIAIRE • 1982 • Balducci Richard • FRN

NOUFOUSS HAIRA • 1968 • Mazhar Ahmed • EGY • TORMENTED SOULS ○ AMES TOURMENTEES

NOUMERO, TO • 1978 • Koundouros Nikos • GRC • NUMBER, THE ○ 1922

NOURISHEE, THE • 1971 • Mimica Vatroslav • YGS

NOUS AURONS TOUTE LA MORT POUR DORMIR • 1977 • Hondo Abib Med • DOC • MRT, FRN

NOUS AUTRES A CHAMPIGNOL • 1956 • Bastia Jean • FRN

NOUS AVONS TOUT FAIT LA MEME CHOSE • 1949 • Sti Rene • FRN

NOUS CHERCHONS UNE FEMME see **FEMME COUPEE EN MORCEAUX, UNE** • 1945

NOUS CONTINUONS LA FRANCE • 1946 • Daquin Louis • FRN

NOUS ET LA REVOLUTION AGRAIRE • 1972 • Allouache Merzak • DCS • ALG

NOUS ETIONS TOUS DES NOMS D'ARBRES • 1983 • Gatti Armand • BLG, FRN

NOUS ETIONS UN SEUL HOMME • 1978 • Vallois Philippe • FRN • WE WERE ONE MAN

NOUS IRONS A DEAUVILLE • 1962 • Rigaud Francis • FRN

NOUS IRONS A MONTE CARLO • 1951 • Boyer Jean • FRN • MONTE CARLO BABY (USA)

NOUS IRONS A PARIS • 1949 • Boyer Jean • FRN • LET'S GO TO PARIS

NOUS IRONS TOUS AU PARADIS • 1977 • Robert Yves • FRN • WE WILL ALL MEET IN PARADISE (USA) ○ PARDON MON AFFAIRE, TOO (UKN)

NOUS LES ETUDIANTS see **AHNA AL-TALAMD'A** • 1959

NOUS LES GOSSES • 1941 • Daquin Louis • FRN • PORTRAIT OF INNOCENCE (USA) ○ US KIDS

NOUS, LES GOSSES see **GUERRE DES GOSSES, LA** • 1936

NOUS LES JEUNES see **ALTITUDE 3200** • 1938

NOUS MAIGRIRONS ENSEMBLE • 1979 • Vocoret Michel • FRN

NOUS NE FAISONS DE MAL A PERSONNE see **NAH'NU LA NAZRA ASH-SHUK** • 1970

NOUS NE FERONS JAMAIS LE CINEMA • 1932 • Cavalcanti Alberto • DOC • FRN

NOUS NE SOMMES PAS MARIES • 1945 • Bernard-Roland • FRN

NOUS NE SOMMES PLUS DES ENFANTS • 1934 • Genina Augusto • FRN

NOUS NE VIEILLIRONS PAS ENSEMBLE • 1972 • Pialat Maurice • FRN, ITL • WE WILL NOT GROW OLD TOGETHER ○ AMANTE GIOVANE, L'(ITL) ○ BREAK-UP ○ WE WON'T GROW OLD TOGETHER

NOUS N'IRONS PLUS AU BOIS • 1951 • Sautet Claude • SHT • FRN

NOUS N'IRONS PLUS AU BOIS • 1954 • Govar Yvan • BLG

NOUS N'IRONS PLUS AU BOIS • 1964 • Etaix Pierre • FRN

NOUS N'IRONS PLUS UN BOIS • 1968 • Dumoulin Georges • FRN • WE WON'T GO TO THE WOODS ANY MORE

NOUS NOUS SOMMES RENCONTRES DANS UN AUTRE REVE • 1980 • Schwarzstein Alain • FRN

NOUS PARLONS, VOUS ECOUTEZ • 1975 • Davaud Michel, Jaulin Robert, Wauthrin Xavier • DOC • FRN

NOUS PRES, NOUS LOIN • 1986 • D'Aix Alain • MTV • CND

NOUS REVIENDRONS see **SA NAUD** • 1972

NOUS SOMMES DE JUIFS ARABES EN ISMAEL • 1977 • Niddam Igaal • DOC • SWT • WE ARE ARAB JEWS IN ISRAEL

NOUS SOMMES LES INGENIEURES see **I WANT TO BE AN ENGINEER** • 1983

NOUS SOMMES TOUS AVEC EUX • 1958 • Shawqi Khalil • SHT • EGY

NOUS SOMMES TOUS DES ASSASSINS • 1952 • Cayatte Andre • FRN, ITL • SIAMO TUTTI ASSASSINI (ITL) ○ ARE WE ALL MURDERERS? (UKN) ○ WE ARE ALL MURDERERS (USA) ○ MURDERERS

NOUVEAU JOURNAL D'UNE FEMME EN BLANC, LE • 1966 • Autant-Lara Claude • FRN • FEMME EN BLANC SE REVOLTE, UNE

NOUVEAU ROCAMBOLE, LE • 1913 • Denola Georges • FRN • NEW ROCAMBOLE, THE

NOUVEAU SEIGNEUR DU VILLAGE, LE • 1908 • Melies Georges • FRN • NEW LORD OF THE VILLAGE, THE

NOUVEAU TESTAMENT, LE • 1936 • Guitry Sacha, Ryder Alexandre • FRN

NOUVEAU VENU, LE • 1979 • de Medeiros Ricardo Beby • BNN • NEWCOMER, THE

NOUVEAU VIETNAM, LE • 1977 • Bertolino Daniel • DOC • CND

NOUVEAUX ARISTOCRATES, LES • 1961 • Rigaud Francis • FRN

NOUVEAUX EXPLOITS DE NICK CARTER, LES • 1909 • Jasset Victorin • SRL • FRN

NOUVEAUX HORIZONS • 1953 • Ichac Marcel • DCS • FRN

NOUVEAUX MAITRES, LES • 1949 • Nivoix Paul • FRN

NOUVEAUX MESSIEURS, LES • 1929 • Feyder Jacques • FRN • NEW GENTLEMEN, THE (USA)

NOUVEAUX MISERABLES, LES • 1947-51 • Verneuil Henri • SHT • FRN

NOUVEAUX PAUVRES, LES see **SOYEZ LES BIENVENUS** • 1940

NOUVEAUX RICHES, LES • 1938 • Berthomieu Andre • FRN

NOUVEAUX ROMANTIQUES, LES • 1978 • Benayat Mohammed • FRN

NOUVEAUX VENUS, LES • 1956-57 • Devlin Bernard • SHT • CND

NOUVEAUX VOYAGES DE GULLIVER, LES • 1956 • Samivel • FRN

NOUVELLE ANTIGONE, LA • 1916 • de Baroncelli Jacques • FRN

NOUVELLE AURORE, LA • 1918 • Violet Edouard-Emile • SRL • FRN

NOUVELLE BATAILLE, LA • 1967 • Essid Hamadi • DOC • TNS

NOUVELLE MISSION DE JUDEX, LA • 1917 • Feuillade Louis • SRL • FRN • NEW MISSION OF JUDEX, THE (USA) ○ FURTHER EXPLOITS OF JUDEX, THE

NOUVELLE PEINE DE MORT, LA • 1907 • Melies Georges • FRN • NEW DEATH PENALTY, A (USA)

NOUVELLE ROUTE DE L'OPIUM, LA • 1975 • Lamour Marianne • DOC • FRN

NOUVELLE TELEVISION, LA • 1985 • Labonte Francois • DOC • CND

NOUVELLE VAGUE • 1989 • Godard Jean-Luc • SWT, FRN • NEW WAVE

NOUVELLES AVENTURES DU CHAT BOTTE, LES • 1958 • Rou Aleksandr • USS

NOUVELLES HISTOIRES DU FLEUVE NIGER • 1967 • Moati Serge • FRN, NGR

NOUVELLES LUTTES EXTRAVAGANTES • 1900 • Melies Georges • FRN • FAT AND LEAN WRESTLING MATCH (USA) ○ WRESTLING SEXTETTE, THE

NOUVO AMORE, UN • 1977 • Ricci Tonino • ITL

NOVA CANCO, LA see **NOVA CANCO: CANET ROCK, LA** • 1975

NOVA CANCO: CANET ROCK, LA • 1975 • Bellmunt Francisco • SPN • NOVA CANCO, LA

NOVA DOMACA ZIVOTINJA • 1964 • Makavejev Dusan • SHT • YGS • NEW DOMESTIC ANIMAL

NOVA IGRACKA • 1964 • Makavejev Dusan • SHT • YGS • NEW TOY

NOVA SCOTIA BYWAYS • 1963 • Perry Margaret • DOC • CND

NOVAIA MOSKVA • 1938 • Medvedkin Alexander • USS

NOVE CESKOSLOVENSKO • 1950 • Beleyev Vassili, Vlcek Vladimir • CZC, USS • NEW CZECHOSLOVAKIA

NOVE OSPITI PER UN DELITTO • 1977 • Baldi Ferdinando • ITL

NOVE RAPAZES E UM CAO • 1963 • Esteves Constantino • PRT

NOVECENTO • 1976 • Bertolucci Bernardo • ITL • 1900 ○ NINETEEN HUNDRED

NOVEL AFFAIR, A (USA) see **PASSIONATE STRANGER, THE** • 1957

NOVEL BURGLARY, A • 1912 • Evans Fred • UKN

NOVEL EXPERIMENT, A • 1911 • *Selig* • USA

NOVEL NAVIGATION • 1909 • FRN

NOVEL, POLITICIAN'S SCHOOL see **SHOSETSU YOSHIDA GAKKO** • 1983

NOVEL ROMANCE, A • 1917 • Millarde Harry • SHT • USA

NOVEL WITH A CONTRABASS see **ROMAN S BASON** • 1949

NOVEL WOOING, A • 1914 • Collins Edwin J.? • UKN

NOVEL: YOSHIDA SCHOOL see **SHOSETSU YOSHIDA GAKKO** • 1983

NOVELA DE UN JOVEN POBRE, LA • 1968 • Cahen Enrique • ARG • STORY OF A POOR YOUNG MAN, THE

NOVELLE GALEOTTE D'AMORE DEL DECAMERONE see **DECAMERON N.3 -LE PIU BELLE DONNE DEL BOCCACCIO** • 1972

NOVELLETTA, LA • 1937 • Comencini Luigi • SHT • ITL

NOVELTY IN SERVANTS • 1915 • *Superba* • USA

NOVELTY SHOP, THE • 1936 • *Mintz Charles (P)* • ANS • USA

NOVEMBER • 1921 • Fleischer Dave • ANS • USA

NOVEMBER see **LISTOPAD** • 1935

NOVEMBER 1828 see **NOPEMBER 1828** • 1978

NOVEMBER CHILDREN • 1971 • MacGregor Sean • USA

NOVEMBER NIGHT see **NOC LISTOPADOWA** • 1979

NOVEMBER PLAN, THE • 1976 • Medford Don • USA • COVER KILL ○ CITY ON ANGELS

NOVEMBERMOND • 1984 • von Grote Alexandra • FRG, FRN • NOVEMBERMOON

NOVEMBERMOON see **NOVEMBERMOND** • 1984

NOVEMBRE A PARIS • 1957 • Reichenbach Francois • SHT • FRN

NOVENTA MINUTOS • 1949 • del Amo Antonio • SPN

NOVIA A LA MEDIDA • 1949 • Martinez Solares Gilberto • MXC

NOVIA DE JUAN LUCERO, LA • 1958 • Alcocer Santos • SPN

NOVIA DE LA MARINA, LA • 1948 • Perojo Benito • ARG

NOVIA DEL MAR, LA • 1947 • Martinez Solares Gilberto • MXC

NOVIA ENSANGRENTADA, LA • 1972 • Aranda Vicente • SPN • BLOOD-SPATTERED BRIDE, THE (USA) ○ BLOODY FIANCEE ○ BLOODY BRIDE, THE ○ 'TIL DEATH DO US PART ○ TILL DEATH DO US PART ○ BLOOD SPLATTERED BRIDE, THE

NOVIA PARA DAVID, UNA • 1985 • Rojas Guillermo Orlando • CUB • LOVE ME THE WAY I AM

NOVIAS IMPACIENTES • 1966 • Delgado Miguel M. • MXC

NOVICE, THE • 1911 • *Selig* • USA

NOVICE, THE see **LETTERE DI UNA NOVIZIA** • 1960

NOVICE, THE see **SUORA GIOVANE, LA** • 1965

NOVICE AT X-RAYS, A (USA) see **RAYONS ROENTGEN, LES** • 1898

NOVICE BULLFIGHTER see **NOVILLERO** • 1936

NOVICE, LA (FRN) see **LETTERE DI UNA NOVIZIA** • 1960

NOVICES, LES • 1970 • Casaril Guy • FRN, ITL • NOVIZIE, LE (ITL)

NOVICIA REBELDE, LA • 1971 • Lucia Luis • SPN

NOVICIO REBELDE, EL • 1968 • Saraceni Julio • ARG • REBELLIOUS NOVICE, THE

NOVILLERO • 1936 • Maicon Boris • MXC • NOVICE BULLFIGHTER

NOVINAR • 1979 • Hadzic Fadil • YGS • JOURNALIST, THE

NOVIO A LA VISTA • 1953 • Bardem Juan Antonio, Berlanga Luis Garcia • SPN • FIANCE IN SIGHT

NOVIO DE MAMA, EL • 1934 • Rey Florian • SPN

NOVIO, MARIDO Y AMANTE • 1948 • Lugones Mario C. • ARG

NOVIO PARA DOS HERMANAS, UN • 1967 • Amadori Luis Cesar • SPN, MXC • BRIDEGROOM FOR TWO SISTERS, A

NOVIOS 68 • 1967 • Lazaga Pedro • SPN • BRIDEGROOM 68

NOVIOS DE LA MUERTE, LOS • 1938 • Marcellini Romolo • ITL

NOVIOS DE LA MUERTE, LOS • 1974 • Gil Rafael • SPN

NOVIOS DE MI MUJER, LOS • 1972 • Fernandez Ramon • SPN

NOVIOS DE MIS HIJAS, LOS • 1964 • Crevenna Alfredo B. • MXC

NOVIOS PARA LAS MUCHACHAS • 1941 • Momplet Antonio • ARG

NOVIOS Y AMANTES • 1971 • *Filman Internacional* • MXC

NOVIYE POKHOZDENIYA SHVEIKA • 1943 • Yutkevich Sergei • USS • NEW ADVENTURES OF SCHWEIK, THE

NOVIYE RASSKAZY BRAVOGO SOLDATA SHVEIKA • 1941 • Yutkevich Sergei • USS • SCHWEIK IN THE CONCENTRATION-CAMP

NOVIZIA, LA • 1975 • Ferretti Piergiorgio • ITL

NOVIZIE, LE (ITL) see **NOVICES, LES** • 1970

NOVOSTI DNYA • 1947-54 • Vertov Dziga • USS • DAILY NEWS

NOVYE PRIKLUCHENIA JANKE PRI DVORE KOVOLA ARTURA • 1989 • Gres Victor • USS • NEW ADVENTURES OF A CONNECTICUT YANKEE AT KING ARTHUR'S COURT, THE

NOVYI ATTRAKTION • 1957 • Dolin V. • USS • THRILLING SHOW, A ○ SAWDUST RING ○ NEW NUMBER, THE

NOVYI BABILON • 1929 • Kozintsev Grigori, Trauberg Leonid • USS • NEW BABYLON ○ NOVYI VAVILON

NOVYI GULLIVER • 1935 • Ptushko Alexander • ANM • USS • NEW GULLIVER, A

NOVYI VAVILON see **NOVYI BABILON** • 1929

NOW • 1965 • Alvarez Santiago • DOC • CUB

NOW • 1971 • Brocka Lino • PHL

NOW see **EMBRACERS, THE** • 1963

NOW ABOUT THESE WOMEN (UKN) see **FOR ATT INTE TALA OM ALLA DESSA KVINNOR** • 1964

NOW AND FOREVER • 1934 • Hathaway Henry • USA • YOU BELONG TO ME

NOW AND FOREVER • 1956 • Zampi Mario • UKN

NOW AND FOREVER • 1982 • Carr Adrian • ASL

NOW AND FOREVER see **SONG OF SURRENDER** • 1949

NOW AND THEN • 1981 • Turnbull Mark • ASL

NOW BARABBAS WAS A ROBBER • 1949 • Parry Gordon • UKN

NOW CINEMA! • 1968 • Bethune Lobert, Torbert Bruce, Mishima Yukio, Taylor John**, Schneider Alan • ANT • USA

NOW CINEMA! (PSYCHOMONTAGE) • 1968 • Kronhausen Eberhard • FRG • PSYCHOMONTAGE (NOW CINEMA!)

NOW DO YOU GET IT WHY I'M CRYING see **BEGRIJPT U NU WAAROM IK HUIL?** • 1970

NOW DON'T GET EXCITED see **NE KOFUN SHICHA IYAYO** • 1931

NOW HARE THIS • 1958 • McKimson Robert • ANS • USA

NOW HEAR THIS • 1963 • Jones Charles M. • ANS • USA

NOW I HAVE TO CALL HIM FATHER • 1911 • Fitzhamon Lewin? • UKN

NOW I KNOW • 1989 • Pappas Robert K. • USA

NOW I LAY ME DOWN see **RACHEL, RACHEL** • 1968

NOW I LAY ME DOWN TO SLEEP • 1913 • *Fearnley Jane* • USA

NOW I'LL TELL • 1934 • Burke Edwin • USA • WHEN NEW YORK SLEEPS (UKN)

NOW I'LL TELL ONE • 1927 • Roach Hal • SHT • USA

NOW I'M A LADY see **GOIN' TO TOWN** • 1935

NOW I'M A WOMAN see **YA SOY UNA MUJER** • 1975

NOW IS THE TIME • 1951 • McLaren Norman, Spottiswoode Raymond • ANS • CND

NOW IT CAN BE SOLD • 1939 • Lord Del • SHT • USA

NOW IT CAN BE TOLD see **HOUSE ON 92ND STREET, THE** • 1945

NOW IT CAN BE TOLD see **SCHOOL FOR DANGER** • 1947

NOW IT CAN BE TOLD see **SECRET DOOR, THE** • 1962

NOW IT'S UP TO YOU see **USTEDES TIENEN LA PALABRA** • 1974

NOW LET'S TALK ABOUT MEN see **QUESTA VOLTA PARLIAMO DI UOMINI** • 1965

NOW, NOT HANDICAPPED NORIKO see **NORIKO WA, IMA** • 1982

NOW OR NEVER • 1921 • Newmeyer Fred, Taylor Sam • SHT • USA

NOW OR NEVER • 1935 • Ray Bernard B. • USA

NOW SHE LETS HIM GO OUT • 1913 • Haldane Bert? • UKN

NOW THAT APRIL'S HERE • 1958 • Davidson William • CND

NOW THAT I WAS BORN A WOMAN see **ONNA TO UMARETA KARANYA** • 1934

NOW THAT SUMMER IS GONE • 1938 • Tashlin Frank • ANS • USA

NOW, VOYAGER • 1942 • Rapper Irving • USA

NOW WATCH THE PROFESSOR • 1912 • *Chamberlain Riley* • USA

NOW WE ARE GOING TO GENEVA see **WE ARE ON THE ROAD TO GENEVA** • 1988

NOW WE SHALL BE HAPPY (USA) see **AHORA SEREMOS FELICES** • 1940

NOW WE WILL CALL YOU BROTHER see **AHORA TE VAMOS A LLAMAR HERMANO** • 1971

NOW WE'LL TELL ONE • 1932 • Parrott James • SHT • USA

NOW WE'RE IN THE AIR • 1927 • Strayer Frank • USA

NOW YOU SEE HIM, NOW YOU DON'T • 1972 • Butler Robert • USA

NOW YOU SEE IT • 1948 • Cassell Richard L. • SHT • USA

NOW YOU SEE IT, NOW YOU DON'T • 1967 • Weis Don • TVM • USA

NOW YOU'RE TALKING • 1940 • Carstairs John Paddy • UKN

NOWHERE TO GO • 1958 • Holt Seth • UKN, USA

NOWHERE TO HIDE • 1977 • Starrett Jack • TVM • USA

NOWHERE TO HIDE • 1987 • Azzopardi Mario • CND

NOWHERE TO RUN • 1977 • Dale Holly • DOC • CND

NOWHERE TO RUN • 1978 • Lang Richard • TVM • USA

NOWHERE WITH NUDNIK • 1967 • Deitch Gene • ANS • USA

NOWOROCZNA NOC • 1965 • Zitzman Jerzy • ANM • PLN • NEW YEAR'S NIGHT ○ NEW YEAR'S EVE

NOWY • 1969 • Ziarnik Jerzy • PLN • NEW MAN, THE

NOWY JANKO MUZYKANT • 1960 • Lenica Jan • ANS • PLN • JOHNNY THE MUSICIAN ○ NEW JANKO THE MUSICIAN ○ JANKO THE MUSICIAN ○ IANKO THE MUSICIAN

NOWY JORK, CZWARTA RANO • 1988 • Krauze Krzysztof • PLN • NEW YORK, 4 A.M.

NOWY PRACOWNIK • 1969 • Ziarnik Jerzy • DOC • PLN • NEW WORKER, THE

NOYONER ALO • 1985 • Islam Baby • BNG • LIGHT OF EYES

NOZ • 1967 • Mitrovic Zika • YGS • KNIFE, THE

NOZ W WODZIE • 1961 • Polanski Roman • PLN • KNIFE IN THE WATER (UKN) ○ LONG SUNDAY, THE ○ YOUNG LOVER, THE

NOZOMI NAKI NI ARAZU • 1949 • Saeki • JPN • HOPE IS NOT DEAD YET

NOZZE DI SANGUE • 1941 • Alessandrini Goffredo • ITL

NOZZE D'ORO • 1911 • Maggi Luigi • ITL

NOZZE VAGABONDE • 1936 • Brignone Guido • ITL

N'TE PROMENE DONC PAS TOUTE NUE • 1906 • Feuillade Louis • FRN

NTESI NANA SHEPEN (1) • 1975 • Lamothe Arthur • DOC • CND • ON DISAIT QUE C'ETAIT NOTRE TERRE

NTESI NANA SHEPEN (2) • 1975 • Lamothe Arthur • DOC • CND

NTESI NANA SHEPEN (3) • 1977 • Lamothe Arthur • DOC • CND

NTESI NANA SHEPEN (4) • 1977 • Lamothe Arthur • DOC • CND

Nth • 1970 • Olean Ellen • ANM • USA

Nth COMMANDMENT, THE • 1923 • Borzage Frank • USA • HIGHER LAW, THE (UKN)

NTTURUDU • 1986 • U'Kset Umban • GNB

NU BORGAR LIVET • 1948 • Molander Gustaf • SWD • LIFE BEGINS NOW

NU COMME UN VER • 1933 • Mathot Leon • FRN • HOMME NU, UN ○ TOUT VA BIEN

NU-FAN T'IEN-T'AIO • 1982 • Pai Ching-Jui • TWN • OFFEND THE LAW OF GOD

NU GAR DEN PA DAGMAR • 1972 • Ornbak Henning • DNM

NU GAR JAG TILL MAXIM • 1910 • Magnusson Charles • SWD • GOING TO THE "MAXIM"

NU-TZU HSUEH-HSAIO • 1983 • Li Mei-Mi • TWN • GIRLS' SCHOOL

NU VREAU SA MA INSOR • 1960 • Marcus Manole • RMN • I DON'T WANT TO GET MARRIED

NUAGE ENTRE LES DENTS, UN • 1973 • Pico Marco • FRN

NUAGES FOUS, LES • 1962 • Lacam Henri • ANS • FRN • MAD CLOUDS, THE

NUBA • 1977 • Riefenstahl Leni • FRN

NUBES DE VERANO see **PARABENS, SENHOR VICENTE** • 1954

NUCFU SA'A JAWAZ • 1969 • Wahab Fatin Abdel • EGY • DEMI-HEURE DE MARIAGE, UNE

NUCLEAIRE + DANGER IMMEDIAT • 1977 • Poljinsky Serge • FRN

NUCLEAR CONSPIRACY, THE see **NEUESBERICHT UBER EINE REISE IN EINE STRAHLENDE ZUKUNFT** • 1986

NUCLEAR COUNTDOWN see **TWILIGHT'S LAST GLEAMING** • 1977

NUCLEAR FREEZE • 1986 • Woodland James • DOC • CND

NUCLEAR FUEL WASTE MANAGEMENT • 1979 • Haldane Don • DOC • CND

NUCLEAR TERROR see **GOLDEN RENDEZVOUS** • 1977

NUCLEAR WINTER • 1985 • Woodland James • DOC • CND

NUDA PER SATANA • 1976 • Batzella Luigi • ITL

NUDE AND THE PRUDE, THE • 1969 • *Emerson Film Enteprises* • USA

NUDE BEAST, THE see **BESTIA DESNUDA, LA** • 1968

NUDE BOMB, THE • 1980 • Donner Clive • USA • RETURN OF MAXWELL SMART, THE

NUDE CALDE E PURE • 1965 • Sabel Virgilio, Santhe Lambert • ITL, FRN

NUDE CAMERA see **BUNNY YEAGER'S NUDE CAMERA** • 1963

NUDE HEAT WAVE see **TOUCHABLES, THE** • 1961

NUDE IN A WHITE CAR (USA) see **TOI LE VENIN** • 1958

NUDE IN CHARCOAL • 1963 • Sarno Joe • USA • SINNERS A LA CARTE ○ MODELS IN CHARCOAL ○ SECRETS OF VENUS

NUDE IN HIS POCKET (USA) see **AMOUR DE POCHE, UN** • 1957

NUDE LAS VEGAS see **BUNNY YEAGER'S NUDE LAS VEGAS** • 1964

NUDE ODYSSEY (USA) see **ODISSEA NUDA** • 1961

NUDE PER L'ASSASSINO • 1975 • Bianchi Andrea • ITL

NUDE RESTAURANT, THE • 1967 • Warhol Andy • USA • ANDY WARHOL'S RESTAURANT

NUDE SCRAPBOOK • 1965 • Mahon Barry • USA

NUDE.. SI MUORE • 1968 • Margheriti Antonio • ITL • YOUNG, THE EVIL AND THE SAVAGE, THE (USA) ○ SETTE VERGINI PER IL DIAVOLO ○ NAKED SHE DIES ○ SEVEN VIRGINS FOR THE DEVIL

NUDE VAMPIRE, THE (UKN) see **VAMPIRE NUE, LA** • 1969

NUDEODEON • 1978 • Girolami Marino • ITL

NUDES, INC. • 1964 • Mahon Barry • USA • BROADWAY PIN-UP HONEYS ○ PIN-UP FACTORY, THE ○ PIN-UP CAMERA

NUDES OF ALL NATIONS (USA) see **NUDES OF THE WORLD** • 1961

NUDES OF THE WORLD • 1961 • Miller Arnold Louis • UKN • SUN, THE PLACE AND THE GIRLS, THE ○ NUDES OF ALL NATIONS (USA)

NUDES ON CREDIT see **LOVE NOW.. PAY LATER** • 1966

NUDES ON THE MOON see **NATURE GIRLS ON THE MOON** • 1960

NUDES ON THE ROCKS see **50,000 B.C.(BEFORE CLOTHING)** • 1963

NUDES ON THE RUN see **RUN SWINGER RUN!** • 1967

NUDES ON TIGER REEF • 1965 • Mahon Barry • USA • GIRLS ON TIGER REEF

NUDI COME DIO LI CREO (ITL) see **NACKT WIE GOTT SIE SCHUF** • 1958

NUDI PER VIVERE • 1964 • Montesi Elio • DOC • ITL

NUDIST CAMP see **NATURE CAMP CONFIDENTIAL** • 1961

NUDIST CONFIDENTIAL see **NATURE CAMP CONFIDENTIAL** • 1961

NUDIST PARADISE • 1959 • Saunders Charles • UKN

NUDIST STORY, THE • 1960 • Herrington Ramsey • UKN

NUDITY REQUIRED • 1989 • Bowen John • USA

NUDNIK ON A SHOESTRING • 1967 • Deitch Gene • ANS • USA

NUDNIK ON A SHOWCASE • 1967 • Deitch Gene • ANS • USA

NUDNIK ON THE BEACH • 1966 • Deitch Gene • ANS • USA

NUDNIK ON THE ROOF • 1966 • Deitch Gene • ANS • USA

NUDNIK'S NUDNICKEL • 1967 • Deitch Gene • ANS • USA

NUDO, CRUDO E.. • 1965 • De Feo Francesco, Bolzoni Adriano • DOC • ITL

NUDO DI DONNA • 1982 • Manfredi Nino, Lattuada Alberto (U/c) • ITL • PORTRAIT OF A WOMAN, NUDE (USA)

NUEROS POTOSIS, LOS • Ruiz Jorge • DCS • BLV • NEW POTOSIS, THE

NUESTRA FAMILIA • 1978 • Saenz Carlos • DOC • CRC

NUESTRA OLIMPIADA EN LA HABANA • 1968 • Massip Jose • DOC • CUB

NUESTRA TIERRA DE PAZ • 1940 • Mom Arturo S. • OUR LAND OF PEACE (USA)

NUESTRAS VIDAS • 1949 • Peon Ramon • MXC

NUESTRO AGENTE EN CASABLANCA • 1966 • Demicheli Tulio • SPN, ITL • NOSTRO AGENTE A CASABLANCA, IL (ITL) ○ KILLER LACKS A NAME, THE (USA)

NUESTRO PASO POR HONG-KONG • 1969 • Comeron Luis Jose • SHT • SPN

NUESTROS BUENOS VECINOS • 1965 • Martinez Arturo • MXC

NUESTROS MARIDOS • 1945 • Urruchua Victor • MXC

NUESTROS ODIOSOS MARIDOS • 1960 • Gomez Landero Humberto • MXC

NUEVA CANCION CHILENA • 1973 • Ruiz Raul • SHT • CHL • NEW CHILEAN SONG

NUEVA CRIATURA, UNA • 1971 • Ciurana Francisco G. • SPN • NEW CREATURE, A

NUEVA ESCUELA, LA • 1973 • Fraga Jorge • CUB • NEW SCHOOL, THE

NUEVA FRANCIA, LA • 1972 • Fresan Juan • ARG • NEW FRANCE, THE

NUEVA MARILYN, LA • 1976 • de la Loma Jose Antonio • SPN

NUEVA OLA, LA see **JUVENTUD SE IMPONE, LA** • 1964

NUEVAS AMISTADES • 1964 • Comas Ramon • SPN

NUEVAS AVENTURAS DE ROBIN DE LOS BOSQUES, LAS (SPN) see **MAGNIFICO ROBIN HOOD, IL** • 1970

NUEVE CARTAS A BERTA • 1967 • Patino Basilio Martin • SPN • NINE LETTERS TO BERTA

NUEVITAS • 1968 • Gomez Manuel Octavio • CUB

NUEVO A LA LUNA see **VOYAGE DANS LA LUNE** • 1909

NUEVO AMANECER • 1953 • Gonzalez Rogelio A. • MXC

NUEVO CAUTO • 1965 • Giral Sergio • SHT • CUB

NUEVO EN ESTA PLAZA • 1966 • Lazaga Pedro • SPN

NUEVO MODO DE VIVIR, UN • 1974 • Blanco Javier • DOC • VNZ • NEW WAY OF LIVING, A

NUEVO MUNDO • 1976 • *Conacine* • MXC

NUEVOS ESPANOLES, LOS • 1974 • Bodegas Roberto • SPN • NEW SPANIARDS, THE

NUEVOS EXTRA TERRESTRES, LOS • 1983 • Simon Piquer • SPN • EXTRA TERRESTRIAL VISITORS

NUGGET IN THE ROUGH, A • 1918 • *Hamilton Shorty* • USA

NUGGET JIM'S PARDNER • 1916 • Borzage Frank • SHT • USA

NUGGET NELL • 1919 • Clifton Elmer • USA

NUGGET NELL'S WARD • 1914 • *Frontier* • USA

NUGGET OF GOLD, A • 1909 • *Lubin* • USA

NUHAWWALU SUDD AL-FURAT • 1970 • Amiralai Omar • SHT • SYR • ESSAI SUR UN BARRAGE DANS LA VALLEE DE L'EUPHRATE

NUISANCE, THE • 1920 • Davey Horace • SHT • USA

NUISANCE, THE • 1932 • Conway Jack • USA • ACCIDENTS WANTED (UKN)

NUIT A L'HOTEL, LA • 1931 • Mittler Leo • FRN

NUIT A MEGEVE, UNE • 1953 • Andre Raoul • FRN

NUIT A PEUR DU SOLEIL, LA see **LAILU YAKHAF ASH-SHAMS, AL-** • 1966

NUIT A SAINT-GERMAINE-DES-PRES, UNE • 1949 • Laviron Jean, Savoie Fred • SHT • FRN

NUIT A TABARIN, UNE • 1947 • Lamac Carl • FRN

NUIT AGITEE, UNE • 1897 • Blache Alice • FRN

NUIT AGITEE, UNE • 1908 • Feuillade Louis • FRN

NUIT AGITEE, UNE • 1912 • Linder Max • FRN

NUIT AMERICAINE, LA • 1973 • Truffaut Francois • FRN, ITL • EFFETTO NOTTE (ITL) ○ DAY FOR NIGHT (UKN)

NUIT AU MOULIN-ROUGE, UN • 1957 • Roy Jean-Claude • FRN

NUIT AU PARADIS, UNE • 1931 • Billon Pierre, Lamac Carl • FRN

NUIT AUX BALEARES • 1956 • Mesnier Paul • FRN

NUIT AVEC HORTENSE, LA • 1988 • Chabot Jean • CND

NUIT BENGALI, LA • 1987 • Klotz Nicolas • IND

NUIT BLANCHE • 1948 • Pottier Richard • FRN

NUIT BLANCHE, LA see **DONNE-MOI TES YEUX** • 1943

NUIT BLANCHE ET ROUGE A LEVRES • 1956 • Vernay Robert • FRN • QUELLE SACREE SOIREE!

NUIT BRULE D'UN SONGE, LA • 1988 • Rodde Michel • SWT

NUIT BULGARE, LA • 1970 • Mitrani Michel • FRN • NUIT DES BULGARES, LA

NUIT CLAIRE, LA • 1979 • Hanoun Marcel • FRN, SWT

NUIT COMME LES AUTRES, UNE see **SERVICE DE NUIT** • 1943

NUIT DE CARNAVAL • 1908 • Melies Georges • FRN • NIGHT WITH MASQUERADERS IN PARIS, A (USA)

NUIT DE CARNAVAL • 1922 • Tourjansky Victor • FRN

NUIT DE DECEMBRE • 1939 • Bernhardt Curtis • FRN • HEURE EXQUISE

NUIT DE FOLIES, UNE • 1934 • Cammage Maurice • FRN

NUIT DE LA MORT, LA • 1980 • Delpard Raphael • FRN

NUIT DE LA POESIE 28 MARS 1980 • 1980 • Labrecque Jean-Claude • CND

NUIT DE LA POESIE, LA • 1970 • Labrecque Jean-Claude, Masse J.-P. • DOC • CND

NUIT DE LA REVANCHE, LA • 1924 • Etievant Henri • FRN

NUIT DE LA SAINT-JEAN, LA • 1922 • Saidreau Robert • FRN

NUIT DE LA SAINT-JEAN, LA see **SCHWEIGEN IM WALDE, DAS** • 1929

NUIT DE L'ECLUSIER, LA • 1988 • Rickenbach Franz • SWT • NIGHT OF THE LOCK-KEEPER, THE

NUIT DE MA VIE, UNE see **LAILATUN MIN UMRI** • 1954

NUIT DE MAI • 1934 • Chomette Henri, Ucicky Gustav • FRN

NUIT DE NOCES • 1935 • Monca Georges, Keroul Maurice • FRN

NUIT DE NOCES • 1949 • Jayet Rene • FRN • UNE NUIT DE NOCES ○ WEDDING NIGHT

NUIT DE NOCES see **LAILAT ZAFAF** • 1966

NUIT DE NOEL, LA • 1911 • Machin Alfred • FRN

NUIT DE SAINT-GERMAINE-DES-PRES, LA • 1977 • Swaim Bob • FRN

NUIT DE SIBYLLE, LA • 1946 • Paulin Jean-Paul • FRN

NUIT DE VARENNES, LA (FRN) see **MONDO MIOVO, IL** • 1982

NUIT D'EPOUVANTE, UNE • 1911 • Jasset Victorin • FRN

NUIT DES ADIEUX, LES • 1965 • Dreville Jean • FRN, USS

NUIT DES BULGARES, LA see **NUIT BULGARE, LA** • 1970

NUIT DES CARESSES, LA • 1975 • Duda Jacques • FRN

NUIT DES ESPIONS, LA • 1959 • Hossein Robert • FRN, ITL • NOTTE DELLE SPIE, LA (ITL) ○ NIGHT ENCOUNTER (USA) ○ DOUBLE AGENTS, THE ○ NIGHT OF THE SPIES, THE

NUIT DES GENERAUX, LA (FRN) see **NIGHT OF THE GENERALS, THE** • 1966

NUIT DES PETRIFIES, LA • 1977 • Brismee Jean • FRN, BLG

NUIT DES TRAQUES, LA • 1959 • Bernard-Roland • FRN

NUIT DES TRAQUES, LA • 1979 • Rollin Jean • FRN

NUIT D'ESPAGNE • 1931 • de La Falaise Henri • FRN

NUIT D'ESPAGNE see **MARIA DE LA NUIT** • 1936

NUIT DOCILE • 1987 • Gilles Guy • FRN

NUIT D'OR • 1976 • Moati Serge • FRN, FRG

NUIT DU 3, LA • 1925 • Vorins Henri • FRN

NUIT DU 11 SEPTEMBRE, LA • 1923 • Bernard-Deschamps • FRN

NUIT DU 13, LA • 1921 • Fescourt Henri • FRN

NUIT DU CARREFOUR, LA • 1932 • Renoir Jean • FRN • NIGHT AT THE CROSSROADS

NUIT DU CIMITIERE, LA • 1973 • Rollin Jean • FRN • NIGHT OF THE CEMETERY, THE ○ CEMETERY NIGHT

NUIT DU TREIZE, LA see **MYSTERE A SHANGAI** • 1950

NUIT DU VOLEUR DE CORBEAU, LA • 1974 • Franju Georges • MTV • FRN

NUIT ELECTRIQUE, LA • 1930 • Deslaw Eugene • FRN • NUITS ELECTRIQUES, LES

NUIT EN AMERIQUE, UNE • 1974 • Chabot Jean • CND

NUIT ENSOLEILLEE, LA • 1981 • Segal Patrick • DOC • FRN

NUIT EST A NOUS, LA • 1929 • Roussell Henry, Froelich Carl • FRN • NIGHT IS OURS, THE

NUIT EST A NOUS, LA • 1953 • Stelli Jean • FRN

NUIT EST MON ROYAUME, LA • 1951 • Lacombe Georges • FRN • NIGHT IS MY KINGDOM

NUIT EST UNE SORCIERE, LA • 1959 • Martin Marcel • SHT • FRN • NIGHT IS A SORCERESS, THE

NUIT ET BROUILLARD • 1955 • Resnais Alain • FRN • NIGHT AND FOG (UKN)

NUIT FANTASTIQUE, LA • 1941 • L'Herbier Marcel • FRN • FANTASTIC NIGHT (USA) ○ TOMBEAU DE MELIES, LE

NUIT INFIDELE, LA • 1968 • d'Ormesson Antoine • FRN • UNFAITHFUL NIGHT (UKN)

NUIT, LA (FRN) see **NOTTE, LA** • 1961

NUIT LA PLUS CHAUDE, LA • 1968 • Pecas Max • FRN • NIGHT OF THE THREE LOVERS, THE (USA) ○ NIGHT OF THE OUTRAGES (UKN)

NUIT LA PLUS LONGUE, LA see **ENFER DANS LA PEAU, L'** • 1965

NUIT MERVEILLEUSE, LA • 1940 • Paulin Jean-Paul • FRN

NUIT NOIRE A CALCUTTA • 1964 • Karmitz Marin • SHT • FRN • NUIT NOIRE, CALCUTTA

NUIT NOIRE, CALCUTTA see **NUIT NOIRE A CALCUTTA** • 1964

NUIT OCCIDENTALE, LA • 1981 • Correa Joao • BLG, NTH

NUIT PORTE JARRETELLES, LA • 1984 • Thevenet Virginie • FRN

NUIT REVEE POUR UN POISSON BANAL, UNE • 1980 • Guillou Bernard • FRN

NUIT S'ACHEVE, LA • 1949 • Mere Pierre • FRN

NUIT SILENCIEUSE • 1936 • Delacroix Rene • FRN

NUIT SUR LA MONTE CHAUVE • 1934 • Alexeieff Alexandre, Parker Claire • ANS • FRN • NIGHT ON BALD MOUNTAIN, A (USA) ○ NIGHT ON A BARE MOUNTAIN, A

NUIT TERRIBLE, UNE • 1896 • Melies Georges • FRN • TERRIBLE NIGHT, A

NUIT, TOUS LES CHATS SONT GRIS, LA • 1977 • Zingg Gerard • FRN • AT NIGHT ALL CATS ARE GRAY

NUIT TRAGIQUE, UNE • 1916 • Burguet Charles • FRN

NUIT TRANSFIGUREE, LA see **DIABLE AU COEUR, LE** • 1977

NUITS ANDALOUSES • 1953 • Cloche Maurice, Blasco Ricardo • FRN, SPN • NOCHES ANDALUZAS (SPN)

NUITS BLANCHES, LES see **PEPE LE MOKO** • 1936

NUITS BLANCHES DE SAINT-PETERSBOURG, LES • 1937 • Dreville Jean • FRN
NUITS BLANCHES (FRN) see **NOTTI BIANCHE, LE** • 1957
NUITS D'ALERTE • 1945 • Mathot Leon • FRN
NUITS D'AMERIQUE, LES (FRN) see **AMERICA DI NOTTE** • 1961
NUITS DE BAL • 1939 • Litvak Anatole • FRN
NUITS DE CABIRIA, LES (FRN) see **NOTTI DI CABIRIA, LE** • 1957
NUITS DE FEU • 1937 • L'Herbier Marcel • FRN • LIVING CORPSE, THE (USA) ○ NIGHTS OF FIRE
NUITS DE LA PLEINE LUNE, LA • 1984 • Rohmer Eric • FRN • FULL MOON IN PARIS (UKN)
NUITS DE L'EPOUVANTE, LES (FRN) see **LAMA NEL CORPO, LA** • 1966
NUITS DE LUCRECE BORGIA, LES (FRN) see **NOTTI DI LUCREZIA BORGIA, LE** • 1959
NUITS DE MONTMARTRE, LES • 1955 • Franchi Pierre • FRN
NUITS DE PAPA, LES see **SERVICE DE NUIT** • 1931
NUITS DE PARIS • 1951 • Baum Ralph • FRN • PARIS NIGHTS (USA)
NUITS DE PARIS see **MIRAGES DE PARIS** • 1932
NUITS DE PIGALLE • 1958 • Jaffe Georges • FRN
NUITS DE PORT-SAID, LES • 1931 • Mittler Leo • FRN
NUITS DE PRINCES • 1929 • L'Herbier Marcel • FRN
NUITS DE PRINCES • 1937 • von Strischewski Wladimir • FRN
NUITS DE RASPOUTINE, LES • 1960 • Chenal Pierre • FRN, ITL • NIGHT THEY KILLED RASPUTIN, THE (USA) ○ NIGHTS OF RASPUTIN (UKN) ○ ULTIMO ZAR, L' (ITL) ○ GIANT MONSTER ○ LAST CZAR, THE
NUITS DE VENISE • 1931 • Billon Pierre, Wiene Robert • FRN • HUIT JOURS DE BONHEUR
NUITS D'ETE EN VILLE • 1990 • Deville Michel • FRN
NUITS D'ORGIE • Baudricourt Michel • FRN
NUITS ELECTRIQUES, LES see **NUIT ELECTRIQUE, LA** • 1930
NUITS ET BARREAUX see **LAILUN WA QIDHBAN** • 1972
NUITS MOSCOVITES, LES • 1934 • Granowsky Alexis • FRN
NUITS ROUGES see **HOMME SANS VISAGE, L'** • 1974
NUITS SAN FIN • 1946 • Severac Jacques • FRN
NUITS SEREINES see **SAJA' AL-LAYL** • 1947
NUITS SUEDOISES • 1976 • Roy Jean-Claude • FRN
NUKE 'EM HIGH see **CLASS OF NUKE 'EM HIGH** • 1986
NUKIASHI SASHIASHI • 1934 • Yoshimura Kozaburo • JPN • SNEAKING
NUKIE'S LULLABY • 1987 • Amitay Jonathan • ANS • CND
NUKKAD • 1987 • Mirza Saeed • IND
NUKKEKAUPPIAS JA KAUNIS LILITH • 1955 • Witikka Jack • FNL • DOLL MERCHANT AND THE BEAUTIFUL LILITH, THE
NULLARBOR HIDEOUT • 1964 • Burstall Tim • SHT • ASL
NUM MAR DE MOLICO • 1965 • Tropa Alfredo • SHT • PRT
NUMAZU HEIGAKKU • 1939 • Imai Tadashi • JPN • NUMAZU MILITARY ACADEMY
NUMAZU MILITARY ACADEMY see **NUMAZU HEIGAKKU** • 1939
NUMBER 1 • 1939-47 • Smith Harry • SHT • USA
NUMBER 2 • 1940-42 • Smith Harry • SHT • USA
NUMBER 3 • 1942-47 • Smith Harry • SHT • USA
NUMBER 4 • 1950 • Smith Harry • SHT • USA
NUMBER 5 • 1950 • Smith Harry • SHT • USA • CIRCULAR TENSIONS
NUMBER 6 • 1951 • Smith Harry • SHT • USA
NUMBER 7 • 1951 • Smith Harry • SHT • USA
NUMBER 8 • 1954 • Smith Harry • SHT • USA
NUMBER 9 • 1954 • Smith Harry • SHT • USA
NUMBER 10 • 1956 • Smith Harry • SHT • USA
NUMBER 10: DIZZY see **SECRET LIVES OF THE BRITISH PRIME MINISTERS: DISRAELI, THE** • 1981
NUMBER 11 • 1956 • Smith Harry • SHT • USA • MIRROR ANIMATIONS
NUMBER 12 • 1943-58 • Smith Harry • USA • HEAVEN & EARTH MAGIC FEATURE ○ MAGIC FEATURE, THE
NUMBER 13 • 1920 • *Franey William* • SHT • USA
NUMBER 13 • 1962 • Smith Harry • ANM • USA
NUMBER 13, WESTBOUND • 1916 • Beal Frank • SHT • USA
NUMBER 14 • 1964-65 • Smith Harry • SHT • USA • LATE SUPERIMPOSITIONS
NUMBER 15 • 1965-66 • Smith Harry • USA
NUMBER 16 • 1967 • Smith Harry • SHT • USA • WOODMAN'S DREAM, THE
NUMBER 17 • 1920 • Beranger George A. • USA
NUMBER 96 • 1974 • Benardos Peter • ASL
NUMBER, THE • 1979 • Boulting Roy • USA
NUMBER, THE see **NOUMERO, TO** • 1978
NUMBER III see **III-ES, A** • 1919
NUMBER ONE • 1916 • *Drew* • SHT • USA
NUMBER ONE • 1969 • Gries Tom • USA • PRO
NUMBER ONE • 1973 • Buffardi Gianni • ITL
NUMBER ONE • 1984 • Blair Les • UKN
NUMBER ONE GUN • 1989 • Shonteff Lindsay • UKN
NUMBER ONE OF THE SECRET SERVICE see **NO.1 OF THE SECRET SERVICE** • 1978
NUMBER ONE QUEEN see **PATTATHU RANI** • 1967
NUMBER ONE WITH A BULLET • 1987 • Smight Jack • USA
NUMBER PLEASE? • 1916 • MacMackin Archer • USA
NUMBER PLEASE! • 1920 • Newmeyer Fred, Taylor Sam • SHT • USA
NUMBER PLEASE • 1931 • King George • UKN
NUMBER PLEASE see **WHAT A NIGHT!** • 1928
NUMBER PLEASE see **NOMMER ASSEBLIEF** • 1981
NUMBER SEVENTEEN • 1928 • von Bolvary Geza • UKN
NUMBER SEVENTEEN • 1932 • Hitchcock Alfred • UKN
NUMBER SIX • 1962 • Tronson Robert • UKN
NUMBER THIRTEEN • 1922 • Hitchcock Alfred • UKN • MRS PEABODY
NUMBERED MEN • 1930 • LeRoy Mervyn • USA • JAILBREAK
NUMBERED WOMAN • 1938 • Brown Karl • USA • PRIVATE NURSE (UKN)
NUMBERS see **WSZYSTKO JEST LICZBA** • 1967
NUMBSKULL EMPTYBROOK IN SPAIN see **UUNO TURHAPURO ESPANJASSA** • 1985
NUMBSKULL EMPTYBROOK IN THE ARMY see **UUNO TURHAPURO ARMEIJAN LEIVISSA** • 1984
NUMBSKULL EMPTYBROOK, IRONMONGER see **RAUTAKAUPPIAS UUNO TURHAPURO** • 1978
NUMBSKULL EMPTYBROOK LOSES HIS MEMORY see **UUNO TURHAPURO MENETTAA MUISTINSA** • 1982
NUMBSKULL EMPTYBROOK MOVES BACK TO THE COUNTRYSIDE see **UUNO TURHAPURO MUUTTAA MAALLE** • 1986
NUMBSKULL EMPTYBROOK'S MARITAL CRISIS see **UUNO TURHAPURON AVIOKRIISI** • 1981
NUMBSKULL EMPTYBROOK'S MEMORY SLOWLY COMES BACK see **UUNO TURHAPURON MUISTI PALAILEE PATKITTAIN** • 1983
NUMERO 121, IL • 1917 • Ghione Emilio • ITL
NUMERO DEUX • 1975 • Godard Jean-Luc, Mieville Anne-Marie • FRN
NUMERO ZERO • 1971 • Eustache Jean • FRN
NUMEROS ZERO • 1981 • Depardon Raymond • DOC • FRN
NUMMISUUTARIT • 1923 • Karu Erkki • FNL • VILLAGE SHOEMAKERS, THE
NUN, THE • 1907 • Fitzhamon Lewin • UKN
NUN, THE (USA) see **SUZANNE SIMONIN, LA RELIGIEUSE DE DIDEROT** • 1965
NUN AND THE COMMISSAR, THE see **OPATICA I KOMESAR** • 1968
NUN AND THE DEVIL, THE (UKN) see **MONACHE DI SANT'ARCANGELO, LE** • 1973
NUN AND THE SERGEANT, THE • 1962 • Adreon Franklin • USA
NUN AT THE CROSSROADS, A (USA) see **ENCRUCIJADA PARA UNA MONJA** • 1967
NUN, MARRIED WOMAN, VIRGIN AND MARTYR see **MONJA, CASADA, VIRGEN Y MARTIR** • 1935
NUN OF MONZA, THE see **MONACA DI MONZA, LA** • 1969
NUNAL SA TUBIG • Bernal Ishmael • PHL • SPECK IN THE WATER
NUN'ALVARES, HEROI E SANTO • 1947 • Coelho Jose Adolfo • SHT • PRT
NUNCA DEBIERON AMARSE • 1951 • Peon Ramon • MXC
NUNCA EN HORAS DE CLASE • 1978 • de la Loma Jose Antonio • SPN
NUNCA ES DEMASIADO TARDE • 1956 • Coll Julio • SPN
NUNCA ES TARDE • 1977 • de Arminan Jaime • SPN • URSULA
NUNCA ES TARDE PARA AMAR • 1952 • Davison Tito • MXC
NUNCA ESTUVE EN VIENA • 1987 • Larreta Antonio • ARG • I NEVER WAS IN VIENNA
NUNCA FOMOS TAO FELIZES • 1984 • Salles Murilo • BRZ • WE HAVE NEVER BEEN SO HAPPY
NUNCA ME HAGAN ESO • 1956 • Baledon Rafael • MXC
NUNCA NOS RENDIREMOS • 1986 • Somarriba Fernando • NCR • WE'LL NEVER SURRENDER
NUNCA PASA NADA • 1963 • Bardem Juan Antonio • SPN • NOTHING EVER HAPPENS (USA)
NUN'S KISS, THE see **NONNE KYSSET** • 1968
NUN'S NIGHT, THE see **NOC NEVESTY** • 1967
NUNS ON THE RUN • 1989 • Lynn Jonathan • UKN
NUN'S STORY, THE • 1959 • Zinnemann Fred • USA
NUNTA DE PIATRA • 1972 • Veroiu Mircea, Pita Dan • RMN • STONE WEDDING, THE
NUNZIO • 1978 • Williams Paul • USA
NUORA, LA • 1916 • Ghione Emilio • ITL
NUORA GIOVANE, LA • 1976 • Russo Luigi • ITL
NUORENA NUKKUNUT • 1937 • Tulio Teuvo • FNL • SILJA – FALLEN ASLEEP WHEN YOUNG
NUORI LUOTSI • 1922 • Karu Erkki • FNL
NUORUUTENI SAVOTAT • 1988 • Niskanen Mikko • FNL • LUMBERCAMP TALES
NUOVE AVVENTURE DEL SCERIFFO EXTRA-TERRESTRE, LE • 1980 • Lupo Michele • ITL • CHISSA PERCHE CAPITANO TUTTO A ME ○ WHY DID YOU PICK ON ME?
NUOVI ANGELI, I • 1962 • Gregoretti Ugo • ITL • NEW ANGELS, THE
NUOVI BARBARI, I • 1983 • Castellari Enzo G. • ITL • WARRIORS OF THE WASTELAND (USA) ○ NEW BARBARIANS, THE
NUOVI MOSTRI, I • 1977 • Monicelli Mario, Risi Dino, Scola Ettore • ITL • VIVA ITALIA (USA) ○ NEW MONSTERS, THE
NUOVO CINEMA PARADISO • 1988 • Tornatore Giuseppe • ITL, FRN • NEW PARADISE CINEMA
NUPITAE • 1969 • Broughton James • SHT • USA
NUR AM RHEIN • 1930 • Mack Max • FRG
NUR AUF DEN BERGEN WOHNT DAS GLUCK • 1923 • *Sing-Film* • FRG
NUR DER NEBEL IST GRAU • 1965 • Menegoz Robert • FRG • ONLY FOG IS GREY
...NUR DER WIND • 1961 • Umgelter Fritz • FRG
NUR DU • 1930 • Wolff Willi • FRG
NUR EIN DIENER • 1919 • Lund Erik • FRG
NUR EIN GASSENMADEL see **NACHTGESTALTEN** • 1929
...NUR EIN KOMODIANT • 1935 • Engel Erich • AUS
NUR EIN SCHMETTERLING • 1918 • Raffay Iwa • FRG
NUR EINE FRAU • 1958 • Balhaus Carl • GDR
NUR EINE LUGE • 1915 • Mack Max • FRG • COLOMBINE
NUR EINE NACHT • 1922 • Walther-Fein Rudolf • FRG
NUR EINE NACHT • 1950 • Kirchhoff Fritz • FRG
NUR EINE TANZERIN • 1926 • Morel-Molander Olof • FRG
NUR EINE ZIRKUSREITERIN ODER DIE GALAVORSTELLUNG DES ZIRKUS CASARE MARSELLI • 1919 • Beck Ludwig • FRG
NUR NICH AUFREGEN • 1953 • Robbeling Harald • FRG
NUR NICHT HEIRATEN • 1915 • Biebrach Rudolf • FRG
NUR NICHT WEICH WERDEN, SUSANNE! • 1934 • von Cserepy Arzen • FRG
NUR TOTE ZEUGEN SCHWEIGEN • 1963 • Martin Eugenio • FRG, SPN, ITL • IPNOSI (ITL) ○ DUMMY OF DEATH ○ HYPNOSIS (USA) ○ HIPNOSIS ○ ONLY THE DEAD ARE SILENT
NUR UM TAUSEND DOLLAR • 1918 • Meinert Rudolf • FRG
NUR ZUM SPASS NUR ZUM SPIEL see **KALEIDOSKOP VALESKA GERT -NUR ZUM SPASS NUR ZUM SPIEL** • 1977
NUREBA • 1967 • Sakao Masanao • JPN • LOVE SCENE
NUREGAMI BOTAN • 1961 • Tanaka Tokuzo • JPN • FANTASTICO
NUREGAMI GONPACHI • 1954 • Osone Tatsuo • JPN
NUREGAMI KENKA TABI • 1960 • Mori Issei • JPN
NUREGAMI SANDO GASA • 1959 • Tanaka Tokuzo • JPN • LORD AND THE GAMBLER, THE
NUREMBERG • 1961 • *Bonnell Lee* • USA
NUREMBERG see **JUDGMENT OF THE PEOPLE** • 1947
NUREMBERG TRIALS, THE (UKN) see **NURNBERGER PROZESS, DER** • 1958
NUREMBURG TRIALS • 1946 • Lorentz Pare • DOC • USA
NUREN FENGQING HUA • 1985 • Tang Jiming • HKG • HONG KONG GRAFFITI
NUREN XIN • 1985 • Guan Jinpeng • HKG • WOMEN
NURETA AIBIKI • 1967 • Maeda Yoichi • JPN • ILLICIT RENDEZVOUS
NURETA FUTARI • 1968 • Masumura Yasuzo • JPN • ONE DAY AT SUMMER'S END
NURETA YOKUJO • 1972 • Kumashiro Tatsumi • JPN • DRENCHED PASSION
NURI BEY MAFIAYA KARSI • 1968 • Aslan Mehmet • TRK • NURI BEY VS. THE MAFIA
NURI BEY VS. THE MAFIA see **NURI BEY MAFIAYA KARSI** • 1968
NURI THE FLEA see **PIRE NURI** • 1968
NURNBERG CAMPAIGN, THE see **SPANILA JIZDA** • 1963
NURNBERGER PROZESS, DER • 1958 • von Podmanitzky Felix • DOC • FRG • HITLER'S EXECUTIONERS (USA) ○ NUREMBERG TRIALS, THE (UKN) ○ EXECUTIONERS, THE ○ NAZI CRIMES AND PUNISHMENT
NURSE • 1980 • Rich David Lowell • TVM • USA
NURSE, THE • 1912 • Brenon Herbert • *Edison* • USA
NURSE, THE • 1912 • Powers P. A. • USA
NURSE, THE • 1921 • Paul Fred • UKN
NURSE, THE see **INFERMIERA, L'** • 1975
NURSE AND MARTYR • 1915 • Moran Percy • UKN
NURSE AND THE COUNTERFEITER, THE • 1914 • *Kalem* • USA
NURSE AT MULBERRY BEND, THE • 1913 • *Joyce Alice* • USA
NURSE BROWN see **ZUSTER BROWN** • 1921
NURSE EDITH CAVELL • 1939 • Wilcox Herbert • USA
NURSE FROM BROOKLYN • 1938 • Simon S. Sylvan • USA
NURSE-MADE • 1970 • *Distripix Inc.* • USA
NURSE MAID, THE • 1932 • *Iwerks Ub (P)* • ANS • USA
NURSE MARJORIE • 1920 • Taylor William D. • USA
NURSE MATES • 1940 • Fleischer Dave • ANS • USA
NURSE OF AN ACHING HEART, THE • 1917 • Mayo Archie • SHT • USA
NURSE ON WHEELS • 1963 • Thomas Gerald • UKN
NURSE SHERRI • 1978 • Adamson Al • USA • BEYOND THE LIVING ○ HOSPITAL OF TERROR
NURSE SISI • 1947 • *Sircar B. N. (P)* • IND
NURSE TO MEET YA • 1955 • Sparber I. • ANS • USA
NURSE TO YOU • 1935 • Parrott Charles, Moffitt Jefferson • SHT • USA
NURSE WILL MAKE IT BETTER see **DEVIL'S WEB** • 1974
NURSEMAID WHO DISAPPEARED, THE • 1939 • Woods Arthur • UKN
NURSEMAID'S DREAM, THE • 1908 • Fitzhamon Lewin • UKN
NURSEMAID'S SURPRISE, THE • 1898 • *Riley Brothers* • UKN
NURSERY CHAIRS • 1928 • Miller Frank • UKN
NURSERY CRIMES • 1943 • Geiss Alec • ANS • USA
NURSERY FAVORITES • 1913 • *Edison* • USA
NURSERY ISLAND • 1936 • Field Mary • UKN
NURSERY RHYME MYSTERIES • 1943 • Cahn Edward L. • USA
NURSERY RHYMES • 1915 • Batley Ethyle • UKN
NURSERY RHYMES see **RIKADLA** • 1949
NURSERY SCANDAL • 1932 • Foster John, Bailey Harry • ANS • USA
NURSERY SCHOOL see **MATERNELLE, LA** • 1933
NURSES see **SESTRICKY** • 1983
NURSES, THE • 1971 • *Matson Maggie* • USA
NURSES ATTENDING THE WOUNDED • 1899 • Ashe Robert • UKN • NURSES ON THE BATTLEFIELD
NURSE'S BROTHER, THE • 1900 • *Mitchell & Kenyon* • UKN
NURSE'S DEVOTION, A • 1912 • Speer Walter Harold • UKN
NURSES OF THE 407TH • 1982 • Kendrick Tony • USA
NURSES ON THE BATTLEFIELD see **NURSES ATTENDING THE WOUNDED** • 1899
NURSES ON THE JOB • 1973 • Boos Walter • FRG
NURSE'S SECRET, THE • 1941 • Smith Noel • USA
NURSIE AND KNIGHT see **NURSIE AND THE KNIGHT** • 1912
NURSIE AND THE KNIGHT • 1912 • *Thanhouser* • USA • NURSIE AND KNIGHT
NURSIE! NURSIE! • 1916 • Butler Alexander • UKN
NURSING A VIPER • 1909 • Griffith D. W. • USA
NURSING SISTERS see **SESTRICKY** • 1983
NURSING THE BABY • 1897 • Smith G. A. • UKN
NUSSKNACKER • 1965 • Liesendahl Heinz • FRG • NUTCRACKER, THE (UKN)
NUSUMARETA KOI • 1951 • Ichikawa Kon • JPN • STOLEN LOVE
NUSUMARETA YOKUJO • 1958 • Imamura Shohei • JPN • STOLEN DESIRE, THE
NUT, THE • 1921 • Reed Theodore • USA
NUT BREAD see **OREKHOVYI KHLEB** • 1980
NUT FACTORY, THE • 1933 • Davis Mannie • ANS • USA
NUT FARM, THE • 1935 • Brown Melville • USA
NUT STUFF • 1918 • Hotaling Arthur D. • SHT • USA
NUTCASE • 1980 • Donaldson Roger • NZL
NUTCRACKER • 1982 • Kawadri Anwar • UKN • NUTCRACKER SWEET (USA)
NUTCRACKER see **NUTCRACKER FANTASY** • 1979
NUTCRACKER, THE • Crommie Dave • USA
NUTCRACKER, THE • 1926 • Ingraham Lloyd • USA • YOU CAN'T FOOL YOUR WIFE
NUTCRACKER, THE • 1953 • Frankel Cyril • UKN
NUTCRACKER, THE • 1986 • Ballard Carroll • USA • NUTCRACKER, THE MOTION PICTURE
NUTCRACKER, THE • 1990 • Schibli Paul • ANM • USA
NUTCRACKER, THE see **DZIADEK DO ORZECHOW** • 1967
NUTCRACKER, THE (UKN) see **NUSSKNACKER** • 1965
NUTCRACKER FANTASIES see **NUTCRACKER FANTASY** • 1979
NUTCRACKER FANTASY • 1979 • Nakamura Takeo • ANM • USA • NUTCRACKER FANTASIES ○ NUTCRACKER
NUTCRACKER SUITE • 1925 • Fleischer Dave • ANS • USA
NUTCRACKER SUITE, THE • 1970 • Webb Robert • UKN

NUTCRACKER SWEET (USA) see **NUTCRACKER** • 1982
NUTCRACKER, THE MOTION PICTURE see **NUTCRACKER, THE** • 1986
NUTRIA, LA • 1971 • Carretero Amaro • ANS • SPN • OTTER, THE
NUTRIA MAN see **TERROR IN THE SWAMP** • 1985
NUTRITION AND GROWTH • 1985 • Beaudry Michel • MTV • CND
NUTS • 1987 • Ritt Martin • USA
NUTS AND JOLTS • 1929 • Lantz Walter • ANS • USA
NUTS AND NOODLES • 1918 • Davis James • SHT • USA
NUTS AND VOLTS • 1964 • Freleng Friz • ANS • USA
NUTS, BOLTS AND BEDROOM SPRINGS • 1975 • Young Gary • ASL
NUTS IN MAY • 1917 • Williamson Robin E. • USA
NUTS IN MAY • 1976 • Leigh Mike • MTV • UKN
NUT'S PROGRESS, A • 1915 • *Zenith Films* • USA
NUTSY YEARS see **SULUDE GODINE** • 1989
NUTTIE COOKIES • 1960 • Learner Keith • UKN
NUTTY AND HIS FATHER • 1914 • *Eclair* • USA
NUTTY BUT NICE • 1940 • White Jules • SHT • USA
NUTTY DELIVERS A MESSAGE TO GARCIA • 1914 • *Eclair* • USA
NUTTY HAS A ROMANCE • 1913 • *Eclair* • USA
NUTTY HAS BIG IDEAS • 1913 • *Eclair* • USA
NUTTY IS DEAD -LONG LIVE NUTTY • 1913 • *Eclair* • USA
NUTTY KNITTERS • 1917 • De Vonde Chester M. • SHT • USA
NUTTY, NAUGHTY CHATEAU (USA) see **CHATEAU EN SUEDE** • 1963
NUTTY NETWORK, THE • 1939 • Davis Mannie • ANS • USA
NUTTY NEWS • 1942 • Clampett Robert • ANS • USA
NUTTY NOTES • 1929 • Lantz Walter, Nolan William • ANS • USA
NUTTY PINE CANYON • 1942 • Lovy Alex • ANS • USA
NUTTY PROFESSOR, THE • 1963 • Lewis Jerry • USA
NUTTY'S GAME • 1912 • *Lubin* • USA
NUUK 250 AR • 1979 • Roos Jorgen • DOC • DNM
NUVOLA DI POLVERE.. UN GRIDO DI MORTE.. ARRIVA SARTANA, UNA • 1970 • Carnimeo Giuliano • ITL, SPN
NUZHNY CHELOVYEK • 1967 • Dolinov B. • USS • NECESSARY MAN, A
NVV CONGRES • 1929 • Ivens Joris • SHT • NTH • CONGRESS DER VAKVEREEINIGINGEN
NY I MOLODEZH! • 1970 • Chkheidze Rezo • USS • OUR YOUTH!
NYA HYSS AV EMIL I LONNEBERGA • 1972 • Hellbom Olle • SWD, FRG
NYA LENSMANNEN, DEN • 1926 • Sinding Leif • NRW
NYAMANTON • 1986 • Sissoko Cheikh Oumar • MLI • LESSONS FROM THE GARBAGE
NYAN-NYAN-NYAN-HOI • 1940 • Akutagawa • JPN • FESTIVAL OF NYAN-NYAN-NYAN
NYAR A HEGYEN • 1967 • Bacso Peter • HNG • SUMMER ON THE HILL
NYARON EGYSZERU • 1963 • Bacso Peter • HNG • NO PROBLEMS IN SUMMER
NYARSAFTON PA SKANSKA SLATTEN • 1961 • Troell Jan • DOC • SWD • NEW YEAR'S EVE ON THE SKANE PLAINS
NYBYGGARNA see **INVANDRARNA** • 1970
NYCKELN OCH RINGEN • 1947 • Henrikson Anders • SWD • KEY AND THE RING, THE
NYE MOZHET BYT! • 1976 • Gaidai Leonid • USS • IT CAN'T BE! ○ IMPOSSIBLE
NYE RAZUM, A STRASTI PRAVYAT MIROM • 1916 • Boleslawski Richard • USS
NYE SAMY UDACHNY DYEN • 1967 • Yegorov Yuri • USS • NOT THE BEST OF DAYS
NYE VENNER • 1956 • Henning-Jensen Astrid • SHT • DNM
NYE ZABUD.. STANTSIYA LUGOVAYA • 1967 • Kurikhin Nikita, Menaker Leonid • USS • DON'T FORGET.. THE LUGOVAYA STATION ○ NE ZABUD.. STANTZIYA LUGOVAGA
NYET I DA • 1967 • Koltsaty Arkadi • USS • NO AND YES
NYETT LIF • 1983 • Bertelsson Thrainn • ICL • NEW LIFE
NYEZHNOST see **NIEJNOSTI** • 1968
NYGIFTA • 1941 • Wallen Sigurd • SWD • NEWLY MARRIED
NYHAVN 17 • 1933 • Schneevoigt George • DNM
NYI BLORONG • 1983 • Gautama Sisworo • INN • SNAKE QUEEN, THE
NYITANY • 1965 • Vadasz Janos • HNG
NYITOTT ABLAK • 1988 • Bednai Nandor, Bodrogi Gyule • HNG • OPEN WINDOW
NYLON NETS • 1963 • Poloka Gennadi, Shenghelia Levan • USS
NYLON NOOSE, THE (USA) see **NYLONSCHLINGE, DIE** • 1963
NYLONSCHLINGE, DIE • 1963 • Zehetgruber Rudolf • DNM, SWT • NYLON NOOSE, THE (USA)
NYMPH, THE • 1916 • *Gilroy Barbara* • SHT • USA
NYMPH OF THE FOOTHILLS, THE • 1918 • Thompson Frederick A. • USA
NYMPH OF THE WAVES • 1903 • *Bartho Cathrina* • USA
NYMPHETTES, LES • 1961 • Zaphiratos Henri-T. • FRN • FIRST TASTE OF LOVE (USA)
NYMPHO • 1965 • Nicola Alfredo • USA
NYMPHO see **WOMAN'S URGE, A** • 1965
NYMPHO, THE (UKN) see **ANDREA -WIE EIN BLATT AUF NACKTER HAUT** • 1968
NYMPHO GIRLS see **DREI SCHWEDINNEN AUF DER REEPERBAHN** • 1980
NYMPHO SUPERSTARS, THE see **FIRST NUDIE MUSICAL, THE** • 1976
NYMPHO WEREWOLF • 1970 • PRT
NYMPHOMANES, LES • 1979 • Bernard-Aubert Claude • FRN
NYMPHS see **NYMPHS ANONYMOUS** • 1968
NYMPHS, THE • 1967 • Keatering Michael • UKN
NYMPHS AND NUISANCES • 1920 • Jones Grover • SHT • USA
NYMPHS ANONYMOUS • 1968 • Conde Manuel S. • USA • NYMPHS
NYMPHS' BATH, THE • 1909 • *Gaumont* • FRN
NYOBO FUNSHITSU • 1928 • Ozu Yasujiro • JPN • WIFE LOST
NYOBO GAKKO • 1961 • Inoue Umeji • JPN • REFRESHER COURSE FOR WIVES
NYOBO SEIFUKU • 1933 • Yamamoto Kajiro • JPN • CONQUEST OF A WIFE
NYOCADIK SZABAD MAJUS 1, A • 1952 • Jancso Miklos • SHT • HNG • EZERKILENCSZAZOTVENKETTO ○ EIGHTH FREE MAY DAY, THE
NYOKA AND THE LOST SECRET OF HIPPOCRATES • 1942 • Witney William • USA • NYOKA AND THE TIGER MAN ○ NYOKA AND THE TIGERMEN
NYOKA AND THE TIGER MAN see **NYOKA AND THE LOST SECRET OF HIPPOCRATES** • 1942
NYOKA AND THE TIGERMEN see **NYOKA AND THE LOST SECRET OF HIPPOCRATES** • 1942
NYOKO • 1960 • Masumura Yasuzo • JPN
NYOLCVAN HUSZAR • 1978 • Sara Sandor • HNG • 80 HUSZARS ○ EIGHTY HUSSARS
NYOM NELKUL • 1983 • Fabry Peter • HNG • NO CLUES
NYONIN AISHU • 1937 • Naruse Mikio • JPN • NEW GRIEF ○ WOMAN'S SORROWS, A
NYONIN MANDARA • 1933 • Ito Daisuke • JPN
NYORDNING PA SJOGARDA • 1944 • Hildebrand Weyler • SWD • NEW ORDER AT SJOGARDA
NYT LEGETOJ • 1977 • Ringaard Peter D. • DNM • NEW TOYS
NYUGATI OVEZET • 1954 • Varkonyi Zoltan • HNG • WEST ZONE ○ WESTERN ZONE
NYUGODJAK BEKEDEN • 1983 • Schiffer Pal • HNG • LET ME REST IN PEACE
NYUJIRANDO NO WAKADAISHO • 1969 • Fukuda Jun • JPN • YOUNG GUY ON MT. COOK (USA)
NYULAK A RUHATARBAN • 1972 • Bacskai-Lauro Istvan • HNG • RABBITS IN THE CLOAKROOM
NYURKA'S LIFE • 1972 • Bobrovsky Anatoli • USS • NIURKA'S LIFE

O

O • Beattie Paul • SHT • USA
O ALTE BURSCHENHERRLICHKEIT • 1925 • Lackner Helene, Rex Eugen • FRG
O ALTE BURSCHENHERRLICHKEIT • 1930 • Randolf Rolf • FRG
O.C. AND STIGGS see **UGLY, MONSTROUS, MIND-ROASTING SUMMER OF O.C. AND STIGGS** • 1985
O CANADA • 1952 • Lambart Evelyn • ANS • CND
O' CANGACEIRO • 1969 • Fago Giovanni • ITL
O DEVCICU • 1918 • Folprecht Josef, Degl Karel • CZC • FOR THE GIRL ○ LITTLE GIRL, THE
O DIESE BAYERN • 1960 • Schroeder Arnulf • FRG
O DIESE MANNER • 1915 • Schonfeld Carl • FRG
O DREAMLAND • 1953 • Anderson Lindsay • SHT • UKN
O DU MEIN OSTERREICH • 1915 • Albes Emil • FRG
O DU MEIN VATERLAND • 1922 • Mack Max • FRG
O DVANACTI MESICKACH • 1960 • Hofman Eduard • ANS • PLN • TWELVE MONTHS, THE
O DWOCH TAKICH CO UKRADLI KSIEZYC • 1962 • Batory Jan • PLN • ABOUT TWO MEN WHO STOLE THE MOON ○ PLUNDERERS OF THE MOON, THE ○ MOON-ROBBERS, THE ○ MOON THIEVES
O, EN SA'N NATT • 1937 • Henrikson Anders • SWD • A, EN SA'N NATT ○ OH, WHAT A NIGHT
O FOR OBLOMOV see **O WIE OBLOMOV** • 1982
O FOR OXYGEN • 1961 • Armstrong John • UKN
"O" GIRLS 1969 see **ORGY GIRL '69** • 1968
O.H.M.S. • 1913 • Butler Alexander? • UKN
O.H.M.S. • 1937 • Walsh Raoul • UKN • YOU'RE IN THE ARMY NOW (USA)
O HAPPY DAY see **SEVENTEEN AND ANXIOUS** • 1970
O. HENRY'S FULL HOUSE • 1952 • Koster Henry, King Henry, Hathaway Henry, Hawks Howard, Negulesco Jean • USA • BAGDAD ON THE SUBWAY
O IRAN • 1989 • Taghvai Nasser • IRN
O, IT'S GREAT TO BE CRAZY • 1918 • *Nestor* • SHT • USA
O JE • 1985 • Drha Vladimir • CZC • OH DEAR
O JUGEND, WIE BIST DU SO SCHON! see **FRAULEIN AUS ARGENTINIEN, DAS** • 1928
O.K. • 1964 • Heynowski Walter, Scheumann Gerhard • GDR
O.K. • 1970 • Verhoeven Michael • FRG
O.K. BILL • 1968 • Avildsen John G. • USA • OKAY BILL
O.K.. CAMERA • 1972 • Rubbo Michael • CND
O.K. CHIEF • 1930 • Mainwaring Bernerd • UKN
O.K. CLEOPATRA • 1971 • Cardona Rene Jr. • VNZ
O.K. CONNERY • 1968 • De Martino Alberto • ITL • OPERATION KID BROTHER (USA)
O.K. END HERE see **O.K. ENDS HERE** • 1963
O.K. ENDS HERE • 1963 • Frank Robert • SHT • USA • O.K. END HERE
O.K. JOHN! • 1947 • Fasano Ugo, D'Erasmo Gianni • ITL
O.K.. LALIBERTE • 1973 • Carriere Marcel • CND
O.K. MISTER • 1978 • Kimiavi Parviz • IRN
O.K. NERO (USA) see **O.K. NERONE** • 1951
O.K. NERONE • 1951 • Soldati Mario • ITL • O.K. NERO (USA) ○ SCANDAL IN THE ROMAN BATH
O.K. PATRON • 1973 • Vital Claude • FRN
O.K. YEVTUSHENKO • 1967 • Madrid Jose Luis • SPN
O KAKA, O KAKA • 1968 • Wenceslao Jose Pepe • PHL
O LA BORSA O LA VITA • 1933 • Bragaglia Carlo Ludovico • ITL • DINAMO DELL'EROISMO, LA
O LABUTI • 1982 • Jires Jaromil • MTV • CZC • ON THE SWAN
O L'AMMAZZO O LA SPOSO (ITL) see **BANG BANG** • 1967
O' LES PETITES STARLETTES • 1979 • Pierson Claude • FRN
O LIUBVI • 1971 • Bogin Mikhail • USS • ABOUT LOVE
O LUCKY MAN! • 1973 • Anderson Lindsay • UKN
O LUNA MY PONY! see **SONO HITO WA MUKASHI** • 1967
O MADCHEN, MEIN MADCHEN, WIE LIEB' ICH DICH! • 1930 • Boese Carl • FRG
O MADIANA • 1978 • Gros-Dubois Constant • FRN
O MALEJ KASI I DUZYM WILKU • 1963 • Nehrebecki Wladyslaw • ANS • PLN • STORY OF LITTLE KASIA AND THE BIG WOLF, THE ○ LITTLE KATE AND BIG WOLF
O MARYSCE A VLCIM HRADKU • 1980 • Pospisilova Vlasta • CZC • MARYSKA AND THE WOLF'S CASTLE
O MILIONARI, KTERY UKRADL SLUNCE • 1948 • Miler Zdenek, Blaha Zbynek, Blahovi Richard • ANS • CZC • MILLIONAIRE WHO STOLE THE SUN, THE
O MIMI SAN • 1914 • Barker Reginald • USA • COURTSHIP OF O SAN, THE
O MISTO NA SLUNCI • 1960 • Vystrcil Frantisek • ANS • CZC • PLACE IN THE SUN, A
O MISU I SATOVIMA • 1969 • Grgic Zlatko, Kolar Boris, Zaninovic Ante • ANS • YGS, FRG • OF MICE AND MEN ○ OF MICE AND BEN
O MODA, MODA • 1969 • Bakhtadze Vaktang • ANS • USS • OH FASHION, FASHION
O, MOET DAT ZO • 1975 • Grasveld Fons • DOC • NTH • OH, I SEE..
O MUSCA CU BANI • 1954 • Popescu-Gopo Ion • RMN • FLY WITH MONEY, A
O, MY DARLING CLEMENTINE • 1943 • McDonald Frank • USA
O-MY THE TENT MOVER • 1917 • Beaudine William • SHT • USA
O.N.Z. W AKCJI • 1949 • Bossak Jerzy • DOC • PLN • U.N. IN ACTION, THE
O NECEM JINEM • 1963 • Chytilova Vera • CZC • ABOUT SOMETHING ELSE ○ ANOTHER WAY OF LIFE ○ SOMETHING DIFFERENT ○ SOMETHING ELSE
O-OKU EMAKI • 1968 • Yamashita Kosaku • JPN • VANITY OF THE SHOGUN'S MISTRESS, THE
O OU L'INVISIBLE ENFANT • 1973 • Duguay Raoul • CND
O! PAGSINTANG LABIS • 1967 • Crisostomo Fely • PHL • OH! SUPREME LOVE
O PANENCE, KTERA PLAKALA • 1954 • Hofman Eduard • ANS • PLN • DOLLY WHO SHED REAL TEARS, THE
O PAR DNU (CZC) see **A QUELQUES JOURS PRES** • 1968
O PICASSO • 1985 • Carle Gilles • DOC • CND
O PICASSO -TABLEAUX D'UNE SUREXPOSITION • 1985 • Hebert Pierre • CND
O POVESTE CA-N BASME see **POVESTE CA-N BASME, O** • 1959
O PYSNE NOCNI KOSILCE • 1950 • Hofman Eduard • ANS • PLN • PROUD NIGHTGOWN, THE
O' RE • 1988 • Magni Luigi • ITL • KING, THE
O RUPAMA CEPOVIMA • 1967 • Zaninovic Ante • YGS • OF HOLES AND CORKS (USA)
O.S.S. • 1946 • Pichel Irving • USA
O.S.S. 117 IS NOT DEAD see **O.S.S. 117 N'EST PAS MORT** • 1956
O.S.S. 117 N'EST PAS MORT • 1956 • Sacha Jean • FRN • O.S.S. 117 IS NOT DEAD
O.S.S. 117 PREND DES VACANCES • 1969 • Kalfon Pierre • FRN, BRZ • OSS 117 TAKES A VACATION
O.S.S. 117 SE DECHAINE • 1963 • Hunebelle Andre • FRN, ITL
O SAISONS, O CHATEAUX • 1957 • Varda Agnes • DCS • FRN
O SAMON CHELOVEKHNOM • 1967 • Yutkevich Sergei • CMP • USS
O SCHWARZWALD, O HEIMAT • 1939 • Boese Carl • FRG • OH, BLACK FOREST, OH HOME (USA)
O SCRISOARE PIERDUTA • 1956 • Iliu Victor • RMN • LAST LETTER, A
O SEVCI MATOUSOVI • 1948 • Cikan Miroslav • CZC • MATTHEW THE SHOEMAKER ○ MATOUS THE SHOEMAKER
O SIFRE • 1967 • Yilmazbas Metin • TRK • THAT CODE
O SKLENICKU VIC see **OSKLENICKU VIC** • 1954
O SLAVE A TRAVE • 1985 • Solan Peter • CZC • ON GLORY AND GRASS
O SNEHURCE • 1972 • Plivova-Simkova Vera • CZC • SNOW-WHITE
O SOLAR MEOW • 1967 • Levitow Abe • ANS • USA
O SOLE MIO • 1929 • Aylott Dave, Symmons E. F. • SHT • UKN
O' SOLE MIO • 1946 • Gentilomo Giacomo • ITL
O SOLE MIO • 1960 • Martin Paul • FRG • GROSSE SCHLAGERBUMMEL, DER
O SUSIE BEHAVE! • 1918 • Santell Alfred • SHT • USA
O T-37 • 1963 • Simoes Quirino • SHT • PRT
O TUTTO O NIENTE • 1968 • Zurli Guido • ITL
O TYM NIE WOLNO ZAPOMNIEC • 1968 • Wionczek Roman • DOC • PLN • THIS MUST NOT BE FORGOTTEN
O.U. WEST • 1925 • Garson Harry • USA
O VECECH NADPRIROZENYCH • 1958 • Krejcik Jiri, Mach Jaroslav, Makovec Milos • CZC • ON MIRACULOUS HAPPENINGS ○ GLORIE ○ HALO, THE ○ MIRACULOUS HAPPENINGS
O WARSZAWIE, ALE INACCZEJ • 1960 • Perski Ludwik (c/d) • DOC • PLN • ABOUT WARSAW BUT DIFFERENTLY
O! WHISKERS! • 1913 • *Crystal* • USA
O WIE OBLOMOV • 1982 • Schroeder Sebastian C. • SWT • O FOR OBLOMOV
O YOU MULE! • 1915 • *Superba* • USA
O, YOU POP • 1914 • *Starlight* • USA
O ZLATE RYBCE see **RYBAR A ZLATA RYBKA** • 1951
?O ZOO! • 1987 • Hoffman Philip • DCS • CND
OABARE JIROCHO IKKA • 1957 • Hidaka Shigeaki • JPN
OAK TREE, TOP EMERGENCY • 1973 • Cocea Dinu • RMN
OAKBANK RACES • 1915 • *West's* • ASL
OAKBANK STEEPLE • 1916 • ASL
OAKBANK STEEPLE • 1917 • *Krischock H. (Ph)* • ASL
OAKBANK STEEPLECHASE • 1918 • *Southern Cross Feature Film Co* • ASL
OAKBANK STEEPLECHASE • 1920 • *Krischock H. (Ph)* • ASL
OAKBANK STEEPLECHASE • 1921 • *Krischock H. (Ph)* • ASL
OAKBANK STEEPLECHASE • 1922 • *Krischock H. (Ph)* • ASL
OAKDALE AFFAIR, THE • 1919 • Apfel Oscar • USA
OAKIE NAVY STORY see **SEA LEGS** • 1930
OAKLAWN HANDICAP, THE • 1915 • McRae Henry • USA
OAKMOUNT HIGH • 1985 • Bond Timothy • TVM • CND
OASE • 1955 • Allegret Yves • FRN, FRG • OASIS
OASIS • 1933 • Hurley Frank • DOC • USA
OASIS see **OASE** • 1955

OASIS, THE • 1984 • Greene Sparky • USA • SAVAGE HUNTER, A
OASIS, THE see **OAZA** • 1972
OASIS OF THE ZOMBIES • 1981 • *Gelin Manuel*
OATH, THE • 1921 • Paul Fred • UKN
OATH, THE • 1921 • Walsh Raoul • USA
OATH AND GUN see **VOTO MAS FUSIL** • 1969
OATH AND THE MAN, THE • 1910 • Griffith D. W. • USA
OATH-BOUND • 1922 • Durning Bernard J. • USA
OATH OF A VIKING, THE • 1914 • Dawley J. Searle • USA
OATH OF CONCHITA, THE • 1913 • *Darkfeather Mona* • USA
OATH OF HATE, THE • 1916 • King Henry • SHT • USA
OATH OF HIS OFFICE, THE • 1912 • *Aoki Tsuru* • USA
OATH OF OBEDIENCE, THE see **BUSHIDO ZANKOKU MONOGATARI** • 1963
OATH OF PIERRE, THE • 1914 • Ayres Sydney • USA
OATH OF SMOKY JOE, THE • 1915 • *Myles Norbert* • USA
OATH OF THE SWORD • 1914 • *Japanese-American* • USA
OATH OF TIMUR, THE see **KLYATVA TIMURA** • 1942
OATH OF VENGEANCE • 1944 • Newfield Sam • USA
OATH OF VENGEANCE, THE • 1920 • *Superior Productions* • SHT • USA
OATH OF YOUTH, THE see **KLIATVA MOLODYCH** • 1944
OATSUI KYUKA • 1968 • Hirayama Mitsunobu • JPN • HOT VACATION
OATSURAE JIROKICHI GOSHI • 1931 • Ito Daisuke • JPN
OAZA • 1972 • Brynych Zbynek • CZC • OASIS, THE
OB ETOM ZABY VAT NELZYA • 1954 • Lukov Leonid • USS • IT MUST NOT BE FORGOTTEN ○ LEST WE FORGET
OBALI • 1976 • Dong Jean-Marie • GBN
OBANTO KOBANTO • 1936 • Toyoda Shiro • JPN
OBANTO KOBANTO • 1955 • Suzuki Hideo • JPN • ROOKIE MANAGER
OBANTO KOBANTO • 1967 • Doi Michiyoshi • JPN • FIGHTING SPIRIT, THE
OBBEDISCO • 1910 • Lolli Alberto Carlo • ITL
OBBIETTIVO RAGAZZE • 1963 • Mattoli Mario • ITL
OBCAN BRYCH • 1958 • Vavra Otakar • CZC • CITIZEN BRYCH
OBCAN KAREL HAVLICEK • 1966 • Jires Jaromil • CZC • CITIZEN KAREL HAVLICEK
OBCHOD NA KORSE • 1965 • Kadar Jan, Klos Elmar • CZC • SHOP ON THE HIGH STREET, THE ○ SHOP ON MAIN STREET
OBDULIA • 1985 • de la Riva Juan Antonio • MXC
OBDURATE FATHER, THE • 1909 • *Vitagraph* • USA
OBEAH • 1934 • Herrick F. Herrick • USA • MYSTERY SHIP, THE (UKN)
OBEDIENT FLAME, THE • 1939 • McLaren Norman • ANS • UKN
OBELIA • 1936 • Hewer H. R. • UKN
"OBEN-OHNE" STORY, DIE • 1965 • Selnig Wolfgang • SWT • TOPLESS STORY, THE (UKN)
OBER, ZAHLEN! • 1957 • Emo E. W. • FRG
OBERAMMERGAU PASSION PLAY (USA) see **PASSION, LA** • 1897
OBERARZT DR. SOLM • 1955 • May Paul • FRG
OBERDAN • 1916 • Serena Gustavo • ITL
OBERST CHABERT see **GRAF CHAGRON** • 1924
OBERST REDL • 1985 • Szabo Istvan • FRG, HNG, AUS • COLONEL REDL (UKN) ○ REDL EZREDES (HNG)
OBERST REDLS ERBEN see **BRANDSTIFTER EUROPAS, DIE** • 1926
OBERST ROKSCHANIN • 1922 • Linnekogel Otto • FRG
OBERWACHTMEISTER BORCK • 1955 • Lamprecht Gerhard • FRG
OBERWACHTMEISTER SCHWENKE • 1935 • Froelich Carl • FRG
OBERWALD MYSTERY, THE see **MISTERO DI OBERWALD, IL** • 1979
OBEY THE LAW • 1926 • Raboch Alfred • USA
OBEY THE LAW • 1933 • Stoloff Ben • USA • EAST OF FIFTH AVENUE (UKN)
OBEY YOUR HUSBAND • 1928 • Hunt Charles J. • USA
OBI O TOKU NATSUKO • 1965 • Tanaka Shigeo • JPN • I'LL CRY ALONE
OBICH • 1973 • Staikov Lyudmil • BUL • AFFECTION ○ LOVE
OBISTOS • 1917 • Balazs Bela • HNG
OBJECT -ALIMONY • 1928 • Dunlap Scott R. • USA • OBJECT -MATRIMONY
OBJECT LESSON • 1941 • Young Christopher • SHT • USA
OBJECT: MATRIMONY • 1909 • *Essanay* • USA
OBJECT MATRIMONY • 1911 • *Hopkins Jack* • USA
OBJECT -MATRIMONY • 1916 • Myers Harry • SHT • USA
OBJECT MATRIMONY • 1959 • Kelly Ron • CND
OBJECT -MATRIMONY see **OBJECT -ALIMONY** • 1928
OBJECT OF BEAUTY, THE • 1990 • Lindsay-Hogg Michael • USA, UKN
OBJECT OF DESIRE • 1983 • Jiune Ji Boung • USA
OBJECTIF 500 MILLIONS • 1966 • Schoendoerffer Pierre • FRN
OBJECTIF HAMBOURG MISSION 083 (FRN) see **M.M.M.83 -MISSIONE MORTALE MOLO 83** • 1966
OBJECTIF TEMPS • 1965 • Meignant Michel • DCS • FRN
OBJECTION see **JESTEM PRZECIW** • 1985
OBJECTIONS OVERCOME • 1909 • *Urban-Eclipse* • USA
OBJECTIONS OVERRULED • 1912 • Dwan Allan • USA
OBJECTIONS OVERRULED • 1913 • Henderson Dell • USA
OBJECTIVE, BURMA • 1945 • Walsh Raoul • USA
OBJECTIVE MOON • 1962 • ANM • FRN • DESTINATION MOON
OBJECTIVE: SABAH • 1968 • Garces Armando • PHL
OBJETIVO BIKINI • 1968 • Ozores Mariano • SPN
OBJETIVO: LAS ESTRELLAS • 1962 • Fernandez Ramon • SPN
OBJEV NA STRAPATE HURCE • 1962 • Stekly Karel • CZC • DISCOVERY ON THE SHAGGY MOUNTAIN
OBJIZDKA • 1968 • Mach Josef • CZC • WAY ROUND, THE ○ DETOUR
OBLACAK I OBLACI • 1962 • Kosmac France • SHT • YGS
OBLACNA PRICA • 1972 • Grgic Zlatko • ANS • YGS • CLOUD AND CLEAR
OBLATYWACZE • 1960 • Amiradzibi Helena • DOC • PLN • TEST PILOTS
OBLIGACION DE ASESINAR, LA • 1937 • Helu Antonio • MXC • OBLIGATION TO ASSASSINATE, THE (USA)
OBLIGATION, THE • 1912 • *Nestor* • USA
OBLIGATION TO ASSASSINATE, THE (USA) see **OBLIGACION DE ASESINAR, LA** • 1937
OBLIGIN' BUCKAROO, THE • 1927 • Thorpe Richard • USA
OBLIGING A FRIEND • 1911 • *Nestor* • USA
OBLIGING YOUNG LADY • 1941 • Wallace Richard • USA
OBLOMOK IMPERII • 1929 • Ermler Friedrich • USS • FRAGMENT OF AN EMPIRE ○ CHIP OF THE EMPIRE, A
OBLOMOV see **NESKOLKO DNEI IZ ZHIZNI I.I. OBLOMOV** • 1980
OBLONG BOX, THE • 1969 • Hessler Gordon • UKN, USA • EDGAR ALLAN POE'S THE OBLONG BOX ○ DANCE, MEPHISTO
OBLONG COUCH, THE see **SAUCY AUSSIE, THE** • 1963
OBMANUTAJA EVA • 1918 • Tourjansky Victor • USS
OBMARU • 1953 • Marx Patricia • SHT • USA
OBON'S DIPPING CONTEST (USA) see **ATOMIC NO OBON, ONNA OYABUN TAIKETSU NO MAKI** • 1961
OBORO KAGO • 1951 • Ito Daisuke • JPN • MYSTERIOUS PALANQUIN, THE
OBORONA TSARITSINA • 1942 • Vasiliev Georgi, Vasiliev Sergei • USS • DEFENCE OF TSARITSIN, THE ○ DEFENSE DE TSARITSYNE, LE
OBOROYO NO ONNA • 1936 • Gosho Heinosuke • JPN • WOMAN OF A PALE NIGHT ○ WOMAN OF THE MIST ○ WOMAN OF A MISTY MOONLIGHT ○ WOMAN OF PALE NIGHT
OBOXU TENGO • 1958 • Watanabe Kunio • JPN • GAY REVENGERS
OBOZ NA PRZEMYSLOWEJ • 1970 • Halladin Danuta • DOC • PLN • CAMP AT PRZEMYSLOWA STREET, THE
OBOZHZHENNIUE KRYLYA • 1915 • Bauer Yevgeni • USS • SINGED WINGS
OBRA DA JUNTA AUTONOMA DAS ESTRADAS, A • 1932 • do Canto Jorge Brum • SHT • PRT
OBRACENI FERDYSE PISTORY • 1931 • Kodicek • CZC • CONVERSION OF FERDYS PISTORA, THE
OBRACUN • 1963 • Mitrovic Zika • YGS • RECKONING, THE
OBRAS DE ARTE • 1938 • Telmo Cottinelli • SHT • PRT
OBRAS MAESTRAS DEL TERROR • 1960 • Carreras Enrique • ARG • MASTER OF HORROR (USA) ○ MASTERWORKS OF TERROR
OBRAZY STAREHO SVETA • 1972 • Hanak Dusan • DCS • CZC • PICTURES OF THE OLD WORLD ○ IMAGES OF AN OLD WORLD
O'BRIEN FINDS A WAY • 1914 • *Warner'S Features* • USA
O'BRIEN'S BUSY DAY • 1912 • *Imp* • USA
O'BRIEN'S INVESTMENT • 1916 • *Jockey* • USA
OB'S STURMT ODER SCHNEIT • 1977 • Berndt Wolfgang, Dorrie Doris • FRG • RAIN OR SHINE
OBSCENE ANIMAL OF ZERO see **ZERO NO INJU** • 1968
OBSCENE COUCH, THE see **SAUCY AUSSIE, THE** • 1963
OBSCENE FAMILY INSIGNIA see **INMON: SHOJO ZUMA KANTSU** • 1967
OBSCENE -THE PETER HERZL CASE see **OBSZON -DER FALL PETER HERZL** • 1981
OBSCENE WIFE see **MIDARAZUMA** • 1968
OBSCENE WIFE see **NEMIDAREZUMA** • 1968
OBSCENITY OF THE VIPER see **JASEI NO IN** • 1920
OBSEQUES SOLENNELLES DE LA COMTESSE DES FLANDRES, MERE DU ROI ALBERT 1er • 1912 • Machin Alfred • FRN
OBSERVATION I, II, III • 1978 • Melancon Andre • CND
OBSESION • 1917 • de la Bandera Manuel • MXC
OBSESION • 1947 • Ruiz-Castillo Arturo • SPN
OBSESION • 1974 • Lara Polop Francisco • SPN
OBSESIONES DE ARMANDO, LAS • 1974 • Delgado Luis Maria • SPN
OBSESSED see **HITTING HOME** • 1988
OBSESSED, THE see **OSSESSA, L'** • 1974
OBSESSED (USA) see **LATE EDWINA BLACK, THE** • 1951
OBSESSED WITH A MARRIED WOMAN • 1985 • Lang Richard • TVM • USA
OBSESSION • Lee Doo-Yong • SKR
OBSESSION • 1948 • Dmytryk Edward • UKN • HIDDEN ROOM, THE (USA)
OBSESSION • 1954 • Delannoy Jean • FRN, ITL • DOMANDA DI GRAZIA (ITL)
OBSESSION • 1968 • Kolar Boris • ANM • YGS
OBSESSION • 1976 • De Palma Brian • USA • DOUBLE RANSOM
OBSESSION • 1983 • Jutrisa Vladimir • ANS • YGS
OBSESSION • 1985 • Ross Jonathan • USA
OBSESSION • 1988 • Eleasari Jacob
OBSESSION see **VASEN** • 1962
OBSESSION see **OPETANIE** • 1973
OBSESSION see **KARVAT** • 1974
OBSESSION see **INJU** • 1977
OBSESSION see **JUNOON** • 1978
OBSESSION see **FENGKUANGDE DAIJIA** • 1988
OBSESSION, AN • 1958 • *Tamiz Edmonde (P)* • SHT • FRN
OBSESSION, THE • 1912 • *Melies* • USA
OBSESSION, THE see **OSSESSA, L'** • 1974
OBSESSION: A TASTE FOR FEAR see **TASTE FOR FEAR, A** • 1987
OBSESSION DE L'OR, L' • 1906 • Nonguet Lucien • FRN
OBSESSION (USA) see **HOMME MYSTERIEUX, L'** • 1933
OBSESSION (USA) see **KUNGSLEDEN** • 1964
OBSESSIONS • 1968 • de la Parra Pim • NTH
OBSESSIONS see **FLESH AND FANTASY** • 1943
OBSESSIONS see **BESESSEN -DAS LOCH IN DER WAND** • 1969
OBSESSIVE LOVE • 1984 • Stern Steven Hilliard • TVM • USA
OBSTACLE, L' • 1918 • Kemm Jean • FRN
OBSTACLE, L' • 1966 • Bouamari Mohamed • ALG
OBSTACLE, THE see **SETE DIAS DE AGONIA** • 1982
OBSTACLE OF AFFECTION, AN see **CHENG-KWAN** • 1968
OBSTACULO, EL • 1945 • Iquino Ignacio F. • SPN
OBSTINATE see **SARSAKHT** • 1968
OBSTINATE MAN, THE see **BOCKERER, DER** • 1981
OBSTINATE SHERIFF, AN • 1915 • *Whitman Velma* • USA
OBSZAR ZAMKNIETY • 1973 • Brzozowski Andrzej • PLN • CLOSED AREA, THE
OBSZON -DER FALL PETER HERZL • 1981 • Stenzel Hans Christof • AUS, FRG • OBSCENE -THE PETER HERZL CASE
OBSZONI TATEN • 1974 • Brummer Alois • FRG • CONFESSIONS OF A MALE ESCORT
OBUROSHIKI see **KIGEKI-OBUROSHIKI** • 1967
OBUS SUR PARIS, UN • 1913 • Fescourt Henri • FRN
OBVIOUS SITUATION, AN • 1930 • Guarino Joseph • UKN • HOURS OF LONELINESS
OBVIOUS THING, THE • 1935 • Riddell James • UKN
OBYKNOVENNYY FASHIZM • 1965 • Romm Mikhail • USS • TRUMPS OVER VIOLENCE (USA) ○ ORDINARY FASCISM
OBYWATEL PISZCYK • 1988 • Kotkowski Andrzej • PLN • CITIZEN P.
OBZALOVANY • 1964 • Kadar Jan, Klos Elmar • CZC • DEFENDANT, THE ○ ACCUSED, THE
OCALENIE • 1959 • Kluba Henryk • SHT • PLN
OCALENIE • 1972 • Zebrowski Edward • PLN • SALVATION
OCALIC MIASTO • 1977 • Lomnicki Jan • PLN, USS • SAVE THE CITY
OCANA, A BRIEF PORTRAIT see **OCANA, UN RETRATO INTERMITENTE** • 1978
OCANA, A GAY PORTRAIT see **OCANA, UN RETRATO INTERMITENTE** • 1978
OCANA: AN INTERMITTENT PORTRAIT see **OCANA, UN RETRATO INTERMITENTE** • 1978
OCANA, UN RETRATO INTERMITENTE • 1978 • Pons Ventura • SPN • OCANA, A BRIEF PORTRAIT ○ INTERMITTENT PORTRAYAL ○ RETRAT INTERMITENT ○ OCANA: AN INTERMITTENT PORTRAIT ○ OCANA, A GAY PORTRAIT
OCARINA SOLO • 1907 • *Walturdaw* • UKN
OCASION, LA • 1978 • Larraz Jose R. • SPN
OCASO • 1967 • Takeda Hernan • CHL • SUNSET
OCASO DE UN PISTOLERO • 1968 • Romero-Marchent Rafael • SPN, ITL • DECLINE OF A SHARPSHOOTER
OCCASIONAL WORK OF A FEMALE SLAVE (UKN) see **GELEGENHEITSARBEIT EINER SKLAVIN** • 1974
OCCASIONALLY YOURS • 1920 • Horne James W. • USA
OCCHI DALLE STELLE • 1978 • Gariazzo Mario • ITL • EYES BEHIND THE STARS (USA) ○ EYES BEYOND THE STARS
OCCHI FREDDI DELLA PAURA, GLI • 1971 • Castellari Enzo G. • ITL, SPN • FRIOS OJOS DEL MIEDO, LOS (SPN) ○ COLD EYES OF FEAR, THE
OCCHI, LA BOCCA, GLI • 1983 • Bellocchio Marco • ITL • EYES, THE MOUTH, THE (USA) ○ YEUX, LA BOUCHE, LES
OCCHI SENZA LUCE, GLI • 1956 • Calzavara Flavio • ITL
OCCHI SENZA VOLTO (ITL) see **YEUX SANS VISAGE, LES** • 1959
OCCHIALI D'ORO, GLI • 1988 • Montaldo Giuliano • ITL • GOLDEN GLASSES, THE ○ GOLD-RIMMED GLASSES, THE
OCCHIO ALLA PENNA • 1981 • Lupo Michele • ITL • BUDDY GOES WEST
OCCHIO ALLA VEDOVA! • 1975 • Pastore Sergio • ITL
OCCHIO DEL MALE, L' • 1982 • Fulci Lucio • ITL • EYE OF THE EVIL DEAD, THE ○ MANHATTAN BABY ○ POSSESSED, THE
OCCHIO DEL RAGNO, L' • 1971 • Montero Roberto Bianchi • ITL, SPN, AUS • OJO DE LA ARANA, EL (SPN) ○ AUGE DER SPINNE, DER (AUS) ○ EYE OF THE SPIDER
OCCHIO DIETRO LA PARETE, L' • 1977 • Petrelli Giuliano • ITL
OCCHIO NEL LABIRINTO, L' • 1972 • Caiano Mario • ITL • EYE OF THE LABYRINTH, THE
OCCHIO PER OCCHIO, DENTE PER DENTE • 1967 • Iglesias Miguel • ITL, SPN • EYE FOR AN EYE, A TOOTH FOR A TOOTH, AN
OCCHIO PER OCCHIO (ITL) see **OEIL POUR OEIL** • 1957
OCCHIO SELVAGGIO, L' • 1967 • Cavara Paolo • ITL • WILD EYE, THE (USA) ○ SAVAGE EYE, THE
OCCIDENT, L' • 1928 • Fescourt Henri • FRN
OCCIDENT, L' • 1937 • Fescourt Henri • FRN
OCCIDENTE Y SABOTAJE • 1962 • Mariscal Ana • SPN
OCCITANIE • 1937 • Millet J. K. Raymond • FRN
OCCULT, THE • 1913 • *American* • USA
OCCULT ROOTS see **CRIME DE SIMAO BOLANDAS, O** • 1980
OCCULTISME ET LA MAGIE, L' • 1952 • Allegret Marc • FRN
OCCUPANTS OF MANOR HOUSE see **KASTELYOK LAKOI** • 1966
OCCUPATI D'AMELIA! • 1924 • D'Ambra Lucio • ITL
OCCUPATI D'AMELIA (ITL) see **OCCUPE-TOI D'AMELIE** • 1949
OCCUPATION • 1969 • *Karezi Jenny* • GRC
OCCUPATION • 1971 • Reid Bill • CND
OCCUPATION, THE see **DAKHAL** • 1982
OCCUPATION IN 26 PICTURES, THE see **OKUPACIJA U 26 SLIKA** • 1977
OCCUPATION IN 26 SCENES, THE see **OKUPACIJA U 26 SLIKA** • 1977
OCCUPATION YEARS, THE see **HERNAMSARIN** • 1967
OCCUPATIONAL HEALTH • 1976-78 • Richardson Boyce • SER • CND
OCCUPE-TOI D'AMELIE • 1912 • Chautard Emile • FRN
OCCUPE-TOI D'AMELIE • 1932 • Weisbach Richard, Viel Marguerite • FRN
OCCUPE-TOI D'AMELIE • 1949 • Autant-Lara Claude • FRN, ITL • OCCUPATI D'AMELIA (ITL) ○ KEEP AN EYE ON AMELIA (UKN) ○ OH AMELIA (USA) ○ LOOK AFTER AMELIA
OCCURRENCE AT OWL CREEK BRIDGE, AN (USA) see **RIVIERE DU HIBOU, LA** • 1961
OCEAN • 1977 • Ferguson Graeme • CND
OCEAN, L' • 1916 • Andreani Henri • FRN
OCEAN, L' • 1931 • de Baroncelli Jacques • FRN
OCEAN, THE • 1974 • Vyshinsky Yu. • USS
OCEAN AT POINT LOOKOUT • 1977 • Cantrill Arthur, Cantrill Corinne • ASL
OCEAN BLUES • 1927 • Christie Al • USA
OCEAN BRUISE • 1965 • Post Howard • ANS • USA
OCEAN HOP, THE • 1927 • Disney Walt • ANS • USA
OCEAN ODDITIES • 1931 • Monkman Noel • DOC • ASL
OCEAN ODYSSEY see **OCEANO** • 1971
OCEAN OF AIR, THE • 1970 • Hoving Hattum • SHT • NTH

OCEAN POINT • 1989 • Bond Jack • UKN
OCEAN SWELLS • 1934 • Stevens George • SHT • USA
OCEAN WAIF, THE • 1916 • Blache Alice • USA
OCEANO • 1971 • Quilici Folco • ITL • OCEAN ODYSSEY
OCEANO CI CHIAMO, L' • 1958 • Roccardi Giovanni, Ferroni Giorgio • DOC • ITL • NOI DELL'OCEANO
OCEANOGRAFIA EN VENEZUELA • 1972 • de la Rosa Antonio • DOC • VNZ
OCEAN'S 11 • 1960 • Milestone Lewis • USA
OCEANS: LIVING IN LIQUID AIR, THE • 1972 • *Document Associates* • SHT • USA
OCEANS OF FIRE • 1986 • Carver Steve • TVM • USA
OCEANS OF LOVE • 1956 • Rasinski Connie • ANS • USA
OCH ALLA DESSA KVINNOR • 1944 • Mattsson Arne • SWD • AND ALL THESE WOMEN
...OCH EFTER SKYMNING KOMMER MORKER • 1947 • Hagberg Rune • SWD
OCHI OCHI • 1973 • Zeman Bronislaw • PLN • OH! OH!
OCHAZUKE NO AJI • 1952 • Ozu Yasujiro • JPN • FLAVOUR OF GREEN TEA OVER RICE, THE ○ TEA AND RICE (USA) ○ TASTE OF GREEN TEA AND RICE, THE
OCHI DE URS • 1983 • Gulea Stere • RMN • BEAR EYE'S CURSE, THE
OCHIBA NIKKI • 1954 • Mizuko Harumi • JPN • DIARY OF FALLEN LEAVES
OCHII DRASULUI MEU • 1963 • Calotescu Virgil • RMN • EYES OF MY CITY, THE
OCHIYO TOSHIGORO • 1937 • Suganuma Kanji • JPN • PRIME OF OCHIYO'S LIFE, THE
OCHIYOGASA • 1935 • Ozaki Jun • JPN • OCHIYO'S UMBRELLA
OCHIYO'S UMBRELLA see **OCHIYOGASA** • 1935
OCHO HOMBRES Y UNA MUJER • 1945 • Soler Julian • MXC
OCHOCIENTAS MIL LEGUAS POR EL AMAZONAS • 1958 • Gomez Muriel Emilio • MXC • 800 LEAGUES OVER THE AMAZON (USA) ○ JANGADA, LA
OCHSE VON KULM, DER • 1955 • Hellberg Martin • GDR • OX OF KULM, THE
OCHSENKRIEG, DER • 1920 • Osten Franz • FRG
OCHSENKRIEG, DER • 1942 • Deppe Hans • FRG
OCHTEND VAN ZES WEKEN, EEN • 1966 • van der Heyde Nikolai • NTH • PRINTEMPS EN HOLLANDE, UN ○ MORNING OF SIX WEEKS, A ○ SPRING IN HOLLAND, A
OCI CIORNIE • 1988 • Mikhalkov Nikita • ITL • DARK EYES ○ BLACK EYES
OCIEL DEL TOA • Landrian Nicolas Guillen • CUB
OCIL 1958 • 1958 • Berr • SHT • FRN
OCTA-MAN • 1971 • Essex Harry • USA • OCTOMAN
OCTAGON, THE • 1980 • Karson Eric • USA
OCTAROON, THE • 1903 • Winslow Dicky? • UKN
OCTAVE OF CLAUDIUS, THE see **BLIND BARGAIN, A** • 1922
OCTAVIA • 1984 • Beaird David • USA
OCTAVO MANDAMIENTO, EL • 1935 • Delgado Fernando • SPN
OCTIABR' DNI • 1958 • Vasiliev Sergei • USS • OCTOBER DAYS ○ DAYS OF OCTOBER, THE ○ JOURS D'OCTOBRE, LES
OCTOBER see **OKTYABR'** • 1928
OCTOBER 4TH • 1925 • Butler Alexander • UKN
OCTOBER '44 see **UNDER EN STEINHIMMEL** • 1974
OCTOBER ALMS • 1978 • Paakspuu Kalli • CND
OCTOBER CINEMA TRUTH • 1923 • Vertov Dziga • USS • YESTERDAY TODAY AND TOMORROW
OCTOBER DAYS see **OCTIABR' DNI** • 1958
OCTOBER DRIVE, THE • 1931 • Lukov Leonid • USS
OCTOBER MAN, THE • 1947 • Baker Roy Ward • UKN • HANGMAN'S NOOSE
OCTOBER MOTH • 1960 • Kruse John • UKN
OCTOBER REVOLUTION see **REVOLUTION D'OCTOBRE** • 1967
OCTOBER SILK • Howard Cecil • USA
OCTOBER WON'T RETURN see **BAO GIO CHO TOI**
OCTOBRE A MADRID • 1967 • Hanoun Marcel • FRN
OCTOBRE A PARIS • 1961 • Panijel Jacques • FRN
OCTOBRE EN AFGHANISTAN • 1966 • Bertolino Daniel, Floquet Francois • DCS • FRN
OCTOMAN see **OCTA-MAN** • 1971
OCTOPUS see **PIEUVRE, LA** • 1926
OCTOPUS, THE • 1915 • Santschi Thomas • USA
OCTOPUS, THE see **FIFTH AVENUE** • 1926
OCTOPUS GANG, THE • 1915 • Martinek H. O. • UKN
OCTOPUS HUNT, THE • 1965 • Devlin Bernard • DCS • CND • CHASSE A LA PIEVRE
OCTOPUSSY • 1983 • Glen John • UKN
OCTOROON, THE • 1909 • *Kalem* • USA
OCTOROON, THE • 1912 • *Australian Photo Play Co* • ASL
OCTOROON, THE • 1913 • Buel Kenean? • USA
OCTOROON, THE • 1919 • ASL
OCTOROON'S SACRIFICE, THE • 1912 • *Republic* • USA
OCTUBRE DE TODOS, EL • 1977 • Alvarez Santiago • DOC • CUB
OCUPACAO DE TERRAS NA BEIRA BAIXA • 1975 • de Macedo Antonio • PRT
OCZAMI PRZYJACIOL • 1970 • Perski Ludwik, Machnacz Leonid • DOC • PLN • THROUGH THE EYES OF FRIENDS
OCZEKIWANIA see **OCZEKIWANIE** • 1962
OCZEKIWANIE • 1962 • Perski Ludwik, Giersz Witold • DOC • PLN • EXPECTATIONS ○ AWAITING ○ OCZEKIWANIA ○ WAITING
OD MOCAMBO SO COPACABANY • 1959 • Wionczek Roman • DOC • PLN • FROM MOCAMBO TO COPACABANA
OD PETKA DO PETKA • 1985 • Vrdoljak Antun • YGS • FROM ONE FRIDAY TO THE NEXT
OD RZEMYCZKA.. • 1961 • Kijowicz Miroslaw • ANS • PLN • HE THAT WILL STEAL A PIN.. ○ FLIGHT, THE
ODA NA RADOST • 1985 • Balik Jaroslav • CZC • ODE TO HAPPINESS
ODA NOBUNAGA • 1955 • Kono Hisashi • JPN
ODA-VISSA • 1962 • Gaal Istvan • SHT • HNG • TO AND FRO
ODAL FEDRANNA • 1980 • Gunnlaugsson Hrafn • ICL, SWD • ANCESTRAL ESTATE ○ FATHER'S ESTATE
ODALISCA NUMERO 13, LA • 1957 • Cortes Fernando • MXC
ODALISQUE, THE • 1914 • Cabanne W. Christy • USA
ODD ACQUAINTANCES • 1916 • *Vitagraph* • SHT • USA
ODD AFFINITY see **SHOKKAKU** • 1969
ODD ANGRY SHOT, THE • 1979 • Jeffrey Tom • ASL
ODD BALLS • 1984 • Lente Miklos • CND • ALL SHOOK UP! ○ ODDBALLS
ODD BIRDS • 1985 • Collachia Jeanne • USA
ODD BIRDS see **PTACI KOHACI** • 1965
ODD CHARGES • 1916 • Miller Frank • UKN
ODD COUPLE, THE • 1968 • Saks Gene • USA
ODD FELLOWS HALL • 1950 • Sutton Denver, Tregillus Leonard • SHT • USA
ODD FREAK, AN • 1916 • Tucker George Loane • UKN
ODD FREAK, AN • 1923 • Haynes Manning • UKN
ODD JOB, THE • 1978 • Medak Peter • UKN
ODD JOB MAN, THE • 1912 • Dwan Allan • USA
ODD JOBS • 1984 • Story Mark • USA
ODD KIND OF LOVE, AN see **MAERKELIG KAERLIGHED, EN** • 1968
ODD KNOTTS • 1913 • *Calvert E. H.* • USA
ODD LOVERS see **KOMEDI I HAGERSKOG** • 1968
ODD MAN OUT • 1915 • Collins Edwin J.? • UKN
ODD MAN OUT • 1947 • Reed Carol • UKN • GANG WAR
ODD NUMBER, THE see **CIFRA IMPAR, LA** • 1961
ODD NUMBERS • 1929 • Jeffrey R. E. • UKN
ODD OBSESSIONS (UKN) see **KAGI** • 1959
ODD SLIPPER, THE • 1915 • King Burton L. • USA
ODD SQUAD, THE • 1985 • Clucher E. B. • ITL
ODD TASTES • 1968 • Davis Don • USA • TASTERS, THE ○ GREAT TASTE
ODD TRIANGLE • 1969 • Sarno Joe • USA
ODD TRICK, THE see **HATTON OF HEADQUARTERS** • 1917
ODD TRICKS • 1924 • Rains Fred • UKN
ODDBALL see **MABOULE** • 1969
ODDBALLS see **ODD BALLS** • 1984
ODDBALLS, THE see **CHUDAKI** • 1974
ODDO • 1967 • Davis Joe • USA
ODDS 777 • 1932 • Schneevoigt George • DNM
ODDS AGAINST • 1915 • Trimble Larry • UKN • LOST AND WON
ODDS AGAINST HER, THE • 1919 • Butler Alexander • UKN
ODDS AGAINST TOMORROW • 1959 • Wise Robert • USA
ODDS AND ENDS • 1959 • Conger Jane Belson • SHT • USA
ODDS AND EVENS see **PARI E DISPARI** • 1978
ODDS AND EVENS see **PARES Y NONES** • 1983
ODDS ON • 1928 • Higgins Arthur • ASL
ODE TO AN OLD TEACHER see **AOGEBA TOTOSHI** • 1966
ODE TO BILLY JOE • 1976 • Baer Max • USA
ODE TO BLAKE • 1969 • Markowitz Murray • SHT • CND
ODE TO HAPPINESS see **ODA NA RADOST** • 1985
ODE TO MOM AND DAD • 1969 • Markowitz Murray • SHT • CND
ODED HANODED • 1933 • Axelrod Nathan • ISR
ODEMARKSPRASTEN • 1946 • Folke Gosta • SWD • CLERGYMAN FROM THE WILDS
ODEN BORTOM HORISON • 1955 • Werner Gosta • SHT • SWD
ODEN JIGOKU • 1960 • Kimura Keigo • JPN • ASSAULT FROM HELL
ODEON see **ALIEN FROM L.A.** • 1988
ODEON 36.72 see **ENTRE ONZE HEURES ET MINUIT** • 1948
ODESDIGRA KLOCKAN, DEN • 1966 • Malmqvist Bertil • SWD • FATEFUL BELL
ODESSA see **ODESSA IN FIAMME** • 1942
ODESSA FILE, THE • 1974 • Neame Ronald • UKN, FRG
ODESSA IN FIAMME • 1942 • Gallone Carmine • ITL • FIAMME IN ORIENTE ○ FIAMME SU ODESSA ○ ODESSA
ODETS • 1924 • Lindlof John • SWD • MAN OF DESTINY
ODETTE • 1915 • Brignone Guido • ITL
ODETTE • 1916 • De Liguoro Giuseppe • ITL
ODETTE • 1916 • Serena Gustavo • ITL
ODETTE • 1928 • Luitz-Morat • FRN
ODETTE • 1934 • Houssin Jacques, Zambon Giorgio • FRN, ITL • DECHEANCE
ODETTE • 1950 • Wilcox Herbert • UKN
ODETTE see **DESARROI** • 1946
ODETTE ET L'HISTOIRE DES FEMMES ILLUSTRES • 1919 • Curtiz Michael • SWD
ODEUR DES FAUVES, L' • 1971 • Balducci Richard • FRN, ITL
ODEUR, GOLD AND INCENSE see **MIRIS, TAMJAN I ZLATO** • 1971
ODHOD OD MASE V LJUTOMERA • 1905 • Grossman Karl • YGS
ODIA IL PROSSIMO TUO • 1968 • Baldi Ferdinando • ITL • HATE YOUR NEIGHBOUR
ODINNADTSATI • 1928 • Vertov Dziga • USS • ELEVENTH HOUR, THE ○ ELEVENTH, THE ○ ELEVENTH YEAR, THE
ODIO • 1935 • Harlan Richard • ARG
ODIO • 1939 • Rowland William • MXC • HATE (USA)
ODIO • 1980 • Mossy Carlo • BRZ • HATRED
ODIO E IL MIO DIO, L' • 1969 • Gora Claudio • ITL
ODIO LE BIONDE • 1980 • Capitani Giorgio • ITL, FRG, FRN • JE HAIS LES BLONDES (FRN) ○ I HATE BLONDES ○ ICH HASSE BLONDINEN
ODIO MI CUERPO • 1973 • Klimovsky Leon • SPN, SWT • I HATE MY BABY
ODIO MORTALE • 1963 • Montemurro Francesco • ITL
ODIO PER ODIO • 1967 • Paolella Domenico • ITL • HATE FOR HATE (UKN) ○ HATRED FOR HATRED
ODIPUSSI • 1988 • Loriot • FRG
ODIRANG • 1984 • SAF
ODISEA DEL GENERAL JOSE, LA • 1968 • Fraga Jorge • CUB • ODYSSEY OF GENERAL JOSE, THE ○ GENERAL JOSE'S ODYSSEY
ODISSEA, L' • 1911 • *Milano* • ITL • HOMER'S ODYSSEY (USA) ○ ADVENTURES OF ULYSSES, THE
ODISSEA DI MONTECASSINO, L' see **GRANDE STRADA, LA** • 1948
ODISSEA NUDA • 1961 • Rossi Franco • ITL, FRN • DIARY OF A VOYAGE IN THE SOUTH PACIFIC ○ NUDE ODYSSEY (USA) ○ LOVE -TAHITI STYLE ○ NAKED ODYSSEY ○ ODYSSEE NUE, L' (FRN)
ODKAZ • 1965 • Schorm Evald • CZC • HERITAGE
ODNA • 1931 • Kozintsev Grigori, Trauberg Leonid • USS • ALONE
ODNA SEMJA • 1943 • Alexandrov Grigori • USS • ONE FAMILY
ODNAZHDI NOCH • 1945 • Barnet Boris • USS • ONE NIGHT
ODONGO • 1956 • Gilling John • UKN
ODOR-ABLE KITTY • 1945 • Jones Charles M. • ANS • USA
ODOR IN THE COURT • 1934 • Holmes Ben • SHT • USA
ODOR OF THE DAY • 1948 • Davis Arthur • ANS • USA
ODORIKO • 1957 • *Kyo Machiko* • JPN • DANCING GIRL
ODOSHI • 1966 • Fukasaku Kinji • JPN • THREAT
ODOUR OF THE BREAST see **CHIBUSA NO KAORI** • 1968
ODPOWIEDZ • 1961 • Drapella Hubert • PLN • ANSWER, THE
ODVAHU PRO VSEDNI DEN see **KAZDY DEN ODVAHU** • 1964
ODVAZNA SLECNA • 1969 • Filip Frantisek • CZC • COURAGEOUS OLD MAID, THE ○ RESOLUTE SPINSTER, THE
ODWIEDZINY O ZMIERZCHU • 1966 • Rybkowski Jan • MTV • PLN • VISIT AT TWILIGHT ○ VISIT AT DUSK, A
ODWIEDZINY PREZYDENTA • 1961 • Batory Jan • PLN • VISIT FROM THE PRESIDENT ○ PRESIDENT'S VISIT, THE
ODWROT • 1969 • Surdel Jerzy • DCS • PLN • RETREAT, THE
ODYGDENS BELONING • 1937 • Lindlof John, Wahlberg Gideon • SWD
ODYSEE DU CAPITAINE STEVE, L' (FRN) see **WALK INTO HELL** • 1957
ODYSSEE D'AMOUR • 1987 • de la Parra Pim • NTH
ODYSSEE DU CAPITAINE STEVE, L' • 1956 • Pagliero Marcello • FRN • VALLEE DU PARADIS, LA
ODYSSEE DU MANHATTAN, L' • 1970 • Gosselin Bernard • DCS • CND
ODYSSEE DU TCHELIOUSKINE, L' • 1934 • Poselsky I. • USS
ODYSSEE NUE, L' (FRN) see **ODISSEA NUDA** • 1961
ODYSSEUS' HEIMKEHR • 1918 • Biebrach Rudolf • FRG
ODYSSEY • 1985 • Tyller Jiri • ANM • CZC, GDR
ODYSSEY 68 • 1968 • Einarson Oddvar • SHT • NRW
ODYSSEY, THE • 1963 • Cantrill Arthur, Cantrill Corinne • ANM • ASL
ODYSSEY IN AUGUST • 1990 • Roscoe Stephen • SHT • CND
ODYSSEY OF GENERAL JOSE, THE see **ODISEA DEL GENERAL JOSE, LA** • 1968
ODYSSEY OF THE NORTH, AN • 1914 • Bosworth Hobart • USA
ODYSSEY OF THE PACIFIC see **EMPEROR OF PERU, THE** • 1981
OEDIPE • 1910 • De Liguoro Giuseppe • ITL
OEDIPUS • 1950-53 • Vickrey Robert • SHT • USA
OEDIPUS ORCA • 1977 • Visconti Eriprando • ITL
OEDIPUS REX • 1957 • Guthrie Tyrone • CND
OEDIPUS REX see **EDIPO RE** • 1967
OEDIPUS THE KING • 1967 • Saville Philip • UKN
OEDIPUS THE KING see **EDIPO RE** • 1967
OEDO GONIN OTOKO • 1951 • Ito Daisuke • JPN • FIVE MEN OF EDO
OEDO NO ONI • 1947 • Hagiwara Ryo • JPN • DEVIL OF EDO
OEDO NO SAIGON • 1928 • *Tsuburaya Eiji (Ph)* • JPN
OEIL, L' • 1982 • Sow Thierno Faty • SNL
OEIL BLEU, L' • 1968 • Sandoz Jacques • SWT • BLUE EYE, THE
OEIL DE LYNX DETECTIVE • 1936 • Ducis Pierre-Jean • FRN
OEIL DU MAITRE, L' • 1957 • Doniol-Valcroze Jacques • FRN
OEIL DU MAITRE, L' • 1979 • Kurc Stephane • FRN
OEIL DU MALIN, L' • 1961 • Chabrol Claude • FRN, ITL • THIRD LOVER, THE (USA)
OEIL DU MONOCLE, L' • 1962 • Lautner Georges • FRN • EYE OF THE MONOCLE, THE (USA)
OEIL EN COULISSES, L' • 1953 • Berthomieu Andre • FRN
OEIL ET FANTASMES SEXUELS, L' • Morgan Charles • FRN
OEIL POUR OEIL • 1918 • Capellani Albert • FRN • EYE FOR AN EYE
OEIL POUR OEIL • 1957 • Cayatte Andre • FRN, ITL • OCCHIO PER OCCHIO (ITL) ○ EYE FOR AN EYE, AN (USA) ○ EYES OF THE SAHARA
OEIL TORVE, L' see **OKO WYKOL** • 1960
OELPRINZ, DER • 1965 • Philipp Harald • FRG, YGS • RAMPAGE AT APACHE WELLS (USA) ○ KRALJ PETROLEJA (YGS) ○ OLPRINZ, DER
O'ER GRIM FIELDS SCARRED • 1911 • *Reliance* • USA
O'ER HILL AND DALE • 1931 • Wright Basil • DOC • UKN
OESTE NEVADA JOE • 1965 • Iquino Ignacio F. • SPN, ITL • SFIDA DEGLI IMPLACABILI, LA (ITL) ○ JOE DEXTER
OEUF, L' • 1971 • Herman Jean • FRN
OEUF, L' • 1971 • Warny Clorinda • ANS • CND
OEUF A LA COQUE, L' • 1963 • Andrieux Marc, Brevent Bernard • ANS • FRN • BOILED EGG (USA) ○ ROOSTER'S EGG, THE
OEUF D'EPINOCHE, L' • 1929 • Painleve Jean • SHT • FRN
OEUF DU SORCIER OU L'OEUF MAGIQUE PROLIFIQUE, L' • 1902 • Melies Georges • FRN • PROLIFIC MAGICAL EGG, THE (USA) ○ EGG IN BLACK ART, THE
OEUFS BROUILLES, LES • 1975 • Santoni Joel • FRN
OEUFS DE L'AUTRUCHE, LES • 1957 • de La Patelliere Denys • FRN • OSTRICH HAS TWO EGGS, THE
OEUVRE AU NOIR, L' • 1988 • Delvaux Andre • BLG, FRN • ABYSS, THE
OEUVRE BIOLOGIQUE DE PASTEUR, L' see **PASTEUR** • 1947
OEUVRE DE JACQUES SERVAL, L' • 1913 • Carre Michel • FRN
OEUVRE IMMORTELLE, L' • 1923 • Duvivier Julien • BLG
OEYAMA SHUTEN DOJI • 1960 • Tanaka Tokuzo • JPN • OGRE IN MT. OE, THE
OF A HOUSE AND A RENTED FLAT see **KE GHAR KE DERA** • 1985
OF A THOUSAND DELIGHTS see **...VAGHE STELLE DELL'ORSA** • 1965
OF AZTEC RACE see **DE RAZA AZTECA** • 1922
OF BEDS AND BROADS see **PARISIENNES, LES** • 1962
OF CASH AND HASH • 1955 • White Jules • SHT • USA
OF CHICANO BLOOD see **DE SANGRE CHICANA** • 1973
OF-COURSE-I-CAN BROTHERS, THE • 1913 • Plumb Hay • UKN
...OF DURF JE NIET? • 1965 • van der Linden Charles Huguenot • SHT • NTH • OR DON'T YOU DARE?
OF FELINE BONDAGE • 1965 • Jones Charles M. • ANS • USA

OF FLESH AND BLOOD (USA) see **GRANDS CHEMINS, LES** • 1963
OF FOX AND HOUNDS • 1940 • Avery Tex • ANS • USA
OF GODS AND THE UNDEAD (USA) see **DEUSES E OS MORTOS, OS** • 1970
OF GREAT EVENTS AND ORDINARY PEOPLE see **DE GRANDS EVENEMENTS ET DES GENS ORDINAIRES** • 1979
OF HOLES AND CORKS (USA) see **O RUPAMA CEPOVIMA** • 1967
OF HUMAN BONDAGE • 1934 • Cromwell John • USA
OF HUMAN BONDAGE • 1946 • Goulding Edmund • USA
OF HUMAN BONDAGE • 1964 • Hughes Ken, Hathaway Henry (U/c) • UKN, USA
OF HUMAN HEARTS • 1938 • Brown Clarence • USA • BENEFITS FORGOT
OF HUMAN RIGHTS • 1950 • van Dongen Helen • NTH
OF LIFE AND LOVE (USA) see **QUESTA E LA VITA** • 1954
OF LOVE AND BANDITS (USA) see **DONNE E BRIGANTI** • 1951
OF LOVE AND DESIRE • 1963 • Rush Richard • USA • FORSAKEN GARDEN, THE ○ IN A SECRET GARDEN
OF LOVE AND LUST (USA) see **GIFTAS** • 1957
OF LOVE AND OTHER LONELY THINGS see **DEL AMOR Y OTRAS SOLEDADES** • 1969
OF MEN AND DEMONS • 1969 • Hubley John, Hubley Faith • ANS • USA
OF MEN AND MONEY see **I RO HA NI HO HE TU** • 1960
OF MEN AND MUSIC • 1950 • Reis Irving, Hammid Alexander • USA
OF MICE AND BEN see **O MISU I SATOVIMA** • 1969
OF MICE AND MAGIC • 1953 • Sparber I. • ANS • USA
OF MICE AND MEN • 1939 • Milestone Lewis • USA
OF MICE AND MEN • 1981 • Badiyi Reza • TVM • USA
OF MICE AND MEN see **O MISU I SATOVIMA** • 1969
OF MICE AND MENACE • 1954 • Kneitel Seymour • ANS • USA
OF PUPS AND PUZZLES • 1941 • Sidney George • SHT • USA
OF PURE BLOOD • 1986 • Sargent Joseph • TVM • USA
OF RICE AND HEN • 1953 • McKimson Robert • ANS • USA
OF SOUND AND FURY see **DE BRUIT ET DE FUREUR** • 1988
OF STARS AND MEN • 1964 • Hubley John • ANM • USA
OF STRAWBERRY, LEMON AND MINT see **DE FRESA, LIMON Y MENTA** • 1977
OF SUCH IS THE KINGDOM • 1913 • *Reliance* • USA
OF THE MARK see **CRAZY LEGS** • 1987
OF THE SAME GENDER • 1968 • Stein Phyllis • USA • SAME GENDER
OF THEE I STING • 1946 • Freleng Friz • ANS • USA
OF UNKNOWN ORIGIN • 1983 • Cosmatos George Pan • USA
OF WAYWARD LOVE (USA) see **AMORE DIFFICILE, L'** • 1962
OFELAS see **VEIVISEREN** • 1987
OFELIA KOMMER TIL BYEN • 1986 • Carlsen Jon Bang • DNM • OPHELIA COMES TO TOWN
OFF BALANCE • 1928 • White Jules • USA
OFF BALANCE see **PHANTOM OF DEATH** • 1987
OFF BEAT • 1986 • Dinner Michael • USA
OFF FOR A BOAT RIDE • 1915 • *Kelly James T.* • USA
OFF FOR THE HOLIDAYS • 1904 • Stow Percy • UKN
OFF FOR THE HOLIDAYS • 1910 • Stow Percy • UKN
OFF-HANDED JAPE, THE • 1966-67 • Nelson Robert • SHT • USA
OFF HIS BEAT • 1925 • Christie Al • USA
OFF HIS BEAT • 1925 • Mayo Archie • SHT • USA
OFF HIS TROLLEY • 1920 • Howe J. A. • SHT • USA
OFF HIS TROLLEY • 1924 • Cline Eddie • SHT • USA
OFF LIMITS • 1952 • Marshall George • USA • MILITARY POLICEMEN (UKN)
OFF LIMITS • 1988 • Bani-Etemad Rakhshan • IRN
OFF LIMITS • 1988 • Crowe Christopher • USA • SAIGON (UKN)
OFF OFF OFF OR ON THE ROOF OF PABLO NERUDA see **OFF OFF OFF OU SUR LE TOIT DE PABLO NERUDA** • 1990
OFF OFF OFF OU SUR LE TOIT DE PABLO NERUDA • 1990 • Fajardo Jorge • CND • OFF OFF OFF OR ON THE ROOF OF PABLO NERUDA
OFF ON see **OFFON** • 1968
OFF ON A COMET • 1979 • Slapczynski Richard • ANM • USA
OFF-SHORE PIRATE, THE • 1921 • Fitzgerald Dallas M. • USA
OFF-SIDE • 1972 • Ferendeles Andrea • ITL
OFF SIDES • 1984 • Lowry Dick • TVM • USA • PIGS VS. FREAKS ○ PIGS VERSUS THE FREAKS, THE
OFF THE AIR • 1980 • Levanon Yaud • ISR
OFF THE BEATEN TRACK • 1960 • Sharples Syd • UKN
OFF THE BEATEN TRACK (UKN) see **BEHIND THE EIGHT BALL** • 1942
OFF THE DOLE • 1935 • Mertz Arthur • UKN
OFF THE EARTH • 1922 • *Universal* • SHT • USA
OFF THE EDGE • 1977 • Firth Michael • DOC • USA
OFF THE HIGHWAY • 1925 • Forman Tom • USA
OFF THE MAIN ROAD • 1970 • Pines James O. • SHT • UKN
OFF THE MAINLAND • 1913 • *Ryno* • USA
OFF THE MINNESOTA STRIP • 1980 • Johnson Lamont • TVM • USA
OFF THE RECORD • 1939 • Flood James • USA • UNFIT TO PRINT (UKN)
OFF THE ROAD • 1913 • Ince Ralph • USA
OFF THE SCENT • 1926 • Barnett Charles • UKN
OFF THE SCENT • 1934 • Samuelson G. B. • UKN
OFF THE TROLLEY • 1919 • Roach Hal • SHT • USA
OFF THE WALL • 1977 • King Rick • USA
OFF THE WALL • 1981 • May Derek • CND
OFF THE WALL • 1983 • Friedberg Rick • USA • SNAKE CANYON PRISON
OFF TO BEDLAM (UKN) see **OMNIBUS DES TOQUES BLANCS ET NOIRS, L'** • 1901
OFF TO BLOOMINGDALE ASYLUM (USA) see **OMNIBUS DES TOQUES BLANCS ET NOIRS, L'** • 1901
OFF TO BUFFALO see **GIVE MY REGARDS TO BROADWAY** • 1948
OFF TO CHINA • 1936 • *Terry Paul/ Moser Frank (P)* • ANS • USA
OFF TO PEORIA • 1930 • Sandrich Mark • SHT • USA
OFF TO PHILADELPHIA • 1929 • Aylott Dave, Symmons E. F. • SHT • UKN
OFF TO THE FRONT • 1914 • ASL
OFF TO THE OPERA • 1952 • Rasinski Connie • ANS • USA
OFF TO THE RACES • 1937 • Strayer Frank • USA
OFF WE GLOW • 1952 • Sparber I. • ANS • USA
OFF YOUR ROCKER • 1980 • Markson Morley, Pall Larry • CND
OFFBEAT • 1961 • Owen Cliff • UKN • DEVIL INSIDE, THE
OFFENCE, THE • 1973 • Lumet Sidney • UKN • SOMETHING LIKE THE TRUTH
OFFEND THE LAW OF GOD see **NU-FAN T'IEN-T'AIO** • 1982
OFFENDERS, THE • 1924 • Holmes Fenwicke L. • USA
OFFENDING KISS, THE • 1915 • Davis Ulysses • USA
OFFENE GRAB, DAS • 1921 • Eichgrun Bruno • FRG
OFFENER HASS GEGEN UNBEKANNT • 1970 • Hauff Reinhard • FRG
OFFENSIVE SYSTEM • 1931 • Kelley Albert • SHT • USA
OFFENTLICHE ROST, DEN • 1988 • Marcussen Leif • ANM • DNM • PUBLIC VOICE, THE
OFFERING, THE • 1967 • Secter David • CND
OFFERING, THE • 1973 • Papadopoulos John • SHT • ASL
OFFERINGS • 1989 • Reynolds Christopher • USA
OFFICE, THE see **URZAD** • 1969
OFFICE AFFAIR, AN see **SLUZHEBNI ROMAN** • 1977
OFFICE BOY, THE • 1930 • Foster John, Bailey Harry • ANS • USA
OFFICE BOY, THE • 1932 • *Iwerks Ub (P)* • ANS • USA
OFFICE BOY'S BIRTHDAY, THE • 1913 • Seay Charles M. • USA
OFFICE BOY'S DREAM, THE • 1908 • Aylott Dave • UKN
OFFICE BOY'S DREAM, THE • 1911 • *Comet* • USA
OFFICE BOY'S REVENGE, THE • 1903 • Porter Edwin S. • USA
OFFICE BOY'S REVENGE, THE • 1904 • Collins Alf? • UKN
OFFICE FAVORITE, THE • 1912 • *Zieman Bennie* • USA
OFFICE GIRL, THE (USA) see **SUNSHINE SUSIE** • 1932
OFFICE LOVE-IN, WHITE COLLAR STYLE • 1968 • Stephen A. C. • USA • SWINGING SECRETARY
OFFICE PARTY • 1989 • Mihalka George • CND
OFFICE PARTY, THE • 1968 • Scott Ron • USA
OFFICE PARTY, THE • 1976 • Grant David • UKN
OFFICE PARTY, THE see **FIRMAFESTEN** • 1973
OFFICE PICNIC, THE • 1972 • Cowan Tom • ASL
OFFICE ROMANCE, AN see **SLUZHEBNI ROMAN** • 1977
OFFICE SCANDAL, THE • 1929 • Stein Paul L. • USA
OFFICE WIFE, THE • 1930 • Bacon Lloyd • USA
OFFICE WIFE, THE • 1934 • King George • UKN
OFFICER 13 • 1933 • Melford George • USA
OFFICER 174 • 1912 • *Baggot King* • USA
OFFICER 444 • 1926 • Wilson Ben, Ford Francis • SRL • USA
OFFICER 666 • 1914 • Powell Frank • USA
OFFICER 666 • 1916 • Niblo Fred • ASL
OFFICER 666 • 1920 • Beaumont Harry • USA
OFFICER AND A GENTLEMAN, AN • 1911 • *Solax* • USA
OFFICER AND A GENTLEMAN, AN • 1914 • Lambart Harry • USA
OFFICER AND A GENTLEMAN, AN • 1984 • Hackford Taylor • USA
OFFICER AND THE LADY, THE • 1941 • White Sam • USA
OFFICER, CALL A COP! • 1917 • Beaudine William • SHT • USA
OFFICER, CALL A COP • 1920 • Lyons Eddie, Moran Lee • SHT • USA
OFFICER CUPID • 1921 • *Sennett Mack (P)* • SHT • USA
OFFICER DUCK • 1939 • Geronimi Clyde • ANS • USA
OFFICER HENDERSON • 1913 • *Solax* • USA • WHAT HAPPENED TO HENDERSON
OFFICER JERRY • 1917 • Fahrney Milton • SHT • USA
OFFICER JIM • 1914 • Ince John • USA
OFFICER JIM • 1926 • McGaugh Wilbur • USA
OFFICER JOHN DONOVAN • 1914 • Brooke Van Dyke • USA
OFFICER KATE • 1914 • Finley Ned • USA
OFFICER MCCUE • 1909 • *Lubin* • USA
OFFICER MURRAY • 1912 • *Clary Charles* • USA
OFFICER O'BRIEN • 1930 • Garnett Tay • USA • BIG SHOT, THE
OFFICER POOCH • 1941 • Hanna William, Barbera Joseph • ANS • USA
OFFICER, SAVE MY CHILD • 1932 • Breslow Lou • SHT • USA
OFFICER WITH A ROSE see **OFICIR SA RUZOM** • 1987
OFFICER'S MESS, THE • 1931 • Haynes Manning • UKN
OFFICER'S MISS, AN • 1917 • *Triangle* • USA
OFFICERS OF FRENCH ARMY LEAVING SERVICE see **DEPART DES OFFICIERS** • 1896
OFFICER'S SWORD, THE see **TISZTI KARDBOJT, A** • 1915
OFFICER'S SWORDKNOT, THE see **TISZTI KARDBOJT, A** • 1915
OFFICIAL 0008 see **MAMOUR-E-0008** • 1967
OFFICIAL 114 see **MAMOUR-E-114** • 1967
OFFICIAL APPOINTMENT, AN • 1912 • Kent Charles • USA
OFFICIAL GOAT PROTECTOR, THE • 1913 • *Chamberlain Riley* • USA
OFFICIAL HISTORY see **HISTORIA OFFICIAL, LA** • 1984
OFFICIAL MOTION PICTURES OF THE JOHNNY BUFF-PANCHO VILLA BOXING EXHIBITION HELD AT ERBET'S FIELD.. • 1922 • *Britton Leon D.* • USA
OFFICIAL OFFICERS • 1925 • Roach Hal • SHT • USA
OFFICIAL POSITION, THE see **SLUZBENI POLOZAJ** • 1964
OFFICIAL SECRET see **SPIES OF THE AIR** • 1939
OFFICIAL STORY, THE (USA) see **HISTORIA OFFICIAL, LA** • 1984
OFFICIAL VERSION, THE (UKN) see **HISTORIA OFFICIAL, LA** • 1984
OFFICIER DE POLICE SANS IMPORTANCE, UN • 1973 • Larriaga Jean • FRN, ITL • REQUIEM PER UN COMMISSARIO DI POLIZIA (ITL)
OFFIZIERSTRAGODIE, EINE see **ROSENMONTAG** • 1924
OFFON • 1968 • Bartlett Scott • SHT • USA • OFF ON
OFFRET • 1985 • Tarkovsky Andrei • SWD, FRN • SACRIFICE, LE (FRN) ○ SACRIFICE, THE
OFFSPRING, THE see **FROM A WHISPER TO A SCREAM** • 1987
OFICINA NO.1 • 1974 • Rojas Abigail • VNZ
OFICIO DE TINIEBLAS • 1978 • Burns Archibaldo • MXC
OFICIO MAS ANTIGUO, EL • 1968 • Alcoriza Luis • MXC
OFICIOS DE CANDIDO, LOS • 1965 • Aguirre Javier • SPN
OFICIR SA RUZOM • 1987 • Sorak Dejan • YGS • OFFICER WITH A ROSE
O'FLANAGAN'S LUCK • 1914 • *Royal* • USA
O'FLYNN, THE • 1948 • Pierson Arthur • USA • FIGHTING O'FLYNN, THE (UKN)
OFRENDA • 1953 • Reiguera Francisco • MXC
OFTEN AN ORPHAN • 1949 • Jones Charles M. • ANS • USA
OG DER ER BAL BAGEFTER • 1971 • Fleming Edward • DNM • AND THERE'S DANCING AFTERWARDS
OGALLALAH • 1911 • *Powers* • USA
O'GARRY OF THE ROYAL MOUNTED • 1915 • Finley Ned • USA
O'GARRY RIDES ALONE • 1918 • *Finley Ned* • SHT • USA
OGGETTI SMARRITI • 1979 • Bertolucci Giuseppe • ITL • ITALIAN WOMAN, AN
OGGI A BERLINO • 1962 • Vivarelli Piero • ITL
OGGI A ME, DOMANI A TE • 1968 • Cervi Tonino • ITL • MY TURN TODAY, YOURS TOMORROW ○ TODAY ITS ME – TOMORROW YOU
OGGI DOMANI DOPODOMANI • 1965 • Ferreri Marco, De Filippo Eduardo, Salce Luciano • ITL, FRN • PARANOIA (USA) ○ OGGI DOMANI E DOPODOMANI ○ TODAY, TOMORROW AND THE DAY AFTER ○ KISS THE OTHER SHEIK ○ BLOND WIFE, THE
OGGI DOMANI E DOPODOMANI see **OGGI DOMANI DOPODOMANI** • 1965
OGGI SPOSI • 1934 • Brignone Guido • ITL • VIAGGIO DI NOZZE ALL'80%
OGGI SPOSI • 1952 • Girolami Marino • ITL
OGHIN-SAMA • 1960 • Tanaka Kinuyo • JPN • LOVE UNDER THE CRUCIFIX
OGIEN • 1971 • Brzozowski Andrzej • PLN • FIRE
OGIFT FADER SOKES • 1953 • Logardt Bengt, Dahlin Hans • SWD • UNMARRIED MOTHERS
OGIN SAMA • 1977 • Kumai Kei • JPN • LOVE AND FAITH (USA) ○ LADY OGIN ○ OGINSAMA
OGINSAMA see **OGIN SAMA** • 1977
OGLEDALO • 1971 • Grgic Zlatko • ANS • YGS • MIRROR, THE
OGNENNYE VERSTY • 1957 • Samsonov Samson • USS • FIERY MILES, THE ○ MILES OF FIRE
OGNI BAKU • 1950 • Heifitz Josif, Zarkhi Alexander • USS • FIRES OF BAKU ○ FLAMES OF BAKU ○ LIGHTS OF BAKU, THE
OGNIOMISTRZ KALEN • 1961 • Petelska Ewa, Petelski Czeslaw • PLN • SERGEANT MAJOR KALEN ○ MOUNTAINS OF FIRE ○ MOUNTAINS ON FIRE
OGNUNO PER SE (ITL) see **GOLD VON SAM COOPER, DAS** • 1968
OGON • 1930 • Donskoi Mark • USS • FIRE
OGON BATTO • 1966 • Sato Hajime • JPN • GOLDEN BAT
OGON KUJYAKU-JO • 1961 • Matsumura Shoji • JPN • ADVENTURES ON THE RYUKYUS ○ GOLDEN PEACOCK CASTLE ○ GOLDEN PEACOCK GARDEN
OGON NO ME • 1966 • Fukuda Jun • JPN
OGON NO TOZOKO • 1966 • Sawashima Tadashi • JPN • GOLDEN COUPLE, THE
OGON NO YARO-DOMO • 1967 • Ezaki Mio • JPN • GOLDEN MOB
OGRE, THE see **OGRO, EL** • 1969
OGRE, THE see **DEMONI 3** • 1988
OGRE AND THE GIRL, THE • 1915 • Greene Clay M. • USA
OGRE IN ATHENS, THE see **DRACOS** • 1956
OGRE IN MT. OE, THE see **OEYAMA SHUTEN DOJI** • 1960
OGRE OF ATHENS, THE see **DRACOS** • 1956
OGRES, THE • 1913 • *Solax* • USA
OGRE'S HOUSE, THE see **CASA DEL OGRO, LA** • 1938
OGRESS, THE see **ORCA, LA** • 1976
OGRESSES, LES (FRN) see **FATE, LE** • 1966
OGRO • 1979 • Pontecorvo Gillo • ITL • OPERATION OGRE ○ OPERACION OGRO
OGRO, EL • 1969 • Rodriguez Ismael • MXC • OGRE, THE
OH • 1968 • Vanderbeek Stan • ANS • USA
OH! ALFIE (USA) see **ALFIE DARLING** • 1975
OH AMELIA (USA) see **OCCUPE-TOI D'AMELIE** • 1949
OH! AMERICA • 1974 • Parbot Michel • DOC • FRN
OH ANNICE see **GOLD CURE, THE** • 1919
OH AUNTIE! • 1916 • Aylott Dave • UKN
OH! BABY • 1911 • *Walton Fred* • USA
OH, BABY • 1915 • *Royal* • USA
OH! BABY! • 1918 • Blystone John G. • SHT • USA
OH, BABY • 1919 • *Christie* • USA
OH, BABY! • 1920 • *Edwards Neely* • SHT • USA
OH, BABY! • 1926 • Knoles Harley • USA
OH BABYLON • 1989 • Ferris Kostas • GRC
OH BILL, BEHAVE! • 1919 • *Parsons Smiling Bill* • SHT • USA
OH BILLY, BEHAVE • 1926 • *Rayart Pictures* • USA
OH, BLACK FOREST, OH HOME (USA) see **O SCHWARZWALD, O HEIMAT** • 1939
OH, BLOODY LIFE! see **TE RONGYOS ELET..!** • 1984
OH, BOBBY, HOW COULD YOU! • 1918 • *Vernon Bobby* • USA
OH, BOY! • 1919 • Capellani Albert • USA
OH BOY! • 1938 • De Courville Albert • UKN
OH BRIDGET • 1925 • Mayo Archie • SHT • USA
OH BROTHER • 1974 • SAF
OH BUOY • 1920 • *Burns Sammy* • USA
OH! CALCUTTA! • 1972 • Aucion Guillaume Martin • USA
OH, CAROL see **COOL IT CAROL!** • 1970
OH! CE BAISER • 1917 • Hervil Rene • FRN
OH DAD! • 1987 • Amitay Jonathan • ANS • CND
OH DAD, POOR DAD, MAMA'S HUNG YOU IN THE CLOSET AND I'M FEELING SO SAD • 1967 • Quine Richard, Mackendrick Alexander • USA
OH, DADDY! • 1915 • Cooley Frank • USA
OH DADDY! • 1922 • Del Ruth Roy • SHT • USA
OH DADDY! • 1935 • Cutts Graham, Melford Austin • UKN
OH DARLING • 1930 • Roberts Stephen • SHT • USA
OH DEAR see **O JE** • 1985
OH DEAR, OH DEAR, OH DEAR see **OJ OJ OJ..** • 1966
OH DEAR UNCLE! • 1939 • Llewellyn Richard • UKN
OH DEM WATERMELONS • 1965 • Nelson Robert • SHT • USA
OH DIESE "LIEBEN" VERWANDTEN! • 1955 • Stockel Joe • FRG, AUS
OH DIESE MANNER • 1941 • Marischka Hubert • FRG
OH, DOCTOR! • 1914 • *Mason Billy* • USA
OH, DOCTOR! • 1915 • *Duncan Bud* • USA

OH, DOCTOR! • 1917 • Arbuckle Roscoe • SHT • USA
OH, DOCTOR! • 1925 • Pollard Harry • USA
OH, DOCTOR! • 1937 • McCarey Ray • USA
OH, DOCTOR see **HIT THE ICE** • 1943
OH DOLCI BACI E LANGUIDE CAREZZE • 1970 • Guerrini Mino • ITL
OH, DU LIEBER AUGUSTIN • 1922 • Breslauer H. K. • AUS
OH, DU LIEBER FRIDOLIN • 1952 • Hamel Peter • FRG
OH, DUCHESS! • 1936 • Lamont Charles • SHT • USA
OH, ETHEL! • 1919 • George Burton • SHT • USA
OH FASHION, FASHION see **O MODA, MODA** • 1969
OH! FATIMAH • 1989 • Badul A. R. • MLY
OH! FOR A CAVE MAN • 1916 • *Rhodes Billie* • USA
OH, FOR A MAN! • 1930 • MacFadden Hamilton • USA
OH! FOR A MAN! (UKN) see **WILL SUCCESS SPOIL ROCK HUNTER?** • 1957
OH FOR A PLUMBER! • 1933 • Newman Widgey R. • UKN
OH FOR A SMOKE! • 1912 • Plumb Hay? • UKN
OH, FOR A WIFE! • 1917 • Davey Forrest • USA
OH, FOR THE LIFE OF A FIREMAN! • 1916 • *Powell Russell* • USA
OH! FRENCHY • 1946 • Gould Dave • SHT • USA
OH GENTLE SPRING • 1942 • Rasinski Connie • ANS • USA
OH, GIRLS! • 1920 • Goldaine Mark • SHT • USA
OH, GOD! • 1977 • Reiner Carl • USA
OH GOD! BOOK II • 1980 • Cates Gilbert • USA
OH GOD, YOU DEVIL! • 1984 • Bogart Paul • USA
OH, GRANDMOTHER'S DEAD! see **TOH, E MORTA LA NONNA!** • 1969
OH HEAVENLY DOG • 1980 • Camp Joe • USA, UKN
OH, HOW I HATE TO GET UP IN THE MORNING • 1924-26 • Fleischer Dave • ANS • USA
OH! HOW I HATE TO GET UP IN THE MORNING • 1932 • Fleischer Dave • ANS • USA
OH, I SEE.. see **O, MOET DAT ZO** • 1975
OH, IS THAT THE WAY IT GOES.. • 1975 • Grasveld Fons • NTH
OH, IS THAT THE WAY IT'S DONE • 1976 • Grasveld Fons • SHT • NTH
OH, IT'S E.Z. • 1919 • *Turner Florence* • USA
OH, IT'S YOU! • 1911 • Stow Percy • UKN
OH JALISCO, DON'T BACK DOWN! see **AY, JALISCO, NO TE RAJES!** • 1941
OH! JEMIMAH! • 1920 • Mannering Cecil • UKN
OH, JO! • 1921 • Jones F. Richard • USA • OLD JO
OH, JOHNNY! • 1919 • Lowry Ira M. • USA
OH, JOHNNY, HOW YOU CAN LOVE! • 1940 • Lamont Charles • USA
OH JONATHAN • 1973 • Wirth Franz Peter • FRG • OH, JONATHAN -OH, JONATHAN!
OH, JONATHAN -OH, JONATHAN! see **OH JONATHAN** • 1973
OH, JUDGE, HOW COULD YOU • 1919 • Hunter T. Hayes • SHT • USA
OH, KAY! • 1928 • LeRoy Mervyn • USA
OH, LA-LA CHERI! see **PARIS COQUIN** • 1955
OH, LADY! LADY! • 1920 • Campbell Maurice • USA
OH! LES FEMMES! see **MAX ET LES FEMMES** • 1912
OH LIFE, WOE STORY, THE A-TEST NEWS! • 1963 • Brakhage Stan • SHT • USA
OH! LOOK WHO'S HERE! • 1914 • MacGregor Norval • USA
OH, LOUISE! • 1919 • *Philipp Adolf* • SHT • USA
OH, LOVELY ISTANBUL see **AH GUZEL ISTANBUL** • 1982
OH, MA MITRAILLEUSE A MUSIQUE see **PLAISIRS DE PARIS** • 1932
OH MABEL • 1924 • Fleischer Dave • ANS • USA
OH, MABEL BEHAVE • 1917 • Sennett Mack, Sterling Ford • USA
OH, MABEL BEHAVE • 1921 • Sennett Mack • SHT • USA
OH, MAN! • 1918 • Curtis Allen • SHT • USA
OH MARY BE CAREFUL • 1921 • Ashley Arthur • USA
OH ME, OH MY • 1969 • Hom Jesper • DNM
OH, MEN! OH, WOMEN! • 1957 • Johnson Nunnally • USA
OH, MIA BELLA MATRIGNA • 1976 • Leoni Guido • ITL
OH, MR. PORTER • 1937 • Varnel Marcel • UKN
OH MUMMY • 1927 • *Christie Al (P)* • SHT • USA
OH MY! • 1915 • Birch Cecil • UKN
OH! MY AUNT • 1913 • Collins Edwin J. • UKN
OH MY AUNT! • 1914 • Hepworth Cecil M. • UKN
OH MY DARLING • 1977 • Ring Borge • ANS • NTH
OH! MY DARLING • 1988 • Bak Cheol-Su • SKR
OH, MY DEAR • 1919 • *Vernon Bobby* • USA
OH MY OPERATION • 1932 • Cozine Ray • USA
OH! MY OPERATION • 1932 • Horne James W. • SHT • USA
OH! MY PAPA • 1968 • Crisostomo Fely • PHL
OH! MY PAPA see **FEUERWERK** • 1959
OH NO DOCTOR! • 1934 • King George • UKN
OH NO, JOHN, NO • 1944 • Munro Grant • ANS • CND
OH NO, MAM'ZELLE see **MAM'ZELLE NITOUCHE** • 1954
OH! OH! see **OCHI OCHI** • 1973
OH, OH, ANTONIO • 1908 • *Warwick Trading Co* • UKN
OH! OH! CLEOPATRA • 1931 • Santley Joseph • USA
OH, OH NURSIE! • 1919 • Lyons Eddie, Moran Lee • SHT • USA
OH! OH! OH! HENERY!! • 1916 • *Yorke Jay C.* • SHT • USA
OH OLSUN • 1974 • Egilmez Ertem • TRK • GOOD FOR YOU!
OH, PETER, PETER! see **VOI, PETER, PETER** • 1972
OH, POP! • 1917 • Jackson Harry • SHT • USA
OH, PROFESSOR, BEHAVE • 1946 • Yates Hal • SHT • USA
OH, PROMISE ME • 1921 • Roach Hal • SHT • USA
OH! QUE MAMBO • 1959 • Berry John • FRN, ITL • GIOVANE LEONE, IL (ITL)
OH! RATS! • 1909 • Porter Edwin S. • USA
OH ROSALINDA! • 1955 • Powell Michael, Pressburger Emeric • UKN, FRG • FLEDERMAUS '55
OH! SABELLA (UKN) see **NONNA SABELLA, LA** • 1957
OH! SAILOR BEHAVE! • 1930 • Mayo Archie • USA • NANCY FROM NAPLES
OH SALOME, OH, OH, OH! • 1909 • *Warwick Trading Co* • UKN
OH, SAMMY! • 1913 • Dillon Eddie • USA
OH, SAY CAN YOU HEAR? • 1937 • Schwarzwald Milton • SHT • USA
OH, SAY, CAN YOU SUE • 1953 • White Jules • SHT • USA
OH SAY, JIM • 1911 • *Powers* • USA
OH SAY YOU CAN SING see **SLIGHTLY SCANDALOUS** • 1946
OH SCHRECK, MEI' HOS IST WEG • 1976 • Frank Hubert • FRG
OH SCISSORS! • 1911 • Wilson Frank? • UKN
OH, SERAFINA! • 1976 • Lattuada Alberto • ITL
OH, SO SICK! • 1910 • *Essanay* • USA
OH! SUCH A BEAUTIFUL OCEAN! • 1913 • *Russell William* • USA
OH, SUCH A NIGHT! • 1912 • Golden Joseph A. • USA
OH, SUN see **SOLEIL O** • 1969
OH! SUPREME LOVE see **O! PAGSINTANG LABIS** • 1967
OH SUSANNA • 1933 • *Terry Paul/ Moser Frank (P)* • ANS • USA
OH SUSANNA • 1952 • Kane Joseph • USA
OH SUSANNA! see **OH SUSANNAH** • 1936
OH SUSANNAH • 1936 • Kane Joseph • USA • OH SUSANNA!
OH, SUSIE, BE CAREFUL • 1919 • Sidney Scott • USA
OH, SUZANNA • 1924-26 • Fleischer Dave • ANS • USA
OH TEACHER • 1924 • Hibbard Fred • USA
OH, TEACHER • 1927 • Disney Walt • ANS • USA
OH, TEACHER • 1932 • Lantz Walter, Nolan William • ANS • USA
OH, TEDDY • 1930 • Taurog Norman • SHT • USA
OH! THAT AWFUL TOOTH see **AT LAST! THAT AWFUL TOOTH** • 1902
OH THAT CAT! • 1907 • Collins Alf? • UKN
OH THAT COLLAR BUTTON • 1902 • Smith G. A. • UKN
OH THAT DOCTOR'S BOY! • 1906 • Martin J. H.? • UKN
OH! THAT FACE! • 1915 • Kellino W. P. • UKN
OH THAT HAT! • 1906 • Jeapes Harold? • UKN
OH, THAT INDIAN! • 1910 • *Powers* • USA
OH, THAT LEMONADE! • 1912 • *Crystal* • USA
OH THAT LIMERICK! • 1907 • Mottershaw Frank • UKN
OH THAT MOLAR! • 1907 • Cooper Arthur • UKN
OH, THAT NASTYA! see **OKH, UZH ETA NASTYA!** • 1973
OH, THAT RAZOR! • 1914 • *Captain Kettle Films* • UKN
OH, THAT TONIC! • 1910 • *Lux* • ITL
OH, THAT TOOTHACHE • 1906 • *Warwick Trading Co* • UKN
OH THAT WOOLLEN UNDERVEST! • 1913 • Kellino W. P. • UKN
OH THE CROCODILE! • 1910 • Rosenthal Joe • UKN
OH! THE WOMEN • 1918 • Grenier George G. • SHT • USA
OH ,THESE DAYS see **ALAYAM, ALAYAM** • 1977
OH, THESE POOR PEOPLE see **ESEK A FIATALOK** • 1967
OH! THIS IS MY WIFE see **AKH! AFTI I YINEKA MOU** • 1967
OH, THOSE BELLS! • 1960 • White Jules • USA
OH THOSE BOYS! • 1908 • Cooper Arthur • UKN
OH, THOSE EYES! • 1912 • Sennett Mack • USA
OH! THOSE MOST SECRET AGENTS see **002 AGENTI SEGRETISSIMI** • 1964
OH THOSE SHOES! • 1921 • *Hearty Harry* • SHT • UKN
OH, TO BE ON THE BANDWAGON see **MAN SKU VAERE NOGET VED MUSIKKEN** • 1969
OH TOMORROW NIGHT see **AH, I MORRON KVALL** • 1919
OH! U BOAT • 1917 • De Vonde Chester M. • SHT • USA
OH, UNCLE! • 1909 • Griffith D. W. • USA
OH, UNCLE! • 1926 • *Sennett Mack (P)* • SHT • USA
OH, WHAT A BOOB! • 1913 • Henderson Dell • USA
OH, WHAT A BOY see **AH, EN SA'N GRABB** • 1939
OH WHAT A DAY! • 1914 • Plumb Hay? • UKN
OH, WHAT A DAY • 1918 • Seiter William A. • USA
OH! WHAT A DREAM • 1913 • *Eclair* • USA
OH! WHAT A DREAM • 1914 • *Columbus* • USA
OH WHAT A DUCHESS! see **MY OLD DUCHESS** • 1933
OH WHAT A FLASH! see **WHAT A FLASH** • 1971
OH WHAT A HAPPY LAND • 1929 • Aylott Dave, Symmons E. F. • SHT • UKN
OH, WHAT A JAM! • 1919 • *Strand* • SHT • USA
OH! WHAT A KISS • 1967 • Conde Conrado • PHL
OH, WHAT A KNIGHT! • 1910 • *Thanhouser* • USA
OH, WHAT A KNIGHT • 1919 • Lehrman Henry • SHT • USA
OH, WHAT A KNIGHT • 1928 • Disney Walt • ANS • USA
OH WHAT A KNIGHT • 1982 • Driessen Paul • ANS • NTH
OH, WHAT A LAWYER see **A, EN SAN ADVOKAT** • 1940
OH! WHAT A LOVELY WAR • 1969 • Attenborough Richard • UKN
OH, WHAT A NIGHT • 1913 • *Reliance* • USA
OH! WHAT A NIGHT • 1914 • *XI Films* • UKN
OH, WHAT A NIGHT • 1919 • Christie Al • SHT • USA
OH, WHAT A NIGHT! • 1926 • Ingraham Lloyd • USA
OH WHAT A NIGHT • 1932 • Thring F. W., Wallace George • SHT • ASL
OH, WHAT A NIGHT! • 1935 • Richardson Frank • UKN
OH, WHAT A NIGHT! • 1937 • Parrott Charles • USA
OH, WHAT A NIGHT • 1944 • Beaudine William • USA
OH, WHAT A NIGHT see **ROUNDERS, THE** • 1914
OH, WHAT A NIGHT see **O, EN SA'N NATT** • 1937
OH, WHAT A NURSE • 1926 • Reisner Charles F. • USA
OH WHAT A PEACH! • 1912 • Collins Edwin J. • UKN
OH! WHAT A SURPRISE! • 1904 • Williamson James • UKN
OH, WHAT A SURPRISE! see **MR. PECKSNIFF FETCHES THE DOCTOR** • 1904
OH! WHAT A SWIM • 1913 • *Crystal* • USA
OH! WHAT A THANKSGIVING DAY! • 1911 • *Pathe* • USA
OH! WHAT A WHOPPER • 1916 • Goldin Sidney M. • SHT • USA
OH! WHAT AN APPETITE • 1908 • *Essanay* • USA
OH, WHAT TIMES, MR. DON SIMON see **AY, QUE TIEMPOS, SENOR DON SIMON!** • 1941
OH! WHAT'S THE USE? • 1914 • *Asher Max* • USA
OH, WHERE IS MY WANDERING BOY TONIGHT? • 1915 • *Mcdermott Marc* • USA
OH, WIFEY BE PLEASED • 1915 • Wilson Frank? • UKN
OH, YEAH! • 1929 • Garnett Tay • USA • NO BRAKES (UKN)
OH YEAH! • 1930 • Baker Eddie • USA
OH, YOU ARE LIKE A ROSE see **ACK, DU AR SOME EN ROS** • 1967
OH, YOU BABY! • 1912 • *Grant Nettie* • USA
OH YOU BEAUTIFUL DOLL • 1926 • Fleischer Dave • ANS • USA
OH YOU BEAUTIFUL DOLL • 1929 • Fleischer Dave • ANS • USA
OH, YOU BEAUTIFUL DOLL • 1949 • Stahl John M. • USA
OH! YOU CITY GIRL • 1915 • *Superba* • USA
OH! YOU EAST LYNN! • 1919 • Howe J. A. • SHT • USA
OH! YOU FLIRT • 1913 • *Imp* • USA
OH! YOU GYPSY GIRL • 1914 • *Crystal* • USA
OH YOU HAVE NO IDEA • 1929 • Aylott Dave, Symmons E. F. • SHT • UKN
OH, YOU HONEYMOON • 1916 • Peacocke Leslie T. • SHT • USA
OH, YOU KID! • 1920 • *Supreme Comedies* • USA
OH! YOU MOTHER-IN-LAW • 1911 • *Powers* • USA
OH! YOU MUMMY • 1914 • Smalley Phillips • USA
OH! YOU PEARL • 1913 • Smalley Phillips • USA
OH! YOU POPPI • 1915 • *Starlight* • USA
OH! YOU PUPPY • 1914 • Smalley Phillips • USA
OH! YOU RUBBER • 1913 • *Bright Lilly* • USA
OH! YOU SCOTCH LASSIE • 1913 • Smalley Phillips • USA
OH, YOU SKELETON • 1910 • *Selig* • USA
OH! YOU STENOGRAPHER • 1911 • *Solax* • USA
OH! YOU SUFFRAGETTE • 1911 • *American* • USA
OH YOU TEACHER • 1911 • *Essanay* • USA
OH, YOU TONY! • 1924 • Blystone John G. • USA
OH! YOU UNBREAKABLE DOLL • 1913 • *Lux* • FRN
OH YOU UNCLE! • 1916 • Greene Clay M. • SHT • USA
OH, YOU WOMEN! • 1919 • Emerson John • USA
OHANAHAN • 1966 • Nomura Yoshitaro • JPN • MISS ONANAHAN
OHANIAN see **KILLER WHO WOULDN'T DIE, THE** • 1976
O'HARA AND THE YOUTHFUL PRODIGAL • 1913 • Brooke Van Dyke • USA
O'HARA AS A GUARDIAN ANGEL • 1913 • Brooke Van Dyke • USA
O'HARA HELPS CUPID • 1913 • Brooke Van Dyke • USA
O'HARA OF THE MOUNTED • 1915 • *Federal* • USA
O'HARA SQUATTER AND PHILOSOPHER • 1912 • Brooke Van Dyke • USA
O'HARA: U.S. TREASURY • 1971 • Webb Jack • TVM • USA • OPERATION COBRA
O'HARA'S GODCHILD • 1913 • Brooke Van Dyke • USA
O'HARA'S WIFE • 1982 • Bartman William S. • USA
OHARU see **SAIKAKU ICHIDAI ONNA** • 1952
OHATARI TANKUI GOTEN • 1958 • Saeki Kozo • JPN • BADGER PALACE, THE
OHAYO • 1959 • Ozu Yasujiro • JPN • TOO MUCH TALK ○ GOOD MORNING
OHE PECHEURS! • Tessier Albert • DCS • CND
OHESO DE SHOBU • 1967 • Seki Koji • JPN • BET WITH A NAVEL, A
OHI • 1969 • Dadiras Dimis • GRC • NO!
OHIME GUSA • 1924 • Ikeda Yoshinobu • JPN • PRINCESS GRASS
OHLEDNUTI • 1968 • Masa Antonin • CZC • LOOKING BACK
OHM, DER NEFFE UND SIE, DER • 1915 • *Rose Berthold* • FRG
OHM KRUGER • 1941 • Steinhoff Hans • FRG
OHMET see **HELLYYS** • 1972
OHMS • 1980 • Lowry Dick • TVM • USA
OHMS -OUR HELPLESS MILLIONS SAVED • 1914 • Moran Percy • UKN
OHNE DATUM • 1962 • Domnick Ottomar • FRG
OHNE DICH KANN ICH NICHT LEBEN see **VERGISS MEIN NICHT** • 1958
OHNE DICH WIRD ES NACHT • 1956 • Jurgens Curd • FRG • WITHOUT YOU IT IS NIGHT
OHNE GELD DURCH DIE WELT • 1929 • Lowenbein Richard • FRG
OHNE HEIMAT see **GEFOLTERTE HERZEN 1** • 1920
OHNE KRIMI GEHT DIE MINI NIE INS BETT • 1962 • Antel Franz • AUS
OHNE MUTTER GEHT ES NICHT • 1958 • Ode Erik • FRG
OHNE NACHSICHT • 1972 • Kotulla Theodor • FRG
OHNE PASS IN FREMDEN BETTEN • 1965 • Brebera Vladimir • GDR
OHNE ZEUGEN • 1919 • Baron Erwin?, Kundert Georg? • AUS
OHNIVE LETO • 1939 • Cap Frantisek, Krska Vaclav • CZC • FIERY SUMMER
OHRFEIGEN • 1969 • Thiele Rolf • FRG
OHTORI-JO HANAYOME • 1957 • Matsuda Sadatsugu • JPN • LORD TAKES A BRIDE, THE
OHYAKU THE FEMALE DEMON • Ishikawa Yoshihiro • JPN
OI ATTEANTI • 1981 • Panoussopoulos George • GRC • FOOLISH LOVE, A
OIL • 1912 • Melies Gaston • USA
OIL • 1920 • North Wilfred • USA • LIQUID GOLD
OIL • 1977 • Dragan Mircea • ITL • OIL: THE BILLION DOLLAR FIRE
OIL 1972 • 1972 • Janabi Mohammed Yusef Al • IRQ
OIL AND ROMANCE • 1925 • Fraser Harry L. • USA
OIL AND WATER • 1913 • Griffith D. W. • USA
OIL CAN HARRY • 1933 • *Terry Paul (P)* • ASS • USA
OIL CAN MYSTERY, THE • 1933 • *Terry Paul/ Moser Frank (P)* • ANS • USA
OIL CAN ROMEO, AN • 1920 • *Byron Lillian* • SHT • USA
OIL CONSPIRACY, THE see **COMPLOT PETROLEO: LA CABEZA DE LA HIDRA** • 1980
OIL COUNTRY ROMANCE, AN • 1911 • Melies Gaston • USA • OIL COUNTY ROMANCE, AN
OIL COUNTY ROMANCE, AN see **OIL COUNTRY ROMANCE, AN** • 1911
OIL FIELD PLOT, THE • 1916 • Horne James W. • SHT • USA
OIL FOR ALADDIN'S LAMP • 1942 • Ivens Joris • SHT • USA
OIL FOR THE 20TH CENTURY • 1951 • Bradford Peter • UKN
OIL FOR THE LAMPS OF CHINA • 1935 • LeRoy Mervyn • USA
OIL HELL OF KILLING WOMEN see **ONNA GOROSHI ABURA JIGOKU** • 1949
OIL LAMPS see **PETROLEJOVE LAMPY** • 1972
OIL ON TROUBLED WATERS • 1913 • Dwan Allan • USA
OIL ON TROUBLED WATERS • 1926 • Barnett Charles • UKN
OIL RAIDER, THE • 1934 • Bennet Spencer Gordon • USA
OIL SMELLER, THE • 1916 • Hartigan P. C. • SHT • USA
OIL, THE BABY AND TRANSYLVANIANS, THE • 1981 • Pita Dan • RMN
OIL: THE BILLION DOLLAR FIRE see **OIL** • 1977
OIL THRU THE DAY • 1964 • Tendlar Dave • ANS • USA
OIL TOWN see **LUCY GALLANT** • 1955
OIL UNDER ICE see **VOYAGEURS, LES** • 1979
OIL UNDERGROUND • 1960 • Staugaard Peter • UKN

OIL WELL CONSPIRACY, THE • 1914 • *Holmes Helen* • USA
OIL WORKERS OF THE CASPIAN SEA see **POVEST O NEFTYANIKAKH KASPIYA** • 1953
OILEY PELOSO THE PUMPH MAN • 1965 • Nelson Robert • SHT • USA
OILFIELD, THE see **OLIEVELD, HET** • 1954
OILING UNCLE • 1920 • Lyons Eddie, Moran Lee • SHT • USA
OILMEN, THE • 1955 • Segaller Denis • UKN
OIL'S WELL • 1929 • Lantz Walter, Nolan William • ANS • USA
OIL'S WELL THAT ENDS WELL • 1949 • Yates Hal • SHT • USA
OIL'S WELL THAT ENDS WELL • 1958 • White Jules • SHT • USA
OILY AMERICAN, THE • 1954 • McKimson Robert • ANS • USA
OILY BIRD, THE • 1954 • Sparber I. • ANS • USA
OILY HARE • 1952 • McKimson Robert • ANS • USA
OILY MAN, THE • 1958 • *Keris* • MLY
OILY MAN STRIKES AGAIN, THE • 1958 • *Keris* • MLY
OILY SCANDAL, AN • 1916 • Frazee Edwin • SHT • USA
OILY TO BED, OILY TO RISE • 1939 • White Jules • SHT • USA
OINARU BAKUSHIN • 1960 • Sekigawa Hideo • JPN • DEVOTION OF THE RAILWAY, THE
OINARU TABIJO • 1960 • Sekigawa Hideo • JPN • THIS LIFE I LOVE ○ GREAT ROAD, THE
OISEAU, L' • 1965 • Vausseur Jacques • ANS • FRN • BIRD, THE
OISEAU BLANC, L' • 1970 • Bendeddouche Jamal • ALG
OISEAU BLANC, L' see **BLEUS DU CIEL, LES** • 1933
OISEAU DE LA SAGESSE, L' • 1966 • Lacam Henri • ANS • FRN • BIRD OF WISDOM (USA)
OISEAU DE MADAME BLOMER, L' • 1978 • Delrieux David • FRN
OISEAU DE NUIT • 1975 • Palacios Bernard • FRN • NIGHT BIRD
OISEAU DE PARADIS, L' • 1962 • Camus Marcel • FRN • DRAGON SKY (USA) ○ BIRD OF PARADISE, THE
OISEAU DE SANG, L' • Brottet Philippe • FRN, SPN • BIRD OF BLOOD, THE
OISEAU EN PAPIER JOURNAL, UN • 1962 • Pappe Julien • ANS • FRN • BIRD OF NEWSPAPER, A
OISEAU MOQUEUR, L' • 1956-62 • Enrico Robert • SHT • FRN
OISEAU RARE, L' • 1973 • Brialy Jean-Claude • FRN
OISEAU RARE, UN • 1935 • Pottier Richard • FRN • DEUX GAGNANTS, LES
OISEAUX BLANCS DE L'ILE D'ORLEANS, LES • 1977 • Letourneau Diane • CND
OISEAUX CLASSIFIES, LES • 1970 • Moreau Michel • DCS • CND
OISEAUX DE NUIT, LES • 1977 • Barnier Luc, Lasfargues Alain • DOC • FRN
OISEAUX DE PASSAGE • 1926 • Roudes Gaston • FRN
OISEAUX VONT MOURIR AU PEROU, LES • 1968 • Gary Romain • FRN • BIRDS COME TO DIE IN PERU, THE (UKN) ○ BIRDS IN PERU (USA)
OISIN • 1969 • Carey Patrick • DOC • IRL
OITO UNIVERSITARIOS • 1967 • Diegues Carlos • MTV • FRN
OJ OJ OJ.. • 1966 • Axelman Torbjorn • SWD • ELLER SANGEN OM DEN ELDRODA HUMMERN ○ OH DEAR, OH DEAR, OH DEAR ○ OJOJOJ, ELLER SANGEN OM DEN ELDRODA HUMMERN ○ POP ○ WELL.. WELL.. ○ SONG OF THE RED LOBSTER, THE
OJA NO KEN • 1959 • Kato Bin • JPN • GAIJIN
OJCIEC • 1967 • Hoffman Jerzy • MTV • PLN • FATHER, THE
OJCIEC KROLOWEJ • 1980 • Solarz Wojciech • PLN
OJCOWIE I DZIECI • 1969 • Lomnicki Jan • DOC • PLN • FATHERS AND CHILDREN
OJEBLIKKET • 1981 • Henning-Jensen Astrid • DNM • MOMENT, THE
OJISAN • 1943 • Shibuya Minoru • JPN • UNCLE
OJO DE AGUA • 1972 • Molinari Oscar • SHT • VNZ
OJO DE CRISTAL, EL • 1955 • Santillan Antonio • SPN
OJO DE DIOS, EL • 1972 • Roche Luis Armando • VNZ • GOD'S EYE
OJO DE LA ARANA, EL (SPN) see **OCCHIO DEL RAGNO, L'** • 1971
OJO DE LA CERRAUDURA, EL • 1964 • Torre-Nilsson Leopoldo • ARG, USA • EAVESDROPPER, THE (UKN)
OJO DE LA MUERTE, EL see **CABEZA VIVIENTE, LA** • 1961
OJO DE LA NOCHE, EL • Berriatua Luciano • SPN
OJO DEL HURACAN, EL • 1970 • Forque Jose Maria • SPN
OJO KICHIZA • 1927 • Kinugasa Teinosuke • JPN
OJO KICHIZA • 1959 • Tanaka Tokuzo • JPN • NAUGHTY ROGUE, THE
OJO TO YUBIWA • 1956 • *Toei Doga* • ANS • JPN • PRINCESS AND THE RING, THE
OJOJOJ, ELLER SANGEN OM DEN ELDRODA HUMMERN see **OJ OJ OJ..** • 1966
OJOS AZULES DE LA MUNECA ROTA, LOS • 1973 • Aured Carlos • SPN • BLUE EYES OF THE BROKEN DOLL, THE ○ HOUSE OF PSYCHOTIC WOMEN, THE ○ HOUSE OF DOOM
OJOS COME PAPA, LOS • 1979 • Chaskel Pedro • DOC • CUB • EYES LIKE DADDY
OJOS DE JUVENTUD • 1948 • Gomez Muriel Emilio • MXC
OJOS DE PERRO • 1982 • Durant Alberto • CUB, PRU • DOG'S EYES
OJOS DEJAN HUELLAS, LOS • 1952 • Saenz De Heredia Jose Luis • SPN
OJOS EN TUS MANOS, LOS • 1956 • Iglesias Miguel • SPN
OJOS MAS LINDO DEL MUNDO • 1943 • Saslavsky Luis • ARG
OJOS NEGROS • 1943 • Soler Fernando • MXC
OJOS PERDIDOS, LOS • 1967 • Garcia Serrano Rafael • SPN • LOST EYES
OJOS SINIESTROS DEL DOCTOR ORLOFF, LOS • 1973 • Franco Jesus • SPN
OJOS TAPATIOS • 1937 • Maicon Boris • MXC
OJOS TAPATIOS • 1960 • Martinez Solares Gilberto • MXC
OJOS VENDADOS, LOS • 1978 • Saura Carlos • SPN • BLINDFOLD ○ BLINDFOLDED EYES
OJOS VERDES see **VESTIDA DE NOVIA** • 1966
OJOSAN • 1930 • Ozu Yasujiro • JPN • YOUNG MISS
OJOSAN • 1937 • Yamamoto Satsuo • JPN • YOUNG MISS
OJOSAN • 1961 • Yuge Taro • JPN • MESDEMOISELLE, LES
OJOSAN KANPAI • 1949 • Kinoshita Keisuke • JPN • HERE'S TO THE GIRLS ○ TOAST TO THE YOUNG MISS, A ○ TOAST TO A YOUNG MISS
OJOSAN NO SAMPOMICHI • 1960 • Horiiki Kiyoshi • JPN
OJOSAN SHACHO • 1954 • Kawashima Yuzo • JPN • YOUNG LADY AS PRESIDENT, A
OJOSAN TOTO • 1956 • Yamamoto Kajiro • JPN • YOUNG LADY ON HER WAY, A
OK KETTEN • 1977 • Meszaros Marta • HNG • MARY AND JULIE ○ TWO OF THEM, THE ○ TWO WOMEN
OKA OORIE KATHA • 1977 • Sen Mrinal • IND • STORY OF A VILLAGE ○ OUTSIDERS, THE
OKAGURA KYODAI • 1946 • Inagaki Hiroshi • JPN
O'KALEMS VISIT TO KILLARNEY, THE • 1912 • Olcott Sidney • USA
OKALHOMA TERROR • 1939 • Bennet Spencer Gordon • USA
OKAME • 1927 • Gosho Heinosuke • JPN • MOON-FACED ○ PLAIN WOMAN, A
OKAMI see **OOKAMI** • 1955
OKAMI TO BUTA TO NINGEN • 1964 • Fukasaku Kinji • JPN • HUMAN WOLVES
OKANDA, DEN • 1913 • Stiller Mauritz • SWD • UNKNOWN WOMAN, THE
OKARINA, DIE • 1919 • Krafft Uwe Jens • FRG
OKASAN • 1952 • Naruse Mikio • JPN • MOTHER
OKASAN NON TOKYO KENBUTSU • 1957 • Murayama Shinji • JPN • MOTHER GOES SIGHTSEEING
OKASARETA BYAKUI • 1967 • Wakamatsu Koji • JPN • VIOLATED ANGELS
OKAVANGO • 1989 • Rubens Percival • SAF
OKAY AMERICA • 1932 • Garnett Tay • USA • PENALTY OF FAME (UKN)
OKAY BILL see **O.K. BILL** • 1968
OKAY BOSS..! • 1977 • Schulhoff Petr • CZC
OKAY FOR SOUND • 1937 • Varnel Marcel • UKN
OKAY SCERIFFO • 1966 • Zane Angio • ITL
OKAY TOOTS! • 1935 • Parrott Charles, Terhune William • SHT • USA
OKEFENOKEE • 1960 • Haig Roul • USA
OKENKO • 1933 • Slavinsky Vladimir • CZC • LITTLE WINDOW
OKEY DOKEY DONKEY • 1958 • Sparber I. • ANS • USA
OKEY KA CHOY • 1967 • To-Chi-Qui • PHL • YOU'RE O.K. CHAP
OKH, UZH ETA NASTYA! • 1973 • Pobedonostseva G. • USS • OH, THAT NASTYA!
OKHOTNIK IZ LALVARA • 1967 • Ai-Artyan A., Dildaryan I. • USS • HUNTER FROM LALVAR
OKIBAM, NON VENDERMI! • 1956 • Fontaine Gianni • ITL
OKICHI, MISTRESS OF A FOREIGNER see **TOJIN OKICHI** • 1931
OKICHI THE STRANGER see **TOJIN OKICHI** • 1931
OKINAWA • 1952 • Jason Leigh • USA
OKINAWA BATTLES see **OKINAWA KESSEN** • 1971
OKINAWA KESSEN • 1971 • Okamoto Kihachi • JPN • BATTLE OF OKINAWA ○ OKINAWA BATTLES
OKINAWA NO SHONEN • 1984 • Shinjo Hiroshi • JPN • OKINAWAN BOYS
OKINAWAN BOYS see **OKINAWA NO SHONEN** • 1984
OKKAR A MILLI • 1982 • Gunnlaugsson Hrafn • ICL • BETWEEN US ○ INTER NOS
OKKOMA HARI • 1967 • Hettiarachchi Wijepala • SLN • EVERYTHING'S ALL RIGHT
OKLAHOMA • 1911 • *Powers* • USA
OKLAHOMA! • 1955 • Zinnemann Fred • USA
OKLAHOMA ANNIE • 1952 • Springsteen R. G. • USA
OKLAHOMA BADLANDS • 1948 • Canutt Yakima • USA
OKLAHOMA BILL • 1910 • *Columbia* • USA
OKLAHOMA BLUES • 1948 • Hillyer Lambert • USA
OKLAHOMA CITY DOLLS, THE • 1981 • Swackhamer E. W. • TVM • USA
OKLAHOMA COWBOY, AN • 1929 • *Acord Art* • USA
OKLAHOMA CRUDE • 1973 • Kramer Stanley • USA
OKLAHOMA CYCLONE • 1930 • McCarthy John P. • USA
OKLAHOMA FRONTIER • 1939 • Beebe Ford • USA
OKLAHOMA JIM • 1931 • Fraser Harry L. • USA
OKLAHOMA JOHN see **RANCH DEGLI SPIETATI, IL** • 1965
OKLAHOMA JUSTICE • 1951 • Collins Lewis D. • USA • OKLAHOMA OUTLAWS
OKLAHOMA KID, THE • 1929 • McGowan J. P. • USA
OKLAHOMA KID, THE • 1939 • Bacon Lloyd • USA
OKLAHOMA OUTLAWS • 1943 • Eason B. Reeves • SHT • USA
OKLAHOMA OUTLAWS see **OKLAHOMA JUSTICE** • 1951
OKLAHOMA RAIDERS • 1943 • Collins Lewis D. • USA • MIDNIGHT RAIDERS (UKN)
OKLAHOMA RENEGADES • 1940 • Watt Nate • USA
OKLAHOMA SHERIFF, THE • 1930 • McGowan J. P. • USA
OKLAHOMA TERRITORY • 1960 • Cahn Edward L. • USA
OKLAHOMA WOMAN, THE • 1956 • Corman Roger • USA
OKLAHOMAN, THE • 1957 • Lyon Francis D. • USA
OKNO Z WIDOKIEM NA MORZE • 1978 • Zaorski Janusz • PLN • WINDOW LOOKING OUT ON THE SEA, THE ○ WINDOW ON THE SEA, THE
OKNO ZABITE DESKAMI • 1972 • Majewski Janusz • MTV • PLN • BOARDED WINDOW, THE
OKO WYKOL • 1960 • Skolimowski Jerzy • SHT • PLN • OEIL TORVE, L'
OKOME • 1951 • Dupont Jacques • SHT • FRN
OKORANA SEVASTOPOLVA • 1911 • Goncharov Vasili M., Khanzhonkov Alexander • USS • DEFENCE OF SEBASTOPOL, THE
OKOS LANY • 1955 • Macskassy Gyula • ANS • HNG • CLEVER GIRL
OKOS MAMA, AZ • 1936 • Martonffy Emil • HNG
OKOTO TO SASUKE • 1935 • Shimazu Yasujiro • JPN • OTOKO AND SASUKE
OKOTO TO SASUKE • 1961 • Kinugasa Teinosuke • JPN • OTOKO AND SASUKE
OKOUZLENA • 1942 • Vavra Otakar • CZC
OKOVANI SOFERI • 1976 • Pavlovic Vladimir • YGS, USS • DRIVERS IN CHAINS
OKRAGLY TYDZIEN • 1977 • Kutz Kazimierz • PLN • WHOLE WEEK, A
OKRAINA • 1933 • Barnet Boris • USS • OUTSIDE THE CITY ○ PATRIOTS (USA) ○ OUTSKIRTS ○ BORDERLINE
OKSIGEN • 1970 • Klopcic Matjaz • YGS • OXYGEN
OKSUZ • 1968 • Olgac Bilge • TRK • ORPHAN, THE
OKTOBER-DAGE • 1970 • Christensen Bent • DNM, PNM • ONLY WAY, THE ○ KOBENHAVN 43
OKTOBERFEST • 1987 • Kresoja Dragan • YGS
OKTOBERI VASARNAP • 1980 • Kovacs Andras • HNG • SUNDAY IN OCTOBER, A
OKTOBERVAART • 1965 • van der Linden Charles Huguenot • SHT • NTH
OKTYABR' • 1928 • Eisenstein Sergei, Alexandrov Grigori • USS • TEN DAYS THAT SHOOK THE WORLD ○ OCTOBER
OKUDZAWA • 1967 • Jaworski Tadeusz • DOC • PLN
OKUMAN CHOJA • 1954 • Ichikawa Kon • JPN • BILLIONAIRE, A
OKUMURA IOKO • 1940 • Toyoda Shiro • JPN • IOKO OKUMURA
OKUNI AND GOHEI see **OKUNI TO GOHEI** • 1952
OKUNI TO GOHEI • 1952 • Naruse Mikio • JPN • OKUNI AND GOHEI
OKUPACIJA U 26 SLIKA • 1977 • Zafranovic Lordan • YGS • OCCUPATION IN 26 PICTURES, THE ○ OCCUPATION IN 26 SCENES, THE
OKUSAMA NI GOYOSIN • 1950 • Nakamura Noboru • JPN
OKUSAMA NI SHIRASU BEKARAZU • 1937 • Shibuya Minoru • JPN • MADAME SHALL NOT KNOW
OKUSAMA SHAKUYOSHO • 1936 • Gosho Heinosuke • JPN • MARRIED LADY BORROWS MONEY, A
OL' GRAY HOSS, THE • 1928 • McGowan Robert • SHT • USA
OL' SWIMMING 'OLE, THE • 1928 • Disney Walt • ANS • USA
OLA & JULIA • 1967 • Halldoff Jan • SWD • OLAF AND JULIA
OLAF -AN ATOM • 1913 • Griffith D. W. • USA
OLAF AND JULIA see **OLA & JULIA** • 1967
OLAF BERNADOTTE • 1918 • Chrisander Nils • FRG
OLAF ERICKSON, BOSS • 1914 • *Leonard Robert* • USA
OLAF LAUGHS LAST • *Brendel El* • SHT • USA
OLANA OF THE SOUTH SEAS • 1914 • *Walcamp Marie* • USA
OLAVI • 1920 • *Lukas Paul* • HNG
OLAVIDE • 1974 • Artero Antonio • SHT • SPN
OLD ABE • 1917 • Chapin Benjamin • SHT • USA
OLD ACQUAINTANCE • 1943 • Sherman Vincent • USA
OLD ACTOR, AN • 1913 • Campbell Colin • USA
OLD ACTOR, THE • 1912 • Griffith D. W. • USA
OLD ACTOR'S STORY, THE • 1922 • Parkinson H. B. • UKN
OLD AGE see **TEMA 13: BATRINETEA** • 1984
OLD AGE AND FOLLY see **ALDERDOM OCH DARSKAP** • 1916
OLD AGE HANDICAP • 1928 • Mattison Frank S. • USA
OLD AGE PENSION • 1935 • Horne James W. • SHT • USA
OLD AGE -THE WASTED YEARS • 1966 • Leacock Richard • DOC • USA
OLD AND NEW TAHITI OR HOW THE INFANT CHIEF WAS SAVED • 1913 • *Bracken Mildred* • USA
OLD AND NEW (USA) see **STAROIE I NOVOIE** • 1929
OLD AND THE NEW, THE • 1915 • Morgan George • USA
OLD AND THE NEW, THE see **STAROIE I NOVOIE** • 1929
OLD AND YOUNG see **OREG ES FIATAL** • 1969
OLD APPOINTMENT, AN • 1912 • Miller Ashley • USA, UKN
OLD ARM CHAIR, THE • 1920 • Nash Percy • UKN
OLD ARMCHAIR, THE • 1913 • Conway Jack • USA
OLD ARMY CHEST, THE • 1909 • *Lubin* • USA
OLD ARMY COAT, THE • 1914 • *Joyce Alice* • USA
OLD ARMY GAME, THE • 1943 • King Jack • ANS • USA
OLD AUNT CHINA • 1959 • Perlov David • UKN
OLD BACHELOR, THE see **GERONTOKOROS, O** • 1967
OLD BACHELOR'S DREAM, THE see **SEN STAREHO MLADENCE** • 1910
OLD BANGUM • 1955 • Bunin Louis • ANM • USA
OLD BARN, THE • 1929 • Sennett Mack • SHT • USA
OLD BARN DANCE, THE • 1938 • Kane Joseph • USA
OLD BATCH, THE • 1915 • *Reliance* • USA
OLD BATTERSEA HOUSE • 1961 • Russell Ken • MTV • UKN
OLD BEECH, THE • 1957 • Kokochashvili Merab • SHT • USS
OLD BELL-RINGER, THE • 1914 • *Mcquarrie Murdock* • USA
OLD BILL see **OLD BILL THROUGH THE AGES** • 1924
OLD BILL, THE • 1932 • Marshall George • SHT • USA • OLD BULL, THE
OLD BILL AND SON • 1940 • Dalrymple Ian • UKN
OLD BILL THROUGH THE AGES • 1924 • Bentley Thomas • UKN • OLD BILL
OLD BILLY • 1911 • *Selig* • USA
OLD BLACK JOE • 1926 • Fleischer Dave • ANS • USA
OLD BLACK JOE • 1929 • Fleischer Dave • ANS • USA
OLD BLACKOUT JOE • 1942 • Sommer Paul, Hubley John • ANS • USA
OLD BONES OF THE RIVER • 1938 • Varnel Marcel • UKN
OLD BOOKKEEPER, THE • 1912 • Griffith D. W. • USA
OLD BOX, AN see **VIEILLE BOITE, UNE** • 1975
OLD BOYFRIENDS • 1979 • Tewkesbury Joan • USA
OLD BULL, THE see **OLD BILL, THE** • 1932
OLD CALIFORNIA • 1914 • *August Edwin* • USA
OLD CAPITAL, THE see **KOTO** • 1963
OLD CAPTAIN, THE • 1911 • *Selig* • USA
OLD CHEMIST, THE • 1915 • *Jefferson Thomas* • USA
OLD CHESS PLAYERS, THE • 1912 • *Lubin* • USA
OLD CHIEF'S DREAM, THE • 1912 • *Republic* • USA
OLD CHINESE OPERA see **STARA CINSKA OPERA** • 1954
OLD CHISHOLM TRAIL, THE • 1942 • Clifton Elmer • USA
OLD CHORISTER, THE • 1904 • Williamson James • UKN
OLD CITY, THE see **GAMLA STAN** • 1931
OLD CLERK, THE • 1913 • McRae Henry • USA
OLD CLOCK ON THE STAIRS, THE • 1912 • *Eclair* • USA
OLD CLOTHES • 1925 • Cline Eddie • USA • RAG MAN, THE
OLD CLOTHES FOR NEW • 1920 • Lyons Eddie, Moran Lee • SHT • USA
OLD CLOTHES SHOP, THE • 1915 • Warren Giles R. • USA
OLD COBBLER, THE • 1914 • MacQuarrie Murdock • USA
OLD CODE, THE • 1915 • *Stowell William* • USA
OLD CODE, THE • 1928 • Wilson Ben • USA
OLD COLLEGE BADGE, THE • 1913 • Raymond Charles • UKN
OLD COLONEL'S GRATITUDE, THE • 1912 • Coleby A. E.? • UKN
OLD COMPOSER AND THE PRIMA DONNA, THE • 1908 • Stow Percy • UKN

OLD CONFECTIONER'S MISTAKE, THE • 1911 • Griffith D. W. • USA
OLD CORRAL, THE • 1936 • Kane Joseph • USA • TEXAS SERENADE (UKN)
OLD CORRAL, THE (UKN) see **SONG OF THE GRINGO** • 1936
OLD COUNTRY, THE • 1921 • Bramble A. V. • UKN
OLD COUNTRY WHERE RIMBAUD DIED, THE see **VIEUX PAYS OU RIMBAUD EST MORT, LE** • 1977
OLD COUPONS • 1913 • O'Sullivan Tony • USA
OLD COWBOY, THE see **STARY KOWBOJ** • 1973
OLD CRAFTSMAN OF THE JARS, THE see **DOK JITAUN NULGURI** • 1969
OLD CROW • 1977 • Obomsawin Alanis • CND
OLD CROWD, THE • 1979 • Anderson Lindsay • MTV • UKN
OLD CURIOSITY SHOP, THE • 1909 • *Essanay* • USA
OLD CURIOSITY SHOP, THE • 1911 • Marston Theodore • USA
OLD CURIOSITY SHOP, THE • 1912 • Powell Frank • UKN
OLD CURIOSITY SHOP, THE • 1913 • Bentley Thomas • UKN
OLD CURIOSITY SHOP, THE • 1921 • Bentley Thomas • UKN
OLD CURIOSITY SHOP, THE • 1934 • Bentley Thomas • UKN
OLD CURIOSITY SHOP, THE see **MISTER QUILP** • 1974
OLD CZECH LEGENDS see **STARE POVESTI CESKE** • 1952
OLD DARK HOUSE, THE • 1932 • Whale James • USA
OLD DARK HOUSE, THE • 1963 • Castle William • UKN, USA
OLD DERELICT, THE • 1914 • *Billington Francelia* • USA
OLD DOC GLOOM • 1916 • *International Film Service* • SHT • USA
OLD DOC YAK • 1913-14 • Smith Sidney • SHS • USA
OLD DOC YAK AND THE ARTIST'S DREAM • 1913 • Smith Sidney • USA
OLD DOCTOR, THE • 1915 • MacQuarrie Murdock • USA
OLD DOCTOR, THE see **VIEJO DOCTOR, EL** • 1940
OLD DR. JUDD • 1912 • *Chamberlain Riley* • USA
OLD DOCTOR'S HUMANITY, THE • 1912 • *Eclair* • USA
OLD DOG TRAY • 1935 • *Terry Paul/ Moser Frank (P)* • ANS • USA
OLD DOLL, THE • 1911 • *Bunny John* • USA
OLD DOLL'S HOUSE see **MIDNIGHT ALIBI** • 1934
OLD DRAC see **VAMPIRA** • 1974
OLD DRACULA (USA) see **VAMPIRA** • 1974
OLD DUTCH • 1915 • Crane Frank H. • USA
OLD ENGLISH • 1930 • Green Alfred E. • USA
OLD ENOUGH • 1984 • Silver Marisa • USA
OLD ENOUGH TO BE HER GRANDPA • 1914 • *American* • USA
OLD EXCUSE, THE • 1911 • *Solax* • USA
OLD FAITHFUL • 1917 • *Baird Leah* • SHT • USA
OLD FAITHFUL • 1935 • Rogers Maclean • UKN
OLD FAMILY BIBLE, THE • 1911 • *Edison* • USA
OLD FASHIONED BOY, AN • 1920 • Storm Jerome • USA • OLD-FASHIONED BOY, AN
OLD-FASHIONED BOY, AN see **OLD FASHIONED BOY, AN** • 1920
OLD-FASHIONED ELOPEMENT, AN • 1912 • *Beaumont Harry* • USA
OLD-FASHIONED GIRL, AN • 1912 • *Weber Lois* • USA
OLD FASHIONED GIRL, AN • 1915 • Crisp Donald • USA
OLD-FASHIONED GIRL, AN • 1916 • Ashley Charles E. • SHT • USA
OLD-FASHIONED GIRL, AN • 1949 • Dreifuss Arthur • USA
OLD-FASHIONED MOTHER, AN • 1912 • *Rex* • USA
OLD FASHIONED MOVIE, AN • *Easy Aces* • SHT • USA
OLD-FASHIONED SCOTTISH REEL • 1903 • Porter Edwin S. • USA
OLD-FASHIONED WAY, THE • 1934 • Beaudine William • USA
OLD-FASHIONED YOUNG MAN, AN • 1917 • Withey Chet • USA
OLD FAVORITE AND THE UGLY GOLLIWOG, THE • 1908 • Stow Percy • UKN
OLD FIDDLER, THE • 1910 • *Kalem* • USA
OLD FIDELITY • 1911 • *Essanay* • USA
OLD FIRE HORSE • 1939 • Donnelly Eddie • ANS • USA
OLD FIRE HORSE, THE • 1914 • France Charles H. • USA
OLD FIRE HORSE AND THE NEW FIRE CHIEF, THE • 1914 • Baker George D. • USA
OLD FISHERMAN'S STORY, THE • 1915 • *Alden Mary* • USA
OLD FLAME, AN • 1930 • *Mintz Charles (P)* • ANS • USA
OLD FLAMES • 1989 • Morahan Christopher • UKN
OLD FLORIST, THE • 1912 • *Essanay* • USA
OLD FLUTE PLAYER, THE • 1914 • Belmore Lionel • USA
OLD FLYNN'S FIDDLE • 1913 • Calvert Charles? • UKN
OLD FOGEY, THE • 1914 • *Eclectic* • USA
OLD FOGEY, THE • 1916 • *Craig Nell* • SHT • USA
OLD FOLK SONG, AN see **HEJ TE ELEVEN FA..** • 1963
OLD FOLKS AT HOME • 1925 • Fleischer Dave • ANS • USA
OLD FOLKS AT HOME, THE • 1907 • Morland John • UKN
OLD FOLKS AT HOME, THE • 1913 • *Thanhouser* • USA
OLD FOLKS AT HOME, THE • 1916 • Withey Chet • USA
OLD FOLKS' CHRISTMAS, THE • 1912 • Tucker George Loane • USA
OLD FOLKS' SACIFICE, THE • 1911 • *Vitagraph* • USA
OLD FOOL, THE • 1923 • Venturini Edward D. • USA
OLD FOOTLIGHT FAVORITE, THE • 1908 • *Melies* • USA
OLD FOOTLIGHT FAVOURITE (?) see **TROP VIEUX!** • 1908
OLD FOURTH WARD, THE • 1917 • Smith David • SHT • USA
OLD FRONTIER, THE • 1950 • Ford Philip • USA
OLD GARDENER, THE • 1912 • Martinek H. O. • UKN
OLD GLAD EYES see **SECRET LIVES OF THE BRITISH PRIME MINISTERS: GLADSTONE, THE** • 1981
OLD GLORY • 1910 • *Vitagraph* • USA
OLD GLORY • 1939 • Jones Charles M. • ANS • USA
OLD GODS ARE STILL ALIVE see **AN LEVA DE GAMLA GUDAR** • 1937
OLD GODS STILL LIVE, THE (USA) see **AN LEVA DE GAMLA GUDAR** • 1937
OLD GOOD-FOR-NOTHING, THE • 1914 • *Aitken Spottiswoode* • USA
OLD GOOD-FOR-NUTHIN', THE • 1915 • Ridgwell George • USA
OLD GORMAN'S GAL • 1913 • *Mackley Arthur* • USA
OLD GRAY MARE, THE • 1913 • Henderson Dell • USA
OLD GRAY MAYOR, THE see **SMART POLITICS** • 1948
OLD GREATHEART see **WAY BACK HOME** • 1931
OLD GREY HARE, THE • 1944 • Clampett Robert • ANS • USA
OLD GREY MARE • 1945 • Crouch William Forest • SHT • USA
OLD GREYHEART (UKN) see **WAY BACK HOME** • 1931
OLD GRINGO • 1989 • Puenzo Luis • USA
OLD GROUCH, THE • 1915 • MacQuarrie Murdock • USA
OLD GROUCHY, THE see **GROUSOUZES, HO** • 1961
OLD GUARD see **VIEUX DE LA VIEILLE, LES** • 1960
OLD GUARD, THE • 1913 • Young James • USA
OLD GUARD, THE • 1941 • Gerasimov Sergei • USS
OLD GUARD, THE see **VECCHIA GUARDIA** • 1933
OLD GUN, THE (USA) see **VIEUX FUSIL, LE** • 1975
OLD GYPSY CUSTOM, AN • 1934 • Edwards Harry J. • SHT • USA
OLD HALL CLOCK, THE • 1909 • *Lubin* • USA
OLD HANNIBAL see **YOU CAN'T BUY EVERYTHING** • 1934
OLD HARTWELL'S CUB • 1918 • Heffron Thomas N. • USA
OLD HAT, THE • 1911 • Bouwmeester Theo • UKN
OLD HEADS AND YOUNG HEARTS • 1910 • *Imp* • USA
OLD HEADS AND YOUNG HEARTS • 1913 • Salter Harry • *Komic* • USA
OLD HEIDELBERG • 1909 • *Essanay* • USA
OLD HEIDELBERG • 1915 • Emerson John • USA • IN OLD HEIDELBERG
OLD HEIDELBERG see **STUDENT PRINCE IN OLD HEIDELBERG, THE** • 1927
OLD HEIDELBERG see **STUDENT'S ROMANCE, THE** • 1935
OLD HIGH CHAIR, THE • 1915 • Conway Jack • SHT • USA
OLD HOKUM • 1931 • *Van Beuren* • ANS • USA
OLD HOME, THE see **SPIRIT OF THE U.S.A., THE** • 1924
OLD HOME WEEK • 1911 • *Thanhouser* • USA
OLD HOME WEEK • 1925 • Heerman Victor • USA
OLD HOMESTEAD, THE • 1916 • Kirkwood James • USA
OLD HOMESTEAD, THE • 1922 • Cruze James • USA
OLD HOMESTEAD, THE • 1935 • Nigh William • USA
OLD HOMESTEAD, THE • 1942 • McDonald Frank • USA
OLD HOMESTEAD: OR, SAVED FROM THE WORKHOUSE, THE • 1905 • Green Tom • UKN
OLD HOUSE, THE • 1927 • Molas Zet • CZC
OLD HOUSE, THE • 1936 • Harman Hugh • ANS • USA
OLD HOUSE PASSING, THE • 1965 • Jordan Larry • SHT • USA
OLD HOUSES • 1978 • Ondaatje Kim • DCS • CND
OLD HUTCH • 1936 • Ruben J. Walter • USA
OLD INDIAN DAYS • 1911 • *Pathe* • USA
OLD INHABITANT see **STAROZHIL** • 1962
OLD IRON • 1938 • Walls Tom • UKN
OLD IRON, NEW HUMOUR see **GLUMA NOVA CU FIER VECHI** • 1965
OLD IRONSIDES • 1926 • Cruze James • USA • SONS OF THE SEA (UKN)
OLD ISAACS, THE PAWNBROKER • 1908 • *Bitzer Billy (Ph)* • USA
OLD ISAACSON'S DIAMONDS • 1915 • *Roland Ruth* • USA
OLD JACKSON'S GIRL • 1914 • *Thompson Dave* • USA
OLD JANE OF THE GAIETY • 1915 • *Thanhouser* • USA
OLD JIM • 1913 • Merwin Bannister • USA
OLD JO see **OH, JO!** • 1921
OLD JOCKEY, THE (UKN) see **STARYI NAYEZHDNIK** • 1940
OLD KENT ROAD, THE • 1912 • *Vitagraph* • USA
OLD KHOTTABYCH see **STARI KHOTTABYCH** • 1956
OLD KING COLE • 1933 • Hand David • ANS • USA
OLD KING KOAL • 1917 • Dyer Anson • ANM • UKN
OLD LADY 31 • 1920 • Ince John • USA
OLD LADY, THE see **PARVI UROK** • 1959
OLD LADY AND THE SHOE, THE • 1929 • *Meglin Kiddies* • SHT • USA
OLD LADY OF TWENTY, AN • 1912 • *Trunnelle Mabel* • USA
OLD LADY THIRTY-ONE see **CAPTAIN IS A LADY, THE** • 1940
OLD LADY WHO LIVED IN A SHOE, THE • 1977 • Pindal Kaj • ANS • CND
OLD LEADER, THE • 1911 • *Powers* • USA
OLD LEGENDS NEVER DIE • 1966 • *Darren James* • MTV • USA
OLD LEGENDS OF CZECHOSLOVAKIA see **STARE POVESTI CESKE** • 1952
OLD LETTER, THE • 1914 • Santschi Thomas • USA
OLD LIE AND THE NEW, THE • 1906 • Martin J. H.? • UKN
OLD LION, THE see **LION DEVENU VIEUX, LE** • 1929
OLD LOCKET, AN • 1914 • Weber Lois • USA
OLD LOS ANGELES • 1948 • Kane Joseph • USA • CALIFORNIA OUTPOST
OLD LOUISIANA • 1937 • Willat Irvin V. • USA • TREASON (UKN)
OLD LOVE see **EINE ALTE LIEBE** • 1959
OLD LOVE, AN (USA) see **VIEJO AMOR, UN** • 1938
OLD LOVE AND THE NEW, THE • 1903 • *Paul R. W.* • UKN
OLD LOVE AND THE NEW, THE • 1910 • Porter Edwin S. • USA
OLD LOVE AND THE NEW, THE • 1912 • *Solax* • USA
OLD LOVE LETTER, AN • 1912 • *Majestic* • USA
OLD LOVE LETTERS • 1909 • *Lubin* • USA
OLD LOVE LETTERS • 1912 • Reid Hal • USA
OLD LOVES AND NEW • 1926 • Tourneur Maurice • USA • DESERT HEALER, THE
OLD LOVE'S BEST, THE • 1914 • *Kb* • USA
OLD LOVES FOR NEW • 1918 • Wells Raymond • USA
OLD MAC • 1961 • Winner Michael • UKN
OLD MACDONALD DUCK • 1941 • King Jack • ANS • USA
OLD MACDONALD HAD A FARM • 1945 • Kneitel Seymour • ANS • USA
OLD MADRID see **WIFE'S ROMANCE, A** • 1923
OLD MAID, THE • 1914 • O'Brien John B. • USA
OLD MAID, THE • 1939 • Goulding Edmund • USA
OLD MAID, THE see **DOMNISOARA AURICA**
OLD MAID, THE see **VIEILLE FILLE, LA** • 1971
OLD MAID AND BONEHEAD • 1910 • *Nestor* • USA
OLD MAID AND FORTUNE TELLER • 1904 • Porter Edwin S. • USA
OLD MAID AND THE BURGLAR, THE • 1910 • *Essanay* • USA
OLD MAID HAVING HER PICTURE TAKEN • 1901 • Porter Edwin S. • USA
OLD MAID IN THE HORSECAR • 1901 • Porter Edwin S. • USA
OLD MAID'S BABY, THE • 1914 • Baker George D. • USA
OLD MAID'S BABY, THE • 1919 • Bertram William • USA
OLD MAID'S DECEPTION, AN • 1913 • Henderson Dell • USA
OLD MAID'S DREAM, THE • 1909 • *Lubin* • USA
OLD MAID'S LAST ATTEMPT, THE • 1913 • *Frontier* • USA
OLD MAID'S PICNIC, THE • 1910 • *Centaur* • USA
OLD MAID'S TEMPERANCE CLUB • 1908 • Porter Edwin S. • USA
OLD MAIDS' TRIUMPH, THE • 1914 • *Powers* • USA
OLD MAID'S VALENTINE, THE • 1900 • Smith G. A. • UKN • VALENTINE, THE
OLD MAID'S VALENTINE, THE • 1910 • *Vitagraph* • USA
OLD MAMMY'S CHARGE • 1913 • *Majestic* • USA
OLD MAMMY'S SECRET CODE • 1913 • Giblyn Charles • USA
OLD MAM'SELLE'S SECRET • 1912 • *Robinson Gertrude* • USA
OLD MAN • 1914 • *Walthall Henry B.* • USA
OLD MAN • 1958 • Frankenheimer John • MTV • USA
OLD MAN, THE • 1931 • Haynes Manning • UKN
OLD MAN AND DOG • 1969 • Armstrong Gillian • SHT • ASL
OLD MAN AND HIS HEN, THE see **KOBUTORI** • 1958
OLD MAN AND JIM, THE • 1911 • Davis Ulysses • USA
OLD MAN AND THE FLOWER, THE • 1962 • Pintoff Ernest • ANS • USA
OLD MAN AND THE SEA, THE • 1958 • Sturges John, King Henry (U/c), Zinnemann Fred (U/c) • USA
OLD MAN HIGGENBOTHAM'S DAUGHTER • 1914 • *Boyle Irene* • USA
OLD MAN IN THE CORNER, THE • 1924 • Croise Hugh • SER • UKN
OLD MAN IS COMING, THE see **GUBBEN KOMMER** • 1939
OLD MAN MINICK see **EXPERT, THE** • 1932
OLD MAN MOTOR-CAR see **DEDECEK AUTOMOBIL** • 1956
OLD MAN OF THE MOUNTAIN, THE • 1933 • Fleischer Dave • SHT • USA
OLD MAN REEVER • 1977 • Shebib Donald • CND
OLD MAN RHYTHM • 1935 • Ludwig Edward • USA
OLD MAN WHO CRIED WOLF, THE • 1973 • Grauman Walter • TVM • USA
OLD MAN WHO TRIED TO GROW YOUNG, THE • 1916 • Heffron Thomas N. • SHT • USA
OLD MANOR, THE see **GAMLA HERRGARDEN, DEN** • 1925
OLD MAN'S BRIDE, THE • 1967 • Gunter George • USA • BRIDE, THE
OLD MAN'S FOLLY, AN • 1911 • *Essanay* • USA
OLD MAN'S FOLLY, AN • 1916 • Eason B. Reeves • SHT • USA
OLD MAN'S LOVE STORY, AN • 1913 • Brooke Van Dyke • USA
OLD MAN'S PENSION DAY, THE • 1909 • Rosenthal Joe • UKN
OLD MANSION, THE see **GUNNAR HEDES SAGA** • 1923
OLD MELODY, THE • 1913 • Shaw Harold • USA
OLD MEMORIES see **VIEJA MEMORIA, LA** • 1977
OLD MEMORIES, THE see **BEAUX SOUVENIRS, LES** • 1982
OLD MEMORY, THE see **VIEJA MEMORIA, LA** • 1977
OLD MEMORY, THE see **VIEJA MEMORIA, LA** • 1985
OLD MEN, THE see **STARZYKI** • 1968
OLD MILL, THE • 1937 • Jackson Wilfred • ANS • USA
OLD MILL, THE see **GAMLA KVARNEN, DE** • 1964
OLD MILL POND, THE • 1936 • Harman Hugh • ANS • USA
OLD MILL STREAM, THE see **GYPSY NIGHT** • 1935
OLD MINERS, THE see **STARZYKI** • 1968
OLD MINER'S DOLL, THE • 1910 • *Yankee* • USA
OLD MODDINGTON'S DAUGHTERS • 1913 • Bowman William J. • USA
OLD MONK'S TALE, THE • 1913 • Dawley J. Searle • USA
OLD MOTHER CLOBBER • 1958 • Rasinski Connie • ANS • USA
OLD MOTHER GREY • 1915 • Powers Francis • USA
OLD MOTHER HUBBARD • 1912 • Cooper Arthur • UKN
OLD MOTHER HUBBARD • 1918 • Edwards Henry • UKN
OLD MOTHER HUBBARD • 1935 • *Iwerks Ub (P)* • ANS • USA
OLD MOTHER RILEY • 1937 • Mitchell Oswald • UKN • ORIGINAL OLD MOTHER RILEY, THE ◦ RETURN OF OLD MOTHER RILEY,THE
OLD MOTHER RILEY AT HOME • 1945 • Mitchell Oswald • UKN
OLD MOTHER RILEY CATCHES A QUISLING see **OLD MOTHER RILEY IN PARIS** • 1938
OLD MOTHER RILEY DETECTIVE • 1943 • Comfort Lance • UKN
OLD MOTHER RILEY, HEADMISTRESS • 1950 • Harlow John • UKN
OLD MOTHER RILEY IN BUSINESS • 1940 • Baxter John • UKN
OLD MOTHER RILEY IN PARIS • 1938 • Mitchell Oswald • UKN • OLD MOTHER RILEY CATCHES A QUISLING
OLD MOTHER RILEY IN SOCIETY • 1940 • Baxter John • UKN
OLD MOTHER RILEY JOINS UP • 1939 • Rogers Maclean • UKN
OLD MOTHER RILEY, M. P. • 1939 • Mitchell Oswald • UKN
OLD MOTHER RILEY MEETS THE VAMPIRE see **MOTHER RILEY MEETS THE VAMPIRE** • 1952
OLD MOTHER RILEY OVERSEAS • 1943 • Mitchell Oswald • UKN
OLD MOTHER RILEY'S CIRCUS • 1941 • Bentley Thomas • UKN
OLD MOTHER RILEY'S GHOSTS • 1941 • Baxter John • UKN
OLD MOTHER RILEY'S JUNGLE TREASURE • 1951 • Rogers Maclean • UKN • JUNGLE TREASURE (USA)
OLD MOTHER RILEY'S NEW LOOK see **OLD MOTHER RILEY'S NEW VENTURE** • 1949
OLD MOTHER RILEY'S NEW VENTURE • 1949 • Harlow John • UKN • MOTHER RILEY'S NEW VENTURE ◦ OLD MOTHER RILEY'S NEW LOOK
OLD MUSIC, THE see **VIEJA MUSICA, LA** • 1985
OLD NEST, THE • 1921 • Barker Reginald • USA
OLD NEW SCOTLAND • 1954 • Perry Margaret • DOC • CND
OLD NIP'S WEDDING see **RUBEZAHLS HOCHZEIT** • 1916
OLD NORRIS' GAL • 1910 • Melies Gaston • USA
OLD NUISANCE, THE • 1913 • Plumb Hay? • UKN
OLD OAKEN BUCKET, THE • 1913 • *Lubin* • USA
OLD OAKEN BUCKET, THE • 1921 • Tully May • USA
OLD OAKEN BUCKET, THE • 1941 • Rasinski Connie • ANS • USA
OLD OAK'S SECRET, THE • 1914 • Thornby Robert T. • USA
OLD OFFENDERS • 1915 • O'Sullivan Tony • USA
OLD OKLAHOMA PLAINS • 1952 • Witney William • USA

OLD OLD FAIRY TALE • 1969 • USS
OLD, OLD SONG, AN • 1913 • *Walters William* • USA
OLD, OLD STORY, THE • 1914 • Batley Ethyle • UKN
OLD, OLD TALE, THE • Kosheverova Nadezhda • USS
OLD ORGAN, THE • 1909 • *Vitagraph* • USA
OLD ORGANIST, THE • 1912 • *Rex* • USA
OLD OVERLAND TRAIL • 1953 • Witney William • USA
OLD PAL WHY DON'T YOU ANSWER ME? • 1922 • *Parkinson H. B.* • SHT • UKN
OLD PARLOR, THE • 1913 • Daly William Robert • USA
OLD PEDDLER, THE • 1911 • *Imp* • USA
OLD PEG LEG'S WILL • 1915 • *Ford Francis* • USA
OLD PEOPLE see **GAMLE, DE** • 1961
OLD PIONEER, THE • 1934 • Ising Rudolf • ANS • USA
OLD PLANTATION, THE • 1935 • Ising Rudolf • ANS • USA
OLD PLAY OF EVERYMAN, THE • 1915 • Gluckstadt Wilhelm • DNM
OLD PROSPECTOR, THE • 1912 • *Nestor* • USA
OLD QUEBEC GATEWAY TO CANADA'S NEW WEALTH • Lavoie Hermenegilde, Lavoie Richard • DCS • CND
OLD RAG DOLL, AN • 1914 • Brenon Herbert • USA
OLD RAGS see **VELHOS SAO OS TRAPOS** • 1980
OLD RAID MULE, THE • 1938 • Parrott Charles • SHT • USA
OLD RASCALS, THE • 1971 • Ryazanov Eldar • USS
OLD RED CAR, THE see **CERVENA AEROVKA** • 1960
OLD RELIABLE • 1914 • Brooke Van Dyke • USA
OLD REPORTER, THE • 1912 • Miller Ashley • USA
OLD RIFLE, THE see **VIEUX FUSIL, LE** • 1975
OLD ROCKIN' CHAIR TOM • 1948 • Hanna William, Barbera Joseph • ANS • USA
OLD ROSES • 1935 • Mainwaring Bernerd • UKN
OLD ST. PAULS • 1914 • Noy Wilfred • UKN • WHEN LONDON BURNED (USA)
OLD SAN FRANCISCO • 1927 • Crosland Alan • USA
OLD SAWBONES • 1935 • Lord Del • SHT • USA
OLD SCHOOL TIE, THE (UKN) see **WE WENT TO COLLEGE** • 1936
OLD SCIENTIST, THE see **VIEUX SAVANT, LE**
OLD SCOUNDREL, AN • 1916 • *Mace Fred* • SHT • USA
OLD SCROOGE • 1910 • *Cines* • ITL
OLD SEA DOG, THE • 1922 • Roach Hal • SHT • USA
OLD SEQUOIA • 1945 • King Jack • ANS • USA
OLD SETERHEND see **OLD SHATTERHAND** • 1964
OLD SHATTERHAND • 1964 • Fregonese Hugo • FRG, FRN, ITL • BATTAGLIA DE FORT APACHE, LA (ITL) ○ CAVALIERS ROUGES, LES (FRN) ○ APACHES' LAST BATTLE ○ SHATTERHAND (USA) ○ OLD SETERHEND
OLD SHELL GAME, THE • 1948 • Kneitel Seymour • ANS • USA
OLD SHERIFF, THE • 1917 • *Kerrigan J. Warren* • SHT • USA
OLD SHOEMAKER, THE • 1909 • *Gaumont* • FRN
OLD SHOEMAKER, THE • 1915 • *Ducrow Tote* • USA
OLD SHOES • 1925 • Stowers Frederick • USA
OLD SILVER WATCH, THE • 1912 • *De Garde Adele* • USA
OLD SIN, THE • 1915 • *Keith June* • USA
OLD SLEUTH, THE DETECTIVE • 1908 • *Kalem* • USA
OLD SMOKEY • 1938 • *Captain And The Kids* • ANS • USA
OLD SOAK, THE • 1926 • Sloman Edward • USA
OLD SOAK, THE see **GOOD OLD SOAK, THE** • 1937
OLD SOLDIER, THE • 1910 • Bouwmeester Theo? • UKN
OLD SOLDIERS • 1938 • Pearson George • SHT • UKN
OLD SOLDIERS NEVER see **SUPPOSE THEY GAVE A WAR AND NOBODY CAME?** • 1970
OLD SOLDIERS NEVER DIE • 1931 • Banks Monty • UKN • SHOW A LEG
OLD SOLDIERS NEVER DIE see **FIXED BAYONETS** • 1951
OLD SOLDIER'S ROMANCE, AN • 1917 • Mong William V. • SHT • USA
OLD SOLDIER'S STORY, THE • 1909 • Olcott Sidney • USA
OLD SONGS AND MEMORIES • 1912 • Campbell Colin • USA
OLD SOUTH, THE • 1940 • Zinnemann Fred • SHT • USA
OLD SPANISH CUSTOM, AN (USA) see **INVADER, THE** • 1936
OLD SPANISH CUSTOMERS • 1932 • Lane Lupino • UKN • TOREADORS DON'T CARE
OLD STAGE COACH, THE • 1912 • *Selig* • USA
OLD STORY, AN • 1966 • de Hert Robbe • BLG
OLD STORY WITH A NEW ENDING, AN • 1910 • Powell Frank, Griffith D. W.? • USA
OLD SUREHAND I • 1965 • Vohrer Alfred • FRG, YGS • LAVIRINT SMRTI (YGS) ○ FLAMING FRONTIER (UKN)
OLD SWEETHEART, THE • 1912 • *Fearnley Jane* • USA
OLD SWEETHEART OF MINE, AN • 1911 • Merwin Bannister • USA
OLD SWEETHEART OF MINE, AN • 1923 • Garson Harry • USA
OLD SWEETHEARTS OF MINE • 1909 • *Vitagraph* • USA
OLD SWIMMIN' HOLE, THE • 1921 • De Grasse Joseph • USA
OLD SWIMMIN' HOLE, THE • 1940 • MacGowan Robert • USA • WHEN YOUTH CONSPIRES (UKN)
OLD SWIMMING HOLE, THE • 1912 • *Reliance* • USA
OLD TESTAMENT, THE (USA) see **VECCHIO TESTAMENTO, IL** • 1963
OLD TEXAS TRAIL, THE • 1944 • Collins Lewis D. • USA • STAGE COACH LINE (UKN)
OLD TIME CINEMA • 1952 • CMP • FRG
OLD TIME MUSIC HALL, AN • 1929 • Aylott Dave • UKN
OLD-TIME NIGHTMARE, THE • 1911 • *Powers* • SHT • USA
OLD TIME SCENE IN THE VILLAGE STOCKS • 1898 • *Paul R. W.* • UKN
OLD-TIMER IN MANILA see **DUGAY NA SA MAYNILA** • 1968
OLD TIMERS • 1936 • *Asher Irving (P)* • SHT • UKN
OLD TIMERS, THE • 1933 • Brice Monte • SHT • USA
OLD TIN CAN, THE see **CANARD EN FER BLANC, LE** • 1967
OLD TOWER, THE • 1967 • Czurko Edward • SHT • PLN
OLD TOYMAKER, THE • 1917 • Holubar Allen • SHT • USA
OLD TOYMAKER'S DREAM, AN • 1913 • Cooper Arthur • UKN
OLD TOYMAKER'S DREAM, THE see **ENCHANTED TOYMAKER, THE** • 1904
OLD TUNE, AN • 1912 • *101 Bison* • USA
OLD TUTOR, THE • 1915 • MacQuarrie Murdock • USA
OLD VIOLIN, THE • 1912 • *Solax* • USA
OLD VS. THE NEW, THE • 1914 • MacGregor Norval • USA
OLD WALLS, THE see **STARYE STENY** • 1974
OLD WATCHMAN, THE • 1916 • Kent Leon D. • SHT • USA
OLD WATER JAR, THE • 1911 • *Vitagraph* • USA
OLD WEDDING DRESS, THE • 1912 • *Essanay* • USA
OLD WELL, THE see **LAO JING** • 1985
OLD WEST, THE • 1952 • Archainbaud George • USA
OLD WIVES FOR NEW • 1918 • De Mille Cecil B. • USA
OLD WIVES' TALE • 1946 • Halas John, Batchelor Joy • ANM • UKN
OLD WIVES' TALE, THE • 1921 • Clift Denison • UKN
OLD WOMAN, THE see **OREG, AZ** • 1971
OLD WOMAN GHOST, THE see **YOBA** • 1976
OLD WOMAN WHO LIVED IN A SHOE, THE • 1903 • *Lubin* • USA
OLD WOMAN WHO LIVED IN A SHOE, THE • *Carroll E. J.* • SHT • ASL
OLD WOMEN OF JAPAN, THE see **NIPPON NO OBACHAN** • 1962
OLD WOOD CARVER, THE • 1913 • von Herkomer Hubert • UKN
OLD WORLD GARDEN, AN • 1929 • Jeffrey R. E. • UKN
OLD WRITING DESK, THE see **CHATOLLETS HEMMELIGHED** • 1913
OLD WYOMING TRAIL, THE • 1937 • Blangsted Folmar • USA
OLD YELLER • 1957 • Stevenson Robert • USA
OLDAS ES KOTES • 1963 • Jancso Miklos • HNG • CANTATA (UKN)
OLDEN AND NEW STYLE CONJURING (USA) see **MAGIE A TRAVERS LES AGES, LA** • 1906
OLDEN DAYS COAT • 1981 • Pittman Bruce • CND
OLDER BROTHER AND YOUNGER SISTER see **ANI IMOTO** • 1977
OLDER BROTHER, YOUNGER SISTER see **ANI IMOTO** • 1953
OLDEST CONFESSION, THE see **HAPPY THIEVES, THE** • 1962
OLDEST LAW, THE • 1918 • Knoles Harley • USA
OLDEST LIVING GRADUATE, THE • 1983 • Hofsiss Jack • MTV • USA
OLDEST PROFESSION, THE (USA) see **PLUS VIEUX METIER DU MONDE, LE** • 1967
OLDEST PROFESSION IN THE WORLD, THE see **PLUS VIEUX METIER DU MONDE, LE** • 1967
OLDRICH A BOZENA • 1985 • Vavra Otakar • CZC • OLDRICH AND BOZENA
OLDRICH AND BOZENA see **OLDRICH A BOZENA** • 1985
OLDURMEK HAKKIMDIR • 1968 • Ergun Nuri • TRK • I HAVE THE RIGHT TO KILL
OLE ANDERS, MARIKEN OG ESPEN • 1978 • Billing Kjell • SHT • NRW
OLE BRANDES AUGEN see **AUGEN DES OLE BRANDIS, DIE** • 1914
OLE DOLE DOFF • Lindberg Lars • ANS • SWD
OLE DOLE DOFF • 1968 • Troell Jan • SWD • EENY MEENY MINY MOE ○ WHO SAW HIM DIE?
OLE HENRY • 1983 • Weiss Ulrich • GDR
OLE MAN RIVER • 1929 • Aylott Dave, Symmons E. F. • SHT • UKN
OLE OPFINDERS OFFER • 1924 • Holger-Madsen, Lauritzen Lau • DNM
OLE REX • 1961 • Hinkle Robert • USA
OLE SWIMMIN' HOLE, THE • 1910 • *Selig* • USA
OLE, THE HYPNOTIST • 1912 • *Imp* • USA
O'LEARY NIGHT see **HAPPY EVER AFTER** • 1954
OLECEKSIN • 1968 • Gorec Ertem • TRK • YOU'LL DIE
OLEG • 1912 • Protazanov Yakov • USS
OLEKO DUNDICH • 1958 • Lukov Leonid • USS, YGS • ALEKZA DUNDIC
OLELKEZO TEKINTETEK • 1982 • Makk Karoly • HNG • CERTAIN KIND OF LOOK, A
OLESYA • 1972 • Ivchenko Boris • USS
OLGA AGAPI MOU • 1968 • Dalianidis Ioannis • GRC • OLGA, MY LOVE
OLGA, MY LOVE see **OLGA AGAPI MOU** • 1968
OLGA ROBARDS • 1989 • Vakopoulos Khristos • GRC • OLGA ROBERTS
OLGA ROBERTS see **OLGA ROBARDS** • 1989
OLGA'S GIRLS • 1964 • Mawra Joseph P. • USA
OLGA'S HOUSE OF SHAME • 1964 • Mawra Joseph P. • USA • 36 HOURS OF TERROR ○ HOUSE OF SHAME
OLGA'S MASSAGE PARLOR see **MME OLGA'S MASSAGE PARLOR** • 1965
OLGA'S PARLOR see **MME OLGA'S MASSAGE PARLOR** • 1965
OLIE KOLONIE • 1975 • SAF
OLIE OP REIS • 1957 • Pendry • DOC • NTH • PATTERN OF SUPPLY
OLIEVELD, HET • 1954 • Haanstra Bert • DOC • NTH • OILFIELD, THE
OLIMPIA • 1930 • Borcosque Carlos • SPN • SI EL EMPERADOR LA SUPIERA
OLIMPIA AGLI AMICI • 1972 • Apra Adriano • MTV • ITL
OLIMPIADA EN MEXICO • 1968 • Isaac Alberto • MXC • OLYMPICS IN MEXICO, THE (USA)
OLIMPIADA W MEKSYKU • 1969 • Byrd Jozef • ANM • PLN • OLYMPIC GAMES IN MEXICO, THE
OLIMPIADI DEI MARITI, LE • 1960 • Bianchi Giorgio • ITL
OLIVE AND THE BURGLAR • 1915 • *Edison* • USA
OLIVE AND THE HEIRLOOM • 1915 • Ridgely Richard • USA
OLIVE IN THE MADHOUSE • 1915 • Ridgely Richard • USA
OLIVE IS DISMISSED • 1914 • Ridgely Richard • USA
OLIVE OYL AND WATER DON'T MIX • 1942 • Fleischer Dave • ANS • USA
OLIVE OYL FOR PRESIDENT • 1948 • Sparber I. • ANS • USA
OLIVE PASSAGER CLANDESTIN • 1931 • de Canonge Maurice • FRN
OLIVE SE MARIE • 1931 • de Canonge Maurice • FRN
OLIVE TREE, THE • 1976 • Metcalfe Edgar • ASL
OLIVE TREES OF JUSTICE, THE (USA) see **OLIVIERS DE LA JUSTICE, LES** • 1962
OLIVEIRA, SUA CULTURA E EXTRACCAO DO AZEITE, A • 1929 • Coelho Jose Adolfo • SHT • PRT
OLIVEIRA, SUA CULTURA E EXTRACCAO DO AZEITE 2, A • 1931 • Coelho Jose Adolfo • SHT • PRT
OLIVER! • 1968 • Reed Carol • UKN
OLIVER & COMPANY • 1989 • Scribner George • ANM • USA
OLIVER CROMWELL • 1911 • Bouwmeester Theo • UKN
OLIVER, JUNCAL 108 • 1900 • Oliver Felix • URG
OLIVER ST.JOHN GOGARTY -SILENCE WOULD NEVER DO • 1988 • Black Donald Taylor • IRL
OLIVER THE EIGHTH • 1934 • French Lloyd • SHT • USA
OLIVER TWIST • 1909 • Blackton J. Stuart • USA
OLIVER TWIST • 1912 • *Goodwin Nat C.* • USA
OLIVER TWIST • 1912 • Bentley Thomas • UKN
OLIVER TWIST • 1916 • Young James • USA
OLIVER TWIST • 1922 • Lloyd Frank • USA
OLIVER TWIST • 1933 • Cowen William J. • USA
OLIVER TWIST • 1940 • Bradley David • USA
OLIVER TWIST • 1948 • Lean David • UKN
OLIVER TWIST • 1982 • Donner Clive • TVM • USA
OLIVER TWIST see **GEHEIMNISSE VON LONDON, DIE** • 1920
OLIVER TWIST, JR. • 1921 • Webb Millard • USA • FORTUNATE FUGITIVE, THE
OLIVER TWIST SADLY TWISTED • 1915 • *Superba* • USA
OLIVER TWISTED • 1917 • Evans Fred, Evans Joe • UKN
OLIVER'S STORY • 1978 • Korty John • USA
OLIVES AND THEIR OIL • 1914 • Sennett Mack • DOC • USA
OLIVE'S BOITHDAY PRESINK • 1941 • Fleischer Dave • ANS • USA
OLIVE'S GREATEST OPPORTUNITY • 1915 • Ridgely Richard • USA
OLIVE'S HERO • 1915 • *Sterling* • USA
OLIVE'S LOVE AFFAIR • 1915 • *Sterling* • USA
OLIVE'S MANUFACTURED MOTHER • 1915 • Ridgely Richard • USA
OLIVE'S OTHER SELF • 1915 • Ridgely Richard • USA
OLIVE'S PET • 1915 • *Sterling* • USA
OLIVE'S SWEEPSTAKES TICKET • 1941 • Fleischer Dave • ANS • USA
OLIVIA • 1950 • Audry Jacqueline • FRN • PIT OF LONELINESS (USA) ○ STRANGE CONDUCT
OLIVIA see **INCANTESIMO TRAGICO** • 1951
OLIVIA see **TASTE OF SIN, A** • 1983
OLIVIA SCRAPBOOK • 1970 • Bonniere Rene • SHT • CND
OLIVIER, L' • 1975 • Akika Ali, Dubroux Daniele, Le Peron Serge, Narboni Jean, Chapouillie Guy, Villain Dominique • DOC • FRN
OLIVIER CROMWELL • 1909 • de Morlhon Camille • FRN
OLIVIER MESSIAEN ET LES OISEAUX • 1973 • Fano Michel, Tual Denise R. • DOC • FRN
OLIVIERS DE LA JUSTICE, LES • 1962 • Blue James • FRN • OLIVE TREES OF JUSTICE, THE (USA)
OLJEEVENTYRET • 1977 • Wam Svend • DCS • NRW
OLLE HENRY IN SAARBRUCKEN • 1984 • Weiss Ulrich • GDR
OLLE TORERO • 1963 • Dovnikovic Borivoj • ANM • YGS
OLLIE THE OWL • 1963 • Kneitel Seymour • ANS • USA
OLLY OAKLEY • 1927 • Cooper George A. • UKN • MUSICAL MEDLEY NO.5
OLLY OLLY OXEN FREE • 1978 • Colla Richard A. • USA • GREAT BALLOON ADVENTURE, THE
OLMEZ AGACI • 1985 • Kurcenli Yusuf • TRK • ETERNAL TREE
OLOKAFTOMA • 1970 • Papaconstantis Dimitris • GRC • HOLOCAUST
OLONGAPO -THE GREAT AMERICAN DREAM • 1988 • Rono Chito • PHL
OLOVENY CHLEB • 1954 • Sequens Jiri • CZC • RED WHITSUN
OLOVNA BRIGADA • 1981 • Cenevski Kiril • YGS • BRIGADE OF LEAD, THE
OLPRINZ, DER see **OELPRINZ, DER** • 1965
OLSEN BANDEN • 1968 • Balling Erik • DNM • OLSEN GANG, THE
OLSEN-BANDEN DERUDA' • 1977 • Balling Erik • DNM
OLSEN-BANDEN GAR AMOK • 1973 • Balling Erik • DNM • OLSEN GANG RUNS AMOK, THE
OLSEN-BANDEN I JYLLAND • 1971 • Balling Erik • DNM
OLSEN-BANDEN OVERGIVER SIG ALDRIG • 1979 • Balling Erik • DNM
OLSEN-BANDEN PA SPANDEN • 1969 • Balling Erik • DNM
OLSEN-BANDEN PA SPORET • 1975 • Balling Erik • DNM
OLSEN-BANDEN SER RODT • 1976 • Balling Erik • DNM • OLSEN GANG SEES RED, THE
OLSEN BANDENS SIDSTE BEDRIFTER • 1974 • Balling Erik • DNM • OLSEN GANG'S LAST ESCAPADE, THE
OLSEN-BANDENS STORE KUP • 1972 • Balling Erik • DNM
OLSEN GANG, THE see **OLSEN BANDEN** • 1968
OLSEN GANG AND DYNAMITE HARRY GO WILD, THE see **OLSENBANDEN OG DYNAMITT-HARRY GAR AMOKKKKKK** • 1974
OLSEN GANG ARE SOARING HIGH, THE see **OLSENBANDEN OG DYNAMITT-HARRY MOT NYE HOYDER** • 1980
OLSEN GANG MEETS KING AND KNIGHT, THE see **OLSENBANDEN MOTER KONGE OG KNEKT** • 1974
OLSEN GANG NEVER GIVES IN, THE see **OLSENBANDEN GIR SEG ALDRI** • 1981
OLSEN-GANG NEVER SURRENDER, THE • 1979 • DNM
OLSEN-GANG NEVER SURRENDERS, THE see **OLSENBANDEN GIR SEG ALDRI** • 1981
OLSEN GANG NO.10, THE see **OLSENBANDEN NR.10** • 1979
OLSEN GANG RUNS AMOK, THE see **OLSEN-BANDEN GAR AMOK** • 1973
OLSEN GANG SEES RED, THE see **OLSEN-BANDEN SER RODT** • 1976
OLSEN GANG STRIKES GOLD, THE see **OLSENBANDEN TAR GULL** • 1973
OLSEN GANG -THEIR FINAL COUP, THE see **OLSENBANDENS ALLER SISTE KUPP** • 1983
OLSEN GANG'S LAST ESCAPADE, THE see **OLSEN BANDENS SIDSTE BEDRIFTER** • 1974
OLSENBANDEN FOR FULL MUSIKK • 1977 • Bohwim Knut • NRW
OLSENBANDEN GIR SEG ALDRI • 1981 • Bohwim Knut • NRW • OLSEN-GANG NEVER SURRENDERS, THE ○ OLSEN GANG NEVER GIVES IN, THE
OLSENBANDEN MOTER KONGE OG KNEKT • 1974 • Bohwim Knut • NRW • OLSEN GANG MEETS KING AND KNIGHT, THE
OLSENBANDEN NR.10 • 1979 • Bohwim Knut • NRW • OLSEN GANG NO.10, THE
OLSENBANDEN OG DATAHARRY • 1978 • Bohwim Knut • NRW

OLSENBANDEN OG DYNAMITT-HARRY GAR AMOKKKKKK • 1974 • Bohwim Knut • NRW • OLSEN GANG AND DYNAMITE HARRY GO WILD, THE

OLSENBANDEN OG DYNAMITT-HARRY MOT NYE HOYDER • 1980 • Bohwim Knut • NRW • OLSEN GANG ARE SOARING HIGH, THE

OLSENBANDEN TAR GULL • 1973 • Bohwim Knut • NRW • OLSEN GANG STRIKES GOLD, THE

OLSENBANDENS ALLER SISTE KUPP • 1983 • Bohwim Knut • NRW • OLSEN GANG -THEIR FINAL COUP, THE

OLSENBANDENS SISTE BEDRIFTER • 1974 • Andersen Knut • NRW

OLSEN'S BIG MOMENT • 1933 • St. Clair Malcolm • USA • OLSEN'S NIGHT OUT

OLSEN'S NIGHT OUT see **OLSEN'S BIG MOMENT** • 1933

OLTRAGGIO, L' • 1920 • Serena Gustavo • ITL

OLTRAGGIO AL PUDORE • 1965 • Amadio Silvio • ITL, FRN • ALL THE OTHER GIRLS DO (USA) ○ CHEATING ITALIAN STYLE ○ TUTTE LE AUTRE REGAZZE LO FANNO

OLTRE IL BENE E IL MALE • 1977 • Cavani Liliana • ITL, FRN, FRG • BEYOND GOOD AND EVIL (UKN) ○ AU-DELA DU BIEN ET DU MAL ○ AL DI LA DEL BENE E DEL MALE ○ SEEDS OF EVIL ○ BEYOND EVIL ○ JENSEITS VON GUT UND BOSE

OLTRE LA PORTA • 1983 • Cavani Liliana • ITL • BEYOND THE DOOR (USA) ○ SECRET BEYOND THE DOOR, THE ○ BEHIND THE DOOR ○ JAIL BIRD ○ BEYOND OBSESSION

OLTRE L'AMORE • 1940 • Gallone Carmine • ITL • PASSIONE

OLTRE LE STELLE • 1979 • D'Angelo Aldo • ITL

OLTRE L'OBLIO • 1948 • Antonioni Michelangelo • DCS • ITL

OLTRE L'OCEANO • 1990 • Gazzara Ben • ITL • BEYOND THE OCEAN

OLU BIR DENIZ • 1989 • Yilmaz Atif • TRK

OLUM SAATI • 1967 • Gorec Ertem • TRK • HOUR OF DEATH, THE

OLUME YALNIZ GIDILAR • 1963 • Yalinkilic Yavuz • TRK • DEAD ONLY PERISH, THE

OLUMSUZ ADAMLAR • 1968 • Atadeniz Yilmaz • TRK • IMMORTAL MAN, THE

OLUMSUZ KADIN • 1967 • Dinler Mehmet • TRK • IMMORTAL WOMAN, THE

OLUNCEYE KADAR • 1967 • Egilmez Ertem • TRK • UNTIL DEATH US DO PART

OLVIDA LOS TAMBORES • 1974 • Gil Rafael • SPN

OLVIDADOS DE DIOS, LOS • 1939 • Pereda Ramon • MXC • THOSE FORGOTTEN BY GOD (USA)

OLVIDADOS, LOS • 1950 • Bunuel Luis • MXC • YOUNG AND THE DAMNED, THE (USA) ○ FORGOTTEN ONES, THE ○ LOST ONES, THE

OLVOVA MYLLARI see **ULVOVA MYLLARI** • 1983

OLYAN, MINT OTTHON • 1978 • Meszaros Marta • HNG • JUST LIKE AT HOME

OLYCKSFAGELN NR.13 • 1942 • Holmberg Tage, Ahren Bjorn • SWD • UNLUCKY FELLOW NO.13

OLYMPIA • 1930 • Feyder Jacques, Barrymore Lionel • USA

OLYMPIA see **SI L'EMPEREUR SAVAIT CA** • 1930

OLYMPIA see **OLYMPISCHE SPIELE 1936** • 1938

OLYMPIA 52 • 1952 • Marker Chris • DOC • FRN

OLYMPIA, FESTIVAL OF THE NATIONS see **OLYMPISCHE SPIELE 1936** • 1938

OLYMPIA-FILM I see **FEST DER VOLKER** • 1938

OLYMPIA-FILM II see **FEST DER SCHONHEIT** • 1938

OLYMPIA (ITL) see **BREATH OF SCANDAL, A** • 1960

OLYMPIA -OLYMPIA • 1972 • Bauer Jochen • FRG

OLYMPIAD • 1971 • Schwartz Lillian, Knowlton Kenneth • ANS • USA

OLYMPIAD see **OLYMPISCHE SPIELE 1936** • 1938

OLYMPIAD '64 • 1964 • Brown Mende (c/d) • USA

OLYMPIAD I VITT • 1948 • Wickman Torgny • DOC • SWD, SWT

OLYMPIAN HOLIDAY see **LOMA** • 1976

OLYMPIC 13 GAGNANT see **ATHLETE INCOMPLET, L'** • 1932

OLYMPIC CAVALCADE • 1948 • Lerner Joseph • DOC • USA

OLYMPIC CHAMP, THE • 1942 • Kinney Jack • ANS • USA

OLYMPIC ELK • 1952 • Algar James • DOC • USA

OLYMPIC EVENTS • 1932 • McCarey Ray • SHT • USA

OLYMPIC GAMES • 1927 • Mack Anthony • SHT • USA

OLYMPIC GAMES, THE (USA) see **OLYMPISCHE SPIELE 1936** • 1938

OLYMPIC GAMES IN MEXICO, THE see **OLIMPIADA W MEKSYKU** • 1969

OLYMPIC GAMES OF 1948, THE see **XIVTH OLYMPIAD -THE GLORY OF SPORT, THE** • 1948

OLYMPIC HERO, THE • 1928 • Neill R. William • USA • ALL AMERICAN

OLYMPIC HONEYMOON • 1936 • Goulding Alf • USA • HONEYMOON MERRY-GO-ROUND

OLYMPIC SKI CHAMPIONS • 1936 • *Smith Pete* • SHT • USA • SKI CHAMPIONS

OLYMPICS IN MEXICO, THE (USA) see **OLIMPIADA EN MEXICO** • 1968

OLYMPIQUE DE MEXICO • 1968 • Sanchez-Ariza Jose (c/d) • MXC

OLYMPISCHE SPIELE 1936 • 1938 • Riefenstahl Leni • FRG • OLYMPIA, FESTIVAL OF THE NATIONS ○ OLYMPIC GAMES, THE (USA) ○ BERLIN OLYMPIAD (UKN) ○ OLYMPIAD ○ OLYMPIA

OM ABBES • 1969 • Abdelwahab Ali • TNS • ABBES' MOTHER

OM DAR B DAR • 1987 • Swaroop Kamal • IND

OM EL AROUSSA see **UM AL-ARUSSA** • 1963

OM KARLEK • 1987 • Arehn Mats • SWD • FILM ABOUT LOVE, A ○ ON LOVE

OM SJU FLICKOR • 1974 • Dahlberg Hans, Seth Carl-Johan • SWD • SEVEN GIRLS

OMAGATSUJI NO KETTO • 1951 • Mori Kazuo • JPN • OMAGATSUJI'S DUEL

OMAGATSUJI'S DUEL see **OMAGATSUJI NO KETTO** • 1951

OMAHA TRAIL, THE • 1942 • Buzzell Edward • USA

OMALA VANGALANGE • 1971 • Faria Antonio • SHT • PRT

O'MALLEY OF THE MOUNTED • 1921 • Hillyer Lambert • USA

O'MALLEY OF THE MOUNTED • 1936 • Howard David • USA

O'MALLEY RIDES ALONE • 1930 • McGowan J. P. • USA

OMAR AND THE OGRES • ANS • USS

OMAR GATLATO see **OMAR KATLATO** • 1977

OMAR KATLATO • 1977 • Allouache Merzak • ALG • OMAR KILLED BY HIS MANHOOD ○ OMAR GATLATO

OMAR KHAYYAM • 1957 • Dieterle William • USA • LOVES OF OMAR KHAYYAM, THE

OMAR KILLED BY HIS MANHOOD see **OMAR KATLATO** • 1977

OMAR MUKHTAR: LION OF THE DESERT see **LION OF THE DESERT** • 1979

OMAR THE TENTMAKER • 1922 • Young James • USA

OMAR'S JOURNEY see **MESHWAR OMAR** • 1986

OMATSURI HANJIRO • 1953 • Inagaki Hiroshi • JPN

OMBLIGO DE LA LUNA, EL • 1985 • Prior Jorge • MXC • NAVEL OF THE MOON, THE

OMBRA, L' • 1919 • Roberti Roberto Leone • ITL

OMBRA, L' • 1955 • Bianchi Giorgio • ITL

OMBRA CHE PARLA, L' • 1918 • Campogalliani Carlo • ITL

OMBRA DEL SOGNO, L' • 1916 • Falena Ugo • ITL

OMBRA DELLA MONTAGNA, L' see **DONNA DELLA MONTAGNA, LA** • 1943

OMBRA DELLA VALLE • 1946 • Barlacchi Cesare • ITL

OMBRA DI UN TRONO, L' • 1921 • Gallone Carmine • ITL

OMBRA DI ZORRO see **CABALGANDO HACIA LA MUERTE** • 1962

OMBRA NELL'OMBRA, UN' • 1979 • Carpi Pier • ITL

OMBRA NERA DEL VESUVIO, L' • 1987 • Steno • MTV • ITL

OMBRAMAGIE • Sassy Jean-Paul • SHT • FRN

OMBRE, L' • 1948 • Berthomieu Andre • FRN

OMBRE AU PAYSAGE see **OUT BEYOND TOWN** • 1948

OMBRE BIANCHE (ITL) see **SAVAGE INNOCENTS, THE** • 1959

OMBRE DE LA NUIT, L' • 1977 • Leconte Jean-Louis • FRN

OMBRE DE LA POMME, L' • 1967 • Lapoujade Robert • ANS • FRN • SHADOW OF THE APPLE, THE

OMBRE DE LA TERRE, L' • 1982 • Louhichi Taieb • TNS, FRN

OMBRE DECHIREE, L' • 1921 • Poirier Leon • FRN

OMBRE DES CHATEAUX, L' • 1977 • Duval Daniel • FRN, IND • SHADOW OF THE CASTLES

OMBRE DU DEUXIEME BUREAU, L' see **NADIA, LA FEMME TRAQUEE** • 1939

OMBRE DU PECHE, L' • 1923 • Protazanov Yakov • FRN

OMBRE D'UN JEU, L' • 1980 • Peres Uziel • FRN • SHADOW OF A GAME, A

OMBRE D'UNE CHANCE, L' • 1974 • Mocky Jean-Pierre • FRN

OMBRE ET LUMIERE • 1950 • Calef Henri • FRN

OMBRE ET LUMIERE DE ROME • 1956 • Ruspoli Mario • SHT • FRN

OMBRE FAMILIERE, L' • 1958 • Pialat Maurice • SHT • FRN

OMBRE ROUGE, L' • 1981 • Comolli Jean-Louis • FRN

OMBRE ROVENTI • 1972 • Caiano Mario • ITL

OMBRE SU TRIESTE • 1952 • Bianchi Nerino Florio • ITL

OMBRE SUL CANAL GRANDE • 1952 • Pellegrini Glauco • ITL

OMBRE SUR LA PRAIRIE see **SHADOW ON THE PRAIRIES** • 1953

OMBRELLE ET PARAPLUIE • 1956 • Tarcali Pierre • FRN • UMBRELLA STORY

OMBRELLONE, L' • 1966 • Risi Dino • ITL, FRN, SPN • WEEKEND, ITALIAN STYLE (USS) ○ PARASOL, EL (SPN) ○ WEEKEND WIVES ○ PARASOL, THE

OMBRES CHINOISES, LES • 1907 • de Chomon Segundo • FRN • CHINESE SHADOWS, THE

OMBRES CHINOISES, LES • 1982 • Ruiz Raul • SHT • FRN • CHINESE SHADOWS

OMBRES DE LA VILLE, LES • 1942 • Tedesco Jean • FRN

OMBRES DE SOIE • 1977 • Stephen Mary • CND • SHADOWS ON SILK

OMBRES NOIRES see **RETOUR A BONHEUR** • 1940

OMBRES QUI PASSANT, LES • 1924 • Volkov Alexander • FRN

OMBRES SUR AFRIQUE, LES • 1948 • Martin Marcel • SHT • FRN

OMBRO CINEMA: LA DANSE • 1968 • Kosower Herbert • ANS • USA

OMBYTE AV TAG • 1943 • Ekman Hasse • SWD • UNEXPECTED MEETING ○ CHANGING TRAINS

OMBYTE FORNOJER • 1939 • Molander Gustaf • SWD • VARIETY IS THE SPICE OF LIFE

OMBYTTA ROLLER • 1921 • Brunius Pauline • SHT • SWD

OMEGA • 1970 • Fox Donald • SHT • USA

OMEGA CONNECTION, THE (USA) see **LONDON CONNECTION, THE** • 1979

OMEGA FACTOR see **SILENT MADNESS** • 1984

OMEGA MAN, THE • 1971 • Sagal Boris • USA • I AM LEGEND

OMEGA SYNDROME, THE • 1987 • Manduke Joe • USA

OMEGAN, THE • 1968 • *Wilder W. Lee/ Navye Vic. N. (P)* • USA, PHL

OMEGANS, THE • 1969 • Wilder W. Lee • USA, PHL

OMELETTE FANTASTIQUE, L' • 1909 • Cohl Emile • ANS • FRN • MAGIC EGGS

OMEN 3: THE FINAL CONFLICT see **FINAL CONFLICT, THE** • 1981

OMEN, THE • 1976 • Donner Richard • UKN, USA

OMEN II see **DAMIEN -OMEN II** • 1978

OMEN OF EVIL see **FINDING KATIE** • 1983

OMENS AND ORACLES • 1913 • Angeles Bert • USA

OMENS OF THE MESA • 1912 • *Thornby Robert* • USA

OMGIVELSER • 1973 • Tuhus Oddvar Bull • NRW • SURROUNDINGS

OMHET • 1972 • Donner Jorn • SWD • TENDERNESS

OMICIDA, L' (ITL) see **MEURTRIER, LE** • 1962

OMICIDIO A SANGUE FREDDO • 1968 • Pastore Sergio • ITL

OMICIDIO PER APPUNTAMENTO • 1967 • Guerrini Mino • ITL

OMICIDIO PER VOCAZIONE • 1968 • Sindoni Vittorio • ITL

OMICIDIO PERFETTO A TERMINI DI LEGGE, UN • 1971 • Ricci Tonino • ITL

OMICRON • 1964 • Gregoretti Ugo • ITL

OMISTASHIPU • 1974 • Lamothe Arthur • DOC • CND

OMITSU NO ENDAN • 1946 • Nakamura Noboru • JPN

OMLADINSKA PRUGA SAMAC-SARAJEVO • 1947 • Jovicic Slobodan, Marjanovic Sida • YGS

OMNIBUS DES TOQUES BLANCS ET NOIRS, L' • 1901 • Melies Georges • FRN • OFF TO BLOOMINGDALE ASYLUM (USA) ○ OFF TO BEDLAM (UKN) ○ ECHAPPES DE CHARENTON

OMOEBA TOKUE KITAMONDA • 1981 • Asama Yoshitaka • JPN • SO FAR FROM HOME

OMOIDE NO YUBIWA • 1968 • Saito Koichi • JPN • WONDERFUL ONES, THE

OMOIDE SUIHEI • 1928 • Tasaka Tomotaka • JPN • RECOLLECTIONS OF A SAILOR

OMOKAGE • 1948 • Gosho Heinosuke • JPN • IMAGE ○ VESTIGE, A

OMOO OMOO • 1949 • Leonard Leon • USA • OMOO OMOO, THE SHARK GOD ○ SHARK GOD, THE (UKN)

OMOO OMOO, THE SHARK GOD see **OMOO OMOO** • 1949

OMOON OR THE CITY IN THE NAME OF GOD (USA) see **CIDADE DO NOME DE DEUS, O** • 1969

OMRE BEDEL KIZ • 1967 • Egilmez Ertem • TRK • GIRL TO LIVE FOR, A

OMRINGAAL • 1960 • Skouen Arne • NRW • SURROUNDED

OMRINGADE HUSET, DET • 1922 • Sjostrom Victor • SWD • HOUSE SURROUNDED, THE (USA) ○ SURROUNDED HOUSE, THE

OMRUMUN TEK GECESI • 1968 • Ergun Nuri • TRK • ONLY NIGHT OF MY LIFE, THE

OMRUNCE AGLADIM • 1967 • Erakalin Ulku • TRK • I'VE CRIED ALL MY LIFE

OMSTRIDTE JORD, DEN • 1915 • Holger-Madsen • DNM • JORDENS HAEVN ○ EARTH'S REVENGE, THE

OMUL IN LODEN • 1979 • Margineanu Nicolae • RMN • MAN IN THE OVERCOAT, THE

ON • 1961 • Djordjevic Purisa • YGS • HE

ON • 1966 • Sjoberg Alf • SWD • ISLAND, THE

ON A BENCH IN A PARK see **PA EN BANK I EN PARK** • 1960

ON A CLEAR DAY YOU CAN COUNT FOREVER • 1971 • Haldane Don • CND

ON A CLEAR DAY YOU CAN SEE FOREVER • 1970 • Minnelli Vincente • USA

ON A COMET see **NA KOMETE** • 1970

ON A COMMON PATH see **KOZOS UTON** • 1953

ON A FALSE SCENT • 1914 • Plumb Hay? • UKN

ON A GOLDEN PLATTER see **MAGASH HAKESSEF** • 1983

ON A JEHO SESTRA • 1931 • Fric Martin, Lamac Carl • CZC • HE AND HIS SISTER

ON A MEADOW see **NA LIVADI** • 1957

ON A MONDAY AFTERNOON see **TARDE.. UN LUNES, UNA** • 1973

ON A PAVING STONE MOUNTED • 1978 • O'Sullivan Thaddeus • UKN

ON A PERDU UNE FEMME NUE see **ON A TROUVE UNE FEMME NUE** • 1934

ON A QUIET EVENING see **V TIHATA VECHER** • 1960

ON A RAISON DE SE REVOLTER • 1973 • Frappier Roger • DOC • CND

ON A RETROUVE LA 7e COMPAGNIE • 1976 • Lamoureux Robert • FRN, FRG

ON A RUNAWAY MOTOR CAR THROUGH PICADILLY CIRCUS • 1899 • *Paul R. W.* • UKN

ON A SEA-BEACH see **PLAZA** • 1964

ON A SILVERY BEACH see **RUPALI SHAIKATEY** • 1977

ON A SMALL ISLAND see **NA MALKIA OSTROV** • 1958

ON A STILL HUNT • 1916 • Miller Rube • USA

ON A SUMMER'S DAY • 1920 • Austin Albert • SHT • USA

ON A SUNDAY AFTERNOON • 1930 • Fleischer Dave • ANS • USA

ON A SUNDAY AFTERNOON (USA) see **DOMINGO EN LA TARDE, UN** • 1938

ON A SUNDAY MORNING see **NIEDZIELNY PORANEC** • 1955

ON A TIGHTROPE see **NA LANE** • 1963

ON A TRAMP STEAMER • 1911 • *Vitagraph* • USA

ON A TROUVE UNE FEMME NUE • 1934 • Joannon Leo • FRN • ON A PERDU UNE FEMME NUE

ON A TUE UN HOMME see **VIVE LA LIBERTE** • 1944

ON A VOLE LA CUISSE DE JUPITER • 1979 • de Broca Philippe • FRN • SOMEBODY'S STOLEN THE THIGH OF JUPITER ○ JUPITER'S THIGH

ON A VOLE LA JOCONDE • 1965 • Deville Michel • FRN, ITL • LADRO DELLA GIOCONDA, IL (ITL) ○ VOLEUR DE LA JOCONDE, LE ○ AVVENTURE DI GOLDEN BOY, LE

ON A VOLE LA MER • 1962 • Salvy • SHT • FRN

ON A VOLE LA TOUR EIFFEL • Image Jean • ANM • FRN

ON A VOLE UN HOMME • 1933 • Ophuls Max • FRN

ON A WALL see **PE UN PERETE** • 1969

ON ACCOUNT OF A DOG • 1915 • *Farrington Reenie* • USA

ON ACCOUNT OF A HANDKERCHIEF • 1912 • *Reliance* • USA

ON AGAIN, OFF AGAIN • 1937 • Cline Eddie • USA • EASY GOING

ON AGAIN-OFF AGAIN FINNEGAN • 1914 • *Joker* • USA

ON-AI GOJU-RYO • 1930 • Inagaki Hiroshi • JPN

ON AN EMPTY BALCONY see **EN EL BALCON VACIO** • 1962

ON AN ISLAND WITH YOU • 1948 • Thorpe Richard • USA

ON ANOTHER MAN'S PASS • 1909 • *Essanay* • USA

ON ANY STREET see **NOTTE BRAVA, LA** • 1959

ON ANY SUNDAY • 1971 • Brown Bruce • DOC • USA

ON ANY SUNDAY II • 1981 • Forsyth Ed, Shoemaker Don • DOC • USA

ON APPROVAL • 1930 • Walls Tom • UKN

ON APPROVAL • 1944 • Brook Clive • UKN

ON ATTEND POLOCHON • 1920 • Machin Alfred • FRN

ON AURA TOUT VU • 1976 • Lautner Georges • FRN • BOTTOM LINE, THE (USA)

ON BITTER CREEK • 1915 • Jones Edgar • USA

ON BOOT HILL (UKN) see **LAST DAYS OF BOOT HILL** • 1947

ON BORROWED TIME • 1939 • Bucquet Harold S. • USA

ON BRIGHTON PIER • 1904 • Collins Alf • UKN

ON BURNING SANDS • 1913 • MacDonald J. Farrell • USA

ON CELEBRATIONS AND GUESTS see **SLAVNOSTI A HOSTECH, O** • 1966

ON CELLOPHANE PAPER • 1975 • Kamal Hussein • EGY

ON CHRISTMAS EVE • 1914 • Collins John H. • USA

ON CIRCUS DAY • 1914 • Fielding Romaine • USA

ON CLOSER INSPECTION • 1953 • Foldes Peter, Foldes Joan • ANM • UKN

ON COMPANY BUSINESS • 1979 • Francovich Allan • DOC • USA

ON CUPID'S HIGHWAY • 1913 • *Nestor* • USA

ON DANGEROUS GROUND • 1915 • Henderson Lucius • USA

ON DANGEROUS GROUND • 1916 • MacQuarrie Murdock • SHT • USA

ON DANGEROUS GROUND • 1917 • Thornby Robert T. • USA

ON DANGEROUS GROUND • 1951 • Ray Nicholas • USA
ON DANGEROUS GROUNDS see **CHOKE CANYON** • 1986
ON DANGEROUS PATHS • 1915 • Collins John H. • USA
ON DANGEROUS ROADS see **PA FARLIGA VAGAR** • 1945
ON DEATH ROW see **HALALRAITELT, A** • 1989
ON DECK • 1927 • Newfield Sam • SHT • USA
ON DEMANDE LE COLONEL • 1955 • Labro Maurice • FRN
ON DEMANDE UN ASSASSIN • 1949 • Neubach Ernst • FRN
ON DEMANDE UN BANDIT • 1947-51 • Verneuil Henri • SHT • FRN
ON DEMANDE UN COMPAGNON • 1933 • May Joe
ON DEMANDE UN HOMME see **MATLUB RAJULUN WAHID** • 1974
ON DEMANDE UN MENAGE • 1945 • Cam Maurice • FRN
ON DEMANDE UNE BRUTE • 1934 • Barrois Charles • SHT • FRN
ON DESERT SANDS • 1915 • *Ayres Sydney* • USA
ON DEVIL'S SERVICE • 1972 • BLG, ITL
ON DISAIT QUE C'ETAIT NOTRE TERRE see **NTESI NANA SHEPEN (1)** • 1975
ON DONOVAN'S DIVISION • 1912 • Edwin Walter • USA
ON DRESS PARADE see **DRESS PARADE** • 1939
ON EDGE • 1926 • Taurog Norman • SHT • USA
ON EFFACE TOUT • 1978 • Vidal Pascal • FRN • WE FORGET EVERYTHING
ON EL CAMINO REAL • 1913 • *Nestor* • USA
ON EL MONTE RANCH • 1912 • *Anderson Broncho Billy* • USA
ON EST AU COTON • 1970 • Arcand Denys, Bernier Pierre • DOC • CND
ON EST LOIN DU SOLEIL • 1970 • Leduc Jacques • CND
ON EST POIVROT, MAIS ON A DU COEUR • 1905 • Blache Alice • FRN
ON EST TOUJOURS TROP BON AVEC LES FEMMES • 1970 • Boisrond Michel • FRN
ON EST VENU LA POUR S'ECLATER • 1979 • Pecas Max • FRN
ON FERTILE LANDS see **BEREKETLI TOPRAKLAR UZERINDE** • 1980
ON FIGHTING WITCHES • 1966 • Shaye Robert • SHT • SWD
ON FIRE • 1987 • Greenwald Robert • TVM • USA
ON FOOT, ON HORSE, AND ON WHEELS (USA) see **A PIED, A CHEVAL ET EN VOITURE** • 1957
ON FORBIDDEN LAND • 1899 • *Warwick Trading Co* • UKN
ON FORBIDDEN PATHS • 1913 • *Frontier* • USA
ON FOREIGN LAND see **POR LA TIERRA AJENA**
ON FOREIGN SHORES see **EN TERRITORIO EXTRANJERO** • 1990
ON FOREIGN SOIL see **TUDA ZEMLJA** • 1957
ON FORTUNE'S WHEEL • 1913 • *Kb* • USA
ON FRIDAY AT ELEVEN see **AN EINEM FREITAG UM HALB ZWOLF** • 1961
ON FURLOUGH • 1927 • Newfield Sam • SHT • USA
ON GIANT'S SHOULDERS • 1979 • Harvey Anthony • TVM • UKN
ON GLORY AND GRASS see **O SLAVE A TRAVE** • 1985
ON GOLDEN POND • 1981 • Rydell Mark • USA
ON GUARD • 1927 • Heath Arch B. • SRL • USA
ON GUARD AT THE BORDER see **NA STRAZY GRANIC** • 1960
ON GUARD FOR NONSENSE see **GOKUDO SHAIN YUKYO DEN** • 1968
ON GUARD FOR THEE • 1981 • Brittain Don • CND
ON GUARD (UKN) see **OUTPOST OF THE MOUNTIES** • 1939
ON HER ACCOUNT • 1918 • *Rhodes Billie* • USA
ON HER BED OF ROSES • 1966 • Zugsmith Albert • USA
ON HER HONOR see **DAZZLING MISS DAVISON, THE** • 1917
ON HER MAJESTY'S SECRET SERVICE • 1969 • Hunt Peter • UKN
ON HER WEDDING DAY • 1912 • *Vitagraph* • USA
ON HER WEDDING DAY • 1913 • *Lubin* • USA
ON HER WEDDING NIGHT • 1915 • Humphrey William • USA
ON HIS FIRST DAY HOME ON LEAVE • 1916 • *Tress Henry* • SHT • UKN
ON HIS GOATMOBILE • 1916 • Hurd Earl • ANS • USA
ON HIS KNEES • 1911 • *Vitagraph* • USA
ON HIS MAJESTY'S SERVICE • 1914 • Tucker George Loane • UKN • 0-18 OR A MESSAGE FROM THE SKY (USA)
ON HIS OWN GROUND see **NA SVOJI ZEMLJI** • 1948
ON HIS WEDDING DAY • 1913 • Sennett Mack • USA
ON HIS WEDDING DAY • 1915 • Davey Horace • USA
ON HOLIDAY • 1950 • Yankov Yanko • BUL
ON ICE • 1933 • Gillstrom Arvid E. • SHT • USA
ON ICE • 1935 • Sharpsteen Ben • ANS • USA
ON ICE AND WATER see **NA IDU I NA VODE** • 1959
ON JOUE OU ON JOUE PAS? • 1986 • Goulet Stella (c/d) • MTV • CND
ON KADIN • 1987 • Goren Serif • TRK • TEN WOMEN
ON KENTUCKY SOIL • 1911 • *Reliance* • USA
ON LAND, AT SEA AND IN THE AIR • 1980 • Driessen Paul • ANM • CND
ON L'APPELAIT CAMBODGE • 1982 • Duckworth Martin • DOC • CND • BACK TO KAMPUCHEA
ON L'APPELLE CATASTROPHE • 1983 • Balducci Richard • FRN
ON L'APPELLE FRANCE • 1967 • Leroy Serge • FRN
ON LE PENSAIT A L'EPREUVE DU FEU see **THEY CALLED IT FIREPROOF** • 1963
ON LEAVE • 1918 • Butler Alexander • UKN
ON LEAVE IN TOKYO • 1953-54 • Devlin Bernard • DCS • CND
ON LIGHT • Sramek Bohuslav, Lhotak K., Sivko V. • ANM • CZC
ON LOCATION • 1912 • Roach Hal • SHT • USA
ON LONESOME MOUNTAIN • 1914 • *Lubin* • USA
ON LOVE see **OM KARLEK** • 1987
ON MIRACULOUS HAPPENINGS see **O VECECH NADPRIROZENYCH** • 1958
ON MONDAY NEXT see **CURTAIN UP** • 1952
ON MOONLIGHT BAY • 1951 • Del Ruth Roy • USA
ON MOONSHINE MOUNTAIN • 1914 • *Lubin* • USA
ON MOUNT ALA-TAU see **V GORACH ALA-TAU** • 1944
ON MOUNTAIN PASS AMAGI see **AMAGI GOE** • 1983
ON MY RESPONSIBILITY see **PE RASPUNDEREA MEA** • 1956
ON MY WAY see **APEN FRAMTID** • 1983
ON MY WAY TO THE CRUSADES, I MET A GIRL WHO.. (USA) see **CINTURA DI CASTITA, LA** • 1967
ON MY WAY TO YOU • 1972 • Mashchenko Nikolay • USS
ON N'AIME QU-UNE FOIS • 1949 • Stelli Jean • FRN • CAILLE, LA
ON N'ARRETE PAS LE PRINTEMPS • 1972 • Gilson Rene • FRN
ON NE BADINE PAS AVEC L'AMOUR • 1908 • Melies Georges • FRN • NO TRIFLING WITH LOVE
ON NE BADINE PAS AVEC L'AMOUR • 1924 • Ravel Gaston • FRN
ON NE BADINE PAS AVEC L'AMOUR • 1961 • Dessailly Jean • FRN
ON NE FERA PAS RIRE DE NOUS AUTRES.. LA COMMUNAUTE URBAINE DE QUEBEC • 1970 • Lavoie Richard • DCS • CND
ON NE MEURT PAS COMME CA • 1946 • Boyer Jean • FRN
ON NE MEURT QUE DEUX FOIS • 1986 • Deray Jacques • FRN • HE DIED WITH HIS EYES OPEN
ON NE ROULE PAS ANTOINETTE • 1936 • Madeux Paul, Christian-Jaque (Spv) • FRN
ON NE SAURAIT PENSER A RIEN see **FEMME DE L'AVIATEUR, LA** • 1980
ON NE TRICHE PAS AVEC LA VIE • 1949 • Delacroix Rene, Vandenberghe Paul • FRN, CND • DOCTEUR LOUISE
ON NE VA PAS SE QUITTER COMME CA • 1980 • Comolli Jean-Louis • FRN
ON N'ENGRAISSE PAS LES COCHONS A L'EAU CLAIRE • 1973 • Lefebvre Jean-Pierre • CND • PIGS ARE SELDOM CLEAN
ON N'ENTERRE PAS LE DIMANCHE • 1959 • Drach Michel • FRN • WE DON'T BURY ON SUNDAYS
ON N'EST PAS DES ANGES • 1982 • Simoneau Guy • CND
ON N'EST PAS DES ANGES.. ELLES NON PLUS • 1980 • Lang Michel • FRN
ON N'EST PAS SERIEUX QUAND ON A 17 ANS • 1974 • Pianko Adam • FRN
ON N'EST PAS SORTI DE L'AUBERGE • 1982 • Pecas Max • FRN
ON NYE KHOTEL UBIVAT • 1967 • Shengelaya Georgi • USS • HE DID NOT WANT TO KILL ◦ ON UBIVAT NE KHOTEL
ON OUR MERRY WAY (UKN) see **MIRACLE CAN HAPPEN, A** • 1948
ON OUR SELECTION • 1920 • Longford Raymond • ASL
ON OUR SELECTION • 1930 • Hall Ken G. • ASL
ON PANTHER CREEK • 1910 • *Lubin* • USA
ON PARADE • 1936 • Pal George • ANS • NTH
ON PAROLE • 1910 • *Powers* • USA
ON PAROLE see **WESTERN WALLOP, THE** • 1924
ON PATROL • 1922 • Del Ruth Roy • SHT • USA
ON PEUT LE DIRE SANS SE FACHER! • 1978 • Coggio Roger • FRN • ONE CAN SAY IT WITHOUT GETTING ANGRY ◦ BELLE EMMERDEUSE, LA
ON PINE MOUNTAIN • 1913 • *Gail Jane* • USA
ON PROBATION • 1912 • *Barnes Justin D.* • USA
ON PROBATION • 1924 • Hutchison Charles • USA
ON PROBATION • 1935 • Hutchison Charles • USA
ON PROBATION see **JOHN SMITH** • 1922
ON PROBATION see **PARTFOGOLT, A** • 1982
ON PURGE BEBE • 1931 • Renoir Jean • FRN
ON RECORD • 1917 • Leonard Robert Z. • USA
ON REGARDAIT TOUJOURS VERS LA MER • 1982 • Kinsey Nicholas • DOC • CND • WE ALWAYS LOOKED OUT TO SEA
ON ROLLER SKATES see **RULLESKOJTERNE** • 1908
ON RUGGED SHORES • 1914 • Christie Al • USA
ON SACRED GROUND • 1980 • Howes Oliver • DOC • ASL
ON SAFARI • 1932 • Holmes F. W. Ratcliffe • UKN
ON SAIT OU ENTRER TONY, MAIS C'EST LES NOTES • 1966 • Fournier Claude • DCS • CND
ON SECRET SERVICE • 1912 • Edwards Walter • USA
ON SECRET SERVICE • 1915 • Bartlett Charles • USA
ON SECRET SERVICE • 1933 • Woods Arthur • UKN • SECRET AGENT (USA) ◦ SPY 77
ON SECRET SERVICE (UKN) see **TRAILIN' WEST** • 1936
ON S'EN FOUT.. ON S'AIME • 1982 • Gerard Michel • FRN
ON SEPARATE PATHS • 1911 • *Selig* • USA
ON S'EST TROMPE D'HISTOIRE D'AMOUR • 1974 • Bertucelli Jean-Louis • FRN
ON SPECIAL DUTY (UKN) see **BULLETS FOR RUSTLERS** • 1940
ON S'PRATIQUE.. C'EST POUR LES OLYMPIQUES • 1976 • Labrecque Jean-Claude • DOC • CND
ON STAGE EVERYBODY • 1945 • Yarbrough Jean • USA
ON SUCH A NIGHT • 1937 • Dupont E. A. • USA
ON SUCH A NIGHT • 1956 • Asquith Anthony • UKN
ON SUNDAYS • 1961 • Baillie Bruce • SHT • USA
ON SUSPICION • 1914 • *Rex* • USA
ON SUSPICION • 1914 • *Lubin* • USA
ON THANKSGIVING DAY • 1908 • Boggs Frank • USA
ON THE AIR • 1932 • McGann William • UKN
ON THE AIR • 1934 • Smith Herbert • UKN
ON THE AIR AND OFF • 1933 • Shores Lynn • SHT • USA
ON THE AIR LIVE WITH CAPTAIN MIDNIGHT • 1979 • Sebastian Beverly, Sebastian Ferdinand • USA • CAPTAIN MIDNIGHT
ON THE ALTAR OF LOVE • 1915 • *Costello Maurice* • USA
ON THE AVENUE • 1937 • Del Ruth Roy • USA
ON THE BALL • 1964 • Tammer Peter • DOC • ASL
ON THE BALTIC • 1970 • Trzos-Rastawiecki Andrzej • DOC • PLN
ON THE BANK OF SOLITUDE see **SUR LE DUNE DE LA SOLITUDE** • 1964
ON THE BANKS OF ALLAN WATER • 1915 • Malins Geoffrey H. • SHT • UKN
ON THE BANKS OF ALLAN WATER • 1916 • Noy Wilfred • UKN
ON THE BANKS OF THE ARAX see **POTU STORONU ARAKSA** • 1947
ON THE BANKS OF THE WABASH • 1923 • Blackton J. Stuart • USA • BANKS OF THE WABASH
ON THE "BATORY" TO POLAND see **NA "BATORYM" DO POLSKI** • 1960
ON THE BEACH • Craig Ray • SHT • USA
ON THE BEACH • 1914 • *Melies* • USA
ON THE BEACH • 1914 • Thornby Robert T. • *Sterling* • USA
ON THE BEACH • 1959 • Kramer Stanley • USA
ON THE BEAM see **IT COMES UP LOVE** • 1943
ON THE BEAT • 1962 • Asher Robert • UKN
ON THE BENCHES IN THE PARK • 1899 • *Haydon & Urry* • UKN
ON THE BLACK HILL • 1987 • Grieve Andrew • UKN
ON THE BORDER • 1909 • Boggs Frank • USA
ON THE BORDER • 1910 • *Powers* • USA
ON THE BORDER • 1913 • Dwan Allan • USA
ON THE BORDER • 1914 • *Hunt Irene* • USA
ON THE BORDER • 1915 • *Adair Robyn* • USA
ON THE BORDER • 1930 • McGann William • USA
ON THE BORDER see **SOVIET BORDER** • 1938
ON THE BORDER LINE • 1912 • *Nestor* • USA
ON THE BORDERLAND OF CIVILIZATION • Johnson Martin E. • USA
ON THE BOTTOM see **NA DNU** • 1969
ON THE BOTTOM RUNG OF HEAVEN see **OP DE BODEM VAN DE HEMEL** • 1965
ON THE BOWERY • 1955 • Rogosin Lionel • USA
ON THE BOWERY see **THIS IS THE BOWERY** • 1941
ON THE BREAD LINE • 1915 • *Majestic* • USA
ON THE BREAST OF THE TIDE • 1914 • *Selig* • USA
ON THE BRINK • 1911 • Porter Edwin S. • USA
ON THE BRINK • 1914 • *Lubin* • USA
ON THE BRINK • 1915 • Buckland Warwick • UKN
ON THE BRINK see **DAMNED, THE** • 1962
ON THE BRINK see **AM RANDE** • 1963
ON THE BRINK OF RUIN • 1913 • *Sais Marin* • USA
ON THE BRINK OF THE ABYSS • 1915 • *Bracey Sidney* • USA
ON THE BRINK OF THE CHASM • 1912 • *Panzer Paul* • USA
ON THE BRINK OF THE PRECIPICE • 1909 • *Urban-Eclipse* • USA
ON THE BRINK OF THE PRECIPICE • 1913 • Buckland Warwick? • UKN
ON THE BRINK OF WAR • 1916 • Horne James W. • SHT • USA
ON THE BROAD STAIRWAY • 1913 • *Sawyer Laura* • USA
ON THE BUSES • 1971 • Booth Harry • UKN
ON THE CACTUS TRAIL • 1912 • *Anderson Broncho Billy* • USA
ON THE CARPET • 1916 • Collins Edwin J.? • UKN
ON THE CARPET (UKN) see **LITTLE GIANT, THE** • 1946
ON THE CHESS BOARD OF FATE • 1914 • *Imp* • USA
ON THE COMET see **NA KOMETE** • 1970
ON THE CORNER OF THE ARBAT AND BUBULINOS STREET • 1973 • Zakharias Manos • USS • CORNER OF ARBAT AND BABULINOS STREET, THE
ON THE COSY SIDE see **STIN ANAPAFTIKI MERIA** • 1981
ON THE CRUISE WITH THE ALBERTINA see **PA KRYSS MED ALBERTINA** • 1938
ON THE CRUISE WITH THE LIGHTNING see **PA KRYSS MED BLIXTEN** • 1927
ON THE DANGER LINE • 1912 • *Barker Florence* • USA
ON THE DAWN ROAD • 1915 • *Roscoe Albert* • USA
ON THE DESERT'S EDGE • 1911 • *Anderson Broncho Billy* • USA
ON THE DIVIDE • 1928 • McGowan J. P. • USA
ON THE DOORSTEPS • 1910 • *Vitagraph* • USA
ON THE DOTTED LINE see **LET WOMEN ALONE** • 1925
ON THE DOUBLE • 1961 • Shavelson Melville • USA
ON THE DUMBWAITER • 1913 • Smiley Joseph • USA
ON THE EAGLE TRAIL • 1915 • Mix Tom • USA
ON THE EARTH see **CHIJO** • 1957
ON THE EDGE • 1949 • Harrington Curtis • SHT • USA
ON THE EDGE • 1985 • Nilsson Rob • USA
ON THE EDGE • 1987 • Damberger Francis • SHT • CND
ON THE EDGE OF THE PRECIPICE • 1912 • *Pathe* • USA
ON THE EDGE OF THE VOID see **SEUIL DU VIDE, LE** • 1971
ON THE EMPTY BALCONY see **EN EL BALCON VACIO** • 1962
ON THE EVE see **NAKANUNYE** • 1959
ON THE EVE OF IVAN KUPALA'S DAY see **IVAN KUPALA'S EVE** • 1968
ON THE EVE OF MATRICULATION see **PRED MATURITOU** • 1932
ON THE EVE OF THE THIRTEENTH see **NOSHTA SRESHTU 13-I** • 1961
ON THE EVE OF WAR see **KAISEN NO ZENYA** • 1943
ON THE EVERYDAY USE OF THE EYES OF DEATH • 1968 • Beavers Robert • SHT • USA
ON THE FARM • 1933 • *White Brian/ Griffiths Sid* • ANM • UKN
ON THE FATEFUL ROADS OF LIFE see **PA LIVETS ODESVAGAR** • 1913
ON THE FIDDLE • 1961 • Frankel Cyril • UKN • OPERATION SNAFU (USA) ◦ OPERATION WAR HEAD ◦ WAR HEAD
ON THE FIRE • 1919 • Roach Hal • SHT • USA • CHEF, THE
ON THE FIRING LINE • 1910 • *Great Western* • USA
ON THE FIRING LINE • 1912 • Ince Thomas H. • USA
ON THE FIRING LINE • 1913 • *Gaumont* • USA
ON THE FISHING BANKS OF SKYE see **FISHING BANKS OF SKYE, THE** • 1934
ON THE FRESH GRASS see **SOBRE LA HERBA VIRGEN** • 1977
ON THE FRINGE OF SOCIETY • 1982 • Udomej Manop • THL
ON THE FRONT PAGE • 1926 • Roach Hal • SHT • USA
ON THE FRONTIER • 1913 • *Bison* • USA
ON THE GAME • 1974 • Long Stanley • UKN
ON THE GO • 1925 • Seiler Lewis • SHT • USA
ON THE GO • 1925 • Thorpe Richard • SHT • USA
ON THE GOLF LINKS • 1915 • *Casino* • USA
ON THE GREAT STEEL BEAM • 1914 • Miller Ashley • USA
ON THE GREAT WHITE TRAIL (UKN) see **RENFREW ON THE GREAT WHITE TRAIL** • 1938
ON THE GREEN PATH see **POR LOS CAMINOS VERDES** • 1989
ON THE HARMFULNESS OF TOBACCO • 1959 • Newman Paul • SHT • USA
ON THE HEIGHTS • 1914 • Edwin Walter • *Edison* • USA
ON THE HEIGHTS • 1914 • Marston A. C.?, Marston Lawrence? • *Ab* • USA
ON THE HIGH CARD • 1921 • *Myers Harry* • USA
ON THE HIGH SEAS • 1914 • *Phillips Dorothy* • USA
ON THE HIGH SEAS • 1915 • *Stanton Richard* • USA
ON THE HIGH SEAS • 1922 • Willat Irvin V. • USA
ON THE HIGHWAY OF LIFE see **NA ESTRADA DA VIDA** • 1981
ON THE HOP • 1913 • Kellino W. P. • UKN

ON THE HUNTING GROUND see **LIECHANG ZHASA** • 1985
ON THE INGURY-RIVER • 1961 • Rondeli David • USS
ON THE INSTALLMENT PLAN • 1911 • *American* • USA
ON THE ISLE OF SAMOA • 1950 • Berke William • USA
ON THE ISLE OF SARNE • 1914 • Ridgely Richard • USA
ON THE JOB • 1913 • *Steppling John* • USA
ON THE JOB • 1915 • Fahrney Milton • USA
ON THE JUMP • 1918 • Roach Hal • *Rolin* • SHT • USA
ON THE JUMP • 1918 • Walsh Raoul • *Fox* • USA
ON THE LAZY LINE • 1914 • Williams C. Jay • USA
ON THE LEDGE • 1914 • *Reliance* • USA
ON THE LEVEL • 1915 • Worthington William • USA
ON THE LEVEL • 1917 • Melford George • USA
ON THE LEVEL • 1930 • Cummings Irving • USA
ON THE LINE • 1976 • Margolis Barbara • USA
ON THE LINE • 1977 • Weiss Barbara N. • USA
ON THE LINE see **RIO ABAJO** • 1982
ON THE LINE OF FIRE -FILM REPORTERS see **NA LINII OGNYA -OPERATORY KINOKHRONIKI** • 1941
ON THE LINE OF PERIL • 1912 • *Vitagraph* • USA
ON THE LITTLE BIG HORN • 1910 • *Nestor* • USA
ON THE LITTLE BIG HORN OR CUSTER'S LAST STAND • 1909 • Boggs Frank • USA
ON THE LITTLE ISLAND see **NA MALKIA OSTROV** • 1958
ON THE LITTLE MILL TRACE • 1915 • Windom Lawrence C. • USA
ON THE LOOKOUT FOR TRAINS see **OSTRE SLEDOVANE VLAKY** • 1966
ON THE LOOSE • 1931 • Roach Hal • SHT • USA
ON THE LOOSE • 1951 • Lederer Charles • USA
ON THE LOVE LINE • 1917 • *Sparkle* • SHT • USA
ON THE MAKE see **DEVIL WITH WOMEN, A** • 1930
ON THE MARRIAGE BROKER JOKE AS CITED BY CLEMENT FREUD IN WIT AND ITS RELATION TO THE UNCONSCIOUS • 1979 • Landow George • USA • CAN THE AVANT-GARDE ARTIST BE WHOLED
ON THE MELLOW SIDE • 1944 • Collins Lewis D. • SHT • USA
ON THE MEXICAN BORDER • 1910 • *Lubin* • USA
ON THE MINUTE • 1914 • Martin E. A. • USA
ON THE MOONLIGHT TRAIL • 1912 • *Essanay* • USA
ON THE MOUNTAIN RANCH • 1913 • Grandon Francis J. • USA
ON THE MOUNTAINS OF ALA-TAU see **V GORACH ALA-TAU** • 1944
ON THE MOVE see **UTKOZBEN** • 1980
ON THE NICKEL • 1979 • Waite Ralph • USA
ON THE NIEMEN RIVER see **NAD NIEMNEM** • 1939
ON THE NIGHT OF THE FIRE • 1939 • Hurst Brian Desmond • UKN • FUGITIVE, THE (USA)
ON THE NIGHT STAGE • 1915 • Barker Reginald • USA • BANDIT AND THE PREACHER, THE
ON THE ODRA see **NAD ODRA** • 1965
ON THE OFFBEAT see **A CONTRATIEMPO** • 1981
ON THE OLD SPANISH TRAIL • 1947 • Witney William • USA
ON THE ORINOCO RIVER see **NAD ORINOKO** • 1970
ON THE OTHER SIDE see **OVERKANT, DE** • 1966
ON THE OTHER SIDE see **ONKRAJ** • 1971
ON THE OTHER SIDE OF CUYUNI see **MAS ALLA DEL CUYUNI** • 1977
ON THE OTHER SIDE OF THE ARAKS see **POTU STORONU ARAKSA** • 1947
ON THE OTHER SIDE OF THE SEA see **PRIKO SINJEG MORA** • 1980
ON THE PAN • 1933 • *Van Beuren* • ANS • USA
ON THE PAVEMENT see **PO TROTOARA** • 1967
ON THE POACHER'S PATH see **NA PYTLACKE STEZCE** • 1981
ON THE POLE see **EDDIE SACHS AT INDIANAPOLIS** • 1961
ON THE POLYNESIAN ISLANDS see **NA WYSPACH POLINEZJI** • 1969
ON THE PRIVATE WIRE • 1915 • *Totten Joseph Byron* • USA
ON THE PUPIL OF HIS EYE • 1912 • *Brooke Van Dyke* • USA
ON THE QUIET • 1918 • Withey Chet • USA
ON THE RAILS • 1940 • Kaplan A., Trakhtenberg Naum • USS
ON THE RAMPAGE • 1916 • *Ovey George* • USA
ON THE RANGER'S ROLL OF HONOR • 1913 • *Frontier* • USA
ON THE RED FRONT see **NA KRASNOM FRONTE** • 1920
ON THE REEF • 1910 • Griffith D. W. • USA
ON THE RESERVE • 1920 • Kellino W. P. • UKN
ON THE RIGHT TRACK • 1948 • Mach Josef • CZC
ON THE RIGHT TRACK • 1981 • Philips Lee • USA
ON THE RIO GRANDE • 1914 • *Little Anna* • USA
ON THE RIVIERA • 1951 • Lang Walter • USA
ON THE ROAD • 1964 • Szczechura Daniel • ANM • PLN
ON THE ROAD AGAIN see **HONEYSUCKLE ROSE** • 1980
ON THE ROAD SPECIAL: THE 1955 SHOW • 1975 • Albury Simon • SHT • UKN
ON THE ROAD TO CALAIS see **ROAD TO CALAIS, THE** • 1914
ON THE ROAD TO HOLLYWOOD • 1982 • Frankfurter Bernhard • DOC • AUS
ON THE ROAD TO KATANGA see **NA PUTU ZA KATANGU** • 1987
ON THE ROAD TO RENO • 1915 • *Johnson Arthur* • USA
ON THE ROAD WITH CIRCUS OZ • 1982 • Friedrichs Zbigniew • DOC • ASL
ON THE ROAD WITH DUKE ELLINGTON • 1967 • Jeremy John • DOC • USA
ON THE ROAD WITH DUKE ELLINGTON • 1974 • Jeremy John • DOC • USA
ON THE ROAD WITH RED MOLE • 1977 • Neill Sam • DOC • NZL
ON THE ROADS OF ARMENIA see **NA DROGACH ARMENII** • 1957
ON THE ROADS OF FATE see **PA LIVETS ODESVAGAR** • 1913
ON THE ROADS TO RUSSIA see **PO RUSI** • 1968
ON THE ROOFS see **SUR LES TOITS** • 1897
ON THE ROOFS OF BUDAPEST see **PESTI HAZTETOK** • 1961
ON THE RUINS OF THE ESTATE see **NA GRAFSKIKH RAZVALINAKH** • 1956
ON THE RUN • 1958 • Morris Ernest • UKN
ON THE RUN • 1963 • Tronson Robert • UKN
ON THE RUN • 1969 • Jackson Pat • UKN
ON THE RUN • 1982 • Brown Mende • ASL
ON THE RUN see **ZGODBA KI JE NI** • 1967
ON THE RUSSIAN FRONTIER • 1914 • Weston Charles • UKN
ON THE SAME PLANET see **NO ODNOI PLANETE** • 1966
ON THE SEA FRONT see **FRENTE AL MAR** • 1980
ON THE SET see **FREE AND EASY** • 1930
ON THE SET see **NA PLANIE** • 1968
ON THE SHELF see **LET WOMEN ALONE** • 1925
ON THE SHORE • 1912 • *Le Saint Edward J.* • USA
ON THE SHOULDERS see **PA DESSA SKULDROR** • 1948
ON THE SIDE (UKN) see **HAUSFRAUEN REPORT** • 1971
ON THE SIDELINES see **SZEPEK ES BOLONDOK** • 1977
ON THE SIDING • Pogacnik Joze • DCS • YGS
ON THE SLOPES OF KILIMANJARO see **NA STOKACH KILIMANDZARO** • 1970
ON THE SOCIETY FILE OF SHANGAHI see **SHANG-HAI SHI-HUI TANG-AN** • 1982
ON THE SOUND • 1963 • Baker Fred • SHT • USA
ON THE SPANISH MAIN • 1917 • Salisbury Edward A. • USA
ON THE SPOT • 1940 • Bretherton Howard • USA
ON THE SPOT • 1954 • Biggs Julian • SER • CND
ON THE SPOT see **GANG BUSTER, THE** • 1931
ON-THE-SQUARE GIRL, THE • 1917 • Fitzmaurice George • USA
ON THE STEEP CLIFF see **U KRUTOGO YARA** • 1962
ON THE STEPS • 1914 • France Charles H. • USA
ON THE STEPS OF THE ALTAR • 1916 • West R. Harley • UKN
ON THE STORMY HILL see **POKPOONGEA UHUNDUCK** • 1960
ON THE STROKE OF FIVE • 1912 • *Thanhouser* • USA
ON THE STROKE OF FIVE • 1914 • Lambart Harry • USA
ON THE STROKE OF NINE see **MURDER ON THE CAMPUS** • 1934
ON THE STROKE OF THREE • 1911 • *Imp* • USA
ON THE STROKE OF THREE • 1924 • Weight F. Harmon • USA • SOLD FOR CASH
ON THE STROKE OF TWELVE • 1915 • Collins John H. • USA
ON THE STROKE OF TWELVE • 1927 • Hunt Charles J. • USA
ON THE SUNNY SIDE • 1942 • Schuster Harold • USA
ON THE SUNNY SIDE see **NA SLUNECNI STRANE** • 1933
ON THE SUNNY SIDE see **PA SOLSIDAN** • 1936
ON THE SUNNY SIDE OF THE STREET • 1959 • Klopcic Matjaz • SHT • YGS
ON THE SUNNY SIDE OF THE STREET see **SUNNY SIDE OF THE STREET** • 1951
ON THE SWAN see **O LABUTI** • 1982
ON THE TABLE TOP • 1915 • *West Billy* • USA
ON THE THIRD DAY • 1983 • O'Toole Stanley • UKN
ON THE THRESHOLD • 1913 • Nicholls George • USA
ON THE THRESHOLD • 1925 • Hoffman Renaud • USA
ON THE THRESHOLD see **NA PROGU** • 1965
ON THE THRESHOLD see **LARS I PORTEN** • 1984
ON THE THRESHOLD OF ART see **KOMEDIANTY** • 1961
ON THE THRESHOLD OF FATE see **STO KATOFLI TIS MIRAS** • 1967
ON THE THRESHOLD OF LIFE see **VINA VLADIMIRA OLMERA** • 1956
ON THE THRESHOLD OF SPACE • 1956 • Webb Robert D. • USA
ON THE THRESHOLD OF SPACE TRAVEL • Goldberger Kurt • DOC • CZC
ON THE TIGER'S BACK see **A CAVALLO DELLA TIGRE** • 1961
ON THE TIGHTROPE see **NA LANE** • 1963
ON THE TOWN • 1949 • Kelly Gene, Donen Stanley • USA
ON THE TOWN see **OP STAP** • 1935
ON THE TRACES OF A LOST FILM • 1968 • Bostan Ion • DOC • RMN
ON THE TRACK see **NA TORACH** • 1972
ON THE TRACK OF OIL see **DINKUM OIL** • 1921
ON THE TRACKS OF THE MISSING • 1979 • Nikolov Margarit • BUL
ON THE TRAIL • 1918 • *Universal* • SHT • USA
ON THE TRAIL see **CHIYARI FUJI** • 1955
ON THE TRAIL OF BLOOD • 1969 • Schulhoff Petr • CZC
ON THE TRAIL OF ELVIS THE CAT • 1987 • Olsson Claes • FNL
ON THE TRAIL OF THE CULPRIT: BLIND HATRED see **DEM TATER AUF DER SPUR: BLINDER HASS** • 1973
ON THE TRAIL OF THE DOCK RATS • 1914 • *K & S Feature Film* • USA
ON THE TRAIL OF THE GERMS • 1912 • *Selig* • USA
ON THE TRAIL OF THE LONESOME PILL • 1917 • *Dunham Phil* • SHT • USA
ON THE TRAIL OF THE LONESOME PINE see **WAITING FOR THE MOON** • 1987
ON THE TRAIL OF THE TIGRESS • 1916 • Bourgeois Paul • SHT • USA
ON THE TURN OF A CARD • 1915 • Humphrey William • USA
ON THE TWELFTH DAY • 1956 • Toye Wendy • UKN
ON THE VERGE • 1912 • *Shamrock* • USA
ON THE VERGE • 1914 • *Frontier* • USA
ON THE VERGE see **GRAN** • 1989
ON THE VERGE OF WAR • 1914 • Turner Otis • USA
ON THE WAR PATH • 1912 • Barker Reginald • USA
ON THE WARPATH • 1909 • *Selig* • USA
ON THE WARPATH • 1911 • *Melford Judson* • USA
ON THE WARSAW HIGHWAY see **NA VARSHAVSKOM TRAKTE** • 1916
ON THE WATCH IN THE FOREST see **DO LESICKA NA CEKANOU** • 1966
ON THE WATERFRONT • 1954 • Kazan Elia • USA
ON THE WAY see **UNTERWEGS** • 1988
ON THE WAY TO PURGATORY see **AKCJA CZYSCIEC** • 1967
ON THE WAY TO SPIDER GATE see **TOCHUKEN KUMOEMON** • 1936
ON THE WAY TO USKUDAR see **KATIP** • 1968
ON THE WESTERN FRONTIER • 1909 • Porter Edwin S. • USA
ON THE WILD SHORE see **NA DIKOM BEREGYE** • 1967
ON THE WILL OF MAN • 1959 • Grigorov Roumen • DOC • BUL
ON THE WRONG SCENT • 1909 • *Essanay* • USA
ON THE WRONG TRACK • 1915 • Beaumont Harry • USA
ON THE WRONG TREK • 1936 • Parrott Charles, Law Harold • SHT • USA
ON THE YARD • 1978 • Silver Raphael D. • USA
ON THEIR OWN • 1940 • Brower Otto • USA
ON THEIR WAY • 1921 • Roach Hal • SHT • USA
ON THEIR WEDDING EVE • 1913 • Costello Maurice • USA
ON THESE EVENINGS • Vesely Herbert • SHT • USA
ON THIN ICE • 1925 • St. Clair Malcolm • USA
ON THIN ICE • 1933 • Vorhaus Bernard • UKN
ON THIN ICE • 1961 • von Cziffra Geza • FRG • BIG FREEZE, THE
ON THIS EARTH see **CHIJO** • 1957
ON THREE MOON CREEK • 1963 • Burstall Tim • SHT • ASL
ON THURSDAYS A MIRACLE see **JUEVES MILAGRO, LOS** • 1957
ON TIME • 1924 • Lehrman Henry • USA
ON TIME FOR WORK • 1913 • *Lubin* • USA
ON TO MARS see **ABBOTT AND COSTELLO GO TO MARS** • 1953
ON TO RENO • 1928 • Cruze James • USA
ON TO THE FRONT! see **TEBYE FRONT** • 1943
ON TO THE POLAR SEA -A YUKON ADVENTURE • 1983 • Raymont Peter, Walker John • CND, USA
ON TOP see **MEN ALLT A HREINU** • 1983
ON TOP OF OLD SMOKY • 1953 • Archainbaud George • USA
ON TOP OF THE UNDERWORLD • 1938 • Delamar Mickey, Kavanagh Denis • SER • UKN
ON TOP OF THE WORLD • 1936 • Davis Redd • UKN • EVERYTHING OKAY
ON TOP OF THE WORLD see **SHAPKA NA TOYAGA** • 1972
ON TOUR see **LITTLE EVA ASCENDS** • 1922
ON TRIAL • 1917 • Young James • USA
ON TRIAL • 1928 • Mayo Archie • USA
ON TRIAL • 1939 • Morse Terry O. • USA
ON TRIAL see **AFFAIRE MAURIZIUS, L'** • 1953
ON UBIVAT NE KHOTEL see **ON NYE KHOTEL UBIVAT** • 1967
ON VALENTINE'S DAY • 1986 • Harrison Ken • TVM • USA
ON VELVET • 1938 • Newman Widgey R. • UKN
ON VOIT BIEN QU'C'EST PAS TOI • 1969 • Zarifian Christian • FRN
ON VOUS PARLE • 1960 • Cayrol Jean, Durand Claude • FRN
ON WINGS OF EAGLES • 1986 • McLaglen Andrew V. • TVM • USA
ON WINGS OF PAPER see **NA PAPIRNATIH AVIONIH** • 1967
ON WINGS OF SONG (UKN) see **LOVE ME FOREVER** • 1935
ON WITH THE DANCE • 1915 • Williams C. Jay • USA
ON WITH THE DANCE • 1920 • Fitzmaurice George • USA
ON WITH THE DANCE • 1927 • Parkinson H. B., Edwards J. Steven • SER • UKN
ON WITH THE MOTLEY see **AMLETO E I SUO CLOWN** • 1920
ON WITH THE NEW • 1938 • Fleischer Dave • ANS • USA
ON WITH THE SHOW • 1929 • Crosland Alan • USA
ON YOUR BACK • 1930 • McClintic Guthrie • USA • CLOTHES AND THE WOMAN
ON YOUR RADIO DIAL • 1935 • Schwarzwald Milton • SHT • USA
ON YOUR TOES • 1927 • Newmeyer Fred • USA
ON YOUR TOES • 1939 • Enright Ray • USA
ON ZE BOULEVARD • 1927 • Millarde Harry • USA
ON ZIZKA'S FORTIFIED WAGON see **NA ZIZKOVE VALECNEM VOZE** • 1968
ON ZIZKA'S WAR WAGON see **NA ZIZKOVE VALECNEM VOZE** • 1968
ONA ZASHCHISHCHAYET RODINU • 1943 • Ermler Friedrich • USS • SHE DEFENDS HER COUNTRY ○ NO GREATER LOVE
ONAN • 1963 • Iimura Takahiko • SHT • JPN
ONAWANDA • 1909 • Blackton J. Stuart (Spv) • USA
ONBORO FILM • 1985 • Tezuka Osamu • ANM • JPN
ONCE • 1963 • Esadze Rezo • SHT • USS • ONE DAY
ONCE • 1973 • Heilig Mort • USA
ONCE • 1980 • Pinsent Gordon • MTV • CND
ONCE • 1990 • Williams Richard • ANM • USA
ONCE A BLACKBIRD SANG see **ZIL PEVCIJ DROZD** • 1972
ONCE A CROOK • 1941 • Mason Herbert • UKN
ONCE A DOCTOR • 1937 • Clemens William • USA
ONCE A GENTLEMAN • 1930 • Cruze James • USA
ONCE A GENTLEMAN see **LET'S LIVE TONIGHT** • 1935
ONCE A HERO • 1987 • Weill Claudia, Inch Kevin • USA
ONCE A HERO (UKN) see **IT HAPPENED IN HOLLYWOOD** • 1937
ONCE A JOLLY SWAGMAN • 1948 • Lee Jack • UKN • MANIACS ON WHEELS (USA)
ONCE A LADY • 1931 • McClintic Guthrie • USA
ONCE A MASON • 1919 • Drew Sidney, Drew Sidney Mrs. • SHT • USA
ONCE A MOTH see **MINSA'Y ISANG GAMU-GAMO** • 1977
ONCE A NIGHT see **NOCHE EMBARAZOSA, UNA** • 1976
ONCE A PLUMBER • 1920 • Lyons Eddie, Moran Lee • USA
ONCE A RAINY DAY see **AKOGARE** • 1966
ONCE A SINNER • 1931 • McClintic Guthrie • USA
ONCE A SINNER • 1950 • Gilbert Lewis* • UKN
ONCE A THIEF-? • 1916 • *Washburn Bryant* • SHT • USA
ONCE A THIEF • 1935 • Pearson George • UKN
ONCE A THIEF • 1951 • Wilder W. Lee • USA
ONCE A THIEF • 1965 • Nelson Ralph • USA, FRN • TUEURS DE SAN FRANCISCO, LES (FRN)
ONCE A THIEF see **HAPPY THIEVES, THE** • 1962
ONCE A WEEK • 1937 • Sziatinay Sandor
ONCE ABOARD THE LUGGER • 1914 • Plumb Hay • UKN
ONCE ABOARD THE LUGGER • 1920 • Ames Gerald, Quiribet Gaston • UKN
ONCE AGAIN • 1982 • Nassenstein Hans • ANS • NTH
ONCE AGAIN • 1986 • Chaudhri Amin • USA
ONCE AGAIN see **PHIR BHI** • 1972
ONCE AGAIN ABOUT LOVE see **YESHCHYO RAZ PRO LYUBOV** • 1968
ONCE AGAIN (USA) see **EK BAAR PHIR** • 1980
ONCE AL ASALTO • 1971 • *Cinema Marte* • MXC
ONCE AND FOR ALWAYS see **SOLE NELLA PELLE, IL** • 1971
ONCE AND FOREVER • 1927 • Stone Phil • USA
ONCE AROUND • 1990 • Hallstrom Lasse • USA
ONCE BEFORE I DIE • 1965 • Derek John • USA, PHL • NO TOYS FOR CHRISTMAS
ONCE BITTEN • 1932 • Hiscott Leslie • UKN
ONCE BITTEN • 1985 • Storm Howard • USA
ONCE BITTEN (USA) see **MORDUS, LES** • 1960
ONCE EVERY TEN MINUTES • 1915 • Roach Hal • USA

ONCE IN A BLUE MOON • 1935 • Hecht Ben, MacArthur Charles • USA • LAUGH LITTLE CLOWN
ONCE IN A LIFETIME • 1925 • Worne Duke • USA
ONCE IN A LIFETIME • 1932 • Mack Russell • USA • MERRY-GO-ROUND
ONCE IN A MILLION • 1936 • Woods Arthur • UKN • WEEKEND MILLIONAIRE (USA)
ONCE IN A NEW MOON • 1935 • Kimmins Anthony • UKN
ONCE IN AUGUST • 1984 • Rubbo Michael • MTV • CND
ONCE IN PARIS.. • 1978 • Gilroy Frank D. • USA
ONCE IN SUMMER • 1936 • Schmein • USS
ONCE IS ENOUGH • 1915 • *La Pearl Harry* • USA
ONCE IS MORE THAN ENOUGH • 1987 • *Ekmongkol Lilit* • THL
ONCE IS NONCE see **EINMAL IST KEINMAL** • 1955
ONCE IS NOT ENOUGH see **JACQUELINE SUSANN'S ONCE IS NOT ENOUGH** • 1974
ONCE MORE see **IMA HITOTABI NO** • 1947
ONCE MORE ABOUT LOVE see **YESHCHYO RAZ PRO LYUBOV** • 1968
ONCE MORE MY DARLING • 1949 • Montgomery Robert • USA
ONCE MORE, WITH FEELING • 1960 • Donen Stanley • USA
ONCE MORE WITH GOSTA EKMAN see **AN EN GANG GOSTA EKMAN** • 1940
ONCE ONE see **EGYSZEREGY** • 1978
ONCE OR TWICE UPON A TIME AND THRICE UPON A SPACE • 1965 • Sens Al • ANS • CND
ONCE OVER • 1923 • Roach Hal • SHT • USA
ONCE OVER, THE • 1915 • Cooley Frank • USA
ONCE-OVER, THE • 1964 • Kneitel Seymour • ANS • USA
ONCE OVER LIGHTLY see **MEANEST GAL IN TOWN, THE** • 1934
ONCE OVER LIGHTLY see **DON'T TELL THE WIFE** • 1937
ONCE PARES DE BOTAS • 1954 • Rovira Beleta Francisco • SPN
ONCE POR CERO • 1970 • Alvarez Santiago • DOC • CUB
ONCE SOMEWHERE see **ORIDATH** • 1986
ONCE THERE WAS A BOY, A PARTISAN, A HORSE.. see **ERASE UN NINO, UN GUERRILLERO, UN COBALLO..** • 1967
ONCE THERE WAS A PRINCESS (UKN) see **MISBEHAVING LADIES** • 1931
ONCE THERE WAS A THRUSH see **ZIL PEVCIJ DROZD** • 1972
ONCE THERE WAS A WAR see **DER VAR ENGANG EN KRIG** • 1966
ONCE THERE WAS (USA) see **BYL SOBIE RAZ** • 1957
ONCE TO EVERY BACHELOR • 1934 • Nigh William • USA
ONCE TO EVERY MAN • 1919 • Hunter T. Hayes • USA
ONCE TO EVERY MAN (UKN) see **FIGHTING HEART, THE** • 1925
ONCE TO EVERY WOMAN • 1920 • Holubar Allen • USA
ONCE TO EVERY WOMAN • 1934 • Hillyer Lambert • USA
ONCE TOO OFTEN • 1904 • Stow Percy • UKN
ONCE UPON A BODY • 1970 • *Chellee Films* • USA
ONCE UPON A BROTHERS GRIMM • 1977 • Campbell Norman • USA
ONCE UPON A COFFEE HOUSE • 1965 • Traube Shepard • USA
ONCE UPON A DEAD MAN • 1971 • Stern Leonard • TVM • USA
ONCE UPON A DREAM • 1949 • Thomas Ralph • UKN
ONCE UPON A DREAM see **THAT NIGHT WITH YOU** • 1945
ONCE UPON A FAMILY • 1980 • Michaels Richard • TVM • USA
ONCE UPON A FRIGHTMARE see **FRIGHTMARE** • 1974
ONCE UPON A GIRL • Jurwich Don • USA
ONCE UPON A HONEYMOON • 1942 • McCarey Leo • USA
ONCE UPON A HORSE • 1958 • Kanter Hal • USA • HOT HORSE
ONCE UPON A HUNT see **TEMPS D'UNE CHASSE, LE** • 1972
ONCE UPON A KNIGHT • 1961 • *James Frank* • USA
ONCE UPON A MIDNIGHT SCARY • 1979 • *Price Vincent* • MTV • USA • VINCENT PRICE'S ONCE UPON A MIDNIGHT SCARY
ONCE UPON A MURDER see **CHIEFS** • 1985
ONCE UPON A PRIME TIME • 1966 • Devlin Bernard • SHT • CND
ONCE UPON A RAILWAY • 1976 • Revesz Gyorgy • HNG
ONCE UPON A RHYME • 1950 • Sparber I. • ANS • USA
ONCE UPON A SATURDAY NIGHT see **DET VAR EN LORDAG AFTEN** • 1968
ONCE UPON A SCOUNDREL • 1973 • Schaefer George • USA
ONCE UPON A SPY • 1980 • Nagy Ivan • TVM • USA
ONCE UPON A STARRY NIGHT • 1978 • Hively Jack • TVM • USA
ONCE UPON A SUMMERTIME • 1941 • Le Borg Reginald • SHT • USA
ONCE UPON A TEXAS TRAIN • 1988 • Kennedy Burt • TVM • USA
ONCE UPON A THURSDAY (UKN) see **AFFAIRS OF MARTHA, THE** • 1942
ONCE UPON A TIME • 1910 • Salter Harry • USA
ONCE UPON A TIME • 1913 • *Reliance* • USA
ONCE UPON A TIME • 1913 • Evans Fred, Evans Joe • UKN
ONCE UPON A TIME • 1915 • Birch Cecil • UKN
ONCE UPON A TIME • 1916 • King Henry • USA
ONCE UPON A TIME • 1918 • Bentley Thomas • UKN
ONCE UPON A TIME • 1922 • Owen Ruth Bryan • USA
ONCE UPON A TIME • 1938 • *Short Films* • SHT • UKN
ONCE UPON A TIME • 1941 • Shepherd Horace • UKN
ONCE UPON A TIME • 1944 • Hall Alexander • USA • YES SIR, THAT'S MY BABY! ○ CURLY
ONCE UPON A TIME • 1957 • Ivanov-Vano Ivan • ANM • USS
ONCE UPON A TIME • ANS • USA
ONCE UPON A TIME see **DER VAR ENGANG** • 1922
ONCE UPON A TIME see **DET VAR EN GANG..** • 1945
ONCE UPON A TIME see **FEE PAS COMME LES AUTRES, UNE** • 1956
ONCE UPON A TIME see **C'ERA UNA VOLTA** • 1967
ONCE UPON A TIME see **GRAND MAGIC CIRCUS, THE** • 1973
ONCE UPON A TIME see **AND ONCE UPON A TIME** • 1975
ONCE UPON A TIME see **ONDANONDU KALADALLI** • 1977
ONCE UPON A TIME A SAILOR see **DET VAR EN GANG EN SJOMAN** • 1951
ONCE UPON A TIME IN AMERICA • 1983 • Leone Sergio • USA, ITL • C'ERA UNA VOLTA IN AMERICA
ONCE UPON A TIME IN GENNARO • 1974 • Shebib Donald • CND
ONCE UPON A TIME IN THE EAST see **IL ETAIT UNE FOIS DANS L'EST** • 1973
ONCE UPON A TIME IN THE WEST (UKN) see **C'ERA UNA VOLTA IL WEST** • 1969
ONCE UPON A TIME IN VIETNAM see **HOW SLEEP THE BRAVE** • 1981
ONCE UPON A TIME.. IS NOW • 1977 • Billington Kevin • MTV • UKN
ONCE UPON A TIME: OR, SOVEREIGN GOOSE PIE • 1921 • *Pistek Theodor* • CZC
ONCE UPON A TIME THERE LIVED SEVEN SIMEONS see **ZHILI-BYLI SEM'SIMEONOV** • 1989
ONCE UPON A TIME THERE WAS.. • 1907 • *Miles Bros.* • USA
ONCE UPON A TIME THERE WAS A DOG • 1983 • Nazarov Eduard • ANS • USS
ONCE UPON A TIME THERE WAS A DOT see **BILA JEDNOM JEDNA TOCKA** • 1964
ONCE UPON A TIME THERE WAS A FULL STOP see **BILA JEDNOM JEDNA TOCKA** • 1964
ONCE UPON A TIME THERE WAS A KING see **THERE ONCE LIVED A KING** • 1954
ONCE UPON A TIME (UKN) see **BYL SOBIE RAZ** • 1957
ONCE UPON A TIME (USA) see **MARIA D'ORO UND BELLO BLUE** • 1976
ONCE UPON A WAR see **DER VAR ENGANG EN KRIG** • 1966
ONCE UPON A WEEKEND • 1987 • Hartman Rivka • ASL
ONCE WAS ENOUGH • 1912 • *Lubin* • USA
ONCE WE WERE see **ERASMOS UNA VEZ** • 1979
ONCE WE WERE DREAMERS see **DREAMERS, THE** • 1988
ONCE YOU KISS A STRANGER • 1969 • Sparr Robert • USA • PERFECT SET-UP, THE ○ SUDDEN DEATH ○ YOU CAN'T WIN THEM ALL
ONCHOUDET EL FOLAD • 1932 • Volpe Mario • EGY
ONCLE DE BOUT DE ZAN, L' • 1916 • Feuillade Louis • FRN
ONCLE DE PEKIN, L' • 1934 • Darmont Jacques • FRN
ONCLE DU CANADA, L' see **PERE CHOPIN, LE** • 1943
ONCLE JANCO see **UNCLE JANCO** • 1967
ONCLE MOSBAH A LA VILLE • 1962 • Khalifa Omar • SHT • TNS
ONCOMING, THE see **VSTRECHNYI** • 1932
ONDA, L' • 1955 • Olmi Ermanno • DOC • ITL
ONDA CIRKELN, DEN • 1967 • Mattsson Arne • SWD • VICIOUS CIRCLE, THE
ONDA OF THE ORIENT • 1916 • McRae Henry • SHT • USA
ONDA OGON • 1947 • Jarrel Stig • SWD • NAR BLODET SJUDER ○ EVIL EYES
ONDANONDU KALADALLI • 1977 • Karnad Girish • IND • ONCE UPON A TIME
ONDATA DI CALORE • 1970 • Risi Nelo • ITL, FRN • DEAD OF SUMMER (USA)
ONDATA DI PIACERE, UNA • 1975 • Deodato Ruggero • ITL • WAVES OF LUST
ONDE BATE O SOL • 1988 • Pinto Joaquim • PRT • WHERE THE SUN BEATS (UKN)
ONDEES BRULANTES • Regis Jack • FRN
ONDER DE BOMEN • 1965 • Langestraat Bob • SHT • NTH • UNDER THE TREES
ONDERAARDS • 1966 • Hin Kees • SHT • NTH
ONDINE • 1908 • Goncharov Vasili M. • USS
ONDINE • 1976 • Thiele Rolf • FRG
ONDOMANE, L' • 1961 • Arcady • SHT • FRN • TELEVISION MANIAC, THE
ONDORT NUMARA • 1985 • Cetin Sinan • TRK • NO.14
ONDRA • 1974 • Keen Lesley H. • UKN
ONDRASZEK • 1959 • Kondek Waclaw • PLN
ONDRASZEK'S SHROVETIDE see **ONDRASZKOWE OSTATKI** • 1968
ONDRASZKOWE OSTATKI • 1968 • Lomnicki Jan • DOC • PLN • ONDRASZEK'S SHROVETIDE ○ SHROVE TUESDAY FOR A ROBBER
ONDSKANS VARDSHUS see **FLYGANDE DRAKEN, DEN** • 1980
ONE • 1958 • Vanderbeek Stan • SHT • USA
ONE, THE see **UNO, L'** • 1965
ONE A.M. • 1916 • Chaplin Charles • SHT • USA
ONE A.M. • 1969 • Godard Jean-Luc • FRN • ONE AMERICAN MOVIE
ONE A MINUTE • 1921 • Nelson Jack • USA
ONE AFTER THE OTHER see **UNO DOPO L'ALTRO** • 1968
ONE AFTERNOON IN KOPPANYMONOSTOR see **DELUTAN KOPPANYMONOSTORBAN, EGY** • 1955
ONE AGAINST MANY • 1919 • *King Anita* • USA
ONE AGAINST ONE • 1912 • O'Sullivan Mr. • USA
ONE AGAINST SEVEN (UKN) see **COUNTER-ATTACK** • 1945
ONE AGAINST THE WORLD • 1939 • Zinnemann Fred • SHT • USA
ONE ALONE • 1929 • Aylott Dave, Symmons E. F. • SHT • UKN
ONE AMERICAN MOVIE see **ONE A.M.** • 1969
ONE AMONG MANY see **EEN BLANDT MANGE** • 1961
ONE AMONG OTHERS see **UNO ENTRE MUCHOS** • 1982
ONE AND ONE (UKN) see **EN OCH EN** • 1978
ONE AND ONLY, THE • 1966 • Lesiewicz Witold • PLN
ONE AND ONLY, THE • 1978 • Reiner Carl • USA
ONE AND ONLY, THE see **YEDINSTVENNAYA** • 1976
ONE AND ONLY, GENUINE, ORIGINAL FAMILY BAND, THE • 1968 • O'Herlihy Michael • USA
ONE AND THE EIGHT, THE see **YIGE HE BAGE** • 1985
ONE ARABIAN NIGHT see **WIDOW TWAN-KEE** • 1923
ONE ARABIAN NIGHT (USA) see **SUMURUN** • 1920
ONE ARMED BANDIT see **ENARMADE BANDITEN, DEN** • 1974
ONE-ARMED BANDIT, THE • 1939 • Lovy Alex • ANS • USA
ONE-ARMED BOXER see **DOP BEY KUAN WAN** • 1972
ONE ARMED BOXER (UKN) see **DOP BEY KUAN WAN** • 1972
ONE-ARMED BOXER VERSUS THE FLYING GUILLOTINE see **MASTER OF THE FLYING GUILLOTINE** • 1975
ONE-ARMED NATAL see **NATAL DA PORTELA** • 1988
ONE ARMED SWORDSMAN, THE • 1968 • Chang Ch'Eh • HKG
ONE AT A TIME • 1924 • Roach Hal • SHT • USA
ONE AWAY see **GITANOS: ESCAPE FROM APARTHEID** • 1976
ONE BAD NIGHT • 1927 • Fryer Bryant • ANS • CND
ONE BAGATELLE see **EGY BAGATELL** • 1975
ONE BEST BET • 1913 • *Brennan John* • USA
ONE BEST BET • 1914 • *Baggot King* • USA
ONE BEST PET, THE • 1920 • *Chester* • SHT • USA
ONE BIG AFFAIR • 1952 • Godfrey Peter • USA
ONE BLOW TOO MANY see **TERRIBLE JOE MORAN** • 1984
ONE BODY TOO MANY • 1944 • McDonald Frank • USA
ONE BORN EVERY MINUTE (UKN) see **FLIM-FLAM MAN, THE** • 1967
ONE BRIDE TOO MANY • 1917 • Moore Matt • SHT • USA
ONE BRIEF SUMMER • 1970 • Mackenzie John • UKN
ONE BUSY HOUR • 1909 • Griffith D. W. • USA
ONE BUT A LION see **EN MET ETT LEJON** • 1940
ONE BY ONE • 1975 • Duboc Claude • DOC • UKN
ONE BY ONE • 1986 • Hinzman Bill • USA • MAJORETTES, THE
ONE CAB'S FAMILY • 1952 • Avery Tex • ANS • USA
ONE CAME HOME see **SPORTING BLOOD** • 1940
ONE CAN SAY IT WITHOUT GETTING ANGRY see **ON PEUT LE DIRE SANS SE FACHER!** • 1978
ONE CANADA/TWO NATIONS • 1968 • Barclay Robert • MTV • CND
ONE CANDLE FOR THE DEVIL see **VELA PARA EL DIABLO, UNA** • 1973
ONE CAN'T ALWAYS TELL • 1913 • *Maurice Mary* • USA
ONE CHANCE IN A MILLION • 1927 • Smith Noel • USA • CHANCE IN A MILLION (UKN)
ONE CHRISTMAS EVE see **ONE WINTER'S NIGHT** • 1914
ONE CLEAR CALL • 1922 • Stahl John M. • USA
ONE COLOMBO NIGHT • 1926 • Edwards Henry • UKN • COLOMBO NIGHT, A
ONE COMPANY • 1943 • Harlow John • SHT • UKN
ONE COOKS, THE OTHER DOESN'T! • 1983 • Michaels Richard • TVM • USA
ONE COULD LAUGH IN FORMER DAYS see **VROEGER KON JE LACHEN** • 1982
ONE CRAZY SUMMER • 1986 • Holland Savage Steve • USA • SUMMER VACATION
ONE CROWDED NIGHT • 1940 • Reis Irving • USA
ONE CYLINDER COURTSHIP, A • 1915 • Davey Horace • USA
ONE CYLINDER LOVE • 1923 • *Sennett Mack (P)* • SHT • USA
ONE-CYLINDER LOVE RIOT, THE • 1920 • Buckingham Thomas • SHT • USA
ONE CYLINDER WONDER, THE • 1949 • *Falcon Films* • SHT • UKN
ONE DAMP DAY • 1917 • Beaudine William • SHT • USA
ONE DANGEROUS NIGHT • 1943 • Gordon Michael • USA
ONE DARK NIGHT • 1939 • Popkin Leo C. • USA
ONE DARK NIGHT see **MIDNIGHT GUEST, THE** • 1923
ONE DARK NIGHT see **REST IN PEACE** • 1982
ONE DAY • 1916 • Clarendon Hal • USA
ONE DAY see **ONCE** • 1963
ONE DAY, 240 HOURS see **ICHINICHI 240 JIKAN** • 1970
ONE DAY A CAT.. see **AZ PRIJDE KOCOUR** • 1963
ONE DAY.. A RIVER see **DIA.. UN RIO, UN** • 1979
ONE DAY AFTER AUGUST see **DIA DESPUES DE AGOSTO, UN** • 1968
ONE DAY AT SUMMER'S END see **NURETA FUTARI** • 1968
ONE DAY BEFORE TOMORROW see **HOW TO STEAL AN AIRPLANE** • 1971
ONE DAY CERTAINLY see **BIR GUN MUTLAKA** • 1976
ONE DAY FOR AN OLD LADY • 1966 • Holly Martin • CZC
ONE DAY, I.. see **ARUHI WATASHI WA** • 1959
ONE DAY I ASKED.. see **DIA YO PREGUNTE.., UN** • 1970
ONE DAY IN IRVINE • 1971 • Littlewood Mark • DCS • UKN
ONE DAY IN PARIS • Korber Serge • FRN
ONE DAY IN POLAND see **JEDEN DZIEN W POLSCE** • 1949
ONE DAY IN SOVIET RUSSIA • 1942 • Marshall Herbert • DOC • UKN
ONE DAY IN SOVIET RUSSIA see **DEN NOVOGO MIRA** • 1940
ONE DAY IN THE LIFE OF A SYRIAN VILLAGE • 1972 • Moazin Marwan Al • SYR
ONE DAY IN THE LIFE OF IVAN DENISOVICH • 1971 • Wrede Caspar • UKN, NRW, USA • DAG I IVAN DENISOVIWICH'S LIV, EN (NRW)
ONE DAY IN THE NEW WORLD see **DEN NOVOGO MIRA** • 1940
ONE DAY MORE • 1972 • Gilic Vlatko • SHT • YGS
ONE DAY MORE, ONE DAY LESS see **PLUSZ MINUSZ EGY NAP** • 1973
ONE DAY MORE OR LESS see **PLUSZ MINUSZ EGY NAP** • 1973
ONE DAY, MY FATHER see **MIA MERA, O PATERAS MOU** • 1968
ONE DAY OF LIFE • 1983 • Dovnikovic Borivoj • ANS • YGS
ONE DAY OF LOVE see **JEDNOG DANA LJUBAV** • 1969
ONE DAY OF WAR see **DEN VOINI** • 1942
ONE DAY SURELY see **BIR GUN MUTLAKA** • 1976
ONE DAY TO LIVE • 1931 • Kelley Albert • SHT • USA
ONE DAY WITH THE RUSSIANS see **DAY WITH THE RUSSIANS, A** • 1961
ONE DAY'S POISON • 1958 • Wilder Donald A. • CND
ONE DEADLY OWNER • 1974 • Fordyce Ian • TVM • UKN
ONE DEADLY SUMMER (USA) see **ETE MEURTRIER, UN** • 1983
ONE DESIGNER TWO DESIGNER • 1979 • Stitt Alexander • SHT • ASL
ONE DESIRE • 1955 • Hopper Jerry • USA
ONE DOES NOT PLAY WITH LOVE see **MAN SPIELT NICHT MIT DER LIEBE!** • 1926
ONE DOLLAR BID • 1918 • Warde Ernest C. • USA
ONE DOLLAR DOWN • 1920 • Goldaine Mark • SHT • USA
ONE DOLLAR, PLEASE • 1916 • *Derr George* • USA
ONE DOLLAR'S WORTH • 1917 • Smith David • SHT • USA
ONE DOWN, TWO TO GO • 1983 • Williamson Fred • USA
ONE DROOPY KNIGHT • 1957 • Lah Michael • ANS • USA
ONE EIGHTH APACHE • 1922 • Wilson Ben • USA
ONE EMBARRASSING NIGHT (UKN) see **MUST WE MARRY?** • 1928
ONE EMBARRASSING NIGHT (USA) see **ROOKERY NOOK** • 1930
ONE ENCHANTED EVENING see **ES WAR EINE RAUSCHENDE BALLNACHT** • 1939
ONE EVENING ON A TRAIN see **SOIR, UN TRAIN, UN** • 1968
ONE EVERY MINUTE • 1919 • Harrison Saul • SHT • USA
ONE EXCITED ORPHAN • 1923 • Phillips Bertram • UKN
ONE EXCITING ADVENTURE • 1934 • Frank Ernst L. • USA
ONE EXCITING KISS see **NORTHWEST OUTPOST** • 1947

ONE EXCITING NIGHT • 1922 • Griffith D. W. • USA
ONE EXCITING NIGHT • 1944 • Forde Walter • UKN • YOU CAN'T DO WITHOUT LOVE (USA)
ONE EXCITING NIGHT • 1945 • Thomas William C. • USA • MIDNIGHT MANHUNT
ONE EXCITING NIGHT see **NIGHT OF ADVENTURE, A** • 1944
ONE EXCITING WEEK • 1946 • Beaudine William • USA
ONE EXTRA DAY see **EXTRA DAY, THE** • 1956
ONE-EYED DRAGON see **DOKUGANRYU MASAMUNE** • 1942
ONE-EYED JACKS • 1961 • Brando Marlon • USA
ONE-EYED MAN, THE see **BORGNE, LE** • 1981
ONE-EYED SOLDIERS • 1967 • Christophe Jean • USA, UKN, YGS
ONE FAIR DAUGHTER • 1913 • Buckland Warwick? • UKN
ONE FAMILY • 1930 • Creighton Walter • UKN
ONE FAMILY see **ODNA SEMJA** • 1943
ONE FATAL HOUR see **FIVE STAR FINAL** • 1931
ONE FATAL HOUR see **TWO AGAINST THE WORLD** • 1936
ONE FIANCE AT A TIME see **EN FASTMAN I TAGET** • 1952
ONE FINE DAY • 1929 • Aylott Dave, Symmons E. F. • SHT • UKN
ONE FINE DAY see **EN VACKER DAG** • 1963
ONE FINE DAY (UKN) see **CERTO GIORNO, UN** • 1968
ONE FLAG AT LAST • 1911 • *Ince Ralph* • USA
ONE FLEW OVER THE CUCKOO'S NEST • 1975 • Forman Milos • USA
ONE FLIGHT UP • 1915 • *Hunt Irene* • USA
ONE FOOT IN HEAVEN • 1941 • Rapper Irving • USA
ONE FOOT IN HELL • 1960 • Clark James B. • USA
ONE FOR ALL (UKN) see **PRESIDENT'S MYSTERY, THE** • 1936
ONE FOR THE BOOK see **VOICE OF THE TURTLE, THE** • 1947
ONE FOR THE MONEY see **SPEEDZONE FEVER** • 1989
ONE FOR THE POT • 1968 • Travers Alfred • SAF
ONE FORGOTTEN, THE • 1915 • Morgan George • USA
ONE FOURTH OF HUMANITY • 1968 • Snow Edgar • USA
ONE FOURTH OF HUMANITY: THE CHINA STORY see **CHINA STORY: ONE-FOURTH OF HUMANITY, THE** • 1968
ONE FRIGHTENED NIGHT • 1935 • Cabanne W. Christy • USA
ONE FROGGY EVENING • 1955 • Jones Charles M. • ANS • USA
ONE FROM THE HEART • 1982 • Coppola Francis Ford • USA
ONE FUNNY KNIGHT • 1957 • Tendlar Dave • ANS • USA
ONE GIRL'S CONFESSION • 1953 • Haas Hugo • USA
ONE GLASS TOO MANY see **OSKLENICKU VIC** • 1954
ONE GLASS TOO MUCH see **OSKLENICKU VIC** • 1954
ONE GLORIOUS DAY • 1922 • Cruze James • USA • EK
ONE GLORIOUS NIGHT • 1924 • Dunlap Scott R. • USA
ONE GLORIOUS SCRAP • 1927 • Lewis Edgar • USA
ONE GOOD COOK • 1915 • *Royal* • USA
ONE GOOD JOKE DESERVES ANOTHER • 1913 • North Wilfred • USA
ONE GOOD REASON • 1973 • Crombie Donald • SHT • ASL
ONE GOOD TURN • 1915 • Wilson Frank • UKN
ONE GOOD TURN • 1917 • Christie Al • *Christie* • SHT • USA
ONE GOOD TURN • 1917 • Smith David • *Broadway Star* • SHT • USA
ONE GOOD TURN • 1931 • Horne James W. • SHT • USA
ONE GOOD TURN • 1936 • Goulding Alf • UKN
ONE GOOD TURN • 1951 • Maude Arthur • UKN
ONE GOOD TURN • 1954 • Carstairs John Paddy • UKN
ONE GOOD TURN, THE • 1913 • *Turner Florence* • USA
ONE GOOD TURN DESERVES ANOTHER • 1909 • Bouwmeester Theo? • UKN
ONE GRAIN OF BARLEY see **HITOTSUBU NO MUGI** • 1958
ONE GREAT VISION • 1953 • Simmons Anthony • SHT • UKN
ONE GUN GARY IN NICK OF TIME • 1939 • Donnelly Eddie • ANS • USA
ONE HAMLET LESS see **AMLETO DI MENO, UN** • 1973
ONE HAM'S FAMILY • 1943 • Avery Tex • ANS • USA
ONE HAND CLAPPING • 1974 • Borris Clay • CND
ONE HAPPY TRAMP • 1914 • *Crystal* • USA
ONE HE-MAN • 1920 • Murray Henry • SHT • USA
ONE HEART AND ONE SOUL • 1956 • Lavoie Richard • DCS • CND
ONE HEAVENLY NIGHT • 1930 • Fitzmaurice George • USA
ONE HONEST MAN • 1915 • Batley Ethyle • UKN
ONE HORSE FARMERS • 1934 • Meins Gus • SHT • USA
ONE HORSE SHOW, THE • 1918 • Lyons Eddie • SHT • USA
ONE HORSE TOWN • 1968 • Smith Paul J. • ANS • USA
ONE HORSE TOWN see **SMALL TOWN GIRL** • 1936
ONE HOUR • 1917 • McAllister Paul, Hollywood Edwin L. • USA
ONE HOUR BEFORE DAWN • 1920 • King Henry • USA • BEHIND RED CURTAINS
ONE HOUR LATE • 1935 • Murphy Ralph • USA • ME WITHOUT YOU
ONE HOUR MARRIED • 1926 • USA
ONE HOUR OF LOVE • 1927 • Florey Robert • USA
ONE HOUR OF ROMANCE see **CONFESSION** • 1937
ONE HOUR PAST MIDNIGHT • 1924 • Rule Beverly C. • USA
ONE HOUR TO DOOMSDAY (UKN) see **CITY BENEATH THE SEA** • 1970
ONE HOUR TO LIVE • 1939 • Schuster Harold • USA
ONE HOUR TO ZERO • 1976 • Summers Jeremy • UKN
ONE HOUR WITH W.C. FIELDS see **BEST OF W. C. FIELDS, THE** • 1969
ONE HOUR WITH YOU • 1932 • Lubitsch Ernst, Cukor George (U/c) • USA
ONE HUNDRED AND ONE DALMATIONS • 1961 • Reitherman Wolfgang, Luske Hamilton, Geronimi Clyde • ANM • USA
ONE HUNDRED BULLETS • 1972 • Calotescu Virgil • RMN
ONE HUNDRED CRIES OF TERROR see **CIEN GRITOS DE TERROR** • 1964
ONE HUNDRED DAYS AFTER CHILDHOOD see **STO DNEI POSLE DETSTVA** • 1975
ONE HUNDRED DAYS IN PALERMO see **CENTO GIORNI A PALERMO** • 1984
ONE HUNDRED DOLLAR BILL, THE • 1911 • *Vitagraph* • USA
ONE HUNDRED DOLLAR ELOPEMENT, THE • 1913 • *Mccoy Gertrude* • USA
ONE HUNDRED DOLLARS • 1915 • *Mulhall Jack* • USA
ONE HUNDRED DOLLARS • 1931 • Lamont Charles • SHT • USA
ONE HUNDRED PERCENT PURE (UKN) see **GIRL FROM MISSOURI, THE** • 1934
ONE HUNDRED PERCENT SERVICE • 1931 • Cozine Ray • USA
ONE HUNDRED TIMES I SHOULDN'T see **CIEN VECES NO DEBO** • 1988
ONE HUNDRED YEARS AFTER • 1911 • *Selig* • USA
ONE HUNDRED YEARS AFTER • 1911 • *Pathe* • FRN
ONE HUNDRED YEARS AGO • 1911 • Mervale Gaston • ASL
ONE HUNDRED YEARS AGO • 1915 • *Julian Rupert* • USA
ONE HUNDRED YEARS FROM NOW • 1929 • Aylott Dave, Symmons E. F. • SHT • UKN
ONE HUNDRED YEARS OF MORMONISM • 1912 • DOC • USA
ONE HUNDRED YEARS OF THE TELEPHONE • 1977 • Bass Saul • SHT • USA
ONE HUSBAND TOO MANY see **YIQI LIANGFU** • 1988
ONE HYSTERICAL NIGHT • 1929 • Craft William James • USA
ONE IN A MILLION • 1934 • Strayer Frank • USA
ONE IN A MILLION • 1936 • Lanfield Sidney • USA
ONE IN A MILLION see **JEDNA Z MILIONU** • 1935
ONE IN A MILLION see **BIGGER THAN LIFE** • 1956
ONE IN A MILLION see **LAKHON MEIN EIK** • 1967
ONE IN A MILLION: THE RON LEFLORE STORY • 1978 • Graham William A. • TVM • USA
ONE INCREASING PURPOSE • 1927 • Beaumont Harry • USA
ONE IS A LONELY NUMBER • 1972 • Stuart Mel • USA
ONE IS BORN A SWINE see **CAROGNE SI NASCE** • 1968
ONE IS BUSINESS, THE OTHER CRIME • 1912 • Griffith D. W. • USA
ONE IS GUILTY • 1934 • Hillyer Lambert • USA
ONE IS LESS THAN ONE see **EINMAL IST KEINMAL** • 1955
ONE IS NOT BORN A SOLDIER see **SOLDATAMI NYE ROZHDAYUTSYA** • 1968
ONE IS ONE • 1969 • Johnson Malcolm • UKN
ONE JUMP AHEAD • 1955 • Saunders Charles • UKN
ONE JUST MAN • 1955 • MacDonald David • UKN
ONE JUST MAN see **GIUSTIZIERE SFIDA LA CITTA, IL** • 1975
ONE KIND OF A FRIEND • 1915 • Ford Francis • USA
ONE KIND OF WIRELESS • 1917 • Harrison Saul • SHT • USA
ONE KISS • 1914 • MacGregor Norval • USA
ONE KISS • 1929 • Aylott Dave, Symmons E. F. • SHT • UKN
ONE LAMP, MANY LAMPS • 1966 • Somlo Tamas • SHT • HNG
ONE LAST CHANCE • 1983 • Hicks Scott • SHT • ASL
ONE LAST FLING • 1949 • Godfrey Peter • USA
ONE LAW BREAKER • 1915 • *Whitman Velma* • USA
ONE LAW FOR ALL • 1920 • Maloney Leo • SHT • USA
ONE LAW FOR BOTH • 1917 • Abramson Ivan • USA
ONE LAW FOR THE WOMAN • 1924 • Henderson Dell • USA
ONE LIFE • 1955 • Godfrey Peter • USA
ONE LIFE see **VIE, UNE** • 1958
ONE LITTLE INDIAN • 1954 • Munro Grant • CND
ONE LITTLE INDIAN • 1962 • Duncan Alma • ANM • CND
ONE LITTLE INDIAN • 1973 • McEveety Bernard • USA
ONE LIVE GHOST • 1936 • Goodwins Leslie • SHT • USA
ONE LOOK SHOOK THE WORLD see **MAPANTSULA** • 1988
ONE LOVE IN THREE NIGHTS see **SZERELEM HAROM EJSZAKAJA, EGY** • 1967
ONE LOVE TOO MANY see **ONNA NO ISSHO** • 1955
ONE LOVELY NIGHT • 1919 • Santell Alfred • SHT • USA
ONE MACHINE TO KILL BAD PEOPLE see **MACCHINA AMMAZZACATTIVI, LA** • 1948
ONE MAD KISS • 1930 • Silver Marcel, Tinling James • USA
ONE MAGIC CHRISTMAS • 1986 • Borsos Philip • CND
ONE-MAMA MAN, A • 1927 • Roach Hal • SHT • USA
ONE MAN • 1977 • Spry Robin • CND
ONE MAN see **EK AADMI** • 1987
ONE MAN, THE see **CRASHIN' THRU** • 1923
ONE MAN BAND • 1965 • Godfrey Bob • SHT • UKN
ONE-MAN BAND, THE (USA) see **HOMME-ORCHESTRE, L'** • 1900
ONE-MAN BAND THAT WENT TO WALL STREET, THE • 1974 • Potterton Gerald • USA
ONE MAN BIKE • 1970 • Keenan Haydn • SHT • ASL
ONE MAN CROWD, THE • 1960 • Keatley Philip • CND
ONE MAN DOG, THE • 1929 • d'Usseau Leon • USA • SLEUTH, THE (UKN)
ONE MAN FORCE • 1989 • Trevillion Dale • USA
ONE MAN GAME, A • 1927 • Laemmle Ernst • USA
ONE MAN IN A MILLION • 1921 • Beban George • USA
ONE MAN JURY • 1978 • Martin Charles • USA
ONE MAN JUSTICE • 1937 • Barsha Leon • USA
ONE MAN LAW • 1931 • Hillyer Lambert • USA
ONE MAN MUTINY (UKN) see **COURT MARTIAL OF BILLY MITCHELL, THE** • 1955
ONE MAN NAVY, THE • 1941 • Davis Mannie • ANS • USA
ONE MAN NEWSPAPER • 1944 • *O'Brien Joseph/ Mead Thomas (P)* • SHT • USA
ONE MAN OUT see **ERIK** • 1990
ONE MAN SHOW • Amar Maurice • CMP • USA
ONE MAN SHOW • 1967 • Breer Robert • USA
ONE MAN TOO MANY see **EN MAN FOR MYCKET** • 1941
ONE MAN TOO MANY see **HOMME DE TROP, UN** • 1967
ONE MAN TRAIL • 1926 • *Montague Monty* • USA
ONE-MAN TRAIL, THE • 1921 • Durning Bernard J. • USA
ONE MAN WANTED see **MATLUB RAJULUN WAHID** • 1974
ONE MAN'S BONUS see **LET'S MAKE A MILLION** • 1937
ONE MAN'S CHINA • 1972 • Greene Felix • DOC • UKN
ONE MAN'S CONFESSION • 1910 • *Centaur* • USA
ONE MAN'S EVIL • 1915 • De Grasse Joseph • USA
ONE MAN'S FATE see **MIEHEN TIE** • 1940
ONE MAN'S GARDEN • 1974 • Winkler Donald • MTV • CND
ONE MAN'S JOURNEY • 1933 • Robertson John S. • USA • DOCTOR, THE
ONE MAN'S LAW • 1940 • Sherman George • USA
ONE MAN'S LOVE • 1912 • *Reliance* • USA
ONE MAN'S STORY • 1948 • Munden Maxwell, Shand Dennis • UKN
ONE MAN'S WAR • 1989 • Toledo Sergio • UKN, USA
ONE MAN'S WAR see **YHDEN MIEHEN SOTA** • 1973
ONE MAN'S WAR see **GUERRE D'UN SEUL HOMME, LA** • 1981
ONE MAN'S WAY • 1964 • Sanders Denis • USA • NORMAN VINCENT PEALE STORY, THE
ONE MARGINAL S see **UM S MARGINAL** • 1983
ONE MEAT BRAWL • 1947 • McKimson Robert • ANS • USA
ONE MILE FROM HEAVEN • 1937 • Dwan Allan • USA
ONE MILLION AC/DC • 1969 • De Priest Ed • USA
ONE MILLION B.C. • 1940 • Roach Hal, Roach Hal Jr. • USA • MAN AND HIS MATE (UKN) ○ CAVE DWELLERS, THE ○ BATTLE OF THE GIANTS ○ CAVE MAN
ONE MILLION DOLLAR PEARL MYSTERY OR THE STOLEN NECKLACE, THE • 1914 • *Dragon* • USA
ONE MILLION DOLLARS • 1915 • Noble John W. • USA
ONE MILLION FOR LAURA see **MILION ZA LAURE** • 1970
ONE MILLION IN JEWELS • 1923 • McGowan J. P. • USA
ONE MILLION POUND NOTE, THE see **EGYMILLIO FONTOS BANKO, AS** • 1916
ONE MILLION YEARS B.C. • 1966 • Chaffey Don • UKN, USA
ONE MINUTE TO MIDNIGHT • 1988 • Curtin Lawrence • USA
ONE MINUTE TO PLAY • 1926 • Wood Sam • USA
ONE MINUTE TO TWELVE see **EINE MINUTE VOR ZWOLF** • 1925
ONE MINUTE TO ZERO • 1952 • Garnett Tay • USA
ONE MOMENT'S TEMPTATION • 1922 • Rooke A. J. • USA
ONE MONTH LATER see **EEN MAAND LATER** • 1987
ONE MONTH TO LIVE • 1911 • *American* • USA
ONE MORE AMERICAN • 1918 • De Mille William C. • USA • LAND OF THE FREE, THE
ONE MORE CHANCE • 1931 • Sennett Mack • SHT • USA
ONE MORE CHANCE • 1981 • Firstenberg Sam • USA
ONE MORE RIVER • 1934 • Whale James • USA • OVER THE RIVER (UKN)
ONE MORE RIVER • 1961 • Poynter Guy K. • SHT • UKN
ONE MORE RIVER • 1963 • Fox Beryl, Leiterman Douglas • DOC • CND
ONE MORE SATURDAY NIGHT • 1986 • Klein Dennis • USA • DATENIGHT
ONE MORE SHOT • 1984 • SAF
ONE MORE SPRING • 1935 • King Henry • USA
ONE MORE TIME • 1931-32 • Ising Rudolf • ANS • USA
ONE MORE TIME • 1970 • Lewis Jerry • UKN, USA
ONE MORE TIME see **IMA HITOTABI NO** • 1947
ONE MORE TOMORROW • 1946 • Godfrey Peter • USA • ANIMAL KINGDOM, THE
ONE MORE TRAIN TO ROB • 1971 • McLaglen Andrew V. • USA • HARK ○ H. FLEET, ROBBER
ONE MORNING see **INTR-O DIMINEATA**
ONE MORNING see **INTR-O DIMINEATA** • 1960
ONE MOTHER'S FAMILY • 1939 • Ising Rudolf • ANS • USA
ONE MOUSE IN A MILLION • 1939 • Rasinski Connie • ANS • USA
ONE MOVE TO HELL see **UNO DI PIU ALL'INFERNO** • 1968
ONE MYSTERIOUS NIGHT • 1944 • Boetticher Budd • USA • BEHIND CLOSED DOORS (UKN)
ONE N—— NIGHT see **ONE NAKED NIGHT** • 1963
ONE NAKED NIGHT • 1963 • *Morris Barbara* • USA • NAKED IN THE NIGHT ○ ONE N—— NIGHT
ONE NEVER KNOWS see **YOU NEVER CAN TELL** • 1951
ONE NEW YORK NIGHT • 1935 • Conway Jack • USA • TRUNK MYSTERY, THE (UKN) ○ ORDER PLEASE
ONE NIGHT • 1915 • *Imp* • USA
ONE NIGHT • 1915 • *Pyramid* • USA
ONE NIGHT • 1918 • Hotaling Arthur D. • SHT • USA
ONE NIGHT see **HER NIGHT OF ROMANCE** • 1924
ONE NIGHT see **EN NATT** • 1931
ONE NIGHT see **ODNAZHDI NOCH** • 1945
ONE NIGHT see **ET RAAT** • 1968
ONE NIGHT.. A TRAIN see **SOIR, UN TRAIN, UN** • 1968
ONE NIGHT, AND THEN • 1910 • Griffith D. W. • USA
ONE NIGHT AT DINNER (USA) see **METTI, UNA SERA A CENA** • 1969
ONE NIGHT AT SUSIE'S • 1930 • Dillon John Francis • USA
ONE NIGHT BRIDE • 1975 • Khan Mumtaz Ali • PKS
ONE NIGHT.. BY ACCIDENT see **SOIR.. PAR HASARD, UN** • 1964
ONE NIGHT IN LISBON • 1941 • Griffith Edward H. • USA
ONE NIGHT IN MALAYSIA see **SEMALAM DI MALAYSIA** • 1975
ONE NIGHT IN PARIS see **PREMIERE** • 1938
ONE NIGHT IN ROME • 1924 • Badger Clarence • USA
ONE NIGHT IN THE TROPICS • 1940 • Sutherland A. Edward • USA • CARIBBEAN HOLIDAY ○ MOONLIGHT IN THE TROPICS
ONE NIGHT OF FAME see **AL DIAVOLO LA CELEBRITA** • 1949
ONE NIGHT OF LOVE • 1934 • Schertzinger Victor • USA
ONE NIGHT OF PASSION see **JONETSU NO ICHIYA** • 1929
ONE NIGHT ONLY • 1919 • Parrott Charles • USA
ONE NIGHT ONLY • 1983 • Bond Timothy • CND
ONE-NIGHT STAND • 1979 • King Allan • CND
ONE NIGHT STAND • 1984 • Duigan John?, Wincer Simon? • ASL
ONE NIGHT STAND see **ALIBIS** • 1977
ONE NIGHT STAND, A • 1915 • McCoy Horace • USA
ONE NIGHT STAND, A • 1918 • Roach Hal • SHT • USA
ONE NIGHT WITH YOU • 1948 • Young Terence • UKN
ONE NOTE TONY • 1947 • Rasinski Connie • ANS • USA
ONE OF MANY • 1917 • Cabanne W. Christy • USA
ONE OF MANY see **UNO ENTRE MUCHOS** • 1982
ONE OF MILLIONS • 1914 • Dawley J. Searle • USA
ONE OF MY WIVES IS MISSING • 1976 • Jordan Glenn • TVM • USA
ONE OF NATURE'S NOBLEMEN • 1911 • *Selig* • USA
ONE OF OUR AIRCRAFT IS MISSING • 1942 • Powell Michael, Pressburger Emeric • UKN
ONE OF OUR DINOSAURS IS MISSING • 1975 • Stevenson Robert • USA
ONE OF OUR GIRLS • 1914 • Heffron Thomas N. • USA
ONE OF OUR OWN • 1975 • Sarafian Richard C. • TVM • USA
ONE OF OUR OWN • 1979 • Fruet William • MTV • CND
ONE OF OUR SPIES IS MISSING • 1966 • Hallenbeck E. Darrell • MTV • USA
ONE OF OURSELVES • 1984 • O'Connor Pat • IRL
ONE OF SIX THOUSAND • 1966 • Kidawa Janusz • DOC • PLN
ONE OF THE BEST • 1927 • Hunter T. Hayes • UKN
ONE OF THE BOSTON BULLERTONS see **PRIVATE AFFAIRS** • 1940
ONE OF THE BRAVEST • 1908 • *Selig* • USA
ONE OF THE BRAVEST • 1912 • *De Forrest Charles* • USA
ONE OF THE BRAVEST • 1914 • Turner Otis • USA
ONE OF THE BRAVEST • 1925 • O'Connor Frank • USA

ONE OF THE BULLDOG BREED • 1909 • Rosenthal Joe • UKN
ONE OF THE DISCARD • 1914 • Ince Thomas H., Sullivan C. Gardner • USA
ONE OF THE FAMILY • 1923 • Roach Hal • SHT • USA
ONE OF THE FAMILY • 1962 • Kneitel Seymour • ANS • USA
ONE OF THE FAMILY • 1964 • Rubens Bernice • UKN
ONE OF THE FINEST • 1910 • *Vitagraph* • USA
ONE OF THE FINEST • 1913 • *Johnstone Lamar* • USA
ONE OF THE FINEST • 1914 • *Bassett Russell* • USA
ONE OF THE FINEST • 1919 • Beaumont Harry • USA
ONE OF THE HONOR SQUAD • 1912 • *Thanhouser* • USA
ONE OF THE MANY see **EN AV DE MANGA** • 1915
ONE OF THE MANY (UKN) see **HE COULDN'T TAKE IT** • 1933
ONE OF THE MISSING • 1969 • Scott Anthony • UKN
ONE OF THE NUTS • 1913 • Calvert Charles? • UKN
ONE OF THE PACK • 1916 • Kent Leon D. • SHT • USA
ONE OF THE RABBLE • 1913 • *Eclair* • USA
ONE OF THE SMITHS • 1931 • Parrott James • SHT • USA
ONE OF THOSE BLIGHTERS • 1983 • Butler Lynton • NZL
ONE OF THOSE THINGS see **HAENDELIGT UHELD** • 1971
ONE OF US • 1970 • Agranovich L. • USS
ONE OF US • 1989 • Barbash Uri • ISR
ONE ON AUNTIE • 1913 • *Nestor* • USA
ONE ON BATTY BILL • 1914 • *Melies* • USA
ONE ON CHARLIE • 1914 • *De Forrest Charles* • USA
ONE ON HENRY • 1916 • Drew Sidney • SHT • USA
ONE ON HIM • 1917 • *Essanay* • SHT • USA
ONE ON IKEY • 1915 • Birch Cecil • UKN
ONE ON JONES • 1912 • *Eclair* • USA
ONE ON MOTHER • 1915 • Matthews H. C. • USA
ONE ON ONE • 1977 • Johnson Lamont • USA
ONE ON RENO • 1911 • Salter Harry • USA
ONE ON ROMANCE • 1913 • Middleton Edwin • USA
ONE ON TOOTY • 1913 • *Eclair* • USA
ONE ON TOP OF THE OTHER (UKN) see **UNA SULL'ALTRA** • 1969
ONE ON WILLIE • 1913 • *Roland Ruth* • USA
ONE OUT OF MANY see **EN AV DE MANGA** • 1915
ONE OUT OF MANY see **E PLURIBUS UNUM** • 1969
ONE OVER ON CUTEY • 1913 • *Vitagraph* • USA
ONE P.M. • 1970 • Pennebaker D. A. • USA • ONE PARALLEL MOVIE
ONE PAGE OF LOVE • 1979 • Roter Ted • USA
ONE PARALLEL MOVIE see **ONE P.M.** • 1970
ONE PARISIAN KNIGHT (UKN) see **OPEN ALL NIGHT** • 1924
ONE PEOPLE see **WAN PIPEL** • 1976
ONE PERFORMANCE ONLY • 1915 • Mullin Eugene • USA
ONE-PIECE BATHING SUIT, THE (UKN) see **MILLION DOLLAR MERMAID** • 1953
ONE PLANET see **NO ODNOI PLANETE** • 1966
ONE PLUS ONE • 1968 • Godard Jean-Luc • FRN • SYMPATHY FOR THE DEVIL (UKN)
ONE PLUS ONE see **JEDEN PLUS JEDEN** • 1971
ONE PLUS ONE EQUALS ONE • 1915 • Johnson Tefft • USA
ONE POLICE PLAZA • 1986 • Jameson Jerry • TVM • USA
ONE POTATO, TWO POTATO • 1957 • Daiken Leslie • UKN
ONE POTATO, TWO POTATO • 1964 • Peerce Larry • USA
ONE POTATO, TWO POTATO see **ECI, PEC, PEC** • 1961
ONE POUND ONLY • 1962 • Gross Yoram • ISR
ONE PRECIOUS YEAR • 1933 • Edwards Henry • UKN
ONE PUNCH O'DAY • 1926 • Brown Harry J. • USA • DRILLS AND THRILLS
ONE QUACK MIND • 1951 • Sparber I. • ANS • USA
ONE QUARTER INCH • 1917 • Roach Hal • SHT • USA
ONE RAINY AFTERNOON • 1936 • Lee Rowland V. • USA
ONE REVOLUTION AROUND THE SUN • 1969 • Burke Martyn • DOC • CND
ONE-ROLE PERFORMANCE, A see **PARASTASI SE PROTO PROSOPO** • 1979
ONE ROMANTIC ADVENTURE OF EDWARD, THE • 1955 • Jordan Larry • SHT • USA
ONE ROMANTIC NIGHT • 1930 • Stein Paul L. • USA • SWAN, THE
ONE ROOM TENANTS (USA) see **WSPOLNY POKOJ** • 1959
ONE-ROUND HOGAN • 1927 • Bretherton Howard • USA
ONE-ROUND O'BRIEN • 1912 • Sennett Mack • USA
ONE ROUND O'BRIEN COMES BACK • 1913 • *Mace Fred* • USA
ONE ROUND O'BRIEN COMES EAST • 1913 • *Apollo* • USA
ONE ROUND O'BRIEN IN THE RING AGAIN • 1914 • *Mace Fred* • USA
ONE ROUND O'BRIEN'S FLIRTATION • 1913 • *Mace Fred* • USA
ONE RUN ELMER • 1935 • Lamont Charles • SHT • USA
ONE RUSSIAN SUMMER (USA) see **GIORNO DEL FURORE, IL** • 1973
ONE SALIVA BUBBLE • 1988 • Lynch David • USA
ONE SATURDAY EVENING.. see **DET VAR EN LORDAG AFTEN** • 1968
ONE SECOND IN MONTREAL • 1969 • Snow Michael • USA
ONE SEPTEMBER NIGHT see **NOCH V SENTYABRE** • 1939
ONE SHALL BE TAKEN • 1914 • Batley Ethyle • UKN
ONE SHE LOVED, THE • 1912 • Griffith D. W. • USA
ONE SHOCKING MOMENT • 1965 • Mikels Ted V. • USA
ONE SHOE MAKES IT MURDER • 1982 • Hale William • TVM • USA
ONE SHOT RANGER • 1925 • *Morrison Pete* • USA
ONE SHOT ROSS • 1917 • Smith Cliff • USA
ONE SILVER DOLLAR (USA) see **DOLLARO BUCATO, UN** • 1965
ONE SILVER PIECE see **JEDEN STRIBRNY** • 1977
ONE SINGLE NIGHT see **EN ENDA NATT** • 1938
ONE SINGS THE OTHER DOES NOT see **UNE CHANTE, L'AUTRE PAS, L'** • 1977
ONE SINGS THE OTHER DOESN'T see **UNE CHANTE, L'AUTRE PAS, L'** • 1977
ONE SMILE IS SUFFICIENT • 1978 • Bassiyouni Mohamed • EGY
ONE SPLENDID HOUR • 1929 • King Burton L. • USA • HER MAD ADVENTURE (UKN)
ONE SPOOKY NIGHT • 1923 • *Sennett Mack (P)* • SHT • USA
ONE SPOOKY NIGHT • 1955 • White Jules • SHT • USA
ONE SPY TOO MANY • 1966 • Sargent Joseph • USA • ALEXANDER THE GREATER AFFAIR, THE
ONE SPY TOO MANY see **WHERE THE SPIES ARE** • 1966
ONE STEP AHEAD OF MY SHADOW • 1933 • Ising Rudolf • ANS • USA
ONE STEP AT A TIME • 1962 • Watson Patrick • DOC • CND
ONE STEP AWAY • 1985 • Fortier Bob • MTV • CND
ONE STEP FORWARD • 1975 • Birman Naum • USS
ONE STEP TO ETERNITY (USA) see **BONNES A TUER** • 1954
ONE STEP TO HELL • 1968 • Howard Sandy, Scolaro Nino • USA, ITL, SPN • CACCIA AI VIOLENTI (ITL) ○ REY DE AFRICA (SPN) ○ KING OF AFRICA
ONE STEP TOO FAR • 1916 • *Hamilton Lloyd V.* • SHT • USA
ONE STOLEN NIGHT • 1923 • Ensminger Robert • USA
ONE STOLEN NIGHT • 1929 • Dunlap Scott R. • USA
ONE STORMY NIGHT • 1922 • Christie Al • USA
ONE-STREET TOWN, A • 1964 • Bazelyan Yakov • USS
ONE SUIT OF CLOTHES • 1914 • *Melies* • USA
ONE SUMMER DAY DOES NOT MEAN LOVE see **EIN SOMMERTAG MACHT KEINE LIEBE** • 1960
ONE SUMMER LOVE see **DRAGONFLY** • 1976
ONE SUMMER OF HAPPINESS see **HON DANSADE EN SOMMAR** • 1951
ONE SUMMER'S DAY • 1917 • Bayley Frank G. • UKN
ONE SUMMER'S SEQUEL • 1915 • Otto Henry • USA
ONE SUNDAY AFTERNOON • 1933 • Roberts Stephen • USA
ONE SUNDAY AFTERNOON • 1948 • Walsh Raoul • USA
ONE SUNDAY MORNING (UKN) see **NIEDZIELNY PORANEC** • 1955
ONE SWALLOW DOESN'T MAKE A SUMMER see **EN FLUGA GOR INGEN SOMMAR** • 1947
ONE SWEDISH SUMMER (USA) see **SOM HAVETS NAKNA VIND** • 1968
ONE TAKE TWO see **FLASHPOINT AFRICA** • 1978
ONE TERRIBLE DAY • 1922 • Roach Hal • SHT • USA
ONE TERRIFIC GUY • 1986 • Antonio Lou • TVM • USA
ONE THAT GOT AWAY, THE • 1957 • Baker Roy Ward • UKN
ONE THING AFTER ANOTHER • 1914 • Trimble Larry • UKN
ONE-THING-AT-A-TIME O'DAY • 1919 • Ince John • USA
ONE THIRD DOWN AND 24 MONTHS TO PAY • 1959 • Macartney-Filgate Terence, McDonnell Fergus • DOC • CND • CARS IN YOUR LIFE, THE
ONE THIRD OF A NATION • 1939 • Murphy Dudley • USA
ONE THOUSAND DOLLARS • 1918 • Webb Kenneth • USA
ONE THOUSAND FACES see **ISANG LIBONG MUKHA** • 1968
ONE THOUSAND MILES AN HOUR • 1917 • Chaudet Louis W. • SHT • USA
ONE THOUSAND TO ONE SHOT • 1914 • *Murray Charles* • USA
ONE THRILLING NIGHT • 1942 • Beaudine William • USA
ONE TIME AROUND see **MOST, THE** • 1962
ONE TO THE MINUTE • 1915 • Dillon John Francis • USA
ONE-TO-THREE • 1914 • *Mason Billy* • USA
ONE TO TWO see **EX-MRS. BRADFORD, THE** • 1936
ONE TOO-EXCITING NIGHT • 1922 • Quiribet Gaston • UKN
ONE TOO MANY • 1916 • *Plump & Runt* • SHT • USA
ONE TOO MANY • 1934 • McGowan Robert • SHT • USA
ONE TOO MANY • 1950 • Kenton Erle C. • USA • KILLER WITH A LABEL (UKN)
ONE TOUCH OF NATURE • 1909 • *Essanay* • USA
ONE TOUCH OF NATURE • 1909 • Griffith D. W. • *Ab* • USA
ONE TOUCH OF NATURE • 1910 • *Solax* • USA
ONE TOUCH OF NATURE • 1911 • Trimble Larry • USA
ONE TOUCH OF NATURE • 1914 • Miller Ashley • USA
ONE TOUCH OF NATURE • 1917 • Griffith Edward H. • USA
ONE TOUCH OF SIN • 1917 • Stanton Richard • USA
ONE TOUCH OF VENUS • 1948 • Seiter William A. • USA
ONE TOUCHING ONE • 1970 • Eden Mark • USA
ONE TRACK MINDS • 1933 • Meins Gus • SHT • USA
ONE TRAVELLER RETURNS • 1914 • Le Saint Edward J. • USA
ONE-TRICK PONY • 1980 • Young Robert Malcolm • USA • ONE TRICK PONY
ONE TRICK PONY see **ONE-TRICK PONY** • 1980
ONE, TWO, THREE • 1912 • Dwan Allan • USA
ONE, TWO, THREE • 1961 • Wilder Billy • USA
ONE, TWO, THREE see **PIERWSZY, DRUGI, TRZECI** • 1964
ONE.. TWO.. THREE.. FIRE! see **PIM, PAM, PUM.., FUEGO!** • 1975
ONE, TWO, THREE, FOUR see **UN, DEUX, TROIS, QUATRE!** • 1960
ONE TWO TWO see **ONE TWO TWO: 122 RUE DE PROVENCE** • 1978
ONE TWO TWO: 122 RUE DE PROVENCE • 1978 • Gion Christian • FRN • CENT VINGT-DEUX RUE DE PROVENCE ○ NEVER LOVE A HOOKER ○ ONE TWO TWO
ONE UP ON FATHER • 1914 • *Heron Andrew (P)* • UKN
ONE WAY AT A TIME • Wolfe Howard • FRN
ONE WAY AT A TIME • 1979 • Colberg Alan • USA
ONE WAY OR ANOTHER see **DE CIERTA MANERA** • 1977
ONE WAY OUT • 1934 • Hillyer Lambert • SHT • USA
ONE WAY OUT • 1955 • Searle Francis • UKN
ONE WAY OUT • 1987 • Kyriazi Paul • USA
ONE WAY PASSAGE • 1932 • Garnett Tay • USA
ONE WAY PENDULUM • 1964 • Yates Peter • UKN
ONE WAY STREET • 1925 • Dillon John Francis • USA
ONE-WAY STREET • 1950 • Fregonese Hugo • USA • DEATH ON A SIDE STREET ○ DEEP END, THE
ONE WAY STREET see **TWO IN A TAXI** • 1941
ONE WAY STREET see **NAUFRAGES DU QUARTIER, LES** • 1980
ONE WAY TICKET • 1935 • Biberman Herbert J. • USA
ONE-WAY TICKET see **PASAJE DE IDA** • 1988
ONE-WAY TICKET FOR LOVE see **KOI NO KATAMICHI-KIPPU** • 1960
ONE-WAY TICKET TO HELL • 1955 • Price Bamlet L. Jr. • USA
ONE WAY TICKET TO LOVE see **KOI NO KATAMICHI-KIPPU** • 1960
ONE WAY TO ADVERTISE • 1915 • Ransom Charles • USA
ONE WAY TO LOVE • 1946 • Enright Ray • USA
ONE WAY TO WIN • 1911 • *Lubin* • USA
ONE-WAY TRAIL, THE • 1920 • Kelsey Fred A. • USA
ONE WAY TRAIL, THE • 1931 • Taylor Ray • USA
ONE WAY WAHINE • 1965 • Brown William O. • USA
ONE WEAK VACATION • 1963 • Kneitel Seymour • ANS • USA
ONE WEEK • 1920 • Keaton Buster, Cline Eddie • SHT • USA
ONE WEEK OF HAPPINESS see **SEMANA DE FELICIDAD, UNA** • 1935
ONE WEEK OF LIFE • 1919 • Henley Hobart • USA
ONE WEEK OF LOVE • 1922 • Archainbaud George • USA
ONE WEEK TO LIVE • 1921 • Hill Sinclair • UKN
ONE WEIRD MOVIE • 1989 • Goren Serif • TRK
ONE WHO CARED, THE • 1914 • *Princess* • USA
ONE WHO HAD TO PAY, THE • 1913 • *Francis Alec B.* • USA
ONE WHO KNOWS ALL, THE see **NALUM THERINDAVAN** • 1968
ONE WHO LOVED HIM BEST, THE • 1914 • Ridgely Richard • USA
ONE WHO PASSED BY • 1916 • Wilson Ben • SHT • USA
ONE WHO REMEMBERED • 1910 • Rains Fred • UKN
ONE WHO SERVES • 1915 • Powers Francis • USA
ONE WIFE TOO MUCH • 1913 • *Crystal* • USA
ONE WILD MOMENT see **MOMENT D'EGAREMENT, UN** • 1978
ONE WILD NIGHT • 1917 • McRae Henry • SHT • USA
ONE WILD NIGHT • 1938 • Forde Eugene J. • USA • HANDLE WITH CARE ○ TIME OUT FOR MURDER
ONE WILD NIGHT • 1951 • Yates Hal • SHT • USA
ONE WILD NIGHT • 1969 • *Cherry Productions* • USA
ONE WILD OAT • 1951 • Saunders Charles • UKN
ONE WILD RIDE • 1925 • Roach Hal • SHT • USA
ONE WILD WEEK • 1921 • Campbell Maurice • USA
ONE WINTER'S NIGHT • 1914 • Collins Edwin J. • UKN • ONE CHRISTMAS EVE
ONE WISH TOO MANY • 1956 • Durst John • UKN
ONE WITH THE FUZZ, THE see **SOME KIND OF A NUT** • 1969
ONE WOMAN, THE • 1916 • Otto Hans • SHT • USA
ONE WOMAN, THE • 1918 • Barker Reginald • USA
ONE WOMAN IDEA, THE • 1929 • Viertel Berthold • USA
ONE WOMAN OR TWO (USA) see **FEMME OU DEUX, UNE** • 1985
ONE WOMAN TO ANOTHER • 1927 • Tuttle Frank • USA
ONE WOMAN'S ANSWER see **WOMAN AGAINST WOMAN** • 1938
ONE WOMAN'S LOVER • Buzzani Sergio • ITL
ONE WOMAN'S REVENGE see **REVENGE** • 1971
ONE WOMAN'S STORY (USA) see **PASSIONATE FRIENDS, THE** • 1948
ONE WOMAN'S WAY • 1915 • MacMackin Archer • USA
ONE WONDERFUL NIGHT • 1914 • Calvert E. H. • USA
ONE WONDERFUL NIGHT • 1922 • Paton Stuart • USA
ONE WONDERFUL SUNDAY see **SUBARASHIKI NICHIYOBI** • 1947
ONE YARD TO GO • 1931 • *Sennett Mack (P)* • SHT • USA
ONE YEAR IN THE LIFE OF A LAPPLAND BOY see **ANTE** • 1977
ONE YEAR LATER • 1933 • Hopper E. Mason • USA
ONE YEAR TO LIVE • 1925 • Cummings Irving • USA
ONE YOU LOVE, THE see **MAN ELSKER, DEN**
ONE ZERO TOO MANY see **EN NOLLA FOR MYCKET** • 1962
ONEICHAN MAKARI TORU • 1959 • Sugie Toshio • JPN • THREE DOLLS FROM HONG KONG (USA) ○ THREE DOLLS GO TO HONG KONG ○ YOUNG GIRL DARES TO PASS
O'NEIL, THE • 1911 • Olcott Sidney • IRL • O'NEILL, THE
O'NEIL OF THE GLEN • 1916 • Kerrigan J. M. • IRL
O'NEILL, THE see **O'NEIL, THE** • 1911
ONE'S A HEIFER • 1984 • Wheeler Anne • MTV • CND
ONES WHO SUFFER, THE • 1912 • *Eyton Bessie* • USA
ONESIME • 1912-14 • Durand Jean • SHS • FRN
ONESIME AUX ENFERS • 1912 • Durand Jean • FRN • SIMPLE SIMON AND THE DEVIL (UKN) ○ SIMPLE SIMON IN HELL
ONESIME CONTRE ONESIME • 1913 • Durand Jean • FRN
ONESIME CORRESPONDANT DE GUERRE • 1913 • Durand Jean • FRN
ONESIME DOUANIER • 1912 • Durand Jean • FRN
ONESIME ET LA MAISON HANTEE • 1913 • Durand Jean • FRN • SIMPLE SIMON AND THE HAUNTED HOUSE
ONESIME ET LE CHAMEAU RECONNAISSANT • 1914 • Durand Jean • FRN
ONESIME ET LE CLUBMAN • 1914 • Durand Jean • FRN • SIMPLE SIMON AND THE CLUBMAN
ONESIME ET L'ENFANT PERDU • 1914 • Durand Jean • FRN
ONESIME HORLOGER • 1912 • Durand Jean • FRN • SIMPLE SIMON CLOCK MAKER
ONESIME TIMIDE • 1913 • Durand Jean • FRN
ONGAKU • 1972 • Masumura Yasuzo • JPN • MUSIC
ONGEWENSTE VREEMDELING • 1974 • Rautenbach Jans • SAF
ONGEWIJDE AARDE • 1967 • van der Heijden Jef • NTH • UNCONSECRATED EARTH
ONGYILKOS • 1970 • Macskassy Gyula, Varnai Gyorgy • ANS • HNG • DON'T KILL YOURSELF
ONI • 1972 • Kawamoto Kihachiro • ANM • JPN • DEMON ○ WITCH, THE
ONI AZAMI • 1927 • Kinugasa Teinosuke • JPN
ONI NO SUMA YAKATA • 1969 • Misumi Kenji • JPN • DEVIL'S TEMPLE, THE
ONI NO UTA • 1975 • Murano Tetsutaro • JPN • DEMON BALLAD
ONI PREZIRU STRAH • 1951 • Cagic Mihailo, Bukumirovic Milos • YGS • THEY DESPISE FEAR
ONI SHLI NA VOSTOK (USS) see **ITALIANO, BRAVA GENTE** • 1964
ONI SRAJALIS ZA RODINOU • 1974 • Bondarchuk Sergei • USS • THEY FOUGHT FOR THE MOTHERLAND (USA) ○ THEY FOUGHT FOR THEIR COUNTRY ○ ONI SRAZHALIS ZA RODINU ○ THEY FOUGHT FOR THEIR MOTHERLAND
ONI SRAZHALIS ZA RODINU see **ONI SRAJALIS ZA RODINOU** • 1974
ONI ZHIVUT RYADOM • 1968 • Roshal Georgi • USS • THEY LIVE CLOSE BY
ONIBABA • 1964 • Shindo Kaneto • JPN • DEVIL WOMAN ○ HOLE, THE ○ DEMON, THE
ONIBI see **ONIBI TORO** • 1958
ONIBI KAGO • 1957 • Hirozu Mitsuo • JPN
ONIBI TORO • 1958 • Kato Bin • JPN • WILL O' THE WISP ○ ONIBI
ONION FIELD, THE • 1979 • Becker Harold • USA
ONION HERO, THE • 1917 • Beaudine William • SHT • USA
ONION MAGNET'S REVENGE, THE • 1917 • *Ham & Bud* • USA

ONION PACIFIC • 1940 • Fleischer Dave • ANS • USA
ONION PATCH, THE • 1915 • MacGregor Norval • USA
ONIONHEAD • 1958 • Taurog Norman • USA
ONIONS AND GARLIC • 1977 • Borenstein Joyce • CND
ONIRO APATILO • 1968 • Arion Giorgos • GRC • DREAMS THAT NEVER CAME TRUE ○ FALSE DREAM
ONIROS • 1967 • Pollet Jean-Daniel • FRN
ONITE AND IONELIS • 1931 • Dunayevas F., Lenartas L. • USS
ONKAPARINGA RACES • 1917 • ASL
ONKEL AUS AMERIKA, DER • 1915 • Hyan Hans • FRG
ONKEL AUS AMERIKA, DER • 1953 • Boese Carl • FRG
ONKEL BRASIG • 1936 • Waschneck Erich • FRG
ONKEL FILSER -ALLERNEUESTE LAUSBUBENGESCICHTEN • 1966 • Jacobs Werner • FRG
ONKEL JOAKIMS HEMMELIGHED • 1967 • Ottosen Carl • DNM • UNCLE JOAKIM'S SECRET
ONKEL OG NEVO see **FADER OG SON** • 1911
ONKEL TOIAS ALS TUGENDWACHTER • 1917 • *Ludl Josef* • FRG
ONKEL TOMS HUTTE • 1965 • von Radvanyi Geza • FRG, FRN, ITL • CASE DE L'ONCLE TOM, LA (FRN) ○ CENTO DOLLARI D'ODIO (ITL) ○ UNCLE TOM'S CABIN (USA) ○ CICA TOMINA KOLIBA (YGS)
ONKELCHENS LIEBLING • 1917 • Kaden Danny • FRG
ONKRAJ • 1971 • Gale Joze • YGS • ON THE OTHER SIDE
ONLY 38 • 1923 • De Mille William C. • USA
ONLY A COFFIN see **SOLO UN ATAUD** • 1966
ONLY A COUNTRY GIRL • 1915 • *Miller Rube* • USA
ONLY A DANCING GIRL see **BARA EN DANSERSKA** • 1927
ONLY A DART • 1908 • Aylott Dave • UKN
ONLY A DOG BUT MORE THAT HUMAN • 1908 • *Urban Trading Co* • UKN
ONLY A DREAM • 1909 • *Gaumont* • FRN
ONLY A DREAM • 1914 • *Melies* • USA
ONLY A DREAM see **BLOTT EN DROM** • 1911
ONLY A FACE AT THE WINDOW • 1903 • Stow Percy • UKN
ONLY A FACTORY GIRL • 1911 • ASL
ONLY A FARMER'S DAUGHTER • 1915 • Jones F. Richard • USA
ONLY A FLOWER GIRL • 1914 • Buckland Warwick? • UKN
ONLY A GIRL see **JUST A GIRL** • 1913
ONLY A HOBO • 1910 • *Atlas* • USA
ONLY A JANITOR • 1919 • Beery Wallace • SHT • USA
ONLY A LIMERICK • 1907 • Coleby A. E.? • UKN
ONLY A MESSENGER BOY • 1915 • Parrott Charles • USA
ONLY A MILL GIRL • 1919 • Willoughby Lewis • UKN
ONLY A MILL GIRL • 1920 • Willoughby Lewis • UKN
ONLY A MILLER'S DAUGHTER • 1912 • *Thanhouser* • USA
ONLY A MOTHER (USA) see **BARA EN MOR** • 1949
ONLY A MOUSE • 1909 • *Empire Films* • UKN
ONLY A PENNY A BOX • 1908 • Collins Alf? • UKN
ONLY A ROOMER • 1916 • Cooper Toby • UKN
ONLY A ROSE • 1916 • King Burton L. • SHT • USA
ONLY A SHOP GIRL • 1922 • Le Saint Edward J. • USA
ONLY A SISTER • 1911 • Melies Gaston • USA
ONLY A SISTER • 1914 • Davis Ulysses • USA
ONLY A SQUAW • 1911 • *Solax* • USA
ONLY A TRAMP • 1909 • Bouwmeester Theo? • UKN
ONLY A TRAMP • 1915 • *Cooper Miriam* • USA
ONLY A TRUMPETER see **BARA EN TRUMPETARE** • 1938
ONLY A WAITER see **BARA EN KYPARE** • 1960
ONLY A WEDDING • 1913 • Kinder Stuart • UKN
ONLY A WOMAN see **NADA MAS QUE UNA MUJER** • 1934
ONLY A WOMAN see **BARA EN KVINNA** • 1941
ONLY A WOMAN (USA) see **ICH BIN AUCH NUR EINE FRAU** • 1962
ONLY AN ICEMAN • 1911 • *Nestor* • USA
ONLY AN OUTCAST • 1912 • Haldane Bert? • UKN
ONLY ANGELS HAVE WINGS • 1939 • Hawks Howard • USA • PLANE NUMBER FOUR
ONLY CHANCE, THE • 1913 • Duncan William • USA
ONLY CHILD • 1987 • Wohl Ira • USA
ONLY CHILD, THE • 1915 • Lessey George A. • USA
ONLY CLUE, THE • 1914 • *Majestic* • USA
ONLY EIGHT HOURS • 1934 • Seitz George B. • USA • SOCIETY DOCTOR
ONLY FIVE YEARS OLD • 1913 • *Selig* • USA
ONLY FOG IS GREY see **NUR DER NEBEL IST GRAU** • 1965
ONLY FOR FUN, ONLY FOR PLAY see **KALEIDOSKOP VALESKA GERT -NUR ZUM SPASS NUR ZUM SPIEL** • 1977
ONLY FOR THEE (USA) see **SOLO PER TE** • 1937
ONLY FUEHRER IS MISSING • 1965 • Vabalas Raimondas • DOC • USS
ONLY FUN AT BULLERBYN see **BARA ROLIGT I BULLERBYN** • 1961
ONLY GAME IN TOWN, THE • 1970 • Stevens George • USA
ONLY GAME IN TOWN, THE • 1979 • Mann Ron • CND
ONLY GIRL, THE • 1932 • Hollander Friedrich • UKN • HEART SONG (USA)
ONLY GIRL IN CAMP, THE • 1911 • *Thanhouser* • USA
ONLY GOD KNOWS • 1974 • Pearson Peter • CND
ONLY HER BROTHER • 1905 • Fitzhamon Lewin • UKN
ONLY HER HUSBAND • 1929 • Lamont Charles • SHT • USA
ONLY HOUSE IN TOWN, THE • 1970 • *Professionals, The* • USA
ONLY IN MY DREAMS • 1970 • Peters Victor • USA
ONLY IN RIO see **BLAME IT ON RIO** • 1983
ONLY IN THE WAY • 1911 • *Thanhouser* • USA
ONLY LIFE, THE see **EKHI ROSTA** • 1941
ONLY MAN, THE • 1915 • Kellino W. P. • UKN
ONLY MAN, THE • 1925 • Parkinson H. B. • UKN • LEADING MAN, THE
ONLY NIGHT OF MY LIFE, THE see **OMRUMUN TEK GECESI** • 1968
ONLY ONCE IN A LIFETIME • 1979 • Grattan Alexander • USA
ONLY ONE, THE see **YEDINSTVENNAYA** • 1976
ONLY ONE DAY LEFT BEFORE TOMORROW see **HOW TO STEAL AN AIRPLANE** • 1971
ONLY ONE GIRL: OR, A BOOM IN SAUSAGES • 1910 • Stow Percy • UKN
ONLY ONE LIFE • 1965 • Lisakovitch Viktor • DOC • USS
ONLY ONE LIFE -THE STORY OF FRIDTJOF NANSEN see **BARE ET LIV -HISTORIEN OM FRIDTJOF NANSEN** • 1968
ONLY ONE NEW YORK • 1964 • Gaisseau Pierre-Dominique • DOC • USA, FRN • NEW-YORK-SUR-MER (FRN) ○ NEW YORK SUR MER
ONLY ONE PAIR • 1916 • Stow Percy? • UKN
ONLY ONE SHIRT • 1914 • *Roland Ruth* • USA
ONLY ONE WINNER see **COOK & PEARY: THE RACE TO THE POLE** • 1983
ONLY ROAD, THE • 1918 • Reicher Frank • USA
ONLY ROAD, THE • 1975 • Pavlovic Vladimir • USS, YGS
ONLY SAPS WORK • 1930 • Gardner Cyril, Knopf Edwin H. • USA • SOCIAL ERRORS
ONLY SKIN DEEP • 1914 • Hevener Jerold T. • USA
ONLY SOME STEPS FROM THE ROOF see **SHAG S KRISHI**
ONLY SON, THE • 1914 • Heffron Thomas N., De Mille Cecil B. • USA
ONLY SON, THE • 1915 • *Trump* • USA
ONLY SON, THE • 1922 • Roach Hal • SHT • USA
ONLY SON, THE see **HITORI MUSUKO** • 1930
ONLY THE BEST see **I CAN GET IT FOR YOU WHOLESALE** • 1951
ONLY THE BRAVE • 1930 • Tuttle Frank • USA
ONLY THE COOL (USA) see **PEAU DE TORPEDO, LA** • 1970
ONLY THE DEAD ARE SILENT see **NUR TOTE ZEUGEN SCHWEIGEN** • 1963
ONLY THE FRENCH CAN (USA) see **FRENCH CANCAN** • 1954
ONLY THE MAID • 1915 • Miller Ashley • USA
ONLY THE MASTER SHALL JUDGE • 1911 • *Powers* • USA
ONLY THE VALIANT • 1951 • Douglas Gordon • USA
ONLY THING, THE • 1925 • Conway Jack • USA
ONLY THING YOU KNOW, THE • 1972 • Mackey Clarke • CND
ONLY TODAY • 1976 • Revach Ze'Ev • ISR
ONLY TWO CAN PLAY • 1962 • Gilliat Sidney • UKN • THAT UNCERTAIN FEELING
ONLY TWO LITTLE SHOES • 1910 • Martinek H. O. • UKN
ONLY VETERAN IN TOWN, THE • 1913 • *Kent Charles* • USA
ONLY WAY, THE • 1913 • North Wilfred • USA
ONLY WAY, THE • 1914 • Pollard Harry • USA
ONLY WAY, THE • 1925 • Wilcox Herbert • UKN • TALE OF TWO CITIES, A
ONLY WAY, THE see **OKTOBER-DAGE** • 1970
ONLY WAY HOME, THE • 1972 • Spradlin G. D. • USA
ONLY WAY OUT, THE • 1915 • *Brice Rosetta* • USA
ONLY WAY OUT, THE • 1926 • Barnett Charles • UKN
ONLY WAY OUT IS DEAD, THE (UKN) see **MAN WHO WANTED TO LIVE FOREVER, THE** • 1970
ONLY WHEN I LARF • 1968 • Dearden Basil • UKN
ONLY WHEN I LAUGH • 1981 • Jordan Glenn • USA • IT HURTS ONLY WHEN I LAUGH (UKN)
ONLY WITH MARRIED MEN • 1974 • Paris Jerry • TVM • USA
ONLY WOMAN, THE • 1924 • Olcott Sidney • USA • SACRIFICE
ONLY WOMAN IN TOWN, THE • 1912 • *Crystal* • USA
ONLY WOMEN HAVE TROUBLE see **KANASHIMI WA ONNA DAKENI** • 1958
ONLY YESTERDAY • 1933 • Stahl John M. • USA
ONLY YOU see **TANGING IKAW** • 1968
ONMITSU SHICHISOKI • 1958 • Matsuda Sadatsugu • JPN • DESTINY OF A CREDENTIAL AGENT
ONNA • 1948 • Kinoshita Keisuke • JPN • WOMAN
ONNA ASARI • 1967 • Mukoi Hiroshi • JPN • SEEKING FOR WOMEN
ONNA BAKARI NO YORU • 1961 • Tanaka Kinuyo • JPN • WOMEN'S NIGHT
ONNA DE ARU KOTO • 1958 • Kawashima Yuzo • JPN • WOMAN UNVEILED
ONNA GA KAIDAN O AGARU TOKI • 1960 • Naruse Mikio • JPN • WHEN A WOMAN ASCENDS THE STAIRS ○ WHEN A WOMAN CLIMBS THE STAIRS
ONNA GOROSHI ABURA JIGOKU • 1949 • Nobuchi Akira • JPN • OIL HELL OF KILLING WOMEN
ONNA GOROSHI ABURA JIGOKU • 1958 • Horikawa Hiromichi • JPN • PRODIGAL SON, THE
ONNA HITORI DAICHI O IKU see **ONNA HITORI DAICHI O YUKU** • 1953
ONNA HITORI DAICHI O YUKU • 1953 • Kamei Fumio • JPN • WOMAN WALKING ALONE ON THE EARTH ○ ONNA HITORI DAICHI O IKU ○ WOMAN WALKS THE EARTH ALONE, A
ONNA KAZOKU • 1961 • Hisamatsu Seiji • JPN • MOONLIGHT IN THE RAIN (USA)
ONNA KEIZU • 1961 • Misumi Kenji • JPN • HER HIDDEN PAST
ONNA KOSO IE O MAMORE • 1939 • Yoshimura Kozaburo • JPN • WOMEN DEFEND THE HOME! ○ WOMEN SHOULD STAY AT HOME
ONNA KYUKETSUKI • 1959 • Nakagawa Nobuo • JPN
ONNA MEKURA HANA TO KIBA • 1968 • Ichimura Hirokazu • JPN • FANGS OF A FEMALE
ONNA NI ASHIATO • 1956 • Shibuya Minoru • JPN • FOOTPRINTS OF A WOMAN
ONNA NO BITAI • 1967 • Yamamoto Shinya • JPN • WOMEN'S COQUETRY
ONNA NO HADA • 1957 • *Kyo Machiko* • JPN • SKIN OF A WOMAN
ONNA NO HAISHO • 1961 • Nakamura Noboru • JPN • LONELY GEISHA, A
ONNA NO HIEZU • 1968 • Hayasaka Hirokiyo • JPN • SECRET ILLUSTRATION OF WOMAN
ONNA NO ISSHO • 1949 • Kamei Fumio • JPN • WOMAN'S LIFE, A
ONNA NO ISSHO • 1953 • Shindo Kaneto • JPN • WOMAN'S LIFE, A ○ LIFE OF A WOMAN, A
ONNA NO ISSHO • 1955 • Nakamura Noboru • JPN • ONE LOVE TOO MANY ○ WOMAN'S LIFE, A
ONNA NO ISSHO • 1962 • Masumura Yasuzo • JPN • LIFE OF A WOMAN
ONNA NO ISSHO • 1967 • Nomura Yoshitaro • JPN • VIE, UN
ONNA NO KAO • 1949 • Imai Tadashi • JPN • WOMAN'S FACE, A
ONNA NO KOYOMI • 1954 • Hisamatsu Seiji • JPN • FIVE SISTERS ○ CALENDAR OF WOMEN
ONNA NO KUNSHO • 1961 • Yoshimura Kozaburo • JPN • DESIGN FOR DYING, A ○ WOMAN'S DECORATION
ONNA NO MACHI • 1940 • Imai Tadashi • JPN • WOMEN'S TOWN ○ WOMEN'S STREET
ONNA NO MISUMI • 1966 • Yoshida Yoshishige • JPN • WOMEN OF THE LAKE ○ LAKE, THE
ONNA NO NAKA NI IRU TANIN • 1966 • Naruse Mikio • JPN • STRANGER WITHIN A WOMAN, THE ○ THIN LINE, THE
ONNA NO REKISHI • 1963 • Naruse Mikio • JPN • WOMAN'S STORY, A ○ WOMAN'S LIFE, A
ONNA NO SAKA • 1960 • Yoshimura Kozaburo • JPN • WOMEN OF KYOTO ○ FENCE OF WOMEN, A ○ WOMAN'S DESCENT
ONNA NO SEME • 1967 • Yamamoto Shinya • JPN • WOMEN'S TORTURE
ONNA NO SHIKI • 1950 • Toyoda Shiro • JPN • FOUR SEASONS OF WOMAN, THE
ONNA NO SHIKIYOKU • 1968 • Miki Hideki • JPN • WOMAN'S CARNAL DESIRE
ONNA NO SONO • 1954 • Kinoshita Keisuke • JPN • GARDEN OF WOMEN, THE ○ ETERNAL GENERATION, THE
ONNA NO SUBETE • 1960 • Yamamoto Kajiro • JPN • WOMAN ALTOGETHER
ONNA NO TAKOBEYA • 1968 • Takeda Ario • JPN • CONCENTRATED SHOCK OF WOMEN, A
ONNA NO TESABAKI • 1968 • Murakami Noboru • JPN • WOMAN'S MANOEUVRING
ONNA NO TORIHIKI • 1967 • Kataoka Hitoshi • JPN • TRAFFIC IN WOMEN
ONNA NO TSUBOFURI • 1968 • Umesawa Kaoru • JPN • SHE GAMBLER
ONNA NO URAMADO • 1960 • Bansho Yoshiaki • JPN • LESSON FOR WIDOWS
ONNA NO URESHINAKI • 1968 • Yakeda Akio • JPN • CRY OF JOY
ONNA NO UZU TO FUCHI TO NAGARE • 1964 • Nakahira Ko • JPN • WHIRLPOOL OF WOMEN (USA) ○ WHIRLPOOL OF FLESH
ONNA NO YOROKOBI • 1967 • Ure Hajime • JPN • PLEASURE OF WOMEN
ONNA NO ZA • 1962 • Naruse Mikio • JPN • WISER AGE, THE (USA) ○ WOMAN'S PLACE, A ○ WOMAN'S STATUS
ONNA ONNA ONNA MONOGATARI • 1963 • Takechi Tetsuji • DOC • JPN • WOMEN.. OH, WOMEN! (USA)
ONNA TO INOCHI O KAKETE BUTTOBASE • 1960 • Magatani Morehei • JPN
ONNA TO KAIZOKU • 1959 • Ito Daisuke • JPN • WOMAN AND THE PIRATES, THE ○ WOMAN AND PIRATES
ONNA TO MISOSHIRO • 1968 • Gosho Heinosuke • JPN • WOMAN AND THE BEANCURD SOUP, A ○ WOMAN AND BEAN SOUP ○ WOMEN AND MISO SOUP
ONNA TO OTOKO NO AJIKURABE • 1968 • Takagi Takeo • JPN • TASTE OF WOMAN, TASTE OF MAN
ONNA TO UMARETA KARANYA • 1934 • Gosho Heinosuke • JPN • NOW THAT I WAS BORN A WOMAN
ONNA TOBA-ARASHI • 1967 • Yuge Taro • JPN • SISTER GAMBLERS, THE
ONNA TOBAKUSHI • 1967 • Yuge Taro • JPN • WOMAN GAMBLER, THE (USA)
ONNA TOBAKUSHI AMADERA KAICHO • 1968 • Tanaka Shigeo • JPN • WOMAN GAMBLER AND THE NUN, THE
ONNA TOBAKUSHI MIDARETSUBO • 1968 • Tanaka Shigeo • JPN • WOMAN GAMBLER'S SUPPLICATION, THE
ONNA TOBAKUSHI NORIKOMU • 1968 • Tanaka Shigeo • JPN • WOMAN GAMBLER COMES, THE
ONNA TOBAKUSHI OKUNOIN KAICHO • 1968 • Inoue Yoshio • JPN • WOMAN GAMBLER'S REVENGE, THE
ONNA TOBAKUSHI TEKKABA YABURI • 1968 • Inoue Yoshio • JPN • WOMAN DICE PLAYER, THE
ONNA TOBAKUSHI ZETSUENJO • 1968 • Tanaka Shigeo • JPN • CHAMPION WOMAN GAMBLER, THE
ONNA TOYO SHIRO • 1953 • *Otowa Nobuko* • JPN • CASTLE CALLED WOMAN
ONNA UKIYO BURO • 1968 • Ida Tan • JPN • HOUSE OF STRANGE LOVES, THE (USA) ○ TOKYO BATH HAREM
ONNA UKIYOZOSHI • 1968 • Ida Tan • JPN • UKIYOE ARTIST
ONNA WA IKUMAN ARITOTEMO • 1966 • Sugie Toshio • JPN • ALTHOUGH THERE ARE MILLIONS OF WOMEN
ONNA WA NIDO UMARERU • 1961 • Kawashima Yuzo • JPN • GEISHA'S DIARY
ONNA WA TEIKO SURU • 1960 • Yuge Taro • JPN • ROCKABILLY LADY
ONNA WA TOMOTO O GYOJIN • 1931 • Naruse Mikio • JPN • LADIES, BE CAREFUL OF YOUR SLEEVES
ONNA WA YORU KESHOSURU • 1961 • Inoue Umeji • JPN • NOCTURNE OF A WOMAN
ONNA-YO AYAMARU NAKARE • 1923 • Kinugasa Teinosuke • JPN
ONNA-YO KIMI NO NA O KEGASU NAKARE • 1930 • Gosho Heinosuke • JPN • WOMAN DON'T MAKE YOU NAME DIRTY ○ WOMEN, DO NOT SHAME YOUR NAMES
ONNA ZEME TARAIMAWASHI • 1968 • Yamashita Osamu • JPN • TORTURING WOMAN BY TURNS
ONNAGA AISHITE NIKUMUTOKI • 1963 • Tomimoto Sokichi • JPN • SHE CAME FOR LOVE
ONNAGOKORO • 1959 • Maruyama Seiji • JPN • WOMAN'S HEART
ONNAGOKORO O DAREGA SHIRU • 1951 • Yamamoto Kajiro • JPN • WHO KNOWS A WOMAN'S HEART
ONNAGOKORO WA HITOSUJI NI • 1954 • Sugie Toshio • JPN • WITH ALL MY HEART
ONNAMAI • 1961 • Ohba Hideo • JPN • ENRAPTURED
ONNANAKASE • 1967 • Sakao Masanao • JPN • WOMEN KILLER
ONNATACHI NO NIWA • 1967 • Nomura Yoshitaro • JPN • AFFAIR OF THE HEART
ONNELLISET LEIKIT see **JUULIA** • 1964
ONNEN SAARI • 1955 • Kurkvaara Maunu • FNL • ISLAND OF HAPPINESS
ONNENPELI • 1965 • Jarva Risto • FNL • GAME OF CHANCE ○ GAME OF LUCK
ONOFRE • 1974 • Delgado Luis Maria • SPN
ONONKA'S VOW • 1910 • Porter Edwin S. • USA
ONORATA FAMIGLIA, UCCIDERE E COSA NOSTRA, L' • 1973 • Ricci Tonino • ITL • BIG FAMILY, THE
ONORATA SOCIETA, L' • 1961 • Pazzaglia Riccardo • ITL

ONORE E GUAPPARIA • 1978 • Longo Tiziano • ITL

ONORE E SANGUE • 1959 • Capuano Luigi • ITL

ONOREVOLE ANGELINA, L' • 1947 • Zampa Luigi • ITL • ANGELINA, M.P. ○ ANGELA

ONOREVOLI, GLI • 1963 • Corbucci Sergio • ITL

ONOVA NESHTO • 1990 • Stoyanov Georgi • BUL • THAT THING

ONRYO SAKURA DAI-SODO • 1957 • Watanabe Kunio • JPN

ONS STAAN 'N DAG OOR • 1942 • SAF

ONSCHERP • 1971 • Andersen Wies • BLG

ONSDAGSVANINNAN • 1946 • Lagerwall Sture, O'Fredericks Alice • SWD

ONSEN ANMA GEISHA • 1968 • Ishii Teruo • JPN • GEISHA MASSEUSES

ONSEN GERIRA DAI SHOGEKI • 1968 • Ichimura Hirokazu • JPN • HOTSPRINGS HOLIDAY (USA) ○ KIGEKI DAI SHOGEKI

ONSET: VARIATION NO.1 • Gruenberger John • SHT • USA

ONSKEDROMMEN • 1950 • Hellander Olle • SHT • SWD

ONTARIO • 1970 • Chapman Christopher • DOC • CND

ONTARIO SURPRISE • 1979 • Vaitiekunas Vince • CND

ONTARIO TOWNS AND VILLAGES see **FACES OF ONTARIO** • 1972-73

ONTBIJT VOOR TWEE • 1973 • van Eyck Robert • BLG • PETIT DEJEUNER POUR DEUX

ONTLUISTERD LAND • 1946 • van der Horst Herman • NTH • TARNISHED LAND

ONTROUW IN DUPLO • 1969 • Langestraat Bob • NTH • INFIDELITY IN DUPLICATE

ONTSTAAN EN VERGAAN see **AARDOLIE** • 1953

ONU ALLAH AFFETSIN • 1970 • Elmas Orhan • TRK

ONWARD BRAZIL see **PRA FRENTE BRASIL** • 1982

ONWARD, CHRISTIAN SOLDIERS • 1906 • Gilbert Arthur • UKN

ONWARD CHRISTIAN SOLDIERS • 1918 • Wilson Rex • UKN

ONWARD TO GLORY AGAIN • 1981 • Stamboulopoulos George • GRC

ONWARDS WITH TIME see **VORWARTS DIE ZEIT** • 1968

ONWETTIGE HUWELIK • 1970 • Schiess Mario • SAF • UNLAWFUL WEDDING

ONYXKOPF, DER • 1917 • May Joe • FRG

ONZE MILLE VIERGES, LES • 1975 • Lipmann Eric • FRN • BISEXUAL (UKN) ○ 11,000 SEXES, THE

OOANA SHOBU • 1968 • Segawa Masaharu • JPN • HOW TO MAKE A BIG HIT

OOG OP AVONTUUR, HET • 1970 • van Gelder Hans • DCS • NTH • ADVENTURES IN PERCEPTION

OOGON NO ME see **HYAPPATSU HYAKUCHU** • 1968

OOH LA-LA! • 1930 • Edwards Harry J. • SHT • USA

OOH.. YOU ARE AWFUL • 1972 • Owen Cliff • UKN • GET CHARLIE TULLY (USA)

OOKA SEIDAN see **SHINPAN OOKA SEIDAN** • 1928

OOKAMI • 1955 • Shindo Kaneto • JPN • PEOPLE CALLED THEM WOLVES ○ OKAMI ○ WOLF ○ WOLVES

OOKA'S TRIAL see **SHINPAN OOKA SEIDAN** • 1928

OOKU MARUHI MONOGATARI • 1967 • Nakajima Sadao • JPN • ZOKU OOKU MARUHI MONOGATARI ○ WOMEN AROUND THE SHOGUN, THE ○ SHOGUN AND HIS MISTRESSES, THE ○ SHOGUN AND HIS MISTRESS, THE

OOM PAH PAH • 1930 • Foster John, Bailey Harry • ANS • USA

OOM PIET SE PLAAS • 1949 • SAF

OOMPAH-PAH • 1965 • ANS • BLG

OOMPAHS, THE • 1952 • Cannon Robert • ANS • USA

OOMPH! • 1969 • Bjorkman Stig • SWD

OONCHA NEECH • 1949 • *Sircar B. N. (P)* • IND

OORLOG EN VREDE -1914-1916-1918 • 1918 • Binger Maurits H., Millar Adelqui • NTH • WAR AND PEACE -1914-1916-1918

OOSHO • 1948 • Ito Daisuke • JPN • CHESS KING, THE ○ KING OF CHESS ○ OSHO ○ CHESS MASTER, THE

OOSHO ICHIDAI • 1955 • Ito Daisuke • JPN • LIFE OF A CHESS-PLAYER, THE

OOTIVARAI URAVU • 1967 • Sridhar C. V. • IND • DESTINATION OOTI

OP DE BODEM VAN DE HEMEL • 1965 • Vrijman Jan • NTH • ON THE BOTTOM RUNG OF HEAVEN

OP HOOP VAN ZEGEN • 1918 • Binger Maurits H. • NTH

OP HOOP VAN ZEGEN • 1987 • Pieters Guido • NTH • GOOD HOPE, THE

OP HOP -HOP OP • 1966 • Hebert Pierre • ANS • CND • OPHOP

OP MED HUMORET • 1943 • Berggreen Ole • DNM • UP WITH HUMOUR

OP OG NED LANGS KYSTEN • 1950 • Lommer Stig • DNM

OP PA FARS HAT • 1985 • Holst Per • DNM • UP ON DADDY'S HAT

OP POP WHAM AND BOP • 1966 • Post Howard • ANS • USA

OP STAP • 1935 • Winar Ernest • NTH • ON THE TOWN

OPADLY LISCIE Z DRZEW • 1975 • Rozewicz Stanislaw • PLN • FALLEN LEAVES FROM THE TREES

OPAL PIN, THE • 1915 • *Sears A. D.* • USA

OPAL RING, AN • 1915 • *Bayne Beverly* • USA

OPAL RING, THE • 1914 • Crane Frank H. • USA

OPAL STEALERS, THE • 1913 • Coleby A. E. • UKN

OPAL'S CURSE, THE • 1914 • O'Sullivan Tony • USA

OPASEN POLET • 1968 • Petrov Dimitar • BUL • PERILOUS FLIGHT

OPATICA I KOMESAR • 1968 • Sipovac Gojko • YGS • NUN AND THE COMMISSAR, THE

OPBRUD • 1987 • Ploug Claus • DNM • CLOSING TIME

OPEN AIR see **FRILUFT** • 1959

OPEN AIR BEDROOM • 1970 • *Kirt Films International* • USA

OPEN AIR MUSEUM, AN • 1973 • Abuladze Tengiz • DOC • USS

OPEN ALL HOURS • 1984 • Lotterby Sydney • MTV • UKN

OPEN ALL NIGHT • 1924 • Bern Paul • USA • ONE PARISIAN KNIGHT (UKN)

OPEN ALL NIGHT • 1934 • Pearson George • UKN

OPEN ANOTHER BOTTLE • 1916 • Goulding Alf • USA

OPEN ANOTHER BOTTLE • 1921 • Roach Hal • SHT • USA

OPEN AT NIGHT see **YORU HIRAKU** • 1931

OPEN BOOK, THE • 1974 • Fetin Vladimir • USS

OPEN CITY (USA) see **ROMA, CITTA APERTA** • 1945

OPEN COUNTRY • 1922 • Hill Sinclair • UKN

OPEN DIALOOG • 1973 • Buyens Frans • BLG • DIALOGUE OUVERT

OPEN DOOR, THE • 1913 • *Broncho* • USA

OPEN DOOR, THE • 1913 • MacGregor Norval • *Selig* • USA

OPEN DOOR, THE • 1914 • Cooper Toby? • UKN

OPEN DOOR, THE • 1915 • *Reliance* • USA

OPEN DOOR, THE • 1919 • Fitzgerald Dallas M. • USA

OPEN DOORS see **PORTE APERTE** • 1990

OPEN DURING ALTERATIONS see **BUSINESS AS USUAL DURING ALTERATIONS** • 1913

OPEN FIRE • 1988 • Mende Roger • USA

OPEN FIRE ON FRANKIE see **FEUER FREI AUF FRANKIE** • 1967

OPEN FROM 6P.M. TO MIDNIGHT see **ABIERTO DE 18 A 24** • 1987

OPEN FUTURE see **APEN FRAMTID** • 1983

OPEN GATE, THE • 1909 • Griffith D. W. • USA

OPEN GATE, THE • 1911 • *Yankee* • USA

OPEN GRAVE, THE • 1964 • Kelly Ron • CND

OPEN HOUSE • 1926 • Lamont Charles • SHT • USA

OPEN HOUSE • 1930 • Fraser Harry L. • USA

OPEN HOUSE • 1953 • Donnelly Eddie • ANS • USA

OPEN HOUSE • 1987 • Mundhra Jag • USA

OPEN, IT'S ME • 1973 • Sharlandgiev Ljobomir • BUL

OPEN LETTER see **ANIHTI EPISOLI** • 1969

OPEN LETTER TO AN EVENING PAPER see **LETTERA APERTA A UN GIORNALE DELLA SERA** • 1970

OPEN PLACES • 1917 • Van Dyke W. S. • USA

OPEN RANGE • 1927 • Smith Cliff • USA

OPEN ROAD, THE • 1911 • Olcott Sidney • USA

OPEN ROAD, THE • 1912 • *Imp* • USA

OPEN ROAD, THE • 1913 • Apfel Oscar • USA

OPEN ROAD, THE see **UPPBROTT** • 1948

OPEN ROAD, THE (USA) see **CHEMINEAU, LE** • 1935

OPEN SEASON • 1974 • Collinson Peter • SWT, SPN • CAZADORES, LOS (SPN) ○ RECON GAME ○ RECON HUNT ○ SHOOT

OPEN SEASON FOR VIRGINS, THE see **SHOJO KAIKIN** • 1968

OPEN SECRET • 1948 • Reinhardt John • USA

OPEN SESAME • 1933 • Horne James W. • SHT • USA

OPEN SKIES see **CEU ABERTO** • 1986

OPEN SPACES • 1926 • Lamont Charles • SHT • USA

OPEN SWITCH, THE • 1913 • *Holmes Stuart* • USA

OPEN SWITCH, THE • 1926 • McGowan J. P. • USA

OPEN SWITCH, THE see **WHISPERING SMITH** • 1926

OPEN THE BARS • 1920 • Morante Milburn, Parrott James • USA

OPEN THE DOOR AND SEE ALL THE PEOPLE • 1964 • Hill Jerome • USA • PEACOCK FEATHERS

OPEN THE DOOR WHEN THE BELL RINGS see **ZVONYAT, OTKROYTE DVER** • 1965

OPEN TO PROPOSALS • 1912 • *Solax* • USA

OPEN TO SEVEN WINDS see **NA SEMI VETRAKH** • 1962

OPEN TRAIL, THE see **RED RIDER, THE** • 1925

OPEN WINDOW see **NYITOTT ABLAK** • 1988

OPEN WINDOW, THE • 1952 • Storck Henri • DOC • UKN • FENETRE OUVERTE, LA

OPEN WINDOW, THE • 1972 • Patterson Richard • SHT • USA

OPEN WINGS see **ABRASASAS** • 1984

OPEN YOUR EYES • 1919 • Hamilton G. P. • USA

OPENED BY MISTAKE • 1915 • *World* • USA

OPENED BY MISTAKE • 1934 • Parrott James • SHT • USA

OPENED BY MISTAKE • 1940 • Archainbaud George • USA

OPENED SHUTTERS • 1921 • Worthington William • USA

OPENED SHUTTERS, THE • 1914 • Turner Otis • USA

OPENING DAY • 1938 • Rowland Roy • SHT • USA

OPENING IN MOSCOW • 1959 • Pennebaker D. A. • USA

OPENING NIGHT • 1933 • *Van Beuren* • ANS • USA

OPENING NIGHT • 1935 • Brown Alex • UKN

OPENING NIGHT • 1978 • Cassavetes John • USA

OPENING NIGHT see **PREMIJERA** • 1957

OPENING NIGHT, THE • 1915 • King Burton L. • USA

OPENING NIGHT, THE • 1927 • Griffith Edward H. • USA • JUDGMENT (UKN)

OPENING OF MISTY BEETHOVEN, THE • 1976 • Metzger Radley H. • USA • MISTY BEETHOVEN

OPENING OF PORT ADELAIDE ELECTRIC TRAMS • 1917 • *Krischock H. (Ph)* • ASL

OPENING OF THE AUCKLAND EXHIBITION • 1898 • Whitehouse A. E. • NZL

OPENING OF THE CARDIFF EXHIBITION BY H.R.H. THE PRINCE OF WALES • 1896 • Acres Birt • UKN

OPENING OF THE KIEL CANAL • 1895 • Acres Birt • UKN

OPENING SPEECH (USA) see **MESDAMES, MESSIEURS** • 1960

OPENING TOMORROW see **JUTRO PREMIERA** • 1962

OPERA • 1973 • Bozzetto Bruno, Manuli Guido • ANS • ITL

OPERA • 1976 • Velissaropoulos Andreas • SHT • GRC

OPERA • 1988 • Argento Dario • ITL

OPERA BALL see **OPERN-BALL, DER** • 1931

OPERA BALL (USA) see **OPERNBALL** • 1939

OPERA CAPER, THE • 1967 • Culhane Shamus, Bakshi Ralph • ANS • USA

OPERA CORDIS • 1968 • Vukotic Dusan • ANS • YGS

OPERA DE QUAT' SOUS, L' • 1930 • Pabst G. W. • FRN • THREEPENNY OPERA, THE

OPERA DE QUATRE PESOS, L' • 1970 • Reichenbach Francois • SHT • FRN

OPERA DEL MONDONGO, LA • 1976 • Arocha Luis Ernesto • DOC • CLM

OPERA DO MALANDRO • 1985 • Guerra Ruy • FRN, BRZ • MALANDRO (USA)

OPERA IN THE VINEYARD see **OPERA VE VINICI** • 1981

OPERA JAKARTA • 1985 • Syumanjaya • INN

OPERA-MOUFFE, L' • 1958 • Varda Agnes • SHT • FRN

OPERA-MUSETTE • 1941 • Lefevre Rene, Renoir Claude • FRN

OPERA NIGHT • 1935 • *Terry Paul/ Moser Frank (P)* • ANS • USA

OPERA PRIMA • 1980 • Trueba Fernando • SPN • FIRST EFFORT

OPERA SCHOOL • 1951 • Parker Gudrun • CND • CLASSE D'OPERA, LA

OPERA SINGER'S ROMANCE, THE • 1915 • Curtis Allen • USA

OPERA VE VINICI • 1981 • Jires Jaromil • CZC • OPERA IN THE VINEYARD

OPERABRANDEN • 1912 • Blom August • DNM • SONG WHICH GRANDMOTHER SANG, THE ○ BEDSTEMODERS VUGGEVISE

OPERACAO DINAMITE • 1967 • Martins Pedro • PRT • OPERATION DYNAMITE

OPERACAO ESTUPEFACIENTES • 1966 • Spiguel Miguel • PRT

OPERACAO OGMA • 1967 • Tropa Alfredo • SHT • PRT

OPERACIJA BEOGRAD • 1968 • Mitrovic Zika • YGS • OPERATION BELGRADE

OPERACIJA TICIJAN • 1963 • Novakovic Rados • YGS, USA • OPERATION TITAN

OPERACION 67 • 1966 • Cardona Rene, Cardona Rene Jr. • MXC

OPERACION ALFA • 1972 • Urteagu Enrique • CHL

OPERACION CABARETERA • 1967 • Ozores Mariano • SPN • OPERATION CABARETERA

OPERACION CARAMBOLA • 1968 • Zacarias Alfredo • MXC • OPERATION CAROM

OPERACION CONTROESPIONAJE (SPN) see **OPERAZIONE CONTROSPIONAGGIO** • 1965

OPERACION DALILA • 1967 • de los Arcos Luis • SPN, USA • OPERATION DELILAH

OPERACION EMBAJADA • 1964 • Palacios Fernando • SPN

OPERACION GOLDMAN (SPN) see **OPERAZIONE GOLDMAN** • 1966

OPERACION H • 1963 • Basterretxea Nestor, Larruquert Fernando • SHT • SPN

OPERACION LADY CHAPLIN (SPN) see **MISSIONE SPECIALE LADY CHAPLIN** • 1966

OPERACION LOTO AZUL see **AGENTE 077 -MISSIONE BLOODY MARY** • 1965

OPERACION MASACRE • 1972 • Cedron Jorge • ARG

OPERACION MATA-HARI • 1968 • Ozores Mariano • SPN • OPERATION MATA-HARI

OPERACION NONGOS see **GALLO CON ESPOLONES, UN** • 1964

OPERACION OGRO see **OGRO** • 1979

OPERACION OSITO • 1971 • Paris Rogelio • DOC • CUB

OPERACION PLUS ULTRA • 1966 • Lazaga Pedro • SPN

OPERACION POKER (SPN) see **OPERAZIONE POKER** • 1965

OPERACION ROMMEL see **HORA CERO: OPERACION ROMMEL** • 1968

OPERACION SAN ANTONIO • 1968 • Carreras Enrique • ARG, SPN • OPERATION SAN ANTONIO

OPERACION SECRETARIA • 1966 • Ozores Mariano • SPN

OPERACION TERROR see **HOMBRE QUE VINO DEL UMMO, EL** • 1970

OPERACION TIBURON • 1965 • de San Anton Jose • MXC, PRC

OPERACION TOISON DE ORO • 1968 • Elorrieta Jose Maria • SPN

OPERACION TURBINA • 1977 • Eguino Antonio • SHT • BLV

OPERACJA V-2 • 1969 • Szmagier Krzysztof • DOC • PLN • V-2 OPERATION, THE ○ OPERATION V-2

OPERASJON COBRA • 1978 • Solum Ola • NRW • OPERATION COBRA

OPERASJON V FOR VANNVIDD • 1970 • Clemens Rolf • NRW • OPERATION M FOR MADNESS

OPERATING ON CUPID • 1915 • Davey Horace • USA

OPERATION ABDUCTION (USA) see **RAPT AU DEUXIEME BUREAU** • 1958

OPERATION ABOLITION • 1962 • *Lewis Fulton* • DOC • USA

OPERATION AMSTERDAM • 1959 • McCarthy Michael • UKN

OPERATION APOLLO see **EPIHIRISIS APOLLON** • 1968

OPERATION ATLANTIS (USA) see **AGENTE SO 3 OPERAZIONE ATLANTIDE** • 1965

OPERATION BELGRADE see **OPERACIJA BEOGRAD** • 1968

OPERATION BETON • 1954 • Godard Jean-Luc • SHT • FRN

OPERATION BIG TEN • Sun John • HKG

OPERATION BIKINI • 1963 • Carras Anthony • USA • SEAFIGHTERS, THE ○ BIKINI BEACH ○ BIKINI

OPERATION BLACK SEPTEMBER • 1976 • Morrison Jack • ISR

OPERATION BOTTLENECK • 1961 • Cahn Edward L. • USA

OPERATION BRAINDRAIN see **BIRDMEN, THE** • 1971

OPERATION BREADBASKET • 1969 • Culp Robert • USA

OPERATION BRUTUS see **AKCJA "BRUTUS"** • 1970

OPERATION BUERRE DE PINOTTES see **PEANUT BUTTER SOLUTION, THE** • 1986

OPERATION BULLSHINE • 1959 • Gunn Gilbert • UKN • GIRLS IN ARMS

OPERATION C.I.A. • 1965 • Nyby Christian • USA • LAST MESSAGE FROM SAIGON

OPERATION CABARETERA see **OPERACION CABARETERA** • 1967

OPERATION CAMEL (USA) see **SOLDATERKAMMERATER PA VAGT** • 1960

OPERATION CAROM see **OPERACION CARAMBOLA** • 1968

OPERATION CAVIAR (USA) see **OPERATION CAVIARE** • 1959

OPERATION CAVIARE • 1959 • von Radvanyi Geza • FRG, FRN • OPERATION CAVIAR (USA)

OPERATION CELLULOID see **EXERCISE GREEN** • 1982

OPERATION CHERRY-STONE see **OPERATION KIRSEBAERSTEN** • 1972

OPERATION COBRA see **O'HARA: U.S. TREASURY** • 1971

OPERATION COBRA see **OPERASJON COBRA** • 1978

OPERATION COLD FEET • 1957 • Lovy Alex • ANS • USA

OPERATION CONSPIRACY see **CLOAK WITHOUT DAGGER** • 1956

OPERATION CORRECTION • 1962 • *American Civil Liberties Union* • DOC • USA

OPERATION COUNTERSPY see **OPERAZIONE CONTROSPIONAGGIO** • 1965

OPERATION CROSS EAGLES • 1969 • Conte Richard • USA, YGS • UNAKRSNA VATRA (YGS)

OPERATION CROSSBOW • 1965 • Anderson Michael • UKN, ITL • OPERAZIONE CROSSBOW (ITL) ○ CODE NAME: OPERATION CROSSBOW ○ GREAT SPY MISSION, THE

OPERATION CUPID • 1960 • Saunders Charles • UKN

OPERATION DAMES • 1958 • Stoumen Louis Clyde • USA • GIRLS IN ACTION (UKN)

OPERATION DAYBREAK • 1975 • Gilbert Lewis* • USA • SEVEN MEN AT DAYBREAK ○ PRICE OF FREEDOM
OPERATION DELILAH see **OPERACION DALILA** • 1967
OPERATION DIAMOND • 1948 • Pilgrim Ronnie • UKN
OPERATION DIAMOND see **YUMINGAI NO JUDAN** • 1963
OPERATION DIPLOMAT • 1953 • Guillermin John • UKN
OPERATION DIPLOMAT PASSPORT (USA) see **PASSEPORT DIPLOMATIQUE, AGENT K8** • 1965
OPERATION DISASTER (USA) see **MORNING DEPARTURE** • 1949
OPERATION DISCOTHEQUE • 1967 • Santiago Pablo • PHL
OPERATION DOUBLE CROSS see **TRAIN D'ENFER** • 1965
OPERATION DYNAMITE see **OPERACAO DINAMITE** • 1967
OPERATION EICHMANN • 1961 • Springsteen R. G. • USA
OPERATION ENEMY FORT (USA) see **YAMANEKO SAKUSEN** • 1962
OPERATION FEAR see **OPERAZIONE PAURA** • 1966
OPERATION GANYMED • 1977 • Erler Rainer • FRG • OPERATION GANYMEDE
OPERATION GANYMEDE see **OPERATION GANYMED** • 1977
OPERATION GAS-OIL • 1955 • de Broca Philippe • SHT • FRN
OPERATION GOLD INGOT (USA) see **EN PLEIN CIRAGE** • 1961
OPERATION GOLDMAN see **OPERAZIONE GOLDMAN** • 1966
OPERATION GOLDSEVEN see **OPERAZIONE GOLDSEVEN** • 1966
OPERATION HAYLIFT • 1950 • Berke William • USA
OPERATION HEARTBEAT (UKN) see **U.M.C.** • 1969
OPERATION: HIT SQUAD • 1987 • van der Merwe Tonie
OPERATION HONG KONG (USA) see **WEISSE FRACHT FUR HONGKONG** • 1964
OPERATION HOURGLASS • 1954 • Hammid Alexander • USA
OPERATION HYDRA • 1980 • Aschner Antonis • AUS
OPERATION IMPOSSIBLE • 1967 • Santiago Cirio H. • PHL
OPERATION INCHON see **INCHON** • 1980
OPERATION KALIMANTAN see **AKCE KALIMANTAN** • 1961
OPERATION KID BROTHER (USA) see **O.K. CONNERY** • 1968
OPERATION KIRSEBAERSTEN • 1972 • Raben Fritz • DNM • OPERATION CHERRY-STONE
OPERATION LA FONTAINE • 1954 • Dewever Jean • FRN
OPERATION LADY CHAPLIN see **MISSIONE SPECIALE LADY CHAPLIN** • 1966
OPERATION LADY MARLENE • 1975 • Lamoureux Robert • FRN, FRG
OPERATION LAUGHTER see **OPERATZIA "Y"** • 1965
OPERATION LEO • 1980 • Hederberg Hans • SWT
OPERATION LEONTINE (USA) see **FAUT PAS PRENDRE LES ENFANTS DU BON DIEU POUR DES CANARDS SAUVAGES** • 1968
OPERATION LOTUS BLEU see **AGENTE 077 -MISSIONE BLOODY MARY** • 1965
OPERATION LOVEBIRDS (USA) see **SLA FORST, FREDE!** • 1965
OPERATION M see **HELL'S BLOODY DEVILS** • 1967
OPERATION M FOR MADNESS see **OPERASJON V FOR VANNVIDD** • 1970
OPERATION MACEDOINE • 1970 • Scandelari Jacques • FRN • MACEDOINE
OPERATION MAD BALL • 1957 • Quine Richard • USA
OPERATION MAGALI • 1952 • Kish Ladislao • FRN
OPERATION MALAYA • 1953 • MacDonald David • DOC • UKN • TERROR IN THE JUNGLE
OPERATION MANHUNT • 1954 • Alexander Jack • CND
OPERATION MASQUERADE see **MASQUERADE** • 1964
OPERATION MATA-HARI see **OPERACION MATA-HARI** • 1968
OPERATION MERMAID see **BAY OF ST. MICHEL, THE** • 1963
OPERATION MJC • 1965 • Pialat Henri • SHT • FRN
OPERATION MONSTERLAND see **KAIJU SOSHINGEKI** • 1968
OPERATION MOONLIGHT see **ZWEI WHISKY UND EIN SOFA** • 1963
OPERATION MURDER • 1957 • Morris Ernest • SPN
OPERATION 'NAM • 1985 • De Angelis Fabrizio • ITL • RAINBOW PROFESSIONALS ○ COBRA MISSION
OPERATION NEGLIGEE see **TSUYOMUSHI ONNA TO YOWAMUSHI OTOKO** • 1968
OPERATION OF THE K-13 GUNSIGHT • 1944 • Hubley John • ANS • USA
OPERATION OGRE see **OGRO** • 1979
OPERATION PACIFIC • 1951 • Waggner George • USA
OPERATION PACIFIC see **MISSION BATANGAS** • 1967
OPERATION PARADISE see **KISS THE GIRLS AND MAKE THEM DIE** • 1966
OPERATION: PARATROOPER • 1989 • De Palma Frank • USA
OPERATION PETTICOAT • 1959 • Edwards Blake • USA
OPERATION PETTICOAT • 1977 • Astin John • TVM • USA • LIFE IN THE PINK ○ PETTICOAT AFFAIR
OPERATION POKER see **OPERAZIONE POKER** • 1965
OPERATION POURQUOI • 1969 • Dansereau Fernand • CND
OPERATION PROXIMA CENTAURI • D'Bomba Jorg • ANM • GDR
OPERATION: RABBIT • 1952 • Jones Charles M. • ANS • USA
OPERATION RAINBOW see **WAKASHACHO RAINBOW SAKUSEN** • 1967
OPERATION REGINA see **LIEH SHIH CHI HUA** • 1975
OPERATION ST. PETER'S (USA) see **OPERAZIONE SAN PIETRO** • 1967
OPERATION SAN ANTONIO see **OPERACION SAN ANTONIO** • 1968
OPERATION SAN GENNARO (FRN) see **OPERAZIONE SAN GENNARO** • 1966
OPERATION SAWDUST • 1953 • Patterson Don • ANS • USA
OPERATION SEAGULL • 1953 • UKN
OPERATION SECRET • 1952 • Seiler Lewis • USA • DANGER FORWARD
OPERATION SKYBOLT see **KATASKOPI STO SARONIKO** • 1968
OPERATION SNAFU (USA) see **ON THE FIDDLE** • 1961
OPERATION SNAFU (USA) see **ROSOLINO PATERNO SOLDATO** • 1970
OPERATION SNATCH • 1962 • Day Robert • UKN
OPERATION STADIUM see **AZCIJA STADION** • 1978
OPERATION STOGIE • 1960 • Morris Ernest • UKN
OPERATION SURVIE • 1960 • Lavoie Richard, Penvion A. H. • DOC • CND
OPERATION SWALLOW see **BATAILLE DE L'EAU LOURDE, LA** • 1947
OPERATION: TAKE NO PRISONERS • 1988 • Shaw Tom • USA • TAKE NO PRISONERS
OPERATION TEUTONIC SWORD see **TEUTONENSCHWERT** • 1958
OPERATION THIRD FORM • 1966 • Eady David • UKN
OPERATION THUNDERBOLT • 1977 • Golan Menahem • ISR • ENTEBBE: OPERATION THUNDERBOLT
OPERATION TIME BOMB (UKN) see **VENT SE LEVE, LE** • 1959
OPERATION TITAN see **OPERACIJA TICIJAN** • 1963
OPERATION TITANIC • 1943 • Litvak Anatole • DOC • USA
OPERATION TONNERRE • 1954 • Sandoz Gerard • FRN
OPERATION UNDERCOVER (UKN) see **REPORT TO THE COMMISSIONER** • 1975
OPERATION V-2 see **OPERACJA V-2** • 1969
OPERATION VIOLIN-CASE see **UNTERNEHMEN GEIGENKASTEN** • 1985
OPERATION W.E.I.R.D. • Guzman Claudio • USA
OPERATION WAR HEAD see **ON THE FIDDLE** • 1961
OPERATION: WAR ZONE • 1988 • Prior David A. • USA
OPERATION WEISSDORN -THE FOURTH REICH • 1989 • Van Rensburg Manie • SAF
OPERATION X see **DOBUNEZUMI SAKUSEN** • 1962
OPERATION X-70 • 1972 • Servais Raoul • ANS • BLG
OPERATION X (USA) see **MY DAUGHTER JOY** • 1950
OPERATION "Y" AND OTHER ADVENTURES OF SHURIK see **OPERATZIA "Y"** • 1965
OPERATION "Y" AND SHURIK'S OTHER ADVENTURES see **OPERATZIA "Y"** • 1965
OPERATION "Y" (UKN) see **AGENTE LOGAN MISSIONE YPOTRON** • 1966
OPERATION YELLOW VIPER • 1966 • SAF
OPERATOR 13 • 1934 • Boleslawski Richard • USA • SPY 13 (UKN)
OPERATOR AND THE SUPERINTENDENT, THE • 1913 • *Nestor* • USA
OPERATOR AT BIG SANDY, THE • 1915 • *Mitchell Rhea* • USA
OPERATOR AT BLACK ROCK, THE • 1914 • McGowan J. P. • USA
OPERATZIA "Y" • 1965 • Gaidai Leonid • USS • OPERATION "Y" AND SHURIK'S OTHER ADVENTURES ○ OPERATION LAUGHTER ○ OPERATION "Y" AND OTHER ADVENTURES OF SHURIK
OPERAZIONE BAALBECK • 1965 • Fregonese Hugo • FRG, FRN • FBI MISSION BALBECK
OPERAZIONE CONTROSPIONAGGIO • 1965 • Iquino Ignacio F. • ITL, SPN, FRN • OPERACION CONTROESPIONAJE (SPN) ○ ASSO DI PICHE ○ ACE OF SPADES ○ AS DE PIC ○ OPERATION COUNTERSPY ○ ASSO DI PICCHE OPERAZIONE CONTROSPIONAGGIO
OPERAZIONE CROSSBOW (ITL) see **OPERATION CROSSBOW** • 1965
OPERAZIONE GOLDMAN • 1966 • Margheriti Antonio • ITL, SPN • OPERACION GOLDMAN (SPN) ○ LIGHTNING BOLT (USA) ○ OPERATION GOLDMAN
OPERAZIONE GOLDSEVEN • 1966 • Leonardi Alberto • ITL, SPN • TECNICA DI UNA SPIA (ITL) ○ OPERATION GOLDSEVEN
OPERAZIONE KAPPA SPARATE A VISTA • 1978 • Petrini Luigi • ITL
OPERAZIONE LADY CHAPLIN see **MISSIONE SPECIALE LADY CHAPLIN** • 1966
OPERAZIONE MITRA • 1955 • Cristallini Giorgio • ITL • INCUBO E FINITO, L'
OPERAZIONE NOTTE • 1955 • Bennati Giuseppe • ITL
OPERAZIONE PARADISO see **KISS THE GIRLS AND MAKE THEM DIE** • 1966
OPERAZIONE PAURA • 1966 • Bava Mario • ITL • CURSE OF THE DEAD (UKN) ○ KILL BABY KILL (USA) ○ CURSE OF THE LIVING DEAD ○ OPERATION FEAR
OPERAZIONE POKER • 1965 • Civirani Osvaldo • ITL, SPN • OPERACION POKER (SPN) ○ OPERATION POKER
OPERAZIONE RICCHEZZA • 1968 • Musy Glori Vittorio • ITL
OPERAZIONE SAN GENNARO • 1966 • Risi Dino • ITL, FRN, FRG • UNSER BOSS IST EIN DAME (FRG) ○ TREASURE OF SAN GENNARO (USA) ○ OPERATION SAN GENNARO (FRN)
OPERAZIONE SAN PIETRO • 1967 • Fulci Lucio • ITL, FRG, FRN • ABENTEUER DES KARDINAL BRAUN, DIE (FRG) ○ AU DIABLE LES ANGES (FRN) ○ OPERATION ST. PETER'S (USA)
OPERAZIONE TRE GATTI GIALLI • 1966 • Parolini Gianfranco • ITL
OPERENE STINY • 1930 • Marten Leo • CZC • FEATHERED SHADOWS, THE ○ FLEDGED SHADOWS
OPERETTA (USA) see **OPERETTE** • 1940
OPERETTE • 1940 • Forst Willi • FRG • OPERETTA (USA)
OPERN-BALL, DER • 1931 • Neufeld Max • AUS • OPERA BALL
OPERNBALL • 1939 • von Bolvary Geza • FRG • OPERA BALL (USA)
OPERNBALL • 1956 • Marischka Ernst • AUS
OPERNREDOUTE • 1931 • Neufeld Max • FRG
OPERNRING see **IM SONNENSCHEIN** • 1936
OPET TWIST, I • 1964 • Vrbanic Ivo • ANS • YGS • TWIST AGAIN (USA)
OPETANIE • 1973 • Lenartowicz Stanislaw • PLN • OBSESSION
OPFER • 1919 • *Toelle Carola* • FRG
OPFER • 1924 • *William Kahn-Film* • FRG
OPFER, DAS • 1918 • May Joe • FRG
OPFER DER CLAUDIA NICOLAJEWNA, DAS • 1920 • *Schroth Heinrich* • FRG
OPFER DER ELLEN LARSEN, DAS • 1921 • Stein Paul L. • FRG
OPFER DER GESELLSCHAFT • 1918 • Grunwald Willy • FRG
OPFER DER HYANEN see **HYANEN DER WELT 1** • 1921
OPFER DER KEUSCHHEIT see **GOTZENDAMMERUNG** • 1920
OPFER DER LEIDENSCHAFT, EIN • *Riemann Johannes* • FRG
OPFER DER LIEBE • *Orfi-Orion-Film* • FRG
OPFER DER LIEBE • 1921 • Eckstein Franz • FRG
OPFER DER LIEBE • 1923 • Hartwig Martin • FRG
OPFER DER NACHT, DAS • 1915 • Ralph Louis • FRG
OPFER DER SCHMACH see **VERLORENE TOCHTER 2** • 1919
OPFER DER YELLA ROGESIUS, DAS • 1918 • Portegg R. • FRG
OPFER DES HERZENS • 1950 • Meyer Johannes • FRG
OPFER EINER FRAU, DAS • 1916 • *Sandten Thea* • FRG
OPFER UM OPFER • 1918 • Mack Max • FRG
OPFERGANG • 1944 • Harlan Veit • FRG • GREAT SACRIFICE, THE (UKN)
OPFINDERS SKAEBNE, EN • 1911 • Blom August • DNM • AEROPLANE INVENTOR, THE
OPHELIA • 1916 • Kaufman Joseph • SHT • USA
OPHELIA • 1962 • Chabrol Claude • FRN, ITL
OPHELIA COMES TO TOWN see **OFELIA KOMMER TIL BYEN** • 1986
OPHIR, DIE STADT DER VERGANGENHEIT see **HERRIN DER WELT 5, DIE** • 1919
OPHOP see **OP HOP -HOP OP** • 1966
OPIATE '67 (USA) see **MOSTRI, I** • 1963
OPICI CISAR • 1955 • Lacko Jan, Tsao Drei • CZC • EMPEROR OF MONKEYS
OPINIAO PUBLICA, A • 1967 • Jabor Arnaldo • DOC • BRZ • PUBLIC OPINION
OPINIONE PUBBLICA • 1954 • Corgnati Maurizio • ITL, FRN
OPIO • 1949 • Peon Ramon • MXC • DROGA MALDITA, LA
OPITSAH -APACHE FOR SWEETHEART • 1912 • *Oakman Wheeler* • USA
OPIUM • 1919 • Reinert Robert • FRG
OPIUM, L' • 1911 • Leprince Rene • FRN
OPIUM AND THE STICK, THE see **OPIUM ET LE BATON, L'** • 1970
OPIUM AND WHIPS see **OPIUM ET LE BATON, L'** • 1970
OPIUM CIGARETTES, THE • 1914 • Kinder Stuart • UKN
OPIUM DEN, THE see **OPIUMHALEN** • 1911
OPIUM DREAMS see **OPIUMS DROMMEN** • 1914
OPIUM ET LE BATON, L' • 1970 • Rachedi Ahmed • ALG • OPIUM AND THE STICK, THE ○ OPIUM AND WHIPS ○ THALA
OPIUM LORD, THE see **KHUN-SA THE OPIUM EMPEROR** • 1983
OPIUM SMOKER'S DREAM • 1906 • *Biograph* • USA
OPIUM SMOKER'S DREAM, THE see **OPIUMS DROMMEN** • 1914
OPIUM SMUGGLER, THE • 1911 • *American* • USA
OPIUM SMUGGLERS, THE • 1912 • *Duncan William* • USA
OPIUM TRAIL, THE see **DEADLY CHINA DOLL** • 1973
OPIUM WAR, THE see **LIN ZEXU** • 1959
OPIUMHALEN • 1911 • Jaenzon Julius • SWD • OPIUM DEN, THE
OPIUMKERINGO • 1943 • Balazs Bela • HNG
OPIUMS DROMMEN • 1914 • Holger-Madsen • DNM • OPIUM DREAMS ○ OPIUM SMOKER'S DREAM, THE
OPKLADA • 1971 • Randic Zdravko • YGS • WAGER, THE
OPLOSSING, DE • 1983 • Francken Sandor • NTH
OPNAME • 1979 • van Zuylen Erik, Kok Marja • NTH • IN FOR TREATMENT
OPOLE REGION, THE see **ZIEMIA OPOLSKA** • 1959
OPONTHOUD, HET • 1969 • Crama Nico • SHT • NTH
OPOWIEDZIAL DZIECIOL SOWIE • 1952 • Nehrebecki Wladyslaw • ANS • PLN • WOODPECKER TOLD THE OWL, THE
OPOWIESC ATLANTYCKA • 1954 • Jakubowska Wanda • PLN • ATLANTIC STORY, AN
OPOWIESC O DRODZE • 1958 • Slesicki Wladyslaw • DOC • PLN • STORY ABOUT THE ROAD ○ TALE OF A JOURNEY
OPOWIESC W CZERWIENI • 1974 • Kluba Henryk • PLN • WRITTEN IN BLOOD
OPPAS, DE • 1981 • Verbrugge Caspar • SHT • NTH
OPPAT MED GRONA HISSEN • 1952 • Larsson Borje • SWD • UP WITH THE GREEN LIFT ○ GRONA HISSEN
OPPENHEIM FAMILY, THE see **SEMLA OPPENHEIM** • 1938
OPPIO PER OPPIO • 1972 • Bozzetto Bruno • ANM • ITL
OPPIUM METS MAGT, I • 1915 • Dinesen Robert • DNM
OPPOL • 1980 • Sethumadhavan K. S. • IND • ELDER SISTER
OPPONENT, THE • 1987 • Martino Sergio • ITL • BLOODFIGHT
OPPORTUNE BURGLAR, THE • 1912 • *Walthall Henry B.* • USA
OPPORTUNITIES FOR THE YOUNG see **VALIBA VIRUNDHU** • 1967
OPPORTUNITY • 1912 • *Bell Gaston* • USA
OPPORTUNITY • 1916 • *Maya Film* • USA
OPPORTUNITY • 1918 • Collins John H. • USA
OPPORTUNITY AND THE MAN • 1911 • Salter Harry • USA
OPPOSING FORCE • 1986 • Karson Eric • USA • HELLCAMP ○ HELL CAMP
OPPOSITE SEX, THE • 1956 • Miller David • USA
OPPRESSED, THE • 1929 • Asselin Henry
OPPRESSION see **PROGON** • 1983
OPPRIMES, LES • 1923 • Roussell Henry • FRN
OPRY HOUSE, THE • 1928 • Disney Walt, Iwerks Ub • ANS • USA
OPSADA • 1956 • Marjanovic Branko • YGS • SIEGE, THE
OPSPORING VAN AARDOLIE, DE • 1954 • Haanstra Bert • DOC • NTH • SEARCH FOR OIL, THE
OPSTEEL • 1968 • Marsili Emilio • SHT • ITL
OPSTINSKO DETE • 1951 • Djordjevic Purisa • YGS • CHILD OF THE COMMUNITY, A
OPTA EMPFANGT • 1936 • Alexeieff Alexandre • FRG
OPTIC TICKLERS • 1966 • Jones Stuart Wynn • ANS • UKN
OPTICAL IMPULSES IN GEOMETRIC PROGRESSION see **IMPULSOS OPTICOS EN PROGRESION GEOMETRICA** • 1971
OPTICAL POEM • 1938 • Fischinger Oskar • ANS • USA
OPTIMIST • 1978 • Czurko Edward • MTV • CND
OPTIMIST, DER • 1938 • Emo E. W. • FRG
OPTIMIST, THE • 1923 • USA
OPTIMIST, THE see **HALLELUJAH, I'M A BUM** • 1933
OPTIMIST, THE (UKN) see **BIG SHOT, THE** • 1931
OPTIMIST AND PESSIMIST see **OPTIMIST I PESIMIST** • 1973
OPTIMIST I PESIMIST • 1973 • Grgic Zlatko • ANS • YGS • OPTIMISTS AND PESSIMISTS ○ OPTIMIST AND PESSIMIST
OPTIMISTIC ORIENTAL OCCULTS, THE • 1916 • *Chamberlain Riley* • USA
OPTIMISTIC TRAGEDY, THE see **OPTIMISTICHESKAYA TRAGEDIYA** • 1964

OPTIMISTICHESKAYA TRAGEDIYA • 1964 • Samsonov Samson • USS • OPTIMISTIC TRAGEDY, THE
OPTIMISTS, THE • 1973 • Simmons Anthony • UKN • OPTIMISTS OF NINE ELMS, THE
OPTIMISTS AND PESSIMISTS see **OPTIMIST I PESIMIST** • 1973
OPTIMISTS OF NINE ELMS, THE see **OPTIMISTS, THE** • 1973
OPTION, L' • Sow Thierno Faty • SNL
OPTION, THE • 1914 • *Maison Edna* • USA
OPTIONS • 1989 • Vila Camilo • USA
OPUS 1 • 1948 • Roos Jorgen • DOC • DNM
OPUS 1 • 1964 • Hebert Pierre • ANS • CND
OPUS 1 • 1972 • Borenstein Joyce • SHT • CND
OPUS 2 • 1964 • Hebert Pierre • ANS • CND
OPUS 3 • 1966 • Hebert Pierre • ANS • CND
OPUS 6 see **OPUS SEIS** • 1969
OPUS 65 see **DIA COMENZO AYER, EL** • 1965
OPUS I • 1922 • Ruttmann Walter • FRG
OPUS II • 1923 • Ruttmann Walter • FRG
OPUS III • 1924 • Ruttmann Walter • FRG
OPUS IV • 1925 • Ruttmann Walter • FRG
OPUS JAZZ • 1963 • Majewski Janusz • SHT • PLN
OPUS SEIS • 1969 • Guzman Patricio • SPN • OPUS 6
OR, L' • 1934 • de Poligny Serge, Hartl Karl • FRN
OR BLANC, L' • 1964 • Shawqi Khalil • SHT • EGY
OR BLEU, L' • Aloisi Gabriel • FRN
OR 'D' UR • 1983 • Chbib Bachar • CND
OR DANS LA MONTAGNE, L' • 1938 • Haufler Max • FRN, SWT • FARINET, ODER DAS FALSCHE GELD ○ FARINET, OU LA FAUSSE MONNAIE ○ FAUX MONNAYEURS
OR DANS LA RUE, L' • 1934 • Bernhardt Curtis • FRN
OR DE L'AVARE, L' • 1916 • Burguet Charles • FRN
OR DES CESARS, L' see **ORO PER I CESARI** • 1963
OR DES MERS, L' • 1932 • Epstein Jean • FRN • GOLD FROM THE SEA
OR DES PHARAONS, L' • 1952 • de Gastyne Marco • FRN • OR DU NIL, L'
OR DON'T YOU DARE? see **...OF DURF JE NIET?** • 1965
OR DU CRISTOBAL, L' • 1939 • Stelli Jean, Becker Jacques (U/c) • FRN
OR DU DUC, L' • 1965 • Baratier Jacques • FRN, ITL
OR DU NIL, L' see **OR DES PHARAONS, L'** • 1952
OR ET LE PLUMB, L' • 1966 • Cuniot Alain • FRN • GOLD AND LEAD
OR FOREVER HOLD YOUR PEACE • 1970 • Nicholson Arch, McCullough Chris • DOC • ASL
OR GRIS, L' • 1981 • Ruiz Raul • DOC • FRN • GREY GOLD
OR LIQUIDE, L' • 1958 • Lanoe Henri • SHT • FRN
OR POUR LES CESARS (FRN) see **ORO PER I CESARI** • 1963
OR QUI BRULE, L' • 1912 • Machin Alfred • NTH
...OR TO BE KILLED see **...NEBO BYT** • 1985
ORA DELLA CRISALIDE, L' • 1973 • Dall'Ara Renato • ITL
ORA DELLA VERITA, L' (ITL) see **MINUTE DE VERITE, LA** • 1952
ORA EGAROJON • 1972 • Islam Chashi Nazrul • BNG • THOSE ELEVEN MEN
ORA NOVE LEZIONE DI CHIMICA see **ORE 9 LEZIONE DI CHIMICA** • 1941
ORA PER VIVERE, UN' see **ANCHE L'INFERNO TREMA** • 1958
ORA PONCIANO! • 1936 • Soria Gabriel • MXC • COME ON, PONCIANO (USA)
ORA PRO NOBIS • 1909 • *Warwick Trading Co* • UKN
ORA PRO NOBIS • 1917 • Wilson Rex • UKN
ORA PRO NOBIS, OR THE POOR ORPHAN'S LAST PRAYER • 1901 • Booth W. R. • UKN • PRO NOBIS ○ FOR US
ORA SUPREMA see **SOLITUDINE** • 1942
ORA TIS DHIKEOSINIS, I • 1967 • Katsimitsoulias Andreas • GRC • HOUR OF JUSTICE, THE
ORA TIS ORGIS, I • 1968 • Grigoriou Grigoris • GRC • HOUR OF WRATH
ORA X -PATTUGLIA SUICIDA • 1969 • Quartararo Gaetano • ITL
'ORACE • 1921 • Merwin Bannister • UKN
'ORACE'S ORDEAL • 1916 • Wilson Frank • UKN
ORACLE, THE • 1953 • Pennington-Richards C. M. • UKN • HORSE'S MOUTH, THE (USA) ○ TO TELL THE TRUTH
ORACLE, THE • 1985 • Findlay Roberta • USA
ORACLE DE DELPHES, L' • 1903 • Melies Georges • FRN • ORACLE OF DELPHI, THE (USA)
ORACLE OF DELPHI, THE (USA) see **ORACLE DE DELPHES, L'** • 1903
ORACLE WINDS, THE see **ASSIFAT AL-AOURAS** • 1967
ORAGE • 1937 • Allegret Marc • FRN • VENIN, LE
ORAGE • 1952 • Billon Pierre, Capitani Giorgio • FRN, ITL • DELIRIO (ITL)
ORAGE, L' • 1917 • de Morlhon Camille • FRN
ORAGE D'ETE • 1949 • Gehret Jean • FRN, ITL
ORAGE EN COLERE BRISE LA VOIX DE LA CASCADE, L' • 1984 • Llorca Denis • FRN
ORAL GENERATION, THE • 1973 • USA
ORAMUNDE • 1931 • Etting Emlen • SHT • USA
ORANG-OUTANG, THE • 1915 • Chaudet Louis W. • USA
ORANG VILLAGE • 1957 • NKR
ORANGE BANDIT, THE • 1914 • *Cummings Dick* • USA
ORANGE GROWER'S DAUGHTER, THE • 1909 • *Kalem* • USA
ORANGE HEIN see **ORANJE HEIN** • 1925
ORANGE PEEL • 1907 • Williamson James • UKN
ORANGE ROAD EXPRESS • 1977 • Omori Kazuki • JPN
ORANGE VALLEY see **SOLOTISTAJA DOLINA** • 1937
ORANGE WATERING TRUCK, THE see **LOCSOLOKOCSI** • 1974
ORANGES AND LEMONS • 1923 • Roach Hal • SHT • USA
ORANGES ARE NOT THE ONLY FRUIT • 1989 • Kidron Beeban • UKN
ORANGES DE JAFFA, LES • 1938 • Alexeieff Alexandre • FRN
ORANJE HEIN • 1925 • Benno Alex • NTH • ORANGE HEIN
ORAO • 1990 • Tadic Zoran • YGS • EAGLE, THE
ORAON • 1955 • *Ghatak Ritwik* • DOC • IND
ORAS-ORAS • 1989 • PHL
ORASUL MEU • 1967 • Popescu-Gopo Ion • RMN • MY CITY
ORATOR • 1969 • Dovnikovic Borivoj, Vunak Dragutin • YGS
ORATOR, THE see **UVODNI SLOVO PRONESE** • 1964
ORATOR, KNIGHT AND COW CHARMER • 1912 • *Thanhouser* • USA
ORATORIO FOR PRAGUE • 1968 • Nemec Jan • DOC • CZC • ORATORIUM FOR PRAGUE
ORATORIUM FOR PRAGUE see **ORATORIO FOR PRAGUE** • 1968
ORAZI E CURIAZI • 1961 • Young Terence, Baldi Ferdinando • ITL • DUEL OF CHAMPIONS (USA) ○ DUEL OF THE CHAMPIONS ○ HORATIO
ORAZI E CURIAZI TRE A DUE • 1977 • Mariuzzo Giorgio • ITL
ORBITA MORTAL (SPN) see **PERRY RHODAN -SOS AUS DEM WELTALL** • 1967
ORCA • 1977 • Anderson Michael • USA • ORCA, THE KILLER WHALE ○ ORCA, KILLER WHALE
ORCA, LA • 1976 • Visconti Eriprando • ITL • PRISONER OF PASSION ○ OGRESS, THE
ORCA, KILLER WHALE see **ORCA** • 1977
ORCA, THE KILLER WHALE see **ORCA** • 1977
ORCHARD OF PERE LAURENT, THE see **LAWRENCE'S ORCHARD** • 1952
ORCHARD STREET • 1956 • Jacobs Ken • USA
ORCHESTERPROBE • 1933 • Valentin Karl, Lamac Carl • FRG
ORCHESTERSZENE • 1928 • Valentin Karl • FRG
ORCHESTRA CONDUCTOR, THE see **DYRYGENT** • 1980
ORCHESTRA LAND • 1964 • Karanovich Anatoli • ANS • USS
ORCHESTRA-MAN • 1971 • Zambrano Roque • SHT • VNZ
ORCHESTRA OF YOUTH see **ORKESTAR JEDNE MLADOSTI** • 1985
ORCHESTRA REHEARSAL (USA) see **PROVA D'ORCHESTRA** • 1979
ORCHESTRA WIVES • 1942 • Mayo Archie • USA
ORCHESTRATION OF COLOUR • 1923 • Richter Hans • FRG
ORCHESTRE ET DIAMANTS • 1961 • Rancy • SHT • FRN
ORCHESTRE ROUGE, L' • 1989 • Rouffio Jacques • FRN
ORCHID DANCER, THE see **DANSEUSE ORCHIDEE, LA** • 1928
ORCHID FOR NO.1, AN see **NO.1 OF THE SECRET SERVICE** • 1978
ORCHID FOR THE TIGER, AN (UKN) see **TIGRE SE PARFUME A LA DYNAMITE, LE** • 1965
ORCHIDEA AZZURRA see **CORTOCIRCUITO** • 1943
ORCHIDEA ROSSO SANGUE, UN' (ITL) see **CHAIR DE L'ORCHIDEE, LA** • 1974
ORCHIDEEN • 1920 • Hacker Gottfried • FRG
ORCHIDS AND ERMINE • 1927 • Santell Alfred • USA
ORCHIDS TO YOU • 1935 • Seiter William A. • USA
ORDEAL • 1958 • Roshal Grigori • USS
ORDEAL • 1973 • Katzin Lee H. • TVM • USA
ORDEAL • 1977 • Ordynsky Vassily • MTV • USS
ORDEAL see **JUNANGE** • 1932
ORDEAL, THE • 1909 • *Edison* • USA
ORDEAL, THE • 1910 • *Nestor* • USA
ORDEAL, THE • 1912 • *Pathe* • USA
ORDEAL, THE • 1914 • *Life Photo Film* • USA
ORDEAL, THE • 1914 • Santschi Thomas • *Selig* • USA
ORDEAL, THE • 1922 • Powell Paul • USA
ORDEAL, THE • 1981 • Pringle Julian • ASL
ORDEAL BY GOLF • 1924 • Wilson Andrew P. • UKN
ORDEAL BY ICE • 1945 • Daly Tom • DOC • CND
ORDEAL BY ICE • 1945 • Gibson Joe, Mayerovitch David • DCS • CND
ORDEAL BY INNOCENCE • 1984 • Davis Desmond • UKN • AGATHA CHRISTIE'S ORDEAL BY INNOCENCE
ORDEAL OF BILL CARNEY, THE • 1981 • London Jerry • TVM • USA
ORDEAL OF DR. MUDD, THE • 1980 • Wendkos Paul • TVM • USA
ORDEAL OF ELIZABETH, THE • 1916 • North Wilfred • USA
ORDEAL OF HELEN GRAY, THE • 1910 • *Powers* • USA
ORDEAL OF PATTY HEARST, THE • 1979 • Wendkos Paul • TVM • USA
ORDEAL OF ROSETTA, THE • 1918 • Chautard Emile • USA
ORDEALS OF DANIEL, THE see **TAN-NI-ERH-TE KU-SHIH** • 1982
ORDEN DE VIVIR • 1971 • *Cima* • MXC
ORDEN: FX 18 DEBE MORIR • 1965 • Cloche Maurice • SPN, FRN, ITL • FX-18 SECRET AGENT ○ ORDER: FX 18 MUST DIE ○ AGENTE X-77 ORDINE DI UCCIDERE
ORDER • 1969 • Kijowicz Miroslaw • ANS • YGS
ORDER AND DISORDER see **POSTAVA K PODPIRANI** • 1963
ORDER: FX 18 MUST DIE see **ORDEN: FX 18 DEBE MORIR** • 1965
ORDER IN THE COURT • 1912 • *Reliance* • USA
ORDER IN THE COURT • 1919 • Roach Hal • SHT • USA
ORDER NI OSANG • 1968 • Navarro Marcelino D. • PHL • ORDER OF OSANG
ORDER OF DEATH • 1983 • Faenza Roberto • ITL • COP KILLERS ○ CORRUPT ○ COPKILLER
ORDER OF MERIT, THE see **POUR LE MERITE** • 1938
ORDER OF OSANG see **ORDER NI OSANG** • 1968
ORDER OF THE BATH, THE • 1915 • *Horseshoe* • UKN
ORDER OF THE BATH, THE • 1915 • Kellino W. P. • *Cricks* • UKN
ORDER OF THE BLACK EAGLE • 1987 • Keeter Worth • USA
ORDER OF THE COURT, AN • 1917 • Hurst Paul C. • SHT • USA
ORDER OF THE DAISY (UKN) see **COMPAGNONS DE LA MARGUERITE, LES** • 1967
ORDER OF THE EAGLE • 1988 • Baldwin Tom • USA
ORDER PLEASE see **ONE NEW YORK NIGHT** • 1935
ORDER TO KILL (USA) see **CLAN DE LOS INMORALES, EL** • 1973
ORDERED TO LOVE (USA) see **LEBENSBORN** • 1961
ORDERLY, THE • 1918 • Gillstrom Arvid E. • USA
ORDERLY, THE see **ORDONNANCE, L'** • 1935
ORDERLY, THE (USA) see **ORDONNANCE, L'** • 1933
ORDERLY ROOM, THE • 1928 • Croise Hugh • UKN
ORDERS • 1915 • Santschi Thomas • USA
ORDERS see **ORDRES, LES** • 1974
ORDERS ARE ORDERS • 1954 • Paltenghi David • UKN
ORDERS IS ORDERS • 1916 • Ford Francis • SHT • USA
ORDERS IS ORDERS • 1933 • Forde Walter • UKN
ORDERS TO KILL • 1958 • Asquith Anthony • UKN
ORDET • 1943 • Molander Gustaf • SWD • WORD, THE
ORDET • 1954 • Dreyer Carl T. • DNM • WORD, THE
ORDINARY BATH, THE • 1985 • Caulfield Paul • DOC • CND
ORDINARY FAMILY, AN see **FAMILIA DE TANTAS, UNA** • 1948
ORDINARY FASCISM see **OBYKNOVENNYY FASHIZM** • 1965
ORDINARY GUY, AN see **ORDINARY HEROES** • 1985
ORDINARY HEROES • 1985 • Cooper Peter H. • USA • ORDINARY GUY, AN
ORDINARY HOUR IN THE EXTRAORDINARY LIFE OF ROBIN BECKETT, AN see **LIFE OF ROBIN BECKETT** • 1963
ORDINARY PEOPLE • 1942 • Holmes J. B., Lee Jack • DOC • UKN
ORDINARY PEOPLE • 1980 • Redford Robert • USA
ORDINARY PEOPLE see **PROSTYE LYUDI** • 1945
ORDINARY STORY, AN see **PROSTAYA ISTORIYA** • 1960
ORDINARY TENDERNESS see **TENDRESSE ORDINAIRE** • 1973
ORDINARY WAYS see **KOZOS UTON** • 1953
ORDINATEUR DES POMPES FUNEBRES, L' • 1976 • Pires Gerard • FRN, ITL
ORDINATEUR ET TETE • 1984 • Beaudry Diane • CND • HEAD START, MEETING THE COMPUTER CHALLENGE
ORDINATIONS • 1954 • Agostini Philippe • FRN
ORDINATIONS • 1955 • Leenhardt Roger • DCS • FRN
ORDINE DELLE 55: ELIMINATE BORMAN! • 1972 • Bardem Juan Antonio • ITL
ORDINE DI UCCIDERE see **TESTA DEL SERPENTE, LA** • 1974
ORDINE FIRMATO IN BIANCO • 1975 • Manera Guido • ITL
ORDINI SONO ORDINI, GLI • 1972 • Giraldi Franco • ITL
ORDNUNG • 1980 • Saless Sohrab Shahid • FRG • ALL IN ORDER
ORDOG, AZ • 1918 • Curtiz Michael • HNG • DEVIL, THE
ORDOGI KISERTETEK • 1986 • Maar Gyula • HNG • TEMPTATIONS OF THE DEVIL
ORDONNANCE, L' • 1921 • Tourjansky Victor • FRN
ORDONNANCE, L' • 1933 • Tourjansky Victor • FRN • ORDERLY, THE (USA) ○ HELENE
ORDONNANCE, L' • 1935 • Schiffrin Simon • FRN • ORDERLY, THE
ORDRE, L' • 1973 • Pollet Jean-Daniel • FRN
ORDRE DES CHOSES, L' • 1974 • Dansereau Fernand, Rossignol Yolande • SHT • CND
ORDRE DES CHOSES OU MORT UN MATIN, L' • 1962 • Lange Henri • SHT • FRN
ORDRE DU ROI • 1909 • Carre Michel • FRN
ORDRE ET BEAUTE PAR L'URBANISME • 1957 • Haesaerts Paul • BLG
ORDRE ET LA SECURITE DU MONDE, L' • 1979 • d'Anna Claude • FRN
ORDRES, LES • 1974 • Brault Michel • CND • ORDERS
ORE 9 LEZIONE DI CHIMICA • 1941 • Mattoli Mario • ITL • ORA NOVE LEZIONE DI CHIMICA
ORE 10 LEZIONE DI CANTO • 1955 • Girolami Marino • ITL
ORE DELL'AMORE, LE • 1963 • Salce Luciano • ITL • HOURS OF LOVE, THE
ORE DI TERRORE • 1971 • Meyer R. • ITL
ORE MO OMAE MO • 1946 • Naruse Mikio • JPN • BOTH YOU AND I
ORE MO OTOKO-SA • 1955 • Yamamoto Kajiro • JPN
ORE NI KAKETA YATSURA • 1962 • Suzuki Seijun • JPN
ORE NI MAKASERO see **HEITAI YAKUZA: ORE NI MAKASERO** • 1967
ORE NI TSUITE-KOI • 1965 • Horikawa Hiromichi • JPN • YOU CAN IF YOU TRY
ORE NO NAMIDA WA AMAKUNAI • 1960 • Harada Hasuo • JPN
ORE NO SENAKA NI HI GA ATARU • 1963 • Nakahira Ko • JPN • I HAVE THE SUN IN MY BACK
ORE NUDE, LE • 1964 • Vicario Marco • ITL • NAKED HOURS, THE
ORE PASSO • 1894 • *Edison* • USA
ORE PLUNDERERS, THE • 1916 • Horne James W. • SHT • USA
ORE RAIDERS, THE • 1927 • Wyler William • SHT • USA
ORE TO AITSU NO MONOGATARI • 1982 • Asama Yoshitaka • JPN • STORY OF ME AND HIM, A
ORE VIOLENTE • 1968 • Labro Maurice • ITL
ORE WA JOYIMBO • 1950 • Inagaki Hiroshi • JPN
ORE WA MATTERU-ZE • 1957 • Kurahara Koreyoshi • JPN • I'LL BE WAITING
ORE WA SHINANAI • 1957 • Iwama Tsuruo • JPN
ORE WA TOKICHIRO • 1955 • Mori Kazuo • JPN
OREA EGIOTISA • 1968 • Konstantinou Panos • GRC • BEAUTIFUL GIRL FROM EGION, A
OREG, AZ • 1971 • Macskassy Gyula, Varnai Gyorgy • ANS • HNG • OLD WOMAN, THE
OREG ES FIATAL • 1969 • Macskassy Gyula, Varnai Gyorgy • ANS • HNG • OLD AND YOUNG
OREGON PASSAGE • 1957 • Landres Paul • USA
OREGON TRAIL, THE • 1936 • Pembroke Scott • USA
OREGON TRAIL, THE • 1939 • Beebe Ford, Goodkind Saul • SRL • USA
OREGON TRAIL, THE • 1945 • Carr Thomas • USA
OREGON TRAIL, THE • 1959 • Fowler Gene Jr. • USA
OREGON TRAIL, THE • 1976 • Sagal Boris • TVM • USA
OREGON TRAIL SCOUTS • 1947 • Springsteen R. G. • USA
OREILLE, L' • 1923 • Cohl Emile • ANS • FRN
OREILLE MENE L'ENQUETE, LES • 1974 • Melancon Andre • SHT • CND
OREKHOVYI KHLEB • 1980 • Zhebrunas Arunas • USS • NUT BREAD
OREMUS ALLELUJA E COSI SIA • 1972 • Caltabiano Alfio • ITL
ORENI MAKASERO • 1958 • Hidaka Shigeaki • JPN
ORENI SAWARUTO ABUNAINE • Hasebe Yasuharu • JPN • IF YOU TOUCH ME ○ DANGER
ORESTE • 1916 • Lolli Alberto Carlo • ITL
ORESTES see **ORESTIS** • 1969
ORESTIS • 1969 • Fotopoulos Vassilis • GRC, USA • ORESTES
ORETACHI NO CHI GA YURUSANAI • 1964 • Suzuki Kiyonori • JPN
ORETACHI NO WEDDING • 1983 • Negishi Kichitaro • JPN • OUR WEDDING
ORETACHI NON KOKYOGAKU • 1978 • Asama Yoshitaka • JPN • OUR OWN ORCHESTRA
ORFANA DEL GHETTO, L' • 1955 • Campogalliani Carlo • ITL
ORFANELLA DELLE STELLE, L' • 1947 • Zannini Giovanni • ITL
ORFEO • 1971 • Leaf Caroline • ANS • USA
ORFEO NEGRO (ITL) see **ORFEU NEGRO** • 1958
ORFEO NOVE • 1973 • Schipa Tito Jr. • ITL

ORFEU NEGRO • 1958 • Camus Marcel • FRN, ITL • ORFEO NEGRO (ITL) ○ BLACK ORPHEUS (USA)
ORFEUS I UNDERJORDEN • 1910 • Magnusson Charles • SWD • ORPHEUS IN THE UNDERWORLD
ORFEUS & JULIE • 1969 • Barfod Bent • SHT • DNM
ORFEUSZ ES EURYDIKE • 1985 • Gaal Istvan • HNG • ORPHEUS AND EURYDICE
ORFF-SCHULWERK, RHYTMISCH-MELODISCHE ERZIEHUNG • 1960 • Tichawsky Heinz, Strobel Hans-Rolf • FRG
ORG • 1979 • Birri Fernando • ARG
ORGAN, THE • 1964 • Uher Stefan • CZC
ORGAN GRINDER, THE • 1912 • *Kalem* • USA
ORGAN GRINDER, THE • 1933 • Ising Rudolf • ANS • USA
ORGAN-GRINDER'S DAUGHTER, THE • 1908 • *Urban* • USA
ORGAN GRINDER'S SWING • 1937 • Fleischer Dave • ANS • USA
ORGAN GRINDER'S WARD, THE • 1912 • *Reliance* • USA
ORGANCHIK • 1933 • Khodateyev Nikolai • USS • MUSIC BOX, THE
ORGANCHIK • 1946 • Khodateyev Nikolai • USS • CANNONBALL, THE
ORGANIC FRAGMENT • 1945 • Fischinger Oskar • ANS • USA
ORGANILLERO, EL • 1955 • Martinez Solares Gilberto • MXC
ORGANILLOS, LOS see **PIANOS MECANICOS, LOS** • 1965
ORGANISATION see **ORGANIZATION** • 1946
ORGANISATION SCIENTIFIQUE DU TRAVAIL, L' • Cantagrel Marc • DOC • FRN
ORGANISED VIOLENCE see **SOSHIKI BORYOKU** • 1967
ORGANISED VIOLENCE (TWO) see **ZOKU SOSHIKI BORYOKU** • 1967
ORGANISING FOR POWER: THE ALINSKY APPROACH • 1968 • Klein Bonnie • SER • CND
ORGANISME DE CONSOLIDATION DU CINEMA, L' • 1959 • Shawqi Khalil • SHT • EGY
ORGANIST, THE • 1913 • *Dragon* • USA
ORGANIST AT ST. VITUS, THE see **VARHANIK U SV. VITA** • 1929
ORGANIST OF ST. VIT, THE see **VARHANIK U SV. VITA** • 1929
ORGANITO DE LA TARDE, EL • 1924 • Ferreyra Jose • ARG
ORGANIVERSE • 1974 • Kohanyi Julius • CND
ORGANIZATION • 1946 • Mulholland Donald • SHT • CND • ORGANISATION
ORGANIZATION, THE • 1971 • Medford Don • USA
ORGANIZER, THE (USA) see **COMPAGNI, I** • 1963
ORGASM see **ORGASMO** • 1968
ORGASMES • Reinhard Pierre B. • FRN
ORGASMO • 1968 • Lenzi Umberto • ITL, FRN • FOLLE ENVIE D'AIMER, UNE (FRN) ○ PARANOIA (UKN) ○ ORGASM
ORGELBAUER VON ST. MARIEN, DER • 1961 • Rieger August • AUS
ORGELSTABE • 1923-27 • Fischinger Oskar • ANM • FRG • STAFFS
ORGIA, LA • 1978 • Bellmunt Francisco • SPN • ORGY, THE
ORGIA DE LOS MUERTOS, LA • 1972 • Merino Jose Luis • SPN, ITL • DRACULA THE TERROR OF THE LIVING DEAD ○ BEYOND THE LIVING DEAD ○ ORGIA DEI MORTI, LA ○ ORGY OF THE DEAD, THE
ORGIA DEI MORTI, LA see **ORGIA DE LOS MUERTOS, LA** • 1972
ORGIA DI SOLE see **AI VOSTRI ORDINA, SIGNORA!** • 1939
ORGIA NOCTURNA DE LOS VAMPIROS, LA • 1972 • Klimovsky Leon • SPN, ITL • VAMPIRES' NIGHT ORGY, THE (USA)
ORGIES ADOLESCENTES • 1976 • Roy Jean-Claude • FRN
ORGIES DU DOCTEUR ORLOFF, LES (FRN) see **SOLO UN ATAUD** • 1966
ORGIES DU GOLDEN SALOON, LES • 1973 • Roussel Gilbert • FRN • FILLES DU GOLDEN SALOON, LES
ORGIES OF DR. ORLOFF, THE see **SOLO UN ATAUD** • 1966
ORGIES POUR NYMPHOMANES • 1981 • Thierry Alain • FRN
ORGOGLIO • 1938 • Elter Marco • ITL • ALBA DI DOMANI
ORGUEIL, L' • 1907 • Dumeny M. M., Legrand • FRN • ARROGANCE ○ PRIDE
ORGUEILLEUX, LES • 1953 • Allegret Yves, Portas Rafael E. • FRN, MXC • PROUD AND THE BEAUTIFUL, THE (USA) ○ ORGULLOSOS, LOS (MXC) ○ PROUD ONES, THE
ORGULLO • 1955 • Mur Oti • SPN
ORGULLO DE MUJER • 1955 • Delgado Miguel M. • MXC
ORGULLOSOS, LOS (MXC) see **ORGUEILLEUX, LES** • 1953
ORGY see **KYOEN** • 1954
ORGY, THE • 1915 • Kaufman Joseph • USA
ORGY, THE see **RANKO** • 1967
ORGY, THE see **ORGIA, LA** • 1978
ORGY AT LIL'S PLACE, THE • 1963 • Nehemiah J. • USA • AT LIL'S PLACE
ORGY AT THE TEAHOUSE see **OZASHIKI 48 TAI** • 1968
ORGY GIRL '69 • 1968 • Canton Robert • USA • "O" GIRLS 1969 ○ ORGY GIRLS
ORGY GIRLS see **ORGY GIRL '69** • 1968
ORGY IN THE OZARKS • 1970 • *Mj Productions* • USA
ORGY OF THE DEAD • 1965 • Stephen A. C. • USA • ORGY OF THE VAMPIRES
ORGY OF THE DEAD, THE see **ORGIA DE LOS MUERTOS, LA** • 1972
ORGY OF THE GOLDEN NUDES see **HONEYMOON OF HORROR** • 1964
ORGY OF THE VAMPIRES see **ORGY OF THE DEAD** • 1965
ORHAZ A KARPATOKBAN • 1914 • Korda Alexander • HNG • WATCH-TOWER IN THE CARPATHIANS
ORI • 1988 • Gerber • BRZ
ORI OKEANIS SAIDUMLOBEA see **TAINA DVUH OKEANOV** • 1955
ORIANA • 1986 • Torres Fina • VNZ
ORIBE'S CRIME see **CRIMEN DE ORIBE, EL** • 1950
ORIDATH • 1986 • Aravindan G. • IND • ONCE SOMEWHERE
ORIENT • 1924 • Righelli Gennaro • FRG, AUS, ITL • ORIENTE (ITL) ○ TOCHTER DER WUSTE, DIE ○ DAUGHTERS OF THE DESERT
ORIENT BY NIGHT (USA) see **NOTTI CALDE D'ORIENTE** • 1962
ORIENT EXPRESS • 1934 • Martin Paul • FRG • SEVEN LIVES WERE CHANGED
ORIENT-EXPRESS see **ORIENTE EXPRESS** • 1954
ORIENT QUI VIENT, L' • 1934 • Leenhardt Roger, Zuber Rene • DCS • FRN
ORIENTAL BLACK ART • 1908 • Melies Georges • FRN
ORIENTAL BLUE • 1975 • Drexler Philip T. • USA
ORIENTAL CARPET, THE see **CINTAMANI A PODVODNIK** • 1965
ORIENTAL DREAMS see **KISMET** • 1944
ORIENTAL HERITAGE • 1956 • Novik William • SHT
ORIENTAL LOVE • 1917 • Wright Walter • SHT • USA
ORIENTAL MYSTIC, THE • 1909 • Blackton J. Stuart • USA
ORIENTAL NIGHT, THE see **NOCHE ORIENTAL, LA** • 1986
ORIENTAL NIGHTS see **ORIENTALISCHE NACHTE** • 1960
ORIENTAL PLAYGIRLS • Chi James Lu • HKG
ORIENTAL ROMANCE, AN • 1915 • *Baggot King* • USA
ORIENTAL ROMEO, AN • 1919 • Robbins Jess • SHT • USA
ORIENTAL RUBY, THE • 1915 • Reehm George E. • USA
ORIENTAL SPASM, THE • 1915 • Fahrney Milton • USA
ORIENTALI, LE • 1960 • Marcellini Romolo • DOC • ITL • WOMAN OF THE ORIENT ○ ORIENTALS, THE
ORIENTALISCHE NACHTE • 1960 • Paul Heinz • FRG • ORIENTAL NIGHTS
ORIENTALS, THE see **ORIENTALI, LE** • 1960
ORIENTAL'S PLOT, THE • 1915 • *Courtot Marguerite* • USA
ORIENTATION, L' • 1974 • Mankiewicz Francis • SHT • CND
ORIENTE ES OCCIDENTE • 1930 • Melford George • USA
ORIENTE EXPRESS • 1954 • Bragaglia Carlo Ludovico • FRN, ITL, FRG • ORIENT-EXPRESS
ORIENTE (ITL) see **ORIENT** • 1924
ORIENTE-OCCIDENTE, DONDE ESTAN LOS LOCOS? • 1968 • Arango Ramiro • SPN
ORIENTE Y SU ESPERANZA • 1970 • Oropeza Daniel • DOC • VNZ • EAST AND ITS HOPES, THE
ORIENTEXPRESS • 1927 • Thiele Wilhelm • FRG
ORIENTEXPRESS • 1944 • Tourjansky Victor • FRG
ORIENTFIEBER • 1923 • Linke Edmund • FRG
ORIGIN OF BEETHOVEN'S MOONLIGHT SONATA • 1909 • *Edison* • USA
ORIGIN OF MAN, THE see **LOST WORLD, THE** • 1960
ORIGIN OF PRINCESS MOON, THE see **TSUKIHIME KEIZU** • 1958
ORIGIN OF SEX -LIBIDO, THE see **SEI NO KIGEN** • 1967
ORIGIN OF THE GANGES RIVER see **GANGAVATAREN** • 1937
ORIGIN OF THE SPECIES, THE see **CLAY** • 1965
ORIGINAL LOCATAIRE, UN • Bowers Charley • FRN • INVENTEUR ACHARNE, UN ○ ECCENTRIC LODGER, AN ○ ENTHUSIASTIC INVENTOR, AN
ORIGINAL OLD MOTHER RILEY, THE see **OLD MOTHER RILEY** • 1937
ORIGINAL SIN • 1988 • Satlof Ron • MTV • USA
ORIGINAL SIN see **PECADO ORIGINAL, EL** • 1964
ORIGINAL SIN, THE (USA) see **APFEL IST AB, DER** • 1948
ORIGINAL WILL, THE • 1913 • *Reliance* • USA
ORIGINE DES KABOULOUKOU, L' • 1962 • Friedman Yona • ANM • FRN
ORIGINES DE LA REVOLUTION TRANQUILLE: DECADE 1929-39 • 1974 • Valcour Pierre • DOC • CND
ORIGINES DE LA REVOLUTION TRANQUILLE: L'UNIVERSITE AU POUVOIR • 1974 • Valcour Pierre • DOC • CND
ORIGINI DELLA FANTASCIENZA, LE • 1963 • Silvestri Dario, Falessi • SHT • ITL • ORIGINS OF SCIENCE FICTION, THE
ORIGINS OF SCIENCE FICTION, THE see **ORIGINI DELLA FANTASCIENZA, LE** • 1963
O'RILEY'S LUCK (UKN) see **ROSE BOWL** • 1936
ORILLA, LA • 1970 • Lucia Luis • SPN
ORILLEROS, LOS • 1975 • Luna Ricardo • ARG • RIVERSIDE MEN
ORILLIA: OUR TOWN • 1974 • Lavut Martin • DOC • CND
ORIN, A BLIND WOMAN see **HANARE GOZE, ORIN** • 1978
ORINOCO CAYMAN, THE see **CAIMAN DEL ORINOCO, EL** • 1979
ORINOCO NEW WORLD see **ORINOKO NUEVO MUNDO** • 1986
ORINOKO NUEVO MUNDO • 1986 • Risquez Diego • VNZ • ORINOCO NEW WORLD
ORIONNEVEL, DE • 1987 • Rood Jurrien • NTH
ORION'S BELT see **ORIONS BELTE** • 1984
ORIONS BELTE • 1984 • Solum Ola • NRW • ORION'S BELT
ORISON • 1967 • Perry Margaret • DOC • CND
ORIZURU OSEN • 1934 • Mizoguchi Kenji • JPN • DOWNFALL OF OSEN, THE (USA) ○ DOWNFALL, THE (UKN) ○ PAPER CRANES FROM OSEN
ORIZZONTALE, L' • 1919 • Righelli Gennaro • ITL
ORIZZONTE DI SANGUE • 1942 • Righelli Gennaro • ITL
ORIZZONTE DIPINTO, L' • 1941 • Salvini Guido • ITL • TEATRO
ORIZZONTE INFUOCATO • 1957 • Montero Roberto Bianchi • ITL
ORIZZONTI DEL SOLE • 1956 • Paolucci Giovanni • ITL
ORKESTAR JEDNE MLADOSTI • 1985 • Pavlovic Sveta • YGS • ORCHESTRA OF YOUTH
ORKIZOME IME ATHOA • 1968 • Paraskhakis Pavlos • GRC • I PLEAD NOT GUILTY
ORLACS HANDE • 1925 • Wiene Robert • AUS • UNHEIMLICHEN HANDE DES DR. ORLAK, DIE ○ HANDS OF ORLAC, THE (USA) ○ SINISTER HANDS OF DR. ORLAK, THE
ORLAK, EL INFIERNO DE FRANKENSTEIN • 1960 • Baledon Rafael • MXC • ORLAK, THE HELL OF FRANKENSTEIN
ORLAK, THE HELL OF FRANKENSTEIN see **ORLAK, EL INFIERNO DE FRANKENSTEIN** • 1960
ORLANDO see **ORLANDO E I PALADINI DI FRANCIA** • 1956
ORLANDO E I PALADINI DI FRANCIA • 1956 • Francisci Pietro • ITL • ROLAND THE MIGHTY (USA) ○ ORLANDO
ORLANDO FURIOSO • 1974 • Ronconi Luca • ITL
ORLEANS COACH, THE • 1912 • *Pathe* • USA
ORLIE PIERKO • 1972 • Holly Martin • CZC • EAGLE'S FEATHERS
ORLOFF AGAINST THE INVISIBLE MAN (USA) see **ORLOFF ET L'HOMME INVISIBLE** • 1970
ORLOFF AND THE INVISIBLE MAN see **ORLOFF ET L'HOMME INVISIBLE** • 1970
ORLOFF ET L'HOMME INVISIBLE • 1970 • Chevalier Pierre • FRN, SPN • ORLOFF Y EL HOMBRE INVISIBLE (SPN) ○ ORLOFF AND THE INVISIBLE MAN ○ ORLOFF AGAINST THE INVISIBLE MAN (USA)
ORLOFF ET TARAKANOWA see **TARAKANOWA** • 1938
ORLOFF Y EL HOMBRE INVISIBLE (SPN) see **ORLOFF ET L'HOMME INVISIBLE** • 1970
ORLOGSMAN • 1943 • Larsson Borje • SWD • MEN-OF-WAR
ORLOV COUPLE, THE see **SUPRUGI ORLOVY** • 1979
ORLOVI RANO LETE • 1966 • Jovanovic Soja • YGS • EAGLES FLY EARLY, THE
ORLOVS, THE see **SUPRUGI ORLOVY** • 1979
ORLOVSKAYA BITVA • 1943 • Gikov G., Stepanova L. • USS • BATTLE OF OREL, THE
ORLOW, DER • 1927 • Fleck Jacob, Fleck Luise • FRG • HEARTS AND DIAMONDS
ORLOW, DER see **DIAMANT DES ZARENS, DER** • 1932
ORMA, L' • 1919 • Mari Febo • ITL
ORME, LE • 1975 • Bazzoni Luigi • ITL
ORME EN PERIL, L' see **DUTCH ELM DISEASE** • 1948
ORMEN • 1966 • Abramson Hans • SWD • SERPENT, THE
ORMENS AGG see **SCHLANGENEI, DAS** • 1977
ORMENS VAG PA HALLEBERGET • 1986 • Widerberg Bo • SWD • SERPENT'S WAY, THE
ORNAMENT DES VERLIEBTEN HERZENS, DAS • 1919 • Reiniger Lotte • ANM • FRG • ORNAMENT OF A LOVING HEART, THE (UKN)
ORNAMENT OF A LOVING HEART, THE (UKN) see **ORNAMENT DES VERLIEBTEN HERZENS, DAS** • 1919
ORNAMENT OF SANKARA see **SANKARABHARANAM** • 1979
ORNAMENTAL SWIMMING • 1937 • Sparling Gordon • DCS • CND • NATATION DE FANTAISIE
ORNITHOLOGY see **ORNITOLOGIJA** • 1970
ORNITOLOGIJA • 1970 • Zaninovic Ante • SHT • YGS • ORNITHOLOGY
ORNUNGAR • 1944 • Johansson Ivar • SWD
ORO BAJO • 1956 • Soffici Mario • ARG
ORO DEI BRAVADOS, L' • 1970 • Romitelli Giancarlo • ITL, FRN • CHAPAGUA (FRN)
ORO DEL MONDO, L' • 1968 • Grimaldi Aldo • ITL • WORLD'S GOLD, THE
ORO DI LONDRA, L' • 1967 • Morandi Guglielmo • ITL • GOLD OF LONDON, THE
ORO DI NAPOLI, L' • 1954 • De Sica Vittorio • ITL • GOLD OF NAPLES ○ EVERY DAY'S A HOLIDAY
ORO DI ROMA, L' • 1961 • Lizzani Carlo • ITL • ROME'S GOLD
ORO, DONNE E MARACAS • 1955 • Tamburella Armando W. • DOC • ITL
ORO ENTRE BARRO • 1940 • Herrera R. • GOLD IN CLAY (USA)
ORO ES TRISTE, EL • 1973 • Sanchez Luis Alfredo • SHT • CLM • GOLD IS SAD
ORO MALDITO see **SE SEI VIVO SPARA** • 1967
ORO NERO • 1942 • Guazzoni Enrico • ITL
ORO PER I CESARI • 1963 • De Toth Andre, Ciuffini Sabatino, Freda Riccardo • ITL, FRN • OR POUR LES CESARS (FRN) ○ OR DES CESARS, L' ○ GOLD FOR THE CESARS
ORO, PLATA, MATA • 1982 • Gallaga Peque • PHL • GOLD, SILVER, BAD LUCK
ORO ROJO • 1978 • Vazquez Figueroa Alberto • SPN
ORO, SANGRE Y SOL • 1925 • Contreras Torres Miguel • MXC • GOLD, BLOOD, AND SUN
ORO VIL • 1941 • Maroto Eduardo G. • SPN
ORO Y MARFIL • 1947 • Delgras Gonzalo • SPN
ORO Y OLATA • 1934 • Peon Ramon • MXC
OROKBEFOGADAS • 1975 • Meszaros Marta • HNG • ADOPTION
OROKOSOK • 1970 • Kovacs Andras • DOC • HNG • HEIRS
OROKSEG • 1980 • Meszaros Marta • HNG, FRN • HERITIERES, LES (FRN) ○ HEIRESSES, THE ○ HERITAGE, THE
OROKU-GUISHI • 1932 • Ito Daisuke • JPN
OROLOGIA A CUCU, L' • 1938 • Mastrocinque Camillo • ITL
OROS • 1960 • Guerra Ruy • SHT • BRZ
OROSIA • 1943 • Rey Florian • SPN
OROSZLAN UGRANI KESZUL, AZ • 1969 • Revesz Gyorgy • HNG • ISLE OF THE LION
O'ROURKE OF THE ROYAL MOUNTED (UKN) see **SASKATCHEWAN** • 1954
OROZCO: EN BUSCA DE UN MURO • 1973 • *Churubusco Azteca* • MXC
ORPHAN, THE • 1911 • *Reliance* • USA
ORPHAN, THE • 1913 • Miller Ashley • USA
ORPHAN, THE • 1920 • Edwards J. Gordon • USA
ORPHAN, THE • 1979 • Ballard John • USA
ORPHAN, THE see **OKSUZ** • 1968
ORPHAN, THE see **INKEDAMA** • 1975
ORPHAN, THE see **FRIDAY THE THIRTEENTH.. THE ORPHAN** • 1979
ORPHAN, THE see **FALATO** • 1988
ORPHAN AT WAR, AN • 1913 • Ford Francis • USA
ORPHAN BOY OF VIENNA, AN see **SINGENDE JUGEND** • 1936
ORPHAN BROTHER, THE see **ANJU TO ZUSHIO-MARU** • 1961
ORPHAN DUCK, THE • 1939 • Rasinski Connie • ANS • USA
ORPHAN EGG, THE • 1953 • Donnelly Eddie • ANS • USA
ORPHAN JOYCE • 1916 • *Fair Joyce* • SHT • USA
ORPHAN MARY AND THE DWARFS see **MARYSIA I KRASNOLUDKI** • 1961
ORPHAN OF THE PECOS • 1937 • Katzman Sam • USA
ORPHAN OF THE RING, THE (UKN) see **KID FROM KOKOMO, THE** • 1939
ORPHAN OF THE SAGE • 1928 • King Louis • USA
ORPHAN OF THE WILDERNESS • 1936 • Hall Ken G. • ASL • CHUT, ORPHAN OF THE WILDERNESS ○ WILDERNESS ORPHAN
ORPHAN SALLY • 1922 • Hemmer Edward L. • USA
ORPHAN TRAIN • 1979 • Graham William A. • TVM • USA
ORPHAN WHO SAVED HIS GRANDFATHER, THE • 1922 • TWN
ORPHANS • 1912 • *Gem* • USA
ORPHANS • 1988 • Pakula Alan J. • USA
ORPHANS see **PODRANKI** • 1977
ORPHANS, THE • 1907 • Williamson James? • UKN
ORPHAN'S BENEFIT • 1934 • Gillett Burt • ANS • USA
ORPHANS' BENEFIT • 1941 • Thomson Riley • ANS • USA
ORPHANS IN THE SURF • 1903 • Porter Edwin S. • USA
ORPHAN'S MINE, THE • 1913 • Dwan Allan • USA

ORPHANS OF THE EARTH • 1984 • Grisolli Paulo Alfonso • MTV • BRZ

ORPHANS OF THE GHETTO • 1922 • *Donaldson Arthur* • USA

ORPHANS OF THE LAW see **REFORMATORY** • 1938

ORPHANS OF THE PLAINS • 1912 • *Pathe* • USA

ORPHANS OF THE STORM • 1921 • Griffith D. W. • USA • TWO ORPHANS, THE

ORPHANS OF THE STREET • 1938 • Auer John H. • USA

ORPHANS OF THE WILDS • 1914 • *Pathe* • USA

ORPHANS' PICNIC • 1936 • Sharpsteen Ben • ANS • USA

ORPHAN'S PLIGHT, AN • 1911 • *Essanay* • USA

ORPHAN'S ROMANCE, AN • 1913 • *Fealy Maude* • USA

ORPHEE • 1950 • Cocteau Jean • FRN • ORPHEUS (USA)

ORPHELIN DE PARIS, L' • 1923 • Feuillade Louis • SRL • FRN

ORPHELIN DU CIRQUE, L' • 1926 • Lannes Georges • FRN

ORPHELINE, L' • 1921 • Feuillade Louis • SRL • FRN

ORPHELINS DE SAINT-VAAST, LES • 1948 • Gourguet Jean • FRN

ORPHEON • 1966 • Meunier Jean-Charles • ANS • FRN

ORPHEUS • 1964 • *Rodrigues Alfred* • FRG

ORPHEUS AND EURYDICE • 1939 • ANM • CZC

ORPHEUS AND EURYDICE • 1962 • Sturlis Edward • ANM • PLN

ORPHEUS AND EURYDICE see **ORFEUSZ ES EURYDIKE** • 1985

ORPHEUS IN DER UNTERWELT • 1973 • Bonnet Horst • GDR

ORPHEUS IN THE UNDERWORLD see **ORFEUS I UNDERJORDEN** • 1910

ORPHEUS SONG FILMS • 1915 • Malins Geoffrey H. • SER • UKN

ORPHEUS (USA) see **ORPHEE** • 1950

ORQUESTA DE SENORITAS • 1941 • Amadori Luis Cesar • ARG

ORQUIDEAS PARA MI ESPOSA • 1953 • Crevenna Alfredo B. • MXC

ORRECHIO, L' • 1946 • Bava Mario • ITL

ORRIBILE SEGRETO DEL DR. HICHCOCK, L' • 1962 • Freda Riccardo • ITL • RAPTUS –THE SECRET OF DR. HICHCOCK (UKN) ○ TERROR OF DR. HICHCOCK, THE ○ HORRIBLE DR. HICHCOCK, THE (USA) ○ HORRIBLE SECRET OF DR. HICHCOCK, THE

ORRORI DEL CASTELLO DI NORIMBERGA, GLI • 1972 • Bava Mario • ITL • TORTURE CHAMBER OF BARON BLOOD, THE ○ BARON BLOOD (USA) ○ BLOOD BARON, THE ○ CHAMBER OF TORTURES, THE ○ THIRST OF BARON BLOOD, THE

ORS AL-DAM • 1977 • Ben Baraka Sohail • MRC • BLOOD WEDDING ○ URS AD-DAM ○ BLOOD HONEYMOON

ORSON WELLES • 1966 • Reichenbach Francois (c/d) • SHT • FRN

ORSZAGUTAR • 1956 • Meszaros Marta • DCS • HNG • WANDERING THE HIGHWAYS

ORTASARK YANIYOR • 1967 • Davutoglu Zafer • TRK • MIDDLE EAST IS BURNING, THE

ORTHOPEDIC PARADISE see **PARAISO ORTOPEDICO** • 1969

ORTLIEB WOMEN, THE see **ORTLIEBSCHEN FRAUEN, DIE** • 1980

ORTLIEBSCHEN FRAUEN, DIE • 1980 • Bondy Luc • FRG • ORTLIEB WOMEN, THE

ORU KAIJU DAISHINGEKI • 1969 • Honda Inoshiro • JPN • GODZILLA'S REVENGE (USA)

ORU THOOVAL PAKSHIKAL • 1988 • Ravindran K. • IND

ORUGA LLAMADA PEPINA, UNA • 1976 • *Conacine* • MXC

ORZEL I RESZKA • 1974 • Filipski Ryszard • PLN • HEADS AND TAILS

ORZOWEI • 1975 • Allegret Yves • FRN

OS MUNDI • 1960 • Hoving Hattum • NTH

OS TIN TELEFTEA STIGMI • 1971 • Retsinas Marios • GRC • TO THE LAST MINUTE

OSA • 1985 • Egorov Oleg • USA

OSAKA 1-2-3 • 1970 • Whitney John • ANS • USA

OSAKA ELEGY (USA) see **NANIWA EREJI** • 1936

OSAKA-JO MONOGATARI • 1961 • Inagaki Hiroshi • JPN • STORY OF THE CASTLE OF OSAKA, THE ○ DAREDEVIL IN THE CASTLE (USA) ○ DEVIL IN THE CASTLE

OSAKA MONOGATARI • 1957 • Mizoguchi Kenji, Yoshimura Kozaburo • JPN • OSAKA STORY, AN

OSAKA NATSU NO JIN • 1937 • Kinugasa Teinosuke • JPN • SUMMER BATTLE OF OSAKA, THE

OSAKA NO ONNA • 1958 • Kinugasa Teinosuke • JPN • WOMAN OF OSAKA, A

OSAKA NO YADO • 1954 • Gosho Heinosuke • JPN • INN AT OSAKA, AN ○ HOTEL AT OSAKA ○ OSAKA STORY ○ INN IN OSAKA, AN ○ INN OF OSAKA

OSAKA STORY see **OSAKA NO YADO** • 1954

OSAKA STORY, AN see **OSAKA MONOGATARI** • 1957

OSAM KILA GRECE • 1981 • Djordjevic Mladomir Purisa • YGS • EIGHT KILOS OF HAPPINESS

OSAMELY JEZDEC • 1966 • Helge Ladislav • CZC • LONELY HORSEMAN, THE

OSAN see **HIYAMESHI TO OSAN TO CHAN** • 1965

OSAN TO BAIDOKU • 1968 • Ogawa Kinya • JPN • SYPHILIS IN LABOUR

OSBEMUTATO • 1974 • Szabo Istvan • MTV • HNG • PREMIERE

OSCAR • 1967 • Molinaro Edouard • FRN

OSCAR, THE • 1966 • Rouse Russell • USA

OSCAR BROWN, JNR. • 1962 • Binder Steve • SHT • USA

OSCAR, CHAMPION DE TENNIS • 1932 • *Tati Jacques* • SHT • FRN

OSCAR, KINA Y EL LASER • 1978 • Blanco Jose Maria • SPN

OSCAR NIEMEYER • Cloue Eric • DOC

OSCAR PER IL SIGNOR ROSSI, UN • 1960 • Bozzetto Bruno • ANS • ITL

OSCAR, THE OYSTER OPENER • 1916 • *Mcnish Frank E.* • SHT • USA

OSCAR WILDE • 1960 • Ratoff Gregory • UKN

OSCAR'S GIFT see **CADEAU D'OSCAR, LE** • 1965

OSCENO DISIDERIO, L' • 1978 • Petroni Giulio • ITL • PENE NEL VENTRE, LE

OSCILLATION • 1926 • Sanderson Challis, Newman Widgey R. • UKN

OSCURA HISTORIA DE LA PRIMA MONTSE, LA • 1977 • Cadena Jordi • SPN

OSCURE VICENDE • 1920 • Serena Gustavo • ITL

OSCURIDAD EN EL CEREBRO, LA • 1971 • Ricci Tonino • SPN, ITL • DARKNESS IN THE BRAIN, THE

OSCUROS SUENOS DE AGOSTO • 1967 • Picazo Miguel • SPN • DARK DREAMS OF AUGUST

OSE NO HANGORO • 1928 • *Tsuburaya Eiji (Ph)* • JPN

OSEKA • 1968 • Pavlovic Vladimir • YGS • LOW-TIDE ○ EBB TIDE ○ HIGH TIDE

OSEMBER, AZ • 1917 • Hinter Cornelius • AUS • PREHISTORIC MAN, THE

OSEN • 1940 • Ermler Friedrich (c/d) • SHT • USS • AUTUMN

OSENNY MARAFON • 1979 • Daneliya Georgi • USS • AUTUMN MARATHON ○ SAD LIFE OF A ROGUE, THE

O'SHAUGHNESSY'S BOY • 1935 • Boleslawski Richard • USA

OSHETIME NE BREGDET • Hakani Hysen • ALB • ECHOES ON THE SHORE

OSHIBKA REZIDYENTA I: PO STAROY LEGYENDYE II: VOZVRASHCHYENIYE BEKASA • 1968 • Dorman Veniamin • USS • SPY'S MISTAKE PART ONE: ACCORDING TO AN OLD LEGEND PART TWO: BEKAS' RETURN, A

OSHIBKI YUNISTI • 1989 • Frumin B. • USS • ERRORS OF YOUTH (UKN)

OSHIDORI KAGO • 1958 • Makino Masahiro • JPN • BULLS-EYE FOR LOVE

OSHIDORI TABI NIKKI • 1929 • Inagaki Hiroshi • JPN • DUCK JOURNEY DIARY

OSHIKIRI SHINKON KI • 1930 • Naruse Mikio • JPN • RECORD OF SHAMELESS NEWLYWEDS, A ○ RECORD OF NEWLYWEDS

OSHO • 1973 • Horikawa Hiromichi • JPN • MASTER HAND (USA)

OSHO see **OOSHO** • 1948

OSINDA • 1976 • Nicolaescu Sergiu • RMN • PUNISHMENT, THE ○ DOOM, THE

OSKLENICKU VIC • 1954 • Pojar Bretislav • ANS • CZC • DROP TOO MUCH, A (USA) ○ O SKLENICKU VIC ○ ONE GLASS TOO MANY ○ ONE GLASS TOO MUCH

OSKLIVA SLECNA • 1959 • Hubacek Miroslav • CZC • PLAIN OLD MAID, THE ○ UGLY SPINSTER, THE

OSLERIZING PAPA • 1905 • *Bitzer Billy (Ph)* • USA

OSLIC, SELEDKA I MEDLA • 1969 • Tuganov Elbert • ANS • USS • DONKEY, THE HERRING AND THE BROOM, THE

OSLO • 1963 • Roos Jorgen • DOC • DNM

OSLOBODILAC • 1971 • Dovnikovic Borivoj • ANS • YGS, USA • LIBERATOR

OSMA VRATA • 1959 • Tanhofer Nikola • YGS • EIGHTH DOOR, THE

OSMAN THE WANDERER see **PIYADE OSMAN** • 1970

OSMANLI KABADAYISI • 1967 • Inanoglu Turker • TRK • OTTOMAN BRAVE, THE

OSMANOGLU • 1967 • Inanoglu Turker • TRK

OSMANTHUS ALLEY see **KUEI-HUA HSIANG** • 1987

OSMJEH 61 • 1961 • Makavejev Dusan • SHT • YGS • SMILE 61

OSMNACTILETA • 1939 • Cikan Miroslav • CZC • EIGHTEEN-YEAR OLD GIRL

OSMONDS, THE • 1973 • *Halas John (P)* • ASS • UKN

OSMY DZIEN TYGODNIA • 1958 • Ford Aleksander • PLN, FRG • EIGHTH DAY OF THE WEEK, THE (USA) ○ ACHTE WOCHENTAG, DER (FRG)

OSOBOYE MNYENIYE • 1968 • Zhilin Viktor • USS • PERSONAL OPINION

OSONE-KE NO ASA • 1946 • Kinoshita Keisuke • JPN • MORNING WITH THE OSONE FAMILY, A ○ MORNING FOR THE OSONE FAMILY

OSOREZAN NO ONNA • 1965 • Gosho Heinosuke • JPN • WOMAN OF THE OSORE MOUNTAINS, A ○ INNOCENT WITCH, AN

OSOSHIKI • 1984 • Itami Juzo • JPN • FUNERAL, THE

OSPEDALE DEL DELITTO, L' • 1950 • Comencini Luigi • ITL

OSPITE, L' • 1971 • Cavani Liliana • ITL • AUCUNE INTIMITE LICITE.. ○ GUEST, THE

OSPITE DI UNA NOTTE, L' • 1939 • Guarino Joseph • ITL

OSRAM • 1958 • Alexeieff Alexandre • SHS • FRN

OSS • 1976 • Mikkelsen Laila • NRW • US

OSS see **LAST ESCAPE, THE** • 1970

OSS 77 OPERAZIONE FIORDILOTO • 1967 • Paolinelli Bruno • ITL

OSS 117 –DOUBLE AGENT (USA) see **NIENTE ROSE PER OSS 117** • 1968

OSS 117 FURIA A BAHIA (ITL) see **FURIA A BAHIA POUR OSS 117** • 1965

OSS 117 MINACCIA BANGKOK (ITL) see **BANCO A BANGKOK** • 1964

OSS 117 –MISSION FOR A KILLER (USA) see **FURIA A BAHIA POUR OSS 117** • 1965

OSS 117 MURDER FOR SALE (UKN) see **NIENTE ROSE PER OSS 117** • 1968

OSS 117 TAKES A VACATION see **O.S.S. 117 PREND DES VACANCES** • 1969

OSS 177 A TOKIO SI MUORE (ITL) see **ATOUT COEUR A TOKYO POUR OSS 117** • 1966

OSS BARONER EMELLAN • 1940 • Johansson Ivar • SWD • BETWEEN US BARONS

OSS EMELLAN • 1969 • Olsson Stellan • SWD • CLOSE TO THE WIND (UKN) ○ IT'S UP TO YOU

OSS TJUVAR EMELLAN ELLER EN BURK ANANAS • 1945 • Molander Olof • SWD • BETWEEN US THIEVES

OSSESSA, L' • 1974 • Gariazzo Mario • ITL • EERIE MIDNIGHT HORROR SHOW, THE ○ DEVIL OBSESSION, THE ○ SEXORCIST, THE ○ TORMENTED ○ ENTER THE DEVIL ○ OBSESSION, THE ○ TORMENTORS, THE ○ OBSESSED, THE

OSSESSIONE • 1943 • Visconti Luchino • ITL • POSTMAN ALWAYS RINGS TWICE, THE

OSSI HAT DIE HOSEN AN • 1928 • Boese Carl • FRG

OSSI'S DIARY see **OSSIS TAGEBUCH** • 1917

OSSIS TAGEBUCH • 1917 • Lubitsch Ernst • FRG • OSSI'S DIARY

OSSUARY, THE see **KOSTNICE** • 1970

OSSUDENI DUSHI • 1975 • Radev Vulo • BUL • DOOMED SOULS ○ DAMNED SOULS

OSTA HASSEN, EL • 1952 • Abu Saif Salah • EGY • FOREMAN HASSAN ○ UST'A H'ASSAN, AL-

OSTACOLO, L' • 1914 • Negroni Baldassare • ITL

OSTAGGIO, L' • 1975 • Valenzano Luigi • ITL

OSTANOVILSIA POEZD • 1983 • Abdrakhitov Vadim • USS • TRAIN STOPS HERE, THE

OSTAP BANDOURA • 1924 • Gardin Vladimir • USS

OSTATNI DNI • 1968 • Passendorfer Jerzy • PLN • LAST DAYS, THE

OSTATNI DZIEN LATA • 1958 • Konwicki Tadeusz, Laskowski Jan • PLN • LAST DAY OF SUMMER, THE

OSTATNI ETAP • 1948 • Jakubowska Wanda • PLN • LAST STOP, THE (USA) ○ LAST STAGE, THE (UKN)

OSTATNI KURS • 1963 • Batory Jan • PLN • DEATH OF A TAXI-DRIVER

OSTATNI PARTEITAG W NORYMBERDZE • 1946 • Bohdziewicz Antoni (c/d) • PLN • LAST PARTEITAG IN NUREMBERG, THE

OSTATNI PO BOGU • 1968 • Komorowski Pawel • PLN • LAST AFTER GOD, THE

OSTATNI STRZAL • 1958 • Rybkowski Jan • PLN • LAST SHOT, THE

OSTENDE, REINE DES PLAGES • 1930 • Storck Henri • DOC • BLG

OSTERMAN WEEKEND, THE • 1983 • Peckinpah Sam • USA

OSTERMANS TESTAMENTE • 1954 • Frisk Ragnar • SWD • OSTERMAN'S WILL

OSTERMAN'S WILL see **OSTERMANS TESTAMENTE** • 1954

OSTERSPAZIERGANG • 1959 • Schamoni Peter • SHT • FRG

OSTIA • 1970 • Citti Sergio • ITL

'OSTLER JOE • 1908 • McCutcheon Wallace • USA

'OSTLER JOE • 1912 • Dawley J. Searle • USA

OSTPREUSSEN UND SEIN HINDENBURG • 1915 • Trautschold Gustav, Schott Richard • FRG • BRUDER IN NOT. OSTPREUSSEN UND SEIN HINDENBERG

OSTRE SLEDOVANE VLAKY • 1966 • Menzel Jiri • CZC • CLOSELY OBSERVED TRAINS (UKN) ○ WELL GUARDED TRAINS ○ ON THE LOOKOUT FOR TRAINS ○ CLOSELY WATCHED TRAINS (USA) ○ SPECIAL PRIORITY TRAINS ○ DIFFICULT LOVE, A

OSTRICH, THE • 1949 • Felstead Bert • UKN

OSTRICH, THE see **PSTROS** • 1960

OSTRICH EGG AND I, THE • 1956 • Lovy Alex • ANS • USA

OSTRICH FEATHERS • 1937 • *Lantz Walter (P)* • ANS • USA

OSTRICH HAS TWO EGGS, THE see **OEUFS DE L'AUTRUCHE, LES** • 1957

OSTRICH TIP, THE • 1916 • *Clifford William* • SHT • USA

OSTROV • 1973 • Hitruck Fedor • USS

OSTROV SOKROVISC • 1971 • Friedman Yevgeni • USS • TREASURE ISLAND

OSTROV STRIBRNYCH VOLAVEK • 1976 • Jires Jaromil • CZC, GDR • ISLAND OF THE SILVER HERONS ○ ISLAND OF SILVER HERONS, THE ○ INSEL DER SILBERREIHER, DIE

OSTROV ZABVENNYA • 1917 • Tourjansky Victor • USS • ISLE OF OBLIVION (USA)

OSTROZNIE YETI • 1958 • Czekalski Andrzej • PLN • BEWARE OF THE YETI

OSTRVA see **VERFUHRUNG AM MEER** • 1963

OSTRVO MUNGOSA see **MONGUZOK SZIGETEN, A** • 1959

OSUDJENI • 1987 • Tadic Zoran • YGS • CONDEMNED, THE

OSUDY DOBREHO VOYAKA SVEJKA • 1954 • Trnka Jiri • ANS • CZC • GOOD SOLDIER SCHWEIK, THE ○ DOBRY VOJAK SVEJK

OSUMI AND HER MOTHER see **OSUMI TO SONO HAHA** • 1924

OSUMI TO SONO HAHA • 1924 • Murata Minoru • JPN • OSUMI AND HER MOTHER

OSVAJANJE SLOBODE • 1980 • Sotra Zdravko • YGS • WINNING FREEDOM ○ WINNING OF FREEDOM

OSVETNIK • 1958 • Vukotic Dusan • ANS • YGS • REVENGER, THE

OSVOBO JDIENNAIA ZEMLIA see **OSVOBOZHDENNAYA ZEMLYA** • 1946

OSVOBOZENI PRAHY • 1976 • Vavra Otakar • CZC • LIBERATION OF PRAGUE

OSVOBOZHDENIE • 1970 • Ozerov Yury • USS, PLN, GDR • LIBERATION ○ GREAT BATTLE, THE

OSVOBOZHDENIYE • 1940 • Dovzhenko Alexander, Solntseva Yulia • USS • LIBERATION

OSVOBOZHDENNAYA FRANTSYA • 1946 • Yutkevich Sergei • DOC • USS • LIBERATED FRANCE ○ FRANCE LIBERATED

OSVOBOZHDENNAYA ZEMLYA • 1946 • Medvedkin Alexander • USS • OSVOBO JDIENNAIA ZEMLIA

OSVOBOZHDYONNY KITAI • 1950 • Gerasimov Sergei, Svilovoi Elena, Setkina Irina, Slavinsky M., Sui Saio-Bin • USS, CHN • LIBERATED CHINA ○ NEW CHINA, THE

OSWALD • 1927-38 • *Lantz Walter (P)* • ASS • USA

OSWALD THE LUCKY RABBIT • 1927 • Disney Walt • ASS • USA

OSWALD THE PLUMBER • 1933 • Lantz Walter, Nolan William • ANS • USA

OSWALT KOLLE: DAS WUNDER DER LIEBE –SEXUALITAT IN DER EHE • 1968 • Gottlieb Franz J. • FRG • MIRACLE OF LOVE, THE (USA) ○ WONDER OF LOVE, THE (UKN) ○ OSWALT KOLLE: THE WONDER OF LOVE –SEXUALITY IN MARRIAGE

OSWALT KOLLE: DAS WUNDER DER LIEBE –SEXUELLE PARTNERSCHAFT • 1968 • Neve Alexis • FRG • SEXUAL PARTNERSHIP (UKN) ○ WUNDER DER LIEBE, DAS ○ OSWALT KOLLE: THE WONDER OF LOVE – SEXUAL PARTNERSHIP

OSWALT KOLLE: DEIN MANN, DAS UNBEKANNTE WESEN • 1970 • Lenz Werner M. • FRG • DEIN MANN, DAS UNBEKANNTE WESEN

OSWALT KOLLE: DEINE FRAU, DAS UNBEKANNTE WESEN • 1969 • Neve Alexis • FRG • DEINE FRAU, DAS UNBEKANNTE WESEN ○ FEMALE SEXUALITY ○ YOUR WIFE –THE UNKNOWN CREATURE

OSWALT KOLLE: THE WONDER OF LOVE –SEXUAL PARTNERSHIP see **OSWALT KOLLE: DAS WUNDER DER LIEBE –SEXUELLE PARTNERSCHAFT** • 1968

OSWALT KOLLE: THE WONDER OF LOVE –SEXUALITY IN MARRIAGE see **OSWALT KOLLE: DAS WUNDER DER LIEBE –SEXUALITAT IN DER EHE** • 1968

OSWALT KOLLE: ZUM BEISPIEL: EHEBRUCH • 1969 • Neve Alexis • FRG • ZUM BEISPIEL: EHEBRUCH ○ ADULTERY
OSWEGO • 1943 • Van Dyke Willard • DOC • USA
OSYENNIYE SVADBY • 1968 • Yashin Boris • USS • AUTUMN WEDDINGS
OSYNLIGA MUREN, DEN • 1944 • Molander Gustaf • SWD • INVISIBLE WALL, THE ○ WALL, THE
OSZ BADACSONYBAN • 1954 • Jancso Miklos • SHT • HNG • AUTUMN IN BADACSONY
OT ORA 40 • 1939 • De Toth Andre • HNG • AT 5:40
OT SNYEGA DO SNYEGA • 1968 • Petrov Yuri • USS • FROM SNOW TO SNOW
OT ZARI DO ZARI • 1976 • Yegiazarov G. • USS • FROM MORNING TO NIGHT
OTAC • 1969 • Vukotic Dusan • ANS • YGS
OTAC • 1973 • Angelovski Kole • YGS • FATHER, THE ○ TATKO
OTAC NA SLUZBENOM PUTU • 1985 • Kusturica Emir • YGS • WHEN FATHER WAS AWAY ON BUSINESS
OTAGE, L' see **SHAITANE EL SAGHIR, EL** • 1963
OTAGES, LES • 1939 • Bernard Raymond • FRN • MAYOR'S DILEMMA, THE (USA) ○ HOSTAGES, THE
OTALIA DE BAHIA see **PASTORES DA NOITE, OS** • 1977
OTAN I YINEKES AGAPOUN • 1967 • Constantinou Panayotis • GRC • WOMEN IN LOVE
OTAN O SYZYGOS TAXEIDEYEI • 1939 • Mizrahi Togo • WHEN THE HUSBAND TRAVELS (USA)
OTANOSHIMI • 1968 • Takagi Osamu • JPN • ENJOYMENT
OTARAANT KVIRIVI see **OTAROVA VDOVA** • 1958
OTAROVA VDOVA • 1958 • Chiaureli Mikhail • USS • OTAR'S WIDOW ○ OTARAANT KVIRIVI ○ WIDOW OF OTAR
OTAR'S WIDOW see **OTAROVA VDOVA** • 1958
OTCHII DOM • 1959 • Kulidjanov Lev • USS • HOME FOR TANYA, A (USA) ○ OUR FATHER'S HOUSE ○ PATERNAL HOME, THE ○ NATIVE HOUSE, THE
OTE-TOI DE MON SOLEIL • 1982 • Jolivet Marc • FRN • DIOGENE
OTEC KONDELIK A ZENICH VEJVARA • 1926 • Anton Karl • CZC • FATHER KONDELIK AND BRIDEGROOM VEJVARA ○ KONDELIK -FATHER, VEJVARA -BRIDEGROOM
OTEC KONDELIK A ZENICH VEJVARA • 1937 • Krnansky M. J. • CZC • FATHER KONDELIK AND BRIDEGROOM VEJVARA
OTEL 'U POGIBSHCHEGO ALPINISTA • 1979 • Kromanov Grigori • USS • DEAD MOUNTAINEER HOTEL, THE
OTELLO • 1907 • Caserini Mario • ITL • OTHELLO
OTELLO • 1909 • Falena Ugo • ITL • OTHELLO
OTELLO • 1909 • Novelli Enrico • ITL • OTHELLO
OTELLO • 1951 • Welles Orson • ITL • OTHELLO (USA)
OTELLO • 1955 • Yutkevich Sergei • USS • OTHELLO
OTELLO • 1974 • Benamou Roger • FRG
OTELLO • 1986 • Zeffirelli Franco • ITL • OTHELLO
OTETS SERGEI • 1918 • Protazanov Yakov • USS • FATHER SERGIUS
OTETS SERGII see **OTYETS SERGII** • 1979
OTETS SOLDATA • 1965 • Chkheidze Revaz • USS • FATHER OF A DEAD SOLDIER (USA) ○ SOLDIER'S FATHER, A ○ JARISKATSIS
OTHELLO • 1918 • Mack Max • FRG
OTHELLO • 1920 • Dyer Anson • ANS • UKN
OTHELLO • 1922 • Buchowetzki Dimitri • FRG
OTHELLO • 1946 • MacKane David • UKN
OTHELLO • 1953 • Deane Charles • UKN
OTHELLO • 1965 • Burge Stuart • UKN
OTHELLO see **OTELLO** • 1907
OTHELLO see **OTELLO** • 1909
OTHELLO see **OTELLO** • 1909
OTHELLO see **OTELLO** • 1955
OTHELLO see **VENETSIANSKIY MAVR** • 1961
OTHELLO see **OTELLO** • 1986
OTHELLO -67 • 1967 • Hitruck Fedor • ANM • USS
OTHELLO IN HARLEM see **PARADISE IN HARLEM** • 1939
OTHELLO IN JONESVILLE • 1913 • Seay Charles M. • USA
OTHELLO (USA) see **OTELLO** • 1951
OTHER • 1980 • Brakhage Stan • SHT • USA
OTHER, THE • 1972 • Mulligan Robert • USA
OTHER, THE see **ANDERE, DER** • 1913
OTHER, THE see **ANDERE, DIE** • 1924
OTHER, THE see **ANDERE, DER** • 1930
OTHER, THE see **ANDERE, DIE** • 1949
OTHER BANK, THE see **DRUGI BRZEG** • 1962
OTHER BOARDING SCHOOL, THE see **OTRA RESIDENCIA, LA** • 1970
OTHER CANTERBURY TALES, THE (UKN) see **ALTRI RACCONTI DI CANTERBURY, GLI** • 1972
OTHER CHRISTOPHER, THE see **OTRO CRISTOBAL, EL** • 1962
OTHER CINDERELLA, THE see **CINDERELLA** • 1977
OTHER CRIME, THE see **OTRO CRIMEN, EL** • 1990
OTHER DOG'S DAY, THE • 1920 • Mannering Cecil • UKN
OTHER FELLOW, THE • 1911 • *Selig* • USA
OTHER FELLOW, OR A FIGHT FOR LOVE, THE • 1909 • *Edison* • USA
OTHER FU MANCHU, THE see **OTRO FU MANCHU, EL** • 1945
OTHER GIRL, THE • 1912 • *101 Bison* • USA
OTHER GIRL, THE • 1913 • *Thanhouser* • USA
OTHER GIRL, THE • 1914 • *Stonehouse Ruth* • USA
OTHER GIRL, THE • 1915 • *Essanay* • USA
OTHER GIRL, THE • 1915 • *Premier* • USA
OTHER GIRL, THE • 1916 • Winter Percy • USA
OTHER GIRL, THE • 1917 • *Price Kate* • USA
OTHER HALF, THE • 1912 • *Cruze James* • USA
OTHER HALF, THE • 1916 • Jaccard Jacques • SHT • USA
OTHER HALF, THE • 1919 • Vidor King • USA
OTHER HALF OF THE NOTE, THE • 1914 • *Boyle Irene* • USA
OTHER HALF OF THE SKY: A CHINA MEMOIR, THE • 1975 • MacLaine Shirley, Weill Claudia • DOC • USA
OTHER HALVES • 1985 • Laing John • NZL
OTHER HAPPINESS, THE see **DRUGOTO SHTASTIE** • 1960
OTHER HELL, THE see **ALTRO INFERNO, L'** • 1981
OTHER ILLUSION, THE see **OTRA ILUSION, LA** • 1989
OTHER JOHNSON, THE • 1910 • *Essanay* • USA
OTHER KID'S SISTER, THE • 1914 • *Eclectic* • USA
OTHER KIND OF LOVE, THE • 1924 • Worne Duke • USA
OTHER KINGDOM, THE • 1984 • Sarin Vic • MTV • CND
OTHER LETTER, THE see **ALLO GRAMMA, TO** • 1976
OTHER LIFE, THE • Odzhagov Rasim • USS
OTHER LIFE OF LYNN STUART, THE see **TRUE STORY OF LYNN STUART, THE** • 1958
OTHER LOVE, THE • 1947 • De Toth Andre • USA
OTHER LOVER, THE • 1985 • Miller Robert Ellis • TVM • USA
OTHER MAN, THE • 1911 • *Nestor* • USA
OTHER MAN, THE • 1912 • *Republic* • USA
OTHER MAN, THE • 1914 • *Bushman Francis X.* • USA
OTHER MAN, THE • 1915 • *Reliance* • USA
OTHER MAN, THE • 1916 • Arbuckle Roscoe • SHT • USA
OTHER MAN, THE • 1918 • Scardon Paul • USA
OTHER MAN, THE • 1970 • Colla Richard A. • TVM • USA
OTHER MAN, THE see **DRUGI CZLOWIEK** • 1961
OTHER MAN, THE see **DRUGI COVEK** • 1989
OTHER MAN'S WIFE, THE • 1915 • Davis Ulysses • USA
OTHER MAN'S WIFE, THE • 1919 • Harbaugh Carl • USA
OTHER MEN'S DAUGHTERS • 1918 • Harbaugh Carl • USA
OTHER MEN'S DAUGHTERS • 1923 • Wilson Ben • USA
OTHER MEN'S GOLD • 1912 • *P & B Film* • UKN
OTHER MEN'S SHOES • 1920 • Lewis Edgar • USA
OTHER MEN'S WIVES • 1919 • Schertzinger Victor • USA
OTHER MEN'S WOMEN • 1931 • Wellman William A. • USA • STEEL HIGHWAY
OTHER MRS. PHIPPS, THE • 1931 • Newall Guy • UKN
OTHER ONE, THE see **UNE ET L'AUTRE, L'** • 1967
OTHER ONE, THE see **CONVERSA ACABADA** • 1982
OTHER PEOPLE, THE see **I LOVE YOU, I HATE YOU** • 1968
OTHER PEOPLE'S BUSINESS • 1914 • Henderson Dell • USA
OTHER PEOPLE'S BUSINESS see **WAY BACK HOME** • 1931
OTHER PEOPLE'S CHILDREN see **ANDRE FOLKS BORN** • 1958
OTHER PEOPLE'S LETTERS see **CIUJYE PISMA** • 1976
OTHER PEOPLE'S MONEY • 1916 • Parke William • USA
OTHER PEOPLE'S MONEY see **ARGENT DES AUTRES, L'** • 1979
OTHER PEOPLE'S SINS • 1931 • Hill Sinclair • UKN
OTHER PERSON, THE • 1921 • Doxat-Pratt B. E. • UKN
OTHER REALMS • 1983 • Cardos John Bud • USA
OTHER SCENE, THE see **ALLI SKINI, I** • 1974
OTHER SELF, THE • 1915 • Kent Leon D. • USA
OTHER SELF, THE see **ANDERE ICH, DAS** • 1918
OTHER SELF, THE see **ANDERE ICH, DAS** • 1941
OTHER SEX, THE • 1967 • Muller Nils R. • SWD
OTHER SHORE, THE see **CHUZHOI BEREG** • 1930
OTHER SHORE, THE see **OTRA ORILLA, LA** • 1966
OTHER SIDE, THE • 1922 • Dierker Hugh • USA
OTHER SIDE OF BONNIE AND CLYDE, THE • 1968 • Buchanan Larry • USA
OTHER SIDE OF HELL, THE • 1978 • Kadar Jan • TVM • USA
OTHER SIDE OF INNOCENCE, THE • 1971 • Power John • MTV • ASL
OTHER SIDE OF JULIE, THE • 1978 • Riverton Anthony • USA
OTHER SIDE OF MADNESS, THE • 1971 • *Klinkett Brian* • USA
OTHER SIDE OF MIDNIGHT, THE • 1977 • Jarrott Charles • USA
OTHER SIDE OF PARADISE, THE • 1967 • Hannam Ken • DOC • ASL
OTHER SIDE OF PARADISE, THE see **FOXTROT** • 1976
OTHER SIDE OF THE BRIDGE, THE see **DINCOLO DE POD** • 1974
OTHER SIDE OF THE COIN, THE • 1978 • Cavadini Fabio • DOC • ASL
OTHER SIDE OF THE DOOR, THE • 1916 • Ricketts Thomas • USA
OTHER SIDE OF THE FENCE, THE • 1913 • *Foy Charlie* • USA
OTHER SIDE OF THE FLAME, THE • 1976 • Bugajski Ryszard • MTV • PLN
OTHER SIDE OF THE HEDGE, THE • 1905 • Fitzhamon Lewin • UKN • OVER THE HEDGE (USA)
OTHER SIDE OF THE LEDGES • 1973 • Defalco Martin • MTV • CND
OTHER SIDE OF THE MEDAL, THE see **DRUGA STRANA MEDALJE** • 1965
OTHER SIDE OF THE MEDAL, THE see **ROVESCIO DELLA MEDAGLIA, IL** • 1974
OTHER SIDE OF THE MOUNTAIN, THE • 1975 • Peerce Larry • USA • WINDOW TO THE SKY, A (UKN)
OTHER SIDE OF THE MOUNTAIN, PART II, THE • 1977 • Peerce Larry • TVM • USA
OTHER SIDE OF THE RAINBOW, THE • 1959 • *Ilyinsky Igor* • USS
OTHER SIDE OF THE UNDERNEATH, THE • 1972 • Arden Jane • UKN • OTHER SIDE OF UNDERNEATH, THE (USA)
OTHER SIDE OF THE WIND, THE • 1970 • Welles Orson
OTHER SIDE OF UNDERNEATH, THE (USA) see **OTHER SIDE OF THE UNDERNEATH, THE** • 1972
OTHER SISTER, THE • 1915 • Smiley Joseph • USA
OTHER SMILE, THE see **ANDERE LACHELN, DAS** • 1978
OTHER STARTED IT BUT SOPHIE FINISHED IT • 1915 • *Essanay* • USA
OTHER STOCKING, THE • 1917 • Clements Roy • SHT • USA
OTHER TIMES see **INYYE NYNCHYE VREMENA** • 1968
OTHER TOMORROW, THE • 1930 • Bacon Lloyd • USA
OTHER TRAIN, THE • 1914 • Pollard Harry • USA
OTHER VICTIM, THE • 1981 • Black Noel • TVM • USA
OTHER VIRGINITY, THE see **OTRA VIRGINIDAD, LA** • 1974
OTHER VOICES • 1970 • Sawyer David H. • DOC • USA
OTHER WISE MAN, THE • 1912 • Dwan Allan • USA
OTHER WOMAN, THE • 1912 • Cox George L. • USA
OTHER WOMAN, THE • 1913 • *Lubin* • USA
OTHER WOMAN, THE • 1913 • *Reliance* • USA
OTHER WOMAN, THE • 1913 • Brooke Van Dyke • *Vitagraph* • USA
OTHER WOMAN, THE • 1918 • Parker Albert • USA
OTHER WOMAN, THE • 1921 • Sloman Edward • USA
OTHER WOMAN, THE • 1931 • Samuelson G. B. • UKN
OTHER WOMAN, THE • 1954 • Haas Hugo • USA
OTHER WOMAN, THE • 1978 • Fahmy Ashraf • EGY
OTHER WOMAN, THE • 1982 • Shavelson Melville • TVM • USA
OTHER WOMAN, THE see **TSUMA TOSHITE ONNA TOSHITE** • 1961
OTHER WOMAN, THE see **MUJER AJENA, LA** • 1988
OTHER WOMAN'S PICTURE, THE • 1915 • *Holmes Gerda* • USA
OTHER WOMAN'S STORY, THE • 1925 • Stanley B. F. • USA
OTHER WOMEN'S CLOTHES • 1922 • Ballin Hugo • USA
OTHER WOMEN'S HUSBANDS • 1926 • Kenton Erle C. • USA
OTHER WORLD OF WINSTON CHURCHILL, THE • 1966 • Stoumen Louis Clyde • DOC • UKN
OTHERS, THE • 1957 • *Churchill Sarah* • MTV • USA
OTHERS AND STALIN see **DRUGOI I STALIN** • 1989
OTHERS' BLOOD, THE see **CHEMINS DE LA VIOLENCE, LES** • 1972
OTHERS WILL FOLLOW see **ZA WAMI POJDA INNI** • 1949
OTHERWISE BILL HARRISON • 1915 • *Totten Joseph Byron* • USA
OTHON (UKN) see **YEUX NE PEUVENT PAS EN TOUT TEMPS SE FERMER OU PEUT-ETRE QU'UN JOUR ROME SE PERMETTRA DE CHOISIR A..** • 1970
OTKLONENIE • 1967 • Ostrovski Grisha, Stoyanov Todor • BUL • SIDE TRACK
OTLEY • 1968 • Clement Dick • UKN
OTO ZIVOT • 1969 • Giersz Witold (c/d) • ANS • PLN, YGS • OTO ZYCIE ○ THAT'S LIFE
OTO ZYCIE see **OTO ZIVOT** • 1969
OTOBUS • 1976 • Okan Tunc • TRK, SWD, SWT • BUS, THE
OTODIK PECSET, AZ • 1977 • Fabri Zoltan • HNG • FIFTH SEAL, THE
OTOKO AND SASUKE see **OKOTO TO SASUKE** • 1935
OTOKO AND SASUKE see **OKOTO TO SASUKE** • 1961
OTOKO AND SASUKE see **SHUNKIN-SHO** • 1976
OTOKO ARITE • 1955 • Maruyama Seiji • JPN • NO TIME FOR TEARS
OTOKO DAIGAKU • 1955 • Tabata Tsuneo • JPN • COLLEGE FOR MEN
OTOKO GA BAKUHATSU SURU • 1959 • Masuda Toshio • JPN • EXPLOSION CAME
OTOKO GA INOCHI O KAKERU TOKI • 1959 • Matsuo Akinori • JPN • WHEN A MAN RISKS HIS LIFE
OTOKO GOKORO • 1925 • Gosho Heinosuke • JPN • MAN'S HEART
OTOKO NAMIDA NON HAMONJO • 1967 • Yamashita Kosaku • JPN • EXPULSION OF TEARS
OTOKO NANTE NANISA • 1967 • Watanabe Yusuke • JPN • OUR INNOCENT CREATURES
OTOKO NARA FURIMUKUNA • 1967 • Nomura Yoshitaro • JPN • PACE THAT THRILLS, THE
OTOKO NARA YUME O MIRO • 1959 • Ushihara Yoichi • JPN • DREAM YOUNG MAN'S DREAM
OTOKO NO CHOSEN • 1968 • Doi Michiyoshi • JPN • HIGH SPEED CHALLENGE
OTOKO NO IKARI O BUCHIMAKERO • 1960 • Matsuo Akinori • JPN
OTOKO NO OKITE • 1968 • Ezaki Mio • JPN • CODE OF MAN, THE
OTOKO NO SHOBU -KANTO ARASHI • 1967 • Yamashita Kosaku • JPN • MEN'S FIGHTING -KANTO ARASHI
OTOKO NO SHOBU: NIO NO IREZUMI • 1967 • Suzuki Noribumi • JPN • MATCH OF MEN: TATTOO OF DEVA KING, THE
OTOKO O SABAKU ONNA • 1948 • Sasaki Yasushi • JPN • MAN JUDGING WOMAN ○ WOMAN WHO CONVICTS MEN, A
OTOKO TAI OTOKO • 1960 • Taniguchi Senkichi • JPN • MAN AGAINST MAN ○ MAN VS. MAN
OTOKO TO ONNA TO INU • 1964 • Kuri Yoji • ANS • JPN • MAN, WOMAN AND DOG
OTOKO TO ONNO NO SHINWA • 1969 • Onchi Hideo • JPN • STAR OF ADAM
OTOKO TO OTOKO NO IKARU MACHI • 1962 • Masuda Toshio • JPN • CITY OF MEN
OTOKO WA TSURAIYO • 1969 • Yamada Yoji • JPN • AM I TRYING! ○ IT'S HARD BEING A MAN ○ TORA-SAN, OUR LOVABLE TRAMP
OTOKO WA TSURAIYO, AIAIGASA • 1975 • Yamada Yoji • JPN • TORA-SAN FINDS A SWEETHEART
OTOKO WA TSURAIYO, HANA MO ARASHI MO TORAJIRO • 1983 • Yamada Yoji • JPN • TORA-SAN, THE EXPERT
OTOKO WA TSURAIYO, HISBISCUS NO HANA • 1981 • Yamada Yoji • JPN • TORASAN GOES TO HISBISCUS LAND
OTOKO WA TSURAIYO, KATSUSHIKA RISSHI-HEN • 1975 • Yamada Yoji • JPN • TORASAN MEETS A LADY SCHOLAR
OTOKO WA TSURAIYO, KUCHIBUE O FUKU TORAJIRO • 1984 • Yamada Yoji • JPN • TORASAN WHISTLING
OTOKO WA TSURAIYO, NANIWA NO KOI NO TORAJIRO • 1982 • Yamada Yoji • JPN • TORASAN'S LOVE IN OSAKA
OTOKO WA TSURAIYO, SHIAWASTE NO AOI TORI • 1987 • Yamada Yoji • JPN • TORASAN, BLUEBIRD OF HAPPINESS
OTOKO WA TSURAIYO, SHIBAMATA YORI AI O KOMETE • 1985 • Yamada Yoji • JPN • TORASAN, FROM SHIBAMATA WITH LOVE
OTOKO WA TSURAIYO, SHIRETOKO BOJO • 1988 • Yamada Yoji • JPN • TORASAN, REMIND SHIRETOKE
OTOKO WA TSURAIYO, TABI TO ONNA TO TORAJIRO • 1984 • Yamada Yoji • JPN • TORASAN'S JOURNEY WITH A LADY
OTOKO WA TSURAIYO, TONDERU TORAJIRO • 1979 • Yamada Yoji • JPN • TORASAN RIDING HIGH
OTOKO WA TSURAIYO, TORAJIRO • 1973 • Yamada Yoji • JPN • TORASAN AND HIS FORGET-ME-NOT
OTOKO WA TSURAIYO, TORAJIRO AJISAI NO KOI • 1983 • Yamada Yoji • JPN • HEARTS AND FLOWERS FOR TORA
OTOKO WA TSURAIYO, TORAJIRO GAMBARE! • 1977 • Yamada Yoji • JPN • TORASAN, HOLD OUT!
OTOKO WA TSURAIYO, TORAJIRO HARU NO YUME • 1979 • Yamada Yoji • JPN • TORASAN DREAMS SPRINGTIME
OTOKO WA TSURAIYO, TORAJIRO JUNJO SHISHU • 1976 • Yamada Yoji • JPN • TORASAN MEETS HIS SCHOOL-MATES
OTOKO WA TSURAIYO, TORAJIRO KAMIFUSEN • 1982 • Yamada Yoji • JPN • TORASAN AND A PAPER BALLOON

OTOKO WA TSURAIYO, TORAJIRO KAMOMEUTA • 1981 • Yamada Yoji • JPN • TORASAN'S SONG OF THE SEAGULL
OTOKO WA TSURAIYO, TORAJIRO KOKORONO TABIJI • 1989 • Yamada Yoji • JPN • TORA-SAN GOES TO VIENNA
OTOKO WA TSURAIYO, TORAJIRO YUYAKE KOYAKE • 1976 • Yamada Yoji • JPN • TORASAN AND THE PAINTER
OTOKO WA TSURAIYO, UWASA NO TORAJIRO • 1978 • Yamada Yoji • JPN • TORASAN AND A LOVELY MAID
OTOKO WA TSURAIYO, WATASHI NO TORASAN • 1973 • Yamada Yoji • JPN • TORASAN LOVES AN ARTIST
OTOKONO ICHIDAIJI • 1960 • Maruyama Seiji • JPN
OTOMAR KORBELAR • 1960 • *Stallich Jan (Ph)* • DOC • CZC
OTOME-GOKORO SANNIN SHIMAI • 1935 • Naruse Mikio • JPN • THREE SISTERS WITH MAIDEN HEARTS
OTON ZUPANCIC • 1951 • Kosmac France • YGS
OTONALES, LAS • 1963 • Seto Javier, Girolami Marino • SPN
OTONO Y EL DESEO, EL • 1970 • *Cine Prods. Internacionale* • MXC
OTONO Y PRIMAVERA • 1947 • Fernandez Bustamente Adolfo • MXC
OTOSHI ANA see **KASHI TO KODOMO** • 1962
OTOSHIMAE • 1967 • Ishii Teruo • JPN • THREE GAMBLERS, THE
OTOTO • 1960 • Ichikawa Kon • JPN • YOUNGER BROTHER ○ HER BROTHER
OTOTO • 1976 • Yamane Shigeyuki • JPN • HER BROTHER
OTPISANI • 1975 • Djordjevic Aleksandar • YGS • WRITTEN OFF
OTRA, LA • 1946 • Gavaldon Roberto • MXC
OTRA ALCOBA, LA • 1976 • de la Iglesia Eloy • SPN
OTRA CARA DEL PLACER, LA • 1978 • Iquino Ignacio F. • SPN
OTRA HISTORIA DE AMOR • 1986 • de Zarate Americo Ortiz • ARG • ANOTHER LOVE STORY
OTRA ILUSION, LA • 1989 • Zambrano Roque • VNZ • OTHER ILLUSION, THE
OTRA IMAGEN, LA • 1973 • Ribas Antoni • SPN
OTRA ORILLA, LA • 1966 • Madrid Jose Luis • SPN • FROM THE OTHER SIDE ○ OTHER SHORE, THE
OTRA PRIMAVERA • 1949 • Crevenna Alfredo B. • MXC
OTRA RESIDENCIA, LA • 1970 • Paso Alfonso • SPN • OTHER BOARDING SCHOOL, THE
OTRA SOMBRA, LA • 1948 • Maroto Eduardo G. • SPN
OTRA VEZ ADIOS • 1981 • Rivas Miguel Angel • SPN • GOODBYE AGAIN
OTRA VEZ, SENORITA • 1968 • Wenceslao Jose Pepe • PHL
OTRA VIDA DEL CAPITAN CONTRERAS, LA • 1954 • Gil Rafael • SPN
OTRA VIRGINIDAD, LA • 1974 • Torres Juan Manuel • MXC • OTHER VIRGINITY, THE
OTRA VUELTA DE TUERCA • 1985 • de la Iglesia Eloy • SPN • TURN OF THE SCREW, THE
OTRA Y YO, LA • 1949 • Momplet Antonio • ARG
OTRANSKY ZAMEK • 1977 • Svankmajer Jan • ANM • CZC • CASTLE OF OTRANTO, THE
OTRO ARBOL DE GUERNICA, EL • 1969 • Lazaga Pedro • SPN
OTRO CRIMEN, EL • 1990 • Morantes Carlos Gonzalez • MXC • OTHER CRIME, THE
OTRO CRISTOBAL, EL • 1962 • Gatti Armand • CUB, FRN • OTHER CHRISTOPHER, THE ○ AUTRE CRISTOBAL, L'
OTRO FU MANCHU, EL • 1945 • Barreiro Ramon • SPN • OTHER FU MANCHU, THE
OTRO YO DE MARCELA, EL • 1950 • de Zavalia Alberto • ARG
OTROKI VO VSELENNOI • 1975 • Viktorov Richard • USS • TEENAGERS IN SPACE
OTROS TIEMPOS • 1959 • Fernandez Cuenca Carlos • SPN
OTSY • 1989 • Syrenko Arkady • USS • FATHERS
OTT IN SPACE • 1962 • Tuganov Elbert • ANS • USS
OTTA GA MITA • 1964 • Masumura Yasuzo • JPN • LOVE AND GREED
OTTAR • 1976 • Vennerod Petter • SHT • NRW
OTTAVA GENERAZIONE • 1977 • Petroni Giulio • ITL
OTTAWA 80 see **OTTAWA FESTIVAL LOGO** • 1980
OTTAWA FESTIVAL LOGO • 1980 • Patel Ishu • ANS • CND • OTTAWA 80
OTTAWA ON THE RIVER • 1939 • Crawley Budge, Crawley Judith • DOC • CND
OTTAWA VALLEY • 1976 • Manatis Janine • MTV • CND
OTTER, THE see **NUTRIA, LA** • 1971
OTTO AND THE NUDE WAVE see **OTTO UND DIE NACKTE WELLE** • 1968
OTTO DER AUSSERFRIESISCHE • 1989 • Waalkes Otto, Wajda Marijan • FRG
OTTO E MEZZO • 1963 • Fellini Federico • ITL • EIGHT AND A HALF ○ 8½
OTTO ER ET NAESEHORN • 1982 • Hammerich Rumle • DNM • OTTO THE RHINO ○ OTTO IS A RHINO
OTTO IS A RHINO see **OTTO ER ET NAESEHORN** • 1982
OTTO IS KEEN ON WOMEN see **OTTO IST AUF FRAUEN SCHARF** • 1968
OTTO IST AUF FRAUEN SCHARF • 1968 • Antel Franz • AUS, FRG, ITL • OTTO IS KEEN ON WOMEN
OTTO LUCK • 1915 • *Bray J. R./ Carlson Wallace A. (P)* • SHS • USA
OTTO MILLIONI DI DOLLARI • 1915 • Serena Gustavo • ITL
OTTO NO TEISO • 1937 • Yamamoto Kajiro • JPN • HUSBAND'S CHASTITY, A
OTTO THE ARTIST • 1916 • McKim Edwin • SHT • USA
OTTO THE BELLBOY • 1916 • McKim Edwin • SHT • USA
OTTO THE COBBLER • 1916 • McKim Edwin • SHT • USA
OTTO, THE FILM • 1986 • *Waalkes Otto* • FRG
OTTO THE GARDENER • 1916 • McKim Edwin • SHT • USA
OTTO THE HERO • 1916 • McKim Edwin • SHT • USA
OTTO THE REPORTER • 1916 • McKim Edwin • SHT • USA
OTTO THE RHINO see **OTTO ER ET NAESEHORN** • 1982
OTTO THE SALESMAN • 1916 • McKim Edwin • SHT • USA
OTTO THE SLEUTH • 1916 • McKim Edwin • SHT • USA
OTTO THE SOLDIER • 1916 • McKim Edwin • SHT • USA
OTTO THE TRAFFIC COP • 1916 • McKim Edwin • SHT • USA
OTTO UND DIE NACKTE WELLE • 1968 • Siegmund Gunther • FRG • OTTO AND THE NUDE WAVE
OTTO YULEVITCH SCHMIDT • 1963 • Schneiderov Vladimir • DOC • USS
OTTOBI KAGO • 1952 • Makino Masahiro • JPN • CAGE FOR HUSBANDS
OTTOCARO WEISS REFORME SON ENTREPRISE see **MORT DU DIRECTEUR DE CIRQUE DE PUCES, LA** • 1974
OTTOKAR, THE WORLD REFORMER • 1976 • Kratzert Hans • GDR
OTTOMAN BRAVE, THE see **OSMANLI KABADAYISI** • 1967
OTTO'S CABARET • 1915 • McKim Edwin • USA
OTTO'S LEGACY • 1916 • McKim Edwin • SHT • USA
OTTO'S VACATION • 1916 • McKim Edwin • SHT • USA
OTVAD HORIZONTA • 1960 • Zhandov Zahari • BUL • BEYOND THE HORIZON
OTVECELI NA DAVNO CHRISANTEMY V SADO • 1916 • Arkatov Alexander • USS • IT'S LONG SINCE THE CHRYSANTHEMUMS BLOOMED IN THE GARDENS
OTYETS SERGII • 1979 • Talankin Igor • USS • FATHER SERGIUS ○ FATHER SERGI ○ OTETS SERGII
OU EST MA RAISON? see **AYNA AQLI?** • 1974
OU EST PASSE TOM? • 1971 • Giovanni Jose • FRN, ITL
OU ETES-VOUS DONC..? • 1968 • Groulx Gilles • CND
OU L'ESPERANCE OU L'AVEUGLE JALOUSIE • 1919 • Protazanov Yakov • USS
OU O INVERNO, OU.. • 1965 • Tropa Alfredo • SHT • PRT
OU SONT PASSEES LES JEUNES FILLES EN FLEUR? • Desvilles Jean • FRN
OU TOUSSENT LES PETIT OISEAUX? • 1974 • Buyens Frans • BLG
OU VA LA VILLE? • 1972 • Regnier Michel • DCS • CND
OU VAS-TU KOUMBA • 1971 • Ferrari Alain, Aure Simon • GBN
OUADHIA, LES • 1964 • Rachedi Ahmed • SHT • ALG
OUANGA (UKN) see **DRUMS OF THE JUNGLE** • 1935
OUANZERBE, CAPITALE DE LA MAGIE see **MAGICIENS NOIRS, LES** • 1949
OUBLIE • 1927 • Dulac Germaine • FRN • PRINCESSE MANDANE, LA
OUBLIE-MOI, MANDOLINE • 1975 • Wyn Michel • FRN
OUBLIETTE, L' • 1912 • Feuillade Louis • FRN
OUBLIETTE, THE • 1914 • Giblyn Charles • USA
OUCH! • 1967 • Bryant Gerard • UKN
OUDER WORDEN • 1975 • van Brakel Nouchka • DOC • NTH • AGEING ○ GROWING OLD
OUDIS ANAMARTITOS • 1967 • Avrameas Nikos • GRC • NONE WITHOUT SIN ○ SINNERS
OUEST • 1963 • Grospierre Louis • DCS • FRN
OUI A L'AMOUR, NON A LA GUERRE • 1969 • Antel Franz • FRN
OUIGOURS -MINORITE NATIONALE -SINKIANG, LES • 1977 • Ivens Joris (c/d) • SHT • FRN
OUIJA BOARD, THE • 1920 • Fleischer Dave • ANS • USA
OUISTITI DE TOTO, L' • 1914 • Cohl Emile • ANS • FRN
OUISTITIS, LES • 1969 • Reichenbach Francois • FRN
OUKAIKON, LE TEMPS DES ERABLES • 1978 • Dinel Pierre • CND
OUPA EN DIE PLAASNOOIENTJIE • 1960 • SAF
OUPA FOR SALE • 1968 • Daneel Richard • SAF • GRANDFATHER FOR SALE
OUR ACQUAINTANCES • 1969 • Gurin Ilya • USS
OUR AGGIE • 1921 • Denton Jack • UKN
OUR AMERICAN PRINCE • 1915 • Vekroff Perry N. • USA
OUR AUNT FROM AFRICA see **KOUKLOS, O** • 1968
OUR BABY • 1913 • *Gem* • USA
OUR BABY • 1914 • Finn Arthur • UKN
OUR BESSIE • 1912 • Haldane Bert? • UKN
OUR BEST • Povh Dusan • SHT • YGS
OUR BETTER SELVES • 1919 • Fitzmaurice George • USA
OUR BETTERS • 1933 • Cukor George • USA
OUR BIT OF THE WORLD see **BETRAYER, THE** • 1921
OUR BLUSHING BRIDES • 1930 • Beaumont Harry • USA
OUR BOY see **VARAN POKJE** • 1936
OUR BOY BADENOV • 1988 • Larry Sheldon • USA
OUR BOYHOOD DAYS • 1906 • Mottershaw Frank • UKN
OUR BOYS • 1915 • Morgan Sidney • UKN
OUR BOYS • 1917 • Berthelet Arthur • SHT • USA
OUR BOYS see **MEIDAN POIKAMME** • 1929
OUR BOYS AT SEA see **MEIDAN POIKAMME MERELLA** • 1933
OUR BOYS IN PURSUIT OF MEXICAN BANDITS • 1916 • *Unicorn* • SHT • USA
OUR BOYS IN UNIFORM see **BEREDSKAPSPOJKAR** • 1941
OUR BUSINESS IS FUN • 1975 • Whyte Michael • UKN
OUR CARIBBEAN COUSINS • 1933 • Sparling Gordon • DCS • CND
OUR CENTURY • Peleshyan Artavazd • USS
OUR CHAMPIONS see **NASHI CHEMPIONY** • 1950
OUR CHILDREN • 1913 • Thornby Robert T. • USA
OUR CHIVALROUS FISH-PEDDLER see **ISSHIN TASUKE EDOKKO MATSURI** • 1967
OUR CISSY • 1973 • Parker Alan • SHT • UKN
OUR CITY see **NGAIO** • 1989
OUR COMBAT • 1939 • Haas Hugo
OUR CONGRESSMAN • 1924 • Wagner Robert • SHT • USA
OUR CONSTRUCTION • 1946 • NKR
OUR CORRESPONDENT • 1959 • Granik Anatoli • USS
OUR COUNTRY • 1944 • Eldridge John • DOC • UKN
OUR COUNTRY see **NAMMA OORU** • 1968
OUR COUNTRY COUSIN • 1914 • Henderson Dell • USA
OUR COUNTRYMEN see **VSICHNI DOBRI RODACI** • 1968
OUR COUNTRY'S YOUTH see **MOLODOST NASHEI STRANY** • 1946
OUR COURTYARD see **NASH DVOR** • 1956
OUR COUSIN FROM ABROAD • 1908 • Fitzhamon Lewin? • UKN
OUR CRAZY FAMILY see **NASE BLAZNIVA RODINA** • 1968
OUR DAD • 1920 • Ingraham Lloyd • USA
OUR DAILY BREAD • 1934 • Vidor King • USA • MIRACLE OF LIFE, THE (UKN) ○ STRUGGLE FOR LIFE
OUR DAILY BREAD • 1946 • Cutts Graham • DCS • UKN
OUR DAILY BREAD see **UNSER TAGLICHES BROT** • 1929
OUR DAILY BREAD see **CITY GIRL** • 1930
OUR DAILY BREAD (USA) see **UNSER TAGLICH BROT** • 1949
OUR DAILY DAY see **DEN NAS KAZDODENNY** • 1969
OUR DAILY WATER • 1976 • Shengelaya Eldar • USS
OUR DANCING DAUGHTERS • 1928 • Beaumont Harry • USA • DANCING DAUGHTERS ○ DANCING GIRL, THE
OUR DARE DEVIL CHIEF • 1915 • Parrott Charles • USA
OUR DARLING NEEDS NOURISHMENT • 1916 • *Unicorn* • USA
OUR DARLING'S CHIPS • 1916 • *Unicorn* • USA
OUR DARLING'S PLAYMATES • 1916 • *Unicorn* • USA
OUR DAUGHTER • 1914 • *Stuart Julia* • USA
OUR DEAR BUDDIES see **KIMI GA WAKAMONO** • 1970
OUR DEFIANT ONES see **NASI FURIANTI** • 1937
OUR DUMB FRIEND • 1930 • *Asfi* • ANS • UKN
OUR ENEMY'S SPY • 1914 • *Walcamp Marie* • USA
OUR EXPLOITS AT WEST POLEY • 1987 • Lawrence Diarmid • UKN
OUR FAIRY PLAY • 1914 • Beggs Lee • USA
OUR FAMILY see **BIZIM AILE** • 1976
OUR FAMILY BUSINESS • 1981 • Collins Robert • TVM • USA • UNDERBOSS, THE
OUR FARMER PRINCE • 1932 • Williamson A. Stanley • UKN
OUR FATHER see **PADRE NUESTRO** • 1984
OUR FATHER'S HOUSE see **OTCHII DOM** • 1959
OUR FATHER'S YOUTH see **YUNOST NASHIKH OTSOV** • 1958
OUR FIGHTING NAVY • 1937 • Walker Norman • UKN • TORPEDOED! (USA) ○ FIGHTING NAVY, THE
OUR FOOLISH FAMILY see **NASE BLAZNIVA RODINA** • 1968
OUR FRIEND, THE ATOM • 1956 • Luske Hamilton • DOC • USA
OUR FRIENDS THE HAYSEEDS • 1917 • Smith Beaumont • ASL
OUR FUNNY FINNY FRIENDS • 1949 • Kneitel Seymour • ANS • USA
OUR GANG • 1923 • McGowan Robert • SHT • USA
OUR GANG see **VARAT GANG** • 1942
OUR GANG COMEDY • 1923-44 • SHS • USA • HAL ROACH'S OUR GANG COMEDY
OUR GANG FOLLIES OF 1936 • 1935 • Meins Gus • SHT • USA
OUR GANG FOLLIES OF 1938 • 1937 • Douglas Gordon • SHT • USA
OUR GIRL FRIDAY • 1953 • Langley Noel • UKN • ADVENTURES OF SADIE (USA)
OUR GIRLS AND THEIR PHYSIQUE • 1920 • Malins Geoffrey H. • SER • UKN
OUR GREAT MIKADO • 1907 • Morland John • UKN
OUR GROUP see **NASZ ZESPOL** • 1955
OUR HAPPINESS ALONE see **NIJU-ISSAI NO CHICHI** • 1964
OUR HEALTH IS NOT FOR SALE • 1978 • Richardson Boyce • DOC • CND
OUR HEART • 1917 • Gardin Vladimir • USS
OUR HEART see **NASHE SERDSTE** • 1946
OUR HEARTS WERE GROWING UP • 1946 • Russell William D. • USA
OUR HEARTS WERE YOUNG AND GAY • 1944 • Allen Lewis • USA
OUR HEAVENLY BODIES (USA) see **WUNDER DER SCHOPFUNG** • 1925
OUR HERITAGE see **THIS ENGLAND** • 1941
OUR HIDDEN WEALTH • 1962 • Porter Eric • ANS • ASL
OUR HITLER see **HITLER: EIN FILM AUS DEUTSCHLAND** • 1977
OUR HOLIDAY • 1967 • Tosheva Nevena • DOC • BUL
OUR HOME IS OUR CASTLE see **BALLADE PA CHRISTIANSHAVN** • 1971
OUR HOME-MADE ARMY • 1914 • *Ab* • USA
OUR HOSPITALITY • 1923 • Keaton Buster, Blystone John G. • USA
OUR HOUSE • 1978 • Armstrong Mary • MTV • CND
OUR HOUSE see **NASH DOM** • 1965
OUR HOUSEMAID • 1910 • *Powers* • USA
OUR HUSBAND • 1935 • Heale Patrick K. • UKN
OUR HUSBANDS see **NOSTRI MARITI, I** • 1966
OUR INCREDIBLE WORLD • 1966 • Abraham Edward Stewart • DOC • UKN • MYSTERY AND THE PLEASURE, THE
OUR INDIA (USA) see **HINDUSTAN HAMARA** • 1950
OUR INDONESIAN FRIEND • 1960 • Karmen Roman • DOC • USS
OUR INNOCENT CREATURES see **OTOKO NANTE NANISA** • 1967
OUR INSTRUCTOR see **WARAREGA KYOKAN** • 1939
OUR INTREPID CORRESPONDENT • 1911 • Stow Percy • UKN
OUR ISLAND NATION • 1937 • Hunt John • UKN • ISLAND NATION, AN
OUR KID see **KOLYOK** • 1959
OUR LADS • 1959 • Vitandis Gheorghe • RMN
OUR LADY OF COMPASSION see **COMPADECIDA, A** • 1969
OUR LADY OF THE PAINTS see **DAME EN COLEURS, LA** • 1984
OUR LADY OF THE PEARLS • 1912 • *Davenport Dorothy* • USA
OUR LADY OF THE SPHERE • Jordan Larry • ANM • USA
OUR LADY OF THE TURKS see **NOSTRA SIGNORA DEI TURCHI** • 1968
OUR LAND see **MAA BHOOMI** • 1979
OUR LAND AUSTRALIA • 1972 • Crombie Donald • DOC • ASL
OUR LAND IS OUR LIFE • 1974 • Ianzelo Tony, Richardson Boyce • DOC • CND
OUR LAND OF PEACE (USA) see **NUESTRA TIERRA DE PAZ** • 1940
OUR LAST DAYS IN MOSCOW see **NOS DERNIERS JOURS A MOSCOU** • 1988
OUR LAST SPRING see **EROICA** • 1960
OUR LATIN THING • 1972 • Gast Leon • DOC • USA
OUR LEADING CITIZEN • 1922 • Green Alfred E. • USA
OUR LEADING CITIZEN • 1939 • Santell Alfred • USA
OUR LIFE IS NOW see **MAMMA** • 1982
OUR LITTLE AFFAIRS see **MI KIS UGYEINK, A** • 1988
OUR LITTLE FAIRY • 1913 • Dwan Allan? • USA
OUR LITTLE GIRL • 1935 • Robertson John S. • USA • HEAVEN'S GATE
OUR LITTLE NELL • 1918 • *Essanay* • SHT • USA
OUR LITTLE NELL • 1924 • Roach Hal • SHT • USA
OUR LITTLE RED RIDING HOOD see **NASE KARKULKA** • 1960
OUR LITTLE TOWN see **MESTECKO NA DLANI** • 1942
OUR LITTLE WIFE • 1918 • Dillon Eddie • USA

OUR LOVE see **AGAPI MAS, I** • 1968
OUR LOVE IS SLIPPING AWAY • 1965 • Miller Arnold Louis • UKN
OUR LOVE LIFE BEGINS ANEW see **PONOVO POCINJE LJUBAVNI ZIVOT** • 1974
OUR LUKE • 1970 • Tammer Peter • DOC • ASL
OUR MAN see **NASZ CZLOWIEK** • 1975
OUR MAN see **NAS CLOVEK** • 1985
OUR MAN FLINT • 1966 • Mann Daniel • USA
OUR MAN FLINT: DEAD ON TARGET • 1978 • Scanlan Joseph L. • TVM • USA
OUR MAN FROM BOND STREET see **MAD MISSION 3: OUR MAN IN BOND STREET** • 1984
OUR MAN IN BAGDAD see **GIOCO DELLE SPIE, IL** • 1966
OUR MAN IN HAVANA • 1960 • Reed Carol • UKN
OUR MAN IN JAMAICA see **A-001 OPERAZIONE GIAMAICA** • 1965
OUR MAN IN MARRAKESH • 1966 • Sharp Don • UKN • BANG! BANG! YOU'RE DEAD (USA) ○ I SPY, I SPY
OUR MAN IN MARRAKESH see **HOMME DE MARRAKECH, L'** • 1966
OUR MAN IN THE CARIBBEAN • 1962 • *Thompson Carlos* • MTV • UKN
OUR MAN IN THE SPACE RACE • 1958 • Watson Patrick • DOC • CND
OUR MARRIAGE see **WATAKUSHI-TACHI NO KEKKON** • 1962
OUR MARSHAL see **NASZ MARSZALEK** • 1947
OUR MEN IN BAGDAD (USA) see **GIOCO DELLE SPIE, IL** • 1966
OUR MEXICAN NEIGHBORS • 1922 • *Church Arthur P.* • DOC • USA
OUR MISS BROOKS • 1956 • Lewis Al • USA
OUR MISS FRED • 1972 • Kellett Bob • UKN
OUR MODERN MAIDENS • 1929 • Conway Jack • USA
OUR MOSCOW • 1939 • Kaufman Mikhail • DOC • USS
OUR MOTHER'S HOUSE • 1967 • Clayton Jack • UKN, USA
OUR MRS. CHESNEY • 1918 • Ince Ralph • USA
OUR MS HAMMOND • 1973 • Woods Grahame • CND
OUR MUTUAL FRIEND • 1922 • Tully May • USA
OUR MUTUAL FRIEND see **NASH OBSHCHII DRUG** • 1961
OUR MUTUAL GIRL MEETS THE RETURNING GIANTS AND THE WHITE SOX see **OUR MUTUAL GIRL NO.10** • 1914
OUR MUTUAL GIRL NO.1 • 1914 • *Phillips Norma* • USA
OUR MUTUAL GIRL NO.2 • 1914 • *Reliance* • USA
OUR MUTUAL GIRL NO.3 • 1914 • *Reliance* • USA
OUR MUTUAL GIRL NO.4 • 1914 • *Reliance* • USA
OUR MUTUAL GIRL NO.5 • 1914 • Noble Jack • USA
OUR MUTUAL GIRL NO.6 • 1914 • *Reliance* • USA
OUR MUTUAL GIRL NO.7 • 1914 • *Reliance* • USA
OUR MUTUAL GIRL NO.8 • 1914 • *Reliance* • USA
OUR MUTUAL GIRL NO.9 • 1914 • *Reliance* • USA
OUR MUTUAL GIRL NO.10 • 1914 • *Reliance* • USA • OUR MUTUAL GIRL MEETS THE RETURNING GIANTS AND THE WHITE SOX
OUR MUTUAL GIRL NO.11 • 1914 • *Reliance* • USA
OUR MUTUAL GIRL NO.12 • 1914 • *Reliance* • USA
OUR MUTUAL GIRL NO.13 • 1914 • *Reliance* • USA
OUR MUTUAL GIRL NO.14 • 1914 • *Reliance* • USA
OUR MUTUAL GIRL NO.15 • 1914 • *Reliance* • USA
OUR MUTUAL GIRL NO.16 • 1914 • *Reliance* • USA
OUR MUTUAL GIRL NO.17 • 1914 • *Reliance* • USA
OUR MUTUAL GIRL NO.18 • 1914 • *Reliance* • USA
OUR MUTUAL GIRL NO.19 • 1914 • *Reliance* • USA
OUR MUTUAL GIRL NO.20 • 1914 • *Reliance* • USA
OUR MUTUAL GIRL NO.21 • 1914 • *Reliance* • USA
OUR MUTUAL GIRL NO.22 • 1914 • *Reliance* • USA
OUR MUTUAL GIRL NO.23 • 1914 • *Reliance* • USA
OUR MUTUAL GIRL NO.24 • 1914 • Noble Jack • USA
OUR MUTUAL GIRL NO.25 • 1914 • *Reliance* • USA
OUR MUTUAL GIRL NO.26 • 1914 • *Reliance* • USA
OUR MUTUAL GIRL NO.27 • 1914 • *Reliance* • USA
OUR MUTUAL GIRL NO.27 • 1914 • *Reliance* • USA
OUR MUTUAL GIRL NO.28 • 1914 • *Reliance* • USA
OUR MUTUAL GIRL NO.29 • 1914 • *Reliance* • USA
OUR MUTUAL GIRL NO.30 • 1914 • *Reliance* • USA
OUR MUTUAL GIRL NO.31 • 1914 • *Reliance* • USA
OUR MUTUAL GIRL NO.32 • 1914 • *Reliance* • USA
OUR MUTUAL GIRL NO.33 • 1914 • *Reliance* • USA
OUR MUTUAL GIRL NO.34 • 1914 • *Reliance* • USA
OUR MUTUAL GIRL NO.35 • 1914 • *Reliance* • USA
OUR MUTUAL GIRL NO.36 • 1914 • Noble Jack • USA
OUR MUTUAL GIRL NO.37 • 1914 • *Reliance* • USA
OUR MUTUAL GIRL NO.38 • 1914 • *Reliance* • USA
OUR MUTUAL GIRL NO.39 • 1914 • *Reliance* • USA
OUR MUTUAL GIRL NO.40 • 1914 • *Reliance* • USA
OUR MUTUAL GIRL NO.41 • 1914 • *Reliance* • USA
OUR MUTUAL GIRL NO.42 • 1914 • *Reliance* • USA
OUR MUTUAL GIRL NO.43 • 1914 • Grey John Wesley • USA
OUR MUTUAL GIRL NO.44 • 1914 • *Reliance* • USA
OUR MUTUAL GIRL NO.45 • 1914 • *Reliance* • USA
OUR MUTUAL GIRL NO.46 • 1914 • *Reliance* • USA
OUR MUTUAL GIRL NO.47 • 1914 • *Reliance* • USA
OUR MUTUAL GIRL NO.48 • 1914 • *Reliance* • USA
OUR MUTUAL GIRL NO.49 • 1914 • *Reliance* • USA
OUR MUTUAL GIRL NO.50 • 1915 • *Reliance* • USA
OUR MUTUAL GIRL NO.51 • 1915 • *Reliance* • USA
OUR MUTUAL GIRL NO.52 • 1915 • *Reliance* • USA
OUR NAGGING WIVES • 1930 • Gillstrom Arvid E. • USA
OUR NEIGHBORS • 1913 • *Selig* • USA
OUR NEIGHBORS -THE CARTERS • 1940 • Murphy Ralph • USA
OUR NEIGHBOR'S WIFE • 1912 • *Cassinelli Dolores* • USA
OUR NEIGHBOUR MISS YAE see **TONARI NO YAECHAN** • 1934
OUR NEW COOK • 1903 • Collins Alf? • UKN
OUR NEW ERRAND BOY • 1905 • Williamson James • UKN
OUR NEW GENERAL SERVANT • 1898 • *Paul R. W.* • UKN
OUR NEW MINISTER • 1910 • *Selig* • USA
OUR NEW MINISTER • 1913 • *Conyers Joseph* • USA
OUR NEW PILLAR BOX • 1907 • Cooper Arthur • UKN • ANIMATED PILLAR BOX, THE
OUR NEW POLICEMAN • 1906 • Fitzhamon Lewin • UKN
OUR NORTHERN CITIZEN • 1956 • Howe John • DOC • CND
OUR NORTHERN NEIGHBOUR • 1942 • Daly Tom • DCS • CND • RUSSIA'S FOREIGN POLICY
OUR OATH see **SLUBUJEMY!** • 1952
OUR OCTOBER see **NASHIAT OKTOMVRI** • 1967
OUR OLD CAR • 1946 • Endfield Cy • SHT • USA
OUR OTHER LIVES • 1916 • Mullin Eugene • SHT • USA
OUR OWN AGE see **WARERU NO JIDAI** • 1959
OUR OWN ORCHESTRA see **ORETACHI NON KOKYOGAKU** • 1978
OUR PALACE • 1953 • Abuladze Tengiz, Chkheidze Revaz • DOC • USS
OUR PARENTS-IN-LAW • 1913 • Smalley Phillips • USA
OUR PEOPLE • 1916 • *Washburn Bryant* • SHT • USA
OUR PEOPLE • 1963 • Mesaros Titus • DOC • RMN
OUR PLANET, THE EARTH • Sienski Maciej • PLN
OUR POOR RELATIONS • 1912 • *Solax* • USA
OUR PROFESSOR, THE ENEMY OF WOMEN see **PAN PROFESOR, NEPRITEL ZEN** • 1913
OUR RED RIDING HOOD see **NASE KARKULKA** • 1960
OUR REGIMENT • 1968 • Mur Oti • USA
OUR RELATIONS • 1936 • Lachman Harry • USA
OUR RUSSIAN ALLIES • 1942 • Marshall Herbert • DOC • UKN
OUR RUSSIAN FRONT • 1942 • Milestone Lewis, Ivens Joris • DCS • USA • REPORT FROM RUSSIA
OUR SCHOOL • 1939 • Rotha Paul • DOC • UKN
OUR SCHOOL • 1962 • Krish John • UKN
OUR SEA see **MARE NOSTRUM** • 1925
OUR SEASIDE HOLIDAY • 1906 • Mottershaw Frank • UKN
OUR SHATTERED DREAMS see **SINTRIMMIA TA ONIRA MAS** • 1967
OUR SHORT LIFE • 1980 • Warneke Lothar • GDR
OUR SILENT LOVE see **ZOKU NAMONAKU MAZUSHIKU UTSUKUSHIKU: CHICHI TO KO** • 1967
OUR SISTER-IN-LAW see **MAA VANDINA** • 1967
OUR SOIL see **TOKA JONE**
OUR SPLENDID DAUGHTER see **NASH MILYI DOKTOR** • 1958
OUR SPORTS CAR DAYS see **NOTRE JEUNESSE EN AUTO SPORT** • 1969
OUR STORY see **NOTRE HISTOIRE** • 1984
OUR STREET WAS PAVED WITH GOLD • 1973 • Kish Albert • DOC • CND
OUR TEACHER see **WARAREGA KYOKAN** • 1939
OUR TEDDY see **FIGHTING ROOSEVELTS, THE** • 1919
OUR TIME • 1974 • Hyams Peter • USA • DEATH OF HER INNOCENCE, THE
OUR TIME NO.1 • 1967 • Arvat Caterina, West Anthony • DCS • UKN
OUR TIMES see **TEMPI NOSTRI** • 1954
OUR TOWN • 1940 • Wood Sam • USA
OUR TOWN see **WAGA MACHI** • 1955
OUR TOWN see **MACHI** • 1961
OUR VERY OWN • 1950 • Miller David • USA
OUR VILLAGE see **IN SAT LA NOI** • 1951
OUR VILLAGE CLUB HOLDS A MARATHON RACE • 1908 • Raymond Charles? • UKN
OUR VILLAGE HEROES • 1911 • Coleby A. E. • UKN
OUR VINES HAVE TENDER GRAPES • 1945 • Rowland Roy • USA • FOR OUR VINES HAVE TENDER GRAPES
OUR VIRGIN ISLAND see **VIRGIN ISLAND** • 1958
OUR VISIT TO CHINA see **KINA VENDEGEI VOLTUNK** • 1957
OUR VOICES SHOULD ALSO BE HEARD • 1971 • Papic Krsto • SHT • YGS
OUR WEALTHY NEPHEW JOHN (USA) see **WEALTHY BROTHER JONATHAN** • 1911
OUR WEDDING see **ORETACHI NO WEDDING** • 1983
OUR WHITE HORSES FROM LIPICANCI see **NASI LIPICANCI** • 1951
OUR WIFE • 1931 • Horne James W. • SHT • USA
OUR WIFE • 1941 • Stahl John M. • USA
OUR WILLIE • 1913 • *Crystal* • USA
OUR WINNING SEASON • 1978 • Ruben Joseph • USA
OUR WIVES • 1913 • Lackaye James • USA
OUR WONDERFUL YEARS see **KAACHAN TO JUICHI-NIN NO KODOMO** • 1966
OUR YOUNG PRESIDENT see **WAKASHACHO DAIFUNSEN** • 1967
OUR YOUTH! see **NY I MOLODEZH!** • 1970
OURAGAN SUR LA MONTAGNE, L' • 1922 • Duvivier Julien • FRN
OURANOS • 1963 • Kanellopoulos Takis • GRC • CIEL, LE ○ HEAVEN
OURS, L' • 1960 • Sechan Edmond • FRN, ITL • TALKING BEAR, THE ○ BEAR, THE
OURS, UN • 1919 • Burguet Charles • FRN
OURS AT THE GATE • 1970 • Filan Ludovit • CZC
OURS ET LA POUPEE, L' • 1970 • Deville Michel • FRN • BEAR AND THE DOLL, THE
OURS ET LA SENTINELLE, L' • 1899 • Melies Georges • FRN • SENTRY'S STRATAGEM, THE
OURS OU TCHEKHOV EST-IL MISOGYNE? • 1977 • Koleva Maria • DCS • FRN
OURSELVES ALONE • 1936 • Summers Walter, Hurst Brian Desmond • UKN • RIVER OF UNREST
OURSIN DANS LA POCHE, UN • 1977 • Thomas Pascal • FRN
OURSINS, LES • 1926 • Sti Rene (c/d) • SHT • FRN
OURSINS, LES • 1929 • Painleve Jean • SHT • FRN
OURSINS, LES • 1953 • Painleve Jean • SHT • FRN • SEA URCHINS
OUSHMAN • 1939 • Kapoor Prithviraj • IND
OUSQUE TU VAS DE MEME? • 1973 • Bobet Jacques • CND
OUT • 1957 • Rogosin Lionel • UNN
OUT • 1982 • Hollander Eli • USA
OUT 1: NOLI ME TANGERE • 1970 • Rivette Jacques • FRN • OUT ONE
OUT 1: SPECTRE • 1970 • Rivette Jacques • FRN • OUT ONE: SPECTRE ○ OUT ONE OUT TWO ○ SPECTRE
OUT AGAIN, IN AGAIN • 1914 • *Tincher Fay* • USA
OUT AGAIN, IN AGAIN • 1917 • Beaudine William • SHT • USA
OUT AGAIN, IN AGAIN • 1948 • Rasinski Connie • ANS • USA
OUT AG'IN, IN AG'IN • 1916 • Semon Larry • SHT • USA
OUT ALL NIGHT • 1927 • Seiter William A. • USA • COMPLETELY AT SEA ○ I'LL BE THERE
OUT ALL NIGHT • 1933 • Taylor Sam • USA • EARLY TO BED ○ NIAGARA FALLS
OUT AND IN • 1913 • Sennett Mack • USA
OUT AND IN • 1918 • *Jaxon* • USA
OUT AND OUT ROUT • 1966 • Larriva Rudy • ANS • USA
OUT AT BIG RANCH see **ALLA EN EL RANCHO GRANDE** • 1936
OUT AT HOME • 1928 • Newfield Sam • SHT • USA
OUT BEYOND TOWN • 1948 • Garceau Raymond • DCS • CND • OMBRE AU PAYSAGE
OUT-BLACKED • 1914 • *Ab* • USA
OUT CALIFORNIA WAY • 1946 • Selander Lesley • USA
OUT COLD • 1988 • Mowbray Malcolm • UKN • STIFFS
OUT FOR A MILLION • 1915 • *Empire* • USA
OUT FOR A STROLL • 1915 • Hotaling Arthur D. • USA
OUT FOR FUN • 1954 • Barclay David • SHT • USA
OUT FOR MISCHIEF • 1910 • *Melies* • USA
OUT FOR THE COIN • 1917 • *Compson Betty* • SHT • USA
OUT FOR THE COUNT • 1916 • Miller Rube • USA
OUT FOR THE DAY • 1909 • *Lubin* • USA
OUT FOR THE DOUGH • 1917 • Beaudine William • SHT • USA
OUT FOR THE NIGHT • 1920 • Christie Al • SHT • USA
OUT-FOXED • 1949 • Avery Tex • ANS • USA
OUT FROM THE SHADOW • 1911 • Griffith D. W. • USA
OUT IN HAPPY HOLLOW • 1914 • *Gibson Margaret* • USA
OUT IN THE RAIN • 1914 • *Blackwell Carlyle* • USA
OUT IN THE RAIN • 1917 • Moss Howard S. • ANM • USA
OUT IN THE WORLD see **V LYUDKYAKH** • 1939
OUT OF A CLEAR BLUE SKY • 1918 • Neilan Marshall • USA
OUT OF A JOB • 1986 • Fortier Bob • MTV • CND
OUT OF AFRICA • 1985 • Pollack Sydney • USA
OUT OF AN OLD MAN'S HEAD see **I HUVET PA EN GAMMAL GUBBE** • 1968
OUT OF BONDAGE • 1915 • *Gish Dorothy* • USA
OUT OF BOREDOM see **SKUKI RADI** • 1968
OUT OF BOUNDS • 1986 • Tuggle Richard • USA
OUT OF CHAOS • 1944 • Craigie Jill • DOC • UKN
OUT OF COLLEGE see **GAKUSO O IDETE** • 1925
OUT OF CONTENTION see **VICTIM, THE** • 1972
OUT OF CONTROL • 1985 • Holzman Allan • USA • CROSSWINDS
OUT OF DARKNESS • 1911 • *Reliance* • USA
OUT OF DARKNESS • 1915 • Melford George • USA
OUT OF DARKNESS • 1941 • Lee Sammy • USA • VOICE OF LIBERTY
OUT OF DARKNESS see **SEDUTO ALLA SUA DESTRA** • 1968
OUT OF EVIL • Krumgold Joseph • ISR
OUT OF EVIL COMETH GOOD • 1912 • Buckland Warwick? • UKN
OUT OF EVIL COMETH GOOD • 1914 • Batley Ethyle • UKN
OUT OF GAS • 1933 • Horne James W. • SHT • USA
OUT OF HIS CLASS • 1913 • *Frontier* • USA
OUT OF HIS ELEMENT • 1912 • Coleby A. E.? • UKN
OUT OF IT • 1969 • Williams Paul • USA
OUT OF IT • 1977 • Cameron Ken • ASL
OUT OF LUCK • 1919 • Clifton Elmer • USA • NOBODY HOME
OUT OF LUCK • 1923 • Sedgwick Edward • USA • SUPERSTITION
OUT OF MIND see **MIND SHADOWS** • 1988
OUT OF MISCHIEF • 1910 • Melies Gaston • USA
OUT OF ORDER • 1916 • Myll Louis • SHT • USA
OUT OF ORDER • 1988 • Turpie Jonnie • UKN
OUT OF ORDER see **ABWARTS: DAS DUELL UBER DER TIEFE** • 1984
OUT OF OUR MINDS • 1984 • Bell John* • MTV • CND
OUT OF PETTICOAT LANE • 1914 • Grandon Francis J. • USA
OUT OF PLACE • 1922 • St. John Al • SHT • USA
OUT OF REACH OF THE DEVIL see **KAM CERT NEMUZE** • 1959
OUT OF ROSENHEIM see **BAGDAD CAFE** • 1988
OUT OF SCALE • 1951 • Hannah Jack • ANS • USA
OUT OF SEASON • 1975 • Bridges Alan • TVM • UKN • WINTER RATES
OUT OF SIGHT • 1966 • Weinrib Lennie • USA
OUT OF SIGHT, OUT OF MIND • 1914 • Henderson Dell • USA
OUT OF SIGHT OUT OF MIND • 1925 • Butler Alexander • UKN
OUT OF SIGHT, OUT OF MIND • 1983 • Dalen Zale R. • TVM • CND
OUT OF SILENCE • 1972 • Forest Leonard • DCS • CND
OUT OF SINGAPORE • 1932 • Hutchison Charles • USA
OUT OF STEP see **CONTREPIED** • 1965
OUT OF STEP see **U RASKO-RAKU** • 1968
OUT OF THE AIR • 1914 • *Turner Fred A.* • USA
OUT OF THE ARCTIC • 1911 • *Solax* • USA
OUT OF THE ASHES • 1915 • Bartlett Charles • USA
OUT OF THE BAG • 1917 • Santell Alfred • SHT • USA
OUT OF THE BANDBOX • 1953 • Redhead Norman • UKN
OUT OF THE BEAST A MAN WAS BORN • 1913 • *Lubin* • USA
OUT OF THE BLACKS, INTO THE BLUES see **EN REMONTANT LE MISSISSIPPI** • 1971
OUT OF THE BLUE • 1931 • Gerrard Gene, Orton John • UKN
OUT OF THE BLUE • 1947 • Jason Leigh • USA
OUT OF THE BLUE • 1980 • Hopper Dennis • CND
OUT OF THE BLUE • 1988 • Peploe Mark • USA
OUT OF THE BODY • 1988 • Trenchard-Smith Brian • ASL
OUT OF THE BORDERS OF TREASON see **STA SINORA TIS PRODOSIAS** • 1968
OUT OF THE BOX • 1944 • Bishop Terry • DCS • UKN
OUT OF THE CHORUS • 1921 • Blache Herbert • USA
OUT OF THE CLOUDS • 1921 • Franchon Leonard • USA
OUT OF THE CLOUDS • 1955 • Dearden Basil, Relph Michael • UKN
OUT OF THE DARK • 1911 • Davis Ulysses • USA
OUT OF THE DARK • 1912 • *Thanhouser* • USA
OUT OF THE DARK • 1988 • Schroeder Michael • USA
OUT OF THE DARK see **VOICE IN THE DARK, A** • 1921
OUT OF THE DARKNESS • 1913 • *Kinemacolor* • USA
OUT OF THE DARKNESS • 1914 • *Rex* • USA
OUT OF THE DARKNESS • 1914 • *American* • USA
OUT OF THE DARKNESS • 1920 • *Mccoy Gertrude* • USA
OUT OF THE DARKNESS • 1985 • Krish John • UKN
OUT OF THE DARKNESS • 1985 • Taylor Jud • TVM • USA
OUT OF THE DARKNESS see **SEDUTO ALLA SUA DESTRA** • 1968
OUT OF THE DARKNESS see **NIGHT CREATURE** • 1978
OUT OF THE DARKNESS (UKN) see **TEENAGE CAVEMAN** • 1958

OUT OF THE DEEP • 1912 • *Wilson Ben* • USA
OUT OF THE DEPTHS • 1911 • *Solax* • USA
OUT OF THE DEPTHS • 1912 • *Bushman Francis X.* • USA
OUT OF THE DEPTHS • 1914 • *Rex* • USA
OUT OF THE DEPTHS • 1914 • *Lubin* • USA
OUT OF THE DEPTHS • 1921 • Thayer Otis B.?, Reicher Frank? • USA
OUT OF THE DEPTHS • 1946 • Lederman D. Ross • USA
OUT OF THE DEPUTY'S HANDS • 1914 • Mackley Arthur • USA
OUT OF THE DREGS • 1914 • *Kb* • USA
OUT OF THE DRIFTS • 1916 • Dawley J. Searle • USA
OUT OF THE DUST • 1920 • McCarthy John P. • USA
OUT OF THE ETHER • 1933 • *Mintz Charles (P)* • ANS • USA
OUT OF THE FAR EAST • 1914 • Crane Frank H. • USA
OUT OF THE FLAMES • 1915 • King Burton L. • USA
OUT OF THE FLOTSAM • 1916 • Melville Wilbert • SHT • USA
OUT OF THE FOG • 1919 • Capellani Albert • USA
OUT OF THE FOG • 1941 • Litvak Anatole • USA • GENTLE PEOPLE, THE
OUT OF THE FOG • 1962 • Tully Montgomery • UKN
OUT OF THE FRYING PAN • 1914 • *Nestor* • USA
OUT OF THE FRYING PAN • 1914 • Plumb Hay? • UKN
OUT OF THE FRYING PAN see **ALL AROUND FRYING PAN** • 1925
OUT OF THE FRYING PAN see **YOUNG AND WILLING** • 1942
OUT OF THE FRYING PAN INTO THE FIRE see **Z BLATA DO LOUZE** • 1934
OUT OF THE GRAVE • 1913 • *White Pearl* • USA
OUT OF THE INKWELL • 1915 • Fleischer Max • ANS • USA
OUT OF THE INKWELL • 1919-23 • *Fleischer Max (P)* • ASS • USA
OUT OF THE INKWELL • 1938 • Fleischer Dave • ANS • USA
OUT OF THE JAWS OF DEATH • 1913 • *Kalem* • USA
OUT OF THE MIST • 1916 • Daly William Robert • SHT • USA
OUT OF THE MIST see **SOHN DER HAGAR, DER** • 1926
OUT OF THE NIGHT • 1910 • Porter Edwin S. • USA
OUT OF THE NIGHT • 1912 • *Bushman Francis X.* • USA
OUT OF THE NIGHT • 1914 • Ince Thomas H., Spencer Richard V. • USA
OUT OF THE NIGHT • 1918 • Kirkwood James • USA
OUT OF THE NIGHT • 1945 • Ulmer Edgar G. • USA • STRANGE ILLUSION (UKN)
OUT OF THE PAST • 1910 • *Vitagraph* • USA
OUT OF THE PAST • 1912 • Collins Edwin J. • UKN
OUT OF THE PAST • 1913 • *Crystal* • USA
OUT OF THE PAST • 1914 • Belmore Lionel • USA
OUT OF THE PAST • 1927 • Fitzgerald Dallas M. • USA
OUT OF THE PAST • 1933 • Hiscott Leslie • UKN
OUT OF THE PAST • 1947 • Tourneur Jacques • USA • BUILD MY GALLOWS HIGH (UKN)
OUT OF THE QUAGMIRE • 1916 • Marston Theodore • SHT • USA
OUT OF THE RAIN • 1917 • *Peter Pan* • ANS • USA
OUT OF THE RAINBOW • 1916 • Ricketts Thomas • SHT • USA
OUT OF THE RUINS • 1915 • Miller Ashley • USA
OUT OF THE RUINS • 1928 • Dillon John Francis • USA
OUT OF THE SEA • 1915 • *Huling Lorraine* • USA
OUT OF THE SHADOW • 1919 • Chautard Emile • USA
OUT OF THE SHADOW • 1961 • Winner Michael • UKN • MURDER ON THE CAMPUS (USA)
OUT OF THE SHADOWS • 1912 • *Tapley Rose* • USA
OUT OF THE SHADOWS • 1916 • King Burton L. • SHT • USA
OUT OF THE SHADOWS • 1931 • Harwood A. R. • SHT • ASL
OUT OF THE SILENCE • 1915 • *Greenwood Reeva* • USA
OUT OF THE SILENT NORTH • 1922 • Worthington William • USA
OUT OF THE SNOW see **OUT OF THE SNOWS** • 1920
OUT OF THE SNOWS • 1920 • Ince Ralph • USA • OUT OF THE SNOW
OUT OF THE STORM • 1913 • North Wilfred • USA
OUT OF THE STORM • 1915 • *Ince John* • USA
OUT OF THE STORM • 1920 • Parke William • USA • TOWER OF IVORY
OUT OF THE STORM • 1926 • Gasnier Louis J. • USA
OUT OF THE STORM • 1948 • Springsteen R. G. • USA
OUT OF THE TIGER'S MOUTH • 1962 • Whelan Tim Jr. • USA
OUT OF THE UNDERWORLD see **NATTEVANDREREN** • 1917
OUT OF THE WAY! see **KHABARDAI** • 1931
OUT OF THE WEST • 1918 • *Hart Neal* • SHT • USA
OUT OF THE WEST • 1926 • De Lacy Robert • USA
OUT OF THE WRECK • 1917 • Taylor William D. • USA
OUT OF THIS WHIRL • 1959 • Kneitel Seymour • ANS • USA
OUT OF THIS WORLD • 1945 • Walker Hal • USA
OUT OF THIS WORLD • 1954 • *Reed Roland (P)* • MTV • USA
OUT OF THIS WORLD • 1954 • Thomas Lowell • DOC • USA
OUT OF THIS WORLD see **HOLD THAT HYPNOTIST** • 1957
OUT OF TIME • 1988 • Butler Robert • TVM • USA
OUT OF TIME (UKN) see **SEBAK MAA EL ZAMAN** • 1988
OUT OF TOUCH • 1972 • Gaisford John • CND
OUT-OF-TOWNERS, THE • 1970 • Hiller Arthur • USA
OUT OF TRUE • 1951 • Leacock Philip • UKN
OUT OF TUNE • 1919 • Parrott Charles • USA
OUT OF WORK • 1909 • Olcott Sidney • USA
OUT OF WORK FOR YEARS • 1975 • Teshigahara Hiroshi • JPN
OUT ON A LIMB • 1950 • Hannah Jack • ANS • USA
OUT ON A LIMB • 1987 • Butler Robert • TVM • USA
OUT ON BAIL • 1922 • Roach Hal • SHT • USA
OUT ON BUSINESS • 1914 • *Crystal* • USA
OUT ON PROBATION see **DADDY O** • 1959
OUT ONE see **OUT 1: NOLI ME TANGERE** • 1970
OUT ONE OUT TWO see **OUT 1: SPECTRE** • 1970
OUT ONE: SPECTRE see **OUT 1: SPECTRE** • 1970
OUT-STEPPING • 1931 • Lamont Charles • SHT • USA
OUT THEY GO • 1976 • Edols Michael • DOC • ASL
OUT TO BORROW MATCHES see **TULITIKKUJA LAINAAMASSA** • 1978
OUT TO PLAY • 1936 • Leacock Philip, Lowenstein Harold • DCS • UKN
OUT TO PUNCH • 1956 • Kneitel Seymour • ANS • USA
OUT TO WIN • 1923 • Clift Denison • UKN
OUT WEST • 1918 • Arbuckle Roscoe • SHT • USA
OUT WEST • 1947 • Bernds Edward • SHT • USA
OUT WEST WITH THE HARDYS • 1938 • Seitz George B. • USA
OUT WEST WITH THE PEPPERS • 1940 • Barton Charles T. • USA
OUT WITH THE TIDE • 1928 • Hutchison Charles • USA • SILENT EVIDENCE (UKN)
OUT YONDER • 1920 • Ince Ralph • USA
OUTBACK • 1971 • Kotcheff Ted • ASL • WAKE IN FRIGHT
OUTBACK • 1988 • Barry Ian • ASL
OUTBACK BOUND • 1988 • Moxey John Llewellyn • TVM • USA
OUTBACK PATROL • 1947 • Robinson Lee • DOC • ASL
OUTBACK VAMPIRES • 1986 • Eggleston Colin • ASL
OUTBREAK see **KITORES** • 1971
OUTBREAK, THE • 1911 • *Selig* • USA
OUTBREAK OF HOSTILITIES • 1981 • Copping David • ASL
OUTCAST • 1917 • Henderson Dell • USA
OUTCAST • 1922 • Withey Chet • USA
OUTCAST • 1928 • Seiter William A. • USA
OUTCAST see **FREDLOS** • 1935
OUTCAST, THE • 1912 • *Bison* • USA
OUTCAST, THE • 1913 • *Ryno* • USA
OUTCAST, THE • 1913 • *Dragon* • USA
OUTCAST, THE • 1915 • O'Brien John B. • USA
OUTCAST, THE • 1934 • Lee Norman • UKN
OUTCAST, THE • 1936 • Florey Robert • USA • HAPPINESS PREFERRED
OUTCAST, THE • 1954 • Witney William • USA • FORTUNE HUNTER, THE (UKN)
OUTCAST, THE see **YE MAMA** • 1987
OUTCAST, THE (UKN) see **MAN IN THE SADDLE** • 1951
OUTCAST, THE (UKN) see **HAKAI** • 1961
OUTCAST AMONG OUTCASTS, AN • 1912 • Griffith D. W. • USA
OUTCAST LADY • 1934 • Leonard Robert Z. • USA • WOMAN OF THE WORLD, A (UKN) ○ GREEN HAT, THE
OUTCAST OF BLACK MESA • 1950 • Nazarro Ray • USA • CLUE, THE (UKN) ○ OUTCASTS OF BLACK MESA
OUTCAST OF THE ISLANDS • 1951 • Reed Carol • UKN
OUTCAST OR HEROINE • 1909 • *Vitagraph* • USA
OUTCAST SOULS • 1928 • Chaudet Louis W. • USA
OUTCASTS see **STVANI LIDE** • 1933
OUTCASTS see **HAKAI** • 1961
OUTCASTS, THE • 1984 • Wynne-Simmons Robert • IRL
OUTCASTS OF BLACK MESA see **OUTCAST OF BLACK MESA** • 1950
OUTCASTS OF POKER FLAT, THE • 1919 • Ford John • USA
OUTCASTS OF POKER FLAT, THE • 1937 • Cabanne W. Christy • USA
OUTCASTS OF POKER FLAT, THE • 1952 • Newman Joseph M. • USA
OUTCASTS OF SOCIETY • 1915 • *Anderson Mignon* • USA
OUTCASTS OF THE CITY • 1958 • Petroff Boris L.
OUTCASTS OF THE TRAIL • 1949 • Ford Philip • USA
OUTCAST'S RETURN, THE see **TUGTHUSFANGE NO.97** • 1914
OUTCAST'S SALVATION, THE • 1910 • *Atlas* • USA
OUTCOME, THE • 1914 • *Imp* • USA
OUTCOME, THE see **ISKHOD** • 1968
OUTCRY see **SOLE SORGE ANCORA, IL** • 1946
OUTCRY, THE (USA) see **GRIDO, IL** • 1957
OUTDOOR PAJAMAS • 1924 • McCarey Leo • SHT • USA
OUTDOORSMAN, THE • 1968 • *Bryant William A./ Payne Ned (P)* • DOC • USA
OUTDOORSTERS, THE see **WHEN NATURE CALLS** • 1985
OUTER AND INNER SPACE • 1966 • Warhol Andy • USA
OUTER EDGE, THE • 1915 • Calvert E. H. • USA
OUTER GALAXY GAZETTE • 1964 • Rasinski Connie • ANS • USA
OUTER GATE, THE • 1937 • Cannon Raymond • USA • BEHIND PRISON BARS
OUTER HEAT see **ALIEN NATION** • 1988
OUTER ISLES, THE • 1932 • George W. H. • UKN
OUTER SHELL, THE • 1913 • *Essanay* • USA
OUTER SPACE CONNECTION, THE • 1975 • Warshofsky Fred • DOC • USA
OUTER SPACE JITTERS • 1957 • White Jules • SHT • USA
OUTER SPACE VISITOR • 1959 • Tendlar Dave • ANS • USA
OUTER TOUCH • 1979 • Warren Norman J. • UKN • SPACED OUT (USA)
OUTFIT, THE • 1973 • Flynn John • USA • GOOD GUYS ALWAYS WIN, THE
OUTGENERALED • 1911 • *Selig* • USA
OUTIL, L' • 1976 • Dansereau Fernand, Rossignol Yolande • DCS • CND
OUTING, THE • 1978 • Lawrence Denny • SHT • ASL
OUTING, THE • 1987 • Daley Tom • USA • LAMP, THE
OUTING, THE see **SCREAM** • 1981
OUTLAND • 1981 • Hyams Peter • USA
OUTLANDER, THE • 1956 • Bare Richard L. • MTV • USA
OUTLAW • 1987 • Cardos John Bud • ITL • OUTLAW OF GOR
OUTLAW, THE • 1908 • *Ab* • USA
OUTLAW, THE • 1912 • *Joyce Alice* • USA
OUTLAW, THE • 1913 • *Patheplay* • USA
OUTLAW, THE • 1913 • Thornby Robert T. • *Vitagraph* • USA
OUTLAW, THE • 1943 • Hughes Howard, Hawks Howard (U/c) • USA
OUTLAW, THE see **HAJDUK** • 1981
OUTLAW, THE see **UTLAGINN** • 1982
OUTLAW AND HIS WIFE, THE see **BERG-EJVIND OCH HANS HUSTRU** • 1918
OUTLAW AND THE BABY, THE • 1912 • Melies Gaston • USA
OUTLAW AND THE CHILD, THE • 1911 • *Anderson Broncho Billy* • USA
OUTLAW AND THE FEMALE DETECTIVE, THE • 1911 • *Bison* • USA
OUTLAW AND THE LADY, THE • 1917 • Kelsey Fred A. • SHT • USA
OUTLAW AND THE LADY, THE (UKN) see **WACO** • 1951
OUTLAW BLUES • 1977 • Heffron Richard T. • USA
OUTLAW BRAND • 1948 • Hillyer Lambert • USA
OUTLAW COLONY, THE • 1912 • Dwan Allan • USA
OUTLAW COLONY, THE • 1916 • *Rancho* • USA
OUTLAW COUNTRY • 1949 • Taylor Ray • USA
OUTLAW DEPUTY, THE • 1911 • *Essanay* • USA
OUTLAW DEPUTY, THE • 1935 • Brower Otto • USA
OUTLAW DOG, THE • 1927 • McGowan J. P. • USA
OUTLAW EXPRESS • 1938 • Waggner George • USA
OUTLAW EXPRESS, THE • 1926 • Maloney Leo • USA
OUTLAW FORCE • 1988 • Heavener David • USA
OUTLAW FURY see **HOSTILE COUNTRY** • 1950
OUTLAW GANG, THE see **DALTON GANG, THE** • 1949
OUTLAW GOLD • 1950 • Fox Wallace • USA
OUTLAW JOSEY WALES, THE • 1976 • Eastwood Clint • USA
OUTLAW JOUKICHI OF MIKOSHIN see **MUSHUKUNIN MIKOSHIN NO JOUKICHI** • 1972
OUTLAW JUSTICE • 1932 • Schaefer Armand • USA
OUTLAW LOVE see **AMOR BANDIDO** • 1980
OUTLAW MOTORCYCLES • 1967 • Moody Titus • USA
OUTLAW OF GOR see **OUTLAW** • 1987
OUTLAW OF RED RIVER (USA) see **PROSCRITO DEL RIO COLORADO, EL** • 1965
OUTLAW OF THE PLAINS • 1946 • Newfield Sam • USA
OUTLAW PLANET see **TERRORE NELLO SPAZIO** • 1965
OUTLAW QUEEN • 1956 • Greene Herbert • USA
OUTLAW REFORMS, THE • 1914 • *Gebhardt Charles* • USA
OUTLAW RIDER, THE see **SE VUOI VIVERE.. SPARA!** • 1968
OUTLAW RIDER, THE (UKN) see **JESSE JAMES** • 1927
OUTLAW RIDERS • 1971 • Houston Tony • USA
OUTLAW ROUNDUP • 1944 • Fraser Harry L. • USA
OUTLAW RULE • 1935 • Luby S. Roy • USA
OUTLAW SAMARITAN, THE • 1911 • *Essanay* • USA
OUTLAW SOLDIERS: LET ME HANDLE IT see **HEITAI YAKUZA: ORE NI MAKASERO** • 1967
OUTLAW STALLION, THE • 1954 • Sears Fred F. • USA • WHITE STALLION, THE
OUTLAW SWORD, THE see **DAI KANBU BURAI** • 1968
OUTLAW TAMER, THE • 1934 • McGowan J. P. • USA
OUTLAW TERRITORY • 1953 • Ireland John, Garmes Lee • USA • HANNAH LEE
OUTLAW TRAIL • 1944 • Tansey Robert • USA
OUTLAW TREASURE • 1955 • Drake Oliver • USA
OUTLAW WOMEN • 1952 • Newfield Sam, Ormond Ron • USA
OUTLAW YET A MAN, AN • 1912 • Thornton F. Martin • UKN
OUTLAWED • 1913 • *Gerrard Film Co.* • USA
OUTLAWED • 1921 • Neitz Alvin J. • USA
OUTLAWED • 1928 • *Hoxie Al* • USA
OUTLAWED • 1929 • Fogwell Reginald • UKN
OUTLAWED • 1929 • Forde Eugene J. • USA
OUTLAWED see **FREDLOS** • 1935
OUTLAWED GUNS • 1935 • Taylor Ray • USA
OUTLAWS • 1986 • Werner Peter • TVM • USA
OUTLAWS see **SZEGENYLEGENYEK (NEHEZELETUEK)** • 1965
OUTLAWS see **BURAIKAN** • 1970
OUTLAWS, THE • 1984 • Frawley James • TVM • USA
OUTLAWS, THE see **PARANOMI, I** • 1958
OUTLAWS, THE see **HAIDUCII** • 1965
OUTLAW'S AWAKENING, THE • 1915 • *Anderson Broncho Billy* • USA
OUTLAW'S BRIDE, THE • 1915 • Mix Tom • USA
OUTLAW'S DAUGHTER, THE • 1914 • *Frontier* • USA
OUTLAW'S DAUGHTER, THE • 1925 • O'Brien John B. • USA
OUTLAW'S DAUGHTER, THE • 1954 • Barry Wesley E. • USA
OUTLAW'S DEPUTIES • 1920 • *Jennings Al* • SHT • USA
OUTLAW'S GRATITUDE, THE • 1913 • *Lubin* • USA
OUTLAW'S HANGMAN see **ESKIYA CELLADI** • 1967
OUTLAWS' HIGHWAY • 1934 • Hill Robert F. • USA • KAZAN, THE FEARLESS (UKN) ○ FIGHTING FURY
OUTLAW'S HONOR, AN • 1915 • *Powers* • USA
OUTLAWS IN THE SKY see **OZORA NO MUHOMONO** • 1960
OUTLAWS IS COMING!, THE • 1965 • Maurer Norman • USA • THREE STOOGES MEET THE GUNSLINGER (UKN)
OUTLAW'S LOVE, THE • 1913 • *Patheplay* • USA
OUTLAW'S NEMESIS, THE • 1914 • *Murray J. S.* • USA
OUTLAWS OF BOULDER PASS • 1942 • Newfield Sam • USA
OUTLAWS OF CAPTAIN ANGHEL SEVENHORSES, THE • 1970 • Cocea Dinu • RMN
OUTLAWS OF LOVE, THE see **FUORILEGGE DEL MATRIMONIO, I** • 1964
OUTLAWS OF PINE RIDGE • 1942 • Witney William • USA
OUTLAWS OF RED RIVER • 1927 • Seiler Lewis • USA
OUTLAWS OF SANTA FE • 1944 • Bretherton Howard • USA
OUTLAWS OF SONORA • 1938 • Sherman George • USA
OUTLAWS OF STAMPEDE PASS • 1943 • Fox Wallace • USA
OUTLAWS OF TEXAS • 1950 • Carr Thomas • USA
OUTLAWS OF THE CHEROKEE TRAIL • 1941 • Orlebeck Lester • USA
OUTLAWS OF THE DEEP • 1920 • Cooper J. Gordon • USA
OUTLAWS OF THE DESERT • 1941 • Bretherton Howard • USA • ARABIAN DESERT OUTLAWS
OUTLAWS OF THE NORTHERN SEA see **HOKKAI YUKYODEN** • 1967
OUTLAWS OF THE ORIENT • 1937 • Schoedsack Ernest B. • USA
OUTLAWS OF THE PANHANDLE • 1941 • Nelson Sam • USA • FARO JACK (UKN)
OUTLAWS OF THE PRAIRIE • 1938 • Nelson Sam • USA
OUTLAWS OF THE RANGE • 1936 • Herman Al • USA • CALL OF JUSTICE, THE (UKN)
OUTLAWS OF THE RIO GRANDE • 1941 • Newfield Sam • USA
OUTLAWS OF THE ROCKIES • 1945 • Nazarro Ray • USA • ROVING ROGUE, A (UKN)
OUTLAWS OF THE SEA • 1923 • Okey Jack • USA
OUTLAWS OF THE WEST (UKN) see **CALL THE MESQUITEERS** • 1938
OUTLAW'S PARADISE • 1927 • *Hoxie Al* • USA
OUTLAW'S PARADISE • 1939 • Newfield Sam • USA
OUTLAW'S REDEMPTION, THE • 1910 • *Atlas* • USA
OUTLAW'S REVENGE, THE see **LIFE OF GENERAL VILLA, THE** • 1914
OUTLAW'S SACRIFICE, AN • 1910 • *Anderson Broncho Billy* • USA
OUTLAW'S SACRIFICE, THE • 1912 • *Mackley Arthur* • USA
OUTLAW'S SACRIFICE, THE • 1919 • *Capital* • SHT • USA
OUTLAW'S SISTER, THE • 1913 • *Nestor* • USA
OUTLAW'S SON • 1954 • McDonald Frank • USA
OUTLAW'S SON, THE • 1957 • Selander Lesley • USA
OUTLAW'S TRAIL, THE • 1911 • Dwan Allan • USA

OUTLINE OF MAN see **GRAFIKA CLOVEKU** • 1957
OUTLINE OF VIOLENCE see **YOGIRI NO BOJO** • 1966
OUTLINED AND OUTWITTED • 1914 • Plumb Hay • UKN
OUTPOST, THE • 1915 • Noy Wilfred • UKN
OUTPOST, THE • 1942 • Davis Mannie • ANS • USA
OUTPOST, THE see **DESIRED WOMAN, THE** • 1927
OUTPOST IN INDO-CHINA (USA) see **FORT-DU-FOU** • 1962
OUTPOST IN MALAYA (USA) see **PLANTER'S WIFE, THE** • 1952
OUTPOST IN MOROCCO • 1949 • Florey Robert • USA
OUTPOST OF HELL (USA) see **DOKURITSU KIKANJUTAI IMADA SHAGEKICHU** • 1963
OUTPOST OF THE MOUNTIES • 1939 • Coleman C. C. Jr. • USA • ON GUARD (UKN)
OUTRAGE • 1950 • Lupino Ida • USA
OUTRAGE • 1964 • Ritt Martin • USA • JUDGMENT IN THE SUN
OUTRAGE • 1973 • Heffron Richard T. • TVM • USA
OUTRAGE! • 1986 • Grauman Walter • TVM • USA
OUTRAGE, THE • 1915 • Hepworth Cecil M. • UKN
OUTRAGEOUS! • 1977 • Benner Richard • CND
OUTRAGEOUS FORTUNE • 1987 • Hiller Arthur • USA
OUTRAGEOUS UNBELIEVABLE MECHANICAL LOVE MACHINE, THE • 1971 • Zugsmith Albert • USA
OUTREMER • 1990 • Rouan Brigitte • FRN
OUTRIDERS, THE • 1950 • Rowland Roy • USA
OUTS AND INS • 1916 • Myll Louis • SHT • USA
OUTSIDE CHANCE • 1978 • Miller Michael • TVM • USA • RETURN TO JACKSON COUNTY JAIL
OUTSIDE CHANCE OF MAXIMILIAN GLICK, THE • 1988 • Goldstein Allan • CND
OUTSIDE DOPE, THE • 1965 • Post Howard • ANS • USA
OUTSIDE IN • 1972 • Baron Allen • USA
OUTSIDE LOOKING IN • 1989 • Duhigg Brendan • SHT • ASL
OUTSIDE MAN, THE (USA) see **HOMME EST MORT, UN** • 1972
OUTSIDE OF PARADISE • 1938 • Auer John H. • USA
OUTSIDE THE CITY see **OKRAINA** • 1933
OUTSIDE THE CITY see **EXTRAMUROS** • 1985
OUTSIDE THE GATES • 1915 • De Grasse Joseph • USA
OUTSIDE THE LAW • 1921 • Browning Tod • USA
OUTSIDE THE LAW • 1930 • Browning Tod • USA
OUTSIDE THE LAW • 1938 • Collins Lewis D. • USA
OUTSIDE THE LAW • 1956 • Arnold Jack • USA
OUTSIDE THE LAW see **I AM THE LAW** • 1938
OUTSIDE THE LAW (UKN) see **CITADEL OF CRIME** • 1941
OUTSIDE THE LAW (USA) see **FUERA DE LA LEY** • 1940
OUTSIDE THE THREE MILE LIMIT • 1940 • Collins Lewis D. • USA • MUTINY ON THE SEAS (UKN) ○ CRIMINAL CARGO ○ ILLICIT CARGO
OUTSIDE THE WALL • 1950 • Wilbur Crane • USA
OUTSIDE THESE WALLS • 1939 • McCarey Ray • USA
OUTSIDE WOMAN, THE • 1921 • *Hawley Wanda* • USA
OUTSIDER • 1987 • Sirovy Zdenek • CZC
OUTSIDER, AN see **VREEMDE VOGEL, EEN** • 1967
OUTSIDER, THE • 1917 • Dowlan William C. • USA
OUTSIDER, THE • 1926 • Lee Rowland V. • USA • DAYBREAK
OUTSIDER, THE • 1931 • Lachman Harry • USA
OUTSIDER, THE • 1939 • Stein Paul L. • UKN
OUTSIDER, THE • 1961 • Mann Delbert • USA • SIXTH MAN, THE
OUTSIDER, THE • 1967 • Ritchie Michael • TVM • USA
OUTSIDER, THE • 1969 • Graham William A. • USA
OUTSIDER, THE • 1979 • Luraschi Tony • NTH, USA
OUTSIDER, THE • 1982 • Sass Barbara • PLN
OUTSIDER, THE see **BERLINGER** • 1976
OUTSIDER, THE (USA) see **GUINEA PIG, THE** • 1948
OUTSIDER IN AMSTERDAM see **GRIJPSTRA & DE GIER** • 1979
OUTSIDERS see **MORI TO MIZUUMI NO MATSURI** • 1958
OUTSIDERS see **CEDDO** • 1977
OUTSIDERS, THE • 1969 • Kuyululu Ayten • MTV • SWD
OUTSIDERS, THE • 1983 • Coppola Francis Ford • USA
OUTSIDERS, THE see **OKA OORIE KATHA** • 1977
OUTSIDERS, THE (UKN) see **BAND A PART** • 1964
OUTSKIRTS see **OKRAINA** • 1933
OUTTAKES • 1977 • Healey Barry • SHT • CND
OUTTAKES • 1984 • Sell Jack M. • USA
OUTWARD BOUND • 1930 • Milton Robert • USA
OUTWARD BOUND see **BETWEEN TWO WORLDS** • 1944
OUTWEST • 1918 • Arbuckle Roscoe • USA • SHERIFF, THE
OUTWITTED • 1909 • *Urban-Eclipse* • USA
OUTWITTED • 1916 • Mitchell Howard M. • SHT • USA
OUTWITTED • 1917 • Baker George D. • *Metro* • USA
OUTWITTED • 1917 • Terwilliger George W. • *Niagara Film Studios* • SHT • USA
OUTWITTED • 1925 • McGowan J. P. • USA
OUTWITTED see **CLAY DOLLARS** • 1921
OUTWITTED BY A CHILD • 1910 • *Walturdaw* • UKN
OUTWITTED BY BILLY • 1913 • *Razeto Stella* • USA
OUTWITTED BY HIS WIFE • 1908 • *Lubin* • USA
OUTWITTED BY HORSE AND LARIAT • 1911 • *Solax* • USA
OUTWITTED FOX, THE • 1957 • Dinov Todor • ANM • BUL
OUTWITTING DAD • 1914 • *Hardy Oliver* • USA
OUTWITTING FATHER • 1911 • *Yankee* • USA
OUTWITTING FATHER • 1912 • *Kalem* • USA
OUTWITTING MAMA • 1913 • Weston Charles? • UKN
OUTWITTING PAPA • 1911 • *Essanay* • USA
OUTWITTING THE HUN • 1918 • Pastrone Giovanni • ITL
OUTWITTING THE PROFESSOR • 1912 • *Wadsworth William* • USA
OUVERT CONTRE X • 1952 • Pottier Richard • FRN
OUVERT POUR CAUSE D'INVENTAIRE • 1946 • Resnais Alain • FRN
OUVERTURE 2012 • 1976 • Blazekovic Milan • ANM • YGS
OUVERTURE POUR LA CONSTRUCTION see **IFTITAH'IYYATUN LI AL-BINA** • 1974
OUVRE-TOI • 1978 • Benazeraf Jose • FRN
OUVREUSE N'A PAS DE CULOTTE, L' • 1980 • Baudricourt Michel • FRN
OVAL DIAMOND, THE • 1916 • Moore W. Eugene • USA
OVAL PORTRAIT, THE • 1934 • *Usc* • SHT • USA
OVAL PORTRAIT, THE • 1972 • *Hendrix Wanda* • TVM • USA
OVCAR • 1972 • Tanovic Bakir • YGS • SHEPHERD, THE
OVEJA NEGRA, LA • 1949 • Rodriguez Ismael • MXC
OVEJA NEGRA, LA • 1987 • Chalbaud Roman • VNZ • BLACK SHEEP, THE
OVER • 1971 • Huisman Michel • BLG, FRN
OVER 18, ..AND READY! • 1969 • Allen Lloyd • USA
OVER 21 • 1945 • Vidor Charles • USA
OVER A CRACKER BOWL • 1912 • Ricketts Thomas • USA
OVER AGAIN see **PUNASHA** • 1961
OVER AND BACK • 1915 • Dillon Eddie • USA
OVER-DEPENDANCY • 1949 • Anderson Robert • DCS • CND • DEPENDANCE
OVER-EXPOSED • 1956 • Seiler Lewis • USA
OVER-EXPOSED • 1969 • Chrisfield W. A. • USA
OVER FORTY • 1982 • Poirier Anne-Claire • CND • BEYOND FORTY
OVER GLAS GESPROKEN • 1957 • Haanstra Bert • NTH • SPEAKING OF GLASS
OVER GRENSEN see **FELDMANN-SAKEN** • 1986
OVER HERE • 1917 • Gove Edgar A. • USA
OVER HERE • 1924 • *Sennett Mack (P)* • SHT • USA
OVER-INCUBATED BABY, AN • 1901 • Booth W. R. • UKN
OVER MY DEAD BODY • 1942 • St. Clair Malcolm • USA
OVER MY DEAD BODY • 1982 • Jensen Ingrid Oustrup • DNM
OVER NIAGARA FALLS • 1914 • *Sterling Camera & Film Co* • USA
OVER NIGHT • 1915 • Young James • USA
OVER NIGHT see **UBER NACHT** • 1973
OVER SECRET WIRES • 1915 • *Chatterton Thomas* • USA
OVER SHE GOES • 1937 • Cutts Graham • UKN
OVER SILENT PATHS • 1910 • Griffith D. W. • USA
OVER THE ANDES • 1944 • Fitzpatrick James • SHT • USA
OVER THE BACK FENCE • 1913 • Williams C. Jay • USA
OVER THE BORDER • 1922 • Stanlaws Penrhyn • USA
OVER THE BORDER • 1950 • Fox Wallace • USA
OVER THE BOUNDING WAVES • 1915 • *Asher Max* • USA
OVER THE BROOKLYN BRIDGE • 1983 • Golan Menahem • USA • MY DARLING SHIKSA ○ ALBY'S DELIGHT
OVER THE CHAFING DISH • 1911 • *Morrison J. W.* • USA
OVER THE CLIFFS • 1913 • *Sheerer Will E.* • USA
OVER THE COUNTER • *Mgm* • SHT • USA
OVER THE CRIB • 1913 • *Lubin* • USA
OVER THE DIVIDE • 1912 • *Williams Clara* • USA
OVER THE EDGE • 1979 • Kaplan Jonathan • USA
OVER THE FENCE • 1917 • Roach Hal • SHT • USA
OVER THE FENCE • 1932 • Breslow Lou • SHT • USA
OVER THE FERRY • 1913 • Buckland Warwick • UKN
OVER THE GARDEN WALL • 1901 • Williamson James • UKN
OVER THE GARDEN WALL • 1910 • *Costello Maurice* • USA
OVER THE GARDEN WALL • 1910 • Fitzhamon Lewin? • UKN
OVER THE GARDEN WALL • 1911 • *Joyce Alice* • USA
OVER THE GARDEN WALL • 1914 • Nash Percy? • *Neptune* • UKN
OVER THE GARDEN WALL • 1914 • Plumb Hay? • *Hepworth* • UKN
OVER THE GARDEN WALL • 1917 • MacGregor Norval • SHT • USA
OVER THE GARDEN WALL • 1918 • *Rhodes Billie* • USA
OVER THE GARDEN WALL • 1919 • Smith David • USA
OVER THE GARDEN WALL • 1920 • *Allen Edgar* • SHT • USA
OVER THE GARDEN WALL • 1934 • Daumery John • UKN
OVER THE GARDEN WALL • 1950 • Blakeley John E. • UKN
OVER THE GOAL • 1937 • Smith Noel • USA
OVER THE HEDGE (USA) see **OTHER SIDE OF THE HEDGE, THE** • 1905
OVER THE HILL • 1917 • Parke William • USA
OVER THE HILL • 1931 • King Henry • USA
OVER THE HILL see **OVER THE HILL TO THE POORHOUSE** • 1920
OVER THE HILL GANG, THE • 1969 • Yarbrough Jean • TVM • USA
OVER THE HILL GANG RIDES AGAIN, THE • 1970 • McCowan George • TVM • USA
OVER THE HILL TO THE POORHOUSE • 1920 • Millarde Harry • USA • OVER THE HILL
OVER THE HILLS • 1911 • Smiley Joseph, Tucker George Loane • USA
OVER THE HILLS TO THE POORHOUSE • 1908 • McCutcheon Wallace • USA
OVER THE HILLS TO THE POORHOUSE • 1912 • *Lubin* • USA
OVER THE LEDGE • 1914 • Lewis Edgar • USA
OVER THE LINE see **PRESTOP** • 1981
OVER THE LITTLE DOG AND THE LITTLE CAT see **PROVIDANI O PEJSKOVI A KOCICCE** • 1955
OVER THE MOON • 1937 • Freeland Thornton, Howard William K.(U/c) • UKN
OVER THE MOON • 1940 • Sherwood Robert E. • USA
OVER THE NORTH MAGNETIC POLE • 1930 • Finnie Richard S. • DOC • CND
OVER THE ODDS • 1961 • Forlong Michael • UKN
OVER THE RIVER (UKN) see **ONE MORE RIVER** • 1934
OVER THE SANTA FE TRAIL • 1947 • Nazarro Ray • USA • NO ESCAPE (UKN)
OVER THE SEAS AND FAR AWAY • 1971 • Sherstobitov Eudgen • USS
OVER THE SEVEN SEAS • 1933 • Vanderbilt William K. • USA
OVER THE SHADING EDGE • 1911 • *Reliance* • USA
OVER THE STICKS • 1929 • Samuelson G. B., Coleby A. E. • UKN
OVER THE SUMMER • 1984 • Sparks Teresa • USA
OVER THE TISSA • 1958 • Vasiliev Dimitri • USS
OVER THE TOP • 1918 • North Wilfred • USA
OVER THE TOP • 1987 • Golan Menahem • USA
OVER THE TRANSOM • 1920 • Fishback Fred C. • SHT • USA
OVER THE WALL • 1938 • McDonald Frank • USA
OVER THE WALL • 1943 • Negulesco Jean • SHT • USA
OVER THE WAVES see **THIS TIME FOR KEEPS** • 1941
OVER THE WIRE • 1910 • *Lubin* • USA
OVER THE WIRE • 1921 • Ruggles Wesley • USA
OVER THE WORLD WITH ROOSEVELT • 1924 • *Ebin Alex B.* • DOC • USA
OVER THERE • 1917 • Kirkwood James • USA
OVER THERE • 1928 • *Super Film Attractions* • DOC • USA
OVER THERE 1914-1918 (USA) see **14-18** • 1962
OVER THEREABOUTS • 1925 • *Sennett Mack (P)* • SHT • USA
OVER-UNDER, SIDEWAYS-DOWN • 1977 • Corr Eugene, Gessner Peter, Wax Steve • USA
OVERALL 1 • 1968 • Reitz Edgar • FRG
OVERALL HERO, AN • 1920 • *Nowell Arthur* • SHT • USA
OVERALL OUTING, AN • 1913 • *Komic* • USA
OVERALL RESPONSIBILITY • 1973 • Natanson Georgi • USS
OVERALLS • 1916 • Halloway Jack • USA
OVERBOARD • 1978 • Newland John • TVM • USA
OVERBOARD • 1987 • Marshall Garry • USA
OVERBOARD see **HEAD WINDS** • 1925
OVERCHARGED • 1912 • Wilson Frank? • UKN
OVERCOAT, THE • 1916 • Berger Rea • USA
OVERCOAT, THE see **CAPPOTTO, IL** • 1952
OVERCOAT, THE (USA) see **SHINEL** • 1926
OVERCOAT, THE (USA) see **MANTEL, DER** • 1955
OVERCOAT, THE (USA) see **SHINEL** • 1960
OVERCOAT SAM • 1937 • Orton Wallace • UKN
OVERCOATS • 1913 • *Solax* • USA
OVERCOME BY AN UNUSUAL FATE IN A BLUE AUGUST SEA see **TRAVOLTI DA UN INSOLITO DESTINO NELL'AZZURRO MARE DI AGOSTO** • 1974
OVERCROWDED OVERSEA OVERSEER, THE • 1916 • *Cooper Claude* • USA
OVERDONE STEAK see **STEAK TROP CUIT, UN** • 1960
OVERDOSE see **SOBREDOSIS** • 1986
OVERDOSE OF DEGRADATION • 1970 • *Hollywood Cinema Associates* • USA
OVERDOSE OF LOVE POTION, AN • 1907 • Stow Percy • UKN
OVERDRAWN AT THE MEMORY BANK • 1983 • Williams Douglas • TVM • USA
OVERDUE TREATMENT, THE • 1973 • Lloyd Ian F. H. • DOC • UKN
OVERFUL SEAT, AN • 1898 • *Riley Brothers* • UKN • WEARY WILLIE
OVERGREPPET (SWD) see **VIOL, LE** • 1967
OVERKANT, DE • 1966 • Wuyts Herman • BLG • ON THE OTHER SIDE
OVERKILL • 1986 • Lommel Ulli • USA
OVERKLASSENS HEMMELIGE SEXGLAEDER • 1974 • Baxter Arnold • DNM • SEXY SISTERS
OVERLAND BOUND • 1930 • Maloney Leo • USA
OVERLAND EXPRESS, THE • 1938 • Eberson Drew • USA
OVERLAND LIMITED, THE • 1925 • O'Neill Frank • USA
OVERLAND MAIL • 1939 • Hill Robert F. • USA
OVERLAND MAIL • 1942 • Beebe Ford, Rawlins John • SRL • USA
OVERLAND MAIL ROBBERY • 1943 • English John • USA
OVERLAND PACIFIC • 1954 • Sears Fred F. • USA
OVERLAND RED • 1920 • Reynolds Lynn • USA
OVERLAND RIDERS • 1946 • Newfield Sam • USA
OVERLAND STAGE, THE • 1927 • Rogell Albert S. • USA
OVERLAND STAGE RAIDERS • 1938 • Sherman George • USA
OVERLAND STAGECOACH • 1942 • Newfield Sam • USA
OVERLAND TELEGRAPH • 1951 • Selander Lesley • USA
OVERLAND TELEGRAPH, THE • 1929 • Waters John • USA • HUMMING WIRES
OVERLAND TO DEADWOOD • 1942 • Berke William • USA • FALLING STONES (UKN)
OVERLAND TO FREMONT • 1910 • *Selig* • USA
OVERLAND TRAIL (UKN) see **TRAIL RIDERS** • 1942
OVERLAND TRAILS • 1948 • Hillyer Lambert • USA
OVERLAND WITH KIT CARSON • 1939 • Nelson Sam, Deming Norman • SRL • USA
OVERLANDERS, THE • 1946 • Watt Harry • UKN
OVERLORD • 1975 • Cooper Stuart • UKN
OVERLORD OF THE NAVY see **FLOTTANS OVERMAN** • 1958
OVERLORDS OF THE UFO • 1970 • DOC • USA
OVERMAN • Phillips Sean • SHT • USA
OVERNIGHT • 1986 • Darcus Jack • CND
OVERNIGHT IN TIROL see **UBERNACHTUNG IN TIROL** • 1973
OVERNIGHT STAY IN THE TYROL see **UBERNACHTUNG IN TIROL** • 1973
OVERNIGHT SUCCESS • 1970 • Draskovic Boro • YGS • INSTANT SUCCESS
OVERNIGHT (USA) see **THAT NIGHT IN LONDON** • 1932
OVERSEAS TO VICTORY • 1919 • *Miller-Hodkinson* • SHT • USA
OVERSEXED • 1974 • Sarno Joe • USA
OVERSHOES OF HAPPINESS see **GALOSE STASTIA** • 1985
OVERSTIMULATED • 1963 • Smith Jack** • USA
OVERTAKING, THE see **SORPASSO, IL** • 1962
OVERTAXED, THE see **TARTASSATI, I** • 1959
OVERTHROWERS see **AIDANKAATAJAT** • 1983
OVERTURE • 1958 • Polidoro Gian Luigi, Singh Krishna • SHT • UNN
OVERTURE TO GLORY • 1940 • Nosseck Max • USA
OVERTURE TO WILLIAM TELL, THE • 1947 • Lundy Dick • ANS • USA
OVERVAL, DE • 1963 • Rotha Paul • NTH • SILENT RAID, THE ○ RESISTANCE
OVERVINTRINGEN • 1965 • Vogel Raymond, Thulin Ingrid • SWD • HIVERNALE
OVERWORKED BOOKKEEPER, THE • 1912 • *Lubin* • USA
OVIRI • 1987 • Carlsen Henning • DNM, FRN • WOLF AT THE DOOR, THE
OVNIS Y VIAJES EXTRATERRESTRES • 1977 • Alcalde Jose Andres • SPN
OVO E A GALINHA, O • 1969 • de Almeida Manuel Faria • SHT • PRT
OVOCE STROMU RAJSKYCH JIME • 1969 • Chytilova Vera • CZC, BLG • WE EAT THE FRUIT OF THE TREES OF PARADISE ○ FRUIT DE PARADIS, LE (BLG) ○ FRUIT OF PARADISE, THE ○ WE'LL EAT THE FRUIT OF PARADISE ○ FRUIT OF THE TREES OF PARADISE, THE
OVOD • 1957 • Fainzimmer Alexander • USS • GADFLY, THE
OVOUTIE O'ROONEY • 1946 • Rieger Jack • USA
OWANA, THE DEVIL WOMAN • 1913 • *Nestor* • USA
OWANEE'S GREAT LOVE • 1911 • *Bison* • USA
OWARINAKI INOCHI O • 1967 • Yoshida Kenji • JPN • WILL TO LIVE, THE
OWD BOB • 1924 • Edwards Henry • UKN
OWD BOB • 1938 • Stevenson Robert • UKN • TO THE VICTOR
OWEEKENO: IN TOUCH WITH THE PAST • 1980 • von Puttkamer Peter • DOC • CND
OWEN MARSHALL, COUNSELLOR AT LAW • 1971 • Kulik Buzz • TVM • USA

OWING MORE • 1912 • *Moore Owen* • USA
OWL, THE • 1973 • Ilic Aleksandar • SHT • YGS
OWL, THE see **BUHO, EL** • 1974
OWL AND THE LEMMING –AN ESKIMO LEGEND, THE see **HIBOU ET LE LEMMING, LE** • 1971
OWL AND THE PUSSY CAT, THE • 1939 • Donnelly Eddie • ANS • USA
OWL AND THE PUSSYCAT, THE • 1934 • *Terry Paul/ Moser Frank (P)* • ANS • USA
OWL AND THE PUSSYCAT, THE • 1953 • Halas John, Borthwick Brian • ANS • UKN
OWL AND THE PUSSYCAT, THE • 1970 • Ross Herbert • USA
OWL AND THE RAVEN –AN ESKIMO LEGEND, THE see **HIBOU ET LE CORBEAU, LE** • 1973
OWL LECTURE see **MIMIZUKO SEPPO** • 1958
OWL WHO MARRIED A GOOSE, THE • 1974 • Leaf Caroline • ANS • CND • MARIAGE DU HIBOU, LE ○ OWL WHO MARRIED THE GOOSE, THE
OWL WHO MARRIED THE GOOSE, THE see **OWL WHO MARRIED A GOOSE, THE** • 1974
OWL WITCH, THE • 1919 • Bertram William • USA
OWL WITCH, THE • 1927 • SHT • USA
OWL'S LEGACY, THE (UKN) see **HERITAGE DE LA CHOUETTE, L'** • 1988
OWLY TO BED • 1959 • Kneitel Seymour • ANS • USA
OWN FLESH AND BLOOD see **RODNAYA KROV** • 1964
OWN YOUR HOME • 1921 • Roach Hal • SHT • USA
OWNER COMES ABOARD, THE • 1940 • Bryce Alex • UKN
OWNER GOES ALOFT, THE • 1942 • Gunn Gilbert • UKN
OWNER OF THE L.L. RANCH, THE • 1911 • Melies Gaston • USA
OWNERLESS FERRYBOAT, THE • 1932 • Ra Un-Gya • KOR
OWNERS, THE see **PROPRIETARII** • 1973
OX AND THE CALF, THE • 1968 • Sibianu Gheorghe • ANM • RMN
OX-BOW INCIDENT, THE • 1956 • Oswald Gerd • MTV • USA
OX OF KULM, THE see **OCHSE VON KULM, DER** • 1955
OXALA • 1981 • Vasconcelos Antonio-Pedro • PRT
OXBOW INCIDENT, THE • 1943 • Wellman William A. • USA • STRANGE INCIDENT (UKN)
OXCART DIARY, AN see **CHIA-CHUANG YI-NIU-CH'E** • 1983
OXED MEN • Furatawa Takui • ANS • JPN
OXFORD AND CAMBRIDGE BOAT RACE, 1901 • 1901 • Paul Robert William • UKN
OXFORD AND CAMBRIDGE BOAT RACE, THE • 1898 • Hepworth Cecil M. • UKN
OXFORD AND CAMBRIDGE UNIVERSITY BOAT RACE • 1895 • Acres Birt • UKN
OXFORD BAGS • 1926 • Walker Norman • UKN
OXFORD BLUES • 1984 • Boris Robert • USA
OXO PARADE • 1948 • Halas John, Batchelor Joy • ANS • UKN
OXYGEN see **OKSIGEN** • 1970
OYABAKA HANAGASSEN • 1953 • *Hidari Sachiko* • JPN • BATTLE OF THE FLOWERS AND THE STUPID FATHER, THE
OYAFUKO DORI • 1958 • Masumura Yasuzo • JPN • DISOBEDIENCE
OYAJI TO SONO KO • 1929 • Gosho Heinosuke • JPN • FATHER AND HIS CHILD ○ FATHER AND HIS SON
OYAKE AKAHACHI • 1937 • Toyoda Shiro • JPN • PUBLIC DISGRACE
OYAKOGUSA • 1967 • Maruyama Seiji • JPN • GREEN LIGHT TO JOY
OYASHIRAZU IN THE ECHIGO REGIME see **ECHIGO TSUTSUISHI OYASHIRAZU** • 1964
OYEBLIKKET • 1977 • Udnaes Sverre • NRW • MOMENT, THE
OYEN-SAN • 1955 • Honda Inoshiro • JPN • MOTHER AND SON
OYOME IN OIDE • 1966 • Honda Inoshiro • JPN • COME MARRY ME
OYSTER DREDGER, THE • 1915 • Chaney Lon • USA
OYSTER MAN, THE • 1950 • Biggs Julian, Palardy Jean • CND
OYSTER PRINCESS, THE see **AUSTERNPRINZESSIN ,DIE** • 1919
OYSTER SHELL, THE see **MUTHU CHIPPI** • 1968
OYSTERMAN'S GOLD, THE • 1909 • *Lubin* • USA
OYSTERS AND PEARLS • 1915 • *Empress* • USA
OYSTERS ARE IN SEASON • 1963 • Rogosin Lionel • SHT • USA
OYU-SAMA • 1951 • Mizoguchi Kenji • JPN • MISS OYU (USA)
OYUKI THE MADONNA (USA) see **MARIA NO OYUKI** • 1935
OYUKI THE VIRGIN (UKN) see **MARIA NO OYUKI** • 1935
OZ • 1976 • Lofven Chris • ASL
OZARK LARK • 1960 • Smith Paul J. • ANS • USA
OZARK ROMANCE, AN • 1918 • Roach Hal • SHT • USA
OZASHIKI 48 TAI • 1968 • Yamamoto Shinya • JPN • ORGY AT THE TEAHOUSE
OZNAMUJE SE RASKAM VASUIM • 1988 • Kachyna Karel • CZC • LET ALL YOUR LOVES KNOW
OZORA NO MUHOMONO • 1960 • Shimazu Shoichi • JPN • OUTLAWS IN THE SKY
OZORA NO SAMURAI • 1976 • Maruyama Seiji • JPN • ZERO PILOT
OZUSHIO • 1952 • Hara Kenkichi • JPN • STORMY WATERS
OZVEGY ES A SZAZADOS, AZ • 1967 • Palasthy Gyorgy • HNG • WIDOW AND THE POLICE OFFICER, THE
OZVEGY MENYASSZONYOK • 1964 • Gertler Viktor • HNG • LADY-KILLER IN TROUBLE
OZZIE NELSON AND HIS ORCHESTRA • 1943 • Negulesco Jean • SHT • USA
OZZIE OF THE CIRCUS • 1929 • Lantz Walter • ANS • USA
OZZIE OF THE MOUNTED • 1928 • *Disney Walt (P)* • ANS • USA
OZZIE OF THE MOUNTED • 1928 • Disney Walt • ANS • USA
OZZIE OSTRICH COMES TO TOWN • 1937 • Davis Mannie, Gordon George • ANS • USA

P

P • 1964 • Keja Jan • SHT • NTH
P + A – I(K) • 1966 • Yalkut Jud • SHT • USA
P & B • 1983 • Alfredson Hans • SWD
P.C. HAWKEYE FALLS IN LOVE • 1912 • Plumb Hay • UKN
P.C. HAWKEYE GOES FISHING • 1912 • Plumb Hay • UKN
P.C. HAWKEYE LEAVES THE FORCE • 1911 • Fitzhamon Lewin • UKN
P.C. HAWKEYE, SPORTSMAN • 1912 • Plumb Hay • UKN
P.C. HAWKEYE TURNS DETECTIVE • 1911 • Fitzhamon Lewin • UKN
P.C. HAWKEYE'S BUSY DAY • 1911 • Fitzhamon Lewin • UKN
P.C. JOSSER • 1931 • Rosmer Milton • UKN • JOSSER P.C.
P.C. NABBEM AND THE ANARCHISTS • 1913 • Collins Edwin J. • UKN
P.C. NABBEM AND THE COINERS • 1914 • Collins Edwin J.? • UKN
P.C. NABBEM'S SMART CAPTURE • 1913 • Collins Edwin J.? • UKN
P.C. PLATT'S PROMOTION • 1913 • Aylott Dave? • UKN
P COMMME PENETRATION • 1976 • Ayranu Lino • FRN
P. HENRY JENKINS AND MARS • 1915 • *Chamberlain Riley* • USA
P.I.– PRIVATE INVESTIGATIONS see **PRIVATE INVESTIGATIONS** • 1987
P.J. • 1967 • Guillermin John • USA • NEW FACE IN HELL (UKN) ○ CRISS CROSS
P.K. AND THE KID • 1982 • Lombardo Lou • USA
P.M.E., VOTRE CLIENT, LA • 1981 • Kinsey Nicholas • DOC • CND
P.O.W. see **SECRET OF BLOOD ISLAND, THE** • 1964
P.O.W. –PRISONERS OF WAR see **SECRET OF BLOOD ISLAND, THE** • 1964
P.O.W. THE ESCAPE • 1986 • Amir Gideon • USA • BEHIND ENEMY LINES
P.. P.. PILL, THE • 1981 • Siponen Frank • FNL
P.P.S. (PROSTITUTES' PROTECTIVE SOCIETY) • 1966 • Mahon Barry • USA • SECRET SOCIETY, THE
P.. RESPECTUEUSE, LA • 1952 • Pagliero Marcello, Brabant Charles • FRN • RESPECTABLE PROSTITUTE, THE (USA) ○ RESPECTFUL PROSTITUTE, THE ○ PUTAIN RESPECTUEUSE, LA
P.S.F. ONE • Gruenberger John • SHT • USA
P.S. I LOVE YOU • 1967 • Wenceslao Jose Pepe • PHL
P.S. I LOVE YOU • 1983 • Suwarnasara Kidd • THL
P.S. TO THE LAUGHING MAN see **P.S. ZUM LACHENDEN MANN** • 1966
P.S. ZUM LACHENDEN MANN • 1966 • Heynowski Walter, Scheumann Gerhard • GDR • P.S. TO THE LAUGHING MAN
P.. SENTIMENTALE, LA • 1958 • Gourguet Jean • FRN
P.T. BARNUM'S ROCKET TO THE MOON see **JULES VERNE'S ROCKET TO THE MOON** • 1967
P.T.T. see **COSTAUD DES P.T.T., LE** • 1931
P4W PRISON FOR WOMEN • 1981 • Dale Holly, Cole Janis • DOC • CND • PRISON FOR WOMEN
PA AND MA ELOPE • 1914 • *Ab* • USA
PA BESOG HOS KONG TINGELING • 1947 • Roos Jorgen, Mertz Albert • DOC • DNM
PA D'ANGEL • 1984 • Bellmunt Francisco • SPN • WAFER
PA DESSA SKULDROR • 1948 • Folke Gosta • SWD • ON THE SHOULDERS
PA DETTA NUMERA VANLIGA SATT • 1916 • Hansen Edmond • SWD • IN THIS WAY WHICH IS SO USUAL NOWADAYS
PA EN BANK I EN PARK • 1960 • Ekman Hasse • SWD • ON A BENCH IN A PARK
PA' EN IGEN AMALIE • 1973 • Kaas Preben • DNM
PA FARLIGA VAGAR • 1945 • Branner Per-Axel • SWD • ON DANGEROUS ROADS
PA HEDER OCH SKOJ • 1956 • Blomgren Bengt • SWD • HONESTLY AND CHEATINGLY
PA KRYSS MED ALBERTINA • 1938 • Branner Per-Axel • SWD • ON THE CRUISE WITH THE ALBERTINA
PA KRYSS MED BLIXTEN • 1927 • Persson Edvard • SWD • ON THE CRUISE WITH THE LIGHTNING
PA KUO LIEN-CHUN • 1975 • Chang Ch'Eh • HKG • BOXER REBELLION
PA LIV OCH DOD • 1943 • Husberg Rolf • SWD • MATTER OF LIFE AND DEATH, A ○ JAGARPLUTONEN
PA LIV OCH DOD • 1986 • Ahrne Marianne • SWD • MATTER OF LIFE AND DEATH, A
PA LIVETS ODESVAGAR • 1913 • Stiller Mauritz • SWD • ON THE FATEFUL ROADS OF LIFE ○ ON THE ROADS OF FATE
PA-PAI CHUANG-SHIH • 1977 • Ting Shan-Hsi • HKG • 800 HEROES
PA PUEN • 1980 • Pakdivijit Chalong • THL
PA' QUE ME SIRVE LA VIDA • 1960 • Salvador Jaime • MXC
PA REESOR • 1954 • Kounavudhi Vichit • THL
PA RYMMEN MED PIPPI LANGSTRUMP • 1970 • Hellbom Olle • SWD, DNM • PIPPI AUSSER RAND UND BAND
PA SANGENS VINGAR see **PRINS GUSTAF** • 1944
PA SAYS • 1913 • Henderson Dell • USA
PA-SHIH CH'I-YU CHIEH LIANG-YUAN • 1978 • Chang Hsing-Yen • HKG • ROMANCE ON THE BUS
PA SOLSIDAN • 1936 • Molander Gustaf • SWD • ON THE SUNNY SIDE
PA TAKES UP PHYSICAL CULTURE • 1907 • Williamson James? • UKN
PA TRUBBEL'S TROUBLES • 1912 • *Missimer Howard* • USA
PA VEJ MOD ET JOB • 1953 • Carlsen Henning • SHT • DNM
PAA LIVETS SKYGGESIDE • 1912 • *Holger-Madsen* • DNM
PAA SLAGET 12 • 1922 • Sandberg Anders W. • DNM
PAALUOTTAMUSMIES • 1971 • Mollberg Rauni • SRL • FNL • SHOP STEWARD, THE
PAAMAJASSA • 1970 • Kassila Matti • FNL • AT HEADQUARTERS
PAANO KUNG WALA KA NA? • 1988 • Chionglo Mel • PHL • WHAT IF YOU GO?
PAAPI • 1953 • *Kapoor Raj* • IND
PAARUNGEN • 1967 • Verhoeven Michael • FRG • DANSE MACABRE ○ COUPLINGS ○ SATANIC GAMES ○ DANCE OF DEATH
PAATHIRA PAATTU • 1967 • Prakash N. • IND • MIDNIGHT SONG
PABERAHNEHA • 1968 • Roshanian Rahim • IRN • BARE FEET
PABLA CASALS BREAKS HIS JOURNEY • 1958 • Sarma V. L. • SHT • UNN
PABLO • 1963 • Massip Jose • CUB
PABLO • 1979 • Casaus Victor • CUB
PABLO AND THE DANCING CHIHUAHUA • 1972 • Perkins Walter • USA
PABLO CASALS • 1955 • Baratier Jacques • FRN
PABLO CASALS MASTER CLASS • 1960 • Hammid Alexander • USA
PABLO CASALS: PUERTO RICAN TESTIMONIES see **PABLO CASALS: TESTIMONIOS PUERTORRIQUENOS** • 1987
PABLO CASALS: TESTIMONIOS PUERTORRIQUENOS • 1987 • Trigo Enrique • DOC • PRC • PABLO CASALS: PUERTO RICAN TESTIMONIES
PABLO PICASSO see **PICASSO** • 1982
PABLO PICASSO, DE 1900 A 1914 • 1959 • Forgue Fabienne • SHT • FRN
PABLO Y CAROLINA • 1955 • de la Serna Mauricio • MXC
PACAR KETINGGALAN KERETA • 1988 • Karya Teguh • INN
PACE THAT KILLS, THE • 1917 • Wells Raymond • SHT • USA
PACE THAT KILLS, THE • 1928 • Parker Norton S., O'Connor William A. • USA
PACE THAT THRILLS, THE • 1925 • Campbell Webster • USA
PACE THAT THRILLS, THE • 1952 • Barsha Leon • USA • CRACK DOWN
PACE THAT THRILLS, THE see **COCAINE FIENDS, THE** • 1936
PACE THAT THRILLS, THE see **OTOKO NARA FURIMUKUNA** • 1967
PACHA, LE • 1968 • Lautner Georges • FRN, ITL • FREDDA ALBA DEL COMMISSARIO JOSS, LA (ITL) ○ SHOWDOWN
PACHIN • 1960 • Ruiz-Castillo Arturo • SPN
PACHIN, ALMIRANTE • 1961 • Alcocer Santos • SPN
PACIENTKA DR. HEGLA • 1940 • Vavra Otakar • CZC • DR. HEGL'S PATIENT
PACIFIC 231 • 1949 • Mitry Jean • SHT • FRN
PACIFIC ADVENTURE (USA) see **SMITHY** • 1946
PACIFIC BANANA • 1980 • Lamond John • ASL
PACIFIC BLACKOUT • 1942 • Murphy Ralph • USA • MIDNIGHT ANGEL
PACIFIC CHALLENGE • 1975 • Amram Robert • DOC • USA
PACIFIC COAST HIGHWAY • 1981 • Higgins William • USA
PACIFIC DESTINY • 1956 • Rilla Wolf • UKN
PACIFIC ENDEAVOUR • 1970 • Dimond Peter • DOC • ASL
PACIFIC HEIGHTS • 1990 • Schlesinger John • USA
PACIFIC INFERNO • 1978 • Bayer Rolf • PHL, USA • DO THEY EVER CRY IN AMERICA?
PACIFIC INFERNO • 1981 • Modica Philippe
PACIFIC LINER • 1938 • Landers Lew • USA
PACIFIC NORTHWEST • 1944 • Van Dyke Willard • DOC • USA
PACIFIC OCEAN, THE see **STILLE OZEAN, DER** • 1983
PACIFIC PALISADES • 1990 • Schmitt Bernard • FRN
PACIFIC PARADISE • 1937 • Sidney George • DCS • USA
PACIFIC RENDEZVOUS • 1942 • Sidney George • USA • SECRET OPERATOR
PACIFIC THRUST • 1945 • Annakin Ken • DCS • UKN
PACIFIC VIBRATIONS • 1971 • Severson John • DOC • USA
PACIFIC WAR, THE (UKN) see **DAITOA SENSO** • 1968
PACIFIC WAR AND HIMEYURI CORPS see **TAIHEIYO SENSO TO HIMEYURI BUTAI** • 1962
PACIFIC WAR AND THE INTERNATIONAL MILITARY TRIBUNE, THE see **DAITOWA SENSO TO KOKUSAI SAIBAN** • 1959
PACIFIST, THE • 1916 • Beaumont Harry • SHT • USA
PACIFIST, THE (USA) see **PACIFISTA, LA** • 1970
PACIFISTA, LA • 1970 • Jancso Miklos • ITL, FRN, FRG • PACIFIST, THE (USA)
PACIORKI JEDNEGO ROZANCA • 1979 • Kutz Kazimierz • PLN • GLASS-BEAD ROSARY, A ○ BEADS OF ONE ROSARY, THE
PACK, THE • 1977 • Clouse Robert • USA • LONG HARD NIGHT, THE (UKN) ○ KILLERS WHO WORE COLLARS ○ LONG DARK NIGHT, THE ○ WE'VE GOT A BONE TO PICK WITH YOU
PACK, THE see **BEHIND THE MASK** • 1958
PACK OF CARDS, A • 1914 • *Lubin* • USA
PACK OF LIES • 1987 • Page Anthony • TVM • UKN
PACK TRAIN • 1953 • Archainbaud George • USA
PACK UP YOUR TROUBLES • 1924-26 • Fleischer Dave • ANS • USA
PACK UP YOUR TROUBLES • 1932 • Marshall George, McCarey Ray • USA • WE'RE IN THE ARMY NOW
PACK UP YOUR TROUBLES • 1939 • Humberstone H. Bruce • USA • WE'RE IN THE ARMY NOW (UKN)
PACK UP YOUR TROUBLES • 1940 • Mitchell Oswald • UKN
PACK UP YOUR TROUBLES • 1944-45 • Jodoin Rene • ANS • CND
PACKAGE, THE • 1989 • Davis Andrew • USA
PACKAGE FOR JASPER, A • 1943 • Pal George • ANS • USA
PACKAGE HOLIDAY, THE • 1981 • Jonsson Bo • SWD
PACKAGE HOLIDAY, THE see **SALLSKAPSRESAN** • 1980
PACKAGE OF TROUBLE, A • 1911 • *Solax* • USA
PACKAGE TOUR see **SALLSKAPSRESAN** • 1980
PACKAGE TOUR, THE • 1984 • Gazdag Gyula • DOC • HNG
PACKAGING STORY • 1964 • Bass Saul • SHT • USA
PACKER JIM'S GUARDIANSHIP • 1915 • Physioc Wray • USA
PACKERS ON THE TRAIL • 1901 • Porter Edwin S. • USA
PACKIN' IT IN • 1982 • Taylor Jud • TVM • USA
PACKING UP • 1927 • Mander Miles • UKN
PACO • 1975 • O'Neil Robert Vincent • USA, CLM
PACO EL ELEGANTE • 1951 • Fernandez Bustamente Adolfo • MXC

PACO L'INFAILLABLE • 1979 • Haudepin Didier • FRN, SPN

PACSIRTA • 1964 • Ranody Laszlo • HNG • SKYLARK ○ LARK, THE

PACT WITH THE DEVIL see **PATTO COL DIAVOLO** • 1948

PACT WITH THE DEVIL see **PACTO DIABOLICO** • 1968

PACTO DE AMOR • 1974 • *Estudios America* • MXC

PACTO DE SANGRE • 1965 • Ortega Juan J. • MXC

PACTO DE SANGRE • 1989 • Roncayolo Malena • VNZ • BLOOD PACT

PACTO DE SILENCIO • 1949 • Roman Antonio • SPN

PACTO DE SILENCIO • 1963 • Roman Antonio • SPN

PACTO DIABOLICO • 1968 • Salvador Jaime • MXC • PACT WITH THE DEVIL ○ DIABOLIC PACT

PACTOLE, LE • 1985 • Mocky Jean-Pierre • FRN

PAD (AND HOW TO USE IT), THE • 1966 • Hutton Brian G. • USA

PAD ITALIJA • 1982 • Zafranovic Lordan • YGS • FALL OF ITALY, THE ○ ISLAND CHRONICLE

PADATIK • 1973 • Sen Mrinal • IND • GUERILLA FIGHTER, THE

PADDINGTON LACE • 1971 • McCullough Chris • SHT • ASL

PADDLE, THE • 1985 • Gosha Hideo • JPN

PADDLE TO THE SEA • 1966 • Mason William • DCS • CND • VOGUE-A-LA-MER

PADDLING IN A KAYAK • 1967 • Csoke Jozsef • DOC • HNG

PADDY • 1969 • Haller Daniel • UKN, IRL • GOODBYE TO THE HILL

PADDY, DER FINDLING ODER DER KAMPF DER VIER • 1923 • Bock-Stieber Gernot • FRG

PADDY O'DAY • 1935 • Seiler Lewis • USA

PADDY O'HARA • 1917 • Edwards Walter • USA • IRISH EYES

PADDY ROLLERS see **MAIN STREET AFTER DARK** • 1944

PADDY THE NEXT BEST THING • 1923 • Cutts Graham • UKN

PADDY THE NEXT BEST THING • 1933 • Lachman Harry • USA

PADDY'S POLITICAL DREAM • 1916 • Dillon John Francis • USA

PADDY'S WAY OF DOING IT • 1908 • Aylott Dave • UKN

PADELLA CALIBRO 38 see **E ALLA FINE LO CHIAMARONO JERUSALEMME L'IMPLACABILE** • 1972

PADENIYE BERLINA • 1949 • Chiaureli Mikhail • USS • FALL OF BERLIN, THE (USA)

PADENIYE DINASTI ROMANOVIKH • 1927 • Shub Esther • USS • FALL OF THE ROMANOV DYNASTY, THE ○ FALL OF THE ROMANOVS, THE

PADIRAC RIVIERE DE LA NUIT • 1948 • Ichac Marcel • DCS • FRN

PADLOCKED • 1926 • Dwan Allan • USA

PADOSAN • 1968 • Sarup Jyoti • IND • NEIGHBOUR

PADRE • 1912 • Pastrone Giovanni • ITL

PADRE, THE • 1911 • *Selig* • USA

PADRE A TODO MAQUINA, UN • 1964 • Salvador Jaime • MXC

PADRE CONTRO HIJO • 1954 • Bustillo Oro Juan • MXC

PADRE COPLILLAS, EL • 1968 • Comas Ramon • SPN

PADRE DE LA CRIATURA, EL • 1972 • Lazaga Pedro • SPN

PADRE DE MAS DE CUATRO • 1938 • O'Quigley Roberto • MXC • FATHER OF MORE THAN FOUR (USA)

PADRE DI FAMIGLIA, IL • 1967 • Loy Nanni • ITL, FRN • HEAD OF THE FAMILY, THE (USA) ○ JEUX D'ADULTES (FRN)

PADRE DIABLO, EL • 1964 • Soler Julian • MXC

PADRE MANOLO, EL • 1967 • Torrado Ramon • SPN • FATHER MANOLO

PADRE MERCADER • 1939 • Amendolla Luis • MXC • MERCHANT FATHER (USA)

PADRE MORELOS, EL • 1942 • Contreras Torres Miguel • MXC

PADRE NUESTRO • 1953 • Gomez Muriel Emilio • MXC

PADRE NUESTRO • 1984 • *Abril Victoria* • SPN • OUR FATHER

PADRE NUESTRO QUE ESTAS EN LA TIERRA • 1971 • *Aldama Julio* • MXC

PADRE PADRONE • 1977 • Taviani Paolo, Taviani Vittorio • ITL • FATHER MASTER (USA)

PADRE PISTOLAS, EL • 1960 • Soler Julian • MXC

PADRE PITILLO, EL • 1954 • de Orduna Juan • SPN

PADRECITO, EL • 1964 • Delgado Miguel M. • MXC

PADRE'S GIFT, THE • 1912 • *Nestor* • USA

PADRE'S SACRIFICE, THE • 1913 • *Majestic* • USA

PADRE'S SECRET, THE • 1910 • Melies Gaston • USA

PADRE'S STRATEGY, THE • 1913 • Melville Wilbert • USA

PADRI E FIGLI • 1957 • Monicelli Mario • ITL, FRN • TAILOR'S MAID, THE (USA) ○ PERES ET FILS (FRN) ○ LIKE FATHER, LIKE SON

PADRINA, LA • 1973 • Vari Giuseppe • ITL

PADRINO ES UN COMPADRE, EL • 1974 • *Cine Vision* • MXC

PADRINO Y SUS AHIJADAS, EL • 1973 • Merino Fernando • SPN

PADRONA E SERVITA, LA • 1976 • Lanfranchi Mario • ITL, FRG • HERRENREITERIN, DIE (FRG) ○ MISTRESS, THE

PADRONE, THE • 1908 • *Kalem* • USA

PADRONE DEL FERRO, IL see **GUERRA DEL FERRO, LA** • 1983

PADRONE DEL MONDO, IL • 1982 • Morrow Dick • ITL • MASTER OF THE WORLD

PADRONE DEL MONDO, IL see **LUCE DEL MONDO, LA** • 1935

PADRONE DEL VAPORE, IL • 1951 • Mattoli Mario • ITL

PADRONE DELLE FERRIERE, IL • 1919 • Pastrone Giovanni • ITL • IRON MASTER, THE

PADRONE DELLE FERRIERE, IL • 1959 • Majano Anton Giulio • ITL, SPN

PADRONE DELLE FERROVIERE, IL • 1918 • Perego Eugenio • ITL

PADRONE E L'OPERAIO, IL • 1975 • Steno • ITL

PADRONE SONO ME, IL • 1956 • Brusati Franco • ITL

PADRONE'S DAUGHTER, THE • 1912 • *Prescott Vivian* • USA

PADRONE'S PLOT, THE • 1913 • *Kalem* • USA

PADRONE'S WARD, THE • 1914 • *Powers* • USA

PADRONI DELLA CITTA, I • 1977 • Di Leo Fernando • ITL, FRG • ZWEI SUPERTYPEN RAUME AUF ○ MISTER SCARFACE ○ BLOOD AND BULLETS

PADUKA PATTABHISHEKAM • 1945 • *Gemini & Rajarajeshwari* • IND

PADUREA SPINZURATILOR • 1965 • Ciulei Liviu • RMN • FOREST OF THE HANGED, THE ○ FOREST OF HANGED MEN ○ LOST FOREST, THE

PADUREANCA • 1988 • Margineanu Nicolae • RMN • FOREST MAIDEN, THE

PAEAN, A see **SANKA** • 1972

PAESE DEI CAMPANELLI, IL • 1954 • Boyer Jean • ITL

PAESE DEL NASCITA MUSSOLINI, IL • 1943 • Emmer Luciano, Gras Enrico • ITL

PAESE DEL SESSO SELVAGGIO, IL • 1972 • Lenzi Umberto • ITL • LAST SURVIVOR, THE (USA) ○ MAN FROM DEEP RIVER, THE ○ DEEP RIVER SAVAGES ○ MONDO CANNIBALE

PAESE DI PAPERINO, IL see **FEE PAS COMME LES AUTRES, UNE** • 1956

PAESE SENZA PACE, IL • 1943 • Menardi Leo • ITL • BARUFFE CHIOZZOTTE, LE

PAFNUCIO SANTO • 1976 • Corkidi Rafael • MXC • ST. PAFNUCIO

PAGADOR DE PROMESSAS, O • 1961 • Duarte Anselmo • BRZ • KEEPER OF PROMISES, THE ○ GIVEN WORD, THE ○ PROMISE, THE

PAGAL • 1941 • Kardar A. R. • IND

PAGAN, THE • 1929 • Van Dyke W. S. • USA

PAGAN AND CHRISTIAN • 1909 • *Edison* • USA

PAGAN GOD, THE • 1919 • Frame Park • USA

PAGAN HELLCAT see **MAEVA** • 1961

PAGAN ISLAND • 1961 • Mahon Barry • USA

PAGAN LADY, THE • 1931 • Dillon John Francis • USA

PAGAN LOVE • 1920 • Ballin Hugo • USA

PAGAN LOVE SONG • 1950 • Alton Robert • USA

PAGAN MOON • 1931-32 • Ising Rudolf • ANS • USA

PAGAN PASSIONS • 1924 • Campbell Colin • USA

PAGANINI • 1910 • *Gance Abel* • FRN

PAGANINI • 1923 • Goldberg Heinz • FRG

PAGANINI see **GERN HAB' ICH DIE FRAUEN GEKUSST** • 1926

PAGANINI see **GERN HAB' ICH DIE FRAU'N GEKUSST** • 1934

PAGANINI STRIKES AGAIN • 1973 • O'Hara Gerry • UKN

PAGANS, THE (USA) see **SACCO DI ROMA, IL** • 1954

PAGARES DE MENDIETA, LOS • 1939 • Torres-Rios Leopoldo • ARG

PAGATI PER MORIRE (ITL) see **ESTOUFFADE A LA CARAIBE** • 1966

PAGBABALIK NI DANIEL BARRION, ANG • 1968 • Garces Armando • PHL • RETURN OF DANIEL BARRION, THE

PAGE, LE • 1912 • Desfontaines Henri • FRN

PAGE BOY AND THE BABY, THE • 1907 • Smith Jack • UKN

PAGE D'AMOUR, UNE • 1965 • Korber Serge • FRN

PAGE D'AMOUR, UNE • 1978 • Rabinowicz Maurice • BLG, FRN • PAGE OF LOVE, A

PAGE DE GLOIRE, UNE • 1915 • Perret Leonce • FRN

PAGE DE NOTRE HISTOIRE, UNE • 1961 • Khalifa Omar • TNS

PAGE FOR CANADIAN HISTORY, A • 1912 • Reid Hal • USA

PAGE FROM LIFE, A • 1914 • Lloyd Frank • USA

PAGE FROM YESTERDAY, A • 1914 • Bellows Walter Clark • USA

PAGE MISS GLORY • 1935 • LeRoy Mervyn • USA

PAGE MISS GLORY • 1936 • Avery Tex • ANS • USA

PAGE MYSTERY, THE • 1917 • Knoles Harley • USA

PAGE OF LOVE, A see **PAGE D'AMOUR, UNE** • 1978

PAGE OF MADNESS, A (UKN) see **KURUTTA IPPEIJI** • 1927

PAGE OUT OF ORDER, A see **KURUTTA IPPEIJI** • 1927

PAGE TIM O'BRIEN see **LOVE IN THE DARK** • 1922

PAGE VOM DALMASSE-HOTEL, DER • 1933 • Janson Victor • FRG

PAGE VOM PALAST-HOTEL, DER • 1957 • Engel Thomas • AUS

PAGEANT see **KOROWOD** • 1967

PAGEANT, DEDICATION, FESTIVAL • 1908 • Melies Gaston • USA • BOSTON NORMAL SCHOOL PAGEANT

PAGEANT OF RUSSIA • 1947 • Yutkevich Sergei • USS

PAGEANT OF SAN FRANCISCO, THE • 1915 • *Pageant* • USA

PAGES D'HISTOIRE • 1916 • Cohl Emile • ANS • FRN

PAGES D'UN CATALOGUE • 1980 • Ruiz Raul • SHT • FRN • PAGES FROM A CATALOGUE

PAGES FROM A CATALOGUE see **PAGES D'UN CATALOGUE** • 1980

PAGES FROM JOSE MARTI'S DIARY see **PAGINAS DEL DIARIO DE JOSE MARTI** • 1971

PAGES FROM THE PAST • 1958 • Kochetov V., Tashkov Yevgyeni • USS

PAGES OF A CALENDAR • Poletika T., Vasilenko V. • ANS • USS

PAGES OF A CULTURE'S HISTORY • 1966 • Stoyanov Yuli • DOC • BUL

PAGES OF BRAVERY • 1959 • Saucan Mircea • RMN

PAGES OF IMMORTALITY • 1965 • Kopalin Ilya • DOC • USS

PAGES OF LIFE • 1922 • Millar Adelqui • UKN

PAGES OF LIFE see **STRANITSY ZHIZN** • 1948

PAGES OF THE PAST • 1964 • Kokochashvili Merab, Shengelaya Eldar, Shengelaya Georgi • USS

PAGINAS DEL DIARIO DE JOSE MARTI • 1971 • Massip Jose • CUB • PAGES FROM JOSE MARTI'S DIARY

PAGINE CHIUSE • 1968 • Da Campo Gianni • ITL

PAGINE DI ORRORE QUOTIDIANO see **ANCHE L'ESTASI** • 1978

PAGING A WIFE • 1925 • Lamont Charles • SHT • USA

PAGING PAGE TWO • 1917 • Baker Graham • SHT • USA

PAGLA THAKUR • 1967 • Sen Hironmoy • IND • MAD SAINT

PAGLIACCI • 1929 • Aylott Dave, Symmons E. F. • SHT • UKN

PAGLIACCI • 1936 • Grune Karl • UKN • CLOWN MUST LAUGH, A (USA)

PAGLIACCI • 1949 • Costa Mario • ITL • LOVE OF A CLOWN (PAGLIACCI) (USA) ○ AMORE TRAGICO

PAGLIACCI, I • 1923 • Samuelson G. B., Summers Walter • UKN

PAGLIACCI, I • 1943 • Hainisch Leopold, Fatigati Giuseppe • ITL, FRG

PAGLIACCI, I • 1970 • von Karajan Herbert • FRG, AUS, SWT

PAGLIACCI SWINGS IT • 1944 • Collins Lewis D. • SHT • USA

PAGO CARA SU MUERTE • 1967 • Klimovsky Leon • SPN

PAGODA • de Castro Eduardo, But Fu • PHL, HNG

PAGODA, THE see **GOJU NO TU** • 1944

PAGODE, DIE • 1914 • May Joe • FRG

PAGODE, DIE • 1917 • Meinert Rudolf • FRG • GEHEIMNIS DER PAGODE, DER

PAGODE, DIE • 1923 • Fekete Alfred • FRG

PAGPUTI NG UWAK, PAGATIM NG TAGAK • 1978 • Castillo Celso Ad. • PHL • WHEN THE CROW TURNS WHITE AND THE HERON TURNS BLACK

PAGU • 1916 • Oswald Richard • FRG

PAH TA LONE GAUNG GYAR • U Ba Shin • BRM

PAHADI HEERA • 1938 • Khan A. M. • IND • KULDIPAK

PAHELA ADMI see **PEHLA ADMI** • 1948

PAHITTIGA JOHANSSON • 1951 • Bolander Hugo • SWD • INGENIOUS JOHANSSON

PAHKAHULLA SUOMI • 1967 • Virtanen Jukka • FNL • CRAZY FINLAND

PAHLI NAZAR • 1945 • *Biswas Anil (M)* • IND

PAI DAENG • 1979 • Cheyaroon Permpol • THL • RED BAMBOO

PAI HUA P'IAO, HSUEH HUA P'IAO • 1977 • Li Hsing • HKG • MELODY FROM HEAVEN

PAI MAO NU • 1970 • Sang Hu • CHN • WHITE-HAIRED GIRL, THE

PAI-SHE CHUAN • 1963 • Yueh Feng • HKG • MADAME WHITE SNAKE ○ MAGIC WHITE SERPENT, THE

PAI TIRANO, O • 1941 • Ribeiro Antonio Lopes • PRT • CRUEL FATHER

PAI-YU LAO-HU • 1977 • Ch'U Yuan • HKG • JADE TIGER

PAID • 1930 • Wood Sam • USA • WITHIN THE LAW (UKN)

PAID BACK • 1911 • *Selig* • USA

PAID BACK • 1922 • Cummings Irving • USA

PAID IN ADVANCE • 1919 • Holubar Allen • USA • GIRL WHO DARED, THE

PAID IN BLOOD • *Cameron Jeff* • USA

PAID IN ERROR • 1938 • Rogers Maclean • UKN

PAID IN FULL • 1910 • *Vitagraph* • USA

PAID IN FULL • 1912 • Dwan Allan • USA

PAID IN FULL • 1914 • Thomas Augustus • USA

PAID IN FULL • 1919 • Chautard Emile • USA

PAID IN FULL • 1950 • Dieterle William • USA • BITTER VICTORY

PAID IN HIS OWN COIN • 1912 • *Buckley May* • USA

PAID TO DANCE • 1937 • Coleman C. C. Jr. • USA

PAID TO KILL (USA) see **FIVE DAYS** • 1954

PAID TO LOVE • 1927 • Hawks Howard • USA • GABY

PAID VACATION, A • 1980 • Thomas Ralph L. • MTV • CND

PAID WITH INTEREST • 1912 • Wilson Frank? • UKN

PAID WITH INTEREST • 1914 • Crisp Donald • USA

PAIDEIA • 1977 • Typaldos Yannis • GRC • EDUCATION

PAIL OF TIME, A see **SPANN AV TID, ET** • 1973

PAILLASSE • 1918 • Magnussen Fritz • SWD

PAILLON DIT LYONNAIS LE JUSTE see **PAPILLON** • 1914

PAIN see **KUTSU** • 1927

PAIN see **ACI** • 1971

PAIN AMER see **PIKRO PSOMI, TO** • 1951

PAIN AND PLEASURE • 1967 • *Arena Sammy* • USA

PAIN AS YOU ENTER • 1924 • Taurog Norman • SHT • USA

PAIN DE BARBARIE, LE • 1934 • Leenhardt Roger • DCS • FRN

PAIN DE BARBARIE, LE • 1948 • Leenhardt Roger • DCS • FRN

PAIN DE LA PASSION, LE • 1952 • Laine Edvin • FNL

PAIN DELLE STELLE • 1947 • Ferroni Giorgio • ITL

PAIN DES JULES, LE • 1959 • Severac Jacques • FRN

PAIN DU CIEL, LE • 1962 • Agostini Philippe • DCS • FRN

PAIN IN THE A..., A (USA) see **EMMERDEUR, L'** • 1973

PAIN IN THE PULLMAN, A • 1936 • Black Preston • SHT • USA

PAIN OF KARA BATTAL, THE see **KARA BATTALIN ACISI** • 1968

PAIN VIVANT, LE • 1954 • Mousselle Jean • FRN

PAINEIS DO PORTO • 1964 • Reis Antonio • SHT • PRT

PAINEL • 1950 • Barreto Victor • BRZ • PANEL

PAINLESS DENTISTRY see **CHARLATAN, LE** • 1901

PAINLESS EXTRACTING • 1916 • *Miller Rube* • USA

PAINLESS EXTRACTING, A • 1907 • Fitzhamon Lewin • UKN

PAINLESS LOVE • 1918 • *Hardy Babe* • SHT • USA

PAINLEV CASE, THE see **SLUCHAYAT PENLEVE** • 1968

PAINS OF LIFE see **HAYAT ACILARI** • 1967

PAINT AND PASSION • 1918 • Rains Fred • SHT • UKN

PAINT AND PERFIDY • 1905 • Fitzhamon Lewin? • UKN

PAINT AND POWDER • 1921 • Roach Hal • SHT • USA

PAINT AND POWDER • 1925 • Stromberg Hunt • USA

PAINT IT BLACK • 1989 • Hunter Tim • USA

PAINT ME A MURDER • 1984 • Cooke Alan • UKN

PAINT POT SYMPHONY • 1949 • Rasinski Connie • ANS • USA

PAINT YOUR WAGON • 1969 • Logan Joshua • USA

PAINTED ANARCHIST, THE • 1915 • *Alhambra* • USA

PAINTED ANGEL, THE • 1929 • Webb Millard • USA • BROADWAY HOSTESS, THE

PAINTED BOATS • 1945 • Crichton Charles • UKN • GIRL ON THE CANAL, THE (USA)

PAINTED BOY, THE • 1964 • Vasilenko N. • ANS • USS

PAINTED DAUGHTERS • 1925 • Whyte F. Stuart • ASL

PAINTED DESERT, THE • 1931 • Higgin Howard • USA

PAINTED DESERT, THE • 1938 • Howard David • USA

PAINTED DOOR, THE • 1973 • Lynch Paul • CND

PAINTED DOOR, THE • 1985 • Pittman Bruce • MTV • CND

PAINTED FACES • 1929 • Rogell Albert S. • USA

PAINTED FACES see **CHAT SIU FUK** • 1988

PAINTED FLAPPER, THE • 1924 • Gorman John • USA

PAINTED HILLS, THE • 1951 • Kress Harold F. • USA • SHEP OF THE PAINTED HILLS

PAINTED HORSES • 1977 • Salvat Keith • SHT • ASL

PAINTED LADY, THE • 1912 • Griffith D. W. • USA

PAINTED LADY, THE • 1914 • Sullivan Frederick • USA

PAINTED LADY, THE • 1924 • Bennett Chester • USA

PAINTED LADY, THE • 1925 • Greenwood Edwin • UKN • RED LIPS

PAINTED LADY BETTY, THE • 1915 • Wilson Frank • UKN

PAINTED LADY'S CHILD, THE • 1914 • Ayres Sydney • USA

PAINTED LIE, THE • 1917 • Wilbur Crane • USA

PAINTED LILY, THE • 1918 • Heffron Thomas N. • USA

PAINTED LIPS • 1918 • Le Saint Edward J. • USA

PAINTED LIPS see **IRODORARERU KUCHIBIRU** • 1929

PAINTED LIPS see **BOQUITAS PINTADAS** • 1974

PAINTED MADONNA, THE • 1917 • Lund O. A. C. • USA

PAINTED PEOPLE • 1924 • Badger Clarence • USA

PAINTED PICTURES • 1930 • Barnett Charles • UKN

PAINTED PONIES • 1927 • Eason B. Reeves • USA

PAINTED POST • 1928 • Forde Eugene J. • USA

PAINTED SMILE, THE • 1962 • Comfort Lance • UKN • MURDER CAN BE DEADLY (USA)

PAINTED SOUL, THE • 1915 • Sidney Scott • USA

PAINTED STALLION, THE • 1937 • Witney William, Taylor Ray • SRL • USA

PAINTED TOWER, THE see **WIEZA MALOWANA** • 1961

PAINTED TRAIL • 1928 • McGowan J. P. • USA

PAINTED TRAIL, THE • 1938 • Hill Robert F. • USA

PAINTED VEIL, THE • 1934 • Boleslawski Richard, Van Dyke W. S. (U/c) • USA

PAINTED WAVES OF LOVE • 1980 • Li Hsing • HKG

PAINTED WOMAN, THE • 1932 • Blystone John G. • USA

PAINTED WORLD, THE • 1914 • Ince Ralph • USA

PAINTED WORLD, THE • 1919 • Ince Ralph • USA

PAINTER, THE • 1917 • *Manson* • USA

PAINTER, THE see **MALAREN** • 1981

PAINTER AND POET see **POET AND PAINTER** • 1951

PAINTER AND THE CITY, THE see **PINTORE A CIDADE, O** • 1956

PAINTER AND THE POINTER, THE • 1944 • Culhane James • ANS • USA

PAINTER AND THE TOWN, THE see **PINTORE A CIDADE, O** • 1956

PAINTER JESUS SOTO see **VUELTA AL ZANJON** • 1974

PAINTERS, THE • 1918 • *Ebony* • SHT • USA

PAINTER'S IDYL, A • 1911 • *Selig* • USA

PAINTER'S MISHAP IN THE BARRACKS, THE see **DOUCHE DE COLONEL, LA** • 1901

PAINTER'S NEPHEW, THE see **NEVEU DU PEINTRE, LA** • 1988

PAINTERS OF QUEBEC • 1944 • Crabtree Grant • DCS • CND • SEPT PEINTRES DU QUEBEC

PAINTERS PAINTING • 1972 • De Antonio Emile • USA

PAINTER'S REVENGE, THE • 1908 • Porter Edwin S. • USA

PAINTER'S RUSE, THE • 1913 • *Powers* • USA

PAINTER'S STUDIO, THE see **ATELIER D'ARTISTE, FARCE DE MODELES** • 1898

PAINTING • 1970 • Tyrlova Hermina • ANM • CZC

PAINTING, THE • 1909 • *Vitagraph* • USA

PAINTING AND PLASTICS • 1948 • Davis James* • SHT • USA

PAINTING FOR THE CAT see **MALOVANI PRO KOCKU** • 1960

PAINTING OF A MIRACULOUS SPIDER, THE see **TOILE D'ARAIGNEE MERVEILLEUSE, LA** • 1908

PAINTING PEOPLE • 1965 • Burstall Tim • DOC • ASL

PAINTING RELATIONS see **PINTANDO RELACIONES**

PAINTING THE CLOUDS WITH SUNSHINE • 1951 • Butler David • USA • GOLD DIGGERS IN LAS VEGAS

PAINTING THE TOWN • 1987 • Graham Trevor • ASL

PAINTING THE TOWN see **HOT HEELS** • 1928

PAINTING WITH LIGHT • 1974 • Siegel Lois • CND

PAINTINGS BY ED EMSHWILLER • 1955-58 • Emshwiller Ed • USA

PAIP'S GIRL see **IMMENSITA, L'** • 1967

PAIR OF ANTIQUE VASES, A • 1911 • Coleby A. E. • UKN

PAIR OF BABY SHOES, A • 1912 • *Lockwood Harold* • USA

PAIR OF BAGS, A • 1912 • Wilson Frank? • UKN

PAIR OF BEARS, A • 1913 • *Joker* • USA

PAIR OF BIRDS, A • 1914 • *Crystal* • USA

PAIR OF BIRDS, A • 1915 • *Pokes & Jabbs* • USA

PAIR OF BOOTS, A • 1912 • *Selig* • USA

PAIR OF BOOTS, A • 1912 • *Lubin* • USA

PAIR OF BRIEFS, A • 1962 • Thomas Ralph • UKN

PAIR OF CUFFS, A • 1914 • *Reliance* • USA

PAIR OF CUPIDS, A • 1918 • Brabin Charles J. • USA

PAIR OF DESPERADOES, A • 1909 • Fitzhamon Lewin? • UKN

PAIR OF DESPERATE SWINDLERS, A • 1906 • Raymond Charles? • UKN

PAIR OF DEUCES, A • 1919 • Goulding Alf • SHT • USA

PAIR OF DUMMIES, A • 1915 • Birch Cecil • UKN

PAIR OF FOILS, A • 1913 • Williams C. Jay • USA

PAIR OF FOOLS, A • 1912 • *White Pearl* • USA

PAIR OF FRAUDS, A • 1913 • *Gale Peter* • UKN

PAIR OF FRAUDS, A • 1914 • Marston Theodore • USA

PAIR OF GLOVES, A • 1911 • *Imp* • USA

PAIR OF GLOVES, A • 1920 • Mannering Cecil • UKN

PAIR OF HANDCUFFS, A • 1912 • Stow Percy • UKN • LINKS OF LOVE

PAIR OF HELLIONS, A • 1924 • Willis Walter • USA

PAIR OF JACKS, A • 1912 • *Conway Jack* • USA

PAIR OF KINGS, A • 1922 • Taurog Norman, Semon Larry • SHT • USA

PAIR OF NEW BOOTS, A • 1911 • Stow Percy • UKN

PAIR OF PANTS, A • 1911 • *Reliance* • USA

PAIR OF PINK PANTHERS, A • 1918 • *Parsons William* • SHT • USA

PAIR OF PRODIGALS, A • 1913 • Thornby Robert T. • USA

PAIR OF QUEENS, A • 1914 • *Mace Fred* • USA

PAIR OF QUEENS, A • 1915 • Baker George D. • USA

PAIR OF SCHEMERS, OR MY WIFE AND MY UNCLE, A • 1910 • *Vitagraph* • USA

PAIR OF SHADOWS • 1916 • Daly William Robert • SHT • USA

PAIR OF SHOES, A • 1911 • *Reliance* • USA

PAIR OF SILK STOCKINGS, A • 1918 • Edwards Walter • USA

PAIR OF SIXES, A • 1918 • Windom Lawrence C. • USA

PAIR OF SKINS, A • 1916 • *Pokes & Jabbs* • USA

PAIR OF SLIPPERS, A • 1909 • *Essanay* • USA

PAIR OF SOCKS, A • 1933 • Lamont Charles • SHT • USA

PAIR OF SPECTACLES, A • 1908 • *Lubin* • USA

PAIR OF SPECTACLES, A • 1916 • Butler Alexander • UKN

PAIR OF STARS, A • 1915 • Birch Cecil • UKN

PAIR OF STOCKINGS, A • 1914 • Bellows Walter Clark • USA

PAIR OF SUICIDES, A • 1912 • *Powers* • USA

PAIR OF TIGHTS, A • 1928 • Yates Hal • SHT • USA

PAIR OF TROUSERS, A • 1912 • Coleby A. E.? • UKN

PAIR OF TRUANTS, A • 1909 • Fitzhamon Lewin • UKN

PAIR OF TWINS, A • 1920 • Russell Albert • SHT • USA

PAIR OF WRITERS, A • 1979 • van Ieperen Ab • SHT • NTH

PAIS CERRADO, TEATRO ABIERTO • 1990 • Balassa Arturo • ARG • CLOSED COUNTRY, OPEN THEATRE

PAIS DE BELLA FLOR, EL • 1975 • Laverde Fernando • SHT • CLM • LAND OF BEAUTIFUL FLOWERS, THE

PAIS DOS TENENTES, O • 1988 • de Andrade Joao Batista • BRZ • LIEUTENANT'S COUNTRY

PAIS PORTATIL • 1977 • Feo Ivan • VNZ • PORTABLE COUNTRY

PAIS QUADRADOS.. FILHOS AVANCADOS • 1970 • Tanko J. B. • BRZ

PAIS, S.A. • 1975 • Forges • SPN • COUNTRY LTD.

PAISA • 1947 • Rossellini Roberto • ITL • PAISAN (USA)

PAISA HI PAISA • 1956 • *Biswas Anil (M)* • IND

PAISAGEM • 1930 • do Canto Jorge Brum • PRT

PAISAGENS DE PORTUGAL • 1952 • Garcia Fernando • SHT • PRT

PAISAN (USA) see **PAISA** • 1947

PAISANELLA see **AVVENTURE IN CITTA** • 1960

PAISTI AG OBAIR • 1973 • Marcus Louis • DCS • IRL • CHILDREN AT WORK

PAIVAA, HERRA KIVI • 1983 • Linnasalo Timo • FNL • HELLO MR. KIVI

PAIX CHEZ SOI, LA • 1921 • Saidreau Robert • FRN

PAIX ET LA VIE, LA • 1962 • Kyrou Ado • FRN

PAIX SUR LE RHIN • 1938 • Choux Jean • FRN

PAIX SUR LES CHAMPS • 1970 • Boigelot Jacques • BLG

PAIXAO DE CRISTO • 1970 • Cobbett William • BRZ

PAIXAO DE CRISTO NA PINTURA ANTIGA PORTUGUESA, A • 1961 • Rosa Baptista • SHT • PRT

PAJA AND JARE, THE LORRY DRIVERS see **PAJA I JARE** • 1974

PAJA I JARE • 1974 • Djukanovic Milo • YGS • PAJA AND JARE, THE LORRY DRIVERS

PAJACYK I PIKUS • 1959 • Nehrebecki Wladyslaw • ANS • PLN • CLOWN AND THE LITTLE DOG, THE ○ PUPPET AND PIKUS, THE ○ CLOWN AND HIS DOG, THE

PAJACYK, PIESEK I PLOMIEN • 1959 • Nehrebecki Wladyslaw • ANS • PLN • CLOWN AND THE LITTLE DOG AND THE FLAME, THE ○ PUPPET, DOG AND FLAME, THE

PAJACYK, PIKUS I KSIEZYC • 1960 • Nehrebecki Wladyslaw • ANS • PLN • LITTLE CLOWN, THE PUP AND THE MOON, THE ○ PUPPET, PIKUS AND THE MOON, THE

PAJAMA GAME, THE • 1957 • Abbott George, Donen Stanley • USA • WHAT LOLA WANTS

PAJAMA GIRL • 1903 • *Bitzer Billy (Ph)* • USA

PAJAMA MARRIAGE, A • 1920 • *Edwards Neely* • USA

PAJAMA PARADE, THE • 1913 • *Majestic* • USA

PAJAMA PARTY • 1964 • Weis Don • USA • MAID AND THE MARTIAN, THE

PAJAMA PARTY, THE • 1931 • Roach Hal • SHT • USA

PAJAMA PARTY IN A HAUNTED HOUSE see **GHOST IN THE INVISIBLE BIKINI, THE** • 1966

PAJAMAS • 1927 • Blystone John G. • USA • PYJAMAS

PAJARERA, LA • 1945 • Gomez Muriel Emilio • MXC

PAJARO DEL FARO, EL • 1971 • Alvarez Santiago • DOC • CUB

PAJARO INDICADOR, EL • 1971 • Carretero Amaro • ANS • SPN • RATEL, THE

PAJAROS DE BADEN-BADEN, LOS • 1974 • Camus Mario • SPN • BIRDS OF BADEN-BADEN, THE

PAKKETUR TIL PARADIS • 1981 • Einarson Eldar • NRW • DESTINATION: PARADISE

PAKLENI OTOK • 1980 • Tadej Vladimir • YGS • HELL'S ISLAND

PAKLIC • 1944 • Cikan Miroslav • CZC • SKELETON KEY, THE

PAKSHIRAJ • 1959 • Tripathi S. N. • IND • SACRED BIRD, THE

PAKT MIT DEM SATAN, DER see **KALTE HERZ, DAS** • 1923

PAKUASHIPU • 1971-77 • Lamothe Arthur • DOC • CND • RIVIERE SECHE, LA

PAL AND GALS • 1954 • White Jules • SHT • USA

PAL FROM TEXAS, THE • 1939 • Webb Harry S. • USA

PAL, FUGITIVE DOG • 1950 • Irving • SHT • USA

PAL JOEY • 1957 • Sidney George • USA

PAL O' MINE • 1936 • Newman Widgey R. • UKN

PAL O'MINE • 1924 • Le Saint Edward J. • USA

PAL UTCAI FIUK, A (HNG) see **BOYS OF PAUL STREET, THE** • 1969

PALABRA DE HONOR • 1939 • Amadori Luis Cesar • ARG

PALABRA ES DE TODOS, LA • 1980 • Susz Pedro • BLV • WORD IS EVERYBODY'S, THE

PALABRAS DE AMOR • 1968 • Ribas Antoni • SPN • TREN DE MATINADA

PALABRAS DE DIOS, LA • 1971 • *Cima* • MXC

PALABRAS DE MAX, LAS • 1977 • Martinez Lazaro Emilio • SPN • WORDS OF MAX, THE ○ WHAT MAX SAID

PALABRAS DE MUJER • 1945 • Diaz Morales Jose • MXC

PALABRE • 1970 • Degelin Emile • BLG

PALABRES SUR LE NIL see **THARTHARA ALA AN-NIL** • 1971

PALAC • 1980 • Junak Tadeusz • PLN

PALACE • 1984 • Molinaro Edouard • FRN

PALACE AND FORTRESS see **DVORETS I KREPOST** • 1925

PALACE OF MYSTERY, THE • 1912 • Kinder Stuart • UKN

PALACE OF NUDES (USA) see **CRIME AU CONCERT MAYOL** • 1954

PALACE OF PLEASURE, THE • 1926 • Flynn Emmett J. • USA

PALACE OF SHAME see **CRIME AU CONCERT MAYOL** • 1954

PALACE OF SNAKES see **YOJA NO MADEN** • 1956

PALACE OF THE ARABIAN NIGHTS, THE (USA) see **PALAIS DES MILLE ET UNE NUITS, LE** • 1905

PALACE OF THE DARKENED WINDOWS, THE • 1920 • Kolker Henry • USA

PALACE SCANDAL • Verhoeven Paul • FRG

PALACES • 1927 • Durand Jean • FRN • BITTER SWEETS

PALACES AND HUTS see **SCHLOSSER UND KATEN** • 1957

PALACES OF A QUEEN • 1966 • Ingrams Michael • DOC • UKN

PALACES OF PEKING see **PEKING PALOTAI** • 1957

PALACIO DA BOLSA • 1950 • Queiroga Perdigao • SHT • PRT

PALACIO DE QUELUZ • 1952 • Mendes Joao • SHT • PRT

PALACIO DOS ANJOS, O • 1970 • Khouri Walter Hugo • BRZ

PALACIO NEGRO • 1976 • Ripstein Arturo • DOC • MXC • BLACK PALACE

PALADIN, DER • 1917 • Rosenhayn Paul • FRG

PALADINI DE FRANCIA, I • 1960 • Luzzati Emmanuele, Gianini Giulio • ANS • ITL • PALADINS OF FRANCE, THE

PALADINI, I see **ARMI E GLI AMORI, LE** • 1983

PALADINI, STORIA D'ARMI E D'AMORI, I see **ARMI E GLI AMORI, LE** • 1983

PALADINS, A STORY OF LOVE AND WAR, THE see **ARMI E GLI AMORI, LE** • 1983

PALADINS OF FRANCE, THE see **PALADINI DE FRANCIA, I** • 1960

PALAIS DE DANSE • 1928 • Elvey Maurice • UKN

PALAIS DES MILLE ET UNE NUITS, LE • 1905 • Melies Georges • FRN • PALACE OF THE ARABIAN NIGHTS, THE (USA)

PALAIS DES PASSIONS, LE see **QASR ASH-SHAWQ**

PALAIS ETRANGERS • 1900 • Melies Georges • FRN

PALAIS IDEAL, LE • 1958 • Kyrou Ado • SHT • FRN

PALAIS ROYALE • 1988 • Lavut Martin • CND

PALAMANASULU • 1968 • Puttanna S. R. • IND • PURE, THE

PALANDAI • 1967 • Singh A. Bhim • IND • FEEDER

PALANGETIYO • 1980 • Obeysekara Vasantha • SLN

PALANQUIN see **PALKI** • 1967

PALANQUIN, THE see **DOCHU SUGOROKU KAGO** • 1927

PALANQUIN DES LARMES, LE • 1986 • Fischer Max • MTV • CND, FRN

PALAVA ENKELI • 1983 • Torhonen Lauri • FNL • BURNING ANGEL, THE

PALAVER • 1926 • Barkas Geoffrey • UKN

PALAVER • 1968 • Degelin Emile • BLG

PALAVER, PALAVER • 1990 • Seiler Alexander J. • DOC • SWT

PALAVOS KOSMOS TOU THANASI, O • 1979 • Katsouridis Dinos • GRC • THANASIS'S CRAZY WORLD

PALAZZO DEI DOGI, IL • 1947 • Pasinetti Francesco • ITL

PALCO ALL'OPERA, UN • 1955 • Marcellini Siro • ITL

PALE ARROW • 1957 • Witney William • USA

PALE ARROW (UKN) see **PAWNEE** • 1957

PALE BETTY see **BLEEKE BET** • 1934

PALE FACE see **VISAGE PALE** • 1986

PALE FACE PUP • 1931 • Foster John, Davis Mannie • ANS • USA

PALE FACE SQUAW, THE • 1913 • *Films Lloyds* • USA

PALE-FACED GIRL, THE • 1970 • Searle Francis • SHT • UKN

PALE FACED PRINCESS, THE • 1910 • *Bison* • USA

PALE FACE'S WOOING, THE • 1909 • *Kalem* • USA

PALE FLOWER see **KAWAITA HANA** • 1964

PALE LIGHT OF SORROW, THE see **LUMINA PALIDA A DURERII** • 1980

PALE OF PREJUDICE, THE • 1914 • *Lubin* • USA

PALE RIDER • 1985 • Eastwood Clint • USA

PALEC BOZY • 1972 • Krauze Antoni • PLN • FINGER OF GOD, THE

PALEFACE • 1933 • *Iwerks Ub (P)* • ANS • USA

PALEFACE, THE • 1921 • Cline Eddie, Keaton Buster • SHT • USA

PALEFACE, THE • 1948 • McLeod Norman Z. • USA

PALEFACE BRAVE, THE • 1914 • *Bartlett Charles* • USA

PALEFACE PRINCESS, THE • 1910 • Melies Gaston • USA • PALEFACED PRINCESS, THE

PALEFACED PRINCESS, THE see **PALEFACE PRINCESS, THE** • 1910

PALEOLITHIC PORNOGRAFFITTI • Gistamano Clarko • ANS • USA

PALEONTHOLOGIE • 1959 • van Gelder Hans • SHT • NTH • SCHAKEL MET HET VERLEDEN ○ STORY IN THE ROCKS

PALERMO • 1938 • Mom Arturo S.

PALERMO ODER WOLFSBURG • 1979 • Schroeter Werner • FRG • PALERMO OR WOLFSBURG

PALERMO OR WOLFSBURG see **PALERMO ODER WOLFSBURG** • 1979

PALESTINA SACRA • 1967 • Pesce Giacomo • ITL

PALESTINE • 1912 • Olcott Sidney • DOC • USA

PALESTINE • 1947 • Carruthers Robin • UKN • THIS MODERN AGE NO.6

PALESTINES, THE see **PALESTINIANS, THE** • 1975

PALESTINIAN, THE • 1977 • Battersby Roy • UKN

PALESTINIAN REVOLT see **FALASTINI AL SAER, AL** • 1970

PALESTINIANS, THE • 1975 • van der Keuken Johan • DOC • NTH • PALESTINES, THE

PALETA DE VELAZQUEZ, LA • 1963 • Castellon Alfredo • SHT • SPN

PALIATSOS, O • 1968 • Karayannis Kostas • GRC • CLOWNS, THE

PALICOVA DCERA • 1941 • Borsky Vladimir • CZC • ARSONIST'S DAUGHTER, THE

PALIKERONG KUTSERO • 1967 • Wenceslao Jose Pepe • PHL • PLAYBOY RIG DRIVER, THE

PALILLO VARGAS HEREDIA • 1943 • Vejar Carlos Jr. • MXC

PALINDROME • 1969 • Frampton Hollis • SHT • USA

PALIO • 1932 • Blasetti Alessandro • ITL

PALIPAT-LIPAT • 1981 • Brocka Lino • PHL

PALISER CASE, THE • 1920 • Parke William • USA

PALISSADES • 1962 • Potignat • SHT • FRN

PALKA-VIRVCHALKA • 1956 • ANS • USS

PALKI • 1967 • Sunny S. U., Paul Mahesh • IND • PALANQUIN

PALLARD THE PUNTER • 1919 • Leigh J. L. V. • UKN

PALLAVA SELVANGAL • 1967 • Rao C. S. • IND • TREASURES OF THE PALLAVAS

PALLAVI • 1976 • Lankesh P. • IND

PALLE ALENE I VERDEN • 1949 • Henning-Jensen Bjarne, Henning-Jensen Astrid • DNM • PALLE ALONE IN THE WORLD (USA)

PALLE ALONE IN THE WORLD (USA) see **PALLE ALENE I VERDEN** • 1949

PALLET ON THE FLOOR • 1984 • Butler Lynton • NZL

PALLI SAMAI • 1932 • *Sircar B. N. (P)* • IND

PALLID DAWN, THE • 1917 • Calvert E. H. • SHT • USA

PALLID HUES IN CLOUDED SKIES • 1911 • *Reliance* • USA

PALLIETER • 1975 • Verhavert Roland • NTH, BLG

PALLISADE • 1986 • McInnes Laurie • SHT • ASL

PALM BEACH • 1979 • Thoms Albie • ASL

PALM BEACH GIRL, THE • 1926 • Kenton Erle C. • USA

PALM BEACH STORY, THE • 1942 • Sturges Preston • USA

PALM COURT ORCHESTRA, THE • 1964 • Halas John • ANS • UKN

PALM SPRINGS • 1936 • Scotto Aubrey • USA • PALM SPRINGS AFFAIR (UKN)

PALM SPRINGS AFFAIR (UKN) see **PALM SPRINGS** • 1936

PALM SPRINGS WEEKEND • 1963 • Taurog Norman • USA
PALM SUNDAY see **VIRAGVASARNAP** • 1969
PALMA DI TU MANO • 1954 • Gavaldon Roberto • MXC
PALMANAM • 1968 • Sethumadhavan K. S. • IND • INNOCENT
PALMER HA MUERTO • 1961 • Fortuny Juan • SPN
PALMES • 1951 • Dupont Jacques • SHT • FRN
PALMIER, LE see **NAKHLA, AN-** • 1976
PALMIER A L'HUILE, LE • 1963 • Rouch Jean • DCS • FRN
PALMIRA • 1963 • Boyadgieva Lada • DOC • BUL
PALMY DAYS • 1931 • Sutherland A. Edward • USA
PALO Y HUESO • 1968 • Sarquis Nicolas • ARG • STICK AND BONE
PALOMA, LA • 1916 • Wolbert William • SHT • USA
PALOMA, LA • 1937 • Contreras Torres Miguel • MXC
PALOMA, LA • 1959 • Martin Paul • FRG
PALOMA, LA • 1974 • Schmid Daniel • SWT
PALOMA, LA see **GROSSE FREIHEIT NMR 7, DIE** • 1944
PALOMA BRAVA • 1960 • Gonzalez Rogelio A. • MXC
PALOMA HERIDA • 1962 • Fernandez Emilio • MXC
PALOMA'S NIGHTS see **NOCHES DE PALOMA, LAS** • 1977
PALOMBELLA ROSCA • 1990 • Moretti Nanni • ITL, FRN • LITTLE RED DOVE
PALOMBIERE, LA • 1983 • Denis Jean-Pierre • FRN
PALOMILLA, LA • 1976 • *Conacite* • MXC • JAGUAR DE OBSIDIANA, EL ○ RESCATE INSOLITO
PALOMILLA BRAVA • 1973 • Ruiz Raul • CHL • BAD GIRL
PALOMINO, THE • 1950 • Nazarro Ray • USA • HILLS OF THE BRAVE (UKN)
PALOMITA BLANCA • 1973 • Ruiz Raul • CHL • LITTLE WHITE DOVE ○ WHITE DOVE
PALOMOS, LOS • 1964 • Fernan-Gomez Fernando • SPN
PALOOKA • 1934 • Stoloff Ben • USA • GREAT SCHNOZZLE, THE (UKN) ○ JOE PALOOKA
PALOOKA FROM PADUCAH • 1934 • Lamont Charles • SHT • USA
PALOS STRIKES AGAIN • 1968 • Dlz • PHL • EEL STRIKES AGAIN
PALS • Homoki-Nagy Istvan • DOC • HNG
PALS • 1910 • Melies Gaston • USA
PALS • 1911 • *Essanay* • USA
PALS • 1911 • *Reliance* • USA
PALS • 1912 • *Pathe* • USA
PALS • 1912 • Dwan Allan • *American* • USA
PALS • 1914 • Wilson Frank • UKN
PALS • 1917 • *Ruge Billy* • USA
PALS • 1925 • McCarthy John P. • USA
PALS • 1933 • Tyer James • ANS • USA • CHRISTMAS NIGHT
PALS • 1987 • Antonio Lou • TVM • USA
PALS see **COLEGAS** • 1983
PALS, THE see **DRUGARCINE** • 1980
PALS AND PETTICOATS • 1920 • Brown Melville, Lord Del • SHT • USA
PALS AND PUGS • 1920 • Robbins Jess • SHT • USA
PALS FIRST • 1918 • Carewe Edwin • USA
PALS FIRST • 1926 • Carewe Edwin • USA
PAL'S GALLANT JOURNEY • 1950 • Irving • SHT • USA
PALS IN BLUE • 1915 • Mix Tom • USA
PALS IN PARADISE • 1926 • Seitz George B. • USA
PALS IN PERIL • 1927 • Thorpe Richard • USA
PAL'S OATH, A • 1911 • *Field Gladys* • USA
PALS OF THE GOLDEN WEST • 1951 • Witney William • USA
PALS OF THE PECOS • 1941 • Orlebeck Lester • USA
PALS OF THE PRAIRIE • 1929 • King Louis • USA
PALS OF THE PRAIRIE • 1934 • Hutchison Charles • SHT • USA
PALS OF THE RANGE • 1910 • *Anderson Broncho Billy* • USA
PALS OF THE RANGE • 1935 • Clifton Elmer • USA
PALS OF THE SADDLE • 1938 • Sherman George • USA
PALS OF THE SILVER SAGE • 1940 • Herman Al • USA
PALS OF THE WEST • 1922 • *Hill R. Lee* • USA • HER HALF BROTHER
PALS OF THE WEST • 1934 • Tansey Robert • SHT • USA
PALS ON THE PRAIRIE see **PRAERIEKAMMERATER** • 1970
PALS OVER MOUNTS AND DALES • Homoki-Nagy Istvan • DOC • HNG
PAL'S RETURN • 1948 • Goodwins Leslie • SHT • USA
PALSIE WALSIE • 1934 • Horne James W. • SHT • USA
PALTOQUET, LE • 1986 • Deville Michel • FRN
PALUDE DEL PECCATO, LA see **PALUDE TRAGICA** • 1953
PALUDE TRAGICA • 1953 • de Orduna Juan • SPN, ITL • PALUDE DEL PECCATO, LA ○ AMORE E FANGO
PALUDISME EN ALGERIE, LE • 1967 • Mazif Sid-Ali • SHT • ALG
PALYGIRLS INTERNATIONAL • 1963 • Wishman Doris • USA • NATURE'S PLAYGIRLS INTERNATIONAL
PALYMUNKASOK • 1957 • Gaal Istvan • SHT • HNG • SURFACEMEN ○ RAILROADERS
PAMBIHIRANG TATLO • 1967 • Villaflor Romy • PHL • WONDERFUL THREE
PAMBRAUN • 1967 • Navarro Rod • PHL
PAMELA • Garnier Pierre-Claude • FRN
PAMELA • 1944 • de Herain Pierre • FRN • PAMELA OU L'ENIGMA DU TEMPLE
PAMELA CONGREVE • 1914 • *Fealy Maude* • USA
PAMELA, D'UN COTE COMME DE L'AUTRE • Antony Michel • FRN
PAMELA OU L'ENIGMA DU TEMPLE see **PAMELA** • 1944
PAMELA, PAMELA YOU ARE.. • 1968 • Rose William L. • USA
PAMELA'S PARTY • 1912 • Plumb Hay • UKN
PAMELA'S PAST • 1916 • *Feely Maude* • USA
PAMET NASEHO DNE • 1963 • Nemec Jan • CZC • MEMORY OF OUR DAY
PAMIATKA Z KALWARII • 1958 • Hoffman Jerzy, Skorzewski Edward • DCS • PLN • SOUVENIR FROM CALVARY, A ○ SOUVENIR OF CALVARY ○ CALVARY ○ KALWARIA
PAMIETNIK GWIEZDNE see **WYCIECZKA W KOSMOS** • 1961
PAMIETNIK PANI HANKI • 1963 • Lenartowicz Stanislaw • PLN • LOST DAYS OF PEACE, THE ○ MRS. HANKA'S DIARY
PAMIETNIKI CHLOPOW • 1952 • Munk Andrzej • DCS • PLN • DIARIES OF THE PEASANTS ○ PEASANT MEMOIRS
PAMPA BARBARA • 1943 • Fregonese Hugo, Demare Lucas • ARG • SAVAGE PAMPAS
PAMPA GRINGA, LA • 1963 • Birri Fernando • DOC • ARG
PAMPA SALVAJE • 1966 • Fregonese Hugo • SPN • SAVAGE PAMPAS
PAMPASREITER see **SCHLUCT DES TODES, DIE** • 1923
PAMPERED YOUTH • 1925 • Smith David • USA • MAGNIFICENT AMBERSONS, THE
PAMPHLET TWILIGHT see **ZETTELDAMMERUNG** • 1979
PAMPOSH • 1953 • Mir Ezra • IND • LOTUS FLOWER
PAMPULIK ALS AFFE • 1912 • *Pallenberg Max* • AUS
PAMPULIK HAT HUNGER • 1913 • *Pallenberg Max* • AUS
PAMPULIK KRIEGT EIN KIND • 1912 • *Pollenberg Max* • AUS
PAMYAT • 1972 • Chukhrai Grigori • USS • REMEMBRANCE ○ MEMORY
PAMYAT SERDTSA • 1958 • Lioznova Tatyana • USS • HEART'S MEMORIES, THE ○ MEMORY OF THE HEART
PAMYATI SERGO ORDZHONIKIDZYE • 1937 • Vertov Dziga, Svilova Elizaveta • USS • IN MEMORY OF SERGEI ORDZHONIKIDZYE
PAN • 1919 • Fejos Paul • HNG
PAN • 1937 • Fjord Olaf • FRG • SCHICKSAL DES LEUTNANT THOMAS GLAHN, DAS
PAN • 1962 • van der Horst Herman • NTH
PAN • Moorse Georg • FRG, ITL
PAN see **KORT AR SOMMAREN** • 1962
PAN-AFRICAN FESTIVAL see **FESTIVAL PAN AFRICAN D'ALGER** • 1970
PAN-AMERICAN EXPOSITION ELECTRIC TOWER • 1901 • *Bitzer Billy (Ph)* • USA
PAN-AMERICAN GAMES • Giraldo Diego Leon • CLM
PAN-AMERICANA • 1945 • Auer John H. • USA
PAN, AMOR Y ANDALUCIA • 1959 • Perojo Benito • SPN
PAN ANATOL SZUKA MILIONA • 1959 • Rybkowski Jan • PLN • MR. ANATOL SEEKS A MILLION
PAN-CHIN PA-LIANG • 1977 • Hui Michael • HKG • PRIVATE EYES, THE
PAN CHOPALI see **ARE GA MINATO NO HIKARI DA** • 1961
PAN DODEK • 1969 • Lomnicki Jan, Bossak Jerzy • PLN • MISTER DODEK
PAN HABETIN OCHAZI • 1949 • Gajer Vaclav • CZC • DEPARTURE OF MR. HABETIN, THE ○ MR. HABETIN DEPARTS
PAN HANDLERS • 1936 • Terhune William • SHT • USA
PAN MICHAEL see **PAN WOLODYJOWSKI** • 1969
PAN NA ROZTRHANI • 1934 • Cikan Miroslav • CZC • VERY BUSY GENTLEMEN
PAN OTEC KARAFIAT • 1935 • Svitak • CZC • MILLER KARAFIAT, THE
PAN-PIEN JEN see **AH YING** • 1983
PAN PLASTYK • 1964 • Latallo Katarzyna • ANM • PLN • MR. ARTIST ○ MISTER DESIGNER
PAN PROFESOR • 1959 • Perski Ludwik • DOC • PLN • PROFESSOR, THE
PAN PROFESOR, NEPRITEL ZEN • 1913 • Steimar Jiri • CZC • OUR PROFESSOR, THE ENEMY OF WOMEN
PAN PROKOUK AKROBATEM • 1959 • Rozkopal Zdenek • CZC • MR. PROKOUK ACROBAT
PAN PROKOUK DETEKTIVEN • 1958 • *Zeman Karel (Sc)* • SHT • CZC • MR. PROKOUK, DETECTIVE ○ MR. PROKOUK, THE DETECTIVE
PAN PROKOUK FILMUJE • 1948 • Zeman Karel • ANS • CZC • MR. PROKOUK MAKES A FILM ○ MR. PROKOUK IS FILMING
PAN PROKOUK HODINAREM • 1972 • *Zeman Karel (Sc)* • ANS • CZC • MR. PROKOUK, THE WATCHMAKER
PAN PROKOUK JEDE NA BRIGADU • 1947 • Zeman Karel • ANS • CZC • MR. PROKOUK LEAVES FOR VOLUNTEER WORK ○ MR. PROKOUK ON A BRIGADE ○ BRIGADY ○ BRIGAD
PAN PROKOUK, PRITEL ZVIRATEK • 1955 • Zeman Karel • ANS • CZC • MR. PROKOUK, FRIEND OF LITTLE ANIMALS ○ MR. PROKOUK THE ANIMAL FANCIER ○ MR. PROKOUK, THE ANIMAL LOVER
PAN PROKOUK URADUJE • 1947 • Zeman Karel • ANS • CZC • MR. PROKOUK AND THE RED TAPE ○ MR. PROKOUK BUREAUCRAT ○ MR. PROKOUK IN THE OFFICE
PAN PROKOUK V POKUSENI • 1947 • Zeman Karel • ANS • CZC • TEMPTATION OF MR. PROKOUK, THE ○ MR. PROKOUK'S TEMPTATION ○ MR. PROKOUK IN TEMPTATION
PAN PROKOUK VYNALEZCEM • 1949 • Zeman Karel • ANS • CZC • MR. PROKOUK THE INVENTOR
PAN RAZITKO A EDISONI • 1980 • Tomanek Jan • CZC • MR. RUBBER STAMP AND EDISONS
PAN REDAKTOR SZALEJE • 1938 • Wencel H. • MR. EDITOR IS CRAZY (USA)
PAN RZEPKA I JEGO CIEN • 1957 • Wajzer Waclaw • PLN • MR. RZEPKA AND HIS SHADOW
PAN SLON • 1960 • Badzian Teresa • ANM • PLN • MR. ELEPHANT
PAN TAU • Polak Jindrich • CZC • MR. TAU (USA)
PAN-TELE-TRON • 1957 • Turpin Digby • UKN
PAN TRABA • 1960 • Zitzman Jerzy • ANS • PLN • MR. TRUMPET
PAN TVARDOVSKI • 1916 • Starevitch Ladislas • USS • MR. TVARDOVSKI (USA)
PAN TVARDOVSKI • 1937 • Szaro Henryk • PLN • DR. FAUSTUS
PAN WOLODYJOWSKI • 1969 • Hoffman Jerzy • PLN • COLONEL WOLODYJOWSKI (UKN) ○ LITTLE KNIGHT, THE ○ PAN MICHAEL
PANACHE • 1976 • Nelson Gary • TVM • USA
PANAMA: DANGER ZONE • 1960 • Rasky Harry • MTV • USA
PANAMA FLO • 1932 • Murphy Ralph • USA
PANAMA HATTIE • 1942 • McLeod Norman Z., Minnelli Vincente (U/c) • USA
PANAMA LADY • 1939 • Hively Jack • USA • SECOND SHOT, THE
PANAMA PASAMA • 1968 • Gopalakrishnan K. S. • IND • LOVE OR WEALTH
PANAMA PATROL • 1939 • Lamont Charles • USA
PANAMA RED • 1976 • Chinn Robert C. • USA
PANAMA SAL • 1957 • Witney William • USA
PANAMERICANA -DREAM ROAD OF THE WORLD see **PANAMERICANA -TRAUMSTRASSE DER WELT** • 1968
PANAMERICANA -TRAUMSTRASSE DER WELT • 1968 • Domnick Hans • DOC • FRG • PANAMERICANA -DREAM ROAD OF THE WORLD
PANAMINT'S BAD MAN • 1938 • Taylor Ray • USA
PANCHA INDERA HARIMAU BERANTAI • 1970 • Kadarisman S. • MLY • CHAINED TIGER
PANCHASHAR • 1968 • Guhathakurta Arup • IND • CUPID
PANCHITA, LA • 1948 • Gomez Muriel Emilio • MXC
PANCHITOS GANG, THE see **BANDA DE LOS PANCHITOS, LA** • 1985
PANCHO LOPEZ • 1956 • Cardona Rene • MXC
PANCHO SE ZENI • 1946 • Hrusinsky Rudolf • CZC • PANCHO TAKES A WIFE
PANCHO TAKES A WIFE see **PANCHO SE ZENI** • 1946
PANCHO VILLA • 1972 • Martin Eugenio • MXC, SPN • DESAFIO DE PANCHO VILLA, EL (SPN)
PANCHO VILLA RETURNS (USA) see **PANCHO VILLA VUELVE** • 1949
PANCHO VILLA VUELVE • 1949 • Contreras Torres Miguel • MXC • PANCHO VILLA RETURNS (USA)
PANCHO VILLA Y LA VALENTINA • 1958 • Rodriguez Ismael • MXC • SOLDIERS OF PANCHO VILLA
PANCHO'S HIDEAWAY • 1964 • Freleng Friz • ANS • USA
PAND EVIL • 1988 • Bechard Gorman • USA
PANDA AND THE MAGIC SERPENT (USA) see **HAKUJA DEN** • 1958
PANDEMONIUM • 1939 • Newman Widgey R. • UKN
PANDEMONIUM • 1982 • Sole Alfred • USA • THURSDAY THE 12TH
PANDEMONIUM • 1987 • Keenan Haydn • ASL
PANDEMONIUM see **SHURA** • 1970
PANDHAYAM • 1967 • Kasilingam A. • IND • GAMBLING
PANDI THEVAN • 1958 • Subrahmanyam K. • IND
PANDILLA, LA • Eguiluz Enrique L. • SHT • SPN
PANDILLA DE LOS ONCE, LA • 1961 • Lazaga Pedro • SPN
PANDILLA EN ACCION, LA • 1959 • Porter Julio • MXC
PANDILLA SE DIVIERTE, LA • 1959 • Porter Julio • MXC
PANDILLERO, EL • 1959 • Baledon Rafael • MXC
PANDORA • 1934 • *Terry Paul/ Moser Frank (P)* • ANS • USA
PANDORA • 1960 • Kumel Harry • SHT • BLG
PANDORA • 1971 • May Derek • CND
PANDORA AND THE FLYING DUTCHMAN • 1951 • Lewin Albert • UKN
PANDORA AND THE KING, THE see **BANDOLA Y EL REY, LA** • 1979
PANDORA'S BOX • 1912 • Baker George D., Trimble Larry • USA
PANDORA'S BOX • 1943 • Rasinski Connie • ANS • USA
PANDORA'S BOX • 1962 • *Miyako Film* • ANS • JPN
PANDORA'S BOX see **BUCHSE DER PANDORA, DIE** • 1929
PANDORE • 1969 • Nys Guy J. • BLG
PANE AMARO, IL see **VERGOGNE DEL MONDO, LE** • 1968
PANE, AMORE E.. • 1955 • Risi Dino • ITL • SCANDAL IN SORRENTO (UKN) ○ BREAD, LOVE AND..
PANE AMORE E ANDALUSIA • 1959 • Seto Javier • SPN, ITL • VIVE AMORE
PANE, AMORE E FANTASIA • 1953 • Comencini Luigi • ITL • BREAD, LOVE AND DREAMS (USA)
PANE AMORE E GELOSIA • 1954 • Comencini Luigi • ITL • BREAD, LOVE AND JEALOUSY ○ FRISKY (USA)
PANE, BURRO E MARMELLATA • 1977 • Capitani Giorgio • ITL
PANE E CIOCCOLATA • 1974 • Brusati Franco • ITL • BREAD AND CHOCOLATE (USA)
PANE, VY JSTE VDOVA • 1971 • Vorlicek Vaclav • CZC • MISTER, YOU ARE A WIDOWER ○ SIR, YOU ARE A WIDOWER ○ YOU ARE A WIDOW, SIR
PANEL see **PAINEL** • 1950
PANEL DOCTOR, THE see **MEDICO DELLA MUTUA, IL** • 1968
PANEL GAME, THE • 1916 • Jaccard Jacques • SHT • USA
PANEL STORY, THE see **PANELSTORY** • 1978
PANELESS WINDOW WASHER, THE • 1937 • Fleischer Dave • ANS • USA
PANELKAPCSOLAT • 1983 • Tarr Bela • HNG • PREFAB PEOPLE, THE
PANELS FOR THE WALLS OF THE WORLD #1 • 1967 • Vanderbeek Stan • SHT • USA
PANELSTORY • 1978 • Chytilova Vera • CZC • STORY FROM A HOUSING ESTATE ○ PREFAB STORY ○ PANEL STORY, THE
PANENSTVI • 1937 • Vavra Otakar • CZC • VIRGINITY ○ INNOCENCE ○ MAIDENHOOD
PANG I BYGGET • 1966 • Frisk Ragnar • SWD • BIG BANG
PANGA • 1989 • Barton Sean • SAF
PANGARAP KO'Y IKAW, ANG • 1967 • Torres Mar S. • PHL • YOU'RE MY DREAM
PANGLIMA BADUL • 1978 • Hassan Hussein Abu • MLY
PANGLIMA MAUT • 1975 • Achnas Naz • MLY • WARRIOR OF DEATH
PANGS OF JEALOUSY • 1917 • *Grandin Ethel* • SHT • USA
PANHANDLE • 1948 • Selander Lesley • USA
PANHANDLE CALIBRE 38 • 1975 • *Wynn Keenan* • ITL
PANHANDLE SCANDAL • 1959 • Lovy Alex • ANS • USA
PANHANDLING ON MADISON AVENUE • 1964 • Kneitel Seymour • ANS • USA
PANI BOVARY TO JA • 1977 • Kaminski Zbigniew • PLN • MADAME BOVARY, IT'S ME ○ MADAME BOVARY THAT'S ME
PANI EDISONI • 1987 • Olmer Vit • CZC • NEW EDISONS, THE
PANI KLUCI • 1975 • Plivova-Simkova Vera • CZC • GENTLEMEN, THE BOYS
PANI TWARDOWSKA • 1956 • Marszalek Lechoslaw • PLN • MRS. TWARDOWSKA
PANIC! • 1914 • Aylott Dave • UKN
PANIC • 1963 • Gilling John • UKN
PANIC see **PANIK** • 1939
PANIC see **PANICO** • 1980
PANIC see **PANIK** • 1984
PANIC AND CALM see **KYOKO TO SHIZUKO** • 1926
PANIC AT LAKEWOOD MANOR • 1977 • Scheerer Robert • USA • IT HAPPENED AT LAKEWOOD MANOR ○ ANTS: PANIC AT LAKEWOOD MANOR ○ ANTS
PANIC AT MADAM TUSSAUD'S • 1948 • Scott Peter Graham • UKN

PANIC BUTTON.. OPERAZIONE FISCO • 1962 • Carnimeo Giuliano, Sherman George • ITL, USA • PANIC BUTTON (USA) ○ LET'S GO BUST
PANIC BUTTON (USA) see **PANIC BUTTON.. OPERAZIONE FISCO** • 1962
PANIC CITY • 1974 • Girdler William • USA • ZEBRA KILLER, THE
PANIC DAYS IN WALL STREET • 1913 • *Childers Naomi* • USA
PANIC IN CHICAGO see **PANIK IN CHIKAGO** • 1931
PANIC IN ECHO PARK • 1977 • Moxey John Llewellyn • TVM • USA
PANIC IN HIGH SCHOOL • 1978 • Ishii Sogo • JPN
PANIC IN NEEDLE PARK • 1971 • Schatzberg Jerry • USA
PANIC IN PARADISE see **PANIK I PARADIS** • 1960
PANIC IN THE CITY • 1968 • Davis Eddie • USA
PANIC IN THE PARLOR, A • 1941 • Roberts Charles E. • USA
PANIC IN THE PARLOR (USA) see **SAILOR BEWARE** • 1956
PANIC IN THE STREETS • 1950 • Kazan Elia • USA
PANIC IN THE WILDERNESS • 1975 • USA
PANIC IN THE YEAR ZERO see **PANIC IN YEAR ZERO** • 1962
PANIC IN YEAR ZERO • 1962 • Milland Ray • USA • PANIC IN THE YEAR ZERO ○ END OF THE WORLD, THE ○ SURVIVAL
PANIC IS ON, THE • 1931 • Parrott James • SHT • USA
PANIC ON A TRAIN see **LUDZIE Z POCIAGU** • 1961
PANIC ON PAGE ONE see **CITY IN FEAR** • 1980
PANIC ON THE 5:22 • 1974 • Hart Harvey • TVM • USA
PANIC ON THE AIR • 1936 • Lederman D. Ross • USA • TRAPPED BY WIRELESS
PANIC ON THE AIR (UKN) see **YOU MAY BE NEXT** • 1935
PANIC ON THE TRANSIBERIAN EXPRESS see **PANICO EN EL TRANSIBERIANO** • 1972
PANIC TRAIN see **PANICO EN EL TRANSIBERIANO** • 1972
PANIC (USA) see **PANIQUE** • 1946
PANICKY PUP • 1933 • Foster John, Bailey Harry • ANS • USA
PANICO • 1980 • Ricci Tonino • ITL • PANIC
PANICO EN EL TRANSIBERIANO • 1972 • Martin Eugenio • SPN, UKN • PANIC ON THE TRANSIBERIAN EXPRESS ○ HORROR EXPRESS (USA) ○ PANIC TRAIN
PANICO NO IMPERIO DO CRIME • 1972 • Fernandes Ary • BRZ
PANIC'S ON, THE • 1922 • De Haven Carter • USA
PANIEKZAAIERS • 1985 • Le Bon Patrick • BLG • SCAREMONGERS, THE
PANIENKA Z OKIENKA • 1964 • Kaniewska Maria • HNG
PANIER A CRABES, LE • 1960 • Lisbona Joseph • FRN
PANIK • 1921 • Piel Harry • FRG
PANIK • 1928 • Piel Harry • FRG
PANIK • 1939 • Willoughby George • SWD • PANIC
PANIK • 1943 • Piel Harry • FRG
PANIK • 1984 • Mannstaedt Per • DOC • DNM • PANIC
PANIK I PARADIS • 1960 • Hasselbalch Hagen • DNM • PANIC IN PARADISE
PANIK IN CHIKAGO • 1931 • Wiene Robert • FRG • PANIC IN CHICAGO
PANIQUE • 1946 • Duvivier Julien • FRN • PANIC (USA)
PANIQUE • 1978 • Lord Jean-Claude • CND
PANITRA SATAN • 1926 • *Excelsior* • IND
PANJE-E-AHANIN • 1968 • Mirsamadzadeh • IRN • IRON FISTS
PANNA A NETVOR • 1978 • Herz Juraj • CZC • BEAUTY AND THE BEAST (USA) ○ MAIDEN AND THE BEAST, THE
PANNA DEGLI AEROMOBILI, LA • 1915 • *Deed Andre* • ITL • BREAKDOWN OF THE AEROMOBILES, THE
PANNA ZAZRACNICA • 1966 • Uher Stefan • CZC • MIRACULOUS VIRGIN, THE ○ MIRACULOUS MAIDEN, THE ○ VIRGINAL MIRACLE-MAKER, THE
PANNAKARAI PILLAI • 1968 • Jambu • IND • RICH BOY, THE
PANNONIAN PEAK, THE see **PANONSKI VRH** • 1989
PANNY I WDOWY • 1990 • Zaorski Janusz • PLN • SPINSTERS AND WIDOWS
PANNY Z WILKO • 1979 • Wajda Andrzej • PLN, FRN • DEMOISELLES DE WILKO, LES (FRN) ○ MAIDS OF WILKO, THE (USA) ○ GIRLS FROM WILKO, THE ○ YOUNG GIRLS OF WILKO, THE (UKN) ○ YOUNG LADIES OF WILKO, THE
PANO • 1979 • Gaucherand Philippe • FRN
PANO VERDE • 1972 • David Mario • ARG • BILLIARD TABLE
PANONSKI VRH • 1989 • Petrovic Eva • YGS • PANNONIAN PEAK, THE
PANOPTICON see **PANOPTIKUM** • 1969
PANOPTICUM 59 • 1959 • Kolm-Veltee H. Walter • AUS
PANOPTIKUM • 1969 • Kijowicz Miroslaw • ANS • PLN • PANOPTICON
PANORAMA • 1975 • Casals Melchor • CUB
PANORAMA BLUE • 1974 • Roberts Alan • USA
PANORAMA CIRCULAIRE • 1900 • Melies Georges • FRN
PANORAMA DE LA SEINE see **VUE PANORAMIQUE PRISE DE LA SEINE** • 1900
PANORAMA DU HAVRE (PRIS D'UN BATEAU) • 1896 • Melies Georges • FRN • PANORAMA OF HAVRE TAKEN FROM A BOAT
PANORAMA DU PORT DE SAINT-HELIER • 1899 • Melies Georges • FRN • BIRD'S-EYE VIEW OF ST. HELIER (JERSEY)
PANORAMA FROM TOP OF A MOVING TRAIN see **PANORAMA PRIS D'UN TRAIN EN MARCHE** • 1898
PANORAMA OF HAVRE TAKEN FROM A BOAT see **PANORAMA DU HAVRE (PRIS D'UN BATEAU)** • 1896
PANORAMA OF RIVER SEINE see **VUE PANORAMIQUE PRISE DE LA SEINE** • 1900
PANORAMA OF RUSSIA (USA) see **PESNI ROSSII** • 1963
PANORAMA OF THE ESPLANADE BY NIGHT • 1901 • Porter Edwin S. • USA
PANORAMA PRIS DU TROTTOIR ROULANT CHAMP DE MARS • 1900 • Melies Georges • FRN
PANORAMA PRIS D'UN TRAIN EN MARCHE • 1898 • Melies Georges • FRN • PANORAMA FROM TOP OF A MOVING TRAIN
PANSAHAR • 1929 • Bose Debaki • IND
PANSY • 1912 • *Selig* • USA
PANSY POST, PROTEAN PLAYER • 1916 • *Keyes Frances* • USA
PANSY'S PAPAS • 1916 • Wolbert William • SHT • USA
PANSY'S PRISON PIES • 1915 • *Keyes Frances* • USA
PANTA RHEI • 1951 • Haanstra Bert • DCS • NTH • ALL THINGS FLOW (UKN) ○ EVERYTHING FLOWS
PANTALASKAS • 1959 • Paviot Paul • FRN
PANTALEON Y LAS VISTADORAS • 1976 • Gutierrez Santos Jose Maria, Vargas Llosa M. • SPN
PANTALON COUPE, LE • 1905 • Blache Alice • FRN
PANTALOON SKIRT, THE • 1911 • *Powers* • USA
PANTALOONS (USA) see **DON JUAN** • 1956
PANTANAL DE SANGUE • 1972 • de Barros Reynaldo Paes • BRZ
PANTANO D'AVIO • 1956 • Olmi Ermanno (Spv) • DOC • ITL
PANTANO DE LAS ANIMAS, EL • 1956 • Baledon Rafael • MXC
PANTANO DE LOS CUERVOS • 1973 • Cano Manuel • SPN
PANTATA BEZOUSEK • 1926 • Lamac Carl • CZC
PANTELEI • 1978 • Stoyanov Georgi • BUL
PANTERA DE MONTE ESCONDIDO, LA • 1960 • Ortega Juan J. • MXC
PANTERA EM MINHA CAMA, UMA • 1972 • Christensen Carlos Hugo • BRZ
PANTERA NEGRA, LA • 1955 • Salvador Jaime • MXC
PANTERA NERA, LA • 1942 • Gambino Domenico M. • ITL
PANTERAS SE COMEN A LOS RICOS • 1969 • Fernandez Ramon • SPN
PANTHEA • 1917 • Dwan Allan • USA
PANTHEON, THE • 1987 • Petrova Malina • DOC • BUL
PANTHER, THE • 1914 • Edwards Walter • USA
PANTHER, THE see **FAHD, AL-** • 1972
PANTHER GIRL OF THE CONGO • 1955 • Adreon Franklin • SRL • USA
PANTHER SQUAD • 1986 • Knight Peter • USA
PANTHER WHO FELT, THE see **PARDALU KTERY VONEL, O** • 1972
PANTHER WOMAN, THE • 1919 • Ince Ralph • USA
PANTHER WOMEN, THE see **MUJERES PANTERAS, LAS** • 1966
PANTHERBRAUT, DIE • 1919 • Lasko Leo • FRG
PANTHERES BLANCHES, LES • 1971 • Jessua Alain • FRN
PANTHER'S CLAW, THE • 1942 • Beaudine William • USA
PANTHER'S MOON (UKN) see **SPY HUNT** • 1950
PANTINS D'AMOUR • 1936 • Kapps Walter • FRN
PANTOFFELHELD, DER • 1922 • Schunzel Reinhold • FRG, AUS
PANTOFFELHELDEN see **MEISTERBOXER, DER** • 1934
PANTOFFELREGERING • 1947 • SAF
PANTOMIMA DELLA MORTE, LA • 1915 • Caserini Mario • ITL
PANTOMIME GIRLS HAVING A LARK • 1902 • Smith G. A. • UKN
PANTOMIMES • 1954 • Paviot Paul • SHT • FRN • PANTOMIMES: MARCEL MARCEAU
PANTOMIMES • 1956 • Lucot Rene • SHT • FRN
PANTOMIMES: MARCEL MARCEAU see **PANTOMIMES** • 1954
PANTOUFLE DE VAIR, LA • 1960 • Rou Aleksandr • USS
PANTOUFLE MYSTERIEUSE, LA see **CENDRILLON** • 1912
PANTRY PANIC see **WHAT'S COOKIN'?** • 1941
PANTRY PIRATE • 1940 • Geronimi Clyde • ANS • USA
PANTS • 1917 • Berthelet Arthur • USA
PANTS AND PANSIES • 1912 • Sennett Mack • USA
PANTS AND PETTICOATS • 1915 • *Morris Reggie* • USA
PANURGE • 1932 • Bernheim Michel • FRN
PANZER TROPHY, THE • 1915 • *Powers* • USA
PANZERGEWOLBE, DAS • 1914 • May Joe • FRG • ARMOURED VAULT, THE
PANZERGEWOLBE, DAS • 1926 • Pick Lupu • FRG • ARMOURED VAULT, THE
PANZERKREUZER SEWASTOPOL see **WEISSE SKLAVEN** • 1936
PAO, O • 1959 • de Oliveira Manoel • PRT • BREAD
PAO, AMOR E TOTOBOLA • 1963 • Campos Henrique • PRT
PAO E AGUA • 1929 • Contreiras Anibal • SHT • PRT
PAO NOSSO • 1940 • Miranda Armando • PRT
PAO-PIAO • 1977 • Ch'En Ming-Hua • HKG • CHINA ARMED ESCORT
PAOLA • 1969 • Bellocchio Marco (c/d) • ITL
PAOLO BARCA, MAESTRO ELEMENTARE PRACTICAMENTE NUDISTA • 1975 • Mogherini Flavio • ITL
PAOLO DE CASPADO see **ENDE DES ABENTEURERS PAOLO DE CASPADO** • 1920
PAOLO E FRANCESCA • 1950 • Matarazzo Raffaello • ITL • FRANCESCA DA RIMINI
PAOLO E FRANCESCA • 1971 • Vernuccio Gianni • ITL
PAOLO IL CALDO • 1973 • Vicario Marco • ITL
PAOLO IL FREDDO • 1974 • Ingrassia Ciccio • ITL
PAOLUZZI STORY, THE • 1981 • Lauder Al • DOC • UKN
PAPA • 1915 • Oxilia Nino • ITL
PAPA see **SON AUTRE AMOUR** • 1933
PAPA, BE GOOD! • 1925 • Roach Hal • SHT • USA
PAPA BY PROXY • 1916 • *Rolma* • SHT • USA
PAPA, CAN YOU HEAR ME SINGING see **TA-TS'O CHE** • 1983
PAPA DIVENTA MAMMA • 1952 • Fabrizi Aldo • ITL
PAPA GETS THE BIRD • 1940 • Harman Hugh • ANS • USA
PAPA HAYDN • 1920 • Frey Karl • FRG
PAPA HELPS THE PAINTERS • 1905 • *Paul R. W.* • UKN
PAPA HULIN • 1921 • Krauss Henry • FRN
PAPA KANN'S NICHT LASSEN • 1921 • Schonfelder Erich • FRG
PAPA LEBONARD • 1945 • Peon Ramon • MXC
PAPA LEBONNARD (ITL) see **PERE LEBONNARD, LE** • 1938
PAPA, LES PETITS BATEAUX • 1971 • Kaplan Nelly • FRN
PAPA LOVES MAMA see **UNEXPECTED FATHER, THE** • 1932
PAPA, MAMA, THE MAID AND I (USA) see **PAPA, MAMAN, LA BONNE ET MOI** • 1954
PAPA, MAMAN, LA BONNE ET MOI • 1954 • Le Chanois Jean-Paul • FRN • PAPA, MAMA, THE MAID AND I (USA)
PAPA, MAMAN, MA FEMME ET MOI • 1956 • Le Chanois Jean-Paul • FRN
PAPA PACIFICO • 1956 • Brignone Guido • ITL
PAPA PAGA see **CATTIVO SOGGETTO, UN** • 1933
PAPA PER UNA NOTTE • 1939 • Bonnard Mario • ITL
PAPA PROSPER see **MIOCHE, LE** • 1936
PAPA PUTS ONE OVER • 1913 • Ince Ralph • USA
PAPA SANS LE SAVOIR • 1931 • Wyler Robert • FRN • FILS A PAPA
PAPA SARTO see **UOMINI NON GUARDANO IL CIELO, GLI** • 1952
PAPA SCORES • 1915 • Birch Cecil • UKN
PAPA SE DESENREDA • 1940 • Zacarias Miguel • MXC
PAPA SE ENREDA OTRA VEZ • 1940 • Zacarias Miguel • MXC
PAPA SOLTERO • 1939 • Harlan Martin • ARG • BACHELOR FATHER (USA)
PAPA, TI RICORDO! • 1954 • Volpe Mario • ITL • FANCIULLA DI POMPEI, LA
PAPA, VOGLIO IMPIEGARMI! see **IMPIEGATA DI PAPA, L'** • 1933
PAPACITO LINDO • 1939 • de Fuentes Fernando • MXC • SUGAR DADDY (USA)
PAPAFLESSAS • 1970 • Andreou Errikos • GRC
PAPAGENO • 1935 • Reiniger Lotte • ANS • FRG • PAPAGONO ○ MAGIC FLUTE, THE
PAPAGENO • 1954 • Reiniger Lotte • ANS • UKN
PAPAGONO see **PAPAGENO** • 1935
PAPAI TRAPLAHAO • 1968 • Lima Victor • BRZ • CLUMSY PAPA
PAPAKOSAM • 1968 • Seshagiri G. V. R. • IND • FOR THE CHILD'S SAKE
PAPANINE ET SES COMPAGNONS • 1938 • Poselsky I. • USS
PAPARAZZI • 1969 • Geller Bruno • USA
PAPARAZZI • 1973 • Rozier Jacques • SHT • FRN
PAPA'S BABY • 1913 • Henderson Dell • USA
PAPA'S BATH • 1903 • Collins Alf? • UKN
PAPA'S BOY • 1914 • Lehrman Henry • USA
PAPA'S BOY • 1927 • Taurog Norman • SHT • USA
PAPA'S CINEMA see **CINEMA DE PAPA, LE** • 1970
PAPA'S DARLING • 1914 • Smallwood Ray C. • USA
PAPA'S DAY OF REST • 1952 • Davis Mannie • ANS • USA
PAPA'S DELICATE CONDITION • 1963 • Marshall George • USA
PAPA'S DOUBLE • 1912 • *Prior Herbert* • USA
PAPA'S DREAM • 1913 • France Charles H. • USA
PAPA'S FIRST OUTING • 1910 • *Essanay* • USA
PAPA'S HELPING HAND • 1913 • *Nestor* • USA
PAPA'S HONEYMOON • 1909 • *Lubin* • USA
PAPAS JUNGE • 1918 • Bolten-Baeckers Heinrich • FRG
PAPA'S LETTER • 1907 • *Walturdaw* • UKN
PAPA'S LETTER • 1914 • Cornwallis Donald • UKN
PAPA'S LITTLE HELPERS • 1952 • Davis Mannie • ANS • USA
PAPA'S LITTLE WEAKNESS • 1914 • Birch Cecil • UKN
PAPAS NEUE FREUNDIN • 1961 • Leopold Georg • GDR
PAPA'S SWEETHEART • 1911 • Merwin Bannister • USA
PAPA'S WIFE • 1915 • Terriss Tom • USA
PAPAYA DEI CARAIBI • 1978 • D'Amato Joe • ITL
PAPELERITO, EL • 1950 • Delgado Agustin P. • MXC
PAPER see **PAPIR** • 1943
PAPER BIRD see **PAPIEROWY PTAK** • 1971
PAPER BIRD, THE see **PAPIRFUGLEN** • 1984
PAPER BOAT IN A SEA OF FIRE see **BANGKANG PAPEL SA DAGAT NG APOY** • 1984
PAPER BOATS • 1949 • Rose Tony • UKN
PAPER BOY • 1971 • Borris Clay • CND
PAPER BRIDGE, THE see **PAPIERNE BRUCKE, DIE** • 1987
PAPER BULLETS • 1941 • Rosen Phil • USA • GANGS INCORPORATED ○ CRIME INC., GANGS INC.
PAPER CHASE, THE • 1952 • *Hall Cameron* • SHT • UKN
PAPER CHASE, THE • 1973 • Bridges James • USA
PAPER COCK-A-DOODLES • 1908 • *Pathe* • SHT • FRN
PAPER COCKEREL, THE • 1965 • Sibianu Gheorghe • ANM • RMN
PAPER CRANES, THE see **SENBAZURU** • 1958
PAPER CRANES FROM OSEN see **ORIZURU OSEN** • 1934
PAPER CUTTING • 1912 • Booth W. R. • UKN
PAPER DOLL, THE • 1913 • *White Pearl* • USA
PAPER DOLLS • 1969 • Hill James • MTV • UKN
PAPER DOLLS • 1982 • Zwick Edward • TVM • USA
PAPER DOLL'S WHISPER OF SPRING, A (USA) see **KAMI NINGYO HARU NO SASAYAKI** • 1926
PAPER FLOWER, THE see **PAPIRFUGLEN** • 1984
PAPER FLOWERS see **KEMBANG KERTAS** • 1985
PAPER GALLOWS see **TORMENT** • 1949
PAPER HANGER, THE • 1920 • *Franey William* • SHT • USA
PAPER HANGER, THE • 1932 • *Mintz Charles (P)* • ANS • USA
PAPER HANGERS, THE • 1937 • Davis Mannie • ANS • USA
PAPER HANGER'S REVENGE, THE • 1918 • Curtis Allen • *Clover* • SHT • USA
PAPER HANGING • 1922 • Dudley Bernard • UKN
PAPER HEART see **CORAZON DE PAPEL** • 1982
PAPER LION • 1968 • March Alex • USA
PAPER MAGIC • 1945 • *Mead Thomas (P)* • SHT • USA
PAPER MAN • 1971 • Grauman Walter • TVM • USA
PAPER MAN, THE see **HOMBRE DE PAPEL, EL** • 1963
PAPER MASK • 1989 • Morahan Christopher • UKN
PAPER MOON • 1973 • Bogdanovich Peter • USA
PAPER NOCTURNE see **PAPIROVE NOKTURNO** • 1949
PAPER ORCHID • 1949 • Baker Roy Ward • UKN
PAPER PEOPLE, THE • 1969 • Gardner David • CND
PAPER PEOPLE LAND • 1939 • Jenkins C. • UKN
PAPER PIGEON see **YORU NO TOGYO** • 1959
PAPER PLANES see **NA PAPIRNATIH AVIONIH** • 1967
PAPER STAR see **PAPERITAHIT** • 1989
PAPER TEARING • 1908 • Booth W. R. • UKN
PAPER TIGER • 1953 • Eason B. Reeves • USA
PAPER TIGER • 1975 • Annakin Ken • UKN
PAPER TIGERS see **TIGRES DE PAPEL** • 1978
PAPER WEDDING, A see **NOCES DE PAPIER, LES** • 1990
PAPER WHEAT • 1979 • Kish Albert • DOC • CND
PAPERBACK HERO • 1972 • Pearson Peter • CND • LAST OF THE BIG GUNS ○ COQ DU VILLAGE, LE
PAPERCITY • 1969 • Bennett John • UKN
PAPERED DOOR, THE • 1915 • Windom Lawrence C. • USA
PAPERHANGER, THE see **WORK** • 1915
PAPERHANGER'S HELPER, THE • 1915 • *Ray Bobby* • SHT • USA
PAPERHANGER'S REVENGE, THE • 1917 • Curtis Allen • *Victor* • SHT • USA
PAPERHOUSE • 1989 • Rose Bernard • UKN
PAPERING THE DEN • 1912 • Henderson Dell • USA
PAPERITAHIT • 1989 • Kaurismaki Mika • FNL • PAPER STAR
PAPERLAND: THE BUREAUCRAT OBSERVED • 1979 • Brittain Don • DOC • CND

PAPESATAN see **SCUSI EMINENZA.. POSSO SPOSARMI?** • 1976
PAPESSE, LA • 1974 • Mercier Mario • FRN
PAPIER PROTEE, LE • 1896 • Melies Georges • FRN • MYSTERIOUS PAPER, THE (USA)
PAPIERENE PETER, DER • 1917 • Gliese Rochus • FRG
PAPIERNE BRUCKE, DIE • 1987 • Beckermann Ruth • AUS • PAPER BRIDGE, THE
PAPIEROWY PTAK • 1971 • Idziak Slawomir • PLN • PAPER BIRD
PAPILIO • 1987 • Svoboda Jiri • CZC
PAPILLON • 1914 • Pouctal Henri • FRN • PAILLON DIT LYONNAIS LE JUSTE
PAPILLON • 1973 • Schaffner Franklin J. • USA
PAPILLON DIT LYONNAIS LE JUSTE see **BACH MILLIONNAIRE** • 1933
PAPILLON FANTASTIQUE, LE • 1910 • Melies Georges • FRN • FANTASTIC BUTTERFLIES, THE
PAPILLON SUR L'EPAULE, UN • 1978 • Deray Jacques • FRN • BUTTERFLY ON THE SHOULDER
PAPILLOTE • 1969 • Hayeem Benjamin • SHT • USA
PAPINTHA • 1910 • *Selig* • USA
PAPION, EL • 1971 • Carretero Amaro • ANS • SPN
PAPIR • 1943 • Henning-Jensen Bjarne • DNM • PAPER
PAPIRFUGLEN • 1984 • Breien Anja • NRW • PAPER FLOWER, THE ○ PAPER BIRD, THE
PAPIROSNITSA OT MOSSELPROMA • 1924 • Jeliabujski Yuri • USS • CIGARETTE-GIRL FROM MOSSELPROM, THE
PAPIROVE NOKTURNO • 1949 • Hofman Eduard • ANS • PLN • PAPER NOCTURNE
PAPITA'S DESTINY • 1913 • Grandon Francis J. • USA
PAP'OCCHIO, IL • 1980 • Arbore Renzo • ITL • POP JESUS SUPERSTAR ○ IN THE POPE'S EYE
PAPOOSE ON THE LOOSE • 1961 • Smith Paul J. • ANS • USA
PAPOUL • 1929 • Allegret Marc • SHT • FRN
PAPPA BOM • 1950 • Kjellgren Lars-Eric • SWD
PAPPA E CICCIA • 1983 • Parenti Neri • ITL
PAPPA LAP • 1972 • Rautenbach Jans • SAF
PAPPA REALE, LA (ITL) see **BONNE SOUPE, LA** • 1964
PAPPA SOKES • 1947 • Mattsson Arne • SWD • FATHER WANTED, A
PAPPA, VARFOR AR DU ARG -DU GJORDE LIKADANT SJALV NAR DU VAR UNG • 1968 • Stivell Arne • SWD • DADDY, WHY ARE YOU ANGRY -YOU DID IT YOURSELF IN YOUR YOUTH
PAPPAGALLI, I • 1956 • Paolinelli Bruno • ITL
PAPPAGALLO DELLA ZIA BERTA, IL • 1912 • Negroni Baldassare • ITL
PAPPAS POJKE • 1937 • Martin Knut • SWD • RICH MAN'S SON, A
PAPPI • 1934 • Rabenalt Arthur M. • FRG
PAPPY'S PUPPY • 1955 • Freleng Friz • ANS • USA
PAPRIKA • 1932 • Boese Carl • FRG
PAPRIKA • 1933 • de Limur Jean • FRN
PAPRIKA • 1934 • Emo E. W. • ITL
PAPRIKA • 1957 • Wilhelm Kurt • FRG
PAPUA AND HER PEOPLE • 1923 • ASL
PAPUA NEW GUINEA INDEPENDENCE CELEBRATIONS • 1975 • Patterson Garry • DOC • ASL
PAPUGA Z CASABLANKI • 1964 • Laskowski Jan • ANS • PLN • PARROT FROM CASABLANCA, THE
PAPY FAIT DE LA RESISTANCE • 1982 • Poire Jean-Marie • FRN
PAQUEBOT LIBERTE, LE • 1950 • Mitry Jean • SHT • FRN
PAQUEBOT TENACITY, LE • 1934 • Duvivier Julien • FRN
PAQUERAS, OS • 1969 • Farias Reginaldo • BRZ • PEEPING TOM, THE
PAQUES ROUGES • 1914 • Feuillade Louis • FRN
PAQUET EMBARRASSANT, UN • 1907 • Feuillade Louis • FRN
PAQUETE, EL FOTOGRAFO PUBLICO NUMERO UNO • 1938 • Iquino Ignacio F. • SPN
PAQUETES DE PAQUITA, LOS • 1954 • Rodriguez Ismael • MXC
PAR A TODO DAR, UN • 1960 • Salvador Jaime • MXC
PAR AVION • 1957 • Breer Robert • SHT • USA
PAR DE ASESINOS, UN • 1970 • Romero-Marchent Rafael • SPN
PAR DE ROBA CHICOS, UN • 1966 • Cardona Rene Jr. • MXC
PAR DE SINVERGUENZAS, UN see **CABALLO QUE CANTA, EL** • 1963
PAR DE ZAPATOS DEL 32, UN • 1973 • Romero-Marchent Rafael • SPN
PAR-DESSUS LE MUR • 1925 • Colombier Piere • FRN
PAR-DESSUS LE MUR • 1961 • Le Chanois Jean-Paul • FRN
PAR DEVANT PAR DERRIERE • Xavier Robert • FRN
PAR DIX-HUIT METRES DE FOND • 1943 • Cousteau Jacques • FRN
PAR HABITUDE • 1923 • Diamant-Berger Henri • FRN
PAR ICI LA MONNAIE • 1973 • Balducci Richard • FRN
PAR JALOUSIE • 1916 • Burguet Charles • FRN
PAR LA FENETRE • 1947 • Grangier Gilles • FRN • JE REVIENDRAI PAR LA FENETRE
PAR L'AMOUR • 1913 • Perret Leonce • FRN
PAR LE FER ET PAR LE FEU (FRN) see **COL FERRO E COL FUOCO** • 1962
PAR LE SANG DES AUTRES • 1973 • Simenon Marc • CND, FRN, ITL • BY THE BLOOD OF OTHERS
PAR LE TROU DE LA SERRURE • 1903 • Zecca Ferdinand • FRN
PAR LEPES A HATAR • 1959 • Keleti Marton • HNG • FEW STEPS TO THE FRONTIER, A
PAR ORDRE DU TZAR • 1953 • Haguet Andre • FRN, FRG
PAR OU T'ES RENTRE.. ON T'A PAS VU SORTIE • 1984 • Clair Philippe • FRN
PAR UN BEAU MATIN D'ETE • 1964 • Deray Jacques • FRN, ITL, SPN • RAPINA AL SOLE (ITL)
PAR UNE BELLE NUIT D'HIVER • 1974 • Beaudin Jean • SHT • CND
PARA-COMMANDO • 1971 • Sauve Alain (c/d) • CND
PARA LA HORCA, UNO • 1972 • *Rosas Priego* • MXC
PARA ONDE VAIS, MARIA? • 1953 • Vitorino Orlando • SHT • PRT
PARA, PEDRO! • 1970 • Dias Pereira • BRZ
PARA QUE EL SOL NO SE APAGUE • 1979 • Pantano Jorge • ARG • LET NOT THE SUN BE PUT OUT
PARA QUE LA CUNA APRIETE • 1950 • Portas Rafael E. • MXC
PARA QUE LA SANGRE? • 1980 • Susz Pedro • BLV • SO WHAT WITH BLOOD?
PARA SIEMPRE AMOR MIO • 1954 • Davison Tito • MXC
PARA TI ES EL MUNDO • 1941 • Buchs Jose • SPN
PARA TODA LA VIDA • 1922 • Perojo Benito • SPN
PARA TODAS HAY • 1964 • Crevenna Alfredo B. • MXC
PARA UM ALBUM DE LISBOA • 1966 • de Almeida Manuel Faria • SHT • PRT
PARA USTED JEFA • 1979 • Murray Guillermo • MXC
PARA VESTIR SANTOS • 1955 • Torre-Nilsson Leopoldo • ARG • TO CLOTHE THE SAINTS ○ SPINSTERS, THE
PARABENS, SENHOR VICENTE • 1954 • Duarte Arthur • PRT, SPN • NUBES DE VERANO
PARABLE, THE • 1978 • Kennedy Michael • CND
PARABLE OF THE LEAVEN • 1990 • Henley Gail • SHT • CND
PARABOLA • 1938 • Bute Mary Ellen, Boyd Rutherford, Nemeth Ted J. • SHT • USA
PARABOLA DEI MARITI, LA see **MARITI -TEMPESTA D'AMORE, I** • 1941
PARABOLO D'ORO • 1956 • De Seta Vittorio • ITL
PARACELSUS • 1943 • Pabst G. W. • FRG
PARACHUTE BATTALION • 1941 • Goodwins Leslie • USA
PARACHUTE JUMPER • 1933 • Green Alfred E. • USA
PARACHUTE MAKER, THE • 1912 • *Panzer Paul* • USA
PARACHUTE NURSE • 1942 • Barton Charles T. • USA
PARACHUTE TO PARADISE • 1968 • Gittler Allan • USA
PARAD ALLE • 1969 • Gutman Ilya • DOC • USS
PARAD PLANYET • 1986 • Abdrakhitov Vadim • USS • PARADE OF THE PLANETS
PARADA • 1962 • Makavejev Dusan • YGS • PARADE, THE
PARADA • 1967 • Wionczek Roman • DOC • PLN • PARADE, THE
PARADA 88 -O LIMITE DE ALERTA • 1980 • de Anchieta Jose, Santos Roberto • BRZ • STOP 88 -THE WARNING LIMIT
PARADA PARAMOUNT • 1930 • de Rochefort Charles • USA
PARADA PECUARIA DE BRAGA • 1940 • Coelho Jose Adolfo • SHT • PRT
PARADA REZERWISTOW • 1934 • Waszynski Michael • PLN
PARADE • 1952 • Eames Charles, Eames Ray • SHT • USA • HERE THEY COME DOWN THE STREET
PARADE • 1960 • Topouzanov Christo • ANM • BUL
PARADE • 1971 • Gemes Jozsef • ANS • HNG
PARADE • 1974 • Tati Jacques • FRN, SWD
PARADE, THE • 1984 • Hunt Peter H. • TVM • USA
PARADE, THE see **PARADA** • 1962
PARADE, THE see **PARADA** • 1967
PARADE D'AMOUR see **LOVE PARADE, THE** • 1929
PARADE DE CHAPEAUX • 1936 • Alexeieff Alexandre • SHT • FRN • HAT PARADE
PARADE DE RIRE • 1946 • Verdier Roger • FRN
PARADE DES GATEAUX, LA • 1948 • Lavoie Hermenegilde • DCS • CND
PARADE DU TEMPS PERDU see **CASSE-PIEDS, LES** • 1948
PARADE EN SEPT NUITS • 1940 • Allegret Marc • FRN
PARADE IN RED SQUARE MOSCOW • 1933 • Karmen Roman • DOC • USS
PARADE OF DISGRACE • 1966 • Kovachev Hristo • DOC • BUL
PARADE OF THE BANDS • 1956 • Carreras Michael • UKN
PARADE OF THE PLANETS see **PARAD PLANYET** • 1986
PARADE OF THE WEST • 1930 • Brown Harry J. • USA • MEDICINE SHOW, THE
PARADE OF THE WOODEN SOLDIERS • 1933 • Fleischer Dave • ANS • USA
PARADE PARAMOUNTU • 1930 • USA
PARADE SUR UN AIR DE CHARLESTON see **SUR UN AIR DE CHARLESTON** • 1926
PARADES • 1972 • Siegel Robert • USA • BREAK LOOSE
PARADES • 1976 • Purdum Richard • UKN • EMBASSY AMERICAN PARADES
PARADIES • 1987 • Dorrie Doris • FRG • PARADISE
PARADIES AUF ERDEN • 1950 • Schonger Hubert • FRG
PARADIES DER DIRNEN, DAS • 1919 • Zelnik Friedrich • FRG
PARADIES DER FLOTTEN SUNDER, DAS • 1968 • Olsen Rolf, Rieger August, von Cziffra Geza • FRG • PARADISE OF SMART SINNERS
PARADIES DER JUNGGESELLEN • 1939 • Hoffmann Kurt • FRG • BACHELOR'S PARADISE (USA)
PARADIES DER MATROSEN • 1959 • Reinl Harald • FRG
PARADIES DER PFERDE, DAS • 1938 • FRG
PARADIES IM SCHNEE, DAS • 1923 • Jacoby Georg • FRG
PARADIES UND FEUEROFEN • 1959 • Viktor Herbert • FRG • PARADISE AND FIERY FURNACE
PARADIESAPFEL, DER • 1922 • Mehlig Willy • FRG
PARADIESGARTEN • 1970 • Schwamm Bernd • FRG
PARADIGME • 1985 • Zanussi Krzysztof • PLN • POUVOIR DU MAL, LE
PARADINE CASE, THE • 1948 • Hitchcock Alfred • USA
PARADING PAJAMAS • 1931 • Fox Wallace • USA
PARADIS • 1980 • Strong Mike • FRN
PARADIS DE SATAN, LE • 1938 • Gandera Felix, Delannoy Jean • FRN
PARADIS DES PILOTES PERDUS, LE • 1948 • Lampin Georges • FRN • HELL OF LOST PILOTS, THE (USA)
PARADIS DES RICHES, LE • 1978 • Barge Paul • FRN
PARADIS DES VOLEURS, LE • 1939 • Marsoudet L. C. • FRN • AVEC LES CHEVAUX DE BOIS ○ ESCAPADE
PARADIS PERDU • 1939 • Gance Abel • FRN • FOUR FLIGHTS TO LOVE (USA) ○ PARADISE LOST (UKN)
PARADIS PERDU, LE see **VERLOREN PARADIJS, HET** • 1978
PARADIS POUR TOUS • 1982 • Jessua Alain • FRN
PARADISE • 1926 • Willat Irvin V. • USA
PARADISE • 1928 • Clift Denison • UKN
PARADISE • Wong James • HKG
PARADISE • 1976 • Hughes Bill • MTV • ASL
PARADISE • 1982 • Gillard Stuart • USA, ISR
PARADISE • 1984 • Patel Ishu • ANS • CND
PARADISE see **CAPTAIN'S PARADISE, THE** • 1953
PARADISE see **PARADISET** • 1955
PARADISE see **PARADISUL** • 1967
PARADISE see **PARADIES** • 1987
PARADISE AHOY see **DAMES AHOY!** • 1930
PARADISE ALLEY • 1920 • *Aubrey Jimmy* • USA
PARADISE ALLEY • 1931 • Argyle John F. • UKN
PARADISE ALLEY • 1961 • Haas Hugo • USA • STARS IN THE BACK YARD
PARADISE ALLEY • 1978 • Stallone Sylvester • USA
PARADISE AMERICA see **AMERIIKAN RAITTI** • 1989
PARADISE AND FIERY FURNACE see **PARADIES UND FEUEROFEN** • 1959
PARADISE AND PURGATORY (USA) see **PARADISO E IL PURGATORIO, IL** • 1911
"PARADISE" BOARDING HOUSE see **PENSIONAT PARADISET** • 1937
PARADISE BRIDE'S SCHOOL, THE see **GOKURAKU HANAYOMEJUKU** • 1936
PARADISE BUNGALOWS see **VIRGIN QUEEN OF ST. FRANCIS HIGH, THE** • 1987
PARADISE CANYON • 1935 • Pierson Carl • USA
PARADISE CONNECTION, THE • 1979 • Preece Michael • TVM • USA
PARADISE EXPRESS • 1937 • Kane Joseph • USA
PARADISE FOR A DAY • 1916 • *Selig* • SHT • USA
PARADISE FOR BUSTER • 1952 • *Keaton Buster* • USA
PARADISE FOR THREE • 1938 • Buzzell Edward • USA • ROMANCE FOR THREE (UKN) ○ THREE MEN IN THE SNOW
PARADISE FOR TWO • 1927 • La Cava Gregory • USA
PARADISE FOR TWO • 1937 • Freeland Thornton • UKN • GAIETY GIRLS, THE (USA)
PARADISE GARDEN • 1917 • Balshofer Fred J. • USA
PARADISE GES.M.B.H. • 1986 • Leytner Nikolaus • AUS • PARADISE LTD.
PARADISE, HAWAIIAN STYLE • 1966 • Moore Michael • USA
PARADISE IN HARLEM • 1939 • Seiden Joseph • USA • OTHELLO IN HARLEM
PARADISE INN • 1985 • Castillo Celso Ad. • PHL
PARADISE IS NOT FOR SALE see **PARADISET ER IKKE TIL SALG** • 1986
PARADISE ISLAND • 1930 • Glennon Bert • USA
PARADISE ISLAND • 1970 • *Stacey Dist.* • USA
PARADISE ISLE • 1937 • Collins Arthur G. • ASL
PARADISE LAGOON (USA) see **ADMIRABLE CRICHTON, THE** • 1957
PARADISE LOST • 1911 • Griffith D. W. • USA
PARADISE LOST • 1951 • Gregory John R. • SHT • USA
PARADISE LOST • 1970 • Lambart Evelyn • ANS • CND
PARADISE LOST see **ELVESZETT PARADICSOM, AZ** • 1962
PARADISE LOST, A see **BRISTET LYKKE** • 1913
PARADISE LOST (UKN) see **PARADIS PERDU** • 1939
PARADISE LTD. see **PARADISE GES.M.B.H.** • 1986
PARADISE MOTEL • 1985 • Medoway Cary • USA • NEW KID IN TOWN
PARADISE NOT YET LOST, OR OONA'S FIFTH YEAR • 1980 • Mekas Jonas • USA
PARADISE NOW • Safran Fred • SHT • USA
PARADISE NOW • 1970 • Rochlin Sheldon • USA
PARADISE OF NINETEEN BRIDES see **GOKURAKU HANAYOMEJUKU** • 1936
PARADISE OF PAPUA, THE see **WITH THE HEADHUNTERS IN PAPUA** • 1923
PARADISE OF SMART SINNERS see **PARADIES DER FLOTTEN SUNDER, DAS** • 1968
PARADISE ON EARTH see **RAJ NA ZIEMI** • 1970
PARADISE PLACE see **PARADISTORG** • 1977
PARADISE POSTPONED • 1986 • Rakoff Alvin • MTV • UKN
PARADISE ROAD • 1965 • Hittelman Carl K. • USA
PARADISE ROAD • 1989 • Scholtz Jan • SAF
PARADISE ROAD see **ULICKA V RAJI** • 1936
PARADISE SQUARE see **PARADISTORG** • 1977
PARADISE TRANSPORT • 1973 • Phelps Richard • NZL
PARADISE (USA) see **PARADISO, IL** • 1912
PARADISE VALLEY (UKN) see **PUEBLO TERROR** • 1931
PARADISET • 1955 • Ragneborn Arne • SWD • PARADISE
PARADISET ER IKKE TIL SALG • 1986 • Ritzau Teit • DOC • DNM • PARADISE IS NOT FOR SALE
PARADISFAGELN • 1916 • Tallroth Konrad • SWD • BIRD OF PARADISE
PARADISIA • 1987 • Page Marcy • ANS • USA
PARADISIO • 1962 • *Howard Arthur* • UKN
PARADISO • 1933 • Brignone Guido • ITL
PARADISO • 1977 • Bricout Christian • FRN
PARADISO, IL • 1912 • *Psiche* • ITL • PARADISE (USA) ○ HEAVEN, THE
PARADISO, IL • 1924 • Palermi Amleto • ITL
PARADISO DELL'UOMO, IL • 1962 • Tomei Giuliano, Hani Susumu • DOC • ITL • GIAPPONE PROIBITO
PARADISO E IL PURGATORIO, IL • 1911 • *Helios* • ITL • PARADISE AND PURGATORY (USA)
PARADISO, HOTEL DU LIBRE-EXCHANGE (FRN) see **HOTEL PARADAISO** • 1966
PARADISO PERDUTO, IL • 1948 • Emmer Luciano, Gras Enrico • ITL • BOSCH
PARADISO RABADO • 1952 • Amadori Luis Cesar • ARG
PARADISO TERRESTRE, IL • 1940 • Emmer Luciano, Gras Enrico • SHT • ITL • EARTHLY PARADISE (USA)
PARADISTORG • 1977 • Lindblom Gunnel • SWD • SUMMER PARADISE (USA) ○ PARADISE SQUARE ○ PARADISE PLACE
PARADISUL • 1967 • Pita Dan • SHT • RMN • PARADISE
PARADOX see **DOOMOORER PHOOL** • 1978
PARADOXICAL BURGLAR, THE • 1915 • *Alhambra* • USA
PARAFERNALIA, O DIA DA CACA • 1970 • Palmeira Francis • BRZ
PARAGINE, LE (ITL) see **PARISIENNES, LES** • 1962
PARAGRAPH 97, WEGEN GRAUSAMKEIT GESCHIEDEN • 1921 • *Stockel Joe* • FRG
PARAGRAPH 144 • 1924 • Jacoby Georg, Lowenstein Hans Otto • AUS • MUSS DIE FRAU MUTTER WERDEN?
PARAGRAPH 175 see **ANDERS ALS DIE ANDERN** • 1919
PARAGUELIA • 1980 • Tassios Pavlos • GRC
PARAHYBA MACHO WOMAN see **PARAHYBA MULHER MACHO** • 1983

PARAHYBA MULHER MACHO • 1983 • Yamasaki Tizuka • BRZ • PARAHYBA MACHO WOMAN
PARAISO • 1952 • Luxemburgo Miguel G. • SPN
PARAISO • 1969 • Alcoriza Luis • MXC
PARAISO AMAZONICO, EL • 1970 • Oropeza Daniel • DOC • VNZ • AMAZON PARADISE, THE
PARAISO ESCONDIDO • 1958 • Sevilla Raphael J., de la Serna Mauricio • MXC
PARAISO ORTOPEDICO • 1969 • Guzman Patricio • SPN • ORTHOPEDIC PARADISE
PARAISO ROBADO • 1960 • Bracho Julio • MXC
PARAISOS PERDIDOS, LOS • 1985 • Patino Basilio Martin • SPN • LOST PARADISES, THE
PARAJAY • 1940 • *Sircar B. N. (P)* • IND
PARAJITO GOMEZ –UNA VIDA FELIZ • 1965 • Kuhn Rodolfo • ARG
PARAKH • 1960 • Roy Bimal • IND
PARALELO EN SIETE • Mitrotti Mario • VNZ
PARALLAX VIEW, THE • 1974 • Pakula Alan J. • USA
PARALLEL see **PARALLELE** • 1924
PARALLEL CORPSE, THE see **PARALLELE LIG, DET** • 1982
PARALLEL FACES see **LANYARCOK TUKORBEN** • 1973
PARALLEL ROUTES see **VIAS PARALELAS** • 1978
PARALLELE • 1924 • Eggeling Viking • ANS • FRG • PARALLEL
PARALLELE LIG, DET • 1982 • Melson Soren, Philip Hans-Erik • DNM • PARALLEL CORPSE, THE
PARALLELES • 1962 • Daquin Louis • SHT • FRN
PARALLELES ET GRAND SOLEIL • 1964 • Dansereau Jean • DOC • CND
PARALLELS • Chigort Liviu • ANS • RMN
PARALLELS • 1980 • Schoenberg Mark • TVM • CND
PARALLELSTRASSE, DIE • 1961 • Khittl Ferdinand • FRG
PARALYSIS • 1972 • Siegel Lois, Jurgens Ray • ANS • CND
PARALYTIC, THE • 1912 • Blache Alice • USA
PARAMATTA see **ZU NEUEN UFERN** • 1937
PARAMEDICS • 1988 • Margolin Stuart • USA
PARAMOUNT EN PARADE • 1930 • de Rochefort Charles • USA
PARAMOUNT ON PARADE • 1930 • Arzner Dorothy, Brower Otto, Goulding Edmund, Heerman Victor, Knopf Edwin H., Lee Rowland V., Lubitsch Ernst, Mendes Lothar, Schertzinger Victor, Sutherland A. Edward, Tuttle Frank • USA
PARAMOUNT OP PARADE • 1930 • USA
PARAMOUNT-REVUE • 1930 • de Rochefort Charles • USA
PARAMOUNT REVUI • 1930 • de Rochefort Charles • USA
PARAMOUNTS STJERNEPARADE • 1930 • USA
PARANINFO, IL • 1934 • Palermi Amleto • ITL • MATCHMAKER, THE (USA)
PARANMA, TO • 1989 • Iliopoulou Vassiliki • GRC • PASSAGE, THE ○ CROSSING, THE
PARANO • 1962 • Dubois Bernard • FRN
PARANOIA • 1967 • Ditvoorst Adriaan • NTH
PARANOIA • 1969 • Lenzi Umberto • ITL, SPN • QUIET PLACE TO KILL, A (UKN)
PARANOIA (UKN) see **ORGASMO** • 1968
PARANOIA (USA) see **OGGI DOMANI DOPODOMANI** • 1965
PARANOIAC • 1963 • Francis Freddie • UKN
PARANOICO, IL • 1975 • Ariza Francisco • SPN
PARANOID MAN, THE see **NEVER SAY DIE** • 1988
PARANOMI, I • 1958 • Koundouros Nikos • GRC • LAWLESS, THE ○ OUTLAWS, THE ○ HUNTED, THE
PARAPLICKO • 1956 • Pojar Bretislav • ANS • CZC • LITTLE UMBRELLA, THE ○ BROLLY, THE
PARAPLUIE FANTASTIQUE, LE • 1903 • Melies Georges • FRN • TEN LADIES IN ONE UMBRELLA (USA) ○ GIRLS IN ONE UMBRELLA, THE
PARAPLUIES DE CHERBOURG, LES • 1964 • Demy Jacques • FRN, FRG • REGENSCHIRME VON CHERBOURG, DIE (FRG) ○ UMBRELLAS OF CHERBOURG, THE (USA)
PARAPSYCHICS • 1974 • Mastorakis Nico • GRC • DEATH HAS BLUE EYES ○ BLUE EYES OF DEATH
PARAPSYCHO -SPEKTRUM DER ANGST • 1975 • Patzak Peter • AUS
PARAQUEDISTAS • 1964 • Simoes Quirino • SHT • PRT
PARAS-PATHAR (USA) see **PARASH PATHAR** • 1957
PARASH PATHAR • 1957 • Ray Satyajit • IND • PHILOSOPHER'S STONE, THE ○ PARAS-PATHAR (USA)
PARASHURAM • 1978 • Sen Mrinal • IND • MAN WITH THE AXE, THE ○ PARASURAM
PARASITE • 1982 • Band Charles • USA
PARASITE, THE • 1912 • *Marsh Mae* • USA
PARASITE, THE • 1913 • *Johnson Arthur* • USA
PARASITE, THE • 1916 • Horne James W. • SHT • USA
PARASITE, THE • 1925 • Gasnier Louis J. • USA
PARASITE, THE see **PARAZIT** • 1960
PARASITE MURDERS, THE • 1975 • Cronenberg David • CND • SHIVERS (UKN) ○ THEY CAME FROM WITHIN ○ FRISSONS
PARASITE OF THE NIGHT, A see **YORU NO KISEICHU** • 1968
PARASITES, THE • 1914 • *Penn M. O.* • USA
PARASITES, THE see **M'SIEUR LA CAILLE** • 1955
PARASITE'S DOUBLE, THE • 1915 • *Lariat* • USA
PARASITES OF LIFE • 1918 • Protazanov Yakov • USS
PARASITES (UKN) see **DRAG** • 1929
PARASOL, THE see **OMBRELLONE, L'** • 1966
PARASOL, EL (SPN) see **OMBRELLONE, L'** • 1966
PARASTASI SE PROTO PROSOPO • 1979 • Grigoratos Dionisis • DOC • GRC • ONE-ROLE PERFORMANCE, A
PARASURAM see **PARASHURAM** • 1978
PARATI • 1968 • Cavalleiro Eliseo Visconti • BRZ
PARATROOP COMMAND • 1959 • Witney William • USA
PARATROOPER • 1988 • Acin Jovan • YGS
PARATROOPER (USA) see **RED BERET, THE** • 1953
PARATROOPERS see **MASSA HA'ALUNKOT** • 1977
PARAVENT MYSTERIEUX, LE • 1903 • Velle Gaston • FRN • MYSTERIOUS FOLDING SCREEN, THE
PARAZIT • 1960 • Lehky Vladimir • ANS • CZC • PARASITE, THE
PARBAJ • 1959 • Macskassy Gyula, Varnai Gyorgy • ANS • HNG • DUEL
PARBESZED • 1963 • Hersko Janos • HNG • DIALOGUE
PARC, LE • 1966 • Yalkut Jud • SHT • USA
PARC INDUSTRIEL, BECANCOUR, LE • 1982 • Beaudry Michel • MTV • CND
PARCEL POST AUTO, A • 1914 • *Mace Fred* • USA
PARCEL POST HUSBAND, A • 1920 • Reisner Charles F. • SHT • USA
PARCEL POST JOHNNIE • 1913 • *Kalem* • USA
PARCEL POST PETE'S NIGHTMARE • 1916 • Moser Frank • ANS • USA
PARCELA, LA • 1921 • Vollrath Ernesto • MXC
PARCELS OR THE BABY • 1913 • Kellino W. P. • UKN
PARCHED LAND, THE • 1978 • Moore Keiron • DOC • UKN
PARCHEGGIO ROSSO • 1972 • Lorenzini Ennio • MTV • ITL
PARCHIS AGAINST THE INVINCIBLE INVENTOR, THE see **PARCHIS VERSUS EL INVENTOR INVENCIBLE, LOS** • 1981
PARCHIS VERSUS EL INVENTOR INVENCIBLE, LOS • 1981 • Sabato Mario • ARG • PARCHIS AGAINST THE INVINCIBLE INVENTOR, THE
PARCOURS, LE see **MICHWAR** • 1973
PARCS ATLANTIQUES • 1967 • Arcand Denys • DCS • CND
PARDA FLORA, LA • 1952 • Klimovsky Leon • SPN
PARDALU KTERY VONEL, O • 1972 • Pojar Bretislav • ANM • CZC • PANTHER WHO FELT, THE
PARDE KE PEECHEY • 1971 • *Em. Ce. R. Films* • IND
PARDESI • 1957 • Abbas Khwaya Ahmad, Pronin Vassily • IND, USS • KHAZDENI ZA TRI MORYA (USS) ○ JOURNEY BEYOND THREE SEAS ○ TRAVELLER, THE ○ KHOZHDENIYE ZA TRI MORYA
PARDESSUS DE DEMI-SAISON, LE • 1917 • Feyder Jacques • FRN
PARDNERS • 1910 • Porter Edwin S. • USA
PARDNERS • 1917 • *Walker Charlotte* • USA
PARDNERS • 1956 • Taurog Norman • USA
PARDNERS see **LONE COWBOY, THE** • 1933
PARDON, THE • 1915 • McKenzie Donald • USA
PARDON ME • 1911 • *Lubin* • USA
PARDON ME • 1922 • Roach Hal • SHT • USA
PARDON ME • 1954 • *Eton Films* • SHT • UKN
PARDON ME FOR BEING A BIT DENSE • 1977 • Thomas Glenna, Stewart Linda • ISR
PARDON ME, YOUR TEETH ARE IN MY NECK see **DANCE OF THE VAMPIRES** • 1967
PARDON MON AFFAIRE, TOO (UKN) see **NOUS IRONS TOUS AU PARADIS** • 1977
PARDON MON AFFAIRE (USA) see **ELEPHANT CA TROMPE ENORMEMENT, UN** • 1977
PARDON MY BACKFIRE • 1953 • White Jules • SHT • USA
PARDON MY BERTH MARKS • 1940 • *Keaton Buster* • SHT • USA
PARDON MY BLOOPER • 1975 • *Dale John* • USA
PARDON MY BRUSH • 1964 • McCarthy John K. • USA
PARDON MY CLUTCH • 1948 • Bernds Edward • SHT • USA
PARDON MY FRENCH • 1921 • Olcott Sidney • USA
PARDON MY FRENCH • 1951 • Vorhaus Bernard • USA, FRN • LADY FROM BOSTON, THE (UKN)
PARDON MY GLOVE • 1922 • Christie Al • USA
PARDON MY GUN • 1930 • De Lacy Robert • USA
PARDON MY GUN • 1943 • Berke William • USA
PARDON MY NERVE! • 1922 • Eason B. Reeves • USA
PARDON MY NIGHTSHIRT • 1956 • White Jules • SHT • USA
PARDON MY PAST • 1945 • Fenton Leslie • USA
PARDON MY PUPS • 1934 • Lamont Charles • SHT • USA
PARDON MY RHYTHM • 1944 • Feist Felix E. • USA
PARDON MY SARONG • 1942 • Kenton Erle C. • USA
PARDON MY SCOTCH • 1935 • Lord Del • SHT • USA
PARDON MY SKI see **HIT THE ICE** • 1943
PARDON MY STRIPES • 1942 • Auer John H. • USA
PARDON MY TRUNK see **BUONGIORNO ELEFANTE** • 1952
PARDON MY WRENCH • 1953 • Yates Hal • SHT • USA
PARDON OUR NERVE • 1939 • Humberstone H. Bruce • USA
PARDON TEVEDTEM (HNG) see **SKANDAL IN BUDAPEST** • 1933
PARDON US • 1931 • Parrott James • USA • JAILBIRDS (UKN)
PARDON US FOR LIVING see **UNDSKYLD VIER HER** • 1981
PARDONED • 1915 • Ricketts Thomas • USA
PARDONNEZ NOS OFFENCES • 1956 • Hossein Robert • FRN • FORGIVE US OUR TRESPASSES
PARDOSI • 1941 • Shantaram Rajaram • IND • NEIGHBOURS
PARE KOSME • 1967 • Thalassinos Errikos • GRC • EVERYTHING AT A LOW PRICE
PARE POUR ACCOSTER • 1950 • Loew Jacques • SHT • FRN
PARED, LA • 1962 • Martin Jorge • ANS • ARG • WALL, THE
PAREEKSHA • 1967 • Bhaskaran P. • IND • TEST
PAREH, HET LIED VAN DER RIJST • 1936 • Franken Mannus • NTH • PAREH, SONG OF THE RICE
PAREH, SONG OF THE RICE see **PAREH, HET LIED VAN DER RIJST** • 1936
PAREIL PAS PAREIL • 1978 • Peres Uziel • FRN, ISR • ALIKE, UNALIKE
PAREJA DISTINTA, UNA • 1973 • Forque Jose Maria • SPN
PARELTHON MIAS YINEKAS, TO • 1968 • Dalianidis Ioannis • GRC • WOMAN'S PAST, A
PAREMA, CREATURE FROM THE STAR-WORLD see **PAREMA, DAS WESEN AUS DER STERNEWELT** • 1922
PAREMA, DAS WESEN AUS DER STERNEWELT • 1922 • Ziffer-Teschenbruck Mano • AUS • PAREMA, CREATURE FROM THE STAR-WORLD
PAREN IZ NASHEGO GORODA • 1942 • Stolper Alexander, Ivanov B. • USS • LAD FROM OUR TOWN (USA) ○ FELLOW FROM OUR TOWN, A
PARENT STRAIN, THE • 1914 • *Lubin* • USA
PARENT TRAP, THE • 1961 • Swift David • USA • PETTICOATS AND BLUEJEANS
PARENT TRAP II • 1986 • Maxwell Ronald F. • USA
PARENTAGE • 1918 • Henley Hobart • USA
PARENTAGE • 1922 • Henley Hobart • USA
PARENTHESIS • 1969 • Kanellopoulos Takis • GRC
PARENTHOOD • 1989 • Howard Ron • USA
PARENTS • 1989 • Balaban Bob • USA
PARENTS see **RODZICE** • 1961
PARENTS, THE see **ELTERN, DIE** • 1973
PARENTS A L'ECOLE • 1954 • Blais Roger • DCS • CND
PARENTS ET ENFANTS • 1978 • Guerin Gerard • FRN
PARENT'S LOVE, A see **DARU DUKA** • 1967
PARENTS NE SONT PAS SIMPLES CETTE ANNEE!, LES • 1983 • Jullian Marcel • FRN
PARENTS ON PROBATION see **BOY TROUBLE** • 1938
PARENTS ON TRIAL • 1939 • Nelson Sam • USA
PARENTS TAKE HEART • 1953 • Windebank P. • UKN
PARENTS TERRIBLES, LES • 1948 • Cocteau Jean • FRN • STORM WITHIN, THE (USA)
PARENTS WANTED • 1931 • Guiol Fred • USA
PARES Y NONES • 1983 • Cuerda Jose Luis • SPN • ODDS AND EVENS
PAREXIYISSI • 1983 • Stavrakas Dimitris • GRC • MISUNDERSTANDING
PARFAIT AMOUR • 1984 • van der Velde Jean • NTH
PARFUM DE LA DAME EN NOIR, LE • 1914 • Chautard Emile • FRN
PARFUM DE LA DAME EN NOIR, LE • 1930 • L'Herbier Marcel • FRN • PERFUME OF THE LADY IN BLACK, THE
PARFUM DE LA DAME EN NOIR, LE • 1949 • Daquin Louis • FRN
PARFUM DER MRS. WORRINGTON, DAS • 1925 • Seitz Franz • FRG
PARFUMS, LES • 1924 • Gremillon Jean • SHT • FRN
PARFUMS REVILLON • 1969 • Reichenbach Francois • SHT • FRN
PARI E DISPARI • 1978 • Corbucci Sergio • ITL • ODDS AND EVENS
PARI ORIGINAL, UN • 1912 • Linder Max • FRN
PARIA, LE • 1968 • Carliez Claude • FRN, SPN • DIAMOND RUSH (UKN)
PARIAHS OF GLORY (USA) see **PARIAS DE LA GLOIRE** • 1963
PARIAS DE LA GLOIRE • 1963 • Decoin Henri • FRN, ITL, SPN • DISPERATI DELLA GLORIA, I (ITL) ○ PARIAS DE LA GLORIA (SPN) ○ PARIAHS OF GLORY (USA)
PARIAS DE LA GLORIA (SPN) see **PARIAS DE LA GLOIRE** • 1963
PARIENTE, EL • 1973 • ARG, FRN, FRG • RELATIVE, THE
PARIGI E SEMPRE PARIGI • 1951 • Emmer Luciano • ITL • PARIS IS ALWAYS PARIS ○ PARIS EST TOUJOURS PARIS
PARIGI MISTERIOSI • 1920 • Serena Gustavo • ITL
PARIGI O CARA • 1962 • Caprioli Vittorio • ITL • DEAR PARIS ○ BELOVED PARIS
PARIGINA, UNA (ITL) see **PARISIENNE, UNE** • 1957
PARIJATAK see **SRI KRISHNA SATYA BHAMA** • 1951
PARIJATHAM • 1950 • Gopalakrishnan K. S. • IND
PARINEETA • 1952 • Roy Bimal • IND
PARIS • Macovet S., Oger Jacques • FRN
PARIS • 1924 • Hervil Rene • FRN
PARIS • 1926 • Goulding Edmund • USA • SHADOWS OF PARIS
PARIS • 1929 • Badger Clarence • USA
PARIS • 1936 • Choux Jean • FRN
PARIS • 1951 • Bernard J.-C. • DCS • FRN
PARIS • 1972 • Bonniere Rene • DCS • CND
PARIS 1900 • 1948 • Vedres Nicole • FRN
PARIS A L'AUTOMNE • 1958 • *Resnais Alain (Ed)* • FRN
PARIS AFTER DARK • 1943 • Moguy Leonide • USA • NIGHT IS ENDING, THE (UKN)
PARIS ASLEEP see **PARIS QUI DORT** • 1924
PARIS AT MIDNIGHT • 1926 • Hopper E. Mason • USA
PARIS AU MOIS D'AOUT • 1966 • Granier-Deferre Pierre • FRN • PARIS IN THE MONTH OF AUGUST (USA) ○ PARIS IN AUGUST (UKN)
PARIS-BEGUIN • 1931 • Genina Augusto • FRN
PARIS BELONGS TO US (USA) see **PARIS NOUS APPARTIENT** • 1958
PARIS-BERLIN • 1935 • Gaudard Lucette • FRN
PARIS BIEN VALE UNA MOZA • 1972 • Lazaga Pedro • SPN
PARIS BIS CEYLON see **FLUG UM DEN ERDBALL, DER** • 1925
PARIS BLUES • 1961 • Ritt Martin • USA
PARIS-BOITE • 1954-55 • Devlin Bernard • DCS • CND
PARIS BOUND • 1929 • Griffith Edward H. • USA
PARIS BRULE-T-IL? • 1966 • Clement Rene • FRN • IS PARIS BURNING? (UKN)
PARIS BY NIGHT • 1989 • Hare David • UKN
PARIS CALLING • 1941 • Marin Edwin L. • USA
PARIS-CAMARGUE • 1935 • Forrester Jack • FRN • VIE EST SI BELLE, LA ○ VIE EST BELLE, LA
PARIS CANAILLE see **PARIS COQUIN** • 1955
PARIS CAPITALE DE LA DANSE • 1949 • Martin Marcel • SHT • FRN
PARIS-CHAMPAGNE • 1962 • Armand Pierre • FRN
PARIS CHANTE TOUJOURS • 1951 • Montazel Pierre • FRN
PARIS CINEMA • 1929 • Mitry Jean, Chenal Pierre • SHT • FRN
PARIS CLANDESTIN • 1957 • Kapps Walter • FRN
PARIS COMMUNE see **ZORI PARISCHA** • 1937
PARIS COQUIN • 1955 • Gaspard-Huit Pierre • FRN • MAID IN PARIS (USA) ○ PARIS CANAILLE ○ PARIS-COQUIN ○ OH, LA-LA CHERI!
PARIS-COQUIN see **PARIS COQUIN** • 1955
PARIS DE ZOLA, LE • 1940 • Tedesco Jean • SHT • FRN
PARIS-DEAUVILLE • 1933 • Delannoy Jean • FRN
PARIS DES MANNEQUINS, LE • 1962 • Reichenbach Francois • SHT • FRN
PARIS DES PHOTOGRAPHES, LE • 1962 • Reichenbach Francois • SHT • FRN
PARIS DES QUATRE SAISONS I-II • 1946-47 • Masson Jean • SHT • FRN
PARIS DES SCANDINAVES, LE • 1964 • Faure Jean-Jacques • SHT • FRN
PARIS D'HIER ET D'AUJOURD'HUI • 1956 • Gibaud Marcel • SHT • FRN
PARIS DOES NOT EXIST see **PARIS N'EXISTE PAS** • 1969
PARIS DOES STRANGE THINGS (USA) see **ELENA ET LES HOMMES** • 1956
PARIS EN CINQ JOURS • 1926 • Colombier Piere, Rimsky Nicolas • FRN
PARIS EN CINQUE HEURES • 1932 • Colombier Piere • FRN
PARIS EROTIKA see **24 HEURES D'UN AMERICAIN A PARIS** • 1964
PARIS EST TOUJOURS PARIS see **PARIGI E SEMPRE PARIGI** • 1951
PARIS-ESTAMBUL SIN REGRESO see **AGENTE 077, DALL'ORIENTE CON FURORE** • 1965

PARIS ET LE DESERT FRANCAIS • 1957 • Leenhardt Roger • DCS • FRN
PARIS EXPOSITION 1900 see **EXPOSITION DE PARIS, L'** • 1900
PARIS EXPRESS see **SOUVENIRS DE PARIS** • 1928
PARIS EXPRESS (USA) see **MAN WHO WATCHED THE TRAINS GO BY, THE** • 1952
PARIS–FERIE • 1957 • Bonnardot Jean-Claude • FRN
PARIS FOLLIES OF 1956 • 1955 • Goodwins Leslie • USA • FRESH FROM PARIS
PARIS FRILLS (USA) see **FALBALAS** • 1945
PARIS GIRLS • 1929 • Roussell Henry • FRN
PARIS GREEN • 1920 • Storm Jerome • USA
PARIS HAT • 1915 • *Alhambra* • USA
PARIS HOLIDAY • 1958 • Oswald Gerd • USA, FRN • A PARIS TOUS LES DEUX (FRN)
PARIS HONEYMOON • 1939 • Tuttle Frank • USA
PARIS HOTEL see **PARIS PALACE HOTEL** • 1956
PARIS IN AUGUST (UKN) see **PARIS AU MOIS D'AOUT** • 1966
PARIS IN SPRING • 1935 • Milestone Lewis • USA • PARIS LOVE SONG (UKN) ○ PARIS IN THE SPRING ○ TWO ON A TOWER
PARIS IN THE MONTH OF AUGUST (USA) see **PARIS AU MOIS D'AOUT** • 1966
PARIS IN THE RAW see **FEMME SPECTACLE, LA** • 1964
PARIS IN THE SPRING see **PARIS IN SPRING** • 1935
PARIS INCIDENT (USA) see **TROIS TELEGRAMMES** • 1950
PARIS INCONNU • 1969 • Chevalier Pierre • FRN
PARIS INTERLUDE • 1934 • Marin Edwin L. • USA • ALL GOOD AMERICANS
PARIS IS ALWAYS PARIS see **PARIGI E SEMPRE PARIGI** • 1951
PARIS IS OURS see **PARIS NOUS APPARTIENT** • 1958
PARIS IS SO LOVELY see **QUE LINDO ES PARIS** • 1989
PARIS JAMAIS VU • 1968 • Lamorisse Albert • FRN • PARIS REDISCOVERED (UKN)
PARIS JE T'AIME • 1962 • Perol Guy • FRN
PARIS, JE T'AIME see **IL EST CHARMANT** • 1931
PARIS LA BELLE • 1959 • Prevert Pierre • SHT • FRN
PARIS LA NUIT • 1904 • Blache Alice • FRN • EXPLOITS D'APACHES A MONTMARTRE
PARIS LA NUIT • 1930 • Diamant-Berger Henri • FRN
PARIS LA NUIT • 1937 • Clement Rene • DCS • FRN
PARIS LA NUIT • 1956 • Baratier Jacques, Valere Jean • FRN
PARIS LAS VEGAS • 1962 • Sala Vittorio • ITL
PARIS–LONDON–BERLIN see **UM EINE MILLION** • 1924
PARIS LOVE SONG (UKN) see **PARIS IN SPRING** • 1935
PARIS MANGE SON PAIN • 1958 • Prevert Pierre • SHT • FRN
PARIS–MEDITERRANEE • 1931 • May Joe • FRN • DEUX DANS UNE VOITURE ○ CHEMIN DU BONHEUR, LE
PARIS MELODIES • 1947-51 • Verneuil Henri • SHT • FRN
PARIS, MES AMOURS • 1935 • Blondeau Alphonse-Lucien • FRN
PARIS MODEL • 1953 • Green Alfred E. • USA
PARIS MUSIC–HALL • 1957 • Cordier Stany • FRN
PARIS–NEW YORK • 1940 • Mirande Yves • FRN
PARIS–NEW YORK–PARIS • 1928 • Peguy Robert • FRN
PARIS N'EXISTE PAS • 1969 • Benayoun Robert • FRN • PARIS DOES NOT EXIST
PARIS NIGHTS (USA) see **NUITS DE PARIS** • 1951
PARIS NOUS APPARTIENT • 1958 • Rivette Jacques • FRN • PARIS BELONGS TO US (USA) ○ PARIS IS OURS
PARIS OH LA LA • 1964 • Weihmayr Franz • DOC • FRG
PARIS ON PARADE • 1938 • Fitzpatrick James A. • DCS • UKN
PARIS OOH–LA–LA! (USA) see **24 HEURES D'UN AMERICAIN A PARIS** • 1964
PARIS PA TO MADER • 1949 • Roos Jorgen • DOC • DNM
PARIS PALACE HOTEL • 1956 • Verneuil Henri • FRN, ITL • PARIS HOTEL
PARIS PENDANT LA GUERRE • 1916 • Diamant-Berger Henri • FRN
PARIS PENDANT LA GUERRE • 1916 • Heuze Andre • FRN
PARIS PICK–UP (USA) see **MONTE–CHARGE, LE** • 1962
PARIS PLANE • 1933 • Carstairs John Paddy • UKN
PARIS PLAYBOYS • 1954 • Beaudine William • USA
PARIS PLAYGIRLS see **SVENSKA FLICKOR I PARIS** • 1960
PARIS PORNO • 1976 • Regis Jack • FRN
PARIS QUI DORT • 1924 • Clair Rene • FRN • CRAZY RAY, THE (USA) ○ RAYON INVISIBLE, LE ○ AT 3.25 ○ INVISIBLE RAY, THE ○ PARIS ASLEEP
PARIS REDISCOVERED (UKN) see **PARIS JAMAIS VU** • 1968
PARIS–SAINT–PETERSBOURG • 1912 • Fescourt Henri • FRN
PARIS SECRET • 1965 • Logereau Edouard • DOC • FRN • PARIS SECRETS ○ SECRET PARIS
PARIS SECRETS see **PARIS SECRET** • 1965
PARIS S'EN VA • 1981 • Rivette Jacques • FRN
PARIS–SOLEIL • 1932 • Hemard Jean • FRN
PARIS, TEXAS • 1984 • Wenders Wim • FRN, FRG
PARIS TOP SECRET • 1969 • Roustang Pierre • FRN, BLG
PARIS–TUNIS • 1963 • Boughedir Ferid • TNS
PARIS UNDERGROUND • 1945 • Ratoff Gregory • USA • MADAME PIMPERNEL (UKN)
PARIS UNDERGROUND see **TOUCHEZ PAS AU GRISBI** • 1953
PARIS UNDERWORLD see **APACHEN, DIE** • 1919
PARIS VU PAR.. 20 ANS APRES • 1984 • Akerman Chantal, Mitterand Frederic, Dubois Bernard, Nordon Vincent, Garrel Philippe, Venault Philippe, Douchet Jean, Rouch Jean, Pollet Jean-Daniel, Rohmer Eric, Godard Jean-Luc, Chabrol Claude • FRN • SIX IN PARIS
PARIS WALTZ, THE (USA) see **VALSE DE PARIS, LA** • 1949
PARIS–WARSAW WITHOUT A VISA see **PARYZ–WARSZAWA BEZ WIZY** • 1967
PARIS WAS MADE FOR LOVERS see **TIME FOR LOVING** • 1971
PARIS WHEN IT SIZZLES • 1964 • Quine Richard • USA • GIRL WHO STOLE THE EIFFEL TOWER, THE ○ TOGETHER IN PARIS
PARISER EHEN see **DR. MONNIER UND DIE FRAUEN** • 1928
PARISER UNTERWELT • 1930 • Heuberger Edmund • FRG
PARISERINNEN • 1921 • Lasko Leo • FRG
PARISERINNEN see **DR. MONNIER UND DIE FRAUEN** • 1928
PARISETTE • 1921 • Feuillade Louis • SRL • FRN
PARISH PRIEST, THE • 1921 • Franz Joseph J. • USA
PARISIAN, THE • 1930 • de Limur Jean • USA
PARISIAN BELLE see **NEW MOON** • 1930
PARISIAN COBBLER, THE see **PARIZHSKY SAPOZHNIK** • 1928
PARISIAN GAIETIES • 1931 • Roberts Stephen • SHT • USA
PARISIAN KNIGHT, A • 1925 • Marshall George • SHT • USA
PARISIAN LOVE • 1925 • Gasnier Louis J. • USA
PARISIAN NIGHTS • 1925 • Santell Alfred • USA
PARISIAN ROMANCE, A • 1916 • Thompson Frederick A. • USA
PARISIAN ROMANCE, A • 1932 • Franklin Chester M. • USA
PARISIAN SCANDAL, A • 1921 • Cox George L. • USA
PARISIAN TIGRESS, THE • 1919 • Blache Herbert • USA
PARISIEN MALGRE LUI (FRN) see **TOTO A PARIGI** • 1958
PARISIENNE, LA (USA) see **PARISIENNE, UNE** • 1957
PARISIENNE, UNE • 1957 • Boisrond Michel • FRN, ITL • PARIGINA, UNA (ITL) ○ PARISIENNE, LA (USA)
PARISIENNE AND THE PRUDES, THE • Gurney Robert Jr. • USA
PARISIENNE LIFE • 1935 • Siodmak Robert • UKN
PARISIENNES, LES • 1962 • Poitrenaud Jacques, Boisrond Michel, Allegret Marc, Barma Claude • FRN, ITL • PARAGINE, LE (ITL) ○ OF BEDS AND BROADS ○ TALES OF PARIS
PARISISKOR • 1928 • Molander Gustaf • SWD • WOMEN OF PARIS
PARISODH • 1968 • Sen Ardhendu • IND • REPAYMENT
PARITRAN • 1951 • *Sircar B. N. (P)* • IND
PARIVAR • 1956 • Sen Asit • IND
PARIVAR • 1968 • Kashyap Keval P. • IND • FAMILY
PARIVARTAN • NPL • CHANGES, THE
PARIVARTAN • 1949 • *Kapoor Raj* • IND
PARIZHSKY SAPOZHNIK • 1928 • Ermler Friedrich • USS • PARISIAN COBBLER, THE
PARK, THE • 1967 • Saunders Richard • UKN
PARK AVENUE DAME see **MURDER IN GREENWICH VILLAGE** • 1937
PARK AVENUE LOGGER • 1937 • Howard David • USA • MILLIONAIRE PLAYBOY (UKN) ○ TALL TIMBER
PARK AVENUE PUSSYCAT • 1956 • Rasinski Connie • ANS • USA
PARK HONEYMOONERS, THE • 1915 • Johnson Tefft • USA
PARK IS MINE, THE • 1985 • Stern Steven Hilliard • TVM • USA
PARK JOHNNIES • 1915 • *L-Ko* • USA
PARK LANE SCANDAL, A • 1915 • Buckland Warwick • UKN
PARK OF GAMES see **PARQUE DE JUEGOS** • 1963
PARK PLAZA 605 • 1953 • Knowles Bernard • UKN • NORMAN CONQUEST (USA)
PARK ROW • 1952 • Fuller Samuel • USA
PARK YOUR BABY • 1939 • *Mintz Charles (P)* • ANS • USA
PARK YOUR CAR • 1920 • Goulding Alf, Roach Hal • SHT • USA
PARKED IN THE PARK • 1920 • *Reynolds Vera* • USA
PARKER • 1985 • Goddard Jim • UKN • BONES
PARKER'S WEEKEND • 1916 • Kellino W. P. • UKN
PARKETTSESSEL 47 • 1926 • Ravel Gaston • FRG
PARKI–PARKA • 1951 • Tessier Albert • DCS • CND
PARKING • 1985 • Demy Jacques • FRN
PARKING SPACE • 1933 • Lantz Walter, Nolan William • SHT • USA
PARKSTONE COMEDIES • 1921 • Aylott Dave • SER • UKN
PARKSTRASSE 13 • 1939 • von Alten Jurgen • FRG • VERHOR UM MITTERNACHT
PARLAMI D'AMORE MARIA • 1977 • Festa Campanile Pasquale • ITL
PARLEMOR • 1961 • Anderberg Torgny • SWD • MOTHER OF PEARL
PARLEZ–MOI D'AMOUR • 1935 • Guissart Rene • FRN
PARLEZ–MOI D'AMOUR • 1975 • Drach Michel • FRN
PARLEZ–NOUS D'AMOUR • 1976 • Lord Jean-Claude • CND
PARLEZ–VOUS? • 1930 • Ray Albert • SHT • USA
PARLEZ–VOUS WOO • 1956 • Kneitel Seymour • ANS • USA
PARLIAMENT STREET • 1968 • Borris Clay • CND
PARLIAMO DI DONNE see **SE PERMETTETE, PARLIAMO DI DONNE** • 1964
PARLOG • 1975 • Vicek Karolj • YGS • NEGLECTED LAND, THE
PARLONS FEMMES (FRN) see **SE PERMETTETE, PARLIAMO DI DONNE** • 1964
PARLONS GRANDMERE • 1989 • Diop Djibril • DOC • SNL
PARLOR, BEDROOM AND BATH • 1920 • Dillon Eddie • USA
PARLOR, BEDROOM AND BATH • 1931 • Sedgwick Edward • USA • ROMEO IN PYJAMAS, A (UKN)
PARLOR, BEDROOM AND WRATH • 1932 • Sweet Harry • USA
PARLOR PESTS • 1929 • Roberts Stephen • SHT • USA
PARLORNA • 1922 • Molander Gustaf • SWD
PARLOUR GAMES see **SALLSKAPSLEK** • 1963
PARMAKLILAR ARKASINDA • 1967 • Inanoglu Turker • TRK • BEHIND THE BARS
PARMAKSIZ SALIH • 1968 • Demirag Turgut • TRK • SALIH WITH NO FINGER
PARMI LES VAUTOURS (FRN) see **UNTER GEIERN** • 1964
PARMIGIANA, LA • 1963 • Pietrangeli Antonio • ITL • GIRL FROM PARMA, THE
PARNELL • 1937 • Stahl John M. • USA
PARNICENJE • 1964 • Lazic Dragoslav • YGS
PAROCHIAL PRINCESS • 1978 • USA
PARODIE DU CID, LA see **RODRIGUEZ AU PAYS DES MERGUEZ** • 1980
PARODY OF THE PAINTER BRUEGHEL • 1974 • Kuri Yoji • ANS • JPN
PAROLA CHE UCCIDE, LA • 1914 • Genina Augusto • ITL
PAROLA DI LADRO • 1957 • Puccini Gianni, Loy Nanni • ITL
PAROLA DI UNA FUORILEGGE.. E LEGGE!, LA • 1975 • Margheriti Antonio • ITL, USA • TAKE A HARD RIDE (USA)
PAROLE! • 1936 • Landers Lew • USA • PAROLED
PAROLE • 1982 • Tuchner Michael • TVM • USA
PAROLE A VENIRE, LE • 1970 • Del Monte Peter • MTV • ITL
PAROLE AUX ENFANTS, LA • 1980 • Melancon Andre • SER • CND
PAROLE DE FLIC • 1986 • Pinheiro Jose • FRN • COP'S HONOUR ○ COP OF HONOUR
PAROLE DONNEE, LA see **DALOKAN** • 1982
PAROLE EST AU FLEUVE, LA • 1961 • Vetusto A., Oswald • SHT • FRN
PAROLE FIXER • 1940 • Florey Robert • USA
PAROLE GIRL • 1933 • Cline Eddie • USA
PAROLE HEIMAT • 1955 • Wilhelm Hans F., Becker Wolfgang, Stapenhorst Fritz • FRG
PAROLE INC. • 1949 • Zeisler Alfred • USA
PAROLE RACKET • 1937 • Coleman C. C. Jr. • USA • FREEDOM FOR SALE
PAROLE VRAIE, LA see **KALIMATU AL–HAQ** • 1953
PAROLED see **PAROLE!** • 1936
PAROLED FROM THE BIG HOUSE • 1938 • Clifton Elmer • USA • MAIN STREET GIRL (UKN)
PAROLED –TO DIE • 1938 • Newfield Sam • USA
PAROLES DU QUEBEC • 1980 • Labrecque Jean-Claude • CND
PAROLES ET MUSIQUE • 1985 • Chouraqui Elie • CND, FRN • LOVE SONGS (USA)
PAROMA • 1984 • Sen Aparna • IND • ULTIMATE WOMAN, THE
PAROVOZ NO.B–100 • 1927 • Kuleshov Lev • USS • LOCOMOTIVE NO.B–100
PAROWOZ PF–47 • 1949 • Has Wojciech J. • DCS • PLN • LOCOMOTIVE PF–47
PAROXISMUS (ITL) see **VENUS IN FURS** • 1970
PARPADO CAIDO, EL see **HEROE A LA FUERZA** • 1963
PARQUE DAS ILUSOES, O • 1963 • Queiroga Perdigao • PRT
PARQUE DE JUEGOS • 1963 • Olea Pedro • SHT • SPN • PARK OF GAMES
PARQUE DE MADRID • 1958 • Cahen Enrique • SPN
PARQUE NACIONAL DA GORONGOSA • 1961 • Spiguel Miguel • SHT • PRT
PARQUES INFANTIS • 1945 • Mendes Joao • SHT • PRT
PARQUES NACIONALES • 1978 • Niehaus Ingo • DOC • CRC
PARRALA, LA • 1940 • Perojo Benito • SPN
PARRANDA • 1977 • Suarez Gonzalo • SPN • BINGE
PARRANDAS see **CAROUSALS** • 1979
PARRANDEROS, LOS • 1962 • Crevenna Alfredo B. • MXC
PARRISH • 1961 • Daves Delmer • USA
PARROT AND CO. see **NOT GUILTY** • 1921
PARROT FROM CASABLANCA, THE see **PAPUGA Z CASABLANKI** • 1964
PARROT OF LONELINESS, THE see **LORO DE LA SOLEDAD, EL** • 1967
PARROT SANG WITH HER OWN BODY, THE • Chung Jin-Woo • SKR
PARROTVILLE FIRE DEPARTMENT, THE • 1934 • Gillett Burt, Muffati Steve • ANS • USA
PARROTVILLE FOLKS • 1934-35 • Gillett Burt, Palmer Tom • ASS • USA
PARROTVILLE OLD FOLKS • 1935 • Gillett Burt, Palmer Tom • ANS • USA
PARROTVILLE POST OFFICE • 1935 • Gillett Burt, Palmer Tom • ANS • USA
PARSHURAM • 1929 • IND
PARSHURAM • 1935 • Bhatt Balwant • IND
PARSIFAL • 1904 • Porter Edwin S. • USA
PARSIFAL • 1912 • Caserini Mario • ITL
PARSIFAL • 1951 • Mangrane Daniel, Serrano De Osma Carlos • SPN • EVIL FOREST, THE
PARSIFAL • 1981 • Syberberg Hans-Jurgen • FRG, FRN
PARSON AND THE BULLY, THE • 1911 • *Martin Owen* • USA
PARSON AND THE MEDICINE MAN, THE • 1912 • *Fischer Margarita* • USA
PARSON AND THE MOONSHINER, THE • 1912 • Kirkwood James • USA
PARSON AND THE OUTLAW, THE • 1957 • Drake Oliver • USA
PARSON CIRA AND PARSON SPIRA see **POP CIRA I POP SPIRA** • 1965
PARSON JAMES • 1912 • *King Burton* • USA
PARSON JIM'S BABY • 1913 • *Kinemacolor* • USA
PARSON LARKIN'S WIFE • 1914 • *Broncho* • USA
PARSON OF PANAMINT, THE • 1915 • Wilson Ben • USA
PARSON OF PANAMINT, THE • 1916 • Taylor William D. • USA
PARSON OF PANAMINT, THE • 1941 • McGann William • USA
PARSON PEPP • 1918 • De Barge C. R. • SHT • USA
PARSON PUTS HIS FOOT IN IT, THE • 1911 • Kinder Stuart • UKN • WITH THE BEST INTENTIONS
PARSON SLIPS A COG, THE • 1915 • *Atlas* • USA
PARSON SUE • 1912 • *Solax* • USA
PARSON WHO FLED THE WEST, THE • 1915 • King Burton L. • USA
PARSONAGE OF DONVIK, THE see **TYRANNISKE FASTMANNEN, DEN** • 1912
PARSON'S BUTTON MATCHER, THE • 1915 • Louis Will • USA
PARSON'S COOKERY LESSON, THE • 1904 • Fitzhamon Lewin • UKN
PARSON'S END, THE see **FARARUV KONEC** • 1968
PARSON'S FIGHT, THE • 1922 • Collins Edwin J. • UKN
PARSON'S HORSE RACE, THE • 1915 • Lessey George A. • USA
PARSON'S POSTER, THE • 1910 • *Actophone* • USA
PARSON'S PRAYER, THE • 1909 • *Bison* • USA
PARSON'S WIDOW, THE see **PRASTANKAN** • 1920
PARSON'S WIFE, THE • 1911 • Fitzhamon Lewin? • UKN
PART 2 SOUNDER • 1976 • Graham William A. • USA • SOUNDER II
PART 2 WALKING TALL • 1975 • Bellamy Earl • USA • LEGEND OF THE LAWMAN (UKN) ○ WALKING TALL: PART 2 ○ WALKING TALL PART 2: VENGEANCE TRAIL
PART DE L'ENFANT, LA • 1943 • Rouquier Georges • SHT • FRN
PART DE L'OMBRAGE, LA • 1945 • Delannoy Jean • FRN • BLIND DESIRE (USA) ○ TROIS AMOURS
PART DES LIONS, LA • 1971 • Larriaga Jean • FRN, ITL
PART DU FEU, LA • 1977 • Perier Etienne • FRN
PART OF HER LIFE, THE • 1912 • *Selig* • USA
PART OF THE FAMILY • 1971 • Ronder Paul • USA
PART TIME HUSBANDS see **WEEKEND HUSBANDS** • 1924
PART TIME PAL • 1947 • Hanna William, Barbera Joseph • ANS • USA
PART–TIME VIRGINS (UKN) see **INTERPLAY** • 1970
PART TIME WIFE • 1930 • McCarey Leo • USA
PART–TIME WIFE • 1934 • *B & S Productions* • UKN
PART–TIME WIFE • 1961 • Varnel Max • UKN
PART TIME WIFE, THE • 1925 • McCarty Henry • USA
PART–TIME WORK OF A DOMESTIC SLAVE (USA) see **GELEGENHEITSARBEIT EINER SKLAVIN** • 1974

PART TWO: THE BEGINNING • 1971 • Lofven Chris • DCS • ASL
PARTAGE DE CATHERINE, LE (FRN) see **BUGIARDA, LA** • 1965
PARTE DEL LEON, LA • 1978 • Aristarain Adolfo • ARG • LION'S SHARE, THE
PARTEA TA DE VINA • 1963 • Muresan Mircea • RMN • YOU ARE GUILTY TOO
PARTED • 1925 • Butler Alexander • UKN
PARTED BY THE SWORD • 1915 • Moran Percy • UKN
PARTED CURTAINS • 1921 • Bracken Bertram • USA
PARTED FROM HIS BRIDE • 1918 • McRae Henry • SHT • USA
PARTED ON THEIR HONEYMOON • 1909 • *Edison* • USA
PARTED TO MEET AGAIN • 1910 • Noy Wilfred • UKN
PARTENAIRES • 1984 • d'Anna Claude • FRN
PARTENZA ORE 7 • 1947 • Mattoli Mario • ITL
PARTFOGOLT, A • 1982 • Schiffer Pal • HNG • ON PROBATION
PARTHENOS, O • 1967 • Dadiras Dimis • GRC • VIRGIN, THE
PARTI SAN LAISSER D'ADDRESSE • 1982 • Veuve Jacqueline • SWT, FRN • NO FORWARDING ADDRESS
PARTIAL ECLIPSE see **NEUPLNE ZATMENI** • 1982
PARTICIPATION, LA • 1965-66 • Garceau Raymond • DCS • CND
PARTICIPATION DES ENSEIGNANTS, LA • 1969 • Lamothe Arthur • DCS • CND
PARTICLES IN SPACE • 1966 • Lye Len • SHT • USA
PARTICULAR COWBOYS, THE • 1914 • *Lubin* • USA
PARTIE DE CAMPAGNE, UNE • 1936 • Renoir Jean • FRN • DAY IN THE COUNTRY, A
PARTIE DE CARTES, UNE • 1896 • Melies Georges • FRN • PLAYING CARDS
PARTIE DE PLAISIR, UNE • 1974 • Chabrol Claude • FRN, ITL • PIECE OF PLEASURE, A (USA) ○ PLEASURE PARTY ○ LOVE MATCH ○ WAY TO PLEASURE, THE
PARTIE DE TRIC-TRAC • 1895 • Lumiere Louis • FRN
PARTIE D'ECARTE • 1895 • Lumiere Louis • FRN • CARD GAME, A ○ CARD PARTY
PARTIE D'ECHECS DE NAPOLEON, LA • 1907 • Jasset Victorin • FRN
PARTIES CARREES CAMPAGNARDES • 1979 • Bernard-Aubert Claude • FRN
PARTIES CHAUDES • 1979 • Bernard-Aubert Claude • FRN
PARTIES FINES • 1977 • Kikoine Gerard • FRN
PARTIES FINES • 1977 • Nudamko Sacha • FRN
PARTIES RAIDES • 1976 • Desvilles Jean • FRN
PARTING see **ROZSTANIE** • 1960
PARTING ETERNAL, THE • 1913 • *Gray Betty* • USA
PARTING GLANCES • 1986 • Sherwood Bill • USA
PARTING HOUR, THE see **AYRILIK SAATI** • 1967
PARTING IS A MALEDICTION see **KATARA INE O HORISMOS** • 1968
PARTING OF THE TRAILS, THE • 1930 • McGowan J. P. • USA
PARTING OF THE WAYS see **LEJANIA** • 1985
PARTING OF THE WAYS, THE • 1912 • Porter Edwin S. • USA
PARTING OF THE WAYS -PSALM 57, THE • 1927 • Barnett Charles • UKN
PARTING TRAILS, THE • 1911 • Dwan Allan • USA
PARTINGS (USA) see **POZEGNANIA** • 1958
PARTIR.. • 1931 • Tourneur Maurice • FRN • PARTIR!
PARTIR • 1971 • Reichenbach Francois • SHT • FRN
PARTIR! see **PARTIR..** • 1931
PARTIR, REVENIR • 1984 • Lelouch Claude • FRN
PARTIRE • 1938 • Palermi Amleto • ITL
PARTIRONO PRETI E TORNARONO.. CURATI • 1973 • Massi Stelvio • ITL
PARTIS POUR LA GLOIRE • 1975 • Perron Clement • CND
PARTISAN see **PARTIZAN** • 1974
PARTISAN SQUADRON, THE see **PARTIZANSKA SKADRILA** • 1980
PARTISAN ZENSHI • 1970 • Tsuchimoto Noriaki • DOC • JPN • PREHISTORY OF THE PARTISANS
PARTISANS, THE see **NARODNIYE MSTITELI** • 1943
PARTISANS, THE see **SISSIT** • 1963
PARTISANS' ESCADRILLE, THE see **PARTIZANSKA SKADRILA** • 1980
PARTISANS IN THE PLAINS OF UKRAINE see **PARTIZANI V STEPYAKH UKRAINY** • 1943
PARTISANS IN THE UKRAINIAN STEPPES, THE see **PARTIZANI V STEPYAKH UKRAINY** • 1943
PARTISANS OF VILNA • 1986 • Waletzky Josh • DOC • USA
PARTITA, LA • 1988 • Vanzina Carlo • ITL • MATCH, THE
PARTITA FOR WOOD INSTRUMENT • 1975 • Zaorski Janusz • PLN
PARTIZAN • 1974 • Jankovic Stole • YGS, USA, LCH • PARTISAN ○ PARTIZANI ○ HELL RIVER
PARTIZAN STORIES see **PARTIZANSKE PRICE** • 1960
PARTIZANI see **PARTIZAN** • 1974
PARTIZANI V STEPYAKH UKRAINY • 1943 • Savchenko Igor • USS • PARTISANS IN THE PLAINS OF UKRAINE ○ PARTISANS IN THE UKRAINIAN STEPPES, THE
PARTIZANSKA SKADRILA • 1980 • Krvavac Hajrudin • YGS • PARTISANS' ESCADRILLE, THE ○ PARTISAN SQUADRON, THE
PARTIZANSKE PRICE • 1960 • Jankovic Stole • YGS • PARTIZAN STORIES ○ POVRATAK ○ CRVENI SAL
PARTIZANSKE SKOLE • 1981 • Latinovic Petar • YGS • SCHOOL FOR PARTISANS
PARTLY CLOUDY • 1916 • Myll Louis • SHT • USA
PARTLY CONFIDENTIAL (UKN) see **THANKS FOR LISTENING** • 1937
PARTNER • 1968 • Bertolucci Bernardo • ITL
PARTNER, THE • 1963 • Glaister Gerald • UKN
PARTNERS • 1912 • *Selig* • USA
PARTNERS • 1912 • Noy Wilfred • UKN
PARTNERS • 1913 • *Eclair* • USA
PARTNERS • 1913 • *Nestor* • USA
PARTNERS • 1916 • Henley Hobart • SHT • USA • MY LADY'S MILLIONS
PARTNERS • 1916 • Wilson Frank • UKN
PARTNERS • 1932 • Allen Fred • USA
PARTNERS • 1977 • Owen Don • CND
PARTNERS • 1982 • Burrows James • USA
PARTNERS • 1982 • Burstall Tim • ASL
PARTNERS see **FOX, THE** • 1921
PARTNERS AGAIN • 1926 • King Henry • USA
PARTNERS AT LAST • 1916 • Dewsbury Ralph • UKN
PARTNERS FOR LIFE • 1912 • Dawley J. Searle • USA
PARTNERS IN CRIME • 1913 • Buckland Warwick? • UKN
PARTNERS IN CRIME • 1913 • Myers Harry • USA
PARTNERS IN CRIME • 1914 • *Ritchie Billie* • USA
PARTNERS IN CRIME • 1928 • Strayer Frank • USA
PARTNERS IN CRIME • 1937 • Murphy Ralph • USA
PARTNERS IN CRIME • 1942 • Launder Frank, Gilliat Sidney • UKN
PARTNERS IN CRIME • 1961 • Duffell Peter • UKN
PARTNERS IN CRIME • 1973 • Smight Jack • TVM • USA
PARTNERS IN CRIME -THE SECRET ADVERSARY • 1983 • Wharmby Tony • TVM • UKN
PARTNERS IN FORTUNE (UKN) see **ROCKIN' IN THE ROCKIES** • 1945
PARTNERS IN TIME • 1946 • Nigh William • USA
PARTNERS OF FATE • 1921 • Durning Bernard J. • USA
PARTNERS OF THE NIGHT • 1920 • Scardon Paul • USA
PARTNERS OF THE PLAINS • 1938 • Selander Lesley • USA
PARTNERS OF THE SUNSET • 1922 • Townley Robert H. • USA
PARTNERS OF THE SUNSET • 1948 • Hillyer Lambert • USA
PARTNERS OF THE TIDE • 1915 • Lessey George A. • USA
PARTNERS OF THE TIDE • 1921 • Jefferson L. V. • USA
PARTNERS OF THE TRAIL • 1931 • Fox Wallace • USA
PARTNERS OF THE TRAIL • 1944 • Hillyer Lambert • USA
PARTNERS PLEASE • 1932 • Richards Lloyd • UKN
PARTNERS THREE • 1919 • Niblo Fred • USA
PARTNERS (UKN) see **AVENGING RIDER, THE** • 1928
PARTOUSE INFERNALE, LA • Benazeraf Jose • FRN
PARTOUSES DU DIABLE • Warren Ken • FRN
PARTOUT PEUT-ETRE OU NULLE PART • 1967 • Hondo Abib Med • SHT • MRT
PARTOUZE FRANCO-SUEDOISE • Law Bernard • FRN
PARTOUZES PERVERSE • Stephen Richard • FRN
PARTS: THE CLONUS HORROR see **CLONUS HORROR, THE** • 1979
PARTY • 1984 • Nihalani Govind • IND
PARTY see **FEEST, HET** • 1963
PARTY see **FESTA** • 1988
PARTY, THE • 1964 • Altman Robert • SHT • USA
PARTY, THE • 1968 • Edwards Blake • USA
PARTY, THE • Megginson R. T. • USA
PARTY, THE • 1974 • Bruhwiler Paul • SWT
PARTY, THE see **VESELICA** • 1960
PARTY, THE see **SERATA** • 1971
PARTY, THE (USA) see **BOUM, LA** • 1980
PARTY AND THE GUESTS, THE see **SLAVNOSTI A HOSTECH, O** • 1966
PARTY ANIMAL • 1983 • Hart Harvey • USA
PARTY ANIMAL, THE • 1984 • Beaird David • USA
PARTY AT KITTY AND STUDS • 1970 • Lewis Morton • USA • PARTY AT KITTY AND STUD'S PLACE ○ ITALIAN STALLION
PARTY AT KITTY AND STUD'S PLACE see **PARTY AT KITTY AND STUDS** • 1970
PARTY CAMP • 1987 • Graver Gary • USA
PARTY CARD, THE • 1936 • Pyriev Ivan • USS
PARTY CRASHERS, THE • 1958 • Girard Bernard • USA
PARTY DRESS, THE • 1912 • *Kent Charles* • USA
PARTY EVERY DAY, A see **ALLE DAGEN FEEST** • 1975
PARTY FEVER • 1938 • Sidney George • SHT • USA
PARTY GIRL • 1930 • Halperin Victor Hugo • USA • DANGEROUS BUSINESS
PARTY GIRL • 1958 • Ray Nicholas • USA
PARTY GIRL • 1969 • *Stacey Dist.* • USA • PARTYGIRLS
PARTY GIRLS • 1969 • Scott Ron • USA
PARTY GIRLS • 1989 • Vincent Chuck • USA
PARTY GIRLS FOR THE CANDIDATE see **CANDIDATE, THE** • 1964
PARTY HUSBAND • 1931 • Badger Clarence • USA
PARTY IN THE BOTANICAL GARDEN, THE see **SLAVNOST V BOTANICKEJ ZAHRADE** • 1969
PARTY IS OVER, THE see **FIN DE FIESTA** • 1960
PARTY LINE • 1988 • Webb William • USA
PARTY, PARTY • 1983 • Winsor Terry • UKN
PARTY PHOTOGRAPHER, THE see **PARTYPHOTOGRAPH, DER** • 1968
PARTY SECRETARY, THE • 1964 • Chebotaryov Vladimir • USS
PARTY SMARTY • 1951 • Kneitel Seymour • ANS • USA
PARTY STOOGE see **STOOGEMANIA** • 1985
PARTY WIRE • 1935 • Kenton Erle C. • USA
PARTYGIRLS see **PARTY GIRL** • 1969
PARTYPHOTOGRAPH, DER • 1968 • Bove Hans Dieter • FRG • PARTY PHOTOGRAPHER, THE
PARTY'S END see **FIM DE FESTA** • 1980
PARTY'S OVER, THE • 1934 • Lang Walter • USA
PARTY'S OVER, THE • 1963 • Hamilton Guy • UKN
PARURE, LA • 1914 • Chautard Emile • FRN
PARVARISH • 1958 • *Kapoor Raj* • IND
PARVI UROK • 1959 • Petrov Valdimir, Vulchanov Rangel • USS, BUL • OLD LADY, THE ○ FIRST LESSON
PARVIAT KURIER (BUL) see **PYERVY KURYER** • 1968
PARYZ-WARSZAWA BEZ WIZY • 1967 • Przybyla Hieronim • PLN • PARIS-WARSAW WITHOUT A VISA
PAS A DEUX • 1987 • Renault Monique, van Dijk Gerrit • ANM • NTH
PAS ASSEZ see **NIET GENOEG** • 1968
PAS BESOIN D'ARGENT • 1933 • Paulin Jean-Paul • FRN
PA'S COMMENTS ON THE MORNING NEWS • 1902 • Smith G. A. • UKN
PAS D'ACCIDENTS see **ACCIDENTS DON'T HAPPEN** • 1946-54
PAS DE BLANC A LA UNE • 1971 • Bouchouchi Youssef • ALG
PAS DE CAVIAR POUR TANTE OLGA • 1965 • Becker Jean • FRN
PAS DE COUP DUR POUR JOHNNY • 1954 • Roussel Emile • FRN
PAS DE DEUX • 1968 • McLaren Norman • SHT • CND • DUO
PAS DE FEMMES • 1932 • Bonnard Mario • FRN
PAS DE JEU SANS SOLEIL • 1972 • Berube Claude • CND
PAS DE LA MULE, LE • 1930 • Epstein Jean • FRN
PAS DE MENTALITE see **AN EINEM FREITAG UM HALB ZWOLF** • 1961
PAS DE PANIQUE • 1965 • Gobbi Sergio • FRN
PAS DE PITIE POUR LES CAVES • 1956 • Lepage Henri • FRN
PAS DE PITIE POUR LES FEMMES • 1950 • Stengel Christian • FRN
PAS DE PROBLEME! • 1975 • Lautner Georges • FRN • DOUX VOYAGE DE MONSIEUR MICHALON, LE
PAS DE REIT POUR MELANIE • 1990 • Beaudry Jean • CND • CASE OF THE WITCH WHO WASN'T, THE
PAS DE ROSES POUR OSS117 see **NIENTE ROSE PER OSS 117** • 1968
PAS DE SOURIS DANS LE BIZENESS • 1954 • Lepage Henri • FRN
PAS DE TEMPS POUR L'AMOUR see **LA WAKT LEB HOB** • 1963
PAS DE VACANCES POUR LES IDOLES • 1965 • Heroux Denis • CND
PAS DE VACANCES POUR MONSIEUR LE MAIRE • 1951 • Labro Maurice • FRN
PAS DE VIOLENCE ENTRE NOUS (FRN) see **QUEM A BETA?** • 1973
PAS DE WEEK-END POUR NOTRE AMOUR • 1949 • Montazel Pierre • FRN
PAS-DESSUS NOS RIVIERES • 1957 • Proulx Maurice • DCS • CND
PAS FOLLE LA GUEPE • 1972 • Delannoy Jean • FRN, FRG, ITL
PAS KOJI JE VOLEO VOZOVE • 1978 • Paskaljevic Goran • YGS • DOG WHO LIKED TRAINS, THE ○ DOG WHO LOVED TRAINS, THE
PA'S MEDICIN • 1912 • *Thanhouser* • USA
PA'S OVERALLS • 1916 • Currier Frank • SHT • USA
PAS PA RYGGEN, PROFESSOR! • 1978 • Okking Jens • DNM • WATCH YOUR BACK, PROFESSOR!
PAS PERDUS, LES • 1964 • Robin Jacques • FRN
PAS POSSIBLES, LES • 1982 • Melancon Andre • SER • CND
PAS QUESTION LE SAMEDI • 1965 • Joffe Alex • FRN, ISR • RAQ LO B'SHABBAT (ISR) ○ IMPOSSIBLE ON SATURDAY (USA) ○ NO QUESTION ON SATURDAY
PAS SI BETE • 1929 • Berthomieu Andre • FRN
PAS SI BETE • 1946 • Berthomieu Andre • FRN
PAS SI MECHANT QUE CA • 1975 • Goretta Claude • FRN, SWT • WONDERFUL CROOK, THE (USA) ○ THIS WONDERFUL CROOK ○ NOT AS WICKED AS THAT
PAS SUR LA BOUCHE • 1931 • Rimsky Nicolas, Evreinoff Nicolas • FRN
PAS UN MOT • 1956 • Portugais Louis • SHT • CND
PAS UN MOT A LA REINE-MERE • 1946 • Cloche Maurice • FRN
PAS VERS LA PAIX see **KHAT'AWAT NAHWA AS-SALAM** • 1975
PASA KIZI • 1967 • Inanoglu Turker • TRK • GENERAL'S DAUGHTER, THE
PASA LA TUNA • 1959 • Elorrieta Jose Maria • SPN
PASACEK Z DOLINY • 1983 • Vlacil Frantisek • CZC • SHEPHERD BOY FROM THE LOWLAND, THE
PASADENA PEACH, THE • 1912 • *Roland Ruth* • USA
PASADO ACUSA, EL • 1938 • Selman David • USA • ACCUSING PAST, THE
PASADO AMENAZA, EL • 1950 • Roman Antonio • SPN
PASADO EL MERIDIANO • Arzuaga Jose Maria • CLM • PASSING THE MERIDIAN
PASAIE DE VENEZUELA • 1956 • Salvia Rafael J. • SPN
PASAJE DE IDA • 1988 • Melendez Agliberto • DMN • ONE-WAY TICKET
PASAJERO DIEZ MIL, EL • 1946 • Morayta Miguel • MXC
PASAJEROS DE UNA PESADILLA • 1984 • Ayala Fernando • ARG • NIGHTMARE PASSENGERS
PASAJEROS DEL JARDIN, LOS • 1982 • Doria Alejandro • ARG • GARDEN TRAVELLERS
PASAJEROS EN TRANSITO • 1976 • *Conacine* • MXC
PASAJEROS, LOS • 1975 • Barrero Jose Antonio • SPN
PASAJES TRES • 1961 • Aguirre Javier • SHT • SPN
PASAK HOLEK • 1929 • Tintner Hans • CZC • PIMP
PASAN KO ANG DAIGDIG • 1988 • Brocka Lino • PHL • I CARRY THE WORLD
PASAPORTE • 1980 • Darino Eduardo • URG • PASSPORT
PASAPORTE PARA LA PAZ • 1975 • Ardavin Cesar • SHT • SPN
PASAPORTE PARA UN ANGEL • 1953 • Seto Javier • SPN
PASARAS DE ESE CARACOL AL FRIO DE AFUERA • 1979 • Marcano Nora • ANS • VNZ • YOU'LL GO FROM THIS SHELL INTO THE COLD OUTSIDE
PASAREA FURTUNII • 1957 • Negreanu Dinu • RMN • STORY PETREL
PASAZADE • 1967 • Inanoglu Turker • TRK • GENERAL'S SON, THE ○ SILAHLI PAZAZADE
PASAZERKA • 1963 • Munk Andrzej • PLN • PASSENGER (UKN) ○ PASSAGERE, LA ○ PASSAGIERIN, DIE ○ VOYAGEURS
PASCAL • 1964-69 • Rohmer Eric • MTV • FRN
PASCAL (USA) see **BLAISE PASCAL** • 1972
PASCALI'S ISLAND • 1989 • Dearden James • UKN, USA
PASCE CORVOS see **SHADOW OF THE RAVEN, THE** • 1988
PASCUAL DUARTE • 1975 • Franco Ricardo • SPN
PASCUALIN • 1965 • Eguiluz Enrique L. • SPN
PASEILLO, EL • 1968 • Mariscal Ana • SPN
PASEO POR LA VIEJA CONSTANTINOPLA • 1967 • Comeron Luis Jose • SHT • SPN
PASEO SOBRE UNA GUERRA ANTIGUA • 1948 • Bardem Juan Antonio, Berlanga Luis Garcia • SPN
PASHA'S DAUGHTER, THE • 1911 • *Garwood William* • USA
PASHA'S NIGHTMARE • 1904 • SHT • USA
PASHA'S WIVES, THE (USA) see **ESCLAVE BLANCHE, L'** • 1939
PASHT • 1965 • Brakhage Stan • USA
PASI SPRE LUNA • 1963 • Popescu-Gopo Ion • RMN • STEPS TO THE MOON ○ FIRST STEPS TO THE MOON ○ STEPS TOWARDS THE MOON
PASION BAJO EL SOL • 1956 • Isasi Antonio • SPN
PASION DE HOMBRE • 1988 • de la Loma Jose Antonio • SPN • MAN OF PASSION, A
PASION DESNUDA, LA • 1952 • Amadori Luis Cesar • ARG
PASION EN EL MAR • 1956 • Ruiz-Castillo Arturo • SPN

PASION INCONFESABLE • 1977 • Torrado Ramon • SPN
PASION JAROCHA • 1949 • Vejar Carlos • MXC
PASION ME DOMINA, UNA • 1959 • Gomez Landero Humberto • MXC
PASION OCULTA • 1966 • Crevenna Alfredo B. • MXC, PRU
PASION SALVAJE see **AMOR SALVAJE** • 1949
PASION SEGUN BERENICE, LA • 1975 • Hermosillo Jaime Humberto • MXC • PASSION ACCORDING TO BERENICE, THE
PASIONERIA • 1951 • Pardave Joaquin • MXC
PASIONES INFERNALES • 1966 • Orol Juan • MXC, PRC • HIJA DEL SOL, LA
PASIONES TORMENTOSAS • 1945 • Orol Juan • MXC
PASJA • 1977 • Rozewicz Stanislaw • PLN • PASSION
PASJI ZIVOT • 1966 • Gasparovic Zdenko • ANS • YGS • DOG'S LIFE, A
PASKUTINE ATOSTOGU DIENA • 1964 • Zhebrunas Arunas • USS
PASLA KONE NA BETONE • 1982 • Uher Stefan • CZC • CONCRETE PASTURES
PASNYOK MARSA • 1914 • *Starevitch Ladislas (P)* • ANS • USS • HEIR OF MARS, THE
PASO, EL • Ancelovici Gaston, Lubbert Orlando • PASSAGE, THE
PASO A LA JUVENTUD • 1957 • Martinez Solares Gilberto • MXC
PASO AL FRENTE, UN • 1960 • Torrado Ramon • SPN
PASO DOBLE • 1985 • Pita Dan • RMN • PASSO DOBLE (PAS IN DOI)
PASODOBLE • 1988 • Garcia Sanchez Jose Luis • SPN
PASOLINI DIRECTS HIS DEATH see **PASOLINI INSZENIERT SEINEN TOD** • 1985
PASOLINI INSZENIERT SEINEN TOD • 1985 • Allahyari Houchang • AUS • PASOLINI DIRECTS HIS DEATH
PASOS DE ANGUSTIA • 1957 • Pamplona Clemente • SPN
PASOS PELIGROSOS see **LA DE LOS OJOS COLOR DEL TIEMPO** • 1952
PASQUA IN SICILIA • 1955 • De Seta Vittorio • ITL • EASTER IN SICILY
PASQUALE • 1916 • Taylor William D. • USA
PASQUALINO CAMMARATA.. CAPITANO DI FREGATA • 1974 • Amendola Mario • ITL
PASQUALINO SETTEBELLEZZE • 1976 • Wertmuller Lina • ITL • SEVEN BEAUTIES –THAT WHAT THEY CALL HIM ○ SEVEN BEAUTIES (USA)
PASS IT ON • 1913 • Wilson Frank? • UKN
PASS KEY, THE • 1909 • *Lubin* • USA
PASS KEY NO.2 • 1912 • *Shields Ernest* • USA
PASS MARK see **ZALICZENIE** • 1968
PASS OF EAGLE'S TAIL see **WASHI-NO-O TOGE** • 1941
PASS OF LOVE AND HATE, THE (USA) see **AIZO TOGE** • 1934
PASS OF MORNING MIST see **ASAGIRI TOGE** • 1936
PASS SARTANA.. E L'OMBRA DELLA TUA MORTE • 1969 • Simonelli Giovanni • ITL
PASS THE AMMO • 1988 • Beaird David • USA
PASS THE BISCUITS MIRANDY • 1943 • Culhane James • ANS • USA
PASS THE DUMPLING • 1927 • *Sennett Mack (P)* • SHT • USA
PASS THE GRAVY • 1928 • McCarey Leo • SHT • USA • LOVE 'EM AND BEAT 'EM
PASS THE HASH, ANN • 1917 • Berthelet Arthur • SHT • USA
PASS THE PRUNES • 1916 • Chaudet Louis W. • SHT • USA
PASS TO LIFE, A see **PUTYOVKHA Z ZHIZN** • 1931
PASS TO ROMANCE (UKN) see **HI, BEAUTIFUL!** • 1944
PASS YOUR EXAM FIRST see **PASSE TON BAC D'ABORD** • 1979
PASSA IL DRAMMA A LILLIPUT • 1918 • D'Ambra Lucio • ITL
PASSA LA MORTE see **TERRA MADRE** • 1931
PASSA LA RUINA • 1919 • Bonnard Mario • ITL
PASSA L'AMORE • 1933 • Palermi Amleto • ITL
PASSADO E O PRESENTE, O • 1972 • de Oliveira Manoel • PRT • PAST AND PRESENT
PASSAGE • 1978 • Paakspuu Kalli • CND
PASSAGE • 1983 • Cantrill Arthur, Cantrill Corinne • DOC • ASL
PASSAGE, THE • 1940 • Ivanov Alexander • USS
PASSAGE, THE • 1979 • Thompson J. Lee • UKN
PASSAGE, THE see **PASO, EL**
PASSAGE, THE see **AFTER THE RAIN** • 1989
PASSAGE, THE see **PARANMA, TO** • 1989
PASSAGE A NIVEAU • 1966 • Sanchez-Ariza Jose • PLN
PASSAGE AU NORD-OUEST • 1971 • Gosselin Bernard • DCS • CND
PASSAGE CLOUTE see **D'AMOUR ET D'EAU FRAICHE** • 1933
PASSAGE DANGEREUX AU MONT-BLANC • 1897 • Melies Georges • FRN • DANGEROUS PASS (MONT BLANC), A
PASSAGE DE VENUS, LE • 1951 • Gleize Maurice • FRN
PASSAGE DES MIRACLES see **ZUQAQ AL-MIDAQQ**
PASSAGE DES TENTES AUX MAISONS, LE see **PATSHIANTSHIUAPA MAK MISTIKUSSIUPAPA** • 1971-77
PASSAGE DU RHIN, LE • 1960 • Cayatte Andre • FRN, ITL, FRG • PASSAGGIO DEL RENO, IL (ITL) ○ JENSEITS DES RHEINS (FRG) ○ TOMORROW IS MY TURN (USA) ○ CROSSING OF THE RHINE, THE
PASSAGE FROM HONG KONG • 1941 • Lederman D. Ross • USA
PASSAGE HOME • 1955 • Baker Roy Ward • UKN
PASSAGE OF LOVE see **I WAS HAPPY HERE** • 1965
PASSAGE OR THE MIDDLE OF THE ROAD see **PASSAGEM OU A MEIO CAMINHO** • 1982
PASSAGE THROUGH MIST • 1989 • Derakhshandeh Pooran • IRN • PASSING THROUGH MIST
PASSAGE TO INDIA, A • 1984 • Lean David • UKN
PASSAGE TO MARSEILLE • 1944 • Curtiz Michael • USA • PASSAGE TO MARSEILLES
PASSAGE TO MARSEILLES see **PASSAGE TO MARSEILLE** • 1944
PASSAGE WEST • 1951 • Foster Lewis R. • USA • HIGH VENTURE (UKN)
PASSAGE WEST see **ESCAPE TO GLORY** • 1940
PASSAGEM DAS HORAS, A • 1971 • Sigueria Jose Rubens • BRZ • PASSING OF THE HOURS
PASSAGEM DE NIVEL • 1965 • Rosa Americo Leite • PRT
PASSAGEM OU A MEIO CAMINHO • 1982 • Melo Jorge Silva • PRT • PASSAGE OR THE MIDDLE OF THE ROAD
PASSAGER, LE • 1926 • de Baroncelli Jacques • FRN
PASSAGER, LE • 1983 • Kinsey Nicholas • MTV • CND
PASSAGER CLANDESTIN, LE • 1960 • Habib Ralph • FRN, AUS • STOWAWAY, THE
PASSAGER DE LA PLUIE, LE • 1969 • Clement Rene • FRN, ITL • UOMO VENUTO DALLA PIOGGIA, L' (ITL) ○ RIDER ON THE RAIN (USA) ○ RIDER IN THE RAIN
PASSAGERE, LA • 1948 • Daroy Jacques • FRN
PASSAGERE, LA see **PASAZERKA** • 1963
PASSAGERS, LES • 1976 • Leroy Serge • FRN, ITL • SHATTERED
PASSAGERS DE LA GRANDE OURSE, LES • 1939 • Grimault Paul • ANS • FRN
PASSAGERS, LES (FRN) see **GHORBA, EL** • 1971
PASSAGES • 1978 • Shapiro Nesya • SHT • CND
PASSAGES FROM "FINNEGAN'S WAKE" • 1967 • Bute Mary Ellen • USA • PASSAGES FROM JAMES JOYCE'S "FINNEGAN'S WAKE" ○ FINNEGAN'S WAKE
PASSAGES FROM JAMES JOYCE'S "FINNEGAN'S WAKE" see **PASSAGES FROM "FINNEGAN'S WAKE"** • 1967
PASSAGGI • 1979 • Fragasso Claudio • ITL
PASSAGGIO DEL RENO, IL (ITL) see **PASSAGE DU RHIN, LE** • 1960
PASSAGIER, DER • 1988 • Brasch Thomas • FRG • WELCOME TO GERMANY
PASSAGIER FABER • 1990 • Schlondorff Volker • FRG • PASSENGER FABER
PASSAGIER IN DER ZWANGSJACKE, DER • 1922 • Walther-Fein Rudolf?, Eichgrun Bruno? • FRG
PASSAGIER VON NR.7, DER • 1921 • Zeyn Willy • FRG
PASSAGIERIN, DIE see **PASAZERKA** • 1963
PASSAGIO A LIVELLO see **ZIA SMEMORATA, LA** • 1941
PASSAIC TEXTILE STRIKE, THE • 1926 • *Russack S. B.* • DOC • USA
PASSANT, LE see **JEU** • 1974
PASSANTE, LA • 1911 • Jasset Victorin • FRN
PASSANTE, LA • 1950 • Calef Henri • FRN
PASSANTE DU SANS-SOUCI, LA • 1982 • Rouffio Jacques • FRN, FRG
PASSAPORTO PER L'ORIENTE • 1952 • Marcellini Romolo • ITL
PASSAPORTO ROSSO • 1935 • Brignone Guido • ITL
PASSARINHO DA RIBEIRA • 1959 • Fraga Augusto • PRT
PASSAROS DE ASAS CORTADAS • 1963 • Ramos Artur • PRT
PASSATO CHE UCCIDE see **TRADIMENTO, IL** • 1951
PASSATORE, IL • 1947 • Coletti Duilio • ITL • BULLET FOR STEFANO, A (USA)
PASSE A VENDRE • 1936 • Pujol Rene • FRN
PASSE DE MONIQUE, LE • 1917 • Feuillade Louis • FRN
PASSE DU DIABLE, LA • 1958 • Dupont Jacques, Schoendoerffer Pierre • FRN
PASSE-MONTAGNE, LE • 1978 • Stevenin Jean-Francois • FRN
PASSE-MURAILLE, LE see **GAROU-GAROU LE PASSE-MURAILLE** • 1950
PASSE SIMPLE, LE • 1977 • Drach Michel • FRN • REPLAY ○ SIMPLE PAST, THE
PASSE TON BAC D'ABORD • 1979 • Pialat Maurice • FRN • GET YOUR DIPLOMA FIRST ○ PASS YOUR EXAM FIRST ○ GRADUATE FIRST ○ DO YOUR EXAMS FIRST
PASSEGGIATA, LA • 1953 • Rascel Renato • ITL
PASSEIO AUSPICIOSO • 1929 • Gaio Afonso • PRT
PASSENGER • 1982 • Sarin Vic • MTV • CND
PASSENGER, THE see **MOSSAFER** • 1975
PASSENGER, THE (USA) see **PROFESSIONE: REPORTER** • 1975
PASSENGER FABER see **PASSAGIER FABER** • 1990
PASSENGER TO LONDON • 1937 • Huntington Lawrence • UKN • BLACK TRUNK, THE
PASSENGER TO TOKYO • 1954 • Hughes Ken • UKN
PASSENGER (UKN) see **PASAZERKA** • 1963
PASSENGERS see **ALLER RETOUR** • 1979
PASSENGERS, THE see **GHORBA, EL** • 1971
PASSENGERS ALIGHTING FROM FERRY BRIGHTON AT MANLY • 1896 • Sestier Marius • ASL
PASSENGERS LANDING AT HARBOUR OF GRANVILLE see **DEBARQUEMENT DE VOYAGEURS PORT DE GRANVILLE** • 1899
PASSENGERS WHO ARE LATE see **SPOZNIENI PRZECHODNIE** • 1962
PASSEPORT 13.444 • 1931 • Mathot Leon • FRN
PASSEPORT DIPLOMATIQUE • 1965 • Vernay Robert • FRN
PASSEPORT DIPLOMATIQUE, AGENT K8 • 1965 • Labrousse Andre • FRN • OPERATION DIPLOMAT PASSPORT (USA)
PASSEPORT POUR LE CANADA see **PASSPORT TO CANADA** • 1949
PASSEPORT POUR LE MONDE • 1958 • Stoloff Victor • DOC • FRN • VOYAGEUR DU BOUT DU MONDE, LE
PASSEPORT POUR L'ENFER see **VISA POUR L'ENFER** • 1958
PASSEPORT POUR L'ENFER (FRN) see **AGENTE 3S3, PASSAPORTO PER L'INFERNO** • 1965
PASSER-BY, THE • 1912 • Apfel Oscar • USA
PASSER-BY, THE • 1915 • Le Saint Edward J. • USA
PASSER-BY, THE see **PRZECHODZEN** • 1966
PASSERBY, THE • 1913 • Neill James • USA
PASSERS-BY • 1916 • Taylor Stanner E. V. • USA
PASSERS-BY • 1920 • Blackton J. Stuart • USA
PASSEURS D'HOMMES • 1937 • Jayet Rene • FRN
PASSEURS D'OR • 1948 • de Meyst E. G. • BLG, FRN
PASSI DI DANZA SU UNA LAMA SI RASOIO • 1973 • Pradeaux Maurizio • ITL, FRN • DEVIL BLADE (FRN) ○ MANIAC AT LARGE
PASSI DI MORTE PERDUTI NEL BUIO • 1977 • Pradeaux Maurizio • ITL
PASSI FURTIVI IN UNA NOTTE BOIA • 1977 • Rigo Vincenzo • ITL
PASSIFLORA • 1986 • Belanger Fernand • DOC • CND
PASSIN' THROUGH see **PASSIN' THRU** • 1921
PASSIN' THRU • 1921 • Seiter William A. • USA • PASSIN' THROUGH
PASSING, THE • 1911 • *Thanhouser* • USA
PASSING, THE • 1983 • Huckert John W. • USA
PASSING CLOUDS see **SPELLBOUND** • 1941
PASSING DAYS see **IDU DANI** • 1968
PASSING FANCY see **DEKIGOKORO** • 1933
PASSING FANCY see **FELHOLJATEK!** • 1984
PASSING GYPSIES • 1912 • *Pathe* • USA
PASSING OF A GROUCH • 1910 • Powell Frank • USA
PASSING OF A SOUL, THE • 1915 • Hepworth Cecil M. • UKN
PASSING OF BLACK EAGLE, THE • 1920 • Ryan Joe • SHT • USA
PASSING OF DIANA, THE • 1914 • Marston Theodore • USA
PASSING OF EVIL, THE see **GRASSHOPPER, THE** • 1970
PASSING OF HELL'S CROWN, THE • 1916 • Jaccard Jacques • SHT • USA
PASSING OF IZZY, THE • 1914 • Nicholls George • USA
PASSING OF J. B. RANDELL & COMPANY, THE • 1912 • *Wilson Benjamin F.* • USA
PASSING OF JOE MARY, THE • 1913 • Thornby Robert T. • USA
PASSING OF MR. QUIN, THE • 1928 • Hiscott Leslie • UKN
PASSING OF PETE, THE • 1916 • Mix Tom • SHT • USA
PASSING OF SAL, THE • 1911 • *Champion* • USA
PASSING OF THE BEAST • 1914 • Reid Wallace • USA
PASSING OF THE HOURS see **PASSAGEM DAS HORAS, A** • 1971
PASSING OF THE OKLAHOMA OUTLAWS, THE • 1915 • Tilghman William • USA
PASSING OF THE OLD FOUR-WHEELER, THE • 1912 • Buckland Warwick • UKN
PASSING OF THE THIRD FLOOR BACK, THE • 1918 • Brenon Herbert • USA
PASSING OF THE THIRD FLOOR BACK, THE • 1935 • Viertel Berthold • UKN
PASSING OF TWO-GUN HICKS, THE • 1914 • Hart William S. • USA • TWO-GUN HICKS
PASSING OF WOLF MACLEAN, THE • 1924 • Hurst Paul C. • USA
PASSING PARADE, THE • 1912 • *Eclair* • USA
PASSING PARADE NO.1 • 1938 • Wrangell Basil • SHT • USA
PASSING SHADOW, THE • 1910 • *Vitagraph* • USA
PASSING SHADOW, THE • 1912 • *Bushman Francis X.* • USA
PASSING SHADOWS • 1934 • Hiscott Leslie • UKN
PASSING SHOW, THE (UKN) see **HOTEL VARIETY** • 1932
PASSING STORM, THE • 1915 • Coyle Walter • USA
PASSING STRANGER, THE • 1954 • Arnold John • UKN
PASSING THE BOMB • 1918 • Curtis Allen • SHT • USA
PASSING THE BUCK • 1919 • Semon Larry • SHT • USA
PASSING THE BUCK • 1932 • Mack Roy • SHT • USA
PASSING THE GRIP • 1917 • Beaudine William • SHT • USA
PASSING THE LOVE OF WOMAN • 1914 • *Powers* • USA
PASSING THE MERIDIAN see **PASADO EL MERIDIANO**
PASSING THROUGH • 1977 • Clark Larry • USA
PASSING THROUGH • 1988 • Hoffman Philip • DOC • CND • TORN FORMATIONS
PASSING THROUGH see **GOOD BAD-MAN, THE** • 1916
PASSING THROUGH MIST see **PASSAGE THROUGH MIST** • 1989
PASSING THROUGH SWEDEN • 1969 • Duckworth Martin • DOC • CND
PASSING TRAINS • 1967 • Gavrilov Eduard, Kremnyov Valeri • USS
PASSION • 1917 • Ridgely Richard • USA
PASSION • 1950 • Lampin Georges • FRN
PASSION • 1954 • Dwan Allan • USA
PASSION • 1982 • Godard Jean-Luc • FRN, SWT • GODARD'S PASSION (USA)
PASSION • 1985 • Doning Olivier • NTH
PASSION see **LIDELSE** • 1945
PASSION see **SZENVEDELY** • 1961
PASSION see **VASEN** • 1962
PASSION see **MANJI** • 1964
PASSION see **VIOLENZA AL SOLE** • 1969
PASSION see **PASJA** • 1977
PASSION see **ZUI AI** • 1987
PASSION, A see **PASSION, EN** • 1969
PASSION, EN • 1969 • Bergman Ingmar • SWD • PASSION OF ANNA, THE (USA) ○ PASSION, A
PASSION, LA • 1897 • *Lear* • FRN
PASSION, LA • 1897 • Hurd • FRN • OBERAMMERGAU PASSION PLAY (USA)
PASSION, LA • 1898 • *Gaumont* • FRN
PASSION, LA • 1902 • Zecca Ferdinand, Nonguet Lucien • FRN • VIE DE JESUS, LA
PASSION, LA • 1906 • *Pathe* • SHT • FRN
PASSION, LA • 1914 • *Normand M.* • FRN • LIFE OF OUR SAVIOUR, THE (USA) ○ LIFE OF CHRIST, THE ○ PASSION PLAY, THE
PASSION, LA • 1960 • Martin Marcel • SHT • FRN
PASSION: A LETTER IN 16MM • 1986 • Rozema Patricia • SHT • CND
PASSION ACCORDING TO BERENICE, THE see **PASION SEGUN BERENICE, LA** • 1975
PASSION AND REVENGE see **GHARAM WA INTIKAM** • 1944
PASSION BEATRICE, LA • 1988 • Tavernier Bertrand • FRN • BEATRICE (USA)
PASSION D'AMOUR (FRN) see **PASSIONE D'AMORE** • 1981
PASSION DE DANSER, LA • 1982 • Letourneau Diane • CND
PASSION DE FEMMES • 1954 • Herwig Hans • FRN
PASSION DE HORITZ, LA • 1897 • *Lumiere* • FRN
PASSION DE JEANNE D'ARC, LA • 1928 • Dreyer Carl T. • FRN • PASSION OF JOAN OF ARC, THE
PASSION DE JESUS, LA • 1907 • de Chomon Segundo • FRN
PASSION DE NOTRE-SEIGNEUR JESUS-CHRIST, LA • 1905 • Zecca Ferdinand, Nonguet Lucien • FRN • VIE ET LA PASSION DE JESUS-CHRIST, LA ○ LIFE AND PASSION OF CHRIST
PASSION D'EVELYNE CLERY, LA see **ROUTE SANS ISSUE** • 1947
PASSION EST MORT DE MICHEL SERVET • 1975 • Goretta Claude • MTV • SWT
PASSION FEVER • 1969 • *Mostest Productions* • YGS
PASSION FILMS • 1899 • Perry Joseph H. • SER • ASL
PASSION FIRE see **JOEN** • 1947
PASSION FLOWER • 1930 • De Mille William C. • USA
PASSION FLOWER • 1986 • Sargent Joseph • TVM • USA
PASSION FLOWER, THE • 1912 • *Wilson Benjamin F.* • USA
PASSION FLOWER, THE • 1916 • *California Motion Picture Co* • USA

PASSION FLOWER, THE • 1921 • Brenon Herbert • USA
PASSION FLOWER HOTEL (USA) see **LEIDENSCHAFTLICHE BLUMCHEN** • 1978
PASSION FOR LIFE see **ECOLE BUISSONIERE, L'** • 1948
PASSION FOR THE SENSES • 1980 • Shindo Kaneto • JPN
PASSION FRUIT • 1921 • Ince John • USA
PASSION HOLIDAY • 1963 • Miles Wynn • USA • MIAMI RENDEZVOUS
PASSION HOTEL • Neutrof Ilja • FRG • HAPPY GIGOLO, THE
PASSION IN A SEASIDE SLUM • Chatterton Bob • USA
PASSION IN HOT HOLLOWS • 1969 • Sarno Joe • USA • HOT HOLLOWS
PASSION IN THE SUN • 1964 • Berry Dale • USA • PASSION OF THE SUN
PASSION ISLAND • 1927 • Haynes Manning • UKN
PASSION ISLAND see **ILE DES PASSIONS, L'** • 1982
PASSION ISLAND (USA) see **ISLA DE LA PASION, LA** • 1941
PASSION OF A WOMAN TEACHER, THE (USA) see **KYOREN NO ONNA SHISHO** • 1926
PASSION OF ANDREW, THE see **STRASTI PO ANDREYU** • 1966
PASSION OF ANNA, THE (USA) see **PASSION, EN** • 1969
PASSION OF JESUS, THE see **ACTO DA PRIMAVERA** • 1963
PASSION OF JOAN OF ARC, THE see **PASSION DE JEANNE D'ARC, LA** • 1928
PASSION OF REMEMBRANCE, THE • 1987 • Blackwood Maureen, Julien Isaac • UKN
PASSION OF ST. FRANCIS, THE • 1932 • Antamoro Giulio • ITL
PASSION OF SLOW FIRE, THE (USA) see **MORT DE BELLE, LA** • 1961
PASSION OF THE SEA see **LOST AND FOUND ON A SOUTH SEA ISLAND** • 1923
PASSION OF THE SUN see **PASSION IN THE SUN** • 1964
PASSION PIT, THE see **SCREAM OF THE BUTTERFLY** • 1965
PASSION PIT, THE see **ICE HOUSE, THE** • 1969
PASSION PLAY, THE • 1897 • Freeman W. W. "doc" • USA
PASSION PLAY, THE • 1898 • *Lubin Sigmund (P)* • USA
PASSION PLAY, THE • 1898 • Vincent L. J. • *Klaw & Erlanger (P)* • USA
PASSION PLAY, THE • 1924 • Buchowetzki Dimitri • FRG
PASSION PLAY, THE • 1928 • *Passion Play Committee* • USA
PASSION PLAY, THE • USA
PASSION PLAY, THE see **PASSION, LA** • 1914
PASSION PLAY GROUND • 1985 • Egoyan Atom • CND
PASSION SEKA • Pacheco Richard • USA
PASSION SELON LES CORAS, LA • 1973 • Reichenbach Francois • SHT • FRN
PASSION SONG, THE • 1928 • Hoyt Harry O. • USA
PASSION STREET see **PASSION STREET, U.S.A.** • 1964
PASSION STREET, U.S.A. • 1964 • Daley Oscar • USA • PASSION STREET ○ BOURBON STREET ○ PASSION STREETS
PASSION STREETS see **PASSION STREET, U.S.A.** • 1964
PASSION (UKN) see **MANJI** • 1964
PASSION (USA) see **VIE DU CHRIST, LA** • 1906
PASSION (USA) see **MADAME DUBARRY** • 1919
PASSION (USA) see **LEIDENSCHAFT** • 1940
PASSION WINS see **A VASEN VITEZI** • 1918
PASSION WITHOUT END see **HATESHINAKI JONETSU** • 1949
PASSION WITHOUT LIMITS, THE see **HATESHINAKI JONETSU** • 1949
PASSIONATE ADVENTURE, THE • 1924 • Cutts Graham • UKN
PASSIONATE ADVENTURE, THE see **TWO LOVERS** • 1928
PASSIONATE AFFAIR see **TENDRE ET VIOLENTE ELISABETH** • 1960
PASSIONATE BREASTS see **GEKIJO NO CHIBUSA** • 1967
PASSIONATE DEMONS, THE (USA) see **LINE** • 1961
PASSIONATE DESIRES see **FUEGO** • 1969
PASSIONATE FRIENDS, THE • 1922 • Elvey Maurice • UKN
PASSIONATE FRIENDS, THE • 1948 • Lean David • UKN • ONE WOMAN'S STORY (USA)
PASSIONATE HEART, THE see **HOROUCI SRDCE** • 1962
PASSIONATE INDUSTRY, THE • 1972 • Long Joan • DOC • ASL
PASSIONATE LIFE OF CLEMENCEAU see **VIE PASSIONNEE DE CLEMENCEAU, LA** • 1953
PASSIONATE PASTIME see **CHESSCETERA** • 1957
PASSIONATE PEOPLE EATER, THE see **LITTLE SHOP OF HORRORS, THE** • 1961
PASSIONATE PILGRIM, THE • 1921 • Vignola Robert G. • USA
PASSIONATE PLUMBER, THE • 1932 • Sedgwick Edward • USA • CARDBOARD LOVER, THE
PASSIONATE QUEST, THE • 1926 • Blackton J. Stuart • USA
PASSIONATE SENTRY, THE (USA) see **WHO GOES THERE?** • 1952
PASSIONATE STRANGER, THE • 1957 • Box Muriel • UKN • NOVEL AFFAIR, A (USA)
PASSIONATE STRANGERS, THE • 1968 • Romero Eddie • PHL
PASSIONATE STRANGERS, THE see **KLEINHOFF HOTEL** • 1977
PASSIONATE SUMMER • 1956 • Cartier Rudolph • UKN • STORM IN JAMAICA
PASSIONATE SUMMER (USA) see **POSSEDEES, LES** • 1955
PASSIONATE SUNDAY see **DARK ODYSSEY** • 1961
PASSIONATE THIEF, THE see **RISATE DI GIOIA** • 1960
PASSIONATE YOUTH • 1925 • Fitzgerald Dallas M. • USA • BLIND MOTHERS (UKN)
PASSIONE • 1953 • Calandri Max • ITL
PASSIONE see **OLTRE L'AMORE** • 1940
PASSIONE A ISNELLO • 1951 • Fasano Ugo • ITL
PASSIONE AFRICANA • 1941 • Righelli Gennaro • ITL
PASSIONE D'AMORE • 1981 • Scola Ettore • ITL, FRN • PASSIONS OF LOVE (USA) ○ PASSION D'AMOUR (FRN)
PASSIONE FATALE • 1950 • Grassi Ernesto • ITL
PASSIONE SECONDO SAN MATTEO, LA (ITL) see **MATTHAUS-PASSION** • 1949
PASSIONE TZIGANE • 1916 • Pasquali Ernesto Maria • ITL
PASSIONELS TAGEBUCH • 1914 • Ralph Louis • FRG
PASSIONNELLE see **POUR UNE NUIT D'AMOUR** • 1946
PASSIONNEMENT • 1932 • Guissart Rene, Mercanton Louis (U/c) • FRN
PASSIONS • Reinhard Pierre B. • FRN
PASSIONS • 1984 • Stern Sandor • TVM • USA
PASSION'S FOOL see **LIEBELEI** • 1927
PASSIONS, HE HAD THREE • 1913 • Lehrman Henry, Sennett Mack (Spv) • USA
PASSIONS IN THE NIGHT see **INIT SA MAGDAMAG** • 1983
PASSIONS NOCTURNES see **LADIES' NIGHT** • 1980
PASSIONS OF LOVE (USA) see **PASSIONE D'AMORE** • 1981
PASSIONS OF MEN, THE • 1913 • Butler Alexander? • UKN
PASSIONS OF MEN, THE • 1914 • Noy Wilfred • UKN
PASSION'S PATHWAY • 1924 • Bracken Bertram • USA
PASSION'S PLAYGROUND • 1920 • Barry J. A. • USA
PASSKEY TO DANGER • 1946 • Selander Lesley • USA
PASSO DOBLE (PAS IN DOI) see **PASO DOBLE** • 1985
PASSOVER MIRACLE, A • 1914 • Olcott Sidney • USA
PASSOVER PLOT, THE • 1977 • Campus Michael • USA, ISR
PASSPORT • 1990 • Daneliya Georgi • FRN
PASSPORT see **PASAPORTE** • 1980
PASSPORT FOR A CORPSE (USA) see **LASCIAPASSARE PER IL MORTO** • 1962
PASSPORT HUSBAND • 1938 • Tinling James • USA
PASSPORT TO ADVENTURE see **PASSPORT TO DESTINY** • 1943
PASSPORT TO ALCATRAZ • 1940 • Collins Lewis D. • USA • ALIEN SABOTAGE (UKN) ○ PASSPORT TO HELL
PASSPORT TO CANADA • 1949 • Blais Roger • DCS • CND • PASSEPORT POUR LE CANADA
PASSPORT TO CHINA (USA) see **VISA TO CANTON** • 1960
PASSPORT TO DESTINY • 1943 • McCarey Ray • USA • MAGNIFICENT ADVENTURE ○ PASSPORT TO ADVENTURE
PASSPORT TO FAME (UKN) see **WHOLE TOWN'S TALKING, THE** • 1935
PASSPORT TO HELL see **PASSPORT TO ALCATRAZ** • 1940
PASSPORT TO HELL see **CITTA SI DEFENDE, LA** • 1951
PASSPORT TO HELL, A • 1932 • Lloyd Frank • USA • BURNT OFFERING (UKN)
PASSPORT TO HELL (UKN) see **AGENTE 3S3, PASSAPORTO PER L'INFERNO** • 1965
PASSPORT TO OBLIVION see **WHERE THE SPIES ARE** • 1966
PASSPORT TO PARADISE • 1932 • Seitz George B. • USA
PASSPORT TO PIMLICO • 1949 • Cornelius Henry • UKN
PASSPORT TO PLEASURE • 1955 • MacIntyre Harold • NZL
PASSPORT TO SHAME • 1959 • Rakoff Alvin • UKN • ROOM 43 (USA)
PASSPORT TO SUEZ • 1943 • De Toth Andre • USA • CLOCK STRUCK TWELVE, THE
PASSPORT TO TERROR • 1989 • Antonio Lou • USA
PASSPORT TO TREASON • 1956 • Baker Robert S. • UKN
PASSWORD IS COURAGE, THE • 1962 • Stone Andrew L. • UKN
PASSWORD "KORN" see **HASLO "KORN"** • 1968
PASSWORD UCCIDETE AGENTE GORDON • 1966 • Grieco Sergio • ITL
PAST • 1950 • Fric Martin • CZC • TRAP, THE
PAST, THE see **CZAS PRZESZLY** • 1961
PAST AND PRESENT see **PASSADO E O PRESENTE, O** • 1972
PAST AND PROMISES • 1917 • Semon Larry • SHT • USA
PAST CARING • 1985 • Eyre Richard • UKN
PAST FORGIVEN, THE • 1913 • *Swayne Marian* • USA
PAST OF MARY HOLMES, THE • 1933 • Thompson Harlan, Vorkapich Slavko • USA • GOOSE WOMAN, THE
PAST ONE AT ROONEY'S • 1917 • Mills Thomas R. • SHT • USA
PAST PERFORMANCE • 1955 • Jones Charles M. • ANS • USA
PAST REDEMPTION • 1913 • Giblyn Charles? • USA
PAST THAT LIVES, THE • 1972 • Bregstein Philo • DOC • NTH
PASTASCIUTTA DEL DESERTO • 1961 • Bragaglia Carlo Ludovico • ITL • SPAGHETTI IN THE DESERT
PASTBISHCHE BAYAKA see **NEBO NASHEGO DETSTVA** • 1967
PASTE • 1916 • Dewsbury Ralph • UKN
PASTE AND PAPER • 1915 • *Mina* • USA
PASTE AND PAPER • 1922 • Roach Hal • SHT • USA
PASTE AND POLITICS • 1916 • Kernan Henry • SHT • USA
PASTE MAKES WASTE • 1968 • Smith Paul J. • ANS • USA
PASTEBOARD CROWN, A • 1922 • Vale Travers • USA • GARDEN OF FOLLY, A
PASTEBOARD LOVER, THE see **FAITHLESS LOVER, THE** • 1928
PASTEL DE SANGRE • 1971 • Bellmunt Francisco, Chavarri Jaime, Martinez Lazaro Emilio, Valles Jose Maria • SPN • BLOOD PUDDING ○ BLOOD PIE
PASTEUR • 1922 • Epstein Jean, Benoit-Levy Jean • FRN
PASTEUR • 1935 • Guitry Sacha, Rivers Fernand • FRN
PASTEUR • 1947 • Rouquier Georges, Painleve Jean • DCS • FRN • OEUVRE BIOLOGIQUE DE PASTEUR, L'
PASTIGENDE KURS • 1986 • Hermansson Bo • NRW • SUCCESS
PASTIMES • 1971 • Shapiro Nesya • CND
PASTIRCI • 1975 • Stiglic France • YGS • SHEPHERDS
PASTO DE FIERAS • 1966 • de Ossorio Amando • SPN
PASTO DELLE BELVE, IL (ITL) see **REPAS DES FAUVES, LE** • 1964
PASTOR ANGELICUS • 1942 • Marcellini Romolo • ITL
PASTOR HALL • 1940 • Boulting Roy • UKN
PASTOR JUSSILAINEN see **PASTORI JUSSILAINEN** • 1955
PASTOR OF VEJLBY, THE • 1931 • Schneevoigt George • DNM
PASTORAL • Kriesberg Irving • ANS • USA
PASTORAL HIDE AND SEEK see **DEN-EN NI SHISU** • 1974
PASTORAL LIFE • 1984 • Bertelsson Thrainn • ICL
PASTORAL SYMPHONY see **SYMPHONIE PASTORALE, LA** • 1946
PASTORALE • 1976 • Ioseliani Otar • USS • SUMMER IN THE COUNTRY, THE
PASTORALE see **PASTORALE 1943** • 1977
PASTORALE 1943 • 1977 • Verstappen Wim • NTH • PASTORALE
PASTORALE D'ETE • 1958 • Hindle Will • SHT • USA
PASTORES DA NOITE, OS • 1977 • Camus Marcel • BRZ, FRN • OTALIA DE BAHIA
PASTORI DI ORGOSOLO • 1958 • De Seta Vittorio • ITL
PASTORI JUSSILAINEN • 1955 • Kassila Matti • FNL • PASTOR JUSSILAINEN
PASTOR'S DAUGHTER, THE see **PRAESTENS DATTER** • 1916
PASTOR'S END see **FARARUV KONEC** • 1968
PASTRY PANIC • 1951 • Davis Mannie • ANS • USA
PASTRY TOWN WEDDING • 1934 • Gillett Burt, Eshbaugh Ted • ANS • USA
PASTURES GREEN • 1916 • Le Viness Carl M. • SHT • USA
PASTURES NEW • 1938 • Alderson John • UKN
PASTURES NEW see **NAMI Z LODEJI** • 1964
PASUNG PUAKA • 1979 • Osman M. • MLY • ACCURSED HANDCUFFS
PAT AND MIKE • 1952 • Cukor George • USA
PAT AND THE FOUR HUNDRED • 1910 • *Essanay* • USA
PAT CASEY'S CASE • 1914 • *Essanay* • USA
PAT CLANCY'S ADVENTURE • 1911 • *O'Connor Edward* • USA
PAT FLANNAGAN'S FAMILY • 1914 • *Reliance* • USA
PAT GARRETT AND BILLY THE KID • 1973 • Peckinpah Sam • USA, MXC
PAT HANNA IN THE GOSPEL ACCORDING TO CRICKET • 1932 • Hanna Pat • SHT • ASL
PAT HOGAN, DECEASED • 1915 • Baker George D. • USA
PAT, THE COWBOY • 1913 • *Brennan John* • USA
PAT, THE SOOTHSAYER • 1912 • *Kalem* • USA
PAT TURNS DETECTIVE • 1918 • *Rooney Pat* • SHT • USA
PAT UND PATACHON IM PARADIES • 1937 • Lamac Carl • AUS
PATA DE PALO • 1950 • Gomez Muriel Emilio • MXC
PATAGONIA IN ARMS see **PATAGONIA REBELDE, LA** • 1974
PATAGONIA REBELDE, LA • 1974 • Olivera Hector • ARG • REBELLION IN PATAGONIA (USA) ○ PATAGONIA IN ARMS
PATAMORPHOSE • 1961 • Boschet Michel • ANM • FRN
PATAPUFETE! • 1967 • Saraceni Julio • ARG
PATATA BOLLENTE, LA • 1979 • Steno • ITL • IT'S BAD TO MIX ○ HOT POTATO
PATATE • 1964 • Thomas Robert • FRN, ITL • FRIEND OF THE FAMILY (USA)
PATATES, LES • 1969 • Autant-Lara Claude • FRN
PATATOMANIE • 1970 • Image Jean • ANS • FRN
PATATRAC • 1931 • Righelli Gennaro • ITL
PATCH MAH BRITCHES • 1935 • *Mintz Charles (P)* • ANS • USA
PATCH OF BLUE, A • 1965 • Green Guy • USA
PATCHED ADONIS, THE • 1914 • *Patheplay* • USA
PATCHED COAT, THE • 1912 • Collins Edwin J.? • UKN
PATCHED SHOE, THE • 1911 • *Solax* • USA
PATCHWORK-COLA see **ARPA-COLA** • 1981
PATCHWORK GIRL OF OZ, THE • 1914 • MacDonald J. Farrell • USA • RAGGEDY GIRL, THE
PATCHWORK QUILT, THE • 1912 • *Vitagraph* • USA
PATCHWORK QUILT, THE • 1913 • France Charles H. • USA
PATCHWORK QUILTS • 1974 • Ondaatje Kim • DCS • CND
PATE KOLO U VOZU • 1958 • Zeman Borivoj • CZC • GRANNY TAKES OVER
PATENT DUCTUS ARTERIOSUS • 1947 • Jackson Pat • DOC • UKN
PATENT FOOD CONVEYOR, THE • 1915 • Williams C. Jay • USA
PATENT GLUE, THE • 1909 • *Walturdaw* • UKN
PATENT HOUSEKEEPER, THE • 1912 • *Edison* • USA
PATENT LEATHER KID, THE • 1927 • Santell Alfred • USA
PATENT LEATHER PUG, THE • 1926 • Rogell Albert S. • USA
PATENTED BY HAM • 1916 • *Hamilton Lloyd V.* • USA
PATENTS PENDING see **HOT HEELS** • 1928
PATENTSCHNAPPSCHLOSS, DAS • 1915 • Peukert Leo • FRG
PATER, LE • 1910 • Feuillade Louis • FRN
PATER VOJTECH • 1928 • Fric Martin • CZC • FATHER VOJTECH
PATER VOJTECH • 1937 • Fric Martin • CZC • FATHER VOJTECH
PATERA KATSE FRONIMA • 1967 • Karayannis Kostas • GRC • BE A GOOD BOY, FATHER
PATERNAL HOME, THE see **OTCHII DOM** • 1959
PATERNAL INSTINCT • 1926 • Barnett Charles • UKN
PATERNAL LOVE • 1915 • Lloyd Frank • USA
PATERNITY • 1981 • Steinberg David • USA
PATER'S PATENT PAINTER • 1909 • Stow Percy • UKN
PATESHESTVIE MEZHDU DVA BRYAGA • 1968 • Vulchanov Rangel • DOC • BUL • VOYAGE BETWEEN TWO SHORES ○ BETWEEN TWO WORLDS
PATH, THE • Myers Richard • SHT • USA
PATH FORBIDDEN, THE • 1914 • *Handworth Octavia* • USA
PATH OF DARKNESS, THE • 1916 • *Darwin Margaret* • USA
PATH OF DUTY, THE • 1910 • *Lubin* • USA
PATH OF GENIUS, THE • 1912 • *Powers* • USA
PATH OF GENIUS, THE • 1914 • Swickard Charles? • USA
PATH OF GLORY, THE • 1934 • Bower Dallas • UKN
PATH OF GROWTH, THE • NKR
PATH OF HAPPINESS, THE • 1916 • *Mersereau Violet* • USA
PATH OF HIS OWN, A • 1979 • Caulfield Paul • MTV • CND
PATH OF HOPE, THE see **CAMMINO DELLA SPERANZA, IL** • 1950
PATH OF THE PADDLE • 1977 • Mason William • SER • CND
PATH OF TRUE LOVE, THE • 1911 • *Turner Florence* • USA
PATH SHE CHOSED, THE • 1920 • Rosen Phil • USA
PATH THAT LEADS TO HEAVEN, THE see **HIMLASPELET** • 1942
PATH THROUGH THE WOOD • 1922 • Pike Oliver • UKN
PATH TO RUIN, THE • 1914 • *Boyle Irene* • USA
PATH TO THE RAINBOW, THE • 1915 • Smiley Joseph • USA
PATH TO TOMORROW • 1964 • Lisakovitch Viktor • DOC • USS
PATH UNDER THE PLANE-TREES, THE see **SUZUKAKE NO SANPOMICHI** • 1959
PATHACHA BHAOO • 1967 • Mane Dutta • IND
PATHALA BHAIRAVI • 1951 • Reddy K. V. • IND
PATHER PANCHALI • 1955 • Ray Satyajit • IND • SONG OF THE ROAD, THE ○ LAMENT OF THE PATH, THE ○ SAGA OF THE ROAD, THE
PATHETIC FALLACY, THE see **AJAANTRIK** • 1958
PATHETIC GAZETTE, THE • 1924 • Brunel Adrian • UKN
PATHETONE PARADE • 1934 • Watts Fred • UKN
PATHETONE PARADE OF 1936 • 1936 • Watts Fred • UKN
PATHETONE PARADE OF 1938 • 1937 • Watts Fred • UKN
PATHETONE PARADE OF 1939 • 1939 • Watts Fred • UKN
PATHETONE PARADE OF 1940 • 1939 • Watts Fred • UKN
PATHETONE PARADE OF 1941 • 1941 • Watts Fred • UKN
PATHETONE PARADE OF 1942 • 1942 • Watts Fred • UKN

PATHEY HOLO DEKHA • 1968 • Adhikari Sachin • IND • THEY MET ON THE WAY
PATHFINDER, THE • 1932 • Sparling Gordon • DCS • CND
PATHFINDER, THE • 1952 • Salkow Sidney • USA
PATHFINDER AND THE MOHICAN, THE • 1956 • Newfield Sam • MTV • CND
PATHFINDER (UKN) see **VEIVISEREN** • 1987
PATHOLOGIE ET LINGUISTIQUE • 1970 • Lavoie Richard • SHT • CND
PATHS AND TRACKS • 1964 • Borisov O., Voitetsky Artur • USS
PATHS INTO THE NIGHT see **WEGE IN DER NACHT** • 1979
PATHS OF ENEMIES • Preobrazhenskaya Olga • USS
PATHS OF FLAME • 1926 • *Kesterton George* • USA
PATHS OF GLORY • 1957 • Kubrick Stanley • USA
PATHS OF HATE see **SENTIERI DELL'ODIO, I** • 1965
PATHS OF SORROW, THE • 1914 • *General* • USA
PATHS OF VIOLENCE, THE see **CHEMINS DE LA VIOLENCE, LES** • 1972
PATHS THAT CROSSED • 1916 • MacDonald J. Farrell • SHT • USA
PATHS TO PARADISE • 1925 • Badger Clarence • USA
PATHWAY FROM THE PAST, THE • 1915 • *Storm Jerome* • USA
PATHWAY OF YEARS, THE • 1913 • *Bushman Francis X.* • USA
PATHWAYS OF LIFE • 1916 • *Gish Lillian* • USA
PATI PARMESHWAR • 1958 • Desai Manoo • IND
PATI PATNI • 1967 • Akbar S. A. • IND • HUSBAND AND WIFE
PATIENCE • 1920 • Leni Paul • FRG
PATIENCE AND FORTITUDE • 1946 • Gould Dave • SHT • USA
PATIENT, THE • 1930 • Taurog Norman • SHT • USA
PATIENT IN ROOM 18, THE • 1938 • Wilbur Crane, Connolly Bobby • USA
PATIENT MASSES, THE see **EVASANA DANA** • 1967
PATIENT PORKY • 1940 • Clampett Robert • ANS • USA
PATIENT VANISHES, THE see **THIS MAN IS DANGEROUS** • 1941
PATIENTS' RIGHTS • 1983 • Armstrong Mary • DOC • CND
PATINOIRE • 1962 • Carle Gilles • DCS • CND
PATIO, O • 1958 • Rocha Glauber • SHT • BRZ
PATIO ANDALUZ • 1952 • Grinan Jorge • SPN
PATIO DAS CANTIGAS, O • 1942 • Ribeiro Francisco • PRT
PATIO IS BEING FLOODED, THE see **PATIO SE ESTA HUNDIENDO, EL** • 1979
PATIO SE ESTA HUNDIENDO, EL • 1979 • Garvizu O. • VNZ • PATIO IS BEING FLOODED, THE
PATIO SERENADE • 1938 • Schwarzwald Milton • SHT • USA
PATISSIEUR ET RAMONEUR • 1904 • Blache Alice • FRN
PATMAN see **MR. PATMAN** • 1980
PATOTA, LA • 1961 • Tinayre Daniel • ARG • TEDDY BOYS
PATRES DU DESORDRE, LES • 1968 • Papatakis Nico • FRN, GRC • THANOS AND DESPINA (USA) ○ SHEPHERDS OF CONFUSION, THE
PATRIA • 1917 • Wharton Leopold, Wharton Theodore, Jaccard Jacques • SRL • USA
PATRIA, AMORE E DOVERE • 1937 • Blasetti Alessandro • ITL
PATRIA BOBA, LA • 1975 • Sanchez Luis Alfredo • SHT • CLM • STUPID FATHERLAND
PATRIA CHICA, LA • 1943 • Delgado Fernando • SPN
PATRIA O MUERTE • 1961 • Hoffman Jerzy, Skorzewski Edward • DOC • PLN
PATRIARCH #1 & #2, THE • 1977 • Jutra Claude • SHT • CND
PATRIARCHI DELLA BIBBIA, I see **PATRIARCHI, I** • 1963
PATRIARCHI, I • 1963 • Baldi Marcello • ITL • PATRIARCHI DELLA BIBBIA, I ○ PATRIARCHS OF THE BIBLE, THE
PATRIARCHS OF THE BIBLE, THE see **PATRIARCHI, I** • 1963
PATRICIA • 1942 • Mesnier Paul • FRN
PATRICIA • 1972 • Dewdney Alexander Keewatin • CND
PATRICIA BRENT, SPINSTER • 1919 • Malins Geoffrey H. • UKN
PATRICIA ET JEAN-BAPTISTE • 1966 • Lefebvre Jean-Pierre • CND
PATRICIA GETS HER MAN • 1937 • Purdell Reginald • UKN
PATRICIA GIVES BIRTH TO A DREAM BY THE DOORWAY • 1962-64 • Jordan Larry • USA
PATRICIA NEAL STORY, THE • 1981 • Harvey Anthony, Page Anthony • TVM • USA
PATRICIA OF THE PLAINS • 1910 • *Anderson Broncho Billy* • USA
PATRICIA'S MOVING PICTURE • 1978 • Klein Bonnie • DOC • CND
PATRICIDE see **U POZERNOVO STOLBA** • 1924
PATRICIO MIRO UNA ESTRELLA • 1934 • Saenz De Heredia Jose Luis • SPN
PATRICK • 1978 • Franklin Richard • ASL
PATRICK, JULIE, FELIX ET TOUS LES AUTRES.. • 1974 • Danis Aime • DCS • CND
PATRICK THE GREAT • 1945 • Ryan Frank • USA
PATRIE • 1914 • Capellani Albert • FRN
PATRIE • 1945 • Daquin Louis • FRN
PATRIMONIO NACIONAL • 1980 • Berlanga Luis Garcia • SPN • NATIONAL HERITAGE
PATRIOT, THE • 1913 • *Moore Eugene* • USA
PATRIOT, THE • 1916 • Smith Cliff, Hart William S. • USA
PATRIOT, THE • 1917 • Drew Sidney, Drew Sidney Mrs. • SHT • USA
PATRIOT, THE • 1928 • Lubitsch Ernst • USA
PATRIOT, THE • 1986 • Harris Frank • USA
PATRIOT, THE see **DARMA KESUMA** • 1971
PATRIOT, THE see **PATRIOTIN, DIE** • 1980
PATRIOT AND THE SPY, THE • 1915 • *Cruze James* • USA
PATRIOT GAME, THE • 1978 • Maccaig Arthur • DOC • FRN
PATRIOTE, LE • 1938 • Tourneur Maurice • FRN • MAD EMPEROR, THE (USA)
PATRIOTEN • 1937 • Ritter Karl • FRG • PATRIOTS (USA)
PATRIOTIC ARABELLA • 1915 • Read James • UKN • ARABELLA SPIES SPIES
PATRIOTIC ENGLISH GIRL, A • 1914 • Bantock Leedham • UKN
PATRIOTIC MRS. BROWN • 1916 • Kellino W. P. • UKN
PATRIOTIC POOCHES • 1943 • Rasinski Connie • ANS • USA
PATRIOTIC POPEYE • 1957 • Kneitel Seymour • ANS • USA
PATRIOTIC SONS, THE • 1912 • *Eclair* • USA
PATRIOTIC WOMAN, THE see **PATRIOTIN, DIE** • 1980
PATRIOTIN, DIE • 1980 • Kluge Alexander • FRG • PATRIOT, THE ○ PATRIOTIC WOMAN, THE
PATRIOTISM • 1918 • West Raymond B. • USA
PATRIOTISM • 1964 • Wieland Joyce • USA
PATRIOTISM see **YUKOKU** • 1965
PATRIOTS, THE see **CHUNG LIEH T'U** • 1975
PATRIOTS (USA) see **OKRAINA** • 1933
PATRIOTS (USA) see **PATRIOTEN** • 1937
PATROCLO E IL SOLDATO CAMILLONE • 1973 • Laurenti Mariano • ITL • PATROCLOOO! ..E IL SOLDATO CAMILLONE, GRAND GROSSO E FRESCONE
PATROCLOOO! ..E IL SOLDATO CAMILLONE, GRAND GROSSO E FRESCONE see **PATROCLO E IL SOLDATO CAMILLONE** • 1973
PATROL, THE see **HASAYARIM** • 1967
PATROL TO THE NORTHWEST PASSAGE • 1937 • Finnie Richard S. • DOC • CND
PATROLLING THE ETHER • 1944 • Burnford Paul • USA
PATROLS • 1943-46 • Monkman John • DOC • UKN
PATRON EST MORT, LE • 1938 • Storck Henri • DOC • BLG
PATRONNE, LA • 1949 • Dhery Robert • FRN
PATRONS / TELEVISION • 1978 • Mordillat Gerard, Philibert Nicolas • SER • FRN
PATROUILLE A L'EST • 1975 • Laskri Amar • ALG
PATROUILLE ANDERSON, LA • 1967 • Schoendoerffer Pierre • FRN • ANDERSON PLATOON, THE ○ SECTION ANDERSON, LA
PATROUILLE BLANCHE • 1941 • Chamborant Christian • FRN
PATROUILLE DE CHOC • 1956 • Bernard-Aubert Claude • FRN • SHOCK PATROL (USA) ○ PATROUILLE SANS ESPOIR ○ DEATH PATROL
PATROUILLE DES SABLES, LA • 1954 • Chanas Rene • FRN, SPN • DESERT FIGHTERS (USA)
PATROUILLE SANS ESPOIR see **PATROUILLE DE CHOC** • 1956
PATRULLA, LA • 1954 • Lazaga Pedro • SPN
PATRULLA DE VALIENTES • 1966 • Vejar Sergio • MXC
PAT'S BIRTHDAY • 1962 • Breer Robert • SHT • USA
PAT'S BREECHES • 1912 • *Champion* • USA
PAT'S DAY OFF • 1912 • Sennett Mack • USA
PAT'S IDEA • 1913 • Melford Mark? • UKN
PAT'S PASTING WAYS • 1916 • Dillon Robert A. • SHT • USA
PAT'S REVENGE • 1914 • Hotaling Arthur D. • USA
PATSANI • 1983 • Asanova Dinara • USS • KIDS
PATSCHULI-MAUSCHEN, DAS • 1918 • Hofer Franz • FRG
PATSHIANTSHIUAPA MAK MISTIKUSSIUPAPA • 1971-77 • Lamothe Arthur • DOC • CND • PASSAGE DES TENTES AUX MAISONS, LE
PATSY • 1917 • Adolfi John G. • USA
PATSY • 1921 • McDermott John • USA
PATSY, THE • 1928 • Vidor King • USA • POLITIC FLAPPER, THE (UKN)
PATSY, THE • 1964 • Lewis Jerry • USA
PATSY, THE see **ADDITION, L'** • 1984
PATSY AMONG THE FAIRIES • 1915 • *Elmer Clarence Jay* • USA
PATSY AMONG THE SMUGGLERS • 1915 • *Elmer Clarence Jay* • USA
PATSY AT COLLEGE • 1915 • *Lubin* • USA
PATSY AT SCHOOL • 1914 • Winter Percy • USA
PATSY AT THE SEASHORE • 1915 • *Lubin* • USA
PATSY IN A SEMINARY • 1915 • *Lubin* • USA
PATSY IN BUSINESS • 1915 • *Lubin* • USA
PATSY IN TOWN • 1915 • *Elmer Clarence Jay* • USA
PATSY MARRIED AND SETTLED • 1915 • *Elmer Clarence Jay* • USA
PATSY OF THE CIRCUS see **CIRCUS GIRL'S ROMANCE, THE** • 1915
PATSY ON A TROLLEY CAR • 1915 • *Lubin* • USA
PATSY ON A YACHT • 1915 • *Elmer Clarence Jay* • USA
PATSY'S ELOPEMENT • 1915 • *Lubin* • USA
PATSY'S FIRST LOVE • 1915 • *Elmer Clarence* • USA
PATSY'S IRISH JOHN see **NO BABIES WANTED** • 1928
PATSY'S LUCK • 1913 • *Nestor* • USA
PATSY'S MISTAKE • 1912 • *Nestor* • USA
PATSY'S PARTNER • 1917 • *Cahill Marie* • SHT • USA
PATSY'S VACATION • 1915 • Winter Percy • USA
PATTATHU RANI • 1967 • Ramanathan S. • IND • NUMBER ONE QUEEN
PATTAYA, DON'T BURN • 1989 • Uncle • THL
PATTE MOUILLE • 1963 • Carle Gilles • DCS • CND
PATTERN FOR MURDER • 1964 • *Mather George* • FRG
PATTERN FOR PLUNDER (USA) see **BAY OF ST. MICHEL, THE** • 1963
PATTERN OF EVIL see **FORNICON -PATTERN OF EVIL** • 1970
PATTERN OF LIFE • 1964 • Collings Geoffrey • ASL
PATTERN OF ROSES, A • 1983 • Clark Lawrence Gordon • UKN
PATTERN OF SUPPLY see **OLIE OP REIS** • 1957
PATTERNS • Shaw-Smith David • DSS • IRL
PATTERNS • 1956 • Cook Fielder • USA • PATTERNS OF POWER (UKN)
PATTERNS FOR A SUNDAY AFTERNOON • 1954 • D'Avino Carmen • ANS • USA
PATTERNS OF LOVE see **JOYO** • 1960
PATTERNS OF POWER (UKN) see **PATTERNS** • 1956
PATTERSON OF THE NEWS • 1916 • Webster Harry Mcrae • SHT • USA
PATTES BLANCHES • 1948 • Gremillon Jean • FRN • WHITE LEGS (UKN)
PATTES DE MOUCHE, LES • 1936 • Gremillon Jean • FRN • LETTRE BRULANTE, UNE ○ FIN DE SIECLE
PATTES DE VELOURS • 1951 • de Vaucorbeil Max • FRN
PATTHAR KE SANAM • 1968 • Nawathe Raja • IND • HEART THAT IS MADE OF STONE, THE
PATTI AND VALLI • 1973 • Daley Sandy • DCS • USA
PATTI ROCKS • 1988 • Morris David Burton • USA
PATTINATHIL BOOTHAM • 1967 • Raman M. V. • IND • GHOST IN THE TOWN
PATTO COL DIAVOLO • 1948 • Chiarini Luigi • ITL • PACT WITH THE DEVIL
PATTON • 1970 • Schaffner Franklin J. • USA • PATTON: A SALUTE TO A REBEL ○ PATTON: LUST FOR GLORY ○ PATTON: SALUTE TO A REBEL
PATTON: A SALUTE TO A REBEL see **PATTON** • 1970
PATTON: LUST FOR GLORY see **PATTON** • 1970
PATTON: SALUTE TO A REBEL see **PATTON** • 1970
PATTUGLIA ANTI-GANG (ITL) see **BRIGADE ANTI-GANGS** • 1966
PATTUGLIA DE PASSO SAN GIACOMO, LA • 1954 • Olmi Ermanno • DOC • ITL
PATTUGLIA DELL'AMBA ALAGI, LA • 1954 • Calzavara Flavio • ITL
PATTUGLIA SPERDUTA, LA • 1952 • Nelli Piero • ITL
PATTY HEARST • 1988 • Schrader Paul • USA • PATTY HEARST: HER OWN STORY
PATTY HEARST: HER OWN STORY see **PATTY HEARST** • 1988
PAUK • 1969 • Marks Aleksandar, Jutrisa Vladimir • ANS • YGS • SPIDER
PAUKER, DER • 1958 • von Ambesser Axel • FRG • CRAMMER, THE
PAUKI • 1942 • Trauberg Ilya, Zemgano I. • USS • SPIDER, THE
PAUL • 1969 • Medveczky Diourka • FRN
PAUL • 1975 • Bugajski Ryszard • MTV • PLN
PAUL AND MICHELE • 1974 • Gilbert Lewis* • UKN, FRN • PAUL ET MICHELE
PAUL AND VIRGINIA • 1910 • *Thanhouser* • USA
PAUL AND VIRGINIA • 1912 • *Rex* • USA
PAUL ANKA see **LONELY BOY** • 1961
PAUL BANNES SCHICKSAL • 1916 • Larsen Viggo • FRG
PAUL BOWLES IN MOROCCO • 1970 • Conklin Gary • DOC • USA
PAUL BUNYAN • 1958 • Clark Les • ANS • USA
PAUL CHEVROLET AND THE ULTIMATE HALLUCINATION see **PAUL CHEVROLET EN DE ULTIEME HALLUCINATIE** • 1986
PAUL CHEVROLET EN DE ULTIEME HALLUCINATIE • 1986 • de la Parra Pim • NTH • PAUL CHEVROLET AND THE ULTIMATE HALLUCINATION
PAUL CLAUDEL • 1951 • Gillet • SHT • FRN
PAUL DELVAUX OR THE FORBIDDEN WOMEN see **PAUL DELVAUX OU LES FEMMES DEFENDUES** • 1970
PAUL DELVAUX OU LES FEMMES DEFENDUES • 1970 • Storck Henri • DOC • BLG • PAUL DELVAUX OR THE FORBIDDEN WOMEN
PAUL DESSAU • 1967 • Cohn-Vossen Richard • DOC • GDR
PAUL-EMILE BORDUAS • 1963 • Godbout Jacques • DCS • CND
PAUL ET MICHELE see **PAUL AND MICHELE** • 1974
PAUL ET VIRGINIE • 1926 • Peguy Robert • FRN
PAUL GAUGUIN • 1957 • Quilici Folco • SHT • ITL
PAUL HORN QUINTET • 1962 • Binder Steve • *Jazz Scene* • SHT • USA
PAUL HORN QUINTET • 1962 • Markas Gary • *Frankly Jazz* • SHT • USA
PAUL JONES, JR. • 1924 • Marshall George • SHT • USA
PAUL KRUGER • 1956 • SAF
PAUL LAWRENCE DUNBAR • 1973 • *Moss Carlton* • USA
PAUL RAYMOND'S EROTICA see **EROTICA** • 1980
PAUL SLEUTH AND THE MYSTIC SEVEN • 1914 • Calvert Charles • UKN • SECRET SEVEN, THE (USA)
PAUL SLEUTH CRIME INVESTIGATOR: THE BURGLARY SYNDICATE • 1912 • Aylott Dave • UKN
PAUL SLEUTH -THE MYSTERY OF THE ASTORIAN CROWN PRINCE • 1912 • Aylott Dave • UKN
PAUL SWAN • 1966 • Warhol Andy • USA
PAUL TEMPLE AND THE CANTERBURY CASE see **CALLING PAUL TEMPLE** • 1948
PAUL TEMPLE RETURNS • 1952 • Rogers Maclean • UKN
PAUL TEMPLE'S TRIUMPH • 1950 • Rogers Maclean • UKN
PAUL TOMKOWICZ: NETTOYEUR D'AIGUILLAGES see **PAUL TOMKOWICZ: STREET RAILWAY SWITCHMAN** • 1954
PAUL TOMKOWICZ: STREET RAILWAY SWITCHMAN • 1954 • Kroitor Roman • DCS • CND • PAUL TOMKOWICZ: NETTOYEUR D'AIGUILLAGES
PAUL UND PAULINE • 1936 • Paul Heinz • FRG
PAUL VALERY • 1960 • Leenhardt Roger • DCS • FRN
PAULA • 1915 • Birch Cecil • UKN
PAULA • 1952 • Mate Rudolph • USA • SILENT VOICE, THE (UKN)
PAULA CAUTIVA • 1963 • Ayala Fernando • ARG
PAULA, HISTORIA DE UMA SUBVERSIVA • 1982 • Ramalho Francisco Jr. • BRZ • PAULA, STORY OF A SUBVERSIVE
PAULA, STORY OF A SUBVERSIVE see **PAULA, HISTORIA DE UMA SUBVERSIVA** • 1982
PAULA (UKN) see **FRAMED** • 1947
PAULCHEN SEMMELMANNS FLEGELJAHRE • 1918 • Schubert Georg • FRG
PAULE PAULAENDER • 1975 • Hauff Reinhard • FRG
PAULETTE see **SEX PERILS OF PAULETTE, THE** • 1965
PAULINA • 1977 • Kawadri Anwar • UKN
PAULINA 1880 • 1972 • Bertucelli Jean-Louis • FRN, FRG
PAULINA S'EN VA • 1969 • Techine Andre • FRN
PAULINE • 1914 • Etievant Henri • FRG
PAULINE A LA PLAGE • 1983 • Rohmer Eric • FRN • PAULINE AT THE BEACH (USA)
PAULINE AT THE BEACH (USA) see **PAULINE A LA PLAGE** • 1983
PAULINE CUSHMAN, THE FEDERAL SPY • 1913 • Eagle Oscar • USA
PAULINE ET L'ORDINATEUR • 1976 • Fehr Francis • FRN
PAULINE'S NECKLACE • 1914 • *Melies* • USA
PAUL'S PERIL • 1920 • Keefe W. E.? • USA
PAUL'S POLITICAL PULL • 1916 • *Hiers Walter* • USA
PAULUS CHANTANT: COQUIN DE PRINTEMPS • 1897 • Melies Georges • FRN • COMEDIAN PAULUS SINGING "COQUIN DE PRINTEMPS" ○ COQUIN DE PRINTEMPS
PAULUS CHANTANT: DERRIERE L'OMNIBUS • 1897 • Melies Georges • FRN • COMEDIAN PAULUS SINGING "DERRIERE L'OMNIBUS" ○ DERRIERE L'OMNIBUS
PAULUS CHANTANT: DUELLISTE MARSEILLAIS • 1897 • Melies Georges • FRN • COMEDIAN PAULUS SINGING "DUELLISTE MARSEILLAIS" ○ DUELLISTE MARSEILLAIS

PAULUS CHANTANT: EN REVENANT D'LA REVUE • 1897 • Melies Georges • FRN • EN REVENNAT D'LA REVUE
PAULUS CHANTANT: PERE LA VICTOIRE • 1897 • Melies Georges • FRN
PAUME, LE see **CRI DU CORMORAN LE SOIR AU-DESSUS DES JONGES, LE** • 1970
PAUMEES DU PETIT MATIN, LES • Rollin Jean • FRN
PAUMES, LES • 1974 • Chouikh Mohamed • ALG
PAUNCH 'N' JUDY • 1940 • *Mintz Charles (P)* • ANS • USA
PAUPER MILLIONAIRE, THE • 1922 • Crane Frank H. • UKN
PAURA, LA • 1954 • Rossellini Roberto • ITL, FRG • ANGST (FRG) ◦ NON CREDO PIU ALL'AMORE ◦ FEAR ◦ INCUBO
PAURA, LA • 1980 • Fulci Lucio • ITL • PAURA NELLA CITTA DEI MORTI VIVENTI ◦ CITY OF THE LIVING DEAD ◦ FEAR ◦ GATES OF HELL, THE ◦ TWILIGHT OF THE DEAD
PAURA D'AMARE • 1942 • Amata Gaetano • ITL • BARBARA E BARBERINA
PAURA D'AMARE, LA • 1918 • Roberti Roberto Leone • ITL
PAURA E AMORE • 1987 • von Trotta Margarethe • ITL, FRG, FRN • FURCHTEN UND LIEBEN ◦ THREE SISTERS
PAURA FA 90, LA • 1951 • Simonelli Giorgio C. • ITL
PAURA IN CITTA • 1976 • Rosati Giuseppe • ITL • HOT STUFF (USA) ◦ FEAR IN THE CITY
PAURA NELLA CITTA DEI MORTI VIVENTI see **PAURA, LA** • 1980
PAUSE • 1964 • Warhol Andy • USA
PAUSE • 1976 • Kubelka Peter • SHT • AUS
PAUSE IN TIME, A see **GAT DE TIJD, EEN** • 1974
PAUVRE JOHN OU LES AVENTURES D'UN BUVEUR DE WHISKY • 1907 • Melies Georges • FRN • SIGHTSEEING THROUGH WHISKY (USA)
PAUVRE MATELOT, LE • 1962 • Reboul Odet • SHT • FRN • POOR SAILOR, THE
PAUVRE POMPIER • 1906 • Blache Alice • FRN
PAUVRE VILLAGE, LE • 1923 • Herve Jean • FRN
PAUVRES GOSSES • 1909 • Perret Leonce • FRN
PAUVRETE, LA • 1960 • Regnier Michel • DCS • CND
PAVAGE MODERNE • 1938 • Leenhardt Roger • DCS • FRN
PAVALAKODI • 1949 • Naidu S. M. Sree Ramulu • IND
PAVAPPETTAVAL • 1967 • Thomas P .a. • IND • THAT POOR GIRL
PAVE, LE • 1905 • Blache Alice • FRN
PAVE DE PARIS, LE • 1961 • Decoin Henri • FRN, ITL • PAVEMENTS OF PARIS, THE
PAVEL CAMRDA'S CAREER see **KARIERA PAVLA CAMRDY** • 1931
PAVEL KORCHAGIN • 1957 • Alov Alexander, Naumov Vladimir • USS
PAVEMENT, THE see **BRUK** • 1971
PAVEMENT BUTTERFLY see **GROSSTADTSCHMETTERLING** • 1929
PAVEMENTS OF PARIS, THE see **PAVE DE PARIS, LE** • 1961
PAVES ROUGES DE MAI 68, LES • Roos Ody, Jaeggi Danielle • DOC • FRN
PAVILION NO.6 see **PAVILON C.6** • 1969
PAVILION VI see **PAVILJON VI** • 1979
PAVILJON VI • 1979 • Pintile Lucian • YGS • PAVILION VI
PAVILLON BRULE, LE • 1941 • de Baroncelli Jacques • FRN
PAVILLON DE LA FRANCE A BRUXELLES • 1959 • Martin Marcel • SHT • FRN
PAVILLON DES ARMEES DE TERRE ET DE MER • 1900 • Melies Georges • FRN
PAVILLON DU QUEBEC, INDUSTRIE 1 • 1967 • Portugais Louis • DCS • CND
PAVILLONENS HEMMELIGHED • 1916 • Mantzius • DNM • SECRET OF THE PAVILION, THE
PAVILON C.6 • 1969 • Balada Ivan • CZC • PAVILION NO.6 ◦ ARK OF FOOLS
PAVILON SELIEM • 1982 • Trancik Dusan • CZC • BEASTS-OF-PREY BUILDING ◦ CAT HOUSE, THE
PAVITRA GANGA • 1932 • *Oriental* • IND • SACRED GANGES, THE (USA)
PAVLE PAVLOVIC • 1976 • Djordjevic Purisa • YGS
PAVLINKA • 1952 • Zarkhi Alexander • USS
PAVLINKA • 1974 • Kachyna Karel • CZC
PAVLOS MELAS • 1973 • Fylaktos Filippos • GRC
PAVLOV/PAVLOVA • 1980 • Moo-Young Ian • UKN
PAVLUKHA • 1962 • Tumanov Semyon, Shchukin Georgi • USS
PAVONE NERO, IL • 1975 • Civirani Osvaldo • ITL
PAVOTS DE L'ENFER, LES • 1970 • Rhomm Patrice • FRN, YGS
PAW • 1959 • Henning-Jensen Astrid • DNM • LURE OF THE JUNGLE, THE ◦ BOY OF THE WORLD ◦ BOY OF TWO WORLDS
PAW, THE see **PRANKE, DIE** • 1931
PAWEL AND GAWEL • 1946 • Potocki R. • ANM • PLN
PAWEL WROBEL • 1971 • Lomnicki Jan • PLN
PAWEOGO • 1983 • Kollo Sanou • BRK • EMMIGRANT, THE
PAWIAK • 1966 • Trzos-Rastawiecki Andrzej • DOC • PLN
PAWN, THE • 1968 • Dillow Jean Carmen • USA
PAWN, THE • 1978 • SAF
PAWN OF FATE, THE • 1916 • Tourneur Maurice • USA • GENIUS -PIERRE, THE
PAWN OF FORTUNE, THE • 1914 • Wharton Leopold • USA
PAWN OF FORTUNE, THE • 1919 • *Howarth Lillian* • USA
PAWN SHOP see **STAMPEN** • 1955
PAWN TICKET 210 • 1922 • Dunlap Scott R. • USA
PAWN TICKET 913 • 1914 • Martin E. A. • USA
PAWNBROKER, THE • 1908 • *Lubin* • USA
PAWNBROKER, THE • 1965 • Lumet Sidney • USA
PAWNBROKER'S DAUGHTER, THE • 1913 • *Joyce Alice* • USA
PAWNBROKER'S HEART, A • 1917 • Cline Eddie • SHT • USA
PAWNED • 1922 • Willat Irvin V. • USA
PAWNED BRACELET, THE • 1913 • Johnson Arthur • USA
PAWNEE • 1957 • Waggner George • USA • PALE ARROW (UKN)
PAWNEE LOVE • 1912 • *Pathe* • USA
PAWNEE ROMANCE, A • 1913 • *Eclair* • USA
PAWNS OF DESTINY • 1914 • Salter Harry • USA
PAWNS OF FATE • 1914 • *Jones Morgan* • USA
PAWNS OF FATE • 1915 • Lloyd Frank • USA
PAWNS OF MARS • 1915 • Marston Theodore • USA
PAWNS OF PASSION see **LIEBESHOLLE** • 1928
PAWNS OF SATAN • 1961 • Greenberg Bob • SHT • USA
PAWNSHOP, THE • 1910 • *Solax* • USA
PAWNSHOP, THE • 1916 • Chaplin Charles • SHT • USA
PAWS, JAWS AND CLAWS see **IT'S SHOWTIME** • 1976
PAW'S NIGHT OUT • 1955 • Smith Paul J. • ANS • USA
PAWS OF THE BEAR • 1917 • Barker Reginald • USA
PAX • 1932 • Elias Francisco, Lemoine Camille • FRN
PAX AETERNA • 1916 • Holger-Madsen • DNM • ETERNAL PEACE
PAX DOMINE • 1924 • Leprince Rene • FRN
PAY AS YOU ENTER • 1928 • Bacon Lloyd • USA
"PAY-AS-YOU-ENTER" MAN, THE • 1913 • *Travers Richard C.* • USA
PAY AS YOU EXIT • 1936 • Douglas Gordon • SHT • USA
PAY CAR, THE • 1909 • Olcott Sidney • USA
PAY DAY • 1918 • Drew Sidney, Drew Sidney Mrs. • USA
PAY DAY • 1922 • Chaplin Charles • SHT • USA
PAY DAY • 1922 • Fleischer Dave • ANS • USA
PAY DAY • 1938 • Hurwitz Leo T., Strand Paul • DOC • USA
PAY-DAY see **ZAHLTAG** • 1972
PAY DIRT • 1916 • Eason B. Reeves, King Henry • USA
PAY FOR YOUR SINS see **KAFERI AN KHATIATAK** • 1933
PAY ME • 1917 • De Grasse Joseph • USA • VENGEANCE OF THE WEST
PAY OFF • 1926 • Henderson Dell • USA
PAY-OFF, THE • 1930 • Sherman Lowell • USA • LOSING GAME, THE (UKN)
PAY-OFF, THE • 1935 • Florey Robert • USA
PAY-OFF, THE • 1942 • Dreifuss Arthur • USA
PAY-OFF, THE • 1971 • Filippov Fyodor • USS
PAY-OFF, THE see **T-BIRD GANG** • 1958
PAY OFF, THE (UKN) see **SADDLES AND SAGEBRUSH** • 1943
PAY-OFF TIME see **DEATH PROMISE** • 1978
PAY OR DIE • 1960 • Wilson Richard • USA
PAY-ROLL, THE • 1911 • *Champion* • USA
PAY ROLL EXPRESS, THE • 1918 • *Gibson Helen* • SHT • USA
PAY THE BABY SITTER • 1969 • *Distripix* • USA
PAY THE CASHIER • 1922 • Roach Hal • SHT • USA
PAY THE DEVIL (UKN) see **MAN IN THE SHADOW** • 1956
PAY THE RENT • 1914 • *Joker* • USA
PAY TRIBUTE TO THE FIRE • 1972 • Okeyev Tolomush • USS • WORSHIP THE FIRE ◦ BOW TO FIRE
PAY YOUR DUES • 1919 • Roach Hal • SHT • USA
PAYABLE ON DEMAND • 1924 • Maloney Leo • USA
PAYASADAS DE LA VIDA • 1934 • Zacarias Miguel • MXC • TRICKS OF LIFE (USA)
PAYDAY • 1973 • Duke Daryl • USA
PAYDAY see **HELL'S HOLE** • 1923
PAYDOS • 1968 • Erakalin Ulku • TRK • DISMISSAL
PAYIN YAUNG • 1969 • Khin Soe • BRM
PAYING BAY • 1964 • *Halas John (P)* • ANS • UKN
PAYING BAY, THE • 1959 • Heyer John • DOC • ASL
PAYING FOR PLAYING • 1977 • Hylkema Hans • SHT • NTH
PAYING FOR SILENCE • 1913 • *Nestor* • USA
PAYING GUEST • 1957 • *Burman S. D. (M)* • IND
PAYING HIM OUT • 1915 • Kellino W. P. • UKN
PAYING HIS DEBT • 1918 • Smith Cliff • USA
PAYING OFF OLD SCORES • 1907 • Stow Percy • UKN
PAYING THE BOARD BILL • 1912 • *Coxen Ed* • USA
PAYING THE LIMIT • 1924 • Gibson Tom • USA
PAYING THE PENALTY • 1913 • *Kinemacolor* • USA
PAYING THE PENALTY • 1913 • Buckland Warwick? • UKN
PAYING THE PENALTY (UKN) see **UNDERWORLD** • 1927
PAYING THE PIPER • 1921 • Fitzmaurice George • USA • MONEY MAD
PAYING THE PIPER • 1947 • McKimson Robert • ANS • USA
PAYING THE PRICE • 1912 • *Lubin* • USA
PAYING THE PRICE • 1913 • *Rex* • USA
PAYING THE PRICE • 1916 • Crane Frank H. • *Paragon* • USA • REPARATION
PAYING THE PRICE • 1916 • Levering Joseph • *Gaumont* • SHT • USA
PAYING THE PRICE • 1924 • *Lynch Owen* • USA
PAYING THE PRICE • 1927 • Selman David • USA
PAYING THE TOLL • 1916 • *Knickerbocker Star* • SHT • USA
PAYMASTER • 1906 • *Bitzer Billy* • USA
PAYMASTER, THE • 1909 • *Bison* • USA
PAYMASTER, THE • 1913 • *Williams Clara* • USA
PAYMASTER'S SON, THE • 1913 • Ince Thomas H. • USA
PAYMENT, THE • 1916 • West Raymond B. • USA
PAYMENT DEFERRED • 1932 • Mendes Lothar • USA
PAYMENT GUARANTEED • 1921 • Cox George L. • USA
PAYMENT IN BLOOD (USA) see **SETTE WINCHESTER PER UN MASSACRO** • 1967
PAYMENT IN FULL • 1915 • Warren Giles R. • USA
PAYMENT IN FULL • 1916 • *Stull Walter* • USA
PAYMENT IN KIND • 1967 • Duffell Peter • UKN
PAYMENT ON DEMAND • 1951 • Bernhardt Curtis • USA • STORY OF A DIVORCE, THE
PAYMENT OVERDUE • 1986 • Benner Richard • MTV • CND
PAYNE AND HILLIARD • 1931 • *First National* • SHT • UKN
PAYO, EL • 1971 • *Cinetelmex* • MXC
PAYOFF • 1989 • Styles Richard • USA
PAYOFF, THE see **MAZZETTA, LA** • 1978
PAYOFF WITH LOVE see **SHUKIN RYOKO** • 1957
PAYROLL • 1961 • Hayers Sidney • UKN • I PROMISE TO PAY
PAYS A COMPRENDRE, UN • 1981 • Dansereau Mireille • CND
PAYS AUX CRANES RASES, LE • 1977 • Behi Ridha • TNS
PAYS BASSARI • 1952 • Gaisseau Pierre-Dominique • FRN
PAYS BEAU, LE • 1972 • Boschet Michel • ANM • FRN
PAYS BLEU, LE • 1977 • Tacchella Jean-Charles • FRN • BLUE COUNTRY, THE (USA)
PAYS DE COCAGNE • 1971 • Etaix Pierre • DOC • FRN • COCAGNE
PAYS DE LA TERRE SANS ARBRES, LE • 1980 • Perrault Pierre • CND • PAYS DE LA TERRE SANS ARBRES OU LE MOUCHOUANIPI, LE
PAYS DE LA TERRE SANS ARBRES OU LE MOUCHOUANIPI, LE see **PAYS DE LA TERRE SANS ARBRES, LE** • 1980
PAYS DES BASQUES, LES see **AU PAYS DES BASQUES** • 1930
PAYS D'OU JE VIENS, LE • 1956 • Carne Marcel • FRN
PAYS DU SOLEIL NAISSANT • 1922 • Rasumny Alexander • USS
PAYS NEUF • 1958 • Dansereau Fernand • CND
PAYS SANS BON SENS! OU WAKE UP, MES BONS AMIS!, UN see **PAYS SON BON SENS!, UN** • 1970
PAYS SANS ETOILES, LE • 1945 • Lacombe Georges • FRN • COUNTRY WITHOUT STARS, THE
PAYS SON BON SENS!, UN • 1970 • Perrault Pierre • DOC • CND • PAYS SANS BON SENS! OU WAKE UP, MES BONS AMIS!, UN
PAYS, UN GOUT, UNE MANIERE, UN • 1976 • Dansereau Fernand, Rossignol Yolande • SHS • CND
PAYS VASTE • 1968 • Labrecque Jean-Claude, Tasker Rex • DCS • CND • CANADA -PAYS VASTE
PAYSAGES DE FLORENCE • 1981 • Jimenez Mary • BLG • CINEMA DE L'AMOUR, LE
PAYSAGES DU SILENCE • 1947 • Cousteau Jacques • FRN • PAYSAGES SOUS-MARINS
PAYSAGES DU SILENCE • 1986 • Junod Blaise • DOC • SWT
PAYSAGES SOUS-MARINS see **PAYSAGES DU SILENCE** • 1947
PAYSAGISTE, LE • 1976 • Drouin Jacques • ANS • CND • MINDSCAPE
PAYSAN ELOQUENT, LE see **FALLAH AL-FACIH, AL-** • 1970
PAYSANNE PERVERTIE, LA • 1959 • Keigel Leonard • FRN
PAYSANNES • 1981 • Guerin Gerard • DOC • FRN
PAYSANS, LES • 1922 • Madzelewski Eugenjusz • PLN
PAYSANS NOIRS • 1947 • Regnier Georges • FRN • FAMORO LE TYRAN
PAZ • 1949 • Diaz Morales Jose • SPN
PAZ EMPIEZA NUNCA, LA • 1960 • Klimovsky Leon • SPN
PAZIENZA HA UN LIMITE.. NOI NO!, LA • 1975 • Morandi Armando • ITL
PAZZA DI GIOIA • 1940 • Bragaglia Carlo Ludovico • ITL • VIAGGIO VERSO IL SOLE
PAZZI DELLA DOMENICA, I • 1955-59 • Taviani Paolo, Taviani Vittorio • DCS • ITL
PAZZO D'AMORE • 1943 • Gentilomo Giacomo • ITL • MANUSCRITTO NELLA BOTTIGLIA
PBL 2 AND PBL 3 • 1968 • Breer Robert • USA
PE RASPUNDEREA MEA • 1956 • Calinescu Paul • RMN • ON MY RESPONSIBILITY
PE UN PERETE • 1969 • Ion Truica • ANS • RMN • ON A WALL
PE UN PICIOR DE PLAI • 1969 • Munteanu Stefan • ANS • RMN • RHAPSODY IN A MAJOR
PEA BROTHERS • 1934 • Roy Gunen, Banerjee Gunamoy • ANS • IND
PEACE see **AMAN** • 1967
PEACE see **HOA-BINH** • 1970
PEACE -A PRAYER FOR THE ROAD see **SHALOM** • 1973
PEACE AND FREEDOM • 1980 • Ballantyne Tanya • CND
PEACE AND QUIET • 1929 • Hill Sinclair • UKN
PEACE AND QUIET • 1931 • Richardson Frank • UKN
PEACE AND QUIET • 1970 • Walton Lloyd A. • CND
PEACE AND QUIET see **MESTA TUT TIKHIYE** • 1967
PEACE AND RIOT • 1919 • *Jester* • SHT • USA
PEACE AT ANY PRICE • 1915 • Birch Cecil • UKN
PEACE AT ANY PRICE • 1916 • Drew Sidney • USA
PEACE CONDFERENCE, THE • 1935 • *Mintz Charles (P)* • ANS • USA
PEACE CONQUERS THE WORLD see **POKOJ ZDOBEDZIE SWIAT** • 1951
PEACE COUNCIL, THE • 1913 • *Panzer Paul* • USA
PEACE FILM, THE see **PEOPLE OF BRITAIN** • 1936
PEACE FOR A GUNFIGHTER • 1967 • Boley Raymond • USA
PEACE GAME, THE (UKN) see **GLADIATORERNA** • 1969
PEACE KILLERS, THE • 1971 • Schwartz Douglas • USA
PEACE OF BRITAIN, THE see **PEOPLE OF BRITAIN** • 1936
PEACE OF MIND • 1930 • *Wilcox Herbert (P)* • SHT • UKN
PEACE OF ROARING RIVER, THE • 1919 • Henley Hobart?, Schertzinger Victor? • USA
PEACE OF THE WORLD see **TENKA TAIHEIKI** • 1928
PEACE OF THE WORLD see **TENKA TAIHEI** • 1955
PEACE OF UTRECH • 1972 • Bonniere Rene • DCS • CND
PEACE OFFERING, THE • 1911 • *Vitagraph* • USA
PEACE OFFERING, THE • 1912 • *Roland Ruth* • USA
PEACE ON EARTH • 1939 • Harman Hugh • ANS • USA
PEACE ON EARTH see **TENKA TAIHEIKI** • 1928
PEACE ON THE WESTERN FRONT • 1930 • Holmes F. W. Ratcliffe • UKN
PEACE, PERFECT PEACE • 1918 • Bocchi Arrigo • UKN
PEACE TIME • 1951 • Braun Vladimir • USS
PEACE-TIME FOOTBALL • 1946 • Davis Mannie • ANS • USA
PEACE TO HIM see **MIR VKHODYASHCHEMU** • 1961
PEACE TO HIM WHO ENTERS (USA) see **MIR VKHODYASHCHEMU** • 1961
PEACE TO THE NEWCOMER see **MIR VKHODYASHCHEMU** • 1961
PEACE TO YOUR HOUSE • 1963 • Yutkevich Sergei • USS
PEACE TOUR (USA) see **FRIEDENSFAHRT** • 1952
PEACE VALLEY see **DOLINA MIRU** • 1956
PEACE WILL CONQUER THE WORLD see **POKOJ ZDOBEDZIE SWIAT** • 1951
PEACE WILL WIN • 1952 • Szelubski Jerzy
PEACE WILL WIN see **POKOJ ZDOBEDZIE SWIAT** • 1951
PEACE WITH HONOR • 1902 • Hepworth Cecil M., Stow Percy • UKN
PEACEABLE KINGDOM, THE • 1971 • Brakhage Stan • USA
PEACEFUL FLAT, A • 1917 • Ray John • SHT • USA
PEACEFUL JONES • 1909 • *Centaur* • USA
PEACEFUL NEIGHBORS • 1939 • Marcus Sid • ANS • USA
PEACEFUL PETERS • 1922 • King Louis • USA
PEACEFUL SEA see **UMI NO WAKADO** • 1955
PEACEFUL VALLEY • 1920 • Storm Jerome • USA
PEACEFUL VICTORY, A • 1913 • *Russell William* • USA
PEACEFUL YEARS, THE • 1948 • Baylis Peter • UKN
PEACEMAKER, THE • 1910 • *Vitagraph* • USA
PEACEMAKER, THE • 1912 • *Selig* • USA
PEACEMAKER, THE • 1913 • *Smalley Phillips* • USA
PEACEMAKER, THE • 1914 • Brooke Van Dyke • USA
PEACEMAKER, THE • 1922 • Coleby A. E. • UKN
PEACEMAKER, THE • 1956 • Post Ted • USA
PEACEMAKERS, THE • 1963 • King Allan • CND
PEACEMAKER'S PAY, THE • 1914 • Hotaling Arthur D. • USA
PEACEMEAL • 1967 • Allotta Albert • SHT • USA
PEACETIME see **BEKEIDO** • 1980
PEACETIME IN PARIS see **SEZONA MIRA U PARIZU** • 1981

PEACETIME SPIES • 1924 • Morrison Lee • UKN
PEACH AND A PAIR, A • 1915 • Christie Al • USA
PEACH AND A PILL, A • 1918 • *Rhodes Billie* • SHT • USA
PEACH AT THE BEACH, THE • 1914 • Neilan Marshall • USA
PEACH BOY see **TAKARAJIMA ENSEI** • 1956
PEACH BRAND, THE • 1914 • *Billington Francelia* • USA
PEACH GANG, THE • 1975 • Graham William A. • TVM • USA
PEACH O'RENO • 1931 • Seiter William A. • USA
PEACH PICKERS, THE • 1916 • *Hamilton Lloyd V.* • SHT • USA
PEACH THIEF, THE see **KRADETSAT NA PRASKOVI** • 1964
PEACHBASKET HAT, THE • 1909 • Griffith D. W. • USA
PEACHES, THE • 1964 • Gill Michael • SHT • UKN
PEACHES AND CREAM • 1982 • McCallum Robert • USA
PEACHES AND PLUMBERS • 1927 • *Sennett Mack (P)* • SHT • USA
PEACHES AND PONIES • 1916 • Ellis Robert • SHT • USA
PEACHY COBBLER, THE • 1950 • Avery Tex • ANS • USA
PEACOCK ALLEY • 1922 • Leonard Robert Z. • USA
PEACOCK ALLEY • 1930 • De Sano Marcel • USA
PEACOCK FAN, THE • 1929 • Rosen Phil • USA
PEACOCK FEATHER FAN, THE • 1914 • Pollard Harry • USA
PEACOCK FEATHERS • 1925 • Gade Svend • USA
PEACOCK FEATHERS see **OPEN THE DOOR AND SEE ALL THE PEOPLE** • 1964
PEACOCK PRINCESS, THE • ANM • CHN
PEACOCK'S PLACE see **AL TROPICO DEL CANCRO** • 1972
PEAK HOUR see **GODZINA SZCZYTU** • 1974
PEAK OF DESTINY see **BERG DES SCHICKSALS, DER** • 1924
PEAK OF FATE see **BERG DES SCHICKSALS, DER** • 1924
PEAKS OF DESTINY see **BERG DES SCHICKSALS, DER** • 1924
PEAKS OF ZELENGORE, THE (USA) see **VRHOVI ZELENGORE** • 1976
PEANUT BATTLE • 1962 • Rasinski Connie • ANS • USA
PEANUT BUTTER SOLUTION, THE • 1986 • Rubbo Michael • CND • SOLUTION BUERRE DE PINOTTES, LA ○ OPERATION BUERRE DE PINOTTES
PEANUT FUNERAL • Bennett David • SHT • USA
PEANUT VENDOR see **EXPERIMENTAL ANIMATION** • 1933
PEANUT VENDOR, THE • 1933 • Fleischer Dave • ANS • USA
PEANUTS AND BULLETS • 1915 • Cogley Nick • USA
PEANUTS AND POLITICS • 1918 • Howe J. A. • SHT • USA
PEANUTS AND POWDER • 1916 • MacMackin Archer • USA
PEAR-TREE OF MISERY, THE see **POIRIER DE MISERE, LE** • 1957
PEARL, THE • 1946 • Fernandez Emilio • USA, MXC
PEARL AND THE POET • 1913 • Smalley Phillips • USA
PEARL AND THE TRAMP • 1913 • Smalley Phillips • USA
PEARL AS A CLAIRVOYANT • 1913 • Smalley Phillips • USA
PEARL AS A DETECTIVE • 1913 • Smalley Phillips • USA
PEARL CRAZY • 1963 • Kuwahara Bob • ANS • USA
PEARL DIVERS, THE • 1960 • *Halas John (P)* • ANS • UKN
PEARL FISHER, THE • 1907 • *Pathe* • FRN
PEARL FOR PEARL • 1922 • Cooper George A. • UKN
PEARL IN THE CROWN see **PERLA W KORONIE** • 1972
PEARL IN THE DESERT, THE • 1964 • Joseph Stanley • DCS • UKN
PEARL IN THE WAVES see **ANO NAMI NO HATEMADE II** • 1961
PEARL LUST • 1936 • Harwood A. R. • ASL
PEARL OF DEATH, THE • 1944 • Neill R. William • USA • SHERLOCK HOLMES AND THE PEARL OF DEATH
PEARL OF GREAT PRICE, A • 1914 • *Truesdell Fred* • USA
PEARL OF GREATER PRICE, A • 1917 • Thayer Otis B. • SHT • USA
PEARL OF LOVE, THE • 1925 • Dadmun Leon E. • USA
PEARL OF PARADISE, THE • 1916 • Pollard Harry • USA
PEARL OF THE ANTILLES, THE • 1915 • Terriss Tom • USA
PEARL OF THE ARMY • 1916 • Jose Edward, Seitz George B. • SRL • USA
PEARL OF THE GOLDEN WEST, THE • 1913 • *Powers* • USA
PEARL OF THE PUNJAB, THE • 1914 • *Craig Nellie* • USA
PEARL OF THE SEA, THE • 1914 • *Maison Edna* • USA
PEARL OF THE SOUTH PACIFIC • 1955 • Dwan Allan • USA
PEARL OF THE SOUTH SEAS • 1927 • Hurley Frank • UKN
PEARL OF THE TLAYUCAN, THE (USA) see **TLAYUCAN** • 1961
PEARLED SERGEANT, THE see **INCILI CAVUS** • 1968
PEARLERS, THE • 1949 • Robinson Lee • DOC • ASL
PEARL'S ADMIRERS • 1913 • Smalley Phillips • USA
PEARLS AND A PEACH • 1918 • *Christie* • USA
PEARLS AND DEVIL-FISH • 1931 • Austin Harold • USA
PEARLS AND GIRLS • 1918 • Davis James • SHT • USA
PEARLS AND PERILS • 1917 • *Mccoy Harry* • SHT • USA
PEARLS AND SAVAGES • 1921 • Hurley Frank • DOC • ASL
PEARLS BRING TEARS • 1937 • Haynes Manning • UKN
PEARL'S DILEMMA • 1913 • Smalley Phillips • USA
PEARL'S HERO • 1913 • Smalley Phillips • USA
PEARL'S MISTAKE • 1913 • Smalley Phillips • USA
PEARLS OF DEATH • 1914 • Evans Joe • UKN
PEARLS OF PAULINE, THE • 1917 • *Pokes & Jabbs* • USA
PEARLS OF ST. LUCIA, THE see **TLAYUCAN** • 1961
PEARLS OF TEMPTATION • 1915 • *Balboa* • USA
PEARLS OF THE CROWN, THE (USA) see **PERLES DE LA COURONNE, LES** • 1937
PEARLS OF THE DEEP (UKN) see **PERLICKY NA DNE** • 1965
PEARLS OF THE MADONNA • 1913 • *Kinemacolor* • USA
PEARLS OF THE SOUTH SEAS see **HOUND OF THE DEEP** • 1926
PEARLS WITHOUT PRICE • 1918 • *Keystone* • SHT • USA
PEARLY YEATS, THE • 1971 • MacKay Bruce • CND
PEASANT, THE see **NHA QUE** • 1989
PEASANT CARELESS • Hempel Johannes • ANM • GDR
PEASANT GIRL'S REVENGE, A • 1912 • Buckland Warwick? • UKN
PEASANT GIRL'S REVENGE, THE • 1906 • Fitzhamon Lewin • UKN
PEASANT ISLAND • 1940 • Taylor Donald • DCS • UKN
PEASANT LETTER see **KADDU BEYKAT** • 1975
PEASANT MEMOIRS see **PAMIETNIKI CHLOPOW** • 1952
PEASANT ON A BICYCLE see **SELYANINUT S KOLELOTO** • 1974
PEASANT PRINCE, THE • 1909 • *Selig* • USA
PEASANT PSALM • 1989 • Verhavert Roland • BLG
PEASANT UPRISING IN 1573, THE see **SELJACKA BUNA 1573** • 1975
PEASANT WITH THE BICYCLE, THE see **SELYANINUT S KOLELOTO** • 1974
PEASANT WOMEN OF RIAZAN see **BABI RIAZANSKIE** • 1927
PEASANTS see **KRESTYANIYE** • 1935
PEASANTS see **KRESTYANYE** • 1972
PEASANTS see **CHLOPI** • 1974
PEASANTS see **CAMPESINOS** • 1976
PEASANTS IN MARCH • Nickel Gitta • DOC • GDR
PEASANT'S LIE, THE • 1914 • *Ab* • USA
PEASANTS OF THE SECOND FORTRESS, THE see **SANRIZUKA -DAINI TORIDE NO HITOBITO** • 1971
PEASANTS' REVOLT 1573, THE see **SELJACKA BUNA 1573** • 1975
PEASANT'S WEDDING, THE • 1939 • Wyckoff Alvin • USA
PEASANT'S WEDDING, THE • 1974 • Kohanyi Julius • CND
PEASHOOTER: OR, A NEW WEAPON FOR THE ARMY, THE • 1905 • Collins Alf? • UKN
PEAU D'ANE • 1908 • Velle Gaston • FRN • DONKEY SKIN
PEAU D'ANE • 1970 • Demy Jacques • FRN • MAGIC DONKEY, THE (UKN) ○ DONKEY SKIN (USA)
PEAU DE BANANE • 1964 • Ophuls Marcel • FRN, ITL • BANANA PEEL (USA) ○ BUCCIA DI BANANA
PEAU DE CHAGRIN • 1913 • Capellani Albert • FRN
PEAU DE CHAGRIN, LA • 1909 • Capellani Albert • FRN • WILD ASS'S SKIN, THE (USA)
PEAU DE CHAGRIN, LA • 1911 • Denola Georges • FRN
PEAU DE CHAGRIN, LA see **SAGRENSKA KOZA** • 1960
PEAU DE CHAGRINS • 1970 • Ramsay Richard • CND
PEAU DE L'OURS, LA • 1957 • Boissol Claude • FRN
PEAU DE PECHE • 1926 • Benoit-Levy Jean, Epstein Marie • FRN • PEAU-DE-PECHE
PEAU-DE-PECHE see **PEAU DE PECHE** • 1926
PEAU DE TORPEDO, LA • 1970 • Delannoy Jean • FRN, ITL • DOSSIER 212 -DESTINAZIONE MORTE (ITL) ○ PILL OF DEATH (UKN) ○ ONLY THE COOL (USA) ○ BLACK TORPEDOES ○ CHILDREN OF MATA HARI
PEAU D'ESPION • 1967 • Molinaro Edouard • FRN, ITL, FRG • CONGIURA DI SPIE (ITL) ○ TO COMMIT A MURDER (USA) ○ GRAUSAME JOB, DER (FRG)
PEAU DOUCE, LA • 1964 • Truffaut Francois • FRN • SOFT SKIN, THE (USA) ○ SILKEN SKIN
PEAU D'UN AUTRE, LA • 1936 • Pujol Rene • FRN
PEAU D'UN FLIC, LA • 1981 • Delon Alain • FRN
PEAU D'UN HOMME, LA • 1950 • Jolivet Rene • FRN
PEAU ET LES OS, LA • 1960 • Panijel Jacques, Sassy Jean-Paul • FRN • MAZUR FILE, THE
PEAU, LA (FRN) see **PELLE, LA** • 1981
PEAU NOIRE • 1930 • d'Esme Jean • DOC • FRN
PEAU SUR L'HERBE, LA • 1931 • Greville Edmond T. • FRN
PEBBLE BY THE WAYSIDE, A see **ROBO NO ISHI** • 1938
PEBBLES see **KIESELSTEINE** • 1983
PECADO • 1950 • Amadori Luis Cesar • MXC • COSAS DE MUJER
PECADO • 1961 • Blake Alfonso Corona • MXC, GTM
PECADO DE AMOR • 1961 • Amadori Luis Cesar • SPN
PECADO DE ANAN Y EVA, EL • 1967 • Zacarias Miguel • MXC • EVA Y ADAN, EL PRIMER PECADO ○ SIN OF ADAM AND EVE, THE (USA)
PECADO DE JUVENTUD • 1961 • de la Serna Mauricio • MXC
PECADO DE LAURA, EL • 1948 • Soler Julian • MXC
PECADO DE QUERERTE, EL • 1949 • Cortes Fernando • MXC
PECADO DE SER MUJER, EL • 1954 • Gomez Urquiza Zacarias • MXC
PECADO DE SER POBRE, EL • 1950 • Rivero Fernando A. • MXC
PECADO DE UNA MADRE, EL • 1943 • Pereda Ramon • MXC
PECADO DE UNA MADRE, EL • 1960 • Blake Alfonso Corona • MXC
PECADO MORTAL • 1954 • Delgado Miguel M. • MXC
PECADO MORTAL • 1971 • Faria Miguel Jr. • BRZ
PECADO MORTAL • 1976 • Diez Miguel Angel • SPN
PECADO ORIGINAL, EL • 1964 • Rodriguez-Soltero Jose • SHT • SPN • ORIGINAL SIN ○ SIN, THE
PECADO POR MES, UN • 1949 • Lugones Mario C. • ARG
PECADOR, EL • 1964 • Baledon Rafael • MXC
PECADOR Y LA BRUJA, EL • 1964 • Buchs Julio • SPN • SINNER AND THE WITCH, THE
PECADORA • 1947 • Diaz Morales Jose • MXC
PECADORA, LA • 1954 • Iquino Ignacio F. • SPN
PECADORAS, LAS • 1968 • Blake Alfonso Corona • MXC • SINNING WOMEN
PECADOS CONYUGALES • 1968 • Forque Jose Maria • SPN
PECADOS DE AMOR • 1933 • Kirkland David • MXC
PECADOS DE UNA CHICA CASI DECENTE, LOS • 1976 • Ozores Mariano • SPN
PECAT • 1955 • Makavejev Dusan • SHT • YGS • SEAL, THE
PECCARO MORTALE • 1975 • Rovira Beleta Francisco • ITL
PECCATI D'ESTATE • 1962 • Bianchi Giorgio • ITL
PECCATI DI GIOVENTU • 1975 • Amadio Silvio • ITL
PECCATI DI MADAME BOVARY, I (ITL) see **NACKTE BOVARY, DIE** • 1969
PECCATI IN FAMIGLIA • 1975 • Gaburro Bruno Alberto • ITL • SINS WITHIN THE FAMILY (UKN) ○ SINS IN THE FAMILY
PECCATO CHE SIA UNA CANAGLIA • 1955 • Blasetti Alessandro • ITL • TOO BAD SHE'S BAD (UKN)
PECCATO D'AMORE (ITL) see **LADY CAROLINE LAMB** • 1972
PECCATO DEGLI ANNI VERDI, IL • 1960 • Trieste Leopoldo • ITL
PECCATO DI ANNA, IL • 1953 • Mastrocinque Camillo • ITL • SIN OF ANNA, THE ○ ANNA'S SIN
PECCATO DI CASTITA • 1956 • Franciolini Gianni • ITL
PECCATO DI ROGELIA SANCHEZ, IL • 1939 • Borghesio Carlo, de Ribon Roberto • ITL, SPN • SANTA ROGELIA (SPN) ○ DONNE DI SPAGNA
PECCATO SENZA MALIZIA • 1975 • Campanelli Theo • ITL
PECCATO VENIALE • 1974 • Samperi Salvatore • ITL • LOVERS AND OTHER RELATIVES ○ VENIAL SIN
PECCATORI DELLA FORESTA NERA, I (ITL) see **CHAMBRE ARDENTE, LA** • 1961
PECCATORI DI PROVINCIA • 1977 • Longo Tiziano • ITL
PECCATORI IN BLUE-JEANS (ITL) see **TRICHEURS, LES** • 1958
PECCATRICE, LA • 1940 • Palermi Amleto • ITL
PECCATRICE, LA • 1975 • Pavoni Pier Ludovico • ITL
PECCATRICE DEL DESERTO, LA • 1959 • Vernuccio Gianni, Sekely Steve • ITL, USA • DESERT DESPERADOES (USA) ○ SINNER, THE (UKN)
PECCATRICE DELL'ISOLA, LA • 1953 • Corbucci Sergio • ITL • ISLAND SINNER, THE (USA)
PECCATRICE SENZA PECCATO • 1923 • Genina Augusto • ITL
PECCATRICI CASTA, LA • 1918 • Righelli Gennaro • ITL
PECES ROJOS, LOS • 1955 • Nieves Conde Jose Antonio • SPN
PECHE, LA • 1937-40 • Tessier Albert • DCS • CND
PECHE, LE see **HARAM, AL-** • 1964
PECHE A L'ANGUILLE, LA • 1975 • Plamondon Leo • DCS • CND
PECHE AU SAUMON ET A LA TRUITE EN GASPESIE, LA • 1939 • Proulx Maurice • DCS • CND
PECHE AUX HARENGS, UNE • 1930 • Storck Henri • DOC • BLG
PECHE AUX POISSONS ROUGES • 1895 • Lumiere Louis • FRN
PECHE DANS LES NUAGES, LA see **SKY FISHING** • 1934
PECHE DE JEUNESSE • 1958 • Duchesne Louis • FRN
PECHE DU CAPITAINE, LA • 1965-66 • Garceau Raymond • DCS • CND
PECHE ET LE CULTE DE LA MER see **MAMY WATER** • 1955
PECHE TRES DOUCE • 1971 • Audy Michel • DCS • CND
PECHERIES, LES • 1965-66 • Garceau Raymond • DCS • CND
PECHES DE JEUNESSE • 1941 • Tourneur Maurice • FRN • SINS OF YOUTH (USA)
PECHEUR DANS LE TORRENT, LE • 1897 • Blache Alice • FRN
PECHEUR D'ISLANDE • 1915 • Pouctal Henri • FRN
PECHEUR D'ISLANDE • 1924 • de Baroncelli Jacques • FRN
PECHEUR D'ISLANDE • 1933 • Guerlais Pierre • FRN
PECHEUR D'ISLANDE • 1959 • Schoendoerffer Pierre • FRN
PECHEURS, LES see **FISHERMEN** • 1959
PECHEURS, LES see **RAYHA WINE** • 1976
PECHEURS DE POMCOUP • 1956 • Forest Leonard • DCS • CND
PECHEURS DU NIGER • 1962 • Rouch Jean • DCS • FRN
PECHKI-LAVOCHKI • 1972 • Shukshin Vassili • USS • PECKI-LOVOCKI
PECHMARIE • 1934 • Engel Erich • FRG
PECHORIN'S NOTES see **ZAPISKI PECHORINA** • 1967
PECHVOGEL, DER see **ZU BEFEHL, HERR UNTEROFFIZIER** • 1931
PECK O' PICKLES • 1916 • Heffron Thomas N. • USA
PECK O' TROUBLE, A • 1953 • McKimson Robert • ANS • USA
PECK OF TROUBLE, A • 1968 • Smith Paul J. • ANS • USA
PECK UP YOUR TROUBLES • 1945 • Freleng Friz • ANS • USA
PECK YOUR OWN HOME • 1960 • Kneitel Seymour • ANS • USA
PECKI-LOVOCKI see **PECHKI-LAVOCHKI** • 1972
PECKING HOLES IN POLES • 1972 • Smith Paul J. • ANS • USA
PECK'S BAD BOY • 1908 • *Essanay* • USA
PECK'S BAD BOY • 1921 • Wood Sam • USA
PECK'S BAD BOY • 1934 • Cline Eddie • USA
PECK'S BAD BOY WITH THE CIRCUS • 1938 • Cline Eddie • USA
PECK'S BAD GIRL • 1918 • Giblyn Charles • USA
PECORA NERA, LA • 1968 • Salce Luciano • ITL • BLACK SHEEP, THE
PECOS BILL • 1946 • *Disney Walt (P)* • ANS • USA
PECOS BILL, KING OF THE COWBOYS • 1986 • Storm Howard • USA
PECOS DANDY, THE • 1934 • Carpenter Horace B.?, Adamson Victor? • USA
PECOS E QUI: PREGA E MUORI • 1967 • Lucidi Maurizio • ITL
PECOS KID, THE • 1935 • Berke William • USA
PECOS PETE • 1955 • Hanna William, Barbera Joseph • ANS • USA
PECOS PETE IN SEARCH OF A WIFE • 1913 • *American* • USA
PECOS PISTOL, THE • 1949 • Cowan Will • SHT • USA
PECOS RIVER • 1951 • Sears Fred F. • USA • WITHOUT RISK (UKN)
PECULIAR CABINET, A see **CABINET PARTICULIER, UN** • 1902
PECULIAR INHERITANCE, A • 1914 • *Melies* • USA
PECULIAR NATURE OF THE WHITE MAN'S BURDEN, THE • 1912 • *Selig* • USA
PECULIAR PATIENTS' PRANKS • 1915 • Roach Hal • USA
PECULIAR PENGUINS • 1934 • Jackson Wilfred • ANS • USA
PECULIAR PEOPLE • 1908 • *Pathe* • FRN
PEDAGOGIC POEM see **PEDAGOGUTCHESKAIA POEMA** • 1956
PEDAGOGICAL INSTITUTION (COLLEGE TO YOU) • 1940 • Fleischer Dave • ANS • USA
PEDAGOGUTCHESKAIA POEMA • 1956 • Maslyukov Alexei, Maievskaia A. • USS • POEM OF YOUTH ○ PEDAGOGIC POEM
PEDAGOSKA BAJKA • 1961 • Makavejev Dusan • SHT • YGS • EDUCATIONAL FAIRY TALE
PEDALES SOBRE CUBA • 1965 • Alvarez Santiago • DOC • CUB • PEDALS OVER CUBA
PEDALS OVER CUBA see **PEDALES SOBRE CUBA** • 1965
PEDANG SAKTI • 1971 • Sudarmadji S. • MLY • INVINCIBLE SWORD, THE
PEDARASI PEDDAMMA KATHA • 1968 • Suryam G. • IND • MAKE-BELIEVE TALES
PEDDA AKKAYYA • 1967 • Subba Rao B. A. • IND • ELDEST SISTER
PEDDLER see **KRAMARZ** • 1990
PEDDLER, THE • 1913 • Lehrman Henry, Sennett Mack (Spv) • USA
PEDDLER, THE • 1917 • Blache Herbert • USA
PEDDLER, THE • 1981 • Glykofridis Panos • GRC • PEDLAR, THE
PEDDLER, THE • 1987 • Makhmalbaf Mohsen • IRN
PEDDLER AND THE LADY, THE (USA) see **CAMPO DE' FIORI** • 1943
PEDDLER OF LIES, THE • 1920 • Dowlan William C. • USA
PEDDLER'S BAG, THE • 1914 • O'Sullivan Tony • USA
PEDDLER'S FIND, THE • 1912 • *Reliance* • USA

PEDDLERS OF EVIL see **PEDDLERS OF SIN** • 1966
PEDDLERS OF SIN • 1966 • *Harris Jerry* • USA • PEDDLERS OF EVIL
PEDDLER'S REWARD, THE • 1909 • *Urban-Eclipse* • USA
PEDDLIN' IN SOCIETY • Righelli Gennaro • ITL
PEDDLING PATRICK PINCHES POULTRY • 1910 • *Wrench Films* • UKN
PEDESTALS • 1985 • Jackson G. Philip • MTV • CND
PEDESTRIAN see **PJESAK** • 1969
PEDESTRIAN, THE • Muresan Mircea • RMN
PEDESTRIAN, THE • 1960 • Lehr George • SHT • USA
PEDESTRIAN, THE (USA) see **FUSSGANGER, DER** • 1974
PEDESTRIAN SAFETY • 1952 • Barclay David • SHT • USA
PEDICAB DRIVER, THE • 1979 • Umboh Wim • INN
PEDICURE, THE see **MAX PEDICURE** • 1914
PEDIGREES, PUPS AND PUSSIES • 1916 • Humphrey Orral • USA
PEDIGUENOS, LOS • 1961 • Leblanc Tony • SPN
PEDLAR, THE • 1982 • Kroeker Allan • CND
PEDLAR, THE see **PEDDLER, THE** • 1981
PEDLAR OF PENMAENMAWR, THE • 1912 • Northcote Sidney • UKN
PEDLAR OF POESY, THE • 1959 • Sens Al • ANS • CND
PEDON MERKKI • 1982 • Pakkasvirta Jaakko • FNL • SIGN OF THE BEAST
PEDRAS DE PORTUGAL • 1933 • Vieira Manuel Luis • SHT • PRT
PEDRO AND LORENZO • 1956 • Tendlar Dave • ANS • USA
PEDRO DIABO AMA ROSA MEIA: NOITE • 1971 • Faria Miguel Jr. • BRZ
PEDRO MICO • 1986 • Fontes Ipojuca • BRZ • PETER MONKEY
PEDRO PARAMO • 1966 • Velo Carlos • MXC
PEDRO SO • 1972 • Tropa Alfredo • PRT
PEDRO SOLL HANGEN • 1941 • Harlan Veit • FRG
PEDRO THE PUNK POET • 1916 • *Yorke Jay C.* • USA
PEDRO'S DILEMMA • 1912 • Sennett Mack • USA
PEDRO'S REVENGE • 1913 • *Lyman Laura* • USA
PEDRO'S TREACHERY • 1913 • *Fielding Romaine* • USA
PEDRUCHO • 1925 • Vorins Henri • FRN
PEE-KOOL-YAR SIT-CHEE-AY-SHUN, A • 1944 • Marcus Sid • ANS • USA
PEE-MAK • Lee Doo-Yong • SKR • HOUSE OF DEATH
PEE WEE KING'S COUNTRY WESTERN HOEDOWN see **COUNTRY WESTERN HOEDOWN** • 1967
PEE-WEE'S BIG ADVENTURE • 1985 • Burton Tim • USA
PEEGEROWCY • 1970 • Gryczelowska Krystyna • DOC • PLN • PEOPLE FROM STATE FARMS
PEEK-A-BOO • 1930 • Newfield Sam • SHT • USA
PEEK-A-BOO (USA) see **AH! LES BELLES BACCHANTES** • 1954
PEEK SNATCHERS, THE • 1965 • *Broadway Roadshow Dist.* • USA
PEEKABOO • 1957 • Kneitel Seymour • ANS • USA
PEEKING IN PEKING • 1931 • Edwards Harry J. • SHT • USA
PEEKING TOM see **PEEPING TOM** • 1933
PEEL • 1983 • Campion Jane • SHT • ASL
PEEP BEHIND THE SCENES, A • 1918 • Malins Geoffrey H., Foss Kenelm • UKN
PEEP BEHIND THE SCENES, A • 1929 • Raymond Jack • UKN
PEEP IN THE DARK, A • Catling Darrell • DCS • UKN
PEEP IN THE DARK, A • 1940 • *Mintz Charles (P)* • ANS • USA
PEEP IN THE DEEP • 1946 • Kneitel Seymour • ANS • USA
PEEP SHOW • 1957 • Russell Ken • SHT • UKN
PEEP SHOW • 1981 • Egoyan Atom • CND
PEEP-SHOW see **SHAHRFARANG** • 1967
PEEP SHOW, THE • 1962 • Pindal Kaj • ANS • CND
PEEP SHOWS OF PARIS see **FRENCH PEEP SHOW** • 1952
PEEPER • 1975 • Hyams Peter • USA • FAT CHANCE
PEEPER, THE • 1961 • Coppola Francis Ford • SHT • USA
PEEPER, THE see **PEEPING TOM** • 1960
PEEPING PENGUINS • 1937 • Fleischer Dave • ANS • USA
PEEPING PETE • 1913 • Sennett Mack, Sterling Ford • USA
PEEPING PHANTOM, THE • 1964 • *All-American Film Producers* • USA • HOW TO SUCCEED WITH GIRLS
PEEPING TOM • 1899 • *Wolff Philipp* • UKN
PEEPING TOM • 1905 • Green Tom? • UKN
PEEPING TOM • 1933 • Santley Joseph • SHT • USA • PEEKING TOM
PEEPING TOM • 1960 • Powell Michael • UKN • FACE OF FEAR ○ PEEPER, THE
PEEPING TOM, THE see **PAQUERAS, OS** • 1969
PEEPING TOM AT THE SEASIDE see **INDISCRET AUX BAINS DE MER, L'** • 1897
PEEPING TOMS • 1973 • Zohar Uri • ISR
PEEPING TOMS, THE see **INDISCRETS, LES** • 1896
PEEPS INTO PUZZLELAND • 1922 • Quiribet Gaston • UKN
PEER GYNT • 1915 • Apfel Oscar • USA
PEER GYNT • 1934 • Wendhausen Fritz • FRG
PEER GYNT • 1941 • Bradley David • USA
PEER GYNT • 1965 • Bradley David • USA
PEER GYNT 1 • 1918 • Oswald Richard, Barnowsky Victor • FRG • PEER GYNTS JUGEND
PEER GYNT 2 • 1918 • Oswald Richard, Barnowsky Victor • FRG • PEER GYNTS WANDERJAHRE UND TOD
PEER GYNTS JUGEND see **PEER GYNT 1** • 1918
PEER GYNTS WANDERJAHRE UND TOD see **PEER GYNT 2** • 1918
PEERLESS PATRIOT see **KOKASHI MUSO** • 1932
PEERS, THE see **ARMI E GLI AMORI, LE** • 1983
PEESUA LAE DOKMAI • 1985 • Mukdasanit Euthana • THL • BUTTERFLY AND FLOWERS
PEFTOUN I SFAIRES SAN TO HALAZI • 1977 • Alevras Nikos • GRC • BULLETS STRIKE LIKE HAILSTONES
PEG LEG PETE • 1932 • *Terry Paul/ Moser Frank (P)* • ANS • USA
PEG LEG PETE, THE PIRATE • 1935 • *Terry Paul/ Moser Frank (P)* • ANS • USA
PEG O' MY HEART • 1919 • De Mille William C. • USA
PEG O' MY HEART • 1922 • Vidor King • USA
PEG O' MY HEART • 1933 • Leonard Robert Z. • USA
PEG O' THE PIRATES • 1918 • Lund O. A. C. • USA
PEG O' THE RING see **ADVENTURES OF PEG O' THE RING, THE** • 1916
PEG O' THE SEA • 1917 • Nowland Eugene • USA
PEG O' THE WILD-WOOD • 1914 • Morrisey Edward • USA
PEG OF OLD DRURY • 1935 • Wilcox Herbert • UKN
PEG OF THE "POLLY P." • 1913 • *Prescott Vivian* • USA
PEG O'THE MOVIES • 1913 • *Wilson Ben F.* • USA
PEG O'THE WILDS • 1914 • *Mersereau Violet* • USA
PEG WOFFINGTON • 1910 • Porter Edwin S. • USA
PEG WOFFINGTON • 1912 • Coleby A. E. • UKN
PEGANDO CON TUBO • 1960 • Salvador Jaime • MXC
PEGANTIN BARU • 1986 • INN
PEGASUS • 1973 • Servais Raoul • ANM • BLG
PEGEEN • 1920 • Smith David • USA
PEGGIE AND THE ROUNDHEADS • 1912 • Coleby A. E. • UKN
PEGGIO PER ME.. MEGLIO PER TE • 1967 • Corbucci Bruno • ITL • WORSE FOR ME.. BETTER FOR YOU
PEGGIORI ANNI DELLA NOSTRA VITA, I • 1950 • Amendola Mario • ITL
PEGGY • 1916 • Giblyn Charles • USA
PEGGY • 1950 • De Cordova Frederick • USA
PEGGY AND PUDDY • 1915 • *Zenith Films* • USA
PEGGY AND THE LAW • 1916 • Ridgwell George • SHT • USA
PEGGY AND THE OLD SCOUT • 1913 • *Pathe* • USA
PEGGY AS PEACEMAKER • 1913 • Batley Ethyle • UKN
PEGGY BECOMES A BOY SCOUT • 1912 • Batley Ethyle • UKN
PEGGY DOES HER DARNDEST • 1919 • Baker George D. • USA
PEGGY GETS RID OF THE BABY • 1912 • Batley Ethyle • UKN
PEGGY LEADS THE WAY • 1917 • Ingraham Lloyd • USA
PEGGY LINN, BURGLAR • 1915 • Taylor William D. • USA
PEGGY MIXES IN • 1918 • *Christie* • USA
PEGGY OF FIFTH AVENUE • 1915 • North Wilfred • USA
PEGGY OF PRIMROSE LANE • 1914 • Le Saint Edward J. • USA
PEGGY OF THE SECRET SERVICE • 1925 • McGowan J. P. • USA
PEGGY ON A SPREE see **PEGGY PA VIFT** • 1946
PEGGY PA VIFT • 1946 • Mattsson Arne • SWD • PEGGY ON A SPREE
PEGGY, PEG AND POLLY • 1950 • Cowan Will • ANS • USA
PEGGY PUTS IT OVER • 1921 • Seyffertitz G. V. • USA
PEGGY REBELS see **MATE OF THE SALLY ANN, THE** • 1917
PEGGY SUE GOT MARRIED • 1986 • Coppola Francis Ford • USA
PEGGY, THE MOONSHINER'S DAUGHTER • 1911 • *Kalem* • USA
PEGGY, THE WILL O' THE WISP see **PEGGY, WILL O' THE WISP** • 1917
PEGGY, WILL O' THE WISP • 1917 • Browning Tod • USA • PEGGY, THE WILL O' THE WISP
PEGGY WISE • 1920 • La Maie Elsier • USA
PEGGY'S BLUE SKYLIGHT • 1985 • Wieland Joyce • SHT • USA
PEGGY'S BURGLAR • 1913 • Ince Ralph • USA
PEGGY'S BURGLAR • 1919 • *Strand* • SHT • USA
PEGGY'S INVITATION • 1913 • *Snow Marguerite* • USA
PEGGY'S NEW PAPA • 1914 • Batley Ethyle • UKN
PEGGY'S PRESENT • 1915 • *Britannia* • UKN
PEGGY'S SWEETHEARTS • 1915 • *L-Ko* • USA
PEGLEG, MUSKET AND SABRE see **SCALAWAG** • 1973
PEGRE DE PARIS, LA • 1906 • Blache Alice • FRN
PEHAVY MAX A STRASIDLA • 1987 • Jakubisko Juraj • CZC, FRG • MAX AND THE GHOSTS
PEHLA ADMI • 1948 • Roy Bimal • IND • PAHELA ADMI
PEHLIVAN • 1964 • Pialat Maurice • SHT • FRN
PEHNIDHIARA, I • 1967 • Kiriakopoulos Hristos • GRC • GAMES
PEI-CH'ING CH'ENG-SHIH • 1989 • Hou Hsiao-Hsien • TWN • CITY OF SADNESS, A (UKN)
PEI-KUO-CH'I-TE JEN • 1981 • Liu Chia-Ch'Ang • HKG • FLAG, THE
PEI NAN HSI TUNG • 1984 • Ts'Ai Chi-Kuang, Lin Ch'Ing-Chieh • TWN, HKG • NORTH SOUTH WEST EAST
PEINE D'AMOUR • 1914 • Fescourt Henri • FRN
PEINE DE MORT A TRAVERS LES AGES, LA see **EXECUTIONS CAPITALES, LES** • 1906
PEINE DU TALION, LA • 1906 • Capellani Albert • FRN
PEINE DU TALION, LA • 1906 • Velle Gaston • FRN
PEINE DU TALION, LA • 1916 • Feuillade Louis • FRN
PEINTRE BARBOUILLARD ET TABLEAU DIABOLIQUE, LE • 1905 • Melies Georges • FRN • MR. DAUBER AND THE MYSTIFYING PICTURES (USA)
PEINTRE ET IVROGNE • 1905 • Blache Alice • FRN
PEINTRE NEO-IMPRESSIONISTE, LE • 1910 • Cohl Emile • ANS • FRN • NEO-IMPRESSIONIST PAINTER, THE (USA)
PEINTRE PAR AMOUR see **MAX PEINTRE PAR AMOUR** • 1912
PEINTRES POPULAIRES DE CHARLEVOIX • 1946 • Palardy Jean • DCS • CND • PRIMITIVE PAINTERS OF CHARLEVOIX
PEINTURE A L'ENVERS • 1898 • Lumiere Louis • FRN • LIGHTNING ARTIST
PEINTURE ALGERIENNE, LA • 1969 • Cherif Hachemi • SHT • ALG
PEINTURE ET LES COCHONS, LA • 1912 • Machin Alfred • NTH
PEINTURE NO.1, LA • 1973 • Duceppe Pierre • DCS • CND
PEIT HEIN • 1968 • Bonniere Rene • DCS • CND
PEITSCHE, DIE • 1916 • Gartner Adolf • FRG
PEITSCHENDE SINNE • 1923 • *Otto Glucksmann & Co* • FRG
PEITSCHENHIEB, DER • 1918 • Moest Hubert • FRG
PEJZAZ POTWOROWSKIEGO • 1966 • Mucha Kazimierz • PLN • POTWOROWSKI'S LANDSCAPE
PEJZAZ Z BOHATEREM • 1970 • Haupe Wlodzimierz • PLN • LANDSCAPE WITH A HERO, THE ○ LANDSCAPE WITH HERO
PEKARUV CISAR • 1951 • Fric Martin • CZC • BAKER'S EMPEROR, THE
PEKING • 1938 • Kamei Fumio • JPN
PEKING BLONDE (USA) see **BLONDE DE PEKIN, LA** • 1968
PEKING EXPRESS • 1951 • Dieterle William • USA
PEKING MAN MYSTERY, THE • 1977 • Rasky Harry • CND
PEKING MEDALLION, THE (UKN) see **SIGILLO DI PECHINO, IL** • 1966
PEKING OPERA BLUES see **DAO MA DAN** • 1987
PEKING PALOTAI • 1957 • Jancso Miklos • SHT • HNG • PALACES OF PEKING
PELE • 1977 • Reichenbach Francois • DOC • FRN, MXC • ROI PELE, LE
PELE-MELE CINEMATOGRAPHIQUE • 1912 • Cohl Emile • ANS • FRN
PELEA CUBANA CONTRA LOS DEMONIOS, UNA • 1971 • Alea Tomas Gutierrez • CUB • CUBAN FIGHT AGAINST THE DEMONS, A ○ CUBAN STRUGGLE AGAINST THE DEMONS, A
PELEGRINO, IL • 1918 • Ghione Emilio • ITL
PELERIN PERDU, LE • 1962 • Jorre Guy • FRN • LOST PILGRIM, THE
PELERINAGE 1963 • 1963 • Khalifa Omar • TNS
PELERINAGE A LA MECQUE see **PELERINS DE LA MECQUE** • 1940
PELERINS DE LA MECQUE • 1940 • Ichac Marcel • DCS • FRN • PELERINAGE A LA MECQUE
PELERINS DE LA MER, LES • 1957 • See Jean-Claude • FRN
PELICAN, LE • 1973 • Blain Gerard • FRN
PELICAN, THE see **"MARRIAGE LICENSE?"** • 1926
PELICAN, THE see **PELICANO, EL** • 1971
PELICAN AND THE SNIPE, THE • 1944 • Luske Hamilton • ANS • USA
PELICANO, EL • 1971 • Carretero Amaro • ANS • SPN • PELICAN, THE
PELICAN'S BILL, THE • 1926 • Lantz Walter • ANS • USA
PELICULA DEL REY, LA • 1986 • Sorin Carlos • ARG • KING'S FILM, THE
PELIGRO DE AMOR • 1976 • Ulloa Jose • SPN
PELIGROS DE JUVENTUD • 1959 • Alazraki Benito • MXC
PELILEO EARTHQUAKE • 1949 • Leacock Richard • DOC • USA
PELL STREET MYSTERY, THE • 1924 • Franz Joseph J. • USA
PELLE, LA • 1981 • Cavani Liliana • ITL, FRN • PEAU, LA (FRN) ○ SKIN, THE
PELLE A SCACCHI, LA • 1969 • Sala Adimaro • ITL • DISTACCO, IL
PELLE DEGLI ALTRI, LA • 1972 • Marzano Marino • ITL • NIGERIA IN FIAMME
PELLE DI BANDITO • 1969 • Livi Piero • ITL
PELLE EROBREREN • 1987 • August Bille • DNM, SWD • PELLE THE CONQUEROR (USA)
PELLE SVANSLOS • 1979 • Lasseby Stig • ANM • SWD • PETEY NO-TAIL ○ PETER-NO-TAIL
PELLE SVANSLOS I AMERIKATT • 1983 • Lasseby Stig • ANM • SWD, DNM • PETER-NO-TAIL IN AMERICA
PELLE THE CONQUEROR (USA) see **PELLE EROBREREN** • 1987
PELLE VIVA • 1964 • Fina Giuseppe • ITL
PELLEAS AND MELISANDE • 1913 • MacDonald Mr. • USA
PELLEGRINI D'AMORE • 1955 • Forzano Andrea • ITL
PELLI ROJU • 1968 • Appa M. • IND • WEDDING DAY, THE
PELLICCIA DI VISONE, UNA • 1956 • Pellegrini Glauco • ITL
PELLY BAY • 1961 • Kelly Ron • DOC • CND
PELO NEL MONDO, IL • 1964 • Margheriti Antonio, Marvi Renato • ITL • GO, GO, GO WORLD! (USA) ○ WEIRD, WICKED WORLD ○ WICKED WORLD
PELOTA DE TRAPO • 1948 • Torres-Rios Leopoldo • ARG
PELOTARI • 1964 • Basterretxea Nestor, Larruquert Fernando • SHT • SPN
PELOTON D'EXECUTION • 1945 • Berthomieu Andre • FRN • RESISTANCE (USA)
PELUDOPOLIS • 1931 • Cristiani Quirino • ANM • ARG
PELUMBA MALAM • 1989 • Adam Abdul Rahman • MLY
PELUQUERO DE SENORAS • 1971 • *Prod. Film. Real* • MXC
PELUSA • 1961 • Seto Javier • SPN
PELVIS • 1977 • Megginson R. T. • USA
PEMBERTON VALLEY, THE • 1957 • King Allan • CND
PEMBURU • 1982 • Razali Rahim • MLY
PEN AND INK VAUDEVILLE • 1924-25 • *Hurd Earl (P)* • ASS • USA
PEN AND THE RIFLE, THE see **PIORO I KARABIN** • 1961
PEN-HI GRAD • 1974 • Wilson Sandra • CND
PEN KNIFE, THE see **SCYZORYK** • 1962
PEN POINT PERCUSSION • 1951 • McLaren Norman • SHT • CND
PEN VULTURE, THE see **PEN VULTURES** • 1918
PEN VULTURES • 1918 • *Hamilton Shorty* • USA • PEN VULTURE, THE
PENA DE MUERTE • 1961 • Forn Josep Maria • SPN • INOCENTE, EL
PENA DE MUERTE • 1973 • Grau Jorge • SPN • DEATH PENALTY
PENAGIH DADAH • 1977 • Sentul Mat • MLY • DRUG ADDICT
PENAL CAMP see **COLONIA PENAL, LA** • 1971
PENAL CODE, THE • 1933 • Melford George • USA
PENAL COLONY, THE see **COLONIA PENAL, LA** • 1971
PENAL SERVITUDE see **KATORGA** • 1928
PENALTIES OF REPUTATION, THE • 1913 • Humphrey William • USA
PENALTY, THE • 1911 • *American* • USA
PENALTY, THE • 1912 • *101 Bison* • USA
PENALTY, THE • 1912 • *Feature Photoplay* • USA
PENALTY, THE • 1915 • Myers Ray • USA
PENALTY, THE • 1920 • Worsley Wallace • USA
PENALTY, THE • 1941 • Bucquet Harold S. • USA • ROOSTY
PENALTY, THE see **AGIR SUC** • 1967
PENALTY OF BEAUTY, THE • 1909 • Fitzhamon Lewin • UKN
PENALTY OF CRIME, THE • 1913 • Smiley Joseph • USA
PENALTY OF FAME, THE see **GUDERNES YNDLING** • 1919
PENALTY OF FAME (UKN) see **OKAY AMERICA** • 1932
PENALTY OF INTEMPERANCE, THE • 1912 • *Mackenzie Donald* • USA
PENALTY OF JEALOUSY, THE • 1913 • *Fielding Romaine* • USA
PENALTY OF SILENCE, THE • 1917 • *Reid Wallace* • SHT • USA
PENALTY OF TREASON, THE • 1916 • Gerrard Douglas • SHT • USA
PENALTY PAID, THE • 1912 • *Pathe* • USA

PENALTY PHASE • 1986 • Richardson Tony • TVM • USA
PENAREK BECHA • Ramlee P. • MLY • RICKSHAW PULLER, THE
PENCE • 1917 • Simavi Sedat • TRK
PENCIL AND INDIA RUBBER see **CERUZA ES RADIR** • 1960
PENCIL AND RUBBER see **CERUZA ES RADIR** • 1960
PENCIL AND THE FIRE-BIRD • Shirman N. • ANS • USS
PENCIL CLUE, THE • 1916 • Ellis Robert • SHT • USA
PENCIL MANIA • 1932 • Foster John, Stallings George • ANS • USA
PENCIL MURDER • 1983 • Thys Guy Lee • BLG
PENDAISON A JEFFERSON CITY • 1911 • Durand Jean • FRN
PENDEKAR • 1976 • Amin M. • MLY • WARRIOR, THE
PENDEKAR SAKTI • 1971 • Kadarisman S. • MLY • AVENGER, THE
PENDENTIF, LE • 1921 • Colombier Piere • FRN
PENDERECKI, LUTOSLAWA • 1977 • Zanussi Krzysztof • PLN
PENDIENTE, EL • 1951 • Klimovsky Leon • SPN
PENDING EXAM see **ASIGNATURA PENDIENTE** • 1977
PENDU, LE • 1906 • Gasnier Louis J. • FRN
PENDULE, A SALOMON, LA • 1961 • Ivernel Vicky • FRN
PENDULUM • 1969 • Schaefer George • USA
PENDULUM, THE (UKN) see **HOOK AND LADDER NO.9** • 1927
PENDULUM OF CHANCE • 1916 • Ricketts Thomas • SHT • USA
PENDULUM OF FATE, THE • 1913 • Kirkland Hardee • USA
PENDULUM OF FATE, THE • 1914 • *Anderson Mignon* • USA
PENE NEL VENTRE, LE see **OSCENO DISIDERIO, L'** • 1978
PENELOPA • 1977 • Uher Stefan • CZC • PENELOPE
PENELOPE • 1966 • Hiller Arthur • USA
PENELOPE see **PENELOPA** • 1977
PENELOPE FOLLE DE SON CORPS • 1974 • Magrou Alain • FRN
PENELOPE OU L'HIVER A KERMAREC • 1972 • Magrou Alain • FRN • PENELOPE (UKN)
PENELOPE PULLS IT OFF • 1975 • Curran Peter • UKN, FRG • SEXY PENELOPE
PENELOPE (UKN) see **PENELOPE OU L'HIVER A KERMAREC** • 1972
PENELOPE'S LOVERS see **MNISTIRES TIS PINELOPIS, I** • 1968
PENENTUAN • 1982 • Jaafar Aziz • MLY
PENETRATION • 1974 • Stuart Falcon • UKN
PENETRATIONS HUMIDES • 1977 • Baudricourt Michel • FRN
PENETRATIONS LUBRIQUES • 1979 • Bernard-Aubert Claude • FRN
PENETRATIONS MULTIPLES • 1978 • Strong Mike • FRN
PENETRATIONS SPECIALES • 1978 • Baudricourt Michel • FRN
PENFOLD'S WINERY AT MAGILL • 1916 • *Marden Frank (Ph)* • ASL
PENGAR • 1945 • Kjellgren Lars-Eric • SWD
PENGAR • 1946 • Poppe Nils • SWD • PENGAR -EN TRAGIKOMISK SAGA ○ MONEY
PENGAR -EN TRAGIKOMISK SAGA see **PENGAR** • 1946
PENGAR FRAN SKYN • 1939 • Hasso Harry • SWD • MONEY FROM THE SKY
PENGE • 1916 • Mantzius • DNM • MONEY
PENGE OG OKONOMI • 1954 • Carlsen Henning • SHT • DNM
PENGENE ELLER LIVET • 1982 • Carlsen Henning • DNM • YOUR MONEY OR YOUR LIFE
PENGENES MAGT • 1915 • Davidsen Hjalmar • DNM
PENGUIN, THE see **PINGWIN** • 1965
PENGUIN FOR YOUR THOUGHTS • 1956 • Kneitel Seymour • ANS • USA
PENGUIN PARADE • 1938 • Avery Tex • ANS • USA
PENGUIN POOL MURDER, THE • 1932 • Archainbaud George • USA • PENGUIN POOL MYSTERY, THE (UKN)
PENGUIN POOL MYSTERY, THE (UKN) see **PENGUIN POOL MURDER, THE** • 1932
PENICILLIN FOR THE GENERAL PRACTITIONER • Massy Jane • DOC • UKN
PENIS • 1965 • Rose A. J. Jr. • USA • 1967
PENITENT, THE • 1912 • *Bayne Beverly* • USA
PENITENT, THE • 1988 • Osmond Cliff • USA
PENITENTES, THE • 1915 • Conway Jack • USA
PENITENTIARY • 1938 • Brahm John • USA
PENITENTIARY • 1979 • Fanaka Jamaa • USA
PENITENTIARY II • 1982 • Fanaka Jamaa • USA
PENITENTIARY III • 1987 • Fanaka Jamaa • USA
PENIZE NEBO ZIVOT • 1932 • Honzl Jindrich • CZC • YOUR MONEY OR YOUR LIFE ○ MONEY OR YOUR LIFE
PENLEVE CASE, THE see **SLUCHAYAT PENLEVE** • 1968
PENN AND TELLER GET KILLED • 1989 • Penn Arthur • USA
PENN ENDRAAL PENN • 1967 • Arurdoss • IND • GIRL IS A GIRL, A
PENN OF PENNSYLVANIA • 1941 • Comfort Lance • UKN • COURAGEOUS MR. PENN, THE (USA)
PENNANT PUZZLE, THE • 1912 • *Lancaster John* • USA
PENNE NERE • 1953 • Biancoli Oreste • ITL
PENNIES FROM HEAVEN • 1936 • McLeod Norman Z. • USA
PENNIES FROM HEAVEN • 1981 • Ross Herbert • USA
PENNILESS MILLIONAIRE, THE • 1921 • Bruun Einar J. • UKN
PENNILESS PRINCE, THE • 1911 • *Imp* • USA
PENNILESS YOUTH see **MIAS PENTARAS NIATA** • 1967
PENNINGTON'S CHOICE • 1915 • Bowman William J. • USA
PENNY see **KISKRACAR** • 1954
PENNY AND ANN • 1974 • Vitale Frank • CND
PENNY AND THE POWNALL CASE • 1948 • Hand Slim • UKN
PENNY ANTE • 1919 • Lyons Eddie, Moran Lee • SHT • USA
PENNY ANTICS • 1955 • Kneitel Seymour • ANS • USA
PENNY ARCADE • 1965 • Hurwitz Harry • SHT • USA
PENNY FOR YOUR THOUGHTS: OR, BIRDS, DOLLS AND SCRATCH -ENGLISH STYLE • 1966 • Winter Donovan • UKN
PENNY GOLD • 1973 • Cardiff Jack • UKN
PENNY-IN-THE-SLOT • 1921 • Roach Hal • SHT • USA
PENNY JOURNEY see **PENNY JOURNEY: THE STORY OF A POST CARD FROM MANCHESTER TO GRAFFHAM** • 1938
PENNY JOURNEY: THE STORY OF A POST CARD FROM MANCHESTER TO GRAFFHAM • 1938 • Jennings Humphrey • DCS • UKN • PENNY JOURNEY
PENNY OF TOP HILL TRAIL • 1921 • Berthelet Arthur • USA
PENNY PALS • 1962 • Kneitel Seymour • ANS • USA
PENNY PARADISE • 1938 • Reed Carol • UKN
PENNY PHILANTHROPIST • 1923 • *Morgan Ralph* • USA
PENNY PHILANTHROPIST, THE • 1917 • McConnell Guy M. • USA
PENNY POINTS TO PARADISE • 1951 • Young Tony • UKN
PENNY POOL, THE • 1937 • Black George • UKN
PENNY PRINCESS • 1952 • Guest Val • UKN
PENNY SERENADE • 1941 • Stevens George • USA
PENNY TO THE RESCUE • 1941 • Jason Will • SHT • USA
PENNY WISDOM • 1937 • Miller David • SHT • USA
PENNY WISE • 1970 • Portici Emilio • USA
PENNY'S PARTY • 1938 • Miller David • SHT • USA
PENNY'S PICNIC • 1938 • Jason Will • SHT • USA
PENNYWHISTLE BLUES • 1951 • Swanson Donald • SAF • MAGIC GARDEN, THE (USA)
PENON DE LAS ANIMAS, EL • 1942 • Zacarias Miguel • MXC • PRECIPICE OF SOULS, THE
PENROD • 1922 • Neilan Marshall • USA
PENROD AND HIS TWIN BROTHER • 1938 • McGann William • USA
PENROD AND SAM • 1923 • Beaudine William • USA
PENROD AND SAM • 1931 • Beaudine William • USA
PENROD AND SAM • 1937 • McGann William • USA
PENROD'S DOUBLE TROUBLE • 1938 • Seiler Lewis • USA
PENS EN POOTJIES • 1974 • SAF
PENSACI, GIACOMINO! • 1936 • Righelli Gennaro • ITL
PENSANDO A TE • 1969 • Grimaldi Aldo • ITL
PENSAR NO FUTURO • 1953 • Mendes Joao • SHT • PRT
PENSER AVANT DE DEPENSER • 1958 • Proulx Maurice • DOC • CND
PENSEUR, LE • 1919 • Poirier Leon • FRN
PENSEZ A CEUX QUI SONT EN-DESSOUS! • 1949 • Decae Henri • SHT • FRN
PENSIERI MORBOSI • 1981 • Regis Jack • ITL • DEEP THOUGHTS
PENSIERO D'AMORE • 1969 • Amendola Mario • ITL
PENSION • 1984 • Chowdbury Rafiqul Bari • BNG
PENSION, LA • 1967 • Fasquel Maurice • SHT • FRN
PENSION CLAUSEWITZ • 1967 • Habib Ralph • FRG
PENSION DE ARTISTAS • 1955 • Fernandez Bustamente Adolfo • MXC
PENSION DES SURDOVES, LA • Plant Claude • FRN
PENSION DU LIBRE AMOUR, LA • 1973 • Matalon Eddy • FRN • HOTEL OF FREE LOVE (UKN)
PENSION GROONEN • 1925 • Wiene Robert • AUS
PENSION JONAS • 1941 • Caron Pierre • FRN
PENSION LAMPEL • 1915 • Mack Max • FRG
PENSION LAUTENSCHLAG • 1920 • Muller-Hagen Carl • FRG
PENSION MIMOSAS • 1934 • Feyder Jacques • FRN
PENSION PRO SVOBODNE PANY • 1967 • Krejcik Jiri • CZC • BOARDING HOUSE FOR SINGLE GENTLEMEN ○ BOARDING HOUSE FOR BACHELORS ○ BOARDING HOUSE FOR GENTLEMEN
PENSION SCHOLLER • 1930 • Jacoby Georg • FRG
PENSION SCHOLLER • 1952 • Jacoby Georg • FRG
PENSION SCHOLLER • 1960 • Jacoby Georg • FRG
PENSIONAT PARADISET • 1937 • Hildebrand Weyler • SWD • SKARGARDSKAVALJERER ○ "PARADISE" BOARDING HOUSE
PENSIONATO, IL • Olmi Ermanno • DCS • ITL
PENSIONE EDELWEISS (ITL) see **SURSIS POUR UN VIVANT** • 1958
PENSIONE PAURA • 1978 • Barilli Francesco • ITL
PENSIONERS, THE • 1912 • Dwan Allan • USA
PENSIONNAIRE, LA see **SPIAGGIA, LA** • 1954
PENTAYIOTISSA'S DAUGHTER see **KORI TIS PENTAYIOTISSAS, I** • 1967
PENTE, LA • 1928 • Andreani Henri • FRN
PENTE, LA • 1931 • Autant-Lara Claude • SHT • FRN
PENTE DOUCE, LA • 1974 • d'Anna Claude • BLG, FRN, ITL
PENTE YINEKES YIA ENAN ANDHRA • 1967 • Silinos Vangelis • GRC • FIVE WOMEN FOR ONE MAN
PENTEK REZI • 1936 • Vajda Ladislao • HNG • FRIDAY ROSE (USA)
PENTHESILEA • 1974 • Mulvey Laura, Wollen Peter • UKN
PENTHOUSE • 1933 • Van Dyke W. S. • USA • CROOKS IN CLOVER (UKN)
PENTHOUSE see **SOCIETY LAWYER** • 1939
PENTHOUSE, THE • 1967 • Collinson Peter • UKN
PENTHOUSE MOUSE • 1963 • Jones Charles M. • ANS • USA
PENTHOUSE PARADISE see **LAURA LANSING SLEPT HERE** • 1988
PENTHOUSE PARTY • 1936 • Nigh William • USA • WITHOUT CHILDREN (UKN)
PENTHOUSE RHYTHM • 1945 • Cline Eddie • USA
PENTICTON PROFILE • 1970 • Wilson Sandra • CND
PENTIMENTO • 1954 • Di Gianni Enzo • ITL
PENTIMENTO • 1978 • Zwartjes Frans • NTH
PENTIMENTO • 1990 • Marshall Tonie • FRN
PENTITO, IL • 1985 • Squitieri Pasquale • ITL • REPENTANT, THE
PENULTIMA DONZELA, A • 1970 • Amaral Fernando • BRZ
PENUMBRA • Knoop John • SHT • USA
PENYAMUN SI BONGKOK • 1972 • Amin M. • MLY • HUNCHBACK ROBBER, THE
PENYAMUN TARBUS • 1979 • Sattar Aziz • MLY • ROBBERS, THE
PENZCSINALO • 1963 • Ban Frigyes • HNG • MONEY-MAKER, THE
PEONIES AND LANTERNS • 1968 • Yamamoto Satsuo • JPN
PEONIES AND STONE LANTERNS see **BOTAN-DORO** • 1955
PEOPLE • 1974 • Zwartjes Frans • DOC • NTH • PEOPLE 74
PEOPLE • 1978 • Damiano Gerard • USA
PEOPLE see **WARAI-NO NINGEN** • 1960
PEOPLE see **LYUDI** • 1966
PEOPLE 74 see **PEOPLE** • 1974
PEOPLE, THE • 1971 • Korty John • TVM • USA
PEOPLE ,THE see **CEDDO** • 1977
PEOPLE ACROSS THE LAKE, THE • 1988 • Seidelman Arthur Allan • TVM • USA
PEOPLE AGAINST O'HARA, THE • 1951 • Sturges John • USA
PEOPLE AND ART see **KIE A MUVESZET** • 1975
PEOPLE AND BEASTS see **LYUDI I ZVERI** • 1962
PEOPLE AND BIRDS see **LUDZIE I PTAKI** • 1972
PEOPLE AND FISH see **LUDZIE I RYBY** • 1962
PEOPLE AND ROBBERS OF CARDAMOM TOWN see **FOLK OG ROVERE I KARDEMOMME BY** • 1988
PEOPLE AND STORMS • 1963 • Kovachev Hristo • DOC • BUL
PEOPLE AND THE NILE see **NASSU WA AN-NIL, AN-** • 1968
PEOPLE AND THEIR GUNS, THE (USA) see **PEUPLE ET SES FUSILS, LE** • 1970
PEOPLE APART • 1957 • Brenton Guy • UKN
PEOPLE ARE BUNNY • 1959 • McKimson Robert • ANS • USA
PEOPLE ARE FUNNY • 1946 • White Sam • USA
PEOPLE BETWEEN, THE • 1947 • McLean Grant • DCS • CND
PEOPLE BETWEEN TWO CHINAS, THE see **HAI-HSIA LIANG-AN** • 1987
PEOPLE CALLED THEM WOLVES see **OOKAMI** • 1955
PEOPLE FROM AFAR • 1977 • Roudarov Nikola • BUL
PEOPLE FROM EMPTY PLACES see **LUDZIE Z PUSTEGO OBSZARU** • 1957
PEOPLE FROM EVERYWHERE, PEOPLE FROM NOWHERE see **GENS DE PARTOUT, GENS DE NULLE PART** • 1981
PEOPLE FROM STATE FARMS see **PEEGEROWCY** • 1970
PEOPLE FROM THE BASE see **LUDZIE Z BAZY** • 1962
PEOPLE FROM THE DEPTHS OF THE FOREST see **FINNSKOGENS FOLK** • 1955
PEOPLE FROM THE EMPTY AREA see **LUDZIE Z PUSTEGO OBSZARU** • 1957
PEOPLE FROM THE METRO see **LIDE Z METRA** • 1974
PEOPLE FROM THE UNDERGROUND see **LIDE Z METRA** • 1974
PEOPLE HAVE THEIR STRIFE NOW AND THEN.. • 1978 • Kennedy Michael • CND
PEOPLE.. HELP! see **YANAS YA HOU!** • 1988
PEOPLE IN BUENOS AIRES see **GENTE EN BUENOS AIRES** • 1974
PEOPLE IN DARKNESS • Ha Won Choi • SKR
PEOPLE IN GLASSHOUSES see **WER IM GLASHAUS LIEBT.. DER GRABEN** • 1970
PEOPLE IN LUCK see **VEINARDS, LES** • 1962
PEOPLE IN THE CITY see **MANNISKOR I STAD** • 1946
PEOPLE IN THE NET see **MENSCHEN IM NETZ** • 1959
PEOPLE IN THE PARK • 1936 • Alexander Donald, Burnford Paul • UKN
PEOPLE IN THE SUBWAY see **LIDE Z METRA** • 1974
PEOPLE IN THE SUN • 1935 • Weiss Jiri • DOC • CZC
PEOPLE IN THE TOWN see **MACHI NO HITOBITO** • 1926
PEOPLE LIKE MARIA • 1958 • Watt Harry • DOC • UKN
PEOPLE LIKE US • 1980 • Coughlan Ian • MTV • ASL
PEOPLE LIKE YOU see **LIDE JAKO TY** • 1960
PEOPLE MAKE PAPERS • 1965 • Schepisi Fred • DOC • ASL
PEOPLE MEET AND SWEET MUSIC FILLS THE HEART (USA) see **MENNESKER MODES OG SOD MUSIK OPSTAR I HJERTET** • 1968
PEOPLE MEET (UKN) see **MENNESKER MODES OG SOD MUSIK OPSTAR I HJERTET** • 1968
PEOPLE MIGHT LAUGH AT US see **MONDE VA NOUS PRENDRE POUR DE SAUVAGES, LE** • 1964
PEOPLE NEXT DOOR, THE • 1970 • Greene David • USA
PEOPLE OF ABRIMES, THE see **LOST CONTINENT, THE** • 1968
PEOPLE OF BERGSLAGEN see **BERGSLAGSFOLKEN** • 1937
PEOPLE OF BRITAIN • 1936 • Rotha Paul • DOC • UKN • PEACE OF BRITAIN, THE ○ PEACE FILM, THE
PEOPLE OF DIMITROVGRAD see **DIMITROVGRADTSI** • 1956
PEOPLE OF FRANCE (USA) see **VIE EST A NOUS, LA** • 1936
PEOPLE OF HALSINGLAND see **HALSINGAR** • 1923
PEOPLE OF HALSINGLAND see **HALSINGAR** • 1933
PEOPLE OF HEMSO see **HEMSOBORNA** • 1919
PEOPLE OF HEMSO, THE see **HEMSOBORNA** • 1944
PEOPLE OF HEMSO, THE see **HEMSOBORNA** • 1955
PEOPLE OF HOGBO FARM see **FOLKET PA HOGBOGARDEN** • 1939
PEOPLE OF HONOUR see **GENTE D'ONORE** • 1968
PEOPLE OF IRELAND • 1973 • Cinema Action • UKN
PEOPLE OF KAJZARJE see **SVET NA KAJZARJU** • 1952
PEOPLE OF NARKE see **NARKINGARNA** • 1923
PEOPLE OF NORRLAND see **NORRLANNINGAR** • 1930
PEOPLE OF ONE HEART see **LIDE JEDNOHO SRDCE** • 1953
PEOPLE OF ROSLAGEN see **ROSPIGGAR** • 1942
PEOPLE OF SIMLANGEN VALLEY see **FOLKET I SIMLANGSDALEN** • 1924
PEOPLE OF SIMLANGEN VALLEY see **FOLKET I SIMLANGSDALEN** • 1948
PEOPLE OF SIN AND BLOOD see **LYUDI GREKHA I KROVI** • 1917
PEOPLE OF SMALAND see **SMALANNINGAR** • 1935
PEOPLE OF THAT LAND, THE see **WAHAN KE LOG** • 1967
PEOPLE OF THE AUSTRALIAN WESTERN DESERT • 1965 • Dunlop Ian • DOC • ASL
PEOPLE OF THE BLUE FIRE • 1961 • Grigoriev Roman • DOC • USS
PEOPLE OF THE BORDER see **GRANSFOLKEN** • 1914
PEOPLE OF THE CUMBERLANDS, THE • 1937 • Kazan Elia, Meyers Sidney, Hill Eugene • DCS • USA
PEOPLE OF THE METRO see **LIDE Z METRA** • 1974
PEOPLE OF THE PEACE • 1958 • Biggs Julian • CND
PEOPLE OF THE PIT, THE • 1915 • Giblyn Charles • USA
PEOPLE OF THE RICE-FIELD see **KOME** • 1957
PEOPLE OF THE ROCKS, THE • 1914 • Somers Dalton • UKN
PEOPLE OF THE SEAL • 1971 • Bolton Laura, Balacki Asen, Brown Quentin • CND
PEOPLE OF THE SLUMS see **PUEBLO DE LATA** • 1973
PEOPLE OF THE VIHORIAT MOUNTAINS • 1956 • Uher Stefan • CZC
PEOPLE OF THE VISTULA see **LUDZIE WISLY** • 1937
PEOPLE OF THE WIND see **BAKHTIARI MIGRATION, THE** • 1975
PEOPLE OF TOMORROW see **MENSEN VAN MORGEN** • 1965
PEOPLE OF VARMLAND see **VARMLANNINGARNA** • 1910
PEOPLE OF VARMLAND see **VARMLANNINGARNA** • 1921
PEOPLE OF VARMLAND see **VARMLANNINGARNA** • 1932
PEOPLE OF VARMLAND see **VARMLANNINGARNA** • 1957
PEOPLE OF YOUNG CHARACTER see **WAKAI HITOTACHI** • 1954
PEOPLE ON A GLACIER see **LIDE NA KRE** • 1937
PEOPLE ON A TRAIN see **LUDZIE Z POCIAGU** • 1961
PEOPLE ON AN ICEBERG see **LIDE NA KRE** • 1937

PEOPLE ON MANOEUVRES see **FOLKET I FALT** • 1953
PEOPLE ON PAPER • 1945 • Morgan Herbert • SHT • USA
PEOPLE ON SUNDAY see **MENSCHEN AM SONNTAG** • 1929
PEOPLE ON THE BRIDGE see **LYUDI NA MOSTU** • 1960
PEOPLE ON THE ICEBERG see **LIDE NA KRE** • 1937
PEOPLE ON THE MOUNTAIN see **EMBEREK A HAVASON** • 1942
PEOPLE ON THE MOVE see **LUDZIE W DRODZE** • 1960
PEOPLE ON THE NERETVA see **LJUDI SA NERETVE** • 1966
PEOPLE ON THE ROAD see **LUDZIE W DRODZE** • 1960
PEOPLE ON WHEELS • 1963 • Sremec Rudolf • DCS • YGS • MEN ON WHEELS
PEOPLE ON WHEELS see **LIDE NA KOLEKACH** • 1966
PEOPLE PEOPLE, THE • 1970 • Coward Roger • UKN
PEOPLE PEOPLE PEOPLE • 1975 • Hubley John • ANS • USA
PEOPLE PREPARING THE STAUFER ANNIVERSARY, THE see **MENSCHEN, DIE DAS STAUFERJAHR VORBEREITEN, DIE** • 1978
PEOPLE SOUP • 1969 • Arkin Alan • SHT • USA
PEOPLE STILL ASK see **MEG KER A NEP** • 1971
PEOPLE THAT TIME FORGOT, THE • 1977 • Connor Kevin • USA, UKN
PEOPLE TOYS see **PEOPLETOYS** • 1974
PEOPLE VS. DR. KILDARE, THE • 1941 • Bucquet Harold S. • USA • MY LIFE IS YOURS (UKN)
PEOPLE VS. JEAN HARRIS, THE • 1981 • Schaefer George • TVM • USA
PEOPLE VS. JOHN DOE, THE • 1916 • Weber Lois • USA
PEOPLE VS. NANCY PRESTON, THE • 1925 • Forman Tom • USA
PEOPLE WANTS TO LIVE, A see **VOLK WILL LEBEN, EIN** • 1939
PEOPLE, WATCH OUT! see **LIDE BDETE** • 1961
PEOPLE WHO OWN THE DARK, THE • 1975 • Klimovsky Leon?, de Ossorio Amando? • SPN
PEOPLE WILL TALK • 1935 • Santell Alfred • USA
PEOPLE WILL TALK • 1951 • Mankiewicz Joseph L. • USA • DOCTOR PRAETORIUS
PEOPLE WITH WINGS see **LEUTE MIT FLUGELN** • 1960
PEOPLE'S AVENGERS, THE see **NARODNIYE MSTITELI** • 1943
PEOPLE'S BANK, THE • 1943 • Parker Gudrun • CND
PEOPLE'S BUILDING see **KENSETSU NO HITOBITO** • 1935
PEOPLE'S CHOICE, THE • 1946 • Fraser Harry L. • USA
PEOPLE'S ENEMY see **PRISON TRAIN** • 1938
PEOPLE'S ENEMY, THE • 1935 • Wilbur Crane • USA
PEOPLE'S ENEMY, THE see **MINSHU NO TEKI** • 1946
PEOPLES OF CANADA • 1940 • Sparling Gordon • CND
PEOPLES OF INDONESIA • 1943 • van Dongen Helen • NTH
PEOPLES OF PAPUA AND NEW GUINEA • 1962 • Dunlop Ian (c/d) • DOC • ASL
PEOPLE'S RAILWAY, THE • 1972 • Brittain Don, Spotton John • CND
PEOPLE'S TEACHER • Chon Sangin • NKR
PEOPLE'S WAR • 1969 • Kramer Robert (c/d) • USA
PEOPLE'S WAY, THE see **VOIE DU PEUPLE, LA**
PEOPLE'S WILL, THE see **FOLKEVILJE** • 1973
PEOPLETOYS • 1974 • MacGregor Sean • USA • HORRIBLE HOUSE ON THE HILL, THE ○ DEVIL TIMES FIVE ○ PEOPLE TOYS ○ TANTRUMS
PEOR QUE LAS FIERAS • 1974 • *Potosi* • MXC
PEOR QUE LOS BUITRES • 1973 • *Cinema Calderon* • MXC
PEPA DONCEL • 1969 • Lucia Luis • SPN
PEPE • 1960 • Sidney George, Delgado Miguel M. • USA, MXC
PEPE, DER PAUKERSCHRECK see **LUMMEL VON DER ERSTEN BANK III, DIE** • 1969
PEPE EL TORO • 1952 • Rodriguez Ismael • MXC
PEPE-HILLO • 1928 • Buchs Jose • SPN
PEPE –HIS TEACHER'S FRIGHT see **LUMMEL VON DER ERSTEN BANK III, DIE** • 1969
PEPE LE MOKO • 1936 • Duvivier Julien • FRN • NUITS BLANCHES, LES ○ CASBAH
PEPE LE PEW • 1947-56 • Jones Charles M. • ASS • USA
PEPEE DU GANGSTER, LA see **PUPA DEL GANGSTER, LA** • 1975
PEPEES AU SERVICE SECRET, LES • 1955 • Andre Raoul • FRN
PEPEES FONT LA LOI, LES • 1954 • Andre Raoul • FRN
PEPELJUGA • 1979 • Grgic Zlatko • ANS • YGS • CINDERELLA
PEPI COLUMBUS • 1954 • Haussermann Ernst • AUS
PEPI, EGYPTILAINEN • 1980 • Partanen Heikki • FNL • PEPI THE EGYPTIAN
PEPI, LUCI AND A WHOLE LOT OF OTHER GIRLS see **PEPI, LUCI, BOM Y ORAS CHICAS DEL MONTON** • 1980
PEPI, LUCI, BOM AND OTHER GIRLS see **PEPI, LUCI, BOM Y ORAS CHICAS DEL MONTON** • 1980
PEPI, LUCI, BOM Y ORAS CHICAS DEL MONTON • 1980 • Almodovar Pedro • SPN • PEPI, LUCI, BOM AND OTHER GIRLS ○ PEPI, LUCI AND A WHOLE LOT OF OTHER GIRLS
PEPI THE EGYPTIAN see **PEPI, EGYPTILAINEN** • 1980
PEPIN DANS LA BOITE, UN • 1978 • Mordillat Gerard, Philibert Nicolas • DOC • FRN
PEPINA REJHOLCOVA • 1932 • Binovec Vaclav • CZC
PEPINO • 1986 • Macina Michael • MTV • CND
PEPITA JIMENEZ • 1945 • Fernandez Emilio • MXC
PEPITA JIMENEZ • 1975 • Moreno Alba Rafael • SPN, USA • BRIDE TO BE
PEPITE D'OR, LA • 1916 • Burguet Charles • FRN
PEPITO AND THE MARVELOUS LAMP see **PEPITO Y LA LAMPARA MARAVILLOSA** • 1971
PEPITO AND THE MONSTER see **PEPITO Y EL MONSTRUO** • 1957
PEPITO AS DEL VOLANTE • 1956 • Rodriguez Joselito • MXC
PEPITO PISCINA • 1976 • Delgado Luis Maria • SPN
PEPITO Y CHABELO DETECTIVES • 1973 • *Churubusco Azteca* • MXC
PEPITO Y CHABELO VS. LOS MONSTRUOS • 1973 • *Churubusco Azteca* • MXC
PEPITO Y EL MONSTRUO • 1957 • Rodriguez Joselito • MXC • PEPITO AND THE MONSTER
PEPITO Y LA LAMPARA MARAVILLOSA • 1971 • Galindo Alejandro • MXC • LITTLE JOE AND THE MARVELOUS LAMP ○ PEPITO AND THE MARVELOUS LAMP
PEPITO Y LOS ROBACHICOS • 1957 • de la Serna Mauricio • MXC
PEPO • 1935 • Bek-Nazarov Amo • USS
PEPOTE see **MI TIO JACINTO** • 1956
PEPPER • 1929 • *B.s.f.p.* • SHT • UKN
PEPPER • 1936 • Tinling James • USA • PUBLIC NUISANCE NO.1
PEPPERING HIS OWN PORRIDGE • 1914 • Birch Cecil • UKN
PEPPERMINT FRAPPE • 1967 • Saura Carlos • SPN
PEPPERMINT FREEDOM see **PEPPERMINT FRIEDEN** • 1982
PEPPERMINT FRIEDEN • 1982 • Rosenbaum Marianne S. W. • FRG • PEPPERMINT FREEDOM
PEPPERMINT SODA see **DIABOLO MENTHE** • 1977
PEPPERMINT TREE, THE • 1954 • *Aries Prod.* • ANS • USA
PEPPERY AFFAIR, A • 1912 • Stow Percy • UKN
PEPPERY SALT • 1936 • Lord Del • SHT • USA
PEPPINO E LA NOBILE DAMA • 1959 • Ballerini Piero, Gramatica Emma • ITL • VECCHIA SIGNORA, LA
PEPPINO E LA VERGINE MARIA • 1975 • *De Carolis Cinzia* • ITL • VIRGIN NAMED MARY, A (USA) ○ VIRTUE AND MAGIC
PEPPINO E VIOLETTA • 1951 • Cloche Maurice, Smart Ralph • ITL, UKN • NEVER TAKE NO FOR AN ANSWER (UKN)
PEPPINO, LE MODELLE E "CHELLA LLA" • 1957 • Mattoli Mario • ITL
PEPPY POLLY • 1919 • Clifton Elmer • USA
PEP'S LEGACY • 1916 • Wolbert William • SHT • USA
PEQUENA ENEMIGA, LA • 1955 • Rodriguez Joselito • MXC
PEQUENA MADRECITA, LA • 1943 • Rodriguez Joselito • MXC
PEQUENA REVANCHA • 1986 • Barrera Olegario • VNZ • SMALL REVENGE
PEQUENECES • 1949 • de Orduna Juan • SPN
PEQUENO CORONEL, EL • 1959 • del Amo Antonio • SPN
PEQUENO MUNDO DE MARCOS, O • 1968 • Vietri Geraldo • BRZ • SMALL WORLD OF MARCO, THE
PEQUENO ROBIN HOOD, EL • 1973 • *Filmicas Re-Al* • MXC
PEQUENO RUISENOR, EL • 1956 • del Amo Antonio • SPN
PEQUENOS AVENTUREROS • 1978 • Mateus Daniel Pires • ARG • LITTLE ADVENTURERS
PEQUENOS GIGANTES, LOS • 1958 • Butler Hugo • MXC
PEQUENOS PRIVILEGIOS, LOS • 1977 • Pastor Julian • MXC • SMALL PRIVILEGES
PER • 1973 • Kristensen Hans • DNM
PER 50,000 MALEDETTI DOLLARI • 1968 • de la Loma Jose Antonio • ITL, SPN, FRG • FOR 50,000 DAMNED DOLLARS
PER AMARE OFELIA • 1974 • Mogherini Flavio • ITL
PER AMORE • 1978 • Giarda Mino • ITL
PER AMORE DI CESARINA • 1976 • Sindoni Vittorio • ITL
PER AMORE DI POPPEA • 1977 • Laurenti Mariano • ITL
PER AMORE O PER FORZA • 1971 • Franciosa Massimo • ITL
PER AMORE.. PER MAGIA • 1967 • Tessari Duccio • ITL • FOR LOVE.. FOR MAGIC ○ BY LOVE.. BY MAGIC
PER ASPERA • 1981 • Rosma Juha • SHT • FNL
PER ASPERA AD ASTRA see **AS ASPERA ED ASTRA** • 1969
PER ASPERA AD ASTRA see **CHEREZ TERNII K ZVEZDAM** • 1981
PER CENTOMILA DOLLARI TI AMMAZZO • 1967 • Fago Giovanni • ITL • FOR 100,000 DOLLARS I'LL KILL YOU
PER FAVORE CHIUDETE LE PERSIANE (ITL) see **BONS VIVANTS, LES** • 1966
PER FAVORE NON SPARATE COL CANNONE see **ASSALTO AL CENTRO NUCLEARE** • 1967
PER FAVORE OCCUPATI DI AMELIA • 1980 • Mogherini Flavio • ITL
PER GRAZIA RICEVUTA • 1971 • Manfredi Nino • ITL
PER IL BENE E PER IL MALE(ITL) see **VIE CONJUGALE: FRANCOISE, LA** • 1964
PER IL GUSTO DI UCCIDERE • 1966 • Valerii Tonino • ITL
PER LE ANTICHE SCALE • 1975 • Bolognini Mauro • ITL • DOWN THE ANCIENT STAIRS (USA) ○ DOWN THE ANCIENT STAIRCASE
PER LE STRADE DEL MONDO see **COEUR DE GUEUX** • 1936
PER LE VIE DELLA CITTA • 1956 • Giachino Luigi Maria • ITL • SATELLITE DEL BUON UMORE, IL
PER MILLE DOLLARI AL GIORNI • 1966 • Amadio Silvio • ITL, SPN • POR MIL DOLARES AL DIA (SPN) ○ RENEGADE GUNFIGHTER (USA) ○ FOR A THOUSAND DOLLARS A DAY
PER.MU.TA.TION.S • 1968 • Whitney John • ANS • USA
PER PIACERE, NON SPARATE COL CANNONE (SPN) see **ASSALTO AL CENTRO NUCLEARE** • 1967
PER POCHI DOLLARI ANCORA • 1966 • Ferroni Giorgio • ITL, FRN, SPN • FORT YUMA GOLD (USA)
PER QUALCHE DOLLARI IN PIU • 1965 • Leone Sergio • ITL, FRG, SPN • FUR EIN PAAR DOLLAR MEHR (FRG) ○ FOR A FEW DOLLARS MORE (USA) ○ MUERTE TENIA UN PRECIO, LA (SPN)
PER QUALCHE DOLLARO IN MENO • 1966 • Mattoli Mario • ITL
PER QUESTA NOTTE • 1977 • Di Carlo Carlo • ITL
PER SALDO MORD see **SWISS CONSPIRACY, THE** • 1975
PER SALVARTI HO PECCATO • 1954 • Costa Mario • ITL
PER UN BREVIARIO DI DOLLARI • 1974 • Bianchi Mario • ITL
PER UN DOLLARO DI GLORIA • 1966 • Cerchio Fernando • ITL, SPN • ESCADRON DE LA MUERTE, EL (SPN) ○ MUTINY AT FORT SHARP
PER UN PUGNO DI CANZONI • 1966 • Merino Jose Luis • ITL
PER UN PUGNO DI DOLLARI • 1964 • Leone Sergio • ITL, FRG, SPN • FUR EINE HANDVOLL DOLLARS (FRG) ○ POR UN PUNADO DE DOLARES (SPN) ○ FOR A FISTFUL OF DOLLARS (USA) ○ FISTFUL OF DOLLARS, A
PER UN PUGNO NELL'OCCHIO • 1965 • Lupo Michele • ITL, SPN
PER UNA BARA PIENA DI DOLLARI • 1971 • Fidani Demofilo • ITL • BARREL FULL OF DOLLARS, A
PER UNA MANCIATA D'ORO • 1966 • Veo Carlo • ITL
PER UNA VALIGIA PIENA DI DONNE • 1964 • Russo Renzo • ITL • KINKY DARLINGS, THE (UKN)
PER UN'ORA D'AMORE • 1914 • Maggi Luigi • ITL
PER UOMINI SOLI • 1939 • Brignone Guido • ITL • FOR MEN ONLY (USA)
PER VIVERE MEGLIO.. DIVERTITEVI CON NOI • 1978 • Mogherini Flavio • ITL
PERADE 1-2, LA • 1934 • Tessier Albert • DCS • CND
PERAHIM • 1973 • Geissendorfer Hans W. • FRG
PERAK A SS • 1946 • Trnka Jiri • ANM • CZC • CHIMNEY SWEEP, THE (USA) ○ SPRINGER AND THE SS MEN ○ DEVIL ON SPRINGS, THE ○ PERAK AGAINST THE SS
PERAK AGAINST THE SS see **PERAK A SS** • 1946
PERCE ET L'ILE BONAVENTURE • 1939 • Proulx Maurice • DCS • CND
PERCE ON THE ROCKS • 1964 • Carle Gilles • DCS • CND
PERCEVAL • 1964-69 • Rohmer Eric • MTV • FRN
PERCEVAL LE GALLOIS • 1978 • Rohmer Eric • FRN, ITL, SWT • PERCEVAL (USA)
PERCEVAL (USA) see **PERCEVAL LE GALLOIS** • 1978
PERCH OF THE DEVIL • 1927 • Baggot King • USA
PERCHE? • 1975 • Dallamano Massimo • ITL • MEDAGLIONE INSANGUINATO, IL ○ NIGHT CHILD (USA)
PERCHE MAMMA TI MANDA SOLA? • 1973 • Balducci Richard • ITL
PERCHE NO? • 1930 • Palermi Amleto • ITL
PERCHE NON CI LASCIATE IN PACE? • 1971 • *Koscina Sylvia* • ITL • WHY DON'T YOU LEAVE US IN PEACE?
PERCHE PAGARE PER ESSERE FELICE • 1971 • Ferreri Marco • DOC • ITL
PERCHE QUELLE STRANE GOCCE DI SANGUE SUL CORPO DI JENNIFER? • 1972 • Carnimeo Giuliano • ITL • EROTIC BLUE (UKN) ○ WHY THOSE STRANGE DROPS OF BLOOD ON THE BODY OF JENNIFER?
PERCHE SI UCCIDE UN MAGISTRATO • 1975 • Damiani Damiano • ITL
PERCHE SI UCCIDONO • 1976 • Macario Mauro • ITL
PERCHERON, LE • 1946 • Proulx Maurice • DCS • CND
PERCIVAL AND HILL • 1928 • *British Film Sound Productions* • SHT • UKN
PERCIVAL CHUBBS AND THE WIDOW • 1912 • *Edison* • USA
PERCIVAL MACKEY TRIO, THE • 1929 • *British Sound Film Production* • SHT • UKN
PERCIVAL'S AWAKENING • 1915 • Hotaling Arthur D. • USA
PERCY • 1925 • Neill R. William • USA • MOTHER'S BOY (UKN)
PERCY • 1970 • Thomas Ralph • UKN
PERCY • 1989 • Merwanji Pervez • IND
PERCY AND HIS SQUAW • 1911 • *Solax* • USA
PERCY ATTENDS A MASQUERADE • 1914 • Collins Edwin J.? • UKN
PERCY GETS A JOB • 1912 • *Percy W. S.* • ASL
PERCY H. BALDWIN, TRIFLER • 1913 • *Moore Owen* • USA
PERCY LEARNS TO WALTZ • 1912 • *Cumpson J. R.* • USA
PERCY LOSES A SHILLING • 1912 • Wilson Frank? • UKN
PERCY MADE GOOD • 1915 • Angeles Bert • USA
PERCY NEEDED A REST • 1914 • Morton Walter • USA
PERCY PIMPERNICKEL –SOUBRETTE • 1914 • Hale Albert W. • USA • PERCY PUMPERNICKEL, SOUBRETTE
PERCY PRYDE AND HIS PHONOFIDDLE ON THE PHONOFILM • 1928 • *De Forest Phonofilm* • SHT • UKN
PERCY PUMPERNICKEL, SOUBRETTE see **PERCY PIMPERNICKEL –SOUBRETTE** • 1914
PERCY THE BANDIT • 1912 • *Nestor* • USA
PERCY, THE COWBOY • 1910 • *Lubin* • USA
PERCY, THE LADY-KILLER • 1914 • *Ab* • USA
PERCY, THE MASHER • 1911 • *Imp* • USA
PERCY THE MECHANICAL MAN • 1916 • *Bray John R. (P)* • USA
PERCY, THE MILLINER • 1914 • *Royal* • USA
PERCY THE POLICEMAN • Murphy Geoff • SER • NZL
PERCY WANTED A MOUSTACHE • 1908 • Rosenthal Joe • UKN
PERCY'S FIRST HOLIDAY • 1914 • *Percy W. S.* • ASL
PERCY'S HALF HOLIDAY • 1906 • *Walurdaw* • UKN
PERCY'S NEW MAMMA • 1913 • *Crystal* • USA
PERCY'S PERSISTENT PURSUIT • 1912 • Stow Percy • UKN
PERCY'S PROGRESS • 1974 • Thomas Ralph • UKN • IT'S NOT THE SIZE THAT COUNTS! (USA) ○ IT'S NOT SIZE THAT COUNTS
PERCY'S WOOING • 1913 • *Neilan Marshall* • USA
PERDEN VIEJITA • 1927 • Ferreyra Jose • ARG
PERDEU-SE UM MARIDO • 1956 • Campos Henrique • PRT
PERDICION DE MUJERES • 1950 • Orol Juan • MXC
PERDIDA • 1949 • Rivero Fernando A. • MXC
PERDIDA • 1980 • Correa Carlos Alberto Prates • BRZ • LOST ONE, THE
PERDIDO POR CEM • 1972 • Vasconcelos Antonio-Pedro • PRT
PERDIZIONE • 1942 • Campogalliani Carlo • ITL • VIE DELL'AMORE, LE
PERDOA-ME POR ME TRAIRES • 1986 • Chediak Braz • BRZ • FORGIVE ME FOR YOUR PORTRAYAL
PERDONAME MI VIDA • 1964 • Delgado Miguel M. • MXC
PERDONAMI • 1953 • Costa Mario • ITL
PERDONO • 1966 • Fizzarotti Ettore Maria • ITL
PERDUE • 1920 • Monca Georges • FRN
PERDUTAMENTE TUO.. MI FIRMO MACALUSO CARMELO FU GIUSEPPE • 1976 • Sindoni Vittorio • ITL
PERE CELEBATAIRE, LE • 1930 • Robison Arthur • FRN
PERE CHOPIN, LE • 1943 • Ozep Fedor, Freedland Georg • CND • MUSIC MASTER, THE ○ ONCLE DU CANADA, L'
PERE DE MADEMOISELLE, LE • 1953 • L'Herbier Marcel, Dagan Robert-Paul • FRN • FATHER OF THE GIRL, THE
PERE ET L'ENFANT, LE see **PREMIER MAI** • 1958
PERE GORIOT • 1915 • Vale Travers • USA
PERE GORIOT, LE • 1921 • de Baroncelli Jacques • FRN
PERE GORIOT, LE • 1944 • Vernay Robert • FRN
PERE HUGO, LE • 1934 • Leenhardt Roger • DCS • FRN
PERE HUGO, LE see **VICTOR HUGO** • 1951
PERE IDEAL, LE • 1973 • Dansereau Mireille • SHT • CND
PERE LA CERISE, LE • 1933 • Peguy Robert • FRN
PERE LA VICTOIRE • 1897 • Melies Georges • FRN
PERE LAMPION, LE • 1934 • Christian-Jaque • FRN
PERE LEBONNARD, LE • 1938 • de Limur Jean • FRN, ITL • PAPA LEBONNARD (ITL)
PERE NOEL A LES YEUX BLEUS, LE • 1966 • Eustache Jean • FRN • SANTA CLAUS HAS BLUE EYES ○ BAD COMPANY ○ FATHER CHRISTMAS HAS BLUE EYES
PERE NOEL EST UNE ORDURE, LE • 1982 • Poire Jean-Marie • FRN
PERE NOEL, PERE NOEL • 1974 • Hebert Pierre • ANS • CND

PERE PREMATURE, LE • 1933 • Guissart Rene • FRN

PERE SERGE, LE • 1945 • Gasnier-Raymond Lucien • FRN

PERE TRANQUILLE, LE • 1948 • Clement Rene • FRN • MR. ORCHID (USA)

PERED OKTYABRE • 1965 • Alexandrov Grigori • USS • BEFORE OCTOBER

PERED SUDOM ISTORII • 1966 • Ermler Friedrich • USS • BEFORE THE JUDGMENT OF HISTORY ○ JUDGEMENT OF HISTORY, THE

PEREGRINA • 1950 • Urueta Chano • MXC

PEREGRINA • 1973 • *Aguila* • MXC

PEREGRINE HUNTERS, THE • 1978 • Petty Cecil • UKN

PEREKLICHKA • 1965 • Khrabrovitsky Daniil • USS • ROLL-CALL

PEREKOP • 1930 • Kavaleridze Ivan • USS

PEREKRESTOK • 1963 • Aimanov Shaken • USS • CROSSROAD

PEREMPUAN • 1988 • Faridah Ida • MLY

PEREPOLOKH • 1976 • Gogoberidze Lana • USS • SCANDAL IN SALKHINETI ○ AURZAURI SALKHINETSHI ○ COMMOTION

PERES ET FILS (FRN) see **PADRI E FIGLI** • 1957

PERFECT • 1985 • Bridges James • USA

PERFECT 36, A • 1918 • Giblyn Charles • USA

PERFECT ALIBI, THE • 1924 • *Maloney Leo* • USA

PERFECT ALIBI, THE see **DOUBLE DANGER** • 1938

PERFECT ALIBI, THE (UKN) see **ALIBI** • 1929

PERFECT ALIBI, THE (USA) see **BIRDS OF PREY** • 1930

PERFECT ANGEL, A • 1912 • *Cosmopolitan* • UKN

PERFECT CLOWN, THE • 1925 • Newmeyer Fred • USA

PERFECT CLUE, THE • 1935 • Vignola Robert G. • USA

PERFECT CONTROL • 1932 • Stoloff Ben • SHT • USA

PERFECT COUPLE, A • 1979 • Altman Robert • USA

PERFECT CRIME see **CRIMEN PERFECTO** • 1977

PERFECT CRIME, A • 1921 • Dwan Allan • USA

PERFECT CRIME, THE • 1925 • Summers Walter • UKN

PERFECT CRIME, THE • 1928 • Glennon Bert • USA

PERFECT CRIME, THE • 1937 • Ince Ralph • UKN • COPPER PROOF

PERFECT CRIME, THE • 1987 • Papnikolas Evris • SHT • GRC

PERFECT CRIME, THE see **INDAGINE SU UN DELITTO PERFETTO** • 1979

PERFECT CRIME, THE (UKN) see **ELLERY QUEEN AND THE PERFECT CRIME** • 1941

PERFECT DAY, A • 1916 • Currier Frank • SHT • USA

PERFECT DAY, A • 1927 • Beauchamp Clem • USA

PERFECT DAY, A • 1929 • Parrott James • SHT • USA

PERFECT DREAMER, THE • 1922 • *Young Producers Filming Co* • USA

PERFECT DRIVER, THE see **KIEROWCA DOSKONALY** • 1971

PERFECT FIT, A • 1921 • Elias Francisco • SHT

PERFECT FLAPPER, THE • 1924 • Dillon John Francis • USA

PERFECT FLAW, THE • 1934 • Haynes Manning • UKN

PERFECT FRIDAY • 1970 • Hall Peter • UKN

PERFECT FURLOUGH, THE • 1958 • Edwards Blake • USA • STRICTLY FOR PLEASURE (UKN)

PERFECT GENTLEMAN see **PERFEKT GENTLEMAN, EN** • 1927

PERFECT GENTLEMAN, A • 1928 • Bruckman Clyde • USA

PERFECT GENTLEMAN, THE • 1935 • Whelan Tim • USA • IMPERFECT LADY, THE (UKN)

PERFECT GENTLEMEN • 1978 • Cooper Jackie • TVM • USA

PERFECT HERO, A • 1990 • Jones James Cellan • UKN

PERFECT HUMAN BEING, A • 1967 • Leth Jorgen • DNM

PERFECT KILLER, THE • Siciliano Mario • ITL

PERFECT LADY • 1924 • Roach Hal • SHT • USA

PERFECT LADY, A • 1918 • Badger Clarence • USA

PERFECT LADY, A see **WOMAN, A** • 1915

PERFECT LADY, THE • 1931 • Rosmer Milton, Jackson Frederick • UKN • LOVELORN LADY, THE

PERFECT LOVE, THE see **PERFECT LOVER, THE** • 1919

PERFECT LOVER, THE • 1919 • Ince Ralph • USA • NAKED TRUTH, THE ○ PERFECT LOVE, THE

PERFECT MARRIAGE see **KANZENNARU KEKKON** • 1967

PERFECT MARRIAGE, THE • 1946 • Allen Lewis • USA

PERFECT MARRIAGE, THE see **BEAU MARIAGE, UN** • 1981

PERFECT MATCH see **TSUIGAI NAMPANGYAU** • 1989

PERFECT MATCH, A • 1916 • Clements Roy • SHT • USA

PERFECT MATCH, A • 1980 • Damski Mel • TVM • USA

PERFECT MATCH, THE • 1987 • Deimel Mark • USA

PERFECT MATE see **MUSUME NO BOKEN** • 1958

PERFECT MODEL, THE • 1918 • *Munson Audrey* • USA

PERFECT MURDER, THE • 1988 • Hai Zafar • IND

PERFECT PEOPLE • 1988 • Green Bruce Seth • TVM • USA

PERFECT SAP, THE • 1927 • Higgin Howard • USA

PERFECT SET-UP • 1936 • Cahn Edward L. • SHT • USA

PERFECT SET-UP, THE see **ONCE YOU KISS A STRANGER** • 1969

PERFECT SNOB, THE • 1941 • McCarey Ray • USA

PERFECT SPECIMEN, THE • 1937 • Curtiz Michael • USA

PERFECT STRANGERS • 1945 • Korda Alexander • UKN • VACATION FROM MARRIAGE (USA)

PERFECT STRANGERS • 1949 • Windust Bretaigne • USA • TOO DANGEROUS TO LOVE (UKN)

PERFECT STRANGERS • 1984 • Cohen Larry • USA • BLIND ALLEY

PERFECT TIMING • 1984 • Bonniere Rene • CND • SWEETHEARTS ○ SOFT FOCUS ○ SOHO BLUES

PERFECT TIMING see **MANNEQUIN** • 1986

PERFECT TRUTH, THE • 1914 • Edwin Walter • USA

PERFECT UNDERSTANDING • 1933 • Gardner Cyril • UKN

PERFECT VILLAIN, A • 1921 • Kenton Erle C. • SHT • USA

PERFECT WEEKEND, A (UKN) see **ST. LOUIS KID** • 1934

PERFECT WOMAN, THE • 1920 • Kirkland David • USA

PERFECT WOMAN, THE • 1949 • Knowles Bernard • UKN

PERFECT WORLD • 1989 • Elling Tom • DNM

PERFECTIONIST, THE • 1986 • Thomson Chris • TVM • ASL

PERFECTIONIST, THE (USA) see **GRAND PATRON, UN** • 1951

PERFECTIONNEMENT DES ENSEIGNANTS, LE • 1969 • Lamothe Arthur • DCS • CND

PERFECTLY FIENDISH FLANAGAN OR THE HART OF THE DREADFUL WEST • 1918 • Harrison Saul • SHT • USA • HART OF THE DREADFUL WEST, THE

PERFECTLY MISMATED • 1934 • Horne James W. • SHT • USA

PERFEKT GENTLEMAN, EN • 1927 • Ekman Gosta, Bryde Vilhelm • SWD • PERFECT GENTLEMAN

PERFIDE.. MA BELLE • 1958 • Simonelli Giorgio C. • ITL • NAPOLI E MILLE CANZONI

PERFIDIA • 1939 • Rowland William • MXC

PERFIDO INCANTO • 1916 • Bragaglia Anton-Giulio • ITL

PERFIDO RICATTO see **VEDI NAPOLI E POI MUORI** • 1952

PERFIDY OF MARY, THE • 1913 • Griffith D. W. • USA

PERFIL DE SATANAS, EL • 1969 • Logar Juan • SPN • PROFILE OF SATAN, THE

PERFORMANCE • 1970 • Roeg Nicolas, Cammell Donald • UKN • PERFORMERS, THE

PERFORMANCE, THE • 1973 • Siegel Lois • CND

PERFORMANCES FRANCAISES • 1953 • Martin Marcel • SHT • FRN

PERFORMER, THE • 1959 • Ginsberg Donald • DOC • CND

PERFORMER, THE • 1987 • Verbrugge Caspar • NTH

PERFORMER, THE see **KOMEDIANT, DE** • 1986

PERFORMERS, THE see **PERFORMANCE** • 1970

PERFORMERS, THE (USA) see **HANA TO NAMIDA TO HONOO** • 1970

PERFORMING PAINTER • 1956 • Whitney John, Crippen Fred • ANS • USA

PERFUME OF THE LADY IN BLACK, THE see **PARFUM DE LA DAME EN NOIR, LE** • 1930

PERFUMED GARDEN, THE • 1970 • Austin Ray • UKN

PERFUMED NIGHTMARE, THE see **MABABANGONG BANGUNGOT** • 1977

PERFUMED WRESTLER, THE • 1915 • MacGregor Norval • USA

PERGOLESI • 1932 • Brignone Guido • ITL

PERHAPS DIOGENES see **MOZDA DIOGEN** • 1968

PERHE see **PYHA PERHE** • 1976

PERICOLO NEGLI ABISSI • 1978 • Vailati Bruno • ITL

PERIGO NAO DORME, O • 1960 • Garcia Fernando • SHT • PRT

PERIGORD NOIR • 1989 • Ribowski Nicolas • FRN

PERIL, THE • 1912 • *Baggot King* • USA

PERIL AU PARADIS • 1964 • Greville Edmond T. • MTV • FRN

PERIL EN LA DEMEURE • 1984 • Deville Michel • FRN • DEATH IN A FRENCH GARDEN (UKN) ○ PERIL (USA)

PERIL FOR THE GUY • 1956 • Hill James • UKN

PERIL FROM THE PLANET MONGO • 1940 • Stephani Frederick • USA

PERIL OF THE CLIFFS, THE • 1912 • *Christy Lillian E.* • USA

PERIL OF THE DANCE HALL, THE • 1913 • *Vignola Robert* • USA

PERIL OF THE FLEET, THE • 1909 • Wormald S.? • UKN

PERIL OF THE PLAINS, THE • 1911 • *Kalem* • USA

PERIL OF THE PLAINS, THE • 1912 • Hamilton G. P. • USA

PERIL OF THE RAIL • 1926 • McGowan J. P. • USA

PERIL (USA) see **PERIL EN LA DEMEURE** • 1984

PERIL WITHIN, THE see **HUN WITHIN, THE** • 1918

PERILOUS CARGO, A • 1913 • *Edwin Walter* • USA

PERILOUS EXPEDITION see **STOT STAR DEN DANSKE SOMAND** • 1948

PERILOUS FLIGHT see **OPASEN POLET** • 1968

PERILOUS HOLIDAY • 1946 • Griffith Edward H. • USA

PERILOUS JOURNEY, A • 1953 • Springsteen R. G. • USA • PERILOUS VOYAGE, A

PERILOUS JOURNEY (UKN) see **BAD BOY** • 1939

PERILOUS LEAP, THE • 1917 • Davis James • SHT • USA

PERILOUS LOVE see **FLAPPER WIVES** • 1924

PERILOUS PEARLS OF PAULINE, THE see **HOT PEARL SNATCH, THE** • 1966

PERILOUS RIDE, A • 1911 • Dawley J. Searle • USA

PERILOUS RIDE, A • 1913 • Melville Wilbert • *Lubin* • USA

PERILOUS RIDE, THE • 1913 • *Majestic* • USA

PERILOUS VOYAGE • 1968 • Graham William A. • TVM • USA • REVOLUTION OF ANTONIO DELEON, THE

PERILOUS VOYAGE, A see **PERILOUS JOURNEY, A** • 1953

PERILOUS WATERS • 1948 • Bernhard Jack • USA

PERILS OF A FISHERMAN, THE • 1907 • Hermansen Hugo • NRW

PERILS OF A PLUMBER • 1916 • Hutchinson Craig • SHT • USA

PERILS OF A WAR MESSENGER, THE • 1911 • *Champion* • USA

PERILS OF BAGAKU • 1961 • *Kobayashi Keiju* • JPN

PERILS OF CHARITY JONES, THE • 1967 • Nicol Alex • MTV • USA

PERILS OF DIVORCE • 1916 • August Edwin • USA

PERILS OF GWENDOLINE, THE see **GWENDOLINE** • 1984

PERILS OF GWENDOLINE IN THE LAND OF THE YIK YAK (USA) see **GWENDOLINE** • 1984

PERILS OF MANDY, THE • 1982 • Rowles Ken • USA

PERILS OF NYOKA • 1942 • Witney William • SRL • USA

PERILS OF OUR GIRL REPORTERS, THE • 1917 • SER • USA

PERILS OF P.K., THE • 1986 • Green Joseph • USA

PERILS OF PARIS, THE (USA) see **TERREUR** • 1924

PERILS OF PAUL • 1920 • *Keefe William* • SHT • USA

PERILS OF PAULINE, THE • 1914 • Mackenzie Donald, Gasnier Louis J. • SRL • USA

PERILS OF PAULINE, THE • 1933 • Taylor Ray • SRL • USA

PERILS OF PAULINE, THE • 1947 • Marshall George • USA

PERILS OF PAULINE, THE • 1967 • Leonard Herbert B., Shelley Joshua • USA

PERILS OF PEARL PUREHEART • 1949 • Donnelly Eddie • ANS • USA

PERILS OF PETERSBORO, THE • 1926 • *Sennett Mack (P)* • SHT • USA

PERILS OF PORK PIE, THE • 1916 • Kellino W. P. • UKN

PERILS OF TEMPTATION, THE • 1915 • *Saunders Jackie* • USA

PERILS OF THE BAKERY • 1917 • *Triangle* • USA

PERILS OF THE BEACH • 1920 • *Reelcraft* • SHT • USA

PERILS OF THE COAST GUARD • 1926 • Apfel Oscar • USA

PERILS OF THE DARKEST JUNGLE see **JUNGLE GOLD** • 1944

PERILS OF THE JUNGLE • 1915 • Martin E. A. • USA

PERILS OF THE PARK • 1916 • Henderson Dell • SHT • USA

PERILS OF THE PARLOR • 1918 • Beery Wallace • SHT • USA

PERILS OF THE PLAINS • 1910 • *Bison* • USA

PERILS OF THE ROYAL MOUNTED • 1942 • Horne James W. • SRL • USA

PERILS OF THE SEA, THE • 1913 • Olcott Sidney, Melford George • USA

PERILS OF THE SECRET SERVICE, THE • 1917 • SER • USA

PERILS OF THE WEST • 1922 • *Hackett William* • USA

PERILS OF THE WHITE LIGHTS • 1914 • *Nilsson Anna Q.* • USA

PERILS OF THE WILDERNESS • 1956 • Bennet Spencer Gordon • SRL • USA

PERILS OF THE WILDS • 1925 • Ford Francis • SRL • USA

PERILS OF THE YUKON • 1922 • Vekroff Perry N., McGowan J. P., Marchant Jay • USA

PERILS OF THUNDER MOUNTAIN, THE • 1919 • Bradbury Robert North, Bowman William J. • SRL • USA

PERIOD OF ADJUSTMENT • 1962 • Hill George Roy • USA

PERIOD OF TWENTY-FIVE YEARS, A see **25 BASANT** • 1986

PERIPETIES D'UNE VISITE EN MONGOLIE • 1937 • Poitevin Jean-Marie • DCS • CND

PERIQUILLO SARNIENTO, EL see **VAGO SIN OFICIO, UN** • 1955

PERISCOPE, LE • 1916 • Gance Abel • FRN

PERISHING SOLICITORS • 1983 • Crichton Charles • SHT • UKN

PERIWINKLE • 1917 • Kirkwood James • USA

PERJANJIAN SYAITAN • 1980 • Sudarmadji S. • MLY

PERJURA • 1938 • Sevilla Raphael J. • MXC

PERJURER, THE • 1916 • *Imp* • SHT • USA

PERJURER, THE • 1958 • Ulmer Edgar G. • FRG

PERJURY • 1921 • Millarde Harry • USA

PERKAWINAN 83 • 1983 • Umboh Wim • INN • WEDDING 83

PERKAWINAN DALAM SEMUSIN • 1976 • Karya Teguh • INN • WOLVES, THE

PERKELE! • 1971 • Donner Jorn • DOC • FNL • FUCK OFF! – IMAGES OF FINLAND (USA) ○ PERKELE! KUVIA SUOMESTA

PERKELE! KUVIA SUOMESTA see **PERKELE!** • 1971

PERKINS' MYSTIC MANOR • 1916 • Humphrey Orral • USA

PERKINS' PEACE PARTY • 1916 • *Chamberlin Riley* • SHT • USA

PERKINS' PEP PRODUCER • 1915 • Smith Sidney • USA

PERKIN'S PHEASANTS • 1916 • Batley Ethyle • UKN

PERLA NEGRA, LA • 1974 • *Universal* • MXC

PERLA NERA, LA • 1922 • Serena Gustavo • ITL

PERLA W KORONIE • 1972 • Kutz Kazimierz • PLN • PEARL IN THE CROWN

PERLE, LA • 1929 • d'Ursel Henri • BLG

PERLE, LA • 1932 • Guissart Rene • FRN

PERLE AUF DUNKLEM GRUNDE, EINE • 1917 • *Smolowa Sybil* • FRG

PERLE DES ORIENTS, DIE • 1921 • Martin Karl Heinz • FRG

PERLE DES REGIMENTS, DIE • 1925 • Jacoby Georg • FRG • STOLZ DER KOMPAGNIE, DER

PERLE DES SERVANTES, LA • 1908 • Melies Georges • FRN • ANGELIC SERVANT, AN (USA)

PERLE DES SUDENS, DIE see **FRAU –DIE NACHTIGALL, DIE** • 1930

PERLE VON TOKAY, DIE • 1954 • Marischka Hubert • AUS

PERLEN BEDEUTEN TRANEN • 1921 • Wilhelm Carl • FRG

PERLEN DER LADY HARRISON, DIE • 1922 • Herald Heinz • FRG

PERLEN DES DR. TALMADGE, DIE • 1924 • Obal Max • FRG

PERLENHALSBAND, DAS • 1917 • Dupont E. A. • FRG

PERLENKETTE, DIE • 1951 • Kulb Karl G. • FRG

PERLENMACHER VON MADRID, DER • 1921 • Frowein Eberhard • FRG • PERLENMACHER VON PARIS, DER

PERLENMACHER VON PARIS, DER see **PERLENMACHER VON MADRID, DER** • 1921

PERLES DE LA COURONNE, LES • 1937 • Guitry Sacha, Christian-Jaque • FRN • PEARLS OF THE CROWN, THE (USA) ○ COLLIER DE PERLES, LE ○ SEPT PERLES DE LA COURONNE, LES

PERLICKY NA DNE • 1965 • Menzel Jiri, Chytilova Vera, Schorm Evald, Nemec Jan, Jires Jaromil • CZC • PEARLS OF THE DEEP (UKN)

PERMANENCIA DEL ARABESCO • 1971 • Chavarri Jaime • SHT • SPN

PERMANENT RECORD • 1988 • Silver Marisa • USA

PERMANENT VACATION • 1981 • Jarmusch Jim • USA

PERMANENT WAVE • 1929 • Lantz Walter, Nolan William • ANS • USA

PERMAN'S EQUESTRIAN BEAR • 1902 • *Warwick Trading Co* • UKN

PERMETTE? ROCCO PAPALEO • 1971 • Scola Ettore • ITL • MY NAME IS ROCCO PAPALEO ○ ROCCO PAPALEO

PERMETTETE, SIGNORA, CHE AMI VOSTRA FIGLIA? • 1974 • Polidoro Gian Luigi • ITL

PERMIAN STRATA • 1969 • Conner Bruce • SHT • USA

PERMINTAAN TERAKHIR • 1974 • Sutan H. M. • MLY • LAST WISH, THE

PERMISO PARA PENSAR • 1988 • Meilij Eduardo • ARG • LICENCE TO THINK

PERMISSION, LA • 1968 • Van Peebles Melvin • FRN • STORY OF A THREE DAY PASS, THE (USA)

PERMISSION TO KILL • 1975 • Frankel Cyril • USA, AUS

PERMISSION TO KILL see **VOLLMACHT ZUM MORD** • 1975

PERMISSIVE • 1970 • Shonteff Lindsay • UKN

PERMIT ME • 1925 • Ray Albert • USA

PERMUTATIONS AND COMBINATIONS • 1976 • Elder Bruce • CND

PERNELLE • 1969 • Ledoux Patrick • BLG

PERNICKETY POLLY ANN see **POLLY ANN** • 1917

PERNIKOVA CHALOUPKA • 1927 • Kokeisl • CZC • BABES IN THE WOOD

PERNIKOVA CHALOUPKA • 1951 • Pojar Bretislav • ANS • CZC • GINGERBREAD HOUSE ○ GINGERBREAD COTTAGE, THE ○ GINGERBREAD HUT

PERO, EN QUE PAIS VIVIMOS? • 1967 • Saenz De Heredia Jose Luis • SPN

PEROLA DO ATLANTICO, A • 1968 • Costa Jose Fonseca • SHT • PRT

PERON: ACTUALIZACION POLITICA Y DOCTRINARIA PARA LA TOMA DEL PODER • 1971 • Solanas Fernando • ARG

PERON: LA REVOLUCION JUSTICIALISTA • 1971 • Solanas Fernando • ARG

PERPETUA • 1922 • Robertson John S., Geraughty Tom • UKN • LOVE'S BOOMERANG (USA)
PERPETUAL MOTION • 1920 • Fleischer Dave • ANS • USA
PERPETUAL MOTION • 1975 • Dinov Todor • ANM • BUL
PERPETUAL MOTION SOLVED • 1914 • *Hilarity* • UKN
PERPETUO AGAINST THE SQUADRON OF DEATH see **PERPETUO CONTRA O ESQUADRAO DA MORTE** • 1967
PERPETUO CONTRA O ESQUADRAO DA MORTE • 1967 • Borges Miguel • BRZ • PERPETUO AGAINST THE SQUADRON OF DEATH
PERPETUUM AND MOBILE, LTD. • 1961 • Mimica Vatroslav • ANS • YGS
PERPLEXED BRIDEGROOM, THE • 1914 • Costello Maurice • USA
PERPLEXING PICKLE PUZZLE, A • 1915 • *Cooper Claude* • USA
PERRA, LA • 1967 • Gomez Muriel Emilio • ARG, MXC • BITCH, THE
PERRA VIDA see **VIDA PERRA** • 1983
PERRI • 1957 • Kenworthy N. Paul, Wright Ralph • USA
PERRO, EL • 1977 • Isasi Antonio • SPN • VENGEANCE
PERRO DE ALAMBRE • 1979 • Cano Manuel • SPN, VNZ • WIRE DOG
PERRO EN ORBITA • 1966 • del Amo Antonio • SPN • DOG IN ORBIT, A
PERRO GANCHO, EL • 1969 • Enriquez Luis B. • PHL • HOODLUMS, THE
PERRO GOLFO • 1962 • Viladomat Domingo • SPN
PERROI VERSHUES • 1984 • Sahatciu Besim • YGS • NABUJALA RIJEKA ○ SWELLING RIVER, THE
PERROQUET VERT, LE • 1928 • Milva • FRN
PERROS CALLEJEROS • 1977 • de la Loma Jose Antonio • SPN
PERROS DE DIOS, LOS • 1973 • del Villar Francisco • MXC
PERROS HAMBRIENTOS, LOS • 1976 • Figueroa Luis • PRU
PERRY GRANT, AGENT OF IRON see **PERRY GRANT AGENTE DI FERRO** • 1966
PERRY GRANT AGENTE DI FERRO • 1966 • Capuano Luigi • ITL • PERRY GRANT, AGENT OF IRON
PERRY MASON AND THE CASE OF THE SINISTER SPIRIT • 1987 • Lang Richard • TVM • USA
PERRY MASON RETURNS • 1985 • Satlof Ron • TVM • USA
PERRY MASON: THE CASE OF THE AVENGING ACE • 1988 • Nyby Christian Ii • TVM • USA
PERRY MASON: THE CASE OF THE LOST LOVE • 1987 • Satlof Ron • TVM • USA
PERRY MASON: THE CASE OF THE MURDERED MADAM • 1987 • Satlof Ron • TVM • USA
PERRY MASON: THE CASE OF THE NOTORIOUS NUN • 1986 • Satlof Ron • TVM • USA
PERRY MASON: THE CASE OF THE SCANDALOUS SCOUNDREL • 1987 • Nyby Christian Ii • TVM • USA
PERRY MASON: THE CASE OF THE SHOOTING STAR • 1986 • Satlof Ron • TVM • USA
PERRY POPGUN • 1962 • Kneitel Seymour • ANS • USA
PERRY RHODAN -SOS AUS DEM WELTALL • 1967 • Zeglio Primo • FRG, ITL, SPN • 4.. 3.. 2.. 1.. MORTE (ITL) ○ ALARM IM WELTALL ○ 4.. 3.. 2.. 1.. DEAD ○ MISSION STARDUST (USA) ○ ORBITA MORTAL (SPN) ○ YOU ONLY LIVE ONCE ○ MORTAL ORBIT
PERRYL • 1970 • Vadim Roger • FRN
PERSECUCION A UN ESPIA (SPN) see **CORRIDA POUR UN ESPION** • 1965
PERSECUCION EN MADRID • 1952 • Gomez Bascuas Enrique • SPN
PERSECUCION HASTA VALENCIA (SPN) see **SAPORE DELLE VENDETTA, IL** • 1968
PERSECUTION • 1973 • Chaffey Don • UKN • TERROR OF SHEBA, THE (USA) ○ GRAVEYARD, THE
PERSECUTION AND ASSASSINATION OF JEAN-PAUL MARAT AS PERFORMED BY THE INMATES OF THE ASYLUM.. • 1966 • Brook Peter • UKN • MARAT/DE SADE
PERSECUTION OF BOB PRETTY, THE • 1916 • Miller Frank • UKN
PERSECUTOR, THE see **PERSEGUIDOR, EL** • 1962
PERSEE L'INVINCIBLE see **PERSEO L'INVINCIBILE** • 1962
PERSEGUIDOR, EL • 1962 • Wilenski Osias • ARG • PERSECUTOR, THE
PERSEO L'INVINCIBILE • 1962 • De Martino Alberto • ITL, SPN • VALLE DE LOS HOMBRES DE PIEDRA, EL (SPN) ○ PERSEE L'INVINCIBLE ○ PERSEUS AGAINST THE MONSTERS (UKN) ○ MEDUSA AGAINST THE SON OF HERCULES (USA) ○ VALLEY OF THE STONE MEN ○ SPN ○ MEDUSA VS. THE SON OF HERCULES
PERSEPHONE • 1951 • de Heusch Luc • BLG
PERSERVING PEGGY • 1912 • *Cosmopolitan* • UKN
PERSEUS AGAINST THE MONSTERS (UKN) see **PERSEO L'INVINCIBILE** • 1962
PERSEVERANCE DOES IT see **TRAGEN VINNER** • 1916
PERSEVERING EDWIN • 1907 • Fitzhamon Lewin • UKN
PERSEVERING PETER • 1913 • Calvert Charles? • UKN
PERSIAN DANCE: EIGHTPENCE A MILE • 1913 • Booth W. R. • UKN
PERSIAN STORY • 1952 • Keene Ralph • UKN
PERSIANE CHIUSE • 1952 • Comencini Luigi • ITL • BEHIND CLOSED SHUTTERS (USA)
PERSIL WAY, THE • 1934 • Asquith Anthony • UKN
PERSISTENCE WINS • 1915 • Cooley Frank • USA
PERSISTENCY • 1916 • Winter Percy • SHT • USA
PERSISTENCY WINS • 1908 • *Lubin* • USA
PERSISTENT AND FINAGLING • 1972 • Rubbo Michael • CND
PERSISTENT DALTON • 1915 • *Lubin* • USA
PERSISTENT LOVER, A • 1912 • Hale Albert W. • USA
PERSISTENT LOVERS, THE • 1914 • *Crystal* • USA
PERSISTENT LOVERS, THE • 1922 • Newall Guy • UKN
PERSISTENT MR. PRINCE, THE • 1914 • North Wilfred • USA
PERSISTENT PERCIVAL • 1916 • Watt Nate • USA
PERSISTENT POET, THE • 1909 • *Lubin* • USA
PERSISTENT POET, THE • 1911 • Wilson Frank? • UKN
PERSISTENT SEED, THE • 1964 • Chapman Christopher • DOC • CND
PERSISTENT SUITOR, A • 1909 • Porter Edwin S. • USA
PERSISTENT SUITOR, A • 1912 • *Selig* • USA
PERSISTENT TROMBONIST, THE • 1908 • *Lubin* • USA
PERSISTENT WOOING, A • 1916 • Myers Harry • USA
PERSON TO BUNNY • 1960 • Freleng Friz • ANS • USA
PERSON UNKNOWN • 1956 • Tully Montgomery • UKN
PERSONA • 1966 • Bergman Ingmar • SWD • MASKS
PERSONAL • 1904 • *Bitzer Billy (Ph)* • USA
PERSONAL AFFAIR • 1953 • Pelissier Anthony • UKN
PERSONAL AFFAIR, A • 1912 • *Edison* • USA
PERSONAL AFFAIR, A • 1940 • Rasumny Alexander • USS
PERSONAL AFFAIR, A see **LICHNOYE DELO** • 1932
PERSONAL AFFAIRS see **LICNE STVARI** • 1980
PERSONAL AID see **ISSHIN TASUKE** • 1930
PERSONAL AND CONFIDENTIAL • 1965 • Nethercott Geoffrey • UKN
PERSONAL BEST • 1982 • Towne Robert • USA
PERSONAL CHOICE • 1989 • Saperstein David • USA
PERSONAL COLUMN (UKN) see **LURED** • 1947
PERSONAL COLUMN (USA) see **PIEGES** • 1939
PERSONAL CONDUCT OF HENRY, THE • 1909 • *Essanay* • USA
PERSONAL EXEMPTIONS • 1988 • Rowe Peter • CND
PERSONAL FOUL • 1987 • Lichtenfeld Ted • USA
PERSONAL HISTORY, ADVENTURES, EXPERIENCE AND OBSERVATION OF DAVID COPPERFIELD THE YOUNGER, THE • 1935 • Cukor George • USA • DAVID COPPERFIELD
PERSONAL HONOUR (UKN) see **HELLO, ANNAPOLIS** • 1942
PERSONAL INTERVIEWS TODAY • 1974 • Shuster S. • USS
PERSONAL MAGNETISM • 1913 • *American* • USA
PERSONAL MAID • 1931 • Mendes Lothar, Bell Monta • USA
PERSONAL MAID'S SECRET • 1935 • Collins Arthur G. • USA
PERSONAL MATTER, A see **LICHNOYE DELO** • 1932
PERSONAL OPINION see **OSOBOYE MNYENIYE** • 1968
PERSONAL OPINION see **SOBSTVENNOYE MNYENIYE** • 1977
PERSONAL PROBLEMS see **NESKOLKO INTERVYU PO LICHNYM VOPROSAM** • 1980
PERSONAL PROPERTY • 1937 • Van Dyke W. S. • USA • MAN IN POSSESSION, THE (UKN)
PERSONAL SECRETARY • 1938 • Garrett Otis • USA
PERSONAL SERVICES • 1987 • Jones Terry • UKN
PERSONAL TEMPEST, A see **SOUKROMA VICHRICE** • 1967
PERSONAL VENDETTA • 1987 • Moxey John Llewellyn • USA
PERSONALITY • 1930 • Heerman Victor • USA
PERSONALITY KID, THE • 1934 • Crosland Alan • USA
PERSONALITY KID, THE • 1946 • Sherman George • USA
PERSONALS, THE • 1981 • Markle Peter • USA
PERSONEL • 1975 • Kieslowski Krzysztof • MTV • PLN • PERSONNEL
PERSONNEL see **PERSONEL** • 1975
PERSONNEL OR PEOPLE • 1969 • Crombie Donald • SHT • ASL
PERSONNEL SELECTION IN THE ARMY, 1944 -OFFICERS • 1946 • Bell Geoffrey • DOC • UKN
PERSONNEL SELECTION -RECRUITS • 1937-45 • Bell Geoffrey • DOC • UKN
PERSONS IN HIDING • 1939 • King Louis • USA
PERSONS UNKNOWN see **SOLITI IGNOTI, I** • 1958
PERSPECTIV, ETT • 1973 • Leijonborg Ingemar • SWD • FUTURE VISION, A
PERSPECTRUM • 1974 • Patel Ishu • ANS • CND
PERSUADER, THE • 1957 • Ross Dick • USA
PERSUADERS, THE • 1971 • Guest Val • UKN
PERSUADERS: LONDON CONSPIRACY, THE • 1976 • Hill James, Greene David • MTV • UKN • LONDON CONSPIRACY, THE
PERSUADERS: MISSION MONTE CARLO, THE • 1975 • Baker Roy Ward, Dearden Basil • MTV • UKN • MISSION MONTE CARLO
PERSUADERS: SPORTING CHANCE, THE • 1972 • Norman Leslie, Medak Peter • MTV • UKN • SPORTING CHANCE
PERSUADERS: THE SWITCH, THE • 1972 • Baker Roy Ward, Guest Val • MTV • UKN • SWITCH, THE
PERSUADING PAPA • 1910 • Fitzhamon Lewin • UKN
PERSUASIVE PEGGY • 1917 • Brabin Charles J. • USA
PERSUASIVE PUSH, THE • 1961 • Bristol Christopher • SHT • USA
PERTENTANGAN • 1982 • Ghani Salleh • MLY
PERU -ISTITUTO DE VERANO • 1956 • Olmi Ermanno (Spv) • DOC • ITL
PERUANERIN, DIE • 1919 • Sauer Fred? • FRG
PERUCKE, DIE • 1925 • Viertel Berthold • FRG
PERUGINA, LA • 1977 • Guida Ernesto • ITL
PERUVIAN CENTAURS • 1908 • PRU
PERVAYA LASTOCHKA see **PIRVELI MERTSKHALI** • 1976
PERVENCHE • 1921 • Wulschleger Henry, Machin Alfred • FRN
PERVERSA, LA • 1953 • Urueta Chano • MXC
PERVERSA CARICIA DE SATAN, LA • Gigo Jorge Luis • SPN • PERVERSE CARESS OF SATAN, THE
PERVERSA SENORA WARD, LA (SPN) see **STRANO VIZIO DELLA SIGNORA WARDH, LO** • 1971
PERVERSE CARESS OF SATAN, THE see **PERVERSA CARICIA DE SATAN, LA**
PERVERSE STATUES, THE • 1908 • *Lux* • FRN
PERVERSE TALES see **CONTES PERVERS** • 1980
PERVERSION • 1974 • Lara Polop Francisco • SPN
PERVERSION CITY, U.S.A. • 1970 • *Able Film Co.* • USA
PERVERSION DE PORNO • 1978 • FRN
PERVERSION STORY see **CALDI AMORE DI UNA MINORENNE, I** • 1969
PERVERSIONS • 1975 • Rafael Peter • FRN
PERVERSIONS PORNO • 1977 • Mulot Claude • FRN
PERVERSIONS SEXUELLES • 1972 • Ruder Ken • FRN, SPN • SEXUAL PERVERSIONS
PERVERSIONS TRES COCHONNES • Baudricourt Michel • FRN
PERVERSIONS TRES INTIMES • 1978 • Baudricourt Michel • FRN
PERVERSITES SUEDOISES • 1977 • Roy Jean-Claude • FRN
PERVERSITY OF FATE, THE • 1910 • *Kalem* • USA
PERVERSOS, LOS • 1965 • Martinez Solares Gilberto • MXC • A GO GO
PERVERT, THE • 1934 • Auer John H. • MXC
PERVERT, THE • 1963 • Kuchar Mike • SHT • USA
PERVERTIDA • 1945 • Diaz Morales Jose • MXC
PERVI DEN • 1955 • Ermler Friedrich • USS • FIRST DAY, THE ○ DEN PERVYI
PERVI REJS V ZVEZDAM • 1961 • Kopalin Ilya • DOC • USS • WITH GAGARIN TO THE STARS ○ FIRST TRIP TO THE STARS
PERVOKLASSNIZA • 1948 • Frez Ilya • USS • FIRST YEAR AT SCHOOL ○ FIRST GRADE, THE
PERVOLA • 1985 • Seunke Orlow • NTH
PERVOROSSIYANYE • 1968 • Ivanov Alexander • USS • RUSSIA'S FIRST COMMUNE
PERVYI DEN MIRA • 1959 • Segel Yakov • USS • DAY THE WAR ENDED, THE (USA) ○ FIRST DAY OF PEACE, THE
PERVYI ESHELON • 1956 • Kalatozov Mikhail • USS • FIRST ECHELON, THE ○ FIRST TRAIN, THE
PERVYI KORNET STRECHNEV • 1928 • Chiaureli Mikhail, Dzigan Yefim • USS • FIRST CORNET STRESHNEV
PERVYI PAREN • 1958 • Paradjanov Sergei • USS • FIRST LAD, THE
PERVYI UCHITEL • 1965 • Konchalovsky Andrei • USS • FIRST TEACHER, THE
PESAR-E-DEHATI • 1967 • Rafiei Aziz • IRN • VILLAGE SON
PESARAN-E-ALAEDIN • 1967 • Motevaselani Mohamad • IRN • ALAEDIN'S SONS
PESCA A MAZZARA DEL VALLO • 1949 • Fallette • SHT • ITL
PESCA DA SARDINHA, A • 1953 • Mendes Joao • SHT • PRT
PESCA DO ATUM • 1939 • de Barros Jose Leitao • SHT • PRT
PESCA DO ATUM, A • 1962 • Queiroga Perdigao • SHT • PRT
PESCA NEL GOLFO • 1933 • Ferroni Giorgio • ITL • FISHING IN THE GULF
PESCA PISCA • 1968 • Duga Irene • SHT • USA
PESCADOR DE COPLAS, EL • 1953 • del Amo Antonio • SPN
PESCADORES DE AMANGAU • 1958 • Spiguel Miguel • SHT • PRT
PESCADORES DE PERLAS • 1938 • Calles Guillermo • MXC • SOL DE GLORIA
PESCADOS see **REDES** • 1934
PESCANDO MILLONES • 1960 • Mur Oti • SPN
PESCATORE DI POSILLIPO, IL see **PESCATORE 'E PUSILLECO** • 1955
PESCATORE 'E PUSILLECO • 1955 • Capitani Giorgio • ITL • PESCATORE DI POSILLIPO, IL
PESCATORELLA • 1947 • Risi Dino • SHT • ITL
PESCATORI • 1942 • Bellini Giacomo P. • ITL
PESCENI GRAD • 1962 • Hladnik Bostjan • YGS • CASTLE IN THE SAND ○ SANDCASTLE
PESCHERECCI • 1957 • De Seta Vittorio • ITL • FISHERMEN
PESCI D'ORO E BIKINI D'ARGENTO • 1962 • Veo Carlo • ITL
PESEN ZA CHOVEKA see **PESSEN ZA CHOVEKA** • 1954
PESKY PELICAN • 1963 • Marcus Sid • ANS • USA
PESMA • 1961 • Novakovic Rados • YGS • POEM, THE
PESN LYUBVI NEDOPETAYA • 1919 • Kuleshov Lev, Polonsky Vitold • USS • UNFINISHED LOVE SONG, THE
PESN O GEROJACH see **KOMSOMOL** • 1932
PESN O KOLTSOVE • 1960 • Gerasimov Vladimir • USS • SONG OF KOLTSOV
PESN PRO KOUPTSA KALACHNIKOVA • 1909 • Goncharov Vasili M. • USS • SONG OF THE MERCHANT KALASHNIKOV
PESN TORZHESTVUYUSHCHEI LIUBVI • 1915 • Bauer Yevgeni • USS • SONG OF TRIUMPHANT LOVE
PESNI ABAYA • 1945 • Roshal Grigori, Aron E. • USS • ABA IBRAHIM KOUMANBAEF ○ SONG OF ABAYA
PESNI RODNOY STORONY • 1953 • Frolov Andrei • USS • FESTIVAL OF RUSSIAN SONG AND DANCES
PESNI ROSSII • 1963 • Uchitel Yefim • USS • PANORAMA OF RUSSIA (USA)
PESNJ O METALLE • 1928 • Heifitz Josif, Zarkhi Alexander • USS • SONG OF STEEL, A
PESNYA KATORZHANINA • 1911 • Protazanov Yakov • USS • PRISONER'S SONG, THE
PESNYA MANSHUK • 1971 • Begalin Mazhit • USS • SONG OF MANSHUK ○ PYESN O MANSHUK
PESNYA O SHCHASTYE • 1934 • Donskoi Mark, Legoshin Vladimir • USS • SONG ABOUT HAPPINESS ○ SONG OF HAPPINESS
PESSEN ZA CHOVEKA • 1954 • Shariliev Borislav • BUL • SONG FOR MAN ○ PESEN ZA CHOVEKA ○ SONG OF MAN
PESSI AND ILLUSIA see **PESSI JA ILLUSIA** • 1983
PESSI JA ILLUSIA • 1983 • Partanen Heikki • FNL • PESSI AND ILLUSIA
PEST, THE • 1917 • Drew Sidney • *Drew* • SHT • USA
PEST, THE • 1917 • Gillstrom Arvid E. • *King Bee* • SHT • USA
PEST, THE • 1919 • Cabanne W. Christy • USA
PEST, THE • 1920 • *Franey William* • SHT • USA
PEST, THE • 1934 • Schwarzwald Milton • SHT • USA
PEST CONTROL • 1950 • Barclay David • SHT • USA
PEST FROM THE WEST • 1939 • Lord Del • SHT • USA
PEST IN FLORENZ, DIE • 1919 • Rippert Otto • FRG • PLAGUE IN FLORENCE, THE
PEST IN THE HOUSE, A • 1947 • Jones Charles M. • ANS • USA
PEST MAN WINS, THE • 1951 • White Jules • SHT • USA
PEST OF FRIENDS, THE • 1927 • *Sennett Mack (P)* • SHT • USA
PEST OF SHOW • 1962 • Hannah Jack • ANS • USA
PEST OF THE NEIGHBORHOOD, THE • 1915 • Castle James W. • USA
PEST PILOT • 1941 • Fleischer Dave • ANS • USA
PEST PUPIL • 1957 • Tendlar Dave • ANS • USA
PEST THAT CAME TO DINNER, THE • 1948 • Davis Arthur • ANS • USA
PEST VAMOOSER, THE • 1915 • Williams C. Jay • USA
PESTALOZZIDORF, DAS see **UNSER DORF** • 1953
PESTALOZZI'S BERG • 1988 • von Gunten Peter • SWT • PESTALOZZI'S MOUNTAIN
PESTALOZZI'S MOUNTAIN see **PESTALOZZI'S BERG** • 1988
PESTE MESE • 1938 • Gaal Bela • HNG • TALES OF BUDAPEST (USA)
PESTI HAZTETOK • 1961 • Kovacs Andras • HNG • ON THE ROOFS OF BUDAPEST
PESTI SZERELEM see **SKANDAL IN BUDAPEST** • 1933
PESTI VE TME • 1987 • Soukup Jaroslav • CZC • FISTS IN THE DARK
PESTICIDE see **RAISINS DE LA MORT, LES** • 1978

PESTILENT CITY • 1965 • Goldman Peter Emanuel • USA
PESTONJI • 1987 • Mehta Vijaya • IND
PESTS, THE see **TO SO GADI** • 1979
PESTS AND PROMISES • 1917 • Semon Larry • SHT • USA
PESTS FOR GUESTS • 1955 • Freleng Friz • ANS • USA
PESTS GOT CAUGHT, THE • Salimov D. • ANS • USS
PESTS OF THE WEST • 1950 • Nichols Charles • ANS • USA
PESTTHEATER see **TOD DES FLOHZIRKUSDIREKTORS ODER OTTOCARO WEISS REFORMIERT SEINE FIRMA, DER** • 1973
PESTY GUEST • 1965 • Marcus Sid • ANS • USA
PESUM DEIVAM • 1967 • Gopalakrishnan K. S. • IND • GOD WHO TALKS, THE
PET, THE • 1917 • McCay Winsor • ANS • USA • MONSTER DOG, THE
PET HEN, THE • 1914 • Kellino W. P. • UKN
PET HOLEK NA KRKU • 1967 • Schorm Evald • CZC • FIVE GIRLS LIKE A MILLSTONE ROUND ONE'S NECK ○ FIVE GIRLS TO DEAL WITH ○ SADDLED WITH FIVE GIRLS ○ LEFT WITH FIVE GIRLS ○ FIVE GIRLS AROUND ONE'S NECK ○ FIVE GIRLS TO COPE WITH
PET MINUTA RAJA • 1959 • Pretnar Igor • YGS • FIVE MINUTES OF PARADISE
PET OF THE BIG HORN RANCH • 1909 • *Selig* • USA
PET OF THE PETTICOATS, THE • 1914 • *Royal* • USA
PET OF THE REGIMENT, THE • 1914 • Wilson Frank? • UKN
PET PEEVE • 1954 • Hanna William, Barbera Joseph • ANS • USA
PET PEEVES • 1947 • Barclay David • SHT • USA
PET PROBLEMS • 1954 • Donnelly Eddie • ANS • USA
PET SEMATARY • 1989 • Lambert Mary • USA
PET SHOP, THE • 1932 • *Mintz Charles (P)* • ANS • USA
PET SMYSLU CLOVECKA • 1912 • Svab-Malostransky Josef • CZC • FIVE SENSES OF MAN, THE
PET STORE, THE • 1933 • Jackson Wilfred • ANS • USA
PET Z MILIONU • 1959 • Brynych Zbynek • CZC • FIVE OUT OF A MILLION
PETAL IN THE CURRENT, THE see **PETAL ON THE CURRENT, THE** • 1919
PETAL ON THE CURRENT, THE • 1919 • Browning Tod • USA • PETAL IN THE CURRENT, THE
PETALS, FLOWERS, WREATHS see **SZIRMOK, VIRAGOK, KOSORUK** • 1985
PETAR DOBROVIC • 1957 • Petrovic Aleksandar • YGS
PETCH SEAN TONG • 1986 • Pakdivijit Chalong • THL • DIAMONDS AND GOLD
PETE AND JOHNNIE see **PETEY AND JOHNNIE** • 1961
PETE FOUNTAIN SEXTET • 1962 • Binder Steve • SHT • USA
PETE GOES TO WAR • 1915 • *Alhambra* • USA
PETE HOTHEAD • 1952 • Parmelee Ted • ANS • USA
PETE JOINS THE FORCE • 1913 • *Lang Pete* • USA
PETE KELLY'S BLUES • 1955 • Webb Jack • USA
PETE MANDELL AND HIS RHYTHM MASTERS NO.1 • 1930 • *Balcon Michael (P)* • SHT • UKN
PETE MANDELL AND HIS RHYTHM MASTERS NO.2 • 1930 • *Balcon Michael (P)* • SHT • UKN
PETE 'N' TILLIE • 1972 • Ritt Martin • USA
PETE, PEARL AND THE POLE (USA) see **PIAZZA PULITA** • 1973
PETE ROLEUM AND HIS COUSINS • 1939 • Losey Joseph, Bay Howard • ANS • USA
PETE SEEGER -A SONG AND A STONE • 1972 • Elfstrom Robert • DOC • USA
PETE SMITH'S SCRAPBOOK • 1942 • *Smith Pete* • SHT • USA
PETE STANDING ALONE • 1982 • Low Colin • CND
PETE, THE ARTIST • 1913 • O'Neil Barry • USA
PETE THE PEDDLE POLISHER • 1915 • *Eclectic* • USA
PETE THE PROWLER • 1917 • Chaudet Louis W. • SHT • USA
PETE TOWNSEND: WHITE CITY see **PETE TOWNSEND: WHITE CITY, THE MUSIC MOVIE** • 1985
PETE TOWNSEND: WHITE CITY, THE MUSIC MOVIE • 1985 • Lowenstein Richard • UKN • WHITE CITY: PETE TOWNSEND ○ PETE TOWNSEND: WHITE CITY ○ WHITE CITY
PETE TRIES THE STAGE • 1913 • O'Neil Barry • USA
PETEC DE CER, UN • 1984 • Munteanu Francisc • RMN • PIECE OF SKY, A
PETER • 1935 • Koster Henry • HNG, AUS
PETER AND PAUL • 1981 • Day Robert • TVM • USA
PETER AND PAUL see **EGYSZEREGY** • 1978
PETER AND PAULA see **CERNY PETR** • 1963
PETER AND PAVLA see **CERNY PETR** • 1963
PETER AND PETRA see **PETER OCH PETRA** • 1989
PETER AND SABINE see **PETER UND SABINE** • 1968
PETER AND THE FLYING CAR see **PETER EN DE VLIEGENDE AUTOBUS** • 1976
PETER AND THE MOON MAN • 1929 • *Health & Cleanliness Council* • SHT • UKN
PETER AND THE WOLF • 1946 • Geronimi Clyde • ANS • USA
PETER AND THE WOLF OR SAND • 1969 • Leaf Caroline • ANS • USA
PETER DER GROSSE • 1922 • Buchowetzki Dimitri • FRG • PETER THE GREAT
PETER, DER MATROSE • 1929 • Schunzel Reinhold • FRG
PETER EN DE VLIEGENDE AUTOBUS • 1976 • van der Meulen Karst • NTH • PETER AND THE FLYING CAR
PETER FELIX -THE BLACK DIAMOND • 1915 • *Fraser Film* • ASL
PETER IBBETSON • 1935 • Hathaway Henry • USA
PETER IBBETSON see **FOREVER** • 1921
PETER IM SCHNEE • 1937 • Lamac Carl • AUS
PETER IN WONDERLAND see **SZARNYAS UGYNOK, A** • 1988
PETER LOVES WORK • 1914 • *Melies* • USA
PETER LUMP • 1916 • Wauer William • FRG
PETER LUNDY AND THE MEDICINE HAT STALLION • 1977 • O'Herlihy Michael • TVM • USA
PETER MAKAROFF • 1913 • *Apex* • USA
PETER MARTINS • 1978 • Leth Jorgen • DOC • NTH
PETER MONKEY see **PEDRO MICO** • 1986
PETER-NO-TAIL see **PELLE SVANSLOS** • 1979
PETER-NO-TAIL IN AMERICA see **PELLE SVANSLOS I AMERIKATT** • 1983
PETER OCH PETRA • 1989 • Jarleman Agneta Elers • SWD • PETER AND PETRA
PETER PAN • 1924 • Brenon Herbert • USA
PETER PAN • 1953 • Luske Hamilton, Geronimi Clyde, Jackson Wilfred • ANM • USA
PETER PAN HANDLED • 1925 • Lantz Walter • ANS • USA
PETER, PAUL AND NANETTE • 1934 • Engels Erich • FRG
PETER PENS POETRY • 1913 • Haldane Bert? • UKN
PETER PEREZ DE PERALVILLO see **GENIAL DETECTIVE PETER PEREZ, EL** • 1952
PETER PICKLES' WEDDING • 1912 • Haldane Bert? • UKN
PETER RABBIT AND TALES OF BEATRIX POTTER (USA) see **TALES OF BEATRIX POTTER** • 1971
PETER SCHIESST DEN VOGEL AB • 1959 • von Cziffra Geza • FRG
PETER SCHLEMIHL • 1915 • Rye Stellan • FRG
PETER STUDIES FORM • 1964 • Strangeway Stan • UKN
PETER STUYVESANT • 1924 • Tuttle Frank • SHT • USA
PETER THE BARBER • 1922 • Dudley Bernard • UKN
PETER THE FIRST see **PYOTR PERVY** • 1937-39
PETER THE GREAT • 1985 • Chomsky Marvin, Schiller Lawrence • MTV • USA
PETER THE GREAT see **PIOTR VELIKY** • 1910
PETER THE GREAT see **PETER DER GROSSE** • 1922
PETER THE GREAT see **PYOTR PERVY** • 1937-39
PETER, THE HERMIT • 1916 • Windom Lawrence C. • SHT • USA
PETER THE PIRATE (USA) see **PIETRO, DER KORSAR** • 1925
PETER THE TRAMP (USA) see **LUFFAR-PETTER** • 1922
PETER TRIES SUICIDE • 1913 • Haldane Bert? • UKN
PETER UND SABINE • 1968 • Rieger August • FRG • PETER AND SABINE ○ HOT BLOOD
PETER VERNON'S SILENCE • 1926 • Longford Raymond • ASL
PETER VINOGRADOF • 1935 • Macheret Alexander • USS
PETER VON SCHOLTEN • 1986 • Kjaeruff-Schmidt Palle • DNM
PETER VOSS, DER HELD DES TAGES • 1959 • Marischka Georg • FRG • MEET PETER VOSS (USA)
PETER VOSS, DER MILLIONENDIEB • 1932 • Dupont E. A. • FRG • PETER VOSS, WHO STOLE MILLIONS
PETER VOSS, DER MILLIONENDIEB • 1945 • Anton Karl • FRG
PETER VOSS, DER MILLIONENDIEB • 1958 • Becker Wolfgang • FRG
PETER VOSS, WHO STOLE MILLIONS see **PETER VOSS, DER MILLIONENDIEB** • 1932
PETERBURGSKAYA NOCH • 1934 • Roshal Grigori, Stroyeva Vera • USS • PETERSBURG NIGHTS ○ SAINT PETERSBURG
PETERBURGSKIYE TRUSHCHOBI • 1915 • Protazanov Yakov, Gardin Vladimir • USS • PETERSBURG SLUMS
PETERING OUT • 1927 • Lantz Walter • ANS • USA
PETERKIN • 1939 • Lovy Alex • ASS • USA
PETERLE • 1943 • Stockel Joe • FRG
PETERMANN IST DAGEGEN • 1937 • Wisbar Frank • FRG
PETERS ERBSCHAFT • 1920 • Trotz Adolf • FRG
PETER'S EVIL SPIRIT • 1914 • *Urban-Eclipse* • FRN
PETERS JUGEND • 1980 • Gerasimov Sergei • USS, FRG
PETER'S LITTLE PICNIC • 1913 • Plumb Hay? • UKN
PETER'S PERFECT PHOTOPLAY • 1916 • *Ross Bud* • SHT • USA
PETER'S PERIL • 1913 • *Gale Peter* • UKN
PETER'S PICTURE POEMS • 1918 • *Dyer Anson (Anm)* • ANS • UKN
PETER'S PLEDGE • 1913 • O'Neil Barry • USA
PETER'S RELATIONS • 1914 • Jackson Harry • USA
PETER'S RIVAL • 1912 • Collins Edwin J.? • UKN
PETERSBURG NIGHTS see **PETERBURGSKAYA NOCH** • 1934
PETERSBURG SLUMS see **PETERBURGSKIYE TRUSHCHOBI** • 1915
PETERSBURGER NACHTE • 1934 • Emo E. W. • FRG • WALZER AN DER NEWA
PETERSBURGER NACHTE • 1958 • Martin Paul • FRG • SCHWARZE AUGEN
PETERSEN • 1974 • Burstall Tim • ASL • JOCK PETERSEN (USA)
PETERSON'S PITIFUL PLIGHT • 1916 • *Delaney Bert* • SHT • USA
PETERVILLE DIAMOND, THE • 1942 • Forde Walter • UKN
PETE'S AWFUL CRIME • 1915 • Curtis Allen • USA
PETE'S DRAGON • 1977 • Chaffey Don • USA
PETE'S HAUNTED HOUSE • 1926 • Lantz Walter • ANS • USA
PETE'S INSURANCE POLICY • 1913 • *Kalem* • USA
PETE'S PANTS • 1917 • *Todd Harry* • SHT • USA
PETE'S PECULIAR PAL • 1916 • *Gayety* • USA
PETE'S PERSIAN PRINCESS • 1916 • *Cooper Claude* • SHT • USA
PETEY AND JOHNNIE • 1961 • Leacock Richard • DOC • USA • PETE AND JOHNNIE
PETEY NO-TAIL see **PELLE SVANSLOS** • 1979
PETEY WHEATSTRAW • 1978 • *Moore Rudy Ray* • USA
PETEY'S SWEETIES see **MR. PETERS' PETS** • 1962
PETFOODS IS A SERIOUS BUSINESS • 1969 • Thoms Albie • DOC • ASL
PETHEROPLIKTOS • 1968 • Kiriakopoulos Hristos • GRC • MY MOTHER-IN-LAW IS A GAMBLER ○ HEN-PECKED
PETI • 1964 • Grgic Zlatko, Statler Pavao • ANS • YGS • FIFTH ONE, THE ○ FIFTH, THE
PETICION, LA • 1976 • Miro Pilar • SPN • ENGAGEMENT, THE ○ DEMAND, THE
PETISTOVKA • 1949 • Fric Martin • CZC • MOTOR CYCLES
PETIT A PETIT • 1970 • Rouch Jean • FRN
PETIT ANGE • 1920 • Luitz-Morat, Regnier Pierre • FRN
PETIT ANGE, LE see **MALAK AS-SAGHIR, AL-** • 1958
PETIT ANGE ET SON PANTIN • 1922 • Luitz-Morat, Vercourt Alfred • FRN
PETIT BABOUIN, LE • 1932 • Gremillon Jean • SHT • FRN
PETIT BAIGNEUR, LE • 1967 • Dhery Robert • FRN, ITL • SI SALVI CHI PUO (ITL) ○ BOUNCING BEAUTY
PETIT BONHEUR • 1972 • Warny Clorinda • ANS • CND
PETIT BOUGNAT, LE • 1969 • Toublanc-Michel Bernard • FRN, ITL
PETIT BOURGOGNE, LA • 1968 • Bulbulian Maurice • DOC • CND
PETIT CAFE, LE • 1919 • Linder Max, Bernard Raymond • FRN
PETIT CAFE, LE • 1930 • Berger Ludwig • FRN
PETIT CAFE, LE • 1962 • Reichenbach Francois • SHT • FRN • SCENES DE LA VIE DE CAFE
PETIT CARAMBOUILLEUR, LE see **TOUT POUR RIEN** • 1933
PETIT CHANTECLER, LE • Rostand Edmond • ANM • FRN
PETIT CHANTECLER, LE • 1910 • Cohl Emile • ANS • FRN
PETIT CHAPERON ROUGE, LE • 1901 • Melies Georges • FRN • RED RIDING HOOD (USA)
PETIT CHAPERON ROUGE, LE • 1928 • Cavalcanti Alberto • FRN • LITTLE RED RIDING HOOD (USA)
PETIT CHAPERON ROUGE, LE see **FILLE A CROQUER, UNE** • 1950
PETIT CHAPERON ROUGE: L'AN 2000 see **PIROSKA ES A FARKAS 2000-BEN** • 1987
PETIT CHAPITEAU, LE • 1963 • Ivens Joris • SHT • CHL, FRN
PETIT CHASSEUR, LE • 1961 • Grospierre Louis • SHT • FRN
PETIT CHOSE, LE • 1923 • Hugon Andre • FRN
PETIT CHOSE, LE • 1938 • Cloche Maurice • FRN
PETIT CIRQUE MEXICAIN, LE • 1975 • Reichenbach Francois • MTV • FRN
PETIT COIN BIEN A MOI, UN • 1918 • Burguet Charles • FRN
PETIT COIN DE PARAPLUIE, UN • 1958 • Menegoz Robert • SHT • FRN
PETIT CON see **P'TIT CON** • 1983
PETIT DEJEUNER POUR DEUX see **ONTBIJT VOOR TWEE** • 1973
PETIT DEMON, LE see **SHAITANE EL SAGHIR, EL** • 1963
PETIT DIABLE, UN • 1896 • Melies Georges • FRN • LITTLE DEVIL, A
PETIT DISCOURS DE LA METHODE • 1963 • Jutra Claude, Patry Pierre • DCS • CND
PETIT ECART, LE • 1931 • Chomette Henri, Schunzel Reinhold • FRN
PETIT ECHO DE LA FORET, LE • Chanowski • ANM • FRN
PETIT ETRANGER, LE see **GHARIB AL SAGHIR, AL** • 1962
PETIT FAUST, LE see **TOUT PETIT FAUST, LE** • 1910
PETIT FIACRE, LE see **AMAXAKI, TO** • 1957
PETIT FILLE AU BOUT DU CHEMIN, LA (FRN) see **LITTLE GIRL WHO LIVES DOWN THE LANE, THE** • 1977
PETIT-FILS, LE see **HAFID, AL-** • 1974
PETIT FRERE DE GREY OWL, LE see **GREY OWL'S LITTLE BROTHER** • 1932
PETIT FRERE ET PETITE SOEUR • 1896-97 • Lumiere Louis • FRN
PETIT GARCON DE L'ENSCENSEUR, LE • 1961 • Granier-Deferre Pierre • FRN
PETIT GOSSE • 1947-49 • Canolle Jean • SHT • FRN
PETIT HAMLET, LE see **HAMLES** • 1960
PETIT HOTEL A LOUER • 1924 • Colombier Piere • FRN
PETIT JACQUES, LE • 1923 • Lannes Georges, Raulet Georges • FRN
PETIT JACQUES, LE • 1934 • Roudes Gaston • FRN
PETIT JACQUES, LE • 1953 • Bibal Robert • FRN
PETIT JIMMY, LE • 1930 • Benoit-Levy Jean, Epstein Marie • FRN • JIMMY BRUITEUR ○ JIMMY
PETIT JOSEPH • 1982 • Barjol Jean-Michel • FRN
PETIT JOUR • 1964 • Pierre • SHT • FRN
PETIT JULES VERNE, LE • 1907 • Velle Gaston • SHT • FRN • LITTLE JULES VERNE, THE ○ JULES VERNE AS A CHILD
PETIT MANUEL D'HISTOIRE DE FRANCE • 1979 • Ruiz Raul • FRN • SHORT HISTORY OF FRANCE
PETIT MARCEL, LE • 1976 • Fansten Jacques • FRN
PETIT MATIN, LE • 1971 • Albicocco Jean-Gabriel • FRN • VIRGIN AND THE SOLDIER, THE
PETIT MILLIONAIRE, LE see **TROIS POUR CENT** • 1933
PETIT MOINEAU DE PARIS, LE • 1923 • Roudes Gaston • FRN
PETIT MONDE DE DON CAMILLO, LE • 1951 • Duvivier Julien • FRN, ITL • PICCOLO MONDO DI DON CAMILLO, IL (ITL) ○ DON CAMILLO ○ LITTLE WORLD OF DON CAMILLO, THE
PETIT MONDE DES ETANGS, LE • 1952 • Colson-Malleville Marie • SHT • FRN
PETIT NOEL • 1960 • Ryssack Eddy • ANS • BLG
PETIT PARADE, LA • 1957 • Kneitel Seymour • ANS • USA
PETIT PEINTRE ET LA SIRENE, LE • 1958 • Image Jean • ANS • FRN • LITTLE PAINTER AND THE MERMAID, THE
PETIT PORT BIEN TRANQUILLE, UN • 1975 • Danis Aime • CND
PETIT POUCET, LE • 1900 • *Pathe* • FRN • TOM THUMB (USA) ○ LITTLE THUMBLET, THE
PETIT POUCET, LE • 1905 • *Pathe* • FRN • TOM THUMB
PETIT POUCET, LE • 1909 • *Pathe* • FRN • TOM THUMB (USA)
PETIT POUCET, LE • 1912 • *C.g.p.c.* • FRN • TOM THUMB (USA)
PETIT POUCET, LE • 1912 • Feuillade Louis • *Pathe* • FRN • TOM THUMB
PETIT POUCET, LE • 1965 • Borowczyk Walerian • ANS • FRN • TOM THUMB
PETIT POUCET, LE • 1972 • Boisrond Michel • FRN • TOM THUMB (USA)
PETIT PRINCE, LE • 1913 • Leprince Rene • FRN
PETIT PROF', LE • 1958 • Carlo-Rim • FRN
PETIT RAMONEUR, LE see **JACK LE RAMONEUR** • 1906
PETIT RESTAURANT DE L'IMPASSE CANIN, LE • 1912 • Fescourt Henri • FRN
PETIT ROI, LE • 1933 • Duvivier Julien • FRN
PETIT ROMAN • 1912 • Linder Max • FRN
PETIT SOLDAT, LE • 1908 • Perret Leonce • FRN • LITTLE SOLDIER, THE
PETIT SOLDAT, LE • 1947 • Grimault Paul • ANS • FRN • LITTLE SOLDIER, THE
PETIT SOLDAT, LE • 1961 • Godard Jean-Luc • FRN • LITTLE SOLDIER, THE
PETIT SOLDAT QUI DEVIENT DIEU, LE • 1908 • Cohl Emile • ANS • FRN
PETIT THEATRE DE JEAN RENOIR, LE • 1969 • Renoir Jean • FRN, ITL, FRG • LITTLE THEATRE OF JEAN RENOIR, THE (USA)
PETIT ZIZI, LE • 1971 • Jabely Jean • ANS • FRN • LITTLE ZIZI, THE
PETITE, LA see **PRETTY BABY** • 1978
PETITE ANDALOUSE, LA • 1914 • Feuillade Louis • FRN
PETITE AURORE L'ENFANT MARTYRE, LA • 1951 • Bigras Jean-Yves • CND • LITTLE AURORE'S TRAGEDY
PETITE BANDE, LA • 1983 • Deville Michel • FRN • LITTLE BUNCH, THE (USA)

PETITE BEARNAISE, LA • 1911 • Perret Leonce • FRN

PETITE BONNE DU PALACE, LA • 1926 • Mercanton Louis • FRN

PETITE BOURGOGNE, LA see **LITTLE BURGUNDY** • 1968

PETITE CHANTEUSE DES RUES, LA • 1924 • Starevitch Ladislas • FRN • LITTLE STREET SINGER, THE (USA)

PETITE CHOCOLATIERE, LA • 1927 • Hervil Rene • FRN

PETITE CHOCOLATIERE, LA • 1931 • Allegret Marc • FRN

PETITE CHOCOLATIERE, LA • 1949 • Berthomieu Andre • FRN

PETITE CUILLERE, LA • 1959 • Vilardebo Carlos • SHT • FRN • LITTLE SPOON, THE (USA)

PETITE DAME DU WAGON-LIT, LA • 1936 • Cammage Maurice • FRN • PETITE FEMME DU WAGON-LIT, LA

PETITE DANSEUSE, LA • 1913 • Feuillade Louis • FRN

PETITE DE MONTPARNASSE, LA • 1931 • de Vaucorbeil Max, Schwarz Hanns • FRN • PILE OU FACE

PETITE ELLI, LA • 1917 • Protazanov Yakov • USS

PETITE ETRANGERE, LA • 1980 • Bernard-Aubert Claude • FRN

PETITE FEMME DANS LE TRAIN, UNE • 1932 • Anton Karl • FRN

PETITE FEMME DU FLORIDA, LA see **MARIUS A PARIS** • 1930

PETITE FEMME DU WAGON-LIT, LA see **PETITE DAME DU WAGON-LIT, LA** • 1936

PETITE FIFI, LA • 1913 • Pouctal Henri • FRN

PETITE FILLE A LA RECHERCHE DU PRINTEMPS, LA • 1971 • Agostini Philippe • FRN

PETITE FILLE EN VELOURS BLEU, LA • 1978 • Bridges Alan • FRN, UKN • LITTLE GIRL IN BLUE VELVET, THE

PETITE FILLE ET LA VIEILLE HORLOGE, LA • 1918-19 • du Plessis Armand • BLG

PETITE FILLE QUI PARLE AUX VACHES, LA see **SALWA** • 1972

PETITE FLEUR • 1986 • Noel Gilles • SHT • CND

PETITE GOSSE • 1910 • de Morlhon Camille • FRN

PETITE HISTOIRE DES GRANDES COOPERATIVES AU QUEBEC • 1976 • Valcour Pierre • DCS • CND

PETITE LILIE, LA see **P'TITE LILIE, LA** • 1927

PETITE LISE, LA • 1930 • Gremillon Jean • FRN

PETITE MAGICIENNE, LA • 1900 • Blache Alice • FRN

PETITE MARCHANDE D'ALLUMETTES, LA • 1928 • Renoir Jean • FRN • LITTLE MATCH GIRL, THE

PETITE MERVEILLE, LA see **AMOUR D'EMMERDEUSE, UN** • 1979

PETITE MOBILISEE, LA • 1918 • Leprieur Gaston • FRN

PETITE MORTE, LA • 1960 • Allen Corey • USA

PETITE NUIT, LA • 1983 • Theberge Andre • CND

PETITE PARADE, LA • 1930 • Starevitch Ladislas • FRN • LITTLE PARADE, THE (USA)

PETITE PESTE • 1938 • de Limur Jean • FRN

PETITE REINE, LA • 1958 • Image Jean • ANS • FRN • LITTLE QUEEN, THE

PETITE ROCQUES, LA • 1915 • Protazanov Yakov • USS

PETITE SAUVAGE, LA • 1935 • de Limur Jean • FRN • CUPIDON AU PENSIONNAT

PETITE SIRENE, LA • 1980 • Andrieux Roger • FRN

PETITE-SOEUR • 1920 • de Carbonnat Louis • FRN

PETITE SUITE • 1961 • Jordan Larry • SHT • USA

PETITE VERTU, LA • 1968 • Korber Serge • FRN

PETITE VOLEUSE, LA • 1988 • Miller Claude • FRN

PETITES ALLIEES, LES • 1936 • Dreville Jean • FRN

PETITES ALLUMEUSES, LES • Baudricourt Michel • FRN

PETITES APHRODITES see **MIKRES APHRODITES** • 1962

PETITES APPRENTIES, LES • 1911 • Feuillade Louis • FRN

PETITES CARDINALES, LES • 1950 • Grangier Gilles • FRN • FAMILLE CARDINAL, LA

PETITES CHATTES SANS CULOTTES • 1980 • Baudricourt Michel • FRN

PETITES COLLEGIENNES, LES • Vernier Gerard • FRN

PETITES CRUAUTES, LES • 1984 • Bouchard Michel • MTV • CND • CRIES OF LOVE, THE

PETITES DU QUAI AUX FLEURS, LES • 1943 • Allegret Marc • FRN

PETITES FILLES, LES • 1978 • Leroi Francis • FRN

PETITES FILLES AU BORDEL • 1980 • Leroi Francis • FRN

PETITES FILLES MODELES, LES • 1952 • Rohmer Eric (c/d) • FRN

PETITES FILLES MODELES, LES • 1972 • Roy Jean-Claude • FRN

PETITES FILLES PAS TRES SAGES • 1981 • Warren Ken • FRN

PETITES FILLES POUR GRAND VICIEUX • Love John • FRN

PETITES FUGUES, LES • 1978 • Yersin Yves • SWT • LITTLE ESCAPES

PETITES GALERES, LES • 1978 • Mongredien Jean-Michel • FRN

PETITES MARIONNETTES, LES • 1918 • Feuillade Louis • FRN

PETITES SAINTES Y TOUCHENT, LES • 1973 • Lemoine Michel • FRN

PETITES SOEURS, LES • 1959 • Patry Pierre • DCS • CND

PETITES SOEURS, LES • 1988 • Groleau • SHT • FRN

PETITES VICIEUSES, LES • 1978 • Baudricourt Michel • FRN

PETITES VICIEUSES FONT LES GRANDES EMMERDEURS, LES • 1976 • Franco Jesus • FRN

PETITS, LES • 1925 • Roudes Gaston, Dumont • FRN

PETITS, LES • 1936 • Remy Constant, Machard Alfred • FRN

PETITS ARPENTS, LES • 1963 • Garceau Raymond • DCS • CND • LITTLE ACRES, THE

PETITS BLANCS AU MANIOC ET A LA SOUCE GOMBOS • 1987 • Bathily Moussa • SNL

PETITS CALINS, LES • 1977 • Poire Jean-Marie • FRN

PETITS CHATS, LES • 1959 • Villa Jacques-R. • FRN • WILD ROOTS OF LOVE (USA)

PETITS COUPEURS DE BOIS VERT, LES • 1904 • Blache Alice • FRN

PETITS DESSOUS DES GRANDS ENSEMBLES, LES • 1975 • Chevreuse Christian • FRN

PETITS ECOLIERES, LES • 1980 • Mulot Claude • FRN

PETITS INVENTEURS, LES • 1975 • Garceau Raymond • DOC • CND

PETITS MATINS, LES • 1961 • Audry Jacqueline • FRN • EARLY MORNINGS ○ GIRL ON THE ROAD

PETITS POULBOTS, LES • 1916 • Diamant-Berger Henri • FRN

PETITS RIENS, LES • 1941 • Leboursier Raymond • FRN

PETITS SLIPS SE DECHAINENT, LES • Pierson Claude • FRN

PETITS SOLEILS, LES see **SHUMUSUN SAGHIRA** • 1968

PETITS VAGABONDS, LES • 1905 • Nonguet Lucien • FRN

PETLA • 1957 • Has Wojciech J. • PLN • NOOSE, THE (USA)

PETOFI '73 • 1973 • Kardos Ferenc • HNG

PETOMANE, IL • 1984 • Festa Campanile Pasquale • ITL • PETOMANIAC, THE ○ WINDBREAKER, THE

PETOMANIAC, THE see **PETOMANE, IL** • 1984

PETOS • 1988 • Kassila Taavi • FNL • BETRAYAL, THE

PETOUCHE see **AH! QUELLE GARE!** • 1932

PETRA • 1937-40 • *Cardiff Jack (Ph)* • DCS • UKN

PETRIA'S WREATH see **PETRIJIN VENAC** • 1981

PETRICA AND SOMEBODY ELSE see **PETRICA SI INCA CINEVA** • 1964

PETRICA AND THE PHANTOMS see **PETRICA SI INCA CINEVA** • 1964

PETRICA SI INCA CINEVA • 1964 • Munteanu Stefan • ANS • RMN • PETRICA AND SOMEBODY ELSE ○ PETRICA AND THE PHANTOMS

PETRIFIED DOG, THE • 1947 • Peterson Sidney • SHT • USA

PETRIFIED FOREST, THE • 1936 • Mayo Archie • USA

PETRIFIED FOREST, THE see **KASEKI NO MORI** • 1973

PETRIFIED MAN, THE see **MAN WHO TURNED TO STONE, THE** • 1957

PETRIJA'S WREATH see **PETRIJIN VENAC** • 1981

PETRIJIN VENAC • 1981 • Karanovic Srdjan • YGS • PETRIJA'S WREATH ○ PETRIA'S WREATH

PETRINA CHRONIA • 1985 • Voulgaris Pantelis • GRC • STONE YEARS

PETROCHEMICALS, THE CATHEDRALS OF THE DESERT see **PETROCHIMIKA, I KATHEDRIKES TIS ERIMOU** • 1981

PETROCHIMIKA, I KATHEDRIKES TIS ERIMOU • 1981 • Katsaros Stathis, Sifianos Giorgos • DOC • GRC • PETROCHEMICALS, THE CATHEDRALS OF THE DESERT

PETROL KRALLARI • 1979 • Alasya Zeki • TRK • KINGS OF PETROL

PETROLE, LE • 1958 • Shawqi Khalil • SHT • EGY

PETROLE, PETROLE • 1981 • Gion Christian • FRN

PETROLEJOVE LAMPY • 1972 • Herz Juraj • CZC • OIL LAMPS

PETROLEO, O • 1970 • de Almeida Manuel Faria • SHT • PRT

PETROLEUM GIRLS see **PETROLEUSES, LES** • 1971

PETROLEUM WAR WILL NOT TAKE PLACE, THE see **HARB AL BATROL LAN TAKA'A** • 1974

PETROLEUMQUELLE, DIE • 1916 • Larsen Viggo • FRG

PETROLEUSES, LES • 1971 • Christian-Jaque, Casaril Guy (U/c) • FRN, ITL, UKN • LEGEND OF FRENCHIE KING, THE (UKN) ○ PISTOLERE, LE (ITL) ○ PETROLEUM GIRLS

PETROLIERS DES SABLES • 1957 • Vilardebo Carlos • SHT • FRN

PETRONELLA • 1927 • Schwarz Hanns • FRG

PETRONELLA • 1985 • Locke Rick • SHT • USA

PETROUCHKA • 1962 • *Fokine Michel* • UKN • PETRUSHKA

PETRUS • 1946 • Allegret Marc • FRN

PETRUSHKA see **PETROUCHKA** • 1962

PETRUSKA • 1916 • Lolli Alberto Carlo • ITL

PETS • 1973 • Nussbaum Raphael • USA • SUBMISSION (UKN)

PETS' TEA PARTY, THE • 1908 • Fitzhamon Lewin • UKN

PETT AND POTT • 1934 • Cavalcanti Alberto • DCS • UKN

PETT RIDGE STORIES • 1924 • *Godal Edward (P)* • SER • UKN

PETTERSSON & BENDEL • 1933 • Branner Per-Axel • SWD

PETTERSSON & BENDELS NYA AFFARER • 1945 • Bergstrand Erik • SWD • NEW AFFAIRS OF PETTERSSON AND BENDELS

PETTERSSON -SVERIGE • 1934 • Wallen Sigurd • SWD • PETTERSSON -SWEDEN

PETTERSSON -SWEDEN see **PETTERSSON -SVERIGE** • 1934

PETTICOAT AFFAIR see **OPERATION PETTICOAT** • 1977

PETTICOAT CAMP • 1912 • *Thanhouser* • USA

PETTICOAT DETECTIVE, A • 1912 • *Powers* • USA

PETTICOAT FEVER • 1936 • Fitzmaurice George • USA

PETTICOAT LARCENY • 1943 • Holmes Ben • USA

PETTICOAT LOOSE • 1922 • Ridgwell George • UKN

PETTICOAT PERFIDY • 1912 • *Majestic* • USA

PETTICOAT PERFIDY • 1913 • Plumb Hay? • UKN

PETTICOAT PILOT, A • 1918 • Sturgeon Rollin S. • USA • MARY 'GUSTA

PETTICOAT PIRATES • 1961 • MacDonald David • UKN

PETTICOAT POLITICS • 1941 • Kenton Erle C. • USA

PETTICOAT RANCH BOSS, A • 1912 • *Shamrock* • USA

PETTICOAT SAFARI • 1969 • SAF

PETTICOAT SHERIFF, THE • 1911 • *Elder Ethel* • USA

PETTICOATS AND BLUEJEANS see **PARENT TRAP, THE** • 1961

PETTICOATS AND PANTS • 1920 • Beaudine William • SHT • USA

PETTICOATS AND POLITICS • 1918 • Mitchell Howard M. • USA

PETTIGREW'S GIRL • 1919 • Melford George • USA • PRIVATE PETTIGREW'S GIRL

PETTIN' IN THE DARK • 1934 • Brown Bernard • ANS • USA

PETTING PREFERRED • 1934 • Gillstrom Arvid E. • SHT • USA

PETTY GIRL, THE • 1950 • Levin Henry • USA • GIRL OF THE YEAR (UKN)

PETTY STORY, THE see **SMASH-UP ALLEY** • 1973

PETUALANG-PETUALANG • 1979 • Noer Arifin C. • INN

PETULIA • 1968 • Lester Richard • UKN, USA

PETUNIA NATIONAL PARK • 1939 • *Captain And The Kids* • ANS • USA

PETZI • 1968 • Antoine Jean • ANM • BLG

PEU, BEAUCOUP, PASSIONNEMENT.., UN • 1970 • Enrico Robert • FRN • LITTLE, A LOT, PASSIONATELY, A

PEU D'AMOUR, UN • 1933 • Steinhoff Hans • FRN • SCAMPOLO

PEU DE FEU, S.V.P., UN • 1904 • Melies Georges • FRN • EVERY MAN HIS OWN CIGAR LIGHTER (USA)

PEU DE SOLEIL DANS L'EAU FROIDE, UN • 1971 • Deray Jacques • FRN, ITL • PO' DI SOLE NELL'AQUA GELIDA, UN (ITL) ○ SUNLIGHT ON COLD WATER (UKN)

PEUPLE, LE • 1915 • Protazanov Yakov • USS

PEUPLE DE CONGO -LEO VAINCRA, LE • Kamba Sebastien • DOC • CNG

PEUPLE EN MARCHE • 1963 • Rachedi Ahmed, Vautier Rene • ALG • FORWARD THE PEOPLE

PEUPLE EST INVINCIBLE, LE • 1969 • Ivens Joris (c/d) • DOC • FRN

PEUPLE ET SES FUSILS, LE • 1970 • Ivens Joris, Loridan Marceline, Sergent Jean-Pierre, Castro Emmanuelle • DOC • FRN • PEOPLE AND THEIR GUNS, THE (USA)

PEUPLE NE PEUT RIEN SANS SES FUSILS, LE • 1969 • Ivens Joris (c/d) • DOC • FRN

PEUPLE PEUT TOUT, LE • 1969 • Ivens Joris (c/d) • DOC • FRN

PEUR, LA • 1909 • Carre Michel • FRN

PEUR, LA • 1936 • Tourjansky Victor • FRN • VERTIGE D'UN SOIR

PEUR, LA see **FOVOS, HO** • 1966

PEUR, LA see **KHAWF, AL-** • 1972

PEUR DE L'EAU, LA • 1913 • Linder Max • FRN

PEUR DES COUPS, LA • 1933 • Autant-Lara Claude • FRN

PEUR ET L'AMOUR, LA • 1967 • Pecas Max • FRN • TORMENT (USA) ○ LOVE + FEAR + TORMENT ○ PEUR ET LE DESIR, LA ○ FEAR AND LOVE

PEUR ET LE DESIR, LA see **PEUR ET L'AMOUR, LA** • 1967

PEUR SUR LA VILLE • 1975 • Verneuil Henri • FRN, ITL • POLIZIOTTO DELLA BRIGATA CRIMINALE, IL (ITL) ○ NIGHT CALLER, THE (UKN) ○ FEAR OVER THE CITY ○ FEAR ON THE CITY

PEUT-ETRE MAURICE RICHARD • 1971 • Gascon Gilles • DOC • CND

PEVITSA • 1971 • Voinov Konstantin • USS • SINGER, THE

PEX QUE FUMA, EL • 1977 • Chalbaud Roman • VNZ • FISH THAT SMOKES, THE ○ SMOKING FISH, THE

PEYOTE QUEEN • 1965 • De Hirsch Storm • SHT • USA

PEYTON PLACE • 1957 • Robson Mark • USA

PEYTON PLACE: THE NEXT GENERATION • 1985 • Elikann Larry • TVM • USA

PEZ DE LOS OJOS DE ORO, EL • 1973 • Ramirez Pedro L. • SPN

PEZZO, CAPOPEZZO E CAPITANO (ITL) see **KANONEN-SERENADE** • 1958

PFAD DER SUNDE, DER • 1916 • Reinert Robert • FRG

PFARRER MIT DER JAZZTROMPETE, DER see **TROMPETEN DER LIEBE** • 1962

PFARRER VON KIRCHFELD, DER • 1926 • Fleck Jacob, Fleck Luise • FRG

PFARRER VON KIRCHFELD, DER • 1955 • Deppe Hans • FRG

PFARRER VON ST. MICHAEL, DER • 1957 • Gluck Wolfgang • FRG

PFARRER VON ST. PAULI, DER • 1970 • Olsen Rolf • FRG

PFARRERS TOCHTERLEIN • 1912 • Biebrach Rudolf • FRG

PFEIFEN see **DYMKY** • 1966

PFEIFEN, BETTEN, TURTELTAUBEN (AUS) see **DYMKY** • 1966

PFINGSTORGEL, DIE • 1938 • Seitz Franz • FRG

PFLICHT ZU LEBEN, DIE • 1919 • Wilhelm Carl • FRG

PFLICHT ZU SCHWEIGEN, DIE • 1927 • Wilhelm Carl • FRG

PHABLE OF A BUSTED ROMANCE, THE • 1916 • Barre Raoul • ANS • USA

PHAEDRA • 1909 • *Pathe* • FRN

PHAEDRA • 1962 • Dassin Jules • USA, FRN, GRC

PHAEDRA WEST see **FEDRA WEST** • 1968

PHAGUN • 1973 • *Burman S. D. (M)* • IND

PHAI DAENG • Cheyaroon Permpol • THL

PHALENES, LES • 1974 • Vallois Philippe • FRN

PHALLIC FOREST, THE • 1972 • Guyatt Kit • ASL

PHALLOCRATES, LES • 1980 • Pierson Claude • FRN

PHANIYAMMA • 1981 • Karanth Prema • IND

PHANTASM • SHT • USA

PHANTASM • 1979 • Coscarelli Don • USA

PHANTASM 2 • 1988 • Coscarelli Don • USA

PHANTASMAGORIA • Opliger Curtis • SHT • USA

PHANTASMES • 1917 • L'Herbier Marcel • FRN

PHANTASMES • Thierry Alain • FRN

PHANTASMES • 1976 • Rollin Jean • FRN

PHANTASMES PORNOGRAPHIQUES • 1976 • Rollin Jean • FRN

PHANTASY, A • 1952 • McLaren Norman • ANS • USA

PHANTASY CARTOON • 1939-49 • *Fleischer* • ASS • USA

PHANTOM • 1922 • Murnau F. W. • FRG

PHANTOM, THE • 1910 • *Pathe* • FRN

PHANTOM, THE • 1916 • Giblyn Charles • USA

PHANTOM, THE • 1926 • Smith Percy • UKN

PHANTOM, THE • 1943 • Eason B. Reeves • SRL • USA

PHANTOM, THE • 1968 • Reilly John Fahey • SHT • UKN

PHANTOM, THE see **FANTASMA, IL** • 1909

PHANTOM, THE see **FANTOMAS SE DECHAINE** • 1965

PHANTOM BAIANO, THE see **BAIANO FANTASMA, O** • 1984

PHANTOM BARON, THE (USA) see **BARON FANTOME, LE** • 1942

PHANTOM BRIDE, THE see **FACE BETWEEN, THE** • 1922

PHANTOM BROADCAST, THE • 1933 • Rosen Phil • USA • PHANTOM OF THE AIR (UKN)

PHANTOM BUCCANEER, THE • 1916 • Haydon J. Charles • USA

PHANTOM BULLET, THE • 1926 • Smith Cliff • USA

PHANTOM BUSTER, THE • 1927 • Bertram William • USA

PHANTOM BUTLER, THE • 1920 • Harbaugh Carl • SHT • USA

PHANTOM CARAVAN • 1954 • Rich Roy • USA

PHANTOM CARRIAGE, THE see **KORKARLEN** • 1921

PHANTOM CARRIAGE, THE see **KORLALEN** • 1958

PHANTOM CAT, THE see **KAIBYO RANBU** • 1956

PHANTOM CHARIOT, THE see **KORKARLEN** • 1921

PHANTOM CHARIOT, THE see **KORLALEN** • 1958

PHANTOM CITY, THE • 1928 • Rogell Albert S. • USA

PHANTOM COWBOY, THE • 1935 • Horner Robert J. • USA

PHANTOM COWBOY, THE • 1941 • Sherman George • USA

PHANTOM CRACKSMAN, THE • 1914 • *Fuller Mary* • USA

PHANTOM CREEPS, THE • 1939 • Beebe Ford, Goodkind Saul • SRL • USA

PHANTOM CRIMINAL, A see **NIHON SEIHANZAISHI: TORIMA** • 1967

PHANTOM DER OPER, DAS • 1915 • Matray Ernst • FRG

PHANTOM DES GROSSEN ZELTES • 1954 • May Paul • FRG

PHANTOM DESPERADO • 1922 • Holt George • USA

PHANTOM EMPIRE • 1935 • Brower Otto, Eason B. Reeves • SRL • USA

PHANTOM EMPIRE, THE • 1988 • Ray Fred Olen • USA

PHANTOM EXPRESS, THE • 1925 • Adolfi John G. • USA

PHANTOM EXPRESS, THE • 1932 • Johnson Emory • USA
PHANTOM EXTRA, THE • 1915 • *Mitchell Rhea* • USA
PHANTOM FAME see **STRICTLY DYNAMITE** • 1934
PHANTOM FATE • 1920 • Harbaugh Carl • SHT • USA
PHANTOM FIEND see **IM STAHLNETZ DES DR. MABUSE** • 1961
PHANTOM FIEND, THE (USA) see **LODGER, THE** • 1932
PHANTOM FLYER, THE • 1928 • Mitchell Bruce • USA • PHANTOM RANGER, THE
PHANTOM FOE • 1920 • Bennet Spencer Gordon • SRL • USA
PHANTOM FOE, THE • 1921 • Millhauser Bertram • SRL • USA
PHANTOM FOE, THE • 1926 • Malins Geoffrey H., Parkinson H. B. • UKN
PHANTOM FORTUNE, THE • 1915 • Otto Henry • USA
PHANTOM FORTUNE, THE • 1923 • Hill Robert F. • SRL • USA
PHANTOM FORTUNES, THE • 1916 • Scardon Paul • USA
PHANTOM FROM 10,000 LEAGUES, THE • 1955 • Milner Dan • USA
PHANTOM FROM SPACE • 1953 • Wilder W. Lee • USA
PHANTOM FUGITIVE, A • 1919 • Jaccard Jacques • SHT • USA
PHANTOM GAMES • 1908 • *Wrench* • UKN
PHANTOM GOLD • 1937 • Kathner Rupert • ASL
PHANTOM GOLD • 1938 • Levering Joseph • USA
PHANTOM GUARD, THE see **GARDE FANTOME, LA** • 1904
PHANTOM GUNSLINGER, THE • 1967 • Zugsmith Albert • USA
PHANTOM HAPPINESS, THE • 1915 • Terwilliger George W. • USA
PHANTOM HONEYMOON, THE • 1919 • Dawley J. Searle • USA
PHANTOM HORSE, THE see **KORKARLEN** • 1921
PHANTOM HORSE, THE see **MABOROSHI NO UMA** • 1955
PHANTOM HORSEMAN, THE • 1924 • Bradbury Robert North • USA • PHANTOM RIDER, THE
PHANTOM HORSEMAN, THE (UKN) see **BORDER OUTLAWS** • 1950
PHANTOM HUSBAND, A • 1917 • Hartman Ferris • USA
PHANTOM IN THE HOUSE, THE • 1929 • Rosen Phil • USA
PHANTOM INDIA (USA) see **INDE FANTOME, L'** • 1969
PHANTOM ISLAND • 1916 • Ford Francis • SHT • USA
PHANTOM JUSTICE • 1924 • Thomas Richard • USA
PHANTOM KILLER see **HAKUCHU NO TORIMA** • 1966
PHANTOM KILLER, THE • 1942 • Beaudine William • USA • MAN AND THE DEVIL
PHANTOM KILLER, THE see **INVISIBLE GHOST, THE** • 1941
PHANTOM KNIGHT, THE • 1911 • *Cines* • ITL
PHANTOM LADY • 1944 • Siodmak Robert • USA
PHANTOM LADY, THE see **DAME FANTOME, LA** • 1904
PHANTOM LIGHT, THE • 1914 • *Walcamo Marie* • SHT • USA
PHANTOM LIGHT, THE • 1935 • Powell Michael • UKN
PHANTOM LOVE (USA) see **AI NO BOREI** • 1977
PHANTOM LOVERS • 1912 • *Pathe* • FRN
PHANTOM LOVERS • 1912 • *Pathe* • USA
PHANTOM LOVERS (UKN) see **FANTASMI A ROMA** • 1961
PHANTOM MEETS THE RETURN OF DR. MABUSE, THE see **IM STAHLNETZ DES DR. MABUSE** • 1961
PHANTOM MELODY, THE • 1920 • Gerrard Douglas • USA
PHANTOM MINE, THE • 1917 • Horne James W. • SHT • USA
PHANTOM MOUSTACHE • 1961 • Kneitel Seymour • ANS • USA
PHANTOM OF 42ND STREET, THE • 1945 • Herman Al • USA
PHANTOM OF CHINATOWN • 1940 • Rosen Phil • USA
PHANTOM OF CRESTWOOD, THE • 1932 • Ruben J. Walter • USA
PHANTOM OF DEATH • 1987 • Deodato Ruggero • ITL • OFF BALANCE
PHANTOM OF FILMORE, THE see **PHANTOM OF THE PARADISE** • 1974
PHANTOM OF HOLLYWOOD, THE • 1974 • Levitt Gene • TVM • USA
PHANTOM OF KENWOOD • USA
PHANTOM OF LIBERTY, THE (UKN) see **FANTOME DE LA LIBERTE, LE** • 1974
PHANTOM OF LOVE, THE see **AI NO BOREI** • 1977
PHANTOM OF MORRISVILLE, THE • Zeman Borivoj • CZC • SON OF HORROR, THE
PHANTOM OF MOULIN ROUGE, THE see **FANTOME DU MOULIN ROUGE, LE** • 1925
PHANTOM OF PARIS see **MYSTERY OF MARIE ROGET, THE** • 1942
PHANTOM OF PARIS, THE • 1931 • Robertson John S. • USA • CHERI-BIBI
PHANTOM OF SANTE FE, THE • 1937 • Jaccard Jacques • USA
PHANTOM OF SOHO, THE see **PHANTOM VON SOHO, DAS** • 1964
PHANTOM OF TERROR see **UCCELLO DALLE PIUME DE CRISTALLO, L'** • 1970
PHANTOM OF THE AIR, THE • 1933 • Taylor Ray • SRL • USA
PHANTOM OF THE AIR (UKN) see **PHANTOM BROADCAST, THE** • 1933
PHANTOM OF THE BRAIN, THE • 1914 • *Searchlight* • UKN
PHANTOM OF THE CONVENT, THE see **FANTASMA DEL CONVENTO, EL** • 1934
PHANTOM OF THE DESERT • 1930 • Webb Harry S. • USA
PHANTOM OF THE FERRIS WHEEL see **FUEGO** • 1964
PHANTOM OF THE FOREST, THE • 1926 • McCarty Henry • USA
PHANTOM OF THE HORSE OPERA • 1961 • Smith Paul J. • ANS • USA
PHANTOM OF THE MALL • 1989 • Friedman Richard • USA
PHANTOM OF THE MOULIN ROUGE, THE see **FANTOME DU MOULIN ROUGE, LE** • 1925
PHANTOM OF THE NORTH, THE • 1929 • Webb Harry S. • USA
PHANTOM OF THE OPERA see **BANYE GESHENG** • 1985
PHANTOM OF THE OPERA, THE • 1925 • Julian Rupert, Sedgwick Edward • USA
PHANTOM OF THE OPERA, THE • 1929 • Julian Rupert, Laemmle Ernst • USA
PHANTOM OF THE OPERA, THE • 1943 • Lubin Arthur • USA
PHANTOM OF THE OPERA, THE • 1962 • Fisher Terence • UKN
PHANTOM OF THE OPERA, THE • 1982 • Markowitz Robert • TVM • USA
PHANTOM OF THE OPERA, THE • 1987 • *Grennell Aiden* • ANM • USA
PHANTOM OF THE OPERA, THE • 1989 • Little Dwight H. • USA
PHANTOM OF THE OPERETTA, THE see **FANTASMA DE LA OPERETA, EL** • 1955
PHANTOM OF THE OPERETTA, THE see **FANTASMA DE LA OPERETA, EL** • 1959
PHANTOM OF THE PARADISE • 1974 • De Palma Brian • USA • PHANTOM OF FILMORE, THE
PHANTOM OF THE PARK, THE see **KISS MEETS THE PHANTOM** • 1978
PHANTOM OF THE PLAINS • 1945 • Selander Lesley • USA
PHANTOM OF THE RANGE • 1928 • Dugan James • USA
PHANTOM OF THE RANGE, THE • 1936 • Hill Robert F. • USA
PHANTOM OF THE RED HOUSE, THE (USA) see **FANTASMA DE LA CASA ROJA, EL** • 1954
PHANTOM OF THE RITZ • 1989 • Plone Allen • USA
PHANTOM OF THE RUE MORGUE • 1954 • Del Ruth Roy • USA
PHANTOM OF THE SNOWS, THE see **MONSTRUO DE LOS VOLCANES, EL** • 1962
PHANTOM OF THE TURF • 1928 • Worne Duke • USA
PHANTOM OF THE VIOLIN, THE see **PHANTOM VIOLIN, THE** • 1914
PHANTOM OF THE WEST • 1931 • Lederman D. Ross • SRL • USA
PHANTOM ON HORSEBACK, THE see **KISERTET LUBLON** • 1977
PHANTOM ON THE HEARTH, THE • 1915 • *Macmillan Violet* • USA
PHANTOM OUTLAW, THE • 1927 • Wyler William • SHT • USA
PHANTOM OUTLAWS • 1944 • Abrahams Derwin • USA
PHANTOM PARADISE • 1912 • Blache Alice • USA
PHANTOM PATROL • 1936 • Hutchison Charles • USA
PHANTOM PICTURE, THE • 1916 • Ward Albert • UKN
PHANTOM PLAINSMEN, THE • 1942 • English John • USA
PHANTOM PLANET, THE • 1961 • Marshall William • USA
PHANTOM POLICE • 1926 • Dillon Robert A. • SRL • USA
PHANTOM PRESIDENT, THE • 1932 • Taurog Norman • USA
PHANTOM RAIDERS • 1940 • Tourneur Jacques • USA
PHANTOM RANCHER, THE • 1940 • Fraser Harry L. • USA
PHANTOM RANGER • 1938 • Newfield Sam • USA
PHANTOM RANGER, THE see **PHANTOM FLYER, THE** • 1928
PHANTOM RIDE -CHAMONIX • 1900 • Paul Robert William • UKN
PHANTOM RIDER, THE • 1910 • *Gaumont* • FRN
PHANTOM RIDER, THE • 1929 • McGowan J. P. • USA
PHANTOM RIDER, THE • 1936 • Taylor Ray • SRL • USA
PHANTOM RIDER, THE • 1946 • Bennet Spencer Gordon, Brannon Fred C. • SRL • USA
PHANTOM RIDER, THE see **PHANTOM HORSEMAN, THE** • 1924
PHANTOM RIDER, THE see **PISTOLERO FANTASMA, EL** • 1967
PHANTOM RIDERS, THE • 1918 • Ford John • USA
PHANTOM RIDES, THE • 1901 • Hepworth Cecil M. • UKN
PHANTOM ROCKET, THE • 1933 • Sherman Frank, Rufle George • ANS • USA
PHANTOM RULER see **INVISIBLE MONSTER, THE** • 1950
PHANTOM SHADOWS • 1925 • Ferguson Al?, Grandon Francis J.? • USA
PHANTOM SHIP, THE • 1908 • Coleby A. E., Martin J. H. • UKN
PHANTOM SHIP, THE • 1913 • Shaw H. W. • USA
PHANTOM SHIP, THE • 1936 • King Jack • ANS • USA
PHANTOM SHIP, THE (USA) see **MYSTERY OF THE MARIE CELESTE, THE** • 1935
PHANTOM SHOT, THE • 1947 • Zampi Mario • UKN
PHANTOM SHOTGUN, THE • 1917 • Harvey Harry • USA
PHANTOM SIGNAL, THE • 1913 • Lessey George A. • USA
PHANTOM SIRENS, THE • 1909 • *Urban-Eclipse* • USA
PHANTOM SKYSCRAPER, THE • 1966 • Bakshi Ralph • ANS • USA
PHANTOM SPEAKS, THE • 1944 • English John • USA
PHANTOM STAGE, THE • 1939 • Waggner George • USA
PHANTOM STAGECOACH, THE • 1957 • Nazarro Ray • USA
PHANTOM STALLION • 1954 • Keller Harry • USA
PHANTOM STOCKMAN • 1953 • Robinson Lee • ASL • CATTLE STATION ○ RETURN OF THE PLAINSMAN
PHANTOM STRIKES, THE (USA) see **GAUNT STRANGER, THE** • 1938
PHANTOM SUBMARINE, THE • 1941 • Barton Charles T. • USA
PHANTOM TERROR, THE • 1921 • *Craft W. J. (P)* • SHT • USA
PHANTOM THIEF, THE • 1915 • Collins John H. • USA
PHANTOM THIEF, THE • 1916 • Stafford Harry G. • USA
PHANTOM THIEF, THE • 1946 • Lederman D. Ross • USA
PHANTOM THUNDERBOLT, THE • 1933 • James Alan • USA
PHANTOM TOLLBOOTH, THE • 1969 • Monahan David, Jones Charles M., Levitow Abe • ANM • USA
PHANTOM TRAILS • 1955 • McDonald Frank • MTV • USA
PHANTOM TREEHOUSE, THE • 1984 • ANM • USA
PHANTOM (UKN) see **SILENT HERO, THE** • 1927
PHANTOM VALLEY • 1948 • Nazarro Ray • USA
PHANTOM VIOLIN, THE • 1914 • Ford Francis • USA • PHANTOM OF THE VIOLIN, THE
PHANTOM VON SOHO, DAS • 1964 • Gottlieb Franz J. • FRG • PHANTOM OF SOHO, THE
PHANTOM WAGON, THE (USA) see **CHARRETTE FANTOME, LA** • 1939
PHANTOM WARNING, THE • 1915 • *Wilson Ben* • USA
PHANTOM WITNESS, THE • 1916 • Sullivan Frederick • SHT • USA
PHANTOME DES GLUCKS • 1929 • Schunzel Reinhold • FRG • MANN IN FESSELN, DER
PHANTOME DES LEBENS • 1919 • Coenen Josef • FRG
PHANTOMS • 1913 • Campbell Colin • USA
PHANTOM'S BRIDGE, THE see **PONTE DEI FANTASMI, IL** • 1912
PHANTOM'S HOTEL, THE see **FANTOM'S HOTEL** • 1932
PHANTOMS, INC. • 1945 • Young Harold • SHT • USA
PHANTOMS OF THE WORKSHOP, THE see **FANTASMAS DEL TALLER, LOS** • 1967
PHANTOM'S SECRET, THE • 1917 • Swickard Charles • USA
PHAR LAP • 1983 • Wincer Simon • ASL • PHAR LAP: HEART OF A NATION
PHAR LAP: HEART OF A NATION see **PHAR LAP** • 1983
PHARAOH, THE see **FARAON** • 1965
PHARAOH'S CURSE • 1957 • Sholem Lee • USA • CURSE OF THE PHARAOH
PHARAOH'S WIFE see **WEIB DES PHARAO, DAS** • 1921
PHARAOHS' WOMAN, THE (USA) see **DONNA DEI FARAOINI, LA** • 1960
PHARMACEUTICAL HALLUCINATIONS OR THE TRICK OF POTARD see **HALLUCINATIONS PHARMACEUTIQUES OU LE TRUC DU POTARD** • 1908
PHARMACIST, THE • 1933 • Ripley Arthur • SHT • USA
PHARMACY FROLICS • 1939 • Schwarzwald Milton • SHT • USA
PHAROS THE WONDER WORKER • 1911 • *Tress Henry (P)* • UKN
PHASE IV • 1973 • Bass Saul • UKN
PHASES OF THE MOON • 1968 • Chomont Tom S. • SHT • USA
PHEDRE • 1908 • Novelli Enrico • ITL
PHEDRE • 1968 • Jourdan Pierre • FRN
PHELA-NDABA • 1970 • Mahomo Nana • SAF • END OF THE DIALOGUE (UKN)
PHENIX CITY STORY, THE • 1955 • Karlson Phil • USA • PHOENIX CITY STORY, THE
PHENIX OU LE COFFRET DE CRISTAL, LE • 1905 • Melies Georges • FRN • CRYSTAL CASKET, THE (USA) ○ COFFRET DE CRISTAL, LE
PHENO WAS HERE • 1982 • Riddiford Richard • NZL
PHENOMENA • 1965 • Belson Jordan • SHT • USA
PHENOMENA see **CREEPERS** • 1985
PHENOMENA 7.7 • 1965 • *Empire Studios* • DOC • USA
PHENOMENAL AND THE TREASURE OF TUTANKAMEN see **FENOMENAL E IL TESORO DI TUTANKAMEN** • 1968
PHENOMENAL CONTORTIONIST, A • 1901 • Porter Edwin S. • USA
PHENOMENAL WRESTLER, THE see **LUCHADOR FENOMENA, EL** • 1952
PHENOMENE, LE • 1978 • Dopff Paul • ANS • FRN
PHENOMENES ELECTRIQUES • 1937 • Grimault Paul • ANS • FRN
PHENOMENON see **FENOMENA** • 1990
PHENOMENON NO.1 • 1965 • Vanderbeek Stan • ANS • USA
PHERA • 1987 • Dasgupta Buddhadeb • IND • RETURN, THE
PHFFFT! • 1954 • Robson Mark • USA
PHI-PHI • 1924 • *Deed Andre* • FRN
PHIL BLOOD'S LEAP • 1913 • Noy Wilfred • UKN
PHIL-FOR-SHORT • 1919 • Apfel Oscar • USA
PHILADELPHIA EXPERIMENT, THE • 1984 • Raffill Stewart • USA
PHILADELPHIA HERE I COME • 1975 • Quested John • USA
PHILADELPHIA STORY, THE • 1940 • Cukor George • USA
PHILAE • 1970 • Awf Samir • SHT • EGY
PHILANTHROPIC TOMMY • 1915 • North Wilfred, Davenport Harry • USA
PHILBERT • 1963 • Donner Richard • SHT • USA
PHILBY, BURGESS AND MACLEAN • 1977 • Flemyng Gordon • MTV • UKN • BURGESS, PHILBY AND MACLEAN: SPY SCANDAL OF THE CENTURY
PHILCAG IN VIETNAM • 1967 • Santiago Clemen T. • PHL
PHILHARMANIACS • 1953 • Kneitel Seymour • ANS • USA
PHILHARMONIKER • 1944 • Verhoeven Paul • FRG
PHILHARMONISTS, LES • 1972 • Leduc Yves • CND
PHILINE • 1945 • Lingen Theo • FRG
PHILIP see **RUN WILD, RUN FREE** • 1969
PHILIP HOLDEN -WASTER • 1916 • Sargent George L. • USA • HIS BROTHER'S KEEPER
PHILIP KENT IN THE LOWER SCHOOL • 1917 • Turbett Ben • SHT • USA
PHILIP MARCH'S ENGAGEMENT • 1913 • *Mason Billy* • USA
PHILIP STEELE • 1912 • *Robinson Gertrude* • USA
PHILIPPE LE BEL ET LES TEMPLIERS • 1910 • Jasset Victorin • FRN
PHILIPPE SOUPAULT • Tavernier Bertrand, Aurenche Jean • DOC • FRN
PHILIPS CAVALCADE • 1964 • Geesink Joop • ANM • NTH
PHILIPS CAVALCADE • 1966 • Keuris Max • NTH
PHILIPS ON PARADE • 1967 • Geesink Joop • ANM • NTH
PHILIPS RADIO • 1931 • Ivens Joris • DOC • NTH • INDUSTRIAL SYMPHONY ○ SYMPHONIE INDUSTRIELLE
PHILISE ME, MARITSA • 1931 • Gaziadis Dimitrios • GRC • KISS ME, MARISA
PHILISTINE IN BOHEMIA, A • 1920 • Griffith Edward H. • SHT • USA
PHILO VANCE RETURNS • 1947 • Beaudine William • USA
PHILO VANCE'S GAMBLE • 1947 • Wrangell Basil • USA
PHILO VANCE'S SECRET MISSION • 1947 • Le Borg Reginald • USA
PHILOSOPHER, THE • 1989 • Thome Rudolf • FRG
PHILOSOPHER, THE see **ADI SHANKARACHARYA** • 1983
PHILOSOPHER'S STONE, THE see **PIERRE PHILOSOPHALE, LA** • 1899
PHILOSOPHER'S STONE, THE see **PARASH PATHAR** • 1957
PHILOSOPHICAL HISTORY see **FILOSOFSKA HISTORIE** • 1937
PHILOSOPHICAL STORY, A see **FILOSOFSKA HISTORIE** • 1937
PHILOSOPHIE DANS LE BOUDOIR, LA • 1969 • Scandelari Jacques • FRN • BEYOND LOVE AND EVIL (USA) ○ PHILOSOPHY OF THE BEDROOM
PHILOSOPHY OF THE BEDROOM see **PHILOSOPHIE DANS LE BOUDOIR, LA** • 1969
PHIL'S BUSY DAY • 1916 • *Dunham Phil* • SHT • USA
PHIL'S VACATION • 1914 • *Royal* • USA
PHINDESELA • 1979 • SAF
PHINDISELA • 1985 • SAF
PHINEAS NEWBORN JNR. TRIO • 1962 • Binder Steve • SHT • USA
PHIR BHI • 1972 • Sinha Shivendra • IND • ONCE AGAIN
PHIR BHI APNA HAI • 1935 • Nene Raja • IND
PHIR SUBAH HOGI • 1958 • *Kapoor Raj* • IND
PHIRINGOTI • 1990 • Barua Jahnu • IND • SPARKS, THE
PHOBIA • *Spillane-Fellows* • USA
PHOBIA • 1980 • Huston John • CND
PHOBIA • 1987 • Dingwall John • ASL

PHOEBE • 1964 • Kaczender George • SHT • CND
PHOEBE OF THE INN • 1912 • Haldane Bert? • UKN
PHOEBE SHOW • 1905 • Porter Edwin S. • USA
PHOELIX • 1979 • Ambrose Anna • UKN
PHOENIX see **FUJICHO** • 1947
PHOENIX 2772 see **HINOTORI 2772 AI NO COSMOZONE** • 1980
PHOENIX, THE • 1910 • *Nobles Milton* • USA
PHOENIX, THE • 1978 • Caan Richard, Arikawa Sadamasa • TWN • WAR OF THE WIZARDS
PHOENIX, THE • 1981 • Hickox Douglas • TVM • USA
PHOENIX, THE see **HI NO TORI** • 1979
PHOENIX AND THE TURTLE, THE • 1972 • Chiappini Luigi V. B. • UKN
PHOENIX BIRD • Carlsen Jon Bang • SHT • DNM
PHOENIX BIRD see **FUGL FONIX** • 1984
PHOENIX CITY STORY, THE see **PHENIX CITY STORY, THE** • 1955
PHOENIX THE NINJA • 1986 • Fong Ho • HKG
PHOENIX THE WARRIOR • 1988 • Hayes Robert • USA
PHONE 1707 CHESTER • 1911 • *Imp* • USA
PHONE CALL FROM A STRANGER, A • 1952 • Negulesco Jean • USA
PHONE MESSAGE, THE • 1916 • Holubar Allen • SHT • USA
PHONE NUMBER 728 see **RUFNUMMER 728** • 1966
PHONE RINGS EVERY NIGHT, THE (USA) see **NACHTS GING DAS TELEPHON** • 1962
PHONEY, THE see **FAUX-CUL, LE** • 1975
PHONEY BALONEY • 1945 • Wickersham Bob • ANS • USA
PHONEY EXPRESS • 1962 • Smith Paul J. • ANS • USA
PHONEY EXPRESS, THE • 1932 • *Iwerks Ub (P)* • ANS • USA
PHONEY MILLIONAIRE, THE see **MILLIONAIRE AL MOUZAYYAF, AL** • 1968
PHONEY NEWS FLASHES • 1955 • Rasinski Connie • ANS • USA
PHONEY PHOTOS • 1918 • Frazee Edwin • SHT • USA
PHONIE FURIEUSE, LA • 1982 • Rached Tahani • CND
PHONIES, THE see **CHANTAS, LOS** • 1975
PHONO-BIO-TABLEAUX FILMS • 1900 • Gibbons Walter • SER • UKN
PHONOGRAPHE, LE • 1969 • Borowczyk Walerian • ANS • FRN
PHONY ALARM, A • 1913 • *Panzer Paul* • USA
PHONY AMERICAN, THE (USA) see **TOLLER HECHT AUF KRUMMEN TOUREN** • 1961
PHONY CANNIBAL, THE • 1915 • *Hamilton Lloyd V.* • USA
PHONY EXPRESS • 1943 • Lord Del • SHT • USA
PHONY PONY • 1969 • Smith Paul J. • ANS • USA
PHONY PRINCE, THE • 1911 • *Kalem* • USA
PHONY RING, THE • 1911 • *Solax* • USA
PHONY SINGER, THE • 1913 • *Roland Ruth* • USA
PHONY STRIKE BREAKERS, THE • 1911 • *Kalem* • USA
PHONY TEETH AND FALSE FRIENDS • 1916 • *Rogers Gene* • SHT • USA
PHOQUES DU ROI D'ORO, LES • 1949 • Cousteau Jacques • FRN • PHOQUES DU SAHARA, LES
PHOQUES DU SAHARA, LES see **PHOQUES DU ROI D'ORO, LES** • 1949
PHOTO FINISH (USA) see **COURTE TETE** • 1956
PHOTO FINNISH-STYLE • 1970 • *Distripix Inc.* • USA
PHOTO HABER see **FOTO HABER** • 1963
PHOTO PHONIES • 1950 • Goodwins Leslie • SHT • USA
PHOTO PORTRAIT • 1970 • Crama Nico • DOC • NTH
PHOTO SOUVENIR • 1960 • Fabiani Henri • SHT • FRN
PHOTOGENIE MECANIQUE, LA • 1924 • Gremillon Jean • SHT • FRN
PHOTOGENIES • 1925 • Epstein Jean • FRN
PHOTOGRAPH, THE see **PHOTOGRAPHIA, H** • 1987
PHOTOGRAPH AND THE BLOTTER, THE • 1913 • Lessey George A. • USA
PHOTOGRAPH FROM AN AREA WINDOW • 1901 • Smith G. A. • UKN
PHOTOGRAPHE • 1895 • Lumiere Louis • FRN
PHOTOGRAPHE, LA • Lean Bruce J. • FRN
PHOTOGRAPHE LASSINE, LE • 1972 • Marconnier Guy • FRN
PHOTOGRAPHER, THE • 1938 • Yarbrough Jean • SHT • USA
PHOTOGRAPHER, THE • 1948 • Van Dyke Willard, Jacoby Irving • DOC • USA
PHOTOGRAPHER, THE • 1974 • Hillman William Byron • USA
PHOTOGRAPHER'S FLIRTATION, THE • 1908 • Fitzhamon Lewin? • UKN
PHOTOGRAPHER'S MISHAP, THE • 1901 • Porter Edwin S. • USA
PHOTOGRAPHIA, H • 1987 • Papatakis Nico • GRC • PHOTOGRAPH, THE
PHOTOGRAPHIC EPISODE, A • 1903 • Collins Alf? • UKN
PHOTOGRAPHIC EXPRESSIONS ILLUSTRATED • 1905 • Jeapes Harold? • UKN
PHOTOGRAPHIE ELECTRIQUE A DISTANCE, LA • 1908 • Melies Georges • FRN • LONG DISTANCE WIRELESS PHOTOGRAPHY (USA)
PHOTOGRAPHIES VIVANTES • 1954 • Borowczyk Walerian • SHT • FRN
PHOTOGRAPHING A GHOST • 1898 • Smith G. A. • UKN
PHOTOGRAPHY • 1898 • *Paul R. W.* • UKN
PHOTOGRAPHY • 1965 • Ratz Gunter • ANM • GDR
PHOTOGRAPHY see **RETUSOR, A** • 1972
PHOTOPLAY WITHOUT A NAME, A • 1915 • Paton Stuart • USA
PHOTOS D'ALIX • 1980 • Eustache Jean • FRN
PHOTOTONE REELS NOS.1-16 • 1928 • Harlow John • SER • UKN
PHRASE, LA • 1972 • Lamothe Arthur • DCS • CND
PHRENOLOGICAL BURLESQUE, A see **PHRENOLOGIE BURLESQUE, LA** • 1901
PHRENOLOGIE BURLESQUE, LA • 1901 • Melies Georges • SHT • FRN • PHRENOLOGIST AND THE LIVELY SKULL, THE (UKN) ○ PHRENOLOGICAL BURLESQUE, A
PHRENOLOGIST, THE • 1910 • *Powers* • USA
PHRENOLOGIST AND THE LIVELY SKULL, THE (UKN) see **PHRENOLOGIE BURLESQUE, LA** • 1901
PHROSO • 1922 • Mercanton Louis • FRN
PHROSO THE MYSTERIOUS MECHANICAL DOLL see **MYSTERIOUS MECHANICAL TOY, THE** • 1903
PHYLLIS • 1971 • Cox Paul • SHT • ASL
PHYLLIS AND THE FOREIGNER • 1915 • Wilson Frank? • UKN
PHYLLIS DIXEY • 1978 • Tuchner Michael • UKN
PHYLLIS OF THE FOLLIES • 1928 • Laemmle Ernst • USA
PHYLLIS OF THE SIERRAS, A • 1915 • *California* • USA
PHYLOGENY • 1968 • Roll Henry • ANS • USA
PHYNX, THE • 1970 • Katzin Lee H. • USA
PHYSICAL • *Anderson Juliet* • USA
PHYSICAL ASSAULT see **PRISONERS** • 1973
PHYSICAL CULTURE • 1911 • Wilson Frank? • UKN
PHYSICAL CULTURE BUG, THE • 1914 • *Komic* • USA
PHYSICAL CULTURE GIRLS • 1903 • *Bitzer Billy (Ph)* • USA
PHYSICAL CULTURE ON THE QUARTER CIRCLE V BAR • 1913 • Duncan William • USA
PHYSICAL CULTURE ROMANCE, A • 1914 • *Edwards Marguerite* • USA
PHYSICAL EDUCATION: GIRLS AGED 11 • 1935 • Holmes J. B. • DOC • UKN
PHYSICAL EVIDENCE • 1989 • Crichton Michael • USA • SMOKE
PHYSICAL FITNESS -THE NEW PERSPECTIVE • 1974 • Sens Al • ANS • CND
PHYSICALLY PRESENT see **DE CUERPO PRESENTE** • 1967
PHYSICIAN, THE • 1928 • Jacoby Georg • UKN
PHYSICIAN OF SILVER GULCH, THE • 1912 • *Lubin* • USA
PHYSICIAN'S HONOR, A • 1912 • *Johnson Arthur* • USA
PHYSIOLOGY AND PREGNANCY see **SEIRI TO NINSHIN** • 1968
PHYSIOPOLIS • 1930 • Dreville Jean • FRN
PI-EROTISCHE BEZIEHUNGEN • 1983 • Kuert Beat • SWT
PI-YUN T'IEN • 1976 • Li Hsing • HKG • POSTERITY AND PERPLEXITY
PIA DE' TOLOMEI • 1941 • Pratelli Esodo • ITL
PIA DE' TOLOMEI • 1958 • Grieco Sergio • FRN, ITL
PIACERE, IL • 1985 • D'Amato Joe • ITL • PLEASURE, THE
PIACERE DELLO SCAPOLO, I • 1960 • Petroni Giulio • ITL
PIACERE E IL MISTERO, IL • 1964 • Peri Enzo • DOC • ITL • PLEASURE AND THE MYSTERY, THE
PIACERE E L'AMORE, IL (ITL) see **RONDE, LA** • 1964
PIACERI CONIUGALI, I (ITL) see **DIFFICULTE D'ETRE INFIDELE, LA** • 1963
PIACERI DEL SABATO NOTTE, I • 1960 • Danza Daniele • ITL • ARABELLA 252104
PIACERI NEL MONDO, I • 1963 • Marinucci Vinicio • ITL
PIACERI PROIBITI, I • 1963 • Andreassi Raffaele • DOC • ITL
PIACEVOLI NOTTI, LE • 1966 • Crispino Armando, Lucignani Luciano • ITL
PIACEVOLI NOTTI DI JUSTINE, LE • 1971 • Antel Franz • ITL
PIAF • 1973 • Casaril Guy • FRN, USA • PIAF -THE EARLY YEARS (USA) ○ SPARROW OF PIGALLE, THE
PIAF -THE EARLY YEARS (USA) see **PIAF** • 1973
PIANETA AZZURRO, IL • 1983 • Piavoli Franco • ITL • BLUE PLANET, THE
PIANETA DEGLI UOMINI SPENTI, IL • 1961 • Margheriti Antonio • ITL • BATTLE OF THE WORLDS (USA) ○ PLANET OF THE LIFELESS MEN ○ GUERRE PLANETARI
PIANETA VENERE • 1972 • Tattoli Elda • ITL • PLANET VENUS, THE
PIANETI CONTRO DI NOI, I • 1961 • Ferrara Romano • ITL, FRN • MONSTRE AUX YEUX VERT, LE (FRN) ○ HANDS OF A KILLER (UKN) ○ PLANETS AGAINST US (USA) ○ MAN WITH THE YELLOW EYES ○ PLANETS AROUND US ○ MONSTER WITH GREEN EYES, THE
PIANGE.. IL TELEFONO • 1975 • De Caro Lucio • ITL
PIANISSIMO • 1963 • D'Avino Carmen • ANS • USA
PIANISTA VENEZOLANA • 1972 • Cosmi Carlo • DOC • VNZ • VENEZUELAN PIANIST
PIANO FOR MRS. CIMINO, A • 1982 • Schaefer George • TVM • USA
PIANO IN MID-AIR, A see **ZONGORA A LEVEGOBEN** • 1976
PIANO LESSON, THE • 1964 • *Svensk* • SHT • SWD
PIANO LESSON, THE see **PIANOLEKTIONEN** • 1966
PIANO, MON AMI • 1957 • Leduc • SHT • FRN
PIANO MOONER • 1942 • Edwards Harry J. • SHT • USA
PIANO MOVER • 1932 • *Mintz Charles (P)* • ANS • USA
PIANO MOVERS, THE see **HIS MUSICAL CAREER** • 1914
PIANO TOONERS • 1932 • Foster John, Rufle George • ANS • USA
PIANOFORTE • 1984 • Comencini Francesca • ITL, FRN
PIANOFORTE • 1984 • Starkiewicz Antoinette • ANS • ASL
PIANOLEKTIONEN • 1966 • Nordin Vera • SWD • PIANO LESSON, THE
PIANORAMA • 1973 • Taylor Richard • SHT • UKN
PIANOS MECANICOS, LOS • 1965 • Bardem Juan Antonio • SPN, ITL, FRN • AMORI DI UNA CALDA ESTATE (ITL) ○ PIANOS MECANIQUES, LES (FRN) ○ UNINHIBITED, THE (USA) ○ ORGANILLOS, LOS ○ PLAYER PIANOS, THE
PIANOS MECANIQUES, LES (FRN) see **PIANOS MECANICOS, LOS** • 1965
PIANTO DELLE ZITELLE, IL • 1959 • Baldi Gian Vittorio • ITL
PIAO-TS'O CH'I-JIH CH'ING • 1984 • Chang Chien-T'Ing • HKG • LET'S MAKE LAUGH
PIAOBU QIYA • Yu Banzheng • CHN • STRANGE ENCOUNTERS
PIASTRE, LA • 1975 • Chartrand Alain • CND
PIATILEKTA • 1929 • Room Abram • USS
PIATKA Z ULICY BARSKIEJ • 1953 • Ford Aleksander • PLN • FIVE BOYS FROM BARSKA STREET ○ FIVE BOYS OF BARSKA STREET
PIATTO PIANGE, IL • 1974 • Nuzzi Paolo • ITL
PIAVE MORMORO.., IL • 1964 • Guerrasio Guido, D'Incerti Vico • DOC • ITL
PIAZZA PULITA • 1973 • Vanzi Luigi • ITL, USA • PETE, PEARL AND THE POLE (USA)
PIAZZA S. SEPOLCRO • 1943 • Forzano Giovacchino • ITL • CRONACA DI DUE SECOLI
PIAZZA SAN MARCO • 1947 • Pasinetti Francesco • ITL
PIAZZA VUOTA, LA • 1973 • Recchia Giuseppe • ITL
PIBE CABEZA, EL • 1975 • Torre-Nilsson Leopoldo • ARG • BIG-HEAD KID
PIC ET PIC ET COLEGRAM • 1970 • Weinberg Rachel • FRN • EENY, MEENY, MINEY, MOE
PIC ET PIC ET CONTREDANSE • 1979 • Goulet Stella • CND
PIC-NIC • 1967 • Radanowicz Georg • SWT
PIC POUR LENINE, UN • 1981 • Germain Bernard • DOC • FRN
PICA SUL PACIFICO, LA • 1959 • Montero Roberto Bianchi • ITL
PICADOR, LE • 1932 • Jaquelux • FRN
PICADOR PORKY • 1937 • Avery Tex • ANS • USA
PICAFLOR • 1935 • Barth-Moglia Luis • ARG
PICAPAU AMARELO • 1974 • Sarno Geraldo • BRZ
PICAR SUSANA, LA • 1944 • Cortes Fernando • MXC
PICARA MOLINERA, LA • 1955 • Klimovsky Leon • SPN, FRN
PICARI, I • 1988 • Monicelli Mario • ITL • ROGUES, THE
PICARO, EL • 1964 • Mariscal Alberto • MXC
PICASSO • 1954 • Emmer Luciano • ITL
PICASSO • 1982 • Rossif Frederic • FRN • PABLO PICASSO
PICASSO LOOK, THE see **REGARD PICASSO, LE** • 1967
PICASSO MYSTERY, THE see **MYSTERE PICASSO, LE** • 1956
PICASSO, ROMANCERO DU PICADOR • 1960 • Desvilles • SHT • FRN
PICASSO SUMMER, THE • 1969 • Bourguignon Serge • USA
PICASSO SUMMER, THE • 1972 • Stalin Robert • USA
PICASSO TRIGGER • 1988 • Sidaris Andy • USA
PICASSO, UN PORTRAIT • 1970 • Quinn Edward • DOC • FRN
PICASSOS AVENTYR • 1978 • Alfredson Hans, Danielsson Tage • SWD • ADVENTURES OF PICASSO, THE
PICASSO'S SCULPTURE • 1967 • Beresford Bruce • DCS • UKN
PICCADILLY • 1929 • Dupont E. A. • UKN
PICCADILLY INCIDENT • 1946 • Wilcox Herbert • UKN • THEY MET AT MIDNIGHT
PICCADILLY JIM • 1920 • Ruggles Wesley • USA
PICCADILLY JIM • 1936 • Leonard Robert Z. • USA
PICCADILLY NIGHTS • 1930 • Arch Albert H. • UKN
PICCADILLY, NULL UHR ZWOLF • 1963 • Zehetgruber Rudolf • FRG • PICCADILLY, ZERO HOUR 12
PICCADILLY PLAYTIME • 1936 • Green Frank • UKN
PICCADILLY ROUNDABOUT • 1944 • Massingham Richard • UKN
PICCADILLY THIRD STOP • 1960 • Rilla Wolf • UKN
PICCADILLY, ZERO HOUR 12 see **PICCADILLY, NULL UHR ZWOLF** • 1963
PICCANIN'S CHRISTMAS, THE • 1917 • SAF
PICCHIATELLI, I • 1958 • Attanasi Antonio • ANM • ITL • THEY'RE CRAZY
PICCIOLA • 1911 • *Normand Mabel* • USA
PICCIONI DI VENEZIA, I • 1942 • Pasinetti Francesco • ITL
PICCOLA DETECTIVE, LA • 1914 • Roberti Roberto Leone • ITL
PICCOLA FONTE • 1918 • Roberti Roberto Leone • ITL
PICCOLA MIA • 1933 • De Liguoro Eugenio • ITL
PICCOLA MOGLIE, UNA • 1944 • Bianchi Giorgio • ITL
PICCOLA OMBRA, LA • 1916 • Falena Ugo • ITL
PICCOLA SANTA • 1954 • Montero Roberto Bianchi • ITL
PICCOLE LABBRA • 1979 • Cattarinich Mimmo • ITL
PICCOLI AVVENTURIERI • 1940 • Calzavara Flavio • ITL • LITTLE ADVENTURES (USA)
PICCOLI FUOCHI • 1985 • Del Monte Peter • ITL • SMALL FIRES
PICCOLI NAUFRAGHI • 1939 • Calzavara Flavio • ITL
PICCOLO • 1959 • Vukotic Dusan • ANS • YGS
PICCOLO ALPINO • 1940 • Biancoli Oreste • ITL
PICCOLO ARCHIMEDE, IL • 1979 • Amelio Gianni • ITL
PICCOLO CERINAIO, IL • 1914 • Genina Augusto • ITL
PICCOLO DIAVOLO, IL • 1988 • Benigni Roberto • ITL • LITTLE DEVIL, THE
PICCOLO EQUIVOCI • 1988 • Tognazzi Ricky • ITL
PICCOLO EROE • 1937 • Blasetti Alessandro • ITL
PICCOLO HOTEL • 1939 • Ballerini Piero • ITL
PICCOLO MONDO ANTICO • 1940 • Soldati Mario • ITL • LITTLE OLD-FASHIONED WORLD
PICCOLO MONDO DI DON CAMILLO, IL (ITL) see **PETIT MONDE DE DON CAMILLO, LE** • 1951
PICCOLO POSTA • 1955 • Steno • ITL
PICCOLO RE, IL • 1940 • Romagnoli Redo • ITL
PICCOLO RIBELLE • 1948 • Cordero Emilio • ITL
PICCOLO SANTO, IL • 1918 • Falena Ugo • ITL
PICCOLO VETRAIO, IL • 1955 • Capitani Giorgio • ITL, FRN
PICCOLO VOM GOLDENEN LOWEN, DER • 1928 • Boese Carl • FRG
PICHIANNI TROUPE • 1934 • *Mgm* • SHT • USA
PICK A STAR • 1937 • Sedgwick Edward • USA • MOVIE STRUCK
PICK AND SHOVEL • 1923 • Roach Hal • SHT • USA
PICK ME UP • 1933 • Horne James W. • SHT • USA
PICK ME UP see **PICK ME UP UR FLICKORNA JACKSON** • 1910
PICK-ME-UP ET UN SPORTSMAN • 1912-14 • Cohl Emile • ANS • USA
PICK ME UP UR FLICKORNA JACKSON • 1910 • Magnusson Charles • SWD • PICK ME UP
PICK-NECKING • 1933 • *Terry Paul/ Moser Frank (P)* • ANS • USA
PICK OUT YOUR HUSBAND • 1920 • Lyons Eddie, Moran Lee • SHT • USA
PICK-POCKET ET POLICEMAN • 1899 • Melies Georges • FRN • DROP TO MUCH, A
PICK-UP • 1933 • Gering Marion • USA • PICK UP
PICK UP • 1968 • Eisenschitz Bernard • SHT • FRN
PICK UP see **PICK-UP** • 1933
PICK-UP, THE • 1968 • Frost R. L. • USA
PICK-UP ARTIST, THE • 1987 • Toback James • USA
PICK-UP GIRLS, THE • Franco Jesus • SPN
PICK-UP SUMMER • 1980 • Mihalka George • CND • PINBALL SUMMER ○ PINBALL PICK-UP
PICKANINNIES AND THE WATER MELON, THE • 1912 • *Imp* • USA
PICKANINNIES AND THE WATER MELONS, THE • 1912 • *Republic* • USA
PICKANINNY, THE • 1921 • Roach Hal • SHT • USA
PICKANINNY BLUES • 1932 • Foster John, Davis Mannie • ANS • USA
PICKET GUARD, THE • 1913 • Dwan Allan • USA
PICKETING FOR LOVE • 1938 • Yarbrough Jean • SHT • USA
PICKING LOCKS • 1937 • Sparling Gordon • DCS • CND • GRANDES ECLUSES, LES
PICKING PEACHES • 1924 • Kenton Erle C. • SHT • USA

PICKING UP THE PIECES • 1985 • Wendkos Paul • TVM • USA
PICKLE GOES IN THE MIDDLE, THE • 1971 • Sullivan James A. • USA
PICKLED HISTORY • 1914 • *Captain Kettle* • UKN
PICKLED LOVE • Tholen Tom • SHT • NTH
PICKLED PEPPERS • 1935 • *Sutton Grady* • SHT • USA
PICKLED PINK • 1965 • Freleng Friz • ANS • USA
PICKLED PUSS • 1948 • Swift Howard • ANS • USA
PICKLES see **SOTTACETTI** • 1972
PICKLES AND DIAMONDS • 1916 • Greene Clay M. • SHT • USA
PICKLES, ART AND SAUERKRAUT • 1914 • Young James • USA
PICKPOCKET • 1959 • Bresson Robert • FRN
PICKPOCKET, THE • 1913 • Baker George D. • USA
PICKPOCKET -A CHASE THROUGH LONDON, THE • 1903 • Collins Alf • UKN
PICKPOCKETS see **VRECKARI** • 1967
PICKUP • 1951 • Haas Hugo, Walden Edgar E. • USA
PICKUP ALLEY (USA) see **INTERPOL** • 1957
PICKUP IN ROME see **GIORNATA BALORDA, LA** • 1960
PICKUP ON 101 • 1972 • Florea John • USA • ECHOES OF THE ROAD (UKN) ○ WHERE THE EAGLE FLIES
PICKUP ON SOUTH STREET • 1953 • Fuller Samuel • USA
PICKWICK PAPERS, THE • 1952 • Langley Noel • UKN
PICKWICK PAPERS, THE • 1985 • Lighthill Brian • MTV • UKN
PICKWICK PAPERS PARTS 1 & 2, THE • 1912 • Trimble Larry • UKN, USA
PICKWICK VERSUS BARDELL • 1913 • Noy Wilfred • UKN
PICNIC • 1948 • Harrington Curtis • SHT • USA
PICNIC • 1955 • Logan Joshua • USA
PICNIC • 1988 • Vestey Paul • ANM
PICNIC • 1989 • Sen Aparna • IND
PICNIC see **PIKNIK** • 1967
PICNIC, THE • 1911 • *Walton Fred* • USA
PICNIC, THE • 1930 • Gillett Burt • ANS • USA
PICNIC AMONG THE POPLARS see **PIKNIK U TOPOLI** • 1982
PICNIC AT HANGING ROCK • 1975 • Weir Peter • ASL
PICNIC DISTURBED, A • 1904 • Mottershaw Frank • UKN
PICNIC IN DAKOTA, A • 1912 • *Crystal* • USA
PICNIC INTERRUPTED BY TRAMPS, A • 1902 • *Warwick Trading Co.* • UKN
PICNIC ON THE GRASS • 1988 • Pjarn Priit • ANM • USS
PICNIC ON THE GRASS (USA) see **DEJEUNER SUR L'HERBE, LE** • 1959
PICNIC ON THE ISLAND, THE • 1913 • Fitzhamon Lewin • UKN
PICNIC PANIC • 1935 • Gillett Burt, Palmer Tom • ANS • USA
PICNIC PANIC • 1946 • Wickersham Bob • ANS • USA
PICNIC PERILS • 1934 • Horne James W. • SHT • USA
PICNIC WITH PAPA • 1952 • Davis Mannie • ANS • USA
PICNICING • 1919 • *Klever Pictures* • SHT • USA
PICNICK MIT WEISMANN • 1968 • Svankmajer Jan • ANM • CZC
PICNICS ARE FUN AND DINO'S SERENADE • 1959 • Keller Lew • ANS • USA
PICO, EL • 1984 • de la Iglesia Eloy • SPN • FIX, THE ○ SHOOT UP, THE
PICOLO ET PICOLETTE • 1963-64 • Image Jean • ASS • FRN
PICONE SENT ME see **MI MANDA PICONE** • 1984
PICOS DE EUROPA I Y II • Eguiluz Enrique L. • SHT • SPN
PICPUS • 1942 • Pottier Richard • FRN • SIGNE PICPUS
PICTORIAL REVUE • 1936 • Watts Fred • UKN
PICTORIAL REVUE OF 1943 • 1943 • Watts Fred • UKN
PICTURA -ADVENTURE IN ART • 1951 • Emmer Luciano, Dupont E. A. • DOC • ITL, FRN, USA
PICTURE, THE • Kozlov G. • USS
PICTURE BRIDES • 1934 • Rosen Phil • USA
PICTURE HUNTERS, THE see **KEPVADASZOK** • 1985
PICTURE IDOL, THE • 1912 • Young James • USA
PICTURE IN THE MIND • 1949 • Stapp Philip, Bryan Julian • ANS • USA
PICTURE MOMMY DEAD • 1966 • Gordon Bert I. • USA • COLOR MOMMY DEAD
PICTURE OF DORIAN GRAY, THE • 1910 • *Psilander Valdemar* • DNM
PICTURE OF DORIAN GRAY, THE • 1913 • Smalley Phillips • SHT • USA
PICTURE OF DORIAN GRAY, THE • 1915 • Moore Mr. • USA
PICTURE OF DORIAN GRAY, THE • 1916 • Durrant Fred W. • UKN
PICTURE OF DORIAN GRAY, THE • 1944 • Lewin Albert • USA
PICTURE OF DORIAN GRAY, THE • 1973 • Jordan Glenn • TVM • USA
PICTURE OF DORIAN GRAY, THE (USA) see **PORTRET DORIANA GREYA** • 1915
PICTURE OF DORIAN GRAY, THE (USA) see **BILDNIS DES DORIAN GRAY, DAS** • 1917
PICTURE OF DORIAN GRAY, THE (USA) see **ELET KIRALYA: DORIAN GRAY, AZ**
PICTURE OF MADAME YUKI, THE (USA) see **YUKI FUJIN EZU** • 1950
PICTURE ON THE WALL, THE • 1915 • *Hamilton Lillian* • USA
PICTURE PALACE PIECANS • 1914 • Kellino W. P. • UKN
PICTURE PAPER • Cripps Erik • DOC • UKN
PICTURE PIONEER • 1946 • *Mead Thomas (P)* • SHT • USA
PICTURE PIRATES • 1916 • Miller Rube • SHT • USA
PICTURE SHOW • 1981 • Straiton John S. • CND
PICTURE SHOW MAN, THE • 1977 • Power John • ASL • TRAVELLING PICTURE SHOW MAN, THE
PICTURE SNATCHER • 1933 • Bacon Lloyd • USA
PICTURE THIEVES, THE • 1910 • Bouwmeester Theo? • UKN
PICTURE WRITER, THE • 1912 • *Vitagraph* • USA
PICTURELAND • 1911 • *Imp* • USA
PICTURES • 1980 • Black Michael • NZL
PICTURES AT AN EXHIBITION • 1972 • Ferguson Nicholas • UKN
PICTURES AT AN EXHIBITION • 1972 • Parker Claire, Alexeieff Alexandre • ANS • CND, FRN • TABLEAUX D'UNE EXPOSITION
PICTURES AT AN EXHIBITION see **KIALLITAS KEPEI, EGY** • 1954
PICTURES FROM AN EXHIBITION • 1963 • Topouzanov Christo • ANM • BUL
PICTURES FROM MEMORY see **SLIKE IZ SJECANJA** • 1988
PICTURES FROM THE 1930'S • 1977 • May Derek • DOC • CND
PICTURES OF AN ANGUISHED YOUTH • 1966 • Klopcic Matjaz • SHT • YGS
PICTURES OF THE ATOM BOMB see **GEMBAKO NO ZU** • 1952
PICTURES OF THE MIDDLE AGES see **IMAGES MEDIEVALES** • 1949
PICTURES OF THE OLD WORLD see **OBRAZY STAREHO SVETA** • 1972
PICTURES OF THE PAST • 1976 • Peippo Antti • SHT • FNL
PICTURES THAT MOVED: AUSTRALIAN CINEMA 1896-1920, THE • 1969 • Anderson Alan • DOC • ASL
PICTURESQUE COLORADO • 1911 • Porter Edwin S. • USA
PICTURESQUE SOUTH AFRICA • 1936 • Fitzpatrick James • SHT • USA
PICTURESQUE SYDNEY • 1910 • *Spencer C. (P)* • ASL
PICTURESQUE WEST, THE • 1899 • *Bitzer Billy (Ph)* • USA
PIDGIN ISLAND • 1916 • Balshofer Fred J. • USA
PIE • 1916 • *Hupp George* • SHT • USA
PIE A LA MAID • 1938 • Lord Del • SHT • USA
PIE-COVERED WAGON, THE • 1932 • Lamont Charles • SHT • USA
PIE EATERS, THE • 1914 • *Lubin* • USA
PIE-EATING COMPETITION, THE • 1902 • *Gaumont* • UKN
PIE-EYED PIPER, THE • 1918 • *Franey William* • SHT • USA
PIE FOR SOPHIE • 1914 • *Joselyn Margaret* • USA
PIE FOR TWO • 1933 • Horne James W. • SHT • USA
PIE IN THE SKY • 1933 • Kazan Elia, Thatcher Mollie Day, Lerner Irving, Steiner Ralph • SHT • USA
PIE IN THE SKY see **TERROR IN THE CITY** • 1966
PIE NOIRE, LA • 1913 • Machin Alfred • NTH
PIE, PIE, BLACKBIRD • 1932 • Mack Roy • SHT • USA
PIE, TRAMP AND THE BULLDOG • 1901 • Porter Edwin S. • USA
PIE WORTH WHILE, A • 1912 • *Lubin* • USA
PIEBALD see **TRAPENI** • 1961
PIEC I POL BLADEGO JOZKA • 1970 • Kluba Henryk • PLN • FIVE AND A HALF OF PALE JOE
PIECAN'S TONIC • 1915 • Evans Joe • UKN
PIECE D'OR, LA • 1964 • Menegoz Robert • FRN
PIECE MANDALA • 1966 • Sharits Paul J. • SHT • USA
PIECE OF AMBER, A • 1915 • *Sherry Barney* • USA
PIECE OF AMBERGRIS, A • 1912 • *Cumpson John* • USA
PIECE OF BREAD, A (UKN) see **SOUSTO** • 1960
PIECE OF CAKE, A • 1948 • Irwin John • UKN
PIECE OF CAKE, A see **C'EST PAS CHINOIS** • 1974
PIECE OF HER ACTION, A • 1968 • Denby Jerry • USA • PIECE OF THE ACTION, A
PIECE OF LACE, A • 1910 • *Conness Robert* • USA
PIECE OF PLEASURE, A (USA) see **PARTIE DE PLAISIR, UNE** • 1974
PIECE OF SKY, A see **PETEC DE CER, UN** • 1984
PIECE OF STRING, THE • 1911 • Smiley Joseph, Tucker George Loane • USA
PIECE OF THE ACTION • 1984 • Weldon John (c/d) • ANM • CND
PIECE OF THE ACTION, A • 1977 • Poitier Sidney • USA
PIECE OF THE ACTION, A see **PIECE OF HER ACTION, A** • 1968
PIECES • 1969 • *Wilson Chellee* • USA
PIECES see **MIL GRITOS TIENE LA NOCHE** • 1982
PIECES OF CHINA • 1926 • *Upham Isaac O.* • DOC • USA
PIECES OF DOG see **PSI KUSY** • 1971
PIECES OF DREAMS • 1970 • Haller Daniel • USA
PIECES OF THE GAME • 1916 • Easton Clem • SHT • USA
PIECZONE GOLABKI • 1966 • Chmielewski Tadeusz • PLN • BOILED BIRDS ○ ROAST PIGEONS ○ BROILED SQUABS
PIEDI, LE • 1974 • Unia Pierre • FRN
PIED-BOY, UN • 1973 • Levie Marc • BLG
PIED DANS LE PLATRE, LES • 1964 • Fabbri Jacques, Lary Pierre • FRN
PIED NICKELES, LES • 1964 • Chambon Jean-Claude • FRN
PIED PIPER, THE • 1907 • Stow Percy • UKN
PIED PIPER, THE • 1924 • Lantz Walter • ANS • USA
PIED PIPER, THE • 1933 • Jackson Wilfred • ANS • USA
PIED PIPER, THE • 1942 • Pichel Irving • USA
PIED PIPER, THE • 1972 • Demy Jacques • UKN, FRG • PIED PIPER OF HAMELIN, THE
PIED PIPER, THE • 1985 • Barta Jiri • ANM • CZC, FRG • PIED PIPER OF HAMELIN, THE
PIED PIPER, THE see **CLOWN AND THE KIDS, THE** • 1968
PIED PIPER, THE see **PIED PIPER OF HAMELIN, THE** • 1985
PIED PIPER MALONE • 1924 • Green Alfred E. • USA • UNCLE JACK
PIED PIPER OF BASIN STREET, THE • 1944 • Culhane James • ANS • USA
PIED PIPER OF GUADALOPE, THE • 1961 • Freleng Friz • ANS • USA
PIED PIPER OF HAMELIN, THE • 1911 • *Pathe* • FRN
PIED PIPER OF HAMELIN, THE • 1911 • Marston Theodore • USA
PIED PIPER OF HAMELIN, THE • 1913 • Lessey George A. • USA
PIED PIPER OF HAMELIN, THE • 1916 • *Edison* • SHT • USA
PIED PIPER OF HAMELIN, THE • 1926 • Tilley Frank • UKN
PIED PIPER OF HAMELIN, THE • 1957 • Windust Bretaigne • MTV • USA
PIED PIPER OF HAMELIN, THE • 1960 • Reiniger Lotte • ANS • UKN
PIED PIPER OF HAMELIN, THE • 1985 • Meyer Nicholas • MTV • USA • PIED PIPER, THE
PIED PIPER OF HAMELIN, THE see **RATTENFANGER VON HAMELN, DER** • 1916
PIED PIPER OF HAMELIN, THE see **PIED PIPER, THE** • 1972
PIED PIPER OF HAMELIN, THE see **PIED PIPER, THE** • 1985
PIED PIPER OF TUCSON, THE see **TODD KILLINGS, THE** • 1971
PIED PIPER PORKY • 1939 • Clampett Robert • ANS • USA
PIED QUI ETREINT, LE • 1916 • Feyder Jacques • FRN
PIEDALU A PARIS • 1951 • Loubignac Jean • FRN
PIEDALU DEPUTE • 1953 • Loubignac Jean • FRN
PIEDALU FAIT DES MIRACLES • 1952 • Loubignac Jean • FRN
PIEDINO IL QUESTURINO • 1974 • Lo Cascio Franco • ITL
PIEDONE A HONG KONG • 1975 • Steno • ITL
PIEDONE D'EGITTO • 1980 • Steno • ITL • FLAT FOOT ON THE NILE
PIEDONE L'AFRICANO • 1978 • Steno • ITL, FRG
PIEDONE LO SBIRRO • 1973 • Steno • ITL, FRG • KNOCK OUT COP, THE (USA) ○ FLATFOOT
PIEDRA DE TOQUE • 1963 • Buchs Julio • SPN
PIEDRA EN EL ZAPATO, UNA • 1955 • Baledon Rafael • MXC
PIEDRA LIBRE • 1976 • Torre-Nilsson Leopoldo • ARG • HIDE AND SEEK ○ FREE FOR ALL
PIEDRA SOBRE PIEDRA • 1970 • Alvarez Santiago • DOC • CUB
PIEDRAS VIVAS • 1956 • Alfonso Raul • SPN
PIEDS NICKELES, LES see **AVENTURES DES PIED NICKELES, LES** • 1947
PIEFKE -DER SCHRECKEN DER KOMPANIE • 1958 • Wehrum Wolfgang • FRG
PIEGE, LE • 1958 • Brabant Charles • FRN, ITL • TRAPPOLA SI CHIUDE, LA (ITL) ○ NO ESCAPE (USA) ○ ANY MAN'S WOMAN
PIEGE, LE see **PIEGES** • 1969
PIEGE A CONS, LE • 1979 • Mocky Jean-Pierre • FRN
PIEGE A FOURRURE • 1977 • Robbe-Grillet Alain • FRN
PIEGE A HOMMES • 1948 • Loubignac Jean • FRN
PIEGE A LOUP, LE see **DOCTEUR POPAUL** • 1972
PIEGE A PUCELLES • 1972 • Leroi Francis • FRN
PIEGE DE L'AMOUR, LE • 1919 • Ryder Alexandre • FRN • LOVE TRAP, THE
PIEGE POUR CENDRILLON • 1965 • Cayatte Andre • FRN, ITL • NON SONO UN'ASSASSINO (ITL) ○ TRAP FOR CINDERELLA, A (USA)
PIEGE POUR UN GARCE see **AMOUR AUX TROUSSES, L'** • 1974
PIEGES • 1939 • Siodmak Robert • FRN • PERSONAL COLUMN (USA) ○ SNARES
PIEGES • 1969 • Baratier Jacques • FRN • PIEGE, LE ○ TRAP
PIEKLO I NIEBO • 1966 • Rozewicz Stanislaw • MTV • PLN • HEAVEN AND HELL ○ HELL AND HEAVEN
PIEL CANELA • 1953 • Ortega Juan J. • MXC
PIEL DE VERANO • 1961 • Torre-Nilsson Leopoldo • ARG • SUMMER SKIN
PIEL DE ZAPA, LA • 1943 • Amadori Luis Cesar • ARG
PIEL DEL AMOR, LA • 1973 • David Mario • ARG • SKIN OF LOVE, THE
PIEL DESNUDA, LA • 1964 • Mistral Jorge • MXC, PRC
PIEL QUEMADA, LA • 1968 • Forn Josep Maria • SPN • BURNT SKIN
PIEN-FU CH'UAN-CHI • 1978 • Ch'U Yuan • HKG • LEGENDS OF THE BAT
PIEN-YUAN JEN • 1981 • Chang Kuo-Ming • HKG • MAN ON THE BRINK
PIER 5, HAVANA • 1959 • Cahn Edward L. • USA
PIER 13 • 1940 • Forde Eugene J. • USA
PIER 13 (UKN) see **ME AND MY GAL** • 1932
PIER 23 • 1951 • Berke William • USA
PIER, THE see **JETEE, LA** • 1962
PIER, THE see **MOLO** • 1969
PIER AT TREPORT DURING A STORM, THE see **TEMPETE SUR LA JETEE DU TREPORT** • 1896
PIER OF PASSION see **JOEN NO HATOBA** • 1951
PIERA'S STORY see **STORIA DI PIERA** • 1983
PIERCING THE VEIL • 1915 • *Alhambra* • USA
PIERETTES GOLDENE TASCHE • 1919 • Kahn William? • FRG
PIERINO COLSPICE ANCORA • 1982 • Girolami Marino • ITL • PIERINO STRIKES AGAIN
PIERINO SALVADANAIO • 1959 • Paolone Filippo • ITL
PIERINO STRIKES AGAIN see **PIERINO COLSPICE ANCORA** • 1982
PIERNA CRECIENTE, FALDA MENGUANTE • 1970 • Aguirre Javier • SPN
PIERNAS DE LA SERPIENTE, LAS • 1970 • Xiol Juan • SPN
PIERNAS DE ORO • 1957 • Galindo Alejandro • MXC
PIERO DELLA FRANCESCA see **INVENZIONE DELLA CROCE, L'** • 1949
PIERO DELLA FRANCESCA -THE NATIVITY • 1966 • Ashton Dudley Shaw • DOC • UKN
PIERPIN • 1936 • Coletti Duilio • ITL
PIERRE • 1972 • Cheminal Dominique • FRN
PIERRE • 1976 • Decorte Jan • BLG
PIERRE A COTON • 1978 • Labrecque Jean-Claude • CND
PIERRE BEAULIEU, AGRICULTEUR 1 & 2 • 1959 • Dansereau Fernand • DCS • CND
PIERRE BERTON • 1967 • Bonniere Rene • DCS • CND
PIERRE BLACKBURN TROMPETTISTE • 1972-73 • Brault Francois • DCS • CND
PIERRE BRISSAC, THE BRAZEN • 1916 • Ricketts Thomas • SHT • USA
PIERRE DANS LA BOUCHE, UNE • 1983 • Leconte Jean-Louis • FRN
PIERRE DE LUNE • Colson-Malleville Marie • DOC • FRN • MOONSTONE
PIERRE ET DJEMILA • 1986 • Blain Gerard • FRN
PIERRE ET JEAN • 1943 • Cayatte Andre • FRN
PIERRE ET MARIE S'EN VONT ENSEMBLE see **GRAND DELIRE, LE** • 1975
PIERRE ET PAUL • 1968 • Allio Rene • FRN
PIERRE FABIEN ET CIE • 1980 • Lombaerts Andre • BLG
PIERRE IMBAULT COR FRANCAIS • 1972-73 • Brault Francois • DCS • CND
PIERRE LAPORTE • 1970 • Beaudry Michel • CND
PIERRE MENDES-FRANCE: UN REPUBLIQUE, UN REGARD • 1978 • Lanzenberg Francois, Seligmann Guy • DOC • FRN
PIERRE MERCURE • 1971 • Gagnon Charles • CND
PIERRE MOLINIER, 7 RUE DES FAUSSETS • 1981 • Simsolo Noel • DOC • FRN
PIERRE OF THE NORTH • 1913 • McRae Henry • *Selig* • USA
PIERRE OF THE NORTH • 1914 • *Essanay* • USA
PIERRE OF THE PLAINS • 1914 • McGill Lawrence • USA
PIERRE OF THE PLAINS • 1942 • Seitz George B. • USA
PIERRE PHILOSOPHALE, LA • 1899 • Melies Georges • FRN • PHILOSOPHER'S STONE, THE
PIERRE PHILOSOPHE, LE • 1912 • *Gance Abel* • FRN
PIERRE ROMAIN-DES FOSSES • 1954 • Deboe Gerard • BLG
PIERRE VALLIERES • 1972 • Wieland Joyce • CND

PIERRES OUBLIEES • 1952 • Grimault Paul • ANS • FRN
PIERRETTE NO.1 • 1924 • Fischinger Oskar • ANM • FRG
PIERRETTE'S DREAM • 1908 • *Pathe* • FRN
PIERROT • 1965 • Leroux Jacques • ANS • FRN
PIERROT ALL'INFERNO • 1908 • *Cines* • ITL • PIERROT IN HELL
PIERROT AND PIERRETTE • 1897 • Acres Birt • UKN
PIERROT AND THE DEVIL'S DICE, THE • 1905 • Martin J. H. • UKN • CONJURING CLOWN, THE
PIERROT AND THE GHOST see **PIERROT ET LE FANTOME** • 1898
PIERROT ASSASSIN • 1903-04 • Blache Alice • FRN
PIERROT DES BOIS • 1954 • Jutra Claude • SHT • CND
PIERROT ET LE FANTOME • 1898 • *Lumiere Louis (P)* • FRN • PIERROT AND THE GHOST
PIERROT IN HELL see **PIERROT ALL'INFERNO** • 1908
PIERROT INAMORATO • 1906 • Velle Gaston • ITL
PIERROT LA TENDRESSE • 1960 • Villiers Francois • FRN
PIERROT LE FOU • 1965 • Godard Jean-Luc • FRN, ITL • BANDITO DELLA 11, IL (ITL) ○ DEMON DE ONZE HEURES, LE
PIERROT MALHEUREUX see **AU CLAIR DE LA LUNE OU PIERROT MALHEUREUX** • 1904
PIERROT, PIERRETTE • 1924 • Feuillade Louis • FRN
PIERROT'S CHRISTMAS • 1900 • Blache Alice • SHT • FRN
PIERROT'S GRIEF see **AU CLAIR DE LA LUNE OU PIERROT MALHEUREUX** • 1904
PIERROT'S PROBLEM • 1902 • *Biograph* • USA
PIERROT'S ROMANCE, THE • 1904 • *Urban Trading Co* • UKN
PIERVAIA LASTOTCHA • 1975 • Mitchedioze Nana • USS
PIERVAIA VESNA • 1950 • Medvedkin Alexander • USS
PIERWSZA KLASA • 1959 • Halladin Danuta • DOC • PLN • CLASS ONE ○ FIRST GRADE
PIERWSZA WYPRAWA • 1964 • Nehrebecki Wladyslaw • ANS • PLN • FIRST EXPEDITION, THE
PIERWSZE DNI • 1951 • Rybkowski Jan • PLN • FIRST DAYS
PIERWSZE LATA • 1949 • Ivens Joris • PLN, CZC, BUL • FIRST YEARS, THE
PIERWSZE POKOLENIE • 1963 • Gryczelowska Krystyna (c/d) • DOC • PLN • FIRST GENERATION, THE
PIERWSZY BIALO-CAERWONY • 1969 • Halladin Danuta • DOC • PLN • FIRST WHITE AND RED, THE
PIERWSZY, DRUGI, TRZECI • 1964 • Szczechura Daniel • ANS • PLN • FIRST, SECOND, THIRD ○ ONE, TWO, THREE ○ SUCCESS
PIERWSZY DZIEN W PRACY • 1969 • Ziarnik Jerzy • DOC • PLN • FIRST DAY AT WORK
PIERWSZY DZIEN WOLNOSCI • 1964 • Ford Aleksander • PLN • FIRST DAY OF FREEDOM, THE
PIERWSZY KROK • 1962 • Karabasz Kazimierz • DCS • PLN • FIRST STEPS, THE ○ FIRST STEP, THE
PIERWSZY PAWILON • 1964 • Majewski Janusz • PLN • FIRST PAVILION, THE
PIERWSZY PLON • 1950 • Has Wojciech J. • DCS • PLN • FIRST HARVEST, THE
PIERWSZY START • 1951 • Buczkowski Leonard • PLN • FIRST START, THE
PIES AND GUYS • 1958 • White Jules • SHT • USA
PIES DE GATO • 1954 • Gonzalez Rogelio A. • MXC
PIESEN O SIVOM HOLUBOVI • 1961 • Barabas Stanislav • CZC • SONG OF THE GREY DOVE
PIESNI NAD WISLA • 1956 • Bossak Jerzy? • DOC • PLN • SONGS OF THE VISTULA
PIET MONDRIAAN • 1973 • Crama Nico • DOC • NTH
PIET SE NIGGIE • 1964 • SAF
PIET SE TANTE • 1959 • SAF
PIETA PER CHI CADE • 1954 • Costa Mario • ITL
PIETA PER CHI RESTA • 1974 • Pinzauti Mario • ITL
PIETRA MICCA • 1938 • Vergano Aldo • ITL
PIETRO, DER KORSAR • 1925 • Robison Arthur • FRG • PETER THE PIRATE (USA) ○ SEA WOLVES
PIETRO THE PIANIST • 1914 • *Selig* • USA
PIETRO WYZEJ • 1938 • Trystan Leon • PLN • APARTMENT ABOVE (USA)
PIETY see **KEGYELET** • 1967
PIEUVRE, LA • 1926 • Painleve Jean • SHT • FRN • OCTOPUS
PIEUVRE, LA see **SUSPECTS, LES** • 1974
PIF LE CHIEN • 1964 • Herman Jean • FRN
PIFFIKINS' PATENT POWDER • 1910 • *Warwick* • UKN
PIG, THE • 1970 • Leviant Michel • ANS • USA
PIG-A-BOO • 1952 • Sparber I. • ANS • USA
PIG ACROSS PARIS (UKN) see **TRAVERSEE DE PARIS, LA** • 1956
PIG HUNT, THE see **GRISJAKTEN** • 1970
PIG IN A PICKLE • 1954 • Smith Paul J. • ANS • USA
PIG WAR, THE see **GUERRA DEL CERDO, LA** • 1975
PIGA BLAND PIGOR, EN • 1924 • Brunius John W. • SWD • MAID AMONG MAIDS
PIGALLE, CARREFOUR DES ILLUSIONS • 1972 • Chevalier Pierre • FRN, ITL, SPN
PIGALLE-SAINT-GERMAINE-DES-PRES • 1950 • Berthomieu Andre • FRN
PIGBIRD • 1981 • Condie Richard • ANS • CND
PIGBOATS see **HELL BELOW** • 1932
PIGEN FRA EGBORG • 1969 • Ottosen Carl • DNM
PIGEN I SOGELYSET • 1959 • Christensen Bent, Anker • DNM • GIRL IN THE SEARCHLIGHT
PIGEN OG DROMMESLOTTET • 1974 • Henriksen Finn • DNM
PIGEN OG PRESSEFOTOGRAFEN • 1962 • Kulle Jarl • DNM • GIRL AND THE PRESS PHOTOGRAPHER, THE
PIGEN SILKE • 1971 • Roos Lise • DOC • DNM • GIRL NAMED SILKE, A
PIGEN UNDEN FAEDRELAND see **MADCHEN OHNE VATERLAND, DAS** • 1912
PIGEON, THE • 1969 • Bellamy Earl • TVM • USA
PIGEON, THE see **PIZHON** • 1929
PIGEON FAIRY, THE • 1906 • *Pathe* • FRN
PIGEON HOLED • 1956 • Lovy Alex • ANS • USA
PIGEON PATROL • 1942 • Lovy Alex • ANS • USA
PIGEON THAT TOOK ROME, THE • 1962 • Shavelson Melville • USA • EASTER DINNER, THE
PIGEON TREE see **GEZI SHU** • 1985
PIGEONS see **SIDELONG GLANCES OF A PIGEON FANCIER** • 1971
PIGER I TROJEN • 1975 • Henriksen Finn • DNM
PIGER I TROJEN 2 • 1976 • Henriksen Finn • DNM
PIGER TIL SOS • 1977 • Henriksen Finn • DNM
PIGMY WORLD, THE • 1909 • *Gaumont* • FRN
PIGPEN (USA) see **PORCILE** • 1969
PIGS • 1984 • Black Cathal • IRL
PIGS see **MIDNIGHT KISS, THE** • 1926
PIGS see **DADDY'S DEADLY DARLING** • 1972
PIG'S A PIG, A • 1913 • *Nestor* • USA
PIGS AND BATTLESHIPS see **BUTA TO GUNKAN** • 1961
PIGS AND PEARLS • 1917 • *La Salle* • USA
PIGS ARE SELDOM CLEAN see **ON N'ENGRAISSE PAS LES COCHONS A L'EAU CLAIRE** • 1973
PIG'S CURLY TAIL, THE • 1926 • Lantz Walter • ANS • USA
PIG'S FEAT, THE • 1963 • Kneitel Seymour • ANS • USA
PIG'S GATE see **SWINKA** • 1990
PIGS IN A POLKA • 1942 • Freleng Friz • ANS • USA
PIGS IS PIGS • 1910 • *Edison* • USA
PIGS IS PIGS • 1914 • Baker George D. • USA
PIGS IS PIGS • 1937 • Freleng Friz • ANS • USA
PIGS IS PIGS • 1954 • Kinney Jack • ANS • USA
PIGS VERSUS THE FREAKS, THE see **OFF SIDES** • 1984
PIGS VS. FREAKS see **OFF SIDES** • 1984
PIGSKIN • 1932 • McCarey Ray • SHT • USA
PIGSKIN CAPERS • 1930 • *Terry Paul/ Moser Frank (P)* • ANS • USA
PIGSKIN CHAMPIONS • 1937 • Clarke Charles G. • SHT • USA
PIGSKIN HERO, A • 1918 • Lyons Eddie, Moran Lee • SHT • USA
PIGSKIN PARADE • 1936 • Butler David • USA • HARMONY PARADE (UKN)
PIGSKIN POLKA • 1937 • Douglas Gordon • SHT • USA
PIGSKIN SKILL • 1948 • Dudley Carl • SHT • USA
PIGSTY (UKN) see **PORCILE** • 1969
PIGTAIL PILOT • 1944 • *O'Brien Joseph/ Mead Thomas (P)* • SHT • USA
PIGULKI DLA AURELII • 1958 • Lenartowicz Stanislaw • PLN • PILLS FOR AURELIA
PILOPIRTTI • 1978 • Huunonen Seppo • FNL • HIDEAWAY
PIJANSTWO • 1958 • Lomnicki Jan • DOC • PLN • DRINKING
PIKANTERIE • 1951 • Braun Alfred • FRG
PIKE MED HVIT BALL see **FYRA GANGER FYRA** • 1965
PIKER'S DREAM OR A RACE TRACK FANTASY, THE • 1907 • Blackton J. Stuart • USA
PIKER'S PEAK • 1957 • Freleng Friz • ANS • USA
PIKKIE • 1972 • SAF
PIKKU PIETARIN PIHA • 1961 • Witikka Jack • FNL • LITTLE PETER'S YARD ○ LITTLE PRESENTS
PIKNIK • 1967 • Sis Vladimir, Smocek Ladislav • CZC • PICNIC
PIKNIK U TOPOLI • 1982 • Amar Zoran • YGS • PICNIC AMONG THE POPLARS
PIKOLO VILAGOS, EGY • 1955 • Mariassy Felix • HNG • GLASS OF BEER, A ○ HALF A PINT
PIKOO • 1980 • Ray Satyajit • IND
PIKOVAYA DAMA • 1910 • Chardynin Pyotr • USS • QUEEN OF SPADES (USA)
PIKOVAYA DAMA • 1916 • Protazanov Yakov • USS • QUEEN OF SPADES, THE
PIKOVAYA DAMA • 1960 • Tikhomirov Roman • USS • QUEEN OF SPADES, THE (USA)
PIKRO PSOMI, TO • 1951 • Grigoriou Grigoris • GRC • PAIN AMER ○ BITTER BREAD
PILA DELLA PEPPA, LA (ITL) see **MAGOT DE JOSEFA, LE** • 1963
PILA ELETTRICA, LA (ITL) see **PILE ELECTRIQUE, LA** • 1906
PILAR GUERRA • 1926 • Buchs Jose • SPN
PILATE AND OTHERS see **PILATUS UND ANDERE -EIN FILM FUR KARFREITAG** • 1972
PILATUS UND ANDERE -EIN FILM FUR KARFREITAG • 1972 • Wajda Andrzej • MTV • FRG • PILATE AND OTHERS
PILDORAS, LAS • 1974 • Cahen Enrique • ARG
PILE DRIVER • 1920 • *Franey William* • SHT • USA
PILE DRIVER, THE see **FATAL MALLET, THE** • 1914
PILE DRIVING see **HEIEN** • 1930
PILE ELECTRIQUE, LA • 1906 • Velle Gaston • FRN, ITL • PILA ELETTRICA, LA (ITL) ○ ELECTRIC BATTERY, THE
PILE OU FACE • 1918 • de Baroncelli Jacques • FRN
PILE OU FACE • 1971 • Fournier Roger • CND
PILE OU FACE • 1980 • Enrico Robert • FRN • HEADS OR TAILS
PILE OU FACE see **PETITE DE MONTPARNASSE, LA** • 1931
PILEBUCK see **SECRET COMMAND, THE** • 1944
PILFERED POKER, THE • 1905 • *Cricks & Sharp* • UKN
PILGRIM, THE • 1910 • *Nestor* • USA
PILGRIM, THE • 1912 • Caserini Mario • ITL
PILGRIM, THE • 1916 • Borzage Frank • SHT • USA
PILGRIM, THE • 1923 • Chaplin Charles • USA
PILGRIM, FAREWELL • 1980 • Roemer Michael • USA
PILGRIM LADY, THE • 1947 • Selander Lesley • USA • INNER CIRCLE, THE
PILGRIM -MESSENGER OF LOVE, THE • 1913 • *August Edwin* • USA
PILGRIM POPEYE • 1951 • Sparber I. • ANS • USA
PILGRIM PORKY • 1940 • Clampett Robert • ANS • USA
PILGRIMAGE • 1933 • Ford John • USA
PILGRIMAGE • 1958 • Macartney-Filgate Terence • DOC • CND
PILGRIMAGE • 1972 • Montresor Beni • USA
PILGRIMAGE, THE • 1912 • *Kalem* • USA
PILGRIMAGE AT NIGHT see **ANYA KORO** • 1959
PILGRIMAGE FOR PEACE: POPE PAUL VI VISITS AMERICA • 1966 • Allensworth Carl • DOC • USA
PILGRIMAGE TO KEVLAAR (USA) see **VALLFARTEN TILL KEVLAAR** • 1921
PILGRIMAGE TO THE VIRGIN see **PROCESI K PANENCE** • 1961
PILGRIMS OF THE NIGHT • 1921 • Sloman Edward • USA
PILGRIM'S PROGRESS, THE • 1912 • *Ambrosio* • ITL
PILKARSKI POKER • 1988 • Zaorski Janusz • PLN • SOCCER POKER
PILL • 1966-67 • Popescu-Gopo Ion • ANM • RMN
PILL, THE • 1923 • *Rock Joe (P)* • SHT • USA
PILL, THE • 1967 • Connell W. Merle • USA
PILL, THE • 1971 • Perlov David • ISR
PILL, THE see **GIRL, THE BODY AND THE PILL, THE** • 1967
PILL, THE see **HAGLOULAH** • 1968
PILL BOX CUPID, A • 1913 • *Lubin* • USA
PILL CAPER, THE • 1967 • Arnold Jack • TVM • USA
PILL MAKER'S MISTAKE, THE • 1906 • Fitzhamon Lewin • UKN
PILL OF DEATH (UKN) see **PEAU DE TORPEDO, LA** • 1970
PILL PEDDLERS • 1953 • Rasinski Connie • ANS • USA
PILL POUNDER, THE • 1923 • La Cava Gregory • SHT • USA
PILL POUNDER, THE see **PILLS FOR PAPA** • 1920
PILLAGE BY PILLAR BOX • 1907 • Fitzhamon Lewin • UKN
PILLANATNYI PEZZAVAR • 1939 • Kanizsay Jozsef • TEMPORARILY BROKE (USA)
PILLAR OF FIRE, THE • 1963 • Frisch Larry • ISR
PILLAR OF FLAME, A • 1915 • Brooke Van Dyke • USA
PILLAR OF PERIL, THE • 1913 • *Frontier* • USA
PILLAR OF SALT see **SOBALVANY** • 1956
PILLAR TO POST • 1947 • Leacock Philip • DOC • UKN
PILLARDS, LES • 1965 • Deray Jacques • FRN, ITL, SPN • ROUTE AUX DIAMANTS, LA
PILLARS OF SOCIETY • 1920 • Wilson Rex • UKN
PILLARS OF SOCIETY, THE • 1911 • *Thanhouser* • USA
PILLARS OF SOCIETY, THE • 1916 • Walsh Raoul • USA
PILLARS OF SOCIETY (UKN) see **STUTZEN DER GESELLSCHAFT** • 1935
PILLARS OF THE SKY • 1956 • Marshall George • USA • TOMAHAWK AND THE CROSS, THE (UKN)
PILLOLA, LA • 1982 • Bozzetto Bruno • ANM • ITL
PILLOLE D'ERCOLE, LE • 1960 • Salce Luciano • ITL • HERCULES' PILLS
PILLORY, THE • 1916 • Sullivan Frederick • USA
PILLOW FIGHT • 1898 • *Riley Brothers* • UKN
PILLOW OF DEATH • 1945 • Fox Wallace • USA
PILLOW OF MIST • 1986 • SKR
PILLOW TALK • 1959 • Gordon Michael • USA
PILLOW TALK see **ROMANTIK PA SENGEKANTEN** • 1973
PILLOW TO POST • 1945 • Sherman Vincent • USA
PILLS AND PILLS • 1914 • *Melies* • USA
PILLS FOR AURELIA see **PIGULKI DLA AURELII** • 1958
PILLS FOR PAPA • 1920 • Santell Alfred • SHT • USA • PILL POUNDER, THE
PILLS OF PERIL • 1916 • Jones F. Richard • SHT • USA
PILLUELO DE MADRID, EL • 1926 • Rey Florian • SPN
PILLULES DU DIABLE, LES see **400 FARCES DU DIABLE, LES** • 1906
PILOT, THE • 1979 • Robertson Cliff • USA • DANGER IN THE SKIES
PILOT IS SAFE, THE • 1941 • Lee Jack • DOC • UKN
PILOT NO.5 • 1942 • Sidney George • USA
PILOT X-15 • 1960 • Macartney-Filgate Terence • DOC • USA
PILOTA RITORNA, UN • 1942 • Rossellini Roberto • ITL
PILOTE DE GUERRE.. PILOTE DE LIGNE • 1949 • Ciampi Yves • FRN
PILOTEN IM PYJAMA • 1968 • Heynowski Walter, Scheumann Gerhard • GDR • PILOTS IN PYJAMAS ○ HILTON HANOI
PILOTOS DE COMBATE • 1970 • *Filmadora Chapultepec* • MXC
PILOTOS DE LA MUERTE • 1962 • Urueta Chano • MXC
PILOTS, THE see **LYOTCHIKI** • 1935
PILOTS IN PYJAMAS see **PILOTEN IM PYJAMA** • 1968
PILSKA JULIA PA BROLLOPSRESAN • 1982 • Whyte Andrew • SWD • HONEYMOON SWEDISH STYLE
PILUK IL TIMIDO • 1968 • Celano Guido • ITL • GIURO.. E IL UCCISE AD UNO AD UNO ○ SWEAR TO KILL THEM ONE BY ONE ○ PILUK THE TIMID
PILUK THE TIMID see **PILUK IL TIMIDO** • 1968
PILVILINNA • 1970 • Rimminen Sakari • FNL • CASTLE OF POT ○ CASTLE OF DREAMS
PILYO SA GIRLS • 1967 • Wenceslao Jose Pepe • PHL • PLAYFUL WITH THE GIRLS
PIM, PAM, PUM... FUEGO! • 1975 • Olea Pedro • SPN • ONE.. TWO.. THREE.. FIRE!
PIM, PAM, PUMMELCHEN • 1969 • Latzke Horst • FRG
PIMP see **PASAK HOLEK** • 1929
PIMP, THE see **MAGNACCIO, IL** • 1968
PIMPERNEL SMITH • 1941 • Howard Leslie • UKN • FIGHTING PIMPERNEL, THE (USA) ○ MISTER V ○ MR. V
PIMPERNEL SVENSSON • 1950 • Lingheim Emil A. • SWD
PIMPLE • 1912-20 • Evans Joe, Evans Fred • SHS • UKN
PIMPLE ACTS • 1915 • Evans Fred, Evans Joe • UKN
PIMPLE, ANARCHIST • 1914 • Evans Fred, Evans Joe • UKN
PIMPLE AND GALATEA • 1914 • Evans Fred, Evans Joe • UKN
PIMPLE AND THE GORILLA • 1913 • Evans Fred, Evans Joe • UKN
PIMPLE AND THE SNAKE • 1912 • Kellino W. P. • UKN
PIMPLE AND THE STOLEN PLANS • 1914 • Evans Fred, Evans Joe • UKN
PIMPLE AS A BALLET DANCER • 1912 • Evans Fred, Evans Joe • UKN
PIMPLE AS A CINEMA ACTOR • 1912 • Evans Fred, Evans Joe • UKN
PIMPLE AS A RENT COLLECTOR • 1912 • Evans Fred, Evans Joe • UKN
PIMPLE AS HAMLET • 1916 • Evans Fred, Evans Joe • SHT • UKN
PIMPLE BEATS JACK JOHNSON • 1914 • Evans Fred, Evans Joe • UKN
PIMPLE BECOMES AN ACROBAT • 1912 • Evans Fred, Evans Joe • UKN
PIMPLE, CHILD STEALER • 1915 • Evans Fred, Evans Joe • UKN
PIMPLE COPPED • 1915 • Evans Fred, Evans Joe • UKN
PIMPLE, COUNTER JUMPER • 1914 • Evans Fred, Evans Joe • UKN
PIMPLE, DETECTIVE • 1913 • Evans Fred, Evans Joe • UKN
PIMPLE DOES THE HAT TRICK • 1913 • Evans Fred, Evans Joe • UKN
PIMPLE DOES THE TURKEY TROT • 1912 • Kellino W. P. • UKN
PIMPLE ELOPES • 1914 • Evans Fred, Evans Joe • UKN
PIMPLE ENDS IT • 1916 • Evans Fred, Evans Joe • SHT • UKN
PIMPLE ENLISTS • 1914 • Evans Fred, Evans Joe • UKN
PIMPLE EXPLAINS • 1915 • Evans Fred, Evans Joe • UKN
PIMPLE GETS A QUID • 1912 • Evans Fred, Evans Joe • UKN

PIMPLE GETS THE HUMP • 1915 • Evans Fred, Evans Joe • UKN
PIMPLE GETS THE JUMPS • 1913 • Evans Fred, Evans Joe • UKN
PIMPLE GETS THE SACK • 1913 • Evans Fred, Evans Joe • UKN
PIMPLE GOES A-BUSKING • 1913 • Evans Fred, Evans Joe • UKN
PIMPLE GOES FISHING • 1913 • Evans Fred, Evans Joe • UKN
PIMPLE GOES TO PARIS • 1914 • Evans Fred, Evans Joe • UKN
PIMPLE HAS ONE • 1915 • Evans Fred, Evans Joe • UKN
PIMPLE -HIMSELF AND OTHERS • 1916 • Evans Fred, Evans Joe • SHT • UKN
PIMPLE -HIS VOLUNTARY CORPS • 1917 • Evans Fred, Evans Joe • SHT • UKN
PIMPLE IN SOCIETY • 1914 • Evans Fred, Evans Joe • UKN
PIMPLE IN THE GRIP OF THE LAW • 1914 • Evans Fred, Evans Joe • UKN
PIMPLE IN THE KILTIES • 1915 • Evans Fred, Evans Joe • UKN
PIMPLE JOINS THE ARMY • 1913 • Evans Fred, Evans Joe • UKN
PIMPLE JOINS THE POLICE FORCE see **ADVENTURES OF PIMPLE -PIMPLE P.C., THE** • 1913
PIMPLE M.P. • 1914 • Evans Fred, Evans Joe • UKN
PIMPLE MEETS CAPTAIN SCUTTLE • 1913 • Evans Fred, Evans Joe • UKN
PIMPLE 'MIDST RAGING BEASTS • 1914 • Evans Fred, Evans Joe • UKN
PIMPLE ON FOOTBALL • 1914 • Evans Fred, Evans Joe • UKN
PIMPLE PINCHED • 1914 • Evans Fred, Evans Joe • UKN
PIMPLE POOR BUT DISHONEST • 1916 • Evans Fred, Evans Joe • SHT • UKN
PIMPLE SEES GHOSTS • 1915 • Evans Fred, Evans Joe • UKN
PIMPLE, SPECIAL CONSTABLE • 1914 • Evans Fred, Evans Joe • UKN
PIMPLE SPLITS THE DIFFERENCE • 1916 • Evans Fred, Evans Joe • SHT • UKN
PIMPLE TAKES A PICTURE • 1913 • Evans Fred, Evans Joe • UKN
PIMPLE, THE BAD GIRL OF THE FAMILY • 1915 • Evans Fred, Evans Joe • UKN
PIMPLE THE SPORT • 1913 • Evans Fred, Evans Joe • UKN
PIMPLE TURNS HONEST • 1914 • Evans Fred, Evans Joe • UKN
PIMPLE UP THE POLE • 1915 • Evans Fred, Evans Joe • UKN
PIMPLE WILL TREAT • 1915 • Evans Fred, Evans Joe • UKN
PIMPLE WINS A BET • 1912 • Evans Fred, Evans Joe • UKN
PIMPLE WRITES A CINEMA PLOT • 1913 • Evans Fred • UKN
PIMPLE'S A WOMAN IN THE CASE • 1916 • Evans Fred, Evans Joe • SHT • UKN
PIMPLE'S ADVICE • 1914 • Evans Fred, Evans Joe • UKN
PIMPLE'S ARM OF THE LAW • 1916 • Evans Fred, Evans Joe • SHT • UKN
PIMPLE'S ART OF MYSTERY • 1915 • Evans Fred, Evans Joe • UKN • FLIVVER'S ART OF MYSTERY (USA)
PIMPLE'S ARTFUL DODGE • 1915 • Evans Fred, Evans Joe • UKN
PIMPLE'S BETTER 'OLE • 1918 • Evans Fred • SHT • UKN
PIMPLE'S BOY SCOUT • 1915 • Evans Fred, Evans Joe • UKN
PIMPLE'S BURGLAR SCARE • 1914 • Evans Fred, Evans Joe • UKN
PIMPLE'S BURLESQUE OF THE STILL ALARM • 1915 • Evans Fred, Evans Joe • UKN • FLIVVER'S STILL ALARM (USA)
PIMPLE'S CHARGE OF THE LIGHT BRIGADE • 1914 • Evans Fred, Evans Joe • UKN
PIMPLE'S CLUTCHING HAND • 1916 • Evans Fred, Evans Joe • SHT • UKN
PIMPLE'S COMPLAINT • 1913 • Evans Fred, Evans Joe • UKN
PIMPLE'S CRIME • 1916 • Evans Fred, Evans Joe • SHT • UKN
PIMPLE'S DILEMMA • 1915 • Evans Fred, Evans Joe • UKN • FLIVVER'S DILEMMA (USA)
PIMPLE'S DOUBLE • 1916 • Evans Fred, Evans Joe • SHT • UKN
PIMPLE'S DREAM OF VICTORY • 1915 • Evans Fred, Evans Joe • UKN
PIMPLE'S EGGS-TRAORDINARY STORY • 1912 • Evans Fred, Evans Joe • UKN
PIMPLE'S ESCAPE FROM PORTLAND • 1914 • Evans Fred, Evans Joe • UKN
PIMPLE'S FIRE BRIGADE • 1912 • Evans Fred, Evans Joe • UKN
PIMPLE'S GOOD TURN • 1915 • Evans Fred, Evans Joe • UKN • FLIVVER'S GOOD TURN (USA)
PIMPLE'S GREAT ADVENTURE • 1916 • Evans Fred, Evans Joe • SHT • UKN
PIMPLE'S GREAT BULL FIGHT • 1913 • Evans Fred, Evans Joe • UKN
PIMPLE'S GREAT FIRE • 1914 • Evans Fred, Evans Joe • UKN
PIMPLE'S HOLIDAY • 1915 • Evans Fred, Evans Joe • UKN
PIMPLE'S HUMANITY • 1914 • Evans Fred, Evans Joe • UKN
PIMPLE'S INFERNO • 1913 • Evans Fred, Evans Joe • UKN
PIMPLE'S IVANHOE • 1913 • Evans Fred, Evans Joe • UKN
PIMPLE'S LADY GODIVA • 1917 • Evans Fred, Evans Joe • SHT • UKN
PIMPLE'S LAST RESOURCE • 1914 • Evans Fred, Evans Joe • UKN
PIMPLE'S LEAP TO FORTUNE • 1914 • Evans Fred, Evans Joe • UKN
PIMPLE'S MERRY WIVES • 1916 • Evans Fred, Evans Joe • SHT • UKN • MERRY WIVES OF PIMPLE, THE
PIMPLE'S MIDNIGHT RAMBLE • 1913 • Evans Fred, Evans Joe • UKN
PIMPLE'S MIDSUMMER NIGHT'S DREAM • 1916 • Evans Fred, Evans Joe • SHT • UKN
PIMPLE'S MILLION DOLLAR MYSTERY • 1915 • Weston Charles • UKN • FLIVVER'S FAMOUS CHEESE HOUND (USA)
PIMPLE'S MONKEY BUSINESS • 1916 • Evans Fred, Evans Joe • SHT • UKN • SOME MONKEY BUSINESS
PIMPLE'S MOTOR BIKE • 1913 • Evans Fred, Evans Joe • UKN
PIMPLE'S MOTOR TOUR • 1915 • Evans Fred, Evans Joe • UKN
PIMPLE'S MOTOR TOUR • 1917 • Evans Fred, Evans Joe • UKN
PIMPLE'S MOTOR TRAP • 1913 • Evans Fred, Evans Joe • UKN
PIMPLE'S MYSTERY OF THE CLOSED DOOR • 1917 • Evans Fred, Evans Joe • SHT • UKN
PIMPLE'S NAUTICAL STORY • 1916 • Evans Fred, Evans Joe • UKN
PIMPLE'S NEW JOB • 1913 • Evans Fred, Evans Joe • UKN
PIMPLE'S PART • 1916 • Evans Fred, Evans Joe • SHT • UKN
PIMPLE'S PAST • 1915 • Weston Charles • UKN • FLIVVER'S TERRIBLE PAST (USA)
PIMPLE'S PERIL • 1915 • Weston Charles • UKN
PIMPLE'S PINK FORMS • 1916 • Evans Fred, Evans Joe • SHT • UKN
PIMPLE'S PITTER-PATTER • 1917 • Evans Fred, Evans Joe • SHT • UKN
PIMPLE'S PRISON • 1914 • Evans Fred, Evans Joe • UKN
PIMPLE'S PROPOSAL • 1914 • Evans Fred, Evans Joe • UKN
PIMPLE'S REST CURE • 1913 • Evans Fred, Evans Joe • UKN
PIMPLE'S RIVAL • 1915 • Evans Fred, Evans Joe • UKN
PIMPLE'S ROAD TO RUIN • 1915 • Evans Fred, Evans Joe • UKN
PIMPLE'S ROMANCE • 1917 • Evans Fred, Evans Joe • SHT • UKN
PIMPLE'S ROYAL DIVORCE • 1915 • Weston Charles • UKN
PIMPLE'S SCRAP OF PAPER • 1915 • Evans Fred, Evans Joe • UKN
PIMPLE'S SENSELESS CENSORING • 1917 • Evans Fred, Evans Joe • SHT • UKN
PIMPLE'S SILVER LAGOON • 1916 • Evans Fred, Evans Joe • SHT • UKN
PIMPLE'S SOME BURGLAR • 1915 • Evans Fred, Evans Joe • UKN
PIMPLE'S SPORTING CHANCE • 1913 • Evans Fred, Evans Joe • UKN
PIMPLE'S STORYETTE • 1915 • Evans Fred, Evans Joe • UKN
PIMPLE'S TABLEAUX VIVANTS • 1917 • Evans Fred, Evans Joe • UKN
PIMPLE'S TENTH COMMANDMENT • 1916 • Evans Fred, Evans Joe • SHT • UKN
PIMPLE'S THE CASE OF JOHNNY WALKER • 1915 • Weston Charles • UKN
PIMPLE'S THE MAN WHO STAYED AT HOME • 1915 • *Evans Fred* • UKN
PIMPLE'S THE WHIP • 1917 • Evans Fred, Evans Joe • SHT • UKN
PIMPLE'S THE WOMAN WHO DID • 1917 • Evans Fred, Evans Joe • SHT • UKN
PIMPLE'S THREE • 1915 • Evans Fred, Evans Joe • UKN
PIMPLE'S THREE MUSKETEERS • 1922 • Evans Fred, Evans Joe • SHT • UKN
PIMPLE'S THREE O'CLOCK RACE • 1915 • Evans Fred, Evans Joe • UKN
PIMPLE'S THREE WEEKS (WITHOUT THE OPTION) • 1915 • Weston Charles • UKN
PIMPLE'S TOPICAL GAZETTE • 1920 • Evans Fred, Evans Joe • SHT • UKN
PIMPLE'S TROUSERS • 1914 • Evans Fred, Evans Joe • UKN
PIMPLE'S UNCLE • 1915 • Evans Fred, Evans Joe • UKN
PIMPLE'S VENGEANCE • 1914 • Evans Fred, Evans Joe • UKN
PIMPLE'S WIFE • 1913 • Evans Fred, Evans Joe • UKN
PIMPLE'S WILL IT -WAS IT -IS IT • 1915 • Evans Fred, Evans Joe • UKN
PIMPLE'S WONDERFUL GRAMOPHONE • 1913 • Evans Fred, Evans Joe • UKN
PIMPLE'S ZEPPELIN SCARE • 1916 • Evans Fred, Evans Joe • UKN
PIN • 1988 • Stern Sandor • CND
PIN FEATHERS • 1933 • Lantz Walter, Nolan William • ANS • USA
PIN PRICKS • 1915 • Birch Cecil • UKN
PIN-UP CAMERA see **NUDES, INC.** • 1964
PIN-UP FACTORY, THE see **NUDES, INC.** • 1964
PIN-UP GIRL • 1944 • Humberstone H. Bruce • USA
PINA MADURA • 1949 • Zacarias Miguel • MXC
PINA YA QETELO • 1982 • SAF
PINBALL • 1977 • Hale Jeffrey • USA
PINBALL PICK-UP see **PICK-UP SUMMER** • 1980
PINBALL SUMMER see **PICK-UP SUMMER** • 1980
PINCE A ONGLES, LA • 1968 • Carriere Jean-Claude • SHT • FRN • NAIL CLIPPERS, THE (UKN) ○ NAILCUTTER, THE
PINCH, THE • 1915 • Lloyd Frank • USA
PINCH HITTER, THE • 1917 • Schertzinger Victor • USA
PINCH HITTER, THE • 1925 • Henabery Joseph • USA
PINCH IN TIME, A • 1948 • Lord Del • SHT • USA
PINCH OF SNUFF, A • 1911 • *Pathe* • USA
PINCH SINGER • 1936 • Newmeyer Fred • SHT • USA
PINCHED • 1917 • Roach Hal • SHT • USA
PINCHED IN THE FINISH • 1917 • *Sterling Ford* • SHT • USA
PINCHER'S LUCKY DAY • 1914 • *Captain Kettle* • UKN
PINCHING APPLES see **MERE, LA** • 1953
PINCUSHION MAN, THE see **BALLOONLAND** • 1935
PINDORAMA • 1970 • Jabor Arnaldo • BRZ
PINE AND GRANITE see **HONKA JA GRANIITTI** • 1977
PINE BOUGHS • 1983 • Lee Chang-Ho • SKR
PINE CANYON IS BURNING • 1977 • Nyby Christian Ii • TVM • USA
PINE RIDGE FEUD • 1909 • Boggs Frank • USA
PINE -THE NEW CASH CROP • 1949 • Clifford William T. • USA
PINE-TREE GROWS IN THE MOUNTAIN, A see **U GORI RASTE ZELEN BOR** • 1972
PINE TREE ON THE MOUNTAIN see **U GORI RASTE ZELEN BOR** • 1972
PINEAPPLE BUTAI • 1960 • *Sugiura Naoki* • JPN • HEY, PINEAPPLE!
PINES IN THE RYE • 1973 • Krinbern I. • USS
PINES OF LORY, THE • 1914 • Miller Ashley • USA
PINES OF ROME, THE • 1941 • Costa Mario • DOC • ITL
PINE'S REVENGE, THE • 1915 • De Grasse Joseph • USA
PING-PONG • 1902 • Williamson James • UKN
PING-PONG • 1950 • *Bendtsen Henning (P)* • ANS • DNM
PING PONG • 1968 • Oelschlegel Gerd • FRG • SCHWEIN HIN -SCHWEIN HER
PING-PONG • 1974 • Carriere Marcel • DCS • CND
PING PONG • 1985 • Liang Puzhi • HKG, UKN
PING PONG E POI • Weisz Frans • NTH
PINGIN OY SKOENNE • 1959 • *Karina Anna* • DNM
PINGUINI CI GUARDANO, I • 1956 • Leoni Guido • ITL
PINGWIN • 1965 • Stawinski Jerzy Stefan • PLN • PENGUIN, THE
PINHAMY • 1979 • Peries Lester James • SHT • SLN
PINI BINDU • 1968 • Palagolla Chula • SLN • DEW DROPS
PINI DI ROMA, I • 1941 • *Stallich Jan (Ph)* • ITL
PINJRE KE PANCHHI • 1968 • Chowdhury Salil • IND • BIRD IN A CAGE
PINK-A-RELLA • 1968 • Pratt Hawley • ANS • USA
PINK AND BLUE BLUES • 1952 • Burness Pete • ANS • USA • PINK BLUE PLUMS
PINK ANGELS, THE • 1971 • *Alderman John* • USA
PINK BLUE PLUMS see **PINK AND BLUE BLUES** • 1952
PINK CADILLAC • 1989 • Van Horn Buddy • USA
PINK CHAMPAGNE • 1980 • Conrad Steve • USA
PINK CHAQUITAS, THE • 1986 • Currie Anthony • CND
PINK DAVINCI • 1975 • McKimson Robert • ANS • USA
PINK DREAMS see **RUZOVE SNY** • 1976
PINK ELEPHANTS • 1926 • Roberts Stephen • SHT • USA
PINK ELEPHANTS • 1937 • Gordon Dan • ANS • USA
PINK-FINGER • 1964 • Freleng Friz • ANS • USA
PINK FLAMINGOS • 1972 • Waters John* • USA
PINK FLOYD see **PINK FLOYD A POMPEII, LES** • 1971
PINK FLOYD A POMPEII, LES • 1971 • Maben D'Adriann • DOC • FRN, FRG, BLG • PINK FLOYD AT POMPEII, THE ○ PINK FLOYD
PINK FLOYD AT POMPEII, THE see **PINK FLOYD A POMPEII, LES** • 1971
PINK FLOYD -THE WALL see **WALL, THE** • 1982
PINK GARTERS • 1912 • *Solax* • USA
PINK GODS • 1922 • Stanlaws Penrhyn • USA
PINK JUNGLE, THE • 1968 • Mann Delbert • USA
PINK MOTEL • 1983 • MacFarland Mike • USA • MOTEL
PINK NARCISSUS • 1971 • Bidgood Jim • USA
PINK NIGHTS • 1985 • Koch Philip • USA
PINK NO CHOHATSU • 1967 • Shindo Takae • JPN • PINK PROVOCATION
PINK OPERA CLOAK, THE • 1913 • *Kroell Adrienne* • USA
PINK ORGASM • Grant David • UKN
PINK PAJAMA GIRL, THE • 1912 • *Keefe Zena* • USA
PINK PAJAMAS • 1918 • *Capitol* • SHT • USA
PINK PAJAMAS • 1918 • Santell Alfred • *Nestor* • SHT • USA
PINK PAJAMAS • 1929 • *Sennett Mack (P)* • SHT • USA
PINK PAJAMAS • 1964 • Freleng Friz • ANS • USA
PINK PALACE, PARADISE BEACH • 1989 • Dor Milan • AUS
PINK PANTHER, THE • 1964 • Edwards Blake • USA
PINK PANTHER STRIKES AGAIN, THE • 1976 • Edwards Blake • USA
PINK PHINK, THE • 1964 • Freleng Friz • ANS • USA
PINK PISTONS • 1966 • Pratt Hawley • ANS • USA
PINK PRANKS • 1971 • Freleng Friz • ANS • USA
PINK PRO, THE • 1976 • McKimson Robert • ANS • USA
PINK PROVOCATION see **PINK NO CHOHATSU** • 1967
PINK PUSSY, THE see **ACOSADA** • 1963
PINK PUSSY CAT, THE see **ACOSADA** • 1963
PINK PUSSY CLUB, THE see **ACOSADA** • 1963
PINK PUSSY (WHERE SIN LIVES), THE (USA) see **ACOSADA** • 1963
PINK SLIP, THE see **ROZOVE KONBINE** • 1932
PINK STRING AND SEALING WAX • 1945 • Hamer Robert • UKN
PINK SWINE • 1964 • Jordan Larry • SHT • USA
PINK TELEPHONE see **MOMOIRO DENWA** • 1967
PINK TELEPHONE, THE (UKN) see **TELEPHONE ROSE, LE** • 1975
PINK TIGHTS • 1920 • Eason B. Reeves • USA
PINK ULYSSES • 1989 • de Kuyper Eric • NTH
PINKERTON MAN, THE • 1911 • *Powers* • USA
PINKIE SE ERFNIS • 1946 • SAF
PINKY • 1949 • Kazan Elia, Ford John (U/c) • USA
PINNACLE see **BLIND HUSBANDS** • 1918
PINNACLE, THE • 1916 • Stanton Richard • SHT • USA
PINNACLE OF FAME • 1943 • Barralet Paul • UKN
PINNE E ARPONIONI • 1952 • Quilici Folco • SHT • ITL
PINNED • 1912 • *Lubin* • USA
PINNING IT ON • 1921 • Roach Hal • SHT • USA
PINO VENEZOLANO, EL • 1974 • Scheuren Jose Vicente • DOC • VNZ
PINOCCHIO • 1911 • Guazzoni Enrico • ITL
PINOCCHIO • 1939 • Luske Hamilton, Sharpsteen Ben • ANM • USA
PINOCCHIO • 1971 • Allen Corey • USA • EROTIC ADVENTURES OF PINOCCHIO
PINOCCHIO • 1976 • Field Ron, Smith Sidney • TVM • USA
PINOCCHIO • 1983 • Medak Peter • MTV • USA
PINOCCHIO • 1985 • Letts Barry • MTV • UKN
PINOCCHIO see **AVVENTURE DI PINOCCHIO, LE** • 1968
PINOCCHIO AND THE EMPEROR OF THE NIGHT • 1987 • Sutherland Hal • ANM • USA
PINOCCHIO DANS L'ESPACE • 1965 • Goossens Ray • ANM • BLG, USA • PINOCCHIO'S ADVENTURES IN OUTER SPACE ○ PINOCCHIO IN OUTER SPACE
PINOCCHIO E LE SUE AVVENTURE • 1958 • Giovannini Attilio • ITL
PINOCCHIO IN OUTER SPACE see **PINOCCHIO DANS L'ESPACE** • 1965
PINOCCHIO (USA) see **TURLIS ABENTEUER** • 1967
PINOCCHIO'S ADVENTURES IN OUTER SPACE see **PINOCCHIO DANS L'ESPACE** • 1965
PINOCCHIO'S STORYBOOK ADVENTURES • 1979 • Merk Ron • USA
PINOCCHIOVA DOBRODRUZSTVI • 1971 • *Stallich Jan (Ph)* • MTV • CZC • ADVENTURES OF PINOCCHIO, THE
PINOT SIMPLE FLIC • 1984 • Jugnot Gerard • FRN
PINS AND NEEDLES • 1921 • Gliddon John • UKN
PINS ARE LUCKY • 1914 • *Hardy Oliver* • USA

PINTAME ANGELITOS BLANCOS • 1954 • Rodriguez Joselito • MXC
PINTANDO RELACIONES • Vera Luis R. • DOC • SWD • PAINTING RELATIONS
PINTER PEOPLE • 1968 • Potterton Gerald • CND
PINTO • 1919 • Schertzinger Victor • USA
PINTO BANDIT, THE • 1944 • Clifton Elmer • USA
PINTO BEN • 1915 • Hart William S. • USA
PINTO CANYON • 1940 • Johnston Raymond K. • USA
PINTO FOR THE PRINCE, A • 1979 • Low Colin, Spotton John • CND
PINTO KID, THE • 1928 • King Louis • USA
PINTO KID, THE • 1941 • Hillyer Lambert • USA • ALL SQUARE (UKN)
PINTO RUSTLERS • 1936 • Webb Harry S. • USA
PINTORE A CIDADE, O • 1956 • de Oliveira Manoel • SHT • PRT • PAINTER AND THE TOWN, THE ◦ PAINTER AND THE CITY, THE
PINTURAS DE MEU IRMAO JULIO, AS • 1967 • de Oliveira Manoel • PRT
PINULOT KA LANG SA LUPA • 1988 • Bernal Ishmael • PHL • I PICKED YOU FROM THE GUTTER
PIO KALOS O MATHITIS, O • 1968 • Andritsos Kostas • GRC • BEST PUPIL, THE
PIO LAMBRO ASTERI, TO • 1967 • Karayannis Kostas • GRC • BRIGHTEST STAR, THE
PIO LAMBRO BOUZOUKI, TO • 1968 • Karayannis Kostas • GRC • BEST BOUZOUKI-PLAYER, THE
PIO X see **UOMINI NON GUARDANO IL CIELO, GLI** • 1952
PIOGGIA D'ESTATE • 1937 • Badiek Michele • ITL
PIOMBI DI VENEZIA, I • 1953 • Callegari Gian Paolo • ITL
PIOMBI DI VENEZIA, I see **VENDICATORE MASCHERATO, IL** • 1964
PIOMBO E LA CARNE, IL • 1965 • Girolami Marino • ITL, FRN, SPN
PION, LE • 1978 • Gion Christian • FRN, FRG
PIONEER BUILDERS see **CONQUERORS, THE** • 1932
PIONEER DAYS • 1911 • *Bison* • USA
PIONEER DAYS • 1917 • Eagle Oscar • SHT • USA
PIONEER DAYS • 1930 • Gillett Burt • ANS • USA
PIONEER DAYS • 1940 • Webb Harry S. • USA
PIONEER JUSTICE • 1947 • Taylor Ray • USA
PIONEER LOVE see **AI NO SENKUSHA** • 1946
PIONEER MARSHAL • 1949 • Ford Philip • USA
PIONEER PEACEMAKER, THE • 1913 • *Mcdonald Hugh* • USA
PIONEER SCOUT, THE • 1928 • Ingraham Lloyd, Werker Alfred L. • USA
PIONEER TRAIL • 1938 • Levering Joseph • USA
PIONEER TRAILS • 1923 • Smith David • USA
PIONEER WOMAN • 1973 • Kulik Buzz • TVM • USA
PIONEERS • 1975 • CHN
PIONEERS, THE • 1916 • Barrett Franklyn • ASL
PIONEERS, THE • 1926 • Longford Raymond • ASL
PIONEERS, THE • 1941 • Herman Al • USA
PIONEERS, THE • 1963 • Burstall Tim • SHT • ASL
PIONEERS, THE see **YUAN** • 1980
PIONEERS CROSSING THE PLAINS IN '49 • 1908 • Porter Edwin S. • USA
PIONEER'S GOLD • 1924 • *Morrison Pete* • USA
PIONEERS IN INGOLSTADT see **PIONIERE IN INGOLSTADT** • 1971
PIONEER'S MISTAKE, THE • 1911 • *Bison* • USA
PIONEERS OF THE FRONTIER • 1940 • Nelson Sam • USA • ANCHOR, THE (UKN)
PIONEERS OF THE WEST • 1927 • *Carter Dick* • USA
PIONEERS OF THE WEST • 1929 • McGowan J. P. • USA
PIONEERS OF THE WEST • 1940 • Orlebeck Lester • USA
PIONEER'S RECOMPENCE, THE • 1913 • *Gebhardt George* • USA
PIONIERE IN INGOLSTADT • 1971 • Fassbinder R. W. • FRG • RECRUITS IN INGOLSTADT ◦ PIONEERS IN INGOLSTADT
PIONIR I DVOJKA • 1949 • Jocic Vera, Jocic Ljubisa • YGS • TRUANT, THE
PIORO I KARABIN • 1961 • Lomnicki Jan • DOC • PLN • PEN AND THE RIFLE, THE
PIORUM KULISTY • 1975 • Piwowarski Radoslaw • PLN • SPHERICAL LIGHTNING
PIOSENKA-WIOSENKA • 1964 • Nehrebecki Wladyslaw • ANS • PLN • SPRING SONG, THE ◦ SPRING MELODY, A
PIOSENKAI DLA KRAKOWA • 1960 • Lomnicki Jan • DOC • PLN • SONGS FOR CRACOW
PIOTR PERVYI see **PYOTR PERVY** • 1937-39
PIOTR VELIKY • 1910 • Goncharov Vasili M., Hansen Kai • USS • PETER THE GREAT
PIOUS CROOKS (UKN) see **HIS LAST HAUL** • 1928
PIOUS UNDERTAKING, A • 1913 • Miller Ashley • USA
PIOVRA, LA • 1918 • Roberti Roberto Leone • ITL
PIOVUTA DAL CIELO • 1953 • De Mitri Leonardo • ITL, FRN
PIP-EYE, PUP-EYE, POOP-EYE AND PEEP-EYE • 1942 • Fleischer Dave • ANS • USA
PIP FROM PITTSBURGH, THE • 1931 • Parrott James • SHT • USA
PIP, SQUEAK AND WILFRED • 1921 • Speed Lancelot, Payne A. B. • ANS • UKN
PIPE, THE • 1912 • *Wilder Marshall P.* • USA
PIPE, CHIEN • 1947-51 • Verneuil Henri • SHT • FRN
PIPE DREAM • 1905 • *Bitzer Billy (Ph)* • USA
PIPE DREAM • 1938 • Harman Hugh • ANS • USA
PIPE DREAM, A • 1915 • *Essanay* • USA
PIPE DREAM, A • 1915 • Castle James W. • *Edison* • USA
PIPE DREAM, THE • 1916 • Myers Harry • SHT • USA
PIPE DREAMS • 1907 • *Lubin* • SHT • USA
PIPE DREAMS • 1916 • *Price Kate* • USA
PIPE DREAMS • 1976 • Verona Stephen F. • USA
PIPE DREAMS AND PRIZES • 1920 • Mann Harry • SHT • USA
PIPE OF DISCONTENT, THE • 1917 • *Keystone* • SHT • USA
PIPE OF PEACE, THE • 1918 • *U.s.m.p.* • USA
PIPE THE WHISKERS • 1918 • Roach Hal • SHT • USA
PIPELINE "FRIENDSHIP" • 1964 • Grigoriev Roman • DOC • USS
PIPENA KUMUDU • 1967 • de Mel Ruby • SLN • FLOWERING LOTUS
PIPER, THE • 1922 • Kenton Erle C. • SHT • USA
PIPER OF STRAKONICE, THE see **STRAKONICKY DUDAK** • 1955
PIPER PRINCE, THE • 1959 • *Dentsu Film* • ANS • JPN
PIPER'S PRICE, THE • 1917 • De Grasse Joseph • USA
PIPER'S TUNE, THE • 1962 • Box Muriel • UKN
PIPES see **DYMKY** • 1966
PIPES DE MADAME SAINT CLAUDE, LES • Ourt Michel • FRN
PIPES OF LUCKNOW, THE • 1926 • Tilley Frank • UKN
PIPES OF PAN, THE • 1914 • De Grasse Joseph • USA
PIPES OF PAN, THE • 1923 • Hepworth Cecil M. • UKN
PIPES OF PARA, THE • 1964 • Brealey Gil • DOC • ASL
PIPI, CACA, DODO see **CHIEDO ASILO** • 1979
PIPI STORM • 1973 • Cavadini Fabio • DOC • ASL
PIPICACADODO (FRN) see **CHIEDO ASILO** • 1979
PIPIN DER KURZE • 1934 • Wolff Carl Heinz • FRG
PIPING HOT • 1925 • Lamont Charles • SHT • USA
PIPING HOT • 1959 • Halas John, Batchelor Joy • ANS • UKN
PIPPA PASSES OR THE SONG OF CONSCIENCE • 1909 • Griffith D. W. • USA
PIPPI AUSSER RAND UND BAND see **PA RYMMEN MED PIPPI LANGSTRUMP** • 1970
PIPPI GOES ON BOARD • 1970 • Hellbom Olle • SWD, FRG
PIPPI IN THE SOUTH SEAS (USA) see **PIPPI LANGSTRUMP PA DE SJU HAVEN** • 1970
PIPPI LANGSTRUMP • 1949 • Gunwall Per • SWD • PIPPI LONG STOCKING
PIPPI LANGSTRUMP • 1969 • Hellbom Olle • SWD, FRG • PIPPI LONGSTOCKING (USA)
PIPPI LANGSTRUMP PA DE SJU HAVEN • 1970 • Hellbom Olle • SWD, FRG • PIPPI IN THE SOUTH SEAS (USA) ◦ PIPPI ON THE SEVEN SEAS
PIPPI LONG STOCKING see **PIPPI LANGSTRUMP** • 1949
PIPPI LONGSTOCKING (USA) see **PIPPI LANGSTRUMP** • 1969
PIPPI ON THE RUN • 1970 • Hellbom Olle • SWD, FRG
PIPPI ON THE SEVEN SEAS see **PIPPI LANGSTRUMP PA DE SJU HAVEN** • 1970
PIPPIN • 1981 • Doby Kathryn • USA
PIPPIN UP TO HIS PRANKS • 1912 • Haldane Bert? • UKN
PIPPO BRICIOLA E NUVOLA BIANCA • 1960 • Zane Angio • ITL
PIQUE • 1916 • Marston Lawrence • SHT • USA
PIQUE ASS • 1922 • Sauer Fred • FRG
PIQUE-ASSIETTES, LES • 1960 • Pontoiseau Roland, Girault Jean • FRN
PIQUE BUBE see **GEHEIMNIS DER SECHS SPIELKARTEN 2, DAS** • 1921
PIQUE DAME • 1918 • Wellin Arthur • FRG • QUEEN OF SPADES
PIQUE DAME • 1927 • Rasumny Alexander • FRG • QUEEN OF SPADES
PIQUE DAME • 1937 • Ozep Fedor • FRN • QUEEN OF SPADES (USA) ◦ DAME DE PIQUE, LA
PIQUE DAME see **SZENZACIO** • 1922
PIQUE-NIQUE • 1973 • Boughedir Ferid • SHT • TNS
PIQUE SIEBEN see **GEHEIMNIS DER SECHS SPIELKARTEN 4, DAS** • 1921
PIQUEURS DE FUTS, LES • 1901 • Melies Georges • FRN • BURGLARS IN THE WINE CELLAR, THE ◦ WINE CELLAR BURGLARS
PIQUEZ SUR LA LIGNEE BRISEE • 1976 • Renaud France Y. Y. • CND
PIR V ZHIRMUNKE • 1941 • Pudovkin V. I. • USS • FEAST AT ZHIRMUNKA
PIRACI RZECZNI • 1965 • Nehrebecki Wladyslaw • ANS • PLN • RIVER PIRATES, THE ◦ PIRATES
PIRACKI SKARB • 1960 • Marszalek Lechoslaw • ANS • PLN • PIRATE'S TREASURE ◦ PIRATE TREASURE, THE ◦ TREASURE OF THE PIRATES, THE
PIRAEUS 7.30 A.M. see **PIREAS ORA 7.30** • 1967
PIRANAS, LAS • 1967 • Berlanga Luis Garcia • ARG, SPN • PIRANHAS, THE (USA) ◦ VICTIMA, LA ◦ BOUTIQUE, LA
PIRANDELLO'S COUNTRY see **TERRA DI PIRANDELLO** • 1951
PIRANHA • 1972 • *Smith William* • MTV • USA • PIRANHA, PIRANHA
PIRANHA • 1978 • Dante Joe • USA
PIRANHA II: FLYING KILLERS • 1981 • Cameron James • NTH • PIRANHA PART TWO: THE SPAWNING (USA)
PIRANHA PART TWO: THE SPAWNING (USA) see **PIRANHA II: FLYING KILLERS** • 1981
PIRANHA, PIRANHA see **PIRANHA** • 1972
PIRANHA WOMEN • 1988 • Athens J. D. • USA • CANNIBAL WOMEN IN THE AVOCADO JUNGLE OF DEATH
PIRANHAS, THE (USA) see **PIRANAS, LAS** • 1967
PIRANHAS DO ASFALTO • 1970 • d'Almeida Neville • BRZ
PIRATA DE DOCE ANOS, UN • 1971 • *Avant* • MXC
PIRATA DEL DIAVOLO, IL • 1963 • Mauri Roberto • ITL, YGS • SARACENS, THE (USA)
PIRATA DELLO SPARVIERO NERO, IL • 1958 • Grieco Sergio • ITL, FRN • PIRATE DE L'EPERVIER NOIR, LE (FRN) ◦ PIRATE OF THE BLACK HAWK, THE (USA)
PIRATA NEGRA, EL • 1954 • Miner Allen H. • MXC, USA, SLV • BLACK PIRATE, THE (USA)
PIRATA SONO IOI, IL • 1940 • Mattoli Mario • ITL
PIRATE, LA • 1984 • Doillon Jacques • FRN
PIRATE, THE • 1948 • Minnelli Vincente • USA
PIRATE, THE • 1978 • Annakin Ken • TVM • USA • HAROLD ROBBIN'S THE PIRATE
PIRATE, THE see **SJOROVAREN** • 1909
PIRATE AND THE SLAVE GIRL, THE (USA) see **SCIMITARRA DEL SARACENO, LA** • 1959
PIRATE BOLD, A • 1916 • Myll Louis • SHT • USA
PIRATE BOLD, A • 1917 • Dillon Robert A. • SHT • USA
PIRATE CITY see **VILLE DES PIRATES, LA** • 1983
PIRATE DE L'EPERVIER NOIR, LE (FRN) see **PIRATA DELLO SPARVIERO NERO, IL** • 1958
PIRATE GOLD • 1913 • *Sweet Blanche* • USA
PIRATE GOLD • 1920 • Seitz George B. • SRL • USA
PIRATE HAUNTS • 1917 • *Grand Feature Film* • USA
PIRATE MOVIE, THE • 1982 • Annakin Ken • USA, ASL
PIRATE OF THE BLACK HAWK, THE (USA) see **PIRATA DELLO SPARVIERO NERO, IL** • 1958
PIRATE REVUE see **PIRATES** • 1930
PIRATE SHIP • 1933 • *Terry Paul/ Moser Frank (P)* • ANS • USA
PIRATE SHIP see **MUTINEERS, THE** • 1949
PIRATE SHIP, THE • 1906 • Fitzhamon Lewin • UKN
PIRATE SHIP, THE • 1908 • Aylott Dave • UKN
PIRATE TREASURE • 1934 • Taylor Ray • SRL • USA
PIRATE TREASURE, THE see **PIRACKI SKARB** • 1960
PIRATEN DER OSTSEEBADER, DIE • 1926 • Arnheim Valy • FRG
PIRATEN DER SCHONHEIT • 1921 • *Hollmann Grete* • FRG
PIRATENE • 1983 • Kolstad Morten • NRW • PIRATES, THE
PIRATES • 1930 • Brooks Marty • USA • PIRATE REVUE
PIRATES • 1985 • Polanski Roman • FRN, ISR
PIRATES see **KAIZUKOSEN** • 1951
PIRATES see **KAIZOKU BAHANSEN** • 1960
PIRATES see **PIRACI RZECZNI** • 1965
PIRATES see **PIRATI** • 1980
PIRATES, THE • 1904 • *Warwick Trading Co* • UKN • BUCCANEERS, THE
PIRATES, THE • 1913 • Baker George D. • USA
PIRATES, THE see **PIRATENE** • 1983
PIRATES BEWARE • 1928 • George Henry W. • USA
PIRATES BOLD • 1915 • Franklin Sidney A., Franklin Chester M. • USA
PIRATE'S DAUGHTER, THE • 1912 • Bosworth Hobart • USA
PIRATES DE LA COTE, LES (FRN) see **PIRATI DELLA COSTA, I** • 1960
PIRATE'S DOWER, THE • 1910 • *Yankee* • USA
PIRATES DU MISSISSIPPI, LES (FRN) see **FLUSSPIRATEN VOM MISSISSIPPI, DIE** • 1963
PIRATES DU RAIL, LES • 1937 • Christian-Jaque • FRN
PIRATES DU RHONE • 1933 • Aurenche Jean (c/d) • SHT • FRN
PIRATE'S FIANCEE see **FIANCEE DU PIRATE, LA** • 1969
PIRATE'S GOLD • 1957 • Donnelly Eddie • ANS • USA
PIRATE'S GOLD, THE • 1908 • Griffith D. W. • USA
PIRATE'S HEART, THE • 1987 • Brauer Jurgen • GDR
PIRATES OF 19.. ,THE see **PIRATES OF 1920, THE** • 1911
PIRATES OF 1920, THE • 1911 • Coleby A. E., Aylott Dave • UKN • PIRATES OF 19.. ,THE
PIRATES OF BLOOD ISLAND (UKN) see **CORSARI DELL'ISOLA DEGLI SQUALI, I** • 1972
PIRATES OF BLOOD RIVER, THE • 1962 • Gilling John • UKN
PIRATES OF CAPRI, THE (USA) see **PIRATI DI CAPRI, I** • 1949
PIRATES OF MONTEREY • 1947 • Werker Alfred L. • USA
PIRATES OF PEACOCK ALLEY, THE • 1914 • Eagle Oscar • USA
PIRATES OF PENZANCE, THE • 1983 • Leach Wilford • USA
PIRATES OF REGENTS CANAL, THE • 1906 • Aylott Dave • UKN
PIRATES OF SPRING COVE, THE see **TRUTH ABOUT SPRING, THE** • 1964
PIRATES OF THE AIR • 1916 • *Voss Fatty* • SHT • USA
PIRATES OF THE COAST (USA) see **PIRATI DELLA COSTA, I** • 1960
PIRATES OF THE HIGH SEAS • 1950 • Bennet Spencer Gordon, Carr Thomas • USA
PIRATES OF THE MISSISSIPPI, THE (USA) see **FLUSSPIRATEN VOM MISSISSIPPI, DIE** • 1963
PIRATES OF THE PLAINS, THE • 1914 • *West Josephine* • USA
PIRATES OF THE PRAIRIE • 1942 • Bretherton Howard • USA
PIRATES OF THE SEVEN SEAS see **QUEER CARGO** • 1938
PIRATES OF THE SKIES • 1939 • McDonough Joseph A. • USA
PIRATES OF THE SKY • 1916 • *Eagle Film* • USA
PIRATES OF THE SKY • 1927 • Andrews Charles • USA
PIRATES OF TORTUGA • 1961 • Webb Robert D. • USA
PIRATES OF TRIPOLI • 1955 • Feist Felix E. • USA
PIRATES ON HORSEBACK • 1941 • Selander Lesley • USA
PIRATES ON LAKE MALAR see **MALARPIRATER** • 1923
PIRATES ON LAKE MALAR see **MALARPIRATER** • 1959
PIRATE'S REVENGE see **VENDETTA DEL CORSARO, LA** • 1951
PIRATE'S TREASURE see **PIRACKI SKARB** • 1960
PIRATI • 1980 • Doubrava Jaroslav, Born Adolf, Macourek Milos • CZC • PIRATES
PIRATI • 1982 • Balik Jaroslav • CZC
PIRATI DEL GOLFO, I • 1940 • Marcellini Romolo • ITL
PIRATI DELLA COSTA, I • 1960 • Paolella Domenico • ITL, FRN • PIRATES DE LA COTE, LES (FRN) ◦ PIRATES OF THE COAST (USA)
PIRATI DELLA MALESIA, I • 1941 • Guazzoni Enrico • ITL
PIRATI DELLA MALESIA, I • 1964 • Lenzi Umberto • ITL
PIRATI DELL'ISOLA VERDE, I • 1970 • Baldi Ferdinando • ITL
PIRATI DI CAPRI, I • 1949 • Ulmer Edgar G., Scotese Giuseppe Maria • ITL • PIRATES OF CAPRI, THE (USA) ◦ MASKED PIRATE, THE (UKN) ◦ CAPTAIN SIROCCO
PIRAVI • 1988 • Shaji • IND
PIRE NURI • 1968 • Guney Yilmaz • TRK • NURI THE FLEA
PIRE O ANEMOS TA ONIRA MOU • 1968 • Kosteletos Odisseas • GRC • DREAMS GONE WITH THE WIND
PIREAS ORA 7.30 • 1967 • Avrameas Nikos • GRC • PIRAEUS 7.30 A.M.
PIRETOS STIN ASFALTO • 1967 • Dimopoulos Dinos • GRC • FEVER ON THE ROADS
PIRI KNOWS EVERYTHING see **PIRI MINDONT TUD** • 1932
PIRI MINDONT TUD • 1932 • Sekely Steve • HNG • PIRI KNOWS EVERYTHING
PIROGOV • 1947 • Kozintsev Grigori • USS
PIROGUES SUR L'OGOOUE • 1947 • Dupont Jacques • SHT • FRN
PIROPO, EL • 1979 • Bernaza Luis Felipe • CUB • FLIRT, THE
PIROS BUGYELLARIS • 1939 • Pasztor Bela • HNG • RED PURSE (USA)
PIROSBETOS HETKOZNAPOK • 1962 • Mariassy Felix • HNG • EVERYDAY -SUNDAY
PIROSKA ES A FARKAS 2000-BEN • 1987 • Meszaros Marta • HNG, CND • PETIT CHAPERON ROUGE: L'AN 2000 ◦ LITTLE RED RIDING HOOD IN 2000 ◦ LITTLE RED RIDING HOOD: YEAR 2000
PIROSKA ES A FARKAS (HNG) see **BYE BYE CHAPERON ROUGE** • 1988
PIROSMANI • 1960 • Shengelaya Georgi • SHT • USS
PIROSMANI • 1970 • Shengelaya Georgi • USS
PIRUETAS JUVENILES • 1943 • Cappelli Giancarlo, Valenti Salvio • ITL, SPN • ROMANZO A PASSO DI DANZA (ITL)

PIRVELI MERTSKHALI • 1976 • Mchedlidze Nana • USS • FIRST SWALLOW, THE ○ PYERVAYA LASTOCHKA ○ FIRST STEP, THE ○ PERVAYA LASTOCHKA
PIRX TEST-FLIGHT see **TEST PILOTA PIRXA** • 1978
PIRY VALTASARA ILI NOCH SO STALINIM • 1989 • Kara Yuri • USS • BALTHASSAR'S FEAST OR MY NIGHT WITH STALIN
PISA Y CRIANZA • 1975 • Ardavin Cesar • SHT • SPN
PISCATORIAL PLEASURES • 1931 • Austin Harold • USA
PISCES DYING • 1969 • Tammer Peter • DOC • ASL
PISCINA, LA • 1976 • Bozzetto Bruno • ANM • ITL
PISCINA, LA (ITL) see **PISCINE, LA** • 1969
PISCINE, LA • 1969 • Deray Jacques • FRN, ITL • PISCINA, LA (ITL) ○ SWIMMING POOL, THE (USA) ○ SINNERS, THE (UKN)
PISEN NEMILOVA-NEHO • 1982 • Weisz Claude • CZC, FRN • CHANSON DU MAL AIME, LA (FRN) ○ SONG OF THE UNLOVED, THE ○ UNLOVABLE ONE, THE
PISEN O HARMONICE • 1974 • Brdecka Jiri • CZC • ACCORDEON SONG
PISEN O SLETU • 1949 • Weiss Jiri • CZC • HIGH FLIES THE HAWK ○ SONG OF THE MEET
PISEN ZIVOTA • 1924 • Krnansky M. J. • CZC • SONG OF LIFE, THE
PISINGANA • 1985 • Pinzon German • CLM
PISITO, EL • 1957 • Ferreri Marco, Ferry Isidoro Martinez • SPN
PISITO DE SOLTERAS • 1972 • Merino Fernando • SPN
PISMA MYORTVOVO CHELOVYEKA • 1986 • Lopouchanski Constantin • USS • LETTERS FROM A DEAD MAN
PISMA S OSTROVA CHUDAKOV • 1967 • Muur Juri • USS • LETTERS FROM THE ISLE OF ECCENTRICS
PISMO-GLAVA • 1984 • Cengic Bato • YGS • HEADS OR TAILS
PISNICKAR • 1932 • Innemann Svatopluk • CZC • SONGSTER, THE
PISO DE SOLTERO • 1963 • Balcazar Alfonso • SPN
PISO PISELLO • 1981 • Del Monte Peter • ITL
PISSARRO • 1976 • Leenhardt Roger • DCS • FRN
PISSENLIT PAR LA RACINE, LE • 1982 • Bedel Jean-Pierre • MTV • CND
PISTE ARGENTEE, LA • 1911 • Roudes Gaston • FRN
PISTE DES GEANTS, LA • 1931 • Couderc Pierre, Walsh Raoul • FRN
PISTE DU NORD, LA • 1939 • Feyder Jacques • FRN • LOI DU NORD, LA
PISTE DU SUD, LA • 1938 • Billon Pierre • FRN
PISTOL, THE see **PISTOLEN** • 1974
PISTOL, THE (USA) see **PISTOLE, DIE** • 1963
PISTOL FOR A HUNDRED COFFINS, A see **PISTOLA PER CENTO BARE, UNA** • 1968
PISTOL FOR RINGO, A (USA) see **PISTOLA PER RINGO, UNA** • 1965
PISTOL HARVEST • 1951 • Selander Lesley • USA
PISTOL JENNY • 1969 • Weidenmann Alfred • FRG
PISTOL PACKIN' MAMA • 1943 • Woodruff Frank • USA
PISTOL PACKIN' NITWITS • 1945 • Edwards Harry J. • SHT • USA
PISTOL-PACKIN' WOODPECKER • 1960 • Smith Paul J. • ANS • USA
PISTOL POINT PROPOSAL, A • 1919 • Holt George • SHT • USA
PISTOL SHOT, A see **VYSTREL** • 1967
PISTOL SHOT, THE see **WYSTRZAL** • 1965
PISTOLA CHIAMATA JENNY, UNA • 1977 • Amendola Toni • ITL
PISTOLA PARA RINGO, UNA (SPN) see **PISTOLA PER RINGO, UNA** • 1965
PISTOLA PER CENTO BARE, UNA • 1968 • Lenzi Umberto • ITL, SPN • PISTOL FOR A HUNDRED COFFINS, A
PISTOLA PER CENTO CROCI, UNA • 1971 • Croccolo Carlo • ITL
PISTOLA PER RINGO, UNA • 1965 • Tessari Duccio • ITL, SPN • PISTOLA PARA RINGO, UNA (SPN) ○ PISTOL FOR RINGO, A (USA) ○ BALLAD OF DEATH VALLEY ○ THE ANGRY GUN
PISTOLAS DE ORO • 1957 • Delgado Miguel M. • MXC
PISTOLAS INVENCIBLES • 1959 • Alazraki Benito • MXC
PISTOLAS NO DISCUTEN, LAS see **PISTOLE NON DISCUTONO, LE** • 1964
PISTOLE, DIE • 1963 • Urchs Wolfgang • ANS • FRG • PISTOL, THE (USA)
PISTOLE NON DISCUTONO, LE • 1964 • Caiano Mario • ITL, SPN, FRG • PISTOLAS NO DISCUTEN, LAS
PISTOLEN • 1974 • Tirl Jiri • SWD • PISTOL, THE
PISTOLERE, LE (ITL) see **PETROLEUSES, LES** • 1971
PISTOLERO see **LAST CHALLENGE, THE** • 1967
PISTOLERO DELL'AVE MARIA, IL • 1969 • Baldi Ferdinando • ITL
PISTOLERO DESCONOCIDO, EL • 1966 • Delgado Miguel M. • MXC • COMANDANTE TIERINA, EL
PISTOLERO FANTASMA, EL • 1967 • *Donahue Troy* • USA • JINETE FANTASMA, EL ○ GHOST GUNMAN, THE ○ PHANTOM RIDER, THE
PISTOLERO OF RED RIVER see **LAST CHALLENGE, THE** • 1967
PISTOLERO SEGNATA DA DIO, IL • 1968 • Ferroni Giorgio • ITL
PISTOLEROS BAJO EL SOL • 1972 • *Filmadora Chapultepec* • MXC
PISTOLEROS DE ARIZONA • 1964 • Balcazar Alfonso • SPN
PISTOLEROS DE CASA GRANDE, LOS • 1964 • Rowland Roy • SPN, USA • GUNFIGHTERS OF CASA GRANDE (USA)
PISTOLEROS DE LA FRONTERA • 1964 • Mariscal Alberto • MXC
PISTOLEROS DEL OESTE • 1964 • Cardona Rene • MXC
PISTOLEROS EN GOLDEN HILL • 1966 • Iquino Ignacio F. • SPN
PISTOLEROS, LOS • 1961 • Alazraki Benito • MXC
PISTOLOCOS, LOS • 1958 • Delgado Miguel M. • MXC
PISTOLS FOR BREAKFAST • 1919 • Roach Hal • SHT • USA
PISTOLS FOR TWO • 1913 • Calvert Charles? • UKN
PISTONNE, LE • 1970 • Berri Claude • FRN • MAN WITH CONNECTIONS, THE (USA)
PIT, A see **ANA** • 1967
PIT, THE • 1915 • Tourneur Maurice • USA
PIT, THE • 1962 • Abrahams Edward • SHT • UKN
PIT, THE • 1981 • Lehman Lewis • TVM • CND • TEDDY
PIT, THE see **ANA** • 1957
PIT, THE see **MIND BENDERS, THE** • 1962
PIT, THE see **TE RUA** • 1990
PIT AND THE PENDULUM, THE • 1913 • Blache Alice • USA
PIT AND THE PENDULUM, THE • 1961 • Corman Roger • USA
PIT AND THE PENDULUM, THE • 1990 • Gordon Stuart • USA
PIT AND THE PENDULUM, THE see **PUITS ET LE PENDULE, LE** • 1912
PIT AND THE PENDULUM, THE see **SCHLANGENGRUBE UND DAS PENDEL, DIE** • 1967
PIT AND THE PENDULUM, THE see **KYVADLO, JAMA A MADEJE** • 1983
PIT AND THE PENDULUM, THE (USA) see **PUITS ET LE PENDULE, LE** • 1963
PIT-BOY'S ROMANCE, A • 1917 • Coleby A. E., Rooke Arthur • UKN
PIT L 23 see **SZYB L 23** • 1932
PIT OF DARKNESS • 1961 • Comfort Lance • UKN
PIT OF DEATH, THE see **KAIDAN OTOSHIANA** • 1968
PIT OF LONELINESS (USA) see **OLIVIA** • 1950
PIT STOP • 1969 • Hill Jack • USA
PIT, THE PENDULUM AND HOPE, THE see **KYVADLO, JAMA A MADEJE** • 1983
PITCAIRN PEOPLE, THE • 1962 • Newington Peter • UKN
PITCH O'CHANCE, THE • 1915 • Borzage Frank • USA
PITCH THAT DEFILES, THE • 1913 • *Majestic* • USA
PITCHING WOO AT THE ZOO • 1944 • Sparber I. • ANS • USA
PITCHMEN • 1985 • Greenwald Barry • CND
PITFALL, THE • 1911 • *Reliance* • USA
PITFALL, THE • 1913 • Giblyn Charles • USA
PITFALL, THE • 1915 • Horne James W. • USA
PITFALL, THE • 1948 • De Toth Andre • USA
PITFALL, THE see **VARIKKUZHI** • 1983
PITFALL, THE see **FALLGROPEN** • 1989
PITFALL, THE (USA) see **KASHI TO KODOMO** • 1962
PITFALL OF THE INSTALLMENT PLAN, THE • 1913 • *Kerrigan J. Warren* • USA
PITFALLS • 1914 • August Edwin • USA
PITFALLS OF A BIG CITY • 1919 • Lloyd Frank • USA
PITFALLS OF A BIG CITY • 1923 • *Sennett Mack (P)* • SHT • USA
PITFALLS OF BUNNY, THE • Davian Joe • USA
PITFALLS OF PASSION • 1927 • Livingstone Leonard • USA
PITHACHE PUNJE • 1913 • Phalke Dada • IND
PITICUL DIN GRADINA DE VARA • 1971 • Bokor Pierre • MTV • RMN
PITIE POUR LE PROF! see **WHY SHOOT THE TEACHER?** • 1976
PITIE POUR LES VAMPS • 1956 • Josipovici Jean • FRN
PITIE POUR MES LARMES see **IRHAM DUMU'I** • 1954
PITIE POUR MON AMOUR see **IRHAM H'UBB** • 1958
PITO PEREZ SE VA DE BRACERO • 1947 • Patino Gomez Alfonso • MXC
PITONG KRUS NG ISANG INA • 1968 • Torres Mar S. • PHL • SEVEN HEADACHES OF A MOTHER
PITONG PASIKLAB SA BAHAY NA TISA • 1963 • San Juan Luis • PHL
PITONG ZAPATA • 1967 • San Juan Luis • PHL • SEVEN ZAPATA
PITOU BOUDREAULT, VIOLONEUX • 1976-77 • Brault Michel, Gladu Andre • DCS • CND
PITOUNE, LA • 1958-60 • Bonniere Rene • DCS • CND
PITS see **UKHABY ZHIZNI** • 1928
PITT: THE YOUNGER GIRL SCANDAL see **SECRET LIVES OF THE BRITISH PRIME MINISTERS: PITT, THE** • 1983
PITTER PATTERNS • 1966 • Goldscholl Morton, Goldscholl Mildred • ANS • USA
PITTORI IN CITTA • 1955-59 • Taviani Paolo, Taviani Vittorio • DCS • ITL
PITTSBURGH • 1942 • Seiler Lewis • USA
PITTSBURGH DOCUMENTS, THE • 1971 • Brakhage Stan • USA
PITTSBURGH KID, THE • 1942 • Townley Jack • USA
PITTSBURGH MILLIONAIRE, A • 1911 • *American* • USA
PITY see **MERHAMET** • 1967
PITY OF IT, THE • 1912 • Campbell Colin • USA
PITY THE CHORUS GIRL see **TROUPING WITH ELLEN** • 1924
PITY THE POOR • 1920 • Physioc Wray • SHT • USA
PITY THE POOR BLIND • 1907 • Martin J. H.? • UKN
PITY THE POOR PIPER • 1974 • King Allan • CND
PITY THE POOR RICH • 1935 • Walker Ian • SHT • UKN • NAT GONELLA AND HIS GEORGIANS
PIU BELLA COPPIA DEL MONDO, LA • 1968 • Mastrocinque Camillo • ITL • MOST BEAUTIFUL COUPLE IN THE WORLD, THE
PIU BELLA DEL REAME, LA • 1990 • Ferrario Cesare • ITL • MOST BEAUTIFUL GIRL IN THE KINGDOM, THE
PIU BELLA SERATA DELLA MIA VITA, LA • 1972 • Scola Ettore • ITL, FRN • PLUS BELLE SOIREE DE MA VIE, LA (FRN)
PIU BELLE NOVELLE DEL BOCCACCIO, LE see **DECAMERON N.4** • 1972
PIU BELLE TRUFFE DEL MONDO, LE see **PLUS BELLES ESCROQUERIES DU MONDE, LES** • 1963
PIU BELLO DI COSI SI MUORE • 1982 • Festa Campanile Pasquale • ITL • YOU CAN'T GET MORE BEAUTIFUL
PIU COMICO SPETTACOLO DEL MONDO, IL • 1953 • Mattoli Mario • ITL
PIU FORTE, LA • 1914 • Falena Ugo • ITL
PIU FORTE.. RAGAZZI! • 1972 • Colizzi Giuseppe • ITL • ALL THE WAY BOYS
PIU GRANDE AMORE, IL see **FOCOLARE SPENTO, IL** • 1925
PIU GRANDE AMORE, IL see **SUOR LETIZIA** • 1956
PIU GRANDE COLPO DEL SECOLO, IL (ITL) see **SOLEIL DES VOYOUS, LE** • 1967
PIU GRANDE COLPO DELLA MALAVITA AMERICANA, IL • 1968 • Reinl Harald • ITL
PIU GRANDE MISTERO D'AMORE, IL • 1956 • Franci Pier Giuseppe • ITL
PIU GRANDE RAPINA DEL WEST, LA • 1967 • Lucidi Maurizio • ITL • GREATEST KIDNAPPING IN THE WEST, THE
PIU TARDI CLAIRE, PIU TARDI.. • 1968 • Rondi Brunello • ITL
PIUME AL VENTO • 1951 • Amadoro Ugo • ITL
PIWO • 1965 • Rozewicz Stanislaw • MTV • PLN • BEER
PIXIE AT THE WHEEL • 1924 • Morrison Lee • SER • UKN
PIXIE LAND • 1938 • Perkins Elmer • ANS • USA
PIXIE PICNIC • 1948 • Lundy Dick • ANS • USA
PIXILLATIONS • 1971 • Schwartz Lillian, Knowlton Kenneth • ANS • USA
PIXOTE see **PIXOTE, A LEI DO MAIS FRACO** • 1981
PIXOTE, A LEI DO MAIS FRACO • 1981 • Babenco Hector • BRZ • PIXOTE: LA LEY DEL MAS DEBIL (UKN) ○ PIXOTE, THE LAW OF THE WEAKER ○ PIXOTE
PIXOTE: LA LEY DEL MAS DEBIL (UKN) see **PIXOTE, A LEI DO MAIS FRACO** • 1981
PIXOTE, THE LAW OF THE WEAKER see **PIXOTE, A LEI DO MAIS FRACO** • 1981
PIYADE OSMAN • 1970 • Goren Serif, Guney Yilmaz • TRK • OSMAN THE WANDERER
PIYAYO, EL • 1955 • Lucia Luis • SPN
PIZEN PETE • 1913 • *Lubin* • USA
PIZHON • 1929 • Donskoi Mark • USS • PIGEON, THE ○ FOP, THE
PIZZA CONNECTION see **ATTACO ALLA PIOURA** • 1985
PIZZA TRIANGLE, THE (UKN) see **DRAMMA DELLA GELOSIA - TUTTI I PARTICOLARI IN CRONACA** • 1970
PIZZA TWEETY PIE, A • 1958 • Freleng Friz • ANS • USA
PIZZICATO PUSSYCAT • 1954 • Freleng Friz • ANS • USA
PJERROT • 1916 • Davidsen Hjalmar • DNM
PJESAK • 1969 • Vunak Dragutin • ANM • YGS • PEDESTRIAN
PJESCANI ZAMAK • 1963 • YGS • SABLE CHATEAU
PLAC A SMICH • 1898 • Krizenecky Jan • CZC • LAUGHING AND CRYING ○ TEARS AND LAUGHTER
PLACA DEL DIAMANT, LA • 1982 • Betriu Francisco • SPN • DIAMOND SQUARE
PLACARD INFERNAL, LE • 1907 • Melies Georges • FRN • BEWILDERING CABINET, THE (USA)
PLACE, THE • 1966 • Sturlis Edward • ANM • PLN
PLACE A OLIVIER GUIMOND • 1966 • Carle Gilles • DOC • CND
PLACE AT THE COAST, THE • 1987 • Ogilvie George • ASL
PLACE ATABA AL-KADRA, LA • 1958 • Wahab Fatin Abdel • EGY
PLACE BEYOND THE WINDS, THE • 1916 • De Grasse Joseph • USA
PLACE CALLED ARDOYNE, A • 1973 • Thompson Philip • DOC • UKN
PLACE CALLED GLORY, A (USA) see **HOLLE VON MANITOBA, DIE** • 1965
PLACE CALLED TODAY, A • 1972 • Schain Don • USA • CITY IN FEAR
PLACE DE LA BASTILLE • 1896 • Melies Georges • FRN
PLACE DE LA CONCORDE • 1896 • Melies Georges • FRN
PLACE DE LA CONCORDE • 1938 • Lamac Carl • FRN
PLACE DE LA REPUBLIQUE • 1973 • Malle Louis, Mozskowicz Fernand • DOC • FRN
PLACE DE L'EQUATION • 1973 • Groulx Gilles • DCS • CND
PLACE DE L'OPERA 1er ASPECT • 1896 • Melies Georges • FRN • PLACE DE L'OPERA 1ST VIEW
PLACE DE L'OPERA 1ST VIEW see **PLACE DE L'OPERA 1er ASPECT** • 1896
PLACE DE L'OPERA 2e ASPECT • 1896 • Melies Georges • FRN • PLACE DE L'OPERA 2ND VIEW
PLACE DE L'OPERA 2ND VIEW see **PLACE DE L'OPERA 2e ASPECT** • 1896
PLACE DE L'OPERA 3RD VIEW see **CARREFOUR DE L'OPERA** • 1898
PLACE DES OUVRIERS DANS L'USINE • 1968 • Dansereau Fernand • DCS • CND
PLACE DU THEATRE-FRANCAIS • 1896 • Melies Georges • FRN
PLACE FOR GOLD, A • 1960 • Wright Basil • DOC • UKN
PLACE FOR LOVERS, A (USA) see **AMANTI** • 1968
PLACE FOR THE SCHOOL, A • 1963 • Jaworski Tadeusz • DOC • PLN
PLACE IN HELL, A see **POSTO ALL'INFERNO, UN** • 1969
PLACE IN THE CROWD, A see **MISTO V HOUFU** • 1964
PLACE IN THE SUN • 1919 • *Blache Margaret* • USA
PLACE IN THE SUN, A • 1914 • Batley Ethyle? • UKN
PLACE IN THE SUN, A • 1916 • Trimble Larry • UKN
PLACE IN THE SUN, A • 1917 • Windom Lawrence C. • SHT • USA
PLACE IN THE SUN, A • 1951 • Stevens George • USA
PLACE IN THE SUN, A see **O MISTO NA SLUNCI** • 1960
PLACE IN THE SUN, A see **LUGAR EN EL SOL, UN** • 1990
PLACE IN THE WORLD, A see **MIEJSCE NA ZIEMI** • 1960
PLACE IN THIS COUNTRY, A • 1972 • Gormley Charles • DCS • UKN
PLACE OF A SKULL, A see **TOPOS KRANIOU** • 1972
PLACE OF HONEYMOONS, THE • 1920 • Buel Kenean • USA
PLACE OF HONOUR, THE • 1921 • Hill Sinclair • UKN
PLACE OF ONE'S OWN, A • 1945 • Knowles Bernard • UKN
PLACE OF REST see **YI-YUAN P'IAO-HSIANG** • 1983
PLACE OF WEEPING, A • 1986 • Roodt Darrell • SAF
PLACE OF WORK WITH TAILPIECE • 1976 • Tait Margaret • UKN
PLACE ON EARTH, A see **MIEJSCE NA ZIEMI** • 1960
PLACE ROYALE -PREMIERE ETAPE • 1971 • Lavoie Richard • DCS • CND
PLACE ST.-AUGUSTIN • 1896 • Melies Georges • FRN
PLACE, THE TIME AND THE MAN, THE • 1914 • *Travers Richard C.* • USA
PLACE TO CALL HOME, A • 1987 • Mayberry Russ • TVM • USA
PLACE TO DIE, A • 1973 • Jefferies Peter • TVM • UKN
PLACE TO GO, A • 1963 • Dearden Basil • UKN
PLACE TO LIVE, A • 1941 • Lerner Irving • USA
PLACE TO STAND, A • 1967 • Chapman Christopher • DOC • CND
PLACE WHERE BOOKS ARE KEPT, A • 1974 • Noonan Chris • DSS • ASL

PLACE WITHOUT LIMITS, THE see **LUGAR SIN LIMITES, EL** • 1976

PLACER DE LA VENGANZA, EL • 1987 • Name Hernando • MXC • SWEETNESS OF REVENGE, THE

PLACER DE MATAR, EL • 1988 • Rotaeta Felix • SPN • PLEASURE OF KILLING, THE

PLACER SANGRIENTO • 1967 • Vieyra Emilio • ARG • DEADLY ORGAN, THE (USA) ○ BLOODY PLEASURE ○ FEAST OF FLESH

PLACERES OCULTOS, LOS • 1977 • de la Iglesia Eloy • SPN • SECRET PLEASURES, THE ○ HIDDEN PLEASURES

PLACES FOR PEOPLE • 1977 • Corcoran Vincent • SHT • IRL

PLACES IN THE HEART • 1984 • Benton Robert • USA • TEXAS PROJECT, THE ○ WAITING FOR MORNING

PLACES.. OR PEOPLE • 1975 • Gormley Charles • DCS • UKN

PLACHE PRIBEHY • 1982 • Flidr Zdenek, Tintera Tomas, Zbornik Dobroslav • CZC • SHY TALES

PLACIDO • 1961 • Berlanga Luis Garcia • SPN

PLACIER EST TENACE, LE see **PLACIERE TENACE, LA** • 1910

PLACIERE TENACE, LA • 1910 • Cohl Emile • ANS • FRN • PLACIER EST TENACE, LE

PLAE GAEW • 1979 • Songsri Cherd • THL • SCAR, THE

PLAFF -DEMASIADO MIEDO A LA VIDA • 1988 • Tabio Juan Carlos • CUB • PLAFF TOO AFRAID OF LIFE (UKN)

PLAFF TOO AFRAID OF LIFE (UKN) see **PLAFF -DEMASIADO MIEDO A LA VIDA** • 1988

PLAGE, LA • 1978 • Gervais Suzanne • ANS • CND

PLAGE DE VILLIERS PAR GROS TEMPS, LA • 1896 • Melies Georges • FRN • BEACH AT VILLIERS IN A GALE, THE

PLAGE DU DESIR, LA see **CAFAJESTES, OS** • 1962

PLAGE PRIVEE • 1971 • Laguionie Jean-Francois • ANS • FRN

PLAGES SANS SUITE • 1980 • Turine Jean-Marc • BLG

PLAGIARIO, EL • 1953 • Gomez Urquiza Zacarias • MXC

PLAGIARISM see **PLAGIO** • 1968

PLAGIO • 1968 • Capogna Sergio • ITL • PLAGIARISM

PLAGUE • 1978 • Hunt Ed • CND • M3: THE GEMINI STRAIN ○ PLAGUE M3: THE GEMINI STRAIN ○ INDUCED SYNDROME ○ MUTATION

PLAGUE • 1985 • Takaishvili Data • ANS • USS

PLAGUE DOGS, THE • 1984 • Rosen Martin • ANM • UKN

PLAGUE IN FLORENCE, THE see **PEST IN FLORENZ, DIE** • 1919

PLAGUE M3: THE GEMINI STRAIN see **PLAGUE** • 1978

PLAGUE OF THE ZOMBIES, THE • 1965 • Gilling John • UKN • ZOMBIES, THE ○ ZOMBIE, THE

PLAGUE ON YOUR CHILDREN, A • 1968 • *Malone Arthur (P)* • UKN

PLAGUE SPOT, THE • 1915 • Marston Theodore • USA

PLAGUE SUMMER • 1951 • Kessler Chester • SHT • USA

PLAGUES AND PUPPY LOVE • 1917 • Semon Larry • SHT • USA

PLAID COAT, THE • 1915 • *Banner* • USA

PLAIN AND FANCY GIRLS • 1925 • McCarey Leo • SHT • USA

PLAIN CLOTHES • 1925 • Edwards Harry J. • SHT • USA

PLAIN CLOTHES • 1988 • Coolidge Martha • USA • GLORY DAYS

PLAIN GIRL'S LOVE, A • 1913 • *Eyton Bessie* • USA

PLAIN JANE • 1913 • *Gail Jane* • USA

PLAIN JANE • 1916 • Miller Charles • USA

PLAIN MAME OR ALL THAT GLITTERS IS NOT GOLD • 1909 • Baker George D. • USA

PLAIN MAN'S GUIDE TO ADVERTISING, THE • 1962 • Godfrey Bob • SHT • UKN

PLAIN MARY • 1914 • *Weber Lois* • USA

PLAIN OLD MAID, THE see **OSKLIVA SLECNA** • 1959

PLAIN PEOPLE see **PROSTYE LYUDI** • 1945

PLAIN SONG, A • 1910 • Griffith D. W. • USA

PLAIN TALE, A • 1911 • *Reliance* • USA

PLAIN WOMAN, A see **OKAME** • 1927

PLAINE, LA • 1970 • Paureilhe Christian • FRN

PLAINLANDS see **POHJANMAA** • 1988

PLAINS ACROSS, THE • 1911 • *Nestor* • USA

PLAINS, MY PLAINS see **SWEEPING FIELDS** • 1957

PLAINS OF BATTLE • 1970 • *Medor W.* • ITL

PLAINS OF HEAVEN, THE • 1983 • Pringle Ian • ASL

PLAINSMAN, THE • 1936 • De Mille Cecil B. • USA

PLAINSMAN, THE • 1966 • Rich David Lowell • USA

PLAINSMAN, THE see **RAIDERS, THE** • 1963

PLAINSMAN AND THE LADY, THE • 1946 • Kane Joseph • USA

PLAINSONG • 1982 • Stabile Ed • USA

PLAISIR, LE • 1951 • Ophuls Max • FRN • HOUSE OF PLEASURE (USA)

PLAISIR A TROIS • 1973 • Franco Jesus • FRN

PLAISIR D'AMOUR • 1968 • Reichenbach Francois • FRN

PLAISIR DE PLAIRE • 1960 • Lecomte Daniel • SHT • FRN

PLAISIR EN FORET • 1960 • Rivard Fernand • DCS • CND

PLAISIRS DE L'INFIDELE, LES • Byron Philippe • FRN

PLAISIRS DE MADAME, LES • Geral Hubert • FRN

PLAISIRS DE PARIS • 1932 • Greville Edmond T. (U/c) • FRN, FRG • VERJUNGTER ADHEMAR (FRG) ○ OH, MA MITRAILLEUSE A MUSIQUE

PLAISIRS DE PARIS • 1952 • Baum Ralph • FRN

PLAISIRS DEFENDUS • 1933 • Cavalcanti Alberto • FRN

PLAISIRS DU TROTTOIR, LES • Byron Philippe • FRN

PLAISIRS FOUS, LES • 1978 • Desvilles Jean • FRN

PLAISIRS PERVERS • 1968 • Benazeraf Jose • FRN

PLAISIRS SOLITAIRES, LES • 1976 • Leroi Francis • FRN • EROTIC PLEASURES: THE BODIES DESIRE ○ EROTIC PLEASURES ○ LONELY PLEASURES

PLAMEN NAD JADRANOM (YGS) see **FLAMMES SUR L'ADRIATIQUE** • 1968

PLAMENY ZIVOTA • 1920 • Binovec Vaclav • CZC • FLAMES OF LIFE, THE

PLAMUZ • 1973 • Rybczynski Zbigniew • PLN

PLAN 9 FROM OUTER SPACE • 1956 • Wood Edward D. Jr. • USA • GRAVE ROBBERS FROM OUTER SPACE

PLAN, THE • 1965-66 • Garceau Raymond • DCS • CND

PLAN DER DREI, DER • 1920 • Neff Wolfgang • FRG

PLAN FOR DESTRUCTION • 1943 • Cahn Edward L. • USA

PLAN FOR LIVING, A • 1975 • Alexander Mike • DOC • UKN

PLAN JAC CERO TRES • 1968 • Bartolome Cecilia • SHT • SPN

PLAN OF BRUSSELS • 1968 • Beavers Robert • USA

PLAN OF GREAT WORKS see **PLAN VELIKH RABOT** • 1930

PLAN SENTIMENTAL, LE • 1978 • Leduc Jacques • DCS • CND

PLAN THAT FAILED, THE • 1911 • *Nestor* • USA

PLAN THAT FAILED, THE • 1912 • *Powers* • USA

PLAN VELIKH RABOT • 1930 • Room Abram • USS • PLAN OF GREAT WORKS ○ FIVE YEAR PLAN, THE

PLANAS, TESTIMONIO DE UN GENOCIDIO • 1971 • Rodriguez Martha, Silva Jorge • CLM

PLANCHE DU DIABLE, LA • 1904 • Melies Georges • FRN • DEVILISH PLANK, THE (USA)

PLANCHER DES VACHES, LE see **SUR LE PLANCHER DES VACHES** • 1939

PLANE CRAZY • 1928 • Disney Walt, Iwerks Ub • ANS • USA

PLANE CRAZY • 1930 • Van Ronkel Jo • SHT • USA

PLANE DAFFY • 1944 • Tashlin Frank • ANS • USA

PLANE DER KALIFORNISCHEN GOLDMINEN ODER DAS ZEICHEN DER DREI KREUZE, DIE see **ZEICHEN DER DREI, DAS** • 1919

PLANE DIPPY • 1936 • Avery Tex • ANS • USA

PLANE DUMB • 1932 • Foster John, Rufle George • ANS • USA

PLANE GOOFY • 1940 • Donnelly Eddie • ANS • USA

PLANE MATES • 1969 • Crombie Donald • SHT • ASL

PLANE NUMBER FOUR see **ONLY ANGELS HAVE WINGS** • 1939

PLANE SAILING • 1937 • Wills Philip, Goldman Bosworth • UKN

PLANE STORY, A • 1916 • Miller Rube • USA

PLANE TALE, A • 1918 • Dyer Anson • ANM • UKN

PLANE TREE ON A ROCK see **CHINARA NA SKALYE** • 1967

PLANES, TRAINS AND AUTOMOBILES • 1987 • Hughes John • USA

PLANET AUSSER KURS • Braun Michael • FRG • PLANET OFF COURSE

PLANET DES TODES, DER see **SCHWEIGENDE STERN, DER** • 1960

PLANET EARTH • 1974 • Daniels Marc • TVM • USA

PLANET MEN see **LOST PLANET, THE** • 1953

PLANET MOUSEOLA • 1960 • Kneitel Seymour • ANS • USA

PLANET OF BLOOD • 1966 • Harrington Curtis • USA • QUEEN OF BLOOD

PLANET OF BLOOD see **TERRORE NELLO SPAZIO** • 1965

PLANET OF DINOSAURS • 1978 • Shea James K. • USA • PLANET OF THE DINOSAURS

PLANET OF HORRORS see **GALAXY OF TERROR** • 1981

PLANET OF OUTLAWS • 1939 • Beebe Ford, Goodkind Saul • USA

PLANET OF STORMS (USA) see **PLANETA BURG** • 1962

PLANET OF TEMPESTS see **PLANETA BURG** • 1962

PLANET OF TERROR see **TERRORE NELLO SPAZIO** • 1965

PLANET OF THE APES • 1968 • Schaffner Franklin J. • USA

PLANET OF THE APES REVISITED see **BENEATH THE PLANET OF THE APES** • 1970

PLANET OF THE DINOSAURS see **PLANET OF DINOSAURS** • 1978

PLANET OF THE LIFELESS MEN see **PIANETA DEGLI UOMINI SPENTI, IL** • 1961

PLANET OF THE MEN see **BENEATH THE PLANET OF THE APES** • 1970

PLANET OF THE VAMPIRES (USA) see **TERRORE NELLO SPAZIO** • 1965

PLANET OF THE WOMEN INVADERS, THE see **PLANETA DE LAS MUJERES INVASORAS, EL** • 1965

PLANET OFF COURSE see **PLANET AUSSER KURS**

PLANET ON THE PROWL see **MISSIONE PIANETA ERRANTE** • 1965

PLANET PEOPLE see **POPLETENA PLANETA** • 1962

PLANET VENUS, THE see **PIANETA VENERE** • 1972

PLANETA ACERO • 1972 • Cosmi Carlo • DOC • VNZ • STEEL PLANET

PLANETA BURG • 1962 • Klushantsev Pavel • USS • PLANET OF STORMS (USA) ○ COSMONAUTS ON VENUS ○ STORM PLANET ○ STORM ON THE PLANET ○ PLANET OF TEMPESTS ○ STORM CLOUDS OF VENUS

PLANETA CIEGO, EL • 1975 • Klimovsky Leon • SPN • BLIND PLANET, THE

PLANETA DE LAS MUJERES INVASORAS, EL • 1965 • Crevenna Alfredo B. • MXC • PLANET OF THE WOMEN INVADERS, THE

PLANETA DEL TERROR, EL • 1972 • Delgado Cruz • SHT • SPN

PLANETARY GIANTS see **GIGANTES PLANETARIOS** • 1965

PLANETE DES FEMMES, LA • 1984 • Deffarge Claude, Troeller Gordian • DOC • FRN

PLANETE FAUVE, LA • 1959 • Delvaux Andre, Brismee Jean, Bettendorf Andre • BLG

PLANETE SAUVAGE, LA • 1973 • Laloux Rene • ANM • FRN, CZC • FANTASTIC PLANET (USA) ○ SAVAGE PLANET, THE

PLANETE VERTE, LA • 1965 • Kamler Piotr • ANS • FRN • GREEN PLANET, THE

PLANETS AGAINST US (USA) see **PIANETI CONTRO DI NOI, I** • 1961

PLANETS AROUND US see **PIANETI CONTRO DI NOI, I** • 1961

PLANETSSCHIEBER • 1920 • Bruck Reinhard • FRG

PLANICIE HEROICA • 1953 • Queiroga Perdigao • PRT

PLANINA NA GNEVOT • 1968 • Georgievski Ljubisa • YGS • MOUNTAIN OF WRATH, THE

PLANK, THE • 1967 • Sykes Eric • UKN

PLANNED CROPS • 1943 • Lye Len • SHT • UKN

PLANNED ELECTRIFICATION • 1940 • Cooper Marcus • DOC • UKN

PLANNED TOWN • Graham Sean • DOC • UKN

PLANO DE EDUCACAO POPULAR • 1953 • Vitorino Orlando • SHT • PRT

PLANQUE, LA • 1961 • Andre Raoul • FRN • WALLS OF FEAR (USA) ○ HIDEOUT, THE ○ BURIED ALIVE

PLANQUE, LA • 1976 • Benazeraf Jose • FRN

PLANQUE TON FRIC, J'ME POINTE! • Pierson Claude • FRN

PLANQUES DU REGIMENT, LES • 1983 • Caputo Michel • FRN

PLANQUEZ-VOUS, LES LACASSES ARRIVENT.. • 1979 • Melancon Andre • CND

PLANS AND PAJAMAS • 1917 • Semon Larry • SHT • USA

PLANS MYSTERIEUX, LES • 1965 • Laliberte Roger • CND • TI-KEN A MOSOU

PLANS OF THE FORTRESS, THE • 1910 • Bouwmeester Theo? • UKN

PLANS OF THE HOUSE, THE • 1913 • *Solax* • USA

PLANT, THE • 1969 • Fisher Albert • SHT • USA

PLANT PESTS AND DISEASES -BROWN ROT see **BROWN ROT** • 1950

PLANTAGE TAMARINE • 1965 • Forlong Michael • NTH

PLANTE, LA • 1983 • Borenstein Joyce, Vamos Thomas • CND

PLANTER, THE • 1917 • Heffron Thomas N. • USA

PLANTER'S DAUGHTER, THE • 1913 • Raymond Charles • UKN

PLANTER'S WIFE, THE • 1908 • Griffith D. W. • USA

PLANTER'S WIFE, THE • 1952 • Annakin Ken • UKN • OUTPOST IN MALAYA (USA)

PLANTEURS DU MUNGO, LES • 1956 • Vilardebo Carlos • SHT • FRN

PLANTING • 1981 • Dalen Zale R. • CND

PLANTING THE SPRING GARDEN • 1912 • Humphrey William • USA

PLANTING TIME • 1912 • *Solax* • USA

PLANTON DU COLONEL, LE • 1897 • Blache Alice • FRN

PLANTS ARE WATCHING, THE see **KIRLIAN WITNESS, THE** • 1981

PLANTS FROM THE DUNES • 1966 • *Nakaya Noboru* • JPN

PLANTS OF THE PANTRY, THE • 1928 • Smith Percy • UKN

PLANUBUNG • 1977 • Petersen Wolfgang • FRG

PLASTER FEUD, A • 1917 • Miller Rube • SHT • USA

PLASTERED IN PARIS • 1928 • Stoloff Ben • USA

PLASTIC AGE, THE • 1925 • Ruggles Wesley • USA

PLASTIC AGE, THE see **RED LIPS** • 1928

PLASTIC BODY SURGERY see **IJO TAIKEN HAKUSHO: JOTAI SEIKEI** • 1967

PLASTIC DOME OF NORMA JEAN, THE • 1970 • Compton Juleen • USA

PLASTIC HAIRCUT • 1963 • Nelson Robert • SHT • USA

PLASTIC IN THE PARK • 1964 • Georgi Katja • ANM • GDR

PLASTIC INEVITABLES (VELVET UNDERGROUND) see **VELVET UNDERGROUND AND NICO, THE** • 1966

PLASTIC JESUS see **PLASTICNI ISUS** • 1972

PLASTIC MILE, THE • 1969 • Ruvinsky Morrie • CND

PLASTIC MOBILES • 1948 • Davis James* • USA

PLASTIC NIGHTMARE, THE • 1988 • Petersen Wolfgang • USA

PLASTIC SHAMROCK • Wilson Mike Raeburn • UKN

PLASTIC SURGERY IN WARTIME • 1941 • Sainsbury Frank • DCS • UKN

PLASTICNI ISUS • 1972 • Stojanovic Lasar • YGS • PLASTIC JESUS

PLASTICS INVENTOR, THE • 1944 • King Jack • ANS • USA

PLASTIKKPOSEN • 1985 • Nicolayssen Hans Otto • NRW • MAGIC BAG, THE

PLASTIQUES • 1963 • Storck Henri • DOC • BLG

PLASTPOSEN • 1987 • Nicolayssen Hans Otto • NRW • ANDERSEN'S RUN

PLATA DULCE • 1982 • Ayala Fernando • ARG • EASY MONEY ○ SWEET CASH

PLATEAU, LE • 1905 • Blache Alice • FRN

PLATERO Y YO • 1968 • Castellon Alfredo • SPN • SILVERSMITH AND I, THE

PLATFORM • 1979 • Sherwin Guy • UKN

PLATILLOS VOLADORES, LOS • 1955 • Soler Julian • MXC • PLATOS VOLADORES, LOS ○ FLYING SAUCERS, THE

PLATINUM • 1988 • Evanchuk Peter • CND

PLATINUM BLONDE • 1931 • Capra Frank • USA

PLATINUM HIGH SCHOOL • 1960 • Haas Charles • USA • RICH, YOUNG AND DEADLY (UKN) ○ TROUBLE AT 16

PLATONISCHE EHE, DIE • 1918 • Leni Paul • FRG

PLATOON • 1987 • Stone Oliver • USA

PLATOON 317 see **317eme SECTION, LA** • 1965

PLATOON LEADER • 1988 • Norris Aaron • USA

PLATOON THE WARRIORS see **PLATOON WARRIORS** • 1987

PLATOON WARRIORS • 1987 • Ko Philip • USA • PLATOON THE WARRIORS

PLATO'S CAVE INN • 1980 • Vanderbeek Stan • USA

PLATO'S: THE MOVIE • 1980 • Sherman Joe • USA

PLATOS VOLADORES, LOS see **PLATILLOS VOLADORES, LOS** • 1955

PLATYPUS COVE • 1983 • Maxwell Peter • ASL

PLAVI 9 • 1950 • Golik Kreso • YGS • BLUE 9, THE

PLAVI SVIJET • 1969 • Kurelec Tomislav • SHT • YGS

PLAY • SHT • FRN

PLAY see **ZABAWA** • 1961

PLAY see **IGRA** • 1962

PLAY see **GRA** • 1968

PLAY 54321 • 1967 • Jurga Andrzej • PLN

PLAY AND LIFE see **JUEGO Y LA VIDA, EL** • 1977

PLAY AND THRILL, WE WILL KILL see **JUGAR, JUGAR VAMOS A MATAR** • 1979

PLAY AND WORK • 1931 • Ptushko Alexander • ANM • USS

PLAY BALL • 1917 • *Pokes & Jabbs* • USA

PLAY BALL • 1925 • Bennet Spencer Gordon • SRL • USA • PLAYING THE GAME

PLAY BALL • 1931 • Foster John, Davis Mannie • ANS • USA

PLAY BALL • 1932 • *Terry Paul/ Moser Frank (P)* • ANS • USA

PLAY BALL • 1933 • *Iwerk Ub (P)* • ANS • USA

PLAY BALL • 1937 • Davis Mannie • ANS • USA

PLAY BOY • 1967 • Battaglia Enzo • ITL

PLAY-BOYS, LES see **HOLD-UP A SAINT-TROP'** • 1960

PLAY DEAD • 1985 • Wittman Peter • USA • SATAN'S DOG

PLAY DIRTY • 1968 • De Toth Andre • UKN • WRITTEN ON THE SAND

PLAY GIRL • 1932 • Enright Ray • USA

PLAY GIRL • 1940 • Woodruff Frank • USA

PLAY GIRL, THE • 1928 • Rosson Arthur • USA

PLAY HOOKEY • 1920 • *Franey William* • SHT • USA

PLAY IN COLORS, A see **FARBENSPIEL** • 1934

PLAY IN THE SUMMER BREEZES (USA) see **SPIEL IM SOMMERWIND** • 1938

PLAY IT AGAIN, SAM • 1972 • Ross Herbert • USA

PLAY IT AS IT LAYS • 1972 • Perry Frank • USA

PLAY IT COOL • 1962 • Winner Michael • UKN

PLAY IT COOL (USA) see **DENKI KURAGE** • 1970

PLAY ME SOMETHING • 1989 • Neat Timothy • UKN

PLAY MISTY FOR ME • 1971 • Eastwood Clint • USA
PLAY MOTEL • 1979 • Gariazzo Mario • ITL
PLAY OF THE SEASON, THE • 1915 • *Hickman Howard* • USA
PLAY OF THE WAVES, THE • 1955 • Pinschewer Julius • ANS • SWT
PLAY PEN GIRLS, THE • 1967 • Burton Victor • USA
PLAY SAFE • 1927 • Henabery Joseph • USA
PLAY SAFE • 1936 • Fleischer Dave • ANS • USA
PLAY SQUARE • 1921 • Howard William K. • USA
PLAY STRAIGHT OR FIGHT • 1918 • Hurst Paul C. • USA
PLAY THE GAME OR LEAVE THE BED • 1971 • Scott John
PLAY THE PIED PIPER • 1941 • *Mintz Charles (P)* • ANS • USA
PLAY UP THE BAND • 1935 • Hughes Harry • UKN
PLAYA DE FORMENTOR • 1964 • Lorente German • SPN
PLAYA DE LAS SEDUCCIONES, LA • 1970 • Gonzalvo Jose Luis • SPN
PLAYA DEL AMOR, LA • 1980 • Aristarain Adolfo • ARG • LOVE BEACH
PLAYA INSOLITO • 1963 • Aguirre Javier • SHT • SPN
PLAYA LLAMADO DESEO, UNA • 1977 • D'Ambrosio Enzo, Morales Humberto • VNZ, ITL • SPIAGGIA DEL DESIDERIO, LA (ITL) ○ BEACH CALLED DESIRE, A ○ TABOO ISLAND
PLAYA PROHIBITA • 1955 • Soler Julian • SPN, MXC
PLAYA VACIA, LA • 1979 • Gavaldon Roberto • MXC
PLAYBACK • 1962 • Lawrence Quentin • UKN
PLAYBIRDS, THE • 1979 • Roe Willy • UKN • SECRETS OF A PLAYGIRL
PLAYBOX ADVENTURE • 1936 • Kellino W. P. • UKN
PLAYBOY, THE (USA) see **KICKING THE MOON AROUND** • 1938
PLAYBOY OF PARIS • 1930 • Berger Ludwig • USA
PLAYBOY OF THE WESTERN WORLD, THE • 1962 • Hurst Brian Desmond • UKN
PLAYBOY PRESIDENT (USA) see **SHACHO DOCHUKI** • 1960
PLAYBOY RIG DRIVER, THE see **PALIKERONG KUTSERO** • 1967
PLAYBOYS see **MANAMALAYO** • 1967
PLAYBOYS, THE • 1989 • O'Brien Jim, Jones Terry • IRL
PLAYER see **SPIELER** • 1989
PLAYER AND THE SAVAGES, THE see **ACTORUL SI SALBATICII** • 1974
PLAYER PIANO • Arkin Alan • USA
PLAYER PIANOS, THE see **PIANOS MECANICOS, LOS** • 1965
PLAYERS • 1979 • Harvey Anthony • USA
PLAYERS see **CLUB, THE** • 1980
PLAYERS see **LILY IN LOVE** • 1985
PLAYERS, THE • 1912 • *Lubin* • USA
PLAYERS, THE • 1912 • Salter Harry • *Victor* • USA
PLAYERS, THE • 1974 • Brittain Don • CND, ASL
PLAYERS, THE see **KOMODIANTEN** • 1941
PLAYERS AGAINST FALLEN ANGELS, THE • 1969 • Fischermann Alberto • ARG
PLAYFUL KIND, THE see **LIONCEAUX, LES** • 1959
PLAYFUL PAN • 1930 • Gillett Burt • ANS • USA
PLAYFUL PELICAN • 1948 • Lundy Dick • ANS • USA
PLAYFUL PEN • 1931 • Disney Walt • ANS • USA
PLAYFUL PEST, THE • 1943 • Sommer Paul • ANS • USA
PLAYFUL PLUTO • 1934 • Gillett Burt • ANS • USA
PLAYFUL POLAR BEARS, THE • 1938 • Fleischer Dave • ANS • USA
PLAYFUL PUP, THE • 1937 • *Lantz Walter (P)* • ANS • USA
PLAYFUL PUSS • 1953 • Davis Mannie • ANS • USA
PLAYFUL ROBOT, THE see **NESTASNI ROBOT** • 1956
PLAYFUL WITH THE GIRLS see **PILYO SA GIRLS** • 1967
PLAYGIRL • 1954 • Pevney Joseph • USA
PLAYGIRL • 1981 • Chionglo Mel • PHL
PLAYGIRL see **BERLIN IST EINE SUNDE WELT** • 1966
PLAYGIRL 70 • 1969 • Chentrens Federico • ITL
PLAYGIRL, THE • 1982 • Findlay Roberta • USA
PLAYGIRL AFTER DARK see **TOO HOT TO HANDLE** • 1960
PLAYGIRL AND THE MINISTER, THE (USA) see **AMOROUS PRAWN, THE** • 1962
PLAYGIRL GANG see **JEZEBELS, THE** • 1975
PLAYGIRL KILLER • 1965 • Santamaria Eric • CND • DECOY FOR TERROR
PLAYGIRLS, THE • 1942 • Negulesco Jean • SHT • USA
PLAYGIRLS AND THE BELLBOY, THE see **MIT EVA FING DIE SUNDE AN** • 1958
PLAYGIRLS AND THE VAMPIRE, THE (USA) see **ULTIMA PREDA DEL VAMPIRO, L'** • 1960
PLAYGIRLS OF FRANKFURT see **IN FRANKFURT SIND DIE NACHTE HEISS** • 1966
PLAYGROUND • 1966 • Sens Al • ANS • CND
PLAYGROUND, THE • 1965 • Hilliard Richard • USA • TAKE ME WHILE I'M WARM
PLAYGROUND EXPRESS • 1955 • Irwin John • UKN
PLAYGROUNDS OF THE MAMMALS • 1932 • Sennett Mack • DOC • USA
PLAYHOUSE, THE • 1921 • Cline Eddie, Keaton Buster • SHT • USA
PLAYING AROUND • 1930 • LeRoy Mervyn • USA • FURIES, THE
PLAYING AT DIVORCE • 1910 • *Vitagraph* • USA
PLAYING AT DOCTORS • 1922 • Dudley Bernard • UKN
PLAYING AT GROWN-UPS see **ZABAWA W DOROSLYCH** • 1966
PLAYING AT LOVE see **JEUX DE L'AMOUR, LES** • 1960
PLAYING AT SOLDIERS see **MALI VOJNICI** • 1968
PLAYING AWAY • 1987 • Ove Horace • UKN
PLAYING BEATIE BOW • 1986 • Crombie Donald • ASL • TIME GAMES
PLAYING BY EAR • 1946 • Barclay David • SHT • USA
PLAYING CARDS see **PARTIE DE CARTES, UNE** • 1896
PLAYING DEAD • 1915 • Drew Sidney • USA
PLAYING DIRTY • 1984 • SAF
PLAYING DOUBLE • 1923 • *Hatton Dick* • USA
PLAYING FIELDS OF BROCK, THE • 1982 • Pyke Roger • CND
PLAYING FOR A FORTUNE • 1914 • *Kalem* • USA
PLAYING FOR FUN • 1936 • Schwarzwald Milton • SHT • USA
PLAYING FOR HIGH STAKES • 1915 • MacDonald Donald • USA
PLAYING FOR KEEPS • 1986 • Weinstein Bob, Weinstein Harvey • USA
PLAYING FOR KEEPS see **LILY IN LOVE** • 1985
PLAYING FOR TIME • 1980 • Mann Daniel • TVM • USA
PLAYING HOOKEY see **RABONA, LA** • 1978
PLAYING HORSE • 1915 • Hotaling Arthur D. • USA
PLAYING IN THE SAND see **SPIEL IM SAND** • 1964
PLAYING IN TOUGH LUCK • 1915 • McKim Edwin • USA
PLAYING IT WILD • 1923 • Duncan William • USA
PLAYING ON THE RAINBOW see **LEK PA REGNBAGEN** • 1958
PLAYING POLITICS • 1936 • *Mintz Charles (P)* • ANS • USA
PLAYING STRAIGHT see **COLLEGE HERO, THE** • 1927
PLAYING THE DEUCE • 1915 • Kellino W. P. • UKN
PLAYING THE ENVIRONMENT GAME • 1973 • Csaky Mick • SHT • UKN
PLAYING THE GAME • 1912 • *Imp* • USA
PLAYING THE GAME • 1915 • North Wilfred • USA
PLAYING THE GAME • 1918 • Schertzinger Victor • USA
PLAYING THE GAME • 1922 • Wynn George • UKN
PLAYING THE GAME see **LOVE'S REDEMPTION** • 1921
PLAYING THE GAME see **PLAY BALL** • 1925
PLAYING THE GAME (UKN) see **CHEER LEADER, THE** • 1928
PLAYING THE GAME (UKN) see **TOUCHDOWN** • 1931
PLAYING THE PIPERS • 1913 • Humphrey William • USA
PLAYING THE PONIES • 1937 • Lamont Charles • SHT • USA
PLAYING THE SAFE GAME • 1915 • McKim Edwin • USA
PLAYING THE THING • 1972 • Morphet Christopher • SHT • UKN
PLAYING TRUANT • 1910 • Martinek H. O. • UKN
PLAYING TRUANT see **SKOLKA SKOLAN** • 1949
PLAYING TRUMPS • 1912 • Blache Alice • USA
PLAYING WITH DEATH see **TARGET EAGLE** • 1982
PLAYING WITH FIRE • 1913 • Angeles Bert • *Vitagraph* • USA
PLAYING WITH FIRE • 1913 • Melville Wilbert • *Lubin* • USA
PLAYING WITH FIRE • 1914 • *Melies* • USA
PLAYING WITH FIRE • 1914 • Santschi Thomas • *Selig* • USA
PLAYING WITH FIRE • 1915 • Myers Harry • USA
PLAYING WITH FIRE • 1916 • Grandon Francis J. • USA
PLAYING WITH FIRE • 1921 • Fitzgerald Dallas M. • USA
PLAYING WITH FIRE • 1985 • Nagy Ivan • TVM • USA
PLAYING WITH FIRE see **THEY'RE PLAYING WITH FIRE** • 1983
PLAYING WITH SOULS • 1925 • Ince Ralph • USA
PLAYING WITH THE DEVIL see **HRATKY S CERTEM** • 1956
PLAYING WITH WATER • 1954 • Heyer John • DOC • ASL
PLAYMATES • 1908 • Porter Edwin S. • USA
PLAYMATES • 1912 • *Gordon Julia Swayne* • USA
PLAYMATES • 1913 • *Powers* • USA
PLAYMATES • 1913 • *Majestic* • USA
PLAYMATES • 1915 • *Sterling* • USA
PLAYMATES • 1916 • *Juvenile Film* • USA
PLAYMATES • 1918 • Parrott Charles • SHT • USA
PLAYMATES • 1941 • Butler David • USA
PLAYMATES • 1972 • Flicker Theodore J. • USA
PLAYMATES, THE see **LEKKAMRATERNA** • 1915
PLAYMATES (USA) see **BAL DES VOYOUS, LE** • 1968
PLAYPEN, THE • 1967 • St. Thomas Warren • USA
PLAYS see **GRY** • 1970
PLAY'S THE THING, THE • 1914 • Sidney Scott • USA
PLAYTHING, THE • 1913 • Kirkwood James • USA
PLAYTHING, THE • 1929 • Knight Castleton • UKN
PLAYTHING OF BROADWAY, THE • 1921 • Dillon John Francis • USA
PLAYTHING OF THE DEVIL • 1974 • *Forsa Marie* • FRG
PLAYTHINGS • 1918 • Gerrard Douglas • USA
PLAYTHINGS OF DESIRE • 1924 • King Burton L. • USA
PLAYTHINGS OF DESIRE • 1933 • *Pinnacle* • USA • MURDER IN THE LIBRARY (UKN)
PLAYTHINGS OF DESTINY • 1921 • Carewe Edwin • USA
PLAYTHINGS OF FATE • 1915 • Reehm George E. • USA
PLAYTHINGS OF HOLLYWOOD • 1931 • O'Connor William A. • USA • LOVE'S MISTAKE (UKN)
PLAYTHINGS OF PASSION • 1919 • Worsley Wallace • USA
PLAYTHINGS OF THE GODS • 1916 • Melville Wilbert • SHT • USA
PLAYTIME • 1967 • Tati Jacques • FRN, ITL
PLAYTIME FOR WORKERS • 1943 • Baim Harold • UKN
PLAYTIME (USA) see **RECREATION, LA** • 1961
PLAYWRIGHT, THE • 1911 • *Essanay* • USA
PLAYWRIGHT, THE • 1911 • *Reliance* • USA
PLAYWRIGHT'S LOVE, THE • 1910 • *Thanhouser* • USA
PLAYWRIGHT'S WRONG, A • 1918 • Raymaker Herman C. • SHT • USA
PLAZA • 1964 • Sturlis Edward • SHT • PLN • BEACH ○ ON A SEA-BEACH
PLAZA DE PUERTO SANTO, LA • 1976 • *Conacite 1* • MXC
PLAZA DEL ORIENTE • 1962 • Cano Mateo • SPN
PLAZA SUITE • 1971 • Hiller Arthur • USA
PLAZOS TRAICIONEROS • 1956 • Orol Juan • MXC
PLEA FOR PASSION, A see **BIGAMO, IL** • 1956
PLEASANT BREAKFAST, A • 1903 • Collins Alf? • UKN
PLEASANT DUTY, A • 1971 • Howe John • CND
PLEASANT JOURNEY, A • 1923 • McGowan Robert • SHT • USA
PLEASANT WAY OF GETTING THIN, A • 1914 • *B & C* • UKN
PLEASANTVILLE • 1975 • Polon Vicki, Locker Kenneth • USA
PLEASE ANSWER • 1940 • Rowland Roy • SHT • USA
PLEASE BE MY WIFE • 1917 • *Leonard Robert* • SHT • USA
PLEASE BELIEVE ME • 1950 • Taurog Norman • USA
PLEASE CONDUCTOR, DON'T PUT ME OFF THE TRAIN • 1907 • Gilbert Arthur • UKN
PLEASE DO NOT DISTURB • 1962 • Mach Josef • CZC
PLEASE DON'T EAT MY MOTHER! • 1972 • Monson Carl • USA • PLEASE NOT MY MOTHER ○ HUNGRY PETS
PLEASE DON'T EAT THE DAISIES • 1960 • Walters Charles • USA
PLEASE, DON'T FIRE THE CANNON see **ASSALTO AL CENTRO NUCLEARE** • 1967
PLEASE DON'T TOUCH THE FLESH FOR HYGIENIC REASONS • 1971 • Chalbaud Roman • VNZ
PLEASE, ELEPHANT see **PROSZE SLONIA** • 1978
PLEASE EXCUSE ME • 1926 • Newfield Sam • SHT • USA
PLEASE EXCUSE ME see **RACTE PROMINOUT** • 1975
PLEASE GET MARRIED • 1919 • Ince John • USA
PLEASE GO 'WAY AND LET ME SLEEP • 1931 • Fleischer Dave • ANS • USA
PLEASE HELP EMILY • 1917 • Henderson Dell • USA
PLEASE HELP ME • 1918 • Lyons Eddie, Moran Lee • SHT • USA
PLEASE HELP THE PORE • 1912 • *Chamberlain Riley* • USA
PLEASE KEEP ME IN YOUR DREAMS • 1937 • Fleischer Dave • ANS • USA
PLEASE MR. BALZAC (USA) see **EN EFFEUILLANT LA MARGUERITE** • 1956
PLEASE MURDER ME • 1956 • Godfrey Peter • USA
PLEASE NOT MY MOTHER see **PLEASE DON'T EAT MY MOTHER!** • 1972
PLEASE, NOT NOW! (USA) see **BRIDE SUR LE COU, LA** • 1961
PLEASE REMIT • 1911 • *Wadsworth William* • USA
PLEASE SIR! • 1971 • Stuart Mark • UKN
PLEASE STAND BY • 1972 • Milton Jack, Milton Joanne • USA
PLEASE TEACHER • 1937 • Dickens Stafford • UKN
PLEASE TEACHER see **THINGS ARE LOOKING UP** • 1935
PLEASE TURN OVER • 1959 • Thomas Gerald • UKN
PLEASED TO EAT YOU • 1950 • Sparber I. • ANS • USA
PLEASED TO MEET CHA! • 1935 • Fleischer Dave • ANS • USA
PLEASING GRANDPA • 1934 • Horne James W. • SHT • USA
PLEASING HER HUSBAND • 1913 • *White Pearl* • USA
PLEASING UNCLE • 1915 • *Princess* • USA
PLEASURE • 1932 • Brower Otto • USA
PLEASURE, THE see **PIACERE, IL** • 1985
PLEASURE AND THE MYSTERY, THE see **PIACERE E IL MISTERO, IL** • 1964
PLEASURE AT HER MAJESTY'S • 1976 • Graef Roger • UKN
PLEASURE BEFORE BUSINESS • 1927 • Strayer Frank • USA
PLEASURE BOUND • 1925 • Taurog Norman • SHT • USA
PLEASURE BUYERS, THE • 1925 • Withey Chet • USA
PLEASURE COVE • 1978 • Bilson Bruce • TVM • USA
PLEASURE CRAZED • 1929 • Gallaher Donald, Klein Charles (Spv) • USA • MASQUERADE
PLEASURE CRUISE • 1933 • Tuttle Frank • USA
PLEASURE DOME • Roy Jean-Claude • FRN
PLEASURE DOMES • 1987 • Fookes Maggi • ANM • ASL
PLEASURE FARM, THE see **WILBUR AND THE BABY FACTORY** • 1970
PLEASURE GAME, THE • 1970 • Vittoli John • USA
PLEASURE GARDEN see **LUSTGARDEN** • 1961
PLEASURE GARDEN, THE • 1926 • Hitchcock Alfred • UKN, FRG • IRRGARTEN DER LEIDENSCHAFT (FRG) ○ GARTEN DER LUST, DER
PLEASURE GARDEN, THE • 1954 • Broughton James • USA
PLEASURE GIRL see **RAGAZZA CON LA VALIGIA, LA** • 1961
PLEASURE GIRLS, THE • 1965 • O'Hara Gerry • UKN
PLEASURE ISLAND • *Roussail Nadine* • FRN
PLEASURE LOVER see **NAKED FURY** • 1960
PLEASURE LOVERS, THE (USA) see **NAKED FURY** • 1960
PLEASURE MACHINE see **PLEASURE MACHINES, THE** • 1969
PLEASURE MACHINE, THE • 1975 • Ferrers Charles • SWT • SEX CONNECTION
PLEASURE MACHINES, THE • 1969 • Garcia Ron • USA • LOVE MACHINES, THE ○ PLEASURE MACHINE ○ LOVE MACHINE
PLEASURE MAD • 1923 • Barker Reginald • USA
PLEASURE OF A BITCH, THE see **ABAZURE NO KARAKU** • 1967
PLEASURE OF HIS COMPANY, THE • 1961 • Seaton George • USA
PLEASURE OF KILLING, THE see **PLACER DE MATAR, EL** • 1988
PLEASURE OF WOMEN see **ONNA NO YOROKOBI** • 1967
PLEASURE OF YOUTH see **SEISHUN NO ETSURAKU** • 1967
PLEASURE PALACE • 1973 • Hunt Ed • CND
PLEASURE PALACE • 1980 • Grauman Walter • TVM • USA
PLEASURE PARTY see **PARTIE DE PLAISIR, UNE** • 1974
PLEASURE PLANTATION • 1970 • Denby Jerry • USA
PLEASURE SEEKERS • 1920 • Archainbaud George • USA
PLEASURE SEEKERS, THE • 1964 • Negulesco Jean • USA
PLEASURE SO DEEP • 1983 • Dirksen Miller • ITL
PLEASURES • 1986 • Miller Sharron • TVM • USA
PLEASURES AND VICES (USA) see **GUEULE D'ANGE** • 1955
PLEASURES ARE PAID FOR see **UNG KAERLIGHED** • 1958
PLEASURES FOR LIFE see **KYO NO INOCHI** • 1957
PLEASURES OF CAMPING, THE • 1912 • *Scardon Paul* • USA
PLEASURES OF LIAISONS, THE see **FURIN NO TANOSHIMI** • 1968
PLEASURES OF PHOTOGRAPHY, THE • 1900 • *Warwick Trading Co* • UKN
PLEASURES OF THE BATH • 1968 • Kunz Werner • DOC • FRG
PLEASURES OF THE FATHER OF THE COUNTRY, THE see **SLASTI OTCE VLASTI** • 1968
PLEASURES OF THE FLESH, THE see **ETSURAKU** • 1965
PLEASURES OF THE RICH • 1926 • Gasnier Louis J. • USA
PLEBEI • 1915 • Protazanov Yakov • USS • PLEBEIAN
PLEBEIAN see **PLEBEI** • 1915
PLEBEYO, EL • 1952 • Gomez Urquiza Zacarias • MXC
PLEDGE IN THE MOONLIGHT, A • 1923 • Yun Paek-Nam • KOR
PLEDGE NIGHT • 1988 • Ziller Paul • USA • HAZING IN HELL
PLEGARIA GAUCHA • 1938 • Irigoyen Julio • ARG
PLEIN AIR • 1956 • Venard Jean • SHT • FRN
PLEIN AUX AS • 1933 • Houssin Jacques • FRN
PLEIN DE SUPER, LE • 1976 • Cavalier Alain • FRN
PLEIN FER • 1990 • Dayan Josee • FRN
PLEIN FEU.. L'AVENTURE • 1969-70 • Bertolino Daniel, Floquet Francois • DCS • CND
PLEIN LES POCHES POUR PAS UN ROND • 1978 • Daert Daniel • FRN
PLEIN SOLEIL • 1960 • Clement Rene • FRN, ITL • IN PIENO SOLE (ITL) ○ PURPLE NOON (USA) ○ BLAZING SUN(UKN) ○ LUST FOR EVIL
PLEIN SUD • 1981 • Beraud Luc • FRN, SPN • HEAT OF DESIRE (USA)
PLEINE BOUCHE • 1978 • *Maillot Francoise* • FRN
PLEINS FEUX • 1958 • Masson Jean • SHT • FRN

PLEINS FEUX SUR L'ASSASSIN • 1961 • Franju Georges • FRN • SPOTLIGHT ON A MURDERER ○ SPOTLIGHT ON MURDER
PLEINS FEUX SUR STANISLAS • 1965 • Dudrumet Jean-Charles • FRN, FRG • RENDEZVOUS DER KILLER (FRG) ○ KILLER SPY (USA)
PLEITO DE SANGRE • 1955 • Gascon Jose • SPN
PLEKKIE IN DIE SON • 1979 • SAF
PLENENO YATO • 1962 • Mundrov Dutcho • BUL • CAPTURED SQUADRON
PLENG SUDTAI • 1987 • Akaraserani Pisan • THL
PLENILUNIO DELLE VERGINI, IL • 1973 • Solvay Paolo • ITL • DEVIL'S WEDDING NIGHT, THE (USA)
PLENTIFUL SUMMER, THE see **SCHEDROYE LETO** • 1951
PLENTY • 1985 • Schepisi Fred • USA
PLENTY BELOW ZERO • 1943 • Wickersham Bob • ANS • USA
PLENTY OF MONEY AND YOU • 1937 • Freleng Friz • ANS • USA
PLENTY ROOM IN PAKISTAN • 1979 • Purdy Jim • DOC • CND
PLES GORILLA • 1968 • Vukotic Dusan • ANS • YGS, USA • GORILLA'S DANCE (USA)
PLES NA KISI • 1961 • Hladnik Bostjan • YGS • DANCING IN THE RAIN ○ DANCE IN THE RAIN ○ DANCE IN RAIN ○ PLES V DESJU
PLES V DESJU see **PLES NA KISI** • 1961
PLETENICE • 1974 • Tadic Zoran • SHT • YGS • BRAIDS
PLEURE PAS LA BOUCHE PLEINE • 1974 • Thomas Pascal • FRN • DON'T CRY WITH YOUR MOUTH FULL ○ SPRING INTO SUMMER
PLEURE PAS, MY LOVE • 1989 • Gatlif Tony • FRN
PLEURS see **HU-MAN** • 1975
PLEYDELL MYSTERY, THE • 1916 • Ward Albert • UKN
PLIO TIS HARAS, TO • 1967 • Laskos Orestis • GRC • SHIP OF JOY
PLISTSKAYA DANCES (USA) see **MAYA PLISETSKAYA** • 1964
PLN see **SCHWEIGENDE STERN, DER** • 1960
PLOCK 1960 • 1960 • Halladin Danuta • DOC • PLN
PLOCK AUTUMN 1961 see **PLOCKA JESIEN 1961** • 1961
PLOCK RUSZA • 1964 • Wionczek Roman • DOC • PLN • PLOCK STARTS
PLOCK STARTS see **PLOCK RUSZA** • 1964
PLOCKA JESIEN 1961 • 1961 • Wionczek Roman • DOC • PLN • PLOCK AUTUMN 1961
PLOD • 1972 • Cort Michael • SHT • UKN
PLOGOFF, DES PIERRES CONTRE DES FUSILS • 1981 • Le Garrec Nicole • DOC • FRN
PLOKHOY KHOROSHYI CHELOVEK • 1974 • Heifitz Josif • USS • GOOD BAD MAN, THE ○ DUEL, THE ○ BAD GOODY, A
PLOMBIER AMOREUX, LE • 1932 • Autant-Lara Claude • FRN
PLOMO SOBRE DALLAS • 1970 • Zabalza Jose Maria • SPN
PLOMO Y SANGRE • 1977 • Bosch Juan • SPN
PLONGE DU "RUBIS", UNE see **SORTIE DU "RUBIS", UNE** • 1950
PLONGEUR FANTASTIQUE, LE • 1906 • Velle Gaston • SHT • FRN • FANTASTIC DIVER, THE
PLOP GOES THE WEASEL • 1953 • McKimson Robert • ANS • USA
PLOT, THE • 1914 • Costello Maurice, Gaillord Robert • USA
PLOT AGAINST BERTIE, THE • 1911 • *Kalem* • USA
PLOT AGAINST HARRY, THE • 1971 • Roemer Michael • USA
PLOT AGAINST THE GOVERNOR, THE • 1913 • *Cruze James* • USA
PLOT AND COUNTERPLOT • 1915 • MacMackin Archer • USA
PLOT AND COUNTERPLOT • 1916 • *Gail Jane* • SHT • USA
PLOT AND PASH • 1912 • Plumb Hay • UKN
PLOT FOR A MILLION, A • 1913 • *Vincent James* • USA
PLOT FOR A SHORT STORY, A see **SYUZHET DLYA NEBOLSHOVO RASKAZA** • 1968
PLOT OF INDIA'S HILLMEN, THE • 1913 • *Kalem* • USA
PLOT OF ROAD, A • 1968 • Iliesu Mirel • DOC • RMN
PLOT SICKENS, THE • 1961 • Kneitel Seymour • ANS • USA
PLOT THAT FAILED, THE • 1909 • Brooke Van Dyke • USA
PLOT THAT FAILED, THE • 1910 • *Powers* • USA
PLOT THAT FAILED, THE • 1912 • *Wolfe Jane* • USA
PLOT THAT FAILED, THE • 1912 • *P & B Films* • UKN
PLOT THAT FAILED, THE • 1914 • *Selig* • USA
PLOT THICKENS, THE • 1936 • Holmes Ben • USA • SWINGING PEARL MYSTERY, THE (UKN)
PLOT THICKENS, THE (UKN) see **HERE COMES COOKIE** • 1935
PLOT TO ASSASSINATE HITLER, THE (USA) see **20 JULI, DER** • 1955
PLOT TO KILL ROOSEVELT, THE (USA) see **TEHERAN** • 1947
PLOT (UKN) see **ATTENTAT, L'** • 1972
PLOTONE DI ESECUZIONE (ITL) see **QUAND SONNERA MIDI** • 1957
PLOTS AND BLOTS • 1924 • Quiribet Gaston • SHT • UKN
PLOTS AND BLOTS • 1925 • Quiribet Gaston • SHT • UKN
PLOTTERS AND PAPERS • 1916 • MacMackin Archer • USA
PLOTZLICHE EINSAMKEIT DES KONRAD STEINER, DIE • 1976 • Gloor Kurt • SWT • SUDDEN LONELINESS OF KONRAD STEINER, THE
PLOTZLICHER REICHTUM DER ARMEN LEUTE VAN KOMBACH, DER • 1970 • Schlondorff Volker • FRG • SUDDEN FORTUNE OF THE POOR PEOPLE OF KOMBACH, THE ○ SUDDEN WEALTH OF THE POOR PEOPLE OF KOMBACH, THE
PLOUFFE, LES • 1981 • Carle Gilles • CND • IL ETAIT UNE FOIS DES GENS HEUREUX: LES PLOUFFE ○ PLOUFFE FAMILY, THE
PLOUFFE FAMILY, THE see **PLOUFFE, LES** • 1981
PLOUGH AND THE STARS, THE • 1936 • Ford John • USA
PLOUGHBOY'S DREAM, THE • 1904 • *Paul R. W.* • UKN
PLOUGHING THE CLOUDS • 1917 • *Pokes & Jabbs* • USA
PLOUGHMAN, THE • 1979 • Purdum Richard • UKN
PLOUGHMAN'S LUNCH, THE • 1982 • Eyre Richard • UKN
PLOUGHSHARE, THE • 1915 • Collins John H. • USA
PLOUM PLOUM TRA LA LA • 1946 • Hennion Robert • FRN • DE PORTE EN PORTE
PLOVEC • 1981 • Kvirikadze Irakli • USS • SWIMMER, THE
PLOW BOY, THE • 1928 • Disney Walt, Iwerks Ub • ANS • USA
PLOW GIRL, THE • 1916 • Leonard Robert Z. • USA
PLOW THAT BROKE THE PLAINS, THE • 1936 • Lorentz Pare • DOC • USA
PLOW WOMAN, THE • 1917 • Swickard Charles • USA
PLOY TALAY • 1986 • Songsri Cherd • THL • GEM FROM THE DEEP, THE ○ SEA GEM, THE
PLUCK see **AMERICAN PLUCK** • 1925
PLUCK AND LUCK • 1916 • *Stull Walter* • SHT • USA
PLUCK AND PLOTTERS • 1918 • Semon Larry • SHT • USA
PLUCK OF THE IRISH (UKN) see **GREAT GUY** • 1936
PLUCK V PLOT • 1922 • Collins Edwin J. • UKN
PLUCKED FROM THE BURNING • 1900 • Booth W. R. • UKN
PLUCKED (USA) see **MORTE HA FATTO L'UOVO, LA** • 1968
PLUCKY AMERICAN GIRL, A • 1910 • Melies Gaston • USA
PLUCKY GIRL, A • 1910 • *Powers* • USA
PLUCKY HOODOO • 1920 • *Van Billy* • SHT • USA
PLUCKY KIDDIE, A • 1910 • Haldane Bert? • UKN
PLUCKY LAD, A • 1910 • Martinek H. O. • UKN
PLUCKY LITTLE GIRL, A • 1909 • Fitzhamon Lewin • UKN
PLUCKY RANCH GIRL, A • 1912 • *Comet* • USA
PLUCKY WESTERN KID, A • 1910 • *Powers* • USA
PLUGG • 1975 • Bourke Terry • ASL
PLUGGED NICKEL, A • 1915 • *Marshall Boyd* • USA
PLUGGET see **SISTA RINGEN** • 1955
PLUIE D'ETE • 1986 • Dauteuil Francois • SHT • CND • SUMMER RAIN
PLUIE D'OR • 1935 • Rozier Willy • FRN
PLUIE ET LE BEAU TEMPS, LA • Coignon Jean • ANS • FRN • RAIN AND GOOD WEATHER
PLUIES ONT TARI, LES see **GAFAT AL-AMTAR** • 1966
PLUK NAUFRAGE DE L'ESPACE • 1974 • Image Jean • ANM • FRN
PLUKOVNIK SVEC • 1929 • Innemann Svatopluk • CZC • COLONEL SVEC
PLUM JUICE see **SOK OD SLJIVA** • 1981
PLUM PUDDING STAKES, THE • 1911 • Martinek H. O. • UKN
PLUM TREE, THE • 1914 • *Bushman Francis X.* • USA
PLUMA AL VIENTO (SPN) see **PLUME AU VENT** • 1952
PLUMAGE OF THE OWL, THE see **PLUMAS DEL MUCARO, LAS** • 1989
PLUMARD EN FOLIE, LE see **LIT, LE** • 1974
PLUMAS DEL MUCARO, LAS • 1989 • Lopez Paco • ANS • PRC • PLUMAGE OF THE OWL, THE
PLUMB • 1988 • Kimiyaei Massoud • IRN
PLUMB CRAZY • 1939 • Yarbrough Jean • SHT • USA
PLUMB DUMB • 1927 • Taurog Norman • SHT • USA
PLUMBER • 1915 • *Starlight* • USA
PLUMBER, THE • 1910 • Wilson Frank? • UKN
PLUMBER, THE • 1911 • *Selig* • USA
PLUMBER, THE • 1914 • Henderson Dell • USA
PLUMBER, THE • 1924 • Cline Eddie • SHT • USA
PLUMBER, THE • 1933 • Lantz Walter, Nolan William • ANS • USA
PLUMBER, THE • 1967 • Culhane Shamus • ANS • USA
PLUMBER, THE • 1980 • Weir Peter • ASL
PLUMBER, THE see **WORK** • 1915
PLUMBER AND PERCY, THE • 1914 • *Komic* • USA
PLUMBER AND THE LADY, THE • 1933 • *Sennett Mack (P)* • SHT • USA
PLUMBER AND THE LUNATICS, THE • 1908 • *Tyler Walter* • UKN
PLUMBER OF SEVILLE, THE • 1957 • Lovy Alex • ANS • USA
PLUMBER WINS THE GIRL, THE • 1915 • *Joker* • USA
PLUMBERS • 1962 • Wdowkowna-Oldak Zofia • ANM • PLN
PLUMBER'S DAUGHTER • 1927 • *Sennett Mack (P)* • SHT • USA
PLUMBER'S HELPERS • 1953 • Rasinski Connie • ANS • USA
PLUMBERS' PICNIC, THE • 1914 • *Malatesta Mary* • USA
PLUMBER'S WATERLOO, A • 1916 • Donaldson R. M. • SHT • USA
PLUMBING FOR GOLD • 1934 • Lamont Charles • SHT • USA
PLUMBING IS A PIPE • 1938 • Fleischer Dave • ANS • USA
PLUMBUM ILI OPASNAYA IGRA • 1986 • Abdrakhitov Vadim • USS • PLUMBUM, OR A DANGEROUS GAME
PLUMBUM, OR A DANGEROUS GAME see **PLUMBUM ILI OPASNAYA IGRA** • 1986
PLUME AU VENT • 1952 • Cuny Louis, Torrado Ramon • FRN, SPN • PLUMA AL VIENTO (SPN)
PLUME COLLECTORS, THE see **SKUPLJACI PERJA** • 1967
PLUME LA POULE • 1946 • Kapps Walter • FRN
PLUMES AU VENT • 1958 • Garceau Raymond • DCS • CND
PLUMP BLOSSOMS see **ERIKLER CICEK ACTI** • 1968
PLUNDER • 1923 • Seitz George B., Bennet Spencer Gordon • SRL • USA
PLUNDER • 1931 • Walls Tom • UKN
PLUNDER • 1967 • Prochazka Vaclav • ANS • CZC
PLUNDER OF THE SUN • 1953 • Farrow John • USA
PLUNDER ROAD • 1957 • Cornfield Hubert • USA
PLUNDERER, THE • 1915 • Lewis Edgar • USA
PLUNDERER, THE • 1924 • Archainbaud George • USA
PLUNDERERS, THE • 1948 • Kane Joseph • USA
PLUNDERERS, THE • 1960 • Pevney Joseph • USA
PLUNDERERS OF PAINTED FLATS • 1959 • Gannaway Albert C. • USA
PLUNDERERS OF THE MOON, THE see **O DWOCH TAKICH CO UKRADLI KSIEZYC** • 1962
PLUNGE INTO DARKNESS • 1977 • Maxwell Peter • MTV • ASL
PLUNGER, THE • 1920 • Henderson Dell • USA
PLUNGING HOOFS • 1929 • McRae Henry • USA
PLURIELLES • 1979 • Lebel Jean-Patrick • FRN
PLUS BEAU GOSSE DE FRANCE, LE • 1937 • Pujol Rene • FRN • MARI DE LA REINE, LE
PLUS BEAU JOUR DE MA VIE.., LE • 1981 • Letourneau Diane • CND
PLUS BEAU QUE MOI, TU MEURS • 1982 • Clair Philippe • FRN, TNS
PLUS BEAUX FRUITS DU MONDE, LES • 1959 • Gruel Henri • ANM • BLG
PLUS BEAUX JOURS, LES • 1957 • de Gastyne Marco • SHT • FRN
PLUS BEAUX JOURS DE MA VIE, LES see **AGMAL IYUM HAYATI** • 1973
PLUS BELLE DES VIES, LA • 1954 • Vermorel Claude • FRN
PLUS BELLE FILLE DU MONDE, LA • 1937 • Kirsanoff Dimitri • FRN • PLUS BELLE FILLE DU MONDE NE PEUT DONNER QUE CE QU'ELLE A, LA
PLUS BELLE FILLE DU MONDE, LA • 1951 • Stengel Christian • FRN
PLUS BELLE FILLE DU MONDE NE PEUT DONNER QUE CE QU'ELLE A, LA see **PLUS BELLE FILLE DU MONDE, LA** • 1937
PLUS BELLE SOIREE DE MA VIE, LA (FRN) see **PIU BELLA SERATA DELLA MIA VITA, LA** • 1972
PLUS BELLES ESCROQUERIES DU MONDE, LES • 1963 • Polanski Roman, Chabrol Claude, Godard Jean-Luc, Gregoretti Ugo, Horikawa Hiromichi • FRN, ITL, JPN • TRUFFE PIU BELLE DEL MONDO, LE (ITL) ○ WORLD'S GREATEST SWINDLES ○ BEAUTIFUL SWINDLERS, THE ○ SEKAI SAGI MONOGATARI ○ PIU BELLE TRUFFE DEL MONDO, LE
PLUS CA CHANGE, PLUS C'EST PAREIL see **GAME IS THE GAME, THE** • 1974
PLUS CA VA, MOINS CA VA • 1977 • Vianey Michel • FRN, SPN
PLUS DE VACANCES POUR LE BON DIEU • 1949 • Vernay Robert • FRN • FACE TO THE WIND ○ NO HOLIDAY FOR THE GOOD GOD
PLUS DE WHISKY POUR CALLAGHAN • 1955 • Rozier Willy • FRN
PLUS FACTOR, THE • 1970 • Schepisi Fred • DCS • ASL
PLUS FORT QUE SON MAITRE • 1896 • Melies Georges • FRN • SMARTER THAN THE TEACHER
PLUS GRAND AMOUR, LE see **FELICIE NANTEUIL** • 1942
PLUS GRAND CRIME, LE see **ENFER DES ANGES, L'** • 1939
PLUS GRAND SUCCES DE RENE CRESTE, LE see **JUDEX** • 1916
PLUS GRANDE RICHESSE, LA • 1974 • Ifticene Mohamed • ALG
PLUS GRANDES NEIGES DU MONDE, LES see **GREATEST SNOW ON EARTH, THE** • 1975
PLUS HEUREUX DES HOMMES, LE • 1952 • Ciampi Yves • FRN
PLUS JAMAIS HIROSHIMA see **NO MORE HIROSHIMA** • 1983
PLUS JAMAIS SEULS • 1970 • Delire Jean • BLG
PLUS JOLI PECHE DU MONDE, LE • 1951 • Grangier Gilles • FRN
PLUS LONGUE NUIT DU DIABLE, LA • 1971 • Brismee Jean • BLG, ITL • NOTTE PIU LONGA DEL DIAVOLO, LA (ITL) ○ DEVIL'S NIGHTMARE (UKN) ○ SERVICE DU DIABLE ○ AU SERVICE DU DIABLE ○ VAMPIRE PLAYGIRLS ○ DEVIL'S LONGEST NIGHT, THE
PLUS / MINUS • Ruutsalo Eino • ANS • FNL
PLUS MORT QUE VIF see **ETRANGE MONSIEUR STEVE, L'** • 1957
PLUS RAPIDE QUE LA MORT • 1925 • Bourgeois Gerard • FRN
PLUS VIEUX METIER DU MONDE, LE • 1967 • Godard Jean-Luc, Bolognini Mauro, de Broca Philippe, Pfleghar Michael, Indovina Franco, Autant-Lara Claude • FRN, ITL, FRG • AMORE ATTRAVERSO I SECOLO, L' (ITL) ○ AMOUR A TRAVERS LES AGES, L' ○ ALTESTE GEWERBE DER WELT, DAS ○ LOVE THROUGH THE CENTURIES ○ OLDEST PROFESSION IN THE WORLD, THE ○ OLDEST PROFESSION, THE (USA)
PLUS VITE • 1966 • Foldes Peter • ANS • FRN • FASTER
PLUSCH UND PLUMOWSKI see **FRAUENHAUS VON RIO, DAS** • 1927
PLUSHETTE'S SWEET REVENGE • 1970 • *Century Cinema Corp.* • USA
PLUSIEURS TOMBENT EN AMOUR • 1980 • Simoneau Guy • DOC • CND
PLUSZ MINUSZ EGY NAP • 1973 • Fabri Zoltan • HNG • ONE DAY MORE, ONE DAY LESS ○ ONE DAY MORE OR LESS
PLUTO AND THE ARMADILLO • 1943 • Geronimi Clyde • ANS • USA
PLUTO AT THE ZOO • 1942 • Geronimi Clyde • ANS • USA
PLUTO, JUNIOR • 1942 • Geronimi Clyde • ANS • USA
PLUTOCRAT see **BUSINESS AND PLEASURE** • 1931
PLUTONIUM BABY • 1987 • Hirschman Ray • USA
PLUTONIUM BABY see **MUTANT KID, THE**
PLUTONIUM INCIDENT, THE • 1980 • Michaels Richard • TVM • USA
PLUTOPIA • 1951 • Nichols Charles • ANS • USA
PLUTO'S BLUE NOTE • 1947 • Nichols Charles • ANS • USA
PLUTO'S CHRISTMAS TREE • 1952 • Hannah Jack • ANS • USA
PLUTO'S DREAM HOUSE • 1940 • Geronimi Clyde • ANS • USA
PLUTO'S FLEDGLING • 1948 • Nichols Charles • ANS • USA
PLUTO'S HEART THROB • 1950 • Nichols Charles • ANS • USA
PLUTO'S HOUSE WARMING • 1947 • Nichols Charles • ANS • USA
PLUTO'S JUDGMENT DAY • 1935 • Hand David • ANS • USA
PLUTO'S KID BROTHER • 1946 • Nichols Charles • ANS • USA
PLUTO'S PARTY • 1952 • Schaffer Milt • ANS • USA
PLUTO'S PLAYMATE • 1941 • Ferguson Norman • ANS • USA
PLUTO'S PURCHASE • 1948 • Nichols Charles • ANS • USA
PLUTO'S QUIN-PUPLETS • 1937 • Sharpsteen Ben • ANS • USA
PLUTO'S SURPRISE PACKAGE • 1949 • Nichols Charles • ANS • USA
PLUTO'S SWEATER • 1949 • Nichols Charles • ANS • USA
PLYMOUTH ADVENTURE • 1952 • Brown Clarence • USA
PLYNA TRATWY • 1962 • Slesicki Wladyslaw • DOC • PLN • RAFTS AFLOAT ○ BOY AND WAVES
PLYWOOD PANIC • 1953 • Smith Paul J. • ANS • USA
PNEUMATIC POLICEMAN, THE • 1908 • Wilson Frank • UKN
PO' DI CIELO, UN • 1956 • Moser Giorgio • ITL
PO' DI SOLE NELL'AQUA GELIDA, UN (ITL) see **PEU DE SOLEIL DANS L'EAU FROIDE, UN** • 1971
PO DI STORIA DEL CAFFE, UN • 1954 • Cerchio Fernando • SHT • ITL
PO: FORZA 50,000 • 1961 • *Olmi Ermanno (P)* • DOC • ITL

PO ISTI POTI SE NE VRACAJ • 1966 • Babic Joze • YGS • DO NOT COME BACK ALONG THE SAME ROAD ○ DO NOT COME ALONG THE SAME ROAD

PO PROSTU ZWYKLI LUDZIE • 1964 • Trzos-Rastawiecki Andrzej • DOC • PLN • SIMPLY ORDINARY PEOPLE

PO RUSI • 1968 • Filippov Fyodor • USS • ON THE ROADS TO RUSSIA ○ ALONG RUSSIAN PATHS ○ THROUGH RUSSIA ○ ALL OVER RUSSIA

PO TROTOARA • 1967 • Marinovich Anton • BUL • ALONG THE PAVEMENT ○ ON THE PAVEMENT

PO UPADKU • 1989 • Trzos-Rastawiecki Andrzej • PLN • AFTER THE FALL

PO WYROKU • 1967 • Gradowski Bohdan • DOC • PLN • AFTER THE SENTENCE

PO ZAKONU • 1926 • Kuleshov Lev • USS • UNEXPECTED, THE ○ BY THE LAW ○ EXPIATION ○ DURA LEX

POACHER, THE • 1909 • *Walturdaw* • UKN

POACHER, THE • 1912 • *Noble Jack* • USA

POACHER, THE • 1929 • Bolton Albert C. • UKN

POACHERS • 1988 • Zahariev Edward • BUL

POACHERS see **FURTIVOS** • 1975

POACHERS see **KRYPSKYTERRE** • 1981

POACHER'S DAUGHTER, THE (USA) see **SALLY'S IRISH ROGUE** • 1958

POACHERS FIGHT FOR LIBERTY, THE • 1912 • Haldane Bert? • UKN

POACHER'S GOD-DAUGHTER, THE see **PYTLAKOVA SCHOVANKA** • 1949

POACHER'S PARDON, THE • 1912 • Olcott Sidney • USA, UKN

POACHER'S REFORM, THE • 1912 • Haldane Bert? • UKN

POACHER'S WIFE, THE • 1910 • *Vitagraph* • USA

POACHING OF BREASTS see **CHIBUSA NO MITSURYOH** • 1968

POBAL • 1970 • Marcus Louis • DOC • IRL

POBEDA • 1938 • Pudovkin V. I., Doller Mikhail • USS • MOTHERS AND SONS ○ VICTORY

POBEDA NA PRAVOBEREZHENOI UKRAINE I IZGNANIYE NEMETSIKH ZA PREDELI UKRAINSKIKH SOVIETSKIKH ZEMEL • 1945 • Dovzhenko Alexander, Solntseva Yulia • USS • VICTORY IN THE UKRAINE AND THE EXPULSION OF THE GERMANS FROM THE BOUNDARIES OF THE UKR. SOV. LAND

POBEDITELI NOCHI • 1927 • Timoshenko S. • USS • VICTORY OF THE NIGHT

POBEL • 1978 • Lindgren Hans • NRW • HOOLIGANS

POBRE CORAZON • 1950 • Diaz Morales Jose • MXC

POBRE DEL POBRE • 1960 • Salvador Jaime • MXC

POBRE DIABLO • 1940 • Benavides Jose Jr. • MXC

POBRE DRACULA, EL • 1976 • Fortuny Juan • SPN

POBRE GARCIA, EL • 1961 • Leblanc Tony • SPN

POBRE HUERFANITA • 1954 • Martinez Solares Gilberto • MXC

POBRE MARIPOSA • 1986 • de la Torre Raul • ARG • POOR BUTTERFLY

POBRE PEREZ, EL • 1937 • Amadori Luis Cesar • ARG • POOR PEREZ

POBRE RICO, EL • 1942 • Iquino Ignacio F. • SPN

POBRE VALBUENA, EL • 1917 • *Noriega Film Co* • MXC

POBRE VALBUENA, EL • 1923 • Buchs Jose • SPN

POBRECITA DRACULIN, EL • 1977 • Fortuny Juan • SPN

POBRES MILLONARIOS • 1957 • Cortes Fernando • MXC

POBRES PARK • 1967 • Camonte Tony • PHL • POOR PARK

POBRES PERO SINVERGUENZAS • 1948 • Gomez Landero Humberto • MXC

POBRES VAN AL CIELO, LOS • 1951 • Salvador Jaime • MXC

POC AR BUILE • 1974 • Marcus Louis • SHT • IRL • WOES OF GOLF

POCAHONTAS • 1908 • Porter Edwin S. • USA

POCAHONTAS • 1910 • *Thanhouser* • USA

POCATELLO KID, THE • 1931 • Rosen Phil • USA

POCCI COUNTS -SOME CHAPTERS IN THE HISTORY OF A FAMILY, THE see **GRAFEN POCCI -EINIGE KAPITEL ZUR GESCHICHTE EINER FAMILIE, DIE** • 1968

POCESTNE PANI PARDUBICKE • 1944 • Fric Martin • CZC • RESPECTABLE LADIES OF PARDUBICKE, THE ○ HONORABLE LADIES OF PARDUBICE, THE ○ VIRTUOUS DAMES OF PARDUBICE, THE

POCETNI UDARAC • 1990 • Bajic Darko • YGS • INITIAL KICK

POCHARD ET L'INVENTEUR, LE • 1902 • Melies Georges • FRN • WHAT BEFELL THE INVENTOR'S VISITOR (UKN) ○ DRUNKARD AND INVENTOR (USA)

POCHARDE, LA • 1921 • Etievant Henri • FRN

POCHARDE, LA • 1936 • Kemm Jean, Bouquet Jean-Louis • FRN

POCHARDE, LA • 1952 • Combret Georges • FRN

POCHARDIANA OU LE REVEUR EVEILLE • 1908 • Melies Georges • FRN • WIDE-AWAKE DREAMER, THE

POCHEMU TY MOLCHISH? • 1967 • Seyidbeili Gasan • USS • WHY DON'T YOU SPEAK UP?

POCHI DOLLARI PER DJANGO • 1966 • Klimovsky Leon • ITL, SPN • FEW DOLLARS FOR DJANGO, A (UKN)

POCHODNE • 1960 • Cech Vladimir • CZC • TORCHES

POCHTOVY ROMAN • 1969 • Matveyev Yevgeni • USS • LOVE BY CORRESPONDENCE

POCIAG • 1959 • Kawalerowicz Jerzy • PLN • NIGHT TRAIN (USA) ○ BALTIC EXPRESS

POCIAG DO HOLLYWOOD • 1988 • Piwowarski Radoslaw • PLN • TRAIN TO HOLLYWOOD

POCIAGIEM PRZYJAZNI DO Z.S.R.R. • 1967 • Wionczek Roman • DOC • PLN • TRAIN OF FRIENDSHIP TO THE U.S.S.R.

POCKET BOXERS • 1903 • Booth W. R. • UKN

POCKET CARTOON, THE • 1941 • Halas John • ANS • UKN

POCKET LOVE, A see **AMOUR DE POCHE, UN** • 1957

POCKET MONEY • 1972 • Rosenberg Stuart • USA

POCKET MONEY see **ARGENT DE POCHE, L'** • 1976

POCKET NOVELTIES • 1928 • Freund Karl • SER • UKN

POCKET POLICEMAN see **AGENT DE POCHE, L'** • 1909

POCKETFUL OF MIRACLES, A • 1961 • Capra Frank • USA

POCKETKNIFE, THE see **SCYZORYK** • 1962

POCKPICKET • 1968 • von Bagh Peter • SHT • FNL

POCO • 1978 • Brooks Dwight • USA • POCO -LITTLE DOG LOST

POCO A POCO • 1975 • Martin Susan • USA

POCO -LITTLE DOG LOST see **POCO** • 1978

POCOMANIA • 1939 • Leonard Arthur • USA • DEVIL'S DAUGHTER, THE

POCZMISTRS • 1967 • Lenartowicz Stanislaw • MTV • PLN

POCZTOWKA Z ZAKOPANEGO • 1960 • Hoffman Jerzy, Skorzewski Edward • DCS • PLN • POSTCARD FROM ZAKOPANE, A ○ POSTCARDS FROM ZAKOPANE

POD GWIAZDA FRYGIJSKA • 1954 • Kawalerowicz Jerzy • PLN • UNDER THE PHRYGIAN STAR

POD IGOTO • 1952 • Dakovski Dako • BUL • UNDER THE YOKE

POD JEDNOU STRECHOU • 1938 • Krnansky M. J. • CZC • UNDER ONE ROOF ○ SAFE HOME

POD JEDNYM DACHEM • 1964 • Wionczek Roman (c/d) • MTV • PLN • UNDER ONE ROOF

POD JEDNYM NIEBEM • 1956 • Weber Kurt • DOC • PLN • UNDER THE SAME SKY

POD JEZEVCI SKALOU • 1981 • Gajer Vaclav • CZC • UNDER THE BADGER'S ROCK

POD PYEPLOM OGON • 1968 • Rakhimov Abdusalom • USS • FIRE UNDER THE ASHES

POD SENKOM HALEBARDE • 1952 • Michieli Coci • YGS • UNDER THE SHADOW OF HALEBARDE

POD SUMNJOM • 1956 • Branko Belan • YGS • SUSPECTED ONE, THE

PODARTA KSIAZKA • 1962 • Giersz Witold • ANS • PLN • TORN BOOK, THE

PODER DE LA CENSURA, EL • 1982 • Vieyra Emilio • ARG • POWER OF CENSORSHIP, THE

PODER DE LAS TINIEBLAS, EL • 1974 • de Ossorio Amando • SPN

PODER DE LAS TINIEBLAS, EL • 1979 • Sabato Mario • ARG • POWER OF DARKNESS, THE

PODER DE LOS HIJOS, EL see **TACOS JOVEN** • 1950

PODER DEL DESEO, EL • 1976 • Bardem Juan Antonio • SPN • POWER OF DESIRE, THE

PODER LOCAL, PODER POPULAR • 1970 • Gomez Sara • DOC • CUB

PODER NEGRO • 1974 • Crevenna Alfredo B. • MXC, VNZ • BLACK POWER

PODER POPULAR, EL see **BATALLA DE CHILE: PART 3, LA** • 1979

PODER SATANICO, EL see **BLUE DEMON CONTRA EL PODER SATANICO** • 1964

PODEROSO INFLUJO DE LA LUNA, EL • 1981 • *Landa Alfredo* • SPN • RISING TIDE OF THE MOON, THE

PODFUK • 1985 • Schmidt Jan • CZC • MEAN BLOW

PODGRODZIE • 1959 • Hoffman Jerzy, Skorzewski Edward • DCS • PLN • BOROUGH, THE

PODGY PORKINS' PLOT • 1915 • Aylott Dave • UKN

PODHALE ON FIRE see **PODHALE W OGNIU** • 1956

PODHALE W OGNIU • 1956 • Batory Jan • PLN • PODHALE ON FIRE

PODKOVA PRO STESTI • 1946 • Zeman Karel • SHT • CZC • HORSESHOE FOR LUCK, A ○ GOOD LUCK HORSESHOE, THE ○ HORSESHOE, THE

PODLIVNE PRATELSTVI HERCE JESENIA • 1985 • Stekly Karel • CZC • UNUSUAL FRIENDSHIP OF THE ACTOR JESENIUS, THE

PODNE • 1968 • Djordjevic Purisa • YGS • NOON

PODNYATAYA TZELINA • 1940 • Raizman Yuli • USS • VIRGIN SOIL UPTURNED

PODOBIZNA • 1948 • Slavicek Jiri • CZC • PORTRAIT, THE

PODPISANIE KAPITULACJI • 1970 • Trzos-Rastawiecki Andrzej • DOC • PLN • SIGNING OF THE CAPITULATION, THE

PODRANKI • 1977 • Gubenko Nikolai • USS • ORPHANS ○ BROKEN WINGS ○ WOUNDED ONE, THE

PODROZ • 1970 • Szczechura Daniel • ANS • PLN • JOURNEY, THE

PODRUGI • 1936 • Arnstam Leo • USS • THREE WOMEN (USA) ○ SONG OF POTEMKIN, THE ○ GIRL FRIENDS, THE ○ FRIENDS

PODSKALAK • 1928 • Prazsky Premysl • CZC

PODVED S RUNENSEM • 1940 • Vavra Otakar • CZC

PODVIG FARKHADA • 1968 • Khachaturov Albert • USS • FARHAD'S ACHIEVEMENT ○ FARKHAD'S FEAT

PODVIG LENINGRADA • 1973 • Yershov Mikhail • USS • FEAT OF LENINGRAD, THE

PODVIG RAZVEDCHIKA • 1947 • Barnet Boris • USS • EXPLOITS OF AN INTELLIGENCE AGENT ○ SCOUT'S EXPLOIT, THE

PODVIG VO IDACH • 1928 • Vasiliev Georgi, Vasiliev Sergei • USS • ICE-BREAKER KRASSNIN, THE ○ EXPLOIT ON THE ICE

PODWOJNE ZYCIE WAZKI • 1958 • Kokesz Stanislaw • DOC • PLN • DOUBLE LIFE OF A DRAGONFLY

POEDINOK • 1957 • Petrov Vladimir • USS • DUEL, THE

POEM see **UTA** • 1972

POEM 8 • 1932 • Etting Emlen • SHT • USA

POEM, THE see **PESMA** • 1961

POEM ABOUT THE COCKROACHES, A • 1987 • Traikova Eldora • DOC • BUL

POEM ABOUT THE SEA see **POEMA O MORE** • 1958

POEM FIELDS NOS.1-8 • 1968 • Vanderbeek Stan, Knowlton Kenneth • ASS • USA

POEM OF AN INLAND SEA see **POEMA O MORE** • 1958

POEM OF JEAN RICHEPIN, THE (USA) see **CANCION DE JEAN RICHEPIN, LA** • 1957

POEM OF LOVE see **POEMA LYUBVI** • 1954

POEM OF THE BLUE STAR, THE • 1961 • *Takarada Akira* • JPN

POEM OF THE SEA (USA) see **POEMA O MORE** • 1958

POEM OF TWO HEARTS, A see **POEMA DVUKH SERDYETS** • 1968

POEM OF YOUTH see **PEDAGOGUTCHESKAIA POEMA** • 1956

POEM POSTERS • 1967 • Ford Charles Henri • SHT • USA

POEMA DE FERNAN GONZALEZ, EL • Eguiluz Enrique L. • SHT • SPN

POEMA DVUKH SERDYETS • 1968 • Yarmatov Kamil • USS • POEM OF TWO HEARTS, A

POEMA LYUBVI • 1954 • Aimanov Shaken • USS • POEM OF LOVE

POEMA O MORE • 1958 • Dovzhenko Alexander, Solntseva Yulia • USS • POEM OF THE SEA (USA) ○ POEM ABOUT THE SEA ○ POEM OF AN INLAND SEA

POEMAT SYMFONICZNY "BAJKA" STANISLAWA MONIUSZKO • 1952 • Munk Andrzej • SHT • PLN • SYMPHONIC POEM FABLE OF STANISLAS MONIUSZKO, THE ○ BAJKA W URSUSIE ○ TALE OF URSUS, THE ○ URSUS ○ URSUSIE

POEME • Greenberg Bob • SHT • USA

POE'S TALES OF TERROR see **TALES OF TERROR** • 1962

POESIE, LA • 1973 • Bertolino Daniel • DCS • CND

POET, THE • 1957 • Barnet Boris • USS

POET, THE see **KEWI** • 1949

POET AND HIS BABIES, A • 1906 • Fitzhamon Lewin • UKN

POET AND MUSE see **RUNOILIJA JA MUUSA** • 1978

POET AND PAINTER • 1951 • Halas John • ASS • UKN • PAINTER AND POET

POET AND PEASANT • 1912 • Ranous William V. • USA

POET AND PEASANT • 1915 • *Briscoe Lottie* • USA

POET AND PEASANT • 1945 • Lundy Dick • ANS • USA

POET AND THE DEVIL, THE • 1983 • Rossenov Ivan • BUL

POET AND THE SOLDIER, THE • 1913 • *Blackwell Carlyle* • USA

POET AND TSAR • 1935 • Levine Moissej • USS

POET GYORGY FALUDY, THE see **FALUDY GYORGY KOLTO** • 1988

POET: IRVING LAYTON OBSERVED • 1986 • Winkler Donald • MTV • CND

POET IV MONTAN see **YVES MONTAND CHANTE** • 1956

POET MAYBE, A see **KANSKE EN DIKTARE** • 1933

POET MUKUNDADAS, THE see **CHARAN KAVI MUKUNDADAS** • 1968

POET NA EKRANE • 1973 • Yutkevich Sergei • MTV • USS • BARYSHNYA I CHULIGAN

POET OF THE PEAKS, THE • 1915 • Eason B. Reeves • USA

POET OF THE PEOPLE, THE • 1911 • *Thanhouser* • USA

POETA E LA LAGUNA, IL • 1920 • Gallone Carmine • ITL

POETE ET SA FOLLE AMANTE, LE • 1916 • Feuillade Louis • FRN

POETEN OG LILLEMOR • 1959 • Balling Erik • DNM

POETIC JUSTICE OF OMAR KHAN • 1915 • Le Saint Edward J. • USA

POETIC LICENSE • 1922 • Cooper George A. • UKN

POETRY IN MOTION • 1983 • Mann Ron • DOC • CND

POETRY OF ADALEN see **ADALENS POESI** • 1928

POETRY OF NATURE • 1939 • Freeman Mervyn • SHT • USA

POET'S BID FOR FAME, THE • 1907 • Cooper Arthur • UKN

POET'S BLOOD see **SANG D'UN POETE, LE** • 1930

POET'S EYE -A TRIBUTE TO WILLIAM SHAKESPEARE, THE • 1964 • Hales Gordon • UKN

POET'S LIFE, A • 1974 • Kawamoto Kihachiro • ANS • JPN

POET'S LONDON • 1959 • Russell Ken • MTV • UKN

POET'S PROGRESS, THE • 1916 • Moore Matt • SHT • USA

POET'S PUB • 1949 • Wilson Frederick • UKN

POET'S RETURN • 1962 • Tourtelot Madeline • USA

POET'S VISION, THE • 1909 • *Gaumont* • FRN

POET'S WINDFALL, THE • 1918 • Edwards Henry • UKN

POEZD IDET NA VOSTOK • 1947 • Raizman Yuli • USS • WESTWARD-BOUND TRAIN, THE ○ TRAIN GOES EAST, THE

POGI • 1967 • Navarro Marcelino D. • PHL • HANDSOME

POGI DOZEN, THE • 1967 • San Juan Luis • PHL • HANDSOME DOZEN, THE

POGLED U NOC • 1979 • Stojanovic Nikola • YGS • LOOKING INTO THE NIGHT

POGLED U ZJENICU SUNCA • 1966 • Bulajic Velko • YGS • GLANCE AT THE PUPIL OF THE SUN, A ○ GLANCE TO THE PUPIL OF THE SUN

POGO SPECIAL BIRTHDAY SPECIAL • 1971 • Jones Charles M. • ANM • USA

POGODA NA JUTRO • 1954 • Urbanowicz Stanislaw • DOC • PLN • TOMORROW'S WEATHER, THE ○ TOMORROW IT WILL BE FINE

POGON ZA ADAMEM see **W POGONI ZA ADAMEM** • 1969

POGONIA ZA LUIZEI • 1969 • *Studio C & D Divulgazione Scientifica* • USS

POGROM • 1919 • Halm Alfred • FRG

POGRZEB KARTOFLA • 1990 • Kolski Jan Jakub • PLN • BURYING THE POTATO

POHADKA MAJE • 1926 • Anton Karl • CZC • MAY STORY, THE ○ FABLE OF MAY ○ ROMANCE ○ MAYTIME TALE, A

POHADKA MAJE • 1940 • Vavra Otakar • CZC • MAY STORY, THE ○ FABLE OF MAY ○ ROMANCE ○ MAY FAIRY TALE ○ FAIRY TALE OF MAY

POHADKA O DRAKOVI • 1953 • Tyrlova Hermina • ANS • CZC • TAMING OF THE DRAGON, THE ○ CRUEL DRAGON

POHADKA O HONZIKOVI A MARENCE • 1980 • Zeman Karel • ANM • CZC • TALE OF JOHN AND MARY, THE

POHADKA O JENICKOVI A MARENCE • 1980 • Zeman Karel • ANM • CZC • STORY OF HANSEL AND GRETEL, THE

POHADKA O MALICKOVI • 1985 • Piesis Gunar • CZC, USS • FAIRY TALE OF MALICEK, THE

POHADKA O NEJBOHATSIM VRABCI • 1960 • Miler Zdenek • ANS • CZC • STORY OF THE RICHEST SPARROW, THE

POHADKA O PUTOVANI • 1982 • Mitta Alexander • CZC, USS • FAIRY-TALE OF PILGRIMAGE, THE

POHADKY TISICE A JEDNE NOCI • 1972 • Zeman Karel • ANM • CZC • ADVENTURES OF SINBAD THE SAILOR, THE ○ TALES OF 1001 NIGHTS ○ THOUSAND AND ONE NIGHTS, A ○ ARABIAN NIGHTS

POHJALAISIA • 1925 • Lahdensuo Jalmari • FNL • NORTHERNERS, THE

POHJAN TAHTEET • 1969 • Kokkonen Ere • FNL • SCRAPS AT THE BOTTOM

POHJANMAA • 1988 • Parikka Pekka • FNL • PLAINLANDS

POHLAD KOCCE USI! • 1985 • Pinkava Josef • CZC • STROKE THE CAT'S EARS!

POHOD • 1968 • Kadijevic Djordje • YGS • EXPEDITION ○ TREK, THE

POHORSKA VESNICE • 1928 • Krnansky M. J. • CZC • MOUNTAIN VILLAGE, THE

POI TI SPOSERO (ITL) see **MONSIEUR DE COMPAGNIE, UN** • 1964

POIDS DE L'ETIQUETTE: L'EPILEPSIE • 1975-77 • Moreau Michel • DCS • CND

POIGNANT STORY • 1962 • *Mori Masayuki* • JPN

POIGNARD FATAL, LE see **FEE CARABOSSE: OU, LE POIGNARD FATAL, LA** • 1906
POIGNARD MALAIS, LE • 1930 • Goupillieres Roger • FRN
POIGNEE DE RIZ, UNE see **MAN OCH KVINNA** • 1939
POIL DE CAROTTE • 1926 • Duvivier Julien • FRN
POIL DE CAROTTE • 1932 • Duvivier Julien • FRN • REDHEAD (USA)
POIL DE CAROTTE • 1951 • Mesnier Paul • FRN
POIL DE CAROTTE • 1972 • Graziani Henri • FRN
POILUS DE LA REVANCHE, LES • 1915 • Perret Leonce • FRN
POINT, THE • 1971 • Wolf Fred • ANM • USA
POINT BLANK • 1967 • Boorman John • USA
POINT BLANK see **PRESSURE POINT** • 1962
POINT DE CHUTE • 1970 • Hossein Robert • FRN
POINT DE FUITE, LE • 1971 • Roy Jean-Louis • SWT
POINT DE JOUR, LE • 1949 • Daquin Louis • FRN
POINT DE MIRE, LE • 1977 • Tramont Jean-Claude • FRN
POINT D'INTERROGATION • 1975 • Bokor Pierre • MTV • RMN
POINT DOLOUREUX, LE • 1978 • Bourgeois Marc • FRN
POINT FINAL A LA LIGNE • 1978 • Gallotte Jean-Francois • FRN
POINT IS TO CHANGE IT, THE (UKN) see **ES KOMMT DRAUF AN, SIE ZU VARANDERN** • 1973
POINT LOMA, OLD TOWN • 1912 • Dwan Allan • DOC • USA
POINT OF DEPARTURE • 1974 • McLennan Don • SHT • ASL
POINT OF DEPARTURE see **ATVALTOZAS** • 1984
POINT OF ESCAPE see **WAR BOY, THE** • 1984
POINT OF FLIGHT see **PUNTO DE FUGA**
POINT OF HONOUR • 1936 • Sparling Gordon • DCS • CND
POINT OF NEW DEPARTURE • 1956 • Villiers David • UKN
POINT OF ORDER! • 1964 • De Antonio Emile • DOC • USA
POINT OF RETURN • 1984 • SAF
POINT OF TERROR • 1971 • Nicol Alex • USA • SCREAM OF TERROR
POINT OF VIEW • 1965 • *Vision Associates* • SHT • USA
POINT OF VIEW see **UHOL POHLADU** • 1985
POINT OF VIEW, THE • 1911 • *Essanay* • USA
POINT OF VIEW, THE • 1920 • Crosland Alan • USA
POINT OF VIEW, THE see **WHITE AND UNMARRIED** • 1921
POINT OF VIEW DOG • 1973 • Spring Sylvia • CND
POINT PELEE, NATURE SANCTUARY • 1952 • Blais Roger • DCS • CND
POINT TO POINT see **NA PRZELAJ** • 1971
POINT TWO TWO see **STONE COLD DEAD** • 1979
POINTE COURTE, LA • 1955 • Varda Agnes • FRN • POINTE-COURTE, LA
POINTE-COURTE, LA see **POINTE COURTE, LA** • 1955
POINTE PELEE • 1976 • Mankiewicz Francis • CND
POINTED FINGER, THE • 1917 • Rice A. W. • SHT • USA
POINTED HEELS • 1929 • Sutherland A. Edward • USA
POINTED JOKE, A • 1914 • Kellino W. P. • UKN
POINTER, THE • 1939 • Geronimi Clyde • ANS • USA
POINTING FINGER, THE • 1919 • Kull Edward?, Morrisey Edward? • USA • NO EXPERIENCE REQUIRED
POINTING FINGER, THE • 1922 • Ridgwell George • UKN
POINTING FINGER, THE • 1933 • Pearson George • UKN
POINTS see **DOTS** • 1940
POINTS FOR PARENTAGE see **PUNKTY ZA POCHODZENIS** • 1983
POINTS OF REFERENCE • 1959 • Leacock Richard • DOC • USA
POINTS WEST • 1929 • Rosson Arthur • USA
POINTSMAN, THE see **WISSELWACHTER, DE** • 1987
POIRIER DE MISERE, LE • 1957 • Coignon Jean • ANS • BLG • PEAR-TREE OF MISERY, THE
POIS FOU, LE • 1972 • Belanger Fernand • MTV • CND
POISON • 1914 • *Frontier* • USA
POISON • 1915 • *Moore Tom* • USA
POISON • 1924 • Chapin James • USA
POISON see **GIFT** • 1966
POISON, LA • 1951 • Guitry Sacha • FRN • POISON (USA)
POISON, LE • 1911 • Feuillade Louis • FRN
POISON AFFAIR, THE see **AFFAIRE DES POISONS, L'** • 1955
POISON DE L'HUMANITE, LE • 1912 • Chautard Emile • FRN
POISON DE L'HUMANITE, LE • 1912-13 • Jasset Victorin • FRN
POISON FOR FAIRIES see **VENENO PARA LAS HADAS** • 1985
POISON IVY • 1913 • Fetterer Harry • USA
POISON IVY • 1985 • Elikann Larry • TVM • USA
POISON IVY (USA) see **MOME VERT-DE-GRIS, LA** • 1952
POISON LABEL, THE • 1911 • Aylott Dave • UKN
POISON OF GOLD, THE see **GULDETS GIFT** • 1916
POISON OR WHISKEY • 1905 • Fitzhamon Lewin • UKN • LOVER'S RUSE, THE (USA)
POISON PEN • 1939 • Stein Paul L. • UKN
POISON PEN, THE • 1919 • August Edwin • USA
POISON ROAD see **CAIRO ROAD** • 1950
POISON (USA) see **POISON, LA** • 1951
POISONED ARROWS • 1911 • *Pathe* • USA
POISONED BIT, THE • 1914 • Kendall Preston • USA
POISONED BOUQUET, THE • 1908 • *Vitagraph* • USA
POISONED BY JEALOUSY • 1915 • West Langdon • USA
POISONED CHOP, THE • 1913 • Ricketts Thomas • USA
POISONED CUP, THE • 1911 • *Reliance* • USA
POISONED CUP, THE • 1917 • Hurst Paul C. • SHT • USA
POISONED DART, THE • 1916 • Horne James W. • SHT • USA
POISONED DARTS, THE • 1913 • Melies Gaston • USA
POISONED DIAMOND, THE • 1934 • Kellino W. P. • UKN
POISONED FLOWER, THE see **ZEHIRLI CICEK** • 1967
POISONED FLUME, THE • 1911 • Dwan Allan • USA
POISONED IVORY • 1934 • Goulding Alf • SHT • USA
POISONED LIFE see **ZEHIRLI HAYAT** • 1967
POISONED LIPS • 1916 • Ford Francis • SHT • USA
POISONED LIPS see **ZEHIRLI DUDAKLAR** • 1967
POISONED PARADISE: THE FORBIDDEN STORY OF MONTE CARLO • 1924 • Gasnier Louis J. • USA
POISONED POOL, THE • 1912 • *Eclair* • USA
POISONED STREAM, THE • 1913 • *Gebhardt George* • USA
POISONED WATERS • 1913 • Fahrney Milton • USA
POISONER, THE (UKN) see **SADDLE LEATHER LAW** • 1944
POISONERS, THE • 1912 • *Champion* • USA
POISONING THE WELL • 1901 • *Mitchell & Kenyon* • UKN
POISONOUS ARROW, THE see **GIFTPILEN** • 1915
POISONOUS DOWRY see **MITGIFT** • 1975
POISONOUS LOVE, A see **FADER OG SON** • 1911
POISONOUS TUSKS see **DOKUGA** • 1967
POISONS • Sajko Mako • DCS • YGS
POISSON CHINOIS, LE see **BATAILLE SILENCIEUSE, LA** • 1937
POISSON D'AVRIL • 1954 • Grangier Gilles • FRN
POISSON DISPUTE, UN • 1912 • Cohl Emile • ANS • FRN
POISSON PROF, THE • SHT • FRN • FISH PROFESSOR, THE
POISSONS, LES • Williams Lloyd Michael • SHT • USA
POITIN • 1978 • Quinn Bob • IRL
POJAT • 1962 • Niskanen Mikko • FNL • BOYS, THE
POJDTE NAMI • 1938 • *Hammid Alexander* • CZC • COME WITH US
POJDTE, PANE, BUDEME SI HRAT! • 1965-67 • Pojar Bretislav • ANM • CZC • COME AND PLAY, SIR
POJEDYNEK • 1964 • Majewski Janusz • PLN • DUEL, THE
POJEDYNEK PROFESOTA FILUTKA • 1956 • Wajzer Waclaw • PLN • PROFESSOR FILUTEK'S DUEL
POJKARNA PA STORHOLMEN • 1932 • Wallen Sigurd • SWD • BOYS OF STORHOLMEN, THE
POJKEN I TRADET • 1961 • Sucksdorff Arne • DOC • SWD • BOY IN THE TREE, THE
POJKEN OCH DRACKEN • 1961 • Widerberg Bo, Troell Jan • SWD • BOY AND THE KITE, THE
POKA .NE. POZDNO • 1958 • Zalakevicius Vitautus • USS • IT'S NOT TOO LATE ○ BEFORE IT'S TOO LATE
POKAL DER FURSTIN, DER • 1920 • Ziener Bruno • FRG
POKER • 1920 • Fleischer Dave • ANS • USA • CARD GAME, THE
POKER • 1951 • Bernhard Gosta • SWD
POKER D'AS • 1928 • Desfontaines Henri • FRN
POKER ALICE • 1987 • Seidelman Arthur Allan • TVM • USA
POKER AT EIGHT • 1935 • Parrott Charles • SHT • USA
POKER D'AS POUR DJANGO • 1968 • Montero Roberto Bianchi • ITL, FRN
POKER DE ASES • 1952 • Cardona Rene • MXC
POKER DE REINAS • 1958 • Alazraki Benito • MXC
POKER DI PISTOLE, UN • 1967 • Vari Giuseppe • ITL • POKER WITH PISTOLS
POKER FACES • 1926 • Pollard Harry • USA
POKER MENTEUSES ET REVOLVER MATIN • 1980 • Van De Putte Christine • FRN
POKER PAYED • 1913 • Smiley Joseph • USA
POKER WIDOWS • 1931 • *Sennett Mack (P)* • SHT • USA • POKER WINDOWS
POKER WINDOWS see **POKER WIDOWS** • 1931
POKER WITH PISTOLS see **POKER DI PISTOLE, UN** • 1967
POKERSPIEL • 1966 • Kluge Alexander • SHT • FRG
POKES AND JABBS • 1915 • *Burns & Stull* • USA
POKES AND JABBS IN A QUIET GAME • 1915 • *Burns & Stull* • USA
POKES AND JABBS IN ONE BUSY DAY • 1915 • *Burns & Stull* • USA
POKES AND JABBS IN TWO FOR A QUARTER • 1915 • *Burns & Stull* • USA
POKFOCI • 1977 • Rozsa Janos • HNG • SPIDER FOOTBALL
POKHALO • 1938 • Balazs Maria • HNG
POKHALO • 1973 • Mihalyfi Imre • HNG • COBWEB
POKHOZDENIYA OKTYABRINI • 1924 • Kozintsev Grigori, Trauberg Leonid • USS • ADVENTURES OF AN OCTOBERITE, THE (USA) ○ ADVENTURES OF OCTYABRINI, THE
POKJANIYEAKA, MONANIEBA • 1984 • Abuladze Tengiz • USS • REPENTANCE
POKKERS UNGER, DE • 1947 • Henning-Jensen Astrid, Henning-Jensen Bjarne • DNM • THOSE BLASTED KIDS
POKKUVARIL • 1981 • Aravindan G. • IND • TWILIGHT
POKLAD NO PTACIM OSTROVE see **POKLAD PTACIHO OSTROVA** • 1952
POKLAD PTACIHO OSTROVA • 1952 • Zeman Karel • CZC • TREASURE OF BIRD ISLAND, THE ○ POKLAD NO PTACIM OSTROVE
POKO • 1981 • Ouedraogo Idrissa • SHT • BRK
POKOJ Z WIDOKIEM NA MORZE • 1977 • Zaorski Janusz • PLN • ROOM WITH A VIEW ON THE SEA, A ○ ROOM OVERLOOKING THE SEA, A
POKOJ ZDOBEDZIE SWIAT • 1951 • Bossak Jerzy, Ivens Joris • DOC • PLN • PEACE WILL CONQUER THE WORLD ○ POKOJ ZWYCIEZY SWIAT ○ PEACE CONQUERS THE WORLD ○ PEACE WILL WIN
POKOJ ZWYCIEZY SWIAT see **POKOJ ZDOBEDZIE SWIAT** • 1951
POKOLENIE • 1954 • Wajda Andrzej • PLN • GENERATION, A (USA) ○ LIGHT IN THE DARKNESS
POKOLENIYE POBEDITELI • 1936 • Stroyeva Vera • USS • GENERATION OF CONQUERORS ○ REVOLUTIONISTS
POKORITELI MORYA • 1959 • Karmen Roman • USS • CONQUERED SEAS
POKPOONGEA UHUNDUCK • 1960 • Hobin Paik • SKR • WUTHERING HEIGHTS ○ ON THE STORMY HILL
POKUS O VRAZDU • 1973 • Sequens Jiri • CZC • ATTEMPTED MURDER
POKUSENI • 1957 • Kachyna Karel • CZC • TEMPTATION
POKUSENI PANI ANTONIE • 1934 • Slavinsky Vladimir • CZC • TEMPTATION OF MRS. ANTONIE, THE
POLACY DO BRONI! • 1945 • Bossak Jerzy • PLN • POLES, TO ARMS!
POLAND'S CHILDREN see **POLENS BORN** • 1947
POLAO E MAKATSANG • 1985 • SAF
POLAR • 1984 • Bral Jacques • FRN
POLAR FRIGHT • 1966 • Smith Paul J. • ANS • USA
POLAR LIFE • 1967 • Ferguson Graeme • DCS • CND
POLAR PALS • 1931 • Foster John, Rufle George • ANS • USA
POLAR PALS • 1939 • Clampett Robert • ANS • USA
POLAR PERILS • 1928 • Roberts Stephen • SHT • USA
POLAR PESTS • 1958 • Avery Tex • ANS • USA
POLAR PESTS • 1958 • Lovy Alex • ANS • USA
POLAR PLAYMATES • 1946 • Swift Howard • ANS • USA
POLAR POWER • 1972 • Gormley Charles • DCS • UKN
POLAR ROMANCE, A • 1915 • Hunt Jay • USA
POLAR STAR, THE • 1919 • Bocchi Arrigo • UKN
POLAR TRAPPERS • 1938 • Sharpsteen Ben • ANS • USA
POLARE • 1976 • Halldoff Jan • SWD • BUDDIES
POLARISED LIGHT • 1960 • Vas Judit • DOC • HNG • POLARIZED LIGHT
POLARIZED LIGHT see **POLARISED LIGHT** • 1960
POLAROID • 1978 • Schouten George • NTH • INSTANT PICTURES (USA)
POLDIEN • 1931 • Heifitz Josif, Zarkhi Alexander • USS • NOON (USA) ○ MIDDAY
POLE POPPENSPALER see **PUPPENSPIELER, DER** • 1945
POLECHKO • 1930 • Medvedkin Alexander • USS
POLEMONTA • 1975 • Mavrikios Dimitris • GRC
POLENBLUT • 1934 • Lamac Carl • FRG, CZC • POLSKA KREV (CZC) ○ POLISH BLOOD (USA)
POLENBLUT see **LETZTEN KOLCZAKS, DIE** • 1920
POLENS BORN • 1947 • Lichtenberg Nicolai • DNM • POLAND'S CHILDREN
POLENTA • 1981 • Simon Maya • SWT
POLEON, THE TRAPPER • 1913 • *Nestor* • USA
POLES, TO ARMS! see **POLACY DO BRONI!** • 1945
POLI ARGA YIA DHAKRIA • 1968 • Glykofridis Panos • GRC • VERY LATE FOR TEARS ○ TEARS OF REMORSE
POLIBEK ZE STADIONU • 1948 • Fric Martin • CZC • KISS FROM THE STADIUM, A
POLICARPO (FRN) see **POLICARPO UFFICIALE DI SCITTURA** • 1959
POLICARPO, MASTER WRITER see **POLICARPO UFFICIALE DI SCITTURA** • 1959
POLICARPO UFFICIALE DI SCITTURA • 1959 • Soldati Mario • ITL, FRN, SPN • POLICARPO (FRN) ○ POLICARPO, MASTER WRITER
POLICE! • 1916 • Chaplin Charles • SHT • USA • CHARLIE THE BURGLAR
POLICE • 1958 • Macartney-Filgate Terence • DOC • CND
POLICE • 1986 • Pialat Maurice • FRN
POLICE 1111 see **POLICE NR.1111** • 1916
POLICE ACADEMY • 1983 • Wilson Hugh • USA
POLICE ACADEMY 2: THEIR FIRST ASSIGNMENT • 1985 • Paris Jerry • USA
POLICE ACADEMY 3: BACK IN TRAINING • 1986 • Paris Jerry • USA
POLICE ACADEMY 4: CITIZENS ON PATROL • 1987 • Drake Jim • USA
POLICE ACADEMY 5: ASSIGNMENT MIAMI • 1988 • Myerson Alan • USA
POLICE ACADEMY 6: CITY UNDER SIEGE • 1989 • Bonerz Peter • USA
POLICE ACCUSE, THE see **POLIZIA ACCUSA: IL SERVIZIO SEGRETO UCCIDE, LA** • 1975
POLICE AMBULANCE see **AGAINST THE LAW** • 1934
POLICE AND SMALL GANGSTERS see **KEISATSU-KAN TO BORYOKU-DAN** • 1959
POLICE ASSASSINS • 1986 • Chung Chi-Man Davi • HKG
POLICE ASSASSINS 2 • 1987 • *Khan Michelle* • HKG
POLICE BULLETS • 1942 • Yarbrough Jean • USA
POLICE CALL • 1933 • Whitman Phil • USA • WANTED (UKN)
POLICE CALL 9000 see **DETROIT 9000** • 1973
POLICE CAN'T MOVE, THE see **POLIZIA HA LE MANI LEGATE, LA** • 1975
POLICE CAR 17 • 1933 • Hillyer Lambert • USA
POLICE CHIEF, THE • 1916 • Heerman Victor • USA • STARS AND BARS
POLICE CONNECTION, THE • 1976 • Gordon Bert I. • USA • DETECTIVE GERONIMO
POLICE COURT • 1932 • King Louis • USA • SON OF MINE (UKN)
POLICE DES MOEURS: LES FILLES DE SAINT TROPEZ • 1986 • Boisserie Nicole • FRN • SAINT TROPEZ VICE
POLICE DIARY see **KEISATSU NIKKI** • 1955
POLICE DOG • 1915 • Anderson Vet • ASS • USA
POLICE DOG • 1955 • Twist Derek • UKN
POLICE DOG STORY, THE • 1961 • Cahn Edward L. • USA
POLICE DOGGED • 1956 • Rasinski Connie • ANS • USA
POLICE FANG: RAZOR HANZO'S TORTURE IN HELL see **GOYOUKIBA: KAMISORI HANZO JIGOKUZEME** • 1973
POLICE FILM see **POLIZEIFILM** • 1968
POLICE FORCE see **POLICE STORY** • 1986
POLICE GIRLS ACADEMY • 1987 • Hieronymous Richard • USA
POLICE IN ACTION: CONFESSIONS OF A LADY COP see **CONFESSIONS OF A LADY COP** • 1988
POLICE IN REALITY, THE see **POLITIET I VIRKELIGHEDEN** • 1987
POLICE INSPECTOR, THE • 1913 • *Belmont* • USA
POLICE INSPECTOR ACCUSES, A see **COMISAR ACUZA, UN** • 1973
POLICE INSPECTOR PALMU see **KOMISARIO PALMU** • 1960-69
POLICE JUDICIAIRE • 1958 • de Canonge Maurice • FRN
POLICE MONDAINE • 1937 • Bernheim Michel, Chamborant Christian • FRN • CEUX DE LA MONDAINE
POLICE MURDERER see **108-GO-SHA** • 1959
POLICE NR.1111 • 1916 • Piel Harry • FRG • POLICE 1111
POLICE NURSE • 1963 • Dexter Maury • USA
POLICE OF THE FUTURE, THE • 1910 • *Gaumont* • USA
POLICE PATROL, THE • 1925 • King Burton L. • USA
POLICE PROTECTION • 1917 • *Myers Harry* • USA
POLICE PYTHON 357 • 1976 • Corneau Alain • FRN, ITL, FRG • CASE AGAINST FERRO, THE (USA)
POLICE RAID see **ZATAH** • 1985
POLICE SECRETE see **BULISS AS-SIRRI, AL-** • 1958
POLICE SQUAD! • 1982 • Abrahams Jim, Zucker David, Zucker Jerry, Dante Joe, Badiyi Reza • TVM • USA
POLICE STORY • 1973 • Graham William A. • TVM • USA • STAKE OUT, THE
POLICE STORY • 1986 • Chan Jackie • HKG • JACKIE CHAN'S POLICE STORY ○ JINGCHA GUSHI ○ POLICE FORCE
POLICE STORY PART II see **GINGTSAT GUSI TSUKTSAP** • 1988
POLICE STORY: THE FREEWAY KILLINGS • 1987 • Graham William A. • TVM • USA • FREEWAY KILLINGS, THE
POLICEJNI HODINA • 1960 • Vavra Otakar • CZC • TIME, GENTLEMEN, PLEASE ○ CLOSING HOUR, THE
POLICEMAN • 1971 • Rossi Sergio • ITL
POLICEMAN • 1978 • Lee Doo-Yong • SKR
POLICEMAN, THE see **VIGILE, IL** • 1960
POLICEMAN, THE (USA) see **HASHOTER AZULAI** • 1971
POLICEMAN AND THE BABY, THE • 1913 • Kirkland Hardee • USA

POLICEMAN OF THE 16TH PRECINCT, THE • 1963 • Sakellarios Alekos • GRC
POLICEMAN THE COOK AND THE COPPER, THE • 1898 • Smith G. A. • UKN
POLICEMAN'S CHRISTMAS EVE, THE • 1909 • *Lubin* • USA
POLICEMAN'S DREAM, A • 1902 • Collins Alf? • UKN
POLICEMAN'S LOT, A • 1985 • Bertelsson Thrainn • ICL
POLICEMAN'S LOVE AFFAIR, THE • 1906 • Cooper Arthur • UKN
POLICEMAN'S SON, A • 1910 • *Imp* • USA
POLICEMAN'S TROUBLES, A see **CAUCHEMAR DU PECHEUR, LE** • 1905
POLICEMAN'S VISION • 1908 • *Pathe* • FRN
POLICEWOMAN • 1974 • Frost Lee • USA
POLICEWOMAN CENTERFOLD • 1983 • Badiyi Reza • TVM • USA
POLICHE • 1928 • Chekhova Olga • USS
POLICHE • 1934 • Gance Abel • FRN
POLICIA BRANCOLA NEL BUIO, LA • 1974 • Colombo Helia • ITL
POLICIAS Y LADRONES • 1956 • Galindo Alejandro • MXC
POLICY MAN • 1938 • *Basie Count* • SHT • USA
POLICY OF PINPRICKS, A • 1913 • Plumb Hay? • UKN
POLIDOR AL CLUB DELLA MORTE • 1912 • *Guillaume Fernando* • ITL • POLIDOR AT THE DEATH CLUB
POLIDOR AT THE DEATH CLUB see **POLIDOR AL CLUB DELLA MORTE** • 1912
POLIJUSCHKA see **POLIKUSKA** • 1958
POLIKUSCHKA (FRG) see **POLIKUSKA** • 1958
POLIKUSHKA • 1919 • Sanin Alexander • USS
POLIKUSKA • 1958 • Gallone Carmine • ITL, FRN, FRG • POLIKUSCHKA (FRG) ○ POLIJUSCHKA
POLIN • 1900-07 • Blache Alice • SER • FRN
POLIO -DIAGNOSIS AND MANAGEMENT • 1948 • Innes Geoffrey • DOC • UKN
POLIOTY VO SNE I NAIAVOU • 1983 • Balayan Roman • USS • FLIGHTS BETWEEN DREAM AND REALITY ○ DREAM FLIGHTS ○ DREAM FLIGHT
POLIS PAULUS PASKASMALL • 1925 • Molander Gustaf • SWD • CONSTABLE PAULUS'S EASTER BOMB
POLISH ALBUM see **ALBUM POLSKI** • 1970
POLISH AND PIE • 1911 • *Sutton Charles* • USA
POLISH BLOOD (USA) see **POLENBLUT** • 1934
POLISH CONTEMPORARY SCULPTURE see **POLSKA PZEZBA WSPOLCZESNA** • 1964
POLISH CUISINE see **KUCHNIA POLSKA** • 1990
POLISH JEW, THE see **JUIF POLONAIS, LE** • 1925
POLISH PASSION see **IT BEGAN ON THE VISTULA** • 1966
POLISH SUITE see **SUITA POLSKA** • 1963
POLISH VAMPIRE IN BURBANK • 1985 • Pirro Mark • USA
POLISHED BURGLAR, A • 1911 • *Essanay* • USA
POLISHING UP • 1914 • Baker George D. • USA
POLISHING UP POLLY • 1915 • King Burton L. • USA
POLITE INVASION, THE • 1960 • Zetterling Mai • DCS • UKN
POLITE LUNATIC, THE • 1905 • Williamson James • UKN
POLITE PARSON, THE • 1909 • Smith Jack ? • UKN
POLITENESS PAYS • 1914 • *Gane Nolan* • USA
POLITENESS PAYS • 1916 • *Junior John* • SHT • USA
POLITIC FLAPPER, THE (UKN) see **PATSY, THE** • 1928
POLITICAL ASYLUM • 1972 • *Brazzi Rossano* • GTM
POLITICAL BOSS, THE • 1914 • *Kalem* • USA
POLITICAL DISCUSSION, A • 1903 • Collins Alf? • UKN
POLITICAL DUEL, A see **DUEL POLITIQUE** • 1899
POLITICAL DYNAMITE • 1962 • Haldane Don • CND
POLITICAL FAVOURITES • 1904 • *Paul R. W.* • UKN
POLITICAL FEUD, A • 1914 • Ince Thomas H., Spencer Richard V.?, Stanton Richard? • USA
POLITICAL KIDNAPPING, A • 1912 • *Kalem* • USA
POLITICAL MESS, A • 1915 • *Joker* • USA
POLITICAL PARTY, A • 1934 • Lee Norman • UKN
POLITICAL PORTRAITS • 1969 • Markopoulos Gregory J. • USA
POLITICAL PULL • 1924 • Roach Hal • SHT • USA
POLITICAL PULL OF JOHN, THE • 1915 • *Thanhouser* • USA
POLITICAL THEATRE see **SOSHI GEKIJO** • 1947
POLITICAL TRAMP, A • 1916 • Chaudet Louis W. • SHT • USA
POLITICIAN, THE • 1913 • *Johnstone Lamar* • USA
POLITICIAN OR VOTE FOR ME, THE • Ravetz Joe • SHT • USA
POLITICIANS • 1970 • Gross Yoram • ANS • ASL
POLITICIANS, THE • 1915 • *Bickel George* • USA
POLITICIANS, THE • 1970 • Ashburne Derek • USA • NAKED ARE THE CHEATERS (UKN)
POLITICIAN'S DREAM, THE • 1911 • Thompson Frederick A. • USA
POLITICIAN'S LOVE STORY, THE • 1909 • Griffith D. W. • USA
POLITICKERS • 1916 • *Cooper Claude* • USA
POLITICS • 1910 • *Selig* • USA
POLITICS • 1931 • Reisner Charles F. • USA
POLITICS see **SIASAT** • 1986
POLITICS AND SUFFRAGETTES • 1914 • *Ab* • USA
POLITICS AND THE PRESS • 1914 • Brooke Van Dyke • USA
POLITICS AT PUMPKIN CORNER see **POLITICS IN PUMPKIN CENTER** • 1917
POLITICS IN PUMPKIN CENTER • 1917 • Santell Alfred • SHT • USA • POLITICS AT PUMPKIN CORNER
POLITICS OF PERSUASION, THE • 1983 • Defalco Martin • MTV • CND
POLITIET I VIRKELIGHEDEN • 1987 • Bonfils Dola • DOC • DNM • POLICE IN REALITY, THE
POLITIK OCH BROTT • 1916 • Magnussen Fritz • SWD
POLITIMESTEREN • 1911 • Blom August • DNM • CONVICTS NO.10 AND NO.13
POLITISCHE TEPPICH, DER • 1922 • Herald Heinz • FRG
POLITZEI • 1988 • Goren Serif • TRK
POLIZEIAKTE 909 • 1934 • Wiene Robert • FRG • FALL TOKERAMO, DER ○ TAIFUN
POLIZEIBERICHT MELDET, DER • 1934 • Jacoby Georg • FRG
POLIZEIBERICHT UEBERFALL see **UBERFALL, DER** • 1928
POLIZEIFILM • 1968 • Wenders Wim • SHT • FRG • POLICE FILM
POLIZEIFUNK MELDET, DER • 1939 • van der Noss Rudolf • FRG
POLIZEIREVIER DAVIDSWACHE (ST. PAULI) • 1964 • Roland Jurgen • FRG • SEVEN CONSENTING ADULTS (USA) ○ HAMBURG -CITY OF VICE (UKN) ○ HAMBURG OFF-LIMITS
POLIZEISPIONIN 77 • 1929 • Wolff Willi • FRG
POLIZIA A VILLABIANCA, LA see **CORTOCIRCUITO** • 1943
POLIZIA ACCUSA: IL SERVIZIO SEGRETO UCCIDE, LA • 1975 • Martino Sergio • ITL • POLICE ACCUSE, THE ○ SILENT ACTION
POLIZIA CHIEDE AIUTO, LA • 1974 • Dallamano Massimo • ITL
POLIZIA E AL SERVIZIO DEL CITTADINO, LA • 1973 • Guerrieri Romolo • ITL
POLIZIA E SCONFITTA, LA • 1977 • Paolella Domenico • ITL
POLIZIA HA LE MANI LEGATE, LA • 1975 • Ercoli Luciano • ITL • POLICE CAN'T MOVE, THE ○ KILLER COP
POLIZIA INCRIMINA, LA LEGGE ASSOLVE, LA • 1973 • Castellari Enzo G. • ITL, SPN • HIGH CRIME (USA)
POLIZIA INTERVIENE: ORDINE DI UCCIDERE!, LA • 1975 • Rosati Giuseppe • ITL • LEFT HAND OF THE LAW, THE
POLIZIA RINGRAZIA, LA • 1972 • Steno • ITL, FRG • LAW ENFORCERS, THE (UKN) ○ EXECUTION SQUAD (USA)
POLIZIA STA A GUARDARE, LA • 1973 • Infascelli Roberto • ITL • GREAT KIDNAPPING, THE
POLIZIA VUOLE GIUSTIZIA, LA see **MILANO TREMA: LA POLIZIA VUOLE GIUSTIZIA** • 1973
POLIZIOTTA, LA • 1974 • Steno • ITL
POLIZIOTTA DELLA SQUADRA DEL BUON COSTUME, LA • 1979 • Tarantini Michele Massimo • ITL
POLIZIOTTA FA CARRIERA, LA • 1976 • Tarantini Michele Massimo • ITL
POLIZIOTTI VIOLENTI • 1976 • Tarantini Michele Massimo • ITL
POLIZIOTTO DELLA BRIGATA CRIMINALE, IL (ITL) see **PEUR SUR LA VILLE** • 1975
POLIZIOTTO E MARCIO, LA • 1974 • Di Leo Fernando • ITL • SHOOT FIRST, DIE LATER (USA)
POLIZIOTTO SCOMODO, UN • 1978 • Massi Stelvio • ITL • CONVOY BUSTERS
POLIZIOTTO SENZA PAURA • 1978 • Massi Stelvio • ITL, AUS • FEARLESS FUZZ ○ FEARLESS
POLIZIOTTO SPRINT • 1977 • Massi Stelvio • ITL
POLIZIOTTO SUPERPIU see **SUPER FUZZ** • 1981
POLIZON A BORDO • 1941 • Rey Florian • SPN
POLJUBAC • 1970 • Pavlinic Zlatko • ANS • YGS • KISS, THE
POLK FILE ON THE AIR • 1988 • Grigoratos Dionisis • GRC
POLKA DES MENOTTES, LES • 1957 • Andre Raoul • FRN
POLKA DOT PUSS • 1949 • Hanna William, Barbera Joseph • ANS • USA
POLKA-GRAPH • 1953 • Bute Mary Ellen, Nemeth Ted J. • ANS • USA
POLKA ON BRAIN • 1909 • *Urban-Eclipse* • USA
POLKA ON THE BRAIN • 1908 • Booth W. R. • UKN
POLLIORKA see **A L'AUBE DU TROISIEME JOUR** • 1962
POLLUTED ONES, THE • 1983 • Lim Kwon-Taek • SKR
POLLUTION • Conrad James • ANS • USA
POLLUTION FRONT-LINE • 1972 • Hewitson Walford • CND
POLLUX AND THE BLUE CAT see **POLLUX ET LE CHAT BLEU** • 1970
POLLUX ET LE CHAT BLEU • 1970 • Danot Serge, Thompson Eric • ANM • FRN, UKN • DOUGAL AND THE BLUE CAT (UKN) ○ POLLUX AND THE BLUE CAT
POLLY • 1921 • Paul Fred • UKN
POLLY ANN • 1917 • Miller Charles • USA • PERNICKETY POLLY ANN
POLLY AT THE RANCH • 1913 • Sturgeon Rollin S. • USA
POLLY FULTON (UKN) see **B.F.'S DAUGHTER** • 1948
POLLY ME LOVE • 1976 • Maxwell Peter • MTV • ASL
POLLY OF THE CIRCUS • 1917 • Horan Charles, Hollywood Edwin L. • USA
POLLY OF THE CIRCUS • 1932 • Santell Alfred • USA
POLLY OF THE FOLLIES • 1922 • Emerson John • USA • GOOD FOR NOTHING
POLLY-OF-THE-POTS-AND-PANS • 1915 • Ince John • USA
POLLY OF THE STORM COUNTRY • 1920 • Rosson Arthur • USA
POLLY PUT THE KETTLE ON • 1917 • Gerrard Douglas • USA
POLLY REDHEAD • 1917 • Conway Jack • USA
POLLY THE GIRL SCOUT • 1911 • Coleby A. E. • UKN
POLLY THE GIRL SCOUT AND GRANDPA'S MEDALS • 1913 • Haldane Bert • UKN
POLLY THE GIRL SCOUT AND THE JEWEL THIEVES • 1913 • Haldane Bert? • UKN
POLLY THE GIRL SCOUT'S TIMELY AID • 1913 • Haldane Bert? • UKN
POLLY-TIX IN WASHINGTON • 1933 • Lamont Charles • SHT • USA • POLLY TIX IN WASHINGTON
POLLY TIX IN WASHINGTON see **POLLY-TIX IN WASHINGTON** • 1933
POLLY WANTS A DOCTOR • 1944 • Swift Howard • ANS • USA
POLLY WITH A PAST • 1920 • De Cordova Leander • USA
POLLYANNA • 1920 • Powell Paul • USA
POLLYANNA • 1960 • Swift David • USA
POLLY'S EXCURSION • 1908 • Coleby A. E. • UKN
POLLY'S PROGRESS • 1914 • Trimble Larry • UKN
POLLY'S TWO FATHERS • 1936 • Hammer Will • UKN
"POLLYWOGS" PICNIC, THE • 1915 • *Hamilton Lloyd V.* • USA
POLNISCHE WIRTSCHAFT • 1928 • Emo E. W. • FRG
POLNOCNA OMSA • 1962 • Krejcik Jiri • CZC • MIDNIGHT MASS
POLO • 1936 • Sidney George • SHT • USA
POLO CHAMPION, THE • 1915 • Hagon M. • UKN
POLO CHAMPIONS, THE • 1914 • *Asher Max* • USA
POLO GAMES, BROOKLYN • 1900 • *Bitzer Billy (Ph)* • USA
POLO JOE • 1936 • McGann William • USA
POLO PHONY, A • 1941 • D'Arcy Harry • SHT • USA
POLO SUBSTITUTE, THE • 1912 • *Bosworth Hobart* • USA
POLONAIS DU CANADA, LES • 1954-55 • Devlin Bernard • DCS • CND
POLONAISE • 1989 • Weisz Frans • NTH
POLONAISE see **POLONEZ** • 1967
POLONAISE, LA • 1971 • Etaix Pierre • SHT • FRN
POLONEZ • 1967 • Gradowski Bohdan • DOC • PLN • POLONAISE
POLONIA-EXPRESS • 1957 • Jung-Alsen Kurt • GDR
POLOWANIE NA MUCHY • 1969 • Wajda Andrzej • PLN • HUNTING FLIES ○ FLIES HUNTING ○ FLY HUNT, THE
POLOWANIE W BIALOWIEZY • 1935 • Bohdziewicz Antoni • SHT • PLN • HUNTING IN THE BIALOWIEZA FOREST
POLSKA KREV (CZC) see **POLENBLUT** • 1934
POLSKA KRONIKA FILMOVA NR 52 A-B see **KRONIKA JUBILEUSZOWA** • 1959
POLSKA PZEZBA WSPOLCZESNA • 1964 • Gordon Konstanty • PLN • POLISH CONTEMPORARY SCULPTURE
POLTERABEND • 1940 • Boese Carl • FRG
POLTERABEND, EIN • 1955 • Bois Curt • GDR
POLTERGEIST • 1982 • Hooper Tobe • USA
POLTERGEIST II • 1986 • Gibson Brian • USA • POLTERGEIST II -THE OTHER SIDE
POLTERGEIST II -THE OTHER SIDE see **POLTERGEIST II** • 1986
POLTERGEIST III • 1988 • Sherman Gary • USA
POLTRON • 1989 • Prelic Svetislav Bata • YGS • POLTROON, THE
POLTROON, THE see **POLTRON** • 1989
POLUDENNY PAROM • 1967 • Kiisk Kaliu • USS • NOON FERRY, THE
POLUDNIK ZERO • 1970 • Podgorski Waldemar • PLN • MERIDIAN ZERO
POLUSTANOK • 1963 • Barnet Boris • USS • WHISTLE STOP
POLVERE DI STELLE • 1973 • Sordi Alberto • ITL
POLVO DE LUX • 1988 • Gonzalez Christian • MXC • LIGHT SPECKS
POLVO ERES • 1974 • Escriva Vicente • SPN
POLVO ROJO • 1982 • Diaz Jesus • CUB • RED DUST
POLVO VENCEDOR DEL SOL • 1979 • de la Riva Juan Antonio • SHT • MXC • DUST, VICTOR OVER THE SUN
POLVORILLA • 1956 • Rey Florian • SPN
POLYECRAN FOR INTERNATIONAL EXPOSITION OF LABOR TURIN see **POLYEKRAN PRO MEZINARODNI VYSTAVU PRACE TURIN** • 1961
POLYECRAN FOR THE BRNO INDUSTRIAL FAIR see **POLYEKRAN PRO BVV** • 1960
POLYEKRAN PRO BVV • 1960 • Jires Jaromil (c/d) • DCS • CZC • POLYECRAN FOR THE BRNO INDUSTRIAL FAIR
POLYEKRAN PRO MEZINARODNI VYSTAVU PRACE TURIN • 1961 • Jires Jaromil (c/d) • DCS • CZC • POLYECRAN FOR INTERNATIONAL EXPOSITION OF LABOR TURIN
POLYESTER • 1981 • Waters John* • USA
POLYGAMOUS POLONIUS • 1960 • Godfrey Bob • ANS • UKN
POLYGAMOUS POLONIUS REVISITED • 1985 • Godfrey Bob • ANS • UKN
POLYKARP APROVIZUJE • 1917 • Kolar J. S. • CZC • POLYKARP ON THE BLACK MARKET
POLYKARP ON THE BLACK MARKET see **POLYKARP APROVIZUJE** • 1917
POLYKARPOVO ZIMNI DOBRODRUZSTVI • 1917 • Kolar J. S. • CZC • POLYKARP'S WINTER ADVENTURE
POLYKARP'S WINTER ADVENTURE see **POLYKARPOVO ZIMNI DOBRODRUZSTVI** • 1917
POLYOLEFINS, THE • 1964 • Pendry Alan • SHT • UKN
POLYORCHIA see **A L'AUBE DU TROISIEME JOUR** • 1962
POM POM GIRLS, THE • 1976 • Ruben Joseph • USA • POM-POM GIRLS, THE
POM-POM GIRLS, THE see **POM POM GIRLS, THE** • 1976
POMAREE SRITHONG • 1987 • Verachon Nantana • THL
POMEGRANATE GIRL see **ANAR-BALA** • 1940
POMEGRANATE TIME see **TAIFU TO ZAKURO** • 1967
POMLADNI VETER • 1976 • Ranfl Rajko • YGS • PROLJETNI VJETAR ○ SPRING WIND
POMME, LA • 1967 • Matton Charles • SHT • FRN
POMME, LA • 1969 • Soutter Michel • SWT
POMME D'ADAM, LA see **TUFFAH'AT ADAM** • 1965
POMME D'AMOUR • 1932 • Dreville Jean • FRN
POMME, LA QUEUE ET LES PEPINS, LA • 1974 • Fournier Claude • CND
POMMIER, LE • 1902 • Blache Alice • FRN
POMMY ARRIVES IN AUSTRALIA • 1913 • Longford Raymond • ASL • POMMY THE FUNNY LITTLE NEW CHUM
POMMY THE FUNNY LITTLE NEW CHUM see **POMMY ARRIVES IN AUSTRALIA** • 1913
POMNI IMJA SVOE • Kolosov Sergei • USS, PLN
POMOCNIK • 1982 • Zahon Zoro • CZC • ASSISTANT, THE
POMODORO, IL • 1961 • Olmi Ermanno (Spv) • DOC • ITL
POMP OF EARTH • 1915 • *Balboa* • USA
POMPADOUR, DIE • 1935 • Harlan Veit, Schmidt-Gentner Willy • FRG
POMPADOURTASKEN see **NAAR FRUEN GAAR PAA EVENTYR** • 1913
POMPEII see **WARRIOR QUEEN** • 1985
POMPERLEYS KAMPF MIT DEM SCHNEESCHUH • 1922 • Fanck Arnold, Holger-Madsen • FRG
POMPEYO EL CONQUISTADOR • 1951 • Cardona Rene • MXC
POMPEY'S DREAM • 1909 • *Pathe* • FRN
POMPIERE DI SERVIZIO, IL • 1906 • Velle Gaston • ITL
POMPIERI DI VIGGIU, I • 1949 • Mattoli Mario • ITL
POMPIERI, I • 1985 • Parenti Neri • ITL • FIREMAN, THE
POMPIERS: ATTAQUE DU FEU • 1895 • Lumiere Louis • FRN
POMPIERS D'OUTREMONT, LES • 1975 • Brault Francois • DCS • CND
POMPON MALENCOUNTREUX, LE • 1903-04 • Blache Alice • FRN
POMPOSA ANG KABAYONG TSISMOSA • 1968 • Pacheco Lauro • PHL • POMPOSA, THE GOSSIPING HORSE
POMPOSA, THE GOSSIPING HORSE see **POMPOSA ANG KABAYONG TSISMOSA** • 1968
POMSTA • 1968 • Brdecka Jiri, Schorm Evald • CZC • REVENGE ○ VENGEANCE
PONCE DE LEON • 1924 • Foy Bryan • SHT • USA
PONCE DE LEON AND THE FOUNTAIN OF YOUTH • 1986 • Larry Sheldon • MTV • USA
PONCHO • 1981 • Uribe Imanol • SPN
PONCHO BLANCO • 1936 • Donadio Francisco P. • ARG
PONCHOS AZULES • 1942 • Barth-Moglia Luis • ARG
PONDEROSO CABALLERO • 1935 • Nosseck Max • SPN
PONEDELJAK ILI UTORAK • 1966 • Mimica Vatroslav • YGS • MONDAY OR TUESDAY
PONGO THE MAN MONKEY • 1906 • *Gaumont* • UKN
PONIRAH see **PONIRAH TERPIDANA** • 1984

PONIRAH TERPIDANA • 1984 • Rahardjo Slamet • INN • PONIRAH
PONJOLA • 1923 • Crisp Donald?, Young James? • USA
PONKY'S BURGLAR • 1913 • Kinder Stuart • UKN
PONKY'S HOUSEBOAT • 1913 • Kinder Stuart • UKN
PONNANA VAZHVU • 1967 • Devan • IND • NEW LEASE OF LIFE
PONOVO POCINJE LJUBAVNI ZIVOT • 1974 • Zafranovic Lordan • YGS • OUR LOVE LIFE BEGINS ANEW
PONT BRULE • 1975 • Henderickx Guido • BLG
PONT DE LA NIEBELE, LE • 1956 • Regnier Michel • DCS • IVC
PONT DE LA TOUR • 1896 • Lumiere Louis • FRN • TOWER BRIDGE
PONT DE SINGES, LE • 1976 • Harris Andre, de Sedouy Alain • DOC • FRN
PONT DE TANCARVILLE, LE • 1959 • Champetier Henri • SHT • FRN
PONT DE VARSOVIE • 1989 • Portabella Pedro • SPN • WARSAW BRIDGE
PONT D'IENA, LE • 1900 • Lumiere Louis • FRN
PONT DU NORD, LE • 1982 • Rivette Jacques • FRN • NORTHERN BRIDGE, THE ○ NORTH BRIDGE
PONT SOUS L'OCEAN, UN see **BRIDGE UNDER THE OCEAN** • 1957
PONT SUR L'ABIME, LE • 1912 • Feuillade Louis • FRN
PONT VERS LE SOLEIL, LE (FRN) see **BRIDGE TO THE SUN** • 1961
PONTCARRAL, COLONEL D'EMPIRE • 1942 • Delannoy Jean • FRN
PONTE DEI FANTASMI, IL • 1912 • Maggi Luigi • ITL • PHANTOM'S BRIDGE, THE
PONTE DEI SOSPIRI, IL • 1940 • Bonnard Mario • ITL
PONTE DEI SOSPIRI, IL • 1964 • Pierotti Piero • ITL, SPN • AVENGER OF VENICE (USA)
PONTE DELLE STREGHE, IL • 1909 • *Vitrotti Giovanni (Ph)* • ITL • BRIDGE OF WITCHES, THE ○ WITCHES' BRIDGE, THE
PONTE DELL'UNIVERSO, IL • 1958 • Cenni Renato • DOC • ITL • CANALE DI PANAMA, IL
PONTE DI VETRO, IL • 1940 • Alessandrini Goffredo • ITL
PONTE SULL'INFINITO, IL • 1941 • Doria Alberto • ITL
PONTI E PORTE DE ROMA • 1949 • Hamza D. A. • SHT • ITL
PONTIANAK • 1957 • Rao B. N. • SNG • VAMPIRE, THE
PONTIANAK GUA MUSANG • 1964 • Rao B. N. • MLY • VAMPIRE OF THE CIVET-CAT CAVE, THE ○ VAMPIRE IN THE CAVE, THE
PONTIANAK KEMBALI • 1963 • Estella Ramon • MLY • VAMPIRE RETURNS, THE
PONTIUS PILATE see **PONZIO PILATO** • 1962
PONTO E VIRGULA • 1929 • Contreiras Anibal • SHT • PRT
PONY BOY see **FOURTH HORSEMAN, THE** • 1932
PONY EXPRESS • 1909 • Porter Edwin S. • USA
PONY EXPRESS • 1925 • Cruze James • USA
PONY EXPRESS • 1953 • Hopper Jerry • USA
PONY EXPRESS, THE • 1911 • *Nestor* • USA
PONY EXPRESS DAYS • 1940 • Eason B. Reeves • SHT • USA
PONY EXPRESS GIRL, THE • 1912 • *Cooper Miriam* • USA
PONY EXPRESS RIDER • 1926 • Horner Robert J. • USA
PONY EXPRESS RIDER • 1976 • Totten Robert • USA
PONY EXPRESS RIDER, THE • 1910 • *Anderson Broncho Billy* • USA
PONY EXPRESS RIDERS, THE • 1916 • Mix Tom • SHT • USA
PONY POST • 1940 • Taylor Ray • USA
PONY SOLDIER • 1952 • Newman Joseph M. • USA • MACDONALD OF THE CANADIAN MOUNTIES (UKN)
PONY WHO PAID THE RENT, THE • 1912 • Fitzhamon Lewin • UKN
PONZIO PILATO • 1962 • Rapper Irving, Callegari Gian Paolo • ITL, FRN • PONTIUS PILATE
POOCH • 1932 • McGowan Robert • SHT • USA
POOCH PARADE • 1940 • *Mintz Charles (P)* • ANS • USA
POOCH THE PUP • 1932-33 • Lantz Walter, Nolan William • ASS • USA
POODLE see **CANICHE** • 1979
POOJA • 1940 • *Biswas Anil (M)* • IND
POOKIE (UKN) see **STERILE CUCKOO, THE** • 1969
POOL OF FLAME, THE • 1916 • Turner Otis • USA
POOL OF LONDON • 1951 • Dearden Basil • UKN
POOL SHARKS, THE • 1915 • Middleton Edwin • USA
POOLS OF THE PAST see **NOTORIOUS MRS. CARRICK, THE** • 1924
POON TANG TRILOGY, THE • Van Meter Ben • SHT • USA • PUNTANG TRILOGY
POONAM KI RAAT • 1965 • Sahu Kishore • IND • NIGHT OF THE FULL MOON
POOP DECK PIRATE • 1961 • Hannah Jack • ANS • USA
POOP GOES THE WEASEL • 1955 • Tendlar Dave • ANS • USA
POOPSIE AND COMPANY see **PUPA DEL GANGSTER, LA** • 1975
POOR ALBERT AND LITTLE ANNIE see **I DISMEMBER MAMA** • 1972
POOR ALGY • 1905 • Porter Edwin S. • USA
POOR AND THE PROUD, THE • Maldoror Sarah • SHT
POOR AUNT MATILDA • 1908 • Stow Percy • UKN
POOR BABY • 1915 • Louis Will • USA
POOR BOOB • 1919 • Crisp Donald • USA
POOR BOOP • 1913 • *Punch* • USA
POOR BUT BEAUTIFUL (USA) see **POVERI MA BELLI** • 1956
POOR BUT DISHONEST • 1915 • *Smith Dick* • USA
POOR BUT HANDSOME see **POVERI MA BELLI** • 1956
POOR BUTTERFLY • 1924 • Roberts Stephen • SHT • USA
POOR BUTTERFLY • 1969 • Gibson Alan • MTV • UKN
POOR BUTTERFLY see **POBRE MARIPOSA** • 1986
POOR CINDERELLA • 1934 • Fleischer Dave • ANS • USA
POOR CLEM • 1915 • Haldane Bert • UKN
POOR COW • 1967 • Loach Kenneth • UKN
POOR, DEAR MARGARET KIRBY • 1921 • Earle William P. S. • USA
POOR DEVIL • 1972 • Scheerer Robert • TVM • USA
POOR ELMER • 1938 • Marcus Sid • ANS • USA
POOR EXCUSE THAT WORKED, A • 1912 • *Lubin* • USA
POOR FELLA ME • 1973 • Beresford Bruce • MTV • ASL
POOR FERDINAND see **STACKARS FERDINAND** • 1941
POOR FINNEY • 1912 • *Rice Herbert* • USA
POOR FISH • 1933 • Santley Joseph • SHT • USA
POOR FISH, A • 1922 • Kenton Erle C. • SHT • USA
POOR FISH, A • 1931 • Sennett Mack • USA
POOR FISH, THE • 1918 • Beaudine William • SHT • USA
POOR FISH, THE • 1924 • McCarey Leo • SHT • USA
POOR FIXER, THE • 1915 • *Farley Dot* • USA
POOR FOLKS' BOY, THE • 1914 • Davis Ulysses • USA
POOR GIRL see **CHUDA HOLKA** • 1929
POOR GIRL, A GHOST STORY • 1986 • Apted Michael • MTV • UKN
POOR GIRLS • 1927 • Craft William James • USA
POOR GIRL'S ROMANCE, A • 1926 • Weight F. Harmon • USA
POOR INNOCENT • 1918 • *Parsons William* • SHT • USA
POOR JAKE'S DEMISE • 1913 • Curtis Allen • USA
POOR JIMMY • 1912 • *Pathe* • USA
POOR JOHN • 1913 • *Komic* • USA
POOR JONES' VACATION • 1912 • *Nestor* • USA
POOR KNIGHT AND THE DUKE'S DAUGHTER, A • 1908 • *Gaumont* • FRN
POOR LITTLE BUTTERFLY • 1938 • Harrison Ben • ANS • USA
POOR LITTLE CHAP HE WAS ONLY DREAMING • 1912-14 • Cohl Emile • ANS • USA
POOR LITTLE MATCH GIRL, THE • 1965 • Meyer Andrew • USA
POOR LITTLE ME • 1935 • Harman Hugh • ANS • USA
POOR LITTLE PEPPINA • 1916 • Olcott Sidney • USA
POOR LITTLE RICH BOY, THE • 1914 • *Eclectic* • USA
POOR LITTLE RICH GIRL • 1965 • Warhol Andy • USA
POOR LITTLE RICH GIRL see **POOR LITTLE RICH GIRL: THE BARBARA HUTTON STORY** • 1987
POOR LITTLE RICH GIRL, A • 1917 • Tourneur Maurice • USA
POOR LITTLE RICH GIRL, THE • 1936 • Cummings Irving • USA
POOR LITTLE RICH GIRL: THE BARBARA HUTTON STORY • 1987 • Jarrott Charles • TVM • USA • POOR LITTLE RICH GIRL
POOR LITTLE RICH MAN • 1915 • *Punchinello* • USA
POOR LITTLE SVEN see **STACKARS LILLA SVEN** • 1947
POOR LITTLE WITCH GIRL • 1965 • Post Howard • ANS • USA
POOR LIZA • Garanina Idea • ANM • USS
POOR MAN'S JOY see **SIROMASHKA RADOST** • 1958
POOR MAN'S STREET see **BEDNATA ULITSA** • 1963
POOR MARIA see **SIROTA MARIJA** • 1968
POOR MARIA see **MARJA PIENI!** • 1972
POOR MARIJA see **SIROTA MARIJA** • 1968
POOR MARJA! see **MARJA PIENI!** • 1972
POOR MEN'S WIVES • 1923 • Gasnier Louis J. • USA
POOR MILLIONAIRE see **POVERI MILIONARI** • 1958
POOR MILLIONAIRE, A see **FATTIG MILJONAR, EN** • 1941
POOR MILLIONAIRE, THE • 1930 • Melford George • USA
POOR MILLIONAIRE, THE (USA) see **ARME MILLIONAR, DER** • 1939
POOR MILLIONAIRES see **STACKARS MILJONARER** • 1936
POOR MILLIONAIRES see **MILLIONAIRHA-YE-GORESNE** • 1967
POOR MOTHER, THE • 1907 • *Pathe* • FRN
POOR MUSICIAN, THE • 1909 • Brooke Van Dyke • USA
POOR NUT, THE • 1927 • Wallace Richard • USA
POOR OLD BILL • 1931 • Banks Monty • UKN
POOR OLD FIDO • 1903 • *Bitzer Billy (Ph)* • USA
POOR OLD MR. AND MRS. BROWN IN THE STOCKS see **IN THE GOOD OLD TIMES** • 1905
POOR OLD MOTHER • 1913 • *Reliance* • USA
POOR OLD PIECAN • 1915 • Evans Joe • UKN
POOR ONES, THE see **ZAVALLILAR** • 1975
POOR OUTLAWS see **SZEGENYLEGENYEK (NEHEZELETUEK)** • 1965
POOR PA: OR, MOTHER'S DAY OUT • 1906 • Green Tom? • UKN
POOR PA PAYS • 1910 • Rosenthal Joe • UKN
POOR PA PAYS • 1913 • Aylott Dave? • UKN
POOR PAPA • 1916 • *Hopper Dewolfe* • USA
POOR PAPA • 1928 • Disney Walt • ANS • USA
POOR PARK see **POBRES PARK** • 1967
POOR PEOPLE see **CHUDI LIDE** • 1939
POOR PEREZ see **POBRE PEREZ, EL** • 1937
POOR PETER PIOUS • 1917 • Chaudet Louis W. • SHT • USA
POOR POLICY • 1915 • Edwards Harry J. • USA
POOR PRETTY EDDIE see **RED NECK COUNTY** • 1975
POOR PRINCESS, THE • 1919 • Sandberg Anders W. • DNM
POOR PRUNE, THE • 1919 • *Burns Sammy* • SHT • USA
POOR RELATION, A • 1912 • *Thanhouser* • USA
POOR RELATION, A • 1915 • *Jefferson Thomas* • USA
POOR RELATION, A • 1921 • Badger Clarence • USA
POOR RELATION, THE • 1912 • *Lubin* • USA
POOR RELATIONS • 1919 • Vidor King • USA
POOR RICH, THE • 1934 • Sedgwick Edward • USA
POOR RICH MAN, THE • 1918 • Brabin Charles J. • USA
POOR SAILOR, THE see **PAUVRE MATELOT, LE** • 1962
POOR SCHMALTZ • 1915 • Ford Hugh • USA
POOR SICK MEN, THE • 1911 • Griffith D. W. • USA
POOR SIMP, THE • 1920 • Heerman Victor • USA
POOR STUDENT, THE • 1910 • *Imp* • USA
POOR WHITE TRASH see **BAYOU** • 1957
POOR WHITE TRASH see **POOR WHITE TRASH: PART II** • 1976
POOR WHITE TRASH: PART II • 1976 • Brownrigg S. F. • USA • SCUM OF THE EARTH ○ POOR WHITE TRASH
POOR WIFE'S DEVOTION, A • 1909 • *Kalem* • USA
POOR WORM, THE see **DOUBLE DEALING** • 1923
POOR WRETCHED SINNER see **ARME SYNDIGE MENNESKE** • 1978
POORLUCK AS A MESSENGER BOY • 1913 • Wilson Frank? • UKN
POORLUCK MINDS THE SHOP • 1914 • Wilson Frank? • UKN
POORLUCK'S EXCURSION TICKETS • 1911 • Fitzhamon Lewin? • UKN
POORLUCK'S FIRST TIFF, THE • 1910 • Fitzhamon Lewin • UKN
POORLUCK'S PICNIC • 1912 • Plumb Hay • UKN
POORLUCKS TAKE PART IN A PAGEANT, THE • 1910 • Fitzhamon Lewin? • UKN
POOVANAM • 1968 • Benegal Shyam • DCS • IND • FLOWER PATH, THE
POOVUM POTTUM • 1968 • Mirasi Dada • IND • FLOWERS AND VERMILION
POP • 1927 • Newman Widgey R. • UKN
POP • 1970 • Kuri Yoji • ANS • JPN
POP see **OJ OJ OJ..** • 1966
POP ALWAYS PAYS • 1940 • Goodwins Leslie • USA • THOUSAND DOLLAR MARRIAGE
POP BUELL -HOOSIER FARMER IN LAOS • 1965 • Van Dyke Willard • DOC • USA
POP CIRA I POP SPIRA • 1965 • Jovanovic Soja • YGS • PARSON CIRA AND PARSON SPIRA ○ IT'S NOT EASY TO GET MARRIED
POP GAME • 1967 • Leroi Francis • FRN • JEU DE LA VIE, LE ○ POP'GAME
POP GEAR • 1965 • Goode Frederic • UKN • GO GO MANIA (USA)
POP GOES MY HEART • 1935 • Freleng Friz • ANS • USA
POP GOES THE EASEL • 1935 • Lord Del • SHT • USA
POP GOES THE EASEL • 1962 • Russell Ken • MTV • UKN
POP 'IM POP • 1950 • McKimson Robert • ANS • USA
POP JESUS SUPERSTAR see **PAP'OCCHIO, IL** • 1980
POP-PIE A LA MODE • 1945 • Sparber I. • ANS • USA
POP SHOW • 1965 • *Mogubgub Fred (Anm)* • ANS • USA
POP TUTTLE, FIRE CHIEF • 1922 • Eddy Robert • USA
POPALONG POPEYE • 1952 • Kneitel Seymour • ANS • USA
POPAS IN TABARA DE VARA • 1958 • Meszaros Marta • DCS • RMN
POPBOCNIK JEHO VYSOSTI • 1933 • Fric Martin • CZC, FRG • ADJUDANT SEINER HOHEIT, DER (FRG) ○ ASSISTANT TO HIS HIGHNESS
POPCORN • 1931 • *Terry Paul/ Moser Frank (P)* • ANS • USA
POPCORN • 1970 • Clifton Peter • DOC • USA • POPCORN: AN AUDIO/VISUAL ROCK THING
POPCORN: AN AUDIO/VISUAL ROCK THING see **POPCORN** • 1970
POPCORN AND POLITICS • 1962 • Kneitel Seymour • ANS • USA
POPCORN STORY, THE • 1950 • Babbitt Art • ANS • USA
POPDOWN • 1968 • Marshall Fred • UKN
POPE GAPONE, LE • 1917 • Protazanov Yakov • USS
POPE JOAN • 1972 • Anderson Michael • UKN • DEVIL'S IMPOSTER, THE
POPE JOHN PAUL II • 1984 • Wise Herbert • TVM • USA
POPE OF GREENWICH VILLAGE, THE • 1984 • Rosenberg Stuart • USA • VILLAGE DREAMS
POPE POPPENSPALER • 1935 • Oertel Curt • FRG
POPEYE • 1955 • *Halas John (P)* • ASS • UKN
POPEYE • 1980 • Altman Robert • USA
POPEYE AND THE PIRATES • 1947 • Kneitel Seymour • ANS • USA
POPEYE DOYLE • 1986 • Levin Peter • TVM • USA
POPEYE FOLLIES: HIS TIMES AND LIFE, THE • 1973 • Fleischer Max • USA
POPEYE FOR PRESIDENT • 1956 • Kneitel Seymour • ANS • USA
POPEYE MAKES A MOVIE • 1950 • Kneitel Seymour • ANS • USA
POPEYE MEETS HERCULES • 1948 • Tytla Bill • ANS • USA
POPEYE MEETS RIP VAN WINKLE • 1941 • Fleischer Dave • ANS • USA
POPEYE PRESENTS EUGENE THE JEEP • 1940 • Fleischer Dave • ANS • USA
POPEYE, THE ACE OF SPACE • 1953 • Kneitel Seymour • ANS • USA
POPEYE THE SAILOR • 1933 • Fleischer Dave • ANS • USA
POPEYE THE SAILOR MEETS ALI BABA'S FORTY THIEVES • 1937 • Fleischer Dave • ANS • USA
POPEYE THE SAILOR MEETS SINBAD THE SAILOR • 1936 • Fleischer Dave • ANS • USA
POPEYE THE SAILOR MEETS WILLIAM TELL • 1940 • Fleischer Dave • ANS • USA
POPEYE'S 20TH ANNIVERSARY • 1954 • Sparber I. • ANS • USA
POPEYE'S MIRTHDAY • 1953 • Kneitel Seymour • ANS • USA
POPEYE'S PAPPY • 1952 • Kneitel Seymour • ANS • USA
POPEYE'S PREMIERE • 1949 • *Paramount* • ANS • USA
POP'GAME see **POP GAME** • 1967
POPI • 1969 • Hiller Arthur • USA
POPIOL I DIAMENT • 1958 • Wajda Andrzej • PLN • ASHES AND DIAMONDS (UKN)
POPIOLY • 1966 • Wajda Andrzej • PLN • ASHES ○ LOST ARMY, THE
POPLAND see **UN, DOS, TRES.., AL ESCONDITE INGLES** • 1969
POPLARS • 1964 • Gaal Istvan • HNG
POPLETENA PLANETA • 1962 • Prochazka Pavel • ANS • CZC • PLANET PEOPLE ○ UPSIDE-DOWN PLANET
POPOLVAR NAJVACSI NA SVETE • 1982 • Tapak Martin • CZC, FRG • BIGGEST LAZYBONES IN THE WORLD, THE
POPOVICH BROTHERS OF SOUTH CHICAGO, THE • 1978 • Godmilow Jill • USA
POPPA KNOWS WORST • 1944 • Holmes Ben • SHT • USA
POPPEA, PROSTITUTA AL SERVIZIO DELL'IMPERO • 1972 • Brescia Alfonso • ITL
POPPIES • 1914 • Kinder Stuart • UKN
POPPIES ARE ALSO FLOWERS see **POPPY IS ALSO A FLOWER, THE** • 1966
POPPIES IN FLANDERS see **POPPIES OF FLANDERS** • 1927
POPPIES OF FLANDERS • 1927 • Maude Arthur • UKN • POPPIES IN FLANDERS
POPPIES (USA) see **GUBIJINSO** • 1935
POPPY • 1917 • Jose Edward • USA
POPPY • 1936 • Sutherland A. Edward, Heisler Stuart (U/c) • USA
POPPY see **GUBIJINSÓ** • 1935
POPPY see **GUBIJINSO** • 1941
POPPY FIELD, THE see **GELINCIK TARLASI** • 1968
POPPY GIRL (UKN) see **POPPY GIRL'S HUSBAND, THE** • 1919
POPPY GIRL'S HUSBAND, THE • 1919 • Hart William S., Hillyer Lambert • USA • POPPY GIRL (UKN)

POPPY IS ALSO A FLOWER, THE • 1966 • Young Terence • USA • DANGER GROWS WILD ○ POPPIES ARE ALSO FLOWERS
POPPY TRAIL, THE • 1920 • Harbaugh Carl • USA
POPPYCOCK! • 1966 • Davidson Carson • SHT • USA
POPPYGUNYA • 1955 • Samsonov Samson • USS • GRASSHOPPER, THE (USA) ○ GADFLY, THE
POPSY POP • 1970 • Herman Jean • FRN, ITL, FRG • FUORI IL MALLOPPO (ITL) ○ BUTTERFLY AFFAIR, THE (USA) ○ 21 CARAT SNATCH, THE
POPSY WOPSY • 1913 • Elvey Maurice • UKN
POPULAR BETTY • 1912 • Young James • USA
POPULAR CRAFTS see **ARTESANIA POPULAR** • 1966
POPULAR JOCULAR DR. BROWN • 1929 • Aylott Dave, Symmons E. F. • SHT • UKN
POPULAR MELODIES • 1933 • Fleischer Dave • ANS • USA
POPULAR NEUROTICS • 1984 • Larry Sheldon • MTV • USA
POPULAR PIECES • 1929 • Aylott Dave • UKN
POPULAR POWER, THE see **BATALLA DE CHILE: PART 3, LA** • 1979
POPULAR SIN, THE • 1926 • St. Clair Malcolm • USA
POPULAR SONG FAVOURITES • 1916 • SHS • UKN
POPULAR TOY, THE see **KAERE LEGETOJ, DET** • 1968
POPULAR VILLAIN, A • 1919 • Howe Kit • SHT • USA
POPULATION EXPLOSION see **EXPLOSION DEMOGRAPHIQUE** • 1967
POPULATION: ONE • 1986 • Daalder Renee • USA
POPULI MORITURI (ITL) see **STERBENDE VOLKER 1** • 1922
POPUTNOVO VYETRA "SINYAYA PTITSA" • 1967 • Yershov Mikhail • USS, YGS • BLUE BIRD OF A FAIR WIND
POQUIANCHIS, LAS • 1976 • Cazals Felipe • MXC • MISERERE
POR ACCIDENTE • 1971 • Giral Sergio • DOC • CUB
POR CAMINOS DE CASTILLA • 1971 • Ardavin Cesar • SHT • SPN
POR CULPA DE UNA MUJER • 1945 • Ugarte Eduardo • MXC
POR EL MISMO CAMINO • 1952 • Galindo Alejandro • MXC
POR ELLAS AUNQUE MAL PAGUEN • 1952 • Bustillo Oro Juan • MXC
POR ESO.. • 1970 • *Almada* • MXC
POR LA PUERTA FALSA • 1950 • de Fuentes Fernando • MXC • FALSE DOOR, THE ○ THROUGH THE FALSE DOOR
POR LA TIERRA AJENA • Littin Miguel • CHL • ON FOREIGN LAND
POR LOS CAMINOS VERDES • 1989 • Vera Marilda • VNZ • ON THE GREEN PATH
POR MIL DOLARES AL DIA (SPN) see **PER MILLE DOLLARI AL GIORNI** • 1966
POR MIS PISTOLAS • 1939 • Bohr Jose • BY MY PISTOLS (USA)
POR MIS PISTOLAS • 1968 • Delgado Miguel M. • MXC • WITH MY GUNS
POR PRIMERA VEZ • 1967 • Cortazar Octavio • DOC • CUB • FOR THE FIRST TIME
POR QUE NACIO EL EJERCITO REBELDE • 1960 • Massip Jose • DOC • CUB
POR QUE PECA LA MUJER • 1951 • Cardona Rene • MXC
POR QUE PECAMOS A LOS CUARENTA? • 1970 • Lazaga Pedro • SPN
POR QUE PERDIMOS LA GUERRA? • 1977 • Galindo Luis, Santillan Diego • SPN • WHY WE LOST THE WAR
POR QUE SEGUIR MATANDO? • 1967 • de la Loma Jose Antonio • SPN, ITL
POR QUE TE ENGANA TU MARIDO? • 1968 • Summers Manuel • SPN • WHY IS YOUR HUSBAND UNFAITHFUL?
POR QUE VIVIR TRISTES? • 1941 • Maroto Eduardo G. • SPN
POR QUE YA NO ME QUIERES? • 1953 • Urueta Chano • MXC
POR QUERER A UNA MUJER • 1951 • Cortazar Ernesto • MXC
POR TI APRENDI A QUERER • 1957 • Diaz Morales Jose • MXC
POR TODO JALISCO • 1972 • *Cima* • MXC
POR UM FIO • 1968 • Silva Fernando Matos • SHT • PRT
POR UN AMOR • 1944 • Diaz Morales Jose • MXC
POR UN AMOR • 1974 • *Cima* • MXC
POR UN PUGNO DI EROI • 1968 • Umgelter Fritz • ITL
POR UN PUNADO DE DOLARES (SPN) see **PER UN PUGNO DI DOLLARI** • 1964
POR UNA MUJER • 1940 • Guzman Roberto • MXC
PORADNIK MATRYMONIALNY • 1968 • Haupe Wlodzimierz • PLN • MATRIMONIAL ADVICE COLUMN ○ GUIDEBOOK TO MATRIMONY
PORANEK MISIA • 1971 • Wilkosz Tadeusz • ANM • PLN • TEDDY BEAR IN THE MORNING
PORC-EPIC, LE see **TOUTE LA FAMILLE ETAIT LA** • 1948
PORCA MISERIA • 1951 • Bianchi Giorgio • ITL
PORCA SOCIETA • 1978 • Russo Luigi • ITL
PORCA VACCA • 1983 • Festa Campanile Pasquale • ITL
PORCELAIN LAMP, THE • 1921 • Blake Ben K. • USA
PORCELAINES TENDRES • 1909 • Cohl Emile • ANS • FRN • SEVRES PORCELAIN
PORCELANAS HOY • 1968 • Ardavin Cesar • SHT • SPN
PORCHERIE (FRN) see **PORCILE** • 1969
PORCI CON LA P38 • 1978 • Pagani Gian Franco • ITL
PORCI CON LE ALI • 1977 • Pietrangeli Paolo • ITL • IF PIGS HAD WINGS
PORCILE • 1969 • Pasolini Pier Paolo • ITL, FRN • PORCHERIE (FRN) ○ PIGPEN (USA) ○ PIGSTY (UKN)
PORCO MONDO • 1978 • Bergonzelli Sergio • ITL
PORCUPINES ARE BORN WITHOUT BRISTLES see **TARALEZHITE SE RAZHDAT BEZ BODLI** • 1971
PORFIRIO DIAZ • 1944 • Sevilla Raphael J., Saavedra Rafael M. • MXC
PORGI L'ALTRA GUANCIA • 1974 • Rossi Franco • ITL, FRN • TURN THE OTHER CHEEK (USA)
PORGY AND BESS • 1959 • Preminger Otto • USA
PORGY'S BOUQUET • 1913 • Williams C. Jay • USA
PORI • 1929 • von Dungern A. • FRG
PORK BUTCHER, THE see **SOUVENIR** • 1988
PORK CHOP HILL • 1959 • Milestone Lewis • USA
PORK CHOP PHOOEY • 1963 • Hanna William, Barbera Joseph • ANS • USA
PORK PLOTTERS, THE • 1916 • Humphrey Orral • USA
PORKALA • 1956 • Donner Jorn • SHT • FNL
PORKULIAR PIGGY • 1944 • Wickersham Bob • ANS • USA • PORKYLIAR PIGGY
PORKY AND DAFFY • 1938 • Clampett Robert • ANS • USA
PORKY AND GABBY • 1937 • Iwerks Ub • ANS • USA
PORKY AND TEABISCUIT • 1939 • Hardaway Ben, Dalton Cal • ANS • USA
PORKY AND THE NORTHWOODS • 1936 • Tashlin Frank • ANS • USA
PORKY AT THE CROCADERO • 1938 • Tashlin Frank • ANS • USA
PORKY CHOPS • 1949 • Davis Arthur • ANS • USA
PORKY IN EGYPT • 1938 • Clampett Robert • ANS • USA
PORKY IN WACKYLAND • 1938 • Clampett Robert • ANS • USA
PORKY PIG'S FEAT • 1943 • Tashlin Frank • ANS • USA
PORKY THE FIREMAN • 1938 • Tashlin Frank • ANS • USA
PORKY THE GIANT KILLER • 1939 • Freleng Friz • ANS • USA
PORKY THE GOB • 1938 • Hardaway Ben, Dalton Cal • ANS • USA
PORKY THE RAINMAKER • 1936 • Avery Tex • ANS • USA
PORKY THE WRESTLER • 1937 • Avery Tex • ANS • USA
PORKYLIAR PIGGY see **PORKULIAR PIGGY** • 1944
PORKY'S • 1982 • Clark Bob • CND • CHEZ PORKY
PORKY'S ANT • 1941 • Jones Charles M. • ANS • USA
PORKY'S BADTIME STORY • 1937 • Clampett Robert • ANS • USA
PORKY'S BASEBALL BROADCAST • 1940 • Freleng Friz • ANS • USA
PORKY'S BEAR FACTS • 1941 • Freleng Friz • ANS • USA
PORKY'S BUILDING • 1937 • Tashlin Frank • ANS • USA
PORKY'S CAFE • 1942 • Jones Charles M. • ANS • USA
PORKY'S DOUBLE TROUBLE • 1937 • Tashlin Frank • ANS • USA
PORKY'S DUCK HUNT • 1937 • Avery Tex • ANS • USA
PORKY'S FIVE AND TEN • 1938 • Clampett Robert • ANS • USA
PORKY'S GARDEN • 1937 • Avery Tex • ANS • USA
PORKY'S HARE HUNT • 1938 • Hardaway Ben, Dalton Cal • ANS • USA
PORKY'S HERO AGENCY • 1937 • Clampett Robert • ANS • USA
PORKY'S HIRED HAND • 1940 • Freleng Friz • ANS • USA
PORKY'S HOTEL • 1939 • Clampett Robert • ANS • USA
PORKY'S II, THE NEXT DAY • 1983 • Clark Bob • CND, USA • CHEZ PORKY II, LE LENDEMAIN
PORKY'S LAST STAND • 1940 • Clampett Robert • ANS • USA
PORKY'S MIDNIGHT MATINEE • 1941 • Jones Charles M. • ANS • USA
PORKY'S MOVIE MYSTERY • 1939 • Clampett Robert • ANS • USA
PORKY'S MOVING DAY • 1936 • King Jack • ANS • USA
PORKY'S NAUGHTY NEPHEW • 1938 • Clampett Robert • ANS • USA
PORKY'S PARTY • 1938 • Clampett Robert • ANS • USA
PORKY'S PASTRY PIRATES • 1942 • Freleng Friz • ANS • USA
PORKY'S PET • 1936 • King Jack • ANS • USA
PORKY'S PHONEY EXPRESS • 1938 • Dalton Cal, Howard Cal • ANS • USA
PORKY'S PICNIC • 1939 • Clampett Robert • ANS • USA
PORKY'S POOCH • 1941 • Clampett Robert • ANS • USA
PORKY'S POOR FISH • 1940 • Clampett Robert • ANS • USA
PORKY'S POPPA • 1938 • Clampett Robert • ANS • USA
PORKY'S POULTRY PLANT • 1936 • Tashlin Frank • ANS • USA
PORKY'S PREVIEW • 1941 • Avery Tex • ANS • USA
PORKY'S PRIZE PONY • 1941 • Jones Charles M. • ANS • USA
PORKY'S RAILROAD • 1937 • Tashlin Frank • ANS • USA
PORKY'S REVENGE • 1985 • Komack James • USA
PORKY'S ROAD RACE • 1937 • Tashlin Frank • ANS • USA
PORKY'S ROMANCE • 1937 • Tashlin Frank • ANS • USA
PORKY'S SNOOZE REEL • 1941 • Clampett Robert, McCabe Norman • ANS • USA
PORKY'S SPRING PLANTING • 1938 • Tashlin Frank • ANS • USA
PORKY'S SUPER SERVICE • 1937 • Iwerks Ub • ANS • USA
PORKY'S TIRE TROUBLE • 1939 • Clampett Robert • ANS • USA
PORN-BROKERS, THE • 1973 • Lindsay John, Bennett Laurie • UKN
PORN FLAKES see **BANG BANG** • 1976
PORNO • 1990 • Koterski Marek • PLN
PORNO BABY • 1969 • Frank Wolfgang • FRG
PORNO BAR • 1977 • FRG
PORNO LIBIDINI DI JUSTINE, LE • 1979 • D'Amato Joe • ITL
PORNO -MADE IN DENMARK • 1972 • *Topsy Film* • DNM
PORNO POP • 1971 • Kronhausen Dr. • DNM
PORNOCHATTES • 1974 • Maria Guy • FRN • TOUCHEZ PAS A MA CHATTE
PORNOCRATES, LES • 1976 • Davy Jean-Francois • FRN
(PORNO)FOLLIE DI NOTTE • 1978 • D'Amato Joe • ITL
PORNOGRAFI • 1971 • Ege Ole • DNM
PORNOGRAFI see **EVIL PLEASURE, THE** • 1966
PORNOGRAFI -THE EVIL PLEASURE see **EVIL PLEASURE, THE** • 1966
PORNOGRAPHER, THE see **JINRUIGAKU NYUMON** • 1966
PORNOGRAPHERS: INTRODUCTION TO ANTHROPOLY, THE see **JINRUIGAKU NYUMON** • 1966
PORNOGRAPHIE INAVOUABLE • 1980 • Bernard-Aubert Claude • FRN
PORNOGRAPHIE SUEDOISE • 1976 • Desvilles Jean • FRN
PORNOGRAPHIE THAILANDAISE • 1977 • Payet Alain • FRN
PORNOGRAPHY: COPENHAGEN 1970 • 1970 • Lyhne Jorgen • DOC • USA • WIDE-OPEN COPENHAGEN 70
PORNOGRAPHY IN DENMARK: A NEW APPROACH • 1970 • De Renzy Alex • DOC • USA • CENSORSHIP IN DENMARK: A NEW APPROACH
PORNOSHOP DELLA SETTIMA STRADA, IL • 1979 • D'Amato Joe • ITL
PORNOTISSIMO • 1977 • Korber Serge • FRN
POROZHNII REIS • 1963 • Vengerov Vladimir • USS • HOME TRIP
PORQUE TE VI LLORAR • 1941 • de Orduna Juan • SPN
PORR I SKANDALSKOLAN • 1972 • SWD
PORRIDGE • 1979 • Clement Dick • UKN • DOING TIME (USA)
PORT ADELAIDE AQUATIC CARNIVAL 1911 • 1911 • *Lyceum Pictures* • ASL
PORT AFRIQUE • 1956 • Mate Rudolph • UKN
PORT ARTHUR • 1936 • Farkas Nicolas • FRG
PORT-ARTHUR • 1936 • Farkas Nicolas • FRN • I GIVE MY LIFE
PORT CHICAGO see **NEWSREEL (PORT CHICAGO)** • 1966
PORT D'ATTACHE • 1942 • Choux Jean • FRN
PORT DE QUEBEC, LE • 1986 • Kinsey Nicholas • DOC • CND
PORT DU DESIR, LE • 1954 • Greville Edmond T. • FRN • HOUSE ON THE WATERFRONT, THE ○ HARBOUR OF DESIRE ○ SAUVEUR D'EPAVES
PORT O' DREAMS (UKN) see **GIRL OVERBOARD** • 1929
PORT OF CALL see **HAMNSTAD** • 1948
PORT-OF-CALL AT ORAN see **ESCALE A ORAN**
PORT OF DESIRE (UKN) see **QUAI DU DESIR** • 1969
PORT OF DESIRE (USA) see **FILLE DE HAMBOURG, LA** • 1958
PORT OF DOOM, THE • 1913 • Dawley J. Searle • USA
PORT OF ESCAPE • 1956 • Young Tony • UKN
PORT OF ESCAPE • 1961 • Calvert John • ASL
PORT OF FORTY THIEVES, THE • 1944 • English John • USA
PORT OF FREEDOM (UKN) see **GROSSE FREIHEIT NMR 7, DIE** • 1944
PORT OF HELL • 1954 • Schuster Harold • USA
PORT OF LONDON • 1930 • Grierson John • DOC • UKN
PORT OF LOST DREAMS • 1935 • Strayer Frank • USA
PORT OF LOST SOULS, THE see **WHITE SLIPPERS** • 1924
PORT OF MISSING GIRLS, THE • 1928 • Cummings Irving • USA
PORT OF MISSING GIRLS, THE • 1938 • Brown Karl • USA
PORT OF MISSING MEN, THE • 1914 • *Daly Arnold* • USA
PORT OF MISSING MICE • 1945 • Donnelly Eddie • ANS • USA
PORT OF MISSING WOMEN, THE • 1913 • *Selig* • USA
PORT OF MISSING WOMEN, THE • 1915 • Weston Charles • UKN
PORT OF NEW YORK • 1949 • Benedek Laslo • USA
PORT OF REVENGE • 1961 • *O'Herlihy Dan* • UKN
PORT OF SEVEN SEAS • 1938 • Whale James • USA • MADELON
PORT OF SHADOWS (UKN) see **QUAI DES BRUMES** • 1938
PORT OF SHAME see **AMANTS DU TAGE, LES** • 1955
PORT OF TEARS, THE see **LIMANI TON DACRION, TO** • 1928
PORT OF WICKEDNESS see **BARBARY COAST** • 1935
PORT SAID • 1948 • Le Borg Reginald • USA
PORT SINISTER • 1953 • Daniels Harold • USA • BEAST OF PARADISE ISLE
PORT SUNLIGHT • 1919 • UKN
PORT WHINES • 1929 • *Mintz Charles (P)* • ANS • USA
PORTA APERTA, LA • 1912 • Del Colle Ubaldo Maria • ITL
PORTA APERTA, LA • 1913 • Pasquali Ernesto Maria • ITL
PORTA DEI SOGNI, LA • 1955 • D'Alessandro Angelo • ITL
PORTA DEL CANNONE, LA • 1969 • Savona Leopoldo • ITL
PORTA DEL CIELO, LA • 1946 • De Sica Vittorio • ITL
PORTA UN BACIONE A FIRENZE • 1957 • Mastrocinque Camillo • ITL
PORTABLE COUNTRY see **PAIS PORTATIL** • 1977
PORTAMI QUELLO CHE HAI E PRENDITI QUELLO CHE VUOI (ITL) see **CAPRICES DE MARIE, LES** • 1969
PORTASI • 1948 • Kubasek Vaclav • CZC
PORTATRICE DI PANE, LA • 1911 • De Montepin S. • ITL
PORTATRICE DI PANE, LA (ITL) see **PORTEUSE DE PAIN, LA** • 1949
PORTATRICE DI PANE, LA (ITL) see **PORTEUSE DE PAIN, LA** • 1963
PORTE, LA • 1964 • Vausseur Jacques • ANS • FRN • DOOR, THE
PORTE APERTE • 1990 • Amelio Gianni • ITL • OPEN DOORS
PORTE DE LILAS • 1957 • Clair Rene • FRN, ITL • QUARTIERE DEI LILLA (ITL) ○ GATES OF PARIS (USA) ○ GATE OF LILACS
PORTE D'OR, LA see **MARLENE** • 1948
PORTE D'ORIENT • 1950 • Daroy Jacques • FRN
PORTE DU LARGE, LA • 1936 • L'Herbier Marcel • FRN • GREAT TEMPTATION, THE ○ DOOR TO THE OPEN SEA
PORTE MONUMENTALE, LA • 1900 • Melies Georges • FRN
PORTE OUVERTE, LA see **BABU AL-MAFTUH, AL-** • 1963
PORTE SILENCE • 1966 • Chabot Jean • SHT • CND
PORTE SULLE SPALLE, LE • 1978 • Passoni Valentino • ITL
PORTE-VEINE, LE • 1937 • Berthomieu Andre • FRN
PORTEFEUILLE, LE • 1967 • Fasquel Maurice • SHT • FRN
PORTENTOSA VIDA DE PADRE VICENTE, LA • 1978 • Mira Carlos • SPN • PORTENTOUS LIFE OF SAINT VINCENT, THE
PORTENTOUS LIFE OF SAINT VINCENT, THE see **PORTENTOSA VIDA DE PADRE VICENTE, LA** • 1978
PORTER, THE • 1917 • *Lust S. B.* • SHT • USA
PORTER, THE see **NEW JANITOR, THE** • 1914
PORTER, THE see **BAARA** • 1979
PORTERS, THE • 1917 • Phillips R. W. • SHT • USA
PORTES CLAQUENT, LES • 1960 • Poitrenaud Jacques, Fermaud Michel • FRN
PORTES DE FEU, LES • 1974 • Bernard-Aubert Claude • FRN
PORTES DE LA NATION, LES • 1954 • Storck Henri • DOC • BLG
PORTES DE LA NUIT, LES • 1946 • Carne Marcel • FRN • GATES OF THE NIGHT (USA) ○ GATES OF NIGHT
PORTES TOURNANTES, LES • 1988 • Mankiewicz Francis • CND • REVOLVING DOORS, THE
PORTEUSE DE PAIN, LA • 1906 • Feuillade Louis • FRN
PORTEUSE DE PAIN, LA • 1912 • Denola Georges • FRN
PORTEUSE DE PAIN, LA • 1923 • Le Somptier Rene • FRN
PORTEUSE DE PAIN, LA • 1934 • Sti Rene • FRN
PORTEUSE DE PAIN, LA • 1949 • Cloche Maurice • FRN, ITL • PORTATRICE DI PANE, LA (ITL)
PORTEUSE DE PAIN, LA • 1963 • Cloche Maurice • FRN, ITL • PORTATRICE DI PANE, LA (ITL) ○ BREAD PEDDLER, THE (USA)
PORTFOLIO • 1990 • Hopkins John* • SHT • CND
PORTIA ON TRIAL • 1937 • Nicholls George Jr. • USA • TRIAL OF PORTIA MERRIMAN, THE (UKN)

PORTICO DE LA GLORIA, EL • 1953 • Salvia Rafael J. • SPN
PORTIERA NUDA, LA • 1975 • Cozzi Luigi • ITL
PORTIERE DI NOTTE, IL • 1974 • Cavani Liliana • ITL • NIGHT PORTER, THE (UKN)
PORTILE ALBASTRE ALE ORASULUI • 1973 • Muresan Mircea • RMN • BLUE GATES OF THE CITY, THE
PORTION D'ETERNITE • 1990 • Favreau Robert • CND • LOOKING FOR ETERNITY
PORTLAND EXPOSE • 1957 • Schuster Harold • USA
PORTNOY'S COMPLAINT • 1972 • Lehman Ernest • USA
PORTO • 1935 • Palermi Amleto • ITL
PORTO, CAPITAL DO TRABALHO • 1961 • Guimaraes Manuel • SHT • PRT
PORTO DE ABRIGO • 1941 • Coelho Jose Adolfo • PRT
PORTO DELLA SPERANZA, IL • 1955 • Liberti Enzo • ITL
PORTO, METROPOLE DO TRABALHO • 1950 • Queiroga Perdigao • SHT • PRT
PORTRAIT • Kristensen Hans • SHT • DNM
PORTRAIT • 1974 • Damiano Gerard • USA
PORTRAIT see **DAVID, CAROL, DON, WILL: A PORTRAIT** • 1966
PORTRAIT see **PORTRE** • 1971
PORTRAIT see **PORTREFILM** • 1975
PORTRAIT, A see **SHOZO** • 1948
PORTRAIT, A see **AL NEIL** • 1979
PORTRAIT, THE • 1910 • *Vitagraph* • USA
PORTRAIT, THE • 1911 • Coleby A. E. • UKN • ZILLAH, A GYPSY ROMANCE
PORTRAIT, THE • 1911 • Ince Thomas H., Tucker George Loane • USA
PORTRAIT, THE • 1913 • *Nesbitt Miriam* • USA
PORTRAIT, THE • 1914 • Young James • USA
PORTRAIT, THE see **PODOBIZNA** • 1948
PORTRAIT, THE see **GIRLS' SCHOOL SCREAMERS** • 1986
PORTRAIT DE BARBARA • 1978 • Reichenbach Francois • MTV • FRN
PORTRAIT DE DIANE DUFRESNE • 1978 • Reichenbach Francois • MTV • FRN
PORTRAIT DE DORIAN GRAY, LE • 1915 • Volkov Alexander • USS
PORTRAIT DE DORIAN GRAY, LE • 1977 • Boutron Pierre • FRN
PORTRAIT DE GROUPE AVEC DAME (FRN) see **GRUPPENBILD MIT DAME** • 1977
PORTRAIT DE HENRI GOETZ • 1947 • Resnais Alain • DCS • FRN
PORTRAIT DE HILDEGARD KNEF • 1974 • Reichenbach Francois • DOC • FRN
PORTRAIT DE JACQUES CHIRAC • 1976 • Reichenbach Francois • MTV • FRN
PORTRAIT DE LA FRANCE • 1957 • Fabiani Henri • SHT • FRN
PORTRAIT DE MARIANNE, LE • 1970 • Goldenberg Daniel • FRN
PORTRAIT DE MIREILLE, LE • 1909 • Perret Leonce • FRN
PORTRAIT DE SON PERE, LE • 1953 • Berthomieu Andre • FRN
PORTRAIT D'HENRI VERNEUIL • 1981 • Halimi Andre • DOC • FRN
PORTRAIT DU CHANOINE LIONEL GROULX, 1878-1978 • 1978 • Valcour Pierre • DOC • CND
PORTRAIT D'UN ASSASSIN • 1949 • Bernard-Roland • FRN
PORTRAIT D'UN HOMME 60% PARFAIT • 1980 • Tresgot Annie • FRN • PORTRAIT OF A SIXTY PERCENT PERFECT MAN ○ BILLY WILDER
PORTRAIT D'UN NOVILLERO see **LOMELIN** • 1965
PORTRAIT D'UN SYNDICALISTE ET DE SA FAMILLE: EDOUARD, CARMEN ET LUCE GAGNON • 1968 • Dansereau Fernand • DCS • CND
PORTRAIT EINER BEWAHRUNG • 1965 • Kluge Alexander • SHT • FRG • PORTRAIT OF ONE WHO PROVED HIS METTLE
PORTRAIT FROM LIFE • 1948 • Fisher Terence • UKN • GIRL IN THE PAINTING, THE ○ JOURNEY INTO YESTERDAY ○ PORTRAIT OF HILDEGARD
PORTRAIT: GERALD SQUIRES OF NEWFOUNDLAND • 1980 • Forest Leonard • DOC • CND
PORTRAIT IN BLACK • 1960 • Gordon Michael • USA
PORTRAIT IN SMOKE (USA) see **WICKED AS THEY COME** • 1956
PORTRAIT IN THE ATTIC, THE • 1915 • Collins John H. • USA
PORTRAIT MYSTERIEUX, LE • 1899 • Melies Georges • FRN • MYSTERIOUS PORTRAIT, A (USA)
PORTRAIT OF A BUSHMAN • 1966 • Holt Niels • SHT • DNM
PORTRAIT OF A BUSINESSMAN see **LIIKEMIEHEN MUOTOKUVA** • 1970
PORTRAIT OF A CHAMPION see **KULDETES** • 1979
PORTRAIT OF A CONDUCTOR, THE see **PORTRET DYRYGENTA** • 1965
PORTRAIT OF A DEAD GIRL see **MCCLOUD: WHO KILLED MISS U.S.A.?** • 1969
PORTRAIT OF A FANATIC see **K'U LIEN** • 1983
PORTRAIT OF A GIRL, A see **LEANYPORTRE** • 1971
PORTRAIT OF A GOON • 1959 • Russell Ken • MTV • UKN
PORTRAIT OF A HARBOR • 1957 • King Allan • CND
PORTRAIT OF A HIT MAN • 1978 • Buckhantz Allan A. • USA • JIM BUCK
PORTRAIT OF A HORSE, THE see **KON** • 1968
PORTRAIT OF A MAN see **FERFIARCKEP** • 1964
PORTRAIT OF A MAN WITH A MEDALLION see **PORTRET MEZCZYZNY Z MEDALONEM** • 1959
PORTRAIT OF A MATADOR • 1958 • Zichy Theodore • UKN
PORTRAIT OF A MINER • 1966 • Mason Richard • DOC • UKN
PORTRAIT OF A MOBSTER • 1961 • Pevney Joseph • USA
PORTRAIT OF A MONK • 1971 • Ljubic Milan • DCS • YGS
PORTRAIT OF A NEW MAN • Sen Mrinal • IND
PORTRAIT OF A REBEL see **WOMAN REBELS, A** • 1936
PORTRAIT OF A REBEL: MARGARET SANGER • 1980 • Vogel Virgil W. • TVM • USA • PORTRAIT OF A REBEL: THE REMARKABLE MRS. SANGER
PORTRAIT OF A REBEL: THE REMARKABLE MRS. SANGER see **PORTRAIT OF A REBEL: MARGARET SANGER** • 1980
PORTRAIT OF A ROADSWEEPER see **GIJS VAN GROENESTEIN, STRAATVEGER** • 1976
PORTRAIT OF A SHOWGIRL • 1982 • Stern Steven Hilliard • TVM • USA
PORTRAIT OF A SINNER (USA) see **ROUGH AND THE SMOOTH, THE** • 1959
PORTRAIT OF A SIXTY PERCENT PERFECT MAN see **PORTRAIT D'UN HOMME 60% PARFAIT** • 1980
PORTRAIT OF A SMALL TOWN, THE see **PORTRET MALEGO MIASTA** • 1961
PORTRAIT OF A SOVIET COMPOSER • 1961 • Russell Ken • MTV • UKN
PORTRAIT OF A STRIPPER • 1979 • Alonzo John A. • TVM • USA
PORTRAIT OF A WOMAN see **FEMME DISPARAIT, UNE** • 1942
PORTRAIT OF A WOMAN, NUDE (USA) see **NUDO DI DONNA** • 1982
PORTRAIT OF A YOUNG MAN • 1932 • Rodakiewicz Henwar • USA
PORTRAIT OF ALANIS • 1966 • Kelly Ron • CND
PORTRAIT OF ALISON • 1955 • Green Guy • UKN • POSTMARK FOR DANGER (USA)
PORTRAIT OF AN AUSTRALIAN • 1962 • Small Rhonda • ASL
PORTRAIT OF AN ESCORT • 1980 • Stern Steven Hilliard • TVM • USA • PROFESSIONAL DATE
PORTRAIT OF AN INDUSTRIAL DESIGNER see **MUOTOILIJAN MAAILMA TIMO SARPANEVA** • 1976
PORTRAIT OF AN UNKNOWN WOMAN (USA) see **BILDNIS EINER UNBEKANNTEN** • 1954
PORTRAIT OF ANITA, THE • 1914 • *Younge Lucille* • USA
PORTRAIT OF CHIEKO see **CHIEKO-SHO** • 1967
PORTRAIT OF CLARE • 1950 • Comfort Lance • UKN
PORTRAIT OF COWARDICE • 1968 • Iliesu Mirel • DOC • RMN
PORTRAIT OF DAVID HOCKNEY • 1972 • Pearce David • UKN
PORTRAIT OF DOLLY GREY, THE • 1916 • Booth W. R. • UKN
PORTRAIT OF FIDEL CASTRO • 1975 • Lollobrigida Gina • DCS • ITL
PORTRAIT OF FRANS HALS see **PORTRET VAN FRANS HALS** • 1963
PORTRAIT OF GEZA ANDA • 1964 • Leacock Richard • DOC • USA
PORTRAIT OF HELL see **JIGOKU-HEN** • 1969
PORTRAIT OF HILDEGARD see **PORTRAIT FROM LIFE** • 1948
PORTRAIT OF INNOCENCE (USA) see **NOUS LES GOSSES** • 1941
PORTRAIT OF JASON • 1967 • Clarke Shirley • DOC • USA
PORTRAIT OF JENNIE • 1948 • Dieterle William • USA • JENNIE (UKN) ○ TIDAL WAVE
PORTRAIT OF LAURA BAYLES see **GRAND OLD GIRL, THE** • 1935
PORTRAIT OF LENIN (USA) see **LENIN V POLSHE** • 1966
PORTRAIT OF LIFE see **EKTI JIBAN** • 1988
PORTRAIT OF LYDIA • 1964 • Straiton John S. • ANS • CND
PORTRAIT OF MADAME CIANETTI, THE • 1970 • Maes J.-Cl. • ANS • BLG
PORTRAIT OF MADAME YUKI (UKN) see **YUKI FUJIN EZU** • 1950
PORTRAIT OF MARIA see **MARIA CANDELARIA** • 1943
PORTRAIT OF MY MOTHER • 1973 • Kreps Bonnie • CND
PORTRAIT OF ONE WHO PROVED HIS METTLE see **PORTRAIT EINER BEWAHRUNG** • 1965
PORTRAIT OF PAUL BURKHARD • 1964 • Leacock Richard • DOC • USA
PORTRAIT OF QUEENIE • 1964 • Orrom Michael • UKN
PORTRAIT OF SEDUCTION • 1977 • Spinelli Anthony • USA
PORTRAIT OF TERESA see **RETRATO DE TERESA** • 1979
PORTRAIT OF THE ARTIST • 1963 • Biggs Julian, Howe John, Burwash Gordon • CND
PORTRAIT OF THE ARTIST AS A YOUNG MAN • 1977 • Strick Joseph • UKN
PORTRAIT OF THE LADY ANNE, THE • 1912 • *La Badie Florence* • USA
PORTRAIT OF THE PATRIOTIC HEROES see **CHUNG LIEH T'U** • 1975
PORTRAIT OF VAN CLIBURN • 1966 • Leacock Richard (c/d) • DOC • USA
PORTRAIT OF YILMAZ GUNEY see **BESUCH AUF IMRALI** • 1979
PORTRAIT ROBOT • 1960 • Paviot Paul • FRN • PORTRAIT ROBOT, OU ECHEC A L'ASSASSIN ○ ECHEC D'UN ASSASSIN, L'
PORTRAIT ROBOT, OU ECHEC A L'ASSASSIN see **PORTRAIT ROBOT** • 1960
PORTRAIT SPIRITE, LE • 1903 • Melies Georges • SHT • FRN • SPIRITUALIST PHOTOGRAPHER, THE (USA)
PORTRAITS • 1968 • Gagne Jacques • SHT • CND
PORTRAITS see **PORTRETY** • 1964
PORTRAITS see **PORTRETI** • 1970
PORTRAITS DE FEMMES • 1975 • Menard Robert • CND
PORTRAITS FOR NOTHING • 1906 • Green Tom? • UKN
PORTRAITS OF PLEASURE • 1974 • Koup Bo • USA
PORTRAITS OF WOMEN see **VISAGES DE FEMMES** • 1969
PORTRAITS OF WOMEN (UKN) see **NAISENKUVIA** • 1970
PORTRE • 1971 • Nepp Jozsef • HNG • PORTRAIT
PORTREFILM • 1975 • Sos Maria • HNG • PORTRAIT
PORTRET DORIANA GREYA • 1915 • Meyerhold Vsevolod • USS • PICTURE OF DORIAN GRAY, THE (USA)
PORTRET DYRYGENTA • 1965 • Perski Ludwik • DOC • PLN • PORTRAIT OF A CONDUCTOR, THE
PORTRET MALEGO MIASTA • 1961 • Slesicki Wladyslaw • DOC • PLN • PORTRAIT OF A SMALL TOWN, THE
PORTRET MEZCZYZNY Z MEDALONEM • 1959 • Lesiewicz Witold • PLN • PORTRAIT OF A MAN WITH A MEDALLION
PORTRET VAN FRANS HALS • 1963 • Dupont Frans • SHT • NTH • PORTRAIT OF FRANS HALS
PORTRETI • 1970 • Pavlinic Zlatko • ANS • YGS • PORTRAITS
PORTRETY • 1964 • Kijowicz Miroslaw • ANS • PLN • PORTRAITS
PORTS OF CALL • 1925 • Clift Denison • USA
PORTS OF SCANDANAVIA: SWEDEN'S EAST COAST • 1949 • Colleran • SHT • SWD
PORTTIKIELTO TAIVAASEEN • 1989 • Suominen Tapio • FNL • BANNED FROM HEAVEN
PORTUGAL • 1976 • Kramer Robert, Spinelli Philip • USA
PORTUGAL ANTIGO E MODERNO • 1954 • Garcia Fernando • SHT • PRT
PORTUGAL DE MES AMOURS (FRN) see **PORTUGAL DO MEU AMOR** • 1968
PORTUGAL DESCONHECIDO • 1968 • de Almeida Manuel Faria • SHT • PRT
PORTUGAL DO MEU AMOR • 1968 • Manzon Jean • DOC • BRZ, FRN • PORTUGAL DE MES AMOURS (FRN) ○ PORTUGAL OF MY LOVE
PORTUGAL EM OSAKA • 1971 • Ribeiro Antonio Lopes • SHT • PRT
PORTUGAL OF MY LOVE see **PORTUGAL DO MEU AMOR** • 1968
PORTUGAL, OITO SECULOS DE HISTORIA • 1940 • Fraga Augusto • SHT • PRT
PORTUGAL, PAIS DE CONTRASTES • 1959 • Garcia Fernando • SHT • PRT
PORTUGAL, ROTEIRO DO SOL • 1961 • Mendes Joao • SHT • PRT
PORTUGAL'S GOOD PEOPLE see **BOM POVO PORTUGUES** • 1981
PORTUGUESA DE NAPOLES, A • 1931 • Costa Henrique • PRT
PORTUGUESA, FUTURO ABIERTO • 1972 • de la Rosa Antonio • DOC • VNZ • PORTUGUESA, OPEN FUTURE
PORTUGUESA, OPEN FUTURE see **PORTUGUESA, FUTURO ABIERTO** • 1972
PORTUGUESE GOODBYE, A see **ADEUS PORTUGUES, UM** • 1985
PORTUGUESE JOE • 1912 • *Cumpson John* • USA
PORTUGUESES NO MUNDO • 1952 • Mendes Joao • SHT • PRT
PORUCHIK KIZHE • 1934 • Fainzimmer Alexander • USS • TSAR WANTS TO SLEEP, THE ○ LIEUTENANT KITE
POSADA SANGRIETA, LA • 1941 • Rivero Fernando A. • MXC • BLOODY INN, THE
POSALJI COVEKA U POLA DVA • 1967 • Ivkov Dragoljub • YGS • SEND A MAN AT HALF-PAST ONE
POSATE LE PISTOLE REVERENDO • 1973 • Savona Leopoldo • ITL
POSAUNIST, DER • 1945 • Boese Carl • FRG
POSEBAN TRETMAN • 1980 • Paskaljevic Goran • YGS • SPECIAL TREATMENT (UKN)
POSEIDON ADVENTURE, THE • 1972 • Neame Ronald • USA
POSEL USVITU • 1949 • Krska Vaclav • CZC • MESSENGER OF DAWN ○ MESSENGER AT DAWN
POSHCHYOCHINA • 1980 • Malyan Ghenrikh • USS • SLAP IN THE FACE, A
POSICION AVANZADA • 1965 • Lazaga Pedro • SPN
POSITIF-NEGATIF, NOTRE FILM • 1970 • Lemaitre Maurice • FRN
POSITION, THE see **MIEJSCE** • 1965
POSITION AND BLACK SWING • 1933 • Marshall George • SHT • USA
POSITION FIRING • 1944 • Hubley John • ANS • USA
POSITION OF TRUST • 1963 • Harris Lionel • UKN
POSITION WANTED • 1924 • Roach Hal • SHT • USA
POSITION WANTED (USA) see **CAMERIERA BELLA PRESENZA OFFRESI** • 1951
POSITIONS see **SABALEROS** • 1959
POSITIONS OF LOVE see **SABALEROS** • 1959
POSITIVE I.D. • 1987 • Anderson Andy • USA
POSITIVE PROOF • 1912 • *Essanay* • USA
POSJET IZ SVEMIRA • 1964 • Grgic Zlatko, Vukotic Dusan • ANS • YGS • VISIT FROM SPACE, A (USA) ○ VISITOR
POSLEDNATA DOUMA • 1973 • Zheljazkova Binka • BUL • LAST WORD, THE
POSLEDNAYA NOCH • 1937 • Raizman Yuli, Vasiliev Dimitri • USS • LAST NIGHT, THE
POSLEDNAYA RELIKVIYA • 1971 • Kromanov Grigori • USS • LAST RELIC, THE ○ LAST RELICS
POSLEDNI BOHEM • 1931 • Innemann Svatopluk • CZC • LAST BOHEMIAN, THE
POSLEDNI DEJSTVI • 1970 • Spata Jan • CZC • LAST ACT, THE
POSLEDNI LETO • 1937 • *Hammid Alexander* • CZC • LAST SUMMER, THE
POSLEDNI LUP • Barta Jiri • ANM • CZC • LAST BOOTY, THE
POSLEDNI MASKARAD • 1934 • Chiaureli Mikhail • USS • LAST MASQUERADE, THE ○ UKANASKNELI MASKARADI
POSLEDNI MEJDAN • 1983 • Zabransky Milos • CZC • LAST BINGE, THE
POSLEDNI MUZ • 1934 • Fric Martin • CZC • LAST MAN, THE
POSLEDNI PROPADNE PEKLU • 1982 • Raza Ludvik • CZC • DEVIL TAKE THE HINDMOST, THE
POSLEDNI RADOST • 1921 • Binovec Vaclav • CZC • LAST JOY, THE
POSLEDNI RUZE OD CASANOVY • 1966 • Krska Vaclav • CZC • CASANOVA'S LAST ROSE ○ LAST ROSE FROM CASANOVA, THE
POSLEDNI TRIK PANA SCHWARZWALLDEA A PANA EDGARA • 1964 • Svankmajer Jan • ANS • CZC • MESSRS. SCHWARZWALD AND EDGAR'S LAST TRICK ○ LAST TRICK, THE ○ LAST TRICK OF MR. SCHWARZWALD AND MR. EDGAR, THE
POSLEDNI VIAK • 1982 • Matula Julius • CZC • LAST TRAIN, THE
POSLEDNI VYSTREL • 1950 • Weiss Jiri • CZC • LAST SHOT, THE
POSLEDNIAT VOYVODA • 1968 • Valchev Nikola • BUL • LAST CHIEFTAIN, THE
POSLEDNII ATTRAKZION • 1929 • Preobrazhenskaya Olga, Pravov Ivan • USS • LAST ATTRACTION, THE
POSLEDNII MESYATS OSENI • 1965 • Derbenev Vadim • USS • LAST MONTH OF AUTUMN, THE
POSLEDNJA POSTAJA • 1972 • Babic Joze • YGS • LAST STOP, THE
POSLEDNJA TRKA • 1979 • Rancic Jovan • YGS • LAST RACE, THE
POSLEDNJI DAN • 1952 • Pogacic Vladimir • YGS • LAST DAY, THE
POSLEDNJI KOLOSEK • 1956 • Mitrovic Zika • YGS • LAST TRACK

POSLEDNJI KRUG U MONCI • 1990 • Boskovic Alexander • YGS • LAST CIRCLE IN MONZA

POSLEDNJI PODVIG DIVERZANTA OBLAKA • 1979 • Mimica Vatroslav • YGS • LAST MISSION OF THE SABOTEUR "CLOUD", THE

POSLEDNO LYATO • 1974 • Hristov Hristo • BUL • LAST SUMMER, THE

POSLEDNY IZ SABUDARA • 1957 • Managadze Shota • USS • LAST FROM SABUDARA, THE

POSLEDNY NAVRAT • 1958 • Kudlac Frantisek • CZC

POSLESLOVIYI • 1983 • Khutsiev Marlen • USS • POSTFACE

POSLIJEPODNE JEDNOG FAZANA • 1973 • Arhanic Marijan • YGS • AFTERNOON OF A PHEASANT

POSLIZG • 1971 • Lomnicki Jan • PLN • SLIP-UP ○ SKID

POSLUSNE HLASIM • 1957 • Stekly Karel • CZC • BEG TO REPORT

POSLYEDNI ZHULIK • 1967 • Mass Vadims, Ebners Janis • USS • LAST SWINDLER, THE

POSOL SOVYETSKOVO SOIUZA • 1970 • Natanson Georgi • USS • AMBASSADOR TO THE SOVIET UNION

POSSE • 1975 • Douglas Kirk • USA

POSSE CAT • 1954 • Hanna William, Barbera Joseph • ANS • USA

POSSE FROM HEAVEN • 1975 • Pine Phillip • USA

POSSE FROM HELL • 1961 • Coleman Herbert • USA

POSSEDEES, LES • 1955 • Brabant Charles • FRN, ITL • ISOLA DELLE DONNE SOLE, L' (ITL) ○ PASSIONATE SUMMER (USA) ○ POSSESSED, THE

POSSEDES, LES • 1988 • Wajda Andrzej • FRN • POSSESSED, THE

POSSESSED • 1931 • Brown Clarence • USA

POSSESSED • 1947 • Bernhardt Curtis • USA

POSSESSED see **JUNOON** • 1978

POSSESSED see **KICHIKU** • 1978

POSSESSED, THE • Duarte Anselmo • BRZ

POSSESSED, THE • 1977 • Thorpe Jerry • TVM • USA

POSSESSED, THE see **POSSEDEES, LES** • 1955

POSSESSED, THE see **MEGSZALLOTTAK** • 1961

POSSESSED, THE see **ENDEMONIADA, LA** • 1975

POSSESSED, THE see **OCCHIO DEL MALE, L'** • 1982

POSSESSED, THE see **POSSEDES, LES** • 1988

POSSESSED, THE (UKN) see **DONNA DEL LAGO, LA** • 1965

POSSESSED BY SPEED see **FARTFEBER** • 1953

POSSESSION • 1919 • Edwards Henry • UKN

POSSESSION • 1973 • Cooper John • TVM • UKN

POSSESSION • 1980 • Zulawski Andrzej • FRN, FRG

POSSESSION, LA • 1929 • Perret Leonce • FRN

POSSESSION DE L'ENFANT, LA • 1909 • Feuillade Louis • FRN

POSSESSION DU CONDAMNE • 1967 • L'Heureux Albert Andre • BLG

POSSESSION OF JOEL DELANEY, THE • 1972 • Hussein Waris • USA

POSSESSO, IL • 1949 • Montero Roberto Bianchi • ITL

POSSESSOR, THE see **SESSO DELLA STREGA, IL** • 1972

POSSESSORS, THE (USA) see **GRANDES FAMILLES, LES** • 1959

POSSIBILITY, A • 1913 • *Gail Jane* • USA

POSSUIDA POR MIL DEMONIOS • 1970 • Frederico Carlos • BRZ

'POSSUM HUNT, THE • 1913 • *Kalem* • USA

POSSUM PADDOCK • 1921 • Villiers Charles • ASL

POSSUM PEARL • 1957 • Kneitel Seymour • ANS • USA

POST 23 • 1941 • Bond Ralph • UKN

POST AS DIRECTOR, THE see **JUYAKU NO ISU** • 1958

POST HASTE • 1933 • Cadman Frank • DOC • UKN

POST HASTE • 1934 • Jennings Humphrey • DCS • UKN

POST-IMPRESSIONISTS, THE • 1913 • Kirkland Hardee • USA

POST MORTEM see **MAINA TADANTA** • 1981

POST MORTEM TECHNIQUE • 1951 • Carlsen Henning • SHT • DNM

POST MORTEMS • 1929 • Pearce A. Leslie • USA

POST NO BILLS • 1914 • Williams C. Jay • USA

POST NO BILLS • 1923 • Roach Hal • SHT • USA

POST NO BILLS see **DEFENSE D'AFFICHER** • 1896

POST OF HONOR, THE • 1930 • Nelson Jack • SHT • USA

POST OFFICE AT ABACHURINA see **ABACHURINA POST-OFFICE** • 1973

POST OFFICE EUROPE see **EUROPA POSTLAGERND** • 1918

POST OFFICE INVESTIGATOR • 1949 • Blair George • USA

POST TELEGRAPHER, THE • 1912 • *Meyers William* • USA

POST WAR INVENTIONS • 1945 • Rasinski Connie • ANS • USA

POSTACKA POHADKA • 1961 • Hofman Eduard • ANS • CZC • POSTMAN'S TALE, THE

POSTAGE DUE • 1924 • Jeske George • SHT • USA

POSTAGE STAMP • 1965 • Zac Pino • ANS • ITL

POSTAL DELIVERY • 1971 • Beech John • UKN

POSTAL INSPECTOR • 1936 • Brower Otto • USA

POSTAL ORDERS • 1932 • Daumery John • UKN

POSTAL SUBSTITUTE, A • 1910 • Melies Gaston • USA

POSTAVA K PODPIRANI • 1963 • Juracek Pavel, Schmidt Jan • CZC • JOSEPH KILIAN (USA) ○ FIGURE TO SUPPORT, A ○ JOSEF KILLIAN ○ ORDER AND DISORDER ○ STATUE TO BE PROPPED, A ○ HUMAN CONDITION, THE

POSTCARD • 1970 • Bonniere Rene • SHT • CND

POSTCARD FROM A JOURNEY see **KARTKA Z PODROZY** • 1983

POSTCARD FROM ZAKOPANE, A see **POCZTOWKA Z ZAKOPANEGO** • 1960

POSTCARDS FROM THE EDGE • 1990 • Nichols Mike • USA

POSTCARDS FROM ZAKOPANE see **POCZTOWKA Z ZAKOPANEGO** • 1960

POSTCARDS WITH FLOWERS see **ILUSTRATE CU FLORI DE CIMP** • 1974

POSTCHI • 1972 • Mehrjui Dariush • IRN • POSTMAN, THE

POSTE-DE-LA-BALEINE • 1967 • Lavoie Richard • DCS • CND

POSTE FRONTIERE • 1973-75 • Bertolino Daniel • DSS • CND

POSTE RESTANTE • 1961 • Vitandis Gheorghe • RMN

POSTE SUD see **FORT DE LA SOLITUDE** • 1947

POSTER CHASE, THE • 1908 • *Urban Trading Co* • UKN

POSTER GIRLS, THE • 1902 • *Biograph* • USA

POSTERITY AND PERPLEXITY see **PI-YUN T'IEN** • 1976

POSTERS see **AFFISSIONI** • 1950

POSTEZ TOT • 1966 • Hebert Pierre • ANS • CND

POSTFACE see **POSLESLOVIYI** • 1983

POSTGRADUATE, THE • 1970 • Kovner Harold • USA

POSTILLON VON LONJUMEAU, DER • 1936 • Lamac Carl • AUS • KONIG LACHELT -PARIS LACHT, DER

POSTLAGERND TURTELTAUBE • 1952 • Buchholz Gerhard T. • FRG

POSTMAN • 1967 • Thomas P. A. • IND

POSTMAN, THE • 1910 • Fitzhamon Lewin? • UKN

POSTMAN, THE • 1912 • *Mace Fred* • USA

POSTMAN, THE • 1913 • Collins Edwin J. • UKN

POSTMAN, THE • 1929 • Tsekhanovsky M. M. • ANS • USS

POSTMAN, THE • 1953 • *O'Brien Dave* • SHT • USA

POSTMAN, THE see **BOUSTAGUY, AL** • 1968

POSTMAN, THE see **POSTCHI** • 1972

POSTMAN ALWAYS RINGS TWICE, THE • 1946 • Garnett Tay • USA

POSTMAN ALWAYS RINGS TWICE, THE • 1981 • Rafelson Bob • USA

POSTMAN ALWAYS RINGS TWICE, THE see **DERNIER TOURNANT, LE** • 1939

POSTMAN ALWAYS RINGS TWICE, THE see **OSSESSIONE** • 1943

POSTMAN AND THE NURSEMAID, THE • 1899 • *Norton C. Goodwin* • UKN

POSTMAN DIDN'T RING, THE • 1942 • Schuster Harold • USA

POSTMAN GOES TO WAR, THE (USA) see **FACTEUR S'EN VA-T-EN GUERRE, LE** • 1966

POSTMAN'S CHRISTMAS BOX, THE • 1906 • Collins Alf? • UKN

POSTMAN'S DILEMMA, THE • 1914 • Kellino W. P. • UKN

POSTMAN'S KNOCK • 1962 • Lynn Robert • UKN

POSTMAN'S TALE, THE see **POSTACKA POHADKA** • 1961

POSTMARK CANADA • 1958 • Fraser Donald • DOC • CND

POSTMARK FOR DANGER (USA) see **PORTRAIT OF ALISON** • 1955

POSTMASTER, THE see **KOLLEJSKII REGISTRATOR** • 1925

POSTMASTER OF PINEAPPLE PLAINS, THE • 1915 • *Mcnish Frank E.* • USA

POSTMASTER'S DAUGHTER, THE see **NOSTALGIE** • 1937

POSTMEISTER, DER • 1940 • Ucicky Gustav • FRG • HER CRIME WAS LOVE

POSTMEISTER, DER • 1955 • von Baky Josef • FRG

POSTO, IL • 1961 • Olmi Ermanno • ITL • SOUND OF TRUMPETS, THE ○ JOB, THE

POSTO ALL'INFERNO, UN • 1969 • Vari Giuseppe • ITL • PLACE IN HELL, A ○ COMMANDO ATTACK

POSTO DI BLOCCO • 1945 • Cerio Ferruccio • ITL

POSTO IDEALE PER UCCIDERE, UN • 1971 • Lenzi Umberto • ITL

POSTPONED • 1915 • Van Wally • USA

POSTRIZINY • 1980 • Menzel Jiri • CZC • CUTTING IT SHORT (UKN) ○ SHORT CUT (USA) ○ CLIPPINGS

POSTWAR JAPANESE see **GENDAIJIN** • 1952

POSTWAR JAPANESE HISTORY see **NIPPON SENGOSHI - MADAMU ONBORO NO SEIKATSU** • 1970

POSTZUG-UBERFALL, DER see **GENTLEMEN BITTEN ZUR KASSE, DIE** • 1965

POSZUKIWACZE • 1962 • Piekutowski Andrzej • PLN • SEARCHERS, THE ○ SEARCH, THE

POT AU FEU • 1965 • Altman Robert • SHT • USA

POT-BOUILLE • 1957 • Duvivier Julien • FRN, ITL • LOVERS IN PARIS (USA) ○ HOUSE OF LOVERS (UKN) ○ LOVERS OF PARIS

POT CARRIERS, THE • 1962 • Scott Peter Graham • UKN

POT GENERATION, THE see **QUINTA DEL PORRO, LA** • 1980

POT LUCK • 1936 • Walls Tom • UKN

POT LUCK PARDS • 1924 • *Morrison Pete* • USA

POT O' GOLD • 1941 • Marshall George • USA • GOLDEN HOUR, THE (UKN) ○ POT OF GOLD

POT OF GOLD see **POT O' GOLD** • 1941

POT OF GOLD, THE • 1917 • *Sais Marin* • SHT • USA

POT! PARENTS! POLICE! • 1975 • Pine Phillip • USA

POT-POURRI • 1929 • Jeffrey R. E. • UKN

POT-POURRI • 1962 • Lamb Derek (c/d) • ANS • CND

POT-POURRI D'ANIMAUX • Tessier Albert • DCS • CND

POTAGE INDIGESTE • 1903 • Blache Alice • FRN

POTAMI, TO • 1960 • Koundouros Nikos • GRC • RIVER, THE ○ RIVIERE, LA

POTASH AND PERLMUTTER • 1923 • Badger Clarence • USA • DR. SUNSHINE (UKN)

POTATO, THE see **KARTOFLER** • 1944

POTATO FRITZ • 1975 • Schamoni Peter • FRG • MASSACRE ON CONDOR PASS ○ MONTANA TRAP

POTATOES see **GAMJA** • 1988

POTE DHEN INE ARGA • 1968 • Ziagos Spiros • GRC • IT'S NEVER TOO LATE

"POTE LARIAT" OF THE FLYING A, THE • 1914 • Hamilton G. P. • USA

POTE TIN KYRIAKI • 1959 • Dassin Jules • GRC • NEVER ON SUNDAY (USA) ○ JAMAIS LE DIMANCHE

POTEM NASTAPI CISZA • 1966 • Morgenstern Janusz • PLN • AND ALL WILL BE QUIET

POTEMKIN (USA) see **BRONENOSETS POTYOMKIN** • 1925

POTENT LOTION • 1955 • *Halas John (P)* • ANS • UKN

POTERE, IL • 1972 • Tretti Augusto • ITL • POWER

POTERE TEMPORALE • 1916 • Ghione Emilio • ITL

POTERE TEMPORALE • 1916 • Negroni Baldassare • ITL

POTERYANNAYA FOTOGRAFIYA • 1959 • Kulidjanov Lev • USS • LOST PHOTOGRAPH, THE

POTE'S POEM • 1915 • Kellino W. P. • UKN

POTHI STON KATARAMENO VALTO • 1967 • Ioannidis Giannis B. • GRC • LUST IN THE SWAMPS (UKN)

POTIFARS HUSTRU • 1911 • Blom August • DNM • VICTIM OF A CHARACTER, THE

POTIFARS HUSTRU • 1917 • Dinesen Robert • DNM

POTIONS AND NOTIONS • 1966 • Culhane Shamus • ANS • USA

POTIPHAR'S WIFE • 1931 • Elvey Maurice • UKN • HER STRANGE DESIRE (USA)

POTIRON • 1921-23 • Mourlan Albert • ASS • FRN

POTLACH • 1988 • Vergitsis Nikos • GRC

POTLUCK PARDS • 1934 • Ray Bernard B. • USA

POTO AND CABENGO • 1979 • Gorin Jean-Pierre • FRG, USA

POTOMOK CHINGIS-KHAN • 1928 • Pudovkin V. I. • USS • HEIR TO GENGHIS KHAN, THE ○ STORM OVER ASIA ○ HEIR TO JENGHIZ KHAN, THE

POTOMOK DJAVOLA • 1917 • Bonc-Tomasevsky M. • USS • DEVIL'S STAIRCASE, THE

POTOP • 1974 • Hoffman Jerzy • PLN • DELUGE, THE (USA) ○ FLOOD, THE

POTPOUREEL • 1972 • Tajchman E. J. • ANS • USA

POTPOURRI • 1968 • Spoecker Peter D. • SHT • USA

POTPOURRI • 1969 • Bush Max Ii • USA

POTPOURRI • 1972 • Kaluza Les • USA

POTR' ET LA FILLE DES EAUX • 1974 • Laguionie Jean-Francois • ANS • FRN

POTRAGA • 1956 • Skrigin Zorz • YGS

POTRAGA ZA BLAGOM • 1974 • Tadej Vladimir • YGS • TREASURE HUNT

POTRAZI VANDU KOS • 1957 • Mitrovic Zika • YGS • LOOK FOR VANDA KOS

POTRET MARIA • 1980 • Salleh Yassin • MLY

POTRO SALVAJE, EL • 1956 • Baledon Rafael • MXC

POTS AND PANS • 1932 • Foster John, Rufle George • ANS • USA

POTS AND PANS PEGGIE • 1917 • Moore W. Eugene • USA

POTS AND POEMS • 1917 • Moore Matt • SHT • USA

POTSDAM, DAS SCHICKSAL EINER RESIDENZ • 1927 • Behrendt Hans • FRG

POTSDAM REBUILDS • 1946 • Huisken Joop • DOC • GDR

POTSELUI MERI PIKFORD • 1927 • Komarov Sergei • USS • KISS OF MARY PICKFORD, THE ○ MARY PICKFORD'S KISS

POTTED PANTOMIMES • 1914 • Kellino W. P. • UKN

POTTED PLAYS NO.1 see **SOCIETY PLAYWRIGHT, THE** • 1912

POTTED PLAYS NO.2 see **BABY, THE** • 1913

POTTED PLAYS NO.3 see **FREEZING MIXTURE** • 1910

POTTED PSALM, THE • 1946 • Peterson Sidney, Broughton James • SHT • USA

POTTER AND THE CLAY, THE • 1914 • Melford George • USA

POTTER OF THE YARD • 1952 • Wall John, Burn Oscar • UKN

POTTERIES see **CSEREPEK** • 1981

POTTERS, THE • 1927 • Newmeyer Fred • USA

POTTER'S CART, THE see **VOITURE DU POTIER, LA** • 1896

POTTER'S CLAY • 1922 • Grenville-Taylor H., Payne Douglas • UKN

POTTERY AT ILZA, THE see **CERAMIKA ILZECKA** • 1951

POTTERY GIRL'S ROMANCE, A • 1918 • Hewitt G. Fletcher • UKN

POTTERY MAKER see **STORY OF A POTTER, THE** • 1925

POTTERY OF ILZECKA, THE see **CERAMIKA ILZECKA** • 1951

POTTERY POETS • 1945 • *Mead Thomas (P)* • SHT • USA

POTTERYMAKER, A see **TOURNEUR EN POTERIE** • 1897

POTTS BUNGLES AGAIN • 1916 • Christie Al • SHT • USA

POTTS IN A PICKLE • 1914 • *Calvert Charles* • USA

POTTSVILLE PALOOKA, THE • 1931 • *Sennett Mack (P)* • SHT • USA

POTTY'S WEDDING DAY • 1915 • *Coronet* • UKN

POTU STORONU ARAKSA • 1947 • Shub Esther • USS • ON THE BANKS OF THE ARAX ○ ACROSS THE ARAX ○ BY THE ARAX ○ ON THE OTHER SIDE OF THE ARAKS ○ ACROSS THE ARAKS

POTUM OF SWAT, THE • 1919 • *Parsons Bill* • SHT • USA

POTWOROWSKI'S LANDSCAPE see **PEJZAZ POTWOROWSKIEGO** • 1966

POTYAUTASOK • 1989 • Soth Sandor • HNG • STOWAWAYS

POU POU • 1960 • Jonouchi Motoharu • SHT • JPN

POUCE • 1971 • Badel Pierre • FRN

POUCETOFS, LES • Danot Serge • FRN

POUDRE DE VITESSE • 1911 • Cohl Emile • ANS • FRN

POUDRE D'ESCAMPETTE, LA • 1971 • de Broca Philippe • FRN, ITL • DARSELA A GAMBE (ITL) ○ TOUCH AND GO (USA) ○ ROUTE AU SOLEIL, LA ○ FRENCH LEAVE

POUGHKEEPSIE REGATTA • 1906 • *Bitzer Billy (Ph)* • USA

POUIC-POUIC • 1963 • Girault Jean • FRN

POUICS • 1910 • Durand Jean • SER • FRN

POULE, LA • 1932 • Guissart Rene • FRN

POULE AUX OEUFS D'OR, LA • 1906 • Velle Gaston, Moreau Gabriel • FRN • CHICKEN THAT LAID GOLDEN EGGS, THE

POULE AUX OEUFS D'OR, LA • 1909 • Velle Gaston • FRN

POULE FANTAISISTE, LA • 1903 • Blache Alice • FRN

POULE MERVEILLEUSE, LA • 1902 • Zecca Ferdinand • FRN

POULE MOUILLEE QUI SE SECHE, UNE • 1912 • Cohl Emile • ANS • FRN

POULE SUR UN MUR, UNE • 1936 • Gleize Maurice • FRN

POULET, LE • 1963 • Berri Claude • SHT • FRN • CHICKEN, THE (USA)

POULET AU VINAIGRE • 1984 • Chabrol Claude • FRN • COP AU VIN

POULETTE GRISE, LA • 1947 • McLaren Norman • ANS • CND • LITTLE GREY HEN, THE

POULIMENOS, O • 1967 • Constantinou Panayotis • GRC • FOR SALE

POULOT N'EST PAS SAGE • 1912 • Cohl Emile • ANS • FRN

POULOU LE MAGNIFIQUE see **ETOILE AUX DENTS, L'** • 1971

POULTRY A LA MODE • 1916 • Miller Rube • SHT • USA

POULTRY PIRATES • 1938 • Freleng Friz • ANS • USA

POUND • 1970 • Downey Robert • USA

POUND FOOLISH • 1926 • Watt Nate, Davis George, Hutton Lucille, Bailey William • USA

POUND FOOLISH • 1940 • Feist Felix E. • SHT • USA

POUND FOR A POUND, A • 1915 • *Roscoe Albert* • USA

POUND OF FLESH see **YI P'ANG JOU** • 1976

POUND PUPPIES AND THE LEGEND OF BIG PAW • 1988 • Decelles Pierre • ANM • USA • POUND PUPPIES: THE LEGEND OF BIG PAW

POUND PUPPIES: THE LEGEND OF BIG PAW see **POUND PUPPIES AND THE LEGEND OF BIG PAW** • 1988

POUNDMAKER'S LODGE -A HEALING PLACE • 1988 • Obomsawin Alanis • DOC • CND

POUPEE, LA • 1899 • *Lumiere* • FRN • DOLL, THE ○ PUPPET, THE

POUPEE, LA • 1920 • Milton Meyrick • UKN • LA POUPEE

POUPEE, LA • 1958 • Baratier Jacques • FRN • HE, SHE OR IT? (UKN) ○ DOLL, THE

POUPEE, LA • 1966 • Laradji Rabah • SHT • ALG
POUPEE ROUGE, LA • 1968 • Leroi Francis • FRN • RED DOLL, THE
POUPEE VIVANTE, LA • 1909 • Melies Georges • FRN • LIVING DOLL, THE (USA)
POUPEES DE ROSEAU • 1981 • Farhati Jalili • MRC • REED DOLLS
POUPEES, LES (FRN) see **BAMBOLE, LE** • 1964
POUPONNIERE, LA • 1932 • Boyer Jean • FRN
POUR AIMER TON PAYS • 1942-43 • Tessier Albert • DCS • CND
POUR AVOIR ADRIENNE see **VOUS SEREZ MA FEMME** • 1932
POUR CENT BRIQUES, T'AS PLUS RIEN! • 1982 • Molinaro Edouard • FRN
POUR CLEMENCE • 1977 • Belmont Charles • FRN • FOR CLEMENCE
POUR DES FUSILS PERDUS • 1967 • Delanjeac Pierre • FRN
POUR DON CARLOS • 1921 • Musidora, Lasseyre Jacques • FRN
POUR EPATER LES POULES • Bowers Charley • SHT • FRN • HOW TO FATTEN CHICKENS
POUR EPOUSER GABY • 1919 • Burguet Charles • FRN
POUR ETRE AIME • 1933 • Tourneur Jacques • FRN
POUR LA DEFENSE • 1919 • Puchalski Eduard • PLN
POUR LA PEAU D'UN FLIC • 1981 • Delon Alain • FRN
POUR LA SUITE DU MONDE • 1963 • Perrault Pierre, Brault Michel • CND • MOONTRAP, THE (USA)
POUR L'ALSACE • 1917 • Desfontaines Henri • FRN
POUR L'AMOUR DE WINNIE • 1919 • Leprieur Gaston • FRN
POUR L'AMOUR DU CIEL (FRN) see **E PIU FACILE CHE UN CAMMELLO** • 1950
POUR LE MAILLOT JAUNE • 1939 • Stelli Jean • FRN
POUR LE MEILLEUR ET POUR LE PIRE • 1975 • Jutra Claude • CND
POUR LE MERITE • 1938 • Ritter Karl • FRG • ORDER OF MERIT, THE
POUR LE MISTRAL • 1966 • Ivens Joris • SHT • FRN
POUR LES BEAUX YEUX see **AMOUR.. AMOUR..** • 1932
POUR LES P'TIOTS • 1908 • Melies Georges • FRN
POUR L'ESPAGNE • 1963 • Rossif Frederic • SHT • FRN
POUR L'ETOILE S.V.P. • 1908 • Melies Georges • FRN
POUR L'HONNEUR D'UN PERE • 1905 • Zecca Ferdinand • FRN
POUR MEMOIRE • 1978 • Born Maurice, Pollet Jean-Daniel • DOC • FRN
POUR MEMOIRE see **MEMORANDUM** • 1967
POUR MON AMOUR see **MIN AGLI HUBBI** • 1959
POUR NE PAS OUBLIER • 1982 • Meneses Pedro • SWT • SO AS NOT TO FORGET
POUR QUE LA CHEVRE PAISSE EN PAIX • 1968 • Nasser George • SHT • LBN
POUR QUE VIVE L'ALGERIE! • 1972 • Kerzabi Ahmed, Rachedi Ahmed, Mazif Sid-Ali, Laradji Rabah, Azizi M., Bouchemaa R. • ALG
POUR QUELQUE CHOSE DE PLUS • 1976 • Bertrand Jean-Claude, Hubinet Jacques • DOC • FRN
POUR QUELQUES ARPENTS DE NEIGE.. • 1962 • Dufaux Georges, Godbout Jacques • DCS • CND • QUELQUES ARPENTS DE NEIGE
POUR QUI LES PRISONS? • 1977 • Lenasz Elia • DOC • FRN
POUR REGNER • 1926 • Luguet Andre • FRN
POUR SECOURER LA SALADE • 1902 • Blache Alice • FRN
POUR SERVICE DE NUIT see **SERVICE DE NUIT** • 1931
POUR SERVIR • 1916 • Burguet Charles • FRN
POUR TOI MON AMOUR • 1971 • Huggert E. • ANM • SWT
POUR TOI, MON ENFANT see **MATERNITE** • 1934
POUR UN AMOUR LOINTAIN • 1968 • Sechan Edmond • FRN
POUR UN BAISER see **VALSE ROYALE** • 1935
POUR UN BOUFFEE DE TABAC • 1915 • Diamant-Berger Henri • FRN
POUR UN MAILLOT JAUNE • 1965 • Lelouch Claude • DOC • FRN • FOR A YELLOW JERSEY (UKN)
POUR UN MONDE PLUS HUMAIN • 1977 • Piquint Jean-Marie • BLG
POUR UN PIANO • 1934 • Chenal Pierre • FRN
POUR UN SOIR • 1931 • Godard Jean • FRN • STELLA MARIS
POUR UN SOU D'AMOUR • 1931 • Gremillon Jean (U/c) • FRN
POUR UN SOURIRE • 1969 • Dupont-Midy Francois • FRN
POUR UNE CULTURE • 1973 • Sauve Alain • CND
POUR UNE EDUCATION DE QUALITE • 1969 • Lamothe Arthur • SER • CND
POUR UNE ETOILE SANS NOM see **MONA, L'ETOILE SANS NOM** • 1966
POUR UNE FEMME see **MIN AGL IMRA'A** • 1959
POUR UNE FORET NOUVELLE • 1985 • Kinsey Nicholas • DOC • CND • FOREST RENEWAL NOW
POUR UNE INFIDELITE • 1972 • Nlanza Ndomanuele Mafuta • ZRE
POUR UNE NUIT D'AMOUR • 1921 • Protazanov Yakov • FRN
POUR UNE NUIT D'AMOUR • 1946 • Greville Edmond T. • FRN • PASSIONNELLE
POUR UNE POIGNEE DE CACAHUETES • 1977 • Chahine Gabriel, Couedic Didier • FRN • RETOUR DE SCRATCH DANS LE + + –, LE
POUR VIVRE HEUREUX • 1932 • della Torre Claudio • FRN
POUR VOS BEAU YEUX • 1929 • Storck Henri • DCS • BLG
POUR X RAISONS • Byron Philippe • FRN
POURQUOI • 1976 • Bernard Anouk • FRN
POURQUOI? • 1985 • Beaudry Michel • MTV • CND
POURQUOI C'EST FAIRE • 1967 • Lavoie Richard • DCS • CND
POURQUOI ISRAEL? • 1973 • Lanzmann Claude • DOC • FRN • ISRAEL WHY?
POURQUOI L'ACTEUR EN RETARD see **ACTEUR EN RETARD, L'** • 1908
POURQUOI L'AMERIQUE? • 1970 • Rossif Frederic • FRN • WHY AMERICA?
POURQUOI L'ETRANGE MONSIEUR ZOLOCK S'INTERESSAIT-IL TANT A LA BANDE DESSINEE? • 1984 • Simoneau Yves • CND • WHY IS THE STRANGE MR. ZOLOCK INTERESTED IN COMIC STRIPS?
POURQUOI PARIS? • 1962 • de La Patelliere Denys • FRN, ITL
POURQUOI PAS.. • 1970 • Cardinal Roger • DCS • CND
POURQUOI PAS? • 1979 • Serreau Coline • FRN • WHY NOT?
POURQUOI PAS? see **CENT MILLE FRANCS POUR UN BAISER** • 1933
POURQUOI PAS NOUS • 1981 • Biraud Maurice, Berny Michel • FRN
POURQUOI PAS TOI see **AMOUREUX DE MARIANNE, LES** • 1953
POURQUOI SANGLOTE LE VIOLON? • 1913 • Protazanov Yakov • USS
POURQUOI VIENS-TU SI TARD? • 1959 • Decoin Henri • FRN • TOO LATE TO LOVE (USA)
POURRIEZ-VOUS M'EXPLIQUER? • 1974 • Brault Francois, Gauvreau J. • SHT • CND
POURSUITE, LA see **ROI SANS DIVERTISSEMENT, UN** • 1962
POURSUITE DU BONHEUR, LA • 1988 • Lanctot Micheline • DOC • CND
POURSUITE IMPLACABLE, LA (FRN) see **REVOLVER** • 1973
POURSUITE MYSTERIEUSE, LA • Lafleur Jean, Svatek Peter • CND
POURVU QU'ON AIT L'IVRESSE • 1957 • Pollet Jean-Daniel • SHT • FRN
POURVU QU'ON AIT L'IVRESSE • 1974 • Bassi Rinaldo • FRN, ITL
POUSADA DAS CHAGAS, A • 1971 • Rocha Paulo • PRT
POUSADAS DE PORTUGAL • 1963 • Rosa Americo Leite • SHT • PRT
POUSSE DES PLANTES, LA • 1913 • Burel Leonce-Henry • SHT • FRN
POUSSE MAIS POUSSE EGAL • 1974 • Heroux Denis • CND
POUSSE-POUSSE • 1974 • Ze-Lecourt Moise • CMR
POUSSEZ-PAS GRAND-PERE DANS LE CACTUS • 1969 • Dague Jean-Claude • FRN
POUSSIERE D'ANGE • 1986 • Niermans Edouard • FRN • ANGEL DUST
POUSSIERE D'EMPIRE • 1983 • Le Lam • VTN, FRN
POUSSIERE SUR LA VILLE • 1965 • Lamothe Arthur • CND
POUSSIERES, LES • 1954 • Franju Georges • DCS • FRN
POUSSIERES DE JUILLET • 1967 • Cherif Hachemi • SHT • ALG
POUSSIN -THE SEVEN SACRAMENTS see **MIND OF NICOLAS POUSSIN -THE SEVEN SACRAMENTS, THE** • 1968
POUTA • 1961 • Kachyna Karel • CZC • COUNTRY DOCTOR, THE ○ FETTERS
POUTING AND BEGUILING see **HNOKE KHAN SU GA MU HMAR PIN** • 1982
POUTNICI • 1988 • Zaoral Zdenek • CZC • WANDERERS
POUTNICI see **ZBEHOVIA A PUTNICI** • 1968
POUVOIR DU MAL, LE see **PARADIGME** • 1985
POUVOIR INTIME • 1983 • Simoneau Yves • CND • INTIMATE POWER
POVERE BIMBE • 1923 • Pastrone Giovanni • ITL
POVERI, BELLI E INNAMORATI • 1968 • Ferrari Giorgio • ITL
POVERI MA BELLI • 1956 • Risi Dino • ITL • POOR BUT BEAUTIFUL (USA) ○ GIRL IN A BIKINI ○ POOR BUT HANDSOME
POVERI MILIONARI • 1958 • Risi Dino • ITL • POOR MILLIONAIRE
POVERO CRISTO • 1976 • Carpi Pier • ITL
POVERO RICCO • 1983 • Festa Campanile Pasquale • ITL
POVERTY AND COMPASSION • 1908 • Bouwmeester Theo • UKN
POVERTY AND NOBILITY (USA) see **MISERIA E NOBILITA** • 1954
POVERTY GULCH • 1918 • *Rancho* • SHT • USA
POVERTY OF RICHES, THE • 1913 • *Rex* • USA
POVERTY OF RICHES, THE • 1921 • Barker Reginald • USA
POVEST O DOBRIH LJUDEH • 1975 • Stiglic France • YGS • STORY OF SOME GOOD PEOPLE, A ○ STORY OF THE GOOD PEOPLE, THE ○ PRICA O DOBRIM LJUDIMA ○ STORY OF GOOD PEOPLE, THE
POVEST O NEFTYANIKAKH KASPIYA • 1953 • Karmen Roman • USS • OIL WORKERS OF THE CASPIAN SEA ○ STORY OF THE CASPIAN OIL MEN ○ CASPIAN STORY ○ CASPIAN OIL WORKERS
POVEST PLAMENNYKH LET • 1960 • Solntseva Yulia • USS • HISTORY OF THE BURNING YEARS, THE ○ CHRONICLE OF FLAMING YEARS ○ FLAMING YEARS, THE ○ TURBULENT YEARS, THE ○ YEARS OF FIRE, THE ○ STORY OF THE TURBULENT YEARS
POVESTE CA-N BASME, O • 1959 • Popescu-Gopo Ion • RMN • PRINCESS IN LOVE, THE ○ O POVESTE CA-N BASME
POVESTE O NASTOYASHCHEM CHELOVEKE • 1948 • Stolper Alexander • USS • STORY OF A REAL MAN
POVESTE SENTIMENTALA • 1961 • Mihu Iulian • RMN • SENTIMENTAL STORY, A
POVESTEA DRAGOSTEI • 1976 • Popescu-Gopo Ion • RMN • STORY OF LOVE, THE
POVIDKY Z PRVNI REPUBLIKY • 1965 • Krejcik Jiri • CZC • TALES FROM THE FIRST REPUBLIC
POVO ORGANIZADO, O • 1976 • van Lieropl Robert • PRT
POVODEN • 1958 • Fric Martin • CZC • FLOOD, THE
POVOROT • 1979 • Abdrakhitov Vadim • USS • TURNING POINT, THE
POVRATAK • 1966 • Pavlovic Zivojin • YGS • HOMECOMING, THE ○ RETURN, THE
POVRATAK • 1980 • Vrdoljak Antun • YGS • RETURN, THE
POVRATAK see **PARTIZANSKE PRICE** • 1960
POVRATAK KATARINE KOZUL • 1989 • Praljak Slobodan • YGS • RETURN OF KATARINA KOZUL, THE
POVRATAK OTPISANIH • 1977 • Djordjevic Aleksandar • YGS • WRITTEN-OFF RETURN, THE
POW POW AT DUCK LAKE • 1967 • Klein Bonnie • DOC • CND
POW WOW • 1959 • Downs Allen, Liebling Jerome • USA
POW WOW TE MORT BEN J'JOUE PU • 1980 • Tremblay Robert • CND • MEDES, LES
POWAQQATSI • 1988 • Reggio Godfrey • USA • NORTH SOUTH
POWDER • 1916 • Maude Arthur • USA
POWDER AND PETROL see **PUDR A BENZIN** • 1931
POWDER AND SHOT see **KRUDT OG KLUNKER** • 1959
POWDER AND SMOKE • 1924 • Roach Hal • SHT • USA
POWDER FLASH OF DEATH, THE • 1913 • Dwan Allan • USA
POWDER MY BACK • 1928 • Del Ruth Roy • USA
POWDER RIVER • 1953 • King Louis • USA
POWDER RIVER GUNFIRE • 1948 • Moore Harold James • SHT • USA
POWDER RIVER RUSTLERS • 1949 • Ford Philip • USA
POWDER TOWN • 1942 • Lee Rowland V. • USA
POWDER TRAIL, THE • 1916 • Ford Francis • SHT • USA
POWDERKEG • 1970 • Heyes Douglas • USA
POWDERSMOKE RANGE • 1935 • Fox Wallace • USA
POWER • 1916 • Wright Fred E. • SHT • USA
POWER • 1920 • *Blinn Holbrook* • SHT • USA
POWER • 1928 • Higgin Howard • USA
POWER • 1980 • Shear Barry, Vogel Virgil W. • TVM • USA
POWER • 1986 • Lumet Sidney • USA
POWER see **POTERE, IL** • 1972
POWER see **ARHONTES** • 1976
POWER, THE • 1967 • Haskin Byron • USA
POWER, THE • 1980 • Carpenter Stephen, Obrow Jeffrey • USA
POWER AMONG MEN • 1958 • Hammid Alexander, Polidoro Gian Luigi, Sarma V. L. • SHT • UNN
POWER AND GLORY (UKN) see **POWER AND THE GLORY, THE** • 1933
POWER AND THE GLORY, THE • 1918 • Windom Lawrence C. • USA
POWER AND THE GLORY, THE • 1933 • Howard William K. • USA • POWER AND GLORY (UKN)
POWER AND THE GLORY, THE • 1941 • Monkman Noel • ASL
POWER AND THE LAND, THE • 1940 • Ivens Joris • SHT • USA
POWER AND THE PRIZE, THE • 1956 • Koster Henry • USA
POWER AND THE TRUTH, THE see **PUTEREA SI ADEVARUL** • 1972
POWER BEHIND THE THRONE, THE • 1912 • St. Loup? • USA
POWER DIVE • 1941 • Hogan James P. • USA
POWER DIVINE, THE • 1923 • Moody H. G.?, Craft William James? • USA
POWER FOR DEFENSE • 1942 • Gercke, Bolte • SHT • USA
POWER FOR THE HIGHLANDS • 1943 • Chambers Jack • DOC • UKN
POWER FROM ABOVE, THE • 1910 • *Electrograff* • USA
POWER FROM FUSION PART 1: THE PRINCIPLES • 1964 • Smith G. Buckland • DOC • UKN
POWER FROM THE RIVER • 1948 • Holmes Cecil • DOC • NZL
POWER GAME • 1982 • Canel Fausto • USA, SPN • SEVENTY-TWO HOURS TO DIE ○ SEVENTY-TWO HOURS OR DIE ○ AMENAZA, LA ○ 72 HOURS OR DIE ○ THREAT, THE
POWER GOD, THE • 1925 • Wilson Ben • SRL • USA
POWER HEADS • 1981 • Anderson John, French Michael • CND
POWER MAKERS, THE • 1957 • Robinson Lee • DOC • ASL
POWER MAN see **POWER WITHIN, THE** • 1979
POWER OF A HYMN, THE • 1912 • *Bodie William* • USA
POWER OF A LIE, THE • 1922 • Archainbaud George • USA
POWER OF A SMILE, THE • 1910 • *Imp* • USA
POWER OF CENSORSHIP, THE see **PODER DE LA CENSURA, EL** • 1982
POWER OF CIVILIZATION, THE • 1913 • *St. Louis Motion Picture* • USA
POWER OF CONSCIENCE, THE • 1912 • *Baggot King* • USA
POWER OF CONSCIENCE, THE • 1913 • Wharton Theodore • USA
POWER OF DARKNESS, THE see **MACHT DER FINSTERNIS, DIE** • 1923
POWER OF DARKNESS, THE see **PODER DE LAS TINIEBLAS, EL** • 1979
POWER OF DECISION, THE • 1917 • Noble John W. • USA
POWER OF DESIRE, THE see **PODER DEL DESEO, EL** • 1976
POWER OF DESTINY see **MOC OSUDU** • 1969
POWER OF DEVOTION, THE • 1911 • *Yankee* • USA
POWER OF EVIL • 1929 • Goldvani M., Barkhoudian P. • USS
POWER OF EVIL, THE • 1916 • Horkheimer H. M., Horkheimer E. D. • USA
POWER OF FASCINATION, THE • 1915 • Madison Cleo • USA
POWER OF GOD, THE see **KUDRAT** • 1970
POWER OF GOLD, THE see **KIZU DARAKE NO SANGA** • 1964
POWER OF GOOD, THE • 1911 • *Essanay* • USA
POWER OF HEREDITY, THE • 1913 • *Leonard Robert* • USA
POWER OF INNOCENCE • 1912 • *Republic* • USA
POWER OF JUSTICE (UKN) see **BEYOND THE SACRAMENTO** • 1940
POWER OF LABOR, THE • 1908 • *Selig* • USA
POWER OF LIFE • 1938 • Lynn Henry
POWER OF LIGHT, THE • 1914 • Johnston Lorimer • USA
POWER OF LOVE, A • 1909 • *Centaur* • USA
POWER OF LOVE, THE • 1911 • *White Pearl* • USA
POWER OF LOVE, THE • 1912 • Dwan Allan • USA
POWER OF LOVE, THE • 1919 • Sandberg Anders W. • DNM
POWER OF LOVE, THE • 1922 • Deverich Nat C. • USA
POWER OF LOVE, THE see **KAERLIGHEDENS STYRKE** • 1911
POWER OF LOVE, THE see **GHODRATE-ESHGH** • 1968
POWER OF MELODY, THE • 1912 • *Von Meter Arthur* • USA
POWER OF MEN IS THE PATIENCE OF WOMEN, THE see **MACHT DER MANNER IST DIE GEDULD DER FRAUEN, DIE** • 1978
POWER OF MIND, THE • 1916 • Ricketts Thomas • SHT • USA
POWER OF MONEY, THE • 1912 • *Solax* • USA
POWER OF MUSIC, THE • 1915 • *Alhambra* • USA
POWER OF MUSIC, THE see **MUSIKENS MAKT** • 1913
POWER OF PIN MONEY, THE • 1917 • Thayer Otis B. • SHT • USA
POWER OF POSSESSION (UKN) see **LAWLESS EMPIRE** • 1945
POWER OF PRAYER • 1913 • *Kinemacolor* • USA
POWER OF PRAYER, THE • 1914 • *Victory* • USA
POWER OF PRAYER, THE • 1915 • *Alhambra* • USA
POWER OF PRAYER, THE • 1915 • Kent Leon D. • *Lubin* • USA
POWER OF PRINT, THE • 1914 • *Patheplay* • USA
POWER OF PUBLICITY, THE • 1915 • *Lorenz John* • USA
POWER OF RIGHT, THE • 1919 • Thornton F. Martin • UKN
POWER OF SILENCE, THE • 1912 • *Johnson Arthur* • USA
POWER OF SILENCE, THE • 1928 • Worsley Wallace • USA
POWER OF SLEEP, THE • 1913 • *Lyon Frank A.* • USA
POWER OF THE ANGELUS, THE • 1915 • Ince Thomas H., Clifford William H. • USA
POWER OF THE CAMERA, THE • 1913 • *Pixley Gus* • USA

POWER OF THE CROSS • 1916 • King Burton L. • SHT • USA
POWER OF THE CROSS, THE • 1912 • *Nestor* • USA
POWER OF THE CROSS, THE • 1913 • Johnson Arthur? • USA
POWER OF THE MIND, THE • 1914 • *Van Trump Jessalyn* • USA
POWER OF THE MOUNTAINS, THE (USA) see **MACHT DER BERGE, DIE** • 1938
POWER OF THE PEOPLE, THE see **BATALLA DE CHILE: PART 3, LA** • 1979
POWER OF THE PRESS • 1943 • Landers Lew • USA
POWER OF THE PRESS see **FREEDOM OF THE PRESS** • 1928
POWER OF THE PRESS, THE • 1909 • Brooke Van Dyke • USA
POWER OF THE PRESS, THE • 1914 • *Barrymore Lionel* • USA
POWER OF THE PRESS, THE • 1928 • Capra Frank • USA
POWER OF THE SEA, THE • 1913 • *Pilot* • USA
POWER OF THE SEA, THE • 1913 • Vale Travers • *Reliance* • USA
POWER OF THE STREET, THE • 1915 • *Edwards Walter* • USA
POWER OF THE SULTAN, THE • 1909 • *Bosworth Hobart* • USA
POWER OF THE WEAK, THE • 1926 • Craft William James • USA
POWER OF THE WHISTLER, THE • 1945 • Landers Lew • USA
POWER OF THOUGHT • 1949 • Donnelly Eddie • ANS • USA
POWER OF THOUGHT, THE • 1912 • *Rex* • USA
POWER OVER MEN • 1929 • Banfield George J. • UKN
POWER PILL, THE • 1968 • Arnold Jack • MTV • USA
POWER PLAY • 1978 • Burke Martyn • CND, UKN • STATE OF SHOCK ○ COUP D'ETAT
POWER SIGNAL LINEMAN • 1953 • Anderson Max • SHT • UKN
POWER THAT RULES, THE • 1913 • Sturgeon Rollin S. • USA
POWER TO FLY • 1953 • Privett Bob • ANS • UKN
POWER TO FORGIVE, THE • 1914 • Stanley George C. • USA
POWER TO KILL, THE • 1914 • Martinek H. O. • UKN
POWER TO KILL, THE see **HIDDEN POWER** • 1939
POWER TO THE PEOPLE • 1972 • Benegal Shyam • DCS • IND
POWER TO WIN, THE • 1942 • Chauvel Charles • DOC • ASL
POWER TRAIN • 1960 • Murakami Jimmy T. • UKN
POWER (USA) see **JEW SUSS** • 1934
POWER WITH PRECISION • 1958 • Rafferty Chips • DOC • ASL
POWER WITHIN, THE • 1921 • Kennedy Lem F. • USA
POWER WITHIN, THE • 1979 • Moxey John Llewellyn • TVM • USA • POWER MAN
POWERED FLIGHT -THE STORY OF THE CENTURY • 1953 • Legg Stuart • DOC • UKN
POWERFUL EYE, THE • 1924 • Laemmle Ernst • SHT • USA
POWERFUL SEA CLAN see **MAMPOU HATTENSHI: UMI NO GOZUKU** • 1942
POWERPLAY see **ZKROCENI ZLEHO MUZE** • 1987
POWERS GIRLS, THE • 1942 • McLeod Norman Z. • USA • HELLO! BEAUTIFUL (UKN)
POWERS OF TEN • 1968 • Eames Charles, Eames Ray • USA
POWERS OF THE AIR, THE • 1914 • *West William* • USA
POWERS THAT PREY • 1918 • King Henry • USA
POWIATOWA LADY MAKBET (PLN) see **SIBIRSKA LEDI MAGBET** • 1962
POWODZ • 1947 • Bossak Jerzy • DOC • PLN • STORM OVER POLAND ○ FLOOD, THE
POWROT • 1960 • Passendorfer Jerzy • PLN • SHADOWS OF THE PAST ○ RETURN TO THE PAST ○ GHOSTS
POWROT • 1969 • Rybkowski Jan • PLN • RETURN, THE
POWROT • 1972 • Kucia Jerzy • PLN • RETURN, THE
POWROT NA STARE MIASTO • 1954 • Bossak Jerzy • DOC • PLN • RETURN TO THE OLD TOWN ○ RETURN TO THE OLD CITY
POWROT NA ZIEMIE • 1967 • Jedryka Stanislaw • PLN • RETURN TO EARTH
POWROT POSLA • 1965 • Wionczek Roman • DOC • PLN • RETURN OF THE ENVOY, THE
POWROT STATKU • 1964 • Marzynski Marian • DOC • PLN • RETURN OF A SHIP ○ RETURN BY BOAT
POWROT WILCZYCY • 1990 • Piestrak Marek • PLN • RETURN OF THE SHE-WOLF
POWSZEDNI DZIEN GESTAPOWCA SCHMIDTA • 1963 • Ziarnik Jerzy • DOC • PLN • DAY IN THE LIFE OF GESTAPO MAN SCHMIDT, A
POWWOW HIGHWAY • 1989 • Wacks Jonathan • USA
POY PYESNYU, POET.. • 1973 • Urusevsky Sergei • USS • SING YOUR SONG, POET..
POYEDINOK • 1945 • Legoshin Vladimir • USS • DUEL
POYEDINOK V GORAKH • 1968 • Rustambekov Kyamil • USS • DUEL IN THE MOUNTAINS
POYISK • 1968 • Khrinyuk Yevgyeni, Zhuk Konstantin • USS • SEARCH
POZAR • 1975 • Giersz Witold • ANS • PLN • FIRE, THE
POZAR, POZAR, COS NARESZCIE DZIEJE SIE! • 1967 • Piwowski Marek • DOC • PLN • FIRE, FIRE, SOMETHING IS HAPPENING AT LAST!
POZEGNANIA • 1958 • Has Wojciech J. • PLN • PARTINGS (USA) ○ LYDIA ATE THE APPLE ○ FAREWELLS
POZEGNANIE JESIENI • 1990 • Trelinski Mariusz • PLN • FAREWELL AUTUMN
POZEGNANIE Z DIABLEM • 1956 • Jakubowska Wanda • PLN • FAREWELL TO THE DEVIL ○ GOODBYE TO THE DEVIL
POZHARAT • 1968 • Belogorski Nyuma • BUL • FIRE, THE
POZNAN NIGHTINGALES, THE see **POZNANSKIE SLOWIKI** • 1966
POZNANSKIE SLOWIKI • 1966 • Przybyla Hieronim • PLN • POZNAN NIGHTINGALES, THE
POZNE POPOLUDNIE • 1964 • Scibor-Rylski Aleksander • PLN • LATE AFTERNOON
POZO, EL • 1964 • de Anda Raul • MXC
POZO, EL • 1972 • Aguirre Javier • SPN • WELL, THE
POZO, EL • 1973 • *Churubusco Azteca* • MXC
POZO DE LOS ENAMORADOS, EL • 1943 • Gan Jose H. • SPN
POZO MUERTO • 1967 • Rebolledo Carlos • VNZ • DEAD PIT
POZOR! • 1959 • Brdecka Jiri • ANS • CZC • LOOK OUT! ○ ATTENTION!
POZOR see **VSTRECHNYI** • 1932
POZOR, VIZITA • 1981 • Kachyna Karel • CZC • WATCH OUT, THE DOCTORS' ROUNDS ○ VIZITA ○ DOCTOR'S ROUND
POZORISNA VEZA • 1981 • Lakovic Milorad • YGS • STAGE CONNECTION
POZZO DEI MIRACOLI, IL • 1941 • Righelli Gennaro • ITL
POZZO DELLE TRE VERITA, IL (ITL) see **PUITS AUX TROIS VERITES, LE** • 1961
PRA FRENTE BRASIL • 1982 • Farias Roberto • BRZ • ONWARD BRAZIL
PRABHU KI LILA • IND
PRACE • 1960 • Kachyna Karel • CZC • SLINGER, THE
PRACTICAL DEMONSTRATION, A • 1914 • *Lubin* • USA
PRACTICAL JOKE, A • 1898 • Smith G. A. • UKN • JOKE ON THE GARDENER, A
PRACTICAL JOKE AND A SAD END, A see **GROV SPOG, EN** • 1908
PRACTICAL JOKE IN A BAR ROOM see **MAIVAISE PLAISANTERIE** • 1901
PRACTICAL JOKE ON THE GARDENER, A see **ARROSEUR ARROSE, L'** • 1895
PRACTICAL JOKER • 1944 • Jason Will • SHT • USA
PRACTICAL JOKERS • 1938 • Sidney George • SHT • USA
PRACTICAL PIG, THE • 1939 • Rickard Dick • ANS • USA
PRACTICAL YOKE • 1966 • Smith Paul J. • ANS • USA
PRACTICALLY YOURS • 1944 • Leisen Mitchell • USA
PRACTICE, THE • 1971 • Hough John • UKN
PRACTICE MAKES PERFECT • 1940 • *Mintz Charles (P)* • ANS • USA
PRACTICE MAKES PERFECT (USA) see **CAVALEUR, LE** • 1979
PRACTICE OF A CRIME see **ENSAYO DE UN CRIMEN** • 1955
PRACTICE OF LOVE, THE see **PRAXIS DER LIEBE, DIE** • 1985
PRACTICE SHOTS • 1931 • Marshall George • SHT • USA
PRACTICE WHAT YOU PREACH • 1917 • *Christie* • USA
PRACTICE WHAT YOU PREACH • 1917 • Chaudet Louis W. • *Nestor* • SHT • USA
PRAERIEKAMMERATER • 1970 • Ottesen Carl • DNM • PALS ON THE PRAIRIE
PRAERIENS SKRAPPE DRENGE • 1970 • Ottosen Carl • DNM
PRAESIDENTEN • 1919 • Dreyer Carl T. • DNM • PRESIDENT, THE
PRAESTEN I VEJLBY • 1920 • Blom August • DNM • VICAR OF VEJLBY, THE ○ LAND OF FATE, THE
PRAESTEN I VEJLBY • 1931 • *Holger-Madsen* • DNM
PRAESTENS DATTER • 1916 • Holger-Madsen • DNM • PASTOR'S DAUGHTER, THE
PRAG • 1937 • Prager Wilhelm • FRG • PRAGUE
PRAGUE see **PRAG** • 1937
PRAGUE see **NAVRAT DOMU** • 1948
PRAGUE 5, THE see **PRAZSKA PETKA** • 1988
PRAGUE ADAMITES, THE see **PRAZSTI ADAMITE** • 1917
PRAGUE AT ZERO HOUR see **PRAHA, NULTA HODINA** • 1962
PRAGUE CASTLE see **NA PRAZSKEM HRADE** • 1932
PRAGUE GALLIVANTER, THE see **PRAZSKY FLAMENDR** • 1941
PRAGUE IN 1549 • Raabeova Hedvika • CZC
PRAGUE NIGHTS see **PRAZSKE NOCI** • 1968
PRAGUE NIGHTS see **PRAZSKE NOCI** • 1968
PRAGUE OF THE JUGENDSTIL PERIOD see **PRAHA SECESNI** • 1974
PRAGUE WAR SECRECY see **VALECNE TAJNOSTI PRAZSKE** • 1926
PRAHA, NULTA HODINA • 1962 • Makovec Milos • CZC • PRAGUE AT ZERO HOUR
PRAHA SECESNI • 1974 • Vlacil Frantisek • SHT • CZC • PRAGUE OF THE JUGENDSTIL PERIOD
PRAHEVALSKY see **PRZHEVALSKII** • 1951
PRAHLAD • 1951 • Burma Phani • IND
PRAHLAD, DEVOTEE TO THE GOD see **BHAKTA PRAHLAD** • 1924
PRAHLAD, DEVOTEE TO THE GOD see **BHAKTA PRAHLAD** • 1924
PRAIA DE PESCADORES • 1930 • de Barros Jose Leitao • PRT
PRAIRIE, THE • 1947 • Wisbar Frank • USA
PRAIRIE, THE • 1989 • Mehrjui Dariush • IRN
PRAIRIE BADMEN • 1946 • Newfield Sam • USA
PRAIRIE CHICKEN, A • 1917 • Moore Vin • SHT • USA
PRAIRIE CHICKENS • 1943 • Roach Hal Jr. • USA
PRAIRIE EN FEU, LA • 1913 • Durand Jean • FRN
PRAIRIE EN FOU, LA • 1907 • Durand Jean • FRN
PRAIRIE EXPRESS • 1947 • Hillyer Lambert • USA
PRAIRIE FLOWER, THE • 1916 • *Utah* • USA
PRAIRIE GUNSMOKE • 1942 • Hillyer Lambert • USA
PRAIRIE HEIRESS, A • 1917 • *Triangle* • USA
PRAIRIE JUSTICE • 1938 • Waggner George • USA
PRAIRIE KING, THE • 1927 • Eason B. Reeves • USA
PRAIRIE LAW • 1940 • Howard David • USA
PRAIRIE MOON • 1938 • Staub Ralph • USA
PRAIRIE MYSTERY, THE • 1922 • Hall George Edwardes • USA
PRAIRIE ON FIRE, THE • 1912 • *Gaumont* • USA
PRAIRIE OUTLAWS • 1948 • Tansey Robert • USA
PRAIRIE PALS • 1943 • Newfield Sam • USA
PRAIRIE PAPAS • 1938 • Townley Jack • SHT • USA
PRAIRIE PIONEERS • 1941 • Orlebeck Lester • USA
PRAIRIE PIRATE, THE • 1925 • Mortimer Edmund • USA • YELLOW SEAL, THE
PRAIRIE PIRATES • 1949 • Cowan Will • SHT • USA
PRAIRIE POSTMISTRESS, THE • 1910 • *Bison* • USA
PRAIRIE RAIDERS • 1947 • Abrahams Derwin • USA • FORGER, THE (UKN)
PRAIRIE ROMEO, A • 1917 • Reynolds Lynn • SHT • USA
PRAIRIE ROUND-UP • 1951 • Sears Fred F. • USA
PRAIRIE RUSTLERS • 1945 • Newfield Sam • USA
PRAIRIE SCHOONERS • 1940 • Nelson Sam • USA • THROUGH THE STORM (UKN)
PRAIRIE SPOONERS • 1941 • D'Arcy Harry • SHT • USA
PRAIRIE STATION • 1941 • Preobrazhenskaya Olga • USS
PRAIRIE STRANGER • 1941 • Hillyer Lambert • USA • MARKED BULLET, THE (UKN)
PRAIRIE THUNDER • 1937 • Eason B. Reeves • USA
PRAIRIE TOWN ROMANCE, A • 1909 • *Selig* • USA
PRAIRIE TRAIL, THE • 1913 • *Bison* • USA
PRAIRIE TRAILS • 1920 • Marshall George • USA
PRAIRIE WIFE, THE • 1925 • Ballin Hugo • USA
PRAIRIE WINTER • 1935 • Cherry Evelyn Spice, Cherry Lawrence W. • DOC • CND
PRAIRIES, THE • 1973 • Kelly Ron • DOC • CND
PRAISE AGENT, THE • 1919 • Crane Frank H. • USA
PRAISE MARX AND PASS THE AMMUNITION • 1970 • Hatton Maurice • UKN
PRAISE THE SEA see **PRIJS DE MAAR** • 1958
PRAK A DRAK • 1960 • Topaldgikov Stefan • ANS • CZC • SLINGSHOT AND THE KITE, THE ○ CATAPAULT AND THE KITE, THE
PRAKTOR KITSOS KALI GASTOUNI • 1967 • Papakostas Giorgos • GRC • AGENT KITSOS CALLS GASTOUNI
PRALAT VON CADORE, DER • 1915 • Albes Emil • FRG
PRAM, THE see **BARNVAGNEN** • 1963
PRAMEELA ARJUN • 1930 • *General Pictures Corp* • IND
PRAMEN LASKY • 1928 • Kokeisl • CZC • SOURCE OF LOVE, THE
PRAMIE FUR IRENE, EINE • 1971 • Sander Helke • FRG
PRAMIEN AUF DEN TOD • 1950 • Jurgens Curd • AUS
PRANA • 1969 • Pena Raul • SPN
PRANAMITHRULU • 1967 • Pulliah P. • IND • CLOSE FRIENDS
PRANCER • 1989 • Hancock John • USA
PRANGASIZ MAHKUMLAR • 1964 • Ariburnu • TRK
PRANK, THE • 1988 • Firstenberg Sam • USA
PRANK WITH A FAKE PYTHON see **SERPENT DE LA RUE DE LA LUNE, LE** • 1908
PRANKE, DIE • 1931 • Steinhoff Hans • FRG • PAW, THE
PRANKE, DIE (FRG) see **UOMO DALL'ARTIGLIO, L'** • 1931
PRANKS • 1909 • Griffith D. W. • USA
PRANKS • 1981 • Obrow Jeffrey, Carpenter Stephen • USA • DORM THAT DRIPPED BLOOD, THE ○ DEATH DORM
PRANKS ON BOARD see **MUCHACHADA DE A BORDO, LA** • 1967
P'RAPS, P'RAPS NOT • 1915 • Collins Edwin J.? • UKN
PRARIEBLUT • 1920 • *Orlanda Martha* • FRG
PRARIEDIVA, DIE • 1920 • Boese Carl • FRG
PRASCHNAS GEHEIMNIS • 1922 • *Andra Fern* • FRG
PRASCOVIA • 1909 • USA
PRASHNAI GULSARA • 1970 • Urusevsky Sergei • USS • AMBLER'S RACE, THE ○ TROTTER'S GAIT, THE ○ BYEG INOKHODTSA
PRASIDENT, DER • 1928 • Righelli Gennaro • FRG • PRESIDENT, THE
PRASIDENT BARRADA • 1920 • Lund Erik • FRG
PRASIDENT IM EXIL, DER • 1969 • Heynowski Walter, Scheumann Gerhard • GDR
PRASTANKAN • 1920 • Dreyer Carl T. • SWD • FOURTH MARRIAGE OF DAME MARGARET, THE ○ PARSON'S WIDOW, THE ○ WITCH WOMAN, THE (USA) ○ YOUTH TO YOUTH
PRASTEN • 1913 • Sjostrom Victor • SWD • CLERGYMAN, THE ○ PRIEST, THE
PRASTEN I UDDARBO • 1958 • Fant Kenne • SWD • CLERGYMAN FROM UDDARBO, THE
PRASTEN SOM SLOG KNOCKOUT • 1943 • Bolander Hugo • SWD • KNOCKOUT CLERGYMAN, THE
PRATA PALOMARIS • 1972 • Faria Andre Luiz De Souza • BRZ
PRATELE NA SIRKACH • 1960 • Kluge Josef • CZC • FRIENDS ON MATCHSTICKS ○ MATCHSTICK PALS, THE
PRATER • 1924 • Felner Peter Paul • FRG • ERLEBNISSE ZWEIER NAHMADCHEN, DIE
PRATER see **WEG DES HERZENS, DER** • 1937
PRATERBUBEN • 1947 • Martin Paul • AUS
PRATERHERZEN • 1953 • Verhoeven Paul • AUS • TINGELTANGEL
PRATERMIZZI • 1927 • Reisch Walter, Ucicky Gustav • AUS
PRATIBAD • 1948 • *Sircar B. N. (P)* • IND
PRATIDWANDI • 1970 • Ray Satyajit • IND • ADVERSARY, THE (UKN) ○ SIDDHARTA AND THE CITY
PRATIMA • 1936 • *Biswas Anil (M)* • IND • PREM MURTI
PRATINIDHI • 1964 • Sen Mrinal • IND • REPRESENTATIVE, THE ○ TWO PLUS ONE
PRATISHODH • 1983 • Dhir S. N. • IND • RETALIATION
PRATISRUTI • 1940 • *Sircar B. N (P)* • IND
PRATO, IL • 1979 • Taviani Paolo, Taviani Vittorio • ITL • MEADOW, THE (USA) ○ FIELD, THE
PRATO MACCHIATO DI ROSSO, IL • 1975 • Ghione Riccardo • ITL
PRATVUSHA • 1979 • Jatla V. N. • IND • DAWN
PRAVDA • 1962 • Babaja Ante • ANS • YGS • JUSTICE
PRAVDA • 1970 • Godard Jean-Luc, Gorin Jean-Pierre, Burron Paul, Rober Jean-Henri • FRN
PRAVE ZACINAME • 1946 • Slavinsky Vladimir • CZC • JUST STARTING
PRAVO NA HRICH • 1932 • Slavinsky Vladimir • CZC • TITLE FOR THE SIN, THE
PRAVO STANJE STVARI • 1964 • Slijepcevic Vladan • YGS • MATTER OF FACTS, A
PRAWDZIE W OCZY • 1970 • Poreba Bohdan • PLN • FACING THE TRUTH
PRAWDZIWY KONIEC WIELKIEJ WOJNY • 1957 • Kawalerowicz Jerzy • PLN • REAL END OF THE GREAT WAR, THE ○ TRUE END OF THE GREAT WAR, THE
PRAWO I PIESC • 1964 • Hoffman Jerzy, Skorzewski Edward • PLN • LAW AND THE FIST, THE
PRAXIS DER LIEBE, DIE • 1985 • Export Valie • AUS, FRG • PRACTICE OF LOVE, THE
PRAY FOR DEATH • 1985 • Hessler Gordon • USA
PRAY FOR THE WILDCATS • 1974 • Lewis Robert Michael • TVM • USA
PRAY TV • 1982 • Markowitz Robert • TVM • USA
PRAY TV see **KGOD** • 1980
PRAYER, THE see **MOLBA** • 1969
PRAYER, THE see **MOLITVA**
PRAYER FOR THE DYING, A • 1987 • Hodges Mike • UKN
PRAYER IN THE NIGHT see **PREGHIERA DELLA NOTTE**
PRAYER OF A HORSE • 1915 • *Macquarrie Murdock* • USA
PRAYER OF A MINER'S CHILD, THE • 1910 • *Bison* • USA
PRAYERS OF MANUELO, THE • 1912 • *Stanley George* • USA
PRAYING MANTIS • 1982 • Gold Jack • TVM • UKN, FRG
PRAYING MANTIS see **T'ANG-LANG** • 1977
PRAZDNIK NOCI • 1917 • Tourjansky Victor • USS
PRAZDNIK SVYATOVO IORGENE • 1930 • Protazanov Yakov • USS • HOLIDAY OF ST. JORGEN, THE ○ FEAST OF ST. JORGEN, THE ○ FESTIVAL AT ST. JURGEN
PRAZDNINY PRO PSA • 1981 • Vosmikova Jaroslava • CZC • DOG'S HOLIDAY ○ HOLIDAY FOR A DOG
PRAZNIK • 1967 • Kadijevic Djordje • YGS • FEAST, THE

PRAZNIK U SARAJEVU • 1990 • Kenovic Ademir • YGS • FESTIVE DAY IN SARAJEVO, A
PRAZNOVANJE POMLADI see **PRIZIVANJE PROLJECA** • 1979
PRAZSKA PETKA • 1988 • Vorel Tomas • CZC • PRAGUE 5, THE
PRAZSKE NOCI • 1968 • Brdecka Jiri, Makovec Milos, Schorm Evald • CZC • NIGHTS OF PRAGUE ○ PRAGUE NIGHTS ○ NIGHTS IN PRAGUE ○ PRAGUE NIGHTS
PRAZSKY FLAMENDR • 1941 • Spelina Karel • CZC • PRAGUE GALLIVANTER, THE
PRAZSTI ADAMITE • 1917 • Fencl Antonin • CZC • PRAGUE ADAMITES, THE
PRE-HYSTERICAL MAN • 1948 • Kneitel Seymour • ANS • USA
PRE ISTINE • 1968 • Rakonjac Kokan • YGS • BEFORE THE TRUTH
PRE-PRODUCTION • 1973 • Le Grice Malcolm • UKN
PRE-RAPHAELITE REVOLT, THE • 1967 • Thompson David* • UKN
PREACHER • 1970 • Prochazka Pavel • UNN
PREACHER AND THE GOSSIPS, THE • 1912 • *Johnson Arthur* • USA
PREACHER MAN • 1971 • Viola Albert T. • USA • PREACHERMAN MEETS WIDDERWOMAN ○ PREACHERMAN
PREACHERMAN • 1971 • *Huxley Amos* • USA
PREACHERMAN see **PREACHER MAN** • 1971
PREACHERMAN MEETS WIDDERWOMAN see **PREACHER MAN** • 1971
PREACHER'S SON, THE • 1918 • Vidor King • SHT • USA
PREACHER'S WIFE, THE • 1910 • *Vitagraph* • USA
PREAMBULE • 1970 • Nold Werner • SHT • CND
PREBET LAPOK • 1978 • Sattar Aziz • MLY
PREBROYVANE NA DIVITE ZAITSI • 1973 • Zahariev Edward • BUL • CENSUS OF HARES, THE ○ HARE CENSUS, THE
PRECIEUSES RIDICULES, LES • 1934 • Perret Leonce • FRN
PRECINCT 45 -LOS ANGELES POLICE (UKN) see **NEW CENTURIONS, THE** • 1972
PRECIO DE LA GLORIA, EL • 1919 • Berra Fernando Orozco • MXC • PRICE OF GLORY, THE
PRECIO DE LA GLORIA, EL • 1947 • Salvador Jaime • MXC
PRECIO DE LA SANGRE, EL • 1959 • Catalan Feliciano • SPN
PRECIO DE UN ASESINO, EL • 1963 • Lluch Miguel • SPN
PRECIO DE UN BESO, EL • 1933 • Silver Marcel • USA • PRICE OF A KISS
PRECIO DE UN HOMBRE, EL • 1966 • Martin Eugenio • SPN, ITL • UGLY ONES, THE (USA) ○ BOUNTY KILLER, THE ○ PRICE OF A MAN, THE
PRECIO DE UNA VIDA, EL • 1944 • Cardona Rene • MXC
PRECIO DEL ABORTO, EL • 1975 • Xiol Juan • SPN
PRECIOSA • 1964 • Ortega Juan J. • MXC
PRECIOUS CARGO, A • 1913 • Plumb Hay • UKN
PRECIOUS GRAIN see **DRAGOTZENNYE ZERNA** • 1948
PRECIOUS JEWELS • 1969 • Stagg William • USA
PRECIOUS METAL VARIATIONS • 1983 • Ehrlich David • ANS • USA
PRECIOUS PACKET, THE • 1916 • Mackenzie Donald • USA
PRECIOUS PARCEL, THE • 1916 • *Plump & Runt* • SHT • USA
PRECIOUS SEEDS, THE see **DRAGOTZENNYE ZERNA** • 1948
PRECIOUS TWINS, THE • 1914 • *Connor Della* • USA
PRECIPICE, THE see **HYOHEKI** • 1958
PRECIPICE OF SOULS, THE see **PENON DE LAS ANIMAS, EL** • 1942
PRECIS • Goel Veronique • SWT
PRECISELY YOURS • 1947 • Bryan Nigel • UKN
PRECISION • 1933 • Sparling Gordon • DCS • CND
PRECISION • 1966 • Dufaux Georges • DCS • CND
PRECO DA VITORIA, O • 1960 • Sampaio Oswaldo • BRZ
PRECONDITIONING • 1984 • Dodd Thomas • DOC • CND
PRECURSOR, THE • 1966 • Wdowkowna-Oldak Zofia • ANM • PLN
PRECURSORES DE LA PINTURA ARGENTINA • 1957 • Torre-Nilsson Leopoldo • SHT • ARG
PRED MATURITOU • 1932 • Vancura Vladislav, Innemann Svatopluk • CZC • BEFORE THE MATRICULATION ○ ON THE EVE OF MATRICULATION
PREDA, LA • 1974 • Paolella Domenico • ITL
PREDA E L'AVVOLTOIO, LA (ITL) see **PRESA Y LA BUITRE, LA** • 1972
PREDATEL • 1926 • Room Abram • USS • TRAITOR
PREDATOR • 1987 • McTiernan John • USA
PREDATOR 2 • 1990 • Hoskins Stephen • USA
PREDATOR, THE see **ALPAGUEUR, L'** • 1976
PREDATORI DEL COBRA D'ORO, I • 1982 • Margheriti Antonio • ITL • RAIDERS OF THE GOLDEN COBRA, THE ○ CACCIATORI DEL COBRA D'ORO, I ○ HUNTERS OF THE GOLDEN COBRA
PREDESTINATION see **SARNEVESHT** • 1968
PREDONI DEL DESERTO, I see **CAVALIERI DEL DESERTO, I** • 1942
PREDONI DEL SAHARA, I • 1966 • Malatesta Guido • ITL
PREDONI DEL SAHARA, I see **CAVALIERI DEL DESERTO, I** • 1942
PREDONI DELLA STEPPA, I • 1964 • Boccia Tanio • ITL • TERROR OF THE STEPPE (USA) ○ MIGHTY KHAN, THE
PREDSEDATEL • 1965 • Saltykov Alexei • USS • CHAIRMAN, THE
PREDSTAVA HAMLETA U MRDUSI DONJOJ • 1974 • Papic Krsto • YGS • VILLAGE PERFORMANCE OF HAMLET, A ○ HAMLET IM DORF MRDUSA DONJA
PREDTUCHA • 1947 • Vavra Otakar • CZC • PREMONITION ○ PRESENTIMENT ○ FORBODINGS
PREET SHIKWA MALA • 1968 • Korde Bal • IND
PREFAB PEOPLE, THE see **PANELKAPCSOLAT** • 1983
PREFAB STORY see **PANELSTORY** • 1978
PREFACE TO A LIFE • 1950 • Resnick • SHT • USA
PREFACE TO LIFE see **COVER TO COVER** • 1936
PREFERE, LE see **ROCK AND TORAH** • 1982
PREFERRED LIST, A • 1933 • Jason Leigh • SHT • USA
PREFETTO DI FERRO, IL • 1977 • Squitieri Pasquale • ITL • IRON PREFECT, THE ○ I AM THE LAW
PREFIERO A TU PAPA • 1952 • Rodriguez Roberto • MXC
PREGA DIO E SCAVATI LA FOSSA • 1968 • Mulargia Edoardo • ITL
PREGA IL MORTO E AMMAZZA IL VIVO • 1971 • Vari Giuseppe • ITL • SHOOT THE LIVING, PRAY FOR THE DEAD ○ TO KILL A JACKAL
PREGHIERA DELLA NOTTE • Bendazzi G., Lagana G. • SHT • ITL • PRAYER IN THE NIGHT ○ NIGHT PRAYER
PREGNANCY see **ARU JOSHI KOKOI NO KIROKU NINSHIN** • 1968
PREGNANCY AND V.D. see **NINSHIN TO SEIBYO** • 1967
PREGNANCY, BIRTH AND ABORTION see **NINSHIN BUNBEN CHUHZETSU** • 1968
PREGNANT PAPA, THE see **LEGENYANA** • 1989
PREHISTORIC HAYSEEDS • 1923 • Smith Beaumont • ASL
PREHISTORIC LOVE STORY, A • 1915 • Bantock Leedham • UKN
PREHISTORIC MAN, THE • 1908 • Booth W. R. • UKN
PREHISTORIC MAN, THE • 1911 • Martinek H. O. • UKN
PREHISTORIC MAN, THE • 1924 • Coleby A. E. • UKN
PREHISTORIC MAN, THE see **OSEMBER, AZ** • 1917
PREHISTORIC PEEPS • 1905 • Fitzhamon Lewin • UKN
PREHISTORIC PERILS see **MIGHTY MOUSE IN PREHISTORIC PERILS** • 1952
PREHISTORIC PLANET see **VOYAGE TO THE PREHISTORIC PLANET** • 1965
PREHISTORIC PLANET WOMEN see **WOMEN OF THE PREHISTORIC PLANET** • 1966
PREHISTORIC PORKY • 1940 • Clampett Robert • ANS • USA
PREHISTORIC POULTRY: THE DINORNIS OR THE GREAT ROARING WHIFFENPOOF • 1917 • O'Brien Willis • ANM • USA
PREHISTORIC SOUND, THE see **SONIDO DE LA MUERTE, EL** • 1966
PREHISTORIC SUPER SALESMAN • 1969 • Smith Paul J. • ANS • USA
PREHISTORIC TIMES: THE WORLD BEFORE MAN • 1953 • *Coronet* • SHT • USA
PREHISTORIC VALLEY (UKN) see **VALLEY OF THE DRAGONS** • 1961
PREHISTORIC WOMEN • 1951 • Tallas Gregg R. • USA
PREHISTORIC WOMEN (USA) see **SLAVE GIRLS** • 1966
PREHISTORIC WORLD see **TEENAGE CAVEMAN** • 1958
PREHISTORY OF THE PARTISANS see **PARTISAN ZENSHI** • 1970
PREHLIDCE VELIM JA • 1969 • Mach Josef • CZC • I COMMAND THE PARADE
PREHYSTERICAL HARE • 1958 • McKimson Robert • ANS • USA
PREIS DER NATIONEN see **MADCHEN MARION, DAS** • 1956
PREIS EINER NACHT, DER • 1967 • Schier G. H. • FRG • PRICE OF A NIGHT, THE
PREIS FURS UBERLEBEN, DER • 1980 • Noever Hans • FRG • PRICE OF SURVIVAL, THE
PREJUDICE • 1915 • Moore Tom • USA
PREJUDICE • 1924 • Belmont Joseph • USA • RITUAL MURDER, THE ○ PROSCRIBED, THE
PREJUDICE • 1949 • Cahn Edward L. • USA
PREJUDICE CONQUERED • 1915 • *Paragon* • USA
PREJUDICE OF PIERRE MARIE • 1911 • Trimble Larry • USA
PREKOBROJNA • 1962 • Bauer Branko • YGS • SUPERNUMERARY GIRL, THE
PREKRASNAJA LJUKANIDA • 1912 • *Starevitch Ladislas (P)* • ANM • USS • BEAUTIFUL LUCANIDAE (USA) ○ BEAUTIFUL STAG BEETLE
PRELAZ PREKO DJAVOLJE KICME see **SPINA DORSALE DEL DIAVOLO, LA** • 1970
PRELIMINARY INVESTIGATION see **VORUNTERSUCHUNG** • 1931
PRELUDE • *Opliger Curtis (P)* • SHT • USA
PRELUDE • 1927 • Knight Castleton • UKN
PRELUDE see **WHEREVER SHE GOES** • 1951
PRELUDE A LA GLOIRE • 1949 • Lacombe Georges • FRN • SYMPHONIE PASSIONNEE ○ ROBERTO
PRELUDE A L'APRES-MIDI D'UN FAUNE • 1938 • Rossellini Roberto • SHT • ITL
PRELUDE AND FUGUE • 1920 • Richter Hans • FRG
PRELUDE ELEVEN see **PRELUDIO 11** • 1963
PRELUDE FOR VOICE, PIANO AND ORCHESTRA • Alexeieff Alexandre • ANS • FRN
PRELUDE POUR VOIX, ORCHESTRE ET CAMERA • 1960 • Arcady • SHT • FRN
PRELUDE TO APOCALYPSE see **TOUBIB, LE** • 1979
PRELUDE TO ECSTASY (USA) see **KUU ON VAARALLINEN** • 1961
PRELUDE TO FAME • 1950 • McDonnell Fergus • UKN
PRELUDE TO SPRING • 1931 • Hoffman John • USA
PRELUDE TO TAURUS • 1972 • *Tiffin Pamela* • USA
PRELUDE TO WAR • 1942 • Litvak Anatole, Capra Frank • DOC • USA • WHY WE FIGHT (PART 1): PRELUDE TO WAR
PRELUDIO 11 • 1963 • Maetzig Kurt • FRG • PRELUDE ELEVEN
PRELUDIO A ESPANA • 1972 • Garcia de Duenas Jesus • DOC • SPN • SPANISH PRELUDE
PRELUDIO D'AMORE • 1946 • Paolucci Giovanni • ITL • SHAMED (USA)
PRELUDIUM • 1941 • Cap Frantisek • CZC
PRELUDY POUSTE • 1982 • Bouassida Abdel Hafidh • CZC, TNS • MIRAGES
PREM BANDHAN • 1936 • *Biswas Anil (M)* • IND
PREM MURTI see **PRATIMA** • 1936
PREM NAGAR • 1974 • *Burman S. D. (M)* • IND
PREM PATRA • 1962 • Roy Bimal • IND
PREM PUJARI • 1970 • *Burman S. D. (M)* • IND
PREM ROG • 1982 • Kapoor Raj • IND
PREMALO PRAMADAM • 1967 • Taliath Joseph Jr. • IND • HAPPINESS IN LOVE
PREMATURE BURIAL, THE • 1962 • Corman Roger • USA
PREMATURE BURIAL, THE see **CRIME OF DR. CRESPI, THE** • 1935
PREMATURE COMPROMISE, THE • 1914 • Brabin Charles J. • USA
PREMATURE MAN, THE see **PREZHDEVRYEMENNY CHELOVYEK** • 1973
PREMEDITATED (USA) see **PREMEDITATION** • 1959
PREMEDITATION • 1912 • Feuillade Louis • FRN
PREMEDITATION • 1959 • Berthomieu Andre • FRN • PREMEDITATED (USA)
PREMENY • 1966 • Kudelka Ladislav • SHT • CZC • CHANGES
PREMIA • 1975 • Mikailyan Sergei • USS • BONUS, THE ○ PRIZE, THE
PREMIER BAL • 1941 • Christian-Jaque • FRN
PREMIER CIGARE, LE • 1896 • Reynaud Emile • FRN
PREMIER CIGARE, UN see **PREMIER CIGARE DU COLLEGIEN, LE** • 1902
PREMIER CIGARE DU COLLEGIEN, LE • 1902 • Zecca Ferdinand • FRN • PREMIER CIGARE, UN
PREMIER COMBAT, LE • 1973 • Corajoud Marie-Jo • SHT • FRN
PREMIER DE CORDEE • 1943 • Daquin Louis • FRN
PREMIER DISTILLATEUR, LE • 1911 • Protazanov Yakov • USS
PREMIER ETE, LE • 1975 • Correa Joao • BLG, FRN • SON PREMIER ETE ○ LOVE CRAZY WOMEN
PREMIER JOUR DE VACANCES DE POULOT, LE • 1912 • Cohl Emile • ANS • FRN
PREMIER MAI • 1958 • Saslavsky Luis • FRN, ITL • FESTA DI MAGGIO (ITL) ○ MAN TO MAN TALK (USA) ○ PERE ET L'ENFANT, LE ○ PREMIER MAY ○ MAYDAY IN PARIS
PREMIER MAY see **PREMIER MAI** • 1958
PREMIER MOT D'AMOUR, LE • 1932 • Guarino Joseph • FRN
PREMIER PAS, LE • 1950 • Chartier • SHT • FRN
PREMIER PRIX DU CONSERVATOIRE • 1942 • Guy-Grand • SHT • FRN
PREMIER RENDEZ-VOUS • 1941 • Decoin Henri • FRN • HER FIRST AFFAIR (USA)
PREMIER VOYAGE • 1979 • Trintignant Nadine • FRN
PREMIERE • 1937 • von Bolvary Geza • AUS
PREMIERE • 1938 • Summers Walter • UKN • ONE NIGHT IN PARIS
PREMIERE see **OSBEMUTATO** • 1974
PREMIERE ANNEE, LA see **PRIMER ANO, EL** • 1972
PREMIERE BRIGADE CRIMINELLE • 1961 • Boutel Maurice • FRN
PREMIERE CIGARETTE, LA • 1904 • Blache Alice • FRN
PREMIERE CROISIERE • 1955 • Renaud • SHT • FRN
PREMIERE DER BUTTERFLY (FRG) see **SOGNO DI BUTTERFLY, IL** • 1939
PREMIERE FOIS, LA • 1976 • Berri Claude • FRN • FIRST TIME, THE (USA)
PREMIERE GAMELLE, LA • 1902 • Blache Alice • FRN
PREMIERE IDYLLE DE BOUCOT, LA • 1920 • Saidreau Robert • FRN
PREMIERE IDYLLE DE BOUT DE ZAN, LA • 1913 • Feuillade Louis • FRN
PREMIERE JOURNEE • 1967 • Laskri Amar • ALG
PREMIERE MELODIE, LA see **LAHN, AL-** • 1957
PREMIERE NUIT, LA • 1958 • Franju Georges • DCS • FRN • FIRST NIGHT, THE
PREMIERE QUESTION SUR LE BONHEUR • 1977 • Groulx Gilles • CND, MXC • PRIMERA PREGUNTA SOBRE LA FELICIDAD (MXC)
PREMIERE SORTIE, LA • 1905 • Linder Max • FRN
PREMIERE SORTIE D'UN COLLEGIEN • 1905 • Gasnier Louis J. • FRN
PREMIERE TOMORROW see **JUTRO PREMIERA** • 1962
PREMIERES ARMES • 1949 • Wheeler Rene • FRN • FIRST WEAPONS (USA) ○ WINNER'S CIRCLE, THE ○ WINNING HIS SPURS
PREMIERES ARMES DE ROCAMBOLE, LES • 1924 • Maudru Charles • FRN
PREMIERES PAGES DU JOURNAL D'ISABELLE • 1980 • Moreau Michel (c/d) • MTV • CND
PREMIERS DESIRS • 1983 • Hamilton David • FRN, FRG
PREMIERS JOURS • 1980 • Warny Clorinda, Gervais Suzanne, Gagnon Lina • ANS • CND • BEGINNINGS
PREMIERS JOURS, LES • 1961 • Herman Jean • FRN
PREMIERS OUTRAGES, LES • 1955 • Gourguet Jean • FRN
PREMIERS PAS DE BEBE • 1896-97 • Lumiere Louis • FRN
PREMIERS PAS D'UNE MAMAN, LES • Navarro Jacques • DOC • FRN
PREMIJERA • 1957 • Kostelac Nikola • ANS • YGS • OPENING NIGHT
PREMIO NOBEL DEL AMOR, EL • 1972 • *Stpc* • MXC
PREMIS DE CONDUIRE, LE • 1973 • Girault Jean • FRN
PREMONITION • 1972 • Rudolph Alan • USA
PREMONITION see **PREDTUCHA** • 1947
PREMONITION, THE • 1975 • Schnitzer Robert Allen • USA
PRENDIMI STRAZIAMI CHE BRUCIO DI PASSIONE • 1976 • Crispino Armando • ITL
PRENDS 10,000 BALLES ET CASSE-TOI • 1980 • Zemmouri Mahmoud • FRN, ALG
PRENDS LA ROUTE • 1936 • Boyer Jean, Chavance Louis • FRN
PRENDS-MOI, COMME UNE CHIENNE • Antony Michel • FRN
PRENDS-MOI JE SUIS ENCORE VIERGE • 1980 • Antony Michel • FRN
PRENDS-MOI PARTOUT • 1977 • Hugues Robert • FRN
PRENDS-MOI VITE • Love John • FRN
PRENDS TA ROLLS.. ET VA POINTERI • 1981 • Balducci Richard • FRN
PRENDS TON PASSE-MONTAGNE, ON VA A LA PLAGE • 1982 • Matalon Eddy • FRN
PRENEZ DES GANTS • 1960 • Billon • SHT • FRN
PRENEZ GARDE A LA PEINTURE • 1898 • Melies Georges • FRN • FRESH PAINT
PRENEZ GARDE A LA PEINTURE • 1932 • Chomette Henri • FRN
PRENEZ LA QUEUE COMME TOUT LE MONDE • 1972 • Davy Jean-Francois • FRN, ITL • LINE UP AND LAY DOWN
PRENOM: CARMEN • 1983 • Godard Jean-Luc • FRN • FIRST NAME: CARMEN
PRENONS LA VILLE • 1973 • Al-Ktari Naceur • SHT • FRN
PRENSES • 1985 • Cetin Sinan • TRK • PRINCESS
PREP AND PEP • 1928 • Butler David • USA • TIGER'S SON
PREPARAT "T" • 1953 • Perski Ludwik • DOC • PLN • PREPARATION "T"
PREPARATI LA BARA • 1968 • Baldi Ferdinando • ITL • PREPARE THE COFFIN

PREPARATION "T" see **PREPARAT "T"** • 1953
PREPARE FOR THE FAIR see **MATSURI NO JUNBI** • 1975
PREPARE THE COFFIN see **PREPARATI LA BARA** • 1968
PREPARED FOR LIFE • 1987 • Kahane Peter, Knauf Thomas • GDR
PREPARED TO DIE • 1923 • Curran William Hughes • USA
PREPAREDNESS • 1916 • *Cub* • USA
PREPAREDNESS • 1916 • Drew Sidney • *Drew* • SHT • USA
PREPAREZ VOS MOUCHOIRS • 1978 • Blier Bertrand • FRN, BLG • GET OUT YOUR HANDKERCHIEFS (USA) ○ GET YOUR HANDKERCHIEFS READY
PREPOTENI, I • 1958 • Amendola Mario • ITL
PREPOTENTI PIU DI PRIMA • 1959 • Mattoli Mario • ITL
PREPPIES • 1984 • Vincent Chuck • USA
PREPPIES see **MAKING THE GRADE** • 1984
PRES DES CIMES • 1921 • Maudru Charles • FRN
PRES D'UN BERCEAU • 1916 • Burguet Charles • FRN
PRESA DEL POTERE DA PARTE DI LUIGI XIV, LA see **PRISE DE POUVOIR PAR DE LOUIS XIV, LA** • 1966
PRESA DI ROMA, LA • 1905 • Alberini Filoteo • ITL
PRESA Y LA BUITRE, LA • 1972 • Romero-Marchent Rafael • SPN, ITL • PREDA E L'AVVOLTOIO, LA (ITL)
PRESAGE see **PRESAGIO** • 1970
PRESAGE see **PRESAGIO** • 1974
PRESAGIO • 1916 • Ghione Emilio • ITL
PRESAGIO • 1970 • Iglesias Miguel • SPN • PRESAGE
PRESAGIO • 1974 • Alcoriza Luis • MXC • PRESAGE
PRESAGIO, IL • 1916 • Genina Augusto • ITL
PRESBYTERIAN CHURCH WAGER, THE see **MCCABE AND MRS. MILLER** • 1971
PRESCOTT KID, THE • 1934 • Selman David • USA
PRESCRIPTION, THE • 1914 • *Melies* • USA
PRESCRIPTION FOR MURDER see **TAKING CARE** • 1988
PRESCRIPTION FOR PERCY • 1954 • Davis Mannie • ANS • USA
PRESCRIPTION FOR ROMANCE • 1937 • Simon S. Sylvan • USA
PRESCRIPTION: MURDER • 1967 • Irving Richard • TVM • USA
PRESCRIPTION SEX • 1970 • *Stacey Dist.* • USA
PRESENCA DE ANITA • 1951 • Jacobi Ruggero • BRZ
PRESENCA DE MARISA • 1988 • Doo John • BRZ • MARISA'S PRESENCE
PRESENCE, THE • 1972 • Brakhage Stan • USA
PRESENCE, THE see **JELENLET** • 1965
PRESENCE D'ALBERT CAMUS • 1962 • Regnier • SHT • FRN
PRESENCE REELLE, LA • 1984 • Ruiz Raul • FRN
PRESENT, THE • 1971 • Higgins Don • DOC • UKN
PRESENT, THE see **CADEAU, LE** • 1961
PRESENT ARMS (UKN) see **LEATHERNECKING** • 1930
PRESENT FOR A SINGLE WOMAN • 1974 • Lacis Eriks • USS
PRESENT FOR HER HUSBAND, A • 1909 • Fitzhamon Lewin • UKN
PRESENT FOR HER HUSBAND, A • 1912 • Wilson Frank • UKN
PRESENT FOR HIS WIFE, A • 1910 • Fitzhamon Lewin? • UKN
PRESENT FROM FATHER, A • 1913 • Stow Percy • UKN
PRESENT FROM INDIA, A • 1911 • Wilson Frank? • UKN
PRESENT FROM UNCLE, A see **UNCLE'S PRESENT** • 1913
PRESENT INDICATIVE see **JELENIDO** • 1972
PRESENTATION OU CHARLOTTE ET SON STEAK • 1951 • Rohmer Eric • SHT • FRN • CHARLOTTE AND HER STEAK
PRESENTIMENT see **PREDTUCHA** • 1947
PRESENTIMENTO • 1957 • Fizzarotti Armando • ITL
PRESENTING LILY MARS • 1943 • Taurog Norman • USA
PRESENTS • 1981 • Snow Michael • CND
PRESERVATION MAN • 1962 • Russell Ken • MTV • UKN
PRESERVING THE WASA • 1965 • Heckford Michael • UKN
PRESIDENT, LE • 1960 • Verneuil Henri • FRN, ITL • MONEY, MONEY, MONEY (USA) ○ PRESIDENT, THE (UKN)
PRESIDENT, THE • 1937 • Bose Nitin • IND
PRESIDENT, THE see **PRAESIDENTEN** • 1919
PRESIDENT, THE see **PRASIDENT, DER** • 1928
PRESIDENT, THE (UKN) see **SURRENDER** • 1927
PRESIDENT, THE (UKN) see **PRESIDENT, LE** • 1960
PRESIDENT ELECT ROOSEVELT, A • 1905 • Melies Gaston • USA
PRESIDENT HAUDECOEUR, LE • 1939 • Dreville Jean • FRN
PRESIDENT INCOG • 1912 • *Republic* • USA
PRESIDENT MCKINLEY'S INAUGURATION • 1897 • *Bitzer Billy (Ph)* • USA
PRESIDENT MUST DIE, THE • 1981 • Conway James L. • USA
PRESIDENT T. R. ROOSEVELT JULY 4TH • 1903 • *Bitzer Billy (Ph)* • USA
PRESIDENT VANISHES, THE • 1934 • Wellman William A. • USA • STRANGE CONSPIRACY (UKN)
PRESIDENTA MUNICIPAL, LA • 1974 • *America* • MXC
PRESIDENTE, LA • 1938 • Rivers Fernand • FRN
PRESIDENTE CAFE FILHO EM LISBOA • 1955 • Ribeiro Antonio Lopes • SHT • PRT
PRESIDENTE DEL BORGOROSSO FOOTBALL CLUB, IL • 1970 • D'Amico Luigi Filippo • ITL
PRESIDENTE DELLA BA.CE.CRE.MI., IL • 1933 • Righelli Gennaro • ITL
PRESIDENTE DI COSTANUEVA, IL • 1928 • Righelli Gennaro • ITL
PRESIDENTESSA, LA • 1952 • Germi Pietro • ITL • LADY PRESIDENT, THE ○ MADEMOISELLE GOBETTE
PRESIDENTESSA, LA • 1977 • Salce Luciano • ITL
PRESIDENT'S ANALYST, THE • 1967 • Flicker Theodore J. • USA • T.P.A.
PRESIDENT'S ANSWER, A • 1918 • *Chapin* • SHT • USA
PRESIDENT'S ANSWER, THE • 1917 • Chapin Benjamin • *Charter* • SHT • USA
PRESIDENT'S BOSS, THE see **HESOKURI SHACHO** • 1955
PRESIDENT'S DEATH, THE see **SMIERC PREZYDENTA** • 1977
PRESIDENT'S LADY, THE • 1953 • Levin Henry • USA
PRESIDENT'S MISTRESS, THE • 1978 • Moxey John Llewellyn • TVM • USA
PRESIDENT'S MYSTERY, THE • 1936 • Rosen Phil • USA • ONE FOR ALL (UKN)
PRESIDENT'S PLANE IS MISSING, THE • 1971 • Duke Daryl • TVM • USA
PRESIDENT'S SPECIAL • 1910 • *Edison* • USA
PRESIDENT'S SPECIAL, THE • 1913 • *Kalem* • USA
PRESIDENT'S SPECIAL, THE • 1914 • Brabin Charles J. • USA
PRESIDENT'S VISIT, THE see **ODWIEDZINY PREZYDENTA** • 1961
PRESIDENT'S WIFE, THE see **ASSASSINATION** • 1987
PRESIDENT'S WOMEN, THE see **FOREPLAY** • 1975
PRESIDIO, EL • 1930 • Wing Ward • USA
PRESIDIO, EL • 1954 • Santillan Antonio • SPN
PRESIDIO, THE • 1988 • Hyams Peter • USA • PRESIDIO: THE SCENE OF THE CRIME, THE (UKN)
PRESIDIO: THE SCENE OF THE CRIME, THE (UKN) see **PRESIDIO, THE** • 1988
PRESOS DESAPARECIDOS • 1979 • Castilla Sergio • CUB, SWD • DISAPPEARED PRISONERS ○ DISAPPEARED, THE
PRESS FOR TIME • 1966 • Asher Robert • UKN
PRESS GANG see **SHADOWS** • 1931
PRESS GANG, THE • 1908 • Blackton J. Stuart • USA
PRESS GANG, THE • 1913 • Henderson Dell • USA
PRESS ILLUSTRATED, THE • 1904 • Fitzhamon Lewin • UKN
PRESSE ET SON EMPIRE, LA see **NEVER A BACKWARD STEP** • 1967
PRESSED DUCK, THE see **CANARD PRESSE, LE** • 1965
PRESSED ROSES • 1910 • *Imp* • USA
PRESSENS MAGT • 1913 • Blom August • DNM • BANKRUN, ET ○ HARVEST OF TEARS, A
PRESSING BUSINESS • 1909 • *Powers* • USA
PRESSING BUSINESS • 1915 • *Pokes & Jabs* • USA
PRESSING HIS SUIT • 1915 • *Imp* • USA
PRESSING HIS SUIT • 1915 • Roach Hal • *Phun Films* • USA
PRESSURE • 1974 • Ove Horace • UKN
PRESSURE BURST! • 1971 • Canes George • SAF
PRESSURE OF GUILT see **SHIRO TO KURO** • 1963
PRESSURE OF THE POSTER, THE • 1915 • Batley Ethyle • UKN
PRESSURE POINT • 1962 • Cornfield Hubert • USA • POINT BLANK
PREST-O, CHANGE-O • 1939 • Jones Charles M. • ANS • USA
PRESTAME QUINCE DIAS • 1970 • Merino Fernando • SPN
PRESTAME TU CUERPO • 1957 • Demicheli Tulio • MXC
PRESTAME TU MARIDO • 1973 • Luzardo Julio • CLM • LEND ME YOUR HUSBAND
PRESTAMELA ESTA NOCHE • 1977 • Demicheli Tulio • SPN
PRESTER JOHN • 1920 • SAF
PRESTIDIGITATEUR D. DEVANT, LE • 1897 • Melies Georges • FRN • D. DEVANT, PRESTIDIGITATEUR ○ D. DEVANT, CONJUROR
PRESTIGE • 1932 • Garnett Tay • USA
PRESTO CHANGO • 1929 • Terry Paul • ANS • USA
PRESTO WILLIE -MAGICIAN • 1914 • *Essanay* • USA
PRESTOP • 1981 • Milcinski Matija • YGS • CRIMINAL OFFENCE ○ PRIJESTRUP ○ OVER THE LINE
PRESTUPLENIE I NAKAZANIE • 1911 • Goncharov Vasili M. • USS • CRIME AND PUNISHMENT
PRESTUPLENIE I NAKAZANIE • 1970 • Kulidjanov Lev • USS • CRIME AND PUNISHMENT
PRESUDA • 1978 • Popov Trajce • YGS • JUDGEMENT
PRESUMED INNOCENT • 1990 • Pakula Alan J. • USA
PRESUMPTION OF STANLEY HAY, M.P., THE • 1925 • Hill Sinclair • UKN
PRETE BELLO, IL • 1990 • Mazzacurati Carlo • ITL, FRN • HANDSOME PRIEST, THE
PRETE, FAI UN MIRACOLO • 1975 • Chiari Mario • ITL
PRETE-MOI TA FEMME • 1936 • Cammage Maurice • FRN
PRETE POUR UN RENDU: OU, UNE BONNE FARCE AVEC MA TETE, UN • 1904 • Melies Georges • FRN • TIT FOR TAT: OR, A GOOD JOKE ON MY HEAD (USA) ○ BONNE FARCE AVEC MA TETE, UNE
PRETE SCOMODO, UN • 1976 • Tosini Pino • ITL
PRETE SPOSATO, IL • 1970 • Vicario Marco • ITL, FRG, SPN
PRETENDER, THE • 1911 • *Yankee* • USA
PRETENDER, THE • 1913 • *Rex* • USA
PRETENDER, THE • 1915 • Kelsey Fred A. • USA
PRETENDER, THE • 1916 • *Klein Robert* • SHT • USA
PRETENDER, THE • 1918 • Smith Cliff • USA
PRETENDER, THE • 1947 • Wilder W. Lee • USA
PRETENDERS, THE • 1915 • Vignola Robert G. • USA
PRETENDERS, THE • 1916 • *Vim* • SHT • USA
PRETENDERS, THE • 1916 • Baker George D. • *Rolfe* • USA
PRETENDERS, THE • 1981 • Stelling Jos • NTH
PRETENDERS, THE see **FUN ON A WEEKEND** • 1947
PRETENDIENTE ARDIENTE, EL see **DUQUESA DEL TEPETATE, LA** • 1951
PRETENSES • 1915 • *Sheehan John* • USA
PRETORA, LA • 1976 • Fulci Lucio • ITL
PRETORE DI PADANIA, IL • 1977 • Lippi Adolfo • ITL
PRETORIA O PRETORIA • 1979 • SAF
PRETRES INTERDITS • 1973 • de La Patelliere Denys • FRN
PRETTY AND TERRIBLE see **HELWA WA CHAKIA** • 1968
PRETTY BABIES • 1918 • Davis James • SHT • USA
PRETTY BABY • 1916 • Chaudet Louis W. • SHT • USA
PRETTY BABY • 1928 • White Jules • USA
PRETTY BABY • 1950 • Windust Bretaigne • USA
PRETTY BABY • 1978 • Malle Louis • USA • PETITE, LA
PRETTY BOY FLOYD • 1960 • Leder Herbert J. • USA
PRETTY BOY FLOYD see **STORY OF PRETTY BOY FLOYD, THE** • 1974
PRETTY BUT WICKED (USA) see **BONITINHA, MAS ORDINARIA** • 1963
PRETTY CLOTHES • 1927 • Rosen Phil • USA
PRETTY DOLLY • 1942 • Holmes Ben • SHT • USA
PRETTY FISHERMAIDEN, THE • 1909 • *Urban-Eclipse* • USA
PRETTY GIRL IN LOWER FIVE, THE • 1913 • *Darnell Jean* • USA
PRETTY GIRLS see **SZEPLEANYOK** • 1987
PRETTY GOOD FOR A HUMAN BEING see **AIKA HYVA IHMISEKSI** • 1977
PRETTY IN PINK • 1986 • Deutch Howard • USA
PRETTY INDIAN GIRL, THE (USA) see **INDIA BONITA, LA** • 1939
PRETTY KILL • 1986 • Kaczender George • USA • PRETTYKILL ○ TOMORROW'S A KILLER
PRETTY LADIES • 1925 • Bell Monta • USA
PRETTY LADY • 1920 • Blystone John G. • SHT • USA
PRETTY LITTLE MILLINER, A • 1909 • *Pathe* • SHT • FRN
PRETTY MAIDS ALL IN A ROW • 1971 • Vadim Roger • USA
PRETTY MRS. SMITH • 1915 • Bosworth Hobart • USA
PRETTY PEACHES • 1978 • De Renzy Alex • USA
PRETTY POISON • 1968 • Black Noel • USA • SHE LET HIM CONTINUE
PRETTY POLICEMAN • 1915 • *Farley Dot* • USA
PRETTY POLLY • 1967 • Green Guy • UKN • MATTER OF INNOCENCE, A
PRETTY ROUGH ON AUNTIE • 1915 • *Heinie & Louie* • USA
PRETTY SISTER OF JOSE • 1915 • Dwan Allan • USA
PRETTY SMART • 1987 • Logothetis Dimitri • USA • BENTLEY ACADEMY, THE
PRETTY SMOOTH • 1919 • Sturgeon Rollin S. • USA
PRETTY SOFT • 1919 • *National Film Corp. Of America* • USA
PRETTY THINGS, THE • 1966 • West Anthony, Arvat Caterina • UKN
PRETTY WOMAN • 1990 • Marshall Garry • USA
PRETTY WOMEN • 1949 • *Red River Dave* • SHT • USA
PRETTYBOY PLAYBOY • 1968 • Chiquito • PHL
PRETTYKILL see **PRETTY KILL** • 1986
PRETZEL AND FLANIGAN • 1916 • *Gayety* • USA
PRETZEL CAPTURES THE SMUGGLERS • 1914 • *Frontier* • USA
PRETZELS • 1930 • *Terry Paul/ Moser Frank (P)* • ANS • USA
PRETZEL'S BABY • 1914 • *Frontier* • USA
PREUSSICHE LIEBESGESCHICHTE • 1938 • Martin Paul • FRG • LIEBESLEGENDE
PREVIEW see **PREVIEW MURDER MYSTERY, THE** • 1936
PREVIEW MURDER MYSTERY, THE • 1936 • Florey Robert • USA • PREVIEW
PREVOYANT DU CANADA, LES • 1958 • Labrecque Jean-Claude • DCS • CND
PREY • 1984 • Warren Norman J. • UKN • ALIEN PREY (USA)
PREY, THE • 1920 • Sargent George L. • USA
PREY, THE • 1980 • Brown Edwin Scott • USA
PREY, THE see **PROOI, DE** • 1984
PREY OF CALL GIRL • Davian Joe • USA
PREY OF PASSIONS see **BUDAK NAFSU** • 1984
PREY OF THE DRAGON, THE • 1921 • Thornton F. Martin • UKN
PREY OF THE WIND, THE see **PROIE DU VENT, LA** • 1926
PREZHDEVRYEMENNY CHELOVYEK • 1973 • Room Abram • USS • UNTIMELY MAN, THE ○ PREMATURE MAN, THE
PREZIL JSEM SVOU SMRT • 1960 • Jasny Vojtech • CZC • I SURVIVED MY DEATH ○ I SURVIVED CERTAIN DEATH
PREZYDENT STARZYNSKI • 1978 • Trzos-Rastawiecki Andrzej • PLN • LORD MAYOR STARZYNSKI
PREZZO DEL PERDONO, IL • 1913 • Lolli Alberto Carlo • ITL
PREZZO DEL POTERE, IL • 1969 • Valerii Tonino • ITL, SPN • MUERTE DE UN PRESIDENTE, LA (SPN) ○ PRICE OF POWER, THE
PREZZO DELLA GLORIA, IL • 1956 • Musu Antonio • ITL
PREZZO DELL'ONORE, IL • 1953 • Baldi Ferdinando • ITL
PRHISTORIC POULTRY • *O'Brien Willis (Anm)* • ANS • USA
PRIBEH LASKY A CTI • 1977 • Vavra Otakar • CZC • STORY OF LOVE AND HONOUR
PRICA BEZ VEZE • 1966 • Zaninovic Ante • ANS • YGS • PURPOSELESS STORY, A ○ CRAZY STORY
PRICA O DOBRIM LJUDIMA see **POVEST O DOBRIH LJUDEH** • 1975
PRICA O FABRICI • 1948 • Pogacic Vladimir • YGS • STORY ABOUT A FACTORY ○ STORY OF A FACTORY
PRICE, THE • 1911 • Porter Edwin S. • USA
PRICE, THE • 1914 • *Lubin* • USA
PRICE, THE • 1914 • *Eclair* • USA
PRICE, THE • 1915 • Golden Joseph A. • USA
PRICE, THE • 1924 • *Alexander James* • ASL
PRICE, THE • 1971 • Cook Fielder • TVM • USA
PRICE DEMANDED, THE • 1913 • O'Neil Barry • USA
PRICE FOR FOLLY, THE • 1915 • Baker George D. • USA
PRICE HE PAID, THE • 1912 • *Bosworth Hobart* • USA
PRICE HE PAID, THE • 1916 • *Unicorn* • SHT • USA
PRICE HE PAID, THE • 1916 • Aylott Dave • UKN
PRICE IS CLARA, THE see **CLARA ES EL PRECIO** • 1974
PRICE MARK, THE • 1917 • Neill R. William • USA
PRICE OF A DINNER, THE • 1906 • *Warwick Trading Co* • UKN
PRICE OF A GIFT, THE • 1914 • Buckland Warwick? • UKN
PRICE OF A GOOD TIME, THE • 1918 • Weber Lois, Smalley Phillips • USA • TIME OF HER LIFE, THE ○ WHIM, THE
PRICE OF A KISS see **PRECIO DE UN BESO, EL** • 1933
PRICE OF A MAN, THE • 1911 • *Ogle Charles* • USA
PRICE OF A MAN, THE see **PRECIO DE UN HOMBRE, EL** • 1966
PRICE OF A NIGHT, THE see **PREIS EINER NACHT, DER** • 1967
PRICE OF A PARTY, THE • 1924 • Giblyn Charles • USA
PRICE OF A ROTTEN TIME, THE • 1918 • Lyons Eddie, Moran Lee • SHT • USA
PRICE OF A RUBY, THE • 1914 • Myers Harry • USA
PRICE OF A SILVER FOX, THE • 1912 • *Hawley Ormi* • USA
PRICE OF A SONG, THE • 1935 • Powell Michael • UKN
PRICE OF A SOUL, THE • 1909 • Porter Edwin S. • USA
PRICE OF A TOWN, THE see **CENA GRADA** • 1971
PRICE OF AMBITION, THE • 1911 • *Kalem* • USA
PRICE OF AMBITION, THE • 1915 • *Grandin Ethel* • USA
PRICE OF APPLAUSE, THE • 1918 • Heffron Thomas N. • USA
PRICE OF ART, THE • 1912 • *Selig* • USA
PRICE OF BEAUTY, THE see **FARLIGE ALDER, DEN** • 1911
PRICE OF BIG BOB'S SILENCE, THE • 1912 • *Vitagraph* • USA
PRICE OF BREAD, THE • 1909 • Gobbett T. J.? • UKN
PRICE OF COAL, THE • 1977 • Loach Kenneth • MTV • UKN
PRICE OF CRIME, THE • 1914 • Hamilton G. P. • USA
PRICE OF CRIME, THE (UKN) see **LAW OF THE CANYON** • 1947
PRICE OF DAILY BREAD, THE • 1987 • Paskievich J., Mirus Michael • DCS • CND
PRICE OF DEATH, THE see **VENDITORE DI MORTE, IL** • 1971
PRICE OF DECEIT • 1912 • *Comet* • USA
PRICE OF DECEPTION, THE • 1913 • Haldane Bert? • UKN
PRICE OF DISHONOR, THE • 1916 • Melville Wilbert • SHT • USA
PRICE OF DIVORCE, THE • 1928 • Hill Sinclair • UKN
PRICE OF FAME, THE • 1910 • *Essanay* • USA

PRICE OF FAME, THE • 1914 • Buckland Warwick? • UKN
PRICE OF FAME, THE • 1915 • Horkheimer H. M. • USA
PRICE OF FAME, THE • 1916 • Brabin Charles J. • USA
PRICE OF FEAR, THE • 1928 • Jason Leigh • USA
PRICE OF FEAR, THE • 1956 • Biberman Abner • USA
PRICE OF FLESH, THE (USA) see **DETOURNEMENT DE MINEURES** • 1959
PRICE OF FOLLY see **WHO PAYS?** • 1915
PRICE OF FOLLY, THE • 1918 • SER • USA
PRICE OF FOLLY, THE • 1937 • Summers Walter • UKN • DOUBLE ERROR
PRICE OF FREEDOM see **OPERATION DAYBREAK** • 1975
PRICE OF GLORY, THE see **PRECIO DE LA GLORIA, EL** • 1919
PRICE OF GOLD, THE • 1911 • *Vitagraph* • USA
PRICE OF GOLD, THE • 1913 • *Phillips Dorothy* • USA
PRICE OF GRATITUDE, THE • 1912 • *Pathe* • USA
PRICE OF GREED, THE • 1955 • Searle Francis, MacDonald David • UKN • BITTER CHANCE, THE ○ RATTAN TRUNK, THE ○ SERPENT BENEATH, THE
PRICE OF HAPPINESS, THE • 1916 • Lawrence Edmund • USA
PRICE OF HER SILENCE, THE • 1914 • Batley Ernest G.? • UKN
PRICE OF HER SILENCE, THE • 1915 • *La Badie Florence* • USA
PRICE OF HER SOUL, THE • 1917 • Apfel Oscar • USA
PRICE OF HIS HEAD, THE • 1918 • *Triangle* • USA
PRICE OF HIS HONOR, THE • 1914 • *Travers Richard C.* • USA
PRICE OF HONOR, THE • 1927 • Griffith Edward H. • USA
PRICE OF HUMAN LIVES, THE • 1913 • France Charles H. • USA
PRICE OF INNOCENCE, THE • 1919 • Kirby Frank Gordon • USA
PRICE OF JEALOUSY, THE • 1910 • *Kalem* • USA
PRICE OF JEALOUSY, THE • 1913 • *Patheplay* • USA
PRICE OF JEALOUSY, THE • 1913 • Melville Wilbert • *Lubin* • USA
PRICE OF JUSTICE, THE • 1915 • *Apex* • USA
PRICE OF JUSTICE, THE (USA) see **BEAUTIFUL JIM** • 1914
PRICE OF LIBERTY, THE see **FRIDEHENS PRIS** • 1960
PRICE OF LOVE, THE see **INTERDIT DE SEJOUR** • 1954
PRICE OF LOVE, THE see **TIMI TIS AGAPIS, I** • 1984
PRICE OF MALICE, THE • 1916 • Lund O. A. C. • USA
PRICE OF MAN, THE see **TSENA CHELOVEKA** • 1928
PRICE OF MONEY, THE • 1912 • Porter Edwin S. • USA
PRICE OF ONE NIGHT, THE see **YHDEN YON HINTA** • 1952
PRICE OF PASSION, THE see **GOOD MOTHER, THE** • 1988
PRICE OF PEACE, THE • 1912 • *Rex* • USA
PRICE OF PIES, THE • 1915 • Hotaling Arthur D. • USA
PRICE OF PLEASURE, THE • 1925 • Sloman Edward • USA
PRICE OF PLEASURE, THE (UKN) see **TROPIC MADNESS** • 1928
PRICE OF POSSESSION, THE • 1921 • Ford Hugh • USA
PRICE OF POWER, THE • 1915 • Conway Jack • USA
PRICE OF POWER, THE • 1916 • *Vitagraph* • USA
PRICE OF POWER, THE • 1916 • *Fine Arts* • USA
PRICE OF POWER, THE see **PREZZO DEL POTERE, IL** • 1969
PRICE OF PRIDE, THE • 1917 • Knoles Harley • USA
PRICE OF REDEMPTION, THE • 1920 • Fitzgerald Dallas M. • USA
PRICE OF SACRILEGE, THE • 1914 • Brenon Herbert • USA
PRICE OF SILENCE, THE • 1913 • *Patheplay* • USA
PRICE OF SILENCE, THE • 1914 • Buel Kenean • USA
PRICE OF SILENCE, THE • 1916 • De Grasse Joseph • USA
PRICE OF SILENCE, THE • 1917 • Lloyd Frank • USA
PRICE OF SILENCE, THE • 1960 • Tully Montgomery • UKN
PRICE OF SILENCE, THE see **AT THE MERCY OF TIBERIUS** • 1920
PRICE OF SUCCESS, THE • 1925 • Gaudio Antonio • USA
PRICE OF SURVIVAL, THE see **PREIS FURS UBERLEBEN, DER** • 1980
PRICE OF THE DRINKS, THE • 1914 • *Ab* • USA
PRICE OF THE FREE, THE • 1913 • Kirkland Hardee • USA
PRICE OF THE NECKLACE, THE • 1914 • Brabin Charles J. • USA
PRICE OF THE PRAIRIE • 1919 • Grandon Francis J. • USA
PRICE OF THINGS, THE • 1930 • Glyn Elinor • UKN
PRICE OF THOUGHTLESSNESS, THE • 1913 • Finley Ned • USA
PRICE OF VANITY, THE • 1911 • *Reliance* • USA
PRICE OF VANITY, THE • 1914 • Lambart Harry • USA
PRICE OF VANITY, THE see **MAN IN DEMAND, THE** • 1955
PRICE OF VENGEANCE, THE • 1985 • Brown Alastair • MTV • CND
PRICE OF VICTORY, THE • 1911 • Porter Edwin S. • USA
PRICE OF VICTORY, THE • 1913 • Ince John • USA
PRICE OF VICTORY, THE • 1916 • Gerrard Douglas • USA
PRICE OF WISDOM, THE • 1935 • Denham Reginald • UKN
PRICE OF YOUTH, THE • 1922 • Wilson Ben • USA
PRICE ON HIS HEAD, A • 1914 • Buckland Warwick? • UKN
PRICE ON HIS HEAD, A • 1916 • Horning Ben • USA
PRICE SHE PAID, THE • 1914 • *Frazer Robert* • USA
PRICE SHE PAID, THE • 1917 • Giblyn Charles • USA
PRICE SHE PAID, THE • 1924 • McRae Henry • USA
PRICE SHE PAYED, THE • 1915 • *Brunette Fritzie* • USA
PRICE WOMAN PAYS, THE • 1919 • Terwilliger George W. • USA
PRICELESS BEAUTY • 1987 • Finch Charles • USA
PRICELESS DAY, A see **AJANDEK EZ A NAP** • 1980
PRICELESS HEAD, A • 1942 • Barnet Boris • USS
PRICELESS TREASURE see **WU CHIA CHIH PAO** • 1976
PRICES UNLIMITED • 1944 • *Errol Leon* • USA
PRICHOZI Z TEMNOT • 1921 • Kolar J. S. • CZC • SPECTRE OF DARKNESS
PRICK UP YOUR EARS • 1987 • Frears Stephen • UKN
PRICKLY PEARS see **FICO D'INDIA** • 1980
PRICKLY PROBLEMS see **HISTOIRES DE Q** • 1974
PRIDE • 1917 • Ridgely Richard • USA
PRIDE • 1980 • Kappeler Friedrich • MTV • SWT
PRIDE see **ORGUEIL, L'** • 1907
PRIDE see **AAN** • 1952
PRIDE AND PO'K CHOPS • 1920 • *Flagg* • USA
PRIDE AND PREJUDICE • 1940 • Leonard Robert Z. • USA
PRIDE AND PREJUDICE • 1980 • Coke Cyril • UKN, ASL
PRIDE AND THE DEVIL • 1917 • Ridgely Richard • USA
PRIDE AND THE MAN • 1917 • Sloman Edward • USA
PRIDE AND THE PASSION, THE • 1957 • Kramer Stanley • USA
PRIDE COMES BEFORE THE FALL see **HOCHMUT KOMMT VOR DEM KNALL** • 1960
PRIDE, LOVE AND SUSPICION see **FIAMMATA, LA** • 1952
PRIDE OF ANGRY BEAR, THE • 1913 • *West William* • USA
PRIDE OF BATTERY B, THE • 1913 • Noy Wilfred • UKN
PRIDE OF DONEGAL, THE • 1929 • Edwards J. Steven • UKN
PRIDE OF INNOCENCE, THE • 1913 • *Pathe* • USA
PRIDE OF ISLANDS, A • 1972 • Marzaroli Oscar • DCS • UKN
PRIDE OF JENNICO, THE • 1914 • Dawley J. Searle • USA
PRIDE OF JESSIE HALLAM, THE • 1981 • Nelson Gary • TVM • USA
PRIDE OF KENTUCKY (UKN) see **STORY OF SEABISCUIT, THE** • 1949
PRIDE OF LEXINGTON, THE • 1911 • *Republic* • USA
PRIDE OF LONESOME • 1913 • Reid Wallace • USA
PRIDE OF MARYLAND • 1951 • Ford Philip • USA
PRIDE OF NATIONS, THE • 1915 • Friese-Greene Claude • UKN
PRIDE OF NEW YORK, THE • 1917 • Walsh Raoul • USA
PRIDE OF PALOMAR, THE • 1922 • Borzage Frank • USA
PRIDE OF PAWNEE, THE • 1929 • De Lacy Robert • USA
PRIDE OF PENGUINS, A • 1975 • Mylne Christopher • DCS • UKN
PRIDE OF PICKSVILLE • 1927 • *Sennett Mack (P)* • SHT • USA
PRIDE OF ST. LOUIS, THE • 1952 • Jones Harmon • USA
PRIDE OF SUNSHINE ALLEY • 1924 • Craft William James • USA
PRIDE OF SWEDEN • 1937 • Fitzpatrick James • SHT • USA
PRIDE OF THE ARMY see **WAR DOGS** • 1942
PRIDE OF THE BLUE GRASS • 1954 • Beaudine William • USA • PRINCE OF THE BLUE GRASS (UKN)
PRIDE OF THE BLUEGRASS • 1939 • McGann William • USA • GANTRY THE GREAT
PRIDE OF THE BOWERY • 1940 • Lewis Joseph H. • USA • HERE WE GO AGAIN (UKN)
PRIDE OF THE BOWERY, THE (UKN) see **MR. HEX** • 1946
PRIDE OF THE CAMPUS • 1962 • *Kayama Yuzo* • JPN
PRIDE OF THE CLAN • 1917 • Tourneur Maurice • USA
PRIDE OF THE FANCY, THE • 1920 • Ward Albert • UKN
PRIDE OF THE FORCE, THE • 1913 • *Nigh William* • USA
PRIDE OF THE FORCE, THE • 1925 • Worne Duke • USA
PRIDE OF THE FORCE, THE • 1933 • Lee Norman • UKN
PRIDE OF THE LEGION, THE • 1932 • Beebe Ford • USA • BIG PAY-OFF, THE
PRIDE OF THE MARINES • 1936 • Lederman D. Ross • USA
PRIDE OF THE MARINES • 1945 • Daves Delmer • USA • FOREVER IN LOVE (UKN) ○ BODY AND SOUL
PRIDE OF THE NAVY • 1939 • Lamont Charles • USA
PRIDE OF THE NORTH, THE • 1920 • Coleby A. E. • UKN
PRIDE OF THE PADDOCK, THE see **MILLION DOLLAR HANDICAP, THE** • 1925
PRIDE OF THE PLAINS • 1944 • Fox Wallace • USA
PRIDE OF THE SOUTH, THE • 1913 • King Burton L. • USA
PRIDE OF THE WEST • 1938 • Selander Lesley • USA
PRIDE OF THE WEST, THE • 1911 • *Powers* • USA
PRIDE OF THE YANKEES • 1932 • *Ruth Babe* • SHT • USA
PRIDE OF THE YANKEES, THE • 1942 • Wood Sam • USA
PRIDE OF THE YARD • 1954 • Donnelly Eddie • ANS • USA
PRIDE'S DEADLY FURY see **WULIN ZHI** • 1983
PRIEHRADA • 1950 • Bielik Palo • CZC • DAM, THE
PRIERE, LA • 1900-07 • Blache Alice • FRN
PRIERE DU MUEZZIN, LA • 1906 • Mesguich Felix • ALG
PRIEST, THE see **PRASTEN** • 1913
PRIEST, THE see **SACERDOTE, EL** • 1978
PRIEST AND EMPRESS see **YOSO** • 1963
PRIEST AND THE BEAUTY, THE see **ANCHIN TO KIYOHIME** • 1960
PRIEST AND THE GOLD MINT see **ZOKU YAKUZA BOZU** • 1968
PRIEST AND THE MAN, THE • 1913 • Dawley J. Searle • USA
PRIEST IN PIGALLE, A see **DESERT DE PIGALLE, LE** • 1957
PRIEST KILLER • 1971 • Colla Richard A. • TVM • USA
PRIEST NICHIREN, THE see **NICHIREN** • 1978
PRIEST OF ISIS, THE see **ULTIMI GIORNI DI POMPEI, GLI** • 1913
PRIEST OF LOVE • 1980 • Miles Christopher • UKN
PRIEST OF THE WILDERNESS, A • 1909 • Olcott Sidney • USA • PRIEST OF WILDERNESS, THE
PRIEST OF WILDERNESS, THE see **PRIEST OF THE WILDERNESS, A** • 1909
PRIEST OR MEDICINE MAN? • 1914 • Montgomery Frank E. • USA
PRIESTER UND DAS MADCHEN, DER • 1958 • Ucicky Gustav • AUS
PRIEST'S END, THE see **FARARUV KONEC** • 1968
PRIESTS' NIGHT see **NOCHE DE CURAS** • 1978
PRIEST'S SUITCASE, THE see **VALITSA TOU PAPA, I** • 1979
PRIEST'S WIFE, THE (UKN) see **MOGLIE DEL PRETE, LA** • 1970
PRIGIONE, LA • 1942 • Cerio Ferruccio • ITL • SERENATA D'AMORE
PRIGIONE D'ACCIAIO, LA • 1914 • Roberti Roberto Leone • ITL
PRIGIONE DI DONNE • 1974 • Rondi Brunello • ITL • SEX LIFE IN A WOMEN'S PRISON
PRIGIONIERA, LA (ITL) see **PRISONNIERE, LA** • 1968
PRIGIONIERA DELLA TORRE DI FUOCO, LA • 1953 • Chili Giorgio W. • ITL
PRIGIONIERA DI AMALFI, LA • 1953 • Cristallini Giorgio • ITL
PRIGIONIERE DELL'ISOLA DEL DIAVOLO, LE • 1962 • Paolella Domenico • ITL, FRN • ILE AUX FILLES PERDUES, L' (FRN) ○ WOMEN OF DEVIL'S ISLAND ○ WOMEN PRISONERS OF DEVIL'S ISLAND, THE
PRIGIONIERI DEL MALE • 1956 • Costa Mario • ITL
PRIGIONIERI DEL MARE • 1960 • Zucchelli Nino • ITL
PRIGIONIERI DELLA TENEBRE • 1953 • Bomba Enrico • ITL
PRIGIONIERI DELL'ORRORE see **SONIDO DE LA MUERTE, EL** • 1966
PRIGIONIERO DEL RE, IL • 1954 • Rivalta Giorgio, Pottier Richard • ITL
PRIGIONIERO DELLA MONTAGNA, IL (ITL) see **FLUCHT IN DIE DOLOMITEN** • 1955
PRIGIONIERO DI SANTA CRUZ, IL • 1941 • Bragaglia Carlo Ludovico • ITL • GIUSTIZIA
PRIHODY MALEHO STENATKA • 1960 • Miler Zdenek • ANS • CZC • PUPPY'S ADVENTURES, THE
PRIJA BANHABI • 1940 • Barua Pramathesh Chandra • IND
PRIJDU HNED • 1942 • Vavra Otakar • CZC
PRIJEKI SUD • 1979 • Ivanda Branko • YGS • COURT MARTIAL
PRIJELA K NAM POUT • 1973 • Plivova-Simkova Vera • CZC • FAIR IS HERE, THE
PRIJESTRUP see **PRESTOP** • 1981
PRIJS DE MAAR • 1958 • van der Horst Herman • NTH • PRAISE THE SEA ○ PRIJS DE ZEE
PRIJS DE ZEE see **PRIJS DE MAAR** • 1958
PRIKLJUCENIJA BURATINO • 1959 • Ivanov-Vano Ivan • ANM • USS • ADVENTURES OF PINOCCHIO, THE
PRIKLYUCHENI V POLUNOSHT • 1964 • Marinovich Anton • BUL • MIDNIGHT ADVENTURE
PRIKO SINJEG MORA • 1980 • Jojic Ljiljana • YGS • ACROSS THE BLUE SEA ○ ON THE OTHER SIDE OF THE SEA
PRILETEL MARSIANIN V OSENNUYU NOCH • 1980 • Shumsky Gennadi • USS • MARTIAN ARRIVES ON AN AUTUMN NIGHT, A
PRIM • 1930 • Buchs Jose • SPN
PRIMA ANGELICA, LA • 1973 • Saura Carlos • SPN • COUSIN ANGELICA (USA)
PRIMA AVENTURA DE PEPE CARVALHO, LA see **TATUAJE** • 1976
PRIMA COMMUNIONE • 1950 • Blasetti Alessandro • ITL • FATHER'S DILEMMA (USA) ○ HIS MAJESTY MR. JONES ○ FIRST COMMUNION
PRIMA DELLA RIVOLUZIONE • 1964 • Bertolucci Bernardo • ITL • BEFORE THE REVOLUTION (USA)
PRIMA DI SERA • 1954 • Tellini Piero • ITL
PRIMA DONNA, LA • 1963 • Lifchitz Philippe • SHT • FRN
PRIMA DONNA, THE • 1913 • *Victor* • USA
PRIMA DONNA, THE • 1915 • *Eclectic* • USA
PRIMA DONNA CHE PASSA, LA • 1940 • Neufeld Max • ITL
PRIMA DONNA'S CAT, THE • 1913 • *Ferel Marion* • USA
PRIMA DONNA'S DUPES, THE • 1912 • Wilson Frank? • UKN
PRIMA DONNA'S HUSBAND,-THE • 1916 • Steger Julius, Golden Joseph A. • USA
PRIMA DONNA'S MOTHER, THE • 1915 • Martin E. A. • USA
PRIMA DONNA'S SPECIAL, THE • 1917 • *Kalem* • USA
PRIMA DRAGOSTE • 1932 • Mihail Jean • RMN
PRIMA E DOPO L'AMORE.. UN GRIDO D'ALLARME • 1972 • Crisci Giovanni • ITL • BEFORE AND AFTER SEX
PRIMA EN LA BANERA UNA • 1976 • Puig Jaime • SPN
PRIMA NOTTE, LA • 1959 • Cavalcanti Alberto • ITL, FRN • NOCES VENITIENNES, LES (FRN)
PRIMA NOTTE DEL DR. DANIELI, INDUSTRIALE COL COMPLESSO DEL GIOCATTOLO • 1970 • Grimaldi Gianni • ITL
PRIMA NOTTE DI NOZZE • 1977 • Prisco Corrado • ITL
PRIMA NOTTE DI QUIETE, LA • 1972 • Zurlini Valerio • ITL, FRN • PROFESSEUR, LE (FRN) ○ FIRST NIGHT OF QUIET ○ INDIAN SUMMER
PRIMA TI PERDONO.. POI TI AMMAZZO • 1970 • Iquino Ignacio F. • ITL, SPN
PRIMA TI SUONO POI TI SPARO • 1975 • Antel Franz • ITL, AUS
PRIMA VERA'S SAGA OF ST. OLAV see **PRIMA VERAS SAGA OM OLAV DEN HELLIGE** • 1984
PRIMA VERAS SAGA OM OLAV DEN HELLIGE • 1984 • Falsk Herodes • NRW • PRIMA VERA'S SAGA OF ST. OLAV
PRIMA VOLTA SULL'ERBA, LA • 1975 • Calderoni Gian Luigi • ITL • DANZA D'AMORE SOTTO GLI OLMI
PRIMADONA • 1985-89 • Osman Aziz M. • MTV • MLY
PRIMADONNA, LA • 1943 • Perilli Ivo • ITL
PRIMAL CALL, THE • 1911 • Griffith D. W. • USA
PRIMAL FEAR see **MOURIR A TUE-TETE** • 1979
PRIMAL INSTINCT, THE • 1916 • Brooke Van Dyke • SHT • USA
PRIMAL LAW, THE • 1921 • Durning Bernard J. • USA
PRIMAL LAW, THE see **PRIMAL LURE, THE** • 1916
PRIMAL LURE, THE • 1916 • Hart William S. • USA • PRIMAL LAW, THE
PRIMAL PLEASURES • 1973 • *Buchman Audrey* • USA
PRIMAL RAGE • 1989 • Rambaldi Vittorio • USA
PRIMAL SCREAM see **HELL FIRE** • 1986
PRIMANEREHRE see **BOYKOTT** • 1930
PRIMANERINNEN • 1951 • Thiele Rolf • FRG
PRIMANERLIEBE • 1927 • Land Robert • FRG
PRIMARY • 1960 • Leacock Richard, Pennebaker D. A. • DOC • USA
PRIMARY SCHOOL see **SZKOLA PODSTAWOWA** • 1972
PRIMATE • 1974 • Wiseman Frederick • USA
PRIMAVERA • 1917 • Leni Paul • FRG
PRIMAVERA DE LA VIDA see **LIVETS VAR** • 1957
PRIMAVERA DE LOS ESCORPIONES, LA • 1970 • *Del Villar* • MXC
PRIMAVERA DEL PAPA, LA • 1949 • Hamza D. A. • SHT • ITL
PRIMAVERA EN EL CORAZON • 1955 • Rodriguez Roberto • MXC
PRIMAVERA ET OTONO • 1932 • Forde Eugene J. • USA
PRIMAVERA IMMORTAL see **SAMRTNO PROLJECE** • 1974
PRIMAVERA MORTAL • 1970 • Iglesias Miguel • SPN
PRIME CUT • 1972 • Ritchie Michael • USA • KANSAS CITY PRIME, THE
PRIME DIRECTIVE • 1990 • Lester Mark L. • USA
PRIME EVIL • 1989 • Findlay Roberta • USA
PRIME MINISTER, THE • 1941 • Dickinson Thorold • UKN • EMPIRE WAS BUILT, AN
PRIME OF LIFE, THE see **TOSHIGORO** • 1968
PRIME OF MISS JEAN BRODIE, THE • 1969 • Neame Ronald • UKN
PRIME OF OCHIYO'S LIFE, THE see **OCHIYO TOSHIGORO** • 1937
PRIME RISK • 1984 • Farkas Michael • USA
PRIME SUSPECT • 1982 • Black Noel • TVM • USA • CRY OF INNOCENCE
PRIME SUSPECT • 1989 • Rutland Mark • USA

PRIME SUSPECT see **AMY PRENTISS: BAPTISM OF FIRE** • 1974
PRIME TIME see **AMERICAN RASPBERRY** • 1980
PRIMEIRA MISSA, A • 1961 • Barreto Victor • BRZ • FIRST MASS, THE
PRIMER ANO, EL • 1972 • Guzman Patricio • DOC • CHL • FIRST YEAR, THE ○ PREMIERE ANNEE, LA
PRIMER CUARTEL, EL • 1966 • Iquino Ignacio F. • SPN
PRIMER FESTIVAL MORTADELLO Y FILEMON • 1967 • Vara Rafael • SPN
PRIMERA AVENTURA, LA see **NINO Y EL LADRON, EL** • 1964
PRIMERA CARGA AL MACHETE, LA • 1968 • Gomez Manuel Octavio • CUB • FIRST CHARGE OF THE MACHETE, THE (UKN) ○ FIRST ASSAULT WITH MACHETES, THE
PRIMERA ENTREGA DE UNA MUJER CASADA • 1971 • Fons Angelino • SPN • FIRST SURRENDER, THE
PRIMERA FUNDACION DE BUENOS AIRES • 1958 • Birri Fernando • ANM • ARG
PRIMERA PREGUNTA SOBRE LA FELICIDAD (MXC) see **PREMIERE QUESTION SUR LE BONHEUR** • 1977
PRIMERAS EXPERIENCAS, LAS • 1976 • Balcazar Alfonso • SPN
PRIMERO EL DOLAR • 1970 • *Noriego Jorge Camargo (P)* • MXC
PRIMERO SOY MEXICANO • 1950 • Pardave Joaquin • MXC
PRIMERO YO • 1963 • Ayala Fernando • ARG
PRIMEROS METROS, LOS • 1980 • *Querejeta Elias (P)* • SPN • FIRST FLEET, THE
PRIMEROSE • 1918 • Caserini Mario • ITL
PRIMEROSE • 1933 • Guissart Rene • FRN
PRIMEVAL TEST, THE • 1913 • Turner Otis • USA
PRIMEVALS • 1989 • Band Charles, Allen David* • USA
PRIMITI TOO TAA • 1988 • Ackerman Ed • ANS • CND
PRIMITIFS DU XIIIe, LES • 1960 • Guilbaud Pierre • SHT • FRN
PRIMITIVE, THE • 1979 • Gautama Sisworo • INN
PRIMITIVE CALL, THE • 1914 • *Chatterton Thomas* • USA
PRIMITIVE CALL, THE • 1917 • Bracken Bertram • USA
PRIMITIVE DESIRES (USA) see **MONTAGNA DEL DIO CANNIBALE, LA** • 1976
PRIMITIVE INSTINCT, THE • 1914 • Melford George • SHT • USA
PRIMITIVE LONDON • 1965 • Miller Arnold Louis • DOC • UKN • SWINGING LONDON EXPOSED ○ PRIMITIVE LONDON EXPOSED ○ SWINGING LONDON EXPOSE ○ SWINGING LONDON ○ LONDON EXPOSED
PRIMITIVE LONDON EXPOSED see **PRIMITIVE LONDON** • 1965
PRIMITIVE LOVE • 1927 • Kleinschmidt Frank E. • USA
PRIMITIVE LOVE (USA) see **AMORE PRIMITIVO, L'** • 1964
PRIMITIVE LOVER, THE • 1922 • Franklin Sidney A. • USA
PRIMITIVE MAN • 1913 • *Kalem* • USA
PRIMITIVE MAN, THE see **BRUTE FORCE** • 1913
PRIMITIVE MAN'S CAREER TO CIVILIZATION, A • 1911 • Kearton Cherry • UKN
PRIMITIVE MONGOLIA AND CHINA • 1947 • Marshall Herbert • DOC • UKN
PRIMITIVE PAINTERS OF CHARLEVOIX see **PEINTRES POPULAIRES DE CHARLEVOIX** • 1946
PRIMITIVE PARADISE • 1961 • Cotlow Lewis • DOC • USA
PRIMITIVE PASSIONS (UKN) see **HEI TIKI** • 1935
PRIMITIVE PLUTO • 1950 • Nichols Charles • ANS • USA
PRIMITIVE SPIRIT, THE • 1915 • *Hinkley William* • USA
PRIMITIVE STRAIN, THE • 1916 • *Arnold Edward* • USA
PRIMITIVE WAY, THE • 1915 • *Santschi Thomas* • USA
PRIMITIVE WOMAN, THE • 1918 • Ingraham Lloyd • USA
PRIMITIVES, THE • 1962 • Travers Alfred • UKN
PRIMITIVOS PORTUGUESES • 1957 • Garcia Fernando • SHT • PRT
PRIMO AMORE • 1941 • Gallone Carmine • ITL
PRIMO AMORE • 1959 • Camerini Mario • ITL • FIRST LOVE (USA)
PRIMO AMORE • 1978 • Risi Dino • ITL
PRIMO APPLAUSO • 1957 • Mercanti Pino • ITL
PRIMO BASILIO, EL • 1934 • de Najera Carlos • MXC
PRIMO BASILIO, O • 1959 • Ribeiro Antonio Lopes • PRT
PRIMO DEL DILUVIO (ITL) see **AVANT LE DELUGE** • 1954
PRIMO PREMIO: MARIA ROSA • 1953 • Grieco Sergio • ITL
PRIMO PREMIO SI CHIAMA IRENE, IL • 1969 • Ragazzi Renzo • ITL • FIRST PRIZE IRENE (UKN) ○ DANIMARCA INCREDIBILE REALTA
PRIMO TANDO A ROMA.. STORIE D'AMORE E D'ALCHIMIA • 1973 • Alberto Juan • ITL
PRIMORDIUM • 1968 • Pantzer Jerry • ANS • USA
PRIMROSE PATH • 1931 • O'Connor William A. • USA
PRIMROSE PATH • 1940 • La Cava Gregory • USA
PRIMROSE PATH, THE • 1915 • Marston Lawrence • USA
PRIMROSE PATH, THE • 1925 • Hoyt Harry O. • USA
PRIMROSE PATH, THE • 1934 • Denham Reginald • UKN
PRIMROSE PATH, THE see **BURNT WINGS** • 1920
PRIMROSE RING, THE • 1917 • Leonard Robert Z. • USA
PRIMULA BIANCA, LA • 1947 • Bragaglia Carlo Ludovico • ITL
PRINC A VECERNICE • 1978 • Vorlicek Vaclav • CZC • PRINCE AND THE EVENING STAR, THE
PRINCE • 1914 • Swickard Charles • USA
PRINCE, THE • 1976 • Michalak Richard • SHT • ASL
PRINCE AND BETTY, THE • 1919 • Thornby Robert T. • USA
PRINCE AND THE BEGGAR MAID, THE • 1921 • Bramble A. V. • UKN
PRINCE AND THE EVENING STAR, THE see **PRINC A VECERNICE** • 1978
PRINCE AND THE GREAT RACE • 1983 • Safran Henri • ASL
PRINCE AND THE NATURE GIRL, THE • 1965 • Wishman Doris • USA
PRINCE AND THE PAUPER, THE • 1909 • Dawley J. Searle • USA
PRINCE AND THE PAUPER, THE • 1915 • Porter Edwin S., Ford Hugh • USA
PRINCE AND THE PAUPER, THE • 1937 • Keighley William • USA
PRINCE AND THE PAUPER, THE • 1962 • Chaffey Don • UKN
PRINCE AND THE PAUPER, THE • 1969 • Geisinger Elliot • USA • ADVENTURES OF THE PRINCE AND THE PAUPER, THE
PRINCE AND THE PAUPER, THE • 1978 • Fleischer Richard • UKN • CROSSED SWORDS (USA)
PRINCE AND THE PAUPER, THE see **SEINE MAJESTAT DAS BETTELKIND** • 1920
PRINCE AND THE PAUPER, THE see **RAJA AUR RUNK** • 1968
PRINCE AND THE POTTER, THE see **RADUGA SEMI NEDESHD** • 1983
PRINCE AND THE PUMPS, THE • 1911 • *Williams Earle* • USA
PRINCE AND THE SHOWGIRL, THE • 1957 • Olivier Laurence, Bushell Anthony • UKN, USA
PRINCE AT THE COURT OF YARRALUMLA, THE • 1987 • Eggleston Colin • ASL
PRINCE AZUR, LE • 1908 • Cohl Emile • ANS • FRN
PRINCE BABOULE • 1938 • Houssin Jacques • FRN • BUSINESS
PRINCE BARBARE, LE • 1988 • Koralnik Pierre • SWT
PRINCE BAYAYA see **BAJAJA** • 1950
PRINCE BEHIND THE SEVEN SEAS, THE see **PRINZ HINTER DEN SIEBEN MEEREN, DER** • 1984
PRINCE BELGE DE L'EUROPE: CHARLES-JOSEPH DE LIGNE • 1962 • Kupissonoff Jacques • SHT • BLG • PRINCE DE LIGNE
PRINCE CHAP, THE • 1916 • Neilan Marshall • USA
PRINCE CHAP, THE • 1920 • De Mille William C. • USA
PRINCE CHARLIE • 1914 • *De Forrest Charles* • USA
PRINCE CHARMANT, LE • 1924 • Tourjansky Victor • FRN
PRINCE CHARMANT, LE • 1941 • Boyer Jean • FRN
PRINCE CHARMING • 1912 • Kirkwood James, Tucker George Loane • USA
PRINCE CHARMING NI LOLA CINDERELLA, MGA • 1969 • Crisostomo Fely • PHL
PRINCE CUCKOO see **PRINZ KUCKUCK** • 1919
PRINCE DE GALLES ET FALLIERES, LE • 1912 • Cohl Emile • ANS • FRN
PRINCE DE LIGNE see **PRINCE BELGE DE L'EUROPE: CHARLES-JOSEPH DE LIGNE** • 1962
PRINCE DE MINUIT • 1934 • Guissart Rene • FRN
PRINCE DE MON COEUR • 1938 • Daniel-Norman Jacques • FRN
PRINCE DEMONIQUE see **AMIR AD-DAHA** • 1963
PRINCE DES SIX JOURS • 1933 • Vernay Robert • FRN
PRINCE DIMITRI see **RESURRECTION** • 1927
PRINCE EHTEJAB see **SHAZDE-EHTEJAB** • 1975
PRINCE EMBETE • 1920 • Monca Georges • FRN
PRINCE EMBETE PAR RIGADIN • 1912 • Monca Georges • FRN
PRINCE FOR A DAY, A • 1917 • Stedman Marshall • SHT • USA
PRINCE FOR CYNTHIA, A • 1953 • Box Muriel • UKN
PRINCE FOR WALES, A • 1969 • Harris Martin D. • DOC • UKN
PRINCE GUSTAF see **PRINS GUSTAF** • 1944
PRINCE HAT BELOW GROUND see **PRINS HATT UNDER JORDEN** • 1963
PRINCE IGOR see **KNYAZ IGOR** • 1970
PRINCE IN A PAWNSHOP, A • 1916 • Scardon Paul • USA
PRINCE IN ADELAIDE, THE • 1920 • *Krischock H. (Ph)* • ASL
PRINCE IN BONDAGE, THE see **PRINCIPE ENCADENADO, EL** • 1960
PRINCE IN DISGUISE, THE • 1915 • Johnson Tefft • USA
PRINCE IN MELBOURNE, THE • 1920 • ASL
PRINCE IN SYDNEY, THE • 1920 • ASL
PRINCE IN WONDERLAND see **WANPAKU OJI NO OROCHITAIJI** • 1963
PRINCE JACK • 1984 • Lovitt Bert • USA
PRINCE JEAN, LE • 1928 • Hervil Rene • FRN
PRINCE JEAN, LE • 1934 • de Marguenat Jean • FRN
PRINCE, KING OF DOGS • 1935 • Feist Felix E. • SHT • USA
PRINCE OF A KING, A • 1923 • Austin Albert • USA
PRINCE OF ABSENCE, THE see **TAVOLLET HERCEGE, A** • 1989
PRINCE OF ADVENTURERS see **CASANOVA** • 1927
PRINCE OF ARCADIA • 1933 • Schwarz Hanns • UKN
PRINCE OF AVENUE A., THE • 1920 • Ford John • USA
PRINCE OF BAVARIA, A • 1914 • Lloyd Frank • USA
PRINCE OF BEL-AIR • 1986 • Braverman Charles • TVM • USA
PRINCE OF BOHEMIA, A • 1914 • *American* • USA
PRINCE OF BROADWAY, THE • 1926 • Gorman John • USA
PRINCE OF CENTRAL PARK, THE • 1977 • Hart Harvey • TVM • USA
PRINCE OF DAFFYDIL • 1920 • Morante Milburn, Diltz Charles • SHT • USA
PRINCE OF DARKNESS • 1987 • Carpenter John • USA
PRINCE OF DARKNESS, THE • 1902 • *Biograph* • USA
PRINCE OF DIAMONDS • 1930 • Brown Karl, Van Buren A. H. • USA
PRINCE OF EVIL, A • 1913 • Ince Ralph • USA
PRINCE OF FOGO, THE see **PRINSEN FRA FOGO** • 1987
PRINCE OF FOXES • 1949 • King Henry • USA
PRINCE OF GRAUSTARK, THE • 1916 • Wright Fred E. • USA
PRINCE OF HEADWAITERS, THE • 1927 • Dillon John Francis • USA
PRINCE OF HEARTS, THE • 1929 • Wheeler Cliff • USA
PRINCE OF HIS RACE, A • 1926 • Calnek Roy • USA
PRINCE OF HOMBURG, THE see **PRINCIPE DI HOMBURG, IL** • 1984
PRINCE OF INDIA, A • 1914 • Wharton Leopold • USA
PRINCE OF KHYBER, A • 1909 • *Empire Films* • UKN
PRINCE OF K'NUTS, THE (UKN) see **HOW TO HANDLE WOMEN** • 1928
PRINCE OF LOVERS, A • 1922 • Calvert Charles • UKN
PRINCE OF MAGICIANS, THE (UKN) see **EXCELSIOR!** • 1901
PRINCE OF PADUA HILLS, THE • 1955 • Landers Lew • MTV • USA
PRINCE OF PEACE • 1930 • Carter Donald • UKN
PRINCE OF PEACE, A • 1915 • Jones Edgar • USA
PRINCE OF PEACE, THE • 1949 • Beaudine William, Daniels Harold • USA
PRINCE OF PEANUTS, THE see **HOW TO HANDLE WOMEN** • 1928
PRINCE OF PENNSYLVANIA • 1988 • Nyswaner Ron • USA
PRINCE OF PEP, THE • 1925 • Nelson Jack • USA • BLACK FLASH, THE
PRINCE OF PILSEN, THE • 1926 • Powell Paul • USA
PRINCE OF PIRATES • 1953 • Salkow Sidney • USA
PRINCE OF PLAYERS • 1955 • Dunne Philip • USA
PRINCE OF ROGUES, THE (USA) see **SCHINDERHANNES** • 1928
PRINCE OF SPACE (USA) see **YUSEI OJI** • 1959
PRINCE OF TEMPTERS, THE • 1926 • Mendes Lothar • USA
PRINCE OF THE BLUE GRASS (UKN) see **PRIDE OF THE BLUE GRASS** • 1954
PRINCE OF THE CITY • 1981 • Lumet Sidney • USA
PRINCE OF THE PLAINS • 1927 • Williamson Robin E. • USA
PRINCE OF THE PLAINS • 1949 • Ford Philip • USA
PRINCE OF THE RUSTLERS • 1936 • Ray Bernard B. • USA
PRINCE OF THE SADDLE • 1926 • *Church Fred* • USA
PRINCE OF THIEVES, THE • 1948 • Bretherton Howard • USA
PRINCE OF WALES • 1933 • UKN
PRINCE OF YESTERDAY, A • 1915 • *Gaumont* • USA
PRINCE OR CLOWN (USA) see **FURST ODER CLOWN** • 1927
PRINCE PARTY, THE • 1914 • *Bushman Francis X.* • USA
PRINCE PISTACHIO • 1921 • Roach Hal • SHT • USA
PRINCE PIWI • 1973 • Quist-Moller Fleming • DNM
PRINCE RUPERT DROPS • 1969 • Frampton Hollis • USA
PRINCE THERE WAS, A • 1921 • Forman Tom • USA
PRINCE VALIANT • 1954 • Hathaway Henry • USA
PRINCE VIOLENT • 1961 • Freleng Friz • ANS • USA
PRINCE WHO WAS A THIEF, THE • 1951 • Mate Rudolph • USA
PRINCE WILLY • 1914 • *Eclair* • USA
PRINCE WITH A DONKEY'S EAR, THE see **PRINCIPE COM ORELHAS DE BURRO, O** • 1980
PRINCE ZILAH, LE • 1926 • Roudes Gaston • FRN
PRINCELY BANDIT, THE • 1916 • Ford Francis • SHT • USA
PRINCES, LES • 1982 • Gatlif Tony • FRN • PRINCES, THE
PRINCES, THE see **PRINCES, LES** • 1982
PRINCE'S COURT MUSICIAN, HAYDN, THE see **ESZTERHAZA MUZSIKUSA, HAYDN** • 1960
PRINCES DE LA CRAVACHE • 1930 • Wion Marcel L. • FRN
PRINCES IN THE TOWER • 1913 • Plumb Hay • UKN
PRINCES IN THE TOWER, THE • 1928 • Banfield George J., Eveleigh Leslie • UKN
PRINCES NOIRS DE SAINT-GERMAIN-DES-PRES, LES • Beye Diogaye • SHT • SNL
PRINCESA DE LOS URSINOS, LA • 1947 • Lucia Luis • SPN
PRINCESS • 1969 • Wuyts Herman • BLG
PRINCESS see **PRENSES** • 1985
PRINCESS, THE see **PRINSESSAN** • 1966
PRINCESS, THE see **ADJ KIRALY KATONAT!** • 1983
PRINCESS ACADEMY, THE • 1987 • Block Bruce • USA, FRN, YGS
PRINCESS AND THE CABBIE, THE • 1981 • Jordan Glenn • TVM • USA
PRINCESS AND THE CALL GIRL, THE • 1984 • Metzger Radley H. • USA
PRINCESS AND THE DRAGON, THE • 1948 • Wasilewski Zenon • ANS • PLN • DRAGON OF CRACOW, THE
PRINCESS AND THE LITTLE DONKEY, THE see **KROLEWNA I OSIOLEK** • 1959
PRINCESS AND THE MAGIC FROG, THE • 1965 • Green Austin • USA • AT THE END OF THE RAINBOW
PRINCESS AND THE MAN, THE • 1913 • Brabin Charles J. • USA
PRINCESS AND THE PEA, THE • 1959 • Georgi Katja • ANS • GDR
PRINCESS AND THE PEA, THE • 1983 • Bill Tony • MTV • USA
PRINCESS AND THE PEASANT, THE • 1910 • Dawley J. Searle • USA
PRINCESS AND THE PIRATE, THE • 1944 • Butler David • USA
PRINCESS AND THE PLUMBER, THE • 1930 • Korda Alexander • USA
PRINCESS AND THE RING, THE see **OJO TO YUBIWA** • 1956
PRINCESS AND THE RIVER see **AMIRA WAL NAHR, AL** • 1986
PRINCESS AND THE WONDERFUL WEAVER, THE • 1968 • Taylor Richard • ANS • UKN
PRINCESS BRIDE, THE • 1987 • Reiner Rob • USA
PRINCESS CHANG PING see **TI-NU HUA** • 1976
PRINCESS CHARMING • 1934 • Elvey Maurice • UKN
PRINCESS CINDERELLA • 1955 • Tofano Sergio • ITL
PRINCESS CLEMENTINA • 1911 • Barker Will? • UKN
PRINCESS COMES ACROSS, THE • 1936 • Howard William K. • USA
PRINCESS DAISY • 1983 • Hussein Waris • TVM • USA
PRINCESS FOR A DAY, A • 1914 • *Wallace Irene* • USA
PRINCESS FROM HOBOKEN, THE • 1927 • Dale Allan • USA
PRINCESS FROM THE MOON see **TAKETORI MONOGATARI** • 1988
PRINCESS GRASS see **OHIME GUSA** • 1924
PRINCESS IN EDO see **SENHIME GOTEN** • 1960
PRINCESS IN LOVE, THE see **POVESTE CA-N BASME, O** • 1959
PRINCESS IN THE VASE, THE • 1908 • Griffith D. W. • USA
PRINCESS IRON FAN • HKG
PRINCESS JASNA AND THE FLYING COBBLER see **PRINCEZNE JASNENCE A LETAJICIM SVCI** • 1987
PRINCESS JONES • 1921 • Seyffertitz G. V. • USA
PRINCESS MERMAID see **NINGYO HIME** • 1974
PRINCESS' NECKLACE, THE • 1917 • France Floyd • USA
PRINCESS NICOTINE OR THE SMOKE FAIRY • 1909 • Blackton J. Stuart, Smith Albert E. • USA
PRINCESS OF ANGKOR WAT see **UTSUKUSHIKI AISHU** • 1958
PRINCESS OF BAGDAD, A • 1913 • Gaskill Charles L. • USA
PRINCESS OF HAPPY CHANCE, THE • 1916 • Elvey Maurice • UKN
PRINCESS OF LORRAINE, THE • 1912 • *Gem* • USA
PRINCESS OF NEW YORK, THE • 1921 • Crisp Donald • USA, UKN
PRINCESS OF PARK ROW, THE • 1917 • Miller Ashley • USA
PRINCESS OF PATCHES, THE • 1917 • Green Alfred E. • USA
PRINCESS OF TAMBOSO, THE • 1976 • Jonas George • MTV • CND
PRINCESS OF THE BLOOD, A • 1916 • Noy Wilfred • UKN
PRINCESS OF THE DARK, A • 1917 • Miller Charles • USA
PRINCESS OF THE DESERT, A • 1914 • Edwin Walter • USA
PRINCESS OF THE HILLS, A • 1912 • *Joyce Alice* • USA

PRINCESS OF THE NILE • 1954 • Jones Harmon • USA
PRINCESS OF THE SEA, THE • 1909 • *Gaumont* • FRN
PRINCESS OF THE VASE • 1908 • *Bitzer Billy (Ph)* • USA
PRINCESS O'HARA • 1935 • Burton David • USA
PRINCESS ON BROADWAY, THE • 1927 • Fitzgerald Dallas M. • USA
PRINCESS O'ROURKE • 1943 • Krasna Norman • USA
PRINCESS PONGYOLA see **HERCEGNO PONGYOLABAN, A** • 1914
PRINCESS PRISCILLA'S FORTNIGHT see **RUNAWAY PRINCESS, THE** • 1929
PRINCESS ROMANOFF • 1915 • Powell Frank • USA • FEDORA
PRINCESS SAYS NO, THE see **UKARE SANDO GASA** • 1959
PRINCESS SEETA see **SEETHA** • 1967
PRINCESS SEN see **SENHIME** • 1954
PRINCESS SNAKE'S TRAVELS see **HEBIHIME DOUCHUH** • 1949
PRINCESS VIRTUE • 1917 • Leonard Robert Z. • USA
PRINCESS WHO HAD NEVER LAUGHED, THE • 1984 • Cullingham Mark • MTV • USA
PRINCESS WITH GOLDEN HAIR • ANS • CZC
PRINCESS WITH HORNS, THE • 1967 • ANS • CZC
PRINCESS WITH THE GOLDEN STAR, THE see **PRINCEZNA SE ZLATOV HVEZDOU** • 1959
PRINCESS WITH THE IRON FAN, THE • 1942 • CHN
PRINCESS YANG, THE see **YOKIHI** • 1955
PRINCESS YANG KWEI FEI, THE see **YOKIHI** • 1955
PRINCESSE, A VOS ORDRES • 1931 • de Vaucorbeil Max, Schwarz Hanns • FRN • SON ALTESSE ORDONNE
PRINCESSE AUX CLOWNS, LA • 1924 • Hugon Andre • FRN
PRINCESSE CLE DE SOL • 1945 • Image Jean • ANS • FRN
PRINCESSE CZARDAS • 1934 • Beucler Andre, Jacoby Georg • FRN • SERENADE
PRINCESSE DE CLEVES, LA • 1960 • Delannoy Jean • FRN, ITL • PRINCIPESSA DI CLEVES, LA (ITL)
PRINCESSE FATALE, LA see **FEE CARABOSSE: OU, LE POIGNARD FATAL, LA** • 1906
PRINCESSE MANDANE, LA see **OUBLIE** • 1927
PRINCESSE MASHA, LA • 1927 • Leprince Rene • FRN
PRINCESSE TAM-TAM • 1935 • Greville Edmond T. • FRN
PRINCESS'S DILEMMA, THE see **PRINSESSE ELENA** • 1913
PRINCETON • 1948 • *Hammid Alexander* • USA
PRINCEZNA SE ZLATOV HVEZDOU • 1959 • Fric Martin • CZC • PRINCESS WITH THE GOLDEN STAR, THE
PRINCEZNE JASNENCE A LETAJICIM SVCI • 1987 • Troska Zdenek • CZC • PRINCESS JASNA AND THE FLYING COBBLER
PRINCIPAL, THE • 1987 • Cain Christopher • USA
PRINCIPAL ENEMY, THE see **ENEMIGO PRINCIPAL, EL** • 1973
PRINCIPAL WIFE see **MIA LUANG** • 1986
PRINCIPE COM ORELHAS DE BURRO, O • 1980 • de Macedo Antonio • PRT • PRINCE WITH A DONKEY'S EAR, THE
PRINCIPE CORONATO CERCASI PER RICCA EREDITIERA • 1970 • Grimaldi Gianni • ITL
PRINCIPE DALLA MASCHERA ROSSA, IL • 1956 • Savona Leopoldo • ITL
PRINCIPE DE LA IGLESIA, UN see **CARDENAL, EL** • 1951
PRINCIPE DEL DESIERTO, EL • 1946 • Rivero Fernando A. • MXC
PRINCIPE DELL'IMPOSSIBILE, IL • 1919 • Genina Augusto • ITL
PRINCIPE DI HOMBURG, IL • 1984 • Lavia Gabriele • ITL • PRINCE OF HOMBURG, THE
PRINCIPE ENCADENADO, EL • 1960 • Lucia Luis • SPN • PRINCE IN BONDAGE, THE
PRINCIPE FUSTO, IL • 1960 • Arena Maurizio • ITL
PRINCIPE GONDOLERO, EL • 1933 • Venturini Edward D.
PRINCIPE RIBELLE, IL • 1950 • Mercanti Pino • ITL
PRINCIPESSA BEBE, LA • 1920 • D'Ambra Lucio • ITL
PRINCIPESSA DEL SOGNO, LA • 1942 • Savarese Roberto, Ricci Maria Teresa • ITL
PRINCIPESSA DELLE CANARIE, LA • 1956 • Moffa Paolo • ITL, SPN • ISLAND PRINCESS, THE ○ ISOLA
PRINCIPESSA DI BAGDAD, LA • 1916 • Negroni Baldassare • ITL
PRINCIPESSA DI BEDFORD, LA • 1914 • Roberti Roberto Leone • ITL
PRINCIPESSA DI CLEVES, LA (ITL) see **PRINCESSE DE CLEVES, LA** • 1960
PRINCIPESSA GIORGIO, LA • 1919 • Roberti Roberto Leone • ITL
PRINCIPESSA MISTERIOSA • 1919 • Brenon Herbert • ITL
PRINCIPESSA NUDA, LA • 1976 • Canevari Cesare • ITL
PRINCIPESSA TARAKANOVA, LA • 1938 • Soldati Mario, Ozep Fedor • ITL
PRINCIPESSINA • 1943 • Gramantieri Tulio • ITL
PRINCIPIO, EL • 1972 • Ortega Gonzalo Martinez • MXC • BEGINNING, THE
PRINCIPIO DA SABEDORIO, O • 1975 • de Macedo Antonio • PRT • RICO O CAMELO E O REINO, O ○ BEGINNING OF WISDOM, THE
PRINCIPLES OF CINEMATOGRAPHY • 1973 • Le Grice Malcolm • UKN
PRINCIPLES OF FLYING, THE • 1973 • Craig Fred • USA
PRINS GUSTAF • 1944 • Bauman Schamyl • SWD • PA SANGENS VINGAR ○ PRINCE GUSTAF ○ UNGA HJARTAN
PRINS HATT UNDER JORDEN • 1963 • Lagerkvist Bengt • SWD • PRINCE HAT BELOW GROUND
PRINS PIWI • 1974 • Quist-Moller Fleming, Refn Anders • DNM
PRINSEN FRA FOGO • 1987 • Tennvik Inge • NRW • PRINCE OF FOGO, THE
PRINSESSA RUUSUNEN • 1949 • Laine Edvin • FNL • SLEEPING BEAUTY
PRINSESSAN • 1966 • Falck Ake • SWD • TIME IN THE SUN, A (USA) ○ PRINCESS, THE
PRINSESSE ELENA • 1913 • Holger-Madsen • DNM • PRINCESS'S DILEMMA, THE
PRINSESSENS HJERTE • 1914 • Davidsen Hjalmar • DNM
PRINT OF DEATH • 1958 • Tully Montgomery • UKN
PRINT OF THE NAILS, THE • 1915 • Nicholls George • USA
PRINTEMPS • 1957 • Bail Rene • DCS • CND
PRINTEMPS, LE • 1909 • Feuillade Louis • FRN
PRINTEMPS, LE • 1967 • Bex Ludo • SHT • BLG
PRINTEMPS, LE • 1971 • Hanoun Marcel • FRN • SPRING
PRINTEMPS A NAGASAKI see **TYPHON SUR NAGASAKI** • 1957
PRINTEMPS A PARIS • 1956 • Roy Jean-Claude • FRN
PRINTEMPS DE LA LIBERTE, LE • 1948 • Gremillon Jean • FRN
PRINTEMPS EN HIVER, UN • 1979 • Deray Jacques • FRN
PRINTEMPS EN HOLLANDE, UN see **OCHTEND VAN ZES WEKEN, EEN** • 1966
PRINTEMPS, L'AUTOMNE ET L'AMOUR ,LE • 1955 • Grangier Gilles • FRN, ITL • MIA MOGLIE NON SI TOCCA (ITL)
PRINTEMPS PERDU • 1989 • Mazari Alain • FRN
PRINTEMPS SOUS LA NEIGE, LE see **BAY BOY, THE** • 1984
PRINTER'S DEVIL, THE • 1923 • Beaudine William • USA
PRINZ DER LEGENDE, DER see **TRAGODIE IM HAUSE HABSBURG** • 1924
PRINZ HINTER DEN SIEBEN MEEREN, DER • 1984 • GDR • PRINCE BEHIND THE SEVEN SEAS, THE
PRINZ KARNEVAL • 1923 • Freisler Fritz • FRG
PRINZ KUCKUCK • 1919 • Leni Paul • FRG • LEBEN UND HOLLENFAHRT EINES WOLLUSTLINGS ○ PRINCE CUCKOO
PRINZ LOUIS FERDINAND • 1927 • Behrendt Hans • FRG
PRINZ OHNE LAND, DER see **FRAU MIT DEN MILLIONEN 2, DIE** • 1923
PRINZ POSTILLION • 1925 • Dammann Gerhard • FRG
PRINZ SAMI • 1917 • Lubitsch Ernst • FRG
PRINZ UND BETTELKNABE see **SEINE MAJESTAT DAS BETTELKIND** • 1920
PRINZ UND DIE KOKOTTE, DER see **PRINZ UND DIE TANZERIN, DER** • 1926
PRINZ UND DIE TANZERIN, DER • 1926 • Eichberg Richard • FRG • PRINZ UND DIE KOKOTTE, DER
PRINZ VERLIEBT SICH, EIN • 1932 • Wiene Conrad
PRINZ VON ARKADIEN, DER • 1932 • Hartl Karl • AUS
PRINZESSCHEN • 1919 • Halm Alfred • FRG
PRINZESSIN AUF URLAUB see **DIEB IM SCHLAFCOUPE, DER** • 1929
PRINZESSIN DAGMAR see **MADCHENPENSIONAT** • 1936
PRINZESSIN ELSE • *Kampers Fritz* • FRG
PRINZESSIN KEHRT HEIM, DIE see **BALLADE** • 1938
PRINZESSIN OLALA • 1928 • Land Robert • FRG • ART OF LOVE, THE
PRINZESSIN SISSY • 1938 • Thiery Fritz • FRG
PRINZESSIN SUWARIN, DIE • 1923 • Guter Johannes • FRG
PRINZESSIN TRULALA • 1926 • Schonfelder Erich • FRG
PRINZESSIN TURANDOT • 1934 • Lamprecht Gerhard • FRG
PRINZESSIN UND DER GEIGER, DIE • 1925 • Cutts Graham • FRG
PRINZESSIN VON NEUTRALIEN, DIE • 1917 • Biebrach Rudolf • FRG
PRINZESSIN VON ST. WOLFGANG, DIE • 1957 • Reinl Harald • FRG
PRIORITIES ON PARADE • 1942 • Rogell Albert S. • USA
PRIORY SCHOOL, THE • 1921 • Elvey Maurice • UKN
PRIPAD BARNABAS KOS • 1964 • Solan Peter • CZC • CASE OF BARNABAS KOS, THE ○ STORY OF BARNABAS KOS
PRIPAD DR. KOVARE • 1949 • Makovec Milos • CZC • CASE OF DR. KOVARE, THE
PRIPAD JESTE REKONCI • 1957 • Rychman Ladislav • CZC • CASE IS NOT CLOSED, THE
PRIPAD LUPINEK • 1960 • Vorlicek Vaclav • CZC • LUPINEK CASE, THE
PRIPAD PRO SELWYN • 1968 • Weiss Jiri • MTV • CZC • JUSTICE FOR SELWYN
PRIPAD PRO ZACINAJICIHO KATA • 1969 • Juracek Pavel • CZC • CASE FOR THE NEW HANGMAN, A ○ CASE FOR A YOUNG HANGMAN, A
PRIRODNA GRANICA • 1971 • Ilic Mihailo • YGS • NATURAL BOUNDARY, THE
PRIS AU COLLET • 1974 • Garceau Raymond • SHT • CND
PRISCILLA • 1912 • *Majestic* • USA
PRISCILLA AND THE PEQUOT • 1911 • *Shannon Irene* • USA
PRISCILLA AND THE UMBRELLA • 1911 • Lehrman Henry, Sennett Mack • USA
PRISCILLA THE RAKE see **SHE WAS ONLY A VILLAGE MAIDEN** • 1933
PRISCILLA'S APRIL FOOL JOKE • 1911 • Lehrman Henry, Sennett Mack (Spv) • USA
PRISCILLA'S CAPTURE • 1912 • Lehrman Henry, Sennett Mack (Spv) • USA
PRISCILLA'S ENGAGEMENT KISS • 1911 • Powell Frank • USA
PRISCILLAS FAHRT INS GLUCK • 1928 • Asquith Anthony • FRG
PRISCILLA'S PRISONER • 1916 • Madison Cleo • SHT • USA
PRISE DE POUVOIR PAR DE LOUIS XIV, LA • 1966 • Rossellini Roberto • MTV • FRN • PRESA DEL POTERE DA PARTE DI LUIGI XIV, LA ○ RISE OF LOUIS XIV, THE (USA) ○ LOUIS XIV SEIZES POWER ○ RISE TO POWER OF LOUIS XIV, THE
PRISE DE POUVOIR PAR PHILIPPE PETAIN, LA • 1979 • Cherasse Jean-A. • DOC • FRN
PRISE DE TOURNAVOS, LA • 1897 • Melies Georges • FRN • SURRENDER OF TOURNAVOS, THE
PRISHOL SOLDAT S FRONTA • 1972 • Gubenko Nikolai • USS • THERE CAME A SOLDIER FROM THE FRONT ○ BACK FROM THE FRONT ○ SOLDIER CAME HOME FROM THE FRONT, A ○ SOLDIER FROM THE WAR RETURNING
PRISHVIN'S PAPER EYES see **BUMAZHNIYE GLAZA PRISHVINA** • 1989
PRISION DE MUJERES • 1976 • Cardona Rene Jr. • MXC
PRISION DE SUENOS • 1948 • Urruchua Victor • MXC
PRISIONERA DEL PASADA • 1954 • Davison Tito • MXC
PRISIONERA DEL RECUERDO • 1952 • Ugarte Eduardo • MXC
PRISIONERAS DE LA TIERRA • 1939 • Soffici Mario • ARG • PRISONERS OF THE EARTH ○ PRISONERS OF EARTH
PRISIONERO TRECE, EL • 1933 • de Fuentes Fernando • MXC • PRISONER NUMBER THIRTEEN
PRISIONEROS DE UNA NOCHE • 1960 • Kohon David Jose • ARG • PRISONERS OF ONE NIGHT ○ PRISONERS OF A NIGHT
PRISIONEROS EN LA CIUDAD • 1968 • de Jaen Antonio • SPN
PRISNE TAJNE PREMIERY • 1967 • Fric Martin • CZC • STRICTLY SECRET PREMIERES ○ RECIPE FOR A CRIME ○ STRICTLY SECRET PREVIEWS
PRISOES DE VIDRO • 1958 • Fraga Augusto • SHT • PRT
PRISON • 1962 • Lapoujade Robert • ANS • FRN
PRISON • 1965 • Warhol Andy • USA
PRISON • 1975 • Geertsen George • CND
PRISON • 1988 • Harlin Renny • USA
PRISON see **KATORGA** • 1928
PRISON see **FANGELSE** • 1949
PRISON, THE see **CONDE, UN** • 1970
PRISON BREAK • 1938 • Lubin Arthur • USA
PRISON BREAKER • 1936 • Brunel Adrian • UKN
PRISON BRIDE see **ROUGOKU NO HANAYOME** • 1939
PRISON CAMP see **FUGITIVE FROM A PRISON CAMP** • 1940
PRISON EN FOLIE, LA • 1930 • Wulschleger Henry • FRN • SOLEIL A L'OMBRE, LE
PRISON FARM • 1938 • King Louis • USA
PRISON FOR CHILDREN • 1987 • Peerce Larry • TVM • USA
PRISON FOR WOMEN see **P4W PRISON FOR WOMEN** • 1981
PRISON GIRLS • 1973 • De Burton Thomas
PRISON MUTINY see **YOU CAN'T BEAT THE LAW** • 1943
PRISON NURSE • 1938 • Cruze James • USA
PRISON OF SEX see **SEIGOKU** • 1968
PRISON ON FIRE see **LONGHU FENGYUN** • 1987
PRISON PANIC, THE • 1930 • Lantz Walter, Nolan William • ANS • USA
PRISON REFORM • 1910 • Coleby A. E., Aylott Dave • UKN
PRISON SANS BARREAUX • 1937 • Moguy Leonide • FRN
PRISON SHADOWS • 1936 • Hill Robert F. • USA
PRISON SHIP • 1945 • Dreifuss Arthur • USA
PRISON SHIP see **PRISON SHIP: THE ADVENTURES OF TARA** • 1987
PRISON SHIP, THE • 1912 • *Nilsson Anna Q.* • USA
PRISON SHIP STAR SLAMMER see **PRISON SHIP: THE ADVENTURES OF TARA** • 1987
PRISON SHIP: THE ADVENTURES OF TARA • 1987 • Ray Fred Olən • USA • PRISON SHIP STAR SLAMMER ○ ADVENTURES OF TARA PART 1, THE ○ STAR SLAMMER ○ PRISON SHIP ○ STAR SLAMMER: THE ESCAPE
PRISON STAIN, THE • 1914 • *Sais Marin* • USA
PRISON SUR LE GOUFFRE, LA • 1912 • Feuillade Louis • FRN
PRISON SURGEON see **THOSE HIGH GREY WALLS** • 1939
PRISON TAINT, THE see **AERELOSE, DEN** • 1916
PRISON TRAIN • 1938 • Wiles Gordon • USA • PEOPLE'S ENEMY
PRISON WARDEN • 1949 • Friedman Seymour • USA
PRISON WITHOUT BARS • 1938 • Hurst Brian Desmond • UKN
PRISON WITHOUT BARS, THE • 1917 • Hopper E. Mason • USA
PRISONER 984 see **NINE EIGHTY FOUR -PRISONER OF THE FUTURE** • 1979
PRISONER, THE • 1923 • Conway Jack • USA
PRISONER, THE • 1928 • Froelich Roman • USA
PRISONER, THE • 1955 • Glenville Peter • UKN
PRISONER, THE • 1984 • Booth Tim • ANS • IRL
PRISONER, THE see **KASSO DEN** • 1978
PRISONER AT KARLSTEN FORT, THE see **FANGEN PA KARLSTENS FASTNING** • 1916
PRISONER AT THE BAR, THE • 1915 • *Karr Darwin* • USA
PRISONER FOR LIFE, A • 1919 • Dillon John Francis • SHT • USA
PRISONER IN THE HAREM, THE • 1913 • *Blache Features* • USA
PRISONER IN THE MIDDLE • 1975 • O'Connor John • USA, ISR • WARHEAD ○ LAST CONFLICT, THE
PRISONER NO.1 see **FANGE NR.1** • 1935
PRISONER NO.113 see **FANGE NR.113** • 1917
PRISONER NUMBER THIRTEEN see **PRISIONERO TRECE, EL** • 1933
PRISONER OF BEZDEZ, THE see **VEZEN NO BEZDEZE** • 1932
PRISONER OF CABANAS, A • 1913 • Campbell Colin • USA
PRISONER OF CORBAL (USA) see **MARRIAGE OF CORBAL, THE** • 1936
PRISONER OF JAPAN • 1942 • Ulmer Edgar G., Ripley Arthur • USA • LAST COMMAND, THE (UKN)
PRISONER OF MARS • 1942 • Anger Kenneth • SHT • USA
PRISONER OF MEXICO, A • 1911 • *Kalem* • USA
PRISONER OF PASSION see **ORCA, LA** • 1976
PRISONER OF RIO • 1988 • Majewski Lech • UKN
PRISONER OF ST. PETERSBURG, THE • 1989 • Pringle Ian • FRG, ASL
PRISONER OF SECOND AVENUE, THE • 1975 • Frank Melvin • USA
PRISONER OF SHARK ISLAND, THE • 1936 • Ford John • USA
PRISONER OF THE BAR, THE • 1915 • Totten Joseph Byron • USA
PRISONER OF THE CANNIBAL GOD (UKN) see **MONTAGNA DEL DIO CANNIBALE, LA** • 1976
PRISONER OF THE CAUCASUS see **KAKAZSKAYA PLENNITZA** • 1967
PRISONER OF THE HAREM, A • 1912 • Olcott Sidney • USA
PRISONER OF THE IRON MASK see **VENGEANCE DU MASQUE DE FER** • 1962
PRISONER OF THE JUNGLE (USA) see **PRISONNIERS DE LA BROUSSE** • 1959
PRISONER OF THE MOHICANS • 1911 • Golden Joseph A. • USA
PRISONER OF THE MOUNTAINS, THE • 1913 • *Joy Ernest* • USA
PRISONER OF THE PINES • 1918 • Warde Ernest C. • USA
PRISONER OF THE VOLGA (USA) see **BATTELLIERI DEL VOLGA, I** • 1959
PRISONER OF WAR • 1954 • Marton Andrew • USA
PRISONER OF WAR see **TARGET UNKNOWN** • 1951
PRISONER OF WAR, THE • 1912 • Dawley J. Searle • USA
PRISONER OF WAR, THE • 1918 • *Hamilton Shorty* • USA
PRISONER OF ZENDA, THE • 1913 • Porter Edwin S., Ford Hugh • USA
PRISONER OF ZENDA, THE • 1915 • Tucker George Loane • UKN
PRISONER OF ZENDA, THE • 1922 • Ingram Rex • USA
PRISONER OF ZENDA, THE • 1937 • Cromwell John, Van Dyke W. S. (U/c) • USA
PRISONER OF ZENDA, THE • 1952 • Thorpe Richard • USA
PRISONER OF ZENDA, THE • 1979 • Quine Richard • USA

PRISONER WITHOUT A NAME, CELL WITHOUT A NUMBER • 1983 • Greene David • TVM • USA • JACOBO TIMERMAN: PRISONER WITHOUT A NAME, CELL WITHOUT A NUMBER
PRISONERS • 1929 • Seiter William A. • USA
PRISONERS • 1973 • Bushnell William H. Jr. • USA • PHYSICAL ASSAULT
PRISONERS • 1983 • Werner Peter • ASL
PRISONERS • 1984 • Werner Peter • USA
PRISONERS IN PETTICOATS • 1950 • *Republic* • USA
PRISONERS OF A NIGHT see **PRISIONEROS DE UNA NOCHE** • 1960
PRISONERS OF ALTONA, THE see **SEQUESTRATI DI ALTONA, I** • 1962
PRISONERS OF CONSCIENCE • 1916 • Mayo Melvin • SHT • USA
PRISONERS OF DEBT –INSIDE THE GLOBAL BANKING CRISIS • 1982 • Raymont Peter • DOC • CND
PRISONERS OF EARTH see **PRISIONERAS DE LA TIERRA** • 1939
PRISONERS OF FREEDOM see **ASIREI HACHOFESH** • 1968
PRISONERS OF HATE see **EHMALOTI TOU MISOUS** • 1971
PRISONERS OF LOVE • 1921 • Rosson Arthur • USA • REINCARNATION
PRISONERS OF MAO see **PRISONNIERS DE MAO** • 1977
PRISONERS OF ONE NIGHT see **PRISIONEROS DE UNA NOCHE** • 1960
PRISONERS OF THE CASBAH • 1953 • Bare Richard L. • USA
PRISONERS OF THE EARTH see **PRISIONERAS DE LA TIERRA** • 1939
PRISONERS OF THE LOST UNIVERSE • 1983 • Marcel Terry • TVM • USA, UKN
PRISONERS OF THE SEA • 1929 • Werner M.
PRISONERS OF THE SEA • 1985 • Pevney Joseph • USA
PRISONERS OF THE STORM • 1926 • Reynolds Lynn • USA
PRISONERS OF THE TOWER • 1946 • Williamson Cecil H. • UKN
PRISONERS OF WAR • 1913 • Melford George • USA
PRISONER'S SONG, THE • 1930 • Fleischer Dave • ANS • USA
PRISONER'S SONG, THE see **PESNYA KATORZHANINA** • 1911
PRISONER'S STORY, THE • 1912 • *Melies* • USA
PRISONNIER, LE see **KASSO DEN** • 1978
PRISONNIER DE MON COEUR • 1931 • Tarride Jean • FRN
PRISONNIER DU CIEL • 1938 • Sti Rene • FRN
PRISONNIER RECALCITRANT, LE • 1900 • Melies Georges • FRN • TRICKY PRISONER, THE (USA)
PRISONNIERE, LA • Lenoir Claudine • SHT • FRN • CAPTIVE, THE
PRISONNIERE, LA • 1968 • Clouzot Henri-Georges • FRN, ITL • PRIGIONIERA, LA (ITL) ○ WOMAN IN CHAINS (USA) ○ FEMALE PRISONER, THE
PRISONNIERE DU DESIR, LA see **FEMME AUX ABOIS, UNE** • 1967
PRISONNIERS, LES see **CAPTURE, THE** • 1955
PRISONNIERS DE LA BROUSSE • 1959 • Rozier Willy • FRN • PRISONER OF THE JUNGLE (USA)
PRISONNIERS DE MAO • 1977 • Belmont Vera • FRN • PRISONERS OF MAO
PRISONS A L'AMERICAINE see **VIOLENCE SUR HOUSTON** • 1969
PRISONS AUSSI, LES • 1971 • Chatelain Helene, Lefort Rene • DOC • FRN
PRISON'S BRIDE, THE see **HAPISHANE GELINI** • 1968
PRISONS DE FEMMES • 1938 • Richebe Roger • FRN
PRISONS DE FEMMES • 1958 • Cloche Maurice • FRN
PRISONS DE L'ESPRIT, LES see **CAPTIVE MINDS: HYPNOSIS AND BEYOND** • 1984
PRISTAV V SRDCI EUROPY • 1939-40 • *Hammid Alexander* • CZC • HARBOR IN THE HEART OF EUROPE
PRISTE BUDEME CHYTREJSI, STAROUSKU • 1983 • Schulhoff Petr • CZC • WE SHALL BE CLEVERER NEXT TIME, OLD CHAP
PRITHVIRAJ SANYUKTA • 1946 • Naqvi Najam • IND
PRITVI PUTRA • 1938 • Desai Jayant • IND
PRIVALOV'S MILLIONS • 1973 • Lapshin Ya. • USS
PRIVARZANIAT BALON • 1967 • Zheljazkova Binka • BUL • ATTACHED BALLOON, THE ○ CAPTIVE BALLOON, THE
PRIVAT KLINIK PROFESSOR LUND see **ARZT OHNE GEWISSEN** • 1959
PRIVATE 69, THE SERGEANT AND I see **69:AN, SERGEANTEN OCH JAG** • 1952
PRIVATE 91 KARLSSON IS DEMOBBED OR SO HE THINKS see **91:AN KARLSSON MUCKAR (TROR HAN)** • 1960
PRIVATE AFFAIRS • 1925 • Hoffman Renaud • USA
PRIVATE AFFAIRS • 1940 • Rogell Albert S. • USA • ONE OF THE BOSTON BULLERTONS
PRIVATE AFFAIRS OF BEL AMI, THE • 1947 • Lewin Albert • USA
PRIVATE AFFAIRS (UKN) see **PUBLIC STENOGRAPHER** • 1933
PRIVATE AFTERNOONS OF PAMELA MANN, THE • 1974 • Metzger Radley H. • USA
PRIVATE AND THE C.O., THE see **ZOKU HEITAI YAKUZA** • 1965
PRIVATE ANGELO • 1949 • Ustinov Peter, Anderson Michael • UKN
PRIVATE ARRANGEMENT • 1970 • Ransom Wes • USA
PRIVATE BANKER, THE • 1916 • Santschi Thomas • SHT • USA
PRIVATE BATTLE, A • 1980 • Lewis Robert • TVM • USA
PRIVATE BENJAMIN • 1980 • Zieff Howard • USA
PRIVATE BOM see **SOLDAT BOM** • 1948
PRIVATE BOX 23 • 1913 • *Eclair* • USA
PRIVATE BROWN • 1909 • *Centaur* • USA
PRIVATE BUCKAROO • 1942 • Cline Eddie • USA
PRIVATE BUNNY • 1914 • Baker George D. • USA
PRIVATE CLINIC OF PROFESSOR LUND, THE see **ARZT OHNE GEWISSEN** • 1959
PRIVATE CLUB (UKN) see **CLUB PRIVE** • 1973
PRIVATE CODE see **CODICE PRIVATO** • 1988
PRIVATE COLLECTION • 1972 • Salvat Keith • ASL
PRIVATE COLLECTIONS (USA) see **COLLECTIONS PRIVEES** • 1975
PRIVATE CONTENTMENT • 1982 • Matalon Vivian • TVM • USA
PRIVATE CONVERSATIONS: ON THE SET OF DEATH OF A SALESMAN • 1986 • Blackwood Christian • USA
PRIVATE DEBTS • 1988 • Cooperstein • SHT • USA
PRIVATE DENNIS HOGAN • 1914 • Lambart Harry • USA
PRIVATE DETECTIVE • 1939 • Smith Noel • USA
PRIVATE DETECTIVE • 1986 • Ottoni Filippo • USA, ITL • DETECTIVE SCHOOL DROPOUTS ○ DUMB DICKS
PRIVATE DETECTIVE 62 • 1933 • Curtiz Michael • USA • MAN KILLER
PRIVATE DINNER, A see **EN CABINET PARTICULIER** • 1897
PRIVATE DUTY NURSES • 1971 • Armitage George • USA
PRIVATE ENTERPRISE, A • 1974 • Smith Peter K. • UKN
PRIVATE ENTRANCE see **EGEN INGANG** • 1956
PRIVATE EYE • 1987 • Tinker Mark • USA
PRIVATE EYE see **DAIN CURSE, THE** • 1978
PRIVATE EYE: BLUE HOTEL see **BLUE HOTEL** • 1987
PRIVATE EYE POOCH • 1955 • Smith Paul J. • ANS • USA
PRIVATE–EYE POPEYE • 1954 • Kneitel Seymour • ANS • USA
PRIVATE EYES • 1953 • Bernds Edward • USA • BOWERY BLOODHOUNDS
PRIVATE EYES, THE • 1980 • Elliott Lang • USA
PRIVATE EYES, THE see **PAN–CHIN PA–LIANG** • 1977
PRIVATE FILES OF J. EDGAR HOOVER, THE • 1978 • Cohen Larry • USA • J. EDGAR HOOVER
PRIVATE FUNCTION, A • 1985 • Mowbray Malcolm • UKN
PRIVATE GALE see **SOUKROMA VICHRICE** • 1967
PRIVATE HECTOR, GENTLEMAN • 1912 • Aylott Dave • UKN
PRIVATE HELL 36 • 1954 • Siegel Don • USA
PRIVATE HISTORY OF A CAMPAIGN THAT FAILED, THE • 1981 • Hunt Peter • TVM • USA
PRIVATE HURRICANE see **SOUKROMA VICHRICE** • 1967
PRIVATE INFORMATION • 1952 • McDonnell Fergus • UKN
PRIVATE INVESTIGATION see **PRIVATE INVESTIGATIONS** • 1987
PRIVATE INVESTIGATION, A see **MISSING PIECES** • 1983
PRIVATE INVESTIGATIONS • 1987 • Dick Nigel • USA • P.I.– PRIVATE INVESTIGATIONS ○ PRIVATE INVESTIGATION
PRIVATE IVAN • Karevsky B.
PRIVATE IVAN BROVKIN see **SOLDAT IVAN BROVKIN** • 1955
PRIVATE IZZY MURPHY • 1926 • Bacon Lloyd • USA
PRIVATE JONES • 1933 • Mack Russell • USA
PRIVATE KEY see **KLYUCH BYEZ PRAVA PEREDACHI** • 1977
PRIVATE LESSON, THE see **LECON PARTICULIERE, LA** • 1968
PRIVATE LESSON, THE see **LEZIONI PRIVATE** • 1975
PRIVATE LESSONS • 1981 • Myerson Alan • USA
PRIVATE LIFE see **CHASTNAYA ZHIZN** • 1983
PRIVATE LIFE, A • 1989 • Gerard Francis • SAF
PRIVATE LIFE OF A CAT, THE • 1945 • Deren Maya, Hammid Alexander • USA
PRIVATE LIFE OF ADAM AND EVE, THE • 1960 • Zugsmith Albert, Rooney Mickey • USA
PRIVATE LIFE OF AN ACTOR, THE (USA) see **COMEDIEN, LE** • 1947
PRIVATE LIFE OF DR. PAUL JOSEPH GOEBBELS, THE see **ENEMY OF WOMEN** • 1944
PRIVATE LIFE OF DON JUAN, THE • 1934 • Korda Alexander • UKN
PRIVATE LIFE OF HELEN OF TROY, THE • 1927 • Korda Alexander • USA • HELEN OF TROY
PRIVATE LIFE OF HENRY VIII, THE • 1933 • Korda Alexander • UKN
PRIVATE LIFE OF LOUIS XIV, THE see **LISELOTTE VON DER PFALZ** • 1935
PRIVATE LIFE OF MUSSOLINI, THE • 1938 • Park John
PRIVATE LIFE OF SHERLOCK HOLMES, THE • 1970 • Wilder Billy • UKN, USA
PRIVATE LIFE OF THE GANNETS, THE • 1934 • Huxley Julian • UKN
PRIVATE LIFE OF THE GODS see **NIGHT LIFE OF THE GODS** • 1935
PRIVATE LIVES • 1931 • Franklin Sidney A. • USA
PRIVATE LIVES OF ELIZABETH AND ESSEX, THE • 1939 • Curtiz Michael • USA • ELIZABETH THE QUEEN ○ ELIZABETH AND ESSEX
PRIVATE MANOEUVRES • 1983 • Shissel Ziv • ISR
PRIVATE MISS JONES see **THOUSANDS CHEER** • 1943
PRIVATE MOMENT, A • 1966 • Malanga Gerard • USA
PRIVATE NAVY OF SGT. O'FARRELL, THE • 1968 • Tashlin Frank • USA
PRIVATE NUMBER • 1936 • Del Ruth Roy • USA • SECRET INTERLUDE (UKN)
PRIVATE NURSE • 1941 • Burton David • USA
PRIVATE NURSE • 1978 • Kikoine Gerard • FRN
PRIVATE NURSE (UKN) see **NUMBERED WOMAN** • 1938
PRIVATE OFFICER, THE • 1914 • *Bushman Francis X.* • USA
PRIVATE OMPONG AND THE SEXY DOZEN • 1968 • Gallardo Cesar Chat • PHL
PRIVATE PARTS • 1972 • Bartel Paul • USA
PRIVATE PARTY see **ET DOGN MED ILSE** • 1971
PRIVATE PARTY, THE • 1987 • Hedayat Hassan • IRN
PRIVATE PEAT • 1918 • Jose Edward • USA
PRIVATE PETTIGREW'S GIRL see **PETTIGREW'S GIRL** • 1919
PRIVATE PLEASURES • 1976 • Gerber Paul • SWD
PRIVATE PLEASURES • Englund Alex C. • USA
PRIVATE PLUTO • 1943 • Geronimi Clyde • ANS • USA
PRIVATE POPSICLE see **PRIVATE POPSICLE: LEMON POPSICLE IV** • 1982
PRIVATE POPSICLE: LEMON POPSICLE IV • 1982 • Davidson Boaz • ISR, FRG • LEMON POPSICLE 4: SAPICHES ○ PRIVATE POPSICLE ○ SAPICHES
PRIVATE POTTER • 1962 • Wrede Caspar • UKN
PRIVATE PRACTICES • 1986 • Dick Kirby • DOC • USA
PRIVATE PROPERTY • 1960 • Stevens Leslie • USA
PRIVATE PROPERTY see **YKSITYISALUE** • 1962
PRIVATE PROPERTY see **YOUNG LADY CHATTERLEY II** • 1984
PRIVATE RELATIONS • 1968 • Crane Larry • USA
PRIVATE RESORT • 1985 • Bowers George • USA
PRIVATE RIGHT, THE • 1967 • Papas Michael • GRC, UKN
PRIVATE ROAD • 1971 • Platt-Mills Barney • UKN
PRIVATE ROAD • 1987 • Nussbaum Raphael • USA • PRIVATE ROAD: NO TRESPASSING ○ NO TRESPASSING
PRIVATE ROAD: NO TRESPASSING see **PRIVATE ROAD** • 1987
PRIVATE SCANDAL • 1931 • Hutchison Charles • USA
PRIVATE SCANDAL • 1934 • Murphy Ralph • USA
PRIVATE SCANDAL, A • 1921 • Franklin Chester M. • USA
PRIVATE SCHOOL • 1983 • Black Noel • USA • PRIVATE SCHOOL FOR GIRLS
PRIVATE SCHOOL FOR GIRLS see **PRIVATE SCHOOL** • 1983
PRIVATE SCREENING see **PROJECTION PRIVEE** • 1973
PRIVATE SECRETARY see **BEHIND OFFICE DOORS** • 1931
PRIVATE SECRETARY see **PRIVATSEKRETARIN, DIE** • 1953
PRIVATE SECRETARY, THE • 1914 • *Grover Leonard* • USA
PRIVATE SECRETARY, THE • 1935 • Edwards Henry • UKN
PRIVATE SESSIONS • 1985 • Pressman Michael • TVM • USA
PRIVATE SHOW • 1985 • Rono Chito • PHL
PRIVATE SMITH • 1913 • *Metcalfe Earl* • USA
PRIVATE SMITH OF THE U.S.A. • 1942 • Vorkapich Slavko • SHT • USA
PRIVATE SNUFFY SMITH see **SNUFFY SMITH, THE YARD BIRD** • 1942
PRIVATE SUPPER AT HELLAR'S, A • 1902 • *Biograph* • USA
PRIVATE TUTOR • 1988 • Olsen William • USA • RETURN TO EDEN ○ BEFORE GOD ○ AFTER SCHOOL ○ QUEST FOR EDEN
PRIVATE VICES AND PUBLIC VIRTUES (UKN) see **VIZI PRIVATI –PUBBLICHE VIRTU** • 1976
PRIVATE VICES, PUBLIC VIRTUES (USA) see **VIZI PRIVATI – PUBBLICHE VIRTU** • 1976
PRIVATE WAR • 1989 • De Palma Frank • USA
PRIVATE WAR OF HARRY FRIGG, THE see **SECRET WAR OF HARRY FRIGG, THE** • 1968
PRIVATE WAR OF MAJOR BENSON, THE • 1955 • Hopper Jerry • USA
PRIVATE WINDSTORM see **SOUKROMA VICHRICE** • 1967
PRIVATE WORE SKIRTS, THE (UKN) see **NEVER WAVE AT A WAC** • 1952
PRIVATE WORLD, A • 1981 • Saretzky Eric • CND
PRIVATE WORLDS • 1935 • La Cava Gregory • USA
PRIVATES 65, 66 AND I see **65, 66 OCH JAG** • 1936
PRIVATE'S AFFAIR, THE • 1959 • Walsh Raoul • USA
PRIVATE'S JOB, THE (USA) see **UNTERNEHMEN MICHAEL** • 1937
PRIVATES ON PARADE • 1983 • Blakemore Michael • UKN
PRIVATE'S PROGRESS • 1956 • Boulting John • UKN
PRIVATE'S STORY, THE see **NOHOTEI MONOGATARI** • 1955
PRIVATION, LA see **HIRMAN, AL–** • 1953
PRIVATSEKRETARIN, DIE • 1931 • Thiele Wilhelm • FRG
PRIVATSEKRETARIN, DIE • 1953 • Martin Paul • FRG • PRIVATE SECRETARY
PRIVATSEKRETARIN HEIRAT, DIE • 1936 • Koster Henry • FRG
PRIVIDENIYA • 1915 • Gardin Vladimir • USS
PRIVIDENIYE, KOTOROYE NE VOZVRASHCHAYETSA • 1930 • Room Abram • USS • GHOST THAT WILL NOT RETURN, THE ○ GHOST THAT NEVER RETURNS, THE
PRIVILEGE • 1967 • Watkins Peter • UKN
PRIVILEGE, THE • 1983 • Knox Alan • UKN
PRIVILEGED • 1982 • Hoffman Michael • UKN
PRIX DE BEAUTE • 1930 • Genina Augusto • FRN • MISS EUROPE
PRIX DE L'EAU, LE • 1966 • Lavoie Richard • DCS • CND
PRIX DE SANG, LE see **HACELDAMA** • 1919
PRIX DU DANGER, LE • 1983 • Boisset Yves • FRN, YGS • PRIZE OF PERIL, THE
PRIX ET PROFITS • 1932 • Allegret Yves • SHT • FRN
PRIYA BANDHABI • 1943 • *Sircar B. N. (P)* • IND
PRIYANGA • 1970 • Jayatilaka Amarnath • SLN
PRIZAK BRODIT PO YEVROPE • 1923 • Gardin Vladimir • USS • SPECTER HAUNTS EUROPE, A
PRIZE, THE • 1959 • Burstall Tim • SHT • ASL
PRIZE, THE • 1963 • Robson Mark • USA
PRIZE, THE see **PREMIA** • 1975
PRIZE, THE see **PUROSKAR** • 1984
PRIZE, THE (USA) see **ROSIER DE MADAME HUSSON, LE** • 1950
PRIZE BABY, THE • 1915 • Hevener Jerold T. • USA
PRIZE EMPLOYER, THE • 1914 • *Ab* • USA
PRIZE ESSAY, THE • 1912 • *Hawley Ormi* • USA
PRIZE FIGHT OR GLOVE CONTEST BETWEEN JOHN BULL AND PRESIDENT KRUGER • 1900 • *Barnes John Sloane* • UKN
PRIZE FIGHTER, THE • 1979 • Preece Michael • USA • PRIZEFIGHTER, THE
PRIZE FIGHTER, THE see **BOKSER** • 1967
PRIZE GUEST, THE • 1939 • Davis Mannie • ANS • USA
PRIZE MAID • Yates Hal • SHT • USA
PRIZE OF ARMS, A • 1962 • Owen Cliff • UKN
PRIZE OF GOLD, A • 1955 • Robson Mark • UKN
PRIZE OF PERIL, THE see **PRIX DU DANGER, LE** • 1983
PRIZE PACKAGE, A • 1912 • *Lubin* • USA
PRIZE PEST, THE • 1951 • McKimson Robert • ANS • USA
PRIZE STORY, THE • 1915 • Myers Harry • USA
PRIZE TRIP, THE see **JUTALOMUTAZAS** • 1975
PRIZE WINNERS, THE • 1916 • *Hardy Babe* • SHT • USA
PRIZED AS A MATE! see **SPOILED ROTTEN** • 1968
PRIZEFIGHTER, THE see **PRIZE FIGHTER, THE** • 1979
PRIZEFIGHTER AND THE LADY, THE • 1933 • Van Dyke W. S., Hawks Howard (U/c) • USA • EVERY WOMAN'S MAN (UKN)
PRIZES AND DECORATIONS see **NAGRODY I ODZNACZENIA** • 1974
PRIZIVANJE PROLJECA • 1979 • Stiglic France • YGS • CELEBRATION IN THE SPRINGTIME ○ PRAZNOVANJE POMLADI ○ RETURN OF SPRING, THE ○ CALL OF SPRING, THE
PRIZZI'S HONOR • 1985 • Huston John • USA
PRKOSNA DELTA • 1981 • Ljubic Vesna • YGS • DEFIANT DELTA, THE
PRLJAVI FILM • 1989 • Sabo Dusan • YGS • DIRTY BUSINESS, THE
PRO see **NUMBER ONE** • 1969
PRO CHUDESA CHELOVYECHSKIYE • 1968 • Monakhov Vladimir • USS • ABOUT HUMAN MIRACLES ○ MIRACLES (UKN)
PRO FOOTBALL • 1934 • McCarey Ray • SHT • USA
PRO KAMARADA • 1941 • Cikan Miroslav • CZC • FOR MY FELLOW

PRO LIOUBOV • 1932 • Medvedkin Alexander • USS • ABOUT LOVE

PRO MEMORIA • 1972 • Sienski Maciej • PLN

PRO NOBIS see **ORA PRO NOBIS: OR, THE POOR ORPHAN'S LAST PRAYER** • 1901

PRO PATRIA • 1914 • Blom August • DNM

PRO PATRIA • 1971 • Sara Sandor • SHT • HNG

PRO-PO KE TA BOUZOUKIA, TO • 1968 • Jackson Stelios, Ikonomou Nikos • GRC • FOOTBALL POOLS AND THE BOUZOUKI, THE

PRO SHOP, THE • 1970 • *Distripix Inc* • USA

PROA AL ENEMIGO • 1971 • Rosado Alfredo Valdes • DOC • CUB

PROBA DE MICROFON • 1980 • Daneliuc Mircea • RMN • MICROPHONE TESTING ○ MICROPHONE TEST

PROBA OGNIA I WODY • 1978 • Olszewski Wlodzimierz • PLN • TRIAL BY FIRE AND WATER

PROBABILITA ZERO • 1969 • Lucidi Maurizio, Argento Dario • ITL • PROBABILITY ZERO

PROBABILITY ZERO see **PROBABILITA ZERO** • 1969

PROBALL CHEERLEADERS • 1979 • Matthews Jack • USA

PROBATION • 1915 • *Majestic* • USA

PROBATION • 1932 • Thorpe Richard • USA • SECOND CHANCE (UKN)

PROBATION • 1987 • Kahane Peter • GDR

PROBATION WIFE, THE • 1919 • Franklin Sidney A. • USA

PROBATIONER, THE • 1913 • Huntley Fred W. • USA

PROBAUT • 1960 • Mariassy Felix • HNG • TEST TRIP

PROBE • 1972 • Mayberry Russ • TVM • USA • SEARCH

PROBLEM, THE • Dudesek Jan • ANM • CZC

PROBLEM, THE • 1915 • Pollard Harry? • USA

PROBLEM CHILD • 1938 • Zamora Rudy • ANS • USA

PROBLEM CHILD • 1955 • Lukashevich Tatyana • USS

PROBLEM GIRLS • 1953 • Dupont E. A. • USA

PROBLEM IN REDUCTION, A • 1912 • *Gardner Helen* • USA

PROBLEM LOVE SOLVED, THE • 1913 • *Thanhouser* • USA

PROBLEM OF THE DAY, THE see **HANANE KADIET EL YOM** • 1944

PROBLEM PAPPY • 1941 • Fleischer Dave • ANS • USA

PROBLEM STUDENTS see **WEN-T'I HSUEH-SHENG** • 1979

PROBLEMAS DE PAPA, LAS • 1954 • Land Kurt • ARG

PROBLEMATISCHE NATUREN • 1916 • Oberlander Hans • FRG

PROBLEMATORIUM • 1967 • Smetana Zdenek • ANS • CZC

PROBLEMS DE LA JEUNESSE • 1964 • Rachedi Ahmed • ALG

PROBLEMS OF SLEEP • 1948 • Massy Jane • UKN

PROBLEMS ON AN IMAGINARY FARM • 1978 • Sens Al • ANS • CND

PROBUZENI • 1959 • Krejcik Jiri • CZC • AWAKENING

PROBUZHDYENIYE • 1968 • Nikolayev Igor, Roshal Marianna, Arsenov Pavel • USS • AWAKENING, THE

PROC? • 1964 • Schorm Evald • CZC • WHY?

PROC? • 1987 • Smyczek Karel • CZC • WHY?

PROC SE NESMEJES? • 1922 • Fiala Eman • CZC • WHY AREN'T YOU LAUGHING?

PROC SE USMIVAS, MONO LISO? • 1966 • Brdecka Jiri • ANS • CZC • WHY DO YOU SMILE, MONA LISA? ○ WHY IS MONA LISA SMILING? ○ MONO LISO?

PROC SEDAJI PTACI NA TELEGRAFNI DRATY • 1948 • Hofman Eduard • ANS • CZC • WHY BIRDS SIT ON TELEGRAPH POLES

PROC UNESCO? • 1958 • Trnka Jiri • ANM • CZC • WHY UNESCO?

PROCEDIMIENTO, EL • 1977 • Benito Carlos • SPN

PROCEDURE, THE see **DIADIKASIA, I** • 1975

PROCEEDINGS IN MARUSIA see **ACTAS DE MARUSIA** • 1974

PROCES AU CRIMINEL, UN • 1973 • Mankiewicz Francis • SHT • CND • PROCES CRIMINEL, UN

PROCES AU VATICAN • 1951 • Haguet Andre • FRN

PROCES CRIMINEL, UN see **PROCES AU CRIMINEL, UN** • 1973

PROCES DE JEANNE D'ARC, LE • 1961 • Bresson Robert • FRN • TRIAL OF JOAN OF ARC, THE (USA)

PROCES DE MARY DUGAN, LE • 1931 • De Sano Marcel • FRN

PROCES, LE (FRN) see **PROZESS, DER** • 1962

PROCES (PROLOGUE), LE • 1962 • Alexeieff Alexandre • FRN

PROCES SOMMAIRE • 1973 • Beaudry Michel • CND

PROCESI K PANENCE • 1961 • Jasny Vojtech • CZC • PILGRIMAGE TO THE VIRGIN

PROCESO • Darino Eduardo • URG

PROCESO A JESUS • 1973 • Saenz De Heredia Jose Luis • SPN • TRIAL OF JESUS

PROCESO A LA LEY • 1962 • Navarro Agustin • ARG • PROCESO DE CONCIENCIA

PROCESO A UNA ESTRELLA • 1966 • Salvia Rafael J. • SPN

PROCESO DE BURGOS, EL • 1980 • Uribe Imanol • DOC • SPN • TRIAL OF BURGOS, THE ○ BURGOS TRIAL, THE

PROCESO DE CONCIENCIA see **PROCESO A LA LEY** • 1962

PROCESO DE CRISTO, EL • 1965 • Bracho Julio • MXC

PROCESO DE GIBRALTAR • 1968 • Manzanos Eduardo • SPN • TRIAL OF GIBRALTAR, THE

PROCESO DE LAS BRUJAS, EL • 1970 • Franco Jesus • SPN, FRG, ITL • HEXENTOTER VON BLACKMOOR, DER (FRG) ○ WITCH KILLER OF BLACKMOOR ○ NIGHT OF THE BLOOD MONSTER (USA) ○ BLOODY JUDGE, THE (UKN) ○ JUEZ SANGRIENTO, EL ○ TRONO DI FUOCO, IL ○ FRG ○ TRIAL OF THE WITCHES, THE

PROCESO DE LAS SENORITAS VIVANCO, EL • 1959 • de la Serna Mauricio • MXC

PROCESO DE MARY DUGAN, EL • 1931 • De Sano Marcel • SPN

PROCESO DO REI, O • Grilo Joao Mario • PRT

PROCESS, THE • 1972 • Brakhage Stan • USA

PROCESS RED • 1966 • Frampton Hollis • USA

PROCESS SERVER, THE see **HE COULDN'T TAKE IT** • 1933

PROCESSES • Davis James* • ANS • USA

PROCESSION, THE • 1959 • Van Dyke Willard • DOC • USA

PROCESSION DE HAKENDOVER, LA • 1953 • Degelin Emile, de Boe Gerard • BLG

PROCESSION OF KANDY, THE see **KANDY PERAHERA** • 1971

PROCESSO, IL (ITL) see **PROZESS, DER** • 1962

PROCESSO A STALIN • 1963 • Lucisano Fulvio, May Renato • DOC • ITL

PROCESSO ALLA CITTA • 1952 • Zampa Luigi • ITL • CITY STANDS TRIAL, THE (USA) ○ TOWN ON TRIAL, A ○ CITY ON TRIAL

PROCESSO ALL'AMORE • 1956 • Liberti Enzo • ITL

PROCESSO CLEMENCEAU, IL • 1918 • Bencivenga • ITL • AFFAIRE CLEMENCEAU, L'

PROCESSO CONTRO IGNOTI • 1952 • Brignone Guido • ITL • GENOESE DRAGNET

PROCESSO DEI VELENI, IL (ITL) see **AFFAIRE DES POISONS, L'** • 1955

PROCESSO DI VERONA, IL • 1962 • Lizzani Carlo • ITL • VERONA TRIAL, THE

PROCESSO E MORTE DI SOCRATE • 1940 • D'Errico Corrado • ITL • DIALOGHI DI PLATONE, I

PROCESSO PER DIRETTISSIMA • 1974 • De Caro Lucio • ITL

PROCESUL ALB • 1965 • Mihu Iulian • RMN • WHITE TRIAL, THE

PROCIDA • 1950 • Fasano Ugo • SHT • ITL

PROCISSAO DOS BEBADOS, A • 1975 • Teles Luis Galvao • PRT

PROCLAMATION see **KIALTO** • 1964

PROCLAMATION DU DOGME DE L'ASSOMPTION • 1951 • Proulx Maurice • DCS • CND

PROCTOR INTERVENES, THE • 1926 • Barnett Charles • UKN

PROCURER, THE • 1968 • Place Graham • USA

PROCURER, THE see **HIMO** • 1965

PROCUREUR HALLERS, LE • 1930 • Wiene Robert • FRN

PRODANA NEVESTA • 1913 • Urban Max • CZC • BARTERED BRIDE, THE

PRODANA NEVESTA • 1933 • Innemann Svatopluk, Kvapil Jaroslav, Pollert • CZC • BARTERED BRIDE, THE

PRODANNYI APPETIT • 1928 • Okhlopkov Nikolai • USS • SOLD APPETITE, THE

PRODE ANSELMO E IL SUO SCUDIERO, IL • 1972 • Corbucci Bruno • ITL

PRODEZZE DI DICKY, LE see **TRAPPOLA D'AMORE** • 1940

PRODIGA, LA • 1946 • Gil Rafael • SPN

PRODIGAL, THE • 1914 • *Moore Tom* • USA

PRODIGAL, THE • 1931 • Pollard Harry • USA • SOUTHERNER, THE

PRODIGAL, THE • 1955 • Thorpe Richard • USA

PRODIGAL, THE • 1984 • Collier James F. • USA

PRODIGAL, THE • 1984 • Kroeker Allan • CND

PRODIGAL BOXER • 1980 • Au Yang Chun • HKG

PRODIGAL BOXER, THE • 1973 • Chai Yang Min • HKG

PRODIGAL BRIDEGROOM, THE • 1926 • Bacon Lloyd, Rodney Earle • SHT • USA

PRODIGAL BROTHER, THE • 1913 • *Pathe* • USA

PRODIGAL DAUGHTER, THE • 1916 • Holubar Allen • SHT • USA

PRODIGAL DAUGHTER, THE • 1930 • Buzzell Edward • SHT • USA

PRODIGAL DAUGHTER, THE see **LEAD KINDLY LIGHT** • 1916

PRODIGAL DAUGHTER, THE (USA) see **FILLE PRODIGUE, LA** • 1980

PRODIGAL DAUGHTERS • 1923 • Wood Sam • USA

PRODIGAL FATHER, THE • 1973 • Petringenaru Adrian • RMN

PRODIGAL HUSBAND, THE • 1914 • *Royal* • USA

PRODIGAL JUDGE, THE • 1922 • Jose Edward • USA

PRODIGAL KNIGHT, A (UKN) see **AFFAIRS OF ANATOL, THE** • 1921

PRODIGAL LIAR, THE • 1919 • Heffron Thomas N. • USA

PRODIGAL PAPA • 1917 • *Gail Jane* • SHT • USA

PRODIGAL PARSON, A • 1908 • *Essanay* • USA

PRODIGAL SON see **EBN AL DAAL, EL** • 1976

PRODIGAL SON, THE • 1908 • *Paul R. W.* • UKN

PRODIGAL SON, THE • 1921 • Gordon Edward R. • UKN

PRODIGAL SON, THE • 1923 • Coleby A. E. • UKN

PRODIGAL SON, THE • 1935 • Trenker Luis • USA

PRODIGAL SON, THE see **ONNA GOROSHI ABURA JIGOKU** • 1958

PRODIGAL SON, THE see **HABEN HA'OVED** • 1968

PRODIGAL SON, THE see **ANAK TUNGGAL** • 1979

PRODIGAL SON, THE see **FILHO PRODIGO, O** • 1980

PRODIGAL SON: OR, RUINED AT THE RACES, THE • 1905 • Williamson James • UKN

PRODIGAL UNCLE, THE • 1917 • De La Parelle M. • SHT • USA

PRODIGAL WIDOW, THE • 1917 • Wilson Ben • SHT • USA

PRODIGAL WIFE, THE • 1912 • *Solax* • USA

PRODIGAL WIFE, THE • 1912 • Haldane Bert? • UKN

PRODIGAL WIFE, THE • 1918 • Reicher Frank • USA

PRODIGAL'S RETURN, THE • 1913 • Wilson Frank? • UKN

PRODIGAL'S RETURN, THE • 1917 • Thayer Otis B. • SHT • USA

PRODLOUZENY CAS • 1984 • Jires Jaromil • CZC • PROLONGED TIME

PRODOSSIA • 1964 • Manoussakis Kostas • GRC • TREACHERY

PRODOTIS, O • 1967 • Maheras Ilias • GRC • TRAITOR, THE

PRODUCERS, THE • 1968 • Brooks Mel • USA

PRODUCER'S DILEMMA, THE • 1947 • Binney Josh • USA

PRODUCT, THE • 1914 • Gaillord Robert, Costello Maurice • USA

PRODUCTION 39 • 1969 • Lokkeberg Pal • NRW

PRODUCTION 337 see **NI LJUGER** • 1969

PRODUCTION SELECTIVE DU RESEAU A 70, LA • 1934 • Storck Henri • DOC • BLG

PRODUCTIVITY IS PEOPLE • 1977 • Robertson Michael • SHT • ASL

PRODUCTIVITY PRIMER • 1964 • Godfrey Bob • ANS • UKN

PRODUITS DE SANTE • 1957 • Lavoie Hermenegilde, Lavoie Richard • DOC • CND

PRODUKSJON NR.4 • 1982 • Tuhus Oddvar Bull • NRW

PROEFKONIJNEN, DE • 1980 • Henderickx Guido • BLG • GUINEA-PIGS, THE

PROEM • 1948 • Tregillus Leonard, Luce Ralph W. Jr. • ANS • USA

PROESTEN I VEJLBY • 1972 • Orsted Claus • DNM • WORKS OF THE DEVIL, THE

PROEZAS DE SATANAS NA VILA DE LEVA-E-TRAZ • 1968 • Soares Paulo Gil • BRZ • SATAN'S FEATS IN THE VILLAGE OF LEVA-E-TRAZ

PROF, LA • Sanders Bob W. • FRN

PROF. BEAN'S REMOVAL • 1913 • Lehrman Henry, Sennett Mack • USA

PROF. DR. GUIDO TERSILLI, PRIMARIO DELLA CLINICA VILLA CELESTE CONVENZIONATA CON LA MUTUE • 1969 • Salce Luciano • ITL

PROF' INGENU, LE see **PROFESSEUR CUPIDON** • 1933

PROF. PUDDENHEAD'S PATENTS -THE AEROCAB AND VACUUM PROVIDER • 1909 • Booth W. R. • UKN

PROF. SCHLEMIEL'S HAT • 1910 • *Gaumont* • FRN

PROFANACION • 1933 • Urueta Chano • MXC

PROFANADORES DE TUMBAS • 1966 • Diaz Morales Jose • MXC • TRAFICANTES DE LA MUERTE, LOS ○ PROFANERS OF TOMBS ○ DEALERS IN DEATH, THE

PROFANAZIONE, LA • 1974 • Longo Tiziano • ITL

PROFANE COMEDY, THE see **SET THIS TOWN ON FIRE** • 1969

PROFANERS OF TOMBS see **PROFANADORES DE TUMBAS** • 1966

PROFE, EL • 1970 • Delgado Miguel M. • MXC

PROFECIA DEL LAGO, LA • 1923 • Velasco Maidana Jose Maria • BLV • PROPHECY OF LAKE TITICACA, THE

PROFESOR CERO, EL • 1942 • Amadori Luis Cesar • ARG

PROFESOR EN DIE PRIKKELPOP see **PROFESSOR AND THE BEAUTY QUEEN, THE** • 1967

PROFESOR EROTICO, EL • 1976 • Cohen Rafael • ARG • EROTIC PROFESSOR, THE

PROFESOR FILUTEK • Nehrebecki Wladyslaw, Wajzer Waclaw • ASS • PLN • PROFESSOR FILUTEK

PROFESOR FILUTEK W PARKU • 1955 • Nehrebecki Wladyslaw • ANS • PLN • PROFESSOR FILUTEK IN THE PARK

PROFESOR ZAZUL • 1962 • Nowicki Marek, Stawicki Jerzy • SHT • PLN

PROFESSER, THE • 1959 • Heyer John • SHT • ASL

PROFESSEUR CUPIDON • 1933 • Beaudoin Robert, Chemel Andre • FRN • PROF' INGENU, LE

PROFESSEUR D'AMOUR, LE • Braguet Jimy • FRN

PROFESSEUR DE MUSIQUE, LE • 1953 • Devlin Bernard • DCS • CND

PROFESSEUR DE PIANO, LE • 1966 • Reichenbach Francois • SHT • FRN

PROFESSEUR ET L'ELEVE, LE • 1972 • Bokor Pierre • MTV • RMN

PROFESSEUR ET LES MATHEMATIQUES, LE • 1971 • Melancon Andre • SHT • CND

PROFESSEUR, LE (FRN) see **PRIMA NOTTE DI QUIETE, LA** • 1972

PROFESSEUR NIMBU, LE • Daix Andre • ANM • FRN

PROFESSEUR RASPOUTINE, LE • Gregory Gerard • FRN

PROFESSION AVENTURIERS • 1973 • Mulot Claude • FRN

PROFESSION GUN, A (UKN) see **MERCENARIO, IL** • 1968

PROFESSION -ORDERLY • 1979 • Kolarov Keran • BUL

PROFESSION: REALISATEUR, AGE: DIX ANS • 1977 • Bellanger Gerard, Serre Daniel • DOC • FRN

PROFESSIONAL, THE (USA) see **PROFESSIONNEL, LE** • 1981

PROFESSIONAL BLONDE see **BLONDE DE PEKIN, LA** • 1968

PROFESSIONAL BRIDE (UKN) see **HARD GUY** • 1941

PROFESSIONAL CO-RESPONDENTS see **NO FUNNY BUSINESS** • 1933

PROFESSIONAL DATE see **PORTRAIT OF AN ESCORT** • 1980

PROFESSIONAL DINER, THE • 1915 • Drew Sidney • USA

PROFESSIONAL GUEST, THE • 1931 • King George • UKN

PROFESSIONAL GUN, A see **DJANGO** • 1966

PROFESSIONAL JEALOUSY • 1907 • *Bitzer Billy (Ph)* • USA

PROFESSIONAL JEALOUSY • 1913 • *Mcdonald Donald* • USA

PROFESSIONAL KILLER see **BERDUGO NG MGA HARI** • 1967

PROFESSIONAL PATIENT, THE • 1917 • Drew Sidney • SHT • USA

PROFESSIONAL SCAPE GOAT, THE • 1914 • Drew Sidney • USA

PROFESSIONAL SOLDIER • 1935 • Garnett Tay • USA

PROFESSIONAL SWEETHEART • 1933 • Seiter William A. • USA • IMAGINARY SWEETHEART (UKN) ○ CARELESS

PROFESSIONALS, THE • 1960 • Sharp Don • UKN

PROFESSIONALS, THE • 1966 • Brooks Richard • USA

PROFESSIONALS FOR A MASSACRE see **PROFESSIONISTI PER UN MASSACRO** • 1968

PROFESSIONE BIGAMO see **WARUM HAB ICH BLOSS 2 X JA GESAGT** • 1969

PROFESSIONE: REPORTER • 1975 • Antonioni Michelangelo • ITL • PASSENGER, THE (USA) ○ FATAL EXIT

PROFESSIONISTI PER UN MASSACRO • 1968 • Cicero Nando • ITL, SPN • PROFESSIONALS FOR A MASSACRE

PROFESSIONNEL, LE • 1981 • Lautner Georges • FRN • PROFESSIONAL, THE (USA)

PROFESSOR • 1920 • *Franey William* • SHT • USA

PROFESSOR, THE • 1911 • *Imp* • USA

PROFESSOR, THE see **PAN PROFESOR** • 1959

PROFESSOR, THE see **CAMORRISTA, IL** • 1986

PROFESSOR AND HIS WAXWORKS, THE • 1907 • *Williams, Brown & Earle* • USA

PROFESSOR AND JADUGAR • 1968 • Sultan • IND • PROFESSOR AND THE MAGICIAN, THE

PROFESSOR AND THE BEAUTY QUEEN, THE • 1967 • Uys Jamie • SAF • PROFESOR EN DIE PRIKKELPOP

PROFESSOR AND THE BUTTERFLY, THE • 1902 • Collins Alf? • UKN

PROFESSOR AND THE LADY, THE • 1912 • Ince Ralph • USA

PROFESSOR AND THE MAGICIAN, THE see **PROFESSOR AND JADUGAR** • 1968

PROFESSOR AND THE NEW HAT, THE • 1911 • Merwin Bannister • USA

PROFESSOR AND THE THOMAS CATS, THE • 1909 • *Vitagraph* • USA

PROFESSOR BALTHASAR • 1967-69 • Grgic Zlatko, Kolar Boris, Zaninovic Ante • ASS • YGS

PROFESSOR BERTONS ERFINDUNG • 1921 • Dessauer Siegfried • FRG

PROFESSOR BEWARE • 1938 • Nugent Elliott • USA

PROFESSOR BOUNDER'S PILLS • 1908 • Coleby A. E. • UKN

PROFESSOR BRIC-A-BRAC'S INVENTIONS • 1908 • *Pathe* • FRN

PROFESSOR COLUMBUS • 1968 • Erler Rainer • FRG

PROFESSOR CREEPS, THE • 1942 • Beaudine William • USA

PROFESSOR DI MI MUJER, EL • 1930 • Florey Robert • SPN • PROFESSOR DI MI SENORA, EL

PROFESSOR DI MI SENORA, EL see **PROFESSOR DI MI MUJER, EL** • 1930

PROFESSOR DIDLITTLE AND THE SECRET FORMULA • 1972 • Chmielewski W. V. • FRG

PROFESSOR DO-MI-SOL-DO see **MAESTRO DO-MI-SOL-DO, IL** • 1906

PROFESSOR ERICHSONS RIVALE • 1916 • Neher Louis • FRG

PROFESSOR FILUTEK see **PROFESOR FILUTEK**

PROFESSOR FILUTEK IN THE PARK see **PROFESOR FILUTEK W PARKU** • 1955

PROFESSOR FILUTEK'S DREAM see **DZIWNY SEN PROFESORA FILUTEKA** • 1956

PROFESSOR FILUTEK'S DUEL see **POJEDYNEK PROFESOTA FILUTKA** • 1956

PROFESSOR GARLAND THE CONJUROR • 1897 • *Prestwich Mfg. Co.* • UKN

PROFESSOR GIVES A LESSON, THE • 1934 • Hillyer Lambert • SHT • USA

PROFESSOR GOES WILD, THE see **SHE'S FOR ME** • 1943

PROFESSOR HAMLER see **DOCENT HAMLER** • 1964

PROFESSOR HANNIBAL see **HANNIBAL TANAR UR** • 1956

PROFESSOR HOSKIN'S PATENT HUSTLER • 1913 • Aylott Dave? • UKN

PROFESSOR JEREMEY'S EXPERIMENT • 1916 • *Humphrey Orral* • SHT • USA

PROFESSOR JIM • 1957 • Cass Henry • UKN

PROFESSOR KRANZ TEDESCO DI GERMANIA • 1978 • Salce Luciano • ITL

PROFESSOR LAROUSSE • 1920 • Greenbaum Mutz • FRG

PROFESSOR LONGHEAD'S BURGLAR TRAP • 1913 • Wilson Frank? • UKN

PROFESSOR LUST • 1967 • Rose Warner • USA

PROFESSOR MAMLOCK • 1938 • Rappaport Herbert, Minkin Adolph • USS

PROFESSOR MAMLOCK • 1961 • Wolf Konrad • GDR

PROFESSOR MATUSA E I SUOI HIPPIES, IL • 1968 • De Maria Luigi • ITL

PROFESSOR, MY SON (USA) see **MIO FIGLIO PROFESSORE** • 1946

PROFESSOR NACHTFALTER • 1951 • Meyer Rolf • FRG

PROFESSOR NARDI • 1925 • *Orbis-Film* • FRG

PROFESSOR NISSENS SELTSAMER TOD • 1917 • Zangenberg Einar • FRG

PROFESSOR NUMBSKULL D.(FOR DAVID) G.(FOR GOLIATH) EMPTYBROOK see **PROFESSORI UUNO D. G. TURHAPURO** • 1976

PROFESSOR OF THE DRAMA • 1903 • *Bitzer Billy (Ph)* • USA

PROFESSOR OFFKEYSKI • 1940 • Rasinski Connie • ANS • USA

PROFESSOR OLDBOY'S REJUVENATOR • 1914 • *Kalem* • USA

PROFESSOR OPTIMO • 1912 • *Wilder Marshall P.* • USA

PROFESSOR PETERSENS PLEJEBORN • 1924 • Lauritzen Lau • DNM • SMUGGLERS, THE

PROFESSOR PIECAN'S DISCOVERY • 1910 • Coleby A. E. • UKN

PROFESSOR POPPER'S PROBLEMS • 1974 • O'Hara Gerry • UKN

PROFESSOR POPPE'S CRAZY ECCENTRICITIES see **PROFESSOR POPPES PRILLIGA PRILLERIER** • 1944

PROFESSOR POPPES PRILLIGA PRILLERIER • 1944 • Linder John Lennart • SWD • PROFESSOR POPPE'S CRAZY ECCENTRICITIES ○ SOM FALLEN FRAN SKYARNA

PROFESSOR POTTER'S MAGIC POTIONS • 1983 • Smith Peter K. • UKN

PROFESSOR PUDDENHEAD'S PATENTS -THE ELECTRIC ENLARGER • 1909 • Booth W. R. • UKN

PROFESSOR REHBEIN UND DER MEISTERRINGER • 1920 • Peukert Leo • FRG

PROFESSOR RICHARD CODMAN'S PUNCH AND JUDY SHOW • 1904 • Codman John • UKN

PROFESSOR ROUFF'S GREAT DISCOVERY • 1911 • *Pathe* • FRN

PROFESSOR SMALL AND MISTER TALL • 1943 • Sommer Paul, Hubley John • ANS • USA

PROFESSOR SNAITH • 1914 • *Ostriche Muriel* • USA

PROFESSOR SPUFF'S ROMANCE • 1914 • *Pathe* • USA

PROFESSOR THIEF see **KIGEKI: DOROBO GAKKO** • 1968

PROFESSOR TOM • 1948 • Hanna William, Barbera Joseph • ANS • USA

PROFESSOR TROMBONE see **RATTO DELLE SABINE, IL** • 1945

PROFESSOR WAMAN M.SC. • 1938 • Vyas Manibhai • IND

PROFESSOR WEISE'S BRAIN SERUM INJECTOR • 1909 • *Lubin Sigmund* • USA

PROFESSOR WILCZUR'S WILL see **TESTAMENT PROFESORA WILCZURA** • 1939

PROFESSOR WILLIAM NUTT • 1913 • Williams C. Jay • USA

PROFESSOR WISEGUY'S TRIP TO THE MOON • 1916 • *Powers* • SHT • USA

PROFESSOR YA-YA'S MEMOIRS • 1964 • Halas John • ANS • UKN

PROFESSOR ZANIKOFF'S EXPERIENCES OF GRAFTING • 1909 • *Lux* • FRN

PROFESSORE VENGA ACCOMPAGNATO DAI SUOI GENITORI • 1974 • Guerrini Mino • ITL

PROFESSOREN see **FORMYDERNE** • 1978

PROFESSORESSA DI LINGUE • 1976 • Fidani Demofilo • ITL

PROFESSORESSA SI SCIENZE NATURALI, LA • 1976 • Tarantini Michele Massimo • ITL

PROFESSORI UUNO D. G. TURHAPURO • 1976 • Kokkonen Ere • FNL • UUNO TURHAPURO II ○ PROFESSOR NUMBSKULL D.(FOR DAVID) G.(FOR GOLIATH) EMPTYBROOK

PROFESSOR'S ANTIGRAVITATIONAL FLUID, THE • 1908 • Fitzhamon Lewin • UKN

PROFESSOR'S AWAKENING, THE • 1914 • Pollard Harry • USA

PROFESSOR'S DAUGHTER, THE • 1913 • Sennett Mack • USA

PROFESSOR'S DAUGHTERS, THE • 1911 • *Pathe* • USA

PROFESSOR'S DILEMMA, THE • 1912 • *Moore Owen* • USA

PROFESSOR'S DREAM, THE • 1909 • Booth W. R. • UKN

PROFESSOR'S FALSE TEETH, THE • 1914 • *B & C* • UKN

PROFESSOR'S GREAT DISCOVERY, THE • 1908 • Williamson James? • UKN

PROFESSOR'S LOVE TONIC, THE • 1909 • *Essanay* • USA

PROFESSOR'S NIGHTMARE, THE • 1915 • Williams C. Jay • USA

PROFESSOR'S PAINLESS CURE, THE • 1915 • Drew Sidney • USA

PROFESSOR'S PECULIAR PRECAUTIONS, THE • 1916 • *Lane Winifred* • USA

PROFESSOR'S PREDICAMENT, THE • 1913 • *Lubin* • USA

PROFESSOR'S ROMANCE, THE • 1911 • *Nestor* • USA

PROFESSOR'S ROMANCE, THE • 1914 • Drew Sidney • USA

PROFESSOR'S SECRET, THE • 1908 • *Gaumont* • FRN

PROFESSOR'S SON, THE • 1912 • *Thanhouser Kid* • USA

PROFESSOR'S STRENGTH TABLETS, THE • 1909 • Stow Percy • UKN

PROFESSOR'S TWIRLY-WHIRLY CIGARETTES, THE • 1909 • Martinek H. O.? • UKN

PROFESSOR'S WARD, THE • 1911 • Salter Harry • USA

PROFESSOR'S WOOING, THE • 1912 • *Bosworth Hobart* • USA

PROFETA, IL • 1967 • Risi Dino • ITL • MR. KINKY (UKN) ○ PROPHET, THE

PROFETA DA FOME, O • 1970 • Capovilla Maurice • BRZ • HUNGER PROPHET, THE

PROFETA DEL GOL (JOHAN CRUYFF STORY), IL • 1976 • Ciotti Sandro • ITL

PROFETA MIMI, EL • 1972 • Estrada Jose • MXC • MIMI THE PROPHET ○ PROPHET MIMI, THE

PROFETA VOLTAL, SZIVEM • 1968 • Zolnay Pal • HNG • YOU'VE BEEN A PROPHET, MY DEAR ○ YOU WERE A PROPHET, MY DEAR

PROFETUL, AURUL SI ARDELE NII • 1978 • Pita Dan • RMN • PROPHET, GOLD AND THE TRANSYLVANIANS, THE

PROFEZIA DI UN DELITTO (ITL) see **MAGICIENS, LES** • 1975

PROFIL DE LA FRANCE • 1939 • Tedesco Jean • SHT • FRN

PROFILE • 1954 • Searle Francis • UKN

PROFILE IN EVIL • 1975 • Hessler Gordon • TVM • USA

PROFILE OF A PROBLEM DRINKER • 1957 • Jackson Stanley R. • DOC • CND

PROFILE OF SATAN, THE see **PERFIL DE SATANAS, EL** • 1969

PROFILE OF TERROR, THE see **SADIST, THE** • 1963

PROFILES OF PLEASURE see **QUNYING LUANWU** • 1988

PROFISSAO, PORTUGUES • 1972 • Lopes Fernando • SHT • PRT

PROFIT AND LOSS • 1915 • Ayres Sydney • USA

PROFIT AND THE LOSS • 1917 • Bramble A. V., Stannard Eliot • UKN

PROFIT BY THEIR EXAMPLE • 1964 • Loach Kenneth • MTV • UKN

PROFIT FROM LOSS • 1915 • Eason B. Reeves • USA

PROFIT OF THE BUSINESS, THE • 1913 • *Lubin* • USA

PROFIT-SHARER, THE see **HABILITADO, EL** • 1972

PROFIT WITHOUT HONOR, A • 1912 • *Rex* • USA

PROFITEER, THE • 1919 • Holbrook John K. • USA

PROFITEERING BLUES, THE • 1920 • *Sterling Merta* • SHT • USA

PROFITEERS, THE • 1919 • Fitzmaurice George • USA

PROFITEERS, THE see **SCHIEBER, DIE** • 1983

PROFLIGATE, THE • 1911 • Boggs Frank, Turner Otis • USA

PROFLIGATE, THE • 1915 • *Calvert E. H.* • USA

PROFLIGATE, THE • 1916 • Ricketts Thomas • SHT • USA

PROFLIGATE, THE • 1917 • Milton Meyrick • UKN

PROFLIGATE SOLDIER, A see **HEITAI GOKUDO** • 1968

PROFOND REGARD, UN see **EXTREME CLOSE-UP** • 1981

PROFOND SECRET, LE see **SHAI'UN FI SADRY** • 1971

PROFONDEURS DE LA MER, LES see **DIEPTE** • 1932

PROFONDO ROSSO • 1975 • Argento Dario • ITL • DEEP RED (USA) ○ DRIPPING DEEP RED ○ HATCHET MURDERS, THE ○ DEEP RED: HATCHET MURDERS

PROFOUND DESIRE OF THE GODS, THE see **KAMIGAMI NO FUKAKI YOKUBO** • 1968

PROFUMO DELLA SIGNORA IN NERA, IL • 1974 • Barilli Francesco • ITL

PROFUMO DI DONNA • 1974 • Risi Dino • ITL • SCENT OF A WOMAN (USA) ○ THAT FEMALE SCENT (UKN) ○ SCENT OF WOMAN

PROFUNDO • 1988 • Llerandi Antonio • CLM, VNZ • DEEP

PROGNOSE INNERDALEN • 1981 • Einarson Oddvar • DOC • NRW • PROGNOSIS INNERDALEN

PROGNOSIS INNERDALEN see **PROGNOSE INNERDALEN** • 1981

PROGON • 1983 • Golubovic Predrag • YGS • OPPRESSION

PROGRAMM • 1976 • Emigholz Heinz • FRG

PROGRAMME DE FORMATION see **CORRECTIONAL PROCESS, THE** • 1964

PROGRAMMED TO KILL see **RETALIATOR** • 1987

PROGRESS OF PEOPLES, THE • 1975 • Moore Keiron • UKN

PROGRESS OF THE RACE • 1903 • Hepworth Cecil M. • UKN

PROGRESS ON PARADE • 1932 • Sparling Gordon • DCS • CND

PROGRESSIVE BOOK AGENT, THE • 1911 • *Powers* • USA

PROGRESSIVE GENTLEMAN, THE • 1974 • Meleh Mabil • SYR

PROGRESSO IN AGRICOLTURA • 1957 • Olmi Ermanno (Spv) • DOC • ITL

PROHIBIDO ENAMORARSE • 1961 • Nieves Conde Jose Antonio • SPN

PROHIBIDO ESTA DE MODA, LO • 1968 • Siro Fernando • ARG • FORBIDDEN IS IN FASHION, THE

PROHIBIDO SONAR • 1965 • Balbuena Silvio F. • SPN

PROHIBITED SEX see **SEXY PROIBITISSIMO** • 1963

PROHIBITION • 1915 • *Bergen Thurlow* • USA

PROHIBITION MONKEY, A • 1920 • Campbell William • SHT • USA

PROIBITISSIMO see **SEXY PROIBITISSIMO** • 1963

PROIBITO • 1955 • Monicelli Mario • ITL • FORBIDDEN ○ DU SANG DANS LE SOLEIL

PROIBITO RUBARE • 1948 • Comencini Luigi • ITL • GUAGLIO ○ NO STEALING

PROIE, LA • 1917 • Monca Georges • FRN

PROIE DU VENT, LA • 1926 • Clair Rene • FRN • PREY OF THE WIND, THE

PROIE POUR L'OMBRE, LA • 1960 • Astruc Alexandre • FRN • SHADOWS OF ADULTERY (USA)

PROISHYESTVIYE, KOTOROVO NIKTO NYE ZAMYETIL • 1968 • Volodin Alexandr • USS • EVENT NO ONE NOTICED, AN

PROJECT 1 • 1969 • Lourie David • SHT • USA

PROJECT 074 • 1953 • De Normanville Peter • UKN

PROJECT A • 1983 • Chan Jackie • HNG

PROJECT A: PART II • 1987 • Chan Jackie • HKG

PROJECT APOLLO • 1968 • Emshwiller Ed • USA

PROJECT GENOCIDE see **STARSHIP INVASIONS** • 1977

PROJECT: KILL • 1977 • Girdler William • USA

PROJECT M 7 (USA) see **NET, THE** • 1953

PROJECT MOONBASE • 1953 • Talmadge Richard • USA

PROJECT OF ENGINEER PRITE, THE see **PROYEKT INZHENERA PRAITA** • 1918

PROJECT REJECT • 1969 • Smith Paul J. • ANS • USA

PROJECT SPEAR • 1964 • Mason Bill • DOC • UKN

PROJECT X • 1949 • Montagne Edward J. • USA

PROJECT X • 1968 • Castle William • USA

PROJECT X • 1987 • Kaplan Jonathan • USA

PROJECT Z • 1968 • Spencer Ronald • SRL • UKN

PROJECTED MAN, THE • 1966 • Curteis Ian • UKN

PROJECTION PRIVEE • 1973 • Leterrier Francois • FRN • PRIVATE SCREENING

PROJECTIONIST, THE • 1971 • Hurwitz Harry • USA

PROKLETI DOMU HAJNU • 1988 • Svoboda Jiri • CZC • INVISIBLES, THE

PROKLETI PRAZNIK • 1958 • Makavejev Dusan • SHT • YGS • DAMNED HOLIDAY

PROKLIATIYE MILLIONI • 1917 • Protazanov Yakov • USS • CURSED MILLIONS ○ DAMNED MILLIONS

PROKOFIEFF -HIS LIFE AND MUSIC see **KOMPOZITOR SERGEY PROKOFYEV** • 1961

PROKURATOR • 1934 • Waszynski Michael • PLN

PROKURATOR MA GLOS • 1965 • Haupe Wlodzimierz • PLN • COUNSEL FOR THE PROSECUTION HAS THE FLOOR, THE

PROKUROR • 1917 • Protazanov Yakov • USS • PUBLIC PROSECUTOR

PROKURORAT • 1968 • Sharlandgiev Ljobomir • BUL • PROSECUTOR, THE

PROLETARPIGEN see **ARME JENNY, DIE** • 1912

PROLIFIC MAGICAL EGG, THE (USA) see **OEUF DU SORCIER OU L'OEUF MAGIQUE PROLIFIQUE, L'** • 1902

PROLJETNI VJETAR see **POMLADNI VETER** • 1976

PROLJETNI ZVUCI • 1960 • Marks Aleksandar, Jutrisa Vladimir • ANS • YGS • SPRING SONGS ○ SPRING TUNES

PROLOG • 1956 • Dzigan Yefim • USS • PROLOGUE

PROLOGO • 1948 • Tomei Giuliano • ITL

PROLOGUE • 1969 • Spry Robin • CND

PROLOGUE see **PROLOG** • 1956

PROLOGUE, THE • 1970 • Rozewicz Stanislaw • PLN

PROLONGED TIME see **PRODLOUZENY CAS** • 1984

PROM • 1970 • Afanasjew Jerzy • PLN • FERRY, THE

PROM NIGHT • 1980 • Lynch Paul • CND • BAL DE L'HORREUR, LE

PROM NIGHT 2: HELLO MARY LOU see **HELLO MARY LOU: PROM NIGHT II** • 1987

PROM NIGHT III: THE LAST KISS • 1990 • Oliver Ron, Simpson Peter • CND

PROM QUEEN • 1987 • Yeshurun Isaac • ISR

PROMENAD I DE GAMLAS LAND • Ahrne Marianne • SWD

PROMENADE • 1967 • Winter Donovan • UKN

PROMENADE DES CONGRESSISTES SUR LE BORD DE LA SAONE • 1895 • Lumiere Louis • FRN

PROMENADE EN CHINE • 1934 • Titayna • DOC • FRN • WALKING THROUGH CHINA

PROMENADE FLAMANDE • 1975 • Hanoun Marcel • SHT • FRN

PROMENADE QUOTIDIENNE AUX INDES • 1959 • Kast Pierre • SHT • FRN

PROMENADE SUR LES ONDES • 1956 • Herwig Hans • SHT • FRN

PROMESA, LA • 1976 • del Pozo Angel • SPN

PROMESA HEROICA • 1939 • Elias Francisco • MXC

PROMESSA, A • 1973 • de Macedo Antonio • PRT

PROMESSA, LA • 1979 • Negrin Alberto • ITL

PROMESSE, LA • 1969 • Freeman Robert, Feyder Paul • FRN • ECHELLE BLANCHE, L' ○ SECRET WORLD (USA)

PROMESSE A L'INCONNUE • 1942 • Berthomieu Andre • FRN

PROMESSE DE JUILLET • 1963 • Hamina Mohamed Lakhdar • DCS • ALG

PROMESSE DE L'AUBE, LA • 1970 • Dassin Jules • FRN, USA • PROMISE AT DAWN (USA)

PROMESSE DI MARINAIO • 1958 • Vasile Turi • ITL

PROMESSES • 1935 • Delacroix Rene • FRN

PROMESSES • 1948 • Petel Pierre • DCS • CND

PROMESSES AUX VINGT ANS • 1958 • Masson Jean • SHT • FRN

PROMESSES DANGEREUSES, LES • 1956 • Gourguet Jean • FRN

PROMESSI SPOSI, I • 1913 • Pasquali Ernesto Maria • ITL

PROMESSI SPOSI, I • 1916 • D'Ambra Lucio • ITL

PROMESSI SPOSI, I • 1916 • Falena Ugo • ITL

PROMESSI SPOSI, I • 1919 • Bonnard Mario • ITL

PROMESSI SPOSI, I • 1941 • Camerini Mario • ITL • SPIRIT AND THE FLESH, THE (USA)

PROMESSI SPOSI, I • 1964 • Maffei Mario • ITL, SPN

PROMETEJ SA OTOKA VISEVICE • 1965 • Mimica Vatroslav • YGS • PROMETHEUS FROM THE ISLAND OF VISEVICA ○ PROMETHEUS FROM VISEVICA ISLAND

PROMETHEE • 1908 • Feuillade Louis • FRN

PROMETHEE • 1935 • Kavaleridze Ivan • USS

PROMETHEE BANQUIER • 1922 • L'Herbier Marcel • FRN

PROMETHEUS • 1919 • Blom August • DNM • BONDS OF HATE

PROMETHEUS • 1965 • Felligi Tamas • HNG

PROMETHEUS • 1965 • Kristl Vlado • ANS • FRG

PROMETHEUS • 1970 • Dinov Todor • ANS • BUL • PROMETHEUS XX

PROMETHEUS BOUND -THE ILLIAC PASSION • 1966 • Markopoulos Gregory J. • USA • ILLIAC PASSION, THE ○ ILIAC PASSION, THE

PROMETHEUS FROM THE ISLAND OF VISEVICA see **PROMETEJ SA OTOKA VISEVICE** • 1965

PROMETHEUS FROM VISEVICA ISLAND see **PROMETEJ SA OTOKA VISEVICE** • 1965
PROMETHEUS SECOND PERSON SINGULAR see **PROMITHEAS SE DEFTERO PROSOPO** • 1975
PROMETHEUS XX see **PROMETHEUS** • 1970
PROMISCUOUS SEX, THE • 1967 • Milligan Andy • USA
PROMISE • 1986 • Jordan Glenn • TVM • USA
PROMISE, THE • 1912 • Dwan Allan • USA
PROMISE, THE • 1913 • Buckland Warwick? • UKN
PROMISE, THE • 1917 • Hunt Jay • USA
PROMISE, THE • 1927 • Hunt Charles J. • USA
PROMISE, THE • 1952 • Walker Norman • UKN
PROMISE, THE • 1969 • Hayes Michael • UKN
PROMISE, THE • 1979 • Cates Gilbert • USA • FACE OF A STRANGER
PROMISE, THE see **KATARA TIS MANAS, I** • 1961
PROMISE, THE see **PAGADOR DE PROMESSAS, O** • 1961
PROMISE AT DAWN (USA) see **PROMESSE DE L'AUBE, LA** • 1970
PROMISE FULFILLED (UKN) see **WILDCAT OF TUCSON** • 1940
PROMISE HER ANYTHING • 1965 • Hiller Arthur • UKN
PROMISE HIM ANYTHING • 1974 • Parone Edward • TVM • USA
PROMISE LAND, THE • 1916 • Windom Lawrence C. • SHT • USA
PROMISE MADE, A see **THANKSGIVING PROMISE, THE** • 1986
PROMISE ME NOTHING (USA) see **VERSPRICH MIR NICHTS** • 1937
PROMISE OF BED, A • 1969 • Ford Derek • UKN • THIS, THAT AND THE OTHER
PROMISE OF HEAVEN see **UITZICHT OP DE HEMEL** • 1961
PROMISE OF LOVE, THE • 1980 • Taylor Don • TVM • USA
PROMISE OF RED LIPS, THE see **ROUGE AUX LEVRES, LE** • 1970
PROMISED A MIRACLE • 1988 • Gyllenhaal Stephen • TVM • USA
PROMISED DREAM, THE • 1978 • Arau Alfonso • MXC, USA
PROMISED LAND • 1988 • Hoffman Michael • USA
PROMISED LAND, THE • 1925 • *Cosray* • USA
PROMISED LAND, THE • 1928 • Hertz Aleksander • PLN
PROMISED LAND, THE see **BRULES, LES** • 1958
PROMISED LAND, THE see **TIERRA PROMETIDA** • 1970
PROMISED LAND, THE (USA) see **TIERRA PROMETIDA, LA** • 1974
PROMISED LAND (USA) see **ZIEMIA OBIECANA** • 1974
PROMISED LANDS • 1974 • Sontag Susan • FRN
PROMISED WOMAN • 1975 • Cowan Tom • ASL
PROMISES FROM TOMORROW see **BELOFTES VAN MORE** • 1981
PROMISES IN THE DARK • 1979 • Hellman Jerome • USA
PROMISES! PROMISES! • 1963 • Donovan King • USA
PROMISES TO KEEP • 1985 • Black Noel • TVM • USA
PROMISES TO KEEP • 1986 • Noyce Phil • ASL
PROMISING LAD, A see **DECKO KOJI OBECAVA** • 1982
PROMISSORY NOTES • 1915 • Jaccard Jacques • USA
PROMITHEAS SE DEFTERO PROSOPO • 1975 • Ferris Kostas • GRC • PROMETHEUS SECOND PERSON SINGULAR
PROMOTER, THE • 1931 • Ceder Ralph • SHT • USA
PROMOTER, THE (USA) see **CARD, THE** • 1952
PROMOTEUR, LE • 1973 • Chapier Henri • FRN
PROMOTION INDUSTRIELLE ET DEUX DE SES ARTISANS, LA • 1968 • Dansereau Fernand • DCS • CND
PROMOTOR, THE • 1911 • *Kalem* • USA
PROMOTOR, THE • 1913 • *Pilot* • USA
PROMOTOR, THE • 1915 • *Edwards Walter* • USA
PROMPT PAYMENT • 1911 • *Thanhouser* • USA
PROMPTED BY JEALOUSY • 1913 • *Selig* • USA
PRONE TO TEMPTATION see **TAKAW TUKSO** • 1986
PRONTO AD UCCIDERE • 1976 • Prosperi Franco • ITL
PRONTO ANTES QUE SE ACABE • 1982 • Galettini Carlos • ARG • QUICK BEFORE IT'S OVER
PRONTO.. C'E UNA CERTA GIULIANA PER TE • 1967 • Franciosa Massimo • ITL • HELLO.. THERE'S SOMEONE CALLED GIULIANA FOR YOU
PRONTO, CHI PARLA? • 1945 • Bragaglia Carlo Ludovico • ITL • VOICE OF LOVE, THE (USA)
PROOF • Devensky David • SHT • USA
PROOF • Reynolds Kevin • USA
PROOF, THE • 1913 • *Nestor* • USA
PROOF, THE • 1915 • Wilson Ben • USA
PROOF OF A MAN, THE • 1914 • *Kerrigan J. Warren* • USA
PROOF OF THE MAN, THE • 1913 • *Nestor* • USA
PROOF OF THE PUDDING, THE • 1914 • Cooper Toby • UKN
PROOF POSITIVE • 1938 • Newman Widgey R. • UKN
PROOI, DE • 1984 • Pieters Vivian • NTH • PREY, THE
PROPAGANDA MESSAGE • 1974 • Nelson Barrie* • CND
PROPAGATION • 1960 • Jodoin Rene • ANS • CND
PROPALO LETO • 1963 • Bykov Rolan • USS • LOST SUMMER, THE
PROPER CHANNELS see **IMPROPER CHANNELS** • 1981
PROPER TIME, THE • 1959 • Laughlin Tom • USA
PROPERTY MAN, THE • 1914 • Chaplin Charles • USA • GETTING HIS GOAT ○ ROUSTABOUT, THE ○ VAMPING VENUS
PROPERTY MAN, THE see **BEFORE THE SHOW** • 1917
PROPERTY THEFT IS NO LONGER A LOSS see **PROPRIETA NON E PIU UN FORTO, LA** • 1973
PROPHECIES OF NOSTRADAMUS: CATASTROPHE 1999 see **NOSTRADAMUS NO DAIYOGEN** • 1974
PROPHECY • 1979 • Frankenheimer John • USA
PROPHECY see **JOSLAT** • 1920
PROPHECY, THE • 1913 • *Essanay* • USA
PROPHECY, THE • 1913 • Edwin Walter • *Edison* • USA
PROPHECY, THE see **YOGEN** • 1982
PROPHECY OF LAKE TITICACA, THE see **PROFECIA DEL LAGO, LA** • 1923
PROPHET, THE see **PROFETA, IL** • 1967
PROPHET, GOLD AND THE TRANSYLVANIANS, THE see **PROFETUL, AURUL SI ARDELE NII** • 1978
PROPHET MIMI, THE see **PROFETA MIMI, EL** • 1972
PROPHET OF THE FIELD, THE see **MEZEI PROFETA** • 1947
PROPHET OF THE HILLS, A • 1915 • Lloyd Frank • USA
PROPHET WITHOUT HONOR • 1939 • Feist Felix E. • SHT • USA
PROPHETESS OF THEBES, THE (USA) see **PROPHETESSE DE THEBES, LA** • 1908
PROPHETESSE DE THEBES, LA • 1908 • Melies Georges • FRN • PROPHESS OF THEBES, THE (USA)
PROPHET'S PARADISE, THE • 1922 • Crosland Alan • USA
PROPIEDAD • 1962 • Soffici Mario • ARG
PROPOSAL, THE • 1910 • Powell Frank • USA
PROPOSAL BY PROXY • 1913 • *Thanhouser* • USA
PROPOSAL UNDER DIFFICULTIES, A • 1912 • *Ridgely Richard* • USA
PROPOSING BILL • 1918 • *Parsons William* • SHT • USA
PROPOSING UNDER DIFFICULTIES • 1910 • *Electograff* • USA
PROPRE A RIEN • 1956 • de Gastyne Marco • SHT • FRN
PROPRE DE L'HOMME, LE • 1960 • Lelouch Claude • FRN • RIGHT OF MAN, THE
PROPRIETA NON E PIU UN FORTO, LA • 1973 • Petri Elio • ITL • PROPERTY THEFT IS NO LONGER A LOSS
PROPRIETARII • 1973 • Creanga Serban • RMN • OWNERS, THE
PROPS • 1923 • Semon Larry • USA
PROPS AND PANIC • 1917 • Fitzgerald Dallas M. • USA
PROPS AND THE SPIRITS • 1925 • *Hurd Earl (P)* • ANS • USA
PROP'S ANGEL • 1913 • Plumb Hay • UKN
PROPS, DROPS AND FLOPS • 1917 • Smith Noel • SHT • USA
PROS.. 2 see **K 2** • 1989
PROS.. 2: A FILM ABOUT PROSTITUTION –LADIES OF THE NIGHT see **K 2** • 1989
PROSCANIE • 1983 • Klimov Elem • USS • FAREWELL TO MATJORA ○ FAREWELL ○ PROSHCHANIE
PROSCRIBED, THE see **PREJUDICE** • 1924
PROSCRIT, LE • 1912 • Feuillade Louis • FRN
PROSCRITO DEL RIO COLORADO, EL • 1965 • Dexter Maury • SPN, ITL • OUTLAW OF RED RIVER (USA) ○ DJANGO, KILLER PER ONORE (ITL)
PROSECUTE THE BLACKHEARTED see **USIGIN ANG MAITIM NA BUDHI** • 1967
PROSECUTING ATTORNEY, THE • 1912 • Campbell Colin • USA
PROSECUTING ATTORNEY, THE • 1913 • *Coombs Guy* • USA
PROSECUTION • 1914 • Davis Ulysses • USA
PROSECUTOR, THE see **PROKURORAT** • 1968
PROSFYGOPOULA • 1938 • Bogris Demetre • GIRL REFUGEE, THE (USA)
PROSHCHANIE see **PROSCANIE** • 1983
PROSHCHAY • 1967 • Pozhenyan Grigori • USS • FAREWELL
PROSHCHAYTE, GOLUBI! • 1961 • Segel Yakov • USS • FAREWELL, DOVES! (USA) ○ GOODBYE DOVES!
PROSHU SLOVA see **JA PRASU SLOVA** • 1975
PROSOCHI KINDINOS • 1983 • Stamboulopoulos George • GRC • CAUTION DANGER
PROSOPO ME PROSOPO see **PROSSOPO ME PROSSOPO** • 1966
PROSOPO TES MEDOUSAS, TO • 1967 • Koundouros Nikos • GRC • FACE OF THE MEDUSA ○ FACE OF MEDUSA, THE
PROSPECCION MINERA EN TAMACURO • 1972 • Lovera Javier • DOC • VNZ
PROSPECTIN' AROUND • 1925 • Barkas Geoffrey • UKN
PROSPECTING BEAR, THE • 1941 • Ising Rudolf • ANS • USA
PROSPECTING FOR PETROLEUM • 1948 • Goldstone Duke • USA
PROSPECTOR, THE • 1912 • *Essanay* • USA
PROSPECTOR, THE • 1917 • Gillstrom Arvid E. • SHT • USA
PROSPECTOR SWEETHEARTS • 1912 • *Pathe* • USA
PROSPECTORS, THE • 1914 • Vale Travers • USA
PROSPECTOR'S DAUGHTER, THE • 1912 • Ince Thomas H. • USA
PROSPECTOR'S LEGACY, THE • 1912 • *Essanay* • USA
PROSPECTOR'S ROMANCE, THE • 1914 • *Warner'S Features* • USA
PROSPECTOR'S TREASURE, THE • 1910 • *Atlas* • USA
PROSPECTOR'S VENGEANCE, THE • 1920 • Eason B. Reeves • SHT • USA
PROSPECT'S AUSTRALIA DAY • 1917 • *Krischock H. (Ph)* • ASL
PROSPERITY • 1932 • Wood Sam • USA
PROSPERITY BLUES • 1932 • *Mintz Charles (P)* • ANS • USA
PROSPERITY RACE, THE • 1962 • Zetterling Mai • DCS • UKN
PROSPERO'S BOOKS • 1990 • Greenaway Peter • UKN
PROSPEROUS TIMES see **BLOMSTRANDE TIDER** • 1979
PROSSENETI, I • 1976 • Rondi Brunello • ITL
PROSSOPO ME PROSSOPO • 1966 • Manthoulis Rovyros • GRC • FACE A FACE ○ FACE TO FACE ○ PROSOPO ME PROSOPO
PROSTACEK • 1945 • Stekly Karel • SHT • CZC
PROSTAYA ISTORIYA • 1960 • Yegorov Yuri • USS • ORDINARY STORY, AN ○ SIMPLE STORY, A
PROSTIA OMENEASCA • 1968 • Sibianu Gheorghe • ANS • RMN
PROSTITUTA AL SERVIZIO DEL PUBBLICO E IN REGOLA CON LE LEGGI STATO, UNA • 1970 • Zingarelli Italo • ITL
PROSTITUTE • 1980 • Garnett Tony • UKN
PROSTITUTE • 1988 • Yu Jin-Sun • SKR
PROSTITUTE, A see **PROSTITUTKA** • 1926
PROSTITUTE, THE see **STORIE DI VITA E MALAVITA** • 1975
PROSTITUTES IN PRISON see **HEISSE TOD, DER** • 1969
PROSTITUTION • 1976 • Davy Jean-Francois • FRN
PROSTITUTION 2 see **SICH VERKAUFEN, DIE** • 1919
PROSTITUTION, DIE • 1919 • Oswald Richard • FRG • GELBE HAUS, DAS
PROSTITUTION, LA • 1962 • Boutel Maurice • FRN
PROSTITUTION CLANDESTINE • Payet Alain • FRN
PROSTITUTION RACKET, THE see **STORIE DI VITA E MALAVITA** • 1975
PROSTITUTKA • 1926 • Frelikh O. • USS • PROSTITUTE, A
PROSTITUZIONE • 1974 • Di Silvestro Rino • ITL
PROSTO DYEVOCHKA • 1967 • Buneyev Boris • USS • JUST A LITTLE GIRL
PROSTOI SLUCHAI • 1932 • Pudovkin V. I. • USS • LIFE IS VERY GOOD ○ SIMPLE CASE, A ○ LIFE IS BEAUTIFUL
PROSTYE LYUDI • 1945 • Kozintsev Grigori, Trauberg Leonid • USS • ORDINARY PEOPLE ○ PLAIN PEOPLE ○ SIMPLE PEOPLE, PLAIN PEOPLE
PROSZE SLONIA • 1978 • Giersz Witold • ANM • PLN • PLEASE, ELEPHANT
PROTAGONISTI, I • 1968 • Fondato Marcello • ITL • PROTAGONISTS, THE
PROTAGONISTS, THE see **PROTAGONISTI, I** • 1968
PROTAR AFFAIR see **AFACEREA PROTAR** • 1956
PROTEA • 1913 • Jasset Victorin • SRL • FRN
PROTEA • 1915 • Bourgeois Gerard • FRN
PROTECK THE WEAKERIST • 1937 • Fleischer Dave • ANS • USA
PROTECT THE SMALL ANIMALS • 1988 • Cohen Chaim • BUL
PROTECTEUR, LE • 1974 • Hanin Roger • FRN, SPN
PROTECTING BIG GAME • 1915 • *Edison* • USA
PROTECTING SAN FRANCISCO FROM FIRE • 1913 • Lehrman Henry • DOC • USA
PROTECTION • 1929 • Stoloff Ben • USA
PROTECTION CIVILE • 1967 • Bedjaoui Ahmed • DCS • ALG
PROTECTION OF FRUIT • 1940 • Tharp Grahame • UKN
PROTECTION OF THE CROSS, THE • 1912 • *Bison* • USA
PROTECTION RACKET (UKN) see **GUN GRIT** • 1936
PROTECTOR, THE • 1985 • Glickenhaus James • USA, HKG
PROTECTORS, THE see **COMPANY OF KILLERS** • 1968
PROTECTORY'S OLDEST BOY, THE • 1913 • *Thanhouser* • USA
PROTEGE, THE see **PROTEGIDO, EL** • 1956
PROTEGE, THE see **STICENIK** • 1966
PROTEGE OF UNCLE SAM, A • 1912 • *Champion* • USA
PROTEGIDAS, LAS • 1975 • Lara Polop Francisco • SPN
PROTEGIDO, EL • 1956 • Torre-Nilsson Leopoldo • ARG • PROTEGE, THE
PROTEST • 1963 • Grenz Ivo • SWD
PROTEST • 1967 • Hadzic Fadil • YGS
PROTEST 68 • 1968 • Gradowski Bohdan • DOC • PLN
PROTEST, THE • 1915 • Hunt Jay • USA
PROTEST AT FORTY-EIGHT YEARS OLD see **YONJU HASSAI NO TEIKO** • 1956
PROTEVOUSSIANIKES PERIPETIES • 1956 • Petropoulakis Yannis • GRC • AVENTURES DANS LA CAPITALE
PROTI VSEM • 1957 • Vavra Otakar • CZC • ALL OUR ENEMIES ○ AGAINST ALL
PROTIV KINGA • 1975 • Jovanovic Dragovan • YGS • AGAINST KING
PROTOCOL • 1984 • Ross Herbert • USA
PROTOCOL FOR A MONTAGE see **PROTOKOLL EINER MONTAGE** • 1974
PROTOKOLL EINER MONTAGE • 1974 • Jahn Sepp, Hirsch Edith • AUS • PROTOCOL FOR A MONTAGE
PROTOKOLL EINER REVOLUTION • 1963 • Lemmer G. • SHT • FRG
PROTOTYPE • 1983 • Greene David • TVM • USA
PROTSESAT • 1968 • Yakimov Yakim • BUL • TRIAL, THE
PROTSESS ESEROV see **PROZESS ESEROV** • 1922
PROTSESS MIRONOVA see **PROZESS MIRONOVA** • 1920
PROTSESS O TROYOKH MILLYONAKH • 1926 • Protazanov Yakov • USS • TRIAL OF THE THREE MILLIONS, THE ○ THREE MILLION CASE, THE ○ THREE THIEVES ○ TRIAL OF THREE MILLIONS
PROTUVA see **SCALAWAG** • 1973
PROUD AND THE BEAUTIFUL, THE (USA) see **ORGUEILLEUX, LES** • 1953
PROUD AND THE DAMNED, THE • 1973 • Grofe Ferde Jr. • TVM • USA • PROUD, DAMNED AND DEAD
PROUD AND THE PROFANE, THE • 1956 • Seaton George • USA
PROUD BULB, THE • 1964 • Buchvarova Radka • BUL
PROUD CANVAS • 1949 • Singer Aubrey • UKN • SAILING TO THE CAPE
PROUD CITY • 1946 • Keene Ralph • DOC • UKN
PROUD CLARISSA • 1911 • Haldane Bert? • UKN
PROUD, DAMNED AND DEAD see **PROUD AND THE DAMNED, THE** • 1973
PROUD FLESH • 1925 • Vidor King • USA
PROUD HEART see **HIS PEOPLE** • 1925
PROUD HERITAGE see **MIRCEA** • 1989
PROUD MEN • 1987 • Graham William A. • TVM • USA
PROUD NIGHTGOWN, THE see **O PYSNE NOCNI KOSILCE** • 1950
PROUD ONES, THE • 1956 • Webb Robert D. • USA
PROUD ONES, THE see **ORGUEILLEUX, LES** • 1953
PROUD ONES, THE (UKN) see **CHEVAL D'ORGEUIL, LE** • 1980
PROUD PRINCESS, THE see **PYSNA PRINCENZNA** • 1952
PROUD REBEL, THE • 1958 • Curtiz Michael • USA
PROUD RIDER, THE • 1972 • Stocki Chester • CND
PROUD SHIPS • 1954 • Armitage Philip • UKN
PROUD STALLION, THE • 1964 • *Kortbova Jorga* • CZC
PROUD STALLION, THE see **TRAPENI** • 1961
PROUD TO BE BRITISH • 1972 • Broomfield Nicholas • DOC • UKN
PROUD TO LIVE • 1980 • Weis Bob • DOC • ASL
PROUD VALLEY, THE • 1940 • Tennyson Pen • UKN • DAVID GOLIATH
PROUDLY SHE MARCHES • 1943 • Beveridge Jane Marsh • DCS • CND
PROVA D'AMORE • 1974 • Longo Tiziano • ITL
PROVA DE FOGO • 1980 • Altberg Marcos • BRZ
PROVA D'ORCHESTRA • 1979 • Fellini Federico • ITL • ORCHESTRA REHEARSAL (USA)
PROVA GENERALE, LA • 1967 • Scavolini Romano • ITL
PROVACATEUR, THE see **PROVOKATOR** • 1928
PROVACI ANCHE TU, LIONEL • 1973 • Montero Roberto Bianchi • ITL
PROVAZ Z OBESENCE • 1927 • Spelina • CZC • ROPE FROM THE HANGED MAN, THE
PROVED GUILTY (UKN) see **WYOMING HURRICANE** • 1944
PROVERBS • 1925 • Butler Alexander • SER • UKN
PROVERKA NA DOROGAKH • 1971 • Gherman Alexei • USS • TRIAL ON THE ROAD, THE
PROVIDANI O PEJSKOVI A KOCICCE • 1955 • Hofman Eduard • ANS • CZC • OVER THE LITTLE DOG AND THE LITTLE CAT
PROVIDENCE • 1977 • Resnais Alain • FRN, UKN, SWT
PROVIDENCE AND MRS. URMY • 1915 • *Bayne Beverly* • USA
PROVIDENCE AND THE TWINS • 1915 • *Majestic* • USA
PROVIDENCE DE NOTRE-DAME DES FLOTS, LA • 1904 • Melies Georges • FRN • PROVIDENCE OF THE WAVES OR THE DREAM OF A POOR FISHERMAN, THE (USA)

PROVIDENCE OF THE WAVES OR THE DREAM OF A POOR FISHERMAN, THE (USA) see **PROVIDENCE DE NOTRE-DAME DES FLOTS, LA** • 1904
PROVIDENTIAL TRAGEDY, A • 1913 • *Nestor* • USA
PROVINCIA VIOLENTA • 1978 • Bianchi Mario • ITL
PROVINCIAL, LE • 1990 • Tarbes Jean-Jacques • FRN
PROVINCIAL ACTORS see **AKTORZY PROWINCJONALNI** • 1979
PROVINCIAL CIRCUS see **DOM BEZ OKIEN** • 1962
PROVINCIALE, IL • 1971 • Salce Luciano • ITL
PROVINCIALE, LA • 1953 • Soldati Mario • ITL • WAYWARD WIFE, THE
PROVINCIALE, LA • 1981 • Goretta Claude • FRN, SWT • GIRL FROM LORRAINE, A (UKN) ○ GIRL FROM THE PROVINCES, THE
PROVINCIALES EN CHALEUR • Roy Jean-Claude • FRN
PROVINCIALI, I • 1959 • Mattoli Mario • ITL
PROVINCIALINA, LA • 1934 • Biancini Ferruccio, Boese Carl • ITL, FRG
PROVING HIS LOVE • 1911 • *Vitagraph* • USA
PROVING HIS WORTH • 1913 • Calvert Charles? • UKN
PROVINZONKEL, DER • 1926 • Noa Manfred • FRG
PROVISIONAL FREEDOM see **LIBERTAD PROVISIONAL** • 1976
PROVOCATION see **DU GAMLA, DU FRIA** • 1970
PROVOCATION, LA • 1969 • Charpak Andre • FRN
PROVOKATOR • 1928 • Turin Victor • USS • PROVACATEUR, THE
PROWL CAR see **BETWEEN MIDNIGHT AND DAWN** • 1950
PROWL GIRLS • 1968 • *Mahon Barry* • USA • RUNAWAY DAUGHTERS
PROWLER, THE • 1951 • Losey Joseph • USA • COST OF LOVING
PROWLER, THE • 1981 • Zito Joseph • USA • ROSEMARY'S KILLER ○ GRADUATION, THE
PROWLERS OF THE EVERGLADES • 1954 • Algar James • DOC • USA
PROWLERS OF THE JUNGLE • 1916 • *Laemmle* • SHT • USA
PROWLERS OF THE NIGHT • 1926 • Laemmle Ernst • USA
PROWLERS OF THE PLAINS see **KNIGHT OF THE TRAILS, A** • 1915
PROWLERS OF THE SEA • 1928 • Adolfi John G. • USA • SEA PROWLERS
PROWLERS OF THE WILD • 1914 • Turner Otis • USA
PROXENETES, LES see **ETTORE LO FUSTO** • 1972
PROXENIO TIS ANNAS, TO • 1971 • Voulgaris Pantelis • GRC • MATCHING OF ANNA, THE ○ ENGAGEMENT OF ANNA
PROXIES • 1921 • Baker George D. • USA
PROXIMA ESTACION, LA • 1981 • Mercero Antonio • SPN • NEXT SEASON, THE
PROXIMA LUNA, UNA • 1965 • Nakatani Carlos • MXC
PROXIMA VEZ QUE VIVAMOS, LA • 1946 • Gomez Bascuas Enrique • SPN
PROXIMA VITIMA, A • 1984 • de Andrade Joao Batista • BRZ • NEXT VICTIM, THE
PROXIMACION AL HOMBRE ORQUESTA • 1973 • Ulive Ugo • VNZ • CLOSE-UP OF THE MAN IN THE ORCHESTRA
PROXIMO OTONO, EL • 1967 • Eceiza Antonio • SPN • NEXT AUTUMN
PROXY HAWKS • 1972 • Darcus Jack • CND
PROXY HUSBAND, A • 1919 • Garwood William • SHT • USA
PROXY LOVER: A FABLE OF THE FUTURE, THE • 1924 • Fleischer Dave • ANS • USA
PROYEKT INZHENERA PRAITA • 1918 • Kuleshov Lev • USS • PROJECT OF ENGINEER PRITE, THE ○ ENGINEER PRITE'S PROJECT
PROZESS, DER • 1948 • Pabst G. W. • AUS • IN NAME DER MENSCHLICHKEIT ○ TRIAL, THE
PROZESS, DER • 1962 • Welles Orson • FRG, FRN, ITL • PROCESSO, IL (ITL) ○ PROCES, LE (FRN) ○ TRIAL, THE (USA)
PROZESS ESEROV • 1922 • Vertov Dziga • USS • TRIAL OF THE SOCIAL REVOLUTIONARIES, THE ○ EZEROV TRIAL, THE ○ PROTSESS ESEROV
PROZESS HAVERS, DER • 1918 • Zeyn Willy • FRG
PROZESS MIRONOVA • 1920 • Vertov Dziga • USS • TRIAL OF MIRONOV, THE ○ MIRONOV TRIAL, THE ○ ACTION AT MIRONOV, THE ○ PROTSESS MIRONOVA
PROZESS WORTH • 1918 • Arnheim Valy • FRG
PROZVAN JE I VB • 1962 • Strbac Milenko • YGS • FIFTH CLASS WAS ALSO CALLED, THE
PRSTYNEK • 1944 • Fric Martin • CZC • WEDDING RING, THE ○ LITTLE RING, THE ○ RING, THE
PRT see **NOCHE DEL TERROR CIEGO, LA** • 1972
PRUDE, THE see **DANGEROUS FLIRT, THE** • 1924
PRUDENCE AND THE PILL • 1968 • Cook Fielder, Neame Ronald • UKN, USA
PRUDENCE OF BROADWAY see **PRUDENCE ON BROADWAY** • 1919
PRUDENCE ON BROADWAY • 1919 • Borzage Frank • USA • PRUDENCE OF BROADWAY
PRUDENCE THE PIRATE • 1916 • Parke William • USA
PRUDE'S FALL, THE • 1924 • Cutts Graham • UKN
PRUEBA DE DIOS see **RENCOR DE LA TIERRA, EL** • 1949
PRULOM • 1946 • Stekly Karel • CZC • BREACH, THE
PRUNE DES BOIS • 1980 • Lobet Marc • BLG
PRUNELLA • 1918 • Tourneur Maurice • USA
PRUNES AND POLITICS • 1944 • Holmes Ben • SHT • USA
PRUNING KNIFE, THE see **WAS SHE JUSTIFIED?** • 1922
PRUNING THE MOVIES • 1914 • *Nestor* • USA
PRUSSIAN CUR, THE • 1918 • Walsh Raoul • USA
PRUSSIAN SPY, THE • 1909 • Griffith D. W. • USA
PRVA LJABAV • 1971 • Calic Zoran • YGS • FIRST LOVE
PRVI GRADJANIN MALE VAROSI • 1966 • Djordjevic Purisa • YGS • FIRST CITIZEN IN A SMALL TOWN, THE
PRVI SPLITSKI ODRED • 1973 • Bercic Vojdrag • YGS • FIRST SPLIT DETACHMENT, THE
PRVNI DEN MEHO SYNA • 1964 • Helge Ladislav • CZC • CHANCE MEETING
PRVNI PARTA • 1959 • Vavra Otakar • CZC • FIRST RESCUE PARTY, THE
PRVNI POLIBENI • 1935 • Slavinsky Vladimir • CZC • FIRST KISS, THE
PRYAMAYA LINIYA • 1968 • Shvyrev Yuri • USS • STRAIGHT COURSE, A ○ STRAIGHT LINE
PRZEBUDZENIE • 1934 • Ford Aleksander • PLN • AWAKENING
PRZECHODZEN • 1966 • Trzos-Rastawiecki Andrzej • DOC • PLN • PASSER-BY, THE
PRZED PODROZA • 1960 • Kwiatowska M. • SHT • PLN • BEFORE THE GREAT TRIP
PRZED PODROZA • 1960 • Wionczek Roman • DOC • PLN • BEFORE A JOURNEY
PRZED TURNIEJEM • 1966 • Marzynski Marian, Szmagier Krzysztof • DOC • PLN • BEFORE THE TOURNAMENT
PRZED WYBORAMI • 1963 • Gryczelowska Krystyna • DOC • PLN • BEFORE THE ELECTION
PRZEDSWIATECZNY WIECZOR • 1966 • Stawinski Jerzy Stefan, Amiradzibi Helena • PLN • CHRISTMAS EVE ○ EVE OF A HOLIDAY
PRZEGLAD KULTURALNY 2/53 • 1952 • Has Wojciech J. • DCS • PLN • CULTURAL REVIEW NO.2/53
PRZEKLADANIEC • 1968 • Wajda Andrzej • MTV • PLN • ROLY-POLY ○ GRAFTING, THE
PRZEKLETA ZIEMIA • 1983 • Czekala Ryszard • PLN • DAMNED SOIL
PRZEMYSL • 1966 • Zanussi Krzysztof • PLN
PRZEOR KODECKI • 1934 • Puchalski Eduard • PLN
PRZEPRASZAM, CZY TU BIJA? • 1977 • Piwowski Marek • PLN • EXCUSE ME, IS IT HERE THEY BEAT UP PEOPLE? ○ EXCUSE ME, DO THEY BEAT HERE? ○ FOUL PLAY
PRZEPRAWA • 1988 • Turov Viktor • PLN, USS • CROSSING
PRZEPROWADZKA DOMINIKA • 1968 • Giersz Witold • ANS • PLN • DOMINIK'S FLITTING ○ REMOVAL OF DOMINIK, THE
PRZERWANY LOT • 1964 • Buczkowski Leonard • PLN • INTERRUPTED FLIGHT
PRZESLUCHANIE • 1981 • Bugajski Ryszard • PLN • INTERROGATION, THE
PRZEZYJMY TO JESZCZE RAZ • 1964 • Perski Ludwik • DOC • PLN • LET US LIVE THROUGH IT ONCE MORE
PRZHEVALSKII • 1951 • Yutkevich Sergei • USS • PRAHEVALSKY
PRZY JACIEL • 1960 • *Skolimowski Jerzy (Sc)* • PLN • FRIEND, A
PRZY TORZE KOLEJOWYM • Brzozowski Andrzej • PLN • BESIDE THE RAILWAY LINE
PRZYGODA NA MARIENSZTACIE • 1954 • Buczkowski Leonard • PLN • ADVENTURE IN WARSAW (USA) ○ ADVENTURE AT MARIENSZTAT ○ MARIENSTADT ADVENTURE, THE
PRZYGODA NOWOROCZNA • 1963 • Wohl Stanislaw • PLN • IT HAPPENED ON THE NEW YEAR DAY ○ NEW YEAR'S EVE
PRZYGODA W PASKI • 1961 • Maliszewska-Kruk Alina • ANS • PLN • ADVENTURE IN STRIPES
PRZYGODA W TERENIE • 1960 • Morgenstern Janusz • SHT • PLN • ADVENTURE IN THE COUNTRY
PRZYGODY GUCIA PINGWINA • 1953 • Nehrebecki Wladyslaw • ANS • PLN • ADVENTURES OF GUCIO THE PENGUIN, THE ○ ADVENTURES OF GUSTAVE THE PENGUIN
PRZYGODY MARYNARZA • 1958 • Giersz Witold • ANS • PLN • SAILOR'S ADVENTURES, A ○ SAILOR'S ADVENTURE, THE
PRZYGODY NA PUSTYNI • 1966 • Nehrebecki Wladyslaw • ANS • PLN • DESERT ADVENTURES
PRZYGODY SINDBADA ZEGLARZA • 1969 • Szczechura Daniel • ASS • PLN • ADVENTURES OF SINDBAD THE SAILOR, THE
PRZYGODY WESOLEGO OBIEZYSWIATA • 1968 • Nehrebecki Wladyslaw • ANS • PLN • ADVENTURES OF THE JOLLY GLOBE TROTTER, THE
PRZYJACIEL • 1963 • Nowicki Marek, Stawicki Jerzy • SHT • PLN • FRIEND, THE
PRZYJAZD RZADU JEDNOSCI NARODOWEJ DO WARSZAWY • 1945 • Bossak Jerzy • DOC • PLN • ARRIVAL OF THE GOVERNMENT OF NATIONAL UNITY IN WARSAW, THE
PRZYPADEK • 1982 • Kieslowski Krzysztof • PLN • CHANCE, THE ○ BLIND CHANCE
PRZYPIS • 1970 • Karabasz Kazimierz • DCS • PLN • FOOTNOTE, THE
PRZYSIEGLAS • 1932 • Nowina-Przybylski Jan • PLN
PSALM, THE see **ZALM** • 1966
PSEFTIS, O • 1968 • Dalianidis Ioannis • GRC • LIAR, THE
PSEUDO PRODIGAL, THE • 1913 • *Cooper Miriam* • USA
PSEUDO SULTAN • 1912 • Trimble Larry • USA
PSEXOANALISIS • 1968 • Olivera Hector • ARG
PSI A LIDE • 1970 • Schorm Evald • CZC • DOGS AND PEOPLE
PSI FACTOR • 1981 • Masters Quentin • USA
PSI KUSY • 1971 • Pojar Bretislav • ANM • CZC • PIECES OF DOG
PSI POHADKA • 1959 • Hofman Eduard • ANS • CZC • TALE OF THE DOG ○ DOG'S TALE, A
PSICANALISTA PER SIGNORA (ITL) see **CONFIDENT DE CES DAMES, LE** • 1959
PSICHA, DIE TANZERIN KATHERINA DER GROSSEN • 1922 • Milikoff Nicolai • FRG
PSIE MIASTECZKO • 1959 • Musialowicz Edward • PLN
PSIHOULA TOU KOSMOU, TA • 1967 • Tegopoulos Apostolos • GRC • CRUMBS OF THE WORLD, THE
PSIHREMIA NAPOLEON • 1968 • Filaktos Filippos • GRC • DON'T LOSE YOUR TEMPER, NAPOLEON ○ SANG-FROID, NAPOLEON
PSIQUE Y SEXO • 1965 • Cahen Enrique, Antin Manuel • ARG
PSOHLAVCI • 1954 • Fric Martin • CZC • DOG'S HEADS ○ DOGHEADS
PSOMI YIA ENA DHRAPETI • 1967 • Asimakopoulos Kostas • GRC • BREAD FOR A FUGITIVE
PSTROS • 1960 • Sramek Bohuslav • ANS • CZC • OSTRICH, THE
PSY • 1980 • de Broca Philippe • FRN
PSYCH-OUT • 1968 • Rush Richard • USA • LOVE CHILDREN, THE
PSYCHE • 1909 • *Pathe* • FRN
PSYCHE • 1947-48 • Markopoulos Gregory J. • SHT • USA
PSYCHE 59 • 1963 • Singer Alexander • UKN
PSYCHE ES NARCISZ • 1981 • Body Gabor • HNG • NARCISSUS AND PSYCHE
PSYCHEDELIC LOVE see **PSYCHEDELIC SEX KICKS** • 1967
PSYCHEDELIC SEX KICKS • 1967 • *Pad Productions* • USA • PYCHEDELICS.. KICKS ○ PSYCHEDELIC LOVE
PSYCHEDELIRIUM • 1969 • Anger Kenneth • FRN
PSYCHIATRE, SON ASILE ET SON FOU • 1972 • Manuel Pierre, Peche Jean-Jacques • BLG
PSYCHIATRIST: GOD BLESS THE CHILDREN, THE • 1970 • Spielberg Steven • TVM • USA • CHILDREN OF THE LOTUS EATERS ○ GOD BLESS THE CHILDREN
PSYCHIATRY IN RUSSIA • 1955 • Maysles Albert • DOC • USA
PSYCHIC, THE (USA) see **SETTE NOTE IN NERO** • 1978
PSYCHIC KILLER • 1975 • Danton Ray • USA • DEATH DEALER, THE
PSYCHIC LOVER, THE • 1969 • Dein Edward • ITL, FRG
PSYCHIC PHENOMENON, THE • 1916 • Ellis Robert • SHT • USA
PSYCHO • 1960 • Hitchcock Alfred • USA
PSYCHO A GO-GO! • 1965 • Adamson Al • USA • FIEND WITH THE ELECTRONIC BRAIN, THE ○ ECHO OF TERROR
PSYCHO-CIRCUS (USA) see **CIRCUS OF FEAR** • 1966
PSYCHO FROM TEXAS • 1982 • Feazall Jim • USA • BUTCHER, THE ○ EVIL/HATE/KILLER ○ HURTING, THE ○ MAMMA'S BOY, THE ○ WHEELER
PSYCHO GIRLS • 1984 • Ciccoritti Gerard • CND
PSYCHO II • 1983 • Franklin Richard • USA
PSYCHO III • 1985 • Perkins Anthony • USA
PSYCHO KILLER (UKN) see **PSYCHO LOVER, THE** • 1970
PSYCHO KILLERS see **FLESH AND THE FIENDS, THE** • 1960
PSYCHO LOVER, THE • 1970 • O'Neil Robert Vincent • USA • PSYCHO KILLER (UKN) ○ LOVING TOUCH, THE ○ LOVELY TOUCH, THE
PSYCHO MANIAC • 1968 • Borlaza Emmanuel • PHL
PSYCHO RIPPER see **SQUARTATORE DI NEW YORK, LO** • 1982
PSYCHO SEX FIEND see **SCREAM.. AND DIE!** • 1973
PSYCHO SISTERS see **SO EVIL MY SISTER** • 1973
PSYCHOCRACY, OR TO SEE OR NOT TO SEE • 1970 • Pojar Bretislav • ANS • CND • TO SEE OR NOT TO SEE
PSYCHODELIC • 1968 • Djurkovic Dejan • SHT • YGS
PSYCHODELIC GIRLS, THE see **SICODELICAS, LAS** • 1968
PSYCHODRAMA • 1969 • Piwowski Marek • DOC • PLN • PYSCHODRAMA, IN OTHER WORDS A FAIRY STORY ABOUT.. ○ PSYCHODRAMA, CYZLI BAJKA O KSIECIU I KOPCIUSZKU WYSTAWIONA W ZAKLADZIE DLA NIELETNICH DZIEWCZAT
PSYCHODRAMA, CYZLI BAJKA O KSIECIU I KOPCIUSZKU WYSTAWIONA W ZAKLADZIE DLA NIELETNICH DZIEWCZAT see **PSYCHODRAMA** • 1969
PSYCHOFARMACA • 1970 • Le Bon Patrick, Henderickx Guido • DOC • BLG
PSYCHOLOGICAL TESTING • 1962 • Kneitel Seymour • ANS • USA
PSYCHOLOGY OF FEAR, THE • 1913 • *Bateman Victory* • USA
PSYCHOMANIA • 1972 • Sharp Don • UKN • DEATH WHEELERS, THE ○ LIVING DEAD, THE ○ FROG, THE
PSYCHOMANIA see **VIOLENT MIDNIGHT** • 1963
PSYCHOMONTAGE NO.1 • 1963 • Kronhausen Phyllis, Kronhausen Eberhard • SHT • UKN
PSYCHOMONTAGE (NOW CINEMA!) see **NOW CINEMA! (PYSCHOMONTAGE)** • 1968
PSYCHOPATH, THE • 1966 • Francis Freddie • UKN • SCHIZO
PSYCHOPATH, THE • 1973 • Brown Larry • USA
PSYCHOPATH, THE see **KILLING KIND, THE** • 1973
PSYCHOS IN LOVE • 1987 • Bechard Gorman • USA
PSYCHOTRONIC MAN, THE • 1980 • Sell Jack M. • USA
PSYCHOUT FOR MURDER (USA) see **SALVARE LA FACCIA** • 1969
PSYCOSISSIMO • 1961 • Steno • ITL
PT 109 • 1963 • Martinson Leslie H. • USA
PT RAIDERS (USA) see **SHIP THAT DIED OF SHAME, THE** • 1955
PTACI KOHACI • 1965 • Lehky Vladimir • ANS • CZC • SAPIENT BIRDS, THE ○ STRANGE BIRDS ○ ODD BIRDS ○ FUNNY BIRDS
PTAK • 1968 • Czekala Ryszard • ANM • PLN • BIRD, THE
PTAKI • 1963 • Karabasz Kazimierz • DCS • PLN • BIRDS, THE
P'TANG YANG KIPPERBANG • 1982 • Apted Michael • TVM • UKN • KIPPERBANG
PTICA I CRVEK • 1977 • Grgic Zlatko • ANS • YGS • BIRD AND THE WORM, THE
P'TIT CON • 1983 • Lauzier Gerard • FRN • PETIT CON
P'TIT PARIGOT, LE • 1926 • Le Somptier Rene • FRN
P'TIT VIENT VITE, LE • 1972 • Carrier Louis-Georges • CND
P'TITE DU SIXIEME, LA • 1917 • Hervil Rene • FRN
P'TITE LILIE, LA • 1927 • Cavalcanti Alberto • FRN • PETITE LILIE, LA
P'TITE VIOLENCE, LA • 1976 • Girard Helene • MTV • CND
P'TITES TETES, LES • 1982 • Menez Bernard, Luret Jean • FRN
PTITSI • 1966 • Andonov Ivan • ANS • HNG
PTITSI I HRUTKI • 1968 • Stoyanov Georgi • ASL • BIRDS AND GREYHOUNDS
PU-SOO-MA • 1983 • Nyunt Win • BRM
PUBELITO, O EL AMOR see **PUEBLITO** • 1962
PUBERTINAGE see **PUBERTINAJE** • 1971
PUBERTINAJE • 1971 • Leder Pablo, Urias Luis, Alcaraz Jose Antonio • MXC • PUBERTINAGE
PUBERTY BLUES • 1982 • Beresford Bruce • ASL
PUBIS ANGELICAL • 1982 • de la Torre Raul • ARG
PUBLIC ACTIVITY see **FURUSATO HARETE** • 1934
PUBLIC AFFAIR, A • 1962 • Girard Bernard • USA
PUBLIC APPROVAL • 1916 • Kent Leon D. • SHT • USA
PUBLIC BE DAMNED • 1917 • Taylor Stanner E. V. • USA
PUBLIC BE HANGED, THE (UKN) see **WORLD GONE MAD, THE** • 1933
PUBLIC BE SOLD, THE see **NO MARRIAGE TIES** • 1933
PUBLIC BENEFACTOR, A see **KIZU DARAKE NO SANGA** • 1964
PUBLIC COWBOY NO.1 • 1937 • Kane Joseph • USA
PUBLIC DEB NUMBER ONE • 1940 • Ratoff Gregory • USA
PUBLIC DEFENDER • 1917 • King Burton L. • USA
PUBLIC DEFENDER, THE • 1931 • Ruben J. Walter • USA • MILLION DOLLAR SWINDLE, THE ○ RECKONER, THE

PUBLIC DISGRACE see **OYAKE AKAHACHI** • 1937
PUBLIC ENEMIES • 1941 • Rogell Albert S. • USA
PUBLIC ENEMY, THE • 1931 • Wellman William A. • USA • ENEMIES OF THE PUBLIC (UKN)
PUBLIC ENEMY NO.1 see **ENNEMI PUBLIC NO.1** • 1953
PUBLIC ENEMY NUMBER ONE • 1981 • Bradbury David • DOC • USA
PUBLIC ENEMY'S WIFE, THE • 1936 • Grinde Nick • USA • G-MAN'S WIFE (UKN)
PUBLIC EYE, THE • 1972 • Reed Carol • USA, UKN • FOLLOW ME (UKN)
PUBLIC GHOST NO.1 • 1935 • Parrott Charles, Law Harold • SHT • USA
PUBLIC HERO NUMBER ONE • 1935 • Ruben J. Walter • USA
PUBLIC IDEAL, THE see **MABODET EL GAMAHIR** • 1967
PUBLIC LIFE OF HENRY THE NINTH, THE • 1935 • Mainwaring Bernerd • UKN
PUBLIC MENACE, THE • 1935 • Kenton Erle C. • USA
PUBLIC NUISANCE NO.1 • 1936 • Varnel Marcel • UKN
PUBLIC NUISANCE NO.1 see **PEPPER** • 1936
PUBLIC OPINION • 1916 • Reicher Frank • USA
PUBLIC OPINION • 1935 • Strayer Frank • USA
PUBLIC OPINION • 1940 • Rotha Paul • DOC • UKN
PUBLIC OPINION see **WOMAN OF PARIS, A** • 1923
PUBLIC OPINION see **THRU DIFFERENT EYES** • 1929
PUBLIC OPINION see **OPINIAO PUBLICA, A** • 1967
PUBLIC PAYS, THE • 1936 • Taggart Errol • SHT • USA
PUBLIC PIGEON NO.1 • 1957 • McLeod Norman Z. • USA
PUBLIC PROSECUTOR see **PROKUROR** • 1917
PUBLIC PROSECUTOR, THE see **NAEB EL AM, EL** • 1945
PUBLIC STENOGRAPHER • 1933 • Collins Lewis D. • USA • PRIVATE AFFAIRS (UKN)
PUBLIC VOICE, THE see **OFFENTLICHE ROST, DEN** • 1988
PUBLIC WEDDING • 1937 • Grinde Nick • USA
PUBLICITE DESTINEE AUX ENFANTS, LA • 1973 • Lavoie Richard • SHT • CND
PUBLICITY MADNESS • 1927 • Ray Albert • USA
PUBLICITY PAYS • 1924 • McCarey Leo • SHT • USA
PUBLIC'S RIGHT TO KNOW, THE • 1974 • Narizzano Silvio • UKN
PUBS AND BEACHES • 1966 • Williams Richard • ANS • UKN
PUCANJ • 1972 • Gapo Branko • YGS • SHOT, THE
PUCANJ • 1978 • Golik Kreso • YGS • SHOT, THE
PUCCINI • 1953 • Gallone Carmine • ITL • HIS TWO LOVES
PUCCINI • 1988 • Kershner Irvin
PUCE A L'OREILLE, LA (FRN) see **FLEA IN HER EAR, A** • 1968
PUCE ET LE PRIVE, LA • 1981 • Kay Roger* • FRN
PUCE MOMENT • 1949 • Anger Kenneth • SHT • USA
PUCE WOMEN • 1948 • Anger Kenneth • USA
PUCERONS, LES • 1955 • Tadie, Lacoste • SHT • FRN
PUCES DE SABLE, LES • 1981 • Laguionie Jean-Francois • ANS • FRN
PUCHAR TATR • 1948 • Has Wojciech J. • DCS • PLN • TATRA CUP, THE
PUCK HETEA JAG • 1951 • Bauman Schamyl • SWD • MY NAME IS PUCK
PUCK'S PRANKS ON A SUBURBANITE • 1906 • Booth W. R.? • UKN
PUDDIN' HEAD • 1941 • Santley Joseph • USA • JUDY GOES TO TOWN (UKN)
PUDDIN' HEAD WILSON see **PUDD'NHEAD WILSON** • 1916
PUDDING AND PIE • 1968 • Blair Leslie • UKN
PUDDING THIEVES, THE • 1967 • Davies Brian • ASL
PUDDLE, MUDDLE, RIDDLE • 1947 • Nieter Hans M. • UKN
PUDDLE PRANKS • 1931 • *Iwerks Ub (P)* • ANS • USA
PUDDLETON POLICE, THE • 1914 • Stow Percy • UKN
PUDD'NHEAD WILSON • 1916 • Reicher Frank • USA • PUDDIN' HEAD WILSON
PUDD'NHEAD WILSON • 1984 • Bridges Alan • TVM • USA
PUDDY THE PUP • 1930 • *Audiocinema* • ASS • USA
PUDDY THE PUP AND THE GYPSIES • 1936 • *Terry Paul (P)* • ANS • USA
PUDDY'S CORONATION • 1937 • Davis Mannie, Gordon George • ANS • USA
PUDELNACKT IN OBERBAYERN • 1968 • Albin Hans • FRG
PUDEUR SINGULIERE, UNE see **DIABLE AU COEUR, LE** • 1977
PUDGE see **UNEXPECTED FATHER, THE** • 1932
PUDGY AND THE LOST KITTEN • 1938 • Fleischer Dave • ANS • USA
PUDGY IN THRILLS AND CHILLS • 1938 • Fleischer Dave • ANS • USA
PUDGY PICKS A FIGHT • 1937 • Fleischer Dave • ANS • USA
PUDGY TAKES A BOW-WOW • 1937 • Fleischer Dave • ANS • USA
PUDGY THE WATCHMAN • 1938 • Fleischer Dave • ANS • USA
PUDR A BENZIN • 1931 • Honzl Jindrich • CZC • POWDER AND PETROL
PUEBLERINA • 1948 • Fernandez Emilio • MXC
PUEBLITO • 1962 • Fernandez Emilio • MXC • PUBELITO, O EL AMOR
PUEBLO • 1973 • Page Anthony • TVM • USA
PUEBLO ARMADO see **PUEBLOS EN ARMAS** • 1961
PUEBLO, CANTO Y ESPERANZA • 1954 • Soler Julian, Crevenna Alfredo B., Gonzalez Rogelio A. • MXC
PUEBLO CHICO • 1974 • Eguino Antonio • BLV • SMALL TOWN
PUEBLO DE LATA • 1973 • Guedez Jesus Enrique • DOC • VNZ • PEOPLE OF THE SLUMS
PUEBLO DE MADERA • 1989 • de la Riva Juan Antonio • MXC • LUMBER TOWN
PUEBLO DE ODIOS • 1969 • Ortega Juan J. • MXC
PUEBLO DE PROSCRITOS see **FUGITIVOS** • 1955
PUEBLO EN ARMAS • 1958 • Contreras Torres Miguel • MXC
PUEBLO FANTASMA, EL • 1963 • Crevenna Alfredo B. • MXC • GHOST TOWN, THE
PUEBLO LEGEND, A • 1912 • Griffith D. W. • SHT • USA
PUEBLO PLUTO • 1949 • Hannah Jack • ANS • USA
PUEBLO QUIETO • 1954 • Peon Ramon • MXC
PUEBLO ROMANCE, A see **HOPI LEGEND, A** • 1913
PUEBLO SIN DIOS, EL • 1954 • Cardona Rene • MXC
PUEBLO TERROR • 1931 • Neitz Alvin J. • USA • PARADISE VALLEY (UKN)
PUEBLOS AND APACHES • 1914 • Miles Mr. • USA
PUEBLOS EN ARMAS • 1961 • Ivens Joris • SHT • CUB • ARMED PEOPLE, AN (USA) ○ CUBA, PUEBLO ARMADO ○ PUEBLO ARMADO ○ ARMED NATION, AN
PUEN-PAENG • 1983 • Songsri Cherd • THL
PUENTE, EL • 1977 • Bardem Juan Antonio • SPN • BRIDGE, THE ○ LONG WEEKEND, THE
PUENTE, EL • 1985 • Urquieta Jose Luis • MXC • BRIDGE, THE
PUENTE AL PROGRESSO • Roncal Hugo • DCS • BLV
PUENTE ALSINA • 1935 • Ferreyra Jose • ARG
PUENTE DE COPLAS • 1961 • Alcocer Santos • SPN
PUENTE DE LA MUERTE, EL • 1910 • de Chomon Segundo • SPN
PUENTE DE LA PAZ, EL • 1957 • Salvia Rafael J. • SPN
PUENTE DEL CASTIGO, EL • 1945 • Delgado Miguel M. • MXC
PUENTE DEL DIABLO, EL • 1955 • Seto Javier • SPN
PUENTE SOBRE EL ELBA, EL (SPN) see **QUEL MALEDETTO PONTE SULL'ELBA** • 1968
PUENTE SOBRE EL TIEMPO, UN • 1963 • Merino Jose Luis • SPN
PUERTA, LA • 1968 • Alcoriza Luis • SHT • MXC • DOOR, THE
PUERTA ABIERTA, LA • 1956 • Ardavin Cesar • SPN
PUERTA CERADA • 1939 • Saslavsky Luis • ARG • CLOSED DOOR (USA)
PUERTA FALSA, LA • 1976 • Sbert Toni • MXC
PUERTA.. JOVEN • 1949 • Delgado Miguel M. • MXC
PUERTA NEGRA, LA • 1989 • Urquieta Jose Luis • MXC • BLACK DOOR, THE
PUERTAS DEL PARAISO, LAS • 1970 • *Marte* • MXC
PUERTAS DEL PRESIDIO, LAS • 1949 • Gomez Muriel Emilio • MXC
PUERTO DE BARCELONA, EL • 1968 • Comeron Luis Jose • SHT • SPN
PUERTO DE LOS SIETE VICIOS, EL • 1951 • Ugarte Eduardo • MXC
PUERTO DE TENTACION • 1950 • Cardona Rene • MXC
PUERTO NUEVO • 1936 • Amadori Luis Cesar, Soffici Mario • ARG
PUFF BALL see **ROYKSOPP** • 1986
PUFNSTUF • 1970 • Morse Hollingsworth • USA • H.R. PUFNSTUF
PUGACHEV • 1938 • Petrov-Bytov P. • USS
PUGACHOV • 1979 • Saltykov Alexei • USS
PUGILATORI • 1951 • Zurlini Valerio • DCS • ITL
PUGILIST, THE see **KNOCK OUT, THE** • 1914
PUGILIST AND THE GIRL, THE • 1912 • *Roland Ruth* • USA
PUGILISTIC POTTS • 1915 • Read James • UKN
PUGILIST'S CHILD, THE • 1910 • *Powers* • USA
PUGILIST'S ROMANCE, A see **KIDNAPPED PUGILIST, THE** • 1914
PUGNI DI ROCCO, I • 1972 • Artale Lorenzo • ITL
PUGNI, DOLLARI E SPINACI • 1978 • Salvi Emimmo • ITL
PUGNI IN TASCA, I • 1965 • Bellocchio Marco • ITL • FIST IN HIS POCKET (USA) ○ FISTS IN THE POCKET
PUGNI, PUPE E MARINAI • 1961 • Danza Daniele • ITL
PUGOWITZA • 1980 • Brauer Jurgen • GDR
PUISHKA see **PYSHKA** • 1934
PUISSANCE MILITAIRE DE LA FRANCE, LA • 1914 • Desfontaines Henri • FRN
PUITS AUX TROIS VERITES, LE • 1961 • Villiers Francois • FRN, ITL • POZZO DELLE TRE VERITA, IL (ITL) ○ THREE FACES OF SIN (USA) ○ TROIS VERITES ○ THREE SINNERS ○ THREE TRUTHS IN THE WELL
PUITS DE JACOB, LES • 1926 • Jose Edward • FRN • DAUGHTER OF ISRAEL (USA)
PUITS DE LA PRIVATION, LES see **BI'R AL-HIRMAN** • 1969
PUITS EN FLAMMES • 1936 • Tourjansky Victor • FRN • VILLE ANATOL ○ ANNAPOLI
PUITS ENCHANTE, LE see **PUITS FANTASTIQUE, LE** • 1903
PUITS ET LE PENDULE, LE • 1912 • Desfontaines Henri • FRN • PIT AND THE PENDULUM, THE
PUITS ET LE PENDULE, LE • 1963 • Astruc Alexandre • FRN • PIT AND THE PENDULUM, THE (USA)
PUITS FANTASTIQUE, LE • 1903 • Melies Georges • FRN • ENCHANTED WELL, THE (USA) ○ PUITS ENCHANTE, LE
PUITS MITOYEN, LES • 1913 • Tourneur Maurice • FRN
PUJARI • 1947 • Aspi • IND
PUJARIN • 1936 • *Sircar B. N. (P)* • IND
PUK OKO SVIJETA • 1964 • Jovanovic • YGS • TRIP AROUND THE WORLD
PUKKELRYGGEDE, DEN see **KAERLIGHEDSLAENGEL** • 1915
PUKOTINA RAJA • 1961 • Pogacic Vladimir • YGS • HEAVEN WITH NO LOVE
PUKOVNIKOVICA • 1973 • Kadijevic Djordje • YGS • COLONEL'S WIFE, THE
PULAKAPINA • 1977 • Niskanen Mikko • FNL • HORSE REBELLION, THE
PULAWY, GODZINA ZERO • 1967 • Wionczek Roman • DOC • PLN • PULAWY ZERO HOUR
PULAWY ZERO HOUR see **PULAWY, GODZINA ZERO** • 1967
PULCHERIE ET SES MEUBLES • 1916 • Cohl Emile • ANS • FRN
PULCINELLA • 1924 • Roudes Gaston • FRN
PULCINELLA • 1973 • Luzzati Emmanuele • ANM • ITL
PULCINELLA CETRULA D'ACERRA • 1961 • Attanasi Antonio • ITL
PULGA EN LA OREJA, LA • 1981 • Guerrero Francisco • ARG • FLEA IN HER EAR, A
PULGA NA BALANCA, UMA • 1953 • Salce Luciano • BRZ
PULGARCITO • 1910 • de Chomon Segundo • SPN • TOM THUMB
PULGARCITO • 1958 • Cardona Rene • MXC • TOM THUMB (USA)
PULL FOR THE SHORE, SAILOR • 1911 • *Sawyer Laura* • USA
PULL MY DAISY • 1959 • Frank Robert, Leslie Alfred • SHT • USA
PULL OF THE SOUTH, THE • 1963 • Watson Patrick • DOC • CND
PULL-OVER ROUGE, LE • 1979 • Drach Michel • FRN • RED SWEATER, THE
PULLING A BONE • 1930 • Bretherton Howard • USA
PULLING DOWN A WALL see **DEMOLITION D'UN MUR** • 1895
PULLING IT OFF see **HE'S MY GIRL** • 1987
PULLMAN BLUNDER, A • 1918 • Hutchinson Craig • SHT • USA
PULLMAN BRIDE, THE • 1917 • Badger Clarence • USA
PULLMAN MYSTERY, THE • 1917 • Swickard Charles • SHT • USA
PULLMAN PARTNERS see **LATEST FROM PARIS, THE** • 1927
PULLMAN PORTER, THE • 1919 • *Arbuckle Roscoe* • SHT • USA
PULMAN NIGHTMARE, A • 1913 • *Thanhouser* • USA
PULNOCNI DOBRODRUZETVI see **PULNOCNI PRIHODA** • 1960
PULNOCNI KOLONA • 1972 • Novak Ivo • CZC • MIDNIGHT TRAIN
PULNOCNI PRIHODA • 1960 • Pojar Bretislav • ANS • CZC • LITTLE TRAIN (USA) ○ MIDNIGHT ADVENTURE ○ IT HAPPENED ○ MIDNIGHT EVENT, THE ○ PULNOCNI DOBRODRUZETVI ○ MIDNIGHT INCIDENT, A
PULP • 1967 • Green Bruce • USA
PULP • 1972 • Hodges Mike • UKN, USA
PULPO HUMANO, EL • 1933 • Bell Jorge • MXC • HUMAN OCTOPUS, THE
PULQUE PETE AND THE OPERA TROUPE • 1912 • *Brennan John E.* • USA
PULSATING GIANT • 1971 • Benegal Shyam • DCS • IND
PULSE • 1969 • Spoecker Peter D. • ANS • USA
PULSE • 1988 • Golding Paul • USA
PULSE OF LIFE, THE • 1917 • Ingram Rex • USA
PULSE OF MADNESS, THE • 1917 • Calvert E. H. • SHT • USA
PULSSCHLAG DES MEERES • 1938 • Rikli Martin • FRG • ETERNAL TIDAL RACE
PULTUSK CODE, THE see **KODEKS PULTUSKI** • 1958
PULVERIZER, THE • 1909 • *Pathe* • USA
PULVERSCHNEE NACH UEBERSEE • 1956 • Leitner Hermann • FRG
PUM • 1979 • Estrada Jose • MXC
PUMA, EL • 1958 • Cardona Rene • MXC
PUMA ACTION, THE see **DAIHAO MEIZHOUBAO** • 1988
PUMA MAN, THE see **UOMO PUMA, L'** • 1980
PUMAMAN, THE see **UOMO PUMA, L'** • 1980
PUMMARO • 1990 • Placido Michele • ITL
PUMP PRIMER • 1970 • *Stacey Dist.* • USA
PUMP TROUBLE • 1953 • Deitch Gene • SHT • USA
PUMP UP THE VOLUME • 1990 • Moyle Allan • USA
PUMPING IRON • 1977 • Butler George, Fiore Robert • DOC • USA
PUMPING IRON II: THE WOMEN • 1985 • Butler George • DOC • USA
PUMPKIN see **KABOCHA** • 1928
PUMPKIN EATER, THE • 1964 • Clayton Jack • UKN
PUMPKIN RACE, THE see **COURSE AUX POTIRONS, LA** • 1907
PUMPKINHEAD • 1988 • Winston Stan • USA • VENGEANCE, THE DEMON
PUMPS • 1913 • Trimble Larry • USA
PUNAHILKKA • 1968 • Berglund Timo • FNL • LITTLE RED RIDING HOOD
PUNAINEN VIIVA • 1959 • Kassila Matti • FNL • RED LINE, THE
PUNARJANMA • 1926 • *Indian Kinema Arts* • IND • INCARNATION (USA)
PUNARJANMA • 1932 • *Sircar B. N. (P)* • IND
PUNASHA • 1961 • Sen Mrinal • IND • OVER AGAIN ○ PUNNASCHA
PUNATUKKA • 1970 • Kurkvaara Maunu • FNL • REDHEAD
PUNCH AND JODY • 1974 • Shear Barry • TVM • USA
PUNCH AND JUDO • 1951 • Sparber I. • ANS • USA
PUNCH AND JUDY • 1898 • *European Blair Camera Co* • UKN
PUNCH AND JUDY • 1901 • *Paul R. W.* • UKN
PUNCH AND JUDY • 1906 • Green Tom • UKN
PUNCH AND JUDY • 1928 • *De Forest Phonofilms* • SHT • UKN
PUNCH AND JUDY see **ANARCHIE CHEZ GUIGNOL, L'** • 1906
PUNCH AND JUDY see **RAVICKARNA** • 1966
PUNCH AND JUDY MAN, THE • 1962 • Summers Jeremy • UKN
PUNCH AND JUDY SHOW, A • 1903 • *Warwick Trading Co* • UKN
PUNCH DRUNKS • 1934 • Breslow Lou • SHT • USA
PUNCH IN THE NOSE, A • 1925 • Roach Hal • SHT • USA
PUNCH OR KARATE, A see **SUNTOK O KARATE** • 1968
PUNCH THE CLOCK • 1922 • Beaudine William • USA
PUNCH THE CLOCK • 1988 • Schlagman Eric L. • USA
PUNCH THE MAGICIAN see **KASPAREK KOUZELNIKEM** • 1927
PUNCH TRUNK • 1953 • Jones Charles M. • ANS • USA
PUNCH-UP IN ISTANBUL see **JERK A ISTAMBUL** • 1967
PUNCHER'S LAW, THE • 1911 • *Essanay* • USA
PUNCHER'S NEW LOVE, THE • 1911 • *Anderson Broncho Billy* • USA
PUNCHI BABA • 1968 • Liyanage Tissa • SLN • LITTLE ONE
PUNCHLINE • 1987 • Seltzer David • USA
PUNCHY COWPUNCHERS • 1950 • Bernds Edward • SHT • USA
PUNCHY DE LEON • 1950 • Hubley John • ANS • USA
PUNCHY PAUNCHO • 1951 • Goodwins Leslie • SHT • USA
PUNCHY POOCH • 1962 • Hannah Jack • ANS • USA
PUNCT SI DE LA CAPAT • 1987 • Visarion Alexa • RMN • STARTING OVER
PUNCTURE PROOF SOCK MAN, THE • 1914 • *Lubin* • USA
PUNCTURED PRINCE, A • 1923 • Fay Hugh • USA
PUNISHED • 1900 • *Paul R. W.* • UKN
PUNISHER, THE • 1989 • Goldblatt Mark • ASL
PUNISHMENT • 1974 • Madsen Olga • NTH
PUNISHMENT see **MOJAZAT** • 1974
PUNISHMENT, THE • 1912 • Griffith D. W. • USA
PUNISHMENT, THE • 1917 • *Leonard Robert* • USA
PUNISHMENT, THE see **OSINDA** • 1976
PUNISHMENT BATTALION (USA) see **STRAFBATAILLON 999** • 1960
PUNISHMENT EXPEDITION • 1971 • Magyar Dezso • HNG
PUNISHMENT ISLAND see **SHOKEI NO SHIMA** • 1966
PUNISHMENT OF ANNE, THE • 1975 • Metzger Radley H. • USA
PUNISHMENT PARK • 1971 • Watkins Peter • USA
PUNISHMENT ROOM see **SHOKEI NO HEYA** • 1956
PUNITION, LA • 1963 • Rouch Jean • DOC • FRN
PUNITION, LA • 1972 • Jolivet Pierre-Alain • FRN, ITL

PUNITION, LA see **IQAB, AL–** • 1947
PUNITION, LA see **TRAFIC DE FILLES** • 1967
PUNK IN LONDON • 1978 • Buld Wolfgang • DOC • FRG
PUNK ROCK MOVIE • 1978 • Letts Don • UKN
PUNKS KOMMT AUS AMERIKA • 1935 • Martin Karl Heinz • FRG
PUNKTCHEN UND ANTON • 1953 • Engel Thomas • AUS
PUNKTUR, PUNKTUR, COMMA, STRIK • 1980 • Jonsson Thorsteinn • ICL • DOT, DOT, COMMA, DASH
PUNKTY ZA POCHODZENIS • 1983 • Trzeciak Franciszek • PLN • POINTS FOR PARENTAGE
PUNNAPRA VAYALAR • 1968 • Kunchako • IND
PUNNASCHA see **PUNASHA** • 1961
PUNOS DE HIERRO • 1927 • Garcia Moreno Gabriel • MXC
PUNOS DE ROCA • 1959 • Baledon Rafael • MXC
PUNOS FRENTE AL CANON • Ancelovici Gaston, Lubbert Orlando • DOC • FISTS BEFORE THE CANNON
PUNT'A A CTYRLISTEK • 1954 • Weiss Jiri • CZC • PUNTA AND THE FOUR–LEAF CLOVER ○ DOGGY AND THE FOUR
PUNTA AND THE FOUR–LEAF CLOVER see **PUNT'A A CTYRLISTEK** • 1954
PUNTANG TRILOGY see **POON TANG TRILOGY, THE**
PUNTER'S MISHAP, THE • 1900 • Hepworth Cecil M. • UKN
PUNTILA • 1970 • Syberberg Hans-Jurgen • SHT • FRG
PUNTILA see **HERR PUNTILA UND SEIN KNECHT MATTI** • 1955
PUNTO DE FUGA • Ruiz Raul • PRT, FRN • POINT OF FLIGHT
PUNTO DEBIL • 1974 • Carbonell Maria L. • VNZ • WEAK POINT
PUNY EXPRESS • 1951 • Lantz Walter • ANS • USA
PUNY SOUL OF PETER RAND, THE • 1915 • Grandon Francis J. • USA
PUNYAL NA GINTO • PHL
PUO UNA MORTA RIVIVERE PER AMORE? see **VENUS IN FURS** • 1970
PUP ON A PICNIC • 1955 • Hanna William, Barbera Joseph • ANS • USA
PUP THE PEACEMAKER • 1915 • King Burton L. • USA
PUPA, LA • 1963 • Orlandini Giuseppe • ITL • EVERY NIGHT OF THE WEEK (UKN) ○ DOLL, THE
PUPA DEL GANGSTER, LA • 1975 • Capitani Giorgio • ITL, FRN • PEPEE DU GANGSTER, LA ○ GANGSTER'S DOLL, THE ○ GET RITA ○ GUN MOLL ○ LADY OF THE EVENING ○ POOPSIE AND COMPANY
PUPIL AND THE PROFESSOR, THE see **TILMIZA WAL OSSTAZ, AL** • 1968
PUPIL GERBER, THE see **SCHULER GERBER, DER** • 1981
PUPILA AL VIENTO • 1949 • Gras Enrico • URG • EYE UPON THE WIND
PUPILLA NELL'OMBRA • 1919 • Bonnard Mario • ITL
PUPILS OF NIKOLAI STREET SCHOOL DURING BREAK • 1904 • FNL
PUPO DAL K.O., IL • 1957 • Saglietto Paolo • ITL
PUPPCHEN • 1918 • Moest Hubert • FRG
PUPPE, DIE • 1919 • Lubitsch Ernst • FRG • DOLL, THE
PUPPE VON LUNAPARK, DIE • 1924 • Speyer Jaap • FRG
PUPPEN DES TODES • 1919 • Bruck Reinhard • FRG
PUPPENFEE, DIE • 1936 • Emo E. W. • AUS
PUPPENHEIM, EIN • 1922 • Viertel Berthold • FRG
PUPPENKONIGIN, DIE • 1924 • Righelli Gennaro • FRG
PUPPENMACHER VON KIANG–NING, DER • 1923 • Wiene Robert • FRG • TRAGIKOMODIE
PUPPENSPIELER, DER • 1945 • Harlan Veit • FRG • POLE POPPENSPALER
PUPPET, THE see **POUPEE, LA** • 1899
PUPPET, THE see **HAMPELMANN, DER** • 1930
PUPPET AND PIKUS, THE see **PAJACYK I PIKUS** • 1959
PUPPET CROWN, THE • 1915 • Melford George • USA
PUPPET, DOG AND FLAME, THE see **PAJACYK, PIESEK I PLOMIEN** • 1959
PUPPET LOVE • 1944 • Kneitel Seymour • ANS • USA
PUPPET MAN, THE • 1921 • Crane Frank H. • UKN • PUPPETS OF FATE
PUPPET MASTER see **PUPPETMASTER** • 1989
PUPPET MURDER CASE, THE • 1935 • *Mintz Charles (P)* • ANS • USA
PUPPET OF WARSAW, THE see **ZOLNIERZ ZWYCIESTWA** • 1953
PUPPET ON A CHAIN • 1970 • Reeve Geoffrey, Sharp Don • UKN
PUPPET PARADE, THE • 1956 • Tyrlova Hermina • ANM • CZC
PUPPET PEOPLE see **CENTRAL BAZAAR** • 1973
PUPPET, PIKUS AND THE MOON, THE see **PAJACYK, PIKUS I KSIEZYC** • 1960
PUPPET PLAYER, THE see **ARAGOUZE, EL** • 1988
PUPPET SHOW • 1936 • Lantz Walter • ANS • USA
PUPPETMASTER • 1989 • Schmoeller David • USA • PUPPET MASTER
PUPPETOON MOVIE, THE • 1987 • *Liebovit Arnold* • CMP • USA
PUPPETOONS • 1943-47 • *Pal George (P)* • ANS • USA
PUPPETRY • 1947 • *Encyclopaedia Britannica* • ANS • USA
PUPPETRY see **BOMMALATTAM** • 1968
PUPPETS • 1916 • *Komedy* • SHT • USA
PUPPETS • 1916 • Browning Tod • USA
PUPPETS • 1926 • Archainbaud George • USA
PUPPET'S DREAM, THE • 1958 • Sens Al • ANS • CND
PUPPET'S HOUR, THE • 1912 • *Halliday Jack* • USA
PUPPET'S NIGHTMARE, THE see **CAUCHEMAR DU FANTOCHE, LE** • 1908
PUPPETS OF FATE • 1912 • Powell Frank • UKN
PUPPETS OF FATE • 1916 • McGill Lawrence • SHT • USA
PUPPETS OF FATE • 1921 • Fitzgerald Dallas M. • USA • SORRENTINA ○ TONY AMERICA
PUPPETS OF FATE • 1933 • Cooper George A. • UKN • WOLVES OF THE UNDERWORLD (USA)
PUPPETS OF FATE see **PUPPET MAN, THE** • 1921
PUPPIES see **STENATA** • 1957
PUPPY AND KITTEN WRITE A LETTER, THE see **JAK PEJSEK A KOCICKOU PSALI PSANI** • 1954
PUPPY AND THE KITTEN MAKE A CAKE, THE see **JAK PEJSEK S KOCICKOU DELALI DORT** • 1951
PUPPY AND THE KITTEN WASH THE FLOOR, THE see **JAK PEJSEK A KOLICKA MYLI PODLAHU** • 1950
PUPPY EXPRESS • 1927 • Lantz Walter • ANS • USA
PUPPY LOVE • 1917 • Stonehouse Ruth • SHT • USA
PUPPY LOVE • 1919 • Neill R. William • USA
PUPPY LOVE • 1932 • *Iwerks Ub (P)* • ANS • USA
PUPPY LOVE • 1933 • Jackson Wilfred • ANS • USA
PUPPY LOVE PANIC, A • 1919 • Davis James • SHT • USA
PUPPY–LOVE SINGERS, THE see **KOIBITO TO YONDE MITAI** • 1968
PUPPY LOVETIME • 1926 • Cline Eddie • SHT • USA
PUPPY TALE • 1954 • Hanna William, Barbera Joseph • ANS • USA
PUPPY'S ADVENTURES, THE see **PRIHODY MALEHO STENATKA** • 1960
PUPS' CHRISTMAS, THE • 1936 • Ising Rudolf • ANS • USA
PUPS IS PUPS • 1930 • McGowan Robert • USA
PUP'S JOKES • 1960 • Nehrebecki Wladyslaw • ANS • PLN
PUPS ON A RAMPAGE • 1900 • Young James • USA
PUPS' PICNIC • 1936 • Ising Rudolf • ANS • USA
PUR SANG • 1931 • Autant-Lara Claude • SHT • FRN
PUR–SANG ARABE, LE • 1962 • Harzallah Ahmed • DCS • TNS
PURA SANGRE • 1982 • Torres Miguel • CUB • PURE BLOOD
PURA VERDAD, LA • 1932 • Romero Manuel • SPN
PURA VIDA! • 1955 • Martinez Solares Gilberto • MXC
PURAN BHAGAT • 1933 • Bose Debaki • IND • DEVOTEE, THE
PURCHASE PRICE, THE • 1913 • *Nestor* • USA
PURCHASE PRICE, THE • 1916 • King Burton L. • SHT • USA
PURCHASE PRICE, THE • 1932 • Wellman William A. • USA • MUD LARK ○ NIGHT FLOWER, THE
PURE S.. • 1975 • Deling Bert • ASL
PURE, THE see **PALAMANASULU** • 1968
PURE AIR see **FRILUFT** • 1959
PURE AMERICA see **TISZTA AMERIKA** • 1987
PURE AND SIMPLE • 1917 • *Watson Harry Jr.* • USA
PURE AND SIMPLE • 1930 • Foster Lewis R. • SHT • USA
PURE AS A LILY (UKN) see **COME UNA ROSA AL NASO** • 1976
PURE BEAUTE • 1954 • Alexeieff Alexandre • SHT • FRN
PURE BLOOD see **PURA SANGRE** • 1982
PURE GOLD • 1910 • *Kalem* • USA
PURE GOLD • 1914 • Davis Ulysses • USA
PURE GOLD AND DROSS • 1913 • *Rex* • USA
PURE GOLD PARTNER, A • 1915 • Reynolds Lynn • USA
PURE GRIT • 1923 • Ross Nat • USA • TEXAS RANGER, A
PURE HELL OF ST. TRINIANS, THE • 1960 • Launder Frank • UKN
PURE IN MIND, THE see **BOY SLAVES** • 1939
PURE LOVE see **JUNJO** • 1930
PURE MEN see **PUROS HOMBRES** • 1977
PURE WHEAT see **TRIGO LIMPIO** • 1967
PURELY PHYSICAL • 1982 • Thornberg Billy • USA
PUREZA • 1940 • de Garcia Eduardo Chianca • BRZ
PURGATION, THE • 1910 • Griffith D. W. • USA
PURGATORIO see **SKARSELD** • 1975
PURGATORIO, IL • 1911 • *Helios* • ITL • PURGATORY (USA)
PURGATORY • 1988 • Denton Lawrence • USA
PURGATORY see **SKARSELD** • 1975
PURGATORY EROICA see **RENGOKU EROICA** • 1970
PURGATORY (USA) see **PURGATORIO, IL** • 1911
PURGE, LA • 1903 • Zecca Ferdinand • FRN
PURIFIED BY FIRE see **AGNI PUTHRI** • 1967
PURIMSPIELER, DER • 1937 • Nowina-Przybylski Jan
PURITAIN, LE • 1937 • Musso Jeff • FRN • PURITAN, THE
PURITAN, THE • 1912 • *Art Films* • UKN
PURITAN, THE • 1914 • Ince John • USA
PURITAN, THE see **PURITAIN, LE** • 1937
PURITAN CONSCIENCE, A • 1915 • *Flamingo* • USA
PURITAN COURTSHIP, A • 1911 • *Pates Gwendolyn* • USA
PURITAN EPISODE, A • 1913 • *Eclair* • USA
PURITAN MAID, THE • 1911 • Martinek H. O. • UKN
PURITAN MAID AND THE ROYALIST REFUGEE, THE • 1908 • Stow Percy • UKN
PURITAN PASSIONS • 1923 • Tuttle Frank • USA • SCARECROW, THE
PURITANS, THE • 1924 • Tuttle Frank • SHT • USA
PURITANS AND INDIANS • 1911 • *Kalem* • USA
PURITY • 1916 • Berger Rea • USA
PURITY AND AFTER • 1978 • Brakhage Stan • SHT • USA
PURITY SQUAD • 1945 • Kress Harold F. • SHT • USA
PURLIE VICTORIOUS see **GONE ARE THE DAYS!** • 1963
PURLOINED MAP, THE see **BIJIN GUMO** • 1960
PURLOINED PUP, THE • 1946 • Nichols Charles • ANS • USA
PURO SICCOME UN ANGELO PAPA MI FECE MONACO • 1969 • Grimaldi Gianni • ITL
PUROS HOMBRES • 1977 • Cortez Cesar • VNZ • PURE MEN
PUROSKAR • 1984 • Jaman C. B. • BNG • PRIZE, THE
PURPLE AND FINE LINEN see **THREE HOURS** • 1927
PURPLE CIPHER, THE • 1920 • Bennett Chester • USA
PURPLE DAWN • 1923 • Seeling Charles R. • USA
PURPLE DAWN, THE • Chinh Kieu • VTN
PURPLE DEATH FROM OUTER SPACE • 1940 • Beebe Ford, Taylor Ray • USA
PURPLE DRESS, THE • 1918 • Justice Martin • USA
PURPLE GANG, THE • 1960 • McDonald Frank • USA
PURPLE HARVEST, THE see **VINTAGE, THE** • 1957
PURPLE HAZE • 1983 • Morris David Burton • USA
PURPLE HAZE (UKN) see **MORE AMERICAN GRAFFITI** • 1979
PURPLE HEART, THE • 1944 • Milestone Lewis • USA
PURPLE HEART DIARY • 1951 • Quine Richard • USA • NO TIME FOR TEARS (UKN)
PURPLE HEARTS see **PURPLE HEARTS: A VIETNAM LOVE STORY** • 1983
PURPLE HEARTS: A VIETNAM LOVE STORY • 1983 • Furie Sidney J. • USA • PURPLE HEARTS
PURPLE HIGHWAY, THE • 1923 • Kolker Henry • USA
PURPLE HILLS, THE • 1915 • MacMackin Archer • USA
PURPLE HILLS, THE • 1961 • Dexter Maury • USA
PURPLE LADY, THE • 1916 • Lessey George A. • USA
PURPLE LILY, THE • 1918 • Kelson George • USA • DEVIL'S DICE, THE
PURPLE LINE, THE • 1960 • Ruppel Karl-Ludwig • ANS • FRG
PURPLE MASK, THE • 1917 • Ford Francis, Cunard Grace • SRL • USA
PURPLE MASK, THE • 1955 • Humberstone H. Bruce • USA
PURPLE MAZE, THE • 1916 • Le Saint Edward J. • SHT • USA
PURPLE MONSTER STRIKES, THE • 1945 • Bennet Spencer Gordon, Brannon Fred C. • SRL • USA • PURPLE SHADOW STRIKES, THE
PURPLE NIGHT, THE • 1915 • Taylor Stanner E. V. • USA
PURPLE NOON (USA) see **PLEIN SOLEIL** • 1960
PURPLE PEOPLE EATER • 1988 • Shayne Linda • USA
PURPLE PHIAL, THE see **ELEVENTH HOUR, THE** • 1922
PURPLE PLAIN, THE • 1954 • Parrish Robert • UKN
PURPLE PRIDE see **ASHES OF VENGEANCE** • 1923
PURPLE RAIN • 1984 • Magnoli Albert • USA
PURPLE RIDERS, THE • 1921 • Bertram William • SRL • USA
PURPLE RIDERS, THE (UKN) see **PURPLE VIGILANTES, THE** • 1938
PURPLE ROSE OF CAIRO, THE • 1984 • Allen Woody • USA
PURPLE SCAR, THE • 1917 • Garcia Al Ernest • SHT • USA
PURPLE SHADOW STRIKES, THE see **PURPLE MONSTER STRIKES, THE** • 1945
PURPLE STREAM, THE • 1961 • Donner Clive • SHT • UKN
PURPLE TAXI (USA) see **TAXI MAUVE, UN** • 1977
PURPLE V, THE • 1943 • Sherman George • USA
PURPLE VIGILANTES, THE • 1938 • Sherman George • USA • PURPLE RIDERS, THE (UKN)
PURPOSELESS STORY, A see **PRICA BEZ VEZE** • 1966
PURPUR UND WASCHBLAU • 1931 • Neufeld Max • AUS • DURCHLAUT, DIE WASCHERIN
PURR CHANCE TO DREAM • 1967 • Washam Ben • ANS • USA
PURSE, THE • 1909 • *Centaur* • USA
PURSE, THE • 1966 • Watson Patricia • CND
PURSE IS WITH ME, THE • 1978 • Aziz Mohamed Abdel • EGY
PURSE SNATCH • 1970 • *Impressive Art Prod.* • USA
PURSE STRINGS • 1933 • Edwards Henry • UKN
PURSUED • 1925 • Henderson Dell • USA
PURSUED • 1934 • King Louis • USA
PURSUED • 1947 • Walsh Raoul • USA
PURSUED, THE • 1985 • Sayf Samir • EGY
PURSUED BY PRISCILLA • 1912 • Collins Edwin J.? • UKN
PURSUER PURSUED, THE • 1914 • *Coxen Ed* • USA
PURSUERS, THE • 1961 • Grayson Godfrey • UKN
PURSUING PACKAGE, THE • 1918 • Santell Alfred • SHT • USA
PURSUING SHADOW, THE • 1915 • *Terriss Tom* • USA
PURSUING SPEAR, THE • 1971 • Kao Pao Shu • HKG
PURSUING VENGEANCE, THE • 1916 • Sabine Martin • USA
PURSUIT • 1935 • Marin Edwin L. • USA
PURSUIT • 1972 • Crichton Michael • TVM • USA • BINARY ○ EXPLOSION
PURSUIT • 1975 • Quillen Thomas • USA
PURSUIT • 1989 • Sharp Ian • TVM • UKN
PURSUIT see **CACCIA TRAGICA** • 1947
PURSUIT see **HAJKA** • 1978
PURSUIT see **PURSUIT OF D.B. COOPER, THE** • 1981
PURSUIT, THE • 1918 • Crisp Donald • USA
PURSUIT, THE see **ROI SANS DIVERTISSEMENT, UN** • 1962
PURSUIT ACROSS THE DESERT • 1961 • Gazcon Gilberto • SPN
PURSUIT AND LOVES OF QUEEN VICTORIA, THE see **MADCHENJAHRE EINER KONIGIN** • 1954
PURSUIT AT DAWN see **AKATSUKI NO TSUISEKI** • 1950
PURSUIT ETERNAL, THE • 1915 • Paton Stuart • USA
PURSUIT OF D.B. COOPER, THE • 1981 • Spottiswoode Roger, Kulik Buzz (U/c) • USA • IN PURSUIT OF D.B. COOPER ○ PURSUIT
PURSUIT OF HAPPINESS, THE • 1934 • Hall Alexander • USA
PURSUIT OF HAPPINESS, THE • 1962 • King Allan • CND
PURSUIT OF HAPPINESS, THE • 1971 • Mulligan Robert • USA
PURSUIT OF HAPPINESS, THE • 1988 • Ansara Martha • ASL
PURSUIT OF HATE, THE • 1914 • *Weber Lois* • USA
PURSUIT OF JANE, THE • 1913 • *Gail Jane* • USA
PURSUIT OF MOONSHINE, THE see **GONKA ZA SAMOGONKOJ** • 1924
PURSUIT OF PAMELA, THE • 1920 • Shaw Harold • UKN
PURSUIT OF PLEASURE, THE • 1915 • *Roland Ruth* • USA
PURSUIT OF POLLY see **IN PURSUIT OF POLLY** • 1918
PURSUIT OF THE GRAF SPREE (USA) see **BATTLE OF THE RIVER PLATE** • 1956
PURSUIT OF THE PHANTOM, THE • 1914 • Bosworth Hobart • USA
PURSUIT OF THE SMUGGLERS, THE • 1913 • *Foxe Earle* • USA
PURSUIT OF VENGEANCE see **MING–YUEH TAO HSUEH–YEH CHIEN–CHOU** • 1978
PURSUIT OF VENUS, THE • 1914 • Collins Edwin J.? • UKN
PURSUIT TO ALGIERS • 1945 • Neill R. William • USA • SHERLOCK HOLMES IN PURSUIT TO ALGIERS
PURUSHARTHAM • 1987 • Mohanan K. R. • IND
PUSAN • 1953 • Ichikawa Kon • JPN • MR. POO ○ MR. PU
PUSANG ITIM • 1959 • Santiago Cirio H. • PHL • MONSTER STRIKES, THE
PUSH BACK THE EDGE • 1952 • Sparling Gordon • DCS • CND
PUSH–BUTTON KITTY • 1952 • Hanna William, Barbera Joseph • ANS • USA
PUSHED TOO FAR • 1988 • Rooney Jack • USA
PUSHER, THE • 1959 • Milford Gene • USA
PUSHER, THE • 1965 • Burke Gregory • USA
PUSHER, THE see **NARCO, EL** • 1985
PUSHER–IN–THE–FACE • 1929 • Florey Robert • USA
PUSHING UP DAISIES see **THEIR BREAKFAST MEANT LEAD** • 1972
PUSHKA see **PYSHKA** • 1934
PUSHOVER • 1954 • Quine Richard • USA
PUSHOVER, THE see **MITO, IL** • 1963
PUSHOVERS, THE • 1989 • Hutton Brian G. • USA
PUSS AND BOOTS • 1915 • Collins Edwin J. • UKN
PUSS–CAFE, THE • 1950 • Nichols Charles • ANS • USA
PUSS GETS THE BOOTS • 1940 • Hanna William, Barbera Joseph • ANS • USA
PUSS IN BOOTS • 1903 • *Lubin* • USA
PUSS IN BOOTS • 1908 • *Pathe* • FRN

PUSS IN BOOTS • 1917 • Morgan Gould • SHT • USA
PUSS IN BOOTS • 1922 • Disney Walt • ANS • USA
PUSS IN BOOTS • 1931 • USA
PUSS IN BOOTS • 1932 • *Weisfeldt M. J. (P)* • USA
PUSS IN BOOTS • 1934 • *Iwerks Ub (P)* • ANS • USA
PUSS IN BOOTS • 1934 • Reiniger Lotte • ANM • FRG
PUSS IN BOOTS • 1936 • *Principal* • SHT • USA
PUSS IN BOOTS • 1938 • Brumberg Valentina, Brumberg L. • ANS • USS
PUSS IN BOOTS • 1938 • Diehle Bros • ANS • FRG
PUSS IN BOOTS • 1954 • *Reiniger Lotte (P)* • ANS • UKN
PUSS IN BOOTS • 1958 • *Dietz Bros.* • SHT • USA
PUSS IN BOOTS • 1984 • Iscove Robert • TVM • USA
PUSS IN BOOTS • 1987 • Marner Eugene • USA
PUSS IN BOOTS see **MASTERKATTEN I STOVLAR** • 1918
PUSS IN BOOTS see **GRAF VON CARABAS, DER** • 1935
PUSS IN BOOTS (USA) see **CHAT BOTTE** • 1902
PUSS IN BOOTS (USA) see **NAGAGUTSU O HAITA NEKO** • 1969
PUSS IN THE WELL • 1914 • *Starlight* • USA
PUSS & KRAM • 1967 • Cornell Jonas • SWD • HUGS AND KISSES ○ PUSS OCH KRAM
PUSS 'N' BOATS • 1966 • Levitow Abe • ANS • USA
PUSS 'N' BOOS • 1954 • Kneitel Seymour • ANS • USA
PUSS 'N' BOOTS • 1903 • Zecca Ferdinand • FRN
PUSS 'N BOOTS • 1983 • Vincent Chuck • USA
PUSS 'N BOOTS (USA) see **CHAT BOTTE, LE** • 1908
PUSS 'N BOOTS (USA) see **GESTIEFELTE KATER, DER** • 1955
PUSS 'N BOOTS (USA) see **GATO CON BOTAS, EL** • 1961
PUSS 'N BOOTY • 1943 • Clampett Robert • ANS • USA
PUSS 'N' TOOTS • 1942 • Hanna William, Barbera Joseph • ANS • USA
PUSS OCH KRAM see **PUSS & KRAM** • 1967
PUSS, PUSS • 1909 • *Gaumont* • FRN
PUSSY CAT • 1969 • Cruz Jose Miranda • PHL
PUSSY CAT STRIKES AGAIN • 1969 • Cruz Jose Miranda • PHL
PUSSY GALORE • 1965 • *Crawford Henry* • USA
PUSSY ON A HOT TIN ROOF • 1961 • Kuchar George, Kuchar Mike • SHT • USA
PUSSY PUMPS UP • 1979 • Starkiewicz Antoinette • ANS • ASL
PUSSY TALK: LE SEXE QUI PARLE see **SEXE QUI PARLE, LE** • 1975
PUSSY TALK (UKN) see **SEXE QUI PARLE, LE** • 1975
PUSSY WILLIE • 1929 • Lantz Walter, Nolan William • ANS • USA
PUSSYCAT see **FASTER, PUSSYCAT! KILL! KILL!** • 1965
PUSSYCAT ALLEY (USA) see **WORLD TEN TIMES OVER, THE** • 1963
PUSSYCAT, PUSSYCAT, I LOVE YOU • 1970 • Amateau Rod • USA
PUSSYCAT SYNDROME • 1983 • Miles Irvin • FRG
PUSSYCATS, THE see **SALUT LES COPINES** • 1966
PUSSYFOOT COMEDY • 1919 • Sandground Maurice • UKN
PUSSY'S BREAKFAST see **KEIRO'S CAT** • 1905
PUSTE OCSY • 1969 • Petelska Ewa, Petelski Czeslaw • PLN • EMPTY EYES
PUSTI SNOVI • 1968 • Jovanovic Soja • YGS • NOTHING BUT DREAMS ○ BARREN DREAMS ○ VAIN DREAMS
PUSTIUL • 1962 • Bostan Elisabeta • RMN • KID, THE
PUSTOLINA see **PUSTOTA** • 1983
PUSTOTA • 1983 • Gale Joze • YGS • WASTELAND, THE ○ PUSTOLINA
PUSTYNIA • 1966 • Kubik Janusz • PLN
PUSTYNYA • 1967 • Khachaturov Eduard • USS • DESERT
PUSZTA – BERGE – BLAUES MEER • 1968 • Dippe Hermann • DOC • FRG • PUSZTA – MOUNTAINS – BLUE SEAS
PUSZTA – MOUNTAINS – BLUE SEAS see **PUSZTA – BERGE – BLAUES MEER** • 1968
PUSZTAI SZEL • 1938 • Sekely Steve • HNG • BEAUTY OF THE PUSTA ○ WINDS OF THE PUSZTA
PUSZTALIEBE see **ZWISCHEN STROM UND STEPPE** • 1938
PUT A PENNY IN THE SLOT • 1909 • Stow Percy • UKN
PUT 'EM UP • 1928 • Lewis Edgar • USA
PUT ENTUZIASTOV • 1930 • Okhlopkov Nikolai • USS • WAY OF THE ENTHUSIASTS
PUT K PRICHALU • 1962 • Daneliya Georgi • USS • WAY TO THE HARBOUR, THE ○ WAY TO THE WHARF, THE
PUT ME AMONG THE GIRLS • 1908 • Aylott Dave • UKN
PUT ME OFF AT WAYVILLE • 1915 • *Neilan Marshall* • USA
PUT ON ICE see **KALTGESTELLT** • 1980
PUT ON THE SPOT see **RIO GRANDE ROMANCE** • 1936
PUT ON YOUR OLD GRAY BONNET • 1929 • Fleischer Dave • ANS • USA
PUT ON YOUR OLD GREY BONNET • 1944-45 • Jodoin Rene • ANS • CND
PUT OUT • 1911 • *Solax* • USA
PUT OUT OR SHUT UP see **SABALEROS** • 1959
PUT PAPA AMONGST THE GIRLS • 1908 • Collins Alf? • UKN
PUT-PUT TROUBLES • 1940 • Thomson Riley • ANS • USA
PUT SOME MONEY IN THE POT • 1949 • Goodwins Leslie • SHT • USA
PUT TO THE TEST • 1913 • Kirkland Hardee • USA
PUT U RAJ • 1971 • Fanelli Mario • YGS • WAY TO PARADISE
PUT UP OR SHUT UP (USA) see **SABALEROS** • 1959
PUT UP YOUR HANDS! • 1919 • Sloman Edward • USA
PUT V SATURN • 1968 • Azarov Vilen • USS • SATURN IS HARDLY VISIBLE ○ ROAD TO SATURN, THE
PUT YOUR DEVIL INTO MY HELL (UKN) see **METTI LO DIAVOLO TUO NE LO MIO INFERNO** • 1972
PUT YOURSELF IN HIS PLACE • 1912 • Marston Theodore • USA
PUT YOURSELF IN HIS PLACE • 1914 • *Frontier* • USA
PUT YOURSELF IN THEIR PLACE • 1913 • Young James • USA
PUTA MISERIA • 1988 • Pons Ventura • SPN • WHAT A LIFE!
PUTAIN D'HISTOIRE D'AMOUR • 1980 • Behat Gilles • FRN
PUTAIN RESPECTUEUSE, LA see **P.. RESPECTUEUSE, LA** • 1952
PUTEREA SI ADEVARUL • 1972 • Marcus Manole • RMN • POWER AND THE TRUTH, THE
PUTESHESTVIE APRELY • 1963 • Derbenev Vadim • USS • JOURNEY INTO APRIL ○ APRIL JOURNEY
PUTESHESTVIE V DRUGOI GOROD • 1968 • Mikailyan Sergei • USS • JOURNEY TO ANOTHER CITY
PUTESHESTVIYE • 1967 • Seleznyova Inessa, Tumanyan Inna, Firsova Jemma • USS • JOURNEY
PUTEVI • 1958 • Petrovic Aleksandar • YGS • ROADS, THE
PUTHIYA BHOOMI • 1968 • Chanakya • IND • NEW EARTH, THE
PUTIFERIO GOES TO WAR see **PUTIFERIO VA ALLA GUERRA** • 1968
PUTIFERIO VA ALLA GUERRA • 1968 • Gavioli Roberto • ANM • ITL • MAGIC BIRD, THE (USA) ○ PUTIFERIO GOES TO WAR
PUTNEY SWOPE • 1969 • Downey Robert • USA
PUTNICI PASSENGERS see **ALLER RETOUR** • 1979
PUTNICI SA SPLENDIDA • 1956 • Strbac Milenko • YGS • TRAVELLERS FROM THE VESSEL "SPLENDID"
PUTNIK DRUGOG RAZREDA • 1973 • Dovnikovic Borivoj • ANM • YGS • SECOND CLASS PASSENGER ○ TRAVELLER SECOND CLASS
PUTOVANI JANA AMOSE • 1983 • Vavra Otakar • CZC • JAN AMOS COMENIUS
PUTOVANJE • 1972 • Zizic Bogdan • SHT • YGS • JOURNEY, THE
PUTOVANJE NA MJESTO NESRECE • 1972 • Berkovic Zvonimir • YGS • TRAVEL TO THE SITE OF THE ACCIDENT ○ JOURNEY TO THE PLACE OF ACCIDENT
PUTRI SEORANG JENDERAL • 1983 • Umboh Wim • INN • GENERAL'S DAUGHTER, THE
PUTSCHLIESEL • 1920 • Schonfelder Erich • FRG
PUTTANA GALERA! • 1977 • Piccioli Gianfranco • ITL
PUTTER, THE • 1931 • Marshall George • SHT • USA
PUTTIN' IT OVER ON PAPA • 1913 • *Panzer Paul* • USA
PUTTIN' ON THE ACT • 1940 • Fleischer Dave • ANS • USA
PUTTIN' ON THE DOG • 1944 • Hanna William, Barbera Joseph • ANS • USA
PUTTIN' ON THE RITZ • 1930 • Sloman Edward • USA
PUTTIN' ON THE RITZ • 1974 • Starkiewicz Antoinette • ANS • UKN
PUTTIN' OUT THE KITTEN • 1937 • *Mintz Charles (P)* • ANS • USA
PUTTING HER FOOT IN IT • 1916 • Davey Horace • SHT • USA
PUTTING HIM ON THE BLACK LIST • 1903 • *Warwick Trading Co* • UKN
PUTTING IT OVER • 1911 • *Essanay* • USA
PUTTING IT OVER • 1915 • *Royal* • USA
PUTTING IT OVER • 1916 • *Beaumont Harry* • SHT • USA
PUTTING IT OVER • 1919 • Crisp Donald • USA • VILLAGE CUT-UP, THE
PUTTING IT OVER • 1922 • Jones Grover • USA
PUTTING IT OVER ON HENRY • 1917 • Drew Sidney • SHT • USA
PUTTING IT TOGETHER • 1970 • Gordon Lee • DOC • CND
PUTTING ON THE 'FLUENCE • 1915 • Birch Cecil • UKN
PUTTING ONE OVER • 1914 • Edwin Walter • USA
PUTTING ONE OVER • 1915 • Giblyn Charles • USA
PUTTING ONE OVER • 1917 • *Rhodes Billie* • SHT • USA
PUTTING ONE OVER • 1919 • Dillon Eddie • USA • CHASING A FORTUNE
PUTTING ONE OVER see **MASQUERADER, THE** • 1914
PUTTING ONE OVER ON IGNATZ • 1917 • Peacocke Leslie T. • SHT • USA
PUTTING PANTS ON PHILIP • 1927 • Bruckman Clyde • SHT • USA
PUTTING PAPA TO SLEEP • 1915 • *Novelty* • USA
PUTTING THE BEE IN HERBERT • 1917 • France Floyd • USA
PUTTING THE PEP IN SLOWTOWN • 1916 • Van Wally • SHT • USA
PUTTY TAT TROUBLE • 1951 • Freleng Friz • ANS • USA
PUTUS SUDAH KASEH SAYANG • 1970 • Ramlee P. • MLY • SO ENDS LOVE
PUTYOVKHA Z ZHIZN • 1931 • Ekk Nikolai, Yanushkevich R. • USS • ROAD TO LIFE, THE ○ PASS TO LIFE, A
PUZZLE • 1923 • Fleischer Dave • ANS • USA
PUZZLE • 1976 • Giraldeau Jacques • ANS • CND
PUZZLE • 1978 • Hessler Gordon • TVM • ASL
PUZZLE see **REBUS** • 1977
PUZZLE CARTOONS • 1914 • Lloyd Sam • ASS • USA
PUZZLE MANIAC, THE • 1906 • Collins Alf? • UKN
PUZZLE OF A DOWNFALL CHILD • 1970 • Schatzberg Jerry • USA
PUZZLE OF HORROR (USA) see **A DOPPIA FACCIA** • 1969
PUZZLE OF THE PEPPER TREE, THE see **MURDER ON A HONEYMOON** • 1935
PUZZLE OF THE RED ORCHID, THE (USA) see **RATSEL DER ROTEN ORCHIDEE, DAS** • 1961
PUZZLE OF THE SILVER HALF-MOONS, THE see **RATSEL DES SILBERN HALBMONDS, DAS** • 1972
PUZZLE WOMAN see **PUZZLED WOMAN, THE** • 1917
PUZZLED • 1913 • Wilson Frank? • UKN
PUZZLED BATHER AND HIS ANIMATED CLOTHES, THE • 1901 • Williamson James • UKN
PUZZLED BY CROSSWORDS • 1925 • Lamont Charles • SHT • USA
PUZZLED PALS • 1933 • Stallings George, Sherman Frank • ANS • USA
PUZZLED WOMAN, THE • 1917 • Ford Francis • SHT • USA • PUZZLE WOMAN
PUZZLES • 1929 • Leni Paul • SHT • USA
PX • 1981 • Brocka Lino • PHL
PYAAR • 1950 • *Kapoor Raj* • IND
PYAAR • 1957 • Dutt Guru • IND • PYAR
PYADOM S NAMI • 1957 • Bergunkev Adolf • USS • NEAR TO US
PYAR see **PYAAR** • 1957
PYASAA • 1957 • *Burman S. D. (M)* • IND
PYAT DNEI -PYAT NOCHEI • 1961 • Arnstam Leo, Thiel Heinz, Golowanow A. • USS, GDR • FUNF TAGE -FUNF NACHTE (GDR) ○ FIVE DAYS -FIVE NIGHTS
PYAT LET BOBBY I POBEDY • 1923 • Vertov Dziga • USS • FIVE YEARS OF STRUGGLE AND VICTORY
PYAT VECHEROV • 1979 • Mikhalkov Nikita • USS • FIVE EVENINGS
PYCHEDELICS.. KICKS see **PSYCHEDELIC SEX KICKS** • 1967
PYERVAYA LASTOCHKA see **PIRVELI MERTSKHALI** • 1976
PYERVY KURYER • 1968 • Yanchev Vladimir • USS, BUL • PARVIAT KURIER (BUL) ○ FIRST COURIER, THE
PYESN O MANSHUK see **PESNYA MANSHUK** • 1971
PYGMALION • 1935 • Engel Erich • FRG
PYGMALION • 1937 • Berger Ludwig • NTH
PYGMALION • 1938 • Asquith Anthony, Howard Leslie • UKN
PYGMALION • 1970 • Grgic Zlatko (c/d) • ANS • YGS
PYGMALION AND GALATEA • 1912 • Neame Elwin • UKN
PYGMALION AND GALATEA see **PYGMALION ET GALATEE** • 1898
PYGMALION ET GALATEE • 1898 • Melies Georges • FRN • PYGMALION AND GALATEA
PYGMEES • 1984 • Adam Raymond • FRN
PYGMIES • 1973 • Hallet Jean-Pierre • DOC
PYGMY HUNT, THE • 1938 • Freleng Friz • ANS • USA
PYGMY ISLAND • 1950 • Berke William • USA
PYHA PERHE • 1976 • Manttari Anssi • FNL • HOLY FAMILY, THE ○ FAMILY, THE ○ PERHE
PYJAMAS see **PAJAMAS** • 1927
PYJAMAS PREFERRED • 1932 • Valentine Val • UKN
PYLON see **TARNISHED ANGELS, THE** • 1957
PYOTR PERVY • 1937-39 • Petrov Vladimir • USS • CONQUESTS OF PETER THE GREAT, THE ○ PETER THE GREAT ○ PETER THE FIRST ○ PIOTR PERVYI
PYOTR RYABINKIN • 1973 • Vyatich-Berezhnykh Damir • USS
PYRAMID, THE • 1961 • Georgi Katja, Georgi Klaus • ANS • GDR
PYRAMID, THE • 1976 • *Brown C. W.* • USA
PYRAMID OF MARS, THE see **DR. WHO: THE PYRAMID OF MARS** • 1975
PYRAMID OF ROSES • 1980 • Chapman Christopher • DOC • CND
PYRAMIDE DE TRIBOULET, LA • 1899 • Melies Georges • FRN • HUMAN PYRAMID, THE
PYRAMIDE DES SONNENGOTTES, DIE • 1965 • Siodmak Robert • FRG, FRN, ITL
PYRAMIDE HUMAINE, LA • 1959 • Rouch Jean • DOC • FRN
PYRET APPLIES FOR A JOB see **PYRET SOKER PLATS**
PYRET SOKER PLATS • Lindgren Lars-Magnus • SHT • SWD • PYRET APPLIES FOR A JOB
PYRO -MAN WITHOUT A FACE see **FUEGO** • 1964
PYRO -THE THING WITHOUT A FACE see **FUEGO** • 1964
PYRO (USA) see **FUEGO** • 1964
PYROMANIAC • Kurson Jane
PYSCHEDELISSIMO • 1969 • Mesnil Christian • BLG
PYSCHO A GO-GO! see **BLOOD OF GHASTLY HORROR** • 1972
PYSCHODRAMA • 1970 • *Mj Productions* • USA
PYSCHODRAMA, IN OTHER WORDS A FAIRY STORY ABOUT.. see **PSYCHODRAMA** • 1969
PYSHKA • 1934 • Romm Mikhail • USS • BALL OF SUET, A (USA) ○ BOULE DE SUIF ○ PUISHKA ○ PUSHKA
PYSNA PRINCEZNA • 1952 • Zeman Borivoj • CZC • PROUD PRINCESS, THE
PYTEL BLECH • 1962 • Chytilova Vera • SHT • CZC • BAG OF FLEAS, A (UKN)
PYTHONESS, THE • 1951 • Halas John • ANS • UKN
PYTLAKOVA SCHOVANKA • 1949 • Fric Martin • CZC • POACHER'S GOD-DAUGHTER, THE ○ KIND MILLIONAIRE, THE
PYX, THE • 1973 • Hart Harvey • CND

Q

Q see **HISTOIRES DE Q** • 1974
Q see **Q -THE WINGED SERPENT** • 1982
Q & A • 1990 • Lumet Sidney • USA
Q-BEC MY LOVE see **Q-BEC MY LOVE OU UN SUCCES COMMERCIAL** • 1969
Q-BEC MY LOVE OU UN SUCCES COMMERCIAL • 1969 • Lefebvre Jean-Pierre • CND • Q-BEC MY LOVE ○ SUCCES COMMERCIAL, UN
Q PLANES • 1939 • Whelan Tim, Woods Arthur • UKN • CLOUDS OVER EUROPE (USA)
Q-RIOSITIES BY "Q" • 1922 • Quiribet Gaston • SHS • UKN • GEMS OF THE SCREEN (USA)
Q-RIOSITIES BY "Q" • 1924 • Quiribet Gaston • SHS • UKN
Q-RIOSITIES BY "Q" • 1925 • Quiribet Gaston • SHS • UKN
Q-SHIPS • 1928 • Barkas Geoffrey, Barringer Michael • UKN • BLOCKADE
Q -THE WINGED SERPENT • 1982 • Cohen Larry • USA • Q
QABUS, AL- • 1971 • Al-Rawi Abdel-Hadi • SHT • IRQ
QADIA 68 • 1968 • Abu Saif Salah • EGY • CASE 68 ○ CADIA, EL ○ QAD'IYYA 68, AL-
QADISIYYA, AL see **QADISSIA, AL-** • 1981
QADISSIA, AL- • 1981 • Abu Saif Salah • IRQ • KADISSIYA, EL ○ QADISIYYA, AL
QAD'IYYA 68, AL- see **QADIA 68** • 1968
QAHIR 1830, AL- • 1969 • Awf Samir • SHT • EGY • CAIRE 1830, LE
QALB LAHU HUKM, AL- • 1956 • Halim Hilmy • EGY • COEUR A SES RAISONS, LE
QALB LAHU WAH'ID, AL- • 1944 • Barakat Henry • EGY • COEUR A SES RAISONS, LE
QALBUN YAHTARIQ • 1959 • el Sheikh Kamal • EGY • COEURS BRULES
QALBY ALA WALADI • 1952 • Barakat Henry • EGY • J'AI PEUR POUR MON ENFANT
QARIATY • 1972 • Louhichi Taieb • SHT • TNS • MON VILLAGE, UN VILLAGE PARMI TANT D'AUTRES ○ MON VILLAGE
QASR ASH-SHAWQ •,Al Imam Hassan • EGY • PALAIS DES PASSIONS, LE
QASUM US WAQT KI • 1976 • Kardar Ajay • PKS • NO GREATER GLORY
QATALA, AL- • 1971 • Fahmy Ashraf • EGY • MEURTRIERS, LES ○ ASSASSINS, LES
QAYAMAT SE QAYAMAT TAK • 1988 • *Khan Aamir* • IND

QB VII • 1974 • Gries Tom • TVM • USA
QI WANG • 1988 • Teng Wenji • CHN • CHESS KING
QI WANG • 1988 • Yen Hao, Xu Ke • HKG • CHESS KING
QIAMAT SEY QIAMAT TAK • 1989 • Khan Mumtaz Ali • PKS
QIANNU YOUHAN • 1988 • Ching Siu-Tong • HKG • CHINESE GHOST STORY, A ○ SINNUI YAUWAN
QIANNU YOUHUN II see **RENJIAN DAO** • 1988
QIN YONG • 1989 • Ching Siu-Tong • CHN, HKG, CND • ENTOMBED WARRIORS, THE ○ TERRA-COTTA WARRIOR, A
QINGCHUN JI • 1985 • Zhang Nuanxin • CHN • SACRIFICE OF YOUTH
QINGCHUN NUCHAO • 1985 • Ts'Ai Chi-Kuang • HKG • GROW UP IN ANGER
QISSAT HUBBI • 1955 • Barakat Henry • EGY • HISTOIRE DE MON AMOUR
QIU JIN • 1983 • Xie Jin • CHN
QIUTIANDE TONGHUA • 1987 • Zhang Wanting • HKG • AUTUMN'S TALE, AN
QIVITOQ • 1956 • Balling Erik • DNM
QRR • 1971 • Alatriste Gustavo • MXC • QUIEN RESULTA RESPONSABLE ○ WHO IS RESPONSIBLE
QUA LA MANO • 1980 • Festa Campanile Pasquale • ITL • GIVE US YOUR HAND ○ GIVE ME FIVE ○ LET'S SHAKE ON IT
QUACK, THE • 1914 • Melville Wilbert • *Lubin* • USA
QUACK, THE • 1914 • Reid Wallace • *Nestor* • USA
QUACK A DOODLE DO • 1950 • Sparber I. • ANS • USA
QUACK DOCTOR, THE • 1920 • Gray George, Bevan Billy • SHT • USA
QUACK, QUACK • 1931 • *Terry Paul/ Moser Frank (P)* • ANS • USA
QUACK QUAKERS, THE • 1916 • Millarde Harry • SHT • USA
QUACK SHOT • 1954 • McKimson Robert • ANS • USA
QUACKER TRACKER, THE • 1967 • Larriva Rudy • ANS • USA
QUACKODILE TEARS • 1962 • Freleng Friz • ANS • USA
QUACKSER FORTUNE HAS A COUSIN IN THE BRONX • 1970 • Hussein Waris • UKN, USA, IRL • FUN LOVING
QUACKY DOODLES • 1917 • *Bray John R. (P)* • ASS • USA
QUACKY DOODLES FAMILY • 1914 • Follett F. M. • ASS • USA
QUADRANTE DELLA FORTUNA, IL see **DANZA DEI MILIONI, LA** • 1940
QUADRANTE D'ORO, IL • 1920 • Ghione Emilio • ITL
QUADRATE • 1934 • Fischinger Oskar • ANS • FRG • SQUARES
QUADRIGA • 1967 • Wicki Bernhard • FRG
QUADRILLE • 1937 • Guitry Sacha • FRN
QUADRILLE • 1955 • Medved Jozef, Krska Karol • CZC
QUADRILLE, LE • 1950 • Rivette Jacques • SHT • FRN
QUADRILLE D'AMOUR • 1934 • Fried Germain, Eichberg Richard • FRN
QUADRILLE REALISTE • 1902 • Blache Alice • FRN
QUADROON • 1972 • Weis Jack • USA
QUADROPHENIA • 1979 • Roddam Franc • UKN
QUAGMIRE, THE • 1916 • Chatterton Thomas • SHT • USA
QUAI DE GRENELLE • 1950 • Reinert Emile Edwin • FRN • MORT A BOIRE, LA ○ DANGER IS A WOMAN ○ SNAKE OF DEATH
QUAI DE LA HAVANE see **GUERRE DE CUBA ET L'EXPLOSION DU MAINE A LA HAVANE** • 1898
QUAI DES BLONDES • 1953 • Cadeac Paul • FRN
QUAI DES BRUMES • 1938 • Carne Marcel • FRN • PORT OF SHADOWS (USA)
QUAI DES ILLUSIONS • 1956 • Couzinet Emile • FRN
QUAI DES ORFEVRES • 1947 • Clouzot Henri-Georges • FRN • JENNY LAMOUR (USA) ○ JOYEUX NOEL
QUAI DU DESIR • 1969 • Maley Jean • FRN • PORT OF DESIRE (UKN)
QUAI DU POINT DU JOUR • 1960 • Faurez Jean • FRN
QUAI NOTRE-DAME • 1960 • Berthier Jacques • FRN
QUAIL HUNT, THE • 1935 • Lantz Walter, Nolan William • ANS • USA
QUAIL SHOOTING, PINEHURST • 1905 • *Bitzer Billy (Ph)* • USA
QUAINT "Q"'S, THE • 1925 • Quiribet Gaston • UKN
QUAIS A MARSEILLES, LES • 1896 • Melies Georges • FRN • DOCKS AT MARSEILLES, THE
QUAKER MOTHER, THE • 1911 • *Costello Maurice* • USA
QUAKERESS, THE • 1913 • West Raymond B. • USA
QUALCOSA DI BLONDA see **AURORA** • 1984
QUALCOSA STRISCIA NEL BUIO • 1971 • Colucci Mario • ITL • SOMETHING IS CRAWLING IN THE DARK (USA) ○ SOMETHING CREEPING IN THE DARK
QUALCUNO DIETRO LA PORTA • 1971 • Gessner Nicolas • ITL, FRN • QUELQU'UN DERRIERE LA PORTE (FRN) ○ SOMEONE BEHIND THE DOOR (USA) ○ TWO MINDS FOR MURDER (UKN) ○ BRAINKILL
QUALCUNO HA TRADITO • 1967 • Prosperi Franco, Zimmer Pierre • ITL, FRN • REQUIEM POUR UNE CANAILLE (FRN) ○ EVERY MAN IS MY ENEMY (USA) ○ SOMEBODY IS A TRAITOR
QUALEN DER NACHT • 1926 • Bernhardt Curtis • FRG
QUALIFIED ADVENTURER, THE • 1925 • Hill Sinclair • UKN
QUALIFYING FOR LENA • 1914 • Williams C. Jay • USA
QUALITE DES IMAGES OPTIQUES • 1956 • Tavano Fred • SHT • FRN
QUALITY OF FAITH, THE • 1916 • Garrick Richard • USA
QUALITY OF FORGIVENESS, THE • 1915 • *Tutt George* • USA
QUALITY OF MERCY • 1913 • MacGregor Norval • *Selig* • USA
QUALITY OF MERCY, THE • 1913 • *Ammex* • USA
QUALITY OF MERCY, THE • 1913 • *Solax* • USA
QUALITY OF MERCY, THE • 1914 • *Eclectic* • USA
QUALITY OF MERCY, THE • 1914 • Buckland Warwick? • UKN
QUALITY OF MERCY, THE • 1915 • Belmore Lionel • USA
QUALITY OF THE ACT, THE • 1956 • Kelly Ron • CND
QUALITY STREET • 1927 • Franklin Sidney A. • USA
QUALITY STREET • 1937 • Stevens George • USA
QUAND C'EST PARTI, C'EST PARTI • 1973 • Heroux Denis • CND, FRN • J'AI MON VOYAGE
QUAND HURLENT LES LOUPS • 1970 • Laferrere Andre • CND
QUAND LA FEMME S'EN MELE • 1958 • Allegret Yves • FRN, ITL, FRG • WHEN A WOMAN MEDDLES (USA)
QUAND LA NUIT TOMBE • 1964 • Sanchez-Ariza Jose • MXC
QUAND LA VIE ETAIT BELLE see **BEBE DE L'ESCADRON, LE** • 1935
QUAND LA VILLE S'EVEILLE • 1975 • Grasset Pierre • FRN
QUAND LE RIDEAU SE LEVE • 1957 • Lelouch Claude • DCS • FRN
QUAND LES EPIS SE COURBENT • 1929 • Dreville Jean • SHT • FRN
QUAND LES FEMMES ONT PRIS LA COLERE • 1977 • Chappdelaine Soizic, Vautier Rene • FRN
QUAND LES FEUILLES TOMBENT • 1911 • Feuillade Louis • FRN
QUAND LES FILLES SE DECHAINENT • 1973 • Maria Guy • FRN • DECHAINEES, LES ○ HOT AND NAKED ○ THRILL SEEKERS
QUAND LES FLEUVES CHANGENT DE CHEMIN • 1958 • Lecomte Daniel • SHT • FRN
QUAND MINUIT SONNERA • 1916 • Burguet Charles • FRN
QUAND MINUIT SONNERA • 1936 • Joannon Leo • FRN
QUAND MURISSENT LES DATTES? • 1968 • Bennani Larbi, Ramdani Abdellaziz • MRC • WHEN DO THE DATES RIPEN?
QUAND NOUS ETIONS DEUX • 1929 • Perret Leonce • FRN
QUAND ON EST BELLE • 1931 • Robison Arthur • FRN • BONNE VIE, LA
QUAND PASSENT LES FAISANS • 1965 • Molinaro Edouard • FRN • ESCROCS, LES
QUAND SONNERA MIDI • 1957 • Greville Edmond T. • FRN, ITL • PLOTONE DI ESECUZIONE (ITL)
QUAND TE TUES-TU? • 1931 • Capellani Roger • FRN
QUAND TE TUES-TU? • 1952 • Couzinet Emile • FRN
QUAND TU DISAIS, VALERY • 1975 • Vautier Rene, Le Garrec Nicole • FRN
QUAND TU LIRAS CETTE LETTRE • 1953 • Melville Jean-Pierre • FRN, ITL • LABBRA PROIBITE (ITL)
QUAND TU SERAS DEBLOQUE, FAIS-MOI SIGNE! • 1981 • Leterrier Francois • FRN
QUAND VIENT L'AMOUR • 1955 • Cloche Maurice • FRN, YGS • KO PRIDE LJUBEZEN
QUAND VIENT L'ETE see **THOUSAND ISLANDS SUMMER** • 1960
QUANDO AS MULHERES PAQUERAM • 1972 • Di Mello Victor • BRZ
QUANDO C'ERA LUI.. CARO LEI! • 1978 • Santi Giancarlo • ITL
QUANDO DICO CHE TI AMO • 1967 • Bianchi Giorgio • ITL • WHEN I SAY I LOVE YOU
QUANDO ERAVAMO MUTI • 1933 • Cassano Riccardo • ITL
QUANDO GLI ANGELI DORMONO • 1947 • Ferraioli • ITL
QUANDO GLI ANGELI PIANGONO • 1958 • Girolami Marino • ITL
QUANDO GLI UOMINI ARMARONO LA CLAVA.. E CON LE DONNE FECERO DIN DON • 1971 • Corbucci Bruno • ITL • WHEN MEN CARRIED CLUBS, WOMEN PLAYED DING DONG! ○ WHEN WOMEN PLAYED DING-DONG
QUANDO I CALIFFI AVEVANO LE CORNA • 1973 • Damiani Amasi • ITL
QUANDO I PICCIOTTI SGARRANO • 1978 • Cappadonna Romolo • ITL
QUANDO IL SOLE SCOTTA (ITL) see **SUR LA ROUTE DE SALINA** • 1969
QUANDO LA PELLE BRUCIA • 1968 • Dall'Ara Renato • ITL
QUANDO LA PREDA E L'UOMO see **SPOGLIATI, PROTESTA, UCCIDI!** • 1973
QUANDO L'AMORE E SENSUALITA • 1973 • De Sisti Vittorio • ITL • WHEN LOVE IS LUST
QUANDO LE DONNE AMANO (ITL) see **ADORABLES CREATURES** • 1952
QUANDO LE DONNE AVEVANO LA CODA • 1970 • Festa Campanile Pasquale • ITL • WHEN WOMEN HAD TAILS (USA)
QUANDO LE DONNE PERSERO LA CODA • 1972 • Festa Campanile Pasquale • ITL, FRG • TOLL TRIEBEN ES DIE ALTEN GERMANEN (FRG) ○ WHEN WOMEN LOST THEIR TAILS (USA)
QUANDO LE DONNE SI CHIAMAVONO MADONNE • 1972 • Grimaldi Aldo • ITL
QUANDO LE PLEIADI TRAMONTANO • 1951 • Carpignano Vittorio • ITL
QUANDO MARTA URLO DALLA TOMBA (ITL) see **MANSION DE LA NIEBLA, LLA** • 1972
QUANDO O CARNAVAL CHEGAR • 1972 • Diegues Carlos • BRZ • WHEN CARNIVAL COMES
QUANDO O MAR GALGOU A TERRA • 1954 • Campos Henrique • PRT
QUANDO OS DEUSES ADORMECEM • 1972 • Marins Jose Mojica • BRZ • WHEN THE GODS FALL ASLEEP
QUANDO SI AMA • 1915 • Campogalliani Carlo • ITL
QUANDO SUONA LA CAMPANA • 1970 • Solvay Paolo • ITL
QUANDO TRAMONTA IL SOLE • 1956 • Brignone Guido • ITL • SUNSET IN NAPLES
QUANN'AMMORE VO'FILA • 1929 • Serena Gustavo • ITL
QUANT'E BELLA LA BERNARDA TUTTA NERA TUTTA CALDA • 1975 • Dandolo Lucio • ITL
QUANTE VOLTE.. QUELLA NOTTE • 1972 • Bava Mario • ITL • FOUR TIMES THAT NIGHT (USA)
QUANTEZ • 1957 • Keller Harry • USA
QUANTO COSTA MORIRE • 1968 • Merolle Sergio • ITL, FRN • COST OF DYING, THE
QUANTO E BELLO LU MURIRE ACCISO • 1976 • Lorenzini Ennio • ITL
QUANTO SEI BELLA ROMA • 1960 • Girolami Marino • ITL, SPN
QUANTRELL'S SON • 1914 • Thornby Robert T. • USA
QUANTRILL'S RAIDERS • 1958 • Bernds Edward • USA
QUARANTA GRADI ALL'OMBRA DEL LENZUOLO • 1976 • Martino Sergio • ITL • SEX WITH A SMILE ○ SEXYCON
QUARANTAINE, LA • 1983 • Poirier Anne-Claire • CND
QUARANTANE • 1923 • Mack Max • FRG
QUARANTE HUIT HEURES D'AMOUR • 1968 • Saint-Laurent Cecil • FRN • 48 HOURS OF LOVE
QUARANTE-QUATRE • 1981 • Smihi Moumen • MRC • RECITS DE LA NUIT, LES ○ TALES OF ONE NIGHT, THE ○ 44
QUARANTIEMES RUGISSANTS, LES • 1982 • de Chalonge Christian • FRN
QUARANTINE • 1988 • Wilkinson Charles • CND
QUARANTINED • 1913 • *Lubin* • USA
QUARANTINED • 1914 • Seay Charles M. • USA
QUARANTINED • 1916 • *Emerald* • SHT • USA
QUARANTINED • 1970 • Penn Leo • TVM • USA • HOUSE ON THE HILL
QUARANTINED BRIDEGROOM, THE • 1917 • Berthelet Arthur • SHT • USA
QUARANTINED RIVALS • 1927 • Mayo Archie • USA
QUARE FELLOW, THE • 1962 • Dreifuss Arthur • UKN, IRL
QUARE FELLOW, THE • 1967 • Hart Harvey • MTV • CND
QUARK • 1981-83 • Bozzetto Bruno • ASS • ITL
QUARREL, THE • 1912 • *Reliance* • USA
QUARREL, THE • 1912 • Golden Joseph A. • *Crystal* • USA
QUARREL, THE • 1914 • *Bright Mildred* • USA
QUARREL, THE • 1915 • *Duncan William* • USA
QUARREL IN A CAFE, A see **ALTERCATION AU CAFE, UNE** • 1896
QUARREL IN LUKASHI, A • 1959 • Muf M. • USS
QUARREL ON THE CLIFF, THE • 1911 • *Prior Herbert* • USA
QUARRELLERS, THE • 1913 • *Solax* • USA
QUARRELSOME ANGLERS, THE • 1898 • Hepworth Cecil M. • UKN • STOLEN DRINK, THE
QUARRELSOME NEIGHBOURS • 1897 • *Paul R. W.* • UKN
QUARRELSOME NEIGHBOURS • 1903 • Williamson James • UKN
QUARRY, THE • 1915 • Marston Lawrence • USA
QUARRY, THE see **AWOL** • 1989
QUARRY MYSTERY, THE • 1914 • Hepworth Cecil M. • UKN
QUART D'HEURE AMERICAIN, LE • 1982 • Galland Philippe • FRN
QUARTA PAGINA • 1943 • Manzari Nicola • ITL
QUARTA PARETE • 1969 • Bolzoni Adriano • ITL
QUARTER BREED, THE • 1916 • Kent Leon D. • SHT • USA
QUARTER DAY EPISODE, A • 1905 • Green Tom? • UKN
QUARTER HOUR OF CITY STATISTICS, A see **VIERTELSTUNDE GROSS-STADTSTATISTIK** • 1933
QUARTER METER, THE • 1913 • *Powers* • USA
QUARTERBACK, THE • 1926 • Newmeyer Fred • USA
QUARTERBACK, THE • 1940 • Humberstone H. Bruce • USA
QUARTERBACK PRINCESS • 1983 • Black Noel • TVM • USA
QUARTERBACK SNEAK see **JOHNNY BE GOOD** • 1988
QUARTERLY BALANCE see **BILANS KWARTALNY** • 1975
QUARTET • 1935 • Ivanov A., Sazonov P. • ANS • USS
QUARTET • 1948 • Annakin Ken, French Harold, Crabtree Arthur, Smart Ralph • UKN • SOMERSET MAUGHAM'S QUARTET
QUARTET • 1971 • *Halas John (P)* • ANS • UKN
QUARTET • 1980 • Ivory James • UKN, FRN
QUARTET, THE see **KWARTECIK** • 1966
QUARTET IN BED see **QUARTETT IM BETT** • 1968
QUARTET THAT SPLIT UP, THE see **KVARTETTEN SOM SPRANGDES** • 1950
QUARTETT IM BETT • 1968 • Schamoni Ulrich • FRG • QUARTET IN BED
QUARTETT ZU FUNFT • 1949 • Lamprecht Gerhard • GDR • VIER MAL LIEBE
QUARTETTO PAZZO • 1947 • Salvini Guido • ITL
QUARTIER CHINOIS • 1946 • Sti Rene • FRN
QUARTIER CHINOIS • 1956-57 • Devlin Bernard • SHT • CND
QUARTIER INTERLOPE see **QUARTIER SANS SOLEIL** • 1939
QUARTIER LATIN • 1928 • Genina Augusto • FRG • LATIN QUARTER
QUARTIER LATIN • 1929 • Genina Augusto • FRN
QUARTIER LATIN • 1939 • Colombier Piere, Chamborant Christian, Esway Alexander (U/c) • FRN
QUARTIER LE REVE see **SYNIKIA TO ONIRO** • 1961
QUARTIER SANS SOLEIL • 1939 • Kirsanoff Dimitri • FRN • QUARTIER INTERLOPE
QUARTIERE DEI LILLA (ITL) see **PORTE DE LILAS** • 1957
QUARTIERI ALTI • 1944 • Soldati Mario • ITL
QUARTO, O • 1969 • Biafora Rubem • BRZ • BEDROOM, THE
QU'AS-TU DONNE A LA PALESTINE? • 1973 • Al-Rawi Abdel-Hadi • SHT • IRQ
QUATERMASS AND THE PIT • 1957 • Cartier Rudolph • MTV • UKN
QUATERMASS AND THE PIT • 1967 • Baker Roy Ward • UKN • FIVE MILLION YEARS TO EARTH (USA)
QUATERMASS CONCLUSION, THE • 1980 • Haggard Piers • TVM • UKN
QUATERMASS EXPERIMENT, THE • 1955 • Guest Val • UKN • CREEPING UNKNOWN, THE (USA) ○ SHOCK
QUATERMASS II • 1956 • Guest Val • UKN • ENEMY FROM SPACE (USA)
QUATIL HASENNA • 1988 • PKS • MURDERERS
QUATORZE JUILLET • 1932 • Clair Rene • FRN • JULY 14TH (USA) ○ FOURTEENTH OF JULY, THE
QUATORZE JUILLET 1953 • 1953 • Gance Abel • FRN
QUATORZE SIECLES APRES LE QORAN • 1968 • Tilmissani Abdel-Qadir At- • SHT • EGY
QUATRE ARTISTES CANADIENS • Tessier Albert • DCS • CND
QUATRE AVENTURES DE REINETTE ET MIRABELLE • 1987 • Rohmer Eric • FRN • AVENTURES DE REINETTE ET MIRABELLE, LES ○ FOUR ADVENTURES OF REINETTE AND MIRABELLE
QUATRE CAVALIERS DE L'APOCALYSE, LES • 1917 • Diamant-Berger Henri • FRN
QUATRE CENT COUPS, LES • 1959 • Truffaut Francois • FRN • 400 BLOWS, THE
QUATRE CENT FARCES DU DIABLE, LES see **400 FARCES DU DIABLE, LES** • 1906
QUATRE CHARLOTS MOUSEQUETAIRES, LES • 1973 • Hunebelle Andre • FRN
QUATRE COEURS see **SI TU VEUX** • 1932
QUATRE DE L'EQUIPE, LES see **AMOUR EN VITESSE, L'** • 1932
QUATRE D'ENTRE ELLES • 1968 • Champion Claude, Reusser Francis, Sandoz Jacques, Yersin Yves, Arnoux Serge, Gorsky Bernard, Lesage Roger, Pasquier Pierre • SWT • FOUR OF THEM ○ VIER FRAU ○ FOUR WOMEN
QUATRE HEURES DU MATIN • 1937 • Rivers Fernand • FRN
QUATRE HEURES DU MATIN • 1951 • Delacroix Rene • SHT • FRN
QUATRE HOMMES AUX POINGS NUS • 1970 • Topart Robert • FRN, ITL, CLM

QUATRE JEUNES ET TROIS BOSS • 1972 • Moreau Michel • DOC • CND
QUATRE JOURS A PARIS • 1954 • Berthomieu Andre • FRN • FOUR DAYS IN PARIS (USA)
QUATRE MATINS • 1987 • Fels Hans • NTH, FRG
QUATRE MOUSQUETAIRES, LES • 1953 • Margaritis Gilles • SHT • FRN
QUATRE MURS, LES • 1963 • Derkaoui Mustafa • SHT • MRC
QUATRE NUITS D'UN REVEUR • 1971 • Bresson Robert • FRN, ITL • FOUR NIGHTS OF A DREAMER (USA)
QUATRE PEINTRES BELGES AU TRAVAIL • 1951 • Haesaerts Paul • BLG
QUATRE PETITS TAILLEURS, LES • 1910 • Cohl Emile • ANS • FRN • FOUR LITTLE TAILORS, THE
QUATRE ROUES DE LA FORTUNE, LES see **ROSE** • 1935
QUATRE SERGENTS DU FORT-CARRE, LES • 1952 • Hugon Andre • FRN
QUATRE SOURIRES, LES • 1958 • Bourguignon Serge • FRN • SOURIRE, LE ○ LANGAGE DU SOURIRE, LE ○ SMILE, THE
QUATRE TEMPS • 1956 • Alexeieff Alexandre • SHT • FRN
QUATRE VAGABONDS, LES • 1931 • Pick Lupu • FRN
QUATRE VERITES • 1962 • Blasetti Alessandro, Bromberger Herve, Clair Rene, Berlanga Luis Garcia • FRN, ITL, SPN • QUATTRO VERITA, LE (ITL) ○ THREE FABLES OF LOVE (USA) ○ CUATRO VERDADES, LAS
QUATRE VEUVES, LES see **INSOUMISES, LES** • 1955
QUATREVINGT-TREIZE • 1914 • Capellani Albert • FRN
QUATRIEME FEMME, LA • 1918 • Rasumny Alexander • USS
QUATRIEME MOUSQUETAIRE, LE (FRN) see **QUATTRO MOSCHETTIERI, I** • 1963
QUATRIEME SEXE, LE • 1962 • Wichard Michel, Gimeno Alfonso, Metzger Radley H. • FRN • FOURTH SEX, THE (USA)
QUATRO CHAVES MAGICAS, AS • 1972 • Salva Alberto • BRZ
QUATTRINI A PALATE see **VENTO DI MILIONI** • 1940
QUATTRO BERSAGLIERI, I see **TRIPOLI BEL SUOL D'AMORE** • 1954
QUATTRO CAPORALI E MEZZO E UN COLONNELLO TUTTO D'UN PEZZO • 1973 • Albertini Bitto • ITL
QUATTRO DEL GETTO TONANTE, I • 1955 • Cerchio Fernando • ITL
QUATTRO DEL PATER NOSTER, I • 1969 • Deodato Ruggero • ITL
QUATTRO DELL'APOCALISSE, I • 1975 • Fulci Lucio • ITL
QUATTRO DELL'AVE MARIA, I • 1968 • Colizzi Giuseppe • ITL • REVENGE IN EL PASO (UKN) ○ FOUR OF THE AVE MARIA, THE ○ ACE HIGH ○ ASSO PIGLIA TUTTO ○ HAVE GUN, WILL TRAVEL ○ REVENGE AT EL PASO
QUATTRO DI BIR EL GOBI, I see **BATTAGLIA, LA** • 1942
QUATTRO DOLLARI DI VENDETTA (ITL) see **CUATRO DOLARES DE VENGANZA** • 1965
QUATTRO DONNE NELLA NOTTE (ITL) see **BONNES A TUER** • 1954
QUATTRO GIORNATE DI NAPOLI, LE • 1962 • Loy Nanni • ITL • BATTAGLIA DI NAPOLI, LA ○ FOUR DAYS OF NAPLES, THE
QUATTRO INESORABILI, I • 1966 • Zeglio Primo • ITL
QUATTRO MARMITTONI ALLE GRANDI MANOVRE • 1974 • Girolami Marino • ITL
QUATTRO MINUTI PER QUATTRO MILIARDI see **QUELLI DELL'ANTIRAPINA** • 1977
QUATTRO MONACI, I • 1962 • Bragaglia Carlo Ludovico • ITL • FOUR MONKS, THE
QUATTRO MOSCHE DE VELLUTO GRIGIO • 1971 • Argento Dario • ITL, FRN • FOUR FLIES ON GREY VELVET (UKN)
QUATTRO MOSCHETTIERI, I • 1936 • Campogalliani Carlo • ITL
QUATTRO MOSCHETTIERI, I • 1963 • Bragaglia Carlo Ludovico • ITL, FRN • QUATRIEME MOUSQUETAIRE, LE (FRN) ○ FOUR MUSKETEERS, THE
QUATTRO NOTTI CON ALBA • 1962 • D'Amico Luigi Filippo • ITL • DESERT WAR (USA)
QUATTRO PASSI FRA LE NUVOLE • 1942 • Blasetti Alessandro • ITL • FOUR STEPS IN THE CLOUDS
QUATTRO PISTOLERI DI SANTA TRINITA, I • 1971 • Cristallini Giorgio • ITL
QUATTRO ROSE ROSSE • 1952 • Malasomma Nunzio • ITL
QUATTRO TASSISTI, I • 1964 • Bianchi Giorgio • ITL
QUATTRO TRAMONTI, I • 1922 • Ghione Emilio • ITL
QUATTRO VERITA, LE (ITL) see **QUATRE VERITES** • 1962
QUATUOR BASILEUS see **BASILEUS QUARTET** • 1982
QUAX, DER BRUCHPILOT • 1941 • Hoffmann Kurt • FRG
QUAX IN FAHRT • 1945 • Weiss Helmut • FRG
QUE ANIMAL TAN TERRIBLE • *Chaney Lon Jr.* • MXC • WHAT A TERRIBLE ANIMAL
QUE ARMAN LAS MUJERES, LA • 1969 • Merino Fernando • SPN
QUE BONITO AMOR! • 1959 • de la Serna Mauricio • MXC
QUE BONITO ES QUERER • 1962 • Crevenna Alfredo B. • MXC
QUE BRAVAS SON LAS COSTENAS • 1954 • Rodriguez Roberto • MXC
QUE CON NINOS SE ACUESTA, EL • 1957 • Gonzalez Rogelio A. • MXC
QUE COSAS TIENE EL AMOR • 1971 • Lorente German • SPN
QUE DIEU VOUS SOIT EN AIDE #1 • 1956-57 • Devlin Bernard • SHT • CND
QUE DIEU VOUS SOIT EN AIDE #2 • 1956-57 • Devlin Bernard • SHT • CND
QUE DIOS ME PERDONE • 1947 • Davison Tito • MXC
QUE ES EL OTONO? • 1977 • Kohon David Jose • ARG • WHAT IS AUTUMN?
QUE ES LA DEMOCRACIA? • 1971 • Alvarez Carlos • CLM • WHAT IS DEMOCRACY? (UKN)
QUE FAIT-ON CE DIMANCHE • 1977 • Essid • FRN
QUE FAREI EU COM ESTA ESPADA? • 1975 • Monteiro Joao Cesar • PRT
QUE HACE UNA CHICA COMO TU EN UN SITIO COMO ESTE? • 1978 • Colomo Fernando • SPN • WHAT'S A GIRL LIKE YOU DOING IN A PLACE LIKE THIS?
QUE HACEMOS CON LOS HIJOS? • 1967 • Lazaga Pedro • SPN
QUE HACER? • 1970 • Ruiz Raul • CHL
QUE HACER CON MIS HIJOS • 1962 • Mariscal Alberto • MXC
QUE HAGO CON LA CRIATURA? • 1935 • Peon Ramon • MXC
QUE HAREMOS CON PAPA? • 1965 • Baledon Rafael • MXC
QUE HAZER • 1972 • Landau Saul, Becket James, Serrano Nina, Ruiz Raul • USA
QUE HE HECHO YO MERECER ESTO? • 1984 • Almodovar Pedro • SPN • WHAT HAVE I DONE TO DESERVE THIS?
QUE HERMANITA! • 1951 • Land Kurt • ARG
QUE HOMBRE TAN SIMPATICO • 1942 • Soler Fernando • MXC
QUE HOMBRE TAN SIN EMBARGO • 1965 • Soler Julian • MXC • WHAT A MAN, WITHOUT A DOUBT
QUE IDIOTAS SON LOS HOMBRES • 1950 • Orol Juan • MXC
QUE LA BETE MEURE • 1969 • Chabrol Claude • FRN, ITL • UCCIDERO UN UOMO (ITL) ○ THIS MAN MUST DIE (USA) ○ KILLER! (UKN)
QUE LA FETE COMMENCE.. • 1975 • Tavernier Bertrand • FRN • LET JOY REIGN SUPREME.. (USA)
QUE L'AMOUR EST BEAU! see **YA SALAM AL-HUBB** • 1962
QUE LES "GROS SALAIRES" LEVENT LE DOIGT! • 1982 • Granier-Deferre Denys • FRN • BETES CURIEUSES, LES ○ BASSE-COUR
QUE LES HOMMES SONT BETES • 1956 • Richebe Roger • FRN
QUE LINDO CHA CHA CHA! • 1954 • Martinez Solares Gilberto • MXC • HOW PRETTY CHA CHA CHA!
QUE LINDO ES MICHOACAN! • 1942 • Rodriguez Ismael • MXC
QUE LINDO ES PARIS • 1989 • Norden Francisco • CLM, FRN • PARIS IS SO LOVELY
QUE ME MATEN EN TUS BRAZOS • 1960 • Baledon Rafael • MXC
QUE ME TOQUEN LAS GOLONDRINAS • 1956 • Morayta Miguel • MXC, ARG
QUE MURIO DE AMOR, EL • 1945 • Morayta Miguel • MXC • HE WHO DIED OF LOVE
QUE NO DEBEN NACER, LOS • 1953 • Delgado Agustin P. • MXC
QUE NO FUIMOS A LA GUERRA, LOS • 1961 • Diamante Julio • SPN • CUANDO ESTALLO LA PAZ
QUE NOCHE AQUELLA • 1957 • de Martino Inigo • MXC
QUE NOCHE DE BODAS, CHICAS! • 1972 • Merino Fernando • SPN
QUE NUNCA AMARON, LOS • 1965 • Diaz Morales Jose • MXC, PRC
QUE NUNCA MUERE, LO • 1954 • Salvador Julio • SPN
QUE PADRE TAN PADRE! • 1960 • Salvador Jaime • MXC
QUE PASA CONTIGO, TIO? • 1977 • del Amo Antonio • SPN
QUE PERRA VIDA • 1961 • Salvador Jaime • MXC
QUE PERSONNE NE SORTE • 1963 • Govar Yvan • FRN, BLG
QUE PEUT-IL AVOIR? • 1912 • Linder Max • FRN
QUE RECIBE LAS BOFETADAS, EL • 1947 • Hardy Boris H. • ARG
QUE RICO EL MAMBO! • 1952 • Lugones Mario C. • ARG
QUE SE CALLEN • 1966 • Cazals Felipe • SHT • MXC • QUIET PLEASE
QUE SEAS FELIZ! • 1956 • Soler Julian • MXC
QUE S'EST-IL PASSE EN MAI? • 1969 • Savignac Jean-Paul • SHT • FRN
QUE TE HA DADO ESA MUJER? • 1951 • Rodriguez Ismael • MXC
QUE TENGA UN AMOR, EL • 1942 • Orellana Carlos • MXC
QUE TIEMPOS AQUELLOS • 1938 • Romero Manuel • THOSE WERE THE DAYS (USA)
QUE VERDE ERA MI PADRE! • 1945 • Rodriguez Ismael • MXC
QUE VIENE MI MARIDO! • 1939 • Urueta Chano • MXC
QUE VIVA CARRANCHO! • 1967 • Balcazar Alfonso • SPN, ITL • MAN FROM CANYON CITY, THE ○ LONG LIVE CARRANCHO!
QUE VIVA MEXICO! • 1931 • Eisenstein Sergei • USA • DEATH DAY ○ EISENSTEIN IN MEXICO ○ TIME IN THE SUN
QUE VIVA TEPITO! • 1980 • Hernandez Mario • MXC • UP WITH TEPITO!
QUE VOLVIERON, LOS • 1946 • Galindo Alejandro • MXC
QUEBEC • 1951 • Templeton George • USA
QUEBEC? • 1966 • Brault Michel, Groulx Gilles • DCS • CND
QUEBEC A L'HEURE DE L'EXPO • 1968 • Carle Gilles • DCS • CND
QUEBEC A VENDRE • 1977 • Garceau Raymond • DOC • CND
QUEBEC AN 2000 • 1968 • Danis Aime, Fournier Claude • DCS • CND
QUEBEC C'EST BON • 1974 • Cardinal Roger • DCS • CND
QUEBEC CONGRES • 1976 • Cardinal Roger • DCS • CND
QUEBEC: DUPLESSIS AND AFTER.. see **QUEBEC: DUPLESSIS ET APRES..** • 1972
QUEBEC: DUPLESSIS ET APRES.. • 1972 • Arcand Denys • DOC • CND • QUEBEC: DUPLESSIS AND AFTER..
QUEBEC ECONOMY IN CRISIS • 1982 • Pearson Peter • MTV • CND
QUEBEC-FETE JUIN 1975 • 1976 • Labrecque Jean-Claude, Jutra Claude • DOC • CND
QUEBEC FORESTIER, LE • 1984 • Kinsey Nicholas • DOC • CND • FORESTS OF QUEBEC, THE
QUEBEC, LA BELLE PROVINCE • 1972 • Beaudry Michel • CND
QUEBEC-PARTY • 1961 • Regnier Michel • DCS • CND
QUEBEC, PATH OF CONQUEST • 1942 • Spottiswoode Raymond • DCS • CND
QUEBEC SAUVAGE • 1973 • Marchand Pierre • DOC • CND
QUEBEC SKI • 1970 • Dansereau Fernand • DOC • CND
QUEBEC SUA JOBBE, LE see **TOUL QUEBEC AU MONDE SUA JOBBE** • 1975
QUEBEC: THE TERCENTENARY CELEBRATIONS • 1908 • Ouimet Leo • CND
QUEBEC USA • 1962 • Jutra Claude, Brault Michel • DCS • CND • VISIT TO A FOREIGN COUNTRY ○ INVASION PACIFIQUE, L'
QUEBEC VU PAR CARTIER-BRESSON, LE • 1969 • Jutra Claude • CND
QUEBEC XXe SIECLE see **HORIZONS OF QUEBEC** • 1952
QUEBECOISES EN FOLIE, LES • Blanc Jack • FRN
QUEBRACHO • 1974 • Wulicher Ricardo • ARG
QUEDA, A • 1978 • Guerra Ruy, Xavier Nelson • BRZ • FALL, THE
QUEEN, THE • 1967 • Simon Frank • DOC • USA
QUEEN, THE see **QUEEN'S AFFAIR, THE** • 1934
QUEEN AND THE CARDINAL, THE (USA) see **JEROME PERREAU** • 1935
QUEEN BEE • 1955 • MacDougall Ranald • USA
QUEEN BEE see **STORIA MODERNA -L'APE REGINA, UNA** • 1963
QUEEN BEE see **JOOBACHI** • 1978
QUEEN BEE, THE see **KROLOWA PSZCZOL** • 1977
QUEEN BESS -HER LOVE STORY see **AMOURS DE LA REINE ELISABETH, LES** • 1912
QUEEN CHRISTINA • 1933 • Mamoulian Rouben • USA
QUEEN CITY ROCKER • 1985 • Morrison Bruce • NZL
QUEEN COTTON • 1941 • Musk Cecil • DCS • UKN
QUEEN DOLL (USA) see **MUNECA REINA** • 1971
QUEEN ELISABETH see **AMOURS DE LA REINE ELISABETH, LES** • 1912
QUEEN ELIZABETH'S DAUGHTER see **KONIGIN ELISABETHS DOCHTER** • 1915
QUEEN FOR A DAY • 1951 • Lubin Arthur • USA • HORSIE
QUEEN FOR A DAY, A • 1911 • *Vitagraph* • USA
QUEEN FOR A DAY, A • 1912 • *Sydmeth Louise* • USA
QUEEN FOR AN HOUR, A • 1915 • Baker George D. • USA
QUEEN FOR CAESAR, A (USA) see **REGINA PER CESARE, UNA** • 1963
QUEEN HIGH • 1930 • Newmeyer Fred • USA
QUEEN IN CHARLOTTETOWN • 1964 • Pearson Peter • DOC • CND
QUEEN IS CROWNED, A • 1953 • Knight Castleton • DOC • UKN
QUEEN KELLY • 1928 • von Stroheim Erich • USA
QUEEN KONG • 1977 • Agrama Frank • ITL, UKN
QUEEN LUISE see **KONIGIN LUISE** • 1911
QUEEN LUISE see **KONIGIN LUISE 1** • 1927
QUEEN MOTHER, THE • 1916 • Noy Wilfred • UKN
QUEEN O' DIAMONDS • 1926 • Withey Chet • USA
QUEEN OF APOLLO • 1970 • Leacock Richard • DOC • USA
QUEEN OF ATLANTIS see **SIREN OF ATLANTIS** • 1949
QUEEN OF BABYLON, THE see **CORTIGIANA DI BABILONIA, LA** • 1955
QUEEN OF BLOOD see **PLANET OF BLOOD** • 1966
QUEEN OF BROADWAY • 1942 • Newfield Sam • USA
QUEEN OF BROADWAY see **KID DYNAMITE** • 1943
QUEEN OF BURLESQUE • 1946 • Newfield Sam • USA
QUEEN OF CIRCUS see **KYOKUBADAN NO JOO** • 1925
QUEEN OF CLUBS see **DAMA SPATHI** • 1966
QUEEN OF CRIME (USA) see **KATE PLUS TEN** • 1938
QUEEN OF DESTINY (USA) see **SIXTY GLORIOUS YEARS** • 1938
QUEEN OF DIAMONDS see **BELLE STARR STORY, THE** • 1968
QUEEN OF EVIL see **SEIZURE** • 1973
QUEEN OF FIST • 1974 • Chien Lung • HKG
QUEEN OF HEARTS • 1936 • Banks Monty • UKN
QUEEN OF HEARTS • 1957 • Halas John, Batchelor Joy • ANM • UKN
QUEEN OF HEARTS • 1989 • Amiel Jon • UKN
QUEEN OF HEARTS see **JACK OF DIAMONDS** • 1912
QUEEN OF HEARTS, THE • 1910 • *Selig* • USA
QUEEN OF HEARTS, THE • 1915 • Worthington William • USA
QUEEN OF HEARTS, THE • 1918 • Lawrence Edmund • USA
QUEEN OF HEARTS, THE • 1923 • Coleby A. E. • UKN
QUEEN OF HEARTS, THE • 1934 • *Iwerks Ub (P)* • ANS • USA
QUEEN OF HEARTS, THE see **MOTHER GOOSE PRESENTS THE QUEEN OF HEARTS** • 1946
QUEEN OF JHANSI see **JHANSI-KI-RANI** • 1953
QUEEN OF JUNGLE LAND, THE • 1915 • Franz Joseph J. • USA
QUEEN OF MAIN STREET see **MISBEHAVING LADIES** • 1931
QUEEN OF MAY, THE • 1912 • *Republic* • USA
QUEEN OF MODERN TIMES, THE (USA) see **GENDAI NO JOO** • 1924
QUEEN OF MY HEART • 1917 • Ward Albert • UKN
QUEEN OF MY HEART see **KONIGIN SEINES HERZENS, DIE** • 1928
QUEEN OF OUTER SPACE • 1958 • Bernds Edward • USA • QUEEN OF THE UNIVERSE
QUEEN OF PELLAGONIA, THE see **DROTTNINGEN AV PELLAGONIEN** • 1927
QUEEN OF QUEENS see **REINA DE REINAS** • 1945
QUEEN OF SEX see **GOLA PROFONDA NERA** • 1977
QUEEN OF SHEBA, THE • 1921 • Edwards J. Gordon • USA
QUEEN OF SHEBA, THE (USA) see **REGINA DI SABA, LA** • 1952
QUEEN OF SHEBA MEETS THE ATOM MAN, THE • 1963 • Rice Ron • USA
QUEEN OF SIN AND THE SPECTACLE OF SODOM AND GOMORRAH, THE see **SODOM UND GOMORRA** • 1922
QUEEN OF SPADES • 1910 • *Deutsche Biograph* • FRG
QUEEN OF SPADES • 1912 • FRN
QUEEN OF SPADES • 1925 • Fraser Harry L. • USA
QUEEN OF SPADES • 1954 • *Woolley Monty* • SHT • USA
QUEEN OF SPADES see **PIQUE DAME** • 1918
QUEEN OF SPADES see **SZENZACIO** • 1922
QUEEN OF SPADES see **PIQUE DAME** • 1927
QUEEN OF SPADES, THE • 1913 • *Cines* • ITL
QUEEN OF SPADES, THE • 1949 • Dickinson Thorold • UKN
QUEEN OF SPADES, THE see **DAMA DI PICCHE, LA** • 1913
QUEEN OF SPADES, THE see **PIKOVAYA DAMA** • 1916
QUEEN OF SPADES, THE see **DAME DE PIQUE, LA** • 1965
QUEEN OF SPADES, THE (USA) see **PIKOVAYA DAMA** • 1960
QUEEN OF SPADES (USA) see **PIKOVAYA DAMA** • 1910
QUEEN OF SPADES (USA) see **PIQUE DAME** • 1937
QUEEN OF SPIES (UKN) see **JOAN OF THE OZARKS** • 1942
QUEEN OF TEMPLE STREET see **MIUGAI WONGHAU** • 1990
QUEEN OF THE AMAZON • 1947 • Finney Edward • USA
QUEEN OF THE AMAZONS see **REGINA DELLE AMAZZONI, LA** • 1960
QUEEN OF THE BAND, THE • 1915 • Myers Ray • USA
QUEEN OF THE BLUES • 1979 • Roe Willy • UKN
QUEEN OF THE BOOGIE • 1947 • *Brooks Hadda* • SHT • USA
QUEEN OF THE BOULEVARDS see **GLANZ UND ELEND DER KURTISANEN** • 1920
QUEEN OF THE BUTTERFLIES, THE (USA) see **REINE DES PAPILLONS, LA** • 1927

QUEEN OF THE CANNIBALS see **REGINA DEI CANNIBALI, LA** • 1979

QUEEN OF THE CHORUS • 1928 • Hunt Charles J. • USA

QUEEN OF THE CIRCUS (USA) see **KYOKUBADAN NO JOO** • 1925

QUEEN OF THE COUNTERFEITERS (USA) see **QUEEN OF THE LONDON COUNTERFEITERS** • 1914

QUEEN OF THE EARTH • 1909 • *Warwick Trading Co* • UKN

QUEEN OF THE EARTH • 1921 • Wynn George • UKN

QUEEN OF THE GORILLAS see **BRIDE OF THE GORILLA** • 1951

QUEEN OF THE GORILLAS see **BRIDE AND THE BEAST, THE** • 1958

QUEEN OF THE GYPSIES • 1979 • Lotyanu Emil • USS

QUEEN OF THE JUNGLE • 1935 • Hill Robert F. • SRL • USA

QUEEN OF THE KITCHEN • 1912 • *Roland Ruth* • USA

QUEEN OF THE LONDON COUNTERFEITERS • 1914 • Youngdeer James • UKN • QUEEN OF THE COUNTERFEITERS (USA)

QUEEN OF THE MARKET PLACE (USA) see **KROLOWA PRZEDMIESCIA** • 1937

QUEEN OF THE MAY, THE • 1910 • Haldane Bert? • UKN

QUEEN OF THE MOB • 1940 • Hogan James P. • USA

QUEEN OF THE MOULIN ROUGE • 1922 • Smallwood Ray C. • USA

QUEEN OF THE NAKED STEEL see **BARBARIAN QUEEN** • 1985

QUEEN OF THE NIGHT • 1986 • Tammer Peter • SHT • ASL

QUEEN OF THE NIGHT CLUBS • 1929 • Foy Bryan • USA

QUEEN OF THE NIGHT CLUBS see **KONIGSLOGE, DIE** • 1929

QUEEN OF THE NIHILISTS • 1910 • *Yankee* • USA

QUEEN OF THE NILE see **SUDAN** • 1945

QUEEN OF THE NILE (USA) see **NEFERTITE REGINA DEL NILO** • 1962

QUEEN OF THE NORTHWOODS • 1929 • Bennet Spencer Gordon, Storey Thomas L. • SRL • USA

QUEEN OF THE PIRATES (USA) see **VENERE DEI PIRATI, LA** • 1960

QUEEN OF THE PRAIRIES • 1910 • *Columbia* • USA

QUEEN OF THE QUARRY, THE • 1909 • Olcott Sidney • USA

QUEEN OF THE RADIO, THE see **RAINHA DO RADIO, A** • 1981

QUEEN OF THE ROAD see **MALKAT HAKVISH** • 1972

QUEEN OF THE SCREEN see **KORLEVA EKRANA** • 1916

QUEEN OF THE SEA, A • 1918 • Adolfi John G. • USA

QUEEN OF THE SEA NYMPHS, THE • 1913 • *Majestic* • USA

QUEEN OF THE SEAS (USA) see **AVVENTURE DI MARY READ, LE** • 1961

QUEEN OF THE SMUGGLERS, THE • 1914 • *Sawyer'S Features* • USA

QUEEN OF THE STARDUST BALLROOM • 1975 • O'Steen Sam • TVM • USA

QUEEN OF THE TARTARS see **REGINA DEI TARTARI, LA** • 1960

QUEEN OF THE UNIVERSE see **QUEEN OF OUTER SPACE** • 1958

QUEEN OF THE VAMPIRES, THE see **REINE DES VAMPIRES, LA** • 1967

QUEEN OF THE WEST • 1952 • Tansey Robert • MTV • USA

QUEEN OF THE WEST see **CATTLE QUEEN** • 1950

QUEEN OF THE WICKED • 1916 • Ward Albert • UKN

QUEEN OF THE YUKON • 1940 • Rosen Phil • USA

QUEEN STEPS OUT, THE • 1951 • Henryson Robert • UKN

QUEEN TOOTHBRUSH • 1962 • *Soyuzmultfilm* • ANS • USS

QUEEN VICTORIA see **SIXTY GLORIOUS YEARS** • 1938

QUEEN VICTORIA'S DIAMOND JUBILEE • 1897 • Paul Robert William • UKN

QUEEN VICTORIA'S VISIT TO DUBLIN • 1900 • Hepworth Cecil M. • UKN

QUEEN WAS IN THE PARLOR, THE • 1931-32 • Ising Rudolf • ANS • USA

QUEEN WAS IN THE PARLOUR, THE • 1927 • Cutts Graham • UKN • FORBIDDEN LOVE ○ FORBIDDEN CARGO

QUEEN WHO RETURNED, A • 1958 • Brealey Gil • DOC • ASL

QUEEN WORLD, THE see **DUTTURU DUNYA** • 1988

QUEEN X • 1917 • O'Brien John B. • USA

QUEENIE • 1921 • Mitchell Howard M. • USA

QUEENIE • 1987 • Peerce Larry • TVM • USA

QUEENIE AND THE CANNIBAL • 1912 • *Imp* • USA

QUEENIE OF THE CIRCUS • 1914 • Raymond Charles • UKN

QUEENIE OF THE NILE • 1915 • Hotaling Arthur D. • USA

QUEENS, THE see **FATE, LE** • 1966

QUEEN'S AFFAIR, THE • 1934 • Wilcox Herbert • UKN • RUNAWAY QUEEN (USA) ○ QUEEN, THE

QUEEN'S DIAMONDS, THE see **THREE MUSKETEERS, THE** • 1974

QUEEN'S EVIDENCE • 1919 • McKay James • UKN

QUEEN'S GUARDS, THE • 1961 • Powell Michael • UKN

QUEEN'S HUSBAND, THE (UKN) see **ROYAL BED, THE** • 1930

QUEEN'S KITTENS • 1938 • Kline Lester • ANS • USA

QUEENS LOGIC • 1990 • Rash Steve • USA

QUEEN'S MUSKETEERS, THE (USA) see **MOUSQUETAIRES DE LA REINE, LES** • 1903

QUEEN'S NECKLACE, THE (USA) see **AFFAIRE DU COLLIER DE LA REINE, L'** • 1945

QUEENS OF EVIL see **DELITTO DEL DIAVOLO, IL** • 1970

QUEEN'S RANSOM, A see **LIEH SHIH CHI HUA** • 1975

QUEEN'S ROYAL TOUR, A • 1954 • Hugham Oxley • DOC • UKN

QUEEN'S SECRET, THE • 1922 • Greenwood Edwin • UKN

QUEEN'S SECRET, THE see **TAINA KOROLEVY** • 1919

QUEEN'S SWORDSMEN, THE (USA) see **ESPADACHINES DE LA REINA, LOS** • 1960

QUEENS UP! • 1920 • Roach Hal • SHT • USA

QUEENS WILD • 1927 • Roberts Stephen • SHT • USA

QUEENS WILD • 1963 • *Bell Virginia* • USA

QUEENSLAND • 1976 • Ruane John • SHT • ASL

QUEENSLAND MEAT INDUSTRY • 1917 • ASL

QUEER CARGO • 1938 • Schuster Harold • UKN • PIRATES OF THE SEVEN SEAS

QUEER DUCKS • 1927 • Beaudine Harold • USA

QUEER ELOPEMENT, A • 1913 • Henderson Dell • USA

QUEER FOLKS • 1911 • *Vitagraph* • USA

QUEER QUARANTINE, A • 1914 • *Beery Wallace* • USA

QUEER.. THE EROTIC, THE (UKN) see **ALTRA FACCIA DEL PECCATO, L'** • 1969

QUEERING CUPID • 1915 • Miller Rube • USA

QUEI DANNATI GIORNI DELL'ODIO E DELL'INFERNO • 1971 • Markson Sean • ITL

QUEI DISPERATI CHE PUZZANO DI SUDORE E DI MORTE • 1970 • Buchs Julio • ITL, SPN • DESESPERADOS, LOS (SPN) ○ BULLET FOR SANDOVAL, A (USA) ○ VENGEANCE IS MINE (UKN)

QUEI DUE • 1935 • Righelli Gennaro • ITL

QUEI POCHI GIORNI D'ESTATE • 1966 • Artale Lorenzo • ITL

QUEI TEMERARI SULLE LORO PAZZE, SCATENATE, SCALCINATE CARRIOLE (ITL) see **MONTE CARLO OR BUST!** • 1969

QUEIMADA! see **QUEMADA!** • 1969

QUEL BANDITO SONO IO! • 1950 • Soldati Mario • ITL

QUEL CALDO MALEDETTO GIORNO DI FUOCO • 1968 • Bianchini Paolo • ITL, SPN • THAT DAMNED HOT DAY OF FIRE ○ AMETRALLADORA, LA ○ GATLING GUN

QUEL CARO DEMETRIO see **GIOCO D'AZZARDO** • 1943

QUEL EST L'ASSASSIN? • 1910 • Linder Max • FRN

QUEL FANTASMA DI MIO MARITO • 1950 • Mastrocinque Camillo • ITL

QUEL FICCANASO DELL'ISPETTORE LAWRENCE • 1974 • Bosch Juan • ITL

QUEL GIORNO DIO NON C'ERA • 1970 • Civirani Osvaldo • ITL • CASO DEFREGGER, IL ○ DIO NON C'ERA

QUEL GRAN PEZZO DELL'UBALDA TUTTA NUDA, TUTTA CALDA • 1972 • Laurenti Mariano • ITL

QUEL MALEDETTO GIORNO DELLA RESA DEI CONTI • 1971 • Garrone Sergio • ITL

QUEL MALEDETTO GIORNO D'INVERNO: DJANGO E SARTANA ALL'ULTIMO SANGUE • 1970 • Fidani Demofilo • ITL

QUEL MALEDETTO PONTE SULL'ELBA • 1968 • Klimovsky Leon • ITL, SPN • PUENTE SOBRE EL ELBA, EL (SPN) ○ LEGION OF NO RETURN, THE (UKN)

QUEL MALEDETTO TRENO BLINDATO • 1978 • Castellari Enzo G. • ITL • INGLORIOUS BASTARDS, THE ○ COUNTERFEIT COMMANDOS

QUEL MOVIMENTO CHE MI PIACE TANTO (DIMMI CHE ILLUSIONE NONE E..) • 1976 • Rossetti Franco • ITL

QUEL NOSTRO GRANDE AMORE • 1966 • Demicheli Tulio • ITL

QUEL POMERIGGIO MALEDETTO • 1977 • Siciliano Mario • ITL

QUEL TESORO DI PAPA • 1959 • Girolami Marino • ITL

QUELE DO PAJEU • 1970 • Duarte Anselmo • BRZ

QUELLA CAROGNA DELL'ISPETTORE STERLING • 1968 • Miraglia Emilio Paolo • ITL • THAT SWINE INSPECTOR STERLING

QUELLA CASA CON LA AL BUIO see **CASA CON LA SCALA NEL BUIO, LA** • 1983

QUELLA CHIARA NOTTE D'OTTOBRE • 1970 • Franciosa Massimo • ITL

QUELLA COROGNA DI FRANK MITRAGLIA • 1968 • Bervi J. • ITL

QUELLA DANNATA PATTUGLIA • 1969 • Montero Roberto Bianchi • ITL • BATTLE OF THE DAMNED

QUELLA ETA MALIZIOSA • 1975 • Amadio Silvio • ITL

QUELLA PICCOLA DIFFERENZA • 1969 • Tessari Duccio • ITL • THAT LITTLE DIFFERENCE

QUELLA PROVINCIA MALIZIOSA • 1975 • Baldanello Gianfranco • ITL

QUELLA SERA SULLA SPIAGGIA (ITL) see **SOIR DE LA PLAGE, UN** • 1961

QUELLA SPORCA STORIA DEL WEST • 1968 • Castellari Enzo G. • ITL • THAT DIRTY STORY OF THE WEST ○ JOHNNY HAMLET

QUELLA STRANA VOGLIA DI AMARE • 1978 • Imperoli Mario • ITL

QUELLA VECCHIA CANAGLIA • 1934 • Bragaglia Carlo Ludovico • ITL

QUELLA VILLA ACCANTO AL CIMITERO • 1982 • Fulci Lucio • USA • HOUSE AT THE END OF THE CEMETERY, THE ○ HOUSE BY THE CEMETERY, THE ○ HOUSE OUTSIDE THE CEMETERY, THE

QUELL'AMORE PARTICOLARE • 1970 • Martinelli Carlo • ITL

QUELLE DROLE DE BLANCHISSERIE • 1912 • Cohl Emile • ANS • FRN

QUELLE DROLE DE GOSSE! • 1935 • Joannon Leo • FRN • SACREE GOSSE, UNE

QUELLE FOLIE! • 1943 • Barakat Henry • EGY

QUELLE JOIE DE VIVRE • 1961 • Clement Rene • FRN, ITL • CHE GIOIA VIVERE (ITL)

QUELLE NOUVELLE! • 1974 • Brault Francois, Gauvreau J. • SHT • CND

QUELLE SACREE SOIREE! see **NUIT BLANCHE ET ROUGE A LEVRES** • 1956

QUELLE SPORCHE ANIME DANNATE • 1971 • Solvay Paolo • ITL

QUELLE STRANE OCCASIONI • 1976 • Magni Luigi, Loy Nanni • ITL

QUELLEN DER LIEBE • 1920 • *Carstennsen Conny* • FRG

QUELLI BELLI SIAMO NOI • 1970 • Mariuzzo Giorgio • ITL

QUELLI CHE CONTANO • 1974 • Bianchi Andrea • ITL

QUELLI CHE NON MUOIONO see **INGIUSTA CONDANNA, L'** • 1952

QUELLI CHE SANNO UCCIDERE (ITL) see **ETRANGERS, LES** • 1968

QUELLI DELLA BANDA BERETTA (ITL) see **GANG DES OTAGES, LE** • 1972

QUELLI DELLA CALIBRO 38 • 1976 • Dallamano Massimo • ITL

QUELLI DELLA MONTAGNA • 1943 • Vergano Aldo • ITL

QUELLI DELL'ANTIRAPINA • 1977 • Siragusa Gianni • ITL • QUATTRO MINUTI PER QUATTRO MILIARDI

QUELLO CHE NON T'ASPETTI see **FABBRICA DELL'IMPREVISTO, LA** • 1943

QUELLO SPORCO DISERTORE • 1971 • Klimovsky Leon • ITL

QUELQUE CHOSE EST ARRIVE DANS MA VIE see **SHAI'UN FI HAYATI** • 1966

QUELQUE JOURS AVEV TOI • 1987 • Sautet Claude • FRN

QUELQUE PART QUELQU'UN • 1972 • Bellon Yannick • FRN • SOMEONE, SOMEWHERE (USA)

QUELQUES ARPENTS DE NEIGE • 1972 • Heroux Denis • CND • REBELS, THE

QUELQUES ARPENTS DE NEIGE see **POUR QUELQUES ARPENTS DE NEIGE..** • 1962

QUELQUES MESSIEURS TROP TRANQUILLES • 1972 • Lautner Georges • FRN

QUELQUES PAS DANS LA VIE (FRN) see **TEMPI NOSTRI** • 1954

QUELQU'UN A TUE • 1933 • Forrester Jack • FRN • CHATEAU DE LA TERREUR, LE ○ SECRET DU VIEUX PRIEURE, LE ○ JEUNE FILLE EFFRAYEE, LA

QUELQU'UN DERRIERE LA PORTE (FRN) see **QUALCUNO DIETRO LA PORTA** • 1971

QUEM A BETA? • 1973 • dos Santos Nelson Pereira • BRZ, FRN • PAS DE VIOLENCE ENTRE NOUS (FRN) ○ QUI EST BETA? ○ WHERE IS BETA? ○ QUEM E BETA? ○ WHO IS BETA?

QUEM E BETA? see **QUEM A BETA?** • 1973

QUEM ESPERA POR SAPATOS DE DEFUNTO MORRE DESCALCO • 1970 • Monteiro Joao Cesar • PRT • WHOEVER WAITS FOR THE SHOES OF A DEAD MAN DIES WITHOUT SHOES

QUEMA DE JUDAS, LA • 1974 • Chalbaud Roman • VNZ • BURNING OF JUDAS, THE ○ GOLPE DE GARCIA ○ FINISHING STROKE

QUEMA EL SUELO • 1951 • Marquina Luis • SPN

QUEMADA! • 1969 • Pontecorvo Gillo • FRN, ITL • BATTLE OF THE ANTILLES ○ QUEIMADA! ○ BURN!

QUEMANDO TRADICIONES • 1971 • Alvarez Santiago • DOC • CUB

QUENCHED THIRST see **UTOLYENIYE ZHAZHDY** • 1968

QUENCHING OF THE THIRST see **UTOLYENIYE ZHAZHDY** • 1968

QUENCHING THIRST see **UTOLYENIYE ZHAZHDY** • 1968

QUENETRA, THE CITY OF DEATH • 1975 • Crammer Jim • USA, SYR

QUENTIN DURWARD (USA) see **ADVENTURES OF QUENTIN DURWARD, THE** • 1956

QUENTIN METHOD, THE see **ROGER & HARRY: THE MITERA TARGET** • 1977

QUENTIN QUAIL • 1946 • Jones Charles M. • ANS • USA

QUERELLE DE BREST • 1982 • Fassbinder R. W. • FRG, FRN • QUERELLE (UKN)

QUERELLE ENFANTINE • 1895 • Lumiere Louis • FRN

QUERELLE (UKN) see **QUERELLE DE BREST** • 1982

QUERELLES DE JARDINS • 1982 • Ruiz Raul • SHT • FRN • GARDEN QUARRELS ○ WAR OF THE GARDENS, THE

QUERIDA, LA • 1975 • Fernan-Gomez Fernando • SPN

QUERIDAS AMIGAS • 1980 • Orgambide Carlos • ARG • DEAR FRIENDS

QUERIDISIMOS VERDUGOS • 1974 • Patino Basilio Martin • SPN • DEAREST EXECUTIONERS

QUERIDO PROFESOR • 1966 • Seto Javier • SPN

QUERIDOS COMPANEROS.. • 1979 • de la Barra Pablo • VNZ, CHL • DEAR COMRADES..

QUERKOPF, DER see **MILLIONENTESTAMENT, DAS** • 1932

QUERO MORRER NO CARNAVAL see **QUIERO MORIR EN CARNAVAL** • 1961

QUERY see **MURDER IN REVERSE** • 1945

QUEST, THE • 1915 • Chaudet Louis W. • *Selig* • USA

QUEST, THE • 1915 • Pollard Harry • *American* • USA

QUEST, THE • 1958 • Jackson Stanley R. • DOC • CND

QUEST, THE • 1976 • Katzin Lee H. • TVM • USA

QUEST, THE • 1982 • Holcomb Rod • TVM • USA

QUEST, THE see **TSUMA YO BARA NO YONI** • 1935

QUEST, THE see **FROG DREAMING** • 1985

QU'EST-CE QUE TU VEUX JULIE? • 1976 • Dubreuil Charlotte • FRN • WHAT DO YOU WANT JULIE?

QU'EST-CE QUI FAIT COURIR DAVID? • 1982 • Chouraqui Elie • FRN

QU'EST-CE QUI FAIT COURIR JACKY? • 1969 • Leszczynski Witold (c/d) • DOC • PLN

QU'EST-CE QUI FAIT COURIR LES CROCODILES? • 1969 • Poitrenaud Jacques • FRN

QU'EST-CE QUI FAIT CRAQUER LES FILLES? • 1982 • Vocoret Michel • FRN

QU'EST-CE QU'ON ATTEND POUR ETRE HEUREUX? • 1982 • Serreau Coline • FRN

QU'EST-CE QU'ON VA DEVENIR? • 1971 • Gauthier Michel • CND

QUEST FOR EDEN see **PRIVATE TUTOR** • 1988

QUEST FOR FIRE • 1981 • Annaud Jean-Jacques • CND, FRN • GUERRE DU FEU, LA (FRN)

QUEST FOR FREEDOM • 1966 • Hilberman David • SHT • USA

QUEST FOR KING SOLOMON'S MINES, THE see **WATUSI** • 1959

QUEST FOR LOVE • 1971 • Thomas Ralph • UKN

QUEST FOR LOVE • 1987 • Nogueira Helena • SAF • FIRE IN THEIR HEARTS

QUEST FOR OIL • 1967 • McCullough Chris • DOC • ASL

QUEST FOR PEACE, THE see **SUPERMAN IV: THE QUEST FOR PEACE** • 1987

QUEST FOR THE BLUEBIRD OF PARADISE, THE • 1923 • Ward J. E. • DOC • ASL

QUEST FOR THE LOST CITY • 1955 • Lamb Dana, Lamb Ginger • DOC • USA

QUEST FOR THE SEVEN CITIES see **GOLD OF THE AMAZON WOMEN** • 1979

QUEST OF HAPPINESS, THE see **DUNUNGEN** • 1919

QUEST OF LIFE, THE • 1916 • Miller Ashley • USA

QUEST OF THE GOLDEN GOAT, THE • 1916 • *Hamilton Lloyd V.* • SHT • USA

QUEST OF THE SACRED GEM, THE • 1914 • Fitzmaurice George • USA

QUEST OF THE WIDOW, THE • 1915 • Davis Ulysses • USA

QUESTA E LA VITA • 1954 • Fabrizi Aldo, Pastina Giorgio, Zampa Luigi, Soldati Mario • ITL • OF LIFE AND LOVE (USA)

QUESTA LIBERTA DI AVERE LE ALI BAGNATE • 1971 • Santini Alessandro • ITL

QUESTA NOSTRA GENTE see **ULTIMA ILLUSIONE** • 1955

QUESTA SPECIE D'AMORE • 1972 • Bevilacqua Alberto • ITL

QUESTA VOLTA PARLIAMO DI UOMINI • 1965 • Wertmuller Lina • ITL • LET'S TALK ABOUT MEN (USA) ○ THIS TIME LET'S TALK ABOUT MEN ○ NOW LET'S TALK ABOUT MEN

QUESTA VOLTA TI FACCIO RICCO • 1974 • Parolini Gianfranco • ITL
QUESTE PAZZE, PAZZE DONNE • 1964 • Girolami Marino • ITL, FRN
QUESTI FANTASMI • 1954 • De Filippo Eduardo • ITL • THESE GHOSTS
QUESTI FANTASMI • 1967 • Castellani Renato • ITL, FRN • GHOSTS –ITALIAN STYLE ○ THREE GHOSTS ○ THESE GHOSTS
QUESTI PAZZI PAZZI ITALIANI • 1965 • Piacentini Tullio • ITL
QUESTI RAGAZZI • 1937 • Mattoli Mario • ITL
QUESTION, LA • 1976 • Heynemann Laurent • FRN
QUESTION, THE • 1911 • *Powers* • USA
QUESTION, THE • 1916 • Handworth Harry • USA
QUESTION, THE • 1917 • Vekroff Perry N. • USA
QUESTION, THE • 1966 • Halas John • UKN
QUESTION, THE • 1970 • *Ghatak Ritwik* • DOC • IND
QUESTION AND ANSWER MAN, THE • 1914 • *Briscoe Lottie* • USA
QUESTION D'ASSURANCE, UNE • 1959 • Kast Pierre • SHT • FRN
QUESTION DE VIE • 1970 • Theberge Andre • CND
QUESTION IN LOVE, A • 1975 • Barakat • EGY
QUESTION IN TOGOLAND • 1957 • Porter • SHT • UNN
QUESTION MARK see **F FOR FAKE** • 1977
QUESTION MARK, THE • 1911 • *Boss Yale* • USA
QUESTION MARK, THE • 1916 • *Davenport Dorothy* • SHT • USA
QUESTION OF ADULTERY, A • 1958 • Chaffey Don • UKN • CASE OF MRS. LORING, THE (USA)
QUESTION OF AGE, A • 1912 • *Pates Gwendoline* • USA
QUESTION OF CLOTHES, A • 1914 • Brooke Van Dyke • *Vitagraph* • USA
QUESTION OF CLOTHES, A • 1914 • Ransom Charles • *Edison* • USA
QUESTION OF CONSCIENCE, A • 1915 • Powell Paul • USA
QUESTION OF COURAGE, A • 1914 • Cabanne W. Christy • USA
QUESTION OF EVIDENCE, A • 1912 • *Herman Charles* • USA
QUESTION OF GUILT, A • 1978 • Butler Robert • TVM • USA
QUESTION OF HAIR, A • 1912 • *Selig* • USA
QUESTION OF HAIR, A • 1912 • *Solax* • USA
QUESTION OF HATS AND GOWNS, A • 1914 • Miller Ashley • USA
QUESTION OF HONESTY, A • 1917 • Thayer Otis B. • SHT • USA
QUESTION OF HONOR, A • 1915 • Eason B. Reeves • USA
QUESTION OF HONOR, A • 1922 • Carewe Edwin • USA
QUESTION OF HONOR, A • 1982 • Taylor Jud • TVM • USA
QUESTION OF HONOUR, A (UKN) see **QUESTIONE D'ONORE, UNA** • 1966
QUESTION OF IDENTITY, A • 1913 • Buckland Warwick? • UKN
QUESTION OF IDENTITY, A • 1914 • Brabin Charles J. • USA
QUESTION OF IDENTITY: WAR OF 1812, A • 1966 • Devlin Bernard • SHT • CND • GUERRE DE 1812, LA
QUESTION OF LEADERSHIP, A • 1981 • Loach Kenneth • UKN
QUESTION OF LIFE, A see **SOMETHING FOR JOEY** • 1977
QUESTION OF LOVE, A • 1978 • Thorpe Jerry • TVM • USA
QUESTION OF LOVING, A see **QUI A TIRE SUR NOS HISTOIRES D'AMOUR?** • 1986
QUESTION OF MODESTY, A • 1911 • *Glynn Elsie* • USA
QUESTION OF PRINCIPLE, A • 1922 • Cooper George A. • UKN
QUESTION OF RAPE, A (UKN) see **VIOL, LE** • 1967
QUESTION OF RIGHT, A • 1914 • *Theby Rosemary* • USA
QUESTION OF RIGHT AND WRONG, A • 1915 • Brooke Van Dyke • USA
QUESTION OF SECONDS, A • 1912 • *Ogle Charles* • USA
QUESTION OF SILENCE, A see **STILTE ROND CHRISTINE M., DE** • 1982
QUESTION OF SIZE, A • 1912 • *Pathe* • USA
QUESTION OF SUSPENSE, A • 1961 • Varnel Max • UKN
QUESTION OF TELEVISION VIOLENCE, THE • 1972 • Ferguson Graeme • DOC • CND
QUESTION OF THE SIXTH, A • 1980 • Parker Graham • MTV • CND
QUESTION OF TODAY, THE • 1928 • Bacon Lloyd • SHT • USA
QUESTION OF TRUST, A • 1920 • Elvey Maurice • UKN
QUESTION ROYALE, LA • 1976 • Mesnil Christian • DOC • BLG
QUESTION SEVEN (USA) see **FRAGE SIEBEN** • 1961
QUESTION TIME • 1984 • Hristov Hristo • BUL
QUESTIONE DI PELLE (ITL) see **TRIPES AU SOLEIL, LES** • 1959
QUESTIONE D'ONORE, UNA • 1966 • Zampa Luigi • ITL, FRN • QUESTION OF HONOUR, A (UKN)
QUESTIONE PRIVATA, UNA • 1966 • Trentin Giorgio • ITL
QUESTIONMARK MOTORIST see **"?" MOTORIST, THE** • 1906
QUESTIONS FOR THE LIVING see **YIGE SIZHE DUI SHENGZHE DE FANGWEN** • 1987
QUESTIONS OF HAIRS, A • 1916 • Stow Percy • UKN
QUESTO AMORE AI CONFINI DEL MONDO • 1960 • Scotese Giuseppe Maria • ITL, ARG
QUESTO E QUELLO • 1984 • Corbucci Sergio • ITL • THIS AND THAT
QUESTO IL PUNTO • Campani Paul • ANS • ITL
QUESTO IMPOSSIBILE OGGETTO • 1973 • Frankenheimer John • ITL, FRN • STORY OF A LOVE STORY, THE (USA) ○ IMPOSSIBLE OBJET, L'(FRN) ○ IMPOSSIBLE OBJECT
QUESTO MONDO MERAVIGLIOSO see **QUESTO NOSTRO MONDO** • 1957
QUESTO MONDO PROIBITO • 1963 • Gabella Fabrizio • ITL
QUESTO NOSTRO MONDO • 1957 • Lazzari Ugo, Negri Angelo • DOC • ITL • QUESTO MONDO MERAVIGLIOSO
QUESTO PAZZO, PAZZO MONDO DELLA CANZONE • 1964 • Corbucci Bruno, Grimaldi Gianni • ITL
QUESTO SI CHE E AMORE • 1978 • Ottoni Filippo • ITL
QUESTO SPORCO MONDO MERAVIGLIOSO • 1971 • Loy Mino, Scattini Luigi • ITL
QUESTOR TAPES, THE • 1974 • Colla Richard A. • TVM • USA
QUETICO • 1958 • Chapman Christopher • DOC • CND
QUETZALCOATL • 1951 • Wisniewski Ray • SHT • USA
QUEUE, THE • 1963 • Donev Donyo • ANM • BUL
QUEUE DE BETON • 1978 • Baudricourt Michel • FRN
QUEUTARDES, LES • 1977 • Stephen Richard • FRN
QUI? • 1970 • Keigel Leonard • FRN, ITL • CADAVERE DAGLI ARTIGLI D'ACCIAIO, IL (ITL) ○ SENSUOUS ASSASSIN, THE (USA) ○ WHO ARE YOU? ○ WHO?
QUI A TIRE SUR NOS HISTOIRES D'AMOUR? • 1986 • Carre Louis • CND • QUESTION OF LOVING, A
QUI A TUE MAX? • 1913 • Linder Max • FRN • MAX ASSASSINE
QUI CA? • 1974 • Brault Francois, Gauvreau J. • SHT • CND
QUI COMINCIA L'AVVENTURA • 1975 • Di Palma Carlo • ITL • LUCKY GIRLS (USA) ○ MIDNIGHT PLEASURES (UKN)
QUI COMMANDE AUS FUSILS • 1969 • Ivens Joris (c/d) • DOC • FRN
QUI EST BETA? see **QUEM A BETA?** • 1973
QUI EST COUPABLE? • 1972 • Bouchouchi Youssef • ALG
QUI ETES-VOUS INSPECTEUR CHANDLER? • 1974 • Lupo Michele • FRN, ITL
QUI ETES-VOUS, M. SORGE? • 1960 • Ciampi Yves • FRN, ITL, JPN • WHO ARE YOU MR. SORGE? (USA) ○ WHO ARE YOU?
QUI ETES-VOUS, POLLY MAGGOO? • 1965 • Klein William • FRN • WHO ARE YOU POLLY MAGGOO?
QUI J'OSE AIMER • Coldefy Jean-Marie • FRN
QUI OSE NOUS ACCUSER? • 1962 • Komor Serge • FRN
QUI? QUOI? POURQUOI? • 1973 • Lamothe Arthur • DCS • CND
QUI SOMMES-NOUS? see **MAN NAHN U** • 1960
QUI TROP EMBRASSE • 1986 • Davila Jacques • FRN
QUI VEUT TUER CARLOS? see **GEHEIMNISSE IN GOLDENEN NYLONS** • 1966
QUICK • 1932 • Siodmak Robert • FRN
QUICK see **QUICK, KOENIG DER CLOWNS** • 1933
QUICK! A PLUMBER • 1911 • *Lubin* • USA
QUICK ACTION • 1921 • Sloman Edward • USA
QUICK AND THE DEAD, THE • 1963 • Totten Robert • USA
QUICK AND THE DEAD, THE • 1987 • Day Robert • TVM • USA
QUICK AS LIGHTNING see **KVICK SOM BLIXTEN** • 1927
QUICK, BEFORE IT MELTS • 1965 • Mann Delbert • USA
QUICK BEFORE IT'S OVER see **PRONTO ANTES QUE SE ACABE** • 1982
QUICK BILLIE • 1970 • Baillie Bruce • USA • QUICK BILLY
QUICK BILLY see **QUICK BILLIE** • 1970
QUICK CHANGE • 1925 • Henderson Dell • USA
QUICK CHANGE • 1990 • Franklin Howard, Murray Bill • USA
QUICK CHANGE see **HOLD-UP** • 1986
QUICK CHANGE MESMERIST, A • 1908 • Booth W. R. • UKN
QUICK DRAW DOG see **HAYAUCHIINU** • 1967
QUICK GUN, THE • 1964 • Salkow Sidney • USA • FAST GUN, THE
QUICK, KOENIG DER CLOWNS • 1933 • Siodmak Robert • FRG • QUICK
QUICK, LET'S GET MARRIED • 1964 • Dieterle William • USA • SEVEN DIFFERENT WAYS ○ CONFESSION, THE
QUICK MILLIONS • 1931 • Brown Rowland • USA
QUICK MILLIONS see **JONES FAMILY IN QUICK MILLIONS** • 1939
QUICK MONEY • 1937 • Killy Edward • USA • TAKING THE TOWN
QUICK ON THE TRIGGER • 1949 • Nazarro Ray • USA • CONDEMNED IN ERROR (UKN)
QUICK ON THE VIGOR • 1950 • Kneitel Seymour • ANS • USA
QUICK RECOVERY, A • 1902 • *Biograph* • USA
QUICK SHAVE AND BRUSH UP • 1900 • Smith G. A. • UKN
QUICK TRIGGER LEE • 1931 • McGowan J. P. • USA
QUICK TRIGGERS • 1918 • *Hart Neal* • SHT • USA
QUICK TRIGGERS • 1928 • Taylor Ray • USA
QUICK TURNOVER • 1976 • USA
QUICK-WIT, THE see **EXIPNAKIAS, O** • 1967
QUICKENING FLAME, THE • 1919 • Vale Travers • USA
QUICKER THAN THE EYE • 1988 • Gessner Nicolas
QUICKER'N A WINK • 1940 • Sidney George • SHT • USA
QUICKER'N LIGHTNIN' • 1925 • Thorpe Richard • USA
QUICKEST WAY, THE • 1913 • *Nestor* • USA
QUICKLY • 1974 • Cavallone Alberto • ITL • SPARI E BACI A COLAZIONE
QUICKSAND • 1950 • Pichel Irving • USA
QUICKSAND see **QUICKSANDS** • 1919
QUICKSAND OF THE FEMALE BODY, THE see **JOTAI NO DORONUMA** • 1968
QUICKSANDS • 1913 • *Kerrigan J. Warren* • USA
QUICKSANDS • 1919 • Schertzinger Victor • USA • QUICKSAND
QUICKSANDS • 1923 • Conway Jack • USA
QUICKSANDS see **BROKEN BARRIER** • 1917
QUICKSANDS see **RUCHOME PIASKI** • 1969
QUICKSANDS, THE • 1914 • *Kalem* • USA
QUICKSANDS, THE • 1914 • Cabanne W. Christy • *Majestic* • USA
QUICKSANDS OF DECEIT • 1916 • Borzage Frank • SHT • USA
QUICKSANDS OF LIFE • 1915 • Leigh J. L. V. • UKN
QUICKSANDS OF SIN • 1913 • *Essanay* • USA
QUICKSANDS OF SOCIETY, THE • 1915 • Vale Travers • USA
QUICKSILVER • 1976 • Theberge Andre • SHT • CND
QUICKSILVER • 1986 • Donnelly Tom • USA
QUICKSILVER PUDDING • 1909 • Collins Alf? • UKN
QUIEN ES LA BESTIA? • 1968 • Arango Ramiro • SPN
QUIEN GRITA VENGANZA? • 1969 • Romero-Marchent Rafael • SPN
QUIEN MATO A EVA? • 1934 • Bohr Jose • MXC
QUIEN ME COMPRA UN LIO? • 1940 • Iquino Ignacio F. • SPN
QUIEN ME QUIERE A MI? • 1936 • Saenz De Heredia Jose Luis, Bunuel Luis (U/c) • SPN
QUIEN PUEDE MATAR A UN NINO? • 1975 • Ibanez Serrador Narciso • SPN • ISLAND OF THE DAMNED (USA) ○ WOULD YOU KILL A CHILD? ○ WHO CAN KILL A CHILD? ○ ISLAND OF DEATH ○ DEATH IS CHILD'S PLAY
QUIEN RESULTA RESPONSABLE see **QRR** • 1971
QUIEN SABE? • 1966 • Damiani Damiano • ITL • BULLET FOR THE GENERAL, A (USA) ○ VIVA BANDITO
QUIEN SOY YO? • 1971 • Fernandez Ramon • SPN
QUIEN TE QUIERE A TI? • 1941 • Aguilar Rolando • MXC
QUIERE CASARSE CONMIGO? • 1967 • Carreras Enrique • ARG, SPN • WOULD YOU LIKE TO MARRY ME?
QUIEREME CON MUSICA • 1956 • Iquino Ignacio F. • SPN
QUIEREME PORQUE ME MUERO • 1953 • Urueta Chano • MXC
QUIERO MORIR EN CARNAVAL • 1961 • Cortes Fernando • MXC, BRZ • QUERO MORRER NO CARNAVAL ○ A RITMO DE BOSSA NOVA
QUIERO SER ARTISTA • 1957 • Davison Tito • MXC
QUIERO VIVIR • 1951 • Gout Alberto • MXC
QUIET AFFAIR, A see **STILLA FLIRT, EN** • 1934
QUIET AMERICAN, THE • 1958 • Mankiewicz Joseph L. • USA
QUIET COOL • 1986 • Borris Clay • USA
QUIET COUNTRY, THE • 1972 • Littlewood Mark • DCS • UKN
QUIET DAY AT MURPHY'S, A • 1914 • Lucas Wilfred • USA
QUIET DAY IN BELFAST, A • 1974 • Bessada Milad • CND
QUIET DAYS IN CLICHY • 1989 • Chabrol Claude • FRN
QUIET DAYS IN CLICHY (USA) see **STILLE DAGE I CLICHY** • 1970
QUIET DEATH, A see **ENAS ISICHOS THANATOS** • 1987
QUIET DON, THE see **TIKHU DON** • 1931
QUIET DUEL, THE see **SHIZUKANARU KETTO** • 1949
QUIET EARTH, THE • 1985 • Murphy Geoff • NZL
QUIET EVENING, A • 1911 • *Reliance* • USA
QUIET EVENING AT HOME, A • 1911 • *American* • USA
QUIET FIGHT, THE see **SHIZUKANARU KETTO** • 1949
QUIET FLOWS THE DON (UKN) see **TIKHII DON** • 1958
QUIET FLOWS THE MEGHNA • 1973 • Kabir Alamgir • BNG
QUIET FOURTH, A • 1941 • D'Arcy Harry • SHT • USA
QUIET FUGITIVE, THE see **TIHIYAT BEGLETS** • 1971
QUIET GUN, THE • 1957 • Claxton William F. • USA
QUIET HOME, A see **CSENDES OTTHON** • 1957
QUIET LITTLE GAME, A • 1915 • *Essanay* • USA
QUIET LITTLE WEDDING, A • 1913 • Sennett Mack • USA
QUIET LONG MELODY • 1966 • Kandelaki Gela • DCS • USS
QUIET MAN, THE • 1952 • Ford John • USA
QUIET NIGHT, A • 1933 • Horne James W. • SHT • USA
QUIET ODESSA see **TIKHAYA ODYESSA** • 1968
QUIET ON THE SET FILMING AGNES OF GOD see **MAKING OF AGNES OF GOD, THE** • 1985
QUIET ONE, THE • 1948 • Meyers Sidney • USA
QUIET PLACE IN THE COUNTRY, A (USA) see **TRANQUILLO POSTO DI CAMPAGNA, UN** • 1968
QUIET PLACE TO KILL, A (UKN) see **PARANOIA** • 1969
QUIET, PLEASE • 1933 • Stevens George • SHT • USA
QUIET PLEASE • 1938 • Neill R. William • UKN
QUIET! PLEASE • 1941 • Fleischer Dave • ANS • USA
QUIET PLEASE! • 1945 • Hanna William, Barbera Joseph • ANS • USA
QUIET PLEASE see **QUE SE CALLEN** • 1966
QUIET PLEASE, MURDER • 1942 • Larkin John • USA
QUIET RACKET, THE • 1966 • Potterton Gerald • CND
QUIET REVOLUTION, A • 1975 • Benegal Shyam • DOC • IND
QUIET ROLLS THE DAY see **EK DIN PRATIDIN** • 1979
QUIET SQUAD, LE • 1967 • McKimson Robert • ANS • USA
QUIET STREET, A • 1922 • Roach Hal • SHT • USA
QUIET SUPPER FOR FOUR, A • 1916 • Christie Al • SHT • USA
QUIET THUNDER • 1988 • Rice David • USA
QUIET TWO, THE see **FUTARI SHIZUKA** • 1922
QUIET VICTORY • 1987 • Campanella Roy Ii • USA • QUIET VICTORY: THE CHARLIE WEDEMEYER STORY
QUIET VICTORY: THE CHARLIE WEDEMEYER STORY see **QUIET VICTORY** • 1987
QUIET WEDDING • 1941 • Asquith Anthony • UKN
QUIET WEEK AT HOME, A see **TICHY TYDEN V DOME** • 1969
QUIET WEEK IN A HOUSE, A see **TICHY TYDEN V DOME** • 1969
QUIET WEEKEND • 1946 • French Harold • UKN
QUIET WOMAN, THE • 1951 • Gilling John • UKN
QUIET WORKER, THE • 1928 • Lamont Charles • SHT • USA
QUIETEST HORSE IN AUSTRALIA, THE • 1908 • ASL
QUIETLY SHOUTING • 1979 • Hughes Bill • DOC • ASL
QUIETOS TODOS! • 1959 • Gomez Urquiza Zacarias • MXC
QUIGLEY DOWN UNDER • 1990 • Wincer Simon • ASL, USA
QU'IL EST JOLI GARCON L'ASSASSIN DE PAPA • 1978 • Caputo Michel • FRN • ARRETE DE RAMER, T'ATTAQUES LA FALAISE
QU'IL ETAIT BON MON PETIT FRANCAIS see **COMO ERA GOSTOSO O MEU FRANCES** • 1971
QUILAS, O MAU DA FITA • 1980 • Costa Jose Fonseca • PRT • QUILAS, THE BAD OF THE PICTURE ○ KILAS, O MAU DA FITA
QUILAS, THE BAD OF THE PICTURE see **QUILAS, O MAU DA FITA** • 1980
QUILLE, LA • 1961 • Herman Jean • FRN
QUILLER MEMORANDUM, THE • 1966 • Anderson Michael • UKN, USA
QUILOMBO • 1984 • Diegues Carlos • BRZ
QUILP see **MISTER QUILP** • 1974
QUILT OF HATHOR see **FRIDAY'S CURSE 4: QUILT OF HATHOR/ THE AWAKENING** • 1987
QUINCANNON, FRONTIER SCOUT • 1956 • Selander Lesley • USA • FRONTIER SCOUT (UKN)
QUINCAS BORBA • 1988 • Filho Roberto Santos • BRZ
QUINCE BAJO LA LONA • 1959 • Navarro Agustin • SPN
QUINCEANERA • 1958 • Crevenna Alfredo B. • MXC
QUINCEVILLE RAFFLE, THE • 1911 • *Essanay* • USA
QUINCY ADAMS SAWYER • 1922 • Badger Clarence • USA
QUINCY ADAMS SAWYER AND MASON'S CORNER FOLKS • 1912 • *Puritan Special Features* • USA
QUINCY'S QUEST • 1979 • Reed Robert • MTV • USA
QUINDICI FORCHE PER UN ASSASSINO • 1968 • Malasomma Nunzio • ITL, SPN • FIFTEEN SCAFFOLDS FOR A MURDERER
QUINIELA, LA • 1959 • Mariscal Ana • SPN
QUININE • 1917 • *International Film Services* • ANS • USA
QUINISCOPIO • 1987 • Padron Juan • ANM • CUB
QUINNEYS • 1919 • Wilson Rex • UKN
QUINNEYS • 1927 • Elvey Maurice • UKN
QUINNS, THE • 1977 • Petrie Daniel • TVM • USA
QUINS see **QUINT CITY, U.S.A.** • 1963

QUINT CITY, U.S.A. • 1963 • Leacock Richard • USA • HAPPY MOTHER'S DAY, MRS. FISHER ○ HAPPY MOTHER'S DAY ○ QUINS
QUINTA DEL PORRO, LA • 1980 • Bellmunt Francisco • SPN • POT GENERATION, THE
QUINTANA • 1969 • Musolino Vincenzo • ITL
QUINTET • 1979 • Altman Robert • USA
QUINTIN SALAZAR • 1968 • Santiago Pablo • PHL
QUINTO COMANDAMENTO, IL see **ALBA DEI FALSI DEI, L'** • 1978
QUINTO DE ALAS • 1968 • Diaz Leody M. • PHL
QUINTO NON AMMAZZARE • 1969 • Klimovsky Leon • ITL
QUINTO PATIO • 1950 • Sevilla Raphael J. • MXC
QUINTRALA, LA • 1955 • del Carril Hugo • ARG
QUINZE ANOS DE OBRAS PUBLICAS • 1948 • Ribeiro Antonio Lopes • SHT • PRT
QUIPROQUO • 1908 • Melies Georges • FRN • MISTAKEN IDENTITY, A (USA)
QUIRINALE, IL • 1947 • Mantici • SHT • ITL
QUIRK • 1976 • USA
QUIT YE LIKE MEN • 1906 • Jeapes Harold? • UKN
QUITE A COMPLICATED GIRL see **RAGAZZA PIUTTOSTA COMPLICATA, UNA** • 1968
QUITE A SHOW see **LEPA PARADA** • 1970
QUITE BY CHANCE • 1987 • Massaro Francesco • ITL
QUITE GOOD CHAPS see **DOST DOBRI CHLAPI** • 1972
QUITE ORDINARY LIFE, A see **KET ELHATAROZAS** • 1976
QUITS • 1911 • Martinek H. O. • UKN
QUITS • 1913 • *A.r. Films* • UKN
QUITS • 1914 • *Melies* • USA
QUITS • 1915 • De Grasse Joseph • *Rex* • USA
QUITS • 1915 • Van Wally • *Vitagraph* • USA
QUITTE OU DOUBLE • 1952 • Vernay Robert • FRN
QUITTE OU DOUBLE see **ROSE** • 1935
QUITTER, THE • 1915 • *Cobb Edmund F.* • USA
QUITTER, THE • 1916 • George Burton • *Bison* • SHT • USA
QUITTER, THE • 1916 • Horan Charles • *Rolfe* • USA
QUITTER, THE • 1929 • Henabery Joseph • USA
QUITTER, THE • 1934 • Thorpe Richard • USA
QUITTER GRANT • 1922 • Collins Edwin J. • UKN
QUITTER THIONVILLE • 1977 • Alkama Mohammed • DOC • FRN
QUIXOTE • 1965 • Baillie Bruce • USA
QUIZ BIZ • 1941 • Jason Will • SHT • USA
QUIZ CRIMES NOS.1-6 • 1943 • Haines Ronald • SHS • UKN
QUIZ WHIZ • 1958 • White Jules • SHT • USA
QULLA, AL- • 1961 • Saleh Tewfik • SHT • EGY • GARGOULETTE, LA
QUNYING LUANWU • 1988 • Ou Dingping • HKG • PROFILES OF PLEASURE
QUO VADIS? • 1901 • Zecca Ferdinand • FRN • WHENCE DOES HE COME
QUO VADIS? • 1912 • Guazzoni Enrico • ITL
QUO VADIS? • 1923 • Annuzio Gabriel D., Jacoby Georg • ITL
QUO VADIS? • 1951 • LeRoy Mervyn • USA
QUO VADIS? • 1974 • Borosak Rudolf, Hrs Vladimir • YGS
QUO VADIS? • 1985 • Rossi Franco • TVM • ITL
QUO VADIS HOMO SAPIENS • 1982 • Popescu-Gopo Ion • ANM • RMN
QUO VADIS, MRS. LUMB? • 1965 • Kelly Ron • CND
QUO VADIS SPIRIDION • 1911 • Dimitracopoulos Spiros • GRC
QUO VADIS ZIVORAD • 1969 • Dukanovic Milo • YGS
QUODLIBET • 1968 • *Biographic* • ANS • UKN
QUOI DE NEUF.. A PIE-IX? • 1973 • Lamothe Arthur • DCS • CND
QUOI DE NEUF, PUSSYCAT? (FRN) see **WHAT'S NEW PUSSYCAT?** • 1965
QUOI? (FRN) see **CHE?** • 1972
QUOTATION FROM U TANT'S REPORT, A see **CYTAT Z RAPORTU U THANTA** • 1972
QUOTE, UNQUOTE see **KLAMMER AUF, KLAMMER ZU** • 1966

R

R—! see **WORST CRIME OF ALL!, THE** • 1966
R-1 • 1927 • Fischinger Oskar • ANS • FRG
R-69 • 1970 • Gagnon Charles • CND
R-69 TWO YEARS LATER • 1976 • Gagnon Charles • DOC • CND
R.A.S. • 1973 • Boisset Yves • FRN, ITL, TNS • R.A.S. NULLA DA SEGNALARE (ITL) ○ R.A.S. RIEN A SIGNALER
R.A.C. INTERNATIONAL RALLY OF GREAT BRITAIN, 1956 • 1956 • Mills Peter • DOC • UKN
R.A.C. INTERNATIONAL T.T. 1955 • 1955 • Mills Peter • DOC • UKN
R.A. KARTINI • 1983 • Syumanjaya • INN
R.A.S. NULLA DA SEGNALARE (ITL) see **R.A.S.** • 1973
R.A.S. RIEN A SIGNALER see **R.A.S.** • 1973
R.C.M.P. • 1960 • Haldane Don • SER • CND
R.C.M.P. AND THE TREASURE OF GENGHIS KHAN • 1948 • Brannon Fred C., Canutt Yakima • USA
R.F.D. 10,000 B.C. • 1917 • O'Brien Willis • ANS • USA • RURAL DELIVERY, TEN THOUSAND B.C.
R.I.P. • 1974 • Funnell Martin • UKN
R.M.C.-67 • 1967 • Perski Ludwik • DOC • PLN
R.N.37 • 1938 • Leenhardt Roger • DCS • FRN
R.O.B.O.T. see **CHOPPING MALL** • 1986
R.O.T.O.R • 1988 • Blaine Cullen • USA
R.P.M. • 1970 • Kramer Stanley • USA • R.P.M. *REVOLUTIONS PER MINUTE ○ REVOLUTIONS PER MINUTE
R.P.M. *REVOLUTIONS PER MINUTE see **R.P.M.** • 1970
R.P.Z. APPELLE BERLIN (FRN) see **GEHEIMAKTION SCHWARZE KAPELLE** • 1960
R.S.V.P. • 1921 • Ray Charles • USA
R.S.V.P. • 1984 • Amero John, Amero Lem • USA
R34 • 1967 • Chambers Jack* • DOC • CND
RA see **RA-EKSPEDISJONEN** • 1971
RA-EKSPEDISJONEN • 1971 • Ehrenborg Lennart • DOC • NRW, SWD • RA EXPEDITIONS, THE ○ RA
RA EXPEDITIONS, THE see **RA-EKSPEDISJONEN** • 1971
RA-MU, KING OF THE SUN • 1934 • Salisbury Edward A. • USA
RA-RA-BOOM-DER-A see **TA-RA-RA-BOOM-DEE-AYE** • 1925
RAAG YAMAN KALYAN, THE • 1972 • Benegal Shyam • DCS • IND
RAAT ANDHERI THI • 1967 • Kumar Shiv • IND • NIGHT WAS DARK, THE
RAAT AUR DIN • 1968 • Bose Satyen • IND • DAY AND NIGHT
RAAT BHORE • 1956 • Sen Mrinal • IND • DAWN, THE ○ NIGHT'S END
RAAZ • 1967 • Dave Ravindra • IND • SECRET ○ MYSTERY
RABA LIOUBVI • 1977 • Mikhalkov Nikita • USS • SLAVE OF LOVE, A ○ RABA LJUBVI ○ RABA LUBVI
RABA LJUBVI see **RABA LIOUBVI** • 1977
RABA LUBVI see **RABA LIOUBVI** • 1977
RABATTEUSE, LA • 1977 • Bernard-Aubert Claude • FRN
RABAUKENKABARETT, DAS • *Hoffmann Jutta* • GDR • NOISY CABARET, THE
RABBI AND THE SHIKSE, THE • 1976 • Silberg Joel • ISR
RABBI GAMLIEL • 1973 • *Banai Yossi* • ISR
RABBI OF NEMIROV, THE • 1965 • Wolman Dan • ISR
RABBI VON KUANG-FU, DER see **HERRIN DER WELT 3, DIE** • 1919
RABBIA, LA • 1963 • Pasolini Pier Paolo, Guareschi Giovanni • DOC • ITL
RABBIT CASE, THE see **CAUSA KRALIK** • 1979
RABBIT EVERY MONDAY • 1951 • Freleng Friz • ANS • USA
RABBIT FIRE • 1951 • Jones Charles M. • ANS • USA
RABBIT HOOD • 1949 • Jones Charles M. • ANS • USA
RABBIT HUNT, THE • 1938 • Kline Lester • ANS • USA
RABBIT MAN, THE see **KANINMANNEN** • 1990
RABBIT OF SEVILLE • 1950 • Jones Charles M. • ANS • USA
RABBIT PUNCH • 1948 • Jones Charles M. • ANS • USA
RABBIT PUNCH • 1955 • Tendlar Dave • ANS • USA
RABBIT RAMPAGE • 1955 • Jones Charles M. • ANS • USA
RABBIT ROMEO • 1957 • McKimson Robert • ANS • USA
RABBIT, RUN • 1970 • Smight Jack • USA
RABBIT SEASONING • 1952 • Jones Charles M. • ANS • USA
RABBIT STEW, THE see **LEGENDA A NYULPAPRIKASROL** • 1975
RABBIT STEW AND RABBITS TOO • 1969 • McKimson Robert • ANS • USA
RABBIT TEST • 1978 • Rivers Joan • USA • SLIGHTLY PREGNANT MAN, THE
RABBIT TRANSIT • 1947 • Freleng Friz • ANS • USA
RABBIT TRAP, THE • 1959 • Leacock Philip • USA
RABBITS see **NIGHT OF THE LEPUS** • 1972
RABBITS ARE THE FRIENDS OF TOADS • 1960 • Knowles Dorothy • USA
RABBIT'S FEAT • 1960 • Jones Charles M. • ANS • USA
RABBITS IN THE CLOAKROOM see **NYULAK A RUHATARBAN** • 1972
RABBITS IN THE TALL GRASS see **KRALICI VE VYSOKE TRAVE** • 1961
RABBIT'S KIN • 1952 • McKimson Robert • ANS • USA
RABBIT'S MONEY, THE see **MONNAIE DE LAPIN, LA** • 1899
RABBITS MOON see **LUNE DES LAPINS, LA** • 1971
RABBITSON CRUSOE • 1956 • Freleng Friz • ANS • USA
RABBLE, THE see **GARAKUTA** • 1964
RABBLE TACTICS see **ZAHYO MONOGATARI** • 1963
RABHI BALKHIE • 1974 • Halil Abdul Khaliq, Nazir Mohamed, Shafaq Toryali, Farani Daoud, Shadan Abdullah • AFG
RABIA, LA see **RAGE, LA** • 1978
RABIA POR DENTRO, LA (MXC) see **RABIA (THE RAGE), LA** • 1962
RABIA (THE RAGE), LA • 1962 • Gold Myron J. • USA, MXC • RABIA POR DENTRO, LA (MXC) ○ RAGE WITHIN, THE
RABID • 1976 • Cronenberg David • CND
RABID HUNTERS • 1932 • Foster John, Stallings George • ANS • USA
RABIHA -TAKIET EL EKHFAA • 1944 • Mustafa Niazi • EGY • MAGIC HAT, THE ○ RABIYA
RABINDRANATH TAGORE • 1961 • Ray Satyajit • DOC • IND • TAGORE
RABINYA • 1970 • Mansurov Bulat • USS • TAKYR, THE SLAVE-GIRL ○ SLAVE-GIRL, THE ○ SLAVE, THE
RABIYA see **RABIHA -TAKIET EL EKHFAA** • 1944
RABLELEK • 1913 • Curtiz Michael • HNG • CAPTIVE SOUL
RABOLIOT • 1945 • Daroy Jacques • FRN
RABONA, LA • 1978 • David Mario • ARG • PLAYING HOOKEY
RABOUCHI POSSELOK • 1965 • Vengerov Vladimir • USS • FACTORY TOWN, A
RABOUILLEUSE, LA • 1943 • Rivers Fernand • FRN
RABOUILLEUSE, LA see **ARRIVISTES, LES** • 1960
RABOUILLEUSE, LA see **TRUBE WASSER** • 1960
RACA • 1961 • Fraga Augusto • PRT
RACCOMANDATO DI FERRO, IL • 1959 • Baldi Marcello • ITL
RACCONTE A DUE PIAZZE (ITL) see **LIT A DEUX PLACES, LE** • 1965
RACCONTI D'ESTATE • 1958 • Franciolini Gianni • ITL, FRN • FEMMES D'UN ETE (FRN) ○ LOVE ON THE RIVIERA (USA) ○ SUMMER TALES ○ GIRLS FOR THE SUMMER
RACCONTI DI CANTERBURY, I • 1972 • Pasolini Pier Paolo • ITL, FRN • CANTERBURY TALES, THE (UKN)
RACCONTI DI CANTERBURY N.2., I • 1974 • Dandolo Lucio • ITL • LUSTY WIVES OF CANTERBURY, THE (UKN)
RACCONTI DI GIOVANI AMORI • 1967 • Olmi Ermanno • ITL
RACCONTI DI VITERBURY, I • 1973 • Caiano Mario • ITL
RACCONTI PROIBITI.. DI NIENTE VESTITI • 1972 • Rondi Brunello • ITL • RACCONTI PROIBITI.. DI NULLA VESTITI ○ MASTER OF LOVE
RACCONTI PROIBITI.. DI NULLA VESTITI see **RACCONTI PROIBITI.. DI NIENTE VESTITI** • 1972
RACCONTI ROMANI • 1955 • Franciolini Gianni • ITL
RACCONTI ROMANI DI UN'EX NOVIZIA • 1973 • Tosini Pino • ITL
RACCONTO DA UN AFFRESCO • 1940 • Emmer Luciano, Gras Enrico • ITL • GIOTTO
RACCONTO DEL NONNO, IL • 1912 • De Liguoro Giuseppe • ITL
RACCONTO DELLA JUNGLA, IL • 1973 • Gibba • ITL
RACCOONS AND THE LOST STAR, THE • 1983 • Gilles Kevin • ANM • USA
RACCOONS' BIG SURPRISE, THE • 1985 • Gilles Kevin • ANM • USA
RACE, THE • Ratz Gunter • ANM • GDR
RACE, THE • 1912 • *Thanhouser* • USA
RACE, THE • 1913 • Thornby Robert T. • *Vitagraph* • USA
RACE, THE • 1914 • Thornby Robert T. • *Keystone* • USA
RACE, THE • 1916 • Melford George • USA
RACE, THE • 1969 • Wolman Dan • ISR
RACE, THE see **CURSA** • 1975
RACE, THE see **DOSTIH** • 1981
RACE AGAINST THE HARVEST see **AMERICAN HARVEST** • 1987
RACE D'EP -UN SIECLE D'IMAGES DE L'HOMOSEXUALITE • 1978 • Soukaz Lionel • DOC • FRN
RACE DES SEIGNEURS, LA • 1974 • Granier-Deferre Pierre • FRN
RACE FOR A BED, A • 1905 • Martin J. H.? • UKN
RACE FOR A BRIDE, A • 1910 • Aylott Dave • UKN
RACE FOR A BRIDE, A • 1910 • Melies Gaston • USA
RACE FOR A BRIDE, A • 1911 • *Bison* • USA
RACE FOR A BRIDE, A • 1914 • *Sterling* • USA
RACE FOR A BRIDE, A • 1914 • *Apollo* • USA
RACE FOR A BRIDE, A • 1922 • Sanderson Challis • UKN
RACE FOR A GOLD MINE, A • 1915 • Mix Tom • USA
RACE FOR A KISS, A • 1904 • Fitzhamon Lewin • UKN
RACE FOR A MINE, A • 1914 • *Balboa* • USA
RACE FOR A ROSE, A • 1908 • Collins Alf? • UKN
RACE FOR LIBERTY, A • 1912 • *Gebhardt George* • USA
RACE FOR LIFE, A • 1913 • *Frontier* • USA
RACE FOR LIFE, A • 1916 • Wolbert William • SHT • USA
RACE FOR LIFE, A • 1928 • Lederman D. Ross • USA
RACE FOR LIFE (UKN) see **SI TOUS LES GARS DU MONDE** • 1955
RACE FOR LIFE (USA) see **MASK OF DUST** • 1954
RACE FOR LOVE, A • 1913 • Fitzhamon Lewin • UKN
RACE FOR MILLIONS • 1907 • Porter Edwin S. • USA
RACE FOR MILLIONS, A see **MONEY MANIAC, THE** • 1921
RACE FOR THE BOMB • 1986 • Eastman Allan • MTV • CND, FRN
RACE FOR THE FARMER'S CUP, THE • 1909 • Fitzhamon Lewin • UKN
RACE FOR THE YANKEE ZEPHYR see **RACE TO THE YANKEE ZEPHYR** • 1981
RACE FOR YOUR LIFE, CHARLIE BROWN • 1977 • Melendez Bill • ANM • USA
RACE GANG see **FOUR DARK HOURS** • 1937
RACE LOVE, THE • 1915 • Mackley Arthur • USA
RACE MEMORIES • 1913 • *Wiggins Lillian* • USA
RACE OF HORSES, A • 1974 • Denton Kit • SHT • ASL
RACE OF THE AGE, THE • 1920 • O'Mohoney J. W.
RACE OF THE RABBIT AND THE HEDGEHOG, THE • Diehle Bros • ANM • FRG
RACE RIOT • 1929 • Lantz Walter, Nolan William • ANS • USA
RACE STREET • 1948 • Marin Edwin L. • USA
RACE SUICIDE • 1916 • Terwilliger George W. • USA
RACE SUICIDE • 1937 • Luby S. Roy • USA
RACE SYMPHONY see **RENNSYMPHONIE** • 1929
RACE, THE SPIRIT OF FRANCO see **RAZA, EL ESPIRITU DE FRANCO** • 1977
RACE TO DANGER see **TREASURE OF THE MOON GODDESS** • 1987
RACE TO THE DRAWBRIDGE, A • 1917 • Davis James • SHT • USA
RACE TO THE POLE, THE see **COOK & PEARY: THE RACE TO THE POLE** • 1983
RACE TO THE YANKEE ZEPHYR • 1981 • Hemmings David • ASL, NZL • TREASURE OF THE YANKEE ZEPHYR (USA) ○ RACE FOR THE YANKEE ZEPHYR
RACE WILD • 1926 • Apfel Oscar • USA
RACE WITH DEATH, A • 1914 • *Rex* • USA
RACE WITH THE DEVIL • 1975 • Starrett Jack • USA
RACE WITH THE LIMITED, A • 1914 • *Rhodes Billie* • USA
RACE WITH TIME, A • 1912 • *Joyce Alice* • USA
RACERS, THE • 1955 • Hathaway Henry • USA • SUCH MEN ARE DANGEROUS (UKN)
RACES see **RAPT** • 1934
RACES IN THE FOREST see **ERDEI SPORTVERSENY** • 1951
RACETRACK • 1933 • Cruze James • USA
RACHE DER AFRIKANERIN, DIE see **ALLEIN IM URWALD** • 1922
RACHE DER GRAFIN BARNETTI, DIE • Piel Harry • FRG
RACHE DER MAUD FERGUSSON, DIE see **HERRIN DER WELT 8, DIE** • 1919
RACHE DER PHARAONEN, DIE • 1925 • Theyer Hans • AUS • REVENGE OF PHARAOH, THE
RACHE DER TOTEN, DIE • 1917 • Oswald Richard • FRG • REVENGE OF THE DEAD
RACHE DES AVENARIUS, DIE • 1917 • *Neumann Lotte* • FRG
RACHE DES BANDITEN, DIE • 1919 • Jutzi Phil • FRG
RACHE DES BASTARDS, DIE • 1919 • Delmont Joseph • FRG
RACHE DES DR. KUNG, DIE • 1968 • Comas Ramon • FRG, ITL, SPN • VENGEANCE OF DR. KUNG, THE
RACHE DES FAKIRS, DIE • 1918 • AUS • REVENGE OF THE FAKIRS, THE
RACHE DES FU MAN CHU, DIE (FRG) see **VENGEANCE OF FU MANCHU, THE** • 1967
RACHE DES HOMUNCULUS, DIE see **HOMUNCULUS 4** • 1916
RACHE DES MARQUIS DOKAMA, DIE • 1922 • Berger Josef • FRG
RACHE DES MESTIZEN, DIE • 1920 • Eichgrun Bruno • FRG
RACHE DES MEXICANERS, DIE • 1920 • Stockel Joe • FRG
RACHE DES MONGOLEN, DIE see **FLIEGENDEN BRIGANTEN 2, DIE** • 1921
RACHE DES TITANEN, DIE • 1919 • Bluen Georg • FRG
RACHE DR THORA WEST, DIE • 1915 • Philippi Siegfried • FRG
RACHE EINER FRAU, DIE • 1921 • Wiene Robert • FRG
RACHE FUR EDDY • 1929 • Tollen Otz • FRG
RACHE IM GOLDTAL, DIE • 1920 • Paster Alfred • FRG

RACHE IST MEIN, DIE • 1914 • *Messter Oskar (P)* • FRG
RACHE IST MEIN, DIE • 1919 • Neuss Alwin • FRG • REVENGE IS MINE
RACHEGOTTIN, DIE • 1917 • Alexander Georg • FRG
RACHEL • 1910 • *Kalem* • USA
RACHEL AND THE BEELZEBUB BOMBARDIERS • 1977 • Ormrod Peter • UKN
RACHEL AND THE STRANGER • 1948 • Foster Norman • USA
RACHEL CADE • 1961 • Douglas Gordon • USA • SINS OF RACHEL CADE, THE
RACHEL PAPERS, THE • 1989 • Harris Damian • UKN
RACHEL, RACHEL • 1968 • Newman Paul • USA • NOW I LAY ME DOWN ○ JEST OF GOD, A
RACHEL RIVER • 1987 • Smolan Sandy • USA
RACHEL'S MAN see **ISH RACHAEL** • 1975
RACHEL'S SIN • 1911 • Fitzhamon Lewin? • UKN
RACHENDE LIEBE • 1917 • Stein Josef • FRG
RACHER, DIE • 1920 • *National-Film* • FRG
RACHER, DIE • 1960 • Anton Karl • FRG • AVENGER, THE (USA)
RACHERIN, DIE • 1919 • Batz Lorenz • FRG
RACHES DES BLUTES, DIE • 1915 • Albes Emil • FRG
RACHMANINOV'S PRELUDE • 1932 • Newman Widgey R. • SHT • UKN
RACIAL INCIDENT see **ZWISCHENFALL IN BENDERATH** • 1956
RACINES DU CRI, LES • 1969 • Arthuys Philippe • FRN
RACINES DU MAL, LES • 1967 • Cam Maurice • FRN
RACING see **RENNEN** • 1961
RACING AGAINST DEATH see **ZAVODYSE SMERTI** • 1981
RACING BLOOD • 1926 • Richardson Frank • USA
RACING BLOOD • 1936 • Hale Rex • USA
RACING BLOOD • 1954 • Barry Wesley E. • USA
RACING BLOOD see **SPEED TO BURN** • 1938
RACING CANINES • 1936 • Miller David • SHT • USA
RACING DEATH • 1917 • *Leonard Robert* • SHT • USA
RACING DRIVERS • 1973 • Maslennikov Igor • USS
RACING FEVER • 1964 • Grefe William • USA
RACING FOOL, THE • 1927 • Brown Harry J. • USA
RACING FOR LIFE • 1924 • McRae Henry • USA
RACING HEARTS • 1923 • Powell Paul • USA
RACING LADY • 1937 • Fox Wallace • USA
RACING LUCK • 1924 • Raymaker Herman C. • USA
RACING LUCK • 1935 • Newfield Sam • USA
RACING LUCK • 1941 • Kathner Rupert • ASL
RACING LUCK • 1948 • Berke William • USA
RACING LUCK see **WEAVERS OF FORTUNE** • 1922
RACING LUCK (UKN) see **RED HOT TIRES** • 1935
RACING MAD • 1928 • Roberts Stephen • SHT • USA
RACING ROMANCE • 1926 • Brown Harry J. • USA • KENTUCKY LUCK
RACING ROMANCE • 1927 • *Barrymore William* • USA
RACING ROMANCE • 1937 • Rogers Maclean • UKN
RACING ROMEO, A • 1927 • Wood Sam • USA
RACING SAYINGS ILLUSTRATED • 1905 • Jeapes Harold? • UKN
RACING STRAIN, THE • 1919 • Flynn Emmett J. • USA
RACING THE CHUTES AT DREAMLAND • 1904 • *Bitzer Billy (Ph)* • USA
RACING WITH THE MOON • 1984 • Benjamin Richard • USA
RACING WORLD • 1968 • Shaw Sam • DCS • USA
RACING YOUTH • 1932 • Moore Vin • USA • BLUE BLAZES ○ SPEED
RACISM • 1972 • Benazeraf Jose • USA
RACK, THE • 1915 • Chautard Emile • USA
RACK, THE • 1956 • Laven Arnold • USA
RACKET, THE • 1928 • Milestone Lewis • USA
RACKET, THE • 1951 • Cromwell John, Ray Nicholas (U/c) • USA
RACKET BUSTER • 1949 • Davis Mannie • ANS • USA
RACKET BUSTERS • 1938 • Bacon Lloyd • USA
RACKET CHEERS • 1930 • Sennett Mack • SHT • USA
RACKET MAN, THE • 1944 • Lederman D. Ross • USA
RACKETEER, THE • 1929 • Higgin Howard • USA • LOVE'S CONQUEST (UKN)
RACKETEER, THE see **RICH PEOPLE** • 1929
RACKETEER RABBIT • 1946 • Freleng Friz • ANS • USA
RACKETEER ROUND-UP • 1934 • Hoyt Robert • USA
RACKETEERS IN EXILE • 1937 • Kenton Erle C. • USA
RACKETEERS OF THE RANGE • 1939 • Lederman D. Ross • USA
RACKETY RAX • 1932 • Werker Alfred L. • USA
RACQUET • 1979 • Winters David • USA
RACS • 1970 • Macskassy Gyula, Varnai Gyorgy • ANS • HNG • BEHIND THE BARS
RACTE PROMINOUT • 1975 • Benes Lubomir • CZC • PLEASE EXCUSE ME
RAD • 1986 • Needham Hal • USA
RAD BIZOM A FELESEGEM • 1939 • Vaszary Janos • I ENTRUST MY WIFE TO YOU (USA)
RAD NA ODREDJENO VREME • 1981 • Jelic Milan • YGS • TEMPORARY WORK
RADANIKA • 1925 • Stranz Fred • FRG
RADAR MEN FROM THE MOON • 1952 • Brannon Fred C. • SRL • USA
RADAR PATROL see **RADAR SECRET SERVICE** • 1950
RADAR PATROL VS. SPY KING • 1950 • Brannon Fred C. • SRL • USA
RADAR SECRET SERVICE • 1950 • Newfield Sam • USA • RADAR PATROL
RADCLIFFE BLUES • 1969 • Weill Claudia • DOC • FRN
RADEAU AVEC BAIGNEURS • 1896-97 • Lumiere Louis • FRN
RADHA AND KRISHNA • 1956 • Bhownagary J. S. • SHT • IND
RADHA KALYANAM • 1935 • *Rajam S.* • IND
RADHA KRISHNA • 1930 • IND
RADHA KRISHNA • 1948 • *Prem Amar* • IND
RADHA KRISHNA • 1954 • *Burman S. D. (M)* • IND
RADHAPURA -ENDSTATION DER VERDAMMTEN • 1968 • Albin Hans, von Rathony Akos? • FRG • RADHAPURA -TERMINUS OF THE DAMNED
RADHAPURA -TERMINUS OF THE DAMNED see **RADHAPURA -ENDSTATION DER VERDAMMTEN** • 1968
RADIANCE OF A THOUSAND SUNS, THE see **BRULERE DE MILLE SOLEILS, LA** • 1964
RADIEUX-CONCERT see **JE T'ADORE, MAIS POURQUOI?** • 1931
RADIO-ACTIVE BOMB, THE • 1923 • *Howard George Bronson* • SHT • USA
RADIO-BALLADE • 1956 • Herwig Hans • SHT • FRN
RADIO BAR • 1937 • Romero Manuel
RADIO BUG, THE • 1926 • Roberts Stephen • SHT • USA
RADIO BUGS • 1944 • Endfield Cy • SHT • USA
RADIO CAB MURDER • 1954 • Sewell Vernon • UKN
RADIO CITY REVELS • 1938 • Stoloff Ben • USA
RADIO COMMITS A BURGLARY, THE see **RADIO TEKEE MURRON** • 1951
RADIO DAYS • 1987 • Allen Woody • USA
RADIO DETECTIVE, THE • 1926 • Craft William James, Crinley William A. • SRL • USA
RADIO DYNAMIC • 1942 • Fischinger Oskar • ANM • FRG
RADIO FLYER, THE • 1924 • Hoyt Harry O. • USA
RADIO FOLLA, LA • 1985 • Bellmunt Francisco • SPN • CRAZY RADIO
RADIO FOLLIES (USA) see **RADIO PARADE OF 1935** • 1934
RADIO GIRL • 1932 • *Terry Paul/ Moser Frank (P)* • ANS • USA
RADIO HAMS • 1939 • Feist Felix E. • SHT • USA
RADIO-HEIRAT, DIE • 1924 • Prager Wilhelm • FRG
RADIO IN BATTLE • Napier-Bell J. B., Anstey Edgar • DOC • UKN
RADIO INTERFERENCE • 1934 • Watt Harry • DCS • UKN
RADIO KING, THE • 1922 • Hill Robert F. • SRL • USA
RADIO KISSES • 1930 • Pearce A. Leslie • SHT • USA
RADIO LOVER • 1936 • Melford Austin, Capon Paul • UKN
RADIO MAD • 1924 • Roach Hal • SHT • USA
RADIO-MANIA • 1923 • Neill R. William • USA • MAN FROM MARS, THE ○ MARS CALLING ○ M.A.R.S.
RADIO MELODIES • 1943 • D'Arcy Harry • SHT • USA
RADIO MELODIES • 1943 • Le Borg Reginald • *Universal* • SHT • USA
RADIO MURDER MYSTERY, THE • 1933 • Brice Monte • SHT • USA
RADIO MURDER MYSTERY, THE (UKN) see **LOVE IS ON THE AIR** • 1937
RADIO NAVIGATION • 1955-57 • Jodoin Rene • ASS • CND
RADIO NIGHTS • 1939 • Shepherd Horace • UKN
RADIO NOW! see **DAESH RADIO!** • 1924
RADIO ON • 1979 • Petit Christopher • UKN
RADIO PARADE • 1933 • De Bear Archie, Beville Richard • UKN • HELLO RADIO
RADIO PARADE OF 1935 • 1934 • Woods Arthur • UKN • RADIO FOLLIES (USA)
RADIO PATROL • 1932 • Cahn Edward L. • USA
RADIO PATROL • 1937 • Beebe Ford, Smith Cliff • SRL • USA
RADIO PATRULLA • 1951 • Cortazar Ernesto • MXC
RADIO PHILIPS • 1977 • Giersz Witold • ANS • PLN
RADIO-QUEBEC COTE-NORD • 1981 • Lesaunier Daniel • MTV • CND
RADIO RACKET • 1931 • Foster John • ANS • USA
RADIO RAMPAGE • 1944 • Roberts Charles E. • SHT • USA
RADIO RANCH • 1935 • Eason B. Reeves, Brower Otto • USA
RADIO REVELS see **CUCKOOS, THE** • 1930
RADIO REVELS OF 1942 (UKN) see **SWING IT SOLDIER** • 1941
RADIO REVUE OF 1937 see **LET'S MAKE A NIGHT OF IT** • 1937
RADIO RHYTHM • 1929 • Santley Joseph • SHT • USA
RADIO RHYTHM • 1931 • Lantz Walter, Nolan William • ANS • USA
RADIO RIOT • 1930 • Fleischer Dave • ANS • USA
RADIO ROCKET BOY • 1973 • Swarthe Robert, Mayer John • USA
RADIO ROMANIA KEEPS BROADCASTING • 1985 • Tanase Dinu • RMN
RADIO RUNAROUND • 1943 • Hillyer Lambert • SHT • USA
RADIO STAR, THE (UKN) see **LOUDSPEAKER, THE** • 1934
RADIO STARS ON PARADE • 1945 • Goodwins Leslie • USA • RADIO STARS ON THE AIR
RADIO STARS ON THE AIR see **RADIO STARS ON PARADE** • 1945
RADIO TEKEE MURRON • 1951 • Kassila Matti • FNL • RADIO COMMITS A BURGLARY, THE
RADIO TROUBADOR • 1938 • Harlan Richard • USA
RADIO VIHOR CALLING ANDJELIJA see **RADIO VIHOR ZOVE ANDJELIJU** • 1980
RADIO VIHOR ZOVE ANDJELIJU • 1980 • Zivanovic Jovan • YGS • RADIO VIHOR CALLING ANDJELIJA
RADIO WONDERFUL • 1972 • Loncraine Richard • UKN
RADIOACTIVE DREAMS • 1984 • Pyun Albert • USA
RADIOBARRED • 1936 • Goodwins Leslie • SHT • USA
RADIOCOMUNICACAOES • 1954 • Mendes Joao • SHT • PRT
RADIOENS BARNDOM • 1949 • *Dreyer Carl T. (Ed)* • DNM
RADIOGRAFIA D'UN COLPO D'ORO (ITL) see **LAS VEGAS, 500 MILLONES** • 1968
RADIOGRAPHY • Topaldgikov Stefan • DOC • BUL
RADISHES AND CARROTS see **DAIKON TO NINJIN** • 1964
RADIUM CITY • 1987 • Langer Carole • DOC • USA
RADIUM MYSTERY, THE see **GREAT RADIUM MYSTERY, THE** • 1919
RADIUM THIEVES, THE • 1915 • Humphrey William • USA
RADON see **SORANO DAIKAIJYU** • 1956
RADUGA • 1941 • Donskoi Mark • USS • RAINBOW
RADUGA SEMI NEDESHD • 1983 • Faisiyev Habibulla • USS • PRINCE AND THE POTTER, THE
RAFAEL EN RAPHAEL • 1974 • Isasi Antonio • SPN
RAFAELA • 1918 • Halm Alfred? • FRG
RAFAELLO, DAS RATSEL VON KOPENHAGEN 1 • 1920 • Neff Wolfgang • FRG • MYSTERIUM VON KOPENHAGEN, DAS
RAFAGA DE PLOMO, UNA • 1965 • Santillan Antonio • SPN, ITL • ROUND OF BULLETS, A
RAFAL U NEBO • 1958 • Bjenjas Vojislav Vanja • YGS • SHOTS IN THE SKY
RAFALE, LA • 1919 • de Baroncelli Jacques • FRN
RAFALES see **MON AMI TIM** • 1932
RAFFERTY AND THE GOLD DUST TWINS • 1975 • Richards Dick • USA • RAFFERTY AND THE HIGHWAY HUSTLERS
RAFFERTY AND THE HIGHWAY HUSTLERS see **RAFFERTY AND THE GOLD DUST TWINS** • 1975
RAFFERTY AT THE HOTEL DE REST • 1915 • Fitzgerald J. A. • USA
RAFFERTY GOES TO CONEY ISLAND • 1915 • Fitzgerald J. A. • USA
RAFFERTY SETTLES THE WAR • 1915 • Fitzgerald J. A. • USA
RAFFERTY STOPS A MARATHON • 1915 • Fitzgerald J. A. • USA
RAFFERTY'S RAFFLE • 1914 • *Mace Fred* • USA
RAFFERTY'S RISE • 1918 • Kerrigan J. M. • UKN
RAFFICA DI COLTELLI see **COLTELLI DEL VENDICATORE, I** • 1967
RAFFICA DI PIOMBO • 1965 • Heusch Paolo • ITL
RAFFINIERTE FRAUEN 1 • 1923 • Heidemann Paul • FRG • SEKTMIEZE
RAFFINIERTE FRAUEN 2 • 1923 • Heidemann Paul • FRG
RAFFINIERTESTE FRAU BERLINS, DIE • 1927 • Osten Franz • FRG
RAFFLE, THE • 1912 • *Solax* • USA
RAFFLE FOR A HUSBAND, A • 1916 • Curtis Allen • SHT • USA
RAFFLES • 1930 • D'Arrast Harry D'Abbadie (U/c), Fitzmaurice George • USA
RAFFLES • 1940 • Wood Sam • USA
RAFFLES • 1958 • Galindo Alejandro • MXC
RAFFLES, DAS RATSEL DER GROSSTADT • 1915 • Matull Kurt • FRG
RAFFLES THE AMATEUR CRACKSMAN • 1905 • Blackton J. Stuart • USA
RAFFLES, THE AMATEUR CRACKSMAN • 1917 • Irving George • USA
RAFFLES, THE AMATEUR CRACKSMAN • 1925 • Baggot King • USA
RAFFLES THE DOG • 1905 • Porter Edwin S. • USA
RAFLE DE CHIENS • 1904 • Blache Alice • FRN
RAFLE EST POUR CE SOIR, LA • 1953 • Dekobra Maurice • FRN
RAFLES SUR LA VILLE • 1957 • Chenal Pierre • FRN • SINNERS OF PARIS (USA) ○ TRAP FOR A KILLER
RAFT, THE • 1972 • Sluizer George • DOC • NTH, BRZ
RAFT OF MEDUSA, THE see **SPLAV MEDUZE** • 1981
RAFT OF THE MEDUSA, THE see **SPLAV MEDUZE** • 1981
RAFTER ROMANCE • 1934 • Seiter William A. • USA
RAFTS AFLOAT see **PLYNA TRATWY** • 1962
RAFTSMEN see **TUTAJOSOK** • 1988
RAG, A BONE AND A HANK OF HAIR, A • 1917 • Bryan Vincent • SHT • USA
RAG. ARTURO DE FANTI BANCARIO-PRECARIO • 1980 • Salce Luciano • ITL • THREE IS A CROWD
RAG BABY, A • 1917 • Richmond J. A. • SHT • USA
RAG BAG, THE • 1913 • *Lubin* • USA
RAG DOG • 1935 • Gillett Burt • ANS • USA
RAG DOLL • 1961 • Comfort Lance • UKN • YOUNG, WILLING AND EAGER (USA)
RAG DOLL see **BEZ BEBEK** • 1987
RAG MAN, THE • 1925 • Cline Eddie • USA
RAG MAN, THE see **OLD CLOTHES** • 1925
RAG-PICKER, THE see **BONNE FARCE, UNE** • 1896
RAG-PICKER CARICATURIST, THE • 1908 • *Pathe Freres* • FRN
RAG-TIME ROMANCE, A • 1919 • Smith Noel • SHT • USA
RAGA • 1959 • Belson Jordan • ANS • USA
RAGA • 1971 • Worth Howard • DOC • USA
RAGA AND THE EMOTIONS • 1971 • Benegal Shyam • DCS • IND
RAGAMUFFIN, THE • 1914 • O'Sullivan Tony • USA
RAGAMUFFIN, THE • 1916 • De Mille William C. • USA
RAGAMUFFIN, THE (UKN) see **HOODLUM, THE** • 1919
RAGAMUFFINS, THE see **TRHANI** • 1936
RAGAN • 1968 • Lelli Luciano • ITL
RAGAN IN RUINS • 1925 • Paul Fred • UKN
RAGANELLA • 1924 • Rosa Silvio Laurenti • ITL
RAGAZZA ALLA PARI, LA • 1976 • Guerrini Mino • ITL
RAGAZZA CHE DORME • 1941 • Forzano Andrea • ITL
RAGAZZA CHE SAPEVA TROPPO, LA • 1962 • Bava Mario • ITL • EVIL EYE, THE (USA) ○ GIRL WHO KNEW TOO MUCH, THE ○ INCUBUS
RAGAZZA CHIAMATA AMORE, UNA (ITL) see **FILLE NOMMEE AMOUR, UNE** • 1968
RAGAZZA CON GLI STIVALI ROSSI, LA (ITL) see **FEMME AUX BOTTES ROUGES, LA** • 1974
RAGAZZA CON LA PISTOLA, LA • 1967 • Monicelli Mario • ITL • GIRL WITH A PISTOL, THE (USA) ○ GIRL WITH THE PISTOL, THE
RAGAZZA CON LA VALIGIA, LA • 1961 • Zurlini Valerio • ITL, FRN • FILLE A LA VALISE, LA (FRN) ○ GIRL WITH A SUITCASE (USA) ○ PLEASURE GIRL
RAGAZZA DAL LIVIDO AZZURRO, LA • 1933 • Emo E. W. • ITL • SIGNORINA DAL LIVIDO AZZURRO, LA
RAGAZZA DAL PIGIAMA GIALLO, LA • 1978 • Mogherini Flavio • ITL
RAGAZZA DALLA PELLE DI CORALLO, LA • 1976 • Civirani Osvaldo • ITL
RAGAZZA DALLA PELLE DI LUNA, LA • 1972 • Scattini Luigi • ITL • SEX OF THEIR BODIES (UKN) ○ MOONSKIN ○ GIRL WITH THE SKIN OF THE MOON, THE
RAGAZZA DALLE MANI DI CORALLO, LA • 1971 • Petrini Luigi • ITL
RAGAZZA DEL BERSAGLIERE, LA • 1967 • Blasetti Alessandro • ITL • BERSAGLIERE'S GIRL, THE
RAGAZZA DEL PAIP'S, LA see **IMMENSITA, L'** • 1967
RAGAZZA DEL PALIO, LA • 1957 • Zampa Luigi • ITL • GIRL AND THE PALIO, THE (USA) ○ LOVE SPECIALIST, THE ○ GIRL WHO RODE IN THE PALIO, THE
RAGAZZA DEL PECCATO, LA (ITL) see **EN CAS DE MALHEUR** • 1958
RAGAZZA DEL PRETE, LA • 1970 • Paolella Domenico • ITL
RAGAZZA DELLA NOTTE, LA (ITL) see **VIVRE LA NUIT** • 1968
RAGAZZA DELLA SALINA, LA (ITL) see **HARTE MANNER -HEISSE LIEBE** • 1956
RAGAZZA DI BUBE, LA • 1963 • Comencini Luigi • ITL, FRN • RAGAZZA, LA (FRN) ○ BEBO'S GIRL (USA)
RAGAZZA DI LATTA, LA • 1970 • Aliprandi Marcello • ITL • GIRL IN TIN, THE ○ TIN GIRL, THE
RAGAZZA DI MILLE MESI, LA • 1961 • Steno • ITL

RAGAZZA DI NOME GIULIO, LA • 1970 • Valerii Tonino • ITL • GIRL CALLED JULES, A (UKN) ○ GIRL NAMED JULIUS, A ○ MODEL LOVE
RAGAZZA DI PASSAGGIO, LA • 1971 • Da Campo Gianni • ITL
RAGAZZA DI PASSAGGIO, LA (ITL) see **FEMME DU GANGE, LA** • 1973
RAGAZZA DI PIAZZA S. PIETRO, LA • 1958 • Costa Mario • ITL, SPN
RAGAZZA DI PRAGA, LA • 1970 • Pastore Sergio • ITL
RAGAZZA DI TRIESTE, LA • 1983 • Festa Campanile Pasquale • ITL • GIRL FROM TRIESTE, THE
RAGAZZA DI TRIESTE, LA (ITL) see **LOUPS CHASSENT LA NUIT, LES** • 1951
RAGAZZA DI VENEZIA, LA see **UOMO DELLA LEGIONE, L'** • 1940
RAGAZZA DI VENT'ANNI, UNA see **VITA TORNA, LA** • 1943
RAGAZZA DI VIA CONDOTTI, LA (ITL) see **CHICA DE VIA CONDOTTI, LA** • 1973
RAGAZZA DI VIA MILLELIRE, LA • 1979 • Serra Gianni • MTV • ITL
RAGAZZA DI VIA VENETO, LA • 1956 • Girolami Marino • ITL
RAGAZZA E IL GENERALE, LA • 1966 • Festa Campanile Pasquale • ITL • GIRL AND THE GENERAL, THE (USA)
RAGAZZA FUORISTRADA, LA • 1973 • Scattini Luigi • ITL
RAGAZZA IN PRESTITO, LA • 1965 • Giannetti Alfredo • ITL, FRN • ENGAGEMENT ITALIANO (USA)
RAGAZZA IN VETRINA, LA • 1960 • Emmer Luciano • ITL, FRN • FILLE DANS LA VITRINE, LA (FRN) ○ GIRL IN THE SHOP WINDOW, THE ○ WOMAN IN THE WINDOW
RAGAZZA, LA (FRN) see **RAGAZZA DI BUBE, LA** • 1963
RAGAZZA MERAVIGLIOSA, LA • 1965 • Grieco Sergio • ITL
RAGAZZA PER L'ESTATE, UNA(ITL) see **FILLE POUR L'ETE, UNE** • 1960
RAGAZZA PIUTTOSTA COMPLICATA, UNA • 1968 • Damiani Damiano • ITL • COMPLICATED GIRL, A (UKN) ○ QUITE A COMPLICATED GIRL
RAGAZZA SOTTO IL LENZUOLO, LA • 1961 • Girolami Marino • ITL • GIRL UNDER THE SHEET, THE
RAGAZZA SPALANCATA, LA • 1975 • Di Nardo Mario • ITL
RAGAZZA TUTTA D'ORO, UNA • 1967 • Laurenti Mariano • ITL
RAGAZZA TUTTA NUDA ASSASSINATA NEL PARCO, UNA • 1972 • Brescia Alfonso • ITL
RAGAZZE AL MARE • 1956 • Biagetti Giuliano • ITL • IN VACANZA AL MARE
RAGAZZE BRIVIDO see **ADORABILI E BUGIARDE** • 1959
RAGAZZE DA MARITO • 1952 • De Filippo Eduardo • ITL
RAGAZZE D'ESTATE see **AMORE A PRIMA VISTA** • 1958
RAGAZZE DI BUONA FAMIGLIA, LE (ITL) see **SAINTES NITOUCHES, LES** • 1962
RAGAZZE DI CAPO VERDE, LE • 1976 • Maraini Dacia • ITL
RAGAZZE DI PIAZZA DI SPAGNA, LE • 1952 • Emmer Luciano • ITL • GIRLS OF THE SPANISH STEPS, THE ○ GIRLS OF THE PIAZZA DI SPAGNA ○ THREE GIRLS FROM ROME
RAGAZZE DI SAN FREDIANO, LE • 1955 • Zurlini Valerio • ITL • GIRLS OF SAN FREDIANO, THE
RAGAZZE D'OGGI • 1955 • Zampa Luigi • ITL, FRN
RAGAZZE IN BIANCO • 1949 • Antonioni Michelangelo • DCS • ITL
RAGAZZI CHE SI AMANO, I • 1963 • Caldana Alberto • ITL
RAGAZZI DEI PARIOLI, I • 1959 • Corbucci Sergio • ITL
RAGAZZI DEL JUKE BOX, I • 1959 • Fulci Lucio • ITL
RAGAZZI DEL MASSACRO, I • 1969 • Di Leo Fernando • ITL
RAGAZZI DELLA DISCOTECA, I see **ANNO DEI GATTI, I** • 1979
RAGAZZI DELLA MARINA • 1958 • De Robertis Francesco • DOC • ITL
RAGAZZI DELLA ROMA VIOLENTA, I • 1976 • Savino Renato • ITL
RAGAZZI DELL'HULLY GULLY, I • 1965 • Giannini Marcello • ITL
RAGAZZI DI BANDIERA GIALLA, I • 1967 • Laurenti Mariano • ITL • LADS OF THE YELLOW FLAG, THE
RAGAZZI DI VIA PANISPERNA, I • 1988 • Amelio Gianni • ITL, FRG • BOYS OF VIA PANISPERNA, THE
RAGAZZINA, LA • 1974 • Imperoli Mario • ITL
RAGAZZINA PERVERSA, LA • 1975 • Freed Gregory • ITL, FRN • FILLE POUR SAINT-TROPEZ, UNE (FRN)
RAGAZZO • 1933 • Perilli Ivo • ITL
RAGAZZO CHE SAPEVA AMARE, IL • 1967 • Dell'Acquila Enzo • ITL
RAGAZZO CHE SORRIDE, IL • 1969 • Grimaldi Aldo • ITL • MATTINO
RAGAZZO DAGLI OCCHI CHIARI, IL • 1970 • Marsili Emilio • ITL • DESERTO BIANCO
RAGAZZO DAL CUORE DI FANGO • 1957 • Corbucci Sergio • ITL • GIOVENTU DISPERATA
RAGAZZO DI BORGATA • 1976 • Paradisi Giulio • ITL • SLUM BOY
RAGAZZO DI CALABRIA, UN • 1988 • Comencini Luigi • ITL, FRN • BOY FROM CALABRIA, A
RAGAZZO E UNA RAGAZZA, UN • 1984 • Risi Marco • ITL • BOY AND A GIRL, A
RAGAZZOLA, LA • 1965 • Orlandini Giuseppe • ITL
RAGBAR • 1972 • Beyzai Bahram • IRN • DOWNPOUR ○ RAINSTORM
RAGE • 1972 • Scott George C. • USA
RAGE • 1980 • Graham William A. • TVM • USA
RAGE • 1984 • Ricci Tonino • ITL
RAGE, LA • 1978 • Anglada Eugeni • SPN • RABIA, LA
RAGE, THE see **MAL, EL** • 1965
RAGE AND GLORY • 1984 • Nesher Avi • ISR
RAGE AT DAWN • 1955 • Whelan Tim • USA • SEVEN BAD MEN
RAGE AU CORPS, LA • 1953 • Habib Ralph • FRN • TEMPEST IN THE FLESH (USA) ○ FIRE IN THE BLOOD
RAGE AU POING, LA • 1974 • Le Hung Eric • FRN
RAGE DE DENTS, UNE • 1900 • Blache Alice • FRN
RAGE DU SEXE, LA • 1977 • Roy Jean-Claude • FRN
RAGE IN HEAVEN • 1941 • Van Dyke W. S. • USA
RAGE OF ANGELS • 1982 • Kulik Buzz • TVM • USA
RAGE OF ANGELS -PART TWO see **RAGE OF ANGELS: THE STORY CONTINUES** • 1986
RAGE OF ANGELS: THE STORY CONTINUES • 1986 • Wendkos Paul • TVM • USA • RAGE OF ANGELS -PART TWO
RAGE OF HONOR • 1986 • Hessler Gordon • USA • WAY OF THE NINJA
RAGE OF PARIS, THE • 1921 • Conway Jack • USA
RAGE OF PARIS, THE • 1938 • Koster Henry • USA
RAGE OF THE BUCCANEERS see **GORDON, IL PIRATO NERO** • 1961
RAGE OF THE SUN AND THE MOON, THE • Juhasz Ferenc • ANS • HNG
RAGE PORNO • Thierry Alain • FRN
RAGE TO KILL • 1987 • Winters David • USA
RAGE TO LIVE, A • 1965 • Grauman Walter • USA
RAGE WITHIN, THE see **RABIA (THE RAGE), LA** • 1962
RAGE WITHIN, THE (UKN) see **DELITTO AL CIRCOLO DEL TENNIS** • 1969
RAGENS RIKE • 1929 • Johansson Ivar • SWD • LAND OF RYE
RAGENS RIKE • 1951 • Johansson Ivar • SWD • LAND OF RYE
RAGEWAR see **DUNGEONMASTER, THE** • 1985
RAGGARE • 1959 • Hellbom Olle • SWD • BLACKJACKETS
RAGGARE GANG see **RAGGARGANGET** • 1962
RAGGARGANGET • 1962 • Frisk Ragnar • SWD • RAGGARE GANG
RAGGAZZA A SAINT TROPEZ, UNA (ITL) see **GENDARME DE SAINT-TROPEZ, LE** • 1964
RAGGED EARL, THE • 1914 • Carleton Lloyd B. • USA
RAGGED EDGE, THE • 1923 • Weight F. Harmon • USA
RAGGED FLAG, A see **RANRU NO HATA** • 1973
RAGGED GIRL OF OZ, THE • 1919 • *Harris Mildred* • USA
RAGGED HEIRESS, THE • 1922 • Beaumont Harry • USA
RAGGED HERO, A • 1908 • *Kalem* • USA
RAGGED LOVER, THE see **BELOVED ROGUE, THE** • 1927
RAGGED MEN see **TRHANI** • 1936
RAGGED MESSENGER, THE • 1917 • Wilson Frank • UKN
RAGGED PRINCE, THE • 1913 • Weston Charles • UKN
RAGGED PRINCESS, THE • 1916 • Adolfi John G. • USA
RAGGED ROAD TO ROMANCE, THE • 1920 • Hayes Ward • SHT • USA
RAGGED ROBIN • 1924 • Mattison Frank S. • USA
RAGGEDY ANN AND ANDY • 1977 • Williams Richard, Potterton Gerald • ANM • USA • RAGGEDY ANN AND ANDY: A MUSICAL ADVENTURE
RAGGEDY ANN AND ANDY: A MUSICAL ADVENTURE see **RAGGEDY ANN AND ANDY** • 1977
RAGGEDY ANN AND RAGGEDY ANDY • 1941 • Fleischer Dave • ANS • USA
RAGGEDY ANNE see **SAVAGE HARBOR** • 1988
RAGGEDY GIRL, THE see **PATCHWORK GIRL OF OZ, THE** • 1914
RAGGEDY MAN • 1981 • Fisk Jack • USA
RAGGEDY QUEEN, THE • 1917 • Marston Theodore • USA
RAGGEDY RAWNEY, THE • 1988 • Hoskins Bob • UKN
RAGGEDY RUG • 1963 • Hanna William, Barbera Joseph • ANS • USA
RAGGEN -DET AR JAG DET • 1936 • Bauman Schamyl • SWD • RAGGEN -THAT'S ME
RAGGEN -THAT'S ME see **RAGGEN -DET AR JAG DET** • 1936
RAGGI MORTALI DEL DR. MABUSE, I (ITL) see **TODESSTRAHLEN DES DR. MABUSE, DIE** • 1964
RAGGING IN THE ARMY • 1904 • *Warwick Trading Co* • UKN
RAGGIO INFERNALE, IL • 1967 • Baldanello Gianfranco • ITL, SPN • NIDO DE ESPIAS (SPN) ○ NEST OF SPIES ○ INFERNAL RAY, THE
RAGINA'S SECRETS • 1969 • Hand Fletcher • USA • DR. BYRD UNLOCKS RAGINA'S SECRETS ○ REGINA'S SECRETS ○ DR. BYRD
RAGING BULL, THE • 1979 • Scorsese Martin • USA
RAGING FURY see **REAL TROUBLE** • 1988
RAGING MOON, THE • 1970 • Forbes Bryan • UKN • LONG AGO TOMORROW (USA)
RAGING SEA, THE • 1969 • Wilde Cornel • USA
RAGING STRAIN, THE • 1932 • Storm Jerome • USA
RAGING TIDE, THE • 1951 • Sherman George • USA
RAGING WATERS (UKN) see **GREEN PROMISE, THE** • 1949
RAGIONE PER MOURIRE, UNA see **RAGIONE PER VIVERE E UNA PER MOURIRE, UNA** • 1972
RAGIONE PER VIVERE E UNA PER MOURIRE, UNA • 1972 • Valerii Tonino • ITL, FRN, SPN • MASSACRE AT FORT HOLMAN (USA) ○ RAGIONE PER MOURIRE, UNA ○ REASON TO LIVE, A REASON TO DIE, A
RAGMAN'S DAUGHTER, THE • 1972 • Becker Harold • UKN • TEA-LEAF, THE
RAGNA ROCK see **RAGNAROCK** • 1973
RAGNAROCK • 1973 • Fraas Arne Philip • DOC • NRW • RAGNA ROCK
RAGNO, IL • 1970 • Cozzi Luigi • ITL
RAGOL DA HAI GANINI, EL • 1967 • Karama Issa • EGY • MY HUSBAND IS IMPOSSIBLE
RAGOL EL LAZI FAKAD ZILLOH, EL • 1968 • el Sheikh Kamal • EGY • MAN WHO LOST HIS SHADOW, THE ○ HOMME QUI PERDIT SON OMBRE, L' ○ RAGUL AK-LAD'I FAQADA D'ILLAHU, AR-
RAGS • 1915 • Kirkwood James • USA
RAGS AND PATRIOTISM • 1914 • *Melies* • USA
RAGS AND RICHES • 1913 • Brenon Herbert • USA
RAGS AND THE GIRL • 1915 • Brooke Van Dyke • USA
RAGS, OLD IRON! • 1910 • *Essanay* • USA
RAGS TO RICHES • 1922 • Worsley Wallace • USA • FROM RAGS TO RICHES
RAGS TO RICHES • 1941 • Kane Joseph • USA
RAGS TO RICHES • 1987 • Green Bruce Seth • TVM • USA
RAGTIME • 1927 • Pembroke Scott • USA • STOLEN MELODY, THE (UKN)
RAGTIME • 1981 • Forman Milos • USA
RAGTIME A LA CARTE • 1913 • *Selsior Films* • UKN
RAGTIME BEAR, THE • 1949 • Hubley John • ANS • USA
RAGTIME COWBOY JOE • 1940 • Taylor Ray • USA
RAGTIME COWBOY PIMPLE • 1915 • Evans Fred, Evans Joe • UKN
RAGTIME MAD • 1913 • Plumb Hay? • UKN
RAGTIME ROMANCE, A • 1913 • Henderson Dell • USA
RAGTIME ROMEO • 1931 • *Iwerks Ub (P)* • ANS • USA
RAGTIME SNAP SHOTS • 1915 • Roach Hal • USA
RAGTIME SUMMER see **AGE OF INNOCENCE** • 1977
RAGTIME TEXAS TOMMY • 1912 • *Selsior Films* • UKN
RAGUL AK-LAD'I FAQADA D'ILLAHU, AR- see **RAGOL EL LAZI FAKAD ZILLOH, EL** • 1968
RAGULUN FI HAYATI see **RAJUL FI HAYATI** • 1961
RAH! RAH! HEIDELBERG • 1926 • Seiler Lewis • SHT • USA
RAH, RAH, RAH! • 1916 • Semon Larry • SHT • USA
RAH! RAH! RAH! • 1928 • Taurog Norman • SHT • USA
RAH RAH RUCKUS • 1964 • Smith Paul J. • ANS • USA
RAHAS DUPATHA • 1967 • Jayamanne Irwin • SLN • SECRET ISLAND, THE
RAHASYA POLICE 115 • 1968 • Panthalu B. R. • IND • SECRET POLICE 115
RAHASYAM • Reddi Sankara • IND
RAHASYAM • 1967 • Ragaviah Vedhantham • IND • MYSTERY
RAHI • 1953 • *Biswas Anil (M)* • IND
RAHSIA • 1987 • Hafsham Othman • MLY • HIDDEN, THE
RAHSIA HATIKU • 1974 • Achnas Naz • MLY • MY HEART'S SECRET
RAI • 1987 • Fettar Sid-Ali • ALG
RA'IA AL-HASNA', AR- • 1972 • Salem Atef • SYR • JOLIE BERGERE, LA
RAICES • 1953 • Alazraki Benito • MXC • ROOTS
RAICES DE SANGRE • 1976 • Trevino Jesus • USA • ROOTS OF BLOOD
RAICES EN EL INFIERNO • 1963 • Gold Myron J. • MXC, USA
RAICES ETERNAS • 1986 • Quinones Noel • DOC • PRC
RAID, THE • 1916 • *Stull Walter* • USA
RAID, THE • 1917 • Marshall George • SHT • USA
RAID, THE • 1954 • Fregonese Hugo • USA
RAID, THE see **BAKUCHIUCHI NAGURIKOMI** • 1968
RAID OF 1915, THE • 1914 • Durrant Fred W. • UKN • IF ENGLAND WERE INVADED
RAID OF THE ARMOURED MOTOR, THE see **MODERN PIRATES, THE** • 1906
RAID OF THE HUMAN TIGERS, THE • 1913 • *Bison* • USA
RAID OF THE RED MARAUDERS, THE • 1914 • *Kalem* • USA
RAID ON A CANTEEN, A • 1905 • Collins Alf • UKN
RAID ON A CLUB, A • 1905 • *Walturdaw* • UKN
RAID ON CAESARS see **LAS VEGAS LADY** • 1976
RAID ON ENTEBBE • 1976 • Kershner Irvin • TVM • USA
RAID ON ROMMEL • 1971 • Hathaway Henry • USA
RAID ON THE INTERESTS see **FAIZE HUCUM** • 1985
RAID PARIS - MONTE CARLO EN 2 HEURES, LE • 1905 • Melies Georges • FRN • ADVENTUROUS AUTOMOBILE TRIP, AN ○ AUTOMOBILE CHASE, THE (USA) ○ VOYAGE AUTOMOBILE PARIS - MONTECARLO EN DEUX HEURES, LE
RAID PARIS NEW YORK EN AUTOMOBILE, LE • 1908 • Melies Georges • FRN • MISHAPS OF THE NEW YORK - PARIS RACE (USA) ○ NEW YORK PARIS EN AUTOMOBILE ○ ENDURANCE CONTEST PARIS-NEW YORK BY AUTOMOBILE, THE
RAID (UKN) see **RAZZIA** • 1947
RAIDER, THE (USA) see **WESTERN APPROACHES** • 1944
RAIDER OF THE RANGE • 1919 • *Universal* • SHT • USA
RAIDERS, THE • 1914 • Barker Reginald? • USA
RAIDERS, THE • 1916 • Mix Tom • *Selig* • SHT • USA
RAIDERS, THE • 1916 • Swickard Charles • *Kb* • USA
RAIDERS, THE • 1921 • Watt Nate • USA
RAIDERS, THE • 1952 • Selander Lesley • USA • RIDERS OF VENGEANCE
RAIDERS, THE • 1963 • Daugherty Herschel • USA • PLAINSMAN, THE
RAIDERS FROM BENEATH THE SEA • 1965 • Dexter Maury • USA
RAIDERS FROM DOUBLE L. RANCH, THE • 1913 • *Roland Ruth* • USA
RAIDERS FROM OUTER SPACE • 1966 • *Darren James* • MTV • USA
RAIDERS IN ACTION • Schvily Benni
RAIDERS OF ATLANTIS see **ATLANTIS INTERCEPTORS** • 1984
RAIDERS OF GHOST CITY • 1944 • Taylor Ray, Collins Lewis D. • SRL • USA
RAIDERS OF LEYTE GULF, THE • 1963 • Romero Eddie • PHL, USA
RAIDERS OF OLD CALIFORNIA • 1957 • Gannaway Albert C. • USA
RAIDERS OF RED GAP • 1943 • Newfield Sam • USA
RAIDERS OF RED ROCK see **FUGITIVE OF THE PLAINS** • 1943
RAIDERS OF SAN JOAQUIN • 1943 • Collins Lewis D. • USA
RAIDERS OF SUNSET GAP, THE • 1918 • *Finley Ned* • SHT • USA
RAIDERS OF SUNSET PASS • 1943 • English John • USA
RAIDERS OF THE BORDER • 1944 • McCarthy John P. • USA
RAIDERS OF THE DESERT • 1941 • Rawlins John • USA
RAIDERS OF THE GOLDEN COBRA, THE see **PREDATORI DEL COBRA D'ORO, I** • 1982
RAIDERS OF THE LIVING DEAD • 1986 • Sherman Samuel M. • USA
RAIDERS OF THE LOST ARK • 1981 • Spielberg Steven • USA
RAIDERS OF THE MEXICAN BORDER • 1912 • *St.louis Motion Picture* • USA
RAIDERS OF THE RANGE • 1942 • English John • USA
RAIDERS OF THE RIVER • 1956 • Haggarty John • UKN
RAIDERS OF THE SEVEN SEAS • 1953 • Salkow Sidney • USA
RAIDERS OF THE SOUTH • 1947 • Hillyer Lambert • USA • SOUTH RAIDERS
RAIDERS OF THE SPANISH MAIN • 1962 • *Morgan Terence* • MTV • UKN
RAIDERS OF THE TREASURE OF TAYOPA see **TAYOPA TREASURE HUNT** • 1974
RAIDERS OF THE WEST • 1942 • Newfield Sam • USA
RAIDERS OF TOMAHAWK CREEK • 1950 • Sears Fred F. • USA • CIRCLE OF FEAR (UKN)
RAIDING THE RAIDERS • 1945 • Rasinski Connie • ANS • USA
RAIGEKITAI SHUTSUDO • 1944 • Yamamoto Kajiro • JPN • TORPEDO SQUADRON MOVES OUT, THE
RAIKHAN • 1940 • Levine Moissej • USS
RAIL • 1967 • Jones Geoffrey • UKN
RAIL, THE • 1959 • Hoffman Jerzy, Skorzewski Edward • PLN

RAIL RIDER, THE • 1916 • Tourneur Maurice • USA
RAIL-RODENTS • 1954 • Tendlar Dave • ANS • USA
RAIL YARD • 1985 • Jackson G. Philip • MTV • CND
RAILPLAN 68 • 1954 • van Gasteren Louis A. • DOC • NTH
RAILROAD, THE see **DEMIRYOLU** • 1980
RAILROAD AND THE WIDOW, THE • 1912 • *Powers* • USA
RAILROAD BANDIT, A • 1916 • McRae Henry • SHT • USA
RAILROAD BUILDER, THE • 1911 • *Thanhouser* • USA
RAILROAD CONSPIRACY, A • 1913 • *Kalem* • USA
RAILROAD DETECTIVE'S DILEMMA, THE • 1913 • *Kalem* • USA
RAILROAD ENGINEER, A • 1912 • *Lubin* • USA
RAILROAD HOLDUP, A • 1915 • *C.k.* • USA
RAILROAD INSPECTOR'S PERIL, THE • 1913 • *Cooper Miriam* • USA
RAILROAD LOCHINVAR, A • 1912 • *Cooper Miriam* • USA
RAILROAD MAN, THE (USA) see **FERROVIERE, IL** • 1956
RAILROAD PICKPOCKET, THE (USA) see **FATALE MEPRISE** • 1900
RAILROAD RAIDERS • 1919 • *Capital* • SHT • USA
RAILROAD RAIDERS, THE • 1917 • McGowan J. P. • SRL • USA
RAILROAD RAIDERS OF '62, THE • 1911 • *Olcott Sidney* • USA
RAILROAD RHYTHM • 1936 • Hopkins A. E. C. • UKN
RAILROAD RHYTHM • 1937 • *Mintz Charles (P)* • ANS • USA
RAILROAD SMASHUP • 1904 • Porter Edwin S. • USA
RAILROAD SMUGGLERS, THE • 1917 • Sidney Scott • USA
RAILROAD TOWN • 1955 • Haldane Don • CND
RAILROAD WOOING, A • 1913 • *Kalem* • USA
RAILROAD WRECK, THE • 1909 • *Phoenix* • USA
RAILROAD WRETCH • 1932 • *Mintz Charles (P)* • ANS • USA
RAILROADED • 1923 • Mortimer Edmund • USA • THICKER THAN WATER
RAILROADED • 1947 • Mann Anthony • USA
RAILROADED TO FAME • 1961 • Tendlar Dave • ANS • USA
RAILROADER, THE • 1919 • Campbell Colin • USA • RAILROADERS, THE
RAILROADERS see **PALYMUNKASOK** • 1957
RAILROADERS, THE • 1958 • Cote Guy-L. • DCS • CND • CHEMINOTS, LES
RAILROADERS, THE see **RAILROADER, THE** • 1919
RAILROADER'S WARNING, A • 1913 • *Vane Denton* • USA
RAILROADIN' • 1929 • McGowan Robert • SHT • USA
RAILRODDER, THE • 1965 • Potterton Gerald • CND
RAILS BENEATH THE PALM TREES see **DES RAILS SOUS LES PALMIERS** • 1951
RAILS IN THE SKY • 1962 • Zahariev Edward • DOC • BUL
RAILS INTO LARAMIE • 1954 • Hibbs Jesse • USA
RAILWAY CHILDREN, THE • 1970 • Jeffries Lionel • UKN
RAILWAY COLLISION, A • 1898 • Paul Robert William • UKN • TERRIBLE RAILWAY ACCIDENT, THE
RAILWAY COLLISION, A • 1900 • Booth W. R. • UKN
RAILWAY DE LA MORT, LE • 1913 • Durand Jean • FRN
RAILWAY JUNCTION • 1961 • Karabasz Kazimierz • PLN
RAILWAY MAIL CLERK, THE • 1910 • *Kalem* • USA
RAILWAY PICKPOCKET, THE see **FATALE MEPRISE** • 1900
RAILWAY STATION see **EESTGAH-E-TRAIN** • 1967
RAILWAY STOP FOR TWO, A see **VOKZAL DLIA DVOIKH** • 1983
RAILWAY TRAFFIC ON THE L.N.W.R. • 1897 • Norton C. Goodwin • UKN • TRAIN ENTERING A STATION
RAILWAY TRAGEDY, A • 1904 • *Gaumont* • UKN
RAILWAY TRAIN see **TETSUWAN KISHA** • 1926
RAILWAY WORKERS, THE see **RALLARE** • 1947
RAILWAYMAN'S PLEDGE, A see **KOLEJARSKI SLOWO** • 1953
RAILWAYMAN'S WORD, A see **KOLEJARSKI SLOWO** • 1953
RAILWAYMEN see **ZELEZNICARI** • 1963
RAIN • 1932 • Milestone Lewis • USA
RAIN • 1965 • Jakubisko Juraj • CZC
RAIN see **REGN** • 1970
RAIN see **KISA** • 1973
RAIN, THE • 1968 • Coignon Jean • ANS • BLG
RAIN AND GOOD WEATHER see **PLUIE ET LE BEAU TEMPS, LA**
RAIN AND SHINE see **REGULAR FELLOW, A** • 1925
RAIN AND SHINE see **VERI AZ ORDOG A FELESEGET** • 1978
RAIN BLACK MY LOVE see **SWAIN** • 1951
RAIN CAME PITTER PATTER DOWN, THE • 1909 • *Warwick Trading Co* • UKN
RAIN DRAIN • 1966 • Bakshi Ralph • ANS • USA
RAIN FOR A DUSTY SUMMER • 1971 • Lubin Arthur • USA, SPN • MIGUEL PRO (SPN)
RAIN IN JULY see **LYULSKI DOZHD** • 1967
RAIN MAKERS, THE • 1951 • Rasinski Connie • ANS • USA
RAIN MAN • 1988 • Levinson Barry • USA
RAIN OF DEATH, THE • 1915 • *Swayne Marion* • USA
RAIN OF PARIS, THE • 1980 • Dinov Todor • ANM • BUL
RAIN OR SHINE • 1930 • Capra Frank • USA
RAIN OR SHINE • 1960 • Rappaport Herbert • USS
RAIN OR SHINE see **OB'S STURMT ODER SCHNEIT** • 1977
RAIN OVER SANTIAGO see **LLUEVE SOBRE SANTIAGO** • 1975
RAIN PEOPLE, THE • 1969 • Coppola Francis Ford • USA
RAIN, RAIN, GO AWAY • 1972 • Smith Paul J. • ANS • USA
RAIN, RAIN, GO AWAY see **SHADOW IN THE SKY** • 1951
RAIN (USA) see **REGEN** • 1929
RAINBOW • 1921 • Jose Edward • USA
RAINBOW • 1978 • Cooper Jackie • TVM • USA
RAINBOW see **RADUGA** • 1941
RAINBOW see **GHOSOGHAZAH** • 1968
RAINBOW see **SPARA, GRINGO, SPARA** • 1968
RAINBOW, THE • 1917 • Dean Ralph • USA
RAINBOW, THE • 1929 • Barker Reginald • USA
RAINBOW, THE • 1989 • Russell Ken • UKN
RAINBOW BEAR, THE • 1970 • Melendez Bill • ANS • USA
RAINBOW BOX, THE • 1917 • Beaumont Harry • SHT • USA
RAINBOW BOYS, THE • 1973 • Potterton Gerald • CND • RAINBOW GANG, THE ○ LOGAN
RAINBOW BRIDGE • 1971 • Wein Chuck • USA
RAINBOW BRIDGE see **WANPAKU OJI NO OROCHITAIJI** • 1963
RAINBOW BRITE AND THE STAR STEALER • 1985 • Deyries Bernard, Yabuki Kimio • ANM • USA
RAINBOW BRITE: MIGHTY MONSTROMURK MENACE • 1983 • Sevush Herb • ANM • USA
RAINBOW CHASERS see **CONFIDENCE** • 1922
RAINBOW CHASERS, THE • 1919 • Malins Geoffrey H. • UKN
RAINBOW-COLOURED STREET see **NANAIRO NO MACHI** • 1952
RAINBOW COMEDIES • 1922 • Dudley Bernard • SHS • UKN
RAINBOW DANCE • 1936 • Lye Len • ANS • UKN
RAINBOW GAME, THE see **LEK PA REGNBAGEN** • 1958
RAINBOW GANG, THE see **RAINBOW BOYS, THE** • 1973
RAINBOW GIRL, THE • 1917 • Sturgeon Rollin S. • USA
RAINBOW ISLAND • 1917 • Roach Hal • SHT • USA
RAINBOW ISLAND • 1944 • Murphy Ralph • USA
RAINBOW JACKET, THE • 1954 • Dearden Basil • UKN
RAINBOW MAN, THE • 1929 • Newmeyer Fred • USA
RAINBOW OF THIS SKY, THE see **KONO TEN NO NIJI** • 1958
RAINBOW ON THE RIVER • 1936 • Neumann Kurt • USA
RAINBOW OVER BROADWAY • 1933 • Thorpe Richard • USA
RAINBOW OVER PARIS see **TOKYO PARIS SEISHUN NO JOKEN** • 1970
RAINBOW OVER SEOUL • 1988 • Kim Ho-Sun • SKR
RAINBOW OVER TEXAS • 1946 • McDonald Frank • USA
RAINBOW OVER THE KINMEN see **KINMON-TO NI KAKERU HASHI** • 1962
RAINBOW OVER THE PACIFIC see **YOAKE NO FUTARI** • 1968
RAINBOW OVER THE RANGE • 1940 • Herman Al • USA
RAINBOW OVER THE ROCKIES • 1947 • Drake Oliver • USA
RAINBOW PARADE • 1935-36 • Gillett Burt, Palmer Tom • ASS • USA
RAINBOW PASS, THE • 1937 • Tourneur Jacques • SHT • USA
RAINBOW PRINCESS, THE • 1916 • Dawley J. Searle • USA
RAINBOW PROFESSIONALS see **OPERATION 'NAM** • 1985
RAINBOW RANCH • 1933 • Fraser Harry L. • USA
RAINBOW RANGE • 1929 • *Cheyenne Bill* • USA
RAINBOW RANGERS • 1924 • Sheldon Forrest • USA
RAINBOW RHYTHM • 1942 • Le Borg Reginald • SHT • USA
RAINBOW RHYTHM see **RAINBOW ROUND THE CORNER** • 1944
RAINBOW RIDERS • 1934 • Cohn Bennett • SHT • USA
RAINBOW RILEY • 1926 • Hines Charles • USA
RAINBOW ROUND MY SHOULDER • 1929 • Aylott Dave, Symmons E. F. • SHT • UKN
RAINBOW 'ROUND MY SHOULDER • 1952 • Quine Richard • USA • CASTLE IN THE AIR
RAINBOW ROUND THE CORNER • 1944 • Gover Victor M. • UKN • RAINBOW RHYTHM
RAINBOW TRAIL, THE • 1918 • Lloyd Frank • USA
RAINBOW TRAIL, THE • 1925 • Reynolds Lynn • USA
RAINBOW TRAIL, THE • 1932 • Howard David • USA
RAINBOW VALLEY • 1935 • Bradbury Robert North • USA
RAINBOW VERDICT, THE • 1971 • Thompson David* • UKN
RAINBOW'S END • 1934 • Spencer Norman • USA
RAINBOW'S END see **A HJARA VERALDAR** • 1983
RAINBOW'S END, THE • 1914 • *Miller'S 101 Ranch* • USA
RAINDROPS AND GIRLS • 1915 • *Sterling* • USA
RAINDROPS, WATERS, WARRIORS see **KAPI, VODE, RATNICI** • 1962
RAINFOX • 1984 • Carlsen Esben Hoilund • DNM
RAINHA DIABA, A • 1974 • Fontoura Antonio Carlos • BRZ
RAINHA DO RADIO, A • 1981 • Goulart Luis Fernando • BRZ • QUEEN OF THE RADIO, THE
RAINHA ISABEL II EM PORTUGAL, A • 1957 • Ribeiro Antonio Lopes • SHT • PRT
RAINING HAPPINESS • 1964 • Kachlik Antonin • CZC
RAINING IN THE MOUNTAINS see **KUNG SHAN LING YU** • 1978
RAINING ON THE MOUNTAIN see **KUNG SHAN LING YU** • 1978
RAINIS • 1949 • Raizman Yuli • USS
RAINMAKER, THE • 1926 • Badger Clarence • USA
RAINMAKER, THE • 1956 • Anthony Joseph • USA
RAINMAKERS • 1897 • *Edison* • SHT • USA
RAINMAKERS see **HOMMES QUI FONT LA PLUIE, LES** • 1951
RAINMAKERS, THE • 1935 • Guiol Fred • USA
RAINS, THE • 1959 • Kazakov S. • USS
RAINS CAME, THE • 1939 • Brown Clarence • USA
RAIN'S HAT, THE • 1978 • Zetterling Mai • MTV • UKN
RAINS OF MY COUNTRY, THE • 1963 • Strbac Milenko • YGS
RAINS OF RANCHIPUR, THE • 1955 • Negulesco Jean • USA
RAINSTORM see **RAGBAR** • 1972
RAINSTORMS AND BRAINSTORMS • 1917 • Hutchinson Craig • SHT • USA
RAINTREE COUNTY, THE • 1957 • Dmytryk Edward • USA
RAINY DAY, A • 1913 • Henderson Dell • USA
RAINY DAY, A • 1919 • *Carr Johnny* • SHT • USA
RAINY DAY, A • 1940 • Harman Hugh • ANS • USA
RAINY DAY, THE • 1915 • *Hawley Ormi* • USA
RAINY DAY FRIENDS • 1986 • Kent Gary • USA
RAINY DAYS • 1928 • Mack Anthony • SHT • USA
RAINY JULY, A (USA) see **DESZCZOWY LUPIEC** • 1958
RAINY KNIGHT, A • 1925 • *Sennett Mack (P)* • SHT • USA
RAINY NIGHT DUEL see **KUROOBI SANGOKUSHI** • 1956
RAINY SEASON, THE see **SADEAIKA** • 1980
RAINY SUNDAY, A see **ESOS VASARNAP** • 1962
RAINY, THE LION KILLER • 1914 • Drew Sidney • USA • HENRY STANLEY, THE LION KILLER
RAISE RAVENS see **CRIA CUERVOS** • 1976
RAISE THE RENT • 1920 • Newmeyer Fred, Roach Hal • SHT • USA
RAISE THE ROOF • 1930 • Summers Walter • UKN
RAISE THE TITANIC • 1980 • Jameson Jerry • USA
RAISED FROM THE RANKS • 1908 • Chart Jack • UKN
RAISED FROM THE RANKS see **GENTLEMAN RANKER, THE** • 1913
RAISIN IN THE SUN, A • 1961 • Petrie Daniel • USA
RAISING A RIOT • 1955 • Toye Wendy • UKN
RAISING ARIZONA • 1987 • Coen Joel • USA
RAISING CAIN • 1924 • Lamont Charles • SHT • USA
RAISING OF LAZARUS, THE • 1948 • *Church-Craft Pics* • SHT • USA
RAISING OF SKIRTS, THE see **LEVANTE DAS SAIAS, O** • 1968
RAISING RAVENS see **CRIA CUERVOS** • 1976
RAISING THE GILHAST POLE • 1973 • Wilson Sandra • CND
RAISING THE ROOF • 1929 • Santley Joseph • SHT • USA
RAISING THE WIND • 1925 • Hiscott Leslie • UKN
RAISING THE WIND • 1961 • Thomas Gerald • UKN • ROOMMATES
RAISING THE WIND see **BIG RACE, THE** • 1934
RAISINS DE LA MORT, LES • 1978 • Rollin Jean • FRN • PESTICIDE
RAISON AVANT LA PASSION, LA • 1969 • Wieland Joyce • DOC • CND • REASON OVER PASSION
RAISON D'ETAT, LA • 1978 • Cayatte Andre • ITL, FRN • STATE REASONS
RAISON DU PLUS FOU, LA see **RAISON DU PLUS FOU EST TOUJOURS LA MEILLEURE, LA** • 1972
RAISON DU PLUS FOU EST TOUJOURS LA MEILLEURE, LA • 1972 • Reichenbach Francois • DOC • FRN • RAISON DU PLUS FOU, LA
RAIZES OCULTAS see **CRIME DE SIMAO BOLANDAS, O** • 1980
RAJ NA ZIEMI • 1970 • Kuzminski Zbigniew • PLN • PARADISE ON EARTH
RAJ NARTIKI • 1940 • Bose Modhu • IND • COURT DANCER, THE
RAJ RAM MEERA • 1933 • Kapoor Prithviraj • IND
RAJA AUR RUNK • 1968 • Atma K. P. • IND • PRINCE AND THE PAUPER, THE
RAJA BHARATHRURHARI • 1949 • Vaidya Ramnik D. • IND
RAJA GOPICHAND • 1938 • Pendharkar Bhal G. • IND
RAJA GOPICHAND see **ALAKH NIRANJAN** • 1950
RAJA HARISCHANDRA • 1923 • IND
RAJA HARISCHANDRA • 1927 • IND
RAJA HARISCHANDRA • 1952 • Singh Hira • NPL, IND
RAJA HARISHCHANDRA see **HARISHCHANDRA** • 1912
RAJA LAUT • 1980 • Lokman Z. • MLY
RAJA SOOYAM • 1965 • Rama Rao N. T. • IND • RAJASUYAM
RAJA VEETU PILLAI • 1967 • Dadamirasi • IND • SON OF A KING
RAJA VIKRAM • 1950 • Urs D. Kempraj • IND
RAJADURGADA RAHASYA • 1967 • Narasimmamoorthy A. C. • IND • MYSTERY OF RAJA-DURGADA, THE
RAJAH, THE • 1911 • Dawley J. Searle • USA
RAJAH, THE • 1919 • Roach Hal • SHT • USA
RAJAH'S AMULET, THE see **EACH TO HIS KIND** • 1917
RAJAH'S CASKET, THE see **ECRIN DU RAJAH, L'** • 1906
RAJAH'S DREAM OR THE BEWITCHED WOOD, THE (USA) see **REVE DU RADJAH OU, LA FORET ENCHANTEE, LE** • 1900
RAJAH'S REVENGE, THE • 1912 • Aylott Dave • UKN
RAJAH'S SACRIFICE, THE • 1915 • Bonavita Jack, Montgomery Frank E. • USA
RAJAH'S TIARA, THE • 1914 • Martinek H. O. • UKN
RAJAH'S TUNIC, THE • 1915 • *Craig Nell* • USA
RAJAH'S VACATION, THE • 1914 • Martin E. A. • USA
RAJAH'S VOW, THE • 1914 • *Kalem* • USA
RAJANIGANDHA • 1974 • Chatterjee Basu • IND
RAJAR, AR- • 1968 • Al-Yassiri Fiasal • SYR • HOMME, L'
RAJASUYAM see **RAJA SOOYAM** • 1965
RAJAT JAYANTI • 1939 • *Sircar B. N. (P)* • IND
RAJATHI • 1967 • Lakshmanan M. • IND
RAJAYOGAM • 1968 • Ramdas Subba • IND • FIT TO BE A KING
RAJGI • 1937 • *Burman S. D. (M)* • IND
RAJO JIGOKU • 1968 • Komori Haku • JPN • INFERNO OF NAKED WOMEN
RAJO TO KENJU • 1957 • Suzuki Seijun • JPN
RAJRANI MEERA • 1933 • *Sircar B. N. (P)* • IND
RAJTUNK IS MULIK • 1960 • Meszaros Marta • DCS • HNG • IT DEPENDS ON US TOO..
RAJU AUR GANGARAM • 1964 • *Biswas Anil (M)* • IND
RAJUL EL MOSTAKBUL • 1947 • Salem Ahmed • EGY • MAN OF THE FUTURE, THE
RAJUL FI HAYATI • 1961 • Shahin Youssef • EGY • MAN IN MY LIFE, THE ○ RAGULUN FI HAYATI
RAK • 1971 • Belmont Charles • FRN
RAK TORAMAN • 1988 • Akaraserani Pisan • THL
RAKA • 1968 • Travers Alfred • SAF
RAKAS • 1961 • Kurkvaara Maunu • FNL • BELOVED ○ DARLING
RAKASTUNUT RAMPA • 1974 • Faven Esko, Laine Tarja • FNL • CRIPPLE IN LOVE
RAKE'S PROGRESS, THE • 1945 • Gilliat Sidney • UKN • NOTORIOUS GENTLEMAN, THE (USA)
RAKE'S ROMANCE, A • 1910 • Coleby A. E. • UKN
RAKEV VE SNU VIDETI.. • 1968 • Mach Jaroslav • CZC • TO SEE A COFFIN IN ONE'S DREAM.. ○ TO SEE A COFFIN IN YOUR DREAM
RAKEVET HA 'EMEK • 1989 • Paz Jonathan • ISR • VALLEY TRAIN, THE
RAKHMANOV'S SISTERS see **SESTRY RAKHMANOVY** • 1954
RAKHTO • 1973 • Gupta Chidamanda Das • IND • BLOOD
RAKHWALA • 1989 • IND
RAKKI-SAN • 1952 • Ichikawa Kon • JPN • MR. LUCKY ○ LUCKY SAN
RAKNA DE LYCKLIGA STUNDERNA BLOTT • 1944 • Carlsten Rune • SWD • COUNT THE HAPPY MOMENTS ONLY
RAKNA MED BRAK • 1957 • Husberg Rolf • SWD • COUNT ON TROUBLE
RAKOCZI HADNAGYA • 1953 • Ban Frigyes • HNG • RAKOCZI'S LIEUTENANT
RAKOCZI INDULO see **RAKOCZY-MARSCH** • 1933
RAKOCZI'S LIEUTENANT see **RAKOCZI HADNAGYA** • 1953
RAKOCZY-MARSCH • 1933 • Frohlich Gustav, Sekely Steve • FRG, HNG, AUS • RAKOCZI INDULO
RAKOON HOSE COMPANY, THE • 1915 • *Edwards John* • USA
RAKTA REKHA • 1968 • Maitra Umaprasad • IND • MARK OF BLOOD
RAKUDAI WA SHITA KEREDO • 1930 • Ozu Yasujiro • JPN • I FAILED BUT.. ○ I FLUNKED BUT..
RAKUGAKI KOKUBAN • 1959 • Shindo Kaneto • JPN • GRAFFITI BLACKBOARD
RAKUGOYARO DAIBAKUSHO • 1967 • Sugie Toshio • JPN • COMIC STORYTELLER'S UPROARIOUS LAUGHTER, A
RAKUGOYARO: ODOROBO • 1967 • Matsubayashi Shue • JPN • COMIC STORYTELLER: THE GREAT BURGLAR, A
RAKUYO-JU • 1987 • Shindo Kaneto • JPN • DECIDUOUS TREE, A
RALLARBLOD • 1978 • Solbakken Erik • NRW • INTRUDERS, THE
RALLARE • 1947 • Mattsson Arne • SWD • NAVVIES ○ RAILWAY WORKERS, THE

RALLIEMENTS MENAGERS • 1951 • Tessier Albert • DCS • CND
RALLY • 1973 • Williams Tony • MTV • NZL
RALLY • 1980 • SAF
RALLY see **BENSAA SUONISSA** • 1971
RALLY see **SAFARI 3000** • 1982
RALLY ROUND THE FLAG • 1909 • Olcott Sidney • USA
RALLY 'ROUND THE FLAG, BOYS! • 1958 • McCarey Leo • USA
RALLYE DES JOYEUSES, LA • 1975 • Nauroy Alain C. • FRN • SEX RALLY
RALLYE DES NEIGES • 1962 • Wilder Donald A. • CND
RALPH BENEFITS BY PEOPLE'S CURIOSITY • 1909 • *Pathe* • FRN
RAM AND SHYAM see **RAM AUR SHYAM** • 1967
RAM AUR SHYAM • 1967 • Chanakya • IND • RAM AND SHYAM
RAM-BUNCTIOUS ENDEAVOUR, A • 1917 • *Reid Wallace* • SHT • USA
RAM DARSHAN • 1950 • Gupta Ramesh • IND
RAM JANMA • 1951 • Bhatt Nanabhai • IND
RAM LAKHAN • 1988 • IND
RAM PRATIGYA • 1949 • Varma Amar • IND
RAM RAJYA • 1967 • Bhatt Vijay • IND • KINGDOM OF RAM, THE
RAM TERI GANGA MAILI • 1985 • Kapoor Raj • IND
RAM VIVAH see **RAMVIVAHA** • 1949
RAMA • Cain Sugar • SHT • USA
RAMA DAMA -IM JAHR DE TRUMMERFRAU • 1990 • Vilsmaier Joseph • FRG • IN THE YEAR OF THE RUBBLE-CLEARING WOMAN
RAMA SUPERMAN INDONESIA • 1974 • INN
RAMADAL • 1958 • Reyes Efren • PHL
RAMADHAN & RAMONA see **KEJARLAH DAKU.. KAU KUTANGKAP** • 1985
RAMANJANEYA YUDDHA • 1939 • Kalyanasundaram A. N. • IND
RAMAR AND THE BURNING BARRIER • 1953 • *Flothow Rudolph (P)* • MTV • USA
RAMAR AND THE DEADLY FEMALES • 1953 • *Flothow Rudolph (P)* • MTV • USA
RAMAR AND THE JUNGLE SECRETS • 1953 • *Flothow Rudolph (P)* • MTV • USA
RAMAR AND THE SAVAGE CHALLENGERS • 1953 • *Flothow Rudolph (P)* • MTV • USA
RAMAR AND THE SEVEN CHALLENGES • 1953 • *Flothow Rudolph (P)* • MTV • USA
RAMAR AND THE UNKNOWN TERROR • 1953 • *Flothow Rudolph (P)* • MTV • USA
RAMAR OF THE JUNGLE (UKN) see **WHITE GODDESS** • 1953
RAMARA • 1916 • *Kaiser-Titz Erich* • FRG
RAMAR'S MISSION TO INDIA • 1953 • *Flothow Rudolph (P)* • MTV • USA
RAMAYANA see **SEETHA DEVI** • 1976
RAMAYVAN • 1987 • Sagar Ramanand • SRL • IND
RAMB-OOH: THE FORCE IS IN YOU • Rogel Van • USA
RAMB-OOH: THE SEX PLATOON • 1988 • Gower Wolfgang • USA
RAMBHAKTA HANUMAN • 1948 • Wadia Homi • IND
RAMBLE IN APHASIA, A • 1918 • Webb Kenneth • SHT • USA
RAMBLES THROUGH HOPLAND • 1913 • Pearson George • DCS • UKN
RAMBLIN' • 1970 • Pennebaker D. A. • SHT • USA
RAMBLIN' GALOOT, THE • 1926 • Bain Fred • USA
RAMBLIN' KID, THE • 1923 • Sedgwick Edward • USA • LONG, LONG TRAIL, THE
RAMBLING RANGER, THE • 1927 • Henderson Dell • USA
RAMBLING ROUND RADIO ROW • 1932-34 • SHS • USA
RAMBO, FIRST BLOOD, PART II • 1985 • Cosmatos George Pan • USA
RAMBO III • 1988 • MacDonald Peter • USA
RAMBO: THE RESCUE • 1986 • ANM • USA
RAMEAU'S NEPHEW see **RAMEAU'S NEPHEW BY DIDEROT (THANX TO DENIS YOUNG) BY WILMA SCHOEN** • 1975
RAMEAU'S NEPHEW BY DIDEROT (THANX TO DENIS YOUNG) BY WILMA SCHOEN • 1975 • Snow Michael • CND • RAMEAU'S NEPHEW
RAMENTAISHI • 1967 • Shima Koji • JPN • NOODLE SELLER, A
RAMER SUMATI • 1947 • *Sircar B. N. (P)* • IND
RAMEURS DES GLACES • 1956 • Rivard Fernand • DCS • CND
RAMI AND JULIET see **RAMI OG JULIE** • 1987
RAMI OG JULIE • 1987 • Clausen Erik • DNM • RAMI AND JULIET
RAMIR • 1958 • Estella Ramon • PHL
RAMKINKAR • 1975 • *Ghatak Ritwik* • DOC • IND
RAMNAGARI • 1977 • Rathod Kantilal • IND
RAMON • 1969 • Shean Alan • ANS • USA
RAMON IL MESSICANO • 1966 • Pradeaux Maurizio • ITL
RAMONA • 1910 • Griffith D. W. • USA
RAMONA • 1916 • Crisp Donald • USA
RAMONA • 1928 • Carewe Edwin • USA
RAMONA • 1936 • King Henry • USA
RAMONA • 1946 • Urruchua Victor • MXC
RAMONA • 1961 • Martin Paul • FRG
RAMONEUR MALGRE LUI • 1912 • Cohl Emile • ANS • FRN
RAMON'S FATHER • 1911 • *Selig* • USA
RAMPAGE • 1963 • Karlson Phil, Hathaway Henry (U/c) • USA • JUNGLE RAMPAGE
RAMPAGE • 1987 • Friedkin William • USA
RAMPAGE AT APACHE WELLS (USA) see **OELPRINZ, DER** • 1965
RAMPANT AGE, THE • 1930 • Rosen Phil • USA
RAMPARTS OF CLAY (USA) see **REMPARTS D'ARGILE** • 1970
RAMPARTS WE WATCH, THE • 1940 • de Rochemont Louis • USA
RAMPER, DER TIERMENSCH • 1927 • Reichmann Max • FRG • STRANGE CASE OF CAPTAIN RAMPER, THE (USA) ○ RAMPER THE BEASTMAN
RAMPER THE BEASTMAN see **RAMPER, DER TIERMENSCH** • 1927
RAMROD • 1947 • De Toth Andre • USA
RAMRODDER, THE • 1969 • Guylder Van • USA • RAMRODDERS
RAMRODDERS see **RAMRODDER, THE** • 1969
RAMSA • 1946 • Xiol Juan • SPN
RAMSBOTTOM RIDES AGAIN • 1956 • Baxter John • UKN
RAMSES see **RAMSES JA UNET** • 1981
RAMSES AND THE DREAMS see **RAMSES JA UNET** • 1981
RAMSES JA UNET • 1981 • Partanen Heikki • DOC • FNL • RAMSES AND THE DREAMS ○ RAMSES
RAMSHACKLE HOUSE • 1924 • Weight F. Harmon • USA
RAMSHACKLED OF SODER see **SODERKAKAR** • 1932
RAMUNTCHO • 1918 • de Baroncelli Jacques • FRN
RAMUNTCHO • 1937 • Barberis Rene • FRN
RAMUNTCHO • 1958 • Schoendoerffer Pierre • FRN
RAMUZ, PASSAGE D'UN POETE • 1959 • Tanner Alain • SHT • SWT
RAMVIVAHA • 1949 • Adib Prem • IND • RAM VIVAH
RAN • 1983 • Kurosawa Akira • JPN
RAN RASA • 1967 • Rathnam E. • SLN • GOLDEN RAYS
RAN SALU • 1967 • Peries Lester James • SLN • SAFFRON ROBE, THE ○ YELLOW ROBE, THE ○ GOLDEN SHAWL
RANA • 1978 • Glomm Lasse • NRW
RANA see **CREATURE FROM SHADOW LAKE, THE** • 1984
RANA: CREATURE FROM SHADOW LAKE see **CREATURE FROM SHADOW LAKE, THE** • 1984
RANA GIRAW • 1967 • Caldera Dharmasiri • SLN • FLIGHT OF PARROTS
RANA: THE LEGEND OF SHADOW LAKE see **CREATURE FROM SHADOW LAKE, THE** • 1984
RANA VERDE, LA • 1957 • Forn Josep Maria • SPN
RANABHERI • 1968 • Satyam Giduthuri • IND • DRUMBEATS OF BATTLE
RANAHANSI • 1953 • *Sircar B. N. (P)* • IND
RANCH, THE • 1988 • Stevens Stella • USA
RANCH CHICKEN, THE • 1911 • Dwan Allan • USA
RANCH DEGLI SPIETATI, IL • 1965 • Balcazar Jaime Jesus, Montero Roberto Bianchi • ITL, SPN, FRG • MAN FROM OKLAHOMA, THE (USA) ○ OKLAHOMA JOHN
RANCH DETECTIVE, THE see **RANGE DETECTIVE, THE** • 1912
RANCH EXILE, THE • 1916 • *Mutual* • USA
RANCH FEUD, THE • 1913 • *Anderson Broncho Billy* • USA
RANCH GIRL, THE • 1911 • Dwan Allan • USA • RANCH GIRL'S RUSTLER, THE
RANCH GIRL AND THE SKY PILOT, THE • 1913 • *Frontier* • USA
RANCH GIRL ON A RAMPAGE • 1912 • *Kalem* • USA
RANCH GIRL'S CHOICE, THE • 1912 • *Nestor* • USA
RANCH GIRL'S LEGACY, THE • 1910 • *Anderson Broncho Billy* • USA
RANCH GIRL'S LOVE, THE • 1912 • *Bison* • USA
RANCH GIRL'S MEASUREMENTS, THE • 1913 • *Frontier* • USA
RANCH GIRL'S MISTAKE, THE • 1912 • *Anderson Broncho Billy* • USA
RANCH GIRL'S PARTNER, THE • 1913 • *Essanay* • USA
RANCH GIRL'S RUSTLER, THE see **RANCH GIRL, THE** • 1911
RANCH GIRL'S TRIAL, THE • 1912 • *Anderson Broncho Billy* • USA
RANCH HAND • 1970 • *Stacey Dist.* • USA
RANCH HOUSE ROMEO • 1939 • Brock Lou • SHT • USA
RANCH KING'S DAUGHTER, THE • 1909 • *Selig* • USA
RANCH LIFE ON THE RANGE • 1912 • Dwan Allan • USA
RANCH-MATES • 1912 • Grandon Francis J. • USA
RANCH OF THE NYMPHOMANIAC GIRLS see **BUMSFIDELEN MADCHEN VON BIRKENHOF, DIE** • 1974
RANCH OF THE NYMPHOMANIACS see **BUMSFIDELEN MADCHEN VON BIRKENHOF, DIE** • 1974
RANCH OWNER'S DAUGHTER, THE • 1909 • Fitzhamon Lewin • UKN • REDSKIN'S OFFER, THE
RANCH OWNER'S LOVE-MAKING, THE • 1913 • Edwin Walter • USA
RANCH RAIDERS, THE • 1910 • *Bison* • USA
RANCH ROMANCE, A • 1914 • *Mcquarrie Murdock* • USA
RANCH STENOGRAPHER, THE • 1913 • *Frontier* • USA
RANCH TENOR, THE • 1911 • Dwan Allan • USA • FOREMAN'S FIXUP, THE
RANCH: THE ALAN WOOD RANCH PROJECT • 1987 • Denure Steven • DCS • CND
RANCH WIDOWER'S DAUGHTERS, THE • 1912 • *Essanay* • USA
RANCH WOMAN, THE • 1912 • *Champion* • USA
RANCHANDI • 1929 • *Kohinoor United Artists* • IND • GODDESS OF WAR, THE (USA)
RANCHEADOR • 1977 • Giral Sergio • CUB • RANCHER, THE ○ SLAVEDRIVER
RANCHER, THE see **RANCHEADOR** • 1977
RANCHERO'S REVENGE, THE • 1913 • Griffith D. W., Cabanne W. Christy • USA
RANCHERS, THE • 1923 • *Elliot George* • USA
RANCHERS AND RASCALS • 1925 • *Maloney Leo* • USA
RANCHER'S FAILING, THE • 1913 • Huntley Fred W. • USA
RANCHER'S LOTTERY, THE • 1912 • *Tennant Dorothy* • USA
RANCHMAN AND THE HUNGRY BIRD, THE • 1912 • *Thanhouser* • USA
RANCHMAN AND THE MISER, THE • 1910 • *Champion* • USA
RANCHMAN'S ANNIVERSARY, THE • 1912 • *Essanay* • USA
RANCHMAN'S AWAKENING, THE • 1912 • *Bison* • USA
RANCHMAN'S BLUNDER, THE • 1913 • *Essanay* • USA
RANCHMAN'S BRIDE, THE • 1910 • *Nestor* • USA
RANCHMAN'S DAUGHTER, THE • 1911 • *Lubin* • USA
RANCHMAN'S DEBT OF HONOR, THE • 1911 • Melies Gaston • USA
RANCHMAN'S DOUBLE, THE • 1913 • *Frontier* • USA
RANCHMAN'S FEUD, THE • 1910 • *Anderson Broncho Billy* • USA
RANCHMAN'S LOVE, THE • 1908 • *Selig* • USA
RANCHMAN'S MARATHON, THE • 1912 • Dwan Allan • USA
RANCHMAN'S MOTHER-IN-LAW, THE • 1911 • *Bison* • USA
RANCHMAN'S NERVE, THE • 1911 • Dwan Allan • USA
RANCHMAN'S PERSONAL, THE • 1910 • *Bison* • USA
RANCHMAN'S REMEDY, THE • 1912 • *Nestor* • USA
RANCHMAN'S RIVAL, THE • 1909 • *Anderson Broncho Billy* • USA
RANCHMAN'S SIMPLE SON, THE • 1910 • *Bison* • USA
RANCHMAN'S SON, THE • 1911 • *Essanay* • USA
RANCHMAN'S TRUST, THE • 1912 • Anderson G. M. • USA
RANCHMAN'S VENGEANCE, THE • 1911 • *American* • USA
RANCHMAN'S WIFE, THE • 1909 • *Bison* • USA
RANCHMAN'S WOOING, THE • 1912 • *Frontier* • USA
RANCHO ALEGRE • 1940 • de Anda Raul • MXC
RANCHO DE LA MUERTE, EL • 1968 • Romero-Marchent Rafael • SPN
RANCHO DE LOS IMPLACABLES, EL • 1964 • Balcazar Alfonso • SPN
RANCHO DE MIS RECUERDOS • 1944 • Contreras Torres Miguel • MXC
RANCHO DELUXE • 1974 • Perry Frank • USA
RANCHO DIABLO • 1968 • Diaz Leody M. • PHL • DEVIL RANCH
RANCHO GRANDE • 1938 • Bustamente Alfonso Rivas
RANCHO GRANDE • 1940 • McDonald Frank • USA
RANCHO NOTORIOUS • 1952 • Lang Fritz • USA
RANCHO SOLO • 1965 • Martinez Arturo • MXC
RANCH'S NEW BARBER, THE • 1911 • *Lubin* • USA
RANCID RANSOM • 1962 • Hanna William, Barbera Joseph • ANS • USA
RANCON, LE • 1961 • Bourguignon Serge • FRN
RANCON, LE • 1984 • Butler Yvan • SWT, FRN
RANCON DU BONHEUR, LA • 1912 • Perret Leonce • FRN
RANCON D'UNE ALLIANCE, LA • 1973 • Kamba Sebastien • CNG
RANCUNE, LA (FRN) see **BESUCH, DER** • 1964
RAND ROVER • 1979 • Sacco Arduino • ITL
RANDEVOU ME MIAN AGNOSTI • 1968 • Georgiadis Vassilis • GRC • APPOINTMENT WITH AN UNKNOWN WOMAN
RANDIN AND CO. • 1913 • *Ambrosio* • ITL
RANDOLPH FAMILY, THE (USA) see **DEAR OCTOPUS** • 1943
RANDOM FLAKES • 1925 • Barkas Geoffrey • UKN
RANDOM HARVEST • 1942 • LeRoy Mervyn • USA
RANDOM WALK TO CLASSICAL RUIN, A • 1971 • Perry Dave • ASL
RANDY RIDES ALONE • 1934 • Fraser Harry L. • USA
RANDY STRIKES OIL (UKN) see **FIGHTING TEXANS, THE** • 1933
RANDY, THE ELECTRIC LADY • 1980 • Schumann Philip • USA
RANG • 1986 • Chakraborty Utpalendu • IND • COLOUR
RANGE BEYOND THE BLUE • 1947 • Taylor Ray • USA
RANGE BLOOD • 1924 • Ford Francis • USA
RANGE BOSS, THE • 1917 • Van Dyke W. S. • USA
RANGE BUSTERS • 1932 • Adamson Victor • USA
RANGE BUSTERS, THE • 1940 • Luby S. Roy • USA
RANGE BUZZARDS • 1925 • Gibson Tom • USA
RANGE COURAGE • 1927 • Laemmle Ernst • USA
RANGE DEADLINE, THE • 1913 • *Nestor* • USA
RANGE DEFENDERS, THE • 1937 • Wright Mack V. • USA
RANGE DETECTIVE, THE • 1912 • Dwan Allan • USA • RANCH DETECTIVE, THE
RANGE FEUD, THE • 1931 • Lederman D. Ross • USA
RANGE GIRL AND THE COWBOY, THE • 1915 • Mix Tom • USA
RANGE JUSTICE • 1911 • *Bison* • USA
RANGE JUSTICE • 1925 • Hayes Ward • USA
RANGE JUSTICE • 1949 • Taylor Ray • USA
RANGE LAND • 1949 • Hillyer Lambert • USA
RANGE LAW • 1913 • *Duncan William* • USA
RANGE LAW • 1931 • Rosen Phil • USA
RANGE LAW • 1944 • Hillyer Lambert • USA
RANGE MASTER, THE • 1955 • Landers Lew • MTV • USA
RANGE PALS • 1911 • *Selig* • USA
RANGE PATROL, THE • 1923 • Moody H. G. • USA
RANGE PIRATE, THE • 1921 • Franchon Leonard • USA
RANGE RAIDERS, THE • 1927 • Hurst Paul C. • USA
RANGE RENEGADES • 1948 • Hillyer Lambert • USA
RANGE RHYTHM • 1942 • Roberts Stephen • SHT • USA
RANGE RIDERS • 1934 • Adamson Victor • USA
RANGE RIDERS see **STRAIGHT SHOOTIN'** • 1927
RANGE RIDERS, THE • 1910 • *Mix Tom* • USA
RANGE RIDERS OF THE GREAT WILD WEST see **WALLOPING WALLACE** • 1924
RANGE ROMANCE, A • 1911 • *Bison* • USA
RANGE SQUATTER, THE see **CLAIM JUMPERS, THE** • 1911
RANGE TERROR, THE • 1925 • Craft William James • USA
RANGE VULTURES • 1925 • *Cuneo Lester* • USA
RANGE WAR • 1939 • Selander Lesley • USA
RANGE WAR, THE • 1917 • Ford John • USA
RANGE WARFARE • 1935 • Luby S. Roy • USA
RANGEKI NO SHICHIBANGAI • 1958 • Sekigawa Hideo • JPN • GUNFIGHT ON SEVENTH STREET
RANGELAND • 1922 • Hart Neal • USA
RANGELAND EMPIRE see **WEST OF THE BRAZOS** • 1950
RANGER, THE • 1918 • *Hamilton Shorty* • USA
RANGER AND HIS GIRL, THE • 1910 • *Lubin* • USA
RANGER AND HIS HORSE, THE • 1912 • Duncan William • USA
RANGER AND THE LADY, THE • 1940 • Kane Joseph • USA
RANGER AND THE LAW, THE • 1921 • Kelly Robert • USA
RANGER BILL • 1925 • *Carter Dick* • USA
RANGER CODE see **RENEGADE RANGER, THE** • 1938
RANGER COURAGE • 1937 • Bennet Spencer Gordon • USA
RANGER DAVE MORGAN • 1920 • Murphy Martin • SHT • USA
RANGER MACHINERY • 1985 • Skagen Peter • DOC • CND
RANGER OF CHEROKEE STRIP • 1949 • Ford Philip • USA
RANGER OF LONESOME GULCH, THE • 1916 • Chatterton Thomas • SHT • USA
RANGER OF PIKE'S PEAK, THE • 1919 • Wells Raymond • SHT • USA
RANGER OF THE BIG PINES • 1925 • Van Dyke W. S. • USA
RANGER OF THE NORTH • 1927 • Storm Jerome • USA
RANGER RIDERS, THE • 1927 • Wilson Ben • USA
RANGERS, THE • 1975 • Nyby Christian Ii • TVM • USA
RANGERS AND RUSTLERS • 1919 • *Steiner William* • USA
RANGERS AT WAR • 1933 • Binney Josh • USA
RANGERS ATTACCO ORA X • 1970 • Montero Roberto Bianchi • ITL, SPN
RANGERS BRIDE, THE • 1910 • *Essanay* • USA
RANGER'S CODE • 1933 • Bradbury Robert North • USA
RANGER'S GIRLS, THE • 1912 • *Melies* • USA
RANGER'S OATH • 1928 • Horner Robert J. • USA

RANGERS OF FORTUNE • 1940 • Wood Sam • USA
RANGER'S REWARD, THE • 1912 • *King Burton* • USA
RANGER'S REWARD, THE • 1914 • *Frontier* • USA
RANGERS RIDE, THE • 1948 • Abrahams Derwin • USA
RANGER'S ROMANCE, THE • 1914 • Mix Tom • USA
RANGER'S ROUNDUP, THE • 1938 • Newfield Sam • USA
RANGERS STEP IN, THE • 1937 • Bennet Spencer Gordon • USA
RANGER'S STRATAGEM, THE • 1911 • *Kalem* • USA
RANGERS TAKE OVER, THE • 1942 • Herman Al • USA
RANGER'S WAY, THE • 1913 • *Nestor* • USA
RANGIKU MONOGATARI • 1956 • Taniguchi Senkichi • JPN
RANGILEY JASOOS • 1989 • Kashmiri Iqbal • PKS
RANGI'S CATCH • 1972 • Forlong Michael • UKN
RANGLE RIVER • 1937 • Badger Clarence • ASL • MEN WITH WHIPS
RANGO • 1931 • Schoedsack Ernest B. • USA
RANGON ALUL • 1960 • Ban Frigyes • HNG • HUSBAND FOR SUSY, A
RANGUN • 1927 • Otsuka • JPN
RANI RADOVI • 1969 • Zilnik Zelimir • YGS • EARLY WORKS (USA)
RANJANG PENGANTIN • 1974 • Karya Teguh • INN • WEDDING, THE
RANK AND FILE, THE • 1971 • Loach Kenneth • MTV • UKN
RANK OUTSIDER, A • 1920 • Garrick Richard • UKN
RANKIN'S SPRINGS IS WEST • 1953 • Powell Geoffrey • ASL
RANKO • 1967 • Wakamatsu Koji • JPN • ORGY, THE
RANKS AND PEOPLE see **CHINY I LIUDI** • 1929
RANNIE ZHURAVLI • 1979 • Shamshiev Bolotbek • USS • EARLY CRANES
RANNSTENSUNGAR • 1944 • Frisk Ragnar • SWD • GUTTER–SNIPES
RANNSTENSUNGAR • 1974 • Anderberg Torgny • SWD
RANNY W LESIE • 1964 • Nasfeter Janusz • PLN • WOUNDED IN THE FOREST ○ WOUNDED IN A FOREST
RANO UTROM • 1965 • Lioznova Tatyana • USS • EARLY IN THE MORNING ○ EARLY MORNING
RANRU NO HATA • 1973 • Yoshimura Kozaburo • JPN • RAGGED FLAG, A
RANSACKED SHOP, THE see **U SNEDENEHO KRAMU** • 1933
RANSOM • 1920 • Wright Mack V. • SHT • USA
RANSOM • 1928 • Seitz George B. • USA
RANSOM • 1955 • Segal Alex • USA • FEARFUL DECISION
RANSOM • 1974 • Wrede Caspar • UKN • TERRORISTS, THE (USA)
RANSOM • 1985 • SAF
RANSOM see **MANIAC** • 1977
RANSOM, THE • 1912 • *Powers* • USA
RANSOM, THE • 1916 • Lawrence Edmund • USA
RANSOM, THE • 1917 • Fahrney Milton • SHT • USA
RANSOM, THE • 1970 • *Stacey Dist.* • USA
RANSOM, THE see **TENGOKU TO JIGOKU** • 1963
RANSOM FOR A DEAD MAN • 1971 • Irving Richard • TVM • USA
RANSOM FOR ALICE • 1977 • Rich David Lowell • TVM • USA
RANSOM IN SARDINIA see **SEQUESTRO DI PERSONA** • 1968
RANSOM MONEY • 1970 • Lee Dewitt • USA
RANSOM NOTE • 1969 • Lester Howard • ANS • USA
RANSOM OF MACK, THE • 1920 • Smith David • SHT • USA
RANSOM OF RED CHIEF, THE • 1911 • Dawley J. Searle • USA
RANSOMED OR A PRISONER OF WAR • 1910 • *Young Clara Kimball* • USA
RANSON'S FOLLY • 1910 • Porter Edwin S. • USA
RANSON'S FOLLY • 1915 • Ridgely Richard • USA
RANSON'S FOLLY • 1926 • Olcott Sidney • USA
RANTOJEN MIEHET • 1971 • Peltomaa Hannu • SHT • FNL • SHADOW OF A CITY, THE
RANTZAU, LES • 1924 • Roudes Gaston • FRN
RAO SAHEB • 1985 • Mehta Vijaya • IND
RAONI • 1980 • Saldanha Luis Carlos, Dutilleux Jean-Pierre • DOC • BRZ, BLG
RAOUL DUGUAY • 1971 • Frappier Roger • DOC • CND
RAOUL WALLENBERG: BETWEEN THE LINES • 1985 • Altmann Karin • DOC • ASL
RAP ATTACK see **KRUSH GROOVE** • 1985
RAPACE, IL (ITL) see **RAPACE, LA** • 1968
RAPACE, LA • 1968 • Giovanni Jose • FRN, ITL, MXC • RAPACE, IL (ITL) ○ BIRDS OF PREY
RAPACES DIURNES ET NOCTURNES, LES • 1913 • Burel Leonce-Henry • SHT • FRN
RAPACITE • 1929 • Berthomieu Andre • FRN
RAPACITY • 1980 • Schumacher Ivan P. • MTV • SWT
RAPATRIEE, LA (FRN) see **RIMPATRIATA, LA** • 1963
RAPAZES DE TAXIS • 1965 • Esteves Constantino • PRT
RAPE • 1969 • Ono Yoko • AUS
RAPE • 1978 • Elam Jo Ann • DOC • USA
RAPE see **VOLDTEKT –TILFELLET ANDERS** • 1971
RAPE, THE • 1982 • Higashi Yoichi • JPN
RAPE, THE see **VIOL, LE** • 1967
RAPE, THE see **NIET VOOR DE POEZEN** • 1972
RAPE, THE (USA) see **AMOK** • 1964
RAPE AND MARRIAGE: THE RIDEOUT CASE • 1980 • Levin Peter • TVM • USA • RIDEOUT CASE, THE
RAPE BECAUSE OF THE CATS, THE see **NIET VOOR DE POEZEN** • 1972
RAPE: FACE TO FACE • 1983 • Bruyere Christian (c/d) • CND, USA
RAPE IN THE DOLL HOUSE • Roman Joseph • ANS • USA
RAPE OF A COUNTRY see **BIJSTERE LAND VAN VELUWEN, HET** • 1948
RAPE OF A SWEET YOUNG GIRL, THE see **VIOL D'UNE JEUNE FILL DOUCE, LE** • 1968
RAPE OF A VIRGIN, THE see **VIASMOS MIAS PATHENOU, O** • 1967
RAPE OF APHRODITE, THE • 1985 • Pantazis Andreas • GRC
RAPE OF CZECHOSLOVAKIA, THE • 1939 • Weiss Jiri • DOC • UKN • SECRET ALLIES
RAPE OF INNOCENCE (USA) see **DUPONT LA JOIE** • 1975
RAPE OF LOVE (USA) see **AMOUR VIOLE, L'** • 1977
RAPE OF MALAYA, THE see **TOWN LIKE ALICE, A** • 1956
RAPE OF RICHARD BECK, THE • 1985 • Arthur Karen • TVM • USA
RAPE OF THE MAIDENS, THE see **RAPIREA FECIOARELOR** • 1968
RAPE OF THE SABINES see **RATTO DELLE SABINE, IL** • 1962
RAPE OF THE SABINES, THE see **RAPTO DE LAS SABINAS, EL** • 1958
RAPE OF THE THIRD REICH, THE see **ENGLAND MADE ME** • 1972
RAPE OF THE VAMPIRES, THE see **VIOL DES VAMPIRES, LES** • 1967
RAPE ON THE MOOR • Konig Hans H. • FRG
RAPE STORIES • 1989 • Strosser • SHT • USA
RAPE, THE REBELLION OF BERTHA MACKENZIE • 1975 • Haldane Don • CND
RAPHAEL LE TATOUE • 1938 • Christian-Jaque • FRN • C'ETAIT MOI
RAPHAEL OU LE DEBAUCHE • 1970 • Deville Michel • FRN
RAPID FIRE • 1989 • Prior David A. • USA
RAPID FIRE ROMANCE • 1926 • Brown Harry J. • USA
"RAPID" POWDER, THE • 1910 • *Pathe* • FRN
RAPID STREAM, A see **HONRYU** • 1926
RAPID TRANSIT • 1971 • Kimball John • ANS • USA
RAPIDE DE NUIT • 1948 • Blistene Marcel • FRN
RAPIDO, EL • 1964 • Salvador Jaime • MXC • MARTIN ROMERO EL RAPIDO
RAPIDO DE LAS 9:15, EL • 1941 • Galindo Alejandro • MXC
RAPIDS, THE • 1923 • Hartford David M. • CND
RAPIER, THE see **ESPADIN, EL** • 1969
RAPINA • 1973 • *Churubusco Azteca* • MXC
RAPINA AL QUARTIERE OVEST • 1962 • Ratti Filippo M. • ITL
RAPINA AL SOLE (ITL) see **PAR UN BEAU MATIN D'ETE** • 1964
RAPIREA FECIOARELOR • 1968 • Cocea Dinu • RMN • RAPE OF THE MAIDENS, THE
RAPIST • 1973 • Zugsmith Albert • USA
RAPIST, THE see **ZOKU NIHON BOKO ANKOKUSHI BOGYAKUMA** • 1967
RAPISTS, THE see **MOGHTASIBOUN, EL** • 1989
RAPISTS –CAN THEY BE STOPPED? • 1985 • Zaritsky John • MTV • CND
RAPORTTI ELI BALLADI LAIVATYTOISTA • 1964 • Kurkvaara Maunu • FNL • REPORT OR BALLAD ABOUT SAILORS' GIRLFRIENDS
RAPPEL IMMEDIAT • 1939 • Mathot Leon • FRN • TANGO D'ADIEU
RAPPELLE-TOI • 1975 • Dansereau Mireille, Cholakian Vartkes • CND
RAPPIN' • 1985 • Silberg Joel • USA
RAPPORTO, IL • 1969 • Massobrio Lionello • ITL
RAPPORTO FULLER BASE A STOCCOLMA see **RAPPORTO FULLER, BASE STOCCOLMA** • 1967
RAPPORTO FULLER, BASE STOCCOLMA • 1967 • Grieco Sergio • ITL, FRN • SVETLAWA UCCIDERA IL 28 SETTEMBRE ○ FULLER REPORT, BASE STOCKHOLM ○ TRAHISON A STOCKHOLM ○ FULLER REPORT ○ RAPPORTO FULLER BASE A STOCCOLMA
RAPPORTPIGEN • 1974 • Thomsen Knud Leif • DNM
RAPPRESAGLIA • 1973 • Cosmatos George Pan • ITL, FRN • MASSACRE IN ROME (UKN) ○ DEATH IN ROME
RAPSODIA BALTYKU • 1935 • Buczkowski Leonard • PLN • BALTIC RHAPSODY
RAPSODIA DE SANGRE • 1957 • Isasi Antonio • SPN • RHAPSODY IN BLOOD
RAPSODIA HUNGARA • 1935 • Miranda Armando • SHT • PRT
RAPSODIA MEXICANA • 1937 • Zacarias Miguel • MXC
RAPSODIA PORTUGUESA • 1958 • Mendes Joao • PRT
RAPSODIA SATANICA • 1915 • Oxilia Nino • ITL • SATAN'S RHAPSODY (USA)
RAPSY AND DOLLY see **RAPSY JA DOLLY** • 1989
RAPSY JA DOLLY • 1989 • Ijas Matti • FNL • RAPSY AND DOLLY ○ DOLLY AND HER LOVER
RAPT • 1934 • Kirsanoff Dimitri • FRN, FRG, SWT • MYSTIC MOUNTAIN, THE (USA) ○ SEPARATION DES RACES, LA ○ RACES ○ FRAUENRAUB
RAPT, LE • 1975 • Franju Georges • MTV • FRN
RAPT AU DEUXIEME BUREAU • 1958 • Stelli Jean • FRN • OPERATION ABDUCTION (USA)
RAPT D'ENFANT PAR LES ROMANICHELS • 1904 • Blache Alice • FRN • VOLEE PAR LES BOHEMIENS
RAPTO, EL • 1953 • Fernandez Emilio • MXC
RAPTO AL SOL • 1955 • Mendez Fernando • MXC
RAPTO DE ELENA, LA DELENTE ITALIANA, EL see **ETTORE LO FUSTO** • 1972
RAPTO DE LAS SABINAS, EL • 1958 • Gout Alberto • MXC, SPN • SHAME OF THE SABINE WOMEN, THE (USA) ○ RAPE OF THE SABINES, THE ○ MATING OF THE SABINE WOMEN, THE
RAPTO DE T.T., EL • 1963 • Viloria Jose Luis • SPN
RAPTO DE UMA ACTRIZ • 1907 • Ferreira Lino • SHT • PRT
RAPTO EN LAS ESTRELLAS • 1971 • Carretero Amaro • ANS • SPN • KIDNAPPING IN THE STARS
RAPTORES, OS • 1969 • Teixeira Aurelio • BRZ • KIDNAPPERS, THE
RAPTURE • 1950 • Alessandrini Goffredo • ITL
RAPTURE • 1965 • Guillermin John • USA, FRN • FLEUR DE L'AGE, LA (FRN)
RAPTURE see **ARREBATO** • 1980
RAPTUS • 1969 • Girolami Marino • ITL
RAPTUS –THE SECRET OF DR. HICHCOCK (UKN) see **ORRIBILE SEGRETO DEL DR. HICHCOCK, L'** • 1962
RAPUNZEL • 1897 • Messter Oskar • FRG
RAPUNZEL • 1979 • *London Women Film Group* • UKN
RAPUNZEL • 1982 • Cates Gilbert • MTV • USA
RAPUNZEL see **STORY OF RAPUNZEL, THE** • 1951
RAPUNZEL LET DOWN YOUR HAIR • 1978 • Shapiro Susan, Ronay Esther, Winham Francine • UKN
RAQ LO B'SHABBAT (ISR) see **PAS QUESTION LE SAMEDI** • 1965
RAQUEL'S MOTEL • 1970 • *Distripix Inc.* • USA
RAQUETTES DES ATCIKAMEG, LES • 1973 • Gosselin Bernard • DCS • CND
RAQUETTEURS, LES • 1958 • Groulx Gilles, Brault Michel • DCS • CND • SNOWSHOERS, THE
RARE ANIMALS • 1921 • Urban Charles • USA
RARE BIRD, A • 1920 • *Banks Monty* • USA
RARE BIRD, THE • 1958 • Sens Al • ANS • CND
RARE BOARDER, A • 1916 • *Stull Walter* • SHT • USA
RARE BOOK MURDER, THE see **FAST COMPANY** • 1938
RARE BREED, A • 1984 • Nelson David • USA
RARE BREED, THE • 1966 • McLaglen Andrew V. • USA
RARE ONES, THE see **RAW ONES, THE** • 1965
RARE SPECIMEN, A • 1910 • Aylott Dave? • UKN
RARIN' ROMEO, A • 1925 • Mayo Archie • SHT • USA
RARIN' TO GO • 1924 • Thorpe Richard • USA • EAGER TO WORK
RAS, AR– • 1976 • Al-Yassiri Fiasal • IRQ • HEAD, THE ○ TETE, LA
RAS EL GUA see **FORT DE LA SOLITUDE** • 1947
RAS LE BOL • Huisman Michel • BLG
RAS LE COEUR • 1979 • Colas Daniel • FRN
RASANBLEMAN • 1979 • D'Aix Alain (c/d) • DOC • CND
RASCAL • 1969 • Tokar Norman • USA
RASCAL, THE see **TSAHPINIS, O** • 1968
RASCAL OF WOLFISH WAYS, A • 1915 • Sennett Mack • USA
RASCAL SNAIL, THE • 1951 • Haupe Wlodzimierz, Bielinska Halina • ANM • PLN
RASCALS • 1938 • Humberstone H. Bruce • USA
RASCALS AND ROBBERS see **RASCALS AND ROBBERS –THE SECRET ADVENTURES OF TOM SAWYER AND HUCK FINN** • 1982
RASCALS AND ROBBERS –THE SECRET ADVENTURES OF TOM SAWYER AND HUCK FINN • 1982 • Lowry Dick • TVM • USA • RASCALS AND ROBBERS
RASCALS OF THE FRONT BENCH I. TO HELL WITH TEACHERS, THE see **LUMMEL VON DER ERSTEN BANK I. ZUR HOLLE MIT DEN PAUKERN, DIE** • 1968
RASCALS OF THE FRONT BENCH II: TO THE DEVIL WITH SCHOOL, THE see **LUMMEL VON DER ERSTEN BANK II: ZUM TEUFEL MIT PER PENNE, DIE** • 1968
RASCAL'S WOLFISH WAY, A • 1915 • Frazee Edwin, Jones F. Richard • USA
RASCEL–FIFI • 1957 • Leoni Guido • ITL
RASCEL MARINE • 1958 • Leoni Guido • ITL
RASCOALA • 1965 • Muresan Mircea • RMN • BLAZING WINTER
RASELJENA OSOBA see **RAZSELJENA OSEBA** • 1982
RASENDE ROLAND, DER • 1915 • Bolten-Baeckers Heinrich • FRG
RASH REVENGE, A • 1913 • *Balboa* • USA
RASHID • 1959 • Shawqi Khalil • SHT • EGY
RASHOKU SAPPOH NUKIMI • 1968 • Komori Haku • JPN • NAKED KILLING
RASHOMON • 1950 • Kurosawa Akira • JPN • IN THE WOODS
RASKE RIVIERA • 1923 • Lauritzen Lau • DNM
RASKENSTAM • 1983 • Hellstrom Gunnar • SWD • CASANOVA OF SWEDEN
RASKEY'S ROAD SHOW • 1915 • Hamilton Lloyd • USA
RASKOLNIKOW • 1923 • Wiene Robert • FRG • CRIME AND PUNISHMENT ○ SCHULD UND SUHNE
RASLOM • 1971 • Saltykov Alexei • USS • BREAKUP
RASMINES BRYLLUP • 1935 • Schneevoigt George • DNM • WEDDING OF RASMINE, THE
RASMUS AND THE TRAMP see **LUFAREN OCH RASMUS** • 1955
RASMUS PA LUFFEN • 1982 • Hellbom Olle • SWD
RASMUS, PONTUS AND TOKER see **RASMUS, PONTUS OCH TOKER** • 1956
RASMUS, PONTUS OCH TOKER • 1956 • Olin Stig • SWD • RASMUS, PONTUS AND TOKER
RASP, THE • 1931 • Powell Michael • UKN
RASPADO, EL • 1964 • Cardona Rene Jr. • MXC, VNZ
RASPBERRY COCKTAIL see **MALINOVY KOKTEJL** • 1982
RASPBERRY ROMANCE, THE • 1925 • Bacon Lloyd • SHT • USA
RASPISANIE NA POSLEZAVTRA • 1980 • Dobrolyubov Igor • USS • TIMETABLE FOR THE DAY AFTER TOMORROW, A
RASPLYUYEV'S GAY DAYS see **VESYOLYYE RASPLYUYEVSKIYE DNI** • 1966
RASPOUTINE • 1953 • Combret Georges • FRN, ITL • RASPUTIN (ITL)
RASPOUTINE see **TRAGEDIE IMPERIALE, LA** • 1937
RASPOUTINE see **SWEDISH SEX CLINIC** • 1981
RASPUTIN • 1917 • Arno • *Saturn* • FRG
RASPUTIN • 1917 • Neufeld Max • *Worldart Films* • FRG • RASPUTIN, THE HOLY SINNER
RASPUTIN • 1925 • AUS
RASPUTIN • 1929 • Larin Nikolai • FRG • RASPUTIN, THE PRINCE OF SINNERS
RASPUTIN see **RASPUTIN, DAMON DER FRAUEN** • 1930
RASPUTIN see **AGONIYA** • 1976
RASPUTIN AND THE EMPRESS • 1932 • Boleslawski Richard • USA • RASPUTIN –THE MAD MONK
RASPUTIN AND THE PRINCESS • 1952 • *Broadway Roadshow Prods.* • SHT • USA
RASPUTIN, DAMON DER FRAUEN • 1930 • Trotz Adolf • FRG • DAMON DER FRAUEN, DER ○ RASPUTIN, DEMON WITH WOMEN ○ RASPUTIN
RASPUTIN (DAS LIEBESLEBEN DES SONDERBAREN HEILIGEN) • 1925 • Gersik R. • AUS • RASPUTIN (THE LOVE LIFE OF A STRANGE HOLY MAN)
RASPUTIN, DEMON WITH WOMEN see **RASPUTIN, DAMON DER FRAUEN** • 1930
RASPUTIN (ITL) see **RASPOUTINE** • 1953
RASPUTIN, THE BLACK MONK • 1917 • Ashley Arthur • USA • RASPUTIN, THE MAD MONK
RASPUTIN: THE HOLY DEVIL (USA) see **RASPUTINS LIEBESABENTEUER** • 1928
RASPUTIN, THE HOLY SINNER see **RASPUTIN** • 1917
RASPUTIN (THE LOVE LIFE OF A STRANGE HOLY MAN) see **RASPUTIN (DAS LIEBESLEBEN DES SONDERBAREN HEILIGEN)** • 1925
RASPUTIN, THE MAD MONK • 1965 • Sharp Don • UKN, USA
RASPUTIN, THE MAD MONK see **RASPUTIN, THE BLACK MONK** • 1917
RASPUTIN –THE MAD MONK see **RASPUTIN AND THE EMPRESS** • 1932
RASPUTIN, THE PRINCE OF SINNERS see **RASPUTIN** • 1929
RASPUTIN (USA) see **TRAGEDIE IMPERIALE, LA** • 1937
RASPUTIN (USA) see **J'AI TUE RASPOUTINE** • 1967

RASPUTINS LIEBESABENTEUER • 1928 • Berger Martin • FRG • RASPUTIN: THE HOLY DEVIL (USA) ○ RASPUTIN'S LOVE ADVENTURE
RASPUTIN'S LOVE ADVENTURE see **RASPUTINS LIEBESABENTEUER** • 1928
RASSENSCHANDE see **KIEDY MILOSC BYLA ZBRODNIA (RASSENSCHANDE)** • 1968
RASSKAZ MOEJ MATERI • 1958 • Raizman Yuli • USS
RASSKAZHI MNYE O SEBYE • 1972 • Mikailyan Sergei • USS • TELL ME ABOUT YOURSELF
RASSKAZY O LENINE • 1957 • Yutkevich Sergei • USS • STORIES ABOUT LENIN
RASSLIN' MATCH, THE • 1934 • Stallings George • ANS • USA
RASSLIN' ROUND • 1934 • *Iwerks Ub (P)* • ANS • USA
RASTAQUOUERE RODRIGUEZ Y PAPANAGAZ, LE • 1906 • Melies Georges • FRN • SEASIDE FLIRTATION, A
RASTELBINDER, DIE • 1927 • Hanus Heinz, Mondet Maurice A., Gottlein Arthur • AUS
RASTHAUS DER GRAUSAMEN PUPPEN, DAS • 1967 • Olsen Rolf • FRG, ITL • LOCANDA DELLE BAMBOLE CRUDELI, LA (ITL) ○ INN OF THE CRUEL DOLLS, THE
RASTRO DE MUERTE • 1980 • Ripstein Arturo • MXC • TRACE OF DEATH, A
RASTUS AMONG THE ZULUS • 1913 • Hotaling Arthur D. • USA
RASTUS AND THE GAME-COCK • 1913 • Sennett Mack • USA
RASTUS IN ZULULAND • 1910 • Hotaling Arthur D. • USA
RASTUS KNEW IT WASN'T • 1914 • *Edwards John* • USA
RASTUS' RIOTOUS RIDE • 1914 • *Harbaugh Carl* • USA
RASUMOFF see **SOUS LES YEUX D'OCCIDENT** • 1936
RASUMOV see **SOUS LES YEUX D'OCCIDENT** • 1936
RASUNA VALEA • 1949 • Calinescu Paul • RMN • VALLEY RESOUNDS, THE
RAT • 1960 • Bulajic Velko • YGS • ATOMIC WAR BRIDE (USA) ○ WAR
RAT, THE • 1914 • *King Henry* • USA
RAT, THE • 1925 • Cutts Graham • UKN
RAT, THE • 1937 • Raymond Jack • UKN
RAT AMONG THE CATS see **FUTARI DAKE NO TORIDE** • 1963
RAT D'AMERIQUE, LE • 1962 • Albicocco Jean-Gabriel • FRN, ITL • SENTIERO DEI DISPERATI, IL (ITL)
RAT DE VILLE ET LE RAT DES CHAMPS, LE • 1926 • Starevitch Ladislas • ANS • FRN • TOWN RAT AND THE COUNTRY RAT, THE (USA) ○ CITY RAT AND THE COUNTRY RAT, THE
RAT DER GOTTER, DER • 1950 • Maetzig Kurt • GDR • COUNCIL OF THE GODS ○ DIVINE COUNCILS
RAT DESTRUCTION • 1942 • Cooper Budge • DOC • UKN
RAT FINK • 1965 • Landis James • USA • MY SOUL RUNS NAKED ○ WILD AND WILLING ○ SWINGING FINK, THE
RAT FINK AND BOBO see **RAT PFINK A BOO BOO** • 1963
RAT FINK AND BOO-BOO see **RAT PFINK A BOO BOO** • 1963
RAT KID ON JOURNEY see **TABISUGATA NEZUMIKOZO** • 1958
RAT LIFE AND DIET IN NORTH AMERICA • 1968 • Wieland Joyce • SHT • USA
RAT MAL, WER HEUT BEI UNS SCHLAFT.. • 1969 • Neve Alexis • FRG • GUESS WHO'S SLEEPING WITH US TONIGHT (UKN)
RAT ON A TRAY, A • 1964 • Tutyshkin Andrey • MTV • USS
RAT PFINK A BOO BOO • 1963 • Steckler Ray Dennis • USA • RAT FINK AND BOBO ○ RAT FINK AND BOO-BOO
RAT RACE, THE • 1960 • Mulligan Robert • USA
RAT SAVIOUR, THE see **IZBAVITELJ** • 1977
RAT-TRAP see **ELIPPATHAYAM** • 1981
RAT WAR see **ROTTASOTA** • 1968
RATA, EL see **ALIAS EL RATA** • 1964
RATACIRE • 1978 • Tatos Alexandru • RMN • WANDERING, THE
RATAI • 1962 • Narusawa Masashige • JPN • BODY, THE (USA)
RATAPAN ANAK TIRI • 1974 • Hassan Sandy Suwardi • INN • WOES OF A STEP-DAUGHTER
RATAPAN RINTIHAN • 1974 • Hassan Sandy Suwardi • INN • CRIES OF DESPAIR
RATAPLAN • 1935 • Elias Francisco • SPN
RATAS, LA • 1963 • Saslavsky Luis • ARG
RATAS DE LA CIUDAD • 1986 • Trujillo Valentin • MXC • CITY RATS
RATAS DEL ASFALTO • 1977 • Villasenor Rafael • MXC
RATAS NO DUERMEN DE NOCHE, LAS • 1973 • Fortuny Juan • SPN, FRN
RATATAA • 1956 • Ekman Hasse • SWD • STAFFEN STOLLE STORY, THE
RATATAPLAN • 1979 • Nichetti Maurizio • ITL
RATBOY • 1986 • Locke Sondra • USA
RATCATCHER, THE see **RATTENFANGER VON HAMELN, DER** • 1916
RATE IT "X" • 1986 • Winer Lucy, De Koenigsberg Paula • DOC • USA
RATE OF CHANGE: THE DIFFERENTIAL CALCULUS • 1937 • Segaller Denis • UKN
RATE OF EXCHANGE • 1975 • Hunter Bill • SHT • ASL
RATED AT $10,000,000 • 1915 • Smiley Joseph • USA
RATEL, THE see **PAJARO INDICADOR, EL** • 1971
RATELRAT, DE • 1987 • Verstappen Wim • NTH • RATTLE RAT
RATEROS ULTIMO MODELO • 1964 • Cortes Fernando • MXC
RATHSKELLER AND THE ROSE, THE • 1918 • Ridgwell George • SHT • USA
RATINGS GAME, THE • 1984 • DeVito Danny • TVM • USA
RATION BORED • 1943 • Hawkins Emery, Schaffer Milt • ANS • USA
RATION FOR THE DURATION • 1943 • Kneitel Seymour • ANS • USA
RATIONING • 1943 • Goldbeck Willis • USA
RATIONS • 1918 • Collins Edwin J.? • UKN
RATNA DEEP • 1947 • Bose Debaki • IND
RATNAKA • 1921 • *Bose Anadi Nath (P)* • IND
RATNAVALI • 1922 • IND
RATNAVALI • 1935 • *Bai Saraswati* • IND
RATNAVALI • 1946 • *Amar* • IND
RATOIUL NEASCULTATOR • 1951 • Popescu-Gopo Ion • ANS • RMN • NAUGHTY DUCK, THE
RATON, EL • 1956 • Urueta Chano • MXC
RATON ARIEL • 1968 • Cruz Abraham • PHL
RATON PASS • 1951 • Marin Edwin L. • USA • CANYON PASS (UKN)
RATOWNICY • 1964 • Raplewski Zbigniew • DOC • PLN • RESCUERS, THE (UKN)
RATS see **RATS: NIGHT OF TERROR** • 1983
RATS, THE • 1900 • *Leno Dan* • UKN
RATS, THE see **RATTEN, DIE** • 1955
RATS, THE see **DEADLY EYES** • 1982
RATS ARE COMING! THE WEREWOLVES ARE HERE!, THE • 1972 • Milligan Andy • USA, UKN
RATS AWAKE, THE see **BUDENJE PACOVA** • 1967
RAT'S KNUCKLES, THE • 1924 • Roach Hal • SHT • USA
RATS: NIGHT OF TERROR • 1983 • Mattei Bruno • ITL, FRN • RATS
RATS OF TOBRUK, THE • 1944 • Chauvel Charles • ASL • FIGHTING RATS OF TOBRUK (USA)
RATS WAKE UP, THE see **BUDENJE PACOVA** • 1967
RATSEL DER GRUNEN SPINNE, DAS • 1960 • Marischka Franz • AUS
RATSEL DER KRIMINALISTIK see **AM NARRENSEIL 2** • 1921
RATSEL DER ROTEN ORCHIDEE, DAS • 1961 • Ashley Helmut • FRG • PUZZLE OF THE RED ORCHID, THE (USA) ○ SECRET OF THE RED ORCHID, THE
RATSEL DER SPHINX, DAS • 1921 • Gartner Adolf • FRG
RATSEL DER UNBEKANNTEN, DAS • 1919 • *Madeleine Magda* • FRG
RATSEL DES BORODUR, DAS • 1926 • Heiland Heinz Karl • FRG
RATSEL DES SILBERN HALBMONDS, DAS • 1972 • FRG, ITL • PUZZLE OF THE SILVER HALF-MOONS, THE
RATSEL EINER NACHT • 1927 • Piel Harry • FRG
RATSEL IM MENSCHEN, DAS • 1920 • Leitner Konrad • FRG
RATSEL UM BEATE • 1938 • Meyer Johannes • FRG
RATSEL VON BANGALOR, DAS • 1917 • von Antalffy Alexander, Leni Paul • FRG
RATSEL VON SENSENHEIM, DAS • 1915 • Del Zopp Rudolf • FRG
RATSELHAFTE FRAU, DIE • 1915 • Schmidthassler Walter • FRG
RATSELHAFTE INSERAT, DAS • 1916 • May Joe • FRG
RATSELHAFTE KLUB, DER • 1919 • Piel Harry • FRG
RATSELHAFTE TOD, DER • 1920 • Hofer Franz • FRG
RATSELHAFTER BLICK, EIN • 1918 • Guter Johannes • FRG
RATSKIN • 1929 • *Mintz Charles (P)* • ANS • USA
RATTAN TRUNK, THE see **PRICE OF GREED, THE** • 1955
RATTE, DIE • 1918 • Piel Harry • FRG
RATTEN, DIE • 1921 • Kobe Hanns • FRG
RATTEN, DIE • 1955 • Siodmak Robert • FRG • RATS, THE
RATTEN ATT ALSKA • 1956 • Pollak Mimi • SWD • RIGHT TO LOVE, THE
RATTEN DER GROSSTADT • 1930 • Neff Wolfgang • FRG
RATTEN DER GROSSTADT 1 • 1920 • Neff Wolfgang • FRG • GEHEIMNISVOLLE NACHT, DIE
RATTENFANGER VON HAMELN, DER • 1916 • Wegener Paul, Gliese Rochus • FRG • PIED PIPER OF HAMELIN, THE ○ RATCATCHER, THE
RATTENLOCH, DAS • 1921 • Obal Max • FRG
RATTENMUHLE, DIE • 1921 • Berger Josef • FRG
RATTENS MUSKETORER • 1945 • Botvid Rolf • SWD
RATTLE OF A SIMPLE MAN • 1964 • Box Muriel • UKN
RATTLE RAT see **RATELRAT, DE** • 1987
RATTLED ROOSTER, THE • 1948 • Davis Arthur • ANS • USA
RATTLER, THE • 1925 • Hurst Paul C. • USA
RATTLER KID see **HOMBRE VINO A MATAR, UN** • 1968
RATTLERS • 1976 • McCauley John • USA
RATTLER'S HISS, THE • 1920 • Eason B. Reeves • SHT • USA
RATTLESNAKE, THE • 1913 • Fielding Romaine • USA
RATTLESNAKES AND GUNPOWDER • 1911 • Dwan Allan • USA
RATTLING ROMEO • 1939 • Lord Del • SHT • USA
RATTLING WHIP, THE • *Wang Fu Yong* • HKG
RATTO DELLE SABINE, IL • 1945 • Bonnard Mario • ITL • PROFESSOR TROMBONE
RATTO DELLE SABINE, IL • 1962 • Bomba Enrico, Pottier Richard • ITL, FRN • ENLEVEMENT DES SABINES, L' (FRN) ○ ROMULUS AND THE SABINES (USA) ○ RAPE OF THE SABINES
RAUB DER DOLLARPRINZESSIN, DER • 1921 • Seitz Franz • FRG
RAUB DER HELENA, DER see **HELENA 1** • 1924
RAUB DER MONA LISA, DER • 1931 • von Bolvary Geza • FRG • THEFT OF THE MONA LISA, THE (USA)
RAUB DER SABINERINNEN, DER • 1919 • Bolten-Baeckers Heinrich • FRG
RAUB DER SABINERINNEN, DER • 1928 • Land Robert • FRG
RAUB DER SABINERINNEN, DER • 1936 • Stemmle R. A. • FRG
RAUB DER SABINERINNEN, DER • 1954 • Hoffmann Kurt • FRG
RAUB IN DER ZENTRALBANK see **GROSSE GELEGENHEIT, DIE** • 1925
RAUBERBANDE, DIE • 1928 • Behrendt Hans • FRG • ROBBER BAND, THE
RAUBERBRAUT, DIE • 1916 • Wiene Robert • FRG
RAUBFISCHER IN HELLAS • 1959 • Hachler Horst • FRG, USA, YGS • AS THE SEA RAGES (USA)
RAULITO, LA • 1975 • Murua Lautaro • ARG
RAUMFALLE, DIE • FRG • SPACE TRAP, THE
RAUMPATROUILLE • Metzinger Theo • FRG • SPACE PATROL
RAUSCH • 1919 • Lubitsch Ernst • FRG • INTOXICATION
RAUSCH EINER NACHT • 1951 • von Borsody Eduard • FRG
RAUSCHGIFT see **WEISSE DAMON, DER** • 1932
RAUSCHGOLD • 1920 • *Albers Hans* • FRG
RAUTAKAUPPIAS UUNO TURHAPURO • 1978 • Kokkonen Ere • FNL • NUMBSKULL EMPTYBROOK, IRONMONGER
RAUTHA SKIKKJAN see **RODA KAPPAN, DEN** • 1967
RAVAGED see **AFTER MEIN KAMPF** • 1961
RAVAGED (UKN) see **ROSE ECORCHEE, LA** • 1970
RAVAGER, THE • 1970 • Nizet Charles • USA
RAVAGERS, THE • 1965 • Romero Eddie • USA
RAVAGERS, THE • 1979 • Compton Richard • USA
RAVEN • 1987 • Lindberg Clas • SWD • FOX, THE
RAVEN, THE • 1912 • *Oliver Guy* • USA
RAVEN, THE • 1915 • Brabin Charles J. • USA
RAVEN, THE • 1935 • Landers Lew • USA
RAVEN, THE • 1942 • Fleischer Dave • ANS • USA
RAVEN, THE • 1953 • *Lippert* • SHT • UKN
RAVEN, THE • 1954 • Jacobs Lewis • SHT • USA
RAVEN, THE • 1963 • Corman Roger • USA
RAVEN, THE see **HRAFNINN FLYGUR** • 1983
RAVEN, THE (USA) see **CORBEAU, LE** • 1943
RAVEN FLIES, THE see **HRAFNINN FLYGUR** • 1983
RAVENGAR • Gasnier Louis J.
RAVENOUS ROGER • 1935 • Field Mary • UKN
RAVENS AND SPARROWS see **WUYA YU MAQUE** • 1949
RAVEN'S DANCE, THE see **KORPINPOLSKA** • 1979
RAVEN'S END see **KVARTERET KORPEN** • 1963
RAVICKARNA • 1966 • Svankmajer Jan • ANM • CZC • PUNCH AND JUDY
RAVIN SANS FOND, LE • 1917 • Feyder Jacques, Bernard Raymond • FRN
RAVINA • 1959 • Biafora Rubem • BRZ
RAVINE, THE (USA) see **CATTURA, LA** • 1969
RAVING WAVING • Jones Stuart Wynn • ANS • UKN
RAVISHED ARMENIA see **AUCTION OF SOULS** • 1919
RAVISHING BARMAID, THE see **SENKYRKA U DIVOKE KRASY** • 1932
RAVISHING IDIOT, A (USA) see **RAVISSANTE IDIOTE, UNE** • 1964
RAVISHING IDIOTS, THE see **RAVISSANTE IDIOTE, UNE** • 1964
RAVISSANTE • 1961 • Lamoureux Robert • FRN, ITL • MOGLI DEGLI ALTRI, LE (ITL)
RAVISSANTE IDIOTE, UNE • 1964 • Molinaro Edouard • FRN, ITL • ADOROBILE IDIOTA (ITL) ○ RAVISHING IDIOT, A (USA) ○ AGENT 38-24-36 (THE WARM-BLOODED SPY) ○ RAVISHING IDIOTS, THE
RAW COUNTRY, THE see **HEART OF THE YUKON, THE** • 1927
RAW COURAGE see **COURAGE** • 1984
RAW DEAL • 1948 • Mann Anthony • USA
RAW DEAL • 1977 • Hagg Russell • ASL
RAW DEAL • 1986 • Irvin John • USA
RAW EDGE • 1956 • Sherwood John • USA
RAW FORCE • 1982 • Murphy Edward • USA, HKG
RAW LOVE • 1965 • Osborne Kent • USA
RAW MATERIAL • 1955 • Biggs Julian • CND
RAW MEAT (USA) see **DEATH LINE** • 1972
RAW ONES, THE • 1965 • Lamb John • DOC • USA • RARE ONES, THE
RAW! RAW! ROOSTER • 1956 • McKimson Robert • ANS • USA
RAW RECRUIT, THE • 1928 • Croise Hugh • UKN
RAW TALENT • 1984 • Revene Larry • USA
RAW TIMBER • 1937 • Taylor Ray • USA
RAW WEEKEND • 1964 • Niehoff Sidney • DOC • USA
RAW WIND IN EDEN • 1958 • Wilson Richard • USA
RAWAAT EL HOB • 1968 • Zulficar Mahmoud • EGY • SPLENDOUR OF LOVE
RAWHEAD • 1987 • Pavlou George • UKN • RAWHEAD REX
RAWHEAD REX see **RAWHEAD** • 1987
RAWHIDE • 1926 • Thorpe Richard • USA
RAWHIDE • 1938 • Taylor Ray • USA
RAWHIDE • 1951 • Hathaway Henry • USA • DESPERATE SIEGE
RAWHIDE HALO, THE • 1960 • Kay Roger • USA • BARB WIRE (THE RAWHIDE HALO) ○ SHOOT OUT AT BIG SAG
RAWHIDE KID, THE • 1928 • Andrews Del • USA
RAWHIDE MAIL • 1934 • Ray Bernard B. • USA
RAWHIDE RANGERS • 1941 • Taylor Ray • USA
RAWHIDE ROMANCE • 1931 • Adamson Victor • USA
RAWHIDE TERROR, THE • 1934 • Mitchell Bruce • USA
RAWHIDE TRAIL, THE • 1958 • Gordon Robert • USA
RAWHIDE YEARS, THE • 1956 • Mate Rudolph • USA
RAY, A see **HIKARI** • 1928
RAY ANTHONY AND HIS ORCHESTRA • 1947 • Foster Harry • SHT • USA
RAY BRADBURY'S NIGHTMARES VOLUME 1 • 1985 • Pittman Bruce, Fruet William • USA
RAY BRADBURY'S NIGHTMARES VOLUME 2 • 1985 • Jackson Douglas, Thomas Ralph L. • USA
RAY BRADBURY'S THE ELECTRIC GRANDMOTHER • 1981 • Black Noel • TVM • USA
RAY DAVIES' RETURN TO WATERLOO see **RETURN TO WATERLOO** • 1985
RAY ELLINGTON AND HIS QUARTET • 1960 • Henryson Robert • UKN
RAY GUN VIRUS • 1966 • Sharits Paul J. • SHT • USA
RAY MASTER L'INAFFERRABILE • 1966 • Sala Vittorio • ITL
RAY MCKINLEY AND HIS ORCHESTRA • 1946 • Foster Harry • *Columbia* • SHT • USA
RAY MCKINLEY AND HIS ORCHESTRA • 1948 • Bonafield Jay • *Rko* • SHT • USA
RAY OF GOD'S SUNSHINE, A • 1913 • *Calvert E. H.* • USA
RAY OF LIGHT see **COLPI DI LUCE** • 1985
RAY OF SUNSHINE, A • 1950 • Shepherd Horace • UKN
RAY OF SUNSHINE, A see **SONNENSTRAHL** • 1933
RAYA • 1981 • Cheyaroon Permpol • THL
RAYA AND SEKINA see **RAYA WA SEKINA** • 1953
RAYA WA SEKINA • 1953 • Abu Saif Salah • EGY • RAYA AND SEKINA
RAYANDO EL SOL • 1945 • Gavaldon Roberto • MXC
RAYES DES VIVANTS • 1952 • Cloche Maurice • FRN
RAYHA WINE • 1976 • Bendeddouche Ghaouti • ALG • PECHEURS, LES ○ ECHEBKA
RAYITO DE LUNA • 1949 • Urueta Chano • MXC
RAYMIE • 1960 • McDonald Frank • USA
RAYMOND MASSEY: ACTOR OF THE CENTURY • 1984 • Rasky Harry • DOC • CND
RAYO, EL • 1936 • Buchs Jose • SPN
RAYO DE JALISCO, EL • 1960 • Peon Ramon • MXC
RAYO DE LUZ, UN • 1960 • Lucia Luis • SPN
RAYO DE SINALOA, EL • 1935 • Gonzalez Julian S. • MXC • HERACLIO BERNAL
RAYO DEL SUR, EL • 1943 • Contreras Torres Miguel • MXC

RAYO DESINTEGRADOR O AVENTURAS DE QUIQUE Y ARTURO EL ROBOT, EL • 1965 • Cervera Pascual • SPN • DISINTEGRATING RAY OR THE ADVENTURES OF QUIQUE AND ARTHUR THE ROBOT, THE
RAYO JUSTICIERO, EL • 1954 • Salvador Jaime • MXC
RAYON DE SOLEIL see **GARDEZ LE SOURIRE** • 1933
RAYON DES AMOURS, LE • 1932 • Greville Edmond T. • FRN
RAYON INVISIBLE, LE see **PARIS QUI DORT** • 1924
RAYON ROENTGEN, LE see **RAYONS ROENTGEN, LES** • 1898
RAYON VERT, LE • 1986 • Rohmer Eric • FRN • SUMMER (USA) ○ GREEN RAY, THE
RAYONS INVISIBLES DE ROENTGEN, LES • 1912 • Comandon Jean • FRN
RAYONS MORTELS DU DOCTEUR MABUSE, LES (FRN) see **TODESSTRAHLEN DES DR. MABUSE, DIE** • 1964
RAYONS ROENTGEN, LES • 1898 • Melies Georges • FRN • NOVICE AT X-RAYS, A (USA) ○ RAYON ROENTGEN, LE ○ RAYONS X, LES ○ X-RAYS, THE
RAYONS X, LES see **RAYONS ROENTGEN, LES** • 1898
RAYS THAT ERASE • 1916 • Collins Edwin J.? • UKN
RAZ, DWA, TRZY • 1967 • Anderson Lindsay • PLN • SINGING LESSON, THE (UKN)
RAZA • 1941 • Saenz De Heredia Jose Luis • SPN
RAZA, EL ESPIRITU DE FRANCO • 1977 • Herralde Gonzalo • SPN • RACE, THE SPIRIT OF FRANCO
RAZAFF LE MALGACHE • 1925 • d'Esme Jean • FRN
RAZBITAYA VAZA • 1913 • Protazanov Yakov • USS • SHATTERED VASE, THE
RAZBOIUL INDEPENDENTEI • 1912 • Brezeanu Grigore • RMN
RAZBUDITE LENOCHKY • 1933 • Kudryavtseva A. • USS • WAKE UP LENOCHKA
RAZBUDITYE MUKHINA • 1968 • Segel Yakov • USS • WAKE MUKHIN UP
RAZBUNAREA HAIDUCILOR • 1968 • Cocea Dinu • RMN • REVENGE OF THE OUTLAWS, THE
RAZEM • 1948 • Bossak Jerzy • DOC • PLN • TOGETHER
RAZGROM NEMETZKIKHY VOISK POD MOSKVOI • 1942 • Kopalin Ilya, Varlamov Leonid • USS • DEFEAT OF THE GERMAN ARMIES NEAR MOSCOW, THE ○ MOSCOW STRIKES BACK (USA)
RAZMEDJA • 1974 • Golik Kreso • YGS • CONFLICT
RAZOBLACHENIE • 1970 • Sabirov Takhir • USS • EXPOSURE
RAZON DE LA CULPA, LA • 1942 • Ortega Juan J. • MXC
RAZOR, THE see **KAMISORI** • 1923
RAZORBACK • 1983 • Mulcahy Russell • ASL
RAZORED IN OLD KENTUCKY • 1930 • Sandrich Mark • SHT • USA
RAZOR'S EDGE, THE • 1946 • Goulding Edmund • USA
RAZOR'S EDGE, THE • 1984 • Byrum John • USA
RAZSELJENA OSEBA • 1982 • Ciglic Marjan • YGS • DISPLACED PERSON, A ○ RASELJENA OSOBA
RAZZA SELVAGGIA • 1980 • Squitieri Pasquale • ITL • SAVAGE BREED
RAZZA VIOLENTA • 1984 • Di Leo Fernando • ITL • VIOLENT BREED, THE
RAZZBERRIES • 1931 • *Terry Paul/ Moser Frank (P)* • ANS • USA
RAZZIA • 1921 • Neff Wolfgang • FRG
RAZZIA • 1931 • Severac Jacques • FRN
RAZZIA • 1947 • Klinger Werner • GDR • RAID (UKN)
RAZZIA • 1972 • de la Loma Jose Antonio • SPN • REDADA, LA
RAZZIA see **KINDER DER STRASSE** • 1928
RAZZIA DER GERECHTIGKEIT see **GEWISSEN DER WELT 2, DAS** • 1921
RAZZIA IN ST. PAULI • 1932 • Hochbaum Werner • FRG
RAZZIA SUR LA CHNOUF • 1954 • Decoin Henri • FRN • RAZZIA (USA) ○ CHNOUF -TO TAKE IT IS DEADLY
RAZZIA (USA) see **RAZZIA SUR LA CHNOUF** • 1954
RAZZLE DAZZLE • 1903 • Porter Edwin S. • USA
R'COON DAWG • 1951 • Nichols Charles • ANS • USA
RDECE KLASJE see **CRVENO KLASJE** • 1971
RDECI BOOGIE ALI KAJ TI JE DEKLICA see **CRVENI BUGI** • 1983
RDZA • 1981 • Zaluski Roman • PLN • RUST, THE
RE • Ryszka Henryk • DOC • PLN
RE-ANIMATOR • 1985 • Gordon Stuart • USA
RE BURLONE • 1935 • Guazzoni Enrico • ITL
RE-CREATION OF BRIAN KENT, THE • 1925 • Wood Sam • USA
RE DEI CRIMINALI, IL see **SUPERARGO EL GIGANTE** • 1967
RE DEI FALSARI, IL (ITL) see **CAVE SE REBIFFE, LE** • 1961
RE DEI SETTE MARI, IL see **DOMINATORE DEI SETTE MARI, IL** • 1962
RE DEK CIRCO, IL • 1941 • Hinrich Hans • ITL
RE DEL FIUME, IL • 1978 • Angeli Ivan • MTV • ITL
RE DELLA MALA, IL • 1974 • Roland Jurgen • ITL
RE DI DANARI see **RE DI DENARI** • 1936
RE DI DENARI • 1936 • Guazzoni Enrico • ITL • RE DI DANARI
RE DI POGGIOREALE, IL • 1961 • Coletti Duilio • ITL, FRN
RE D'INGHILTERRA NON PAGA, IL • 1941 • Forzano Giovacchino • ITL
RE-ENACTMENT, THE see **RECONSTITUIREA** • 1968
RE-ENCOUNTERS • 1989 • Espindola Luisa Fernanda • SHT • RMN
RE-ENTRY • 1964 • Belson Jordan • ANS • USA
RE FANTASMA, IL • 1914 • Falena Ugo • ITL
RE-INFORCER, THE • 1949 • Lewis Jerry • SHT • USA
RE LEAR • 1910 • De Liguoro Giuseppe, Lo Savio Girolamo • ITL
RE: LONE see **ANGAENDE LONE** • 1970
RE: LUCKY LUCIANO (USA) see **LUCKY LUCIANO** • 1973
RE-MADE MAID, THE • 1916 • *Gayety* • USA
RE MIZERABURU • 1950 • Ito Daisuke • JPN • LES MISERABLES
RE SI DIVERTE, IL • 1941 • Bonnard Mario • ITL • KING'S JESTER, THE (USA)
RE-TAGGED • 1913 • *Essanay* • USA
RE-TOUCHER, THE see **RETUSOR, A** • 1972
RE-UNION (UKN) see **IN LOVE WITH LIFE** • 1934
REACH FOR GLORY • 1962 • Leacock Philip • UKN
REACH FOR THE SKY • 1956 • Gilbert Lewis* • UKN
REACH FOR TOMORROW see **LET NO MAN WRITE MY EPITAPH** • 1960
REACHING FOR THE MOON • 1917 • Emerson John • USA
REACHING FOR THE MOON • 1931 • Goulding Edmund • USA
REACHING FOR THE MOON • 1933 • Fleischer Dave • ANS • USA
REACHING FOR THE SKY see **AHAS GAUWA** • 1974
REACHING FOR THE STARS see **ADVENTURES IN SPACE** • 1964
REACHING FOR THE STARS (USA) see **GRIFF NACH DEN STERNEN** • 1955
REACHING FOR THE SUN • 1941 • Wellman William A. • USA
REACHING OUT • 1968 • Garland Patrick, Knight Derrick • DCS • UKN
REACHING OUT • 1980 • Yates Rebecca, Salzman Glen • CND
REACHOUT see **HOTLINE** • 1982
REACTEUR NUCLEAIRE, LE • 1966 • Otero Manuel, Leroux Jacques • SHT • FRN
REACTION: A PORTRAIT OF A SOCIETY IN CRISIS • 1973 • Spry Robin • DOC • CND
REACTOR • 1985 • Brescia Alfonso • ITL
REACTOR, THE • 1989 • Heavener David • USA • DEADLY REACTOR
READER OF MINDS, THE • 1914 • *Thanhouser* • USA
READIN' AND WRITIN' • 1932 • McGowan Robert • SHT • USA
READIN', RITIN' AND RHYTHM • 1939 • Schwarzwald Milton • SHT • USA
READIN', RITIN' AND RHYTHMETIC • 1948 • Kneitel Seymour • ANS • USA
READIN' 'RITIN' AND 'RITHMETIC • 1951 • Cowan Will • SHT • USA
READIN' 'RITIN' 'RITHMETIC • 1926 • Eddy Robert • USA
READIN', WRITHING AND 'RITHMETIC • 1964 • Kneitel Seymour • ANS • USA
READIN', WRITIN' AND 'RITHMETIC • 1912 • *Miller Walker* • USA
READING BETWEEN THE LINES • 1990 • Davis Martha • DOC • CND
READING LESSON, THE see **LEESPLANKJE, HET** • 1973
READY AYE READY • 1912 • ASL
READY FOR ANYTHING! • 1968 • Darcia • USA
READY FOR LOVE • 1934 • Gering Marion • USA
READY FOR RENO • 1915 • *Griffith Ray* • USA
READY FOR SLAUGHTER • 1983 • King Allan • TVM • USA
READY FOR THE GRAVE • 1990 • Steindler Milan • CZC
READY FOR THE PEOPLE • 1964 • Kulik Buzz • USA
READY MADE FAMILY, A • 1915 • *Wise Thomas A.* • USA
READY MADE MAID, A • 1915 • Metcalfe Earl • USA
READY MIX • 1980 • Lunney Brendon • DOC • ASL
READY MONEY • 1914 • Apfel Oscar • USA
READY MONEY RINGFIELD • 1918 • *Farnum Dustin* • SHT • USA
READY, SET, ZOOM • 1955 • Jones Charles M. • ANS • USA
READY TO RIDE • 1950 • Cowan Will • SHT • USA
READY WHEN YOU ARE, MR. MCGILL! • 1977 • Newell Mike • UKN
READY, WILLING AND ABLE • 1937 • Enright Ray • USA
READY WILLING BUT UNABLE • *Brendel El* • SHT • USA
READY WOOLEN AND ABLE • 1960 • Jones Charles M. • ANS • USA
REAL ADVENTURE, THE • 1922 • Vidor King • USA
REAL AGATHA, THE • 1914 • Travers Richard C. • USA
REAL AMERICAN HERO, A • 1978 • Antonio Lou • TVM • USA
REAL AUSTRALIAN SERIES • 1910 • ASL
REAL BLOKE, A • 1935 • Baxter John • UKN • NAVVY, THE
REAL BRUCE LEE, THE • 1979 • Markovic Jim • HKG
REAL DESEJO • 1989 • Sava Augusto • BRZ • REAL DESIRE
REAL DESIRE see **REAL DESEJO** • 1989
REAL DR. KAY, THE • 1916 • Louis Will • SHT • USA
REAL END OF THE GREAT WAR, THE see **PRAWDZIWY KONIEC WIELKIEJ WOJNY** • 1957
REAL ESTATE DEAL, A • 1912 • Henderson Dell • USA
REAL ESTATE FRAUD, THE • 1912 • Dwan Allan • USA
REAL ESTATERS • 1916 • *Cooper Claude* • SHT • USA
REAL FOLKS • 1918 • Edwards Walter • USA
REAL GAME, THE • 1980 • Cohen Avi • ISR
REAL GENIUS • 1985 • Coolidge Martha • USA
REAL GIRL, A (UKN) see **HARDBOILED** • 1929
REAL GLORY, THE • 1939 • Hathaway Henry • USA
REAL GONE GIRLS, THE see **MAN FROM O.R.G.Y., THE** • 1970
REAL GONE WOODY • 1954 • Smith Paul J. • ANS • USA
REAL HELPMATE, A • 1914 • Kendall Preston • USA
REAL IMPOSTOR, THE • 1913 • *Lubin* • USA
REAL INSIDE • 1984 • Weldon John (c/d) • ANM • CND
REAL ITALIAN PIZZA • 1971 • Rimmer David • CND
REAL LIFE • 1979 • Brooks Albert • USA
REAL LIFE • 1983 • Megahy Francis • UKN
REAL LIFE IN THE FOREST • 1950 • Zguridi Alexander • DOC • USS
REAL LIVE TEDDY BEAR, A • 1910 • Wilson Frank? • UKN
REAL LOVE AND COUNTERFEIT MONEY • 1916 • *Jockey* • USA
REAL MCCOY, THE • 1930 • Doane Warren • SHT • USA
REAL MEN • 1987 • Feldman Dennis • USA
REAL MEN DON'T EAT GUMMY BEARS see **GUMMI BARCHEN KUSST MAN NICHT** • 1989
REAL MISS LOVELEIGH, THE • 1914 • *White Leo* • USA
REAL MOTHER, THE • 1913 • *Reliance* • USA
REAL PESTS! see **TO SO GADI** • 1979
REAL SEA, THE • 1965 • Bocharov Edvard • USS
REAL SEA SERPENT, THE • 1905 • Williamson James • SHT • UKN
REAL STORY see **TRUE STORY** • 1964
REAL STUFF, THE • 1986 • Zaritsky John • MTV • CND
REAL SWORD FIGHT see **SHINKEN SHOBU** • 1969
REAL THING, THE • 1913 • Plumb Hay? • UKN
REAL THING, THE • 1966 • Saroff Raymond • USA
REAL THING, THE • 1980 • Djaya Sjuman • INN
REAL THING AT LAST, THE • 1916 • MacBean L. C. • UKN
REAL THING IN COWBOYS, THE • 1914 • Mix Tom • USA
REAL TIME see **ECHTZEIT** • 1983
REAL TROUBLE • 1988 • Grossman Douglas • USA • RAGING FURY
REAL TRUTH, THE see **ZIVA ISTINA** • 1973
REAL WOMAN, A (USA) see **MULHER DE VERDADE** • 1954
REALANGO 18 • 1963 • Torres Oscar • CUB
REALE DISSOLUTO, IL • Mussio Magdalo • ANS • ITL • ROYAL DISSOLUTE, THE
REALI DI FRANCIA, I • 1960 • Costa Mario • ITL • ATTACK OF THE MOORS (USA)
REALIDADE INTERNACIONAL -TANGER, UMA • 1953 • Ribeiro Antonio Lopes • SHT • PRT
REALIDADES PORTUGUESAS • 1962 • Spiguel Miguel • SHT • PRT
REALISATION see **ESZMELES** • 1985
REALISMO SOCIALISTA • 1973 • Ruiz Raul • CHL • SOCIALIST REALISM
REALISTIC REHEARSAL, A • 1912 • *Paige Mabel* • USA
REALITES MALGACHES • Muntcho Monique • FRN
REALITIES • 1930 • Mainwaring Bernerd • UKN
REALITY, THE see **RZECZYWISTOSC** • 1961
REALITY AND FICTION • 1977 • Lejter Herman • VNZ
REALITY IN REVOLT • 1981 • Sens Al • SHT • CND
REALITY OF KAREL APPEL, THE see **WERKELIJKHEID VAN KAREL APPEL, DE** • 1962
REALIZADOR • 1975 • Alvarez Santiago • DOC • CUB
REALIZATION • 1916 • Ricketts Thomas • SHT • USA
REALIZATION, THE • 1911 • Porter Edwin S. • USA
REALIZATION OF A CHILD'S DREAM, THE • 1912 • *Champion* • USA
REALIZATION OF A NEGRO'S AMBITION, THE • 1917 • *Lincoln M.p.* • USA
REALLY BIG FAMILY, A • 1967 • Grasshoff Alex • DOC • USA
REALLY EXCEPTIONAL see **ECCEZZZIUNALE.. VERAMENTE** • 1982
REALLY IMPORTANT PERSON, A • 1947 • Wrangell Basil • SHT • USA
REALLY SCENT • 1959 • Jones Charles M. • ANS • USA
REALM BETWEEN THE LIVING AND THE DEAD, THE see **YINYANG JIE** • 1988
REALM OF MAN see **MANNISKORS RIKE** • 1949
REALTA ROMANZESCA • 1969 • Proia Gianni • ITL
REALTIONSHIP WRECKER see **KOWASHIYA JINROKU** • 1968
REAP THE WILD WIND • 1942 • De Mille Cecil B. • USA
REAPERS, THE • 1916 • King Burton L. • USA
REAPERS OF THE WHIRLWIND • 1915 • MacDonald J. Farrell • USA
REAPING, THE • 1913 • *Broncho* • USA
REAPING, THE • 1915 • Calvert E. H. • *Essanay* • USA
REAPING, THE • 1915 • King Burton L. • *Selig* • USA
REAPING FOR THE WHIRLWIND • 1914 • *Roland Ruth* • USA
REAPING THE WHIRLWIND • 1912 • *Nestor* • USA
REAR ADMIRAL RICHARD E. BYRD'S SECOND GREAT ANTARCTIC EXPEDITION INTO LITTLE AMERICA • 1935 • *Faralla Dario (P)* • DOC • USA • LITTLE AMERICA
REAR CAR, THE see **MURDER IN THE PRIVATE CAR** • 1934
REAR DELIVERIES • Higgins William • FRN
REAR GUARD see **COMMAND, THE** • 1954
REAR GUNNER, THE • 1943 • Enright Ray • DCS • USA
REAR RAVENS see **CRIA CUERVOS** • 1976
REAR WINDOW • 1954 • Hitchcock Alfred • USA
REARGUARD see **VALAHOL MAGYARORSZAGON** • 1988
REARVIEW MIRROR • 1984 • Antonio Lou • TVM • USA
REASON, THE • 1912 • *Gem* • USA
REASON AND EMOTION • 1943 • Roberts Bill • ANS • USA
REASON AND EMOTION see **ROZUM A CIT** • 1962
REASON, DEBATE AND A TALE see **JUKTI, TAKKO AAR GAPPO** • 1974
REASON FOR NOT DIVORCING see **WAKARENU RIYUU** • 1988
REASON OVER PASSION see **RAISON AVANT LA PASSION, LA** • 1969
REASON TO DIE, A • 1989 • Spring Tim • SAF
REASON TO LIVE, A • 1985 • Levin Peter • TVM • USA
REASON TO LIVE, A REASON TO DIE, A see **RAGIONE PER VIVERE E UNA PER MOURIRE, UNA** • 1972
REASON WHY, THE • 1911 • Melies Gaston • USA
REASON WHY, THE • 1918 • Vignola Robert G. • USA
REASON WHY, THE see **DI'ASIMANDON AFORMIN** • 1974
REASONABLE DOUBT • 1936 • King George • UKN
REASONABLE DOUBT, A • 1963 • Watson Patrick • DOC • CND
REASONABLE FORCE • 1983 • Rowe Peter • TVM • CND
REASONABLE FORCE • 1988 • Goddard Jim • UKN
REASONS OF STATE see **RECURSO DEL METODO, EL** • 1978
REAZIONE A CATENA • 1971 • Bava Mario • ITL • TWITCH OF THE DEATH NERVE ○ BLOODBATH BAY OF DEATH ○ CARNAGE (USA) ○ ANTEFATTO, L' ○ ECOLOGIA DEL DELITTO ○ ECOLOGY OF A CRIME ○ BAY OF BLOOD ○ BLOOD BATH
REB SPIKES AND HIS FOLLIES ENTERTAINERS • 1927 • Foy Bryan • SHT • USA
REBANO DE LOS ANGELES, EL • 1979 • Bolivar Cesar • VNZ • FLOCK OF ANGELS, THE
REBECCA • 1913 • Andreani Henri • FRN
REBECCA • 1940 • Hitchcock Alfred • USA
REBECCA OF SUNNYBROOK FARM • 1917 • Neilan Marshall • USA
REBECCA OF SUNNYBROOK FARM • 1932 • Santell Alfred • USA
REBECCA OF SUNNYBROOK FARM • 1938 • Dwan Allan • USA
REBECCA THE JEWESS (USA) see **IVANHOE** • 1913
REBECCA'S DAUGHTER • 1989 • Forsyth Bill • USA
REBECCA'S WEDDING DAY • 1914 • Dillon Eddie • USA
REBEL • 1985 • Jenkins Michael • ASL
REBEL see **NO PLACE TO HIDE** • 1975
REBEL, DIE • 1975 • SAF
REBEL, THE • 1915 • Matthews J. E. • ASL
REBEL, THE • 1933 • Knopf Edwin H., Trenker Luis • USA
REBEL, THE • 1960 • Day Robert • UKN • CALL ME GENIUS (USA)
REBEL, THE see **REBELL, DER** • 1932
REBEL, THE see **CITA DE AMOR, UNA** • 1956
REBEL, THE see **MOUTAMARRED, AL** • 1968
REBEL, THE (UKN) see **BUSHWHACKERS, THE** • 1951
REBEL, THE (UKN) see **AMAKUSA SHIRO TOKISADA** • 1962

REBEL AGAINST THE LIGHT see **SANDS OF BEERSHEBA** • 1965
REBEL ANGEL • 1962 • Douglas Lamont • USA
REBEL CITY • 1953 • Carr Thomas • USA
REBEL FLIGHT TO CUBA see **ABSCHIED VON DEN WOLKEN** • 1959
REBEL GIRLS • 1957 • *Del Mar Eddie* • PHL
REBEL GLADIATORS, THE (USA) see **URSUS GLADIATORE RIBELLE** • 1963
REBEL HIGH • 1987 • Jakobs Harry • USA
REBEL IN THE RING • 1964 • Lawrence Jay O. • USA
REBEL IN TOWN • 1956 • Werker Alfred L. • USA
REBEL JESUS • 1972 • Buchanan Larry • USA
REBEL LIEUTENANT, THE • Ferroni Giorgio • ITL, FRN
REBEL LOVE • 1984 • Bagby Milton Jr. • USA
REBEL NUN, THE (UKN) see **FLAVIA LA MONACA MUSULMANA** • 1974
REBEL OF THE ROAD see **HOT ROD** • 1979
REBEL RABBIT • 1949 • McKimson Robert • ANS • USA
REBEL ROUSERS • 1970 • Cohen Martin B. • USA
REBEL SET, THE • 1959 • Fowler Gene Jr. • USA
REBEL SON, THE • 1938 • De Courville Albert, Brunel Adrian (U/c) • UKN • TARAS BULBA
REBEL SOULS (USA) see **ALMAS REBELDES** • 1937
REBEL TROUBLE • 1962 • Tendlar Dave • ANS • USA
REBEL WAVES • 1989 • Schaeffer Franky • USA
REBEL WITH A CAUSE see **LONELINESS OF THE LONG DISTANCE RUNNER, THE** • 1962
REBEL WITH A CAUSE (UKN) see **CHE GUEVARA, EL** • 1968
REBEL WITHOUT A CAUSE • 1955 • Ray Nicholas • USA
REBEL WITHOUT CLAWS, THE • 1961 • Freleng Friz • ANS • USA
REBELDE, EL • 1943 • Salvador Jaime • MXC
REBELDE SIN CASA • 1957 • Alazraki Benito • MXC
REBELDES A GO GO see **JUVENTUD SIN LEY** • 1965
REBELDES DE ARIZONA, LOS • 1970 • Zabalza Jose Maria • SPN
REBELDES EN CANADA • 1968 • de Ossorio Amando • SPN, ITL • REBELS IN CANADA
REBELDIA • 1953 • Nieves Conde Jose Antonio • SPN
REBELDIA • 1978 • Velasco Andres • SPN
REBELIAO EM VILA RICA • 1958 • Santo Pereira Jose Geraldo, Santo Pereira Jose Renato • BRZ
REBELION • 1934 • Gomez Manuel G. • MXC
REBELION DE LA SIERRA, LA • 1957 • Gavaldon Roberto • MXC
REBELION DE LAS MUERTAS, LA • 1972 • Klimovsky Leon • SPN, ITL • VENGEANCE OF THE ZOMBIES (USA) ○ REVOLT OF THE DEAD ONES, THE ○ VENDETTA DEI MORTI VIVENTI, LA ○ REBELLION OF THE DEAD WOMEN, THE
REBELION DE LOS ADOLESCENTES, LA • 1957 • Diaz Morales Jose • MXC
REBELION DE LOS BUCANEROS, LA • 1972 • Merino Jose Luis • SPN
REBELION DE LOS COLGADOS, LA • 1953 • Crevenna Alfredo B., Fernandez Emilio • MXC • REVOLT OF THE HANGED ○ REBELLION OF THE HANGED, THE
REBELION DE LOS ESCLAVOS, LA (SPN) see **RIVOLTA DEGLI SCHIAVI, LA** • 1961
REBELION DE LOS FANTASMAS, LA • 1946 • Fernandez Bustamente Adolfo • MXC • REBELLION OF THE GHOSTS ○ REVOLT OF THE GHOSTS
REBELL, DER • 1932 • Bernhardt Curtis, Trenker Luis • FRG • REBEL, THE
REBELLE, LE • 1930 • Millar Adelqui • FRN • GENERAL, LE
REBELLE, LE • 1981 • Blain Gerard • FRN
REBELLE, LE see **SERMENTS** • 1931
REBELLE, LE see **MOUTAMARRED, AL** • 1968
REBELLEN, DIE (FRG) see **FLASHPOINT AFRICA** • 1978
REBELLENLIEBE • 1919 • Heiland Heinz Karl • FRG
REBELLES, LES see **MONTS EN FLAMMES, LES** • 1931
REBELLION • 1936 • Shores Lynn • USA • TREASON (UKN)
REBELLION see **HANRAN** • 1954
REBELLION see **JOIUCHI –HAIRYOZUMA SHIMATSU** • 1967
REBELLION see **VEERA PURAN APPU** • 1978
REBELLION see **RED BERETS, THE** • 1982
REBELLION, THE • 1918 • *Boy City Film* • SHT • USA
REBELLION A ROMANS, UNE • 1981 • Venault Philippe • FRN
REBELLION IN CUBA see **CHIVATO** • 1961
REBELLION IN PATAGONIA (USA) see **PATAGONIA REBELDE, LA** • 1974
REBELLION OF JAPAN see **UTAGE** • 1967
REBELLION OF KITTY BELLE, THE • 1914 • Cabanne W. Christy • USA
REBELLION OF MANDY, THE • 1912 • *Essanay* • USA
REBELLION OF MR. MINOR, THE • 1917 • Drew Sidney, Drew Sidney Mrs. • SHT • USA
REBELLION OF THE DEAD WOMEN, THE see **REBELION DE LAS MUERTAS, LA** • 1972
REBELLION OF THE GHOSTS see **REBELION DE LOS FANTASMAS, LA** • 1946
REBELLION OF THE HANGED, THE see **REBELION DE LOS COLGADOS, LA** • 1953
REBELLIOUS BARRIER see **MYATYEZHNAYA ZASTAVA** • 1967
REBELLIOUS BLOSSOM, A • 1911 • Salter Harry • USA
REBELLIOUS BRIDE, THE • 1919 • Reynolds Lynn • USA • UNKISSED BRIDE, THE
REBELLIOUS DAUGHTERS • 1938 • Yarbrough Jean • USA
REBELLIOUS GIRL, THE see **DON'T** • 1925
REBELLIOUS NOVICE, THE see **NOVICIO REBELDE, EL** • 1968
REBELLIOUS ONE, THE see **WILD SEED, THE** • 1965
REBELLIOUS PUPIL, THE • 1913 • *Laughlin Anna* • USA
REBELLIOUS SCHOOLGIRLS • 1907 • Fitzhamon Lewin • UKN
REBELLIOUS WALKING STICK, THE • 1906 • *Pathe* • USA
REBELOTE • 1983 • Richard Jacques • FRN
REBELS see **FELLAGHAS** • 1970
REBELS, THE • 1979 • Mayberry Russ • TVM • USA
REBELS, THE see **MOUTAMARRIDOUNE, AL** • 1968
REBELS, THE see **QUELQUES ARPENTS DE NEIGE** • 1972
REBELS IN CANADA see **REBELDES EN CANADA** • 1968
REBEL'S NET, THE • 1917 • *Ford Francis* • SHT • USA
REBELS ON THE HIGH SEA see **SHUJINSAN** • 1956
REBELS ON THE LOOSE (USA) see **RINGO E GRINGO CONTRO TUTTI** • 1966
REBIRTH • 1963 • Clark Dan • SHT • USA
REBIRTH OF A NATION see **BAATH OMAR** • 1965
REBIRTH OF THE SOIL, THE see **YOMIGAERU DAICHI** • 1970
REBORN see **RENACER** • 1980
REBOUND • 1931 • Griffith Edward H. • USA
REBOUND, THE • 1918 • *Roland Ruth* • SHT • USA
REBOZO DE SOLEDAD, EL • 1952 • Gavaldon Roberto • MXC • SOLEDAD
REBRO ADAMOVO • 1956 • Marinovich Anton • BUL • RIB OF ADAM, A ○ ADAM'S RIB
REBUILDING OF ROME AND NEXOS, THE see **RONNES OG NEXOS GENOPBYGNING** • 1954
REBUKED INDIAN, THE • 1911 • *Pathe* • USA
REBUS • 1968 • Zanchin Nino • ITL, FRG, SPN • HEISSES SPIEL FUR HARTE MANNER (FRG) ○ APPOINTMENT IN BEIRUT
REBUS • 1977 • Zygadlo Tomasz • PLN • PUZZLE
REBYATA S NASHEGO DVORA • 1959 • Saltykov Alexei • USS • BOYS FROM OUR COURTYARD
REBYU NO SHIMAI • 1929 • Shimazu Yasujiro • JPN • REVUE SISTERS
RECADO, O • 1972 • Costa Jose Fonseca • PRT
RECALLING OF JOHN GREY, THE • 1915 • Wilson Frank • UKN
RECAPTURED LOVE • 1930 • Adolfi John G. • USA • FAME
RECARDO • Costa Jose Fonseca • PRT • ERRAND
RECE DO GORY • 1967 • Skolimowski Jerzy • PLN • HANDS UP!
RECEIVED PAYMENT • 1922 • Maigne Charles • USA • MILTON MYSTERY, THE
RECEIVERS • 1938 • Delamar Mickey, Kavanagh Denis • UKN
RECEIVER'S DOOM, THE • 1909 • Coleby A. E. • UKN
RECEIVING TELLER, THE • 1912 • *Handworth Octavia* • USA
RECENT CONFEDERATE VICTORY, A • 1914 • Ince John • USA
RECEP THE ENRAGED see **KUDUZ RECEP** • 1967
RECEPTION • 1957 • Corman Roger • USA
RECEPTION • 1967 • Jackson Douglas • CND
RECEPTION OF BRITISH FLEET • 1905 • *Bitzer Billy (Ph)* • USA
RECESS • 1969 • Johnson Rule Royce • USA
RECESS • 1969 • Scott Michael • SHT • CND
RECETARIO • 1975 • Ardavin Cesar • SHT • SPN
RECHERCHE • Hirsch Hy • SHT • USA
RECHERCHE VISUELLE POUR ACCOMPAGNER UNE TRAME MUSICALE • 1969 • Coderre Laurent • ANM • CND
RECHNUNG –EISKALT SERVIERT, DIE • 1966 • Ashley Helmut • FRG, FRN
RECHT AUF GLUCK, DAS • 1919 • Ziener Bruno • FRG
RECHT AUF LIEBE, DAS • 1929 • Fleck Jacob, Fleck Luise • FRG • SEXUALNOT
RECHT AUF LIEBE, DAS • 1939 • Stockel Joe • FRG • RIGHT TO LOVE, THE (USA)
RECHT AUF SUNDE, DAS • 1923 • *Nathan S.* • FRG • GOLD IM DSCHAGGAGEBIET, DAS
RECHT DER FREIEN LIEBE, DAS • 1920 • Speyer Jaap • FRG
RECHT DER UNGEBORENEN, DAS • 1929 • Trotz Adolf • FRG
RECHT ZU LEBEN, DAS • 1927 • Wohlmuth Robert • AUS
RECIEN CASADAS, LAS • 1960 • Diaz Morales Jose • MXC
RECIEN CASADOS.. NO MOLESTAR • 1950 • Cortes Fernando • MXC
RECIEN LLEGADO ESCRIBIO SU EPITAFIO • 1977 • Brell Alfred S. • SPN
RECIF DE CORAIL, LE • 1938 • Gleize Maurice • FRN
RECIPE FOR A CRIME see **PRISNE TAJNE PREMIERY** • 1967
RECIPE TO COOK A CLOWN • 1978 • Siegel Lois • CND
RECIT DE NOTRE PAYS, UN see **HIKAYAT MIN BALADNA** • 1969
RECIT DU COLONEL, LA • 1908 • Feuillade Louis • FRN
RECITAL IN GRADINA CU PITICI • 1987 • Nicolae Cristiana • RMN • VIOLIN SOLO IN THE ELVES' GARDEN ○ RECITAL IN THE DWARFS' GARDEN
RECITAL IN THE DWARFS' GARDEN see **RECITAL IN GRADINA CU PITICI** • 1987
RECITATION BY JAMES WELCH • 1913 • Booth W. R.? • UKN
RECITS DE LA NUIT, LES see **QUARANTE–QUATRE** • 1981
RECKLESS • 1935 • Fleming Victor • USA
RECKLESS • 1981 • Milicevic Djordje • CND • RECKLESS AND IN LOVE
RECKLESS • 1984 • Foley James • USA
RECKLESS AGE • 1944 • Feist Felix E. • USA
RECKLESS AGE, THE • 1924 • Pollard Harry • USA
RECKLESS AGE, THE (UKN) see **DRAGSTRIP RIOT** • 1958
RECKLESS AND IN LOVE see **RECKLESS** • 1981
RECKLESS BUCKAROO, THE • 1935 • Fraser Harry L. • USA
RECKLESS CHANCES • 1922 • McGowan J. P. • USA
RECKLESS COURAGE • 1925 • Gibson Tom • USA • FLYING COURAGE (UKN)
RECKLESS COURAGE, A see **MAN IN THE SADDLE, THE** • 1928
RECKLESS DISREGARD • 1985 • Hart Harvey • TVM • USA, CND • JUDGEMENT, THE
RECKLESS DRIVER, THE • 1946 • Culhane James • ANS • USA
RECKLESS ENDANGERMENT • 1988 • Kaplan Jonathan • USA
RECKLESS HOUR, THE • 1931 • Dillon John Francis • USA
RECKLESS LADY, THE • 1926 • Higgin Howard • USA
RECKLESS LIVING • 1931 • Gardner Cyril • USA • TWENTY GRAND
RECKLESS LIVING • 1938 • McDonald Frank • USA
RECKLESS MOLLYCODDLE, THE • 1927 • *Holt Richard* • USA
RECKLESS MOMENT, THE • 1949 • Ophuls Max • USA • BLANK WALL, THE
RECKLESS MONEY • 1926 • *Dudley Sherman H. Jr.* • USA
RECKLESS ONE, THE see **INOCHISHIRAZU NO AITSU** • 1967
RECKLESS PERIOD see **MUTEPPO JIDAI** • 1928
RECKLESS RANGER • 1937 • Bennet Spencer Gordon • USA
RECKLESS REDDY REFORMS • 1911 • *Joyce Alice* • USA
RECKLESS RIDER, THE • 1931 • Schaefer Armand • USA • LAW DEMANDS, THE (UKN)
RECKLESS RIDING BILL • 1924 • Morrow Frank • USA
RECKLESS ROADS • 1935 • Lynwood Burt • USA
RECKLESS ROMANCE • 1924 • Sidney Scott • USA
RECKLESS ROMEO, A see **CREAM PUFF ROMANCE, A** • 1916
RECKLESS ROMEOS • 1916 • *Stull Walter* • USA
RECKLESS ROMEOS see **FLIRTING WITH DANGER** • 1934
RECKLESS ROSIE • 1929 • Burns Neal • USA • RITZY ROSIE
RECKLESS ROSIE (UKN) see **NAUGHTY BABY** • 1928
RECKLESS ROVER, A • 1918 • *Ebony* • SHT • USA
RECKLESS SEX, THE • 1920 • Christie Al • USA
RECKLESS SEX, THE • 1925 • Neitz Alvin J. • USA
RECKLESS SPEED • 1924 • Craft William James • USA
RECKLESS TACTICS OF THE SPIDERS see **THE SPIDERS NO GOGO MUKOUMIZUSAKUSEN** • 1967
RECKLESS WIVES • 1921 • *Murray Myra* • USA
RECKLESS WRESTLERS • 1916 • Roach Hal • SHT • USA
RECKLESS YOUTH • 1922 • Ince Ralph • USA
RECKLESS YOUTH (UKN) see **DAUGHTERS OF DESIRE** • 1929
RECKONER, THE see **PUBLIC DEFENDER, THE** • 1931
RECKONING, THE • 1908 • Griffith D. W. • USA
RECKONING, THE • 1912 • *101 Bison* • USA
RECKONING, THE • 1912 • *Republic* • USA
RECKONING, THE • 1915 • *Ramona* • USA
RECKONING, THE • 1932 • Fraser Harry L. • USA
RECKONING, THE • 1970 • Gold Jack • UKN
RECKONING, THE • 1984 • SAF
RECKONING, THE see **FINAL RECKONING, THE** • 1914
RECKONING, THE see **OBRACUN** • 1963
RECKONING, THE (UKN) see **SAY IT WITH SABLES** • 1928
RECKONING DAY • 1919 • King Burton L. • USA
RECKONING DAY, THE • 1915 • *Calvert E. H.* • USA
RECKONING DAY, THE • 1918 • Pollard Harry • USA
RECLAIMED • 1918 • Webster Harry Mcrae • USA
RECLAMATION • 1911 • *Powers* • USA
RECLAMATION, THE • 1916 • Sloman Edward • USA
RECLAMATION OF JIM THE LOAFER, THE • 1913 • *Durrant Edward* • UKN
RECLAMATION OF SNARKY, THE • 1911 • Haldane Bert? • UKN
RECLINING ACT • Pavlinic Zlatko • ANS • YGS
RECLUTA CON NINO • 1956 • Ramirez Pedro L. • SPN
RECLUTA –FUERZAS ARMADAS • 1972 • Blanco Javier • DOC • VNZ • ARMED FORCES
RECOGIDA, LA • 1972 • *Elias Augusto* • MXC
RECOGNITION, THE • 1912 • Dwan Allan • USA
RECOIL • 1953 • Gilling John • USA
RECOIL • 1963 • Wendkos Paul • TVM • USA
RECOIL, THE • 1912 • *Reliance* • USA
RECOIL, THE • 1915 • *Gallagher Ray* • USA
RECOIL, THE • 1916 • *Puritan* • USA
RECOIL, THE • 1917 • Fitzmaurice George • USA
RECOIL, THE • 1921 • *Chesebro George* • USA
RECOIL, THE • 1922 • Malins Geoffrey H. • UKN
RECOIL, THE • 1924 • Hunter T. Hayes • USA
RECOILING VENGEANCE, A • 1916 • MacGregor Norval • SHT • USA
RECOLLECTIONS • 1977 • Leszczynski Witold • PLN
RECOLLECTIONS FROM CHILDHOOD see **AMINTIRI DIN COPILARIE** • 1964
RECOLLECTIONS OF A SAILOR see **OMOIDE SUIHEI** • 1928
RECOLLECTIONS OF BOYHOOD see **RECOLLECTIONS OF BOYHOOD: AN INTERVIEW WITH JOSEPH WELCH** • 1954
RECOLLECTIONS OF BOYHOOD: AN INTERVIEW WITH JOSEPH WELCH • 1954 • Van Dyke Willard • DOC • USA • RECOLLECTIONS OF BOYHOOD
RECOLLECTIONS OF THE YELLOW HOUSE (UKN) see **RECORDACOES DE CASA AMARELA** • 1989
RECOMMENDATION FOR MERCY • 1976 • Markowitz Murray • CND
RECOMPENSA • 1977 • Duarte Arthur • PRT, BRZ • REWARD
RECOMPENSE • 1925 • Beaumont Harry • USA
RECOMPENSE, LA (FRN) see **REWARD, THE** • 1965
RECON GAME see **OPEN SEASON** • 1974
RECON HUNT see **OPEN SEASON** • 1974
RECONCILED • 1912 • *Bison* • USA
RECONCILED AT RENO • 1912 • *Comet* • USA
RECONCILED BY BURGLARS • 1912 • *Mackenzie Donald* • USA
RECONCILED IN BLOOD • 1914 • *Selig* • USA
RECONCILIATION, THE • 1908 • Williamson James? • UKN
RECONSTITUIREA • 1968 • Pintile Lucian • RMN • RECONSTITUTION, THE ○ RE-ENACTMENT, THE ○ RECONSTRUCTION, THE
RECONSTITUTION see **ANAPARASTASIS** • 1970
RECONSTITUTION, THE see **RECONSTITUIREA** • 1968
RECONSTRUCTED REBEL, A • 1912 • Campbell Colin • USA
RECONSTRUCTION see **ANAPARASTASIS** • 1970
RECONSTRUCTION, THE see **RECONSTITUIREA** • 1968
RECONSTRUCTION OF RONNIE AND NEXOS, THE see **RONNES OG NEXOS GENOPBYGNING** • 1954
RECORD BREAKER, THE • 1915 • *Pullen Eddie* • USA
RECORD CITY • 1977 • Steinmetz Dennis • USA
RECORD DU MONDE • 1930 • Boudrioz Robert • FRN
RECORD HOP • 1957 • *Universal* • SHT • USA
RECORD OF A CRIME see **ZAPIS ZBRODNI** • 1975
RECORD OF A LIVING BEING see **IKIMONO NO KIROKU** • 1955
RECORD OF A TENEMENT GENTLEMAN see **NAGAYA SHINSHI–ROKU** • 1948
RECORD OF LOVE see **AIJO NO KEIFU** • 1961
RECORD OF LOVE AND DESIRE see **AIYOKU NO YORU** • 1930
RECORD OF MY LOVE, A see **WAGA AI NO KI** • 1941
RECORD OF NEWLYWEDS see **OSHIKIRI SHINKON KI** • 1930
RECORD OF SHAMELESS NEWLYWEDS, A see **OSHIKIRI SHINKON KI** • 1930
RECORD OF THREE GENERATIONS OF PRESIDENTS, THE see **SHACHO SANDAIKI** • 1958
RECORD OF YOUTH, A see **SHONEN–KI** • 1951
RECORD PARTY • 1947 • Cowan Will • SHT • USA
RECORD ROMANCE, A • 1912 • *Weston Helen* • USA
RECORD RUN, THE see **DANGER LIGHTS** • 1930
RECORD SNEEZE, THE • 1905 • Collins Alf? • UKN
RECORDACOES DE CASA AMARELA • 1989 • Monteiro Joao Cesar • PRT • RECOLLECTIONS OF THE YELLOW HOUSE (UKN)
RECORDAR ES VIVIR • 1940 • Rivero Fernando A. • MXC

RECORDED LIVE • 1982 • Korican Michael, Rowsome Andrew C., Travessos Almerinda • CND
RECORDING OF A LIVING BEING see **IKIMONO NO KIROKU** • 1955
RECORDING OF MOVEMENT, THE see **JAK LIDE ZAJALI POHYB** • 1962
RECORDING OF WANDERING, A see **HOROKI** • 1962
RECORDS AU GOUFFRE DE LA PIERRE-SAINT-MARTIN • 1951-55 • Tazieff Haroun • SHT • FRN
RECOURS DE LA METHODE, LE see **RECURSO DEL METODO, EL** • 1978
RECOURS EN GRACE • 1960 • Benedek Laslo • FRN, ITL • TRA DUE DONNE (ITL)
RECOURSE TO THE METHOD, THE see **RECURSO DEL METODO, EL** • 1978
RECOVERY see **GENESUNG** • 1956
RECOVERY see **JELBESZED** • 1975
RECREATION • 1914 • Chaplin Charles • USA • SPRING FEVER
RECREATION, LA • 1961 • Moreuil Francois • FRN • PLAYTIME (USA) ○ LOVE PLAY
RECREATION A LA MARTINIERE • 1895 • Lumiere Louis • FRN
RECREATION I • 1957 • Breer Robert • SHT • USA
RECREATION II • 1957 • Breer Robert • SHT • USA
RECREATION OF AN HEIRESS, THE • 1910 • Powell Frank • USA
RECRUIT, THE • 1918 • Seiter William A. • SHT • USA
RECRUITING DAZE • 1940 • Lovy Alex • ANS • USA
RECRUITS • 1986 • Zielinski Rafal • USA
RECRUITS IN INGOLSTADT see **PIONIERE IN INGOLSTADT** • 1971
RECSK 1950-53: THE STORY OF A SECRET FORCED LABOUR CAMP see **RECSK 1950-1953 THE HUNGARIAN GULAG** • 1988
RECSK 1950-1953 THE HUNGARIAN GULAG • 1988 • Boszormenyi Geza, Gyarmathy Livia • DOC • HNG • RECSK 1950-53: THE STORY OF A SECRET FORCED LABOUR CAMP
RECTA FINAL, LA • 1964 • Enrique Taboada Carlos • MXC
RECTO-VERSO • Dark Tony • USA
RECTOR'S STORY, THE • 1914 • *Hill Lee* • USA
RECUERDO DE AQUELLA NOCHE, EL • 1944 • Urueta Chano • MXC
RECUERDO DE BANGKOK • 1967 • Comeron Luis Jose • SHT • SPN
RECUERDOS DE MI VALLE • 1944 • Morayta Miguel • MXC
RECUERDOS DE UN ANGEL • 1948 • Cahen Enrique • ARG
RECUERDOS DEL PORVENIR, LOS • 1968 • Ripstein Arturo • MXC • MEMORIES OF THE FUTURE
RECUPERANTI, I • 1970 • Olmi Ermanno • ITL • SCAVENGERS, THE
RECURSO DEL METODO, EL • 1978 • Littin Miguel • MXC, CUB, FRN • RESORT OF THE METHOD, THE ○ REASONS OF STATE ○ VIVA EL PRESIDENTE ○ RECOURS DE LA METHODE, LE ○ RECOURSE TO THE METHOD, THE
RECYCLAGE, LE • 1969 • Lamothe Arthur • DCS • CND
RED • 1969 • Carle Gilles • CND
RED, LA • 1953 • Fernandez Emilio • MXC • ROSANNA (USA) ○ NET, THE
RED ACE, THE • 1918 • Jaccard Jacques • SRL • USA
RED ACES • 1929 • Wallace Edgar • UKN
RED AGITATION • Pak Hak • NKR
RED ALERT • 1977 • Hale William • TVM • USA
RED AND BLACK see **ROSSO E NERO** • 1954
RED AND BLACK see **KRAASNOYE I CHYORNOYE** • 1976
RED AND BLACK see **CRVENI I CRNI** • 1985
RED AND BLACK (USA) see **CZERWONE I CZARNE** • 1963
RED AND BLUE • 1967 • Richardson Tony • UKN
RED-AND-BLUE PARADISE see **RODBLATT PARADIS** • 1972
RED AND GOLD see **CZERWONE I ZLOTE** • 1971
RED AND GREEN see **SHU TO MIDORI** • 1956
RED AND PETE, PARTNERS • 1913 • O'Sullivan Tony • USA
RED AND THE BLACK, THE see **CZERWONE I CZARNE** • 1963
RED AND THE WHITE, THE (USA) see **CSILLAGOSOK, KATONAK** • 1967
RED AND WHITE • 1932 • Zhelyabuzhsky A.
RED AND WHITE ROSES • 1913 • Brooke Van Dyke?, Ince Ralph? • USA
RED ANGEL, THE see **ANGE ROUGE, L'** • 1948
RED ANGEL, THE see **AKAI TENSHI** • 1966
RED ANTS • 1988 • Boudouris Vassilis • GRC
RED APPLE, THE see **KRASNOYE YABLOKO** • 1975
RED APPLES see **MERE ROSII** • 1976
RED ARMY, THE • 1936 • Jones Andrew Miller • UKN
RED ARMY DAYS see **GORJACE D ENEKI** • 1935
RED ARMY'S BRIDGE, THE • 1964 • Chien Yun-Ta • ANS • CHN
RED AVENGER, THE • 1911 • *Bison* • USA
RED BADGE OF COURAGE, THE • 1951 • Huston John • USA
RED BADGE OF COURAGE, THE • 1974 • Philips Lee • TVM • USA
RED BALL EXPRESS • 1952 • Boetticher Budd • USA
RED BALLOON, THE see **BALLON ROUGE, LE** • 1956
RED BAMBOO see **PAI DAENG** • 1979
RED BARN CRIME: OR, MARIA MARTIN, THE • 1908 • *Haggar & Sons* • UKN
RED BARN MYSTERY, THE • 1908 • *Williams, Brown & Earle* • USA
RED BARON, THE (UKN) see **VON RICHTOFEN AND BROWN** • 1971
RED BARRIER, THE • 1912 • *Morey Harry T.* • USA
RED BARRY • 1938 • Beebe Ford, James Alan • SRL • USA
RED BAT see **BENI KOMORI** • 1931
RED BEARD see **HUNG TU-TZU** • 1958
RED BEARD see **AKAHIGE** • 1965
RED BELLS see **KRASNYE KOLOKOLA** • 1981
RED BELLS: I'VE SEEN THE BIRTH OF THE NEW WORLD • 1983 • Bondarchuk Sergei • USS, MXC
RED BELLS: MEXICO IN FLAMES see **KRASNYE KOLOKOLA** • 1981
RED BERET, THE • 1953 • Young Terence • UKN • PARATROOPER (USA)
RED BERET (HIGHWAY PATROL) • 1968 • Cruz Jose Miranda • PHL
RED BERETS, THE • 1982 • Siciliano Mario • ITL • REBELLION
RED BICYCLE see **AKAI JITENSHIA** • 1954
RED BLOOD • 1926 • McGowan J. P. • USA
RED BLOOD AND BLUE • 1925 • Hutchinson James C. • USA
RED BLOOD AND YELLOW • 1919 • *Anderson Broncho Billy* • USA
RED BLOOD OF COURAGE, THE • 1915 • Santschi Thomas • USA
RED BLOOD OF COURAGE, THE • 1935 • English John • USA
RED BLOODED AMERICAN GIRL • 1990 • Blyth David • USA
RED BOOGIE see **CRVENI BUGI** • 1983
RED BOOGIE, OR WHAT'S UP, GIRL? see **CRVENI BUGI** • 1983
RED BULL, DER LETZTE APACHE • 1920 • Jutzi Phil • FRG
RED CANYON • 1949 • Sherman George • USA • BLACK VELVET
RED CHURCH • 1976 • Winkler Paul • ASL
RED CIRCLE, THE • 1916 • MacDonald Sherwood • SRL • USA
RED CIRCLE, THE • 1922 • Ridgwell George • UKN
RED CIRCLE, THE (UKN) see **CERCLE ROUGE, LE** • 1970
RED CIRCLE, THE (USA) see **ROTE KREIS, DER** • 1959
RED CLAY • 1927 • Laemmle Ernst • USA
RED CLOAK, THE see **AKAI JINBAORI** • 1958
RED CLOAK, THE (USA) see **MANTELLO ROSSO, IL** • 1955
RED CLOUD, THE INDIAN GAMBLER • 1908 • *Kalem* • USA
RED CLOUD'S SECRET • 1911 • Melies Gaston • USA
RED CLUB, THE • 1914 • DNM
RED COUNTESS, THE see **VOROS GROFNO, A** • 1984
RED COURAGE • 1921 • Eason B. Reeves • USA
RED CRAG see **LIE HUOZHONG YONGSHENG** • 1965
RED CROSS HEROINE • 1909 • *Bison* • USA
RED CROSS MARTYR, A • 1911 • Trimble Larry • USA
RED CROSS MARTYR, A • 1912 • Reid Hal • USA
RED CROSS NURSE, THE • 1914 • *Columbus* • USA
RED CROSS ON WHITE FIELD • 1967 • Orthel Rolf • DOC • NTH
RED CROSS PANORAMA • 1957 • Bilcock David Sr. • DOC • ASL
RED CROSS PLUCK • 1914 • Batley Ethyle • UKN
RED CROSS SEAL, THE • 1910 • *Edison* • USA
RED CROSSED • 1918 • *Mason Billy* • USA
RED CULOTTES, THE (USA) see **CULOTTES ROUGES, LES** • 1963
RED CUNT, THE see **SEXE ENRAGE, LE** • 1970
RED DAISY • 1989 • Vafeas Vassilis • GRC
RED DANCE, THE • 1928 • Walsh Raoul • USA • RED DANCER OF MOSCOW, THE (UKN)
RED DANCER OF MOSCOW, THE (UKN) see **RED DANCE, THE** • 1928
RED DANUBE, THE • 1949 • Sidney George • USA
RED DAWN • 1984 • Milius John • USA
RED DAWN see **MORGENROT** • 1933
RED DAY, THE see **RODA DAGEN** • 1931
RED DESERT • 1950 • Beebe Ford • USA
RED DESERT, THE (USA) see **DESERTO ROSSO, IL** • 1964
RED DESERT PENITENTIARY • 1987 • Sluizer George • NTH
RED DETACHMENT OF WOMEN, THE • 1970 • CHN
RED DETACHMENT OF WOMEN, THE see **HUNG SIK LEUNG DJE CHING** • 1960
RED DEVILS, THE • 1911 • Drew Sidney • USA
RED DICE • 1926 • Howard William K. • USA
RED DOCKERS see **MUELLE ROJO** • 1989
RED DOLL, THE see **POUPEE ROUGE, LA** • 1968
RED DRAGON see **MANHUNTER** • 1986
RED DRAGON, THE • 1945 • Rosen Phil • USA
RED DRAGON (USA) see **GEHEIMNIS DER DREI DSCHUNKEN, DAS** • 1965
RED DUST • 1932 • Fleming Victor • USA
RED DUST see **POLVO ROJO** • 1982
RED DYE • 1914 • Henderson Dell • USA
RED EAGLE • 1911 • *Vitagraph* • USA
RED EAGLE, THE LAWYER • 1912 • *Pathe* • USA
RED EAGLE'S LOVE AFFAIR • 1910 • *Lubin* • USA
RED EARTH see **VOROS FOLD** • 1983
RED EARTH see **TERRE ROUGE** • 1988
RED EARTH, THE see **RODE ENGE, DE** • 1945
RED EARTH, THE see **CRVENA ZEMLJA** • 1976
RED EMMA • 1976 • King Allan • CND
RED ENSIGN • 1934 • Powell Michael • UKN • STRIKE! (USA)
RED EYES see **YEUX ROUGES, LES** • 1982
RED FEATHER'S FRIENDSHIP • 1911 • *Powers* • USA
RED FERN AND THE KID • 1910 • *Bison* • USA
RED FLAG see **RED FLAG: THE ULTIMATE GAME** • 1981
RED FLAG: THE ULTIMATE GAME • 1981 • Taylor Don • TVM • USA • RED FLAG
RED FLESH see **AKAI NIKU** • 1967
RED FLOWER • Chon Sangin • NKR
RED FLYER, THE (UKN) see **VALERI CHKALOV** • 1941
RED FOAM • 1920 • Ince Ralph • USA
RED FORK RANGE • 1931 • Neitz Alvin J. • USA
RED FURY • 1947 • Parker Benjamin R. • SHT • USA
RED FURY, THE • 1985 • Dayton Lyman D. • USA
RED GARTERS • 1954 • Marshall George • USA
RED GIRL, THE • 1908 • Griffith D. W. • USA
RED GIRL AND THE CHILD, THE • 1910 • Youngdeer James • USA
RED GIRL'S FRIENDSHIP, A • 1910 • *Bison* • USA
RED GIRL'S HEART, A • 1911 • *Bison* • USA
RED GIRL'S ROMANCE, A • 1910 • *Bison* • USA
RED GIRL'S SACRIFICE, THE • 1913 • *Bison* • USA
RED GLADES, THE see **RED MEADOWS** • 1966
RED GLASS, A see **AKAI GURASU** • 1966
RED GLOVE, THE • 1919 • McGowan J. P. • SRL • USA
RED GLOW OVER KLADNO see **RUDA ZARE NAD KLADNEM** • 1955
RED GODDESS, THE • 1917 • *Darkfeather Mona* • SHT • USA
RED GOLD • 1930 • *Lyons Cliff (Tex)* • USA
RED GROOMS' TARGET DISCOUNT STORE • 1970 • Grooms Red, Kraning Al • SHT • USA
RED GROUND, THE • 1954 • Dickinson Thorold • SHT • UKN • HAKARKA HA A DOM
RED GROUP OF ASAKUSA see **ASAKUSA KURENAI DAN** • 1952
RED GUARDS IN HONG KONG • 1987 • Mak Johnny • HKG
RED GUARDS OF LAKE HONG see **HONGHU CHIWEIDUI** • 1961
RED HAIR • 1928 • Badger Clarence • USA
RED-HAIRED ALIBI • 1932 • Cabanne W. Christy • USA
RED-HAIRED CUPID, A • 1918 • Smith Cliff • USA
RED HAND, THE (USA) see **ROTE HAND, DIE** • 1960
RED HANDKERCHIEF see **AKAI HANKACHI** • 1964
RED HANGMAN, THE see **BOIA SCARLATTO, IL** • 1965
RED HAWK'S LAST RAID • 1910 • *Kalem* • USA
RED HAWK'S SACRIFICE • 1914 • *Kalem* • USA
RED HEAD AND MA'S SUITORS • 1914 • *Selig* • USA
RED HEAD INTRODUCES HERSELF • 1914 • MacGregor Norval • USA
RED-HEADED BABY • 1931-32 • Ising Rudolf • ANS • USA
RED-HEADED LEAGUE, THE • 1921 • Elvey Maurice • UKN
RED HEADED MONKEY, THE • 1950 • Davis Mannie • ANS • USA
RED-HEADED STRANGER • 1986 • Witliff William • USA
RED-HEADED WOMAN • 1932 • Conway Jack • USA
RED HEART, THE • 1913 • *Crystal* • USA
RED HEAT • 1984 • Collector Robert • USA
RED HEAT • 1988 • Hill Walter • USA
RED HEELS (USA) see **SPIELZEUG VON PARIS, DAS** • 1925
RED HELL • 1962 • Faralla William D. • USA
RED HICKS DEFIES THE WORLD • 1913 • Henderson Dell • USA
RED HORNET, THE see **CHINESE RING, THE** • 1947
RED HORSE, THE see **CRVENIOT KONJ** • 1981
RED HORSES WIN THE RACE, THE see **RODE HESTE VINDER LOBET, DE** • 1968
RED HOT • 1989 • Haggis Paul • USA
RED HOT see **USIJANJE** • 1979
RED, HOT AND BLUE • 1949 • Farrow John • USA
RED, HOT AND SEXY see **BEACH BUNNIES** • 1977
RED HOT BULLETS • 1927 • Roberts Stephen • SHT • USA
RED-HOT COURTSHIP, A • 1912 • *Lubin* • USA
RED HOT DOLLARS • 1919 • Storm Jerome • USA
RED HOT FINISH, A • 1920 • Watson William • SHT • USA
RED HOT HOOFS • 1926 • De Lacy Robert • USA
RED HOT HOTTENTOTTS • 1920 • Roach Hal • SHT • USA
RED HOT IN BED (UKN) see **HARLIS** • 1975
RED HOT LEATHER • 1926 • Rogell Albert S. • USA
RED HOT MAMA • 1934 • Fleischer Dave • ANS • USA
RED HOT MUSIC • 1937 • Davis Mannie, Gordon George • ANS • USA
RED HOT RANGERS • 1947 • Avery Tex • ANS • USA
RED HOT RHYTHM • 1929 • McCarey Leo • USA
RED HOT RIDING HOOD • 1943 • Avery Tex • ANS • USA
RED HOT RILEY (UKN) see **LIFE OF RILEY, THE** • 1927
RED HOT ROMANCE • 1922 • Fleming Victor • USA
RED HOT ROMANCE, A • 1913 • Sennett Mack • USA
RED HOT SPEED • 1929 • Henabery Joseph • USA
RED HOT TIRES • 1925 • Kenton Erle C. • USA
RED HOT TIRES • 1935 • Lederman D. Ross • USA • RACING LUCK (UKN)
RED HOT TRAIL, THE • 1920 • Wright Mack V. • SHT • USA
RED HOT ZORRO • 1973 • Roussel Gilbert • FRN
RED HOUSE, THE • 1947 • Daves Delmer • USA • NO TRESPASSING
RED INDIAN, THE see **INDIANER, DER** • 1988
RED INGLE AND HIS NATURAL SEVEN • 1948 • Cowan Will • SHT • USA
RED INK see **VOROS TINTA** • 1959
RED INK TRAGEDY • 1912 • *Bunny John* • USA
RED INN, THE see **AUBERGE ROUGE, L'** • 1950
RED INN, THE (USA) see **AUBERGE ROUGE, L'** • 1923
RED KIMONO • 1925 • Lang Walter • USA
RED KISS (USA) see **ROUGE BAISER** • 1986
RED LANE, THE • 1920 • Reynolds Lynn • USA
RED LANTERN, THE • 1919 • Capellani Albert • USA
RED LANTERNS (USA) see **KOKKINA PHANARIA** • 1962
RED-LETTER DAYS see **UNNEPNAPOK** • 1967
RED LIE, THE • 1916 • Julian Rupert • SHT • USA
RED LIGHT • 1949 • Del Ruth Roy • USA
RED LIGHT see **SOMEWHERE I'LL FIND YOU** • 1942
RED LIGHT, THE • 1913 • Buckland Warwick • UKN
RED LIGHT, THE see **SPIONEN FRA TOKIO** • 1910
RED-LIGHT BASES see **AKASEN KICHI** • 1953
RED-LIGHT DISTRICT see **AKASEN KICHI** • 1953
RED-LIGHT DISTRICT see **AKASEN CHITAI** • 1956
RED LIGHT STING, THE • 1984 • Holcomb Rod • TVM • USA • RED-LIGHT STING, THE
RED-LIGHT STING, THE see **RED LIGHT STING, THE** • 1984
RED LIGHT STREET see **KIRMIZI FENER SOKAGI** • 1968
RED LIGHTS • 1923 • Badger Clarence • USA
RED LIGHTS AHEAD • 1937 • Reed Roland • USA
RED LILY, THE • 1924 • Niblo Fred • USA
RED LINE 7000 • 1965 • Hawks Howard • USA
RED LINE, THE see **PUNAINEN VIIVA** • 1959
RED LION see **AKAGE** • 1969
RED LIPS • 1928 • Brown Melville • USA • CREAM OF THE EARTH (UKN) ○ PLASTIC AGE, THE
RED LIPS see **PAINTED LADY, THE** • 1925
RED LIPS see **AKAI KUCHIBIRU IMADA KIEZU** • 1947
RED LIPS see **ROSSETTO, IL** • 1960
RED LIPS, THE see **ROUGE AUX LEVRES, LE** • 1970
RED LIPS (USA) see **LABBRA ROSSE** • 1960
RED LOVE • 1925 • Lewis Edgar • USA
RED MAJESTY • 1929 • Noice Harold • DOC • USA
RED MAN, THE • 1909 • *World Film* • USA
RED MAN COMETH • 1970 • *Able Film Co.* • USA
RED MAN'S BURDEN, THE • 1912 • Merwin Bannister • USA
RED MAN'S GRATITUDE, A • 1911 • *Bison* • USA
RED MAN'S HEART, A • 1914 • *Majestic* • USA
RED MAN'S HONOR, THE • 1910 • *Pathe* • USA
RED MAN'S LOVE, A • 1909 • *Powers* • USA
RED MAN'S LOVE, A • 1912 • *Chester Virginia* • USA
RED MAN'S PENALTY, THE • 1911 • *Bison* • USA
RED MAN'S WAY, THE • 1910 • *Selig* • USA
RED MAN'S WRATH, THE • 1911 • *Bison* • USA
RED MANTLE, THE see **RODA KAPPAN, DEN** • 1967
RED MARGARET, MOONSHINER • 1913 • Dwan Allan • USA

RED MARK, THE • 1928 • Cruze James • USA
RED MARK OF MADNESS, THE see **ROSSO SEGNO DELLA FOLLIA, IL** • 1969
RED MASK see **KIZIL MASKE** • 1968
RED MASK see **KIZIL MASKE** • 1968
RED MASK, THE • 1913 • *Ray Charles* • USA
RED MAY see **VOROS MAJUS** • 1968
RED MEADOWS • 1966 • Lotyanu Emil • USS • RED GLADES, THE
RED MEADOWS (USA) see **RODE ENGE, DE** • 1945
RED MEAT see **I LOVED A WOMAN** • 1933
RED MEN TELL NO TALES • 1931 • Buzzell Edward • SHT • USA
RED MENACE, THE • 1949 • Springsteen R. G. • USA • ENEMY WITHIN, THE (UKN)
RED MILL, THE • 1926 • Arbuckle Roscoe • USA
RED MONARCH • 1983 • Gold Jack • TVM • USA
RED MORNING • 1935 • Fox Wallace • USA • GIRL OF THE ISLANDS ○ KARA
RED MOUNTAIN • 1951 • Dieterle William, Farrow John (U/c) • USA
RED NECK COUNTY • 1975 • Robinson Richard • USA • HOOTCH COUNTY BOYS, THE ○ HEARTBREAK MOTEL ○ REDNECK COUNTY ○ POOR PRETTY EDDIE
RED NICHOLS AND HIS FIVE PENNIES • 1950 • Cowan Will • SHT • USA
RED NICHOLS AND HIS WORLD FAMOUS PENNIES • 1936 • Henabery Joseph • SHT • USA
RED NIGHTS • 1987 • Hanooka Itzhak • USA
RED NIGHTS OF THE GESTAPO, THE see **LUNGHE NOTTI DELLA GESTAPO, LE** • 1977
RED NOSES • 1932 • Horne James W. • USA
RED NOVEMBER see **ROTE NOVEMBER, DER** • 1968
RED OLD HILLS OF GEORGIA, THE • 1913 • *Edison* • USA
RED ORCHIDS (USA) see **ROTE ORCHIDEEN** • 1938
RED OVER RED see **COME SPY WITH ME** • 1967
RED PADDY see **SEMERAH PADI**
RED PANTIES see **AKAI PANTI** • 1959
RED PARTISANS see **KRASNYE PARTIZANY** • 1924
RED PEACOCK see **BENI-KUJAKO** • 1955
RED PEACOCK, THE (USA) see **ARME VIOLETTA** • 1920
RED PEARLS • 1930 • Forde Walter • UKN
RED PEONY GAMBLER, THE see **HIBOTAN BAKUTO** • 1968
RED PERIL see **KIZIL TEHLIKE** • 1967
RED PIERS see **JOTAI SAMBASHI** • 1959
RED PLAIN see **DASHTE SORKH** • 1968
RED PLANET MARS • 1952 • Horner Harry • USA • MIRACLE FROM MARS
RED PLANET MARS see **MISSION MARS** • 1968
RED PLEASURE see **AKAI KAIRAKU** • 1968
RED PONY, THE • 1949 • Milestone Lewis • USA
RED PONY, THE • 1973 • Totten Robert • TVM • USA
RED POPPIES FROM ISSYK-KUL • 1973 • Shamshiev Bolotbek • USS • RED POPPIES OF ISSYK-KUL, THE
RED POPPIES OF ISSYK-KUL, THE see **RED POPPIES FROM ISSYK-KUL** • 1973
RED POSTER, THE see **AFFICHE ROUGE, L'** • 1977
RED POTTAGE • 1918 • Milton Meyrick • UKN
RED PRESNYA see **KRASNAYA PRESNYA** • 1926
RED PSALM (UKN) see **MEG KER A NEP** • 1971
RED PURSE (USA) see **PIROS BUGYELLARIS** • 1939
RED RAIDERS, THE • 1927 • Rogell Albert S. • USA
RED RAIN see **JACK'S BACK** • 1988
RED, RED HEART, THE • 1918 • Lucas Wilfred • USA
RED REQUIEM see **VOROS REKVIEM** • 1975
RED RIDER, THE • 1920 • SER • USA
RED RIDER, THE • 1925 • Smith Cliff • USA • OPEN TRAIL, THE
RED RIDER, THE • 1934 • Landers Lew • SRL • USA
RED RIDERS OF CANADA • 1928 • De Lacy Robert • USA
RED RIDING HOOD • 1931 • Foster John, Bailey Harry • ANS • USA
RED RIDING HOOD • Miler Zdenek • ANS • CZC
RED RIDING HOOD see **LITTLE RED RIDING HOOD** • 1987
RED RIDING HOOD OF THE HILLS • 1914 • *Essanay* • USA
RED RIDING HOOD RIDES AGAIN • 1941 • Marcus Sid • ANS • USA
RED RIDING HOOD (USA) see **PETIT CHAPERON ROUGE, LE** • 1901
RED RIDING HOODLUM • 1957 • Smith Paul J. • ANS • USA
RED RIDING HOODWINKED • 1955 • Freleng Friz • ANS • USA
RED RIDINGHOOD AND THE WOLF • 1926 • *Dilley Perry Jay (P)* • ANS • USA
RED RINGS OF FEAR see **ENIGMA ROSSO** • 1978
RED RIVER • 1948 • Hawks Howard • USA
RED RIVER • 1985 • Lavut Martin • MTV • CND
RED RIVER • 1988 • Michaels Richard • TVM • USA
RED RIVER -BLACK SHEEP see **KIZILIRMAK -KARAKOYOUN** • 1967
RED RIVER RANGE • 1939 • Sherman George • USA
RED RIVER RENEGADES • 1946 • Carr Thomas • USA
RED RIVER ROBIN HOOD • 1942 • Selander Lesley • USA
RED RIVER SHORE • 1953 • Keller Harry • USA
RED RIVER VALLEY • 1936 • Eason B. Reeves • USA
RED RIVER VALLEY • 1941 • Kane Joseph • USA
RED ROCK OUTLAW • 1950 • Pond Elmer S. • USA
RED ROCKET • 1987 • Strayer Colin • DCS • CND
RED ROOF, THE see **LANGKHA DEANG** • 1987
RED ROOF OF EATOHARB, THE see **ITOHABU NO AKAI YANE** • 1977
RED ROPE, THE • 1937 • Luby S. Roy • USA
RED ROSE • 1982 • IND
RED ROSE see **MAWAR MERAH** • 1987
RED ROSE, THE see **ROSE OF BLOOD, THE** • 1917
RED ROSE, THE see **BARON AND THE ROSE, THE** • 1940
RED ROSE, THE see **ROSA ROSSA, LA** • 1973
RED ROSE STANDS FOR SADNESS, BLACK ROSE FOR LOVE • 1989 • Soloviev Sergei • USS
RED ROSES FOR THE FUHRER see **ROSE ROSSE PER IL FUHRER** • 1968
RED ROSES OF PASSION • 1967 • Sarno Joe • USA
RED ROWANBERRIES see **JARZEBINA CZERWONA** • 1969
RED RUNS THE RIVER • 1963 • Stenholm Katherine • USA
RED SAILS see **ALYE PARUSA** • 1961
RED SALUTE • 1935 • Lanfield Sidney • USA • ARMS AND THE GIRL (UKN) ○ HER ENLISTED MAN ○ RUNAWAY DAUGHTER
RED SAMSON, THE see **VOROS SAMSON, A** • 1917
RED SANDS, THE • 1969 • Khamraev Ali, Akbarkhodzhaev K. • USS
RED SATURDAY see **BLOODY KIDS** • 1980
RED SAUNDERS PLAYS CUPID see **FIGHTING GRINGO, THE** • 1917
RED SAUNDERS' SACRIFICE • 1912 • *Williams Clara* • USA
RED SCARF, THE see **SELVI BOYLUM AL YAZMALIM** • 1979
RED SCORPION • 1989 • Zito Joseph • USA
RED SEA ADVENTURE • 1952 • Haas Hans • FRG • UNDER THE RED SEA
RED SHADOW, THE • 1932 • Neumann Kurt • SHT • USA
RED SHED, THE see **CERVENA KULNA** • 1968
RED SHEIK, THE (USA) see **SCEICCO ROSSO, LO** • 1962
RED SHIRTS see **CAMICIE ROSSE** • 1952
RED SHOES • 1985 • Kroeker Allan • MTV • CND
RED SHOES, THE • 1948 • Powell Michael, Pressburger Emeric • UKN
RED SHOES, THE • 1970 • Bonniere Rene • SHT • CND
RED SIGNALS • 1927 • McGowan J. P. • USA
RED SKELETON • 1921 • Hai Fang Kwan • CHN
RED SKIES OF MONTANA • 1952 • Newman Joseph M., Hathaway Henry (U/c) • USA • SMOKE JUMPERS
RED SKY AT MORNING • 1944 • Arthur Hartney • ASL
RED SKY AT MORNING • 1970 • Goldstone James • USA • THAT SAME SUMMER
RED SNOW • 1952 • Petroff Boris L. • USA
RED SNOW-BALL TREE, THE see **KALINA KRASNAYA** • 1974
RED SONG see **MEG KER A NEP** • 1971
RED SONJA • 1985 • Fleischer Richard • USA
RED SORGHUM see **HONG GAOLIANG** • 1987
RED SPIDER, THE • 1988 • Jameson Jerry • TVM • USA
RED SPIDERS, THE • 1914 • *Warner'S Features* • USA
RED SPORT ON THE MARCH see **ROTSPORT MARSCHIERT** • 1930
RED SQUARE • 1964 • Kandelaki Gela • SHT • USS
RED SQUARE see **KRASNAYA PLOSHAD** • 1971
RED STAIN see **RUDA STOPA** • 1963
RED STAIN, THE • 1913 • UKN
RED STAIN, THE • 1917 • Cochrane George • SHT • USA
RED STALLION, THE • 1947 • Selander Lesley • USA
RED STALLION IN THE ROCKIES • 1949 • Murphy Ralph • USA
RED STAR HIDDEN BY THE MOON, THE see **MEGHEY DHAAKA TAARA** • 1959
RED STAR INN, THE • 1909 • Melies Gaston • USA
RED STAR'S HONOR • 1911 • *Powers* • USA
RED STEPHANO, THE • 1915 • Davis Ulysses • USA
RED SUN (UKN) see **SOLEIL ROUGE** • 1971
RED SUNDOWN • 1956 • Arnold Jack • USA
RED SWEATER, THE see **PULL-OVER ROUGE, LE** • 1979
RED SWEENEY'S DEFEAT • 1913 • Hamilton G. P.? • USA
RED SWEENEY'S MISTAKE • 1913 • *Blackwell Carlyle* • USA
RED SWORD, THE • 1929 • Vignola Robert G. • USA • THREE DAYS TO LIVE (UKN)
RED TANKS • 1942 • Maiman R.
RED TAPE • 1915 • *Ideal* • USA
RED TASSELLED SWORD, THE see **HUNG YING TAO** • 1976
RED TENT, THE see **KRASNAYA PALATKA** • 1969
RED TERROR, THE • 1961 • *Hoffberg Productions* • FRG
RED, THE MEDIATOR • 1914 • *Reliance* • USA
RED, THE RED AND THE RED, THE see **ROUGE, LE ROUGE ET LE ROUGE, LE**
RED THREAD OF MARRIAGE, THE see **TALI MERAH PERKAWINAN** • 1983
RED TIDE, THE see **BLOODTIDE** • 1984
RED TOMAHAWK • 1967 • Springsteen R. G. • USA
RED TOWER, THE see **RODA TORNET, DET** • 1914
RED TRACTOR, THE • 1964 • Tendlar Dave • ANS • USA
RED TRAIL • 1923 • *Swinburne Nora* • USA
RED TRAIL see **RUDA STOPA** • 1963
RED TRAIN, THE (USA) see **TRAIN ROUGE, LE** • 1973
RED TYPE • ANS • UKN
RED VASE, THE see **KIZIL VAZO** • 1961
RED VENGEANCE • 1917 • *Big U* • SHT • USA
RED VIOLIN, THE • 1975 • Kiisk Kaliu • USS
RED VIPER, THE • 1919 • Tyrol Jacques • USA
RED VIRGIN, THE • 1915 • Kent Leon D. • USA
RED WAGON • 1934 • Stein Paul L. • UKN
RED WARNING, THE • 1923 • Bradbury Robert North • USA
RED WATER see **AKAI MIZU** • 1963
RED WEDDING see **NOCES ROUGES, LES** • 1972
RED WHEAT, THE see **CRVENO KLASJE** • 1971
RED, WHITE AND BLACK, THE see **SOUL SOLDIERS** • 1970
RED, WHITE AND BLEW • 1917 • Fahrney Milton • USA
RED, WHITE AND BLUE • 1970 • Baron Allen • USA
RED, WHITE AND BLUE see **ROOKIES** • 1927
RED, WHITE AND BLUE BLOOD • 1918 • Brabin Charles J. • USA
RED, WHITE AND BLUE LINE, THE • 1955 • Ford John • SHT • USA
RED, WHITE AND BOO • 1955 • Sparber I. • ANS • USA
RED, WHITE AND ZERO • 1979 • Brook Peter, Anderson Lindsay, Richardson Tony • UKN
RED WHITSUN see **OLOVENY CHLEB** • 1954
RED WIDOW, THE • 1916 • Durkin James • USA
RED WINE • 1928 • Cannon Raymond • USA • LET'S MAKE WHOOPEE
RED WING AND THE PALEFACE • 1912 • *Wolfe Jane* • USA
RED WING AND THE WHITE GIRL • 1910 • *Bison* • USA
RED WING'S CONSTANCY • 1910 • *Bison* • USA
RED WING'S GRATITUDE • 1909 • Youngdeer James • USA
RED WING'S LOYALTY • 1910 • *Bison* • USA
RED WINS • 1915 • MacGregor Norval • USA
RED WOMAN, THE • 1917 • Hopper E. Mason • USA
RED ZONE see **ZONA ROJA** • 1975
REDADA, LA see **RAZZIA** • 1972
REDBIRD WINS • 1914 • *Rich Vivian* • USA
REDCOAT'S ROMANCE, THE • 1930 • Levigard Josef • SHT • USA
REDDING • 1929 • Franken Mannus • NTH
REDDY'S REDEMPTION • 1911 • *American* • USA
REDEEMED • 1912 • *Majestic* • USA
REDEEMED CLAIM, THE • 1913 • *Anderson Broncho Billy* • USA
REDEEMED CRIMINAL, THE • 1911 • *Essanay* • USA
REDEEMED (USA) see **AS YE REPENT** • 1915
REDEEMER, THE • 1976 • Gochis Constantine S. • USA • REDEEMER.. SON OF SATAN, THE
REDEEMER, THE see **IZBAVITELJ** • 1977
REDEEMER, THE (USA) see **MISTERIOS DEL ROSARIO, LOS** • 1959
REDEEMER.. SON OF SATAN, THE see **REDEEMER, THE** • 1976
REDEEMING LOVE • 1917 • Taylor William D. • USA
REDEEMING SIN, THE • 1925 • Blackton J. Stuart • USA
REDEEMING SIN, THE • 1929 • Bretherton Howard • USA
REDEMPTION • 1909 • Jasset Victorin • FRN
REDEMPTION • 1912 • Jasset Victorin • FRN
REDEMPTION • 1913 • *Thanhouser* • USA
REDEMPTION • 1914 • Brenon Herbert • USA
REDEMPTION • 1916 • *Buffalo* • SHT • USA
REDEMPTION • 1917 • Steger Julius, Golden Joseph A. • USA
REDEMPTION • 1930 • Niblo Fred • USA
REDEMPTION • 1947 • Grezhov B. • BUL
REDEMPTION, THE • 1912 • *Reliance* • USA
REDEMPTION, THE • 1913 • *Kalem* • USA
REDEMPTION OF A COWARD, THE • 1911 • *Champion* • USA
REDEMPTION OF A PAL, THE • 1914 • Otto Henry • USA
REDEMPTION OF A RETAILER • 1961 • Sewell Bill • UKN
REDEMPTION OF BEN FARLAND, THE • 1912 • *Burns Robert* • USA
REDEMPTION OF BRONCHO BILLY, THE • 1913 • *Anderson Broncho Billy* • USA
REDEMPTION OF DAVE DARCEY, THE • 1916 • Scardon Paul • USA
REDEMPTION OF DAVID CORSON, THE • 1914 • *Farnum William* • USA
REDEMPTION OF "GREEK JOE", THE • 1912 • *Mong William* • USA
REDEMPTION OF HELENE, THE • 1916 • Sloman Edward • SHT • USA
REDEMPTION OF HIS NAME, THE • 1918 • Moran Percy • UKN
REDEMPTION OF RAILROAD JACK, THE • 1913 • Martin E. A. • USA
REDEMPTION OF RAWHIDE, THE • 1911 • Melies Gaston • USA
REDEMPTION OF RED MULLIN, THE • 1917 • Thayer Otis B. • SHT • USA
REDEMPTION OF RED RUBE, THE • 1912 • *Thornby Robert* • USA
REDEMPTION OF RIVERTON, THE • 1912 • *Lawrence Florence* • USA
REDEMPTION OF SLIVERS, THE • 1912 • *Calvert E. H.* • USA
REDEMPTION OF THE JASON, THE • 1915 • Cooley Frank • USA
REDEMPTION OF WHITE HAWK, THE • 1912 • *Bison* • USA
REDENZIONE • 1915 • Gallone Carmine • ITL
REDENZIONE • 1942 • Albani Marcello • ITL
REDENZIONE • 1952 • Casserini Piero • ITL
REDENZIONE, LA • 1958 • Chiarissi Vincenzo • DOC • ITL
REDES • 1934 • Zinnemann Fred, Gomez Muriel Emilio • MXC • PESCADOS ○ WAVE, THE ○ NETS
REDEZCUBRIMIENTO DE MEXICO, EL • 1977 • Cortes Fernando • MXC
REDHEAD • 1919 • Maigne Charles • USA
REDHEAD • 1934 • Brown Melville • USA
REDHEAD • 1941 • Cahn Edward L. • USA
REDHEAD see **PUNATUKKA** • 1970
REDHEAD, THE (USA) see **ROTE, DIE** • 1962
REDHEAD AND THE COWBOY, THE • 1950 • Fenton Leslie • USA
REDHEAD FROM MANHATTAN • 1943 • Landers Lew • USA
REDHEAD FROM WYOMING, THE • 1952 • Sholem Lee • USA • CATTLE KATE
REDHEAD (USA) see **POIL DE CAROTTE** • 1932
REDHEADS ON PARADE • 1935 • McLeod Norman Z. • USA
REDHEADS PREFERRED • 1926 • Dale Allan • USA
REDINGOTE, LA • 1908 • Perret Leonce • FRN
REDL EZREDES (HNG) see **OBERST REDL** • 1985
REDMAN AND THE CHILD, THE • 1908 • Griffith D. W. • USA
REDMAN AND THE RENEGADES, THE • 1956 • Newfield Sam • MTV • CND • REDMEN AND THE RENEGADES, THE
REDMAN'S DEVOTION, A • 1910 • *Bison* • USA
REDMAN'S FRIENDSHIP, A • 1912 • *Pathe* • USA
REDMAN'S LOYALTY, A • 1912 • *Gerhardt George* • USA
REDMAN'S PERSECUTION, THE • 1910 • *Bison* • USA
REDMAN'S VIEW, THE • 1909 • Griffith D. W. • USA
REDMEN AND THE RENEGADES, THE see **REDMAN AND THE RENEGADES, THE** • 1956
REDNECK • 1972 • Narizzano Silvio • UKN, ITL • SENZA RAGIONE (ITL)
REDNECK COUNTY see **RED NECK COUNTY** • 1975
REDNESS OF THE LIPS, THE see **ROUGE AUX LEVRES, LE** • 1970
REDONDO • 1985 • Busteros Raul • MXC • ROUND
REDRESS, THE see **DESFORRA, A** • 1967
REDS • 1981 • Beatty Warren • USA • JOHN READ AND LOUISE BRYANT STORY, THE
RED'S CONQUEST • 1911 • *Selig* • USA
REDSKIN • 1929 • Schertzinger Victor • USA
REDSKIN BLUES • 1932 • Foster John, Stallings George • ANS • USA
REDSKIN RAIDERS, THE • 1912 • *Kalem* • USA
REDSKIN RECKONING, A • 1914 • *Bison* • USA
REDSKIN RHUMBA • 1948 • Cowan Will • SHT • USA
REDSKINS AND REDHEADS • 1941 • D'Arcy Harry • SHT • USA
REDSKINS AND THE RENEGADES, THE • 1914 • *Darkfeather Mona* • USA
REDSKIN'S APPEAL, A • 1912 • *Gebhardt George* • USA
REDSKIN'S BRAVERY, A • 1911 • *Bison* • USA
REDSKIN'S MERCY, A • 1913 • *Patheplay* • USA

REDSKIN'S OFFER, THE see **RANCH OWNER'S DAUGHTER, THE** • 1909
REDSKIN'S SECRET, THE • 1911 • *Bison* • USA
REDTOPS AND TYRANNOS, THE see **RODTOTTERNE OG TYRANNOS** • 1988
REDUCING • 1930 • Reisner Charles F. • USA
REDUCING • 1952 • Barclay David • SHT • USA
REDUCING CREME • 1934 • *Iwerk Ub (P)* • ANS • USA
REDWING • 1908 • Gilbert Arthur • UKN
REDWOOD FOREST TRAIL • 1950 • Ford Philip • USA
REDWOOD LANE • 1916 • Hunt Jay • USA
REDWOOD SAP • 1951 • Lantz Walter • ANS • USA
REED • 1966 • Mesaros Titus • DOC • RMN
REED, THE • 1960 • Abesadze Otar • SHT • USS
REED CASE, THE • 1917 • Holubar Allen • USA
REED DOLLS see **POUPEES DE ROSEAU** • 1981
REED MEXICO INSURGENT see **REED, MEXICO INSURGENTE** • 1971
REED, MEXICO INSURGENTE • 1971 • Leduc Paul • MXC • REED MEXICO INSURGENT ○ JOHN REED
REEDS AT THE FOOT OF THE MOUNTAIN see **GAOSHANXIADE HUA HUAN** • 1985
REEDS THAT RUSTLE IN THE WIND see **KAZE NI SOYOGU ASHI** • 1951
REEF, THE • 1976 • Heyer John • DOC • ASL
REEF OF STARS, THE • 1924 • SAF
REEFER AND THE MODEL • 1988 • Comerford Joe • IRL
REEFER MADNESS see **BURNING QUESTION, THE** • 1940
REEL BOAT • 1981 • Ohlsson Terry • SHT • ASL
REEL DES OUVRIERS • 1976-77 • Brault Michel, Gladu Andre • DCS • CND
REEL EATER, THE • 1958 • *Johnson Dave* • SHT • USA
REEL HORROR • 1985 • Hagen Ross, Hagen Claire • USA
REEL O' LAFFS • 1920 • MacCullough Jack • USA
REEL REDSKINS • 1916 • *Unicorn* • USA
REEL VIRGINIAN, THE • 1924 • *Sennett Mack (P)* • SHT • USA • WEST VIRGINIAN, THE
REEN KOM WEER, DIE • 1963 • SAF
REET, PETITE AND GONE • 1947 • Crouch William Forest • SHT • USA
REFEREE • 1920 • *Franey William* • USA
REFEREE, THE • 1922 • Ince Ralph • USA
REFERENCE • 1986 • Hristov Hristo • BUL
REFERENDUM • 1953 • Garceau Raymond • DCS • CND • TEMPEST IN TOWN
REFERENDUM • 1962 • Rachedi Ahmed • ALG
REFIFI ENTRE LAS MUJERES • 1956 • Cortes Fernando • MXC
REFINERIA NACIONAL DE MORON • 1974 • Camacho Carlos Antonio • DOC • VNZ
REFINERY, THE see **TASFIE-KHANEH** • 1978
REFINING FIRES • 1915 • Pollard Harry? • USA
REFLECTING SKIN, THE • 1989 • Ridley Phillip • UKN
REFLECTION see **ZRCADLENI** • 1965
REFLECTION OF A DESIRE see **REFLEJO DE UN DESEO** • 1986
REFLECTION OF FEAR, A • 1973 • Fraker William A. • USA • LABYRINTH ○ AUTUMN CHILD
REFLECTIONS • 1973 • Ricketson James • SHT • ASL
REFLECTIONS • 1984 • Billington Kevin • UKN
REFLECTIONS see **ZRCADLENI** • 1965
REFLECTIONS see **TUKORKEPEK** • 1976
REFLECTIONS FROM THE FIRELIGHT • 1912 • *Imp* • USA
REFLECTIONS IN A GOLDEN EYE • 1967 • Huston John • USA
REFLECTIONS IN A MIRROR see **TUKORKEPEK** • 1976
REFLECTIONS NO.11 • 1951 • Davis James* • SHT • USA
REFLECTIONS OF MURDER • 1974 • Badham John • TVM • USA
REFLECTIONS OF NEW YORK • 1963 • Radkai Paul • SHT • USA
REFLECTIONS ON A LEADERSHIP CONVENTION • 1977 • Raymont Peter • DOC • CND
REFLECTIONS ON BLACK • 1955 • Brakhage Stan • SHT • USA
REFLECTIONS ON LIGHT AND SPEED see **REFLETS DE LUMIERE ET DE VITESSE** • 1925
REFLECTIVE • 1985 • Jackson G. Philip • MTV • CND
REFLEJO DE UN DESEO • 1986 • Soto Ivonne Maria • PRC • REFLECTION OF A DESIRE
REFLET DE CLAUDE MERCOEUR, LE • 1923 • Duvivier Julien • FRN
REFLETS DE LUMIERE ET DE VITESSE • 1925 • Chomette Henri • SHT • FRN • REFLECTIONS ON LIGHT AND SPEED
REFLEXFILM • 1947 • Roos Jorgen • DOC • DNM
REFLEXION • 1971 • Jahn Sepp, Hirsch Edith • AUS
REFLEXION SUR LA GUERRE DU VIETNAM • 1967 • Fettar Sid-Ali • ALG
REFLEXION SUR UN VOYAGE see **INDE FANTOME, L'** • 1969
REFLUX • 1961 • Gegauff Paul • FRN
REFORM see **LIFE'S MOCKERY** • 1928
REFORM CANDIDATE, THE • 1911 • *Brower Robert* • USA
REFORM CANDIDATE, THE • 1914 • *Johnstone Lamar* • USA
REFORM CANDIDATE, THE • 1915 • Lloyd Frank • USA
REFORM GIRL • 1933 • Newfield Sam • USA
REFORM SCHOOL • 1939 • Popkin Leo C. • USA
REFORM SCHOOL GIRL • 1957 • Bernds Edward • USA
REFORM SCHOOL GIRLS • 1986 • Desimone Tom • USA
REFORMA AGRARIA EN MARCHA, LA • 1974 • Scheuren Jose Vicente • DOC • VNZ
REFORMATION • 1915 • Otto Henry • USA
REFORMATION, THE • 1913 • *Broncho* • USA
REFORMATION, THE • 1913 • *Kb* • USA
REFORMATION, THE see **LAEREAAR, ET** • 1914
REFORMATION DELAYED, A • 1916 • Mayo Melvin • USA
REFORMATION OF CALLIOPE, THE • 1913 • *Eclair* • USA
REFORMATION OF CHRISTOPHER WINKLE, THE • 1914 • *Searchlight* • UKN
REFORMATION OF DAD, THE • 1913 • Parker Lem B. • USA
REFORMATION OF DOG HOLE, THE • 1916 • Horne James W. • SHT • USA
REFORMATION OF HAM, THE • 1914 • Neilan Marshall • USA
REFORMATION OF JACK ROBBINS, THE • 1911 • Melies Gaston • USA
REFORMATION OF KID HOGAN, THE • 1912 • *Hawley Ormi* • USA
REFORMATION OF MARY, THE • 1912 • *Solax* • USA
REFORMATION OF PETER AND PAUL, THE • 1915 • *Thanhouser* • USA
REFORMATION OF ST. JULES, THE • 1949 • Gilkison Anthony • UKN
REFORMATION OF SIERRA SMITH • 1912 • Dwan Allan • USA • LOST WATCH, THE
REFORMATION OF THE GANG, THE see **GANG, THE** • 1914
REFORMATORY • 1938 • Collins Lewis D. • USA • ORPHANS OF THE LAW
REFORMATORY see **ZAKIAD** • 1990
REFORMED BY STRATEGY • 1912 • *Comet* • USA
REFORMED OUTLAW, THE • 1912 • *101 Bison* • USA
REFORMED OUTLAW, THE • 1913 • Fielding Romaine • USA
REFORMED SANTA CLAUS, A • 1911 • *Vitagraph* • USA
REFORMED WOLF • 1954 • Rasinski Connie • ANS • USA
REFORMER, THE • 1915 • Middleton Edwin • USA
REFORMER, THE see **YAKUSA SENSEI** • 1960
REFORMER AND THE REDHEAD, THE • 1950 • Panama Norman, Frank Melvin • USA
REFORMERS, THE • 1916 • *Hardy Babe* • SHT • USA
REFORMERS, OR THE LOST ART OF MINDING ONE'S BUSINESS, THE • 1913 • Griffith D. W. • USA
REFORMES DE PORTENT BIEN, LES • 1979 • Clair Philippe • FRN
REFORMING A HUSBAND • 1909 • *Lubin* • USA
REFORMING RUBBERING ROSIE • 1916 • *Cunningham Arthur* • USA
REFORMING THE OUTLAW • 1915 • *Alhambra* • USA
REFRACTIONS NO.1 • 1951 • Davis James* • SHT • USA
REFRAINS POPULAIRES DE PODDOUBNO • 1957 • Rappaport Herbert • USS
REFRESHER COURSE FOR WIVES see **NYOBO GAKKO** • 1961
REFRIGERATOR CAR'S CAPTIVE, THE • 1914 • *Kalem* • USA
REFUGE • 1915 • Matthews H. C. • USA
REFUGE • 1923 • Schertzinger Victor • USA
REFUGE see **ZUFLUCHT** • 1928
REFUGE, LE • 1930 • Mathot Leon • FRN
REFUGE, THE • 1910 • *Reliance* • USA
REFUGE ENGLAND • 1959 • Vas Robert • SHT • UKN
REFUGE OF FEAR (UKN) see **REFUGIO DEL MIEDO, EL** • 1973
REFUGEE • 1963 • Ernst Franz • SHT • DNM
REFUGEE • 1983 • Srichue Siwat • THL • VIETNAM COMMANDOS
REFUGEE see **BOMEI KI** • 1955
REFUGEE, THE • 1915 • *Thanhouser* • USA
REFUGEE, THE • 1918 • Hepworth Cecil M. • UKN
REFUGEE, THE • 1940 • Vorhaus Bernard • USA • THREE FACES WEST
REFUGEE FROM DEAD CAVE see **REFUGIADOS DE LA CUEVA DEL MUERTE, LOS** • 1983
REFUGEES see **FLUCHTLINGE** • 1933
REFUGEES, THE • 1915 • MacMackin Archer • USA
REFUGEES IN MADRID see **REFUGIADOS EN MADRID** • 1938
REFUGES • 1963 • Languepin Jean-Jacques, Vernadet R. • SHT • FRN
REFUGIADOS DE LA CUEVA DEL MUERTE, LOS • 1983 • Alvarez Santiago • CUB • REFUGEE FROM DEAD CAVE
REFUGIADOS EN MADRID • 1938 • Galindo Alejandro • MXC • REFUGEES IN MADRID
REFUGIO DEL MIEDO, EL • 1973 • Ulloa Jose • SPN • REFUGE OF FEAR (UKN) ○ SURVIVORS OF THE LAST RACE
REFUSAL, THE see **FALL JAGERSTATTER, DER** • 1972
REFUSE • 1981 • Danielsson Tage • SWD
REGAIN • 1937 • Pagnol Marcel • FRN • HARVEST (USA) ○ ARSULE
REGAINED REPUTATION, A • 1913 • *Reliance* • USA
REGAINING THE WIND • 1926 • Miller Frank • UKN
REGAL CAVALCADE (USA) see **ROYAL CAVALCADE** • 1935
REGALO DE NAVIDAD • 1967 • Cosmi Carlo • VNZ • CHRISTMAS PRESENT
REGALO DE REYES • 1942 • del Rio Mario • MXC
REGALO DE REYES, EL • 1919 • Buchs Jose, Roesset Julio • SPN
REGALO DI NATALE • 1987 • Avati Pupi • ITL • CHRISTMAS PRESENT
REGAN'S DAUGHTER • 1914 • Marston Theodore • USA
REGARD, LE • 1912 • Fescourt Henri • FRN
REGARD, LE • 1976 • Hanoun Marcel • FRN • EXTASE
REGARD DE LA MAIN • 1972 • Bouguermouh Abderrahmane • ALG
REGARD DE L'ARTISTE, LE see **NADHRATU AL-FANNAN** • 1970
REGARD DES AUTRES, LE • 1980 • Solanas Fernando • DOC • FRN
REGARD PICASSO, LE • 1967 • Kaplan Nelly • FRN • PICASSO LOOK, THE
REGARD SUR LA FOLIE • 1962 • Ruspoli Mario • DOC • FRN • LOOK AT MADNESS
REGARDE, ELLE A LES YEUX GRANDS OUVERTS • 1979 • Le Masson Yann • DOC • FRN
REGARDE SUR LE MONDE, UN • Chalais Francois • DOC • FRN
REGARDING VASSILIS • 1987 • Tsiolis Stavros • GRC
REGARDS SUR LA BELGIQUE ANCIENNE • 1936 • Storck Henri • DOC • BLG
REGARDS SUR LE PAKISTAN • 1959 • Kast Pierre • SHT • FRN
REGARDS SUR L'INDOCHINE • 1954 • Rouy • SHT • FRN
REGARDS SUR L'OCCULTISME • 1965 • Cote Guy-L. • DOC • CND
REGATA TORBAY-CASCAIS, A • 1943 • Ribeiro Antonio Lopes • SHT • PRT
REGATES DE SAN FRANCISCO, LES • 1959 • Autant-Lara Claude • FRN, ITL
REGATTAFURST, DER • 1923 • Wenter Adolf • FRG
REGEMENTETS ROS • 1952 • Jarrel Bengt • SWD • ROSE OF THE REGIMENT
REGEN • 1929 • Ivens Joris, Franken Mannus • NTH • RAIN (USA)
REGENERATES, THE • 1917 • Hopper E. Mason • USA
REGENERATING LOVE, THE • 1915 • Terwilliger George W. • USA
REGENERATION • 1911 • *Gardner Helen* • USA
REGENERATION • 1912 • *St. Louis Motion Picture* • USA
REGENERATION • 1914 • *Kalem* • USA
REGENERATION • 1914 • Reid Wallace • *Powers* • USA
REGENERATION • 1923 • *Mayo Stella* • USA
REGENERATION • 1988 • Stephens Russel • CND
REGENERATION, THE • 1910 • *American* • USA
REGENERATION, THE • 1915 • Walsh Raoul • USA
REGENERATION ISLE see **LOVE'S REDEMPTION** • 1921
REGENERATION OF APACHE KID • 1911 • *Selig* • USA
REGENERATION OF FATHER, THE see **REJUVENATION OF FATHER, THE** • 1910
REGENERATION OF JIM HALSEY, THE • 1916 • Campbell Colin • SHT • USA
REGENERATION OF JOHN STORM, THE • 1913 • *Prescott Vivian* • USA
REGENERATION OF MARGARET, THE • 1916 • Brabin Charles J. • SHT • USA
REGENERATION OF NANCY, THE • 1913 • *Lubin* • USA
REGENERATION OF REGINALD, THE • 1917 • *Herz Ralph* • SHT • USA
REGENERATION OF WORTHLESS DAN, THE • 1912 • *Nestor* • USA
REGENERATOR • 1986 • Eastman G. L. • USA
REGENSCHIRME VON CHERBOURG, DIE (FRG) see **PARAPLUIES DE CHERBOURG, LES** • 1964
REGENT, THE see **REGENTA, LA** • 1974
REGENTA, LA • 1974 • Suarez Gonzalo • SPN • REGENT, THE
REGENT'S PARK MYSTERY, THE • 1924 • Croise Hugh • UKN
REGGAE • 1971 • Ove Horace • DOC • UKN
REGGAE A L'HEURE H. • 1959 • Herman Jean • FRN
REGGAE SUNSPLASH • 1980 • Paul Stephan • FRG, JMC
REGGIA SUL FIUME, LA • 1940 • Salvi Alberto • ITL
REGGIE BREAKS THE COLLEGE RULES • 1912 • *Comet* • USA
REGGIE MIXES IN • 1916 • Cabanne W. Christy • USA • MYSTERIES OF NEW YORK (UKN)
REGGIE, THE DAREDEVIL • 1914 • *Ab* • USA
REGGIE, THE SQUAW MAN • 1914 • *Kalem* • USA
REGGIE'S ENGAGEMENT • 1910 • *Lubin* • USA
REGGIMENTO ROYAL CRAVATE, IL • 1922 • Gallone Carmine • ITL
REGG'S AND BACON • 1976 • Stolen Will • UKN
REGI IDOK FOCIJA • 1974 • Sandor Pal • HNG • FOOTBALL OF THE GOOD OLD DAYS
REGICIDE -ANATOMY OF AN ASSASSINATION see **KIRALYGILKOSSAG -EGY MERENYLET ANATOMIAJA** • 1984
REGIME PRISIONAL PORTUGUES • 1954 • Semedo Artur, Mendes Joao • SHT • PRT
REGIME SANS PAIN • 1984 • Ruiz Raul • FRN
REGIMENT, LE • 1896 • Melies Georges • FRN • FRENCH REGIMENT GOING TO THE PARADE
REGIMENT MODERNE, LA • 1906 • Blache Alice • FRN
REGIMENT OF FROCKS AND FRILLS • 1907 • Gilbert Arthur • UKN
REGIMENT OF TWO, A • 1913 • Ince Ralph, Baker George D. • USA
REGIMENTAL BALL, THE • 1911 • *Thanhouser* • USA
REGIMENTAL PALS • 1912 • *Bison* • USA
REGIMENTAL PET, THE see **STOLEN AIRSHIP PLANS, THE** • 1912
REGIMENTSMUSIK • 1945 • Rabenalt Arthur M. • FRG
REGIMENTSTOCHTER, DIE • 1928 • Behrendt Hans • FRG
REGIMENTSTOCHTER, DIE • 1953 • AUS
REGIMENTSTOCHTER, DIE see **TOCHTER DES REGIMENTS, DIE** • 1933
REGINA • 1987 • Piscicelli Salvatore • ITL
REGINA AMSTETTEN • 1954 • Neumann Kurt • FRG
REGINA AND THE MEN see **REGINA JA MIEHET** • 1983
REGINA COELI • 1955 • Haesaerts Paul • BLG
REGINA DEI CANNIBALI, LA • 1979 • Martin Frank • ITL • DR. BUTCHER M.D. (MEDICAL DEVIATE) ○ QUEEN OF THE CANNIBALS ○ MEDICAL DEVIATE ○ ZOMBIE HOLOCAUST ○ ISLAND OF THE LAST ZOMBIES, THE
REGINA DEI TARTARI, LA • 1960 • Grieco Sergio • ITL, FRN • REINE DES BARBARES, LA (FRN) ○ HUNS, THE (USA) ○ QUEEN OF THE TARTARS
REGINA DEL CARBONE, LA • 1919 • Righelli Gennaro • ITL
REGINA DEL DESERTO, LA see **NEL SEGNO DI ROMA** • 1959
REGINA DELLA SCALA • 1937 • Salvini Guido, Mastrocinque Camillo • ITL
REGINA DELLE AMAZZONI, LA • 1960 • Sala Vittorio • ITL • COLOSSUS AND THE AMAZONS (USA) ○ COLOSSUS AND THE AMAZON QUEEN ○ QUEEN OF THE AMAZONS
REGINA DELLE POVERA GENTE, LA • 1958 • Ramirez Pedro L. • ITL, SPN
REGINA DELL'ORO, LA • 1913 • Roberti Roberto Leone • ITL
REGINA DI NAVARRA, LA • 1942 • Gallone Carmine • ITL • ALLEGRA REGINA, L'
REGINA DI SABA, LA • 1952 • Francisci Pietro • ITL • QUEEN OF SHEBA, THE (USA)
REGINA IN BERLINA, CON BONAVENTURA E CENERENTOLA see **CENERENTOLA E IL SIGNOR BONAVENTURA** • 1942
REGINA JA MIEHET • 1983 • Manttari Anssi • FNL • REGINA AND THE MEN
REGINA MARGOT, LA (ITL) see **REINE MARGOT, LA** • 1954
REGINA PER CESARE, UNA • 1963 • Pierotti Piero, Tourjansky Victor • ITL, FRN • QUEEN FOR CAESAR, A (USA)
REGINA VON EMMERITZ AND GUSTAVUS ADOLPHUS see **REGINA VON EMMERITZ OCH GUSTAV II ADOLPH** • 1910
REGINA VON EMMERITZ OCH GUSTAV II ADOLPH • 1910 • Linden Gustaf M. • SWD • REGINA VON EMMERITZ AND GUSTAVUS ADOLPHUS
REGINALD KING AND HIS ORCHESTRA • 1936 • Shepherd Horace • SHT • UKN
REGINALD'S COURTSHIP • 1913 • Williams C. Jay • USA
REGINALD'S REVENGE • 1915 • *Premier* • USA
REGINA'S SECRETS see **RAGINA'S SECRETS** • 1969
REGINE • 1934 • Waschneck Erich • FRG

REGINE • 1956 • Braun Harald • FRG
REGINE, LE see **DELITTO DEL DIAVOLO, IL** • 1970
REGINE, DIE TRAGODIE EINER FRAU • 1927 • Waschneck Erich • FRG
REGION 80 • 1970 • Bulbulian Maurice • DOC • CND
REGION CENTRALE, LA • 1971 • Snow Michael • CND • CENTRAL REGION, THE
REGIONAL PROGRAM • 1972 • Singh Hardev • CND
REGISTERED NURSE • 1934 • Florey Robert • USA
REGISTERED POUCH, THE • 1917 • Morton Walter • USA
REGISTERED WOMAN see **WOMAN OF EXPERIENCE, A** • 1931
REG'LAR FELLERS • 1941 • Dreifuss Arthur • USA
REGLE DE QUATRE, LA • 1975 • Danis Aime • DCS • CND
REGLE DU JEU, LA • 1939 • Renoir Jean • FRN • CAPRICES DE MARIANNE, LES ○ CHASSE EN SOLOGNE, LA ○ RULES OF THE GAME, THE ○ FAIR PLAY
REGLEMENT INTERIEUR, LE • 1980 • Vuillermet Michel • FRN
REGLEMENTS DE COMPTES • 1962 • Chevalier Pierre • FRN
REGLES, RITES • 1982 • Fleischer Alain • FRN
REGN • 1970 • Lokkeberg Vibeke • SHT • NRW • RAIN
REGNE DE KARAKOCHE, LE see **HUKMU KARAKUCH** • 1953
REGNE DU JOUR, LE • 1966 • Perrault Pierre • DOC • CND
REGNO DI NAPOLI see **NEAPOLITANISCHE GESCHWISTER** • 1978
REGOLAMENTO DI CONTI (ITL) see **HOMMES, LES** • 1973
REGRESA UN DESCONOCIDO • 1961 • Bosch Juan • SPN
REGRESO, EL • 1950 • Torres-Rios Leopoldo • ARG
REGRESO AL SILENCIO • 1967 • Kramarenco Naum • CHL • RETURN TO SILENCE
REGRESO DE AL CAPONE, EL • 1969 • Zabalza Jose Maria • SPN
REGRESO DE COMETA, EL • 1988 • Arino Luis • SPN • RETURN OF THE COMET, THE
REGRESO DE LOS SIETE MAGNIFICOS, EL (SPN) see **RETURN OF THE SEVEN** • 1966
REGRESO DE LOS VILLALOBOS, EL see **AQUI ESTAN LOS VILLALOBOS** • 1959
REGRESO DEL AMATEUR DE BIBLIOTECAS, EL • Ruiz Raul • SHT • FRN • RETURN OF THE LIBRARY AMATEUR, THE
REGRESO DEL MONSTRUO, EL • 1959 • Rodriguez Joselito • MXC • RETURN OF THE MONSTER, THE
REGRESSO A TERRA DO SOL • 1966 • Costa Jose Fonseca • SHT • PRT
REGRET see **LITOST** • 1970
REGRETS see **MIREN** • 1963
REGULAR AS CLOCKWORK see **NE JOUEZ PAS AVEC LES MARTIANS** • 1967
REGULAR CUT-UPS • 1919 • Morris Charles • SHT • USA
REGULAR FELLOW, A • 1919 • Cabanne W. Christy • USA
REGULAR FELLOW, A • 1925 • Sutherland A. Edward • USA • HE'S A PRINCE ○ RAIN AND SHINE
REGULAR GIRL, A • 1919 • Young James • USA
REGULAR PAL, A • 1920 • Roach Hal • SHT • USA
REGULAR PATSY, A • 1918 • *Mason Billy* • USA
REGULAR RIP, A • 1914 • Henderson Dell • USA
REGULAR SCOUT, A • 1926 • Kirkland David • USA
REHABILITATED • 1917 • *Kerrigan J. Warren* • USA
REHABILITATION • 1905 • Blache Alice • FRN
REHABILITATION DES HABITATIONS • 1972 • Regnier Michel • DCS • CND
REHEARSAL • 1953 • Blais Roger • DCS • CND • REPETITION
REHEARSAL, THE • 1910 • *Powers* • USA
REHEARSAL, THE • 1915 • MacDonald J. Farrell • USA
REHEARSAL, THE • 1974 • Dassin Jules
REHEARSAL FOR A CRIME see **ENSAYO DE UN CRIMEN** • 1955
REHEARSAL FOR MURDER • 1982 • Greene David • TVM • USA
REHEARSAL FOR SIN see **SHOCKING SEX, THE** • 1964
REHEARSALS FOR EXTINCT ANATOMIES • 1987 • Quay Brothers • ANM • UKN
REHEARSING A PLAY • 1905 • Fitzhamon Lewin • UKN
REHLA ILAL KAMAR • 1959 • Wahab Hamada Abdel • EGY • JOURNEY TO THE MOON
REI DA FORCA, O • 1922 • de Albuquerque Ernesto • PRT
REI DA PILANTRAGEM, O • 1969 • Campos Jacy • BRZ • KING OF TROUBLE, THE
REI DA VELA, O • 1984 • Correa Jose Celso Martinez • BRZ • KING OF THE CANDLE
REI DAS BERLENGAS, O • 1977 • Semedo Artur • PRT • ANJINHOS NAO VOAM, OS ○ KING OF BERLENG, THE ○ ANGELS DON'T FLY
REI PELE, O • 1962 • Christensen Carlos Hugo • ARG
REICH MIR DIE HAND, MEIN LEBEN • 1955 • Hartl Karl • AUS • LIFE AND LOVES OF MOZART, THE (USA)
REICHSGRAFIN GISELA • 1918 • Mendel Georg Victor • FRG
REIFE KIRSCHEN • 1972 • Seemann Horst • GDR
REIFENDE JUGEND • 1933 • Froelich Carl • FRG
REIFENDE JUGEND • 1955 • Erfurth Ulrich • FRG
REIFEZEIT • 1976 • Saless Sohrab Shahid • FRG • COMING OF AGE, THE ○ TIME OF MATURING
REIGATE SQUIRES, THE • 1912 • Treville Georges • UKN
REIGATE SQUIRES, THE • 1922 • Ridgwell George • UKN
REIGEN • 1974 • Schenk Otto • FRG, AUS • DANCE OF LOVE (UKN) ○ RONDE, LA
REIGEN, DER • 1920 • Oswald Richard • FRG • WERDEGANG, EIN
REIGN BEHIND A CURTAIN see **CHUI LIAN TING ZHENG** • 1983
REIGN OF NAPLES, THE see **NEAPOLITANISCHE GESCHWISTER** • 1978
REIGN OF NUMBERS see **WSZYSTKO JEST LICZBA** • 1967
REIGN OF TERROR • 1949 • Mann Anthony • USA • BLACK BOOK, THE
REIGN OF THE VAMPIRE • 1970 • Le Grice Malcolm • UKN
REIGNING BEAUTY, THE see **CH'ING-CH'ENG-CHIH LIEN** • 1984
REIJIN • 1946 • *Hara Setsuko* • JPN • BEAUTY
REILLY: ACE OF SPIES • 1983 • Goddard Jim • MTV • UKN • REILLY: THE ACE OF SPIES
REILLY OF THE RAINBOW DIVISION see **RILEY OF THE RAINBOW DIVISION** • 1928
REILLY: THE ACE OF SPIES see **REILLY: ACE OF SPIES** • 1983
REILLY'S WASH DAY • 1919 • Jones F. Richard • SHT • USA
REIMEI HACHIGATSU JUGO-NICHI • 1952 • Sekigawa Hideo • JPN • DAWN FIFTEENTH OF AUGUST
REIMEI IZEN • 1931 • Kinugasa Teinosuke • JPN • BEFORE DAWN
REIN see **KNUT FORMOS SISTE JAKT** • 1973
REINA BARBARA, LA see **BARBARIAN QUEEN** • 1985
REINA DE LA OPERETA, LA • 1945 • Benavides Jose Jr. • MXC
REINA DE MEXICO, LA • 1940 • Mendez Fernando • MXC
REINA DE REINAS • 1945 • Contreras Torres Miguel • MXC • QUEEN OF QUEENS
REINA DE REINAS see **VIRGEN QUE FORJO UNA PATRIA, LA** • 1942
REINA DEL CHANTECLER, LA • 1962 • Gil Rafael • SPN
REINA DEL CIELO, LA • 1958 • Salvador Jaime • MXC
REINA DEL MAMBO, LA • 1950 • Pereda Ramon • MXC
REINA DEL RIO, LA • 1938 • Cardona Rene • MXC
REINA DEL TABARIN, LA • 1960 • Franco Jesus • SPN
REINA DEL TROPICO, LA • 1945 • de Anda Raul • MXC
REINA MORA, LA • 1922 • Buchs Jose • SPN
REINA MORA, LA • 1936 • Ardavin Eusebio F. • SPN
REINA MORA, LA • 1954 • Alfonso Raul, Ardavin Eusebio F. • SPN
REINA SALVAJE see **BARBARIAN QUEEN** • 1985
REINA SANTA • 1946 • Gil Rafael • SPN
REINA ZANAHORIA • 1978 • Suarez Gonzalo • SPN
REINCARNATE, THE • 1971 • Haldane Don • CND • DARK SIDE, THE
REINCARNATION • 1915 • *La Badie Florence* • USA
REINCARNATION see **PRISONERS OF LOVE** • 1921
REINCARNATION see **UJRAELOK** • 1921
REINCARNATION, THE see **CURSE OF THE CRIMSON ALTAR** • 1968
REINCARNATION, THE see **T'OU-T'AI JEN** • 1976
REINCARNATION DE SERGE RENARDIER, LE • 1921 • Duvivier Julien • FRN
REINCARNATION OF A SOUL, THE • 1913 • *August Edwin* • USA
REINCARNATION OF ISABEL, THE • 1973 • Polselli Renato • ITL • GHASTLY ORGIES OF COUNT DRACULA
REINCARNATION OF KARMA, THE • 1912 • Brooke Van Dyke • USA
REINCARNATION OF PETER PROUD, THE • 1974 • Thompson J. Lee • USA
REINCIDENTE, EL • 1978 • de la Cerda Clemente • VNZ • SOY UN DELINCUENTE II ○ RELAPSE, THE
REINDEER see **KNUT FORMOS SISTE JAKT** • 1973
REINDEER PEOPLE see **SARVTID** • 1943
REINDEER TIME see **SARVTID** • 1943
REINE DE BIARRITZ, LA • 1934 • Toulout Jean • FRN
REINE DE LA NUIT, LA see **MALIKAT AL-LAYL** • 1971
REINE DE SABA, LA • 1913 • Andreani Henri • FRN
REINE DES BARBARES, LA (FRN) see **REGINA DEI TARTARI, LA** • 1960
REINE DES PAPILLONS, LA • 1927 • Starevitch Ladislas • ANM • FRN • QUEEN OF THE BUTTERFLIES, THE (USA)
REINE DES VAMPIRES, LA • 1967 • Rollin Jean • FRN • QUEEN OF THE VAMPIRES, THE
REINE ELISABETH, LA see **AMOURS DE LA REINE ELISABETH, LES** • 1912
REINE LUMIERE, LA • 1921 • Navarre Rene • FRN
REINE MARGOT, LA • 1910 • de Morlhon Camille • FRN
REINE MARGOT, LA • 1914 • Desfontaines Henri • FRN
REINE MARGOT, LA • 1954 • Dreville Jean • FRN, ITL • REGINA MARGOT, LA (ITL) ○ WOMAN OF EVIL, A
REINE SUNDERIN, DIE • 1921 • Moest Hubert • FRG
REINES DU PEEPSHOW, LES • Ricaud Michel • FRN
REINO DE LOS GANGSTERS • 1947 • Orol Juan • MXC
REIS DOOR HET ZAND • 1982 • Hamelberg Andreas • NTH • JOURNEY THROUGH SAND
REISE, DIE • 1986 • Imhoof Markus • SWT
REISE AUF DEN MOND • 1959 • Stanzl Karl • ANS • AUS • TRIP TO THE MOON
REISE DAS LAND, DIE • 1987 • Hoffmann Frank, Kieffer Paul • LXM
REISE DER HOFFNUNG • 1989 • Koller Xavier • SWT, FRG, ITL • JOURNEY OF HOPE
REISE IN DIE VERGANGENHEIT • 1943 • Zerlett Hans H. • FRG
REISE IN JENSEITS -DIE WELT DES UBERNATURLICHEN • 1975 • Olsen Rolf • DOC • FRG • JOURNEY INTO THE BEYOND ○ JOURNEY INTO BEYOND ○ JOURNEY INTO THE UNKNOWN
REISE INS EHEBETT • 1966 • Hasler Joachim • GDR
REISE INS GLUCK, DIE see **ZWEI IN EINEM AUTO** • 1931
REISE INS GLUCK, EINE • 1958 • Schleif Wolfgang • FRG
REISE INS JENSEITS, DIE • 1916 • Gartner Adolf • FRG
REISE NACH AFRIKA, DIE • 1928 • Reiniger Lotte • ANS • FRG • DR. DOLITTLE'S TRIP TO AFRICA
REISE NACH LYON, DIE • 1980 • von Alemann Claudia • FRG
REISE NACH MARRAKESH, DIE • 1949 • Eichberg Richard • FRG
REISE NACH TILSIT, DIE • 1939 • Harlan Veit • FRG • SUN IS RISING, THE
REISE NACH WIEN, DIE • 1973 • Reitz Edgar • FRG • JOURNEY TO VIENNA
REISE OHNE WIEDERKEHR • 1990 • von Grote Alexandra • FRG • JOURNEY WITHOUT RETURN
REISE UM DIE ERDE IN 80 TAGEN, DIE • 1919 • Oswald Richard • FRG • ROUND THE WORLD IN 80 DAYS
REISEN TIL JULESTJERNEN • 1976 • Solum Ola • NRW
REISEN TIL MELONIA • 1989 • Ahlin Per • ANM • NRW, SWD • VOYAGE TO MELONIA ○ RESAN TILL MELONIA
REISENS INS LANDESINNERE • 1988 • von Gunten Peter • DOC • SWT • JOURNEYS LAND (UKN)
REITER OHNE KOPF 1, DER • 1921 • Piel Harry • FRG • TODESFALLE, DIE
REITER OHNE KOPF 2, DER • 1921 • Piel Harry • FRG • GEHEIMNISVOLLE MACHT, DIE
REITER OHNE KOPF 3, DER • 1921 • Piel Harry • FRG • HARRY PEELS SCHWERSTER SIEG
REITER VON DEUTSCH-OSTAFRIKA, DIE • 1934 • Selpin Herbert • FRG
REITERATE THE WARNING! see **VARUJ!** • 1947
...REITET FUR DEUTSCHLAND • 1941 • Rabenalt Arthur M. • FRG
REIVERS, THE • 1969 • Rydell Mark • USA • YELLOW WINTON FLYER, THE
REIZENDE FAMILIE, EINE • 1945 • Waschneck Erich • FRG • DANKE ES GEHT MIR GUT
REIZENDE FAMILIE, EINE see **MEISTERDETEKTIV, DER** • 1944
REJEANNE PADOVANI • 1973 • Arcand Denys • CND
REJECTED BY PA • 1904 • Collins Alf? • UKN
REJECTED LOVER'S LUCK, THE • 1913 • Duncan William • USA
REJECTED WOMAN, THE • 1924 • Parker Albert • USA
REJOICE WHILE YOU ARE YOUNG see **GLAD DIG I DIN UNGDOM** • 1939
REJS • 1970 • Piwowski Marek • PLN • TRIP DOWN THE RIVER, A ○ CRUISE, THE ○ VOYAGE
REJSEFEBER • 1944 • Lauritzen Lau Jr. • SHT • DNM
REJSENDE • 1923 • Lauritzen Lau • DNM
REJTOZKODO, A • 1985 • Kezdi-Kovacs Zsolt • HNG • ABSENTEE, THE
REJUVENATION • 1912 • *Cruze James* • USA
REJUVENATION OF AUNT MARY, THE • 1914 • Dillon Eddie • USA
REJUVENATION OF AUNT MARY, THE • 1916 • Henderson Dell • SHT • USA
REJUVENATION OF AUNT MARY, THE • 1927 • Kenton Erle C. • USA
REJUVENATION OF DAN, THE • 1913 • Kinder Stuart? • UKN
REJUVENATION OF FATHER, THE • 1910 • *Lubin* • USA • REGENERATION OF FATHER, THE
REJUVENATION OF LIZA JANE, THE • 1915 • Curtis Allen • USA
REJUVENATION OF SALLY DIDET, OR WHAT ADVERTISING DID TO HELP ONE POOR SOUL, THE • 1917 • *Allardice J. D.* • USA
REJUVENATOR, THE • 1917 • *U.s.m.p.* • USA
REJUVENATOR, THE • 1988 • Jones Brian Thomas • USA • JUVENATRIX: A CLASSIC TALE OF HORROR ○ SKINDEEP
REJUVENATOR, THE see **CHUNG-SHEN TA SHIH** • 1981
REJUVENATORS, THE • 1918 • *Passing Show Comedies* • USA
REKA • 1933 • Rovensky Josef • CZC • ECSTASY OF YOUNG LIFE (USA) ○ RIVER, THE ○ YOUNG LOVE
REKA CARUJE • 1945 • Krska Vaclav • CZC • SPELL OF THE RIVER, THE ○ MAGIC OF THE RIVER
REKA ZIVOTA A SMRTI • 1939-40 • Klos Elmar • CZC • RIVER OF LIFE AND DEATH, THE
REKAVA • 1957 • Peries Lester James • SLN • LINE OF DESTINY ○ LINE OF LIFE, THE
REKISHI • 1940 • Uchida Tomu • JPN • HISTORY
REKISHI, KAKU KYORAN NO JIDAI • 1984 • Hani Susumu • DOC • JPN • HISTORY, AGE OF NUCLEAR MADNESS, THE
REKOPIS ZNALEZIONY W SARAGOSSIE • 1965 • Has Wojciech J. • PLN • SARAGOSSA MANUSCRIPT, THE (USA) ○ ADVENTURES OF A NOBLEMAN ○ MANUSCRIPT FOUND IN SARAGOSSA ○ DIARY FOR IN SARAGOSSA, A
REKRUTTSKOLEN • Wam Svend • SHT • NRW
REKTOR PA SENGEKANTEN • 1972 • Hilbard John • DNM • DANISH BED AND BOARD (UKN) ○ BEDSIDE HEAD
REKVIJEM • 1971 • Damjanovic Caslav • YGS • REQUIEM ○ LAST TRAIN TO BERLIN ○ LAST RAMPAGE, THE
RELACION MATRIMONIAL Y OTRAS COSAS • 1975 • Vidal Alberto • SPN
RELACIONES CASI PUBLICAS • 1969 • Saenz De Heredia Jose Luis • SPN
RELAPSE, THE see **REINCIDENTE, EL** • 1978
RELATION PEDAGOGIQUE • 1973 • Labrecque Jean-Claude • SER • CND
RELATIONS see **BANDHAVYALU** • 1968
RELATIONS (USA) see **TUMULT** • 1969
RELATIONSHIP, THE • 1988 • Derakhshandeh Pooran • IRN
RELATIONSHIP BEFORE MARRIAGE see **KONZEN KOJYOKI** • 1968
RELATIVE, THE see **PARIENTE, EL** • 1973
RELATIVE SECRETS see **DIXIE LANES** • 1988
RELATIVES • 1985 • Bowman Anthony • ASL
RELATIVES see **ROKONOK** • 1954
RELATIVITY • 1966 • Emshwiller Ed • USA
RELATIVITY see **YOUNG IDEAS** • 1924
RELATO POLICIACO • 1954 • Isasi Antonio • SPN
RELATOS DE TIERRA SECA • 1979 • Cordido Ivork • VNZ • STORIES FROM TIERRA SECA ○ TALES OF DROUGHTY SOIL
RELAX BABY • 1973 • Franco Jesus
RELAX FREDDY • 1967 • Balling Erik • DNM
RELAXE-TOI, CHERIE • 1964 • Boyer Jean • FRN, ITL • HO UNA MOGLIE PAZZA, PAZZA, PAZZA (ITL)
RELAY • 1967 • Khrabrovitsky Daniil • USS
RELAY, THE see **STAFETA** • 1969
RELAY EVENT, A see **BIEG** • 1971
RELAY RACE see **STAFETA** • 1969
RELAZIONI PERICOLOSE (ITL) see **LIAISONS DANGEREUSES, LES** • 1959
RELEASE • 1972 • Taghvai Nasser • SHT • IRN
RELEASE OF DAN FORBES, THE • 1916 • MacDonald Donald • SHT • USA
RELENTLESS • 1948 • Sherman George • USA • THREE WERE THOROUGHBREDS
RELENTLESS • 1977 • Katzin Lee H. • TVM • USA
RELENTLESS • 1989 • Lustig William • USA
RELENTLESS LAW, THE see **RELENTLESS OUTLAW, THE** • 1912
RELENTLESS OUTLAW, THE • 1912 • Dwan Allan • USA • RELENTLESS LAW, THE
RELEVE, LA • 1934 • Delacroix Rene • FRN
RELEVE, LA • 1938 • Epstein Jean • FRN
RELEVE, LA see **UNTEL PERE ET FILS** • 1940
RELEVO, EL • 1973 • Forque Jose Maria • SPN, FRN, VNZ • RELIEF, THE
RELEVO PARA UN PISTOLERO • 1964 • Torrado Ramon • SPN
RELIABLE HENRY • 1917 • Drew Sidney • SHT • USA
RELIABLE MAN, THE • 1968 • Bottcher Jurgen • DOC • GDR
RELIC, THE • 1914 • *Broncho* • USA

RELIC OF OLD JAPAN, A • 1914 • Barker Reginald, Ince Thomas H. (Spv) • USA
RELIC OF THE OLDEN DAYS, A • 1914 • *Frontier* • USA
RELICARIO, EL • 1926 • Contreras Torres Miguel • MXC
RELICARIO, EL • 1933 • de Banos Ricardo • SPN • RELIQUARY, THE (USA)
RELICARIO, EL • 1970 • Gil Rafael • SPN
RELIEF • Weiss Peter • SHT • SWD
RELIEF, THE see **RELEVO, EL** • 1973
RELIEF IN THE WHITE WIND • 1988 • Korabov Nicolai • BUL
RELIEF OF LUCKNOW, THE • 1912 • Dawley J. Searle • USA
RELIGIEUSE, LA (UKN) see **SUZANNE SIMONIN, LA RELIGIEUSE DE DIDEROT** • 1965
RELIGIEUSE DE DIDEROT, LA see **SUZANNE SIMONIN, LA RELIGIEUSE DE DIDEROT** • 1965
RELIGION AND GUN PRACTICE • 1913 • Duncan William • USA
RELIGIOUS RACKETEERS see **MYSTIC CIRCLE MURDER, THE** • 1939
RELIQUARY, THE (USA) see **RELICARIO, EL** • 1933
RELIQUIAS PORTUGUESAS DO BRASIL • 1959 • de Barros Jose Leitao • SHT • PRT
RELITTO, IL • 1961 • Paolucci Giovanni, Cacoyannis Michael • ITL • WASTREL, THE (USA)
RELOJ DEL ANTICUARIO, EL • 1925 • Ardavin Eusebio F. • SPN • DEL RASTRO A LA CASTELLANA
RELUCTANT ASTRONAUT, THE • 1967 • Montagne Edward J. • USA
RELUCTANT BRIDE, THE • 1955 • Cass Henry • UKN • TWO GROOMS FOR A BRIDE (USA)
RELUCTANT BRIDEGROOM, THE • 1905 • Fitzhamon Lewin • UKN
RELUCTANT CINDERELLA, A • 1913 • Williams C. Jay • USA
RELUCTANT DEBUTANTE, THE • 1958 • Minnelli Vincente • USA
RELUCTANT DRAGON, THE • 1941 • Werker Alfred L., Luske Hamilton, Handley Jim, Beebe Ford, Verity Erwin, Blystone Jasper • USA
RELUCTANT HEROES • 1951 • Raymond Jack • UKN
RELUCTANT HEROES, THE • 1971 • Day Robert • TVM • USA • RELUCTANT HEROES OF HILL 656, THE (UKN) ○ EGGHEAD ON HILL 656, THE
RELUCTANT HEROES OF HILL 656, THE (UKN) see **RELUCTANT HEROES, THE** • 1971
RELUCTANT INSPECTORS, THE see **REVIZORY PONEVOLE** • 1954
RELUCTANT MILLIONAIRE see **MUZ Z NEZNAMA** • 1939
RELUCTANT NUDIST, THE • 1963 • Pelc Stanley • UKN • SANDY, THE RELUCTANT NATURE GIRL (USA) ○ SANDY, THE RELUCTANT NUDIST
RELUCTANT PUP, THE • 1953 • Davis Mannie • ANS • USA
RELUCTANT RECRUIT, THE • 1971 • Smith Paul J. • ANS • USA
RELUCTANT SADIST, THE see **JEG –EN MARKI** • 1967
RELUCTANT SAINT, THE • 1962 • Dmytryk Edward • USA, ITL • CRONACHE DI UN CONVENTO (ITL) ○ JOSEPH DESA
RELUCTANT SPY, THE (USA) see **HONORABLE STANISLAS AGENT SECRET, L'** • 1963
RELUCTANT VIRGIN, THE see **NO, SONO VERGINE!** • 1971
RELUCTANT WIDOW, THE • 1950 • Knowles Bernard • UKN
REMAINDER OF THE SHIPWRECK, THE see **RESTOS DEL NAUFRAGIO, LOS** • 1977
REMAINS OF THE SHIPWRECK, THE see **RESTOS DEL NAUFRAGIO, LOS** • 1977
REMAINS OF THE WRECK, THE see **RESTOS DEL NAUFRAGIO, LOS** • 1977
REMAINS TO BE SEEN • 1953 • Weis Don • USA
REMAINS TO BE SEEN • 1983 • Aaron Jane • USA
REMAJA KEDUA • 1984 • Sirait Edward Pesta • INN • SECOND YOUTH
REMAKING OF A MAN, THE • 1910 • *Powers* • USA
REMANDO AL VIENTO • 1988 • Suarez Gonzalo • SPN, NRW • ROWING IN THE WIND ○ ROWING WITH THE WIND
REMARKABLE ANDREW, THE • 1942 • Heisler Stuart • USA
REMARKABLE MR. KIPPS, THE see **KIPPS** • 1941
REMARKABLE MR. PENNYPACKER, THE • 1959 • Levin Henry • USA
REMARKABLE ROCKET, THE • 1975 • Potterton Gerald • USA
REMBETIKO • 1984 • Ferris Kostas • GRC
REMBRANDT • 1936 • Korda Alexander • UKN
REMBRANDT • 1942 • Steinhoff Hans, Rohrig Walter • FRG
REMBRANDT see **TRAGODIE EINES GROSSEN, DIE** • 1920
REMBRANDT see **REMBRANDT FECIT 1669** • 1977
REMBRANDT ALS ETSER • 1966 • Janssen U. • SHT • NTH
REMBRANDT DE LA RUE LEPIC, LE • 1911 • Durand Jean • FRN
REMBRANDT, ETC. AND JANE • 1976 • Brakhage Stan • SHT • USA
REMBRANDT FECIT 1669 • 1977 • Stelling Jos • NTH • REMBRANDT
REMBRANDT, PAINTER OF MEN see **REMBRANDT, SCHILDER VAN DER MENS** • 1956
REMBRANDT, SCHILDER VAN DER MENS • 1956 • Haanstra Bert • NTH • REMBRANDT, PAINTER OF MEN
REMBRANDT, THE THREE CROSSES • 1968 • Ashton Dudley Shaw • DOC • UKN
REMBRANDT VOGELVRIJ • 1970 • Damen Ermie • NTH
REMBULAN DAN MATAHARI • 1980 • Rahardjo Slamet • INN • TIME TO MEND, A
REMEDIAL READING COMPREHENSION • 1970 • Landow George • USA
REMEDY see **DERMAN** • 1985
REMEDY, THE • 1915 • *Victor* • USA
REMEDY FOR RICHES • 1940 • Kenton Erle C. • USA
REMEMBER • 1916 • Burguet Charles • FRN
REMEMBER • 1926 • Selman David • USA
REMEMBER? • 1939 • McLeod Norman Z. • USA
REMEMBER BELGIUM • 1915 • Batley Ethyle • UKN
REMEMBER LAST NIGHT • 1934 • Whale James • USA
REMEMBER MARY MAGDALEN • 1914 • Dwan Allan • USA
REMEMBER ME THIS WAY • 1975 • Inkpen Ron, Foster Bob • UKN
REMEMBER ME (UKN) see **HORSEMEN OF THE SIERRAS** • 1949
REMEMBER MY NAME • 1978 • Rudolph Alan • USA
REMEMBER PEARL HARBOR • 1942 • Santley Joseph • USA
REMEMBER REMEMBER THE FIFTH OF NOVEMBER • 1907 • Collins Alf? • UKN
REMEMBER THAT FACE! see **MERKEN SIESICH DIESES GESICHT** • 1985
REMEMBER THAT FACE (UKN) see **MOB, THE** • 1951
REMEMBER THE DAY • 1941 • King Henry • USA
REMEMBER THE NIGHT • 1940 • Leisen Mitchell • USA
REMEMBER THE POKER PLAYING MONKEYS • 1977 • Jacoby • USA
REMEMBER THE UNICORN see **GEORGE IN CIVVY STREET** • 1946
REMEMBER TOMORROW see **DANGEROUSLY THEY LIVE** • 1942
REMEMBER WHEN? • 1925 • Edwards Harry J. • SHT • USA
REMEMBER WHEN • 1937 • MacDonald David • UKN • RIDING HIGH
REMEMBER WHEN? • 1974 • Kulik Buzz • TVM • USA
REMEMBRANCE • 1922 • Hughes Rupert • USA
REMEMBRANCE • 1927 • Wynne Bert • UKN
REMEMBRANCE see **PAMYAT** • 1972
REMEMBRANCE OF LOVE • 1982 • Smight Jack • TVM • USA
REMEMBRANCE OF LOWRY • 1961 • Robertson George C. • CND
REMEMBRANCES OF O.K. see **ERINNERUNGEN** • 1986
REMENY JOGA, A • 1982 • Kezdi-Kovacs Zsolt • HNG • RIGHT TO HOPE, THE
REMENYKEDOK • 1971 • Renyi Tamas • HNG • CHARMING FAMILY, A
REMERCIEMENTS AU PUBLIC see **VUE DE REMERCIEMENTS AU PUBLIC** • 1900
REMI • 1979 • Dezaki Osamu • ANM • JPN
REMINGTON • 1989 • Kozole Damjan • YGS
REMINGTON CALIBRE 12 • 1972 • Heynowski Walter, Scheumann Gerhard • GDR
REMINISCENCE see **BAKASIN MO SA GUNITA** • 1968
REMINISCENCE OF THE WAR, A • 1899 • *Norton C. Goodwin* • UKN
REMINISCENCES see **SMRITICHITRE** • 1983
REMINISCENCES FROM A JOURNEY TO LITHUANIA • 1972 • Mekas Jonas • USA
REMISELEGEPLADSEN • 1972 • Beckendorff Leif • DNM • DEPOT PLAYGROUND, THE
REMITTANCE MAN, THE • 1912 • Melies Gaston • USA
REMITTANCE MAN, THE • 1913 • Lincoln W. J. • ASL
REMITTANCE WOMAN, THE • 1923 • Ruggles Wesley • USA
REMO E ROMOLO (STORIA DI DUE FIGLI DI UNA LUPA) • 1976 • Castellacci Mario, Pingitore Pier Francesco • ITL
REMO: UNARMED AND DANGEROUS see **REMO WILLIAMS: THE ADVENTURE BEGINS** • 1985
REMO WILLIAMS: THE ADVENTURE BEGINS • 1985 • Hamilton Guy • USA • REMO WILLIAMS ..UNARMED AND DANGEROUS ○ REMO: UNARMED AND DANGEROUS ○ REMO WILLIAMS: THE ADVENTURE CONTINUES
REMO WILLIAMS: THE ADVENTURE CONTINUES see **REMO WILLIAMS: THE ADVENTURE BEGINS** • 1985
REMO WILLIAMS ..UNARMED AND DANGEROUS see **REMO WILLIAMS: THE ADVENTURE BEGINS** • 1985
REMODELING HER HUSBAND • 1920 • Gish Lillian • USA
REMOLINO • 1959 • Gazcon Gilberto • MXC
REMOLINO DE PASION • 1945 • Momplet Antonio • MXC
REMONSTRANCES see **MOTFORESTILLING** • 1973
REMONTONS LES CHAMPS-ELYSEES • 1938 • Guitry Sacha, Bibal Robert • FRN
REMORQUES • 1940 • Gremillon Jean • FRN • STORMY WATERS (UKN)
REMORSE • 1903 • Williamson James • UKN
REMORSE • 1914 • *Murray J. S.* • USA
REMORSE • 1917 • *Mathew'S Photo Play* • ASL
REMORSE • 1989 • Howard Simon • SHT • UKN
REMORSELESS LOVE • 1921 • Ince Ralph • USA
REMOTE CONTROL • 1930 • Grinde Nick, St. Clair Malcolm, Sedgwick Edward • USA
REMOTE CONTROL • 1988 • Lieberman Jeff • USA
REMOUS • 1934 • Greville Edmond T. • FRN • WHIRLPOOL
REMOVAL OF DOMINIK, THE see **PRZEPROWADZKA DOMINIKA** • 1968
REMOVAL OF TONSILS AND ADENOIDS (MR. GEORGE WAUGH'S METHOD) • 1929 • Griffith John • DOC • UKN
REMOVALISTS, THE • 1975 • Jeffrey Tom • ASL
REMPART DES BEGUINES, LE • 1972 • Casaril Guy • FRN, ITL • AMORI IMPOSSIBILI, GLI (ITL) ○ BEGUINES, THE (UKN)
REMPART DU BRABANT • 1919 • Bergerat Theo • FRN
REMPARTS D'ARGILE • 1970 • Bertucelli Jean-Louis • FRN, ALG • RAMPARTS OF CLAY (USA)
REMUCH CEMETERY, THE see **CMENTARZ REMUCH** • 1962
REN-AIBYO KANJA • 1961 • Edagawa Hiroshi • JPN
REN BESKED OM SNAVS • 1962 • Carlsen Henning • SHT • DNM
REN DAO ZHONGNIAN • 1983 • Sun Yu, Wang Qimin • CHN • AT MIDDLE AGE
REN-NYO: A PRIEST AND HIS MOTHER • 1981 • Kawamoto Kihachiro • ANM • JPN
RENA • 1939 • Waszynski Michael • PLN
RENA RAMA SANNINGEN • 1939 • Hildebrand Weyler • SWD • NOTHING BUT THE TRUTH
RENACER • 1980 • Luna Bigas • SPN, USA • REBORN ○ BLOODY MARY ○ RENACIDA
RENACIDA see **RENACER** • 1980
RENAI HIJOJI • 1933 • Yamamoto Kajiro • JPN • LOVE CRISIS
RENAI SANBAGARASU • 1949 • Nakamura Noboru • JPN • LOVE TRIO
RENAI SUKII-JUTSU • 1934 • Yamamoto Kajiro • JPN
RENAI TOKKYU • 1954 • Sugie Toshio, Suzuki • JPN • LOVE EXPRESS
RENAISSANCE • 1933 • Harrington Curtis • SHT • USA
RENAISSANCE • 1963 • Borowczyk Walerian • ANS • FRN
RENAISSANCE • 1965 • Ruspoli Mario • FRN
RENAISSANCE • 1970 • Lagrange Yvan • FRN
RENAISSANCE AT CHARLEROI, THE • 1917 • Mills Thomas R. • USA
RENAISSANCE DU HAVRE • 1948 • Camus Marcel • SHT • FRN
RENAISSANCE DU RAIL, LA • 1949 • Chaperot Georges • DOC • FRN
RENAISSANCE SONGS • 1969 • Iliesu Mirel • SHT • RMN
RENALDO & CLARA • 1978 • Dylan Bob • USA
RENA'S PET PIRATE • 1915 • *Thistle* • USA
RENATE IM QUARTETT • 1939 • Verhoeven Paul • FRG
RENATES LIEBESGESCHICHTE • 1915 • Del Zopp Rudolf • FRG
RENAULT, TEHERAN 28 • 1990 • Shayeghi Siamak • IRN
RENBO KOUTA • 1924 • Yamamoto Kajiro • JPN
RENCONTRE • 1978 • Coderre Laurent • ANM • CND
RENCONTRE • 1980 • Payer Roch Christophe • CND
RENCONTRE, LA • 1914 • Feuillade Louis • FRN
RENCONTRE, LA • 1974 • Dansereau Fernand, Rossignol Yolande • SHT • CND
RENCONTRE A PARIS • 1956 • Lampin Georges • FRN
RENCONTRE AVEC UNE FEMME REMARQUABLE LAURE GAUDREAULT • 1984 • Cadrin-Rossignol Iolande • CND
RENCONTRES • 1960 • Mitry Jean • SHT • FRN
RENCONTRES • 1962 • Agostini Philippe • FRN
RENCONTRES A MITZIC • 1963 • Carriere Marcel, Dufaux Georges • DCS • CND
RENCONTRES AVEC LE PRESIDENT HO CHI MINH • 1970 • Ivens Joris (c/d) • SHT • FRN
RENCONTRES DANS L'INVISIBLE • 1958 • Lavoie Richard • DCS • CND
RENCONTRES SUR LE RHIN • 1953 • Bonniere Rene • SHT • FRN
RENCOR DE LA TIERRA, EL • 1949 • Crevenna Alfredo B. • MXC • PRUEBA DE DIOS ○ TORBELLINO
REND MIG I REVOLUTIONEN • 1970 • Balling Erik • DNM
REND MIG I TRADIONERNE • 1979 • Fleming Edward • DNM • TRADITIONS, UP YOURS!
RENDAS E PANOS • 1959 • Ribeiro Antonio Lopes • SHT • PRT
RENDERING ACCOUNTS see **AJUSTE DE CUENTAS**
RENDEZ-MOI MA PEAU • 1980 • Schulmann Patrick • FRN
RENDEZ-MOI MON PAYS • 1986 • Rached Tahani • MTV • CND
RENDEZ-VOUS • 1932 • Boese Carl • FRG
RENDEZ VOUS • 1976 • Walton Lloyd A. • DOC • CND
RENDEZ-VOUS • 1985 • Techine Andre • FRN
RENDEZ-VOUS 10H30 • 1985 • Sauve Alain • SHT • CND
RENDEZ-VOUS, LE • 1961 • Delannoy Jean • FRN, ITL
RENDEZ-VOUS, LE see **MIAD, AL-** • 1955
RENDEZ-VOUS A ANTIBES-JUAN-LES-PINS see **ANTIPOLIS** • 1952
RENDEZ-VOUS A BRAY • 1971 • Delvaux Andre • FRN, FRG, BLG • RENDEZVOUS AT BRAY (UKN)
RENDEZ-VOUS A GRENADE • 1951 • Pottier Richard • FRN
RENDEZ-VOUS A MELBOURNE • 1956 • Lucot Rene • FRN • MELBOURNE RENDEZVOUS (USA)
RENDEZ-VOUS A PARIS • 1946 • Grangier Gilles • FRN
RENDEZ-VOUS AT THE GRINDING ROOM see **DOSTAVENICKO VE MLYNICI** • 1898
RENDEZ-VOUS AU CRESPUSCULE see **LIQA' FI AL-GHURUB** • 1959
RENDEZ-VOUS AU TAS DE SABLE • 1990 • Grousset Didier • FRN
RENDEZ-VOUS AU TROPIQUE DU CANCER • 1968 • Tolbi Abdelaziz • ALG
RENDEZ-VOUS AUX CHAMPS-ELYSEES see **RENDEZ-VOUS CHAMPS-ELYSEES** • 1937
RENDEZ-VOUS AVEC LA CHANCE • 1949 • Reinert Emile Edwin • FRN • LIT A DEUX PLACES, LE
RENDEZ-VOUS AVEC L'HISTOIRE • 1965 • Essid Hamadi • DOC • TNS
RENDEZ-VOUS AVEC L'INCONNU see **MAWID MA'A AL-MAGHUL** • 1959
RENDEZ-VOUS CHAMPS-ELYSEES • 1937 • Houssin Jacques • FRN • CONTROLEUR DES CHAMPS-ELYSEES, LE ○ RENDEZ-VOUS AUX CHAMPS-ELYSEES
RENDEZ-VOUS D'AMOUR see **HAWID GHARAM** • 1955
RENDEZ-VOUS D'ANNA, LES • 1978 • Akerman Chantal • FRN, FRG, BLG • MEETINGS OF ANNA, THE
RENDEZ-VOUS D'ASNIERES, LE • 1962 • Gruel Henri • SHT • FRN
RENDEZ-VOUS DE JUILLET • 1949 • Becker Jacques • FRN
RENDEZ-VOUS DE MINUIT, LE • 1961 • Leenhardt Roger • FRN • RENDEZVOUS AT MIDNIGHT
RENDEZ-VOUS DU DIABLE, LES • 1958 • Tazieff Haroun • DOC • FRN • AU RENDEZ-VOUS DU DIABLE ○ VOLCANO
RENDEZ-VOUS EN FORET, LE • 1972 • Fleischer Alain • FRN • MEETING IN THE FOREST, THE
RENDEZ-VOUS IN WIEN • 1936 • Janson Victor • AUS
RENDEZ-VOUS IN WIEN • 1959 • Weiss Helmut • AUS • WHISKY, WODKA, WIENERIN
RENDEZ-VOUS SAUVAGE, LE • Lenoir Claudine • SHT • FRN • WILD RENDEZVOUS, THE
RENDEZVOUS • 1923 • Neilan Marshall • USA
RENDEZVOUS • 1935 • Howard William K. • USA • BLACK CHAMBER
RENDEZVOUS • 1965 • *Ghatak Ritwik* • DOC • IND
RENDEZVOUS see **WAY TO THE STARS, THE** • 1945
RENDEZVOUS see **SVIDANIE** • 1963
RENDEZVOUS 24 • 1946 • Tinling James • USA
RENDEZVOUS, THE • 1949 • Gilkison Anthony • UKN
RENDEZVOUS A MARSEILLE see **RETOUR A MARSEILLE** • 1979
RENDEZVOUS AT BRAY (UKN) see **RENDEZ-VOUS A BRAY** • 1971
RENDEZVOUS AT MIDNIGHT • 1935 • Cabanne W. Christy • USA
RENDEZVOUS AT MIDNIGHT see **RENDEZ-VOUS DE MINUIT, LE** • 1961
RENDEZVOUS AT ORCHARD BRIDGE • 1954 • Xie Jin • CHN
RENDEZVOUS AT SALZKAMMERGUT • 1948 • Stoger Alfred • AUS
RENDEZVOUS DER KILLER (FRG) see **PLEINS FEUX SUR STANISLAS** • 1965
RENDEZVOUS HOTEL • 1979 • Hunt Peter • TVM • USA
RENDEZVOUS HOTEL, A see **AVEC RIYOKAN** • 1968

RENDEZVOUS IN BLACK • 1956 • Frankenheimer John • MTV • USA
RENDEZVOUS IN SPACE • 1964 • Capra Frank • SHT • USA
RENDEZVOUS IN SPACE see **ZVYOZDNYYE BRATYA** • 1962
RENDEZVOUS IN TRAVERS see **TREFFEN IN TRAVERS** • 1988
RENDEZVOUS (UKN) see **DARLING, HOW COULD YOU?** • 1951
RENDEZVOUS WITH ANNIE • 1946 • Dwan Allan • USA • CORPORAL DOLAN GOES A.W.O.L. ○ CORPORAL DOLAN AWOL
RENDEZVOUS WITH DEATH see **CH'ING T'IEH** • 1981
RENDEZVOUS WITH FORGOTTEN YEARS see **STEVNEMOTE MED GLEMTE AR** • 1957
RENDEZVOUS WITH THE DEVIL • 1965 • USA
RENDEZVOUS WITH THE PAST see **VSTRYECHA S PROSHLYM** • 1967
RENDS-MOI LA CLE! • 1980 • Pires Gerard • FRN
RENE HAGGARD JOURNEYS ON • 1915 • *Wilson Ben* • USA
RENE LA CANNE • 1976 • Girod Francis • FRN, ITL • TRE SIMPATHICE CAROGNE
RENE LERICHE, CHIRURGIEN DE LA DOULEUR • 1948 • Lucot Rene • FRN
RENE LEVESQUE: LE VRAI CHEF • 1976 • Brault Michel • SHT • CND
RENE LEVESQUE POUR LE VRAI • 1973 • Brault Michel • SHT • CND
RENE LEVESQUE VOUS PARLEZ: LES 6 MILLIARDS • 1969 • Brault Michel • SHT • CND
RENE MAGRITTE • 1968 • Beresford Bruce • SHT • UKN
RENE SIMARD AU JAPON • 1974 • Larouche Laurent • DOC • CND
RENEGADE • 1934 • Scott Ewing • USA
RENEGADE • 1987 • Clucher E. B. • ITL
RENEGADE, THE • 1908 • *Kalem* • USA
RENEGADE, THE • 1912 • *American* • USA
RENEGADE, THE • 1912 • *Nestor* • USA
RENEGADE, THE • 1915 • Swickard Charles • USA
RENEGADE, THE • 1943 • Newfield Sam • USA • CODE OF THE PLAINS
RENEGADE, THE see **LIGHT OF VICTORY, THE** • 1919
RENEGADE GIRL • 1947 • Berke William • USA
RENEGADE GIRLS see **CAGED HEAT** • 1974
RENEGADE GUNFIGHTER (USA) see **PER MILLE DOLLARI AL GIORNI** • 1966
RENEGADE HOLMES M.D. • 1925 • Wilson Ben • USA
RENEGADE KNIGHTS • 1988 • Nelson Dusty • USA
RENEGADE POSSE see **BULLET FOR A BADMAN** • 1964
RENEGADE PRIEST, THE see **DEFROQUE, LE** • 1953
RENEGADE RANGER, THE • 1938 • Howard David • USA • RANGER CODE
RENEGADE ROUNDUP • 1944 • Abrahams Derwin • USA
RENEGADE TRAIL, THE • 1939 • Selander Lesley • USA
RENEGADES • 1918 • Hopper E. Mason • USA
RENEGADES • 1930 • Fleming Victor • USA
RENEGADES • 1946 • Sherman George • USA
RENEGADES • 1974 • Noyce Phil • DOC • ASL
RENEGADES • 1989 • Sholder Jack • USA
RENEGADES, THE • 1912 • *Lubin* • USA
RENEGADES, THE • 1982 • Spottiswoode Roger • TVM • USA
RENEGADES, THE • 1988 • Patterson John • USA
RENEGADE'S HEART, THE • 1913 • Dwan Allan • USA
RENEGADES OF SONORA • 1948 • Springsteen R. G. • USA
RENEGADES OF THE RIO GRANDE • 1945 • Bretherton Howard • USA • BANK ROBBERY (UKN)
RENEGADES OF THE SAGE • 1949 • Nazarro Ray • USA • FORT, THE (UKN)
RENEGADES OF THE WEST • 1932 • Robinson Casey • USA
RENEGADE'S SISTER, THE • 1914 • *Miller'S 101 Ranch* • USA
RENEGADE'S VENGEANCE, THE • 1914 • *Selig* • USA
RENEGADO BLANCO, EL • 1959 • Mendez Fernando • MXC
RENEGATE, LA • 1947 • Severac Jacques • FRN
RENFREW OF THE MOUNTED IN SKY BANDITS see **SKY BANDITS** • 1940
RENFREW OF THE ROYAL MOUNTED • 1937 • Herman Al • USA
RENFREW OF THE ROYAL MOUNTED IN CRASHIN' THRU see **CRASHIN' THRU** • 1939
RENFREW OF THE ROYAL MOUNTED IN FIGHTING MAD see **FIGHTING MAD** • 1939
RENFREW OF THE ROYAL MOUNTED IN YUKON FLIGHT see **YUKON FLIGHT** • 1940
RENFREW ON THE GREAT WHITE TRAIL • 1938 • Herman Al • USA • ON THE GREAT WHITE TRAIL (UKN)
RENFREW VALLEY BARN DANCE see **JOHN LAIR'S RENFRO VALLEY BARN DANCE** • 1966
RENGO KANTAI • 1982 • Matsubayashi Shue • JPN • COMBINED FLEET, THE
RENGO KANTAI SHIREICHOKAN YAMAMOTO ISOROKU • 1968 • Maruyama Seiji • JPN • ADMIRAL YAMAMOTO ○ YAMAMOTO ISOROKU
RENGOKU EROICA • 1970 • Yoshida Yoshishige • JPN • HEROIC PURGATORY ○ PURGATORY EROICA
RENJIAN DAO • 1988 • Ching Siu-Tong • HKG • CHINESE GHOST STORY II, A ○ SINNUI YAUWAN II ○ QIANNU YOUHUN II
RENNEN • 1961 • Kluge Alexander, Kruntorad Paul • SHT • FRG • RACING
RENNEN DES TODES, DAS • 1924 • *Reinwald Grete* • FRG
RENNFAHRER • 1961 • Kluge Alexander • SHT • FRG
RENNFIEBER • 1917 • Oswald Richard • FRG
RENNIE • 1982 • Norman Ron • USA
RENNSYMPHONIE • 1929 • Richter Hans • FRG • RACE SYMPHONY
RENO • 1923 • Hughes Rupert • USA • LAW AGAINST LAW
RENO • 1930 • Crone George J. • USA
RENO • 1939 • Farrow John • USA
RENO -ALL CHANGE • 1919 • *Harrison Jimmie* • USA
RENO AND THE DOC • 1984 • Dennis Charles • CND
RENO DIVORCE, A • 1927 • Graves Ralph • USA
RENO ROMANCE, A • 1910 • Salter Harry • USA
RENOVATION URBAINE • 1972 • Regnier Michel • DCS • CND
RENSEN RENSHO • 1930 • Uchida Tomu • JPN • SUCCESSIVE VICTORIES
RENSHENG • 1985 • Wu Tianming • CHN • LIFE
RENT-A-COP • 1988 • London Jerry • USA
"RENT-A-GIRL" • 1965 • Rose William L. • USA • RENTED
RENT COLLECTOR, THE • 1908 • Williamson James? • UKN
RENT COLLECTOR, THE • 1921 • Taurog Norman, Semon Larry • SHT • USA
RENT DAY • 1907 • Hough Harold • UKN
RENT DODGERS, THE • 1920 • Brown Melville • SHT • USA
RENT FREE • 1922 • Higgin Howard • USA
RENT IN A-REAR, THE • 1913 • Stow Percy • UKN
RENT JUMPERS, THE • 1915 • Cogley Nick • USA
RENTADICK • 1972 • Clark Jim, Loncraine Richard • UKN
RENTAK DESA • 1989 • Razali Rahim • MLY • COUNTRY FROLIC
RENTED see **"RENT-A-GIRL"** • 1965
RENTED LIPS • 1988 • Downey Robert • USA
RENTED MAN, THE • 1917 • Baldwin Ruth Ann • SHT • USA
RENTED RIOT, A • 1937 • Yarbrough Jean • SHT • USA
RENTED TROUBLE • 1922 • Santell Alfred • SHT • USA
RENTMAN, THE • 1986 • Hutchens Ross • SHT • ASL
RENTREE DES CLASSES • 1955 • Rozier Jacques • SHT • FRN
RENUNCIA POR MOTIVOS DE SALUD • 1975 • Baledon Rafael • MXC
RENUNCIATION • 1910 • *Vitagraph* • USA
RENUNCIATION, THE • 1909 • Griffith D. W. • USA
RENUNCIATION, THE • 1913 • *Nestor* • USA
RENUNCIATION, THE • 1914 • *Payne Edna* • USA
RENVOYE DU PARADIS see **TARID EL FARDAWSE** • 1965
RENZ CIRCUS, THE see **ZIRKUS RENZ** • 1943
REOU-TAKH • 1972 • Traore Mahama Johnson • SNL
REP JE ULAZNICA • 1959 • Vukotic Dusan • ANS • YGS • MY TAIL IS MY TICKET ○ MY TAIL'S MY TICKET
REPAID • 1914 • Edwards Walter • USA
REPAID • 1916 • Ricketts Thomas • SHT • USA
REPAID WITH INTEREST • 1910 • *Defender* • USA
REPAIRING A PUNCTURE • 1897 • Welford Walter D. • UKN
REPARATION • 1911 • *Essanay* • USA
REPARATION • 1912 • *Republic* • USA
REPARATION see **PAYING THE PRICE** • 1916
REPARATION, THE • 1914 • Le Saint Edward J. • USA
REPAS A L'ECOLE, LE • 1967 • Lavoie Richard • DCS • CND
REPAS DE BEBE, LE see **DEJEUNER DE BEBE, LE** • 1895
REPAS DE BEBE, LE see **GOUTER DE BEBE, LE** • 1896
REPAS DES FAUVES, LE • 1964 • Christian-Jaque • FRN, ITL, SPN • PASTO DELLE BELVE, IL (ITL)
REPAS EN FAMILLE • 1896-97 • Lumiere Louis • FRN
REPAS FANTASTIQUE, LE • 1900 • Melies Georges • FRN • FANTASTICAL MEAL, A (USA)
REPAS IMPOSSIBLE, LE see **REPAS INFERNAL, LE** • 1901
REPAS INFERNAL, LE • 1901 • Zecca Ferdinand • FRN • REPAS IMPOSSIBLE, LE ○ SOUPIERE, LA ○ INFERNAL MEAL, THE
REPAST see **MESHI** • 1951
REPATRIADO, EL • 1974 • *Cima* • MXC
REPAYING THE DEBT • 1912 • Fitzhamon Lewin • UKN
REPAYMENT see **PARISODH** • 1968
REPEAL see **GAY BRIDE, THE** • 1934
REPEAT DIVE • 1981 • Dotan Shimon • ISR
REPEAT PERFORMANCE • 1947 • Werker Alfred L. • USA
REPEAT WITH US THE FOLLOWING EXERCISE see **REPITAN CON NOSOTROS EL SIGUIENTE EJERCICIO** • 1972
REPEATER • 1982 • Monger Chris • UKN
REPEATER, THE • 1912 • *Russell William* • USA
REPEATER, THE • 1972 • Keach Stacy • SHT • USA
REPEATING THE HONEYMOON • 1918 • Peacocke Leslie T. • SHT • USA
REPENT AT LEISURE • 1941 • Woodruff Frank • USA
REPENTANCE • 1914 • *Glickman William* • USA
REPENTANCE • 1916 • Calvert E. H. • SHT • USA
REPENTANCE • 1922 • Gordon Edward R. • UKN
REPENTANCE see **POKJANIYEAKA, MONANIEBA** • 1984
REPENTANCE, O GOD • 1975 • Reda Aly • EGY
REPENTANCE OF DR. BLINN, THE • 1915 • Smith David • USA
REPENTANT, THE • 1916 • Kent Leon D. • USA
REPENTANT, THE see **PENTITO, IL** • 1985
REPERAGES • 1978 • Soutter Michel • SWT, FRN
REPETITION see **REHEARSAL** • 1953
REPETITION DANS UN CIRQUE • 1903 • Blache Alice • FRN
REPETITION GENERALE, LA • 1980 • Schroeter Werner • FRG
REPITAN CON NOSOTROS EL SIGUIENTE EJERCICIO • 1972 • Kleinman Edgardo • ARG • REPEAT WITH US THE FOLLOWING EXERCISE
REPLAY see **PASSE SIMPLE, LE** • 1977
REPLICA DI UN DELITTO • 1972 • Amadio Silvio, Goslar Jurgen? • ITL • VIOLENCE (USA) ○ REPLICA OF A CRIME ○ AMUCK
REPLICA OF A CRIME see **REPLICA DI UN DELITTO** • 1972
REPMANAD • 1979 • Aberg Lars • SWD • CALL-UP, THE
REPO • 1981 • Vafeas Vassilis • GRC • DAY OFF
REPO MAN • 1984 • Cox Alex • USA
REPONSES DE FEMMES • 1975 • Varda Agnes • FRN
REPORT • 1961 • Balik Jaroslav • CZC • NOTES FROM THE GALLOWS
REPORT • 1963-67 • Conner Bruce • SHT • USA
REPORT, THE • 1988 • Nikolov Milen • BUL
REPORT, THE see **GOZARESH** • 1977
REPORT, THE see **TAQRIR, AL** • 1986
REPORT ABOUT GUYANA see **REPORTAJE SOBRE GUAYANA** • 1973
REPORT FROM BIAFRA • 1968 • van Gasteren Louis A. • DOC • NTH
REPORT FROM CHINA see **YOAKE NO KUNI** • 1967
REPORT FROM HANEDA • 1967 • Ogawa Shinsuke • JPN
REPORT FROM KURNESH • Xhako Marianthi • DOC • ALB
REPORT FROM MILLBROOK • 1966 • Mekas Jonas • USA • MILLBROOK REPORT, THE
REPORT FROM RUSSIA see **OUR RUSSIAN FRONT** • 1942
REPORT FROM THE ALEUTIANS • 1942 • Huston John • DOC • USA
REPORT FROM THE UNITED STATES ON PRESIDENT THEODORE ROOSEVELT • 1907 • *Jaenzon Julius (Ph)* • SWD
REPORT FROM THE VIETNAM WAR see **KOREGA BETONAMU SENSODA** • 1968
REPORT II see **REPORTAZ NR.2** • 1930
REPORT NO.1 see **REPORTAZ NR.1** • 1930
REPORT OF COMRADE STALIN ON PROPOSED CONSTITUTION OF THE USSR TO THE 8TH EXTRAORDINARY CONGRESS OF.. • 1937 • Alexandrov Grigori • USS
REPORT ON A MURDER • 1987 • Najafi Mohammad-Ali • IRN
REPORT ON ABNORMAL EXPENSES: BLUE VIOLATION see **IJO TAIKEN HOKUKU HAKUSHO: AOI BOKO** • 1967
REPORT ON PROSTITUTION see **HUNENREPORT** • 1972
REPORT ON THE CHAIRMAN OF A FARMER'S COOPERATIVE see **RIPORT EGY TSZ-ELNOKROL** • 1960
REPORT ON THE PARTY AND THE GUESTS, A (USA) see **SLAVNOSTI A HOSTECH, O** • 1966
REPORT ON THE SITUATION IN LEBANON • 1976 • Yasri Faisal • LBN
REPORT OR BALLAD ABOUT SAILORS' GIRLFRIENDS see **RAPORTTI ELI BALLADI LAIVATYTOISTA** • 1964
REPORT STRAIGHT FROM THE FRYING PAN, A see **REPORTAZ PROSTO Z PATELNI** • 1960
REPORT TO JUDY • 1944 • *Universal* • SHT • USA
REPORT TO MOTHER see **AMMA ARIYAN** • 1986
REPORT TO THE COMMISSIONER • 1975 • Katselas Milton • USA • OPERATION UNDERCOVER (UKN)
REPORT TO THE STOCKHOLDERS • Mills Bob • SHT • USA
REPORTAGE 57 • 1959 • Veiczi Janos • GDR
REPORTAGE SUR LES INDIENS D'AMAZONE • 1967 • Baratier Jacques • SHT • FRN
REPORTAGE SUR ORLY • 1964 • Godard Jean-Luc • DCS • UKN
REPORTAGE SUR "PARIS BRULE-T-IL?" • 1966 • Reichenbach Francois • SHT • FRN
REPORTAJE • 1953 • Fernandez Emilio • MXC
REPORTAJE SOBRE EL TABACO, UN • 1971 • Bernaza Luis Felipe • DOC • CUB
REPORTAJE SOBRE GUAYANA • 1973 • Brandler Alfredo • DOC • VNZ • REPORT ABOUT GUYANA
REPORTAJE SOBRE UN CRIMEN • 1972 • *A.a. Mexicanos* • MXC
REPORTAZ NR.1 • 1930 • Jakubowska Wanda • DOC • PLN • REPORT NO.1
REPORTAZ NR.2 • 1930 • Jakubowska Wanda • DOC • PLN • REPORT II
REPORTAZ PROSTO Z PATELNI • 1960 • Hoffman Jerzy, Skorzewski Edward • DCS • PLN • REPORT STRAIGHT FROM THE FRYING PAN, A
REPORTED MISSING • 1922 • Lehrman Henry • USA
REPORTED MISSING • 1937 • Carruth Milton • USA
REPORTER, THE • 1911 • *Pathe* • USA
REPORTER, THE • 1911 • *Selig* • USA
REPORTER, THE • 1926 • Seiler Lewis • SHT • USA
REPORTER JIMMIE INTERVENES • 1914 • Le Saint Edward J. • USA
REPORTER ON THE CASE, THE • 1914 • Le Saint Edward J. • USA
REPORTERO, EL • 1966 • Baledon Rafael • MXC, VNZ
REPORTERS • 1981 • Depardon Raymond • DOC • FRN
REPORTER'S ROMANCE, THE • 1911 • *Solax* • USA
REPORTER'S SCOOP, THE • 1913 • *Siegmann George* • USA
REPOS DU GUERRIER, LE • 1962 • Vadim Roger • FRN, ITL • RIPOSO DEL GUERIERO, IL (ITL) ○ LOVE ON A PILLOW (USA) ○ WARRIOR'S REST
REPPS UND WEBBS • 1925 • *Axa-Film* • FRG
REPRESENTATIVE, THE see **PRATINIDHI** • 1964
REPRIEVE see **SHIKKO YUYO** • 1950
REPRIEVE see **CONVICTS FOUR** • 1962
REPRIEVE, THE • 1908 • Brooke Van Dyke • USA
REPRIEVE, THE • 1913 • Lincoln W. J. • ASL
REPRIEVED (UKN) see **SING SING NIGHTS** • 1934
REPRIMAND, LA • 1966 • Fraikin Marcel • BLG
REPRIMIDO, EL • 1974 • Ozores Mariano • SPN
REPRISAL • 1915 • Otto Henry • USA
REPRISAL! • 1956 • Sherman George • USA
REPRISAL, THE • 1916 • Daly William Robert • SHT • USA
REPROACH OF ANNESLEY, THE • 1915 • *Ritchie Franklin* • USA
REPROBATE, THE • 1913 • *Reliance* • USA
REPRODUCTION INTERDITE • 1956 • Grangier Gilles • FRN • SCHEMER, THE (USA)
REPROUVES, LES • 1936 • Severac Jacques • FRN
REPTILE, THE • 1965 • Gilling John • UKN
REPTILICUS • 1961 • Pink Sidney, Bang Paul • DNM, USA
REPUBBLICA DI MUSSOLINI (R.S.I.), LA • 1976 • Grimaldi Angelo • ITL
REPUBLIC IN FLAMES • 1969 • Georgievski Ljubisa • YGS
REPUBLIC IN THE FOREST, THE • Todorov Dimiter • ANM • BUL
REPUBLIC OF SHKID see **RESPUBLIKA SHKID** • 1967
REPUBLIC OF SIN see **FIEVRE MONTE A EL PAO, LA** • 1959
REPUBLIC WILL NEVER FORGET, THE • 1989 • CHN
REPUBLICAN MARRIAGE, A • 1911 • *Gaillord Robert* • USA
REPUBLICANS -THE NEW BREED • 1964 • Leacock Richard • DOC • USA
REPUBLIK DER BACKFISCHE, DIE • 1928 • David Constantin J. • FRG
REPUBLIKA BABSKA • 1969 • Przbyl Henryk • PLN • WOMEN'S REPUBLIC, THE
REPUBLIQUE EST MORTE A DIEN-BIEN-PHU, LA • 1975 • Kanapa Jerome • DOC • FRN
REPUESTA DE OCTUBRE, LA • 1973 • Guzman Patricio • DOC • CHL • RESPONSE IN OCTOBER, THE
REPULO ARANY • 1932 • Sekely Steve • HNG
REPULSION • 1965 • Polanski Roman • UKN
REPUTATION • 1917 • O'Brien John B. • USA
REPUTATION • 1921 • Paton Stuart • USA • FALSE COLORS
REPUTATION (UKN) see **LADY WITH A PAST** • 1932
REQUEST TAKE OFF • 1972 • Vekhotko A., Troshchenko N. • USS
REQUIEM • Nameth Ronald • SHT • USA
REQUIEM • Povh Dusan • SHT • YGS
REQUIEM • 1970 • Dell Jeff • SHT • USA
REQUIEM • 1982 • Fabri Zoltan • HNG
REQUIEM see **REKVIJEM** • 1971
REQUIEM A L'AUBE • 1976 • Desbordes Olivier • FRN

REQUIEM DLA 500,000 • 1963 • Bossak Jerzy, Kazimierczak Waclaw • DOC • PLN • REQUIEM FOR 500,000
REQUIEM FOR 500,000 see **REQUIEM DLA 500,000** • 1963
REQUIEM FOR A CITY BLOCK • 1960 • Kohanyi Julius • CND
REQUIEM FOR A GUNFIGHTER • 1965 • Bennet Spencer Gordon • USA
REQUIEM FOR A HEAVYWEIGHT • 1962 • Nelson Ralph • USA • BLOOD MONEY (UKN)
REQUIEM FOR A LONE MAN see **REQUIEM POR UN HOMBRE SOLO** • 1969
REQUIEM FOR A REVOLUTIONARY see **VOROS REKVIEM** • 1975
REQUIEM FOR A SECRET AGENT see **CHEF SCHICKT SEINEN BESTEN MANN, DER** • 1966
REQUIEM FOR A SPANISH PEASANT see **REQUIEM POR UN CAMPESINO ESPANOL** • 1985
REQUIEM FOR A VILLAGE • 1975 • Raeburn Michael, Gladwell David • UKN
REQUIEM FOR MOZART (USA) see **MOTSART I SALYERI** • 1962
REQUIEM FOR PORK-CHOP • 1975 • Lavut Martin • DOC • CND
REQUIEM IN THE HUNGARIAN MANNER see **N.N. A HALAL ANGYALA** • 1970
REQUIEM PARA EL GRINGO • 1968 • Merino Jose Luis • SPN, ITL • REQUIEM PER UN GRINGO (ITL)
REQUIEM PARA UN SOLTERO • 1972 • *Estudios America* • MXC
REQUIEM PER UN AGENTE SEGRETO (ITL) see **CHEF SCHICKT SEINEN BESTEN MANN, DER** • 1966
REQUIEM PER UN COMMISSARIO DI POLIZIA (ITL) see **OFFICIER DE POLICE SANS IMPORTANCE, UN** • 1973
REQUIEM PER UN GRINGO (ITL) see **REQUIEM PARA EL GRINGO** • 1968
REQUIEM POR UN CAMPESINO ESPANOL • 1985 • Betriu Francisco • SPN • REQUIEM FOR A SPANISH PEASANT
REQUIEM POR UN CANALLA • 1966 • Orozco Fernando • MXC, CLM
REQUIEM POR UN EMPLEADO • 1977 • Merino Fernando • SPN
REQUIEM POR UN HOMBRE SOLO • 1969 • Garrido Jose Carlos • SHT • SPN • REQUIEM FOR A LONE MAN
REQUIEM POUR UN CAID • 1964 • Cloche Maurice • FRN
REQUIEM POUR UN VAMPIRE see **VIERGES ET VAMPIRES** • 1972
REQUIEM POUR UNE CANAILLE (FRN) see **QUALCUNO HA TRADITO** • 1967
REQUIESCANT • 1967 • Lizzani Carlo • ITL, FRG • MOGEN SIE IN FRIEDEN RUH'EN (FRG) ○ LET THEM REST
REQUIN, LE • 1929 • Chomette Henri • FRN
REQUINS DE GIBRALTAR, LES • 1947 • Reinert Emile Edwin • FRN
REQUINS DU PETROLE, LES • 1933 • Decoin Henri, Katscher Rudolf • FRN
REQUISITOIRE, LE • 1930 • Buchowetzki Dimitri • FRN • HOMICIDE
REQUITED FEELINGS (UKN) see **NAGRODZONE UCZUCIA** • 1958
REQUITED LOVE • 1912 • *Stonehouse Ruth* • USA
REQUITTAL, THE • 1912 • *Solax* • USA
RESA DEI CONTI, LA • 1967 • Sollima Sergio • ITL, SPN • HALCON Y LA PRESA, EL (SPN) ○ BIG GUNDOWN, THE (USA) ○ RETURN OF THE COUNTS
RESA DI TITI, LA • 1946 • Bianchi Giorgio • ITL
RESA I NATTEN • 1954 • Faustman Erik • SWD • NIGHT JOURNEY
RESA I TONER • 1959 • Lewin Gosta • SWD
RESA MED FAR • 1968 • Sjoman Vilgot • SHT • SWD • JOURNEY WITH FATHER
RESACA • 1934 • Santana Alberto • PRU
RESAN • 1967 • Klyvare Berndt • SWD • JOURNEY, THE
RESAN • 1977 • Josephson Erland • SWD • TWO
RESAN BORT • 1945 • Sjoberg Alf • SWD • JOURNEY OUT
RESAN TILL DEJ • 1953 • Olin Stig • SWD • JOURNEY TO YOU, THE
RESAN TILL MELONIA see **REISEN TIL MELONIA** • 1989
RESBALOSOS, LOS • 1959 • Delgado Miguel M. • MXC
RESCAPEE DU LUSITANIA, LA • 1917 • Perret Leonce • USA
RESCAPES DE LA PREHISTOIRE, LES • 1973-74 • Valcour Pierre • DOC • CND
RESCATE • 1974 • Alvarez Santiago • DOC • CUB
RESCATE, EL • 1964 • Gomez Urquiza Zacarias • MXC
RESCATE INSOLITO see **PALOMILLA, LA** • 1976
RESCUE • 1958 • Blais Roger • DCS • CND
RESCUE see **BROKEN JOURNEY** • 1948
RESCUE, THE • 1914 • *Hellar Mildred* • USA
RESCUE, THE • 1915 • *Empire* • USA
RESCUE, THE • 1917 • Park Ida May • USA
RESCUE, THE • 1929 • Brenon Herbert • USA
RESCUE, THE • 1984 • Pounchev Borislav • BUL
RESCUE, THE • 1988 • Fairfax Ferdinand • USA
RESCUE A DROWNING MAN see **SPASITYE UTOPAYUSHCHEVO** • 1968
RESCUE AT LATRABJARG see **BJORGUNARAFREKID VID LATRABJARG** • 1946
RESCUE CO-ORDINATOR CENTER, THE • 1958 • Blais Roger • DCS • CND
RESCUE DOG • 1947 • Nichols Charles • ANS • USA
RESCUE FROM DROWNING • 1898 • *Paul R. W.* • UKN
RESCUE FROM GILLIGAN'S ISLAND • 1978 • Martinson Leslie H. • TVM • USA
RESCUE FROM OUTER SPACE see **SUPAH JAIYANTO 2** • 1957
RESCUE ME • 1988 • Harshaw Jubel • USA
RESCUE OF MR. HENPECKED, THE • 1911 • *Thanhouser* • USA
RESCUE OF MOLLY FINNEY, THE • 1910 • *Kalem* • USA
RESCUE OF THE PIONEER'S DAUGHTER, THE • 1910 • *Bison* • USA
RESCUE ON THE RIVER see **SAUVETAGE EN RIVIERE** • 1896
RESCUE PARTY • 1952 • Kroitor Roman • CND
RESCUE SQUAD • 1935 • Bennet Spencer Gordon • USA
RESCUE SQUAD, THE • 1963 • Bell Colin • UKN
RESCUED BY A RANCH GIRL • 1914 • *Warner'S Features* • USA
RESCUED BY LIFEBOAT • 1906 • Collins Alf • UKN
RESCUED BY ROVER • 1905 • Fitzhamon Lewin • UKN
RESCUED BY WIRELESS • 1912 • *Imp* • USA
RESCUED BY WIRELESS • 1914 • McRae Henry • USA
RESCUED FROM AN EAGLE'S NEST • 1907 • Dawley J. Searle, Porter Edwin S. • USA
RESCUED FROM THE BURNING STAKE • 1913 • *St.louis Motion Picture Co* • USA
RESCUED FROM THE DESERT • 1911 • *Melford Judson* • USA
RESCUED IN MID AIR • 1906 • Stow Percy • UKN
RESCUED IN TIME • 1911 • *Standing Jack* • USA
RESCUER, THE • Soloviev Sergei • USS
RESCUERS • 1985 • SAF
RESCUERS, THE • 1977 • Reitherman Wolfgang, Lounsbery John, Stevens Art • ANM • USA
RESCUERS, THE (UKN) see **RATOWNICY** • 1964
RESCUERS DOWN UNDER, THE • 1990 • Butoy Hendel, Gabriel Michael • ANM • USA
RESCUING AN HEIRESS • 1916 • Buss Harry • UKN
RESCUING ANGEL, THE • 1919 • Edwards Walter • USA
RESCUING DAVE • 1913 • *Mason Billy* • USA
RESCUING UNCLE • 1917 • MacGregor Norval • USA
RESEARCH FOR BUILDING • 1970 • Williamson Tom • SHT • UKN
RESEARCH INTO A TRUE VIRGIN see **JUN SHOJO SHIRABE** • 1968
RESEAU SECRET • 1967 • Bastia Jean • FRN • SECRET CONNECTION
RESECTION OF THE LUNGS • 1961 • Goldberger Kurt • DOC • CZC
RESEMBLANCE OF NAKED SPACES • Minh Rinh • VTN
RESENDE • 1969 • Guimaraes Manuel • SHT • PRT
RESERVE HAT RUH • 1931 • Obal Max • FRG
RESERVED FOR LADIES (USA) see **SERVICE FOR LADIES** • 1932
RESERVEHELD, DER • 1965 • Luderer Wolfgang • GDR
RESERVIERT FUR DEN TOD • 1963 • Thiel Heinz • GDR
RESERVIST BEFORE AND AFTER THE WAR, A • 1902 • Williamson James • UKN
RESHMA AUR SHERA • 1971 • Dutt Sunil • IND
RESIDENCE ON EARTH see **RESIDENCIA EN LA TIERRA** • 1979
RESIDENCIA, LA • 1969 • Ibanez Serrador Narciso • SPN • HOUSE THAT SCREAMED, THE (USA) ○ BOARDING SCHOOL, THE
RESIDENCIA EN LA TIERRA • 1979 • Lubbert Orlando, Barckhausen Christiane • DCS • FRG • RESIDENCE ON EARTH
RESIDENCIA PARA ESPIAS • 1966 • Franco Jesus • SPN, FRN
RESIDENT PATIENT, THE • 1921 • Elvey Maurice • UKN
RESIGNATION • 1911 • *Imp* • USA
RESIGNATION • 1912 • *Reliance* • USA
RESISTANCE • 1976 • McMullen Ken, Rodrigues Chris • UKN
RESISTANCE see **OVERVAL, DE** • 1963
RESISTANCE see **UNDERGROUND** • 1970
RESISTANCE AND OHM'S LAW • 1944 • Cukor George • DOC • USA
RESISTANCE (USA) see **PELOTON D'EXECUTION** • 1945
RESISTENZA, UNA NAZIONE CHE RISORGE • 1976 • Giannarelli Ansano • ITL
RESOLUTE SPINSTER, THE see **ODVAZNA SLECNA** • 1969
RESOLUTIONS DE BOUT DE ZAN, LES • 1914 • Feuillade Louis • FRN
RESOLVE, LE • 1915 • *Greenwood Winnifred* • USA
RESORT OF THE METHOD, THE see **RECURSO DEL METODO, EL** • 1978
RESOUNDING CRY, THE see **BRADO RETUMBANTE** • 1968
RESOURCEFUL BILLY • 1915 • *Santa Barbara* • USA
RESOURCEFUL DENTIST, A • 1902 • Collins Alf? • UKN
RESOURCEFUL LOVER, A • 1916 • *Judy* • USA
RESOURCEFUL LOVERS • 1911 • Sennett Mack • USA
RESOURCEFUL ROBERT • 1910 • *Lubin* • USA
RESOURCEFUL SCOUT, THE (USA) see **SCOUT'S STRATEGY, A** • 1911
RESPECT BY PROXY see **RESPECTABLE BY PROXY** • 1920
RESPECT THE LAW • 1941 • Newman Joseph M. • SHT • USA
RESPECTABLE BY PROXY • 1920 • Blackton J. Stuart • USA • RESPECT BY PROXY
RESPECTABLE LADIES OF PARDUBICKE, THE see **POCESTNE PANI PARDUBICKE** • 1944
RESPECTABLE LIFE, A see **ANSTANDIGT LIV, ETT** • 1979
RESPECTABLE PROSTITUTE, THE (USA) see **P.. RESPECTUEUSE, LA** • 1952
RESPECTFUL PROSTITUTE, THE see **P.. RESPECTUEUSE, LA** • 1952
RESPIRATORS • 1915 • Batley Ernest G.? • UKN
RESPLENDENCE OF THE RACE see **FULGURACION DE LA RAZA** • 1922
RESPONDENT, THE see **SPENDERS, THE** • 1921
RESPONSABILITE LIMITEE? see **COLPEVOLI, I** • 1957
RESPONSE IN OCTOBER, THE see **REPUESTA DE OCTUBRE, LA** • 1973
RESPONSIBILITY see **DAR LA CARA** • 1962
RESPONSIVE EYE, THE • 1965 • De Palma Brian • DCS • USA
RESPUBLIKA SHKID • 1967 • Poloka Gennadi • USS • REPUBLIC OF SHKID ○ SHKID REPUBLIC, THE
RESPUESTA, LA • 1969 • Forn Josep Maria • SPN • ANSWER, THE
RESSALAH MIN EMRAA MAGHOOLA • 1962 • Abu Saif Salah • EGY • LETTER FROM AN UNKNOWN WOMAN ○ RISSA MEN IMRAA MAGHOULA ○ RISALA MIN IMRA'A MAJHULA
REST CURE, THE • 1910 • *Atlas* • USA
REST CURE, THE • 1913 • Hotaling Arthur D. • USA
REST CURE, THE • 1917 • *Pokes & Jabbs* • SHT • USA
REST CURE, THE • 1923 • Coleby A. E. • UKN
REST CURE, THE • 1936 • Wilbur Crane • USA
REST DAY, THE • 1927 • White Jules • USA
REST IN PEACE • 1934 • Auer John H. • MXC
REST IN PEACE • 1982 • McLoughlin Tom • USA • ONE DARK NIGHT ○ ENTITY FORCE, THE ○ NIGHT OF DARKNESS
REST IN PIECES • 1987 • Braunstein Joseph • USA
REST IS SILENCE, THE (UKN) see **REST IST SCHWEIGEN, DER** • 1959
REST IST SCHWEIGEN, DER • 1959 • Kautner Helmut • FRG • REST IS SILENCE, THE (UKN)
REST OF THE STORY, THE see **ANANTARAM** • 1986
REST RESORT • 1937 • *Lantz Walter (P)* • ANS • USA
RESTAURANT • 1965 • Warhol Andy • USA
RESTAURANT, THE • 1920 • Fleischer Dave • ANS • USA
RESTAURANT INTIM • 1950 • Faustman Erik • SWD • INTIMATE RESTAURANT, THE
RESTAURANT RIOT, A • 1920 • Howe J. A. • SHT • USA
RESTE AVEC NOUS, ON S'TIRE • 1981 • Tarantini Michele Massimo • FRN, ITL
RESTING PLACE • 1986 • Korty John • TVM • USA • HALLMARK HALL OF FAME
RESTITUTION • 1915 • Otto Henry • USA
RESTITUTION • 1918 • Gaye Howard • USA
RESTLESS • 1985 • Lewiston Denis • NZL
RESTLESS see **MAN-TRAP** • 1961
RESTLESS see **BELOVED, THE** • 1971
RESTLESS BREED, THE • 1957 • Dwan Allan • USA
RESTLESS DAUGHTERS see **UNRUHIGE TOCHTER** • 1967
RESTLESS KNIGHTS • 1935 • Lamont Charles • SHT • USA
RESTLESS NATIVES • 1986 • Hoffman Michael • UKN
RESTLESS NIGHT, THE (USA) see **UNRUHIGE NACHT** • 1958
RESTLESS ONE, THE • 1965 • Ross Dick • USA
RESTLESS ONES, THE see **NEMIRNI** • 1967
RESTLESS ONES, THE see **NEPOSYEDY** • 1968
RESTLESS PORT, THE • 1966 • van der Linden Charles Huguenot • NTH
RESTLESS SAX, THE • 1931 • *Mintz Charles (P)* • ANS • USA
RESTLESS SEX, THE • 1920 • Leonard Robert Z. • USA
RESTLESS SOULS • 1919 • Dowlan William C. • USA
RESTLESS SOULS • 1922 • Ensminger Robert • USA
RESTLESS SPIRIT, THE • 1913 • Dwan Allan • USA
RESTLESS THREE, THE • 1919 • Bruce Robert C. • USA
RESTLESS WIVES • 1924 • La Cava Gregory • USA
RESTLESS WOMAN, THE • 1914 • Vale Travers • USA
RESTLESS YEARS, THE • 1958 • Kautner Helmut • USA • WONDERFUL YEARS, THE (UKN)
RESTLESS YOUTH • 1928 • Cabanne W. Christy • USA • WAYWARD YOUTH (UKN)
RESTLESS YOUTH see **TREVOZHNAYA MOLODOST** • 1955
RESTLESS YOUTH see **JIWA REMAJA** • 1975
RESTLESS YOUTH (UKN) see **HEART OF BROADWAY, THE** • 1928
RESTORATION, THE • 1909 • Griffith D. W. • USA
RESTORATION, THE • 1910 • *Thanhouser* • USA
RESTORATION, THE • 1912 • Balshofer Fred J. • USA
RESTORATION OF THE "NIGHT WATCH", THE • 1977 • Kok Theo • SHT • NTH
RESTORED BY REPENTANCE • 1908 • *Lubin* • USA
RESTOS DEL NAUFRAGIO, LOS • 1977 • Franco Ricardo • VNZ, SPN • REMAINDER OF THE SHIPWRECK, THE ○ REMAINS OF THE SHIPWRECK, THE ○ REMAINS OF THE WRECK, THE
RESULT, THE see **RESULTAT** • 1966
RESULT OF A PICNIC, THE (USA) see **HOW MARY DECIDED** • 1911
RESULT OF EATING HORSE FLESH • 1908 • *Pathe* • FRN
RESULTAT • 1966 • Zaninovic Ante • ANS • YGS • RESULT, THE
RESURRECCION • 1931 • Selman David • USA
RESURRECCION • 1943 • Martinez Solares Gilberto • MXC
RESURRECTED • 1989 • Greengrass Paul • UKN
RESURRECTED, THE see **UJRAELOK** • 1921
RESURRECTED MONSTER, THE see **MONSTRUO RESUCITADO, EL** • 1953
RESURRECTIO • 1931 • Blasetti Alessandro • ITL • RESURRECTION
RESURRECTION • 1909 • Calmettes Andre • FRN
RESURRECTION • 1909 • Griffith D. W. • USA
RESURRECTION • 1912 • *Walls Blanche* • USA
RESURRECTION • 1913 • *Cummings Irving* • USA
RESURRECTION • 1918 • Jose Edward • USA
RESURRECTION • 1923 • L'Herbier Marcel • FRN
RESURRECTION • 1927 • Carewe Edwin • USA • PRINCE DIMITRI
RESURRECTION • 1931 • Carewe Edwin • USA
RESURRECTION • 1980 • Petrie Daniel • USA
RESURRECTION see **RESURREZIONE** • 1917
RESURRECTION see **RESURRECTIO** • 1931
RESURRECTION see **WE LIVE AGAIN** • 1934
RESURRECTION see **FUKKATSU** • 1950
RESURRECTION see **AUFERSTEHUNG** • 1958
RESURRECTION see **VOSKRESENIE** • 1961
RESURRECTION, A see **EN OPSTANDELSE** • 1914
RESURRECTION, THE • 1916 • *Pathe* • SHT • USA
RESURRECTION, THE • 1986 • Manttari Anssi • FNL
RESURRECTION DAY see **FUKKATSU NO HI** • 1979
RESURRECTION DU BOUIF, LA • 1922 • Pouctal Henri • FRN
RESURRECTION OF BRONCHO BILLY, THE • 1970 • Carpenter John (c/d) • SHT • USA
RESURRECTION OF CALEB WORTH, THE • 1914 • Miller Ashley • USA
RESURRECTION OF CLAYTON ZACHARY WHEELER, THE see **RESURRECTION OF ZACHARY WHEELER, THE** • 1973
RESURRECTION OF DAN PACKARD, THE • 1916 • Smithson Frank • SHT • USA
RESURRECTION OF EVE • 1973 • Mitchell Jim, Mitchell Artie • USA
RESURRECTION OF GOLD BAR, THE • 1917 • Horne James W. • SHT • USA
RESURRECTION OF HOLLIS, THE • 1916 • Davenport Harry • SHT • USA
RESURRECTION OF JOHN, THE • 1911 • *Edison* • USA
RESURRECTION OF LAZARUS, THE • 1910 • *Eclair* • USA
RESURRECTION OF LOVE see **GHIAMAT ESHGHE** • 1974
RESURRECTION OF LOVE, THE (USA) see **AI NI YOMIGAERU HI** • 1922
RESURRECTION OF ZACHARY WHEELER, THE • 1973 • Wynn Bob • TVM • USA • RESURRECTION OF CLAYTON ZACHARY WHEELER, THE
RESURRECTION SYNDICATE, THE see **NOTHING BUT THE NIGHT** • 1972

RESURREZIONE • 1917 • Caserini Mario • ITL • RESURRECTION
RESURREZIONE • 1944 • Calzavara Flavio • ITL
RESURREZIONE see **AUFERSTEHUNG** • 1958
RETABLO PARA ROMEO Y JULIETA, UN • 1971 • Reboiro Antonio Fernandez • CUB • NEW ROMEO AND JULIET, A
RETAGGIO DI SANGUE • 1956 • Calandri Max • ITL
RETAGGIO D'ODIO • 1915 • Negroni Baldassare • ITL
RETALHOS DA VIDA DE UM MEDICO • 1962 • do Canto Jorge Brum • PRT
RETALIATION • 1911 • *Yankee* • USA
RETALIATION see **SHIMA WA MORATTA** • 1968
RETALIATION see **PRATISHODH** • 1983
RETALIATION, THE see **DESQUITE, EL** • 1982
RETALIATOR • 1987 • Holzman Allan • USA • PROGRAMMED TO KILL
RETALIATOR II: OUT ON BAIL • 1989 • Hessler Gordon • USA
RETAPEUR DE CERVELLE, LE • 1911 • Cohl Emile • ANS • FRN • BRAIN INSPECTOR, THE ○ BRAINS REPAIRED
RETARDED LIFE • 1960 • Goldberger Kurt • DOC • CZC
RETE, LA • 1970 • Serra Gianni • MTV • ITL
RETE PIENA DI SABBIA, UNA • 1967 • Ruffo Elio • ITL
RETENEZ-MOI.. OU JE FAIS UN MALHEUR • 1983 • Gerard Michel • FRN
RETEZ • 1981 • Svoboda Jiri • CZC • CHAIN, THE
RETICENCIAS see **. . .** • 1972
RETIK THE MOON MENACE • 1966 • Brannon Fred C. • USA
RETINAL CAPSULE • 1968 • Markson Morley • CND
RETIRED PLAYBOY, A see **KATI KOURASMENA PALLIKARIA** • 1967
RETIREMENT OF MR. NAPOLEON, THE see **KIGEKI KAKUEKITEISHA** • 1965
RETO A LA VIDA • 1953 • Bracho Julio • MXC
RETORNO, EL • 1926 • Bertoni Romulo • CRC
RETORNO A LA JUVENTAD • 1953 • Bustillo Oro Juan • MXC • RETURN TO YOUTH
RETORNO A LA VERDAD • 1956 • del Amo Antonio • SPN
RETORNO A QUINTO PATIO • 1951 • Diaz Morales Jose • MXC
RETORNO DE CLINT EL SOLITARIO, EL • 1972 • Balcazar Alfonso • SPN
RETORNO DE LAS TINIEBLAS, EL • 1976 • Iglesias Miguel • SPN
RETORNO DE LOS VAMPIROS, EL • Zabalza Jose Maria • SPN • RETURN OF THE VAMPIRES, THE
RETORNO DE WALPURGIS, EL • 1973 • Aured Carlos • SPN • BLACK HARVEST OF COUNTESS DRACULA, THE ○ CURSE OF THE DEVIL ○ RETURN OF WALPURGIS, THE
RETORNO DEL HOMBRO LOBO, EL • 1980 • Molina Jacinto • SPN
RETOUR see **APRES L'ORAGE** • 1941
RETOUR, LE • 1928 • Machin Alfred • FRN
RETOUR, LE • 1946 • Cartier-Bresson Henri • FRN
RETOUR, LE • 1956-57 • Devlin Bernard • SHT • CND
RETOUR, LE • 1961 • Goretta Claude • SHT • SWT
RETOUR, LE • 1971 • Fares Tewfik • ALG
RETOUR, LE • 1973 • Solo Randrasana Ignace • MDG
RETOUR A BONHEUR • 1940 • Jayet Rene • FRN • ENFANT DANS LA TOURMENTE, L' ○ VOIX DU BONHEUR, LA ○ OMBRES NOIRES
RETOUR A DIEPPE • 1954-55 • Devlin Bernard • DCS • CND
RETOUR A DRESDEN see **RETURN TO DRESDEN** • 1986
RETOUR A LA BIEN-AIMEE • 1979 • Adam Jean-Francois • FRN
RETOUR A LA RAISON, LE • 1923 • Ray Man • SHT • FRN • RETURN TO REASON, THE
RETOUR A LA TERRE • 1938 • *Tati Jacques* • SHT • FRN
RETOUR A LA TERRE, LE • 1977 • Gosselin Bernard, Perrault Pierre • DOC • CND
RETOUR A LA TERRE, LE see **AWDA ILA AR-RIF, AL** • 1939
RETOUR A LA VIE • 1948 • Lampin Georges, Clouzot Henri-Georges, Dreville Jean, Cayatte Andre • FRN • RETURN TO LIFE
RETOUR A LA VIE see **ACHRAROUMES** • 1978
RETOUR A L'AUBE • 1938 • Decoin Henri • FRN • SHE RETURNED AT DAWN (USA)
RETOUR A MARSEILLE • 1979 • Allio Rene • FRN, FRG • RENDEZVOUS A MARSEILLE
RETOUR A NEW YORK • 1962 • Reichenbach Francois • SHT • FRN
RETOUR AU CANTONNEMENT • 1896 • Melies Georges • FRN • RETURN TO THE BARRACKS
RETOUR AU PARADIS • 1935 • de Poligny Serge • FRN • VACANCES
RETOUR AUX CHAMPS, LE • 1918 • de Baroncelli Jacques • FRN
RETOUR D'AFRIQUE, LE • 1973 • Tanner Alain • SWT, FRN • RETURN FROM AFRICA
RETOUR DE BONHEUR • 1930 • Jayet Rene, Revol Claude • FRN • RETURN OF HAPPINESS
RETOUR DE CHRISTOPHE COLON, LE • 1982 • Saire Jean-Pierre • FRN
RETOUR DE DON CAMILLO, LE • 1953 • Duvivier Julien • FRN, ITL • RITORNO DI DON CAMILLO, IL (ITL) ○ RETURN OF DON CAMILLO, THE
RETOUR DE FLAMME • 1942 • Fescourt Henri • FRN
RETOUR DE JEAN-MAURICE, LE • 1987 • Demontaut Philippe • FRN
RETOUR DE LA FILLE DU DRAGON, LE • Isoppo Daniel • FRN • RETURN OF THE DRAGON'S DAUGHTER, THE ○ RETURN OF THE DRAGON GIRL, THE
RETOUR DE L'IMMACULEE CONCEPTION, LE • 1971 • Forcier Andre • CND • GRANDS ENFANTS, LES
RETOUR DE MANIVEL, LE • 1916 • Feuillade Louis • FRN
RETOUR DE MANIVELLE • 1957 • de La Patelliere Denys • FRN • THERE'S ALWAY'S A PRICE TAG (USA)
RETOUR DE MARTIN GUERRE, LE • 1982 • Vigne Daniel • FRN • RETURN OF MARTIN GUERRE, THE (UKN)
RETOUR DE SCRATCH DANS LE + + –, LE see **POUR UNE POIGNEE DE CACAHUETES** • 1977
RETOUR DE SURCOUF, LE • 1965 • FRN
RETOUR DE TIEMAN, LE • 1970 • Kouyate Djibril • SHT • MLI • RETURN OF TIEMAN, THE
RETOUR DES BIDASSES EN FOLIE, LE • 1982 • Vocoret Michel • FRN
RETOUR DES CHAMPS • 1899-00 • Blache Alice • FRN
RETOUR DES VEUVES, LE • 1978 • Bernard-Aubert Claude • FRN
RETOUR DU BISON, LE see **RETURN OF THE BUFFALO, THE** • 1934
RETOUR DU CONSCRIT, LE • 1944 • Gelinas Gratien • SHT • CND
RETOUR DU DOCTEUR MABUSE, LE see **IM STAHLNETZ DES DR. MABUSE** • 1961
RETOUR DU FILS PRODIGUE, LE see **AWDAT AL IBN AL DAL** • 1976
RETOUR DU GRAND BLOND, LE • 1975 • Robert Yves • FRN • RETURN OF THE TALL BLOND MAN WITH ONE BLACK SHOE (USA) ○ RETURN OF THE TALL BLOND, THE
RETOUR D'ULYSSE, LE • 1908 • Le Bargy Charles, Calmettes Andre • FRN • RETURN OF ULYSSES, THE
RETOUR D'UN AVENTURIER, LE • 1966 • Alassane Moustapha • NGR, FRN • RETURN OF THE ADVENTURER, THE ○ RETURN OF AN ADVENTURER
RETOUR D'UNE PROMENADE EN MER • 1896-97 • Lumiere Louis • FRN
RETOUR EN FORCE • 1979 • Poire Jean-Marie • FRN
RETOUR MADRID • 1968 • Haanstra Bert • SHT • NTH • RETURN TICKET TO MADRID
RETRACING STEPS • 1988 • Blackwood Michael • USA
RETRANSMISION, LA • 1974 • Diez Miguel Angel • SHT • SPN
RETRAT INTERMITENT see **OCANA, UN RETRATO INTERMITENTE** • 1978
RETRATO, EL • 1963 • Valdes Oscar, Solas Humberto • CUB
RETRATO DE FAMILIA • 1976 • Gimenez-Rico Antonio • SPN • FAMILY PORTRAIT
RETRATO DE TERESA • 1979 • Vega Pastor • CUB • PORTRAIT OF TERESA
RETREADS • 1989 • Connell James • USA
RETREAT • 1971 • Patterson Garry • SHT • ASL
RETREAT, THE see **ODWROT** • 1969
RETREAT FROM EDEN, THE • 1912 • *Solax* • USA
RETREAT FROM KISKA see **TAIHEIYO KISEKI NO SAKUSEN KISUKA** • 1965
RETREAT, HELL! • 1952 • Lewis Joseph H. • USA
RETRIBUTION • 1910 • *Defender* • USA
RETRIBUTION • 1912 • *Powers* • USA
RETRIBUTION • 1912 • *Republic* • USA
RETRIBUTION • 1913 • *Kalem* • USA
RETRIBUTION • 1913 • *Lubin* • USA
RETRIBUTION • 1913 • *Thanhauser* • USA
RETRIBUTION • 1913 • *Solax* • USA
RETRIBUTION • 1913 • Reid Wallace, Robards Willis • *Nestor* • USA
RETRIBUTION • 1913 • Wilson Frank? • UKN
RETRIBUTION • 1914 • *Fischer Margarita* • USA
RETRIBUTION • 1914 • Batley Ethyle • UKN
RETRIBUTION • 1915 • Le Saint Edward J. • USA
RETRIBUTION • 1916 • Batley Ernest G. • UKN
RETRIBUTION • 1921 • Lionello Armand • ASL
RETRIBUTION • 1988 • Magar Guy • USA
RETRIBUTION see **CHILD THOU GAVEST ME, THE** • 1921
RETRIBUTION see **DEFEND YOURSELF** • 1925
RETRIBUTION OF YSOBEL, THE • 1913 • *Frontier* • USA
RETRIEVERS, THE see **HOT AND DEADLY** • 1981
RETROGRESSION • 1913 • *Buckham Hazel* • USA
RETROSCENA • 1939 • Blasetti Alessandro • ITL
RETROUVAILLES, LES • 1971 • Bouchouchi Youssef • ALG
RETTE, DEN • 1913 • Davidsen Hjalmar • DNM
RETTEN SEJRER • 1917 • Holger-Madsen • DNM • JUSTICE VICTORIOUS
RETTER DER MENSCHHEIT • 1919 • *Haack Kate* • FRG
RETURN • 1985 • Silver Andrew • USA
RETURN see **ZAVRACHTANE** • 1967
RETURN see **ALBUM POLSKI** • 1970
RETURN see **RITORNO** • 1973
RETURN, THE • 1911 • Porter Edwin S. • USA
RETURN, THE • 1914 • *Frazer Robert* • USA
RETURN, THE • 1916 • Bertram William • *Mustang* • SHT • USA
RETURN, THE • 1916 • Heffron Thomas N. • *Selig* • SHT • USA
RETURN, THE • 1921 • Paul Fred • UKN
RETURN, THE • 1970 • *Stacey Dist.* • USA
RETURN, THE • 1973 • *Dullea Keir* • MTV • USA
RETURN, THE • 1973 • Rydman Sture • SHT • UKN
RETURN, THE • 1975 • Haddad Marwan • DOC • SYR
RETURN, THE • 1980 • Clark Greydon • USA • ALIEN'S RETURN, THE ○ EARTHRIGHT
RETURN, THE see **KOM TILLBAKA, DE** • 1962
RETURN, THE see **POVRATAK** • 1966
RETURN, THE see **POWROT** • 1969
RETURN, THE see **POWROT** • 1972
RETURN, THE see **RUCKKEHR** • 1977
RETURN, THE see **POVRATAK** • 1980
RETURN, THE see **PHERA** • 1987
RETURN, THE see **RUCKKEHR, DIE** • 1990
RETURN A TICKET TO CAIRO • 1975 • Abnudi Atiat Al- • UKN
RETURN ATTACK, A see **SEI SIMPATICHE CAROGNE** • 1968
RETURN BY BOAT see **POWROT STATKU** • 1964
RETURN ENGAGEMENT • 1978 • Hardy Joseph • TVM • USA
RETURN ENGAGEMENT • 1983 • Rudolph Alan • USA
RETURN FARE TO LAUGHTER • 1950 • Anderson James M. • UKN
RETURN FROM AFRICA see **RETOUR D'AFRIQUE, LE** • 1973
RETURN FROM HELL see **INTOARCEREA DIN IAD** • 1984
RETURN FROM LIMBO see **WOMEN ARE LIKE THAT** • 1938
RETURN FROM NOWHERE • 1944 • Burnford Paul • USA
RETURN FROM THE ASHES • 1965 • Thompson J. Lee • UKN, USA
RETURN FROM THE BEYOND (USA) see **MISTERIOS DE LA MAGIA NEGRA** • 1957
RETURN FROM THE PAST • 1967 • Hewitt David L. • USA • DR. TERROR'S GALLERY OF HORRORS ○ GALLERY OF HORRORS ○ BLOOD SUCKERS, THE
RETURN FROM THE RIVER KWAI • 1989 • McLaglen Andrew V. • UKN
RETURN FROM THE SEA • 1954 • Selander Lesley • USA
RETURN FROM THE SUN • 1956 • Casparius Hans G. • SHT • UKN
RETURN FROM WITCH MOUNTAIN • 1978 • Hough John • USA
RETURN HOME • 1989 • Argall Ray • ASL
RETURN HOME see **NAVRAT DOMU** • 1948
RETURN OF A CITIZEN see **AWDAT MOWATINE** • 1987
RETURN OF A MAN CALLED HORSE • 1976 • Kershner Irvin • USA
RETURN OF A SHIP see **POWROT STATKU** • 1964
RETURN OF A SMILE see **VOZVRASHCHYENIYE ULYBKI** • 1968
RETURN OF A STRANGER • 1937 • Hanbury Victor • UKN • FACE BEHIND THE SCAR, THE (USA) ○ RETURN OF THE STRANGER
RETURN OF A STRANGER • 1962 • Varnel Max • UKN
RETURN OF A SWORDSMAN • 1966 • HKG
RETURN OF AN ADVENTURER see **RETOUR D'UN AVENTURIER, LE** • 1966
RETURN OF BATMAN, THE see **BATMAN AND ROBIN** • 1949
RETURN OF BECKY, THE • 1912 • *Bayne Beverly* • USA
RETURN OF BEN CASEY, THE • 1988 • Scanlan Joseph L. • TVM • USA, CND
RETURN OF BOSTON BLACKIE, THE • 1927 • Hoyt Harry O. • USA
RETURN OF BRUCE • Velasco Joseph • HKG, PHL
RETURN OF BULLDOG DRUMMOND, THE • 1934 • Summers Walter • UKN
RETURN OF CAL CLAUSON, THE • 1914 • *Reliance* • USA
RETURN OF CAPTAIN AMERICA, THE see **CAPTAIN AMERICA** • 1944
RETURN OF CAPTAIN INVINCIBLE • 1982 • Mora Philippe • ASL • LEGEND IN LEOTARDS
RETURN OF CAPTAIN JOHN, THE • 1912 • *Imp* • USA
RETURN OF CAPTAIN KLYDE, THE see **KAPTAJN KLYDE OG HANS VENNER VENDER TILBAGE** • 1981
RETURN OF CAPTAIN MARVEL see **ADVENTURES OF CAPTAIN MARVEL** • 1941
RETURN OF CAPTAIN NEMO, THE see **AMAZING CAPTAIN NEMO, THE** • 1978
RETURN OF CAROL DEANE, THE • 1938 • Woods Arthur • UKN
RETURN OF CASEY JONES, THE • 1933 • McCarthy John P. • USA • TRAIN 2419
RETURN OF CHANDU, THE • 1934 • Taylor Ray • SRL • USA
RETURN OF CHARLIE CHAN, THE see **CHARLIE CHAN (HAPPINESS IS A WARM CLUE)** • 1971
RETURN OF COMPANY D • 1911 • *Bison* • USA
RETURN OF COUNT YORGA • 1971 • Kelljan Bob • USA • ABOMINABLE COUNT YORGA, THE
RETURN OF CRIME, THE • 1913 • *Tennant Barbara* • USA
RETURN OF DANIEL BARRION, THE see **PAGBABALIK NI DANIEL BARRION, ANG** • 1968
RETURN OF DANIEL BOONE, THE • 1941 • Hillyer Lambert • USA • MAYOR'S NEST, THE (UKN)
RETURN OF DESPERADO, THE • 1988 • Swackhamer E. W. • TVM • USA • RETURN OF THE DESPERADO, THE ○ TOWN CALLED BEAUTY, A
RETURN OF DJAMOKA, THE see **CAMOKANIN DONUSU** • 1968
RETURN OF DR. FU MANCHU, THE • 1930 • Lee Rowland V. • USA • NEW ADVENTURES OF DR. FU MANCHU, THE ○ INSIDIOUS DR. FU MANCHU, THE
RETURN OF DR. MABUSE, THE see **IM STAHLNETZ DES DR. MABUSE** • 1961
RETURN OF DR. SATAN see **DR. SATAN Y LA MAGIA NEGRA, EL** • 1967
RETURN OF DR. X, THE • 1939 • Sherman Vincent • USA
RETURN OF DON CAMILLO, THE see **RETOUR DE DON CAMILLO, LE** • 1953
RETURN OF DRACULA, THE • 1958 • Landres Paul • USA • FANTASTIC DISAPPEARING MAN, THE (UKN) ○ CURSE OF DRACULA
RETURN OF "DRAW" EGAN, THE • 1916 • Hart William S. • USA
RETURN OF EVE, THE • 1916 • Berthelet Arthur • USA
RETURN OF FRANK CANNON, THE • 1980 • Allen Corey • TVM • USA
RETURN OF FRANK JAMES, THE • 1940 • Lang Fritz • USA
RETURN OF FRANKENSTEIN, THE see **BRIDE OF FRANKENSTEIN** • 1935
RETURN OF GENTLEMAN JOE, THE • 1915 • *Craig Nell* • USA
RETURN OF GIANT MAJIN, THE (USA) see **DAIMAJIN IKARU** • 1966
RETURN OF GILBERT AND SULLIVAN, THE • 1950 • *Allen Irving (P)* • USA
RETURN OF GODZILLA, THE see **GOJIRA NO GYAKUSHYU** • 1955
RETURN OF GOOPY AND BAGHA, THE see **GOOPY BAGHA PHIRE ELO** • 1990
RETURN OF HAPPINESS see **RETOUR DE BONHEUR** • 1930
RETURN OF HELEN REDMOND, THE • 1914 • Ricketts Thomas • USA
RETURN OF JACK BELLEW, THE • 1914 • Thornby Robert T. • USA
RETURN OF JACK SLADE, THE • 1955 • Schuster Harold • USA • TEXAS ROSE (UKN) ○ SON OF SLADE
RETURN OF JAMES JEROME, THE • 1916 • Sloman Edward • SHT • USA
RETURN OF JESSE JAMES, THE • 1950 • Hilton Arthur • USA
RETURN OF JIMMY VALENTINE, THE • 1936 • Collins Lewis D. • USA
RETURN OF JOACHIM STILLER, THE see **KOMST VAN JOACHIM STILLER, DE** • 1976
RETURN OF JOE FORRESTER, THE • 1975 • Vogel Virgil W. • TVM • USA
RETURN OF JOHN BOSTON, THE • 1916 • Byrne Jack • SHT • USA
RETURN OF JOHN GRAY, THE • 1912 • *Walthall Henry B.* • USA
RETURN OF JOSEY WALES, THE • 1986 • Parks Michael • TVM • USA
RETURN OF KATARINA KOZUL, THE see **POVRATAK KATARINE KOZUL** • 1989

RETURN OF KID BARKER, THE • Emery Robert J. • USA
RETURN OF KING LAPUSNEANU, THE see **INTOARCEREA LUI VODA LAPUSNEANU** • 1980
RETURN OF KIT CARSON, THE • 1933 • Schaefer Armand, Clark Colbert • USA
RETURN OF LADY LINDA, THE • 1913 • Lund O. A. C. • USA
RETURN OF LIFE, THE • 1912 • *Majestic* • USA
RETURN OF MAGELLAN, THE • 1974 • Nicolae Cristiana • RMN • MAGELLAN'S RETURN
RETURN OF MAJIN, THE see **DAIMAJIN IKARU** • 1966
RETURN OF MARCUS WELBY, M.D., THE • 1984 • Singer Alexander • TVM • USA
RETURN OF MARTIN DONNELLY, THE • 1915 • Humphrey William • USA
RETURN OF MARTIN GUERRE, THE (UKN) see **RETOUR DE MARTIN GUERRE, LE** • 1982
RETURN OF MARY, THE • 1918 • Lucas Wilfred • USA
RETURN OF MAXIM, THE see **VOZVRASHCHENIYE MAKSIMA** • 1937
RETURN OF MAXWELL SMART, THE see **NUDE BOMB, THE** • 1980
RETURN OF MICKEY SPILLANE'S MIKE HAMMER, THE • 1986 • Danton Ray • TVM • USA
RETURN OF MR. H., THE see **MADMEN OF MANDORAS, THE** • 1964
RETURN OF MR. MOTO, THE • 1965 • Morris Ernest • UKN • MR. MOTO AND THE PERSIAN OIL CASE
RETURN OF MONTE CRISTO, THE • 1946 • Levin Henry • USA • MONTE CRISTO'S REVENGE (UKN)
RETURN OF NATHAN BECKER, THE • 1933 • Milman R. M.
RETURN OF OCTOBER, THE • 1948 • Lewis Joseph H. • USA • DATE WITH DESTINY, A (UKN)
RETURN OF O'GARRY, THE • 1918 • Finley Ned • SHT • USA
RETURN OF OLD MOTHER RILEY,THE see **OLD MOTHER RILEY** • 1937
RETURN OF PETER BLIMM, THE • 1913 • *Lubin* • USA
RETURN OF PETER GRIMM, THE • 1926 • Schertzinger Victor • USA
RETURN OF PETER GRIMM, THE • 1935 • Nicholls George Jr. • USA
RETURN OF RAFFLES, THE • 1932 • Markham Mansfield • UKN
RETURN OF RICHARD NEAL, THE • 1915 • *Bushman Francis X.* • USA
RETURN OF RINGO, THE (UKN) see **RITORNO DI RINGO, IL** • 1965
RETURN OF RUSTY, THE • 1946 • Castle William • USA
RETURN OF SABATA (UKN) see **E TORNATO SABATA.. HAI CHIUSO UN'ALTRA VOLTE** • 1971
RETURN OF "ST. LUCAS", THE see **VOZVRASHCHENIE "SVYATOVO LUKI"** • 1971
RETURN OF ST. LUKE, THE see **VOZVRASHCHENIE "SVYATOVO LUKI"** • 1971
RETURN OF SANDOKAN see **SANDOKAN CONTRO IL LEOPARDO DI SARAWAK** • 1965
RETURN OF SHERLOCK HOLMES, THE • 1929 • Dean Basil, Brook Clive • USA
RETURN OF SHERLOCK HOLMES, THE • 1986 • Connor Kevin • UKN
RETURN OF SINANOGLU, THE see **SINANOGLUNUN DONUSU** • 1968
RETURN OF "SOAPWEED SCOTTY", THE • 1917 • King Burton L. • SHT • USA
RETURN OF SOPHIE LANG, THE • 1936 • Archainbaud George • USA
RETURN OF SPRING, THE see **PRIZIVANJE PROLJECA** • 1979
RETURN OF SUPERBUG • 1979 • Zehetgruber Rudolf • FRG
RETURN OF T.R.H. THE PRINCE AND PRINCESS OF WALES • 1903 • Paul Robert William • UKN
RETURN OF TA-WA-WA • 1910 • *Melies* • USA
RETURN OF TARZAN, THE • 1920 • Revier Harry • USA • REVENGE OF TARZAN, THE
RETURN OF THE 38 GANG, THE see **RITORNANO QUELLI DELLA CALIBRO 38** • 1977
RETURN OF THE ADVENTURER, THE see **RETOUR D'UN AVENTURIER, LE** • 1966
RETURN OF THE ALIEN'S DEADLY SPAWN see **DEADLY SPAWN, THE** • 1983
RETURN OF THE APE MAN • 1944 • Rosen Phil • USA
RETURN OF THE BAD MEN • 1948 • Enright Ray • USA
RETURN OF THE BEVERLY HILLBILLIES, THE • 1981 • Leeds Robert • TVM • USA
RETURN OF THE BIG CAT • 1975 • Leetch Tom • USA • BIG CAT, THE
RETURN OF THE BIONIC BOY, THE see **DYNAMITE JOHNSON** • 1978
RETURN OF THE BIRDS • Ninh Nguyen Hai • VTN
RETURN OF THE BLIND DEAD (USA) see **ATAUD DE LOS MUERTOS SIN OJOS, EL** • 1973
RETURN OF THE BOOMERANG see **ADAM'S WOMAN** • 1970
RETURN OF THE BUFFALO, THE • 1934 • Sparling Gordon • DCS • CND • RETOUR DU BISON, LE
RETURN OF THE CHINESE BOXER • 1974 • Wang Yu • HKG
RETURN OF THE CISCO KID, THE • 1939 • Leeds Herbert I. • USA
RETURN OF THE COMET, THE see **REGRESO DE COMETA, EL** • 1988
RETURN OF THE CORSICAN BROTHERS (UKN) see **BANDITS OF CORSICA, THE** • 1953
RETURN OF THE COUNTS see **RESA DEI CONTI, LA** • 1967
RETURN OF THE DEADLY BLADE see **FEI TAO, YU CHIEN FEI TAO** • 1981
RETURN OF THE DESPERADO, THE see **RETURN OF DESPERADO, THE** • 1988
RETURN OF THE DIRTY SEVEN, THE see **SHICHININ NONYAJU CHI NO SENGEN** • 1967
RETURN OF THE DRAGON • 1975 • Foster Norman • USA
RETURN OF THE DRAGON GIRL, THE see **RETOUR DE LA FILLE DU DRAGON, LE**
RETURN OF THE DRAGON (USA) see **MENG LUNG KUO CHIANG** • 1972
RETURN OF THE DRAGON'S DAUGHTER, THE see **RETOUR DE LA FILLE DU DRAGON, LE**
RETURN OF THE DURANGO KID • 1945 • Abrahams Derwin • USA • STOLEN TIME (UKN)
RETURN OF THE ELUSIVE AVENGERS, THE see **KORONA RUSSKOI IMPERII** • 1971
RETURN OF THE ENVOY, THE see **POWROT POSLA** • 1965
RETURN OF THE EVIL DEAD see **ATAUD DE LOS MUERTOS SIN OJOS, EL** • 1973
RETURN OF THE FIVE MASKED MEN, THE see **MASKELI BESLERIN DONUSU** • 1968
RETURN OF THE FLY, THE • 1959 • Bernds Edward • USA
RETURN OF THE FROG, THE • 1938 • Elvey Maurice • UKN
RETURN OF THE FRONTIERSMAN • 1950 • Bare Richard L. • USA
RETURN OF THE GIANT MONSTERS, THE (USA) see **GAMERA TAI GYAOS** • 1967
RETURN OF THE GOLEM, THE see **CISARUV PEKAR** • 1951
RETURN OF THE GUNFIGHTER • 1966 • Neilson James • TVM • USA • AS I RODE DOWN TO LAREDO
RETURN OF THE HERO see **ROAD BACK, THE** • 1937
RETURN OF THE HEROES see **ASLANLARIN DONUSU** • 1966
RETURN OF THE HULK, THE • 1977 • Levi Alan J. • TVM • USA • RETURN OF THE INCREDIBLE HULK, THE
RETURN OF THE IKONS • 1965 • Boyadgieva Lada • DOC • BUL
RETURN OF THE INCREDIBLE HULK see **INCREDIBLE HULK RETURNS, THE** • 1988
RETURN OF THE INCREDIBLE HULK, THE see **RETURN OF THE HULK, THE** • 1977
RETURN OF THE ISLANDER, THE see **AN TOILEANACH A DFHILL** • 1971
RETURN OF THE JEDI • 1983 • Marquand Richard • USA
RETURN OF THE KILLER TOMATOES • 1987 • De Bello John • USA
RETURN OF THE KING.. A STORY OF THE HOBBITS, THE* • 18980 • Kubo Akiyuki, Rankin Arthur Jr., Bass Jules • ANM • USA, JPN
RETURN OF THE KUNG FU DRAGON • 1978 • Yu Chik-Lim • HKG
RETURN OF THE LASH • 1947 • Taylor Ray • USA
RETURN OF THE LIBRARY AMATEUR, THE see **REGRESO DEL AMATEUR DE BIBLIOTECAS, EL**
RETURN OF THE LIVING DEAD • 1985 • O'Bannon Dan • USA • NIGHT OF THE LIVING DEAD
RETURN OF THE LIVING DEAD see **MESSIAH OF EVIL** • 1975
RETURN OF THE LIVING DEAD, THE • 1983 • Hooper Tobe • USA
RETURN OF THE LIVING DEAD PART II • 1988 • Wiederhorn Ken • USA
RETURN OF THE LONE WOLF see **LONE WOLF RETURNS, THE** • 1926
RETURN OF THE MAGIC HAT see **AWDET TAKIET EL EKHFAA** • 1946
RETURN OF THE MAN FROM U.N.C.L.E. • 1982 • Austin Ray • TVM • USA • RETURN OF THE MAN FROM U.N.C.L.E. (THE FIFTEEN YEARS LATER AFFAIR)
RETURN OF THE MAN FROM U.N.C.L.E.(THE FIFTEEN YEARS LATER AFFAIR) see **RETURN OF THE MAN FROM U.N.C.L.E.** • 1982
RETURN OF THE MISSUS, THE • 1906 • Green Tom? • UKN
RETURN OF THE MOD SQUAD, THE • 1979 • McCowan George • TVM • USA
RETURN OF THE MOHICANS • 1948 • Beebe Ford, Eason B. Reeves • USA
RETURN OF THE MONSTER, THE see **REGRESO DEL MONSTRUO, EL** • 1959
RETURN OF THE MONSTER MAKER • 1958 • Glut Don • SHT • USA
RETURN OF THE MUSKETEERS, THE • 1989 • Lester Richard • UKN, FRN, SPN
RETURN OF THE ONE ARMED SWORDSMAN • 1968 • Chang Ch'Eh • HKG
RETURN OF THE OUTLAW see **KAETTEKITA GOKUDO** • 1968
RETURN OF THE PINK PANTHER • 1975 • Edwards Blake • UKN, USA
RETURN OF THE PLAINSMAN see **PHANTOM STOCKMAN** • 1953
RETURN OF THE PRODIGAL, THE • 1923 • Coleby A. E. • UKN
RETURN OF THE PRODIGAL SON see **AWDAT AL IBN AL DAL** • 1976
RETURN OF THE PRODIGAL SON, THE see **NAVRAT ZTRACENEHO SYNA** • 1966
RETURN OF THE RANGERS, THE • 1943 • Clifton Elmer • USA
RETURN OF THE RAT, THE • 1929 • Cutts Graham • UKN
RETURN OF THE REBELS • 1981 • Nosseck Noel • TVM • USA
RETURN OF THE REINDEER • 1973 • Mylne Christopher • DOC • UKN
RETURN OF THE RIDDLE MAN • 1927 • Hill Robert F. • SRL • USA
RETURN OF THE SCARLET PIMPERNEL, THE • 1937 • Schwarz Hanns • UKN
RETURN OF THE SECAUSUS SEVEN, THE • 1980 • Sayles John • USA
RETURN OF THE SECRET SOCIETY see **BABETTE IN RETURN OF THE SECRET SOCIETY** • 1968
RETURN OF THE SEVEN • 1966 • Kennedy Burt • USA, SPN • REGRESO DE LOS SIETE MAGNIFICOS, EL (SPN)
RETURN OF THE SHAGGY DOG, THE • 1987 • Gillard Stuart • TVM • USA
RETURN OF THE SHE-WOLF see **POWROT WILCZYCY** • 1990
RETURN OF THE SIX-MILLION-DOLLAR MAN AND THE BIONIC WOMAN, THE • 1987 • Austin Ray • TVM • USA
RETURN OF THE SOLDIER • 1982 • Bridges Alan • UKN
RETURN OF THE SPIRIT, THE see **AWDIT EL ROH** • 1969
RETURN OF THE STRANGER see **RETURN OF A STRANGER** • 1937
RETURN OF THE STREETFIGHTER • 1976 • Osawa Shigehiro • JPN
RETURN OF THE SWAMP THING, THE • 1989 • Wynorski Jim • USA
RETURN OF THE TALL BLOND, THE see **RETOUR DU GRAND BLOND, LE** • 1975
RETURN OF THE TALL BLOND MAN WITH ONE BLACK SHOE (USA) see **RETOUR DU GRAND BLOND, LE** • 1975
RETURN OF THE TEENAGE WEREWOLF • 1959 • Glut Don • SHT • USA
RETURN OF THE TERROR • 1934 • Bretherton Howard • USA
RETURN OF THE TEXAN • 1952 • Daves Delmer • USA
RETURN OF THE TIGER • 1973 • Shaw James Fung • HKG • SILENT KILLER FROM ETERNITY
RETURN OF THE TWINS' DOUBLE, THE • 1914 • *Ford Francis* • USA
RETURN OF THE VAMPIRE, THE • 1943 • Landers Lew, Neumann Kurt • USA
RETURN OF THE VAMPIRES, THE see **RETORNO DE LOS VAMPIROS, EL**
RETURN OF THE VIGILANTES, THE (UKN) see **VIGILANTES RETURN, THE** • 1947
RETURN OF THE VIKINGS • 1945 • Frend Charles • DOC • UKN
RETURN OF THE WHISTLER, THE • 1948 • Lederman D. Ross • USA
RETURN OF THE WOLF MAN • 1957 • Glut Don • SHT • USA
RETURN OF THE WORLD'S GREATEST DETECTIVE, THE • 1976 • Hargrove Dean • TVM • USA
RETURN OF THE ZOMBIES • 1984 • *Cooper Stan* • USA
RETURN OF THOMAS, THE • 1969 • Ne'Eman Yehuda • SHT • ISR
RETURN OF THUNDER CLOUD'S SPIRIT, THE • 1913 • McRae Henry • USA
RETURN OF TIEMAN, THE see **RETOUR DE TIEMAN, LE** • 1970
RETURN OF TIN-TIN-TIN, THE • 1947 • Nosseck Max • USA
RETURN OF TONY, THE • 1913 • *Baggot King* • USA
RETURN OF TRIGGER DAWSON, THE • 1955 • Landers Lew • MTV • USA
RETURN OF ULYSSES, THE see **RETOUR D'ULYSSE, LE** • 1908
RETURN OF VASSILI BORTNIKOV, THE see **VOZVRASHCHENIE VASSILIYA BORTNIKOVA** • 1953
RETURN OF WALPURGIS, THE see **RETORNO DE WALPURGIS, EL** • 1973
RETURN OF WIDOW POGSON'S HUSBAND • 1911 • *Vitagraph* • USA
RETURN OF WILD BILL, THE • 1940 • Lewis Joseph H. • USA • FALSE EVIDENCE (UKN)
RETURN OF WILDFIRE, THE • 1948 • Taylor Ray • USA • BLACK STALLION (UKN)
RETURN OF WILLIAM MARR, THE • 1912 • *Bushman Francis X.* • USA
RETURN TICKET TO MADRID see **RETOUR MADRID** • 1968
RETURN TO ACTION • 1946 • Gunn Gilbert • DOC • UKN
RETURN TO AFRICA see **ESCAPE FROM ANGOLA** • 1976
RETURN TO BOGGY CREEK • 1977 • Moore Tom* • USA
RETURN TO CAMPUS • 1975 • Cornsweet Harold • USA
RETURN TO DEPARTURE • 1987 • Tougas Kirk • CND
RETURN TO DRESDEN • 1986 • Duckworth Martin • MTV • CND • RETOUR A DRESDEN
RETURN TO EARTH • 1976 • Taylor Jud • TVM • USA
RETURN TO EARTH see **POWROT NA ZIEMIE** • 1967
RETURN TO EDEN see **PRIVATE TUTOR** • 1988
RETURN TO FANTASY ISLAND • 1978 • McCowan George • USA
RETURN TO GLANNASCAUL • 1951 • Edwards Hilton • UKN
RETURN TO HEAVEN see **TENGOKU SONOHI-GAERI** • 1930
RETURN TO HORROR HIGH • 1987 • Froehlich Bill • USA
RETURN TO JACKSON COUNTY JAIL see **OUTSIDE CHANCE** • 1978
RETURN TO KANSAS CITY • 1978 • Fox Beryl • DOC • CND
RETURN TO KING SOLOMON'S MINES see **WATUSI** • 1959
RETURN TO LIFE • 1938 • Kline Herbert, Cartier-Bresson Henri • USA
RETURN TO LIFE • 1960 • Krish John • UKN
RETURN TO LIFE see **RETOUR A LA VIE** • 1948
RETURN TO LIFE see **ACHRAROUMES** • 1978
RETURN TO MACON COUNTY see **HIGHWAY GIRL** • 1975
RETURN TO MACON COUNTY LINE see **HIGHWAY GIRL** • 1975
RETURN TO MANHOOD see **NANBANJI NO SEMUSHI-OTOKO** • 1957
RETURN TO MAYBERRY • 1986 • Sweeney Bob • TVM • USA
RETURN TO OZ • 1964 • Rankin Arthur Jr. • ANM • USA
RETURN TO OZ • 1985 • Murch Walter • USA
RETURN TO PARADISE • 1953 • Robson Mark • USA
RETURN TO PEYTON PLACE • 1961 • Ferrer Jose • USA
RETURN TO REASON, THE see **RETOUR A LA RAISON, LE** • 1923
RETURN TO SALEM'S LOT, A • 1987 • Cohen Larry • USA
RETURN TO SENDER • 1963 • Hales Gordon • UKN
RETURN TO SILENCE see **REGRESO AL SILENCIO** • 1967
RETURN TO SNOWY RIVER PART II (USA) see **MAN FROM SNOWY RIVER II, THE** • 1987
RETURN TO SYLVAN • 1986 • Nichol Robert L. • SHT • CND
RETURN TO THE 36TH CHAMBER see **SHAO-LIN TA-P'ENG HSIAO-TZU** • 1980
RETURN TO THE BARRACKS see **RETOUR AU CANTONNEMENT** • 1896
RETURN TO THE CAPITAL see **KIKYO** • 1950
RETURN TO THE DREAMING • 1973 • Holmes Cecil • DOC • ASL
RETURN TO THE EDGE OF THE WORLD • 1978 • Powell Michael • UKN
RETURN TO THE HORRORS OF BLOOD ISLAND see **BEAST OF BLOOD** • 1970
RETURN TO THE LAND OF OZ • Kolar Boris • ANM • USA, YGS
RETURN TO THE OLD CITY see **POWROT NA STARE MIASTO** • 1954
RETURN TO THE OLD TOWN see **POWROT NA STARE MIASTO** • 1954
RETURN TO THE PAST see **POWROT** • 1960
RETURN TO TO-WA-WA, THE • 1910 • Melies Gaston • USA
RETURN TO TREASURE ISLAND • 1954 • Dupont E. A. • USA • BANDIT ISLAND OF KARABEI
RETURN TO WARBOW • 1958 • Nazarro Ray • USA
RETURN TO WATERLOO • 1985 • Davies Ray • UKN • RAY DAVIES' RETURN TO WATERLOO
RETURN TO YESTERDAY • 1940 • Stevenson Robert • UKN
RETURN TO YOUTH see **RETORNO A LA JUVENTAD** • 1953

RETURN TO YOUTH AND TROUBLE, A • 1916 • *Drew Lillian* • SHT • USA
RETURN WITH ME see **GAA MED MIG HJEM** • 1941
RETURNED ENGAGEMENT, A • 1935 • Jason Leigh • SHT • USA
RETURNED TO THE FOLD • 1911 • *Yankee* • USA
RETURNING, THE • 1983 • Bender Joel • USA
RETURNING, THE • 1990 • Day John • NZL
RETURNING HOME • 1975 • Petrie Daniel • TVM • USA
RETUSOR, A • 1972 • Zolnay Pal • HNG • RE-TOUCHER, THE ○ FOTOGRAFIA ○ PHOTOGRAPHY
REUBEN IN THE SUBWAY • 1905 • *Bitzer Billy (Ph)* • USA
REUBEN, REUBEN • 1951 • Cowan Will • SHT • USA
REUBEN, REUBEN • 1983 • Miller Robert Ellis • USA
REUBEN'S BUSY DAY • 1914 • *Connors Buck* • USA
REUB'S LITTLE GIRL • 1913 • Martinek H. O. • UKN • COASTGUARD'S HAUL, THE
REUNION • 1922 • Fleischer Dave • ANS • USA
REUNION • 1932 • Campbell Ivar • UKN
REUNION • 1936 • Taurog Norman • USA • HEARTS IN REUNION (UKN)
REUNION • 1980 • Mayberry Russ • TVM • USA
REUNION • 1984 • Langman Chris • ASL
REUNION • 1986 • K'O Yi-Cheng • TWN
REUNION • 1989 • Schatzberg Jerry • USA
REUNION see **TILL WE MEET AGAIN** • 1936
REUNION see **REUNION IN FRANCE** • 1942
REUNION see **SAIKAI** • 1953
REUNION see **MILAN** • 1967
REUNION, THE • 1916 • Parke William • SHT • USA
REUNION, THE • 1982 • Kroeker Allan • CND
REUNION, THE (USA) see **RIMPATRIATA, LA** • 1963
REUNION AT FAIRBOROUGH • 1985 • Wise Herbert • TVM • USA
REUNION D'OFFICIERS • 1896 • Melies Georges • FRN • FRENCH OFFICERS' MEETING
REUNION IN FRANCE • 1942 • Dassin Jules • USA • MADEMOISELLE FRANCE (UKN) ○ REUNION
REUNION IN RENO • 1951 • Neumann Kurt • USA
REUNION IN RHYTHM • 1937 • Douglas Gordon • SHT • USA
REUNION IN VIENNA • 1932 • Franklin Sidney A. • USA
REUNITED • 1910 • *Imp* • USA
REUNITED • 1915 • *Eclair* • USA
REUNITED AT THE GALLOWS • 1909 • *Bison* • USA
REUNITED BY SANTA CLAUS • 1909 • *Powers* • USA
REUNITED BY THE SEA • 1912 • *Crane Frank* • USA
REUSSITE DE MEI-THEBRE • 1972 • Kossoko Yaya • SHT • NGR
REV. DELL'S SECRET, THE • 1924 • Ramster P. J. • ASL • REVEREND DELL'S SECRET, THE
REV. GOODLEIGH'S COURTSHIP, THE • 1911 • *Imp* • USA
REV. JOHN WRIGHT OF MISSOURI, THE • 1910 • *Nestor* • USA
REVAK, LO SCHIAVO DI CARTAGINE • 1960 • Mate Rudolph • ITL • REVAK, SLAVE OF CARTHAGE ○ BARBARIANS, THE ○ REVAK THE REBEL ○ BARBARIAN, THE ○ FREEDOM FOR REBEL
REVAK, SLAVE OF CARTHAGE see **REVAK, LO SCHIAVO DI CARTAGINE** • 1960
REVAK THE REBEL see **REVAK, LO SCHIAVO DI CARTAGINE** • 1960
REVAMP • Hudiberg Peter • SHT • USA
REVANCH • 1930 • *Romm Mikhail (Sc)* • USS • REVANCHE
REVANCHA • 1948 • Gout Alberto • MXC
REVANCHE • 1984 • Vergitsis Nikos • GRC
REVANCHE see **REVANCH** • 1930
REVANCHE, LA • 1916 • *Lincoln W. J.* • ASL
REVANCHE, LA • 1974 • Bulbulian Maurice • DCS • CND
REVANCHE, LA • 1981 • Lary Pierre • FRN
REVANCHE DE FITZIGLI, LA • 1920-23 • Rastrelli Amedee • FRN
REVANCHE DE ROGER-LA-HONTE, LA • 1946 • Cayatte Andre • FRN
REVANCHE DES HUMANOIDES, LA • 1982 • Barille Albert • ANM • FRN
REVANCHE DU MAUDIT, LA • 1929 • Leprince Rene • FRN • GHOST SHIP, THE
REVANSA • 1978 • Nicolaescu Sergiu • RMN • REVENGE
REVE, LE • 1922 • de Baroncelli Jacques • FRN
REVE, LE • 1930 • de Baroncelli Jacques • FRN
REVE, LE • 1976 • Foldes Peter • CND
REVE A LA LUNE • 1905 • Zecca Ferdinand, Velle Gaston • FRN • AMANT DE LA LUNE, L' ○ DREAM OF THE MOON ○ LOVER OF THE MOON
REVE AU COIN DU FEU • 1894 • Reynaud Emile • FRN
REVE BLOND, UN • 1932 • Martin Paul • FRN
REVE DANS LA LUNE, LA • 1905 • Zecca Ferdinand • FRN
REVE D'ARTISTE • 1898 • Melies Georges • FRN • ARTIST'S DREAM, THE (USA)
REVE DE DRANEM, LE • 1908 • Zecca Ferdinand • FRN
REVE DE FETARD • 1908 • Jasset Victorin • FRN
REVE DE GILBERTO, LE see **GILBERTO'S DREAM** • 1980
REVE DE L'ASTRONOME, LE see **HOMME DANS LA LUNE, L'** • 1898
REVE DE L'HOROLOGER, LE • 1904 • Melies Georges • FRN • CLOCK MAKER'S DREAM, THE (USA)
REVE DE NOEL, LE • 1900 • Melies Georges • FRN • CHRISTMAS DREAM, THE (USA)
REVE DE RIP, LE see **LEGENDE DE RIP VAN WINCKLE, LA** • 1905
REVE DE SHAKESPEARE, LE • 1907 • Melies Georges • SHT • FRN • SHAKESPEARE WRITING JULIUS CAESAR (USA) ○ MORT DU JULIUS CESAR, LA ○ SHAKESPEARE ECRIVANT LA MORT DE JULES CESAR ○ DREAM OF SHAKESPEARE, THE ○ DEATH OF JULIUS CAESAR, THE
REVE DE SINGE • 1978 • Ferreri Marco • FRN, ITL • CIAO MASCHIO (ITL) ○ BYE BYE MONKEY ○ CIAO MALE ○ CIAO SCIMMIA
REVE D'ENFANT • 1910 • Cohl Emile • ANS • FRN • CHILD'S DREAM, THE
REVE DES APACHES, LE • 1908 • Feuillade Louis • FRN
REVE DU CHASSEUR, LA • 1904 • Blache Alice • FRN
REVE DU GARCON DE CAFE, LE see **SONGE D'UN GARCON DE CAFE, LE** • 1910
REVE DU MAITRE DE BALLET, LE • 1903 • Melies Georges • FRN • DREAM OF THE BALLET MASTER, THE (UKN) ○ BALLET MASTER'S DREAM, THE
REVE DU PARIA, LE • 1902 • Melies Georges • FRN • DREAM OF A HINDU BEGGAR, THE (USA)
REVE DU PAUVRE • 1898 • Melies Georges • FRN • BEGGAR'S DREAM, THE (USA)
REVE DU RADJAH OU, LA FORET ENCHANTEE, LE • 1900 • Melies Georges • FRN • RAJAH'S DREAM OR THE BEWITCHED WOOD, THE (USA)
REVE D'UN BUVEUR, LE • 1898 • *Pathe* • FRN • DRINKER'S DREAM, THE
REVE D'UN FUMEUR D'OPIUM, LE • 1908 • Melies Georges • FRN • DREAM OF AN OPIUM FIEND, THE (USA)
REVE D'UN GARCON DE CAFE • 1913 • Cohl Emile • ANS • FRN • WAITER'S DREAM, THE
REVE D'UNE NUIT, LA see **HILM LAYLA** • 1949
REVE ENFANTIN • 1910 • Cohl Emile • ANS • FRN • REVES INFANTINS
REVE ET REALITE • 1901 • Zecca Ferdinand • FRN
REVE ETERNEL • 1934 • Chomette Henri, Fanck Arnold • FRN • ROI DU MONT BLANC, LE
REVE INTERDIT, LE • 1915 • Capellani Albert • FRN
REVE PLUS LONG QUE LA NUIT, UN • 1976 • de Saint-Phalle Niki • FRN
REVEALED BY THE POT • 1909 • Polaski Benjamin • HKG
REVEIL, LE • 1925 • de Baroncelli Jacques • FRN
REVEIL DES AVEUGLES, LE • 1975-77 • Moreau Michel • DCS • CND
REVEIL DU DIMANCHE see **KYRIAKATIKO XYPNIMA** • 1953
REVEIL DU JARDINIER, LE • 1904 • Blache Alice • FRN
REVEIL D'UN MONSIEUR PRESSE, LE • 1901 • Melies Georges • FRN • HOW HE MISSED HIS TRAIN (USA)
REVEILLE • 1924 • Pearson George • UKN
REVEILLE! • 1976-77 • Brault Michel, Gladu Andre • DCS • CND
REVEILLE see **REVELJ** • 1917
REVEILLE, DAS GROSSE WECKEN • 1925 • Kaufmann Fritz • FRG
REVEILLE-TOI, CHERIE • 1960 • Magnier Claude • FRN
REVEILLE WITH BEVERLY • 1943 • Barton Charles T. • USA
REVEILLON • 1982 • Labonte Francois • CND
REVEILLON CHEZ BOB • 1984 • Granier-Deferre Denys • FRN
REVELACION • 1947 • Obregon Antonio • SPN
REVELATEUR, LE • 1968 • Garrel Philippe • FRN
REVELATION • 1918 • Baker George D. • USA
REVELATION • 1924 • Baker George D. • USA • IN A MONASTERY GARDEN
REVELATION, LA • 1971 • Lavalle Alain, Matalon Eddy? • FRN • SEX IS BEAUTIFUL (UKN)
REVELATION, THE • 1912 • *Nestor* • USA
REVELATION, THE • 1913 • Balshofer Fred J. • USA
REVELATION, THE • 1974 • Khalzanov B. • USS
REVELATION, THE see **APENBARINGEN** • 1977
REVELATIONS • 1916 • Maude Arthur • USA
REVELER, THE • 1914 • Campbell Colin • USA
REVELJ • 1917 • Klercker Georg • SWD • REVEILLE
REVELLER, THE see **FETARD, LE**
REVELRY see **ROUNDERS, THE** • 1914
REVENANT, LE • 1903 • Melies Georges • FRN • MR. JONES' COMICAL EXPERIENCE WITH A GHOST ○ APPARITION, THE (USA) ○ GHOST AND THE CANDLE, THE
REVENANT, LE • 1908 • Jasset Victorin • FRN
REVENANT, LE • 1913 • Feuillade Louis • FRN • GHOST, THE
REVENANT, LE see **SOLILOQUES DU PAUVRE, LES** • 1951
REVENANT, UN • 1946 • Christian-Jaque • FRN • LOVER'S RETURN, A (USA) ○ GHOST, A
REVENANTE, LA • 1918 • de Baroncelli Jacques • FRN • GHOST, THE
REVENGE • Poplavskaya Irina • USS
REVENGE! • 1904 • Collins Alf • UKN
REVENGE • 1906 • Larsen Viggo • DNM
REVENGE • 1918 • Browning Tod • USA
REVENGE • 1928 • Carewe Edwin • USA
REVENGE • Neufeld Max • AUS
REVENGE • 1969 • Tosini Pino • ITL
REVENGE • 1971 • Hayers Sidney • UKN • INN OF THE FRIGHTENED PEOPLE (USA) ○ TERROR FROM UNDER THE HOUSE
REVENGE • 1971 • Taylor Jud • TVM • USA • THERE ONCE WAS A WOMAN ○ ONE WOMAN'S REVENGE
REVENGE • 1979 • De Martino Alberto • ITL • VIGILANTE 2 ○ STREET LAW
REVENGE • 1985 • SAF
REVENGE • 1986 • Lewis Christopher • USA
REVENGE • 1989 • Scott Anthony • USA
REVENGE see **ALLT HAMNAR SIG** • 1917
REVENGE see **ZEMSTA** • 1957
REVENGE see **MEGALOS DHIHASMOS** • 1968
REVENGE see **POMSTA** • 1968
REVENGE see **FATTO DI SANGUE FRA DUE UOMINI PER CAUSA DI UNA VEDOVA (SI SOSPETTANO MOVENTI POLITICI)** • 1978
REVENGE see **REVANSA** • 1978
REVENGE see **UTU** • 1983
REVENGE, THE see **ADAUCHI** • 1964
REVENGE AT DAYBREAK see **JEUNE FOLLE, LA** • 1952
REVENGE AT EL PASO see **QUATTRO DELL'AVE MARIA, I** • 1968
REVENGE AT MONTE CARLO • 1933 • Eason B. Reeves • USA • MYSTERY AT MONTE CARLO (UKN)
REVENGE CHAMPION, THE see **ADAUCHI SANSHU** • 1931
REVENGE FOR A RAPE • 1976 • Galfas Timothy • TVM • USA
REVENGE IN EL PASO (UKN) see **QUATTRO DELL'AVE MARIA, I** • 1968
REVENGE IS MINE • 1985 • SAF
REVENGE IS MINE see **RACHE IST MEIN, DIE** • 1919
REVENGE IS MY DESTINY • 1973 • Adler Joseph • TVM • USA
REVENGE IS SWEET • 1911 • *Lubin* • USA
REVENGE IS SWEET • 1912 • *Edison* • USA
REVENGE IS SWEET • 1913 • Collins Edwin J.? • UKN
REVENGE IS SWEET see **HAMNDEN AR LJUV** • 1915
REVENGE IS SWEET see **BABES IN TOYLAND** • 1934
REVENGE OF AL CAPONE, THE • 1988 • Pressman Michael • TVM • USA
REVENGE OF ASIA • 1983 • Ishii Sogo • JPN
REVENGE OF BLACK EAGLE (USA) see **VENDETTA DI AQUILA NERA, LA** • 1952
REVENGE OF DR. DEATH, THE see **MADHOUSE** • 1974
REVENGE OF DRACULA • 1958 • Glut Don • SHT • USA
REVENGE OF DRACULA see **DRACULA -PRINCE OF DARKNESS** • 1965
REVENGE OF DRACULA see **DRACULA VS. FRANKENSTEIN** • 1971
REVENGE OF FRANKENSTEIN, THE • 1958 • Fisher Terence • UKN
REVENGE OF GENERAL LING, THE (USA) see **WIFE OF GENERAL LING** • 1937
REVENGE OF HERCULES, THE see **VENDETTA DI ERCOLE, LA** • 1960
REVENGE OF IVANHOE, THE (USA) see **RIVINCITA DI IVANHOE, LA** • 1965
REVENGE OF KAMALI ZEYBEK, THE see **KAMALI ZEYBEGIN INTIKAMI** • 1967
REVENGE OF KING KONG, THE see **KINGO KONGO NO GYAKUSHU** • 1967
REVENGE OF LADY MORGAN, THE see **VENDETTA DI LADY MORGAN, LA** • 1966
REVENGE OF MILADY, THE see **FOUR MUSKETEERS, THE** • 1975
REVENGE OF MR. THOMAS ATKINS, THE • 1914 • Tucker George Loane • UKN
REVENGE OF PHARAOH, THE see **RACHE DER PHARAONEN, DIE** • 1925
REVENGE OF SPARTACUS, THE see **VENDETTA DI SPARTACUS, LA** • 1964
REVENGE OF TARZAN, THE see **RETURN OF TARZAN, THE** • 1920
REVENGE OF THE BARBARIANS see **HRAFNINN FLYGUR** • 1983
REVENGE OF THE BARBARIANS (USA) see **VENDETTA DEI BARBARI, LA** • 1961
REVENGE OF THE BLACK EAGLE (UKN) see **VENDETTA DI AQUILA NERA, LA** • 1952
REVENGE OF THE BLACK HAWK, THE see **KARA ATMACANIN INTIKAMI** • 1968
REVENGE OF THE BLOOD BEAST, THE • 1966 • Reeves Michael • UKN, ITL • SORELLA DI SATANA, LA (ITL) ○ SHE BEAST, THE (USA) ○ LAGO DI SATANA, IL ○ SISTER OF SATAN
REVENGE OF THE CHEERLEADERS • 1976 • Lerner Richard • USA • HOTS 3
REVENGE OF THE COLOSSAL BEASTS • 1962-69 • Carpenter John • SHT • USA
REVENGE OF THE COLOSSAL MAN see **WAR OF THE COLOSSAL BEAST** • 1958
REVENGE OF THE CONQUERED (USA) see **DRAKUT IL VENDICATORE** • 1962
REVENGE OF THE CREATURE • 1955 • Arnold Jack • USA
REVENGE OF THE DEAD • 1975 • Lee Evan • USA
REVENGE OF THE DEAD see **RACHE DER TOTEN, DIE** • 1917
REVENGE OF THE DEAD see **NIGHT OF THE GHOULS** • 1959
REVENGE OF THE DEAD see **ZEDER** • 1983
REVENGE OF THE DRAGON • 1972 • Shen Chiang • HKG • REVENGE OF THE DRAGONS
REVENGE OF THE DRAGONS see **REVENGE OF THE DRAGON** • 1972
REVENGE OF THE DRUNKEN MASTER • Ho Godfrey • HKG
REVENGE OF THE EARWIG • 1958 • Beresford Bruce • ASL
REVENGE OF THE FAKIRS, THE see **RACHE DES FAKIRS, DIE** • 1918
REVENGE OF THE GIANTS, THE see **DEVLERIN INTIKAMI** • 1967
REVENGE OF THE GLADIATORS see **VENDETTA DEI GLADIATORI, LA** • 1965
REVENGE OF THE GLADIATORS (USA) see **VENDETTA DI SPARTACUS, LA** • 1964
REVENGE OF THE GODS • 1966 • *Darren James* • MTV • USA
REVENGE OF THE HOUSE OF USHER • 1980 • USA
REVENGE OF THE INNOCENTS see **SOUTH BRONX HEROES** • 1985
REVENGE OF THE KINEMATOGRAPH CAMERAMAN see **MEST' KINEMATOGRAFICESKOGO OPERATORA** • 1912
REVENGE OF THE LIVING DEAD see **LAMA NEL CORPO, LA** • 1966
REVENGE OF THE LOONEY SPOONS • 1965 • Vanderbeek Stan • ANS • USA
REVENGE OF THE MASTER, THE see **EFENIN INTIKAMI** • 1967
REVENGE OF THE MASTERS, THE see **EFELERIN OCU** • 1968
REVENGE OF THE MUSKETEERS (USA) see **D'ARTAGNAN CONTRO I TRE MOSCHETTIERI** • 1963
REVENGE OF THE MYSTERONS FROM MARS • 1981 • Burgess Brian, Lynn Robert, Turner Kenneth • ANM • UKN
REVENGE OF THE NERDS • 1984 • Kanew Jeff • USA
REVENGE OF THE NERDS 2 see **REVENGE OF THE NERDS, II: NERDS IN PARADISE** • 1987
REVENGE OF THE NERDS, II: NERDS IN PARADISE • 1987 • Roth Joe • USA • REVENGE OF THE NERDS 2
REVENGE OF THE NINJA • 1984 • Firstenberg Sam • USA • NINJA II: REVENGE OF THE NINJA
REVENGE OF THE OUTLAWS, THE see **RAZBUNAREA HAIDUCILOR** • 1968
REVENGE OF THE PATRIOTS • 1981 • *Li Bruce* • HKG
REVENGE OF THE PIRATES (USA) see **VENDETTA DEL CORSARO, LA** • 1951
REVENGE OF THE SCREAMING DEAD see **MESSIAH OF EVIL** • 1975
REVENGE OF THE SERPENTS see **YILANLARIN OCU** • 1985
REVENGE OF THE SILK MASKS, THE • 1912 • *Eclair* • USA
REVENGE OF THE STEEPLEJACK, THE • 1915 • *Anderson Mignon* • USA
REVENGE OF THE STEPFORD WIVES • 1980 • Fuest Robert • TVM • USA
REVENGE OF THE STOLEN STARS • 1985 • Lommel Ulli • USA
REVENGE OF THE TEENAGE VIXENS FROM OUTER SPACE • 1985 • Farrell Jeff • USA

REVENGE OF THE TEENAGE WEREWOLF • 1960 • Glut Don • SHT • USA
REVENGE OF THE THE PINK PANTHER • 1978 • Edwards Blake • UKN, USA
REVENGE OF THE VAMPIRE see **DENDAM PONTIANAK** • 1957
REVENGE OF THE VAMPIRE (UKN) see **MASCHERA DEL DEMONIO, LA** • 1960
REVENGE OF THE ZOMBIES • 1943 • Sekely Steve • USA • CORPSE VANISHED, THE (UKN)
REVENGE OF THE ZOMBIES • 1981 • Menga Horace • HKG
REVENGE OF URSUS (USA) see **VENDETTA DI URSUS, LA** • 1961
REVENGE OF YUKINOJO, THE see **YUKINOJO HENGE** • 1935
REVENGE OF YUKINOJO, THE see **YUKINOJO HENGE** • 1963
REVENGE OR? • 1919 • Kennedy Aubrey M. • USA
REVENGE RIDER, THE • 1935 • Selman David • USA
REVENGE SQUAD see **HIT AND RUN** • 1982
REVENGE! (UKN) see **END OF THE TRAIL** • 1936
REVENGEFUL SERVANT GIRL, THE • 1914 • Williams C. Jay • USA
REVENGEFUL SPIRIT OF EROS, THE see **EROGAMI NO ONRYO** • 1930
REVENGER, THE see **HAMNAREN** • 1915
REVENGER, THE see **OSVETNIK** • 1958
REVENGER, THE see **FUKUSHUKI** • 1968
REVENGERS, THE • 1972 • Mann Daniel • USA, MXC
REVENTON, EL • 1975 • Burns Archibaldo • MXC
REVENUE AGENT • 1950 • Landers Lew • USA
REVENUE AGENT, THE • 1915 • *Anderson Broncho Billy* • USA
REVENUE AND THE GIRL, THE • 1911 • *Sais Marin* • USA
REVENUE MAN AND THE GIRL, THE • 1911 • Griffith D. W. • USA
REVENUE OFFICER'S DEPUTY, THE • 1914 • Kelsey Fred A. • USA
REVENUE OFFICER'S LAST CASE, THE • 1911 • *Powers* • USA
REVER OU ENVOL • 1971 • Reichenbach Francois • SHT • FRN
REVERBERATION • 1969 • Gehr Ernie • SHT • USA
REVEREND DELL'S SECRET, THE see **REV. DELL'S SECRET, THE** • 1924
REVEREND SALAMANDER UNATTACHED, THE • 1915 • *Essanay* • USA
REVERENDO COLT • 1970 • Klimovsky Leon • ITL
REVERIE • 1931 • *Coles Joyce* • SHT • USA
REVERIE POUR CLAUDE DEBUSSY • 1951 • Mitry Jean • SHT • FRN
REVERIES DE DEBUSSY • 1951 • Mitry Jean • SHT • FRN
REVERON • 1951 • Benacerraf Margot, Nadler Henry • SHT • VNZ
REVERSAL OF FORTUNE • 1989 • Schroeder Barbet • USA
REVERSAL ROTATION • 1976 • Sinden Tony • UKN
REVERSE BE MY LOT, THE • 1938 • Stross Raymond • UKN
REVERSE OF THE MEDAL, THE • 1923 • Cooper George A. • UKN
REVERSIBLE DIVERS • 1901 • Porter Edwin S. • USA
REVERSING A SHAVE • 1905 • Green Tom? • UKN
REVERSING DARWIN'S THEORY see **DOCTOR'S EXPERIMENT, THE** • 1908
REVES D'AMOUR • 1946 • Stengel Christian • FRN • DREAMS OF LOVE (USA)
REVES DE PRINTEMPS see **FRUHLINGSRAUSCHEN** • 1929
REVES D'UN FUMEUR D'OPIUM • 1906 • Jasset Victorin • SHT • FRN • DREAMS OF AN OPIUM SMOKER
REVES INFANTINS see **REVE ENFANTIN** • 1910
REVETEMENT DES ROUTES, LE • 1923 • Gremillon Jean • SHT • FRN
REVETEMENTS ROUTIERS • 1938 • Leenhardt Roger • DCS • FRN
REVEUR EVEILLE, LE • 1908 • Melies Georges • FRN
REVISITED • 1974 • Borenstein Joyce • CND
REVISOR • 1933 • Fric Martin • CZC • GOVERNMENT INSPECTOR ○ INSPECTOR GENERAL, THE ○ ACCOUNTANT ○ INSPECTOR, THE
REVISTA DEL CENTENARIO, LA • 1910 • Alsina Julio R. • ARG
REVISTA NACIONAL • 1911 • *Navascue Y Camus* • MXC
REVIVAL • 1963 • Shebib Donald • CND
REVIVED see **UJRAELOK** • 1921
REVIVISCENCE D'UN CHIEN • 1929 • Painleve Jean • SHT • FRN
REVIZOR • 1952 • Petrov Vladimir • USS • INSPECTOR GENERAL, THE
REVIZORY PONEVOLE • 1954 • Solntseva Yulia • USS • RELUCTANT INSPECTORS, THE ○ UNWILLING INSPECTORS
REVNOST • 1963 • Dinov Todor • BUL
REVOLT see **SCARLET DAWN** • 1932
REVOLT, THE • 1916 • O'Neil Barry • USA
REVOLT, THE • 1935 • Bacon Lloyd • USA
REVOLT, THE see **ISAYAN** • 1980
REVOLT AT FORT LARAMIE • 1957 • Selander Lesley • USA
REVOLT IN HUNGARY see **HUNGARN IN FLAMMEN** • 1957
REVOLT IN THE BIG HOUSE • 1958 • Springsteen R. G. • USA
REVOLT IN THE DESERT • 1937 • Korda Zoltan • USA
REVOLT IN THE REFORMATORY see **REVOLTE IM ERZIEHUNGDHAUS** • 1929
REVOLT IN TOYLAND see **VZPOURA HRACEK** • 1947
REVOLT OF JOB, THE see **JOB LAZADASA** • 1983
REVOLT OF MAMIE STOVER, THE • 1956 • Walsh Raoul • USA
REVOLT OF MR. WIGGS, THE • 1915 • Stratton Edmund F. • USA
REVOLT OF SHEIK SALEH AL ALI, THE see **THAWRA AL SHEIKH SALEH AL ALI** • 1985
REVOLT OF THE BARBARIANS (USA) see **RIVOLTA DEI BARBARI, LA** • 1965
REVOLT OF THE DEAD ONES, THE see **REBELION DE LAS MUERTAS, LA** • 1972
REVOLT OF THE DEMONS see **REVOLT OF THE ZOMBIES** • 1936
REVOLT OF THE FISHERMEN, THE see **VOSTANIYE RYBAKOV** • 1934
REVOLT OF THE GHOSTS see **REBELION DE LOS FANTASMAS, LA** • 1946
REVOLT OF THE HANGED see **REBELION DE LOS COLGADOS, LA** • 1953
REVOLT OF THE LIVING, THE see **MONDE TREMBLERA, LE** • 1939
REVOLT OF THE MAMELUKES see **MAMALIK, AL-** • 1965
REVOLT OF THE MERCENARIES (USA) see **RIVOLTA DEI MERCENARI, LA** • 1962
REVOLT OF THE MINAMATA VICTIMS see **MINAMATA IKKI** • 1972
REVOLT OF THE PRAETORIANS (USA) see **RIVOLTA DEI PRETORIANI, LA** • 1965
REVOLT OF THE ROBOTS see **AELITA** • 1924
REVOLT OF THE SLAVES, THE (USA) see **RIVOLTA DEGLI SCHIAVI, LA** • 1961
REVOLT OF THE TARTARS see **MICHELE STROGOFF** • 1956
REVOLT OF THE TOYS see **VZPOURA HRACEK** • 1947
REVOLT OF THE VOLGA see **VENDICATORE, IL** • 1959
REVOLT OF THE ZOMBIES • 1936 • Halperin Victor Hugo • USA • REVOLT OF THE DEMONS
REVOLT OF TOYS, THE see **VZPOURA HRACEK** • 1947
REVOLT OVER KASAN see **BULAT BATYR** • 1927
REVOLTA DEI TEENAGERS, LA (ITL) see **MONDO TEENO** • 1967
REVOLTE, DIE • 1969 • Hauff Reinhard • FRG
REVOLTE, LE • 1938 • Mathot Leon, Bibal Robert • FRN
REVOLTE AU PENITENCIER DE FILLES • 1983 • Roussel Gilbert • FRN, ITL • WOMEN'S PRISON MASSACRE (USA)
REVOLTE DES GUEUX, LA • 1912 • Machin Alfred • NTH
REVOLTE DES INDIENS APACHES, LA (FRN) see **WINNETOU I** • 1963
REVOLTE DES VIVANTS, LES see **MONDE TREMBLERA, LE** • 1939
REVOLTE DU CUIRASSE POTEMKINE, LA see **EVENEMENTS D'ODESSA, LES** • 1905
REVOLTE IM ERZIEHUNGDHAUS • 1929 • Asagaroff Georg • FRG • REVOLT IN THE REFORMATORY
REVOLTE SUR LA VOLGA see **VENDICATORE, IL** • 1959
REVOLTEE, LA • 1919 • Leprieur Gaston • FRN
REVOLTEE, LA • 1947 • L'Herbier Marcel • FRN • STOLEN AFFECTIONS (USA)
REVOLTEES DE L'ALBATROS, LES (FRN) see **AMMUTINAMENTO, L'** • 1962
REVOLTES, LES see **MANTELLO ROSSO, IL** • 1955
REVOLTES DE LOMANACH, LES • 1953 • Pottier Richard • FRN, ITL • EROE DELLA VANDEA, L' (ITL)
REVOLTES DU DANAE, LES • 1952 • Peclet Georges • FRN
REVOLTOSA, LA • 1924 • Rey Florian • SPN
REVOLTOSA, LA • 1950 • Diaz Morales Jose • SPN
REVOLTOSA, LA • 1963 • Diaz Morales Jose • SPN, MXC
REVOLTOSO, EL • 1951 • Martinez Solares Gilberto • MXC
REVOLUCAO DE LISBOA • 1915 • de Albuquerque Ernesto • SHT • PRT
REVOLUCAO DE MAIO, A • 1937 • Ribeiro Antonio Lopes • PRT
REVOLUCAO ESCUTURAL see **BEIJO DE VIDA, O** • 1976
REVOLUCAO NA PAZ, UMA • 1949 • Ribeiro Antonio Lopes • SHT • PRT
REVOLUCION • 1932 • Moreno Antonio • MXC • SOMBRA DE PANCHO VILLA, LA
REVOLUCION • 1963 • Sanjines Jorge • BLV
REVOLUCION, LA • 1973 • de la Torre Raul • ARG • REVOLUTION, THE
REVOLUCION, LA • 1978 • *Briceno Rafael* • VNZ • REVOLUTION, THE
REVOLUCION DE LAS FLORES, LA • 1968 • Covacevich Alvaro • CHL, USA • REVOLUTION OF THE FLOWERS, THE ○ NEW LOVE
REVOLUCION DE MAYO • 1910 • Gallo Mario • ARG
REVOLUCION EN VERACRUZ, LA • 1911 • MXC
REVOLUCION MATRIMONIAL, LA • 1975 • Nieves Conde Jose Antonio • SPN • MATRIMONIAL REVOLUTION, THE
REVOLUCNI ROK 1848 • 1948 • Krska Vaclav • CZC • REVOLUTIONARY YEAR 1848, THE
REVOLUTION • 1968 • O'Connell Jack • DOC • USA
REVOLUTION • 1985 • Hudson Hugh • UKN, NRW
REVOLUTION see **KING'S ROMANCE, THE** • 1914
REVOLUTION, THE see **REVOLUCION, LA** • 1973
REVOLUTION, THE see **REVOLUCION, LA** • 1978
REVOLUTION DER JUGEND • 1929 • Wiene Conrad • FRG
REVOLUTION D'OCTOBRE • 1967 • Rossif Frederic • FRN • OCTOBER REVOLUTION
REVOLUTION DU DANSAGE, LA • 1976-77 • Brault Michel, Gladu Andre • DCS • CND
REVOLUTION DU YEMEN, LA see **THAWRAT AL-YAMAN** • 1966
REVOLUTION FOR THE HELL OF IT • 1970 • Levy Jacques • USA
REVOLUTION FRANCAISE, LA • 1989 • Enrico Robert, Heffron Richard • FRN, USA • FRENCH REVOLUTION, THE
REVOLUTION IN RUSSIA see **EVENEMENTS D'ODESSA, LES** • 1905
REVOLUTION IN THE VILLAGE see **GAMPERILAYA** • 1964
REVOLUTION INDUSTRIELLE • 1970 • Lamothe Arthur • CND
REVOLUTION IS GREEN, THE see **REVOLUTION IST GRUN, DIE** • 1981
REVOLUTION IS IN YOUR HEAD, THE • 1970 • Rosenthal Eugene • DOC • USA
REVOLUTION IST GRUN, DIE • 1981 • Grusch Werner • AUS • REVOLUTION IS GREEN, THE
REVOLUTION MARRIAGE, A see **REVOLUTIONSBRYLLUP** • 1914
REVOLUTION MUNICIPALE, LA • 1970 • Savard Claude, Lavoie Richard, Dupont Jacques • CND
REVOLUTION OF ANTONIO DELEON, THE see **PERILOUS VOYAGE** • 1968
REVOLUTION OF THE FLOWERS, THE see **REVOLUCION DE LAS FLORES, LA** • 1968
REVOLUTIONARY, THE • 1970 • Williams Paul • UKN
REVOLUTIONARY, THE see **EPANASTATIS POPOLAROS** • 1971
REVOLUTIONARY, THE (USA) see **AMAKUSA SHIRO TOKISADA** • 1962
REVOLUTIONARY FAMILY, A see **GEMING JIATING** • 1960
REVOLUTIONARY ROMANCE, A • 1911 • Blache Alice • USA
REVOLUTIONARY ROMANCE, A • 1913 • *Eyton Bessie* • USA
REVOLUTIONARY YEAR 1848, THE see **REVOLUCNI ROK 1848** • 1948
REVOLUTIONEN I VANDKANTEN • 1971 • Winding Thomas • DNM • LOST IN THE SAND
REVOLUTIONENS BORN • 1981 • Mogensen Michael, Jensen Helle Toft • DOC • DNM • CHILDREN OF THE REVOLUTION, THE
REVOLUTIONIST see **REVOLUTSIONER** • 1917
REVOLUTIONIST, THE (USA) see **KING'S ROMANCE, THE** • 1914
REVOLUTIONISTS see **POKOLENIYE POBEDITELI** • 1936
REVOLUTIONISTS, THE • 1912 • *Lubin* • USA
REVOLUTIONNAIRE, LE • 1965 • Lefebvre Jean-Pierre • CND
REVOLUTIONS PER MINUTE see **R.P.M.** • 1970
REVOLUTIONSBRYLLUP • 1909 • *Blom August* • DNM • WEDDING DURING THE FRENCH REVOLUTION, A
REVOLUTIONSBRYLLUP • 1914 • Blom August • DNM • REVOLUTION MARRIAGE, A
REVOLUTIONSBRYLLUP • 1927 • Sandberg Anders W. • DNM • MARRIAGE UNDER TERROR
REVOLUTIONSHOCHZEIT • 1928 • Sandberg Anders W. • FRG
REVOLUTIONSHOCHZEIT • 1937 • Zerlett Hans H. • FRG
REVOLUTSIONER • 1917 • Bauer Yevgeni • USS • REVOLUTIONIST
REVOLVER • 1973 • Sollima Sergio • ITL, FRN, FRG • POURSUITE IMPLACABLE, LA (FRN) ○ BLOOD IN THE STREETS (USA)
REVOLVER, THE • 1969 • Buchvarova Radka • ANS • BUL
REVOLVER AUX CHEVEUX ROUGES, LE • 1974 • Geilfus Frederic • BLG • MAN ALIVE
REVOLVER DE BRINQUEDO • 1980 • Calmon Antonio • BRZ • TOY GUN
REVOLVER DES CORPORALS, DER • 1967 • Losansky Rolf • GDR • CORPORAL'S REVOLVER, THE ○ CORPORAL'S GUN, THE
REVOLVER EN GUARDIA • 1960 • Urueta Chano • MXC
REVOLVER SANGRIENTO, EL • 1963 • Delgado Miguel M. • MXC
REVOLVING DOORS, THE • 1910 • *Imp* • USA
REVOLVING DOORS, THE see **PORTES TOURNANTES, LES** • 1988
REVOLVING TABLE, THE • 1903 • Stow Percy? • UKN
REVUE A LA CARTE • 1935 • Schwarzwald Milton • SHT • USA
REVUE AT THE SODRAN THEATRE see **SODRANS REVY** • 1951
REVUE BLANCHE, LA • 1966 • Ferreux • SHT • FRN
REVUE MONTMARTROISE • 1932 • Cavalcanti Alberto • FRN
REVUE NA ZAKAZKU • 1982 • Podskalsky Zdenek • CZC, USS • REVUE TO ORDER
REVUE NAVAL A CHERBOURG • 1896 • Melies Georges • FRN • NAVAL REVIEW AT CHERBOURG, A
REVUE PARADE • 1938 • Hopwood R. A. • UKN
REVUE SISTERS see **REBYU NO SHIMAI** • 1929
REVUE TO ORDER see **REVUE NA ZAKAZKU** • 1982
REVYKOBING KALDER • 1973 • Hedman Trine, Hedman Werner • DNM
REWARD • 1980 • Swackhamer E. W. • USA
REWARD see **RECOMPENSA** • 1977
REWARD, THE • 1914 • *Jones Edgar* • USA
REWARD, THE • 1915 • Barker Reginald • *Reliance* • USA
REWARD, THE • 1915 • Drew Sidney • *Vitagraph* • USA
REWARD, THE • 1915 • Webster Harry Mcrae • *Imp* • USA
REWARD, THE • 1916 • *Stull Walter* • USA
REWARD, THE • 1960 • *Halas John (P)* • ANS • UKN
REWARD, THE • 1965 • Bourguignon Serge • USA, FRN • RECOMPENSE, LA (FRN)
REWARD, THE see **BELONNINGEN** • 1981
REWARD FOR BRONCHO BILLY, THE • 1912 • *Anderson Broncho Billy* • USA
REWARD OF CHIVALRY, THE • 1916 • Worthington William • SHT • USA
REWARD OF COURAGE • 1913 • Dwan Allan • USA
REWARD OF MERIT • 1909 • *Empire Films* • UKN
REWARD OF PATIENCE, THE • 1916 • Vignola Robert G. • USA
REWARD OF PERSEVERANCE, THE • 1912 • Haldane Bert? • UKN
REWARD OF SERVICE, THE • 1913 • *Lubin* • USA
REWARD OF THE FAITHLESS, THE • 1917 • Ingram Rex • USA
REWARD OF THRIFT, THE • 1914 • Finley Ned, Johnson Tefft • USA
REWARD OF VALOUR, THE • 1912 • Dwan Allan • USA
REWARDED FEELINGS see **NAGRODZONE UCZUCIA** • 1958
REWARDS OF VIRTUE, THE • 1983 • Hatton Maurice • UKN
REWI'S LAST STAND • 1939 • Hayward Rudall C. • NZL
REX HARRISON PRESENTS SHORT STORIES OF LOVE • 1971 • Laven Arnold (c/d) • MTV • USA • THREE FACES OF LOVE (UKN)
REX MUNDI see **TANZENDE TOD, DER** • 1925
REXIE THE POLYGOT • 1967 • Marszalek Lechoslaw • ANS • PLN
REY, EL • 1975 • *Aguila* • MXC
REY DE AFRICA (SPN) see **ONE STEP TO HELL** • 1968
REY DE JOROPO, EL see **ALIAS EL REY DE JOROPO** • 1978
REY DE LA CABEZA ELASTICA, EL • de Chomon Segundo • SPN • KING WITH THE ELASTIC HEAD, THE
REY DE LA CARRETERA, EL • 1954 • Fortuny Juan • SPN
REY DE LAS FINANZAS, EL • 1944 • Torrado Ramon • SPN
REY DE LOS CAMPOS DE CUBA, EL • 1913 • Quesada Enrique Diaz • CUB
REY DE LOS GITANOS, EL • 1933 • Strayer Frank • USA • KING OF THE GYPSIES
REY DE LOS VIVOS, EL • 1949 • Cahen Enrique • ARG • AVIVATO
REY DE MEXICO, EL • 1955 • Baledon Rafael • MXC
REY DEL BARRIO, EL • 1949 • Martinez Solares Gilberto • MXC • KING OF THE NEIGHBORHOOD, THE
REY DEL TOMATE, EL • 1962 • Delgado Miguel M. • MXC
REY QUE RABIO, EL • 1929 • Buchs Jose • SPN
REY QUE RABIO, EL • 1939 • Buchs Jose • SPN

REY SE DIVIERTE, EL • 1944 • de Fuentes Fernando • MXC
REYES DEL VOLANTE, LOS • 1964 • Morayta Miguel • MXC
REYES MAGOS • 1974 • Varela Miguel Angel • DOC • VNZ • MAGIC KINGS
REYHANEH • 1989 • Raisian • IRN
REYNA NG KARATE • 1967 • Marquez Artemio • PHL • KARATE QUEEN
REYNARD THE FOX • 1903 • *Lubin* • USA
REYNARD THE FOX see **ROMAN DE REYNARD, LE** • 1938
REZA POR TU ALMA Y MUERE • 1970 • Demicheli Tulio • SPN
REZERVAT • 1990 • Zahariev Edward • BUL • NATURE RESERVE
REZZOU, LE • 1938 • Leenhardt Roger • DCS • FRN
RHADPURA -ENDSTATION DER VERDAMMTEN • 1969 • FRG
RHAPSODIE • 1954 • Berneis Peter • FRG, FRN
RHAPSODIE ARLESIENNE • Des Vallieres Jean • SHT • FRN
RHAPSODIE DE SATURNE • 1947 • Image Jean • ANS • FRN
RHAPSODIE DER LIEBE • 1929 • Sekely Steve • FRG, AUS
RHAPSODIE IN BLEI (FRG) see **TREASURE OF SAN TERESA, THE** • 1959
RHAPSODY • 1954 • Vidor Charles • USA
RHAPSODY see **BLUE DANUBE, THE** • 1932
RHAPSODY IN A MAJOR see **PE UN PICIOR DE PLAI** • 1969
RHAPSODY IN AUGUST • 1990 • Kurosawa Akira • JPN
RHAPSODY IN BLACK AND BLUE • 1932 • Scotto Aubrey • SHT • USA
RHAPSODY IN BLOOD see **RAPSODIA DE SANGRE** • 1957
RHAPSODY IN BLUE • 1945 • Rapper Irving • USA
RHAPSODY IN BOGOTA • 1974 • Arzuaga Jose Maria • SHT • CLM
RHAPSODY IN BREW • 1933 • Gilbert Billy • SHT • USA
RHAPSODY IN RIVETS • 1941 • Freleng Friz • ANS • USA
RHAPSODY IN STEEL • 1935 • Goodman F. Lyle • SHT • USA
RHAPSODY IN TWO LANGUAGES • 1934 • Sparling Gordon • DCS • CND
RHAPSODY IN WOOD • 1947 • Pal George • ANS • USA
RHAPSODY IN WOOD • 1960 • Calinescu Bob • ANM • RMN
RHAPSODY IN ZOO • 1937 • Schwarzwald Milton • SHT • USA
RHAPSODY.. MOTION PAINTING III • Rogers Roger Bruce • SHT • USA
RHAPSODY OF A RIVER • Marcus Louis • DOC • IRL
RHAPSODY OF STEEL • 1959 • Urbano Carl • ANS • USA
RHAPSODY RABBIT • 1946 • Freleng Friz • ANS • USA
RHEA SYLVIA • 1908 • Novelli Enrico • ITL
RHEINGOLD • 1978 • Schilling Niklaus • FRG
RHEINISCHE BRAUTFAHRT • 1939 • Lippl Alois J. • FRG
RHEINISCHES MADCHEN BEIM RHEINISCHEN WEIN, EIN • 1927 • Guter Johannes • FRG
RHEINLANDMADEL, DAS • 1930 • Meyer Johannes • FRG
RHEINSBERG • 1967 • Hoffmann Kurt • FRG
RHEINZAUBER see **DES RHEINES UND DER LIEBE WELLEN. RHEINZAUBER** • 1925
RHIN, FLEUVE INTERNATIONAL, LE • 1952 • Bourguignon Serge, Zwobada Andre • FRN
RHINEMANN EXCHANGE, THE • 1977 • Kennedy Burt • TVM • USA
RHINESTONE • 1984 • Clark Bob • USA
RHINO! • 1964 • Tors Ivan • USA, SAF
RHINO • 1989 • Isaacs Ronnie • SAF
RHINOCEROS • 1973 • O'Horgan Tom • USA
RHINOCEROS, THE see **RINOCERONTE, EL** • 1971
RHINOCEROS (USA) see **NASHORNER, DIE** • 1963
RHINOCEROSES see **NASHORNER, DIE** • 1963
RHODA'S BURGLAR • 1915 • *Bowles Donald* • USA
RHODE ISLAND MURDERS, THE see **DEMON MURDER CASE, THE** • 1983
RHODE ISLAND RED • 1968 • Rainer Yvonne • SHT • USA
RHODES OF AFRICA • 1936 • Viertel Berthold • UKN, SAF • RHODES (USA)
RHODES (USA) see **RHODES OF AFRICA** • 1936
RHODESIA COUNTDOWN • 1969 • Raeburn Michael • UKN
RHUBARB • 1951 • Lubin Arthur • USA
RHUBARB • 1970 • Sykes Eric • UKN
RHUBARB AND RASCALS • 1914 • Plumb Hay • UKN
RHUMBA RHYTHMS • 1941 • Le Borg Reginald • SHT • USA
RHYME OF VENGEANCE, A see **AKUMA NO TEMARI-UTA** • 1977
RHYTHM • Calinescu Bob • ANM • RMN
RHYTHM • 1953 • Lye Len • ANS • USA
RHYTHM see **RITMOS** • 1978
RHYTHM 21 see **RHYTHMUS 21** • 1921
RHYTHM 23 see **RHYTHMUS 23** • 1923
RHYTHM 1934 see **RYTMUS 1934** • 1980
RHYTHM, A see **IQA** • 1970
RHYTHM AND BLUES REVIEW • 1955 • *Basie Count* • CMP • USA
RHYTHM AND WEEP • 1946 • White Jules • SHT • USA
RHYTHM BARBARIAN, THE see **BARBARO DEL RITMO, EL** • 1963
RHYTHM CAFE • 1938 • Schwarzwald Milton • SHT • USA
RHYTHM HITS THE ICE (UKN) see **ICE-CAPADES REVUE** • 1942
RHYTHM IN A RIFF • 1945 • Anderson Leonard • USA
RHYTHM IN LIGHT • 1936 • Bute Mary Ellen, Nemeth Ted J. • SHT • USA
RHYTHM IN THE AIR • 1936 • Woods Arthur • UKN
RHYTHM IN THE AIR see **TWENTY MILLION SWEETHEARTS** • 1934
RHYTHM IN THE BOW • 1935 • Hardaway Ben • ANS • USA
RHYTHM IN THE CLOUDS • 1937 • Auer John H. • USA
RHYTHM IN THE RANKS • 1941 • Pal George • ANS • USA
RHYTHM INN • 1951 • Landres Paul • USA
RHYTHM JAMBOREE • 1940 • Ceballos Larry • SHT • USA
RHYTHM MASTERS • 1949 • Cowan Will • SHT • USA
RHYTHM 'N' GREENS • 1964 • Miles Christopher • UKN
RHYTHM OF A CITY see **MANNISKOR I STAD** • 1946
RHYTHM OF CRIME, THE see **RITAM ZLOCINA** • 1982
RHYTHM OF INDIA • 1958 • Medori Alfredo • UKN
RHYTHM OF THE ISLANDS • 1943 • Neill R. William • USA
RHYTHM OF THE MAMBO • 1949 • Cowan Will • SHT • USA
RHYTHM OF THE PEOPLE • 1962 • Hettiarachi P. • DOC • SLN
RHYTHM OF THE RIO GRANDE • 1940 • Herman Al • USA
RHYTHM OF THE SADDLE • 1938 • Sherman George • USA
RHYTHM ON THE RAMPAGE • 1937 • Yarbrough Jean • SHT • USA
RHYTHM ON THE RANCH (UKN) see **ROOTIN' TOOTIN' RHYTHM** • 1937
RHYTHM ON THE RANGE • 1936 • Taurog Norman • USA
RHYTHM ON THE RESERVATION • 1939 • Fleischer Dave • ANS • USA
RHYTHM ON THE RIVER • 1940 • Schertzinger Victor • USA
RHYTHM ON THE RIVER (UKN) see **FRESHMAN LOVE** • 1936
RHYTHM PARADE • 1942 • Bretherton Howard, Gould Dave • USA
RHYTHM RACKETEER • 1937 • Seymour James • UKN
RHYTHM REVEL • 1941 • Ceballos Larry • SHT • USA
RHYTHM ROMANCE see **SOME LIKE IT HOT** • 1939
RHYTHM ROUND-UP • 1945 • Keays Vernon • USA • HONEST JOHN (UKN)
RHYTHM SERENADE • 1943 • Wellesley Gordon • UKN
RHYTHM WRANGLERS • 1937 • Roberts Charles E. • SHT • USA
RHYTHME ET VARIATIONS • 1930 • Dulac Germaine • SHT • FRN
RHYTHMES DE PARIS • 1947-51 • Verneuil Henri • SHT • FRN
RHYTHMETIC • 1956 • Lambart Evelyn, McLaren Norman • ANS • CND • RYTHMETIC
RHYTHMITIS • *Leroy Hal* • SHT • USA
RHYTHMS • 1963 • Iliesu Mirel • DOC • RMN
RHYTHMS AND IMAGES • 1966 • Calotescu Virgil • DOC • RMN
RHYTHMUS • 1921-27 • Richter Hans • ASS • FRG • FILM IN RHYTHM
RHYTHMUS 21 • 1921 • Richter Hans • ANS • FRG • RHYTHM 21 ○ FILM IST RHYTHMUS
RHYTHMUS 23 • 1923 • Richter Hans • SHT • FRG • RHYTHM 23
RHYTHMUS 25 • 1925 • Richter Hans • FRG
RIACHUELO • 1934 • Barth-Moglia Luis • ARG
RIADOM S NAMI • 1931 • *Romm Mikhail (Sc)* • USS
RIASZTOLOVES • 1977 • Bacso Peter • HNG • ALARM SHOT
RIATA see **DEADLY TRACKERS, THE** • 1973
RIB OF ADAM, A see **REBRO ADAMOVO** • 1956
RIBA • 1976 • Grgic Zlatko • ANS • YGS • FISH, THE
RIBALD TALES OF ROBIN HOOD, THE • 1969 • Kanter Richard • USA • ROBIN HOOD
RIBALTA, LA • 1912 • Caserini Mario • ITL
RIBATEJO • 1949 • Campos Henrique • PRT
RIBATEJO • 1957 • Queiroga Perdigao • SHT • PRT
RIBBON, THE • 1972 • van Heyningen Matthijs • SHT • NTH
RIBBON OF STEEL • 1985 • Beecroft Stuart • MTV • CND
RIBBONS AND BOXING GLOVES • 1914 • *Ab* • USA
RIBEIRA DA SAUDADE, A • 1962 • Mendes Joao • PRT
RIBELLE DI AMALFI, IL see **LEONE DI AMALFI, IL1** • 1951
RIBELLE DI CASTELMONTE, IL • 1965 • De Angelis Vertunio • ITL
RIBLJE OKO • 1979 • Marusic Josko • YGS • FISHEYE
RIBOLOV • 1972 • Grgic Zlatko • ANS • YGS • FISHING TRIP, THE
RIBON O MUSUBU FUJIN • 1939 • Yamamoto Satsuo • JPN • LADY WITH A RIBBON, A
RIBUT BARAT • 1980 • Ghani Salleh • MLY
RIBUT DI HUJUNG SENJA • 1980 • Osmera Ed • MLY
RIC AND GIAN IN THE CONQUEST OF THE WEST see **RIC E GIAN ALLA CONQUISTA DEL WEST** • 1967
RIC E GIAN ALLA CONQUISTA DEL WEST • 1967 • Civirani Osvaldo • ITL • RIC AND GIAN IN THE CONQUEST OF THE WEST
RICAIN, LE • 1978 • Pallardy Jean-Marie • FRN
RICARDO • 1968 • Amin-E-Amini • IRN
RICATTO ALLA MALA (ITL) see **VERANO PARA MATAR, UN** • 1973
RICATTO DI UN COMMISSARIO DI POLIZIA A UN GIOVANE INDIZIAT DI REATO (ITL) see **AVEUX LES PLUS DOUX, LES** • 1970
RICATTO DI UN PADRE, IL • 1957 • Vari Giuseppe • ITL
RICCHEZZA SENZA DOMANI • 1939 • Poggioli Ferdinando M. • ITL
RICCHI E POVERI • 1949 • Rossi Aldo • ITL • BRISCOLA
RICCO see **AJUSTE DE CUENTAS** • 1973
RICE • 1964 • Van Dyke Willard, Galentine Wheaton • DOC • USA
RICE see **KOME** • 1957
RICE, THE see **MESHI** • 1951
RICE AND OLD SHOES • 1912 • *Buckley May* • USA
RICE AND OLD SHOES • 1922 • St. Clair Malcolm • SHT • USA
RICE BOWL see **WAN**
RICE GIRL (USA) see **RISAIA, LA** • 1956
RICE GIRLS see **RISAIA, LA** • 1956
RICE INDUSTRY OF JAPAN, THE • 1913 • Melies Gaston • DOC • USA
RICH AND FAMOUS • 1981 • Cukor George • USA
RICH AND IDLE see **HAYATA DONUS** • 1967
RICH AND RESPECTABLE (USA) see **AB MORGEN SIND WIR REICH UND EHRLICH** • 1977
RICH AND STRANGE • 1931 • Hitchcock Alfred • UKN • EAST OF SHANGHAI
RICH AND THE POOR, THE • 1911 • *American* • USA
RICH ARE ALWAYS WITH US, THE • 1932 • Green Alfred E. • USA
RICH BITCH • *Cantudo Maria* • ITL
RICH BOY, THE see **PANNAKARAI PILLAI** • 1968
RICH BRIDE, THE see **BOGOTAYA NEVESTA** • 1937
RICH BUT HONEST • 1927 • Ray Albert • USA
RICH FULL LIFE, THE (UKN) see **CYNTHIA** • 1947
RICH GIRL, POOR GIRL • 1921 • Harris Harry B. • USA
RICH HALL'S VANISHING AMERICA • 1986 • Rash Steve • MTV • USA
RICH IDLER, THE • 1916 • Smith David • SHT • USA
RICH KIDS • 1979 • Young Robert Malcolm • USA
RICH MAN, A see **RIG MAND, EN** • 1979
RICH MAN, POOR GIRL • 1938 • Schunzel Reinhold • USA
RICH MAN, POOR MAN • 1918 • Dawley J. Searle • USA
RICH MAN, POOR MAN • 1922 • Roach Hal • SHT • USA
RICH MAN, POOR MAN • 1975 • Greene David, Segal Alex • MTV • USA
RICH MAN WITHOUT A PENNY, A see **ENAS APENTAROS LEFTAS** • 1967
RICH MAN'S DARLING, A • 1918 • Jones Edgar • USA
RICH MAN'S FOLLY • 1931 • Cromwell John • USA
RICH MAN'S PLAYTHING • 1917 • Harbaugh Carl • USA
RICH MAN'S SON, A see **PAPPAS POJKE** • 1937
RICH MEN'S SONS • 1927 • Graves Ralph • USA
RICH MEN'S WIVES • 1922 • Gasnier Louis J. • USA
RICH MR. ROCKAMORGAN, THE • 1913 • *Champion* • USA
RICH PEOPLE • 1929 • Griffith Edward H. • USA • RACKETEER, THE
RICH REVENGE, A • 1910 • Griffith D. W. • USA
RICH SLAVE, THE • 1920 • Fielding Romaine • USA
RICH UNCLE, THE • 1913 • Smalley Phillips • USA
RICH VEIN see **BOLSHAYA RUDA** • 1964
RICH, YOUNG AND DEADLY (UKN) see **PLATINUM HIGH SCHOOL** • 1960
RICH, YOUNG AND PRETTY • 1951 • Taurog Norman • USA
RICHARD • 1972 • Hurwitz Harry, Yerby Lorees • USA
RICHARD HAMILTON • 1969 • Scott James • UKN
RICHARD HUTTER • Burkhardt Georg • FRG
RICHARD II • 1978 • Giles David • MTV • UKN
RICHARD III • 1908 • Ranous William V., Blackton J. Stuart (Spv) • USA
RICHARD III • 1911 • Benson F. R. • UKN
RICHARD III • 1913 • Dudley M. B. • USA
RICHARD III • 1913 • Warde Frederick • USA
RICHARD III • 1955 • Olivier Laurence, Bushell Anthony • UKN
RICHARD III • 1986 • Ruiz Raul • FRN
RICHARD KIMBER AND HIS ORCHESTRA • 1942 • Negulesco Jean • SHT • USA
RICHARD KRAFT AT THE PLAYBOY CLUB • 1963 • Landow George • USA
RICHARD MORTENSENS BEVAEGELIGE MALERI • 1944 • Roos Jorgen • DOC • DNM
RICHARD PRYOR -HERE AND NOW • 1983 • Pryor Richard • USA
RICHARD PRYOR IS BACK LIVE IN CONCERT • 1979 • Margolis Jeff • USA
RICHARD PRYOR -LIVE AND SMOKIN' • 1985 • Blum Michael • USA
RICHARD PRYOR LIVE IN CONCERT • 1979 • Margolis Jeff • USA
RICHARD PRYOR LIVE ON THE SUNSET STRIP • 1982 • Layton Joe • USA
RICHARD TAUBER STORY, THE see **DU BIST DIE WELT FUR MICH** • 1953
RICHARD THE BRAZEN • 1917 • Vekroff Perry N. • USA
RICHARD, THE LION-HEARTED • 1923 • Withey Chet • USA
RICHARD WAGNER • 1912 • Froelich Carl • FRG
RICHARD'S THINGS • 1980 • Harvey Anthony • UKN
RICHE POUR UN JOUR • 1965 • Boughedir Ferid, Murali Mustafa • SHT • TNS
RICHELIEU • 1914 • Dwan Allan • USA
RICHELIEU see **CARDINAL'S CONSPIRACY, THE** • 1909
RICHELIEU OR THE CONSPIRACY • 1909 • Blackton J. Stuart • USA
RICHER THAN THE EARTH (UKN) see **WHISTLE AT EATON FALLS, THE** • 1951
RICHES see **FOOL'S GOLD, A** • 1916
RICHES AND MISERY OR, THE GRASSHOPPER AND THE ANT see **RICHESSE ET MISERE; OU, LA CIGALE ET LA FOURMI** • 1899
RICHES AND ROGUES • 1913 • Weston Charles? • UKN
RICHES AND ROMANCE see **AMAZING QUEST OF ERNEST BLISS, THE** • 1936
RICHES OF THE EARTH • 1959 • Goldsmith Sidney • ANM • CND
RICHESSE DES AUTRES, LA • 1973 • Bulbulian Maurice, Gauthier Michel • DOC • CND
RICHESSE ET MISERE; OU, LA CIGALE ET LA FOURMI • 1899 • Melies Georges • FRN • RICHES AND MISERY OR, THE GRASSHOPPER AND THE ANT ○ WANDERING MINSTREL, THE
RICHESSES DU NIL see **NIL ARZAQ, AN-** • 1972
RICHEST CAT IN THE WORLD, THE • 1986 • Beeman Greg • TVM • USA
RICHEST GIRL, THE • 1918 • Capellani Albert • USA
RICHEST GIRL IN THE WORLD • 1915 • Le Saint Edward J. • USA
RICHEST GIRL IN THE WORLD, THE • 1934 • Seiter William A. • USA
RICHEST GIRL IN THE WORLD, THE (USA) see **VERDENS RIGESTE PIGE** • 1958
RICHEST MAN IN THE WORLD, THE • 1930 • Wood Sam • USA • SINS OF THE CHILDREN ○ FATHER'S DAY
RICHEST MAN IN TOWN, THE • 1941 • Barton Charles T. • USA
RICHIAMO, IL • 1979 • Del Monte Peter • ITL
RICHIAMO DEL CUORE, IL • 1930 • Salvatori Jack • ITL
RICHIAMO DEL GHIACCIAIO, IL • 1952 • Langini Osvaldo • ITL
RICHIAMO DEL LUPO, IL • 1975 • Baldanello Gianfranco • ITL, SPN • GREAT ADVENTURE, THE (USA) ○ CALL OF THE WOLF
RICHIAMO DEL SANGUE • 1947 • Vajda Ladislao, Bucchi Valentino • ITL
RICHIAMO DELLA FORESTA, IL (ITL) see **CALL OF THE WILD** • 1972
RICHIAMO DELL'ALPE SPLENDENTE, IL • 1947 • Casara Severino • ITL
RICHIAMO NELLA TEMPESTA, IL • 1952 • Palella Oreste • ITL • AMANTI DELL'INFINITO, GLI
RICHIE see **DEATH OF RICHIE, THE** • 1977
RICHIE BROCKELMAN: MISSING 24 HOURS • 1976 • Averback Hy • TVM • USA
RICHLER OF ST. URBAIN • 1971 • Owen Don • CND
RICHTER, DER • 1917 • *De Carli Bruno* • FRG
RICHTER UND SEIN HENKER, DER • 1976 • Schell Maximilian • FRG, ITL • END OF THE GAME (USA) ○ GETTING AWAY WITH MURDER ○ JUDGE AND HIS HANGMAN, THE ○ MURDER ON THE BRIDGE ○ DECEPTION ○ GIUDICE E I SUO BOIA, IL
RICHTER VON ZALAMEA, DER • 1920 • Berger Ludwig • FRG

RICHTER VON ZALAMEA, DER • 1955 • Hellberg Martin • GDR • JUDGE OF ZALAMEA, THE
RICHTERIN, DIE • 1917 • von Woringen Paul • FRG
RICHTERIN VON SOLVIGSHOLM, DIE • 1916 • Justitz Emil • FRG
RICHTHOFEN, DER ROTE RITTER DER LUFT • 1927 • Kertesz Desider, Joseph Peter • FRG • RICHTHOFEN: THE RED KNIGHT OF THE AIR (USA)
RICHTHOFEN: THE RED KNIGHT OF THE AIR (USA) see **RICHTHOFEN, DER ROTE RITTER DER LUFT** • 1927
RICHTIGE MANN, DER • 1982 • Berner Dieter • AUS • ACCURATE MAN, THE
RICHU • 1985 • Yu Banzheng • CHN • SUNRISE
RICKETY GIN • 1927 • Disney Walt • ANS • USA
RICK'S REDEMPTION • 1913 • *Garwood William* • USA
RICKSHAW • 1960 • King Allan • CND
RICKSHAW MAN, THE see **MUHOMATSU NO ISSHO** • 1943
RICKSHAW MAN, THE see **MUHOMATSU NO ISSHO** • 1958
RICKSHAW MAN, OR THE LIFE OF RECKLESS MATSU see **MUHOMATSU NO ISSHO** • 1943
RICKSHAW PULLER, THE see **PENAREK BECHA**
RICKSHAW, THE DETECTIVE • 1911 • *Reliance* • USA
RICKY 1 • 1986 • Naud William T. • USA • HEART TO WIN
RICKY GOES TO CAMP • 1982 • Frizzell John • CND
RICO see **AJUSTE DE CUENTAS** • 1973
RICO O CAMELO E O REINO, O see **PRINCIPIO DA SABEDORIO, O** • 1975
RICOCHET • 1963 • Moxey John Llewellyn • UKN
RICOCHET ROMANCE • 1954 • Lamont Charles • USA
RICOCHETS see **SHTEI ETZBAOTH ME'TZIDON** • 1985
RICOMINCIO DA TRE • 1980 • Troisi Massimo • ITL • STARTING AGAIN AT THREE (UKN)
RICORDAMI • 1956 • Baldi Ferdinando • ITL
RICORDATI DI NAPOLI • 1958 • Mercanti Pino • ITL
RID I NATT! • 1942 • Molander Gustaf • SWD • RIDE TONIGHT!
RIDDANCE see **SZABAD LELEGZET** • 1973
RIDDAREN AV IGAR see **EROTIKON** • 1920
RIDDER VAN DIE GROOTPAD • 1976 • SAF
RIDDLE GAWNE • 1918 • Hart William S., Hillyer Lambert • USA
RIDDLE IN RASCALS, A • 1916 • Beaudine William • SHT • USA
RIDDLE ME THIS see **GUILTY AS HELL** • 1932
RIDDLE OF LUMEN, THE • 1972 • Brakhage Stan • USA
RIDDLE OF THE GREEN UMBRELLA, THE • 1914 • Buel Kenean • USA
RIDDLE OF THE OLD OWL, THE • 1981 • Bonin Laurier • MTV • CND
RIDDLE OF THE RANGE, THE see **RUTH OF THE RANGE** • 1923
RIDDLE OF THE RINGS, THE • 1915 • Horne James W. • USA
RIDDLE OF THE SANDS, THE • 1978 • Maylam Tony • UKN, USA
RIDDLE OF THE SILK STOCKINGS, THE • 1915 • Lessey George A. • USA
RIDDLE OF THE TIN SOLDIER, THE • 1913 • *Joyce Alice* • USA
RIDDLE OF THE WALL, THE see **TAYINSTVENNAYA STENA** • 1968
RIDDLE OF THE WOODEN LEG, THE • 1915 • *Hutton Leona* • USA
RIDDLE RANCH • 1936 • Hutchison Charles • USA
RIDDLE RIDER, THE • 1924 • Craft William James • SRL • USA
RIDDLE TRAIL, THE • 1928 • *Lyons Cliff (Tex)* • USA
RIDDLE: WOMAN, THE • 1920 • Jose Edward • USA
RIDDLES IN RHYTHM • 1956 • *Universal* • SHT • USA
RIDDLES OF THE SPHINX • 1978 • Wollen Peter, Mulvey Laura • UKN
RIDE, THE • 1963 • Potterton Gerald • CND
RIDE A CROOKED MILE • 1938 • Green Alfred E. • USA • ESCAPE FROM YESTERDAY (UKN)
RIDE A CROOKED TRAIL • 1958 • Hibbs Jesse • USA
RIDE A NORTHBOUND HORSE • 1969 • Totten Robert • TVM • USA
RIDE A RECKLESS MILE see **GREAT DAN PATCH, THE** • 1949
RIDE A VIOLENT MILE • 1957 • Warren Charles Marquis • USA
RIDE A WHITE HORSE • 1968 • Evans Bob • ASL
RIDE A WILD PONY • 1975 • Chaffey Don • ASL, USA
RIDE A WILD STUD • 1969 • Ekard Revilo • USA • RIDE THE WILD STUD
RIDE ALONG, KID • 1920 • *Mccullough Ralph* • SHT • USA
RIDE AND KILL (UKN) see **CAVALCA E UCCIDI** • 1963
RIDE BACK, THE • 1957 • Miner Allen H. • USA
RIDE BENE CHI RIDE ULTIMO • 1977 • Aleandri Marco, Chiari Walter, Bramieri Gino, Caruso Pino • ITL
RIDE BEYOND VENGEANCE • 1966 • McEveety Bernard • USA • NIGHT OF THE TIGER, THE
RIDE CLEAR OF DIABLO • 1954 • Hibbs Jesse • USA
RIDE, COWBOY, RIDE • 1939 • Amy George • SHT • USA
RIDE 'EM, COWBOY • 1936 • Selander Lesley • USA • COWBOY ROUND-UP
RIDE 'EM COWBOY • 1941 • Lubin Arthur • USA
RIDE 'EM, COWGIRL • 1939 • Diege Samuel • USA
RIDE 'EM HIGH • 1927 • Thorpe Richard • USA
RIDE 'EM PLOW BOY! • 1928 • Disney Walt • ANS • USA
RIDE FOR A BRIDE, A • 1911 • Raymond Charles? • UKN
RIDE FOR A BRIDE, A • 1913 • Nicholls George • USA
RIDE FOR LIFE, A • 1912 • *Bison* • USA
RIDE FOR LIFE, A • 1917 • *Pokes & Jabbs* • SHT • USA
RIDE FOR LIFE, A see **BUSHRANGER'S RANSOM, A** • 1911
RIDE FOR YOUR LIFE • 1924 • Sedgwick Edward • USA
RIDE FOR YOUR LIFE • 1968 • Spry Robin • CND
RIDE HARD, RIDE WILD • 1970 • Peterssons Elov • DNM
RIDE HIM, BOSKO • 1933 • Harman Hugh • ANS • USA
RIDE HIM, COWBOY • 1932 • Allen Fred • USA • HAWK, THE (UKN)
RIDE IN A PINK CAR • 1978 • Emery Robert J. • USA
RIDE IN THE WHIRLWIND • 1966 • Hellman Monte • USA • RIDE THE WHIRLWIND
RIDE, KELLY, RIDE • 1941 • Foster Norman • USA
RIDE LONESOME • 1959 • Boetticher Budd • USA
RIDE, MISTER? • 1970 • Hallstrom Don • USA
RIDE OF THE VALKYRIES, THE • 1907 • Jeapes Harold? • UKN
RIDE ON, VAQUERO! • 1941 • Leeds Herbert I. • USA
RIDE OUT FOR VENGEANCE • 1957 • Girard Bernard • USA
RIDE, RANGER, RIDE • 1936 • Kane Joseph • USA
RIDE, ROXIE, RIDE • Moberly Luke • USA
RIDE, RYDER, RIDE • 1949 • Collins Lewis D. • USA
RIDE, TENDERFOOT, RIDE • 1940 • McDonald Frank • USA
RIDE THE HIGH COUNTRY • 1962 • Peckinpah Sam • USA • GUNS IN THE AFTERNOON (UKN)
RIDE THE HIGH IRON • 1956 • Weis Don • USA
RIDE THE HIGH WIND • 1965 • Millin David • SAF
RIDE THE MAN DOWN • 1952 • Kane Joseph • USA
RIDE THE PINK HORSE • 1947 • Montgomery Robert • USA
RIDE THE TIGER • 1971 • Montgomery George • USA
RIDE THE WHIRLWIND see **RIDE IN THE WHIRLWIND** • 1966
RIDE THE WILD STUD see **RIDE A WILD STUD** • 1969
RIDE THE WILD SURF • 1964 • Taylor Don • USA
RIDE THE WIND • 1967 • Witney William • TVM • USA
RIDE TO DEATH, THE • 1910 • *Powers* • USA
RIDE TO GLORY see **BLADE RIDER: ATTACK OF THE INDIAN NATION** • 1965
RIDE TO HANGMAN'S TREE, THE • 1967 • Rafkin Alan • USA
RIDE TONIGHT! see **RID I NATT!** • 1942
RIDE, VAQUERO! • 1953 • Farrow John • USA • VAQUERO
RIDE WITH UNCLE JOE, A • 1943 • Annakin Ken • DCS • UKN
RIDEAU CRAMOISI, LE • 1952 • Astruc Alexandre • FRN • CRIMSON CURTAIN, THE
RIDEAU HALL • 1962 • Barclay Robert • MTV • CND
RIDEAU ROUGE, LE • 1952 • Barsacq Andre • FRN • CE SOIR ON JOUE MACBETH
RIDEAUX BLANCS, LES • 1966 • Franju Georges • SHT • FRN
RIDENDO E SCHERZANDO • 1978 • Aleandri Marco • ITL
RIDEOUT CASE, THE see **RAPE AND MARRIAGE: THE RIDEOUT CASE** • 1980
RIDER ABOVE THE CITY see **VSADNIK NAD GORODOM** • 1967
RIDER FROM TUCSON • 1950 • Selander Lesley • USA
RIDER IN BLUE see **RYTTARE I BLATT** • 1959
RIDER IN THE NIGHT, THE (USA) see **RUITER IN DIE NAG, DIE** • 1963
RIDER IN THE RAIN see **PASSAGER DE LA PLUIE, LE** • 1969
RIDER OF DEATH VALLEY, THE • 1932 • Rogell Albert S. • USA • DESTRY OF DEATH VALLEY
RIDER OF MYSTERY RANCH, THE • 1924 • *Mix Art* • USA
RIDER OF REVENGE • 1971 • Hsiung Ting-Wu • HKG
RIDER OF SILHOUETTE, THE • 1915 • Easton Clem • USA
RIDER OF THE KING LOG, THE • 1921 • Hoyt Harry O. • USA
RIDER OF THE LAW • 1919 • Ford John • USA
RIDER OF THE LAW • 1927 • Hurst Paul C. • USA
RIDER OF THE LAW, THE • 1935 • Bradbury Robert North • USA
RIDER OF THE PLAINS • 1931 • McCarthy John P. • USA • GREATER LOVE, THE (UKN)
RIDER OF THE PLAINS, THE • 1915 • *Empire* • USA
RIDER OF THE PLAINS (UKN) see **WAR PAINT** • 1926
RIDER OF THE SKULLS, THE see **CHARRO DE LAS CALAVERAS, EL** • 1965
RIDER OF THE WHITE HORSE, THE (USA) see **SCHIMMELREITER, DER** • 1934
RIDER ON A DEAD HORSE • 1962 • Strock Herbert L. • USA
RIDER ON THE RAIN (USA) see **PASSAGER DE LA PLUIE, LE** • 1969
RIDER ON THE WHITE HORSE, THE see **SCHIMMELREITER, DER** • 1934
RIDERA • 1967 • Corbucci Bruno • ITL • CUORE MATTO ○ YOU'LL LAUGH ○ MAD HEART
RIDERE, RIDERE, RIDERE • 1955 • Anton Edoardo, Paolella Domenico • ITL
RIDERLESS BICYCLE, THE • 1906 • *Pathe* • FRN
RIDERS see **VSADNIKI** • 1939
RIDERS AT NIGHT • 1923 • *Williams Big Boy* • USA
RIDERS FROM NOWHERE • 1940 • Johnston Raymond K. • USA
RIDERS IN THE DARK • 1989 • Parmet Philip • USA
RIDERS IN THE SKY • 1949 • English John • USA
RIDERS IN THE SKY see **NEBESTI JEZDCI** • 1968
RIDERS OF BLACK MOUNTAIN • 1940 • Newfield Sam • USA
RIDERS OF BLACK RIVER • 1939 • Deming Norman • USA
RIDERS OF BORDER BAY • 1925 • *Kesterson George* • USA
RIDERS OF CAPISTRANO • 1955 • Landers Lew • MTV • USA
RIDERS OF DEATH VALLEY • 1941 • Beebe Ford, Taylor Ray • SRL • USA
RIDERS OF DESTINY • 1933 • Bradbury Robert North • USA
RIDERS OF MYSTERY • 1925 • Bradbury Robert North • USA
RIDERS OF PASCO BASIN • 1940 • Taylor Ray • USA
RIDERS OF SANTA FE • 1944 • Fox Wallace • USA • MILE A MINUTE (UKN) ○ RIDERS OF THE SANTA FE
RIDERS OF THE BADLANDS • 1942 • Bretherton Howard • USA
RIDERS OF THE BLACK HILLS • 1938 • Sherman George • USA
RIDERS OF THE CACTUS • 1931 • Kirkland David • USA
RIDERS OF THE DARK • 1928 • Grinde Nick • USA
RIDERS OF THE DAWN • 1920 • Conway Jack • USA • DESERT OF WHEAT, THE
RIDERS OF THE DAWN • 1937 • Bradbury Robert North • USA
RIDERS OF THE DAWN • 1945 • Drake Oliver • USA
RIDERS OF THE DEADLINE • 1943 • Selander Lesley • USA
RIDERS OF THE DESERT • 1932 • Bradbury Robert North • USA
RIDERS OF THE DUSK • 1949 • Hillyer Lambert • USA
RIDERS OF THE FRONTIER • 1939 • Bennet Spencer Gordon • USA
RIDERS OF THE GOLDEN GULCH • 1932 • Smith Cliff • USA
RIDERS OF THE KITCHEN RANGE • 1925 • Roach Hal • SHT • USA
RIDERS OF THE LAW • 1922 • Bradbury Robert North • USA
RIDERS OF THE LONE STAR • 1947 • Abrahams Derwin • USA
RIDERS OF THE NEW FOREST • 1946 • Leacock Philip • UKN
RIDERS OF THE NIGHT • 1918 • Collins John H. • USA
RIDERS OF THE NORTH • 1931 • McGowan J. P. • USA
RIDERS OF THE NORTHLAND • 1942 • Berke William • USA • NEXT IN LINE (UKN)
RIDERS OF THE NORTHWEST MOUNTED • 1943 • Berke William • USA
RIDERS OF THE PLAINS • 1910 • Porter Edwin S. • USA
RIDERS OF THE PLAINS • 1924 • Jaccard Jacques • SRL • USA
RIDERS OF THE PONY EXPRESS • 1949 • Salle Michael • USA
RIDERS OF THE PURPLE COWS • 1924 • *Sennett Mack (P)* • SHT • USA
RIDERS OF THE PURPLE SAGE • 1918 • Lloyd Frank • USA
RIDERS OF THE PURPLE SAGE • 1925 • Reynolds Lynn • USA
RIDERS OF THE PURPLE SAGE • 1931 • MacFadden Hamilton • USA
RIDERS OF THE PURPLE SAGE • 1941 • Tinling James • USA
RIDERS OF THE RANGE • 1923 • Thayer Otis B. • USA
RIDERS OF THE RANGE • 1950 • Selander Lesley • USA
RIDERS OF THE RIO • 1931 • Tansey Robert • USA • LAW OF THE RIO (UKN)
RIDERS OF THE RIO GRANDE • 1929 • McGowan J. P. • USA
RIDERS OF THE RIO GRANDE • 1943 • Bretherton Howard • USA
RIDERS OF THE ROCKIES • 1937 • Bradbury Robert North • USA
RIDERS OF THE SAGE • 1939 • Webb Harry S. • USA
RIDERS OF THE SAND STORM • 1925 • *Williams Big Boy* • USA
RIDERS OF THE SANTA FE see **RIDERS OF SANTA FE** • 1944
RIDERS OF THE STORM • 1929 • McGowan J. P. • USA
RIDERS OF THE STORM (USA) see **AMERICAN WAY, THE** • 1986
RIDERS OF THE TIMBERLINE • 1941 • Selander Lesley • USA
RIDERS OF THE WEST • 1927 • Wilson Ben • USA
RIDERS OF THE WEST • 1942 • Bretherton Howard • USA
RIDERS OF THE WHISTLING PINES • 1949 • English John • USA
RIDERS OF THE WHISTLING SKULL, THE • 1937 • Wright Mack V. • USA • GOLDEN TRAIL, THE (UKN)
RIDERS OF THE WITCH, THE see **JINETES DE LA BRUJA, LOS** • 1965
RIDERS OF VENGEANCE • 1919 • Ford John • USA
RIDERS OF VENGEANCE • 1928 • Horner Robert J. • USA
RIDERS OF VENGEANCE see **RAIDERS, THE** • 1952
RIDERS TO THE SEA • 1935 • Hurst Brian Desmond • UKN
RIDERS TO THE STARS • 1954 • Carlson Richard • USA
RIDERS UP • 1924 • Cummings Irving • USA • WHEN JOHNNY COMES MARCHING HOME
RIDES AND SLIDES • 1923 • Raymaker Herman C. • USA
RIDGEWAY OF MONTANA • 1915 • McRae Henry • USA
RIDGEWAY OF MONTANA • 1924 • Smith Cliff • USA
RIDI NIMNAYA • 1978 • Nihalsingha D. B. • SLN
RIDI PAGLIACCIO! • 1941 • Mastrocinque Camillo • ITL
RIDICULE AND TEARS see **LOJEN OCH TARAR** • 1913
RIDIN' COMET • 1925 • Wilson Ben • USA
RIDIN' DEMON, THE • 1929 • Taylor Ray • USA
RIDIN' DOUBLE see **RIDING DOUBLE** • 1924
RIDIN' DOWN THE CANYON • 1942 • Kane Joseph • USA
RIDIN' DOWN THE TRAIL • 1947 • Bretherton Howard • USA
RIDIN' EASY • 1925 • Hayes Ward • USA
RIDIN' FOOL • 1924 • *Cuneo Lester* • USA
RIDIN' FOOL, THE • 1931 • McCarthy John P. • USA
RIDIN' FOR JUSTICE • 1931 • Lederman D. Ross • USA
RIDIN' GENT, A • 1926 • Cohn Bennett • USA
RIDIN' GENTS • 1934 • Cohn Bennett • SHT • USA
RIDIN' KID FROM POWDER RIVER, THE • 1924 • Sedgwick Edward • USA • SADDLE HAWK, THE
RIDIN' LAW • 1930 • Webb Harry S. • USA
RIDIN' LUCK • 1927 • Gordon Edward R. • USA
RIDIN' MAD • 1924 • Jaccard Jacques • USA
RIDIN' ON • 1936 • Ray Bernard B. • USA • UNSEEN ENEMY, THE (UKN)
RIDIN' ON A RAINBOW • 1941 • Landers Lew • USA
RIDIN' PRETTY • 1925 • Rosson Arthur • USA
RIDIN' RASCAL, THE • 1926 • Smith Cliff • USA
RIDIN' ROMEO, A • 1921 • Marshall George • USA
RIDIN' ROWDY, THE • 1927 • Thorpe Richard • USA
RIDIN' SPEED • 1931 • Adamson Victor • USA
RIDIN' STRAIGHT • 1926 • *Reeves Bob* • USA
RIDIN' STREAK, THE • 1925 • Andrews Del • USA
RIDIN' THE CHEROKEE TRAIL • 1941 • Bennet Spencer Gordon • USA
RIDIN' THE LONE TRAIL • 1937 • Newfield Sam • USA
RIDIN' THE OUTLAW TRAIL • 1951 • Sears Fred F. • USA
RIDIN' THE RANGE • 1939 • Townley Jack • USA
RIDIN' THE TRAIL • 1940 • Johnston Raymond K. • USA
RIDIN' THE WIND • 1925 • Andrews Del, Werker Alfred L. • USA
RIDIN' THROUGH see **STRAIGHT THROUGH** • 1925
RIDIN' THRU • 1923 • *Hatton Dick* • USA
RIDIN' THRU • 1935 • Webb Harry S. • USA
RIDIN' THUNDER • 1925 • Smith Cliff • USA • RIDING THUNDER
RIDIN' WEST • 1924 • Webb Harry S. • USA
RIDIN' WILD • 1922 • Ross Nat • USA
RIDIN' WILD • 1925 • De La Mothe Leon • USA
RIDIN' WILD see **SAGEBRUSH TRAIL, THE** • 1922
RIDING AVENGER, THE • 1936 • Fraser Harry L. • USA
RIDING DOUBLE • 1924 • Maloney Leo • USA • RIDIN' DOUBLE
RIDING FAST • 1987 • Milicevic Djordje • CND
RIDING FOOL • 1924 • Carpenter Horace B. • USA
RIDING FOR A FALL see **MANEGES** • 1949
RIDING FOR A KING • 1926 • West Walter • USA
RIDING FOR FAME • 1928 • Eason B. Reeves • USA
RIDING FOR LIFE • 1926 • McGowan J. P. • USA
RIDING FOR LOVE • 1926 • Wyler William • SHT • USA
RIDING HIGH • 1943 • Marshall George • USA • MELODY INN (UKN)
RIDING HIGH • 1950 • Capra Frank • USA
RIDING HIGH • 1980 • Cramer Ross • UKN • HEAVY METAL (USA) ○ VERY HEAVY METAL
RIDING HIGH see **REMEMBER WHEN** • 1937
RIDING HOOD AND RED see **CAPERUCITA Y ROJA** • 1976
RIDING ON AIR • 1937 • Sedgwick Edward • USA
RIDING ON THE EDGE • 1988 • Fargo James • USA
RIDING ON TOP OF A CAR • 1907 • Morland John • UKN

RIDING RENEGADE, THE • 1928 • Fox Wallace • USA
RIDING RIVALS • 1926 • Thorpe Richard • USA
RIDING ROMANCE • 1926 • McGowan J. P. • USA
RIDING SHOTGUN • 1954 • De Toth Andre • USA
RIDING SPEED • 1934 • Wilsey Jay • USA
RIDING TALL see **SQUARES** • 1972
RIDING THE CALIFORNIA TRAIL • 1947 • Nigh William • USA • CISCO AND THE ANGEL
RIDING THE GOAT • 1916 • *King Cole* • USA
RIDING THE RAILS • 1938 • Fleischer Dave • ANS • USA
RIDING THE SUNSET TRAIL • 1941 • Tansey Robert • USA
RIDING THE WIND • 1942 • Killy Edward • USA
RIDING THROUGH NEVADA • 1943 • Berke William • USA
RIDING THUNDER see **RIDIN' THUNDER** • 1925
RIDING TO FAME • 1927 • Barringer A. B. • USA
RIDING TO WIN (UKN) see **THOROUGHBRED, THE** • 1930
RIDING TORNADO, THE • 1932 • Lederman D. Ross • USA
RIDING WEST • 1944 • Berke William • USA • FUGITIVE FROM TIME (UKN)
RIDING WILD • 1919 • Harvey Harry • SHT • USA
RIDING WILD • 1935 • Selman David • USA
RIDING WITH BUFFALO BILL • 1954 • Bennet Spencer Gordon • SRL • USA
RIDING WITH DEATH • 1921 • Jaccard Jacques • USA
RIDOLF IN THE LION'S CAGE see **FRIDOLF I LEJONKULAN** • 1933
RIE REISE NACH SUNDEVIT • 1966 • Carow Heiner • GDR • JOURNEY TO SUNDEVIT
RIEDLAND • 1976 • Bolliger Wilfried • MTV • SWT
RIEL • 1979 • Bloomfield George • TVM • CND
RIEN A LOUER MONSIEUR LEBUREAU • 1920 • Luitz-Morat • FRN
RIEN DE RIEN see **TUFA DE VENETIA** • 1977
RIEN N'A D'IMPORTANCE see **SHAIA YUHIM, LA** • 1973
RIEN NE VA PLUS • 1963 • Bacque Jean • FRN
RIEN NE VA PLUS • 1979 • Ribes Jean-Michel • FRN
RIEN N'EST IMPOSSIBLE A L'HOMME • 1910 • Cohl Emile • ANS • FRN • NOTHING IS IMPOSSIBLE TO THE MAN
RIEN QUE DES HEURES • 1926 • Cavalcanti Alberto • FRN
RIEN QUE DES MENSONGES • 1932 • Anton Karl • FRN • TROIS POINTS C'EST TOUT ○ FRANCS-MACONS ○ CERCLE VICIEUX, LE
RIEN QUE LA VERITE • 1931 • Guissart Rene • FRN
RIEN QU'UN JEU • 1983 • Sauriol Brigitte • CND • JUST A GAME
RIEN QU'UNE NUIT see **LAILATUN WAHIDA** • 1968
RIENIE • 1980 • SAF
RIESENRAD, DAS • 1961 • von Radvanyi Geza • FRG
RIESENSCHMUGGEL, DER • 1920 • Hofer Franz • FRG
RIFF-RAFF see **GOLFOS, LOS** • 1959
RIFF RAFF GIRLS (USA) see **DU RIFIFI CHEZ LES FEMMES** • 1959
RIFF-RAFF (USA) see **CANAILLES, LES** • 1959
RIFF RAFFY DAFFY • 1948 • Davis Arthur • ANS • USA
RIFFPIRATEN • 1920 • de Jeer Ott • FRG
RIFFRAFF • 1935 • Ruben J. Walter • USA
RIFFRAFF • 1947 • Tetzlaff Ted • USA • MR. FIX
RIFFRAFF AND RIVALRY • 1917 • Baker Graham • SHT • USA
RIFIFI AD AMSTERDAM • 1966 • Grieco Sergio • ITL, SPN • RIFIFI EN AMSTERDAM (SPN) ○ RIFIFI IN AMSTERDAM (USA)
RIFIFI EN AMSTERDAM (SPN) see **RIFIFI AD AMSTERDAM** • 1966
RIFIFI EN LA CIUDAD • 1963 • Franco Jesus • SPN
RIFIFI FOR GIRLS see **DU RIFIFI CHEZ LES FEMMES** • 1959
RIFIFI FRA LE DONNE (ITL) see **DU RIFIFI CHEZ LES FEMMES** • 1959
RIFIFI IN AMSTERDAM • 1962 • Korporaal John • NTH
RIFIFI IN AMSTERDAM (USA) see **RIFIFI AD AMSTERDAM** • 1966
RIFIFI IN PARIS (UKN) see **DU RIFIFI A PANAMA** • 1966
RIFIFI IN TOKYO (USA) see **DU RIFIFI A TOKYO** • 1963
RIFIFI INTERNACIONALE (ITL) see **DU RIFIFI A PANAMA** • 1966
RIFIFI (USA) see **DU RIFIFI CHEZ LES HOMMES** • 1955
RIFLE AND THE FISHING ROD, THE see **STRZELBA I WEDKA** • 1966
RIFLE BILL, -LE ROI DE LA PRAIRIE • 1908 • Jasset Victorin • FRN
RIFLE IMPLACABLE, EL • 1964 • Delgado Miguel M. • MXC
RIFLEMEN, THE (USA) see **CARABINIERS, LES** • 1962
RIFLES, THE see **FUZIS, OS** • 1964
RIFT, THE • 1989 • Simon Piquer • USA
RIG 20 • 1952 • Riley Ronald H., Villiers David • UKN
RIG MAND, EN • 1979 • Carlsen Jon Bang • DOC • DNM • RICH MAN, A
RIG MOVE • 1964 • Higgins Don • DCS • UKN
RIGADIN • 1912-14 • Monca Georges • SER • FRN
RIGADIN AND HIS SONS see **RIGADIN ET SES FILS** • 1912
RIGADIN ET SES FILS • 1912 • Monca Georges • FRN • RIGADIN AND HIS SONS
RIGADIN PEINTRE CUBISTE • 1912 • Monca Georges • FRN • WHIFFLES CUBIST PAINTER
RIGAS FERREOS • 1970 • Sakellarios Alekos • GRC
RIGHT ABOUT FACE see **SWING FEVER** • 1943
RIGHT AFTER BROWN • 1919 • Green Alfred E. • USA
RIGHT AGE TO MARRY, THE • 1935 • Rogers Maclean • UKN
RIGHT AMOUNT, THE • 1986 • Dodd Thomas • MTV • CND
RIGHT AND THE WRONG, THE see **RIGHT AND WRONG, THE** • 1970
RIGHT AND WRONG, THE • 1970 • Kumar Harbance • T&T • RIGHT AND THE WRONG, THE
RIGHT AND WRONG OF IT, THE • 1914 • Ince Ralph • USA
RIGHT APPROACH, THE • 1961 • Butler David • USA
RIGHT BY THE BLUE SEA see **U SAMOVA SINEVO MORYA** • 1936
RIGHT CANDIDATE FOR ROSEDALE, THE • 1979 • Klein Bonnie • DOC • CND
RIGHT CAR BUT THE WRONG BERTH, THE • 1916 • *Russell Dan* • SHT • USA
RIGHT CLUE, THE • 1912 • *Daly W. R.* • USA
RIGHT CROSS • 1950 • Sturges John • USA
RIGHT DECISION, THE • 1910 • *Edison* • USA
RIGHT DIRECTION, THE • 1916 • Hopper E. Mason • USA
RIGHT DOPE, THE • 1914 • Dillon Eddie • USA
RIGHT ELEMENT, THE • 1919 • Wilson Rex • UKN
RIGHT FOR RIGHT'S SAKE • 1913 • *Sawyer Laura* • USA
RIGHT GIRL, THE • 1910 • Salter Harry • USA
RIGHT GIRL?, THE • 1915 • Ince Ralph • USA
RIGHT GUY see **GOOD LUCK, MR. YATES** • 1943
RIGHT-HAND MAN, THE • 1986 • Drew Di • ASL • RIGHT HAND MAN, THE
RIGHT HAND MAN, THE see **RIGHT-HAND MAN, THE** • 1986
RIGHT HAND OF THE DEVIL, THE • 1963 • Katcher Aram • USA
RIGHT HAND PATH, THE • 1917 • King Burton L. • SHT • USA
RIGHT IS MIGHT • 1911 • Haldane Bert? • UKN
RIGHT LINE, THE • 1961 • Cobham David, Reid Noel Cunningham • UKN
RIGHT MAN, THE • 1913 • Thompson Frederick A. • USA
RIGHT MAN, THE • 1917 • McRae Henry • SHT • USA
RIGHT MAN, THE • 1925 • Harvey John • USA
RIGHT MAN, THE see **HER FIRST ROMANCE** • 1940
RIGHT MAN, THE see **MEGFELELO EMBER, A** • 1959
RIGHT NAME BUT THE WRONG MAN, THE • 1911 • *Selig* • USA
RIGHT NUMBER BUT THE WRONG HOUSE, THE • 1913 • *Edison* • USA
RIGHT OF A MOTHER, THE see **ANA HAKKI ODENMEZ** • 1968
RIGHT OF A SEIGNEUR, THE • 1915 • *Vitagraph* • USA
RIGHT OF ASYLUM • 1978 • Cervera Pascual • MTV • SPN
RIGHT OF CHOICE • 1988 • Tsanev Emil • BUL
RIGHT OF LOVE • 1910 • Salter Harry • USA
RIGHT OF MAN, THE see **PROPRE DE L'HOMME, LE** • 1960
RIGHT OF MARY BLAKE, THE • 1916 • *Bluebird* • USA
RIGHT OF MIGHT, THE • 1917 • Barber George • SHT • USA
RIGHT OF THE PEOPLE, THE • 1986 • Bloom Jeffrey • TVM • USA
RIGHT OF THE STRONGEST, THE • 1924 • Lewis Edgar • USA
RIGHT OF WAY • 1911 • Melies Gaston • USA
RIGHT OF WAY • 1911 • Wilson Frank? • UKN
RIGHT OF WAY • 1983 • Schaefer George • TVM • USA
RIGHT OF WAY, THE • 1913 • *Patheplay* • USA
RIGHT OF WAY, THE • 1913 • MacMackin Archer • *Essanay* • USA
RIGHT OF WAY, THE • 1914 • Brooke Van Dyke • USA
RIGHT OF WAY, THE • 1915 • Noble Jack • USA
RIGHT OF WAY, THE • 1920 • Dillon John Francis • USA
RIGHT OF WAY, THE • 1931 • Lloyd Frank • USA
RIGHT-OF-WAY CASEY • 1917 • Marshall George • SHT • USA
RIGHT OF YOUTH, THE see **UNGDOMMENS RET** • 1911
RIGHT OFF THE BAT • 1915 • Reticker Hugh • USA
RIGHT OFF THE BAT • 1958 • Kneitel Seymour • ANS • USA
RIGHT OFF THE REEL • 1915 • Curtis Allen • USA
RIGHT ON! • 1971 • Danska Herbert • USA
RIGHT ON, MAN! see **TAALTA TULLAAN, ELAMA!** • 1979
RIGHT OR WRONG • 1911 • Melies Gaston • USA
RIGHT OUT OF HISTORY: THE MAKING OF JUDY CHICAGO'S DINNER PARTY • 1980 • Demetrakis Johanna • USA • MAKING OF JUDY CHICAGO'S DINNER PARTY, THE
RIGHT PERSON, THE • 1955 • Cotes Peter • UKN
RIGHT ROAD, THE • 1913 • Grandon Francis J. • USA
RIGHT SHALL PREVAIL • 1912 • *Champion* • USA
RIGHT STUFF, THE • 1983 • Kaufman Philip • USA
RIGHT THAT FAILED, THE • 1922 • Veiller Bayard • USA • KEEP OFF THE GRASS
RIGHT TO DIE • 1987 • Wendkos Paul • TVM • USA
RIGHT TO BE BORN, THE • 1968 • Weschler Lazar
RIGHT TO BE BORN, THE see **DERECHO DE NACER, EL** • 1951
RIGHT TO BE HAPPY, THE • 1916 • Julian Rupert • USA • SCROOGE THE SKINFLINT (UKN) ○ CHRISTMAS CAROL, A
RIGHT TO DIE, THE • 1914 • *Broncho* • USA
RIGHT TO HAPPINESS see **MELODIE DER LIEBE** • 1932
RIGHT TO HAPPINESS, THE • 1914 • MacGregor Norval • USA
RIGHT TO HAPPINESS, THE • 1915 • MacMackin Archer • USA
RIGHT TO HAPPINESS, THE • 1919 • Holubar Allen • USA
RIGHT TO HAPPINESS, THE see **DERECHO A LA FELICIDAD, EL** • 1968
RIGHT TO HOPE, THE • 1981 • Kezdi-Kovacs Zsolt • HNG
RIGHT TO HOPE, THE see **REMENY JOGA, A** • 1982
RIGHT TO KILL? • 1985 • Erman John • TVM • USA
RIGHT TO KILL, THE • 1937 • Nigh William • USA
RIGHT TO LABOR, THE • 1909 • *Lubin* • USA
RIGHT TO LABOR, THE • 1910 • *Yankee* • USA
RIGHT TO LIE, THE • 1919 • Carewe Edwin • USA
RIGHT TO LIVE, THE • 1915 • *Stone George* • USA
RIGHT TO LIVE, THE • 1921 • Coleby A. E. • UKN
RIGHT TO LIVE, THE • 1933 • Parker Albert • UKN
RIGHT TO LIVE, THE • 1935 • Keighley William • USA • SACRED FLAME, THE (UKN)
RIGHT TO LIVE, THE (UKN) see **FOREVER YOURS** • 1944
RIGHT TO LOVE, THE • 1920 • Fitzmaurice George • USA
RIGHT TO LOVE, THE • 1930 • Wallace Richard • USA
RIGHT TO LOVE, THE see **FESCHE ERZHERZOG, DER** • 1926
RIGHT TO LOVE, THE see **RATTEN ATT ALSKA** • 1956
RIGHT TO LOVE, THE see **DROIT D'AIMER, LE** • 1972
RIGHT TO LOVE, THE (USA) see **RECHT AUF LIEBE, DAS** • 1939
RIGHT TO ROMANCE, THE • 1933 • Santell Alfred • USA • BEAUTIFUL
RIGHT TO STRIKE, THE • 1923 • Paul Fred • UKN
RIGHT TO SURVIVE, A • 1973 • Walker Giles • MTV • CND
RIGHT TO THE HEART • 1942 • Forde Eugene J. • USA • YOU CAN'T ALWAYS TELL
RIGHT TO THE HEART see **JUSQU'AU COEUR** • 1968
RIGHT TO THE HEART see **MITTEN INS HERZ** • 1984
RIGHT UP IN FRONT OF FATHER • 1910 • *Lubin* • USA
RIGHT WAY, THE • 1921 • Olcott Sidney • USA • WITHIN PRISON WALLS ○ MAKING GOOD
RIGHTED WRONG, THE • 1915 • *Victory* • USA
RIGHTEOUS REVENGE, THE • 1919 • Kim Do-San • KOR
RIGHTEOUS WAR • 1950 • DOC • NKR
RIGHTFUL HEIR, THE • 1913 • Dawley J. Searle • USA
RIGHTFUL HEIR, THE • 1914 • Edwards Walter? • USA • SATAN MCALLISTER'S HEIR
RIGHTFUL THEFT, A • 1915 • *Majestic* • USA
RIGHTS OF A SAVAGE, THE • 1912 • *Fischer Margarita* • USA
RIGHTS OF FATHERS, THE • 1931 • Stroyeva Vera • USS
RIGHTS OF MAN, THE • 1915 • Pratt Jack • USA
RIGOLBOCHE • 1936 • Christian-Jaque • FRN
RIGOLETTO • 1910 • Falena Ugo • ITL
RIGOLETTO • 1922 • Wynn George • UKN
RIGOLETTO • 1927 • Parkinson H. B. • UKN
RIGOLETTO • 1947 • Gallone Carmine • ITL
RIGOLETTO see **KONIG AMUSIERT SICH, DER** • 1918
RIGOLETTO, ACT TWO • 1926 • *Deforest Phonofilm* • SHT • UKN
RIGOLETTO E LA SUA TRAGEDIA • 1956 • Calzavara Flavio • ITL
RIGOLLO THE MAN OF MANY FACES • 1910 • *Urban Trading Co* • UKN
RIGOR MORTIS • 1981 • Maas Dick • NTH
RIH AL-JANUB • 1975 • Riad Mohamed Slimane • ALG • VENT DU SUD ○ RYAH EL JANOBV ○ SOUTH WIND, THE ○ WIND FROM THE SOUTH
RIH AL SADD • 1986 • Bouzid Nouri • TNS • MAN OF ASHES ○ RIH ESSED
RIH ESSED see **RIH AL SADD** • 1986
RIHAEE • 1988 • Arunaraje • IND
RIHLA AL-AKHIRA, AR- • 1966 • Siddik Khalid • SHT • KWT • DERNIER VOYAGE, LE
RIHLA LADHIDHA • 1970 • Wahab Fatin Abdel • EGY • VOYAGE SYMPATHETIQUE, UN
RIH'LAT AL-UMR • 1974 • Arafa Saad • EGY • VOYAGE D'UNE VIE, LE
RIISUMINEN • 1986 • Torhonen Lauri • FNL • UNDRESSING
RIJALUM YAH'FURUNA A'MAKIN FI AL-ARD • 1971 • Jamil Mohammed Shoukry • EGY • CEUX QUI FOUILLENT LES ENTRAILLES DU SOL
RIJALUN TAHTA ASH-SHAMS • 1970 • Maleh Nabil • SYR • DES HOMMES SOUS LE SOLEIL
RIKA, THE MIXED-BLOOD GIRL see **KONKETSUJI RIKA** • 1973
RIKADLA • 1949 • Hofman Eduard • ANS • PLN • NURSERY RHYMES
RIKI-TIKI-TAVY • 1975 • Jones Charles M. • ANM • USA
RIKISHA MAN, THE (USA) see **MUHOMATSU NO ISSHO** • 1958
RIKKI-TIKKI-TAVI • Snezhko-Blotskaya A. • ANS • USS
RIKKI-TIKKI-TAVI • 1975 • Zguridi Alexander • USS
RIKKY AND PETE • 1987 • Tass Nadia • ASL
RIKO NA OYOME-SAN • 1958 • Imaizumi Kenjyu • JPN • IMAGE WIFE
RIKOS JA RANGAISTUS • 1983 • Kaurismaki Aki • FNL • CRIME AND PUNISHMENT
RIKU NO NINGYO • 1926 • Abe Yutaka • JPN • MERMAID ON LAND, A
RIKUGUN • 1944 • Kinoshita Keisuke • JPN • ARMY, THE
RIKUGUN CHOHO 33 • 1968 • Kobayashi Tsuneo • JPN • ARMY INTELLIGENCE 33
RIKUGUN NAKANO GAKKO • 1966 • Masumura Yasuzo • JPN • SCHOOL OF SPIES, THE
RIKUGUN NAKANO GAKKO: MITSUMEI • 1967 • Inoue Akira • JPN • SECRET ASSIGNMENT
RIKUGUN NAKANO GAKKO -RYO SANGO SHIREI • 1967 • Tanaka Tokuzo • JPN • ASSIGNMENT DRAGON NO.3
RIKUGUN NAKANO GOKKO KAISEN ZENYA • 1968 • Inoue Akira • JPN • NIGHT BEFORE PEARL HARBOR, THE
RIKUGUN ZANGYAKU MONOGATARI • 1963 • *Mikuni Rentaro* • JPN • STORY OF ARMY CRUELTY, A
RIKYU • 1989 • Teshigahara Hiroshi • JPN
RILEY AND SCHULTZE • 1912 • Sennett Mack • USA
RILEY OF THE RAINBOW DIVISION • 1928 • Ray Robert • USA • FLAPPERS IN KHAKI (UKN) ○ REILLY OF THE RAINBOW DIVISION
RILEY THE COP • 1928 • Ford John • USA
RILEY'S DECOYS • 1913 • *Ab* • USA
RILKA: OR, THE GYPSY QUEEN see **ROMANY LASS, A** • 1918
RILTRATTO DI PINA • 1966 • Baldi Gian Vittorio • ITL
RIM OF THE CANYON • 1949 • English John • USA
RIM OF THE DESERT, THE • 1915 • *Balboa* • USA
RIMACS RHUMBA ORCHESTRA, THE • 1935 • Henabery Joseph • SHT • USA
RIMAL MIN ZAHAB see **RIMALUN MIN DHAHAB** • 1966
RIMALUN MIN DHAHAB • 1966 • Shahin Youssef • SPN • SABLES D'OR ○ RIMAL MIN ZAHAB ○ SAND OF GOLD
RIMASE UNO SOLO E FU LA MORTE PER TUTTI • 1971 • Mulargia Edoardo • ITL
RIME OF THE ANCIENT MARINER • 1953 • Shull William M. • SHT • USA
RIME OF THE ANCIENT MARINER • 1967 • ANS • USA
RIMES • 1954 • Alexeieff Alexandre • SHT • FRN
RIMFIRE • 1949 • Eason B. Reeves • USA
RIMINI RIMINI • 1987 • Corbucci Sergio • ITL
RIMORSO • 1953 • Grottini Armando • ITL
RIMPATRIATA, LA • 1963 • Damiani Damiano • ITL, FRN • RAPATRIEE, LA (FRN) ○ REUNION, THE (USA) ○ GET-TOGETHER, THE
RIMROCK JONES • 1918 • Crisp Donald • USA
RIMSKII-KORSAKOV • 1953 • Roshal Grigori, Kozansky Grigori • USS • RIMSKY-KORSAKOV
RIMSKY-KORSAKOV see **RIMSKII-KORSAKOV** • 1953
RINA EN UN CAFE • 1897 • Gelabert Fructuoso • SPN
RINALDO RINALDINI • 1927 • Obal Max • FRG
RINCON BRUJO • 1949 • Gout Alberto • MXC
RINCON CERCA DEL CIELO, UN • 1952 • Gonzalez Rogelio A. • MXC
RINCON DE LAS VIRGENES, EL • 1972 • Isaac Alberto • MXC • NEST OF VIRGINS, THE ○ DELL OF THE VIRGINS, THE ○ CORNER OF THE VIRGINS, THE
RINCON PARA QUERERNOS, UN • 1964 • Iquino Ignacio F. • SPN
RINDERCELLA • 1970 • Burton Hardi • USA • RINDERCELLA AND HER FELLA ○ CINDERELLER AND HER FELLER
RINDERCELLA AND HER FELLA see **RINDERCELLA** • 1970
RINE DES RESQUILLEUSES, LA • 1936 • Glass Max, de Gastyne Marco • FRN
RING • 1977 • Petrini Luigi • ITL
RING, EL • 1966 • Valdes Oscar • DOC • CUB
RING, LE • 1901 • Lumiere Louis • FRN
RING, THE • 1914 • *Majestic* • USA
RING, THE • 1914 • Smalley Phillips • *Crystal* • USA

RING, THE • 1927 • Hitchcock Alfred • *Bip* • UKN
RING, THE • 1927 • Parkinson H. B. • *Song Films* • SHT • UKN
RING, THE • 1927 • Raizman Yuli, Gavronsky A. • USS • DUTY AND LOVE ○ CIRCLE, THE
RING, THE • 1952 • Neumann Kurt • USA
RING, THE see **PRSTYNEK** • 1944
RING, THE see **BOXING RING, THE** • 1959
RING-A-DING RHYTHM (USA) see **IT'S TRAD, DAD** • 1962
RING AND THE BELLE • 1941 • Lord Del • SHT • USA
RING AND THE BOOK, THE • 1914 • *Ab* • USA
RING AND THE MAN, THE • 1914 • Powers Francis • USA
RING AND THE RAJAH, THE • 1914 • Shaw Harold • UKN
RING AND THE RINGER, THE • 1918 • De Barge C. R. • SHT • USA
RING AROUND THE CLOCK (USA) see **VOGLIAMOCI BENE** • 1950
RING AROUND THE MOON • 1936 • Lamont Charles • USA
RING AROUND THE ROSY • 1915 • *Royal* • USA
RING DER BAJADERE, DER • 1928 • Stuart Henry • FRG
RING DER DREI WUNSCHE, DER • 1918 • Wellin Arthur? • FRG
RING DER GIUDITTA FOSCARI, DER • 1917 • Halm Alfred • FRG
RING DES HAUSES STILLFRIED, DER • 1918 • Hanus Emerich • FRG
RING DES SCHICKSALS, DER • 1916 • Eichberg Richard • FRG
RING MADNESS • 1939 • D'Arcy Harry • SHT • USA
RING MASTERS, THE • 1969 • Lerman Richard • SHT • USA
RING OF A SPANISH GRANDEE, THE • 1912 • *Snow Marguerite* • USA
RING OF BRIGHT WATER • 1969 • Couffer Jack • UKN
RING OF DEATH see **DETECTIVE, UN** • 1969
RING OF DESIRE • 1981 • Balakoff Pierre • USA
RING OF DESTINY, THE • 1915 • Madison Cleo • USA
RING OF DUCHESS ANN, THE • 1970 • PLN
RING OF FEAR • 1954 • Grant James Edward, Wellman William A. (U/c) • USA
RING OF FIRE • 1961 • Stone Andrew L. • USA
RING OF LOVE • 1911 • *Solax* • USA
RING OF PASSION • 1978 • Lewis Robert Michael • TVM • USA
RING OF SORROW, THE • 1913 • *Brunette Fritzie* • USA
RING OF SPIES • 1963 • Tronson Robert • UKN • RING OF TREASON (USA)
RING OF STEEL • 1940 • Cummins G. Thomas • UKN
RING OF STEEL • 1942 • Kanin Garson • DOC • USA
RING OF TERROR • 1962 • Paylow Clark • USA
RING OF THE BORGIAS, THE • 1915 • West Langdon • USA
RING OF TREASON (USA) see **RING OF SPIES** • 1963
RING-RING BOI • 1964 • Kuri Yoji • ANS • JPN • RING RING BOY
RING RING BOY see **RING-RING BOI** • 1964
RING RIVALS • 1917 • Smith Noel • SHT • USA
RING SELLER, THE see **BAIYYA AL-KHAWATIM** • 1965
RING THAT WASN'T, THE • 1914 • Aylott Dave • UKN
RING UP MARTIN 224466 • 1966 • Vosmik Milan • CZC • MARTIN SPEAKING
RING UP THE CURTAIN • 1919 • Roach Hal • SHT • USA
RING UP THE CURTAIN (UKN) see **BROADWAY TO HOLLYWOOD** • 1933
RINGADING KID • 1963 • Kneitel Seymour • ANS • USA
RINGARDS, LES • 1978 • Pouret Robert • FRN
RINGENDE SEELEN • 1918 • Illes Eugen • FRG
RINGER, THE • 1928 • Maude Arthur • UKN
RINGER, THE • 1931 • Forde Walter • UKN
RINGER, THE • 1952 • Hamilton Guy • UKN
RINGER, THE • 1979 • *Bridges Jeff* • USA
RINGER, THE see **AMERICAN SUCCESS COMPANY, THE** • 1979
RINGING HIS BELLE • 1920 • Davey Horace • SHT • USA
RINGING THE CHANGES • 1913 • Stow Percy • UKN
RINGING THE CHANGES • 1929 • Hiscott Leslie • UKN
RINGMASTER, THE • 1933 • Starevitch Ladislas • ANS • FRN
RINGO A CAMINHO DO INFERNO • 1972 • Rosa Sebastiao • BRZ • CUM-QUIBUS
RINGO AND HIS GOLDEN PISTOL see **JOHNNY ORO** • 1966
RINGO E GRINGO CONTRO TUTTI • 1966 • Corbucci Bruno • ITL, SPN • REBELS ON THE LOOSE (USA)
RINGO EN NEBRASKA • 1965 • Roman Antonio • SPN, ITL • RINGO NEL NEBRASKA (ITL) ○ NEBRASKA IL PISTOLERO ○ GUNMAN CALLED NEBRASKA, A
RINGO GESTAPO'YA KARSI • 1967 • Okcugil Cevat • TRK • RINGO VS. THE GESTAPO
RINGO IL CAVALLIERE SOLITARIO • 1968 • Romero-Marchent Rafael • ITL, SPN • RINGO, THE LONE HORSEMAN
RINGO IL VOLTO DELLA VENDETTA • 1966 • Caiano Mario • ITL
RINGO KAZIM • 1967 • Inanoglu Turker • TRK
RINGO KID see **RINGO KIT** • 1967
RINGO KIT • 1967 • Davutoglu Zafer • TRK • RINGO KID
RINGO NEL NEBRASKA (ITL) see **RINGO EN NEBRASKA** • 1965
RINGO, THE LONE HORSEMAN see **RINGO IL CAVALLIERE SOLITARIO** • 1968
RINGO VS. THE GESTAPO see **RINGO GESTAPO'YA KARSI** • 1967
RINGS AND ROBBERS • 1914 • *Ab* • USA
RINGS AND THINGS • 1920 • Santell Alfred • SHT • USA
RINGS AROUND THE WORLD • 1966 • Cates Gilbert • DOC • USA
RINGS OF PASSION • 1975 • *Wade Johnny* • USA
RINGS ON HER FINGERS • 1942 • Mamoulian Rouben • USA
RINGSIDE • 1949 • McDonald Frank • USA
RINGSIDE • 1960 • Gunwall Per • SWD
RINGSIDE MAISIE • 1941 • Marin Edwin L. • USA • CASH AND CARRY (UKN)
RINGTAILED RHINOCEROS, THE • 1915 • Terwilliger George W. • USA
RINGVALL ON ADVENTURES see **RINGVALL PA AVENTYR** • 1913
RINGVALL PA AVENTYR • 1913 • Klercker Georg • SWD • RINGVALL ON ADVENTURES
RINK, THE • 1916 • Chaplin Charles • SHT • USA
RINNEGATI DI CAPTAIN KIDD, I • 1963 • Montero Roberto Bianchi, Schleif Wolfgang • ITL, FRG
RINNEGATO see **GRANDE APPELLO, IL** • 1936
RINNEGO MIO FIGLIO see **ZAPPATORE, LO** • 1950
RINOCERONTE, EL • 1971 • Castello Amaro • ANS • SPN • RHINOCEROS, THE
RINTY OF THE DESERT • 1928 • Lederman D. Ross • USA
RIO • 1939 • Brahm John • USA
RIO 70 (USA) see **SUMURU** • 1968
RIO '80 see **FUTURE WOMEN** • 1975
RIO ABAJO • 1982 • Borau Jose Luis • SPN • ON THE LINE
RIO BABILONIA • 1982 • d'Almeida Neville • BRZ • RIO BABYLON
RIO BABYLON see **RIO BABILONIA** • 1982
RIO BRAVO • 1959 • Hawks Howard • USA
RIO CONCHOS • 1964 • Douglas Gordon • USA
RIO DAS MORTES • 1970 • Fassbinder R. W. • FRG
RIO DAS MORTES • 1971 • Schlondorff Volker • MTV • FRG
RIO DE FIERAS • 1970 • *Jalisco* • MXC
RIO DE LAS ANIMAS, EL • 1963 • Ortega Juan J. • MXC
RIO DE MACHADO DE ASSIS • 1964 • dos Santos Nelson Pereira • SHT • BRZ
RIO DE ORO • 1970 • *Cinemobile* • MXC
RIO ESCONDIDO • 1947 • Fernandez Emilio • MXC • HIDDEN RIVER
RIO, FORTY DEGREES see **RIO, QUARENTA GRAUS** • 1955
RIO GRANDE • 1920 • Carewe Edwin • USA
RIO GRANDE • 1938 • Nelson Sam • USA
RIO GRANDE • 1950 • Ford John • USA
RIO GRANDE PATROL • 1950 • Selander Lesley • USA
RIO GRANDE RAIDERS • 1946 • Carr Thomas • USA
RIO GRANDE RANGER • 1938 • Bennet Spencer Gordon • USA
RIO GRANDE ROMANCE • 1936 • Hill Robert F. • USA • FRAMED (UKN) ○ PUT ON THE SPOT
RIO GUADALQUIVIR • 1956 • Manzanos Eduardo, Zeglio Primo • SPN, ITL • DIMENTICA IL MIO PASSATO (ITL) ○ CONSUELA
RIO GUANIAMO • 1971 • Thome Rudolf • FRG
RIO HONDO • 1965 • Gonzalez Rogelio A. • MXC
RIO LOBO • 1970 • Hawks Howard • USA
RIO MALDITO • 1961 • Xiol Juan • SPN
RIO NEGRO • 1977 • Perez Manuel • CUB • BLACK RIVER
RIO NEGRO • 1989 • Lichy Atahualpa • FRN, VNZ, SPN • BLACK RIVER
RIO NO WAKADAISHO • 1968 • Iwauchi Katsumi • JPN • YOUNG GUY IN RIO
RIO NUDO • 1969 • Albert Sinte S. • USA
RIO, QUARENTA GRAUS • 1955 • dos Santos Nelson Pereira • BRZ • RIO, FORTY DEGREES
RIO QUE NOS LLEVA, EL • 1988 • de Real Antonio • SPN • RIVER THAT WAS, THE
RIO RATTLER • 1935 • Ray Bernard B. • USA
RIO RITA • 1929 • Reed Luther • USA
RIO RITA • 1942 • Simon S. Sylvan • USA
RIO VEREO 77 • 1976 • Howard John • DOC • UKN
RIO Y LA MUERTE, EL • 1954 • Bunuel Luis • MXC • RIVER AND DEATH, THE (USA) ○ DEATH AND THE RIVER
RIO ZONA NORTE • 1957 • dos Santos Nelson Pereira • BRZ • RIO, ZONE NORD
RIO, ZONE NORD see **RIO ZONA NORTE** • 1957
RIOM LE BEAU • 1966 • Guilbert • SHT • FRN
RIO'S ROAD TO HELL • 1931 • Pollard Bud • USA
RIOT • 1969 • Kulik Buzz • USA
RIOT, THE • 1913 • *Nestor* • USA
RIOT, THE • 1913 • Sennett Mack • *Keystone* • USA
RIOT, THE see **BOUNA** • 1975
RIOT AND REVEL ON ORDER see **SUS OG DUS PA BY'N** • 1968
RIOT AT LAUDERDALE see **HELL'S PLAYGROUND** • 1967
RIOT IN CELL BLOCK 11 • 1954 • Siegel Don • USA
RIOT IN JUVENILE PRISON • 1959 • Cahn Edward L. • USA
RIOT IN RHYTHM • 1950 • Kneitel Seymour • ANS • USA
RIOT IN RHYTHM • 1957 • Cowan Will • SHT • USA
RIOT IN RUBEVILLE, A • 1914 • *De Grey Sid* • USA
RIOT ON 42ND STREET • 1988 • Kincaid Tim • USA
RIOT ON PIER SIX (UKN) see **NEW ORLEANS UNCENSORED** • 1955
RIOT ON SUNSET STRIP • 1967 • Dreifuss Arthur • USA
RIOT PATROL see **DEVIL'S PARTY, THE** • 1938
RIOT SQUAD • 1932 • Webb Harry S. • USA
RIOT SQUAD • 1941 • Finney Edward • USA
RIOTOUS BRUIN, THE see **RUINED BRUIN, THE** • 1961
RIOTOUS SKIN OF THE OUTLAW see **ZANKYO ABAREHADA** • 1967
RIP CAN WINKLE • 1924 • *Foy Bryan/ Brice Monte (P)* • SHT • USA
RIP OF THE FLESH, A see **NIKU NO HOKOROBI** • 1968
RIP-OFF • 1972 • Shebib Donald • CND
RIP OFF see **LOVE AND THE MIDNIGHT AUTO SUPPLY** • 1978
RIP-OFF, THE see **CONTRORAPINA** • 1979
RIP ROARIN' BUCKAROO • 1936 • Hill Robert F. • USA
RIP ROARIN' ROBERTS • 1924 • Thorpe Richard • USA
RIP ROARING LOGAN • 1928 • Horner Robert J. • USA
RIP ROARING RILEY • 1935 • Clifton Elmer • USA • MYSTERY OF DIAMOND ISLAND, THE (UKN)
RIP-ROARING RIVALS • 1918 • Curtis Allen • SHT • USA
RIP SEW AND STITCH • 1953 • White Jules • SHT • USA
RIP SNORTER, THE • 1925 • Hayes Ward • USA
RIP & STITCH TAILORS • 1919 • St. Clair Malcolm, Watson William • SHT • USA
RIP-TIDE, THE • 1923 • Pratt Jack • USA
RIP VAN WINKLE • 1896 • McCutcheon Wallace • USA
RIP VAN WINKLE • *Rufus Rose Co.* • ANM • USA
RIP VAN WINKLE • Nicholson Nick, Muir Roger
RIP VAN WINKLE • 1903 • *Lubin Sigmund* • USA
RIP VAN WINKLE • 1903 • Collins Alf • UKN
RIP VAN WINKLE • 1908 • Turner Otis • USA
RIP VAN WINKLE • 1910 • *Columbia* • USA
RIP VAN WINKLE • 1910 • Marston Theodore • *Thanhouser* • USA
RIP VAN WINKLE • 1912 • *Reliance* • USA
RIP VAN WINKLE • 1912 • *Union Features* • USA
RIP VAN WINKLE • 1912 • *Eclair* • FRN
RIP VAN WINKLE • 1912 • Kent Charles, Blackton J. Stuart (Spv) • *Vitagraph* • USA
RIP VAN WINKLE • 1912 • Lincoln W. J. • ASL
RIP VAN WINKLE • 1912 • Reid Hal • USA
RIP VAN WINKLE • 1914 • *World Comedy* • USA
RIP VAN WINKLE • 1914 • Kinder Stuart • UKN • FORGOTTEN
RIP VAN WINKLE • 1914 • Middleton Edwin • USA
RIP VAN WINKLE • 1921 • Lascelle Ward • USA
RIP VAN WINKLE • 1934 • Terry Paul, Moser Frank • ANS • USA
RIP VAN WINKLE • 1978 • Vinton Will • ANS • USA
RIP VAN WINKLE • 1985 • Coppola Francis Ford • MTV • USA
RIP VAN WINKLE see **RIP VAN WYK** • 1960
RIP VAN WINKLE BADLY RIPPED • 1915 • *Browning Will* • USA
RIP VAN WINKLE (USA) see **LEGENDE DE RIP VAN WINCKLE, LA** • 1905
RIP VAN WYK • 1957 • Nofal Emil • SAF
RIP VAN WYK • 1960 • Uys Jamie • SAF • RIP VAN WINKLE
RIPA DRACULUI • 1957 • Mihail Jean • RMN • DEVIL'S RAVINE, THE
RIPACSOK • 1981 • Sandor Pal • HNG • SALAMON & STOCK SHOW, THE
RIPE AND MARRIAGEABLE see **MI WA JUKUSHITARI** • 1959
RIPE EARTH • 1938 • Boulting Roy • DCS • UKN
RIPENING SEED, THE see **BLE EN HERBE, LE** • 1953
RIPETENTE FA L'OCCHIETO AL PRESIDE, LA • 1980 • Laurenti Mariano • ITL
RIPORT EGY TSZ-ELNOKROL • 1960 • Meszaros Marta • DCS • HNG • REPORT ON THE CHAIRMAN OF A FARMER'S COOPERATIVE
RIPOSO DEL GUERIERO, IL (ITL) see **REPOS DU GUERRIER, LE** • 1962
RIPOUX, LES • 1984 • Zidi Claude • FRN • MY NEW PARTNER (USA) ○ COP, LE
RIPOUX CONTRE RIPOUX • 1990 • Zidi Claude • FRN
RIPPED OFF (USA) see **UOMO DALLA PELLE DURA, UN** • 1972
RIPPER, THE • 1985 • Lewis Christopher • USA
RIPPING TIME, A • 1918 • Lyons Eddie, Moran Lee • SHT • USA
RIPPLES ON DEAD WATER see **SI SHUI WEI LAN** • 1989
RIPPLING ROMANCE • 1945 • Wickersham Bob • ANM • USA
RIPS AND RUSHES • 1917 • Semon Larry • SHT • USA
RIP'S DREAM see **LEGENDE DE RIP VAN WINCKLE, LA** • 1905
RIPTIDE • 1934 • Goulding Edmund • USA
RIPTIDE (USA) see **SI JOLIE PETITE PLAGE, UNE** • 1948
RIPUDIATA • 1955 • Chili Giorgio W. • ITL
RIRES DE PARIS • 1952 • Lepage Henri • FRN • SINS OF PARIS (USA)
RIRI ET NONO • 1929-33 • Daroy Jacques • SHT • FRN
RISA DE LA CIUDAD, LA • 1962 • Gazcon Gilberto • MXC
RISAIA, LA • 1956 • Matarazzo Raffaello • ITL, FRN • FILLE DE LA RIZIERE, LA (FRN) ○ RICE GIRL (USA) ○ RICE GIRLS
RISALA • 1966 • Ben Aicha Sadok • SHT • TNS • LETTRE, UNE
RISALA MIN IMRA'A MAJHULA see **RESSALAH MIN EMRAA MAGHOOLA** • 1962
RISALA MIN ZAMAN AL HARB • 1984 • Alawiya Burhan • DOC • LBN • WARTIME LETTER
RISALAH, AL- • 1976 • Akkad Moustapha • LBN • MOHAMMAD, MESSENGER OF GOD (USA) ○ MESSAGE, THE (UKN)
RISALAT GAHRAM • 1953 • Barakat Henry • EGY • MESSAGE D'AMOUR
RISATE DI GIOIA • 1960 • Monicelli Mario • ITL • PASSIONATE THIEF, THE
RISCATTO, IL • 1954 • Girolami Marino • ITL
RISE AGAINST THE SWORD see **ABARE GOEMON** • 1966
RISE AND FALL OF A JAZZ GIRL, THE see **JAZU MUSUME NI EIKO ARE** • 1958
RISE AND FALL OF EMILY SPROD, THE • 1964 • Godfrey Bob • ANS • UKN
RISE AND FALL OF HORATIO, THE see **HORACIJEV USPON I PAD** • 1969
RISE AND FALL OF IDI AMIN, THE • 1981 • Patel Sharad • UKN, KNY • AMIN: THE RISE AND FALL
RISE AND FALL OF IVOR DICKIE, THE • 1977 • Katz James C. • UKN
RISE AND FALL OF LEGS DIAMOND, THE • 1960 • Boetticher Budd • USA
RISE AND FALL OF LOVE see **JONETSU NO FUCHIN** • 1926
RISE AND FALL OF MCDOO, THE • 1913 • Henderson Dell • USA
RISE AND FALL OF MICKEY MAHONE, THE • 1912 • *Pathe* • USA
RISE AND FALL OF OFFICER 13, THE • 1915 • Davey Horace • USA
RISE AND FALL OF ROCK'N'ROLL, THE see **KAKO JE PROPAO ROKENROL** • 1989
RISE AND FALL OF SHINSENGUMI, THE see **KOBO SHINSENGUMI** • 1930
RISE AND FALL OF SQUIZZY TAYLOR, THE • 1969 • Buesst Nigel • DOC • ASL
RISE AND FALL OF THE GREAT LAKES • 1970 • Mason William • SHT • CND
RISE AND FALL OF THE THIRD REICH, THE • 1967 • Kaufman Jack • DOC • USA
RISE AND FALL OF WEARY WILLY, THE • 1911 • Dawley J. Searle • USA
RISE AND RISE OF CASANOVA, THE (UKN) see **CASANOVA E COMPAGNI** • 1978
RISE AND RISE OF MICHAEL RIMMER, THE • 1970 • Billington Kevin • USA
RISE AND SHINE • 1941 • Dwan Allan • USA
RISE, FAIR SUN see **ASAYAKE NO UTA** • 1973
RISE OF A NATION, THE • 1916 • *Puritan* • SHT • USA
RISE OF CATHERINE THE GREAT, THE see **CATHERINE THE GREAT** • 1934
RISE OF DUTON LANG, THE • 1955 • Evans Osmond • ANS • USA
RISE OF HELGA, THE (UKN) see **SUSAN LENOX, HER FALL AND RISE** • 1931

RISE OF JENNIE CUSHING, THE • 1917 • Tourneur Maurice • USA • RISE OF JENNY CUSHING, THE
RISE OF JENNY CUSHING, THE see **RISE OF JENNIE CUSHING, THE** • 1917
RISE OF KODOKAN, THE see **HANA NO KODOKAN** • 1953
RISE OF LOUIS XIV, THE (USA) see **PRISE DE POUVOIR PAR DE LOUIS XIV, LA** • 1966
RISE OF OFFICER 174, THE • 1913 • *Baggot King* • USA
RISE OF OFFICER CASEY, THE • 1914 • *Lubin* • USA
RISE OF ROSCOE PAYNE, THE see **NO TRESPASSING** • 1922
RISE OF SUSAN, THE • 1916 • Taylor Stanner E. V. • USA
RISE OF THE JOHNSONS, THE • 1914 • *Edwards John* • USA
RISE TO POWER OF LOUIS XIV, THE see **PRISE DE POUVOIR PAR DE LOUIS XIV, LA** • 1966
RISEN FROM THE ASHES • 1914 • *Rex* • USA
RISEN SOUL OF JIM GRANT, THE • 1913 • Brabin Charles J. • USA
RISHU • 1960 • Ohba Hideo • JPN • STUDY
RISHYA SHRUNGA • 1976 • Prasad V. R. K. • IND • FERTILITY GOD, THE
RISING DAMP see **RISING DAMP -THE MOVIE** • 1980
RISING DAMP -THE MOVIE • 1980 • McGrath Joseph • UKN • RISING DAMP
RISING GENERATION, THE • 1928 • Knoles Harley, Dewhurst George • UKN
RISING IN THE WORLD see **MIRAI NO SHUSSE** • 1927
RISING OF THE MOON, THE • 1957 • Ford John • IRL, UKN
RISING SEA, THE • 1953 • Ranody Laszlo (c/d) • HNG
RISING SUN see **TS'AN-TUNG-TE CHAN-CHENG** • 1980
RISING SUN, THE see **GUNES DOGGARKEN** • 1985
RISING SUN IS SHINING, THE see **ASAHI WA KAGAYAKU** • 1929
RISING TARGET • 1976 • Frank Barbara • DOC • USA
RISING TIDE see **HAVET STIGER** • 1990
RISING TIDE, THE • 1933 • Rotha Paul • DOC • UKN
RISING TIDE, THE • 1949 • Palardy Jean • DCS • CND • MAREE MONTANTE
RISING TIDE OF THE MOON, THE see **PODEROSO INFLUJO DE LA LUNA, EL** • 1981
RISING TO FAME (UKN) see **HIS RISE TO FAME** • 1927
RISK, THE see **STEPIEN RISKA** • 1969
RISK, THE (USA) see **SUSPECT** • 1960
RISKS AND ROUGHNECKS • 1917 • Semon Larry • SHT • USA
RISKY BUSINESS • 1920 • Harris Harry B. • USA
RISKY BUSINESS • 1926 • Hale Alan • USA
RISKY BUSINESS • 1939 • Lubin Arthur • USA
RISKY BUSINESS • 1983 • Brickman Paul • USA
RISKY DRIVER, THE see **JEZDEC FORMULE RISK** • 1973
RISKY ROAD, THE • 1918 • Park Ida May • USA
RISO AMARO • 1949 • De Santis Giuseppe • ITL • BITTER RICE (UKN)
RISQUE DE VIVRE, LE • 1977 • Calderon Gerald • DOC • FRN
RISQUES DU FLIRT, LES • 1912 • Fescourt Henri • FRN
RISQUES DU METIER, LES • 1967 • Cayatte Andre • FRN
RISSA MEN IMRAA MAGHOULA see **RESSALAH MIN EMRAA MAGHOOLA** • 1962
RISTIGOUCHE 1760 • 1984 • Kinsey Nicholas • DOC • CND
RISTIKON VARJOSSA • 1945 • Laine Edvin • FNL • IN THE SHADOW OF PRISON BARS
RISTO VANARIN PIILOKAMERA • 1978 • Vanari Risto • FNL • RISTO VANARI'S CANDID CAMERA
RISTO VANARI'S CANDID CAMERA see **RISTO VANARIN PIILOKAMERA** • 1978
RISVEGLIO DI UNA CITTA • 1933 • Zampa Luigi • DOC • ITL
RITA AND DUNDI • 1976 • Thoms Albie • SHT • ASL
RITA DA CASCIA • 1942 • Leonviola Antonio • ITL
RITA FLEES.. HE RUNS.. THEY ESCAPE see **FELDMARESCIALLA, LA** • 1967
RITA FUGGE.. LUI CORRE.. EGLI SCAPPA see **FELDMARESCIALLA, LA** • 1967
RITA HAYWORTH: THE LOVE GODDESS • 1983 • Goldstone James • USA
RITA IN THE WEST see **RITA NEL WEST** • 1967
RITA, LA FIGLIA AMERICANA • 1965 • Vivarelli Piero • ITL
RITA LA ZANZARA • 1966 • Wertmuller Lina • ITL • RITA THE MOSQUITO (USA)
RITA NEL WEST • 1967 • Baldi Ferdinando • ITL • RITA IN THE WEST
RITA, SUE AND BOB TOO • 1987 • Clarke Alan • UKN
RITA THE MOSQUITO (USA) see **RITA LA ZANZARA** • 1966
RITA (USA) see **LETTERE DI UNA NOVIZIA** • 1960
RITAM ZLOCINA • 1982 • Tadic Zoran • YGS • RHYTHM OF CRIME, THE
RITCHIE, TRAMP CYCLIST • 1899 • *Warwick Trading Co* • UKN
RITE, THE (UKN) see **RITEN** • 1969
RITEN • 1969 • Bergman Ingmar • SWD • RITE, THE (UKN) ○ RITUAL, THE
RITES AND RITUALS OF NEW GUINEA • 1974 • Bittman Roman • DOC • CND
RITES OF LOVE AND DEATH see **YUKOKU** • 1965
RITES OF PASSAGE • 1980 • Jackson G. Philip • MTV • CND
RITES OF PASSAGE see **BERNICE BOBS HER HAIR** • 1976
RITES OF SUMMER see **WHITE WATER SUMMER** • 1987
RITI, MAGIE NERE E SEGRETE ORGE NEL '300 • 1973 • Polselli Renato • ITL
RITI SEGRETI • 1974 • Cangini Gabriella • ITL
RITMOS • 1978 • de Pedro Manuel • SHT • VNZ • RHYTHM
RITMOS DEL CARIBE • 1950 • Ortega Juan J. • MXC
RITORNA IL CAPATAZ • 1954 • Simonelli Giorgio C. • ITL
RITORNA ZA-LA MORT see **FUMERIO D'OPPIO, LA** • 1947
RITORNANO QUELLI DELLA CALIBRO 38 • 1977 • Vari Giuseppe • ITL • RETURN OF THE 38 GANG, THE ○ GANGSTERS
RITORNO • 1940 • von Bolvary Geza • ITL • MELODIE DI SOGNO
RITORNO • 1973 • Amico Gianni • ITL • RETURN
RITORNO ALLA TERRA • 1934 • Franchini Mario • ITL
RITORNO ALLA VITA • 1957 • Nieves Conde Jose Antonio • ITL, SPN
RITORNO DEL GLADIATORE PIU FORTE DEL MONDO • 1971 • Albertini Bitto • ITL
RITORNO DELLA MAMMA, IL • 1915 • Falena Ugo • ITL
RITORNO DI ARSENIO LUPIN, IL (ITL) see **SIGNE ARSENE LUPIN** • 1959
RITORNO DI CASANOVA, IL • 1978 • Festa Campanile Pasquale • MTV • ITL
RITORNO DI DON CAMILLO, IL (ITL) see **RETOUR DE DON CAMILLO, LE** • 1953
RITORNO DI RINGO, IL • 1965 • Tessari Duccio • ITL, SPN • RETURN OF RINGO, THE (UKN)
RITORNO DI SABATA, IL see **E TORNATO SABATA.. HAI CHIUSO UN'ALTRA VOLTE** • 1971
RITORNO DI ZANNA BIANCA, IL • 1974 • Fulci Lucio • ITL
RITRATTI DI DONNE AFRICANE • 1977 • Maraini Dacia • MTV • ITL
RITRATTO DI BORGHESIA IN NERO • 1978 • Cervi Tonino • ITL • NEST OF VIPERS
RITRATTO DI PINA • 1961 • Baldi Gian Vittorio • ITL
RITRATTO DI PROVINCIA IN ROSSO • 1976 • Leto Marco • ITL
RITRO VARSI • 1947 • Palella Oreste • ITL
RITROVARSI ALL'ALBA • 1955 • Pizzi Adolfo • ITL
RITSAR BEZ BRONYA • 1966 • Shariliev Borislav • USS • KNIGHT WITHOUT ARMOUR
RITT IN DIE FREIHEIT • 1936 • Hartl Karl • FRG
RITT IN DIE SONNE, DER • 1926 • Jacoby Georg • FRG
RITT UNTER WASSER, DER • 1921 • Piel Harry • FRG
RITTER BLAUBART • 1973 • Felsenstein Walter • GDR
RITTER DER NACHT • 1928 • Reichmann Max • FRG
RITTMEISTER WRONSKI • 1954 • Erfurth Ulrich • FRG
RITUAL • 1973 • Pittman Bruce • CND
RITUAL • 1977 • Cox Paul • SHT • ASL
RITUAL, A see **GHATASHRADDHA** • 1977
RITUAL, THE see **RITEN** • 1969
RITUAL IN TRANSFIGURED TIME • 1946 • Deren Maya • SHT • USA
RITUAL MURDER, THE see **PREJUDICE** • 1924
RITUAL OF EVIL • 1969 • Day Robert • TVM • USA
RITUAL OF LOVE see **A CHACUN SON PARADIS** • 1951
RITUALMORD, DER see **GEACHTETEN, DIE** • 1919
RITUALS • 1976 • Carter Peter • CND • CREEPER, THE
RITUALS see **RITUELEN** • 1988
RITUELEN • 1988 • Curiel Herbert • NTH • RITUALS
RITZ, THE • 1976 • Lester Richard • UKN
RITZY • 1927 • Rosson Richard • USA
RITZY HOTEL • 1932 • *Mintz Charles (P)* • ANS • USA
RITZY ROSIE see **RECKLESS ROSIE** • 1929
RIUSCIRA IL NOSTRO EROE A RITROVARE IL PIU GRANDE DIAMANTE DE MONDO? • 1971 • Malatesta Guido • ITL
RIUSCIRA L'AVVOCATO FRANCO BENENATO A SCONFIGGERE IL SUO ACERRIMO NEMICO IL PRETORE CICCIO DE INGRAS • 1971 • Guerrini Mino • ITL
RIUSCIRANNO I NOSTRI EROI A RITROVARE L'AMICO MISTERIOSAMENTE SCOMPARSO IN AFRICA? • 1968 • Scola Ettore • ITL • WILL OUR FRIEND SUCCEED IN FINDING THEIR FRIEND.. ○ WILL OUR HEROES BE ABLE TO FIND THEIR FRIEND WHO HAS MYSTERIOUSLY DISAPPEARED IN AFRICA?
RIVA DEI BRUTI, LA • 1930 • Camerini Mario • ITL
RIVAGE DE L'AMOUR see **SHAT'I' AL-GHARAM** • 1948
RIVAGE DE L'AMOUR see **SHAT'I' AL-HUBB** • 1960
RIVAGE DES SECRETS, LE see **SHAT'I AL-ASRAR** • 1958
RIVAL, LA • 1954 • Urueta Chano • MXC
RIVAL, THE • 1916 • Hertz Aleksander • PLN
RIVAL ANARCHISTS, THE • 1914 • Reed Langford • UKN
RIVAL ARTISTS • 1916 • Ellis Robert • SHT • USA
RIVAL ARTISTS, THE • 1911 • *Nestor* • USA
RIVAL BARBERS • 1905 • Williamson James • UKN
RIVAL BARBERS, THE • 1914 • *Nigh William* • USA
RIVAL BILL-STICKERS, THE • 1897 • *Paul R. W.* • UKN
RIVAL CANDIDATES • 1916 • *Buffalo* • USA
RIVAL CANDIDATES, THE • 1911 • *Edison* • USA
RIVAL CAPTAINS, THE • 1916 • Batley Ethyle • UKN
RIVAL CLOTHIERS, THE • 1900 • *Warwick Trading Co* • UKN
RIVAL COLLECTORS, THE • 1914 • *Melies* • USA
RIVAL CONSTABLES, THE • 1912 • *Pathe* • USA
RIVAL COOKS, THE • 1910 • *Selig* • USA
RIVAL CYCLISTS, THE • 1908 • Williamson James? • UKN
RIVAL DE CHERUBIN • 1911 • Perret Leonce • FRN
RIVAL DE SATAN • 1910 • Bourgeois Gerard • FRN • RIVAL OF SATAN
RIVAL DENTISTS, THE • 1914 • *Moran Lee* • USA
RIVAL DRAMATISTS, THE • 1911 • *Selig* • USA
RIVAL DUPE, LE • 1911 • Carre Michel • FRN
RIVAL ENGINEERS, THE • 1912 • *Kalem* • USA
RIVAL FAKERS • 1916 • *Hamilton Lloyd V.* • SHT • USA
RIVAL MADE TO MEASURE see **GEGNER NACH MASS** • 1963
RIVAL MASHERS, THE see **THOSE LOVE PANGS** • 1914
RIVAL MESMERIST, THE • 1909 • Fitzhamon Lewin? • UKN
RIVAL MINERS, THE • 1910 • Melies Gaston • USA
RIVAL MUSIC HALL ARTISTES, THE see **TOM TIGHT ET DUM DUM** • 1903
RIVAL MUSICIANS, THE • 1913 • Kellino W. P. • UKN
RIVAL OF PERPETUA, THE • 1915 • *Shubert* • USA
RIVAL OF SATAN see **RIVAL DE SATAN** • 1910
RIVAL PAINTERS, THE • 1905 • Haggar William • UKN
RIVAL PILOTS, THE • 1916 • McRae Henry • SHT • USA
RIVAL PITCHERS, THE • 1913 • *Majestic* • USA
RIVAL QUEENS, THE • 1916 • Louis Will • SHT • USA
RIVAL RAILROAD'S PLOT, THE • 1914 • McGowan J. P. • USA
RIVAL REFLECTIONS • 1914 • Furniss Harry • UKN
RIVAL ROGUES • 1916 • Miller Rube • USA
RIVAL ROMEOS • 1917 • *Hamilton Lloyd V.* • SHT • USA
RIVAL ROMEOS • 1928 • Disney Walt • ANS • USA
RIVAL ROMEOS • 1951 • Donnelly Eddie • ANS • USA
RIVAL SALESMEN, THE • 1913 • *Steppling John* • USA
RIVAL SCULPTORS, THE • 1911 • *Edison* • USA
RIVAL SERVANTS, THE see **TO TJENESTEPIGER** • 1910
RIVAL SNOW SHOVELLERS, THE • 1902 • *Mitchell & Kenyon* • UKN
RIVAL SPORTSMEN, THE • 1905 • Fitzhamon Lewin • UKN
RIVAL STAGE LINES, THE • 1914 • Mix Tom • USA
RIVAL STATE LINES, THE • 1911 • *Selig* • USA
RIVAL SUITORS see **FATAL MALLET, THE** • 1914
RIVAL WAITERS • 1915 • *Hoffman George* • USA
RIVAL WORLD, THE see **STRIJD ZONDER EINDE** • 1954
RIVALE, LA • 1957 • Majano Anton Giulio • ITL
RIVALE, LA • 1974 • Gobbi Sergio • FRN
RIVALE DELL'IMPERATRICE, LA • 1951 • Comin Jacopo, Salkow Sidney • ITL
RIVALE DI PAPA, IL • 1916 • Campogalliani Carlo • ITL
RIVALEN • 1923 • Piel Harry • FRG
RIVALEN DER LIEBE see **ZWEI BRUDER** • 1929
RIVALEN DER LUFT • 1934 • Wisbar Frank • FRG
RIVALEN DER MANEGE • 1958 • Philipp Harald • FRG • BIMBO THE GREAT (USA)
RIVALEN IM WELTREKORD see **ACHTUNG! LIEBE! LEBENSGEFAHR!** • 1929
RIVALI • 1962 • Vrbanic Ivo • ANM • YGS • RIVALS
RIVALITA • 1953 • Biagetti Giovanni • ITL • MEDICO CONDOTTO
RIVALITE see **RIVALITE DE MAX, LE** • 1913
RIVALITE D'AMOUR • 1908 • Melies Georges • FRN • TRAGEDY IN SPAIN, A
RIVALITE DE MAX, LE • 1913 • Linder Max • FRN • RIVALITE
RIVALRY • 1914 • *Anderson Mignon* • USA
RIVALRY, THE • 1975 • *Hill Arthur* • TVM • USA
RIVALRY AND WAR • 1914 • Beery Wallace • USA
RIVALRY IN THE OILFIELDS • 1910 • *Bison* • USA
RIVALS • 1915 • *Kalem* • USA
RIVALS • 1972 • Shah Krishna • USA • DEADLY RIVALS ○ DEADLY THIEF, THE
RIVALS see **RIVALI** • 1962
RIVALS see **STRANGER AT JEFFERSON HIGH, THE** • 1981
RIVALS, THE • 1903 • Collins Alf? • UKN
RIVALS, THE • 1906 • Fitzhamon Lewin • UKN
RIVALS, THE • 1907 • Porter Edwin S. • USA
RIVALS, THE • 1909 • *Lux* • FRN
RIVALS, THE • 1909 • Fitzhamon Lewin? • UKN
RIVALS, THE • 1911 • *Powers* • USA
RIVALS, THE • 1912 • *Essanay* • USA
RIVALS, THE • 1912 • *Selig* • USA
RIVALS, THE • 1912 • Sennett Mack • *Keystone* • USA
RIVALS, THE • 1913 • Franklin Sidney A., Franklin Chester M. • *Majestic* • USA
RIVALS, THE • 1913 • Marston Theodore • *Kinemacolor* • USA
RIVALS, THE • 1915 • *Komic* • USA
RIVALS, THE • 1916 • *Vim* • USA
RIVALS, THE • 1916 • *Utah* • USA
RIVALS, THE • 1963 • Varnel Max • UKN
RIVALS, THE see **NATIZILI, I** • 1967
RIVALS AND REVENGE • 1917 • Hevener Jerold T. • USA
RIVALS (DUEL SCENE), THE • 1914 • *Williams Eric* • UKN
RIVALS FOR A WEEK • 1908 • *Lubin* • USA
RIVALS OF THE DRAGON • 1981 • Yeung Kwan, Yu Florence • HKG
RIVALS OUTWITTED, THE • 1913 • *Majestic* • USA
RIVAUX DE LA PISTE • 1932 • de Poligny Serge • FRN
RIVE DROITE, RIVE GAUCHE • 1984 • Labro Philippe • FRN
RIVE GAUCHE • 1931 • Korda Alexander • FRN
RIVELAZIONE E FATALITA • 1914 • Falena Ugo • ITL
RIVELAZIONI DI UN MANIACO SESSUALE AL CAPO DELLA SQUADRA MOBILE • 1972 • Montero Roberto Bianchi • ITL • CONFESSIONS OF A SEX MANIAC (USA) ○ SO SWEET, SO DEAD
RIVELAZIONI DI UNO PSICHIATRA SUL MONDO PERVERSA DEL SESSO • 1973 • Polselli Renato • ITL
RIVER 70 see **SUMURU** • 1968
RIVER, THE • 1928 • Borzage Frank • USA • FEMME AU CORBEAU, LA
RIVER, THE • 1938 • Lorentz Pare • DOC • USA
RIVER, THE • 1951 • Renoir Jean • UKN, FRN, IND • FLEUVE, LE (FRN)
RIVER, THE • 1984 • Rydell Mark • USA
RIVER, THE see **REKA** • 1933
RIVER, THE see **POTAMI, TO** • 1960
RIVER, THE see **GORGOPOTAMOS, O** • 1968
RIVER, THE see **IRMAK** • 1973
RIVER, THE see **NAHR, AL** • 1977
RIVER AFLAME see **VALURILE DUNARI** • 1959
RIVER AND DEATH, THE (USA) see **RIO Y LA MUERTE, EL** • 1954
RIVER AND WOMAN see **NADI-O-NARI** • 1965
RIVER BANK see **GANGA ADDARA**
RIVER BANK, THE • Naumov Vladimir • USS
RIVER BEAT • 1954 • Green Guy • UKN
RIVER BOY • 1967 • Black Noel • SHT • USA
RIVER CALLED TITAS, A see **TITAS EKTI NADIR NAAM** • 1973
RIVER CHANGES, THE • 1956 • Crump Owen • FRG
RIVER DEATH • 1977 • Huston Jimmy • USA
RIVER ELEGY see **HE SHANG** • 1988
RIVER FLOWS TOWARDS THE EAST, THE see **YIJIANG CHUNSHUI XIANG DONG LIU** • 1947
RIVER FOR DEATH see **RIVER OF DEATH** • 1988
RIVER FUEFUKI, THE see **FUEFUKI-GAWA** • 1960
RIVER GANG • 1945 • David Charles • USA • FAIRY TALE MURDER (UKN)
RIVER GANGES, THE see **GANGA** • 1960
RIVER GIRL, THE see **DONNA DEL FIUME, LA** • 1955
RIVER GODDESS, THE • 1916 • Moore Matt • SHT • USA
RIVER GRAY AND THE RIVER GREEN, THE • 1919 • Bruce Robert C. • USA
RIVER HOUSE see **RUEN PAE** • 1989
RIVER HOUSE GHOST, THE • 1932 • Richardson Frank • UKN
RIVER HOUSE MYSTERY, THE • 1926 • Coleby A. E. • UKN
RIVER HOUSE MYSTERY, THE • 1935 • Foulsham Fraser • UKN
RIVER INN, THE see **ROADHOUSE NIGHTS** • 1930
RIVER LADY • 1948 • Sherman George • USA
RIVER MELODIES • 1948 • Parker Benjamin R. • SHT • USA
RIVER MUSIC • 1961 • Hammid Alexander • USA
RIVER NIGER, THE • 1976 • Shah Krishna • USA • RIVER NIGER: GHETTO WARRIORS, THE
RIVER NIGER: GHETTO WARRIORS, THE see **RIVER NIGER, THE** • 1976
RIVER OF ASPIRATION, THE • VTN
RIVER OF BLOOD, THE see **AGUAS BAJAN TURBIAS, LAS** • 1951
RIVER OF DEATH • 1988 • Carver Steve • USA • RIVER FOR DEATH

RIVER OF DESTINY • 1954 • UKN
RIVER OF DESTINY see **FORLORN RIVER** • 1927
RIVER OF DIAMONDS • 1989 • Smawley Robert • SAF
RIVER OF DOLLARS, A see **FIUME DI DOLLARI, UN** • 1967
RIVER OF EVIL (USA) see **UND DER AMAZONAS SCHWEIGT** • 1963
RIVER OF FOREVER see **CHIKUMAGAWA ZESSHO** • 1967
RIVER OF GOLD, THE • 1970 • Friedkin David • TVM • USA
RIVER OF LIFE • 1977 • Bertolino Daniel • DCS • CND
RIVER OF LIFE AND DEATH, THE see **REKA ZIVOTA A SMRTI** • 1939-40
RIVER OF LIGHT, THE • 1921 • Aylott Dave • UKN
RIVER OF MISSING MEN • 1937 • Collins Lewis D. • USA
RIVER OF MYSTERY • 1969 • Stanley Paul • TVM • USA
RIVER OF NO RETURN • 1954 • Preminger Otto • USA
RIVER OF OBLIVION • 1986 • SKR
RIVER OF POISON (UKN) see **SOUTH OF DEATH VALLEY** • 1949
RIVER OF ROMANCE • 1929 • Wallace Richard • USA • MAGNOLIA
RIVER OF ROMANCE, THE • 1915 • *Lorenz John* • USA
RIVER OF ROMANCE, THE • 1916 • Otto Henry • USA
RIVER OF STARS, THE • 1921 • Thornton F. Martin • UKN
RIVER OF THREE JUNKS, THE (USA) see **RIVIERE DES TROIS JONQUES, LA** • 1956
RIVER OF TOMBS, THE • Luzardo Julio • CLM
RIVER OF UNREST see **OURSELVES ALONE** • 1936
RIVER PATROL • 1948 • Hart Ben R. • UKN
RIVER PIRATE, THE • 1928 • Howard William K. • USA
RIVER PIRATES • 1905 • *Bitzer Billy (Ph)* • USA
RIVER PIRATES, THE • 1913 • *Boyle Irene* • USA
RIVER PIRATES, THE see **PIRACI RZECZNI** • 1965
RIVER (PLANET EARTH) • 1977 • Raymont Peter • DOC • CND
RIVER –POEM OF WRATH, THE see **KAWA, ANO URAGIRI GA OMOKU** • 1967
RIVER RAT, THE • 1984 • Rickman Tom • USA
RIVER RENDEZVOUS see **DUNAPARTI RANDEVU** • 1937
RIVER RIBBER • 1945 • Sommer Paul • ANS • USA
RIVER RIVALS • 1967 • Booth Harry • SRL • UKN
RIVER "SCHOONERS", THE see **VOITURES D'EAU, LES** • 1968
RIVER SOLO FLOWS see **BUGAWAN SOLO** • 1951
RIVER SPEAKS, A • 1957 • Casparius Hans G. • SHT • UKN
RIVER THAMES –YESTERDAY • 1937-40 • *Cardiff Jack (Ph)* • DCS • UKN
RIVER THAT WAS, THE see **RIO QUE NOS LLEVA, EL** • 1988
RIVER TO CROSS • 1950 • Shearman John • UKN
RIVER WANGANUI, THE • 1913 • Melies Gaston • DOC • USA
RIVER WITHOUT A BRIDGE PARTS 1 & 2, THE see **HASHI NO NAI KAWA** • 1969
RIVER WITHOUT BRIDGES see **HASHI NO NAI KAWA** • 1969
RIVER WITHOUT BUOYS, THE see **MEIYOUHANGBIAODE HELIU** • 1985
RIVER WOLVES, THE • 1934 • Pearson George • UKN
RIVER WOMAN, THE • 1928 • Henabery Joseph • USA
RIVERBOAT MISSION • 1962 • Tendlar Dave • ANS • USA
RIVERBOAT RHYTHM • 1946 • Goodwins Leslie • USA
RIVERMAN, THE • 1983 • Hall Ivan • SAF
RIVERRUN • 1970 • Korty John • USA
RIVERS AND LANDSCAPES see **SWISS TRIP** • 1934
RIVER'S EDGE • 1987 • Hunter Tim • USA
RIVER'S EDGE, THE • 1957 • Dwan Allan • USA
RIVER'S END • 1920 • Heerman Victor • USA
RIVER'S END • 1940 • Enright Ray • USA • DOUBLE IDENTITY
RIVER'S END, THE • 1920 • Neilan Marshall • USA
RIVER'S END, THE • 1930 • Curtiz Michael • USA
RIVERS OF FIRE AND ICE, THE see **AFRICAN SAFARI** • 1968
RIVER'S SECRET, THE • 1914 • *Melies* • USA
RIVERSIDE MELODIES • 1929 • *Shepherd Alice* • UKN
RIVERSIDE MEN see **ORILLEROS, LOS** • 1975
RIVERSIDE MURDER, THE • 1935 • Parker Albert • UKN
RIVERSIDE ROMANCE, A • 1913 • Kinder Stuart • UKN
RIVES, LES • 1972 • Regnier Michel • DCS • CND
RIVETER, THE • 1940 • Lundy Dick • ANS • USA
RIVETS (UKN) see **FAST WORKERS** • 1924
RIVIERA DU BRENTA • 1952 • Pialat Maurice • SHT • FRN
RIVIERA EXPRESS see **ACCROCHE-COEUR, L'** • 1938
RIVIERA, TODAY'S EDEN, THE see **DU COTE DE LA COTE** • 1958
RIVIERE, LA see **POTAMI, TO** • 1960
RIVIERE DES TROIS JONQUES, LA • 1956 • Pergament Andre • FRN • RIVER OF THREE JUNKS, THE (USA)
RIVIERE DU GOUFFRE • 1958-60 • Bonniere Rene • DCS • CND
RIVIERE DU HIBOU, LA • 1961 • Enrico Robert • SHT • FRN • OCCURRENCE AT OWL CREEK BRIDGE, AN (USA) ○ INCIDENT AT OWL CREEK
RIVIERE LA PAIX • 1961 • Garceau Raymond • DCS • CND
RIVIERE SECHE, LA see **PAKUASHIPU** • 1971-77
RIVINCITA DI IVANHOE, LA • 1965 • Boccia Tanio • ITL • REVENGE OF IVANHOE, THE (USA)
RIVKIN: BOUNTY HUNTER • 1981 • Harris Harry • TVM • USA
RIVOLTA DEGLI SCHIAVI, LA • 1961 • Malasomma Nunzio • ITL, SPN, FRG • REBELION DE LOS ESCLAVOS, LA (SPN) ○ SKLAVEN ROMS, DIE (FRG) ○ REVOLT OF THE SLAVES, THE (USA)
RIVOLTA DEI BARBARI, LA • 1965 • Malatesta Guido • ITL • REVOLT OF THE BARBARIANS (USA)
RIVOLTA DEI COSACCHI, LA see **FABBRO DEL CONVENTO, IL** • 1949
RIVOLTA DEI GLADIATORI, LA • 1958 • Cottafavi Vittorio • ITL, SPN • WARRIOR AND THE SLAVE, THE (USA) ○ SPARTAN GLADIATORS ○ WARRIOR AND THE SLAVE GIRL, THE
RIVOLTA DEI MERCENARI, LA • 1962 • Costa Piero • ITL, SPN • REVOLT OF THE MERCENARIES (USA) ○ MERCENARIOS, LOS (SPN)
RIVOLTA DEI PRETORIANI, LA • 1965 • Brescia Alfonso • ITL • REVOLT OF THE PRAETORIANS (USA)
RIVOLTA DEI SETTE, LA • 1965 • De Martino Alberto • ITL • SPARTAN GLADIATORS, THE
RIVOLUZIONE A CUBA • 1965 • Malaspina Luciano • DOC • ITL
RIVOLUZIONE SESSUALE, LA • 1968 • Ghione Riccardo • ITL • SEXUAL REVOLUTION, THE
ROACHES SERENADE • Weill Claudia • SHT • USA
ROAD, THE • 1965 • Iliesu Mirel • DOC • RMN
ROAD, THE • 1967 • Li Hsing • HKG
ROAD, THE • 1983 • Chen Lizhou • CHN
ROAD, THE see **STRADA, LA** • 1954
ROAD, THE see **DOROGA** • 1955
ROAD, THE see **MICHI** • 1956
ROAD, THE see **VOIE, LA** • 1967
ROAD, THE see **DROGA** • 1971
ROAD A YEAR LONG, THE (USA) see **STRADA LUNGA UN ANNO, LA** • 1958
ROAD AGENT • 1926 • McGowan J. P. • USA
ROAD AGENT • 1941 • Lamont Charles • USA • TEXAS ROAD AGENT
ROAD AGENT • 1952 • Selander Lesley • USA
ROAD AGENT, THE • 1917 • *Triangle Komedy* • USA
ROAD AGENTS, THE • 1909 • *Essanay* • USA
ROAD AGENT'S LOVE, THE • 1912 • *Anderson Broncho Billy* • USA
ROAD BACK, THE • 1937 • Whale James • USA • RETURN OF THE HERO
ROAD BACK, THE see **CESTA ZPATKY** • 1958
ROAD BEGINS AT MANGISHLAK, THE • 1966 • Lisakovitch Viktor • DOC • USS
ROAD BETWEEN, THE • 1917 • Levering Joseph • USA
ROAD BUILDER, THE see **NIGHT DIGGER, THE** • 1971
ROAD CALLED STRAIGHT, THE • 1919 • Lowry Ira M. • USA
ROAD DEMON • 1938 • Brower Otto • USA
ROAD DEMON, THE • 1921 • Reynolds Lynn • USA
ROAD FOR YOUTH, THE see **DROGA MLODYCH** • 1935
ROAD FROM M.I.S., THE • 1959 • Williams Derek • UKN
ROAD GAMES • 1981 • Franklin Richard • ASL
ROAD GANG • 1936 • King Louis • USA • INJUSTICE (UKN)
ROAD GANGS see **SPACEHUNTER: ADVENTURES IN THE FORBIDDEN ZONE** • 1983
ROAD HOGS IN TOYLAND • 1911 • Cooper Arthur • SHT • UKN
ROAD HOME, THE • 1987 • Kaszubowski Jerzy
ROAD HOME, THE see **SYNI** • 1946
ROAD HOUSE • 1928 • Rosson Richard?, McGuinness James Kevin? • USA
ROAD HOUSE • 1934 • Elvey Maurice • UKN
ROAD HOUSE • 1948 • Negulesco Jean • USA
ROAD HOUSE • 1989 • Herrington Rowdy • USA
ROAD HOUSE GIRL (USA) see **WHEEL OF FATE** • 1953
ROAD HUSTLERS, THE • 1968 • Jackson Larry E. • USA
ROAD I TRAVEL WITH YOU, THE see **KIMI TO YUKU MICHI** • 1936
ROAD IN INDIA, A • 1937-40 • *Cardiff Jack (Ph)* • DCS • UKN
ROAD LORE • 1963 • McCullough Chris • SHT • ASL
ROAD MOVIE • 1974 • Strick Joseph • USA
ROAD NORTH, THE • Kamarof A.
ROAD OF AMBITION, THE • 1920 • Earle William P. S. • USA
ROAD OF ANTHRACITE, THE • 1903 • Porter Edwin S. • USA
ROAD OF LIFE see **ESTRADA DA VIDA** • 1968
ROAD OF MANY TURNINGS, THE • 1916 • Brooke Van Dyke • USA
ROAD OF PROGRESS see **FUNDACOMUN, UN CAMINO** • 1972
ROAD OF THE BURNING VAN see **DOROGA GORYASHCHEVO FURGONA** • 1967
ROAD OF THE GIANTS, THE see **STRADA DEI GIGANTI, LA** • 1960
ROAD OF TRANSGRESSION, THE • 1913 • *Calvert E. H.* • USA
ROAD OF TRUTH, THE • 1956 • Frid Ya. • USS
ROAD O'STRIFE • 1915 • Ince John, Hansel Howell • SRL • USA
ROAD RACERS see **ROADRACERS** • 1959
ROAD RAIDERS • 1989 • Lang Richard • USA
ROAD REBELS • 1963 • Calarco Reno D. • USA
ROAD RUNNER AND COYOTE • 1948 • Jones Charles M. • ASS • USA
ROAD SENSE • 1951 • McCarthy Michael, Tambling Richard • UKN
ROAD SENSE • 1969 • Mason Bill • DOC • UKN
ROAD SHOW • 1941 • Roach Hal, Douglas Gordon, Roach Hal Jr. • USA
ROAD SHOW, THE see **CHASING RAINBOWS** • 1930
ROAD THROUGH THE DARK, THE • 1918 • Mortimer Edmund • USA
ROAD THROUGH THE DAYS • 1972 • Terziev Ivan • BUL
ROAD TO ALCATRAZ • 1945 • Grinde Nick • USA
ROAD TO ANDALAY • 1964 • Freleng Friz • ANS • USA • TEQUILA MOCKING BIRD
ROAD TO ARCADY, THE • 1922 • King Burton L. • USA
ROAD TO BAGDAD, THE see **BAGDAT YOLU** • 1968
ROAD TO BALI • 1952 • Walker Hal • USA • ROAD TO HOLLYWOOD
ROAD TO BROADWAY, THE • 1926 • Mitchell Howard M. • USA
ROAD TO CALAIS, THE • 1914 • Weston Charles • UKN • ON THE ROAD TO CALAIS
ROAD TO CANTERBURY, THE • 1952 • Eady David • UKN
ROAD TO CORINTH, THE see **ROUTE DE CORINTHE, LA** • 1967
ROAD TO CRIME see **NA SENDA DO CRIME** • 1954
ROAD TO DEATH OF OLD REALES, THE see **CAMINO HACIA LA MUERTE DEL VIEJO REALES, EL**
ROAD TO DENVER, THE • 1955 • Kane Joseph • USA
ROAD TO DISHONOUR, THE see **HAI-TANG** • 1930
ROAD TO DIVORCE, THE • 1920 • Rosen Phil • USA
ROAD TO EIN HAROD • 1989 • Eran Doron • ISR
ROAD TO ETERNITY see **NINGEN NO JOKEN II** • 1959
ROAD TO ETERNITY, THE • 1917 • Smith David • SHT • USA
ROAD TO FAME, THE • 1915 • *Kingston Winnifred* • USA
ROAD TO FAME, THE • 1916 • King Burton L. • SHT • USA
ROAD TO FORT ALAMO, THE (USA) see **STRADA PER FORT ALAMO, LA** • 1965
ROAD TO FORTUNE, THE • 1930 • Varney-Serrao Arthur • UKN
ROAD TO FRANCE, THE • 1918 • Henderson Dell • USA
ROAD TO 'FRISCO, THE (UKN) see **THEY DRIVE BY NIGHT** • 1940
ROAD TO GLORY, THE • 1926 • Hawks Howard • USA
ROAD TO GLORY, THE • 1936 • Hawks Howard • USA • WOODEN CROSSES ○ ZERO HOUR
ROAD TO GOD see **KAMI E NO MICHI** • 1928
ROAD TO HAPPINESS • 1942 • Rosen Phil • USA
ROAD TO HAPPINESS, THE • 1910 • *Lubin* • USA
ROAD TO HAPPINESS, THE • 1956 • NKR
ROAD TO HAPPINESS, THE see **LYKKEN** • 1916
ROAD TO HAPPINESS, THE see **GOLDENE SCHMETTERLING, DER** • 1926
ROAD TO HEALTH, THE • 1938 • Salt Brian • UKN
ROAD TO HEAVEN, THE • 1922 • Sanderson Challis • UKN
ROAD TO HEAVEN, THE see **HIMLASPELET** • 1942
ROAD TO HOLLYWOOD • 1947 • Pollard Bud • USA
ROAD TO HOLLYWOOD see **ROAD TO BALI** • 1952
ROAD TO HOLLYWOOD, THE • 1933 • Pollard Bud • SHT • USA
ROAD TO HONG KONG, THE • 1962 • Panama Norman • UKN, USA • ROAD TO THE MOON
ROAD TO HONOUR, THE see **DARK ROAD, THE** • 1917
ROAD TO HOPE, THE see **CAMMINO DELLA SPERANZA, IL** • 1950
ROAD TO IMMORTALITY, THE • 1958 • Tovstonogov G., Chiginsky A. • USS
ROAD TO KATMANDU, THE (UKN) see **CHEMINS DE KATMANDOU, LES** • 1969
ROAD TO KLOCKRIKE see **VAGEN TILL KLOCKRIKE** • 1953
ROAD TO LENIN, THE • 1970 • Reisch Gunter • GDR, USS
ROAD TO LIFE, THE • 1956 • Maslyukov Alexei, Mayevskaya M. • USS
ROAD TO LIFE, THE see **PUTYOVKHA Z ZHIZN** • 1931
ROAD TO LONDON, THE • 1921 • Mullin Eugene • USA, UKN
ROAD TO LOVE, A • 1909 • Porter Edwin S. • USA
ROAD TO LOVE, THE • 1916 • Sidney Scott • USA
ROAD TO MANDALAY, THE • 1926 • Browning Tod • USA
ROAD TO MOROCCO • 1942 • Butler David • USA
ROAD TO NASHVILLE • 1966 • Zens Will • USA
ROAD TO NOWHERE, THE see **YOU CAN'T GET AWAY WITH IT** • 1923
ROAD TO PARADISE, THE • 1931 • Beaudine William • USA • AT BAY
ROAD TO PEACE, THE see **BEKE UTJA, A** • 1917
ROAD TO PLAINDALE, THE • 1914 • Henderson Dell?, Jefferson William? • USA
ROAD TO RENO, THE • 1931 • Wallace Richard • USA
ROAD TO RENO, THE • 1938 • Simon S. Sylvan • USA
ROAD TO RICHMOND, THE • 1910 • *Selig* • USA
ROAD TO RIO • 1947 • McLeod Norman Z. • USA
ROAD TO RIO see **THAT NIGHT IN RIO** • 1941
ROAD TO RISE AND FALL see **EIKO EN MICHI** • 1950
ROAD TO ROMANCE, THE • 1927 • Robertson John S. • USA • ROMANCE (UKN)
ROAD TO ROMANCE, THE see **SMILE, BROTHER, SMILE** • 1927
ROAD TO RUIN, THE • 1908 • *Selig* • USA
ROAD TO RUIN, THE • 1911 • Haldane Bert? • UKN
ROAD TO RUIN, THE • 1913 • Dwan Allan • USA
ROAD TO RUIN, THE • 1913 • Gray George?, Haldane Bert? • UKN
ROAD TO RUIN, THE • 1913 • Lincoln W. J. • ASL
ROAD TO RUIN, THE • 1914 • *Warner'S Features* • USA
ROAD TO RUIN, THE • 1920 • Edwards Harry J. • SHT • USA
ROAD TO RUIN, THE • 1928 • Parker Norton S. • USA
ROAD TO RUIN, THE • 1934 • Shyer Melville, Reid Dorothy • USA
ROAD TO RUSSIA • 1944 • Hurley Frank • UKN
ROAD TO ST. TROPEZ (UKN) see **ROUTE DE ST. TROPEZ, LA** • 1966
ROAD TO SALINA (USA) see **SUR LA ROUTE DE SALINA** • 1969
ROAD TO SATURN, THE see **PUT V SATURN** • 1968
ROAD TO SHAME, THE (USA) see **DES FEMMES DISPARAISSENT** • 1959
ROAD TO SINGAPORE • 1940 • Schertzinger Victor • USA
ROAD TO SINGAPORE, THE • 1931 • Green Alfred E. • USA
ROAD TO SUCCESS, THE • 1912 • Dwan Allan • USA
ROAD TO SUCCESS, THE see **VIA DEL EXITO, LA** • 1977
ROAD TO THE BARRICADES, THE see **CESTA K BARIKADAM** • 1946
ROAD TO THE BIG HOUSE • 1947 • Colmes Walter • USA
ROAD TO THE DAWN, THE • 1913 • *Johnson Arthur* • USA
ROAD TO THE FUTURE, THE • 1986 • Skagen Peter • DOC • CND
ROAD TO THE HEART, THE • 1909 • Griffith D. W. • USA
ROAD TO THE MOON see **ROAD TO HONG KONG, THE** • 1962
ROAD TO THE REICH • 1945 • Daly Tom • DOC • CND
ROAD TO THE SOUTH, THE • 1981 • van der Keuken Johan • DOC • NTH
ROAD TO THE STARS see **DOROGA K ZVEZDAM** • 1957
ROAD TO TIBET • 1956 • Sis Vladimir, Vanis Josef • DOC • CZC
ROAD TO UMINARI see **UMINARI KAIDO** • 1934
ROAD TO UNITY, THE see **DROGA DO JEDNOSCI** • 1948
ROAD TO UTOPIA • 1945 • Walker Hal • USA
ROAD TO YESTERDAY, THE • 1914 • Marston Lawrence • USA
ROAD TO YESTERDAY, THE • 1925 • De Mille Cecil B. • USA
ROAD TO ZANZIBAR, THE • 1941 • Schertzinger Victor • USA
ROAD TRIP see **JOCKS** • 1987
ROAD WARRIOR, THE (USA) see **MAD MAX 2** • 1981
ROAD WEST, THE see **DROGA NA ZACHOD** • 1961
ROAD WITHOUT SLEEP see **DOROGA BEZ SNA** • 1946
ROADBLOCK • 1951 • Daniels Harold • USA
ROADFILM • 1970 • Lawder Standish D. • ANS • USA
ROADHOUSE see **WILD COMPANY** • 1930
ROADHOUSE 66 • 1984 • Robinson John Mark • USA
ROADHOUSE GIRL see **MARILYN** • 1953
ROADHOUSE MURDER, THE • 1932 • Ruben J. Walter • USA
ROADHOUSE NIGHTS • 1930 • Henley Hobart • USA • RIVER INN, THE
ROADHOUSE QUEEN • 1933 • *Sennett Mack (P)* • SHT • USA
ROADIE • 1980 • Rudolph Alan • USA
ROADKILL • 1990 • McDonald Bruce • CND
ROADRACERS • 1959 • Swerdloff Arthur • USA • ROAD RACERS
ROADS • 1964 • Iliesu Mirel • DOC • RMN

ROADS • 1973 • *Halas John (P)* • ANS • UKN
ROADS, THE see **PUTEVI** • 1958
ROADS ACROSS BRITAIN • 1939 • Cole Sidney • DOC • UKN
ROADS AND LIVES • 1956 • Bazelyan L. • USS
ROADS OF BATTLE, THE see **TAISTELUJEN TIE** • 1960
ROADS OF DESTINY • 1921 • Lloyd Frank • USA
ROADS OF EXILE, THE (UKN) see **CHEMINS DE L'EXIL, OU LES DERNIERES ANNEES DE JEAN-JACQUES ROUSEAU, LES** • 1978
ROADS OF MEN, THE see **CESTY MUZU** • 1972
ROADS OF WAR, THE • 1958 • Saakov Leon • USS
ROADS THAT LEAD HOME, THE • 1913 • *Solax* • USA
ROADS TO RESOURCES • 1973 • Maunder Paul • NZL
ROADS TO THE SOUTH, THE see **ROUTES DU SUD, LES** • 1978
ROADS WE TAKE, THE • 1920 • Smith David • SHT • USA
ROADSIDE IMPRESARIO, A • 1917 • Crisp Donald • USA
ROADSIDE INN, A see **HOTEL DES VOYAGEURS DE COMMERCE, L'** • 1906
ROADSWEEPER see **GIJS VAN GROENESTEIN, STRAATVEGER** • 1976
ROADWAYS • 1937 • Legg Stuart, Coldstream William • DOC • CND
ROAMIN' HOLIDAY • 1937 • Douglas Gordon • SHT • USA
ROAMIN' ROMAN • 1964 • Smith Paul J. • ANS • USA
ROAMIN' VANDALS • 1934 • Jason Leigh, Yates Hal • SHT • USA
ROAMIN' WILD • 1936 • Ray Bernard B. • USA
ROAMING BATHTUB, THE • 1919 • Griffin Frank C. • SHT • USA
ROAMING COWBOY, THE • 1937 • Hill Robert F. • USA
ROAMING IN THE GLOAMING • 1931 • Pearson George • SHT • UKN
ROAMING LADY • 1936 • Rogell Albert S. • USA
ROAMING ROMEO • 1928 • George Henry W. • USA
ROAMING ROMEO • 1933 • Gillstrom Arvid E. • SHT • USA
ROAMING ROMEO, A • 1916 • *Victor* • SHT • USA
ROAMING ROMEO, A • 1920 • *Mann Hank* • SHT • USA
ROANOAK • 1986 • Egleson Jan • TVM • USA
ROAR • 1981 • Marshall Noel • USA
ROAR AND EARTH see **BAKUON TO DAICHI** • 1957
ROAR, NAVY, ROAR • 1942 • *O'Brien Joseph/ Mead Thomas (P)* • SHT • USA
ROAR OF HAMMER RAPIDS, THE see **HAMMARFORSENS BRUS** • 1948
ROAR OF THE CROWD • 1953 • Beaudine William • USA
ROAR OF THE DRAGON • 1932 • Ruggles Wesley • USA
ROAR OF THE IRON HORSE • 1951 • Bennet Spencer Gordon, Carr Thomas • SRL • USA
ROAR OF THE PRESS, THE • 1941 • Rosen Phil • USA
ROARIN' BRONCS • 1927 • Thorpe Richard • USA
ROARIN' DAN • 1920 • Rosen Phil • SHT • USA
ROARIN' GUNS • 1936 • Newfield Sam • USA
ROARIN' LEAD • 1936 • Wright Mack V., Newfield Sam • USA
ROARING ADVENTURE, A • 1925 • Smith Cliff • USA
ROARING BILL • 1913 • *Eclair* • USA
ROARING BILL ATWOOD • 1926 • Cohn Bennett • USA
ROARING CHALLENGE • 1955 • Landers Lew • MTV • USA
ROARING CITY • 1951 • Berke William • USA
ROARING CROWD, THE see **INDIANAPOLIS SPEEDWAY** • 1939
ROARING FIRE • 1981 • Suzuki Norry • JPN
ROARING FIRES • 1927 • Lackey W. T.?, Barringer A. B.? • USA
ROARING FORTIES, THE see **ROBES OF SIN** • 1924
ROARING FRONTIERS • 1941 • Hillyer Lambert • USA
ROARING GAME, THE • 1952 • Sparling Gordon • DCS • CND • SPORT DU TONNERRE, UN
ROARING GUNS • 1930 • *Hoxie Al* • USA
ROARING GUNS • 1944 • Negulesco Jean • SHT • USA
ROARING LION, THE • 1923 • Kenton Erle C. • SHT • USA
ROARING LIONS AND WEDDING BELLS • 1917 • Campbell William • SHT • USA
ROARING LIONS ON THE MIDNIGHT EXPRESS • 1918 • Lehrman Henry • SHT • USA
ROARING LOVE AFFAIR, A • 1920 • Robbins Jess • SHT • USA
ROARING OAKS • 1919 • Millhauser Bertram • SRL • USA
ROARING RAILS • 1924 • Forman Tom • USA
ROARING RANCH • 1930 • Eason B. Reeves, Rosson Arthur • USA
ROARING RANGERS • 1946 • Nazarro Ray • USA • FALSE HERO (UKN)
ROARING RIDER • 1926 • Thorpe Richard • USA
ROARING ROAD • 1926 • Hurst Paul C. • USA
ROARING ROAD, THE • 1919 • Cruze James • USA
ROARING SIX GUNS • 1937 • McGowan J. P. • USA
ROARING TIMBER • 1937 • Rosen Phil • USA
ROARING TIMBER see **COME AND GET IT!** • 1936
ROARING TWENTIES, THE • 1939 • Walsh Raoul, Litvak Anatole • USA
ROARING WEST, THE • 1935 • Taylor Ray • SRL • USA
ROARING WESTWARD • 1949 • Drake Oliver • USA
ROARING YEARS, THE see **ANNI RUGGENTI** • 1962
ROARS OF SPRING see **HARU NO TODOROKI** • 1952
ROAST PIGEONS see **PIECZONE GOLABKI** • 1966
ROB 'EM GOOD • 1923 • Stromberg Hunt • USA
ROB ROY • 1911 • Vivian Arthur • UKN
ROB ROY • 1913 • *Eclair* • USA
ROB ROY • 1922 • Kellino W. P. • UKN
ROB ROY THE HIGHLAND ROGUE • 1953 • French Harold • UKN • ROB ROY (USA)
ROB ROY (USA) see **ROB ROY THE HIGHLAND ROGUE** • 1953
ROB YOUR NEIGHBOUR see **RUBA AL PROSSIMO TUO** • 1968
ROBBEKALLEPAUL see **ROBBY KALLE PAUL** • 1988
ROBBER, THE • 1918 • Harvey Harry • SHT • USA
ROBBER AND THE JEW, THE • 1908 • Smith Jack ? • UKN
ROBBER BAND, THE see **RAUBERBANDE, DIE** • 1928
ROBBER BARON, THE • 1910 • *Kalem* • USA
ROBBER BARON IN THE COUNTRY • D'Bomba Jorg • ANM • GDR
ROBBER-CATCHING MACHINE, THE • 1911 • *Eclair* • FRN
ROBBER KITTEN, THE • 1935 • Hand David • ANS • USA
ROBBER OF ANGKOR, THE • 1913 • Melies Gaston • USA
ROBBER RUMCAJZ • Capek Ladislav • ASS • CZC
ROBBER SAGA, THE see **SENGOKU GUNTODEN** • 1959
ROBBER SPIDER, THE see **ROVEDDERKOPPEN** • 1915
ROBBER SYMPHONY, THE (UKN) see **GEHETZTE MENSCHEN** • 1932
ROBBER SYPHONY, THE • 1936 • Feher Friedrich • UKN
ROBBERS see **ATRACADORES, LOS** • 1961
ROBBERS, THE • 1913 • Edwin Walter, Dawley J. Searle • USA
ROBBERS, THE see **PENYAMUN TARBUS** • 1979
ROBBERS OF SACRED MOUNTAIN see **FALCON'S GOLD** • 1985
ROBBERS OF THE RANGE • 1941 • Killy Edward • USA
ROBBERS OF THE SACRED MOUNTAIN see **FALCON'S GOLD** • 1985
ROBBERS' ROOST • 1933 • King Louis • USA
ROBBER'S ROOST • 1955 • Salkow Sidney • USA
ROBBER'S RUSE: OR, FOILED BY FIDO, THE • 1909 • Coleby A. E. • UKN
ROBBER'S TALE, THE see **LOUPEZNICKA POHADKA** • 1964
ROBBERY • 1897 • *Paul R. W.* • UKN
ROBBERY • 1967 • Yates Peter • UKN
ROBBERY • 1985 • Thornhill Michael • ASL
ROBBERY, THE see **LISTIA STIN ATHINA** • 1969
ROBBERY AT OLD BURNSIDE BANK • 1912 • Wilson Frank? • UKN
ROBBERY AT PINE RIVER, THE • 1914 • *Broncho* • USA
ROBBERY AT THE RAILROAD STATION, THE • 1912 • *Champion* • USA
ROBBERY OF A MAIL CONVOY BY BANDITS • 1904 • *Urban Trading Co* • UKN
ROBBERY OF THE CITIZEN'S BANK, THE • 1908 • *Lubin* • USA
ROBBERY OF THE MAIL COACH • 1903 • Mottershaw Frank • UKN • COACH HOLDUP IN DICK TURPIN'S DAY, A ○ JACK SHEPPARD (USA)
ROBBERY ROMAN STYLE (USA) see **SUPER-RAPINA A MILANO** • 1965
ROBBERY UNDER ARMS • 1907 • MacMahon Charles • ASL
ROBBERY UNDER ARMS • 1920 • Brampton Kenneth • ASL
ROBBERY UNDER ARMS • 1957 • Lee Jack • UKN
ROBBERY UNDER ARMS • 1985 • Hannam Ken, Crombie Donald • ASL
ROBBERY WITH VIOLENCE • 1905 • Collins Alf? • UKN
ROBBERY WITH VIOLENCE • 1959 • Barnett Ivan • UKN
ROBBIE AND THE REDSKINS • 1911 • *Kalem* • USA
ROBBING CLEOPATRA'S TOMB (USA) see **CLEOPATRE** • 1899
ROBBING H.M. MAILS • 1906 • Cooper Arthur • UKN
ROBBING THE FISHES • 1916 • Louis Will • SHT • USA
ROBBING THE WIDOWED AND FATHERLESS • 1909 • Bouwmeester Theo? • UKN
ROBBINS, CHAMPION OF ALL CHAMPIONS • 1902 • *Warwick Trading Co* • UKN
ROBBO see **ROBIN AND THE 7 HOODS** • 1964
ROBBY • 1968 • Bluemke Ralph C. • USA
ROBBY KALLE PAUL • 1988 • Levy Dani • SWT, FRG • ROBBEKALLEPAUL
ROBE, THE • 1953 • Koster Henry • USA
ROBE NOIRE POUR UN TUEUR, UNE • 1980 • Giovanni Jose • FRN
ROBE OF HONOE • 1918 • *Walthall Henry B.* • USA
ROBE ROUGE, LA • 1912 • Pouctal Henri • FRN
ROBE ROUGE, LA • 1933 • de Marguenat Jean • FRN
ROBERT ADAM • 1974 • Grigor Murray • DOC • UKN
ROBERT ALS LOHENGRIN • 1915 • Eichberg Richard • FRG
ROBERT AND BERTRAM see **ROBERT UND BERTRAM** • 1961
ROBERT AND FANNY see **MANDAGARNA MED FANNY** • 1977
ROBERT BALDWIN • 1960 • Howe John • CND
ROBERT EMMET • 1911 • Dawley J. Searle • USA
ROBERT EN BERTRAND • 1983 • Blancke Cor, Linthout Ronny • BLG
ROBERT ET ROBERT • 1978 • Lelouch Claude • FRN
ROBERT ET SONIA DELAUNEY, PRISE DE VUE POUR UNE MONOGRAPHE • 1972 • Raynaud Patrick • DOC • FRN
ROBERT FROST.. A LOVE LETTER TO THE WORLD • 1964 • Clarke Shirley • DOC • USA • ROBERT FROST: A LOVER'S QUARREL WITH THE WORLD
ROBERT FROST: A LOVER'S QUARREL • 1962 • Macartney-Filgate Terence • DOC • USA
ROBERT FROST: A LOVER'S QUARREL WITH THE WORLD see **ROBERT FROST.. A LOVE LETTER TO THE WORLD** • 1964
ROBERT HALE'S AMBITION • 1913 • Eagle Oscar • USA
ROBERT HAVING HIS NIPPLE PIERCED • 1973 • Daley Sandy • DOC • USA
ROBERT JOX • 1990 • Gordon Stuart • USA
ROBERT KLIPPEL • 1978 • Salvat Keith • DOC • ASL
ROBERT KOCH, DER BEKAMPFER DES TODES • 1939 • Steinhoff Hans • FRG • ROBERT KOCH (USA)
ROBERT KOCH (USA) see **ROBERT KOCH, DER BEKAMPFER DES TODES** • 1939
ROBERT MACAIRE AND BERTRAND see **ROBERT MACAIRE ET BERTRAND** • 1906
ROBERT MACAIRE ET BERTRAND • 1905 • Blache Alice • FRN • MORT DE ROBERT MACAIRE ET BERTRAND
ROBERT MACAIRE ET BERTRAND • 1906 • Melies Georges • FRN • ROBERT MACAIRE AND BERTRAND
ROBERT MACAIRE OR THE TWO VAGABONDS • 1910 • *Actophone* • USA
ROBERT MCBRYDE AND ROBERT COLQUHOUN • 1959 • Russell Ken • MTV • UKN
ROBERT MEYER -DER ARZT AUS HEILBRON • 1955 • Spiess Helmut • GDR
ROBERT THE DEVIL • 1910 • *Gaumont* • UKN
ROBERT, THE DEVIL: OR, FREED FROM SATAN'S POWER • 1910 • *Gaumont* • FRN
ROBERT THORNE FORECLOSES • 1915 • King Burton L. • USA
ROBERT UND BERTRAM • 1915 • Mack Max • FRG
ROBERT UND BERTRAM • 1928 • Walther-Fein Rudolf • FRG
ROBERT UND BERTRAM • 1939 • Zerlett Hans H. • FRG
ROBERT UND BERTRAM • 1961 • Deppe Hans • FRG • ROBERT AND BERTRAM
ROBERTA • 1935 • Seiter William A. • USA
ROBERTA FLACK • 1971 • Powell David W. • SHT • USA
ROBERTE • 1978 • Zucca Pierre • FRN, CND
ROBERTO see **PRELUDE A LA GLOIRE** • 1949
ROBERTO CARLOS EM RITMO DE AVENTURA • 1967 • Farias Roberto • BRZ
ROBERTO EL DIABLO • 1956 • Lazaga Pedro • SPN
ROBERTO ROSSELLINI, UN RICORDO • 1978 • D'Alessandro Angelo • MTV • ITL
ROBERT'S CAPTURE • 1913 • *Coventry Tom* • UKN
ROBERT'S LAST SUPPER • 1912 • Haldane Bert? • UKN
ROBERT'S LESSON • 1913 • Smalley Phillips • USA
ROBES OF SIN • 1924 • Allen Russell • USA • ROARING FORTIES, THE
ROBESPIERRE • 1913 • *Shay William* • USA
ROBIN • 1979 • Aldrich Hank • USA
ROBIN AND MARIAN • 1976 • Lester Richard • USA
ROBIN AND THE 7 HOODS • 1964 • Douglas Gordon • USA • ROBBO
ROBIN CRUSOE • 1968 • *Fearless Productions* • USA
ROBIN HOOD • 1908 • *Kalem* • USA
ROBIN HOOD • 1912 • Arnaud Etienne, Blache Herbert • USA
ROBIN HOOD • 1913 • Marston Theodore • USA
ROBIN HOOD • 1922 • Dwan Allan • USA • DOUGLAS FAIRBANKS IN ROBIN HOOD
ROBIN HOOD • 1933 • *Terry Paul/ Moser Frank (P)* • ANS • USA
ROBIN HOOD • 1972 • Sutherland Hal • *Filmation* • ANM • USA
ROBIN HOOD • 1973 • Reitherman Wolfgang • *Disney* • ANM • USA
ROBIN HOOD see **RIBALD TALES OF ROBIN HOOD, THE** • 1969
ROBIN HOOD AND HIS MERRY MEN • 1908 • Stow Percy • UKN
ROBIN HOOD AND HIS MERRY MEN see **STORY OF ROBIN HOOD, THE** • 1952
ROBIN HOOD AND THE PIRATES (USA) see **ROBIN HOOD E I PIRATI** • 1961
ROBIN HOOD AND THE SORCERER • 1983 • Sharp Ian • TVM • UKN • ROBIN HOOD, THE LEGEND ○ ROBIN OF SHERWOOD
ROBIN HOOD DAFFY • 1958 • Jones Charles M. • ANS • USA
ROBIN HOOD E I PIRATI • 1961 • Simonelli Giorgio C. • ITL • ROBIN HOOD AND THE PIRATES (USA)
ROBIN HOOD EL ARQUERO INVENCIBLE • 1971 • Merino Jose Luis • SPN, ITL • ROBIN HOOD L'INVINCIBILE ARCIERE (ITL)
ROBIN HOOD, FRECCIA, FAGIOLI E KARATE • 1976 • Ricci Tonino • ITL, SPN
ROBIN HOOD IN AN ARROW ESCAPE • 1936 • Davis Mannie, Gordon George • ANS • USA
ROBIN HOOD, JR. • 1923 • Bricker Clarence • USA
ROBIN HOOD, JR. • 1934 • *Iwerks Ub (P)* • ANS • USA
ROBIN HOOD JUNIOR • 1975 • McCarthy Matt, Black John • UKN
ROBIN HOOD L'INVINCIBILE ARCIERE (ITL) see **ROBIN HOOD EL ARQUERO INVENCIBLE** • 1971
ROBIN HOOD MAKES GOOD • 1939 • Jones Charles M. • ANS • USA
ROBIN HOOD NUNCA MUERE • 1974 • Bellmunt Francisco • SPN
ROBIN HOOD OF EL DORADO • 1936 • Wellman William A. • USA
ROBIN HOOD OF MONTEREY • 1947 • Cabanne W. Christy • USA
ROBIN HOOD OF TEXAS • 1947 • Selander Lesley • USA
ROBIN HOOD OF THE PECOS • 1941 • Kane Joseph • USA
ROBIN HOOD OF THE RANGE • 1943 • Berke William • USA
ROBIN HOOD OUTLAWED • 1912 • Raymond Charles • UKN
ROBIN HOOD, THE LEGEND see **ROBIN HOOD AND THE SORCERER** • 1983
ROBIN HOOD WINKED • 1948 • Kneitel Seymour • ANS • USA
ROBIN HOODLUM • 1946 • Hubley John • ANS • USA
ROBIN HOOD'S MEN • 1924 • *Regent Films* • SHT • UKN
ROBIN HOODWINKED • 1958 • Hanna William, Barbera Joseph • ANS • USA
ROBIN HOODWINKED • 1967 • Culhane Shamus • ANS • USA
ROBIN HOODY WOODY • 1963 • Smith Paul J. • ANS • USA
ROBIN OF SHERWOOD see **ROBIN HOOD AND THE SORCERER** • 1983
ROBIN RODENTHOOD • 1955 • Tendlar Dave • ANS • USA
ROBINSON • 1957 • de Gastyne Marco • SHT • FRN
ROBINSON • 1969 • Moorse Georg • FRG
ROBINSON see **HAGYJATOK ROBINSONT** • 1989
ROBINSON AND CRUSOE see **WHY SAILORS GO WRONG** • 1928
ROBINSON CHARLEY • 1948 • Halas John, Batchelor Joy • ANS • UKN
ROBINSON CRUSOE • 1910 • Blom August • DNM
ROBINSON CRUSOE • 1913 • Turner Otis • USA
ROBINSON CRUSOE • 1916 • Marion George F. • USA
ROBINSON CRUSOE • 1917 • *Leonard Robert* • SHT • USA
ROBINSON CRUSOE • 1922 • Hill Robert F., Eason B. Reeves • SRL • USA • ADVENTURES OF ROBINSON CRUSOE
ROBINSON CRUSOE • 1925 • Lantz Walter • ANS • USA
ROBINSON CRUSOE • 1927 • Wetherell M. A. • UKN
ROBINSON CRUSOE • 1933 • *Terry Paul/ Moser Frank (P)* • ANS • USA • SHIPWRECKED BROTHERS
ROBINSON CRUSOE • 1946 • Andrievski Alexander • USS
ROBINSON CRUSOE • 1950 • Musso Jeff • FRN • NAUFRAGE DU PACIFIQUE, LE
ROBINSON CRUSOE • 1972 • Gibba • ANM • ASL
ROBINSON CRUSOE • 1974 • McTaggart James • TVM • UKN
ROBINSON CRUSOE see **AVENTURES DE ROBINSON CRUSOE, LES** • 1902
ROBINSON CRUSOE see **AVENTURAS DE ROBINSON CRUSOE, LAS** • 1952
ROBINSON CRUSOE see **ROBINSON CRUSOE AND THE TIGER** • 1969
ROBINSON CRUSOE AND SON • 1932 • Edwards Harry J. • SHT • USA
ROBINSON CRUSOE AND THE TIGER • 1969 • Cardona Rene Jr. • MXC • ROBINSON CRUSOE
ROBINSON CRUSOE ISLE • 1934 • Lantz Walter, Nolan William • ANS • USA

ROBINSON CRUSOE JR. • 1941 • McCabe Norman • ANS • USA
ROBINSON CRUSOE OF CLIPPER ISLAND • 1936 • Wright Mack V., Taylor Ray • SRL • USA
ROBINSON CRUSOE OF MYSTERY ISLAND • 1936 • Wright Mack V., Taylor Ray • USA • S.O.S. CLIPPER ISLAND (UKN)
ROBINSON CRUSOE ON MARS • 1964 • Haskin Byron • USA
ROBINSON CRUSOE UND SEINE WILDEN SKLAVINNEN • 1971 • Franco Jesus • FRG, FRN • SEXY DARLINGS, THE (UKN)
ROBINSON CRUSOELAND (UKN) see **ATOLL K** • 1952
ROBINSON CRUSOE'S BROADCAST • 1938 • Foster John • ANS • USA
ROBINSON, EIN • 1940 • Fanck Arnold • FRG • TAGEBUCH EINES MATROSEN, DAS
ROBINSON ET LE TRIPORTEUR • 1959 • Pinoteau Jack • FRN, SPN • MONSIEUR ROBINSON CRUSOE (USA)
ROBINSON GIRL see **ROBINSONKA** • 1974
ROBINSON GRUESOME • 1958 • Smith Paul J. • ANS • USA
ROBINSON I ROSLAGEN • 1948 • Bauman Schamyl • SWD • ROBINSON OF ROSLAGEN
ROBINSON I SKARGARDEN • 1920 • Carlsten Rune • SWD • MODERN ROBINSON, A (USA) ○ ROBINSON IN THE ARCHIPELAGO
ROBINSON IN THE ARCHIPELAGO see **ROBINSON I SKARGARDEN** • 1920
ROBINSON JUNIOR • 1931 • Machin Alfred • FRN • BLACK AND WHITE
ROBINSON OF ROSLAGEN see **ROBINSON I ROSLAGEN** • 1948
ROBINSON SOLL NICHT STERBEN • 1957 • von Baky Josef • FRG • GIRL AND THE LEGEND, THE (USA)
ROBINSONKA • 1974 • Kachyna Karel • CZC • ROBINSON GIRL
ROBINSON'S PLACE see **DU COTE DE ROBINSON** • 1964
ROBO, EL • 1965 • Fraga Jorge • CUB
ROBO AL TREN CORREO, EL • 1964 • Urueta Chano • MXC
ROBO DE DIAMANTES (SPN) see **RUN LIKE A THIEF** • 1967
ROBO DE LAS MOMIAS DE GUANAJUATO, EL • 1972 • Novaro Tito • MXC • THEFT OF THE MUMMIES OF GUANAJUATO, THE
ROBO DEL TREN, EL (MXC) see **TRAIN ROBBERS, THE** • 1973
ROBO NO ISHI • 1938 • Tasaka Tomotaka • JPN • PEBBLE BY THE WAYSIDE, A ○ STONE ON ROADSIDE, A
ROBO NO ISHI • 1960 • Hisamatsu Seiji • JPN • WAYSIDE PEBBLE
ROBOCOP • 1987 • Verhoeven Paul* • USA
ROBOCOP II • 1990 • Kershner Irvin • USA
ROBOJOX • 1988 • Gordon Stuart • USA
ROBOT • 1960 • Dobrila Sasa • ANS • YGS
ROBOT, THE • 1932 • Fleischer Dave • ANS • USA
ROBOT HOLOCAUST • 1985 • Kincaid Tim • USA
ROBOT HUMANO, EL • 1959 • Portillo Rafael • MXC • ROBOT VS. THE AZTEC MUMMY, THE (USA) ○ AZTEC ROBOT VS. THE HUMAN ROBOT, THE ○ MOMIA AZTECA CONTRA EL ROBOT HUMANO, LA
ROBOT MONSTER • 1953 • Tucker Phil • USA • MONSTERS FROM THE MOON ○ MONSTER FROM MARS
ROBOT OF REGALIO • 1954 • *Reed Roland (P)* • MTV • USA
ROBOT ORDONNATEUR, LE • 1970 • Moreau Michel • DCS • CND
ROBOT RABBIT • 1953 • Freleng Friz • ANS • USA
ROBOT RINGER • 1962 • Kneitel Seymour • ANS • USA
ROBOT RIVAL • 1964 • Kneitel Seymour • ANS • USA
ROBOT VS. THE AZTEC MUMMY, THE (USA) see **ROBOT HUMANO, EL** • 1959
ROBOT WRECKS • 1941 • Cahn Edward L. • SHT • USA
ROBOTECH: THE MOVIE • 1986 • Macek Carl, Noburo Ishiguro • ANM • USA
ROBOTER, DER • 1969 • *Defa* • ANS • FRG • COMPUTER, THE
ROBOTNICY '80 • 1980 • Chodakowski Andrzej, Zajaczkowski Andrzej • PLN • WORKERS '80
ROBOTS • 1932 • Deslaw Eugene • FRN
ROBOTS IN TOYLAND • 1965 • Rasinski Connie • ANS • USA
ROBOTS OF DEATH, THE see **AUTOMATAS DE LA MUERTE, LOS** • 1961
ROBSON'S REVOLVING HEEL PADS • 1909 • *Graphic* • UKN
ROBUS see **YEKEBEZAN** • 1967
ROBUST PATIENT, A • 1911 • *Selig* • USA
ROBUST ROMEO, A • 1914 • Henderson Dell • USA
ROC-A-BYE SINBAD • 1964 • Rasinski Connie • ANS • USA
ROCAMBOLE • 1914 • Denola Georges • FRN
ROCAMBOLE • 1923 • Maudru Charles • FRN
ROCAMBOLE • 1932 • Rosca Gabriel • FRN
ROCAMBOLE • 1946 • Peon Ramon • MXC
ROCAMBOLE • 1947 • de Baroncelli Jacques • FRN, ITL
ROCAMBOLE • 1963 • Borderie Bernard • FRN, ITL
ROCAMBOLE VS. LA SECTA DEL ESCORPION • 1965 • Gomez Muriel Emilio • MXC
ROCAMBOLE VS. LAS MUJERES ARPIAS • 1965 • Gomez Muriel Emilio • MXC • ROCAMBOLE VS. THE HARPY WOMEN
ROCAMBOLE VS. THE HARPY WOMEN see **ROCAMBOLE VS. LAS MUJERES ARPIAS** • 1965
ROCCE INSANGUINATE see **ALTURA** • 1951
ROCCIA INCANTATA, LA • 1950 • Morelli Giulio • ITL
ROCCO AND HIS BROTHERS (USA) see **ROCCO E I SUOI FRATELLI** • 1960
ROCCO E I SUOI FRATELLI • 1960 • Visconti Luchino • ITL, FRN • ROCCO ET SES FRERES (FRN) ○ ROCCO AND HIS BROTHERS (USA)
ROCCO E LE SORELLE • 1961 • Simonelli Giorgio C. • ITL
ROCCO ET SES FRERES (FRN) see **ROCCO E I SUOI FRATELLI** • 1960
ROCCO PAPALEO see **PERMETTE? ROCCO PAPALEO** • 1971
ROCHE AUX MOUETTES, LA • 1932 • Monca Georges • FRN
ROCHE DE FEU, LA • 1956 • Tavano Fred • SHT • FRN
ROCHESTERSTREET 29 see **SILBERKONIG 4, DER** • 1921
ROCHEUSES 1950 • 1950 • Tessier Albert • DCS • CND
ROCHIA ALBA DE DANTELA • 1989 • Pita Dan • RMN • WHITE LACE DRESS, THE
ROCINANTE • 1987 • Guedes Ann, Guedes Eduardo • UKN
ROCIO • 1980 • Ruiz Fernando • DOC • SPN
ROCIO AND JOSE see **ROCIO Y JOSE** • 1983
ROCIO DE LA MANCHA • 1963 • Lucia Luis • SPN
ROCIO Y JOSE • 1983 • Garcia Pelayo Gonzalo • SPN • ROCIO AND JOSE
ROCK '70 see **GROUPIES** • 1970
ROCK-A-BYE • 1974 • Bensimon Jacques • DOC • CND
ROCK-A-BYE BABY • 1920 • Roach Hal • SHT • USA
ROCK-A-BYE BABY • 1958 • Tashlin Frank • USA
ROCK-A-BYE BEAR • 1952 • Avery Tex • ANS • USA
ROCK-A-BYE COWBOY • 1933 • Stevens George • SHT • USA
ROCK-A-BYE GATOR • 1962 • Hannah Jack • ANS • USA
ROCK-A-DOODLE • 1990 • Bluth Don • ANM • IRL
ROCK ALL NIGHT • 1958 • Corman Roger • USA
ROCK AND TORAH • 1982 • Grynbaum Marc-Andre • FRN • PREFERE, LE
ROCK AROUND THE CLOCK • 1956 • Sears Fred F. • USA
ROCK AROUND THE WORLD (USA) see **TOMMY STEELE STORY, THE** • 1957
ROCK, BABY, ROCK IT • 1957 • Sporup Murray Douglas • USA
ROCK BOY • 1985 • I Du-Yong • SKR
ROCK CITY • 1981 • Clifton Peter • DOC • UKN
ROCK CITY see **SOUND OF THE CITY** • 1973
ROCK CONVERT, THE see **ROCK TERITO** • 1988
ROCK 'EM COWBOY • 1957 • Staub Ralph • SHT • USA
ROCK HOUND MAGOO • 1957 • Burness Pete • ANS • USA
ROCK HOUNDS, THE • 1968 • Tendlar Dave • ANS • USA
ROCK ISLAND TRAIL • 1950 • Kane Joseph • USA • TRANSCONTINENT EXPRESS (UKN)
ROCK KIDS see **YAOGUN QINGNIAN** • 1988
ROCK 'N' RODENT • 1967 • Levitow Abe • ANS • USA
ROCK 'N ROLL • 1959 • Robinson Lee • DOC • ASL
ROCK 'N' ROLL • 1978 • De Sisti Vittorio • ITL
ROCK 'N' ROLL COWBOYS • 1987 • Stewart Rob • ASL
ROCK 'N' ROLL DIGGER see **ROKKIDIGGARI** • 1982
ROCK 'N' ROLL HIGH SCHOOL • 1979 • Arkush Allan • USA
ROCK 'N' ROLL JAMBOREE see **ROCK 'N' ROLL REVUE** • 1956
ROCK 'N' ROLL MOM • 1988 • Schultz Michael • TVM • USA
ROCK 'N' ROLL NIGHTMARE see **EDGE OF HELL** • 1986
ROCK 'N' ROLL REVUE • 1956 • Kohn Joseph • USA • HARLEM ROCK 'N' ROLL (UKN) ○ ROCK 'N' ROLL JAMBOREE
ROCK 'N' ROLL SWINDLE, THE see **GREAT ROCK 'N' ROLL SWINDLE, THE** • 1980
ROCK 'N' ROLL WOLF • 1978 • Bostan Elisabeta • RMN, FRN, USS
ROCK 'N ROLL WRESTLING WOMEN VS. THE AZTEC MUMMY • 1986 • Cardona Rene, San Fernando Manuel • MXC, USA
ROCK 'N' RULE • 1983 • Smith Clive A. • ANM • CND • ROCK & RULE
ROCK OF AGES • 1902 • *Biograph* • USA
ROCK OF AGES • 1902 • Porter Edwin S. • *Edison* • USA
ROCK OF AGES • 1912 • *Theby Rosemary* • USA
ROCK OF AGES • 1918 • Phillips Bertram • UKN
ROCK OF AGES • 1928 • Parkinson H. B., Edwards J. Steven • UKN
ROCK OF FRIENDSHIP, THE (UKN) see **WYOMING** • 1928
ROCK OF HOPE, THE • 1914 • *Myers Harry* • USA
ROCK OF RICHES, THE • 1916 • Smalley Phillips, Weber Lois • SHT • USA
ROCK ON REJKJAVIK • 1982 • Fridriksson Fridrik Thor • ICL
ROCK POOLS • 1936 • Field Mary • UKN
ROCK PRETTY BABY • 1956 • Bartlett Richard • USA
ROCK RIVER RENEGADES • 1942 • Luby S. Roy • USA
ROCK, ROCK, ROCK! • 1956 • Price Will • USA
ROCK & RULE see **ROCK 'N' RULE** • 1983
ROCK SHOW • 1981 • *Wings* • UKN • ROCKSHOW
ROCK TERITO • 1988 • Xantus Janos • HNG • ROCK CONVERT, THE
ROCK YOU SINNERS • 1957 • Kavanagh Denis • UKN
ROCKABILLY BABY • 1957 • Claxton William F. • USA
ROCKABILLY LADY see **ONNA WA TEIKO SURU** • 1960
ROCKABYE • 1932 • Cukor George • USA
ROCKABYE • 1986 • Michaels Richard • TVM • USA
ROCKABYE LEGEND see **LEGEND OF ROCKABYE POINT, THE** • 1955
ROCKABYE RHYTHM • 1945 • Collins Lewis D. • SHT • USA
ROCKED TO SLEEP • 1920 • Dieltz Charles, Luddy I. • SHT • USA
ROCKER, LE • 1975 • Dussault Louis • CND
ROCKERS • 1978 • Bafaloukos Theodoros • JMC
ROCKET ATTACK, U.S.A. • 1960 • Mahon Barry • USA
ROCKET BYE BABY • 1956 • Jones Charles M. • ANS • USA
ROCKET FROM CALABUCH (USA) see **CALABUIG** • 1956
ROCKET FROM FENWICK, A see **MOUSE ON THE MOON, THE** • 1963
ROCKET GIBRALTAR • 1988 • Petrie Daniel • USA
ROCKET GIRL • 1962 • IND
ROCKET MAN, THE • 1954 • Rudolph Oscar • USA
ROCKET RACKET • 1962 • Hannah Jack • ANS • USA
ROCKET RACKET, THE • 1966 • Post Howard • ANS • USA
ROCKET SHIP see **SPACESHIP TO THE UNKNOWN** • 1936
ROCKET SHIP (UKN) see **MARS ATTACKS THE WORLD** • 1938
ROCKET SHIP X-M • 1950 • Neumann Kurt • USA • EXPEDITION MOON ○ ROCKETSHIP X-M
ROCKET SQUAD • 1956 • Jones Charles M. • ANS • USA
ROCKET TARZAN • 1963 • Patel B. J. • IND
ROCKET TO MARS • 1946 • Tytla Bill • ANS • USA
ROCKET TO NOWHERE see **KLAUN FERDINAND A RAKETA** • 1962
ROCKET TO THE MOON see **CAT WOMEN OF THE MOON** • 1953
ROCKET TO THE MOON see **JULES VERNE'S ROCKET TO THE MOON** • 1967
ROCKETEERS • 1932 • Foster John, Rufle George • ANS • USA
ROCKETMAN FLIES AGAIN • 1966 • Glut Don • SHT • USA
ROCKETS GALORE • 1958 • Relph Michael • UKN • MAD LITTLE ISLAND (USA)
ROCKETS IN THE DUNES • 1960 • Hammond William C. • UKN
ROCKETS MUST NOT TAKE OFF, THE • 1964 • Shvachko A., Timonishin Anton • USS
ROCKETS OF THE FUTURE • 1948 • Parker Benjamin R. • SHT • USA
ROCKETSHIP • 1944 • Beebe Ford, Hill Robert F. • USA
ROCKETSHIP X-M see **ROCKET SHIP X-M** • 1950
ROCKETTES see **LEGS** • 1982
ROCKFORD FILES, THE • 1974 • Heffron Richard T. • TVM • USA
ROCKIN' IN THE ROCKIES • 1945 • Keays Vernon • USA • PARTNERS IN FORTUNE (UKN)
ROCKIN' ROAD TRIP • 1986 • Olsen William • USA
ROCKIN' THE BLUES • 1957 • Rosenblum Arthur • USA
ROCKIN' THROUGH THE ROCKIES • 1940 • White Jules • SHT • USA
ROCKIN' WITH SEKA see **ROCKING WITH SEKA** • 1980
ROCKING CHAIR REBELLION • 1981 • Larry Sheldon • MTV • USA
ROCKING HORSE, THE • 1962 • Scott James • UKN
ROCKING HORSE WINNER, THE • 1949 • Pelissier Anthony • UKN
ROCKING MOON • 1926 • Melford George • USA
ROCKING SILVER • 1984 • Clausen Erik • DNM
ROCKING THE FOUNDATIONS • 1986 • Fiske Pat • DOC • ASL
ROCKING WITH SEKA • 1980 • Zigowitz Ziggy Jr. • USA • ROCKIN' WITH SEKA ○ SEKA'S CRUISE
ROCKINGHAM SHOOT, THE • 1988 • Hickey Kieran • IRL
ROCKINGHORSE see **SUSETZ** • 1977
ROCK'N ROLL HOT WAX see **AMERICAN HOT WAX** • 1978
ROCKPEOPLE, THE see **SKALNI PLEMENO** • 1944
ROCKS OF VALPRE, THE • 1919 • Elvey Maurice • UKN
ROCKS OF VALPRE, THE • 1935 • Edwards Henry • UKN • HIGH TREASON (USA)
ROCKSHOW see **ROCK SHOW** • 1981
ROCKULA • 1989 • Bercovici Luca • USA
ROCKY • 1948 • Karlson Phil • USA
ROCKY • 1976 • Avildsen John G. • USA
ROCKY EDEN • 1949 • Sparling Gordon • DCS • CND
ROCKY HORROR PICTURE SHOW, THE • 1975 • Sharman Jim • USA, UKN
ROCKY II • 1979 • Stallone Sylvester • USA
ROCKY III • 1982 • Stallone Sylvester • USA
ROCKY IV • 1985 • Stallone Sylvester • USA
ROCKY JONES, SPACE RANGER • 1952 • Beaudine William, Morse Hollingsworth • SER • USA
ROCKY MOUNTAIN • 1950 • Keighley William • USA
ROCKY MOUNTAIN GRANDEUR • 1937 • Smith • SHT • USA
ROCKY MOUNTAIN MYSTERY • 1935 • Barton Charles T. • USA • FIGHTING WESTERNER
ROCKY MOUNTAIN RANGERS • 1940 • Sherman George • USA
ROCKY RHODES • 1934 • Raboch Alfred • USA
ROCKY ROAD, THE • 1910 • Griffith D. W. • USA
ROCKY ROAD OF LOVE, THE • 1914 • Baker George D. • USA
ROCKY ROAD TO RUIN, THE • 1943 • Sommer Paul • ANS • USA
ROCKY V: THE FINAL BELL • 1990 • Avildsen John G. • USA
ROCKY'S KNIFE see **ROCKYS MESSER** • 1967
ROCKYS MESSER • 1967 • Mock Joachim • FRG • ROCKY'S KNIFE
ROCNIK JEDENADVACET • 1957 • Gajer Vaclav • CZC • BORN IN 1921 ○ BORN 1921
ROCOCO COMES TO THE ISLAND OF THE HUZZIS • Karner Andi, Werner Hans • ANM • AUS
ROCZNICA • 1969 • Trzos-Rastawiecki Andrzej • DOC • PLN • ANNIVERSARY, THE
ROD • 1973 • Robertson Michael • SHT • USA
ROD, THE see **MAULA BUX** • 1988
ROD FLASH CONQUERS INFINITY • 1973 • Burtt Benjamin, Anderson Richard • SHT • USA
ROD STEWART AND FACES AND KEITH RICHARDS • 1977 • Grod Roger • DOC • UKN
RODA DAGEN • 1931 • Edgren Gustaf • SWD • RED DAY, THE
RODA HASTARNA, DE • 1954 • Johansson Ivar • SWD
RODA KAPPAN, DEN • 1967 • Axel Gabriel • SWD, DNM, ICL • RODE KAPPE, DEN (DNM) ○ HAGBARD AND SIGNE (USA) ○ RED MANTLE, THE ○ RAUTHA SKIKKJAN
RODA PRESA, A • 1954 • Mendes Joao • SHT • PRT
RODA TORNET, DET • 1914 • Stiller Mauritz • SWD • RED TOWER, THE ○ MASTER, THE
RODA TRIANGELN • 1937 • *Europa Film* • SWD
RODAN see **SORANO DAIKAIJYU** • 1956
RODAS DE LISBOA • 1945 • Ribeiro Francisco • SHT • PRT
RODBLATT PARADIS • 1972 • Tuhus Oddvar Bull • NRW • RED-AND-BLUE PARADISE
RODDA KALBI • 1958 • Zoulfakar Ezeldin • EGY
RODE ENGE, DE • 1945 • Ipsen Bodil, Lauritzen Lau Jr. • DNM • RED MEADOWS (USA) ○ RED EARTH, THE
RODE ENKE, DEN see **ROVEDDERKOPPEN** • 1915
RODE HESTE VINDER LOBET, DE • 1968 • Meineche Annelise • DNM • RED HORSES WIN THE RACE, THE
RODE KAPPE, DEN (DNM) see **RODA KAPPAN, DEN** • 1967
RODE RUBIN, DEN see **SANGEN OM DEN RODE RUBIN** • 1970
RODELHEXE, DIE • 1921 • Terner Rudolf • FRG
RODELKAVALIER, DER • 1918 • Lubitsch Ernst • FRG
RODENDANSKA PRICA • 1969 • Grgic Zlatko, Kolar Boris, Zaninovic Ante • ANS • YGS, FRG • ARTS AND FLOWERS
RODENT TO STARDOM • 1967 • Lovy Alex • ANS • USA
RODEO • 1952 • Beaudine William • USA
RODEO, THE • 1929 • *Sennett Mack (P)* • SHT • USA
RODEO DOUGH • 1931 • *Mintz Charles (P)* • ANS • USA
RODEO DOUGH • 1940 • Lee Sammy • SHT • USA
RODEO GIRL • 1980 • Cooper Jackie • TVM • USA
RODEO KING AND THE SENORITA • 1951 • Ford Philip • USA
RODEO MIXUP, A • 1924 • Ford Francis • USA • WINGS OF THE WEST
RODEO RHYTHM • 1942 • Newmeyer Fred • USA
RODEO RIDER • 1971 • Woods Grahame • CND
RODEO ROMEO • 1946 • Sparber I. • ANS • USA
RODERICK'S RIDE • 1912 • *Selig* • USA
RODH VRIKSHA • 1985 • Khosla Raj • SHT • IND
RODIN • 1942 • Lucot Rene • FRN
RODIN • 1970 • Kohanyi Julius • CND

RODNAYA KROV • 1964 • Yershov Mikhail • USS • TIES OF BLOOD, THE ○ YOUR OWN BLOOD ○ BLOOD TIES ○ OWN FLESH AND BLOOD

RODNEY see **KEEP 'EM ROLLING** • 1934

RODNEY FAILS TO QUALIFY • 1924 • Wilson Andrew P. • UKN

RODNEY STEPS IN • 1931 • Newall Guy • UKN

RODNEY STONE • 1920 • Nash Percy • UKN

RODNEY'S BOX • Heinz John • ANS • USA

RODNIA • 1983 • Mikhalkov Nikita • USS • FAMILY RELATIONS ○ KIN

RODOGUNE • 1911 • de Morlhon Camille • FRN

RODOLPHE BRESDIN • 1962 • Kaplan Nelly • FRN

RODRIGO D. see **RODRIGO D. –NO FUTURO** • 1989

RODRIGO D. –NO FUTURE see **RODRIGO D. –NO FUTURO** • 1989

RODRIGO D. –NO FUTURO • 1989 • Gaviria Victor • CLM • RODRIGO D. –NO FUTURE ○ RODRIGO D.

RODRIGUEZ AU PAYS DES MERGUEZ • 1980 • Clair Philippe • FRN, TNS • PARODIE DU CID, LA

RODRIGUEZ, SUPERNUMERARIO • 1948 • Cahen Enrique • ARG

RODS OF WRATH • 1915 • Penn M. O. • USA

RODTOTTERNE OG TYRANNOS • 1988 • Johansen Svend • DNM • REDTOPS AND TYRANNOS, THE

RODZICE • 1961 • Ziarnik Jerzy • DOC • PLN • PARENTS

RODZINA • 1971 • Halladin Danuta • DOC • PLN • FAMILY, THE

RODZINA • 1975 • Wojciechowski Krzysztof • PLN • FAMILY, A

RODZINA CZLOWIECZA • 1966 • Slesicki Wladyslaw • DOC • PLN • FAMILY OF MAN, THE

RODZINA INDONEZYJSKA • 1973 • Giersz Witold • ANS • PLN • INDONESIAN FAMILY, AN

ROEI NO UTA • 1938 • Mizoguchi Kenji (c/d) • JPN • SONG OF THE CAMP (USA)

ROGACIANO EL HUAPANGUERO • 1957 • Morayta Miguel • MXC

ROGELIA • 1962 • Gil Rafael • SPN

ROGER AND ME • 1989 • Moore Michael • DOC • USA

ROGER CORMAN: HOLLYWOOD'S WILD ANGEL • 1978 • Blackwood Christian • DOC • USA

ROGER & HARRY: THE MITERA TARGET • 1977 • Starrett Jack • TVM • USA • QUENTIN METHOD, THE ○ LOVE FOR RANSOM

ROGER-LA-HONTE • 1922 • de Baroncelli Jacques • FRN

ROGER LA HONTE • 1932 • Roudes Gaston • FRN

ROGER-LA-HONTE • 1945 • Cayatte Andre • FRN

ROGER LA HONTE see **TRAPPOLA PER L'ASSASSINO** • 1966

ROGER, THE PRIDE OF THE RANCH • 1913 • *Nestor* • USA

ROGER THE STOOLIE see **STOOLIE, THE** • 1972

ROGER TOUHY, GANGSTER • 1944 • Florey Robert • USA • LAST GANGSTER, THE (UKN)

ROGNEDA • 1911 • Protazanov Yakov • USS

ROGOPAG see **ROGOPAG LAVIAMOCI IL CERVELLO** • 1963

ROGOPAG LAVIAMOCI IL CERVELLO • 1963 • Rossellini Roberto, Godard Jean-Luc, Gregoretti Ugo, Pasolini Pier Paolo • ITL, FRN • ROGOPAG

ROGUE, THE • 1918 • Gillstrom Arvid E. • SHT • USA

ROGUE AND RICHES • 1920 • Franklin Harry L. • USA • ROUGE AND RICHES

ROGUE COP • 1954 • Rowland Roy • USA • KELVANEY

ROGUE IN LOVE, A • 1916 • Merwin Bannister • UKN

ROGUE IN LOVE, A • 1922 • Brouett Albert • UKN

ROGUE LION see **MAKULU** • 1972

ROGUE MALE • 1976 • Donner Clive • TVM • UKN

ROGUE OF THE RANGE • 1936 • Luby S. Roy • USA

ROGUE OF THE RIO GRANDE • 1930 • Bennet Spencer Gordon • USA

ROGUE OF THE RIO GRANDE see **LUCKY CISCO KID** • 1940

ROGUE RIVER • 1950 • Rawlins John • USA

ROGUE SONG, THE • 1929 • Barrymore Lionel • USA

ROGUE SYNDICATE, THE • 1915 • *Courtot Marguerite* • USA

ROGUE WITH A HEART, THE • 1916 • Hill Robert F. • SHT • USA

ROGUES see **TRUHANES** • 1984

ROGUES, THE see **PICARI, I** • 1988

ROGUES AND ROMANCE • 1920 • Seitz George B. • USA

ROGUES' GALLERY • 1945 • Herman Al • USA

ROGUE'S GALLERY • 1968 • Horn Leonard • USA

ROGUES' GALLERY, THE • 1913 • Lucas Wilfred • USA

ROGUES' GALLERY (UKN) see **DEVIL'S TRAIL, THE** • 1942

ROGUE'S MARCH • 1952 • Davis Allan • USA

ROGUE'S NEMESIS • 1916 • Horne James W. • SHT • USA

ROGUE'S NEST, THE • 1917 • MacDonald Donald • SHT • USA

ROGUES OF LONDON • 1915 • Haldane Bert? • UKN

ROGUES OF PARIS • 1913 • Blache Alice • USA

ROGUES OF SHERWOOD FOREST • 1950 • Douglas Gordon • USA

ROGUES OF THE TURF • 1910 • *Walturdaw* • UKN

ROGUES OF THE TURF • 1913 • Noy Wilfred • USA

ROGUES OF THE WEST see **TROUBLE BUSTER, THE** • 1925

ROGUE'S PAWN, THE • 1916 • Ellis Robert • SHT • USA

ROGUE'S REGIMENT • 1948 • Florey Robert • USA

ROGUE'S ROMANCE, A • 1919 • Young James • USA

ROGUE'S TAVERN, THE • 1936 • Hill Robert F. • USA

ROGUE'S TRIAL, THE see **COMPADECIDA, A** • 1969

ROGUES' TRICKS (USA) see **DOUCHE D'EAU BOUILLANTE, LA** • 1907

ROGUE'S WIFE, A • 1915 • Nash Percy • UKN

ROGUE'S YARN • 1957 • Sewell Vernon • UKN

ROHFILM • 1968 • Hein Wilhelm, Hein Birgit • FRG

ROI, LE • 1936 • Colombier Piere • FRN • ROI S'AMUSE, LE

ROI, LE • 1949 • Sauvajon Marc-Gilbert • FRN • ROYAL AFFAIR, A (USA)

ROI BIS, LE • 1932 • Beaudoin Robert • FRN

ROI DE CAMARGUE • 1934 • de Baroncelli Jacques • FRN

ROI DE CAMARGUE, LE • 1921 • Hugon Andre • FRN

ROI DE COEUR, LE • 1966 • de Broca Philippe • FRN, ITL • TUTTI PAZZI MENO IO (ITL) ○ KING OF HEARTS (USA)

ROI DE LA COUTURE, LE see **COUTURIER DE MON COEUR** • 1935

ROI DE LA MER, LE • 1917 • de Baroncelli Jacques • FRN

ROI DE LA MONTAGNE, LE • 1915 • Perret Leonce • FRN

ROI DE LA PEDALE, LE • 1925 • Champreux Maurice • FRN

ROI DE LA VITESSE, LE • 1924 • Diamant-Berger Henri • FRN

ROI DE L'AIR, LE • 1913 • Zecca Ferdinand (c/d) • FRN

ROI DE PARIS, LE • 1922 • Maudru Charles, de Marsan Maurice • FRN

ROI DE PARIS, LE • 1930 • Mittler Leo • FRN

ROI DE PERFUMS, LE • 1910 • *Gance Abel* • FRN

ROI DE THULE, LE • 1910 • Feuillade Louis • FRN • LURED BY A PHANTOM OR THE KING OF THULE (USA)

ROI DES AULNES, LE • 1908 • de Chomon Segundo • FRN • KING OF THE ALDERS, THE

ROI DES AULNES, LE • 1930 • Iribe Marie-Louise • FRN • ERL KING, THE

ROI DES BRICOLEURS, LE • 1977 • Mocky Jean-Pierre • FRN

ROI DES CAMELOTS, LE • 1950 • Berthomieu Andre • FRN

ROI DES CHAMPS-ELYSEES, LE • 1934 • Nosseck Max • FRN

ROI DES CONS, LE • 1981 • Confortes Claude • FRN

ROI DES DOLLARS, LE see **MAIN DU PROFESSEUR HAMILTON, LA** • 1903

ROI DES FACTEURS, LE see **COSTAUD DES P.T.T., LE** • 1931

ROI DES GALEJEURS, LE • 1940 • Rivers Fernand • FRN

ROI DES MEDIUMS, LE • 1910 • Melies Georges • FRN • APPARITIONS FANTOMATIQUES

ROI DES MONTAGNES, LE see **VOLEUR DE FEMMES** • 1963

ROI DES PALACES ,LE • 1932 • Gallone Carmine • FRN

ROI DES RESQUILLEURS, LE • 1930 • Colombier Piere • FRN

ROI DES RESQUILLEURS, LE • 1945 • Devaivre Jean • FRN

ROI DES TIREURS, LE • 1905 • Melies Georges • FRN • KING OF THE SHARPSHOOTERS, THE (USA)

ROI DU BLA-BLA-BLA, LE • 1950 • Labro Maurice • FRN

ROI DU CAMEMBERT, LE • 1931 • Mourre Antoine • FRN

ROI DU CIRAGE, LE • 1931 • Colombier Piere • FRN

ROI DU CIRQUE, LE (FRN) see **ZIRKUSKONIG, DER** • 1924

ROI DU MAQUILLAGE, LE • 1904 • Melies Georges • FRN • KING OF THE MACKEREL FISHERS, THE ○ UNTAMEABLE WHISKERS, THE (USA)

ROI DU MONT BLANC, LE see **REVE ETERNEL** • 1934

ROI DU VILLAGE, LE • 1962 • Gruel Henri • ANM • FRN • MOISE ET L'AMOUR

ROI ES MORT EN EXIL, LE • 1970 • de Medeiros Ricardo Beby • BNN

ROI ET L'OISEAU, LE • 1967 • Grimault Paul • ANM • FRN

ROI ET L'OISEAU, LE • 1979 • Grimault Paul • ANM • FRN • KING AND THE BIRD, THE ○ KING AND MISTER BIRD, THE

ROI LEAR AU VILLAGE, LE • 1911 • Feuillade Louis • FRN

ROI PANDORE, LE • 1949 • Berthomieu Andre • FRN

ROI PELE, LE see **PELE** • 1977

ROI S'AMUSE, LE see **ROI, LE** • 1936

ROI SANS DIVERTISSEMENT, UN • 1962 • Leterrier Francois • FRN • POURSUITE, LA ○ PURSUIT, THE

ROI S'ENNUIE, LE see **ECHEC AU ROI** • 1931

ROIS DE LA FLOTTE, LES • 1938 • Pujol Rene • FRN

ROIS DU SPORT, LES • 1937 • Colombier Piere • FRN

ROIS MAUDITS, LES • Barma Claude • MTV • FRN

ROJO • 1964 • Tsuchimoto Noriaki • JPN • ALONG MY ROAD

ROJO NO REIKAN • 1921 • Murata Minoru • JPN • SOULS ON THE ROAD

ROJO Y NEGRO • 1942 • Arevalo Carlos • SPN

ROK 1946 • 1946 • Bossak Jerzy • DOC • PLN • YEAR 1946, THE

ROK 1949 • 1949 • Bossak Jerzy • DOC • PLN • YEAR 1949, THE

ROK FRANKA W. • 1967 • Karabasz Kazimierz • DOC • PLN • YEAR OF FRANEK W., A ○ FRANK W'S YEAR ○ YEAR IN FRANK'S LIFE, A

ROK PIERWSWY • 1960 • Lesiewicz Witold • PLN • YEAR ONE ○ FIRST YEAR, THE

ROK SPOKOJNEGO SLONCA • 1985 • Zanussi Krzysztof • PLN • YEAR OF THE QUIET SUN, THE ○ YEAR OF QUIET SUN, A

ROKH • 1975 • Sadeghi Ali Akbar • IRN • ROOK, THE ○ CHESS

ROKKIDIGGARI • 1982 • Lehmuskallio Jouko • FNL • ROCK 'N' ROLL DIGGER

ROKONOK • 1954 • Mariassy Felix • PLN • RELATIVES

ROKOVAYA OSHIBKA • 1989 • Khubov Nikita • USS • FATEFUL MISTAKE

ROKUDENASHI • 1960 • Yoshida Yoshishige • JPN • GOOD-FOR-NOTHING

ROKUJO YUKIYAMA TSUMUGI • 1965 • Matsuyama Zenzo • JPN • DARK THE MOUNTAIN SNOW (USA)

ROKUMEIKAN • 1985 • Ichikawa Kon • JPN • ROKUMEIKAN, HIGH SOCIETY OF MEIJI

ROKUMEIKAN, HIGH SOCIETY OF MEIJI see **ROKUMEIKAN** • 1985

ROLAND THE MIGHTY (USA) see **ORLANDO E I PALADINI DI FRANCIA** • 1956

ROLANDA POLONKSY, SCULPTOR • 1971 • Niskin Lionel • UKN

ROLANDE MET DE BLES • 1970 • Verhavert Roland • BLG

ROLE, THE see **BHUMIKA** • 1976

ROLE DES FEMMES DANS LE MONDE DU TRAVAIL, LE • 1968 • Dansereau Fernand • DCS • CND

ROLE EFFACE DE MARIE, LE • 1978 • Mongredien Jean-Michel • FRN

ROLE OF MY FAMILY IN WORLD REVOLUTION, THE see **ULOGA MOJE PORODICE U SVETSKOJ REVOLUCIJI** • 1971

ROLF LIEBERMANN • Calderon Gerald • DOC • FRN

ROLL ALONG, COWBOY • 1938 • Meins Gus • USA

ROLL-CALL see **PEREKLICHKA** • 1965

ROLL-CALL see **APEL** • 1971

ROLL CALL see **APEL** • 1971

ROLL-CALL FOR THE DEAD see **APEL POLEGLYCH** • 1957

ROLL CALL FOR THE INSURGENTS • 1961 • Kidawa Janusz • DOC • PLN

ROLL, FREDDY, ROLL • 1975 • Persky Bill • TVM • USA

ROLL OF THUNDER • 1978 • Smight Jack • TVM • USA

ROLL ON, TEXAS MOON • 1946 • Witney William • USA

ROLL ON (UKN) see **LAWLESS PLAINSMEN** • 1942

ROLL, THUNDER, ROLL • 1949 • Collins Lewis D. • USA

ROLL, WAGONS, ROLL • 1940 • Herman Al • USA

ROLL YOUR OWN • 1921 • *International Film Service* • ANS • USA

ROLL YOUR PEANUT • 1914 • *Joker* • USA

ROLLAND GARROS • 1975 • Reichenbach Francois • MTV • FRN

ROLLED STOCKINGS • 1927 • Rosson Richard • USA

ROLLENDE HOTEL, DAS • 1918 • Piel Harry • FRG

ROLLENDE KORRIDOR, DER • 1920 • Herbig Paul • FRG

ROLLENDE KUGEL, DIE • 1919 • Biebrach Rudolf • FRG

ROLLENDE KUGEL, DIE • 1927 • Schonfelder Erich • FRG

ROLLENDE RAD, DAS • 1935 • Reiniger Lotte • ANS • FRG

ROLLENDE SCHICKSAL, DAS • 1923 • Osten Franz • FRG

ROLLER AND THE VIOLIN, THE see **KATOK I SKRIPKA** • 1961

ROLLER BLADE see **ROLLERBLADE** • 1986

ROLLER BOOGIE • 1979 • Lester Mark L. • USA

ROLLER DERBY (UKN) see **DERBY** • 1971

ROLLER MANIA • 1980 • Webb William • DOC • UKN

ROLLER SKATE see **DANCE MOVIE** • 1963

ROLLERBABIES • 1976 • Stevens Carter • USA

ROLLERBALL • 1975 • Jewison Norman • USA

ROLLERBLADE • 1986 • Jackson Donald G. • USA • ROLLER BLADE

ROLLERCOASTER • 1977 • Goldstone James • USA

ROLLICKING ADVENTURES OF ELIZA FRASER, THE • 1976 • Burstall Tim • ASL • ELIZA FRASER ○ FAITHFUL NARRATIVE OF THE CAPTURE, SUFFERINGS AND MIRACULOUS ESCAPE OF ELIZA FRASER, A

ROLLICKING ROD'S BIG LARK • 1912 • *Nestor* • USA

ROLLIN' PLAINS • 1938 • Herman Al • USA

ROLLIN' WESTWARD • 1939 • Herman Al • USA

ROLLING ACROSS THE ATLANTIC see **TRAVERSEE DE L'ATLANTIQUE A LA RAME** • 1978

ROLLING ALONG • 1930 • Ray Albert • SHT • USA

ROLLING ALONG see **MUSIC GOES ROUND, THE** • 1936

ROLLING ALONG HAVING MY UPS AND DOWNS • 1929 • Aylott Dave, Symmons E. F. • SHT • UKN

ROLLING CARAVANS • 1938 • Levering Joseph • USA

ROLLING DOWN THE GREAT DIVIDE • 1942 • Newfield Sam • USA

ROLLING HOME • 1926 • Seiter William A. • USA

ROLLING HOME • 1938 • Ince Ralph • UKN

ROLLING HOME • 1947 • Berke William • USA

ROLLING HOME • 1974 • Witzig Paul • ASL

ROLLING HOME TO TEXAS • 1940 • Herman Al • USA

ROLLING IN MONEY • 1934 • Parker Albert • UKN

ROLLING MAN • 1972 • Hyams Peter • TVM • USA

ROLLING MILL, THE see **WALCOWNIA** • 1956

ROLLING RICE BALL, THE • *Gakken Company* • ANM • JPN

ROLLING ROAD, THE • 1927 • Cutts Graham • UKN

ROLLING SEA see **BARANDE HAV** • 1951

ROLLING STONE, A • 1919 • Parrott Charles • USA

ROLLING STONES • 1916 • Henderson Dell • USA

ROLLING STONES • 1936 • *Terry Paul/ Moser Frank (P)* • ANS • USA

ROLLING STONES ROCK AND ROLL CIRCUS, THE • 1968 • Lindsay-Hogg Michael • USA

ROLLING THUNDER • 1977 • Flynn John • USA

ROLLING TO RUIN • 1916 • Kernan Henry • SHT • USA

ROLLING VENGEANCE • 1987 • Stern Steven Hilliard • USA

ROLLOVER • 1981 • Pakula Alan J. • USA

ROLY-POLY see **PRZEKLADANIEC** • 1968

ROM • 1989 • Karamaggio Menelaos • DOC • GRC

ROMA • 1972 • Fellini Federico • ITL, FRN • FELLINI-ROMA (FRN) ○ FELLINI'S ROMA (USA)

ROMA • 1990 • Antonioni Michelangelo • SHT • ITL

ROMA A MANO ARMATA • 1976 • Lenzi Umberto • ITL

ROMA BENE • 1971 • Lizzani Carlo • ITL

ROMA, CITTA APERTA • 1945 • Rossellini Roberto • ITL • OPEN CITY (USA) ○ ROME, OPEN CITY ○ CITTA APERTA

ROMA, CITTA LIBERA • 1948 • Pagliero Marcello • ITL • NOTTE PORTA CONSIGLIO, LA

ROMA COME CHICAGO • 1968 • De Martino Alberto • ITL • ROME LIKE CHICAGO (USA) ○ BANDITI A ROMA ○ BANDITS IN ROME

ROMA CONTRA ROMA • 1963 • Vari Giuseppe • ITL • WAR OF THE ZOMBIES, THE (USA) ○ NIGHT STAR –GODDESS OF ELECTRA ○ ROME AGAINST ROME

ROMA DROGATA LA POLIZIA NON PUO INTERVENIRE • 1976 • Marcaccini Lucio • ITL

ROMA L'ALTRA FACCIA DELLA VIOLENZA • 1976 • Girolami Marino • ITL

ROMA – MONTEVIDEO • 1948 • Antonioni Michelangelo • DCS • ITL

ROMA, ORE 11 • 1952 • De Santis Giuseppe • ITL • ROME ELEVEN O'CLOCK

ROMA PORTUGUESA • 1957 • Duarte Arthur • SHT • PRT

ROMA RIVUOLE CESARE • 1973 • Jancso Miklos • ITL, HNG • ROME WANTS ANOTHER CAESAR (USA)

ROMA VIOLENTA • 1975 • Girolami Marino • ITL • STREET KILLERS (UKN) ○ FORCED IMPACT

ROMAGEM A DIO • 1959 • Spiguel Miguel • SHT • PRT

ROMAIN KALBRIS • 1923 • Monca Georges • FRN

ROMAN, THE • 1910 • Turner Otis • USA

ROMAN AUS DEN BERGEN, EIN see **GEIER-WALLY, DIE** • 1921

ROMAN BOXERA • 1921 • Binovec Vaclav • CZC • CASHEL BYRON'S PROFESSION

ROMAN CANDLES • 1966 • Waters John* • USA

ROMAN COWBOY, A • 1917 • Mix Tom • SHT • USA

ROMAN D'AMOUR • 1904 • Nonguet Lucien, Zecca Ferdinand • FRN

ROMAN D'AMOUR see **SI TU VEUX** • 1932

ROMAN D'AMOUR ET D'AVENTURES • 1918 • Mercanton Louis, Hervil Rene • FRN

ROMAN DE LA MIDINETTE, LE • 1915 • Feuillade Louis • FRN

ROMAN DE MAX, LE • 1912 • Linder Max • FRN

ROMAN DE REYNARD, LE • 1938 • Starevitch Ladislas • ANM • FRN • STORY OF THE FOX, THE (USA) ○ ADVENTURES OF REYNARD ○ REYNARD THE FOX ○ TALE OF THE FOX, THE

ROMAN DE SOEUR LOUISE, LE • 1908 • Feuillade Louis • FRN

ROMAN DE WERTHER, LE • 1938 • Ophuls Max • FRN • WERTHER

ROMAN DER CHRISTINE VON HERRE, DER • 1921 • Berger Ludwig • FRG

ROMAN DER LILIAN HAWLEY, DER • 1924 • Koebner Franz W. • FRG
ROMAN DU MOUSSE, LE • 1914 • Perret Leonce • FRN
ROMAN D'UN JEUNE HOMME PAUVRE, LE • 1911 • Capellani Albert • FRN
ROMAN D'UN JEUNE HOMME PAUVRE, LE • 1911 • Denola Georges • FRN
ROMAN D'UN JEUNE HOMME PAUVRE, LE • 1927 • Ravel Gaston • FRN
ROMAN D'UN JEUNE HOMME PAUVRE, LE • 1935 • Gance Abel • FRN
ROMAN D'UN SPAHI, LE • 1914 • Pouctal Henri • FRN
ROMAN D'UN SPAHI, LE • 1936 • Bernheim Michel • FRN
ROMAN D'UN TRICHEUR, LE • 1936 • Guitry Sacha • FRN • STORY OF A CHEAT, THE (USA) ○ MEMOIRES D'UN TRICHEUR, LES ○ CHEAT, THE (UKN)
ROMAN D'UN VOLEUR DE CHEVAUX, LE (FRN) see **ROMANCE OF A HORSETHIEF** • 1972
ROMAN D'UNE PAUVRE FILLE, LE • 1911 • Bourgeois Gerard • FRN
ROMAN EINER ARMEN SUNDERIN, DER • 1922 • Eichberg Richard • FRG
ROMAN EINER HALBWELTDAME, DER • 1922 • Dessauer Siegfried • FRG
ROMAN EINER JUNGEN EHE • 1952 • Maetzig Kurt • GDR • STORY OF A YOUNG COUPLE
ROMAN EINER NACHT • 1933 • Boese Carl • FRG
ROMAN EINER SIEBZEHN JAHRIGEN • 1955 • Verhoeven Paul • FRG
ROMAN EINES ARZTES • 1939 • von Alten Jurgen • FRG
ROMAN EINES DIENSTMADCHENS, DER • 1921 • Schunzel Reinhold • FRG, AUS
ROMAN EINES FRAUENARZTES • 1954 • Harnack Falk • FRG
ROMAN EINES PFERDES, DER see **ARABELLA** • 1924
ROMAN EINES SPIELERS see **SPIELER, DER** • 1938
ROMAN EINES ZIRKUSKINDES, DER see **SPRUNG INS LEBENS, DER** • 1924
ROMAN HOLIDAY • 1953 • Wyler William • USA
ROMAN HOLIDAY • 1987 • Nosseck Noel • TVM • USA
ROMAN KARMEN, WHOM WE KNOW AND DO NOT KNOW* • Grigoriev I., Pumpyanskaya S., Semyonov T. • DOC • USS
ROMAN LEGION HARE • 1955 • Freleng Friz • ANS • USA
ROMAN LOVE TEMPLE • 1970 • *Topar Productions* • USA
ROMAN MONTALBAN • 1967 • Herrera Armando A. • PHL
ROMAN NUMERAL SERIES I-IX • 1979-81 • Brakhage Stan • SER • USA
ROMAN O RUZI • 1972 • Brdecka Jiri • SHT • CZC • STORY OF A ROSE
ROMAN PUNCH • 1930 • *Terry Paul/ Moser Frank (P)* • ANS • USA
ROMAN S BASON • 1949 • Trnka Jiri • ANS • CZC • STORY OF THE BASS-CELLO, THE ○ STORY OF A DOUBLE BASS, THE ○ NOVEL WITH A CONTRABASS
ROMAN SCANDAL, A • 1920 • Christie Al • SHT • USA
ROMAN SCANDALS • 1933 • Tuttle Frank • USA
ROMAN SCANDALS '73 see **FRATELLO HOMO, SORELLA BONA** • 1972
ROMAN SIGNORINA see **BELLA DI ROMA, LA** • 1955
ROMAN SPRING OF MRS. STONE, THE • 1962 • Quintero Jose • USA, UKN • WIDOW AND THE GIGOLO, THE
ROMAN ZAIR see **BABY LOVE -LEMON POPSICLE V** • 1983
ROMANA, LA • 1954 • Zampa Luigi • ITL • WOMAN OF ROME
ROMANCE • 1920 • Withey Chet • USA
ROMANCE • 1930 • Brown Clarence • USA
ROMANCE • 1932 • *Terry Paul/ Moser Frank (P)* • ANS • USA
ROMANCE • 1965 • Pojar Bretislav • ANM • CZC
ROMANCE • 1987 • Mazzucco Massimo • ITL
ROMANCE • 1988 • Bianchi Sergio • BRZ
ROMANCE see **POHADKA MAJE** • 1926
ROMANCE see **POHADKA MAJE** • 1940
ROMANCE see **ROMANS** • 1940
ROMANCE, THE • 1913 • Dwan Allan • USA
ROMANCE A LA CARTE • 1915 • *Duncan Bud* • USA
ROMANCE A LA CARTE • 1938 • Rogers Maclean • UKN
ROMANCE A L'INCONNUE • 1930 • Barberis Rene • FRN
ROMANCE A TROIS • 1942 • Richebe Roger • FRN
ROMANCE AND ARABELLA • 1919 • Edwards Walter • USA
ROMANCE AND BRASS TACKS • 1918 • Justice Martin • SHT • USA
ROMANCE AND BRIGHT LIGHTS see **ROMANCE OF THE UNDERWORLD** • 1928
ROMANCE AND DUTY • 1913 • *Joy Ernest* • USA
ROMANCE AND DYNAMITE • 1918 • Davis James • SHT • USA
ROMANCE AND RASCALS • 1918 • Semon Larry • SHT • USA • ROMANS AND RASCALS
ROMANCE AND REALITY • 1912 • *Fischer Marguerite* • USA
ROMANCE AND REALITY • 1921 • Lambart Harry • UKN
ROMANCE AND RHYTHM • 1940 • *Baker Kenny* • USA
ROMANCE AND RHYTHM (UKN) see **COWBOY FROM BROOKLYN, THE** • 1938
ROMANCE AND RICHES (USA) see **AMAZING QUEST OF ERNEST BLISS, THE** • 1936
ROMANCE AND RINGS • 1919 • *Drew Sidney* • SHT • USA
ROMANCE AND RIOT • 1916 • Ellis Robert • USA
ROMANCE AND ROSES • 1917 • MacGregor Norval • SHT • USA
ROMANCE AND ROUGHHOUSE • 1916 • Semon Larry • SHT • USA
ROMANCE AND RUSTLERS • 1925 • Wilson Ben • USA
ROMANCE AND UPPERCUTS • 1911 • *Nestor* • USA
ROMANCE AS A REMEDY • 1915 • Smiley Joseph • USA
ROMANCE AT CATALINA, A • 1912 • *Melies* • USA
ROMANCE AT RANDOM • 1916 • *Julian Rupert* • SHT • USA
ROMANCE AT THE STUDIO: GUIDANCE TO LOVE see **SATSUEIJI ROMANSU-RENAI ANNAI** • 1932
ROMANCE DA EMPREGADA • 1988 • Barreto Bruno • BRZ • STORY OF FAUSTA, THE
ROMANCE DE FIERAS • 1953 • Rodriguez Ismael • MXC
ROMANCE DE LUXE • 1930 • Roberts Stephen • SHT • USA
ROMANCE DE PARIS • 1941 • Boyer Jean • FRN
ROMANCE DEL ANICETO Y LA FRANCISCA • 1967 • Favio Leonardo • ARG • BALLAD OF ANICETO AND FRANCISCA, THE
ROMANCE DEL PALMAR, EL • 1939 • Peon Ramon • MXC
ROMANCE DO LUACHIMO, O • 1968 • Rosa Baptista • PRT
ROMANCE EN PUERTO RICO • 1961 • Pereda Ramon • MXC, PRC
ROMANCE EXPRESS (USA) see **TOKKYU NIPPON** • 1961
ROMANCE FOR BUGLE see **ROMANCE PRO KRIDLOVKU** • 1966
ROMANCE FOR THE FLUGELHORN see **ROMANCE PRO KRIDLOVKU** • 1966
ROMANCE FOR THREE (UKN) see **PARADISE FOR THREE** • 1938
ROMANCE FOR TRUMPET see **ROMANCE PRO KRIDLOVKU** • 1966
ROMANCE FROM DARKNESS see **ROMANCE Z TEMNOT** • 1987
ROMANCE IN A GIPSY CAMP • 1908 • *Lubin* • USA
ROMANCE IN A GLASS HOUSE see **I LIVE FOR LOVE** • 1935
ROMANCE IN A MINOR KEY see **ROMANZE IN MOLL** • 1943
ROMANCE IN BEAR CREEK • 1915 • *Reynolds Marie* • USA
ROMANCE IN BUDAPEST see **SKANDAL IN BUDAPEST** • 1933
ROMANCE IN FLANDERS, A • 1937 • Elvey Maurice • UKN • LOST ON THE WESTERN FRONT (USA) ○ WIDOW'S ISLAND
ROMANCE IN LESVOS see **EROTES STI LESVO** • 1967
ROMANCE IN MANHATTAN • 1934 • Roberts Stephen • USA
ROMANCE IN OLD KENTUCKY, A • 1912 • *Eclair* • USA
ROMANCE IN PARIS see **KING AND THE CHORUS GIRL, THE** • 1937
ROMANCE IN PARIS, A see **AMOUR A PARIS, UN** • 1987
ROMANCE IN RHYTHM • 1934 • Huntington Lawrence • UKN • NIGHT CLUB MURDER
ROMANCE IN THE DARK • 1938 • Potter H. C. • USA
ROMANCE IN THE RAIN • 1934 • Walker Stuart • USA
ROMANCE IN THE ROCKIES • 1910 • *Lubin* • USA
ROMANCE, INCORPORATED see **HONEYMOON AHEAD** • 1945
ROMANCE IS SACRED (UKN) see **KING AND THE CHORUS GIRL, THE** • 1937
ROMANCE LAND • 1923 • Sedgwick Edward • USA
ROMANCE OF A BATHING GIRL, THE see **GOODBYE KISS, THE** • 1928
ROMANCE OF A BEANERY • 1915 • McKim Edwin • USA
ROMANCE OF A DIXIE BELLE, THE • 1911 • *Gaunthier Gene* • USA
ROMANCE OF A DOUBLE BASS • 1976 • Young Robert • UKN
ROMANCE OF A DRY TOWN, THE • 1912 • *Kalem* • USA
ROMANCE OF A FISHER BOY, THE • 1913 • *Excelsior* • USA
ROMANCE OF A FISHERMAID • 1909 • *Bison* • USA • FISHERMAID'S ROMANCE, A
ROMANCE OF A GAMBLER • 1912 • *Nestor* • USA
ROMANCE OF A HANDKERCHIEF, THE • 1915 • Brooke Van Dyke • USA
ROMANCE OF A HORSETHIEF • 1972 • Polonsky Abraham, Hanzekovic Fedor (Itl Vers) • USA, FRN, YGS • ROMAN D'UN VOLEUR DE CHEVAUX, LE (FRN) ○ RUNNING BEAR ○ ROMANZO DI UN LADRO DI CAVALLO (ITL)
ROMANCE OF A JEWESS • 1908 • Griffith D. W. • USA
ROMANCE OF A MILLION DOLLARS, THE • 1926 • Terriss Tom • USA
ROMANCE OF A MOVIE STAR • 1920 • Garrick Richard • UKN
ROMANCE OF A PHOTOGRAPH, THE • 1914 • Salter Harry • USA
ROMANCE OF A POOR YOUNG MAN, THE • 1914 • *Cecil Edward* • USA
ROMANCE OF A QUEEN, THE (UKN) see **THREE WEEKS** • 1924
ROMANCE OF A RICKSHAW • 1912 • *Walker Lillian* • USA
ROMANCE OF A ROGUE • 1928 • Baggot King • USA
ROMANCE OF A ROYALIST MAID, THE • 1912 • Thornton F. Martin • UKN • FOR LOVE AND THE KING
ROMANCE OF A SELF-MADE WIDOW, THE see **SELF MADE WIDOW** • 1917
ROMANCE OF A SNAKE CHARMER • 1910 • *Bison* • USA
ROMANCE OF A STRANDED ACTRESS, THE • 1909 • *Essanay* • USA
ROMANCE OF A TAXICAB • 1908 • *Essanay* • USA
ROMANCE OF A WAR NURSE • 1908 • Porter Edwin S. • USA
ROMANCE OF A WILL, THE see **KAERLIGHEDENS TRIUMF** • 1914
ROMANCE OF AN ACTOR, THE • 1914 • *August Edwin* • USA
ROMANCE OF AN ACTRESS see **LIFE OF AN ACTRESS** • 1927
ROMANCE OF AN ACTRESS, THE • 1915 • *Harte Betty* • USA
ROMANCE OF AN AMERICAN DUCHESS, THE • 1915 • *Travers Richard C.* • USA
ROMANCE OF AN ANVIL, A • 1910 • *Champion* • USA
ROMANCE OF AN EGG • 1908 • *Bitzer Billy (Ph)* • USA
ROMANCE OF AN OLD MAID, THE • 1912 • *Bainbridge Rolinda* • USA
ROMANCE OF AN UMBRELLA, THE • 1909 • *Costello Maurice* • USA
ROMANCE OF ANNIE LAURIE, THE • 1920 • Somers Gerald • UKN
ROMANCE OF BILL GOAT HILL, A • 1916 • Reynolds Lynn • USA
ROMANCE OF BOND COVE • 1911 • Salter Harry • USA
ROMANCE OF BOOK & SWORD, THE see **SHU JIAN EN CHOU LU** • 1988
ROMANCE OF BRITISH HISTORY, THE • 1922 • *Godal Edward (P)* • SHS • UKN
ROMANCE OF CIRCLE RANCH, THE • 1910 • Melies Gaston • USA
ROMANCE OF COYOTE HILL • 1914 • *Miller'S 101 Ranch* • USA
ROMANCE OF DANCING, THE • 1938 • Parsons Herbert R. • SHS • UKN
ROMANCE OF DIGESTION, THE • 1937 • Feist Felix E. • SHT • USA
ROMANCE OF ELAINE, THE • 1915 • Seitz George B., Golden Joseph A., Wharton Leopold, Wharton Theodore • SRL • USA
ROMANCE OF ERIN • 1913 • *Domino* • USA
ROMANCE OF HAPPY VALLEY, THE • 1919 • Griffith D. W. • USA
ROMANCE OF HAWAII, A • 1915 • *Victor* • USA
ROMANCE OF HAYMAKING, A • 1910 • *London Cinematograph Co* • UKN
ROMANCE OF HEFTY BURKE, THE • 1911 • *Edison* • USA
ROMANCE OF HINE-MOA, THE • 1926 • Pauli Gustav • UKN
ROMANCE OF LADY HAMILTON, THE • 1919 • Haldane Bert • UKN
ROMANCE OF LONELY ISLAND, THE • 1911 • *Thanhouser* • USA
ROMANCE OF LOST VALLEY, THE see **GRUB STAKE, THE** • 1923
ROMANCE OF LOVERS, THE see **ROMANS O VLYUBLYONNYKH** • 1975
ROMANCE OF MARGARET CATCHPOLE see **ROMANTIC STORY OF MARGARET CATCHPOLE** • 1911
ROMANCE OF MAYFAIR, A • 1925 • Bentley Thomas • UKN
ROMANCE OF MEXICO, A • 1915 • Fielding Romaine • USA
ROMANCE OF OLD BAGDAD, A • 1922 • Foss Kenelm • UKN
ROMANCE OF OLD CALIFORNIA, A • 1915 • Physioc Wray • USA
ROMANCE OF OLD ERIN, A • 1910 • Olcott Sidney • USA
ROMANCE OF OLD HOLLAND, A • 1914 • *Broncho* • USA
ROMANCE OF OLD MADRID, A • 1909 • *Edison* • USA
ROMANCE OF OLD MEXICO, A • 1909 • *Vitagraph* • USA
ROMANCE OF PUCK FAIR, A • 1916 • Kerrigan J. M. • IRL
ROMANCE OF RADIUM, THE • 1937 • Tourneur Jacques • SHT • USA
ROMANCE OF RAILS AND POWER, A • 1918 • *Essanay* • SHT • USA
ROMANCE OF RICHES, A see **SQUIRE OF LONG HADLEY, THE** • 1925
ROMANCE OF RIO GRANDE see **ROMANCE OF THE RIO GRANDE** • 1929
ROMANCE OF ROBERT BURNS • 1936 • Wilbur Crane • USA
ROMANCE OF ROSY RIDGE, THE • 1947 • Rowland Roy • USA • MISSOURI STORY, THE
ROMANCE OF ROWENA, THE • 1913 • Williams C. Jay • USA
ROMANCE OF RUNNIMEDE • 1928 • Dunlap Scott R. • ASL
ROMANCE OF SEVILLE, A • 1929 • Walker Norman • UKN
ROMANCE OF SUNSHINE VALLEY • 1914 • Miller Charles • USA
ROMANCE OF TARZAN, THE • 1918 • Lucas Wilfred, Meredyth Bess • USA
ROMANCE OF TERESA HENNERT, THE see **ROMANS TERESY HENNERT** • 1978
ROMANCE OF THE 60'S, A • 1911 • *Standing Jack* • USA
ROMANCE OF THE AIR, THE • 1919 • Revier Harry • USA
ROMANCE OF THE ALPS, A • 1908 • *Vitagraph* • USA
ROMANCE OF THE ALPS, A • 1915 • *Marsh Marguerite* • USA
ROMANCE OF THE BACKWOODS, A • 1915 • Myers Harry • USA
ROMANCE OF THE BORDER, A • 1912 • *Payne Edna* • USA
ROMANCE OF THE BURKE & WILLS EXPEDITION OF 1860, A • 1918 • Tinsdale A. C. • ASL
ROMANCE OF THE CAVE DWELLERS, A • 1911 • Porter Edwin S. • USA
ROMANCE OF THE COAST, A • 1912 • *Clayton Ethel* • USA
ROMANCE OF THE EVERGLADE, A • 1914 • France Charles H. • USA
ROMANCE OF THE FOREST RESERVE, A • 1914 • Duncan William • USA
ROMANCE OF THE HILLS, A • 1913 • *Selbie Evelyn* • USA
ROMANCE OF THE HOLLOW TREE, THE • 1916 • *Arey Wayne* • SHT • USA
ROMANCE OF THE ICE FIELDS, A • 1912 • Apfel Oscar • USA
ROMANCE OF THE LIMBERLOST • 1938 • Nigh William • USA
ROMANCE OF THE MEXICAN REVOLUTION, A • 1914 • *Shenfield Jordan* • USA
ROMANCE OF THE MUMMY, THE • 1910 • *Pathe* • FRN
ROMANCE OF THE NAVY, A • 1915 • *Hawley Ormi* • USA
ROMANCE OF THE NIGHT, A • 1915 • *Stonehouse Ruth* • USA
ROMANCE OF THE NILE • 1924 • *Kerman Films* • USA
ROMANCE OF THE NORTHWEST, A • 1914 • *Lubin* • USA
ROMANCE OF THE OLD MILL • 1908 • *Selig* • USA
ROMANCE OF THE OZARKS, A • 1913 • *Larkin Dollie* • USA
ROMANCE OF THE POTATO • 1939 • Lee Sammy • SHT • USA
ROMANCE OF THE PRAIRIE, A • 1910 • *Bison* • USA
ROMANCE OF THE PUEBLO, A • 1914 • *Ab* • USA
ROMANCE OF THE RAILS, A • 1912 • *Lessey George* • USA
ROMANCE OF THE RAILS, A • 1913 • *Frontier* • USA
ROMANCE OF THE RANCHO see **SOUTH OF MONTEREY** • 1946
ROMANCE OF THE REDWOODS • 1939 • Vidor Charles • USA
ROMANCE OF THE REDWOODS, A • 1917 • De Mille Cecil B. • USA
ROMANCE OF THE RIO GRANDE • 1929 • Santell Alfred • USA • ROMANCE OF RIO GRANDE
ROMANCE OF THE RIO GRANDE • 1941 • Leeds Herbert I. • USA
ROMANCE OF THE RIO GRANDE, A • 1911 • Campbell Colin • USA
ROMANCE OF THE ROCKIES • 1937 • Bradbury Robert North • USA
ROMANCE OF THE ROCKY COAST • 1909 • *Lubin* • USA
ROMANCE OF THE ROSARY, THE see **ROSARY, THE** • 1922
ROMANCE OF THE SAWDUST RING, A • 1914 • *Borzage Paul* • USA
ROMANCE OF THE SEA, A • 1914 • *Broncho* • USA
ROMANCE OF THE SOUTH, A • 1910 • *Exclusive Films* • USA
ROMANCE OF THE U.S. NAVY, A • 1912 • *Thanhouser* • USA
ROMANCE OF THE UNDERWORLD • 1928 • Cummings Irving • USA • ROMANCE AND BRIGHT LIGHTS
ROMANCE OF THE UNDERWORLD, A • 1918 • Kirkwood James • USA
ROMANCE OF THE UTAH PIONEERS, THE • 1913 • Farney Charles • USA
ROMANCE OF THE WASTELAND • 1924 • *Mix Art* • USA
ROMANCE OF THE WEST • 1930 • Tansey Robert, Tansey John • USA • SPORTING JUSTICE (UKN)
ROMANCE OF THE WEST • 1935 • Staub Ralph • SHT • USA
ROMANCE OF THE WEST • 1946 • Tansey Robert • USA
ROMANCE OF THE WEST, A • 1912 • *Essanay* • USA
ROMANCE OF THE WESTERN HILLS, A • 1910 • Griffith D. W. • USA
ROMANCE OF TRAINED NURSE, THE • 1910 • *Kalem* • USA

ROMANCE OF TRANSPORTATION IN CANADA, THE • 1952 • Koenig Wolf, Low Colin • CND • SPORTS ET TRANSPORTS

ROMANCE OF WALL STREET, A • 1911 • *Vitagraph* • USA • STOCK EXCHANGE TRAGEDY, A

ROMANCE OF WASTDALE, A • 1921 • Elvey Maurice • UKN

ROMANCE OF YUSHIMA, THE see **YUSHIMA NO SHIRAUME** • 1955

ROMANCE ON BAR O, THE • 1911 • *Essanay* • USA

ROMANCE ON THE BEACH see **CRI DE LA CHAIR, LE** • 1963

ROMANCE ON THE BUS see **PA-SHIH CH'I-YU CHIEH LIANG-YUAN** • 1978

ROMANCE ON THE HIGH SEAS • 1948 • Curtiz Michael • USA • IT'S MAGIC (UKN)

ROMANCE ON THE LAZY K • 1910 • *Lubin* • USA

ROMANCE ON THE ORIENT EXPRESS • 1985 • Clark Lawrence Gordon • TVM • USA

ROMANCE ON THE RANGE • 1942 • Kane Joseph • USA

ROMANCE ON THE RUN • 1938 • Meins Gus • USA

ROMANCE PRO KRIDLOVKU • 1966 • Vavra Otakar • CZC • ROMANCE FOR THE FLUGELHORN ○ ROMANCE FOR TRUMPET ○ ROMANCE FOR BUGLE

ROMANCE PROMOTORS, THE • 1920 • Bennett Chester • USA

ROMANCE RANCH • 1924 • Mitchell Howard M. • USA

ROMANCE RIDES THE RANGE • 1936 • Fraser Harry L. • USA

ROMANCE ROAD • 1925 • Windermere Fred • USA

ROMANCE SENTIMENTALE • 1930 • Eisenstein Sergei, Alexandrov Grigori • SHT • FRN

ROMANCE SIN PALABRAS • 1948 • Torres-Rios Leopoldo • ARG

ROMANCE SONAMBULO • 1958 • Wilenski Osias • ARG

ROMANCE TROPICAL • 1934 • Viguie Juan E.

ROMANCE (UKN) see **ROAD TO ROMANCE, THE** • 1927

ROMANCE WITHOUT FINANCE • 1945 • Crouch William Forest • SHT • USA

ROMANCE Z TEMNOT • 1987 • Pojar Bretislav, Drouin Jacques • ANM • CZC, CND • ROMANCE FROM DARKNESS

ROMANCES OF THE PRIZE RING • 1926 • Parkinson H. B., Malins Geoffrey H. • SHS • UKN

ROMANCING ALONG • 1938 • Goodwins Leslie • SHT • USA

ROMANCING THE STONE • 1984 • Zemeckis Robert • USA

ROMANETO • 1980 • Soukup Jaroslav • CZC

ROMANOFF AND JULIET • 1961 • Ustinov Peter • USA • DIG THAT JULIET

ROMANS • 1940 • Ohberg Ake • SWD • ROMANCE

ROMANS AND RASCALS see **ROMANCE AND RASCALS** • 1918

ROMAN'S AWAKENING, THE see **BACK TO LIFE AFTER 2000 YEARS** • 1910

ROMANS O VLYUBLYONNYKH • 1975 • Konchalovsky Andrei • USS • LOVERS' ROMANCE, A ○ ROMANCE OF LOVERS, THE

ROMANS TERESY HENNERT • 1978 • Gogolewski Ignacy • PLN • ROMANCE OF TERESA HENNERT, THE ○ TERESA HENNERT'S ROMANCE

ROMANTIC ADVENTURE, A see **ROMANTYCZNA PRZYGODA** • 1963

ROMANTIC ADVENTURESS, A • 1920 • Knoles Harley • USA

ROMANTIC AGE, THE • 1927 • Florey Robert • USA

ROMANTIC AGE, THE • 1949 • Greville Edmond T. • UKN • NAUGHTY ARLETTE (USA)

ROMANTIC AGE, THE see **HER FIRST ROMANCE** • 1951

ROMANTIC AGE, THE (UKN) see **SISTERS UNDER THE SKIN** • 1934

ROMANTIC AGONY, THE see **VAARWEL** • 1973

ROMANTIC COMEDY • 1983 • Hiller Arthur • USA

ROMANTIC ENGLAND • 1929 • Parkinson H. B. • UKN

ROMANTIC ENGLISHWOMAN, THE (UKN) see **ANGLAISE ROMANTIQUE, UNE** • 1974

ROMANTIC JOSIE • 1914 • Beggs Lee • USA

ROMANTIC JOURNEY, THE • 1916 • Fitzmaurice George • USA

ROMANTIC LANDSCAPE IN ENGLAND • 1980 • Kohanyi Julius • MTV • CND

ROMANTIC MELODIES • 1932 • Fleischer Dave • ANS • USA

ROMANTIC MISFORTUNE • 1916 • *Hippo* • USA

ROMANTIC MR. HINKLIN, THE see **YOU CAN'T FOOL YOUR WIFE** • 1940

ROMANTIC REDSKINS • 1910 • *American* • USA

ROMANTIC REGGIE • 1915 • Drew Sidney • USA

ROMANTIC ROGUE • 1927 • Brown Harry J. • USA

ROMANTIC ROSA see **WHAT HAPPENED TO ROSA** • 1920

ROMANTIC STORY, A see **ROMANTIKUS TORTENET** • 1966

ROMANTIC STORY OF MARGARET CATCHPOLE • 1911 • Longford Raymond • ASL • ROMANCE OF MARGARET CATCHPOLE

ROMANTIC VAQUERO see **VALIANT HOMBRE, THE** • 1949

ROMANTICA AVVENTURA, UNA • 1940 • Camerini Mario • ITL

ROMANTICI A VENEZIA • 1947 • Emmer Luciano, Gras Enrico • ITL • ROMANTICS IN VENICE ○ VENISE ET SES AMANTS

ROMANTICISM see **ROMANTIKA** • 1972

ROMANTICISMO • 1913 • Caserini Mario • ITL

ROMANTICISMO • 1951 • Fracassi Clemente • ITL

ROMANTICS see **ROMANTIKI** • 1941

ROMANTICS, THE see **ROMANTYCZNI** • 1970

ROMANTICS IN VENICE see **ROMANTICI A VENEZIA** • 1947

ROMANTIK PA SENGEKANTEN • 1973 • Hilbard John • DNM • DANISH PILLOW TALK (USA) ○ BEDSIDE ROMANCE ○ PILLOW TALK

ROMANTIKA • 1972 • Kezdi-Kovacs Zsolt • HNG • ROMANTICISM

ROMANTIKI • 1941 • Donskoi Mark • USS • CHILDREN OF THE SOVIET ARCTIC ○ ROMANTICS

ROMANTIKUS TORTENET • 1966 • Macskassy Gyula • ANS • HNG • ROMANTIC STORY, A

ROMANTISCHE BRAUTFAHRT • 1944 • Hainisch Leopold • FRG

ROMANTYCZNA PRZYGODA • 1963 • Marszalek Lechoslaw • PLN • ROMANTIC ADVENTURE, A

ROMANTYCZNI • 1970 • Rozewicz Stanislaw • PLN • ROMANTICS, THE

ROMANY, THE • 1923 • Pearson George • UKN

ROMANY LASS, A • 1918 • Thornton F. Martin • UKN • RILKA: OR, THE GYPSY QUEEN

ROMANY LOVE • 1931 • Paul Fred • UKN

ROMANY RHYTHM • 1938 • Parsons Herbert R. • UKN

ROMANY ROB'S REVENGE • 1910 • *Bison* • USA

ROMANY ROSE, A • 1917 • Stedman Marshall • SHT • USA

ROMANY RYE see **LIFE LINE, THE** • 1919

ROMANY RYE, THE • 1914 • Taylor Stanner E. V. • USA

ROMANY RYE, THE • 1915 • Nash Percy • UKN

ROMANY TRAGEDY, A • 1911 • Griffith D. W. • USA

ROMANY WIFE, THE • 1910 • *Kalem* • USA

ROMANY'S REVENGE, THE • 1907 • Mottershaw Frank • UKN

ROMANZA RUSA • 1934 • Rey Florian • SPN

ROMANZE IN MOLL • 1943 • Kautner Helmut • FRG • ROMANCE IN A MINOR KEY

ROMANZE IN VENEDIG • 1962 • von Borsody Eduard • AUS

ROMANZO, IL • 1913 • Martoglio Nino • ITL

ROMANZO A PASSO DI DANZA (ITL) see **PIRUETAS JUVENILES** • 1943

ROMANZO D'AMORE • 1950 • Coletti Duilio • ITL • ALL FOR LOVE

ROMANZO DELLA MIA VITA, IL • 1953 • De Felice Lionello • ITL • LUCIANO TAJOLI

ROMANZO DI UN GIOVANE POVERO, IL • 1943 • Brignone Guido • ITL

ROMANZO DI UN GIOVANE POVERO, IL • 1958 • Girolami Marino • ITL, SPN

ROMANZO DI UN GIOVANE POVERO, IL • 1974 • Canevari Cesare • ITL

ROMANZO DI UN LADRO DI CAVALLO (ITL) see **ROMANCE OF A HORSETHIEF** • 1972

ROMANZO DI UNA GIOVANE POVERA, IL • 1919 • Palermi Amleto • ITL

ROMANZO DI UNA VESPA • 1919 • Caserini Mario • ITL

ROMANZO DI UN'EPOCA • 1941 • Emmer Luciano • ITL

ROMANZO POPOLARE • 1974 • Monicelli Mario • ITL

ROMAREI, DAS MADCHEN MIT DEN GRUNEN AUGEN • 1958 • Reinl Harald • FRG

ROMARIAS • 1953 • Vitorino Orlando • SHT • PRT

ROMARIN • 1936 • Hugon Andre • FRN

ROMARZO see **BOMARZO** • 1949

ROME '78 • 1978 • Nares James • USA

ROME 1585 (USA) see **MASNADIERI, I** • 1962

ROME 2033 see **ROME 2033: THE FIGHTER CENTURIONS** • 1983

ROME 2033: THE FIGHTER CENTURIONS • 1983 • Fulci Lucio • ITL • NEW GLADIATORS, THE ○ ROME 2033

ROME ADVENTURE • 1962 • Daves Delmer • USA • LOVERS MUST LEARN

ROME AGAINST ROME see **ROMA CONTRA ROMA** • 1963

ROME ELEVEN O'CLOCK see **ROMA, ORE 11** • 1952

ROME EXPRESS • 1932 • Forde Walter • UKN

ROME EXPRESS • 1949 • Stengel Christian • FRN

ROME LIKE CHICAGO (USA) see **ROMA COME CHICAGO** • 1968

ROME, OPEN CITY see **ROMA, CITTA APERTA** • 1945

ROME – PARIS – ROME see **SIGNORI, IN CARROZZA!** • 1951

ROME-ROMEO • 1990 • Fleischer Alain • FRN

ROME SYMPHONY • 1937-40 • *Cardiff Jack (Ph)* • DCS • UKN

ROME WANTS ANOTHER CAESAR (USA) see **ROMA RIVUOLE CESARE** • 1973

ROMEK I ANKA • 1964 • Fiwek Wojciech • PLN

ROMELIO'S SECRET see **SECRETO DE ROMELIO, EL** • 1989

ROMEO • 1989 • Horst Rita • NTH

ROMEO AND JULIET • Calinescu Bob • ANM • RMN

ROMEO AND JULIET • 1908 • *Tearle Godfrey* • UKN

ROMEO AND JULIET • 1908 • Blackton J. Stuart • USA • ROMEO AND JULIETTE

ROMEO AND JULIET • 1911 • Marston Theodore • USA

ROMEO AND JULIET • 1912 • *Pathe* • USA

ROMEO AND JULIET • 1914 • Vale Travers • USA

ROMEO AND JULIET • 1915 • Kellino W. P. • UKN

ROMEO AND JULIET • 1916 • Edwards J. Gordon • *Fox* • USA

ROMEO AND JULIET • 1916 • Noble John W., Bushman Francis X. • *Quality* • USA

ROMEO AND JULIET • 1917 • Dayton Helena Smith • ANS • USA

ROMEO AND JULIET • 1919 • Dyer Anson • ANS • UKN

ROMEO AND JULIET • 1920 • Moore Vin • SHT • USA

ROMEO AND JULIET • 1924 • *Sennett Mack (P)* • SHT • USA

ROMEO AND JULIET • 1933 • *Terry Paul/ Moser Frank (P)* • ANS • USA

ROMEO AND JULIET • 1936 • Cukor George • USA

ROMEO AND JULIET • 1958 • Tyrlova Hermina • ANM • CZC

ROMEO AND JULIET • 1966 • Czinner Paul • UKN

ROMEO AND JULIET • 1968 • Zeffirelli Franco • UKN, ITL • ROMEO E GIULIETTA (ITL)

ROMEO AND JULIET • 1978 • Rakoff Alvin • TVM • USA

ROMEO AND JULIET see **SHUHADDAA EL GHARAM** • 1944

ROMEO AND JULIET see **ROMEO I DZULETTA** • 1955

ROMEO AND JULIET -1971 see **WHAT BECAME OF JACK AND JILL?** • 1971

ROMEO AND JULIET AT THE END OF NOVEMBER • 1971 • Balik Jaroslav • MTV • CZC

ROMEO AND JULIET IN OUR TOWN • 1910 • *Selig* • USA

ROMEO AND JULIET OF TODAY see **KAKO SU SE VOLELI ROMEO I JULIJA** • 1967

ROMEO AND JULIET (UKN) see **GIULIETTA E ROMEO** • 1954

ROMEO AND JULIET (USA) see **ROMEO E GIULIETTA** • 1908

ROMEO AND JULIET (USA) see **GIULIETTA E ROMEO** • 1964

ROMEO AND JULIETTE see **ROMEO AND JULIET** • 1908

ROMEO E GIULIETTA • 1908 • Caserini Mario • ITL • ROMEO AND JULIET (USA)

ROMEO E GIULIETTA (ITL) see **ROMEO AND JULIET** • 1968

ROMEO I DZULETTA • 1955 • Arnstam Leo, Lavrovskiy Leonid • USS • BALLET OF ROMEO AND JULIET, THE ○ ROMEO AND JULIET

ROMEO IN PYJAMAS • 1913 • *Solax* • USA

ROMEO IN PYJAMAS, A (UKN) see **PARLOR, BEDROOM AND BATH** • 1931

ROMEO IN RHYTHM • 1940 • Ising Rudolf • ANS • USA

ROMEO, JULIE A TMA • 1960 • Weiss Jiri • CZC • ROMEO, JULIET AND THE DARKNESS ○ SWEET LIGHT IN A DARK ROOM ○ ROMEO, JULIET AND DARKNESS ○ SWEET LIGHT IN THE DARK WINDOW

ROMEO, JULIET AND DARKNESS see **ROMEO, JULIE A TMA** • 1960

ROMEO, JULIET AND THE DARKNESS see **ROMEO, JULIE A TMA** • 1960

ROMEO MONK, A • 1932 • Foster John, Davis Mannie • ANS • USA

ROMEO OF THE COAL WAGON • 1916 • *Teare Ethel* • SHT • USA

ROMEO PRIS AU PIEGE • 1905 • Blache Alice • FRN

ROMEO ROBIN, A • 1930 • Foster John, Davis Mannie • ANS • USA

ROMEO UND JULIA AUF DEM DORFE • 1941 • Trommer Hans, Schmidely Valerien • SWT

ROMEO UND JULIA IM SCHNEE • 1920 • Lubitsch Ernst • FRG

ROMEO VS. JULIET see **ROMEO VS. JULIETA** • 1968

ROMEO VS. JULIETA • 1968 • Soler Julian • MXC • ROMEO VS. JULIET

ROMEO Y JULIETA • 1943 • Delgado Miguel M. • MXC

ROMEOS AND JOLLY JULIETS • 1919 • Watson William • SHT • USA

ROMEO'S DAD • 1920 • Terwilliger George W. • SHT • USA

ROMEOW AND JULIECAT • 1947 • Pal George • ANS • USA

ROMERO • 1989 • Duigan John • USA

ROME'S GOLD see **ORO DI ROMA, L'** • 1961

ROMIOS EHI FILOTIMO, O • 1968 • Sakellarios Alekos • GRC • ROMIOS HAS AMBITION ○ DUTY

ROMIOS HAS AMBITION see **ROMIOS EHI FILOTIMO, O** • 1968

ROMMEL -DESERT FOX (UKN) see **DESERT FOX, THE** • 1951

ROMMEL RUFT KAIRO • 1959 • Schleif Wolfgang • FRG

ROMMEL'S TREASURE (USA) see **TESORO DI ROMMEL, IL** • 1965

ROMOLA • 1925 • King Henry • USA

ROMOLO E REMO • 1961 • Corbucci Sergio • ITL • DUEL OF THE TITANS (USA) ○ ROMULUS AND REMUS

ROMP IN A SWAMP • 1959 • Smith Paul J. • ANS • USA

ROMP OF FANNY HILL see **FANNY HILL** • 1964

ROMPIBALLE, IL (ITL) see **EMMERDEUR, L'** • 1973

ROMPIMIENTO, EL • 1938 • Gomez Antonio Delgado • VNZ

ROMUALD ET JULIETTE • 1989 • Serreau Coline • FRN • ROMUALD & JULIETTE (UKN)

ROMUALD & JULIETTE (UKN) see **ROMUALD ET JULIETTE** • 1989

ROMULUS AND REMUS see **ROMOLO E REMO** • 1961

ROMULUS AND THE SABINES (USA) see **RATTO DELLE SABINE, IL** • 1962

ROMY. ANATOMIE EINES GESICHTS • 1965 • Syberberg Hans-Jurgen • DOC • FRG • ROMY. ANATOMY OF A FACE

ROMY. ANATOMY OF A FACE see **ROMY. ANATOMIE EINES GESICHTS** • 1965

RONA JAFFE'S MAZES & MONSTERS • 1982 • Stern Steven Hilliard • TVM • USA • MAZES AND MONSTERS

RONAN'S COUNTRY • 1967 • Holmes Cecil • DOC • ASL

RONDA ESPANOLA • 1951 • Vajda Ladislao • SPN

RONDA REVOLUCIONARIA • 1976 • *Conacine* • MXC

RONDALLA • 1949 • Urruchua Victor • MXC

RONDE, LA • 1950 • Ophuls Max • FRN

RONDE, LA • 1964 • Vadim Roger • FRN, ITL • PIACERE E L'AMORE, IL (ITL) ○ CIRCLE OF LOVE (USA)

RONDE, LA see **REIGEN** • 1974

RONDE AUX MILLIONS, LA see **FOIS DANS LA VIE, UNE** • 1933

RONDE CARREE • 1961 • Jodoin Rene • ANS • CND

RONDE DE NUIT • 1949 • Campaux Francois • FRN

RONDE DE NUIT • 1983 • Missiaen Jean-Claude • FRN

RONDE DE NUIT, LA • 1925 • Silver Marcel • FRN

RONDE DES HEURES, LA • 1930 • Ryder Alexandre • FRN

RONDE DES HEURES, LA • 1949 • Ryder Alexandre • FRN

RONDE ENFANTINE • 1896-97 • Lumiere Louis • FRN

RONDE INFERNALE, LA • 1928 • Luitz-Morat • FRN

RONDEROS, LOS • 1986 • Eyde Marianne • PRU

RONDINI IN VOLO • 1950 • Capuano Luigi • ITL

RONDO • 1958 • Leszczynski Witold • SHT • PLN • ROUNDABOUT

RONDO • 1966 • Berkovic Zvonimir • YGS

RONDO • 1966 • Kijowicz Miroslaw • ANS • PLN • ROUNDABOUT, THE

RONDOM HET OUDEKERKSPLEIN.. • 1968 • Kerbosch Roeland • DOC • NTH • ROUND ABOUT THE OLD CHURCH SQUARE

RONDS DE CUIR, LES • 1967 • Riad Mohamed Slimane • ALG

RONIN CALLED NEMURI, THE see **NEMURI KYOSHIRO ONNA JIGOKU** • 1968

RONINGAI • 1928 • Makino Masahiro • JPN • STREET OF MASTERLESS SAMURAI, THE ○ JOBLESS SAMURAI

RONJA ROVERDATTER • 1984 • Danielsson Tage • NRW, SWD • RONJA ROVERDATTER (SWD) ○ RONJA, THE ROBBER'S DAUGHTER

RONJA ROVERDATTER (SWD) see **RONJA ROVERDATTER** • 1984

RONJA, THE ROBBER'S DAUGHTER see **RONJA ROVERDATTER** • 1984

RONNES OG NEXOS GENOPBYGNING • 1954 • *Dreyer Carl T.* • DNM • RECONSTRUCTION OF RONNIE AND NEXOS, THE ○ REBUILDING OF ROME AND NEXOS, THE

RONNY • 1931 • Le Bon Roger, Schunzel Reinhold • FRN

RONNY • 1931 • Schunzel Reinhold • FRG

RONTAS ES REMENYSEG • 1982 • Moldovan Domokos • HNG • BEWITCHED BY HOPE

RONTGENSTRAHLEN • 1936 • Rikli Martin • FRG • X-RAYS

ROOF, THE • 1933 • Cooper George A. • UKN

ROOF, THE • 1978 • Andonov Ivan • BUL

ROOF, THE see **TETTO, IL** • 1956

ROOF GARDEN, THE • 1905 • *Gaumont* • UKN • ROOFTOP GARDENS

ROOF GARDEN, THE see **TERRAZA, LA** • 1963

ROOF GARDEN ROUGH HOUSE, A • 1919 • Davis James • SHT • USA

ROOF NEEDS MOWING, THE • 1970 • Armstrong Gillian • SHT • ASL

ROOF OF THE WHALE, THE see **TOIT DE LA BALEINE, LE** • 1981

ROOF-TILE OF THE TEMPYO ERA, A see **TEMPYO NO IRAKA** • 1979

ROOF TREE, THE • 1921 • Dillon John Francis • USA

ROOFS AND RIOTS • 1918 • McCray Roy • SHT • USA

ROOFS AT DAWN see **HAJNALI HAZTETOK** • 1986

ROOFSPACE • 1979 • von Puttkamer Peter • SHT • CND

ROOFTOP GARDENS see **ROOF GARDEN, THE** • 1905
ROOFTOP RAZZLE DAZZLE • 1964 • Smith Paul J. • ANS • USA
ROOFTOPS • 1989 • Wise Robert • USA
ROOFTOPS OF LONDON • 1936 • Keene Ralph, Burnford Paul • UKN
ROOFTOPS OF NEW YORK • 1960 • McCarty Robert • SHT • USA
ROOFTREE see **TVARBALK** • 1967
ROOGIE'S BUMP • 1954 • Young Harold • USA • KID COLOSSUS, THE (UKN)
ROOIE SIEN • 1974 • Weisz Frans • NTH
ROOK, THE see **SOMETHING FOR EVERYONE** • 1970
ROOK, THE see **ROKH** • 1975
ROOKERY NOOK • 1930 • Walls Tom, Haskin Byron • UKN • ONE EMBARRASSING NIGHT (USA)
ROOKIE, THE • 1916 • *Cub* • SHT • USA
ROOKIE, THE • 1916 • Davenport Harry • *Vitagraph* • SHT • USA
ROOKIE, THE • 1919 • *Miller-Hodgkinson* • SHT • USA
ROOKIE, THE • 1932 • Cline Eddie • SHT • USA
ROOKIE, THE • 1959 • O'Hanlon George • USA
ROOKIE, THE • 1990 • Eastwood Clint • USA
ROOKIE BEAR • 1941 • Ising Rudolf • ANS • USA
ROOKIE COP, THE • 1939 • Howard David • USA • SWIFT VENGEANCE (UKN) ○ G-DOG
ROOKIE FIREMAN • 1950 • Friedman Seymour • USA
ROOKIE MANAGER see **OBANTO KOBANTO** • 1955
ROOKIE OF THE YEAR • 1955 • Ford John • MTV • USA
ROOKIE REVIEW • 1941 • Freleng Friz • ANS • USA
ROOKIES • 1927 • Wood Sam • USA • RED, WHITE AND BLUE
ROOKIES, THE • 1971 • Taylor Jud • TVM • USA
ROOKIES COME HOME (UKN) see **BUCK PRIVATES COME HOME** • 1947
ROOKIES IN BURMA • 1943 • Goodwins Leslie • USA
ROOKIES ON PARADE • 1941 • Santley Joseph • USA • JAMBOREE (UKN)
ROOKIE'S RETURN, THE • 1921 • Nelson Jack • USA
ROOKIES (UKN) see **BUCK PRIVATES** • 1941
ROOM • 1974 • Lander Ned • ASL
ROOM 11 • 1970 • Irwin Bud • USA
ROOM 13 (USA) see **ZIMMER 13** • 1964
ROOM 23 • 1923 • Cline Eddie • SHT • USA
ROOM 23 see **BEDROOM BLUNDER, A** • 1917
ROOM 43 (USA) see **PASSPORT TO SHAME** • 1959
ROOM 257 • 1912 • *Majestic* • USA
ROOM, THE • Gerstein Mordi • SHT • USA
ROOM, THE • 1959 • D'Avino Carmen • SHT • USA
ROOM, THE • 1987 • Altman Robert • USA
ROOM, THE see **CHAMBRE, LA** • 1966
ROOM, THE see **HEYA** • 1967
ROOM AND BIRD • 1951 • Freleng Friz • ANS • USA
ROOM AND BOARD • 1921 • Crosland Alan • USA
ROOM AND BOARD see **ROOM AND BROAD** • 1968
ROOM AND BOARD -A DOLLAR AND A HALF • 1915 • Lehrman Henry • USA
ROOM AND BORED • 1943 • Wickersham Bob • ANS • USA
ROOM AND BORED • 1962 • Smith Paul J. • ANS • USA
ROOM AND BROAD • 1968 • Place Graham • USA • ROOM AND BOARD
ROOM AND WRATH • 1956 • Lovy Alex • ANS • USA
ROOM AT THE END OF THE UNIVERSE • 1989 • Glickenhaus James • USA
ROOM AT THE TOP • 1959 • Clayton Jack • UKN
ROOM BETWEEN, THE • 1915 • Levering Joseph • USA
ROOM FOR A STRANGER see **ADULTEROUS AFFAIR** • 1966
ROOM FOR MEN see **MIEJSLE DLA CZLOWIEKA** • 1972
ROOM FOR ONE see **MIEJSCE DLA JEDNEGO** • 1965
ROOM FOR ONE MORE • 1952 • Taurog Norman • USA • EASY WAY, THE
ROOM FOR RENT • 1968 • Tapawan Chito B. • PHL
ROOM FOR TWO • 1940 • Elvey Maurice • UKN
ROOM IN THE HOUSE • 1955 • Elvey Maurice • UKN
ROOM IN TOWN, A see **CHAMBRE EN VILLE, UNE** • 1982
ROOM MATES • 1933 • Stevens George • SHT • USA
ROOM MATES • 1971 • Marks Arthur • USA
ROOM OF MYSTERY, THE • 1917 • *Van Margaret* • SHT • USA
ROOM OVERLOOKING THE SEA, A see **POKOJ Z WIDOKIEM NA MORZE** • 1977
ROOM RENT AND ROMANCE • 1916 • Clements Roy • SHT • USA
ROOM RUNNERS • 1932 • *Iwerks Ub (P)* • ANS • USA
ROOM SERVICE • 1938 • Seiter William A. • USA
ROOM TO LET • 1950 • Grayson Godfrey • UKN
ROOM TO MOVE see **RUNNING GAME, THE** • 1982
ROOM UPSTAIRS, THE • 1987 • Margolin Stuart • TVM • USA
ROOM UPSTAIRS, THE (USA) see **MARTIN ROUMAGNAC** • 1946
ROOM WITH A VIEW, A • 1986 • Ivory James • UKN
ROOM WITH A VIEW ON THE SEA, A see **POKOJ Z WIDOKIEM NA MORZE** • 1977
ROOM WITH CRY see **SZOBA KIALTASSAL** • 1990
ROOM WITH THICK WALLS see **KABE ATSUKI HEYA** • 1953
ROOMMATE, THE • 1984 • Cox Nell • TVM • USA
ROOMMATES • 1971 • *Mason Dan* • USA
ROOMMATES • 1982 • Vincent Chuck • USA
ROOMMATES see **RAISING THE WIND** • 1961
ROOMMATES see **MARCH OF THE SPRING HARE** • 1969
ROOMMATES SOCIABLE • 1969 • Glick Wizard • USA
ROOMS AND RUMORS • 1918 • Semon Larry • SHT • USA
ROOMS FOR RENT • 1915 • *Victor* • USA
ROONEY • 1958 • Pollock George • UKN
ROONEY, THE BRIDE • 1915 • Ransom Charles • USA
ROONEY'S SAD CASE • 1915 • Drew Sidney • USA
ROOP LEHKA • 1962 • Hussain Mohd • IND
ROOPBAN • 1965 • Salahuddin • BNG
ROOPKUMARI • 1956 • Vyas Manibhai • IND
ROOSEVELT, MAN OF DESTINY • 1946 • *Universal* • SHT • USA
ROOSEVELT STORY, THE • 1947 • *Levine Martin (P)* • DOC • USA
ROOSEVELT SYKES • 1972 • Buba P., Nelson • SHT • USA
ROOSEVELT SYKES: THE HONEYDRIPPER • 1961 • Bruynoghe Yannick • SHT • BLG
ROOST THE KIDDER • 1912 • *Holmes Stuart* • USA
ROOSTER • 1982 • Mayberry Russ • TVM • USA
ROOSTER • 1983 • Mack Brice • USA • ROOSTER: SPURS OF DEATH
ROOSTER, THE • 1970 • Zohar Uri • ISR
ROOSTER, THE • 1989 • Shin Seung Soo • SKR
ROOSTER, THE see **TUPPEN** • 1981
ROOSTER COGBURN • 1975 • Millar Stuart • USA • ROOSTER COGBURN AND THE LADY
ROOSTER COGBURN AND THE LADY see **ROOSTER COGBURN** • 1975
ROOSTER: SPURS OF DEATH see **ROOSTER** • 1983
ROOSTER'S EGG, THE see **OEUF A LA COQUE, L'** • 1963
ROOSTY see **PENALTY, THE** • 1941
ROOT, THE • 1963 • Kim Soo-Yong • SKR
ROOT, THE see **KORZEN** • 1965
ROOT OF ALL EVIL, THE • 1915 • *Aitken Spottiswoode* • USA
ROOT OF ALL EVIL, THE • 1919 • Ridgwell George • USA
ROOT OF ALL EVIL, THE • 1947 • Williams Brock • UKN
ROOT OF EVIL, THE • 1912 • Griffith D. W. • USA
ROOT OF EVIL, THE • 1914 • *Turner William H.* • USA
ROOTIN' TOOTIN' RHYTHM • 1937 • Wright Mack V. • USA • RHYTHM ON THE RANCH (UKN)
ROOTLESS, THE see **GHUDDI** • 1979
ROOTS • 1934 • Field Mary • UKN
ROOTS • 1963 • Iliesu Mirel • DOC • RMN
ROOTS • 1977 • Greene David, Chomsky Marvin, Moses Gilbert, Erman John • TVM • USA
ROOTS see **RAICES** • 1953
ROOTS IN A PARCHED GROUND • 1989 • Clark Matt • USA
ROOTS: KUNTA KINTE'S GIFT • 1988 • Hooks Kevin • TVM • USA • KUNTE KINTE'S GIFT ○ ROOTS: THE GIFT
ROOTS OF AMERICAN MUSIC: COUNTRY AND URBAN MUSIC • 1971 • Garfias Robert • USA
ROOTS OF BLOOD see **RAICES DE SANGRE** • 1976
ROOTS OF EVIL see **BLUT DES BOSEN, DIE** • 1979
ROOTS OF GRIEF see **FRIHETENS MURAR** • 1978
ROOTS OF HEAVEN, THE • 1958 • Huston John • USA
ROOTS OF STONE • Arzuaga Jose Maria • CLM
ROOTS OF THE RISING SUN, THE • 1971 • Radev Vulo • BUL
ROOTS, ROCK & REGGAE • 1978 • Marre Jeremy • DOC • UKN
ROOTS: THE GIFT see **ROOTS: KUNTA KINTE'S GIFT** • 1988
ROOTS: THE NEXT GENERATIONS • 1978 • Erman John, Richards Lloyd, Brown George Stanford, Dubin Charles S. • TVM • USA
ROOTY TOOT TOOT • 1952 • Hubley John • ANS • USA
ROPAVEJERO, EL • 1946 • Gomez Muriel Emilio • MXC
ROPE • 1948 • Hitchcock Alfred • USA
ROPE • 1960 • Elster Michael • UKN
ROPE see **ROPE OF FLESH** • 1965
ROPE, THE see **UZE** • 1976
ROPE AND BREASTS see **NAWA TO CHUBASA** • 1967
ROPE AND CHAIN see **HIMO TO KUSARI** • 1968
ROPE AROUND THE NECK (USA) see **CORDE AU COU, LA** • 1964
ROPE FROM THE HANGED MAN, THE see **PROVAZ Z OBESENCE** • 1927
ROPE HANGS FROM THE SKY, THE see **SOGA PENDE DEL CIELO, LA** • 1979
ROPE LADDER TO THE MOON • 1969 • Palmer Tony • UKN
ROPE OF FLESH • 1965 • Meyer Russ • USA • MUDHONEY! ○ MUD HONEY ○ ROPE
ROPE OF SAND • 1949 • Dieterle William • USA
ROPE TRICK • 1967 • Godfrey Bob • ANS • UKN
ROPED • 1919 • Ford John • USA
ROPED AND TIED • 1911 • *Nestor* • USA
ROPED AND TIED • 1918 • *Hart Neal* • SHT • USA
ROPED BY RADIO • 1925 • *Kesterson George* • USA
ROPED IN • 1911 • Melies Gaston • USA
ROPED IN • 1912 • *Stedman Myrtle* • USA
ROPED IN • 1917 • Marshall George • SHT • USA
ROPED IN see **CAUGHT** • 1931
ROPED INTO SCANDAL • 1917 • Hutchinson Craig • SHT • USA
ROPES see **FALSE KISSES** • 1921
ROPIN' FOOL, THE • 1922 • Badger Clarence • SHT • USA
ROPIN' RIDIN' FOOL, THE • 1925 • *Morrison Pete* • USA
ROPING A BRIDE • 1915 • Mix Tom • USA
ROPING A SWEETHEART • 1916 • Mix Tom • SHT • USA
ROPING HER ROMEO • 1917 • Fishback Fred C., Del Ruth Hampton • SHT • USA
ROPING WILD BEARS • 1934 • Frank W. Earle • USA
ROPOTAMO • 1957 • Yonchev Lyuben • BUL
ROPPA NO SHINKON RYOKO • 1940 • Yamamoto Kajiro • JPN
ROQUEVILLARD, LES • 1922 • Duvivier Julien • FRN
ROQUEVILLARD, LES • 1943 • Dreville Jean • FRN
RORKE'S DRIFT • 1914 • Ridgely Richard • USA
RORO MENDUT • 1983 • Prijono Ami • INN
RORY O'MOORE see **RORY O'MORE** • 1911
RORY O'MORE • 1911 • Olcott Sidney • USA • RORY O'MOORE
RORY O'THE BOGS • 1913 • MacDonald J. Farrell • USA
ROSA • 1974 • Cosmi Carlo • VNZ
ROSA • 1981 • Samperi Salvatore • ITL
ROSA see **ROZA** • 1981
ROSA AND LIN see **ROSA UND LIN** • 1971
ROSA AND THE AUTHOR • 1915 • *Anderson Augusta* • USA
ROSA BLANCA • 1961 • Gavaldon Roberto • MXC
ROSA BLANCA, LA • 1953 • Fernandez Emilio • MXC, CUB • MOMENTOS DE LA VIDA DI MARTI
ROSA BLANCA, LA • 1972 • Gavaldon Roberto • MXC
ROSA DE ALFAMA • 1953 • Campos Henrique • PRT
ROSA DE FRANCIA • 1935 • Wiles Gordon • USA • ROSE OF FRANCE
ROSA DE LAS NIEVES • 1944 • Orona Vicente • MXC
ROSA DE LIMA • 1962 • Elorrieta Jose Maria • SPN • ROSA OF LIMA
ROSA DE LOS VIENTOS, LA • 1981 • Guzman Patricio • SPN, VNZ, CUB • ROSE OF THE WINDS ○ COMPASS ROSE, THE
ROSA DE MADRID • 1927 • Ardavin Eusebio F. • SPN
ROSA DE XOCHIMILCO • 1938 • Vejar Carlos • MXC
ROSA DEL CARIBE • 1944 • Benavides Jose Jr. • MXC
ROSA DI BAGDAD, LA • 1949 • Domenghini Anton Gino • ANM • ITL • SINGING PRINCESS, THE (USA) ○ ROSE OF BAGDAD, THE
ROSA DI SANGUE (ITL) see **ANGELICA** • 1939
ROSA DI TEBE • 1912 • Novelli Amleto • ITL • ROSE OF THEBES, THE
ROSA DIAMANT, DER • 1925 • Gliese Rochus • FRG • LIFE'S SHADOWS
ROSA DO ADRO, A • 1919 • PRT
ROSA DO ADRO, A • 1938 • de Garcia Eduardo Chianca • PRT
ROSA, LA TEQUILERA • 1966 • Cortes Fernando • MXC, PRC
ROSA LA TERCIOPELO see **CARNE DE CABARET** • 1939
ROSA LUXEMBURG • 1986 • von Trotta Margarethe • FRG
ROSA OF LIMA see **ROSA DE LIMA** • 1962
ROSA PANTOFFELCHEN, DAS • 1916 • Oberlander Hans • FRG
ROSA PANTOFFELCHEN, DAS • 1927 • Hofer Franz • FRG
ROSA PER TUTTI, UNA • 1967 • Rossi Franco • ITL • EVERY MAN'S WOMAN (UKN) ○ ROSE FOR EVERYONE, A ○ EVERYMAN'S WOMAN
ROSA ROJA, LA • 1960 • Serrano De Osma Carlos • SPN
ROSA ROSSA, LA • 1912 • Maggi Luigi • ITL
ROSA ROSSA, LA • 1973 • Giraldi Franco • ITL • RED ROSE, THE
ROSA TRIKOT, DAS • 1919 • Lasko Leo • FRG
ROSA UND LIN • 1971 • Emmerich Klaus • FRG • ROSA AND LIN
ROSAIRE, LE • 1934 • Ravel Gaston, Lekain Tony • FRN
ROSAL BENDITO, EL • 1936 • Bustillo Oro Juan • MXC
ROSALBA • 1954 • Gomez Landero Humberto • MXC
ROSALBA, LA FANCIULLA DI POMPEI • 1952 • Montillo Natale • ITL
ROSALEEN DHU • 1920 • Powers William • UKN
ROSALES, LA • 1984 • Lypszyc Raul • ARG
ROSALIE • 1937 • Van Dyke W. S. • USA
ROSALIE • 1966 • Borowczyk Walerian • ANS • FRN
ROSALIE AND SPIRITUALISM see **ROSALIE FAIT DU SPIRITISME** • 1911
ROSALIE FAIT DU SPIRITISME • 1911 • Bosetti Romeo • SHT • FRN • ROSALIE AND SPIRITUALISM
ROSALIE GOES SHOPPING • 1989 • Adlon Percy • FRG
ROSALIE (UKN) see **NOT SO DUMB** • 1930
ROSALIND AT REDGATE • 1919 • *Stonehouse Ruth* • SHT • USA
ROSALINDA • 1944 • Aguilar Rolando • MXC
ROSALYNNE AND THE LIONS (UKN) see **ROSELYNE ET LES LIONS** • 1989
ROSAMUNDA NON PARLA.. SPARA (ITL) see **ELLE CAUSE PLUS.. ELLE FLINGUE** • 1972
ROSANNA (USA) see **RED, LA** • 1953
ROSANNA'S DREAM • 1912 • *Reliance* • SHT • USA
ROSARIO • 1935 • Zacarias Miguel • MXC
ROSARIO, EL • 1943 • Ortega Juan J. • MXC
ROSARIO DE AMOZOC, EL • 1938 • Bohr Jose • MXC
ROSARIO, LA CORTIJERA • 1923 • Buchs Jose • SPN
ROSARY, THE • 1910 • Salter Harry • USA
ROSARY, THE • 1911 • Baker R. E. • USA
ROSARY, THE • 1913 • Smalley Phillips • USA
ROSARY, THE • 1915 • Campbell Colin • USA
ROSARY, THE • 1916 • *Puritan* • SHT • USA
ROSARY, THE • 1921 • Newall Guy • USA
ROSARY, THE • 1922 • Storm Jerome • USA • ROMANCE OF THE ROSARY, THE
ROSARY, THE • 1928 • Parkinson H. B., Edwards J. Steven • SHT • UKN
ROSARY MURDERS, THE • 1987 • Walton Fred • USA
ROSAS • 1972 • Antin Manuel • ARG
ROSAS DE OTONO • 1943 • de Orduna Juan • SPN
ROSAS DEL MILAGRO, LAS • 1959 • Soler Julian • MXC • MIRACLE OF THE ROSES, THE ○ MIRACULOUS ROSES, THE
ROSAURA A LAS DIEZ • 1958 • Soffici Mario • ARG
ROSAURO CASTRO • 1950 • Gavaldon Roberto • MXC
ROSC -THE POETRY OF VISION • 1979 • Scott Ciarin • SHT • IRL
ROSE • 1935 • Rouleau Raymond • FRN • QUATRE ROUES DE LA FORTUNE, LES ○ QUITTE OU DOUBLE
ROSE see **ROZA** • 1962
ROSE, LA • 1916 • de Baroncelli Jacques • FRN
ROSE, THE • 1979 • Rydell Mark • USA
ROSE, THE see **ROZA** • 1973
ROSE AMONG THE BRIARS, A • 1915 • *Saunders Jackie* • USA
ROSE AND THE DAGGER, THE • 1911 • Porter Edwin S. • USA
ROSE AND THE RING, THE • 1978 • Reiniger Lotte • ANM • CND
ROSE AND THE THORN, THE • 1914 • Lambart Harry • USA
ROSE AT SIXTEEN, A • 1913 • *Frontier* • USA
ROSE AT THE DOOR, THE • 1914 • Ridgely Richard • USA
ROSE BERND • 1919 • Halm Alfred • FRG
ROSE BERND • 1957 • Staudte Wolfgang • FRG • SINS OF ROSE BERND, THE (USA)
ROSE BLANCHE, LA • 1913 • Feuillade Louis • FRN
ROSE BOWL • 1936 • Barton Charles T. • USA • O'RILEY'S LUCK (UKN)
ROSE BOWL STORY, THE • 1952 • Beaudine William • USA
ROSE BUDS IN THE RAINBOW see **NIJI NO MAKANO LEMMON** • 1968
ROSE BUSH OF THE MEMORIES, THE • 1914 • *Cooper Miriam* • USA
ROSE CAFE, THE • 1987 • Suissa Daniele J. • CND • MAN WHO GUARDS THE GREENHOUSE, THE
ROSE COLORED SCARF, THE • 1916 • Worthington William • SHT • USA
ROSE DE FER, LA • 1972 • Rollin Jean • FRN
ROSE DE LA MER, LA • 1946 • de Baroncelli Jacques • FRN
ROSE DE SANG, LA see **ANGELICA** • 1939
ROSE DEL MARTIRIO, LA • 1918 • Falena Ugo • ITL
ROSE DELLA MADONNA, LE • 1914 • Maggi Luigi • ITL
ROSE DER WILDNIS, DIE • 1916 • Schmidthassler Walter • FRG

ROSE DES FLANDRES, LA • 1918-19 • du Plessis Armand • BLG
ROSE DI DANZICA, LE • 1979 • Bevilacqua Alberto • ITL • ROSES OF DANZICA, THE
ROSE D'OR, LA • 1910 • Velle Gaston • SHT • FRN • GOLD ROSE, THE
ROSE DREAMS see **RUZOVE SNY** • 1976
ROSE DU SOUK, LA see **SIROCCO** • 1930
ROSE ECORCHEE, LA • 1970 • Mulot Claude • FRN • RAVAGED (UKN) ○ BLOOD ROSE, THE ○ FLAYED ROSE, THE ○ H COMME HORREUR
ROSE EFFEUILLEE, LA • 1926 • Pallu Georges • FRN
ROSE EFFEUILLEE, LA • 1936 • Pallu Georges • FRN
ROSE ET LANDRY • 1963 • Godbout Jacques, Rouch Jean • DCS • CND
ROSE ET LE BLANC, LE • 1979 • Pansard-Besson Robert • FRN • AVENTURES DE HOLLY AND WOOD, LES
ROSE ET LE RESEDA, LA • 1945 • Michel Andre • SHT • FRN
ROSE ET LE SEL, LA • 1964 • Champion • SHT • FRN
ROSE ET LINE • Leroi Francis • FRN
ROSE ET MONSIEUR CHARBONNEAU • 1976 • Cote Guy-L. • DOC • CND
ROSE FOR EVERYONE, A see **ROSA PER TUTTI, UNA** • 1967
ROSE FRANCE • 1919 • L'Herbier Marcel • FRN
ROSE GARDEN, THE • 1989 • Rademakers Fons • FRG, USA
ROSE GARDEN OF SIX ACRES see **HATHOLDAS ROZSAKERT** • 1979
ROSE IN THE MUD, A see **WARUI YATSU HODO YOKU NEMURU** • 1960
ROSE LEAVES • 1910 • *Vitagraph* • USA
ROSE LEAVES • 1915 • *Reliance* • USA
ROSE MARIE • 1927 • Hubbard Lucien • USA
ROSE MARIE • 1936 • Van Dyke W. S. • USA • INDIAN LOVE CALL
ROSE MARIE • 1954 • LeRoy Mervyn • USA
ROSE MONDAY see **ROSENMONTAG** • 1924
ROSE MONDAY see **ROSENMONTAG** • 1930
ROSE MONDAY see **ROSENMONTAG** • 1955
ROSE O' MY HEART • 1914 • Santschi Thomas • USA
ROSE O' PARADISE • 1918 • Young James • USA
ROSE O' SALEM-TOWN • 1910 • Griffith D. W. • USA
ROSE O' THE RIVER • 1912 • Buckland Warwick • UKN
ROSE O' THE RIVER see **ROSE OF THE RIVER** • 1919
ROSE O' THE SEA • 1922 • Niblo Fred • USA
ROSE O' THE SHORE • 1915 • Physioc Wray • USA
ROSE OF BAGDAD, THE see **ROSA DI BAGDAD, LA** • 1949
ROSE OF BLOOD, THE • 1917 • Edwards J. Gordon • USA • RED ROSE, THE
ROSE OF CALIFORNIA, THE • 1912 • *Imp* • USA
ROSE OF CIMARRON • 1952 • Keller Harry • USA
ROSE OF FRANCE see **ROSA DE FRANCIA** • 1935
ROSE OF ITALY, A • 1916 • Beaumont Harry • SHT • USA
ROSE OF KENTUCKY, THE • 1911 • Griffith D. W. • USA
ROSE OF KILDARE, THE • 1927 • Fitzgerald Dallas M. • USA • FORGOTTEN VOWS (UKN)
ROSE OF LOVE, THE • 1916 • *Hiawatha* • USA
ROSE OF MAY, THE • 1913 • Kirkland Hardee • USA
ROSE OF MONTEREY see **ROSE OF THE GOLDEN WEST** • 1927
ROSE OF NOME • 1920 • Le Saint Edward J. • USA
ROSE OF OLD MEXICO, A • 1913 • Dwan Allan, Reid Wallace • USA
ROSE OF OLD ST. AUGUSTINE, THE • 1911 • *Selig* • USA
ROSE OF PARIS, THE • 1924 • Cummings Irving • USA
ROSE OF RHODESIA, THE • 1917 • SAF
ROSE OF SAN JUAN • 1913 • *Ayres Sydney* • USA
ROSE OF SANTA ROSA • 1948 • Nazarro Ray • USA
ROSE OF SHARON, THE • 1913 • *Essanay* • USA
ROSE OF SHARON AND THE OLD MEN OF KNOHULT, THE see **SARONS ROS OCH GUBBARNA I KNOHULT** • 1968
ROSE OF SURREY • 1913 • Trimble Larry • UKN
ROSE OF THE ALLEY • 1914 • *Balboa* • USA
ROSE OF THE ALLEY • 1916 • Horan Charles, Dowlan William C. • USA
ROSE OF THE BOWERY • 1927 • Bracken Bertram • USA
ROSE OF THE CIRCUS • 1911 • Blache Alice • USA
ROSE OF THE DESERT • 1925 • *Williams Big Boy* • USA
ROSE OF THE GOLAN, THE see **FLEUR DU GOLAN, LA** • 1974
ROSE OF THE GOLDEN WEST • 1927 • Fitzmaurice George • USA • ROSE OF MONTEREY
ROSE OF THE ISLANDS • 1912 • *Champion* • USA
ROSE OF THE MISTY POOL, THE • 1915 • *Michelena Beatriz* • USA
ROSE OF THE NIGHT, THE see **WICKED DARLING, THE** • 1919
ROSE OF THE PHILLIPINES, A • 1910 • *Imp* • USA
ROSE OF THE RANCH, THE • 1910 • *Lubin* • USA
ROSE OF THE RANCHO • 1914 • De Mille Cecil B., Apfel Oscar • USA
ROSE OF THE RANCHO • 1936 • Gering Marion, Florey Robert (U/c) • USA
ROSE OF THE REGIMENT see **REGEMENTETS ROS** • 1952
ROSE OF THE RIO GRANDE • 1938 • Nigh William • USA
ROSE OF THE RIO GRANDE see **GOD'S COUNTRY AND THE MAN** • 1931
ROSE OF THE RIVER • 1919 • Thornby Robert T. • USA • ROSE O' THE RIVER
ROSE OF THE SEA see **UMI NO BARA** • 1945
ROSE OF THE SOUTH • 1916 • Scardon Paul • USA
ROSE OF THE TENDERLOIN, A • 1909 • Dawley J. Searle • USA
ROSE OF THE TENEMENTS • 1926 • Rosen Phil • USA
ROSE OF THE WEST • 1919 • Millarde Harry • USA
ROSE OF THE WINDS see **ROSA DE LOS VIENTOS, LA** • 1981
ROSE OF THE WORLD • 1918 • Tourneur Maurice • USA
ROSE OF THE WORLD • 1925 • Beaumont Harry • USA
ROSE OF THE YUKON • 1949 • Blair George • USA
ROSE OF THEBES, THE see **ROSA DI TEBE** • 1912
ROSE OF THISTLE ISLAND see **ROSEN PA TISTELON** • 1945
ROSE OF THISTLE ISLAND, THE see **ROSEN PA TISTELON** • 1915
ROSE OF TRALEE • 1937 • Mitchell Oswald • UKN
ROSE OF TRALEE • 1942 • Burger Germain • UKN
ROSE OF VERSAILLES, THE see **BERUSAIYU NO BARA** • 1978
ROSE OF WASHINGTON SQUARE • 1939 • Ratoff Gregory • USA
ROSE OF WOLFVILLE, THE • 1918 • Bradbury Robert North • SHT • USA
ROSE OF YESTERDAY, A • 1914 • *Frontier* • USA
ROSE OF YESTERYEAR, THE • 1914 • *Leonard Marion* • USA
ROSE ON HIS ARM, THE see **TAIYO TO BARA** • 1956
ROSE, PIERROT ET LA LUCE, LA • 1982 • Gagnon Claude • CND
ROSE ROSSE PER ANGELICA • 1966 • Steno • ITL
ROSE ROSSE PER IL FUHRER • 1968 • Di Leo Fernando • ITL • CODE NAME RED ROSES (USA) ○ RED ROSES FOR THE FUHRER
ROSE ROUGE, LA • 1914 • Pouctal Henri • FRN
ROSE ROUGE, LA • 1950 • Pagliero Marcello • FRN
ROSE SCARLATTE • 1940 • De Sica Vittorio • ITL • DUE DOZZINE DI ROSE SCARLATTE
ROSE STREET • 1958 • Tait Margaret, Pirie Alex • UKN
ROSE TATTOO, THE • 1955 • Mann Daniel • USA
ROSE-TINTED DREAMS see **RUZOVE SNY** • 1976
ROSE TREE, THE see **GUL AGACI** • 1967
ROSE VON DSCHIANDUR, DIE • 1918 • Halm Alfred • FRG
ROSE VON STAMBUL, DIE • 1919 • *Massary Fritz* • FRG
ROSE VON STAMBUL, DIE • 1953 • Anton Karl • FRG
ROSEANNA • 1967 • Abramson Hans • SWD
ROSEANNA MCCOY • 1949 • Reis Irving, Ray Nicholas • USA
ROSEBUD • 1974 • Preminger Otto • USA
ROSEBUD BEACH HOTEL, THE • 1985 • Hurwitz Harry • USA • BIG LOBBY, THE
ROSEL VOM SCHWARZWALD, DIE • 1956 • Schundler Rudolf • FRG
ROSELAND • 1971 • Hobbs C. F. • USA
ROSELAND • 1977 • Ivory James • USA
ROSELYN • 1915 • Lambart Harry • USA
ROSELYNE ET LES LIONS • 1989 • Beineix Jean-Jacques • FRN • ROSALYNNE AND THE LIONS (UKN)
ROSEMARY • 1915 • Bowman William J., Balshofer Fred J. • USA
ROSEMARY CLIMBS THE HEIGHTS • 1919 • Ingraham Lloyd • USA
ROSEMARY -FOR REMEMBRANCE • 1910 • *Lubin* • USA
ROSEMARY IS PREGNANT AGAIN • 1969 • *Gunter Productions* • USA
ROSEMARY, THAT'S FOR REMEMBRANCE • 1914 • Grandon Francis J. • USA
ROSEMARY (USA) see **ROZMARING** • 1940
ROSEMARY (USA) see **MADCHEN ROSEMARIE, DAS** • 1958
ROSEMARY'S BABY • 1968 • Polanski Roman • USA
ROSEMARY'S BABY II see **LOOK WHAT'S HAPPENED TO ROSEMARY'S BABY** • 1976
ROSEMARY'S KILLER see **PROWLER, THE** • 1981
ROSEN AUS DEM SUDEN • 1926 • Froelich Carl • FRG
ROSEN AUS DEM SUDEN • 1934 • Janssen Walter • FRG • ROSES FROM THE SOUTH (USA)
ROSEN AUS DEM SUDEN • 1954 • Antel Franz • FRG
ROSEN BLUHEN AUF DEM HEIDEGRAB • 1927 • Porten Franz • FRG
ROSEN BLUHEN AUF DEM HEIDEGRAB • 1952 • Konig Hans H. • FRG
ROSEN BLUH'N AUF DEM HEIDEGRAB • 1929 • Blachnitzky Curt • FRG
ROSEN DER LIEBE see **LIEBLING DER WELT** • 1949
ROSEN, DIE DER STERM ENTBLATTERT • 1917 • Matull Kurt? • FRG
ROSEN FUR BETTINA • 1956 • Pabst G. W. • FRG • LICHT IN DER FINSTERNIS ○ BALLERINA
ROSEN FUR DEN STAATSANWALT • 1959 • Staudte Wolfgang • GDR • ROSES FOR THE PROSECUTOR
ROSEN IM HERBST • 1955 • Jugert Rudolf • FRG • EFFI BRIEST
ROSEN IN TIROL • 1940 • von Bolvary Geza • FRG
ROSEN PA TISTELON • 1915 • Klercker Georg • SWD • ROSE OF THISTLE ISLAND, THE
ROSEN PA TISTELON • 1945 • Ohberg Ake • SWD • ROSE OF THISTLE ISLAND
ROSEN-RESLI • 1954 • Reinl Harald • FRG
ROSENBERGS MUST NOT DIE, THE • 1981 • Lorenzi Stellio • FRN
ROSENCRANTZ AND GUILDENSTERN see **ROSENCRANTZ AND GUILDENSTERN ARE DEAD** • 1990
ROSENCRANTZ AND GUILDENSTERN ARE DEAD • 1990 • Stoppard Tom • UKN • ROSENCRANTZ AND GUILDENSTERN
ROSENDA • 1948 • Bracho Julio • MXC
ROSENKAVALIER, DER • 1926 • Wiene Robert • AUS
ROSENKAVALIER, DER • 1962 • Czinner Paul • UKN
ROSENKRANZ, DER • 1918 • Alexander Georg • FRG
ROSENMONTAG • 1924 • Meinert Rudolf • FRG • OFFIZIERSTRAGODIE, EINE ○ ROSE MONDAY
ROSENMONTAG • 1930 • Steinhoff Hans • FRG • ROSE MONDAY
ROSENMONTAG • 1955 • Birgel Willy • FRG • ROSE MONDAY
ROSENTOPF CASE, THE see **FALL ROSENTOPF, DER** • 1918
ROSES AND THORNS • 1915 • King Burton L. • USA
ROSES ARE FOR THE RICH • 1987 • Miller Michael • TVM • USA
ROSES ARE RED • 1947 • Tinling James • USA
ROSES BLOOM TWICE, THE • 1978 • Stevens David • MTV • ASL
ROSES FOR ROSIE • 1913 • *Lubin* • USA
ROSES FOR THE PROSECUTOR see **ROSEN FUR DEN STAATSANWALT** • 1959
ROSES FROM THE SOUTH (USA) see **ROSEN AUS DEM SUDEN** • 1934
ROSE'S HOUSE • 1977 • Borris Clay • CND
ROSES IN THE DUST • 1921 • Calvert Charles • UKN
ROSE'S MEMORY, THE see **MEMORIES OF A ROSE, THE** • 1962
ROSES NOIRES • 1935 • Boyer Jean, Martin Paul • FRN
ROSES OF DANZICA, THE see **ROSE DI DANZICA, LE** • 1979
ROSES OF MEMORY • 1915 • Taylor Edward C. • USA
ROSES OF PICARDY • 1918 • *Rosenfeld David (P)* • UKN
ROSES OF PICARDY • 1927 • Elvey Maurice • UKN
ROSES OF REMEMBRANCE • 1913 • *Nestor* • USA
ROSES OF THE VIRGIN, THE • 1910 • *Kalem* • USA
ROSES OF YESTERDAY • 1913 • Kirkland Hardee • USA
ROSE'S REVENGE • 1913 • *Chamberlain Riley* • USA
ROSES ROUGES ET PIMENTS VERTS • 1973 • Rovira Beleta Francisco • FRN, ITL, SPN • LONELY WOMAN, THE (USA)
ROSE'S STORY, THE • 1911 • Smiley Joseph, Tucker George Loane • USA
ROSETTI AND RYAN: MEN WHO LOVE WOMEN • 1977 • Astin John • TVM • USA
ROSI AND THE BIG CITY see **ROSI UND DIE GROSSE STADT** • 1980
ROSI UND DIE GROSSE STADT • 1980 • Behrens Gloria • FRG • ROSI AND THE BIG CITY
ROSIE • 1912 • *Eclair* • USA
ROSIE! • 1968 • Rich David Lowell • USA
ROSIE DIXON: NIGHT NURSE • 1977 • Cartwright Justin • UKN
ROSIE O'GRADY • 1917 • Collins John H. • USA
ROSIE THE RIVETER • 1944 • Santley Joseph • USA • IN ROSIE'S ROOM (UKN)
ROSIE THE RIVETER • 1980 • Fields Connie • USA • LIFE AND TIMES OF ROSIE THE RIVETER, THE
ROSIE: THE ROSEMARY CLOONEY STORY • 1982 • Cooper Jackie • TVM • USA
ROSIER DE MADAME HUSSON, LE • 1931 • Bernard-Deschamps • FRN • VIRTUOUS ISADORE, THE
ROSIER DE MADAME HUSSON, LE • 1950 • Boyer Jean • FRN • PRIZE, THE (USA)
ROSIER MIRACULEUX, LE • 1904 • Melies Georges • SHT • FRN • WONDERFUL ROSE TREE, THE (USA)
ROSIERE DE PESSAC, LA • 1969 • Eustache Jean • DOC • FRN
ROSIERE DE PESSAC II, LA • 1979 • Eustache Jean • DOC • FRN
ROSIERE DES HALLES, LA • 1935 • de Limur Jean • FRN • VIERGE DES HALLES, LA
ROSIE'S MANY THORNS • 1915 • *Federal* • USA
ROSIE'S RANCHO • 1917 • *Henry Gale* • USA
ROSINA FUMO VIENE IN CITTA PER FARSI IL CORREDO • 1972 • Gora Claudio • ITL
ROSITA • 1923 • Lubitsch Ernst • USA
ROSITA'S CROSS OF GOLD • 1913 • *Reliance* • USA
ROSL VOM TRAUNSEE, DIE see **DU BIST ENTZUCKEND, ROSEMARIE** • 1933
ROSLYN AND BLAGICA • 1979 • Ricketson James • DOC • ASL
ROSLYN ROMANCE • 1971 • Baillie Bruce • USA
ROSMUNDA E ALBOINO • 1961 • Campogalliani Carlo • ITL • SWORD OF THE CONQUEROR (USA)
ROSOLINO PATERNO SOLDATO • 1970 • Loy Nanni • ITL • THERE'S NO BUSINESS LIKE WAR BUSINESS ○ OPERATION SNAFU (USA)
ROSOR VARJE KVALL • 1939 • *Paramount* • SWD, DNM
ROSPIGGAR • 1942 • Bauman Schamyl • SWD • PEOPLE OF ROSLAGEN
ROSS SMITH FLIGHT, THE • 1920 • Hurley Frank • DOC • ASL
ROSSA, LA • 1956 • Capuano Luigi • ITL
ROSSA, LA (ITL) see **ROTE, DIE** • 1962
ROSSA DALLA PELLE CHE SCOTTA, LA • 1972 • Russo Renzo • ITL
ROSSA DEL BAR, LA • 1985 • Pons Ventura • SPN • RUBIA DEL BAR, LA ○ BLONDE IN THE BAR ○ BLONDE GIRL AT THE BAR
ROSSETTO, IL • 1960 • Damiani Damiano • ITL, FRN • JUEX PRECOCES (FRN) ○ LIPSTICK (USA) ○ RED LIPS ○ COLONNA INFAME, LA
ROSSIGNOL EST MORT, LE • 1947-49 • Canolle Jean • SHT • FRN
ROSSIGNOL ET LES CLOCHES, LE • 1951 • Delacroix Rene • CND
ROSSINI • 1943 • Bonnard Mario • ITL
ROSSITER CASE, THE • 1951 • Searle Francis • UKN
ROSSIYA NIKOLAI II I LEV TOLSTOY • 1928 • Shub Esther • USS • RUSSIA OF NICHOLAS II AND LEV TOLSTOY, THE
ROSSO • 1985 • Kaurismaki Mika • FNL
ROSSO E NERO • 1954 • Paolella Domenico • ITL • RED AND BLACK
ROSSO SEGNO DELLA FOLLIA, IL • 1969 • Bava Mario • ITL, SPN • HACHA PARA LA LUNA DE MIEL, UNA (SPN) ○ HATCHET FOR A HONEYMOON (USA) ○ BLOOD BRIDES (UKN) ○ ACCETTA PER LA LUNA DI MIELE, UN' ○ RED MARK OF MADNESS, THE ○ SPN ○ AXE FOR THE HONEYMOON, AN
ROSSZEMBEREK • 1979 • Szomjas Gyorgy • HNG • BAD GUYS ○ WRONGDOERS
ROSTRO AL MAR • 1949 • Serrano De Osma Carlos • SPN
ROSTRO DE LA MUERTE, EL • 1963 • Salvador Jaime • MXC • FACE OF DEATH, THE
ROSTRO DEL ASESINO, EL • 1965 • Lazaga Pedro • SPN • FACE OF THE MURDERER, THE
ROSTRO HUMANO DE CARACAS, EL • 1973 • Blanco Javier • DOC • VNZ • HUMAN FACE OF CARACAS, THE
ROSTRO INFERNAL • 1961 • Crevenna Alfredo B. • MXC • INCREDIBLE FACE OF DR. B., THE (USA) ○ HELL FACE
ROSTRO OCULTO, EL • 1964 • de la Cerda Clemente • VNZ • HIDDEN FACE, THE
ROSTROS • 1977 • Galvan Juan Antonio • SPN
ROSTROS OLVIDADOS • 1952 • Bracho Julio • MXC
ROSY DAWN, THE see **ZA RANNICH CERVANKU** • 1934
ROSY LA BOURRASQUE (FRN) see **TEMPORALE ROSY** • 1979
ROSY RAPTURE • 1915 • Nash Percy • UKN
ROT IST DIE LIEBE • 1957 • Hartl Karl • FRG
ROTA DE COLOMBO, A • 1969 • Costa Jose Fonseca • SHT • PRT
ROTAGG • 1946 • Mattsson Arne • SWD • BAD EGGS
ROTAIE • 1929 • Camerini Mario • ITL
ROTATION • 1949 • Staudte Wolfgang • GDR
ROTE, DIE • 1962 • Kautner Helmut • FRG, ITL • ROSSA, LA (ITL) ○ REDHEAD, THE (USA)
ROTE FADEN, DER • 1915 • von Woringen Paul • FRG
ROTE FADEN, DER • 1923 • *Stuart Webbs-Film* • FRG
ROTE FLEDERMAUS, DIE • 1921 • Seitz Franz • FRG
ROTE HAND, DIE • 1960 • Meisel Kurt • FRG, ITL • MANO ROSSO, LA (ITL) ○ RED HAND, THE (USA)

ROTE HENKER, DER • 1919 • Biebrach Rudolf • FRG
ROTE HEXE, DIE • 1920 • Feher Friedrich • FRG
ROTE KATZE DIE • 1921 • Capello Carlo • FRG
ROTE KREIS, DER • 1928 • Zelnik Friedrich • FRG • CRIMSON CIRCLE, THE (USA)
ROTE KREIS, DER • 1959 • Roland Jurgen • FRG • RED CIRCLE, THE (USA) ○ CRIMSON CIRCLE, THE
ROTE LIPPEN SOLL MAN KUSSEN see **GANZE WELT IST HIMMELBLAU, DIE** • 1964
ROTE MARIANNE, DIE • 1922 • Berger Friedrich • FRG
ROTE MAUS, DIE • 1925 • Meinert Rudolf • FRG
ROTE MUHLE • 1940 • von Alten Jurgen • FRG
ROTE MUHLE, DIE • 1921 • Boese Carl • FRG
ROTE MUTZE, DIE see **HEIRATSSCHWINDLER** • 1937
ROTE NACHT, DIE • 1921 • Speyer Jaap • FRG
ROTE NOVEMBER, DER • 1968 • Machalz Alfons • GDR • RED NOVEMBER
ROTE ORCHIDEEN • 1938 • Malasomma Nunzio • FRG • RED ORCHIDS (USA)
ROTE PLAKAT, DAS • 1920 • Justitz Emil • FRG
ROTE PRINZ, DER • 1954 • Schott-Schobinger Hans • AUS
ROTE RAUSCH, DER • 1962 • Schleif Wolfgang • FRG
ROTE REDOUTE, DIE • 1920 • Kobe Hanns • FRG
ROTE REITER, DER • 1919 • Stranz Fred • FRG
ROTE REITER, DER • 1923 • Koebner Franz W. • FRG
ROTE REITER, DER • 1935 • Randolf Rolf • FRG
ROTE ROSEN, ROTE LIPPEN, ROTER WEIN • 1953 • Martin Paul • FRG
ROTE SARAFAN, DER • 1919 • Zickel Martin • FRG
ROTE SCHATTEN, DER • 1921 • Attenberger Toni • FRG
ROTE SONNE • 1970 • Thome Rudolf • FRG
ROTE SPUREN • 1920 • Larsen Viggo • FRG
ROTE STREIFEN, DER • 1916 • Gad Urban • FRG
ROTE STRUMPF, DER • 1980 • Tumler Wolfgang • FRG
ROTEIRO DAS CATARATAS • 1957 • Spiguel Miguel • SHT • PRT
ROTEN SCHUHE, DIE • 1917 • Moest Hubert • FRG
ROTER MOHN • 1956 • Antel Franz • AUS
ROTHAUSGASSE, DIE • 1928 • Oswald Richard • FRG
ROTHCHILD • 1933 • de Gastyne Marco • FRN
ROTHENBURGER, DIE • 1918 • Pick Lupu • FRG • LIEB UND SEELE
ROTHKO CONSPIRACY, THE • 1983 • Watson Paul • TVM • UKN
ROTHSCHILD, DIE • 1940 • Waschneck Erich • FRG
ROTI • 1941 • Khan Mehboob • IND • BREAD
ROTI • 1988 • Idrees M. • PKS
ROTLICHT! • 1987 • Odermatt Urs • SWT
ROTMANAD • 1970 • Halldoff Jan • SWD • WHAT ARE YOU DOING AFTER THE ORGY? ○ DOG DAYS
ROTORUA LOOKABOUT • 1969 • Hutt Peter • DOC • NZL
ROTSPORT MARSCHIERT • 1930 • Blum Victor • DOC • FRG • RED SPORT ON THE MARCH
ROTTA SUD • 1947 • De Robertis Francesco • ITL
ROTTASOTA • 1968 • Kurkvaara Maunu • FNL • RAT WAR
ROTTEN APPLE, THE • 1963 • Hayes John • USA • 5 MINUTES TO LOVE ○ IT ONLY TAKES 5 MINUTES
ROTTEN BLOOD see **ZKAZENA KREV** • 1913
ROTTEN TO THE CORE • 1965 • Boulting John • UKN
ROTTERDAM – AMSTERDAM • 1918 • Larsen Viggo • FRG
ROTTERDAM –EUROPOORT • 1966 • Ivens Joris • SHT • NTH, FRN • ROTTERDAM –EUROPORT ○ FLYING DUTCHMAN, THE
ROTTERDAM –EUROPORT see **ROTTERDAM –EUROPOORT** • 1966
ROTTERDAM METROPOLIS • 1966 • Alsemgeest Peter • NTH
ROTTERS, THE • 1921 • Bramble A. V. • UKN
ROTTWEILER see **DOGS OF HELL** • 1982
ROTTWEILER: THE DOGS OF HELL see **DOGS OF HELL** • 1982
ROUBLE A DEUX FACES, LE • 1969 • Perier Etienne • FRN, SPN • RUBLO DE LAS DOS CARAS, EL (SPN) ○ TELEPHONE ROUGE, LE ○ DAY THE HOT LINE GOT HOT, THE (USA) ○ HOT LINE, THE
ROUE, LA • 1922 • Gance Abel • FRN • WHEEL, THE
ROUE, LA • 1956 • Haguet Andre • FRN • WHEELS OF FATE
ROUE DE LA FORTUNE, LA • 1938 • Storck Henri • DOC • BLG
ROUE'S HEART, THE • 1909 • Griffith D. W. • USA
ROUGE see **YANZHI KOU** • 1988
ROUGE AND RICHES see **ROGUE AND RICHES** • 1920
ROUGE AUX LEVRES, LE • 1970 • Kumel Harry • BLG, FRN, FRG • DAUGHTERS OF DARKNESS (USA) ○ LEVRES ROUGES, LES ○ PROMISE OF RED LIPS, THE ○ ERZEBETH ○ RED LIPS, THE ○ BLUT AN DEN LIPPEN ○ REDNESS OF THE LIPS, THE ○ FRN ○ BLOOD ON HER LIPS
ROUGE BAISER • 1986 • Belmont Vera • FRN • RED KISS (USA)
ROUGE DE CHINE, LE • 1976 • Richard Jacques • FRN
ROUGE EST MIS, LE • 1952 • Barrere, Knapp • SHT • FRN
ROUGE EST MIS, LE • 1957 • Grangier Gilles • FRN • SPEAKING OF MURDER (USA)
ROUGE ET LE BLANC, LE • 1971 • Autant-Lara Claude • FRN
ROUGE ET LE NOIR, LE • 1926 • Righelli Gennaro • ITL
ROUGE ET LE NOIR, LE • 1954 • Autant-Lara Claude • FRN, ITL • UOMO E IL DIAVOLO, L' (ITL) ○ ROUGE ET NOIR (USA) ○ SCARLET AND BLACK
ROUGE ET LE NOIR, LE see **CORRIERE DEL RE, IL** • 1948
ROUGE ET LE NOIR, LE see **KRAASNOYE I CHYORNOYE** • 1976
ROUGE ET NOIR see **GEHEIME KURIER, DER** • 1928
ROUGE ET NOIR (USA) see **ROUGE ET LE NOIR, LE** • 1954
ROUGE, LE ROUGE ET LE ROUGE, LE • Andrien Jean-Jacques • BLG • RED, THE RED AND THE RED, THE
ROUGE MIDI • 1984 • Guediguian Robert • FRN
ROUGE OF THE NORTH see **YUAN NU** • 1988
ROUGE VENETIEN • 1989 • Perier Etienne • FRN, ITL • VENETIAN RED (UKN)
ROUGED LIPS • 1923 • Shaw Harold • USA
ROUGH AND READY • 1918 • Stanton Richard • USA
ROUGH AND READY • 1924 • Taurog Norman • SHT • USA
ROUGH AND READY • 1927 • Rogell Albert S. • USA
ROUGH AND READY • 1930 • *Montana Bill* • USA
ROUGH AND READY REGGIE • 1917 • Jackson Harry • SHT • USA
ROUGH AND THE SMOOTH, THE • 1959 • Siodmak Robert • UKN • PORTRAIT OF A SINNER (USA)
ROUGH AND TUMBLEWEED • 1961 • Smith Paul J. • ANS • USA
ROUGH BOYS see **ANGELS DIE HARD** • 1970
ROUGH BUT ROMANTIC • 1915 • Blystone John G. • USA
ROUGH COMPANY (UKN) see **VIOLENT MEN, THE** • 1954
ROUGH CUT • 1980 • Siegel Don • USA, UKN • ROUGHCUT
ROUGH DAY FOR THE QUEEN see **RUDE JOURNEE POUR LA REINE** • 1973
ROUGH DIAMOND see **GANGA BRUTA** • 1932
ROUGH DIAMOND, A • 1912 • Noy Wilfred • UKN
ROUGH DIAMOND, A • 1913 • *Mills Thomas R.* • USA
ROUGH DIAMOND, THE • 1921 • Sedgwick Edward • USA
ROUGH DIAMONDS see **ZWARE JONGENS** • 1983
ROUGH GOING • 1925 • Van Wally • USA
ROUGH HOUSE, THE • 1917 • Arbuckle Roscoe • SHT • USA
ROUGH HOUSE RHYTHM • 1931 • Sweet Harry • SHT • USA
ROUGH HOUSE ROSIE • 1927 • Strayer Frank • USA • ROUGH–HOUSE ROSIE
ROUGH–HOUSE ROSIE see **ROUGH HOUSE ROSIE** • 1927
ROUGH ICE FLOWER see **LU–PING HUA** • 1989
ROUGH IDEA OF LOVE • 1930 • Sennett Mack • USA
ROUGH JUSTICE • 1984 • Yalden-Tomson Peter • MTV • CND
ROUGH KNIGHT, A • *Hopper De Wolfe* • USA
ROUGH LIFE see **NA PRZELAJ** • 1971
ROUGH LOVER, THE • 1918 • De Grasse Joseph • USA
ROUGH NECK, THE • 1916 • *Essanay* • SHT • USA
ROUGH NECK, THE • 1916 • Mayo Melvin • *Lubin* • SHT • USA
ROUGH NECKING • 1934 • Stevens George • SHT • USA
ROUGH NIGHT IN JERICHO • 1967 • Laven Arnold • USA
ROUGH NIGHT ON THE BRIDGE, A • 1910-12 • Melies Gaston • USA
ROUGH NIGHTS IN PARADISE • 1985 • SAF
ROUGH ON HUSBANDS • 1918 • *Sterling Merta* • SHT • USA
ROUGH ON RATS • 1912 • *Prior Herbert* • USA
ROUGH ON RATS • 1933 • Bailey Harry • ANS • USA
ROUGH ON RENTS • 1942 • Holmes Ben • SHT • USA
ROUGH ON ROMEO • 1922 • Roach Hal • SHT • USA
ROUGH ON RUBES • 1920 • *Reynold Vera* • USA
ROUGH ON THE CONJURER • 1905 • *Walturdaw* • UKN
ROUGH ON THE POLICEMAN • 1905 • *Walturdaw* • UKN
ROUGH ON UNCLE • 1915 • *Dangerfield Winnie* • UKN
ROUGH PARTY, A • 1925 • Lamont Charles • SHT • USA
ROUGH PASSAGE, A • 1922 • Barrett Franklyn • ASL
ROUGH PLATEAU see **DRSNA PLANINA** • 1980
ROUGH RIDE WITH NITROGLYCERINE, A • 1912 • Duncan William • USA
ROUGH RIDERS • 1927 • Fleming Victor • USA • TRUMPET CALL, THE (UKN)
ROUGH RIDERS OF CHEYENNE • 1945 • Carr Thomas • USA
ROUGH RIDERS OF DURANGO • 1951 • Brannon Fred C. • USA
ROUGH RIDER'S ROMANCE, THE • 1910 • *Kalem* • USA
ROUGH RIDERS' ROUNDUP • 1939 • Kane Joseph • USA
ROUGH RIDIN' • 1924 • Thorpe Richard • USA
ROUGH RIDIN' JUSTICE • 1945 • Abrahams Derwin • USA • DECOY (UKN)
ROUGH RIDIN' RED • 1928 • King Louis • USA
ROUGH RIDING • 1954 • *Smith Pete* • SHT • USA
ROUGH RIDING HOOD • 1966 • Marcus Sid • ANS • USA
ROUGH RIDING RANGER • 1935 • Clifton Elmer • USA • SECRET STRANGER, THE (UKN)
ROUGH RIDING RHYTHM • 1937 • McGowan J. P. • USA
ROUGH RIDING ROMANCE • 1919 • Rosson Arthur • USA
ROUGH RIDING ROMEO (UKN) see **FLAMING GUNS** • 1932
ROUGH ROMANCE • 1930 • Erickson A. F. • USA
ROUGH SEA see **MAR BRAVO** • 1981
ROUGH SEA AT DOVER • 1896 • Paul Robert William • UKN
ROUGH SEAS • 1921 • Roach Hal • SHT • USA
ROUGH SEAS • 1931 • Parrott James • SHT • USA
ROUGH SHOD • 1922 • Eason B. Reeves • USA
ROUGH SHOD FIGHTER, A • 1927 • *Russell William* • USA
ROUGH SHOOT • 1952 • Parrish Robert • UKN • SHOOT FIRST (USA)
ROUGH SKETCH see **WE WERE STRANGERS** • 1949
ROUGH SKETCH FOR A PROPOSED FILM DEALING WITH THE POWERS OF TEN AND THE RELATIVE SIZE OF THINGS IN.. • 1969 • Eames Charles • SHT • USA
ROUGH STUFF • 1917 • Smith Noel • SHT • USA
ROUGH STUFF • 1925 • Henderson Dell • USA
ROUGH TIME FOR THE BROKER, A • 1904 • Fitzhamon Lewin • UKN
ROUGH, TOUGH AND READY • 1945 • Lord Del • USA • MEN OF THE DEEP (UKN)
ROUGH, TOUGH WEST, THE • 1952 • Nazarro Ray • USA
ROUGH TOUGHS AND ROOF TOPS • 1917 • Semon Larry • SHT • USA
ROUGH TREATMENT see **BEZ ZNIECZULENIA** • 1978
ROUGH WATERS • 1930 • Daumery John • USA
ROUGH WEATHER COURTSHIP, A • 1910 • *Vitagraph* • USA
ROUGHCUT see **ROUGH CUT** • 1980
ROUGHEST AFRICA • 1923 • Roach Hal • SHT • USA
ROUGHING THE CUB • 1913 • Angeles Bert • USA
ROUGHLY SPEAKING • 1945 • Curtiz Michael • USA
ROUGHLY SQUEAKING • 1946 • Jones Charles M. • ANS • USA
ROUGHNECK, THE • 1915 • Hart William S., Smith Cliff • USA • CONVERT, THE
ROUGHNECK, THE • 1919 • Apfel Oscar • USA
ROUGHNECK, THE • 1924 • Conway Jack • USA • THORNS OF PASSION (UKN)
ROUGHNECK LOVER see **LOVIN' THE LADIES** • 1930
ROUGHNECKS • 1960 • Cote Guy-L. • DCS • CND • MAITRES–SONDEURS, LES
ROUGHSHOD • 1949 • Robson Mark • USA
ROUGOKU NO HANAYOME • 1939 • Arai Ryohei • JPN • PRISON BRIDE
ROULEMENT A BILLE, LE • 1924 • Gremillon Jean • SHT • FRN
ROULETABILLE • 1922 • Fescourt Henri • FRN • ROULETABILLE CHEZ LES BOHEMIENS
ROULETABILLE 1 • 1912 • Tourneur Maurice • FRN • MYSTERE DE LA CHAMBRE JAUNE, LE
ROULETABILLE 1 • 1946 • Chamborant Christian • FRN • ROULETABILLE JOUR ET GAGNE
ROULETABILLE 2 • 1912 • Tourneur Maurice • FRN • DERNIERE INCARNATION DE LARSAN, LA
ROULETABILLE 2 • 1946 • Chamborant Christian • FRN • ROULETABILLE CONTRE LA DAME DE PIQUE ○ ROULETTE TABLE VS. THE QUEEN OF SPADES
ROULETABILLE AVIATEUR • 1932 • Sekely Steve • FRN
ROULETABILLE CHEZ LES BOHEMIENS see **ROULETABILLE** • 1922
ROULETABILLE CONTRE LA DAME DE PIQUE see **ROULETABILLE 2** • 1946
ROULETABILLE JOUR ET GAGNE see **ROULETABILLE 1** • 1946
ROULETTE • 1924 • Taylor Stanner E. V. • USA
ROULETTE see **WHEEL OF CHANCE** • 1928
ROULETTE, LA • 1957 • Patry Pierre • DCS • CND
ROULETTE CHINOISE (FRN) see **CHINESISCHES ROULETT** • 1976
ROULETTE TABLE VS. THE QUEEN OF SPADES see **ROULETABILLE 2** • 1946
ROULI–ROULANT • 1966 • Jutra Claude • DCS • CND • DEVIL'S TOY, THE
ROULOTTE E ROULETTE • 1960 • Vasile Turi • ITL
ROUMANIE, TERRE D'AMOUR • 1930 • de Morlhon Camille • FRN
ROUMI, LE • 1969 • Boughedir Ferid • TNS
ROUND see **REDONDO** • 1985
ROUND ABOUT THE OLD CHURCH SQUARE see **RONDOM HET OUDEKERKSPLEIN..** • 1968
ROUND MIDNIGHT • 1986 • Tavernier Bertrand • FRN, USA
ROUND OF BULLETS, A see **RAFAGA DE PLOMO, UNA** • 1965
ROUND RAINBOW CORNER • 1950 • Neall Frank • UKN
ROUND ROBIN • 1976 • USA
ROUND THE BEND • 1966 • Negus-Fancey O. • UKN
ROUND THE WORLD IN 80 DAYS see **REISE UM DIE ERDE IN 80 TAGEN, DIE** • 1919
ROUND THE WORLD IN TWO HOURS VIA THE ALL RED ROUTE • 1914 • *Australian Films* • ASL • ALL RED ROUTE, THE
ROUND TRIP • 1967 • Gaisseau Pierre-Dominique • USA
ROUND TRIP $5.98 • 1910 • *Capitol* • USA
ROUND TRIP IN MODERN ART • 1949 • Rogers Roger Bruce • ANM • USA
ROUND TRIP TO MARS • 1957 • Smith Paul J. • ANS • USA
ROUND–UP, THE • 1917 • Ford John • USA
ROUND UP, THE • 1920 • Melford George • USA • ROUND–UP, THE
ROUND–UP, THE • 1941 • Selander Lesley • USA
ROUND–UP, THE see **ROUND UP, THE** • 1920
ROUND–UP, THE see **SZEGENYLEGENYEK (NEHEZELETUEK)** • 1965
ROUND–UP AT DAWN, THE • 1911 • *Kalem* • USA
ROUND–UP TIME IN TEXAS • 1937 • Kane Joseph • USA
ROUNDABOUT • 1962 • Robin Georges • UKN
ROUNDABOUT see **RONDO** • 1958
ROUNDABOUT, THE see **RONDO** • 1966
ROUNDABOUT, THE see **KARUSEL** • 1971
ROUNDED CORNERS • 1922 • Arthur George K. • UKN
ROUNDER, THE • 1930 • Nugent John Charles • USA
ROUNDERS, THE • 1914 • Chaplin Charles • USA • OH, WHAT A NIGHT ○ TWO OF A KIND ○ REVELRY ○ LOVE THIEF, THE
ROUNDERS, THE • 1964 • Kennedy Burt • USA
ROUNDING UP AND BRANDING CATTLE • 1904 • Porter Edwin S. • USA
ROUNDING UP AT THE "YEGGMAN" • 1904 • Porter Edwin S. • USA
ROUNDING UP BOWSER • 1914 • *Imp* • USA
ROUNDING UP THE COUNTERFEITERS • 1913 • *Kalem* • USA
ROUNDING UP THE LAW • 1922 • Seeling Charles R. • USA
ROUPEL • 1970 • *Paris James (P)* • GRC
ROUSSALKA • 1910 • Goncharov Vasili M. • USS
ROUSTABOUT • 1964 • Rich John • USA
ROUSTABOUT, THE • 1922 • Roach Hal • SHT • USA
ROUSTABOUT, THE see **PROPERTY MAN, THE** • 1914
ROUTE 11 TO DANGER • 1957 • Selander Lesley • USA
ROUTE, LA • 1972 • Bizot Jean-Francois • FRN
ROUTE AU SOLEIL, LA see **POUDRE D'ESCAMPETTE, LA** • 1971
ROUTE AUX DIAMANTS, LA see **PILLARDS, LES** • 1965
ROUTE DANS SILLAGE • 1963 • Menegoz Robert • SHT • FRN
ROUTE DE CORINTHE, LA • 1967 • Chabrol Claude • FRN, ITL, GRC • WHO'S GOT THE BLACK BOX? (USA) ○ ROAD TO CORINTH, THE
ROUTE DE L'OUEST, LA • 1964 • Arcand Denys • DCS • CND
ROUTE DE L'OUEST, LA see **GOIN' DOWN THE ROAD** • 1970
ROUTE DE NOUMEA, LA see **ROUTE DU BAGNE, LA** • 1945
ROUTE DE ST. TROPEZ, LA • 1966 • Sarne Mike • FRN, UKN • ROAD TO ST. TROPEZ (UKN)
ROUTE DE SALINA, LA see **SUR LA ROUTE DE SALINA** • 1969
ROUTE DE SUEDE, LA • 1952 • Demarne Pierre • SHT • FRN
ROUTE DES CIMES, LA • 1957 • Languepin Jean-Jacques • FRN
ROUTE DES EPICES, LA • 1950 • Novik William • SHT • FRN
ROUTE DU BAGNE, LA • 1945 • Mathot Leon • FRN • ROUTE DE NOUMEA, LA ○ FEMMES POUR NOUMEA ○ MANON 326
ROUTE DU BONHEUR, LA • 1952 • Labro Maurice, Simonelli Giorgio C. • ITL, FRN • SALUTI E BACI (ITL) ○ AMICAL SOUVENIR
ROUTE DU DEVOIR, LA • 1918 • Monca Georges • FRN
ROUTE DU FER, LA • 1972 • Lamothe Arthur • DCS • CND
ROUTE ENCHANTEE, LA • 1938 • Caron Pierre • FRN
ROUTE EST BELLE, LA • 1929 • Florey Robert • FRN
ROUTE ETERNELLE, LA • Colson-Malleville Marie • DOC • FRN • ETERNAL ROAD, THE
ROUTE HEUREUSE, LA • 1935 • Lacombe Georges • FRN
ROUTE IMPERIALE, LA • 1935 • L'Herbier Marcel • FRN
ROUTE INCONNUE, LA • 1948 • Poirier Leon • FRN

ROUTE NAPOLEON, LA • 1953 • Delannoy Jean • FRN
ROUTE OF DEPARTURE • 1987 • el Deek Bashir • EGY
ROUTE SANS ISSUE • 1947 • Stelli Jean • FRN • PASSION D'EVELYNE CLERY, LA
ROUTE SECRETE, LA • 1960 • Leherissey Jean • SHT • FRN
ROUTES BARREES • 1956 • Collet • SHT • FRN
ROUTES DE FRANCE, LES • 1954 • Bonniere Rene • DCS • FRN
ROUTES DU QUEBEC, LES • 1951 • Proulx Maurice • DCS • CND
ROUTES DU SUD, LES • 1978 • Losey Joseph • FRN, SPN • ROADS TO THE SOUTH, THE
ROUTINE see **RUTINA** • 1979
ROUTINE JOB • 1946 • Gunn Gilbert • DOC • UKN
ROUZHAYE TARIKE YEK MATHAR • 1967 • Zarandi Mohamad Ali • IRN • DARK DAYS OF A MOTHER, THE
ROVEDDERKOPPEN • 1915 • Blom August • DNM • RODE ENKE, DEN ○ ROBBER SPIDER, THE ○ WHITE WIDOW, THE
ROVER, THE see **AVVENTURIERO, L'** • 1967
ROVER AND ME • 1949 • Chisnell Frank • UKN
ROVER DANGERFIELD • 1990 • George James, Seeley Bob • ANM • USA
ROVER DRIVES A CAR • Hepworth Cecil M. • UKN
ROVER MAKES GOOD • 1953 • Dooley John • UKN
ROVER TAKES A CALL • 1905 • Fitzhamon Lewin • UKN
ROVER THE PEACEMAKER • 1911 • Fitzhamon Lewin • UKN
ROVER'S BIG CALL • 1942 • Glazer Herbert • SHT • USA
ROVER'S RESCUE • 1940 • White Volney • ANS • USA
ROVER'S RIVAL • 1937 • Clampett Robert • ANS • USA
ROVESCIO DELLA MEDAGLIA, IL • 1974 • Bizzarri Alvaro • SWT • OTHER SIDE OF THE MEDAL, THE
ROVESNIK VEKA • 1960 • Samsonov Samson • USS • AS OLD AS THE CENTURY ○ MAN OF THE CENTURY
ROVING ROGUE, A (UKN) see **OUTLAWS OF THE ROCKIES** • 1945
ROVING TUMBLEWEEDS • 1939 • Sherman George • USA • WASHINGTON COWBOY
ROW, THE see **AWANTURA** • 1971
ROW AND JOY ABOUT KUNNEMANN (USA) see **KRACH UND GLUCK UM KUNNEMANN** • 1937
ROW BOAT ROMANCE • 1914 • Avery Charles • USA
ROW IN A LAUNDRY, A • 1903 • Collins Alf? • UKN
ROW ROW ROW • 1930 • Fleischer Dave • ANS • USA
ROW, ROW, ROW YOUR BOAT • 1944 • Munro Grant • ANS • CND
ROWAN TREE, THE see **JARZEBINA CZERWONA** • 1969
ROWDY, THE • 1921 • Kirkland David • USA
ROWDY AND HIS NEW PAL • 1912 • *Lessey George* • USA
ROWDY ANN • 1919 • Christie Al • SHT • USA
ROWDY COMES HOME • 1913 • *Reliance* • USA
ROWDY STARTS SOMETHING • 1913 • *Punch* • USA
ROWDYMAN, THE • 1972 • Carter Peter • CND
ROWER • 1957 • Polanski Roman • PLN • BICYCLE, THE
ROWIESNICY • 1962 • Lomnicki Jan • DOC • PLN • CONTEMPORARIES
ROWING IN THE WIND see **REMANDO AL VIENTO** • 1988
ROWING TO WIN • 1922 • Parkinson H. B. • UKN
ROWING WITH THE WIND see **REMANDO AL VIENTO** • 1988
ROWLANDSON'S ENGLAND • 1955 • Hawkesworth John • SHT • UKN
ROXANA see **EROTIC ODYSSEY** • 1976
ROXANNE • 1987 • Schepisi Fred • USA
ROXIE HART • 1942 • Wellman William A. • USA
ROY COLT & WINCHESTER JACK • 1970 • Bava Mario • ITL
ROY TASH • 1966 • Bonniere Rene • DCS • CND
ROYAL AFFAIR, A (USA) see **ROI, LE** • 1949
ROYAL AFFAIR IN VERSAILLES (USA) see **SI VERSAILLES M'ETAIT CONTE** • 1955
ROYAL AFRICAN RIFLES • 1953 • Selander Lesley • USA • STORM OVER AFRICA (UKN)
ROYAL AMERICAN, THE • 1927 • Brown Harry J. • USA
ROYAL BABBLE, THE see **KUNGLIGA PATRASKET** • 1945
ROYAL BALLET, THE • 1960 • Czinner Paul • UKN
ROYAL BALLET GIRL, THE (USA) see **K.U.K. BALLETTMADEL, DAS** • 1926
ROYAL BANNERS OVER OTTAWA • 1939 • Sparling Gordon • DCS • CND
ROYAL BED, THE • 1930 • Sherman Lowell • USA • QUEEN'S HUSBAND, THE (UKN)
ROYAL BLOOD • 1916 • *Plump & Runt* • USA
ROYAL BLUFF, THE • 1931 • Roberts Stephen • SHT • USA
ROYAL BOX, THE • 1914 • Eagle Oscar • USA
ROYAL BOX, THE • 1930 • Foy Bryan • USA
ROYAL CAFE • 1936 • Schwarzwald Milton • SHT • USA
ROYAL CAT NAP • 1958 • Hanna William, Barbera Joseph • ANS • USA
ROYAL CAVALCADE • 1935 • Brenon Herbert, Bentley Thomas, Varnel Marcel, Lee Norman, Summers Walter, Kellino W. P. • UKN • REGAL CAVALCADE (USA)
ROYAL CHILDREN see **KONIGSKINDER** • 1962
ROYAL DEMAND, A • 1933 • Minzenty Gustave • UKN
ROYAL DEMOCRAT, A • 1919 • Conway Jack • USA • NOBLE WANDERER, THE
ROYAL DISSOLUTE, THE see **REALE DISSOLUTO, IL**
ROYAL DIVORCE, A • 1923 • Butler Alexander • UKN
ROYAL DIVORCE, A • 1938 • Raymond Jack • UKN
ROYAL EAGLE • 1936 • Cooper George A., Ridley Arnold • UKN
ROYAL ENGLAND, A STORY OF AN EMPIRE'S THRONE • 1911 • Stormont Leo, Coleby A. E. • UKN
ROYAL FAMILY • 1969 • Cawston Richard • UKN
ROYAL FAMILY, A • 1915 • Nigh William • USA
ROYAL FAMILY OF BROADWAY, THE • 1930 • Cukor George, Gardner Cyril • USA • THEATRE ROYAL
ROYAL FLASH • 1975 • Lester Richard • UKN
ROYAL FLESH • 1968 • De Serge Carlton • USA • UNDERCOVER SCANDALS OF HENRY VIII, THE ○ HENRY VIII
ROYAL FLUSH (UKN) see **TWO GUYS FROM MILWAUKEE** • 1946
ROYAL FOUR FLUSH, THE • 1925 • Roach Hal • SHT • USA
ROYAL FOUR FLUSHER • 1947 • Kneitel Seymour • ANS • USA
ROYAL FOUR FLUSHER, THE • 1930 • Buzzell Edward • SHT • USA
ROYAL GAME, THE see **SCHACHNOVELLE, DIE** • 1960
ROYAL GOOD TIME, A • 1934 • Stallings George • ANS • USA
ROYAL HERITAGE • 1952 • Pine Diana • UKN
ROYAL HUNT, THE see **KUNGAJAKT** • 1944
ROYAL HUNT, THE see **MRIGAYAA** • 1976
ROYAL HUNT OF THE SUN, THE • 1969 • Lerner Irving • UKN, USA
ROYAL HUNTING, THE see **CHASSE ROYALE, LA** • 1969
ROYAL JELLY see **JALEA REAL** • 1981
ROYAL JOHANSSON see **KUNGLIGA JOHANSSON** • 1934
ROYAL JOURNEY • 1951 • Bairstow David • DOC • CND • VOYAGE ROYAL
ROYAL LOVE • 1915 • Nash Percy • UKN
ROYAL MERCY see **TSARKA MILOST** • 1962
ROYAL MISTAKE, THE see **KRALOVSKY OMYL** • 1968
ROYAL MOUNTED PATROL, THE • 1941 • Hillyer Lambert • USA • GIANTS A'FIRE (UKN)
ROYAL MOUNTED RIDES AGAIN, THE • 1945 • Taylor Ray, Collins Lewis D. • SRL • USA
ROYAL OAK, THE • 1923 • Elvey Maurice • UKN
ROYAL ONTARIO MUSEUM • 1972 • Bonniere Rene • DCS • CND
ROYAL OUTCAST, A • 1909 • *Selig* • USA
ROYAL PAUPER, THE • 1917 • Turbett Ben • USA
ROYAL PROVINCE, THE • 1967 • Perry Margaret • DOC • CND
ROYAL RAG • 1954 • Brealey Gil • DOC • ASL
ROYAL RAZZ, THE • 1924 • McCarey Leo • SHT • USA
ROYAL REGATTA see **KOLOLYEVSKAYA REGATA** • 1967
ROYAL REMEMBRANCES • 1929 • Hepworth Cecil M. • UKN
ROYAL RIDER, THE • 1929 • Brown Harry J. • USA
ROYAL RIVER • 1951 • Smith Brian • UKN • DISTANT THAMES
ROYAL RIVER • 1958 • Sparling Gordon • DCS • CND • FLEUVE SOUVERAIN, UN
ROYAL RODEO • 1939 • Amy George • SHT • USA
ROYAL ROGUE, A • 1917 • Kerr Robert, Hartman Ferris • SHT • USA
ROYAL ROMANCE, A • 1913 • Miller Ashley • USA
ROYAL ROMANCE, A • 1917 • Vincent James • USA
ROYAL ROMANCE, A • 1930 • Kenton Erle C. • USA
ROYAL ROMANCE OF CHARLES AND DIANA, THE • 1982 • Levin Peter • TVM • USA
ROYAL SCANDAL see **HOSE, DIE** • 1927
ROYAL SCANDAL, A • 1945 • Preminger Otto, Lubitsch Ernst • USA • CZARINA (UKN)
ROYAL STANDARD, THE • 1907 • Gilbert Arthur • UKN
ROYAL STIRLING • 1971 • Littlewood Mark • DCS • UKN
ROYAL SURVIVOR, A • 1914 • *Melies* • USA
ROYAL TOUR OF QUEEN ELIZABETH, THE • 1954 • *Gordon Craig (P)* • DOC • UKN
ROYAL TRACK, THE see **KUNGSLEDEN** • 1964
ROYAL WALTZ, THE (USA) see **KONIGSWALZER** • 1935
ROYAL WEDDING • 1950 • Donen Stanley • USA • WEDDING BELLS (UKN)
ROYAL WEDDING, THE • 1896 • Acres Birt • UKN
ROYAL WEDDING AT WINDSOR, THE • 1905 • Hepworth Cecil M. • UKN
ROYAL WELCOME • 1951 • Sparling Gordon • DCS • CND
ROYAL WILD WEST, THE • 1914 • Drew Sidney • USA
ROYAL WISHBONE, THE • 1910 • *Yankee* • USA
ROYALIST'S WIFE, THE • 1909 • Raymond Charles? • UKN
ROYAUME DES FEES, LE • 1903 • Melies Georges • FRN • FAIRYLAND, THE (USA) ○ KINGDOM OF THE FAIRIES, THE ○ WONDERS OF THE DEEP ○ AU PAYS DES FEES
ROYAUME DES MIROIRS DEFORMANTS, LE • 1963 • Rou Aleksandr • USS
ROYAUME VOUS ATTEND, UN • 1975 • Perrault Pierre, Gosselin Bernard • DOC • CND
ROYKSOPP • 1986 • Breien Anja • NRW • PUFF BALL
ROZ GARAN • 1968 • AFG • DAY BY DAY
ROZA • 1962 • Majewski Janusz • PLN • ROSE
ROZA • 1973 • Szpakowicz Piotr • PLN • ROSE, THE
ROZA • 1981 • Christophis Christophoros • GRC • ROZA –THE NATURE OF THE UNIVERSE ○ ROSA
ROZA –THE NATURE OF THE UNIVERSE see **ROZA** • 1981
ROZBIJEMY ZABAWA • 1957 • Polanski Roman • PLN • BREAKING UP THE DANCE ○ BREAKING UP THE PARTY ○ BREAK UP THE PARTY ○ BREAKING THE PARTY ○ BREAK UP THE DANCE
ROZBITKOWIE • 1969 • Giersz Witold (c/d) • ANS • PLN • CASTAWAYS, THE
ROZDESTVO OBITATELEJ LESA • 1912 • Starevitch Ladislas • USS • CHRISTMAS OF THE FOREST'S INHABITANTS (USA) ○ CHRISTMAS NIGHT ○ CHRISTMAS AT THE FOX'S BOARDING HOUSE ○ BIRTH OF THE HOSTS OF THE FOREST, THE ○ CHRISTMAS EVE
ROZEKI MONO • 1928 • *Tsuburaya Eiji (Ph)* • JPN
ROZHAI DUSHWAR • 1974 • Latifi Wali • AFG • DIFFICULT DAYS
ROZHOVORY • 1969 • Schorm Evald • MTV • CZC • DIALOGUES
ROZINA SEBRANEC • 1945 • Vavra Otakar • CZC • ROZINA, THE FOUNDLING
ROZINA, THE FOUNDLING see **ROZINA SEBRANEC** • 1945
ROZKAZ: OCALIC MIASTO • 1976 • Lomnicki Jan • PLN
ROZMARING • 1940 • Martonffy Emil • HNG • ROSEMARY (USA)
ROZMARNE LETO • 1967 • Menzel Jiri • CZC • CAPRICIOUS SUMMER
ROZMARY LASKY • 1970 • Kabrt Josef • CZC • CAPRICES OF LOVE, THE
ROZMOWA • 1974 • Andrejew Piotr • PLN • CONVERSATION, THE ○ TALK, THE
ROZNICA 1965–66 • 1966 • Gryczelowska Krystyna • DOC • PLN • DIFFERENCE 1965–66, A
ROZOVE KONBINE • 1932 • Marten Leo • CZC • PINK SLIP, THE
ROZSA BOKOR • 1937 • Vajda Ladislao • HNG
ROZSTANIE • 1960 • Has Wojciech J. • PLN • GOODBYE TO THE PAST ○ PARTING
ROZTOMILY CLOVEK • 1941 • Fric Martin • CZC • CHARMING MAN, A
ROZUM A CIT • 1962 • Brdecka Jiri • ANS • CZC • SENTIMENT AND REASON ○ REASON AND EMOTION
ROZWODOW NIE BEDZIE • 1963 • Stawinski Jerzy Stefan • PLN • NO MORE DIVORCES ○ VOYAGERS
RR • 1981 • Brakhage Stan • USA
RUANDA–URANDI • 1955 • de Heusch Luc • BLG
RUB IT IN • 1970 • *Distripix Inc.* • USA
RUB OUT THE KILLERS see **SATSUJINSHA O KESE** • 1964
RUBA AL PROSSIMO TUO • 1968 • Maselli Francesco • ITL • FINE PAIR, A (USA) ○ COPPIA TRANQUILLA, UNA ○ ROB YOUR NEIGHBOUR
RUBACUORI • 1931 • Brignone Guido • ITL
RUBAIYAT OF A SCOTCH HIGH BALL, THE • 1918 • Justice Martin • SHT • USA
RUBAIYAT OF OMAR KHAYYAM, THE • 1922 • Earle Ferdinand P. • USA
RUBBER • 1936 • Rutten Gerard • NTH
RUBBER CEMENT • 1975 • Breer Robert • USA
RUBBER GUN, THE • 1976 • Moyle Allan • CND
RUBBER HEADS • 1908 • *Pathe* • SHT • FRN
RUBBER HEELS • 1927 • Heerman Victor • USA
RUBBER MADNESS • 1980 • Wynne Cordell • MTV • CND
RUBBER MAN, THE • 1909 • *Lubin Sigmund* • USA
RUBBER RACKETEERS • 1942 • Young Harold • USA
RUBBER TARZAN see **GUMMI TARZAN** • 1981
RUBBER TIRES • 1927 • Hale Alan • USA • 10,000 REWARD
RUBBER TWICE see **DVAKRAT KAUCEK** • 1939-40
RUBBERFACE AS A SPECIAL CONSTABLE • 1916 • *Cricks* • UKN
RUBBERNECK, THE • 1924 • Roach Hal • SHT • USA
RUBBING IT IN • 1917 • Drew Sidney, Drew Sidney Mrs. • USA
RUBE, THE • 1914 • Farnum Marshall • USA
RUBE, THE • 1925 • *Burns Sammy* • USA
RUBE AND FENDER • 1903 • Porter Edwin S. • USA
RUBE AND MANDY AT CONEY ISLAND • 1903 • Porter Edwin S. • USA
RUBE AND THE BARON, THE • 1913 • Sennett Mack • USA
RUBE AND THE BOOB, THE • 1913 • *Neilan Marshall* • USA
RUBE BOSS, THE • 1913 • *Mace Fred* • USA
RUBE BROWN IN TOWN • 1907 • *Bitzer Billy (Ph)* • USA
RUBE CONDUCTOR, A • 1915 • *Punchinello* • USA
RUBE COUPLE AT A COUNTY FAIR • 1904 • Porter Edwin S. • USA
RUBE DETECTIVE, THE • 1912 • *Kalem* • USA
RUBE GOLDBERG CARTOON • *Barre Raoul (P)* • ASS • USA
"RUBE" MARQUAND WINS • 1912 • *Kalem* • USA
RUBE, THE INTERLOPER • 1914 • *Kalem* • USA
RUBENS • 1947 • Haesaerts Paul, Storck Henri • BLG
RUBENS • 1977 • Verhavert Roland • BLG
RUBES AND ROBBERS • 1919 • Pratt Gilbert • SHT • USA
RUBES AND ROMANCE • 1920 • *Howell Alice* • SHT • USA
RUBES AND THE BUNCO MEN, THE • 1909 • *Essanay* • USA
RUBE'S DELIRIUM • 1915 • *Deer* • USA
RUBE'S DUCK, THE • 1914 • *Lubin* • USA
RUBES' EASTER AT ATLANTIC CITY, THE • 1912 • *Lubin* • USA
RUBE'S HOTEL TANGLE • 1916 • Miller Rube • USA
RUBES IN THE THEATRE • 1901 • Porter Edwin S. • USA
RUBE'S MISTAKE • 1912 • *Lubin* • USA
RUBE'S SLEEP PRODUCER, THE • 1915 • *Luna* • USA
RUBEZAHL, HERR DER BERGE • 1957 • Kobler Erich • FRG
RUBEZAHLS HOCHZEIT • 1916 • Wegener Paul • FRG • OLD NIP'S WEDDING
RUBIA DEL BAR, LA see **ROSSA DEL BAR, LA** • 1985
RUBIA MIREYA, LA • 1948 • *Lamas Fernando* • ARG
RUBIA'S JUNGLE • 1970 • de la Parra Pim • NTH
RUBICON • 1931 • Weinshtak Vladimir
RUBICON see **ETTER RUBICON** • 1987
RUBIN–SALAMANDER, DER • 1918 • Biebrach Rudolf • FRG
RUBLO DE LAS DOS CARAS, EL (SPN) see **ROUBLE A DEUX FACES, LE** • 1969
RUBOG SA GUNTO • 1971 • Brocka Lino • PHL
RUBY • 1967 • Tapawan Chito B. • PHL
RUBY • 1970 • Bartlett Richard • USA
RUBY • 1977 • Harrington Curtis • USA
RUBY see **RUBY GENTRY** • 1952
RUBY AND OSWALD • 1978 • Stuart Mel • TVM • USA • FOUR DAYS IN DALLAS
RUBY AND RATA • 1990 • Preston Gaylene • NZL
RUBY CIRCLE, THE • 1914 • *Leonard Robert* • USA
RUBY GENTRY • 1952 • Vidor King • USA • RUBY
RUBY LIPS • 1928 • Parrott James • SHT • USA
RUBY, THE THIEF see **KAITO, RUBY** • 1989
RUCAK • 1972 • Grgic Zlatko • ANS • YGS • LUNCH, THE
RUCHE MERVEILLEUSE, LA • 1905 • Velle Gaston • SHT • FRN • MARVELOUS HIVE, THE
RUCHOME PIASKI • 1969 • Slesicki Wladyslaw • DOC • PLN • QUICKSANDS ○ SHIFTING SANDS ○ MOVING SAND
RUCKBLICK AUS DEM JAHRE 3000 • 1921 • Oswald Richard • FRG
RUCKENDEKOLLETE, DAS • 1975 • Nemec Jan • SWT, FRN, FRG • DECOLLETE DANS LE DOS, LE (FRN)
RUCKKEHR • 1977 • Jasny Vojtech • AUS • RETURN, THE
RUCKKEHR, DIE • 1990 • von Trotta Margarethe • FRG • RETURN, THE
RUCKKEHR DER TRUPPEN VON DER FRUHJAHRSPARADE, DIE • 1900 • Messter Oskar • FRG
RUCKUS • 1980 • Kleven Max • USA • LONER, THE
RUDA STOPA • 1963 • Miler Zdenek • ANS • CZC • RED STAIN ○ RED TRAIL
RUDA ZARE NAD KLADNEM • 1955 • Vlcek Vladimir • CZC • RED GLOW OVER KLADNO
RUDD FAMILY GOES TO TOWN, THE see **DAD AND DAVE COME TO TOWN** • 1938
RUDDIGORE • 1967 • Batchelor Joy • ANM • UKN
RUDD'S NEW SELECTION • 1921 • Longford Raymond • ASL
RUDE AWAKENING • 1908 • Melies Georges • FRN
RUDE AWAKENING • 1982 • Sasdy Peter • TVM • UKN
RUDE AWAKENING • 1989 • Grunwalt David, Russo Aaron • USA
RUDE AWAKENING, A • 1914 • *Beauty* • USA
RUDE BOY • 1980 • Hazan Jack, Mingay David • UKN
RUDE HOSTESS, A • 1909 • Griffith D. W. • USA
RUDE INTRUDER, THE • 1972 • Smith Paul J. • ANS • USA

RUDE JOURNEE POUR LA REINE • 1973 • Allio Rene • FRN, SWT • ROUGH DAY FOR THE QUEEN
RUDI NA KRTINACH • 1911 • Longen Emil Arthur • CZC • RUDI THE GODFATHER
RUDI NA ZALATECH • 1911 • Longen Emil Arthur • CZC • RUDI THE SEDUCER OF WOMEN
RUDI SPORTSMANEM • 1911 • Longen Emil Arthur, Pech Antonin • CZC • RUDI THE SPORTSMAN
RUDI THE GODFATHER see **RUDI NA KRTINACH** • 1911
RUDI THE SEDUCER OF WOMEN see **RUDI NA ZALATECH** • 1911
RUDI THE SPORTSMAN see **RUDI SPORTSMANEM** • 1911
RUDOBELSKAYA REPUBLIC see **RUDOBELSKAYA RESPUBLIKA** • 1971
RUDOBELSKAYA RESPUBLIKA • 1971 • Kalinin Nikolai • USS • RUDOBELSKAYA REPUBLIC
RUDOLPH AND FROSTY'S CHRISTMAS IN JULY • 1979 • USA
RUDOLPH THE RED-NOSED REINDEER • 1948 • Fleischer Max • ANS • USA
RUDOLPH THE RED-NOSED REINDEER • 1967 • *Ives Burl* • ANM • USA
RUD'S HEIRESS • 1913 • Duncan William • USA
RUDY VALLEE AND CONNECTICUT YANKEES • 1929 • Santley Joseph • SHT • USA
RUDY VALLEE MELODIES • 1932 • Fleischer Dave • ANS • USA
RUDYARD KIPLING'S JUNGLE BOOK • 1942 • Korda Zoltan • USA • JUNGLE BOOK, THE (UKN)
RUE, LA see **STREET, THE** • 1976
RUE BARBARE • 1983 • Behat Gilles • FRN • STREET OF THE DAMNED ○ STREET OF THE LOST
RUE CASES-NEGRES • 1983 • Palcy Euzhan • FRN • SUGAR CANE ALLEY ○ BLACK SHACK ALLEY
RUE CHINOISE, LA • 1956 • Loriquet • SHT • FRN
RUE DE LA PAIX • 1926 • Diamant-Berger Henri • FRN • SINS OF FASHION
RUE DE L'ENFER, LA • 1977 • Favre Bernard • DOC • FRN
RUE DE L'ESTRAPADE • 1953 • Becker Jacques • FRN • FRANCOISE STEPS OUT (UKN)
RUE DE PARIS (USA) see **RUE DES PRAIRIES** • 1959
RUE DES AMOURS FACILES, LA (FRN) see **VIA MARGUTTA** • 1960
RUE DES BOUCHES PEINTES, LA • 1955 • Vernay Robert • FRN
RUE DES CASCADES • 1964 • Delbez Maurice • FRN
RUE DES NATIONS, LA • 1900 • Melies Georges • FRN
RUE DES PRAIRIES • 1959 • de La Patelliere Denys • FRN, ITL • MIO FIGIO (ITL) ○ RUE DE PARIS (USA) ○ STREETS OF PARIS
RUE DES SAUSSAIES • 1950 • Habib Ralph • FRN • 11, RUE DES SAUSSAIES
RUE DU PAVE D'AMOUR, LA • 1923 • Hugon Andre • FRN
RUE DU PIED-DE-GRUE • 1979 • Grand-Jouan Jean-Jacques • BLG, FRN
RUE HAUTE • 1976 • Ernotte Andre • FRN, BLG
RUE JEANNE MANCE • 1978 • Ballantyne Tanya • CND
RUE LEPIC SLOW RACE, THE • 1968 • Miles Christopher • SHT • UKN
RUE SANS JOIE, LA • 1938 • Hugon Andre • FRN
RUE SANS LOI, LA • 1950 • Gibaud Marcel • FRN
RUE SANS NOM, LA • 1934 • Chenal Pierre • FRN
RUEDA DE LA VIDA, LA • 1942 • Ardavin Eusebio F. • SPN
RUEDA DE SOSPECHOSOS • 1964 • Fernandez Ramon • SPN
RUEE DES VIKINGS, LA (FRN) see **INVASORI, GLI** • 1961
RUELLE DES FOU see **DARB AL-MAHABIL** • 1955
RUELLE DES IDIOTS see **DARB AL-MAHABIL** • 1955
RUEN PAE • 1989 • Kounavudhi Vichit • THL • RIVER HOUSE
RUES DE HONG KONG • 1964 • Guillemot Claude • SHT • FRN
RUF, DER • 1949 • von Baky Josef • FRG • LAST ILLUSION, THE ○ CALL, THE
RUF AN DAS GEWISSEN • 1945 • Anton Karl • FRG • RUF DES GEWISSENS
RUF AUS DEM AETHER • 1951 • Pabst G. W., Klaren Georg C. • FRG
RUF AUS DEM JENSEITS, DER • 1920 • Kirsch Richard • FRG
RUF AUS DER FERNE, DER • 1925 • *Elro-Film* • FRG
RUF DER BERGE • 1954 • Wieser Eduard • AUS, SWT
RUF DER GOTTER • 1957 • Wawrzyn Dietrich • FRG
RUF DER LIEBE, DER • 1916 • Biebrach Rudolf • FRG
RUF DER SIBYLLA, DER • 1984 • Klopfenstein Clemens • SWT
RUF DER WALDER • 1965 • Antel Franz • AUS
RUF DER WILDGANSE, DER • 1961 • Hinrich Hans • AUS
RUF DER WILDNIS see **TUMULTO DE PAIXOES** • 1958
RUF DER WILDNIS (FRG) see **CALL OF THE WILD** • 1972
RUF DES GEWISSENS see **RUF AN DAS GEWISSEN** • 1945
RUF DES NORDENS, DER • 1929 • Malasomma Nunzio • FRG
RUF DES SCHICKSALS, DER • 1922 • Guter Johannes • FRG
RUFFHOUSE • 1916 • Miller Rube • USA
RUFFIAN, LE • 1982 • Giovanni Jose • FRN
RUFFIANS, THE see **CANAILLES, LES** • 1959
RUFFLED SURFACE • 1963 • Gajer Vaclav • CZC
RUFNUMMER 728 • 1966 • Ford Aleksander • FRG • PHONE NUMBER 728
RUFUS • 1974 • Meyering Samuel • NTH
RUFUS JONES FOR PRESIDENT • 1933 • Mack Roy • SHT • USA
RUG NAAR DE ZEE, DE • 1966 • Terpstra Erik • SHT • NTH
RUG SI FLACARA • 1980 • Petringenaru Adrian • RMN • STAKE AND THE FLAME, THE
RUGANTINO • 1973 • Festa Campanile Pasquale • ITL
RUGBY • 1934 • McCarey Ray • SHT • USA
RUGGED BEAR • 1953 • Hannah Jack • ANS • USA
RUGGED COAST, THE • 1913 • *August Edwin* • USA
RUGGED ISLAND, THE • 1934 • Brown Jenny • UKN
RUGGED O'RIORDANS, THE see **SONS OF MATTHEW** • 1949
RUGGED PATH, THE • 1918 • *Villis Marjorie* • UKN
RUGGED WATER • 1925 • Willat Irvin V. • USA
RUGGLES OF RED GAP • 1918 • Windom Lawrence C. • USA
RUGGLES OF RED GAP • 1923 • Cruze James • USA
RUGGLES OF RED GAP • 1935 • McCarey Leo • USA
RUGIADA DI SANGUE • 1915 • Negroni Baldassare • ITL
RUGMAKER'S DAUGHTER • 1915 • Bosworth Hobart • USA
RUH EL JASSAD, EL • 1948 • Rafla Hilmy • EGY • SPIRIT OF THE BODY, THE
RUHHAL, AL- • 1975 • Mazif Sid-Ali • ALG • NOMADES, LES
RUHIGES HEIM MIT KUCHENBENUTZUNG • 1929 • Wilhelm Carl • FRG • MADEL VON DER OPERETTE, DAS
RUHM UND FRAUENGUNST • 1918 • Osten Franz • FRG
RUHUNU KUMARI • 1968 • Tampoe W. M. S. • SLN • RUHUNU PRINCESS, THE
RUHUNU PRINCESS, THE see **RUHUNU KUMARI** • 1968
RUIDO DEL SILENCIO, EL • 1963 • Zabalza Jose Maria • SPN
RUIN OF MANLEY, THE • 1914 • Ricketts Thomas • USA
RUINAS DE BABILONIA, LAS • 1959 • Torrado Ramon • SPN, FRG • LOWE VON BABYLON, DER (FRG)
RUINE-BABINES, LES • 1976-77 • Brault Michel, Gladu Andre • DCS • CND
RUINED • 1968 • *Mitam Productions* • USA
RUINED see **KHANE-KHARAB** • 1975
RUINED BRUIN, THE • 1961 • McCarthy John K. • USA • BARE AND THE SHAPELY, THE ○ RIOTOUS BRUIN, THE
RUINED BY A DUMBWAITER • 1918 • *Keystone* • USA
RUINED BY LOVE • 1920 • Clemens James • USA
RUINED LIFE, A • 1911 • Coleby A. E. • UKN
RUINED MAP, THE (USA) see **MOETSUKITA CHIZU** • 1968
RUINED SHOPKEEPER, THE see **U SNEDENEHO KRAMU** • 1933
RUINING RANDALL'S REPUTATION • 1916 • *Chamberlin Riley* • USA
RUINS, THE see **KHANDAR** • 1983
RUINS OF PALMYRA AND BAALBEK • 1937-40 • *Cardiff Jack (Ph)* • DCS • UKN
RUISENOR DE LAS CUMBRES, EL • 1958 • del Amo Antonio • SPN
RUISENOR DEL BARRIO, EL • 1951 • Salvador Jaime • MXC
RUISSEAU, LE • 1929 • Hervil Rene • FRN
RUISSEAU, LE • 1938 • Lehmann Maurice, Autant-Lara Claude • FRN
RUITER IN DIE NAG, DIE • 1963 • Perold Jan • SAF • RIDER IN THE NIGHT, THE (USA)
RUKA • 1964 • Trnka Jiri • ANM • CZC • HAND, THE
RUKMANI HARAN • 1934 • *Imperial* • IND
RUKMANI HARAN • 1937 • Lakshmi Bharat • IND
RUKMANI KALYANAM • 1937 • *Shantakumari* • IND
RUKMINI • 1939 • Banerjee Jyotish • IND
RUKMINI HARAN • *Kohinoor* • IND
RULE 'EM AND WEEP • 1932 • Sweet Harry • SHT • USA
RULE G • 1915 • *Tabler Percy Dempsey* • USA
RULE OF REASON, THE • 1917 • Davenport Charles E. • SHT • USA
RULE OVER NIGHT see **YORU NO NAWABARI** • 1967
RULE SIXTYTHREE • 1915 • Baker Richard Foster • USA
RULE THYSELF • 1913 • Williams C. Jay • USA
RULER, THE (USA) see **HERRSCHER, DER** • 1937
RULER OF MEN, A • 1920 • Smith David • SHT • USA
RULER OF THE ROAD • 1918 • Warde Ernest C. • USA
RULER OF THE WORLD see **HERR DER WELT, DER** • 1934
RULERS, THE see **ARHONTES** • 1976
RULERS OF THE SEA • 1939 • Lloyd Frank • USA
RULES AND DISPLACEMENT OF ACTIVITIES PART I • 1974 • Parr Mike • ASL
RULES AND DISPLACEMENT OF ACTIVITIES, PART II • 1976 • Parr Mike • ASL
RULES OF MARRIAGE, THE • 1982 • Katselas Milton • TVM • USA
RULES OF THE GAME, THE see **REGLE DU JEU, LA** • 1939
RULETERO A TODA MARCHA • 1962 • Baledon Rafael • MXC
RULING CLASS, THE • 1972 • Medak Peter • UKN
RULING PASSION, THE • 1910 • Melies Gaston • USA
RULING PASSION, THE • 1911 • Griffith D. W. • USA
RULING PASSION, THE • 1912 • *Reliance* • USA
RULING PASSION, THE • 1916 • Brenon Herbert • USA
RULING PASSION, THE • 1922 • Weight F. Harmon • USA
RULING PASSIONS • 1918 • Schomer Abraham S. • USA
RULING POWER, THE • 1915 • Belmore Lionel • USA
RULING VOICE, THE • 1931 • Lee Rowland V. • USA • UPPER UNDERWORLD
RULLESKOJTERNE • 1908 • *Holger-Madsen* • DNM • ON ROLLER SKATES
RUM AND WALL PAPER • 1915 • Avery Charles • USA
RUM RUNNER see **BOULEVARD DU RHUM** • 1971
RUM RUNNERS, THE • 1923 • *Maloney Leo* • USA
RUMAENSK BLOD OR SOSTRENE CORRODI • 1913 • *Christensen Benjamin* • DNM
RUMAH PUAKA • 1957 • *Menado Marina* • MLY • DIMANA GAJAH BERDIRI TEGAK ○ HAUNTED HOUSE ○ WHERE THE ELEPHANT STOOD
RUMANIA • 1947 • Beleyev Vassili • USS
RUMBA • 1935 • Gering Marion • USA
RUMBA • 1939 • McLaren Norman • ANS • CND
RUMBA, LA • 1978 • Valdes Oscar • DOC • CUB
RUMBA CALIENTE • 1952 • Martinez Solares Gilberto • MXC
RUMBA LAND • 1939 • Ceballos Larry • USA
RUMBLE FISH • 1983 • Coppola Francis Ford • USA
RUMBLE ON THE DOCKS • 1956 • Sears Fred F. • USA
RUMBO • 1949 • Torrado Ramon • SPN
RUMBO A BELEN • 1967 • Ochoa Jose • SPN
RUMBO A BRASILIA • 1960 • de la Serna Mauricio • BRZ, MXC • EN ROUTE TO BRASILIA
RUMBO AL CAIRO • 1935 • Perojo Benito • SPN • BOUND FOR CAIRO (USA)
RUMBURAK • 1985 • Vorlicek Vaclav • CZC, FRG
RUMEUR D'AMOUR see **ICHAAT AL-HUBB** • 1960
RUMEURS • 1946 • Daroy Jacques • FRN • RUMORS (USA)
RUMIANTSEV CASE, THE see **DELO RUMYANTSEVA** • 1955
RUMMAGE SALE, THE • 1911 • *American* • USA
RUMMAGE SALE, THE • 1914 • Le Saint Edward J. • USA
RUMMELPLATZ DER LIEBE • 1954 • Neumann Kurt • FRG • CIRCUS OF LOVE
RUMMIES AND RAZORS • 1918 • Semon Larry • SHT • USA
RUMMY, THE • 1916 • Powell Paul • USA
RUMMY, THE • 1933 • Lord Del • SHT • USA
RUMMY ACT OF OMAR K.M., THE • 1916 • Humphrey Orral • USA
RUMMY ROMANCE, A • 1917 • Davis James • SHT • USA
RUMOR OF WAR, A • 1980 • Heffron Richard T. • TVM • USA
RUMORS OF EVENING • 1958 • Frankenheimer John • MTV • USA
RUMORS (USA) see **RUMEURS** • 1946
RUMOUR • 1940 • Peake Bladon • UKN
RUMOUR • 1970 • Hodges Mike • TVM • UKN
RUMOUR, THE see **GERUCHT, HET** • 1960
RUMOURS OF GLORY: BRUCE COCKBURN LIVE • 1982 • Lavut Martin • CND
RUMPELSTILTSKIN • 1915 • West Raymond B. • USA
RUMPELSTILTSKIN • 1952 • Wilder William • SHT • USA
RUMPELSTILTSKIN • 1982 • Andolino Emile • TVM • USA
RUMPELSTILTSKIN • 1986 • van Lamsweerde Pino • ANS
RUMPELSTILTSKIN • 1987 • Irving David • USA • RUMPLESTILTSKIN
RUMPELSTILZCHEN • 1923 • AUS
RUMPELSTILZCHEN • 1955 • Fredersdorf Herbert B. • FRG • RUMPESTILTSKIN (USA)
RUMPELSTILZCHEN see **ZAUBERMANNCHEN, DAS** • 1960
RUMPESTILTSKIN (USA) see **RUMPELSTILZCHEN** • 1955
RUMPLESTILTSKIN see **RUMPELSTILTSKIN** • 1987
RUMPUS see **TOLPAR** • 1978
RUMPUS IN THE HAREM • 1956 • White Jules • SHT • USA
RUMUZ GONCAGUL • 1987 • Tozum Irfan • TRK • SIGNED ROSEBUD
RUN • 1990 • Burrowes Geoff • USA
RUN A CROOKED MILE • 1969 • Levitt Gene • TVM • USA
RUN ACROSS THE RIVER • 1961 • Chambers Everett • USA
RUN AFTER ME UNTIL I CATCH YOU see **COURS APRES MOI QUE JE T'ATTRAPE** • 1976
RUN, ANGEL, RUN! • 1969 • Starrett Jack • USA
RUN, APPALOOSA, RUN • 1966 • Lansburgh Larry • USA
RUN, CHRISSIE, RUN • 1984 • Langman Chris • ASL
RUN, COUGAR, RUN • 1972 • Courtland Jerome • USA
RUN COUNTER RUN • 1972 • Zaorski Janusz • PLN
RUN 'EM RAGGED • 1920 • *Pollard Snub* • SHT • USA
RUN FOR COVER • 1955 • Ray Nicholas • USA • COLORADO
RUN FOR FREEDOM • 1984 • SAF
RUN FOR THE HILLS • 1953 • Landers Lew • USA
RUN FOR THE MONEY, A • 1909 • *Powers* • USA
RUN FOR THE ROSES • 1978 • Levin Henry • USA • THOROUGHBREDS, THE ○ THOROUGHBRED
RUN FOR THE SUN • 1956 • Boulting Roy • USA
RUN FOR YOUR LIFE • 1984 • Webb William • USA
RUN FOR YOUR LIFE • 1990 • Kovachev Oleg • BUL
RUN FOR YOUR LIFE see **LUTE, EL** • 1987
RUN FOR YOUR LIFE see **SWEET REVENGE** • 1987
RUN FOR YOUR MONEY, A • 1949 • Frend Charles • UKN • LARK, THE
RUN FOR YOUR WIFE (USA) see **MES FEMMES AMERICAINES** • 1966
RUN GENTA RUN see **HADAKAKKO** • 1961
RUN, GIRL, RUN • 1928 • *Sennett Mack (P)* • SHT • USA
RUN HERO RUN see **HELL WITH HEROES, THE** • 1968
RUN HOME SLOW • 1965 • *Mccambridge Mercedes* • USA
RUN IF YOU CAN • 1987 • Stone Virginia Lively • USA
RUN LIKE A THIEF • 1967 • Glasser Bernard • USA, SPN • ROBO DE DIAMANTES (SPN) ○ DIAMOND COUNTRY ○ DIAMOND HUNTERS
RUN LOVER RUN see **AI-CH'ING CH'ANG P'AO** • 1976
RUN, MAN, RUN see **CORRI, UOMO, CORRI** • 1968
RUN, MIKI, RUN see **MY CHAMPION** • 1981
RUN OF THE ARROW • 1957 • Fuller Samuel • USA
RUN ON GOLD, A (UKN) see **MIDAS RUN** • 1969
RUN ON PERCY, THE • 1915 • Smith Sidney • USA
RUN ON THE BANK, THE • 1912 • *Bison* • USA
RUN OR BURN see **WHITEWATER SAM** • 1978
RUN, PSYCHO, RUN • 1969 • Rondi Brunello • ITL
RUN, RABBIT, RUN see **LAUF, HASE, LAUF** • 1979
RUN REBECCA RUN • 1982 • Maxwell Peter • ASL
RUN! RUN! • 1920 • Kellino W. P. • UKN
RUN, RUN, JOE • 1974 • Colizzi Giuseppe • ITL, SPN, FRN
RUN, RUN, SWEET ROAD RUNNER • 1965 • Larriva Rudy • ANS • USA
RUN SHADOW RUN see **COVER ME BABE** • 1970
RUN, SHEEP, RUN • 1935 • Harman Hugh • ANS • USA
RUN SILENT, RUN DEEP • 1958 • Wise Robert • USA
RUN, SIMON, RUN • 1970 • McCowan George • TVM • USA
RUN, STRANGER, RUN see **HAPPY MOTHER'S DAY, LOVE GEORGE** • 1973
RUN SWINGER RUN! • 1967 • Mahon Barry • USA • NUDES ON THE RUN
RUN THE WILD RIVER • 1971 • Currey Jack • DOC • USA
RUN TO BE CAUGHT see **FUSS, HOGY UTOLERJENEK** • 1972
RUN TO EARTH BY BOY SCOUTS • 1911 • Aylott Dave? • UKN
RUN TO EARTH (UKN) see **UNTAMED JUSTICE** • 1929
RUN TO FREEDOM • 1989 • Bernard Laurens • SAF
RUN, VIRGIN, RUN (UKN) see **JUNGFRAUEN VON BUMSHAUSEN, DIE** • 1969
RUN, WAITER, RUN see **VRCHNI, PRCHNI** • 1981
RUN WILD, RUN FREE • 1969 • Sarafian Richard C. • UKN • PHILIP ○ WHITE COLT, THE
RUN WITH THE DEVIL (USA) see **VIA MARGUTTA** • 1960
RUN WITH THE WIND • 1966 • Shonteff Lindsay • UKN
RUNA AND THE BLACK HAND • 1913 • *Reliance* • USA
RUNA PLAYS CUPID • 1913 • *Reliance* • USA
RUNAROUND • 1970 • *Cosmos Films* • USA
RUNAROUND, THE • 1931 • Craft William James • USA • WAITING FOR THE BRIDE (UKN) ○ WAITING AT THE CHURCH
RUNAROUND, THE • 1946 • Lamont Charles • USA
RUNAWAY • 1964 • O'Shea John • NZL
RUNAWAY • 1969 • Lawder Standish D. • ANS • USA
RUNAWAY! • 1973 • Rich David Lowell • TVM • USA • RUNAWAY TRAIN, THE (UKN)
RUNAWAY • 1984 • Crichton Michael • USA
RUNAWAY, THE • 1913 • *Thanhouser* • USA
RUNAWAY, THE • 1914 • *Frontier* • USA
RUNAWAY, THE • 1917 • Henderson Dell • USA
RUNAWAY, THE • 1924 • Fleischer Dave • ANS • USA
RUNAWAY, THE • 1926 • De Mille William C. • USA
RUNAWAY, THE • 1958 • *Brasseur Pierre* • FRN
RUNAWAY, THE • 1964 • Young Tony • UKN
RUNAWAY, THE (UKN) see **ATITHI** • 1966

RUNAWAY BARGE, THE • 1975 • Sagal Boris • TVM • USA
RUNAWAY BLACKIE • 1933 • Bailey Harry • ANS • USA
RUNAWAY BOY, THE see **BARI THEKEY PALIYE** • 1959
RUNAWAY BRIDE, THE • 1930 • Crisp Donald • USA • COOKING HER GOOSE
RUNAWAY BUS, THE • 1954 • Guest Val • UKN
RUNAWAY CLOSET, THE • 1915 • *Sterling* • USA
RUNAWAY COLT, A • 1917 • Richmond J. A. • SHT • USA
RUNAWAY DAUGHTER see **RED SALUTE** • 1935
RUNAWAY DAUGHTERS • 1956 • Cahn Edward L. • USA
RUNAWAY DAUGHTERS see **PROWL GIRLS** • 1968
RUNAWAY ENCHANTRESS, THE see **SEA TIGER, THE** • 1927
RUNAWAY ENGINE, THE • 1911 • *Kalem* • USA
RUNAWAY EXPRESS, THE • 1926 • Sedgwick Edward • USA
RUNAWAY FREIGHT, THE • 1913 • *Holmes Helen* • USA
RUNAWAY FREIGHT, THE • 1914 • *Pallette Eugene* • USA
RUNAWAY GIRL • 1966 • Petroff Hamil • USA
RUNAWAY GIRLS • 1928 • Sandrich Mark • USA
RUNAWAY GIRLS see **JUNGEN AUSREISSERINNEN, DIE** • 1971
RUNAWAY HOLIDAY, A • 1929 • Harman Bobby • UKN
RUNAWAY HORSE, THE • 1907 • Zecca Ferdinand • FRN
RUNAWAY JANE • 1915 • Eagle Oscar • SRL • USA
RUNAWAY KIDS, THE • 1908 • Fitzhamon Lewin • UKN
RUNAWAY KNOCK, THE • 1898 • Smith G. A. • UKN
RUNAWAY KNOCK AND THE SUFFERING MILKMAN, THE • 1898 • *Riley Brothers* • UKN
RUNAWAY LADIES • 1935 • de Limur Jean • UKN
RUNAWAY MATCH, THE • 1903 • Collins Alf • UKN • MARRIAGE BY MOTOR
RUNAWAY MELODY • 1979 • Burke Louis • SAF • FOLLOW THAT RAINBOW
RUNAWAY MOUSE • 1954 • Davis Mannie • ANS • USA
RUNAWAY PRINCESS, THE • 1914 • *Fealy Maude* • USA
RUNAWAY PRINCESS, THE • 1929 • Asquith Anthony, Wendhausen Frederick • UKN, FRG • PRINCESS PRISCILLA'S FORTNIGHT
RUNAWAY QUEEN (USA) see **QUEEN'S AFFAIR, THE** • 1934
RUNAWAY RAILWAY • 1965 • Darnley-Smith Jan • UKN
RUNAWAY ROMANY • 1917 • Lederer George W. • USA
RUNAWAY STREETCAR, THE see **ILUSION VIAJA EN TRANVIA, LA** • 1953
RUNAWAY TRAIN, THE • 1985 • Konchalovsky Andrei • USA
RUNAWAY TRAIN, THE (UKN) see **RUNAWAY!** • 1973
RUNAWAY UNCLE, THE • 1913 • *Eclair* • USA
RUNAWAY VAN, THE • 1906 • Stow Percy • UKN
RUNAWAY WIFE, THE • 1915 • *Baird Stewart* • USA
RUNAWAYS see **SOUTH BRONX HEROES** • 1985
RUNAWAYS, THE • 1912 • *Buckley May* • USA
RUNAWAYS, THE • 1913 • Barker Reginald? • USA
RUNAWAYS, THE • 1915 • Franklin Sidney A., Franklin Chester M. • USA
RUNAWAYS, THE • 1972 • Webber Bickford Otis • USA • YOU CAN'T RUN AWAY FROM SEX (UKN)
RUNAWAYS, THE • 1975 • Harris Harry • TVM • USA
RUND UM DEN ALEXANDERPLATZ • 1925 • Schonfelder Erich? • FRG
RUND UM EINE MILLION • 1933 • Neufeld Max • FRG
RUNNER • 1962 • Owen Don • SHT • CND • COUREUR, LE
RUNNER, THE • 1977 • Dimsey Ross • ASL
RUNNER, THE • 1990 • Jones Chris • UKN
RUNNER STUMBLES, THE • 1979 • Kramer Stanley • USA
RUNNERS • 1983 • Sturridge Charles • UKN
RUNNIN' ON EMPTY • 1982 • Clark John • ASL • FAST LANE FEVER (USA) ○ WILD WHEELS
RUNNIN' STRAIGHT • 1920 • Flaven Art • SHT • USA
RUNNING • 1976 • De Bruyn Dirk • ASL
RUNNING • 1979 • Stern Steven Hilliard • USA, CND
RUNNING A CINEMA • 1921 • *Buxton Dudley (Anm)* • ANS • UKN
RUNNING ACROSS THE WAVES see **BEGUSHCHAYA PO VOLNAM** • 1967
RUNNING AWAY BACKWARDS • 1964 • King Allan • CND • COMING OF AGE IN IBIZA
RUNNING AWAY OF DORIS, THE • 1912 • *Edison* • USA
RUNNING BEAR see **ROMANCE OF A HORSETHIEF** • 1972
RUNNING BRAVE • 1983 • Shebib Donald • CND
RUNNING CANON, THE see **ZANBOURAK** • 1973
RUNNING DOGS • 1987 • Todorov Lyudmil • BUL
RUNNING FAWN'S CHIEF • 1911 • *Powers* • USA
RUNNING FENCE • 1978 • Maysles Albert, Maysles David, Zwerin Charlotte • DOC • USA
RUNNING FIGHT, THE • 1915 • *Heming Violet* • USA
RUNNING FOR SHERIFF • 1954 • Hines William Everett • USA
RUNNING FROM THE GUNS see **FREE ENTERPRISE** • 1986
RUNNING FROM THE GUNS (USA) see **FREE ENTERPRISE** • 1948
RUNNING GAME, THE • 1982 • Keenan Haydn (c/d) • ASL • ROOM TO MOVE
RUNNING HOLLYWOOD • 1932 • Lamont Charles • SHT • USA
RUNNING HOT • 1983 • Griffiths Mark • USA
RUNNING IN MADNESS, DYING IN LOVE see **KYOSO JOSHIKO** • 1970
RUNNING, JUMPING AND STANDING STILL FILM, THE • 1960 • Lester Richard • SHT • UKN
RUNNING MAN • 1981 • Brittain Don • MTV • CND
RUNNING MAN, THE • 1963 • Reed Carol • UKN, USA
RUNNING MAN, THE • 1987 • Glaser Paul Michael • USA
RUNNING MAN, THE see **CITY'S EDGE, THE** • 1983
RUNNING MATES • 1986 • Neff Thomas L. • USA
RUNNING ON EMPTY • 1988 • Lumet Sidney • USA
RUNNING OUT • 1982 • Day Robert • TVM • USA
RUNNING OUT OF LUCK • 1985 • Temple Julien • USA • SHE'S THE BOSS
RUNNING ROCKET • 1988 • Lynch David • USA
RUNNING SCARED • 1972 • Hemmings David • UKN
RUNNING SCARED • 1980 • Glicker Paul • USA
RUNNING SCARED • 1984 • Fortier Bob • MTV • CND
RUNNING SCARED • 1986 • Hyams Peter • USA
RUNNING SILENT see **SILENT RUNNING** • 1972
RUNNING TARGET • 1956 • Weinstein Marvin R. • USA • MY BROTHER DOWN THERE
RUNNING THROUGH THE WAVES see **BEGUSHCHAYA PO VOLNAM** • 1967
RUNNING TIME • 1974 • Ransen Mort • CND
RUNNING TO INDIA • 1966 • Robertson George C. • CND
RUNNING WATER • 1922 • Elvey Maurice • UKN
RUNNING WILD • 1919 • *Capital* • SHT • USA
RUNNING WILD • 1921 • Roach Hal • SHT • USA
RUNNING WILD • 1927 • La Cava Gregory • USA
RUNNING WILD • 1955 • Biberman Abner • USA
RUNNING WILD • 1973 • McCahon Robert • USA
RUNNING WITH CHARLES PADDOCK • 1932 • Breslow Lou • SHT • USA
RUNNING WITH THE DEVIL • 1972 • Sullivan Ron • USA
RUNNING YOUNG • 1983 • SAF
RUNOILIJA JA MUUSA • 1978 • Pakkasvirta Jaakko • FNL • ELAMAN KOREUS ○ POET AND MUSE ○ ELEGANCE OF LIFE, THE
RUNON KUNINGAS JA MUUTTOLINTU • 1940 • Saakka Toivo • FNL • KING OF POETS AND THE BIRD OF PASSAGE, THE
RUNS GOOD • 1970 • O'Neill Patrick • SHT • USA
RUNT, THE • 1915 • Campbell Colin • USA
RUNT, THE • 1936 • *Terry Paul/ Moser Frank (P)* • ANS • USA
RUNT PAGE • 1932 • Nazarro Ray • SHT • USA
RUNWAY, THE see **BARI THEKEY PALIYE** • 1959
RUNWAY, THE see **JETEE, LA** • 1962
RUOTA DEL VIZIO, LA • 1920 • Genina Augusto • ITL
RUPA • 1971 • Grgic Zlatko • ANS • YGS • HOLE, THE
RUPALI SHAIKATEY • 1977 • Kabir Alamgir • BNG • ON A SILVERY BEACH ○ LONER, THE
RUPERT MURDOCH • 1967 • Hannam Ken • DOC • ASL
RUPERT OF COLE SLAW • 1924 • Pembroke Percy • SHT • USA • RUPERT OF HEE-HAW
RUPERT OF HEE-HAW see **RUPERT OF COLE SLAW** • 1924
RUPERT OF HENTZAU • 1915 • Tucker George Loane • UKN
RUPERT OF HENTZAU • 1923 • Heerman Victor • USA
RUPERT THE RUNT • 1940 • Davis Mannie • ANS • USA
RUPERT'S RUBE RELATION • 1916 • *Chamberlin Riley* • USA
RUPIMONO see **813: THE ADVENTURES OF ARSENE LUPIN** • 1922
RUPKATHA • 1950 • *Sircar B. N. (P)* • IND
RUPLEKHA • 1934 • *Sircar B. N. (P)* • IND
RUPTURE • 1961 • Etaix Pierre, Carriere Jean-Claude • SHT • FRN • BREAK, THE
RUPTURE, LA • 1970 • Chabrol Claude • FRN, ITL, BLG • ALL'OMBRA DEL DELITTO (ITL) ○ BREAKUP, THE (USA) ○ JOUR DES PARQUES, LE ○ HALLUCINATION
RUPTURES DE FIBRES • 1931 • Painleve Jean • SHT • FRN
RURAL AFFAIR, A • 1914 • *Sterling* • USA
RURAL CO-OP • 1947 • Lorentz Pare • SHT • USA
RURAL COMMUNITY see **GROMADA** • 1950
RURAL CONQUEROR, A • 1911 • Salter Harry • USA
RURAL DELIVERY, TEN THOUSAND B.C. see **R.F.D. 10,000 B.C.** • 1917
RURAL DEMON, A • 1914 • Lehrman Henry, Sennett Mack • USA
RURAL DEMONS, THE • 1914 • *Ritchie Billie* • USA
RURAL ELOPEMENT, A • 1909 • Griffith D. W. • USA
RURAL FREE DELIVERY ROMANCE, A • 1914 • *Princess* • USA
RURAL HAPPINESS (USA) see **GLUCK AUF DEN LANDE** • 1940
RURAL HUNGARY • 1939 • Fitzpatrick James • SHT • USA
RURAL INSTITUTE see **SELSKAYA UCHITELNITSA** • 1947
RURAL RHAPSODY • 1946 • Mead Thomas • SHT • USA
RURAL RIOT, A • 1918 • Davis James • SHT • USA
RURAL ROMANCE, A • 1913 • *Reliance* • USA
RURAL ROMANCE, A • 1914 • *Princess* • USA
RURAL ROMANCE, A • 1914 • *Sterling* • USA
RURAL ROMANCE, A • 1916 • *Hutton Lucille* • SHT • USA
RURAL ROMANCE, A • 1920 • *West Billy* • SHT • USA
RURAL ROMEO, A • 1910 • *Imp* • USA
RURAL ROMEOS • 1914 • *Albuquerque* • USA
RURAL ROUGHNECKS • 1916 • *Lloyd Harold* • USA • LUKE, THE RURAL ROUGHNECK
RURAL SCHOOL • 1940 • Pearson George • DCS • UKN
RURAL SCHOOL: CHILDREN, 8-11 • 1936 • Jones Andrew Miller • UKN
RURAL SWEDEN • 1938 • Fitzpatrick James • SHT • USA
RURAL THIRD DEGREE, A • 1913 • Nicholls George, Sennett Mack (Spv) • USA
RURAL TRAGEDY, A • 1909 • *Edison* • USA
RURI NO KISHI see **RYURI NO KISHI** • 1956
RUSA, LA • 1988 • Camus Mario • SPN • RUSSIAN SPY, THE
RUSALKA • 1962 • Kaslik Vaclav • CZC
RUSALOCHKA • 1976 • Bychkov Vladimir • USS, BUL • MALKATA ROUSSALKA ○ LITTLE MERMAID, THE
RUSCELLO DI RIPASOTTILE, IL • 1941 • Rossellini Roberto • SHT • ITL
RUSE, THE • 1915 • Hart William S., Smith Cliff • USA
RUSE, THE • 1916 • Mullin Eugene • SHT • USA
RUSE DU GRAND-PERE • 1916 • Burguet Charles • FRN
RUSE OF THE RATTLER, THE • 1921 • McGowan J. P. • USA
RUSES DU DIABLE, LES • 1965 • Vecchiali Paul • FRN • DEVIL'S TRICKS, THE
RUSES, RHYMES AND ROUGHNECKS • 1915 • Roach Hal • USA
RUSH • 1984 • Ricci Tonino • ITL • RUSH: THE ASSASSIN
RUSH HOUR • 1941 • Asquith Anthony • UKN
RUSH HOUR, THE • 1927 • Hopper E. Mason • USA
RUSH HOURS see **GODZINY SZCZYTU** • 1967
RUSH ORDERS • 1921 • Roach Hal • SHT • USA
RUSH: THE ASSASSIN see **RUSH** • 1984
RUSH TO JUDGMENT • 1967 • De Antonio Emile • USA
RUSHIN' BALLET • 1937 • Douglas Gordon • SHT • USA
RUSHIN' DANCERS, THE • 1917 • Chaudet Louis W. • SHT • USA
RUSHING BUSINESS • 1916 • *Stull Walter* • SHT • USA
RUSHING BUSINESS • 1927 • Newfield Sam • SHT • USA
RUSHING ROULETTE • 1965 • McKimson Robert • ANS • USA
RUSHING THE LUNCH COUNTER • 1915 • *Hamilton Lloyd V.* • USA
RUSHING TIDE, THE • 1928 • Hayle Gerald M. • ASL
RUSK see **SKORPAN** • 1957
RUSKAN JALKEEN • 1979 • Laine Edvin • FNL • AFTER THE AUTUMN LEAVES ○ WINTER OF BLACK SNOW
RUSLAN AND LUDMILLA (USA) see **RUSLAN I LJUDMILA** • 1914
RUSLAN I LIUDMILA • 1970 • Ptushko Alexander • USS
RUSLAN I LJUDMILA • 1914 • Starevitch Ladislas • USS • RUSLAN AND LUDMILLA (USA)
RUSS MEYER'S "UP" see **UP** • 1976
RUSS MEYER'S VIXEN • 1969 • Meyer Russ • USA • VIXEN
RUSS MORGAN AND HIS ORCHESTRA • 1949 • *Universal* • SHT • USA
RUSSELL AFFAIR, THE • 1928 • Ramster P. J. • ASL
RUSSIA • 1972 • Holcomb Theodore • DOC • USA
RUSSIA see **SONG OF RUSSIA** • 1943
RUSSIA AFLAME • 1943 • Chauvel Charles • DOC • ASL
RUSSIA HOUSE, THE • 1990 • Schepisi Fred • UKN, USA
RUSSIA IN THE 70'S • 1970 • Francisco Clay • DOC • USA
RUSSIA -LAND OF TOMORROW • 1919 • Sandground Maurice • UKN
RUSSIA OF NICHOLAS II AND LEV TOLSTOY, THE see **ROSSIYA NIKOLAI II I LEV TOLSTOY** • 1928
RUSSIA ON PARADE • 1946 • Beleyev Vassili, Vensher Ivan, Poselsky I., Marcellini Romolo, Cortese Leonardo, Lisizian Tamara • USS
RUSSIA -THE LAND OF OPPRESSION • 1910 • Porter Edwin S. • USA
RUSSIA THROUGH THE SHADOWS • 1922 • *Broms Allan S. (P)* • USA
RUSSIAN ADVENTURE see **CINERAMA'S RUSSIAN ADVENTURE** • 1966
RUSSIAN BALLERINA see **BALERINA** • 1947
RUSSIAN DRESSING • 1933 • *Mintz Charles (P)* • ANS • USA
RUSSIAN DRESSING • 1938 • Yarbrough Jean • SHT • USA
RUSSIAN FIELD • 1972 • Moskalenko N. • USS
RUSSIAN FOREST, THE • 1964 • Petrov Vladimir • USS
RUSSIAN LESSON • 1942 • Moffat Ivan • UKN
RUSSIAN LION, THE • 1910 • *Vitagraph* • USA
RUSSIAN LULLABY • 1931 • Fleischer Dave • ANS • USA
RUSSIAN MIRACLE, THE see **RUSSICHE WUNDER, DAS** • 1963
RUSSIAN PEASANT, THE • 1912 • *Humphries William* • USA
RUSSIAN QUESTION, THE see **RUSSKI VOPROZ** • 1947
RUSSIAN REVELS • 1943 • Le Borg Reginald • SHT • USA
RUSSIAN REVOLUTION, THE • 1927 • *Collwyn Pictures* • DOC • USA
RUSSIAN RHAPSODY • 1944 • Clampett Robert • ANS • USA
RUSSIAN ROCKET TO THE MOON see **DOROGA K ZVEZDAM** • 1957
RUSSIAN ROMANCE, A • 1909 • *Tiger* • USA
RUSSIAN ROULETTE • 1975 • Lombardo Lou • USA
RUSSIAN ROULETTE see **TWO BEFORE ZERO** • 1962
RUSSIAN SAILOR -IVAN NIKULIN • 1944 • Savchenko Igor • USS • IVAN NIKULIN -RUSSIAN SAILOR
RUSSIAN SOLDIER, THE • 1985 • Millar Gavin • TVM • UKN
RUSSIAN SOUVENIRS see **RUSSKI SUVENIR** • 1960
RUSSIAN SPY, THE see **RUSA, LA** • 1988
RUSSIAN SURPRISE, A • 1904 • *Paul R. W.* • UKN
RUSSIAN WOMEN, THE see **ZHENSHCHINY** • 1965
RUSSIAN WONDER, THE see **RUSSICHE WUNDER, DAS** • 1963
RUSSIANS ARE COMING, THE • 1987 • Carow Heiner • GDR
RUSSIANS ARE COMING, THE RUSSIANS ARE COMING, THE • 1966 • Jewison Norman • USA
RUSSIANS AT WAR • 1942 • *Van Dongen Helen* • CMP • NTH
RUSSIA'S FIRST COMMUNE see **PERVOROSSIYANYE** • 1968
RUSSIA'S FOREIGN POLICY see **OUR NORTHERN NEIGHBOUR** • 1942
RUSSICHE WUNDER, DAS • 1963 • Thorndike Andrew, Thorndike Annelie • GDR • RUSSIAN WONDER, THE ○ RUSSIAN MIRACLE, THE
RUSSKI SUVENIR • 1960 • Alexandrov Grigori • USS • RUSSIAN SOUVENIRS
RUSSKI VOPROZ • 1947 • Romm Mikhail • USS • RUSSIAN QUESTION, THE
RUSSKIES • 1987 • Rosenthal Rick • USA
RUSSLAND 1 • 1924 • *Sphinx-Film* • FRG • TOLSTOI, DER FRIEDENSAPOSTEL
RUSSLAND 2 • 1924 • *Sphinx-Film* • FRG • VOM DIEB ZUM BEHERRSCHER
RUSSLAND 3 • 1924 • *Sphinx-Film* • FRG • THRONSTURZER, DER
RUST see **RYD** • 1990
RUST, THE see **RDZA** • 1981
RUST NEVER SLEEPS • 1979 • Young Neil • USA
RUSTAM AND SUHRAB • Kimyagarov Boris • USS
RUSTIC AND THE NUN, THE see **JECA E A FREIRA, O** • 1968
RUSTIC CHIVALRY (USA) see **NOBLEZA BATURRA** • 1935
RUSTIC FLIRT, A • 1909 • *Walturdaw* • UKN
RUSTIC HEARTS • 1913 • *Lubin* • USA
RUSTIC HEROINE, OR IN THE DAYS OF KING GEORGE, A • 1908 • *Vitagraph* • USA
RUSTIC MAIDEN, THE • 1912 • *Tennant Barbara* • USA
RUSTIC ROMANCE, A • 1911 • *Urban Trading Co* • UKN
RUSTIC ROMEO, A • 1919 • *Christie* • USA
RUSTICATING • 1917 • *Myers Harry* • USA
RUSTING WORLD see **DECLIN** • 1980
RUSTLE OF A SKIRT, THE • 1915 • *Fuller Mary* • USA
RUSTLE OF SILK, THE • 1923 • Brenon Herbert • USA
RUSTLER OUTWITTED, THE • 1914 • *Frontier* • USA
RUSTLER SHERIFF, THE • 1911 • Dwan Allan • USA
RUSTLERS • 1949 • Selander Lesley • USA
RUSTLERS, THE • 1911 • *Selig* • USA
RUSTLERS, THE • 1919 • Barker Reginald • SHT • USA
RUSTLER'S DAUGHTER, THE • 1912 • Melies Gaston • USA
RUSTLER'S END, THE • 1928 • *Hoxie Al* • USA
RUSTLER'S HIDEOUT • 1944 • Newfield Sam • USA
RUSTLER'S HIDEOUT see **RUSTLER'S ROUND-UP** • 1946
RUSTLERS OF DEVIL'S CANYON • 1947 • Springsteen R. G. • USA
RUSTLERS OF RED DOG • 1935 • Landers Lew • SRL • USA
RUSTLERS OF THE BADLANDS • 1945 • Abrahams Derwin • USA • BY WHOSE HAND? (UKN)
RUSTLERS OF THE NIGHT • 1921 • Franchon Leonard • USA
RUSTLERS ON HORSEBACK • 1950 • Brannon Fred C. • USA
RUSTLER'S PARADISE • 1935 • Fraser Harry L. • USA
RUSTLERS' RANCH • 1926 • Rogell Albert S. • USA
RUSTLERS' RANCH • 1926 • Smith Cliff • USA
RUSTLER'S RANSOM • 1950 • *Universal* • SHT • USA

RUSTLER'S REFORMATION, THE • 1913 • Duncan William • USA

RUSTLER'S RETRIBUTION, THE • 1916 • *Sunset* • USA

RUSTLER'S RHAPSODY • 1985 • Wilson Hugh • USA

RUSTLER'S ROUND-UP • 1933 • McRae Henry • USA

RUSTLER'S ROUND-UP • 1946 • Fox Wallace • USA • RUSTLER'S HIDEOUT

RUSTLER'S SPURS, THE • 1913 • *Essanay* • USA

RUSTLER'S STEP-DAUGHTER, THE • 1913 • *Selbie Evelyn* • USA

RUSTLER'S VALLEY • 1937 • Watt Nate • USA

RUSTLER'S VINDICATION, THE • 1917 • *Mix Tom* • USA

RUSTLING A BRIDE • 1919 • Willat Irvin V. • USA

RUSTLING FOR CUPID • 1926 • Cummings Irving • USA

RUSTLING OF LEAVES: INSIDE THE PHILIPPINE REVOLUTION, THE • 1988 • Wild Netti • DOC • CND

RUSTOM-E-BAGHDAD • 1963 • Patel B. J. • IND

RUSTY FLAME see **SABITA HONOO** • 1977

RUSTY KATE, THE FARMER'S DAUGHTER • 1916 • Kennedy Aubrey M. • SHT • USA

RUSTY KNIFE see **SABITA NAIFU** • 1958

RUSTY LEADS THE WAY • 1948 • Jason Will • USA

RUSTY REGGIE'S RECORD • 1916 • *Cooper Claude* • SHT • USA

RUSTY RIDES ALONE • 1933 • Lederman D. Ross • USA

RUSTY ROMEOS • 1957 • White Jules • SHT • USA

RUSTY SAVES A LIFE • 1949 • Friedman Seymour • USA

RUSTY'S BIRTHDAY • 1949 • Friedman Seymour • USA

RUTA DE LOS NARCOTICOS, LA • 1962 • Forn Josep Maria • SPN

RUTEN • 1927 • Ito Daisuke • JPN • WANDERING

RUTEN • 1960 • Fukuda Seiichi • JPN • WANDERING

RUTEN NO OHI • 1960 • Tanaka Kinuyo • JPN • WANDERING PRINCESS, A

RUTERAS, LAS • 1968 • Tankel Ignacio • ARG

RUTH • 1912 • Wilson Frank? • UKN

RUTH ETTING • 1929 • Santley Joseph • SHT • USA

RUTH HALBFASS see **MORAL DER RUTH HALBFASS, DIE** • 1971

RUTH OF THE RANGE • 1923 • Warde Ernest C., Van Dyke W. S. • SRL • USA • RIDDLE OF THE RANGE, THE

RUTH OF THE ROCKIES • 1920 • Marshall George • SRL • USA

RUTH RIDLEY RETURNS • 1916 • Hollingsworth Alfred • SHT • USA

RUTHERFORD COUNTY LINE • 1985 • McIntyre Thom • USA

RUTHLESS • 1948 • Ulmer Edgar G. • USA

RUTHLESS FOUR, THE (USA) see **GOLD VON SAM COOPER, DAS** • 1968

RUTHLESS PEOPLE • 1986 • Abrahams Jim, Zucker David, Zucker Jerry • USA

RUTH'S REMARKABLE RECEPTION • 1916 • *Keyes Francis* • SHT • USA

RUTILO EL FORASTERO • 1962 • Morayta Miguel • MXC

RUTINA • 1979 • Quiroz Livio • VNZ • ROUTINE

RUTLES, THE • 1978 • Idle Eric, Weis Gary • TVM • USA, UKN • RUTLES (A.K.A. ALL YOU NEED IS CASH), THE ○ ALL YOU NEED IS CASH

RUTLES (A.K.A. ALL YOU NEED IS CASH), THE see **RUTLES, THE** • 1978

RUTS see **UKHABY ZHIZNI** • 1928

RUTS OF FOG see **SURCOS DE NIEBLA** • 1978

RUTSCHBAHN • 1928 • Eichberg Richard • FRG

RUTSUBO NA NAKKA NI • 1924 • Ito Daisuke • JPN

RUUSUJEN AIKA • 1969 • Jarva Risto • FNL • TIME OF ROSES (USA) ○ TIME OF THE ROSES

RUY BLAS • 1909 • Blackton J. Stuart (Spv) • USA

RUY BLAS • 1914 • Henderson Lucius • USA

RUY BLAS • 1947 • Billon Pierre • FRN, ITL

RUYI • 1983 • Huang Jianzhong • CHN • AS-YOU-WISH

RUZENA NASKOVA • 1960 • Fric Martin • CZC

RUZGAR GIBI GECTI • 1968 • Sonay Suat • TRK • GONE WITH THE WIND

RUZOVE SNY • 1976 • Hanak Dusan • CZC • ROSE-TINTED DREAMS ○ PINK DREAMS ○ ROSE DREAMS

RX MURDER (USA) see **FAMILY DOCTOR** • 1958

RYADOVOI ALEXANDER MATROSOV • 1948 • Lukov Leonid • USS • ALEXANDER MATROSOV

RYAH EL JANOBV see **RIH AL-JANUB** • 1975

RYAN WHITE STORY, THE • 1988 • Herzfeld John • TVM • USA

RYAN'S DAUGHTER • 1970 • Lean David • UKN

RYAN'S FOUR • 1982 • Bleckner Jeff • TVM • USA

RYBAR A ZLATA RYBKA • 1951 • Trnka Jiri • CZC • GOLDEN FISH, THE (USA) ○ O ZLATE RYBCE ○ GOLD FISH, A

RYD • 1990 • Oskarsson Larus • ICL • RUST

RYE ON THE ROCKS • 1969 • Haldane Don • CND

RYGGSKOTT • 1921 • Brunius Pauline • SWD

RYKMENTIN MURHEENKRYYNI • 1938 • Sarkka Toivo, Norta Yrjo • FNL

RYMDINVASION I LAPPLAND • 1958 • Vogel Virgil W., Warren Jerry (Usa Version) • SWD, USA • INVASION OF THE ANIMAL PEOPLE (USA) ○ SPACE INVASION OF LAPLAND ○ TERROR IN THE MIDNIGHT SUN (UKN)

RYNOX • 1931 • Powell Michael • UKN

RYOJIN NIKKI • 1964 • Nakahira Ko • JPN • HUNTER'S DIARY, THE

RYOJU • 1961 • Gosho Heinosuke • JPN • HUNTING RIFLE

RYOKI SHIKIJO YAWA • 1968 • Umesawa Kaoru • JPN • BIZARRE NIGHT STORY OF SEXUAL DESIRE

RYOMA ANSATSU • 1974 • Kuroki Kazuo • JPN • ASSASSINATION OF RYOMA

RYOOK NAM-MAI • 1960 • Chu Yong-Sop • KOR • BROTHERS AND SISTERS ○ MOTHER'S CARESS

RYOSHOKU • 1967 • Kataoka Hitoshi • JPN • DEBAUCHERY

RYOSO • 1948 • Nakamura Noboru • JPN • TRAVELLING SPIRIT

RYS • 1981 • Rozewicz Stanislaw • PLN • SMILE OF THE EVIL EYE, THE

RYSKA SNUVAN • 1937 • Edgren Gustaf • SWD • COLD IN THE HEAD, A

RYSOPIS • 1964 • Skolimowski Jerzy • PLN • IDENTIFICATIONS MARKS -NONE

RYTHME DE ROTTERDAM • 1952 • Bruisse Ytzen • DOC • NTH

RYTHMES see **IQA** • 1970

RYTHMES DE CHINE • 1956 • Philippe Anne • SHT • BLG

RYTHMETIC see **RHYTHMETIC** • 1956

RYTMUS 1934 • 1980 • Balik Jaroslav • CZC • RHYTHM 1934

RYTSAR MECHTY • 1964 • Derbenev Vadim • USS • DREAM KNIGHT, THE ○ KNIGHT OF THE DREAM, THE

RYTTARE I BLATT • 1959 • Mattsson Arne • SWD • RIDER IN BLUE

RYURI NO KISHI • 1956 • Shindo Kaneto • JPN • FISHING BOAT, THE ○ BOAT, THE ○ RURI NO KISHI ○ BANK OF DEPARTURE

RYUSEI KARATE UCHI • 1956 • Saeki Kiyoshi • JPN

RYYSYRANNAN JOOSEPPI • 1955 • Hallstrom Roland • FNL • JOSEPH OF RYYSYRANTA

RYZHIK • 1960 • Frez Ilya • USS • GINGER

RZECZ NIEPOSPOLITA • 1962 • Lomnicki Jan • DOC • PLN • UNCOMMONWEALTH

RZECZYWISTOSC • 1961 • Bohdziewicz Antoni • PLN • REALITY, THE

S

S 077 SPIONAGGIO A TANGERI • 1965 • Tallas Gregg R. • ITL, SPN • MARC MATO, AGENTE S.077 (SPN) ○ ESPIONAGE IN TANGIERS (USA)

S-A FURAT O BOMBA • 1961 • Popescu-Gopo Ion • RMN • BOMB WAS STOLEN, A

S.A.R.L. • Christian-Jaque • FRN

S A S 181 ANTWORTET NICHT • 1959 • Balhaus Carl • GDR

S.A.S. A SAN SALVADOR • 1982 • Coutard Raoul • FRN • TERMINATE WITH EXTREME PREJUDICE ○ SAS A SAN SALVADOR

S BERNARDO see **SAO BERNARDO** • 1972

S. CARLINO • 1950 • Fasano Ugo • SHT • ITL

S CERTY NEJSOU ZERTY • 1985 • Bocan Hynek • CZC • DEVILS ARE NOT TO BE TRIFLED WITH

S DETSA NA MORE • 1972 • Petrov Dimitar • BUL • WITH CHILDREN AT THE SEASIDE

S' EHO PANDA STI KARDIA MOU • 1967 • Arion Giorgos • GRC • I HAVE YOU ALWAYS IN MY HEART

S FOR SEX (UKN) see **CHALEURS** • 1970

S.I. • 1913 • Gad Urban • FRG, DNM

S.I.D. CONTRA KOCESKY • 1968 • Merino Jose Luis • SPN

S.K. TWINS IN WHO'S WHO, THE • 1914 • Kingsley Pierce • USA

'S NACHTS ALS ALLE KINDEREN SLAPEN • 1966 • van der Hoeven Jan • SHT • NTH

S.O.S. • 1914 • Batley Ethyle • UKN

S.O.S. • 1918 • *American Standard* • USA

S.O.S. • 1928 • Hiscott Leslie • UKN

S.O.S. • 1939 • Eldridge John • DOC • UKN

S.O.S. • 1975 • *Divine Honeysuckle* • USA • SCREW ON THE SCREEN

S.O.S. • 1976 • Jankovics Marcell • ANM • HNG

S.O.S. see **SCHIFF IN NOT S.O.S.** • 1928

S.O.B. • 1980 • Edwards Blake • USA

S.O.B.'S, THE see **SPINA DORSALE DEL DIAVOLO, LA** • 1970

S.O.S. ABUELITA • 1958 • Klimovsky Leon • SPN

S.O.S. AVALANCHE see **HIGH ICE** • 1980

S.O.S. CLIPPER ISLAND (UKN) see **ROBINSON CRUSOE OF MYSTERY ISLAND** • 1936

S.O.S. CLUB • 1969 • *Mitam Productions* • USA

S.O.S. COASTGUARD • 1937 • Witney William, James Alan • SRL • USA

S.O.S. COASTGUARD • 1942 • Witney William, James Alan • USA

S.O.S. CONSPIRACION BIKINI • 1966 • Cardona Rene Jr. • MXC, ECD

S.O.S. DIE INSEL DER TRANEN • 1923 • Mendes Lothar • FRG

S.O.S. EISBERG • 1933 • Fanck Arnold • FRG

S.O.S. FOCH • 1931 • Arroy • SHT • FRN

S.O.S. FONSKA • 1968 • Le Bon Patrick, Henderickx Guido, de Hert Robbe • BLG

S.O.S. GLETSCHERPILOT • 1958 • Vicas Victor • SWT

S.O.S. HELICOPTERE • 1959 • Lelouch Claude • DOC • FRN

S.O.S. ICEBERG • 1933 • Garnett Tay • USA

S.O.S. ICEBERG (UKN) see **NORDPOL -AHOI!** • 1933

S.O.S. ICICLE • 1933 • Lantz Walter, Nolan William • ANS • USA

S.O.S. INVASION • 1968 • Balbuena Silvio F. • SPN

S.O.S. KINDTAND • 1943 • Henning-Jensen Bjarne • DNM • S. O.S. MOLARS

S.O.S. MEDICO see **XXX MEDICO** • 1940

S.O.S MEDITERRANEAN see **ALERTE EN MEDITERRANEE** • 1938

S.O.S. MOLARS see **S.O.S. KINDTAND** • 1943

S.O.S. NORONHA • 1956 • Rouquier Georges • FRN

S.O.S. OVER THE TAYGA • 1976 • Koltsaty Arkadi, Perov Valentin • USS

S.O.S. PACIFIC • 1959 • Green Guy • UKN

S.O.S. PERILS OF THE SEA • 1925 • Hogan James P. • USA

S.O.S. POSEIDON • 1977 • Dragan Mircea

S.O.S. RADIO SERVICE • 1934 • Cavalcanti Alberto • DOC • FRN

S.O.S. SAHARA • 1938 • de Baroncelli Jacques • FRN, FRG

S.O.S. SUBMARINE see **UOMINI SUL FONDO** • 1941

S.O.S. SWEDES AT SEA see **SOS -EN SEGERSALLSKAPSRESA** • 1989

S.O.S. TIDAL WAVE • 1939 • Auer John H. • USA • TIDAL WAVE (UKN)

S.O.S. TITANIC • 1979 • Hale William • TVM • USA

S.O.S. TUBERCULOSE-CANCER-POLYMYELITE • 1960 • Regnier Michel • DCS • CND

S.P.F.C. see **TAKING OFF** • 1971

S.P.L.A.S.H. • 1980 • Mills Michael • CND

S.P.O.O.K.S • 1989 • Thomas Anthony • USA

S.P.Q.R. • 1971 • Koch Volker • FRG

S.S. GIRLS • 1976 • *Carrara Gabriele* • ITL

S.S. IONIAN see **HER LAST TRIP** • 1939

S.T.A.B. see **SPOILERS, THE** • 1976

S TEBOU ME BAVI SVET • 1982 • Polednakova Marie • CZC • WITH YOU THE WORLD THRILLS ME ○ WITH YOU THE WORLD IS FUN

S.V.D. • 1927 • Kozintsev Grigori, Trauberg Leonid • USS • CLUB OF THE BIG IDEAS, THE ○ CLUB OF THE BIG DEED, THE ○ SOYUZ VELIKOGO DELA

S VEROM U BOGA • 1932 • Popovic Mihailo • YGS • WITH FAITH IN GOD

S VYLOUCENIM VEREJNOSTI • 1933 • Fric Martin • CZC • CLOSED DOORS

S & W • 1967 • Hein Wilhelm • FRG

S.W.A.L.K. see **MELODY** • 1971

S.W.A.T. • 1988 • Hulette Donald • USA

S.W.B. • 1969 • Pires Gerard • FRN

S-X BY ADVERTISEMENT • 1969 • Reed Joel M. • USA • SEX BY ADVERTISEMENT

S2S BASE MORTE CHIAMA SUNIPER (ITL) see **MALEDICTION DE BELPHEGOR, LA** • 1967

SA DAGGA • 1982 • Thiam Momar • SNL • TROUBADOUR, THE

SA GOSSE • 1920 • Desfontaines Henri • FRN

SA KABILANG BUHAY • Salumbides Vicente • PHL

SA LILIM NG WATAWAT • 1967 • Marquez Artemio • PHL • UNDER THE FLAG

SA MAJESTE see **CAHIBU AL-JALALA** • 1963

SA MAJESTE L'AMOUR see **SON ALTESSE L'AMOUR** • 1931

SA MAJESTE LE CHAUFFEUR DE TAXI • 1919 • Luitz-Morat • FRN

SA MANLULUPIG DI KA PASISIIL • 1968 • Feleo Ben • PHL • NEVER SHALL INVADERS CONQUER

SA-MANN BRAND • 1933 • Seitz Franz • FRG

SA MEILLEURE CLIENTE • 1932 • Colombier Piere • FRN

SA MORI RANIT DIN DRAGOSTE DE VIATA • 1983 • Veroiu Mircea • RMN • FATALLY INJURED BY LOVE OF LIFE ○ TO DIE FROM LOVE OF LIFE

SA NAUD • 1972 • Riad Mohamed Slimane • ALG • NOUS REVIENDRONS ○ SANAOUD ○ SAFARI

SA NUIT DE NOCES see **MARIONS-NOUS** • 1931

SA TEKH KTO V MORE • 1948 • Fainzimmer Alexander • USS • FOR THOSE WHO ARE AT SEA

SA TETE • 1929 • Epstein Jean • FRN

SA TUKTAS EN AKTA MAN • 1941 • Arvedson Ragnar • SWD • TO CHASTISE A HUSBAND

SA TUKTAS KARLEKEN • 1955 • Fant Kenne • SWD • LOVE CHASTISED

SA VAXTE VAR VARLD • 1963 • Gunwall Per • SWD

SA ZIMBEASCA TOTI COPIII • 1957 • Meszaros Marta • DCS • RMN

SAAD HINDUSTANI • 1971 • Abbas Khwaya Ahmad • IND

SAAD THE ORPHAN • 1985 • Fahmy Ashraf • EGY

SAADIA • 1953 • Lewin Albert • USA

SAALIK, EL • 1985 • Abdel-Sayed Daoud • EGY • VAGABONDS, THE

SAAN DARATING ANG UMAGA • 1983 • de los Reyes Maryo • PHL • WHERE DOES MORNING COME FROM?

SAAT EL TAHRIR DAKKAT BARRA YA ISTI'MAR • 1974 • Srour Heini, Piironen Paavo, Huopainen Heikki, Nousiainen Heikki, Nissi Timo • LBN • HEURE DE LA LIBERATION A SONNE, L' ○ HOUR OF THE LIBERATION HAS SOUNDED, THE ○ TIME OF LIBERATION HAS COME, THE ○ DAMNED RADICALS

SAATANAN SUOMALAINEN • 1973 • Tolonen Asko • FNL • DAMNED FINN

SAATHI • 1968 • Sridhar C. V. • IND • COMPANION

SABA • 1929 • Chiaureli Mikhail • USS

SABADO A LA NOCHE CINE • 1960 • Ayala Fernando • ARG

SABADO, CHICA Y MOTEL.., QUE LIO AQUEL! • 1976 • Merino Jose Luis • SPN

SABADO DE GLORIA • 1978 • Miro Pilar • SPN

SABADO EN LA PLAYA • 1966 • Farre Estaban • SPN

SABADO NEGRO • 1958 • Delgado Miguel M. • MXC

SABAH AL-KHAYR YA ZAWGATI • Shukry Abdel Moneim • EGY • BONJOUR MA FEMME CHERIE!

SABAH YILDIZI • 1968 • Inanoglu Turker • TRK • MORNING STAR, THE

SABAHSIZ GECELER • 1968 • Gorec Ertem • TRK • NIGHTS WITHOUT MORNING

SABAKA (UKN) see **HINDU, THE** • 1953

SABALEROS • 1959 • Bo Armando • ARG • PUT UP OR SHUT UP (USA) ○ PUT OUT OR SHUT UP ○ POSITIONS ○ POSITIONS OF LOVE

SABAR OPARAY • 1955 • Agradoot • IND

SABASH THAMBI • 1967 • Jambu • IND • BRAVO -MY BROTHER

SABAT AYAM FIL GANNA • 1969 • Wahab Fatin Abdel • EGY • SABATU AYYAM FI AL-JANNA ○ SEPT JOURS AU PARADIS

SABATA see **EHI AMICO.. C'E SABATA, HAI CHIUSO** • 1969

SABATO, DOMENICA E VENERDI • 1979 • Castellano, Pipolo, Festa Campanile Pasquale, Martino Sergio • ITL

SABATU AYYAM FI AL-JANNA see **SABAT AYAM FIL GANNA** • 1969

SABBAT OF THE BLACK CAT • 1973 • Marsden Ralph • ASL

SABBATH see **AKELARRE** • 1984

SABELA DE CAMBADOS • 1948 • Torrado Ramon • SPN

SABER DANCE, THE see **DANSE DES SABRES, LA**

SABIAN DEMASIADO • 1962 • Lazaga Pedro • SPN

SABINA • 1916 • *Trautmann Ludwig* • FRG

SABINA, LA • 1979 • Borau Jose Luis • SPN, SWD

SABINE • 1982 • van Nie Rene • NTH

SABINE KLEIST, 7 JAHRE • 1982 • Dziuba Helmut • GDR • SABINE KLEIST -SEVEN YEARS OLD

SABINE KLEIST -SEVEN YEARS OLD see **SABINE KLEIST, 7 JAHRE** • 1982

SABINE UND DER ZUFALL see **MEIN MANN DARF ES NICHT WISSEN** • 1944

SABINE UND DIE 100 MANNER • 1960 • Thiele Wilhelm • FRG

SABINE WULFF • Stranka Erwin • GDR

SABIOS ARBOLES, MAGIOCS ARBOLES • 1988 • Delano Jack • ANS • PRC • WISE TREES, MAGICAL TREES

SABIRNI CENTAR • 1989 • Markovic Goran • YGS • COLLECTING POINT, THE
SABISHI MURA see **SABISHIKI MURA** • 1924
SABISHIKI MURA • 1924 • Kinugasa Teinosuke • JPN • LONELY VILLAGE ○ SABISHI MURA
SABISHIKI RANBOMONO • 1927 • Gosho Heinosuke • JPN • LONELY ROUGHNECK, THE ○ LONELY HOODLUM
SABITA HONOO • 1977 • Sadanaga • JPN • RUSTY FLAME
SABITA KNIFE see **SABITA NAIFU** • 1958
SABITA NAIFU • 1958 • Masuda Toshio • JPN • SABITA KNIFE ○ RUSTY KNIFE
SABITA PENDANT • 1967 • Ezaki Mio • JPN • STAINED PENDANT, THE
SABLAZAN • 1984 • Jovanovic Dragovan • YGS • SCANDAL
SABLE BLESSING, THE • 1916 • Sargent George L. • USA
SABLE CHATEAU see **PJESCANI ZAMAK** • 1963
SABLE CICADA • 1939 • Poh Richard • CHN
SABLE LORCHA, THE • 1915 • Ingraham Lloyd • USA
SABLE VERT, LE • 1962 • Shawqi Khalil • SHT • EGY
SABLES • 1927 • Kirsanoff Dimitri • FRN • SAND
SABLES D'OR see **RIMALUN MIN DHAHAB** • 1966
SABLES OF DEATH see **LADY IN FURS, THE** • 1925
SABOR A SANGRE • 1977 • Hernandez Mario • MXC
SABOR DE LA VENGANZA, EL • 1963 • Romero-Marchent Joaquin Luis • SPN
SABOR DO PECADO, O • 1967 • Silveira Mozael • BRZ • TASTE OF SIN, THE
SABOTAGE • 1924 • Neff Wolfgang? • FRG
SABOTAGE • 1936 • Hitchcock Alfred • UKN • WOMAN ALONE, A (USA) ○ WOMAN ALONE, THE
SABOTAGE • 1939 • Young Harold • USA • SPIES AT WORK (UKN)
SABOTAGE • 1952 • Jonsson Eric • SWD
SABOTAGE • 1967 • van Brakel Nouchka • SHT • NTH
SABOTAGE see **MENACE** • 1934
SABOTAGE see **TRAPPED IN THE SKY** • 1939
SABOTAGE see **SE OPP FOR SPIONER!** • 1944
SABOTAGE see **MUKHARRIBUN, AL–** • 1965
SABOTAGE AT SEA • 1942 • Hiscott Leslie • UKN
SABOTAGE SQUAD • 1942 • Landers Lew • USA
SABOTAGGIO IN MARE see **MIZAR** • 1953
SABOTEUR • 1942 • Hitchcock Alfred • USA
SABOTEUR, THE see **MORITURI** • 1965
SABOTEUR, CODE NAME MORITURI see **MORITURI** • 1965
SABOTEURS, DIE • 1974 • SAF
SABOTEURS, LES see **MUKHARRIBUN, AL–** • 1965
SABOTIER DU VAL-DE-LOIRE, LE • 1955 • Demy Jacques • SHT • FRN
SABRA • 1934 • Ford Aleksander • PLN • CHALUTZIM
SABRA • 1970 • de La Patelliere Denys • FRN, ITL, ISR • DEATH OF A JEW (USA)
SABRAS QUE TE QUIERO • 1958 • Davison Tito • MXC
SABRE AND FOIL • 1969 • Kaczender George • SHT • CND
SABRE AND THE ARROW, THE (UKN) see **LAST OF THE COMANCHES** • 1952
SABRE JET • 1953 • King Louis • USA
SABRINA • 1954 • Wilder Billy • USA • SABRINA FAIR (UKN)
SABRINA FAIR (UKN) see **SABRINA** • 1954
SABRINA'S WONDERFUL LEGS see **BELLISSIME GAMBE DI SABRINA, LE** • 1958
SABRINE • 1975 • Mustafa Hassam Eddin • EGY
SABTE YAR • 1972 • Gorec Ertem • TRK
SABU AND THE MAGIC RING • 1957 • Blair George • USA
SABU BANAT, AS– • 1960 • Salem Atef • EGY • SEPT FILLES, LES
SABU PRINCIPE LADRO see **BUONGIORNO ELEFANTE** • 1952
SABUR DULU DONG • 1990 • INN
SAC AU DOS • 1896 • Melies Georges • FRN • SACKS UP!
SAC DE BILLES, UN • 1976 • Doillon Jacques • FRN • BAG OF MARBLES, A
SACCO AND VANZETTI (USA) see **SACCO E VANZETTI** • 1971
SACCO BELLO, UN • 1979 • Verdone Carlo • ITL
SACCO DI ROMA, IL • 1910 • Guazzoni Enrico • ITL
SACCO DI ROMA, IL • 1954 • Cerio Ferruccio • ITL • PAGANS, THE (USA) ○ BARBARIANS, THE
SACCO DI ROMA E CLEMENTO VII, IL • 1920 • Guazzoni Enrico • ITL
SACCO E VANZETTI • 1971 • Montaldo Giuliano • ITL, FRN • SACCO AND VANZETTI (USA)
SACCO IN PLYPAC, IL • 1961 • Olmi Ermanno (Spv) • DOC • ITL
SACERDOTE, EL • 1978 • de la Iglesia Eloy • SPN • PRIEST, THE
SACHE AUGUST SCHULZE, DIE see **KINDER VON GERICHT** • 1931
SACHE, DIE SICH VERSTEHT, EINE • 1971 • Bitomsky Hartmut, Farocki Harun • FRG
SACHE MIT SCHORRSIEGEL, DIE • 1928 • Speyer Jaap • FRG • CONSCIENCE
SACHE MIT STYX, DIE • 1942 • Anton Karl • FRG • WER DIE HEIMAT LIEBT
SACHI–DULAL • 1934 • *Bulu* • IND
SACHTA POHRBENYCH IDEI • 1921 • Myzet Rudolf • CZC • SHAFT OF BURIED HOPES, THE ○ MINE OF BURIED IDEALS
SACHVERSTANDIGEN, DIE • 1974 • Kuckelmann Norbert • FRG • EXPERTS, THE
SACI, O • 1952 • Nanni Rodolfo • BRZ
SACK, THE see **HOGY SZALADNAK FAK** • 1966
SACK, THE see **WOREK** • 1967
SACKCLOTH AND SCARLET • 1925 • King Henry • USA
SACKED! see **AFSKEDENS TIME** • 1973
SACKETTS, THE • 1979 • Totten Robert • TVM • USA • DAYBREAKERS, THE ○ LOUIS L'AMOUR'S THE SACKETTS
SACKS UP! see **SAC AU DOS** • 1896
SACRAMENT, THE • 1989 • Claus Hugo • BLG
SACRAMENT OF CONFIRMATION, THE • 1924 • Payne John M. • UKN
SACRE BLEU CROSS • 1967 • McKimson Robert • ANS • USA
SACRE D'EDOUARD VII, LE • 1902 • Melies Georges • FRN • COURONNEMENT D'EDOUARD VII, LE ○ CORONATION OF EDWARD VII, THE
SACRE LEONCE • 1935 • Christian-Jaque • FRN
SACRED AND OBSCENE see **SAGRADO Y OBSCENO** • 1976
SACRED AND PROFANE LOVE • 1921 • Taylor William D. • USA
SACRED AND PROFANE LOVE see **CHAINED** • 1934
SACRED BIRD, THE see **PAKSHIRAJ** • 1959
SACRED BRACELET, THE • 1915 • Melville Wilbert • USA
SACRED DRAMAS • 1928 • Parkinson H. B., Edwards J. Steven • SER • UKN
SACRED(?) ELEPHANT, THE • 1911 • Martinek H. O. • UKN
SACRED FLAME, THE • 1919 • Schomer Abraham S. • USA
SACRED FLAME, THE • 1929 • Mayo Archie • USA
SACRED FLAME, THE (UKN) see **RIGHT TO LIVE, THE** • 1935
SACRED FOUNTAIN, THE (USA) see **FONTAINE SACREE OU LA VENGEANCE DE BOUDHA, LA** • 1901
SACRED GANGES, THE • 1937-40 • *Cardiff Jack (Ph)* • DCS • UKN
SACRED GANGES, THE (USA) see **PAVITRA GANGA** • 1932
SACRED GROUND • 1983 • Pierce Charles B. • USA
SACRED HEARTS • 1985 • Rennie Barbara • UKN
SACRED HOPE see **SANTA ESPERANZA** • 1981
SACRED MOUNTAIN, THE (USA) see **MONTANA SAGRADA, LA** • 1972
SACRED OATH, THE • 1916 • *Lily* • USA
SACRED ORDER, THE • 1923 • Coleby A. E. • UKN
SACRED PROTECTOR, THE see **HITO HADA KANNON** • 1937
SACRED RUBY, THE • 1920 • Waite Glenn • USA
SACRED SAND, THE see **SVETI PESAK** • 1968
SACRED SILENCE • 1919 • Millarde Harry • USA
SACRED SOLDIERS MARCHED, THE see **YUKIYUKITE SHINGUN** • 1988
SACRED, THE SELFISH AND THE VAGABOND, THE see **BANAL, GANID, AT ANG PUSAKAL, ANG** • 1968
SACRED TIGER OF AGRA, THE • 1915 • Carleton Lloyd B. • USA
SACRED TURQUOIS OF THE ZUNI, THE • 1910 • Olcott Sidney • USA
SACRED WIVES OF VENGEANCE, THE • 1973 • Ch'U Yuan • HKG • KILLER, THE (UKN)
SACREE GOSSE, UNE see **QUELLE DROLE DE GOSSE!** • 1935
SACREE JEUNESSE • 1958 • Berthomieu Andre • FRN
SACRES GENDARMES • 1980 • Launois Bernard • FRN
SACRIFACE • 1968 • Douglas James* • SHT • USA
SACRIFICE • 1913 • Jasset Victorin • FRN
SACRIFICE • 1913 • Kirkland Hardee • *Vitagraph* • USA
SACRIFICE • 1917 • Reicher Frank • USA
SACRIFICE • 1929 • Peers Victor • UKN
SACRIFICE • 1971 • Salvat Keith • SHT • ASL
SACRIFICE! • 1972 • Lenzi Umberto • ITL
SACRIFICE see **ONLY WOMAN, THE** • 1924
SACRIFICE see **FURTHER ADVENTURES OF TENNESSEE BUCK** • 1987
SACRIFICE, THE • 1909 • Griffith D. W. • USA
SACRIFICE, THE • 1911 • Brooke Van Dyke • USA
SACRIFICE, THE • 1912 • *Buckley May* • USA
SACRIFICE, THE • 1913 • *Kalem* • USA
SACRIFICE, THE • 1913 • *Patheplay* • USA
SACRIFICE, THE • 1914 • *Reliance* • USA
SACRIFICE, THE • 1914 • Pollard Harry • *Beauty* • USA
SACRIFICE, THE • 1915 • *Ramona* • USA
SACRIFICE, THE • 1916 • *Supreme* • USA
SACRIFICE, THE • 1916 • Beal Frank • *Selig* • USA
SACRIFICE, THE • 1978 • Alianak Hrant • CND
SACRIFICE, THE see **ADAK** • 1980
SACRIFICE, THE see **OFFRET** • 1985
SACRIFICE AREA • 1981 • Damen Ermie, Schuurman Otto • DOC • NTH
SACRIFICE AT THE SPILLWAY, THE • 1913 • *Tracy Herbert* • USA
SACRIFICE D'ABRAHAM, LE • 1911 • Andreani Henri • FRN
SACRIFICE D'HONNEUR see **VEILLE D'ARMES** • 1935
SACRIFICE FOR WORK, A • 1907 • Cooper Arthur? • UKN
SACRIFICE, LE (FRN) see **OFFRET** • 1985
SACRIFICE OF A WOMAN see **FRAUENOPFER** • 1922
SACRIFICE OF JONATHAN GRAY, THE • 1915 • MacQuarrie Murdock • USA
SACRIFICE OF KATHLEEN, THE • 1914 • Brooke Van Dyke • USA
SACRIFICE OF SILVER CLOUD, THE • 1911 • *Bison* • USA
SACRIFICE OF YOUTH see **QINGCHUN JI** • 1985
SACRIFICE SURHUMAIN • 1913 • de Morlhon Camille • FRN
SACRIFICE TO CIVILIZATION, A • 1911 • *Bosworth Hobart* • USA
SACRIFICED KILLER, THE see **KURBANLIK KATIL** • 1967
SACRIFICIAL FIRES • 1914 • *Balboa* • USA
SACRIFICIAL HORSE see **ASWAMEDHER GHORA** • 1981
SACRIFIEE, LA • 1955 • Belisle Benjamin • CND
SACRIFIES, LES • 1982 • Touita Okacha • FRN
SACRILEGE • 1914 • Burguet Charles • FRN
SACRILEGIOUS HERO, THE see **SHIN HEIKE MONOGATARI** • 1955
SAD DEVIL, A • 1912 • *Selig* • USA
SAD DOG'S STORY, A • 1915 • Mackey Johnny, Ridgely Richard • USA
SAD HORSE, THE • 1959 • Clark James B. • USA
SAD IDIOT, THE see **KANASHIKI HAKUCHI** • 1924
SAD LIFE OF A ROGUE, THE see **OSENNY MARAFON** • 1979
SAD LITTLE GHOST, THE see **DUHOVITA PRICA** • 1978
SAD LITTLE GUINEA PIGS • 1938 • *Mintz Charles (P)* • ANS • USA
SAD LOVE OF ZERO see **LOVES OF ZERO, THE** • 1928
SAD NIGHT BIRD • 1977 • el Elmi Yehia • EGY
SAD SACK, THE • 1957 • Marshall George • USA
SAD SACK, THE see **TIRE-AU-FLANC 1962** • 1961
SAD SEA WAVES, THE • 1916 • *Christie* • USA
SAD SONG OF THE DEFEATED, THE see **HAIZAN NO UTA WA KANASHI** • 1922
SAD SONG OF YELLOW SKIN • 1970 • Rubbo Michael • DOC • CND • SAD SONGS FOR YELLOW SKINS ○ JAUNE EN PERIL, LE ○ STREETS OF SAIGON, THE
SAD SONGS FOR YELLOW SKINS see **SAD SONG OF YELLOW SKIN** • 1970
SAD SPEECH see **KANASHITI KOTABA** • 1952
SAD STORY OF A BARMAID see **JOKYU AISHI** • 1930
SAD TUNE see **SATSUMA HIKYAKU** • 1938
SAD YOUNG MEN, THE see **JOVENES VIEJOS, LOS** • 1961
SADA', AS– • 1973 • Fahmy Ashraf • EGY • ECHO, L'
SADAN ER DE ALLE • 1968 • Thomsen Knud Leif • DNM • THEY ALL DO IT (UKN) ○ THEY ARE ALL LIKE THAT
SADAN ER JEG OSSE • 1979 • Roos Lise • DNM • I'M LIKE THAT TOO
SADAN ER PORNO • 1971 • Lenz Werner M. • DOC • DNM
SADAN GOR DE DET • 1972 • Orsted Ole • DNM
SADAN GOR DE DET –OGSA • 1973 • *Stromberg Soren* • DNM
SADAT • 1983 • Michaels Richard • TVM • USA
SADAT'S ETERNAL EGYPT • 1980 • Hyatt Gordon • DOC • USA
SADDER BUT WISER • 1914 • *Royal* • USA
SADDLE ACES • 1935 • Fraser Harry L. • USA
SADDLE BUSTER, THE • 1932 • Allen Fred • USA
SADDLE COURAGE • 1935 • Clifton Elmer • USA
SADDLE CYCLONES • 1925 • Thorpe Richard • USA
SADDLE GIRTH, THE • 1917 • Mix Tom • SHT • USA
SADDLE HAWK, THE • 1925 • Sedgwick Edward • USA
SADDLE HAWK, THE see **RIDIN' KID FROM POWDER RIVER, THE** • 1924
SADDLE JUMPERS • 1927 • Wilson Ben • USA
SADDLE KING, THE • 1920 • Laemmle Edward • SHT • USA
SADDLE KING, THE • 1929 • Wilson Ben • USA
SADDLE LEATHER LAW • 1944 • Kline Benjamin • USA • POISONER, THE (UKN)
SADDLE LEGION • 1951 • Selander Lesley • USA
SADDLE MATES • 1928 • Thorpe Richard • USA
SADDLE MOUNTAIN ROUNDUP • 1941 • Luby S. Roy • USA
SADDLE PALS • 1947 • Selander Lesley • USA
SADDLE SERENADE • 1945 • Drake Oliver • USA
SADDLE SILLY • 1941 • Jones Charles M. • ANS • USA
SADDLE-SORE WOODY • 1964 • Smith Paul J. • ANS • USA
SADDLE THE WIND • 1958 • Parrish Robert • USA
SADDLE TRAMP • 1950 • Fregonese Hugo • USA
SADDLED WITH FIVE GIRLS see **PET HOLEK NA KRKU** • 1967
SADDLEMATES • 1941 • Orlebeck Lester • USA
SADDLES AND SAGEBRUSH • 1943 • Berke William • USA • PAY OFF, THE (UKN)
SADE 76 • 1976 • Scandelari Jacques • FRN
SADEAIKA • 1980 • Rimminen Sakari • FNL • RAINY SEASON, THE
SADEQ THE KURD • 1972 • Taghvai Nasser • IRN
SADE'S JUSTINE see **JUSTINE DE SADE** • 1970
SADGATI • 1981 • Ray Satyajit • IND • DELIVERANCE
SADHU AUR SHAITAAN • 1968 • Bhimsingh A. • IND • SAINT AND THE DEVIL, THE
SADIE • 1980 • Chinn Robert C. • USA
SADIE AND SON • 1987 • Moxey John Llewellyn • TVM • USA
SADIE GOES TO HEAVEN • 1917 • Van Dyke W. S. • USA
SADIE HAWKINS DAY • 1944 • Wickersham Bob • ANS • USA
SADIE LOVE • 1919 • Robertson John S. • USA
SADIE MCKEE • 1934 • Brown Clarence • USA
SADIE THOMPSON • 1928 • Walsh Raoul • USA
SADIQUE, LE • 1967 • FRN
SADIQUE AUX DENTS ROUGES, LE • 1970 • Van Belle Jean-Louis • FRN, BLG • SADIST WITH RED TEETH, THE
SADISMO • 1967 • *Billitteri Salvatore (P)* • CMP • CND
SADIST, THE • 1963 • Landis James • USA • PROFILE OF TERROR, THE ○ FACE OF TERROR, THE
SADIST, THE see **BUMMER** • 1973
SADIST, THE (UKN) see **TRAFRACKEN** • 1966
SADIST WITH RED TEETH, THE see **SADIQUE AUX DENTS ROUGES, LE** • 1970
SADISTEROTICA • 1967 • Franco Jesus • SPN
SADISTIC LOVER, THE • 1966 • Gunter George • USA
SADJA • 1918 • Lund Erik • FRG
SADKO • 1953 • Ptushko Alexander, Landis James (Usa Vers) • USS, USA • MAGIC VOYAGE OF SINBAD, THE (USA) ○ SONG OF INDIA
SADNESS REDUCED TO GO see **TRISTESSE MODELE REDUIT** • 1988
SADO • 1977 • Higashi Yoichi • JPN • BOY CALLED THIRD BASE, THE ○ THIRD BASE
SADO–NO TAMAGO • 1966 • Kuri Yoji • ANS • JPN • EGGS, THE (USA)
SADOL KANDULU • 1967 • Perera Senator Reggie • SLN • TEARS OF THE OUTCASTS
SADONO KUNI ONDEKO–ZA • 1977 • Shinoda Masahiro • JPN • SADO'S ONDEKA–ZA
SADO'S ONDEKA–ZA see **SADONO KUNI ONDEKO–ZA** • 1977
SAELFANGST I NORDGRONLAND, EN • 1955 • Henning-Jensen Bjarne • DNM
SAETA DEL RUISENOR • 1957 • del Amo Antonio • SPN • FLAMENCO
SAETA RUBIA • 1956 • Seto Javier • SPN
SAETTA, PRINCIPE PER UN GIORNO • 1925 • Camerini Mario • ITL
SAFAK SOKMESIN • 1968 • Gorec Ertem • TRK • LET THERE BE NO DAWN
SAFAR • 1972 • Beyzai Bahram • SHT • IRN
SAFARBALEK • 1967 • Barakat Henry • LBN
SAFARE SANG • 1977 • Kimiyaei Massoud • IRN • JOURNEY OF A STONE ○ TRAVEL OF THE STONE, THE ○ SAFAREH SANGUE
SAFAREH SANGUE see **SAFARE SANG** • 1977
SAFARI • 1940 • Griffith Edward H. • USA
SAFARI • 1951 • Holmes Cecil • ANM • ASL
SAFARI • 1956 • Young Terence • UKN
SAFARI see **SA NAUD** • 1972
SAFARI 3000 • 1982 • Hurwitz Harry • USA • TWO IN THE BUSH ○ RALLY
SAFARI CANADIEN: DU COTE DU YUKON • 1969 • Cardinal Roger • DOC • CND
SAFARI DIAMANTS (FRN) see **FUR EINE HANDVOLL DIAMANTEN** • 1966
SAFARI –DIE REISE • 1987 • Pevny Wilhelm • AUS • SAFARI –THE VOYAGE
SAFARI DRUMS • 1953 • Beebe Ford • USA • BOMBA AND THE SAFARI DRUMS (UKN)
SAFARI EXPRESS • 1976 • Tessari Duccio • ITL
SAFARI FOTOGRAFICO, UM • 1972 • de Almeida Manuel Faria • SHT • PRT
SAFARI IN ALASKA • 1965 • Hayes Ron • DOC • USA

SAFARI MOJA (ALASKA TO AFRICA) • 1970 • *Taber Willy* • DOC • USA
SAFARI RALLY see **SEIMILA CHILOMETRI DI PAURA** • 1978
SAFARI SENZA RITORNO • 1981 • Birkinshaw Alan • ITL • INVADERS OF THE LOST GOLD
SAFARI SO GOOD • 1947 • Sparber I. • ANS • USA
SAFARI -THE VOYAGE see **SAFARI -DIE REISE** • 1987
SAFARI TO SUCCESS • 1960 • Carter Danny • UKN
SAFARI TOPOLOGIQUE, LE • 1970 • Moreau Michel • DCS • CND
SAFE, THE • 1930 • Aylott Dave • UKN
SAFE, THE • 1932 • *Baddeley Angela* • SHT • UKN
SAFE ADVENTURE, A • 1915 • *Ab* • USA
SAFE AFFAIR, A • 1931 • Wynne Herbert • UKN
SAFE AT HOME • 1941 • Allen Ethan
SAFE AT HOME • 1954 • Barclay David • SHT • USA
SAFE AT HOME! • 1962 • Doniger Walter • USA
SAFE BET, A see **IT'S A BET** • 1935
SAFE BLOWER, THE • 1942 • Haines Ronald • UKN
SAFE-BREAKERS see **KASARI** • 1958
SAFE CLOTHING • 1949 • Bairstow David • DOC • CND • HABITS SANS DANGER
SAFE-CRACKER, THE see **KASAR** • 1974
SAFE DANGER, A • 1918 • *Richards Chris* • SHT • USA
SAFE DISASTER, A • 1918 • *Triangle* • USA
SAFE FOR DEMOCRACY see **LIFE'S GREATEST PROBLEM** • 1919
SAFE GUARDED • 1924 • *Hart Neal* • USA
SAFE HOME see **POD JEDNOU STRECHOU** • 1938
SAFE IN HELL • 1931 • Wellman William A. • USA • LOST LADY, THE (UKN)
SAFE IN JAIL • 1913 • Sennett Mack • USA
SAFE IN THE SAFE • 1916 • *Russell Dan* • SHT • USA
SAFE INVESTMENT, A • 1915 • Drew Sidney • *Vitagraph* • USA
SAFE INVESTMENT, A • 1915 • Hotaling Arthur D. • *Lubin* • USA
SAFE JOURNEY • Goldberger Kurt • DOC • CZC
SAFE LOSS, A • 1916 • Miller Rube • USA
SAFE PASSAGE • 1985 • Bittman Roman • CND
SAFE PLACE, A • 1971 • Jaglom Henry • USA
SAFE PROPOSITION, A • 1912 • *Selig* • USA
SAFE PROPOSITION, A • 1916 • *Turpin Ben* • SHT • USA
SAFE PROPOSITION, A • 1932 • Hiscott Leslie • UKN
SAFE RISK, A • 1916 • Smith Sidney • SHT • USA
SAFE TRANSPORT OF RADIO ACTIVE MATERIAL • 1964 • Sewell George • DOC • UKN
SAFECRACKER, THE • 1957 • Milland Ray • USA, UKN
SAFERNDRI, DIE TANZERIN VON DSCHIAPUR • 1918 • Bluen Georg • FRG • TANZERIN VON DSCHIAPUR, DIE
SAFETY BOOTS • 1965 • Dunning George • ANM • UKN
SAFETY CURTAIN, THE • 1918 • Franklin Sidney A. • USA
SAFETY FIRST • 1915 • *Starlight* • USA
SAFETY FIRST • 1915 • *Empire* • USA
SAFETY FIRST • 1915 • Dillon Eddie • *Komic* • USA
SAFETY FIRST • 1915 • Fahrney Milton • *Mina* • USA
SAFETY FIRST • 1916 • *L-Ko* • SHT • USA
SAFETY FIRST • 1916 • Wehen Rex • *Moon Film* • SHT • USA
SAFETY FIRST • 1917 • Drew Sidney, Drew Sidney Mrs. • SHT • USA
SAFETY FIRST • 1926 • Paul Fred • UKN
SAFETY FIRST • 1928 • Croise Hugh • UKN
SAFETY FIRST • 1938 • Bindley Victor • DOC • ASL
SAFETY FIRST AMBROSE • 1916 • Fishback Fred C. • SHT • USA
SAFETY FIRST AND LAST • 1915 • Clements Roy • USA
SAFETY IN NUMBERS • 1930 • Schertzinger Victor • USA
SAFETY IN NUMBERS • 1938 • St. Clair Malcolm • USA
SAFETY LAST • 1923 • Newmeyer Fred, Taylor Sam • USA
SAFETY MATCH, THE see **SVEDSKAYA SPICKA** • 1954
SAFETY PIN SMUGGLERS • 1917 • *Hamilton Lloyd V.* • USA
SAFETY SECOND • 1950 • Hanna William, Barbera Joseph • ANS • USA
SAFETY SLEUTH • 1944 • Jason Will • SHT • USA
SAFETY SPIN • 1953 • Burness Pete • ANS • USA
SAFETY SUIT FOR SKATERS, THE • 1908 • Fitzhamon Lewin? • UKN
SAFETY SUPERVISOR, THE • 1951 • Mulholland Donald • SHT • CND
SAFETY WORST • 1915 • *Hardy Oliver* • USA
SAFFO, VENERE DI LESBO • 1960 • Francisci Pietro • ITL, FRN • WARRIOR EMPRESS, THE (USA) ○ SAPHO, VENUS OF LESBOS ○ SAPHO
S'AFFRANCHIR • 1913 • Feuillade Louis • FRN
SAFFRON ROBE, THE see **RAN SALU** • 1967
SAFIR GEHANNAM • 1944 • Wahby Youssef • EGY • AMBASSADOR OF HELL, THE ○ AMBASSADOR FROM HELL, THE
SAFIYE SULTAN • 1953 • *Efi Film* • TRK
SAFO 1963 see **AMOR Y SEXO** • 1963
SAFRANA OU LE DROIT A LA PAROLE • 1977 • Sokhona Sidney • DOC • FRN
SAFTEST OF THE FAMILY, THE • 1931 • Pearson George • SHT • UKN
SAG DET I TONER • 1929 • Adolphson Edvin, Jaenzon Julius • SWD • SAY IT WITH MUSIC ○ DREAM WALTZ, THE
SAG DET MED BLOMMAR • 1952 • Kjellgren Lars-Eric • SWD • SAY IT WITH FLOWERS
SAG' DIE WAHRHEIT • 1946 • Weiss Helmut • FRG
SAG' ENDLICH JA • 1945 • Weiss Helmut • FRG
SAG JA, MUTTI see **SINGENDEN ENGEL VON TIROL, DIE** • 1958
SAG' MIR, WER DU BIST • 1933 • Jacoby Georg • FRG
SAGA, EN • 1938 • Schneevoigt George • DNM
SAGA DE LOS DRACULA, LA • 1972 • Klimovsky Leon • SPN • SAGA OF DRACULA (USA) ○ DRACULA'S SAGA ○ DRACULA SAGA, THE ○ DRACULA: THE BLOODLINE CONTINUES ○ SAGA OF THE DRACULAS, THE
SAGA DE MADIANA, LA • 1983 • Lethem Roland • BLG
SAGA OF ANATAHAN, THE see **ANATAHAN** • 1954
SAGA OF DEATH VALLEY • 1939 • Kane Joseph • USA
SAGA OF DRACULA (USA) see **SAGA DE LOS DRACULA, LA** • 1972
SAGA OF GOSTA BERLING, THE see **GOSTA BERLINGS SAGA** • 1924
SAGA OF H.M.S. BOUNTY, THE see **MUTINY ON THE BOUNTY** • 1983
SAGA OF HEMP BROWN, THE • 1958 • Carlson Richard • USA
SAGA OF JEREMIAH JOHNSON, THE see **JEREMIAH JOHNSON** • 1972
SAGA OF SATCHMO see **SATCHMO THE GREAT** • 1957
SAGA OF TANEGASHIMA see **TEPPO DENRAIKI** • 1968
SAGA OF THE DRACULAS, THE see **SAGA DE LOS DRACULA, LA** • 1972
SAGA OF THE FLYING HOSTESSES, THE see **COPACABANA PALACE** • 1962
SAGA OF THE GREAT BUDDHA see **DAIBUTSU KAIGEN** • 1952
SAGA OF THE ROAD, THE see **PATHER PANCHALI** • 1955
SAGA OF THE SIBERIAN LAND, THE see **SKAZANIYE O ZEMLYE SIBIRSKOI** • 1947
SAGA OF THE TAIRA CLAN see **SHIN HEIKE MONOGATARI** • 1955
SAGA OF THE VAGABONDS see **SENGOKU GUNTODEN** • 1959
SAGA OF THE VIKING WOMEN AND THEIR VOYAGE TO THE WATERS OF THE GREAT SEA SERPENT, THE see **VIKING WOMEN AND THE SEA SERPENT, THE** • 1957
SAGA OF THE WEST see **WHEN A MAN'S A MAN** • 1935
SAGA OF WINDWAGON SMITH, THE • 1961 • Nichols Charles • ANS • USA
SAGACITY VERSUS CRIME • 1913 • Martinek H. O. • UKN
S'AGAPO • 1970 • Vouyouklakis Takis • GRC • I LOVE YOU
SAGAR SANGAME • 1935-47 • Bose Debaki • IND
SAGARA JALAYA • 1988 • Peries Sumitra • SLN
SAGARANA: O DUELO • 1974 • Thiago Paulo • BRZ
SAGARIKA • 1950 • Agradoot • IND
SAGE BRUSH GAL, THE • 1915 • Sturgeon Rollin S. • USA
SAGE BRUSH HAMLET, A • 1919 • Franz Joseph J. • USA
SAGE BRUSH LAW • 1917 • Horne James W. • SHT • USA
SAGE-BRUSH LEAGUE, THE • 1919 • Grant Harry A. • USA
SAGE-BRUSH PHRENOLOGIST, THE • 1911 • Dwan Allan • USA
SAGE-BRUSH TOM • 1915 • Mix Tom • USA
SAGE DES TODES, DIE • 1981 • Franco Jesus • FRG, SPN • BLOODY MOON
SAGE-FEMME DE PREMIERE CLASSE • 1902 • Blache Alice • FRN
SAGE-FEMME, LE CURE ET LE BON DIEU, LA (FRN) see **JESSICA** • 1962
SAGE FROM THE SEA, THE see **KONDURA** • 1977
SAGE HEN, THE • 1921 • Lewis Edgar • USA
SAGE, THE CHERUB AND THE WIDOW, THE • 1910 • *Vitagraph* • USA
SAGE VOM HUND VON BASKERVILLE, DIE • 1915 • Oswald Richard • FRG
SAGE VON ALTEN HIRTEN XEUDI UND SEINEM FREUND REIMAN, DIE • 1973 • Siber H. J. • SWT
SAGEBRUSH FAMILY TRAVELS WEST, THE • 1940 • Newfield Sam • USA
SAGEBRUSH GENTLEMAN, A • 1920 • Sowders Edward • SHT • USA
SAGEBRUSH GOSPEL • 1924 • Hatton Richard • USA
SAGEBRUSH HEROES • 1945 • Kline Benjamin • USA
SAGEBRUSH LADY, THE • 1925 • Carpenter Horace B.?, Davey Horace? • USA
SAGEBRUSH LAW • 1942 • Nelson Sam • USA
SAGEBRUSH POLITICS • 1930 • Adamson Victor • USA
SAGEBRUSH SADIE • 1928 • Disney Walt • ANS • USA
SAGEBRUSH SERENADE • 1939 • Roberts Charles E. • SHT • USA
SAGEBRUSH TRAIL • 1933 • Schaefer Armand • USA
SAGEBRUSH TRAIL, THE • 1922 • Thornby Robert T. • USA • RIDIN' WILD
SAGEBRUSH TROUBADOUR, THE • 1935 • Kane Joseph • USA
SAGEBRUSHER, THE • 1920 • Sloman Edward • USA
SAGES ET LES FOUS, LES see **JULIE ETAIT BELLE** • 1976
SAGINA • 1974 • *Burman S. D. (M)* • IND
SAGINAW TRAIL, THE • 1953 • Archainbaud George • USA
SAGITTARIUS V • 1969 • Lerman Richard • SHT • USA
SAGOLANDET • 1988 • Troell Jan • SWD • LAND OF DREAMS, THE
SAGRADA FAMILIA, A • 1972 • Monteiro Joao Cesar • PRT
SAGRADO Y OBSCENO • 1976 • Chalbaud Roman • VNZ • SACRED AND OBSCENE
SAGRARIO • 1933 • Peon Ramon • MXC
SAGRENSKA KOZA • 1960 • Kristl Vlado, Vrbanic Ivo • ANS • YGS • PEAU DE CHAGRIN, LA ○ SKIN OF SORROW, THE
SAGS PA STAN, DET • 1941 • Lindberg Per • SWD • TALK OF THE TOWN
SAGUARO see **SAPEVANO SOLO UCCIDERE** • 1968
SAGUENAY • 1948 • Blais Roger • DCS • CND
SAGUENAY • 1962 • Chapman Christopher • DOC • CND
SAH ISMAIL • 1968 • Kiran Adnan • TRK • SHAH ISMAIL
SAHAJATRI • 1951 • Agradoot • IND
SAHARA • 1919 • Rosson Arthur • USA
SAHARA • 1943 • Korda Zoltan • USA • SOMEWHERE IN SAHARA
SAHARA • 1983 • McLaglen Andrew V. • USA
SAHARA, AN IV • 1960 • Gerard • SHT • FRN
SAHARA BRULE, LE • 1960 • Gast Michel • FRN
SAHARA CROSS • 1977 • Valerii Tonino • ITL
SAHARA D'AUJOURD'HUI • 1957 • Gout Pierre • DOC • FRN
SAHARA HARE • 1955 • Freleng Friz • ANS • USA
SAHARA LA DETERMINATION D'UN PEUPLE • 1976 • Sanchez-Ariza Jose • SPN
SAHARA LOVE • 1926 • Hill Sinclair • UKN
SAHARA N'EST PAS A VENDRE, LE • 1977 • Saab Jocelyne • DOC • FRN
SAHARAN VENTURE • 1965 • Woof Harry • DCS • UKN
SAHARY DJELI • 1911 • *Warwick Trading Co* • UKN
SAHEIJI FINDS A WAY see **BAKUMATSU TAIYODEN** • 1958
SAHERA EL SAGHIRA, EL • 1963 • EGY • SMALL WITCH, THE
SAHHAR, AS- • 1969 • Badie Mustapha • ALG • ENNEMI PUBLIC, L' ○ CHARLATAN, LE
SAHIN • 1967 • Kovac Ctibor • CZC
SAHIR AN-NISSA' • 1958 • Wahab Fatin Abdel • EGY • SEDUCTEUR, LE
SAI COSA FACEVA STALIN ALLE DONNE? • 1969 • Liverani Maurizio • ITL • DO YOU KNOW WHAT STALIN DID TO WOMEN?
SAIBOGU 009 • 1966 • Serikawa Yugo • JPN • CYBORG 009
SAIBOGU 009 -KAIJU SENSO • 1967 • Serikawa Yugo • JPN • CYBORG 009 -KAIJU SENSO ○ CYBORG 009 -UNDERGROUND DUEL
SAID EFFENDI • 1959 • Husni Kameran • IRQ
"SAID" EIN VOLK IN KETTEN • 1923 • Linke Edmund • FRG
SAID O'REILLY TO MCNAB • 1937 • Beaudine William • UKN • SEZ O'REILLY TO MCNAB (USA)
SAID POEM, A • 1976 • Soul Veronika • ANS • CND
SAIDA A ENLEVE MANNEKEN PIS • 1913 • Machin Alfred • NTH
SAIGNEE, LA • 1971 • Mulot Claude • FRN, ITL • A DENTI STRETTI (ITL) ○ MANHUNT FOR MURDER (USA) ○ CONTRACT, THE
SAIGNEUR EST AVEC NOUS, LE • 1975 • Lethem Roland • BLG
SAIGO NI WARAU OTOKO • 1949 • Yasuda Kimiyoshi • JPN • FINAL LAUGHTER
SAIGO NO JOITO • 1945 • Inagaki Hiroshi • JPN • LAST PARTY OF CHAUVINISTS, THE ○ LAST ABDICATION
SAIGO NO KIRIFUDA • 1960 • Nomura Yoshitaro • JPN • GRAVE TELLS ALL, THE
SAIGO NO NIHONHEI • 1960 • Iizuka Masuichi • JPN • LAST OF THE IMPERIAL ARMY, THE ○ LAST JAPANESE SOLDIER, THE ○ SAIGO NO NIPPONHEI
SAIGO NO NIPPONHEI see **SAIGO NO NIHONHEI** • 1960
SAIGO NO SHINPAN • 1965 • Horikawa Hiromichi • JPN • LAST JUDGEMENT
SAIGON • 1948 • Fenton Leslie • USA
SAIGON • 1959 • King Allan • CND
SAIGON see **SAIGON: PORTRAIT OF A CITY** • 1967
SAIGON COMMANDOS • 1987 • Henderson Clark • USA
SAIGON: PORTRAIT OF A CITY • 1967 • Fox Beryl • DOC • CND • SAIGON
SAIGON: THE YEAR OF THE CAT • 1983 • Frears Stephen • UKN
SAIGON (UKN) see **OFF LIMITS** • 1988
SAIHAIEN BOLAN DE BAD see **SAYEHAYE BOLANDE BAD** • 1978
SAIJO KATAGI • 1959 • Nakahira Ko • JPN • TALENTED WOMAN, THE
SAIKAI • 1953 • Kimura Keigo • JPN • REUNION ○ MEETING AGAIN
SAIKAI • 1974 • Saito Koichi • JPN • MEETING AGAIN
SAIKAKU ICHIDAI ONNA • 1952 • Mizoguchi Kenji • JPN • LIFE OF OHARU, THE (USA) ○ LIFE OF A WOMAN BY SAIKAKU ○ OHARU ○ KOSHOKU ICHIDAI ONNA
SAIKAKU'S FIVE WOMEN see **KOSHOKU GO-NIN ONNA** • 1948
SAIKO SHUKON FUJIN • 1959 • Masumura Yasuzo • JPN • MOST VALUABLE MADAM, THE
SAIKUN SHIN SENJUTSU • 1932 • Yamamoto Kajiro • JPN • NEW STRATEGY
SAIL A CROOKED SHIP • 1961 • Brecher Irving S. • USA
SAIL AWAY • 1979 • MacKay Bruce • MTV • CND, USA
SAIL INTO DANGER • 1957 • Hume Kenneth • UKN
SAILAAB • 1956 • Dutt Guru • IND
SAILBOAT • 1967 • Wieland Joyce • SHT • USA
SAILING see **ZEILEN** • 1962
SAILING 1000 MILES UP THE RIVER AMAZON • 1936 • Dalrymple J. Blake • DOC • UKN
SAILING ALONG • 1924 • Lamont Charles • SHT • USA
SAILING ALONG • 1938 • Hale Sonnie • UKN
SAILING AND VILLAGE BAND • 1958 • Keller Lew • ANS • USA
SAILING FOR TOMORROW see **MING-T'IEN CHIH YU WO** • 1982
SAILING IN THE SKY • 1955 • Rivard Fernand • DCS • CND
SAILING OF THE SHIP KOFUKU-GO, THE see **KOFUKU-GO SHUPPAN** • 1981
SAILING, SAILING OVER THE BOUNDING MAIN • 1926 • Fleischer Dave • ANS • USA
SAILING TO BROOKLYN • 1974 • Cameron Ken • SHT • ASL
SAILING TO THE CAPE see **PROUD CANVAS** • 1949
SAILING UNDER FALSE COLORS • 1913 • *Frontier* • USA
SAILING WITH A SONG • 1949 • Cowan Will • SHT • USA
SAILING ZERO • 1964 • Kneitel Seymour • ANS • USA
SAILOR • 1968 • Crombie Donald • DOC • ASL
SAILOR, THE • 1919 • Kenton Erle C. • SHT • USA
SAILOR AND THE DEVIL, THE • 1967 • Williams Richard • ANS • UKN
SAILOR BE GOOD • 1933 • Cruze James • USA • TARS AND FEATHERS
SAILOR BEWARE • 1951 • Walker Hal • USA
SAILOR BEWARE • 1956 • Parry Gordon • UKN • PANIC IN THE PARLOR (USA)
SAILOR FROM GIBRALTAR, THE • 1967 • Richardson Tony • UKN
SAILOR FROM THE COMET • 1958 • Annensky Isider • USS
SAILOR FUKU TO KIKANJU • 1982 • Somai Shinji • JPN • SCHOOLGIRL WITH A MACHINE-GUN, A
SAILOR GEORGE • 1928 • Newfield Sam • SHT • USA
SAILOR GOES ASHORE, A see **SJOMAN GAR I LAND, EN** • 1937
SAILOR IN A DRESS-COAT see **SJOMAN I FRACK, EN** • 1942
SAILOR IN PHILIPPINES • 1908 • *Kalem* • USA
SAILOR IZZY MURPHY • 1927 • Lehrman Henry • USA
SAILOR JACK'S REFORMATION • 1911 • Olcott Sidney • USA
SAILOR-MADE MAN, A • 1921 • Newmeyer Fred • USA
SAILOR MAID • 1937 • Lamont Charles • SHT • USA
SAILOR MOUSE • 1938 • Lovy Alex • ANS • USA
SAILOR OF THE KING (USA) see **SINGLE-HANDED** • 1953
SAILOR OF THE SEA see **SINGLE-HANDED** • 1953
SAILOR ON A HORSE see **SJOMAN TILL HAST, EN** • 1940
SAILOR PAPA, A • 1925 • Roach Hal • SHT • USA
SAILOR TAKES A WIFE, THE • 1945 • Whorf Richard • USA • JOHN AND MARY
SAILOR TRAMP, A • 1922 • Thornton F. Martin • UKN
SAILOR WHO FELL FROM GRACE WITH THE SEA, THE • 1976 • Carlino Lewis John • UKN
SAILOR WITH THE GOLDEN FISTS, THE see **MARINO DE LOS PUNOS DE ORO, EL** • 1968

SAILORS, THE see **NAFTIS TOU EGEOU, O** • 1968
SAILOR'S ADVENTURE, THE see **PRZYGODY MARYNARZA** • 1958
SAILOR'S ADVENTURES, A see **PRZYGODY MARYNARZA** • 1958
SAILORS ALL • 1943 • Vorkapich Slavko • SHT • USA
SAILORS AND SEXTANTS see **HEJ DU GLADA SOMMAR** • 1965
SAILOR'S BELT, THE • 1909 • *Urban-Eclipse* • USA
SAILORS BEWARE! • 1927 • Yates Hal, Guiol Fred • SHT • USA
SAILOR'S BRIDE, A • 1911 • Noy Wilfred • UKN
SAILOR'S CHARACTER, A • 1971 • Zhuravlyov Vasili • USS
SAILOR'S CHILD • 1909 • *Bison* • USA
SAILOR'S CONSOLATION • 1951 • Halas John • ANS • UKN
SAILOR'S COURTSHIP, A • 1906 • Collins Alf? • UKN
SAILOR'S DANCE see **SJOMANSDANSEN** • 1911
SAILOR'S DEPARTURE, THE • 1898 • *Paul R. W.* • UKN
SAILORS DO CARE • 1944 • Gilbert Lewis* • DCS • UKN
SAILORS DON'T CARE • 1928 • Kellino W. P. • UKN
SAILORS DON'T CARE • 1940 • Mitchell Oswald • UKN
SAILORS DON'T CRY • 1989 • Didden Marc • BLG
SAILOR'S HEART, A • 1912 • Lucas Wilfred? • USA
SAILOR'S HOLIDAY • 1929 • Newmeyer Fred • USA
SAILOR'S HOLIDAY • 1944 • Berke William • USA
SAILOR'S HOME, THE • 1936 • *Terry Paul/ Moser Frank (P)* • ANS • USA
SAILOR'S HORNPIPE • 1898 • *Levi, Jones & Co* • UKN
SAILOR'S LADY • 1940 • Dwan Allan • USA
SAILOR'S LASS, A • 1907 • Fitzhamon Lewin • UKN
SAILOR'S LIFE see **BUHAY MARINO** • 1967
SAILOR'S LOVE LETTER, THE • 1911 • *Prior Herbert* • USA
SAILOR'S LUCK • 1933 • Walsh Raoul • USA
SAILORS OF THE GUARD • 1933 • Fryer Bryant • ANS • CND
SAILORS OF THE SEVEN SEAS • 1920 • Revier Harry • SRL • USA
SAILORS ON DECK see **MARINAI IN COPERTA** • 1967
SAILORS ON LEAVE • 1941 • Rogell Albert S. • USA
SAILOR'S RETURN, THE • 1898 • *Paul R. W.* • UKN
SAILOR'S RETURN, THE • 1977 • Gold Jack • UKN
SAILOR'S SACRIFICE, A • 1910 • Bouwmeester Theo? • UKN
SAILOR'S SMILING SPIRIT, THE • 1916 • *Chamberlin Riley* • USA
SAILOR'S SONG • 1913 • Booth W. R.? • UKN
SAILOR'S SONG see **LIED DER MATROSEN, DAS** • 1958
SAILOR'S SWEETHEART, A • 1927 • Bacon Lloyd • USA
SAILOR'S SWEETHEART, A see **LOVE DARES ALL** • 1913
SAILOR'S SWEETHEART, THE • 1905 • *Cricks & Sharp* • UKN
SAILORS TAKE CARE • 1933 • *Premier* • SHT • UKN
SAILORS THREE • 1940 • Forde Walter • UKN • THREE COCKEYED SAILORS (USA)
SAILORS' THREE CROWNS, THE see **TROIS COURONNES DANOIS DES MATELOTS, LES** • 1982
SAILOR'S WEDDING, THE • 1905 • Stow Percy • UKN
SAILOR'S WIFE see **SARENG BOU** • 1977
SAILORS WITHOUT A SEA • 1958 • Uher Stefan • CZC
SAILOR'S WIVES • 1928 • Henabery Joseph • USA
SAIMAA GESTURE, THE see **SAIMAA-ILMIO** • 1982
SAIMAA-ILMIO • 1982 • Kaurismaki Aki, Kaurismaki Mika • FNL • SAIMAA GESTURE, THE
SAINT see **MAULA SAIN** • 1988
SAINT ALLIANCE, THE see **SANTA ALIANCA, A** • 1977
SAINT AND HER FOOL, THE (USA) see **HEILIGE UND IHR NARR, DIE** • 1928
SAINT AND THE BRAVE GOOSE, THE • 1978 • Frankel Cyril • MTV • UKN
SAINT AND THE DEVIL, THE see **SADHU AUR SHAITAAN** • 1968
SAINT AND THE SINGER, THE • 1914 • *Powers* • USA
SAINT AND THE SIWASH, THE • 1912 • Stedman Marshall • USA
ST. ANDREWS BY THE NORTHERN SEA • 1973 • Littlewood Mark • DOC • UKN
SAINT ARUNAGIRI • 1937 • *Sundari A.* • IND
ST. BENNY THE DIP • 1951 • Ulmer Edgar G. • USA • ESCAPE IF YOU CAN (UKN)
SAINT BERNARD see **SAO BERNARDO** • 1972
ST. CHRISTOPHER'S • 1967 • Platt-Mills Barney • UKN
SAINT COHEN • 1973 • Dayan Assaf • ISR
SAINT CONDUIT LE BAL, LE see **SAINT MENE LA DANSE, LE** • 1960
SAINT DAY OF TIATIRA see **DIA SANTO DE TIATIRA, EL** • 1970
SAINT-DENIS DANS LE TEMPS • 1969 • Carriere Marcel • CND
SAINT-DENIS GARNEAU • 1960 • Dansereau Jean, Portugais Louis • DCS • CND
SAINT, DEVIL AND WOMAN • 1916 • Sullivan Frederick • USA
ST. ELIZABETH'S SQUARE • 1965 • Bahna Vladimir • CZC
ST. ELMO • 1910 • *Thanhouser* • USA
ST. ELMO • 1914 • *Balboa* • USA
ST. ELMO • 1923 • Storm Jerome • USA • ST. ELMO MURRAY
ST. ELMO • 1923 • Wilson Rex • UKN
ST. ELMO MURRAY see **ST. ELMO** • 1923
ST. ELMO'S FIRE • 1985 • Schumacher Joel • USA
SAINT FAMILY see **SKORPION, PANNA I LUCZNIK** • 1972
ST. FRANCIS OF ASSISI (USA) see **SAN FRANCISCO DE ASIS** • 1943
SAINT-FRANCOIS • 1939 • Bartosch Berthold • ANM • FRN
SAINT FROM THE OUTSKIRTS OF TOWN, THE see **SVATEJ Z KREJCARKU** • 1969
SAINT FROM THE SUBURBS, THE see **SVATEJ Z KREJCARKU** • 1969
ST. GEORGE AND THE 7 CURSES (UKN) see **MAGIC SWORD, THE** • 1962
ST. GEORGE AND THE DRAGON • 1910 • *Edison* • USA
ST. GEORGE AND THE DRAGON • 1912 • *Milano* • ITL
ST. GEORGE AND THE DRAGON • 1929 • *Whitehall Films* • SHT • UKN
ST. GEORGE AND THE DRAGON see **MAGIC SWORD, THE** • 1962
SAINT-GERMAIN-DES-PRES • 1953 • Pagliero Marcello • SHT • FRN
SAINT-GERMAIN-EN-LAYE CITY ROYALE • 1956 • Poitrenaud Jacques • SHT • FRN
ST. HELENA AND ITS MAN OF DESTINY • 1936 • Fitzpatrick James • SHT • USA
ST. HELENA (DER GEFANGENE KAISER) see **NAPOLEON AUF ST. HELENA** • 1929
ST. HELENS • 1981 • Pintoff Ernest • USA • ST. HELENS: KILLER VOLCANO ○ KILLER VOLCANO
ST. HELENS: KILLER VOLCANO see **ST. HELENS** • 1981
SAINT IN LONDON, THE • 1939 • Carstairs John Paddy • UKN
SAINT IN NEW YORK, THE • 1938 • Holmes Ben • USA
SAINT IN PALM SPRINGS, THE • 1941 • Hively Jack • USA
ST. IVES • 1959 • Kelly Ron • CND
ST. IVES • 1976 • Thompson J. Lee • USA
SAINT JACK • 1979 • Bogdanovich Peter • USA
SAINT JOAN • 1927 • Newman Widgey R. • UKN
SAINT JOAN • 1957 • Preminger Otto • UKN
SAINT JOAN THE MAID see **MERVEILLEUSE VIE DE JEANNE D'ARC, LA** • 1928
ST. JOHN'S FIRE (USA) see **JOHANNISFEUER** • 1939
SAINT JOHNSON see **LAW AND ORDER** • 1932
ST. JOSEPH'S TAPER • 1913 • *Bracken Mildred* • USA
ST. JUDE OF THE BORDER see **IN 'N OUT** • 1986
ST. LAWRENCE, THE • 1973 • Owen Don • DOC • CND
ST. LAWRENCE SEAWAY, THE • 1958 • Howe John • DOC • CND
ST. LAZARE RAILROAD STATION see **GARE SAINT-LAZARE, LA** • 1896
ST. LOUIS BLUES • 1929 • Murphy Dudley • SHT • USA
ST. LOUIS BLUES • 1939 • Walsh Raoul • USA • BEST OF THE BLUES
ST. LOUIS BLUES • 1958 • Reisner Allen • USA
ST. LOUIS EXPOSITION • 1902 • *Bitzer Billy (Ph)* • USA
ST. LOUIS GAL • 1938 • *Mckinney Nina Mae* • USA
ST. LOUIS KID • 1934 • Enright Ray • USA • PERFECT WEEKEND, A (UKN)
ST. LOUIS SQUARE • 1984 • Castillo Nardo • CND
ST. LOUIS WOMAN • 1935 • Ray Albert • USA
ST. MARTIN'S LANE • 1938 • Whelan Tim • UKN • SIDEWALKS OF LONDON (USA)
ST. MATTHEW PASSION (USA) see **MATTHAUS-PASSION** • 1949
SAINT-MAURICE EN IMAGES, LE • 1938 • Tessier Albert • DCS • CND
ST. MAWR • 1988 • Russell Ken • UKN
SAINT MEETS THE TIGER, THE • 1941 • Stein Paul L. • UKN
SAINT MENE LA DANSE, LE • 1960 • Nahum Jacques • FRN • DANCE OF DEATH, THE (USA) ○ SAINT CONDUIT LE BAL, LE
ST. MICHAEL HAD A ROOSTER see **SAN MICHELE AVEVA UN GALLO** • 1972
ST. MORITZ BLITZ • 1961 • Smith Paul J. • ANS • USA
SAINT NICHOLAS • Noman Theo Van Haren • NTH
ST. PAFNUCIO see **PAFNUCIO SANTO** • 1976
SAINT-PAUL-DE-VENCE • 1949 • Mariaud Robert • SHT • FRN
ST. PAULI BETWEEN NIGHT AND MORNING see **ST. PAULI ZWISCHEN NACHT UND MORGEN** • 1967
ST. PAULI ZWISCHEN NACHT UND MORGEN • 1967 • Benazeraf Jose • FRG • ST. PAULI BETWEEN NIGHT AND MORNING
ST. PETER'S UMBRELLA see **SZENT PETER ESERNYOJE** • 1917
SAINT PETERSBURG see **PETERBURGSKAYA NOCH** • 1934
SAINT PRAHLADA see **BHAKTA PRAHLADA** • 1967
SAINT PREND L'AFFUT, LE • 1966 • Christian-Jaque • FRN, ITL • SANTO PRENDE LA MIRA, IL (ITL) ○ SAINT VERSUS.., THE (USA)
SAINT SIMEON OF THE DESERT see **SIMON DEL DESIERTO** • 1965
SAINT STRIKES BACK, THE • 1939 • Farrow John • USA
SAINT TAKES OVER, THE • 1940 • Hively Jack • USA
SAINT-TROPEZ see **SAINT-TROPEZ, DEVOIR DE VACANCES** • 1952
SAINT-TROPEZ BLUES • 1960 • Moussy Marcel • FRN, ITL
SAINT-TROPEZ, DEVOIR DE VACANCES • 1952 • Paviot Paul • SHT • FRN • SAINT-TROPEZ
SAINT TROPEZ VICE see **POLICE DES MOEURS: LES FILLES DE SAINT TROPEZ** • 1986
SAINT TURKARAM • 1920 • *Kalanidhi* • IND
SAINT-VAL MYSTERY, THE see **MYSTERE SAINT-VAL, LE** • 1944
ST. VALENTINE'S DAY MASSACRE, THE • 1967 • Corman Roger • USA
SAINT VERSUS.., THE (USA) see **SAINT PREND L'AFFUT, LE** • 1966
SAINT VOYOU, PRIEZ POUR NOUS • 1979 • Beni Alphonse • FRN, CMR
SAINT WENCELAUS see **SVATY VACLAV** • 1929
SAINTE-ANNE DE ROQUEMAURE • 1942 • Proulx Maurice • DCS • CND
SAINTE ET LE FOU, LA see **HEILIGE UND IHR NARR, DIE** • 1928
SAINTE FAMILLE, LA • 1973 • Marchou • FRN
SAINTE ODILE • 1913 • Ravel Gaston • FRN
SAINTED DEVIL, A • 1924 • Henabery Joseph • USA
SAINTED SISTERS, THE • 1948 • Russell William D. • USA
SAINTES NITOUCHES, LES • 1962 • Montazel Pierre • FRN, ITL • RAGAZZE DI BUONA FAMIGLIA, LE (ITL) ○ YOUNG GIRLS OF GOOD FAMILIES ○ JEUNES FILLES DE BONNE FAMILLE, LES ○ WILD LIVING
SAINTLY ALLIANCE, THE see **SANTA ALIANCA, A** • 1977
SAINTLY SINNER, THE • 1917 • Wells Raymond • USA
SAINTLY SINNERS • 1962 • Yarbrough Jean • USA
SAINTS, LES see **BIENHEUREUX, LES** • 1982
SAINTS, THE • Barfod Bent • ANS • DNM
SAINT'S ADVENTURE, THE • 1917 • Berthelet Arthur • USA
SAINTS AND SINNERS • 1911 • Porter Edwin S. • USA
SAINTS AND SINNERS • 1915 • *American* • USA
SAINTS AND SINNERS • 1915 • Brooke Van Dyke • *Broadway Star* • USA
SAINTS AND SINNERS • 1916 • Kirkwood James • USA
SAINTS AND SINNERS • 1949 • Arliss Leslie • UKN
SAINTS ARE MARCHING OUT, THE • 1970 • Fleischmann George • DOC • IRL
SAINT'S DOUBLE TROUBLE, THE • 1940 • Hively Jack • USA
SAINT'S GIRL FRIDAY, THE (USA) see **SAINT'S RETURN, THE** • 1953
SAINT'S RETURN, THE • 1953 • Friedman Seymour • UKN • SAINT'S GIRL FRIDAY, THE (USA)
SAINT'S VACATION, THE • 1941 • Fenton Leslie • UKN
SAIR-E-PARISTAN see **SHAN-E-KHUDA** • 1934
SAISON CINQUIEME • 1967 • Gagne Jean • SHT • CND
SAISON DANS LA VIE D'EMMANUEL, UNE • 1972 • Weisz Claude • FRN
SAISON IN KAIRO • 1933 • Schunzel Reinhold • FRG
SAISON IN OBERBAYERN see **HOTEL ALLOTRIA** • 1956
SAISON IN SALZBURG • 1952 • Marischka Ernst • AUS
SAISON IN SALZBURG see **...UND DIE MUSIK SPIELT DAZU** • 1943
SAISONARBEITER, DER • 1972 • Bizzarri Alvaro • SWT
SAISONS, LES see **SEASONS, THE** • 1953
SAIT-ON JAMAIS • 1957 • Vadim Roger • FRN, ITL • COLPO DA DUE MILIARDI, UN (ITL) ○ WHEN THE DEVIL DRIVES (UKN) ○ NO SUN IN VENICE (USA)
SAITANE see **SARTANI** • 1972
SAIYIDAT AL-QASR • 1958 • el Sheikh Kamal • EGY • DAME DU CHATEAU, LA
SAIYIDAT AL-QIT'AR see **SAYIDAT EL KITAR** • 1951
SAIYU-KI • 1960 • Yabushita Taiji, Tezuka Osamu • ANM • JPN • ALAKAZAM THE GREAT (USA) ○ SAIYU-KI: THE ENCHANTED MONKEY
SAIYU-KI: THE ENCHANTED MONKEY see **SAIYU-KI** • 1960
SAJA' AL-LAYL • 1947 • Barakat Henry • EGY • NUITS SEREINES
SAJENKO, THE SOVIET • 1929 • Behn-Grund Friedl • FRG
SAKAFLIAS, O • 1967 • Kontaxis Vasilis • GRC • BANDIT, THE
SAKARIBA BLUES • 1968 • Konishi Michio • JPN • BLUE NEON
SAKASU GONINGUMI • 1935 • Naruse Mikio • JPN • FIVE MEN IN THE CIRCUS
SAKE TO ONNA TO YARI • 1960 • Uchida Tomu • JPN • WINE, WOMEN AND A LANCE ○ SAKI WOMAN AND A LANCE
SAKEBU AZIA • 1932 • Uchida Tomu • JPN • ASIA CALLING
SAKHA PRASAKHA • 1990 • Ray Satyajit • IND, FRN • FAMILY REUNION
SAKHAROV • 1984 • Gold Jack • TVM • UKN
SAKHTE IRAN • 1978 • Naderi Amir • IRN • MADE IN IRAN
SAKI WOMAN AND A LANCE see **SAKE TO ONNA TO YARI** • 1960
SAKIMA AND THE MASKED MARVEL • 1943 • Bennet Spencer Gordon • USA
SAKKA MAT, EL see **SAQQA' MAT, AS-** • 1977
SAKR, EL • 1950 • Abu Saif Salah • EGY • FALCON, THE ○ SAQR, AS-
SAKUNTHALAI • 1967 • Kunchako • IND • SHAKUNTALA
SAKURA DANCE see **SAKURA ONDO** • 1934
SAKURA KILLERS • 1986 • Ward Richard • USA
SAKURA NO KUNI • 1941 • Shibuya Minoru • JPN • CHERRY COUNTRY
SAKURA NO MORI NO MANKAI NO SHITA • 1974 • Shinoda Masahiro • JPN • UNDER THE FALL OF THE CHERRY BLOSSOMS ○ UNDER THE CHERRY BLOSSOMS
SAKURA ONDO • 1934 • Gosho Heinosuke • JPN • CHERRY BLOSSOM CHORUS ○ SAKURA DANCE
SAKURA-TAI CHIRU • 1988 • Shindo Kaneto • JPN • SAKURA THEATRE GROUP HAS GONE
SAKURA THEATRE GROUP HAS GONE see **SAKURA-TAI CHIRU** • 1988
SAKURADA-MON • 1961 • Nishiyama Masaki • JPN • CHERRY TREE GATE
SAKYA see **SHAKA** • 1962
SAL-A-MALLE-EK • 1965 • Daniel P., Nadeau G. • SHT • FRN
SAL GORDA • 1983 • Trueba Fernando • SPN • BAD TASTE
SAL GROGAN'S FACE • 1922 • Collins Edwin J. • UKN
SAL OF SINGAPORE • 1929 • Higgin Howard • USA
SAL SANTEN, REBEL • 1982 • van den Berg Rudolf • DOC • NTH
SAL ZTRACENYCH KROKU • 1958 • Jires Jaromil • SHT • CZC • HALL OF LOST FOOTSTEPS, THE
SALA DE GUARDIA • 1952 • Demicheli Tulio • ARG • EMERGENCY WARD
SALAAM, BOMBAY! see **CHAL, BOMBAY, CHAL** • 1988
SALACION, LA see **ENCUENTRO: LA SALACION, EL** • 1965
SALADIN see **NASSER SALAH-EL-DINE, EL** • 1963
SALADIN AND THE GREAT CRUSADES see **NASSER SALAH-EL-DINE, EL** • 1963
SALAHEDDIN • 1952 • *Assis* • EGY
SALAINEN ELAMANI • 1972 • Peranne Antti • ANS • FNL • MY SECRET LIFE
SALAIRE DE LA PEUR, LE • 1953 • Clouzot Henri-Georges • FRN, ITL • VITE VENDUTE (ITL) ○ WAGES OF FEAR, THE (USA) ○ SALARIO DELLA PAURA, IL
SALAIRE DU PECHE, LE • 1956 • de La Patelliere Denys • FRN
SALAK MILYONER • 1974 • Egilmez Ertem • TRK • STUPID MILLIONAIRE, THE
SALAKO • 1975 • Yilmaz Atif • TRK
SALAM AFTER DEATH • Shamshum George • LBN
SALAM ALA AL-HABAIB • 1958 • Halim Hilmy • EGY • BONJOUR A CELLE QUE J'AIME
SALAMA FI KHAYR • 1937 • Mustafa Niazi • EGY • SALAMA SAUVE
SALAMA SAUVE see **SALAMA FI KHAYR** • 1937
SALAMANDER, THE • 1915 • Donaldson Arthur • USA
SALAMANDER, THE • 1916 • *Sainpolis John* • USA
SALAMANDER, THE • 1928 • Roshal Grigori • USS, FRG
SALAMANDER, THE • 1981 • Zinner Peter • USA, UKN, ITL
SALAMANDER, THE (UKN) see **SALAMANDRE, LA** • 1971
SALAMANDRA DEL DESERTO, LA • 1971 • Freda Riccardo • ITL, ISR
SALAMANDRE, LA • 1971 • Tanner Alain • SWT • SALAMANDER, THE (UKN)
SALAMANDRE, LE • 1969 • Cavallone Alberto • ITL
SALAMANDRE D'OR, LA • 1962 • Regamey Maurice • FRN, ITL
SALAMAT AL JALIL • 1985 • Wadii Yusuf • DOC • SYR • INTEGRITY OF THE HONOURABLE, THE
SALAMBO • 1961 • Grieco Sergio • ITL, FRN • LOVES OF SALAMMBO, THE (USA) ○ SALAMMBO (FRN)
SALAMBO see **SALAMMBO** • 1925

SALAMISM • 1968 • Villareal Mitos • PHL
SALAMMBO • 1925 • Marodon Pierre • FRN • KAMPF UM KARTHAGO, DER ○ SALAMBO
SALAMMBO (FRN) see **SALAMBO** • 1961
SALAMON & STOCK SHOW, THE see **RIPACSOK** • 1981
SALAMONICO • 1972 • Steinhardt Alfred • ISR
SALARIED MEN'S LOYAL RONIN STORY see **SALARY-MAN CHUSHINGURA** • 1960
SALARIO DEL CRIMEN, EL • 1964 • Buchs Julio • SPN
SALARIO DELLA PAURA, IL see **SALAIRE DE LA PEUR, LE** • 1953
SALARIO MINIMO • 1971 • Gonzaga Adhemar • BRZ
SALARIO PARA MATAR (SPN) see **MERCENARIO, IL** • 1968
SALARY, 200 A MONTH • 1937 • Balogh Bela • HNG
SALARY-MAN CHUSHINGURA • 1960 • Sugie Toshio • JPN • MASTERLESS FORTY-SEVEN, THE ○ SARAIIMAN CHUSHINGURA ○ SALARIED MEN'S LOYAL RONIN STORY
SALARY-MAN MEJIRO SANPEI -HUSBAND'S SIGH see **SALARY-MAN MEJIRO SANPEI -TEISHUNO TAMEIKINO** • 1960
SALARY-MAN MEJIRO SANPEI -NYOBONO KAONI MAKI • 1960 • Suzuki Hideo • JPN • SALARY-MAN MEJIRO SANPEI -WIFE'S HONOUR
SALARY-MAN MEJIRO SANPEI -TEISHUNO TAMEIKINO • 1960 • Suzuki Hideo • JPN • SALARY-MAN MEJIRO SANPEI -HUSBAND'S SIGH
SALARY-MAN MEJIRO SANPEI -WIFE'S HONOUR see **SALARY-MAN MEJIRO SANPEI -NYOBONO KAONI MAKI** • 1960
SALASIL MIN HARIR • 1962 • Barakat Henry • EGY • CHAINES DE SOIE
SALAUDS VONT EN ENFER, LES • 1955 • Hossein Robert • FRN • WICKED GO TO HELL, THE
SALAVAT YULAEV • 1941 • Protazanov Yakov • USS
SALAVIINANPOLTTAJAT • 1907 • Sparre Louis, Puro Teuvo • FNL • MOONSHINERS, THE
SALAZAR E A NACAO • 1940 • Ribeiro Antonio Lopes • SHT • PRT
SALE AFFAIRE, UNE • 1980 • Bonnot Alain • FRN
SALE HISTOIRE, UNE • 1977 • Eustache Jean • FRN • DIRTY STORY, A
SALE OF A HEART, THE • 1913 • Costello Maurice, Gaillord Robert • USA
SALE REVEUR • 1978 • Perier Jean-Marie • FRN • DIRTY DREAMER
SALE TEMPS POUR LES MOUCHES see **COMMISSAIRE SAN ANTONIO** • 1966
SALEM ALEIKUM • 1959 • von Cziffra Geza • FRG
SALEM CAME TO SUPPER see **NIGHT VISITOR, THE** • 1970
SALEM COMES TO SUPPER see **NIGHT VISITOR, THE** • 1970
SALEM'S LOT • 1979 • Hooper Tobe • TVM • USA • SALEM'S LOT: THE MOVIE
SALEM'S LOT: THE MOVIE see **SALEM'S LOT** • 1979
SALERNO BEACHHEAD see **WALK IN THE SUN, A** • 1946
SALESLADY • 1938 • Collins Arthur G. • USA
SALESLADY, THE • 1915 • *Snow Marguerite* • USA
SALESLADY, THE • 1916 • Thompson Frederick A. • USA
SALESLADY OF DREAMS see **VENDEDORA DE FANTASIAS, LA** • 1950
SALESLADY'S MATINEE IDOL, THE • 1909 • *Edison* • USA
SALESMAN • 1969 • Maysles Albert, Maysles David, Zwerin Charlotte • DOC • USA
SALESMAN, THE • 1923 • St. John Al • SHT • USA
SALESMAN, THE • 1960 • *Halas John (P)* • ANS • UKN
SALESMAN, THE see **SEEMABADHA** • 1972
SALESMAN COMES, THE • *Hunter Jackie* • USA
SALESMANSHIP see **ELADAS MUVESZETE, AZ** • 1960
SALESMANSHIP AHOY • 1935 • Boasberg Al • SHT • USA
SALGA DE LA COCINA • 1931 • Infante Jorge • SPN
SALIDA DE MISA DE DOCE EN LA IGLESIA DEL PILAR EN ZARAGOZA • 1896 • Jimeno Eduardo • SPN
SALIENT, THE • 1970 • Carter Peter • CND
SALIH WITH NO FINGER see **PARMAKSIZ SALIH** • 1968
SALIM ET SALIMA • 1963 • Bouchouchi Youssef • SHT • ALG
SALIM LANGDA PE MAT RO • 1989 • Mirza Saeed • IND
SALIUT, MARIA! • 1970 • Heifitz Josif • USS • SALUTE MARYA ○ MARIA ○ SALUTE, MARIA!
SALKA VALKA • 1954 • Mattsson Arne • SWD, ICL
SALLAH SHABATI • 1964 • Kishon Ephraim • ISR • SALLAH (USA)
SALLAH (USA) see **SALLAH SHABATI** • 1964
SALLE A MANGER FANTASTIQUE • 1898 • Melies Georges • FRN • DINNER UNDER DIFFICULTIES, A (USA)
SALLE DE BAIN, LA • 1988 • Lvoff John • FRN
SALLIE'S SURE SHOT • 1913 • Duncan William • USA
SALLIIKO AITI • Kaarresalo-Kasari Eila • SHT • FNL • WOULD MOMMA ALLOW?
SALLSKAPSLEK • 1963 • Anderberg Torgny • SWD • PARLOUR GAMES ○ GAME OF TRUTH
SALLSKAPSRESAN • 1980 • Aberg Lars • SWD • CHARTER TRIP, THE ○ PACKAGE TOUR ○ PACKAGE HOLIDAY, THE
SALLY • 1925 • Green Alfred E. • USA
SALLY • 1929 • Dillon John Francis • USA
SALLY AND FREEDOM • 1981 • Lindblom Gunnel • SWD
SALLY AND SAINT ANNE • 1952 • Mate Rudolph • USA
SALLY ANN'S STRATEGY • 1912 • Edwin Walter • USA
SALLY BISHOP • 1916 • Pearson George • UKN
SALLY BISHOP • 1923 • Elvey Maurice • UKN
SALLY BISHOP • 1932 • Hunter T. Hayes • UKN
SALLY CASTLETON, SOUTHERNER • 1915 • West Langdon • USA
SALLY IN A HURRY • 1917 • North Wilfred • USA
SALLY IN OUR ALLEY • 1900 • Gibbons Walter • UKN
SALLY IN OUR ALLEY • 1913 • *Morris Flora* • UKN
SALLY IN OUR ALLEY • 1913 • Campbell Colin • USA
SALLY IN OUR ALLEY • 1916 • Trimble Larry • UKN
SALLY IN OUR ALLEY • 1916 • Vale Travers • USA
SALLY IN OUR ALLEY • 1921 • Rowden W. C. • SHT • UKN
SALLY IN OUR ALLEY • 1927 • Lang Walter • USA
SALLY IN OUR ALLEY • 1931 • Elvey Maurice • UKN
SALLY, IRENE AND MARY • 1925 • Goulding Edmund • USA
SALLY, IRENE AND MARY • 1938 • Seiter William A. • USA
SALLY OF THE SAWDUST • 1925 • Griffith D. W. • USA
SALLY OF THE SCANDALS • 1928 • Shores Lynn • USA
SALLY OF THE SUBWAY • 1932 • Seitz George B. • USA
SALLY SCRUGGS, HOUSEMAID • 1913 • *Leonard Robert* • USA
SALLY SWING • 1938 • Fleischer Dave • ANS • USA
SALLY, THE WITCH see **MAHOTSUKAI SARI** • 1968
SALLY'S BEAUX • 1910 • *Powers* • USA
SALLY'S BIZNIZ see **17 OP** • 1988
SALLY'S BLIGHTED CAREER • 1919 • Christie Al • SHT • USA
SALLY'S ELOPEMENT • 1914 • Pollard Harry • USA
SALLY'S GUARDIAN • 1913 • *Kalem* • USA
SALLY'S IRISH ROGUE • 1958 • Pollock George • UKN • POACHER'S DAUGHTER, THE (USA)
SALLY'S ROMANCE • 1913 • Miller Ashley • USA
SALLY'S SHOULDERS • 1928 • Shores Lynn • USA
SALMON FISHING, QUEBEC • 1905 • *Bitzer Billy (Ph)* • USA
SALMON LOAFER • 1963 • Marcus Sid • ANS • USA
SALMON POACHERS -A MIDNIGHT MELEE, THE • 1905 • Haggar William • UKN
SALMON YEGGS • 1958 • Smith Paul J. • ANS • USA
SALO O LE CENTOVENTI GIORNATE DI SODOMA • 1975 • Pasolini Pier Paolo • ITL • SALO -THE 120 DAYS OF SODOM (USA) ○ SALO OR THE 120 DAYS OF SODOM
SALO OR THE 120 DAYS OF SODOM see **SALO O LE CENTOVENTI GIORNATE DI SODOMA** • 1975
SALO -THE 120 DAYS OF SODOM (USA) see **SALO O LE CENTOVENTI GIORNATE DI SODOMA** • 1975
SALOM, BAKHOR • 1963 • Khamraev Ali • SHT • USS
SALOME • 1902 • Messter Oskar • FRG
SALOME • 1908 • Blackton J. Stuart • USA
SALOME • 1919 • Edwards J. Gordon • USA
SALOME • 1922 • Bryant Charles • USA
SALOME • 1922 • Wiene Robert • FRG
SALOME • 1923 • Strauss Malcolm • USA • MALCOLM STRAUSS' SALOME ○ STRAUSS' SALOME
SALOME • 1940 • Catalan Feliciano • SPN
SALOME • 1952 • Dieterle William • USA • SALOME, THE DANCE OF THE SEVEN VEILS
SALOME • 1971 • Schroeter Werner • FRG
SALOME • 1972 • Bene Carmelo • ITL
SALOME • 1972 • Brzozowski Andrzej • MTV • PLN
SALOME • 1978 • Almodovar Pedro • SPN
SALOME • 1980 • Brakhage Stan • SHT • USA
SALOME • 1981 • Guillen Laurice • PHL
SALOME • 1986 • d'Anna Claude • FRN, ITL
SALOME '73 • 1964 • Fiory Odoardo • ITL
SALOME AND DELILAH • 1964 • Warhol Andy • USA
SALOME CRAZE • 1909 • *Phoenix* • USA
SALOME DANCE, THE • 1908 • *Lubin* • USA
SALOME DANCE MUSIC, THE • 1909 • *Warwick Trading Co* • UKN
SALOME MAD • 1909 • Bouwmeester Theo? • *Hepworth* • UKN
SALOME MAD • 1909 • Coleby A. E. • *Cricks & Martin* • UKN
SALOME OF THE TENEMENTS • 1925 • Olcott Sidney • USA
SALOME, THE DANCE OF THE SEVEN VEILS see **SALOME** • 1952
SALOME VS. SHENANDOAH • 1919 • Kenton Erle C., Grey Ray • SHT • USA
SALOME, WHERE SHE DANCED • 1945 • Lamont Charles • USA
SALOME'S LAST DANCE • 1988 • Russell Ken • UKN
SALOMIEN • 1972 • SAF
SALOMOS DOM • 1914 • Breidahl Axel • SWD • KING SOLOMON'S JUDGMENT
SALOMY JANE • 1914 • Dawley J. Searle, Beyfuss Alex E. • USA
SALOMY JANE • 1923 • Melford George • USA • LAW OF THE SIERRAS, THE
SALOMY JANE (UKN) see **WILD GIRL** • 1932
SALON DE BAILE see **DANCING** • 1951
SALON DE BELLEZA • 1951 • Diaz Morales Jose • MXC
SALON DE COIFFURE • 1908 • Melies Georges • FRN • IN THE BARBER SHOP (USA)
SALON DE MASSAGE • 1970 • *Jo-Jo Dist.* • USA
SALON DE MAYO • 1970 • Hernandez Bernabe • CUB
SALON DORA GREEN • 1933 • Galeen Henrik • FRG • FALLE, DIE
SALON DU LIVRE, LE • 1981 • Bedel Jean-Pierre • MTV • CND
SALON KITTY • 1976 • Brass Tinto • ITL, FRN, FRG • MADAM KITTY (USA)
SALON MEXICO • 1948 • Fernandez Emilio • MXC
SALON NAUTIQUE • 1954 • de Broca Philippe • SHT • FRN
SALONIQUE, NID D'ESPIONS see **MADEMOISELLE DOCTEUR** • 1936
SALONPIRATEN • 1915 • Schmidthassler Walter • FRG
SALONWAGEN E 417 • 1939 • Verhoeven Paul • FRG
SALOON BAR • 1940 • Forde Walter • UKN
SALOON NEXT DOOR, THE • 1910 • *Imp* • USA
SALOONKEEPER'S NIGHTMARE, THE • 1908 • *Gaumont* • FRN
SALOPERIE DE ROCK AND ROLL • 1979 • Delamarre Jean-Noel • FRN
SALOPES ET VICIEUSES • 1978 • Bernard-Aubert Claude • FRN
SALSA • 1976 • Masucci Jerry, Gast Leon • DOC • USA
SALSA see **SALSA: THE MOTION PICTURE** • 1988
SALSA POUR GOLDMAN see **AINAMA** • 1980
SALSA: THE MOTION PICTURE • 1988 • Davidson Boaz • USA • SALSA
SALT • Carbonell Maria L. • DCS • VNZ
SALT see **SO** • 1974
SALT AND PEPPER • 1968 • Donner Richard • UKN, USA
SALT AND PEPPER • 1979 • Revach Ze'Ev • ISR
SALT AND SWEET • 1963 • Kidawa Janusz • DOC • PLN
SALT COD • 1954 • Spotton John, Warson Allan • CND
SALT FOR SVANETIA see **SOL SVANETII** • 1930
SALT IS MORE PRECIOUS THAN GOLD see **SOL NAD ZLATO** • 1982
SALT IS WORTH MORE THAN GOLD see **SOL NAD ZLATO** • 1982
SALT LAKE RAIDERS • 1950 • Brannon Fred C. • USA
SALT LAKE TRAIL • 1926 • *Kesterson George* • USA
SALT MAKEREL MINE, A • 1914 • *Kalem* • USA
SALT OF THE BLACK COUNTRY see **SOL ZIEMI CZARNEJ** • 1969
SALT OF THE BLACK EARTH see **SOL ZIEMI CZARNEJ** • 1969
SALT OF THE EARTH • 1917 • Harrison Saul • USA
SALT OF THE EARTH • 1954 • Biberman Herbert J. • USA
SALT OF THE EARTH see **SEL DE LA TERRE, LE** • 1950
SALT OF THE SEA see **VOLTINITSA** • 1956
SALT ON THE BIRD'S TAIL, THE • 1910 • Melies Gaston • USA
SALT, SALIVA, SPERM AND SWEAT • 1987 • Brophy Philip • SHT • ASL
SALT TO THE DEVIL (USA) see **GIVE US THIS DAY** • 1949
SALT WATER • 1974 • Sinclair Arturo • SHT • PRU
SALT WATER DAFFY • 1941 • Lantz Walter • ANS • USA
SALT WATER SPRAY AND TOUGH OLD BOYS see **SALTSTANK OCH KRUTGUBBAR** • 1946
SALT WATER TABBY • 1947 • Hanna William, Barbera Joseph • ANS • USA
SALT WATER TAFFY • 1930 • *Terry Paul/ Moser Frank (P)* • ANS • USA
SALT WOES, THE • 1986 • Dodd Thomas • DOC • CND
SALTA GUBBAR OCH SEXTANTER see **HEJ DU GLADA SOMMAR** • 1965
SALTANAT • 1955 • Pronin Vassily • USS
SALTARELLA, LA • 1912 • Burguet Charles • FRN
SALTARELLO see **KENNST DU DAS LAND** • 1931
SALTED MINE, THE • 1911 • *Bison* • USA
SALTED MINE, THE • 1912 • *King Burton* • USA
SALTIMBANCHI • 1981 • Bostan Elisabeta • RMN • CLOWNS, THE
SALTIMBANCHI, I (ITL) see **SALTIMBANQUES, LES** • 1930
SALTIMBANCOS • 1951 • Guimaraes Manuel • PRT
SALTIMBANQUES, LES • 1930 • Jaquelux, Land Robert • FRN, FRG, ITL • SALTIMBANCHI, I (ITL) ○ GAUKLER (FRG)
SALTO • 1965 • Konwicki Tadeusz • PLN
SALTO, O • 1967 • de Chalonge Christian • FRN • VOYAGE OF SILENCE (USA) ○ SAUT, LE
SALTO A LA GLORIA • 1959 • Klimovsky Leon • SPN • JUMP TO GLORY
SALTO DE TEQUENDAMA, EL • 1971 • Mitrotti Mario • VNZ
SALTO MORTAL • 1961 • Ozores Mariano • SPN
SALTO MORTALE • 1931 • Dupont E. A. • FRG • TRAPEZE (UKN) ○ CIRCUS OF SIN, THE
SALTO MORTALE • 1931 • Dupont E. A. • FRN
SALTO MORTALE • 1953 • Tourjansky Victor • FRG
SALTO NEL VUOTO • 1979 • Bellocchio Marco • ITL, FRN • LEAP IN THE DARK, A (USA) ○ LEAP INTO THE VOID (UKN) ○ SAUT DANS LE VIDE, LE
SALTSTANK OCH KRUTGUBBAR • 1946 • Bauman Schamyl • SWD • SALT WATER SPRAY AND TOUGH OLD BOYS ○ AUGUST KARLSSONS ATERKOMST
SALTY • 1974 • Browning Ricou • USA
SALTY MCGUIRE • 1937 • Davis Mannie, Gordon George • ANS • USA
SALTY O'ROURKE • 1945 • Walsh Raoul • USA
SALTY ROSE see **SLANA RUZE** • 1982
SALTY SAUNDERS • 1923 • Hart Neal • USA
SALTY SQUAB • Szoboszlay Peter • ANS • HNG
SALUDOS AMIGOS • 1942 • Jackson Wilfred, Roberts Bill, Luske Hamilton, Kinney Jack • ANM • USA • GREETINGS, FRIENDS
SALUDOS HOMBRE • 1969 • Sollima Sergio • ITL
SALUT A LA FRANCE see **SALUTE TO FRANCE** • 1944
SALUT BERTHE! • 1968 • Lefranc Guy • FRN
SALUT DE DRANEM, LE • 1901 • Zecca Ferdinand • FRN
SALUT I FORCA AL CANUT • 1979 • Bellmunt Francisco • SPN • HEALTHY LUST AND FUN
SALUT J'ARRIVE • 1981 • Poteau Gerard • FRN
SALUT JERUSALEM • 1972 • Chapier Henri • DOC • FRN • COLLINES DE SION, LES
SALUT LA PUCE • 1982 • Balducci Richard • FRN
SALUT L'ARTISTE • 1973 • Robert Yves • FRN, ITL • BIT PLAYER, THE
SALUT LES COPINES • 1966 • Bastid Jean-Loup • FRN • PUSSYCATS, THE
SALUT LES CUBAINS • 1963 • Varda Agnes • DCS • FRN • HELLO CUBANS
SALUT LES FRANGINES • 1974 • Gerard Michel • FRN
SALUT LES POURRIS • 1977 • Di Leo Fernando • FRN
SALUT MALENCONTREUX see **SALUT MALENCONTREUX D'UN DESERTEUR** • 1896
SALUT MALENCONTREUX D'UN DESERTEUR • 1896 • Melies Georges • FRN • SOLDIER'S UNLUCKY SALUTATION, A ○ SALUT MALENCONTREUX
SALUT TORONTO • 1965 • Perron Clement • DCS • CND
SALUT, VOLEURS! • 1973 • Cassenti Frank • FRN
SALUTARY LESSON, A • 1910 • Griffith D. W. • USA
SALUTE • 1929 • Ford John • USA
SALUTE E MALATA O I POVERI MUOIONO PRIMA, LA • 1971 • Bertolucci Bernardo • SHT • ITL
SALUTE FOR THREE • 1943 • Murphy Ralph • USA
SALUTE JOHN CITIZEN • 1942 • Elvey Maurice • UKN
SALUTE, MARIA! see **SALIUT, MARIA!** • 1970
SALUTE MARYA see **SALIUT, MARIA!** • 1970
SALUTE OF THE JUGGER • 1989 • Peoples David Webb • ASL
SALUTE THE TOFF • 1952 • Rogers Maclean • UKN • BRIGHTHAVEN EXPRESS (USA)
SALUTE TO DUKE ELLINGTON • 1950 • Cowan Will • SHT • USA
SALUTE TO FRANCE • 1944 • Kanin Garson, Renoir Jean • USA • SALUT A LA FRANCE
SALUTE TO PIONEERS see **BOU VAN 'N NASIE, DIE** • 1939
SALUTE TO ROMANCE (UKN) see **ANNAPOLIS SALUTE** • 1937
SALUTE TO SONG • 1957 • *Universal* • SHT • USA
SALUTE TO THE FARMERS • 1941 • Tully Montgomery • DCS • UKN
SALUTE TO THE MARINES • 1943 • Simon S. Sylvan • USA
SALUTE TO THE SPANISH PIONEERS • 1936 • Karmen Roman • DOC • USS
SALUTE TO VICTORY • 1945 • Hawes Stanley • DCS • CND
SALUTI E BACI (ITL) see **ROUTE DU BONHEUR, LA** • 1952
SALUUT EN DE KOST • 1974 • Le Bon Patrick • BLG • GOODBYE AND THANK YOU ○ AU REVOIR ET MERCI
SALVADOR • 1986 • Stone Oliver • USA

SALVADOR ALLENDE GOSSENS: UN TEMOIGNAGE • 1974 • Bulbulian Maurice • DCS • CND
SALVADOR VALERO • 1973 • Santana Juan, Torija Alberto, Toro Fernando • VNZ
SALVAGE • 1919 • Bashame E. R. • UKN
SALVAGE • 1921 • King Henry • USA
SALVAGE see **TERROR ISLAND** • 1920
SALVAGE see **GIRL OVERBOARD** • 1929
SALVAGE 1 • 1979 • Philips Lee • TVM • USA
SALVAGE GANG, THE • 1958 • Krish John • UKN
SALVAGE WITH A SMILE • 1940 • Brunel Adrian • DOC • UKN
SALVAJE ANDA SUELTO, UN (MXC) see **SAVAGE IS LOOSE, THE** • 1974
SALVAJES DE PUENTE SAN GIL, LOS • 1967 • Ribas Antoni • SPN • WILD ONES OF SAN GIL BRIDGE, THE ○ SAVAGES OF ST. GIL'S BRIDGE
SALVAJES, LOS • 1957 • Baledon Rafael • MXC • SAVAGES, THE
SALVARE LA FACCIA • 1969 • Brazzi Rossano, Kneeland Ted • ITL, ARG • DADDY SAID THE WORLD WAS LOVELY ○ PSYCHOUT FOR MURDER (USA) ○ SAVE YOUR FACE
SALVATE MIA FIGLIA • 1951 • Corbucci Sergio • ITL
SALVATION • 1959 • Kluba Henryk • PLN
SALVATION! • 1987 • B. Beth • USA • SALVATION! HAVE YOU SAID YOUR PRAYERS TODAY
SALVATION see **OCALENIE** • 1972
SALVATION ARMY LASS, THE • 1909 • Griffith D. W. • USA
SALVATION! HAVE YOU SAID YOUR PRAYERS TODAY see **SALVATION!** • 1987
SALVATION HUNTERS, THE • 1925 • von Sternberg Josef • USA
SALVATION JANE • 1927 • Rosen Phil • USA
SALVATION JOAN • 1916 • North Wilfred • USA
SALVATION NELL • 1915 • Beyfuss Alex E. • USA
SALVATION NELL • 1921 • Webb Kenneth • USA
SALVATION NELL • 1931 • Cruze James • USA • MEN WOMEN LOVE (UKN)
SALVATION OF NANCE O'SHAUGNESSY, THE • 1914 • Campbell Colin • USA
SALVATION SAL • 1913 • Thornby Robert T. • USA
"SALVATION" SMITH • 1910 • *Powers* • USA
SALVATION SUE • 1912 • *Champion* • USA
SALVATION SUE • 1919 • *Christie* • USA
SALVATIONIST, THE • 1912 • *Pate Gwendolyn* • USA
SALVATOR ROSA see **AVVENTURA DI SALVATOR ROSA, UN** • 1940
SALVATOR STABLE, THE see **STAJNIA NA SALWATORZE** • 1967
SALVATORE GIULIANO • 1962 • Rosi Francesco • ITL • SALVATORE GIULIANO: THE DREADED MAFIA ○ DREADED MAFIA, THE
SALVATORE GIULIANO: THE DREADED MAFIA see **SALVATORE GIULIANO** • 1962
SALVIAMO IL PANORAMA see **AMORE E CHIACCHIERE** • 1957
SALVO D'ACQUISTO • 1975 • Guerrieri Romolo • ITL
SALWA • 1972 • Shahin Youssef • SHT • EGY • PETITE FILLE QUI PARLE AUX VACHES, LA
SALZ UND BROT see **HARTE MANNER -HEISSE LIEBE** • 1956
SALZBURG CONNECTION, THE • 1972 • Katzin Lee H. • USA
SALZBURG EVERYMAN, THE see **JEDERMANN** • 1961
SALZBURG PILGRIMAGE • 1956 • Czinner Paul • SHT • UKN
SALZBURGER GESCHICHTEN • 1957 • Hoffmann Kurt • FRG
SAM • 1959 • Pogacic Vladimir • YGS • ALONE
SAM ADAMS • 1974 • Carter Peter • CND
SAM AND HIS MUSKET • 1935-36 • *Dyer Anson (P)* • ANS • UKN
SAM AND THE BULLY • 1914 • Hotaling Arthur D. • USA
SAM COOPER'S GOLD see **GOLD VON SAM COOPER, DAS** • 1968
SAM DAVIS, THE HERO OF TENNESSEE • 1915 • *The Connor Producing Co* • USA
SAM, GRACE, DOUG AND THE DOG • 1976 • Lavut Martin • CND
SAM HILL: WHO KILLED THE MYSTERIOUS MR. FOSTER • 1971 • Cook Fielder • TVM • USA • WHO KILLED THE MYSTERIOUS MR. FOSTER
SAM "LIGHTNING" HOPKINS • 1971 • Peavy Charles D. • SHT • USA
SAM LLOYD'S FAMOUS PUZZLES • 1917 • O'Brien Willis • USA
SAM MARLOWE, PRIVATE EYE see **MAN WITH BOGART'S FACE, THE** • 1980
SAM NA SAM • 1977 • Hostenko Andrzej • PLN • SUPERIMPOSITION
SAM PEPYS JOINS THE NAVY • 1941 • Searle Francis • SHT • UKN
SAM POSROD MIASTA • 1965 • Bielinska Halina • PLN • ALONE IN THE TOWN ○ ALONE IN A CITY
SAM REMO, LA GRANDE SFIDA • 1960 • Vivarelli Piero • ITL
SAM SIMPKINS, SLEUTH • 1912 • *Missimer Howard* • USA
SAM SMALL LEAVES TOWN • 1937 • Goulding Alf • USA • IT'S SAM SMALL AGAIN
SAM SMITH see **SAM SMITH GENUINE ENGLAND** • 1976
SAM SMITH GENUINE ENGLAND • 1976 • Ashton Dudley Shaw • DOC • UKN • SAM SMITH
SAM SOBIE STEREM • 1971 • Latallo Katarzyna • PLN • STEERING MY OWN DESTINY
SAM THOMPSON • 1986 • Black Donald Taylor • IRL
SAM WHISKEY • 1969 • Laven Arnold • USA • WHISKEY'S RENEGADES
SAMA JUGA BO HONG • 1986 • Umam Chaerul • INN
SAMA NO AJI see **SAMMA NO AJI** • 1962
SAMA HOUSS! • 1989 • Arafa Sherif • EGY • SILENCE!
SAMAC • 1958 • Mimica Vatroslav • ANS • YGS • ALONE ○ LONELY MAN, THE
SAMAD AND THE IRON CURTAIN GIANT see **SAMAD JA FOOLAD ZAREH DIV** • 1972
SAMAD BE SHAHR MIRAVAD • 1978 • Sayyad Parviz • IRN • SAMAD GOES TO TOWN
SAMAD GOES TO TOWN see **SAMAD BE SHAHR MIRAVAD** • 1978
SAMAD JA FOOLAD ZAREH DIV • 1972 • Moghadam Jalal • IRN • SAMAD AND THE IRON CURTAIN GIANT
SAMADHI • 1967 • Belson Jordan • SHT • USA
SAMAN • 1977 • Zolnay Pal • HNG • SHAMAN
SAMAN WAL KARIF, EL • 1967 • Mustafa Hassam Eddin • EGY
SAMANISHVILI'S STEPMOTHER • 1974 • Shengelaya Eldar • USS
SAMANKA see **ILE DES PASSIONS, L'** • 1982
SAMANTHA see **NEW KIND OF LOVE, A** • 1963
SAMANTHY SURPRISES SMETHPORT • 1915 • *Brunswick-Balke-Collender Co* • USA
SAMANYOLU • 1967 • Aksoy Orhan • TRK • MILKY WAY, THE
SAMAR • 1962 • Montgomery George • USA
SAMARA • 1956 • Ismail Mahmud • EGY
SAMARAA'S ART • 1978 • Saleh Tewfik • IRQ
SAMARANG • 1933 • Wing Ward • USA
SAMARITAN, THE see **DU SKAL ELSKE DIN NAESTE** • 1915
SAMARITAN, THE see **HARP IN HOCK, A** • 1927
SAMARITAN, THE (UKN) see **SOUL OF THE SLUMS** • 1931
SAMARITAN OF COOGAN'S TENEMENT, THE • 1912 • *Johnson Arthur* • USA
SAMARITAN: THE MITCH SNYDER STORY • 1986 • Heffron Richard T. • TVM • USA
SAMARITAN'S COURTSHIP, THE • 1910 • *Lubin* • USA
SAMBA • 1928 • Bruckner August • FRG
SAMBA • 1964 • Gil Rafael • SPN
SAMBA -CREATION OF THE WORLD see **SAMBA DA CRIACAO DO MUNDO** • 1982
SAMBA DA CRIACAO DO MUNDO • 1982 • de Figueiredo Vera • BRZ • SAMBA -CREATION OF THE WORLD
SAMBA LE GRAND • 1977 • Alassane Moustapha • ANS • NGR
SAMBIZANGA • 1972 • Maldoror Sarah • CNG, FRN
SAMBO • 1902 • Williamson James • UKN
SAMBO • 1951 • Tamburella Paolo William • ITL
SAMBO'S WEDDING DAY • 1919 • Hutchinson Craig • SHT • USA
SAME • 1964 • Tasaka Tomotaka • JPN • SHARKS, THE
SAME AELLIN • 1972 • Host Per, Vibe-Muller Titus • NRW • LAPPLANDER'S LIFE, THE
SAME GENDER see **OF THE SAME GENDER** • 1968
SAME-JAKKI • 1957 • Host Per • NRW • LAPLANDERS, THE ○ LAST OF THE NOMADS
SAME OLD STORY, THE • 1913 • *Carney Augustus* • USA
SAME OLD STORY, THE see **HISTOIRE COMME UNE AUTRE, UNE** • 1981
SAME OLD TALE, THE • 1905 • Green Tom • UKN
SAME PLAYER SHOOTS AGAIN • 1967 • Wenders Wim • SHT • FRG
SAME PLAYER SHOOTS AGAIN see **NAAKT OVER DE SCHUTTING** • 1973
SAME SKIN, THE see **COUNTRY DANCE** • 1969
SAME TIME, NEXT YEAR • 1978 • Mulligan Robert • USA
SAMEDI -LE VENTRE DE LA NUIT • 1978 • Leduc Jacques • DOC • CND
SAMEDI SOIR • 1960 • Andrei Yannick • FRN • NIGHT OUT
SAMEDI SOIR • 1977 • Labonte Francois • CND
SAMEERA • 1982 • Shukla Vinay • IND
SAMEZAYA • 1930 • Inagaki Hiroshi • JPN
SAMHALLETS DOM • 1912 • Jaenzon Julius • SWD • CONDEMNED BY SOCIETY ○ JUSTICE OF SOCIETY, THE
SAMI DER SEEFAHRER • May Joe • AUS
SAMI NA SWIECIE • 1958 • Halladin Danuta • DOC • PLN • ALONE IN THE WORLD
SAMI SWOI • 1967 • Checinski Sylwester • PLN • WE ARE ALL FRIENDS ○ ALL FRIENDS HERE
SAMIDARE ZOSHI • 1924 • Mizoguchi Kenji • JPN • CHRONICLE OF THE MAY RAIN (USA) ○ MAY RAIN AND SILK PAPER
SAMII MEDLENNII POEZD • 1963 • Uskov Valeri, Krasnopolsky Vladimir • USS • SLOWEST TRAIN, THE
SAMII YUNII PIONER • 1925 • Derzhavin • USS • VERY YOUNG PIONEER, A
SAMJHANA • Pradhan Shambhu • NPL
SAMMA NO AJI • 1962 • Ozu Yasujiro • JPN • AUTUMN AFTERNOON, AN ○ TASTE OF MACKEREL, THE ○ SAMA NO AJI ○ TASTE OF FISH, THE ○ WIDOWER, THE
SAMMENSVERGELSEN • 1984 • Gundersen Ivar Axel • NRW • DEVIL TO PAY, THE
SAMMIE JOHNSIN • 1916 • Messmer Otto • ASS • USA • SAMMY JOHNSIN
SAMMIE JOHNSIN AND HIS WONDERFUL LAMP • 1916 • Messmer Otto • ANS • USA
SAMMIE JOHNSIN, MAGICIAN • 1916 • Messmer Otto • ANS • USA
SAMMON TARINA • 1974 • Nelimarkka Riitta • ANM • FNL • TALE OF THE SAMPO, THE
SAMMY AND ROSIE GET LAID • 1987 • Frears Stephen • UKN
SAMMY DAVIS SHOW, THE • 1962 • Markas Gary • SHT • USA
SAMMY GOING SOUTH • 1963 • Mackendrick Alexander • UKN • BOY TEN FEET TALL, A (USA) ○ BOY IS TEN FEET TALL, A
SAMMY IN SIBERIA • 1919 • Roach Hal • SHT • USA
SAMMY JOHNSIN see **SAMMIE JOHNSIN** • 1916
SAMMY ORPHEUS OR THE PIED PIPER OF ANIMALDOM • 1912 • Campbell Colin • USA • SAMMY ORPHEUS OR THE PIED PIPER OF THE JUNGLE
SAMMY ORPHEUS OR THE PIED PIPER OF THE JUNGLE see **SAMMY ORPHEUS OR THE PIED PIPER OF ANIMALDOM** • 1912
SAMMY STOPS THE WORLD • 1979 • Shapiro Mel • USA • STOP THE WORLD, I WANT TO GET OFF
SAMMY, THE CUB REPORTER • 1915 • *Banner* • USA
SAMMY THE WAY OUT SEAL • 1963 • Tokar Norman • USA
SAMMY VERSUS CUPID • 1916 • *Burns Sammy* • USA
SAMMY'S AUTOMATON • 1914 • *Eclipse* • USA
SAMMY'S DOUGH-FUL ROMANCE • 1916 • *Burns Sammy* • USA
SAMMY'S FLYING ESCAPADE • 1912 • *Eclipse* • FRN
SAMMY'S REVENGE • 1912 • Rains Fred • UKN
SAMMY'S SCANDALOUS SCHEME • 1915 • *Burns Sammy* • USA
SAMMY'S SEMI-SUICIDE • 1916 • *Hiers Walter* • SHT • USA
SAMMY'S SUCKER • 1907 • Booth W. R. • UKN
SAMMY'S SUPER T-SHIRT • 1978 • Summers Jeremy • UKN
SAMMY'S VACATION • 1914 • *Crystal* • USA
SAMNA • 1975 • Patel Jabbar • IND
SAMO JEDNOM SE LJUBI • 1981 • Grlic Rajko • YGS • MELODY HAUNTS MY MEMORY, THE (USA) ○ YOU ONLY LIVE ONCE ○ MELODY HAUNTS MY REVERIE, THE
SAMO LJUDI • 1957 • Bauer Branko • YGS • TRACES ○ JUST PEOPLE
SAMOA, QUEEN OF THE JUNGLE see **SAMOA, REGINA DELLA GIUNGLA** • 1968
SAMOA, REGINA DELLA GIUNGLA • 1968 • Malatesta Guido • ITL • SAMOA, QUEEN OF THE JUNGLE
SAMOGONSHCHIKI • 1961 • Gaidai Leonid • USS • MOONSHINERS ○ BOOTLEGGERS ○ ALCOHOLMAKERS, THE
SAMOLUB • 1966 • Nehrebecki Wladyslaw • ANS • PLN • EGOIST, THE
SAMONIKLI • 1964 • Pretnar Igor • YGS
SAMOTNOSC WE DWOJE • 1968 • Rozewicz Stanislaw • PLN • LONELINESS FOR TWO ○ TWO WERE LONELY, THE ○ LONELINESS TETE A TETE
SAMOURAI, LE • 1967 • Melville Jean-Pierre • FRN, ITL • FRANK COSTELLO FACCIA D'ANGELO (ITL) ○ GODSON, THE (USA) ○ SAMURAI, THE
SAMOVOLNE POHYBY ROSTLIN • 1959 • Calabek Jan • CZC • SPONTANEOUS MOVEMENT OF PLANTS
SAMPAN • 1968 • Bourke Terry • USA, HKG
SAMPO • 1959 • Ptushko Alexander, Sebelious Gregg • USS, FNL • DAY THE EARTH FROZE, THE (USA)
SAMPO LAPPELILL • 1949 • Husberg Rolf • SWD • SAMPO THE LITTLE LAPP
SAMPO THE LITTLE LAPP see **SAMPO LAPPELILL** • 1949
SAMPOORNA RAMAYANA • 1961 • Mistry Babhubhai • IND
SAMRAT ASHOK • 1948 • Lall K. B. • IND
SAMRTNO PROLJECE • 1974 • Petrovic Stevan, Iglesias Miguel • YGS, SPN, USA • PRIMAVERA IMMORTAL ○ MORIBUND SPRING
SAM'S BOY • 1922 • Haynes Manning • UKN
SAM'S DESPONDENCY • 1913 • *Gem* • USA
SAM'S KID • 1922 • SAF
SAM'S SON • 1984 • Landon Michael • USA
SAM'S SONG • 1971 • Leondopoulos Jordan • USA • SWAP, THE
SAM'S SWEETHEART • 1915 • Humphrey William • USA
SAMSARA see **LUNHUI** • 1988
SAMSKARA • 1972 • Reddy Pattabhi Rama • IND • FUNERAL RITES
SAMSON • 1914 • Johnston Lorimer, Hamilton G. P. • USA
SAMSON • 1915 • Lewis Edgar • USA
SAMSON • 1936 • Tourneur Maurice • FRN
SAMSON • 1961 • Wajda Andrzej • PLN
SAMSON AGAINST THE SHEIK (USA) see **MACISTE CONTRO LO SCEICCO** • 1962
SAMSON AND DELILAH • Aurocha Luis Ernesto • SHT
SAMSON AND DELILAH • 1903 • Zecca Ferdinand • FRN
SAMSON AND DELILAH • 1910 • Zecca Ferdinand • FRN
SAMSON AND DELILAH • 1922 • Collins Edwin J. • UKN
SAMSON AND DELILAH • 1927 • Parkinson H. B. • UKN
SAMSON AND DELILAH • 1949 • De Mille Cecil B. • USA
SAMSON AND DELILAH • 1984 • Philips Lee • TVM • USA
SAMSON AND DELILAH (USA) see **SAMSON UND DELILA** • 1922
SAMSON AND LEBLEB see **SAMSUN WA LEBLEB** • 1951
SAMSON AND SALLY • 1984 • Hastrup Jannik • ANM • DNM
SAMSON AND THE MIGHTY CHALLENGE (USA) see **ERCOLE, SANSONE, MACISTE E URSUS: GLI INVINCIBILE** • 1965
SAMSON AND THE SEA BEASTS (USA) see **SANSONE CONTRO I PIRATI** • 1963
SAMSON AND THE SEVEN CHALLENGES see **ERCOLE, SANSONE, MACISTE E URSUS: GLI INVINCIBILE** • 1965
SAMSON AND THE SEVEN MIRACLES OF THE WORLD (USA) see **MACISTE ALLA CORTE DEL GRAN KHAN** • 1961
SAMSON AND THE SLAVE QUEEN (USA) see **ZORRO CONTRO MACISTE** • 1964
SAMSON AND THE TREASURE OF THE INCAS see **SANSONE E IL TESORO DEGLI INCAS** • 1964
SAMSON AND THE VAMPIRE WOMAN see **SANTO CONTRA LAS MUJERES VAMPIROS** • 1961
SAMSON IN KING SOLOMON'S MINES (USA) see **MACISTE NELLE MINIERE DI RE SALOMONE** • 1964
SAMSON IN THE WAX MUSEUM (USA) see **SANTO EN EL MUSEO DE CERA** • 1963
SAMSON, JR. • 1946 • *Mead Thomas (P)* • SHT • USA
SAMSON SCRAP • 1962 • Deitch Gene • ANS • USA
SAMSON, SEIN EIGENER MORDER • 1919 • Bey Mouhssinn • FRG
SAMSON UND DELILA • 1922 • Korda Alexander • AUS • SAMSON AND DELILAH (USA)
SAMSON (USA) see **SANSONE** • 1962
SAMSON VS. THE BLACK PIRATE see **SANSONE CONTRO IL CORSARO NERO** • 1962
SAMSON VS. THE GIANT KING (USA) see **MACISTE ALLA CORTE DELLO ZAR** • 1964
SAMSON VS. THE PIRATES see **SANSONE CONTRO I PIRATI** • 1963
SAMSON VS. THE VAMPIRE WOMEN (USA) see **SANTO CONTRA LAS MUJERES VAMPIROS** • 1961
SAMSUN EL KABIR • 1948 • el Tehmessani Kamal • EGY • MIGHTY SAMSON, THE
SAMSUN WA LEBLEB • 1951 • Shawkat Saifeddine • EGY • SAMSON AND LEBLEB
SAMTPFOTCHEN DRECT SEIN LETZTES DING • 1969 • FRG
SAMUEL BILIBID • 1967 • Chiquito • PHL
SAMUEL FULLER AND THE BIG RED ONE • 1978 • Ockersen Thijs • DOC • NTH
SAMUEL LOUNT • 1985 • Keane Laurence • CND
SAMUEL OF POSEN • 1910 • *Selig* • USA
SAMURAI • 1965 • Kuri Yoji • ANS • JPN
SAMURAI • 1965 • Okamoto Kihachi • JPN • SAMURAI ASSASSIN
SAMURAI • 1979 • Corbucci Sergio • ITL, USA
SAMURAI • 1979 • Katzin Lee H. • TVM • USA
SAMURAI see **MIYAMOTO MUSASHI** • 1954
SAMURAI, THE see **SAMOURAI, LE** • 1967
SAMURAI AND ORPHANS see **SEKI NO YATAPPE** • 1963
SAMURAI ASSASSIN see **SAMURAI** • 1965

SAMURAI BANNERS see **FURIN KAZAN** • 1969
SAMURAI FROM NOWHERE (USA) see **DOJO YABURI** • 1964
SAMURAI GOLD SEEKERS see **KEDAMONO NO KEN** • 1965
SAMURAI JOKER see **HANA NO OEDO MUSEKININ** • 1965
SAMURAI NO KO • 1963 • Wakasughi Mitsuo • JPN • YOUNG SAMURAI, THE ○ SON OF A SAMURAI
SAMURAI (PART III) (USA) see **KETTO GANRYU JIMA** • 1955
SAMURAI (PART II)(USA) see **ICHIJOJI NO KETTO** • 1955
SAMURAI PIRATE (USA) see **DAITOZOKU** • 1963
SAMURAI REBELLION see **JOIUCHI -HAIRYOZUMA SHIMATSU** • 1967
SAMURAI REINCARNATION see **MAKAI TENSHO** • 1981
SAMURAI SAGA see **ARU KENGO NO SHOGAI** • 1959
SAMURAI SPY see **IBUN SARUTOBI SASUKE** • 1965
SAMURAI VAGABONDS see **TONOSAMA YAJIKITA** • 1960
SAMURAI'S LOVE see **BANCHO SARA YASHIKI -OKIKU TO HARIMA** • 1954
SAMVETSOMMA ADOLF • 1936 • Wallen Sigurd • SWD • CONSCIENTIOUS ADOLF ○ MALAJLUCKAN
SAMVITTIGHEDSKVALER • 1920 • Fonss Olaf • DNM
SAMVITTIGHEDSNAG see **HVEM VAR FORBRYDEREN?** • 1912
SAMYAN SAN SEIGAI • 1989 • Sin Gei-Yin • HKG • HEART INTO HEARTS
SAMYAN SEIGAI • 1988 • Sin Gei-Yin • HKG • HEART TO HEARTS
SAN • 1966 • Djordjevic Purisa • YGS • DREAM, THE
SAN AGUSTIN • 1974 • Blanco Javier • DOC • VNZ
SAN ANTONE • 1952 • Kane Joseph • USA
SAN ANTONE AMBUSH • 1949 • Ford Philip • USA
SAN ANTONE KID, THE • 1944 • Bretherton Howard • USA
SAN ANTONIO • 1945 • Butler David, Walsh Raoul (U/c) • USA
SAN ANTONIO NE PENSE QU'A CA • 1981 • Seria Joel • FRN
SAN ANTONIO ROSE • 1941 • Lamont Charles • USA
SAN BABILA ORE VENTI UN DELITTO INUTILE • 1976 • Lizzani Carlo • ITL
SAN BENEDETTO DOMINATORE DEI BARBARI see **SOLE DI MONTECASSINO, IL** • 1945
SAN-CHIAO HSI-T'I • 1982 • Sung Hsiang-Ju • TWN • HELPLESS TASTE, THE
SAN CLEMENTE • 1981 • Depardon Raymond, Ristelhueber Sophie • FRN
SAN DEMETRIO - LONDON • 1943 • Frend Charles • UKN
SAN DIEGO • 1912 • Dwan Allan • DOC • USA
SAN DIEGO, I LOVE YOU • 1944 • Le Borg Reginald • USA
SAN DOMINGO • 1970 • Syberberg Hans-Jurgen • FRG
SAN FELIPE DE JESUS • 1949 • Bracho Julio • MXC
SAN FERNANDO VALLEY • 1944 • English John • USA
SAN FERRY ANN • 1965 • Summers Jeremy • UKN
SAN FRANCESCO see **FRANCESCO** • 1988
SAN FRANCISCO • 1906 • *Bitzer Billy (Ph)* • USA
SAN FRANCISCO • 1936 • Van Dyke W. S. • USA
SAN FRANCISCO • 1945 • Van Dyke Willard • DOC • USA
SAN FRANCISCO • 1968 • Stern Anthony • DCS • UKN
SAN FRANCISCO • 1984 • Charles Freddy • BLG
SAN FRANCISCO CELEBRATION, THE • 1913 • Sennett Mack • DOC • USA
SAN FRANCISCO COWBOY • 1969 • *A.a.f. Productions* • USA
SAN FRANCISCO DE ASIS • 1943 • Gout Alberto • MXC • ST. FRANCIS OF ASSISI (USA)
SAN FRANCISCO DISASTER, THE • 1906 • *Sheffield Photo Co.* • UKN
SAN FRANCISCO DOCKS • 1940 • Lubin Arthur • USA
SAN FRANCISCO EARTHQUAKE, THE • 1906 • Blackton J. Stuart • USA
SAN FRANCISCO INTERNATIONAL • 1970 • Moxey John Llewellyn • TVM • USA • SAN FRANCISCO INTERNATIONAL AIRPORT (UKN)
SAN FRANCISCO INTERNATIONAL AIRPORT (UKN) see **SAN FRANCISCO INTERNATIONAL** • 1970
SAN FRANCISCO NIGHTS • 1928 • Neill R. William • USA • DIVORCE (UKN) ○ FRUIT OF DIVORCE, THE
SAN FRANCISCO STORY, THE • 1952 • Parrish Robert • USA
SAN FRANCISCO SUMMER 1967 • 1968 • Shebib Donald • CND
SAN GENNARO • 1947 • Emmer Luciano, Gras Enrico • ITL
SAN GIOVANNI DECOLLATO • 1940 • Palermi Amleto • ITL
SAN GOTTARDO see **SAN GOTTARDO EINE SZENISCHE DOKUMENTATION** • 1977
SAN GOTTARDO EINE SZENISCHE DOKUMENTATION • 1977 • Herman Villi • SWT • SAN GOTTARDO
SAN KYODAI NO KETTO • 1960 • Tanaka Shigeo • JPN • THREE BROTHERS AND THE UNDERWORLD
SAN MARCO • 1913 • Maggi Luigi • ITL
SAN MARTIN DE PORRES • 1974 • *Clasa* • MXC
SAN MASSENZA • 1955 • Olmi Ermanno • DOC • ITL • CIMEGO
SAN MICHELE AVEVA UN GALLO • 1972 • Taviani Paolo, Taviani Vittorio • ITL • ST. MICHAEL HAD A ROOSTER
SAN MINIATO, LUGLIO '44 • 1954 • Taviani Paolo, Taviani Vittorio • DCS • ITL
SAN PABLO EN EL ARTE • 1966 • Ardavin Cesar • SHT • SPN
SAN PASQUALE BAYLONNE, PROTETTORE DELLE DONNE • 1976 • D'Amico Luigi Filippo • ITL • SEX FOR SALE (UKN)
SAN PEDRO BUMS, THE • 1977 • Shear Barry • TVM • USA
SAN PIETRO see **BATTLE OF SAN PIETRO, THE** • 1944
SAN QUENTIN • 1937 • Bacon Lloyd • USA
SAN QUENTIN • 1946 • Douglas Gordon • USA
SAN REMO CANTA • 1956 • Paolella Domenico • ITL
SAN RIFLE EN LA HABANA see **THIEF IN SILK** • 1952
SAN SALVATORE • 1956 • Jacobs Werner • FRG
SAN SHAO-YEH-TE CHIEN • 1978 • Ch'U Yuan • HKG • DEATH DUEL
SAN SIMEON DEL DESIERTO see **SIMON DEL DESIERTO** • 1965
SAN SIMON DE LOS MAGUEYES • 1972 • *Churubusco Azteca* • MXC
SAN TOY • 1900 • *Tempest Marie* • UKN
SANA ULA HOB • 1976 • Abu Saif Salah, Salem Atef, Mustafa Niazi, Rafla Hilmy • EGY • FIRST-YEAR LOVE ○ SANA ULA HUBB
SANA ULA HUBB see **SANA ULA HOB** • 1976
SANADA FUUNROKU • 1963 • Kato Tai • JPN • SASUKE AND HIS COMEDIANS
SANANGUAGAT INUIT MASTERWORKS OF 1000 YEARS • 1974 • May Derek • DOC • CND
SANAOUD see **SA NAUD** • 1972
SANATORIUM see **SANATORIUM POD KLEPSYDRA** • 1973
SANATORIUM BENEATH THE OBITUARY, A see **SANATORIUM POD KLEPSYDRA** • 1973
SANATORIUM POD KLEPSYDRA • 1973 • Has Wojciech J. • PLN • HOURGLASS SANATORIUM, THE (USA) ○ SANATORIUM ○ SANATORIUM BENEATH THE OBITUARY, A ○ SANDGLASS, THE
SANATORIUM TOTAL VERRUCKT • 1954 • Elling Alwin • FRG
SANBA GARASU SANDAIKAI • 1959 • Bansho Yoshiaki • JPN • TOKYO OMNIBUS
SANBAYAKU ROKUJUGO-YA • 1948 • Ichikawa Kon • JPN • THREE HUNDRED AND SIXTY FIVE NIGHTS
SANBIKI NO AKUTO • 1968 • Matsuo Akinori • JPN • THREE ROGUES
SANBIKI NO ONNA TOBAKUSHI • 1967 • Tanaka Shigeo • JPN • THOROUGHBRED WOMEN GAMBLERS
SANBIKI NO TANUKI • 1966 • Suzuki • JPN • THREE BADGERS
SANCHEZ DEBEN MORIR, LOS • 1965 • Delgado Miguel M. • MXC
SANCTA MARIA • 1941 • Neville Edgar, Faraldo Pier Luigi • ITL, SPN
SANCTA SIMPLICITAS • 1968 • Popescu-Gopo Ion • RMN
SANCTIMONIOUS SPINSTERS' SOCIETY, THE • 1913 • Martinek H. O.? • UKN
SANCTUARY • 1916 • Harris Claude • UKN
SANCTUARY • 1961 • Richardson Tony • USA
SANCTUARY see **SANTUARIO** • 1951
SANCTUARY see **AZYL** • 1978
SANCTUARY see **LAST RITES** • 1988
SANCTUARY AND PLAYGROUND • 1939 • Oliver Bill • DOC • CND
SANCTUARY OF FEAR • 1979 • Moxey John Llewellyn • TVM • USA • GIRL IN THE PARK ○ FATHER BROWN, DETECTIVE ○ FATHER BROWN
SANCTUARY OF THE SEA • 1980 • Stoneman John • MTV • USA
SANCULOTTO, IL see **IO SONO LA PRIMULA ROSSA** • 1954
SAND • 1920 • Hillyer Lambert • USA
SAND see **SABLES** • 1927
SAND AND STONE • 1967 • Kidawa Janusz • DOC • PLN
SAND BARRIER, THE • 1978 • Jubenvill Ken • SHT • CND
SAND BLIND • 1925 • Jaccard Jacques • USA
SAND CASTLE see **KASTILYONG BUHANGIN** • 1981
SAND CASTLE, THE • 1969 • Hill Jerome • USA
SAND CASTLE, THE see **CHATEAU DE SABLE, LE** • 1977
SAND CASTLES see **SANDCASTLES** • 1972
SAND HILL LOVERS, THE • 1914 • *Kerrigan J. Warren* • USA
SAND LARK, THE • 1916 • Horkheimer H. M., Horkheimer E. D. • SHT • USA
SAND, LOVE AND SALT (USA) see **HARTE MANNER -HEISSE LIEBE** • 1956
SAND MAN, THE • 1920 • Newmeyer Fred, Roach Hal • SHT • USA • SANDMAN, THE
SAND OF GOLD see **RIMALUN MIN DHAHAB** • 1966
SAND OF KUROBE, THE see **KUROBE NO TAIYO** • 1968
SAND PEBBLES, THE • 1966 • Wise Robert • USA
SAND RAT, THE • 1915 • Daly William Robert • USA
SAND, SCAMPS AND STRATEGY • 1916 • Semon Larry • SHT • USA
SAND STORM, THE • 1912 • *Fielding Romaine* • USA
SAND (UKN) see **WILL JAMES' SAND** • 1949
SAND-WOMAN see **SUNA NO ONNA** • 1964
SANDA TAI GAILA see **FURANKENSHUTAIN NO KAIJU -SANDA TAI GAILAH** • 1966
SANDA VS. GAILA see **FURANKENSHUTAIN NO KAIJU -SANDA TAI GAILAH** • 1966
SANDA WONG • 1951 • De Leon Gerardo • PHL
SANDAI KAIJU CHIKYU SAIDAI NO KESSEN • 1965 • Honda Inoshiro • JPN • GHIDRAH -THE THREE-HEADED MONSTER (USA) ○ GREATEST BATTLE ON EARTH, THE ○ MONSTER OF MONSTERS GHIDORAH ○ GHIDORAH ○ GODZILLA VS. MONSTER ZERO ○ BIGGEST FIGHT ON EARTH, THE
SANDAKAN HACHIBAN SHOKAN, BOHKYO • 1975 • Kumai Kei • JPN • SANDAKAN NO.8 ○ BROTHEL NO.8 ○ BOKYO
SANDAKAN NO.8 see **SANDAKAN HACHIBAN SHOKAN, BOHKYO** • 1975
SANDAL, THE • 1969 • Austin Ray • UKN
SANDAL KEEPER, THE (USA) see **HORAFUKI TAIKOKI** • 1964
SANDALWOOD CRADLE see **CHANDAN KA PALNA** • 1967
SANDANJU NO OTOKO • 1961 • Suzuki Seijun • JPN
SANDCASTLE • 1967 • Vidugiris A., Bronstein Y. • SHT • USS
SANDCASTLE see **PESCENI GRAD** • 1962
SANDCASTLES • 1972 • Post Ted • TVM • USA • SAND CASTLES ○ GODS MUST WAIT, THE
SANDE ANSIGT, DET • 1951 • Ipsen Bodil, Lauritzen Lau Jr. • DNM
SANDE KAERLIGHED, DEN • 1912 • Blom August • DNM • FLUGTEN GENNEM SKYERNE ○ FUGITIVES, THE
SANDERS see **COAST OF SKELETONS** • 1964
SANDERS OF THE RIVER • 1935 • Korda Zoltan • UKN • BOSAMBO (USA)
SANDERS OF THE RIVER • 1964 • SAF
SANDESAYA • 1960 • Peries Lester James • SLN • MESSAGE, THE
SANDFLOW • 1936 • Selander Lesley • USA
SANDGLASS, THE see **SANATORIUM POD KLEPSYDRA** • 1973
SANDGRAFIN, DIE • 1927 • Steinhoff Hans • FRG
SANDGRASS PEOPLE, THE • 1989 • Roets Koos • SAF
SANDHYA RAG • 1977 • Saika Bhabendranath • IND • EVENING SONG
SANDINO • 1988 • Littin Miguel • NCR, SPN, MXC
SANDMAN, THE • 1909 • *Edison* • USA
SANDMAN, THE • 1913 • *Kinemacolor* • USA
SANDMAN, THE see **SAND MAN, THE** • 1920
SANDMAN TALES • 1933 • *Mintz Charles (P)* • ANS • USA
SANDOK, IL MACISTE DELLA GIUNGLA • 1964 • Lenzi Umberto • ITL, FRN • SANDOK, THE GIANT OF THE JUNGLE ○ TEMPLE OF THE WHITE ELEPHANTS ○ TEMPIO DELL'ELEFANTE BIANCO, IL
SANDOK, THE GIANT OF THE JUNGLE see **SANDOK, IL MACISTE DELLA GIUNGLA** • 1964
SANDOKAN • 1964 • Lenzi Umberto • SPN, FRN, ITL • SANDOKAN, LE TIGRE DE BORNEO (FRN) ○ SANDOKAN THE GREAT (USA) ○ SANDOKAN, LA TIGRE DI MOMPRACEM (ITL)
SANDOKAN • 1974 • Solimo Sarjo • MLY • SANDOKAN TIGER OF MALAYA ○ SANDOKAN, HARIMAU MALAYA ○ TIGER OF MALAYA
SANDOKAN • 1976 • Sollima Sergio • ITL
SANDOKAN AGAINST THE LEOPARD OF SARAWAK (USA) see **SANDOKAN CONTRO IL LEOPARDO DI SARAWAK** • 1965
SANDOKAN, ALLA RISCOSSA • 1964 • Capuano Luigi • ITL • SANDOKAN FIGHTS BACK (USA) ○ SANDOKAN STRIKES BACK
SANDOKAN ALLA RISCOSSA • 1977 • Sollima Sergio • ITL
SANDOKAN CONTRO IL LEOPARDO DI SARAWAK • 1965 • Capuano Luigi • ITL, FRG • SANDOKAN AGAINST THE LEOPARD OF SARAWAK (USA) ○ RETURN OF SANDOKAN
SANDOKAN FIGHTS BACK (USA) see **SANDOKAN, ALLA RISCOSSA** • 1964
SANDOKAN, HARIMAU MALAYA see **SANDOKAN** • 1974
SANDOKAN, LA TIGRE DI MOMPRACEM (ITL) see **SANDOKAN** • 1964
SANDOKAN, LE TIGRE DE BORNEO (FRN) see **SANDOKAN** • 1964
SANDOKAN STRIKES BACK see **SANDOKAN, ALLA RISCOSSA** • 1964
SANDOKAN THE GREAT (USA) see **SANDOKAN** • 1964
SANDOKAN TIGER OF MALAYA see **SANDOKAN** • 1974
SANDPIPER, THE • 1965 • Minnelli Vincente • USA • FLIGHT OF THE SANDPIPER, THE
SANDPIT GENERALS, THE see **WILD PACK, THE** • 1971
SANDRA • 1924 • Sawyer Arthur H. • USA
SANDRA • 1952 • Orol Juan • MXC, CUB • MUJER DE FUEGO, LA
SANDRA -THE MAKING OF A WOMAN • 1970 • Graver Gary • USA • I AM SANDRA
SANDRA (USA) see **...VAGHE STELLE DELL'ORSA** • 1965
SANDS OF BEERSHEBA • 1965 • Ramati Alexander • USA, ISR • MORDEI HA'OR (ISR) ○ REBEL AGAINST THE LIGHT
SANDS OF DEE, THE • 1912 • Griffith D. W. • USA
SANDS OF ECSTASY • 1968 • Stouffer Larry • USA • SANDS OF EXTASY
SANDS OF EXTASY see **SANDS OF ECSTASY** • 1968
SANDS OF FATE • 1914 • Crisp Donald • USA
SANDS OF IWO JIMA • 1949 • Dwan Allan • USA
SANDS OF LIFE, THE • 1914 • *Balboa* • USA
SANDS OF SACRIFICE • 1917 • Sloman Edward • USA
SANDS OF THE DESERT • 1918 • *Hart Neal* • SHT • USA
SANDS OF THE DESERT • 1960 • Carstairs John Paddy • UKN
SANDS OF THE KALAHARI • 1965 • Endfield Cy • UKN, SAF
SANDS OF TIME • 1915 • Campbell Colin • USA
SANDS OF TIME, THE • 1913 • Johnston Lorimer • USA
SANDS OF TIME, THE • 1919 • Ayrton Randle • UKN
SANDSTONE • 1977 • Dana Jonathan • DOC • USA
SANDSTORM, THE see **TRISHAGNI** • 1988
SANDU FOLLOWS THE SUN (USA) see **CHELOVEK IDYOT ZA SOLNTSEM** • 1962
SANDUI YINGYANG YIZHANG CHUANG • 1988 • Cheung Chi-Kue • HKG • COUPLES, COUPLES, COUPLES
SANDWICH • 1980 • Bozzetto Bruno • ANM • ITL
SANDWICH, LE • 1975 • Abnudi Atiat Al- • EGY
SANDWICH MAN, THE • 1966 • Hartford-Davis Robert • UKN
SANDWICH MAN, THE see **ERH-TZU-TE TA WAN-OU** • 1983
SANDWICH SHINDIG • 1968 • Conde Conrado • PHL
SANDWICHES, THE • 1899 • Smith G. A. • UKN • HUNGRY COUNTRYMAN, THE
SANDY • 1918 • Melford George • USA
SANDY • 1926 • Beaumont Harry • USA
SANDY • 1982 • Nerval Michel • FRN
SANDY AND SHORTY START SOMETHING • 1914 • Thornby Robert T. • USA
SANDY AND SHORTY WORK TOGETHER • 1913 • Thornby Robert T. • USA
SANDY AT HOME • 1916 • Page Will • UKN
SANDY BURKE OF THE U-BAR-U • 1919 • Lowry Ira M. • USA
SANDY CLAWS • 1955 • Freleng Friz • ANS • USA
SANDY GETS HER MAN • 1940 • Garrett Otis, Smith Paul Gerard • USA • FIREMAN SAVE MY CHILD
SANDY GETS SHORTY A JOB • 1913 • Thornby Robert T. • USA
SANDY IS A LADY • 1940 • Lamont Charles • USA
SANDY LAND see **BALUCHARI** • 1968
SANDY MCPHERSON'S QUIET FISHING TRIP • 1908 • Porter Edwin S. • USA
SANDY, REFORMER • 1916 • MacQuarrie Murdock • SHT • USA
SANDY STEPS OUT • 1938 • Comfort Lance • SHT • UKN
SANDY TAKES A BOW (UKN) see **UNEXPECTED FATHER** • 1939
SANDY THE FIREMAN • 1930 • *Powell Sandy* • SHT • UKN
SANDY THE LOST POLICEMAN • 1931 • *Powell Sandy* • SHT • UKN
"SANDY" THE POACHER • 1909 • *Lubin* • USA
SANDY, THE RELUCTANT NATURE GIRL (USA) see **RELUCTANT NUDIST, THE** • 1963
SANDY, THE RELUCTANT NUDIST see **RELUCTANT NUDIST, THE** • 1963
SANDY THE SEAL • 1969 • Lynn Robert • UKN
SANDY, THE SUBSTITUTE • 1910 • *Edison* • USA
SANDY'S NEW KILT • 1912 • Aylott Dave? • UKN
SANDY'S SUSPICION • 1916 • Page Will • UKN
SANE ASYLUM, A • 1912 • Porter Edwin S. • USA
SANE FOURTH OF JULY, A • 1911 • *Edison* • USA
SAN'ELENA PICCOLA ISOLA • 1943 • Simoni Renato • ITL
SANFTE LAUF, DER • 1967 • Senft Haro • FRG • SMOOTH CAREER, THE ○ SMOOTH SAILING
SANG, LE • 1971 • Pollet Jean-Daniel • FRN
SANG A LA TETE, LE • 1956 • Grangier Gilles • FRN
SANG ACCUSATEUR, LE • 1975 • Franju Georges • MTV • FRN

SANG D'ALLAH, LE see **AU SEUIL DU HAREM** • 1922
SANG DE L'ACONA, LE see **SANG DU FLAMBOYANT, LE** • 1980
SANG DE L'EXIL, LE • 1970 • Ifticene Mohamed • ALG
SANG DES AUTRES, LE • 1983 • Chabrol Claude • CND, FRN • BLOOD OF OTHERS, THE
SANG DES AUTRES, LE see **CHEMINS DE LA VIOLENCE, LES** • 1972
SANG DES BETES, LE • 1949 • Franju Georges • DCS • FRN • BLOOD OF BEASTS, THE ○ BLOOD OF THE BEASTS
SANG DES FINOELS, LE • 1922 • Monca Georges, Pansini Rose • FRN
SANG DES PARIAS, LE • 1973 • Kola Djim Mamadou • BRK • BLOOD OF THE PARIAS, THE
SANG DU FLAMBOYANT, LE • 1980 • Migeat Francois • SWT, FRN • SANG DE L'ACONA, LE
SANG DU SIPOULLE ET L'ELECTOPHORESE, LE • 1958 • Painleve Jean • SHT • FRN
SANG D'UN POETE, LE • 1930 • Cocteau Jean • FRN • BLOOD OF A POET, THE (USA) ○ VIE D'UN POETE, LA ○ POET'S BLOOD
SANG ET LA ROSE, LE see **ET MOURIR DE PLAISIR** • 1960
SANG ET LUMIERES • 1954 • Rouquier Georges • FRN, SPN • LOVE IN A HOT CLIMATE (USA) ○ BEAUTY AND THE BULLFIGHTER ○ SANGRE Y LUCES (SPN)
SANG-FROID, NAPOLEON see **PSIHREMIA NAPOLEON** • 1968
SANG GURU • 1981 • Sirait Edward Pesta • INN • TEACHER, THE ○ TOPAZ
SANGA-ARI • 1962 • Matsuyama Zenzo • JPN • THERE ARE MOUNTAINS AND RIVERS ○ MOTHER COUNTRY
SANGAL • 1987 • *Siddiqui Arifa* • PKS • CHAIN
SANGAM • 1964 • Kapoor Raj • IND • UNION
SANGAREE • 1953 • Ludwig Edward • USA
SANGAWUNU MENIKE • 1967 • Wanaguru Dudley • SLN • HIDDEN GEM
SANGE SABOUR • 1968 • Kassaei Abas • IRN • ADAMANT, THE
SANGEN OM DEN ELDRODA BLOMMAN • 1918 • Stiller Mauritz • SWD • SONG OF THE SCARLET FLOWER ○ FLAME OF LIFE, THE ○ ACROSS THE RAPIDS
SANGEN OM DEN ELDRODA BLOMMAN • 1934 • Branner Per-Axel • SWD • SONG OF THE SCARLET FLOWER
SANGEN OM DEN ELDRODA BLOMMAN • 1956 • Molander Gustaf • SWD • SONG OF THE SCARLET FLOWER, THE
SANGEN OM DEN RODE RUBIN • 1970 • Meineche Annelise • DNM • SONG OF THE RED RUBY, THE (UKN) ○ RODE RUBIN, DEN
SANGEN OM STOCKHOLM • 1947 • Ahrle Elof • SWD • ALICE BABS I TOPPFORM ○ SONG ABOUT STOCKHOLM
SANGEN TILL HENNE • 1934 • Johansson Ivar • SWD • SONG TO HER, THE (USA)
SANGEN TILL LIVET • 1943 • Sinding Leif • NRW
SANGER IHRER HOHEIT, DER see **STIMME DES HERZENS, DIE** • 1937
SANGERIN, DIE • 1921 • *Schaeff Emmy* • FRG
SANGKAMMARTJUVEN • 1959 • Gentele Goran • SWD • THIEF IN THE BEDROOM, A
SANGOO KASHI MEE • 1967 • Mane Anant • IND
SANGRE • 1978 • Fernandez Ramon • SPN
SANGRE DE NOSTRADAMUS, LA • 1960 • Curiel Federico, Segar Stig (Usa Vers) • MXC • BLOOD OF NOSTRADAMUS, THE (USA)
SANGRE DE VIRGENES • 1967 • Vieyra Emilio • ARG • BLOOD OF THE VIRGINS
SANGRE EN EL BARRIO • 1951 • Fernandez Bustamente Adolfo • MXC • CRUCERO 33
SANGRE EN EL RING • 1960 • Curiel Federico • MXC
SANGRE EN EL RUEDO • 1952 • Contreras Torres Miguel • MXC, SPN
SANGRE EN EL RUEDO • 1968 • Gil Rafael • SPN
SANGRE EN LA BARRACA • 1962 • Orol Juan • MXC
SANGRE EN LAS MONTANAS • 1938 • Contreras Jaime L. • MXC
SANGRE EN RIO BRAVO • 1965 • Rodriguez Roberto • MXC
SANGRE HERMANA • 1914 • MXC • BLOOD OF BROTHERS
SANGRE MANDA, LA • 1933 • Bohr Jose, Sevilla J. • MXC
SANGRE NEGRA • 1948 • Chenal Pierre • ARG • NATIVE SON (USA)
SANGRE TORERA • 1949 • Pardave Joaquin • MXC
SANGRE Y ACERO • 1956 • Demare Lucas • ARG
SANGRE Y ARENA • 1988 • Elorrieta Javier • SPN • BLOOD AND SAND
SANGRE Y FUEGO • 1983 • Giral Sergio • CUB • BLOOD AND FIRE
SANGRE Y LUCES (SPN) see **SANG ET LUMIERES** • 1954
SANGSUE • 1973 • Ousseini Inoussa • SHT • NGR
SANGUE, O • Costa Pedro • PRT
SANGUE A CA' FOSCARI • 1948 • Calandri Max • ITL
SANGUE BLEU • 1914 • Oxilia Nino • ITL
SANGUE CHIAMA SANGUE • 1968 • Capuano Luigi • ITL • BLOOD CALLS BLOOD
SANGUE DI NOMAD see **VENDETTA DI ZINGARA** • 1952
SANGUE DI SBIRRO • 1977 • Brescia Alfonso • ITL
SANGUE DI ZINGARA • 1956 • Basaglia Maria • ITL
SANGUE E LA ROSA, IL (ITL) see **ET MOURIR DE PLAISIR** • 1960
SANGUE E LA SFIDA, IL • 1962 • Iquino Ignacio F. • ITL • BLOOD AND DEFIANCE (USA)
SANGUE MINEIRO • 1929 • Mauro-Humberto • BRZ • MINAS BLOOD ○ BLOOD OF MINAS
SANGUE PIU FANGO UGUALE LOGOS PASSIONE • 1974 • De Giorgi Elsa • ITL
SANGUE SUL DESERTO • 1949 • Vernuccio Gianni • EGY
SANGUE SUL SAGRATO • 1952 • Alessandrini Goffredo, Nesci Michele • ITL
SANGUE TOUREIRO • 1958 • Fraga Augusto • PRT
SANGUISUGA CONDUCE LA DANZA, LA • 1975 • Rizzo Alfredo • ITL
SANGYO SUPAI • 1968 • Kudo Eiichi • JPN • INDUSTRIAL SPY
SANIA ALBASTRA • 1987 • Carmazan Ioan • RMN • BLUE SLEIGH, THE
SANITARIUM, THE • 1910 • *Selig* • USA • CLINIC, THE
SANITARIUM SCANDAL, A • 1917 • Beaudine William • SHT • USA
SANITARIUM SCRAMBLE, A • 1916 • Eason B. Reeves • SHT • USA
SANITARY GULCH • 1913 • *Pilot* • USA
SANJAR • 1961 • Ranitovic Branko • ANS • YGS • DREAMER, THE
SANJU -SANGENDO TOSHIYA MONOGATARI • 1945 • Naruse Mikio • JPN • TALE OF ARCHERY AT THE SANJUSANGENDO, A
SANJURO see **TSUBAKI SANJURO** • 1962
SANJUSAN-GOSHA OHTOH NASHI • 1955 • Taniguchi Senkichi • JPN • NO RESPONSE FROM CAR 33
SANKA • 1972 • Shindo Kaneto • JPN • SONG OF PRAISE ○ PAEAN, A
SANKARABHARANAM • 1979 • Viswanath K. • IND • ORNAMENT OF SANKARA
SANMEN KIJI • 1931 • Uchida Tomu • JPN • STORIES OF HUMAN INTEREST
SANNA • 1984 • SAF
SANNIKOV'S LAND see **ZEMLYA SANNIKOVA** • 1973
SANNIN NO BAKUTO • 1967 • Ozawa Shigehiro • JPN • THREE GAMBLERS
SANNIN NO JOSEI • 1935 • Toyoda Shiro • JPN • THREE WOMEN
SANNIN NO KAOYAKU • 1960 • Inoue Umeji • JPN • LAST BETRAYAL, THE
SANRI-ZUKA SERIES NO.6 -THE COMMUNITY OF HETA see **SANRIZUKA, HETA BURAKU** • 1972
SANRIZUKA -DAINI TORIDE NO HITOBITO • 1971 • Ogawa Shinsuke • JPN • SANRIZUKA -PEOPLE OF THE SECOND FORTRESS ○ PEASANTS OF THE SECOND FORTRESS, THE
SANRIZUKA, HETA BURAKU • 1972 • Ogawa Shinsuke • JPN • SANRI-ZUKA SERIES NO.6 -THE COMMUNITY OF HETA
SANRIZUKA NO FUYU • 1970 • Ogawa Shinsuke • JPN • WINTER IN NARITA
SANRIZUKA NO NATSU • 1968 • Ogawa Shinsuke • DOC • JPN • SUMMER IN NARITA
SANRIZUKA -PEOPLE OF THE SECOND FORTRESS see **SANRIZUKA -DAINI TORIDE NO HITOBITO** • 1971
SANS DEVANT DERRIERE • 1974 • CND • AS USUAL
SANS FAMILLE • 1913 • *Fromet Maria* • FRN
SANS FAMILLE • 1925 • Monca Georges, Keroul Maurice • FRN • NO RELATIONS
SANS FAMILLE • 1934 • Allegret Marc • FRN
SANS FAMILLE • 1957 • Michel Andre • FRN, ITL • SENZA FAMIGLIA (ITL) ○ ADVENTURES OF REMI, THE
SANS LAISSER D'ADRESSE • 1950 • Le Chanois Jean-Paul • FRN
SANS LE JOUG • 1911 • Feuillade Louis • FRN
SANS LENDEMAIN • 1939 • Ophuls Max • FRN • THERE'S NO TOMORROW (USA) ○ DUCHESSE DE TILSITT, LA ○ MAQUILLAGE ○ NO TOMORROW
SANS LUNES DEL VALEDOR, EL • 1906 • MXC
SANS MERE • 1908 • Jasset Victorin • FRN
SANS MOBILE APPARENT • 1971 • Labro Philippe • FRN, ITL • WITHOUT APPARENT MOTIVE (USA) ○ SENZA MOVENTE (ITL)
SANS PAROLE • Gilbert Nicole • BLG
SANS SOLEIL • 1982 • Marker Chris • DOC • FRN • SUNLESS
SANS SOMMATION • 1972 • Gantillon Bruno • FRN, ITL, FRG
SANS TAMBOUR, NI TROMPETTE • 1949 • Blanc Roger • FRN
SANS TAMBOUR NI TROMPETTE (FRN) see **GANS VON SEDAN, DIE** • 1959
SANS TOIT NI LOI • 1985 • Varda Agnes • FRN • VAGABONDE ○ VAGABOND (USA)
SANSAR • Bose Debaki • IND
SANSAR SIMANTE • 1966 • *Ghatak Ritwik* • IND
SANSATIE DER TOEKOMST, DE see **TELEVISIE** • 1931
SANSHIRO • 1955 • Nakagawa Nobuo • JPN • STRAY SHEEP
SANSHIRO AT GINZA see **GINZA SANSHIRO** • 1950
SANSHIRO OF GINZA see **GINZA SANSHIRO** • 1950
SANSHIRO SUGATA see **SUGATA SANSHIRO** • 1945
SANSHO DAYU • 1954 • Mizoguchi Kenji • JPN • SANSHO THE BAILIFF (USA) ○ SUPERINTENDENT SANSHO, THE ○ BAILIFF, THE
SANSHO THE BAILIFF (USA) see **SANSHO DAYU** • 1954
SANSKAR • 1958 • *Biswas Anil (M)* • IND
SANSONE • 1962 • Parolini Gianfranco • ITL • SAMSON (USA)
SANSONE CONTRO I PIRATI • 1963 • Boccia Tanio • ITL • SAMSON AND THE SEA BEASTS (USA) ○ SAMSON VS. THE PIRATES
SANSONE CONTRO IL CORSARO NERO • 1962 • Capuano Luigi • ITL • HERCULES AND THE BLACK PIRATES (USA) ○ SAMSON VS. THE BLACK PIRATE
SANSONE E IL TESORO DEGLI INCAS • 1964 • Pierotti Piero • ITL • HERCULES AND THE TREASURE OF THE INCAS (USA) ○ LOST TREASURE OF THE AZTECS ○ SAMSON AND THE TREASURE OF THE INCAS
SANSSOUCI see **FRIDERICUS REX (EIN KONIGSSCHICKSAL) 3** • 1923
SANSUI YAU SEUNGFUNG • 1989 • Guan Jinpeng • HKG
SANT DNYANESHWAR • 1940 • Damle V., Fatehlal S. • IND
SANT GORA KUMBHAR • 1967 • Thakur Raja • IND
SANT HANDER INTE HAR • 1950 • Bergman Ingmar • SWD • THIS CAN'T HAPPEN HERE (UKN) ○ HIGH TENSION (USA) ○ THIS DOESN'T HAPPEN HERE
SANT JANABAI • 1938 • Devare Narayan, Sarpotdai N. D. • IND
SANT NAMDEO • 1938 • Apte Baburao • IND
SANT SAKHU • 1941 • Damle V., Fatehlal S. • IND
SANT THUKARAM • 1963 • Nadkarni Sundarao • IND
SANT TULSIDAS • 1939 • Desai Jayant • IND
SANT TURKARAM • 1936 • Damle V., Fatehlal S. • IND • TUKARAM
SANTA • 1918 • Peredo Luis G. • MXC
SANTA • 1931 • Moreno Antonio • MXC
SANTA • 1943 • Foster Norman • MXC
SANTA ALIANCA, A • 1977 • Geada Eduardo • PRT • SAINTLY ALLIANCE, THE ○ SAINT ALLIANCE, THE
SANTA AND THE ICE CREAM BUNNY • 1972 • *R & S Film Enterprises* • USA
SANTA AND THE THREE BEARS • 1970 • Benedict Tony • ANM • USA
SANTA ANNA WINDS • 1988 • Cimino Michael • USA
SANTA ANTERO • 1980 • Guimaraes Dordio • PRT
SANTA BARBARA • 1978 • Correa Luis De Miranda • SPN, VNZ
SANTA CANDIDA • 1945 • Amadori Luis Cesar • ARG
SANTA CATALINA ISLANDS • 1914 • Sennett Mack • DOC • USA
SANTA CATALINA, MAGIC ISLE OF THE PACIFIC • 1911 • Dwan Allan • DOC • USA
SANTA CHIKITA • 1959 • Sakellarios Alekos • GRC
SANTA CLAUS • 1898 • Smith G. A. • UKN • VISIT OF SANTA CLAUS, THE
SANTA CLAUS • 1912 • Thornton F. Martin, Callum R. H., Booth W. R. • UKN
SANTA CLAUS • 1913 • *Kinemacolor* • USA
SANTA CLAUS • 1925 • *Kleinschmidt F. E.* • SHT • USA
SANTA CLAUS • 1926 • Cooper George A. • UKN
SANTA CLAUS • 1959 • Cardona Rene • MXC
SANTA CLAUS see **SANTA CLAUS -THE MOVIE** • 1985
SANTA CLAUS AND THE CHILDREN • 1898 • *Paul R. W.* • UKN
SANTA CLAUS AND THE CLUBMAN • 1911 • *Shaw Harold M.* • USA
SANTA CLAUS AND THE MINER'S CHILD, THE • 1909 • *Centaur* • USA
SANTA CLAUS' BUSY DAY • 1906 • SHT • FRN
SANTA CLAUS CONQUERS THE MARTIANS • 1964 • Webster Nicholas • USA
SANTA CLAUS HAS BLUE EYES see **PERE NOEL A LES YEUX BLEUS, LE** • 1966
SANTA CLAUS' MISTAKE • 1905 • Collins Alf? • UKN
SANTA CLAUS -THE MOVIE • 1985 • Szwarc Jeannot • UKN • SANTA CLAUS
SANTA CLAUS V.C. • 1914 • *Pennant Films* • UKN
SANTA CLAUS VERSUS CUPID • 1915 • Louis Will • USA
SANTA CLAUS VISITS THE LAND OF MOTHER GOOSE see **MAGIC LAND OF MOTHER GOOSE, THE** • 1966
SANTA DEL BARRIO, LA • 1948 • Urueta Chano • MXC
SANTA DICA DO SERTAO • 1989 • del Pino Carlos • BRZ
SANTA ESPERANZA • 1981 • Alarcon Sebastian • USS • SACRED HOPE
SANTA FE • 1951 • Pichel Irving • USA
SANTA FE BOUND • 1936 • Webb Harry S. • USA
SANTA FE MARSHAL • 1940 • Selander Lesley • USA
SANTA FE PASSAGE • 1955 • Witney William • USA
SANTA FE PETE • 1925 • Webb Harry S. • USA
SANTA FE RIDES • 1937 • Ray Bernard B. • USA
SANTA FE SADDLEMATES • 1945 • Carr Thomas • USA • SANTE FE SADDLEMATES
SANTA FE SATAN see **CATCH MY SOUL** • 1974
SANTA FE SCOUTS • 1943 • Bretherton Howard • USA
SANTA FE STAMPEDE • 1938 • Sherman George • USA
SANTA FE TRAIL • 1936 • Ray Bernard B. • USA
SANTA FE TRAIL • 1940 • Curtiz Michael • USA
SANTA FE TRAIL, THE • 1930 • Brower Otto, Knopf Edwin H. • USA • LAW RIDES WEST, THE (UKN) ○ SPANISH ACRES
SANTA FE UPRISING • 1946 • Springsteen R. G. • USA
SANTA IS ARRIVING see **SANTA IS COMING** • 1969
SANTA IS COMING • 1969 • *Fleetan Films* • USA • SANTA IS ARRIVING
SANTA LUCIA • 1956 • Jacobs Werner • FRG
SANTA LUCIA LUNTANA • 1951 • Vergano Aldo • ITL
SANTA MARIA see **GEHEIMNIS DER SANTA MARIA, DAS** • 1921
SANTA MARIA. DAS GEHEIMNIS EINER BRIGG see **GEHEIMNIS DER SANTA MARIA, DAS** • 1921
SANTA NOTTE • 1947 • Bava Mario • ITL
SANTA ROGELIA (SPN) see **PECCATO DI ROGELIA SANCHEZ, IL** • 1939
SANTA SANGRE • 1989 • Jodorowsky Alejandro • ITL
SANTA VISITS THE MAGIC LAND OF MOTHER GOOSE see **MAGIC LAND OF MOTHER GOOSE, THE** • 1966
SANTAJ • 1981 • Saizescu Geo • RMN • BLACKMAIL
SANTAN • Thapa Prakesh • NPL
SANTANDER, LA CIUDAD EN LLAMAS • 1944 • Marquina Luis • SPN
SANTARELLINA • 1911 • Caserini Mario • ITL
SANTARELLINA see **DIAVOLO VA IN COLLEGIO, IL** • 1944
SANTARELLINA (ITL) see **MAM'ZELLE NITOUCHE** • 1954
SANTA'S CHRISTMAS CIRCUS • 1966 • Wiziarde Frank • USA
SANTA'S CHRISTMAS ELF • 1971 • *Cinetron* • USA
SANTA'S SURPRISE • *Fleet* • ANS • USA
SANTA'S SURPRISE • 1947 • Kneitel Seymour • ANS • USA
SANTA'S TOY SHOP • 1929 • Hogan Tom • SHT • USA
SANTA'S WORKSHOP • 1932 • Jackson Wilfred • ANS • USA
SANTE AFRIQUE • 1976 • Regnier Michel • DSS • CND
SANTE FE SADDLEMATES see **SANTA FE SADDLEMATES** • 1945
SANTEE • 1973 • Nelson Gary • USA • TURN OF THE BADGE
SANT'ELENA PICCOLA ISOLA • 1943 • Simoni Renato, Scarpelli Umberto • ITL • NAPOLEONE A SANT'ELENA
SANTH WAHATE KRISHNA MAI • 1967 • Pathak Madhukar • IND
SANTIAGO • 1956 • Douglas Gordon • USA • GUN RUNNER, THE (UKN)
SANTIAGO • 1970 • Brocka Lino • PHL
SANTO AGAINST BLUE DEMON IN ATLANTIS see **SANTO CONTRA BLUE DEMON EN LA ATLANTIDA** • 1968
SANTO AGAINST THE BLACK MAGIC see **SANTO CONTRA LA MAGIA NEGRA** • 1972
SANTO AGAINST THE ZOMBIES see **SANTO CONTRA LOS ZOMBIES** • 1961
SANTO AND BLUE DEMON VS. DRACULA AND THE WOLF MAN (USA) see **SANTO Y BLUE DEMON CONTRA DRACULA Y EL HOMBRE LOBO** • 1972
SANTO AND DRACULA'S TREASURE see **VAMPIRO Y EL SEXO, EL** • 1968
SANTO AND THE BLUE DEMON VS. THE MONSTERS see **SANTO Y BLUE DEMON CONTRA LOS MONSTRUOS** • 1968

SANTO ATACA LAS BRUJAS • 1964 • Diaz Morales Jose • MXC • ATACAN LAS BRUJAS ○ SANTO ATTACKS THE WITCHES ○ WITCHES ATTACK, THE

SANTO ATTACKS THE WITCHES see **SANTO ATACA LAS BRUJAS** • 1964

SANTO CONTRA BLUE DEMON EN LA ATLANTIDA • 1968 • Soler Julian • MXC • SANTO AGAINST BLUE DEMON IN ATLANTIS

SANTO CONTRA CAZDORES DE CABEZAS • 1969 • *Milton Nadia* • MXC • SANTO VS. THE HEAD HUNTERS

SANTO CONTRA CEREBRO DEL MAL • 1958 • Rodriguez Joselito • MXC, CUB

SANTO CONTRA EL BARON BRAKOLA • 1965 • Diaz Morales Jose • MXC • BARON BRAKOLA, EL ○ SANTO VS. BARON BRAKOLA

SANTO CONTRA EL CEREBRO DIABOLICO • 1961 • Curiel Federico • MXC • SANTO VS. THE DIABOLICAL BRAIN

SANTO CONTRA EL DR. MUERTE • 1973 • Romero-Marchent Rafael • SPN

SANTO CONTRA EL ESPECTRO see **ESPECTRO DEL ESTRANGULADOR, EL** • 1963

SANTO CONTRA EL ESTRANGULADOR • 1965 • Cardona Rene • MXC • SANTO VS. THE STRANGLER

SANTO CONTRA EL REY DEL CRIMEN • 1961 • Curiel Federico • MXC • SANTO VS. THE KING OF CRIME

SANTO CONTRA HOMBRES INFERNALES • 1958 • Rodriguez Joselito • MXC, CUB

SANTO CONTRA LA HIJA DE FRANKENSTEIN • 1971 • Delgado Miguel M. • MXC • SANTO VS. FRANKENSTEIN'S DAUGHTER ○ HIJA DE FRANKENSTEIN, LA ○ DAUGHTER OF FRANKENSTEIN, THE ○ SANTO VS. THE DAUGHTER OF FRANKENSTEIN

SANTO CONTRA LA INVASION DE LOS MARCIANOS • 1966 • Crevenna Alfredo B. • MXC • SANTO VERSUS THE MARTIAN INVASION ○ SANTO EL ENMASCARADO DE PLATA VS. LA INVASION DE LOS MARCIANOS

SANTO CONTRA LA MAGIA NEGRA • 1972 • Crevenna Alfredo B. • MXC • SANTO AGAINST THE BLACK MAGIC

SANTO CONTRA LAS MUJERES VAMPIROS • 1961 • Blake Alfonso Corona • MXC • SAMSON VS. THE VAMPIRE WOMEN (USA) ○ SAMSON AND THE VAMPIRE WOMAN ○ SANTO VS. THE VAMPIRE WOMEN

SANTO CONTRA LOS ASESINOS DE LA MAFIA • 1969 • Bengoa Manuel • SPN • SANTO VS. THE MAFIA MURDERERS

SANTO CONTRA LOS JINETES DEL TERROR • 1969 • Cardona Rene • MXC • SANTO VS. THE RIDERS OF TERROR

SANTO CONTRA LOS MONSTRUOS DE FRANKENSTEIN see **SANTO Y BLUE DEMON CONTRA LOS MONSTRUOS** • 1968

SANTO CONTRA LOS VILLANOS DEL RING • MXC • SANTO VS. THE VILLAINS OF THE RING

SANTO CONTRA LOS ZOMBIES • 1961 • Alazraki Benito • MXC • INVASION OF THE ZOMBIES (USA) ○ SANTO AGAINST THE ZOMBIES ○ SANTO VS. THE ZOMBIES

SANTO DE LA ESPADA, EL • 1970 • Torre-Nilsson Leopoldo • ARG • KNIGHT OF THE SWORD, THE

SANTO DISONORE • 1949 • Brignone Guido • ITL

SANTO EL ENMASCARADO DE PLATA VS. LA INVASION DE LOS MARCIANOS see **SANTO CONTRA LA INVASION DE LOS MARCIANOS** • 1966

SANTO EL ENMASCARADO DE PLATA VS. LOS VILLANOS DEL RING • 1966 • Crevenna Alfredo B. • MXC

SANTO EN EL HOTEL DE LA MUERTE • 1961 • Curiel Federico • MXC • HOTEL DE LA MUERTE ○ SANTO IN THE HOTEL OF THE DEAD

SANTO EN EL MUSEO DE CERA • 1963 • Blake Alfonso Corona • MXC • SAMSON IN THE WAX MUSEUM (USA) ○ SANTO IN THE WAX MUSEUM

SANTO EN EL TESORO DE DRACULA see **VAMPIRO Y EL SEXO, EL** • 1968

SANTO EN LA VENGANZA DE LA MOMIA • 1971 • Cardona Rene • MXC • SANTO IN THE MUMMY'S REVENGE

SANTO EN LA VENGANZA DE LAS MUJERES VAMPIRO • 1968 • Curiel Federico • MXC • VENGANZA DE LAS MUJERES VAMPIRO, LA ○ VENGEANCE OF THE VAMPIRE WOMEN, THE ○ SANTO IN THE REVENGE OF THE VAMPIRE WOMEN

SANTO FRENTE A LA MUERTE • Orozco Fernando • MXC • SANTO IN FRONT OF DEATH

SANTO IN FRONT OF DEATH see **SANTO FRENTE A LA MUERTE**

SANTO IN THE HOTEL OF THE DEAD see **SANTO EN EL HOTEL DE LA MUERTE** • 1961

SANTO IN THE MUMMY'S REVENGE see **SANTO EN LA VENGANZA DE LA MOMIA** • 1971

SANTO IN THE REVENGE OF THE VAMPIRE WOMEN see **SANTO EN LA VENGANZA DE LAS MUJERES VAMPIRO** • 1968

SANTO IN THE WAX MUSEUM see **SANTO EN EL MUSEO DE CERA** • 1963

SANTO-KACHO • 1959 • Nagashiro Ryosuke • JPN • THIRD CLASS THIEF

SANTO MODICO • 1929 • Mazoyer Robert • FRN

SANTO OFICIO, EL • 1972 • Ripstein Arturo • MXC • HOLY OFFICE, THE

SANTO PATRONO, IL • 1972 • Albertini Bitto • ITL

SANTO PRENDE LA MIRA, IL (ITL) see **SAINT PREND L'AFFUT, LE** • 1966

SANTO VERSUS THE MARTIAN INVASION see **SANTO CONTRA LA INVASION DE LOS MARCIANOS** • 1966

SANTO VS. BARON BRAKOLA see **SANTO CONTRA EL BARON BRAKOLA** • 1965

SANTO VS. CAPULINA • 1971 • *Clasa-Mohme* • MXC

SANTO VS. DRACULA Y EL HOMBRE LOBO, EL • 1972 • *Cinema Calderon* • MXC

SANTO VS. EL ATOMO VIVIENTE • 1971 • *Filmadora Chapultepec* • MXC

SANTO VS. FRANKENSTEIN'S DAUGHTER see **SANTO CONTRA LA HIJA DE FRANKENSTEIN** • 1971

SANTO VS. LA MAFIA DEL VICIO • MXC • SANTO VS. THE MAFIA OF VICE

SANTO VS. THE DAUGHTER OF FRANKENSTEIN see **SANTO CONTRA LA HIJA DE FRANKENSTEIN** • 1971

SANTO VS. THE DIABOLICAL BRAIN see **SANTO CONTRA EL CEREBRO DIABOLICO** • 1961

SANTO VS. THE HEAD HUNTERS see **SANTO CONTRA CAZDORES DE CABEZAS** • 1969

SANTO VS. THE KING OF CRIME see **SANTO CONTRA EL REY DEL CRIMEN** • 1961

SANTO VS. THE MAFIA MURDERERS see **SANTO CONTRA LOS ASESINOS DE LA MAFIA** • 1969

SANTO VS. THE MAFIA OF VICE see **SANTO VS. LA MAFIA DEL VICIO**

SANTO VS. THE RIDERS OF TERROR see **SANTO CONTRA LOS JINETES DEL TERROR** • 1969

SANTO VS. THE STRANGLER see **SANTO CONTRA EL ESTRANGULADOR** • 1965

SANTO VS. THE VAMPIRE WOMEN see **SANTO CONTRA LAS MUJERES VAMPIROS** • 1961

SANTO VS. THE VILLAINS OF THE RING see **SANTO CONTRA LOS VILLANOS DEL RING**

SANTO VS. THE ZOMBIES see **SANTO CONTRA LOS ZOMBIES** • 1961

SANTO Y BLUE DEMON CONTRA DRACULA Y EL HOMBRE LOBO • 1972 • Delgado Miguel M. • MXC • SANTO AND BLUE DEMON VS. DRACULA AND THE WOLF MAN (USA)

SANTO Y BLUE DEMON CONTRA LOS MONSTRUOS • 1968 • Martinez Solares Gilberto • MXC • SANTO CONTRA LOS MONSTRUOS DE FRANKENSTEIN ○ SANTO AND THE BLUE DEMON VS. THE MONSTERS

SANTO Y BLUE DEMON EN EL MUNDO DE LOS MUERTOS • 1969 • Martinez Solares Gilberto • MXC • MUNDO DE LOS MUERTES, EL ○ WORLD OF THE DEAD, THE

SANTO Y BLUE DEMON VS. DR. FRANKENSTEIN • 1973 • *Cinema Calderon* • MXC

SANTO Y EL AGUILA REAL • 1971 • Crevenna Alfredo B. • MXC

SANTO Y MANTEQUILLA EN LA V. LLORENA • 1974 • *Cinema Calderon* • MXC

SANTOS INOCENTES, LOS • 1984 • Camus Mario • SPN • HOLY INNOCENTS, THE

SANTOS REYES, LOS • 1958 • Baledon Rafael • MXC

SANTOS ROTOS, LOS • 1971 • Mitrotti Elio • VNZ • BROKEN SAINTS, THE

SANTOS VEGA VUELVE • 1947 • Torres-Rios Leopoldo • ARG

SANTRALPA • 1949 • Agradoot • IND

SANTUARIO • 1951 • Barreto Victor • BRZ • SANCTUARY

SANTUARIO NO SE RINDE, EL • 1949 • Ruiz-Castillo Arturo • SPN

SANZU NO KAWA NO UBAGURAMA see **SHOGUN ASSASSIN** • 1980

SAO BERNARDO • 1972 • Hirszman Leon • BRZ • SAINT BERNARDO ○ S BERNARDO

SAO PAULO EN FESTA • 1954 • Barreto Victor • BRZ

SAO PAULO: SINFONIA DE UNA METROPOLI • 1929 • Kememy Adalbert • BRZ

SAO PEDRO DA COVA • 1976 • Simoes Rui • PRT

SAOBRACAJNI ZNACI • 1968 • Vunak Dragutin • ANM • YGS • TRAFFIC SIGNS

SAOIRSE? • 1961 • Morrison George • IRL • FREEDOM

SAP, THE • 1926 • Kenton Erle C. • USA

SAP, THE • 1929 • Mayo Archie • USA

SAP ABROAD, THE (UKN) see **SAP FROM SYRACUSE, THE** • 1930

SAP FROM SYRACUSE, THE • 1930 • Sutherland A. Edward • USA • SAP ABROAD, THE (UKN)

SAP OF THE EARTH see **SEVE DE LA TERRE** • 1955

SAP TAKES A WRAP, THE • 1939 • Lord Del • SHT • USA

SAPAGKA'T AKO'Y PANGIT LAMANG • 1968 • de Guzman Armando • PHL • BECAUSE I'M UGLY

SAPERA • 1939 • Bose Debaki • IND • SNAKE CHARMER (USA)

SAPEVANO SOLO UCCIDERE • 1968 • Boccia Tanio • ITL • SAGUARO

SAPHEAD, THE • 1920 • Blache Herbert • USA

SAPHEAD'S REVENGE, A • 1915 • *Griffith Ray* • USA

SAPHEAD'S SACRIFICE, A • 1920 • Hutchinson Craig • USA

SAPHO • 1900 • *Lubin* • SHT • USA

SAPHO • 1908 • Novelli Enrico • ITL

SAPHO • 1912 • Chautard Emile • FRN

SAPHO • 1913 • *Guyon Cecile* • FRN

SAPHO • 1913 • Cabanne W. Christy • USA • SAPPHO

SAPHO • 1917 • Ford Hugh • USA

SAPHO • 1934 • Perret Leonce • FRN

SAPHO see **SAFFO, VENERE DI LESBO** • 1960

SAPHO 63 see **AMOR Y SEXO** • 1963

SAPHO OU LA FUREUR D'AIMER • 1970 • Farrel Georges • FRN, ITL • SEX IS MY GAME

SAPHO-UP-TO-DATE • 1915 • *Superba* • USA

SAPHO, VENUS OF LESBOS see **SAFFO, VENERE DI LESBO** • 1960

SAPICHES see **PRIVATE POPSICLE: LEMON POPSICLE IV** • 1982

SAPIENT BIRDS, THE see **PTACI KOHACI** • 1965

SAPLINGS, THE see **SAZHENTSY** • 1973

SAPNON KA SAUDGAR • 1968 • *Kapoor Raj* • IND

SAPORE DELLE VENDETTA, IL • 1968 • Coll Julio • ITL, SPN • PERSECUCION HASTA VALENCIA (SPN) ○ NARCO MEN, THE (USA) ○ TASTE OF REVENGE, THE

SAPORE DI MARE • 1983 • Vanzina Carlo • ITL • TASTE OF SEA, A

SAPORE DI MARE 2 UN ANNO DOPO • 1984 • Cortini Bruno • ITL • TASTE OF SEA 2, ONE YEAR LATER, A

SAPPHIRE • 1959 • Dearden Basil • UKN

SAPPHO • 1913 • *Roberts Florence* • USA

SAPPHO • 1917 • Chautard Emile • USA

SAPPHO • 1921 • Buchowetzki Dimitri • FRG • SAPPHO OR DIE GESCHLOSSENE KETTE ○ MAD LOVE

SAPPHO • 1922 • *Parkinson H. B.* • UKN

SAPPHO see **SAPHO** • 1913

SAPPHO '68 • 1968 • Anders Jan • USA

SAPPHO DARLING • 1968 • Steele Gunnar

SAPPHO OR DIE GESCHLOSSENE KETTE see **SAPPHO** • 1921

SAPPORO, CROISSANCE PLANIFIEE • 1974 • Regnier Michel • DOC • CND

SAPPORO ORIMPIKKU • 1972 • Shinoda Masahiro • DOC • JPN • SAPPORO WINTER OLYMPICS

SAPPORO WINTER OLYMPICS see **SAPPORO ORIMPIKKU** • 1972

SAPPY BIRTHDAY • 1942 • Edwards Harry J. • SHT • USA

SAPPY BULLFIGHTERS • 1959 • White Jules • SHT • USA

SAPPY HOMIENS • 1956 • Salkin Leo • ANS • USA

SAPPY PAPPY • 1942 • Edwards Harry J. • SHT • USA

SAPROFITA, IL • 1974 • Nasca Sergio • ITL

SAPS AT SEA • 1940 • Douglas Gordon • USA • TWO'S COMPANY

SAPS IN CHAPS • 1942 • Freleng Friz • ANS • USA

SAPTE ARTE see **SEPTE ARTE** • 1958

SAPTE ZILE • 1973 • Veroiu Mircea • RMN • SEVEN DAYS

SAPUREY • 1939 • *Sircar B. N. (P)* • IND

SAPVILLE'S STALWART SON • 1916 • *Cooper Claude* • USA

SAQI • 1952 • Rawail H. S. • IND

SAQQA' MAT, AS- • 1977 • Abu Saif Salah • EGY, TNS • WATERBEARER IS DEAD, THE ○ SAKKA MAT, EL ○ WATER-CARRIER IS DEAD, THE

SAQR, AS- • 1965 • Siddik Khalid • SHT • KWT • FALCON, THE ○ FAUCON, LE

SAQR, AS- see **SAKR, EL** • 1950

SAQUEADORES DEL DOMINGO, LOS (SPN) see **HOMME DE MARRAKECH, L'** • 1966

SARA AKASH • 1970 • Chatterjee Basu • IND • WHOLE SKY, THE

SARA DANE • 1982 • Hardy Rod, Conway Gary • MTV • ASL

SARA LAR SIG FOLKVETT • 1937 • Molander Gustaf • SWD • SARA LEARNS MANNERS

SARA LEARNS MANNERS see **SARA LAR SIG FOLKVETT** • 1937

SARAB, AS- • 1970 • Shinnawi Anwar Ash- • EGY • MIRAGE, LE

SARABA HAKOBUNE • 1984 • Terayama Shuji • JPN • FAREWELL TO THE ARK

SARABA ITOSHIKI HITOYO • 1988 • Harada Masato • JPN • FAREWELL TO MY SWEETHEART

SARABA MOSUKUWA GURENTAI • 1968 • Horikawa Hiromichi • JPN • GOODBYE MOSCOW

SARABA NATSU NO HIKARI • 1968 • Yoshida Yoshishige • JPN • FAREWELL TO SUMMER LIGHT

SARABA RABAURU • 1954 • *Tsuburaya Eiji* • JPN

SARABAND FOR DEAD LOVERS • 1948 • Dearden Basil, Relph Michael • UKN • SARABAND (USA)

SARABAND FOR THE 17TH REGIMENT • 1976 • Pogacnik Joze • SHT • YGS

SARABAND (USA) see **SARABAND FOR DEAD LOVERS** • 1948

SARABANDE ET VARIATIONS • 1964 • Vuilleme Gilbert • SWT

SARACEN BLADE, THE • 1954 • Castle William • USA

SARACENS, THE (USA) see **PIRATA DEL DIAVOLO, IL** • 1963

SARACINESCA • 1918 • Roberti Roberto Leone • ITL

SARAGOSSA MANUSCRIPT, THE (USA) see **REKOPIS ZNALEZIONY W SARAGOSSIE** • 1965

SARAH • 1975 • SAF

SARAH • 1982 • Dugowson Maurice • FRN

SARAH AND SON • 1930 • Arzner Dorothy • USA

SARAH DIT, LEILA DIT • 1983 • Buyens Frans • BLG

SARAH JACKSON • 1980 • MacDonald Ramuna • MTV • CND

SARAH LAWRENCE • 1940 • Van Dyke Willard • DOC • USA

SARAH, MY DEAR see **SARIKA, DRAGAM** • 1971

SARAH T. -PORTRAIT OF A TEENAGE ALCOHOLIC • 1975 • Donner Richard • TVM • USA

SARAH VAUGHN AND HERB JEFFRIES • 1950 • Cowan Will • SHT • USA • KID ORY AND HIS CREOLE JAZZ BAND ○ MAHOGANY MUSIC

SARAHANDRI • 1922 • Painter Baburao • IND

SARAH'S HERO • 1911 • Stow Percy • UKN

SARAIIMAN CHUSHINGURA see **SALARY-MAN CHUSHINGURA** • 1960

SARAJEVO • 1955 • Kortner Fritz • AUS • UM THRON UND LIEBE

SARAJEVO ASSASSINATION, THE see **SARAJEVSKI ATENTAT** • 1975

SARAJEVO (UKN) see **DE MAYERLING A SARAJEVO** • 1940

SARAJEVSKI ATENTAT • 1968 • Hadzic Fadil • YGS • ASSASSINATION OF CROWN PRINCE FERDINAND ○ ASSASSINATION AT SARAJEVO

SARAJEVSKI ATENTAT • 1975 • Bulajic Velko • YGS, CZC • ATENTAT U SARAJEVU ○ SARAJEVO ASSASSINATION, THE ○ DAY THAT SHOOK THE WORLD, THE ○ ASSASSINATION IN SARAJEVO ○ ASSASSINATION AT SARAJEVO ○ ASSASSINATION

SARANA • 1967 • Pieris Asoka • SLN • HAVEN

SARANDA • 1970 • Mollica Nino • ITL

SARANG BANK SONNIM KWA OMONI • 1962 • Shin Sang-Okk • KOR • MY MOTHER AND THE ROOMER

SARANNO UOMINI • 1957 • Siano Silvio • ITL, SPN

SARANSH • 1984 • Bhatt Mahesh • IND • GIST

SARARIIMAN AKUTO JUTSU • 1968 • Sugawa Eizo • JPN • HOW TO BE THE WORST OF OFFICE WORKERS

SARASWATHI SABATHAM • 1966 • Nagarajan A. P. • IND

SARASWATI CHANDRA • 1969 • Saraya Govind • IND

SARAT • 1974 • Ovadia George • ISR

SARATI LE TERRIBLE • 1923 • Mercanton Louis, Hervil Rene • FRN

SARATI LE TERRIBLE • 1937 • Hugon Andre • FRN

SARATOGA • 1937 • Conway Jack • USA

SARATOGA-KOFFER, DER • 1918 • Meinert Rudolf • FRG

SARATOGA TRUNK • 1945 • Wood Sam • USA

SARAVA BRASIL DOS MIL ESPIRITOS • 1972 • Schneider Miguel O. • DOC • BRZ

SARDANAPALO • 1910 • De Liguoro Giuseppe • ITL

SARDAR PATEL • 1990 • Mehta Ketan • IND

SARDINIAN PROJECT, THE • Chambers Jack • DOC • UKN

SARDONICUS see **MR. SARDONICUS** • 1961

SARENG BOU • 1977 • Mamun Abdullah Al • BNG • SURVIVORS, THE ○ SAILOR'S WIFE

SARG AUS HONGKONG, EIN • 1964 • Kohler Manfred R. • FRG, FRN • COFFIN FROM HONG KONG, A (USA)

SARG BLEIBT HEUTE ZU, DER • 1967 • Comas Ramon • FRG, SPN • COFFIN STAYS SHUT TODAY, THE

SARGA ARNYEK • 1920 • *Lukas Paul* • HNG

SARGA CSIKO • 1937 • Pasztor Bela • HNG

SARGAM • 1950 • *Kapoor Raj* • IND
SARGE • 1970 • Colla Richard A. • USA • SARGE: THE BADGE OR THE CROSS ○ BADGE OR THE CROSS, THE
SARGE GOES TO COLLEGE • 1947 • Jason Will • USA
SARGE: THE BADGE OR THE CROSS see **SARGE** • 1970
SARGENTO GETULIO • 1982 • Penna Hermano • BRZ • SERGEANT GETULIO
SARGENTO PEREZ, EL • 1971 • *Cineprod Internacionale* • MXC
SARGIE'S PLAYMATE, THE • 1931 • Edwards Harry J. • SHT • USA
SARI MERSEDES • 1987 • Okan Tunc • TRK, FRN, SWT • FIKRIMIN INCE GULU ○ YELLOW MERCEDES, THE
SARIE MARAIS • 1931 • SAF
SARIE MARAIS • 1949 • SAF
SARIKA, DRAGAM • 1971 • Sandor Pal • HNG • SARAH, MY DEAR
SARIKAT SAYFEYA • 1987 • Nassrallah Yousry • EGY • SOMERSAULT
SARILHOS DE FRALDAS • 1966 • Esteves Constantino • PRT
SARIPINAR 1914 see **SEY SARSILIYOR** • 1986
SARJA • 1987 • Dutta Raj • IND
SARK YILDIZI • 1967 • Tengiz Asaf • TRK • EASTERN STAR, THE
SARKARI PRASER • 1926 • Painter Baburao • IND
SARMASIK GULLERI • 1968 • Saydam Nejat • TRK • CLIMBING ROSES
SARMISTHA • 1939 • Mitra Naresh • IND
SARNEVESHT • 1968 • Aghanikyan Hekmat • IRN • PREDESTINATION
SARONG GIRL • 1943 • Dreifuss Arthur • USA
SARONS ROS OCH GUBBARNA I KNOHULT • 1968 • Ohlsson Ake • SWD • ROSE OF SHARON AND THE OLD MEN OF KNOHULT, THE
SARRAOUNIA • 1986 • Hondo Abib Med • BRK
SARRE, PLEINS FEUX • 1951 • Alekan Henri, Bonniere Rene • SHT • FRN
SARSAKHT • 1968 • Poorsaeid Esmaeil • IRN • OBSTINATE
SARTANA • 1967 • Cardone Alberto • ITL, FRG
SARTANA, ANGEL OF DEATH see **SONO SARTANA IL VOSTRO BECCHINO** • 1969
SARTANA BETE UM DEINEN TOD see **...SE INCONTRI SARTANA PREQA PER LA TUA MORTE** • 1968
SARTANA NELLA VALLE DEGLI AVVOLTOI • 1970 • Mauri Roberto • ITL
SARTANA NEVER FORGIVES see **SARTANA NO PERDONE** • 1968
SARTANA NO PERDONE • 1968 • Balcazar Alfonso • SPN, ITL • SARTANA NON PERDONA (ITL) ○ SARTANA NEVER FORGIVES ○ SONORA
SARTANA NON PERDONA (ITL) see **SARTANA NO PERDONE** • 1968
SARTANA, PRAY FOR YOUR DEATH see **...SE INCONTRI SARTANA PREQA PER LA TUA MORTE** • 1968
SARTANI • 1972 • Ganda Oumarou • SHT • NGR • SAITANE ○ SATAN
SARTORI STRESS • 1984 • Gobron Jean-Noel • BLG
SARTRE PAR LUI-MEME • 1976 • Astruc Alexandre, Contat Michel • DOC • FRN
SARU BIMA • 1967 • Ramachandran L. S. • SLN • FERTILE LAND
SARUMBA • 1950 • Gering Marion • USA, CUB
SARUTALI • 1968 • Popescu-Gopo Ion • ANS • RMN • KISS ME QUICK
SARUTOBI see **IBUN SARUTOBI SASUKE** • 1965
SARUTUL • 1965 • Bratu Lucian • RMN • KISS, THE
SARVTID • 1943 • Sucksdorff Arne • DCS • SWD • REINDEER TIME ○ REINDEER PEOPLE
SAS A SAN SALVADOR see **S.A.S. A SAN SALVADOR** • 1982
SASABUE OMON • 1969 • Tanaka Tokuzo • JPN • GIRL WITH BAMBOO LEAVES
SASAKI KOJIRO • 1951 • Inagaki Hiroshi • JPN • KOJIRO SASAKI
SASAKI KOJIRO • 1967 • Inagaki Hiroshi • JPN • KOJIRO
SASAME YUKI • 1983 • Ichikawa Kon • JPN • FINE SNOW
SASAMEYUKI • 1950 • Abe Yutaka • JPN • MAKIOKA SISTERS, THE
SASAMEYUKI • 1959 • Shima Koji • JPN • MAKIOKA SISTERS, THE
SASAYAKU SHIBIJIN • 1963 • Murayama Sadao • JPN • WHISPERING DEAD BEAUTY
SASAYASHI NO JOE • 1967 • Saito Koichi • JPN • WHISPERING JOE (USA)
SASEK A KRALOVNA • 1987 • Chytilova Vera • CZC • JESTER AND THE QUEEN, THE
SASHA -LITTLE SASHA see **SASHA -SASHENKA** • 1967
SASHA -SASHENKA • 1967 • Chetverikov Vitali • USS • SASHA -LITTLE SASHA ○ ACTING ACTRESS
SASHA'S FIRST STEPS IN LIFE • 1956 • Schweitzer Mikhail • USA
SASHKA LE SEMINARISTE • 1915 • Protazanov Yakov • USS
SASIEDZI • 1969 • Scibor-Rylski Aleksander • PLN • NEIGHBOURS, THE
SASKATCHEWAN • 1954 • Walsh Raoul • USA • O'ROURKE OF THE ROYAL MOUNTED (UKN)
SASKATCHEWAN -45° BELOW • 1969 • Kent Larry • CND
SASKATCHEWAN JUBILEE • 1965 • Crawley Budge • DOC • CND
SASKATCHEWAN -LAND ALIVE • 1980 • Chapman Christopher • DOC • CND
SASKATCHEWAN TRAVELLER • 1956 • Haldane Don • SHT • CND
SASKATOON, LA MESURE • 1974 • Regnier Michel • DOC • CND
SASKIN HAFIYE KILLINGE KARSI • 1967 • Baytan Natuk • TRK • STUNNED DETECTIVE VS. KILLING
SASOM I EN SPEGEL • 1961 • Bergman Ingmar • SWD • THROUGH A GLASS DARKLY (UKN)
SASORI • 1967 • Mizukawa Junzo • JPN • SCORPION
SASQUATCH • 1978 • Ragozzini Ed • USA
SASQUATCH SUMMER • 1983 • Woodland James • CND
SASSO IN BOCCA, IL • 1970 • Ferrara Giuseppe • ITL • SECRET DOSSIER OF THE MAFIA ○ STONE IN THE MOUTH
SASSY CATS • 1933 • *Mintz Charles (P)* • ANS • USA
SASUKE AGAINST THE WIND • 1973 • Shinoda Masahiro • JPN
SASUKE AND HIS COMEDIANS see **SANADA FUUNROKU** • 1963
SATAN see **BRENN, HEXE, BRENN** • 1969
SATAN see **SARTANI** • 1972
SATAN AND THE WOMAN • 1928 • King Burton L. • USA
SATAN BUG, THE • 1965 • Sturges John • USA
SATAN DEFEATED • 1911 • *Pathe* • FRN
SATAN DIKTATOR • 1920 • Linke Edmund • FRG
SATAN EN PRISON • 1907 • Melies Georges • FRN • SATAN IN PRISON (USA)
SATAN FINDS MISCHIEF • 1908 • *Pathe Freres* • FRN
SATAN GOES TO TOWN see **DIABO DESCEU A VILA, O** • 1979
SATAN IN HIGH HEELS • 1962 • Intrator Jerald • USA
SATAN IN PRISON (USA) see **SATAN EN PRISON** • 1907
SATAN IN SABLES • 1925 • Flood James • USA
SATAN IN SOFIA • 1921 • Gendov Vassil • BUL
SATAN IN SYDNEY • 1918 • Smith Beaumont • ASL
SATAN IS DEAD.. AND WELL AND LIVING IN LONDON see **SATANIC RITES OF DRACULA, THE** • 1973
SATAN JUNIOR • 1919 • Blache Herbert • USA • DIANA ARDWAY
SATAN LEADS THE DANCE see **ET SATAN CONDUIT LE BAL** • 1962
SATAN LOCKT MIT LIEBE, DER • 1960 • Jugert Rudolf • FRG
SATAN MCALLISTER'S HEIR see **RIGHTFUL HEIR, THE** • 1914
SATAN MET A LADY • 1936 • Dieterle William • USA
SATAN MIT DEN ROTEN HAAREN, DER • 1964 • Stummer Alfons • FRG
SATAN MURDERS, THE • 1974 • Swift Lela • TVM • USA
SATAN NEVER SLEEPS • 1962 • McCarey Leo • USA, UKN • DEVIL NEVER SLEEPS, THE ○ FLIGHT FROM TERROR ○ CHINA STORY
SATAN NO TSUME • 1959 • Wakabayashi Eijiro • JPN • MAJIN NO TSUME ○ CLAWS OF SATAN, THE
SATAN OF ALL HORRORS see **SATANAS DE TODOS LOS HORRORES** • 1972
SATAN ON A RAMPAGE • 1911 • *Eclipse* • SHT • FRN
SATAN ON EARTH • 1918 • *Gaumont* • SHT • USA
SATAN ON MISCHIEF BENT • 1911 • *Urban* • USA
SATAN OPIUM • 1915 • Dessauer Siegfried • FRG
SATAN OR THE DRAMA OF HUMANITY (USA) see **SATANA** • 1911
SATAN SANDERSON • 1915 • Noble John W. • USA
SATAN TOWN • 1926 • Mortimer Edmund • USA
SATAN TRIUMPHANT • Mosjoukine Ivan • FRN
SATAN TRIUMPHANT see **SATANA LIKUYUSHCHII** • 1917
SATANA • 1911 • Maggi Luigi • ITL • SATAN OR THE DRAMA OF HUMANITY (USA)
SATANA LIKUYUSHCHII • 1917 • Protazanov Yakov • USS • SATAN TRIUMPHANT
SATANAS • 1916 • Feuillade Louis • FRN
SATANAS • 1919 • Murnau F. W. • FRG
SATANAS DE TODOS LOS HORRORES • 1972 • Soler Julian • MXC • SATAN OF ALL HORRORS
SATANIC GAMES see **PAARUNGEN** • 1967
SATANIC RITES OF DRACULA, THE • 1973 • Gibson Alan • UKN • SATAN IS DEAD.. AND WELL AND LIVING IN LONDON ○ DRACULA AND HIS VAMPIRE BRIDE ○ COUNT DRACULA AND HIS VAMPIRE BRIDE ○ DRACULA IS DEAD AND WELL AND LIVING IN LONDON
SATANICO, EL • 1966 • Diaz Morales Jose • MXC, PRC
SATANICO PANDEMONIO • 1973 • *Hollywood* • MXC
SATANIK • 1967 • Vivarelli Piero • ITL, SPN
SATANIS, THE DEVIL'S MASS • 1970 • Laurent Ray • DOC • USA
SATANIST, THE • 1968 • Spencer Zoltan G. • USA • SUCCUBUS
SATANISTS, THE (UKN) see **ANGELI BIANCHI.. ANGELI NERI** • 1969
SATAN'S AMAZON • 1915 • Coleby A. E. • UKN
SATAN'S BED • 1965 • Smith Marshall, Tamijian • USA
SATAN'S BLACK WEDDING • 1976 • Miller Phillip • USA
SATAN'S BLADE • 1984 • Castillo Scott Jr. • USA
SATAN'S BREW (USA) see **SATANSBRATEN** • 1976
SATAN'S CASTLE • 1913 • *Ambrosio* • ITL
SATAN'S CHEERLEADERS • 1976 • Clark Greydon • USA
SATAN'S CHILDREN • 1975 • Wiezycki Joe • USA
SATAN'S CHOICE • 1965 • Shebib Donald • CND
SATAN'S CLAW see **SATAN'S SKIN** • 1970
SATAN'S CRADLE • 1949 • Beebe Ford • USA
SATAN'S DOG see **PLAY DEAD** • 1985
SATAN'S FEATS IN THE VILLAGE OF LEVA-E-TRAZ see **PROEZAS DE SATANAS NA VILA DE LEVA-E-TRAZ** • 1968
SATAN'S FIVE WARNINGS see **CINCO ADVERTENCIAS DE SATANAS, LAS** • 1938
SATAN'S FIVE WARNINGS see **CINCO ADVERTENCIAS DE SATANAS, LAS** • 1945
SATAN'S FIVE WARNINGS see **CINCO ADVERTENCIAS DE SATANAS, LAS** • 1969
SATAN'S HARVEST • 1970 • Montgomery George • SAF
SATAN'S LOVERS see **AMANTES DEL DIABLO, LES** • 1971
SATAN'S MEMOIRS (USA) see **HERZOGIN SATANELLA** • 1919
SATAN'S MISTRESS see **DEVIL'S MATE, THE** • 1966
SATAN'S MISTRESS see **DARK EYES** • 1980
SATAN'S PRIVATE DOOR • 1917 • Haydon J. Charles • USA
SATAN'S RHAPSODY (USA) see **RAPSODIA SATANICA** • 1915
SATAN'S RIVAL • 1911 • *Pathe* • FRN
SATAN'S SADISTS • 1970 • Adamson Al • USA
SATAN'S SATELLITES • 1958 • Brannon Fred C. • USA
SATAN'S SCHOOL FOR GIRLS • 1973 • Rich David Lowell • TVM • USA
SATAN'S SISTER • 1925 • Pearson George • UKN
SATAN'S SKIN • 1970 • Haggard Piers • UKN • BLOOD ON SATAN'S CLAW (USA) ○ DEVIL'S TOUCH, THE ○ SATAN'S CLAW
SATAN'S SLAVE see **SATAN'S SLAVES** • 1976
SATAN'S SLAVES • 1976 • Warren Norman J. • UKN • SATAN'S SLAVE
SATAN'S SMITHY • 1909 • *Pathe* • SHT • FRN
SATAN'S STORIES • Svitacek Vladimir, Hornicek Miroslav • CZC
SATAN'S SUPPER see **CATACLYSM** • 1972
SATAN'S SWORD see **DAIBOSATSU TOGE** • 1960
SATAN'S TEMPTATION see **VASVASE SHITAN** • 1967
SATAN'S TRIANGLE • 1975 • Roley Sutton • TVM • USA
SATAN'S VICTIM (USA) see **SAYTANI CHAKKAR** • 1933
SATAN'S WAITIN' • 1954 • Freleng Friz • ANS • USA
SATAN'S WOMAN see **DEVIL'S MATE, THE** • 1966
SATANSBRATEN • 1976 • Fassbinder R. W. • FRG • SATAN'S BREW (USA)
SATANSKETTEN • 1921 • Lasko Leo • FRG
SATANSKORAAL • 1959 • SAF
SATAR KHAN • 1973 • Hatami Ali • IRN
SATCHEL GAME, THE • 1913 • *Harlow John* • USA
SATCHMO THE GREAT • 1957 • *Murrow Edward R./ Friendly Fred W. (P)* • DOC • USA • SAGA OF SATCHMO
SATDEE NIGHT • 1973 • Armstrong Gillian • SHT • ASL
SATELITE CHIFLADO, EL • 1956 • Saraceni Julio • ARG • WHISTLE SATELLITE, THE
SATELLITE • 1970 • Schifano Mario • ITL
SATELLITE DE VENUS, LE • 1977 • Kaplan Nelly • FRN
SATELLITE DEL BUON UMORE, IL see **PER LE VIE DELLA CITTA** • 1956
SATELLITE IN THE SKY • 1956 • Dickson Paul • UKN • FLAME IN THE SKY
SATELLITE OF BLOOD see **FIRST MAN INTO SPACE** • 1959
SATELLITES OF THE SUN • 1974 • Goldsmith Sidney • CND
SATH SAMUDURU • 1967 • Gunasinghe Siri • SLN • SEVEN SEAS
SATHI • 1938 • *Sircar B. N. (P)* • IND
SATHYAM THAVARATHE • 1968 • Selvaraj Pondy • IND • ABIDE BY TRUTH
SATHYAMAY JAYAM • 1967 • Rama Rao P. N. • IND • VICTORY LIES IN TRUTH
SATI • 1987 • Sen Aparna • IND
SATI see **DAKSHYA YAGNA** • 1923
SATI see **DAKSHA YAGNA** • 1934
SATI AHALYA • 1949 • Painter Vasant • IND
SATI MANAHANDA • 1923 • Phalke Dada • IND
SATI PADMINI • 1923 • Painter Baburao • IND
SATI PARVATI • 1919 • *Narayandas D./ Patel M. (P)* • IND
SATI PINGALA • 1937 • Kale D. K. • IND
SATI SAVITRI • 1926 • *Maharashtra* • IND
SATI SAVITRI • 1932 • Shah • IND
SATI SAVITRI • 1933 • Reddy H. M. • IND
SATI SAVITRI • 1934 • *East India Film* • IND
SATI SAVITRI • 1948 • IND
SATI SULOCHANA • 1920 • *Hindustan* • IND
SATI SULOCHANA • 1934 • *Bharat Laxmi* • IND
SATI SULOCHANA • 1934 • *South India Movietone* • IND
SATI SULOCHANA • 1936 • *Shree Godawari Cinetone* • IND
SATI SULOCHANA • 1937 • IND
SATI SULOCHANA see **SATI VIJAY** • 1948
SATI TARA • 1925 • *Hindustan* • IND • WAR BETWEEN WALI AND SUGRIVA
SATI TULASI • 1949 • *Iyyangar Pandurang* • IND
SATI VIJAY • 1930 • IND
SATI VIJAY • 1948 • Parmar K. J. • IND • SATI SULOCHANA
SATI VIRMATI • 1921 • *National* • IND
SATI VRINDA • Gajbar Bal • IND
SATIEMANIA • 1978 • Gasparovic Zdenko • YGS
SATIN AND CALICO • 1917 • Blackton J. Stuart • SHT • USA
SATIN AND GINGHAM • 1912 • *Lubin* • USA
SATIN GIRL, THE • 1923 • Rosson Arthur • USA
SATIN MUSHROOM, THE • 1969 • Brown Don • USA • SOFT WARM EXPERIENCE, A
SATIN SLIPPER, THE • 1985 • de Oliveira Manoel • PRT
SATIN SUITE • Drexler Philip T. • USA
SATIN VENGEANCE see **NAKED VENGEANCE** • 1986
SATIN WOMAN, THE • 1927 • Lang Walter • USA
SATIRICOSISSIMO • 1970 • Laurenti Mariano • ITL
SATIRISTS, THE see **SATYRYCY** • 1953
SATISFACTION see **SWEET LITTLE ROCK AND ROLLER** • 1987
SATISFIED CUSTOMERS • 1954 • Rasinski Connie • ANS • USA
SATISFIERS OF ALPHA BLUE see **ALPHA BLUE** • 1981
SATOGASHI GA KOWARERU TOKI • 1967 • Imai Tadashi • JPN • WHEN THE SUGAR COOKIE CRUMBLES ○ SATOSHI GA KOWARERU TOKI ○ WHEN THE SUGAR CAKE BREAKS ○ WHEN THE COOKIE CRUMBLES ○ WHEN SUGAR COOKIES ARE BROKEN
SATOMI HAKKEN DEN • 1955 • Kono Hisashi • JPN
SATOMI HAKKEN-DEN • 1959 • Uchide Kokichi • JPN • EIGHT BRAVE BROTHERS
SATOMI HAKKEN DEN • 1984 • Fukasaku Kinji • JPN • LEGEND OF THE DOGS OF SATOMI
SATORI • 1973 • Higashi Yoichi • JPN • JAPANESE DEMON, A
SATOSHI GA KOWARERU TOKI see **SATOGASHI GA KOWARERU TOKI** • 1967
SATRAPIS, O • 1968 • Andritsos Kostas • GRC • DESPOT, THE
SATRIA • 1971 • Rojik Omar • MLY • CHIVALROUS HUNCHBACK, THE
SATSUEIJI ROMANSU-RENAI ANNAI • 1932 • Gosho Heinosuke • JPN • ROMANCE AT THE STUDIO: GUIDANCE TO LOVE ○ STUDIO ROMANCE, A
SATSUJINKEN 2 • 1973 • Ozawa Shigehiro • JPN
SATSUJINKYO SHIDAI • 1966 • Kuri Yoji • ANS • JPN • AU FOU!
SATSUJINKYOJIDAI • 1967 • Okamoto Kihachi • JPN • EPOCH OF MURDER MADNESS ○ AGE OF ASSASSINS, THE
SATSUJINSHA NO KAO • 1950 • Kinugasa Teinosuke • JPN • FACE OF A MURDERER, THE
SATSUJINSHA O KESE • 1964 • Masuda Toshio • JPN • RUB OUT THE KILLERS
SATSUMA HIKYAKU • 1938 • Ito Daisuke • JPN • SAD TUNE
SATSUMA HIKYAKU-TOKAI HEN • 1932 • Ito Daisuke • JPN • MESSENGER TO SATSUMA
SATSUMA NO MISSHI see **KURAMA TENGU: SATSUMA NO MISSHI** • 1941
SATTAWIS DOWN • 1973 • Kaul Awtar Krishan • IND • TWENTY-SEVEN DOWN -VARANASI EXPRESS ○ 27 DOWN
SATU KUNINKAASTA JOLLA EI OLLUT SYNDANTA see **KUNINGAS JOLLA EI OLLUT SYNDANTA** • 1983

SATU TITEK DIGARISON • 1971 • Amin M. • MLY
SATUJA VALLASTA • 1970-72 • Partanen Heikki, Rautoma Riitta • ASS • FNL • FABLES ABOUT POWER
SATURDAY • 1919 • Kellette John William • SHT • USA
SATURDAY see **SOBOTA** • 1944
SATURDAY AFTERNOON • 1926 • Edwards Harry J. • SHT • USA
SATURDAY AFTERNOON BLOOD SACRIFICE: TV PLUG: LITTLE COBRA DANCE • 1957 • Jacobs Ken • SHT • USA
SATURDAY ANGEL see **DOYOBI NO TENSHI** • 1954
SATURDAY EVENING see **SUBOTOM UVECE** • 1957
SATURDAY EVENING DANCE see **TANZ AM SONNABEND – MORD?** • 1962
SATURDAY EVENING PUSS • 1950 • Hanna William, Barbera Joseph • ANS • USA
SATURDAY EVENINGS see **LORDAGSKVALLAR** • 1933
SATURDAY HOLIDAY, A • 1913 • Dillon Eddie • USA
SATURDAY IN THE LIFE OF GRAZYNA A. AND JERZY T., A see **SOBOTA GRAZYNY A. I JERZEGO T.** • 1969
SATURDAY ISLAND • 1951 • Heisler Stuart • UKN • ISLAND OF DESIRE (USA)
SATURDAY, JULY 27, 1963 see **1963. JULIUS 27. SZOMBAT** • 1963
SATURDAY LOVELY SATURDAY • 1971 • *Crowther Leslie* • UKN
SATURDAY MEN, THE • 1962 • Fletcher John • UKN
SATURDAY MORNING • 1922 • Roach Hal • SHT • USA
SATURDAY MORNING • 1971 • MacKenzie Kent • DOC • USA
SATURDAY NIGHT • 1922 • De Mille Cecil B. • USA
SATURDAY NIGHT • 1950 • York Derek • UKN
SATURDAY NIGHT AND SUNDAY MORNING • 1960 • Reisz Karel • UKN
SATURDAY NIGHT AT THE BATHS • 1976 • Buckley David • USA
SATURDAY NIGHT BATH IN APPLE VALLEY • 1965 • Myhers John • USA • SATURDAY NIGHT IN APPLE VALLEY
SATURDAY NIGHT DANCE, THE see **BALUL DE SIMBATA SEARA** • 1968
SATURDAY NIGHT FEVER • 1977 • Badham John • USA
SATURDAY NIGHT IN APPLE VALLEY see **SATURDAY NIGHT BATH IN APPLE VALLEY** • 1965
SATURDAY NIGHT KID, THE • 1929 • Sutherland A. Edward • USA
SATURDAY NIGHT OUT • 1964 • Hartford-Davis Robert • UKN
SATURDAY NIGHT REVUE • 1937 • Lee Norman • UKN
SATURDAY NIGHT SQUARE DANCE • 1949 • *Boyd Jim* • SHT • USA
SATURDAY NIGHT SWING CLUB, THE • 1938 • French Lloyd • SHT • USA
SATURDAY SHOPPING • 1903 • Hepworth Cecil M. • UKN • SATURDAY'S SHOPPING (USA)
SATURDAY THE 14TH • 1981 • Cohen Howard R. • USA
SATURDAY THE 14TH STRIKES BACK • 1988 • Cohen Howard R. • USA
SATURDAY TRAIN, THE see **TRENO DEL SABATO, IL** • 1964
SATURDAY'S CHILDREN • 1929 • La Cava Gregory • USA
SATURDAY'S CHILDREN • 1940 • Sherman Vincent • USA
SATURDAY'S HERO • 1951 • Miller David • USA • IDOLS IN THE DUST (UKN) ○ HERO, THE
SATURDAY'S HEROES • 1937 • Killy Edward • USA
SATURDAY'S LESSON • 1929 • McGowan Robert • SHT • USA
SATURDAY'S MILLIONS • 1933 • Sedgwick Edward • USA
SATURDAY'S SHOPPING (USA) see **SATURDAY SHOPPING** • 1903
SATURDAY'S WAGES • 1905 • Stow Percy • UKN
SATURN 3 • 1980 • Donen Stanley • UKN
SATURN IS HARDLY VISIBLE see **PUT V SATURN** • 1968
SATURNIN • 1939 • Noe Yvan • FRN • SATURNIN DE MARSEILLE
SATURNIN DE MARSEILLE see **SATURNIN** • 1939
SATURNIN ET COMPAGNIE • Tourane Jean • SHT • FRN
SATURNIN ET LE VACA VACA • Tourane Jean • FRN
SATURNIN OU LE BON ALLUMEUR • 1921 • Feuillade Louis • FRN
SATY DELAJI CLOVECKA • 1912 • Urban Max, Sedlacek Jara • CZC • CLOTHES MAKE MAN
SATYAJIT RAY –FILM MAKER • 1982 • Benegal Shyam • DOC • IND
SATYAM, SHIVAM, SUNDARAM • 1977 • Kapoor Raj • IND
SATYAVAN SAVITRI • 1913 • Phalke Dada • IND
SATYAWAN SAVITRI • 1949 • Vyas Manibhai • IND
SATYR AND THE LADY, THE • 1911 • *Thanhouser* • USA
SATYRE, LE see **MONSIEUR SANS-GENE** • 1935
SATYRICON • 1969 • Polidoro Gian Luigi • ITL
SATYRICON see **FELLINI-SATYRICON** • 1969
SATYRYCY • 1953 • Perski Ludwik • DOC • PLN • SATIRISTS, THE
SAUCE AND SENORITAS • 1920 • Brown Melville • SHT • USA
SAUCE FOR THE GANDER • 1915 • *Osterman Kathryn* • USA
SAUCE FOR THE GANDER • 1916 • Horne James W. • SHT • USA
SAUCE FOR THE GOOSE • 1913 • Lytton L. Rogers, Young James • USA
SAUCE FOR THE GOOSE • 1917 • *Triangle* • USA
SAUCE FOR THE GOOSE • 1917 • Christie Al • *Christie* • USA
SAUCE FOR THE GOOSE • 1918 • Edwards Walter • USA
SAUCEPAN JOURNEY, THE see **KASTRULLRESAN** • 1950
SAUCY AUSSIE, THE • 1963 • Bowley Walter • USA • OBSCENE COUCH, THE ○ OBLONG COUCH, THE
SAUCY MADELINE • 1918 • Jones F. Richard • SHT • USA
SAUCY SAUSAGES • 1929 • Lantz Walter, Nolan William • ANS • USA
SAUCY SUE • 1909 • *Lubin* • USA
SAUERBRUCH • 1954 • Hansen Rolf • FRG • DAS WAR MEIN LEBEN
SAUERKRAUT SYMPHONY, A • 1916 • *Hamilton Lloyd V.* • USA
SAUL ALINSKY WENT TO WAR • 1968 • Brittain Don, Pearson Peter • CND
SAUL AND DAVID • 1909 • Blackton J. Stuart • USA
SAUL AND DAVID (USA) see **SAUL E DAVID** • 1965
SAUL E DAVID • 1965 • Baldi Marcello • ITL, SPN • SAUL Y DAVID ○ SAUL AND DAVID (USA)
SAUL Y DAVID see **SAUL E DAVID** • 1965
SAULO DE TARSO • 1966 • Ardavin Cesar • SHT • SPN
SAUMON ATLANTIQUE, LE see **A PROPOS D'UNE RIVIERE** • 1955
SAUR SEPUH • 1989 • INN
SAUSAGE MACHINE, THE • 1897 • *Biograph* • USA
SAUSAGES • 1905 • Williamson James • UKN
SAUSALITO • 1948 • Stauffacher Frank • SHT • USA
SAUSALITO • 1967 • Warhol Andy • USA
SAUT, LE see **SALTO, O** • 1967
SAUT A LA COUVERTURE • 1895 • Lumiere Louis • FRN • BRIMADE DANS UNE CASERNE
SAUT DANS LE VIDE, LE see **SALTO NEL VUOTO** • 1979
SAUT DE L'ANGE, LE • 1971 • Boisset Yves • FRN, ITL • DA PARTE DEGLI AMICI FIRMATO MAFIA (ITL) ○ COBRA (UKN) ○ ANGEL'S LEAP ○ CODE NAME: COBRA
SAUT HUMIDIFIE DE M. PICK • 1900 • Blache Alice • FRN
SAUTE MA VILLE • 1968 • Akerman Chantal • SHT • BLG
SAUTELA BHAI • 1962 • *Biswas Anil* • IND
SAUTER-FINEGAN ORCHESTRA, THE • 1955 • *Universal* • SHT • USA
SAUTERELLE see **GRANDE SAUTERELLE, LA** • 1967
SAUVAGE, LE • 1975 • Rappeneau Jean-Paul • FRN, ITL • LOVERS LIKE US (USA) ○ CALL ME SAVAGE (UKN) ○ SAVAGE, THE
SAUVAGE ET BEAU • 1984 • Rossif Frederic • DOC • FRN
SAUVE QUI PEUT • 1980 • Godard Jean-Luc • FRN, SWT • EVERY MAN FOR HIMSELF (USA) ○ SLOW MOTION (UKN) ○ SAUVE QUI PEUT (LA VIE) ○ VIE, LA
SAUVE QUI PEUT (LA VIE) see **SAUVE QUI PEUT** • 1980
SAUVETAGE, UN • 1913 • Pouctal Henri • FRN
SAUVETAGE EN RIVIERE • 1896 • Melies Georges • FRN • RESCUE ON THE RIVER
SAUVEUR D'EPAVES see **PORT DU DESIR, LE** • 1954
SAUVONS NOS BEBES • 1918 • Dorval Henri • CND
SAUVONS NOS SOLS see **LAND IN TRUST** • 1948
SAVAGE! • 1962 • Jones Arthur A. • USA • MISSION TO HELL
SAVAGE • 1972 • Spielberg Steven • TVM • USA • WATCH DOG
SAVAGE! • 1973 • Santiago Cirio H. • PHL
SAVAGE, THE • 1911 • *Nestor* • USA
SAVAGE, THE • Youngdeer James • USA
SAVAGE, THE • 1917 • Julian Rupert • USA
SAVAGE, THE • 1926 • Newmeyer Fred • USA
SAVAGE, THE • 1952 • Marshall George • USA • WARBONNET
SAVAGE, THE see **MACHISMO –40 GRAVES FOR 40 GUNS** • 1970
SAVAGE, THE see **SAUVAGE, LE** • 1975
SAVAGE AFRICA • 1962 • SAF
SAVAGE AMERICAN, THE see **TALISMAN, THE** • 1966
SAVAGE ATTACK AND REPULSE • 1899 • *Warwick Trading Co* • UKN
SAVAGE ATTRACTION (USA) see **HOSTAGE** • 1983
SAVAGE BEES, THE • 1976 • Geller Bruce • TVM • USA
SAVAGE BREED see **RAZZA SELVAGGIA** • 1980
SAVAGE BRIDGE • 1976 • Crawford Herold • USA
SAVAGE CURSE, THE • 1974 • Sichel John • TVM • UKN
SAVAGE DAWN • 1985 • Nuchtern Simon • USA
SAVAGE DEATH see **VAHSI OLUM** • 1967
SAVAGE DRUMS • 1951 • Berke William • USA
SAVAGE ENCOUNTER • 1980 • Buys Bernard • SAF
SAVAGE EYE, THE • 1960 • Strick Joseph, Meyers Sidney, Maddow Ben • USA
SAVAGE EYE, THE see **OCCHIO SELVAGGIO, L'** • 1967
SAVAGE FRONTIER • 1953 • Keller Harry • USA
SAVAGE GIRL, THE • 1933 • Fraser Harry L. • USA
SAVAGE GIRL'S DEVOTION, A • 1911 • *Bison* • USA
SAVAGE GUNS, THE • 1962 • Carreras Michael • USA, SPN • TIERRA BRUTAL (SPN)
SAVAGE HARBOR • 1988 • Monson Carl • USA • RAGGEDY ANNE
SAVAGE HARVEST • 1981 • Collins Robert • USA
SAVAGE HEART see **CORAZON SALVAJE** • 1968
SAVAGE HORDE, THE • 1950 • Kane Joseph • USA
SAVAGE HUNT, THE • 1981 • Scavolini Romano • ITL
SAVAGE HUNTER, A see **OASIS, THE** • 1984
SAVAGE IN THE CITY • Shadow John • HKG
SAVAGE INNOCENTS, THE • 1959 • Ray Nicholas, Bandini Baccio • UKN, ITL, FRN • DENTS DU DIABLE, LES (FRN) ○ OMBRE BIANCHE (ITL)
SAVAGE INSTINCT, THE • 1917 • Young James • USA
SAVAGE INTRUDER, THE • 1977 • Wolfe Donald • USA
SAVAGE IS LOOSE, THE • 1974 • Scott George C. • USA, MXC • SALVAJE ANDA SUELTO, UN (MXC)
SAVAGE ISLAND • 1985 • Mulargia Edoardo, Beardsley Nicholas • USA, ITL, SPN • ESCAPE FROM HELL
SAVAGE ISLANDS see **NATE AND HAYES** • 1983
SAVAGE JUSTICE • 1988 • Romero Joey • USA
SAVAGE LAND, THE see **THIS SAVAGE LAND** • 1968
SAVAGE LOVE • 1924 • Christie Al • USA
SAVAGE MAN, SAVAGE BEAST see **ULTIME GRIDA DALLA SAVANA** • 1975
SAVAGE MESSIAH • 1972 • Russell Ken • UKN
SAVAGE MUTINY • 1953 • Bennet Spencer Gordon • USA
SAVAGE PAMPAS see **PAMPA BARBARA** • 1943
SAVAGE PAMPAS see **PAMPA SALVAJE** • 1966
SAVAGE PASSIONS • 1927 • *Calhoun Alice* • USA
SAVAGE PLANET, THE see **PLANETE SAUVAGE, LA** • 1973
SAVAGE PRINCESS (UKN) see **AAN** • 1952
SAVAGE RED –OUTLAW WHITE • 1974 • Hunt Paul • USA
SAVAGE SAM • 1963 • Tokar Norman • USA
SAVAGE SARAH • 1988 • Ginnane Anthony I. • ASL
SAVAGE SEA, THE • 1975 • Stoneman John • MTV • CND
SAVAGE SEVEN, THE • 1968 • Rush Richard • USA
SAVAGE SISTERS • 1974 • Romero Eddie • USA
SAVAGE SOLDIER • Phillip Stu • USA
SAVAGE SPLENDOR • 1949 • Denis Armand • DOC • USA
SAVAGE SPORT • 1974 • Van Der Watt Keith • SAF
SAVAGE STREETS • 1985 • Steinmann Danny • USA
SAVAGE SUNDAY see **LOW BLOW** • 1986
SAVAGE TRIANGLE (USA) see **GARCON SAUVAGE, LE** • 1951
SAVAGE WATER • 1982 • Kener Paul W. • USA
SAVAGE WEEKEND • 1976 • Paulsen David • USA • KILLER BEHIND THE MASK ○ UPSTATE MURDERS, THE
SAVAGE WEEKEND • 1979 • Kirby John Mason • USA
SAVAGE WILD, THE • 1970 • Eastman Gordon • DOC • USA • WILD ARCTIC
SAVAGE WILDERNESS • 1955 • Mann Anthony • USA • LAST FRONTIER, THE (UKN)
SAVAGE WOMAN, THE • 1918 • Mortimer Edmund • USA
SAVAGE WORLD, THE • 1976 • Eastman Gordon • USA
SAVAGE/LOVE • 1981 • Clarke Shirley • USA
SAVAGES • 1972 • Ivory James • USA
SAVAGES • 1974 • Katzin Lee H. • TVM • USA
SAVAGES, THE see **SALVAJES, LOS** • 1957
SAVAGES FROM HELL see **BIG ENOUGH N' OLD ENOUGH** • 1968
SAVAGES OF ST. GIL'S BRIDGE see **SALVAJES DE PUENTE SAN GIL, LOS** • 1967
SAVAGES OF THE SEA • 1925 • Mitchell Bruce • USA
SAVALAN • 1989 • Samadi Yadollah • IRN
SAVAMALA • 1983 • Mitrovic Zika • YGS
SAVANA VIOLENTA • 1976 • Climati Antonio, Morra Mario • ITL
SAVANNAH SMILES • 1983 • De Moro Pierre • USA
SAVANT ET LE CHIMPANZE, LE • 1900 • Melies Georges • FRN • DOCTOR AND THE MONKEY, THE (USA)
SAVARONA SYNDROME, THE see **LONELY PROFESSION, THE** • 1969
SAVATE, LA • 1938 • Miller David • SHT • USA
SAVE A LITTLE SUNSHINE • 1938 • Lee Norman • UKN
SAVE AND PROTECT • 1988 • Sokurov Alexander
SAVE ME, SADIE • 1920 • Beaudine William • SHT • USA
SAVE THE CHILDREN • 1973 • Lathan Stan • DOC • USA • BROTHERS AND SISTERS IN CONCERT
SAVE THE CHILDREN FUND FILM, THE • 1971 • Loach Kenneth • SHT • UKN
SAVE THE CITY see **OCALIC MIASTO** • 1977
SAVE THE COUPONS • 1915 • Van Deusen Courtlandt • USA
SAVE THE DOG! • 1988 • Aaron Paul • TVM • USA • GO FOR BROKE
SAVE THE DROWNING MAN see **SPASITYE UTOPAYUSHCHEVO** • 1968
SAVE THE LADY • 1982 • Thau Leon • ASL
SAVE THE SHIP • 1923 • Roach Hal • SHT • USA
SAVE THE TIGER • 1973 • Avildsen John G. • USA
SAVE WHAT YOU CAN • 1985 • Marzouk Said • EGY
SAVE YOUR FACE see **SALVARE LA FACCIA** • 1969
SAVE YOUR MONEY • 1921 • Roach Hal • SHT • USA
SAVED! • 1904 • *Biograph* • USA
SAVED AT THE ALTAR • 1912 • *Pathe* • USA
SAVED BY A BURGLAR • 1909 • Booth W. R.? • UKN
SAVED BY A CAT • 1912 • *Karr Darwin* • USA
SAVED BY A CHILD (USA) see **LEFT IN TRUST** • 1911
SAVED BY A DREAM • 1909 • Williamson James? • UKN
SAVED BY A DREAM • 1914 • Batley Ethyle? • UKN
SAVED BY A DREAM • 1915 • Myers Harry • USA
SAVED BY A LIE • 1906 • Stow Percy • UKN
SAVED BY A PILLAR BOX • 1906 • Collins Alf? • UKN
SAVED BY A SCENT • 1915 • Curtis Allen • USA
SAVED BY A SHOWER • 1915 • *Asher Max* • USA
SAVED BY A SKIRT • 1915 • Davey Horace • USA
SAVED BY A SONG • 1916 • Wilson Ben • SHT • USA
SAVED BY A VISION • 1910 • *Atlas* • USA
SAVED BY A WATCH • 1914 • Mix Tom • USA
SAVED BY A WOMAN • 1901 • *Mitchell & Kenyon* • UKN
SAVED BY AIRSHIP • 1913 • *Reliance* • USA
SAVED BY AN AUTO • 1912 • *American* • USA
SAVED BY CARLO • 1909 • Coleby A. E. • UKN
SAVED BY FIRE • 1912 • *Selig* • USA
SAVED BY FIRE • 1912 • Northcote Sidney • UKN
SAVED BY HER HORSE • 1915 • Mix Tom • USA
SAVED BY HIS HORSE • 1913 • *Pathe* • USA
SAVED BY HIS OWN CHILD • 1910 • *Phoenix* • USA
SAVED BY HIS SWEETHEART • 1909 • *Lubin* • USA
SAVED BY HIS SWEETHEART • 1910 • Fitzhamon Lewin • UKN
SAVED BY LOVE • 1908 • Porter Edwin S. • USA
SAVED BY PARCEL POST • 1913 • *Irwin Wallace* • USA
SAVED BY RADIO • 1922 • Craft William James • USA • SAVED BY WIRELESS
SAVED BY TELEPHONE • 1912 • *Blackwell Carlyle* • USA
SAVED BY TELEPHONE • 1915 • *Myles Norbert A.* • USA
SAVED BY THE BELL • 1950 • Kneitel Seymour • ANS • USA
SAVED BY THE BELLE • 1939 • Parrott Charles • SHT • USA
SAVED BY THE BIOSCOPE • 1909 • *Wrench Films* • UKN
SAVED BY THE BOYS IN BLUE • 1914 • *Sawyer'S Features* • USA
SAVED BY THE ENEMY • 1913 • *Edison* • USA
SAVED BY THE FLAG • 1910 • Trimble Larry • USA
SAVED BY THE JUVENILE COURT • 1913 • *Columbine* • USA
SAVED BY THE PONY EXPRESS • 1911 • *Selig* • USA
SAVED BY THE SUN • 1914 • Calvert Charles? • UKN
SAVED BY THE TELEGRAPH • 1909 • Fitzhamon Lewin • UKN
SAVED BY THE TELEGRAPH CODE • 1908 • Stow Percy • UKN
SAVED BY THE UNION JACK • 1914 • *Bamberger Joseph (P)* • UKN
SAVED BY THEIR CHEEILD • 1914 • *Ab* • USA
SAVED BY WIRELESS • 1915 • Wright Walter • USA
SAVED BY WIRELESS see **SAVED BY RADIO** • 1922
SAVED FROM A LIFE OF CRIME • 1914 • Marston Theodore • USA
SAVED FROM A TERRIBLE DEATH • 1908 • Fitzhamon Lewin • UKN
SAVED FROM A VAMP • 1918 • *L-Ko* • SHT • USA
SAVED FROM COURT MARTIAL • 1912 • Melford George • USA
SAVED FROM DISGRACE • 1915 • *Empire* • USA
SAVED FROM HERSELF • 1915 • *A.a.a.* • UKN
SAVED FROM HIMSELF • 1910 • *Defender* • USA
SAVED FROM HIMSELF • 1911 • Griffith D. W. • USA
SAVED FROM HIMSELF • 1915 • *Saunders Jackie* • USA
SAVED FROM SIN • 1913 • *Scardon Paul* • USA
SAVED FROM THE BURNING WRECK • 1907 • Coleby A. E.? • UKN

SAVED FROM THE HAREM • 1915 • Melville Wilbert, Sloman Edward • USA
SAVED FROM THE REDMEN • 1910 • *Bison* • USA
SAVED FROM THE SEA • 1907 • *Cricks & Sharp* • UKN
SAVED FROM THE SEA • 1908 • *Gaumont* • UKN
SAVED FROM THE SEA • 1909 • ASL
SAVED FROM THE SEA • 1909 • Fitzhamon Lewin? • UKN
SAVED FROM THE SEA • 1920 • Kellino W. P. • UKN
SAVED FROM THE SNOW • 1911 • *Eyton Bessie* • USA
SAVED FROM THE SPY • 1914 • *Captain Kettle Film* • UKN
SAVED FROM THE TITANIC • 1912 • *Gibson Dorothy* • USA
SAVED FROM THE TORRENTS • 1911 • *Bushman Francis X.* • USA
SAVED FROM THE VAMPIRE • 1915 • Henderson Dell • USA
SAVED FROM THE VIGILANTES • 1913 • Duncan William • USA
SAVED IN MID-AIR • 1913 • *Royal Film* • USA
SAVELLI, LA see **FANATISME** • 1934
SAVER OF THE ENVIRONMENT • 1973 • Greve Bredo • SHT • NRW
SAVERIO EL CRUEL • 1977 • Wulicher Ricardo • ARG • SAVERIO THE CRUEL
SAVERIO THE CRUEL see **SAVERIO EL CRUEL** • 1977
SAVETIER ET LE FINANCIER, LE • 1909 • Feuillade Louis • FRN
SAVEUR, LE • 1970 • Mardore Michel • FRN • SAVIOUR, THE (UKN)
SAVING AN AUDIENCE • 1912 • Brooke Van Dyke • USA
SAVING FLAME, THE • 1914 • *Billington Francelia* • USA
SAVING GRACE • 1986 • Young Robert Malcolm • USA
SAVING GRACE, THE • 1914 • Cabanne W. Christy • USA
SAVING LIE, THE • 1913 • *Patheplay* • USA
SAVING MABEL'S DAD • 1913 • Sennett Mack • USA
SAVING OF BILL BLEWETT, THE • 1936 • *Grierson John (P)* • DOC • UKN
SAVING OF DAN, THE • 1911 • Davis Ulysses • USA
SAVING OF FAUST, THE • 1911 • *Pathe* • FRN
SAVING OF YOUNG ANDERSON, THE • 1914 • *Reliance* • USA
SAVING PRESENCE, THE • 1914 • O'Sullivan Tony • USA
SAVING RAFFLES • 1917 • Evans Fred, Evans Joe • UKN
SAVING SIGN, THE • 1911 • *Kalem* • USA
SAVING SISTIE SUSIE • 1921 • Christie Al • USA
SAVING SONG, THE • 1941 • *Hylton Jack* • SHT • UKN
SAVING SUSIE FROM THE SEA • 1916 • *Smith Dick* • SHT • USA
SAVING THE CHILD • 1914 • *Joker* • USA
SAVING THE COLOURS • 1914 • Weston Charles • UKN
SAVING THE DESPATCHES • 1904 • *Cricks & Sharp* • UKN
SAVING THE FAMILY NAME • 1916 • Weber Lois, Smalley Phillips • USA
SAVING THE FAST MAIL • 1917 • Davis James • SHT • USA
SAVING THE GAME • 1912 • Seay Charles M. • USA
SAVING THE ROYAL MAIL • 1912 • Fitzhamon Lewin • UKN
SAVING THE SPECIAL • 1911 • *Gordon Julia Swayne* • USA
SAVINGS OF BILL BLEWETT, THE • 1937 • Watt Harry • DOC • UKN
SAVIOUR, THE see **CHIU-SHIH-CHE** • 1981
SAVIOUR, THE (UKN) see **SAVEUR, LE** • 1970
SAVITRI • 1934 • *India Film Ind.* • IND
SAVITRI • 1934 • *East India* • IND
SAVITRI • 1937 • Osten Franz • IND
SAVITRI • 1961 • *Biswas Anil (M)* • IND
SAVITRI SATYAVAN • 1933 • *Rajalaxmi T. P.* • IND
SAVITRI SATYAWAN • 1923 • IND
SAVOIR-FAIRE S'IMPOSE, LE • 1971 • Poirier Anne-Claire • DSS • CND
SAVOLTA AFFAIR, THE see **VERDAD SOBRE EL CASO SAVOLTA, LA** • 1980
SAVOY-HOTEL 217 • 1936 • Ucicky Gustav • FRG • MORD IM SAVOY
SAVOYAN BOY, THE see **GARCON SAVOYARD, LE** • 1967
SAW MILL HERO, A • 1911 • *Kalem* • USA
SAW MILL MYSTERY, THE • 1937 • Rasinski Connie • ANS • USA
SAW WOOD • 1913 • *Punch* • USA
SAWAN • 1945 • Khosla Dwarka • IND
SAWDUST • 1923 • Conway Jack • USA
SAWDUST AND SALOME • 1914 • Brooke Van Dyke • USA
SAWDUST AND SOCIETY • 1917 • *Greater Pictures* • SHT • USA
SAWDUST AND TINSEL (UKN) see **GYCKLARNAS AFTON** • 1953
SAWDUST DOLL, THE • 1919 • Bertram William • USA
SAWDUST LOVE • 1916 • *Armstrong Billy* • USA
SAWDUST PARADISE, THE • 1928 • Reed Luther • USA
SAWDUST RING see **NOVYI ATTRAKTION** • 1957
SAWDUST RING, THE • 1917 • Powell Paul, Miller Charles • USA
SAWDUST TRAIL, THE • 1924 • Sedgwick Edward • USA
SAWMILL, THE • 1921 • Semon Larry, Taurog Norman • SHT • USA
SAWMILL HAZARD, A • 1913 • *Hollister Alice* • USA
SAWNEY SAM'S DILEMMA • 1914 • *Barker* • UKN
SAWRANA -OUR REVOLUTION • 1978 • Sabatier Christian • DOC • ETH
SAWT MINA AL-MAHDI • 1956 • Salem Atef • EGY • VOIX DU PASSE, UNE
SAXOFONE • 1978 • Pozzetto Renato • ITL • SAXOPHONE
SAXON CHARM, THE • 1948 • Binyon Claude • USA • CHARMING MATT SAXON, THE
SAXOPHON-SUSI • 1928 • Lamac Carl • FRG • SUZY SAXOPHONE
SAXOPHONE see **SAXOFONE** • 1978
SAY A LITTLE PRAYER • 1987 • Rothkrans Patricia • SHT • ASL
SAY ABRACADABRA • 1952 • Baim Harold • UKN
SAY "AH!" JASPER • 1944 • Pal George • ANS • USA
SAY AMEN, SOMEBODY • 1983 • Nierenberg George T. • DOC • USA • SAY AMEN, SOMEONE
SAY AMEN, SOMEONE see **SAY AMEN, SOMEBODY** • 1983
SAY ANYTHING • 1989 • Crowe Cameron • USA
SAY ANYTHING • 1989 • Hough John • USA
SAY BOW WOW • 1964 • Brealey Gil • SHT • ASL
SAY GOODBYE, MAGGIE COLE • 1972 • Taylor Jud • TVM • USA
SAY HELLO TO YESTERDAY • 1970 • Rakoff Alvin • UKN
SAY IN YOUR COMMUNITY WITH THE AUSTRALIAN ASSISTANCE PLAN, A • 1975 • Howes Oliver • DOC • ASL
SAY IT AGAIN • 1926 • La Cava Gregory • USA
SAY IT IN FRENCH • 1938 • Stone Andrew L. • USA
SAY IT WITH BABIES • 1926 • Roach Hal • SHT • USA
SAY IT WITH DIAMONDS • 1923 • De Haven Carter • USA
SAY IT WITH DIAMONDS • 1927 • Nelson Jack • USA
SAY IT WITH DIAMONDS • 1935 • Davis Redd • UKN
SAY IT WITH FLOWERS • 1934 • Baxter John • UKN
SAY IT WITH FLOWERS see **SAG DET MED BLOMMAR** • 1952
SAY IT WITH MUSIC • 1932 • Raymond Jack • UKN
SAY IT WITH MUSIC see **SAG DET I TONER** • 1929
SAY IT WITH SABLES • 1928 • Capra Frank • USA • RECKONING, THE (UKN)
SAY IT WITH SONGS • 1929 • Bacon Lloyd • USA • LITTLE PAL
SAY-MAMA • 1985 • SAF
SAY NOTHING • Noren Andrew • SHT • USA
SAY ONE FOR ME • 1959 • Tashlin Frank • USA
SAY THAT YOU LOVE ME see **DI QUE ME QUIERES** • 1939
SAY UNCLE • 1944 • Holmes Ben • USA
SAY WHAT THEY MAY see **DIGAN LO QUE DIGAN** • 1968
SAY YES • 1986 • Yust Larry • USA
SAY YOU WANT ME • 1977 • Howes Oliver • SHT • ASL
SAY! YOUNG FELLOW • 1918 • Henabery Joseph • USA
SAYAMARO THE GREAT THIEF see **KAITO SAYAMARO** • 1928
SAYANG ANAKKU SAYANG • 1975 • Sulong Jamil • MLY • MY BELOVED CHILDREN
SAYAT NOVA • 1969 • Paradjanov Sergei • USS • COLOR OF THE POMEGRANATE (USA) ◦ TSVET GRANATA
SAYEHAYE BOLANDE BAD • 1978 • Farmanara Bahman • IRN • LONG SHADOWS OF THE WIND, THE ◦ TALL SHADOWS OF THE WIND ◦ SAIHAIEN BOLAN DE BAD ◦ SHADOWS OF THE WIND, THE
SAYIDAT EL KITAR • 1951 • Shahin Youssef • EGY • LADY OF THE TRAIN, THE ◦ SAIYIDAT AL-QIT'AR ◦ LADY IN THE TRAIN, THE
SAYILI KABADAYILAR • 1965 • Kazankaya Hasan • TRK
SAYONARA • 1957 • Logan Joshua • USA
SAYONARA KONNICHIWA • 1959 • Ichikawa Kon • JPN • GOODBYE AND GOOD DAY! ◦ GOODBYE, GOOD DAY
SAYONARA MY DARLING • 1968 • de Villa Jose • PHL • GOODBYE MY DARLING
SAYON'S BELL • 1943 • Shimizu Hiroshi • JPN
SAYS WHO? see **HVEM HAR BESTEMT..?** • 1978
SAYTANI CHAKKAR • 1933 • *Shree Narayan* • IND • SATAN'S VICTIM (USA)
SAYYID AT-TAQADDUMI, AS- • 1973 • Maleh Nabil • SYR • MONSIEUR LE PROGRESSISTE
SAZAA • 1952 • Mistry Fali • IND
SAZEN TANGE see **TANGE SAZEN** • 1934
SAZHENTSY • 1973 • Chkheidze Revaz • USS • SAPLINGS, THE
SAZISH • 1976 • Afzal Kaukab • PKS • CONSPIRACY, THE
SB ZATVARA KRUG • 1975 • Stamenkovic Miomir • YGS • SECURITY SERVICE CLOSES IN, THE
SBAGLIO DI ESSERE VIVO, LO • 1945 • Bragaglia Carlo Ludovico • ITL • MY WIDOW AND I (USA)
SBANDATA, LA • 1974 • Malfatti Alfredo • ITL
SBANDATI, GLI • 1956 • Maselli Francesco • ITL • STRAGGLERS, THE
SBANDATO! • 1956 • Morroni Antero • ITL
SBARCO DI ANZIO, LO • 1968 • Dmytryk Edward • ITL • BATTLE FOR ANZIO, THE ◦ ANZIO LANDING, THE ◦ ANZIO
SBARRA, LA see **ISPETTORE VARGAS, L'** • 1940
SBATTI IL MOSTRO IN PRIMA PAGINA • 1972 • Bellocchio Marco • ITL • STICK THE MONSTER ON THE FIRST PAGE ◦ MONSTER ON PAGE ONE, THE ◦ STRIKE THE MONSTER ON PAGE ONE
SBERNE SUROVOSTI • 1965 • Herz Juraj • CZC • JUNK SHOP, THE
SBIRRO, LA TUA LEGGE E LENTA.. LA MIA NO! • 1979 • Massi Stelvio • ITL
SBOGOM, PRIYATELI! • 1970 • Shariliev Borislav • BUL • FAREWELL, FRIENDS!
SBOHEM OFELIE • 1980 • Doubkova Dagmar • CZC • GOODBYE OPHELIA
SCAB WAITER, THE • 1914 • *Melies* • USA
SCABIES see **SVRAB** • 1969
SCABIES see **LA GALE** • 1989
SCACCO ALLA MAFIA • 1970 • Sabatini Lorenzo • ITL • MORTE IMPROVVISA, LA
SCACCO ALLA REGINA • 1969 • Festa Campanile Pasquale • ITL, FRG • CHECK TO THE QUEEN
SCACCO INTERNAZIONALE • 1968 • Rosati Giuseppe • ITL • LAST CHANCE, THE
SCACCO MATTO • 1919 • Campogalliani Carlo • ITL
SCACCO TUTTO MATTO, UNO see **SEI SIMPATICHE CAROGNE** • 1968
SCALA, LA • 1931 • Righelli Gennaro • ITL
SCALA DI GIACOBBE, LA • 1920 • Falena Ugo • ITL
SCALA -TOTAL VERRUCKT • 1958 • Ode Erik • FRG
SCALAWAG • 1973 • Douglas Kirk • USA, ITL, YGS • PEGLEG, MUSKET AND SABRE ◦ PROTUVA
SCALAWAG, THE • 1912 • *Conway Jack* • USA
SCALDINO, LO • 1919 • Genina Augusto • ITL
SCALE IN HI-FI see **ESCALA EN HI-FI** • 1963
SCALES OF JUSTICE, THE • 1909 • Brooke Van Dyke • USA
SCALES OF JUSTICE, THE • 1913 • Eagle Oscar • USA
SCALES OF JUSTICE, THE • 1914 • Heffron Thomas N. • USA
SCALES OF JUSTICE, THE • 1914 • Lord Alfred • UKN • BRITISH BULLDOG CONQUERS, A
SCALES OF JUSTICE, THE • 1915 • *Edwards Walter* • USA
SCALES OF LOVE, THE see **NERACA KASIH** • 1983
SCALLAWAG, THE • 1914 • Fitzhamon Lewin • UKN
SCALLYWAG, THE • 1921 • Sanderson Challis • UKN
SCALLYWAG FOOLS THE MISSUS • 1913 • *A.r. Films* • UKN
SCALP • 1985 • Carle Gilles • CND
SCALP MERCHANT, THE • 1978 • Rubie Howard • MTV • ASL
SCALP TREATMENT • 1952 • Lantz Walter • ANS • USA
SCALP TROUBLE • 1939 • Clampett Robert • ANS • USA
SCALPEL • 1976 • Grissmer John • USA • FALSE FACE
SCALPEL see **BAD FOR EACH OTHER** • 1953
SCALPEL, PLEASE see **SKALPEL, PROSIM** • 1985
SCALPHUNTERS, THE • 1968 • Pollack Sydney • USA
SCALPLOCK • 1966 • Goldstone James • TVM • USA
SCALPS • 1983 • Ray Fred Olen • USA
SCAMP, THE • 1957 • Rilla Wolf • UKN • STRANGE AFFECTION (USA)
SCAMP, THE see **SOWIZDRZAL SWIETOKRZYSKI** • 1977
SCAMP FROM SWIETYKRZYZ MOUNTAINS, THE see **SOWIZDRZAL SWIETOKRZYSKI** • 1977
SCAMPOLO • 1929 • Genina Augusto • FRN
SCAMPOLO • 1941 • Malasomma Nunzio • ITL
SCAMPOLO • 1958 • Weidenmann Alfred • FRG • MADCHEN SCAMPOLO, DAS
SCAMPOLO see **MADCHEN DER STRASSE, DAS** • 1928
SCAMPOLO see **PEU D'AMOUR, UN** • 1933
SCAMPOLO '53 • 1954 • Bianchi Giorgio • ITL, FRN • FEMMES MENENT LE JEU, LES (FRN)
SCAMPOLO, EIN KIND DER STRASSE • 1932 • Steinhoff Hans • AUS, FRG • UM EINEN GROSCHEN LIEBE
SCAMPS AND SCANDALS • 1919 • Semon Larry • SHT • USA
SCANDAL • 1915 • Weber Lois, Smalley Phillips • USA
SCANDAL • 1916 • Davis Will S. • USA
SCANDAL • 1917 • Giblyn Charles • USA
SCANDAL? • 1929 • Perestiani Ivan • USS
SCANDAL • 1929 • Ruggles Wesley • USA • HIGH SOCIETY (UKN)
SCANDAL • 1989 • Caton-Jones Michael • UKN
SCANDAL see **SKYANDURU** • 1950
SCANDAL see **BADNAM** • 1969
SCANDAL see **CH'OU WEN** • 1975
SCANDAL see **SABLAZAN** • 1984
SCANDAL '64 see **CHRISTINE KEELER AFFAIR, THE** • 1964
SCANDAL, LE • 1916 • de Baroncelli Jacques • FRN
SCANDAL, THE • 1923 • Rooke Arthur • UKN
SCANDAL, THE see **SKANDALEN** • 1913
SCANDAL, THE see **ESCANDALO, EL** • 1986
SCANDAL AT SCOURIE • 1953 • Negulesco Jean • USA
SCANDAL AT SEA, A • 1915 • *Russell Dan* • USA
SCANDAL EVERYWHERE • 1917 • Hutchinson Craig • SHT • USA
SCANDAL FOR SALE • 1932 • Mack Russell • USA • HOT NEWS ◦ AMBITION ◦ SCANDAL SHEET
SCANDAL IN A SMALL TOWN • 1988 • Page Anthony • TVM • USA
SCANDAL IN BOHEMIA, A • 1921 • Elvey Maurice • UKN
SCANDAL IN BUDAPEST see **SKANDAL IN BUDAPEST** • 1933
SCANDAL IN DENMARK (USA) see **DER KOM EN SOLDAT** • 1969
SCANDAL IN HICKVILLE, A • 1915 • Davis Ulysses • USA
SCANDAL IN MONTMARTRE see **MOME PIGALLE, LA** • 1955
SCANDAL IN PARIS, A see **FRAU AUF DER FOLTER, DIE** • 1928
SCANDAL IN PARIS, A (UKN) see **THIEVE'S HOLIDAY** • 1946
SCANDAL IN SALKHINETI see **PEREPOLOKH** • 1976
SCANDAL IN SORRENTO (UKN) see **PANE, AMORE E..** • 1955
SCANDAL IN THE FAMILY • 1915 • *Selby Gertrude* • USA
SCANDAL IN THE FAMILY see **ESCANDALO EN LA FAMILIA** • 1968
SCANDAL IN THE FAMILY see **SCANDOLO IN FAMIGLIA** • 1976
SCANDAL IN THE HOUSE OF POLIDOR see **SCANDOLO IN CASA POLIDOR** • 1912
SCANDAL IN THE ROMAN BATH see **O.K. NERONE** • 1951
SCANDAL INC. see **SCANDAL INCORPORATED** • 1956
SCANDAL INCORPORATED • 1956 • Mann Edward • USA • SCANDAL INC.
SCANDAL MONGER, THE • 1911 • *Yankee* • USA
SCANDAL MONGERS • 1918 • Weber Lois, Smalley Phillips • USA
SCANDAL MONGERS, THE • 1911 • *Lubin* • USA
SCANDAL OF COLONEL REDL, THE see **AFERA PLUKOVNIKA REDLA** • 1930
SCANDAL OVER THE TEACUPS • 1900 • Smith G. A. • UKN
SCANDAL PROOF • 1925 • Mortimer Edmund • USA
SCANDAL SHEET • 1940 • Grinde Nick • USA
SCANDAL SHEET • 1952 • Karlson Phil • USA • DARK PAGE, THE (UKN)
SCANDAL SHEET • 1985 • Rich David Lowell • TVM • USA
SCANDAL SHEET see **SCANDAL FOR SALE** • 1932
SCANDAL STREET • 1925 • Bennett Whitman • USA
SCANDAL STREET • 1931 • Cromwell John • USA • UNFIT TO PRINT
SCANDAL STREET • 1938 • Hogan James P. • USA
SCANDALE • 1948 • Le Henaff Rene • FRN
SCANDALE • 1982 • Mihalka George • CND • SCANDALS
SCANDALE, LE • 1934 • L'Herbier Marcel • FRN
SCANDALE, LE • 1966 • Chabrol Claude • FRN • CHAMPAGNE MURDERS, THE (USA)
SCANDALE AU VILLAGE, UN • 1913 • Feuillade Louis • FRN
SCANDALE AUX CHAMPS-ELYSEES • 1948 • Blanc Roger • FRN
SCANDALE AUX GALERIES, UN • 1937 • Sti Rene • FRN • ET AVEC CA, MADAME
SCANDALE.. NUDI • 1964 • Di Gianni Enzo • ITL
SCANDALI AL MARE • 1961 • Girolami Marino • ITL
SCANDALO A MILANO see **DIFENDO IL MIO AMORE** • 1956
SCANDALO PERBENE, UNO • 1984 • Festa Campanile Pasquale • ITL • BOURGEOIS SCANDAL, A
SCANDALO SEGRETO • 1990 • Vitti Monica • ITL • SECRET SCANDAL
SCANDALOSA GILDA • 1985 • Lavia Gabriele • ITL • SCANDALOUS GILDA
SCANDALOUS • 1983 • Cohen Rob • UKN
SCANDALOUS • 1988 • Young Robert William • USA
SCANDALOUS ADVENTURES OF BURAIKAN, THE (USA) see **BURAIKAN** • 1970
SCANDALOUS BOYS AND THE FIRE CHUTE, THE • 1908 • Stow Percy • UKN
SCANDALOUS GILDA see **SCANDALOSA GILDA** • 1985
SCANDALOUS JOHN • 1971 • Butler Robert • USA
SCANDALOUS TONGUES • 1922 • Schertzinger Victor • USA

SCANDALS see **SCANDALE** • 1982
SCANDALS OF 1933 • 1933 • Goldberg Jack • SHT • USA
SCANDALS OF CLOCHEMERLE, THE (USA) see **CLOCHEMERLE** • 1947
SCANDALS OF PARIS (USA) see **THERE GOES SUSIE** • 1934
SCANDINAVIAN SCANDAL, A • 1913 • *Sindelar Pearl* • USA
SCANDOLO • 1975 • Samperi Salvatore • ITL • SUBMISSION (USA)
SCANDOLO IN CASA POLIDOR • 1912 • *Guillaume Fernando* • SHT • ITL • SCANDAL IN THE HOUSE OF POLIDOR
SCANDOLO IN FAMIGLIA • 1976 • Andrei Marcello • ITL • SCANDAL IN THE FAMILY
SCANDOLO, LO • 1966 • Gobbi Anna • ITL
SCANDOLO PER BENE • 1940 • Pratelli Esodo • ITL
SCANIAN GUERRILLA see **SNAPPHANAR** • 1942
SCANNERS • 1980 • Cronenberg David • CND
SCANO BOA • 1961 • Dall'Ara Renato • ITL
SCANSATI.. A TRINITA ARRIVA ELDORADO • 1972 • Fidani Demofilo • ITL
SCANTY PANTIES • 1961 • Hornick Jay • USA
SCANZONATISSIMO • 1963 • Verde Dino • ITL
SCAPA FLOW • 1930 • Lasko Leo • FRG
SCAPEGOAT, THE • 1912 • *Selig* • USA
SCAPEGOAT, THE • 1913 • *Gem* • USA
SCAPEGOAT, THE • 1913 • Johnston Lorimer • *American* • USA
SCAPEGOAT, THE • 1914 • Mix Tom • USA
SCAPEGOAT, THE • 1915 • Haydon J. Charles? • USA
SCAPEGOAT, THE • 1959 • Hamer Robert • UKN, USA
SCAPEGOAT, THE • 1960 • *Halas John (P)* • ANS • UKN
SCAPEGOAT, THE see **SYNTIPUKKI** • 1935
SCAPEGOAT, THE (USA) see **FORNARETTO DI VENEZIA, IL** • 1963
SCAPEGRACE, THE • 1913 • *Lubin* • USA
SCAPEGRACE, THE • 1913 • Collins Edwin J. • UKN
SCAPEGRACE, THE • 1916 • Byrne Jack • SHT • USA
SCAPOLO, LO • 1956 • Pietrangeli Antonio • ITL • ALBERTO IL CONQUISTATORE ○ BACHELOR, THE
SCAPPAMENTO APERTO (ITL) see **ECHAPPEMENT LIBRE** • 1964
SCAPRICCIATIELLO • 1956 • Capuano Luigi • ITL
SCAR, A see **BLIZNA** • 1976
SCAR, THE • 1912 • *Republic* • USA
SCAR, THE • 1913 • *Rex* • USA
SCAR, THE • 1914 • O'Sullivan Tony • USA
SCAR, THE • 1915 • Humphrey William • USA
SCAR, THE • 1919 • Crane Frank H. • USA
SCAR, THE see **PLAE GAEW** • 1979
SCAR, THE (UKN) see **HOLLOW TRIUMPH** • 1948
SCAR HANAN • 1925 • Wilson Ben, Linden Eddie, Cunliff Don • USA
SCAR OF CONSCIENCE, THE see **BRAND OF CAIN, THE** • 1915
SCAR OF SHAME, THE • 1927 • Peregini Frank • USA
SCARAB • 1983 • Jaffe Stephen-Charles • USA, SPN
SCARAB MURDER CASE, THE • 1936 • Hankinson Michael • UKN
SCARAB RING, THE • 1921 • Jose Edward • USA
SCARABEA see **SCARABEA –WIEVIEL ERDE BRAUCHT DER MENSCH?** • 1968
SCARABEA –HOW MUCH LAND DOES A MAN NEED? see **SCARABEA –WIEVIEL ERDE BRAUCHT DER MENSCH?** • 1968
SCARABEA –WIEVIEL ERDE BRAUCHT DER MENSCH? • 1968 • Syberberg Hans-Jurgen • FRG • SCARABEA –HOW MUCH LAND DOES A MAN NEED? ○ SCARABEA
SCARABEE D'OR, LE • 1911 • Desfontaines Henri • ITL • GOLDEN BEETLE, THE (USA)
SCARABUS • 1971 • Frydman Gerald • ANS • BLG
SCARABUS II • 1973 • Frydman Gerald • SHT • BLG
SCARAMOUCHE • 1923 • Ingram Rex • USA
SCARAMOUCHE • 1952 • Sidney George • USA
SCARAMOUCHE • 1963 • Isasi Antonio • FRN, SPN, ITL • MASCARA DE SCARAMOUCHE, LA (SPN) ○ ADVENTURES OF SCARAMOUCHE,THE ○ AVVENTURE DI SCARAMOUCHE, LE (ITL)
SCARAMOUCHE see **AVVENTURE E GLI AMORI DI SCARAMOUCHE, LE** • 1976
SCARAMOUCHES • 1910 • Fitzhamon Lewin • UKN
SCARE THE GIRLS OFF see **SCARE THEIR PANTS OFF** • 1968
SCARE THEIR PANTS OFF • 1968 • Maddox John • USA • HE SCARED THE GIRLS OFF ○ SCARE THE GIRLS OFF ○ SCARE THEM OFF
SCARE THEM OFF see **SCARE THEIR PANTS OFF** • 1968
SCARECROW • 1920 • Keaton Buster, Cline Eddie • SHT • USA
SCARECROW • 1971 • Sharad John S. • SHT • UKN
SCARECROW • 1973 • Schatzberg Jerry • USA
SCARECROW see **STRASILO** • 1957
SCARECROW, THE • 1911 • Wilson Frank • UKN
SCARECROW, THE • 1914 • *Royal* • USA
SCARECROW, THE • 1916 • Birch Cecil • UKN
SCARECROW, THE • 1981 • Pillsbury Sam • NZL
SCARECROW, THE • 1986 • Bykov Rolan • USS
SCARECROW, THE see **PURITAN PASSIONS** • 1923
SCARECROW, THE (USA) see **EPOUVANTAIL, L'** • 1921
SCARECROW, THE (USA) see **EPOUVANTAIL, L'** • 1943
SCARECROW AND THE CHAPERONE, THE • 1914 • *Universal* • USA
SCARECROW IN A GARDEN OF CUCUMBERS • 1972 • *Woodlawn Holly* • USA
SCARECROW OF ROMNEY MARSH, THE see **DR. SYN –ALIAS THE SCARECROW** • 1963
SCARECROW PUMP • 1904 • Porter Edwin S. • USA
SCARECROWS • 1988 • Wesley William • USA
SCARECROW'S SECRET, THE • 1914 • *Frontier* • USA
SCARED CROWS, THE • 1939 • Fleischer Dave • ANS • USA
SCARED SILLY • 1927 • Lamont Charles • SHT • USA
SCARED STIFF • 1919 • Lyons Eddie, Moran Lee • SHT • USA
SCARED STIFF • 1926 • Horne James W. • SHT • USA
SCARED STIFF • 1931 • Edwards Harry J. • SHT • USA
SCARED STIFF • 1945 • McDonald Frank • USA • TREASURE OF FEAR
SCARED STIFF • 1953 • Marshall George • USA
SCARED STIFF • 1987 • Friedman Richard • USA

SCARED STRAIGHT see **SCARED STRAIGHT! ANOTHER STORY** • 1980
SCARED STRAIGHT! ANOTHER STORY • 1980 • Michaels Richard • TVM • USA • SCARED STRAIGHT
SCARED TO DEATH • 1947 • Cabanne W. Christy • USA
SCARED TO DEATH • 1947 • Mattox Walt • USA
SCARED TO DEATH • 1980 • Malone William • USA • TERROR FACTOR
SCARED! (UKN) see **WHISTLING IN THE DARK** • 1932
SCAREDY CAT • 1948 • Jones Charles M. • ANS • USA
SCAREHEADS • 1931 • Newmeyer Fred • USA
SCAREHEADS • 1931 • Smith Noel • USA • SPEED REPORTER, THE (UKN)
SCAREM MUCH • 1924 • *Sennett Mack (P)* • SHT • USA
SCAREMAKER, THE see **GIRLS' NITE OUT** • 1983
SCAREMONGERS, THE see **MISS KNOWALL** • 1940
SCAREMONGERS, THE see **PANIEKZAAIERS** • 1985
SCARF see **BANDANA** • 1968
SCARF, THE • 1951 • Dupont E. A. • USA • DUNGEON, THE
SCARF OF MIST, THIGH OF SATIN • 1967 • Sarno Joe • USA • SCARF OF MIST, WOMEN OF SATIN
SCARF OF MIST, WOMEN OF SATIN see **SCARF OF MIST, THIGH OF SATIN** • 1967
SCARF PIN, THE • 1913 • *Faust Martin* • USA
SCARFACE • 1932 • Hawks Howard • USA • SHAME OF A NATION, THE (UKN) ○ SCARFACE, SHAME OF A NATION
SCARFACE • 1983 • De Palma Brian • USA
SCARFACE AND APHRODITE • 1963 • Zimmerman Vernon • SHT • USA
SCARFACE MOB, THE • 1962 • Karlson Phil • MTV • USA • UNTOUCHABLES: THE SCARFACE MOB
SCARFACE, SHAME OF A NATION see **SCARFACE** • 1932
SCARLATINE, LA • 1983 • Aghion Gabriel • FRN
SCARLET AND BLACK see **ROUGE ET LE NOIR, LE** • 1954
SCARLET AND GOLD • 1925 • Grandon Francis J. • USA
SCARLET AND GREEN see **SIN TO MIDORI** • 1937
SCARLET AND THE BLACK, THE • 1982 • London Jerry • TVM • USA
SCARLET ANGEL • 1952 • Salkow Sidney • USA
SCARLET ARROW, THE • 1928 • Taylor Ray • USA
SCARLET BARONESS, THE (USA) see **FEUERROTE BARONESSE, DIE** • 1959
SCARLET BLADE, THE • 1963 • Gilling John • UKN • CRIMSON BLADE, THE (USA)
SCARLET BRAND • 1932 • McGowan J. P. • USA
SCARLET BUCCANEER, THE (UKN) see **SWASHBUCKLER** • 1976
SCARLET CAMELIA see **GOBEN NO TSUBAKI** • 1965
SCARLET CAR, THE • 1918 • De Grasse Joseph • USA
SCARLET CAR, THE • 1923 • Paton Stuart • USA
SCARLET CHASTITY, THE • 1916 • Melville Wilbert • SHT • USA
SCARLET CLAW, THE • 1944 • Neill R. William • USA • SHERLOCK HOLMES AND THE SCARLET CLAW
SCARLET CLUE, THE • 1945 • Rosen Phil • USA • CHARLIE CHAN AND THE SCARLET CLUE
SCARLET COAT, THE • 1955 • Sturges John • USA
SCARLET CRYSTAL, THE • 1917 • Swickard Charles • USA
SCARLET DAREDEVIL, THE (USA) see **TRIUMPH OF THE SCARLET PIMPERNEL, THE** • 1928
SCARLET DAWN • 1932 • Dieterle William • USA • REVOLT
SCARLET DAYDREAM • 1966 • Takechi Tetsuji • JPN
SCARLET DAYS • 1919 • Griffith D. W. • USA
SCARLET DOVE, THE • 1928 • Gregor Arthur • USA
SCARLET DOVE, THE see **TULIPUNAINEN KYYHKYNEN** • 1961
SCARLET DROP, THE • 1918 • Ford John • USA • HILL BILLY, THE (UKN)
SCARLET EMPRESS, THE • 1934 • von Sternberg Josef • USA
SCARLET EXECUTIONER, THE see **BOIA SCARLATTO, IL** • 1965
SCARLET EYE, THE (USA) see **TEMPESTA SU CEYLON** • 1963
SCARLET FEVER see **SKARLATINA** • 1924
SCARLET FLOWER see **SHU NO KAFUN** • 1960
SCARLET HAIR see **MAKKA NA UBUGE** • 1968
SCARLET HEAVEN see **FORBIDDEN** • 1949
SCARLET HONEYMOON, THE • 1925 • Hale Alan • USA
SCARLET HORSEMAN, THE • 1946 • Taylor Ray, Collins Lewis D. • SRL • USA
SCARLET HOUR, THE • 1956 • Curtiz Michael • USA
SCARLET HOURS see **NIGHT ANGEL** • 1931
SCARLET JUNGLE, THE see **SCOTLAND YARD JAGT DOKTOR MABUSE** • 1963
SCARLET KISS, THE • 1920 • Goodwins Fred • UKN
SCARLET LADY, THE • 1915 • Nicholls George • USA
SCARLET LADY, THE • 1922 • West Walter • UKN
SCARLET LADY, THE • 1928 • Crosland Alan • USA • SCARLET WOMAN, THE (UKN)
SCARLET LETTER, THE • 1907 • Olcott Sidney • USA
SCARLET LETTER, THE • 1911 • Smiley Joseph, Tucker George Loane • USA
SCARLET LETTER, THE • 1913 • Miles David • USA
SCARLET LETTER, THE • 1917 • Harbaugh Carl • USA
SCARLET LETTER, THE • 1920 • *Selznick* • SHT • USA
SCARLET LETTER, THE • 1922 • Sanderson Challis • UKN
SCARLET LETTER, THE • 1926 • Sjostrom Victor • USA
SCARLET LETTER, THE • 1934 • Vignola Robert G. • USA
SCARLET LETTER, THE (USA) see **SCHARLACHROTE BUCHSTABE, DER** • 1972
SCARLET LILY, THE • 1923 • Schertzinger Victor • USA
SCARLET MARK, THE • 1916 • Henderson Lucius • SHT • USA
SCARLET NEGLIGEE • 1968 • Scott Ron • USA
SCARLET OATH, THE • 1916 • Powell Frank, Vale Travers • USA
SCARLET PAGES • 1930 • Enright Ray • USA
SCARLET PIMPERNEL, THE • 1917 • Stanton Richard • USA
SCARLET PIMPERNEL, THE • 1935 • Young Harold • UKN
SCARLET PIMPERNEL, THE • 1982 • Donner Clive • TVM • USA, UKN
SCARLET PIMPERNEL, THE see **ELUSIVE PIMPERNEL, THE** • 1950
SCARLET PUMPERNICKEL, THE • 1950 • Jones Charles M. • ANS • USA
SCARLET RIDER, THE • 1920 • Jaccard Jacques • SHT • USA

SCARLET RIVER • 1933 • Brower Otto • USA
SCARLET ROAD, THE • 1916 • *Duncan Malcolm* • USA
SCARLET ROAD, THE • 1918 • Le Saint Edward J. • USA
SCARLET ROSE see **HI NO BARA** • 1948
SCARLET RUNNER, THE • 1916 • Van Wally, Earle William P. S. • SRL • USA
SCARLET SAIL OF PARIS, THE • 1973 • Khutsiev Marlen • DOC • USS
SCARLET SAINT, THE • 1925 • Archainbaud George • USA
SCARLET SCORPION, THE see **ESCORPIAO ESCARLATE, O** • 1989
SCARLET SEAS • 1929 • Dillon John Francis • USA
SCARLET SHADOW, THE • 1919 • Leonard Robert Z. • USA
SCARLET SIN, THE • 1915 • Turner Otis, Bosworth Hobart • USA
SCARLET SPEAR, THE • 1954 • Breakston George, Stahl C. Ray • UKN
SCARLET STREAK, THE • 1926 • McRae Henry • SRL • USA
SCARLET STREET • 1945 • Lang Fritz • USA
SCARLET THREAD • 1951 • Gilbert Lewis* • UKN
SCARLET TRAIL, THE • 1919 • Lawrence John S. • USA
SCARLET WEB, THE • 1954 • Saunders Charles • UKN
SCARLET WEEKEND, A • 1932 • Melford George • USA
SCARLET WEST, THE • 1925 • Adolfi John G. • USA
SCARLET WOMAN, THE • 1916 • Lawrence Edmund • USA
SCARLET WOMAN, THE see **FEMME ECARLATE, LA** • 1969
SCARLET WOMAN, THE (UKN) see **SCARLET LADY, THE** • 1928
SCARLET WOOING, THE • 1920 • Morgan Sidney • UKN
SCARLET YOUTH • 1928 • Curran William Hughes • USA
SCARLETT BUCKANEER see **SWASHBUCKLER** • 1976
SCARLETT O'HARA WAR, THE • 1980 • Erman John • TVM • USA
SCARPE AL SOLE, LE • 1935 • Elter Marco • ITL
SCARPE GROSSE • 1940 • Falconi Dino • ITL
SCARRED • Mattoli Mario • ITL
SCARRED • 1984 • Turko Rosemarie • USA • STREET LOVE
SCARRED FACE, THE • 1928 • Paul Fred • UKN
SCARRED HANDS • 1923 • Smith Cliff • USA
SCARS • 1915 • King Burton L. • USA
SCARS • 1972 • Winkler Paul • ASL
SCARS AND BARS • 1918 • Smith Noel • SHT • USA
SCARS AND STRIPES FOREVER • 1916 • *Ritchie Billie* • SHT • USA
SCARS OF DRACULA, THE • 1970 • Baker Roy Ward • UKN
SCARS OF HATE • 1923 • Moody H. G. • USA
SCARS OF JEALOUSY • 1923 • Hillyer Lambert • USA
SCARS OF LOVE • 1919 • *Austral Photoplays* • ASL
SCARS OF POSSESSION • 1914 • *Bushman Francis X.* • USA
SCARS OF THE NIGHT see **SIGNS OF NIGHT** • 1988
SCARS OF THE PAST see **ZDE JSOU LVI** • 1958
SCARY CROWS • 1937 • *Mintz Charles (P)* • ANS • USA
SCARY TIME, A • 1960 • Clarke Shirley • USA
SCASSINATORI, GLI (ITL) see **CASSE, LE** • 1971
SCAT BURGLARS, THE • 1937 • Rowson Leslie • UKN
SCAT CATS • 1957 • Hanna William, Barbera Joseph • ANS • USA
SCATENATO, LO • 1967 • Indovina Franco • ITL • CATCH AS CATCH CAN (USA) ○ UNCHAINED, THE ○ TUTTI FRUTTI
SCATTERBRAIN • 1940 • Meins Gus • USA
SCATTERED BODY AND THE WORLD UPSIDE DOWN, THE see **CUERTO REPARTIDO Y EL MUNDO AL REVES** • 1975
SCATTERED CLOUDS see **MIDARE-GUMO** • 1967
SCATTERGOOD BAINES • 1941 • Cabanne W. Christy • USA
SCATTERGOOD MEETS BROADWAY • 1941 • Cabanne W. Christy • USA
SCATTERGOOD PULLS THE STRINGS • 1941 • Cabanne W. Christy • USA
SCATTERGOOD RIDES HIGH • 1942 • Cabanne W. Christy • USA
SCATTERGOOD SURVIVES A MURDER • 1942 • Cabanne W. Christy • USA
SCATTERGOOD SWINGS IT see **CINDERELLA SWINGS IT** • 1943
SCAVA IN FONDO ALL'AMORE • 1976 • Cavallone Alberto • ITL
SCAVENGER HUNT • 1979 • Schultz Michael • USA
SCAVENGERS • 1988 • McLachlan Duncan • USA
SCAVENGERS, THE • 1959 • Cromwell John • USA, PHL • CITY OF SIN
SCAVENGERS, THE • 1967 • SAF
SCAVENGERS, THE • 1969 • Frost R. L. • USA • GRABBERS, THE
SCAVENGERS, THE see **RECUPERANTI, I** • 1970
SCEICCO BIANCO, LO • 1952 • Fellini Federico • ITL • WHITE SHEIK, THE
SCEICCO LA VEDE COSI, LO • 1974 • Moffa Paolo (c/d) • ITL
SCEICCO ROSSO, LO • 1962 • Cerchio Fernando • ITL, FRN • RED SHEIK, THE (USA) ○ CHEIK ROUGE, LE (FRN)
SCELERATS, LES • 1960 • Hossein Robert • FRN • TORMENT
SCENARIO • 1985 • Mavroidis Dinos • GRC
SCENARIO BUG, THE • 1916 • O'Hara Charles C. • SHT • USA
SCENARIO EDITOR'S DREAM, THE • 1914 • *Powers* • USA
SCENARIO WRITER, THE • 1913 • *Majestic* • USA
SCENE D'ESCAMOTAGE • 1897-98 • Blache Alice • FRN
SCENE EN CABINET PARTICULIER VUE A TRAVERS LE TROU DE LA SERRURE, UNE see **CABINET PARTICULIER, UN** • 1902
SCENE FROM MELBURY HOUSE, THE • 1973 • UKN
SCENE NUN, TAKE ONE • 1964 • Hatton Maurice • SHT • UKN
SCENE OF HIS CRIME, THE • 1914 • *Apollo* • USA
SCENE OF THE CRIME • 1949 • Rowland Roy • USA
SCENE OF THE CRIME (USA) see **LIEU DU CRIME, LE** • 1985
SCENE ON BRIGHTON PIER see **EARLY FASHIONS ON BRIGHTON PIER** • 1898
SCENENS BORN • 1913 • *Christensen Benjamin* • DNM
SCENER TIL EN FILM • 1973 • Nicolayssen Hans Otto • SHT • NRW • SCENES FOR A FILM
SCENER UR ETT AKTENSKAP • 1973 • Bergman Ingmar • MTV • SWD • SCENES FROM A MARRIAGE (USA)
SCENES BETWEEN TWO WELL-KNOWN COMEDIANS • 1900 • Smith Jack • UKN
SCENES DE GREVE EN VENDEE • 1970 • FRN

SCENES DE LA VIE CRUELLE • 1912-14 • Zecca Ferdinand, Leprince Rene • FRN
SCENES DE LA VIE DE CAFE see **PETIT CAFE, LE** • 1962
SCENES DE MENAGE • 1954 • Berthomieu Andre • FRN
SCENES D'ENFANTS • 1896-97 • Lumiere Louis • FRN
SCENES DIRECTOIRE • 1904 • Blache Alice • SER • FRN
SCENES DU HAUT-SAINT-MAURICE • 1932 • Tessier Albert • DCS • CND
SCENES FOR A FILM see **SCENER TIL EN FILM** • 1973
SCENES FROM A MALL • 1990 • Mazursky Paul • USA
SCENES FROM A MARRIAGE (USA) see **SCENER UR ETT AKTENSKAP** • 1973
SCENES FROM A MURDER (USA) see **ASSASSINO E AL TELEFONO, L'** • 1972
SCENES FROM THE BATTLEFIELD OF GETTYSBURG • 1908 • *Lubin* • USA
SCENES FROM THE CLASS STRUGGLE IN BEVERLY HILLS • 1989 • Bartel Paul • USA
SCENES FROM THE GOLDMINE • 1987 • Rocco Marc • USA
SCENES FROM THE LIFE OF SHOCK-WORKERS see **SLIKE IZ ZIVOTA UDARNIKA** • 1973
SCENES FROM THE PORTUGUESE CLASS STRUGGLE • 1977 • Kramer Robert, Spinelli Philip • USA
SCENES FROM UNDER CHILDHOOD: SECTION NO.1 • 1967 • Brakhage Stan • USA
SCENES FROM UNDER CHILDHOOD: SECTION NO.2 • 1969 • Brakhage Stan • USA
SCENES FROM UNDER CHILDHOOD: SECTION NO.3 • 1969 • Brakhage Stan • USA
SCENES FROM UNDER CHILDHOOD: SECTION NO.4 • 1970 • Brakhage Stan • USA
SCENES IN AN ORPHANS' ASYLUM • 1903 • Porter Edwin S. • USA
SCENES OF BATTLE see **BARWY WALKI** • 1965
SCENES OF OTHER DAYS • 1913 • *Prior Herbert* • USA
SCENIC ROUTE, THE • 1978 • Rappaport Mark • USA
SCENINGANG • 1956 • Ekerot Bengt • SWD • STAGE ENTRANCE
SCENT-IMENTAL OVER YOU • 1947 • Jones Charles M. • ANS • USA
SCENT-IMENTAL ROMEO • 1950 • Jones Charles M. • ANS • USA
SCENT OF A WOMAN (USA) see **PROFUMO DI DONNA** • 1974
SCENT OF ALMONDS see **DAKH NA BADEMI, S** • 1967
SCENT OF HEATHER, A • 1981 • Drexler Philip T. • USA
SCENT OF INCENSE, THE see **KOGE** • 1964
SCENT OF LOVE • 1970 • *Stacey Dist.* • USA
SCENT OF MYSTERY • 1960 • Cardiff Jack • USA • HOLIDAY IN SPAIN (UKN)
SCENT OF QUINCE, THE • 1982 • Idrizovic Mirza • YGS
SCENT OF THE EARTH, THE see **MIRIS ZEMLJE** • 1979
SCENT OF THE MATTERHORN, THE • 1961 • Jones Charles M. • ANS • USA
SCENT OF VIOLETS, THE • 1985 • Gavala Maria • GRC
SCENT OF WILD FLOWERS, THE see **MIRIS POLJSKOG CVECA** • 1977
SCENT OF WOMAN see **PROFUMO DI DONNA** • 1974
SCENT SPRAY, THE • 1905 • Collins Alf • UKN
SCENTED ENVELOPES, THE • 1923 • Coleby A. E. • UKN
SCENTED ROMANCE, A • 1919 • *West Billy* • SHT • USA
SCENTED SOAP • 1929 • Aylott Dave, Symmons E. F. • SHT • UKN
SCENTING A TERRIBLE CRIME • 1913 • Dillon Eddie • USA
SCENTRALIZOWANA KONTROLA PRZEBIEGU PRODUKCJI • 1951 • Has Wojciech J. • DCS • PLN • CENTRALISED CONTROL OF FLOW OF PRODUCTION
SCEPTER OF SUSPICION • 1917 • King Henry • USA
SCEPTICAL COWBOY, THE • 1909 • *Centaur Film* • USA
SCEPTRE AND THE MACE, THE • 1957 • Howe John • CND
SCERIFFA, LA • 1959 • Montero Roberto Bianchi • ITL
SCERIFFO DI ROCKSPRING, LO • 1971 • Sabatini Mario • ITL
SCERIFFO E L'EXTRATERRESTRE,LO see **SCERIFFO EXTRATERRESTRE.. POCO EXTRA E MOLTO TERRESTRE, UNO** • 1979
SCERIFFO EXTRATERRESTRE.. POCO EXTRA E MOLTO TERRESTRE, UNO • 1979 • Lupo Michele • ITL • SHERIFF AND THE SATELLITE KID, THE (USA) ○ SCERIFFO E L'EXTRATERRESTRE,LO ○ CHISSA PERSCHE.. CAPITANO TUTTO A ME
SCERIFFO TUTTO D'ORO, UNO • 1966 • Civirani Osvaldo • ITL
SCHAATSENRIJDEN • 1929 • Ivens Joris • NTH • SKATING ○ SKATERS, THE
SCHAB NESHINI DOR DJAHANNAM • 1957 • Khotschikian Samuel • IRN • NIGHT IN HELL, A
SCHABERNACK • 1936 • Emo E. W. • FRG
SCHACH DEM LEBEN see **DAMON DES "GRAND HOTEL MAJESTIC", DER** • 1920
SCHACH DEM ZUFALL • 1961 • Schamoni Peter • SHT • FRG
SCHACHMATT • 1931 • Asagaroff Georg • FRG
SCHACHNOVELLE, DIE • 1960 • Oswald Gerd • FRG • BRAINWASHED (USA) ○ THREE MOVES TO FREEDOM ○ ROYAL GAME, THE
SCHACKO KLAK • 1989 • Kieffer Paul, Feitler Frank • LXM
SCHADEL DER PHARAONENTOCHTER, DER • 1920 • Tollen Otz • FRG
SCHAFER VOM TRUTZBERG, DER • 1959 • von Borsody Eduard • FRG
SCHAFFNERIN DER LINIE 6, DIE • 1915 • Schonwald Gustav • FRG
SCHAKEL MET HET VERLEDEN see **PALEONTHOLOGIE** • 1959
SCHAM see **MADCHEN AM KREUZ** • 1929
SCHAM DICH, BRIGITTE see **WIR WERDEN DAS KIND SCHON SCHAUKELN** • 1952
SCHAMANS OF THE BLIND COUNTRY • 1981 • Oppitz Michael • FRG
SCHAMLOS • 1968 • Saller Eddy • AUS, FRG, FRN • SHAMELESS
SCHAMLOSE SEELEN ODER EIN MADCHENSCHICKSAL • 1922 • Neff Wolfgang • FRG
SCHANDE • 1922 • Dessauer Siegfried • FRG
SCHANDFLECK, DER • 1917 • Fleck Jacob, Fleck Luise • AUS
SCHARFE HEINRICH DIE BUMSFIDELEN ABENTEUER EINER JUNGEN EHE • 1971 • Thiele Rolf • FRG
SCHARFE SCHUSSE AUF JAMAICA see **A-001 OPERAZIONE GIAMAICA** • 1965
SCHARFER SCHUSS, EIN • 1917 • *Kaiser-Titz Erich* • FRG
SCHARLACHROTE BUCHSTABE, DER • 1972 • Wenders Wim • FRG, SPN • LETRA ESCARLATA, LA (SPN) ○ SCARLET LETTER, THE (USA)
SCHARLACHROTE BUCHSTABE, DER see **E, DER SCHARLACHROTE BUCHSTABE** • 1918
SCHARLACHROTE DSCHUNKE, DIE see **SCOTLAND YARD JAGT DOKTOR MABUSE** • 1963
SCHARLATAN, DER see **NAMENLOS** • 1923
SCHASEN see **SISTA RINGEN** • 1955
SCHASTE see **STCHASTIE** • 1934
SCHATJES • 1983 • van Hemert Ruud • NTH • DARLINGS ○ SWEETHEARTS
SCHATTEN • 1923 • Robison Arthur • FRG • SCHATTEN, EINE NACHTLICHE HALLUZINATION ○ WARNING SHADOWS
SCHATTEN, DER • 1918 • Dupont E. A. • FRG • LEBENDER SCHATTEN, DER
SCHATTEN AM FENSTER, DER • 1915 • *Speyer Eva* • FRG
SCHATTEN AUS DEM TOTENREICH • 1920 • Kalden Hans? • FRG
SCHATTEN DER ENGEL • 1976 • Schmid Daniel • SWT • SHADOWS OF ANGELS
SCHATTEN DER GABY LEED, DER • 1921 • Boese Carl • FRG
SCHATTEN DER MANEGE • 1931 • Paul Heinz • FRG
SCHATTEN DER NACHT • 1918 • Kahn William • FRG • FALL DUIF, DER
SCHATTEN DER NACHT • 1950 • York Eugen • FRG
SCHATTEN DER NACHT see **WENN MENSCHEN IRREN** • 1926
SCHATTEN DER UNTERWELT • 1931 • Piel Harry • FRG
SCHATTEN DER VERGANGENHEIT • 1917 • Oswald Richard • FRG
SCHATTEN DER VERGANGENHEIT • 1919 • von Woringen Paul • FRG
SCHATTEN DER VERGANGENHEIT • 1922 • Biebrach Rudolf • FRG
SCHATTEN DER VERGANGENHEIT • 1936 • Hochbaum Werner • AUS • SHADOWS OF THE PAST (USA)
SCHATTEN DER WELTSTADT • 1925 • Wolff Willi • FRG • WELTSTADTNACHE
SCHATTEN DER WUSTE • 1989 • *Stokowski Oliver* • FRG
SCHATTEN DES GLUCKS • *Von Schlettow Hans Adalbert* • FRG
SCHATTEN DES HERRN MONITOR, DIE • 1950 • York Eugen • FRG
SCHATTEN DES MEERES see **IM SCHATTEN DES MEERES** • 1912
SCHATTEN DES TOTEN, DER • 1926 • Weiss Bruno • FRG
SCHATTEN, EINE NACHTLICHE HALLUZINATION see **SCHATTEN** • 1923
SCHATTEN EINER STUNDE • 1920 • Rippert Otto • FRG
SCHATTEN JENER NACHT, DIE • 1922 • *Von Schlettow Adalbert* • FRG
SCHATTEN UBER DEN INSELN • 1952 • Meyer Otto • GDR
SCHATTEN UBER NEAPEL • 1951 • Wolff Hans • FRG, ITL • CAMORRA
SCHATTEN UBER ST. PAULI • 1938 • Kirchhoff Fritz • FRG • HAFENDROSCHKE "JUNGE LIEBE"
SCHATTEN UBER TIRAN-KOMMANDO SINAI see **HA'MATARAH TIRAN** • 1968
SCHATTEN UND LICHT • 1977 • Lhotzky Georg • AUS • SHADOWS AND LIGHT
SCHATTEN WERDEN LANGER, DIE • 1962 • Vajda Ladislao • FRG, SWT • SHADOWS GROW LONGER, THE (USA) ○ GIRLS IN THE SHADOWS ○ DEFIANT DAUGHTERS
SCHATTENKINDER DES GLUCKS • 1922 • Osten Franz • FRG
SCHATTENREITER • 1974 • Moorse Georg • FRG • SHADOW RIDER
SCHATTENSPIELER, DER • 1919 • Beck Ludwig • FRG
SCHATZ, DER • 1923 • Pabst G. W. • FRG • ALTEE SPIEL UM GOLD UND LIEBE, EIN ○ TREASURE, THE
SCHATZ DER AZTEKEN, DER • 1921 • Heiland Heinz Karl • FRG
SCHATZ DER AZTEKEN, DER • 1965 • Siodmak Robert • FRG, FRN, ITL
SCHATZ DER GESINE JAKOBSEN, DER • 1923 • Walther-Fein Rudolf • FRG
SCHATZ IM BERGE, DER • 1917 • Zeyn Willy • FRG
SCHATZ IM SILBERSEE, DER • 1962 • Reinl Harald • FRG, FRN, YGS • TRESOR DU LAC D'ARGENT, LE (FRN) ○ BLAGO U SREBRNOM JEZERU (YGS) ○ TREASURE OF SILVER LAKE (USA)
SCHATZ, MACH' KASSE • 1926 • Basch Felix • FRG
SCHATZ VOM TOPLITZSEE, DER • 1959 • Antel Franz • FRG • SCHUSSE IM MORGENGRAUEN
SCHATZKAMMER DER RESIDENZ • 1959 • Borel Victor • FRG
SCHATZKAMMER IM SEE 1, DIE • 1921 • Werckmeister Hans • FRG • BRILLANTENMARDER
SCHATZKAMMER IM SEE 2, DIE • 1921 • Werckmeister Hans • FRG • CLUB DER ZWOLF, DER
SCHAUKEL, DIE • 1983 • Adlon Percy • FRG • SWING, THE
SCHAUPLATZE • 1967 • Wenders Wim • SHT • FRG • LOCATIONS
SCHAUSPIELER DER HERZOGIN, DER • 1920 • Stein Paul L. • FRG
SCHAUT AUF DIESE STADT • 1962 • Gass Karl • DOC • GDR • LOOK AT THIS CITY ○ BERLIN WALL, THE
SCHECK AUFS LEBEN, DER • 1924 • Kahn William • FRG
SCHEDROYE LETO • 1951 • Barnet Boris • USS • BOUNTIFUL SUMMER (USA) ○ PLENTIFUL SUMMER, THE
SCHEDRYI VECHER • 1980 • Muratov Alexander • USS • GENEROUS EVENING
SCHEHERAZADE • 1982 • Lucas Stephen • USA • SCHEHERAZADE ONE THOUSAND AND ONE NIGHTS
SCHEHERAZADE ONE THOUSAND AND ONE NIGHTS see **SCHEHERAZADE** • 1982
SCHEHERAZADE (USA) see **SHEHEREZADE** • 1963
SCHEIDUNGSGRUND, DER • 1937 • Lamac Carl • FRG, CZC
SCHEIDUNGSGRUND, EIN • 1915 • Del Zopp Rudolf • FRG
SCHEIDUNGSGRUND LIEBE • 1960 • Frankel Cyril • FRG
SCHEIDUNGSREISE • 1938 • Deppe Hans • FRG
SCHEIN UND SEIN • 1915 • *Eggerth Otto* • FRG
SCHEINE DES TODES • 1922 • Mendes Lothar • FRG
SCHEINHEILIGE FLORIAN, DER • 1941 • Stockel Joe • FRG
SCHEINTOTE CHINESE, DER • 1928 • Reiniger Lotte • ANS • FRG
SCHEISSKERL • 1969 • Muehl Otto • FRG
SCHEITERHAUFEN, DER • 1945 • Rittau Gunther • FRG
SCHEMA D'UNE IDENTIFICATION • 1945 • Resnais Alain • FRN
SCHEME, THE • 1912 • *Missimer Howard* • USA
SCHEME OF SHIFTLESS SAM SMITH, THE • 1913 • *Brennan John* • USA
SCHEME THAT FAILED, THE • 1911 • *Solax* • USA
SCHEME THAT FAILED, THE • 1911 • *Lubin* • USA
SCHEME THAT FAILED, THE • 1914 • *Komic* • USA
SCHEME THAT FAILED, THE • 1916 • *Juvenile Film* • USA
SCHEMER, THE see **VIVIDOR, EL** • 1978
SCHEMER, THE (UKN) see **SWING THE WESTERN WAY** • 1947
SCHEMER, THE (USA) see **REPRODUCTION INTERDITE** • 1956
SCHEMER SKINNY'S SCANDAL • 1917 • *Rolin* • USA
SCHEMER SKINNY'S SCHEMES • 1917 • *Rolin* • USA
SCHEMERS, THE • 1912 • *Powers* • USA
SCHEMERS, THE • 1912 • *Imp* • USA
SCHEMERS, THE • 1913 • Baker George D. • USA
SCHEMERS, THE • 1916 • *Essanay* • SHT • USA
SCHEMERS, THE • 1916 • *Vim* • USA
SCHEMERS, THE • 1916 • *Drew* • SHT • USA
SCHEMERS, THE • 1917 • Terwilliger George W. • SHT • USA
SCHEMERS, THE • 1922 • *Reol Productions* • USA
SCHEMERS: OR, THE JEWELS OF HATE, THE • 1914 • Wilson Frank? • UKN
SCHEMING GAMBLER'S PARADISE, THE (USA) see **TRIPOT CLANDESTIN, LE** • 1905
SCHEMING SCHEMERS • 1956 • White Jules • SHT • USA
SCHEMING WOMAN, THE • 1913 • *Karr Darwin* • USA
SCHENK MIR DAS LEBEN • 1927 • Fery Klaus • FRG
SCHENKE ZUR EWIGEN LIEBE, DIE • 1945 • Weidenmann Alfred • FRG
SCHERBEN • 1921 • Pick Lupu • FRG • SHATTERED
SCHERBEN BRINGEN GLUCK • 1957 • Marischka Ernst • AUS • 7 JAHRE PECH
SCHERZI DA PRETE • 1978 • Pingitore Pier Francesco • ITL
SCHERZO • 1932 • Cortez Stanley • SHT • USA
SCHERZO • 1939-41 • McLaren Norman • ANS • USA
SCHERZO • 1983 • Wertmuller Lina • ITL • JOKE OF DESTINY, A (USA) ○ JOKE ○ JOKE OF DESTINY, LYING IN WAIT AROUND THE CORNER LIKE A BANDIT, A
SCHEUSAL, DAS see **DUVAD** • 1959
SCHEVEN CONTRA FECHTENBERG • 1915 • Larsen Viggo • FRG
SCHIAFFO, LO (ITL) see **GIFLE, LA** • 1974
SCHIAFFONI E KARATI • 1974 • Margheriti Antonio • ITL • HERCULES VS. KING FU (USA) ○ MR. HERCULES AGAINST KARATE
SCHIAVA DEL PECCATO • 1954 • Matarazzo Raffaello • ITL
SCHIAVA DI BAGDAD, LA (ITL) see **SHEHEREZADE** • 1963
SCHIAVA DI ROMA, LA • 1961 • Grieco Sergio • ITL • CONQUISTA DELLE GALLIE, LA ○ SLAVE OF ROME, THE ○ SLAVE WARRIOR
SCHIAVA IO CE L'HO E TU NO, LA • 1973 • Capitani Giorgio • ITL • MY DARLING SLAVE
SCHIAVE BIANCHE • 1962 • Clement Michel, Scarpelli Umberto • ITL
SCHIAVE BIANCHE, LA see **TRATTA DELLE BIANCHE, LA** • 1952
SCHIAVE DI CARTAGINE, LE • 1956 • Brignone Guido • ITL • SWORD AND THE CROSS, THE
SCHIAVE ESISTONO ANCORA, LE • 1964 • Malenotti Roberto, Quilici Folco • DOC • ITL, FRN • SLAVE TRADE IN THE WORLD TODAY (USA) ○ ESCLAVES EXISTENT TOUJOURS, LES (FRN)
SCHIAVI PIU FORTI DEL MONDO, GLI • 1964 • Lupo Michele • ITL • SEVEN SLAVES AGAINST THE WORLD (USA) ○ SEVEN SLAVES AGAINST ROME
SCHIAVITU (ITL) see **ESCLAVE, L'** • 1953
SCHICHIBAN ME NO MISSHI • 1958 • Mori Issei • JPN
SCHICK DEINE FRAU NICHT NACH ITALIEN • 1960 • Grimm Hans • FRG
SCHICKSAL • 1924 • Basch Felix • FRG
SCHICKSAL • 1942 • von Bolvary Geza • FRG
SCHICKSAL AM BERG • 1950 • Hess Ernst • FRG
SCHICKSAL AM LENKRAD • 1953 • Vergano Aldo • AUS
SCHICKSAL AM STROM • 1944 • Paul Heinz • FRG
SCHICKSAL AUS ZWEITER HAND • 1949 • Staudte Wolfgang • FRG • ZUKUNFT AUS ZWEITER HAND
SCHICKSAL DER AENNE WOLTER, DER see **WEG, DER ZUR VERDAMMNIS FUHRT 1, DER** • 1918
SCHICKSAL DER CAROLA VAN GELDERN, DAS • 1919 • Wolff Ludwig?, Froelich Carl? • FRG
SCHICKSAL DER GABRIELE STARK, DAS • 1915 • *Messter-Film* • FRG
SCHICKSAL DER JULIA TOBALDI, DAS • 1916 • *Morena Erna* • FRG
SCHICKSAL DER MARIA KEITH, DAS • 1919 • Walther-Fein Rudolf • FRG
SCHICKSAL DER RENATE JONGK, DAS • 1918 • Wolff Carl Heinz • FRG
SCHICKSAL DER RENATE LANGEN, DAS • 1931 • Walther-Fein Rudolf • FRG • SEIN LETZTER BRIEF
SCHICKSAL DES EDGAR MORTON see **DAMON DER WELT 1** • 1919
SCHICKSAL DES LEUTNANT THOMAS GLAHN, DAS see **PAN** • 1937
SCHICKSAL DES THOMAS BALT, DAS see **WEG ZU GOTT, DER** • 1923
SCHICKSAL EINER ARZTIN, DAS see **FRAU AM SCHEIDEWEGE, DIE** • 1938
SCHICKSAL EINER MILLIARDARSTOCHTER, DAS • 1923 • *Vicor-Film* • FRG • HEMMUNGSLOS
SCHICKSAL EINER NACHT, DAS • 1927 • Schonfelder Erich • FRG
SCHICKSAL EINER SCHONEN FRAU, DAS • 1932 • Wiene Conrad • FRG, AUS • MADAME BLAUBERT
SCHICKSAL IN KETTEN • 1946 • Hoesch Eduard • AUS • WEITE WEG, DER
SCHICKSALS-DOLCH, DER • 1919 • Aichinger Hanns Raimund • FRG

SCHICKSALSSTUNDE, DER • 1920 • *Marion Oscar* • FRG
SCHICKSALSSTUNDE AUF SCHLOSS SVANESKJOLD, DIE • 1915 • Rippert Otto • FRG
SCHICKSALSTAG, DER • 1921 • Licho Adolf Edgar • FRG
SCHICKSALSWENDE see **FRIDERICUS REX (EIN KONIGSSCHICKSAL) 4** • 1923
SCHICKSALSWURFEL • 1929 • Osten Franz • FRG • THROW OF THE DICE ○ THROW OF DICE, A
SCHIEBER • 1920 • Noa Manfred • FRG
SCHIEBER, DIE • 1983 • Zell Hannes, Balik Jaroslav • AUS, CZC • PROFITEERS, THE
SCHIEBERKONIG, DER • 1920 • Moest Hubert • FRG
SCHIELENDE GLUCK, DAS see **ZEZOWATE SZCZESCIE** • 1960
SCHIESSUBUNG, DIE • 1975 • Kuckelmann Norbert • FRG • SHOOTING EXERCISE, THE
SCHIFF DER VERLORENEN MENSCHEN, DAS • 1929 • Tourneur Maurice • FRG • NAVIRE DES HOMMES PERDUS, LE ○ SHIP OF LOST MEN, THE
SCHIFF IN NOT • 1925 • Sauer Fred • FRG
SCHIFF IN NOT • 1936 • Ruttmann Walter • FRG
SCHIFF IN NOT S.O.S. • 1928 • Gallone Carmine • FRG • S.O.S. ○ SHIPWRECK
SCHIFF OHNE HAFEN, DAS • 1932 • Piel Harry • FRG • GESPENSTERSCHIFF, DAS
SCHIFFBRUCHIGEN, DIE • 1922 • Noa Manfred • FRG
SCHIFFE UND MENSCHEN • 1920 • Boese Carl • FRG
SCHIJN VAN TWIJFEL, EEN • 1975 • Orthel Rolf • DOC • NTH • SHADOW OF A DOUBT ○ WESTERBORK
SCHILTEN • 1980 • Kuert Beat • SWT
SCHIMANSKI 2 • 1987 • Gies Hajo • FRG • CRACK CONNECTION, THE ○ ZABOU
SCHIMANSKI ON THE KILLER'S TRACK • 1986 • Gies Hajo • FRG
SCHIMBUL DE MIINE • 1959 • Meszaros Marta • DCS • RMN
SCHIMMELKRIEG IN DER HOLLEDAU, DER • 1937 • Lippl Alois J. • FRG
SCHIMMELREITER, DER • 1934 • Oertel Curt, Deppe Hans • FRG • RIDER OF THE WHITE HORSE, THE (USA) ○ RIDER ON THE WHITE HORSE, THE
SCHINDERHANNES • 1928 • Bernhardt Curtis • FRG • PRINCE OF ROGUES, THE (USA)
SCHINDERHANNES, DER • 1958 • Kautner Helmut • FRG • DUEL IN THE FOREST (USA)
SCHIPP SCHIPP HURRAH! • 1915 • Karfiol William • FRG
SCHIRINS HOCHZEIT • 1975 • Sanders Helma • FRG • SCHIRIN'S WEDDING
SCHIRIN'S WEDDING see **SCHIRINS HOCHZEIT** • 1975
SCHIRM MIT DEM SCHWAN, DER • 1915 • Froelich Carl • FRG
SCHIROKKO • 1918 • Heuberger Edmund • FRG
SCHIZO • 1976 • Walker Pete • UKN • BLOOD OF THE UNDEAD
SCHIZO see **PSYCHOPATH, THE** • 1966
SCHIZO see **ALL WOMAN** • 1967
SCHIZOID • 1980 • Paulsen David • USA
SCHIZOID (USA) see **LUCERTOLA CON LA PELLE DI DONNA, UNA** • 1971
SCHLACHT AN DEN NERETVA, DIE see **BITKA NA NERETVI** • 1969
SCHLACT UM BERLIN • 1973 • Baske Franz • DOC • FRG • BATTLE OF BERLIN, THE (USA)
SCHLACT VON BADEMUNDE, DIE • 1921 • Mayring Philipp L. • FRG
SCHLAFWAGENKONTROLLEUR, DER • 1935 • Eichberg Richard • FRG, FRN • CONTROLEUR DES WAGON-LITS, LE (FRN)
SCHLAG AUF SCHLAG • 1959 • von Cziffra Geza • FRG
SCHLAGENDE WETTER • 1923 • Grune Karl • FRG
SCHLAGER-REVUE 1962 • 1961 • Engel Thomas • AUS
SCHLAGERPARADE • 1953 • Ode Erik • FRG
SCHLAGERPARADE 60 • 1960 • Marischka Franz • AUS
SCHLAGERRAKETEN • 1960 • Ode Erik • FRG
SCHLANGENEI, DAS • 1977 • Bergman Ingmar • FRG, USA • SERPENT'S EGG, THE (USA) ○ ORMENS AGG
SCHLANGENGRUBE UND DAS PENDEL, DIE • 1967 • Reinl Harald • FRG • BLOOD DEMON, THE (UKN) ○ PIT AND THE PENDULUM, THE ○ TORTURE CHAMBER OF DR. SADISM, THE ○ SNAKE PIT AND THE PENDULUM, THE
SCHLANGENRING, DER • 1917 • Wolff Carl Heinz • FRG
SCHLEICHENDE GIFT, DAS • 1920 • Philippi Siegfried • FRG
SCHLEIER DER FAVORITIN, DER see **CURARE ODER DER INDISCHE DOLCH** • 1915
SCHLEIER FIEL, DER • 1960 • May Paul • FRG
SCHLEIERTANZERIN, DIE • 1929 • Burguet M. C. • FRG
SCHLEMIHL • 1915 • Oswald Richard • FRG • LEBENSBILD, EIN
SCHLEMIHL, DER • 1931 • Nosseck Max • FRG
SCHLEMMERORGIE, DIE see **WHO IS KILLING THE GREAT CHEFS OF EUROPE?** • 1978
SCHLEPPZUG M17 • 1933 • George Heinrich • FRG • TUGBOAT M17
SCHLESISCHE TOR, DAS • 1983 • Klopfenstein Clemens • DOC • SWT
SCHLEUSE, DIE • 1962 • Kramer Harry • SHT • FRG
SCHLIEREN • 1959 • De Normanville Peter • UKN
SCHLOCK • 1972 • Landis John • USA • BANANA MONSTER, THE
SCHLOSS, DAS • 1968 • Noelte Rudolf • FRG, SWT • CASTLE, THE (USA)
SCHLOSS DES SCHRECKENS, DAS • 1919 • Dengel Edy • FRG
SCHLOSS DES SCHRECKENS, DAS see **GEHEIMNIS DER SCHWARZEN KOFFER, DAS** • 1962
SCHLOSS EINOD • 1919 • Lund Erik • FRG
SCHLOSS GRIPSHOLM • 1963 • Hoffmann Kurt • FRG
SCHLOSS HUBERTUS • 1934 • Deppe Hans • FRG
SCHLOSS HUBERTUS • 1954 • Weiss Helmut • FRG
SCHLOSS HUBERTUS • 1973 • Reinl Harald • FRG
SCHLOSS IM SUDEN, DAS • 1933 • von Bolvary Geza • FRG
SCHLOSS IN FLANDERN, DAS • 1936 • von Bolvary Geza • FRG • CASTLE IN FLANDERS, A
SCHLOSS IN TIROL, DAS • 1957 • von Radvanyi Geza • FRG
SCHLOSS TAMARE • 1915 • von Woringen Paul • FRG
SCHLOSS UND HUTTE • 1915 • Del Zopp Rudolf • FRG
SCHLOSS VOGELOD • 1921 • Murnau F. W. • FRG • HAUNTED CASTLE (USA) ○ VOGELOD: THE HAUNTED CASTLE ○ VOGELOD CASTLE ○ CASTLE VOGELOD
SCHLOSS VOGELOD • 1936 • Obal Max • FRG • VOGELOD CASTLE
SCHLOSSER UND KATEN • 1957 • Maetzig Kurt • GDR • CASTLES AND COTTAGES ○ PALACES AND HUTS
SCHLOSSFRAU VON RADOMSK, DIE • 1915 • *Stuart Webbs-Film* • FRG
SCHLOSSHERR VON HOHENSTEIN, DER • 1917 • Oswald Richard • FRG
SCHLUCT DES TODES, DIE • 1923 • Albertini Luciano, Bertoni Francis A. • FRG • PAMPASREITER
SCHLUMMERNDE VULKAN, DER • 1921 • Bauer James • FRG
SCHLUSSAKKORD • 1936 • Sirk Douglas • FRG • FINAL ACCORD (UKN) ○ NINTH SYMPHONY
SCHLUSSAKKORD • 1960 • Liebeneiner Wolfgang • FRG
SCHLUSSEL, DER see **SLEUTEL, DE** • 1963
SCHLUSSEL, DIE • 1974 • Gunther Egon • GDR • KEYS, THE
SCHLUSSEL UM DEN HALS.., DEN • 1959 • Tichawsky Heinz, Strobel Hans-Rolf • FRG
SCHMEERGUNTZ • 1965 • Nelson Gunvor, Wiley Dorothy • SHT • USA
SCHMETTERLINGE WEINEN NICHT • 1970 • Uberall Klaus • SWT, FRG • BUTTERFLIES DON'T CRY
SCHMETTERLINGSSCHLACHT, DIE • 1924 • Eckstein Franz • FRG
SCHMIDT THE SPY • 1916 • *Sydney Lewis* • SHT • UKN
SCHMIED VON KOCHEL 1, DER see **TRAGODIE EINES VOLKES 1, DIE** • 1922
SCHMIED VON KOCHEL 2, DER see **TRAGODIE EINES VOLKES 2, DIE** • 1922
SCHMIED VON ST. BARTOLONA, DER • 1955 • Michel Max • FRG
SCHMIEDE DES GRAUENS, DIE • 1920 • Attenberger Toni • FRG
SCHMINKE • 1922 • Kaufmann Fritz • FRG
SCHMUCK DER GRAFIN, DER • 1916 • *Gotz Kurt* • FRG
SCHMUCK DER HERZOGIN, DER • 1916 • Philippi Siegfried • FRG
SCHMUCK DES RAJAH, DER • 1918 • Gad Urban • FRG
SCHMUGGLER VON BERNINA, DIW • 1924 • Zurn Walther • FRG
SCHMUGGLER VON SAN DIEGO, DIE • 1920 • Arnheim Valy • FRG
SCHMUGGLERBRAUT VON MALORCA, DIE • 1929 • Behrendt Hans • FRG • MADCHEN VON VALENCIA, DAS ○ GIRL OF VALENCIA
SCHMUGGLERIN, DIE • 1920 • Burg Eugen • FRG
SCHMUGGLERMADONNA, DIE see **MARIZZA, GENANNT DIE SCHMUGGLERMADONNA** • 1920
SCHMUTZ • 1986 • Manker Paulus • AUS • MR. DIRT
SCHMUTZIGER ENGEL • 1958 • Vohrer Alfred • FRG • IMPERFECT ANGEL (USA) ○ DIRTY ANGEL (UKN) ○ FALLEN ANGEL
SCHMUTZIGES GELD see **SONG** • 1928
SCHNEEGLOCKCHEN BLUHN IN SEPTEMBER • 1974 • Ziewer Christian • FRG • SNOWDROPS BLOOM IN SEPTEMBER
SCHNEEPIRATEN • 1925 • *Drehwa-Film* • FRG
SCHNEESCHUHBANDITEN • 1928 • Krafft Uwe Jens • FRG
SCHNEEWITTCHEN • 1928 • Zengerling Aloys Alfons • FRG
SCHNEEWITTCHEN UND DIE SIEBEN GAUKLER • 1962 • Hoffmann Kurt • FRG, SWT • SNOW WHITE AND THE SEVEN JUGGLERS
SCHNEEWITTCHEN UND DIE SIEBEN ZWERGE • ANS • FRG
SCHNEEWITTCHEN UND DIE SIEBEN ZWERGE • 1956 • Kobler Erich • FRG • SNOW WHITE AND THE SEVEN DWARFS ○ SNOW WHITE (USA)
SCHNEEWITTCHEN UND ROSENROT • 1955 • Kobler Erich • FRG • SNOW WHITE AND ROSE RED (USA)
SCHNEIDER VON ULM, DER • 1978 • Reitz Edgar • FRG • TAILOR FROM ULM, THE
SCHNEIDER WIBBEL • 1920 • Noa Manfred • FRG
SCHNEIDER WIBBEL • 1931 • Henckels Paul • FRG
SCHNEIDER WIBBEL • 1939 • de Kowa Viktor • FRG
SCHNEIDERKOMTESS, DIE • 1922 • Mack Max • FRG • IST ARBEIT SCHANDE?
SCHNEIDER'S ANTI-NOISE CRUSADE • 1909 • Griffith D. W. • USA
SCHNELLER ALS DER TOD • 1925 • Piel Harry • FRG
SCHNITTE • 1966 • Grobe Peter • FRG
SCHNITZ, THE TAILOR • 1913 • Sennett Mack • USA
SCHNOOK, THE see **SWINGIN' ALONG** • 1962
SCHODAMI W GORE.. • 1988 • Domalik Andrzej • PLN • STAIRWAY TO HEAVEN ○ UPSTAIRS..
SCHODY • 1964 • Hofman Eduard • ANS • CZC • LADDER, THE ○ STEPS, THE
SCHODY • 1967 • Schabenbeck Stefan • PLN • STAIRCASE ○ STAIRS
SCHOLAR, THE • 1918 • Gillstrom Arvid E. • SHT • USA
SCHOLAR IN SOCIETY: NORTHROP FRYE IN CONVERSATION • 1984 • Winkler Donald • MTV • CND
SCHON IST DIE LIEBE AM KONIGSSEE • 1960 • Albin Hans • FRG
SCHON IST DIE MANOVERZEIT • 1938 • Schonfelder Erich • FRG • KARTOFFELSUPP, KARTOFFELSUPP
SCHON IST DIE WELT • 1957 • von Bolvary Geza • FRG
SCHON IST ES, VERLIEBT ZU SEIN! • 1934 • Janssen Walter • FRG
SCHON IST JEDER TAG, DEN DU MIR SCHENSKT, MARIE LOUISE • 1933 • Reiber Willy • FRG • SONNE GEHT AUF, DIE
SCHON MUSS MAN SEIN • 1951 • von Rathony Akos • FRG
SCHON WIE DIE SUNDE (FRG) see **CAROLINE CHERIE** • 1967
SCHONE ABENTEUER, DAS • 1924 • Noa Manfred • FRG
SCHONE ABENTEUER, DAS • 1932 • Schunzel Reinhold • FRG
SCHONE ABENTEUER, DAS • 1959 • Hoffmann Kurt • FRG • BEAUTIFUL ADVENTURE, THE
SCHONE ARTHUR, DER • 1915 • Haase Magnus • FRG
SCHONE FRAULEIN SCHRAGG, DAS • 1937 • Deppe Hans • FRG
SCHONE GEHEIMNIS, DAS • 1919 • Del Zopp Rudolf • FRG
SCHONE JOLAN, DIE • 1918 • Meinert Rudolf • FRG
SCHONE LUGNERIN, DIE • 1959 • von Ambesser Axel • FRG, FRN
SCHONE LURETTE, DIE • 1960 • Kolditz Gottfried • GDR
SCHONE MADEL, DAS • 1922 • Mack Max • FRG
SCHONE MEISTERIN, DIE • 1956 • Schundler Rudolf • FRG
SCHONE MISS LILIAN, DIE • 1920 • Eckstein Franz • FRG
SCHONE MULLERIN, DIE • 1954 • Liebeneiner Wolfgang • FRG
SCHONE PRINZESSIN VON CHINA, DIE • 1916 • Gliese Rochus • FRG
SCHONE SUNDERIN, DIE see **UND WANDERN SOLLST DU RUHELOS..** • 1915
SCHONE TIER, DAS see **MARIZZA, GENANNT DIE SCHMUGGLERMADONNA** • 1920
SCHONE TOLZERIN, DIE • 1952 • Haussler Richard • FRG
SCHONEN BEINE DER SABRINA, DIE (FRG) see **BELLISSIME GAMBE DI SABRINA, LE** • 1958
SCHONEN TAGE VON ARANJUEZ • 1933 • Meyer Johannes • FRG
SCHONEN WILDEN VON IBIZA, DIE • Gotz Siggi • FRG • BEAUTIFUL AND WILD ON IBIZA ○ SEX ON THE ROCKS
SCHONER GIGOLO -ARMER GIGOLO • 1978 • Hemmings David • FRG, USA, UKN • JUST A GIGOLO (USA)
SCHONER TAG, EIN • 1943 • Mayring Philipp L. • FRG
SCHONHEITSFLECKCHEN, DAS • 1936 • Hansen Rolf • FRG
SCHONSTE FRAU DER WELT, DIE • 1924 • Eichberg Richard • FRG
SCHONSTE FRAU VON PARIS, DIE • 1928 • Fleck Jacob, Fleck Luise • FRG
SCHONSTE GESCHENK, DAS • 1916 • Lubitsch Ernst • FRG
SCHONSTE MANN IM STAATE, DER • 1931 • Boese Carl • FRG
SCHONSTE TAG MEINES LEBENS, DER • 1939 • Lindtberg Leopold • DOC • SWT
SCHONSTE TAG MEINES LEBENS, DER • 1957 • Neufeld Max • AUS
SCHONSTEN BEINE VON BERLIN, DIE • 1927 • Wolff Willi • FRG
SCHONZEIT FUR FUCHSE • 1966 • Schamoni Peter • FRG • CLOSE TIME FOR FOXES ○ CLOSE SEASON FOR FOXES
SCHOOL • 1972 • Elffers Joost • SHT • NTH
SCHOOL see **SZKOLA** • 1958
SCHOOL BEGINS • 1928 • Mack Anthony • SHT • USA
SCHOOL BELLS see **HEARTS OF MEN** • 1915
SCHOOL BIRDS • 1937 • Davis Mannie, Gordon George • ANS • USA
SCHOOL BOY'S MEMORIES OR KIDS AT SCHOOL • 1915 • *Liberty* • USA
SCHOOL DAY MEMORIES • 1915 • *Fisher Harry* • USA
SCHOOL DAYS • 1913 • *Pilot* • USA
SCHOOL DAYS • 1917 • Moss Howard S. • ANM • USA
SCHOOL DAYS • 1920 • Semon Larry, Peebles Mort, Taurog Norman • SHT • USA
SCHOOL DAYS • 1921 • Nigh William • USA
SCHOOL DAYS • 1932 • *Iwerks Ub (P)* • ANS • USA
SCHOOL DAYS • 1932 • Fleischer Dave • ANS • USA
SCHOOL DAYS see **THINGS ARE LOOKING UP** • 1935
SCHOOL DAZE • 1942 • *Terry Paul (P)* • ANS • USA
SCHOOL DAZE • 1988 • Lee Spike • USA
SCHOOL FOR CATS see **KOCICI SKOLA** • 1960
SCHOOL FOR CHARM • 1953-54 • Devlin Bernard • DCS • CND
SCHOOL FOR DANGER • 1947 • Baird Edward • UKN • NOW IT CAN BE TOLD
SCHOOL FOR DEAFMUTES see **ESCUELA DE SORDOMUDOS** • 1967
SCHOOL FOR FATHERS see **SKOLA OTCU** • 1957
SCHOOL FOR GIRLS • 1934 • Nigh William • USA
SCHOOL FOR HUSBANDS • 1937 • Marton Andrew • UKN
SCHOOL FOR HUSBANDS, A • 1917 • Melford George • USA
SCHOOL FOR JIVE see **MR. BIG** • 1943
SCHOOL FOR LOVE see **SCHOOL FOR SEX** • 1969
SCHOOL FOR LOVE (USA) see **FUTURES VEDETTES** • 1955
SCHOOL FOR MERMAIDS • 1945 • *O'Brien Joseph/ Mead Thomas (P)* • SHT • USA
SCHOOL FOR OFFENDERS • 1965 • Hanibal Jiri • CZC
SCHOOL FOR PARTISANS see **PARTIZANSKE SKOLE** • 1981
SCHOOL FOR RANDLE • 1949 • Blakeley John E. • UKN
SCHOOL FOR SABOTAGE see **THEY CAME TO BLOW UP AMERICA** • 1943
SCHOOL FOR SCANDAL see **SHKOLA ZLOSLOVIYA** • 1952
SCHOOL FOR SCANDAL, THE • 1914 • Buel Kenean • USA
SCHOOL FOR SCANDAL, THE • 1923 • Greenwood Edwin • *B & C* • SHT • UKN
SCHOOL FOR SCANDAL, THE • 1923 • Phillips Bertram • *B.p. Productions* • UKN
SCHOOL FOR SCANDAL, THE • 1930 • Elvey Maurice • UKN
SCHOOL FOR SCOUNDRELS see **SCHOOL FOR SCOUNDRELS OR HOW TO WIN WITHOUT ACTUALLY CHEATING** • 1960
SCHOOL FOR SCOUNDRELS OR HOW TO WIN WITHOUT ACTUALLY CHEATING • 1960 • Hamer Robert • UKN • SCHOOL FOR SCOUNDRELS
SCHOOL FOR SECRETS • 1946 • Ustinov Peter • UKN • SECRET FLIGHT (USA)
SCHOOL FOR SEX • 1969 • Walker Pete • UKN • SCHOOL FOR LOVE
SCHOOL FOR SEX see **NIKUTAI NO GAKKO** • 1965
SCHOOL FOR SONS-IN-LAW, THE see **ECOLE DES GENDRES, L'** • 1897
SCHOOL FOR STARS • 1935 • Pedelty Donovan • UKN
SCHOOL FOR STRUMPETS see **ECOLE DES COCOTTES, L'** • 1957
SCHOOL FOR SUICIDE see **SELVMORDSSKOLEN** • 1964
SCHOOL FOR SWING • 1936 • Schwarzwald Milton • SHT • USA
SCHOOL FOR THIEVES see **SCUOLA DI LADRI** • 1987
SCHOOL FOR UNCLAIMED GIRLS (USA) see **SMASHING BIRD I USED TO KNOW, THE** • 1969
SCHOOL FOR VANDALS • 1987 • Finbow Colin, Wells Orlando • UKN
SCHOOL FOR VIOLENCE (UKN) see **HIGH SCHOOL HELLCATS** • 1959
SCHOOL FOR VIRGINS • 1975 • von Cziffra Geza • ITL

SCHOOL FOR VIRGINS (UKN) see **JOSEFINE: DAS LIEBESTOLLE KATZCHEN** • 1972
SCHOOL FOR WIVES • 1925 • Halperin Victor Hugo • USA
SCHOOL GIRLS • 1977 • Howard Kenneth • FRG
SCHOOL HOLIDAYS, THE • 1963 • Kokochashvili Mikhail • USS
SCHOOL HOUSE SCANDAL, A see **SCHOOLHOUSE SCANDAL, A** • 1919
SCHOOL IN COLOGNE • 1948 • Wallace Graham • UKN, FRG
SCHOOL IN THE MAILBOX • 1946 • Hawes Stanley • DOC • ASL
SCHOOL IS NOT AN ISLAND, THE • 1974 • Noonan Chris • DOC • ASL
SCHOOL KIDS' PICNIC, THE • 1913 • *Majestic* • USA
SCHOOL LEAVERS, THE see **MATURZYSCI** • 1972
SCHOOL MARM OF COYOTE COUNTY, THE • 1911 • Melies Gaston • USA
SCHOOL-MARM'S RIDE FOR LIFE, THE • 1910 • *Defender* • USA
SCHOOL OF COURAGE see **SKOLA MUZESTVA** • 1957
SCHOOL OF ECHOES see **YAMABIKO GAKKO** • 1952
SCHOOL OF FATHERS see **SKOLA OTCU** • 1957
SCHOOL OF FREEDOM see **JIYU GAKKU** • 1951
SCHOOL OF HARD KNOCKS • 1970 • *Kirt Films International* • USA
SCHOOL OF LOVE • 1969 • *Cherry Productions* • USA
SCHOOL OF LOVE see **NIKUTAI NO GAKKO** • 1965
SCHOOL OF SEX see **NIKUTAI NO GAKKO** • 1965
SCHOOL OF SPIES, THE see **RIKUGUN NAKANO GAKKO** • 1966
SCHOOL OF SUICIDE see **SELVMORDSSKOLEN** • 1964
SCHOOL OF WORK, THE • 1959 • Stiopul Savel • RMN
SCHOOL OUTING, A see **GITA SCOLASTICA, UNA** • 1984
SCHOOL PALS • 1923 • Seiler Lewis, Stoloff Ben • SHT • USA
SCHOOL PLAY • 1969 • Rydell Charles • USA
SCHOOL PRINCIPAL, THE • 1913 • Johnson Arthur • USA
SCHOOL SPIRIT • 1985 • Holleb Alan • USA
SCHOOL TEACHER AND THE WAIF, THE • 1912 • Griffith D. W. • USA
SCHOOL TEACHER AT ANGEL CAMP, THE • 1914 • *Frontier* • USA
SCHOOL TEACHER FROM VIGEVANO, THE see **MAESTRO DI VIGEVANO, IL** • 1963
SCHOOL THAT LEARNED TO EAT, THE • 1948 • Lassee Fred • USA
SCHOOL, THE BASIS OF LIFE see **SKOLA ZAKLAD ZIVOTA** • 1938
SCHOOL, THE BEGINNING OF LIFE see **SKOLA ZAKLAD ZIVOTA** • 1938
SCHOOL WALTZ see **SHKOLNI VALS** • 1978
SCHOOL WHERE LIFE BEGINS see **SKOLA ZAKLAD ZIVOTA** • 1938
SCHOOL WITHOUT BLACKBOARDS see **SZKOLA BEZ TABLIC** • 1960
SCHOOLBOY DREAMS • 1940 • *Mintz Charles (P)* • ANS • USA
SCHOOLBOY PENITENTIARY (UKN) see **LITTLE RED SCHOOLHOUSE, THE** • 1936
SCHOOLBOYS' PRANKS • 1907 • Green Tom? • UKN
SCHOOLBOYS' REVOLT, THE • 1908 • Fitzhamon Lewin • UKN
SCHOOLDAYS see **DAIGAKU NO SAMURAI-TACHI** • 1957
SCHOOLGIRL DIARY • Mattoli Mario • ITL
SCHOOLGIRL REBELS • 1915 • Wilson Frank? • UKN
SCHOOLGIRL REPORT NO.1 see **SCHULMADCHEN-REPORT 12** • 1978
SCHOOLGIRL WITH A MACHINE-GUN, A see **SAILOR FUKU TO KIKANJU** • 1982
SCHOOLHOUSE SCANDAL, A • 1919 • Cline Eddie • SHT • USA • SCHOOL HOUSE SCANDAL, A
SCHOOLING see **SKOLOVANJE** • 1970
SCHOOLING OF MARY ANN, THE • 1914 • Le Saint Edward J. • USA
SCHOOLMA'AM, THE • 1913 • *Patheplay* • USA
SCHOOLMA'AM OF SNAKE, THE • 1911 • Dwan Allan • USA
SCHOOLMA'AM OF STONE GULCH, THE • 1912 • *Roland Ruth* • USA
SCHOOLMA'AM'S COURAGE, THE • 1911 • *Reliance* • USA
SCHOOLMARM'S SHOOTING MATCH, THE • 1913 • *Selig* • USA
SCHOOLMASTER, THE (UKN) see **HOOSIER SCHOOLMASTER, THE** • 1935
SCHOOLMASTER HOFER see **HAUPTLEHRER HOFER** • 1975
SCHOOLMASTER OF MARIPOSA, THE • 1910 • *Selig* • USA
SCHOOLMASTER'S PORTRAIT, THE • 1898 • *Riley Brothers* • UKN
SCHOOLMATES see **COMPAGNI DI SCUOLA** • 1988
SCHOOLMISTRESS, THE see **TANITONO** • 1945
SCHOOLMISTRESS ON THE SPREE see **LARARINNA PA VIFT** • 1941
SCHOOLS, THE • 1962 • *Cawston Richard (P)* • UKN
SCHOOLS AND SCHOOLS • 1918 • Justice Martin • SHT • USA
SCHOOL'S OUT • 1930 • McGowan Robert • SHT • USA
SCHOOLTIME BLUES see **SULI-BULI** • 1983
SCHOONER GANG, THE • 1937 • Hackney W. Devenport • UKN
SCHOONER THE BETTER, THE • 1946 • Swift Howard • ANS • USA
SCHOPFER, DER • 1928 • Boudrioz Robert • FRG • ZWISCHEN LIEBE UN PFLICHT
SCHORFHEIDE • 1937 • Schulz Ulrich K. T. • FRG
SCHORNSTEIN NR.4 (FRG) see **VOLEUSE, LA** • 1966
SCHORPIOEN, DE • 1984 • Verbong Ben • NTH • NEVER KILL A SCORPION ○ SCORPION, THE
SCHOT IS TE BOORD, HET • 1952 • van der Horst Herman • DOC • NTH • SHOOT THE NETS
SCHOTIS • 1942 • Maroto Eduardo G. • SPN
SCHPOUNTZ, LE • 1937 • Pagnol Marcel • FRN • HEARTBEAT (USA)
SCHRAGE OTTO, DER • 1957 • von Cziffra Geza • FRG
SCHRAGE VOGEL see **SPIELST DU MIT SCHRAGEN VOGELN** • 1968
SCHRAMMELN • 1944 • von Bolvary Geza • FRG
SCHRECKEN DER GARNISON, DER • 1931 • Boese Carl • FRG
SCHRECKEN DER MILLIONARE, DER • 1920 • Neff Wolfgang • FRG
SCHRECKEN DER MILLIONARE, DER see **SENSATIONELLEN ERLEBNISSE GEHEIMAGENTEN. ERSTES ERLEBNIS: DER SCHRECKEN DER MILLIONARE** • 1923
SCHRECKEN DER WESTKUSTE, DER • 1925 • Stein Josef, Boese Carl • FRG
SCHRECKEN DES MEERES, DER • 1924 • Osten Franz • FRG
SCHRECKEN VOM HEIDEKRUG, DER • 1934 • Boese Carl • FRG
SCHRECKENSNACHT AUF SCHLOSS DRACHENEGG, DIE • 1920 • Leffler Robert • FRG
SCHRECKENSNACHT IM HAUSE CLARQUE, DIE • 1920 • Hartt Hanns Heinz • FRG
SCHRECKENSNACHT IM IRRENHAUSE IVOY, DIE • 1919 • von Cserepy Arzen, Tollen Otz • FRG
SCHRECKENSNACHT IN DER MENAGERIE, DIE • 1921 • Wendt Ernst • FRG
SCHRECKENSTAGE DER FINANZKREISE see **AM NARRENSEIL 1** • 1921
SCHRECKLICHE MADCHEN, DAS • 1990 • Verhoeven Michael • FRG • NASTY GIRL, THE
SCHREI AUS DER TIEFE, DER • 1922 • Dessauer Siegfried • FRG
SCHREI DER SCHWARZEN WOLFE, DER • 1972 • Reinl Harald • FRG • CRY OF THE BLACK WOLVES
SCHREI DES GEWISSENS, DER • 1919 • Illes Eugen • FRG
SCHREI IN DER NACHT, EIN • 1915 • Neuss Alwin • FRG
SCHREI IN DER WUSTE, DER • 1924 • Stockel Joe • FRG • MARCCO, DER SCHREI IN DER WUSTE
SCHREI NACH GLUCK, DER • 1925 • *Hofer-Film* • FRG
SCHREI NACH LUST • 1968 • Schlesinger Gunter • FRG • LIEBE ALS KODER ○ CRY FOR LUST ○ LOVE AS BAIT
SCHREIE IN DER NACHT • 1968 • Margheriti Antonio • FRG, ITL
SCHREIN DER MEDICI, DER • 1920 • Herbig Paul • FRG
SCHRIJVER EN DE DOOD, DE • 1988 • Driessen Paul • ANM • NTH • WRITER, THE
SCHRITT FUR SCHRITT • 1960 • Veiczi Janos • GDR • STEP BY STEP
SCHRITT INS REICH DER FREIHEIT -ZUM BEISPIEL IN PERU • 1978 • Strobel Hans Rolf • DOC • FRG
SCHRITT VOM WEGE, DER • 1939 • Grundgens Gustaf • FRG • FALSE STEP, THE (USA) ○ EFFIE BRIEST
SCHRITT VOM WEGE, EIN • 1919 • Meinert Rudolf • FRG
SCHRITTE INS REICH FREIHEIT -ZUM BEISPIEL IN TANSANIA • 1978 • Strobel Hans Rolf • DOC • FRG
SCHTROUMPF A TOUT FAIRE • 1966 • Ryssack Eddy, Rosy Maurice • ANS • BLG
SCHTROUMPF AND THE DRAGON, THE see **SCHTROUMPF ET LE DRAGON, LE** • 1963
SCHTROUMPF ET LE DRAGON, LE • 1963 • Ryssack Eddy, Rosy Maurice • ANS • BLG • SCHTROUMPF AND THE DRAGON, THE
SCHTROUMPF ET L'OEUF, LE • 1960 • Ryssack Eddy • ANS • BLG
SCHTROUMPF VOLANT, LE • 1963 • Ryssack Eddy, Rosy Maurice • ANS • BLG • FLYING SCHTROUMPF, THE
SCHTROUMPFS, LES • 1960 • Ryssack Eddy, Rosy Maurice • ASS • BLG
SCHTROUMPFS NOIRS, LES • 1961 • Ryssack Eddy • ANS • BLG
SCHUBERT see **SINFONIA D'AMORE** • 1955
SCHUBERT'S FRUHLINGSTRAUM • 1931 • Oswald Richard • FRG
SCHUBERT'S SERENADE (USA) see **SERENADE** • 1939
SCHUBERTS UNVOLLENDETE SYMPHONIE see **LEISE FLEHEN MEINE LIEDER** • 1933
SCHUCHTERNE CASANOVA, DER • 1936 • Lamac Carl • FRG
SCHUCHTERNE FELIX, DER • 1935 • Boese Carl • FRG
SCHUDSCHEIN DES PANDOLA, DER see **MARINELEUTNANT VON BRINKEN** • 1918
SCHUH DES PATRIARCHEN, DER • 1988 • Moll Bruno • SWT
SCHUHE EINER SCHONEN FRAU, DIE • 1922 • Hanus Emerich • FRG
SCHUHPALAST PINKUS • 1916 • Lubitsch Ernst • FRG • SHOE SALON PINKUS
SCHULD, DIE • 1919 • Biebrach Rudolf • FRG
SCHULD, DIE • 1924 • Berger Josef • FRG
SCHULD ALLEIN IST DER WEIN • 1949 • Kirchhoff Fritz • FRG
SCHULD DER GABRIELE ROTTWEIL, DIE • 1944 • Rabenalt Arthur M. • FRG
SCHULD DER LAVINIA MORLAND, DIE • 1920 • May Joe • FRG
SCHULD DES DR. HOMMA, DIE • 1951 • Verhoeven Paul • FRG
SCHULD DES GRAFEN WERONSKI, DIE • 1921 • Biebrach Rudolf • FRG
SCHULD UND SUHNE • 1922 • Biebrach Rudolf • FRG
SCHULD UND SUHNE see **RASKOLNIKOW** • 1923
SCHULDIG • 1913 • Oberlander Hans • FRG
SCHULDIG • 1927 • Meyer Johannes • FRG
SCHULDIG? see **EDES ANNA** • 1958
SCHULDIGE, DIE • 1921 • Sauer Fred • FRG
SCHULDLOSE VERDACHT, DER • 1918 • *Widal Maria* • FRG
SCHULE DES LEBENS see **GLUCKLICHER MENSCH, EIN** • 1943
SCHULE FUR EHEGLUCK • 1954 • Schelkopf Toni, Geis Rainer • FRG
SCHULER GERBER, DER • 1981 • Gluck Wolfgang • AUS, FRG • PUPIL GERBER, THE
SCHULER-REPORT-JUNGE, JUNGE WAS DIE MADCHEN ALLES VON UNS WOLLEN! • 1971 • Schroeder Eberhard • FRG
SCHULERFILM • 1982 • Jacusso Nino, Rickenbach Franz • SWT
SCHULFREUND, DER • 1960 • Siodmak Robert • FRG • MEIN SCHULFREUND
SCHULMADCHEN PORNO • 1978 • *Love Film* • FRG
SCHULMADCHEN-REPORT • 1970 • Hofbauer Ernst • FRG
SCHULMADCHEN-REPORT 2 • 1970 • Hofbauer Ernst • FRG
SCHULMADCHEN-REPORT 3 -WAS ELTERN NICHT MAL AHNEN • 1971 • Hofbauer Ernst • FRG
SCHULMADCHEN-REPORT 4 • 1972 • Hofbauer Ernst • FRG
SCHULMADCHEN-REPORT 5 • 1974 • Hofbauer Ernst • FRG
SCHULMADCHEN-REPORT 6 • 1974 • Hofbauer Ernst • FRG
SCHULMADCHEN-REPORT 7 • 1974 • Hofbauer Ernst • FRG
SCHULMADCHEN-REPORT 8 • 1974 • Hofbauer Ernst • FRG
SCHULMADCHEN-REPORT 9 • 1975 • Boos Walter • FRG
SCHULMADCHEN-REPORT 10 • 1976 • Hofbauer Ernst • FRG • SCHULMADCHEN-REPORT 10 -IRGENDWANN FANGT JEDE AN ○ YOUNG BEDMATES
SCHULMADCHEN-REPORT 10 -IRGENDWANN FANGT JEDE AN see **SCHULMADCHEN-REPORT 10** • 1976
SCHULMADCHEN-REPORT 11 • 1976 • Hofbauer Ernst • FRG • CONFESSIONS OF A NAKED VIRGIN ○ SCHULMADCHEN-REPORT 11 TEIL: PROBIEREN GEHT UBER STUDIEREN
SCHULMADCHEN-REPORT 11 TEIL: PROBIEREN GEHT UBER STUDIEREN see **SCHULMADCHEN-REPORT 11** • 1976
SCHULMADCHEN-REPORT 12 • 1978 • Boos Walter • FRG • BLUE FANTASIES ○ SCHOOLGIRL REPORT NO.1
SCHULTZ HAS THE SMALL POX • 1911 • *Lubin* • USA
SCHULTZ' LADY FRIEND • 1915 • *Asher Max* • USA
SCHULTZ THE BARBER • 1914 • *Joker* • USA
SCHULTZ THE PAPER HANGER • 1914 • *Joker* • USA
SCHULTZ'S LOTTERY TICKET • 1913 • *Crystal* • USA
SCHUSS AM NEBELHORN, DER • 1933 • Beck-Gaden Hanns • FRG • GEWISSEN DES SEBASTIAN GEYER, DAS
SCHUSS DURCHS FENSTER • 1950 • Breuer Siegfried • AUS
SCHUSS -GEGENSCHUSS • 1984 • Kuhn Christoph • SWT
SCHUSS IM MORGENGRAUEN • 1932 • Zeisler Alfred • FRG
SCHUSS IM PAVILLON, DER • 1925 • Obal Max • FRG
SCHUSS IM TONFILMATELIER, DER • 1930 • Zeisler Alfred • FRG
SCHUSS IM TRAUM, DER • 1915 • Mack Max • FRG
SCHUSS IN DEN SCHATTEN, DER • 1925 • *Continental-Film* • FRG
SCHUSS IN DER PARISER OPER, DER see **FRAU MIT DEN MILLIONEN 1, DIE** • 1923
SCHUSS UM MITTERNACHT • 1944 • Zerlett Hans H. • FRG
SCHUSS VON DER KANZEL, DER • 1942 • Lindtberg Leopold • SWT
SCHUSSE AN DER GRENZE • 1933 • Hubler-Kahla J. A. • FRG
SCHUSSE AUS DEM GEIGENKASTEN • 1965 • Umgelter Fritz • FRG, FRN • TREAD SOFTLY (UKN)
SCHUSSE IM 3/4-TAKT • 1965 • Weidenmann Alfred • AUS
SCHUSSE IM MORGENGRAUEN see **SCHATZ VOM TOPLITZSEE, DER** • 1959
SCHUSSE IN DER NACHT see **GROSSE BLUFF, DER** • 1933
SCHUSSE IN KABINE 7 • 1938 • Boese Carl • FRG
SCHUSSE IN MARIENBAD • 1974 • Toman Ivo • GDR, CZC
SCHUSSE UNTERM GALGEN • 1968 • Seemann Horst • GDR • SHOTS UNDER THE GALLOWS
SCHUT, DER • 1964 • Siodmak Robert • FRG, FRN, ITL • SHOOT, THE (USA) ○ YELLOW DEVIL, THE
SCHUTZE LIESCHEN MULLER • 1956 • Konig Hans H. • FRG
SCHUTZENFEST IN SCHILDA • 1931 • Trotz Adolf • FRG
SCHUTZENGRABEN • Ralph Louis? • FRG
SCHUTZENKONIG, DER • 1932 • Seitz Franz • FRG
SCHUTZENKONIG WIRD DER FELIX • 1934 • Boese Carl • FRG
SCHUTZENLIESEL • 1954 • Schundler Rudolf • FRG
SCHUTZENLIESL • 1926 • Walther-Fein Rudolf • FRG
SCHUZKA SE STINY • 1982 • Svoboda Jiri • CZC • MEETING WITH SHADOWS, A
SCHWABEMADLE, DAS • 1919 • Lubitsch Ernst • FRG
SCHWACHE STUNDE, DIE • 1943 • Slavinsky Vladimir • FRG
SCHWACHE STUNDE, EINE • 1919 • Gartner Adolf • FRG
SCHWANENSEE • 1967 • Branss Truck • FRG, AUS • SWAN LAKE (UKN)
SCHWARZ AUF WEISS • 1943 • Emo E. W. • FRG
SCHWARZ UND WEISS WIE TAGE UND NACHTE • 1978 • Petersen Wolfgang • FRG • BLACK AND WHITE LIKE DAY AND NIGHT
SCHWARZ WEISS BLUES see **SCHWARZ-WEISS BLUS** • 1962
SCHWARZ-WEISS BLUS • 1962 • Verhavert Roland • DOC • BLG • SCHWARZ WEISS BLUES
SCHWARZ-WEISS-ROTE HIMMELBETT, DAS • 1962 • Thiele Rolf • FRG
SCHWARZBROT UND KIPFERL see **...UND DIE LIEBE LACHT DAZU** • 1957
SCHWARZE ABT, DER • 1963 • Gottlieb Franz J. • FRG • BLACK ABBOT, THE (USA)
SCHWARZE AMULETT, DAS • 1920 • Weigert August • FRG
SCHWARZE AUGEN • 1951 • von Bolvary Geza • FRG
SCHWARZE AUGEN see **PETERSBURGER NACHTE** • 1958
SCHWARZE BLITZ, DER • 1958 • Grimm Hans • FRG
SCHWARZE BOOT, DAS • 1920 • *May-Jong Mabel* • FRG
SCHWARZE CHAUFFEUR, DER • 1917 • May Joe • FRG
SCHWARZE DOMINO, DER • 1929 • Janson Victor • FRG
SCHWARZE ENGEL, DER • 1973 • Schroeter Werner • FRG • BLACK ANGEL
SCHWARZE ERDE • 1923 • Hofer Franz • FRG
SCHWARZE FRACHT • 1956 • Riefenstahl Leni • DOC • FRG • BLACK FREIGHT
SCHWARZE GALEERE, DIE • 1962 • Hellberg Martin • GDR • BLACK GALLEON, THE
SCHWARZE GAST, DER • 1920 • Neff Wolfgang • FRG
SCHWARZE GESICHT, DAS • 1922 • Osten Franz • FRG
SCHWARZE GOTT, DER • 1921 • Halm Alfred • FRG
SCHWARZE GRAF, DER • 1920 • Tollen Otz • FRG
SCHWARZE HAND • 1909 • Rye Stellan • FRG
SCHWARZE HAND, DIE see **MIR KOMMT KEINER AUS** • 1917
SCHWARZE HANNE, DIE • 1926 • Hamburger Ludwig • FRG
SCHWARZE HARLEKIN, DER • 1922 • Seitz Franz • FRG
SCHWARZE HUSAR, DER • 1915 • Piel Harry • FRG
SCHWARZE HUSAR, DER • 1932 • Lamprecht Gerhard • FRG • BLACK HUSSAR
SCHWARZE JACK, DER • 1921 • Stranz Fred • FRG
SCHWARZE KAPELLE, DIE see **GEHEIMAKTION SCHWARZE KAPELLE** • 1960
SCHWARZE KASSETTE, DIE • 1920 • *Colani Victor* • FRG
SCHWARZE KATZE, DIE • 1919 • Oswald Richard • FRG
SCHWARZE KOBRA, DIE • 1963 • Zehetgruber Rudolf • AUS • BLACK COBRA, THE (USA)
SCHWARZE KUGEL, DIE • 1917 • Schmidthassler Walter • FRG
SCHWARZE KUVERT, DAS • 1922 • Piel Harry • FRG
SCHWARZE LO, DIE • 1917 • Mack Max • FRG

SCHWARZE LOCK, DIE • 1918 • Grunwald Willy • FRG
SCHWARZE MARION, DIE • 1919 • Krafft Uwe Jens • FRG
SCHWARZE MONTAG, DER • 1922 • *Moja Hella* • FRG
SCHWARZE MORITZ, DER • 1916 • Taufstein, Berg • FRG
SCHWARZE NELKE, DIE • 1915 • *Seefeld Eddy* • FRG
SCHWARZE NYLONS -HEISSE NACHTE • 1958 • Marno Erwin • FRG • INDECENT (USA) ○ WAYLAID WOMEN ○ ALL BAD
SCHWARZE PANTHER • 1966 • Mach Josef • GDR
SCHWARZE PANTHER VON RATANA, DER • 1963 • Roland Jurgen • FRG • BLACK PANTHER OF RATANA (USA) ○ KILLER PANTHER, THE
SCHWARZE PANTHERIN, DIE • 1921 • Guter Johannes • FRG
SCHWARZE PERLE, DIE • 1986 • Mamin Ueli • SWT
SCHWARZE PERLEN • 1919 • Lund Erik • FRG
SCHWARZE PIERROT, DER • 1917 • *Neumann Lotte* • FRG
SCHWARZE PIERROT, DER • 1926 • Piel Harry • FRG
SCHWARZE ROSE, ROSEMARIE • 1962 • Ardavin Cesar • FRG, SPN
SCHWARZE ROSE VON CRUSKA, DIE • 1920 • Schafer Willy, Brandt Heinrich • FRG
SCHWARZE ROSEN • 1935 • Martin Paul • FRG
SCHWARZE SCHACHDAME, DIE • 1922 • Herald Heinz • FRG
SCHWARZE SCHAF, DAS • 1943 • Zittau Friedrich • FRG
SCHWARZE SCHAF, DAS • 1960 • Ashley Helmut • FRG
SCHWARZE SCHMACH, DIE • 1921 • Boese Carl • FRG
SCHWARZE SPINNE, DIE • 1920 • Philippi Siegfried • FRG
SCHWARZE SPINNE, DIE • 1984 • Rissi Mark M. • SWT • BLACK SPIDER, THE
SCHWARZE STERN, DER • 1922 • Bauer James • FRG
SCHWARZE TANNER, DER • 1986 • Koller Xavier • SWT
SCHWARZE TRAUM, DER • 1911 • Gad Urban • FRG, DNM • SORTE DROM, DEN ○ BLACK DREAM, THE
SCHWARZE WALFISCH, DER • 1934 • Wendhausen Fritz • FRG
SCHWARZEN ADLER VON SANTA FE, DIE • 1962 • Hofbauer Ernst • FRG, FRN, ITL • BLACK EAGLE OF SANTA FE (UKN) ○ BLACK EAGLES OF SANTA FE
SCHWARZER JAGER JOHANNA • 1934 • Meyer Johannes • FRG • SPIONE DES KAISERS, DER
SCHWARZER KATER: LOVERS • 1980 • Hall Russell • UKN • LOVERS
SCHWARZER KIES • 1961 • Kautner Helmut • FRG • BLACK GRAVEL
SCHWARZER SAMT • 1964 • Thiel Heinz • GDR • BLACK VELVET
SCHWARZER STERN IN WEISSEN NACHT (FRG) see **HOMME SE PENCHE SUR SON PASSE, UN** • 1958
SCHWARZER ZWIEBACK see **CHORNYYE SUKHARI** • 1972
SCHWARZFAHRT INS GLUCK • 1938 • Boese Carl • FRG • LITTLE SINNER, THE (USA) ○ KLEINE SUNDERIN, DIE
SCHWARZWALDMADEL • 1920 • Wellin Arthur • FRG
SCHWARZWALDMADEL • 1929 • Janson Victor • FRG
SCHWARZWALDMADEL • 1933 • Zoch Georg • FRG
SCHWARZWALDMADEL • 1950 • Deppe Hans • FRG
SCHWARZWALDMELODIE • 1956 • von Bolvary Geza • FRG
SCHWARZWALZER KIRSCH • 1958 • von Bolvary Geza • FRG
SCHWEBENDE JUNGFRAU, DIE • 1931 • Boese Carl • FRG
SCHWECHATER • 1958 • Kubelka Peter • SHT • AUS
SCHWEDENMADEL (FRG) see **SOMMARFLICKAN** • 1956
SCHWEDISCHE JUNGFRAU, DIE • 1965 • Wilhelm Kurt • FRG
SCHWEDISCHE NACHTIGALL, DIE • 1941 • Brauer Peter P. • FRG
SCHWEIGEN AM STARNBERGER SEE, DAS see **LUDWIG II, KONIG VON BAYERN** • 1919
SCHWEIGEN DER GROSSTADT, DAS see **WEISSE SKLAVIN 2, DIE** • 1921
SCHWEIGEN IM WALDE 1 • 1918 • von Woringen Paul • FRG • ERBFOLGESTREIT, EIN
SCHWEIGEN IM WALDE 2 • 1918 • von Woringen Paul • FRG • AUSSERGERICHTLICHE EINIGUNG, EINE
SCHWEIGEN IM WALDE, DAS • 1929 • Dieterle William • FRG • SILENCE DANS LA FORET, LE ○ NUIT DE LA SAINT-JEAN, LA
SCHWEIGEN IM WALDE, DAS • 1937 • Deppe Hans • FRG
SCHWEIGEN IM WALDE, DAS • 1955 • Weiss Helmut • FRG
SCHWEIGENDE ENGEL, DER • 1954 • Reinl Harald • FRG
SCHWEIGENDE MUND, DER • 1951 • Hartl Karl • FRG
SCHWEIGENDE STERN, DER • 1960 • Maetzig Kurt • GDR, PLN • FIRST SPACESHIP ON VENUS (USA) ○ MILCZACA GWIAZDA (PLN) ○ SILENT PLANET, THE ○ SPACESHIP VENUS DOES NOT REPLY ○ SPACESHIP TO VENUS ○ SILENT PLANET, THE ○ PLN ○ PLANET DES TODES, DER
SCHWEIGEPFLICHT • 1916 • Heymann Robert • FRG
SCHWEIJKS FLEGELJAHRE • 1964 • Liebeneiner Wolfgang • AUS
SCHWEIK AS A CIVILIAN see **SVEJK V CIVILU** • 1927
SCHWEIK AT THE FRONT see **SVEJK NA FRONTE** • 1926
SCHWEIK IN CIVILIAN LIFE see **SVEJK V CIVILU** • 1927
SCHWEIK IN RUSSIAN CAPTIVITY see **SVEJK V RUSKEM ZAJETI** • 1927
SCHWEIK IN THE CONCENTRATION-CAMP see **NOVIYE RASSKAZY BRAVOGO SOLDATA SHVEIKA** • 1941
SCHWEIK'S NEW ADVENTURES • 1943 • Lamac Carl • UKN • IT STARTED AT MIDNIGHT
SCHWEIK'S YEARS OF INDISCRETION see **TRIALS OF PRIVATE SCHWEIK** • 1964
SCHWEIN HIN -SCHWEIN HER see **PING PONG** • 1968
SCHWEITZER • 1989 • Hofmeyr Gray • SAF
SCHWEIZER FILM, DER • 1989 • *Buache Freddy (P)* • DOC • SWT • SWITZERLAND AND THE SILVER SCREEN
SCHWEIZER NAMENS NOTZLI, EIN • 1988 • Ehmck Gustav, Roderer Walter • SWT
SCHWEIZERMACHER, DIE • 1979 • Lyssy Rolf • SWT • FAISEURS DE SUISSES, LES ○ SWISSMAKERS, THE
SCHWERE JUNGE, DER • 1921 • Noa Manfred • FRG • ZIRKUSMADEL, DAS
SCHWERE JUNGENS -LEICHTE MADCHEN • 1927 • Boese Carl • FRG
SCHWERE TAGE see **UND DENNOCH KAM DAS GLUCK** • 1923
SCHWERER FALL, EIN • 1927 • Basch Felix • FRG
SCHWERES OPFER, EIN • 1911 • Stark Kurt • FRG
SCHWERT UND HERD • 1916 • Mendel Georg Victor • FRG
SCHWERVERBRECHER, DER • 1918 • Seitz Franz • FRG
SCHWESTER VERONIKA • 1926 • Lamprecht Gerhard • FRG
SCHWESTER VOM ROTEN KREUZ, DIE • 1915 • *Sandten Thea* • FRG
SCHWESTERN, DIE • 1915 • *Speyer Eva* • FRG
SCHWESTERN ODER DIE BALANCE DES GLUCKS • 1980 • von Trotta Margarethe • FRG • SISTERS, OR THE BALANCE OF HAPPINESS (USA)
SCHWIEGEN DES DICHTERS • 1987 • Lilienthal Peter • FRG
SCHWIEGERSOHNE • 1926 • Steinhoff Hans • AUS
...SCHWIERIG SICH ZU VERLOBEN • 1983 • Heymann Karl-Heinz • GDR • DIFFICULT TO GET ENGAGED
SCHWITZKASTEN • 1978 • Cook John • AUS • SWEAT BOX
SCHWUR, DER • 1919 • Lund Erik • FRG
SCHWUR DER RENATE RABENEAU, DER • 1916 • Rippert Otto • FRG
SCHWUR DES PETER HERGATZ, DER • 1921 • Halm Alfred • FRG
SCHWUR DES SOLDATEN POOLEY, DER • 1962 • Jung-Alsen Kurt • FRG, UKN • STORY OF PRIVATE POOLEY, THE (UKN) ○ SURVIVOR, THE (USA)
SCI-BOTS 1: CONFLICT • Terry Jim • ANM • JPN
SCI-BOTS 2: STRIKE BACK • Terry Jim • ANM • JPN
SCIALLE MALEDETTO DI CATERINA II, LA • 1921 • Rosa Silvio Laurenti • ITL
SCIALO, LO • 1979 • Zurlini Valerio • ITL
SCIANA CZAROWNIC • 1967 • Komorowski Pawel • PLN • WALL OF WITCHES, THE ○ WITCHES' WALL, THE
SCIANTOSA, LA • 1970 • Giannetti Alfredo • ITL • CHANTEUSE, THE
SCIANY • 1988 • Dumala Piotr • ANM • PLN • WALLS, THE
SCIARADA PER QUATTRO SPIE (ITL) see **AVEC LA PEAU DES AUTRES** • 1966
SCIENCE • 1911 • *Baggot King* • USA
SCIENCE CLOSER TO LIFE see **NAUKA BLIZEJ ZYCIA** • 1951
SCIENCE ET AGRICULTURE see **SCIENCE HELPS THE FARMER** • 1948
SCIENCE FICTION • 1970 • Kijowicz Miroslaw • ANS • PLN
SCIENCE FRICTION • 1959 • Vanderbeek Stan • ANS • USA
SCIENCE FRICTION • 1963 • Marcus Sid • ANS • USA
SCIENCE GOES WITH PEOPLE see **VEDA JDE S LIDEM** • 1952
SCIENCE HELPS THE FARMER • 1948 • Garceau Raymond • DCS • CND • SCIENCE ET AGRICULTURE
SCIENCE IN THE ORCHESTRA • 1950 • Strasser Alex • UKN
SCIENCE JOINS AN INDUSTRY • 1946 • Hill James • DCS • UKN
SCIENCE OF CRIME, THE • 1914 • Vale Travers • USA
SCIENCE OF THE SOAP BUBBLES • 1921 • Urban Charles • USA
SCIENCE PRODIGIEUSE DES PHARAONS, LA • 1976 • Robert Denis • DOC • CND
SCIENCE WORKERS • 1966 • Grigorov Roumen • DOC • BUL
SCIENCES CLOSER TO LIFE, THE see **NAUKA BLIZEJ ZYCIA** • 1951
SCIENTIFIC CARDPLAYER, THE see **SCOPONE SCIENTIFICO, LO** • 1972
SCIENTIFIC MOTHER, A • 1915 • *Falstaff* • USA
SCIENTIFICALLY STUNG • 1946 • *Meads Thomas (P)* • SHT • USA
SCIENTIFIQUIZ • 1949 • *Smith Pete* • SHT • USA
SCIENTIST'S DOLL, THE • 1914 • *Anderson Mignon* • USA
SCIENTIST'S NIGHTMARE, THE • 1910 • *Pathe* • FRN
SCIENTISTS OF TOMORROW • 1968 • *Ghatak Ritwik* • DOC • IND
SCIENZA FATALE • 1913 • Lolli Alberto Carlo • ITL
SCIMITAR OF THE PROPHET, THE • 1913 • *Foxe Earle* • USA
SCIMITARRA DEL SARACENO, LA • 1959 • Pierotti Piero • ITL, FRN • PIRATE AND THE SLAVE GIRL, THE (USA) ○ VENGEANCE DU SARRASIN, LA
SCINTILLATING SIN see **VIOLATED PARADISE** • 1963
SCIOPEN • 1983 • Odorisio Luciano • ITL
SCIOPERO DEI MILIONI, LO • 1948 • Matarazzo Raffaello • ITL • ABBASSO LA FORTUNA
SCIPIONE DETT ANCHE L'AFRICANO • 1971 • Magni Luigi • ITL
SCIPIONE L'AFRICANO • 1937 • Gallone Carmine • ITL • DEFEAT OF HANNIBAL, THE ○ SPICIO AFRICANUS
SCIPPATORI, GLI see **ULTIMA VOLTA, L'** • 1976
SCIPPO, LO • 1966 • Cicero Nando • ITL
SCISSERE • 1983 • Mettler Peter • CND
SCISSORS • 1962 • *Ghatak Ritwik* • DOC • IND
SCISSORS • 1967 • Dewdney Alexander Keewatin • ANS • CND
SCISSORS • 1970 • Vystrcil Frantisek • ANM • CZC
SCISSORS AND THE LITTLE BOY, THE • 1965 • Topouzanov Christo • ANS • BUL
SCISSORS AND THE LITTLE GIRL, THE • 1966 • Topouzanov Christo • ANS • BUL
SCIUSCIA • 1946 • De Sica Vittorio • ITL • SHOE SHINE (USA) ○ SHOESHINE
SCOBIE MALONE • 1975 • Ohlsson Terry • ASL
SCOCCIATORE, LO see **VIA PADOVA 46** • 1954
SCOFFER, THE • 1920 • Dwan Allan • USA
SCOGGIE • 1974 • Scott Cynthia • MTV • CND
SCOGLIERA DEL PECCATO, LA • 1951 • Montero Roberto Bianchi • ITL
SCOMUNICATE DI SAN VALENTINO, LE • 1973 • Grieco Sergio • ITL
SCONOSCIUTO DI SAN MARINO, LO • 1947 • Cottafavi Vittorio, Waszynski Michael • ITL • STRANGER FROM SAN MARINO, THE
SCONTENTI, GLI • 1961 • Lipartiti Giuseppe • ITL
SCONTRI STELLARI OLTRE LA TERZA DIMENSIONE • 1979 • Cozzi Luigi • ITL, USA • STARCRASH (USA)
SCOOBY-DOO AND THE GHOUL SCHOOL • 1988 • Nicholas Charles B. • ANM • USA
SCOOP • 1978 • Perris Anthony • MTV • CND
SCOOP • 1987 • Millar Gavin • TVM • UKN
SCOOP, THE • 1912 • *Storey Edith* • USA
SCOOP, THE • 1934 • Rogers Maclean • UKN
SCOOP, THE • 1985 • SAF
SCOOP, THE (UKN) see **HONOR OF THE PRESS** • 1932
SCOOP AT BELVILLE, THE • 1915 • *Huling Lorraine* • USA
SCOOPED BY A HENCOOP • 1914 • *Lyons Eddie* • USA
SCOOPED BY CUPID • 1914 • *Victor* • USA
SCOPE TWO • Stockert Hank • SHT • USA
SCOPERTA, LA • 1969 • Piccon Elio • ITL
SCOPONE SCIENTIFICO, LO • 1972 • Comencini Luigi • ITL • SCIENTIFIC CARDPLAYER, THE
SCORCHED EARTH see **BRENT JORD** • 1971
SCORCHED HEAT • 1988 • Borg Peter • USA
SCORCHED WINGS • 1916 • Shaw Brinsley • SHT • USA
SCORCHER, THE • 1927 • Brown Harry J. • USA
SCORCHING FLAME, THE • 1918 • Robi Armand • CND
SCORCHING FURY • 1952 • Freers Rick • USA
SCORCHING SANDS • 1923 • Roach Hal • SHT • USA
SCORCHY • 1976 • Avedis Howard • USA
SCORE • 1973 • Metzger Radley H. • USA, YGS
SCORE, THE • 1973 • Hynd John • DOC • USA
SCORE, THE see **LYFTET** • 1977
SCORE FOR WOODWIND • 1969 • Jaworski Tadeusz • PLN
SCORING see **YESTERDAY** • 1980
SCORNED AND SWINDLED • 1984 • Wendkos Paul • TVM • USA
SCORPIO • 1973 • Winner Michael • USA
SCORPIO '70 • 1970 • Sullivan Ron • USA • BLACK REVENGE
SCORPIO LETTERS, THE • 1968 • Thorpe Richard • TVM • USA
SCORPIO NIGHTS • 1985 • Gallaga Peque • PHL
SCORPIO RISING • 1966 • Anger Kenneth • USA
SCORPIO SCARAB • 1972 • *Hamilton George* • USA
SCORPION • 1986 • Riead William • USA • SUMMONS, THE
SCORPION see **SASORI** • 1967
SCORPION, LE • 1964 • Hanin Serge • FRN, ITL • SCORPIONE, LO (ITL)
SCORPION, THE • 1989 • Awad Adel • EGY
SCORPION, THE see **SKORPIO, A** • 1918
SCORPION, THE see **SCHORPIOEN, DE** • 1984
SCORPION THUNDERBOLT • Ho Godfrey • HKG
SCORPION WOMAN, THE • 1989 • Zanke Susanne • AUS
SCORPIONE, LO (ITL) see **SCORPION, LE** • 1964
SCORPION'S DANCE • 1986 • Keso Lasse • FNL
SCORPION'S STING, THE • 1915 • Vignola Robert G. • USA
SCORPION'S STING, THE (USA) see **DEVIL'S BONDMAN, THE** • 1915
SCORTICATELI VIVI • 1979 • Siciliano Mario • ITL
SCOTCH • 1930 • Sennett Mack • SHT • USA
SCOTCH HIGHBALL • 1930 • *Terry Paul/ Moser Frank (P)* • ANS • USA
SCOTCH HOP • MacLaine Christopher • SHT • USA
SCOTCH ON THE ROCKS (USA) see **LAXDALE HALL** • 1952
SCOTCH REEL • 1898 • *Levi, Jones & Co* • UKN
SCOTCH TAPE • 1962 • Smith Jack** • USA
SCOTCHED IN SCOTLAND • 1954 • White Jules • SHT • USA
SCOTLAND FOR SPORT • 1958 • Fairbairn Kenneth • DOC • UKN
SCOTLAND FOREVER • 1914 • Lambart Harry • USA
SCOTLAND YARD • 1930 • Howard William K. • USA • "DETECTIVE CLIVE", BART. (UKN)
SCOTLAND YARD • 1941 • Foster Norman • USA
SCOTLAND YARD • 1947 • DOC • UKN • THIS MODERN AGE NO.2
SCOTLAND YARD COMMANDS see **LONELY ROAD, THE** • 1936
SCOTLAND YARD DRAGNET (USA) see **HYPNOTIST, THE** • 1957
SCOTLAND YARD HUNTS DR. MABUSE see **SCOTLAND YARD JAGT DOKTOR MABUSE** • 1963
SCOTLAND YARD INSPECTOR (USA) see **LADY IN THE FOG** • 1952
SCOTLAND YARD INVESTIGATOR • 1945 • Blair George • USA
SCOTLAND YARD JAGT DOKTOR MABUSE • 1963 • May Paul • FRG • DR. MABUSE VS. SCOTLAND YARD (USA) ○ SCHARLACHROTE DSCHUNKE, DIE ○ SCOTLAND YARD VS. DR. MABUSE ○ SCOTLAND YARD HUNTS DR. MABUSE ○ SCARLET JUNGLE, THE
SCOTLAND YARD MYSTERY, THE • 1934 • Bentley Thomas • UKN • LIVING DEAD, THE (USA)
SCOTLAND YARD VS. DR. MABUSE see **SCOTLAND YARD JAGT DOKTOR MABUSE** • 1963
SCOTT FREE • 1976 • Wiard William • TVM • USA
SCOTT JOPLIN • 1977 • Kagan Jeremy Paul • USA
SCOTT JOPLIN, KING OF RAGTIME COMPOSERS • 1977 • Anderson Amelia • DCS • USA
SCOTT OF THE ANTARCTIC • 1948 • Frend Charles • UKN
SCOTTIE AND THE FROGS • 1915 • Birch Cecil • UKN
SCOTTIE FINDS A HOME • 1935 • Gillett Burt • ANS • USA
SCOTTIE LOVES ICE CREAM • 1915 • Birch Cecil • UKN
SCOTTIE SMITH • 1970 • Henkel Peter • SAF
SCOTTIE TURNS THE HANDLE • 1915 • Birch Cecil • UKN
SCOTTIE'S DAY OUT • 1915 • Birch Cecil • UKN
SCOTTISH COVENANTERS, THE • 1909 • Perry Joseph H. • ASL
SCOTTISH MAZURKA • 1943 • Nieter Hans M. • DCS • UKN
SCOTTSBORO • 1934 • Hurwitz Leo T. • DOC • USA
SCOTTY OF THE BOY SCOUTS see **SCOTTY OF THE SCOUTS** • 1926
SCOTTY OF THE SCOUTS • 1926 • Worne Duke • USA • SCOTTY OF THE BOY SCOUTS
SCOTTY WEED'S ALIBI • 1915 • *Ridgely Cleo* • USA
SCOUMOUNE, LA • 1973 • Giovanni Jose • FRN, ITL • CLAN DEI MARSIGLIESI, IL (ITL) ○ HIT MAN, THE (UKN) ○ KILLER MAN (USA) ○ SCOUNDREL ○ MAFIA WARFARE
SCOUNDREL see **NARAZUMONO** • 1956
SCOUNDREL see **SCOUMOUNE, LA** • 1973
SCOUNDREL, A see **AKUTO** • 1965
SCOUNDREL, THE • 1935 • MacArthur Charles, Hecht Ben • USA • MIRACLE ON 49TH STREET
SCOUNDREL, THE • 1987 • Mustafiev Vagif • USS
SCOUNDREL, THE see **MARIES DE L'AN II, LES** • 1970
SCOUNDREL IN WHITE (UKN) see **DOCTEUR POPAUL** • 1972
SCOUNDRELS, THE see **GOLFOS, LOS** • 1959
SCOUNDRELS, THE see **CANALLAS, LOS** • 1968
SCOUNDREL'S TALE, THE • 1916 • *Griffith Raymond* • USA
SCOUNDREL'S TOLL, A • 1916 • Cavender Glen • SHT • USA
SCOURGE, THE • 1922 • Malins Geoffrey H. • UKN • FORTUNE'S FOOLS
SCOURGE, THE see **BICZ BOZY** • 1967
SCOURGE OF GOD, THE see **BICZ BOZY** • 1967

SCOURGE OF THE DESERT, THE • 1915 • Hart William S., Smith Cliff • USA
SCOURGE OF THE LITTLE C, THE see **TUMBLING RIVER** • 1927
SCOUT • 1953 • NKR
SCOUT, THE • 1989 • Hatamikia Ebrahim • IRN
SCOUT, THE • 1989 • Ritchie Michael • USA
SCOUT FELLOW • 1951 • Kneitel Seymour • ANS • USA
SCOUT WITH THE GOUT, A • 1947 • Tytla Bill • ANS • USA
SCOUTING FOR TROUBLE • 1960 • Kneitel Seymour • ANS • USA
SCOUTING FOR WASHINGTON • 1917 • Griffith Edward H. • SHT • USA
SCOUTMASTER MAGOO • 1958 • Cannon Robert • ANS • USA
SCOUTMASTER'S MOTTO, THE • 1911 • Wilson Frank? • UKN
SCOUTS • Cadinot Jean-Daniel • FRN
SCOUTS, THE see **HASAYARIM** • 1967
SCOUTS AT A RALLY see **HARCERZE NA ZLOCIE** • 1953
SCOUT'S EXPLOIT, THE see **PODVIG RAZVEDCHIKA** • 1947
SCOUT'S HONOR • 1980 • Levin Henry • TVM • USA
SCOUT'S MOTTO, THE • 1914 • Aylott Dave • UKN
SCOUTS OF THE AIR see **DANGER FLIGHT** • 1939
SCOUT'S STRATEGY, A • 1911 • Coleby A. E. • UKN • RESOURCEFUL SCOUT, THE (USA)
SCOUTS TO THE RESCUE • 1909 • Aylott Dave • UKN
SCOUTS TO THE RESCUE • 1939 • Taylor Ray, James Alan • SRL • USA
SCOUTS TO THE RESCUE • 1956 • Rasinski Connie • ANS • USA
SCOWLS OF PARIS see **GRIMACI PARIZHI** • 1924
SCRAGS • 1930 • Sanderson Challis • UKN
SCRAM • 1932 • McCarey Ray • SHT • USA
SCRAMBLE • 1961 • UKN
SCRAMBLE • 1970 • Eady David • UKN
SCRAMBLE see **MR. BILLION** • 1977
SCRAMBLED ACHES see **SCRAMBLED ARCHES** • 1957
SCRAMBLED ARCHES • 1957 • Jones Charles M. • ANS • USA • SCRAMBLED ACHES
SCRAMBLED BRAINS • 1951 • White Jules • SHT • USA
SCRAMBLED EGGS • 1939 • Lovy Alex • ANS • USA
SCRAMBLED HEARTS • 1917 • *Ritchie Billie* • SHT • USA
SCRAMBLED HONEYMOON, A • 1916 • *Perez Tweedledum* • SHT • USA
SCRAMBLED ROMANCE, A • 1920 • Hayes Ward • SHT • USA
SCRAMBLED WIVES • 1921 • Griffith Edward H. • USA
SCRAMBLES • 1960-63 • Emshwiller Ed • SHT • USA
SCRAP COLLECTORS LTD. see **SUKURAPPU SHUDAN** • 1968
SCRAP FOR VICTORY • 1943 • Rasinski Connie • ANS • USA
SCRAP HAPPY • 1943 • Jason Will • SHT • USA
SCRAP IN BLACK AND WHITE • 1903 • Porter Edwin S. • USA
SCRAP IRON • 1921 • Ray Charles • USA
SCRAP OF PAPER, A • 1914 • Vale Travers • USA
SCRAP OF PAPER, A see **THREE GREEN EYES** • 1919
SCRAP OF PAPER, THE • 1920 • Collins Tom • USA
SCRAP OF PAPER AND A PIECE OF STRING, A • 1964 • Korty John • ANM • USA
SCRAP THE JAPS • 1942 • Kneitel Seymour • ANS • USA
SCRAPBOOK FOR 1922 • 1947 • Baylis Peter, Baily Leslie • UKN
SCRAPING BOTTOM see **BORN TO WIN** • 1971
SCRAPPER, THE • 1917 • Ford John • SHT • USA
SCRAPPER, THE • 1922 • Henley Hobart • USA
SCRAPPER, THE • 1959 • Sanishvili Nikolai • USS
SCRAPPILY MARRIED • 1916 • Beaudine William • SHT • USA
SCRAPPILY MARRIED • 1930 • Pearce A. Leslie • USA
SCRAPPILY MARRIED • 1940 • Ripley Arthur • SHT • USA
SCRAPPILY MARRIED • 1945 • Kneitel Seymour • ANS • USA
SCRAPPIN' KID, THE • 1926 • Smith Cliff • USA
SCRAPPY • 1933-39 • *Mintz Charles* • ASS • USA
SCRAPPY BILL • 1909 • *Centaur* • USA
SCRAPPY BIRTHDAY • 1949 • Lundy Dick • ANS • USA
SCRAPPY HAPPY DAFFY • 1943 • Tashlin Frank • ANS • USA
SCRAPPY'S ADDED ATTRACTION • 1939 • *Mintz Charles (P)* • ANS • USA
SCRAPPY'S ART GALLERY • 1934 • *Mintz Charles (P)* • ANS • USA
SCRAPPY'S BAND CONCERT • 1937 • *Mintz Charles (P)* • ANS • USA
SCRAPPY'S BIG MOMENT • 1935 • *Mintz Charles (P)* • ANS • USA
SCRAPPY'S BOY SCOUTS • 1936 • *Mintz Charles (P)* • ANS • USA
SCRAPPY'S CAMERA TROUBLES • 1936 • *Mintz Charles (P)* • ANS • USA
SCRAPPY'S DOG SHOW • 1934 • *Mintz Charles (P)* • ANS • USA
SCRAPPY'S EXPEDITION • 1934 • *Mintz Charles (P)* • ANS • USA
SCRAPPY'S GHOST STORY • 1935 • *Mintz Charles (P)* • ANS • USA
SCRAPPY'S MUSIC LESSON • 1937 • *Mintz Charles (P)* • ANS • USA
SCRAPPY'S NEWS FLASHES • 1937 • *Mintz Charles (P)* • ANS • USA
SCRAPPY'S PARTY • 1933 • *Mintz Charles (P)* • ANS • USA
SCRAPPY'S PLAYMATES • 1938 • *Mintz Charles (P)* • ANS • USA
SCRAPPY'S PONY • 1936 • *Mintz Charles (P)* • ANS • USA
SCRAPPY'S RELAY RACE • 1934 • *Mintz Charles (P)* • ANS • USA
SCRAPPY'S RODEO • 1939 • *Mintz Charles (P)* • ANS • USA
SCRAPPY'S SIDE SHOW • 1939 • *Mintz Charles (P)* • ANS • USA
SCRAPPY'S TELEVISION • 1934 • *Mintz Charles (P)* • ANS • USA
SCRAPPY'S THEME SONG • 1934 • *Mintz Charles (P)* • ANS • USA
SCRAPPY'S TOY SHOP • 1934 • *Mintz Charles (P)* • ANS • USA
SCRAPPY'S TRAILER • 1935 • *Mintz Charles (P)* • ANS • USA
SCRAPPY'S TRIP TO MARS • 1938 • *Mintz Charles (P)* • ANS • USA
SCRAPS see **SPARROWS** • 1926
SCRAPS AT THE BOTTOM see **POHJAN TAHTEET** • 1969
SCRAPS OF PAPER • 1918 • *Arbuckle Fatty* • SHT • USA • FATTY ARBUCKLE IN A LIBERTY LOAN APPEAL
SCRATCH • 1982 • Patin Claude • FRN
SCRATCH, THE • 1913 • *Carney Augustus* • USA
SCRATCH A TIGER • 1969 • Pratt Hawley • ANS • USA
SCRATCH AS SCRATCH CAN • 1909 • Aylott Dave • UKN
SCRATCH AS SCRATCH CAN • 1931 • Sandrich Mark • SHT • USA
SCRATCH HARRY • 1970 • Matter Alex • USA • EROTIC THREE, THE (UKN)
SCRATCH MEAL • 1936 • Elton Arthur • UKN
SCRATCH MY BACK • 1920 • Olcott Sidney • USA
SCRATCH OF A PEN, A • 1915 • *Eclectic* • USA
SCRATCH PAD • 1960 • Hirsch Hy • SHT • FRN
SCRATCH, SCRATCH, SCRATCH • 1955 • White Jules • SHT • USA
SCRATCHED • 1916 • Kelsey Fred A. • SHT • USA
SCRAWAN ANGJUR KEBIMBAYAM see **SECAWAN ANGGUR KEBIMBANGAN** • 1985
SCREAM • 1981 • Quisenberry Byron • USA • OUTING, THE
SCREAM, THE see **KRZYK** • 1983
SCREAM, THE (USA) see **URLO, L'** • 1965
SCREAM.. AND DIE! • 1973 • Larraz Jose R. • UKN • HOUSE THAT VANISHED, THE (UKN) ○ DON'T GO INTO THE BEDROOM ○ PSYCHO SEX FIEND ○ DON'T GO IN THE BEDROOM
SCREAM AND SCREAM AGAIN • 1969 • Hessler Gordon • UKN, USA • SCREAMER
SCREAM, BABY, SCREAM • 1969 • Adler Joseph • USA
SCREAM BLACULA SCREAM • 1973 • Kelljan Bob • USA • BLACULA II
SCREAM BLOODY MURDER • 1972 • Emery Robert J., Ray Marc B. • USA
SCREAM FOR HELP • 1984 • Winner Michael • USA, UKN
SCREAM FREE see **FREE GRASS** • 1969
SCREAM FROM SILENCE, A see **MOURIR A TUE-TETE** • 1979
SCREAM GREATS, VOL.1 • 1986 • Santostefano Damon • DOC • USA
SCREAM IN SOCIETY, A • 1920 • Moore Vin • SHT • USA
SCREAM IN THE DARK • 1935 • *Commodore* • USA • SCREAM IN THE NIGHT (UKN)
SCREAM IN THE DARK, A • 1943 • Sherman George • USA
SCREAM IN THE NIGHT, A • 1919 • King Burton L., De Cordova Leander • USA
SCREAM IN THE NIGHT (UKN) see **SCREAM IN THE DARK** • 1935
SCREAM IN THE STREETS, A • 1972 • Monson Carl • USA • GIRLS IN THE STREETS
SCREAM OF DEATH see **GRITO DE LA MUERTE, EL** • 1958
SCREAM OF FEAR (USA) see **TASTE OF FEAR** • 1961
SCREAM OF SILENCE, A see **MOURIR A TUE-TETE** • 1979
SCREAM OF TERROR see **POINT OF TERROR** • 1971
SCREAM OF THE BUTTERFLY • 1965 • Lobato Ebar • USA • FOUR CORNERED TRIANGLE ○ PASSION PIT, THE
SCREAM OF THE DEMON LOVER see **IVANNA** • 1970
SCREAM OF THE WOLF • 1974 • Curtis Dan • TVM • USA
SCREAM, PRETTY PEGGY • 1973 • Hessler Gordon • TVM • USA
SCREAM SHOW see **DEAD-TIME STORIES: VOLUME 2** • 1987
SCREAM TIME see **SCREAMTIME** • 1983
SCREAM TO A WHISPER, A • 1988 • Bergman Robert • USA
SCREAM (UKN) see **NIGHTMARE HOUSE** • 1973
SCREAMER • 1974 • O'Riordan Shaun • TVM • UKN
SCREAMER see **SCREAM AND SCREAM AGAIN** • 1969
SCREAMERS • 1979 • Miller Dan T., Martino Sergio • ITL, USA • ISLE OF THE FISH MEN
SCREAMERS see **ISOLA DEGLI UOMINI PESCE, L'** • 1979
SCREAMING DEAD, THE see **DRACULA CONTRA EL DR. FRANKENSTEIN** • 1971
SCREAMING EAGLES • 1956 • Haas Charles • USA
SCREAMING HEAD, THE see **NACKTE UND DER SATAN, DIE** • 1959
SCREAMING JETS • 1951 • Blais Roger • DCS • CND • AVIONS A REACTIONS
SCREAMING MIMI • 1958 • Oswald Gerd • USA
SCREAMING SHADOW, THE • 1920 • Wilson Ben, Worne Duke • SRL • USA
SCREAMING SKULL, THE • 1958 • Nicol Alex • USA
SCREAMING SKULL, THE • 1973 • Monty Gloria • TVM • USA
SCREAMING TIGER, THE • 1973 • *Wang Yu* • HKG
SCREAMING WOMAN, THE • 1972 • Smight Jack • TVM • USA
SCREAMING WOMAN, THE • 1986 • Pittman Bruce • MTV • CND
SCREAMS FROM THE SECOND FLOOR see **NIKAI NO HIMAI** • 1931
SCREAMS OF A WINTER'S NIGHT • 1979 • Wilson James L. • USA
SCREAMTIME • 1983 • Beresford Al • UKN • SCREAM TIME
SCREEN -ENTRANCE EXIT • 1974 • Le Grice Malcolm • UKN
SCREEN FOLLIES • 1919 • *Dahme A. A./ Seel Luis (P)* • ANS • USA
SCREEN MUSICAL FOR CHILDREN, A see **LASTEN ELOKUVAMUSIKAALI** • 1973
SCREEN OF DEATH, THE see **CLUM PERDESI** • 1960
SCREEN OF PINS see **NEZ, LE** • 1963
SCREEN PLAYLETS • 1926 • *Gaumont* • SHS • UKN
SCREEN PLAYLETS • 1927 • *Gaumont* • SHS • UKN
SCREEN SNAPSHOTS • 1940-56 • Staub Ralph • SHS • USA
SCREEN STRUCK • 1937 • Huntington Lawrence • UKN
SCREEN STRUCK see **STAGE STRUCK** • 1925
SCREEN TEST • 1965 • Warhol Andy • USA • SCREEN TEST #2
SCREEN TEST • 1986 • Auster Sam • USA
SCREEN TEST #2 see **SCREEN TEST** • 1965
SCREEN TEST NUMBER ONE • 1965 • Warhol Andy • USA
SCREEN TESTS see **ZDJECIA PROBNE** • 1978
SCREEN TIME see **SENDETID** • 1979
SCREEN VAUDEVILLE NUMBER ONE • 1934 • *Burnaby Davy* • SHT • USA
SCREENED VAULT, THE • 1917 • Ellis Robert • SHT • USA
SCREENTEST GIRLS, THE • 1969 • S. Zoltan • USA
SCREW LOOSE • 1984 • George Leslie • USA
SCREW ON THE SCREEN see **S.O.S.** • 1975
SCREWBALL • 1957 • Kuchar George, Kuchar Mike • SHT • USA
SCREWBALL, THE • 1943 • Lovy Alex • ANS • USA
SCREWBALL ACADEMY • 1987 • Blanchard John • USA • LOOSE ENDS
SCREWBALL FOOTBALL • 1939 • Avery Tex • ANS • USA
SCREWBALL HOTEL • 1988 • Zielinski Rafal • USA
SCREWBALL SQUIRREL • 1944 • Avery Tex • ANS • USA
SCREWBALLS • 1983 • Zielinski Rafal • CND
SCREWBALLS II: LOOSE SCREWS see **LOOSE SCREWS** • 1985
SCREWDRIVER, THE • 1941 • Lantz Walter • ANS • USA
SCREWY SQUIRREL • 1944-45 • Avery Tex • ASS • USA
SCREWY TRUANT • 1945 • Avery Tex • ANS • USA
SCRIBBLE, THE see **CARBANICA** • 1982
SCRIBBLING KITTEN, THE see **KONEKO NO RAKUGAKI** • 1957
SCRIBE, THE • 1966 • *Keaton Buster* • CND
SCRIM • 1976 • Bijl Jacob • MTV • NTH, FRG, SWD
SCROGGINS AND THE FLY PEST • 1911 • Aylott Dave? • UKN
SCROGGINS AND THE WALTZ DREAM • 1911 • Aylott Dave? • UKN
SCROGGINS GETS THE SOCIALIST CRAZE • 1911 • Aylott Dave? • UKN
SCROGGINS GOES IN FOR CHEMISTRY AND DISCOVERS A MARVELLOUS POWDER • 1911 • Coleby A. E. • UKN
SCROGGINS HAS HIS FORTUNE TOLD • 1911 • Coleby A. E. • UKN • SCROGGINS VISITS A PALMIST (USA)
SCROGGINS PLAYS GOLF • 1911 • Coleby A. E.? • UKN
SCROGGINS PUTS UP FOR BLANKSHIRE • 1910 • Coleby A. E. • UKN
SCROGGINS TAKES THE CENSUS • 1911 • Aylott Dave • UKN
SCROGGINS VISITS A PALMIST (USA) see **SCROGGINS HAS HIS FORTUNE TOLD** • 1911
SCROGGINS WINS THE FIDDLE-FADDLE PRIZE • 1911 • Coleby A. E. • UKN • FOOL'S FANCY (USA)
SCROLL'S SECRET, THE (USA) see **INAZUMA KOTENGU** • 1958
SCROOGE • 1913 • Bantock Leedham • UKN
SCROOGE • 1922 • Wynn George • UKN
SCROOGE • 1923 • Greenwood Edwin • UKN
SCROOGE • 1928 • Croise Hugh • UKN
SCROOGE • 1935 • Edwards Henry • UKN
SCROOGE • 1951 • Hurst Brian Desmond • UKN • CHRISTMAS CAROL, A (USA)
SCROOGE • 1970 • Neame Ronald • UKN
SCROOGE MCDUCK AND MONEY • 1967 • Luske Hamilton • ANS • USA
SCROOGE: OR, MARLEY'S GHOST • 1901 • Booth W. R. • UKN
SCROOGE THE SKINFLINT (UKN) see **RIGHT TO BE HAPPY, THE** • 1916
SCROOGED • 1988 • Donner Richard • USA
SCRUB, THE • 1915 • *Domino* • USA
SCRUB LADY, THE • 1914 • *Chamberlain Riley* • USA
SCRUB LADY, THE • 1917 • *Dressler Marie* • SHT • USA
SCRUB ME, MAMA, WITH A BOOGIE BEAT • 1941 • Lantz Walter • ANS • USA
SCRUBBERS • 1982 • Zetterling Mai • UKN
SCRUFFY • 1938 • Faye Randall • UKN
SCRUFFY • 1980 • *Young Alan* • ANM • USA
SCRUGGS see **GAME CALLED SCRUGGS, A** • 1965
SCRUPLES • 1981 • Day Robert • TVM • USA
SCUAIPA • 1979 • Cordido Ivork • VNZ
SCUBA DUBA DO • 1966 • Bakshi Ralph • ANS • USA
SCUDDHA-HOO, SCUDDA HAY • 1948 • Herbert F. Hugh • USA • SUMMER LIGHTNING (UKN)
SCUFFLE IN BAGDAD FOR X-27 see **GIOCO DELLE SPIE, IL** • 1966
SCUGNIZZI • 1990 • Loy Nanni • ITL • NEOPOLITAN BOYS
SCUGNIZZO, LO • 1979 • Brescia Alfonso • ITL
SCULACCIATA, LA • 1974 • Festa Campanile Pasquale • ITL
SCULLION'S DREAM • 1907 • *Pathe* • FRN
SCULLION'S JOKE ON THE CHEF (USA) see **FARCE DE MARMITON** • 1900
SCULPTEUR AVEUGLE, LE • 1913 • Chautard Emile • FRN
SCULPTEUR MODERNE • 1909 • de Chomon Segundo • FRN
SCULPTOR • 1963 • Fiering Alvin • SHT • USA
SCULPTOR'S DREAM • 1929 • *Tellegan Paul* • USA
SCULPTOR'S DREAM, THE • 1910 • Coleby A. E.? • UKN
SCULPTOR'S DREAM, THE see **MARBLE HEART, THE** • 1909
SCULPTOR'S JEALOUS MODEL, THE • 1904 • *Paul R. W.* • UKN
SCULPTOR'S LOVE, THE • 1909 • Brooke Van Dyke • USA
SCULPTOR'S MODEL, THE • 1915 • Nicholls George • USA
SCULPTOR'S NIGHTMARE, THE • 1908 • Griffith D. W. • SHT • USA
SCULPTOR'S WELSH RABBIT DREAM, THE • 1908 • Porter Edwin S. • USA
SCULPTRESS OF POLICKA, THE • 1970 • Bocek Jaroslav • ANM • CZC
SCULPTUREI, LA • 1973 • Bertolino Daniel • DCS • CND
SCULPTURE AUJOURD'HUI • 1965 • Geilfus Frederic • DOC • BLG
SCULPTURE AUSTRALIA '69 • 1969 • Burstall Tim • DOC • ASL
SCULPTURE OF DAVID LYNN, THE • 1961 • Baillie Bruce • SHT • USA • DAVID LYNN'S SCULPTURE
SCULPTURE OF RENAISSANCE • 1967 • Czurko Edward • DCS • PLN
SCUM • 1978 • Clarke Alan • UKN
SCUM OF THE EARTH! • 1963 • Lewis Herschell G. • USA • DEVIL'S CAMERA
SCUM OF THE EARTH see **POOR WHITE TRASH: PART II** • 1976
SCUMBUSTERS see **ASSAULT OF THE KILLER BIMBOS** • 1988
SCUOLA DEI TIMIDI, LA • 1942 • Bragaglia Carlo Ludovico • ITL
SCUOLA DELLE VERGINI, LA • 1969 • Zachar Jozef • ITL
SCUOLA DI BALLO (ITL) see **DANCE ACADEMY** • 1988
SCUOLA DI LADRI • 1987 • Castellano, Pipolo • ITL • SCHOOL FOR THIEVES
SCUOLA DI SEVERINO, LA • 1949 • Guerrini • SHT • ITL
SCUOLA ELEMENTARE • 1955 • Lattuada Alberto • ITL, FRN
SCURTA ISTORIE • 1956 • Popescu-Gopo Ion • ANS • RMN • SHORT HISTORY, A (USA) ○ BRIEF HISTORY

SCUSATE IL RITARDO • 1983 • Troisi Massimo • ITL • SORRY I'M LATE
SCUSI EMINENZA.. POSSO SPOSARMI? • 1976 • Bugnatelli Salvatore • ITL • PAPESATAN
SCUSI, FACCIAMO L'AMORE? • 1968 • Caprioli Vittorio • ITL, FRN • ET SI ON FAISANT L'AMOUR (FRN) ○ LISTEN, LET'S MAKE LOVE (USA) ○ EXCUSE ME, SHALL WE MAKE LOVE?
SCUSI, LEI CONOSCE IL SESSO? • 1968 • De Sisti Vittorio • ITL • EXCUSE ME, DO YOU LIKE SEX? (UKN) ○ EXCUSE ME, ARE YOU FAMILIAR WITH SEX?
SCUSI LEI E FAVOREVOLE O CONTRARIO? • 1966 • Sordi Alberto • ITL
...SCUSI, MA LEI LE PAGA LE TASSE? • 1971 • Guerrini Mino • ITL
SCUSI, SI POTREBBE EVITARE IL SERVIZIO MILITAIRE? • 1974 • Petrini Luigi • ITL
SCUTTLERS, THE • 1920 • Edwards J. Gordon • USA
SCYZORYK • 1962 • Lorek Leszek • ANM • PLN • POCKETKNIFE, THE ○ PEN KNIFE, THE
SE • 1948 • Lorentz Svend Aage • DNM • EYE, THE ○ LOOK
SE ABRE EL ABISMO • 1945 • Chenal Pierre • ARG
SE ACABARON LAS MUJERES • 1946 • Peon Ramon • MXC
SE ALQUILA MARIDO • 1961 • Delgado Miguel M. • MXC
SE ARMO EL BELEN • 1969 • Saenz De Heredia Jose Luis • SPN
SE, EXZELLENZ DER REVISOR • 1922 • Zelnik Friedrich • FRG
SE FOSSI DEPUTATO • 1949 • Simonelli Giorgio C. • ITL
SE HA FUGADO UN PRESO • 1933 • Perojo Benito • SPN
...SE INCONTRI SARTANA PREGA PER LA TUA MORTE • 1968 • Parolini Gianfranco • ITL, FRG • SARTANA, PRAY FOR YOUR DEATH ○ SARTANA BETE UM DEINEN TOD ○ ...IF YOU MEET SARTANA PRAY FOR YOUR DEATH
SE INFIEL Y NO MIRES CON QUIEN • 1985 • Trueba Fernando • SPN • BE WANTON AND TREAD NO SHAME ○ BE UNFAITHFUL AND DON'T CARE WITH WHOM
SE IO FOSSI ONESTO • 1942 • Bragaglia Carlo Ludovico • ITL
SE JAVANMARD • 1968 • Reypoor Bahram • IRN • THREE GENEROUS MEN
SE KI, SE BE • 1918 • Korda Alexander • HNG • NEITHER AT HOME OR ABROAD ○ NOT IN –OR OUT ○ NEITHER IN NOR OUT
SE LA LLEVO EL REMINGTON • 1948 • Urueta Chano • MXC
SE LE FUE EL NOVIO • 1945 • Salvador Julio • SPN
SE LE PASO LA MANO • 1952 • Soler Julian • MXC • HIS HAND SLIPPED
SE LLAMABA S.N. • 1978 • Correa Luis De Miranda • VNZ • IT WAS CALLED S.N. ○ NAME WAS S.N., THE
SE LOS CHUPO LA BRUJA • 1957 • Salvador Jaime • MXC • WITCH HAS SUCKED THEM UP, THE
SE MUEVE • 1977 • Feo Ivan, Llerandi Antonio • DOC • VNZ • IT MOVES
SE NECESITA CHICO • 1963 • Mercero Antonio • SPN
SE NON AVESSI PIU TE • 1965 • Fizzarotti Ettore Maria • ITL
SE NON SON MATTI NO LI VOGLIAMO • 1941 • Pratelli Esodo • ITL • COMPAGNIA DEI MATTI, LA
SE OPP FOR SPIONER! • 1944 • Holmgren Per Gosta • SWD • WATCH OUT FOR SPIES! ○ SABOTAGE
SE PERMETTETE, PARLIAMO DI DONNE • 1964 • Scola Ettore • ITL, FRN • LET'S TALK ABOUT WOMEN (USA) ○ PARLONS FEMMES (FRN) ○ PARLIAMO DI DONNE
SE QUELL'IDIOTA CI PENSASSE.. • 1939 • Giannini Nino • ITL
SE RAMATAN ILUSIONES • 1944 • Lugones Mario C. • ARG
SE SEGURA, MALANDRO! • 1979 • Carvana Hugo • BRZ • HOLD ON, SWINDLE!
SE SEI BRUTTA NON TI SPOSA see **BELLE O BRUTTE SI SPOSAN TUTTE..** • 1939
SE SEI VIVO SPARA • 1967 • Questi Giulio • ITL, SPN • DJANGO KILL (UKN) ○ DANJO KILL (IF YOU LIVE SHOOT) ○ ORO MALDITO
SE SOLICITA MUCHACHA DE BUENA PRESENCIA Y JOVEN CON MOTO PROPIO • 1977 • Anzola Alfredo J. • VNZ • GOOD-LOOKING GIRL AND YOUNG MAN WITH OWN MOTORCYCLE NEEDED
SE SOLICITA MUCHACHA DE BUENA PRESENCIA Y MOTORIZADO CON MOTO PROPIA • Anzola Alfredo J. • VNZ • TO HIRE: GOOD LOOKING GIRL AND MESSENGER WITH BIKE OF HIS OWN
SE SOLICITAN MODELOS • 1954 • Urueta Chano • MXC
SE TI INCONTRO TI AMMAZZO • 1971 • Crea Gianni • ITL
SE TUTTE LE DONNE DEL MONDO (ITL) see **KISS THE GIRLS AND MAKE THEM DIE** • 1966
SE VENDE UN PALACIO • 1942 • Vajda Ladislao • SPN
SE VINCESSI CENTO MILIONI! • 1954 • Campogalliani Carlo, Moscovini Carlo • ITL
SE VIVE UNA VEZ • 1965 • Gonzalez Arturo • SPN
SE VUOI VIVERE.. SPARA! • 1968 • Garrone Sergio • ITL • IF YOU WANT TO LIVE.. SHOOT! ○ OUTLAW RIDER, THE
SEA, THE • 1932 • Jakubowska Wanda • DOC • PLN
SEA, THE see **MARE, IL** • 1962
SEA, THE see **MORETO** • 1967
SEA AND POISON see **UMI TO DOKUYAKU** • 1987
SEA AND THE DAYS, THE see **MER ET LES JOURS, LA** • 1959
SEA AROUND US, THE • 1953 • *Allen Irwin (P)* • DOC • USA
SEA BALLET • 1970 • UKN
SEA BAT, THE • 1930 • Ruggles Wesley • USA
SEA BATHING see **BAIGNADE EN MER** • 1896
SEA BATHING see **BAINS EN MER** • 1896-97
SEA–BATTLE OF MARACAIBO, THE see **BATALLA NAVAL DE MARACAIBO, LA** • 1974
SEA BEAST, THE • 1926 • Webb Millard • USA
SEA BRAT • 1915 • *Reliance* • USA
SEA BREAKING ON THE ROCKS see **EFFET DE MER SUR LES ROCHERS** • 1896
SEA CHASE, THE • 1955 • Farrow John • USA
SEA CITY –GREENOCK • 1975 • Henson Laurence • DOC • UKN
SEA CLIFF, LONG ISLAND • 1929 • *Williams Allen* • DOC • USA
SEA COAST OF BOHEMIA, THE • 1914 • *Imp* • USA
SEA COASTS OF NEW ZEALAND, THE • 1908 • Barrett Franklyn • DOC • NZL
SEA DEVIL, THE see **HAVETS DJAVUL** • 1937
SEA DEVILS • 1931 • Levering Joseph • USA
SEA DEVILS • 1937 • Stoloff Ben • USA
SEA DEVILS • 1953 • Walsh Raoul • UKN
SEA DOG, THE • 1913 • Barker Reginald? • USA
SEA DOGS, THE • 1916 • *Plump & Runt* • USA
SEA DOGS AND LAND RATS • 1916 • *Selby Gertrude* • SHT • USA
SEA DOG'S LOVE, A • 1913 • Henderson Dell • USA
SEA DOGS OF AUSTRALIA • 1913 • Keith Martyn? • ASL
SEA DOG'S TALE, A • 1926 • Sennett Mack • SHT • USA
SEA EAGLE see **HAVSGAMARNA** • 1915
SEA EAGLE, THE see **EAGLE OF THE SEA, THE** • 1926
SEA ETERNAL, THE • 1913 • Johnson Arthur • USA
SEA FEVER (USA) see **EN RADE** • 1927
SEA FIEND, THE (UKN) see **DEVIL MONSTER** • 1935
SEA FIGHTERS, THE see **TIGER OF THE SEA** • 1964
SEA FIGHTING IN GREECE see **COMBAT NAVAL EN GRECE** • 1897
SEA FLIGHT • 1982 • Cox Peter • DOC • ASL
SEA FLOWER, THE • 1918 • Campbell Colin • USA
SEA FOR YOURSELF • 1940 • Trego Charles T. • SHT • USA
SEA FORT • 1940 • Dalrymple Ian • DOC • UKN
SEA FURY • 1929 • Melford George • USA
SEA FURY • 1958 • Endfield Cy • UKN
SEA GATE, THE • 1974 • Tarasov S. • USS
SEA GEM, THE see **PLOY TALAY** • 1986
SEA GHOST, THE • 1915 • *Dowling Joseph* • USA
SEA GHOST, THE • 1931 • Nigh William • USA
SEA GOD, THE • 1930 • Abbott George • USA
SEA GOING BIRDS • 1932 • *Sennett Mack (P)* • SHT • USA
SEA GOT IN YOUR BLOOD, THE • 1968 • Millar David • CND
SEA GULL, THE • 1914 • Sturgeon Rollin S. • USA
SEA GULL, THE • 1969 • Lumet Sidney • UKN, USA
SEA GULL, THE see **WOMAN OF THE SEA, A** • 1926
SEA GULL, THE (USA) see **GABBIANO, IL** • 1977
SEA GYPSIES, THE • 1978 • Raffill Stewart • USA • SHIPWRECK! (UKN) ○ SHIPWRECKED
SEA HARVEST • 1973 • Knudsen Vilhjalmur • DCS • ICL
SEA HAWK, THE • 1924 • Lloyd Frank • USA
SEA HAWK, THE • 1940 • Curtiz Michael • USA
SEA HORNET, THE • 1951 • Kane Joseph • USA
SEA HORSE, THE • 1918 • Clokey Art • SHT • USA
SEA HORSE, THE (UKN) see **HIPPOCAMPE GEOLOGIQUE, L'** • 1933
SEA HORSES • 1926 • Dwan Allan • USA
SEA HOUND, THE • 1947 • Eason Walter B., Wright Mack V. • SRL • USA
SEA–HUNTER, A • 1955 • Nemolyaev V. • USS
SEA IS AT OUR GATES, THE • 1985 • Bittman Roman • MTV • CND
SEA KILLER see **BEYOND THE REEF** • 1981
SEA LEGS • 1930 • Heerman Victor • USA • OAKIE NAVY STORY
SEA LILY, THE • 1916 • Cochrane George • SHT • USA
SEA LILY, THE see **LIS DE MER, LE** • 1970
SEA LION, THE • 1921 • Lee Rowland V. • USA
SEA LIONS OF THE PACIFIC • 1935 • Oliver Bill • DOC • CND
SEA–LOVING SON SAILS AWAY, THE see **TAIYOJI** • 1929
SEA MAIDEN, THE • 1913 • *Charleson Mary* • USA
SEA MASTER, THE • 1917 • Sloman Edward • USA
SEA MATES • 1916 • Powers Francis • SHT • USA
SEA MYSTERY, A • 1916 • *Lee Robert* • SHT • USA
SEA NYMPH • 1980 • Stoneman John • CND
SEA NYMPHS • 1916 • Davey Horace • USA
SEA NYMPHS see **VIOLATED PARADISE** • 1963
SEA NYMPHS, THE • 1914 • Sennett Mack • USA
SEA OF BLOOD • NKR
SEA OF FIREWORKS see **UMI NO HANABI** • 1951
SEA OF GENKAI, THE see **GENKAI–NADA** • 1975
SEA OF GRASS, THE • 1946 • Kazan Elia • USA
SEA OF LOST SHIPS • 1953 • Kane Joseph • USA
SEA OF LOVE • 1989 • Becker Harold • USA
SEA OF RAVENS, THE see **MOR' VRAN** • 1930
SEA OF ROSES, A see **MAR DE ROSAS** • 1979
SEA OF SAND • 1958 • Green Guy • UKN • DESERT PATROL (USA)
SEA OF YOUTH, THE • 1966 • Ogawa Shinsuke • JPN
SEA PANTHER, THE • 1918 • Heffron Thomas N. • USA
SEA PIRATE, THE (USA) see **SURCOUF, L'EROE DEI SETTE MARI** • 1966
SEA PROWLERS see **PROWLERS OF THE SEA** • 1928
SEA QUEST see **BLUE FIN** • 1978
SEA RACKETEERS • 1937 • MacFadden Hamilton • USA • LOVE AHOY
SEA RAIDERS • 1923 • Griffith Edward H. • USA
SEA RAIDERS • 1941 • Beebe Ford, Rawlins John • SRL • USA
SEA RIDER, THE • 1920 • Hollywood Edwin L. • USA
SEA ROUTE, A • 1963 • Chkheidze Revaz • USS
SEA ROVER'S SUMMER • 1949 • Sparling Gordon • DCS • CND
SEA SALTS • 1949 • Hannah Jack • ANS • USA
SEA SANCTUARY • 1973 • Stoneman John • MTV • UKN
SEA SCAMPS • 1926 • Lamont Charles • SHT • USA
SEA SCOUTS • 1939 • Lundy Dick • ANS • USA
SEA SERPENT, THE • 1986 • Greens Gregory • SPN
SEA SERPENT'S DESIRE, A • 1918 • *Franey William* • SHT • USA
SEA SHADOW • 1965 • *Bradley Lisa* • SHT • USA
SEA SHALL NOT HAVE THEM, THE • 1954 • Gilbert Lewis* • UKN
SEA SHORE ROMEO, A • 1915 • Wilson Ben • USA
SEA SIRENS • 1919 • *Vernon Bobby* • SHT • USA
SEA SOLDIERS' SWEETIES • 1932 • Edwards Harry J. • SHT • USA
SEA SPOILERS, THE • 1936 • Strayer Frank • USA
SEA SPRITES • 1961 • Blais Roger • DCS • CND • SIRENES MODERNES
SEA SQUAW, THE • 1925 • *Sennett Mack (P)* • SHT • USA
SEA STORIES see **MORSKIYE RASSKAZY** • 1967
SEA TIGER, THE • 1927 • Dillon John Francis • USA • RUNAWAY ENCHANTRESS, THE
SEA TIGER, THE • 1952 • McDonald Frank • USA
SEA URCHIN, THE • 1913 • August Edwin • USA
SEA URCHIN, THE • 1926 • Cutts Graham • UKN
SEA URCHIN, THE • 1936 • Durden J. V. • UKN
SEA URCHINS see **OURSINS, LES** • 1953
SEA VULTURES see **HAVSGAMARNA** • 1915
SEA VULTURES, THE • 1911 • *Yankee* • USA
SEA WAIF, THE • 1913 • *Ryno* • USA
SEA WAIF, THE • 1918 • Reicher Frank • USA
SEA WALL, THE see **BARRAGE CONTRE LE PACIFIQUE** • 1958
SEA WALL, THE (UKN) see **WEST OF DODGE CITY** • 1947
SEA–WOLF, THE • 1913 • Bosworth Hobart • USA
SEA WOLF, THE • 1920 • Melford George • USA
SEA WOLF, THE • 1926 • Ince Ralph • USA
SEA WOLF, THE • 1930 • Santell Alfred • USA
SEA WOLF, THE • 1941 • Curtiz Michael • USA
SEA WOLF, THE • 1973 • Staudte Wolfgang • FRG
SEA WOLVES see **PIETRO, DER KORSAR** • 1925
SEA WOLVES, THE • 1910 • *Bison* • USA
SEA WOLVES, THE • 1980 • McLaglen Andrew V. • UKN, USA
SEA WOMAN, THE see **WHY WOMEN LOVE** • 1925
SEA WOOF, THE • 1919 • *Capitol* • SHT • USA
SEA WYF AND BISCUIT see **SEAWIFE** • 1957
SEABIRD, LANDBIRD • 1980 • von Puttkamer Peter • SHT • CND
SEABIRDS OF SCOTLAND • 1973 • Palmer Eric • DOC • UKN
SEABO • 1978 • Huston Jimmy • USA
SEABOUND TRAIN, A • 1990 • Slabakov Andrei • BUL
SEADOGS OF AUSTRALIA • 1914 • *Mccullagh J. S. (P)* • ASL
SEADOGS OF GOOD QUEEN BESS • 1922 • Greenwood Edwin • UKN
SEAFARERS, THE • 1953 • Kubrick Stanley • DCS • USA
SEAFIGHTERS, THE see **OPERATION BIKINI** • 1963
SEAGULL • NKR
SEAGULL see **GUNGCAIL** • 1978
SEAGULL, THE • 1983 • Chung Jin-Woo • SKR
SEAGULL, THE (UKN) see **CHAIKA** • 1971
SEAGULL ISLAND see **SECRET OF SEAGULL ISLAND, THE** • 1981
SEAGULLS see **MAKER** • 1989
SEAGULLS, THE see **MAKENE**
SEAGULLS DIE IN THE HARBOUR see **MEEUWEN STERVEN IN DE HAVEN** • 1955
SEAGULLS OVER SORRENTO • 1954 • Boulting John, Boulting Roy • UKN • CREST OF THE WAVE (USA)
SEAL, THE see **PECAT** • 1955
SEAL HUNTING IN THE ARCTIC see **SWILIN' RACKET, THE** • 1928
SEAL ISLAND • 1948 • Algar James • DOC • USA
SEAL ISLAND • 1976 • Spencer Ronald • UKN
SEAL OF SILENCE, THE • 1913 • Ince Thomas H. • USA
SEAL OF SILENCE, THE • 1918 • Mills Thomas R. • USA
SEAL OF SOLOMON, THE see **AZIMAT** • 1958
SEAL OF THE CHURCH, THE • 1910 • Melies Gaston • USA
SEAL OF TIME, THE • 1912 • *Leonard Marion* • USA
SEAL ON THE LOOSE • 1970 • Smith Paul J. • ANS • USA
SEAL SKINNERS • 1939 • *Captain And The Kids* • ANS • USA
SEAL SKINS • 1932 • Pratt Gilbert, Lightfoot Morey • SHT • USA
SEALED CARGO • 1951 • Werker Alfred L. • USA • GAUNT WOMAN, THE
SEALED ENVELOPE, THE • 1912 • *Powers* • USA
SEALED ENVELOPE, THE • 1919 • Gerrard Douglas • USA
SEALED HEARTS • 1919 • Ince Ralph • USA
SEALED INSTRUCTIONS • 1909 • *Selig* • USA
SEALED LIPS • 1912 • *Solax* • USA
SEALED LIPS • 1915 • Ince John • USA
SEALED LIPS • 1925 • Gaudio Antonio • USA
SEALED LIPS • 1931 • Neumann Kurt • SHT • USA
SEALED LIPS • 1941 • Waggner George • USA • BEYOND THE LAW
SEALED LIPS see **LEVRES CLOSES** • 1906
SEALED LIPS see **FORSEGLADE LAPPAR** • 1927
SEALED LIPS (UKN) see **AFTER TONIGHT** • 1933
SEALED OASIS, THE • 1914 • Le Saint Edward J. • USA
SEALED ORDERS • 1914 • *Victor* • USA
SEALED ORDERS • 1914 • Melville Wilbert • *Lubin* • USA
SEALED PACKAGE, THE • 1914 • Santschi Thomas • USA
SEALED ROOM • 1909 • Griffith D. W. • USA
SEALED ROOM, THE • 1926 • Shirley Arthur • ASL
SEALED SOIL, THE • 1978 • Nabili Marva • IRN
SEALED VALLEY • 1915 • McGill Lawrence • USA
SEALED VERDICT • 1948 • Allen Lewis • USA
SEALED WITH A KISS see **LIANG HSAIO–WU–CHIH** • 1981
SEALS see **KAMERAJAGD AUF SEEHUNDE** • 1937
SEALSKIN COAT, THE • 1916 • Ellis Robert • USA
SEAMAN NUMBER SEVEN see **HAI–YUAN CH'I–HAO** • 1972
SEAMEN see **HOMBRES DEL MAR** • 1977
SEAMSTRESS, THE see **SVADLENKA** • 1936
SEANCE • 1959 • Belson Jordan • ANS • USA
SEANCE • 1970 • Heffner Avram • SHT • ISR
SEANCE DE LA RUE DU COUVENT, LA • 1979 • Melancon Andre • CND
SEANCE DE PRESTIDIGITATION • 1896 • Melies Georges • FRN • CONJURING (USA)
SEANCE ON A WET AFTERNOON • 1964 • Forbes Bryan • UKN
SEAPREME COURT, THE • 1954 • Kneitel Seymour • ANS • USA
SEARA VERMELHA • 1963 • D'Aversa Alberto • BRZ • VIOLENT LAND, THE
SEARCH see **POYISK** • 1968
SEARCH see **PROBE** • 1972
SEARCH see **ISKANJA** • 1980
SEARCH, THE • 1948 • Zinnemann Fred • USA, SWT • GEZEICHNETEN, DIE (SWT)
SEARCH, THE see **POSZUKIWACZE** • 1962
SEARCH, THE see **BUSCA, LA** • 1967
SEARCH, THE see **BUSQUEDA, LA** • 1972
SEARCH, THE see **ANVESHANE** • 1978
SEARCH, THE see **SHODH** • 1979
SEARCH AND DESTROY • 1979 • Fruet William • CND • STRIKING BACK
SEARCH AND DESTROY • 1988 • Ingvordsen J. Christian • USA
SEARCH AND RESEARCH • 1967 • Marquis Eric • DCS • UKN
SEARCH AREAS • 1958 • Blais Roger • DCS • CND

SEARCH FOR A BETTER LIFE, THE see **ZITONTAS TI TIHI STA XENA** • 1967
SEARCH FOR BEAUTY • 1934 • Kenton Erle C. • USA
SEARCH FOR BRIDIE MURPHY, THE • 1956 • Langley Noel • USA
SEARCH FOR DANGER • 1949 • Bernhard Jack • USA
SEARCH FOR FISH see **GYOEI NO MURE** • 1984
SEARCH FOR ICARUS • 1963 • Mideke Michael • SHT • USA
SEARCH FOR INTIMACY, THE • 1987 • Kennedy Michael • DCS • CND
SEARCH FOR LEARNING, A • 1966 • Shebib Donald • CND
SEARCH FOR MISERY • 1964 • Kuwahara Bob • ANS • USA
SEARCH FOR OIL, THE see **OPSPORING VAN AARDOLIE, DE** • 1954
SEARCH FOR OIL IN NIGERIA • 1960 • Nesbitt Frank, Ozoude Adolph • DOC • NGR
SEARCH FOR PARADISE • 1957 • Lang Otto • DOC • USA
SEARCH FOR PEACE • 1968 • *Shaw Mason* • ANT • USA, NTH
SEARCH FOR SOLUTIONS, THE • 1979 • Jackson Michael • DOC • USA
SEARCH FOR THE EVIL ONE • 1967 • Kane Joseph • USA
SEARCH FOR THE GODS • 1975 • Taylor Jud • TVM • USA
SEARCH FOR THE MOTHER LODE: THE LAST GREAT TREASURE see **MOTHER LODE** • 1980
SEARCH FOR VENUS AROUND THE WORLD see **AROUND THE WORLD WITH NOTHING ON** • 1963
SEARCH FOR WILD GINSENG • Chung Jin-Woo • SKR
SEARCH IN THE DEEP • 1968 • Watson Patrick • DOC • CND
SEARCH IN THE ISLAND • 1990 • Sabbaghzadeh Mehdi • IRN
SEARCH INTO DARKNESS • 1962 • Van Dyke Willard • DOC • USA
SEARCH ME! • 1916 • Dillon John Francis • USA
SEARCH OPERATION • 1958 • Blais Roger • DCS • CND
SEARCH, THE SCIENTIFIC DETECTIVE • 1914 • *Ab* • USA
SEARCHED IN VAIN see **ANVESHICHU KANDETHIYILLA** • 1967
SEARCHER, THE • 1989 • Motevaselani Mohamad • IRN • SEEKER, THE
SEARCHERS, THE • 1956 • Ford John • USA
SEARCHERS, THE see **POSZUKIWACZE** • 1962
SEARCHERS OF THE VOODOO MOUNTAIN • 1984 • Suarez Bobby A. • USA
SEARCHING EYE, THE • 1964 • Bass Saul • SHT • USA
SEARCHING FOR CRIMINALS see **DAR JOSTOJOYE TABAHCARAN** • 1967
SEARCHING FOR EILEEN see **ZOEKEN NAAR EILEEN** • 1987
SEARCHING FOR MAYRA see **ALLA RICERCA DI MAYRA** • 1972
SEARCHING FOR VENUS see **AROUND THE WORLD WITH NOTHING ON** • 1963
SEARCHING LOOK, A • 1961 • Danek Oldrich • CZC
SEARCHING THE HEARTS OF STUDENTS see **CESTA DO HUBIN STUDAKOVY DUSE** • 1939
SEARCHING WIND, THE • 1946 • Dieterle William • USA
SEARCHMASTER, THE • 1958 • Blais Roger • DCS • CND
SEAS BENEATH, THE • 1931 • Ford John • USA
SEASHELL AND THE CLERGYMAN, THE see **COQUILLE ET LE CLERGYMAN, LA** • 1928
SEASHORE • 1971 • Rimmer David • CND
SEASHORE BABY • 1904 • *Bitzer Billy (Ph)* • USA
SEASHORE FROLICS • 1903 • Porter Edwin S. • USA
SEASICK SAILORS • 1951 • Davis Mannie • ANS • USA
SEASIDE ADVENTURE • 1952 • Davis Mannie • ANS • USA
SEASIDE COMEDY, A • 1911 • Bouwmeester Theo • UKN
SEASIDE EPISODE, A • 1909 • Coleby A. E. • UKN
SEASIDE FLIRT, A • 1914 • *Crystal* • USA
SEASIDE FLIRTATION, A see **RASTAQUOUERE RODRIGUEZ Y PAPANAGAZ, LE** • 1906
SEASIDE GIRL, A • 1907 • Fitzhamon Lewin • UKN
SEASIDE INTRODUCTION, A • 1911 • Fitzhamon Lewin • UKN
SEASIDE LODGINGS • 1906 • Martin J. H.? • UKN
SEASIDE ROMEOS • 1917 • *Hamilton Lloyd V.* • USA
SEASIDE SAMARITAN, A • 1913 • *August Edwin* • USA
SEASIDE SIREN, A • 1920 • Beaudine William • SHT • USA
SEASIDE SWINGERS (USA) see **EVERY DAY'S A HOLIDAY** • 1964
SEASIDE VIEWS • 1906 • Green Tom? • UKN
SEASIDE VILLAGE • 1965 • Kim Soo-Yong • SKR
SEASON, THE • 1966 • MacDonald Donald*
SEASON FOR ASSASSINS see **TEMPO DEGLI ASSASSINI, IL** • 1976
SEASON FOR GIRLS, A see **MUSUME NO KISETSU** • 1968
SEASON FOR LOVE, THE (USA) see **MORTE-SAISON DES AMOURS, LA** • 1961
SEASON IN HAKKARI, A see **HAKKARI'DE BIR MEVSIM** • 1987
SEASON OF CHILDREN, THE • 1917 • Windom Lawrence C. • SHT • USA
SEASON OF DREAMS see **STACKING** • 1987
SEASON OF LOVE, THE see **MORTE-SAISON DES AMOURS, LA** • 1961
SEASON OF MONSTERS see **SZORNYEK EVADJA** • 1987
SEASON OF PASSION (USA) see **SUMMER OF THE 17TH DOLL** • 1959
SEASON OF SEX CRIMINALS, THE see **CHIKAN NO KISETSU** • 1968
SEASON OF THE SUN see **TAIYO NO KISETSU** • 1956
SEASON OF THE WITCH see **JACK'S WIFE** • 1973
SEASONAL IDYLL, A see **IDILIO DE ESTACION, UN** • 1978
SEASONAL WIND, THE see **KISETSU-FU** • 1977
SEASONAL WORKERS • 1964 • Sremec Rudolf • DCS • YGS
SEASONS see **ANOTIMPURI** • 1963
SEASONS, THE • 1953 • Chapman Christopher • DCS • CND • SAISONS, LES
SEASONS, THE see **FOUR SEASONS** • 1970
SEASONS, THE see **GODISNJA DOBA** • 1980
SEASON'S GREETINKS • 1933 • Fleischer Dave • ANS • USA
SEASONS IN THE MIND • 1970 • Pearson Peter • CND
SEASON'S MEMOIRS see **SHEET GRISHMAR SMRITI** • 1983
SEASONS OF MEIJI see **MEIJI HARU AKI** • 1968
SEASONS OF OUR LOVE see **STAGIONI DEL NOSTRO AMORE, LE** • 1966
SEASON'S OPENING see **ZACIATOK SEZONY** • 1987
SEASONS WE WALKED TOGETHER, THE see **FUTARI DE ARUITA IKU-HARU-AKI** • 1962
SEAT, THE see **FOTEL** • 1963
SEAT OF PASSION, PARK OF PLEASURE • 1969 • *Athena Productions* • USA
SEAT OF THE TROUBLE • 1914 • *Powers* • USA
SEAT OF YOUTH see **SIENEN NO ISU** • 1962
SEATED AT HIS RIGHT see **SEDUTO ALLA SUA DESTRA** • 1968
SEATED AT HIS RIGHT HAND see **SEDUTO ALLA SUA DESTRA** • 1968
SEATED ON HIS RIGHT see **SEDUTO ALLA SUA DESTRA** • 1968
SEATS OF THE MIGHTY, THE • 1914 • Hunter T. Hayes • USA
SEATS TWO • 1970 • Zwartjes Frans • SHT • NTH
SEAWARDS THE GREAT SHIPS • 1959 • *Grierson John (P)* • DOC • UKN
SEAWATCH • 1980 • Ohlsson Terry (c/d) • SHT • ASL
SEAWEED • 1909 • *Warwick Trading Co* • UKN
SEAWEED CHILDREN, THE see **MALACHI'S COVE** • 1974
SEAWEED SANDWICH • 1970 • *Merrill H. Glenn (P)* • DOC • USA
SEAWIFE • 1957 • McNaught Bob • UKN • SEA WYF AND BISCUIT
SEBAK MAA EL ZAMAN • 1988 • Kawadri Anwar • EGY, UKN • OUT OF TIME (UKN)
SEBASTIAN • 1967 • Greene David • UKN • MISTER SEBASTIAN
SEBASTIAN AND THE SPARROW • 1988 • Hicks Scott, Bennett Bill? • ASL
SEBASTIAN, DER TRIBUN DES KAISERS • 1919 • Frey Karl? • FRG
SEBASTIAN KNEIPP -EIN GROSSES LEBEN • 1958 • Liebeneiner Wolfgang • AUS • WASSERDOKTOR, DER
SEBASTIANE • 1976 • Jarman Derek, Humfress Paul • UKN
SEBASTOPOL • 1939 • Vajda Ladislao • FRN
SEBENING KACA • 1986 • INN
SEBRING, LA CINQUIEME HEURE • 1966 • Fournier Claude • DCS • CND
SECANGKIR KOPI PAHIT • 1985 • Karya Teguh • INN • MEROBEK ANGAN-ANGAN ○ BITTER COFFEE ○ TORN DREAM
SECAWAN ANGGUR KEBIMBANGAN • 1985 • Umboh Wim • INN • SCRAWAN ANGJUR KEBIMBAYAM
SECH SCHWEDINNEN IM PENSIONAT • 1980 • Dietrich Erwin C. • SWT, FRN • UNTAMED SEX
SECH TAGE HEIMATURLAUB • 1941 • von Alten Jurgen • FRG
SECHERESSE see **VIDAS SECAS** • 1963
SECHS KUMMERBUBEN, DIE • 1968 • Schnyder Franz • SWT • SIX UNFORTUNATES, THE
SECHS MADCHEN SUCHEN NACHT QUARTIER • 1928 • Behrendt Hans • FRG
SECHS PISTOLEN JAGEN PROFESSOR Z • 1967 • Coll Julio • FRG, SPN, PRT • SIX GUNS ARE CHASING PROFESSOR Z
SECHS SCHWEDINNEN AUF IBIZA • *Albert Marianne* • FRG • MORE DESIRES WITHIN YOUNG GIRLS
SECHS WOCHEN UNTER DEN APACHEN see **ACHTUNG HARRY! AUGEN AUF!!** • 1926
SECHSE KOMMEN DURCH DIE WELT • 1972 • Simon Rainer • GDR
SECHZEHN TOCHTER UND KEIN PAPA • 1928 • Trotz Adolf • FRG • FRITZ UND FRITZI
SECKS • Zuckerman Michael T. • USA
SECLUDED ROADHOUSE, THE • 1926 • *Barrymore William* • USA
SECLUSION NEAR A FOREST see **NA SAMOTE U LESA** • 1976
SECOND ADVENTURE OF BONEHEAD -INITIATED INTO THE ROYAL GAZEBOS • 1910 • *Centaur* • USA
SECOND AWAKENING OF CHRISTA KLAGES, THE see **ZWEITE ERWACHEN DER CHRISTA KLAGES, DER** • 1978
SECOND BEGINNING, THE • 1915 • King Burton L. • USA
SECOND BEST BED, THE • 1938 • Walls Tom • UKN
SECOND BEST SECRET AGENT IN THE WHOLE WIDE WORLD, THE (USA) see **LICENSED TO KILL** • 1965
SECOND BOTTLE, THE • 1965 • Donev Donyo • ANM • BUL
SECOND BREATH (UKN) see **DEUXIEME SOUFFLE, LE** • 1966
SECOND BUREAU • 1936 • Hanbury Victor • UKN
SECOND CHANCE • 1947 • Tinling James • USA
SECOND CHANCE • 1950 • Beaudine William • USA
SECOND CHANCE • 1953 • Mate Rudolph • USA
SECOND CHANCE • 1971 • Tewkesbury Peter • USA
SECOND CHANCE SEA • 1976 • Hubley Faith • ANS • USA
SECOND CHANCE (UKN) see **PROBATION** • 1932
SECOND CHANCE (UKN) see **SI C'ETAIT A REFAIRE** • 1975
SECOND CHANCES see **THIS RECKLESS AGE** • 1932
SECOND CHILDHOOD • 1914 • MacGregor Norval • USA
SECOND CHILDHOOD • 1936 • Meins Gus • SHT • USA
SECOND CHOICE • 1930 • Bretherton Howard • USA
SECOND CHORUS • 1940 • Potter H. C. • USA
SECOND CLASS MAIL • Snowden Alison • ANM • CND
SECOND CLASS PASSENGER see **PUTNIK DRUGOG RAZREDA** • 1973
SECOND CLUE, THE • 1914 • Pollard Harry? • USA
SECOND COMING, THE see **MESSIAH OF EVIL** • 1975
SECOND COMING OF EVA, THE • 1975 • Ahlberg Mac • SWD
SECOND COMING OF SUZANNE, THE • 1974 • Barry Michael • USA • SUZANNE
SECOND COMMANDMENT, THE • 1915 • Buel Kenean • USA
SECOND DANCE, THE see **ANDRA DANSEN** • 1983
SECOND DEGREE, THE • 1981 • Colelli Ralph • USA
SECOND FACE • 1954 • Rich Roy • USA • DOUBLE PROFILE
SECOND FACE, THE • 1950 • Bernhard Jack • USA
SECOND FACE OF DR. JEKYLL, THE see **SON OF DR. JEKYLL, THE** • 1951
SECOND FIDDLE • 1923 • Tuttle Frank • USA
SECOND FIDDLE • 1939 • Lanfield Sidney • USA
SECOND FIDDLE • 1957 • Elvey Maurice • UKN
SECOND FIDDLE see **MEN ARE SUCH FOOLS** • 1932
SECOND FIDDLE TO A STEEL GUITAR • 1965 • Duncan Victor • USA
SECOND FLOOR MYSTERY, THE • 1930 • Del Ruth Roy • USA • SECOND STORY MYSTERY, THE ○ SECOND STORY MURDER, THE
SECOND GENERATION, THE • 1914 • *Pathe* • USA
SECOND GENERATION, THE see **DRUGA GENERACIJA** • 1983
SECOND GREATEST SEX, THE • 1955 • Marshall George • USA
SECOND GROOM, THE see **ARIS EL THANI, EL** • 1967
SECOND HALF, THE see **NESSEF EL AKHAR, AL** • 1967
SECOND-HAND HEARTS see **HAMSTER OF HAPPINESS, THE** • 1979
SECOND HAND KISSES • 1931 • Foster Lewis R. • SHT • USA
SECOND HAND LOVE • 1923 • Wellman William A. • USA
SECOND HAND ROSE • 1922 • Ingraham Lloyd • USA
SECOND-HAND VIRGIN see **JUNGFRAU AUS ZWEITER HAND** • 1967
SECOND HAND WIFE • 1933 • MacFadden Hamilton • USA • ILLEGAL DIVORCE, THE (UKN)
SECOND HOMECOMING, THE • 1913 • *Nestor* • USA
SECOND HONEYMOON • 1930 • Rosen Phil • USA
SECOND HONEYMOON • 1937 • Lang Walter • USA
SECOND HONEYMOON, A • 1911 • *Costello Maurice* • USA
SECOND HUNDRED YEARS, THE • 1927 • Guiol Fred • SHT • USA
SECOND I, THE • 1964 • Donev Donyo • ANM • BUL
SECOND IN COMMAND, THE • 1915 • Bowman William J. • USA
SECOND JOURNEY, THE • 1981 • Cantrill Arthur, Cantrill Corinne • DOC • ASL
SECOND KILLING OF THE DOG, THE • 1988 • Babenco Hector • USA
SECOND LAWYER see **DRUHA SMENA** • 1940
SECOND LIEUTENANT, THE • 1915 • Aylott Dave • UKN
SECOND LIFE, A see **DAINAI NO JINSEI** • 1948
SECOND MATE, THE • 1929 • Edwards J. Steven • UKN
SECOND MATE, THE • 1951 • Baxter John • UKN
SECOND MR. BUSH, THE • 1940 • Carstairs John Paddy • UKN
SECOND MOVE WITH A PAWN, THE see **DRUHA TAH PESCEM** • 1985
SECOND MRS. FENWAY, THE see **HER HONOR THE GOVERNOR** • 1926
SECOND MRS. ROEBUCK, THE • 1914 • O'Brien Jack, Cabanne W. Christy • USA
SECOND MRS. TANQUERAY, THE • 1914 • *Crawley Constance* • USA
SECOND MRS. TANQUERAY, THE • 1916 • Paul Fred • UKN
SECOND MRS. TANQUERAY, THE • 1952 • Bower Dallas • UKN
SECOND PART see **DRUHA SMENA** • 1940
SECOND PENALTY, THE • 1914 • Thornton F. Martin? • UKN
SECOND POWER, THE (USA) see **SEGUNDO PODER, EL** • 1977
SECOND SERVE • 1986 • Page Anthony • TVM • USA
SECOND SEX, THE • 1968 • Masumura Yasuzo • JPN
SECOND SHIFT, THE see **DRUHA SMENA** • 1940
SECOND SHIFT, THE see **ANDRE SKIFTET, DET** • 1978
SECOND SHOT, THE • 1913 • *Wilbur Crane* • USA
SECOND SHOT, THE • 1915 • Terwilliger George W. • USA
SECOND SHOT, THE see **PANAMA LADY** • 1939
SECOND SHOT, THE see **ZWEITE SCHUSS, DER** • 1943
SECOND SHOT, THE (UKN) see **BITTER SWEETS** • 1928
SECOND SIGHT • 1911 • *Moore Owen* • USA
SECOND SIGHT • 1914 • Finley Ned • USA
SECOND SIGHT • 1938 • *Fidelity* • SHT • UKN
SECOND SIGHT • 1989 • Zwick Joel • USA
SECOND SIGHT: A LOVE STORY • 1984 • Korty John • TVM • USA
SECOND SIN, THE • 1966 • Millin David • SAF
SECOND SISTER see **MAJHLI DIDI** • 1968
SECOND SON, THE • 1915 • Wright Fred E. • USA
SECOND SON CROW see **JINANBO KARASU** • 1955
SECOND SOUFFLE, LE • 1959 • Bellon Yannick • FRN
SECOND SOUFFLE, UN • 1978 • Blain Gerard • FRN, FRG • SECOND WIND
SECOND SPRING, A see **ZWEITE FRUHLING, DER** • 1975
SECOND STAIN, THE • 1922 • Ridgwell George • UKN
SECOND STAR TO THE RIGHT • 1980 • Annett Paul • UKN • NEVER NEVER LAND
SECOND STORY MURDER, THE see **SECOND FLOOR MYSTERY, THE** • 1930
SECOND STORY MYSTERY, THE see **SECOND FLOOR MYSTERY, THE** • 1930
SECOND STORY RINGER, THE • 1916 • *Vitagraph* • SHT • USA
SECOND STRING, THE • 1915 • Wilson Frank • UKN
SECOND THOUGHTS • 1938 • Parker Albert • UKN • CRIME OF PETER FRAME, THE
SECOND THOUGHTS • 1983 • Turman Lawrence • USA
SECOND TIME AROUND, THE • 1961 • Sherman Vincent • USA • STAR IN THE WEST ○ CALICO SHERIFF, THE ○ MOTHER OUGHT TO MARRY
SECOND TIME LUCKY • 1984 • Anderson Michael • NZL
SECOND TO NONE • 1926 • Raymond Jack • UKN
SECOND TOUCH see **TWEE VROUWEN** • 1978
SECOND TOUR (USA) see **DRUHA SMENA** • 1940
SECOND TRACK, THE see **ZWEITE GLEIS, DAS** • 1962
SECOND VICTORY, THE • 1987 • Thomas Gerald • UKN
SECOND VOYAGE DE NOCES • Debest Maxime • FRN
SECOND WIFE • 1930 • Mack Russell • USA
SECOND WIFE • 1936 • Killy Edward • USA
SECOND WIFE, THE • 1914 • *Selig* • USA
SECOND WIFE, THE see **ZAWGA AL THANIA, AL** • 1967
SECOND WIND • 1976 • Shebib Donald • TVM • USA
SECOND WIND see **DEUXIEME SOUFFLE, LE** • 1966
SECOND WIND see **SECOND SOUFFLE, UN** • 1978
SECOND WOMAN, THE • 1949 • Kern James V. • USA • ELLEN (UKN)
SECOND WORLD WAR DOCUMENTARY see **NIITAKAYAMA NOBORE** • 1968
SECOND YOUTH • 1924 • Parker Albert • USA
SECOND YOUTH see **REMAJA KEDUA** • 1984
SECONDA B • 1934 • Alessandrini Goffredo • ITL
SECONDA MOGLIE, LA • 1922 • Palermi Amleto • ITL
SECONDE VERITE, LA • 1965 • Christian-Jaque • FRN, ITL • AMANTE INFEDELE (ITL)
SECONDHAND GIRL see **MADCHEN AUS ZWEITER HAND, EIN** • 1976
SECONDO PONZIO PILATO • 1988 • Magni Luigi • ITL • ACCORDING TO PONTIUS PILATE

SECONDO TRAGICO FANTOZZI, IL • 1976 • Salce Luciano • ITL
SECONDS • 1966 • Frankenheimer John • USA
SECOURS AUX NAUFRAGES • 1903-04 • Blache Alice • FRN
SECRET see **RAAZ** • 1967
SECRET, LE • 1974 • Enrico Robert • FRN • SECRET, THE
SECRET, THE • 1911 • *Lubin* • USA
SECRET, THE • 1917 • Ford John • USA
SECRET, THE • 1918 • Edwards Henry • UKN
SECRET, THE • 1955 • Endfield Cy • UKN
SECRET, THE see **SECRET, LE** • 1974
SECRET, THE see **FENG CHIEH** • 1980
SECRET, THE see **SECRETO, EL** • 1988
SECRET, THE see **SEGRETO, IL** • 1990
SECRET ADMIRER • 1985 • Greenwalt David • USA
SECRET AFFAIRS • 1982 • Cukor George • USA
SECRET AFRICA see **AFRICA SEGRETA** • 1969
SECRET AFRICAN FOREST see **FORET SECRETE D'AFRIQUE** • 1968
SECRET AGENT • 1943 • Kneitel Seymour • ANS • USA
SECRET AGENT 077 see **WEISSE FRACHT FUR HONGKONG** • 1964
SECRET AGENT 777 OPERATION MYSTERY see **AGENTE SEGRETO 777 OPERAZIONE MISTERO** • 1965
SECRET AGENT, THE • 1911 • *Lubin* • USA
SECRET AGENT, THE • 1915 • *Haines Robert T.* • USA
SECRET AGENT, THE • 1936 • Hitchcock Alfred • UKN
SECRET AGENT F.O.B. see **UNDER THE COUNTER SPY** • 1954
SECRET AGENT FIREBALL (USA) see **SPIE UCCIDONO A BEIRUT, LE** • 1965
SECRET AGENT OF JAPAN • 1942 • Pichel Irving • USA
SECRET AGENT SUPER DRAGON(USA) see **NEW YORK CHIAMA SUPERDRAGO** • 1966
SECRET AGENT SVENSSON see **HEMLIGA SVENSSON** • 1933
SECRET AGENT (UKN) see **GEHEIMAGENT, DER** • 1932
SECRET AGENT (USA) see **ON SECRET SERVICE** • 1933
SECRET AGENT WOODY • 1967 • Smith Paul J. • ANS • USA
SECRET AGENT X-9 • 1937 • Beebe Ford, Smith Cliff • SRL • USA
SECRET AGENT X-9 • 1945 • Taylor Ray, Collins Lewis D. • SRL • USA
SECRET ALLIES see **RAPE OF CZECHOSLOVAKIA, THE** • 1939
SECRET ARMY (UKN) see **ENEMY AGENT** • 1940
SECRET ASSIGNMENT see **RIKUGUN NAKANO GAKKO: MITSUMEI** • 1967
SECRET BEYOND THE DOOR • 1947 • Lang Fritz • USA
SECRET BEYOND THE DOOR, THE see **OLTRE LA PORTA** • 1983
SECRET BRIDE, THE • 1934 • Dieterle William • USA • CONCEALMENT (UKN)
SECRET BRIGADE • 1951 • Sablin V. Korsh
SECRET CALL, THE • 1931 • Walker Stuart • USA
SECRET CAVE, THE • 1953 • Durst John • UKN
SECRET CELLAR, THE • 1916 • *Baggot King* • SHT • USA
SECRET CEREMONY • 1968 • Losey Joseph • UKN
SECRET CINEMA, THE • 1968 • Bartel Paul • USA
SECRET CODE, THE • 1915 • *Kalem* • USA
SECRET CODE, THE • 1918 • Parker Albert • USA
SECRET CODE, THE • 1942 • Bennet Spencer Gordon • SRL • USA
SECRET CODE, THE see **SECRETUL CIFRULUI** • 1959
SECRET COMMAND, THE • 1944 • Sutherland A. Edward • USA • BY SECRET COMMAND ○ PILEBUCK
SECRET CONCLAVE, THE (USA) see **UOMINI NON GUARDANO IL CIELO, GLI** • 1952
SECRET CONNECTION see **RESEAU SECRET** • 1967
SECRET COURIER, THE see **GEHEIME KURIER, DER** • 1928
SECRET CRIME, A • 1914 • *Kalem* • USA
SECRET DE D'ARTAGNAN, LE • 1962 • Marcellini Siro • FRN, ITL • COLPO SEGRETO DI D'ARTAGNAN, IL (ITL) ○ SECRET MARK OF D'ARTAGNAN, THE (USA)
SECRET DE GENEVIEVE, LE • 1916 • de Morlhon Camille • FRN
SECRET DE MADAME CLAPAIN, LE • 1943 • Berthomieu Andre • FRN • ETRANGE MADAME CLAPAIN, L'
SECRET DE MAYERLING, LE • 1948 • Delannoy Jean • FRN • SECRET OF MAYERLING, THE (USA)
SECRET DE MONTE-CRISTO, LE • 1948 • Valentin Albert • FRN
SECRET DE POLICHINELLE, LE • 1923 • Hervil Rene • FRN
SECRET DE POLICHINELLE, LE • 1936 • Berthomieu Andre • FRN
SECRET DE ROSETTE LAMBERT, LE • 1920 • Bernard Raymond • FRN
SECRET DE SOEUR ANGELE, LE • 1956 • Joannon Leo • FRN, ITL • SEGRETO DI SUOR ANGELA, IL ○ SISTER ANGELE'S SECRET (USA)
SECRET DECREE see **DIEXUE HEIGU** • 1985
SECRET DES HOMMES BLEUS, LE see **TRESOR DES HOMMES BLEUS, LE** • 1960
SECRET DES SELENITES, LE • 1981 • Image Jean • ANM • FRN • MOON MADNESS ○ MOONTREK
SECRET DES TEMPLIERS, LE • 1975 • Franju Georges • MTV • FRN
SECRET DES WORONZEFF, LE • 1934 • Beucler Andre, Robison Arthur • FRN
SECRET D'HELENE MARIMON, LE • 1953 • Calef Henri • FRN, ITL • TRADIMENTO DI ELENA MARIMON, IL (ITL)
SECRET DIARY FROM A WOMEN'S PRISON (UKN) see **DIARIO SEGRETO DI UN CARCERE FEMMINILE** • 1973
SECRET DIARY OF A GIRL STUDENT see **JOSHIGAKUSEI GOKUHI NIKKI** • 1968
SECRET DIARY OF A MINOR, THE see **DIARIO SEGRETO DI UNA MINORENNE, IL** • 1968
SECRET DIARY OF ADRIAN MOLE AGED 13 3/4, THE • 1985 • Sasdy Peter • MTV • UKN
SECRET DIARY OF SIGMUND FREUD, THE • 1984 • Greene Danford B. • USA
SECRET DISCOVERY OF AUSTRALIA, THE • 1983 • Burton Geoff, Caulfield Michael • DOC • ASL
SECRET DOCUMENT -VIENNA (USA) see **FUSILLE A L'AUBE** • 1950
SECRET DOOR, THE • 1962 • Kay Gilbert L. • UKN, USA • NOW IT CAN BE TOLD
SECRET DOSSIER OF THE MAFIA see **SASSO IN BOCCA, IL** • 1970
SECRET DR L'EMERALDE, LE • 1936 • de Canonge Maurice • FRN • ENIGMATIQUE GENTLEMAN, L'
SECRET DREAMS OF MONA Q, THE • 1977 • Kaufman Charles • USA
SECRET DU CHEVALIER D'EON, LE • 1960 • Audry Jacqueline • FRN, ITL • STORIE D'AMORE PROIBITE (ITL) ○ CAVALIERE E LA CZARINA, IL ○ SECRET OF THE CHEVALIER D'EON, THE
SECRET DU DOCTEUR, LE • 1930 • de Rochefort Charles • FRN
SECRET DU DOCTEUR, LE see **HYDROTHERAPIE FANTASTIQUE** • 1909
SECRET DU FLORIDA, LE • 1946 • Houssin Jacques • FRN • AVENTURE SUR LA COTE ○ LARGUEZ LES VOILES
SECRET DU FORCAT, LE • 1913 • Feuillade Louis • FRN
SECRET DU LONE STAR, LE • 1919 • de Baroncelli Jacques • FRN
SECRET DU MEDECIN, LE see **HYDROTHERAPIE FANTASTIQUE** • 1909
SECRET DU VIEUX PRIEURE, LE see **QUELQU'UN A TUE** • 1933
SECRET D'UNE FEMME, LE see **SIRRU IMRA'A** • 1960
SECRET D'UNE MERE, LE • 1952 • Gourguet Jean • FRN
SECRET D'UNE NUIT, LE • 1934 • Gandera Felix • FRN
SECRET D'UNE VIE, LE see **FEMME SANS IMPORTANCE, UNE** • 1937
SECRET ENEMIES • 1943 • Stoloff Ben • USA
SECRET EVIDENCE • 1941 • Nigh William • USA
SECRET EXECUTIONERS • *Wong Chen-Li* • HKG
SECRET FILE 1413 (USA) see **DOSSIER 1413** • 1959
SECRET FILE, ASSIGNMENT ABROAD • 1959 • Dreifuss Arthur • USA
SECRET FILE: HOLLYWOOD • 1962 • Cushman Ralph • USA • SECRET FILES OF HOLLYWOOD
SECRET FILE, U.S.A. • 1955 • Dreifuss Arthur • USA
SECRET FILES OF DETECTIVE "X", THE • 1968 • Hilliard Richard • USA • FILES OF DETECTIVE X
SECRET FILES OF HOLLYWOOD see **SECRET FILE: HOLLYWOOD** • 1962
SECRET FLIGHT (USA) see **SCHOOL FOR SECRETS** • 1946
SECRET FOE, THE • 1916 • Reynolds Lynn • USA
SECRET FORMULA, THE • 1913 • Golden Joseph A. • USA
SECRET FORMULA, THE • 1914 • *Blackwell Carlyle* • USA
SECRET FORMULA, THE • 1915 • MacDonald Donald • USA
SECRET FORMULA, THE (USA) see **FORMULA SECRETA, LA** • 1965
SECRET FOUR, THE • 1921 • Russell Albert, Vekroff Perry N. • USA
SECRET FOUR, THE see **FOUR JUST MEN, THE** • 1939
SECRET FOUR, THE (UKN) see **KANSAS CITY CONFIDENTIAL** • 1953
SECRET FRENCH PROSTITUTION REPORT (UKN) see **DOSSIER PROSTITUTION** • 1969
SECRET FURY, THE • 1950 • Ferrer Mel • USA • BLIND SPOT
SECRET GAME, THE • 1917 • De Mille William C. • USA
SECRET GAME, THE (UKN) see **JEUX INTERDITS** • 1948
SECRET GAMES see **JEUX INTERDITS** • 1948
SECRET GARDEN, THE • 1919 • Clonebaugh G. Butler • USA
SECRET GARDEN, THE • 1949 • Wilcox Fred M. • USA
SECRET GARDEN, THE • 1975 • Brooking Dorothea • MTV • UKN
SECRET GARDEN, THE • 1987 • Grint Alan • TVM • UKN
SECRET GIFT, THE • 1920 • Franklin Harry L. • USA
SECRET HEART, THE • 1946 • Leonard Robert Z. • USA
SECRET HISTORY OF THE CHING COURT, THE • 1950 • Chu Shih-Ling • HKG
SECRET HONOR • 1984 • Altman Robert • USA
SECRET HOUR, THE • 1928 • Lee Rowland V. • USA • BEGGARS OF LOVE
SECRET ILLUSTRATION OF WOMAN see **ONNA NO HIEZU** • 1968
SECRET INFORMATION see **TAREKOMI** • 1968
SECRET INGREDIENT, THE see **TANJI SASTOJACK** • 1987
SECRET INTENTIONS see **SECRETAS INTENCIONES, LAS** • 1969
SECRET INTERLUDE (UKN) see **PRIVATE NUMBER** • 1936
SECRET INTERLUDE (UKN) see **VIEW FROM POMPEY'S HEAD, THE** • 1955
SECRET INVASION, THE • 1964 • Corman Roger • USA, YGS • DUBIOUS PATRIOTS
SECRET ISLAND, THE see **RAHAS DUPATHA** • 1967
SECRET JOURNEY, THE • 1939 • Baxter John • UKN • AMONG HUMAN WOLVES
SECRET KILLING see **MURDER ONCE REMOVED** • 1971
SECRET KINGDOM, THE • 1917 • Marston Theodore, Brabin Charles J. • SRL • USA
SECRET KINGDOM, THE • 1925 • Hill Sinclair • UKN • BEYOND THE VEIL
SECRET LAND, THE • 1948 • *Dull Orville O. (P)* • DOC • USA
SECRET LIE, THE (UKN) see **INTO NO MAN'S LAND** • 1928
SECRET LIFE, A • 1914 • Noy Wilfred • UKN
SECRET LIFE OF AN AMERICAN WIFE, THE • 1968 • Axelrod George • USA
SECRET LIFE OF HERNANDO CORTEZ, THE • 1969 • Chamberlain John • UKN
SECRET LIFE OF JOHN CHAPMAN, THE • 1976 • Rich David Lowell • TVM • USA
SECRET LIFE OF PLANTS, THE • 1978 • Green Walon • DOC • USA
SECRET LIFE OF WALTER MITTY, THE • 1947 • McLeod Norman Z. • USA
SECRET LIVES • 1937 • Greville Edmond T. • UKN • I MARRIED A SPY (USA)
SECRET LIVES OF THE BRITISH PRIME MINISTERS: ASQUITH, THE • 1983 • Cunliffe David • MTV • UKN • ASQUITH: THE TAX SCANDAL ○ SIR HENRY ASQUITH ○ ASQUITHS, THE
SECRET LIVES OF THE BRITISH PRIME MINISTERS: DISRAELI, THE • 1981 • Rakoff Alvin • MTV • UKN • BENJAMIN DISRAELI ○ NUMBER 10: DIZZY ○ DISRAELI ○ DIZZY
SECRET LIVES OF THE BRITISH PRIME MINISTERS: GLADSTONE, THE • 1981 • Wise Herbert • MTV • UKN • GLADSTONE: THE PROSTITUTE SCANDAL ○ OLD GLAD EYES
SECRET LIVES OF THE BRITISH PRIME MINISTERS: LLOYD GEORGE • 1983 • Wise Herbert • MTV • UKN • LLOYD GEORGE: THE MENAGE A TROIS SCANDAL ○ DAVID LLOYD GEORGE ○ WOMAN OF STYLE, A
SECRET LIVES OF THE BRITISH PRIME MINISTERS: MACDONALD, THE • 1983 • Reynolds David • MTV • UKN • JAMES RAMSAY MACDONALD ○ MACDONALD ○ UNDERDOG
SECRET LIVES OF THE BRITISH PRIME MINISTERS: PITT, THE • 1983 • Reynolds David • MTV • UKN • PITT: THE YOUNGER GIRL SCANDAL ○ BLOODLINE
SECRET LIVES OF THE BRITISH PRIME MINISTERS: THE DUKE OF WELLINGTON, THE see **SECRET LIVES OF THE BRITISH PRIME MINISTERS: THE IRON DUKE, THE** • 1983
SECRET LIVES OF THE BRITISH PRIME MINISTERS: THE IRON DUKE, THE • 1983 • Glenister John • MTV • UKN • WELLINGTON: THE DUEL SCANDAL ○ DUKE OF WELLINGTON, THE ○ SECRET LIVES OF THE BRITISH PRIME MINISTERS: THE DUKE OF WELLINGTON, THE ○ IRON DUKE, THE
SECRET LODE, THE • 1914 • *Kb* • USA
SECRET LOVE • 1916 • Leonard Robert Z. • USA
SECRET LOVE LIFES OF ROMEO AND JULIET, THE see **SECRET SEX LIVES OF ROMEO AND JULIET, THE** • 1969
SECRET LOVE OF MARILYN MONROE, THE see **THIS YEAR'S BLONDE** • 1980
SECRET MAN, THE • 1917 • Ford John • USA
SECRET MAN, THE • 1958 • Kinnoch Ronald • UKN
SECRET MARK OF D'ARTAGNAN, THE (USA) see **SECRET DE D'ARTAGNAN, LE** • 1962
SECRET MARRIAGE • 1919 • *Maclaren Mary* • USA
SECRET MARRIAGE, A see **HEMLIGT GIFTERMAL, ETT** • 1912
SECRET MARRIAGE, THE • 1913 • *Boyle Irene* • USA
SECRET MARRIAGE, THE • 1914 • Melville Wilbert • USA
SECRET MEETING (USA) see **MARIE-OCTOBRE** • 1958
SECRET MENACE • 1931 • Kahn Richard C. • USA
SECRET MESSAGE, THE • 1915 • *Courtot Marguerite* • USA
SECRET MISSION • 1923 • Bentley Thomas • UKN
SECRET MISSION • 1942 • French Harold • UKN
SECRET MISSION see **TONIGHT WE RAID CALAIS** • 1943
SECRET MISSION see **SEKRETNAYA MISSIYA** • 1950
SECRET MISSION IN THE CARIBBEAN see **MISION SECRETA EN EL CARIBE** • 1971
SECRET MOTIVE (UKN) see **LONDON BLACKOUT MURDERS** • 1942
SECRET NATION, THE see **NACION CLANDESTINA, LA** • 1989
SECRET NEST, THE • 1914 • Morrisey Edward • USA
SECRET NIGHT CALLER, THE • 1975 • Jameson Jerry • TVM • USA
SECRET NINJA, ROARING TIGER • Ho Godfrey • HKG
SECRET OF A BALANCED ROCK, THE • 1913 • *Frontier* • USA
SECRET OF A WIFE see **TSUMA NO HIMITSU** • 1924
SECRET OF A WOMAN TEACHER see **JOKYOSHI NO HIMITSU** • 1967
SECRET OF BEAUTY see **SEKRET KRASOTY** • 1955
SECRET OF BLACK CANYON, THE • 1925 • Hayes Ward • USA
SECRET OF BLACK MOUNTAIN, THE • 1917 • Hoffman Otto • USA
SECRET OF BLOOD, THE see **TAJEMSTVI KRVE** • 1953
SECRET OF BLOOD ISLAND, THE • 1964 • Lawrence Quentin • UKN • P.O.W. -PRISONERS OF WAR ○ P.O.W.
SECRET OF CASTLE MUNROE, THE see **SEGRETO DEL CASTELLO DI MONROE, IL** • 1914
SECRET OF CHARLES DICKENS • 1981 • Larry Sheldon • MTV • USA
SECRET OF CONVICT LAKE, THE • 1951 • Gordon Michael • USA
SECRET OF DEATH ISLAND see **GEHEIMNIS DER TODESINSEL, DAS** • 1967
SECRET OF DEATH VALLEY, THE • 1906 • *Lubin* • SHT • USA
SECRET OF DEEP HARBOR • 1961 • Cahn Edward L. • USA
SECRET OF DR. ALUCARD, THE see **TASTE OF BLOOD, A** • 1967
SECRET OF DR. CHALMERS, THE see **CRYSTALBRAIN L'UOMO DAL CERVELLO DI CRISTALLO** • 1970
SECRET OF DR. IBRAHIM, THE see **SERR EL DOKTOR IBRAHIM** • 1936
SECRET OF DR. KILDARE, THE • 1939 • Bucquet Harold S. • USA
SECRET OF DR. ORLOFF, THE see **SECRETO DEL DR. ORLOFF, EL** • 1964
SECRET OF DORIAN GRAY, THE see **DIO CHIAMATO DORIAN, IL** • 1970
SECRET OF ETERNAL NIGHT • 1956 • Vasiliev Dimitri • USS
SECRET OF EVE, THE • 1917 • Vekroff Perry N. • USA
SECRET OF FATOUMA, THE • 1928 • Dedoncloit • TNS
SECRET OF FYLFOT, THE see **SHINOBI NO MANJI** • 1968
SECRET OF G 32 (UKN) see **FLY BY NIGHT** • 1942
SECRET OF LINDA HAMILTON (UKN) see **SECRETS OF A SORORITY GIRL** • 1946
SECRET OF LOST RIVER, THE • 1915 • *Borzage Frank* • USA
SECRET OF MADAME BLANCHE, THE • 1933 • Brabin Charles J. • USA • LADY, THE
SECRET OF MADAME X, THE • 1971 • Starkiewicz Antoinette • ANS • ASL
SECRET OF MAGIC ISLAND, THE (USA) see **FEE PAS COMME LES AUTRES, UNE** • 1956
SECRET OF MAYERLING, THE (USA) see **SECRET DE MAYERLING, LE** • 1948
SECRET OF MONTE CRISTO, THE (USA) see **TREASURE OF MONTE CRISTO, THE** • 1961
SECRET OF MY SUCCESS, THE • 1965 • Stone Andrew L. • UKN, USA
SECRET OF MY SUCCESS, THE • 1987 • Ross Herbert • USA
SECRET OF NAVAJO CAVE • 1976 • Flocker James T. • USA

SECRET OF NIKOLA TESLA, THE see **TAJNA NIKOLE TESLE** • 1981
SECRET OF NIMH, THE • 1982 • Bluth Don • ANM • USA
SECRET OF OUTER SPACE ISLAND see **FEE PAS COMME LES AUTRES, UNE** • 1956
SECRET OF OUTLAW FLATS, THE • 1953 • McDonald Frank • MTV • USA
SECRET OF PADRE ANTONIO, THE • 1913 • *Frontier* • USA
SECRET OF PANCHO VILLA, THE see **SECRETO DE PANCHO VILLA, EL** • 1954
SECRET OF PROFESSOR INSAROV'S PORTRAIT, THE • 1913 • Bauer Yevgeni • USS
SECRET OF ST. IVES, THE • 1949 • Rosen Phil • USA
SECRET OF ST. JOB FOREST, THE see **SZENTJOBI ERDO TITKA, A** • 1917
SECRET OF SANTA VITTORIA, THE • 1969 • Kramer Stanley • USA
SECRET OF SEAGULL ISLAND, THE • 1981 • Ungaro Nestore • MTV • ITL • SEAGULL ISLAND
SECRET OF SECRETS see **HICHU NO HI** • 1968
SECRET OF STAMBOUL, THE • 1936 • Marton Andrew • UKN • SPY IN WHITE, THE
SECRET OF STORM COUNTRY, THE • 1917 • Miller Charles • USA
SECRET OF SUCCESS, THE (UKN) see **SEKRET USPEKHA** • 1965
SECRET OF THE AIR, THE • 1914 • Brenon Herbert • UKN, USA • ACROSS THE ATLANTIC (USA)
SECRET OF THE AMERICA DOCK, THE see **GEHEIMNIS DER AMERIKA-DOCKS, DAS** • 1918
SECRET OF THE ATTIC see **BALLAGO IDO** • 1975
SECRET OF THE BIG NARRATOR see **TAJEMSTVI VELIKEHO VYPRAVECE** • 1972
SECRET OF THE BLACK DRAGON, THE • 1985 • Rothemund Sigi • NTH, FRG, USA
SECRET OF THE BLACK TRUNK, THE (USA) see **GEHEIMNIS DER SCHWARZEN KOFFER, DAS** • 1962
SECRET OF THE BLACK WIDOW see **GEHEIMNIS DER ROTEN KATZE, DAS** • 1949
SECRET OF THE BLACK WIDOW, THE (USA) see **GEHEIMNIS DER SCHWARZEN WITWE, DAS** • 1963
SECRET OF THE BLUE MEN, THE see **TRESOR DES HOMMES BLEUS, LE** • 1960
SECRET OF THE BLUE ROOM • 1933 • Neumann Kurt • USA • SECRETS OF THE BLUE ROOM
SECRET OF THE BORGIAS, THE • 1917 • Ellis Robert • SHT • USA
SECRET OF THE BULB, THE • 1913 • Bowman William J. • USA
SECRET OF THE CELLAR, THE • 1915 • Castle James W. • USA
SECRET OF THE CHATEAU • 1935 • Thorpe Richard • USA
SECRET OF THE CHEVALIER D'EON, THE see **SECRET DU CHEVALIER D'EON, LE** • 1960
SECRET OF THE CHINESE CARNATION, THE (USA) see **GEHEIMNIS DER CHINESISCHEN NELKE, DAS** • 1964
SECRET OF THE DEAD, THE • 1915 • *Domino* • USA
SECRET OF THE FOREST, THE • 1956 • Conyers Darcy • UKN
SECRET OF THE GOLDEN HILL see **THANGAMALAI RAHASYAM** • 1957
SECRET OF THE GOLDEN SHOES, THE • 1959 • Dinov Todor • ANM • BUL
SECRET OF THE GREEN PINS, THE see **COSA AVETE FATTO A SOLANGE?** • 1972
SECRET OF THE HILLS, THE • 1921 • Bennett Chester • USA
SECRET OF THE INCAS • 1954 • Hopper Jerry • USA
SECRET OF THE INN see **VARDSHUSETS HEMLIGHET** • 1917
SECRET OF THE KANIYUT CAVE see **TAYNA PESHCHYERY KANIYUTA** • 1968
SECRET OF THE KING • 1916 • *Nordisk* • DNM
SECRET OF THE LOCH, THE • 1934 • Rosmer Milton • UKN • LOCH NESS MONSTER, THE ○ LOCH NESS MYSTERY, THE
SECRET OF THE LOCKET, THE • 1909 • *Edison* • USA
SECRET OF THE LOST VALLEY, THE • 1917 • Horne James W. • SHT • USA
SECRET OF THE MAGIC HAT, THE see **SIRR TAKIEET EL EKHFA** • 1960
SECRET OF THE MINE, THE • 1913 • *Vernon Film Co* • USA
SECRET OF THE MISER'S CAVE, THE • 1912 • *Wolf Jane* • USA
SECRET OF THE MONASTERY, THE see **AMADERA MARUHI MONOGATARI** • 1968
SECRET OF THE MONASTERY (UKN) see **KLOSTRET I SENDOMIR** • 1920
SECRET OF THE MOOR, THE • 1919 • Willoughby Lewis • UKN
SECRET OF THE MOUNTAIN, THE • 1914 • *Eclectic* • USA
SECRET OF THE MOUNTAIN LAKE • Rou Aleksandr • USS
SECRET OF THE MUMMY, THE see **SECRETO DE LA MOMIA EGIPCIA, EL** • 1972
SECRET OF THE NIGHT, THE • 1916 • Calvert E. H. • SHT • USA
SECRET OF THE NINJA see **SHINOBI NO MANJI** • 1968
SECRET OF THE OLD CASTLE, THE see **TAGEMNICA STAREGO ZAMKU** • 1956
SECRET OF THE OLD PIT, THE • 1956 • Berestowski • PLN
SECRET OF THE OLD WRITING DESK, THE see **CHATOLLETS HEMMELIGHED** • 1913
SECRET OF THE OPAL MINE, THE • 1911 • *Yankee* • USA
SECRET OF THE PALM, THE • 1911 • *Imp* • USA
SECRET OF THE PARADISE HOTEL see **HOTELL PARADISETS HEMLIGHET** • 1931
SECRET OF THE PAVILION, THE see **PAVILLONENS HEMMELIGHED** • 1916
SECRET OF THE PHANTOM KNIGHT see **CHOPPY AND THE PRINCESS** • 1984
SECRET OF THE PUEBLO, THE • 1923 • Hart Neal • USA
SECRET OF THE PURPLE REEF • 1960 • Witney William • USA
SECRET OF THE RED ORCHID, THE see **RATSEL DER ROTEN ORCHIDEE, DAS** • 1961
SECRET OF THE SACRED FOREST, THE • 1970 • Du Pont Michael • USA
SECRET OF THE SAFE, THE • 1921 • Paul Fred • UKN
SECRET OF THE SAHARA • 1987 • Negrin Alberto • ITL
SECRET OF THE SAHARA see **STEEL LADY, THE** • 1953
SECRET OF THE SECRET WEAPON, THE see **SECRETUL ARMEI SECRETE** • 1989
SECRET OF THE SHAOLIN POLES, THE • *Meng Fei* • HKG
SECRET OF THE SKIES • 1934 • Harwood A. R. • ASL
SECRET OF THE SPHINX (USA) see **SFINGE SORRIDE PRIMA DI MORIRE STOP -LONDRA, LA** • 1964
SECRET OF THE STILL, THE • 1911 • *Kalem* • USA
SECRET OF THE SUBMARINE, THE • 1916 • Sargent George L. • SRL • USA
SECRET OF THE SWAMP, THE • 1916 • Reynolds Lynn • USA
SECRET OF THE SWORD, THE see **HE-MAN AND SHE-RA: THE SECRET OF THE SWORD*** • 1985
SECRET OF THE TELEGIAN (USA) see **DENSO NINGEN** • 1960
SECRET OF THE THREE JUNKS, THE see **GEHEIMNIS DER DREI DSCHUNKEN, DAS** • 1965
SECRET OF THE THREE SWORD POINTS, THE see **SEGRETO DELLE TRE PUNTE, IL** • 1953
SECRET OF THE URN see **TANGE SAZEN HIEN LAI-GIRI** • 1966
SECRET OF THE WHISTLER • 1946 • Sherman George • USA
SECRET OF THE WILL, THE • 1914 • *Nilsson Anna Q.* • USA
SECRET OF THE YELLOW MONKS, THE see **GEHEIMNIS DER GELBEN MONCHE, DAS** • 1966
SECRET OF TREASURE ISLAND, THE • 1938 • Clifton Elmer • SRL • USA
SECRET OF TREASURE MOUNTAIN • 1956 • Friedman Seymour • USA
SECRET OF TWO OCEANS, THE see **TAINA DVUH OKEANOV** • 1955
SECRET OF WENDEL SAMSON, THE see **SECRET OF WENDELL SAMPSON, THE** • 1966
SECRET OF WENDELL SAMPSON, THE • 1966 • Kuchar Mike • USA • SECRET OF WENDEL SAMSON, THE
SECRET OF YOLANDA, THE see **AHAVA ILEMETH** • 1982
SECRET OF YOUTH, THE • 1956 • Fetin Vladimir • SHT • USS
SECRET OPERATOR see **PACIFIC RENDEZVOUS** • 1942
SECRET ORCHARD • 1915 • Reicher Frank • USA
SECRET ORDER OF HORNS, THE • 1911 • *Powers* • USA
SECRET ORDERS • 1926 • Withey Chet • USA
SECRET PARIS see **PARIS SECRET** • 1965
SECRET PARTNER, THE • 1961 • Dearden Basil • UKN • SLEEPING PARTNER, THE
SECRET PASSAGE see **KIETA NIKKOSEN** • 1960
SECRET PASSION, THE see **FREUD** • 1963
SECRET PASSION OF SALVADOR DALI, THE • 1961 • Mekas Jonas • USA
SECRET PATH, THE • Weiler Kurt • ANM • GDR
SECRET PATROL • 1936 • Selman David • USA
SECRET PEOPLE • 1952 • Dickinson Thorold • UKN
SECRET PERIL, THE • 1919 • Neitz Alvin J. • SHT • USA
SECRET PLACE, THE • 1957 • Donner Clive • UKN
SECRET PLACES • 1985 • Barron Zelda • UKN
SECRET PLEASURES, THE see **PLACERES OCULTOS, LOS** • 1977
SECRET POLICE 115 see **RAHASYA POLICE 115** • 1968
SECRET POLICEMAN'S BALL • 1980 • Graef Roger • UKN
SECRET POLICEMAN'S OTHER BALL, THE • 1982 • Graef Roger, Temple Julien • UKN
SECRET POLICEMAN'S PRIVATE PARTS, THE • 1984 • Graef Roger, Temple Julien • UKN
SECRET POWER see **GEHEIME MACHT, DIE** • 1927
SECRET PROFESSIONNEL • 1958 • Andre Raoul • FRN
SECRET RENDEZVOUS, A see **MIKKAI** • 1960
SECRET RITES • 1971 • Ford Derek • UKN
SECRET ROOM, THE • 1915 • Moore Tom • *Kalem* • USA
SECRET ROOM, THE • 1915 • Powell Paul • *Lubin* • USA
SECRET SCANDAL see **SCANDALO SEGRETO** • 1990
SECRET S'CIETY • 1919 • Harvey John Joseph • SHT • USA
SECRET SCROLLS (PART I) (USA) see **YAGYU BUGEICHO** • 1957
SECRET SCROLLS (PART II) see **YAGYU BUGEICHO -SORYU HIKEN** • 1958
SECRET SERVANTS • 1917 • Beaudine William • SHT • USA
SECRET SERVICE • 1913 • Calvert Charles • UKN
SECRET SERVICE • 1919 • Ford Hugh • USA
SECRET SERVICE • 1932 • Ruben J. Walter • USA
SECRET SERVICE DAN • 1919 • *Capitol* • SHT • USA
SECRET SERVICE IN DARKEST AFRICA • 1943 • Bennet Spencer Gordon • SRL • USA • MANHUNT IN THE AFRICAN JUNGLE
SECRET SERVICE INVESTIGATOR • 1948 • Springsteen R. G. • USA
SECRET SERVICE MAN, THE • 1912 • *Law Rodman* • USA
SECRET SERVICE OF THE AIR • 1939 • Smith Noel • USA
SECRET SERVICE SAM • 1913 • Hall Edward • USA
SECRET SERVICE SNITZ • 1914 • *Sterling Ford* • USA
SECRET SERVICE STEVE • 1912 • *Atlas* • USA
SECRET SERVICE WOMAN • 1909 • *Bison* • USA
SECRET SEVEN, THE • 1916 • Humphrey William • SHT • USA
SECRET SEVEN, THE • 1940 • Moore James • USA • MARCH OF CRIME
SECRET SEVEN, THE (USA) see **PAUL SLEUTH AND THE MYSTIC SEVEN** • 1914
SECRET SEVEN, THE (USA) see **INVINCIBILI SETTE, GLI** • 1964
SECRET SEX LIVES OF ROMEO AND JULIET, THE • 1969 • Stootsberry A. P. • USA • SECRET LOVE LIFES OF ROMEO AND JULIET, THE ○ SEX LIFE OF ROMEO AND JULIET, THE
SECRET SHAOLIN KUNG FU, THE see **INVINCIBLE SHAOLIN KUNG FU**
SECRET SHARER, THE • 1953 • Brahm John • USA
SECRET SIN, THE • 1915 • Reicher Frank • USA
SECRET SINNERS • 1933 • Ford Wesley • USA
SECRET SIX, THE • 1931 • Hill George W. • USA
SECRET SOCIETY, THE • 1965 • Johnsen S. N. • USA
SECRET SOCIETY, THE see **P.P.S. (PROSTITUTES' PROTECTIVE SOCIETY)** • 1966
SECRET SOLVAY FILE, THE see **GEHEIMAKTEN SOLVAY** • 1952
SECRET SORROW • 1921 • *Verwayen Percy* • USA
SECRET STORM • 1977 • Ansara Martha • DOC • ASL
SECRET STORY OF CRUELTY -WOMAN TORTURE see **ZANNIN MARUHI ONNA ZEME** • 1968
SECRET STRANGER, THE (UKN) see **ROUGH RIDING RANGER** • 1935
SECRET STRINGS • 1918 • Ince John • USA
SECRET STUDIO, THE • 1927 • Schertzinger Victor • USA
SECRET SUPPER OF THE SEDMATSI, THE see **TAINATA VECHERIA NA SEDMATSITE** • 1957
SECRET TENT, THE • 1956 • Chaffey Don • UKN
SECRET TREASURE, THE • 1913 • *Patheplay* • USA
SECRET TREATY, THE • 1914 • *Eclair* • USA
SECRET TREATY, THE see **TREDIE MAGT, DEN** • 1912
SECRET TUNNEL, THE • 1947 • Hammond William C. • UKN
SECRET TURKISH BATH see **MARUHI TORUKO BURO** • 1968
SECRET VALLEY • 1937 • Bretherton Howard • USA • GANGSTER'S BRIDE, THE (UKN)
SECRET VALLEY • 1980 • Bourke Terry (c/d) • MTV • ASL
SECRET VENTURE • 1955 • Springsteen R. G. • UKN
SECRET VOICE, THE • 1936 • Pearson George • UKN
SECRET WAR OF HARRY FRIGG, THE • 1968 • Smight Jack • USA • PRIVATE WAR OF HARRY FRIGG, THE ○ MEANWHILE, FAR FROM THE FRONT
SECRET WAR OF JACKIE'S GIRLS, THE • 1980 • Hessler Gordon • TVM • USA
SECRET WAY, THE • 1958 • Schulz Kurt Herbert • ANM • GDR
SECRET WAYS, THE • 1961 • Karlson Phil • USA
SECRET WEAPON • 1988 • Dolgy Mike • USA
SECRET WEAPON see **SHERLOCK HOLMES AND THE SECRET WEAPON** • 1942
SECRET WEAPONS see **SEXPIONAGE** • 1984
SECRET WEDDING see **BODA SECRETA** • 1988
SECRET WEDDING, THE • 1912 • *Santschi Tom* • USA
SECRET WELL, THE • 1915 • *Sais Marin* • USA
SECRET WIRE, THE • 1916 • Ricketts Thomas • SHT • USA
SECRET WITNESS • 1931 • Freeland Thornton • USA
SECRET WOMAN, THE • 1918 • Coleby A. E. • UKN
SECRET WOMAN, THE (UKN) see **SHANGHAI ROSE** • 1929
SECRET WORLD OF ODILON REDON, THE • 1973 • Cross Stephen • UKN
SECRET WORLD (USA) see **PROMESSE, LA** • 1969
SECRETAIRES TRES PARTICULIERES • 1980 • Pirau Reine • FRN
SECRETARIA PARA TODO • 1958 • Iquino Ignacio F. • SPN
SECRETARIA PARTICULAR • 1952 • Diaz Morales Jose • MXC
SECRETARIA PELIGROSA • 1955 • Orol Juan • MXC, SPN
SECRETARIAS, LAS • 1968 • Lazaga Pedro • SPN
SECRETARIES SPREAD • 1970 • *Kirt Film International* • USA
SECRETARY, THE • 1966 • Jaworski Tadeusz • DOC • PLN
SECRETARY, THE • 1967 • Bottcher Jurgen • DOC • GDR
SECRETARY, THE • 1972 • *Gamble Josh* • USA
SECRETARY, THE see **KATIP** • 1968
SECRETARY OF FRIVOLOUS AFFAIRS, THE • 1915 • Ricketts Thomas • USA
SECRETARY OF THE DISTRICT COMMITTEE see **SEKRETAR RAIKON** • 1942
SECRETARY TROUBLE • 1948 • Yates Hal • SHT • USA
SECRETARY'S CRIME, THE • 1909 • Coleby A. E. • UKN
SECRETAS INTENCIONES, LAS • 1969 • Eceiza Antonio • SPN • SECRET INTENTIONS
SECRETE ENFANCE • 1977 • Seligmann Guy • DOC • FRN
SECRETO, EL • 1988 • Roche Luis Armando • VNZ • SECRET, THE
SECRETO DE BILL NORTH, EL see **ASSASSINIO MADE IN ITALY** • 1963
SECRETO DE JUAN PALOMO, EL • 1946 • Morayta Miguel • MXC
SECRETO DE LA MOMIA EGIPCIA, EL • 1972 • Gelabert Alejandro Marti • SPN, FRN • SECRET OF THE MUMMY, THE
SECRETO DE LA MONJA, EL • 1939 • Sevilla Raphael J. • MXC
SECRETO DE LA SOLTERONA, EL • 1944 • Delgado Miguel M. • MXC
SECRETO DE LAS ESMERALDAS, EL • 1965 • Almeida Sebastian • SPN
SECRETO DE LOS HOMBRES AZULES, EL (SPN) see **TRESOR DES HOMMES BLEUS, LE** • 1960
SECRETO DE MONICA, EL • 1961 • Forque Jose Maria • SPN
SECRETO DE MUERTE see **GEMMA** • 1949
SECRETO DE PANCHO VILLA, EL • 1954 • Baledon Rafael • MXC • SECRET OF PANCHO VILLA, THE
SECRETO DE PAPA, EL • 1959 • Merida Jose C. • SPN
SECRETO DE ROMELIO, EL • 1989 • Cortes Busi • MXC • ROMELIO'S SECRET
SECRETO DE TOMY, EL • 1963 • del Amo Antonio • SPN
SECRETO DE UNA MUJER, EL • 1954 • Morayta Miguel • MXC
SECRETO DEL CAPITAN O'HARA, EL • 1964 • Ruiz-Castillo Arturo • SPN
SECRETO DEL DOCTEUR, EL • 1930 • de Rochefort Charles • SPN
SECRETO DEL DR. ORLOFF, EL • 1964 • Franco Jesus • SPN, AUS • DR. ORLOFF'S MONSTER (USA) ○ MISTRESSES OF DR. JEKYLL ○ DR. ORLOFF'S SECRET ○ SECRET OF DR. ORLOFF, THE
SECRETO DEL SACERDOTE, EL • 1940 • Rodriguez Joselito • MXC
SECRETO DEL TEXANO, EL • 1965 • Crevenna Alfredo B. • MXC
SECRETO DEL ZORRO, EL • 1970 • Merino Jose Luis • SPN
SECRETO ENTRE MUJERES • 1948 • Urruchua Victor • MXC
SECRETO ETERNO • 1942 • Orellana Carlos • MXC
SECRETO ETERNO • 1970 • *Filmadora Chapultepec* • MXC
SECRETO INCONFESABLE DE UN CHICO BIEN, EL • 1975 • Grau Jorge • SPN
SECRETO PROFESIONAL • 1954 • Pardave Joaquin • MXC
SECRETOS DE ALCOBA • 1976 • Lara Polop Francisco • SPN
SECRETOS DEL BUZON, LOS • 1948 • Catrani Catrano • ARG
SECRETOS DEL SEXO DEBIL, LOS • 1960 • Diaz Morales Jose • MXC
SECRETS • 1924 • Borzage Frank • USA
SECRETS • 1933 • Borzage Frank, Neilan Marshall (U/c) • USA
SECRETS • 1942 • Blanchar Pierre • FRN • FOL ETE, LE
SECRETS • 1971 • Saville Philip • UKN
SECRETS • 1973 • Jones Phillip • USA

SECRETS • 1977 • Wendkos Paul • TVM • USA
SECRETS • 1983 • Millar Gavin • UKN
SECRETS see **HIMEGOTO** • 1967
SECRETS see **HEIMLICHKEITEN** • 1968
SECRETS see **CONFIDENCIAS** • 1982
SECRETS see **HEMLIGHETEN** • 1983
SECRETS D'ALCOVE • 1954 • Delannoy Jean, Decoin Henri, Franciolini Gianni, Habib Ralph • FRN, ITL • LETTO, IL (ITL) ○ BED, THE (USA)
SECRETS DE FAMILLE see **COUP DE FEU DANS LA NUIT** • 1942
SECRETS DE LA MER ROUGE, LES • 1937 • Pottier Richard • FRN
SECRETS DE LA PRESTIDIGITATION DEVOILES, LES • 1904 • Blache Alice • FRN
SECRETS DE PARIS • 1939 • Masson Jean • SHT • FRN
SECRETS D'ETAT • 1914 • Burguet Charles • FRN
SECRETS DU MAROC • 1953 • Leherissey Jean • SHT • FRN
SECRETS OF A BEAUTY PARLOR • 1917 • Williams Harry • SHT • USA
SECRETS OF A CALL GIRL (UKN) see **ANNA QUEL PARTICOLARE PIACERE** • 1973
SECRETS OF A CO-ED • 1943 • Lewis Joseph H. • USA • SILENT WITNESS (UKN)
SECRETS OF A DOOR TO DOOR SALESMAN • 1973 • Rilla Wolf • UKN • NAUGHTY WIVES (USA)
SECRETS OF A FRENCH MAID, THE • Dietrich Erwin C. • SWT
SECRETS OF A GIRL FRIDAY see **SEX WITH THE STARS** • 1980
SECRETS OF A GREAT NARRATOR, THE see **TAJEMSTVI VELIKEHO VYPRAVECE** • 1972
SECRETS OF A MARRIED MAN • 1984 • Graham William A. • TVM • USA
SECRETS OF A MODEL • 1940 • Newfield Sam • USA
SECRETS OF A MOTHER AND DAUGHTER • 1983 • Beaumont Gabrielle • TVM • USA
SECRETS OF A NURSE • 1938 • Lubin Arthur • USA
SECRETS OF A PLAYGIRL see **PLAYBIRDS, THE** • 1979
SECRETS OF A SECRETARY • 1931 • Abbott George • USA
SECRETS OF A SENSUOUS NURSE, THE (USA) see **INFERMIERA, L'** • 1975
SECRETS OF A SEXY GAME see **CONFESSIONS FROM THE DAVID GALAXY AFFAIR** • 1979
SECRETS OF A SORORITY GIRL • 1946 • Landers Lew?, Wisbar Frank? • USA • SECRET OF LINDA HAMILTON (UKN)
SECRETS OF A SOUL • Hoffmann Kurt • FRG
SECRETS OF A SOUL see **GEHEIMNISSE EINER SEELE** • 1926
SECRETS OF A SOUL see **CONFESSIONS OF AN OPIUM EATER** • 1962
SECRETS OF A SUPER STUD • 1975 • Lewis Morton M. • UKN
SECRETS OF A WINDMILL GIRL • 1966 • Miller Arnold Louis • UKN
SECRETS OF A WOMEN'S TEMPLE see **HIROKU ONNADERA** • 1969
SECRETS OF AN ACTRESS • 1938 • Keighley William • USA
SECRETS OF AN UNCOVER MODEL • 1965 • Seymour Maurice • USA
SECRETS OF BUDDHA (UKN) see **HEISSER HAFEN HONGKONG** • 1962
SECRETS OF CAVELLI, THE see **HOHE SCHULE** • 1934
SECRETS OF CHINATOWN • 1934 • Newmeyer Fred • CND • BLACK ROBE, THE
SECRETS OF DR. MABUSE (USA) see **TODESSTRAHLEN DES DR. MABUSE, DIE** • 1964
SECRETS OF DRACULA, THE see **MANUGANG NI DRAKULA, MGA** • 1964
SECRETS OF F.P.1 see **F.P.1** • 1932
SECRETS OF HOLLYWOOD • 1933 • Merrick George M. • USA
SECRETS OF HOUSE NO.5, THE • 1912 • *Pathe* • USS
SECRETS OF LADY TRUCKERS • Segall Stuart • USA
SECRETS OF LIFE • 1934 • Field Mary • SER • UKN
SECRETS OF LIFE • 1957 • Algar James • DOC • USA
SECRETS OF LOVE • 1987 • Kumel Harry • BLG
SECRETS OF MONTE CARLO • 1951 • Blair George • USA
SECRETS OF NAKED GIRLS see **MATRATZEN TANGO** • 1972
SECRETS OF NATURE • 1928 • Field Mary, Woods Arthur • SER • UKN
SECRETS OF NATURE • 1948 • Zguridi Alexander • DOC • USS
SECRETS OF NAUGHTY SUSAN see **MIJN NACHTEN MET SUSAN, OLGA, ALBERT, JULIE, PIET & SANDRA** • 1974
SECRETS OF PARIS, THE • 1922 • Webb Kenneth • USA
SECRETS OF SCOTLAND YARD • 1944 • Blair George • USA
SECRETS OF SEX • 1969 • Balch Anthony • UKN • BIZARRE (USA)
SECRETS OF SOCIETY, THE see **LADY AUDLEY'S SECRET** • 1915
SECRETS OF SWEET SIXTEEN: WHAT SCHOOLGIRLS DON'T TELL • 1974 • Rott Claus • FRG • WHAT SCHOOLGIRLS DON'T TELL
SECRETS OF THE BERMUDA TRIANGLE • 1977 • Brittain Don • CND
SECRETS OF THE BLUE ROOM see **SECRET OF THE BLUE ROOM** • 1933
SECRETS OF THE CITY see **STADT IST VOLLER GEHEIMNISSE, DIE** • 1955
SECRETS OF THE CONFESSION • 1906 • de Banos Ricardo • SPN
SECRETS OF THE DEATH ROOM see **LOVE ME DEADLY** • 1972
SECRETS OF THE EAST see **GEHEIMNISSE DES ORIENTS** • 1928
SECRETS OF THE FRENCH POLICE • 1932 • Sutherland A. Edward • USA
SECRETS OF THE GODS • 1976 • Sachs William • USA
SECRETS OF THE LONE WOLF • 1941 • Dmytryk Edward • USA • SECRETS (UKN)
SECRETS OF THE NAZI CRIMINALS (USA) see **KRIGSFORBRYTARE** • 1962
SECRETS OF THE NAZI WAR CRIMINALS see **KRIGSFORBRYTARE** • 1962
SECRETS OF THE NIGHT • 1925 • Blache Herbert • USA • NIGHT CAP, THE
SECRETS OF THE NIGHT see **NIGHTCAP, THE** • 1917
SECRETS OF THE ORIENT (USA) see **GEHEIMNISSE DES ORIENTS** • 1928
SECRETS OF THE PHANTOM CAVERNS see **WHAT WAITS BELOW** • 1983
SECRETS OF THE PIRATE'S INN • 1969 • Nelson Gary • MTV • USA
SECRETS OF THE RANGE • 1928 • Horner Robert J. • USA
SECRETS OF THE RED BEDROOM see **SEXPIONAGE** • 1984
SECRETS OF THE REEF • 1956 • Ritter Lloyd, Lerner Murray, Young Robert • DOC • USA
SECRETS OF THE SATIN BLUES see **FOLIES D'ELODIE, LES** • 1981
SECRETS OF THE UNDERGROUND • 1943 • Morgan William • USA
SECRETS OF THE WASTE LAND • 1941 • Abrahams Derwin • USA
SECRETS OF THE WISE FISHERMAN • 1958 • Antonov L. • USS
SECRETS OF THREE HUNGRY WIVES • 1978 • Hessler Gordon • TVM • USA
SECRETS OF VENUS see **NUDE IN CHARCOAL** • 1963
SECRETS OF WOMEN (USA) see **KVINNORS VANTAN** • 1952
SECRETS OF WU SIN • 1933 • Thorpe Richard • USA
SECRETS OF YOUNG NURSES see **YOUNG NURSES, THE** • 1973
SECRET'S PRICE, THE • 1915 • *Drew Lillian* • USA
SECRETS (UKN) see **SECRETS OF THE LONE WOLF** • 1941
SECRETUL ARMEI SECRETE • 1989 • Tatos Alexandru • RMN • SECRET OF THE SECRET WEAPON, THE
SECRETUL CIFRULUI • 1959 • Bratu Lucian • RMN • SECRET CODE, THE
SECTE DE MARRAKECH, LA see **BRIGADE MONDAINE: LA SECTE DE MARRAKECH** • 1979
SECTION ANDERSON, LA see **PATROUILLE ANDERSON, LA** • 1967
SECTION DES DISPARUS • 1956 • Chenal Pierre • FRN, ARG
SECTION FOREMAN, THE • 1912 • *Imp* • USA
SECTION SPECIALE • 1975 • Costa-Gavras • FRG, ITL, FRN • SPECIAL SECTION (USA)
SECUENTE • 1983 • Tatos Alexandru • RMN • SEQUENCES
SECUESTRADOR, EL see **SEQUESTRADOR, EL** • 1958
SECUESTRO • 1976 • Klimovsky Leon • SPN
SECUESTRO, EL • 1972 • *Cima* • MXC
SECUESTRO A LA ESPANOLA • 1972 • Cano Mateo • SPN
SECUESTRO DE UN MILLON DE DOLARES, EL • 1970 • *Batjac Productions* • MXC
SECUESTRO DIABOLICO • 1957 • Urueta Chano • MXC
SECUESTRO EN ACAPULCO • 1960 • Curiel Federico • MXC
SECUESTRO EN LA CIUDAD • 1964 • Delgado Luis Maria • SPN
SECUESTRO SENSACIONAL • 1942 • Donadio Francisco P. • ARG
SECURING EVIDENCE • 1911 • Porter Edwin S. • USA
SECURITE DU TRAVAIL DANS LES INDUSTRIES SIDERURGIQUES • 1948 • Tedesco Jean • SHT • FRN
SECURITE ET HYGIENE DU TRAVAIL DANS LA FABRICATION DU SUCRE ET DE L'ALCOOL • 1952 • Dumas • SHT • FRN
SECURITY RISK • 1954 • Schuster Harold • USA
SECURITY SERVICE CLOSES IN, THE see **SB ZATVARA KRUG** • 1975
SECURITY UNLIMITED see **MO-TENG PAO-PIAO** • 1981
SED DE AMOR • 1958 • Blake Alfonso Corona • MXC • THIRST FOR LOVE
SEDA, SANGRE Y SOL • 1941 • Rivero Fernando A. • MXC • SILK, BLOOD AND SUN
SEDAM PLAMENCICA • 1975 • Stalter Pavao • YGS, ITL • SEVEN LITTLE FLAMES
SEDDOK BLOOD FIEND see **SEDDOK, L'EREDE DI SATANA** • 1961
SEDDOK, L'EREDE DI SATANA • 1961 • Majano Anton Giulio • ITL • ATOM AGE VAMPIRE (USA) ○ SEDDOK, SON OF SATAN ○ SEDDOK BLOOD FIEND ○ BLOOD FIEND
SEDDOK, SON OF SATAN see **SEDDOK, L'EREDE DI SATANA** • 1961
SEDE DE AMAR: CAPUZES NEGROS • 1980 • Reichenbach Francois • BRZ • LUST FOR LOVING: BLACK HOODS
SEDGE HAT, THE see **YATARO-GASA** • 1932
SEDIA A ROTELLE, LA (ITL) see **MEURTRE EST UN MEURTRE, UN** • 1972
SEDIA DEL DIAVOLO, LA • 1912 • *Film D'Arte Italiana* • ITL • DEVIL'S CHAIR, THE
SEDIA ELETTRICA • 1969 • Fidani Demofilo • ITL
SEDICENNI, LE • 1966 • Petrini Luigi • ITL
SEDICIANNI • 1973 • Longo Tiziano • ITL
SEDIM NA KONARI, A JE MI DOBRE • 1989 • Jakubisko Juraj • CZC • SITTING ON A BRANCH, ENJOYING MYSELF ○ SITTING ON A BRANCH AND I FEEL FINE
SEDM HAVRANU • 1967 • Cech Vladimir • CZC • SEVEN RAVENS
SEDMI KONTINENT • 1966 • Vukotic Dusan • YGS, CZC • SEVENTH CONTINENT, THE (USA) ○ SEDMY KONTINENT (CZC) ○ SIEDMA PEVNINA
SEDMIKRASKY • 1966 • Chytilova Vera • CZC • DAISIES
SEDMINA • 1969 • Klopcic Matjaz • YGS • GREETINGS TO MARIA ○ FUNERAL FEAST
SEDMOY SPUTNIK • 1968 • Aronov Grigori, German Aleksei • USS • SEVENTH FELLOW-TRAVELLER, THE
SEDMY DEN, OSMA NOC see **DEN SEDMY, OSMA NOC** • 1969
SEDMY KONTINENT • 1960 • Gajer Vaclav • CZC • SEVENTH CONTINENT, THE
SEDMY KONTINENT (CZC) see **SEDMI KONTINENT** • 1966
SEDOTTA E ABBANDONATA • 1964 • Germi Pietro • ITL, FRN • SEDUITE ET ABANDONNEE (FRN) ○ SEDUCED AND ABANDONED (USA)
SEDOTTI E BIDONATI • 1964 • Bianchi Giorgio • ITL
SEDOV EXPEDITION see **SEDOVCHY** • 1940
SEDOVCHY • 1940 • Karmen Roman • USS • SEDOV EXPEDITION ○ SEDOVITES, THE
SEDOVITES, THE see **SEDOVCHY** • 1940
SEDUCCION, LA • 1980 • Ripstein Arturo • MXC • SEDUCTION, THE
SEDUCED • 1985 • Freedman Jerrold • TVM • USA
SEDUCED AND ABANDONED (USA) see **SEDOTTA E ABBANDONATA** • 1964
SEDUCED IN SODOM (UKN) see **FILLE DE LA MER MORTE, LA** • 1966
SEDUCER, THE see **UOMO DI PAGLIA, L'** • 1957
SEDUCER, THE see **MOUTON ENRAGE, LE** • 1974
SEDUCER -MAN OF STRAW, THE see **UOMO DI PAGLIA, L'** • 1957
SEDUCERS, THE • 1962 • Ferguson Graeme • USA
SEDUCERS, THE see **DEATH GAME** • 1977
SEDUCERS, THE (USA) see **TOP SENSATION** • 1969
SEDUCTEUR, LE see **SAHIR AN-NISSA'** • 1958
SEDUCTEUR INGENU, LE see **TOUTE LA FAMILLE ETAIT LA** • 1948
SEDUCTEURS, LES (FRN) see **SUNDAY LOVERS** • 1980
SEDUCTIO • 1988 • Chbib Bachar • CND
SEDUCTION • 1979 • USA
SEDUCTION see **EROTIKON** • 1929
SEDUCTION see **CINDERELLA** • 1937
SEDUCTION see **YUWAKU** • 1948
SEDUCTION see **SEDUZIONE, LA** • 1973
SEDUCTION, THE • 1982 • Schmoeller David • USA • SEDUCTION: A FATAL OBSESSION, THE
SEDUCTION, THE see **SEDUCCION, LA** • 1980
SEDUCTION, THE see **VERLOCKUNG, DIE** • 1988
SEDUCTION: A FATAL OBSESSION, THE see **SEDUCTION, THE** • 1982
SEDUCTION BY THE SEA (USA) see **VERFUHRUNG AM MEER** • 1963
SEDUCTION OF GINA, THE • 1984 • Freedman Jerrold • TVM • USA
SEDUCTION OF INGA, THE • 1973 • Sarno Joe • USA, SWD • NAGON ATT ALSKA (SWD)
SEDUCTION OF JOE TYNAN, THE • 1979 • Schatzberg Jerry • USA • SENATOR, THE
SEDUCTION OF JULIA, THE see **JULIA, DU BIST ZAUBERHAFT** • 1962
SEDUCTION OF LYNN CARTER, THE • 1974 • Brown Wes • USA
SEDUCTION OF MIMI, THE (USA) see **MIMI METALLURGICO FERITO NELL'ONORE** • 1972
SEDUCTION OF MISS LEONA, THE • 1980 • Hardy Joseph • TVM • USA
SEDUCTION OF THE SOUTH (USA) see **BRIGANTI ITALIANI, I** • 1961
SEDUCTOR, EL • 1955 • Urueta Chano • MXC
SEDUCTRESS, THE see **TEACHER, THE** • 1974
SEDUITE ET ABANDONNEE (FRN) see **SEDOTTA E ABBANDONATA** • 1964
SEDUTA SPIRITICA • 1949 • Risi Dino • ITL
SEDUTO ALLA SUA DESTRA • 1968 • Zurlini Valerio • ITL • OUT OF DARKNESS ○ BLACK JESUS ○ OUT OF THE DARKNESS ○ SEATED AT HIS RIGHT ○ SEATED ON HIS RIGHT ○ SEATED AT HIS RIGHT HAND
SEDUTTORE, IL • 1954 • Rossi Franco • ITL
SEDUZIONE, LA • 1973 • Di Leo Fernando • ITL • SEDUCTION
SEE A PIN AND PICK IT UP • 1909 • Porter Edwin S. • USA
SEE AMERICA THIRST • 1930 • Craft William James • USA
SEE CHINA AND DIE • 1982 • Cohen Larry • TVM • USA • MOMMA THE DETECTIVE ○ HEARSAY
SEE HEAR MY LOVE see **ECOUTE VOIR..** • 1978
SEE, HEAR, TALK, THINK, DREAM AND ACT FILM, THE • 1965 • Sens Al • ANS • CND • SEE, HEAR, WALK, TALK, THINK AND ACT FILM, THE
SEE, HEAR, WALK, TALK, THINK AND ACT FILM, THE see **SEE, HEAR, TALK, THINK, DREAM AND ACT FILM, THE** • 1965
SEE HERE MY LOVE see **ECOUTE VOIR..** • 1978
SEE HERE, PRIVATE HARGROVE • 1943 • Ruggles Wesley • USA
SEE HOW SHE RUNS • 1978 • Heffron Richard T. • TVM • USA
SEE HOW THEY COME • 1968 • Hennigar William K. • USA • SEE HOW THEY COME AND GO ○ SEE HOW THEY GO
SEE HOW THEY COME AND GO see **SEE HOW THEY COME** • 1968
SEE HOW THEY GO see **SEE HOW THEY COME** • 1968
SEE HOW THEY RUN • 1955 • Arliss Leslie • UKN
SEE HOW THEY RUN • 1965 • Rich David Lowell • TVM • USA • WIDOW MAKERS, THE
SEE HOW THEY RUN see **BRIGHT ROAD** • 1953
SEE HOW WE RUN • 1984 • Nicolle Douglas • DOC • CND
SEE LUCIAN see **VLEPE LOUKIANOS** • 1969
SEE MY LAWYER • 1921 • Christie Al • USA
SEE MY LAWYER • 1945 • Cline Eddie • USA
SEE NAPLES AND DIE (USA) see **VEDI NAPOLI E POI MUORI** • 1952
SEE NO EVIL • 1988 • Cowan Paul • DOC • CND
SEE NO EVIL, HEAR NO EVIL • 1988 • Hiller Arthur • USA
SEE NO EVIL (USA) see **BLIND TERROR** • 1971
SEE RUFT, THE • 1942 • Kollner H. F. • FRG
SEE-SAW, THE see **INVISIBLE BOND, THE** • 1920
SEE-SAW OF LIFE, THE • 1913 • *Imp* • USA
SEE SAW SEEMS • 1966 • Vanderbeek Stan • SHT • USA
SEE THE MAN RUN • 1971 • Allen Corey • TVM • USA
SEE THE MUSIC see **MARION BROWN** • 1970
SEE THE WORLD • 1934 • *Terry Paul/ Moser Frank (P)* • ANS • USA
SEE YA LATER GLADIATOR • 1968 • Lovy Alex • ANS • USA
SEE YOU AT MAO see **BRITISH SOUNDS** • 1969
SEE YOU IN HELL, DARLING (UKN) see **AMERICAN DREAM, AN** • 1966
SEE YOU IN HELL, FELLOWS! see **DO VIDENIA V PEKLE, PRIATELIA** • 1970
SEE YOU IN HELL, FRIENDS see **DO VIDENIA V PEKLE, PRIATELIA** • 1970
SEE YOU IN JAIL • 1927 • Henabery Joseph • USA
SEE YOU IN THE FUNNY PAPERS • 1983 • Munro Grant • CND
SEE YOU IN THE MORNING • 1989 • Pakula Alan J. • USA
SEE YOU IN THE NEXT WAR see **NASVIDENJE V NASLEDNJI VOJNI** • 1981
SEE YOU LATER • 1928 • *Douglas Earl* • USA
SEE YOU OUTSIDE see **A LA SALIDA NOS VEMOS** • 1985

SEE YOU TOMORROW • 1987 • Scherer Gene • USA
SEE YOU TOMORROW (UKN) see **DO WIDZENIA DO JUTRA** • 1960
SEE YOU TONIGHT • 1934 • Beaudine William • SHT • USA
SEE YOUR DOCTOR • 1939 • Wrangell Basil • SHT • USA
SEED • 1931 • Stahl John M. • USA
SEED, THE see **KIMEN** • 1973
SEED AND THE HARVEST • 1914 • Vignola Robert G. • USA
SEED OF INNOCENCE • 1980 • Davidson Boaz • USA • TEN MOTHERS
SEED OF MAN, THE (USA) see **SEME DELL'UOMO, IL** • 1969
SEED OF TERROR see **GRAVE OF THE VAMPIRE** • 1972
SEED OF THE FATHERS, THE • 1913 • *Leonard Marion* • USA
SEEDING OF SARAH BURNS, THE • 1979 • Stern Sandor • TVM • USA
SEEDING THE FUTURE see **SIEMBRA DEL FUTURO** • 1978
SEEDLING, THE (UKN) see **ANKUR** • 1974
SEEDS • 1968 • Milligan Andy • USA
SEEDS, THE • 1959 • Kelly Ron • CND
SEEDS OF CHAOS • 1914 • Webster Harry Mcrae • USA
SEEDS OF DISCOVERY • 1970 • *Nasa* • SHT • USA
SEEDS OF EVIL see **GARDENER, THE** • 1974
SEEDS OF EVIL see **OLTRE IL BENE E IL MALE** • 1977
SEEDS OF FREEDOM • 1929 • Roshal Grigori • USS
SEEDS OF FREEDOM • 1943 • Burger Hans
SEEDS OF JEALOUSY • 1914 • *Balboa* • USA
SEEDS OF JEALOUSY • 1914 • *Princess* • USA
SEEDS OF JEALOUSY • 1916 • *Darkfeather Mona* • SHT • USA
SEEDS OF REDEMPTION • 1917 • Hill Robert F. • SHT • USA
SEEDS OF SILVER • 1913 • Huntley Fred W. • USA
SEEDS OF VENGEANCE • 1920 • Sellers Oliver L. • USA
SEEDS OF WEALTH • 1913 • O'Neil Barry • USA
SEEFAHRT, DIE IST LUSTIG, EINE • 1935 • Elling Alwin • FRG • FAHRT INS BLAUE, DIE
SEEFAHRT IST NOT! • 1921 • Biebrach Rudolf • FRG
SEEIN' RED WHITE 'N' BLUE • 1943 • Gordon Dan • ANS • USA
SEEIN' THINGS • 1909 • Melies Georges • FRN
SEEIN' THINGS • 1924 • Roach Hal • SHT • USA
SEEING DOUBLE • 1913 • North Wilfred • USA
SEEING DOUBLE • 1917 • *Dudley Charles* • USA
SEEING DOUBLE • 1920 • Reardon James • UKN
SEEING GHOSTS • 1948 • Davis Mannie • ANS • USA
SEEING HANDS • 1943 • Fritsch Gunther V. • SHT • USA
SEEING IS BELIEVING • 1912 • *Calvert E. H.* • USA
SEEING IS BELIEVING • 1934 • Davis Redd • UKN
SEEING IT THROUGH • 1920 • Mitchell Claude H. • USA
SEEING IT THROUGH (UKN) see **MOTH, THE** • 1934
SEEING LONDON IN ONE DAY • 1910 • Bouwmeester Theo • UKN
SEEING NELLIE HOME • 1924 • McCarey Leo • SHT • USA
SEEING NELLIE HOME • 1943 • Holmes Ben • SHT • USA
SEEING REDS: STORIES OF AMERICAN COMMUNISTS • 1983 • Reichert Julia, Klein James • DOC • USA
SEEING STARS • 1927 • Roberts Stephen • SHT • USA
SEEING STARS • 1932 • *Mintz Charles (P)* • ANS • USA
SEEING STARS • 1938 • Boulting Roy • DCS • UKN
SEEING STARS AND STRIPES • 1914 • *Reliance* • USA
SEEING THINGS • 1917 • Clements Roy • *Nestor* • SHT • USA
SEEING THINGS • 1917 • Jackson Harry • *Klever* • SHT • USA
SEEING THINGS • 1919 • Santell Alfred • SHT • USA
SEEING'S BELIEVING • 1922 • Beaumont Harry • USA
SEEK AND THOU SHALT FIND • 1908 • Melies Georges • FRN
SEEKADETT, DER • 1926 • Boese Carl • FRG
SEEKER, THE see **SEARCHER, THE** • 1989
SEEKERS, THE • 1916 • Turner Otis • USA
SEEKERS, THE • 1954 • Annakin Ken • UKN • LAND OF FURY (USA)
SEEKERS, THE • 1979 • Hayers Sidney • MTV • USA
SEEKERS AFTER ROMANCE • 1915 • *Ab* • USA
SEEKING AN INSPIRATION • 1915 • *Paton Stuart* • USA
SEEKING AN OVERSOUL • 1918 • Baker Graham • SHT • USA
SEEKING FOR WOMEN see **ONNA ASARI** • 1967
SEEKING MY DESTINY • 1974 • Manasarova A. • USS
SEELAVATHI • 1967 • Unni P. B. • IND
SEELE DES KINDES, DIE see **LIEBE UND LEBEN 1** • 1918
SEELE EINER FRAU, DIE • 1916 • *Andra Fern* • FRG
SEELE SAITEN SCHWINGEN NICHT, DER • 1917 • Andra Fern
SEELEN, DIE SICH NACHTS BEGEGNEN • 1915 • Illes Eugen • FRG
SEELEN IM STURM • 1920 • Illes Eugen • FRG
SEELENBRAU, DER • 1950 • Ucicky Gustav • AUS
SEELENKAUFER, DER • 1919 • Pick Lupu • FRG
SEELENVERKAUFER • 1919 • Boese Carl • FRG
SEELENWANDERUNG • 1964 • Erler Rainer • FRG • TRANSMIGRATION OF SOULS ○ WANDERINGS OF A SOUL
SEELISCHE KONSTRUKTIONEN • 1927 • Fischinger Oskar • ANS • FRG • SPIRITUAL CONSTRUCTIONS
SEEMABADHA • 1972 • Ray Satyajit • IND • COMPANY LIMITED ○ SALESMAN, THE
SEEMS LIKE OLD TIMES • 1980 • Sandrich Jay • USA • NEIL SIMON'S SEEMS LIKE OLD TIMES
SEEN AT THE CHIROPODIST'S • 1907 • Cooper Arthur • UKN
SEEN FROM THE GALLERY • 1915 • *Wadsworth William* • USA
SEEN THROUGH THE MAKE-UP • 1915 • Ransom Charles • USA
SEER OF BOND STREET, THE (USA) see **SPIRITUALISM EXPOSED** • 1913
SEER OF THE DEAD, THE see **HALOTTLATO, A** • 1978
SEER WAS HERE • 1978 • Jutra Claude • MTV • CND
SEER WHO WALKS ALONE, THE • 1985 • Aravindan G. • DOC • IND
SEERESS, THE • 1903 • *Biograph* • USA
SEESAW AND THE SHOES, THE • 1945 • Foster Douglas • SHT • USA • MOMENTS THAT MADE HISTORY
SEESCHLACHT, DIE • 1917 • Oswald Richard • FRG
SEESCHLACHT BEIM SKAGERRAK • 1926 • Noa Manfred • FRG
SEETA • 1933 • Bose Debaki • IND
SEETA • 1934 • Kapoor Prithviraj • IND
SEETA • 1935 • *Bhaduri Sisir* • IND
SEETA HARAN • 1930 • *Asian Film Co* • IND
SEETA SWAYAMVAR • 1948 • *Khote Durga* • IND
SEETEUFEL 1, DER • 1923 • Heiland Heinz Karl • FRG
SEETEUFEL 2, DER • 1923 • Heiland Heinz Karl • FRG
SEETHA • 1967 • Nagarajan A. P. • IND • PRINCESS SEETA
SEETHA DEVI • 1976 • Sandrasagara Manik • SLN, IND, PKS • RAMAYANA
SEETHA KALYANAM • 1977 • Bapu • IND • SITA'S WEDDING ○ SITA KALYANAM ○ SITA SWAYAMVAR
SEETHA RAMA JANANAM • 1945 • *Prathibha* • IND
SEFILLER • 1967 • Davutoglu Zafer • TRK • MISERABLE ONES, THE
SEFUL SECTORULUI SUFLETE • 1967 • Vitandis Gheorghe • RMN • CHIEF OF THE SOULS' DEPARTMENT, THE ○ SOULS DEPARTMENT, THE
SEGANANA • 1985 • SAF
SEGANTINI, IL PITTORE DELLA MONTAGNA • 1948 • Risi Dino • SHT • ITL
SEGER I MORKER • 1954 • Folke Gosta • SWD • VICTORY IN DARKNESS ○ VICTORY IN THE DARK
SEGESVAR • 1974 • Lanyi Andras • HNG • MYTH–MAKERS, THE
SEGITSEG • 1970 • Macskassy Gyula, Varnai Gyorgy • ANS • HNG • HELP
SEGITSEG OROKOLTEM! • 1937 • Sekely Steve • HNG • HELP! I'VE INHERITED ○ HELP, I'M AN HEIRESS
SEGNALE VIENE DAL CIELO, IL • 1951 • Carpignano Vittorio • ITL
SEGNI PARTICOLARI: BELLISSIMO • 1984 • Castellano, Pipolo • ITL • IDENTIFYING FEATURES: VERY HANDSOME
SEGNO DEL COYOTE, IL • 1963 • Caiano Mario • ITL, SPN
SEGNO DEL VENDICATORE, IL • 1962 • Mauri Roberto • ITL
SEGNO DI VENERE, IL • 1955 • Risi Dino • ITL • SIGN OF VENUS
SEGNO DI ZORRO, IL • 1963 • Caiano Mario • ITL, FRN, SPN • DUEL AT THE RIO GRANDE (USA) ○ SIGNE DE ZORRO, LE
SEGODNYA • 1924 • Vertov Dziga • USS • TODAY ○ SEVODIYA
SEGODNYA • 1930 • Shub Esther • USS • CANNONS OR TRACTORS ○ TODAY ○ SEVODNYA
SEGODNYA OTPUSKA NYE BUDYET • 1959 • Tarkovsky Andrei • SHT • USS • THERE WILL BE NO LEAVE TONIGHT ○ THERE WILL BE NO LEAVE TODAY
SEGOPOTSO • 1989 • Chesselet, Matthew • SAF
SEGREDO DAS ASAS, O • 1944 • Mauro-Humberto • BRZ
SEGREDO DO CORCUNDA, O • 1924 • Traversa Alberto • BRZ
SEGRETAGENTISSIMO see **SEGRETISSIMO** • 1967
SEGRETARIA PER TUTTI, LA • 1933 • Palermi Amleto • ITL
SEGRETARIA PRIVATA, LA • 1931 • Alessandrini Goffredo • ITL
SEGRETARIA PRIVATA DI MIO PADRE, LA • 1977 • Laurenti Mariano • ITL
SEGRETI CHE SCOTTANO (ITL) see **GEHEIMNISSE IN GOLDENEN NYLONS** • 1966
SEGRETI DELLA NOTTE, I • 1958 • Mattoli Mario • ITL
SEGRETI DELLE CITTA PIU NUDE DEL MUNDO, I • 1971 • Martino Luciano • ITL
SEGRETISSIMO • 1967 • Cerchio Fernando • ITL • SHARK WEARS PERFUME, THE ○ SEGRETAGENTISSIMO
SEGRETO, IL • 1990 • Maselli Francesco • ITL • SECRET, THE
SEGRETO DEI FRATI GIALLI, IL (ITL) see **GEHEIMNIS DER GELBEN MONCHE, DAS** • 1966
SEGRETO DEI SOLDATI DI ARGILLA, IL • 1970 • Ferguson R. • ITL
SEGRETO DEL CASTELLO DI MONROE, IL • 1914 • Genina Augusto • ITL • SECRET OF CASTLE MUNROE, THE
SEGRETO DEL DR. CHALMERS, IL (SPN) see **CRYSTALBRAIN L'UOMO DAL CERVELLO DI CRISTALLO** • 1970
SEGRETO DEL DOTTORE, IL • 1930 • Salvatori Jack • ITL
SEGRETO DEL GAROFANO CINESE, IL (ITL) see **GEHEIMNIS DER CHINESISCHEN NELKE, DAS** • 1964
SEGRETO DEL VESTITO ROSSO, IL see **ASSASSINIO MADE IN ITALY** • 1963
SEGRETO DELLA GROTTA AZZURRA, IL • 1922 • Gallone Carmine • ITL
SEGRETO DELLA SIERRA DORADO, IL • 1957 • Belli Pino • DOC • ITL
SEGRETO DELLE ROSE, IL • 1958 • Principe Albino • ITL
SEGRETO DELLE TRE PUNTE, IL • 1953 • Bragaglia Carlo Ludovico • ITL • SECRET OF THE THREE SWORD POINTS, THE
SEGRETO DELLO SPARVIERO NERO, IL • 1961 • Paolella Domenico • ITL
SEGRETO DI BUDDA, IL (ITL) see **HEISSER HAFEN HONGKONG** • 1962
SEGRETO DI DON GIOVANNI, IL • 1947 • Costa Mario, Mastrocinque Camillo? • ITL
SEGRETO DI STATO • 1914 • Rosa Silvio Laurenti • ITL
SEGRETO DI SUOR ANGELA, IL see **SECRET DE SOEUR ANGELE, LE** • 1956
SEGRETO DI VILLA PARADISO, IL • 1940 • Gambino Domenico M. • ITL • NOTTE A VILLA PARADISO, UNA ○ VILLA PARADISO
SEGRETO INVIOLABILE, IL • 1939 • De Gomar Julio F. • ITL
SEGUA, LA • 1984 • Yglesias Antonio • CRC
SEGUGIO, IL (ITL) see **ACCROCHE-TOI, Y A DU VENT** • 1961
SEGUIN • 1982 • Trevino Jesus • TVM • USA
SEGUIRE TUS PASOS • 1968 • Morayta Miguel?, Crevenna Alfredo B.? • MXC, PRU • I'LL FOLLOW IN YOUR STEPS
SEGUME.. VENI CONMIGO • 1973 • Saslavsky Luis • ARG • COME ALONG.. FOLLOW ME
SEGUNDA DECLARACION DE LA HABANA • 1965 • Alvarez Santiago • DOC • CUB
SEGUNDA MUJER, LA • 1952 • Diaz Morales Jose • MXC
SEGUNDO EXPOSICAO NACIONAL DE FLORICULTURA • 1941 • Coelho Jose Adolfo • SHT • PRT
SEGUNDO FESTIVAL MORTADELO Y FILEMON • 1969 • Vara Rafael • SPN
SEGUNDO LOPEZ, AVENTURERO URBANO • 1952 • Mariscal Ana • SPN
SEGUNDO PODER, EL • 1977 • Forque Jose Maria • SPN • SECOND POWER, THE (USA)
SEGURA EST EL INFIERNO • 1986 • Alcalde Jose Andres • VNZ • HELL FOR SURE
SEHENDE LIEBE see **SEHNENDE LIEBE** • 1920
SEHNENDE LIEBE • 1920 • Walther-Fein Rudolf • FRG • SEHENDE LIEBE
SEHNSUCHT • 1920 • Murnau F. W. • FRG • BAJAZZO
SEHNSUCHT 202 • 1932 • Neufeld Max • FRG
SEHNSUCHT DER VERONIKA VOSS, DIE • 1982 • Fassbinder R. W. • FRG • VERONICA VOSS
SEHNSUCHT DES HERZENS • 1951 • Martin Paul • FRG • FRUHLINGSROMANZE
SEHNSUCHT HAT MICH VERFUHRT • 1959 • Ten Haaf Wilm • FRG
SEHNSUCHT JEDER FRAU, DIE • 1930 • Sjostrom Victor • USA
SEI BAMBINE E IL PERSEO • 1939 • Forzano Giovacchino • ITL
SEI DONNE PER L'ASSASSINO • 1964 • Bava Mario • ITL, FRN, FRG • SIX FEMMES POUR L'ASSASSIN (FRN) ○ BLOOD AND BLACK LACE (USA) ○ BLUTIGE SEIDE (FRG) ○ FASHION HOUSE OF DEATH ○ SIX WOMEN FOR THE MURDERER
SEI GEGRUSST, DU MEIN SCHONES SORRENT • 1930 • Mengon Romano • FRG
SEI GETREU BIS IN DEN TOD • 1918 • Stein Josef • FRG
SEI GIA CADAVERE AMIGO.. TI CERCA GARRINGO • 1971 • Iquino Ignacio F. • ITL
SEI JELLATO AMICO.. HAI INCONTRATO SACRAMENTO • 1972 • Cristallini Giorgio • ITL
SEI MOGLI DI BARBABLU, LE • 1950 • Bragaglia Carlo Ludovico • ITL • SIX WIVES OF BLUEBEARD, THE
SEI NO AKUTOKU • 1968 • Kitami Ichiroh • JPN • VICE OF SEX
SEI NO BOHRYOKU • 1968 • Okuwaki Toshio • JPN • VIOLENCE OF SEX
SEI NO HAITO • 1968 • Umesawa Kaoru • JPN • SHARE OF SEX, THE
SEI NO HARENCHI • 1968 • Nishimura Leo • JPN • SHAMELESS SEX
SEI NO HORO • 1967 • Wakamatsu Koji • JPN • VAGABOND OF SEX
SEI NO ISHOKU TAIKEN • 1968 • Tachibana Akira • JPN • EXTRAORDINARY EXPERIENCE OF SEX
SEI NO KAIDAN • 1968 • Nishihara Giichi • JPN • STEPS IN SEX
SEI NO KIGEN • 1967 • Shindo Kaneto • JPN • ORIGIN OF SEX –LIBIDO, THE ○ LIBIDO
SEI NO SAN-AKU • 1967 • Ogawa Kinya • JPN • THREE EVILS OF SEX
SEI NO URAOMOTE • 1968 • Uchida Yusuke • JPN • BOTH SIDES OF SEX
SEI ORE DI TEMPO • 1954 • Rolvy Sasy • ITL
SEI PER OTTO QUARANTOTTO see **TUTTA LA CITTA CANTA** • 1944
SEI SIMPATICHE CAROGNE • 1968 • Fiz Robert • ITL, SPN • ATRACO DE IDA Y VUELTA, UN (SPN) ○ IT'S YOUR MOVE (USA) ○ SCACCO TUTTO MATTO, UNO ○ MAD CHECKMATE ○ RETURN ATTACK, A
SEI TSINGAM • 1989 • Luk Jamie • HKG • FOUR LOVES
SEI TU L'AMORE • 1930 • Sabato Alfredo
SEI UNA CAROGNA.. E T'AMMAZZO • 1972 • Esteba M. • ITL
SEI ZARTLICH, PINGUIN • 1982 • Hajek Peter • FRG, AUS • BE GENTLE, PENGUIN
SEICHITAI • 1968 • Adachi Masao • JPN • SEX ZONE
SEIDO NO KIRISUTO • 1955 • Shibuya Minoru • JPN • CHRIST IN BRONZE
SEIEN, SHISHOGIRI • 1968 • Komori Haku • JPN • ATTACK POINT OF WOMEN
SEIFENBLASEN • 1915 • Bolten-Baeckers Heinrich • FRG
SEIFENBLASEN • 1933 • Dudow Slatan • FRG • SOAP BUBBLES ○ BULLES DE SAVON
SEIFENBLASEN • 1985 • Ninaus Alfred • AUS • SOAP–BUBBLES
SEIGENKI • 1973 • Narishima Toichiro • JPN • TIME WITHIN MEMORY (USA) ○ TIME WITHOUT MEMORY
SEIGI NO TSUWAMONO • 1927 • Tasaka Tomotaka • JPN • SOLDIER'S JUSTICE
SEIGIHA • 1957 • Shibuya Minoru • JPN • CASE OF HONOUR, A
SEIGNEURS DE LA FORET, LES • 1959 • Sielmann Heinz, Brandt Henry • DOC • BLG • LORDS OF THE FOREST
SEIGOKU • 1968 • Matsubara Jiro • JPN • PRISON OF SEX
SEIHA • 1983 • Nakajima Sadao • JPN • CONQUEST
SEIHAN • 1967 • Ogawa Kinya • JPN • SEX CRIMINAL
SEIHANZAI • 1967 • Wakamatsu Koji • JPN • SEX CRIMES
SEIKATSU TO MIZU • 1952 • Hani Susumu (c/d) • DOC • JPN • WATER IN OUR LIFE
SEIKATSUSEN ABC • 1931 • Shimazu Yasujiro • JPN • ABC LIFELINE
SEIKI NO DAIJAKUTEN • 1968 • Wada Yoshinori • JPN • GREAT DIRECT
SEILERGASSE 8 • 1960 • Kunert Joachim • FRG • NO.8 SEILER STREET ○ DREI, DIE
SEIMEI NO KANMURI • 1936 • Uchida Tomu • JPN
SEIMILA CHILOMETRI DI PAURA • 1978 • Albertini Bitto • ITL, KNY • 6,000 KM PI PAURA ○ SAFARI RALLY
SEIN BESTER FREUND • 1918 • May Joe? • FRG
SEIN BESTER FREUND • 1937 • Piel Harry • FRG • HIS BEST FRIEND (USA)
SEIN BESTER FREUND • 1962 • Trenker Luis • FRG
SEIN CHEF • 1925 • *Otto Gebuhr-Film* • FRG
SEIN EINZIGER SOHN • 1917 • Wellin Arthur • FRG
SEIN ERSTES KIND • 1915 • Del Zopp Rudolf • FRG
SEIN FUNFTER FALL • 1917 • Meinert Rudolf • FRG
SEIN GROSSER FALL • 1926 • Wendhausen Fritz • FRG
SEIN GROSSTER BLUFF • 1927 • Piel Harry • FRG • ER ODER ICH ○ BIG BLUFF, THE
SEIN IST DAS GERICHT • 1922 • Lange Bruno • FRG
SEIN LEBENSLICHT • 1921 • Neufeld Max • AUS
SEIN LETZTE MASKE • 1916 • Oswald Richard • FRG
SEIN LETZTER BERICHT: AUS DEM VATERHAUS VERSTOSSEN • 1917 • Illes Eugen • FRG

SEIN LETZTER BRIEF see **SCHICKSAL DER RENATE LANGEN, DAS** • 1931
SEIN LETZTER SEITENSPRUNG • 1918 • Larsen Viggo • FRG
SEIN LETZTER TRICK • 1920 • Brunner Rolf • FRG
SEIN LETZTES EDELWEISS • 1930 • Seitz Franz • FRG
SEIN LETZTES MODELL • 1937 • van der Noss Rudolf • FRG, HNG
SEIN LIEBESLIED • 1931 • von Bolvary Geza • FRG
SEIN SCHEIDUNGSGRUND • 1931 • Zeisler Alfred • FRG
SEIN SCHWIERIGSTER FALL • 1915 • May Joe • FRG
SEIN SEITENSPRUNG • 1915 • Ostermayr Peter • FRG
SEIN SOHN • 1941 • Brauer Peter P. • FRG
SEIN TODFEIND • 1917 • Piel Harry • FRG
SEIN WEIB • 1918 • Mack Max • FRG
SEINE A RENCONTRE PARIS, LA • 1957 • Ivens Joris • FRN • SEINE MEETS PARIS, THE
SEINE BEICHTE • 1919 • Moest Hubert • FRG
SEINE BESTE ROLLE • 1943 • Slavinsky Vladimir • FRG
SEINE DREI FRAUEN • 1920 • Gerdes Herbert • FRG • DREI FRAUEN
SEINE EIGENE FRAU • 1915 • Schonwald Gustav • FRG
SEINE ET SES MARCHANDS, LA • 1953 • Gibaud Marcel • SHT • FRN
SEINE EXZELLENZ VON MADAGASKAR 1 • 1921 • Jacoby Georg • FRG • MADCHEN AUS DER FREMDE, DAS
SEINE EXZELLENZ VON MADAGASKAR 2 • 1921 • Jacoby Georg • FRG • STUBBS, DER DETEKTIV
SEINE FRAU, DIE UNBEKANNTE • 1923 • Christensen Benjamin • FRG, DNM • WILBUR CRAWFORDS WUNDERSAMES ABENTEUER ○ HIS MYSTERIOUS ADVENTURE (USA)
SEINE FREUNDIN ANNETTE • 1930 • Basch Felix • FRG
SEINE HOHEIT, DER DIENSTMANN • 1930 • Neufeld Max • FRG
SEINE HOHEIT DER DIENSTMANN see **BEIDEN SEEHUNDE, DIE** • 1934
SEINE HOHEIT, DER EINTANZER • 1927 • Leiter Karl • AUS • ENTFESSELTE WIEN, DAS
SEINE KLEINE MADONNA • 1917 • Schubert Georg • FRG
SEINE KOKETTE FRAU • 1916 • Moest Hubert • FRG
SEINE MAJESTAT DAS BETTLEKIND • 1920 • Korda Alexander • AUS • PRINCE AND THE PAUPER, THE ○ PRINZ UND BETTELKNABE
SEINE MEETS PARIS, THE see **SEINE A RENCONTRE PARIS, LA** • 1957
SEINE MUTTER see **EHRE DEINE MUTTER** • 1928
SEINE NEUE NASE • 1917 • Lubitsch Ernst • FRG
SEINE OFFIZIELLE FRAU see **ESKAPADE** • 1936
SEINE STARKSTE WAFFE • 1928 • Piel Harry • FRG
SEINE TOCHTER IST DER PETER • 1936 • Helbig Heinz • AUS • HIS DAUGHTER IS PETER (USA)
SEINE TOCHTER IST DER PETER • 1955 • Frohlich Gustav • AUS
SEINEN NO KI • 1960 • Masuda Toshio • JPN • DAY OF YOUTH
SEINEN VATER ERSCHOSS ER NICHT, DAS WAR SEIN FEHLER • 1971 • Geissendorfer Hans W. • FRG
SEINER HOHEIT BRAUTFAHRT • 1919 • Hofer Franz • FRG
SEINERZEIT ZU MEINER ZEIT • 1944 • Barlog Boleslav • FRG
SEINES BRUDERS LEIBEIGENER • 1921 • *Hubner Hubert* • FRG • LEIBEIGENSCHAFT
SEINS DE GLACE, LES • 1974 • Lautner Georges • FRN, ITL • ESECUTORE OLTRE LA LEGGE (ITL) ○ SOMEONE IS BLEEDING (UKN) ○ ICY BREASTS (USA)
SEIRI TO NINSHIN • 1968 • Ogawa Kinya • JPN • PHYSIOLOGY AND PREGNANCY
SEIRYU NA DOKUTSU • JPN • CAVE OF THE BLUE DRAGON
SEIS DIAS PARA MORIR • 1966 • Gomez Muriel Emilio • MXC
SEIS PASAJES AL INFIERNO • 1975 • Siro Fernando • ARG • SIX TICKETS TO HELL
SEIS SUEGRAS DE BARBA AZUL, LAS • 1945 • Christensen Carlos Hugo • ARG • SIX MOTHER-IN-LAWS OF BLUEBEARD, THE
SEISAKU NO TSUMA • 1924 • Murata Minoru • JPN
SEISAKU NO TSUMA • 1965 • Masumura Yasuzo • JPN • WIFE OF SEISAKU, THE
SEISEI DODO • 1959 • Horiuchi Manao • JPN
SEISHOKU NO ISHIZUE • 1978 • Moritani Shiro • JPN • FOUNDATION OF THE ORDINATION, THE
SEISHU HANAOKA'S WIFE see **HANAOKA SEISHU NO TSUMA** • 1967
SEISHUN • 1925 • Gosho Heinosuke • JPN • YOUTH
SEISHUN • 1968 • Ichikawa Kon • DCS • JPN • TOURNAMENT ○ YOUTH
SEISHUN DAITORYO • 1966 • Ezaki Mio • JPN • YOUTH PRESIDENT
SEISHUN KAIDAN • 1955 • Ichikawa Kon • JPN • YOUTH'S GHOST STORY, THE ○ GHOST STORY OF YOUTH
SEISHUN KORO • 1957 • Mizuko Harumi • JPN
SEISHUN MUSEN RYOKO • 1958 • Nakagawa Nobuo • JPN • JOURNEY OF YOUTH
SEISHUN NO ETSURAKU • 1967 • Kimata Akitaka • JPN • PLEASURE OF YOUTH
SEISHUN NO KAZE • 1968 • Nishimura Shogoro • JPN • SOCIETY, THE
SEISHUN NO KIRYU • 1942 • Fushimizu Osamu • JPN • CURRENTS OF YOUTH
SEISHUN NO MON • 1974 • Urayama Kirio • JPN • GATE OF THE YOUTH, THE ○ GATE OF YOUTH, THE
SEISHUN NO MON, JIRITSU HEN • 1976 • Urayama Kirio • JPN • GATE OF YOUTH: INDEPENDENCE, THE ○ GATE OF YOUTH, PART 2, THE
SEISHUN NO MON, JIRITSU HEN • 1982 • Kurahara Koreyoshi • JPN • GATE OF YOUTH II, THE
SEISHUN NO OTO • 1954 • Sekigawa Hideo • JPN • SOUTH OF YOUTH
SEISHUN NO SATSUJIN-SHA • 1976 • Hasegawa Kazuhiko • JPN • KILLER OF YOUTH, A ○ KILLER YOUTH, THE ○ MURDERER OF YOUTH ○ YOUTH KILLER, THE
SEISHUN NO UMI • 1967 • Nishimura Shogoro • JPN • BLACK SHEEP, THE
SEISHUN NO YUME IMA IZUKO • 1932 • Ozu Yasujiro • JPN • WHERE NOW ARE THE DREAMS OF YOUTH ○ WHERE ARE THE DREAMS OF YOUTH
SEISHUN NO YUMEJI • 1922 • Mizoguchi Kenji • JPN • DREAM PATH OF YOUTH, THE (USA) ○ DREAMS OF YOUTH
SEISHUN O FUKINARASE • 1960 • Masuda Toshio • JPN
SEISHUN TARO • 1967 • Nakahira Ko • JPN • YOUTHFUL TARO ○ TARO'S YOUTH
SEISHUN TOWA NANDA • 1965 • Masuda Toshio • JPN
SEISHUN ZANKOKU MONOGATARI • 1960 • Oshima Nagisa • JPN • STORY OF CRUELTY OF YOUTH, A ○ CRUEL STORY OF YOUTH ○ CRUEL TALES OF YOUTH ○ NAKED YOUTH
SEISHUN ZENIGATA HEIJI • 1953 • Ichikawa Kon • JPN • YOUTH OF HEIJI ZENIGATA, THE
SEITENSPRUNGE • 1930 • Sekely Steve • FRG
SEITENSPRUNGE • 1940 • Stoger Alfred • FRG
SEITENSPRUNGE IM SCHNEE • 1950 • Breuer Siegfried • AUS
SEITENSTRASSE DER PROSTITUTION • 1967 • Ammann Gerhard • FRG • BY-WAY OF PROSTITUTION
SEITSEMAN VELJESTA • 1939 • Ilmari Wilho • FNL
SEITSEMAN VELJESTA • 1976 • Nelimarkka Riitta, Seeck Jaakko • FNL • SEVEN BROTHERS
SEIZE THE DAY • 1986 • Cook Fielder • USA
SEIZE THE TIME see **AFFERRA IL TEMPO** • 1973
SEIZOROI KENKA WAKASHU • 1955 • Saeki Kiyoshi • JPN
SEIZURE • 1973 • Stone Oliver • CND • QUEEN OF EVIL
SEIZURE: THE STORY OF KATHY MORRIS • 1980 • Isenberg Gerald I. • TVM • USA
SEJNANE • 1974 • Ben Ammar Abdul Latif • TNS
SEKAI DAI SENSO • 1961 • Matsubayashi Shue • JPN • LAST WAR, THE (USA) ○ FINAL WAR, THE
SEKAI O KAKERU KOI • 1959 • Takizawa Eisuke • JPN • LOVE AND DEATH
SEKAI SAGI MONOGATARI see **PLUS BELLES ESCROQUERIES DU MONDE, LES** • 1963
SEKA'S CRUISE see **ROCKING WITH SEKA** • 1980
SEKCJA ZWLOK • 1973 • Czekala Ryszard • ANM • PLN • AUTOPSY
SEKE DO ROU • 1968 • Parvisi Khosrow • IRN • TWO-SIDED COIN
SEKEBEKWA • 1985 • SAF
SEKI NO YATAPPE • 1935 • Inagaki Hiroshi, Yamanaka Sadao • JPN
SEKI NO YATAPPE • 1959 • Kado Satoshi • JPN
SEKI NO YATAPPE • 1963 • Yamashita Kosaku • JPN • SAMURAI AND ORPHANS
SEKIDOO KAKERU OTOKO • 1968 • Saito Buichi • JPN • DIAMOND OF THE ANDES
SEKIREI NO KYOKO • 1951 • Toyoda Shiro • JPN • WAGTAIL TUNE
SEKISHUN • 1967 • Nakamura Noboru • JPN • THREE FACES OF LOVE
SEKISHUN-CHO • 1959 • Kinoshita Keisuke • JPN • BIRD OF SPRINGS PAST, THE ○ BIRD MISSING SPRING, THE
SEKKA TOMURAI ZASHI • 1982 • Takabayashi Yoichi • JPN
SEKKA TOMURAI ZASHI IREZUMI • 1981 • Takabayashi Yoichi • JPN • IREZUMI (SPIRIT OF TATTOO) (USA)
SEKKUSU CHEKKU-DAINI NO SEI • 1968 • Masumura Yasuzo • JPN • SEX CHECK DAI-NI NO SEI ○ SEX CHECK, THE
SEKRET KRASOTY • 1955 • Segel Yakov • USS • SECRET OF BEAUTY
SEKRET O SPEHA see **SEKRET USPEKHA** • 1965
SEKRET USPEKHA • 1965 • Lavrovskiy Leonid, Shelenkov Aleksandr • USS • SECRET OF SUCCESS, THE (UKN) ○ BOLSHOI BALLET 67 (USA) ○ SEKRET O SPEHA
SEKRETAR DER KONIGIN, DER • 1916 • Wiene Robert • FRG
SEKRETAR RAIKON • 1942 • Pyriev Ivan • USS • SECRETARY OF THE DISTRICT COMMITTEE ○ WE WILL COME BACK
SEKRETARIN DES GESANDTEN, DIE • 1919 • Ziener Bruno • FRG
SEKRETNAYA MISSIYA • 1950 • Romm Mikhail • USS • SECRET MISSION
SEKSDAGESLOBET see **6 DAGESLOBET** • 1958
SEKSMISJA • 1984 • Machulski Juliusz • PLN • SEX MISSION
SEKSOLATKI • 1971 • Hubner Zygmunt • PLN
SEKSTET • 1964 • Hovmand Annelise • DNM • SEXTET
SEKTMIEZE see **RAFFINIERTE FRAUEN 1** • 1923
SEKUNDA STRAHA • 1969 • Vunak Dragutin • ANM • YGS
SEKWETTE, DIE • 1916 • Mack Max • FRG
SEL DE LA TERRE, LE • 1950 • Rouquier Georges • SHT • FRN • SALT OF THE EARTH
SELAMSIZ BANDOSU • 1987 • Colgecen Nesli • TRK • TOWN BAND, THE
SELBIN TROUPE OF MARVELLOUS CLEVER ACROBATS, THE • 1902 • *Warwick Trading Co* • UKN
SELBSTMORDERKLUB, DER • 1920 • Oswald Richard • FRG • SUICIDE CLUB, THE
SELCOR • 1975 • Traikov Atanas • BUL • VILLAGE CORRESPONDENT, THE
SELECTING HIS HEIRESS • 1911 • Humphrey William • USA
SELECTION INTERVIEW, A • 1970 • Holmes Cecil • SHT • ASL
SELF see **NAAN** • 1967
SELF-ACCUSED • 1913 • *Imp* • USA
SELF ACCUSED • 1914 • Weston Charles • UKN
SELF CONTROL • 1938 • King Jack • ANS • USA
SELF-CONVICTED • 1913 • *Lubin* • USA
SELF DEFENCE • 1916 • Roos Charles G., Roos Leonard Halley • CND
SELF DEFENCE see **JU-JITSU TO THE RESCUE** • 1913
SELF DEFENCE see **SIEGE** • 1982
SELF DEFENSE • 1933 • Rosen Phil • USA
SELF-DEFENSE • 1942 • Anderson Philip • USA
SELF DEFENSE -FOR COWARDS • 1962 • *Snyder William L. (P)* • ANS • USA
SELF-HYPNOTIZED • 1915 • *Royal* • USA
SELF-MADE FAILURE, A • 1924 • Beaudine William • USA
SELF-MADE HERO, A • 1910 • Salter Harry • USA
SELF-MADE HERO, A • 1917 • *St. John Al* • USA
SELF-MADE LADY • 1932 • King George • UKN
SELF-MADE LADY, A • 1918 • Kirkland David • SHT • USA
SELF-MADE MAIDS • 1950 • McCollum Hugh • SHT • USA
SELF-MADE MAN, A • 1922 • Lee Rowland V. • USA
SELF-MADE MONGREL, A • 1945 • *Paramount Noveltoon* • ANS • USA
SELF MADE WIDOW • 1917 • Vale Travers • USA • ROMANCE OF A SELF-MADE WIDOW, THE
SELF-MADE WIFE, THE • 1923 • Dillon John Francis • USA
SELF OBLITERATION • 1968 • Yalkut Jud • ANS • USA
SELF-PORTRAIT • 1961 • Glover Guy • CND • AUTO-PORTRAIT
SELF SERVICE • 1974 • Bozzetto Bruno • ANS • ITL
SELF SERVICE DU NU • 1972 • Gantillon Bruno • ANT • FRN
SELF STARTER, THE • 1926 • Brown Harry J. • USA
SELF TRIO • 1976 • Emshwiller Ed • USA
SELFISH GIANT, THE • 1962 • *Reiner-Film* • ANS • FRG
SELFISH GIANT, THE • 1969 • Allen David • ANM • USA
SELFISH GIANT, THE • 1971 • Sander Peter • ANS • USA
SELFISH WOMAN, THE • 1916 • Hopper E. Mason • USA
SELFISH YATES • 1918 • Hart William S. • USA
SELIGE EXZELLENZ, DIE • 1927 • Thiele Wilhelm, Licho Adolf Edgar • FRG • HIS LATE EXCELLENCY
SELIGE EXZELLENZ, DIE • 1935 • Zerlett Hans H. • FRG • TAGEBUCH DER BARONIN W., DAS
SELIMA • 1934 • *Burman S. D. (M)* • IND
SELINA-ELLA • 1915 • Aylott Dave • UKN
SELINA OF THE WEEKLIES • 1915 • Aylott Dave • UKN
SELINA'S FLIGHT FOR FREEDOM • 1914 • Collins Edwin J.? • UKN
SELINUNTE • 1951 • Birri Fernando • SHT • ARG
SELINUNTE, I TEMPI CORICATI • 1955 • Birri Fernando • ITL
SELJACKA BUNA 1573 • 1975 • Mimica Vatroslav • YGS • PEASANT UPRISING IN 1573, THE ○ PEASANTS' REVOLT 1573, THE ○ ANNO DOMINO 1573
SELKVINNEN • 1953 • Sinding Leif • NRW
SELL A MILLION • 1975 • SAF
SELL 'EM COWBOY • 1924 • Hayes Ward • USA • ALIAS TEXAS PETE OWENS (UKN)
SELLA D'ARGENTO • 1978 • Fulci Lucio • ITL
SELLAISENA KUIN SINA MINUT HALUSIT • 1944 • Tulio Teuvo • FNL
SELLERS OF GIRLS (USA) see **MARCHANDS DE FILLES** • 1957
SELLING OF AMERICA, THE see **BEER** • 1985
SELLING OLD MASTER • 1911 • *Edison* • USA
SELLING OUT • 1972 • Jaworski Tadeusz • DOC • CND
SELLO A PECSETGYURUN • 1967 • Mihalyfi Imre • HNG • WATER-NYMPH ON THE SIGNET RING
SELLOUT, THE • 1951 • Mayer Gerald • USA • COUNTY LINE
SELLOUT, THE • 1975 • Collinson Peter • UKN, ITL, ISR • ...E POI NON RIMASE NESSUNO (ITL) ○ MELIMOT BEYERUSHALAIM ○ SPIA SENZA DOMANI, LA
SELSKAYA UCHITELNITSA • 1947 • Donskoi Mark • USS • VILLAGE SCHOOLTEACHER, THE ○ VILLAGE TEACHER ○ EMOTIONAL EDUCATION, AN ○ RURAL INSTITUTE ○ VARVARA
SELSKII VRACH • 1952 • Gerasimov Sergei • USS • VILLAGE DOCTOR, THE ○ COUNTRY DOCTOR, THE
SELTSAME FRAULEIN SYLVIA, DAS • 1945 • Martin Paul • FRG
SELTSAME GAST, DER • 1923 • *Eiko-Film* • FRG
SELTSAME GESCHICHTE DES BARONS TORELLI, DIE • 1918 • Oswald Richard • FRG
SELTSAME GESCHICHTE DES BRANDNER KASPER, DIE • 1949 • von Baky Josef • FRG • STRANGE STORY OF BRANDNER KASPER, THE ○ TOR ZUM PARADIES, DAS
SELTSAME GRAFIN, DIE • 1961 • von Baky Josef • FRG • STRANGE COUNTESS, THE (USA)
SELTSAME KOPFE • 1916 • Wieder Konrad • FRG
SELTSAME LEBEN DES HERRN BRUGGS, DAS • 1951 • Engel Erich • FRG
SELTSAME MENSCHEN • 1917 • Hofer Franz • FRG
SELTSAME MENSCHEN • 1923 • *Apollo-Film* • FRG
SELTSAME NACHT DER HELGA WANGEN, DIE • 1928 • Holger-Madsen • FRG
SELTSAME VERGANGENHEIT DER THEA CARTER, DIE • 1929 • Levigard Josef • FRG
SELTSAMEN ABENTEUER DES HERRN FRIDOLIN B., DIE • 1948 • Staudte Wolfgang • GDR • STRANGE ADVENTURES OF HERR FRIDOLIN B.
SELTSAMER FALL, EIN • 1914 • *Oswald Richard (Sc)* • FRG • DR. JEKYLL AND MR. HYDE
SELTSAMER GAST, EIN • 1936 • Lamprecht Gerhard • FRG
SELTSAMES ERLIBNIS, EIN see **WER WAR ES?** • 1920
SELVA DE FUEGO, LA • 1945 • de Fuentes Fernando • MXC • JUNGLE FIRE
SELVA TRAGICA • 1964 • Farias Roberto • BRZ
SELVAGGIA • 1959 • De Bassan Aldo • ITL
SELVI BOYLUM AL YAZMALIM • 1979 • Yilmaz Atif • TRK • RED SCARF, THE
SELVMORDSSKOLEN • 1964 • Thomsen Knud Leif • DNM • SCHOOL FOR SUICIDE ○ SCHOOL OF SUICIDE
SELYANINUT S KOLELOTO • 1974 • Kirkov Lyudmil • BUL • PEASANT ON A BICYCLE ○ PEASANT WITH THE BICYCLE, THE
SEM NYANEK • 1962 • Bykov Rolan • USS • SEVEN NURSEMAIDS
SEM SCIAGOV ZA GORIZONT • 1968 • Sobolev F. • USS
SEM SOBRA DE PECADO • 1983 • Costa Jose Fonseca • PRT
SEMAFORO EN ROJO • 1963 • Soler Julian • MXC, CLM
SEMAINE DANS LA VIE DE CAMARADES, UNE • 1976 • Gagne Jean • DOC • CND
SEMAINE DE BONTE, OU LES SEPT ELEMENTS CAPITAUX, UNE • 1961 • Desvilles • SHT • FRN
SEMAINE DE VACANCES, UNE • 1981 • Tavernier Bertrand • FRN • WEEK'S VACATION, A (USA) ○ WEEK'S HOLIDAY, A (UKN)
SEMAINE EN FRANCE, UNE • 1963 • Guillemot Claude, Chambon Jean-Claude • SHT • FRN
SEMALAM DI MALAYSIA • 1975 • Pelamonia Nico • MLY • ONE NIGHT IN MALAYSIA
SEMAMBU KUNING • 1972 • Rojik Omar • MLY • YELLOW BAMBOO, THE
SEMANA DE FELICIDAD, UNA • 1935 • Nosseck Max • SPN • ONE WEEK OF HAPPINESS
SEMANA DEL ASESINO, LA • 1972 • de la Iglesia Eloy • SPN • CANNIBAL MAN, THE ○ APARTMENT ON THE 13TH FLOOR ○ WEEK OF THE ASSASSIN, THE

SEME DELL'UOMO, IL • 1969 • Ferreri Marco • ITL • SEED OF MAN, THE (USA)
SEME DI CAINO, IL • 1972 • Masi Marco • ITL
SEMEINYE FOTOGRAFI • 1989 • Kuik Valentin • USS • FAMILY ALBUM
SEMEJANTE A PEDRO • 1970 • Bellmunt Francisco • SHT • SPN
SEMENTE SELECCIONADA DE TRIGO E ARROZ • 1953 • Coelho Jose Adolfo • SHT • PRT
SEMERAH PADI • Ramlee P. • IND • RED PADDY
SEMERO SINOVEI MOIKH • 1971 • Taghizade Tofic • USS • MY SEVEN SONS
SEMERO SMELYKH • 1936 • Gerasimov Sergei • USS • SEVEN BRAVE MEN ○ BOLD SEVEN, THE ○ BRAVE SEVEN, THE
SEMEUR DE RUINES, LE • 1913 • Jasset Victorin • FRN
SEMI-TOUGH • 1977 • Ritchie Michael • USA
SEMIDIOSES, LOS • 1954 • Perla Alejandro • SPN
SEMINAR, DER • 1967 • Nekes Werner • FRG
SEMINARISTA, EL • 1949 • Rodriguez Roberto • MXC
SEMINARISTE • 1970 • Sanchez-Ariza Jose • PLN
SEMINARISTE, LE • 1976 • Leoni Guido • ITL
SEMINARY SCANDAL • 1916 • Christie Al • USA
SEMINARY SCANDAL, A • 1920 • *Merriam Charlotte* • USA
SEMINO MORTE.. LO CHIAMAVANO CASTIGO DI DIO • 1972 • Mauri Roberto • ITL
SEMINOLE • 1953 • Boetticher Budd • USA
SEMINOLE HALF-BREED, THE see **SEMINOLE HALF-BREEDS, THE** • 1910
SEMINOLE HALF-BREEDS, THE • 1910 • Olcott Sidney • USA • SEMINOLE HALF-BREED, THE
SEMINOLE UPRISING • 1955 • Bellamy Earl • USA
SEMINOLE'S SACRIFICE, THE • 1911 • *Selig* • USA
SEMINOLE'S TRUST, THE • 1910 • *Kalem* • USA
SEMINOLE'S VENGEANCE, OR THE SLAVE CATCHER'S OF FLORIDA, THE • 1909 • Olcott Sidney • USA
SEMIRAMIS • 1909 • de Morlhon Camille • FRN
SEMIRAMIS see **IO SEMIRAMIDE** • 1963
SEMIRAMIS, QUEEN OF BABYLON • 1910 • *Pathe* • FRN
SEMLA OPPENHEIM • 1938 • Roshal Grigori • USS • OPPENHEIM FAMILY, THE
SEMMELWEISS • 1939 • De Toth Andre • HNG
SEMMELWEISS • 1952 • Ban Frigyes • HNG
SEMMELWEISS • 1980 • Tuhus Oddvar Bull • NRW, YGS
SEMMELWEISS -REITER DER MUTTER • 1950 • Klaren Georg C. • FRG • STUNDE DER ENTSCHEIDUNG ○ DR. SEMMELWEISS
SEMMERETSDAMEN see **SUFFRAGETTEN, DIE** • 1913
SEMNUL SARPELUI • 1981 • Veroiu Mircea • RMN • IN THE SIGN OF THE SERPENT
SEMPRE PIU DIFFICILE • 1943 • Angiolillo Renato, Ballerini Piero • ITL
SEMYA POLENOVIKH • 1916 • Boleslawski Richard • USS
SEMYA TARASSA see **NEPOKORENNYE** • 1945
SEN BENIMSIN • 1967 • Erakalin Ulku • TRK • YOU ARE MINE
S'EN FOUT LA MORT • 1990 • Denis Claire • FRN
SEN GIN • 1935 • Ogate Tomio • JPN • CHOICE SILVER
SEN NO RIKYU • 1989 • Kumai Kei • JPN
SEN NOCI • 1985 • Sis Vladimir • CZC • NIGHT DREAM
SEN NOCI SVATOJANSKE • 1959 • Trnka Jiri • ANM • CZC • MIDSUMMER NIGHT'S DREAM, A
SEN STAREHO MLADENCE • 1910 • Krizenecky Jan • CZC • OLD BACHELOR'S DREAM, THE ○ BACHELOR'S DREAM, THE
SEN TURKULERINI SOYLE • 1985 • Goren Serif • TRK • SING YOUR SONGS
SEN YAN'S DEVOTION • 1924 • Coleby A. E. • UKN
SENAL DEL VAMPIRO, LA • 1943 • ARG • SIGN OF THE VAMPIRE, THE ○ MARK OF THE VAMPIRE, THE
SENALES EN LA VENTANA • 1974 • Chavarri Jaime • SHT • SPN
SENATE PAGE BOYS see **ADVENTURE IN WASHINGTON** • 1941
SENATOR, DER see **JAHRE VERGEHEN, DIE** • 1944
SENATOR, THE • 1916 • Golden Joseph A. • USA
SENATOR, THE see **SEDUCTION OF JOE TYNAN, THE** • 1979
SENATOR WAS INDISCREET, THE • 1947 • Kaufman George S. • USA • MR. ASHTON WAS INDISCREET (UKN)
SENATOR'S BILL, THE • 1914 • *Leonard Robert* • USA
SENATOR'S BROTHER, THE • 1914 • Humphrey William • USA
SENATOR'S DAUGHTER, THE • 1979 • Flowers Don • USA
SENATOR'S DISHONOR, THE • 1913 • *Davenport E. L.* • USA
SENATOR'S DOUBLE, THE • 1910 • Salter Harry • USA
SENATOR'S LADY, THE • 1914 • *Maison Edna* • USA
SENBAZURU • 1953 • Yoshimura Kozaburo • JPN • THOUSAND CRANES, A
SENBAZURU • 1958 • Kimura Sotoji • JPN • PAPER CRANES, THE
SENBAZURU • 1969 • Masumura Yasuzo • JPN • THOUSAND CRANES
SENBAZURU HICHO • 1959 • Misumi Kenji • JPN • THOUSAND CRANES FLYING, A
SEND A GORILLA • 1988 • Read Melanie • NZL
SEND A MAN AT HALF-PAST ONE see **POSALJI COVEKA U POLA DVA** • 1967
SEND ANOTHER COFFIN see **SLIGHTLY HONORABLE** • 1940
SEND 'EM BACK HALF DEAD • 1933 • Davis Redd • UKN
SEND FOR PAUL TEMPLE • 1946 • Argyle John F. • UKN
SEND HOME NO.7 (USA) see **SKICKA HEM NR.7** • 1937
SEND IN THE CLOWNS see **T'AI-SHANG T'AI-HSIA** • 1983
SEND ME NO FLOWERS • 1964 • Jewison Norman • USA
SEND NO.7 HOME see **SKICKA HEM NR.7** • 1937
SEND YOUR ELEPHANT TO CAMP • 1962 • Bartsch Art • ANS • USA
SENDA IGNORADA • 1946 • Nieves Conde Jose Antonio • SPN
SENDA OSCURA, LA • 1947 • Barth-Moglia Luis • ARG
SENDA PROHIBIDA • 1959 • Crevenna Alfredo B. • MXC
SENDA TORCIDA • 1963 • Santillan Antonio • SPN
SENDAS DEL DESTINO • 1939 • Ortega Juan J. • MXC
SENDAS MARCADAS • 1961 • Bosch Juan • SPN
SENDER, THE • 1983 • Christian Roger • UKN
SENDEROS DE FE • 1939 • Barth-Moglia Luis • ARG
SENDETID • 1979 • Risan Leidulv • SHT • NRW • SCREEN TIME
SENDING DER LYSISTRATA, DIE • 1961 • Kortner Fritz • FRG
SENDO KOUTA • 1923 • Ikeda Gishun • JPN • SONG OF THE BOATMAN, THE
SENDUNG DES JOGHI, DIE see **INDISCHE GRABMAL I, DAS** • 1921
SENECHAL LE MAGNIFIQUE • 1957 • Boyer Jean • FRN, ITL • CAPITANO DELLA LEGIONE, IL (ITL) ○ SENECHAL THE MAGNIFICENT (USA) ○ HIS GREATEST ROLE
SENECHAL THE MAGNIFICENT (USA) see **SENECHAL LE MAGNIFIQUE** • 1957
SENGO ZANKOKU MONOGATARI • 1968 • Takechi Tetsuji • JPN • MASS VIOLATION, THE
SENGOKU BURAI • 1952 • Inagaki Hiroshi • JPN • SWORD FOR HIRE ○ MERCENARIES, THE
SENGOKU GUNTODEN • 1959 • Sugie Toshio • JPN • SAGA OF THE VAGABONDS ○ ROBBER SAGA, THE
SENGOKU JIEITAI • 1979 • Saito Mitsumasa • JPN • SLIP OF THE BATTLE FIELD, THE ○ DAY OF THE APOCALYPSE ○ TIME SLIP ○ TELE ○ TIME WARS
SENGOKU YARO • 1963 • Okamoto Kihachi • JPN • WARRING CLANS (USA)
SENHIME • 1954 • Kimura Keigo • JPN • PRINCESS SEN
SENHIME GOTEN • 1960 • Misumi Kenji • JPN • PRINCESS IN EDO
SENHOR, O • 1959 • Campos Antonio • SHT • PRT
SENHORES DA TERRA, OS • 1971 • Thiago Paulo • BRZ • MASTERS OF THE LAND
SENI AFFEDEMEN • 1967 • Sagiroglu Duygu • TRK • I CAN'T FORGIVE YOU
SENI KALBIME GONDUM • 1982 • Tuna Feyzi • TRK • BURIED IN MY HEART
SENI KAYBEDERESEN • 1961 • Yilmaz Atif • TRK • IF I LOSE YOU
SENILITA • 1962 • Bolognini Mauro • ITL, FRN • WHEN A MAN GROWS OLD
SENINLE SONDEFA • 1980 • Tuna Feyzi • TRK • LAST TIME WITH YOU, THE
SENIOR PROM • 1958 • Rich David Lowell • USA
SENIOR TRIP • 1981 • Johnson Kenneth • TVM • USA
SENIOR WEEK • 1987 • Goldman Stuart • USA
SENIOR YEAR • 1974 • Donner Richard • TVM • USA
SENIORCHEF, DER • 1942 • Brauer Peter P. • FRG
SENIORITY VERSUS ABILITY • 1968 • Devlin Bernard • DCS • CND • ANCIENNETE ET COMPETENCE
SENIORS • 1978 • Amateau Rod • USA
SENIORS, JUNIORS, COLLEAGUES see **UWAYAKU SHITAYAKU GODOYAKU** • 1959
SENJA MERAH • 1982 • Abu-Hassan Hussein • MLY
SENJIN • 1935 • Ogata Juzaburo • JPN • BATTLE DUST
SENJO NI NAGARERU UTA • 1965 • Matsuyama Zenzo • JPN • WE WILL REMEMBER
SENK FILIA, A • 1917 • Curtiz Michael • HNG • SENKI FIA, A ○ NOBODY'S SON
SEN'KA AFRIKANEC • 1927 • Ivanov-Vano Ivan • ANS • USS • SENKA THE AFRICAN
SENKA NO HATE • 1950 • Yoshimura Kozaburo • JPN • END OF WAR DISASTERS ○ HEIGHT OF BATTLE, THE ○ END OF BATTLE FIRE, THE
SENKA THE AFRICAN see **SEN'KA AFRIKANEC** • 1927
SENKETSU NO TOBA • 1968 • Nomura Takeshi • JPN • BROKEN VOW, THE
SENKI FIA, A see **SENK FILIA, A** • 1917
SENKYAKU BANRAI • 1962 • Nakamura Noboru • JPN
SENKYRKA U DIVOKE KRASY • 1932 • Innemann Svatopluk • CZC • RAVISHING BARMAID, THE
SENNIN BURAKU • 1960 • Magatani Morehei • JPN • INVITATION TO THE ENCHANTED TOWN
SENOR ALCALDE, EL • 1922 • Castilla Enrique • MXC
SENOR ALCALDE, EL • 1938 • Martinez Solares Gilberto • MXC
SENOR AMERICANO • 1929 • Brown Harry J. • USA
SENOR DAREDEVIL • 1926 • Rogell Albert S. • USA
SENOR DE LA SALLE, EL • 1964 • Amadori Luis Cesar • SPN
SENOR DE OSANTO, EL • 1972 • *Churubusco Azteca* • MXC
SENOR DOCTOR, EL • 1965 • Delgado Miguel M. • MXC
SENOR DROOPY • 1949 • Avery Tex • ANS • USA
SENOR ESTA SERVIDO, EL • 1975 • Isla Sinesio • SPN
SENOR ESTEVE, EL • 1948 • Neville Edgar • SPN
SENOR FOTOGRAFO, EL • 1952 • Delgado Miguel M. • MXC
SENOR GOBERNADOR, EL • 1950 • Cortazar Ernesto • MXC
SENOR GRINGO see **FURY IN PARADISE** • 1955
SENOR JIM • 1936 • Jaccard Jacques • USA • MURDER IN THE DARK (UKN)
SENOR MUCAMO, UN • 1940 • Discepolo Enrique Santos • ARG
SENOR PRESIDENTE, EL • 1970 • Madanes Marcos • ARG
SENOR PRESIDENTE, EL see **SR. PRESIDENTE, EL** • 1983
SENOR TORMENTA, EL • 1962 • Fernandez Fernando • MXC
SENORA AMA • 1954 • Bracho Julio • MXC, SPN
SENORA BOLERO • 1989 • Vera Marilda • VNZ • LADY BOLERO
SENORA CASADA NECEISITA MARIDO • 1935 • Tinling James • USA • MARRIED WOMAN NEEDS A HUSBAND, A
SENORA DE ENFRENTE, LA • 1945 • Martinez Solares Gilberto • MXC
SENORA DE FATIMA, LA • 1951 • Gil Rafael • SPN
SENORA DE INTENDENTE, LA • 1967 • Bo Armando • ARG • DIRECTOR'S WIFE, THE
SENORA DE NADIE • 1982 • Bemberg Maria Luisa • ARG • NOBODY'S WIFE
SENORA DOCTOR • 1973 • Ozores Mariano • SPN
SENORA ESTUPENDA, UNA • 1968 • Martin Eugenio • SPN, MXC • AMAZING WOMAN, AN
SENORA LLAMADA ANDRES, UNA • 1970 • Buchs Julio • SPN • LADY CALLED ANDREW, A
SENORA MOVIDA, UNA • 1958 • Cardona Rene • MXC
SENORA MUERTE, LA • 1968 • Salvador Jaime • MXC • DEATH WOMAN, THE (UKN) ○ MRS. DEATH (USA) ○ MADAME DEATH
SENORA TENTACION • 1947 • Diaz Morales Jose • MXC
SENORELLA AND THE GLASS HUARACHE • 1964 • Freleng Friz • ANS • USA
SENORES GENERALES, SENORES CORONELES • Dagron Alfonso Gumucio • BLV
SENORITA • 1921 • Gliddon John • UKN
SENORITA • 1927 • Badger Clarence • USA
SENORITA, THE • 1909 • *Selig* • USA
SENORITA DE TREVELEZ, LA • 1935 • Neville Edgar • SPN
SENORITA FILLIS, QUEEN OF THE REVOLVING GLOBE • 1903 • *Urban Trading Co* • UKN
SENORITA FROM THE WEST • 1945 • Strayer Frank • USA • HAVE A HEART
SENORITA INUTIL, LA • 1921 • Buchs Jose • SPN
SENORITAS • 1958 • Mendez Fernando • MXC
SENORITA'S BUTTERFLY, THE • 1912 • *Lubin* • USA
SENORITA'S CONQUEST, THE • 1911 • *Gibson Frances* • USA
SENORITAS DE MALA COMPANIA, LAS • 1973 • Nieves Conde Jose Antonio • SPN
SENORITAS DE UNIFORME • 1976 • Delgado Luis Maria • SPN
SENORITA'S REMORSE, THE • 1912 • *Lubin* • USA
SENORITA'S REPENTANCE, THE • 1913 • Duncan William • USA
SENORITA'S SACRIFICE, THE • 1911 • *Yankee* • USA
SENORITAS VIVANCO, LAS • 1958 • de la Serna Mauricio • MXC
SENORITO OCTAVIO, EL • 1950 • Mihura Jeronimo • SPN
SENORITO Y LAS SEDUCTORAS • 1970 • Fernandez Ramon • SPN
SENOR'S SILVER BUCKLE, THE • 1915 • Otto Henry • USA
SENRYO-JISHI • 1958 • Uchida Tomu • JPN • THIEF IS SHOGUN'S KIN, THE
SENRYO KOISHI • 1935 • Inagaki Hiroshi • JPN
SENS DE LA MORT, LE • 1922 • Protazanov Yakov • FRN
SENSACIONAL Y EXTRANO CASO DEL HOMBRE Y LA BESTIA, EL see **EXTRANO CASO DEL HOMBRE Y LA BESTIA, EL** • 1951
SENSATION • 1937 • Hurst Brian Desmond • UKN
SENSATION see **SZENZACIO** • 1922
SENSATION see **MISLEADING LADY, THE** • 1932
SENSATION see **TOP SENSATION** • 1969
SENSATION GENERATION • 1969 • *King Sherry* • USA • SENSATIONAL GENERATION
SENSATION HUNTERS • 1933 • Vidor Charles • USA
SENSATION HUNTERS • 1946 • Cabanne W. Christy • USA
SENSATION IM SAVOY • 1950 • von Borsody Eduard • FRG
SENSATION IM WINTERGARTEN • 1929 • Righelli Gennaro • FRG
SENSATION IN SAN REMO • 1951 • Jacoby Georg • FRG
SENSATION SEEKERS • 1927 • Weber Lois • USA
SENSATIONAL FISHING SCENE • 1899 • *Haydon & Urry* • UKN
SENSATIONAL GENERATION see **SENSATION GENERATION** • 1969
SENSATIONAL SHEATH GOWN, THE • 1908 • *Lubin* • USA
SENSATIONELLEN ERLEBNISSE GEHEIMAGENTEN. ERSTES ERLEBNIS: DER SCHRECKEN DER MILLIONARE • 1923 • *Kuhnast-Film* • FRG • SCHRECKEN DER MILLIONARE, DER
SENSATIONS • 1973 • Seguin Robert • CND
SENSATIONS • 1975 • Ferro Alberto • NTH
SENSATIONS • 1977 • Shillingford Peter, Grant David • UKN
SENSATIONS • 1988 • Vincent Chuck • USA
SENSATIONS see **SENSATIONS OF 1945** • 1944
SENSATIONS OF 1945 • 1944 • Stone Andrew L. • USA • SENSATIONS
SENSATIONS-PROZESS • 1928 • Feher Friedrich • FRG
SENSATIONSPROZESS CASSILLA • 1939 • von Borsody Eduard • FRG
SENSE AND SENSIBILITY • 1980 • Bennett Rodney • MTV • UKN
SENSE OF COMMUNITY, A • 1983 • Rodgers Bob • DOC • CND
SENSE OF FREEDOM, A • 1981 • Mackenzie John • UKN
SENSE OF HUMOR, A • 1913 • Seay Charles M. • USA
SENSE OF HUMUS, A • 1976 • Chapman Christopher • DOC • CND
SENSE OF LOSS, A • 1972 • Ophuls Marcel • DOC • USA, SWT
SENSE OF MUSIC • 1983 • Walker John • CND
SENSE OF PLACE, A • 1975 • Bonniere Rene • DOC • CND
SENSE OF RESPONSIBILITY, A • 1971 • Ball Alan • ANS • UKN
SENSEI NO TSUSHINBO • 1977 • Takeda Kazunari • JPN • TEACHER'S MARK CARD, THE
SENSELESS • 1962 • Rice Ron • SHT • USA
SENSES see **SENSI** • 1987
SENSI • 1987 • Lava Gabriele • ITL • SENSES
SENSITIVE, PASSIONATE MAN, A • 1977 • Newland John • TVM • USA
SENSITIVE SPOT see **CITLIVA MISTA** • 1987
SENSIZ YASAYAMAM • 1980 • Erksan Metin • TRK • I CANNOT LIVE WITHOUT YOU
SENSO • 1954 • Visconti Luchino • ITL • WANTON COUNTESS, THE ○ WANTON CONTESSA, THE ○ SENTIMENT
SENSO TO HEIWA • 1947 • Kamei Fumio, Yamamoto Satsuo • JPN • WAR AND PEACE
SENSO TO NINGEN • 1970 • Yamamoto Satsuo • JPN • HUMAN BEING AND WAR ○ BATTLE OF MANCHURIA, THE ○ MEN AND WAR
SENSO TO NINGEN, KAKETSU-HEN • 1973 • Yamamoto Satsuo • JPN • WAR AND PEOPLE NO.3
SENSOMMER • 1988 • Skolmen Roar • NRW • INDIAN SUMMER ○ SUMMER'S ENDING ○ GULT OG SORT ○ YELLOW AND BLACK
SENSUAL FIRE • 1979 • Tobalina Carlos • USA
SENSUAL JUNGLE (UKN) see **CAUTIVA DE LA SELVA, LA** • 1968
SENSUAL PARADISE (UKN) see **TOGETHER** • 1972
SENSUAL PLEASURES, THE • Li Han-Hsiang • HKG
SENSUAL SORCERESS see **DIABLE EST PARMI NOUS, LE** • 1972
SENSUAL WOMAN, THE see **SENSUALLY LIBERATED FEMALE, THE** • 1970
SENSUALIDAD • 1950 • Gout Alberto • MXC • SENSUALITY
SENSUALIDAD • 1973 • Lorente German • SPN
SENSUALIST, THE • 1966 • Goldman Peter Emanuel • USA • SENSUALISTS, THE
SENSUALIST, THE see **TURKS FRUITS** • 1973
SENSUALISTS, THE see **SENSUALIST, THE** • 1966

SENSUALITA • 1952 • Fracassi Clemente • ITL • BAREFOOT SAVAGE, THE (USA) ○ ENTICEMENT (UKN)
SENSUALITA: E UN ATTIMO DI VITA, LA • 1975 • Marracini Dante • ITL
SENSUALITY see **SENSUALIDAD** • 1950
SENSUALLY LIBERATED FEMALE, THE • 1970 • *New World Studio* • USA • SEXUALLY LIBERATED FEMALE, THE ○ SENSUAL WOMAN, THE ○ WOMAN AND LOVER ○ SEXUOUS FEMALE, THE
SENSUELLA • 1971 • Tulio Teuvo • FNL
SENSUIKAN E-57 KOFUKUSEZU • 1959 • Matsubayashi Shue • JPN • SUBMARINE E-57 NEVER SURRENDERS
SENSUOUS ASSASSIN, THE (USA) see **QUI?** • 1970
SENSUOUS DETECTIVE, THE • Dimitri M. M. • USA
SENSUOUS FLYGIRLS, THE • 1976 • Zuba Constantine, Berland Nicholas • USA
SENSUOUS NURSE, THE see **INFERMIERA, L'** • 1975
SENSUOUS SORCERESS • 1973 • Beaudin Jean • CND
SENSUOUS VAMPIRES see **VAMPIRE HOOKERS** • 1978
SENTA AUF ABWEGEN • 1959 • Hellberg Martin • GDR • SENTA GOES ASTRAY
SENTA GOES ASTRAY see **SENTA AUF ABWEGEN** • 1959
SENTADOS AL BORDE DE LA MANANA CON LOS PIES COLGADOS • 1978 • Betancor Antonio Jose • SPN
SENTENCE, LA • 1959 • Valere Jean • FRN
SENTENCE, THE see **MAN WHO TALKED TOO MUCH, THE** • 1940
SENTENCE, THE see **WYROK** • 1961
SENTENCE IS DEATH, THE • 1914 • Somers Dalton • UKN
SENTENCE OF DEATH, THE • 1913 • Pearson George • UKN
SENTENCE OF DEATH, THE • 1927 • Mander Miles • UKN • HIS GREAT MOMENT
SENTENCE SUSPENDED (UKN) see **MILITARY ACADEMY WITH THAT 10TH AVENUE GANG** • 1950
SENTENCED FOR LIFE • 1911 • ASL
SENTENCED FOR LIFE • 1960 • Varnel Max • UKN
SENTENCED FOR LIFE • 1979 • Barbash Uri • MTV • ISR
SENTENCED TO SOFT LABOR see **BREATHLESS MOMENT, THE** • 1924
SENTENCIA • 1949 • Gomez Muriel Emilio • MXC
SENTENCIA CONTRA UNA MUJER • 1960 • Isasi Antonio • SPN
SENTENCIADO A MUERTE • 1950 • Urruchua Victor • MXC
SENTENCING DILEMMA • 1985 • Pacheco Bruno-Lazaro • DOC • CND
SENTENZA DI MORTE • 1967 • Lanfranchi Mario • ITL • DEATH SENTENCE (UKN)
SENTIERI DELL'ODIO, I • 1965 • Girolami Marino • ITL • PATHS OF HATE
SENTIERO DEI DISPERATI, IL (ITL) see **RAT D'AMERIQUE, LE** • 1962
SENTIERO DELL'ODIO, IL • 1952 • Grieco Sergio • ITL • TERRA D'ODIO
SENTIMENT see **SENSO** • 1954
SENTIMENT AND REASON see **ROZUM A CIT** • 1962
SENTIMENT AND SONG (UKN) see **SONG OF THE PRAIRIE** • 1945
SENTIMENTAL BLOKE • 1932 • Thring F. W. • ASL
SENTIMENTAL BLOKE, THE • 1919 • Longford Raymond • ASL
SENTIMENTAL BURGLAR, A • 1914 • Costello Maurice, Gaillord Robert • USA
SENTIMENTAL EXPERIMENT see **TENTATIVO SENTIMENTALE, UN** • 1963
SENTIMENTAL JOURNALIST see **NAKIMUSHI KISHA** • 1950
SENTIMENTAL JOURNEY • 1943 • Brook Peter • UKN
SENTIMENTAL JOURNEY • 1946 • Lang Walter • USA
SENTIMENTAL JOURNEY • 1984 • Goldstone James • TVM • USA
SENTIMENTAL JOURNEY (USA) see **VOYAGE EN DOUCE, LE** • 1980
SENTIMENTAL LADY, THE • 1915 • Olcott Sidney • USA
SENTIMENTAL REASONS • 1984 • Montesi Jorge • CND
SENTIMENTAL (REQUIEM FOR A FRIEND) see **SENTIMENTAL (REQUIEM PARA UN AMIGO)** • 1981
SENTIMENTAL (REQUIEM PARA UN AMIGO) • 1981 • Renan Sergio • ARG • SENTIMENTAL (REQUIEM FOR A FRIEND)
SENTIMENTAL SISTER, THE • 1914 • Kirkwood James • USA
SENTIMENTAL SOPHIE • 1915 • *Essanay* • USA
SENTIMENTAL STORY, A see **POVESTE SENTIMENTALA** • 1961
SENTIMENTAL STORY, A see **SENTIMENTALNYI ROMAN** • 1976
SENTIMENTAL SWORDSMAN, THE see **TO-CH'ING CHIEN-K'O WU-CH'ING CHIEN** • 1978
SENTIMENTAL SWORDSMAN AND THE RUTHLESS BLADE, THE see **TO-CH'ING CHIEN-K'O TUAN-CH'ING TAO** • 1979
SENTIMENTAL TOMMY • 1915 • Cooper Toby? • UKN
SENTIMENTAL TOMMY • 1921 • Robertson John S. • USA
SENTIMENTALNYI ROMAN • 1976 • Maslennikov Igor • USS • SENTIMENTAL STORY, A
SENTIMIENTOS -MIRTA DE LINIERS A ESTAMBUL • 1987 • Coscia Jorge, Guillermo Saura • ARG • FEELINGS -MIRTA FROM LINIERS TO ISTANBUL
SENTINEL, THE • 1977 • Winner Michael • USA
SENTINEL ASLEEP, THE • 1911 • *Pickford Mary* • USA
SENTINEL OF THE SEA • 1981 • Stoneman John • MTV • CND
SENTINELLE DI BRONZO • 1937 • Marcellini Romolo • ITL
SENTINELLE ENDORMIE, LA • 1965 • Dreville Jean • FRN, ITL
SENTINELLES DE L'EMPIRE • 1938 • d'Esme Jean • DOC • FRN
SENTINELS OF SILENCE • 1971 • *Welles Orson (N)* • USA
SENTINELS OF THE SEA see **MAILMAN, THE** • 1923
SENTINELS UNDER THE NEON LIGHTS • 1963 • Wang Ping, Ko Hsin • CHN
SENTIVANO UNO STRANO, ECCITANTE, PERICOLOSO PUZZO DI DOLLARI • 1973 • Alfaro Italo • ITL
SENTRY'S STRATAGEM, THE see **OURS ET LA SENTINELLE, L'** • 1899
SENYORA, LA • 1987 • Cadena Jordi • SPN • LADY, THE
SENYUM DAN TANIS • 1974 • Rizal A. • INN • SMILES AND TEARS
SENYUM DIPAGI BULAN SEPTEMBER • 1974 • Umboh Wim • INN • SMILES ON A SEPTEMBER MORNING
SENZA BANDIERA • 1951 • De Felice Lionello • ITL
SENZA BUCCIA • 1979 • Aliprandi Marcello • ITL • SKIN DEEP ○ WITHOUT THE PEEL
SENZA CIELO • 1940 • Guarini Alfredo • ITL • DEA BIANCA, LA
SENZA COLPA • 1915 • Gallone Carmine • ITL
SENZA COLPA • 1920 • Serena Gustavo • ITL
SENZA DIO, I • 1972 • Montero Roberto Bianchi • ITL, SPN • SIN DIOS, LOS (SPN)
SENZA FAMIGLIA see **SENZA FAMIGLIA NULLA TENENTI CERCANO AFFETTO** • 1972
SENZA FAMIGLIA (ITL) see **SANS FAMILLE** • 1957
SENZA FAMIGLIA NULLA TENENTI CERCANO AFFETTO • 1972 • Gassman Vittorio • ITL • WITHOUT FAMILY, OR.. ○ SENZA FAMIGLIA
SENZA LUCE -NESSUNO SPAZIO • 1987 • Pfaffli Andres • DOC • SWT
SENZA MOVENTE (ITL) see **SANS MOBILE APPARENT** • 1971
SENZA NOME, I (ITL) see **CERCLE ROUGE, LE** • 1970
SENZA PIETA • 1921 • Ghione Emilio • ITL
SENZA PIETA • 1948 • Lattuada Alberto • ITL • WITHOUT PITY
SENZA RAGIONE (ITL) see **REDNECK** • 1972
SENZA SAPERE NIENTE DI LEI • 1969 • Comencini Luigi • ITL
SENZA SCRUPOLI • 1985 • Valerii Tonino • ITL • NO SCRUPLES
SENZA SOLE NE LUNA • 1964 • Ricci Luciano • ITL
SENZA TITOLO • 1978 • Carrubba Franco • ITL
SENZA UNA DONNA • 1943 • Guarini Alfredo • ITL
SENZA VELI • 1953 • Gallone Carmine • ITL
SENZA VIA D'USCITA • 1971 • Sciume Piero • ITL • NO EXIT (USA)
SEOBE • 1989 • Petrovic Aleksandar • YGS, FRN • MIGRATIONS
SEPARACION MATRIMONIAL • 1973 • Fons Angelino • SPN
SEPARATE BEDS see **BASATRHAYE JODAGANE** • 1968
SEPARATE BEDS (UKN) see **WHEELER DEALERS, THE** • 1963
SEPARATE FROM SARAH • 1916 • *Dunkinson Harry* • SHT • USA
SEPARATE PEACE, A • 1972 • Peerce Larry • USA
SEPARATE ROOMS see **NOTRE HISTOIRE** • 1984
SEPARATE TABLES • 1958 • Mann Delbert • USA
SEPARATE TABLES • 1983 • Schlesinger John • TVM • USA
SEPARATE VACATIONS • 1986 • Anderson Michael • CND
SEPARATE WAYS • 1981 • Avedis Howard • USA • VALENTINE
SEPARATI IN CASA • 1985 • Pazzaglia Riccardo • ITL • DIVORCED AT HOME
SEPARATION • 1968 • Bond Jack • UKN
SEPARATION DES RACES, LA see **RAPT** • 1934
SEPIA CINDERELLA • 1947 • Leonard Arthur • USA
SEPOLCRO DEI RE, IL • 1961 • Cerchio Fernando • ITL, FRN • VALLEE DES PHARAONS, LA (FRN) ○ CLEOPATRA'S DAUGHTER (USA) ○ DAUGHTER OF CLEOPATRA ○ TOMB OF THE KING, THE
SEPOLCRO INDIANO, IL (ITL) see **INDISCHE GRABMAL, DAS** • 1959
SEPOLTA VIVA, LA • 1949 • Brignone Guido • ITL • BURIED ALIVE
SEPOLTA VIVA, LA • 1973 • Lado Aldo • ITL
SEPOY'S WIFE, THE • 1910 • *Young Clara Kimball* • USA
SEPPUKU • 1962 • Kobayashi Masaki • JPN • HARAKIRI
SEPPUN NO TANIMA • 1959 • Nomura Kosho • JPN
SEPT BARRES D'OR, LES • 1910 • Melies Georges • FRN • SEVEN INGOTS OF GOLD, THE
SEPT CHATEAUX DU DIABLE, LES • 1901 • Zecca Ferdinand • FRN • SEVEN CASTLES OF THE DEVIL, THE
SEPT DE TREFLE, LE • 1921 • Navarre Rene • FRN
SEPT EPEES POUR LE ROI see **SETTE SPADE DEL VENDICATORE, LE** • 1963
SEPT FILLES, LES see **SABU BANAT, AS-** • 1960
SEPT FOIS FEMME (FRN) see **WOMAN TIMES SEVEN** • 1967
SEPT FOIS PAR JOUR.. • 1971 • Heroux Denis • CND, ISR • SEVEN TIMES A DAY
SEPT GARS ET UNE GARCE • 1966 • Borderie Bernard • FRN, ITL, RMN • SEPT HOMMES ET UNE GARCE ○ SEVEN GUYS AND A GAL
SEPT HOMMES see **SEPT HOMMES.. UNE FEMME** • 1936
SEPT HOMMES EN OR (FRN) see **SETTE UOMINI D'ORO** • 1965
SEPT HOMMES ET UNE GARCE see **SEPT GARS ET UNE GARCE** • 1966
SEPT HOMMES POUR TOBROUK (FRN) see **BATTAGLIA DEL DESERTO, LA** • 1969
SEPT HOMMES.. UNE FEMME • 1936 • Mirande Yves • FRN • SEPT HOMMES
SEPT JOURS AILLEURS • 1968 • Karmitz Marin • FRN • SEVEN DAYS SOMEWHERE ELSE
SEPT JOURS AU PARADIS see **SABAT AYAM FIL GANNA** • 1969
SEPT MORTS SUR ORDONNANCE • 1976 • Rouffio Jacques • FRN, FRG, SPN
SEPT PECHES CAPITAUX, LES • 1900 • Melies Georges • FRN • SEVEN CAPITAL SINS, THE (USA)
SEPT PECHES CAPITAUX, LES • 1910 • Feuillade Louis • SER • FRN
SEPT PECHES CAPITAUX, LES • 1951 • Rossellini Roberto, Dreville Jean, Dhomme Sylvain, Chabrol Claude, De Filippo Eduardo, Allegret Yves, Vadim Roger, Godard Jean-Luc, Autant-Lara Claude, Bloettler Ugo, de Broca Philippe, Demy Jacques, Lacombe Georges, Carlo-Rim, Molinaro Edouard • FRN, ITL • SETTE PECCATI CAPITALI, I (ITL) ○ SEVEN CAPITAL SINS, THE ○ SETTE PECCATI CAPITALI, I ○ SEVEN DEADLY SINS, THE ○ SEVEN DEADLY SINS ○ SEVEN CAPITAL SINS
SEPT PEINTRES DU QUEBEC see **PAINTERS OF QUEBEC** • 1944
SEPT PERLES DE LA COURONNE, LES see **PERLES DE LA COURONNE, LES** • 1937
SEPTE ARTE • 1958 • Popescu-Gopo Ion • ANS • RMN • SEVEN ARTS, THE ○ SAPTE ARTE
SEPTEMBER • 1988 • Allen Woody • USA
SEPTEMBER see **SEPTEMBRIE** • 1978
SEPTEMBER 16 see **DEN NASHEY ZHIZNI** • 1960
SEPTEMBER 30, 1955 • 1977 • Bridges James • USA • 24 HOURS OF THE REBEL ○ 9/30/55 ○ NINE THIRTY FIFTY-FIVE
SEPTEMBER '51 • 1984 • Quint Raymond • SHT • ASL
SEPTEMBER 1939 see **WRZESIEN -TAK BYLO** • 1961
SEPTEMBER AFFAIR • 1950 • Dieterle William • USA
SEPTEMBER FIVE AT SAINT-HENRI see **A SAINT-HENRI LE CINQ SEPTEMBRE** • 1962
SEPTEMBER GUN • 1983 • Taylor Don • TVM • USA
SEPTEMBER HEROES, THE see **SEPTEMVRIITSI** • 1954
SEPTEMBER -HOW IT WAS see **WRZESIEN -TAK BYLO** • 1961
SEPTEMBER IN THE RAIN • 1937 • Freleng Friz • ANS • USA
SEPTEMBER LOVE • 1979 • Pakdivijit Chalong • THL
SEPTEMBER LOVE see **SEPTEMBERLIEBE** • 1961
SEPTEMBER MORN • 1914 • *Arling Charles* • USA
SEPTEMBER MORNING, A • 1916 • *Griffith Ray* • SHT • USA
SEPTEMBER NIGHTS see **ZARIJOVE NOCI** • 1957
SEPTEMBER STORM • 1960 • Haskin Byron • USA
SEPTEMBER THOUGHTS • 1961 • Gass Karl • DOC • GDR
SEPTEMBER WHEAT • 1981 • Krieg Peter • DOC
SEPTEMBERLIEBE • 1961 • Maetzig Kurt • GDR • SEPTEMBER LOVE
SEPTEMBRE CHILIEN • 1973 • Muel Bruno, Robichet Theo • DOC • FRN
SEPTEMBRIE • 1978 • Ursu Timotei • RMN • SEPTEMBER
SEPTEMBRISTS see **SEPTEMVRIITSI** • 1954
SEPTEMVRIITSI • 1954 • Zhandov Zahari • BUL • SEPTEMBER HEROES, THE ○ SEPTEMBRISTS
SEPTIEME CIBLE, LA • 1984 • Pinoteau Claude • FRN
SEPTIEME CIEL, LE • 1957 • Bernard Raymond • FRN, ITL • VEDOVA ELETTRICA, LA (ITL)
SEPTIEME COMMANDEMENT, LE • 1957 • Bernard Raymond • FRN
SEPTIEME JOUR DE SAINT-MALO, LE • 1959 • Mesnier Paul • FRN
SEPTIEME JURE, LE • 1962 • Lautner Georges • FRN • SEVENTH JUROR, THE (USA)
SEPTIEME PORTE, LA • 1946 • Zwobada Andre • FRN
SEPTIEMO PARALELO see **SETTIMO PARALELLO** • 1962
SEPTIMA PAGINA • 1950 • Vajda Ladislao • SPN
SEPTIMA'S IDEAL see **IDEAL SEPTIMY** • 1938
SEPTIMO DE CABALLERIA, EL • 1965 • Martin Eugenio • SPN
SEPULCRALES, LAS • 1970 • Aznar Tomas • SHT • SPN
SEPUTIH HATINYA SEMERAH BIBIRNYA • 1981 • Rahardjo Slamet • INN • AS WHITE AS HER HEART, AS RED AS HER LIPS
SEQUEL TO THE DIAMOND IN THE SKY • 1916 • Sloman Edward • SRL • USA
SEQUENCE • 1980 • Winning David • CND
SEQUENCES see **SECUENTE** • 1983
SEQUENCES INTERDITES • 1975 • Benazeraf Jose • FRN
SEQUESTRADOR, EL • 1958 • Torre-Nilsson Leopoldo • ARG • KIDNAPPER, THE ○ SECUESTRADOR, EL
SEQUESTRATI DI ALTONA, I • 1962 • De Sica Vittorio • ITL, FRN • SEQUESTRES D'ALTONA, LES (FRN) ○ CONDEMNED OF ALTONA, THE (USA) ○ PRISONERS OF ALTONA, THE
SEQUESTREE, LA • 1908 • Cohl Emile • ANS • FRN
SEQUESTRES D'ALTONA, LES (FRN) see **SEQUESTRATI DI ALTONA, I** • 1962
SEQUESTRO DI PERSONA • 1968 • Mingozzi Gianfranco • ITL • ISLAND OF CRIME (UKN) ○ RANSOM IN SARDINIA ○ UNLAWFUL RESTRAINT
SEQUOIA • 1934 • Franklin Chester M. • USA
SERA C'INCONTRAMMO, UNA • 1975 • Schivazappa Piero • ITL
SERA DI MAGGIO, UNA • 1955 • Pastina Giorgio • ITL
SERAA FIL MINAA • 1955 • Shahin Youssef • EGY • STRUGGLE IN THE PORT ○ SIRAUN FI AL-MINA ○ STRUGGLE ON THE PIER
SERAA FIL WADA • 1953 • Shahin Youssef • EGY • STRUGGLE IN THE VALLEY ○ BLAZING SUN, THE ○ SIRAUN FI AL-WADI
SERAA MAAL MALAIKA • 1961 • Tewfik Hassan • EGY • STRUGGLE WITH THE ANGELS
SERAFINO • 1968 • Germi Pietro, Kresel Lee (Eng. Version) • ITL, FRN • SERAFINO OU L'AMOUR AUX CHAMPS (FRN)
SERAFINO OU L'AMOUR AUX CHAMPS (FRN) see **SERAFINO** • 1968
SERAGLIO • 1958 • Reiniger Lotte • ANS • UKN
SERAGLIO see **SURREAL** • 1976
SERAIL see **SURREAL** • 1976
SERAMPANG TIGA • 1980 • Sasakul Ismail • MLY
SERANGAN FAJAR • 1981 • Noer Arifin C. • INN • DAWN, THE
SERAPHIN • 1949 • Gury Paul • CND
SERAPHIN OU LES JAMBES NUES • 1921 • Feuillade Louis • FRN
SERAPHINE'S LOVE AFFAIR • 1914 • Seay Charles M. • USA
SERAPHITA'S DIARY • 1982 • Wiseman Frederick • USA
SERATA • 1971 • Ursianu Malvina • RMN • PARTY, THE ○ EVENING
SERATA D'HONORE DI BUFFALO, LA • 1916 • Campogalliani Carlo • ITL
SERATA DI GALA see **FORZA BRUTA, LA** • 1941
SERAYDAR • 1975 • Haritash Khosrow • IRN • GUARDIAN, THE
SERBARILOR GALANTE (RMN) see **FETES GALANTES, LES** • 1965
SERBIAN LADY MACBETH see **SIBIRSKA LEDI MAGBET** • 1962
SERDCE SOLOMONA • 1932 • Gerasimov Sergei, Kressin M. • USS • HEART OF SOLOMON, THE ○ SOLOMON'S HEART
SERDTSE MATERI • 1966 • Donskoi Mark • USS • HEART OF A MOTHER (UKN) ○ SONS AND MOTHERS (USA) ○ MOTHER'S HEART, A ○ SERDZE MATERI
SERDTSYE BETSYA YNOV • 1956 • Room Abram • USS • HEART BEATS ANEW, THE ○ HEART BEATS AGAIN, THE ○ NEW HEART, A
SERDZE MATERI see **SERDTSE MATERI** • 1966
SERE CUALQUIER COSA PERO TE QUIERO • 1986 • Galettini Carlos • ARG • I LOVE YOU, NO MATTER WHAT I AM
SEREBRISTAYA PYL • 1953 • Room Abram • USS • SIERIEBRISTAYA PYL ○ SILVER DUST

SEREGETI DARF NICHT STERBEN • 1959 • Grzimek Michael, Grzimek Bernard • DOC • FRG • SERENGETI SHALL NOT DIE (USA) ○ THEY SHALL NOT DIE
SERENA • Lincoln Fred
SERENA • 1962 • Maxwell Peter • UKN
SERENADE • 1921 • Walsh Raoul • USA
SERENADE • 1927 • D'Arrast Harry D'Abbadie • USA
SERENADE • 1937 • Forst Willi • FRG
SERENADE • 1939 • Boyer Jean • FRN • SCHUBERT'S SERENADE (USA) ○ SERENADE ETERNELLE
SERENADE • 1956 • Mann Anthony • USA
SERENADE see **PRINCESSE CZARDAS** • 1934
SERENADE, THE • 1904 • *Warwick Trading Co* • UKN
SERENADE, THE • 1916 • *Plump & Runt* • USA
SERENADE A DEUX • 1948 • Masson Jean • SHT • FRN
SERENADE AU BOURREAU • 1951 • Stelli Jean • FRN
SERENADE AU TEXAS • 1958 • Pottier Richard • FRN
SERENADE AUX NUAGES • 1945 • Cayatte Andre • FRN
SERENADE BY MOONLIGHT see **SERENATA A LA LUZ DE LA LUNA** • 1979
SERENADE BY PROXY, A • 1913 • Miller Ashley • USA
SERENADE EINER GROSSEN LIEBE • 1959 • Mate Rudolph • FRG, USA, ITL • FOR THE FIRST TIME (USA)
SERENADE ETERNELLE see **SERENADE** • 1939
SERENADE FOR MURDER see **GIRL ON THE SPOT** • 1946
SERENADE FOR TWO SPIES (USA) see **SERENADE FUR ZWEI SPIONE** • 1965
SERENADE FROM "FAUST" • 1906 • Gilbert Arthur • UKN
SERENADE FUR ZWEI SPIONE • 1965 • Pfleghar Michael, Cardone Alberto • FRG, ITL • SINFONIA PER DUE SPIE (ITL) ○ SERENADE FOR TWO SPIES (USA)
SERENADE IN SWING • 1942 • Le Borg Reginald • SHT • USA
SERENADE OF THE WEST (UKN) see **GIT ALONG, LITTLE DOGIES** • 1937
SERENADE OF THE WEST (UKN) see **COWBOY SERENADE** • 1942
SERENADE (UKN) see **BROADWAY SERENADE** • 1939
SERENADERS, THE • 1945 • Negulesco Jean • SHT • USA
SERENAL • 1959 • McLaren Norman • ANS • CND
SERENATA A LA LUZ DE LA LUNA • 1979 • Jover Carlos, Salgot Jose Antonio • SPN • SERENADE BY MOONLIGHT
SERENATA A MARIA • 1957 • Capuano Luigi • ITL
SERENATA AL VENTO • 1956 • De Marchi Luigi • ITL
SERENATA AMARA • 1953 • Mercanti Pino • ITL
SERENATA D'AMORE • 1965 • Lattanzi Franco • ITL
SERENATA D'AMORE see **PRIGIONE, LA** • 1942
SERENATA DI SCHUBERT, LA • 1920 • Serena Gustavo • ITL
SERENATA EN ACAPULCO • 1950 • Urueta Chano • MXC
SERENATA EN MEXICO • 1955 • Urueta Chano • MXC
SERENATA EN NOCHE DE LUNA • 1965 • Soler Julian • MXC
SERENATA ESPANOLA • 1947 • de Orduna Juan • SPN
SERENATA PER SEDICI BIONDE • 1957 • Girolami Marino • ITL
SERENATA TRAGICA • 1951 • Guarino Joseph • ITL • GUAPPARIA
SERENATA ZIGANA • 1929 • Negroni Baldassare • ITL
SERENATELLA SCIUE SCIUE • 1958 • Campogalliani Carlo • ITL
SERENDIPITY • Kolar Boris • ANS • YGS
SERENE SIAM • 1937 • Fitzpatrick James • SHT • USA
SERENE VELOCITY • 1970 • Gehr Ernie • SHT • USA
SERENGETI SHALL NOT DIE (USA) see **SEREGETI DARF NICHT STERBEN** • 1959
SERENISSIMUS LERNT TANGO • 1914 • Rye Stellan • FRG
SERENISSIMUS UND DIE LETZTE JUNGFRAU • 1928 • Mittler Leo • FRG
SERENITY • 1962 • Markopoulos Gregory J. • USA
SERENYI, DIE • 1918 • Halm Alfred • FRG
SEREZHA • 1960 • Daneliya Georgi, Talankin Igor • USS • SUMMER TO REMEMBER, A (USA) ○ SPLENDID DAYS, THE ○ SERYOZHA (THE SPLENDID DAYS) ○ SERYOZHA
SERF-ACTRESS, A • 1963 • Tikhomirov G. V. • USS
SERFS see **NONGNU** • 1964
SERGE ET REAL • 1963-64 • Fournier Claude • DCS • CND
SERGE PANINE • 1913 • Pouctal Henri • FRN
SERGE PANINE • 1915 • Physioc Wray • USA
SERGE PANINE • 1922 • Maudru Charles, de Marsan Maurice • FRN
SERGE PANINE • 1938 • Mere Charles, Schiller Paul • FRN
SERGEANT 45 • 1967 • Dantes Tony • PHL
SERGEANT, THE • 1910 • *Selig* • USA
SERGEANT, THE • 1968 • Flynn John • USA
SERGEANT, THE • 1990 • Kimiyaei Massoud • IRN
SERGEANT, THE see **KREK** • 1967
SERGEANT BERRY • 1938 • Selpin Herbert • FRG
SERGEANT BLUE see **GATLING GUN, THE** • 1972
SERGEANT BYRNE OF THE N.W.M.P. • 1912 • Campbell Colin • USA
SERGEANT DEADHEAD • 1965 • Taurog Norman • USA • SERGEANT DEADHEAD THE ASTRONUT!
SERGEANT DEADHEAD THE ASTRONUT! see **SERGEANT DEADHEAD** • 1965
SERGEANT DILLON'S BRAVERY • 1911 • *Solax* • USA
SERGEANT GETULIO see **SARGENTO GETULIO** • 1982
SERGEANT HAMMON OF THE R.C.M.P. • 1920 • Craft William James • USA
SERGEANT HOFMEYER • 1914 • *Sterling Ford* • USA
SERGEANT JIM (USA) see **DOLINA MIRU** • 1956
SERGEANT JIM'S HORSE • 1915 • *Kb* • USA
SERGEANT KLEMS see **SERGENTE KLEMS, IL** • 1971
SERGEANT LIGHTNING AND THE GORGONZOLA GANG • 1915 • Read James • UKN
SERGEANT MADDEN • 1939 • von Sternberg Josef • USA
SERGEANT MAJOR KALEN see **OGNIOMISTRZ KALEN** • 1961
SERGEANT MATLOVICH VS. THE U.S. AIR FORCE • 1978 • Leaf Paul • TVM • USA
SERGEANT MIKE • 1945 • Levin Henry • USA
SERGEANT MURPHY • 1938 • Eason B. Reeves • USA
SERGEANT RUTLEDGE • 1960 • Ford John • USA • TRIAL OF SERGEANT RUTLEDGE, THE
SERGEANT RYKER • 1967 • Kulik Buzz • USA • COURT MARTIAL OF SGT. RYKER, THE ○ CASE AGAINST PAUL RYKER, THE ○ TORN BETWEEN TWO VALUES
SERGEANT STEINER see **BREAKTHROUGH** • 1978
SERGEANT WAS A LADY, THE • 1961 • Glasser Bernard • USA
SERGEANT WHITE'S PERIL • 1911 • *Lubin* • USA
SERGEANT X • 1931 • von Strischewski Wladimir • FRG • GEHEIMNIS DES FREMDENLEGIONARS, DAS ○ LEGION OF THE LOST
SERGEANT X OF THE FOREIGN LEGION (USA) see **SERGENT X** • 1959
SERGEANT YORK • 1941 • Hawks Howard • USA
SERGEANT'S BOY, THE • 1912 • Barker Reginald • USA
SERGEANT'S DAUGHTER • 1913 • *Foxe Earle* • USA
SERGEANT'S DAUGHTER, THE • 1910 • *Solax* • USA
SERGEANT'S DAUGHTER, THE • 1911 • Noy Wilfred • UKN
SERGEANT'S SECRET, THE • 1913 • *Ray Charles* • USA
SERGEANTS THREE • 1962 • Sturges John • USA • BADLANDS ○ SOLDIERS THREE
SERGEI EISENSTEIN, POSTSCRIPT • Epners A. • DOC • USS
SERGEI EISENSTEIN, PREFACE • Epners A. • DOC • USS
SERGEI YESENIN • 1971 • Urusevsky Sergei • DOC • USS
SERGENT BAKARY WOOLEN • 1966 • Akin Lamine • GUN
SERGENT X • 1959 • Borderie Bernard • FRN • SERGEANT X OF THE FOREIGN LEGION (USA)
SERGENT X, LE • 1931 • von Strischewski Wladimir • FRN • VIVE LA LEGION ○ ISOLES, LES ○ DESERT, LE
SERGENTE D'ISPEZIONE • 1959 • Savarese Roberto • ITL
SERGENTE KLEMS, IL • 1971 • Grieco Sergio • ITL, SPN • MAN OF LEGEND (USA) ○ SERGEANT KLEMS
SERGENTE ROMPIGLIONI, IL • 1973 • Ferretti Piergiorgio • ITL
SERGENTE ROMPIGLIONI DIVENTA.. CAPORALE, IL • 1975 • Laurenti Mariano • ITL
SERGEY LAZO • 1968 • Gordon Alexander • USS
SERGO ORDZHONIKIDZE • 1937 • Vertov Dziga • USS
SERGYL CHEZ LES FILLES • 1951 • Daroy Jacques • FRN
SERGYL ET LE DICTATEUR • 1948 • Daroy Jacques • FRN
SERIAL • 1980 • Persky Bill • USA
SERIE 4 • 1972 • Gregoire Normand • CND
SERIE NOIRE • 1954 • Foucaud Pierre • FRN • INFILTRATOR, THE (USA)
SERIE NOIRE • 1979 • Corneau Alain • FRN
SERIEUX, COMME LE PLAISIR • 1975 • Benayoun Robert • FRN • JE SERAI SERIEUX COMME LE PLAISIR ○ SERIOUS AS PLEASURE
SERIGNE HASSANE • 1972 • Aw Tidiane • SNL
SERIOUS AS PLEASURE see **SERIEUX, COMME LE PLAISIR** • 1975
SERIOUS CHARGE • 1959 • Young Terence • UKN • IMMORAL CHARGE ○ TOUCH OF HELL, A
SERIOUS GAME see **ALLVARSAMMA LEKEN, DEN** • 1945
SERIOUS SIXTEEN • 1910 • Griffith D. W. • USA
SERIS, LOS • 1972 • Cazals Felipe • DOC • MXC
SERMENT DE DOLORES, LE • 1914 • Bourgeois Gerard • FRN
SERMENTS • 1931 • Fescourt Henri • FRN • REBELLE, LE
SERMENTS see **EN NATT** • 1931
SERMOES • 1989 • Bressane Julio • BRZ • SERMONS
SERMONS see **SERMOES** • 1989
SERP I MOLOT • 1921 • Gardin Vladimir • USS • SICKLE AND HAMMER
SERPE • 1919 • Roberti Roberto Leone • ITL
SERPENT, LE • 1973 • Verneuil Henri • FRN, ITL, FRG • SERPENTE, IL (ITL) ○ SERPENT, THE (UKN) ○ NIGHT FLIGHT FROM MOSCOW
SERPENT, THE • 1912 • *Republic* • USA
SERPENT, THE • 1916 • Walsh Raoul • USA • FIRES OF HATE (UKN)
SERPENT, THE • 1918 • Stahl John M. • USA
SERPENT, THE see **ORMEN** • 1966
SERPENT, THE (UKN) see **SERPENT, LE** • 1973
SERPENT AND THE RAINBOW, THE • 1988 • Craven Wes • USA
SERPENT BENEATH, THE see **PRICE OF GREED, THE** • 1955
SERPENT DE LA RUE DE LA LUNE, LE • 1908 • Melies Georges • FRN • SNAKE OF MOON STREET, THE ○ PRANK WITH A FAKE PYTHON
SERPENT-GOD, THE see **DIOS SERPIENTE, EL** • 1970
SERPENT IN THE FOG, THE see **SERPIENTE EN LA NIEBLA, LA** • 1978
SERPENT IN THE HOUSE, A • 1916 • Daly William Robert • SHT • USA
SERPENT ISLAND • 1954 • Gordon Bert I. • USA
SERPENT OF THE NILE • 1953 • Castle William • USA
SERPENT OF THE SLUMS, THE • 1914 • *K & S Feature Film* • USA
SERPENT PRINCESS, THE see **HEBI HIME-SAMA** • 1940
SERPENT WARRIORS • 1986 • Rasmussen Niels • USA
SERPENTARIO, EL • 1971 • Carretero Amaro • ANS • SPN
SERPENTE, IL (ITL) see **SERPENT, LE** • 1973
SERPENTE A SONAGLI, IL • 1935 • Matarazzo Raffaello • ITL
SERPENTELLO • 1897 • *Velograph Syndicate* • UKN
SERPENTIN • 1919-20 • Durand Jean • SER • FRN
SERPENTIN A DRESS BOUBOULE • 1920 • Durand Jean • SHT • FRN
SERPENTIN A ENGAGE BOUBOULE • 1920 • Durand Jean • SHT • FRN
SERPENTIN AU HAREM • 1919 • Durand Jean • SHT • FRN
SERPENTIN ET LES CONTREBANDIERS • 1919 • Durand Jean • SHT • FRN
SERPENTIN FAIT DE LA PEINTURE • 1920 • Durand Jean • SHT • FRN
SERPENTIN LE BONHEUR EST A TOI • 1919 • Durand Jean • SHT • FRN
SERPENTIN MANOEUVRE • 1919 • Durand Jean • SHT • FRN
SERPENTIN REPORTER • 1919 • Durand Jean • SHT • FRN
SERPENTINE DANCE, A see **DANSE SERPENTINE** • 1896
SERPENTINE DANCE -ANNABELLE • 1897 • Dickson W. K. L. • USA • ANNABELLE THE DANCER
SERPENTINE DANCER • 1902 • Collins Alf? • UKN
SERPENTS, THE • 1912 • Ince Ralph • USA
SERPENT'S EGG, THE (USA) see **SCHLANGENEI, DAS** • 1977
SERPENT'S EYES, THE • 1912 • *Rex* • USA
SERPENT'S TOOTH, THE • 1908 • Fitzhamon Lewin? • UKN
SERPENT'S TOOTH, THE • 1915 • Van Wally • USA
SERPENT'S TOOTH, THE • 1917 • Sturgeon Rollin S. • USA
SERPENT'S WAY, THE see **ORMENS VAG PA HALLEBERGET** • 1986
SERPICO • 1974 • Lumet Sidney • USA, ITL
SERPICO: THE DEADLY GAME • 1976 • Collins Robert • TVM • USA • DEADLY GAME, THE
SERPIENTE DE LA LUNA DE LOS PIRATAS, LA • 1972 • Jorge Jean-Louis • DMN
SERPIENTE EN LA NIEBLA, LA • 1978 • Cordido Ivork • VNZ • SERPENT IN THE FOG, THE
SERR EL DOKTOR IBRAHIM • 1936 • Aptekman Alexandre • EGY • SECRET OF DR. IBRAHIM, THE
SERRA BRAVA • 1948 • Miranda Armando • PRT
SERRA DA ESTRELA -GOUVEIA • 1944 • Miranda Armando • SHT • PRT
SERSANT EN DIE TIGER MOTH, DIE • 1973 • SAF
SERSERI • 1967 • Ergun Nuri • TRK • TRAMP, THE
SERSERILER KRALI • 1967 • Dinler Mehmet • TRK • KING OF TRAMPS
SERTANEJO, O • 1954 • Barreto Victor • BRZ
SERTORIO • 1977 • Faria Antonio • PRT
SERUM DU DOCTEUR HORMET, LE • 1929 • Painleve Jean • SHT • FRN
SERVA PADRONA, LA • 1934 • Mannini Giorgio • ITL
SERVANT, THE • 1963 • Losey Joseph • UKN
SERVANT, THE see **GERO** • 1927
SERVANT, THE (UKN) see **SLUGA** • 1988
SERVANT GIRL'S LEGACY, THE • 1914 • Hotaling Arthur D.? • USA
SERVANT IN THE HOUSE, A • 1920 • Conway Jack • USA
SERVANT IN THE HOUSE, THE • 1915 • *Power Tyrone* • USA
SERVANT OF ALL • 1962 • Fox Beryl, Leiterman Douglas • DOC • CND
SERVANT OF THE RICH, A • 1914 • Ince John • USA
SERVANT PROBLEM, OR HOW MR. BULLINGTON RAN THE HOUSE, THE • 1912 • *Turner Florence* • USA
SERVANT QUESTION, THE • 1914 • *Essanay* • USA
SERVANT QUESTION, THE • 1914 • *Komic* • USA
SERVANT QUESTION, THE • 1920 • Henderson Dell • USA
SERVANT QUESTION OUT WEST, THE • 1914 • Duncan William • USA
SERVANTE, LA • 1930 • Choux Jean • FRN
SERVANTE, LA • 1969 • Bertrand Jacques-Paul • FRN
SERVANTE ET MAITRESSE • 1977 • Gantillon Bruno • FRN
SERVANTES DU BON DIEU, LES • 1978 • Letourneau Diane • CND • SERVANTS OF THE GOOD LORD, THE ○ HANDMAIDENS OF GOD, THE
SERVANTES IZ MALOGA MISTA • 1983 • Marusic Daniel • YGS • CERVANTES FROM A SMALL TOWN
SERVANTS, THE see **CH'IANG-NEI CH'IANG-WAI** • 1980
SERVANTS ALL • 1936 • Bryce Alex • UKN
SERVANTS' ENTRANCE • 1934 • Lloyd Frank • USA
SERVANTS' ENTRANCE • 1988 • Medak Peter • USA
SERVANT'S NECK, THE see **GERO NO KUBI** • 1955
SERVANTS OF THE GOOD LORD, THE see **SERVANTES DU BON DIEU, LES** • 1978
SERVANT'S REVENGE, A • 1909 • *Lubin* • USA
SERVANTS SUPERCEDED • 1911 • Stow Percy • UKN
SERVANTS SUPERCEDED • 1914 • *Royal* • USA
SERVES HIM RIGHT • 1977 • Josephson Erland • SWD
SERVEZ-VOUS, MESDAMES • 1972 • Pradier Jean-Paul • FRN
SERVIAN TRAGEDY, THE • 1903 • Winslow Dicky • UKN
SERVICE, THE see **SERVICIO, EL** • 1978
SERVICE DE LUXE • 1938 • Lee Rowland V. • USA
SERVICE DE NUIT • 1931 • Fescourt Henri • FRN • THEODORE EST FATIGUE ○ NUITS DE PAPA, LES ○ POUR SERVICE DE NUIT
SERVICE DE NUIT • 1943 • Faurez Jean, Randone Belisario L. • FRN, ITL • TURNO DI NOTTE (ITL) ○ NUIT COMME LES AUTRES, UNE
SERVICE DE SAUVETAGE SUR LA COTE BELGE, LE • 1930 • Storck Henri • DOC • BLG
SERVICE DU DIABLE see **PLUS LONGUE NUIT DU DIABLE, LA** • 1971
SERVICE FOR FARMERS • 1958 • UKN, VNZ
SERVICE FOR LADIES • 1927 • D'Arrast Harry D'Abbadie • USA • HEAD WAITER, THE
SERVICE FOR LADIES • 1932 • Korda Alexander • UKN • RESERVED FOR LADIES (USA)
SERVICE OF LOVE, A • 1917 • Robertson John S. • SHT • USA
SERVICE PRECIPITE • 1903 • Blache Alice • FRN
SERVICE SECRET • 1914 • Bernard-Deschamps • FRN
SERVICE STAR, THE • 1918 • Miller Charles • USA • FLAG OF MOTHERS, THE
SERVICE (UKN) see **LOOKING FORWARD** • 1933
SERVICE UNDER JOHNSTON AND LEE • 1911 • *Champion* • USA
SERVICE WITH A GUILE • 1946 • Tytla Bill • ANS • USA
SERVICE WITH A SMILE • 1934 • Mack Roy • SHT • USA
SERVICE WITH A SMILE • 1937 • Fleischer Dave • ANS • USA
SERVICE WITH A SMILE • 1964 • Kneitel Seymour • ANS • USA
SERVICE WITH THE COLORS • 1940 • Eason B. Reeves • SHT • USA
SERVICER, THE • 1974 • Capetanis Leon • USA, FRG
SERVICIO, EL • 1978 • Cortes Alberto • MXC • SERVICE, THE
SERVICIO EN LA MAR • 1950 • Suarez De Lozo Luis • SPN
SERVICIO SECRETO • 1959 • Martinez Arturo • MXC
SERVING A SUMMONS • 1907 • Coleby A. E. • UKN
SERVING THE WRIT • 1907 • Fitzhamon Lewin? • UKN
SERVING TWO MASTERS • 1921 • *Earle Josephine* • USA
SERVIZIO DI SCORTA see **SI PUO ESSERE PIU BASTARDI DELL'ISPETTORE CLIFF?** • 1973
SERVUS BAYERN • 1977 • Achternbusch Herbert • FRG
SERYOZHA see **SEREZHA** • 1960
SERYOZHA (THE SPLENDID DAYS) see **SEREZHA** • 1960
SES • 1986 • Okten Zeki • TRK • VOICE, THE
SES ANCETRES • 1915 • Cohl Emile • ANS • FRN
SES PORTUGUESAS • 1959 • Ribeiro Antonio Lopes • SHT • PRT
SES SOLDATE • 1975 • SAF
(SESAME STREET PRESENTS) FOLLOW THAT BIRD see **FOLLOW THAT BIRD** • 1985
SESION CONTINUA • 1984 • Garci Jose Luis • SPN • DOUBLE FEATURE
SESIR • 1976 • Grgic Zlatko • ANS • YGS • HAT, THE

SESSION WITH THE COMMITTEE, A see **COMMITTEE, THE** • 1968
SESSIONS • 1983 • Pearce Richard • TVM • USA
SESSJUK AIRMATA IBU • 1980 • Rahim A. • MLY
SESSO DEGLI ANGELI, IL • 1968 • Liberatore Ugo • ITL, FRG • GESCHLECHT DER ENGEL, DAS (FRG) ○ SEX OF ANGELS, THE (USA) ○ SEX OF THE ANGELS
SESSO DEL DIAVOLO, IL • 1971 • Brazzi Oscar • ITL • TRITTICO
SESSO DELLA STREGA, IL • 1972 • Pannaccio Elo • ITL • SEX OF THE WITCH (USA) ○ WITCH'S SEX, THE ○ POSSESSOR, THE ○ SEX OF A WITCH
SESSO E VOLENTIERI • 1982 • Risi Dino • ITL • SEX AND VIOLENCE
SESSO IN CONFESSIONALE • 1974 • De Sisti Vittorio • ITL
SESSO IN TESTA • 1974 • Ammirata Sergio • ITL • SEX IN THE HEAD ○ SEX ON THE BRAIN
SESSO MATTO • 1973 • Risi Dino • ITL • HOW FUNNY CAN SEX BE (USA) ○ SESSOMATTO ○ MAD SEX
SESSO PROFONDO • 1980 • Martin Frank • ITL • FLYING SEX
SESSO (USA) see **NEL LABIRINTO DEL SESSO** • 1969
SESSOMATTO see **SESSO MATTO** • 1973
SEST CERNYCH DIVEK ANEB PROC ZMIZEL ZATIC? • 1969 • Rychman Ladislav • CZC • SIX BLACK GIRLS
SEST MEDVEDU S CIBULKOU • 1972 • Lipsky Oldrich • CZC • SIX BEARS AND A CLOWN
SESTA BRZINA • 1982 • Sotra Zdravko • YGS • SIXTH GEAR
SESTIG JAAR VAN JOH VORSTER • 1976 • SAF
SESTNACTILETA • 1918 • Palous Jan A. • CZC • TEENAGER, THE
SESTO CONTINENTE • 1954 • Quilici Folco • DOC • ITL • SIXTH CONTINENT ○ BLUE CONTINENT ○ LOST CONTINENT, THE
SESTRA ANGELIKA • 1932 • Fric Martin • CZC • SISTER ANGELICA
SESTRICKY • 1983 • Kachyna Karel • CZC • NURSING SISTERS ○ NURSES
SESTRIERES • 1949 • Cote Guy-L. • DCS • UKN
SESTRY • 1957 • Roshal Grigori • USS • SISTERS
SESTRY • 1970 • Schorm Evald • MTV • CZC • SISTERS
SESTRY RAKHMANOVY • 1954 • Yarmatov Kamil • USS • RAKHMANOV'S SISTERS
SESZELE • 1990 • Linda Boguslaw • PLN • SEYCHELLES
SET, THE • 1970 • Brittain Frank • ASL
SET 'EM UP • 1939 • Feist Felix E. • SHT • USA
SET FREE • 1918 • Browning Tod • USA
SET FREE • 1927 • Rosson Arthur • USA
SET IN MOTION • 1982 • Paakspuu Kalli • CND
SET THIS TOWN ON FIRE • 1969 • Rich David Lowell • USA • TO SET THIS TOWN ON FIRE ○ PROFANE COMEDY, THE
SET-TO BETWEEN JOHN BULL AND PAUL KRUGER • 1901 • *Warwick Trading Co* • UKN
SET TO MUSIC see **SING A JINGLE** • 1944
SET-UP, THE • 1926 • Smith Cliff • USA
SET-UP, THE • 1949 • Wise Robert • USA
SET-UP, THE • 1963 • Glaister Gerald • UKN
SETARE HAYE HAFTASEMOON • 1968 • Madani Hosain • IRN • STARS IN THE SKY, THE
SETE BALAS PARA SELMA • 1967 • de Macedo Antonio • PRT • SEVEN BULLETS FOR SELMA
SETE DELL'ORO, LA • 1919 • Mari Febo • ITL
SETE DIAS DE AGONIA • 1982 • de Oliveira Denoy • BRZ • SEVEN DAYS OF AGONY ○ ENCALHE, O ○ OBSTACLE, THE
SETEA • 1960 • Dragan Mircea • RMN • THIRST
SETENTA VECES SIETE • 1962 • Torre-Nilsson Leopoldo • ARG • FEMALE: SEVENTY TIMES SEVEN (USA) ○ SEVENTY TIMES SEVEN ○ FEMALE, THE
SETENTA VECES SIETE • 1967 • Acaso Felix • SPN
SETH'S SWEETHEART • 1914 • Ransom Charles • USA
SETH'S TEMPTATION • 1910 • Olcott Sidney • USA
SETH'S WOODPILE • 1913 • France Charles H. • USA
SETHU BANDHAN • 1937 • Padmanabhan R. • IND
SETHUBANDAN see **SETU BANDHAN** • 1932
SETINGGAN • 1980 • Sattar Aziz • MLY
SETIPANA • 1978 • SAF
SETKANI V BUKURESTI • 1954 • *Stellich Jan (Ph)* • CZC • MEETING IN BUCHAREST, THE
SETKANI V CERVENI • 1977 • Kachyna Karel • CZC • ENCOUNTER IN JULY, AN ○ MEETING IN JULY
SETOUCHI SHONEN YAKYUDAN • 1984 • Shinoda Masahiro • JPN • BOYS' BASEBALL TEAM OF SETOUCHI ○ MACARTHUR'S CHILDREN
SETRELE PISMO • 1920 • Rovensky Josef • CZC • FADED WRITING, THE
SETT BANAT WA ARISS • 1968 • Ziada El Sayad • EGY • 6 GIRLS AND A BRIDEGROOM
SETTE ANNI DI FELICITA • 1942 • Marischka Ernst, Savarese Roberto • ITL, FRG • SIEBEN JAHRE GLUCK (FRG)
SETTE BASCHI ROSSI • 1968 • Siciliano Mario • ITL, FRG • CONGO HELL (UKN) ○ SEVEN RED BERETS
SETTE CADAVERI PER SCOTLAND YARD (ITL) see **JACK, EL DESTRIPADOR DE LONDRES** • 1971
SETTE CANNE E UN VESTITO see **SETTE CANNE, UN VESTITO** • 1950
SETTE CANNE, UN VESTITO • 1950 • Antonioni Michelangelo • DCS • ITL • SETTE CANNE E UN VESTITO
SETTE CANZONI PER SETTE SORELLE • 1957 • Girolami Marino • ITL
SETTE CERVELLI PER UN COLPO PERFETTO • 1972 • Pigaut Roger • ITL
SETTE CINESI D'ORO, LE • 1967 • Cascino Vincenzo • ITL • SEVEN GOLDEN CHINESE, THE
SETTE COLT PER SETTE CAROGNE • 1968 • Chardon Richard • ITL
SETTE CONTADINI, I • 1957 • Petri Elio • SHT • ITL
SETTE CONTRO LA MORTE • 1965 • Ulmer Edgar G. • ITL, FRG • HELDEN -HIMMEL UND HOLLE (FRG) ○ CAVERN, THE (USA) ○ NEUNZIG NACHTE UND EIN TAG
SETTE CONTRO TUTTI • 1965 • Lupo Michele • ITL
SETTE CROCI A SAN RAMON • 1972 • Degli Espinosa Francesco • ITL
SETTE DEL GRUPPO, I • 1974 • Crea Gianni • ITL
SETTE DEL TEXAS, I • 1964 • Romero-Marchent Joaquin Luis • ITL, SPN
SETTE DELL'ORSA MAGGIORE, I • 1953 • Coletti Duilio • ITL • HELL RAIDERS OF THE DEEP (USA) ○ HUMAN TORPEDOES
SETTE DI MARSA MATRUH, I see **LUNGA NOTTE DEI DISERTORI, LA** • 1970
SETTE DOLLARI SUL ROSSO see **SIETE DOLARES AL ROJO** • 1968
SETTE DONNE D'ORO CONTRO 2-07 • 1966 • Cascino Vincenzo • ITL
SETTE DONNE PER I MACGREGOR • 1967 • Giraldi Franco • ITL, SPN, FRN • SIETE MUJERES PARA LOS MACGREGOR (SPN) ○ UP THE MACGREGORS (USA)
SETTE DONNE PER UNA STRAGE • 1967 • Parolini Gianfranco • ITL
SETTE EROICHE CAROGNE (ITL) see **COMANDO AL INFIERNO** • 1968
SETTE FALSARI, I (ITL) see **MONNAIE DE SINGE** • 1965
SETTE FATICHE DI ALI BABA, LE • 1963 • Salvi Emimmo • ITL • SEVEN TASKS OF ALI BABA, THE (USA) ○ ALI BABA AND THE SACRED CROWN
SETTE FOLGORI DI ASSUR, LE • 1962 • Amadio Silvio • ITL • WAR GODS OF BABYLON (USA) ○ 7TH THUNDERBOLT (UKN) ○ SEVENTH THUNDERBOLT, THE
SETTE GIORNI ALL'ALTRO MONDO • 1936 • Mattoli Mario • ITL
SETTE GIORNI CENTO LIRE • 1933 • Malasomma Nunzio • ITL
SETTE GLADIATORI, I • 1962 • Lazaga Pedro • ITL, SPN • SIETE ESPARTANOS, LOS (SPN) ○ GLADIATORS SEVEN (USA)
SETTE MAGNIFICI CORNUTI, I • 1974 • Russo Luigi • ITL
SETTE MAGNIFIQUE PISTOLE, LE • 1966 • Guerrieri Romolo • ITL
SETTE MONACHE A KANSAS CITY • 1973 • Zeani Marcello • ITL
SETTE MONACI D'ORO, I • 1966 • Rossi Bernardo • ITL
SETTE NANI ALLA RISCOSSA, I • 1952 • Tamburella Paolo William • ITL • SEVEN DWARFS TO THE RESCUE, THE (USA)
SETTE NOTE IN NERO • 1978 • Fulci Lucio • ITL • PSYCHIC, THE (USA)
SETTE ORA DI FUOCO (ITL) see **AVENTURAS DEL OESTE** • 1964
SETTE ORCHIDEE MASCHIATE DI ROSSO • 1972 • Lenzi Umberto • ITL
SETTE ORE DI FUOCO • 1965 • Romero-Marchent Joaquin Luis • ITL, SPN, FRG
SETTE ORE DI GUAI • 1951 • Metz Vittorio, Marchesi Marcello • ITL
SETTE ORE DI VIOLENZA PER UNA SOLUZIONE IMPREVISTA • 1973 • Tarantini Michele Massimo • ITL
SETTE PECCATI CAPITALI, I see **SEPT PECHES CAPITAUX, LES** • 1951
SETTE PECCATI CAPITALI, I (ITL) see **SEPT PECHES CAPITAUX, LES** • 1951
SETTE PECCATI DI PAPA, I (ITL) see **J'AVAIS SEPT FILLES** • 1954
SETTE PECCATI, I • 1920 • Serena Gustavo • ITL
SETTE PECCATI, I • 1942 • Kish Ladislao • ITL
SETTE PISTOLAS PARA LOS MACGREGOR (SPN) see **SETTE PISTOLE PER I MACGREGOR** • 1966
SETTE PISTOLAS PER EL GRINGO (ITL) see **SIETE PISTOLAS PARA EL GRINGO** • 1967
SETTE PISTOLE PER I MACGREGOR • 1966 • Giraldi Franco • ITL, SPN • SEVEN GUNS FOR THE MACGREGORS (USA) ○ SETTE PISTOLAS PARA LOS MACGREGOR (SPN)
SETTE PISTOLE PER UN MASSACRO • 1967 • Caiano Mario • ITL
SETTE SCIALLI DI SETA GIALLA • 1972 • Pastore Sergio • ITL • CRIMES OF THE BLACK CAT (UKN)
SETTE SFIDE, LE • 1961 • Zeglio Primo • ITL • SEVEN REVENGES, THE (USA)
SETTE SPADE DEL VENDICATORE, LE • 1963 • Freda Riccardo • ITL, FRN • SEVENTH SWORD, THE (USA) ○ SETTE SPADE PER IL RE ○ SEPT EPEES POUR LE ROI
SETTE SPADE PER IL RE see **SETTE SPADE DEL VENDICATORE, LE** • 1963
SETTE STRANI CADAVERI • 1973 • D'Amato Joe • ITL
SETTE UOMINI D'ORO • 1965 • Vicario Marco • ITL, SPN, FRN • SIETE HOMBRES DE ORO (SPN) ○ SEPT HOMMES EN OR (FRN) ○ SEVEN GOLDEN MEN (USA)
SETTE UOMINI E UN CERVELLO • 1968 • Brazzi Rossano • ITL, ARG • SEVEN MEN AND A BRAIN ○ CRIMINAL SYMPHONY
SETTE VERGINI PER IL DIAVOLO see **NUDE.. SI MUORE** • 1968
SETTE VIPERE, LE • 1965 • Polselli Renato • ITL
SETTE VOLTE DONNA (ITL) see **WOMAN TIMES SEVEN** • 1967
SETTE WINCHESTER PER UN MASSACRO • 1967 • Castellari Enzo G. • ITL • SEVEN WINCHESTERS FOR A MASSACRE ○ PAYMENT IN BLOOD (USA) ○ FINAL DEFEAT, THE
SETTIMA DONNA, LA • 1978 • Prosperi Franco • ITL • TERROR
SETTIMANA AL MARE, LA • 1980 • Laurenti Mariano • ITL • WEEK AT SEA
SETTIMANA BIANCA, LA • 1980 • Laurenti Mariano • ITL
SETTIMANA COME UN'ALTRA, UNA • 1979 • Costatini Daniele • ITL
SETTIMO PARALELLO • 1962 • Marcelli Elia • DOC • ITL, VNZ • SETTIMO PARALELLO: TIERRA BRAVA ○ SEPTIEMO PARALELO
SETTIMO PARALELLO: TIERRA BRAVA see **SETTIMO PARALELLO** • 1962
SETTING BACK THE HANDS OF TIME • 1910 • *Pathe* • FRN
SETTING FIRES FOR SCIENCE • 1958 • Brittain Don • DOC • CND
SETTING SON, THE • 1930 • Foster Lewis R. • SHT • USA
SETTING SUN see **ARU RAKUJITSU** • 1959
SETTING THE FASHION • 1916 • Ellis Robert • SHT • USA
SETTING THE STYLE • 1914 • Baker George D. • USA
SETTLED AT THE SEASIDE • 1915 • Wright Walter • USA
SETTLED IN FULL • 1920 • Malins Geoffrey H. • UKN
SETTLED OUT OF COURT • 1910 • *Selig* • USA
SETTLED OUT OF COURT • 1912 • *Forde Victoria* • USA
SETTLED OUT OF COURT • 1915 • MacMackin Archer • USA
SETTLED OUT OF COURT • 1920 • *Christie* • SHT • USA
SETTLED OUT OF COURT • 1925 • Cooper George A. • UKN
SETTLEMENT see **SIEDLISZCZE** • 1960
SETTLEMENT, THE • 1983 • Rubie Howard • ASL
SETTLEMENT AND CONFLICT • 1967 • Brault Michel • SHT • CND
SETTLEMENT OF LOVE see **AIJO NO KESSAN** • 1956
SETTLEMENT WORKERS, THE • 1909 • *Selig* • USA
SETTLER, THE see **ABATIS, L'** • 1952
SETTLERS, THE see **INVANDRARNA** • 1970
SETTLER'S WIFE, THE • 1911 • *Nestor* • USA
SETTLING A BOUNDARY DISPUTE • 1910 • *Atlas* • USA
SETU BANDHAN • 1932 • Phalke Dada • IND • SETHUBANDAN ○ BRIDGING OF LANKA, THE ○ BRIDGE ACROSS THE SEA
SEUIL DU VIDE, LE • 1971 • Davy Jean-Francois • FRN • ON THE EDGE OF THE VOID ○ THRESHOLD OF THE VOID, THE
SEUILS INTERDITS • 1972 • Behi Ridha • SHT • TNS • FORBIDDEN STEPS
SEUL A CORPS PERDU • 1961 • Maley Jean • FRN • A CORPS PERDU
SEUL AMOUR, UN • 1943 • Blanchar Pierre • FRN
SEUL DANS LA NUIT • 1945 • Stengel Christian • FRN • ASSASSIN CHANTAIT, L'
SEUL DANS PARIS • 1951 • Bromberger Herve • FRN
SEUL LE VENT CONNAIT LA RESPONSE (FRN) see **ANTWORT KENNT NUR DER WIND, DIE** • 1975
SEUL OU AVEC D'AUTRES • 1962 • Heroux Denis, Arcand Denys, Venne Stephane • CND
SEULE FOIS DANS LA VIE, UNE see **FOIS DANS LA VIE, UNE** • 1933
SEULE NUIT DANS LE STUDIO, UNE • 1973 • Bokor Pierre • MTV • RMN
SEULS • 1981 • Reusser Francis • SWT • LONERS
SEULS AU MONDE • 1951 • Chanas Rene • FRN
SEULS LES ENFANTS ETAIENT PRESENTS see **DON'T LET THE ANGELS FALL** • 1968
SEUNG GIN HO • 1989 • Sin Gei-Yin • HKG • HAPPY TOGETHER
SEUNS VAN DIE WOLKE • 1975 • SAF
SEVDA • 1967 • Burckin Selahattin • TRK • LOVE
SEVE DE LA TERRE • 1955 • Alexeieff Alexandre • ANS • FRN • SAP OF THE EARTH
SEVEMEZ KIMSE SENI • 1968 • Egilmez Ertem • TRK • NO ONE CAN LOVE YOU
SEVEN • 1979 • Sidaris Andy • USA
SEVEN AGAINST THE SUN • 1964 • Millin David • SAF
SEVEN AGAINST THE WALL • 1958 • Schaffner Franklin J. • MTV • USA
SEVEN AGES • 1905 • Porter Edwin S. • USA
SEVEN AGES OF MAN, THE • 1914 • Vernon Charles • UKN
SEVEN ALONE • 1975 • Bellamy Earl • USA
SEVEN AND SEVENTY • 1915 • *Big U* • USA
SEVEN ANGRY MEN • 1955 • Warren Charles Marquis • USA
SEVEN ARTS, THE see **SEPTE ARTE** • 1958
SEVEN BAD MEN see **RAGE AT DAWN** • 1955
SEVEN BALD PATES • 1920 • Beaudine William • SHT • USA
SEVEN BARS OF GOLD • 1912 • *Melies* • USA
SEVEN BEAUTIES -THAT WHAT THEY CALL HIM see **PASQUALINO SETTEBELLEZZE** • 1976
SEVEN BEAUTIES (USA) see **PASQUALINO SETTEBELLEZZE** • 1976
SEVEN BEAUTIFUL GIRLS see **SJU VACKRA FLICKOR** • 1956
SEVEN BLACK BRASSIERES see **SJU SVARTA BE-HA** • 1954
SEVEN BLOWS OF THE DRAGON • Chang Ch'Eh • HKG
SEVEN BRAVE MEN see **SEMERO SMELYKH** • 1936
SEVEN BRIDES FOR SEVEN BROTHERS • 1954 • Donen Stanley • USA
SEVEN BRIDES FOR SEVEN BROTHERS • 1982 • Sheldon James • TVM • USA
SEVEN BRIDES OF CORPORAL ZBRUYEV, THE • 1971 • Melnikov Vitali • USS
SEVEN BROTHERS see **SEITSEMAN VELJESTA** • 1976
SEVEN BULLETS FOR SELMA see **SETE BALAS PARA SELMA** • 1967
SEVEN CAPITAL SINS see **SEPT PECHES CAPITAUX, LES** • 1951
SEVEN CAPITAL SINS, THE see **SEPT PECHES CAPITAUX, LES** • 1951
SEVEN CAPITAL SINS, THE (USA) see **SEPT PECHES CAPITAUX, LES** • 1900
SEVEN CASTLES OF THE DEVIL, THE see **SEPT CHATEAUX DU DIABLE, LES** • 1901
SEVEN CERVI BROTHERS, THE see **7 FRATELLI CERVI, I** • 1967
SEVEN CHANCES • 1925 • Keaton Buster • USA
SEVEN CITIES OF GOLD • 1955 • Webb Robert D. • USA
SEVEN CITIES OF LOVE see **HAFT SHAHR-E-ESHGH** • 1967
SEVEN CITIES TO ATLANTIS see **WARLORDS OF ATLANTIS** • 1978
SEVEN COLORED RING, THE see **NANAIRO YUBI WA** • 1918
SEVEN CONSENTING ADULTS (USA) see **POLIZEIREVIER DAVIDSWACHE (ST. PAULI)** • 1964
SEVEN CRYSTAL BALLS, THE see **TINTIN: THE SEVEN CRYSTAL BALLS**
SEVEN DARING GIRLS (USA) see **INSEL DER AMAZONEN** • 1960
SEVEN DAYS • 1910 • *Selig* • USA
SEVEN DAYS • 1914 • Henderson Dell? • USA
SEVEN DAYS • 1916 • *Mailes Charles H.* • SHT • USA
SEVEN DAYS • 1925 • Sidney Scott • USA
SEVEN DAYS see **SAPTE ZILE** • 1973
SEVEN DAYS A WEEK • 1967 • Kohout Pavel • CZC
SEVEN DAYS ASHORE • 1944 • Auer John H. • USA
SEVEN DAYS IN JANUARY see **SIETE DIAS DE ENERO** • 1978
SEVEN DAYS IN MAY • 1964 • Frankenheimer John • USA
SEVEN DAYS LEAVE • 1930 • Wallace Richard, Cromwell John • USA • MEDALS (UKN)
SEVEN DAYS' LEAVE • 1942 • Whelan Tim • USA
SEVEN DAYS OF AGONY see **SETE DIAS DE AGONIA** • 1982

SEVEN DAYS.. SEVEN NIGHTS (UKN) see **MODERATO CANTABILE** • 1960
SEVEN DAYS SOMEWHERE ELSE see **SEPT JOURS AILLEURS** • 1968
SEVEN DAYS TO LONG • 1970 • Hennigar William K. • USA
SEVEN DAYS TO NOON • 1950 • Boulting John • UKN
SEVEN DEAD IN THE CAT'S EYES see **MORTE NEGLI OCCHI DEL GATTO, LA** • 1973
SEVEN DEADLY PILLS • 1964 • Jackson Pat • UKN
SEVEN DEADLY SINS • 1917 • SER • USA
SEVEN DEADLY SINS see **SEPT PECHES CAPITAUX, LES** • 1951
SEVEN DEADLY SINS, THE see **SEPT PECHES CAPITAUX, LES** • 1951
SEVEN DEATHS IN THE CAT'S EYE see **MORTE NEGLI OCCHI DEL GATTO, LA** • 1973
SEVEN DIALS MYSTERY, THE • 1980 • Wharmby Tony • TVM • UKN
SEVEN DIFFERENT WAYS see **QUICK, LET'S GET MARRIED** • 1964
SEVEN DOLLARS ON RED see **SIETE DOLARES AL ROJO** • 1968
SEVEN DOLLARS TO KILL see **SIETE DOLARES AL ROJO** • 1968
SEVEN DOORS OF DEATH see **ALDILA, L'** • 1981
SEVEN DOORS TO DEATH • 1944 • Clifton Elmer • USA
SEVEN DOORS TO DEATH • 1983 • Fulci Lucio • ITL
SEVEN DWARFS TO THE RESCUE, THE (USA) see **SETTE NANI ALLA RISCOSSA, I** • 1952
SEVEN FACES • 1929 • Viertel Berthold • USA
SEVEN FACES OF A NO-GOOD, THE see **7 FACES DE UM CAFAJESTE, AS** • 1968
SEVEN FACES OF DR. LAO, THE • 1964 • Pal George • USA
SEVEN FACES OF DR. SI BAGO, THE • Martinez Tony Blade, Espiritu Romy • PHL
SEVEN FAIRIES • 1964 • Li Han-Hsiang • TWN
SEVEN FOOTPRINTS TO SATAN • 1929 • Christensen Benjamin • USA
SEVEN FORGOTTEN MEN see **IKARI NO KOTO** • 1958
SEVEN FRECKLES see **SIEBEN SOMMERSPROSSEN**
SEVEN FROM THE RHINE see **SIEBEN VON RHEIN** • 1954
SEVEN GIRLS see **SEVEN SWEETHEARTS** • 1942
SEVEN GIRLS see **OM SJU FLICKOR** • 1974
SEVEN GIRLS FOR SEVEN BOYS see **HAFAT DOKHTAR BARYE HAFAT PESAR** • 1968
SEVEN GOLDEN CHINESE, THE see **SETTE CINESI D'ORO, LE** • 1967
SEVEN GOLDEN MEN STRIKE AGAIN (USA) see **GRANDE COLPO DEI 7 UOMINI D'ORO, IL** • 1966
SEVEN GOLDEN MEN (USA) see **SETTE UOMINI D'ORO** • 1965
SEVEN GRAVES FOR ROGAN • 1981 • Cimber Matt • USA • MARIO PUZO'S SEVEN GRAVES FOR ROGAN ○ TIME TO DIE, A
SEVEN GUNS FOR THE MACGREGORS (USA) see **SETTE PISTOLE PER I MACGREGOR** • 1966
SEVEN GUNS TO MESA • 1958 • Dein Edward • USA
SEVEN GUYS AND A GAL see **SEPT GARS ET UNE GARCE** • 1966
SEVEN HEADACHES OF A MOTHER see **PITONG KRUS NG ISANG INA** • 1968
SEVEN HILLS OF ROME, THE • 1957 • Rowland Roy • USA, ITL • ARRIVEDERCI ROMA (ITL)
SEVEN HOURS OF GUNFIRE see **AVENTURAS DEL OESTE** • 1964
SEVEN HOURS TO JUDGMENT • 1988 • Bridges Beau • USA
SEVEN HUNDRED MILLION, THE • 1964 • Watson Patrick • DOC • CND
SEVEN IN DARKNESS • 1969 • Caffey Michael • TVM • USA
SEVEN IN THE SUN (USA) see **AVVENTURIERI DEI TROPICI, GLI** • 1960
SEVEN INGOTS OF GOLD, THE see **SEPT BARRES D'OR, LES** • 1910
SEVEN INTO SNOWY • 1977 • Shepherd Antonio • USA
SEVEN JOURNEYS (USA) see **IN JENEN TAGEN** • 1947
SEVEN KEYS • 1962 • Jackson Pat • UKN
SEVEN KEYS TO BALDPATE • 1915 • Luke Monty • ASL
SEVEN KEYS TO BALDPATE • 1917 • Ford Hugh • USA
SEVEN KEYS TO BALDPATE • 1925 • Newmeyer Fred • USA
SEVEN KEYS TO BALDPATE • 1929 • Barker Reginald • USA
SEVEN KEYS TO BALDPATE • 1935 • Hamilton William, Killy Edward • USA
SEVEN KEYS TO BALDPATE • 1947 • Landers Lew • USA
SEVEN KINDS OF TROUBLE see **BELANIN YEDI TURLUSU** • 1969
SEVEN LADIES see **LIFE'S BIG LITTLE MAN** • 1990
SEVEN LITTLE AUSTRALIANS • 1939 • Collins Arthur G. • ASL
SEVEN LITTLE FLAMES see **SEDAM PLAMENCICA** • 1975
SEVEN LITTLE FOYS, THE • 1955 • Shavelson Melville • USA
SEVEN LIVELY ARTS • 1959 • Hubley John • ANS • USA
SEVEN LIVES OF THE CAT, THE see **SIETE VIDAS DEL GATO, LAS** • 1970
SEVEN LIVES WERE CHANGED see **ORIENT EXPRESS** • 1934
SEVEN MAD MEN (USA) see **SIETE LOCOS, LOS** • 1973
SEVEN MADMEN, THE see **SIETE LOCOS, LOS** • 1973
SEVEN MAGNIFICENT FIGHTS see **HAI-YUAN CH'I-HAO** • 1972
SEVEN MAGNIFICENT GLADIATORS, THE • 1983 • Mattei Bruno • ITL
SEVEN MEN AND A BRAIN see **SETTE UOMINI E UN CERVELLO** • 1968
SEVEN MEN AT DAYBREAK see **OPERATION DAYBREAK** • 1975
SEVEN MEN FROM NOW • 1956 • Boetticher Budd • USA
SEVEN MILES FROM ALCATRAZ • 1942 • Dmytryk Edward • USA
SEVEN MINUTES, THE • 1971 • Meyer Russ • USA
SEVEN MINUTES IN HEAVEN • 1986 • Feferman Linda • USA
SEVEN MONSTERS • 1971 • Cayard Bruce • ANS • USA
SEVEN MYSTERIES see **KAIDAN HONJO NANFUSHIGI** • 1957
SEVEN NIGHTS IN JAPAN • 1976 • Gilbert Lewis* • UKN, FRN
SEVEN NO-GOODS, THE see **YEDI BELALILAR** • 1970
SEVEN NOTES see **7 NOTAS** • 1973
SEVEN NOTES BREAK THE SILENCE see **SYEM NOT V TISHINYE** • 1967
SEVEN NOTES IN SILENCE see **SYEM NOT V TISHINYE** • 1967
SEVEN NURSEMAIDS see **SEM NYANEK** • 1962
SEVEN OF CLUBS see **MAKKHETES** • 1916
SEVEN PEARLS, THE • 1917 • Mackenzie Donald • SRL • USA
SEVEN-PER-CENT SOLUTION, THE • 1976 • Ross Herbert • USA
SEVEN PISTOLS FOR EL GRINGO see **SIETE PISTOLAS PARA EL GRINGO** • 1967
SEVEN RAVENS • 1937 • Diehle Bros • ANM • FRG
SEVEN RAVENS see **SEDM HAVRANU** • 1967
SEVEN RAVENS, THE • 1952 • Diehle Bros • ANM • FRG
SEVEN RAVENS, THE (USA) see **SIEBEN RABEN, DIE** • 1969
SEVEN RED BERETS see **SETTE BASCHI ROSSI** • 1968
SEVEN REVENGES, THE (USA) see **SETTE SFIDE, LE** • 1961
SEVEN SAMURAI, THE (USA) see **SHICHININ NO SAMURAI** • 1954
SEVEN SEALED ORDERS • 1914 • *Essanay* • USA
SEVEN SEAS see **SATH SAMUDURU** • 1967
SEVEN SEAS TO CALAIS (USA) see **DOMINATORE DEI SETTE MARI, IL** • 1962
SEVEN SECOND LOVE AFFAIR, THE • 1966 • *Stewart Rick* • DOC • USA
SEVEN SECRETS OF SU-MARU, THE see **SUMURU** • 1968
SEVEN, SEVENTEEN AND SEVENTY • 1910 • Fitzhamon Lewin? • UKN
SEVEN SINNERS • 1925 • Milestone Lewis • USA
SEVEN SINNERS • 1936 • De Courville Albert • UKN • DOOMED CARGO (USA) ○ WRECKER, THE
SEVEN SINNERS • 1940 • Garnett Tay • USA • CAFE OF SEVEN SINNERS (UKN) ○ DOOMED CARGO
SEVEN SISTERS see **HOUSE ON SORORITY ROW** • 1983
SEVEN SISTERS, THE • 1915 • Olcott Sidney • USA
SEVEN SLAPS (USA) see **SIEBEN OHRFEIGEN** • 1937
SEVEN SLAVES AGAINST ROME see **SCHIAVI PIU FORTI DEL MONDO, GLI** • 1964
SEVEN SLAVES AGAINST THE WORLD (USA) see **SCHIAVI PIU FORTI DEL MONDO, GLI** • 1964
SEVEN SORROWS see **SIETE DOLORES** • 1968
SEVEN SPIES IN THE TRAP see **SIETE ESPIAS EN LA TRAMPA** • 1967
SEVEN STEPS FROM NOW see **YEDI ADIM SONRA** • 1968
SEVEN SURPRISES • 1963 • Jutra Claude, Faille Albert, Carpentier Eduardo, Munro Grant • ANT • CND
SEVEN SURVIVORS • 1963 • Vigars N. R. H. • UKN
SEVEN SUSPECTS FOR MURDER (UKN) see **CHAT ET LA SOURIS, LE** • 1975
SEVEN SWANS, THE • 1918 • Dawley J. Searle • USA
SEVEN SWEETHEARTS • 1942 • Borzage Frank • USA • SEVEN GIRLS
SEVEN TASKS OF ALI BABA, THE (USA) see **SETTE FATICHE DI ALI BABA, LE** • 1963
SEVEN THIEVES • 1960 • Hathaway Henry • USA
SEVEN THUNDERS • 1957 • Fregonese Hugo • UKN • BEASTS OF MARSEILLES, THE (USA)
SEVEN TILL FIVE • 1933 • McLaren Norman • ANS • UKN
SEVEN TIMES A DAY see **SEPT FOIS PAR JOUR..** • 1971
SEVEN TIMES DEATH see **HOUSE OF THE SEVEN CORPSES, THE** • 1973
SEVEN TIMES SEVEN (USA) see **7 VOLTE 7** • 1968
SEVEN UP see **SLICE OF LIFE** • 1982
SEVEN-UPS, THE • 1973 • D'Antoni Philip • USA
SEVEN VERY BRAVE MEN see **SIETE BRAVISIMOS, LOS** • 1968
SEVEN VIRGINS FOR THE DEVIL see **NUDE.. SI MUORE** • 1968
SEVEN WAVES AWAY • 1956 • Sale Richard • UKN • ABANDON SHIP (USA)
SEVEN WAYS FROM SUNDOWN • 1960 • Keller Harry • USA
SEVEN WERE SAVED • 1947 • Pine William H. • USA
SEVEN WILD LIONS see **YEDI DAGIN ASLANI** • 1966
SEVEN WINCHESTERS FOR A MASSACRE see **SETTE WINCHESTER PER UN MASSACRO** • 1967
SEVEN WINDS see **NA SEMI VETRAKH** • 1962
SEVEN WITNESSES see **HUNT THE MAN DOWN** • 1950
SEVEN WOMEN • 1965 • Ford John • USA
SEVEN WOMEN FOR SATAN see **WEEK-ENDS MALEFIQUES DU COMTE ZAROFF, LES** • 1975
SEVEN WOMEN FROM HELL • 1961 • Webb Robert D. • USA
SEVEN WONDERS OF HONJO, THE see **HONJO NANA FUSHIGI** • 1957
SEVEN WONDERS OF THE WORLD • 1956 • Tetzlaff Ted, Thomas Lowell, Garnett Tay, Marton Andrew, Thompson Walter, Mantz Paul • USA
SEVEN YEAR ITCH, THE • 1955 • Wilder Billy • USA
SEVEN YEARS BAD LUCK • 1913 • Miller Ashley • USA
SEVEN YEARS BAD LUCK • 1921 • Linder Max • USA
SEVEN YEARS IN TIBET • 1956 • Nieter Hans M. • UKN
SEVEN YEARS OF COURAGE • DOC • NTH
SEVEN ZAPATA see **PITONG ZAPATA** • 1967
SEVENDE HORISON, DIE • 1958 • SAF
SEVENTEEN • 1916 • Vignola Robert G. • USA
SEVENTEEN • 1940 • King Louis • USA
SEVENTEEN see **SYTTEN** • 1965
SEVENTEEN see **SODACHI-ZAKARI** • 1967
SEVENTEEN AND ANXIOUS • 1970 • Brynych Zbynek • FRG • O HAPPY DAY
SEVENTEEN AND FAIR OF HAIR see **BATTAGLIA DEI MODS, LA** • 1966
SEVENTEEN MOMENTS OF SPRING • 1974 • Lioznova Tatyana • MTV • USS
SEVENTEEN YEARS OLD see **SJUTTON AR** • 1957
SEVENTH AGE, THE • 1975 • Ricketson James • DOC • ASL
SEVENTH AGE, THE see **GAMLE, DE** • 1947
SEVENTH ANNIVERSARY OF THE RED ARMY, THE • 1925 • Vertov Dziga • USS
SEVENTH BANDIT, THE • 1926 • Dunlap Scott R. • USA
SEVENTH BROTHER, THE • Pojar Bretislav • CZC
SEVENTH BULLET • 1972 • Khamraev Ali • USS
SEVENTH CAVALRY • 1956 • Lewis Joseph H. • USA • 7TH CAVALRY
SEVENTH COLUMN • 1943 • Jason Will • SHT • USA
SEVENTH COMMANDMENT, THE • 1915 • *Courtot Marguerite* • USA
SEVENTH CONTINENT, THE see **SEDMY KONTINENT** • 1960
SEVENTH CONTINENT, THE (UKN) see **SIEBENTE KONTINENT, DER** • 1989
SEVENTH CONTINENT, THE (USA) see **SEDMI KONTINENT** • 1966
SEVENTH CROSS, THE • 1944 • Zinnemann Fred • USA
SEVENTH DAWN, THE • 1964 • Gilbert Lewis* • UKN, USA • WHEREVER LOVE TAKES ME ○ THIRD ROAD, THE
SEVENTH DAY, THE • 1909 • Griffith D. W. • USA
SEVENTH DAY, THE • 1914 • Weston Charles • UKN
SEVENTH DAY, THE • 1915 • Louis Will • USA
SEVENTH DAY, THE • 1922 • King Henry • USA
SEVENTH DAY, EIGHTH NIGHT see **DEN SEDMY, OSMA NOC** • 1969
SEVENTH DAY OF CREATION, THE • Georgiadis Vassilis • GRC
SEVENTH DAY, THE EIGHTH NIGHT, THE see **DEN SEDMY, OSMA NOC** • 1969
SEVENTH FAIRY, THE see **CH'I-HSIEN NU**
SEVENTH FAIRY SISTER, THE see **CH'I-HSIEN NU**
SEVENTH FELLOW-TRAVELLER, THE see **SEDMOY SPUTNIK** • 1968
SEVENTH FLOOR, THE (USA) see **FISCHIO AL NASO, IL** • 1967
SEVENTH HEAVEN • 1937 • King Henry • USA
SEVENTH HEAVEN • 1972 • Bocharov Edvard • USS
SEVENTH HEAVEN, THE see **SJUNDE HIMLEN** • 1956
SEVENTH JUROR, THE (USA) see **SEPTIEME JURE, LE** • 1962
SEVENTH LOVE, THE • 1975 • Andonov Ivan • BUL
SEVENTH MATCH, THE • 1982 • Gross Yoram • ANM • ASL
SEVENTH NOON, THE • 1915 • *Glendinning Ernest* • USA
SEVENTH PERSON, THE • 1919 • *Walsh George* • USA
SEVENTH PRELUDE, THE • 1914 • *Essanay* • USA
SEVENTH SEAL, THE (UKN) see **SJUNDE INSEGLET, DET** • 1957
SEVENTH SHERIFF, THE • 1923 • Hatton Richard • USA
SEVENTH SIGN, THE • 1988 • Schultz Carl • USA • BOARDER, THE
SEVENTH SIN, THE • 1917 • *Vitagraph* • SHT • USA
SEVENTH SIN, THE • 1917 • Marston Theodore • *Mcclure* • USA
SEVENTH SIN, THE • 1957 • Neame Ronald, Minnelli Vincente (U/c) • USA
SEVENTH SON, THE • 1912 • Reid Hal • USA
SEVENTH SURVIVOR, THE • 1941 • Hiscott Leslie • UKN
SEVENTH SWORD, THE (USA) see **SETTE SPADE DEL VENDICATORE, LE** • 1963
SEVENTH THUNDERBOLT, THE see **SETTE FOLGORI DI ASSUR, LE** • 1962
SEVENTH VEIL, THE • 1945 • Bennett Compton • UKN
SEVENTH VICTIM, THE • 1943 • Robson Mark • USA
SEVENTH VOYAGE OF SINBAD, THE • 1958 • Juran Nathan • USA
SEVENTH WORD, THE • 1915 • Noy Wilfred • UKN
SEVENTIES PEOPLE, THE see **70-TALETS MANNISKOR** • 1975
SEVENTY AND SEVEN • 1917 • *Paul Ellis* • SHT • USA
SEVENTY FIVE CENTS AN HOUR see **SIXTY CENTS AN HOUR** • 1923
SEVENTY-SEVEN, PARK LANE • 1931 • De Courville Albert • UKN
SEVENTY TIMES SEVEN see **SETENTA VECES SIETE** • 1962
SEVENTY-TWO DESPERATE REBELS, THE • Lin Bin • HKG • 72 DESPERATE REBELS, THE
SEVENTY TWO HOURS see **SIEDEMDZIESIAT DWIE GODZINY** • 1970
SEVENTY-TWO HOURS OR DIE see **POWER GAME** • 1982
SEVENTY-TWO HOURS TO DIE see **POWER GAME** • 1982
SEVENTY YEARS VENEZUELA see **VENEZUELA SETENTA ANOS** • 1971
SEVER DO VOUGA -UMA EXPERIENCIA • 1971 • Rocha Paulo • PRT
SEVERA, A • 1931 • de Barros Jose Leitao • PRT
SEVERAL AFRICAS • 1975 • Andermann Andrea • MTV • ITL
SEVERAL INTERVIEWS ON PERSONAL MATTERS see **NESKOLKO INTERVYU PO LICHNYM VOPROSAM** • 1980
SEVERAL INTERVIEWS ON PRIVATE MATTERS see **NESKOLKO INTERVYU PO LICHNYM VOPROSAM** • 1980
SEVERANCE • 1989 • Steinberg David • USA
SEVERE LESSON, A • 1912 • *Republic* • USA
SEVERE TEST, A • 1913 • *Solax* • USA
SEVERED ARM, THE • 1974 • Alderman Thomas S. • USA
SEVERED HAND, THE • 1914 • Lucas Wilfred • USA
SEVERED HAND, THE • 1916 • *Madison Cleo* • USA
SEVERED HEAD, A • 1970 • Clement Dick • UKN
SEVERED HEADS see **CABEZAS CORTADAS** • 1970
SEVERED THONG, THE • 1914 • *Alden Mary* • USA
SEVERNI PRISTAV • 1953 • Makovec Milos • CZC
SEVERNOE SIIANIE • 1926 • Foregger • USS • MIRAGE IN THE NORTH
SEVERO TORELLI • 1914 • Feuillade Louis • FRN
SEVGILI MUHAFIZIN • 1970 • Conturk Remzi • TRK • MY DEAR BODYGUARD
SEVILLA DE MIS AMORES • 1930 • Novarro Ramon • USA • SINGER OF SEVILLE, THE ○ SEVILLANA, LA
SEVILLANA, LA see **SEVILLA DE MIS AMORES** • 1930
SEVILLANE, LA • 1941 • Hugon Andre • FRN
SEVILLE DE MES AMOURS see **CHANTEUR DE SEVILLE, LE** • 1930
SEVMEKTEN KORKUYORUM • 1968 • Saydam Nejat • TRK • AFRAID TO LOVE
SEVODIYA see **SEGODNYA** • 1924
SEVODNYA see **SEGODNYA** • 1930
SEVODNYA -NOVYI ATTRAKSION • 1964 • Dudko Apollinari, Kosheverova Nadezhda • USS • LOVE AND TIGERS
SEVRES PORCELAIN see **PORCELAINES TENDRES** • 1909
SEWER see **KANAL** • 1957
SEWER, THE • 1912 • Warren Edward • USA
SEWERS OF GOLD see **GREAT RIVIERA BANK ROBBERY, THE** • 1979
SEWERS OF PARIS, THE see **EGOUTS DU PARADIS, LES** • 1978
SEWING GIRL, THE • 1910 • *Powers* • USA
SEX • 1920 • Niblo Fred • USA
SEX see **ANDY WARHOL'S WOMEN** • 1971
SEX A LA BOUCHE, LE • 1977 • Desvilles Jean • FRN
SEX A TRAVERS LE MONDE, LE • Debest Maxime • FRN
SEX-A-VISION • 1985 • Morehead Ned • USA

SEX-ABENTEUER DER DREI MUSKETIERE • 1975 • Dietrich Erwin C. • FRG • SEX-ADVENTURES OF THE THREE MUSKETEERS, THE
SEX ACADEMY • *Longley Tamara* • SPN • MADAME OLGA'S PUPILS
SEX ADS • 1966 • Pearson Peter • DOC • CND
SEX ADVENTURES OF A SINGLE MAN, THE (UKN) see **BENGELCHEN LIEBT KREUZ UND QUER** • 1968
SEX-ADVENTURES OF THE THREE MUSKETEERS, THE see **SEX-ABENTEUER DER DREI MUSKETIERE** • 1975
SEX AGENT see **IN DER HOLLE IST NOCH PLATZ** • 1961
SEX AIRLINES • *Spelvin Georgina* • USA
SEX AND ASTROLOGY • 1970 • *New World Studios* • USA
SEX AND NOT YET SIXTEEN see **SEX UND NOCH NICHT SECHZEHN** • 1968
SEX AND THE ANIMALS see **LOVE AND THE ANIMALS** • 1969
SEX AND THE COLLEGE GIRL • 1964 • Adler Joseph • USA • FUN LOVERS, THE
SEX AND THE MARRIED DETECTIVE see **COLUMBO: SEX AND THE MARRIED DETECTIVE** • 1989
SEX AND THE MARRIED WOMAN • 1977 • Arnold Jack • TVM • USA
SEX AND THE OTHER WOMAN • 1972 • Long Stanley • UKN
SEX AND THE SINGLE GAY • 1970 • Rocco Pat • USA
SEX AND THE SINGLE GIRL • 1964 • Quine Richard • USA
SEX AND THE SINGLE PARENT • 1979 • Cooper Jackie • TVM • USA
SEX AND THE SINGLE SAILOR (USA) see **HOW TO PICK UP A GIRL** • 1967
SEX AND THE TEENAGER see **TO FIND A MAN** • 1972
SEX AND THE VAMPIRE (UKN) see **FRISSON DES VAMPIRES, LE** • 1970
SEX AND VIOLENCE see **SESSO E VOLENTIERI** • 1982
SEX APPEAL • 1986 • Vincent Chuck • USA
SEX AT 7,000 FEET see **FREUDE AM FLIEGEN** • 1977
SEX AT NIGHT see **IMPASSE DES VERTUS** • 1955
SEX AT THE OLYMPICS • 1973 • Boos Walter • FRG
SEX BOAT • 1980 • Frazer David I., Svetlana • USA
SEX BOX, THE see **LOVE BOX, THE** • 1972
SEX BUSINESS, MADE IN PASSING • 1969 • Syberberg Hans-Jurgen • DOC • FRG
SEX BY ADVERTISEMENT see **S-X BY ADVERTISEMENT** • 1969
SEX CAN BE DIFFICULT see **AMORE DIFFICILE, L'** • 1962
SEX CANNIBAL, THE • 1969 • Hunt Ed • USA
SEX CHANGE see **CAMBIO DE SEXO** • 1977
SEX CHARADE • 1970 • Franco Jesus
SEX CHARGE see **ACH JODEL MIR NOCH EINEN -STOSZTRUPP VENUS BLAST ZUM ANGRIFF** • 1973
SEX CHECK, THE see **SEKKUSU CHEKKU-DAINI NO SEI** • 1968
SEX CHECK DAI-NI NO SEI see **SEKKUSU CHEKKU-DAINI NO SEI** • 1968
SEX CIRCUS • 1969 • Goetz Tommy • USA
SEX CLINIC see **CLINIC XCLUSIVE** • 1971
SEX CLINIC GIRLS • 1976 • Bo Reimer • USA
SEX CLUB INTERNATIONAL • 1967 • Mahon Barry • USA • LUCKY BANG BANG'S SEX CLUB INTERNATIONAL
SEX COMES AND GOES see **SEXO VA, SEXO VIENE** • 1977
SEX CONNECTION see **PLEASURE MACHINE, THE** • 1975
SEX CONNECTION, THE • 1969 • Ferrer Charles • FRG
SEX CRIMES see **SEIHANZAI** • 1967
SEX CRIMINAL see **SEIHAN** • 1967
SEX CURES THE CRAZY • 1968 • *Century Cinema Corp* • USA
SEX CYCLE, THE • 1966 • Sarno Joe • USA • SEX CYCLES, THE
SEX CYCLES, THE see **SEX CYCLE, THE** • 1966
SEX DEMONS, THE see **DEMONS, LES** • 1973
SEX DENS OF BANGKOK • *Wong Angela May* • SWT
SEX DIARY see **LETTO IN PIAZZA, IL** • 1976
SEX DRIVE • 1968 • Shinagawa Shoji • JPN
SEX EN GROS • 1971 • Vest Nils • DOC • DNM
SEX EXPERT see **NEWAZASHI** • 1968
SEX EXPRESS • 1975 • Ford Derek • UKN
SEX FAMILY ROBINSON • 1968 • Vair Linda • USA
SEX FAMILY ROBINSON ON THE FARM • 1969 • Vair Linda • USA • FAMILY ROBINSON ON THE FARM
SEX FARM • 1974 • Miller Arnold Louis • UKN
SEX FEVER see **INSEL DER 1,000 FREUDEN, DIE** • 1977
SEX FEVER ON AN ISLAND OF 1,000 DELIGHTS see **INSEL DER 1,000 FREUDEN, DIE** • 1977
SEX FOLLIES • Sachmann Kurt
SEX FOR SALE (UKN) see **SAN PASQUALE BAYLONNE, PROTETTORE DELLE DONNE** • 1976
SEX FREAKS • 1974 • von Hellen M. C. • USA
SEX GAMES see **COMMUTER HUSBANDS** • 1972
SEX GARAGE • 1973 • USA
SEX HUNGRY GIRLS see **GARCES, LES** • 1973
SEX HYGIENE • 1941 • Ford John • DOC • USA
SEX I KOBENHAVN • 1970 • Wolter Erling • DNM
SEX IN BUSINESS see **HONOR AMONG LOVERS** • 1931
SEX IN CHAINS (USA) see **GESCHLECHT IN FESSELN** • 1928
SEX IN FETTERS see **GESCHLECHT IN FESSELN** • 1928
SEX IN SWEDEN • 1977 • Ahlberg Mac • SWD • MOLLY
SEX IN THE AFTERNOON see **ALTA INFEDELTA** • 1964
SEX IN THE CLASSROOM • 1971 • Di Leo Fernando • ITL
SEX IN THE GRASS (UKN) see **LIEBESQUELLE, DIE** • 1965
SEX IN THE HEAD see **SESSO IN TESTA** • 1974
SEX IN THE OFFICE (UKN) see **EROTIK IM BERUF** • 1971
SEX IN THE SNOW (UKN) see **APRES-SKI** • 1971
SEX IS A PLEASURE (UKN) see **TOLLDREISTEN GESCHICHTEN DES HONORE DE BALZAC** • 1969
SEX IS A WOMAN see **DEATH IS A WOMAN** • 1966
SEX IS BEAUTIFUL (UKN) see **REVELATION, LA** • 1971
SEX IS GAMES, PEOPLE PLAY see **GAME PEOPLE PLAY, THE** • 1967
SEX IS MY GAME see **SAPHO OU LA FUREUR D'AIMER** • 1970
SEX IS NOT FOR VIRGINS (UKN) see **FLEISSIGEN BIENEN VOM FROHLICHEN BOCK, DIE** • 1970
SEX IS THE GAME PEOPLE PLAY see **GAME PEOPLE PLAY, THE** • 1967
SEX IS THE NAME OF THE GAME (UKN) see **INTIMIDADES DE UNA PROSTITUTA** • 1972
SEX ISN'T SIN (UKN) see **LOVE IN A FOUR LETTER WORLD** • 1970
SEX-JACK • 1971 • Wakamatsu Koji • JPN
SEX JOYU ZANKOKUSHI • 1968 • Mukoi Hiroshi • JPN • CRUEL STORY OFF SEX FILM ACTORS, A
SEX KILLER see **GIRL KILLER, THE** • 1967
SEX KITTENS GO TO COLLEGE • 1960 • Zugsmith Albert • USA • TEACHER WAS A SEXPOT ○ BEAUTY AND THE ROBOT
SEX, LIES AND VIDEOTAPE • 1989 • Sodebergh Steven • USA
SEX LIFE IN A CONVENT (UKN) see **KLOSTERSCHULERINNEN, DIE** • 1971
SEX LIFE IN A CONVENT (USA) see **INTERNO DI UN CONVENTO** • 1977
SEX LIFE IN A WOMEN'S PRISON see **PRIGIONE DI DONNE** • 1974
SEX LIFE OF ROMEO AND JULIET, THE see **SECRET SEX LIVES OF ROMEO AND JULIET, THE** • 1969
SEX LIFE OF THE POLYP, THE • 1928 • Chalmers Thomas • SHT • USA
SEX, LOVE AND MARRIAGE see **LOVE AND MARRIAGE** • 1970
SEX, LOVE, MURDER see **HERZBUBE** • 1972
SEX LURE, THE • 1916 • Abramson Ivan • USA • GIRL WHO DID NOT CARE, THE
SEX MACHINE • Saller Eddy • FRG
SEX MACHINE see **WILBUR AND THE BABY FACTORY** • 1970
SEX MACHINE, THE (USA) see **CONVIENE FAR BENE L'AMORE** • 1975
SEX MADNESS • 1929 • *Richardson Jack* • USA
SEX MADNESS • 1934 • Esper Dwain • USA
SEX MANIAC see **VISITA DEL VICIO, LA** • 1978
SEX, MAO, LSD.. OR SO IS LIFE • 1971 • Antic Jovan • SHT • YGS
SEX MISSION see **SEKSMISJA** • 1984
SEX MONSTER see **LUCHADORAS CONTRA EL ROBOT ASESINO, LAS** • 1969
SEX NEST, THE • 1971 • *Arent Eddie*
SEX NO SHINPI • 1968 • Yamashita Osamu • JPN • MYSTERY OF SEX
SEX O NO SEX • 1974 • Diamante Julio • SPN
SEX O'CLOCK NEWS, THE • 1986 • Vanderbes Romano • USA • GUIDE TO AMERICA
SEX O'CLOCK, U.S.A. • 1976 • Reichenbach Francois • DOC • FRN, USA
SEX ODYSSEY • 1970 • *Distripix, Inc.* • USA
SEX OF A WITCH see **SESSO DELLA STREGA, IL** • 1972
SEX OF ANGELS, THE (USA) see **SESSO DEGLI ANGELI, IL** • 1968
SEX OF THE ANGELS see **SESSO DEGLI ANGELI, IL** • 1968
SEX OF THE WITCH (USA) see **SESSO DELLA STREGA, IL** • 1972
SEX OF THEIR BODIES (UKN) see **RAGAZZA DALLA PELLE DI LUNA, LA** • 1972
SEX ON THE BRAIN see **SESSO IN TESTA** • 1974
SEX ON THE GROOVE TUBE see **CASE OF THE FULL MOON MURDERS** • 1971
SEX ON THE ROCKS see **SCHONEN WILDEN VON IBIZA, DIE**
SEX OR BUST • 1973 • Lieberman Art • USA
SEX, PART ENEMY NO.1 see **SEX -PARTIJSKI NEPRLJATELJ BR.1** • 1990
SEX -PARTIJSKI NEPRLJATELJ BR.1 • 1990 • Sabo Dusan • YGS • SEX, PART ENEMY NO.1
SEX PERILS OF PAULETTE, THE • 1965 • Wishman Doris • USA • SEX PERILS OF PAULINE ○ PAULETTE
SEX PERILS OF PAULINE see **SEX PERILS OF PAULETTE, THE** • 1965
SEX PLAY see **GAMES GIRLS PLAY** • 1974
SEX POWER • 1970 • Chapier Henri • FRN
SEX QUARTET see **FATE, LE** • 1966
SEX RACKETEERS, THE see **MAN OF VIOLENCE** • 1970
SEX RALLY see **RALLYE DES JOYEUSES, LA** • 1975
SEX RITUALS OF THE OCCULT • 1970 • *Fine Products* • USA
SEX RULES • 1988 • Karmel Pip • SHT • ASL
SEX SAUVAGE • Baudricourt Michel • FRN
SEX SECRETS OF THE SEX THERAPIST, THE • 1986 • *Ashby Debee* • UKN
SEX SEEKERS, THE • 1969 • *American Film Production Co* • USA
SEX SERVICE (UKN) see **CAROSELLO DI NOTTE** • 1964
SEX SHOP • 1972 • Berri Claude • FRN, ITL, FRG
SEX SHUFFLE, THE • 1968 • Scott Ron • USA • LOVE SHUFFLE, THE
SEX SLAVES see **INSEL DER 1,000 FREUDEN, DIE** • 1977
SEX SLEUTH • *Jess Marilyn* • FRN
SEX SYMBOL, THE • 1974 • Rich David Lowell • TVM • USA
SEX TAPES SCANDAL, THE • 1989 • Nosseck Noel • USA
SEX THIEF, THE • 1973 • Campbell Martin • UKN
SEX THROUGH A WINDOW see **EXTREME CLOSE-UP** • 1973
SEX TO THE END see **TROLL** • 1973
SEX TRIP, THE • 1969 • *Cherry Productions* • USA
SEX UND NOCH NICHT SECHZEHN • 1968 • Baumgartner Peter • FRG • SEX AND NOT YET SIXTEEN ○ ...UND NOCH NICHT 16 ○ ...AND NOT YET 16
SEX VICTIMS, THE • 1973 • Robbins Derek?, Ford Sam? • UKN
SEX WISH • 1976 • McCoy Tim • USA
SEX WITH A SMILE see **QUARANTA GRADI ALL'OMBRA DEL LENZUOLO** • 1976
SEX WITH A STRANGER see **ETRANGERE, L'** • 1968
SEX WITH THE STARS • 1980 • Kawadri Anwar • UKN • CONFESSIONS OF THE NAUGHTY NYMPHOS ○ SECRETS OF A GIRL FRIDAY
SEX WITHOUT LOVE (UKN) see **CHARNELLES, LES** • 1975
SEX WORLD • 1978 • Spinelli Anthony • USA
SEX ZONE see **SEICHITAI** • 1968
SEXAGERS • 1972 • Hubner Zygmunt • PLN
SEXANALYSED, THE see **NEUROTICOS, LOS** • 1972
SEXE DE ANGES, LE (FRN) see **VOCI BIANCHE, LE** • 1964
SEXE ENRAGE, LE • 1970 • Lethem Roland • SHT • BLG • RED CUNT, THE ○ ENRAGED SEX, THE
SEXE FAIBLE, LE • 1934 • Siodmak Robert • FRN • WEAKER SEX, THE
SEXE NU, LE • 1974 • Benazeraf Jose • FRN • NAKED SEX (UKN)
SEXE QUI PARLE, LE • 1975 • Mulot Claude • FRN • PUSSY TALK (UKN) ○ PUSSY TALK: LE SEXE QUI PARLE
SEXES ENCHAINES, LES see **GESCHLECHT IN FESSELN** • 1928
SEXIER THAN SEX • 1974 • Dittmer Hans, Gilbert David • SWD, UKN
SEXIER THAN SEX see **BAKSMALLA** • 1973
SEXIEST STORY EVER TOLD, THE • 1970 • Ren-Mart • USA
SEXLINGAR • 1942 • Bolander Hugo, Soderblom Ake • SWD • SEXTUPLETS
SEXO AMOR Y FANTASIA • 1976 • Xiol Juan • SPN
SEXO ATACA, EL • 1978 • Summers Manuel • SPN
SEXO FUERTE, EL • 1945 • Gomez Muriel Emilio • MXC • SUPER-HEMBRAS, LAS ○ STRONGER SEX, THE ○ SUPER FEMALES
SEXO VA, SEXO VIENE • 1977 • Almodovar Pedro • SPN • SEX COMES AND GOES
SEXOANALIZADOS, LOS see **NEUROTICOS, LOS** • 1972
SEXOLOGOS • 1969 • Dezard Daniele, Meignant Michel • DOC • FRN • LIBERTE, EGALITE, SEXUALITE
SEXOLOID • 1979 • Vicari Angelo • ITL
SEXORCIST, THE see **OSSESSA, L'** • 1974
SEXPERIENCIAS • 1968 • Nunes Jose Maria • SPN
SEXPERT • 1976 • Sarno Joe • USA • ABIGAIL LESLIE IS BACK IN TOWN ○ MISTY
SEXPERTS -TOUCHED BY TEMPTATION • 1965 • Nehemiah J. • USA • TOUCHED BY TEMPTATION ○ LOVE EXPERTS, THE
SEXPIONAGE • 1984 • Taylor Don • TVM • USA • SECRETS OF THE RED BEDROOM ○ SECRET WEAPONS
SEXPLOITERS, THE • 1965 • Ruban Al C. • USA • EXPLOITERS, THE
SEXPLOITERS, THE see **KIGEKI HACHURUI** • 1968
SEXPLORER, THE • 1975 • Ford Derek • UKN • DIARY OF A SPACE VIRGIN ○ GIRL FROM STARSHIP VENUS
SEXPOT • 1988 • Vincent Chuck • USA
SEX'S VENGEANCE see **VENGANZA DEL SEXO, LA** • 1967
SEXTA CARRERA, LA • 1953 • Delgado Miguel M. • MXC
SEXTANERIN, DIE • Innemann Svatopluk • ERSTE LIEBE ○ FIRST LOVE
SEXTANKA • 1932 • Innemann Svatopluk • CZC
SEXTEEN • 1975 • Locke Peter • USA
SEXTERMINATORS, THE • 1970 • Grant John A. • USA • SIX TERMINATORS, THE
SEXTET • 1964 • *Berman Harry (P)* • USA • SIX WOMEN AND A MAN ○ SIXTET
SEXTET see **SEKSTET** • 1964
SEXTETTE • 1978 • Hughes Ken, Rapper Irving • USA
SEXTETTEN KARLSSON • 1945 • Ahrle Elof • SWD • KVARTERETS BUSUNGAR
SEXTON BLAKE • 1909 • Carlile C. Douglas • UKN
SEXTON BLAKE • 1928 • *Banfield George J. (P)* • SER • UKN
SEXTON BLAKE AND THE BEARDED DOCTOR • 1935 • Cooper George A. • UKN
SEXTON BLAKE AND THE HOODED TERROR • 1938 • King George • UKN
SEXTON BLAKE AND THE MADEMOISELLE • 1935 • Bryce Alex • UKN
SEXTON BLAKE, GAMBLER • 1928 • Banfield George J. • UKN • BLAKE -THE GAMBLER
SEXTON BLAKE V. BARON KETTLER • 1912 • Moss Hugh • UKN
SEXTON OF LONGWYN, THE • 1908 • *Lubin* • USA
SEXTON PIMPLE • 1915 • Evans Fred, Evans Joe • UKN
SEXTROVERT, THE (UKN) see **DESIRELLA** • 1970
SEXTUPLETS see **SEXLINGAR** • 1942
SEXUAL DESIRE • 1975 • Peeters Barbara, Deerson Jacques • USA
SEXUAL DESIRES see **COLEGIALAS LESBIANAS Y EL PLACER DE PERVERTIR** • 1982
SEXUAL DEVIANTS • *Stone Amanda*
SEXUAL ENCOUNTER GROUP • 1970 • De Renzy Alex • DOC • USA
SEXUAL EXPLOITS OF NAUGHTY PENNY, THE • 1978 • Vincent Chuck • USA
SEXUAL EXTASY see **NACKT UND HEISS AUF MYKONOS** • 1979
SEXUAL FANTASIES see **I TVILLINGERNES TEGN** • 1975
SEXUAL FREEDOM • 1984 • Brusadori Giovanni • ITL
SEXUAL FREEDOM IN DENMARK • 1970 • von Hellen M. C. • USA • DANSK SEXUALITET
SEXUAL FREEDOM IN MARRIAGE • 1970 • *Distripix Inc.* • USA
SEXUAL HEIGHTS • Tobalina Carlos • USA
SEXUAL INADEQUACIES see **NEL LABIRINTO DEL SESSO** • 1969
SEXUAL LIFE OF FRANKENSTEIN, THE • 1970 • Novak Harry? • USA
SEXUAL MEDITATION: FAUN'S ROOM YALE • 1972 • Brakhage Stan • USA
SEXUAL MEDITATION: HOTEL • 1972 • Brakhage Stan • USA
SEXUAL MEDITATION NO.1: MOTEL • 1970 • Brakhage Stan • USA
SEXUAL MEDITATION: OFFICE SUITE • 1972 • Brakhage Stan • USA
SEXUAL MEDITATION: OPEN FIELD • 1972 • Brakhage Stan • USA
SEXUAL MEDITATION: ROOM WITH VIEW • 1971 • Brakhage Stan • USA
SEXUAL PARTNERSHIP (UKN) see **OSWALT KOLLE: DAS WUNDER DER LIEBE -SEXUELLE PARTNERSCHAFT** • 1968
SEXUAL PERVERSIONS see **PERVERSIONS SEXUELLES** • 1972
SEXUAL PERVERSITY IN CHICAGO see **ABOUT LAST NIGHT** • 1986
SEXUAL PRACTICES IN SWEDEN • 1970 • Hansen Karl • SWD
SEXUAL REVOLUTION, THE see **RIVOLUZIONE SESSUALE, LA** • 1968
SEXUALLY LIBERATED FEMALE, THE see **SENSUALLY LIBERATED FEMALE, THE** • 1970
SEXUALLY YOURS (UKN) see **SEXUELLEMENT VOTRE** • 1974
SEXUALNOT see **RECHT AUF LIEBE, DAS** • 1929
SEXUALNOT see **EROS IN KETTEN** • 1930
SEXUELLEMENT VOTRE • 1974 • Pecas Max • FRN • SEXUALLY YOURS (UKN)
SEXUOUS FEMALE, THE see **SENSUALLY LIBERATED FEMALE, THE** • 1970

SEXUS (USA) see **ENFER DANS LA PEAU, L'** • 1965

SEXY! • 1963 • Russo Renzo, Russo Giuseppe • DOC • ITL

SEXY A TAHITI • 1961 • Bonsignori Umberto • ITL

SEXY AD ALTA TENSIONE • 1963 • De Fina P. V. Oscar, Vincenzo Pasquale • DOC • ITL

SEXY ADVENTURES OF LIPPS AND MCCAINE, THE see **LIPPS AND MCCAINE** • 1978

SEXY AL NEON • 1962 • Fecchi Ettore • DOC • FRN, ITL

SEXY AL NEON BIS • 1963 • Fecchi Ettore • DOC • FRN, ITL

SEXY BLUES • 1974 • Franco Jesus

SEXY CAT • 1972 • Perez Tabernero Julio • SPN

SEXY CHE SCOTTA • 1963 • Macchi Franco • DOC • ITL

SEXY DARLINGS, THE (UKN) see **ROBINSON CRUSOE UND SEINE WILDEN SKLAVINNEN** • 1971

SEXY DOZEN, THE see **CHARLEY'S TANTE NACKT** • 1969

SEXY FOLLIE • 1963 • Montero Roberto Bianchi • DOC • ITL

SEXY GANG • 1967 • Henry-Jacques • FRN • MICHELLE (USA) ○ ADORABLES CANAILLES

SEXY GIRL (ITL) see **VOULEZ-VOUS DANSER AVEC MOI** • 1960

SEXY MAGICO • 1963 • Loy Mino, Scattini Luigi • DOC • ITL

SEXY NEL MONDO • 1963 • Montero Roberto Bianchi • DOC • ITL

SEXY NUDO • 1963 • Montero Roberto Bianchi • ITL

SEXY PARTY (UKN) see **DELITTO ALLO SPECCHIO** • 1964

SEXY PENELOPE see **PENELOPE PULLS IT OFF** • 1975

SEXY PROIBITISSIMO • 1963 • Martinelli Marcello • ITL • MOST PROHIBITED SEX, THE ○ PROHIBITED SEX ○ PROIBITISSIMO ○ FORBIDDEN FEMININITY ○ SEXY SUPER INTERDIT

SEXY PROIBITO • 1963 • Civirani Osvaldo • DOC • ITL

SEXY SECRETS OF THE KISSOGRAM GIRLS, THE • *Donna* • KISSOGRAM GIRLS

SEXY SHOW (USA) see **CAROSELLO DI NOTTE** • 1964

SEXY SINNERS (UKN) see **DECAMERON PROIBITISSIMO** • 1972

SEXY SISTERS see **OVERKLASSENS HEMMELIGE SEXGLAEDER** • 1974

SEXY SUPER INTERDIT see **SEXY PROIBITISSIMO** • 1963

SEXY SUSAN KNOWS HOW see **FRAU WIRTIN BLAST AUCH GERN TROMPETE** • 1972

SEXY SUSAN SINS AGAIN see **FRAU WIRTIN HAT AUCH EINEN GRAFEN** • 1968

SEXYCON see **QUARANTA GRADI ALL'OMBRA DEL LENZUOLO** • 1976

SEXYRELLA • 1968 • Mulot Claude • FRN • BIEN FAIRE ET LES SEDUIRE

SEY SARSILIYOR • 1986 • Yilmaz Atif • TRK • SARIPINAR 1914 ○ DEGIRMEN

SEY SEYETI • 1980 • Beye Diogaye • SNL • MAN, SOME WOMEN, A

SEYCHELLES see **SESZELE** • 1990

SEYH AHMET • 1968 • Gorec Ertem • TRK • SHEIK AHMET

SEYIT HAN see **SEYYIT KHAN** • 1968

SEYMOUR HICKS AND ELLALINE TERRISS • 1913 • Bantock Leedham • UKN

SEYMOUR HICKS EDITS "THE TATLER" • 1907 • *Urban Trading Co* • UKN

SEYMOUR HOUSE PARTY, THE • 1915 • Reehm George E. • USA

SEYN SAMIL • 1967 • Baytan Natuk • TRK • SHEIK SHAMIL

SEYTAN KAFESI • 1968 • Yalaz Suat • TRK • DEVIL'S CAGE, THE

SEYTAN KAYALIKLARI • 1970 • Filmer • TRK • DEVIL CRAG

SEYTANIN OGLU • 1967 • Duru Yilmaz • TRK • BUYUK CELLATLAR ○ DEVIL'S SON, THE ○ GREAT HANGMEN, THE

SEYYIT HAN "TOPRAGIN GELINI" see **SEYYIT KHAN** • 1968

SEYYIT KHAN • 1968 • Guney Yilmaz • TRK • SEYYIT HAN "TOPRAGIN GELINI" ○ BRIDE OF THE EARTH ○ SEYIT HAN

SEZ O'REILLY TO MCNAB (USA) see **SAID O'REILLY TO MCNAB** • 1937

SEZONA MIRA U PARIZU • 1981 • Golubovic Predrag • YGS, FRN • PEACETIME IN PARIS

SFERES DHEN YIRIZOUN PISO, I • 1967 • Foskolos Nikos • GRC • BULLETS DO NOT TURN BACK

SFIDA, LA • 1958 • Rosi Francesco • ITL, SPN • CHALLENGE, THE

SFIDA A RIO BRAVO • 1965 • Demicheli Tulio • ITL, SPN, FRN • JENNIE LEES HA UNA NUOVA PISTOLA (SPN) ○ DUEL A RIO BRAVO (FRN) ○ GUNMEN OF THE RIO GRANDE (USA) ○ DESAFIO EN RIO BRAVO ○ DUEL AT RIO BRAVO ○ SHERIFF DEL O.K. CORRAL, EL

SFIDA AL DIAVOLO • 1965 • Veggezzi Giuseppe • ITL • KATARSIS ○ CATHARSIS ○ FAUST

SFIDA AL RE DI CASTIGLIA • 1964 • Baldi Ferdinando • ITL, SPN • TYRANT OF CASTILE, THE (USA)

SFIDA DEGLI IMPLACABILI, LA (ITL) see **OESTE NEVADA JOE** • 1965

SFIDA DEI GIGANTI, LA • 1965 • Lucidi Maurizio • ITL • CHALLENGE OF THE GIANT, THE

SFIDA DEI MACKENNA, LA • 1970 • Klimovsky Leon • ITL • CHALLENGE OF THE MCKENNAS, THE

SFIDA NELLA CITTA DELL'ORO • 1960 • Medori Alfredo, Kugelstadt Hermann • ITL

SFIDA SUL FONDO • 1976 • Coletti Melchiade • ITL

SFIDA VIENE DA BANGKOK, LA • 1965 • Parolini Gianfranco • ITL, FRG, FRN • DIAMANTENHOLLE AM MEKONG, DIE (FRG) ○ MISSION TO HELL (USA) ○ CAVE OF DIAMONDS

SFINGE, LA • 1919 • Roberti Roberto Leone • ITL

SFINGE DAGLI OCCHI VERDI, LA • 1918 • Mari Febo • ITL

SFINGE D'ORO, LA • 1967 • Scattini Luigi • ITL, SPN, EGY • ESFINGE DE CRISTAL, LA (SPN) ○ GLASS SPHINX, THE (USA) ○ SFINGE TUTTA D'ORO, UNA ○ ALL-GOLD SPHINX, THE

SFINGE SORRIDE PRIMA DI MORIRE STOP -LONDRA, LA • 1964 • Tessari Duccio • ITL, FRG • HEISSE SPUR KAIRO-LONDON (FRG) ○ SECRET OF THE SPHINX (USA)

SFINGE TUTTA D'ORO, UNA see **SFINGE D'ORO, LA** • 1967

SFINXEN • 1913 • Davidsen Hjalmar • DNM

SFINXEN SON • 1915 • Dinesen Robert • DNM

SFIRSITUL NOPTI • 1982 • Veroiu Mircea • RMN • END OF THE NIGHT, THE ○ END OF NIGHT, THE

SGARBO, LO • 1975 • Girolami Marino • ITL

SGARRO ALLA CAMORRA • 1973 • Fizzarotti Ettore Maria • ITL

SGARRO, LO • 1962 • Siano Silvio • ITL, FRN

SGT. PEPPER'S LONELY HEARTS CLUB BAND • 1978 • Schultz Michael • USA, FRG

SGUARDO DAL PONTE, UNO (ITL) see **VU DU PONT** • 1962

SH! DON'T WAKE THE BABY • 1915 • *Gerard Joseph J.* • USA

SH-H-H-H-H • 1955 • Avery Tex • ANS • USA

SH! NOT A WORD • 1915 • Cooper Toby • UKN

SH! THE OCTOPUS • 1937 • McGann William • USA

SHA HSIAO-TZU • 1976 • Chang Ch'Eh • HKG • MAD BOY, THE

SHA-JEN-CHE SZU • 1981 • Mou Tun-Fei • HKG • STING OF DEATH, THE

SHA-LU CHAN-CH'ANG-TE PIEN-YUAN • 1987 • Li Tao-Ming Li • SHT • TWN

SHA LUNG CH'UN-HAI • 1989 • Chu Yen-P'Ing • TWN • DUMB DRAGONS GO TO SEA

SHA OU • 1981 • Zhang Nuanxin • CHN • DRIVE TO WIN, THE

SHA-SHOU HAO (HKG) see **BATTLE CREEK BRAWL** • 1980

SHAB-E-FERESHTEGAN • 1968 • Fazeli Reza • IRN • NIGHT OF ANGELS, THE

SHABA NO KAZE • 1928 • Uchida Tomu • JPN • WIND OF THIS WORLD

SHABAB IMRA'A see **CHABAB EMRAA** • 1956

SHABAB MAGNOUN GEDDAN • 1967 • Mustafa Niazi • EGY • MAD.. MAD.. YOUTHS

SHABASH • 1949 • Mallick P. • ANM • IND

SHABBIES, THE • 1915 • North Wilfred • USA

SHABBY TIGER, THE see **MASQUERADE** • 1964

SHABISTAN • 1951 • Mitra B. • IND

SHABNAM • 1949 • *Burman S. D. (M)* • IND

SHABON MUSUME • 1927 • Tasaka Tomotaka • JPN • SOAP GIRL

SHACHO DOCHUKI • 1960 • Matsubayashi Shue • JPN • PLAYBOY PRESIDENT (USA)

SHACHO GUOJOKI • 1966 • Matsubayashi Shue • JPN • FIVE GENTS AT SUNRISE

SHACHO HANJOKI • 1968 • Matsubayashi Shue • JPN • FIVE GENTS AND KARATE GRANDPA

SHACHO NINPOCHI • 1965 • Matsubayashi Shue • JPN • FIVE GENT'S TRICK BOOK

SHACHO SANDAIKI • 1958 • Matsubayashi Shue • JPN • RECORD OF THREE GENERATIONS OF PRESIDENTS, THE ○ SHACHOU SANDAI-KI

SHACHO SEN-ICHIYA • 1967 • Matsubayashi Shue • JPN • DISCOVER JAPAN WITH FIVE GENTS ○ ZOKU SHACHO SENICHIYA ○ FIVE GENTS PREFER GEISHA

SHACHOU KOUKOU-KO • 1962 • Sugie Toshio • JPN • STORY OF THE COMPANY PRESIDENT'S OVERSEAS TRAVELS

SHACHOU SANDAI-KI see **SHACHO SANDAIKI** • 1958

SHACHTERY see **CHAKHTIERY** • 1936

SHACK NEXT DOOR, THE • 1914 • *Universal* • USA

SHACK OUT ON 101 • 1955 • Dein Edward • USA

SHACKLED • 1918 • Barker Reginald?, Worsley Wallace • USA

SHACKLED LIGHTNING • 1925 • *Merrill Frank* • USA

SHACKLES • 1916 • Cochrane George • SHT • USA

SHACKLES OF FEAR • 1924 • Ferguson Al • USA

SHACKLES OF GOLD • 1922 • Brenon Herbert • USA

SHACKLES OF TRUTH • 1917 • Sloman Edward • USA

SHACKLETON'S EXPEDITION TO THE ANTARCTIC see **SOUTHWARD ON THE 'QUEST'** • 1923

SHADA KALO • 1953 • Bose Amal • IND • DR. JEKYLL AND MR. HYDE (USA)

SHADE OF AUTUMN, THE • 1912 • *Gaumont* • USA

SHADES OF LOVE: CHAMPAGNE FOR TWO • 1987 • Furey Lewis • USA • CHAMPAGNE FOR TWO

SHADES OF PUFFING BILLY • 1967 • Colacino Antonio • ASL

SHADES OF RED • 1982 • Rimmer David • CND

SHADES OF SHAKESPEARE • 1919 • Christie Al • SHT • USA

SHADEY • 1985 • Saville Philip • UKN

SHADOW • Lindberg Lars • ANS • SWD

SHADOW, THE • 1913 • Turner Otis • USA

SHADOW, THE • 1914 • *Joyce Alice* • USA

SHADOW, THE • 1916 • *American* • USA

SHADOW, THE • 1916 • Holubar Allen • *Victor* • SHT • USA

SHADOW, THE • 1921 • Davis J. Charles, Brown Jack W. • USA

SHADOW, THE • 1921 • Micheaux Oscar • USA

SHADOW, THE • 1933 • Cooper George A. • UKN

SHADOW, THE • 1937 • Coleman C. C. Jr. • USA • CIRCUS SHADOW, THE (UKN) ○ CARNIVAL LADY

SHADOW, THE • 1940 • Horne James W. • SRL • USA

SHADOW, THE • 1967 • Crisostomo Fely • PHL

SHADOW, THE • 1972 • Kosheverova Nadezhda • USS

SHADOW, THE • 1977 • Godfrey Bob • ANS • UKN

SHADOW, THE see **SKUGGAN** • 1953

SHADOW, THE see **CIEN** • 1956

SHADOW, THE see **STIN** • 1960

SHADOW AND THE SHADE, THE • 1915 • Le Saint Edward J. • USA

SHADOW ARMY see **ARMEE DES OMBRES, L'** • 1969

SHADOW BETWEEN, THE • 1920 • Dewhurst George • UKN

SHADOW BETWEEN, THE • 1931 • Walker Norman • UKN

SHADOW BOX, THE • 1980 • Newman Paul • TVM • USA

SHADOW CATCHER, THE • 1974 • McLuhan Teri • DOC • USA

SHADOW CHASERS • 1985 • Johnson Kenneth • TVM • USA

SHADOW DANCING • 1988 • Furey Lewis • CND • STAGE FRIGHT

SHADOW DETECTIVE STORIES • 1931-32 • *Universal* • SHS • USA

SHADOW DREAM • 1987 • Poskaitis Rimas • USA

SHADOW GIRL, THE (USA) see **CLOWNESSE FANTOME, LA** • 1902

SHADOW HOUSE • 1972 • Dixon Ken • USA

SHADOW IN LIGHT see **STIN VE SVETLE** • 1928

SHADOW IN THE MIST see **KUSHIRO NO YORU** • 1968

SHADOW IN THE SKY • 1951 • Wilcox Fred M. • USA • RAIN, RAIN, GO AWAY

SHADOW IN THE STREETS, A • 1975 • Donner Richard • TVM • USA

SHADOW LADY, THE (USA) see **DAME FANTOME, LA** • 1904

SHADOW LAUGHS, THE • 1933 • Hoerl Arthur • USA

SHADOW LINE, THE see **LIGNE D'OMBRE, LA** • 1971

SHADOW LINE, THE see **SMUGA CIENIA** • 1976

SHADOW MAN • 1988 • Andreyev Pyotr • NTH

SHADOW MAN (USA) see **STREET OF SHADOWS** • 1953

SHADOW OF A CITY, THE see **RANTOJEN MIEHET** • 1971

SHADOW OF A CRIME, THE • 1914 • *White Pearl* • USA

SHADOW OF A DOUBT • 1943 • Hitchcock Alfred • USA

SHADOW OF A DOUBT see **SCHIJN VAN TWIJFEL, EEN** • 1975

SHADOW OF A GAME, A see **OMBRE D'UN JEU, L'** • 1980

SHADOW OF A KILLER see **CON LA RABBIA AGLI OCCHI** • 1976

SHADOW OF A MAN • 1955 • McCarthy Michael • UKN

SHADOW OF A SMILE see **TORMENTO** • 1972

SHADOW OF A WOMAN • 1946 • Santley Joseph • USA

SHADOW OF ANOTHER TIME see **DVA DNYA** • 1927

SHADOW OF BLACKMAIL (UKN) see **WIFE WANTED** • 1946

SHADOW OF CHIKARA, THE see **WISHBONE CUTTER** • 1978

SHADOW OF CHINATOWN • 1936 • Hill Robert F. • SRL • USA • SHADOWS OF CHINATOWN

SHADOW OF DARKNESS see **YAMI NO KAGEBOSHI** • 1938

SHADOW OF DEATH • 1923 • Bentley Thomas • UKN

SHADOW OF DEATH • 1939 • Marks Harry S. • UKN

SHADOW OF DEATH see **BRAINWAVES** • 1982

SHADOW OF DEATH see **DESTROYER** • 1988

SHADOW OF DOUBT • 1935 • Seitz George B. • USA

SHADOW OF DOUBT, THE • 1916 • Physioc Wray • USA

SHADOW OF DREAM • 1990 • Delir Hossein • IRN

SHADOW OF EGYPT, THE • 1924 • Morgan Sidney • UKN • SHADOW OF THE MOSQUE, THE

SHADOW OF EVIL • 1921 • Reardon James • UKN

SHADOW OF EVIL (USA) see **BANCO A BANGKOK** • 1964

SHADOW OF FEAR • 1963 • Morris Ernest • UKN

SHADOW OF FEAR, THE • 1915 • Humphrey William • USA

SHADOW OF FEAR (USA) see **BEFORE I WAKE** • 1954

SHADOW OF GUILT, THE • 1914 • *Kalem* • USA

SHADOW OF KARAKORUM, THE see **IM SCHATTEN DES KARAKORUM** • 1955

SHADOW OF LIGHTNING RIDGE • 1920 • Lucas Wilfred • ASL

SHADOW OF MIKE EMERALD, THE • 1935 • Rogers Maclean • UKN

SHADOW OF NAZARETH, THE • 1913 • *Warner'S Features* • USA

SHADOW OF NIGHT, THE see **MODERN OTHELLO, A** • 1917

SHADOW OF ROSALIE BYRNES, THE • 1920 • Archainbaud George • USA

SHADOW OF SHAME, THE • 1913 • *Wilbur Crane* • USA

SHADOW OF SISA, THE see **ANINO NI SISA** • 1968

SHADOW OF SUSPICION • 1944 • Beaudine William • USA

SHADOW OF TERROR • 1945 • Landers Lew • USA

SHADOW OF THE APPLE, THE see **OMBRE DE LA POMME, L'** • 1967

SHADOW OF THE BAT, THE see **SOMBRA DEL MURCIELAGO, LA** • 1966

SHADOW OF THE CASTLES see **OMBRE DES CHATEAUX, L'** • 1977

SHADOW OF THE COBRA • 1989 • Joffe Mark • TVM • ASL

SHADOW OF THE CROSS, THE • 1912 • *Stonehouse Ruth* • USA

SHADOW OF THE DESERT see **SHADOW OF THE EAST, THE** • 1924

SHADOW OF THE EAGLE • 1950 • Salkow Sidney • UKN • EAGLE AND THE LAMB, THE

SHADOW OF THE EAGLE, THE • 1932 • Beebe Ford • SRL • USA

SHADOW OF THE EAST, THE • 1924 • Archainbaud George • USA • SHADOW OF THE DESERT

SHADOW OF THE GUILLOTINE (USA) see **MARIE-ANTOINETTE** • 1955

SHADOW OF THE HAWK • 1976 • McCowan George • CND

SHADOW OF THE LAW • 1930 • Gasnier Louis J., Marcin Max • USA

SHADOW OF THE LAW, THE • 1908 • *Selig* • USA

SHADOW OF THE LAW, THE • 1926 • Worsley Wallace • USA

SHADOW OF THE MOSQUE, THE see **SHADOW OF EGYPT, THE** • 1924

SHADOW OF THE PAST • 1950 • Zampi Mario • UKN

SHADOW OF THE PAST, A • 1912 • *Little Anna* • USA

SHADOW OF THE PAST, A • 1913 • Ince Thomas H. • USA

SHADOW OF THE PEACOCK • 1987 • Noyce Phil • ASL

SHADOW OF THE RAVEN, THE • 1988 • Gunnlaugsson Hrafn • ICL, SWD • PASCE CORVOS

SHADOW OF THE THIN MAN • 1941 • Van Dyke W. S. • USA

SHADOW OF THE TIGER • Yeung Kuen • HKG • DUEL OF THE SEVEN TIGERS

SHADOW OF THE WEREWOLF (UKN) see **NACHT DER VAMPIRE** • 1970

SHADOW OF THEIR WINGS see **WINGS FOR THE EAGLE** • 1942

SHADOW OF TIME • 1964 • Kotowski Jerzy • ANS • PLN • SHADOWS OF TIME

SHADOW OF TRAGEDY, THE • 1914 • Johnson Arthur • USA

SHADOW OF TREASON • 1963 • Breakston George • USA

SHADOW OF WAVES see **NAMIKAGE** • 1965

SHADOW OF ZORRO, THE (USA) see **CABALGANDO HACIA LA MUERTE** • 1962

SHADOW ON THE BLIND, THE • 1912 • *Furniss Harry* • USA

SHADOW ON THE HILL, THE (UKN) see **FIGLIO DELL'UOMO, IL** • 1955

SHADOW ON THE LAND • 1968 • Sarafian Richard C. • TVM • USA

SHADOW ON THE MOUNTAIN see **SHADOW ON THE MOUNTAIN AN EXPERIMENT ON THE WELSH HILLS** • 1931

SHADOW ON THE MOUNTAIN AN EXPERIMENT ON THE WELSH HILLS • 1931 • Elton Arthur • DOC • UKN • SHADOW ON THE MOUNTAIN

SHADOW ON THE PRAIRIES • 1953 • Blais Roger • DCS • CND • OMBRE SUR LA PRAIRIE

SHADOW ON THE SNOW see **ARNYEK A HAVON** • 1990

SHADOW ON THE WALL • 1949 • Jackson Pat • USA • DEATH IN THE DOLL'S HOUSE

SHADOW ON THE WALL, A • 1914 • *Melies* • USA

SHADOW ON THE WALL, THE • 1925 • Eason B. Reeves • USA
SHADOW ON THE WINDOW • 1957 • Asher William • USA
SHADOW OVER ELVERON • 1968 • Goldstone James • TVM • USA
SHADOW PLAY • 1986 • Shadburne Susan • USA
SHADOW RANCH • 1930 • King Louis • USA
SHADOW RANGER • 1926 • *Kesterson George* • USA
SHADOW RETURNS, THE • 1946 • Rosen Phil • USA
SHADOW RIDER see **SCHATTENREITER** • 1974
SHADOW RIDERS, THE • 1982 • McLaglen Andrew V. • TVM • USA • LOUIS L'AMOUR'S THE SHADOW RIDERS
SHADOW RIVER • 1933 • Sparling Gordon • DCS • CND
SHADOW SINISTER, THE • 1916 • Rice A. W. • SHT • USA
SHADOW STRIKES, THE • 1937 • Shores Lynn • USA
SHADOW VALLEY • 1947 • Taylor Ray • USA
SHADOW VS. THE 1000 EYES OF DR. MABUSE, THE see **TAUSEND AUGEN DES DR. MABUSE, DIE** • 1960
SHADOW WARRIOR, THE see **KAGEMUSHA** • 1980
SHADOW WITHIN, THE see **KAGE NO KURUMA** • 1970
SHADOW WORLD • 1983 • ANM • USA
SHADOWED • 1914 • Smalley Phillips • USA
SHADOWED • 1946 • Sturges John • USA • GLOVED HAND, THE
SHADOWED see **GIRL IN THE WEB, THE** • 1920
SHADOWED EYES • 1939 • Rogers Maclean • UKN
SHADOWED LIVES • 1914 • *Rex* • USA
SHADOWED SHADOW, A • 1916 • Beaudine William • SHT • USA
SHADOWED (UKN) see **LOOK OUT GIRL, THE** • 1928
SHADOWGRAPH MESSAGE, THE • 1913 • *Essanay* • USA
SHADOWGRAPH MESSAGE, THE • 1915 • *Edwards Walter* • USA
SHADOWING HENRY • 1917 • Drew Sidney, Drew Sidney Mrs. • SHT • USA
SHADOWLANDS • 1985 • Stone Norman • UKN
SHADOWMAN (UKN) see **HOMME SANS VISAGE, L'** • 1974
SHADOWPLAY • 1982 • Stapleton Oliver • UKN
SHADOWS • 1913 • Carleton Lloyd B. • USA
SHADOWS • 1914 • *Essanay* • USA
SHADOWS • 1914 • *Imp* • USA
SHADOWS • 1915 • Travers Henry • USA
SHADOWS • 1915 • Weston Harold • UKN
SHADOWS • 1916 • Eason B. Reeves • SHT • USA
SHADOWS • 1919 • Barker Reginald • USA
SHADOWS • 1922 • Forman Tom • USA • CHING, CHING, CHINAMAN
SHADOWS • 1923 • Fleischer Dave • ANS • USA
SHADOWS • 1931 • Esway Alexander • UKN • MY WIFE'S FAMILY ○ PRESS GANG
SHADOWS • 1959 • Cassavetes John • USA
SHADOWS • 1982 • Irvine Royden • ASL
SHADOWS see **HEART IN PAWN, A** • 1919
SHADOWS ACROSS THE SNOW see **SKUGGOR OVER SNON** • 1945
SHADOWS AND LIGHT see **SCHATTEN UND LICHT** • 1977
SHADOWS AND SUNSHINE • 1910 • *Lubin* • USA
SHADOWS AND SUNSHINE • 1914 • *Princess* • USA
SHADOWS AND SUNSHINE • 1916 • King Henry • USA
SHADOWS FROM LIGHT • 1984 • Dwoskin Stephen • UKN
SHADOWS FROM THE PAST • 1915 • Ridgely Richard • USA
SHADOWS GROW LONGER, THE (USA) see **SCHATTEN WERDEN LANGER, DIE** • 1962
SHADOWS IN A ROOM see **BLAZING MAGNUM** • 1977
SHADOWS IN PARADISE • 1986 • Kaurismaki Aki • FNL
SHADOWS IN SUNLIGHT see **MAHIRU NO ANKOKU** • 1956
SHADOWS IN SWING • 1941 • Le Borg Reginald • SHT • USA
SHADOWS IN THE NIGHT • 1944 • Forde Eugene J. • USA • CRIME DOCTOR'S RENDEZVOUS, THE
SHADOWS IN THE STORM • 1989 • Tannen Terrell • USA
SHADOWS OF A GREAT CITY • 1913 • Wilson Frank • UKN
SHADOWS OF A GREAT CITY, THE • 1915 • *Thurston Adelaide* • USA
SHADOWS OF A HOT SUMMER see **STINY HORKEHO LETA** • 1977
SHADOWS OF ADULTERY (USA) see **PROIE POUR L'OMBRE, LA** • 1960
SHADOWS OF ANGELS see **SCHATTEN DER ENGEL** • 1976
SHADOWS OF CHINATOWN • 1926 • Hurst Paul C. • USA
SHADOWS OF CHINATOWN see **SHADOW OF CHINATOWN** • 1936
SHADOWS OF CONSCIENCE • 1921 • McCarthy John P. • USA
SHADOWS OF DARKNESS see **MR. PATMAN** • 1980
SHADOWS OF DOUBT • 1916 • *Supreme* • USA
SHADOWS OF FEAR (USA) see **THERESE RAQUIN** • 1928
SHADOWS OF FIRE • 1947 • *Republic* • USA
SHADOWS OF FORGOTTEN ANCESTORS (USA) see **TINE ZABUTYKH PREDKIV** • 1965
SHADOWS OF HER PEST • 1918 • *Farley Dot* • SHT • USA
SHADOWS OF LIFE • 1913 • Smalley Phillips, Weber Lois • USA
SHADOWS OF OUR ANCESTORS see **TINE ZABUTYKH PREDKIV** • 1965
SHADOWS OF OUR FORGOTTEN ANCESTORS see **TINE ZABUTYKH PREDKIV** • 1965
SHADOWS OF PARIS • 1924 • Brenon Herbert • USA
SHADOWS OF PARIS see **PARIS** • 1926
SHADOWS OF SING SING • 1934 • Rosen Phil • USA
SHADOWS OF SINGAPORE (UKN) see **MALAY NIGHTS** • 1932
SHADOWS OF SUSPICION • 1916 • MacDonald Donald • SHT • USA
SHADOWS OF SUSPICION • 1919 • Carewe Edwin • USA
SHADOWS OF THE CAT, THE • 1961 • Gilling John • UKN
SHADOWS OF THE HARBOR • 1915 • Cullison Webster • USA
SHADOWS OF THE HOT SUMMER see **STINY HORKEHO LETA** • 1977
SHADOWS OF THE MOULIN ROUGE, THE • 1914 • Blache Alice • USA
SHADOWS OF THE NIGHT • 1928 • Lederman D. Ross • USA • DEADLINE, THE
SHADOWS OF THE NORTH • 1923 • Hill Robert F. • USA • SKYLINE OF SPRUCE, THE
SHADOWS OF THE ORIENT • 1937 • Lynwood Burt • USA
SHADOWS OF THE PAST • 1911 • *Selig* • USA
SHADOWS OF THE PAST • 1914 • Ince Ralph • USA
SHADOWS OF THE PAST • 1919 • Ince Ralph • USA
SHADOWS OF THE PAST • 1920 • *Ridgeway Fritzi* • SHT • USA
SHADOWS OF THE PAST • 1928 • Lang Walter • USA
SHADOWS OF THE PAST see **POWROT** • 1960
SHADOWS OF THE PAST, THE • 1913 • *Billington Francelia* • USA
SHADOWS OF THE PAST (USA) see **SCHATTEN DER VERGANGENHEIT** • 1936
SHADOWS OF THE RANGE • 1942 • English John • USA
SHADOWS OF THE SEA • 1922 • Crosland Alan • USA
SHADOWS OF THE WEST • 1920 • Hurst Paul C. • USA
SHADOWS OF THE WEST • 1949 • Taylor Ray • USA
SHADOWS OF THE WIND, THE see **SAYEHAYE BOLANDE BAD** • 1978
SHADOWS OF THE YOSHIWARA see **JUJIRO** • 1928
SHADOWS OF TIME see **SHADOW OF TIME** • 1964
SHADOWS OF TOMBSTONE • 1953 • Witney William • USA
SHADOWS OF YOSHIWARA see **JUJIRO** • 1928
SHADOWS ON SILK see **OMBRES DE SOIE** • 1977
SHADOWS ON THE RANGE • 1946 • Hillyer Lambert • USA
SHADOWS ON THE SAGE • 1942 • Orlebeck Lester • USA
SHADOWS ON THE SNOW see **SKUGGOR OVER SNON** • 1945
SHADOWS ON THE STAIRS • 1941 • Lederman D. Ross • USA
SHADOWS ON THE WALL • 1987 • Poole Patrick C. • USA
SHADOWS OVER CHINATOWN • 1946 • Morse Terry O. • USA
SHADOWS OVER SHANGHAI • 1938 • Lamont Charles • USA
SHADOWS RUN BLACK • 1984 • Heard Howard • USA
SHADY LADY • 1945 • Waggner George • USA
SHADY LADY, THE • 1929 • Griffith Edward H. • USA
SHAFFER JAMES P. see **HUMMINGBIRD** • 1968
SHAFT • 1971 • Parks Gordon • USA
SHAFT, THE • 1969 • Tomblin Barry • UKN
SHAFT IN AFRICA • 1973 • Guillermin John • USA
SHAFT OF BURIED HOPES, THE see **SACHTA POHRBENYCH IDEI** • 1921
SHAFT'S BIG SCORE • 1972 • Parks Gordon • USA
SHAG • 1989 • Barron Zelda • UKN
SHAG S KRISHI • *Nikolaiev Mitia* • USS • ONLY SOME STEPS FROM THE ROOF
SHAGAI, SOVIET! • 1926 • Vertov Dziga • USS • STRIDE, SOVIET!
SHAGGY • 1948 • Tansey Robert • USA
SHAGGY D. A., THE • 1977 • Stevenson Robert • USA
SHAGGY DOG, THE • 1959 • Barton Charles T. • USA
SHAGI V NOCHI • 1963 • Vabalas Raimondas • USS • FOOTSTEPS IN THE NIGHT ○ FOOTSTEPS IN THE DARK
SHAGIRD • 1967 • Ganguly Samir • IND • BACHELOR
SHAH ISMAIL see **SAH ISMAIL** • 1968
SHAHEEN • 1985 • Siddik Khalid • KWT, ITL • FALCON, THE
SHAHEN SHAI • 1953 • *Burman S. D. (M)* • IND
SHAHENSHAH • 1953 • IND
SHAHENSHAH • 1988 • *Bachchan Amitabh* • IND
SHAHID REJAI SCHOOL • 1989 • Zargar Karim • IRN
SHAHRAHE ZENDEGI • 1968 • Ghaderi Iraj • IRN • LIFE'S HIGHWAY
SHAHRE GHESSEH • 1973 • Anvar Manoutchehr • IRN • CITY OF TALES
SHAHRFARANG • 1967 • Ossanlu Parviz • IRN • PEEP-SHOW
SHAH'S MAGIC BEARD, THE • 1967 • Nowicki Bogdan • ANM • PLN
SHAIA YUHIM, LA • 1973 • Kamal Hussein • EGY • RIEN N'A D'IMPORTANCE
SHAIF-E-SULEMANI see **TILISMI TALWAR** • 1934
SHAIL BALA • 1932 • *Gohar Miss* • IND
SHAITAN AS-SAHRA see **SHAITAN EL SAHARA** • 1954
SHAITAN EL SAHARA • 1954 • Shahin Youssef • EGY • DEVIL OF THE DESERT, THE ○ SHAITAN AS-SAHRA
SHAITAN, IL DIAVOLO DEL DESERTO (ITL) see **FORTUNE CARREE** • 1954
SHAITANE EL SAGHIR, EL • 1963 • el Sheikh Kamal • EGY • SMALL DEVIL, THE ○ SHAYTAN AS-SAGHIR, ASH- ○ PETIT DEMON, LE ○ OTAGE, L'
SHAI'UN FI HAYATI • 1966 • Barakat Henry • EGY • QUELQUE CHOSE EST ARRIVE DANS MA VIE
SHAI'UN FI SADRY • 1971 • el Sheikh Kamal • EGY • PROFOND SECRET, LE
SHAI'UN MINA AL-ADHAB • 1969 • Abu Saif Salah • EGY • CERTAINE DOULEUR, UNE
SHAI'UN MINA AL-KHAWF • 1969 • Kamal Hussein • EGY • SOUPCON DE PEUR, UN
SHAKA • 1962 • Misumi Kenji • JPN • LIFE OF BUDDHA, THE ○ BUDDHA ○ SAKYA
SHAKA ZULU • 1986 • Faure William C. • MTV • SAF
SHAKE-A-BOOM • 1967 • Cayado Tony • PHL
SHAKE 'EM UP • 1921 • Roach Hal • SHT • USA
SHAKE HANDS WITH MURDER • 1944 • Herman Al • USA
SHAKE HANDS WITH THE DEVIL • 1959 • Anderson Michael • UKN
SHAKE, RATTLE AND ROCK! • 1956 • Cahn Edward L. • USA
SHAKE YOUR POWDER PUFF • 1934 • Freleng Friz • ANS • USA
SHAKEDOWN • 1936 • Selman David • USA
SHAKEDOWN • 1950 • Pevney Joseph • USA
SHAKEDOWN • 1988 • Glickenhaus James • USA • BLUE JEAN COP
SHAKEDOWN, THE • 1929 • Wyler William • USA
SHAKEDOWN, THE • 1960 • Lemont John • UKN • NAKED MIRROR, THE
SHAKEDOWN, THE see **BIG SHAKEDOWN, THE** • 1934
SHAKEDOWN ON THE SUNSET STRIP • 1988 • Grauman Walter • TVM • USA
SHAKER RUN • 1985 • Morrison Bruce • NZL
SHAKERS, THE • 1946 • *Holm Hanya* • USA
SHAKESPEARE • 1934 • Holmes J. B. • UKN
SHAKESPEARE AND KRONBERG see **SHAKESPEARE OG KRONBERG** • 1951
SHAKESPEARE ECRIVANT LA MORT DE JULES CESAR see **REVE DE SHAKESPEARE, LE** • 1907
SHAKESPEARE OG KRONBERG • 1951 • Roos Jorgen • DOC • DNM • HAMLET'S CASTLE ○ SHAKESPEARE AND KRONBERG
SHAKESPEARE WALLAH • 1966 • Ivory James • IND
SHAKESPEARE -WITH TIN EARS • 1933 • Goodwins Leslie • SHT • USA
SHAKESPEARE WRITING JULIUS CAESAR (USA) see **REVE DE SHAKESPEARE, LE** • 1907
SHAKESPEARE'S THEATER: THE GLOBE PLAYHOUSE • 1953 • Jordan William, Jordan Mildred • DOC • USA
SHAKESPERIAN SPINACH • 1940 • Fleischer Dave • ANS • USA
SHAKEY: AN EXPERIMENT IN ROBOT PLANNING AND LEARNING • 1975 • *Hart Peter/ Nilsson Hans (P)* • SHT • USA
SHAKHMATNAYA GORYACHKA • 1925 • Pudovkin V. I., Shpikovsky Nikolai • USS • CHESS FEVER ○ CHAKHMATNAIA GORIATCHKA
SHAKIEST GUN IN THE WEST, THE • 1968 • Rafkin Alan • USA
SHAKKAR • 1988 • Islam Nazaral • PKS • CIRCLES ○ FRAUD
SHAKKET EL TALABA • 1967 • Radwan Tolba • EGY • STUDENT FLAT
SHAKSHI GOPAL • 1949 • Mukherjee Chitra • IND
SHAKUNTALA • 1931 • Kapoor Prithviraj • IND
SHAKUNTALA • 1943 • Shantaram Rajaram • IND
SHAKUNTALA • 1945 • *Prithvi* • IND
SHAKUNTALA • 1947 • Shantaram Victor • IND
SHAKUNTALA see **SAKUNTHALAI** • 1967
SHALAKO! • 1968 • Dmytryk Edward • UKN, FRG
SHALIMAR • 1978 • Shah Krishna • USA, IND
SHALL A WOMAN OBEY see **WOMAN WHO OBEYED, THE** • 1923
SHALL CUCKOO SING AT NIGHT? • Chung Jin-Woo • SKR
SHALL CURFEW RING TONIGHT • 1914 • Murphy J. A.?, Smiley Joseph? • USA
SHALL NEVER HUNGER • 1912 • *Johnson Arthur* • USA
SHALL THE CHILDREN PAY (UKN) see **WHAT PRICE INNOCENCE?** • 1933
SHALL WE DANCE • 1937 • Sandrich Mark • USA
SHALL WE DANCE • 1989 • Koca Bogdan • SHT • ASL
SHALL WE DANCE FIRST? see **SKAL VI DANSE FORST?** • 1979
SHALL WE FORGIVE HER? • 1917 • Ashley Arthur • USA
SHALL WE PLAY HIDE AND SEEK • 1970 • Hedegaard Tom • DNM
SHALLOW BOX TRICK, THE see **BOITE A MALICE, LA** • 1903
SHALLOW GRAVE • 1987 • Styles Richard • USA
SHALOM • 1973 • Yosha Yaki • ISR • PEACE -A PRAYER FOR THE ROAD
SHAM • 1921 • Heffron Thomas N. • USA
SHAM, THE see **KLIPPET** • 1982
SHAM BATTLE SHENANIGANS • 1942 • Rasinski Connie • ANS • USA
SHAM REALITY, THE • 1916 • Ford Francis • SHT • USA
SHAM SUFFRAGETTE, THE • 1913 • *Powers* • USA • BILLY THE SUFFRAGETTE
SHAM SWORD SWALLOWER, THE • 1906 • Williamson James • UKN
SHAMAN see **SAMAN** • 1977
SHAMAN, THE • 1987 • Yakub Michael • USA
SHAMAN PSALM • 1981 • Broughton James • USA
SHAME • 1918 • Noble John W. • USA
SHAME • 1921 • Flynn Emmett J. • USA
SHAME • 1987 • Jodrell Steve • ASL
SHAME see **VSTRECHNYI** • 1932
SHAME see **INTRUDER, THE** • 1961
SHAME see **STUD** • 1967
SHAME see **UTANC** • 1973
SHAME, THE see **SKAMMEN** • 1968
SHAME OF A NATION, THE (UKN) see **SCARFACE** • 1932
SHAME OF MARY BOYLE, THE (USA) see **JUNO AND THE PAYCOCK** • 1929
SHAME OF PATTI SMITH, THE see **CASE OF PATTI SMITH, THE** • 1962
SHAME OF THE BULLCON, THE • 1917 • Curtis Allen • SHT • USA
SHAME OF THE JUNGLE • 1975 • Szulzinger Boris, Picha • ANM • BLG, FRN
SHAME OF THE SABINE WOMEN, THE (USA) see **RAPTO DE LAS SABINAS, EL** • 1958
SHAME ON YOU see **HARAM ALEK** • 1953
SHAME ON YOU, SWINE see **VERGOGNA, SCHIFOSI!** • 1968
SHAME, SHAME, EVERYBODY KNOWS HER NAME • 1969 • Jacoby Joseph • USA
SHAMED (USA) see **PRELUDIO D'AMORE** • 1946
SHAMEFUL see **NERO SU BIANCO** • 1969
SHAMEFUL BEHAVIOR? • 1926 • Kelley Albert • USA
SHAMEFUL DREAM see **HAZUKASHII YUME** • 1927
SHAMEFUL SUMMER • 1969 • Bastac Branislav • YGS
SHAMEFUL TECHNIQUE see **HAZUKASHII GIKO** • 1967
SHAMELESS see **MY MAN AND I** • 1952
SHAMELESS see **SCHAMLOS** • 1968
SHAMELESS, THE • 1962 • Martin Jay • USA • NAKED SEARCH, THE ○ BAREST HEIRESS, THE
SHAMELESS DESIRE • 1967 • Bronislau Serge • USA • SHAMELESS DESIRES
SHAMELESS DESIRES see **SHAMELESS DESIRE** • 1967
SHAMELESS OLD LADY, THE (USA) see **VIEILLE DAME INDIGNE, LA** • 1964
SHAMELESS SEX see **SEI NO HARENCHI** • 1968
SHAMELESS WIDOW, A see **VIUDA DESCOCADA** • 1980
SHAMESTRICKEN MAN, THE see **SHARMSAR**
SHAMING, THE see **GOOD LUCK, MISS WYCKOFF** • 1979
SHAMING OF THE TRUE, THE • 1930 • Creighton Walter • UKN
SHAMISEN AND MOTORCYCLE see **SHAMISEN TO OTOBAI** • 1961
SHAMISEN TO OTOBAI • 1961 • Shinoda Masahiro • JPN • LOVE OLD AND NEW ○ LOVE NEW AND OLD ○ SHAMISEN AND MOTORCYCLE
SHAMPOO • 1975 • Ashby Hal • USA
SHAMROCK ALLEY • 1927 • Lamont Charles • SHT • USA
SHAMROCK AND ROLL • 1969 • McKimson Robert • ANS • USA
SHAMROCK AND THE ROSE, THE • 1927 • Nelson Jack • USA
SHAMROCK HANDICAP, THE • 1926 • Ford John • USA
SHAMROCK HILL • 1949 • Dreifuss Arthur • USA
SHAMROCK TOUCH, THE see **LUCK OF THE IRISH, THE** • 1948

SHAMS AL-RABIH • 1968 • Lahalolo Latif • MRC • SPRING SUN, THE
SHAMS FI YAUM GHAIM • 1985 • Shahin Mohammed • SYR • SUN ON A CLOUDY DAY
SHAMS OF SOCIETY • 1921 • Walsh Thomas B. • USA
SHAMS WA ADH-DHIBA, ASH- • 1976 • Behi Ridha • NTH, TNS • HYENA'S SUN ○ SOLEIL DES HYENES
SHAMUS • 1959 • Marquis Eric • UKN
SHAMUS • 1973 • Kulik Buzz • USA
SHAMUS O'BRIEN • 1912 • Turner Otis • USA
SHAMUS O'BRIEN: OR, SAVED FROM THE SCAFFOLD • 1905 • Green Tom? • UKN
SHAMWARI • 1979 • Harding Clive • SAF
SHAN-CHUNG CH'UAN-CHI • 1978 • Hu King • HKG • LEGEND OF THE MOUNTAIN (USA)
SHAN-E-KHUDA • 1934 • *Bibbo* • IND • SAIR-E-PARISTAN
SHAN-KO LIEN • 1964 • Lo Chen • HKG • SHEPHERD GIRL, THE (USA)
SHAN KOU • 1981 • Yu Yunk'Ang • HKG • BEAST, THE
SHANABO FIL MASSIADA • 1968 • Mustafa Hassam Eddin • EGY • SHANABO IN A TRAP
SHANABO IN A TRAP see **SHANABO FIL MASSIADA** • 1968
SHANE • 1953 • Stevens George • USA
SHANG-HAI SHI-HUI TANG-AN • 1982 • Wang Chu-Chin • TWN • ON THE SOCIETY FILE OF SHANGAHI
SHANG-HSING LIEH-CH'E • 1982 • Sung Hsiang-Ju • TWN • UP TRAIN, THE
SHANGANI PATROL • 1971 • Millin David • SAF
SHANGHAI • 1935 • Flood James • USA
SHANGHAI • 1938 • Kamei Fumio • JPN
SHANGHAI • 1985 • Fleury Pieter • DOC • NTH
SHANGHAI BOUND • 1927 • Reed Luther • USA
SHANGHAI CHEST, THE • 1948 • Beaudine William • USA
SHANGHAI COBRA, THE • 1945 • Karlson Phil • USA • CHARLIE CHAN IN THE SHANGHAI COBRA
SHANGHAI DOCUMENT, THE see **SHANGHAISKY DOKUMENT** • 1928
SHANGHAI DRAMA, THE see **DRAME DE SHANGHAI, LE** • 1938
SHANGHAI EXPRESS • 1932 • von Sternberg Josef • USA
SHANGHAI GESTURE, THE • 1941 • von Sternberg Josef • USA
SHANGHAI JOE see **MIO NOME E SHANGHAI JOE, IL** • 1973
SHANGHAI LADY • 1929 • Robertson John S. • USA • GIRL FROM CHINA, THE (UKN)
SHANGHAI MADNESS • 1933 • Blystone John G. • USA
SHANGHAI MOON see **SHANGHAI NO TSUKI** • 1941
SHANGHAI NO TSUKI • 1941 • Naruse Mikio • JPN • MOON OVER SHANGHAI, THE ○ SHANGHAI MOON
SHANGHAI ROSE • 1929 • Pembroke Scott • USA • SECRET WOMAN, THE (UKN)
SHANGHAI STORY, THE • 1954 • Lloyd Frank • USA
SHANGHAI SURPRISE, THE • 1986 • Goddard Jim • UKN, USA
SHANGHAI VANCE KING • 1984 • Fukasaku Kinji • JPN
SHANGHAI WOODY • 1971 • Smith Paul J. • ANS • USA
SHANGHAIED • 1909 • *Essanay* • USA
SHANGHAIED • 1910 • *Defender* • USA
SHANGHAIED • 1912 • Campbell Colin • USA
SHANGHAIED • 1913 • *Champion* • USA
SHANGHAIED • 1915 • *Monty* • USA
SHANGHAIED • 1915 • Chaplin Charles • *Essanay* • USA • CHARLIE ON THE OCEAN ○ CHARLIE THE SAILOR
SHANGHAIED • 1927 • Ince Ralph • USA
SHANGHAIED • 1934 • Gillett Burt • ANS • USA
SHANGHAIED BABY, THE • 1915 • Terwilliger George W. • USA
SHANGHAIED COWBOYS, THE • 1912 • *Nestor* • USA
SHANGHAIED JONAH, A • 1917 • *Armstrong Billy* • SHT • USA
SHANGHAIED LOVE • 1931 • Seitz George B. • USA
SHANGHAIED LOVERS • 1924 • Del Ruth Roy • SHT • USA
SHANGHAIED SHIPMATES • 1936 • King Jack • ANS • USA
SHANGHAISKY DOKUMENT • 1928 • Blyokh Yakov • USS • SHANGHAI DOCUMENT, THE ○ CHINESE DOCUMENT, A
SHANGO LA PISTOLA INFALLIBILE • 1970 • Mulargia Edoardo
SHANGRI-LA • 1961 • *Randall Dick (P)* • USA
SHANHAI NO ONNA • 1952 • Inagaki Hiroshi • JPN • LADY FROM SHANGHAI ○ WOMAN OF SHANGHAI
SHANI • 1988 • Rizvi Saeed • PKS
SHANK ZAHRAN • 1967 • Shukry Mamduh • EGY
SHANKAR-PARVATI • 1944 • Doshi Chaturbhuj • IND
SHANKAR'S VICTORY see **JAI SHANKAR** • 1951
SHANKS • 1974 • Castle William • USA • SHOCK
SHANKS AND CHIVALRY • 1916 • Semon Larry • SHT • USA
SHANLINZHONGTOU YIGE NUREN • 1988 • Wang Junzheng • CHN • FIRST WOMAN IN THE FORESTS, THE
SHANNON OF THE SIXTH • 1914 • Melford George • USA
SHANNONS OF BROADWAY, THE • 1929 • Flynn Emmett J. • USA
SHANNON'S WOMEN • 1969 • Rotsler William • USA • LOVE, HOLLYWOOD STYLE
SHANTATA, COURT CHALU AHE • 1970 • Karnad Girish • IND
SHANTET HAMZA • 1967 • el Saifi Hassan • EGY • HAMZA'S SUITCASE
SHANTUNG MAN IN HONGKONG see **HSIAO SHANTUNG TAO HSIANGKANG** • 1975
SHANTY AT TREMBLING HILL, THE • 1914 • *Bushman Francis X.* • USA
SHANTY TRAMP • 1967 • Prieto Joseph G. • USA
SHANTY WHERE OLD SANTA CLAUS LIVES, THE • 1933 • Ising Rudolf • ANS • USA
SHANTYTOWN • 1943 • Santley Joseph • USA
SHANTYTOWN HONEYMOON • 1972 • *Brooke Ashley* • USA
SHAO-LIN SAN-SHIH-LIU FANG • 1977 • Liu Chia-Liang • HKG • 36TH CHAMBER OF SHAOLIN, THE ○ MASTER KILLER
SHAO-LIN SZU • 1981 • Chang Hsing-Yen • HKG • SHAOLIN TEMPLE, THE
SHAO-LIN TA-P'ENG HSIAO-TZU • 1980 • Liu Chia-Liang • HKG • RETURN TO THE 36TH CHAMBER
SHAO NU SHIH CHIEH • 1977 • Ch'En Yao-Ch'I • HKG • YOUNG GIRL'S TEN RULES, A
SHAOLIN AVENGERS see **FANG SHIH-YU HU HU-CH'IEN** • 1976
SHAOLIN CHALLENGES NINJA see **HUANG FEI-HUNG YU LU A-TS'AI** • 1978
SHAOLIN CHAMBER OF DEATH • 1984 • Chen Chi Hua • HKG • SHAOLIN WOODEN MEN
SHAOLIN DEATH SQUAD • 1977 • Kuo Joseph • HKG • SHAOLIN KIDS, THE
SHAOLIN DEVIL AND SHAOLIN ANGEL • *Chen Sing* • HKG • SHAOLIN DEVIL, SHAOLIN ANGEL
SHAOLIN DEVIL, SHAOLIN ANGEL see **SHAOLIN DEVIL AND SHAOLIN ANGEL**
SHAOLIN DRUNK FIGHTER see **SHAOLIN DRUNKEN FIGHTER** • 1986
SHAOLIN DRUNKEN FIGHTER • 1986 • Tao Man Po • HKG • SHAOLIN DRUNK FIGHTER
SHAOLIN HU HO CHEN T'IEN-HSIA • 1976 • Wang Yu • HKG • TIGER AND CRANE FISTS
SHAOLIN INVINCIBLE STICKS • Lee Tso Nam • HKG
SHAOLIN IRON CLAWS • Ko Shih Hao • HKG
SHAOLIN KIDS, THE see **SHAOLIN DEATH SQUAD** • 1977
SHAOLIN MANTIS see **T'ANG-LANG** • 1977
SHAOLIN MARTIAL ARTS • 1974 • Chang Ch'Eh • HKG
SHAOLIN SZU SHIH-PA T'UNG JEN • 1976 • Kuo Nanhung • HKG • 18 BRONZEMEN, THE
SHAOLIN TEMPLE • Chang Ch'Eh • HKG
SHAOLIN TEMPLE 2 • Kuo Joseph • HKG • SHAOLIN TEMPLE STRIKES BACK
SHAOLIN TEMPLE, THE see **SHAO-LIN SZU** • 1981
SHAOLIN TEMPLE STRIKES BACK see **SHAOLIN TEMPLE 2**
SHAOLIN: THE BLOOD MISSION • 1984 • Leung Wing Chan • HKG
SHAOLIN TZU-TI • 1975 • Chang Ch'Eh • HKG • MEN FROM THE MONASTERY ○ DRAGON'S TEETH, THE
SHAOLIN WARRIOR • Li Chao • HKG
SHAOLIN WOODEN MEN see **SHAOLIN CHAMBER OF DEATH** • 1984
SHAOLIN WU TSU • 1975 • Chang Ch'Eh • HKG • FIVE SHAOLIN MASTERS
SHAOLIN'S SILVER SPEAR • 1975 • Sung Ting Mei • HKG
SHAONIAN FAN • 1985 • Zhang Liang • CHN • JUVENILE DELINQUENTS
SHAOYEDE MONAN • 1988 • Wu Yi-Gong, Zhang Jianya • CHN • TRIBULATIONS OF A YOUNG MASTER, THE
SHAPE AHOY • 1945 • Sparber I. • ANS • USA
SHAPE OF FILMS TO COME • 1968 • Van Dyke Willard • DOC • USA
SHAPE OF NIGHT, THE see **YORU NO HENRIN** • 1964
SHAPE OF QUALITY, THE • 1965 • Schepisi Fred • DOC • ASL
SHAPE OF THINGS TO COME, THE see **THINGS TO COME** • 1936
SHAPE OF THINGS TO COME, THE see **H.G. WELLS' THE SHAPE OF THINGS TO COME** • 1979
SHAPE UP • 1985 • Tobias Marice • USA
SHAPER • 1981 • Lofven Chris • SHT • ASL
SHAPES AND SCRAPES • 1920 • Moore Vin • SHT • USA
SHAPING THE WORLD • 1961 • Goldscholl Morton, Goldscholl Mildred • ANM • USA
SHAPKA NA TOYAGA • 1972 • Kirkov Lyudmil • BUL • ON TOP OF THE WORLD ○ HAT ON A STICK
SHAPP FOR GOVERNOR • 1966 • Patry Pierre • DCS • USA • CANDIDAT GOUVERNEUR, MILTON SHAPP
SHAQUE • 1976 • Vikas Aruna • IND • TRIAL, THE
SHARAD OF ATLANTIS • 1936 • Eason B. Reeves, Kane Joseph • USA
SHARADA • 1958 • *Kapoor Raj* • IND
SHARAF EL BADAWI • 1918 • *Italo-Egyptian Cine Co.* • EGY
SHARAZ • 1968 • Elorrieta Jose Maria • ITL
SHARDS see **CSEREPEK** • 1981
SHARE AND SHARE ALIKE • 1925 • Bennett Whitman • USA
SHARE CROPPER see **HARI HONDAL BARGADAR** • 1981
SHARE OF SEX, THE see **SEI NO HAITO** • 1968
SHARE OUT, THE • 1962 • Glaister Gerald • UKN
SHARE THE WEALTH • 1936 • Lord Del • SHT • USA
SHARED ROOM see **WSPOLNY POKOJ** • 1959
SHARI' AL-BAHLAWAN see **SHARIAH EL BAHLAWANE** • 1949
SHARIAH EL BAHLAWANE • 1949 • Abu Saif Salah • EGY • STREET OF THE PUPPET SHOW ○ SHARI' AL-BAHLAWAN
SHARID, ASH- • 1941 • Barakat Henry • EGY • DELINQUANT, LE
SHARIK AND SHURIK • 1960 • Makhnach Leonid • DOC • USS
SHARING RICHARD • 1988 • Bonerz Peter • TVM • USA
SHARK! • 1969 • Fuller Samuel, Portillo Rafael • USA, MXC • ARMA DE DOS FILOS, UN (MXC) ○ MANEATER ○ CAINE
SHARK! • 1982 • Stoneman John • MTV • CND
SHARK, THE • 1920 • Henderson Dell • USA
SHARK AND THE SARDINES, THE • de Arma Jesus • ANS • CUB
SHARK BOY OF BORA BORA see **BEYOND THE REEF** • 1981
SHARK FEEDER, THE see **HAIFISCHFUTTERET, DER**
SHARK FISHERMEN see **TIBURONEROS** • 1962
SHARK GOD, THE • 1913 • *Champion* • USA
SHARK GOD, THE (UKN) see **OMOO OMOO** • 1949
SHARK HUNTER, THE • 1984 • Castellari Enzo G. • ITL
SHARK HUNTER, THE see **CACCIATORE DE SQUALI, IL** • 1979
SHARK KILL • 1976 • Graham William A. • TVM • USA
SHARK MASTER, THE • 1921 • Granville Fred Leroy • USA
SHARK MONROE • 1918 • Hart William S. • USA
SHARK REEF • 1985 • Kool Allen • CND
SHARK REEF (UKN) see **SHE-GODS OF SHARK REEF** • 1956
SHARK RIVER • 1953 • Rawlins John • USA
SHARK WEARS PERFUME, THE see **SEGRETISSIMO** • 1967
SHARK WHO KNEW TOO MUCH, THE see **HAJEN SOM VISSTE FOR MYCKET** • 1989
SHARKEY'S MACHINE • 1981 • Reynolds Burt • USA
SHARKFIGHTERS, THE • 1956 • Hopper Jerry • USA
SHARKS, THE see **SAME** • 1964
SHARKS AND SWORDFISH • 1931 • *Smith Pete* • SHT • USA
SHARK'S CAVE (UKN) see **FOSSA MALEDETTA, LA** • 1978
SHARKS IS SHARKS • 1917 • De Lorme L. E., Hancock H. E. • ANS • USA
SHARK'S PARADISE • 1986 • Jenkins Michael • ASL
SHARK'S TREASURE • 1974 • Wilde Cornel • USA • TREASURE, THE
SHARMA AND BEYOND • 1984 • Gilbert Brian • UKN
SHARMEELEE • 1971 • *Burman S. D. (M)* • IND
SHARMSAR • IRN • SHAMESTRICKEN MAN, THE
SHARON: PORTRAIT OF A MISTRESS • 1977 • Greenwald Robert • TVM • USA
SHARON, VESTIDA DE ROJO • 1968 • Lorente German • SPN
SHARON'S BABY see **I DON'T WANT TO BE BORN** • 1975
SHARP LEFT BEHIND THE MOON • Ratz Gunter • ANM • GDR
SHARP PRACTICE • 1912 • Noy Wilfred • UKN
SHARP SHOOTERS • 1928 • Blystone John G. • USA • THREE NAVAL RASCALS (UKN)
SHARP-WITTED THIEF, THE • 1910 • Fitzhamon Lewin • UKN
SHARPER THAN THE SHARPEST see **SHITT SUTT KA JIN JIN LE** • 1983
SHARPIES • 1978 • Moore Michael • SAF
SHARPIES see **HAURI** • 1987
SHARPS AND CHAPS • 1912 • *Nestor* • USA
SHARPS AND FLATS • 1915 • Birch Cecil • UKN
SHARPS WANT A FLAT, THE • 1914 • *Asher Max* • USA
SHARPSHOOTER see **MARKO ASINTADO** • 1967
SHARPSHOOTER, THE • 1913 • Giblyn Charles • USA
SHARPSHOOTER, THE • 1978 • DNM
SHARPSHOOTERS • 1938 • Tinling James • USA
SHARPSHOOTERS see **STRELTZI** • 1967
SHARPSHOOTERS, THE • Donev Boniu • ANS • BUL
SHASATSU-MA • 1970 • Adachi Masao • JPN • YOUNG MAN WITH A GUN
SHASHOU QING • 1988 • Yan Xueshu • CHN, HKG • KILLER'S LOVE
SHASO • 1989 • Masuda Toshio • JPN • COMPANY EXECUTIVES
SHAT'I AL-ASRAR • 1958 • Salem Atef • EGY • RIVAGE DES SECRETS, LE
SHAT'I' AL-GHARAM • 1948 • Barakat Henry • EGY • RIVAGE DE L'AMOUR
SHAT'I' AL-HUBB • 1960 • Barakat Henry • EGY • RIVAGE DE L'AMOUR
SHATRANJ KE KHILARI • 1977 • Ray Satyajit • IND • CHESS PLAYERS, THE (USA)
SHATRANJE BAAD • 1975 • Aslani Mohammad Reza • IRN • CHESS OF WIND, THE
SHATTER see **CALL HIM MR. SHATTER** • 1975
SHATTERED • 1990 • Johnson Lamont • USA • VOICES WITHIN
SHATTERED • 1990 • Petersen Wolfgang • USA
SHATTERED see **SCHERBEN** • 1921
SHATTERED see **SOMETHING TO HIDE** • 1971
SHATTERED see **PASSAGERS, LES** • 1976
SHATTERED DREAM, A • 1911 • Melies Gaston • USA
SHATTERED DREAMS • 1922 • Scardon Paul • USA • CLAY
SHATTERED DREAMS • 1988 • Schonfeld Victor • UKN
SHATTERED FAITH • 1923 • Ormont Jesse J. • USA
SHATTERED IDEALS • 1917 • *Big U* • SHT • USA
SHATTERED IDOLS • 1922 • Sloman Edward • USA • BRIDE OF THE GODS
SHATTERED IDYLL, A • 1916 • Aylott Dave • UKN
SHATTERED INNOCENCE • 1988 • Stern Sandor • TVM • USA
SHATTERED LIVES • 1925 • McCarty Henry • USA
SHATTERED MEMORIES • 1915 • Leonard Robert Z. • USA
SHATTERED NERVES • 1916 • Wilson Ben • USA
SHATTERED REPUTATIONS • 1923 • *Walker Johnnie* • USA
SHATTERED ROMANCE, A • 1915 • *Wiggins Lillian* • USA
SHATTERED SILENCE see **LOVE IS NEVER SILENT** • 1985
SHATTERED SILENCE, THE • 1967 • Parker Morten • DOC • CND
SHATTERED SPIRITS • 1986 • Greenwald Robert • TVM • USA
SHATTERED TREE, THE • 1914 • Wilson Ben • USA
SHATTERED VASE, THE see **RAZBITAYA VAZA** • 1913
SHATTERED VOWS • 1984 • Bender Jack • TVM • USA
SHATTERHAND (USA) see **OLD SHATTERHAND** • 1964
SHAUGHRAUN, THE • 1912 • Olcott Sidney • USA
SHAVE BY INSTALMENTS ON THE UNEASY SYSTEM, A • 1905 • Martin J. H.? • UKN
SHAVE, PLEASE see **CHCIALBYM SIE OGOLIC** • 1967
SHAVED AND TRIMMED • 1915 • *Zenith Films* • USA
SHAVED IN MEXICO • 1915 • Blystone John G. • USA
SHAVING MUGS • 1953 • Kneitel Seymour • ANS • USA
SHAWL DER KAISERIN KATHERINA II, DER • 1920 • Halden Karl • FRG
SHA(W)LY NOT? • 1914 • Aylott Dave? • UKN
SHAWNIGAN • 1964 • Robertson George C. • CND
SHAWQ • 1976 • Fahmy Ashraf • EGY • DESIRE
SHAYATIN EL TALATA, EL • 1964 • Mustafa Hassam Eddin • EGY • THREE DEVILS, THE
SHAYATINE EL JAU • 1955 • Mustafa Niazi • EGY • SKY-DEVILS, THE
SHAYO NO OMOKAGE • 1967 • Saito Kosei • JPN • LONELY LIFE, THE
SHAYTAN AS-SAGHIR, ASH- see **SHAITANE EL SAGHIR, EL** • 1963
SHAZDE-EHTEJAB • 1975 • Farmanara Bahman • IRN • PRINCE EHTEJAB
SHCHIT I MYECH. I: BYEZ PRAVA BYT SOBOY • 1968 • Basov Vladimir • USS • SHIELD AND THE SWORD. PART ONE: NO RIGHT TO BE ONE'S SELF, THE
SHCHIT I MYECH. II: PRIKAZANO VYZHIT • 1968 • Basov Vladimir • USS • SHIELD AND THE SWORD. PART TWO: THE ORDER -STAY ALIVE, THE
SHCHIT I MYECH. III: OBZHALOVANIYU NYE PODLEZHIT • 1968 • Basov Vladimir • USS • SHIELD AND THE SWORD. PART THREE: NOT SUBJECT TO APPEAL, THE
SHCHIT I MYECH. IV: POSLYEDNI RUBYEZH • 1968 • Basov Vladimir • USS • SHIELD AND THE SWORD. PART FOUR: THE LAST FRONTIER, THE
SHCHORS • 1939 • Solntseva Yulia, Dovzhenko Alexander • USS • SHORS
SHE • 1908 • Porter Edwin S. • USA
SHE • 1911 • Marston Theodore • USA
SHE • 1916 • Barker Will, Lucoque H. Lisle • UKN
SHE • 1917 • Buel Kenean • USA
SHE • 1925 • De Cordova Leander • UKN
SHE • 1935 • Pichel Irving, Holden Lansing C. • USA
SHE • 1965 • Day Robert • UKN
SHE • 1970 • Nickel Gitta • GDR

S*H*E • 1980 • Lewis Robert • TVM • USA
SHE • 1983 • Nesher Avi • ITL
SHE see **KANOJO** • 1926
SHE see **ELLES** • 1966
SHE see **AVAL** • 1967
SHE ALWAYS GETS THEIR MAN • 1962 • Grayson Godfrey • UKN
SHE AND FEAR see **ELLA Y EL MIEDO** • 1968
SHE AND HE see **KANOJO TO KARE** • 1963
SHE AND HE see **BLAHO LASKY** • 1966
SHE AND HE (UKN) see **ASSOLUTO NATURALE, L'** • 1969
SHE AND I see **WATASHI TO KANOJO** • 1929
SHE AND THE THREE see **SIE UND DIE DREI** • 1922
SHE AND THE THREE (USA) see **SIE UND DIE DREI** • 1935
SHE ASKED FOR IT • 1937 • Kenton Erle C. • USA
SHE ASKED FOR TROUBLE • 1912 • Plumb Hay? • UKN
SHE BEAST, THE (USA) see **REVENGE OF THE BLOOD BEAST, THE** • 1966
SHE CAME BY BUS see **SHE CAME ON THE BUS** • 1969
SHE CAME FOR LOVE see **ONNAGA AISHITE NIKUMUTOKI** • 1963
SHE CAME LIKE A WIND see **HON KOM SOM EN VIND** • 1952
SHE CAME ON THE BUS • 1969 • Ledger Curt • USA • SHE CAME BY BUS ○ SICK ONES, THE
SHE CAME, SHE SAW, SHE CONQUERED • 1911 • *Vitagraph* • USA
SHE CAME, SHE SAW, SHE CONQUERED • 1916 • Ellis Robert • SHT • USA
SHE CAME TO THE VALLEY • 1979 • Band Albert • USA
SHE CLIMBS TO CONQUER • 1932 • Oliver Bill • DOC • CND
SHE CONQUERED see **HON SEGRADE** • 1916
SHE COULDN'T GET AWAY FROM IT • 1915 • *Farley Dot* • USA
SHE COULDN'T GROW UP • 1918 • *Rhodes Billie* • USA
SHE COULDN'T HELP IT • 1921 • Campbell Maurice • USA • IN THE BISHOP'S CARRIAGE
SHE COULDN'T SAY NO • 1930 • Bacon Lloyd • USA
SHE COULDN'T SAY NO • 1939 • Cutts Graham • UKN
SHE COULDN'T SAY NO • 1941 • Clemens William • USA
SHE COULDN'T SAY NO • 1954 • Bacon Lloyd • USA • BEAUTIFUL BUT DANGEROUS (UKN) ○ SHE HAD TO SAY YES
SHE COULDN'T TAKE IT • 1935 • Garnett Tay • USA • WOMAN TAMER (UKN)
SHE-CREATURE, THE • 1956 • Cahn Edward L. • USA
SHE CRIED • 1912 • *Turner Florence* • USA
SHE CRIED MURDER! • 1973 • Daugherty Herschel • TVM • USA
SHE DANCES ALONE • 1981 • Dornhelm Robert • USA, AUS
SHE DEFENDS HER COUNTRY see **ONA ZASHCHISHCHAYET RODINU** • 1943
SHE DEMONS • 1958 • Cunha Richard E. • USA
SHE DEVIL • 1989 • Seidelman Susan • USA • LIFE AND LOVES OF A SHE-DEVIL, THE
SHE DEVIL see **SHE-DEVIL, THE** • 1957
SHE DEVIL, THE • 1916 • *Brockwell Gladys* • SHT • USA
SHE DEVIL, THE • 1918 • Edwards J. Gordon • USA
SHE-DEVIL, THE • 1957 • Neumann Kurt • USA • SHE DEVIL
SHE-DEVIL ISLAND • 1937 • *Grand National* • USA
SHE-DEVILS ON WHEELS • 1968 • Lewis Herschell G. • USA
SHE DID HER BIT • 1918 • Blystone John G. • SHT • USA
SHE DID IT HIS WAY! • 1968 • Graham Ronald • USA
SHE DIDN'T DO IT • 1918 • *Triangle* • USA
SHE DIDN'T SAY NO! • 1958 • Frankel Cyril • UKN
SHE DIDN'T STAY IN BED see **SHE SHOULD HAVE STAYED IN BED** • 1963
SHE DIDN'T WANT A SHEIK see **SHEIK STEPS OUT, THE** • 1937
SHE DIDN'T WANT TO DO IT • 1915 • Cooper Toby? • UKN
SHE DIED WITH HER BOOTS ON see **WHIRLPOOL** • 1970
SHE DONE HIM RIGHT • 1940 • Beaudine William • USA
SHE DONE HIM WRONG • 1933 • Lantz Walter, Nolan William • ANS • USA
SHE DONE HIM WRONG • 1933 • Sherman Lowell • USA
SHE DREAMT OF ONIONS • 1911 • Coleby A. E.? • UKN
SHE DRIVES ME CRAZY see **CRAZY HORSE** • 1988
S'HE EE CLIT SOAK • 1971 • Quillen Thomas • USA
SHE FELL AMONG THIEVES • 1978 • Donner Clive • TVM • UKN
SHE FELL FAINTING IN HER ARMS • 1903 • *Bitzer Billy (Ph)* • USA
SHE FREAK • 1967 • Mabe Byron • USA • ALLEY OF NIGHTMARES ○ SHE-FREAK ○ FREAKS!
SHE-FREAK see **SHE FREAK** • 1967
SHE GAMBLER see **ONNA NO TSUBOFURI** • 1968
SHE GAVE HIM A ROSE • 1914 • *Lubin* • USA
SHE GETS HER MAN • 1935 • Nigh William • USA
SHE GETS HER MAN • 1945 • Kenton Erle C. • USA
SHE-GODS OF SHARK REEF • 1956 • Corman Roger • USA • SHARK REEF (UKN)
SHE GOES TO WAR • 1929 • King Henry • USA
SHE GOT HER MAN (UKN) see **MAISIE GETS HER MAN** • 1942
SHE GOT THE MONEY • 1911 • *Essanay* • USA
SHE GOT WHAT SHE ASKED FOR see **BELLEZZA DI IPPOLITA, LA** • 1962
SHE GOT WHAT SHE WANTED • 1930 • Cruze James • USA • DISCONTENT
SHE HAD TO CHOOSE • 1934 • Ceder Ralph • USA
SHE HAD TO EAT • 1937 • St. Clair Malcolm • USA
SHE HAD TO SAY YES • 1933 • Berkeley Busby, Amy George • USA
SHE HAD TO SAY YES see **SHE COULDN'T SAY NO** • 1954
SHE HAS LIVED HER DESTINY see **KANOJO NO UNMEI** • 1924
SHE HAS WHAT IT TAKES • 1943 • Barton Charles T. • USA • BROADWAY DADDIES
SHE, HE AND ANDERSSON see **HON, HAN OCH ANDERSSON** • 1926
SHE HIRED A HUSBAND • 1919 • Dillon John Francis • USA
SHE-HSING TIAO SHOU • 1978 • Yuan Ho-P'ing • HKG • SNAKE IN THE EAGLE'S SHADOW ○ SNAKE IN EAGLE'S SHADOW ○ SNAKES IN EAGLE SHADOW ○ EAGLE'S SHADOW, THE
SHE IS A BIG GIRL NOW see **AYA THANG LOKU LAMAYEK** • 1974
SHE IS A PIPPIN • 1912 • Henderson Dell • USA
SHE IS AWAY • 1975 • Elder Bruce • CND
SHE IS BICIMIDINE see **ELLE EST BICIMIDINE** • 1927
SHE IS LIKE A RAINBOW • Kothuys Anton • NTH
SHE IS MY DAISY • 1907 • Gilbert Arthur • UKN
SHE-KILLING, THE see **DISI KILLING** • 1967
SHE KNEW ALL THE ANSWERS • 1941 • Wallace Richard • USA • GIRL'S BEST FRIEND IS WALL STREET, A
SHE KNEW NO OTHER WAY • 1977 • Efstratiadis Omiris • GRC
SHE KNEW TOO MUCH • 1988 • Lynch Paul • USA
SHE KNEW WHAT SHE WANTED • 1936 • Bentley Thomas • UKN
SHE KNOWS Y'KNOW • 1962 • Tully Montgomery • UKN
SHE LANDED A BIG ONE • 1914 • *Beery Wallace* • USA
SHE LEARNED ABOUT SOLDIERS • 1934 • Marshall George • USA
SHE LET HIM CONTINUE see **PRETTY POISON** • 1968
SHE LIVES! • 1973 • Hagmann Stuart • TVM • USA
SHE LOST HER YOU KNOW WHAT see **TURM DER VERBOTENEN LIEBE, DER** • 1968
SHE LOVED A FIREMAN • 1938 • Farrow John • USA
SHE LOVED A SAILOR • 1916 • Heerman Victor • USA
SHE LOVED HIM PLENTY • 1918 • Jones F. Richard • SHT • USA
SHE LOVED THEM BOTH • 1915 • Ayres Sydney • USA
SHE LOVES AND LIES • 1920 • Withey Chet • USA
SHE LOVES ME NOT • 1918 • Roach Hal • SHT • USA
SHE LOVES ME NOT • 1934 • Nugent Elliott • USA
SHE LOVES ME, SHE LOVES ME NOT.. • 1964 • Khamraev Ali • USS
SHE, LUCIFER AND I see **ELLA, LUCIFER Y YO** • 1952
SHE MADE HER BED • 1934 • Murphy Ralph • USA • BABY IN THE ICE BOX, THE
SHE MADE HERSELF BEAUTIFUL • 1914 • *Lubin* • USA
SHE MAN, THE • 1967 • Clark Bob • USA • FIXATION
SHE-MAO-HO HUN-HSING CH'UAN • 1980 • Luo Wen, Hsiao Lung • HKG • LACKEY AND THE LADY TIGER
SHE MARRIED A COP • 1939 • Salkow Sidney • USA
SHE MARRIED AN ARTIST • 1937 • Gering Marion • USA
SHE MARRIED FOR LOVE • 1914 • *Bell Eva* • USA
SHE MARRIED HER BOSS • 1935 • La Cava Gregory • USA
SHE MARRIED HER HUSBAND • 1917 • Moore Matt • SHT • USA
SHE-ME • 1919 • Perez Marcel • USA
SHE MEANT NO HARM see **HER ADVENTUROUS NIGHT** • 1946
SHE MOB • 1968 • *Castle Marni* • USA
SHE MONSTER OF THE NIGHT see **FRANKENSTEIN'S DAUGHTER** • 1959
SHE MUST BE SEEING THINGS • 1988 • McLaughlin Sheila • USA
SHE MUST BE UGLY • 1913 • Hotaling Arthur D. • USA
SHE MUST ELOPE • 1913 • Hotaling Arthur D. • USA
SHE MUST HAVE SWALLOWED IT • 1912 • Stow Percy • UKN
SHE NEEDED A DOCTOR • 1917 • *Moran Polly* • SHT • USA
SHE NEVER KNEW • 1911 • *Yankee* • USA
SHE NEVER KNEW • 1912 • *Kent Charles* • USA
SHE NEVER KNEW • 1913 • Brenon Herbert • USA
SHE NEVER KNEW • 1915 • *American* • USA
SHE ONLY DANCED ONE SUMMER see **HON DANSADE EN SOMMAR** • 1951
SHE OR NO ONE see **HON ELLER INGEN** • 1934
SHE PLAYED WITH FIRE (USA) see **FORTUNE IS A WOMAN** • 1957
SHE REMINDS ME OF YOU • 1934 • Fleischer Dave • ANS • USA
SHE RETURNED AT DAWN (USA) see **RETOUR A L'AUBE** • 1938
SHE SERVED HIM RIGHT • 1931 • Buzzell Edward • SHT • USA
SHE SHALL HAVE MURDER • 1950 • Birt Daniel • UKN
SHE SHALL HAVE MUSIC • 1935 • Hiscott Leslie • UKN
SHE SHOULD HAVE STAYED IN BED • 1963 • Mahon Barry • USA • SHE DIDN'T STAY IN BED
SHE SHOULD HAVE STAYED IN BED see **JE SUIS FRIGIDE.. POURQUOI?** • 1972
SHE SHOULD WORRY • 1913 • *Asher Max* • USA
SHE-SICK SAILORS • 1944 • Kneitel Seymour • ANS • USA
SHE SIGHED BY THE SEASIDE • 1921 • Kenton Erle C. • SHT • USA
SHE SLEPT THROUGH IT ALL • 1913 • *Baggot King* • USA
SHE STAYED KISSED see **KISSES FOR BREAKFAST** • 1941
SHE STEPS OUT see **HARMONY AT HOME** • 1930
SHE STOOPS TO CONQUER • 1910 • *Thanhouser* • USA
SHE STOOPS TO CONQUER • 1914 • Tucker George Loane • UKN
SHE STOOPS TO CONQUER • 1923 • Greenwood Edwin • UKN
SHE, THE ONLY ONE see **HON, DEN ENDA** • 1926
SHE THOUGHT IT WAS HIM see **HON TRODDE DET VAR HAN** • 1943
SHE TIAO YING-HSIUNG CH'UAN • 1977 • Chang Ch'Eh • HKG • BRAVE ARCHERS, THE
SHE TOOK A CHANCE • 1915 • Williams C. Jay • USA
SHE TOOK MOTHER'S ADVICE • 1909 • *Lubin* • USA
SHE WAITS • 1971 • Mann Delbert • TVM • USA • NIGHT OF THE EXORCIST
SHE WALKETH ALONE • 1915 • Eason B. Reeves • USA
SHE WANG-TZU • 1976 • Chen Lo • HKG • SNAKE PRINCE
SHE WANTED A BOARDER • 1912 • *Vitagraph* • USA
SHE WANTED A BOW-WOW • 1910 • *Essanay* • USA
SHE WANTED A COUNT • 1914 • *Lubin* • USA
SHE WANTED A FORD • 1916 • *Russell Dan* • SHT • USA
SHE WANTED A MAN WITH BRAINS • 1911 • *Champion* • USA
SHE WANTED A MILLIONAIRE • 1932 • Blystone John G. • USA
SHE WANTED TO BE A WIDOW • 1915 • MacGregor Norval • USA
SHE WANTED TO KNOW • 1914 • *Lubin* • USA
SHE WANTED TO MARRY A HERO • 1910 • *Thanhouser* • USA
SHE WAS A HIPPY VAMPIRE see **WILD WORLD OF BATWOMAN, THE** • 1966
SHE WAS A LADY • 1934 • MacFadden Hamilton • USA
SHE WAS A PEACH • 1914 • *Lubin* • USA
SHE WAS A VISITOR • Deitch Donna • SHT • USA
SHE WAS AN ACROBAT'S DAUGHTER • 1937 • Freleng Friz • ANS • USA
SHE WAS FAIR GAME • 1985 • Andreacchio Mario • ASL • FAIR GAME
SHE WAS HIS MOTHER • 1915 • Brenon Herbert • USA
SHE WAS LIKE A WILD CHRYSANTHEMUM see **NOGIKU NO GOTOKI KIMI NARIKI** • 1955
SHE WAS NOT AFRAID • 1911 • *Solax* • USA
SHE WAS ONLY A VILLAGE MAIDEN • 1933 • Maude Arthur • UKN • PRISCILLA THE RAKE
SHE WAS ONLY A WORKING GIRL • 1914 • Christie Al • USA
SHE WAS SOME VAMPIRE • 1916 • Curtis Allen • SHT • USA
SHE WAS THE OTHER • 1911 • Hotaling Arthur D.? • USA
SHE WAS VICTORIOUS see **HON SEGRADE** • 1916
SHE WASN'T HUNGRY, BUT.. • 1919 • Beery Wallace • SHT • USA
SHE WENT TO THE RACES • 1945 • Goldbeck Willis • USA
SHE WHO DARES (UKN) see **THREE RUSSIAN GIRLS** • 1943
SHE WHO DID NOT BEND see **AFTI POU DHEN LIYISE** • 1967
SHE WHO LAST LAUGHS • 1916 • Semon Larry • SHT • USA
SHE WILL NEVER KNOW • 1913 • *American* • USA
SHE WINKED • 1915 • MacMackin Archer • USA
SHE-WOLF see **MOTHER'S MILLIONS** • 1931
SHE WOLF, THE • 1913 • Davenport Charles E. • *Reliance* • USA
SHE WOLF, THE • 1913 • Ford Francis • *Bison* • USA
SHE WOLF, THE • 1919 • Smith Cliff • SHT • USA • SHE-WOLF, THE
SHE-WOLF, THE see **SHE WOLF, THE** • 1919
SHE-WOLF, THE see **LUPA, LA** • 1953
SHE-WOLF, THE see **LOBA, LA** • 1964
SHE-WOLF, THE see **VALCHITSATA** • 1965
SHE-WOLF, THE see **WILCZYCA** • 1983
SHE-WOLF, THE (USA) see **U KRUTOGO YARA** • 1962
SHE-WOLF AND THE DOVE, THE see **LOBA Y LA PALOMA, LA** • 1973
SHE-WOLF OF DEVIL'S MOOR, THE see **WOLFIN VOM TEUFELSMOOR, DIE** • 1978
SHE-WOLF OF LONDON • 1946 • Yarbrough Jean • USA • CURSE OF THE ALLENBYS, THE (UKN)
SHE-WOLF OF WALL STREET see **MOTHER'S MILLIONS** • 1931
SHE WOLVES • 1925 • Elvey Maurice • USA
SHE-WOLVES, THE see **LOUVES, LES** • 1957
SHE WON A PRIZE • 1916 • Baker George D. • SHT • USA
SHE WORE A YELLOW RIBBON • 1949 • Ford John • USA
SHE WOULD BE A BUSINESS MAN • 1910 • *Centaur* • USA
SHE WOULD BE A COWBOY • 1915 • *Kalem* • USA
SHE WOULD BE A SUFFRAGETTE • 1908 • Williamson James? • UKN
SHE WOULD BE AN ACTRESS • 1909 • *Greene Kempton* • USA
SHE WOULD BE WED: OR, LEAP YEAR PROPOSAL • 1908 • Coleby A. E. • UKN
SHE WOULD SING • 1905 • *Cricks & Sharp* • UKN • SISTER MARY JANE'S TOP NOTE
SHE WOULD TALK • 1911 • Aylott Dave • UKN
SHE WOULDN'T SAY YES • 1946 • Hall Alexander • USA
SHE WRONGED HIM RIGHT • 1934 • Fleischer Dave • ANS • USA
SHE WROTE A PLAY • 1914 • *Eclair* • USA
SHE WROTE A PLAY AND PLAYED IT • 1916 • Curtis Allen • SHT • USA
SHE WROTE THE BOOK • 1946 • Lamont Charles • USA • LOVE TAKES A HOLIDAY
SHEBA • 1919 • Hepworth Cecil M. • UKN
SHEBA BABY • 1975 • Girdler William • USA
SHEBA Y EL DIABLO • 1970 • Elorrieta Jose Maria • SPN
SHECH THEKE SHURU • 1968 • Chitrasathi • IND • STARTING FROM THE END
SHECHAVATAR • 1954 • Thakur Ramchandra • IND
SHED NO TEARS • 1948 • Yarbrough Jean • USA
SHEDDING THE LOAD • 1952 • *Hall Cameron* • SHT • UKN
SHEENA, QUEEN OF THE JUNGLE • 1984 • Guillermin John • USA • SHEENA (UKN)
SHEENA (UKN) see **SHEENA, QUEEN OF THE JUNGLE** • 1984
SHEEP AHOY • 1954 • Jones Charles M. • ANS • USA
SHEEP DOG, THE • 1949 • Nichols Charles • ANS • USA
SHEEP EATERS, THE see **LAMPAANSYOJAT** • 1972
SHEEP HAS FIVE LEGS, THE see **MOUTON A CINQ PATTES, LE** • 1954
SHEEP HERDER, THE • 1914 • *Victor* • USA
SHEEP IN THE DEEP, A • 1962 • Jones Charles M. • ANS • USA
SHEEP IN THE MEADOW • 1939 • Davis Mannie • ANS • USA
SHEEP RUNNERS, THE • 1914 • Farnum Marshall • USA
SHEEP SHAPE • 1946 • Sparber I. • ANS • USA
SHEEP STEALER, THE • 1908 • *Tyler Walter* • UKN
SHEEP STEALERS ANONYMOUS • 1963 • Hanna William, Barbera Joseph • ANS • USA
SHEEP TRAIL • 1926 • Fraser Harry L. • USA
SHEEP WRECKED • 1958 • Lah Michael • ANS • USA
SHEEPDOG OF THE HILLS • 1941 • Burger Germain • UKN
SHEEPISH WOLF, THE • 1942 • Freleng Friz • ANS • USA
SHEEPISH WOLF, THE • 1963 • Kneitel Seymour • ANS • USA
SHEEPMAN, THE • 1958 • Marshall George • USA • STRANGER WITH A GUN
SHEEPMAN'S DAUGHTER, THE • 1911 • Dwan Allan • USA
SHEEPMAN'S ESCAPE, THE • 1912 • *Anderson Broncho Billy* • USA
SHEEPMAN'S TRIUMPH, A • 1911 • *Kalem* • USA
SHEEPMATES • 1934 • Thring F. W. • ASL
SHEEP'S CLOTHING • 1914 • Seay Charles M. • USA
SHEEP'S CLOTHING see **SIN SHIP, THE** • 1931
SHEEPSKIN TROUSERS: OR, NOT IN THESE • 1912 • Stow Percy • UKN
SHEER BLUFF • 1921 • Richardson Frank • UKN
SHEER LUCK • 1931 • Mitchell Bruce • USA
SHEER MADNESS see **HELLER WAHN** • 1983
SHEER SPORT • 1972 • Hebert Marc • CND
SHEER TRICKERY • 1924 • Brunel Adrian • UKN
SHEESH GREESHMAM CHITRA see **SHEET GRISHMAR SMRITI** • 1983

SHEET GRISHMAR SMRITI • 1983 • Dasgupta Buddhadeb • IND • SEASON'S MEMOIRS ○ SHEESH GREESHMAM CHITRA

SHEFFIELD BLADE, A • 1918 • Roberts Harry, Bamberger Joseph J. • UKN

SHEHAR AUR SAPNA • 1963 • Abbas Khwaya Ahmad • IND • CITY AND THE DREAM, THE

SHEHERAZADE see **GEHEIMNISSE DES ORIENTS** • 1928

SHEHERAZADE • 1963 • Gaspard-Huit Pierre • FRN, ITL, SPN • SCHIAVA DI BAGDAD, LA (ITL) ○ SCHEHERAZADE (USA)

SHEHERAZADE • 1989 • de Broca Philippe • FRN

SHEIK, THE • 1921 • Melford George • USA

SHEIK, THE • 1922 • Wynn George • SHT • UKN

SHEIK AHMET see **SEYH AHMET** • 1968

SHEIK AHMET, EAGLE OF THE DESERT see **COL KARTALI SEYH AHMET** • 1968

SHEIK OF ARABY, THE • 1926 • Mander Miles • UKN

SHEIK OF ARABY, THE see **MAN WHO TURNED WHITE, THE** • 1919

SHEIK OF MOJAVE, THE • 1928 • *"cheyenne Bill"* • USA

SHEIK SHAMIL see **SEYN SAMIL** • 1967

SHEIK STEPS OUT, THE • 1937 • Pichel Irving • USA • SHE DIDN'T WANT A SHEIK

SHEIKCHILLI • 1940 • IND • GHANCHAKKAR

SHEIKH CHILLI • 1937 • *Kapoor R. P.* • SHT • IND

SHEIKH CHILLI • 1956 • Thakur Ramchandra • IND

SHEIK'S WIFE, THE • 1922 • Roussell Henry • FRN

SHEILA LEVINE IS DEAD AND LIVING IN NEW YORK • 1975 • Furie Sidney J. • USA

SHEILA SCOTT • 1968 • Bonniere Rene • DCS • CND

SHEILA'S CHRISTMAS • 1977 • Borris Clay • CND

SHELAGH DELANEY'S SALFORD • 1960 • Russell Ken • MTV • UKN

SHE'LL BE SWEET see **MAGEE AND THE LADY** • 1977

SHE'LL BE WEARING PINK PYJAMAS • 1985 • Goldschmidt John • UKN

SHE'LL FOLLOW YOU ANYWHERE • 1971 • Rea David C. • UKN

SHELL FORTY-THREE • 1916 • Barker Reginald • USA

SHELL GAME • 1975 • Jordan Glenn • TVM • USA

SHELL GAME, THE • 1918 • Baker George D. • USA

SHE'LL HAVE TO GO • 1962 • Asher Robert • UKN • MAID FOR MURDER (USA)

SHELL OF LIFE, THE • 1914 • *Lubin* • USA

SHELL SHOCK • 1964 • Hayes John • USA

SHELL SHOCK ROCK • 1979 • Davis John • DOC • UKN

SHELL-SHOCKED EGG, THE • 1948 • McKimson Robert • ANS • USA

SHELL SHOCKED SAMMY • 1923 • Mattison Frank S. • USA

SHELLEY • 1987 • Bruyere Christian • CND

SHELLEY, CIVIL ENGINEER • 1968 • Tammer Peter (c/d) • DOC • ASL

SHELLGAME • 1985 • Yalden-Tomson Peter • MTV • CND

SHELLING THE RED CROSS • 1900 • *Mitchell & Kenyon* • UKN

SHELLS • 1916 • *Krischock H. (Ph)* • ASL

SHELLS, THE • 1913 • Smith Frank L. • USA

SHELLS AND SHIVERS • 1917 • Semon Larry • SHT • USA

SHELLS HAVE NEVER SPOKEN, THE • 1962 • Calotescu Virgil • DOC • RMN

SHELLS, MORE SHELLS • 1915 • Evans Joe • UKN

SHELLSHOCK • 1988 • Sharon Yoel • ISR

SHELLY MANNE AND HIS MEN • 1962 • Binder Steve • SHT • USA

SHELLY MANNE QUINTET • 1962 • Markas Gary • SHT • USA

SHELTER • 1966 • Nicholson Arch • DOC • ASL

SHELTER, THE (UKN) see **MIKLAT, HA** • 1989

SHELTER OF YOUR ARMS, THE see **TURKS FRUITS** • 1973

SHELTERED DAUGHTERS • 1921 • Dillon Eddie • USA

SHELTERED IN THE WOODS • 1910 • *Essanay* • USA

SHELTERED LADY, THE see **LADY IN A JAM** • 1942

SHELTERED UNDER THE STARS AND STRIPES • 1909 • *Bison* • USA

SHELTERING AN INGRATE • 1914 • Ricketts Thomas • USA

SHELTERING SKY, THE • 1989 • Bertolucci Bernardo • UKN, USA

SHELTLANDSGJENGEN (NRW) see **SUICIDE MISSION** • 1956

SHEN-TIAO • 1981 • Chang Ch'Eh • HKG • BRAVE ARCHER AND HIS MATE

SHEN T'OU MIAO T'AN SHOU TUO-TUO • 1980 • Liang Puzhi • HKG • ITCHY FINGERS

SHENANDOAH • 1911 • *Champion* • USA

SHENANDOAH • 1913 • Buel Kenean • USA

SHENANDOAH • 1965 • McLaglen Andrew V. • USA • FIELDS OF HONOR

SHENANIGANS • 1977 • Jacoby Joseph • USA • GREAT GEORGIA BANK HOAX, THE ○ GREAT BANK HOAX, THE

SHENGSI XIAN • 1985 • Liang Puzhi • HKG • LIFE AND DEATH (A STRUGGLE) ○ ISLAND, THE

SHENTAN ZHUGULI • 1987 • Chen Xinjian • HKG • INSPECTOR CHOCOLATE

SHEP COMES HOME • 1948 • Beebe Ford • USA

SHEP OF THE PAINTED HILLS see **PAINTED HILLS, THE** • 1951

SHEP, THE HERO • 1913 • McGill Lawrence • USA

SHEP THE SENTINEL • 1915 • *Farrington Rene* • USA

SHEPHERD see **GOKUL** • 1947

SHEPHERD, THE • 1922 • Barsky • USS

SHEPHERD, THE • 1955 • Biggs Julian • CND

SHEPHERD, THE • 1970 • ANS • USA

SHEPHERD, THE see **OVCAR** • 1972

SHEPHERD BOY FROM THE LOWLAND, THE see **PASACEK Z DOLINY** • 1983

SHEPHERD GIRL, THE (USA) see **SHAN-KO LIEN** • 1964

SHEPHERD KING, THE • 1923 • Edwards J. Gordon • USA

SHEPHERD KING, THE see **GOKUL CHA RAJA** • 1950

SHEPHERD LASSIE OF ARGYLE, THE • 1914 • Trimble Larry • UKN

SHEPHERD OF SOULS, THE • 1915 • Wilson Frank • UKN

SHEPHERD OF THE HILLS • 1928 • Rogell Albert S. • USA

SHEPHERD OF THE HILLS • 1941 • Hathaway Henry • USA

SHEPHERD OF THE HILLS, THE • 1920 • Wright Harold Bell • USA

SHEPHERD OF THE HILLS, THE • 1964 • Parker Ben • USA • THUNDER MOUNTAIN

SHEPHERD OF THE NIGHT FLOCK • 1972-77 • Stoney George C. • USA

SHEPHERD OF THE OZARKS • 1942 • McDonald Frank • USA • SUSANNA (UKN)

SHEPHERD OF THE ROUNDHOUSE • 1943 • *O'Brien Joseph/ Mead Thomas (P)* • SHT • USA

SHEPHERD OF THE SOUTHERN CROSS • 1914 • Butler Alexander • ASL

SHEPHERD -PSALM 23, THE • 1927 • Barnett Charles • UKN

SHEPHERDESS AND THE CHIMNEY SWEEP, THE • Atamanov Lev • ANM • USS

SHEPHERDESS AND THE CHIMNEY SWEEP, THE see **BERGERE ET LE RAMONEUR, LA** • 1953

SHEPHERDS see **PASTIRCI** • 1975

SHEPHERD'S DOG, THE • 1909 • Fitzhamon Lewin • UKN

SHEPHERD'S FLUTE, THE • 1909 • *Gaumont* • SHT • FRN

SHEPHERD'S FLUTE, THE • 1912 • *Halliday Jack* • USA

SHEPHERDS OF CONFUSION, THE see **PATRES DU DESORDRE, LES** • 1968

SHEPPER-NEWFOUNDER, THE • 1930 • McCarey Leo • USA

SHEP'S RACE WITH DEATH • 1914 • *Thanhouser* • USA

SHER-E-JUNGLE see **ZAMBO** • 1937

SHER KA PANJA • 1936 • *Biswas Anil (M)* • IND

SHER MOUNTAIN KILLINGS MYSTERY, THE • 1989 • Martin Vince • ASL

SHERBROOKE LA REINE DES CANTONS DE L'EST • 1952 • Lavoie Hermenegilde • DOC • CND

SHERIDAN'S PRIDE • 1914 • *Joker* • USA

SHERIDAN'S RIDE • 1913 • Turner Otis • USA

SHERIFF, LE see **JUGE FAYARD DIT "LE SHERIF", LE** • 1977

SHERIFF, THE • 1910 • *Selig* • USA

SHERIFF, THE • 1911 • *Anderson Broncho Billy* • USA

SHERIFF, THE • 1913 • Franklin Sidney A., Franklin Chester M. • USA

SHERIFF, THE • 1918 • Arbuckle Roscoe, Cavender Glen • SHT • USA

SHERIFF, THE • 1970 • Rich David Lowell • TVM • USA

SHERIFF, THE see **OUTWEST** • 1918

SHERIFF AND HIS MAN, THE • 1912 • *Essanay* • USA

SHERIFF AND HIS SON, THE • 1910 • *Champion* • USA

SHERIFF AND MISS JONES • 1910 • *Powers* • USA

SHERIFF AND THE DETECTIVE, THE • 1910 • *Champion* • USA

SHERIFF AND THE MAN, THE • 1911 • Salter Harry • USA

SHERIFF AND THE RUSTLER, THE • 1913 • *Selig* • USA

SHERIFF AND THE SATELLITE KID, THE (USA) see **SCERIFFO EXTRATERRESTRE.. POCO EXTRA E MOLTO TERRESTRE, UNO** • 1979

SHERIFF AT MUSCATINE, THE • 1914 • *Kb* • USA

SHERIFF DEL O.K. CORRAL, EL see **SFIDA A RIO BRAVO** • 1965

SHERIFF FOR AN HOUR • 1914 • *Reliance* • USA

SHERIFF JIM'S LAST SHOT • 1912 • *Vitagraph* • USA

SHERIFF NELL'S COMEBACK • 1920 • Cline Eddie • SHT • USA

SHERIFF NELL'S TUSSLE • 1918 • Campbell William • SHT • USA

SHERIFF NO DISPARA, EL • 1965 • Monter Jose Luis • SPN

SHERIFF OF BISBEE, THE • 1914 • *Kb* • USA

SHERIFF OF BLACK GULCH, THE • 1910 • *Bison* • USA

SHERIFF OF CIMARRON • 1945 • Canutt Yakima • USA

SHERIFF OF COCHISE, THE • 1913 • *Essanay* • USA

SHERIFF OF FRACTURED JAW, THE • 1958 • Walsh Raoul • UKN

SHERIFF OF GOPHER FLATS, THE see **GALLOPING GALLAGHER** • 1924

SHERIFF OF HOPE ETERNAL, THE • 1921 • Wilson Ben • USA

SHERIFF OF LAS VEGAS • 1944 • Selander Lesley • USA

SHERIFF OF MEDICINE BOW, THE • 1948 • Hillyer Lambert • USA

SHERIFF OF PINE MOUNTAIN, THE • 1916 • Wilson Ben • SHT • USA

SHERIFF OF PLUMAS, THE • 1916 • Ellsworth Warren • SHT • USA

SHERIFF OF RED ROCK GULCH, THE • 1915 • MacQuarrie Murdock • USA

SHERIFF OF REDWOOD VALLEY • 1946 • Springsteen R. G. • USA

SHERIFF OF SAGE VALLEY • 1942 • Newfield Sam • USA • BILLY THE KID, SHERIFF OF SAGE VALLEY

SHERIFF OF STONE GULCH, THE • 1913 • *Kalem* • USA

SHERIFF OF STONY BUTTE, THE • 1912 • Morty Frank • USA

SHERIFF OF SUN-DOG, THE • 1922 • Wilson Ben, King Louis • USA

SHERIFF OF SUNDOWN • 1944 • Selander Lesley • USA

SHERIFF OF TOMBSTONE • 1941 • Kane Joseph • USA

SHERIFF OF TOMBSTONE, THE see **GALLOPING GALLAGHER** • 1924

SHERIFF OF TUOLUMNE, THE • 1911 • *Selig* • USA

SHERIFF OF WICHITA • 1949 • Springsteen R. G. • USA

SHERIFF OF WILLOW CREEK, THE • 1915 • Cooley Frank • USA

SHERIFF OF WILLOW GULCH, THE • 1914 • *Ab* • USA

SHERIFF OF YAWAPAI COUNTY, THE • 1913 • Duncan William • USA

SHERIFF OUTWITTED, THE • 1912 • *Comet* • USA

SHERIFF OUTWITTED, THE • 1912 • *Nestor* • USA

SHERIFF PRO TEM, THE • 1913 • *Bracken Mildred* • USA

SHERIFF TEDDY • 1957 • Carow Heiner • GDR

SHERIFF TERRIBLE, EL • 1962 • Momplet Antonio • SPN

SHERIFF WAS A LADY, THE (USA) see **FREDDY UND DAS LIED DER PRARIE** • 1964

SHERIFF'S ADOPTED CHILD, THE • 1912 • Morty Frank • USA

SHERIFF'S BABY, THE • 1913 • Griffith D. W. • USA

SHERIFF'S BLUNDER, THE • 1916 • Mix Tom • SHT • USA

SHERIFF'S BROTHER, THE • 1911 • *Bison* • USA

SHERIFF'S BROTHER, THE • 1911 • *Essanay* • USA

SHERIFF'S BROTHER, THE • 1912 • *Panzer Paul* • USA

SHERIFF'S CAPTIVE, THE • 1911 • *American* • USA

SHERIFF'S CAPTURE, THE • 1910 • *Lubin* • USA

SHERIFF'S CHILD, THE • 1913 • *Essanay* • USA

SHERIFF'S CHOICE, THE • 1914 • Mackley Arthur • USA

SHERIFF'S CHUM, THE • 1911 • *Anderson Broncho Billy* • USA

SHERIFF'S DAUGHTER, THE • 1910 • *Centaur* • USA

SHERIFF'S DAUGHTER, THE • 1910 • Fitzhamon Lewin • UKN

SHERIFF'S DAUGHTER, THE • 1912 • *Lubin* • USA

SHERIFF'S DAUGHTER, THE • 1912 • Melies Gaston • USA

SHERIFF'S DAUGHTER, THE see **TICKET TO TOMAHAWK, A** • 1950

SHERIFFS DE LA FRONTERA, LOS • 1964 • Cardona Rene • MXC

SHERIFF'S DECISION, THE • 1911 • *Essanay* • USA

SHERIFF'S DEPUTY, THE • 1914 • *Frontier* • USA

SHERIFF'S DEVOTION, THE • 1913 • *Gaumont* • USA

SHERIFF'S DILEMMA, THE • 1915 • O'Sullivan Tony • USA

SHERIFF'S DUTY, THE • 1916 • Mix Tom • SHT • USA

SHERIFF'S FRIEND, THE • 1911 • *Vitagraph* • USA

SHERIFF'S GIRL • 1926 • Wilson Ben • USA

SHERIFF'S GIRL, THE • 1909 • *Centaur* • USA

SHERIFF'S HONEYMOON, THE • 1913 • *Essanay* • USA

SHERIFF'S INHERITANCE, THE • 1912 • *Essanay* • USA

SHERIFF'S LASH, THE • 1929 • *Lyons Cliff "tex"* • USA

SHERIFF'S LONE HAND, THE see **COWBOY AND THE FLAPPER, THE** • 1924

SHERIFF'S LOVE, THE • 1911 • *Bison* • USA

SHERIFF'S LUCK, THE • 1912 • *Mackley Arthur* • USA

SHERIFF'S MASTER, THE • 1914 • *Reliance* • USA

SHERIFF'S MISTAKE, THE • 1911 • *Mersereau Violet* • USA

SHERIFF'S MISTAKE, THE • 1912 • *Lubin* • USA

SHERIFF'S MYSTERIOUS AIDE, THE • 1912 • *Bison* • USA

SHERIFF'S OATH, THE • 1919 • Rosen Phil • SHT • USA

SHERIFF'S PRISONER, THE • 1912 • *Lubin* • USA

SHERIFF'S PRISONER, THE • 1914 • Walsh Raoul • USA

SHERIFF'S REWARD, THE • 1912 • *Bison* • USA

SHERIFF'S REWARD, THE • 1913 • *Pathe* • USA

SHERIFF'S REWARD, THE • 1914 • Mix Tom • USA

SHERIFF'S RIVAL, THE • 1913 • *Frontier* • USA

SHERIFF'S ROUND-UP, THE • 1912 • *Conway Jack* • USA

SHERIFF'S SACRIFICE, THE • 1910 • *Anderson Broncho Billy* • USA

SHERIFF'S SECRET, THE • 1931 • Hogan James P. • USA

SHERIFF'S SISTER, THE • 1911 • *Kalem* • USA

SHERIFF'S SISTER, THE • 1914 • *Broncho* • USA

SHERIFF'S SISTERS, THE • 1911 • Dwan Allan • USA

SHERIFF'S SON, THE • 1913 • *Essanay* • USA

SHERIFF'S SON, THE • 1919 • Schertzinger Victor • USA

SHERIFF'S STORY, THE • 1913 • *Mackley Arthur* • USA

SHERIFF'S STORY, THE • 1914 • *Allard Arthur* • USA

SHERIFF'S STORY, THE • 1915 • *Coyle Walter* • USA

SHERIFF'S STREAK OF YELLOW, THE • 1915 • *Hart William S.* • USA

SHERIFF'S SWEETHEART, THE • 1911 • *American* • USA

SHERIFF'S TRAP, THE • 1915 • Morgan George • USA

SHERIFF'S WARNING, THE • 1913 • *Nestor* • USA

SHERIFF'S WIFE, THE • 1913 • Mackley Arthur • USA

SHERLOCK AMBROSE • 1918 • Fredericks Walter S. • SHT • USA

SHERLOCK AND ME • 1988 • Eberhardt Thom • USA, UKN • WITHOUT A CLUE

SHERLOCK BONEHEAD • 1914 • Neilan Marshall • USA

SHERLOCK BOOB, THE • 1914 • Mitchell Bruce • USA • BOOB DETECTIVE, THE

SHERLOCK BROWN • 1922 • Veiller Bayard • USA

SHERLOCK HOLMES • 1912 • Treville Georges • SER • UKN

SHERLOCK HOLMES • 1916 • Berthelet Arthur • USA

SHERLOCK HOLMES • 1922 • Parker Albert • USA • MORIARTY

SHERLOCK HOLMES • 1932 • Howard William K. • USA

SHERLOCK HOLMES • 1937 • Engels Erich • FRG • GRAUE DAME, DIE

SHERLOCK HOLMES AND SPIDER WOMAN • 1944 • Neill R. William • USA • SHERLOCK HOLMES AND THE SPIDER WOMAN ○ SPIDER WOMAN (UKN)

SHERLOCK HOLMES AND THE BASKERVILLE CURSE • 1984 • Graham Ed • ANM • USA • SHERLOCK HOLMES IN THE BASKERVILLE CURSE

SHERLOCK HOLMES AND THE BASKERVILLE CURSE see **SHERLOCK HOLMES: THE BASKERVILLE CURSE** • 1983

SHERLOCK HOLMES AND THE DEADLY NECKLACE see **SHERLOCK HOLMES UND DAS HALSBAND DES TODES** • 1962

SHERLOCK HOLMES AND THE MISSING REMBRANDT (USA) see **MISSING REMBRANDT, THE** • 1932

SHERLOCK HOLMES AND THE PEARL OF DEATH see **PEARL OF DEATH, THE** • 1944

SHERLOCK HOLMES AND THE SCARLET CLAW see **SCARLET CLAW, THE** • 1944

SHERLOCK HOLMES AND THE SECRET CODE (UKN) see **DRESSED TO KILL** • 1946

SHERLOCK HOLMES AND THE SECRET WEAPON • 1942 • Neill R. William • USA • SHERLOCK HOLMES FIGHTS BACK ○ SECRET WEAPON

SHERLOCK HOLMES AND THE SPIDER WOMAN see **SHERLOCK HOLMES AND SPIDER WOMAN** • 1944

SHERLOCK HOLMES AND THE VALLEY OF FEAR see **SHERLOCK HOLMES: THE VALLEY OF FEAR** • 1983

SHERLOCK HOLMES AND THE VOICE OF TERROR • 1942 • Rawlins John • USA

SHERLOCK HOLMES AND THE WOMAN IN GREEN see **WOMAN IN GREEN, THE** • 1945

SHERLOCK HOLMES BAFFLED • 1903 • *Biograph* • SHT • USA

SHERLOCK HOLMES ET LE COLLIER DE LA MORT (FRN) see **SHERLOCK HOLMES UND DAS HALSBAND DES TODES** • 1962

SHERLOCK HOLMES FACES DEATH • 1943 • Neill R. William • USA

SHERLOCK HOLMES' FATAL HOUR (USA) see **SLEEPING CARDINAL, THE** • 1931

SHERLOCK HOLMES FIGHTS BACK see **SHERLOCK HOLMES AND THE SECRET WEAPON** • 1942

SHERLOCK HOLMES' FINAL HOUR see **SLEEPING CARDINAL, THE** • 1931

SHERLOCK HOLMES FIVE see **DROSKE 519** • 1909

SHERLOCK HOLMES GIRL, THE • 1914 • France Charles H. • USA

SHERLOCK HOLMES GROSSTER FALL (FRG) see **STUDY IN TERROR, A** • 1965

SHERLOCK HOLMES: HOUND OF THE BASKERVILLES see **HOUND OF THE BASKERVILLES, THE** • 1972
SHERLOCK HOLMES IN NEW YORK • 1976 • Sagal Boris • TVM • USA
SHERLOCK HOLMES IN PURSUIT TO ALGIERS see **PURSUIT TO ALGIERS** • 1945
SHERLOCK HOLMES IN TERROR BY NIGHT see **TERROR BY NIGHT** • 1946
SHERLOCK HOLMES IN THE BASKERVILLE CURSE see **SHERLOCK HOLMES AND THE BASKERVILLE CURSE** • 1984
SHERLOCK HOLMES IN THE GREAT MURDER MYSTERY • 1908 • *Crescent* • DNM
SHERLOCK HOLMES IN WASHINGTON • 1943 • Neill R. William • USA
SHERLOCK HOLMES, JR. • 1911 • Porter Edwin S. • USA
SHERLOCK HOLMES: MURDER BY DECREE (USA) see **MURDER BY DECREE** • 1979
SHERLOCK HOLMES' SMARTER BROTHER see **ADVENTURE OF SHERLOCK HOLMES' SMARTER BROTHER, THE** • 1975
SHERLOCK HOLMES SOLVES "THE SIGN OF THE FOUR" • 1913 • *Benham Harry* • USA
SHERLOCK HOLMES: THE BASKERVILLE CURSE • 1983 • Nicholas Alex • ANM • UKN • SHERLOCK HOLMES AND THE BASKERVILLE CURSE ○ BASKERVILLE CURSE, THE
SHERLOCK HOLMES: THE MASKS OF DEATH • 1984 • *Cushing Peter* • MTV • UKN
SHERLOCK HOLMES' THE SIGN OF FOUR • 1983 • Davis Desmond • UKN • SIGN OF FOUR, THE (USA)
SHERLOCK HOLMES: THE VALLEY OF FEAR • 1983 • ANM • UKN • SHERLOCK HOLMES AND THE VALLEY OF FEAR ○ VALLEY OF FEAR, THE
SHERLOCK HOLMES (UKN) see **ADVENTURES OF SHERLOCK HOLMES, THE** • 1939
SHERLOCK HOLMES UND DAS HALSBAND DES TODES • 1962 • Fisher Terence • FRG, ITL, FRN • SHERLOCK HOLMES ET LE COLLIER DE LA MORT (FRN) ○ VALLEY OF FEAR, THE (UKN) ○ SHERLOCK HOLMES AND THE DEADLY NECKLACE
SHERLOCK I • 1908 • *Holger-Madsen* • DNM
SHERLOCK II • 1908 • DNM
SHERLOCK III • 1908 • *Holger-Madsen* • DNM
SHERLOCK JONES • 1975 • van der Heyde Nikolai • NTH
SHERLOCK JR. • 1924 • Keaton Buster • USA
SHERLOCK PINK • 1976 • McKimson Robert • ANS • USA
SHERLOCK SLEUTH • 1925 • Roach Hal • SHT • USA
SHERLOCK THE BOOB DETECTIVE • 1915 • Mitchell Bruce • USA
SHERMAN SAID IT • 1933 • Parrott Charles • SHT • USA
SHERMAN WAS RIGHT • 1914 • *Simon Louis* • USA
SHERMAN WAS RIGHT • 1918 • *Mason Dan* • USA
SHERMAN WAS RIGHT • 1932 • *Terry Paul/ Moser Frank (P)* • ANS • USA
SHERMAN'S MARCH • 1986 • McElwee Ross • USA
SHERNI • Malhotra Harmesh • IND
SHERRY • 1920 • Lewis Edgar • USA
SHERRY'S HOUSE OF NUDES see **CHERRY'S HOUSE OF NUDES** • 1964
SHE'S A-1 IN THE NAVY • 1943 • *O'Brien Joseph/ Mead Thomas (P)* • SHT • USA
SHE'S A BOY • 1927 • Lamont Charles • SHT • USA
SHE'S A COUSIN OF MINE • 1915 • *Mica* • USA
SHE'S A GOOD GIRL see **SPRUNG INS GLUCK, DER** • 1927
SHE'S A GREAT GREAT GIRL • 1929 • Aylott Dave, Symmons E. F. • SHT • UKN
SHE'S A HE • 1930 • Newfield Sam • SHT • USA
SHE'S A LADY • 1973 • Ohlsson Terry • SHT • ASL
SHE'S A LASSIE FROM LANCASHIRE • 1908 • *Walturdaw* • UKN
SHE'S A PIPPIN • 1915 • *Aubrey James* • USA
SHE'S A RAILROADER • 1978 • Tranter Barbara • SHT • CND
SHE'S A SHEIK • 1927 • Badger Clarence • USA
SHE'S A SOLDIER TOO • 1944 • Castle William • USA
SHE'S A SWEETHEART • 1945 • Lord Del • USA • HELLO MOM
SHE'S A VAMP • 1920 • *Roubert Matty* • USA
SHE'S ALL MINE see **SHE'S OIL MINE** • 1941
SHE'S BACK • 1989 • Kincaid Tim • USA • DEAD AND MARRIED
SHE'S BACK ON BROADWAY • 1953 • Douglas Gordon • USA • BACK ON BROADWAY
SHE'S BEEN AWAY • 1989 • Hall Peter • UKN
SHE'S DANGEROUS • 1937 • Foster Lewis R., Carruth Milton • USA
SHE'S DOING IT AGAIN • 1969 • Bertini Victor?, Burton Victor? • USA
SHE'S DONE IT AGAIN • 1910 • *Thanhouser* • USA
SHE'S DRESSED TO KILL • 1979 • Trikonis Gus • TVM • USA • SOMEONE'S KILLING THE WORLD'S GREATEST MODELS
SHE'S EVERYWHERE • 1919 • Terwilliger George W. • SHT • USA
SHE'S FOR ME • 1943 • Le Borg Reginald • USA • PROFESSOR GOES WILD, THE
SHE'S GOT EVERYTHING • 1938 • Santley Joseph • USA • SHE'S GOT THAT SWING
SHE'S GOT THAT SWING see **SHE'S GOT EVERYTHING** • 1938
SHE'S GOTTA HAVE IT • 1986 • Lee Spike • USA
SHE'S HAVING A BABY • 1988 • Hughes John • USA
SHE'S IN THE ARMY • 1942 • Yarbrough Jean • USA
SHE'S IN THE ARMY NOW • 1981 • Averback Hy • TVM • USA
SHE'S MONIQUE MY LOVE see **MONIQUE MY LOVE** • 1969
SHE'S MY BABY • 1927 • Windermere Fred • USA
SHE'S MY DAISY • 1931 • Pearson George • SHT • UKN
SHE'S MY GIRL! • 1928 • Newfield Sam • SHT • USA
SHE'S MY LOVELY (UKN) see **GET HEP TO LOVE** • 1942
SHE'S MY WEAKNESS • 1930 • Brown Melville • USA
SHE'S NO LADY • 1937 • Vidor Charles • USA
SHE'S OIL MINE • 1941 • *Keaton Buster* • SHT • USA • SHE'S ALL MINE
SHE'S OUT OF CONTROL • 1989 • Dragoti Stan • USA • DADDY'S LITTLE GIRL
SHE'S PROUD AND SHE'S BEAUTIFUL • 1908 • Gilbert Arthur • UKN
SHE'S SEVENTEEN AND ANXIOUS see **EMANUELLE PERCHE VIOLENZA ALLA DONNE?** • 1977
SHE'S THE BOSS see **RUNNING OUT OF LUCK** • 1985
SHE'S THE ONLY ONE see **HON, DEN ENDA** • 1926
SHE'S WORKING HER WAY THROUGH COLLEGE • 1952 • Humberstone H. Bruce • USA
SHESHET HAYAMIM • 1968 • Hameiri Yaacov, Herbst Itzhak • DOC • ISR • SIX DAYS TO ETERNITY (USA)
SHESTAYA CHAST MIRA • 1926 • Vertov Dziga • USS • SIXTH PART OF THE WORLD, A ○ SIXTH OF THE EARTH, A
SHESTOE IULYA see **SHESTOYE IYULYA** • 1968
SHESTOYE IYULYA • 1968 • Karasik Yuli • USS • SIXTH OF JULY, THE (UKN) ○ SHESTOE IULYA
SHEVGYACHYA SHENGA • 1955 • Athavale Shantaram • IND
SHHH.. • 1963 • Ross Jane • USA
SHI NO DANGAI • 1951 • Taniguchi Senkichi • JPN • DEATH CLIFF
SHI NO HOKO • 1926 • Tasaka Tomotaka • JPN
SHI NO MACHI O NOGARATE • 1952 • *Wakao Ayako* • JPN • ESCAPE FROM THE DEAD STREET
SHIAWASE • 1974 • Onchi Hideo • JPN • HAPPINESS
SHIBAIDO • 1944 • Naruse Mikio • JPN • THEATRE ○ WAY OF DRAMA, THE
SHIBIJIN YASHIKI • 1954 • Arai Ryohei • JPN • DEATH PEOPLE'S MANSION
SHIBIL • 1968 • Zhandov Zahari, Petkanova Magda • BUL
SHIBIRE-KURAGE • 1972 • Masumura Yasuzo • JPN • HOT LITTLE GIRL, THE
SHICHIMENCHO NO YUKUE • 1924 • Mizoguchi Kenji • JPN • TURKEYS: WHEREABOUTS UNKNOWN ○ TURKEYS IN A ROW ○ TRACE OF A TURKEY, THE
SHICHININ NO ONNASURI • 1958 • Horiuchi Manao • JPN
SHICHININ NO SAMURAI • 1954 • Kurosawa Akira • JPN • SEVEN SAMURAI, THE (USA) ○ MAGNIFICENT SEVEN, THE
SHICHININ NO YAJU • 1967 • Ezaki Mio • JPN • DIRTY SEVEN, THE
SHICHININ NON TSUISEKI-SHA • 1958 • Murayama Shinji • JPN • TOKYO PATROL -SEVEN DETECTIVES
SHICHININ NONYAJU CHI NO SENGEN • 1967 • Ezaki Mio • JPN • RETURN OF THE DIRTY SEVEN, THE
SHIDO MONOGATARI • 1941 • Kumagai Hisatora • JPN • INSTRUCTIVE STORY
SHIELD, THE • 1972 • Kelly Ron • CND
SHIELD AND THE SWORD. PART FOUR: THE LAST FRONTIER, THE see **SHCHIT I MYECH. IV: POSLYEDNI RUBYEZH** • 1968
SHIELD AND THE SWORD. PART ONE: NO RIGHT TO BE ONE'S SELF, THE see **SHCHIT I MYECH. I: BYEZ PRAVA BYT SOBOY** • 1968
SHIELD AND THE SWORD. PART THREE: NOT SUBJECT TO APPEAL, THE see **SHCHIT I MYECH. III: OBZHALOVANIYU NYE PODLEZHIT** • 1968
SHIELD AND THE SWORD. PART TWO: THE ORDER -STAY ALIVE, THE see **SHCHIT I MYECH. II: PRIKAZANO VYZHIT** • 1968
SHIELD-BEARER, THE see **GIERMEK** • 1964
SHIELD FOR MURDER • 1954 • O'Brien Edmond, Koch Howard W. • USA
SHIELD OF FAITH, THE • 1956 • Walker Norman • UKN
SHIELD OF HONOR, THE • 1927 • Johnson Emory • USA • ARM OF THE LAW, THE
SHIELD OF INNOCENCE, THE • 1914 • *Melies* • USA
SHIELD OF SILENCE, THE • 1925 • Maloney Leo • USA
SHIELD OF THE CONDOR see **ESCUDO DEL CONDOR, EL** • 1988
SHIELDING SHADOW, THE • 1917 • Gasnier Louis J., Mackenzie Donald • SRL • USA
SHIFROVANNY DOKUMENT • 1928 • Ptushko Alexander • ANS • USS • DOCUMENT IN CIPHER
SHIFSHUF NAIM • 1981 • Davidson Boaz • ISR, FRG • HOT BUBBLEGUM: LEMON POPSICLE III ○ HOT BUBBLEGUM
SHIFT • 1972-74 • Gehr Ernie • USA
SHIFT THE GEAR, FRECK • 1919 • *World* • SHT • USA
SHIFTING FORTUNE, A • 1913 • *Victor* • USA
SHIFTING SANDS • 1918 • *Balboa* • SHT • USA
SHIFTING SANDS • 1918 • Parker Albert • *Triangle* • USA
SHIFTING SANDS • 1923 • Granville Fred Leroy • USA
SHIFTING SANDS see **RUCHOME PIASKI** • 1969
SHIFTING SHADOWS • 1917 • Calvert E. H. • SHT • USA
SHIFTS • 1931 • Kelley Albert • SHT • USA
SHIFTY SHOPLIFTER, THE • 1918 • Curtis Allen • SHT • USA
SHIFTY'S CLAIM • 1911 • *Bison* • USA
SHIGA NAOYA • 1958 • Hani Susumu • DOC • JPN
SHIH-BA PAN WU-YI • 1981 • Liu Chia-Liang • HKG • LEGENDARY WEAPONS OF CHINA ○ LEGENDARY WEAPONS OF KUNG FU
SHIH CHING YU-HUN • Sung Ts'Un-Shou • HKG • GHOST OF THE MIRROR
SHIH-SAN NU NI • 1977 • Chang Mei-Chun • HKG • 13 GOLDEN NUNS
SHIH SAN SHOU • 1977 • Ch'En Le-Yi • HKG • THREE POEMS
SHIH-TI CH'U-MA • 1980 • Chan Jackie • HKG • YOUNG MASTER, THE
SHIH-TZU-LU K'OU • 1977 • Chin Han • HKG • CROSSROAD
SHIIKU • 1961 • Oshima Nagisa • JPN • CATCH, THE ○ BREEDING
SHIJIP KANUN NAL • 1957 • Lee Byung • KOR • WEDDING DAY, THE
SHIKAMO KARERA WA YUKU PART I & II • 1931 • Mizoguchi Kenji • JPN • AND YET THEY GO ON (USA) ○ NEVERTHELESS THEY GO ON
SHIKAR • 1968 • Ram Atma • IND • HUNT
SHIKARI • 1945 • *Burman S. D.(M)* • IND
SHIKARI • 1964 • *Singh K. N.* • IND
SHIKI NATSUKO • 1981 • Higashi Yoichi • JPN • NATSUKO, HER SEASON
SHIKI NO AIYOKU • 1958 • Nakahira Ko • JPN • FOUR SEASONS OF LOVE, THE
SHIKIDO JINGI • 1968 • Miki Hideki • JPN • MANNER AND JUSTICE OF SEX
SHIKIJO SHINDAN • 1968 • Kataoka Hitoshi • JPN • DIAGNOSIS OF SEXUAL DESIRE
SHIKIYOKU NO HATE • 1968 • Ezaki Mio • JPN • AT LUST'S END
SHIKKO YUYO • 1950 • Saburi Shin • JPN • REPRIEVE
SHILLING FOR CANDLES, A see **YOUNG AND INNOCENT** • 1937
SHILLING SHORT OF HIS WAGES, A • 1907 • Collins Alf? • UKN
SHILLINGBURY BLOWERS, THE • 1979 • Guest Val • UKN • ...AND THE BAND PLAYED ON
SHILPI • 1957 • Agradoot • IND
SHIMA NO ONNA • 1920 • Kotani H. • JPN • ISLAND WOMAN
SHIMA TO RATAI JIKEN • 1931 • Gosho Heinosuke • JPN • NAKED MURDER CASE OF THE ISLAND ○ ISLAND OF NAKED SCANDAL
SHIMA WA MORATTA • 1968 • Hasebe Yasuharu • JPN • RETALIATION
SHIMAI • 1955 • Hieki Mioji • JPN
SHIMAI NO YAKUSOKU • 1940 • Yamamoto Satsuo • JPN • END OF ENGAGEMENT
SHIMANA PERIYE • 1978 • Kabir Alamgir • BNG • BEYOND THE FRINGE ○ ACROSS THE FRINGE
SHIMIZU MINATO NI KITA OTOKO • 1960 • Makino Masahiro • JPN
SHIMIZU NO ABAREMBO • 1959 • Matsuo Akinori • JPN • WILD REPORTER
SHIMMERING LIGHT • 1978 • Chaffey Don • TVM • ASL • SURF
SHIMMERING OVER THE WAVES see **BEGUSHCHAYA PO VOLNAM** • 1967
SHIMMY LAGANO BELLE TARANTELLE E TARALUCCI E VINO see **SHIMMY LAGANO TARANTELLE E VINO** • 1978
SHIMMY LAGANO TARANTELLE E VINO • 1978 • Wertmuller Lina • ITL • SHIMMY LAGANO BELLE TARANTELLE E TARALUCCI E VINO
SHIMMY SHEIK, THE • 1923 • Brunel Adrian • SHT • UKN
SHIMPU GROUP, THE see **KAMIKAZE REN** • 1933
SHIMPU-REN see **KAMIKAZE REN** • 1933
SHIN ABASHIRI BANGAICHI • 1968 • Makino Masahiro • JPN • MAN FROM ABASHIRI STRIKES AGAIN, THE
SHIN BAKA JIDAI • 1946 • Taniguchi Senkichi • JPN • THESE FOOLISH TIMES
SHIN HEIKE MONOGATARI • 1955 • Mizoguchi Kenji • JPN • NEW TALES OF THE TAIRA CLAN (UKN) ○ TAIRA CLAN, THE (USA) ○ SACRILEGIOUS HERO, THE ○ SAGA OF THE TAIRA CLAN ○ SHIN-HEIKE MONOGATARI ○ TALES OF THE TAIRA CLAN
SHIN-HEIKE MONOGATARI see **SHIN HEIKE MONOGATARI** • 1955
SHIN HEIKE MONOGATARI: SHIZUKA TO YOSHITSUNE • 1956 • Shima Koji • JPN • NEW TALE OF GENJI: SHIZUKA AND YOSHITSUNE
SHIN HEITAI YAKUZA • 1966 • Tanaka Tokuzo • JPN • HOODLUM SOLDIER DESERTS AGAIN, THE
SHIN IREZUMI MUZAN TEKKA NO JINGI • 1968 • Sekigawa Hideo • JPN • DEVIL IN THE FLESH ○ DEVIL IN MY FLESH
SHIN JINSEI YONJUHATTE URAMOMOTE • 1968 • Higashimoto Kaoru • JPN • ALL THE TRICKS IN LIFE
SHIN JOJI NO RIREKISHO • 1967 • Yamashita Osamu • JPN • NEW PERSONAL HISTORY OF LOVE AFFAIRS
SHIN JOSEI KAGAMI • 1928 • Gosho Heinosuke • JPN • NEW KIND OF WOMAN, A ○ NEW WOMAN'S GUIDANCE
SHIN JOSEI MONDO • 1955 • *Kyo Machiko* • JPN • NEW WOMAN'S DIALOGUE
SHIN MEOTO ZENZAI • 1963 • Toyoda Shiro • JPN • NEW MARITAL RELATIONS
SHIN NIPPON CHIN DOCHU • 1959 • Magatani Morehei (c/d) • JPN
SHIN NO SHIKOTEI • 1963 • Tanaka Shigeo • JPN • GREAT WALL OF CHINA, THE ○ GREAT WALL, THE
SHIN ONNA DAIGAKU • 1960 • Hisamatsu Seiji • JPN
SHIN ONNA ONNA ONNA MONOGATARI • 1964 • Tamura Taijiro • JPN • IT'S A WOMAN'S WORLD
SHIN ONO GA TSUMI • 1926 • Mizoguchi Kenji • JPN • MY FAULT (USA) ○ IT'S MY FAULT ○ MY FAULT CONTINUED ○ MY FAULT NEW VERSION
SHIN OTOKO WA TSURAIYO • 1970 • Kobayashi Shunichi • JPN • TORA-SAN'S GRAND SCHEME
SHIN YOROKOBI MO KANASHIMA MO IKUTOSHITSUKI • 1985 • Kinoshita Keisuke • JPN • LIGHTHOUSE KEEPER'S FAMILY
SHINA NINGYO • 1981 • Terayama Shuji • JPN, FRN • FRUITS DE LA PASSION, LES (FRN) ○ FRUITS OF PASSION, THE
SHINA NO YORU • 1940 • Fushimizu Osamu • JPN • CHINA NIGHT
SHINANO FUDOK • 1941 • Kamei Fumio • JPN
SHINBONE ALLEY • 1971 • Wilson John D., Detiege David • ANM • USA • ARCHY AND MEHITABEL
SHINDIG, THE • 1930 • Gillett Burt • ANS • USA
SHINDO • 1936 • Gosho Heinosuke • JPN • NEW ROAD, THE ○ NEW WAY
SHINDOBADDO NO BOKEN • 1968 • Yabushita Taiji, Kuroda Masao, Kita Morio • JPN • ADVENTURES OF SINDBAD, THE
SHINE • 1942 • Berne Josef • SHT • USA
SHINE BRIGHT, MY STAR • 1969 • Mitta Alexander • USS • SHINE, O SHINE, MY STAR
SHINE 'EM UP • 1922 • Roach Hal • SHT • USA
SHINE GIRL, THE • 1916 • Parke William • USA
SHINE, O SHINE, MY STAR see **SHINE BRIGHT, MY STAR** • 1969
SHINE ON HARVEST MOON • 1932 • Fleischer Dave • ANS • USA
SHINE ON, HARVEST MOON • 1938 • Kane Joseph • USA
SHINE ON, HARVEST MOON • 1944 • Butler David • USA
SHINE ON MY SHOES see **LUCES DE MIS ZAPATOS** • 1973
SHINE ON YOUR SHOES • 1946 • Gould Dave • SHT • USA
SHINEL • 1926 • Kozintsev Grigori, Trauberg Leonid • USS • OVERCOAT, THE (USA) ○ CLOAK, THE

SHINEL • 1960 • Batalov Alexei • USS • OVERCOAT, THE (USA) ○ CLOAK, THE
SHINES AND MONKEYSHINES • 1918 • Howe J. A. • SHT • USA
SHING A LING LOO, PRETTY GIRL • 1967 • Wenceslao Jose Pepe • PHL
SHINGAPORU SOKOGEKI • 1943 • Shima Koji • JPN • ALL-OUT ATTACK ON SINGAPORE ○ ATTACK ON SINGAPORE
SHINING, THE • 1980 • Kubrick Stanley • USA
SHINING ADVENTURE, THE • 1925 • Ballin Hugo • USA
SHINING FUTURE, THE • 1944 • Prinz Leroy • SHT • USA
SHINING HOUR, THE • 1938 • Borzage Frank • USA
SHINING IN THE RED SUNSET (USA) see **AKAI YUKI NO TERASARETE** • 1925
SHINING LIGHT FROM LUND see **LJUSET FRAN LUND** • 1955
SHINING SEASON, A • 1979 • Margolin Stuart • TVM • USA
SHINING STAR see **THAT'S THE WAY OF THE WORLD** • 1975
SHINING SUN BECOMES CLOUDED, THE see **TERU HI KUMORU HI** • 1926
SHINING VICTORY • 1941 • Rapper Irving • USA • WINGED VICTORY
SHINJI FUJIN • 1950 • Yamamoto Kajiro • JPN
SHINJITSU ICHIRO • 1937 • Tasaka Tomotaka • JPN
SHINJU TEN NO AMIJIMA • 1969 • Shinoda Masahiro • JPN • DOUBLE SUICIDE AT AMIJIMA ○ DOUBLE SUICIDE
SHINJU YOIMACHIGUSA • 1925 • Kinugasa Teinosuke • JPN
SHINJUKU DOROBO NIKKI • 1969 • Oshima Nagisa • JPN • DIARY OF A SHINJUKU BURGLAR (USA) ○ DIARY OF A SHINJUKU THIEF(UKN)
SHINJUKU MAD • 1970 • Wakamatsu Koji • JPN
SHINJUKU NO HADA • 1968 • Saimura Kazuhiko • JPN • NAKED FACE OF SHINJUKU, THE
SHINJUKU SODACHI • 1968 • Hase Kazuo • JPN • YOUNG REBELS OF SHINJUKU
SHINKANSEN DAIBABUHA • 1975 • Sato Junya • JPN • NEGATIVE CONTACT ○ BULLET TRAIN, THE
SHINKEN SHOBEI see **SHINKEN SHOBU** • 1969
SHINKEN SHOBU • 1969 • Uchida Tomu • JPN • SWORDS OF DEATH ○ SHINKEN SHOBEI ○ REAL SWORD FIGHT
SHINKON NANATSU NO TANOSHIMI • 1958 • Edagawa Hiroshi • JPN • AMUSEMENT OF SEVEN MARRIED COUPLES
SHINKON TAKUAN FUFU • 1954 • Mizuko Harumi • JPN
SHINKON URA OMOTE • 1937 • Yamamoto Kajiro • JPN
SHINKU CHITAI • 1952 • Yamamoto Satsuo • JPN • VACUUM ZONE
SHINOBI NINJA • 1984 • Chuen Lik, Gotho Syuji • JPN
SHINOBI NO MANJI • 1968 • Suzuki Noribumi • JPN • SECRET OF FYLFOT, THE ○ SECRET OF THE NINJA
SHINOBI NO MONO • 1963 • Yamamoto Satsuo • JPN • BAND OF ASSASSINS, A
SHINOBU-GAWA • 1972 • Kumai Kei • JPN • LONG DARKNESS, THE
SHINOBU ITO • 1972 • Deme Masanobu • JPN
SHINPAN OOKA SEIDAN • 1928 • Ito Daisuke • JPN • OOKA'S TRIAL ○ OOKA SEIDAN
SHINPAN YOTSUYA KAIDAN • 1928 • Ito Daisuke • JPN • YOTSUYA GHOST STORY NEW EDITION
SHINPEN TANGE GAZEN -SEKISHU NO MAKI • 1939 • Yamamoto Satsuo • JPN
SHINRAN • 1960 • Tasaka Tomotaka • JPN
SHINREI JAKOUNEKO • 1940 • Arai Ryohei • JPN
SHINSAI KAIGI • 1949 • Chiba Yasuki • JPN • DIVINE COUNCIL
SHINSENGUMI • 1934 • Inagaki Hiroshi • JPN
SHINSENGUMI • 1970 • Sawashima Tadashi • JPN • BAND OF ASSASSINS (USA)
SHINSENGUMI ONITAICHO • 1954 • Kono Juichi • JPN • LAST OF THE SAMURAI
SHINSENGUMI SHIMATSUKI • 1963 • Misumi Kenji • JPN • NEW CLASS MANAGEMENT
SHINSETSU • 1942 • Gosho Heinosuke • JPN • NEW SNOW
SHINYA NO CHOSEN • 1959 • Murayama Shinji • JPN • CHALLENGE AT MIDNIGHT
SHIOBARA TASUKE • 1930 • *Tsuburaya Eiji (Ph)* • JPN
SHIOKARI TOGE • 1973 • Nakamura Noboru • JPN • LOVE STOPPED THE RUNAWAY TRAIN
SHIOSAI • 1954 • Taniguchi Senkichi • JPN • SOUND OF WAVES, THE ○ SURF
SHIP, THE see **NAVE** • 1940
SHIP, THE see **BATEN** • 1961
SHIP-A-HOOEY • 1954 • Sparber I. • ANS • USA
SHIP AHOY • 1919 • Parrott Charles • USA
SHIP AHOY! • 1920 • Griffin Frank C. • SHT • USA
SHIP AHOY • 1930 • Foster John • ANS • USA
SHIP AHOY • 1942 • Buzzell Edward • USA
SHIP AHOY! see **SKEPP OHOJ!** • 1931
SHIP AHOY, WOODY • 1969 • Smith Paul J. • ANS • USA
SHIP AND THE ISLAND, THE • 1973 • Henning-Jensen Bjarne • DNM
SHIP AND THE STARS, THE • 1975 • Henning-Jensen Bjarne • DNM
SHIP ANGELICA, THE see **SHIP OF ANJELICA, THE** • 1988
SHIP BOUND FOR INDIA, A see **SKEPP TILL INDIALAND** • 1947
SHIP COMES IN, A • 1928 • Howard William K. • USA • HIS COUNTRY (UKN)
SHIP COMES TO ANTWERP, A • 1953 • Curtis Martin • UKN
SHIP FROM SHANGHAI, THE • 1929 • Brabin Charles J. • USA
SHIP IN HARBOUR • 1955 • Haldane Don • CND
SHIP IS BORN, A • 1942 • Negulesco Jean • SHT • USA
SHIP IS BORN, A see **NARODZINY STATKU** • 1961
SHIP OF ANJELICA, THE • 1988 • Bozorgnia Mohammad-Reza • IRN • SHIP ANGELICA, THE
SHIP OF CONDEMNED WOMEN, THE (USA) see **NAVE DELLE DONNE MALEDETTE, LA** • 1953
SHIP OF DOOM, THE • 1917 • Gittens Wyndham • USA
SHIP OF ETHER see **SHIP OF THE ETHER** • 1935
SHIP OF FOOLS • 1965 • Kramer Stanley • USA
SHIP OF HEAVEN, THE see **HIMMELSKIBET** • 1917
SHIP OF JOY see **PLIO TIS HARAS, TO** • 1967
SHIP OF LOST MEN, THE see **SCHIFF DER VERLORENEN MENSCHEN, DAS** • 1929
SHIP OF SOULS • 1925 • Miller Charles • USA
SHIP OF THE ETHER • 1935 • Pal George • ANS • NTH • ETHER SHIP ○ SHIP OF ETHER
SHIP OF THE MONSTERS, THE see **NAVE DE LOS MONSTRUOS, LA** • 1959
SHIP OF WANTED MEN • 1933 • Collins Lewis D. • USA
SHIP OF ZOMBIES see **BUQUE MALDITO, EL** • 1974
SHIP, OY, OY! • 1918 • Curtis Allen • SHT • USA
SHIP SAFETY see **WATERTIGHT** • 1943
SHIP SAILS ON, THE see **E LA NAVE VA** • 1983
SHIP THAT DIED, THE • 1938 • Tourneur Jacques • SHT • USA
SHIP THAT DIED OF SHAME, THE • 1955 • Dearden Basil, Relph Michael • UKN • PT RAIDERS (USA)
SHIP TO HEAVEN, A see **HIMMELSKIBET** • 1917
SHIP TO INDIA, A (UKN) see **SKEPP TILL INDIALAND** • 1947
SHIP WAS LOADED, THE (USA) see **CARRY ON ADMIRAL** • 1957
SHIPBUILDERS, THE • 1943 • Baxter John • UKN
SHIPMATES • 1909 • Martinek H. O.? • UKN
SHIPMATES • 1926 • Croise Hugh • UKN
SHIPMATES • 1931 • Pollard Harry • SHT • USA
SHIPMATES FOREVER • 1935 • Borzage Frank • USA
SHIPMATES O' MINE • 1936 • Mitchell Oswald • UKN
SHIPPING A CLOCK • 1913 • *Elmer Clarence* • USA
SHIPPU! KURAMA TENGU • 1956 • *Arashi Kanjuro* • JPN • HURRY! KURAMA!
SHIPS ATTACKING FORTS see **KORABLI SHTURMUYUT BASTIONY** • 1953
SHIP'S CAFE • 1935 • Florey Robert • USA
SHIP'S CONCERT • 1937 • Hiscott Leslie • UKN
SHIP'S HUSBAND, THE • 1910 • *Edison* • USA
SHIPS OF HATE • 1931 • McCarthy John P. • USA
SHIPS OF THE NIGHT • 1928 • Worne Duke • USA
SHIP'S REGISTER see **HAJONAPLO** • 1987
SHIPS STORM THE BASTIONS, THE see **KORABLI SHTURMUYUT BASTIONY** • 1953
SHIPS THAT MEET see **SKEPP SOM MOTAS** • 1916
SHIPS THAT PASS IN THE NIGHT • 1921 • Nash Percy • UKN
SHIPS WITH WINGS • 1941 • Nolbandov Sergei • UKN
SHIPWRECK • 1931 • Lantz Walter, Nolan William • ANS • USA
SHIPWRECK see **SCHIFF IN NOT S.O.S.** • 1928
SHIPWRECK see **NAUFRAGIO** • 1977
SHIPWRECK ISLAND (USA) see **DOS ANOS DE VACACIONES** • 1962
SHIPWRECK! (UKN) see **SEA GYPSIES, THE** • 1978
SHIPWRECKED • 1911 • *Selig* • USA
SHIPWRECKED • 1913 • *Nilsson Anna Q.* • USA
SHIPWRECKED • 1926 • Henabery Joseph • USA
SHIPWRECKED • 1984 • Bennett Bill • DCS • ASL
SHIPWRECKED see **SEA GYPSIES, THE** • 1978
SHIPWRECKED BROTHERS see **ROBINSON CRUSOE** • 1933
SHIPWRECKED MAX see **SKEPPSBRUTNE MAX** • 1936
SHIPWRECKS see **WRAKI** • 1957
SHIPYARD • 1934 • Rotha Paul • DOC • UKN
SHIPYARD AT THE ADRIATIC SEA see **CANTIERI DELL'ADRIATICO, I** • 1933
SHIPYARD SALLY • 1939 • Banks Monty • UKN
SHIPYARD SYMPHONY • 1943 • Donnelly Eddie • ANS • USA
SHIR HASHIRIM • Lynn Henry
SHIRAI GONPACHI • 1928 • *Tsuburaya Eiji (Ph)* • JPN
SHIRAK • 1988 • Mehrjui Dariush • IRN
SHIRALEE, THE • 1957 • Norman Leslie • UKN
SHIRANUI-KAI • 1974 • Tsuchimoto Noriaki • DOC • JPN
SHIRANUI KENGYO • 1960 • Mori Issei • JPN
SHIRASAGI • 1941 • Shimazu Yasujiro • JPN • SNOWY HERON
SHIRASAGI • 1959 • Kinugasa Teinosuke • JPN • WHITE HERON, THE ○ SNOWY HERON
SHIRATORI WA KANASHI KARAZUYA • 1949 • Toyoda Shiro • JPN
SHIRAYURI WA NAGEKU • 1925 • Mizoguchi Kenji • JPN • WHITE LILY LAMENTS, THE (USA) ○ LAMENT OF A WHITE LILY
SHIRAZ • 1928 • Osten Franz • FRG
SHIRIBOE SONICHI • 1969 • Misumi Kenji • JPN • BARKING-DONKEY SONICHI
SHIRIKURAE MAGOICHI • 1969 • Misumi Kenji • JPN • MAGOICHI SAGA, THE
SHIRIN FARHAD • 1980 • Sharad Abdus • BNG • LEGEND OF LOVE
SHIRKER'S NIGHTMARE, THE • 1914 • Booth W. R. • UKN
SHIRLEY • 1922 • Bramble A. V. • UKN
SHIRLEY KAYE • 1917 • Kaufman Joseph • USA
SHIRLEY OF THE CIRCUS • 1922 • Lee Rowland V. • USA
SHIRLEY TEMPLE STORY • 1976 • Padros Antoni • SPN
SHIRLEY THOMPSON VERSUS THE ALIENS • 1971 • Sharman Jim • ASL
SHIRLEY VALENTINE • 1989 • Gilbert Lewis* • UKN
SHIRLEY YORKE see **STORY OF SHIRLEY YORKE, THE** • 1948
SHIRO TO KURO • 1963 • Horikawa Hiromichi • JPN • PRESSURE OF GUILT ○ WHITE AND BLACK
SHIRO TOKISADA FROM AMAKUSA see **AMAKUSA SHIRO TOKISADA** • 1962
SHIRO ZUKIN ARAWARU • 1949 • Wagaki Hiroshi • JPN
SHIROGANE SHINJU • 1956 • Shindo Kaneto • JPN • GEISHA'S SUICIDE, A ○ SILVER DOUBLE SUICIDE ○ GIN-SHINJU
SHIROI AKUMA • 1958 • Saito Buichi • JPN • BUDDING OF LOVE
SHIROI ASA • 1964 • Teshigahara Hiroshi • SHT • JPN • WHITE MORNING
SHIROI GAKE • 1960 • Imai Tadashi • JPN • WHITE CLIFF, THE ○ CLIFF, THE
SHIROI HADA TO KIIROI TAICHO • 1961 • Horiuchi Manao • JPN • INTERNEES OF KAMPALI ○ WOMEN BEHIND BARBED WIRE
SHIROI HASHI • 1956 • Ohba Hideo • JPN • WHITE BRIDGE
SHIROI HATO • 1960 • Tabata Tsuneo • JPN • WHITE PIGEON
SHIROI HEKIGA • 1942 • *Tsuburaya Eiji* • JPN
SHIROI KAIKAN • 1968 • Fukuda Seiichi • JPN • WHITE PLEASURE
SHIROI KIBA • 1960 • Gosho Heinosuke • JPN • WHITE FANGS ○ WHITE FANG
SHIROI KONA NO KYOFU • 1960 • Murayama Shinji • JPN • CHASE AFTER OPIUM DEALERS, THE
SHIROI KYOTO • 1966 • Yamamoto Satsuo • JPN • GREAT WHITE TOWER, THE
SHIROI MAGYO • 1956 • Nakamura Noboru • JPN • WHITE DEVIL-FISH
SHIROI MICHI, SHINRAN • 1987 • Mikuni Rentaro • JPN • WHITE ROAD, AN ETERNAL PRIEST, SHINRAN
SHIROI YAJU • 1950 • Naruse Mikio • JPN • WHITE BEAST
SHIROIKOYA KOMAKO • 1960 • Misumi Kenji • JPN • WHAT PRICE LOVE
SHIROKI HYOGA NO HATENI • 1978 • Kadota Ryutaro • DOC • JPN • BEYOND THE WHITE GLACIER
SHIROTORI • 1965 • Masuda Toshio • JPN
SHIRT OF HER BACK, THE • 1961 • Gary Ken • USA
SHIRTS • 1914 • Storrie Kelly • UKN
SHIRTS • 1919 • Kenton Erle C. • SHT • USA
SHIRTS AND SHOCKS • 1913 • *Majestic* • USA
SHIRTS / SKINS • 1973 • Graham William A. • TVM • USA
SHISHI NO ZA • 1953 • Ito Daisuke • JPN • LION'S DANCE
SHISHIM SHA'OT LE'SUEZ • 1967 • Jaeger Kobi • ISR • SIXTY HOURS TO SUEZ
SHISHIMARU IPPEI • 1955 • Hagiwara Ryo • JPN
SHISHKABUGS • 1962 • Freleng Friz • ANS • USA
SHISHUNKI see **ADOLESCENTI, LE** • 1964
SHISSHUN NO TECHNIQUE • 1968 • Miki Eisuke • JPN • TECHNIQUE OF A FAINT
SHITAMACHI • 1957 • Chiba Yasuki • JPN • DOWNTOWN
SHITANAMEZURI • 1968 • Hayasaka Hiroshi • JPN • APPETITE
SHITO NO DENSETSU • 1963 • Kinoshita Keisuke • JPN • LEGEND OR WAS IT?, A ○ LEGEND OF A DUEL TO THE DEATH
SHITOYAKANA KEDAMONO • 1963 • Kawashima Yuzo • JPN • ELEGANT BEAST
SHITOYAKANA KEMONO • 1963 • Kawashima Yuzo • JPN • SOFT BEAST
SHITT SUTT KA JIN JIN LE • 1983 • Nyunt Win • BRM • SHARPER THAN THE SHARPEST
SHITTO • 1949 • Yoshimura Kozaburo • JPN • JEALOUSY
SHIV KANYA • 1953 • Desai Dhirubhai • IND
SHIV LEELA • 1922 • IND
SHIV LEELA • 1951 • Ghanekar G. B. • IND
SHIVA RATRI • 1921 • *Madan J. F. (P)* • IND
SHIVA UND DIE GALGEN BLUME • 1945 • Steinhoff Hans • FRG
SHIVER AND SHAKE • 1922 • Roach Hal • SHT • USA
SHIVER-FEVER • Munteanu Stefan • ANM • RMN
SHIVER ME TIMBERS • 1934 • Fleischer Dave • ANS • USA
SHIVER MY TIMBERS • 1931 • McGowan Robert • SHT • USA
SHIVER ON THE SKIN, A see **BRIVIDO SULLA PELLE, UN** • 1966
SHIVERING SHAKESPEARE • 1930 • Mack Anthony, McGowan Robert (Spv) • SHT • USA
SHIVERING SHERLOCKS • 1948 • Lord Del • SHT • USA
SHIVERING SPOOKS • 1926 • Roach Hal • SHT • USA
SHIVERS • 1934 • Ripley Arthur • SHT • USA
SHIVERS IN SUMMER see **FRENESIA DELL'ESTATE** • 1964
SHIVERS (UKN) see **PARASITE MURDERS, THE** • 1975
SHIVERS (USA) see **DRESZCZE** • 1981
SHIWU GUAN • 1956 • Tao Jin • CHN • FIFTEEN STRINGS OF CASH
SHIZI JIETOU • 1937 • Shen Xiling • CHN • CROSSROADS
SHIZUKA GOSEN • 1938 • *Yamada Isuzu* • JPN • SILENT MUTUAL ELECTION
SHIZUKANARU KETTO • 1949 • Kurosawa Akira • JPN • SILENT DUEL, THE ○ QUIET DUEL, THE ○ QUIET FIGHT, THE
SHIZUKANARU KYODEN • 1959 • Sekigawa Hideo • JPN • SILENT MURDER, THE
SHKID REPUBLIC, THE see **RESPUBLIKA SHKID** • 1967
SHKOLA ZLOSLOVIYA • 1952 • Room Abram • USS • SCHOOL FOR SCANDAL
SHKOLNI VALS • 1978 • Lyubimov Pavel • USS • SCHOOL WALTZ
SHLOSHA YAMIN VE YELED • 1966 • Zohar Uri • ISR • NOT MINE TO LOVE (USA) ○ THREE DAYS AND A CHILD
SHNEI KUNI LEMEL • 1965 • Becker Israel • ISR • FLYING MATCHMAKER, THE (USA)
SHO O SUTEYI, MACHI E DEYO • 1971 • Terayama Shuji • JPN • THROW AWAY YOUR BOOKS, LET'S GO INTO THE STREETS! ○ THROW AWAY BOOKS, LET'S GO INTO THE STREETS!
SHOAH • 1985 • Lanzmann Claude • DOC • FRN
SHOAL LIGHT, THE • 1915 • Sidney Scott • USA
SHOBOSHI TO SONO MUSUME • 1959 • Shima Koji • JPN
SHOBUINU • 1967 • Inoue Yoshio • JPN • SILENT GUN, THE
SHOCHIKU FOLLIES see **TOKYO ODORI** • 1959
SHOCK • 1934 • Pomeroy Roy J. • USA
SHOCK • 1946 • Werker Alfred L. • USA
SHOCK see **QUATERMASS EXPERIMENT, THE** • 1955
SHOCK see **SHANKS** • 1974
SHOCK see **SHOCK TRANSFERT SUSPENCE HYPNOS** • 1977
SHOCK, THE • 1923 • Hillyer Lambert • USA • BITTERSWEET
SHOCK CHAMBER • 1985 • TVM • CND
SHOCK CORRIDOR • 1963 • Fuller Samuel • USA • LONG CORRIDOR ○ STRAIGHTJACKET
SHOCK-ING COMPLAINT, A • 1912 • Aylott Dave • UKN
SHOCK PATROL (USA) see **PATROUILLE DE CHOC** • 1956
SHOCK PUNCH, THE • 1925 • Sloane Paul • USA
SHOCK TO THE SYSTEM, A • 1989 • Egleson Jan • USA
SHOCK TRANSFERT SUSPENCE HYPNOS • 1977 • Bava Mario • ITL • ALL 33 DI VIA OROLOGIO FA SEMPRE FREDDO ○ TRANSFERT SUSPENCE HYPNOS ○ BEYOND THE DOOR 2 ○ SUSPENSE ○ SHOCK
SHOCK TREATMENT • 1964 • Sanders Denis • USA
SHOCK TREATMENT • 1981 • Sharman Jim • USA
SHOCK TREATMENT • 1987 • Doyle Julian • USA
SHOCK TREATMENT see **TRAITEMENT DE CHOC** • 1972
SHOCK TROOP • 1988 • Ingvordsen J. Christian • USA
SHOCK TROOP see **STOSSTRUPP 1917** • 1934
SHOCK TROOPS see **HOMME DE TROP, UN** • 1967
SHOCK TROOPS see **MUZ KTORY LUZE** • 1968
SHOCK (USA) see **TRAITEMENT DE CHOC** • 1972
SHOCK WAVE see **STRANDED** • 1987
SHOCK WAVES see **DEATH CORPS** • 1970

SHOCKER • 1989 • Craven Wes • USA
SHOCKER see **STADT OHNE MITLEID** • 1961
SHOCKING • 1976 • Mulot Claude • FRN
SHOCKING ACCIDENT, A • 1983 • Scott Anthony • UKN
SHOCKING AFFAIR • 1949 • Yates Hal • SHT • USA
SHOCKING BAD FORM • 1914 • Aylott Dave • UKN
SHOCKING HER FUTURE MOTHER-IN-LAW • 1912 • *Majestic* • USA
SHOCKING HIS FLOCK • 1912 • *Majestic* • USA
SHOCKING INCIDENT • 1903 • *Bitzer Billy (Ph)* • USA
SHOCKING JOB, A • 1913 • Aylott Dave • UKN • SHOCKS AND SHORTS
SHOCKING MISS PILGRIM, THE • 1947 • Seaton George • USA
SHOCKING NIGHT, A • 1921 • Lyons Eddie, Moran Lee • USA
SHOCKING PINK • 1965 • Freleng Friz • ANS • USA
SHOCKING SEX, THE • 1964 • *Mishkin William* • USA • REHEARSAL FOR SIN
SHOCKING STOCKINGS • 1915 • Dillon Eddie • USA
SHOCKPROOF • 1949 • Sirk Douglas • USA • LOVERS, THE
SHOCKS AND SHORTS see **SHOCKING JOB, A** • 1913
SHOCKS OF DOOM • 1919 • Houry Henri • SHT • USA
SHOCKTRAUMA • 1982 • Till Eric • TVM • CND
SHOD WITH FIRE • 1920 • Flynn Emmett J. • USA
SHODDY, THE TAILOR • 1915 • Louis Will • USA
SHODH • 1979 • Chaudhuri Biplab Ray • IND • SEARCH, THE
SHODO SATSUJIN, MUSUKO YO • 1979 • Kinoshita Keisuke • JPN • IMPULSIVE KILLER ○ MY SON
SHOE COMPOT • 1985 • Barkan Yehuda • ISR
SHOE INVENTOR, THE see **IZUMITELJ CIPELA** • 1967
SHOE MUST GO ON, THE • 1960 • Kneitel Seymour • ANS • USA
SHOE SALON PINKUS see **SCHUHPALAST PINKUS** • 1916
SHOE SHINE (USA) see **SCIUSCIA** • 1946
SHOEBLACK OF PICCADILLY • 1920 • Greening L. Stuart • UKN
SHOEFLIES • 1965 • Post Howard • ANS • USA
SHOEIN' HOSSES • 1934 • Fleischer Dave • ANS • USA
SHOELESS JOE see **FIELD OF DREAMS** • 1989
SHOEMAKER AND THE DOLL, THE • 1913 • *Garwood William* • USA
SHOEMAKER AND THE ELVES • 1962 • *Coronet* • ANS • USA, JPN
SHOEMAKER AND THE ELVES, THE • 1934 • *Mintz Charles (P)* • ANS • USA
SHOEMAKER AND THE ELVES, THE (USA) see **HEINZELMANNCHEN** • 1956
SHOEMAKER AND THE HATTER, THE • 1949 • Halas John, Batchelor Joy • ANS • UKN
SHOEMAKER OF COEPENICK, THE • 1908 • *Vitagraph* • USA
SHOEMAKER'S ELEVENTH, THE • 1914 • *Wilson Ben* • USA
SHOES • 1916 • Weber Lois • USA
SHOES, THE • 1961 • Pintoff Ernest • SHT • USA
SHOES OF THE FISHERMAN, THE • 1968 • Anderson Michael • USA, ITL
SHOES THAT DANCED, THE • 1918 • Borzage Frank • USA
SHOES WITH RHYTHM • 1937 • Schwarzwald Milton • SHT • USA
SHOESHINE see **SCIUSCIA** • 1946
SHOESHINE AND BARBER SHOP • 1894 • Dickson W. K. L. • USA
SHOESHINE JASPER • 1946 • Pal George • ANS • USA
SHOESTRING • 1980 • Camfield Douglas • MTV • UKN
SHOGUN • 1981 • London Jerry • TVM • USA, JPN
SHOGUN AND HIS MISTRESS, THE see **OOKU MARUHI MONOGATARI** • 1967
SHOGUN AND HIS MISTRESSES, THE see **OOKU MARUHI MONOGATARI** • 1967
SHOGUN AND THE FISHMONGER see **IEMITSU TO HIKOZA TO ISSHIN TASUKE** • 1961
SHOGUN AND THREE THOUSAND WOMEN, THE see **TOKUGAWA ONNA KEIZU** • 1968
SHOGUN ASSASSIN • 1980 • Misumi Kenji, Weisman David, Houston Robert • USA, JPN • SANZU NO KAWA NO UBAGURAMA ○ BABY CART AT THE RIVER STYX ○ KOSURE OOKAMI ○ KOSURE OOKAMI N.2
SHOGUN TO HEI see **SHOGUN TO SAMBO TO HEI** • 1942
SHOGUN TO SAMBO TO HEI • 1942 • Taguchi Tetsu • JPN • GENERAL, STAFF OFFICER AND SOLDIERS ○ SHOGUN TO HEI ○ GENERALS AND SOLDIERS
SHOGUN TRAVELS INCOGNITO see **TENKA NO FUKU SHOGUN** • 1959
SHOGUN WARRIORS: GRANDIZER • 1982 • ANM • JPN
SHOGUN'S HOLIDAY see **EDOKKO MATSURI** • 1958
SHOGUN'S SAMURAI, THE • 1979 • Fukasaku Kinji • JPN
SHOGUN'S SHADOW see **GEKITOTSU** • 1989
SHOHAR-E-AHOU RHANOM • 1968 • Molapoor Davoud • IRN • MRS. AHOU'S HUSBAND
SHOHIN-SHUSOKU • 1924 • Kinugasa Teinosuke • JPN
SHOHIN-SHUTO • 1924 • Kinugasa Teinosuke • JPN
SHOJO GA MITA • 1966 • Misumi Kenji • JPN • VIRGIN WITNESS, THE
SHOJO GEBA-GEBA • 1970 • Wakamatsu Koji • JPN • VIOLENT VIRGIN, THE
SHOJO KAIKIN • 1968 • Tsuzuki Yohnosuke • JPN • OPEN SEASON FOR VIRGINS, THE
SHOJO MIREN • 1967 • Mukoi Kan • JPN • ATTACHMENT OF A VIRGIN
SHOJO NO JYAKUTEN • 1968 • Kataoka Hitoshi • JPN • VIRGIN'S WEAK POINT, THE
SHOJO NO KETSUMIYAKU • 1967 • Yamashita Osamu • JPN • VEIN OF VIRGINS, A
SHOJO NO SHI • 1927 • Gosho Heinosuke • JPN • DEATH OF A MAIDEN ○ DEATH OF A VIRGIN
SHOJO NYUYO • 1930 • Gosho Heinosuke • JPN • GIRL NYUYO, THE ○ WE NEED VIRGINS ○ VIRGINS WANTED
SHOJO SEITAI • 1967 • Komori Haku • JPN • ECOLOGY OF A VIRGIN
SHOJO SHOMEISHO • 1967 • Mukoi Hiroshi • JPN • CERTIFICATE OF VIRGINITY
SHOJO WA SHINJI NO GOTOKU • 1947 • Nakamura Noboru • JPN
SHOJO-YO SAYONARA • 1933 • Gosho Heinosuke • JPN • GOODBYE MY GIRL ○ VIRGIN, GOODBYE
SHOJO ZAKURA • 1967 • Okuwaki Toshio • JPN • VIRGIN CHERRY
SHOJO ZANKOKU • 1967 • Watanabe Yuzuru • JPN • VIRGIN CRUELTY
SHOKEI NO HEYA • 1956 • Ichikawa Kon • JPN • PUNISHMENT ROOM
SHOKEI NO SHIMA • 1966 • Shinoda Masahiro • JPN • PUNISHMENT ISLAND ○ CAPTIVE'S ISLAND
SHOKKAKU • 1969 • Shindo Kaneto • JPN • STRANGE AFFINITY ○ ODD AFFINITY ○ TENTACLES
SHOKOH-E-JAVANMARDI • 1968 • Riyahi Esmaeil • IRN • MAGNIFICENCE OF BRAVERY, THE
SHOKUTAKU NO NAI IE • 1985 • Kobayashi Masaki • JPN • FAMILY WITHOUT A DINNER TABLE ○ EMPTY TABLE, THE
SHOLAY • 1975 • Sippy Ramesh • IND • EMBERS
SHOLEHAYE KHASHM • 1968 • Safaei Reza • IRN • FLAME OF ANGER, THE
SHOMETSU • 1978 • Kuri Yoji • ANS • JPN
SHON, THE PIPER • 1913 • Turner Otis • USA
SHONEN • 1969 • Oshima Nagisa • JPN • BOY
SHONEN HYORYUKI • 1960 • Sekigawa Hideo • JPN • DRIFTING BOYS
SHONEN JACK TO MAHOTSUKAI • 1967 • Yabushita Taiji • ANM • JPN • JACK AND THE WITCH (USA) ○ IT'S A WONDROUS, WONDROUS, WONDROUS, WONDROUS WORLD
SHONEN-KI • 1951 • Kinoshita Keisuke • JPN • RECORD OF YOUTH, A ○ YOUTH
SHONEN SARUTOBI SASUKE • 1960 • Daikubara Akira, Yamamoto Sanze • ANM • JPN • MAGIC BOY (USA) ○ ADVENTURES OF A LITTLE SAMURAI
SHONEN TANTEIDAN • 1959 • Wakabayashi Eijiro • JPN • BOY DETECTIVES, THE
SHONEN TANTEIDAN -KABUTOMUSHI NO YOKI & TETTO NO KAIJIN • 1957 • Sekigawa Hideo • JPN • 20 FACES
SHONIN NO ISU • 1965 • Yamamoto Satsuo • JPN • WITNESS SEAT, THE
SHOO FLY • 1915 • King Burton L. • USA
SHOOT • 1976 • Hart Harvey • CND, USA
SHOOT see **OPEN SEASON** • 1974
SHOOT, THE (USA) see **SCHUT, DER** • 1964
SHOOT AND CRY • 1988 • Klodawsky Helen • DOC • CND
SHOOT FIRST, DIE LATER (USA) see **POLIZIOTTO E MARCIO, LA** • 1974
SHOOT FIRST, LAUGH LAST see **UOMO, UN CAVALLO, UNA PISTOLA, UN** • 1968
SHOOT FIRST (USA) see **ROUGH SHOOT** • 1952
SHOOT, GRINGO, SHOOT see **SPARA, GRINGO, SPARA** • 1968
SHOOT IT: BLACK, SHOOT IT: BLUE • 1974 • McGuire Dennis • USA
SHOOT LOUD, LOUDER.. I DON'T UNDERSTAND see **SPARA FORTE, PIU FORTE.. NON CAPISCO** • 1966
SHOOT ON SIGHT • 1920 • Roach Hal • SHT • USA
SHOOT OUT • 1971 • Hathaway Henry • USA
SHOOT-OUT AT BEAVER FALLS • 1970 • August Harry • USA • SHOWDOWN AT BEAVER FALLS
SHOOT OUT AT BIG SAG see **RAWHIDE HALO, THE** • 1960
SHOOT OUT AT MEDICINE BEND • 1957 • Bare Richard L. • USA
SHOOT! SHOOT AGAIN! see **UDARI YESHCHYO UDARI** • 1968
SHOOT STRAIGHT • 1923 • Roach Hal • SHT • USA
SHOOT THE LIVING, PRAY FOR THE DEAD see **PREGA IL MORTO E AMMAZZA IL VIVO** • 1971
SHOOT THE MOON • 1962 • Grooms Red, Burckhardt Rudy • SHT • USA
SHOOT THE MOON • 1982 • Parker Alan • USA
SHOOT THE NETS see **SCHOT IS TE BOORD, HET** • 1952
SHOOT THE PIANIST see **TIREZ SUR LE PIANISTE** • 1960
SHOOT THE PIANO PLAYER (USA) see **TIREZ SUR LE PIANISTE** • 1960
SHOOT THE SUN DOWN • 1981 • Leeds David • USA
SHOOT THE WORKS • 1934 • Ruggles Wesley • USA • THANK YOUR STARS (UKN)
SHOOT TO KILL • 1947 • Berke William • USA
SHOOT TO KILL • 1961 • Winner Michael • UKN
SHOOT TO KILL • 1988 • Spottiswoode Roger • USA • DEADLY PURSUIT (UKN) ○ MOUNTAIN KING, THE
SHOOT UP, THE see **PICO, EL** • 1984
SHOOTDOWN • 1989 • Pressman Michael • TVM • USA
SHOOTER • 1988 • Nelson Gary • TVM • USA
SHOOTERS • 1989 • Yuval Peter • USA
SHOOTIN' FOOL, THE • 1920 • *Gibson Hoot* • SHT • USA
SHOOTIN' FOR LOVE • 1923 • Sedgwick Edward • USA
SHOOTIN' INJUNS • 1925 • Roach Hal • SHT • USA
SHOOTIN' IRONS • 1927 • Rosson Richard • USA
SHOOTIN' IRONS see **WEST OF TEXAS** • 1943
SHOOTIN' KID, THE • 1920 • Gibson Ed Hoot • SHT • USA
SHOOTIN' MAD • 1919 • Robbins Jess • USA
SHOOTIN' SQUARE • 1924 • *Perrin Jack* • USA
SHOOTIN' STARS • 1960 • Kneitel Seymour • ANS • USA
SHOOTING, THE • 1967 • Hellman Monte • USA
SHOOTING, THE see **BAD BLOOD** • 1980
SHOOTING A BOER SPY • 1899 • Ashe Robert • UKN
SHOOTING A RUSSIAN SPY • 1904 • *Cricks & Sharp* • UKN
SHOOTING AT RANDOM • 1916 • *Heinie & Louie* • USA
SHOOTING AT THE KARASH PASS see **VISTRIL V GORACH** • 1970
SHOOTING BIG GAME WITH A CAMERA • 1928 • *Patterson Frederick Beck* • DOC • USA
SHOOTING EXERCISE, THE see **SCHIESSUBUNG, DIE** • 1975
SHOOTING GALLERY, THE • Stepanek Miroslav • ANS • CZC
SHOOTING HIGH • 1940 • Green Alfred E. • USA
SHOOTING HIS 'ART OUT • 1916 • Kirkland David • SHT • USA
SHOOTING IN THE HAUNTED WOODS • 1909 • *Gaumont* • SHT • FRN
SHOOTING MATCH, A • 1914 • *Sterling Ford* • USA
SHOOTING OF DAN MCGOO • 1945 • Avery Tex • ANS • USA
SHOOTING OF DAN MCGREW, THE • 1915 • Blache Herbert • USA
SHOOTING OF DAN MCGREW, THE • 1924 • Badger Clarence • USA
SHOOTING OF DAN MCGREW, THE • 1966 • Graham Ed • ANS • USA
SHOOTING OF DORREGO, THE see **FUSILAMIENTO DE DORREGO, EL** • 1908
SHOOTING OF TRAITOR ERNST S., THE see **ERSCHIESSUNG DES LANDESVERRATERS ERNST S., DIE** • 1976
SHOOTING PARTY, THE • 1918 • *Anderson Mignon* • SHT • USA
SHOOTING PARTY, THE • 1984 • Bridges Alan • UKN
SHOOTING PARTY, THE (USA) see **HUNTING ACCIDENT, THE** • 1978
SHOOTING RANGE see **CELLOVOLDE** • 1989
SHOOTING SHOWDOWN see **TWO-FISTED SHERIFF** • 1937
SHOOTING STAR • 1984 • Rosma Juha • MTV • FNL
SHOOTING STAR, THE • 1915 • *Historical Feature Film* • USA
SHOOTING STAR, THE • 1917 • *Essanay* • SHT • USA
SHOOTING STAR, THE see **TINTIN: THE SHOOTING STAR** • 1987
SHOOTING STARS • 1928 • Bramble A. V., Asquith Anthony • UKN
SHOOTING STARS • 1937 • Humphris Eric • UKN
SHOOTING STARS • 1983 • Lang Richard • TVM • USA
SHOOTING STRAIGHT • 1927 • Wyler William • USA
SHOOTING STRAIGHT • 1930 • Archainbaud George • USA • DEAD GAME
SHOOTING THE CHUTES see **MONTAGNE RUSSES NAUTIQUES** • 1898
SHOOTING UP THE MOVIES • 1916 • Mix Tom • SHT • USA
SHOOTING WILD • 1927 • Sandrich Mark • SHT • USA
SHOOTIST, THE • 1976 • Siegel Don • USA
SHOOTOUT IN A ONE DOG TOWN • 1973 • Kennedy Burt • TVM • USA
SHOP ANGEL • 1932 • Hopper E. Mason • USA
SHOP AROUND THE CORNER, THE • 1939 • Lubitsch Ernst • USA
SHOP AT SLY CORNER, THE • 1947 • King George • UKN • CODE OF SCOTLAND YARD, THE (USA)
SHOP GIRL, THE see **WINIFRED THE SHOP GIRL** • 1916
SHOP GIRL'S BIG DAY, THE • 1913 • *Farley Dot* • USA
SHOP-GIRLS OF PARIS (USA) see **AU BONHEUR DES DAMES** • 1943
SHOP LIFTER, THE • 1915 • *Thanhouser* • USA
SHOP, LOOK AND LISTEN • 1940 • Freleng Friz • ANS • USA
SHOP NUN, THE • 1915 • Levering Joseph • USA
SHOP ON MAIN STREET see **OBCHOD NA KORSE** • 1965
SHOP ON THE HIGH STREET, THE see **OBCHOD NA KORSE** • 1965
SHOP SOILED see **CROWDED DAY, THE** • 1954
SHOP SPOILED (USA) see **CROWDED DAY, THE** • 1954
SHOP STEWARD, A • 1978 • Blagg Linda • DOC • ASL
SHOP STEWARD, THE see **PAALUOTTAMUSMIES** • 1971
SHOP WINDOWS see **ZA VITRINOI UNIVERMAGA** • 1955
SHOPGIRLS: OR, THE GREAT QUESTION • 1914 • Trimble Larry • UKN
SHOPLIFTER see **I WAS A SHOPLIFTER** • 1950
SHOPLIFTER, THE • 1905 • Mottershaw Frank • UKN
SHOPPING MALL • 1985 • Barnard Michael • USA
SHOPPING WITH WIFIE • 1932 • Stafford Babe • SHT • USA
SHOPPINGTOWN • 1987 • Caesar David • ASL
SHOPSOILED GIRL, THE • 1915 • Bantock Leedham • UKN
SHOPWORN • 1932 • Grinde Nick • USA
SHOPWORN ANGEL, THE • 1928 • Wallace Richard • USA
SHOPWORN ANGEL, THE • 1938 • Potter H. C. • USA
SHORE ACRES • 1914 • Pratt Jack • USA
SHORE ACRES • 1920 • Ingram Rex • USA
SHORE LEAVE • 1925 • Robertson John S. • USA
SHORES AND PEOPLE • Grigorov Roumen • DOC • BUL
SHORES OF AMERICA, THE see **AMERIIKAN RAITTI** • 1989
SHORES OF HOPE, THE see **BYEREG NADYEZHDY** • 1967
SHORES OF PHOS: A FABLE, THE • 1972 • Brakhage Stan • USA
SHORI NO HI MADE • 1945 • Naruse Mikio • JPN • VICTORY IN THE SUN ○ UNTIL VICTORY DAY
SHORI TO HAIBOKU • 1960 • Inoue Umeji • JPN • VICTORY OR DEFEAT
SHORISHA • 1957 • Inoue Umeji • JPN • CHAMPION
SHORS see **SHCHORS** • 1939
SHORT AND SUITE • 1959 • McLaren Norman • ANS • CND
SHORT AND TALL STORY see **SHORT TALL STORY** • 1970
SHORT AND VERY SHORT FILMS • 1976 • Emshwiller Ed • CMP • USA
SHORT CHANGE • 1923 • Mayo Archie • SHT • USA
SHORT CHANGED • 1986 • Ogilvie George • ASL
SHORT CIRCUIT • 1964 • Wise David • ANS • USA
SHORT CIRCUIT • 1986 • Badham John • USA
SHORT CIRCUIT 2 • 1988 • Johnson Kenneth • USA
SHORT CUT TO HELL • 1957 • Cagney James • USA
SHORT CUT (USA) see **POSTRIZINY** • 1980
SHORT DAY'S WORK, A see **KROTKI DZIEN PRACI** • 1982
SHORT ENCOUNTERS see **KOROTKIYE VSTRYECHI** • 1968
SHORT ENCOUNTERS, LONG FAREWELLS see **KOROTKIYE VSTRYECHI** • 1968
SHORT EYES • 1977 • Young Robert Malcolm • USA • SLAMMER
SHORT FILM ABOUT KILLING, A (UKN) see **KROTKI FILM O ZABIJANIU** • 1988
SHORT FILM ABOUT LOVE, A (UKN) see **KROTKI FILM O MILOSCI** • 1988
SHORT FILMS 75 • 1975 • Brakhage Stan • USA
SHORT FILMS 76 • 1976 • Brakhage Stan • USA
SHORT FUSE see **GOOD TO GO** • 1986
SHORT GRASS • 1950 • Selander Lesley • USA
SHORT HEAD see **COURTE TETE** • 1956
SHORT HISTORY, A (USA) see **SCURTA ISTORIE** • 1956
SHORT HISTORY OF FRANCE see **PETIT MANUEL D'HISTOIRE DE FRANCE** • 1979
SHORT IN THE SADDLE • 1963 • Smith Paul J. • ANS • USA
SHORT IS THE SUMMER (USA) see **KORT AR SOMMAREN** • 1962
SHORT KILTS • 1924 • Jeske George • SHT • USA
SHORT LIFE AND A MERRY ONE, A • 1913 • France Charles H. • USA
SHORT MEETINGS see **KOROTKIYE VSTRYECHI** • 1968

SHORT MEETINGS AND LONG FAREWELLS see **KOROTKIYE VSTRYECHI** • 1968
SHORT MEMORY see **MEMOIRE COURTE, LA** • 1979
SHORT ORDERS • 1923 • Roach Hal • SHT • USA
SHORT SEVEN • 1969 • Severijn Jonne • SHT • NTH
SHORT SHAVE • 1965 • Snow Michael • USA
SHORT SIGHTED CRIME, A • 1916 • *Perez Tweedledum* • USA
SHORT-SIGHTED ERRAND BOY, THE • 1910 • Fitzhamon Lewin? • UKN
SHORT-SIGHTED JANE • 1907 • Collins Alf? • UKN
SHORT-SIGHTED SAMMY • 1905 • Martin J. H.? • UKN
SHORT SKIRTS • 1921 • Harris Harry B. • USA
SHORT SKIRTS AND DEEP WATER • 1917 • Curtis Allen • SHT • USA
SHORT SKIRTS (UKN) see **BARE KNEES** • 1928
SHORT SNORTS ON SPORTS • 1948 • Lovy Alex • ANS • USA
SHORT-STOP'S DOUBLE, THE • 1913 • France Charles H. • USA
SHORT STORIES ABOUT CHILDREN, WHICH.. • 1961 • Khamraev Ali, Makhmudov M. • USS
SHORT TALL STORY • 1970 • Halas John • ANS • UKN • SHORT AND TALL STORY
SHORT TERM SHERIFF • 1964 • Tendlar Dave • ANS • USA
SHORT TRAIN, THE • 1970 • Dalen Zale R. • CND
SHORT VISION, A • 1956 • Foldes Joan, Foldes Peter • ANS • UKN
SHORT WALK TO DAYLIGHT • 1972 • Shear Barry • TVM • USA
SHORT WEIGHT • 1922 • Goulding Alf • USA
SHORT WORK see **KURZER PROZESS** • 1967
SHORTAGE • 1990 • Cohen Chaim • BUL
SHORTENIN' BREAD • 1950 • Sparber I. • ANS • USA
SHORTEST DAY, THE (USA) see **GIORNO PIU CORTO, IL** • 1963
SHORTY • 1914 • Miller Ashley • USA
SHORTY AMONG THE CANNIBALS • 1915 • *Hamilton Jack "shorty"* • USA
SHORTY AND SHERLOCK HOLMES • 1914 • *Hamilton Shorty* • USA
SHORTY AND THE ARIDVILLE TERROR • 1914 • *Broncho* • USA
SHORTY AND THE FORTUNE TELLER • 1914 • Ince Thomas H. • USA
SHORTY AND THE YELLOW RING • 1917 • Gray Bob • SHT • USA
SHORTY AT THE SHORE • 1910 • *Lubin* • USA
SHORTY BAGS THE BULLION THIEVES • 1917 • Gray Bob • SHT • USA
SHORTY ESCAPES MATRIMONY • 1914 • Ford Francis • USA
SHORTY FALLS INTO A TITLE • 1914 • *Broncho* • USA
SHORTY GETS IN TROUBLE • 1914 • Ford Francis • USA
SHORTY GOES TO COLLEGE • 1917 • Gray Bob • SHT • USA
SHORTY HOOKS A LOAN SHARK • 1917 • Gray Bob • SHT • USA
SHORTY IN THE TIGER'S DEN • 1917 • Gray Bob • SHT • USA
SHORTY INHERITS A HAREM • 1915 • *Hamilton Shorty* • USA
SHORTY JOINS THE SECRET SERVICE • 1917 • Gray Bob • SHT • USA
SHORTY LANDS A MASTER CROOK • 1917 • Gray Bob • SHT • USA
SHORTY LAYS A JUNGLE GHOST • 1917 • Gray Bob • SHT • USA
SHORTY MAKES A BET • 1914 • *Ab* • USA
SHORTY PROMOTES HIS LOVE AFFAIR • 1917 • Gray Bob • SHT • USA
SHORTY REDUCES THE HIGH COST OF LIVING • 1917 • Gray Bob • SHT • USA
SHORTY ROGERS AND HIS GIANTS • 1962 • Binder Steve • *Meadowlane Production* • SHT • USA
SHORTY ROGERS AND HIS GIANTS • 1962 • Markas Gary • *Frankly Jazz* • SHT • USA
SHORTY SOLVES A WIRELESS MYSTERY • 1917 • Gray Bob • SHT • USA
SHORTY TRAILS THE MOONSHINERS • 1917 • Gray Bob • SHT • USA
SHORTY TRAPS A LOTTERY KING • 1917 • Gray Bob • SHT • USA
SHORTY TURNS ACTOR • 1915 • *Hamilton Shorty* • USA
SHORTY TURNS JUDGE • 1914 • Ford Francis • USA
SHORTY TURNS WILD MAN • 1917 • Gray Bob • SHT • USA
SHORTY UNEARTHS A TARTAR • 1917 • Gray Bob • SHT • USA
SHORTY'S ADVENTURES IN THE CITY • 1915 • *Hamilton Shorty* • USA
SHORTY'S LONG SUIT • 1920 • Cooper G., Hayes Ward • SHT • USA
SHORTY'S RANCH • 1915 • *Broncho* • USA
SHORTY'S SACRIFICE • 1914 • Ford Francis • USA
SHORTY'S SECRET • 1915 • *Broncho* • USA
SHORTY'S STRATEGY • 1914 • Ford Francis • USA
SHORTY'S TRIP TO MEXICO • 1914 • Ford Francis • USA
SHORTY'S TROUBLED SLEEP • 1915 • *Hamilton Jack "shorty"* • USA
SHOSENA • 1972 • Demicheli Tulio • SPN
SHOSETSU YOSHIDA GAKKO • 1983 • Moritani Shiro • JPN • NOVEL, POLITICIAN'S SCHOOL ○ NOVEL: YOSHIDA SCHOOL
SHOT, THE • 1915 • Le Viness Carl M. • USA
SHOT, THE see **SKOTTET** • 1914
SHOT, THE see **WYSTRZAL** • 1965
SHOT, THE see **VYSTREL** • 1967
SHOT, THE see **SKOTTET** • 1969
SHOT, THE see **PUCANJ** • 1972
SHOT, THE see **BIG RIP-OFF, THE** • 1975
SHOT, THE see **PUCANJ** • 1978
SHOT AND BOTHERED • 1966 • Larriva Rudy • ANS • USA
SHOT AT SUNRISE • 1915 • *Rogers Irene* • USA
SHOT GUN CUPID, A • 1913 • *Princess* • USA
SHOT IN A BAR-ROOM see **ITCHING FOR REVENGE** • 1915
SHOT IN THE AIR, A see **TIRO AL AIRE** • 1980
SHOT IN THE DARK, A • 1912 • *Bison* • USA
SHOT IN THE DARK, A • 1915 • Wilson Ben • USA
SHOT IN THE DARK, A • 1933 • Pearson George • UKN
SHOT IN THE DARK, A • 1935 • Lamont Charles • USA
SHOT IN THE DARK, A • 1941 • McGann William • USA
SHOT IN THE DARK, A • 1960 • Greene David • MTV • CND
SHOT IN THE DARK, A • 1964 • Edwards Blake • UKN, USA
SHOT IN THE DUMBWAITER • 1918 • Lyons Eddie, Moran Lee • SHT • USA
SHOT IN THE EXCITEMENT • 1914 • Henderson Dell • USA
SHOT IN THE FACTORY, THE see **LAUKAUS TEEHTAALLA** • 1972
SHOT IN THE FRACAS • 1914 • *Warner'S Features* • USA
SHOT IN THE FRACAS • 1915 • *Eclectic* • USA
SHOT IN THE FRACAS • 1916 • Miller Rube • SHT • USA
SHOT IN THE FRONTIER • 1954 • White Jules • SHT • USA
SHOT IN THE GET-AWAY • 1920 • Watson William • SHT • USA
SHOT IN THE HEAD see **FEJLOVES** • 1968
SHOT IN THE KITCHEN • 1920 • *Romayne Super-Film* • USA
SHOT IN THE MOUNTAINS KARASH-KARASH, A see **VISTRIL V GORACH** • 1970
SHOT IN THE NIGHT, A • 1910 • *Capitol* • USA
SHOT IN THE NIGHT, A • 1914 • *Purdee Stephen* • USA
SHOT IN THE NIGHT, A • 1923 • *Holeby Walter* • USA
SHOT IN THE WEST • 1917 • Chaudet Louis W. • SHT • USA
SHOT IN TIME, A • 1910 • *Bison* • USA
SHOT ON THE KARASH PASS, A see **VISTRIL V GORACH** • 1970
SHOT THAT FAILED, THE • 1912 • *Mersereau Violet* • USA
SHOTDOWN • 1989 • Worsdale Andrew • SAF
SHOTGUN • 1955 • Selander Lesley • USA
SHOTGUN JONES • 1914 • Campbell Colin • USA
SHOTGUN MAN AND THE STAGE DRIVER, THE • 1913 • Duncan William • USA
SHOTGUN NO OTOKO • 1961 • Suzuki Kiyonori • JPN
SHOTGUN PASS • 1931 • McGowan J. P. • USA
SHOTGUN RANCHMAN, THE • 1912 • *Mackley Arthur* • USA
SHOTGUN ROMANCE, A • 1915 • *Ovey George* • USA
SHOTGUN WEDDING, A • 1920 • Fishback Fred C. • SHT • USA
SHOTGUN WEDDING, THE • 1963 • Petroff Boris L. • USA
SHOTGUNS THAT KICK • 1914 • Arbuckle Roscoe, Dillon Eddie • USA
SHOTS IN THE SKY see **RAFAL U NEBO** • 1958
SHOTS ON THE STAVE see **IMPUSCATURI PE PORTATIV** • 1967
SHOTS UNDER THE GALLOWS see **SCHUSSE UNTERM GALGEN** • 1968
SHOULD A BABY DIE? • 1916 • *Donaldson Arthur* • USA
SHOULD A DOCTOR TELL? • 1923 • Butler Alexander • UKN
SHOULD A DOCTOR TELL? • 1923 • Ramster P. J. • ASL
SHOULD A DOCTOR TELL? • 1930 • Haynes Manning • UKN
SHOULD A GIRL MARRY? • 1928 • Pembroke Scott • USA
SHOULD A GIRL MARRY? • 1939 • Hillyer Lambert • USA • GIRL FROM NOWHERE, THE
SHOULD A GIRL PROPOSE? • 1926 • Ramster P. J. • ASL
SHOULD A HUSBAND FORGIVE? • 1919 • Walsh Raoul • USA
SHOULD A MOTHER TELL? • 1915 • Edwards J. Gordon • USA
SHOULD A MOTHER TELL • 1925 • Butler Alexander • UKN
SHOULD A WIFE FORGIVE? • 1915 • *Lorraine Lillian* • USA
SHOULD A WIFE WORK? • 1922 • Plympton Horace G. • USA
SHOULD A WOMAN DIVORCE? • 1914 • Abramson Ivan • USA
SHOULD A WOMAN TELL? • 1920 • Ince John • USA
SHOULD A WOMAN TELL? (UKN) see **WANDERING FIRES** • 1925
SHOULD CROONERS MARRY? • 1933 • Stevens George • SHT • USA
SHOULD DR. KILDARE TELL? see **DR. KILDARE'S CRISIS** • 1940
SHOULD DUMMIES WED? • 1920 • Del Ruth Roy • SHT • USA
SHOULD GIRLS KISS SOLDIERS? • 1918 • Ramster P. J. • SHT • ASL
SHOULD HUSBANDS BE WATCHED • 1925 • McCarey Leo • SHT • USA
SHOULD HUSBANDS COME FIRST? • 1927 • Roach Hal • SHT • USA
SHOULD HUSBANDS MARRY? • *Herbert Hugh* • SHT • USA
SHOULD HUSBANDS WORK? • 1939 • Meins Gus • USA
SHOULD LADIES BEHAVE? • 1933 • Beaumont Harry • USA • VINEGAR TREE, THE
SHOULD LANDLORDS LIVE? • 1924 • Roach Hal • SHT • USA
SHOULD MARRIED MEN GO HOME? • 1928 • Parrott James • SHT • USA
SHOULD MEN WALK HOME? • 1926 • McCarey Leo • SHT • USA
SHOULD PARENTS TELL? see **STORY OF BOB AND SALLY, THE** • 1948
SHOULD SAILORS MARRY? • 1925 • Roach Hal • SHT • USA
SHOULD SHE HAVE TOLD? • 1916 • McDermott John • SHT • USA
SHOULD SHE OBEY? • 1917 • Siegmann George • USA
SHOULD SLEEPWALKERS MARRY? • 1927 • *Sennett Mack (P)* • SHT • USA
SHOULD TAILORS TRIFLE? • 1920 • Buckingham Thomas • SHT • USA
SHOULD TALL MEN MARRY? • 1926 • Bruckman Clyde • SHT • USA
SHOULD WAITERS MARRY? • 1920 • Buckingham Thomas • SHT • USA
SHOULD WE EAT PIE? • 1915 • Benton Curtis • USA
SHOULD WIVES WORK? • 1937 • Goodwins Leslie • SHT • USA
SHOULD WOMEN DRIVE? • 1928 • Yates Hal • SHT • USA
SHOULD WOMEN TELL • 1919 • Gerrard Douglas • USA
SHOULDER • 1964 • Warhol Andy • SHT • USA
SHOULDER ARMS • 1918 • Chaplin Charles • SHT • USA
SHOUT! • 1985 • Robinson Ted • MTV • ASL • SHOUT: THE STORY OF JOHNNY O'KEEFE
SHOUT, A see **SURAKH** • 1973
SHOUT, THE • 1978 • Skolimowski Jerzy • UKN
SHOUT, THE see **GRITO, EL** • 1968
SHOUT AT THE DEVIL • 1976 • Hunt Peter • UKN
SHOUT FROM THE ABYSS, A see **CRI DANS L'ABIME, UN** • 1922
SHOUT IT FROM THE HOUSE TOPS (USA) see **CRIEZ-LE SUR LES TOITS** • 1932
SHOUT OF DOLORES, THE see **GRITO DE DOLORES, EL** • 1908
SHOUT OUT AT THE NINTH • 1917 • Griffith Edward H. • SHT • USA
SHOUT: THE STORY OF JOHNNY O'KEEFE see **SHOUT!** • 1985
SHOVE OFF • 1931 • Cline Eddie • SHT • USA
SHOVE THY NEIGHBOR • 1957 • Rasinski Connie • ANS • USA
SHOVEL UP A BIT MORE COAL see **STOKER, THE** • 1935
SHOW see **LAONIANG GOUSAO** • 1985
SHOW 5000 • 1969 • Al-Ktari Naceur • SHT • ITL
SHOW, THE • 1922 • Fleischer Dave • ANS • USA
SHOW, THE • 1922 • Taurog Norman, Semon Larry • SHT • USA
SHOW, THE • 1926 • Browning Tod • USA
SHOW A LEG see **OLD SOLDIERS NEVER DIE** • 1931
SHOW BARDOT • 1968 • Matalon Eddy, Reichenbach Francois • MTV • FRN • SPECIAL BARDOT
SHOW BIZ BEAGLE • 1972 • Smith Paul J. • ANS • USA
SHOW BIZ BUGS • 1957 • Freleng Friz • ANS • USA
SHOW BOAT • 1929 • Pollard Harry • USA
SHOW BOAT • 1936 • Whale James • USA
SHOW-BOOTH, A • Garanina Idea • ANM • USS
SHOW-BUS • 1981 • Schatzberg Jerry • USA
SHOW BUSINESS • 1932 • White Jules • SHT • USA
SHOW BUSINESS • 1944 • Marin Edwin L. • USA
SHOW BUSINESS see **FOOTLIGHT FEVER** • 1941
SHOW BUSTERS, THE • 1914 • Middleton Mr. • USA
SHOW-DOWN, THE • 1917 • Reynolds Lynn • USA
SHOW FLAT • 1936 • Mainwaring Bernerd • UKN
SHOW FOLKS • 1928 • Stein Paul L. • USA
SHOW FOR SALE • 1937 • Schwarzwald Milton • SHT • USA
SHOW GIRL • 1928 • Santell Alfred • USA
SHOW GIRL, THE • 1911 • *Vitagraph* • USA
SHOW GIRL, THE • 1927 • Hunt Charles J. • USA
SHOW GIRL IN HOLLYWOOD • 1930 • LeRoy Mervyn • USA
SHOW GIRL'S GLOVE, THE • 1914 • *Joyce Alice* • USA
SHOW-GIRL'S STRATAGEM, THE • 1911 • Salter Harry • USA
SHOW GOES ON, THE • 1937 • Dean Basil • UKN
SHOW GOES ON, THE (USA) see **THREE MAXIMS, THE** • 1936
SHOW IS ON, THE see **CIRKUS BUDE** • 1954
SHOW LEADER • 1966 • Baillie Bruce • USA
SHOW LIFE see **SONG** • 1928
SHOW ME A STRONG TOWN AND I'LL SHOW YOU A STRONG BANK • 1965 • De Palma Brian • SHT • USA
SHOW ME THE WAY TO GO HOME • 1932 • Fleischer Dave • ANS • USA
SHOW MUST GO ON, THE see **THREE MAXIMS, THE** • 1936
SHOW OF FORCE • 1989 • Barreto Bruno • BRZ
SHOW OF STARS, THE • 1929 • Adolfi John G. • USA
SHOW OF THE YEAR • 1966 • USA
SHOW OFF, THE • 1926 • St. Clair Malcolm • USA • SHOW-OFF, THE
SHOW-OFF, THE • 1934 • Reisner Charles F. • USA
SHOW-OFF, THE • 1946 • Beaumont Harry • USA
SHOW-OFF, THE see **SHOW OFF, THE** • 1926
SHOW-OFF, THE see **MEN ARE LIKE THAT** • 1930
SHOW-OFF, THE see **BHALE MONAGADU** • 1968
SHOW PEOPLE • 1928 • Vidor King • USA • BREAKING INTO THE MOVIES
SHOW THEM NO MERCY • 1935 • Marshall George • USA • TAINTED MONEY (UKN) ○ SNATCHED
SHOW TIME • 1932 • *Mintz Charles (P)* • ANS • USA
SHOW TIME • 1948 • Blair George • USA
SHOW WORLD see **BROADWAY TO HOLLYWOOD** • 1933
SHOWA GENROKU HARENCHI BUSHI • 1968 • Ichimura Yasukazu, Hasebe Toshiaki • JPN • NEVER SAY DIE
SHOWA GENROKU TOKYO 196X-NEN • 1968 • Onchi Hideo • JPN • TOKYO 196X
SHOWA KARESUSUKI • 1974 • Nomura Yoshitaro • JPN • ELEGY FOR OUR TIME
SHOWA NO INOCHI • 1968 • Masuda Toshio • JPN • STORMY ERA (USA) ○ MAN OF A STORMY ERA
SHOWA SHINSENGUMI • 1932 • Tasaka Tomotaka, Murata Minoru • JPN
SHOWA ZANKYODEN: CHIZOME NO KARAJISHI • 1967 • Makino Masahiro • JPN • DRAGON TATTOO: FULL OF BLOOD
SHOWBOAT • 1951 • Sidney George • USA
SHOWBOAT NINETEEN EIGHTY EIGHT see **1988: THE REMAKE** • 1978
SHOWCASE • 1972 • Miller Arnold Louis • UKN
SHOWDOWN • 1942 • Sparber I. • ANS • USA
SHOWDOWN • 1963 • Springsteen R. G. • USA • IRON COLLAR, THE
SHOWDOWN • 1973 • Seaton George • USA
SHOWDOWN see **PACHA, LE** • 1968
SHOWDOWN, THE • 1915 • *Reliance* • USA
SHOWDOWN, THE • 1928 • Schertzinger Victor • USA
SHOWDOWN, THE • 1940 • Bretherton Howard • USA
SHOWDOWN, THE • 1950 • McGowan Dorrell, McGowan Stuart E. • USA
SHOWDOWN, THE (UKN) see **WEST OF ABILENE** • 1940
SHOWDOWN AT ABILENE • 1956 • Haas Charles • USA
SHOWDOWN AT BEAVER FALLS see **SHOOT-OUT AT BEAVER FALLS** • 1970
SHOWDOWN AT BOOT HILL • 1958 • Fowler Gene Jr. • USA
SHOWDOWN AT DAWN see **AKATSUKI NO CHIHEISEN** • 1959
SHOWDOWN AT ULCER GULCH • 1958 • USA
SHOWDOWN FOR ZATOICHI (USA) see **ZATO ICHI JIGOKUTABI** • 1967
SHOWDOWN IN THE STORM see **ARASHI NO NAKA O TSUPPASHIRE** • 1958
SHOWER OF GOLD see **GULDREGN** • 1988
SHOWER OF KNIVES see **COLTELLI DEL VENDICATORE, I** • 1967
SHOWER OF SLIPPERS, A • 1913 • Seay Charles M. • USA
SHOWER OF TENDER SKIN, A see **YAWAHADA SHIGURE** • 1967
SHOWGIRLS • 1986 • McCallum Robert • USA
SHOWGIRL'S LUCK • 1931 • Dawn Norman • ASL
SHOWING OFF • 1931 • *Mintz Charles (P)* • ANS • USA

SHOWING SOME SPEED • 1916 • Myll Louis • SHT • USA
SHOWING UNCLE • 1911 • *Essanay* • USA
SHOWING UP OF LARRY THE LAMB, THE • 1962 • *Halas John (P)* • ANS • UKN
SHOWMAN • 1962 • Maysles Albert, Maysles David • DOC • USA
SHOWMAN, THE • 1930 • ANS • USA
SHOWMAN'S DREAM, THE • 1914 • Lyndhurst F. L. • UKN
SHOWMAN'S TREASURE, THE • 1907 • Cooper Arthur? • UKN
SHOW'S THE THING, THE • 1936 • Stross Raymond • UKN
SHOWTIME • 1938 • !werks Ub • ANS • USA • SNOWTIME
SHOWTIME • 1959 • Brealey Gil • DOC • ASL
SHOWTIME (USA) see **GAIETY GEORGE** • 1945
SHOYA GA NIKUI • 1968 • Chiba Takashi • JPN • SPITEFUL BRIDAL NIGHT, A
SHOZO • 1948 • Kinoshita Keisuke • JPN • PORTRAIT, A
SHOZO, A CAT AND TWO WOMEN see **NEKO TO SHOZO TO FUTARI NO ONNA** • 1956
SHQYPNIA –LAND OF THE MOUNTAIN EAGLE • 1935 • Barbrook Leslie • UKN
SHRAGA KATAN • 1979 • Revach Ze'Ev • ISR • LITTLE MAN
SHRAVAN KUMAR • 1948 • Daryani Ram • IND
SHREE DNYANESHWAR • 1921 • *National* • IND
SHREE GANESH • 1963 • *Wadia* • IND
SHREE GANESH JANMA • 1951 • Desai Jayant • IND
SHREE GANESH VIVAH • 1955 • *Sapru* • IND
SHREE GOURANG LEELA • 1934 • *Radha Film* • IND
SHREE JAGANNATH • 1950 • Mitra C. R. • IND
SHREE KRISHNA BHAGWAN • 1935 • Ahmed W. Z. • IND • LIFE OF SHREE KRISHNA BHAGWAN
SHREE KRISHNA BHAKTA PIPAJI • 1922 • *National* • IND
SHREE KRISHNA DARSHAN • 1950 • Sheik A. R. • IND
SHREE KRISHNA JANMA see **SHRI KRISHNA JANMA** • 1918
SHREE KRISHNARJUN YUDDHA • 1945 • Sinha Mohan • IND
SHREE KRISHNAVTAR • 1922 • IND • INCARNATION OF KRISHNA
SHREE RAM AVTAR • 1950 • Garchar W. • IND
SHREE VISHNU BHAGWAN • 1951 • Nene Raja • IND
SHREW, THE see **HIRCIN KADIN** • 1967
SHRI 420 • 1955 • Kapoor Raj • IND • MISTER 420
SHRI GANESH • 1962 • Dharwadkar S. S. • IND
SHRI KRISHNA BHAGWAN • 1944 • *Shalimar Pics* • IND
SHRI KRISHNA JANMA • 1918 • Phalke Dada • IND • BIRTH OF LORD KRISHNA, THE ○ KRISHNA JANMA ○ SHREE KRISHNA JANMA
SHRI KRISHNA RUKMINI • 1949 • Desai Dhirubhai • IND
SHRI KRISHNA SHISHTAI • 1928 • *Hindustan* • IND
SHRIEK, THE • 1933 • Lantz Walter, Nolan William • ANS • USA
SHRIEK IN THE NIGHT, A • 1915 • Jaccard Jacques • SHT • USA
SHRIEK IN THE NIGHT, A • 1933 • Ray Albert • USA
SHRIEK OF ARABY, THE • 1923 • Jones F. Richard • USA
SHRIEK OF THE MUTILATED • 1976 • Findlay Michael • USA
SHRIKE, THE • 1955 • Ferrer Jose • USA
SHRIKES, THE see **MOZU** • 1961
SHRIMAN SATYAVADI • 1960 • *Kapoor Raj* • IND
SHRIMANJI • 1968 • Dayal Ram • IND • SIGNOR, THE
SHRIMANT MEHUNA PAHIJE • 1967 • Shamshir A. • IND
SHRIMP, THE • 1930 • Rogers Charles • SHT • USA
SHRIMP FISHERMAN • 1953 • Hammid Alexander • DOC • USA
SHRIMPS FOR A DAY • 1934 • Meins Gus • SHT • USA
SHRINE OF HAPPINESS, THE • 1916 • Bracken Bertram • USA
SHRINE OF THE SEVEN LAMPS, THE • 1923 • Coleby A. E. • UKN
SHRINE OF VICTORY, THE see **GREEK TESTAMENT** • 1942
SHRINER'S DAUGHTER, THE • 1913 • *Greenwood Winnifred* • USA
SHRINKING RAWHIDE, THE • 1912 • *Bosworth Hobart* • USA
SHROUD OF SNOW, THE see **YUKI NO MOSHO** • 1967
SHROVE TUESDAY FOR A ROBBER see **ONDRASZKOWE OSTATKI** • 1968
SHRUTI AND THE GRACES IN INDIAN MUSIC, THE • 1972 • Benegal Shyam • DCS • IND
SHTE DOIDAT NOVI DNI • 1945 • Marinovich Anton • BUL • NEW DAYS WILL COME
SHTEI ETZBAOTH ME'TZIDON • 1985 • Cohen Eli • ISR • RICOCHETS
SHTO SLUCHILOS S ANDRESOM LAPETEUSOM? • 1967 • Kromanov Grigori • USS • WHAT'S THE MATTER WITH ANDRES LAPETEUS? ○ WHAT HAPPENED WITH ANDRES LAPETEUS
SHTORM • 1957 • Dubson M. • USS • STORM
SHU JIAN EN CHOU LU • 1988 • Hsu An-Hua • HKG, CHN • ROMANCE OF BOOK & SWORD, THE ○ BOOK AND THE SWORD, THE
SHU NO KAFUN • 1960 • Ohba Hideo • JPN • SCARLET FLOWER
SHU SHAN • 1983 • Hsu K'O • HKG • ZU WARRIORS FROM THE MAGIC MOUNTAIN
SHU TO MIDORI • 1956 • Nakamura Noboru • JPN • MIDNIGHT VISITOR ○ RED AND GREEN
SHUANG CHO • 1990 • Huang Yu-Shan • TWN
SHUBUN see **SKYANDURU** • 1950
SHUCHU NIKKI • 1924 • Ito Daisuke • JPN • DIARY OF A DRUNKARD, THE
SHUDDERS • 1984 • Rosma Juha • SHT • FNL
SHUDDERS see **KISS OF THE TARANTULA, THE** • 1972
SHUEN • 1964 • Kurahara Koreyoshi • JPN • FLAME OF DEVOTION, THE
SHUFFLE • 1981 • Ishii Sogo • JPN
SHUFFLE OFF TO BUFFALO • 1933 • Freleng Friz • ANS • USA
SHUFFLE RHYTHM • 1942 • Le Borg Reginald • SHT • USA
SHUFFLE THE QUEENS • 1920 • Beaudine William • SHT • USA
SHUHADDAA EL GHARAM • 1944 • Salim Kamel • EGY • ROMEO AND JULIET
SHUI-CHING JEN • 1981 • Hua Shan • HKG • CRYSTALMAN
SHUI LIAN TING ZHENG • 1983 • Li Han-Hsiang • HKG, CHN • BEHIND THE SCREEN
SHUJINSAN • 1956 • Inagaki Hiroshi • JPN • REBELS ON THE HIGH SEA
SHUK RAMBA • 1953 • Desai Dhirubhai • IND
SHUKAIDO • 1949 • Nakamura Noboru • JPN • BEGONIA
SHUKIN RYOKO • 1957 • Nakamura Noboru • JPN • PAYOFF WITH LOVE
SHUKUJI • 1985 • Kuriyama Tomio • JPN • CONGRATULATORY SPEECH
SHUKUJO TO HIJE • 1931 • Ozu Yasujiro • JPN • LADY AND HER FAVOURITES, THE ○ LADY AND THE BEARD, THE
SHUKUJO WA NANI O WASURETAKA • 1937 • Ozu Yasujiro • JPN • WHAT DID THE LADY FORGET?
SHUKUZU • 1953 • Shindo Kaneto • JPN • GEISHA GIRL GINKO, A ○ GINKO THE GEISHA ○ EPITOME
SHULAMITE, THE • 1915 • Tucker George Loane • UKN
SHULAMITE, THE see **FOLLY OF DESIRE, THE** • 1916
SHULAMITE, THE (UKN) see **UNDER THE LASH** • 1921
SHUMPUDEN DEN see **SHUNPU-DEN** • 1965
SHUMUSUN SAGHIRA • 1968 • Hamada Khalid • SHT • SYR • PETITS SOLEILS, LES
SHUNDEINI • 1958 • Abe Yutaka • JPN • STORY OF A NUN
SHUNKIN MONOGATARI • 1954 • Ito Daisuke • JPN • STORY OF SHUNKIN
SHUNKIN-SHO • 1976 • Nishikawa Katsumi • JPN • OTOKO AND SASUKE
SHUNKO • 1960 • Murua Lautaro • ARG
SHUNPU-DEN • 1965 • Suzuki Seijun • JPN • SHUMPUDEN DEN ○ JOY GIRLS
SHUNSETSU • 1950 • Yoshimura Kozaburo • JPN • SPRING SNOW
SHURA • 1970 • Matsumoto Toshio • JPN • DEMONS (USA) ○ PANDEMONIUM
SHURAJO HIBUN • 1952 • Kinugasa Teinosuke • JPN
SHUSHIN IMADA KIEZU • 1949 • Shibuya Minoru • JPN • DEVOTION NOW VANISHED
SHUSSE KOMORIUTA • 1967 • Takamori Ryuichi • JPN • LULLABY FOR MY SON
SHUSSE TAIKOKI • 1938 • Inagaki Hiroshi • JPN • GREAT POWER RISING IN THE WORLD, A ○ TOYOTOMI'S RECORD OF PROMOTION
SHUT MY BIG MOUTH • 1942 • Barton Charles T. • USA
SHUT UP AND DEAL • 1959 • Donne John • USA
SHUT UP.. I'M CRYING • 1970 • Siegler R. • SHT • USA
SHUTDOWN • 1979 • Sky Laura • DOC • CND
SHUTEYE POPEYE • 1952 • Sparber I. • ANS • USA
SHUTSUGOKU YONJUHACHI JIKAN • 1969 • Mori Issei • JPN • 48-HOUR PRISON BREAK
SHUTTER BUG • 1963 • Smith Paul J. • ANS • USA
SHUTTER BUGGED CAT • 1967 • Ray Tom • ANS • USA
SHUTTERED ROOM, THE • 1967 • Greene David • UKN
SHUTTERED WINDOWS see **VOLETS CLOS, LES** • 1972
SHUTTLE, THE • 1918 • Sturgeon Rollin S. • USA
SHUTTLE COMMAND • 1985 • Battle Murray • SHT • CND
SHUTTLE OF FATE, THE • 1912 • *Santschi Tom* • USA
SHUTTLE OF LIFE, THE • 1920 • Williams D. J. • UKN
SHUU • 1956 • Naruse Mikio • JPN • SUDDEN RAIN
SHUZENJI MONOGATARI • 1955 • Nakamura Noboru • JPN • MASK OF DESTINY, THE (USA) ○ MASK AND DESTINY, THE
SHVEDSKI KRALE • 1968 • Kirkov Lyudmil • BUL • STEEL KINGS
SHWE EIN THE • 1932 • *British Burma Film Co* • BRM
SHY ANTON see **BLYGE ANTON** • 1940
SHY DECEIVER, THE see **FUKEBA TOBUYONA OTOKODAGA** • 1968
SHY PEOPLE • 1981 • Konchalovsky Andrei • USA
SHY TALES see **PLACHE PRIBEHY** • 1982
SHY THIRTY CENTS • 1916 • Miller Rube • USA
SHYLOCK • 1910 • Desfontaines Henri • FRN
SHYLOCK OF WALL STREET see **NONE SO BLIND** • 1923
SHYLOCK VON KRAKAU, DER • 1913 • Wilhelm Carl • FRG
SHYNESS • 1953 • Jackson Stanley R. • DOC • CND
SHYNESS OF SHORTY, THE • 1910 • *Edison* • USA
SI ADELITA SE FUERA CON OTRO • 1948 • Urueta Chano • MXC
SI AND SUE, ACROBATS • 1915 • Hotaling Arthur D. • USA
SI BUTA • 1974 • MLY • BLIND WARRIOR, THE
SI CA VOUS CHANTE • 1951 • Loew Jacques • FRN
SI C'ETAIT A REFAIRE • 1975 • Lelouch Claude • FRN • IF I HAD TO DO IT ALL OVER AGAIN ○ SECOND CHANCE (UKN)
SI DOEL ANAK MODERN • 1976 • Jaya Syuman • INN
SI DON JUAN ETAIT UNE FEMME see **DON JUAN 1973, OU SI DON JUAN ETAIT UNE FEMME** • 1973
SI DOUCES, SI PERVERSES (FRN) see **COSI DOLCE.. COSI PERVERSA** • 1969
SI EL EMPERADOR LA SUPIERA see **OLIMPIA** • 1930
SI EL EMPERADOR LO SUPIERA • 1930 • Franklin Chester M. • USA
SI ELLE DIT OUI.. JE NE DIS PAS NON! • 1982 • Vital Claude • FRN
SI ESTAS MUERTO POR QUE BAILAS • 1970 • Herrero Pedro Mario • SPN
SI FA COSI • 1934 • Giovannetti Adriano • ITL
SI FULANO FUESE MENGANO • 1971 • Ozores Mariano • SPN
SI JAMAIS JE TE PINCE • 1920 • Monca Georges • FRN
SI J'AVAIS QUATRE DROMADAIRES • 1966 • Marker Chris • FRN, FRG • IF I HAD FOUR DROMEDARIES
SI JE SUIS COMME CA, C'EST LA FAUTE DE PAPA • 1978 • Santoni Joel • FRN • WHEN I WAS A KID, I DIDN'T CARE (USA)
SI JE TE CHERCHE, JE ME TROUVE • 1974 • Diamantis Roger • FRN
SI J'ETAIS LE PATRON • 1934 • Pottier Richard • FRN
SI J'ETAIS RICHE see **LAW KUNTU GHANI** • 1942
SI J'ETAIS ROI!!! • 1910 • Melies Georges • FRN
SI J'ETAIS UN ESPION • 1966 • Blier Bertrand • FRN • BREAKDOWN (USA) ○ IF I WERE A SPY
SI JEUNESSE SAVAIT.. • 1947 • Cerf Andre • FRN • IF YOUTH ONLY KNEW..
SI JOLI VILLAGE, UN • 1978 • Perier Etienne • FRN • INVESTIGATION, THE
SI JOLIE PETITE PLAGE, UNE • 1948 • Allegret Yves • FRN • RIPTIDE (USA) ○ SUCH A PRETTY LITTLE BEACH
SI JONES LOOKING FOR JOHN SMITH see **LOOKING FOR JOHN SMITH** • 1906
SI KABAYAN • 1989 • *Petet Didi* • INN • SI KEBAYAN
SI KEBAYAN see **SI KABAYAN** • 1989
SI LE ROI SAVAIT CA • 1956 • Canaille Caro, Anton Edoardo • FRN, ITL • AL SERVIZIO DELL'IMPERATORE (ITL)
SI LE SOLEIL NE REVENAIT PAS • 1987 • Goretta Claude • SWT
SI LE VENT TE FAIT PEUR • 1959 • Degelin Emile • BLG • IF THE WIND FRIGHTENS YOU
SI L'EMPEREUR SAVAIT CA • 1930 • Feyder Jacques • FRN • OLYMPIA
SI LES CAVALIERS.. • Mahamane Bakabe • NGR • IF THE HORSEMEN..
SI MA GUEULE VOUS PLAIT • 1981 • Caputo Michel • FRN
SI MAMAD • 1974 • Jaya Syuman • INN
SI MARITA AT ANG PITONG DUWENDE • 1960 • de Guzman Susana • PHL
SI ME HAN DE MATAR MANANA • 1946 • Zacarias Miguel • MXC
SI ME VIERA DON PORFIRIO • 1950 • Cortes Fernando • MXC
SI MELATI • 1954 • Effendy Basuki, Gras Enrico • INN
SI MENJE • 1950 • Effendy Basuki • INN
SI.. MI VIDA • 1952 • Mendez Fernando • MXC
SI MOH PAS-DE-CHANCE • 1971 • Smihi Moumen • SHT • MRC
SI MUORE SOLO UNA VOLTA • 1967 • Romitelli Giancarlo • ITL
SI NOUS BUVIONS UN COUP • 1909 • Cohl Emile • ANS • FRN • ET SI NOUS BUVIONS UN COUP
SI PARIS NOUS ETAIT CONTE • 1955 • Guitry Sacha • FRN
SI PITIANG • 1952 • Sukardi Kotot • INN
SI PODEMOS • 1973 • Jordan Josefina, Donda Franca • DOC • VNZ • WE CAN
SI PUO ESSERE PIU BASTARDI DELL'ISPETTORE CLIFF? • 1973 • Dallamano Massimo • ITL, UKN • BLUE MOVIE BLACKMAIL (UKN) ○ SERVIZIO DI SCORTA ○ SUPERBITCH
SI PUO FARE.. AMIGO • 1972 • Lucidi Maurizio • ITL, SPN, FRN • BIG AND THE BAD, THE (UKN) ○ CAN BE DONE AMIGO
SI PUO FARE MOLTO CON SETTE DONNE • 1971 • Piccioni Fabio • ITL
SI PUTS ONE OVER • 1914 • *Belmont Claude* • USA
SI QUIERES VIVIR.. DISPARA • 1975 • Elorrieta Jose Maria • SPN
SI QUIERO • 1965 • de Anda Raul • MXC
SI REGNE EN METRE • 1977 • Beaudry Michel • CND
SI SALVI CHI PUO (ITL) see **PETIT BAIGNEUR, LE** • 1967
SI SALVI CHI VUOLE • 1979 • Faenza Roberto • ITL
SI SALVO SOLO L'ARETINO PIETRO CON UNA MANO AVANTI E L'ALTRA DIETRO • 1972 • Amadio Silvio • ITL • ARETINO'S STORIES OF THE THREE LUSTFUL DAUGHTERS (UKN)
SI, SENOR • 1919 • Roach Hal • SHT • USA
SI SHUI WEI LAN • 1989 • Ling Zhifeng • CHN • RIPPLES ON DEAD WATER
SI SIGNORA see **SISSIGNORA** • 1942
SI SIMPLE HISTOIRE, UNE • 1970 • Ben Ammar Abdul Latif • TNS • SIMPLE STORY LIKE THIS, A
SI T'AS BESOIN DE RIEN.. FAIS-MOI SIGNE • 1986 • Clair Philippe • FRN
SI TE DICEN QUE CAI • 1989 • Aranda Vicente • SPN • IF THEY TELL YOU I FELL
SI TE HUBIERAS CASADA • 1948 • Tourjansky Victor
SI TITI ETAIT LE PATRON • 1920 • de Carbonnat Louis • FRN
SI TOUS LES AMOUREUX DU MONDE.. • 1964 • Brainin Gregoire • FRN
SI TOUS LES GARS DU MONDE • 1955 • Christian-Jaque • FRN, FRG • IF ALL THE GUYS IN THE WORLD (USA) ○ RACE FOR LIFE (UKN) ○ IF EVERY GUY IN THE WORLD
SI TU ES SAGE.. • 1974 • Sauve Alain • MTV • CND
SI TU M'AIMES see **MIRAGES** • 1937
SI TU REVIENS • 1937 • Daniel-Norman Jacques • FRN
SI TU VEUX • 1932 • Hugon Andre • FRN • EXCURSIONS DANS LA VILLE ○ ROMAN D'AMOUR ○ QUATRE COEURS
SI USTED NO PUEDE, YO SI • 1950 • Soler Julian • MXC
SI VERSAILLES M'ETAIT CONTE • 1955 • Guitry Sacha • FRN • ROYAL AFFAIR IN VERSAILLES (USA) ○ VERSAILLES (UKN) ○ AFFAIR IN VERSAILLES
SI VIVIERAMOS JUNTOS • 1982 • Skarmeta Antonio • IF WE LIVED TOGETHER
SI VOLVEMOS A VERNOS • 1967 • Regueiro Francisco • SPN • IF WE SEE EACH OTHER AGAIN ○ SMASHING UP ○ IF WE MEET AGAIN
SI VOLVIERAS A MI • 1953 • Crevenna Alfredo B. • MXC
SI VOUS CHERCHEZ UN LOGEMENT • 1953 • Novik William • SHT • FRN
SI VOUS N'AIMEZ PAS CELA, N'EN DEGOUTEZ PAS LES AUTRES • 1977 • Lewin Raymond • FRN
SI VOUS NE M'AIMEZ PAS • 1916 • Feuillade Louis • FRN
SI YO FUERA DIPUTADO • 1951 • Delgado Miguel M. • MXC
SI YO FUERA MILLONARIO • 1962 • Soler Julian • MXC
SI YO FUERA UNA CUALQUIERA • 1949 • Cortazar Ernesto • MXC
SIAM • 1954 • Wright Ralph • USA
SIAM, THE LAND OF CHANG • 1929 • *Holmes Burton* • DOC • USA
SIAMO DONNE • 1953 • Franciolini Gianni, Visconti Luchino, Rossellini Roberto, Zampa Luigi, Guarini Alfredo, Seiler Alexander J., Kovach June, Gnant Rob • ITL • WE, THE WOMEN
SIAMO QUATTRO MARZIANI see **MARZIANI HANNO DODICI MANI, I** • 1964
SIAMO RICCHI E POVERI • 1954 • Marcellini Siro • ITL
SIAMO TUTTI ASSASSINI (ITL) see **NOUS SOMMES TOUS DES ASSASSINS** • 1952
SIAMO TUTTI BEAT see **SOLDATI E CAPELLONI** • 1967
SIAMO TUTTI IN LIBERTA PROVVISORIA • 1971 • Scarpelli Manilo • ITL
SIAMO TUTTI INQUILINI • 1953 • Mattoli Mario • ITL
SIAMO TUTTI MILANESI • 1954 • Landi Mario • ITL
SIAMO TUTTI NECESSARI (ITL) see **TODOS SOMOS NECESARIOS** • 1956
SIAMO TUTTI POMICIONI • 1963 • Girolami Marino • ITL

SIAMO UOMINI O CAPORALI! • 1955 • Mastrocinque Camillo • ITL
SIAMOI AND JALLALI see **SIAMOI WA JALLALI** • 1978
SIAMOI WA JALLALI • 1978 • Shaban Abbas • AFG • SIAMOI AND JALLALI
SIASAT • 1986 • PKS • POLITICS
SIAVACCH A PERSEPOLIS see **SIAVASH IN PERSEPOLIS** • 1966
SIAVASH IN PERSEPOLIS • 1966 • Rahnema Ferydoun • IRN • SIAVACCH A PERSEPOLIS ○ KING'S BOOK, THE ○ BOOK OF KINGS, THE
SIBAD • 1967 • Santos Teodorico C. • PHL • FAST ONE, THE
SIBERIA • 1926 • Schertzinger Victor • USA
SIBERIAD, THE see **SIBIRIADA** • 1979
SIBERIADE see **SIBIRIADA** • 1979
SIBERIAN LADY MACBETH see **SIBIRSKA LEDI MAGBET** • 1962
SIBERIAN PATROL see **TOMMY** • 1931
SIBERIAN SINGING • 1961 • Makhnach Leonid • DOC • USS
SIBERIANA see **SIBIRIADA** • 1979
SIBERIANS, THE see **SIBIRYAKI** • 1940
SIBIRIADA • 1979 • Konchalovsky Andrei • USS • SIBERIAD, THE ○ SIBERIADE ○ SIBERIANA
SIBIRSKA LEDI MAGBET • 1962 • Wajda Andrzej • YGS, PLN • POWIATOWA LADY MAKBET (PLN) ○ FURY IS A WOMAN (USA) ○ SIBERIAN LADY MACBETH ○ SERBIAN LADY MACBETH
SIBIRSKY PATROL see **TOMMY** • 1931
SIBIRYAKI • 1940 • Kuleshov Lev • USS • SIBERIANS, THE
SIBLING RIVALRY • 1990 • Reiner Carl • USA
SIBYL'S SCENARIO • 1916 • Horkheimer H. M., Horkheimer E. D. • SHT • USA
SIC 'EM, SAM • 1918 • Parker Albert • SHT • USA
SIC 'EM TOWSER • 1918 • Roach Hal • SHT • USA
SICARI DI HITLER, I (ITL) see **GEHEIMAKTION SCHWARZE KAPELLE** • 1960
SICARIO 77 VIVO O MORTO • 1966 • Guerrini Mino • ITL • KILLER 77 ALIVE OR DEAD
SICARIO, IL • 1961 • Damiani Damiano • ITL
SICH VERKAUFEN, DIE • 1919 • Oswald Richard • FRG • PROSTITUTION 2
SICILIA BAROCCA • 1951 • Carpignano Vittorio • ITL
SICILIA ELLENICA • 1955 • Manera Guido • ITL
SICILIAN, THE • 1987 • Cimino Michael • USA
SICILIAN CHECKMATE see **VIOLENZA: QUINTO POTERE, LA** • 1972
SICILIAN CLAN, THE (UKN) see **CLAN DES SICILIENS, LE** • 1969
SICILIAN CONNECTION, THE see **AFYON-OPPIO** • 1972
SICILIAN CONNECTION, THE see **ATTACO ALLA PIOURA** • 1985
SICILIAN CROSS, THE (UKN) see **ESECUTORI, GLI** • 1976
SICILIAN STORY see **INESORABILI, GLI** • 1951
SICILIANS, THE • 1964 • Morris Ernest • UKN
SICILIEN, LE • 1958 • Chevalier Pierre • FRN
SICK ABED • 1920 • Wood Sam • USA
SICK ANIMALS • 1970 • Breban Nicolae • RMN
SICK KITTEN, THE see **LITTLE DOCTOR AND THE SICK KITTEN, THE** • 1901
SICK MAN FROM THE EAST, THE • 1911 • *Vitagraph* • USA
SICK ONES, THE see **SHE CAME ON THE BUS** • 1969
SICK, SICK, SICK WORLD see **IT'S A SICK, SICK, SICK WORLD** • 1965
SICK, SICK SIDNEY • 1958 • Bartsch Art • ANS • USA
SICK, SICK WORLD see **IT'S A SICK, SICK, SICK WORLD** • 1965
SICK STOCKRIDER, THE • 1913 • Lincoln W. J. • ASL
SICK TRANSIT • 1966 • Post Howard • ANS • USA
SICKLE AND HAMMER see **SERP I MOLOT** • 1921
SICKLE FIGHT see **BRIGA DE FOICE** • 1980
SICKLE OR THE CROSS, THE • 1951 • Strayer Frank • USA
SICODELICAS, LAS • 1968 • Martinez Solares Gilberto • MXC, PRU • PSYCHODELIC GIRLS, THE
SID AND NANCY • 1986 • Cox Alex • UKN
SID NEE'S FINISH • 1914 • *Bracy Sidney* • USA
SIDA: ESPEJO DE LA SOLEDAD • 1988 • Muratti Jose E. • DOC • PRC • AIDS: MIRROR OF LONELINESS
SIDASTI BOERINN I DALNUM • 1949 • Gislason Oskar • ICL • LAST FARM IN THE VALLEY, THE
SIDDHARTA AND THE CITY see **PRATIDWANDI** • 1970
SIDDHARTHA • 1972 • Rooks Conrad • USA, IND
SIDDHESHWARI • 1989 • Kaul Mani • DOC • IND
SIDE-BOARD FOLDING-BED, THE • 1909 • *Lubin* • USA
SIDE-BY-SIDE • 1958 • Bergunkev Adolf • USS
SIDE BY SIDE • 1975 • Beresford Bruce • ASL
SIDE BY SIDE • 1988 • Bender Jack • TVM • USA
SIDE BY SIDE: THE TRUE STORY OF THE OSMOND FAMILY • 1982 • Mayberry Russ • TVM • USA
SIDE CAR • U Myint Soe • BRM
SIDE-CAR THAMAR BA KHET • 1978 • Khin Soe • BRM • TRISHAW-MAN BA KHET
SIDE LIGHTS OF THE SAWDUST RING see **STORE HJERTE, DET** • 1924
SIDE SEAT PAINTINGS SLIDES SOUND FILM • 1970 • Snow Michael • CND
SIDE SHOW • 1931 • Del Ruth Roy • USA
SIDE SHOW • 1981 • Conrad William • TVM • USA
SIDE SHOW, THE (UKN) see **TWO FLAMING YOUTHS** • 1927
SIDE SHOW FAKIR • 1938 • Schwarzwald Milton • SHT • USA
SIDE SHOW OF LIFE, THE • 1924 • Brenon Herbert • USA • SIDESHOW OF LIFE, THE
SIDE STREET • 1929 • St. Clair Malcolm • USA • THREE BROTHERS (UKN)
SIDE STREET • 1949 • Mann Anthony • USA
SIDE STREET ANGEL • 1937 • Ince Ralph • UKN
SIDE STREET STORY (USA) see **NAPOLI, MILIONARIA** • 1950
SIDE STREETS • 1933 • Campbell Ivar • UKN
SIDE STREETS • 1934 • Green Alfred E. • USA • WOMAN IN HER THIRTIES (UKN) ○ FUR COATS
SIDE TRACK see **OTKLONENIE** • 1967
SIDE-TRACKED • 1916 • *Plump & Runt* • SHT • USA
SIDE TRACKED BY SISTER • 1913 • *Majestic* • USA
SIDECAR BOYS • 1974 • Bellamy Earl • USA • SIDECAR RACERS (UKN) ○ TEAM, THE
SIDECAR RACERS (UKN) see **SIDECAR BOYS** • 1974
SIDEHACKERS, THE see **FIVE THE HARD WAY** • 1969
SIDEKICKS • 1974 • Kennedy Burt • TVM • USA
SIDELONG GLANCES OF A PIGEON FANCIER • 1971 • Dexter John • USA • PIGEONS
SIDEREAL CRUISES see **CROISIERES SIDERALES** • 1941
SIDESHOW • 1950 • Yarbrough Jean • USA
SIDESHOW '69 • 1968 • Molina Hector C. • PHL
SIDESHOW, THE • 1928 • Kenton Erle C. • USA
SIDESHOW OF LIFE, THE see **SIDE SHOW OF LIFE, THE** • 1924
SIDESHOW WRESTLERS (?) see **HIGH-LIFE TAYLOR** • 1908
SIDESTREET • 1977 • Pearson Peter (c/d) • SER • CND
SIDEWALK COWBOY, THE • 1968 • *Lake Sam* • USA • MATINEE COWBOY
SIDEWALK STORIES • 1990 • Lane Charles • USA
SIDEWALKS • 1961 • Menken Marie • SHT • USA
SIDEWALKS OF LONDON (USA) see **ST. MARTIN'S LANE** • 1938
SIDEWALKS OF NEW YORK • 1920 • Craft William James • USA
SIDEWALKS OF NEW YORK • 1923 • Park Lester • USA
SIDEWALKS OF NEW YORK, THE • 1929 • Fleischer Dave • ANS • USA
SIDEWALKS OF NEW YORK, THE • 1931 • White Jules, Myers Zion • USA
SIDEWINDER ONE • 1977 • Bellamy Earl • USA
SIDI-BEL-ABBES • 1953 • Alden-Delos Jean • FRN
SIDI BOU SAID • 1964 • Essid Hamadi • SHT • TNS
SIDI-BRAHIM • 1939 • Didier Marc • FRN • DIABLES BLEUS, LES
SIDNEY SHELDON'S BLOODLINE • 1979 • Young Terence • USA • BLOODLINE
SIDNEY SHORR: A GIRL'S BEST FRIEND • 1981 • Mayberry Russ • TVM • USA
SIDNEY THE ELEPHANT • 1957-63 • *Terrytoons* • ASS • USA
SIDNEY'S FAMILY TREE • 1958 • Bartsch Art • ANS • USA
SIDNEY'S WHITE ELEPHANT • 1963 • Bartsch Art • ANS • USA
SIDONIE PANACHE • 1934 • Wulschleger Henry • FRN, ALG
SID'S LONG COUNT • 1930 • Newfield Sam • SHT • USA
SIDSTE DANS, DEN • 1922 • Sandberg Anders W. • DNM
SIDSTE FLEKSNES, DEN see **SISTE FLEKSNES, DEN** • 1974
SIDSTOFFER • 1907 • Larsen Viggo • DNM
SIE • 1954 • Thiele Rolf • FRG
SIE FANDEN IHREN WEG • 1962 • Vesely Herbert • FRG
SIE KANN NICHT NEIN SAGEN • 1914 • *Oswald Richard (Sc)* • FRG • YOU CAN'T SAY NO
SIE KANNTEN SICH ALLE • 1958 • Groschopp Richard • GDR • EHRLICHE NAME, DER
SIE LIEBTEN SICH EINEN SOMMER • 1973 • Reinl Harald • FRG
SIE NANNTEN IHN AMIGO • 1958 • Carow Heiner • GDR • THEY CALLED HIM AMIGO
SIE NANNTEN IHN GRINGO • 1966 • Rowland Roy • FRG, SPN, ITL • LEY DEL FORESTERO, LA (SPN) ○ MAN CALLED GRINGO, A (UKN)
SIE NANNTEN IHN KRAMBAMBULI • 1972 • Antel Franz • FRG, AUS • THEY CALLED HIM KRAMBAMBULI
SIE SIND FREI, DR. KORCZAK see **MARTYRER -DR. KORCZAK UND SEINE KINDER, DER** • 1974
SIE UND DIE DREI • 1922 • Dupont E. A. • FRG • SHE AND THE THREE
SIE UND DIE DREI • 1935 • Janson Victor • FRG • SHE AND THE THREE (USA)
SIEBEN BRIEFE • 1944 • Slavinsky Vladimir • FRG
SIEBEN JAHR PECH • 1940 • Marischka Ernst • FRG
SIEBEN JAHRE GLUCK (FRG) see **SETTE ANNI DI FELICITA** • 1942
SIEBEN MANNER DER SU-MARU, DIE (FRG) see **SUMURU** • 1968
SIEBEN OHRFEIGEN • 1937 • Martin Paul • FRG • SEVEN SLAPS (USA)
SIEBEN RABEN, DIE • 1969 • Wiemer Christel • ANS • FRG • SEVEN RAVENS, THE (USA)
SIEBEN SOMMERSPROSSEN • Zschoche Hermann • GDR • SEVEN FRECKLES
SIEBEN TAGE FRIST • 1969 • Vohrer Alfred • FRG
SIEBEN TOCHTER DER FRAU GYURKOVICS, DIE (FRG) see **FLICKORNA GYURKOVICS** • 1926
SIEBEN TODSUNDEN, DIE • 1920 • *Tzatschewa Manja* • FRG
SIEBEN UND ZWANZIG MINUTEN, FUNF UND VIERZIG SEKONDEN • 1960 • Dahlmann Gerd • FRG
SIEBEN VON RHEIN • 1954 • Thorndike Andrew, Thorndike Annelie • GDR • SEVEN FROM THE RHINE
SIEBENMAL IN DER WOCHE • 1957 • Philipp Harald • FRG
SIEBENTE GEBOT, DAS see **GEHEIMNISSE VON LONDON, DIE** • 1920
SIEBENTE GROSSMACHT, DIE • 1919 • Grunwald Willy • FRG
SIEBENTE JUNGE, DER • 1926 • Osten Franz • FRG
SIEBENTE JUNGE, DER • 1941 • Lippl Alois J. • FRG • LIEBESURLAUB
SIEBENTE KONTINENT, DER • 1989 • Haneke Michael • AUS • SEVENTH CONTINENT, THE (UKN)
SIEBENTE KUSS, DER • 1918 • *Worner Hilde* • FRG
SIEBENTE NACHT, DIE • 1922 • Teuber Arthur • FRG
SIEBENTE OPFER, DAS • 1964 • Gottlieb Franz J. • FRG
SIEBENTE TAG, DER • 1920 • Stahl-Nachbaur Ernst • FRG
SIEBZEHN JAHR, BLONDES HAAR see **BATTAGLIA DEI MODS, LA** • 1966
SIEBZEHNJAHRIGE, EINE • 1934 • Rabenalt Arthur M. • FRG
SIEBZEHNJAHRIGEN, DIE • 1919 • Henning Hanna • FRG
SIEBZEHNJAHRIGEN, DIE • 1928 • Asagaroff Georg • FRG
SIECLE A SOIF, LE • 1958 • Vogel Raymond • SHT • FRN
SIECLE D'ACIER, LE • 1939 • Tedesco Jean • SHT • FRN
SIECLE D'OR: L'ART DES PRIMITIFS FLAMANDS, UN • 1953 • Haesaerts Paul • BLG • GOLDEN CENTURY ○ GOLDEN AGE, THE
SIECLE S'EST ECOULE, UN • 1945 • Palardy Jean • DCS • CND
SIEDEMDZIESIAT DWIE GODZINY • 1970 • Trzos-Rastawiecki Andrzej • DOC • PLN • SEVENTY TWO HOURS
SIEDLISZCZE • 1960 • Gryczelowska Krystyna • DOC • PLN • SETTLEMENT
SIEDMA PEVNINA see **SEDMI KONTINENT** • 1966
SIEG DER HERZEN • 1944 • Ruhmann Heinz • FRG
SIEG DER JUGEND, DER • 1927 • Sauer Fred • FRG
SIEG DER LIEBE see **AN HEILIGEN WASSER** • 1952
SIEG DES ERFINDERS, DER • 1915 • Albes Emil • FRG
SIEG DES GLAUBENS • 1933 • Riefenstahl Leni • DOC • FRG • VICTORY OF THE FAITH ○ VICTORY OF FAITH
SIEG DES HERZENS, DER • 1915 • Biebrach Rudolf? • FRG
SIEG DES MAHARADSCHA, DER • 1923 • Delmont Joseph • FRG
SIEG IM WESTEN • 1941 • Noldan Svend • FRG • VICTORY IN THE WEST
SIEGA VERDE • 1960 • Gil Rafael • SPN
SIEGE • 1925 • Gade Svend • USA
SIEGE • 1969 • Tofano Gilberto • ISR
SIEGE • 1977 • Friel Deirdre • MTV • IRL
SIEGE • 1978 • Pearce Richard • TVM • USA
SIEGE • 1982 • Donovan Paul • CND • SELF DEFENCE
SIEGE, THE • 1970 • Muresan Mircea • RMN
SIEGE, THE • 1975 • Yershov Mikhail • USS
SIEGE, THE see **OPSADA** • 1956
SIEGE AND FALL OF THE ALAMO, THE • 1913 • *Mathews H. C.* • USA
SIEGE AT FIREBASE GLORIA, THE see **FORWARD FIREBASE GLORIA** • 1988
SIEGE AT RED RIVER, THE • 1954 • Mate Rudolph • USA
SIEGE DE CALAIS, LE • 1911 • Andreani Henri • FRN • SIEGE OF CALAIS, THE
SIEGE DE SYRACUSE, LE (FRN) see **ASSEDIO DI SIRACUSA, L'** • 1960
SIEGE OF ALCAZAR see **ASSEDIO DELL'ALCAZAR, L'** • 1940
SIEGE OF BESZTERCZE, THE see **BESZTERCE OSTROMA** • 1948
SIEGE OF CALAIS, THE see **SIEGE DE CALAIS, LE** • 1911
SIEGE OF FIREBASE GLORIA, THE see **FORWARD FIREBASE GLORIA** • 1988
SIEGE OF FORT BISMARCK (USA) see **CHINTAO YOSAI BAKUGEKI MEIREI** • 1963
SIEGE OF HELL STREET, THE see **SIEGE OF SIDNEY STREET, THE** • 1960
SIEGE OF LIEGE, THE • 1914 • *Mina* • USA
SIEGE OF PETERSBURG, THE • 1912 • *Hallam Harry* • USA
SIEGE OF PINCHGUT, THE • 1959 • Watt Harry • ASL • FOUR DESPERATE MEN (USA)
SIEGE OF SIDNEY STREET, THE • 1960 • Baker Robert S. • UKN • SIEGE OF HELL STREET, THE
SIEGE OF SYRACUSE (USA) see **ASSEDIO DI SIRACUSA, L'** • 1960
SIEGE OF THE SAXONS, THE • 1963 • Juran Nathan • UKN
SIEGE OF THE SOUTH • 1931 • Hurley Frank • DOC • ASL • WITH MAWSON TO THE FROZEN SOUTH
SIEGEL GOTTES, DAS • 1949 • Stoger Alfred • AUS
SIEGER, DER • 1932 • Hinrich Hans, Martin Paul • FRG • VICTOR, THE
SIEGER, DIE • 1918 • Biebrach Rudolf • FRG • VICTOR, THE
SIEGER, DIE • 1922 • Ruttmann Walter • FRG • VICTOR, THE
SIEGERIN, DIE • 1919 • *Wolter Hilde* • FRG
SIEGERIN WEIB • 1918 • *Synd Lu* • FRG
SIEGFRIED • PHL
SIEGFRIED see **NIBELUNGEN 1, DIE** • 1924
SIEGFRIED see **ZYGFRYD** • 1986
SIEGFRIED DER MATROSE see **STORCHS TREIKT, DER** • 1931
SIEGFRIED UND DAS SAGENHAFTE LIEBESLEBEN DER NIBELUNGEN • 1971 • Hoven Adrian, Friedman David F. (Usa Vers.) • FRG, USA • LONG SWIFT SWORD OF SIEGFRIED, THE (USA) ○ MAIDEN QUEST ○ EROTIC ADVENTURES OF SIEGFRIED, THE (UKN) ○ TERRIBLE QUICK SWORD OF SIEGFRIED, THE
SIEGFRIED (USA) see **SIGFRIDO** • 1912
SIEGFRIED (USA) see **SIGFRIDO** • 1959
SIEGFRIED'S DEATH see **NIBELUNGEN 1, DIE** • 1924
SIEGFRIEDS TOD see **NIBELUNGEN 1, DIE** • 1924
SIEKIEREZADA • 1986 • Leszczynski Witold • PLN • AXILIAD
SIEMBRA DEL FUTURO • 1978 • Blanco Javier • SHT • VNZ • SEEDING THE FUTURE
SIEMBRO VIENTO EN MI CIUDAD • 1979 • Perez Fernando • DOC • CUB • I PLANT THE WIND IN MY CITY
SIEMPRE EN LA ARENA • 1957 • Torrado Ramon, Magon Barry • SPN
SIEMPRE EN MI RECUERDO • 1962 • Balbuena Silvio F., Cano Manuel • SPN
SIEMPRE ES DOMINGO • 1961 • Palacios Fernando • SPN
SIEMPRE ESTARE CONTIGO • 1958 • Soler Julian • MXC
SIEMPRE HAY UN MANANA • 1961 • Morayta Miguel • MXC • VIDA DEL PADRE LAMBERT, LA
SIEMPRE LISTO EN LAS TINIEBLAS • 1939 • *Cantinflas* • SHT • MXC • ALWAYS READY IN THE DARKNESS
SIEMPRE MUJERES • 1942 • Arevalo Carlos • SPN
SIEMPRE TE AMARE • 1971 • *Filma Chapultepec* • MXC
SIEMPRE TRIUNFA EL AMOR • 1974 • Cohen Rafael • ARG • LOVE ALWAYS WINS
SIEMPRE TUYA • 1950 • Fernandez Emilio • MXC • ALWAYS YOURS
SIEMPRE VUELVEN DE MADRUGADA • 1948 • Mihura Jeronimo • SPN
SIEN BESTER FREUND • 1929 • Piel Harry • FRG • ABENTEUER MIT FUNFZEHN HINDEN, EIN ○ HIS BEST FRIEND (USA)
SIEN JOU MORE • 1970 • SAF
SIENEN NO ISU • 1962 • Nishikawa Katsumi • JPN • SEAT OF YOUTH
SIENER IN DIE SUBURBS • 1973 • Swart Francois • SAF
SIERAAD UIT AS • 1970 • SAF
SIERIEBRISTAYA PYL see **SEREBRISTAYA PYL** • 1953
SIERO DELLA VERITA • 1951 • Milani Mario, Risi Dino • DOC • ITL
SIERPEN -KRONIKA MIESIACA JERZEGO T. • 1972 • Karabasz Kazimierz • DOC • PLN • AUGUST -A MONTH IN THE LIFE OF JERZY T.
SIERRA • 1950 • Green Alfred E. • USA
SIERRA BARON • 1958 • Clark James B. • USA
SIERRA CHICA • 1938 • Irigoyen Julio • ARG
SIERRA DE RONDA • 1934 • Rey Florian • SPN
SIERRA DE TERUEL (SPN) see **ESPOIR** • 1939
SIERRA DEL TERROR, LA • 1955 • Salvador Jaime • MXC

SIERRA FALCON • 1967 • Chapier Henri • DCS • FRN
SIERRA JIM'S REFORMATION • 1914 • O'Brien Jack • USA
SIERRA LEONE • 1988 • Schrader Uwe • FRG
SIERRA MAESTRA • 1969 • Giannarelli Ansano • ITL
SIERRA MALDITA • 1954 • del Amo Antonio • SPN
SIERRA MORENA • 1944 • Elias Francisco • MXC
SIERRA PASSAGE • 1951 • McDonald Frank • USA
SIERRA STRANGER • 1957 • Sholem Lee • USA
SIERRA SUE • 1941 • Morgan William • USA
SIERVO DE DIOS, EL • 1968 • Navarro Agustin • VNZ, SPN • GOD'S SERVANT
SIESTA • 1977 • Sevcik Igor • ANM • CZC
SIESTA • 1988 • Lambert Mary • USA, UKN
SIESTA, LA • 1976 • Grau Jorge • SPN
SIESTA SAMBA • 1975 • Sjoman Vilgot • SWD
SIESTA VETA • 1985 • Uher Stefan • CZC • SIXTH SENTENCE, THE
SIETE BRAVISIMOS, LOS • 1968 • Klimovsky Leon • SPN • SEVEN VERY BRAVE MEN
SIETE CHACALES • 1974 • Madrid Jose Luis • SPN
SIETE DE COPAS, EL • 1960 • Gavaldon Roberto • MXC
SIETE DE PANCHO VILLA, LOS • 1966 • Elorrieta Jose Maria • SPN
SIETE DIAS DE ENERO • 1978 • Bardem Juan Antonio • SPN • SEVEN DAYS IN JANUARY
SIETE DISPAROS AL AMANECER • 1974 • Elorrieta Jose Maria • SPN
SIETE DOLARES AL ROJO • 1968 • Cardone Alberto • SPN, ITL • SETTE DOLLARI SUL ROSSO ○ SEVEN DOLLARS ON RED ○ SEVEN DOLLARS TO KILL
SIETE DOLORES • 1968 • Enriquez Luis B. • PHL • SEVEN SORROWS
SIETE ESPARTANOS, LOS (SPN) see **SETTE GLADIATORI, I** • 1962
SIETE ESPIAS EN LA TRAMPA • 1967 • Amendola Mario • SPN, ITL • TRAPPOLA PER 7 SPIE (ITL) ○ SEVEN SPIES IN THE TRAP
SIETE GRITOS EN EL MAR • 1954 • Amadori Luis Cesar • ARG
SIETE HOMBRES DE ORO (SPN) see **SETTE UOMINI D'ORO** • 1965
SIETE LEGUAS, EL • 1955 • de Anda Raul • MXC
SIETE LIBERO? see **ULTIMA CARROZZELLA, L'** • 1943
SIETE LOCOS, LOS • 1973 • Torre-Nilsson Leopoldo • ARG • SEVEN MAD MEN (USA) ○ SEVEN MADMEN, THE
SIETE MACHOS, EL • 1950 • Delgado Miguel M. • MXC
SIETE MAGNIFICAS, LAS • 1966 • Zehetgruber Rudolf, Pink Sidney • SPN, AUS, ITL • FRAUEN, DIE DURCH DIE HOLLE GEHEN (AUS) ○ DONNE ALLA FRONTIERA (ITL) ○ TALL WOMEN, THE (USA) ○ WOMEN WHO GO THROUGH HELL
SIETE MINUTOS PARA MORIR • 1966 • Fernandez Ramon • SPN
SIETE MUJERES • 1944 • Perojo Benito • ARG
SIETE MUJERES • 1953 • Bustillo Oro Juan • MXC
SIETE MUJERES PARA LOS MACGREGOR (SPN) see **SETTE DONNE PER I MACGREGOR** • 1967
SIETE NINOS DE ECIJA, LOS • 1946 • Morayta Miguel • MXC
SIETE PECADOS • 1957 • Diaz Morales Jose • MXC
SIETE PISTOLAS PARA EL GRINGO • 1967 • Xiol Juan • SPN, ITL • SETTE PISTOLAS PER EL GRINGO (ITL) ○ SEVEN PISTOLS FOR EL GRINGO
SIETE VIDAS DEL GATO, LAS • 1970 • Lazaga Pedro • SPN • SEVEN LIVES OF THE CAT, THE ○ CAT'S SEVEN LIVES, THE
SIF, DAS WEIB, DAS DEN MORD BEGING see **ARME KLEINE SIF** • 1927
SIGFRIDO • 1912 • Caserini Mario • ITL • SIEGFRIED (USA)
SIGFRIDO • 1959 • Gentilomo Giacomo • ITL • SIEGFRIED (USA) ○ LEGGENDA DEI NIBELUNGHI, LA ○ DRAGON'S BLOOD
SIGGE NILSSON AND I see **SIGGE NILSSON OCH JAG** • 1938
SIGGE NILSSON OCH JAG • 1938 • Wallen Sigurd • SWD • SIGGE NILSSON AND I
SIGHET, SIGHET • 1967 • Becker Harold • SHT • USA
SIGHT, THE • 1985 • Mankiewicz Francis • MTV • CND
SIGHT FOR SQUAW EYES, A • 1963 • Kneitel Seymour • ANS • USA
SIGHT OF THE BLIND • 1915 • *Eclair* • USA
SIGHT UNSEEN, A • 1914 • Taylor Stanner E. V. • USA
SIGHTSEEING THROUGH WHISKY (USA) see **PAUVRE JOHN OU LES AVENTURES D'UN BUVEUR DE WHISKY** • 1907
SIGILLO DI PECHINO, IL • 1966 • Hill James, Winterstein Franz • ITL, FRG, FRN • HOLLE VON MACAO, DIE (FRG) ○ PEKING MEDALLION, THE (UKN) ○ CORRUPT ONES, THE (USA) ○ CORROMPUS, LES ○ HELL TO MACAO
SIGILLO ROSSO • 1951 • Calzavara Flavio • ITL
SIGMA III • 1966 • Whiteman Albert W. • USA
SIGN, THE • 1913 • *Calvert E. H.* • USA
SIGN HERE, PLEASE • 1973 • Papadimitrakis Lambros • SHT • GRC
SIGN INVINCIBLE, THE see **SIGN INVISIBLE, THE** • 1918
SIGN INVISIBLE, THE • 1918 • Lewis Edgar • USA • SIGN INVINCIBLE, THE
SIGN O' THE TIMES • 1987 • Prince • USA
SIGN OF AQUARIUS • 1970 • Emery Robert J. • USA • GHETTO FREAKS
SIGN OF CANCER, THE see **ZNAMENI RAKA** • 1967
SIGN OF DEATH, THE see **SIGNO DE LA MUERTE, EL** • 1939
SIGN OF DISASTER see **ZNAK BEDY** • 1986
SIGN OF FOUR, THE • 1923 • Elvey Maurice • UKN
SIGN OF FOUR, THE • 1932 • Lee Rowland V., Cutts Graham • UKN
SIGN OF FOUR, THE (USA) see **SHERLOCK HOLMES' THE SIGN OF FOUR** • 1983
SIGN OF LEO, THE see **SIGNE DU LION, LE** • 1959
SIGN OF THE BEAST see **PEDON MERKKI** • 1982
SIGN OF THE BROKEN SHACKLES, THE • 1915 • Millarde Harry • USA
SIGN OF THE CACTUS, THE • 1925 • Smith Cliff • USA
SIGN OF THE CLAW, THE • 1926 • Eason B. Reeves • USA
SIGN OF THE CRAB, THE see **ZNAMENI RAKA** • 1967
SIGN OF THE CROSS, THE • 1904 • Haggar William • UKN
SIGN OF THE CROSS, THE • 1914 • Thompson Frederick A. • USA
SIGN OF THE CROSS, THE • 1932 • De Mille Cecil B. • USA
SIGN OF THE CROSS, THE see **DIABLE AU CONVENT, LE** • 1899
SIGN OF THE CUCUMBER, THE • 1917 • Smith Dick • SHT • USA
SIGN OF THE DAGGER (UKN) see **TRAIL TO LAREDO** • 1948
SIGN OF THE GLADIATOR (USA) see **NEL SEGNO DI ROMA** • 1959
SIGN OF THE HELMET, THE • 1911 • *Powers* • USA
SIGN OF THE LION see **SIGNE DU LION, LE** • 1959
SIGN OF THE PAGAN • 1954 • Sirk Douglas • USA
SIGN OF THE POPPY, THE • 1916 • Swickard Charles • USA
SIGN OF THE RAM • 1948 • Sturges John • USA
SIGN OF THE ROSE, THE • 1915 • Ince Thomas H. • USA
SIGN OF THE ROSE, THE • 1922 • Garson Harry • USA
SIGN OF THE SCARF • 1917 • Ellis Robert • USA
SIGN OF THE SNAKE, THE • 1913 • Giblyn Charles • USA
SIGN OF THE SPADE, THE • 1916 • MacQuarrie Murdock • USA
SIGN OF THE THREE LABELS, THE • 1911 • Seay Charles M. • USA
SIGN OF THE VAMPIRE, THE see **SENAL DEL VAMPIRO, LA** • 1943
SIGN OF THE VAMPIRE, THE see **VAMPYROS LESBOS –DIE ERBIN DES DRACULA** • 1971
SIGN OF THE VIRGIN (USA) see **SOUHVEZDI PANNY** • 1966
SIGN OF THE WOLF • 1941 • Bretherton Howard • USA
SIGN OF THE WOLF, THE • 1931 • Sheldon Forrest, Webb Harry S. • SRL • USA
SIGN OF VENUS see **SEGNO DI VENERE, IL** • 1955
SIGN OF ZORRO, THE • 1960 • Foster Lewis R., Foster Norman • MTV • USA
SIGN OFF • 1971 • Conner Ian • SHT • USA
SIGN ON THE DOOR, THE • 1921 • Brenon Herbert • USA
SIGN PLEASE • 1933 • Rawlins John* • SHT • UKN
SIGN PLEASE • 1936 • *Wise Vic* • SHT • UKN
SIGN WRITER, THE • 1897 • Smith G. A. • UKN • AWKWARD SIGNWRITER, THE
SIGNAL • 1918 • Arkatov Alexander • USS
SIGNAL • 1971 • Kamei Takehiko • ANS • JPN
SIGNAL see **LASSATOK FELEIM!** • 1968
SIGNAL 7 • 1983 • Nilsson Rob • USA
SIGNAL, THE • 1913 • Lessey George A. • USA
SIGNAL, THE • 1914 • *Lubin* • USA
SIGNAL, THE see **MAYAK** • 1942
SIGNAL CODE, THE • 1912 • *Thanhouser* • USA
SIGNAL FIRE, THE • 1912 • *Vitagraph* • USA
SIGNAL FIRES • 1926 • *Church Fred* • USA
SIGNAL FIRES IN SHANGHAI see **NOROSHI WA SHANGHAI NI AGARU** • 1944
SIGNAL IN DER NACHT • 1937 • Schneider-Edenkoben Richard • FRG
SIGNAL LIGHT • 1912 • *Lynch Baby* • USA
SIGNAL–MASTER • 1943-46 • Monkman John • DOC • UKN
SIGNAL OF DISTRESS, THE • 1912 • *Turner Florence* • USA
SIGNAL ROUGE, LE • 1948 • Neubach Ernst • FRN
SIGNAL THROUGH THE FLAMES • 1984 • Rochlin Sheldon, Harris Maxine • DOC • USA
SIGNAL TOWER, THE • 1924 • Brown Clarence • USA
SIGNALE –EIN WELTRAUMABENTEUR • 1970 • Kolditz Gottfried • GDR, PLN • SIGNALS –AN ADVENTURE IN SPACE ○ SIGNALS –A SPACE ADVENTURE ○ SIGNALS –A WORLD–DREAM ADVENTURE
SIGNALET • 1966 • Gammeltoft Ole • SHT • DNM
SIGNALI NAD GRADOM • 1960 • Mitrovic Zika • YGS • SIGNALS OVER THE CITY
SIGNALS, THE see **SYGNALY** • 1959
SIGNALS –A SPACE ADVENTURE see **SIGNALE –EIN WELTRAUMABENTEUR** • 1970
SIGNALS –A WORLD–DREAM ADVENTURE see **SIGNALE –EIN WELTRAUMABENTEUR** • 1970
SIGNALS –AN ADVENTURE IN SPACE see **SIGNALE –EIN WELTRAUMABENTEUR** • 1970
SIGNALS IN THE NIGHT • 1913 • Martinek H. O.? • UKN
SIGNALS OVER THE CITY see **SIGNALI NAD GRADOM** • 1960
SIGNAUX DANS L'OMBRE • 1955 • Lacombe Georges • FRN
SIGNE, LA • 1969 • Rouch Jean • DCS • FRN
SIGNE ARSENE LUPIN • 1959 • Robert Yves • FRN, ITL • RITORNO DI ARSENIO LUPIN, IL (ITL) ○ SIGNED, ARSENE LUPIN (USA)
SIGNE DE LA BALANCE, LE • Vandercoille Alain • DOC • FRN
SIGNE DE ZORRO, LE see **SEGNO DI ZORRO, IL** • 1963
SIGNE DU LION, LE • 1959 • Rohmer Eric • FRN • SIGN OF LEO, THE ○ SIGN OF THE LION
SIGNE FURAX • 1981 • Simenon Marc • FRN
SIGNE ILLISIBLE • 1942 • Chamborant Christian • FRN
SIGNE PICPUS see **PICPUS** • 1942
SIGNE REYNARD • Soutter Michel • SWT
SIGNED, ARSENE LUPIN (USA) see **SIGNE ARSENE LUPIN** • 1959
SIGNED JUDGEMENT (UKN) see **COWBOY FROM LONESOME RIVER, THE** • 1944
SIGNED ROSEBUD see **RUMUZ GONCAGUL** • 1987
SIGNED, SEALED AND CLOBBERED • 1958 • Rasinski Connie • ANS • USA
SIGNES DE TERRE, SIGNES DE CHAIR • 1984 • Cuneo Anne • SWT
SIGNES EXTERIEURS DE RICHESSE • 1983 • Monnet Jacques • FRN
SIGNET OF SHEBA, THE see **SPORTING CHANCE, A** • 1919
SIGNET RING, THE • 1917 • Howard George Bronson • USA
SIGNING OF THE CAPITULATION, THE see **PODPISANIE KAPITULACJI** • 1970
SIGNING OFF • 1936 • Schwarzwald Milton • SHT • USA
SIGNING PEACE AT PRETORIA • 1902 • *Bromhead A. C.* • UKN
SIGNO DE LA MUERTE, EL • 1939 • Urueta Chano • MXC • SIGN OF DEATH, THE
SIGNO DEL VAMPIRO, EL see **VAMPYROS LESBOS –DIE ERBIN DES DRACULA** • 1971
SIGNOR, THE see **SHRIMANJI** • 1968
SIGNOR BRUSCHINO, IL • 1967 • Sala Vittorio • ITL
SIGNOR MAX, IL • 1937 • Camerini Mario • ITL • MR. MAX (USA)
SIGNOR MINISTRO LI PRESE TUTTI E SUBITO, IL • 1978 • Alessandrini Sergio • ITL
SIGNOR POTTI'S LOVE AFFAIR • 1911 • Coleby A. E. • UKN
SIGNOR ROBINSON MOSTRUOSA STORIA D'AMORE E D'AVVENTURE • 1976 • Corbucci Sergio • ITL
SIGNOR ROSSI • Bozzetto Bruno • ASS • ITL • MR. ROSSI
SIGNOR ROSSI A VENEZIA, IL • 1974 • Bozzetto Bruno • ANM • ITL
SIGNOR ROSSI AL CAMPING, IL • 1970 • Bozzetto Bruno • ANM • ITL
SIGNOR ROSSI AL MARE, IL • 1964 • Bozzetto Bruno • ANS • ITL
SIGNOR ROSSI AL SAFARI FOTOGRAFICO, IL • 1972 • Bozzetto Bruno • ANM • ITL
SIGNOR ROSSI CERCA LA FELICITA, IL • 1976 • Bozzetto Bruno • ANM • ITL • MISTER ROSSI LOOKS FOR HAPPINESS
SIGNOR ROSSI COMPERA L'AUTOMOBILA, IL • 1966 • Bozzetto Bruno • ANS • ITL, SWT • MR. ROSSI BUYS A CAR (USA)
SIGNOR ROSSI VA A SCIARE, IL • 1963 • Bozzetto Bruno • ANS • ITL
SIGNORA ARLECCHINO, LA • 1918 • Caserini Mario • ITL • MADAMA ARLECCHINO
SIGNORA DALLE CAMELIE, LA • 1909 • Falena Ugo • ITL • CAMILLE (USA)
SIGNORA DALLE CAMELIE, LA • 1914 • Negroni Baldassare • ITL
SIGNORA DALLE CAMELIE, LA • 1915 • Serena Gustavo • ITL • LADY OF THE CAMELLIAS, THE
SIGNORA DALLE CAMELIE, LA • 1948 • Gallone Carmine • ITL • LOST ONE, THE (USA) ○ TRAVIATA, LA
SIGNORA DALLE CAMELIE, LA (ITL) see **DAME AUX CAMELIAS, LA** • 1953
SIGNORA DALLE CAMILIE, LA see **DAME AUX CAMELIAS, LA** • 1981
SIGNORA DEGLI ORRORI, LA • 1977 • Bolognini Mauro • ITL • BLACK JOURNAL (USA)
SIGNORA DELLA NOTTE, LA • 1985 • Schivazappa Piero • ITL • LADY OF THE NIGHT
SIGNORA DELL'OVEST, UNA • 1942 • Koch Carl • ITL • CAROVANE ○ CAROVANA
SIGNORA DI MONTECARLO, LA • 1938 • Soldati Mario, Berthomieu Andre • ITL
SIGNORA DI TUTTI, LA • 1934 • Ophuls Max • ITL
SIGNORA E SERVITA, LA • 1946 • Giannini Nino • ITL • SIGNORE E SERVITO, IL
SIGNORA E STATA VIOLENTATA, LA • 1973 • Sindoni Vittorio • ITL
SIGNORA FORTUNA • 1937 • Righelli Gennaro • ITL • LADY LUCK
SIGNORA GIOCA BENE A SCOPA?, LA • 1974 • Carnimeo Giuliano • ITL
SIGNORA IN NERO, LA • 1943 • Malasomma Nunzio • ITL
SIGNORA PARADISO, LA • 1934 • Guazzoni Enrico • ITL
SIGNORA SENZA CAMILIE, LA • 1953 • Antonioni Michelangelo • ITL • LADY WITHOUT CAMELIAS, THE (UKN) ○ CAMILLE WITHOUT CAMELIAS (USA) ○ WOMAN WITHOUT CAMELIAS, THE
SIGNORA SENZA PACE, LA • 1919 • Negroni Baldassare • ITL
SIGNORE, LE • 1960 • Vasile Turi • ITL
SIGNORE A DOPPIO PETTO, IL • 1941 • Calzavara Flavio • ITL
SIGNORE DELLA TAVERNA, IL • 1940 • Palermi Amleto • ITL
SIGNORE DESIDERA?, IL • 1933 • Righelli Gennaro • ITL
SIGNORE E SERVITO, IL see **SIGNORA E SERVITA, LA** • 1946
SIGNORE E SIGNORI • 1966 • Germi Pietro • ITL, FRN • BIRDS, THE BEES AND THE ITALIANS, THE (USA) ○ MESDAMES ET MESSIEURS ○ BELLES DAMES, VILAINS MESSIEURS ○ CES MESSIEURS DAMES ○ LADIES AND GENTLEMEN
SIGNORE E SIGNORI BUONANOTTE • 1976 • Comencini Luigi, Loy Nanni, Monicelli Mario, Scola Ettore, Magni Luigi • ITL
SIGNORE PREFERISCONO IL MAMBO, LE (ITL) see **CES DAMES PREFERENT LE MAMBO** • 1957
SIGNORI DI NASCE • 1960 • Mattoli Mario • ITL
SIGNORI, IN CARROZZA! • 1951 • Zampa Luigi • ITL • ROME – PARIS – ROME
SIGNORI LA FESTA E FINITA • 1914 • Serena Gustavo • ITL
SIGNORINA, LA • 1942 • Kish Ladislao • ITL
SIGNORINA CICLONE, LA • 1916 • D'Ambra Lucio • ITL
SIGNORINA CICLONE, LA • 1916 • Genina Augusto • ITL
SIGNORINA DAL LIVIDO AZZURRO, LA see **RAGAZZA DAL LIVIDO AZZURRO, LA** • 1933
SIGNORINA DELL'AUTOBUS, LA • 1933 • Malasomma Nunzio • ITL
SIGNORINA MADRE DI FAMIGLIA, LA • 1924 • Gallone Carmine • ITL
SIGNORINE DELLA VILLA ACCANTO, LE • 1942 • Rosmino Gian Paolo • ITL
SIGNORINE DELLO 04, LE • 1955 • Franciolini Gianni • ITL
SIGNORINELLA • 1950 • Mattoli Mario • ITL
SIGNORINETTE • 1943 • Zampa Luigi • ITL
SIGNOS DEL ZODIACO, LOS • 1962 • Vejar Sergio • MXC • SIGNS OF THE ZODIAC, THE
SIGNPOST TO MURDER • 1964 • Englund George • USA
SIGNPRESS CONTRO SCOTLAND YARD (ITL) see **MISTER ZEHN PROZENT –NIEZEN UND MONETEN** • 1967
SIGNS OF CONQUEST • 1989 • Irvin John • USA
SIGNS OF LIFE • 1989 • Coles John David • USA
SIGNS OF LIFE (USA) see **LEBENSZEICHEN** • 1967
SIGNS OF NIGHT • 1988 • Kokkinopoulos Panos • GRC • SCARS OF THE NIGHT
SIGNS OF THE TIMES • 1961 • Craig Ray • SHT • USA
SIGNS OF THE ZODIAC, THE see **SIGNOS DEL ZODIACO, LOS** • 1962
SIGNS OF TROUBLE • 1917 • Bailey William • SHT • USA
SIGNS ON THE ROAD see **ZNAKI NA DRODZE** • 1971
SIGNUM LAUDIS • 1979 • Holly Martin • CZC
SIGUEME CORAZON • 1951 • de Anda Raul • MXC
SIGUIENDO PISTAS • 1959 • Gomez Urquiza Zacarias • MXC
SIGURD DRAKEDREPER • 1988 • Jorfald Knut W., Rasmussen Lars • NRW • SIGURD THE DRAGONSLAYER
SIGURD THE DRAGONSLAYER see **SIGURD DRAKEDREPER** • 1988

SIJE • 1971 • Babic Nikola • SHT • YGS
SIJILLUS AMAL • 1974 • Nahhass Hashim An- • SHT • EGY • BILAN DE TRAVAIL
SIKANDAR • 1941 • Kapoor Prithviraj, Modi Sohrab M. • IND • ALEXANDER THE GREAT
SIKATOR • 1966 • Renyi Tamas • HNG • DEADLOCK
SIKER: CIRKUSZ • 1970 • Macskassy Gyula, Varnai Gyorgy • ANS • HNG • SUCCESS: THE CIRCUS
SIKHS, THE • 1979 • Singh Hardev • DOC • CND
SIKIT PUNYA GILA • 1982 • Ismail Raja • MLY
SIKKIM, TERRE SECRETE • 1957 • Bourguignon Serge • DOC • FRN
SIKKIN • 1971 • Ray Satyajit • DOC • IND
SIKKIN, AS- • 1970 • Hamada Khalid • SYR • KNIFE, THE
SIKO HOREPSE SITAKI • 1967 • Stratzalis Kostas • GRC • LET'S DANCE THE SIRTAKI
SIKUSILARMIUT • 1974 • Raymont Peter • DOC • CND
S'IL VOUS PLAIT.. LA MER? • 1979 • Lancelot Martine • FRN
SILAHA YEMINLIYDIM • 1965 • Inci Kemal • TRK
SILAHLARI ELLERINDE OLDULER • 1967 • Tuna Feyzi • TRK • THEY DIED WITH THEIR GUNS ON
SILAHLARIN KANUNU • 1966 • Atadeniz Yilmaz • TRK
SILAHLI PAZAZADE see **PASAZADE** • 1967
SILAHSIZ DOGUSELIM • 1967 • Olgac Bilge • TRK • LET US FIGHT WITHOUT ARMS
SILAS AT THE SEASIDE • 1916 • Evans Joe • UKN
SILAS MARNER • 1911 • Marston Theodore • USA
SILAS MARNER • 1913 • Brabin Charles J. • USA
SILAS MARNER • 1916 • Warde Ernest C. • USA
SILAS MARNER • 1985 • Foster Giles • TVM • UKN
SILAS Q. PINCH, SENSATIONALIST • 1914 • *Solograph* • UKN
SILAS SIMPLE'S LOVE AFFAIR • 1915 • *Piccadilly* • UKN
SILAS WARNER • 1911 • *Vitagraph* • USA
SILBERKONIG 1, DER • 1921 • Lund Erik • FRG • 13. MARZ, DER
SILBERKONIG 2, DER • 1921 • Lund Erik • FRG • MANN DER TAT, DER
SILBERKONIG 3, DER • 1921 • Lund Erik • FRG • CLAIM 36
SILBERKONIG 4, DER • 1921 • Lund Erik • FRG • ROCHESTERSTREET 29
SILBERMOVE, DIE • 1921 • Sauer Fred • FRG
SILBERNE FESSEL, DIE • 1920 • Illes Eugen • FRG
SILBERNE KUGEL, DIE • 1915 • Oswald Richard • FRG
SILBERTUNNEL, DER • 1915 • Delmont Joseph • FRG
SILENCE • Muresan Mircea • RMN
SILENCE • 1915 • *American* • USA
SILENCE • 1926 • Brooke Hugh, Greenidge John • UKN
SILENCE • 1926 • Julian Rupert • USA
SILENCE • 1931 • Gasnier Louis J., Marcin Max • USA
SILENCE • 1962 • Topouzanov Christo • ANS • BUL
SILENCE • 1964 • Basov Vladimir • USS
SILENCE • 1970 • Engel Jules • SHT • USA
SILENCE • 1974 • Korty John • USA • CRAZY JACK AND THE BOY ○ CRY SILENCE
SILENCE • 1990 • Hosseini Ali Sajjadi • IRN
SILENCE see **DERNIERE BERCEUSE, LA** • 1930
SILENCE see **TISHINA** • 1964
SILENCE! see **SAMAA HOUSS!** • 1989
SILENCE see **TISHINA** • 1990
SILENCE, LE • 1920 • Delluc Louis • FRN
SILENCE, THE • 1975 • Hardy Joseph • TVM • USA
SILENCE, THE (UKN) see **MILCZENIE** • 1963
SILENCE, THE (UKN) see **TYSTNADEN** • 1963
SILENCE, THE (USA) see **TWO MINUTES** • 1939
SILENCE AND CRY (USA) see **CSEND ES KIALTAS** • 1968
SILENCE D'AILLEURS, LE • 1990 • Mouyal Guy • FRN
SILENCE DANS LA FORET, LE see **SCHWEIGEN IM WALDE, DAS** • 1929
SILENCE DE LA MER, LE • 1947 • Melville Jean-Pierre • FRN
SILENCE DE MORT see **VIE PERDU, UNE** • 1933
SILENCE DES ORGANES, LE • 1975 • Cristiani Jean-Noel • DOC • FRN
SILENCE EST D'OR, LE • 1946 • Clair Rene • FRN • MAN ABOUT TOWN (USA) ○ SILENCE IS GOLDEN
SILENCE ET FEUDE BROUSSE • 1973 • de Medeiros Ricardo Beby • BNN
SILENCE FOR SILENCE • 1913 • *Lubin* • USA
SILENCE HAS NO WINGS (USA) see **TOBENAI CHINMOKU** • 1966
SILENCE IN THE NORTH see **SILENCE OF THE NORTH** • 1981
SILENCE IS GOLDEN see **SILENCE EST D'OR, LE** • 1946
SILENCE IS KILLING • 1976 • Muller John • MTV • CND
SILENCE OF CHRISTINE M., THE see **STILTE ROND CHRISTINE M., DE** • 1982
SILENCE OF DEAN MAITLAND • 1914 • Longford Raymond • ASL
SILENCE OF DEAN MAITLAND, THE • 1934 • Hall Ken G. • ASL
SILENCE OF DR. EVANS, THE see **MOLCHANIYE DOKTORA IVENSA** • 1973
SILENCE OF DOCTOR IVENS, THE see **MOLCHANIYE DOKTORA IVENSA** • 1973
SILENCE OF DONALD LANG, THE see **DUMMY** • 1979
SILENCE OF JASPER HOLT, THE • 1915 • Collins Edwin J.? • UKN
SILENCE OF JOHN GORDON, THE • 1914 • Pollard Harry • USA
SILENCE OF MADNESS, THE see **GALSKAPENS STILLHET** • 1984
SILENCE OF MARTHA, THE see **MARTHA'S VINDICATION** • 1916
SILENCE OF RICHARD WILTON, THE • 1913 • Buckland Warwick? • UKN
SILENCE OF THE HEART • 1984 • Michaels Richard • TVM • USA
SILENCE OF THE HEART, THE see **GOLU HADAWATHA** • 1968
SILENCE OF THE LAMBS, THE • 1990 • Demme Jonathan • USA
SILENCE OF THE NORTH • 1981 • King Allan • CND • SILENCE IN THE NORTH ○ COMES A TIME
SILENCE.. ON TOURNE • 1976 • Coggio Roger • FRN
SILENCE SELLERS, THE • 1917 • King Burton L. • USA
SILENCE THE WITNESS see **TESTIMONE DEVE TACERE, IL** • 1974
SILENCE (USA) see **CHINMOKU** • 1972
SILENCER, THE • 1988 • Sotos Jim • USA
SILENCERS, THE • 1966 • Karlson Phil • USA
SILENCIEUX, LE • 1972 • Pinoteau Claude • FRN, ITL • UOMO CHE NON SEPPE TACERE, L' (ITL) ○ SILENT ONE, THE ○ ESCAPE TO NOWHERE ○ MAN WHO DIED TWICE, THE
SILENCIO • 1962 • Nunes Jose Maria • SPN
SILENCIO DE TUMBO, UN • 1972 • Franco Jesus • SPN
SILENCIO SUBLIME • 1935 • Peon Ramon • MXC
SILENCIOSO, EL • 1966 • Mariscal Alberto • MXC
SILENE SMUTNA PRINCEZNA • 1968 • Zeman Borivoj • CZC • EVER-SO-SAD PRINCESS, THE ○ MADLY SAD PRINCESS, THE ○ AWFULLY SAD PRINCESS, THE
SILENT ACCUSER, THE • 1914 • *Eclectic* • FRN
SILENT ACCUSER, THE • 1915 • Kaufman Joseph • USA
SILENT ACCUSER, THE • 1924 • Franklin Chester M. • USA
SILENT ACCUSER, THE see **LOVE PIRATE, THE** • 1923
SILENT ACTION see **POLIZIA ACCUSA: IL SERVIZIO SEGRETO UCCIDE, LA** • 1975
SILENT ASSASSINS • 1987 • Thomas Scott, Young Lee Doo • USA
SILENT AVENGER, THE • 1920 • Duncan William • SRL • USA
SILENT AVENGER, THE • 1927 • Hogan James P. • USA
SILENT BARRICADE, THE see **NEMA BARIKADA** • 1949
SILENT BARRIER, THE • 1920 • Worthington William • USA
SILENT BARRIERS (USA) see **GREAT BARRIER, THE** • 1937
SILENT BATTLE • 1963 • McCullough Chris • DOC • ASL
SILENT BATTLE, THE • 1915 • Kent Leon D. • USA
SILENT BATTLE, THE • 1916 • Conway Jack • USA
SILENT BATTLE, THE • 1939 • Mason Herbert • UKN • CONTINENTAL EXPRESS (USA)
SILENT BELL, THE see **MADEMOISELLE FIFI** • 1944
SILENT CALL, THE • 1912 • *Nestor* • USA
SILENT CALL, THE • 1912 • *Majestic* • USA
SILENT CALL, THE • 1921 • Trimble Larry • USA
SILENT CALL, THE • 1961 • Bushelman John • USA
SILENT CASTLE, THE • 1912 • *Gaumont* • FRN
SILENT CLUES see **MILCZACE SLADY** • 1961
SILENT CO-ED, THE • 1915 • *Falstaff* • USA
SILENT CODE, THE • 1935 • Paton Stuart • USA
SILENT COMMAND, THE • 1915 • Leonard Robert Z. • USA
SILENT COMMAND, THE • 1923 • Edwards J. Gordon • USA
SILENT CONFLICT • 1948 • Archainbaud George • USA
SILENT CRY see **NEMA KIALTAS** • 1982
SILENT CRY, THE • 1977 • Dwoskin Stephen • UKN, FRG, FRN
SILENT DEATH see **VOODOO ISLAND** • 1957
SILENT DEATH, THE • 1914 • Ridgely Richard • USA
SILENT DUEL see **DUEL I HESHTUR** • 1967
SILENT DUEL, THE see **SHIZUKANARU KETTO** • 1949
SILENT DUST • 1949 • Comfort Lance • UKN
SILENT ENEMY, THE • 1930 • Carver H. P. • USA
SILENT ENEMY, THE • 1958 • Fairchild William • UKN
SILENT EVIDENCE • 1922 • Calvert Charles • UKN
SILENT EVIDENCE (UKN) see **OUT WITH THE TIDE** • 1928
SILENT FLUTE, THE (UKN) see **CIRCLE OF IRON** • 1978
SILENT FLYER, THE • 1926 • Craft William James • SRL • USA
SILENT GIRLS, THE see **TAVSE PIGER, DE** • 1986
SILENT GUARDIAN, THE • 1926 • Bletcher William • USA
SILENT GUN, THE • 1969 • Caffey Michael • TVM • USA
SILENT GUN, THE see **SHOBUINU** • 1967
SILENT HERO, THE • 1927 • Worne Duke • USA • PHANTOM (UKN)
SILENT HERO, THE • 1988 • Driscoll Richard • USA, UKN • SILENT HEROES
SILENT HEROES • 1913 • Edwards Walter? • USA
SILENT HEROES see **SILENT HERO, THE** • 1988
SILENT HOUSE, THE • 1913 • *Ramo* • USA
SILENT HOUSE, THE • 1929 • Forde Walter • UKN
SILENT HUNT • 1990 • Poorahmad Kiumars • IRN
SILENT INVASION, THE • 1962 • Varnel Max • UKN
SILENT JIM • 1912 • *Francis Alec B.* • USA
SILENT JOY • 1986 • Hanak Dusan • CZC
SILENT KILL see **ASTRAL FACTOR** • 1976
SILENT KILLER FROM ETERNITY see **RETURN OF THE TIGER** • 1973
SILENT LADY, THE • 1917 • Wilson Elsie Jane • USA
SILENT LIE, THE • 1917 • Walsh Raoul • USA
SILENT LOVE see **TINGBUDAODE SHUOHUA** • 1985
SILENT LOVE, A see **STILLE LIEFDE, EEN** • 1977
SILENT LOVER, THE • 1926 • Archainbaud George • USA • MEN OF THE DAWN
SILENT LOVERS, THE • 1980 • Erman John • TVM • USA
SILENT MADNESS • 1984 • Nuchtern Simon • USA • NIGHT KILLER ○ OMEGA FACTOR
SILENT MAJORITY, THE see **TAUSE FLERTALL, DET** • 1977
SILENT MAN, THE • 1915 • Kent Leon D. • USA
SILENT MAN, THE • 1916 • Baggot King • SHT • USA • SILENT STRANGER, THE
SILENT MAN, THE • 1917 • Hart William S. • USA
SILENT MAN OF TIMBER GULCH, THE • 1916 • Leonard Robert Z. • SHT • USA
SILENT MASTER, THE • 1917 • Perret Leonce • USA
SILENT MEMBER, THE • 1916 • Leonard Robert Z. • USA
SILENT MEN • 1933 • Lederman D. Ross • USA
SILENT MESSAGE, THE • 1910 • *Anderson Broncho Billy* • USA
SILENT MESSENGER, THE • 1914 • *Hunter Alison* • UKN
SILENT MESSENGER, THE • 1914 • Hamilton G. P.? • USA
SILENT MOVIE • 1976 • Brooks Mel • USA
SILENT MURDER, THE see **SHIZUKANARU KYODEN** • 1959
SILENT MUSIC • Albers Rudy • SHT • USA
SILENT MUTUAL ELECTION see **SHIZUKA GOSEN** • 1938
SILENT MYSTERY, THE • 1918 • Ford Francis • SRL • USA
SILENT NIGHT see **CICHA NOC** • 1978
SILENT NIGHT see **MAGDALENE** • 1989
SILENT NIGHT, BLOODY NIGHT • 1972 • Gershuny Theodore • USA • NIGHT OF THE DARK FULL MOON ○ ZORA ○ DEATH HOUSE
SILENT NIGHT, DEADLY NIGHT • 1984 • Sellier Charles E. Jr. • USA
SILENT NIGHT, DEADLY NIGHT PART II • 1987 • Harry Lee • USA
SILENT NIGHT, EVIL NIGHT see **BLACK CHRISTMAS** • 1975
SILENT NIGHT, LONELY NIGHT • 1969 • Petrie Daniel • TVM • USA
SILENT NUMBER • 1973 • Rubie Howard • MTV • ASL
SILENT ONE, THE • 1984 • Mackay Yvonne • NZL
SILENT ONE, THE see **SILENCIEUX, LE** • 1972
SILENT PAL • 1925 • McCarty Henry • USA
SILENT PARTNER • 1944 • Blair George • USA
SILENT PARTNER, THE • 1917 • Neilan Marshall • USA
SILENT PARTNER, THE • 1923 • Maigne Charles • USA
SILENT PARTNER, THE • 1927 • Wyler William • SHT • USA
SILENT PARTNER, THE • 1978 • Duke Daryl • CND • ARGENT DE LA BANQUE, L' ○ DOUBLE DEADLY
SILENT PASSENGER, THE • 1935 • Denham Reginald • UKN
SILENT PATHS, THE see **MALCHALIVITE PATEKI** • 1967
SILENT PERIL, THE • 1914 • *Walcamp Marie* • USA
SILENT PLANET, THE see **SCHWEIGENDE STERN, DER** • 1960
SILENT PLANET, THE see **SCHWEIGENDE STERN, DER** • 1960
SILENT PLAYGROUND, THE • 1963 • Goulder Stanley • UKN
SILENT PLEA, THE • 1915 • Belmore Lionel • USA
SILENT POWER, THE • 1926 • O'Connor Frank • USA
SILENT PRISONER, THE • 1917 • *Grandin Ethel* • SHT • USA
SILENT RAGE • 1982 • Miller Michael • USA
SILENT RAID, THE see **OVERVAL, DE** • 1963
SILENT RAIDERS • 1954 • Bartlett Richard • USA
SILENT REACH • 1982 • Rubie Howard • MTV • ASL
SILENT REBELLION see **MY PALIKARI** • 1982
SILENT RIDER, THE • 1918 • Smith Cliff • USA
SILENT RIDER, THE • 1927 • Reynolds Lynn • USA
SILENT ROAD • 1962 • Rotha Paul • UKN
SILENT ROLL CALL, THE see **NIJEMA PROZIVKA** • 1974
SILENT RUINS • Homoki-Nagy Istvan • DOC • HNG
SILENT RUNNING • 1972 • Trumbull Douglas • USA • RUNNING SILENT
SILENT SALESMAN, THE • 1974 • Robertson Michael • DOC • ASL
SILENT SANDERSON • 1925 • Dunlap Scott R. • USA
SILENT SANDY • 1914 • Kirkwood James • USA
SILENT SCREAM • 1979 • Harris Denny • USA
SILENT SCREAM • 1990 • Hayman David • UKN
SILENT SCREAM, THE • 1980 • Gibson Alan • TVM • UKN
SILENT SELBY • 1916 • Chatterton Thomas • SHT • USA
SILENT SENTENCE • 1983 • Spangler Larry • USA
SILENT SENTENCE see **KNIFE FOR THE LADIES, A** • 1973
SILENT SENTINEL • 1929 • Neitz Alvin J. • USA
SILENT SENTINEL, THE • 1918 • Harvey Harry • SHT • USA
SILENT SHAME, THE • 1916 • McGill Lawrence?, Hansel Howell? • SHT • USA
SILENT SHELDON • 1925 • Webb Harry S. • USA
SILENT SIGNAL, THE • 1911 • Blache Alice • USA
SILENT SIGNAL, THE • 1912 • *Phillips L. C.* • USA
SILENT SONG • 1967 • Jarrott Charles • MTV • UKN
SILENT SOUND SENSE STARS SUBOTNICK & SENDER • 1962 • Brakhage Stan • SHT • USA
SILENT STRANGER, THE • 1924 • Rogell Albert S. • USA • STEP DOWN TO TERROR (UKN)
SILENT STRANGER, THE • 1975 • Vanzi Luigi • ITL
SILENT STRANGER, THE see **SILENT MAN, THE** • 1916
SILENT STRANGER, THE (UKN) see **STEP DOWN TO TERROR** • 1958
SILENT STRENGTH • 1919 • Scardon Paul • USA
SILENT TEMPEST, THE • 1989 • Yalcin Oguz • TRK
SILENT TONGUE, THE • 1911 • Merwin Bannister • USA
SILENT TONGUE, THE • 1915 • Louis Will • USA
SILENT TRAIL • 1928 • McGowan J. P. • USA
SILENT TRAIL, THE • 1916 • Bartlett Charles • SHT • USA
SILENT TRAILS • 1914 • Sturgeon Rollin S. • USA
SILENT TWEETMENT • 1946 • Wickersham Bob • ANS • USA
SILENT VALLEY • 1935 • Ray Bernard B. • USA
SILENT VALLEY, THE • 1914 • Baggot King • USA
SILENT VICTORY: THE KITTY O'NEIL STORY • 1979 • Antonio Lou • TVM • USA
SILENT VILLAGE, THE • 1943 • Jennings Humphrey • UKN
SILENT VOICE see **AMAZING GRACE AND CHUCK** • 1987
SILENT VOICE, THE • 1915 • Bowman William J., Balshofer Fred J. • USA
SILENT VOICE, THE see **MAN WHO PLAYED GOD, THE** • 1922
SILENT VOICE, THE (UKN) see **MAN WHO PLAYED GOD, THE** • 1932
SILENT VOICE, THE (UKN) see **PAULA** • 1952
SILENT VOW, THE • 1922 • Duncan William • USA
SILENT W, THE • 1915 • North Wilfred • USA
SILENT WARNING, THE • 1913 • *Kalem* • USA
SILENT WATCHER, THE • 1924 • Lloyd Frank • USA
SILENT WAY, THE • 1914 • Otto Henry • USA
SILENT WEAPON, THE • 1961 • Duffell Peter • UKN
SILENT WEEK IN THE HOUSE see **TICHY TYDEN V DOME** • 1969
SILENT WIFE • 1965 • Li Hsing • HKG
SILENT WIRES • 1924 • *Hutchison Charles* • USA
SILENT WITNESS • 1917 • Lambart Harry?, Bacon Gerald F.? • USA
SILENT WITNESS • 1932 • Varnel Marcel, Hough R. Lee • USA
SILENT WITNESS • 1942 • Yarbrough Jean • USA • ATTORNEY FOR THE DEFENCE (UKN)
SILENT WITNESS • 1985 • Miller Michael • TVM • USA
SILENT WITNESS, A • 1912 • Barrett Franklyn • ASL
SILENT WITNESS, A • 1913 • Wilson Frank? • UKN
SILENT WITNESS, THE • 1912 • *Heming Violet* • USA
SILENT WITNESS, THE • 1914 • *Victor* • USA
SILENT WITNESS, THE • 1914 • Edwards Walter? • *Broncho* • USA
SILENT WITNESS, THE • 1915 • *Reliance* • USA
SILENT WITNESS, THE • 1954 • Tully Montgomery • UKN
SILENT WITNESS, THE • 1962 • Kennedy Ken • USA
SILENT WITNESS, THE • 1978 • Wolfe David W. • DOC • USA
SILENT WITNESS (UKN) see **SECRETS OF A CO-ED** • 1943
SILENT WOMAN, THE • 1918 • Blache Herbert • USA
SILENT WORLD, THE see **MONDE DU SILENCE, LE** • 1956
SILENT YEARS • 1921 • Gasnier Louis J. • USA • MA'MSELLE JO
SILENTLY I SCREAM • 1972 • *Mar Sally* • USA
SILENY KANKAN • 1982 • Balik Jaroslav • CZC, AUS • CRAZY CAN-CAN, THE
SILENZIO see **CANZONE DELL'AMORE, LA** • 1930

SILENZIO: SI GIRA! • 1944 • Campogalliani Carlo • ITL • MUSICA PER TUTTI
SILENZIO.. SI SPARA (ITL) see **CA VA BARDER** • 1954
SILENZIO: SI UCCIDE • 1972 • Zurli Guido • ITL
SILESIA IN BLACK AND GREEN see **KONCERT NA EKRENIE SLASK** • 1956
SILFURTUNGLID • 1978 • Gunnlaugsson Hrafn • MTV • ICL • SILVER MOON
SILHOUETTE DES TEUFELS, DIE • 1917 • May Joe • FRG
SILHOUETTEN • 1936 • Reiniger Lotte • ANS • FRG
SILHOUETTEN AAN DE HORIZON • 1966 • Moonen Jan • NTH
SILHOUETTENSCHNEIDER, DER • 1920 • Frowein Eberhard • FRG
SILHOUETTES • 1908 • *Pathe* • FRN
SILHOUETTES • 1936 • Reisch Walter • USA
SILHOUETTES see **SILOUETTES** • 1968
SILHUETAS DA VIDA • 1955 • Mendes Joao • SHT • PRT
SILICATES, THE see **ISLAND OF TERROR** • 1965
SILJA -FALLEN ASLEEP WHEN YOUNG see **NUORENA NUKKUNUT** • 1937
SILJA -FALLEN ASLEEP WHEN YOUNG see **SILJA -NUORENA NUKKUNUT** • 1956
SILJA -NUORENA NUKKUNUT • 1956 • Witikka Jack • FNL • SILJA -FALLEN ASLEEP WHEN YOUNG
SILK • 1986 • Santiago Cirio H. • USA
SILK, BLOOD AND SUN see **SEDA, SANGRE Y SOL** • 1941
SILK BOUQUET, THE • 1926 • *Wong Anna May* • USA • DRAGON HORSE, THE
SILK EXPRESS, THE • 1933 • Enright Ray • USA
SILK HAT HARRY • 1918 • La Cava Gregory • ASS • USA
SILK HAT KID • 1935 • Humberstone H. Bruce • USA
SILK HOSE AND HIGH PRESSURE • 1915 • Lehrman Henry • USA
SILK HOSIERY • 1921 • Niblo Fred • USA
SILK HUSBANDS AND CALICO WIVES • 1920 • Green Alfred E. • USA
SILK LEGS • 1927 • Rosson Arthur • USA
SILK-LINED BURGLAR, THE • 1919 • Dillon John Francis • USA
SILK NOOSE, THE (USA) see **NOOSE, THE** • 1948
SILK STOCKING ROMANCE, A • 1915 • *Deer* • USA
SILK STOCKING SAL • 1924 • Browning Tod • USA
SILK STOCKINGS • 1920 • *Ovey George* • USA
SILK STOCKINGS • 1927 • Ruggles Wesley • USA
SILK STOCKINGS • 1957 • Mamoulian Rouben • USA
SILKEN AFFAIR, THE • 1956 • Kellino Roy • UKN
SILKEN LADY, THE (UKN) see **LIFE'S CROSSROADS** • 1928
SILKEN PUSSYCAT, THE • 1977 • Chinn Robert C. • USA • JADE PUSSYCAT, THE
SILKEN SHACKLES • 1926 • Morosco Walter • USA
SILKEN SKIN see **PEAU DOUCE, LA** • 1964
SILKEN SPIDER, THE • 1916 • Borzage Frank • SHT • USA
SILKEN THREADS • 1928 • Eveleigh Leslie • UKN
SILKLESS BANK NOTE, THE • 1920 • Cooper J. Gordon, Harbaugh Carl • SHT • USA
SILKS AND SADDLES • 1921 • Wells John • ASL
SILKS AND SADDLES • 1929 • Hill Robert F. • USA • THOROUGHBREDS (UKN) ○ FROG, THE
SILKS AND SADDLES • 1936 • Hill Robert F. • USA • COLLEGE RACEHORSE (UKN)
SILKS AND SATINS • 1916 • Dawley J. Searle • USA
SILKS AND SULKIES • 1950 • Petel Pierre • DCS • CND • COURSES SOUS HARNAIS
SILKWOOD • 1983 • Nichols Mike • USA • CHAIN REACTION
SILLONS D'AFRIQUE • 1943 • Tedesco Jean • SHT • FRN
SILLY BILLIES • 1936 • Guiol Fred • USA • WILD WEST, THE
SILLY HILLBILLY • 1949 • Sparber I. • ANS • USA
SILLY SAMMY • 1911 • Stow Percy • UKN
SILLY SCANDALS • 1931 • Fleischer Dave • ANS • USA
SILLY SCIENCE • 1960 • Kneitel Seymour • ANS • USA
SILLY SEALS • 1938 • Kline Lester • ANS • USA
SILLY SEX, THE • 1913 • *Reliance* • USA
SILLY SULTAN, A • 1916 • Chaudet Louis W. • SHT • USA
SILLY SUPERSTITION • 1939 • Gillett Burt • ANS • USA
SILLY SYMPHONY • *Disney Walt (P)* • ASS • USA
SILLY YOUNGER BROTHER AND CLEVER ELDER BROTHER see **GUTEI KENKEI** • 1931
SILNICE SPIVA • 1937 • *Hammid Alexander* • CZC • HIGHWAY SINGS, THE
SILNYI CHELOVEK • 1916 • USS • STRONG MAN, THE
SILNYYE DUKHOM • 1967 • Georgiev Viktor • USS • STRONG IN SPIRIT
SILOM OTAC • 1970 • Jovanovic Soja • YGS • FATHER BY FORCE
SILOUETTES • 1968 • Zois Kostis • GRC • SILHOUETTES
SILT • 1931 • Birt Daniel • DCS • UKN
SILTALAN PEHTOORI • 1933 • Orko Risto • FNL • STEWARD OF SILTALA, THE
SILURAMENTO DELL'OCEANIA, IL • 1917 • Genina Augusto • ITL
SILURI UMANI • 1955 • Leonviola Antonio • ITL
SILVER BADGE COMEDIES • 1920 • Ross Jack • SER • UKN
SILVER BANDIT, THE • 1950 • Clifton Elmer • USA
SILVER BEARS • 1977 • Passer Ivan • USA, UKN
SILVER BELL, THE • 1914 • *Ray Charles* • USA
SILVER BLAZE • 1912 • Treville Georges • UKN
SILVER BLAZE • 1923 • Ridgwell George • UKN
SILVER BLAZE • 1937 • Bentley Thomas • UKN • MURDER AT THE BASKERVILLES (USA)
SILVER BOOTS see **GIN NO BOOTS** • 1967
SILVER BRIDGE, THE • 1920 • Cairns Dallas • UKN
SILVER BUDDHA, THE • 1923 • Coleby A. E. • UKN
SILVER BULLET • 1949 • *Universal* • SHT • USA
SILVER BULLET • 1985 • Attias Daniel • USA • STEPHEN KING'S SILVER BULLET
SILVER BULLET, THE • 1935 • Ray Bernard B. • USA
SILVER BULLET, THE • 1942 • Lewis Joseph H. • USA
SILVER BUTTE • 1949 • Cowan Will • SHT • USA
SILVER CANDLESTICKS, THE • 1914 • *Kb* • USA
SILVER CANYON • 1951 • English John • USA
SILVER CAR, THE • 1921 • Smith David • USA
SILVER CHAINS (UKN) see **KID FROM AMARILLO, THE** • 1951
SILVER CHALICE, THE • 1954 • Saville Victor • USA
SILVER CIGARETTE CASE, THE • 1913 • Brooke Van Dyke • USA
SILVER CITY • 1951 • Haskin Byron • USA • HIGH VERMILION (UKN)
SILVER CITY • 1968 • Wenders Wim • SHT • FRG
SILVER CITY • 1984 • Turkiewicz Sophia • ASL
SILVER CITY BONANZA • 1951 • Blair George • USA
SILVER CITY KID • 1944 • English John • USA
SILVER CITY RAIDERS • 1943 • Berke William • USA • LEGAL LARCENY (UKN)
SILVER CITY (UKN) see **ALBUQUERQUE** • 1948
SILVER CLOUD'S SACRIFICE • 1910 • *Kalem* • USA
SILVER COMES THROUGH • 1927 • Ingraham Lloyd • USA • SILVER KING COMES THRU ○ SILVER COMES THRU
SILVER COMES THRU see **SILVER COMES THROUGH** • 1927
SILVER CORD, THE • 1933 • Cromwell John • USA
SILVER CROSS, THE • 1913 • *Solax* • USA
SILVER DARLINGS, THE • 1947 • Elder Clarence, Evans Clifford • UKN
SILVER DEVIL (UKN) see **WILD HORSE** • 1930
SILVER DOLLAR • 1932 • Green Alfred E. • USA
SILVER DOLLAR, THE • 1909 • *Lubin* • USA
SILVER DOUBLE SUICIDE see **SHIROGANE SHINJU** • 1956
SILVER DRAGON NINJA • Kong Don • HKG
SILVER DREAM RACER • 1980 • Wickes David • UKN
SILVER DUST see **SEREBRISTAYA PYL** • 1953
SILVER FINGERS • 1926 • McGowan J. P. • USA
SILVER FLEET, THE • 1943 • Sewell Vernon, Wellesley Gordon • UKN
SILVER FOX, THE see **SREBURNATA LISITSA** • 1990
SILVER FOX AND SAM DAVENPORT, THE • 1962 • Schloss Henry • USA
SILVER FROM ACROSS THE BORDER see **HOPEAA RAJAN TAKAA** • 1963
SILVER GIRL, THE • 1919 • Keenan Frank, Howe Eliot • USA
SILVER GLOBE, THE see **NA SREBRNYM GLOBIE** • 1977
SILVER GOAT, THE see **EZUST KECSKE, AZ** • 1916
SILVER GREYHOUND, THE • 1919 • Merwin Bannister • UKN
SILVER GREYHOUND, THE • 1932 • McGann William • UKN
SILVER GRINDSTONE, THE • 1913 • Duncan William • USA
SILVER HAIRPIN, A • NKR
SILVER HERMIT FROM SHAOLIN TEMPLE • 1985 • Roc T'len • HKG
SILVER HORDE, THE • 1920 • Lloyd Frank • USA
SILVER HORDE, THE • 1930 • Archainbaud George • USA
SILVER KEY, THE (UKN) see **GIRL IN THE CASE** • 1944
SILVER KING, THE • 1919 • Irving George • USA
SILVER KING, THE • 1929 • Hunter T. Hayes • UKN
SILVER KING COMES THRU see **SILVER COMES THROUGH** • 1927
SILVER LINING see **LOOK FOR THE SILVER LINING** • 1949
SILVER LINING, THE • 1910 • *Nestor* • USA
SILVER LINING, THE • 1911 • Haldane Bert • UKN
SILVER LINING, THE • 1914 • *Balboa* • USA
SILVER LINING, THE • 1915 • Eason B. Reeves • USA
SILVER LINING, THE • 1919 • Coleby A. E. • UKN
SILVER LINING, THE • 1921 • West Roland • USA
SILVER LINING, THE • 1927 • Bentley Thomas • UKN
SILVER LINING, THE • 1932 • Crosland Alan • UKN • THIRTY DAYS
SILVER LODE • 1954 • Dwan Allan • USA
SILVER LOVING CUP, THE • 1914 • Crane Frank H. • USA
SILVER MEDAL OF LOVE see **KOINA NO GINPEI** • 1961
SILVER MOON see **SILFURTUNGLID** • 1978
SILVER MOON'S RESCUE • 1912 • *Pathe* • USA
SILVER MOUTH see **SOLVMUNN** • 1982
SILVER NEEDLE IN THE SKY • 1954 • *Reed Roland (P)* • MTV • USA
SILVER ON THE SAGE • 1939 • Selander Lesley • USA
SILVER OX see **BOI DE PRATA** • 1982
SILVER-PLATED GUN, THE • 1913 • Dwan Allan • USA
SILVER PLUME MINE • 1910 • *Nestor* • USA
SILVER QUEEN • 1942 • Bacon Lloyd • USA
SILVER RAIDERS • 1950 • Fox Wallace • USA
SILVER RANGE • 1946 • Hillyer Lambert • USA
SILVER RIVER • 1948 • Walsh Raoul • USA
SILVER ROSARY, THE • 1928 • Clift Denison • UKN
SILVER SANDS (UKN) see **WESTERN CARAVANS** • 1939
SILVER SCREEN • 1989 • Parry Michael • USA
SILVER SKATES • 1943 • Goodwins Leslie • USA
SILVER SKATES, THE see **HANS BRINKER** • 1979
SILVER SKIES see **STRIBRNA OBLAKA** • 1938
SILVER SLAVE, THE • 1927 • Bretherton Howard • USA
SILVER SLIPPERS see **CHEREVICHKI** • 1945
SILVER SNUFF BOX, THE • 1914 • Marston Theodore • USA
SILVER SOIL • 1939 • Heyer John • DOC • ASL
SILVER SPOON, THE • 1934 • King George • UKN
SILVER SPURS • 1922 • McCarty Henry, Meehan James Leo • USA
SILVER SPURS • 1936 • Taylor Ray • USA
SILVER SPURS • 1943 • Kane Joseph • USA
SILVER STALLION • 1941 • Finney Edward • USA
SILVER STAR, THE • 1955 • Bartlett Richard • USA
SILVER STREAK • 1976 • Hiller Arthur • USA
SILVER STREAK, THE • 1935 • Atkins Thomas
SILVER STREAK, THE • 1945 • Donnelly Eddie • ANS • USA
SILVER TAIL AND HIS SQUAW • 1911 • *Powers* • USA
SILVER TENOR: OR, THE SONG THAT FAILED, THE • 1904 • Collins Alf • UKN
SILVER THREADS • 1961 • Kollanyi Agoston • HNG
SILVER THREADS AMONG THE GOLD • 1911 • Porter Edwin S. • USA
SILVER THREADS AMONG THE GOLD • 1915 • Kingsley Pierce • USA
SILVER THREADS AMONG THE GOLD • 1921 • Rowden W. C. • SHT • UKN
SILVER TONGUED ORATOR, THE • 1913 • *Cruze James* • USA
SILVER TOP • 1938 • King George • UKN
SILVER TRAIL, THE • 1937 • Ray Bernard B. • USA
SILVER TRAILS • 1948 • Cabanne W. Christy • USA
SILVER TREASURE, THE • 1926 • Lee Rowland V. • USA • NOSTROMO
SILVER VALLEY • 1927 • Stoloff Ben • USA
SILVER WEDDING, THE • 1906 • *Am & B* • USA
SILVER WHIP, THE • 1953 • Jones Harmon • USA
SILVER WIND, THE see **STRIBRNY VITR** • 1954
SILVER WINGS • 1922 • Carewe Edwin, Ford John • USA
SILVER WING'S DREAM • 1911 • *Bison* • USA
SILVER WING'S TWO SUITORS • 1912 • *Pathe* • USA
SILVER WOLF, THE • 1916 • SAF
SILVERADO • 1985 • Kasdan Lawrence • USA
SILVERFISH KING, THE • 1974 • Sauer John, Sauer Pat • USA
SILVERIA • 1958 • Silos Octavio • PHL
SILVERSMITH AND I, THE see **PLATERO Y YO** • 1968
SILVERTIP see **I SLAGBJORNENS SPAR** • 1931
SILVERY DUST • 1951 • USS
SILVERY MOON • 1933 • Foster John, Davis Mannie • ANS • USA
SILVERY WIND, THE see **STRIBRNY VITR** • 1954
SILVESTERNACHT AM ALEXANDERPLATZ • 1939 • Schneider-Edenkoben Richard • FRG
SILVESTERPUNSCH • 1960 • Reisch Gunter • GDR • NEW YEAR PUNCHBOWL
SILVESTRE • 1980 • Monteiro Joao Cesar • PRT • SYLVESTER
SILVIA AND LOVE see **SILVIA E L'AMORE** • 1968
SILVIA E L'AMORE • 1968 • Bergonzelli Sergio • ITL • SILVIA AND LOVE
SILVIO • 1981 • Cespedes Leonardo, Soto Juan, Ocampo Gaston • DOC • SWD
SILVIO PELLICO IL MARTIRE DELLO SPIETZBERG • 1915 • Pavanelli Livio • ITL
SIM TJONG • 1970 • Shin Sang-Okk • HKG
SIMAO BOLANDA'S CRIME see **CRIME DE SIMAO BOLANDAS, O** • 1980
SIMAO O CAOLHO • 1952 • Cavalcanti Alberto • BRZ • SIMON THE ONE-EYED (USA)
SIMARRON BROTHERS • 1968 • Cayado Tony • PHL
SIMBA • 1955 • Hurst Brian Desmond • UKN
SIMBA, THE KING OF BEASTS see **SIMBA, THE KING OF BEASTS: A SAGA OF THE AFRICAN VELDT** • 1928
SIMBA, THE KING OF BEASTS: A SAGA OF THE AFRICAN VELDT • 1928 • Johnson Martin E. • DOC • USA • SIMBA, THE KING OF BEASTS
SIMBAD E IL CALIFFO DI BAGDAD • 1973 • Francisci Pietro • ITL
SIMBAD EL MAREADO • 1950 • Martinez Solares Gilberto • MXC
SIMBATA MORTILOR • 1968 • Calotescu Virgil • RMN • ALL SOULS DAY
SIMCHON FAMILY, THE (USA) see **MISHPACHAT SIMCHON** • 1964
SIMENON • 1967 • Bonniere Rene • DCS • CND
SIMFONIJA LJUBVI ISMERTI • 1914 • Tourjansky Victor • USS • SYMPHONY OF LOVE AND DEATH
SIMFONIYA DONBASA see **ENTUZIAZM** • 1931
SIMHA SWAPNA • 1968 • Subba Rao W. R. • IND • NIGHTMARE
SIMHASAN • 1979 • Patel Jabbar • IND
SIMILTUDE DES LONGUEURS ET DES VITESSES • 1958 • Painleve Jean • SHT • FRN
SIMIO BLANCO, EL • 1974 • *Conacine* • MXC
SIMITRIO • 1960 • Gomez Muriel Emilio • MXC • JUEGO DE NINOS
SIMME 'E NAPULE, PAISA see **TORNA A NAPOLI** • 1949
S'IMMOLER DANS L'OMBRE • 1953 • Lavoie Hermenegilde • DOC • CND
SIMON • 1956 • Zadek Peter • SHT • UKN
SIMON • 1962 • Grospierre Louis • SHT • FRN
SIMON • 1980 • Brickman Marshall • USA
SIMON AND LAURA • 1955 • Box Muriel • UKN
SIMON BEYERS • 1947 • SAF
SIMON BLANCO • 1974 • *Aguilar* • MXC
SIMON BOLIVAR • 1941 • Contreras Torres Miguel • MXC • LIFE OF SIMON BOLIVAR, THE (USA)
SIMON BOLIVAR • 1968 • Blasetti Alessandro • ITL, SPN, VNZ • EPOPEYA DE SIMON BOLIVAR, LA
SIMON, CONTAMOS CONTIGO • 1972 • Fernandez Ramon • SPN
SIMON DEL DESIERTO • 1965 • Bunuel Luis • MXC • SIMON OF THE DESERT (USA) ○ SAN SIMEON DEL DESIERTO ○ SAINT SIMEON OF THE DESERT
SIMON FROM BACKABO see **SIMON I BACKABO** • 1934
SIMON I BACKABO • 1934 • Edgren Gustaf • SWD • SIMON FROM BACKABO
SIMON, KING OF THE WITCHES • 1971 • Kessler Bruce • USA
SIMON MENYHERT SZULTESE • 1954 • Varkonyi Zoltan • HNG • BIRTH OF MENYHERT SIMON, THE
SIMON OF THE DESERT (USA) see **SIMON DEL DESIERTO** • 1965
SIMON, SIMON • 1970 • Stark Graham • UKN
SIMON SYNDAREN • 1955 • Hellstrom Gunnar • SWD • SIMON THE SINNER
SIMON THE CELLARER • 1899 • *Wolff Philipp* • UKN
SIMON THE CELLARER • 1902 • Moss Hugh • SHT • UKN
SIMON THE JESTER • 1915 • Jose Edward • USA
SIMON THE JESTER • 1925 • Melford George • USA
SIMON THE MONK • 1930 • *Sullivan-Powers* • ASS • USA
SIMON THE ONE-EYED (USA) see **SIMAO O CAOLHO** • 1952
SIMON THE SINNER see **SIMON SYNDAREN** • 1955
SIMON THE SWISS (UKN) see **VOYOU, LE** • 1970
SIMONA • 1974 • Longchamps Patrick • ITL, BLG • HISTOIRE DE L'OEIL, L' (BLG) ○ STORY OF THE EYE, THE
SIMONA UN CORPO PER TUTTI see **MIA MOGLIE UN CORPO PER L'AMORE** • 1972
SIMONE • 1918 • de Morlhon Camille • FRN
SIMONE BARBES OU LA VERTU • 1979 • Treilhou Marie-Claude • FRN
SIMONE DE BEAUVOIR • 1978 • Dayan Josee, Ribowska Malka • DOC • FRN
SIMONE E MATTEO UN GIOCO DA RAGAZZI • 1975 • Carnimeo Giuliano • ITL
SIMONE EST COMME CA • 1932 • Anton Karl • FRN
SIMONE EVRARD: OR, DEATHLESS DEVOTION • 1923 • Greenwood Edwin • UKN
SIMONE MARTINI • 1957 • Andreassi Raffaele • SHT • ITL
SIMON'S SWIMMING SOUL-MATE • 1915 • *Hastings Carey* • USA

SIMOUN, LE • 1933 • Gemier Firmin • FRN
SIMP, THE • 1920 • Hartman Ferris • SHT • USA
SIMP, THE • 1921 • *Dudley Sherman H. Jr.* • USA
SIMP AND SATIN • 1920 • Morante Milburn • SHT • USA
SIMP AND THE SOPHOMORE, THE • 1915 • Louis Will • USA
SIMP SIMPSON AND THE SPIRITS • 1914 • *Selig* • USA
SIMPARELE • 1974 • Solas Humberto • CUB
SIMPATICO MASCALZONE • 1959 • Amendola Mario • ITL
SIMPATICO MASCALZONE, UN • 1919 • Campogalliani Carlo • ITL
SIMPKINS' DREAM OF A HOLIDAY • 1911 • Bouwmeester Theo, Booth W. R.? • UKN
SIMPKINS GETS THE WAR SCARE • 1914 • Wilson Frank? • UKN
SIMPKINS' LITTLE SWINDLE • 1914 • Plumb Hay? • UKN
SIMPKIN'S SATURDAY OFF • 1907 • Fitzhamon Lewin • UKN
SIMPKINS, SPECIAL CONSTABLE • 1914 • Plumb Hay? • UKN
SIMPKINS' SUNDAY DINNER • 1914 • Plumb Hay? • UKN
SIMPLE CASE, A see **PROSTOI SLUCHAI** • 1932
SIMPLE CASE OF MONEY, A (USA) see **MILLIONNAIRES D'UN JOUR** • 1949
SIMPLE CHARITY • 1910 • Griffith D. W. • USA
SIMPLE EVENT, A see **YEK ETTEFAGHE SADEH** • 1973
SIMPLE FAITH • 1914 • *Victor* • USA
SIMPLE FATHER, THE see **HAZOBABAS, O** • 1968
SIMPLE HISTOIRE, UNE • 1959 • Hanoun Marcel • FRN • SIMPLE STORY, A
SIMPLE HISTOIRE D'AMOUR • Colson-Malleville Marie • DOC • FRN • SIMPLE LOVE STORY, A
SIMPLE IKE DECIDES TO MARRY • 1911 • *Kalem* • USA
SIMPLE JUSTICE • 1988 • Del Prete Deborah • USA
SIMPLE LIFE • 1905 • *Bitzer Billy (Ph)* • USA
SIMPLE LIFE, THE • 1912 • *Majestic* • USA
SIMPLE LIFE, THE • 1912 • *Pathe* • USA
SIMPLE LIFE, THE • 1913 • *Nestor* • USA
SIMPLE LIFE, THE • 1919 • Semon Larry • SHT • USA
SIMPLE LIFE, THE • 1926 • Parkinson H. B. • UKN
"SIMPLE LIFE" CURE, THE • 1914 • Plumb Hay? • UKN
SIMPLE LIVES • 1911 • *Comet* • USA
SIMPLE LOVE, A see **FAPADOS SZERELEM** • 1959
SIMPLE LOVE, THE • 1912 • Dwan Allan • USA
SIMPLE LOVE STORY, A see **SIMPLE HISTOIRE D'AMOUR**
SIMPLE MAID, A • 1912 • *Pathe* • USA
SIMPLE MELODY, A see **ENKEL MELODI, EN** • 1974
SIMPLE-MINDED FELLOW, THE see **TA MENG CH'ENG** • 1976
SIMPLE-MINDED MURDERER, THE see **ENFALDIGE MORDAREN, DEN** • 1982
SIMPLE PAST, THE see **PASSE SIMPLE, LE** • 1977
SIMPLE PEOPLE, PLAIN PEOPLE see **PROSTYE LYUDI** • 1945
SIMPLE POLLY • 1915 • De Grasse Joseph • USA
SIMPLE QUESTION D'ETIQUETTE, UNE • 1973 • Cardinal Pierre • DCS • CND
SIMPLE SAPHO • 1917 • Curtis Allen • SHT • USA
SIMPLE SHANKAR see **BHOLA SHANKAR** • 1951
SIMPLE SIMON • 1922 • Edwards Henry • UKN
SIMPLE SIMON • 1935 • *Iwerks Ub (P)* • ANS • USA
SIMPLE SIMON AND THE CLUBMAN see **ONESIME ET LE CLUBMAN** • 1914
SIMPLE SIMON AND THE DEVIL (UKN) see **ONESIME AUX ENFERS** • 1912
SIMPLE SIMON AND THE HAUNTED HOUSE see **ONESIME ET LA MAISON HANTEE** • 1913
SIMPLE SIMON AT THE RACES • 1909 • Wormald S.? • UKN
SIMPLE SIMON CLOCK MAKER see **ONESIME HORLOGER** • 1912
SIMPLE SIMON IN HELL see **ONESIME AUX ENFERS** • 1912
SIMPLE SIMON'S SCHOOLING • 1916 • *Cooper Claude* • USA
SIMPLE SIMON'S SURPRISE PARTY (USA) see **INVITES DE M. LATOURTE, LES** • 1904
SIMPLE SIREN • 1945 • Sommer Paul • ANS • USA
SIMPLE SIS • 1927 • Raymaker Herman C. • USA
SIMPLE SONGS • 1974 • *Preston Billy* • USA
SIMPLE SOULS • 1920 • Thornby Robert T. • USA
SIMPLE STORY, A • 1931 • Stolper Alexander • USS
SIMPLE STORY, A see **SIMPLE HISTOIRE, UNE** • 1959
SIMPLE STORY, A see **PROSTAYA ISTORIYA** • 1960
SIMPLE STORY, A see **SZERU TORTENET, EGY** • 1975
SIMPLE STORY, A see **HISTOIRE SIMPLE, UNE** • 1978
SIMPLE STORY LIKE THIS, A see **SI SIMPLE HISTOIRE, UNE** • 1970
SIMPLE TAILOR, THE • 1934 • Vilner V.
SIMPLE THINGS, THE • 1953 • Nichols Charles • ANS • USA
SIMPLEMENTS VIVIR • 1970 • Galindo Alejandro • MXC • SIMPLY TO LIVE
SIMPLET • 1942 • Fernandel, Carlo-Rim • FRN
SIMPLETTE • 1919 • Hervil Rene • FRN
SIMPLICIO • 1978 • Rubartelli Franco • VNZ
SIMPLY KILLING • 1931 • Taurog Norman • SHT • USA
SIMPLY ORDINARY PEOPLE see **PO PROSTU ZWYKLI LUDZIE** • 1964
SIMPLY TERRIFIC • 1938 • Neill R. William • UKN
SIMPLY TO LIVE see **SIMPLEMENTS VIVIR** • 1970
SIMPSON AND GODLEE STORY, THE • 1956 • Casparius Hans G. • SHT • UKN
SIMPSON LINE, THE • 1953 • Fletcher Trevor • UKN
SIMPSON'S SKATE • 1910 • *Weston Frank* • USA
SIM'S VOYAGE see **VOYAGE DE SIM, LA** • 1966
SIMULADORA, LA • 1955 • Lugones Mario C. • ARG
SIMULANG WALANG HANGGAN • 1968 • Sibal Jose Flores • PHL • BEGINNING OF ETERNITY
SIN • 1915 • Brenon Herbert • USA
SIN see **GREKH** • 1916
SIN see **SYND** • 1928
SIN see **SYND** • 1948
SIN see **BELOVED, THE** • 1971
SIN, THE • 1951 • Makarczynski Tadeusz • DOC • PLN
SIN, THE see **PECADO ORIGINAL, EL** • 1964
SIN, THE see **BIANCO, ROSSO E..** • 1972
SIN, THE see **GOOD LUCK, MISS WYCKOFF** • 1979
SIN, THE (USA) see **HAKAI** • 1961
SIN AGAFAYE • 1967 • Lahalolo Latif • SHT • MRC
SIN ALIENTO, SIN RESPIRO, SIN VERGUENZA • 1976 • Lara Polop Francisco • SPN
SIN ALLEY (USA) see **BUNDFALD** • 1957
SIN CA PEUT VOUS FAIRE PLAISIR • 1948 • Daniel-Norman Jacques • FRN
SIN CARGO • 1926 • Gasnier Louis J. • USA
SIN DIOS, LOS (SPN) see **SENZA DIO, I** • 1972
SIN EGEN SLAV • 1917 • Tallroth Konrad • SWD • SLAVE TO YOURSELF
SIN FIN • 1970 • de la Cerda Clemente • VNZ • WITHOUT END
SIN FIN -LA MUERTE NO ES NINGUNA SOLUCION • 1987 • Pauls Christian • ARG • WITHOUT END OR LOOP – DEATH IS NO SOLUTION
SIN FLOOD, THE • 1922 • Lloyd Frank • USA
SIN FLOOD (UKN) see **WAY OF ALL MEN, THE** • 1930
SIN IN THE CITY • 1966 • *Ass. Film Dist. Of California* • USA
SIN IN THE SUBURBS • 1964 • Sarno Joe • USA
SIN LA SONRISA DE DIOS • 1955 • Salvador Julio • SPN
SIN MAGAZINE • 1965 • *Hudson Jed* • USA
SIN MORS HUS • 1973 • Blom Per • NRW • HIS MOTHER'S HOUSE ○ MORS HUS ○ MOTHER'S HOUSE
SIN NOW.. PAY LATER see **INFERNO ADDOSSO, L'** • 1959
SIN NOW.. PAY LATER see **LOVE NOW.. PAY LATER** • 1966
SIN OF A WOMAN, THE • 1912 • Rolfe Alfred • ASL
SIN OF ABBY HUNT see **SONG OF SURRENDER** • 1949
SIN OF ADAM AND EVE, THE (USA) see **PECADO DE ANAN Y EVA, EL** • 1967
SIN OF ANNA, THE see **PECCATO DI ANNA, IL** • 1953
SIN OF ESTHER WATERS, THE see **ESTHER WATERS** • 1948
SIN OF FATHER MOURET, THE see **FAUTE DE L'ABBE MOURET, LA** • 1970
SIN OF HAROLD DIDDLEBOCK, THE • 1946 • Sturges Preston • USA • MAD WEDNESDAY (UKN)
SIN OF INNOCENCE • 1986 • Seidelman Arthur Allan • TVM • USA
SIN OF INNOCENCE, THE • 1918 • *Roland Ruth* • SHT • USA
SIN OF JESUS, THE • 1961 • Frank Robert • USA
SIN OF KATARINA PADYCHOVA, THE • 1974 • Holly Martin • CZC
SIN OF MADELON CLAUDET, THE • 1931 • Selwyn Edgar • USA • LULLABY, THE (UKN)
SIN OF MARTHA QUEED, THE • 1921 • Dwan Allan • USA • SINS OF THE PARENTS (UKN)
SIN OF MONA KENT, THE • 1961 • Hundt Charles J. • USA • SINS OF MONA KENT, THE ○ MONA KENT
SIN OF NORA MORAN, THE • 1933 • Goldstone Phil • USA
SIN OF OLGA BRANDT, THE • 1914 • De Grasse Joseph • USA
SIN OF ST. ANTHONY, THE see **SINS OF ST. ANTHONY, THE** • 1920
SIN OF THE SABBATH • 1915 • *Ritchie Billie* • USA
SIN OF THE WORLD, THE • 1919 • Ricketts Thomas • USA
SIN ON THE BEACH (USA) see **CRI DE LA CHAIR, LE** • 1963
SIN SHIP, THE • 1931 • Wolheim Louis • USA • SHEEP'S CLOTHING
SIN SIND DIE FRAUEN • 1950 • Stockel Joe • FRG • DORFMONARCH, DER
SIN SISTER, THE • 1929 • Klein Charles • USA
SIN SNIPER, THE see **STONE COLD DEAD** • 1979
SIN, SUFFER AND REPENT • 1966 • Lewis Herschell G. • USA
SIN, SUN AND SEX see **BAL DES VOYOUS, LE** • 1968
SIN SYNDICATE, THE see **ZERO GIRLS** • 1965
SIN TAKES A HOLIDAY • 1930 • Stein Paul L. • USA
SIN THAT WAS HIS, THE • 1920 • Henley Hobart • USA
SIN TO MIDORI • 1937 • Shimazu Yasujiro • JPN • SCARLET AND GREEN
SIN TOWN • 1929 • Cooper J. Gordon • USA
SIN TOWN • 1942 • Enright Ray • USA
SIN UN ADIOS • 1970 • Escriva Vicente • SPN
SIN UNATONED • 1917 • *Leonard Robert* • SHT • USA
SIN UNIFORME • 1948 • Vajda Ladislao • SPN
SIN UNPARDONABLE, A • 1911 • *Pathe* • USA
SIN VENTURA, LA • 1947 • Davison Tito • MXC
SIN WITH REBATE see **SUNDE MIT RABATT** • 1968
SIN WOMAN, THE • 1917 • Lederer George W. (Spv) • USA
SIN YE DO, THE • 1916 • Edwards Walter • USA
SIN YOU SINNERS • 1963 • Farrar Anthony • USA
SINAATUNA • 1959 • Saleh Tewfik • SHT • EGY • NOTRE INDUSTRIE
SINAI COMMANDOS (USA) see **HA'MATARAH TIRAN** • 1968
SINAI FIELD MISSION • 1978 • Wiseman Frederick • DOC • USA
SINAIA • 1962 • Lengyel Ivan • ISR • CLOUDS OVER ISRAEL (USA)
SINAIS DE VIDA • 1983 • Rocha Luis Filipe • PRT
SINANOGLU • 1968 • Yalinkilic Yavuz • TRK
SINANOGLUNUN DONUSU • 1968 • Yalinkilic Yavuz • TRK • RETURN OF SINANOGLU, THE
SINATLE CHVENS PANJREBSHI • 1969 • Mgeladze Georgi • USS • LIGHT IN OUR WINDOWS
SINATRA • 1988 • Betriu Francisco • SPN
SINBAD • 1936 • Pal George • ANS • NTH
SINBAD see **SZINDBAD** • 1971
SINBAD AGAINST THE 7 SARACENS see **SINBAD CONTRO I 7 SARACENI** • 1965
SINBAD, ALI BABA AND ALLADIN • 1963 • Arora P. N. • IND
SINBAD AND THE EYE OF THE TIGER • 1977 • Wanamaker Sam • USA, UKN
SINBAD CONTRO I 7 SARACENI • 1965 • Salvi Emimmo • ITL • ALI BABA AND THE SEVEN SARACENS (USA) ○ SINBAD AGAINST THE 7 SARACENS
SINBAD NO BOKEN • 1962 • Yabushita Taiji • JPN • ADVENTURES OF SINBAD, THE (USA) ○ SINDBAD NO BOKEN
SINBAD OF THE SEVEN SEAS • 1987 • Castellari Enzo G. • ITL
SINBAD THE SAILOR • 1919 • Dawn Norman • SHT • USA
SINBAD THE SAILOR • 1935 • *Uwerks Ub (P)* • ANS • USA
SINBAD THE SAILOR • 1947 • Wallace Richard • USA
SINBAD THE SAILOR • 1952 • *Wadia Homi/ Bhatt Nana-Bhai (P)* • IND
SINBAD THE SAILOR • 1955 • *Luce Ralph (Ph)* • ANS • USA
SINBAD'S GOLDEN VOYAGE see **GOLDEN VOYAGE OF SINBAD, THE** • 1973
SINCE DADDY WAS TAKEN AWAY • 1909 • *Warwick Trading Co* • UKN
SINCE YOU WENT AWAY • 1944 • Cromwell John, De Toth Andre (U/c) • USA
SINCERE HEART see **MAGOKORO** • 1953
SINCERELY CHARLOTTE • 1986 • Huppert Caroline • FRN
SINCERELY VIOLET • 1987 • Ransen Mort • CND
SINCERELY YOURS • 1955 • Douglas Gordon • USA
SINCERITY • 1913 • *Kirkwood James* • USA
SINCERITY • 1973 • Brakhage Stan • USA
SINCERITY see **MAGOKORO** • 1939
SINCERITY see **MAGOKORO** • 1953
SINCERITY II • 1975 • Brakhage Stan • USA
SINCERITY III • 1978 • Brakhage Stan • SHT • USA
SINCERITY IV • 1980 • Brakhage Stan • SHT • USA
SINCERITY V • 1980 • Brakhage Stan • SHT • USA
SINDACALISTA, IL • 1972 • Salce Luciano • ITL
SINDBAD • 1945 • ANS • USS
SINDBAD see **SZINDBAD** • 1971
SINDBAD BURIED see **SINDBAD POGRZEBANY** • 1969
SINDBAD NO BOKEN see **SINBAD NO BOKEN** • 1962
SINDBAD POGRZEBANY • 1969 • Szczechura Daniel • ANS • PLN • SINDBAD BURIED
SINDBAD THE SAILOR • 1930 • IND
SINDBAD THE SAILOR • 1939 • IND
SINDBAD THE SAILOR • 1946 • *Patel Shanta* • IND
SINDERELLA • 1972 • *Grant David H./ Inkpen Ron (P)* • ANS • UKN
SINDERELLA see **SINDERELLA AND THE GOLDEN BRA** • 1964
SINDERELLA AND THE GOLDEN BRA • 1964 • Minardi Loel • USA • CINDERELLA AND THE GOLDEN DRESS ○ CINDY AND HER GOLDEN DRESS ○ CINDERELLA AND THE GOLDEN —— ○ SINDERELLA
SINDHOOR • *Rnfc* • NPL • VERMILION MARK
SINDICATO DE LA MUERTE, EL • 1953 • Orol Juan • MXC, CUB • ANTESALA DE LA MUERTE, LA
SINDICATO DE TELEMIRONES • 1953 • Cardona Rene • MXC
SINDUR DIONA MUSAY • 1985 • Bhuiyan Jahanara • BNG
SINEFIASMENOI ORIZONTES • 1968 • Papanikolaou Mihalis • GRC • CLOUDY SKIES
SINEGORIYA • 1945 • Garin Erast • USS • LAND OF THE BLUE MOUNTAINS, THE
SINEKLI BAKKAL • 1967 • Dinler Mehmet • TRK • FLIES' GROCERY, THE
SINEWS OF STEEL • 1927 • O'Connor Frank • USA
SINEWS OF THE DEAD • 1914 • Melies Gaston • USA
SINEWS OF WAR, THE • 1913 • *Ray Charles* • USA
SINFONIA AMAZONICA • 1952 • ANM • BRZ • BRAZIL SYMPHONY (USA)
SINFONIA D'AMORE • 1955 • Pellegrini Glauco • ITL • SCHUBERT
SINFONIA DE OTONO • 1964 • Briz Jose • SHT • SPN
SINFONIA DE UNA VIDA • 1945 • Gorostiza Celestino • MXC
SINFONIA DEL HAGAR • 1947 • Iquino Ignacio F. • SPN
SINFONIA FATALE • 1947 • Stoloff Victor • ITL
SINFONIA MAGICA • 1946 • Pagot Nino, Pagot Tony • ITL
SINFONIA PER DUE SPIE (ITL) see **SERENADE FUR ZWEI SPIONE** • 1965
SINFONIA PER UN MASSACRO (ITL) see **SYMPHONIE POUR UN MASSACRE** • 1963
SINFUL ANGEL • 1963 • Kazansky Gennadi • USS
SINFUL BED, THE • 1974 • von Anutroff Ilja • FRG
SINFUL BLOOD see **HRISNA KREV** • 1929
SINFUL DAVEY • 1969 • Huston John • UKN
SINFUL DWARF, THE • 1973 • Raski Vidal • USA
SINFUL LIFE, A • 1989 • Schreiner William • USA • IMMACULATE CONCEPTION OF BABY BUMP, THE
SINFUL MARRIAGE, THE • 1917 • Calvert E. H. • SHT • USA
SING • 1988 • Baskin Richard • USA
SING A JINGLE • 1944 • Lilley Edward • USA • LUCKY DAYS (UKN) ○ SET TO MUSIC
SING A LITTLE • 1951 • Ladouceur Jean-Paul • ANS • CND
SING A SONG • 1932 • Fleischer Dave • ANS • USA
SING A SONG, FOR HEAVEN'S SAKE • 1966 • Van Court Ulf • USA
SING A SONG OF SEX see **NIHON SHUNKAKU** • 1967
SING A SONG OF SIX PINTS • 1947 • White Jules • SHT • USA
SING, ABER SPIEL NICHT MIT MIR • 1963 • Nachmann Kurt • AUS
SING AGAIN OF MICHIGAN • 1951 • Sparber I. • ANS • USA
SING ALONG WITH ME • 1952 • Scott Peter Graham • UKN
SING AND BE HAPPY • 1937 • Tinling James • USA
SING AND BE HAPPY • 1946 • Kemp Matty • SHT • USA
SING AND LIKE IT • 1934 • Seiter William A. • USA • SO YOU WON'T SING, EH?
SING AND SWING (USA) see **LIVE IT UP** • 1963
SING ANOTHER CHORUS • 1941 • Lamont Charles • USA
SING AS WE GO • 1934 • Dean Basil • UKN
SING AS YOU SWING • 1937 • Davis Redd • UKN • LET THE PEOPLE LAUGH ○ SWING TEASE ○ MUSIC BOX, THE
SING, BABIES, SING • 1933 • Fleischer Dave • ANS • USA
SING, BABY, SING • 1936 • Lanfield Sidney • USA
SING BEAST SING • 1980 • Newland Marvin • CND
SING, BING, SING • 1933 • Stafford Babe • SHT • USA
SING BOY SING • 1957 • Ephron Henry • USA • SINGIN' IDOL, THE
SING, COWBOY, SING • 1937 • Bradbury Robert North • USA
SING, DANCE, PLENTY HOT • 1940 • Landers Lew • USA • MELODY GIRL (UKN)
SING FOR THE HARLEQUIN see **SING VIR DIE HARLEKYN** • 1979
SING FOR YOUR SUPPER • 1941 • Barton Charles T. • USA
SING, HELEN, SING • 1943 • Roush Leslie • SHT • USA
SING LEE AND THE BAD MAN • 1912 • *Panzer Paul* • USA
SING ME A LOVE SONG • 1936 • Enright Ray • USA • COME UP SMILING (UKN)
SING ME A LOVE SONG (UKN) see **MANHATTAN MOON** • 1935
SING ME A SONG OF TEXAS • 1945 • Keays Vernon • USA • FORTUNE HUNTER (UKN)
SING, NEIGHBOR, SING • 1944 • McDonald Frank • USA
SING OR SWIM • 1948 • Kneitel Seymour • ANS • USA
SING, ROSA, SING • 1919 • *Lyons Eddie* • SHT • USA
SING-SING • 1971 • Schroeder Barbet • DOC • FRN
SING SING • 1984 • Corbucci Sergio • ITL

SING SING NIGHTS • 1934 • Collins Lewis D. • USA • REPRIEVED (UKN)
SING SING PRISON • 1931 • *Terry Paul/ Moser Frank (P)* • ANS • USA
SING SING THANKSGIVING • 1973 • Hoffman David, Wiland Harry • DOC • USA
SING SINNER SING • 1933 • Christy Howard • USA
SING, SISTER, SING • 1935 • Parrott James • SHT • USA
SING, SISTERS, SING • 1933 • Fleischer Dave • ANS • USA
SING VIR DIE HARLEKYN • 1979 • Hamman F. C. • SAF • SING FOR THE HARLEQUIN
SING WHILE YOU DANCE • 1946 • Lederman D. Ross • USA
SING WHILE YOU WORK • 1949 • Parker Benjamin R. • SHT • USA
SING WHILE YOU'RE ABLE • 1937 • Neilan Marshall • USA
SING WITH THE COMMODORES #1, 2, 3 • 1950 • Blais Roger • SHT • CND
SING, YOU DANCERS • 1930 • Taurog Norman • SHT • USA
SING YOU SINNERS • 1938 • Ruggles Wesley • USA
SING YOUNG PEOPLE see **UTAE WAKODOTACHI** • 1963
SING YOUR HEART OUT • 1979 • Nesher Avi • ISR
SING YOUR SONG, POET.. see **POY PYESNYU, POET..** • 1973
SING YOUR SONGS see **SEN TURKULERINI SOYLE** • 1985
SING YOUR WAY HOME • 1945 • Mann Anthony • USA
SING YOUR WORRIES AWAY • 1942 • Sutherland A. Edward • USA
SINGAL L'ANTILOPE SACREE • 1967 • Coutard Raoul • SHT • FRN
SINGAPORE • 1947 • Brahm John • USA
SINGAPORE MUTINY, THE • 1928 • Ince Ralph • USA • WRECK OF THE SINGAPORE, THE (UKN)
SINGAPORE NO YOWA FUKETE • 1967 • Ichimura Hirokazu • JPN • UNDER THE STAR OF SINGAPORE
SINGAPORE, SINGAPORE (USA) see **CINQ GARS POUR SINGAPOUR** • 1967
SINGAPORE STORY, THE • 1952 • Eason B. Reeves • USA
SINGAPORE TIGER • 1986 • BRM
SINGAPORE WOMAN • 1941 • Negulesco Jean • USA
SINGAPORE, ZERO HOUR see **GOLDSNAKE ANONIMA KILLERS** • 1966
SINGAPUR, HORA CERO (SPN) see **GOLDSNAKE ANONIMA KILLERS** • 1966
SINGAREE • 1910 • Blom August • DNM
SINGE EN HIVER, UN • 1962 • Verneuil Henri • FRN • MONKEY IN WINTER, A (USA) ○ IT'S HOT IN HELL
SINGED • 1927 • Wray John Griffith • USA • LOVE OF WOMEN
SINGED WINGS • 1922 • Stanlaws Penrhyn • USA
SINGED WINGS see **OBOZHZHENNIUE KRYLYA** • 1915
SINGENDE ENGEL • 1947 • Ucicky Gustav • AUS • SINGING ANGELS (USA)
SINGENDE HAUS, DAS • 1948 • Antel Franz • AUS
SINGENDE HOTEL, DAS • 1953 • von Cziffra Geza • FRG
SINGENDE JUGEND • 1936 • Neufeld Max • AUS • ORPHAN BOY OF VIENNA, AN
SINGENDE JUGEND see **MIT MUSIK DURCHS LEBEN OU SINGENDE JUGEND** • 1938
SINGENDE KLINGENDE BAUMCHEN, DAS • 1965 • Stefani Franceq • FRG • SINGING TINKLING TREELET, THE ○ LITTLE SINGING TREE, THE
SINGENDE STADT, DIE • 1930 • Gallone Carmine • FRG
SINGENDE TOR, DER • 1939 • Meyer Johannes • FRG, ITL
SINGENDEN ENGEL VON TIROL, DIE • 1958 • Lehner Alfred • AUS • SAG JA, MUTTI
SINGER, THE see **PEVITSA** • 1971
SINGER AND THE DANCER, THE • 1977 • Armstrong Gillian • ASL
SINGER JIM MCKEE • 1924 • Smith Cliff • USA
SINGER MIDGET'S SCANDAL • 1921 • Cline Eddie • SHT • USA
SINGER MIDGET'S SIDE SHOW • 1921 • Cline Eddie • SHT • USA
SINGER NOT THE SONG, THE • 1961 • Baker Roy Ward • UKN
SINGER OF NAPLES, THE (USA) see **CANTANTE DE NAPOLES, EL** • 1935
SINGER OF SEVILLE, THE see **CALL OF THE FLESH** • 1930
SINGER OF SEVILLE, THE see **SEVILLA DE MIS AMORES** • 1930
SINGERIES HUMAINES • 1910 • Cohl Emile • ANS • FRN • JOLLY WHIRL, THE
SINGIN' IDOL, THE see **SING BOY SING** • 1957
SINGIN' IN THE CORN • 1946 • Lord Del • USA • GIVE AND TAKE (UKN)
SINGIN' IN THE RAIN • 1952 • Kelly Gene, Donen Stanley • USA
SINGIN' THE BLUES • 1948 • Parker Benjamin R. • SHT • USA
SINGING: A JOY IN ANY LANGUAGE • 1982 • Ianzelo Tony (c/d) • DOC • CND
SINGING ALONG • 1949 • *Universal* • SHT • USA
SINGING ANGELS (USA) see **SINGENDE ENGEL** • 1947
SINGING BANDIT, THE • 1937 • Schwarzwald Milton • SHT • USA
SINGING BARBERS, THE • 1946 • Moore Harold James • SHT • USA
SINGING BLACKSMITH, THE see **YANKEL DEM SCHMIDT** • 1938
SINGING BOXER, THE • 1933 • *Sennett Mack (P)* • SHT • USA
SINGING BUCKAROO, THE • 1937 • Gibson Tom • USA
SINGING CHAMPIONS • 1952 • Blais Roger • DCS • CND • VOIX D'ACADIE
SINGING CITY see **CITTA CANORA, LA** • 1952
SINGING COP, THE • 1938 • Woods Arthur • UKN • MUSIC AND MYSTERY
SINGING COWBOY, THE • 1936 • Wright Mack V. • USA
SINGING COWBOYS • 1986 • Proikov Proiko • ANM • BUL
SINGING COWGIRL, THE • 1939 • Diege Samuel • USA
SINGING DAYS, THE see **GIORNI CANTATI, I** • 1979
SINGING DUDE, THE • 1940 • *Morgan Dennis* • SHT • USA
SINGING EARTH, THE see **ZEM SPIEVA** • 1933
SINGING FOOL, THE • 1928 • Bacon Lloyd • USA
SINGING FOR LOVE see **AI WA OSHIMINAKU** • 1967
SINGING GUNMAN, THE see **BAKUDAN-OTOKO TO IWARERU AITSU** • 1967
SINGING GUNS • 1950 • Springsteen R. G. • USA
SINGING HILL, THE • 1941 • Landers Lew • USA
SINGING IN THE AIR • 1937 • Yarbrough Jean • SHT • USA
SINGING IN THE DARK • 1956 • Nosseck Max
SINGING KETTLE, THE see **THIS IS THE LIFE** • 1933
SINGING KID, THE • 1936 • Keighley William • USA
SINGING LAND, THE see **ZEM SPIEVA** • 1933
SINGING LESSON see **TRALLANDE JANTA, EN** • 1942
SINGING LESSON, THE (UKN) see **RAZ, DWA, TRZY** • 1967
SINGING MAKES LIFE BEAUTIFUL see **DALOLVA SZEP AZ ELET** • 1950
SINGING MARINE, THE • 1937 • Enright Ray • USA
SINGING MUSKETEER, THE (UKN) see **THREE MUSKETEERS, THE** • 1939
SINGING NUN, THE • 1966 • Koster Henry • USA
SINGING ON THE TRAIL • 1946 • Nazarro Ray • USA • LOOKIN' FOR SOMEONE (UKN)
SINGING ON THE TREADMILL • Gazdag Gyula • HNG
SINGING ONE THINKS NO HARM see **TKO PJEVA, ZLO NE MISLI** • 1971
SINGING OUTLAW, THE • 1937 • Lewis Joseph H. • USA
SINGING PLUMBER, THE • 1932 • *Sennett Mack (P)* • SHT • USA
SINGING PRINCESS, THE (USA) see **ROSA DI BAGDAD, LA** • 1949
SINGING RIVER • 1921 • Giblyn Charles • USA
SINGING SAP, THE • 1930 • Lantz Walter, Nolan William • ANS • USA
SINGING SAPS • 1930 • Foster John, Davis Mannie • ANS • USA
SINGING SHERIFF, THE • 1944 • Goodwins Leslie • USA
SINGING SPURS • 1948 • Nazarro Ray • USA
SINGING STREET, THE • 1952 • McIsaac Nigel • UKN
SINGING TAXI DRIVER (USA) see **TAXI DI NOTTE** • 1950
SINGING TEACHER, THE see **UCHITEL PENIYA** • 1972
SINGING THROUGH see **BE CAREFUL MR. SMITH** • 1935
SINGING THRUSH, THE see **ZIL PEVCIJ DROZD** • 1972
SINGING TINKLING TREELET, THE see **SINGENDE KLINGENDE BAUMCHEN, DAS** • 1965
SINGING VAGABOND, THE • 1935 • Pierson Carl • USA
SINGING WOOD • 1958 • Makarczynski Tadeusz • DOC • PLN
SINGITHI SURATHAL • 1968 • Rajapakse Kingsley • SLN • YOUNG FROLICS
SINGLE ACT, THE • 1914 • Powell Paul • USA
SINGLE AND MARRIED • 1914 • Sandberg Anders W. • DNM
SINGLE BARS, SINGLE WOMEN • 1984 • Winer Harry • TVM • USA
SINGLE CODE, THE • 1917 • Ricketts Thomas • USA
SINGLE GIRLS, THE • 1974 • Sebastian Ferdinand, Sebastian Beverly • USA
SINGLE HANDED • 1914 • *Valdez Reina* • USA
SINGLE HANDED • 1923 • Sedgwick Edward • USA • HEADS UP
SINGLE-HANDED • 1953 • Boulting Roy • UKN • SAILOR OF THE KING (USA) ○ BROWN ON RESOLUTION ○ ABLE SEAMAN BROWN ○ SAILOR OF THE SEA
SINGLE-HANDED see **CAPCANA** • 1973
SINGLE-HANDED see **YKSINTEOIN** • 1989
SINGLE-HANDED JIM • 1913 • Hamilton G. P.? • USA
SINGLE-HANDED SANDERS • 1932 • Nosler Lloyd • USA • WYOMING (UKN)
SINGLE LIFE • 1921 • Collins Edwin J. • UKN
SINGLE MAN, A • 1928 • Beaumont Harry • USA
SINGLE MAN, THE • 1919 • Bramble A. V. • UKN
SINGLE REGRET, A • 1982 • Fortier Bob • MTV • CND
SINGLE ROOM FURNISHED • 1968 • Ottaviano Matteo • USA
SINGLE SAILOR see **HOW TO PICK UP A GIRL** • 1967
SINGLE SHOT BARTON (UKN) see **LION'S DEN, THE** • 1936
SINGLE SHOT PARKER see **HEART OF TEXAS RYAN, THE** • 1917
SINGLE SIN, THE • 1931 • Nigh William • USA
SINGLE STANDARD, THE • 1914 • *Griffith Film* • USA
SINGLE STANDARD, THE • 1929 • Robertson John S. • USA
SINGLE SWINGERS ONLY see **FOR SINGLE SWINGERS ONLY** • 1968
SINGLE TRACK, THE • 1921 • Campbell Webster • USA
SINGLE WIVES • 1924 • Archainbaud George • USA
SINGLE WOMAN AND THE DOUBLE STANDARD, THE • 1963 • Fox Beryl • DOC • CND
SINGLES see **DANGEROUS LOVE** • 1989
SINGLES, THE • 1967 • Johnsen S. N. • USA • SINGLES ONLY
SINGLES ONLY see **SINGLES, THE** • 1967
SINGLETON'S PLUCK see **LAUGHTERHOUSE** • 1984
SINGOALLA • 1949 • Christian-Jaque • FRN, SWD • GYPSY FURY (USA) ○ WIND IS MY LOVER, THE ○ MASK AND THE SWORD, THE
SINGSONG GIRL RED PEONY • 1930 • Chang Shih-Chuan • CHN
SINGULAR CYNIC, A • 1914 • Salter Harry • USA
SINGUR • 1968 • Marcus Manole • RMN • ALL ALONE
SINHA MOCA • 1953 • Payne Tom, Sampaio Oswaldo • BRZ
SINHALESE DANCE, A • 1950 • Peries Lester James • SHT • SLN
SINHASAN • 1934 • Jagirdar Gajanan • IND
SINHASTA OR THE PATH OF IMMORTALITY • 1968 • Benegal Shyam • DCS • IND
SINHEGARH • 1923 • Painter Baburao • IND
SININEN VIIKKO • 1954 • Kassila Matti • FNL • BLUE WEEK
SINISTER GUEST, THE see **UNHEIMLICHE GAST, DER** • 1922
SINISTER HANDS • 1932 • Schaefer Armand • USA
SINISTER HANDS OF DR. ORLAK, THE see **ORLACS HANDE** • 1925
SINISTER HOUSE see **MUSS 'EM UP** • 1936
SINISTER HOUSE (UKN) see **WHO KILLED DOC ROBBIN?** • 1948
SINISTER INVASION see **INVASION SINIESTRA** • 1968
SINISTER JOURNEY • 1948 • Archainbaud George • USA
SINISTER MAN, THE • 1961 • Donner Clive • UKN
SINISTER MONK, THE (USA) see **UNHEIMLICHE MONCH, DER** • 1965
SINISTER STREET • 1922 • Beranger George A. • UKN
SINISTER STUFF • 1934 • Muffati Steve • ANS • USA • VILLAIN PURSUES HER
SINISTER URGE, THE • 1961 • Wood Edward D. Jr. • USA • YOUNG AND IMMORAL, THE
SINISTER WISH, THE see **UNHEIMLICHEN WUNSCHE, DIE** • 1939
SINJI GALEB • 1953 • Bauer Branko • YGS • BLUE SEAGULL, THE
SINK OR SWIM • 1921 • Roach Hal • SHT • USA
SINK OR SWIM • 1938 • Delamar Mickey, Kavanagh Denis • SHT • UKN
SINK OR SWIM • 1952 • Rasinski Connie • ANS • USA
SINK THE BISMARCK! • 1960 • Gilbert Lewis* • UKN
SINKING IN THE BATHTUB • 1930 • Harman Hugh, Ising Rudolf • ANS • USA
SINKING OF THE LUSITANIA, THE • 1918 • McCay Winsor • ANM • USA
SINLESS SINNER, A • 1919 • Brenon Herbert • USA
SINLESS SINNER, A • 1919 • McKay James • UKN • MIDNIGHT GAMBOLS (USA)
SINNER, THE • 1911 • *Thanhouser* • USA
SINNER, THE • 1915 • Revier Harry • USA
SINNER, THE see **SUNDERIN, DIE** • 1951
SINNER, THE see **GREZHNITSA** • 1962
SINNER, THE see **DELANCEY STREET: THE CRISIS WITHIN** • 1975
SINNER, THE (UKN) see **PECCATRICE DEL DESERTO, LA** • 1959
SINNER AND THE WITCH, THE see **PECADOR Y LA BRUJA, EL** • 1964
SINNER IN PARADISE see **KAETTE KITA YOPPARAI** • 1968
SINNER MUST PAY, THE see **VANITY** • 1915
SINNER OF MAGDALA, THE • 1950 • Contreras Torres Miguel • MXC
SINNER OR SAINT • 1923 • Windom Lawrence C. • USA
SINNER TAKE ALL • 1936 • Taggart Errol • USA
SINNERS • 1920 • Webb Kenneth • USA
SINNERS see **OUDIS ANAMARTITOS** • 1967
SINNERS, THE see **AU ROYAUME DES CIEUX** • 1949
SINNERS, THE see **NACHTLOKAL ZUM SILBERMOND, DAS** • 1959
SINNERS, THE see **TERBABAS** • 1972
SINNERS, THE (UKN) see **PISCINE, LA** • 1969
SINNERS A LA CARTE see **NUDE IN CHARCOAL** • 1963
SINNER'S BLOOD • 1969 • Douglas Neil • USA
SINNERS GO TO HELL see **NO EXIT** • 1962
SINNER'S HOLIDAY • 1930 • Adolfi John G. • USA • WOMEN IN LOVE
SINNER'S HOLIDAY see **CHRISTMAS EVE** • 1947
SINNERS IN HEAVEN • 1924 • Crosland Alan • USA
SINNERS IN LOVE • 1928 • Melford George • USA
SINNERS IN PARADISE • 1938 • Whale James • USA
SINNERS IN SILK • 1924 • Henley Hobart • USA • FREE LOVE
SINNERS IN THE CINEMA PARADISE see **SYNDARE I FILMPARADISET** • 1956
SINNERS IN THE SUN • 1932 • Hall Alexander • USA
SINNERS OF PARIS (USA) see **RAFLES SUR LA VILLE** • 1957
SINNER'S PARADE • 1928 • Adolfi John G. • USA
SINNER'S REPENTANCE, A • 1909 • Bouwmeester Theo? • UKN
SINNER'S SACRIFICE, A • 1910 • *Bison* • USA
SINNERS TO HELL see **ISI NERAKA** • 1960
SINNERS TO HELL see **JIGOKU** • 1960
SINNESRAUSCH • 1920 • Philippi Siegfried • FRG
SINNING URGE, THE (UKN) see **BRANT BARN** • 1967
SINNING WOMEN see **PECADORAS, LAS** • 1968
SINNUI YAUWAN see **QIANNU YOUHAN** • 1988
SINNUI YAUWAN II see **RENJIAN DAO** • 1988
SINO ANG DAPAT SISIHIN • 1967 • de Villa Jose • PHL • WHO'S TO BE BLAMED
SINO ANG MAY KARAPATAN • 1968 • de Jesus Ding M. • PHL • WHO HAS THE RIGHT?
SINS • 1985 • Hickox Douglas • MTV • USA
SINS IN THE FAMILY see **PECCATI IN FAMIGLIA** • 1975
SINS OF A BROTHER • 1917 • *Brenon Herbert* • SHT • USA
SINS OF A FATHER, THE • 1923 • Greenwood Edwin • UKN
SINS OF AMBITION • 1918 • Abramson Ivan • USA
SINS OF BABYLON, THE see **MACISTE, L'EROE PIU GRANDE DEL MONDO** • 1963
SINS OF CASANOVA see **AVVENTURE DI GIACOMO CASANOVA, LE** • 1954
SINS OF DESIRE see **ANDRE CORNELIS** • 1927
SINS OF DORIAN GRAY, THE • 1983 • Maylam Tony • TVM • USA
SINS OF FASHION see **RUE DE LA PAIX** • 1926
SINS OF HARVEY CLARE, THE • 1914 • *Britannia Films* • UKN • VICTIMS OF BLACKMAIL
SINS OF HER PARENTS • 1916 • Lloyd Frank • USA
SINS OF HIS FATHER • 1920 • Gerrard Douglas • USA
SINS OF JEZEBEL • 1953 • Le Borg Reginald • USA
SINS OF KITTY see **URSULA** • 1967
SINS OF LOLA MONTES, THE (USA) see **LOLA MONTES** • 1955
SINS OF MAN • 1936 • Ratoff Gregory, Brower Otto • USA
SINS OF MEN • 1916 • Vincent James • USA
SINS OF MONA KENT, THE see **SIN OF MONA KENT, THE** • 1961
SINS OF PARIS (USA) see **RIRES DE PARIS** • 1952
SINS OF POMPEI see **DERNIERS JOURS DE POMPEI, LES** • 1948
SINS OF RACHEL, THE • 1975 • Fontaine Richard • USA
SINS OF RACHEL CADE, THE see **RACHEL CADE** • 1961
SINS OF ROME (USA) see **SPARTACO** • 1952
SINS OF ROSANNE, THE see **SINS OF ROZANNE** • 1920
SINS OF ROSE BERND, THE (USA) see **ROSE BERND** • 1957
SINS OF ROZANNE • 1920 • Forman Tom • USA • SINS OF ROSANNE, THE
SINS OF ST. ANTHONY, THE • 1920 • Cruze James • USA • SIN OF ST. ANTHONY, THE
SINS OF SOCIETY, THE • 1915 • Eagle Oscar • USA
SINS OF SODOM see **ALL THE SINS OF SODOM** • 1968
SINS OF THE BORGIAS (USA) see **LUCRECE BORGIA** • 1953
SINS OF THE CHILDREN • 1918 • Lopez John S. • USA
SINS OF THE CHILDREN see **RICHEST MAN IN THE WORLD, THE** • 1930
SINS OF THE CHILDREN see **IN HIS STEPS** • 1936
SINS OF THE CHILDREN, THE see **BORNENES SYND** • 1916
SINS OF THE FATHER • 1911 • *Lubin* • USA
SINS OF THE FATHER • 1913 • *Champion* • USA

SINS OF THE FATHER • 1983 • Hook Harry • UKN
SINS OF THE FATHER • 1985 • Werner Peter • TVM • USA
SINS OF THE FATHER see **SINS OF THE FATHERS** • 1928
SINS OF THE FATHER see **HOME IS THE HERO** • 1959
SINS OF THE FATHER, THE • 1912 • *Panzer Paul* • USA
SINS OF THE FATHER, THE • 1913 • Edwards Walter • *Kb* • USA
SINS OF THE FATHERS • 1909 • *Vitagraph* • USA
SINS OF THE FATHERS • 1928 • Berger Ludwig • USA • SINS OF THE FATHER
SINS OF THE FATHERS • 1949 • Rosen Phil • USA
SINS OF THE FLESHAPOIDS • 1965 • Kuchar Mike • USA
SINS OF THE MOTHER, THE • 1918 • Chester George Randolph, Chester George Randolph Mrs. • USA
SINS OF THE MOTHERS • 1915 • Ince Ralph • USA
SINS OF THE MOTHERS, THE • 1919 • Ince Ralph • USA
SINS OF THE PARENTS • 1914 • *Adler Sarah* • USA
SINS OF THE PARENTS (UKN) see **SIN OF MARTHA QUEED, THE** • 1921
SINS OF THE PAST • 1984 • Hunt Peter H. • TVM • USA
SINS OF YOUTH, THE • 1919 • Batley Ernest G. • UKN
SINS OF YOUTH (USA) see **PECHES DE JEUNESSE** • 1941
SIN'S PAY DAY • 1932 • Seitz George B. • USA
SIN'S PENALTY • 1916 • Wolbert William • SHT • USA
SINS THAT YE SIN, THE • 1915 • *Bondhill Gertrude* • USA
SINS WITHIN THE FAMILY (UKN) see **PECCATI IN FAMIGLIA** • 1975
SINS YE DO, THE • 1924 • Granville Fred Leroy • UKN
SINTFLUT • 1927 • Berger Josef • FRG
SINTFLUT, DIE • 1917 • Oswald Richard • FRG
SINTHIA • 1970 • Rose Kendall S. • USA
SINTHIA, THE DEVIL'S DOLL • 1970 • Christian Sven • USA • DEVIL'S DOLL, THE
SINTOMAS (SPN) see **SYMPTOMS** • 1974
SINTRA • 1949 • Mendes Joao • SHT • PRT
SINTRA • 1958 • Mendes Joao • SHT • PRT
SINTRA, CENARIO DE FILME ROMANTICO • 1933 • do Canto Jorge Brum • SHT • PRT
SINTRIMMIA TA ONIRA MAS • 1967 • Doukas Kostas • GRC • OUR SHATTERED DREAMS
SINVERGUENZA • 1940 • Torres-Rios Leopoldo • ARG
SINVERGUENZA, EL • 1971 • *Gamo* • MXC
SINYAYA PTITSA • 1975 • Cukor George • USS, USA • BLUE BIRD, THE (USA)
SINYAYA TETRAD • 1963 • Kulidjanov Lev • USS • BLUE NOTEBOOK, THE
SIOUX BLOOD • 1929 • Waters John • USA
SIOUX CITY SUE • 1946 • McDonald Frank • USA
SIOUX LOVER'S STRATEGY, A • 1911 • *Pathe* • USA
SIOUX ME • 1939 • Hardaway Ben, Dalton Cal • ANS • USA
SIOUX ME • 1965 • Marcus Sid • ANS • USA
SIOUX SPY, A • 1911 • *Bison* • USA
SIOUX'S CAVE OF DEATH, THE • 1912 • *Pathe* • USA
SIOUX'S REWARD, A • 1910 • *Bison* • USA
SIP OF LOVE, A see **BIR UDUM SEVGI** • 1985
SIPOLO MACSKAKO • 1971 • Gazdag Gyula • HNG • WHISTLING COBBLESTONES
SIPPSCHAFT, DIE • 1920 • Wilhelm Carl • FRG
SIQUEIROS • 1968 • Csoke Jozsef • DOC • HNG
SIR ARNE'S TREASURE see **HERR ARNES PENGAR** • 1919
SIR ARNE'S TREASURE see **HERR ARNES PENNIGAR** • 1954
SIR FRANCIS DRAKE see **DOMINATORE DEI SETTE MARI, IL** • 1962
SIR FRANCIS DRAKE ,IL RE DEI SETTE MARI see **DOMINATORE DEI SETTE MARI, IL** • 1962
SIR GALAHAD OF TWILIGHT • 1914 • Taylor William D.? • USA
SIR GEORGE AND THE HEIRESS • 1911 • *Edison* • USA
SIR HENRY ASQUITH see **SECRET LIVES OF THE BRITISH PRIME MINISTERS: ASQUITH, THE** • 1983
SIR HENRY AT RAWLINSON END • 1980 • Roberts Steve • UKN
SIR IRVING AND JEAMES • 1956 • Kneitel Seymour • ANS • USA
SIR JAMES MORTIMER'S WAGER • 1916 • Seldon-Truss Leslie • UKN • WAGER, THE
SIR JOHN GREIFT EIN! see **MARY** • 1931
SIR LUMBERJACK • 1926 • Garson Harry • USA
SIR OR MADAM • 1928 • Boese Carl • UKN
SIR PERCY AND THE PUNCHERS • 1911 • Melies Gaston • USA
SIR ROSS & SIR KEITH SMITH • 1920 • ASL
SIR ROSS SMITH FLIGHT • 1920 • *Hurley Frank (Ph)* • ASL
SIR RUPERT'S WIFE • 1922 • Sanderson Challis • UKN
SIRI SIRI • 1968 • Rubbo Michael • CND
SIR THOMAS LIPTON OUT WEST • 1913 • Sennett Mack • DOC • USA
SIR, YOU ARE A WIDOWER see **PANE, VY JSTE VDOVA** • 1971
SIRA AL-ABT'AL • 1961 • Saleh Tewfik • EGY • COMBAT HEROIQUE ○ LUTTES DES HEROS
SIRAUN FI AL-GABAL • 1960 • Mustafa Hassam Eddin • EGY • BATAILLE SUR LA MONTAGNE
SIRAUN FI AL-MINA see **SERAA FIL MINAA** • 1955
SIRAUN FI AL-WADI see **SERAA FIL WADA** • 1953
SIRAUN FI AN-NIL • 1959 • Salem Atef • EGY • DUEL SUR LE NIL
SIRE LE ROY N'A PLUS RIEN DIT • 1964 • Rouquier Georges • DCS • CND, FRN
SIREN, THE • 1914 • Reid Wallace • USA
SIREN, THE • 1915 • Davis Ulysses • USA
SIREN, THE • 1917 • West Roland • USA
SIREN, THE • 1927 • Haskin Byron • USA
SIREN CALL, THE • 1922 • Willat Irvin V. • USA
SIREN OF ATLANTIS • 1949 • Tallas Gregg R. • USA • ATLANTIS THE LOST CONTINENT ○ QUEEN OF ATLANTIS ○ ATLANTIS
SIREN OF BAGDAD • 1953 • Quine Richard • USA
SIREN OF CORSICA, A • 1915 • Smiley Joseph • USA
SIREN OF IMPULSE, A • 1912 • Griffith D. W. • USA
SIREN OF SEVILLE, THE • 1924 • Storm Jerome, Stromberg Hunt • USA
SIREN OF THE DESERT, A • 1914 • *Lubin* • USA
SIREN OF THE JUNGLE, A • 1916 • Swickard Charles • USA
SIREN OF THE SAHARA, THE • 1976 • Salman Mohammed • SYR
SIREN OF THE TROPICS • 1937 • Goldberg Dave, Goldberg Jack • USA
SIRENA • 1947 • Stekly Karel • CZC • STRIKE, THE
SIRENA DEL GOLFO, LA • 1959 • Ferronetti Ignazio • ITL
SIRENA DEL GOLFO, LA see **MA CHI TE LO FARE?** • 1948
SIRENA NEGRA, LA • 1947 • Serrano De Osma Carlos • SPN
SIRENE • 1968 • Servais Raoul • ANS • BLG
SIRENE, LA • 1904 • Melies Georges • FRN • MERMAID, THE (USA)
SIRENE, LA • 1907 • Feuillade Louis • FRN
SIRENE, LA see **NADAHA, EL** • 1974
SIRENE, LE • 1911 • *A. Croce & Co* • ITL • SIRENS, THE
SIRENE DES TROPIQUES, LA • 1927 • Etievant Henri, Nalpas • FRN
SIRENE DU MISSISSIPPI, LA • 1969 • Truffaut Francois • FRN, ITL • MIA DROGA SI CHIAMA JULIE, LA (ITL) ○ MISSISSIPPI MERMAID (USA)
SIRENES • 1961 • Degelin Emile • BLG
SIRENES MODERNES see **SEA SPRITES** • 1961
SIRENS, THE see **SIRENE, LE** • 1911
SIREN'S NECKLACE, THE • 1909 • Brooke Van Dyke • USA
SIRENS OF THE SEA • 1917 • Holubar Allen • USA • DARLINGS OF THE GODS (UKN)
SIRENS OF THE SUDS • 1919 • Watson William • SHT • USA
SIREN'S REIGN, THE • 1915 • Vignola Robert G. • USA
SIREN'S SONG, THE • 1915 • Revier Harry • USA
SIREN'S SONG, THE • 1919 • Edwards J. Gordon • USA
SIRIPALA AND RANMENIKA • 1977 • Jayatilaka Amarnath • SLN
SIRIUS NO DENSETSU • 1982 • Hata Masami • JPN • LEGEND OF SIRIUS, A
SIRIUS REMEMBERED • 1959 • Brakhage Stan • SHT • USA
SIRK, AS- see **CIRK, AL** • 1968
SIRKUS FANDANGO • 1954 • Skouen Arne • NRW • CIRCUS FANDANGO
SIROCCO • 1930 • Severac Jacques • FRN • ROSE DU SOUK, LA ○ SIROCO
SIROCCO • 1951 • Bernhardt Curtis • USA
SIROCCO see **SIROKKO** • 1969
SIROCCO D'HIVER see **SIROKKO** • 1969
SIROCCO (USA) see **MAISON DU MALTAIS, LA** • 1938
SIROCO see **SIROCCO** • 1930
SIROKKO • 1969 • Jancso Miklos • HNG, FRN • WINTER WIND (USA) ○ SIROCCO D'HIVER ○ TELI SIROKKO ○ SIROCCO ○ WINTER SIROCCO
SIROKO JE LISCE • 1981 • Latinovic Petar • YGS • LEAVES ARE WIDE, THE
SIROMA SAM AL' SAM BESAN • 1971 • Ivkov Dragoljub • YGS • I'M POOR BUT ANGRY ○ I'M POOR BUT STUPID
SIROMASHKA RADOST • 1958 • Marinovich Anton • BUL • POOR MAN'S JOY
SIROTA MARIJA • 1968 • Lazic Dragoslav • YGS • POOR MARIJA ○ POOR MARIA
SIRPPI JA KITARA • 1988 • Mykkanen Marjaana • DOC • FNL • FROM RUSSIA WITH ROCK
SIRR TAKIEET EL EKHFA • 1960 • Mustafa Niazi • EGY • SECRET OF THE MAGIC HAT, THE
SIRRU IMRA'A • 1960 • Salem Atef • EGY • SECRET D'UNE FEMME, LE
SIRUP • 1989 • Ryslinge Helle • DNM • SYRUP
SIRUTONDA NAYANAR • 1935 • *Sundarappa* • IND
SIS • 1914 • *Princess* • USA
SIS • 1915 • Ridgwell George • USA
SIS • 1989 • Livaneli Zulfu • TRK, SWT, SWD • MIST (UKN) ○ FOG
SIS HOPKINS • 1919 • Badger Clarence • USA
SIS HOPKINS • 1941 • Santley Joseph • USA
SI'S SURPRISE PARTY • 1912 • *Solax* • USA
SIS THE DETECTIVE • 1916 • Ellis Robert • USA
SI'S WONDERFUL MINERAL SPRING • 1914 • Neilan Marshall • USA
SISA • 1951 • De Leon Gerardo • PHL
SISIFUS • 1974 • Sinclair Arturo • SHT • PRU
SISIMUT • 1966 • Roos Jorgen • DOC • DNM
SISIPHUS see **SIZIF** • 1967
SISKA • 1962 • Kjellin Alf • SWD
SISS DOBBINS, OIL MAGNATE • 1914 • *Maison Edna* • USA
SISSI • 1932 • Reiniger Lotte • ANS • FRG
SISSI • 1956 • Marischka Ernst • AUS • FOREVER MY LOVE
SISSI, DIE JUNGE KAISERIN • 1956 • Marischka Ernst • AUS • FOREVER MY LOVE
SISSI SCHICKSALJAHRE EINER KAISERIN • 1957 • Marischka Ernst • AUS • FOREVER MY LOVE
SISSIGNORA • 1942 • Poggioli Ferdinando M. • ITL • SI SIGNORA
SISSIGNORE • 1968 • Tognazzi Ugo • ITL • YESSIR!
SISSIT • 1963 • Niskanen Mikko • FNL • GUERILLAS ○ PARTISANS, THE
SISSY SHERIFF • 1967 • Smith Paul J. • USA
SISSYBELLE • 1913 • Parker Lem B. • USA
SISSY'S HOT SUMMER • 1981 • *Royalle Candida* • USA
SISTA AVENTYRET, DEN • 1975 • Halldoff Jan • SWD • LAST ADVENTURE, THE
SISTA BUDET • 1980 • Dahl Christer • SWD, NRW • DON'T GET CAUGHT
SISTA LEKEN, DEN • 1983 • Lindstrom Jon • SWD, FNL • LAST GAME ○ LAST SUMMER, THE
SISTA NATTEN • 1957 • Larsson Borje • SWD • MORD I MARSTRAND ○ LAST NIGHT
SISTA PARET UT • 1956 • Sjoberg Alf • SWD • LAST PAIR OUT ○ LAST COUPLE OUT
SISTA RINGEN • 1955 • Skoglund Gunnar • SWD • LAST FORM ○ SCHASEN ○ PLUGGET
SISTA STEGEN, DE (SWD) see **MATTER OF MORALS, A** • 1960
SISTE FLEKSNES, DEN • 1974 • Hermansson Bo • NRW • SIDSTE FLEKSNES, DEN
SISTE KAROLEN, DEN see **ELI SJURSDOTTER** • 1938
SISTEMA PELEGRIN, EL • 1951 • Iquino Ignacio F. • SPN
SISTEMA TUNEL • 1978 • Blanco Javier • DCS • VNZ • TUNNEL SYSTEM
SISTEMAZIONE PIU COMODA, UNA • 1978 • Voi Pierluigi • ITL
SISTEMO L'AMERICA E TORNO • 1974 • Loy Nanni • ITL
SISTER, THE • 1911 • Olcott Sidney • USA
SISTER ACT see **FOUR DAUGHTERS** • 1938
SISTER AGAINST SISTER • 1917 • Vincent James • USA
SISTER AGAINST SISTER (USA) see **SORELLA CONTRO SORELLA** • 1920
SISTER ANGELE'S SECRET (USA) see **SECRET DE SOEUR ANGELE, LE** • 1956
SISTER ANGELICA see **SESTRA ANGELIKA** • 1932
SISTER BALONIKA • 1968 • Keatley Philip • CND
SISTER CECILIA see **HVOR SORGERNE GLEMMES** • 1916
SISTER CITROEN see **SOR CITROEN** • 1967
SISTER GAMBLERS, THE see **ONNA TOBA-ARASHI** • 1967
SISTER-IN-LAW • 1979 • Yukol Prince Chatri • THL
SISTER-IN-LAW, THE • 1975 • Ruben Joseph • USA
SISTER KENNY • 1946 • Nichols Dudley • USA
SISTER MARGARET AND THE SATURDAY NIGHT BABIES • 1987 • Wendkos Paul • TVM • USA
SISTER MARY JANE'S TOP NOTE • 1907 • Fitzhamon Lewin • UKN
SISTER MARY JANE'S TOP NOTE see **SHE WOULD SING** • 1905
SISTER OF SATAN see **REVENGE OF THE BLOOD BEAST, THE** • 1966
SISTER OF SIX, A • 1916 • Franklin Chester M., Franklin Sidney A. • USA
SISTER OF SIX, A see **FLICKORNA GYURKOVICS** • 1926
SISTER, SISTER • 1982 • Berry John • TVM • USA
SISTER, SISTER • 1987 • Condon Bill • USA
SISTER STELLA L. • 1984 • De Leon Mike • PHL
SISTER STREET FIGHTERS see **SISTER STREETFIGHTER** • 1976
SISTER STREETFIGHTER • 1976 • Yamaguchi Kazuhiko • JPN • SISTER STREET FIGHTERS
SISTER SUSIE'S SEWING SHIRTS FOR SOLDIERS • 1915 • Buss Harry • UKN
SISTER SUSIE'S SEWING SHIRTS FOR SOLDIERS • 1917 • Noy Wilfred • UKN
SISTER TERESA • 1974 • Millin David • SAF • SUSTER THERESA
SISTER TO ASSIST 'ER, A • 1913 • Booth W. R.? • UKN
SISTER TO ASSIST 'ER, A • 1922 • Dewhurst George • UKN
SISTER TO ASSIST 'ER, A • 1927 • Dewhurst George • UKN
SISTER TO ASSIST 'ER, A • 1930 • Dewhurst George • UKN
SISTER TO ASSIST 'ER, A • 1938 • Newman Widgey R., Dewhurst George • UKN
SISTER TO ASSIST 'ER, A • 1948 • Dewhurst George • UKN
SISTER TO CAIN, A • 1916 • Sloman Edward • SHT • USA
SISTER TO CARMEN • 1913 • Gaskill Charles L. • USA
SISTER TO JUDAS • 1933 • Hopper E. Mason • USA
SISTER TO SALOME, A • 1920 • Le Saint Edward J. • USA
SISTER YE-YE see **SOR YE-YE** • 1968
SISTERHOOD see **ADDICTED TO HIS LOVE** • 1988
SISTERHOOD, THE • 1988 • Santiago Cirio H. • USA
SISTERHOOD, THE see **LADIES CLUB, THE** • 1986
SISTERLY SCHEME, A • 1919 • Drew Sidney Mrs. (Spv) • SHT • USA
SISTERS • 1910 • Merwin Bannister • USA
SISTERS • 1912 • Salter Harry • USA
SISTERS • 1914 • *Powers* • USA
SISTERS • 1914 • Davis Ulysses • *Vitagraph* • USA
SISTERS • 1915 • Nash Percy? • UKN
SISTERS • 1922 • Capellani Albert • USA
SISTERS • 1930 • Flood James • USA
SISTERS • 1973 • De Palma Brian • USA • BLOOD SISTERS
SISTERS see **SYSTRARNA** • 1912
SISTERS see **KYODAI** • 1955
SISTERS see **SESTRY** • 1957
SISTERS see **AKKA NAGO** • 1968
SISTERS see **SESTRY** • 1970
SISTERS see **FILMREGENY -HAROM NOVER** • 1978
SISTERS see **SOME GIRLS** • 1988
SISTERS, THE • 1911 • Noy Wilfred • UKN
SISTERS, THE • 1913 • *Imp* • USA
SISTERS, THE • 1914 • Cabanne W. Christy • *Majestic* • USA
SISTERS, THE • 1938 • Litvak Anatole • USA
SISTERS, THE • 1965 • Andreou Errikos • GRC • MAKE ME A WOMAN
SISTERS, THE see **FRONA** • 1954
SISTERS, THE (UKN) see **SORELLE, LE** • 1969
SISTERS ALL • 1913 • Trimble Larry • USA
SISTERS AND I, THE see **KOTO YUSHU: ANE IMOUTO** • 1967
SISTER'S BURDEN, A • 1915 • Vignola Robert G. • USA
SISTER'S DEVOTION, A • 1910 • *Bison* • USA
SISTER'S DEVOTION, A • 1912 • *American* • USA
SISTERS HENGLER SPECIALTY DANCERS, THE • 1896 • *Paul R. W.* • UKN
SISTERS IN ARMS • 1918 • West Walter • UKN
SISTERS IN LEATHER • 1969 • Crilly Spence • USA • SISTERS IN LEATHERETTE
SISTERS IN LEATHERETTE see **SISTERS IN LEATHER** • 1969
SISTER'S LOVE, A • 1909 • Brooke Van Dyke • USA
SISTER'S LOVE, A • 1912 • Griffith D. W. • USA
SISTERS OF CORRUPTION see **CORRUPCION DE CHRIS MILLER, LA** • 1972
SISTERS OF DEATH • 1978 • Mazzuca Joseph A. • USA
SISTERS OF EVE • 1928 • Pembroke Scott • USA • AVARICE (UKN)
SISTERS OF NISHIJIN see **NISHIJIN NO SHIMAI** • 1952
SISTERS OF THE GION (USA) see **GION NO SHIMAI** • 1936
SISTERS OF THE GOLDEN CIRCLE • 1918 • Webb Kenneth • SHT • USA
SISTERS, OR THE BALANCE OF HAPPINESS (USA) see **SCHWESTERN ODER DIE BALANCE DES GLUCKS** • 1980
SISTER'S PEST • 1930 • Van Ronkel Jo • SHT • USA
SISTER'S SACRIFICE, A • 1910 • *Imp* • USA
SISTER'S SACRIFICE, A • 1910 • *Vitagraph* • USA
SISTER'S SOLACE, THE • 1915 • *Anderson Augusta* • USA
SISTERS UNDER THE SKIN • 1934 • Burton David • USA • ROMANTIC AGE, THE (UKN)
SISYPHUS • 1971 • Holwill Donald • ANS • UKN
SISYPHUS • 1974 • Jankovics Marcell • ANM • HNG
SISYPHUS (USA) see **SIZIF** • 1967

SIT EL NAZRA, EL • 1968 • Eddin Ahmed Dia • EGY • HEADMISTRESS, THE
SIT TIGHT • 1931 • Bacon Lloyd • USA
SITA KALYANAM see **SEETHA KALYANAM** • 1977
SITA SWAYAMVAR see **SEETHA KALYANAM** • 1977
SITA VANVAS • 1949 • Jani Pranbhai • IND
SITARON SE AAGEY • 1958 • *Burman S. D. (M)* • IND
SITA'S WEDDING see **SEETHA KALYANAM** • 1977
SITE BETTER, A • 1970 • Wilkins Bert • UKN • ELECTRICITY SUPPLY –EARLY WARNING
SITE IN THE SEA, A • 1971 • Sachs Gloria • UKN
SITE OF A SKULL see **TOPOS KRANIOU** • 1972
SITFONGDIK NUIYAN see **SUTFONGDIK NUIYAN** • 1989
SITHA GIYA THANE • 1967 • Ranasinghe Herbert • SLN • WHERE THE HEART IS
SITHAPAHARANAM • 1939 • *Ramayana* • IND
SITIADOS EN LA CIUDAD • 1955 • Lluch Miguel • SPN
SITKA SUE • *Vague Vera* • SHT • USA
SITSIRITSIT ALIBANGBANG • 1967 • Villaflor Romy • PHL
SITTER–DOWNERS, THE • 1937 • Lord Del • SHT • USA
SITTIN' ON A BACKYARD FENCE • 1933 • Duval Earl • ANS • USA
SITTING BULL • 1954 • Salkow Sidney • USA
SITTING BULL AT THE "SPIRIT LAKE MASSACRE" • 1927 • Bradbury Robert North • USA • WITH SITTING BULL AT THE "SPIRIT LAKE MASSACRE"
SITTING BULL –THE HOSTILE SIOUX INDIAN CHIEF • 1914 • *American Rotograph Co* • USA
SITTING DUCKS • 1980 • Jaglom Henry • USA
SITTING IN LIMBO • 1986 • Smith John N. • CND
SITTING IN THE PARK • 1967 • de Villa Jose • PHL
SITTING ON A BRANCH AND I FEEL FINE see **SEDIM NA KONARI, A JE MI DOBRE** • 1989
SITTING ON A BRANCH, ENJOYING MYSELF see **SEDIM NA KONARI, A JE MI DOBRE** • 1989
SITTING ON THE MOON • 1936 • Staub Ralph • USA
SITTING PRETTY • 1924 • McCarey Leo • SHT • USA
SITTING PRETTY • 1933 • Brown Harry J. • USA
SITTING PRETTY • 1948 • Lang Walter • USA
SITTING TARGET • 1971 • Hickox Douglas • UKN
SITTLICHKEITSVERBRECHER, DER • 1963 • Schnyder Franz • SWT • MOLESTERS, THE (USA)
SITUATION DE TRANSITION • 1966 • Beloufa Farouq • ALG
SITUATION DU THEATRE AU QUEBEC • 1969 • Gagne Jacques • DOC • CND
SITUATION EST GRAVE.. MAIS PAS DESESPEREE • 1976 • Besnard Jacques • FRN
SITUATION HOPELESS –BUT NOT SERIOUS • 1965 • Reinhardt Gottfried • USA
SITUATION OF MARRIAGE, THE see **KEKKON NO SEITAI** • 1941
SITUATION OF THE HUMAN WORLD, THE see **HITO NO YO NO SUGATA** • 1928
SITUATION ZERO • 1988 • Harper Stanley • DOC • KMP
SITUATIONS • Chanowski Thijs • NTH
SITUM • 1984 • Vikas Aruna • IND • CIRCUMSTANCE
SITZMARKS THE SPOT • 1948 • Sparling Gordon • DCS • CND
SIU NAMYAN CHOWGEI • 1988 • Chan Gordon • HKG • YUPPIE FANTASIA, THE
SIU NGOU GONGWU • 1990 • Hu King, Xu Ke • HKG • SWORDSMAN
SIUNATTI HULLUUS • 1975 • Mollberg Rauni • MTV • FNL • BLESSED MADNESS
SIUZHET DLYA NEBLOSHOVO RASSKAZA see **SYUZHET DLYA NEBOLSHOVO RASKAZA** • 1968
SIVA • 1968 • Levine Charles I. • SHT • USA
SIVA L'INVISIBLE • 1904 • Melies Georges • FRN • INVISIBLE SIVA, THE (USA)
SIVOOKY DEMON • 1919 • Binovec Vaclav • CZC • GREY EYED DEMON
SIVOUSHKO • 1962 • Dinov Todor • ANS • BUL • GREYSKIN ○ LITTLE GREY THING
SIX AGAINST THE ROCK • 1987 • Wendkos Paul • TVM • USA
SIX AND A HALF BY ELEVEN (A KODAK) see **SIX ET DEMI–ONZE (UN KODAK)** • 1927
SIX AND A HALF DOZEN • 1921 • Paul Fred • UKN
SIX BAGATELLES see **HAT BAGATELL** • 1988
SIX BEARS AND A CLOWN see **SEST MEDVEDU S CIBULKOU** • 1972
SIX BEST CELLARS, THE • 1920 • Crisp Donald • USA
SIX BLACK GIRLS see **SEST CERNYCH DIVEK ANEB PROC ZMIZEL ZATIC?** • 1969
SIX BLACK HORSES • 1962 • Keller Harry • USA
SIX BRAVE MEN • ANS • USA
SIX BRIDGES TO CROSS • 1955 • Pevney Joseph • USA
SIX CANDLES • 1960 • Barden E. • UKN
SIX CENT LOAF, THE • 1915 • *La Badie Florence* • USA
SIX CENT MILLE FRANCS PAR MOIS • 1925 • Peguy Robert, Koline Nicolas • FRN
SIX CENT MILLE FRANCS PAR MOIS • 1933 • Joannon Leo • FRN
SIX CHARACTERS IN SEARCH OF AN AUTHOR • 1972 • Wendkos Paul • TVM • USA
SIX CHEVAUX BLEUS • 1967 • Joulia Philippe • FRN • ZOSSIA
SIX COLUMN see **LOVE WAR, THE** • 1970
SIX CYLINDER ELOPEMENT, A • 1912 • *Chamberlain Riley* • USA
SIX CYLINDER LOVE • 1917 • Mix Tom • SHT • USA
SIX CYLINDER LOVE • 1923 • Clifton Elmer • USA
SIX CYLINDER LOVE • 1931 • Freeland Thornton • USA
SIX–DAY BIKE RIDER • 1934 • Bacon Lloyd • USA
SIX DAY RACE, THE see **6 DAGESLOBET** • 1958
SIX DAYS • 1923 • Brabin Charles J. • USA
SIX DAYS, THE see **6 DAGESLOBET** • 1958
SIX DAYS A WEEK (USA) see **BUGIARDA, LA** • 1965
SIX DAYS TO ETERNITY (USA) see **SHESHET HAYAMIM** • 1968
SIX DIRECTIONS OF BOXING, THE • 1979 • Hsu Tyrone • HKG
SIX ET DEMI–ONZE (UN KODAK) • 1927 • Epstein Jean • FRN • SIX AND A HALF BY ELEVEN (A KODAK)
SIX ET DOUZE • 1968 • Rechiche Majid, Tazi Mohamed • SHT • MRC
SIX FACES OF TERYLENE • 1964 • Evans David • DCS • UKN
SIX FEET FOUR • 1919 • King Henry • USA
SIX FEMMES POUR L'ASSASSIN (FRN) see **SEI DONNE PER L'ASSASSINO** • 1964
SIX–FIFTY, THE • 1923 • Ross Nat • USA
SIX FOOT ROMANCE, A • 1914 • *Lubin* • USA
SIX GUN DECISION • 1953 • McDonald Frank • MTV • USA
SIX GUN FOR HIRE • 1946 • Fraser Harry L. • USA
SIX GUN GOLD • 1942 • Howard David • USA
SIX GUN GOSPEL • 1943 • Hillyer Lambert • USA
SIX–GUN GOSPEL • 1948 • Nazarro Ray • USA
SIX GUN JUSTICE • 1930 • Nelson Jack • SHT • USA
SIX GUN JUSTICE • 1935 • Hill Robert F. • USA
SIX GUN LAW • 1948 • Nazarro Ray • USA
SIX GUN LAW see **ELFEGO BACA: SIX GUN LAW** • 1962
SIX GUN MAN • 1946 • Fraser Harry L. • USA
SIX–GUN MESA • 1950 • Fox Wallace • USA
SIX GUN MUSIC • 1949 • Watt Nate • SHT • USA
SIX–GUN RHYTHM • 1939 • Newfield Sam • USA
SIX GUN SERENADE • 1947 • Beebe Ford • USA
SIX–GUN TRAIL • 1938 • Newfield Sam • USA
SIX GUNS ARE CHASING PROFESSOR Z see **SECHS PISTOLEN JAGEN PROFESSOR Z** • 1967
SIX HEURES A PERDRE • 1946 • Joffe Alex, Levitte Jean • FRN
SIX HITS AND A MISS • 1942 • Negulesco Jean • SHT • USA
SIX HOURS TO LIVE • 1932 • Dieterle William • USA
SIX HUNDRED YEARS OF BYDGOSZCZ see **600–LECIE BYDGOSZCZY** • 1946
SIX IN PARIS see **PARIS VU PAR.. 20 ANS APRES** • 1984
SIX INCHES TALL (UKN) see **ATTACK OF THE PUPPET PEOPLE** • 1958
SIX JOURS DE LA CREATION, LES • 1961 • Mayo Nine • FRN
SIX LESSONS FROM MADAME LA ZONGA • 1941 • Rawlins John • USA
SIX LOOP–PAINTINGS • 1970 • Spinello Barry • SHT • USA
SIX MEN, THE • 1951 • Law Michael • UKN
SIX MILLION DOLLAR MAN, THE • 1973 • Irving Richard • TVM • USA • CYBORG
SIX MOIS DE VACANCES see **AGAZAT NUCF SANA** • 1962
SIX MONTHS TO LIVE • 1915 • *Wilson Ben* • USA
SIX MOTHER–IN–LAWS OF BLUEBEARD, THE see **SEIS SUEGRAS DE BARBA AZUL, LAS** • 1945
SIX NAPOLEONS, THE • 1922 • Ridgwell George • UKN
SIX O'CLOCK • 1912 • *Costello Maurice* • USA
SIX OF A KIND • 1934 • McCarey Leo • USA
SIX OR NINE • 1915 • *Wilson Ben* • USA
SIX PACK • 1982 • Petrie Daniel • USA
SIX PACK ANNIE • 1975 • *Bloom Lindsay* • USA
SIX PENGUINS, THE • 1970 • Panov Asparough • ANS • BUL
SIX PETITES BOUGIES • 1962 • Cotton • SHT • FRN
SIX PETITES FILLES EN BLANC • 1941 • Noe Yvan • FRN
SIX REELS OF FILM TO BE SHOWN IN ANY ORDER • 1971 • Salt Barry • UKN
SIX SHES AND A HE • 1964 • *Hamilton Joel* • USA
SIX–SHOOTER ANDY • 1918 • Franklin Sidney A. • USA • SIX SHOOTER ANDY
SIX SHOOTER ANDY see **SIX–SHOOTER ANDY** • 1918
SIX–SHOOTER JUSTICE • 1917 • Kelsey Fred A. • SHT • USA
SIX SHOOTERS IN LARIAT • 1931 • Hogan James P. • USA
SIX SHOOTIN' ROMANCE, A • 1926 • Smith Cliff • USA
SIX SHOOTIN' SHERIFF • 1938 • Fraser Harry L. • USA
SIX–SIDED TRIANGLE, THE • 1963 • Miles Christopher • UKN
SIX–SMURF FLUTE, THE see **FLUTE A SIX SCHTROUMPFS, LA** • 1975
SIX SUSPECTS (USA) see **DAIROKU NO YOGISHA** • 1960
SIX TERMINATORS, THE see **SEXTERMINATORS, THE** • 1970
SIX TICKETS TO HELL see **SEIS PASAJES AL INFIERNO** • 1975
SIX UNFORTUNATES, THE see **SECHS KUMMERBUBEN, DIE** • 1968
SIX WAR YEARS • 1975 • King Allan • CND
SIX WEEKS • 1982 • Bill Tony • USA
SIX WEEKS OF HAPPINESS see **HAT HET BOLDOGSAG** • 1939
SIX WIVES OF BLUEBEARD, THE see **SEI MOGLI DI BARBABLU, LE** • 1950
SIX WOMEN • 1974 • Bennett Mike • USA
SIX WOMEN AND A MAN see **SEXTET** • 1964
SIX WOMEN FOR THE MURDERER see **SEI DONNE PER L'ASSASSINO** • 1964
SIX YEARS see **ZES JAREN** • 1946
SIXES AND NINES • 1913 • Hotaling Arthur D. • USA
SIXIEME ETAGE • 1939 • Cloche Maurice • FRN
SIXIEME FACE DU PENTAGONE, LA • 1967 • Mørker Chris, Reichenbach Francois • FRN
SIXPENCE • 1985 • SAF
SIXTEEN CANDLES • 1984 • Hughes John • USA
SIXTEEN FATHOMS DEEP • 1934 • Schaefer Armand • USA
SIXTEEN FLYING FINGERS • 1960 • Henryson Robert • UKN
SIXTEEN YEARS LATER see **16 ANOS DESPUES** • 1979
SIXTEENTH WIFE, THE • 1917 • Brabin Charles J. • USA
SIXTET see **SEXTET** • 1964
SIXTH AND MAIN • 1977 • Cain Christopher • USA
SIXTH COMMANDMENT see **SJATTE BUDET** • 1947
SIXTH COMMANDMENT, THE • 1912 • Collins Edwin J. • UKN
SIXTH COMMANDMENT, THE • 1913 • Bowman William J. • USA
SIXTH COMMANDMENT, THE • 1924 • Cabanne W. Christy • USA
SIXTH CONTINENT see **SESTO CONTINENTE** • 1954
SIXTH DAY, THE see **YOM EL SADES, EL** • 1986
SIXTH DEGREE, THE • 1925 • Diamant-Berger Henri • USA
SIXTH GEAR see **SESTA BRZINA** • 1982
SIXTH MAN, THE see **OUTSIDER, THE** • 1961
SIXTH OF JULY, THE (UKN) see **SHESTOYE IYULYA** • 1968
SIXTH OF THE EARTH, A see **SHESTAYA CHAST MIRA** • 1926
SIXTH PART OF THE WORLD, A see **SHESTAYA CHAST MIRA** • 1926
SIXTH SENTENCE, THE see **SIESTA VETA** • 1985
SIXTH SHOT, THE see **SJATTE SKOTTET** • 1943
SIXTY CENTS AN HOUR • 1923 • Henabery Joseph • USA • SEVENTY FIVE CENTS AN HOUR
SIXTY CYCLES see **60 CYCLES** • 1964
SIXTY–EIGHT see **'68** • 1988
SIXTY–FOUR DAY HERO • 1987 • Rosso Franco • UKN
SIXTY GLORIOUS YEARS • 1938 • Wilcox Herbert • UKN • QUEEN OF DESTINY (USA) ○ QUEEN VICTORIA
SIXTY HOURS TO SUEZ see **SHISHIM SHA'OT LE'SUEZ** • 1967
SIXTY SADDLES FOR GOBI see **DESTINATION GOBI** • 1953
SIXTY SECOND ASSASSIN • 1981 • *Li John* • HKG
SIXTY–SEVEN DAYS see **UZICKA REPUBLIKA** • 1974
SIXTY YEARS A QUEEN • 1913 • Haldane Bert • UKN
SIXTYNINE • 1969 • Donner Jorn • FNL, SWD • 69
SIZE M • 1970 • Sinden Tony • UKN
SIZIF • 1967 • Marks Aleksandar, Jutrisa Vladimir • ANS • YGS • SISYPHUS (USA) ○ SISIPHUS
SIZILIANISCHE BLUTRACHE • 1920 • Gartner Adolf • FRG
SIZZLE • 1981 • Medford Don • TVM • USA
SIZZLE • 1981 • Vincent Chuck • USA • SIZZLE PANTS
SIZZLE BEACH see **SIZZLE BEACH USA** • 1986
SIZZLE BEACH USA • 1986 • Brander Richard • USA • MALIBU HOT SUMMER ○ SIZZLE BEACH
SIZZLE PANTS see **SIZZLE** • 1981
SIZZLE WITH SISSIE • 1946 • Crouch William Forest • SHT • USA
S/J FOSSILEA • 1973 • Mulders Jean • BLG
SJAELENS VEN see **SJAELETYVEN** • 1915
SJAELETYVEN • 1915 • Holger-Madsen • DNM • UNWILLING SINNER, THE ○ SJAELENS VEN ○ HIS INNOCENT DUPE
SJATTE BUDET • 1947 • Jarrel Stig • SWD • SIXTH COMMANDMENT
SJATTE SKOTTET • 1943 • Ekman Hasse • SWD • SIXTH SHOT, THE
SJECAS LI SE DOLLY BELL? • 1981 • Kusturica Emir • YGS • DO YOU REMEMBER DOLLY BELL?
SJETTE TRAEKNING • 1936 • Schneevoigt George • DNM
SJOCHARMORER • 1939 • Rodin Gosta • SWD • CHARMERS AT SEA
SJOMAN GAR I LAND, EN • 1937 • Arvedson Ragnar • SWD • SAILOR GOES ASHORE, A
SJOMAN I FRACK, EN • 1942 • Arvedson Ragnar • SWD • SAILOR IN A DRESS–COAT
SJOMAN TILL HAST, EN • 1940 • Lingheim Emil A. • SWD • SAILOR ON A HORSE
SJOMANSDANSEN • 1911 • Nylander N. H., Magnusson Charles • SWD • SAILOR'S DANCE
SJOROVAREN • 1909 • Magnusson Charles • SWD • PIRATE, THE
SJORS AND SJIMMIE IN THE LAND OF THE GIANTS see **SJORS EN SJIMMIE IN HET LAND DER REUZEN** • 1967
SJORS EN SJIMMIE IN HET LAND DER REUZEN • 1967 • van der Linden H. J. • NTH • SJORS AND SJIMMIE IN THE LAND OF THE GIANTS
SJOSALAVAR • 1949 • Gunwall Per • SWD • SPRING AT SJOSALA
SJOV I GADEN • 1969 • Ottosen Carl • DNM
SJOVE AR, DE • 1959 • Kjaerulff-Schmidt Palle • DNM • FUNNY YEARS, THE
SJU DAGAR FOR ELIZABETH • 1927 • Sinding Leif • NRW
SJU SVARTA BE–HA • 1954 • Bernhard Gosta • SWD • SEVEN BLACK BRASSIERES
SJU VACKRA FLICKOR • 1956 • Bergstrom Hakan • SWD • SEVEN BEAUTIFUL GIRLS
SJUNDE HIMLEN • 1956 • Ekman Hasse • SWD • SEVENTH HEAVEN, THE
SJUNDE INSEGLET, DET • 1957 • Bergman Ingmar • SWD • SEVENTH SEAL, THE (UKN)
SJUTTON AR • 1957 • Kjellin Alf • SWD • SEVENTEEN YEARS OLD
SKA' VI LEGE SKJUL? • 1970 • Hedegaard Tom • DNM, NRW
SKABENGA • 1953 • Michael George • SAF • SKABENKA ○ AFRICAN FURY
SKABENKA see **SKABENGA** • 1953
SKADU VAN GISTER • 1961 • SAF
SKADUS VAN GISTER • 1974 • SAF
SKADUWEES OOR BRUGPLASS see **HOUSE OF THE LIVING DEAD, THE** • 1973
SKAEBNEBAELTET • 1912 • *Christensen Benjamin* • DNM
SKAEBNES VEJE • 1913 • Holger-Madsen • DNM • UNDER KAERLIGHEDENS AAG ○ IN THE BONDS OF PASSION
SKAEBNESVANGRE LOGN, DEN see **FRU POTIFAR** • 1911
SKAEBNESVANGRE OPFINDELSE, DEN • 1910 • Blom August • DNM • DR. JEKYLL AND MR. HYDE ○ JEKYLL AND HYDE
SKAEVE DAGE I THY • 1970 • Ammundsen Kjeld, Nielsen Gregers, Preisler Ebbe, Broby Finn, Hansen Dino Raymond, Jorgensen Teij • DNM
SKAG • 1980 • Perry Frank • TVM • USA
SKAL VI DANSE FORST? • 1979 • Olsen Annette • DNM • SHALL WE DANCE FIRST?
SKAL VI VAEDDE EN MILLION • 1932 • Schneevoigt George • DNM
SKALNI PLEMENO • 1944 • Korbelar Otomar • CZC • ROCKPEOPLE, THE
SKALNI SEVCI • 1931 • Longen • CZC • DIE–HARD SHOEMAKERS, THE
SKALPEL, PROSIM • 1985 • Svoboda Jiri • CZC • SCALPEL, PLEASE
SKAMMEN • 1968 • Bergman Ingmar • SWD • SHAME, THE
SKANDAL IM GRANDHOTEL see **FURST SEPPL** • 1932
SKANDAL IM MADCHENPENSIONAT • 1953 • Kobler Erich • FRG
SKANDAL IM VIKTORIA–CLUB, DER • 1919 • Eriksen Erich • FRG
SKANDAL IN BADEN–BADEN • 1928 • Waschneck Erich • FRG
SKANDAL IN BUDAPEST • 1933 • von Bolvary Geza, Sekely Steve • FRG, HNG • PARDON TEVEDTEM (HNG) ○ ROMANCE IN BUDAPEST ○ PESTI SZERELEM ○ SCANDAL IN BUDAPEST
SKANDAL IN DER BOTSCHAFT • 1950 • Ode Erik • FRG
SKANDAL IN DER PARKSTRASSE • 1932 • Wenzler Franz • FRG
SKANDAL IN ISCHL • 1957 • Thiele Rolf • AUS
SKANDAL UM DIE FLEDERMAUS • 1936 • Selpin Herbert • FRG
SKANDAL UM DR. VLIMMEN • 1956 • Rabenalt Arthur M. • FRG

SKANDAL UM DODO • 1959 • von Borsody Eduard • AUS
SKANDAL UM EVA • 1930 • Pabst G. W. • FRG • EVA SCANDAL, THE
SKANDAL UM HAHN • 1938 • Seitz Franz • FRG
SKANDALEN • 1913 • Klercker Georg • SWD • SCANDAL, THE
SKANDERBEG see **VELIKII VOIN ALBANII SKANDERBEG** • 1953
SKANINGAR • 1944 • Benktsson Benkt-Ake • SWD
SKANOR–FALSTERBO • 1939 • Lingheim Emil A. • SWD • SMALL TOWNS OF SKANOR–FALSTERBO
SKANSEN • 1978 • Giersz Witold • ANS • PLN • ETHNOGRAPHICAL MUSEUM
SKANSENVAR • 1946 • Werner Gosta • SHT • SWD • SPRING AT SKANSEN
SKAPANI W OGNIU • 1963 • Passendorfer Jerzy • PLN • CHRISTENED BY FIRE
SKARABEUS • 1976 • Voyame Pierre, Joray Niggi • SWT
SKARB • 1949 • Buczkowski Leonard • PLN • TREASURE, THE
SKARB CZARNEGO JACKA • 1961 • Giersz Witold • ANS • PLN • BLACK JACK'S TREASURE
SKARB KAPITANA MARTENSA • 1957 • Passendorfer Jerzy • PLN • CAPTAIN MARTEN'S TREASURE
SKAREDA DEDINA • 1975 • Kachyna Karel • CZC • UGLY VILLAGE, THE
SKARGARDSFLIRT • 1935 • Bornebusch Arne • SWD • FLIRTATION IN THE ARCHIPELAGO
SKARGARDSKAVALJERER see **PENSIONAT PARADISET** • 1937
SKARGARDSNATT, EN • 1953 • Logardt Bengt • SWD • NIGHT IN THE ARCHIPELAGO, A
SKARLATINA • 1924 • Ermler Friedrich • DOC • USS • SCARLET FEVER
SKARPRETTEREN • 1972 • Reuter-Christiansen Ursula • DNM • EXECUTIONER, THE
SKARSELD • 1975 • Meschke Michael • SWD • A DIVINE COMEDY –PURGATORY ○ PURGATORIO ○ PURGATORY
SKARSLIPAREN • 1913 • Klercker Georg • SWD • KNIFE GRINDER
SKA'RU' ME' PA FEST? • 1966 • Fellbom Claes • SWD
SKAT VAN ISSIE • 1972 • SAF
SKATE see **BLADES OF STEEL** • 1987
SKATE AT SEA, A • 1919 • Moore Vin • SHT • USA
SKATE FOR A BRIDE, A • 1916 • Metcalfe Earl • SHT • USA
SKATEBOARD • 1978 • Gage George • USA
SKATERDATER • 1966 • Black Noel • USA
SKATERS, THE see **SCHAATSENRIJDEN** • 1929
SKATERS ON THE AMSTEL • 1974 • Kohanyi Julius • MTV • CND
SKATETOWN U.S.A. • 1979 • Levey William A. • USA
SKATING see **SCHAATSENRIJDEN** • 1929
SKATING BUG, THE • 1911 • *Pickford Mary* • USA
SKATING CRAZE AT MOODYVILLE, THE • 1916 • *Judy* • USA
SKATING HOUNDS • 1929 • Terry Paul • ANS • USA
SKATING INSTRUCTORS • 1926 • Fisher Bud • ANS • USA
SKATING MASTER, THE • 1914 • *Noel Billy* • USA
SKATING ON THIN ICE • 1980 • Reid Bill • DOC • CND
SKATING ON THIN ICE see **SKATING ON THIN UYS** • 1985
SKATING ON THIN UYS • 1985 • Uys Pieter-Dirk • SAF • SKATING ON THIN ICE
SKATING RINK • 1927 • Ivanov-Vano Ivan, Cherkez D. • ANS • USS
SKATING RINK, THE • 1916 • *Bambrick Gertrude* • SHT • USA
SKATING RINK AND THE VIOLIN, THE • 1959 • Konchalovsky Andrei, Tarkovsky Andrei • USS
SKAZANIYE O ZEMLYE SIBIRSKOI • 1947 • Pyriev Ivan • USS • SAGA OF THE SIBERIAN LAND, THE ○ TALES OF SIBERIAN LAND ○ TALE OF SIBERIA, A ○ SONG OF SIBERIA ○ SYMPHONY OF LIFE ○ STORY OF SIBERIAN LAND, A
SKAZANY • 1976 • Trzos-Rastawiecki Andrzej • PLN • CONDEMNED
SKAZKA MORTA • 1915 • Tourjansky Victor • USS
SKAZKA O CARE DURANDAE • 1934 • Ivanov-Vano Ivan • ANS • USS • TALES OF TSAR DURANDAI ○ CZAR DURANDAI, THE
SKAZKA O KONKE–GORBUNKE • 1961 • Radunskiy Aleksandr, Tulubyeva Zoya • USS • LITTLE HUMPBACKED HORSE, THE (USA) ○ KONIOK GORBUNOK
SKAZKA O RYBAKE I RYBKE • 1913 • Starevitch Ladislas, Ivanov-Gaj A. • USS • FABLE OF THE FISHERMAN AND THE FISH, THE
SKAZKA O RYBAKE I RYBKE • 1937 • Ptushko Alexander • ANS • USS • TALE OF THE FISHERMAN AND THE LITTLE FISH ○ FISHMONGER AND THE FISH
SKAZKA O SPJASCEJ CAREVNE I SEMI BOGATYRIACH • 1914 • Cardynin P. • USS • SLEEPING BEAUTY (USA)
SKAZKA O TSARE SALTANE • 1967 • Ptushko Alexander • USS • TALE OF TSAR SALTAN, THE ○ TALES OF CZAR TSALTAN ○ TALE OF CZAR SALTAN, THE
SKAZKA STRANSTVILI • 1983 • Mitta Alexander • USS • STORY OF THE VOYAGES, THE
SKEDADDLE GOLD • 1927 • Thorpe Richard • USA
SKEEZER • 1982 • Hunt Peter H. • TVM • USA
SKEIN • 1974 • Brakhage Stan • USA
SKEIN OF LIFE, THE • 1915 • MacDonald Donald • USA
SKELETHAANDEN see **JUVELERERNES SKROEK** • 1915
SKELETHAANDENS SIDSTE BEDRIFT see **JUVELERERNES SKROEK** • 1915
SKELETHANDEN • 1915 • Schneevoigt George • DNM
SKELETON, THE • 1910 • *Vitagraph* • USA
SKELETON, THE • 1912 • *Powers* • USA
SKELETON, THE • 1914 • Reid Wallace • USA
SKELETON CANYON RAID, THE • 1917 • Horne James W. • SHT • USA
SKELETON COAST • 1987 • Cardos John Bud • USA
SKELETON DANCE, THE • 1928 • Disney Walt, Iwerks Ub • ANS • USA
SKELETON DANCE, MARIONETTES • 1898 • *Edison* • USA
SKELETON FROLIC • 1937 • Iwerks Ub • ANS • USA
SKELETON IN THE CLOSET, THE • 1913 • *Blackwell Carlyle* • USA
SKELETON KEY, THE see **PAKLIC** • 1944
SKELETON KEYS • 1925 • Butler Alexander • UKN
SKELETON OF MRS. MORALES, THE see **ESQUELETO DE LA SENORA MORALES, EL** • 1959
SKELETON ON HORSEBACK see **BILA NEMOC** • 1937
SKELETON SETS THE TRAP see **KOSTUR POSTAVLJA ZAMKU** • 1962
SKELETON'S HAND, THE see **JUVELERERNES SKROEK** • 1915
SKELETT, DAS • 1916 • Eichberg Richard • FRG
SKELETT DES HERRN MARKUTIUS, DAS • 1920 • Janson Victor • FRG
SKELETTREITER VON COLORADO, DER • 1920 • Stockel Joe • FRG
SKELLEY AND THE TURKEY • 1914 • Dillon Eddie • USA
SKELLEY BUYS A HOTEL • 1914 • Dillon Eddie • USA
SKELLEY'S BIRTHDAY • 1914 • Dillon Eddie • USA
SKELLEY'S SKELETON • 1913 • *Ab* • USA
SKELLY'S SKELETON • 1916 • MacMackin Archer • USA
SKELM VAN DIE LIMPOPO • 1962 • SAF
SKELMS • 1979 • Scholtz Jan • SAF • THIEVES
SKELTROS • 1921 • Rosa Silvio Laurenti • ITL
SKEPIOEN, DIE • 1946 • SAF
SKEPP KOMMER LASTAT, ETT • 1932 • Alfe Thure • SWD
SKEPP OHOJ! • 1931 • Edgren Gustaf • SWD • SHIP AHOY!
SKEPP SOM MOTAS • 1916 • Sjostrom Victor • SWD • SHIPS THAT MEET ○ MEETING SHIPS
SKEPP TILL INDIALAND • 1947 • Bergman Ingmar • SWD • SHIP TO INDIA, A (UKN) ○ SHIP BOUND FOR INDIA, A ○ FRUSTRATION (USA) ○ LAND OF DESIRE, THE
SKEPPAR JANSSON • 1945 • Wallen Sigurd • SWD • SKIPPER JANSSON
SKEPPAR MUNTERS BRAVADER • 1950 • Ohberg Ake • SWD • YOUNG AND IN LOVE ○ UNG OCH KAR
SKEPPARE I BLASVADER • 1951 • Olsson Gunnar • SWD • SKIPPER IN STORMY WEATHER
SKEPPARFROJD see **TVA HJARTAN OCH EN SKUTA** • 1932
SKEPPARGATAN 40 • 1925 • Edgren Gustaf • SWD • 40 SKIPPER'S STREET
SKEPPARKARLEK • 1931 • Johansson Ivar • SWD • SKIPPER LOVE
SKEPPSBRUTNE MAX • 1936 • Wallen Sigurd, Schulz Fritz • SWD • SHIPWRECKED MAX
SKEPTICAL COWBOY, THE • *Centaur* • USA
SKERTSO DIAVOLA • 1918 • Tourjansky Victor • USS
SKETCH, A • 1963 • Tosheva Nevena • DOC • BUL
SKETCH LIFE • 1988 • Daniels Stan • USA
SKETCH OF DANIEL see **ESBOZO DE DANIEL** • 1986
SKETCH OF MADAME YUKI see **YUKI FUJIN EZU** • 1950
SKETCH ON THE ROAD, A see **GAIJO NO SUKECHI** • 1925
SKETCH WITH THE THUMB PRINT, THE • 1912 • *Furniss Harry* • USA
SKETCHES • 1976 • Brakhage Stan • SHT • USA
SKETCHES • 1990 • Israel Neal • USA
SKETCHES FOR A DIRECTOR'S PORTRAIT see **SZKICE SO PORTRETU REZYSERA** • 1970
SKETCHES OF A KILLER • 1978 • *Macrae Meredith* • USA
SKETCHES OF A STRANGLER • 1978 • Leder Paul • USA
SKETCHES OF SCOTLAND • 1949 • Stringer G. Henry • UKN
SKETCHY SKIING • 1932 • Sparling Gordon • DCS • CND
SKEZAG • 1971 • Freedman Joel L., Messina Philip F. • USA
SKI, LE • Lavoie Hermenegilde • DCS • CND
SKI, LE • 1908 • Cohl Emile • ANS • FRN
SKI A QUEBEC • 1950 • Proulx Maurice • DCS • CND
SKI BATTALION • 1938 • Muzykant R., Muzykant Yu. • USS
SKI BIRDS • 1939 • Trego Charles T. • SHT • USA
SKI BUM, THE • 1971 • Clark Bruce • USA
SKI CHAMP, THE • 1958 • Grimm Hans • FRG
SKI CHAMPIONS see **OLYMPIC SKI CHAMPIONS** • 1936
SKI CHASE, THE see **WEISSE RAUSCH, DER** • 1931
SKI CROSS COUNTRY • 1983 • Nicolle Douglas • MTV • CND
SKI DANCE see **FIRE AND ICE** • 1987
SKI EXTREM • 1968 • Gorter Jurgen Jr. • FRG • SKI RECORDS
SKI–FASZINATION • 1965 • Bogner Willy • DOC • FRG
SKI FEVER • 1967 • Siodmak Curt • USA, AUS, CZC • LEIBESSPIELE IM SCHNEE (AUS)
SKI FOR TWO • 1944 • Culhane James • ANS • USA • WOODY PLAYS SANTA
SKI IN THE SKY • 1949 • Sparling Gordon • DCS • CND
SKI LIFT TO DEATH • 1978 • Wiard William • TVM • USA
SKI–NAPPER • 1964 • Marcus Sid • ANS • USA
SKI ON THE WILD SIDE • 1967 • Miller Warren • DOC • USA
SKI PARTY • 1965 • Rafkin Alan • USA
SKI PATROL • 1940 • Landers Lew • USA
SKI RAIDERS, THE (UKN) see **SNOW JOB** • 1972
SKI RECORDS see **SKI EXTREM** • 1968
SKI RESORT, THE • 1960 • *Halas John (P)* • ANS • UKN
SKI SKILL • 1937 • *Smith Pete* • SHT • USA
SKI SKILL • 1946 • Blais Roger • DCS • CND • DESCENTES ET VIRAGES
SKI TOTAL • 1962 • Ertaud Jacques • FRN
SKI TROOP ATTACK • 1960 • Corman Roger • USA
SKIACHTRA, I • 1985 • Manousakis Manousos • GRC • ENCHANTRESS, THE
SKIBET ER LADET MED • 1945 • Henning-Jensen Astrid • DOC • DNM
SKICKA HEM NR.7 • 1937 • Wahlberg Gideon, Bauman Schamyl • SWD • SEND HOME NO.7 (USA) ○ SEND NO.7 HOME
SKID see **SMYK** • 1960
SKID see **POSLIZG** • 1971
SKID KIDS • 1953 • Chaffey Don • UKN
SKID PROOF • 1923 • Dunlap Scott R. • USA
SKID ROW • 1956 • King Allan • DOC • CND
SKID ROW STOPGAP • 1954 • Brusseau William E. • USA
SKIDDING HEARTS • 1917 • Wright Walter • SHT • USA
SKIDDING THRONES • 1919 • Lyons Eddie, Moran Lee • SHT • USA
SKIDOO • 1964 • Biggs Julian • CND
SKIDOO • 1968 • Preminger Otto • USA
SKIDS AND SCALLAWAGS • 1918 • Semon Larry • SHT • USA
SKIERRI –LAND OF THE DWARF BIRCH see **SKIERRI – VAIVAISKOIVUJEN MAA** • 1983
SKIERRI –VAIVAISKOIVUJEN MAA • 1983 • Lehmuskallio Markku • FNL • SKIERRI –LAND OF THE DWARF BIRCH
SKIES ABOVE see **CIEL SUR LA TETE, LE** • 1964
SKIES OF DEATH, THE see **CIELOS DE LA MUERTE, LOS** • 1977
SKIEUR DE L'EVEREST, LE see **MAN WHO SKIED DOWN EVEREST, THE** • 1974
SKIFAHRT INS GLUCK • 1924 • *Alpenfilm* • FRG
SKIING ON THE SUMMIT see **GO GO WAKADAISHO** • 1967
SKILABOD TIL SONDRU • 1983 • Palsdottir Kristin • ICL • NOTE FOR SANDRA, A ○ MESSAGE TO SANDRA
SKILFUL SLEIGHER'S STRATEGY, THE • 1916 • *Swan William* • USA
SKILLED HANDS READY see **VAKMAN PARAAT** • 1956
SKILLS UNLIMITED • 1964 • Browne K. R. • UKN
SKILSMISSENS BORN • 1939 • Christensen Benjamin • DNM • CHILDREN OF DIVORCE, THE
SKIMPY IN THE NAVY • 1949 • Dickens Stafford • UKN
SKIN • 1965 • Linder Carl • SHT • USA
SKIN • 1987 • Henderickx Guido • BLG
SKIN see **HUD** • 1986
SKIN, THE see **PELLE, LA** • 1981
SKIN COLOUR OF THE MOON see **HADAIRO NO TSUKI** • 1957
SKIN DEEP • 1922 • Hillyer Lambert • USA
SKIN DEEP • 1929 • Enright Ray • USA
SKIN DEEP • 1968 • Cox Paul • SHT • ASL
SKIN DEEP • 1988 • Edwards Blake • USA
SKIN DEEP see **SKINDEEP** • 1978
SKIN DEEP see **SENZA BUCCIA** • 1979
SKIN DEEP IN LOVE • 1967 • Sarno Joe • USA • DEEP IN LOVE
SKIN FLICKER see **SKINFLICKER** • 1972
SKIN GAME • 1971 • Bogart Paul, Douglas Gordon (U/c) • USA
SKIN GAME, A • 1915 • Daly William Robert • USA
SKIN GAME, THE • 1920 • Doxat-Pratt B. E. • UKN
SKIN GAME, THE • 1931 • Hitchcock Alfred • UKN
SKIN GAME, THE see **KIL 1** • 1964
SKIN GAMES see **KIL 1** • 1964
SKIN OF A WOMAN see **ONNA NO HADA** • 1957
SKIN OF LOVE, THE see **PIEL DEL AMOR, LA** • 1973
SKIN OF SORROW, THE see **SAGRENSKA KOZA** • 1960
SKIN OF YOUR EYE • 1973 • Cantrill Arthur, Cantrill Corinne • ASL
SKIN ON SKIN • 1981 • Spinelli Anthony • USA
SKIN SKIN (UKN) see **KAPY SELAN ALLA** • 1967
SKIN TO SKIN (UKN) see **VON HAUT ZU HAUT** • 1969
SKIN TRICK see **ZOKU: MIDAREGAMI HADAIROJIGAKE** • 1967
SKINDEEP • 1978 • Steven Geoff • NZL • SKIN DEEP
SKINDEEP see **REJUVENATOR, THE** • 1988
SKINFLICKER • 1972 • Bicat Tony • UKN • SKIN FLICKER
SKINFLINT, THE • 1912 • *West William H.* • USA
SKINFLINT, THE • 1915 • *Princess* • USA
SKINFOLKS • 1964 • Marcus Sid • ANS • USA
SKINHEADS • 1989 • Clark Greydon • USA
SKINNAY ENNIS AND HIS ORCHESTRA • 1941 • Negulesco Jean • SHT • USA
SKINNAY ENNIS AND HIS ORCHESTRA • 1949 • Cowan Will • SHT • USA
SKINNER STEPS OUT • 1929 • Craft William James • USA
SKINNER'S BABY • 1917 • Beaumont Harry • USA
SKINNER'S BIG IDEA • 1928 • Shores Lynn • USA
SKINNER'S BUBBLE • 1917 • Beaumont Harry • USA
SKINNER'S DRESS SUIT • 1917 • Beaumont Harry • USA
SKINNER'S DRESS SUIT • 1926 • Seiter William A. • USA
SKINNERS IN SILK • 1925 • *Sennett Mack (P)* • SHT • USA
SKINNING SKINNERS • 1921 • Nigh William • USA
SKINNY AND OTHERS see **CHDY I INNI** • 1967
SKINNY GETS A GOAT • 1917 • Roach Hal • SHT • USA
SKINNY ROUTS A ROBBER • 1917 • *Rolin* • SHT • USA
SKINNY, SCHOOL AND SCANDAL • 1919 • Harvey John Joseph • SHT • USA
SKINNY THE MOOCHER • 1939 • Lord Del • SHT • USA
SKINNY'S FALSE ALARM • 1917 • Roach Hal • SHT • USA
SKINNY'S FINISH • 1908 • Porter Edwin S. • USA
SKINNY'S LOVE TRIANGLE • 1917 • *Rolin* • SHT • USA
SKINNY'S SHIPWRECKED SAND–WITCH see **SKINNY'S SHIPWRECKED SANDWICH** • 1917
SKINNY'S SHIPWRECKED SANDWICH • 1917 • Roach Hal • SHT • USA • SKINNY'S SHIPWRECKED SAND–WITCH
SKINNY'S SICK • 1919 • *Briggs* • SHT • USA
SKINOUSSA, PAYSAGE AVEC LA CHUTE D'ICARE • 1979 • Baronnet Jean • DOC • FRN
SKINS • 1989 • Mastroianni Armand • USA
SKINTIGHT • 1981 • De Priest Ed • USA
SKIP THE MALOO! • 1931 • Parrott James • SHT • USA
SKIP TRACER • 1977 • Dalen Zale R. • CND
SKIP–TRACER see **SQUEEZE, THE** • 1987
SKIPALONG ROSENBLOOM • 1951 • Newfield Sam • USA • SQUARE SHOOTER, THE
SKIPPER see **TODD KILLINGS, THE** • 1971
SKIPPER, THE • 1988 • *Barkan Yehuda* • ISR
SKIPPER, THE • 1989 • Keglevic Peter • FRG
SKIPPER & CO see **SKIPPER OG CO.** • 1974
SKIPPER IN STORMY WEATHER see **SKEPPARE I BLASVADER** • 1951
SKIPPER JANSSON see **SKEPPAR JANSSON** • 1945
SKIPPER LOVE see **SKEPPARKARLEK** • 1931
SKIPPER NEXT TO GOD see **MAITRE APRES DIEU** • 1950
SKIPPER OF THE OSPREY • 1933 • Walker Norman • UKN
SKIPPER OF THE OSPREY, THE • 1916 • Miller Frank • UKN
SKIPPER OG CO. • 1974 • Henning-Jensen Bjarne • DNM • SKIPPER & CO
SKIPPER SIMPSON'S DAUGHTER • 1915 • MacMackin Archer • USA
SKIPPER SURPRISED HIS WIFE, THE • 1950 • Nugent Elliott • USA
SKIPPERS AND SCHEMERS • 1918 • Howe J. A. • SHT • USA
SKIPPER'S DAUGHTERS, THE • 1909 • *Selig* • USA
SKIPPER'S MATE, THE • 1917 • SER • USA
SKIPPER'S WOOING, THE • 1922 • Haynes Manning • UKN
SKIPPER'S YARN, THE • 1910 • *Edison* • USA
SKIPPING CHEESES, THE see **FROMAGES AUTOMOBILES, LES** • 1907
SKIPPY • 1932 • Taurog Norman • USA
SKIPPY AND THE THREE R'S • 1954 • Rusinow Irving • USA
SKIRKER'S SON, THE • 1918 • ASL
SKIRL OF THE PIBROCH, THE • 1908 • Aylott Dave? • UKN
SKIRMISH see **ALL'S FAIR** • 1989

SKIRMISH BY THE CYCLE CORPS • 1899 • *Warwick Trading Co* • UKN
SKIRT DANCE • 1898 • *Cinematograph Co* • UKN
SKIRT SHY • 1929 • Rogers Charles • SHT • USA
SKIRT SHY see **LEAP YEAR** • 1921
SKIRT STRATEGY • 1917 • *Depp Harry* • SHT • USA
SKIRTS • 1916 • *Tincher Fay* • SHT • USA
SKIRTS • 1917 • *Gibson Margaret* • USA
SKIRTS • 1921 • Del Ruth Hampton • USA
SKIRTS AHOY! • 1952 • Lanfield Sidney • USA
SKIRTS AND CINDERS • 1916 • McKim Edwin • SHT • USA
SKIRTS (USA) see **LITTLE BIT OF FLUFF, A** • 1928
SKIS DE FRANCE • 1947 • Ichac Marcel • DCS • FRN
SKI'S THE LIMIT, THE • 1949 • Sparber I. • ANS • USA
SKITCH HENDERSON AND THE MODERNAIRES • 1950 • *Universal* • SHT • USA
SKITS ON PLAYS • 1908 • *Tyler Walter* • UKN
SKITS ON SONGS • 1908 • *Tyler Walter* • UKN
SKITTLE ALLEY, THE see **BOWLING ALLEY, THE** • 1963
SKIWAYS • 1940 • Sparling Gordon • DCS • CND
SKJULT VIDEN • 1978 • Hartkopp Christian • DOC • DNM • HIDDEN KNOWLEDGE
SKJULTE SKAT, DEN see **DR. NICOLA I** • 1909
SKJULTE VIRKELIGHED, DEN • 1987 • Henriksen Morten • DNM • HIDDEN REALITY, THE
SKLAVEN DER LIEBE • 1924 • Boese Carl • FRG • HOCHZEIT VON VALENI, DIE
SKLAVEN DER PFLICHT • 1915 • Larsen Viggo • FRG
SKLAVEN DER SEELEN • 1919 • Rothauser Eduard • FRG • ER SELBST -SEIN GOTT
SKLAVEN DER SINNE see **IRRENDE SEELEN** • 1921
SKLAVEN DES 20 JAHRHUNDERTS see **GEFANGENE, DER** • 1920
SKLAVEN DES KAPITALS • 1919 • *Haack Kate* • FRG
SKLAVEN DES XX. JAHRHUNDERTS see **GEFANGENE, DER** • 1920
SKLAVEN FREMDEN WILLENS • 1919 • Eichberg Richard • FRG
SKLAVEN ROMS, DIE (FRG) see **RIVOLTA DEGLI SCHIAVI, LA** • 1961
SKLAVENKARAWANE, DIE • 1958 • Marischka Georg • FRG
SKLAVENKONIGIN, DIE • 1924 • Curtiz Michael • AUS • MOON OVER ISRAEL ○ MOON OF ISRAEL
SKLENIKOVA VENUSA • 1985 • Tapak Martin • CZC • HOTHOUSE VENUS, A
SKLO, SKLO, SKLO • 1961 • Bernat Miro • CZC • GLASS, GLASS, GLASS
SKOGEN AR VAR ARVIDEL • 1944 • Johansson Ivar • SWD • FOREST IS OUR INHERITANCE, THE
SKOK • 1968 • Kutz Kazimierz • PLN • START, THE ○ LEAP, THE
SKOK • 1978 • Szczechura Daniel • ANS • PLN
SKOKIE • 1981 • Wise Herbert • TVM • USA
SKOLA MUZESTVA • 1957 • Basov Vladimir, Korchagin M. • USS • SCHOOL OF COURAGE
SKOLA OTCU • 1957 • Helge Ladislav • CZC • SCHOOL OF FATHERS ○ SCHOOL FOR FATHERS
SKOLA ZAKLAD ZIVOTA • 1938 • Fric Martin • CZC • SCHOOL, THE BEGINNING OF LIFE ○ SCHOOL WHERE LIFE BEGINS ○ SCHOOL, THE BASIS OF LIFE
SKOLKA SKOLAN • 1949 • Bauman Schamyl • SWD • PLAYING TRUANT
SKOLOVANJE • 1970 • Bourek Zlatko, Sacer Zlatko • ANS • YGS • SCHOOLING
SKOMAGERPRINSEN • 1921 • Davidsen Hjalmar • DNM
SKOMAKARE BLIV VID DIN LAST • 1915 • Sjostrom Victor • SWD • COBBLER STICK TO YOUR LAST ○ KEEP TO YOUR TRADE ○ COBBLER STAY AT YOUR BENCH
SKONA HELENA • 1951 • Edgren Gustaf • SWD • HELEN OF TROY
SKONA SUSANNA OCH GUBBARNA • 1959 • Strandmark Erik • SWD • BEAUTIFUL SUSAN AND THE OLD MEN
SKONHEDEN OG UDYRET • 1983 • Malmros Nils • DNM • BEAUTY AND THE BEAST
SKONHETSVARD I DJUNGELN • 1936 • Fejos Paul • DCS • SWD, DNM • BEAUTY CARE IN THE JUNGLE
SKONNE EVELYN, DEN • 1916 • Sandberg Anders W. • DNM • EVELYN THE BEAUTIFUL
SKOOL DAZE • 1970 • *Stacey Dist.* • USA
SKOOLPLAY • 1977 • Brown Alan • UKN
SKOPJE 1963 • 1964 • Bulajic Velko • YGS
SKORPAN • 1957 • Lagerkvist Hans • SWD • RUSK
SKORPIO, A • 1918 • Curtiz Michael • HNG • SCORPION, THE
SKORPION, PANNA I LUCZNIK • 1972 • Kondratiuk Andrzej • PLN • SAINT FAMILY
SKOTINI KATASKEVI MIAS ILIOGRAFIAS • 1976 • Dimogerontakis Dimitris • GRC • DARK MAKING OF AN HELIOGRAPHY, THE
SKOTININS, THE see **GOSPODA SKOTININY** • 1927
SKOTTET • 1914 • Stiller Mauritz • SWD • SHOT, THE
SKOTTET • 1969 • Fellbom Claes • SWD • ACCIDENTAL KILLER ○ SHOT, THE
SKOVENS BORN • 1917 • Holger-Madsen • DNM
SKRACKEN HAR TUSEN OGON • 1971 • Wickman Torgny • SWD • FEAR HAS A THOUSAND EYES
SKRALLAN, RUSKPRICK AND KNORRHANE see **SKRALLAN, RUSKPRICK OCH KNORRHANE** • 1967
SKRALLAN, RUSKPRICK OCH KNORRHANE • 1967 • Hellbom Olle • SWD • SKRALLAN, RUSKPRICK AND KNORRHANE
SKRAMMELLEGEPLADSEN • 1966 • Lund-Sorensen Sune • DNM • JUNK PLAYGROUND, THE
SKRAPHANDLERE • 1976 • Hermansson Bo • NRW
SKRATTBOMBEN • 1954 • Larsson Borje • SWD • BOMB OF LAUGHTER
SKRBNIK • 1974 • Borosak Rudolf, Fabiani Leo • YGS • GUARDIAN, THE
SKRIFT I SNE • 1965 • Hansen Bang • NRW
SKRIVANCI NA NITICH • 1969 • Menzel Jiri • CZC • LARKS ON A THREAD ○ LARKS ON A STRING ○ SKYLARKS ON A STRING
SKRIVANCI PISEN • 1933 • Innemann Svatopluk • SONG OF THE LARK ○ LARK'S SONG, THE
SKRZYDLA • 1966 • Pulchny Leonard • ANM • PLN • WINGS
SKUD I MORKET, ET see **TRUET LYKKE** • 1915
SKUGGAN • 1953 • Fant Kenne • SWD • SHADOW, THE
SKUGGOR OVER SNON • 1945 • Sucksdorff Arne • DCS • SWD • SHADOWS ACROSS THE SNOW ○ SHADOWS ON THE SNOW
SKUKI RADI • 1968 • Voitetsky Artur • USS • FOR BOREDOM'S SAKE ○ TO BANISH BOREDOM ○ OUT OF BOREDOM
SKULL, THE • 1913 • Ranous William V. • USA
SKULL, THE • 1914 • Crane Frank H. • USA
SKULL, THE • 1965 • Francis Freddie • UKN
SKULL, THE see **CALAVERA, LA** • 1954
SKULL: A NIGHT OF TERROR see **NIGHT OF RETRIBUTION** • 1987
SKULL AND CROWN • 1935 • Clifton Elmer • USA
SKULL AND THE CROWN, THE • 1914 • Martin E. A. • USA
SKULL COMMANDOS • 1967 • Cayado Tony • PHL
SKULL ISLAND see **MOST DANGEROUS GAME, THE** • 1932
SKULLDUGGERY • 1960 • Vanderbeek Stan • ANS • USA
SKULLDUGGERY • 1970 • Douglas Gordon • USA
SKULLDUGGERY • 1983 • Richter Ota • USA
SKUNKED AGAIN • 1936 • Davis Mannie, Gordon George • ANS • USA
SKUPLJACI PERJA • 1967 • Petrovic Aleksandar • YGS • I EVEN MET HAPPY GYPSIES (USA) ○ SREO SAM CAK I SRECNE CIGANE ○ I EVEN MET SOME HAPPY GYPSIES ○ HAPPY GIPSIES..! ○ PLUME COLLECTORS, THE ○ SOME GYPSIES ARE HAPPY
SKVENEI ANEKDOT • 1965 • Alov Alexander, Naumov Vladimir • USS • UGLY STORY, AN ○ BAD JOKE
SKY • 1962 • Carey Patrick • DOC • CND
SKY see **AASMAN** • 1990
SKY ABOVE BERLIN, THE see **HIMMEL UBER BERLIN, DER** • 1987
SKY ABOVE HEAVEN (USA) see **CIEL SUR LA TETE, LE** • 1964
SKY ABOVE, THE MUD BELOW, THE see **CIEL ET LA BOUE, LE** • 1961
SKY BANDITS • 1940 • Staub Ralph • USA • RENFREW OF THE MOUNTED IN SKY BANDITS
SKY BANDITS see **GUNBUS** • 1987
SKY BATTALION, THE see **NEBESKI ODRED** • 1961
SKY BEGINS ON THE 3RD FLOOR, THE see **CERUL INCEPE LA ETAJUL III** • 1967
SKY BELONGS TO US, THE • 1964 • Gedris Marionas Vintzo • SHT • USS
SKY BEYOND HEAVEN see **CIEL SUR LA TETE, LE** • 1964
SKY BEYOND THE CLOUDS, THE • 1973 • Yegorov Yuri • USS
SKY BIKE, THE • 1967 • Frend Charles • UKN
SKY BLUE see **AZUL CELESTE** • 1990
SKY-BLUE STEPPE, THE see **V LASUREVOI STEPI** • 1971
SKY BOUND • 1926 • Roberts Stephen • SHT • USA
SKY BOY • 1929 • Rogers Charles, McCarey Leo • SHT • USA
SKY BRIDE • 1932 • Roberts Stephen • USA
SKY CALLS, THE see **NEBO ZOVYOT** • 1959
SKY COMMANDO • 1953 • Sears Fred F. • USA
SKY DEVILS • 1932 • Sutherland A. Edward • USA
SKY-DEVILS, THE see **SHAYATINE EL JAU** • 1955
SKY DRAGON • 1949 • Selander Lesley • USA
SKY-EYE • 1920 • Kennedy Aubrey M. • USA
SKY FISHING • 1934 • Sparling Gordon • DCS • CND • PECHE DANS LES NUAGES, LA
SKY FULL OF MOON • 1952 • Foster Norman • USA
SKY GIANT • 1938 • Landers Lew • USA • GROUND CREW ○ NORTHERN FLIGHT
SKY HAS NO BARS, THE see **CERUL N-ARE GRATII** • 1962
SKY HAWK, THE • 1929 • Blystone John G. • USA
SKY HEIST • 1976 • Katzin Lee H. • TVM • USA
SKY HIGH • 1922 • Reynolds Lynn • USA
SKY HIGH • 1931 • Mack Roy • SHT • USA
SKY HIGH • 1951 • Newfield Sam • USA
SKY HIGH see **SKYHIGH** • 1985
SKY HIGH CORRAL • 1926 • Smith Cliff • USA
SKY HIGH IN NEW ZEALAND • 1961 • Bowie Ronald • NZL
SKY-HIGH SAUNDERS • 1927 • Mitchell Bruce • USA
SKY HUNTERS, THE • 1915 • *Mayo Edna* • USA
SKY IS CLEAR, THE see **SORA WA HARETARI** • 1925
SKY IS FALLING, THE • 1947 • Davis Mannie • ANS • USA
SKY IS FALLING, THE • 1973 • Narizzano Silvio • USA • BLOODBATH
SKY IS MINE, THE see **TEN TO CHI O KAKERU OTOKO** • 1959
SKY IS OUR ROOF, THE see **KAMIENNE NIEBO** • 1959
SKY IS OUR ROUTE, THE see **KAMIENNE NIEBO** • 1959
SKY IS THE LIMIT, THE • 1915 • *Starlight* • USA
SKY JUMPER, THE • 1925 • Marshall George • SHT • USA
SKY LARK, THE • 1920 • *Lytell Bert* • USA
SKY LARKS • 1934 • Lantz Walter • ANS • USA
SKY MONSTER, THE • 1914 • *Universal* • USA
SKY MURDER • 1940 • Seitz George B. • USA
SKY OF OUR CHILDHOOD, THE see **NEBO NASHEGO DETSTVA** • 1967
SKY OF STONE, A see **KAMIENNE NIEBO** • 1959
SKY OVER HOLLAND • 1967 • Ferno John • SHT • NTH
SKY PARADE, THE • 1936 • Lovering Otho • USA
SKY PATROL • 1939 • Bretherton Howard • USA
SKY PILOT • 1924 • Lantz Walter • ANS • USA
SKY PILOT, THE • 1911 • *Talmadge Norma* • USA
SKY PILOT, THE • 1921 • Vidor King • USA
SKY PILOT'S INTEMPERANCE, THE • 1911 • Dwan Allan • USA
SKY PIRATE • 1939 • Waggner George • USA • MYSTERY PLANE (UKN)
SKY PIRATE, THE • 1914 • Arbuckle Roscoe, Dillon Eddie • USA
SKY PIRATE, THE • 1926 • *Washburn Bryant* • USA
SKY PIRATE, THE • 1970 • Meyer Andrew • USA
SKY PIRATES • 1938 • Pal George • ANS • NTH
SKY PIRATES • 1976 • Pennington-Richards C. M. • UKN
SKY PIRATES • 1986 • Eggleston Colin • ASL
SKY PIRATES see **GUNBUS** • 1987
SKY PLUMBER, THE • 1924 • Roach Hal • SHT • USA
SKY PRINCESS, THE • 1942 • Pal George • ANS • USA
SKY RACKET • 1937 • *Victory* • USA • FLIGHT INTO DANGER (UKN)
SKY RAIDER, THE • 1925 • Hunter T. Hayes • USA
SKY RAIDERS • 1941 • Beebe Ford, Taylor Ray • SRL • USA
SKY RAIDERS, THE • 1931 • Cabanne W. Christy • USA
SKY RAIDERS, THE • 1938 • Foulsham Fraser • UKN
SKY RANGER, THE • 1921 • Seitz George B. • SRL • USA • MAN WHO STOLE THE MOON, THE ○ MAN WHO STOLE THE EARTH, THE
SKY RIDER, THE • 1928 • Neitz Alvin J. • USA
SKY RIDERS • 1976 • Hickox Douglas • USA
SKY SCIENCE • 1943 • Jason Will • SHT • USA
SKY SCRAPER! see **CHOKOSO NO AKEBONO** • 1969
SKY SCRAPING • 1930 • Fleischer Dave • ANS • USA
SKY SCRAPPERS • 1928 • Disney Walt • ANS • USA
SKY SCRAPPERS • 1957 • Tendlar Dave • ANS • USA
SKY SHINES, THE see **SORA WA HARETARI** • 1925
SKY SHIP see **HIMMELSKIBET** • 1917
SKY SKIDDER, THE • 1929 • Mitchell Bruce • USA
SKY SKIERS • 1951 • Trego Charles T. • SHT • USA
SKY SKIPPERS • 1930 • Foster John, Bailey Harry • ANS • USA
SKY SOCIALIST, THE • 1965 • Jacobs Ken • USA
SKY SPIDER, THE • 1931 • Thorpe Richard • USA
SKY SPLITTER, THE • 1922 • Miller Ashley, Norling J. A. • SHT • USA
SKY TERROR see **SKYJACKED** • 1972
SKY, THE EARTH, THE see **CIEL, LA TERRE, LE** • 1965
SKY THROUGH THE LEAVES, THE see **KROZ GRANJE NEBO** • 1958
SKY THROUGH THE TREES, THE see **KROZ GRANJE NEBO** • 1958
SKY TRAP, THE • 1979 • Courtland Jerome • TVM • USA
SKY TROOPER • 1942 • King Jack • ANS • USA
SKY WEST AND CROOKED • 1965 • Mills John • UKN • GYPSY GIRL (USA) ○ BATS WITH BABY FACES
SKY WHERE HARUO FLEW, THE see **HARUO NO TONDA SORA** • 1977
SKY WITHOUT STARS (USA) see **HIMMEL OHNE STERNE** • 1955
SKY WITHOUT SUN see **NIEBO BEZ SLONCA** • 1966
SKYANDURU • 1950 • Kurosawa Akira • JPN • SCANDAL ○ SHUBUN
SKYBOUND • 1935 • Johnston Raymond K. • USA
SKYDDSANGELN • 1990 • Osten Suzanne • SWD • GUARDIAN ANGEL, THE
SKYDIVERS, THE • 1963 • Francis Coleman • USA
SKYFIRE • 1920 • Hart Neal • USA
SKYFIRE see **BLAZING ARROWS** • 1922
SKYGGEN AF EMMA • 1987 • Kragh-Jacobsen Soren • DNM • EMMA'S SHADOW
SKYHAWK • 1974 • Cheng Chang Ho • HKG
SKYHIGH • 1985 • Mastorakis Nico • USA • SKY HIGH
SKYHOOK • 1958 • Hill James • UKN
SKYJACKED • 1972 • Guillermin John • USA • SKY TERROR ○ AIRBORNE
SKYLARK • 1941 • Sandrich Mark • USA
SKYLARK see **PACSIRTA** • 1964
SKYLARK GROWING UP see **HABARI NO TAKEKURABE** • 1958
SKYLARKING • 1923 • *Sennett Mack (P)* • SHT • USA
SKYLARKS • 1936 • Freeland Thornton • UKN
SKYLARKS ARE THE FIRST TO RETURN see **ZHAVORONKI PRILETAYUT PYERVYMI** • 1968
SKYLARKS FLY HOME FIRST see **ZHAVORONKI PRILETAYUT PYERVYMI** • 1968
SKYLARKS ON A STRING see **SKRIVANCI NA NITICH** • 1969
SKYLDIG, IKKE SKYLDIG • 1953 • Roos Jorgen • DOC • DNM • GUILTY THOUGH INNOCENT
SKYLIGHT ROOM, THE • 1917 • Justice Martin • USA
SKYLIGHT SLEEP • 1916 • Roach Hal • SHT • USA
SKYLINE • 1931 • Taylor Sam • USA
SKYLINE see **LINEA DEL CIELO, LA** • 1984
SKYLINE OF SPRUCE, THE see **SHADOWS OF THE NORTH** • 1923
SKYLINE SERENADE • 1941 • Le Borg Reginald • SHT • USA
SKYLINER • 1949 • Berke William • USA
SKYMNINGSLJUS • 1951 • Werner Gosta • SHT • SWD
SKYRIDER • 1976 • Halas John • ANS • UKN
SKYROCKET, THE • 1926 • Neilan Marshall • USA • LOVE OR LIMELIGHT
SKY'S NO LIMIT, THE • 1984 • Rich David Lowell • TVM • USA • STAR CHASERS
SKY'S THE LIMIT • 1925 • Irving I. W., Fraser Harry L.? • USA
SKY'S THE LIMIT, THE • 1937 • Garmes Lee, Buchanan Jack • UKN
SKY'S THE LIMIT, THE • 1943 • Griffith Edward H. • USA
SKY'S THE LIMIT, THE • 1965 • Tendlar Dave • ANS • USA
SKY'S THE LIMIT, THE • 1975 • Leetch Tom • USA
SKYSCRAPER • 1928 • Higgin Howard • USA
SKYSCRAPER, THE • 1958 • Clarke Shirley, Van Dyke Willard, Jacoby Irving • USA
SKYSCRAPER CAPER • 1968 • Lovy Alex • ANS • USA
SKYSCRAPER SOULS • 1932 • Selwyn Edgar • USA
SKYSCRAPER STORY, THE see **CHOKOSO NO AKEBONO** • 1969
SKYSCRAPER SYMPHONY • 1928 • Florey Robert • USA
SKYSCRAPER WILDERNESS see **BIG CITY, THE** • 1937
SKYTTEN • 1977 • Hedegaard Tom, Ernst Franz • DNM
SKYWARD • 1980 • Howard Ron • TVM • USA
SKYWATCH (USA) see **LIGHT UP THE SKY** • 1960
SKYWAY • 1933 • Collins Lewis D. • USA
SKYWAY TO DEATH • 1974 • Hessler Gordon • TVM • USA
SKYWAYMAN, THE • 1920 • Hogan James P. • USA • DAREDEVIL, THE (UKN)
SLA FORST, FREDE! • 1965 • Balling Erik • DNM • OPERATION LOVEBIRDS (USA)
SLABSIDES • 1911 • *Kalem* • USA
SLACHTVEE • 1980 • Conrad Patrick • BLG • CARNE, LA
SLACK-BAKED BREAD see **ZAKALEC** • 1977
SLACKER, THE • 1917 • *Emerald* • USA • SLACKER'S HEART, A
SLACKER, THE • 1917 • Cabanne W. Christy • *Metro* • USA
SLACKER'S HEART, A see **SLACKER, THE** • 1917
SLAD MAGNETYCZNY • 1978 • Leszczynski Witold • PLN • MAGNETIC TRACK
SLADE (UKN) see **JACK SLADE** • 1953
SLADKE HRY JEDNOHO LETA see **SLADKE HRY MINULEHO LETA** • 1969

SLADKE HRY MINULEHO LETA • 1969 • Herz Juraj • CZC • SWEET GAMES OF LAST SUMMER (UKN) ○ SLADKE HRY JEDNOHO LETA
SLADKE STAROSTI • 1985 • Herz Juraj • CZC • SWEET WORRIES
SLADKY CAS KALIMAGDORY see **SUSSE ZEIT MIT KALIMAGDORA, DIE** • 1968
SLADY • 1974 • Giersz Witold • ANS • PLN • FOOTPRINTS
SLAEGTEN • 1978 • Refn Anders • DNM • HERITAGE ○ BARON, THE
SLAET OP TEN TROMMLE • Franken Mannus • NTH
SLAG FOR SLAG • 1958 • *Gunwall Per (Edt)* • SWD
SLAG'S PLACE • 1965 • Naden David, Furdivall Gwyneth • UKN
SLAGSKAMPEN • 1984 • Clegg Tom • SWD, UKN, NRW • INSIDE MAN, THE
SLAGSMAL I GAMLA STOCKHOLM • 1897 • Florman Ernest • SWD
SLAKTEN AR BAST • 1944 • Falck Ragnar • SWD • YOUR RELATIVES ARE BEST
SLAKTEN AR VARST • 1936 • Henrikson Anders • SWD • YOUR RELATIVES ARE WORST
SLALOM • 1936 • Obal Max • FRG
SLALOM • 1965 • Salce Luciano • ITL, FRN, EGY
SLAM BANG JIM • 1920 • Sloman Edward • USA
SLAM BANG JIM see **SNAP JUDGMENT** • 1917
SLAM DANCE see **SLAMDANCE** • 1987
SLAM-DUNK • 1986 • Brown Jim • USA
SLAMARKE DIVOJKE • 1971 • Skrabalo Ivo • YGS • STRAW GIRLS
SLAMBERT • 1966 • Quist-Moller Fleming, Hastrup Jannik • ANS • DNM
SLAMDANCE • 1987 • Wang Wayne • USA • SLAM DANCE
SLAMENY KLOBOUK • 1972 • Lipsky Oldrich • CZC • STRAW HAT, THE
SLAMET TINGGAL JEANETTE • 1988 • Umboh Wim • INN
SLAMMER see **SHORT EYES** • 1977
SLAMMER see **WHO'S THAT GIRL?** • 1987
SLAMMER GIRLS • 1987 • Vincent Chuck • USA • BIG SLAMMER, THE
SLAMS, THE • 1973 • Kaplan Jonathan • USA
SLANA RUZE • 1982 • Majewski Janusz • CZC • SALTY ROSE
SLANDER • 1916 • Davis Will S. • USA
SLANDER • 1956 • Rowland Roy • USA
SLANDER see **IFTIRA** • 1968
SLANDER HOUSE • 1938 • Lamont Charles • USA
SLANDER THE WOMAN • 1923 • Holubar Allen • USA • WHITE FRONTIER, THE
SLANDERERS, THE • 1924 • Ross Nat • USA
SLANDER'S TONGUE • 1913 • Miller Ashley • USA
SLANT • 1958 • Romero George A. • SHT • USA
SLANT AR EN SLANT, INTE SANT?, EN • Lindgren Lars-Magnus • SHT • SWD • COIN IS A COIN, A
SLANTSETO I SYANKATA • 1962 • Vulchanov Rangel, Petrov Valeri • BUL • SUN AND SHADOW ○ SLANTZETO I SIANKATA
SLANTZETO I SIANKATA see **SLANTSETO I SYANKATA** • 1962
SLAP, THE (USA) see **GIFLE, LA** • 1974
SLAP HAPPY HUNTERS • 1941 • Donnelly Eddie • ANS • USA
SLAP HAPPY LION • 1947 • Avery Tex • ANS • USA
SLAP-HAPPY MOUSE, THE • 1956 • McKimson Robert • ANS • USA
SLAP HAPPY PAPPY • 1940 • Clampett Robert • ANS • USA
SLAP HAPPY SLEUTHS • 1950 • McCollum Hugh • SHT • USA
SLAP IN THE FACE • 1975 • Thiele Rolf • FRG
SLAP IN THE FACE, A see **POSHCHYOCHINA** • 1980
SLAP SHOT • 1977 • Hill George Roy • USA
SLAPHAPPY VALLEY • 1939 • Lovy Alex • ANS • USA
SLAPP FANGARNE LOSS -DET AR VARI • 1976 • Danielsson Tage • SWD • LET THE PRISONERS GO -FOR IT'S SPRING
SLAPPIEST DAYS OF OUR LIFE, THE • 1952 • CMP • USA
SLAPSHOTS • 1974 • Horowitz Irving • USA
SLAPSTICK see **SLAPSTICK (OF ANOTHER KIND)** • 1984
SLAPSTICK (OF ANOTHER KIND) • 1984 • Paul Steven • USA • SLAPSTICK
SLASH • Gale John • USA
SLASHED YOSABURO see **KIRARE YOSABURO** • 1960
SLASHER, THE • 1958 • Kuchar George, Kuchar Mike • SHT • USA
SLASHER, THE (USA) see **COSH BOY** • 1952
SLASTI OTCE VLASTI • 1968 • Stekly Karel • CZC • PLEASURES OF THE FATHER OF THE COUNTRY, THE ○ JOYS OF THE FATHER OF HIS COUNTRY, THE
SLATE & WYN AND BLANCHE MCBRIDE • 1986 • McLennan Don • ASL • SLATE, WYN & ME (USA) ○ SLATE, WYN AND MCBRIDE
SLATE, WYN AND MCBRIDE see **SLATE & WYN AND BLANCHE MCBRIDE** • 1986
SLATE, WYN & ME (USA) see **SLATE & WYN AND BLANCHE MCBRIDE** • 1986
SLATES OF THE TENPYO PERIOD see **TEMPYO NO IRAKA** • 1979
SLATTERY'S HURRICANE • 1949 • De Toth Andre • USA
SLAUGHTER • 1972 • Starrett Jack • USA
SLAUGHTER see **DOGS** • 1977
SLAUGHTER, THE • 1976 • *Monarch* • USA, ARG • SNUFF
SLAUGHTER HIGH see **APRIL FOOL'S DAY** • 1985
SLAUGHTER HOTEL see **EATEN ALIVE** • 1976
SLAUGHTER HOTEL (USA) see **BESTIA UCCIDE A SANGUE FREDDO, LA** • 1971
SLAUGHTER IN BROAD DAYLIGHT see **HAKUCHU NO ZANSATSU** • 1967
SLAUGHTER IN SAN FRANCISCO • 1973 • Lowe William • HKG
SLAUGHTER OF THE VAMPIRES, THE see **STRAGE DEI VAMPIRI, LA** • 1962
SLAUGHTER ON TENTH AVENUE • 1957 • Laven Arnold • USA
SLAUGHTER TRAIL • 1951 • Allen Irving • USA
SLAUGHTERDAY • 1981 • Patzak Peter • USA
SLAUGHTERERS see **APOCALISSE DOMANI** • 1980
SLAUGHTERHOUSE • 1987 • Roessler Rick • USA
SLAUGHTERHOUSE FIVE • 1972 • Hill George Roy • USA
SLAUGHTERHOUSE ROCK • 1988 • Logothetis Dimitri • USA • HELL ISLAND
SLAUGHTER'S BIG RIP-OFF • 1973 • Douglas Gordon • USA
SLAVA • 1959 • Pojar Bretislav • ANS • CZC • GLORY ○ FAME
SLAVA SOVETSKIM GEROINYAM • 1938 • Vertov Dziga, Svilova Elizaveta • USS • TO THE GLORY OF SOVIET HEROINES ○ FAMOUS SOVIET HEROES
SLAVA TROVDOU • 1949 • Medvedkin Alexander • USS
SLAVE, THE • 1909 • Griffith D. W. • USA
SLAVE, THE • 1916 • *Rex* • SHT • USA
SLAVE, THE • 1917 • Gillstrom Arvid E. • *Kingbee* • SHT • USA
SLAVE, THE • 1917 • Nigh William • *Fox* • USA
SLAVE, THE • 1918 • Bocchi Arrigo • UKN
SLAVE, THE see **RABINYA** • 1970
SLAVE, THE (USA) see **ESCLAVE, L'** • 1953
SLAVE, THE (USA) see **FIGLIO DI SPARTACUS, IL** • 1962
SLAVE, THE (USA) see **FEMME AUX ABOIS, UNE** • 1967
SLAVE AUCTION, THE • 1918 • *Chapin* • SHT • USA
SLAVE FACTORY, THE see **DOREI KOJO** • 1968
SLAVE GIRL • 1947 • Lamont Charles • USA • FLAME OF TRIPOLI
SLAVE GIRL, THE • 1915 • Browning Tod • USA
SLAVE GIRL, THE see **CAPTAIN KIDD AND THE SLAVE GIRL** • 1954
SLAVE-GIRL, THE see **RABINYA** • 1970
SLAVE GIRLS • 1966 • Carreras Michael • UKN • PREHISTORIC WOMEN (USA)
SLAVE GIRLS FROM BEYOND INFINITY • 1987 • Dixon Ken • USA
SLAVE GIRLS OF SHEBA (USA) see **VERDI BANDIERE DI ALLAH, LE** • 1964
SLAVE ISLAND see **WAHAL DUPATHA** • 1968
SLAVE MARKET, THE • 1917 • Ford Hugh • USA
SLAVE MERCHANTS, THE see **ANTHAR L'INVINCIBILE** • 1965
SLAVE OF CORRUPTION, A • 1916 • *Saunders Jackie* • SHT • USA
SLAVE OF DESIRE • 1923 • Baker George D. • USA • MAGIC SKIN, THE
SLAVE OF DESIRE see **ESCLAVA DEL DESEO** • 1968
SLAVE OF FASHION, A • 1925 • Henley Hobart • USA • NOTHING TO WEAR
SLAVE OF FEAR, A • 1917 • Kelsey Fred A. • SHT • USA
SLAVE OF LOVE • Khamdamov Rustam • USS
SLAVE OF LOVE, A see **RABA LIOUBVI** • 1977
SLAVE OF LOVE, THE see **GHULAM ISHQ** • 1978
SLAVE OF MAMMON, A • 1915 • *Santa Barbara* • USA
SLAVE OF PARADISE, THE see **ESCLAVA DEL PARAISO, LA** • 1968
SLAVE OF ROME, THE see **SCHIAVA DI ROMA, LA** • 1961
SLAVE OF SATAN, A • 1913 • *Patheplay* • USA
SLAVE OF SLAVE see **ALIPIN NG BUSABOS** • 1968
SLAVE OF THE CANNIBAL GOD see **MONTAGNA DEL DIO CANNIBALE, LA** • 1976
SLAVE OF THE VAMPIRE • 1959 • Glut Don • SHT • USA
SLAVE OF VANITY, A • 1920 • Otto Henry • USA • IRIS
SLAVE QUEEN OF BABYLON (USA) see **IO SEMIRAMIDE** • 1963
SLAVE SHIP • 1937 • Garnett Tay • USA
SLAVE TO DRINK, A • 1909 • *Kalem* • USA
SLAVE TO YOURSELF see **SIN EGEN SLAV** • 1917
SLAVE TRADE IN THE WORLD TODAY (USA) see **SCHIAVE ESISTONO ANCORA, LE** • 1964
SLAVE TRADING IN A HAREM see **VENTE D'ESCLAVES AU HAREM** • 1897
SLAVE WARRIOR see **SCHIAVA DI ROMA, LA** • 1961
SLAVE WIDOW see **DOREI MIBOJIN** • 1967
SLAVE WOMAN, THE see **CORTIGIANA DI BABILONIA, LA** • 1955
SLAVEDRIVER see **RANCHEADOR** • 1977
SLAVER, THE • 1927 • Revier Harry • USA
SLAVERS • 1978 • Goslar Jurgen • FRG
SLAVERS, THE • 1977 • Kent Larry • CND
SLAVERS OF THE THAMES • 1915 • Moran Percy • UKN
SLAVERY DAYS -THE NEW MASTER • 1906 • Hough Harold • UKN
SLAVERY OF FOXICUS, THE • 1914 • *Neilan Marshall* • USA
SLAVES • 1969 • Biberman Herbert J. • USA
SLAVES DEVOTION, A • 1913 • Giblyn Charles • USA
SLAVES OF BABYLON • 1953 • Castle William • USA
SLAVES OF BEAUTY • 1927 • Blystone John G. • USA
SLAVES OF CHINATOWN see **WHITE SLAVES OF CHINATOWN** • 1964
SLAVES OF DESTINY • 1924 • Elvey Maurice • UKN • MIRANDA OF THE BALCONY
SLAVES OF LOVE • 1969 • Nizet Charles • USA
SLAVES OF NEW YORK • 1989 • Ivory James • USA
SLAVES OF PRIDE • 1920 • Terwilliger George W. • USA
SLAVES OF SCANDAL • 1924 • *Lee-Bradford Corp.* • USA
SLAVES OF THE INVISIBLE MONSTER • 1950 • Brannon Fred C. • USA
SLAVES OF THE NIGHT see **EJSZAKA RABJA, AZ** • 1914
SLAVES OF THE SIN-DICATE • 1967 • *Mitam Productions* • USA • SLAVES OF THE SYNDICATE
SLAVES OF THE SYNDICATE see **SLAVES OF THE SIN-DICATE** • 1967
SLAVES (UKN) see **BLACKSNAKE!** • 1973
SLAVEY STUDENT, THE • 1915 • Collins John H. • USA
SLAVEY'S DREAM, THE • 1904 • Fitzhamon Lewin • UKN
SLAVEY'S INFINITY, THE • 1911 • Salter Harry • USA
SLAVEY'S LEGACY, THE see **LADY SLAVEY, THE** • 1916
SLAVEY'S ROMANCE, THE • 1914 • *Victor* • USA
SLAVICA • 1947 • Afric Vjekoslav • YGS
SLAVNOST V BOTANICKEJ ZAHRADE • 1969 • Havetta Elo • CZC • FETE IN THE BOTANICAL GARDENS, THE ○ PARTY IN THE BOTANICAL GARDEN, THE
SLAVNOSTI A HOSTECH, O • 1966 • Nemec Jan • CZC • REPORT ON THE PARTY AND THE GUESTS, A (USA) ○ PARTY AND THE GUESTS, THE ○ ON CELEBRATIONS AND GUESTS
SLAVNOSTI SNEZENEK • 1983 • Menzel Jiri • CZC • SNOWDROP FESTIVITIES, THE
SLAY IT WITH FLOWERS • 1943 • Wickersham Bob • ANS • USA
SLAYER, THE • 1982 • Cardone J. S. • USA
SLAYGROUND • 1983 • Bedford Terry • UKN
SLAYING OF THE SERPENT, THE see **KALYA MARDAN** • 1919
SLAYRIDE • 1972 • Chomsky Marvin • USA
SLEAZEMANIA: THE SPECIAL EDITION • 1986 • CMP • USA
SLECNA GOLEM • 1973 • Balik Jaroslav • CZC • MISS GOLEM
SLECNA OD VODY • 1959 • Zeman Borivoj • CZC • YOUNG LADY FROM THE RIVERSIDE, THE ○ YOUNG LADY FROM THE RIVER BANK, THE
SLEDGE • 1970 • Morrow Vic, Gentili Giorgio • ITL, USA • MAN CALLED SLEDGE, A (UKN)
SLEDGE, THE • 1955 • Szemes Mihaly • HNG
SLEDGE HAMMER • 1984 • Prior David A. • USA
SLEDGE PATROL SIRIUS, THE see **SLOEDEPATRULJEN SIRIUS** • 1980
SLEEP • 1964 • Warhol Andy, Morrissey Paul • USA
SLEEP AND DEATH see **IPNOS KE THANATOS** • 1975
SLEEP, BEAUTIFUL SLEEP • 1915 • Louis Will • USA
SLEEP DEEP see **SLEEP WELL** • 1966
SLEEP, GENTLE SLEEP • 1911 • *Edison* • USA
SLEEP HAPPY • 1951 • Lantz Walter • ANS • USA
SLEEP IS LOVELY see **I LOVE YOU, I HATE YOU** • 1968
SLEEP IS LOVELY see **NEGATIVES** • 1968
SLEEP MY LOVE • 1948 • Sirk Douglas • USA
SLEEP NO MORE see **INVASION OF THE BODY SNATCHERS** • 1956
SLEEP OF CYMA ROGET • 1920 • Gaskill Charles L. • USA
SLEEP OF DEATH, THE see **FLYGANDE DRAKEN, DEN** • 1980
SLEEP, SLEEP, MY LOVE see **DUERME, DUERME, MI AMOR** • 1974
SLEEP WALKER, THE • 1911 • *Vitagraph* • USA
SLEEP WALKER, THE see **SLEEPWALKER, THE** • 1922
SLEEP WELL • 1966 • Lindberg Lars • ANS • SWD • SLEEP DEEP
SLEEP WELL see **SUSS GOTT** • 1956
SLEEP WELL, PROFESSOR OLIVER • 1989 • Patterson John • TVM • USA
SLEEPAWAY CAMP • 1983 • Hiltzik Robert • USA • NIGHTMARE VACATION
SLEEPAWAY CAMP 2 see **UNHAPPY CAMPERS** • 1988
SLEEPAWAY CAMP II: UNHAPPY CAMPERS see **UNHAPPY CAMPERS** • 1988
SLEEPAWAY CAMP III • 1989 • Simpson Michael A. • USA • TEENAGE WASTELAND
SLEEPBREAKERS, THE • 1910 • Collins Alf • UKN
SLEEPER • 1973 • Allen Woody • USA
SLEEPER, THE • 1909 • *Pathe* • FRN
SLEEPER, THE • 1912 • *Lubin* • USA
SLEEPERS EAST • 1934 • MacKenna Kenneth • USA
SLEEPERS WEST • 1941 • Forde Eugene J. • USA
SLEEPING BEAUTY • 1903 • *Lubin* • USA
SLEEPING BEAUTY • 1920 • Vasiliev Dimitri, Vasiliev Nikolai • USS
SLEEPING BEAUTY • Pal George • ANS • NTH
SLEEPING BEAUTY • 1947 • *Films For Children* • USA
SLEEPING BEAUTY • 1952 • *March Of Time* • SHT • USA
SLEEPING BEAUTY • 1952 • Wilder William • *World Tv* • SHT • USA
SLEEPING BEAUTY • 1959 • *Fonteyn Margot* • UKN
SLEEPING BEAUTY • 1959 • Geronimi Clyde • ANM • USA
SLEEPING BEAUTY • 1959 • Kahl Milt • ANM • USA
SLEEPING BEAUTY • 1960 • *Halas John (P)* • ANS • UKN
SLEEPING BEAUTY • 1961 • Tang Huang • HKG
SLEEPING BEAUTY • 1963 • Just Erika • GDR
SLEEPING BEAUTY • 1983 • Kagan Jeremy Paul • MTV • USA
SLEEPING BEAUTY • 1987 • Irving David • USA • CANNON MOVIE TALES: SLEEPING BEAUTY
SLEEPING BEAUTY see **BELLE AU BOIS DORMANT, LA**
SLEEPING BEAUTY see **BELLE AU BOIS DORMANT, LA** • 1915
SLEEPING BEAUTY see **DORNROSCHEN** • 1917
SLEEPING BEAUTY see **DORNROSCHEN** • 1922
SLEEPING BEAUTY see **DORNROSCHEN** • 1929
SLEEPING BEAUTY see **BELLE AU BOIS DORMANT, LA** • 1935
SLEEPING BEAUTY see **PRINSESSA RUUSUNEN** • 1949
SLEEPING BEAUTY see **NEMURERU BIJO** • 1968
SLEEPING BEAUTY see **DORNROSCHEN**
SLEEPING BEAUTY, THE • 1912 • Neame Elwin • UKN
SLEEPING BEAUTY, THE • 1913 • *Venus Feature* • USA
SLEEPING BEAUTY, THE • 1953 • Sremec Rudolf • SHT • YGS
SLEEPING BEAUTY, THE • 1954 • Reiniger Lotte • ANS • UKN
SLEEPING BEAUTY, THE see **SPYASHCHAYA KRASAVITSA** • 1930
SLEEPING BEAUTY, THE (USA) see **SPYASHCHAYA KRASAVITSA** • 1964
SLEEPING BEAUTY AND SNOW WHITE see **DORNWITTCHEN UND SCHNEEROSCHEN** • 1970
SLEEPING BEAUTY (USA) see **BELLE AU BOIS DORMANT, LA** • 1902
SLEEPING BEAUTY (USA) see **BELLE AU BOIS DORMANT, LA** • 1908
SLEEPING BEAUTY (USA) see **SKAZKA O SPJASCEJ CAREVNE I SEMI BOGATYRIACH** • 1914
SLEEPING BEAUTY (USA) see **BELLA ADORMENTATA, LA** • 1942
SLEEPING BEAUTY (USA) see **DORNROSCHEN** • 1955
SLEEPING CAR • 1933 • Litvak Anatole • UKN • LOVE AND LET LOVE
SLEEPING CAR, THE see **VAGON LI** • 1977
SLEEPING-CAR DWELLING see **COCHE CAMA ALOJAMIENTO** • 1968
SLEEPING CAR MURDERS, THE see **COMPARTIMENTS TUEURS** • 1965
SLEEPING CAR TO TRIESTE • 1948 • Carstairs John Paddy • UKN
SLEEPING CARDINAL, THE • 1931 • Hiscott Leslie • UKN • SHERLOCK HOLMES' FATAL HOUR (USA) ○ SHERLOCK HOLMES' FINAL HOUR
SLEEPING CITY, THE • 1950 • Sherman George • USA • CONFIDENTIAL SQUAD
SLEEPING CUTIE, THE • 1930 • Foster Lewis R. • SHT • USA
SLEEPING DOGS • 1977 • Donaldson Roger • NZL
SLEEPING DRAGON • 1975 • *Lui Raymond* • PHL
SLEEPING EMBER see **BRAZA DORMIDA** • 1928

SLEEPING FIRES • 1917 • Ford Hugh • USA
SLEEPING FIST • Yeh Yang-Ju • HKG
SLEEPING LION, THE • 1919 • Julian Rupert • USA
SLEEPING LOVERS, THE • 1899 • Williamson James • UKN
SLEEPING MEMORY, A • 1917 • Baker George D. • USA
SLEEPING PARTNER, THE see **SECRET PARTNER, THE** • 1961
SLEEPING PARTNERS • 1930 • Hicks Seymour • UKN
SLEEPING PORCH, THE • 1929 • Pearce A. Leslie • USA
SLEEPING PRINCESS, THE • 1939 • Gillett Burt • ANS • USA
SLEEPING SENTINEL, THE • 1914 • *Lubin* • USA
SLEEPING TIGER, THE • 1954 • Losey Joseph • UKN
SLEEPING TONIC, THE • 1909 • *Essanay* • USA
SLEEPING WORDS OF THE BRIDE see **HANAYOME NO NEGOTO** • 1933
SLEEPING WORDS OF THE BRIDEGROOM see **HANAMUKO NO NEGOTO** • 1934
SLEEPLESS NIGHT • 1948 • Rasinski Connie • ANS • USA
SLEEPLESS NIGHTS • 1932 • Bentley Thomas • UKN • GOOD NIGHT, DARLING
SLEEPLESS NIGHTS see **NOTTI BIANCHE, LE** • 1957
SLEEPLESS TUESDAY • 1945 • Yates Hal • SHT • USA
SLEEPLESS YEARS see **ALMATLAN EVEK** • 1959
SLEEPWALK • 1986 • Driver Sara • USA
SLEEPWALKER, THE • 1909 • Bouwmeester Theo? • UKN
SLEEPWALKER, THE • 1915 • Sandberg Anders W. • DNM
SLEEPWALKER, THE • 1917 • Jackson Harry • SHT • USA
SLEEPWALKER, THE • 1922 • Le Saint Edward J. • USA • SLEEP WALKER, THE ○ LOVE COMPLEX, THE
SLEEPWALKER, THE • 1925 • Seiler Lewis • SHT • USA
SLEEPWALKER, THE • 1942 • Geronimi Clyde • ANS • USA
SLEEPWALKER, THE see **SOMNABULIST, THE** • 1903
SLEEPWALKER, THE see **BONIFACE SOMNAMBULE** • 1950
SLEEPWALKERS see **LUNATYCY** • 1959
SLEEPWALKERS see **SONAMBULOS** • 1978
SLEEPY BETRAYERS see **STILLE BETRUGER** • 1989
SLEEPY GRASS • 1972 • Burke Martyn • CND
SLEEPY HEAD • 1914 • *Komic* • USA
SLEEPY HEAD • 1976 • *Spelvin Georgina* • USA
SLEEPY HEAD, THE • 1921 • Roach Hal • SHT • USA
SLEEPY HOLLOW • 1911 • *Nestor* • USA
SLEEPY JONES • 1910 • *Powers* • USA
SLEEPY LAGOON • 1943 • Santley Joseph • USA
SLEEPY ROMANCE, A • 1913 • *Lubin* • USA
SLEEPY SAM, THE SLEUTH • 1915 • *Norman Richard Edward* • USA
SLEEPY SAM'S AWAKENING • 1910 • Coleby A. E.? • UKN
SLEEPY TIME CHIMES • 1971 • Smith Paul J. • ANS • USA
SLEEPY TIME DONALD • 1947 • King Jack • ANS • USA
SLEEPY TIME DOWN SOUTH • 1932 • Fleischer Dave • ANS • USA
SLEEPY TIME POSSUM • 1951 • McKimson Robert • ANS • USA
SLEEPY-TIME SQUIRREL • 1954 • Lundy Dick • ANS • USA
SLEEPY TIME TOM • 1951 • Hanna William, Barbera Joseph • ANS • USA
SLEEPY TRAMPS, THE • 1911 • *Lubin* • USA
SLEEPYTIME BEAR • 1969 • Smith Paul J. • ANS • USA
SLEEPYTIME GAL • 1942 • Rogell Albert S. • USA
SLEIGH BELLS • 1928 • Disney Walt • ANS • USA
SLEIGH BELLS, THE • 1907 • Olcott Sidney • USA
SLENDER THREAD, THE • 1965 • Pollack Sydney • USA
SLENDER TRAP, THE • 1986 • Clark Barry • USA
SLEPOY MUZYKANT • 1961 • Lukashevich Tatyana • USS • SOUND OF LIFE (USA)
SLESAR I KANTZLER • 1923 • Gardin Vladimir, Preobrazhenskaya Olga • USS • LOCKSMITH AND CHANCELLOR
SLEUFOOT'S SEVENTH SUICIDE • 1913 • *Patheplay* • USA
SLEUTEL, DE • 1963 • Houwer Rob • SHT • NTH, FRG • SCHLUSSEL, DER ○ KEY, THE
SLEUTH • 1972 • Mankiewicz Joseph L. • USA, UKN
SLEUTH, THE • 1922 • Semon Larry, Roach Hal • SHT • USA
SLEUTH, THE (UKN) see **ONE MAN DOG, THE** • 1929
SLEUTH BUT SURE • 1956 • Tendlar Dave • ANS • USA
SLEUTH SLAYER, THE • 1984 • Huston Jimmy • USA
SLEUTHING • 1913 • Angeles Bert • USA
SLEUTHS • 1918 • Jones F. Richard • SHT • USA
SLEUTHS, THE • 1916 • *Pokes & Jabbs* • USA
SLEUTHS AND SLICKERS • 1918 • Howe J. A. • SHT • USA
SLEUTHS AND SURPRISES • 1918 • Kernan Henry • SHT • USA
SLEUTHS AT THE FLORAL PARADE, THE • 1913 • Sennett Mack • USA
SLEUTH'S LAST STAND, THE • 1913 • Sennett Mack • USA
SLEUTHS UNAWARES • 1913 • Thornby Robert T. • USA
SLEZI • 1914 • Bauer Yevgeni • USS • TEARS
SLI SOLDATI • 1957 • Trauberg Leonid • USS • SOLDIERS MARCHED ON, THE ○ SOLDIERS WERE MARCHING ○ SOLDIERS MARCH, THE
SLICE OF LIFE • 1982 • Lamond John • ASL • SEVEN UP
SLICE OF LIFE, A • 1914 • Taylor William D.? • USA
SLICE OF LIFE, A (UKN) see **TEMPI NOSTRI** • 1954
SLICK CHICK, THE • 1962 • McKimson Robert • ANS • USA
SLICK DETECTIVE, A • 1920 • *Tusun Comedies* • USA
SLICK HARE • 1947 • Freleng Friz • ANS • USA
SLICK TARTAN • 1949 • Chisnell Frank • UKN
SLICKED-UP PUP • 1951 • Hanna William, Barbera Joseph • ANS • USA
SLICKER, THE • 1920 • St. John Al • SHT • USA
SLICKING THE SLICKERS • 1916 • *Humphrey Orral* • USA
SLICK'S ROMANCE • 1911 • *Selig* • USA
SLIDE, BABY, SLIDE • 1932 • Stoloff Ben • SHT • USA
SLIDE DONALD SLIDE • 1949 • Hannah Jack • ANS • USA
SLIDE, KELLY, SLIDE • 1927 • Sedgwick Edward • USA
SLIDE, SPEEDY, SLIDE • 1931 • *Sennett Mack (P)* • SHT • USA
SLIDES • 1919 • Fleischer Dave • ANS • USA
SLIGHT CASE OF LARCENY, A • 1953 • Weis Don • USA
SLIGHT CASE OF MURDER, A • 1938 • Bacon Lloyd • USA
SLIGHT MISTAKE, A • 1911 • Humphrey William • USA
SLIGHT MISTAKE, A • 1913 • *Lubin* • USA
SLIGHT MISTAKE, A • 1914 • *Melies* • USA
SLIGHT MISUNDERSTANDING, A • 1913 • *Majestic* • USA
SLIGHTLY AT SEA • 1940 • D'Arcy Harry • SHT • USA
SLIGHTLY DAFFY • 1944 • Freleng Friz • ANS • USA
SLIGHTLY DANGEROUS • 1943 • Ruggles Wesley • USA • CARELESS
SLIGHTLY DIFFERENT WORLD, A see **TROCHE INNY SWIAT** • 1959
SLIGHTLY FRENCH • 1949 • Sirk Douglas • USA
SLIGHTLY HONORABLE • 1940 • Garnett Tay • USA • SEND ANOTHER COFFIN
SLIGHTLY MARRIED • 1932 • Thorpe Richard • USA
SLIGHTLY MISTAKEN • 1915 • Curtis Allen • USA
SLIGHTLY PREGNANT MAN, THE see **EVENEMENT LE PLUS IMPORTANT DEPUIS QUE L'HOMME A MARCHE SUR LA LUNE, L'** • 1973
SLIGHTLY PREGNANT MAN, THE see **RABBIT TEST** • 1978
SLIGHTLY SCANDALOUS • 1946 • Jason Will • USA • OH SAY YOU CAN SING
SLIGHTLY SCARLET • 1930 • Gasnier Louis J., Knopf Edwin H. • USA
SLIGHTLY SCARLET • 1956 • Dwan Allan • USA
SLIGHTLY STATIC • 1935 • Terhune William • SHT • USA
SLIGHTLY TEMPTED • 1940 • Landers Lew • USA
SLIGHTLY TERRIFIC • 1944 • Cline Eddie • USA
SLIGHTLY USED • 1927 • Mayo Archie • USA
SLIGHTLY WORN GOWN, THE • 1915 • Humphrey William • USA
SLIJK • 1971 • Conrad Patrick • BLG
SLIKE IZ SJECANJA • 1988 • Dragic Nedeljko • ANM • YGS • PICTURES FROM MEMORY
SLIKE IZ ZIVOTA UDARNIKA • 1973 • Cengic Bato • YGS • SCENES FROM THE LIFE OF SHOCK-WORKERS
SLIKOVNICA PCELARA • 1958 • Makavejev Dusan • DOC • YGS • BEEKEEPER'S SCRAPBOOK
SLIM • 1937 • Enright Ray • USA
SLIM AND THE BANDIT • 1913 • *Frontier* • USA
SLIM AND THE BOYS AT BREEZY BEACH • 1913 • *Frontier* • USA
SLIM AND THE DYNAMITERS • 1914 • *Frontier* • USA
SLIM AND THE INDIANS • 1914 • *Frontier* • USA
SLIM AND THE MONEY POTS • 1914 • *Frontier* • USA
SLIM AND THE MUMMY • 1914 • *Warner'S Features* • USA
SLIM AND THE OTHERS see **CHDY I INNI** • 1967
SLIM AND THE PETTICOATS • 1913 • *Frontier* • USA
SLIM BECOMES A COOK • 1914 • *Frontier* • USA
SLIM BECOMES A DETECTIVE • 1913 • *Frontier* • USA
SLIM BECOMES AN EDITOR • 1914 • *Frontier* • USA
SLIM CARTER • 1957 • Bartlett Richard • USA
SLIM DRISCOLL, SAMARITAN • 1913 • Bowman William J. • USA
SLIM DUSTY MOVIE, THE • 1984 • Stewart Rob • ASL
SLIM, FAT OR MEDIUM • 1915 • Clements Roy • USA
SLIM FINGERS • 1929 • Levigard Josef • USA
SLIM GETS THE REWARD • 1913 • *Frontier* • USA
SLIM HIGGINS • 1915 • Mix Tom • USA
SLIM HOGAN'S GETAWAY • 1914 • *Reliance* • USA
SLIM JIM'S LAST CHANCE • 1911 • *Kalem* • USA
SLIM JOINS THE ARMY • 1914 • *Frontier* • USA
SLIM OBSESSION • 1984 • Shebib Donald • MTV • CND
SLIM PRINCESS, THE • 1915 • Calvert E. H. • USA
SLIM PRINCESS, THE • 1920 • Schertzinger Victor • USA
SLIM PROPOSES -BUT • 1913 • *Frontier* • USA
SLIM SHOULDERS • 1922 • Crosland Alan • USA
SLIM SLAM'EM SLAMMED • 1914 • Hopper E. Mason • USA
SLIM THE BRAVE AND SOPHIE THE FAIR • 1915 • *Potel Victor* • USA
SLIM TO THE RESCUE • 1914 • *Frontier* • USA
SLIME CITY • 1988 • Lamberson Gregory • USA
SLIME PEOPLE, THE • 1962 • Hutton Robert • USA
SLIM'S LAST TRICK • 1913 • *Frontier* • USA
SLIM'S STRATEGY • 1914 • *Frontier* • USA
SLING SHOT 6 7/8 • 1951 • Lantz Walter • ANS • USA
SLINGER, THE see **PRACE** • 1960
SLINGREVALSEN • 1981 • Carlsen Esben Hoilund • DNM • STEPPING OUT
SLINGSHOT AND THE KITE, THE see **PRAK A DRAK** • 1960
SLINGSHOT KID, THE • 1927 • King Louis • USA
SLINK PINK • 1967 • Freleng Friz • ANS • USA
SLIOZY KAPALI • 1982 • Daneliya Georgi • USS • TEARS ARE FLOWING, THE
SLIP, THE • 1912 • *Stowell William* • USA
SLIP AT THE SWITCH, A • 1932 • Sandrich Mark • SHT • USA
SLIP OF THE BATTLE FIELD, THE see **SENGOKU JIEITAI** • 1979
SLIP OF THE TONGUE • 1970 • *Distripix Inc* • USA
SLIP UP • 1974 • Walters Robert • USA • EAGER FINGERS, EAGER LIPS ○ LOVE-IN ARRANGEMENTS
SLIP-UP see **POSLIZG** • 1971
SLIP UP SOME REDSKIN • 1951 • Kneitel Seymour • ANS • USA
SLIPHORN KING OF POLAROO • 1945 • Lundy Dick • ANS • USA
SLIPPER see **TOFFLAN -EN LYCKLIG KOMEDI** • 1967
SLIPPER -A HAPPY COMEDY, THE see **TOFFLAN -EN LYCKLIG KOMEDI** • 1967
SLIPPER AND THE ROSE, THE • 1976 • Forbes Bryan • UKN • SLIPPER AND THE ROSE -THE STORY OF CINDERELLA, THE (USA) ○ STORY OF CINDERELLA, THE
SLIPPER AND THE ROSE -THE STORY OF CINDERELLA, THE (USA) see **SLIPPER AND THE ROSE, THE** • 1976
SLIPPERY BURGLAR, THE see **FORCE DOIT RESTER A LA LOI** • 1899
SLIPPERY FEET • 1925 • Beaudine Harold • USA
SLIPPERY JIM • 1906 • Zecca Ferdinand • SHT • FRN
SLIPPERY JIM • 1912 • *Solax* • USA
SLIPPERY JIM THE BURGLAR • 1906 • Green Tom? • UKN
SLIPPERY JIM'S REPENTANCE • 1908 • Brooke Van Dyke • USA
SLIPPERY JOB, A • 1902 • *Mitchell & Kenyon* • UKN
SLIPPERY MCGEE see **SLIPPY MCGEE** • 1923
SLIPPERY MCGEE see **SLIPPY MCGEE** • 1948
SLIPPERY PEARLS, THE (UKN) see **STOLEN JOOLS, THE** • 1931
SLIPPERY PIMPLE • 1913 • Evans Fred, Evans Joe • UKN
SLIPPERY ROAD • 1928 • Taurog Norman • SHT • USA
SLIPPERY SADIE • 1914 • *Starlight* • USA
SLIPPERY SILKS • 1936 • Black Preston • SHT • USA
SLIPPERY SLICKERS • 1920 • Roach Hal • SHT • USA
SLIPPERY SLIM AND THE CLAIM AGENT • 1914 • *Essanay* • USA
SLIPPERY SLIM AND THE FORTUNE TELLER • 1914 • *Essanay* • USA
SLIPPERY SLIM AND THE GREEN-EYED MONSTER • 1914 • *Essanay* • USA
SLIPPERY SLIM AND THE IMPERSONATOR • 1914 • *Potel Victor* • USA
SLIPPERY SLIM AND THE STORK • 1914 • *Potel Victor* • USA
SLIPPERY SLIM -DIPLOMAT • 1914 • *Potel Victor* • USA
SLIPPERY SLIM GETS CURED • 1914 • *Essanay* • USA
SLIPPERY SLIM GETS SQUARE • 1914 • *Essanay* • USA
SLIPPERY SLIM REPENTS • 1913 • Henderson Dell • USA
SLIPPERY SLIM, THE MORTGAGE AND SOPHIE • 1914 • *Essanay* • USA
SLIPPERY SLIM'S DILEMMA • 1914 • *Essanay* • USA
SLIPPERY SLIM'S INHERITANCE • 1914 • *Potel Victor* • USA
SLIPPERY SLIM'S STRATAGEM • 1914 • *Potel Victor* • USA
SLIPPERY SLIM'S WEDDING DAY • 1915 • *Potel Victor* • USA
SLIPPERY SLIPPERS • 1962 • Hanna William, Barbera Joseph • ANS • USA
SLIPPERY VISITOR, A • 1906 • Cooper Arthur • UKN
SLIPPERY WHEN WET • 1959 • Brown Bruce • USA
SLIPPERY WHEN WET • 1976 • Anderson Karl • USA
SLIPPING FEET • 1920 • Blystone John G. • SHT • USA
SLIPPING FINGERS • 1913 • *Clary Charles* • USA
SLIPPING INTO DARKNESS • 1988 • Gaver Eleanor • USA • TAKEN BY FORCE
SLIPPING IT OVER ON FATHER • 1916 • Dillon John Francis • USA
SLIPPING WIVES • 1927 • Guiol Fred • SHT • USA
SLIPPY MCGEE • 1923 • Ruggles Wesley • USA • SLIPPERY MCGEE
SLIPPY MCGEE • 1948 • Kelley Albert • USA • SLIPPERY MCGEE
SLIPS AND SLACKERS • 1917 • Semon Larry • SHT • USA
SLIPS AND SLOPS • 1915 • Aylott Dave • UKN
SLIPSTREAM • 1973 • Acomba David • CND • VOIX DANS LA NUIT, UNE
SLIPSTREAM • 1989 • Lisberger Steven • UKN
SLITHER • 1973 • Zieff Howard • USA
SLITHIS • 1978 • Traxler Stephen • USA • SPAWN OF THE SLITHIS
SLJEMOVI • 1967 • Ristic Zika • YGS • HELMETS
SLNKO, DAZD, LALIE POLNE • 1972 • Havetta Elo • CZC • SUN, RAIN AND FIELD LILY ○ LILIES OF THE FIELD
SLNKO V SIETI • 1962 • Uher Stefan • CZC • SUNSHINE IN A NET
SLOANE • 1984 • Rosenthal Dan • USA
SLOANE AFFAIR, THE • 1972 • Jackson Douglas • CND
SLOBODA ILI STRIP • 1973 • Zilnik Zelimir • YGS • FREEDOM OR STRIP
SLOCHTEREN AAN DE LIJN • 1966 • Orthel Rolf • SHT • NTH
SLOCUM DISASTER • 1904 • *Bitzer Billy (Ph)* • USA
SLOCUM HARRIERS, THE • 1919 • Sandground Maurice • UKN
SLOEDEPATRULJEN SIRIUS • 1980 • Roos Jorgen • DOC • DNM • SLEDGE PATROL SIRIUS, THE
SLOGAN • 1969 • Grimblat Pierre • FRN
SLON I VEREVOCHKA • 1945 • Frez Ilya • USS • ELEPHANT AND THE SKIPPING ROPE, THE
SLONCE WSCHODZI RAZ NA DZIEN • 1967 • Kluba Henryk • PLN • SUN RISES ONCE A DAY, THE
SLONECZNE WZGORZE • 1963 • Gryczelowska Krystyna • DOC • PLN • SUNNY HILL
SLOPE IN THE SUN, A see **HI NO ATARU SAKAMICHI** • 1967
SLOPER'S NEW HAT • 1911 • Kinder Stuart? • UKN
SLOPER'S VISIT TO BRIGHTON • 1898 • Williamson James • UKN
SLOPPY BILL OF THE ROLLICKING R see **JOLLY BILL OF THE ROLLICKING R** • 1911
SLOPPY JALOPY • 1952 • Burness Pete • ANS • USA
SLOSHTON QUARTETTE, THE • 1908 • Collins Alf? • UKN
SLOT I ET SLOT, ET • 1955 • Dreyer Carl T. • DCS • DNM • CASTLE WITHIN A CASTLE
SLOTH • 1917 • Marston Theodore • USA
SLOVO DLYA ZASHCHITY • 1977 • Abdrakhitov Vadim • USS • SPEECH FOR THE DEFENCE
SLOW AND SURE • 1923 • St. John Al • SHT • USA
SLOW AS LIGHTNING • 1923 • Jones Grover • USA
SLOW ATTACK see **ENDSTATION FREIHEIT** • 1981
SLOW BEAU • 1930 • *Mintz Charles (P)* • ANS • USA
SLOW BULLET • 1988 • Wright Allen • USA
SLOW BURN • 1986 • Chapman Matthew • USA
SLOW BUT SURE • 1914 • *Wilson Ben* • USA
SLOW BUT SURE • 1934 • *Terry Paul/ Moser Frank (P)* • ANS • USA
SLOW DANCE WORLD • 1987 • Besen Ellen, Baumholz Lonny • ANS • CND
SLOW DANCING IN THE BIG CITY • 1978 • Avildsen John G. • USA
SLOW DESCENT INTO HELL, A see **YOUR TICKET IS NO LONGER VALID** • 1980
SLOW DOWN • 1967 • Heffner Avram • SHT • ISR
SLOW DYNAMITE • 1925 • Mattison Frank S. • USA
SLOW EXPRESS, THE • 1918 • Clements Roy • SHT • USA
SLOW MOTION • 1973 • Pindal Kaj • ANS • CND
SLOW MOTION see **USPORENO KRETANJE** • 1980
SLOW MOTION (UKN) see **SAUVE QUI PEUT** • 1980
SLOW RUN • 1968 • Kardish Larry • CND
SLOW SUMMER see **LANGSAMER SOMMER** • 1976
SLOW VS. BONER • 1984 • SAF
SLOWCE M • 1964 • Brdecka Jiri • ANS • CZC • LETTER M ○ MINSTREL'S SONG
SLOWEST TRAIN, THE see **SAMII MEDLENNII POEZD** • 1963
SLUBUJEMY! • 1952 • Bossak Jerzy • DOC • PLN • WE SWEAR! ○ OUR OATH
SLUBY ULANSKIE • 1935 • Kranicz Mieczyslaw • PLN • LOVE IN THE ARMY
SLUCAJ HARMS • 1987 • Pesic Slobodan D. • YGS • HARMS CASE, THE
SLUCAJ POSPANOG BOKSERA • 1961 • Grgic Zlatko • ANS • YGS • CASE OF THE SLEEPY BOXER, THE

SLUCHAI NA SHAKHTE 8 • 1957 • Basov Vladimir • USS • CASE OF PIT NO.8, THE
SLUCHAI NA STADIONE • 1929 • Ptushko Alexander • ANS • USS • EVENT IN THE STADIUM
SLUCHAI V VULKANYE • 1941 • Kuleshov Lev, Khokhlova • USS • INCIDENT ON A VOLCANO
SLUCHAYAT PAINLEVE see **SLUCHAYAT PENLEVE** • 1968
SLUCHAYAT PENLEVE • 1968 • Stoyanov Georgi • BUL • PENLEVE CASE, THE ○ SLUCHAYAT PAINLEVE ○ PAINLEV CASE, THE
SLUG IN THE HEATER, A see **BALLE DANS LE CANON, UNE** • 1958
SLUGA • 1988 • Abdrakhitov Vadim • USS • SERVANT, THE (UKN)
SLUGGARD, THE see **KRECEK** • 1946
SLUGGARD'S SURPRISE, THE • 1900 • Hepworth Cecil M. • UKN
SLUGGER'S WIFE, THE • 1985 • Ashby Hal • USA
SLUGS, THE MOVIE • 1988 • Simon Piquer • USA
SLUICE • 1978 • Brakhage Stan • SHT • USA
SLUM • 1952 • Roos Jorgen • DOC • DNM
SLUM BOY see **RAGAZZO DI BORGATA** • 1976
SLUMBER PARTY '57 • 1976 • Levey William A. • USA • TEENAGE SLUMBER PARTY
SLUMBER PARTY IN HORROR HOUSE see **GHOST IN THE INVISIBLE BIKINI, THE** • 1966
SLUMBER PARTY MASSACRE • 1984 • Jones Amy • USA • SLUMBER PARTY MURDERS
SLUMBER PARTY MASSACRE II • 1987 • Brock Deborah • USA
SLUMBER PARTY MURDERS see **SLUMBER PARTY MASSACRE** • 1984
SLUMBERING FIRES (UKN) see **BUCKING BROADWAY** • 1918
SLUMBERING MEMORY, THE • 1916 • *Buffalo* • SHT • USA
SLUMBERLAND • 1908 • Brooke Van Dyke • USA
SLUMBERLAND EXPRESS • 1936 • *Lantz Walter (P)* • ANS • USA
SLUMBERVILLE'S SCARE • 1914 • *Lubin* • USA
SLUMP IS OVER, THE see **CRISE EST FINIE, LA** • 1934
SLUMP OF LIFE • 1978 • Sani Asrul • INN
SLUMRANDE TONER • 1978 • Bergenstrahle Johan • SWD • FOR YOUR PLEASURE
SLUMS OF BERLIN see **VERRUFENEN, DIE** • 1925
SLUMS OF HUMANITY, THE • 1916 • *Puritan* • USA
SLUT • 1966 • Forsberg • SHT • SWD • END, THE
SLUT, THE • 1965 • Milor Nicholas • USA • URSULA THE SLUT ○ URSULA THE HUSSY ○ URSULA
SLUZBENI POLOZAJ • 1964 • Hadzic Fadil • YGS • OFFICIAL POSITION, THE
SLUZHEBNI ROMAN • 1977 • Ryazanov Eldar • USS • OFFICE AFFAIR, AN ○ OFFICE ROMANCE, AN
SLUZHILI DVA TOVARISHCHA • 1968 • Karelov Yevgyeni • USS • TWO FRIENDS IN THE ARMY ○ THERE SERVED TWO COMRADES ○ TWO COMRADES-IN-ARMS ○ SOLDIER FRIENDS
SLYEDSTVIYE PRODOLZHAYETSYA • 1967 • Atakishiyev Alisettar • USS • INVESTIGATION CONTINUES, THE
SLYUBIMYMI NE RASSTAVAITES • 1980 • Arsenov Pavel • USS • DON'T LEAVE YOUR LOVED ONES
SLZY, KTERE SVET NEVIDI • 1961 • Fric Martin • MTV • CZC • TEARS THE WORLD CAN'T SEE
SMAAK VAN WATER, DE • 1982 • Seunke Orlow • NTH • TASTE OF WATER, THE
SMACK AND THISTLE • 1989 • Ikoli Tunde • UKN
SMAEKLAASEN • 1908 • *Holger-Madsen* • DNM • SPRING LOCK, THE
SMALA, LA • 1984 • Hubert Jean-Loup • FRN
SMALANNINGAR • 1935 • Rodin Gosta • SWD • PEOPLE OF SMALAND
SMALL ADVENTURE, A see **CHIISANA BOKEN RYOKO** • 1963
SMALL BACHELOR, THE • 1927 • Seiter William A. • USA
SMALL BACK ROOM, THE • 1948 • Powell Michael, Pressburger Emeric • UKN • HOUR OF GLORY (USA)
SMALL BALL TOSSED BY A DWARF, THE • 1981 • Lee Won-So • SKR
SMALL BAND JAZZ • 1961 • Henryson Robert • SHT • UKN
SMALL BANKNOTE • 1966 • Krukowski Waclaw • ANM • PLN
SMALL CHANGE • 1917 • *Compson Betty* • SHT • USA
SMALL CHANGE (USA) see **ARGENT DE POCHE, L'** • 1976
SMALL CHILD'S FIRST ADVENTURE, A see **CHIISANA BOKEN RYOKO** • 1963
SMALL CIRCLE OF FRIENDS, A • 1980 • Cohen Rob • USA
SMALL CZECHOSLOVAK ICON see **CESKOSLOVENSKY JEZISEK** • 1918
SMALL DEVIL, THE see **SHAITANE EL SAGHIR, EL** • 1963
SMALL DIVER, THE • Doicheva Zdenka • ANS • BUL
SMALL FIRES see **PICCOLI FUOCHI** • 1985
SMALL FRY • 1939 • Fleischer Dave • ANS • USA
SMALL HOTEL • 1957 • MacDonald David • UKN
SMALL HOURS, THE • 1962 • Chaitin Norman C. • USA • FLAMING DESIRE
SMALL IS BEAUTIFUL -IMPRESSIONS OF FRITZ SCHUMACHER • 1978 • Brittain Don, Kiefer Douglas, Howells Barrie • DOC • CND
SMALL KILLING, A • 1981 • Stern Steven Hilliard • TVM • USA
SMALL MAGNETIC HAND, THE • 1916 • Bartlett Charles • SHT • USA
SMALL MAN, THE • 1935 • Baxter John • UKN
SMALL MERMAID, A see **MALA SIRENA** • 1968
SMALL MIRACLE, THE • 1973 • Szwarc Jeannot • TVM • USA
SMALL ONE, THE • 1978 • Bluth Don • ANS • USA
SMALL ONE, THE see **MALY** • 1970
SMALL ONE, THE see **CABITO, EL** • 1977
SMALL POX SCARE AT GULCH HOLLOW, THE • 1913 • *Frontier* • USA
SMALL PRIVILEGES see **PEQUENOS PRIVILEGIOS, LOS** • 1977
SMALL PROPELLER, THE • 1967 • Spencer John • SHT • UKN
SMALL REVENGE see **PEQUENA REVANCHA** • 1986
SMALL SALESMAN, THE see **EMBORAKOS, O** • 1967
SMALL SPACE see **CHIISANA KUKAN** • 1964
SMALL STRANGER, THE see **GHARIB AL SAGHIR, AL** • 1962
SMALL TALK • 1929 • McGowan Robert • SHT • USA
SMALL TIME ACT • 1913 • Nicholls George • USA
SMALL TIMERS • 1929 • SHT • USA
SMALL TOWN see **PUEBLO CHICO** • 1974
SMALL TOWN, THE see **MIASTECZKO** • 1956
SMALL TOWN BOY • 1937 • Tryon Glenn • USA
SMALL TOWN CALLED HISBISCUS, A see **FURONG ZHEN** • 1985
SMALL TOWN DEB • 1941 • Schuster Harold • USA
SMALL TOWN GIRL • 1936 • Wellman William A. • USA • ONE HORSE TOWN
SMALL TOWN GIRL • 1952 • Kardos Leslie • USA
SMALL TOWN GIRL, A • 1915 • Dwan Allan • USA
SMALL TOWN GIRL, A • 1917 • Adolfi John G. • USA
SMALL TOWN GIRLS • 1979 • Janovich Tom • USA • ECSTASY GIRLS
SMALL TOWN GUY, THE • 1917 • Windom Lawrence C. • USA
SMALL TOWN IDOL, A • 1920 • Kenton Erle C. • USA
SMALL TOWN IN TEXAS, A • 1976 • Starrett Jack • USA
SMALL TOWN LAWYER (UKN) see **MAIN STREET LAWYER** • 1939
SMALL TOWN MASSACRE see **DEAD KIDS** • 1981
SMALL TOWN PRINCESS, A • 1927 • *Sennett Mack (P)* • SHT • USA
SMALL-TOWN QUINTET, THE see **SVEN KLANGS KVINTETT** • 1976
SMALL TOWN SINNERS (USA) see **KLEINSTADTSUNDER** • 1927
SMALL TOWN STORY • 1953 • Tully Montgomery • UKN
SMALL TOWN STUFF • 1916 • MacGregor Norval • SHT • USA
SMALL TOWNS OF SKANOR-FALSTERBO see **SKANOR-FALSTERBO** • 1939
SMALL TRAIN, A see **MALI VLAK** • 1959
SMALL VILLAGE BY THE RIVER, A • Ngiem Phu My • VTN
SMALL VOICE, THE • 1948 • McDonnell Fergus • UKN • HIDEOUT, THE (USA)
SMALL WARS see **HURUB SAGHIRA** • 1983
SMALL WESTERN see **MALY WESTERN** • 1960
SMALL WISHES • 1989 • Karamati Masud • IRN
SMALL WITCH, THE see **SAHERA EL SAGHIRA, EL** • 1963
SMALL WONDER see **FIRST TIME, THE** • 1952
SMALL WORLD IN THE DARK, A see **KLEINE WELT IM DUNKELEM, EINE** • 1938
SMALL WORLD OF MARCO, THE see **PEQUENO MUNDO DE MARCOS, O** • 1968
SMALL WORLD OF SAMMY LEE, THE • 1963 • Hughes Ken • UKN
SMALLEST SHOW ON EARTH, THE • 1956 • Dearden Basil • UKN • BIG TIME OPERATORS (USA)
SMALLEST WORM, THE • 1915 • Wilson Frank? • UKN
SMALLPOX ON THE CIRCLE U • 1914 • *Eclair* • USA
SMANIA ADDOSSO, LA • 1963 • Andrei Marcello • ITL, FRN • EYE OF THE NEEDLE, THE (USA)
SMARA • 1982 • Gruber Steff • SWT
SMARAGD DES RADJAH VON PANLANZUR, DER see **ABENTEUER EINES ERMORDETEN 2, DIE** • 1921
SMARKULA • 1963 • Buczkowski Leonard • PLN • TEENAGER
SMART • 1985 • Kraanen Joost • DOC • NTH
SMART • 1990 • Chaudhry Haider • PKS
SMART ALEC • 1951 • Guillermin John • UKN
SMART ALEC see **HOLLYWOOD DREAMING** • 1987
SMART ALECKS • 1942 • Fox Wallace • USA
SMART BLONDE • 1937 • McDonald Frank • USA
SMART CAPTURE, A • 1904 • Collins Alf? • UKN
SMART CAPTURE, A • 1907 • Fitzhamon Lewin • UKN
SMART GIRL • 1935 • Scotto Aubrey • USA
SMART GIRLS DON'T TALK • 1948 • Bare Richard L. • USA
SMART GUY • 1944 • Hillyer Lambert • USA • YOU CAN'T BEAT THE LAW
SMART GUYS, THE see **SMATTES, LES** • 1972
SMART MONEY • 1931 • Green Alfred E. • USA
SMART NYAMA • 1963 • Piskov Hristo • BUL • THERE IS NO DEATH
SMART POLITICS • 1948 • Jason Will • USA • OLD GRAY MAYOR, THE
SMART SET, A • 1919 • Bramble A. V. • UKN
SMART SET, THE • 1928 • Conway Jack • USA
SMART SEX, THE • 1921 • Granville Fred Leroy • USA • GIRL AND THE GOOSE, THE
SMART STEPPERS • 1929 • Roberts Stephen • SHT • USA
SMART WOMAN • 1931 • La Cava Gregory • USA • NANCY'S PRIVATE AFFAIR
SMART WOMAN • 1948 • Blatt Edward A. • USA
SMART WORK • 1931 • Arbuckle Roscoe • USA
SMARTER THAN THE TEACHER see **PLUS FORT QUE SON MAITRE** • 1896
SMARTEST GIRL IN TOWN, THE • 1936 • Santley Joseph • USA • MILLION DOLLAR PROFILE
SMARTGRANSEN • 1983 • Elers-Jarlemann Agneta • DOC • SWD • BEYOND SORROW, BEYOND PAIN
SMARTY • 1934 • Florey Robert • USA • HIT ME AGAIN (UKN)
SMARTY CAT • 1955 • Hanna William, Barbera Joseph • ANS • USA
SMASH AND GRAB • 1937 • Whelan Tim • UKN • LARCENY STREET (USA)
SMASH HIT • 1989 • Stewart John • USA
SMASH PALACE • 1981 • Donaldson Roger • NZL
SMASH-UP • 1947 • Heisler Stuart • USA • WOMAN DESTROYED, A (UKN) ○ SMASH-UP, THE STORY OF A WOMAN
SMASH-UP • 1963 • Mariassy Felix • HNG
SMASH-UP ALLEY • 1973 • Lasko Edward J. • USA • PETTY STORY, THE
SMASH-UP IN INTERSTATE FIVE • 1973 • Moxey John Llewellyn • TVM • USA
SMASH-UP, THE STORY OF A WOMAN see **SMASH-UP** • 1947
SMASH YOUR BAGGAGE • 1933 • Mack Roy • SHT • USA
SMASHED BACK • 1927 • *Hollywood Producers Finance Ass.* • USA
SMASHED IN THE CAREER • 1917 • Lehrman Henry • SHT • USA
SMASHING BARRIERS • 1919 • Duncan William, Smith Cliff? • SRL • USA
SMASHING BARRIERS • 1923 • Duncan William • USA
SMASHING BIRD I USED TO KNOW, THE • 1969 • Hartford-Davis Robert • UKN • SCHOOL FOR UNCLAIMED GIRLS (USA) ○ HOUSE OF UNCLAIMED WOMEN
SMASHING JOB, A • 1946 • Hughes Harry • UKN
SMASHING OF THE REICH (USA) see **GUERRE INCONNUE, LA** • 1961
SMASHING STROKE, THE • 1917 • Conway Jack? • SHT • USA
SMASHING THE CRIME SYNDICATE (UKN) see **HELL'S BLOODY DEVILS** • 1967
SMASHING THE MONEY RING • 1939 • Morse Terry O. • USA
SMASHING THE PLOT • 1918 • *Ruge Billy* • SHT • USA
SMASHING THE RACKETS • 1938 • Landers Lew • USA
SMASHING THE SPY RING • 1939 • Cabanne W. Christy • USA • INTERNATIONAL SPY
SMASHING THROUGH • 1918 • Clifton Elmer • USA
SMASHING THROUGH • 1928 • Kellino W. P. • UKN
SMASHING THROUGH (UKN) see **CHEYENNE CYCLONE** • 1932
SMASHING TIME • 1913 • *Lubin* • USA
SMASHING TIME • 1967 • Davis Desmond • UKN
SMASHING UP see **SI VOLVEMOS A VERNOS** • 1967
S'MATTER, PETE? • 1927 • Lantz Walter • ANS • USA
SMATTES, LES • 1972 • Labrecque Jean-Claude • CND • SMART GUYS, THE
SMEDE OKO SLO OKO • 1967 • Argus Robert • YGS • BROWN EYE EVIL EYE
SMEDER PA LUFFEN • 1949 • Faustman Erik • SWD • VAGABOND BLACKSMITHS
SMEKKELAARMEIDER • 1961 • de Meyst E. G. • BLG
SMEKMANAD • 1972 • Lundberg Claes • SWD • HONEYMOON
SMELL OF HONEY!, THE see **SMELL OF HONEY, A SWALLOW OF BRINE!, A** • 1966
SMELL OF HONEY, A SWALLOW OF BRINE!, A • 1966 • Elliott B. Ron • USA • TASTE OF HONEY, A SWALLOW OF BRINE, A ○ SMELL OF HONEY!, THE
SMELL OF POISON, THE see **DOKUYAKU NO NIOU ONNA** • 1967
SMELL OF THE YUKON, THE • 1919 • Lyons Eddie, Moran Lee • SHT • USA
SMELYE LYUDI • 1950 • Yudin Konstantin • USS • BRAVE MEN, THE
SMEMORATO DI COLLEGNO LO • 1962 • Corbucci Sergio • ITL
SMEMORATO, LO • 1936 • Righelli Gennaro • ITL
SMEMORATO, LO • 1965-68 • Salce Luciano • ITL, FRN
SMERTELNI VRAG • 1971 • Matveyev Yevgeni • USS • DEADLY ENEMY ○ SWORN ENEMIES
SMERTENS BORN • 1977 • Thomsen Christian Braad • DNM • CHILDREN OF PAIN
SMESNY PAN • 1969 • Kachyna Karel • CZC • MAN OF THE STREET ○ FUNNY MAN, THE ○ FUNNY OLD MAN, THE
SMIC SMAC SMOC • 1971 • Lelouch Claude • FRN
SMIERC DZIECIOROBA • 1990 • Nowak Wojciech • PLN • DEATH OF A KIDMAKER
SMIERC PREZYDENTA • 1977 • Kawalerowicz Jerzy • PLN • DEATH OF A PRESIDENT, THE ○ DEATH OF THE PRESIDENT ○ PRESIDENT'S DEATH, THE
SMIERC PROWINCJALA • 1966 • Zanussi Krzysztof • SHT • PLN • DEATH OF A PROVINCIAL
SMIERC W SRODKOWYM POKOJU • 1965 • Trzos-Rastawiecki Andrzej • MTV • PLN • DEATH IN THE MIDDLE ROOM
SMIFFY AT BLACKPOOL see **JOHN WILLIE AT BLACKPOOL** • 1913
SMIL • 1916 • Holger-Madsen • DNM • BEGGAR MAN OF PARIS, THE ○ FATHER SORROW ○ FARS SORG
SMIL EMIL • 1969 • Hom Jesper • DNM • SMILE, EMIL!
SMIL MAND • 1972 • Schmidt Aase • DNM
SMILE • 1974 • Ritchie Michael • USA
SMILE 61 see **OSMJEH 61** • 1961
SMILE, THE • Ursianu Malvina • RMN
SMILE, THE see **QUATRE SOURIRES, LES** • 1958
SMILE, THE see **US MIECH** • 1965
SMILE, BROTHER, SMILE • 1927 • Dillon John Francis • USA • ROAD TO ROMANCE, THE
SMILE BROUGHT BACK, A see **VOZVRASHCHYENIYE ULYBKI** • 1968
SMILE DARN YA SMILE • 1931-32 • Ising Rudolf • ANS • USA
SMILE, EMIL! see **SMIL EMIL** • 1969
SMILE FOR AUNTIE • 1980 • Deitch Gene • USA
SMILE IN THE STORM, A • 1937 • Vorhaus Bernard, Sokal H. R. • USA
SMILE, JENNY, YOU'RE DEAD • 1974 • Thorpe Jerry • TVM • USA
SMILE OF A CHILD, A • 1911 • Griffith D. W. • USA
SMILE OF OUR EARTH, THE see **DAICHI WA HOHOEMU** • 1925
SMILE OF THE EVIL EYE, THE see **RYS** • 1981
SMILE OF THE LAMB, THE see **HYIUCH HAGDI** • 1985
SMILE ON A DECEMBER MORNING • 1975 • Umboh Wim • INN
SMILE ORANGE • 1976 • Rhone Trevor • JMC
SMILE PLEASE • 1924 • *Sennett Mack (P)* • SHT • USA
SMILE RETURNED, THE see **VOZVRASHCHYENIYE ULYBKI** • 1968
SMILE WHEN YOU SAY "I DO" • 1973 • Funt Allen • TVM • USA
SMILE WINS, THE • 1923 • Jeske George • SHT • USA
SMILE WINS, THE • 1927 • Roach Hal • SHT • USA
SMILE, YOU'RE ON CAMERA • 1979 • ISR
SMILER, THE • 1920 • *Gibson Hoot* • SHT • USA
SMILER HAS STAGE FEVER (USA) see **CHARLEY SMILER IS STAGE STRUCK** • 1911
SMILES • 1919 • Gillstrom Arvid E. • USA
SMILES • 1929 • Fleischer Dave • ANS • USA
SMILES • 1964 • Avildsen John G. • SHT • USA
SMILES AND TEARS see **LOJEN OCH TARAR** • 1913
SMILES AND TEARS see **SENYUM DAN TANIS** • 1974
SMILES ARE TRUMPS • 1922 • Marshall George • USA
SMILES OF A SUMMER'S NIGHT (UKN) see **SOMMARNATTENS LEENDE** • 1955
SMILES OF FORTUNE • 1914 • Hotaling Arthur D. • USA
SMILES ON A SEPTEMBER MORNING see **SENYUM DIPAGI BULAN SEPTEMBER** • 1974
SMILEY • 1956 • Kimmins Anthony • UKN, ASL
SMILEY GETS A GUN • 1958 • Kimmins Anthony • UKN, ASL

SMILEY'S PEOPLE • 1982 • Langton Simon • MTV • UKN, USA
SMILIN' ALONG • 1932 • Argyle John F. • UKN
SMILIN' AT TROUBLE • 1925 • Garson Harry • USA • SMILING AT TROUBLE
SMILIN' GUNS • 1929 • McRae Henry • USA
SMILIN' KID, THE • 1920 • Gibson Ed Hoot • SHT • USA
SMILIN' ON • 1923 • Craft William James • USA
SMILIN' THRO' • 1922 • *Parkinson H. B.* • SHT • UKN
SMILIN' THROUGH • 1922 • Franklin Sidney A. • USA • SMILING THROUGH
SMILIN' THROUGH • 1932 • Franklin Sidney A. • USA
SMILIN' THROUGH • 1941 • Borzage Frank • USA
SMILING AGAIN see **UJRA MOSOLYOGNAK** • 1954
SMILING ALL THE WAY • 1920 • Butler Fred J., McClung Hugh • USA
SMILING ALONG (USA) see **KEEP SMILING** • 1938
SMILING AT TROUBLE see **SMILIN' AT TROUBLE** • 1925
SMILING BANDIT, THE • 1916 • *Rancho* • USA
SMILING BILLY • 1927 • Worne Duke • USA
SMILING BOB • 1912 • Melies Gaston • USA
SMILING CHARACTER, A see **HOHOEMU HINSEI** • 1930
SMILING DAN • 1913 • Miller Charles? • USA
SMILING EARTH, THE (USA) see **DAICHI WA HOHOEMU** • 1925
SMILING EYES see **GULEN GOZLER** • 1977
SMILING GHOST, THE • 1941 • Seiler Lewis • USA
SMILING IRISH EYES • 1929 • Seiter William A. • USA
SMILING JIM • 1922 • Franz Joseph J. • USA
SMILING LAND, THE • 1952 • Gajer Vaclav • CZC
SMILING LIEUTENANT, THE • 1931 • Lubitsch Ernst • USA
SMILING LIFE, A see **HOHOEMU HINSEI** • 1930
SMILING MADAME BEAUDET, THE (USA) see **SOURIANTE MADAME BEAUDET, LA** • 1922
SMILING NIKKATSU see **HOHOEMU NIKKATSU** • 1932
SMILING TERROR, THE • 1929 • Levigard Josef • USA
SMILING THROUGH see **SMILIN' THROUGH** • 1922
SMITE OF CONSCIENCE, THE • 1917 • Terwilliger George W. • SHT • USA
SMITH • 1917 • Elvey Maurice • UKN
SMITH! • 1969 • O'Herlihy Michael • USA
SMITH • 1977 • Brown Alan • MTV • UKN
SMITH BABY'S BIRTHDAY • 1928 • Whitman Phil • USA
SMITH, JAMES O. ORGANIST U.S.A. • 1965 • Wildenhahn Klaus • DOC • FRG
SMITH OF MINNESOTA • 1942 • Landers Lew • USA
SMITH, OUR FRIEND • 1946 • Lassally Walter (c/d) • SHT • UKN
SMITH SERIES, THE • 1976 • Lavut Martin • CND
SMITHEREENS • 1982 • Seidelman Susan • USA
SMITH'S ARMY LIFE • 1928 • *Sennett Mack (P)* • SHT • USA
SMITH'S BABY • 1926 • Cline Eddie • SHT • USA
SMITH'S BURGLAR see **BURGLAR, THE** • 1928
SMITH'S CANDY SHOP • 1927 • *Sennett Mack (P)* • SHT • USA
SMITH'S CATALINA ROWBOAT RACE • 1928 • *Sennett Mack (P)* • SHT • USA • CATALINA ROWBOAT RACE
SMITH'S COOK • 1927 • *Sennett Mack (P)* • SHT • USA
SMITH'S COUSIN • 1927 • *Sennett Mack (P)* • SHT • USA
SMITH'S CUSTOMER • 1927 • Bacon Lloyd • SHT • USA
SMITH'S FARM DAYS • 1928 • Whitman Phil • SHT • USA
SMITH'S FISHING TRIP • 1927 • *Sennett Mack (P)* • SHT • USA
SMITH'S HOLIDAY • 1928 • Goulding Alf • SHT • USA
SMITH'S KINDERGARTEN • 1927 • *Sennett Mack (P)* • SHT • USA
SMITH'S LANDLORD • 1926 • *Sennett Mack (P)* • SHT • USA
SMITH'S MARMALADE • 1911 • *Powers* • USA
SMITH'S MODISTE SHOP • 1927 • *Sennett Mack (P)* • SHT • USA
SMITH'S NEW HOME • 1927 • Bacon Lloyd • SHT • USA
SMITHS OF LONDON, THE • 1952 • Hopkinson Peter • UKN
SMITH'S PETS • 1927 • *Sennett Mack (P)* • SHT • USA
SMITH'S PICNIC • 1926 • *Sennett Mack (P)* • SHT • USA
SMITH'S PONY • 1927 • Goulding Alf • SHT • USA
SMITH'S RESTAURANT • 1928 • *Sennett Mack (P)* • SHT • USA
SMITH'S SURPRISE • 1927 • Bacon Lloyd • SHT • USA
SMITH'S UNCLE • 1926 • *Sennett Mack (P)* • SHT • USA
SMITH'S VACATION • 1926 • Cline Eddie • SHT • USA
SMITH'S VISITOR • 1926 • *Sennett Mack (P)* • SHT • USA
SMITH'S WIVES • 1935 • Haynes Manning • UKN
SMITHSON BECOMES A COWBOY • 1911 • *Urban Trading Co* • UKN
SMITHY • 1924 • Jeske George • SHT • USA
SMITHY • 1933 • King George • UKN
SMITHY • 1946 • Hall Ken G. • ASL • PACIFIC ADVENTURE (USA) ○ SOUTHERN CROSS (UKN)
SMITHY'S GRANDMA PARTY • 1913 • *Beery Wallace* • USA
SMITTEN KITTEN • 1952 • Hanna William, Barbera Joseph • ANS • USA
SMMIS • 1976 • Cardinal Roger • DCS • CND
SMOG • 1962 • Rossi Franco • ITL
SMOK-XPEDITION • 1969 • Nehrebecki Wladyslaw • ANS • PLN • DRAGON EXPEDITION, THE
SMOKE • 1962 • Kramer Joseph • USA
SMOKE • 1970 • McEveety Vincent • TVM • USA
SMOKE • 1971 • Axelman Torbjorn • SWD
SMOKE see **KEMURI** • 1925
SMOKE see **DIM** • 1967
SMOKE see **FUST** • 1970
SMOKE see **PHYSICAL EVIDENCE** • 1989
SMOKE AND FLESH • 1968 • Mangine Joe • USA
SMOKE BELLEW • 1929 • Dunlap Scott R. • USA
SMOKE EATERS, THE • 1926 • Hutchison Charles • USA
SMOKE FROM LONE BILL'S CABIN, THE • 1913 • *Vitagraph* • USA
SMOKE IN THE WIND • 1971 • Kane Joseph • USA
SMOKE JUMPERS • 1951 • Newman Joseph M. • DCS • USA
SMOKE JUMPERS see **RED SKIES OF MONTANA** • 1952
SMOKE LIGHTNING • 1933 • Howard David • USA
SMOKE MENACE • 1937 • Taylor John • DOC • UKN
SMOKE OF EVIL • 1967 • *Inter-American Film Dist.* • USA
SMOKE OF NIGHT see **YORU NO EMMACHO** • 1961
SMOKE OF POTATO HAULM see **DYM BRAMBOROVE NATE** • 1976
SMOKE OF THE FORTY FIVE, THE • 1911 • Dwan Allan • USA
SMOKE RINGS • 1943 • Dreifuss Arthur • SHT • USA
SMOKE RINGS • 1986 • Bittman Roman • MTV • CND
SMOKE SIGNAL • 1955 • Hopper Jerry • USA
SMOKE SIGNAL, THE • 1920 • Murphy Martin • SHT • USA
SMOKE TREE RANGE • 1937 • Selander Lesley • USA
SMOKED HAMS • 1947 • Lundy Dick • ANS • USA
SMOKED HUSBAND, A • 1908 • Griffith D. W. • USA
SMOKED OUT • 1904 • *Warwick Trading Co* • UKN
SMOKED OUT • 1923 • Beebe Ford, Maloney Leo • USA
SMOKED TO A FINISH • 1913 • *Kalem* • USA
SMOKER, THE • 1910 • Griffith D. W.?, Powell Frank? • USA
SMOKER'S JOKE, THE • 1907 • Cooper Arthur? • UKN
SMOKES AND LOLLIES • 1978 • Armstrong Gillian • DCS • ASL
SMOKESCREEN • 1964 • O'Connolly Jim • UKN
SMOKEY ADVENTURE, A • 1916 • Millarde Harry • USA
SMOKEY AND THE BANDIT • 1977 • Needham Hal • USA
SMOKEY AND THE BANDIT II • 1980 • Needham Hal • USA • SMOKEY AND THE BANDIT RIDE AGAIN (UKN)
SMOKEY AND THE BANDIT III • 1983 • Lowry Dick • USA
SMOKEY AND THE BANDIT RIDE AGAIN (UKN) see **SMOKEY AND THE BANDIT II** • 1980
SMOKEY AND THE GOODTIME OUTLAWS • 1978 • Grasshoff Alex • USA • GOODTIME OUTLAWS, THE
SMOKEY AND THE HOTWIRE GANG • 1979 • Cardoza Anthony • USA
SMOKEY BITES THE DUST • 1981 • Griffith Charles B. • USA
SMOKEY JOE • 1945 • Rasinski Connie • ANS • USA
SMOKEY JOE'S REVENGE • 1974 • Spencer Ronald • UKN
SMOKEY MOUNTAIN MELODY • 1948 • Nazarro Ray • USA
SMOKEY SMITH • 1935 • Bradbury Robert North • USA
SMOKEY SMOKES • 1920 • La Cava Gregory • ANS • USA
SMOKEY SMOKES (AND) LAMPOONS • 1920 • La Cava Gregory • ANS • USA
SMOKING FISH, THE see **PEX QUE FUMA, EL** • 1977
SMOKING GUNS • 1927 • *Roosevelt Buddy* • USA
SMOKING GUNS • 1934 • James Alan • USA • DOOMED TO DIE (UKN)
SMOKING GUNS (UKN) see **BILLY THE KID'S SMOKING GUNS** • 1942
SMOKING LAMP, THE see **LAMPE QUI FILE, LA** • 1909
SMOKING MIRROR • 1989 • Coronado Celestino • UKN
SMOKING OUT OF BELLA BUTTS, THE • 1915 • Baker George D. • USA
SMOKING TRAIL, THE • 1924 • Bertram William • USA
SMOKY • 1933 • Forde Eugene J. • USA
SMOKY • 1946 • King Louis • USA
SMOKY • 1966 • Sherman George • USA
SMOKY CANYON • 1952 • Sears Fred F. • USA
SMOKY LOVE AFFAIR, A • 1917 • *Compson Betty* • USA
SMOKY MOUNTAIN CHRISTMAS, A • 1986 • Winkler Henry • TVM • USA
SMOKY RIVER SERENADE • 1947 • Abrahams Derwin • USA • THREAT, THE (UKN)
SMOKY STORY, A • 1912 • Calvert Charles? • UKN
SMOKY TRAILS • 1939 • Ray Bernard B. • USA
SMOLDERING EMBERS • 1920 • Keenan Frank • USA
SMOOTH AS SATIN • 1925 • Ince Ralph • USA
SMOOTH AS SILK • 1946 • Barton Charles T. • USA • NOTORIOUS GENTLEMAN
SMOOTH CAREER, THE see **SANFTE LAUF, DER** • 1967
SMOOTH MOVES • 1984 • Sellier Charles E. Jr. • USA • SNOWBALLING
SMOOTH RUNNING • 1948-51 • Harris Roy • DOC • UKN
SMOOTH SAILING see **SANFTE LAUF, DER** • 1967
SMOOTH TALK • 1985 • Chopra Joyce • USA
SMORGASBROAD see **INTERNATIONAL SMORGASBROAD** • 1965
SMORGASORD • 1983 • Lewis Jerry • USA • CRACKING UP
SMOTHERED VOICES • 1977 • Hormasji Homi • IND
SMOULDERING, THE • 1915 • Beal Frank • USA
SMOULDERING EMBERS see **BRASA ADORMECIDA** • 1988
SMOULDERING FIRES • 1915 • *Kerrigan J. Warren* • USA
SMOULDERING FIRES • 1925 • Brown Clarence • USA
SMOULDERING FLAME, THE • 1916 • Campbell Colin • USA
SMOULDERING SPARK, THE • 1914 • Taylor William D.? • USA
SMOULDERING SPARK, THE • 1917 • Campbell Colin • SHT • USA
SMRITICHITRE • 1983 • Mehta Vijaya • IND • REMINISCENCES ○ MEMORY EPISODES
SMRT GOSPODINA GOLUZE • 1983 • Nikolic Zivko • YGS, AUS, CZC • DEATH OF MR. GOLUZA, THE
SMRT KRASNYCH SRNCU • 1987 • Kachyna Karel • CZC • FORBIDDEN DREAMS
SMRT MOUCHY • 1975 • Kachyna Karel • CZC • DEATH OF THE FLY, THE
SMRT PANA BALTISBERGA • 1965 • Menzel Jiri • CZC • DEATH OF MR. BALTISBERGER, THE
SMRT SI RIKA ENGELCHEN • 1963 • Kadar Jan, Klos Elmar • CZC • DEATH CALLS ITSELF ENGELCHEN ○ DEATH IS CALLED ENGELCHEN
SMRT TALENTOVANEHO SEVCE • 1982 • Schmidt Jan • CZC • DEATH OF A TALENTED COBBLER, THE
SMRTICI VUNE • 1970 • Bedrich Vaclav • CZC • DEADLY ODOUR, THE ○ DEADLY PERFUME
SMUDGE • 1922 • Ray Charles • USA
SMUDGE THE GREAT DETECTIVE • 1913 • Calvert Charles? • UKN
SMUG FIT see **NOT JUST ANOTHER AFFAIR** • 1982
SMUGA CIENIA • 1976 • Wajda Andrzej • MTV • PLN, UKN • SHADOW LINE, THE
SMUGGLARNE • 1913 • Stiller Mauritz • SWD • SMUGGLERS, THE
SMUGGLED CARGO • 1939 • Auer John H. • USA
SMUGGLED DIAMONDS, THE • 1915 • *La Badie Florence* • USA
SMUGGLED LACES, THE • 1913 • *Crystal* • USA
SMUGGLER, THE • 1911 • *Thanhouser* • USA
SMUGGLER, THE • 1912 • Hotaling Arthur D. • USA
SMUGGLER, THE • 1913 • *Kalem* • USA
SMUGGLER, THE • 1913 • *Patheplay* • USA
SMUGGLER, THE • 1915 • Walsh Raoul • USA
SMUGGLER, THE • Fulci Lucio • ITL
SMUGGLER AND THE GIRL, THE see **DIAMOND SMUGGLERS, THE** • 1911
SMUGGLERS see **CSEMPESZEK** • 1958
SMUGGLERS see **NA-TZU HAN**
SMUGGLERS see **AMANTE DELL'ORSA MAGGIORE, L'** • 1971
SMUGGLERS, THE • 1904 • Barker Will? • UKN
SMUGGLERS, THE • 1911 • *Kalem* • USA
SMUGGLERS, THE • 1912 • *Nestor* • USA
SMUGGLERS, THE • 1915 • Evans Fred • UKN
SMUGGLERS, THE • 1916 • *Ab* • SHT • USA
SMUGGLERS, THE • 1916 • Olcott Sidney • *Famous Players* • USA
SMUGGLERS, THE • 1968 • Hayes Alfred • TVM • USA
SMUGGLERS, THE see **SMUGGLARNE** • 1913
SMUGGLERS, THE see **PROFESSOR PETERSENS PLEJEBORN** • 1924
SMUGGLERS, THE see **SMUGLERE** • 1968
SMUGGLERS, THE (USA) see **MAN WITHIN, THE** • 1947
SMUGGLERS, THE (USA) see **CONTREBANDIERES, LES** • 1968
SMUGGLER'S CAVE, THE • 1914 • Waller Wallett • UKN
SMUGGLER'S CAVE, THE • 1915 • Eason B. Reeves • USA
SMUGGLER'S CHILD, THE • 1913 • *Solax* • USA
SMUGGLERS COVE • 1948 • Beaudine William • USA
SMUGGLER'S DAUGHTER, THE • 1912 • Barker Reginald • USA
SMUGGLER'S DAUGHTER, THE • 1913 • Collins Edwin J. • UKN
SMUGGLER'S DAUGHTER, THE • 1913 • Lucas Wilfred • *Rex* • USA
SMUGGLER'S DAUGHTER, THE • 1913 • Myers Harry • *Lubin* • USA
SMUGGLER'S DAUGHTER, THE • 1914 • Hevener Jerold T. • USA
SMUGGLER'S DAUGHTER, THE • 1915 • *Hamilton Lillian* • USA
SMUGGLER'S DAUGHTER OF ANGLESEA, THE • 1912 • Northcote Sidney • UKN
SMUGGLER'S GAME, THE • 1910 • *Selig* • USA
SMUGGLER'S GOLD • 1951 • Berke William • USA
SMUGGLERS' HARVEST • 1938 • Phipps John R. • UKN
SMUGGLERS IN DINNER-JACKET see **SMUGLERE I SMOKING** • 1956
SMUGGLER'S ISLAND • 1915 • Ford Francis • USA
SMUGGLER'S ISLAND • 1951 • Ludwig Edward • USA
SMUGGLER'S LASS, THE • 1915 • Clark Jack J. • USA
SMUGGLER'S LAST DEAL, THE • 1913 • *Kalem* • USA
SMUGGLER'S LOVE, A • 1915 • *Harte Betty* • USA
SMUGGLERS OF DEATH see **KRAL SUMAVY** • 1959
SMUGGLERS OF LONE ISLE, THE • 1914 • *Sais Marin* • USA
SMUGGLERS OF SANTA CRUZ, THE • 1916 • MacDonald Donald • SHT • USA
SMUGGLERS OF SLIGO, THE • 1914 • Cabanne W. Christy • USA
SMUGGLER'S PRISONER, THE • 1912 • *Melies* • USA
SMUGGLER'S REVENGE, THE • 1912 • *Union Films* • UKN
SMUGGLER'S SISTER, THE • 1913 • *Siegmann George* • USA
SMUGGLER'S SISTER, THE • 1914 • Campbell Colin • USA
SMUGGLER'S STEPDAUGHTER, THE • 1911 • Fitzhamon Lewin • UKN
SMUGGLER'S WARD, THE • 1915 • MacDonald J. Farrell • USA
SMUGGLER'S WIFE, THE • 1914 • O'Sullivan Tony • USA
SMUGGLING SHIP see **MITSUYUSEN** • 1954
SMUGLERE • 1968 • Clemens Rolf • NRW • SMUGGLERS, THE
SMUGLERE I SMOKING • 1956 • Andersen Bjarne • NRW • SMUGGLERS IN DINNER-JACKET
SMUKKE-ARNE OG ROSA • 1967 • Methling Sven • DNM • HANDSOME ARNE AND ROSA
SMULTRONSTALLET • 1957 • Bergman Ingmar • SWD • WILD STRAWBERRIES (UKN)
SMURFS AND THE MAGIC FLUTE, THE see **FLUTE A SIX SCHTROUMPFS, LA** • 1975
SMUT PEDDLARS, THE see **SMUT PEDDLER, THE** • 1965
SMUT PEDDLER, THE • 1965 • Rose Warner • USA • SMUT PEDDLARS, THE
SMUTECNI SLAVNOST • 1970 • Sirovy Zdenek • CZC • FUNERAL RITES ○ FUNERAL CEREMONIES
SMUTSIG HISTORIA, EN • 1984 • Donner Jorn • FNL • DIRTY STORY
SMUTSIGA FINGRAR • 1972 • Mattsson Arne • SWD • DIRTY FINGERS (USA)
SMYATENIYE CHUVSTV • 1978 • Arsenov Pavel • USS • TUMULT
SMYERT ROSTOVSHCHIKA • 1967 • Sabirov Takhir • USS • DEATH OF A USURER
SMYK • 1960 • Brynych Zbynek • CZC • SKID
SMYKKETYVEN • 1989 • Breien Anja • NRW • TWICE UPON A TIME
SNACK BAR BUDAPEST • 1988 • Brass Tinto • ITL
SNACKA GAR JU.. • 1982 • Andree Ulf • SWD • TALK'S CHEAP
SNADJI SE DRUZE • 1982 • Makarovic Berislav • YGS • FIND A WAY, COMRADE
SNAFU • 1945 • Moss Jack • USA • WELCOME HOME (UKN)
SNAHA • 1954 • Marinovich Anton • BUL • DAUGHTER-IN-LAW
SNAIL, THE • 1918 • *Hamilton Shorty* • USA
SNAILBURG VOLUNTEERS, THE • 1915 • MacGregor Norval • USA
SNAILS, THE (UKN) see **ESCARGOTS, LES** • 1965
SNAIL'S STRATEGY see **ESTRATEGIA DEL CARACOL** • 1989
SNAIPER • 1932 • Timoshenko S. • USS • SNIPER
SNAKE, THE • 1913 • *Bison* • USA
SNAKE, THE • 1919 • Kennedy Aubrey M. • USA
SNAKE AND CRANE: ARTS OF SHAOLIN • 1984 • Chen Chi Hua • HKG
SNAKE BITE, THE • 1911 • *Lubin* • USA
SNAKE CANYON PRISON see **OFF THE WALL** • 1983
SNAKE CHARMER, THE • 1914 • *Eclair* • USA
SNAKE CHARMER (USA) see **SAPERA** • 1939
SNAKE-DEVIL ISLAND • 1956 • USA
SNAKE FANG • 1989 • Kimiyaei Massoud • IRN
SNAKE FIST FIGHTER • 1981 • Chin Hsin • HKG
SNAKE GIRL AND THE SILVER-HAIRED WITCH, THE see **HEBIMUSUME TO HAKUHATSUKI** • 1968

SNAKE IN EAGLE'S SHADOW see **SHE-HSING TIAO SHOU** • 1978
SNAKE IN THE EAGLE'S SHADOW see **SHE-HSING TIAO SHOU** • 1978
SNAKE IN THE GRASS • 1911 • Melies Gaston • USA
SNAKE IN THE MONKEY'S SHADOW see **HOU HSING K'OU SHOU** • 1979
SNAKE MAN, THE • 1910 • *Lux* • FRN
SNAKE MAN, THE • 1972 • Loon Ti • KMP
SNAKE OF DEATH see **QUAI DE GRENELLE** • 1950
SNAKE OF MOON STREET, THE see **SERPENT DE LA RUE DE LA LUNE, LE** • 1908
SNAKE PEOPLE • 1968 • Ibanez Juan, Hill Jack • USA, MXC • MUERTE VIVIENTE, LA (MXC) ○ ISLE OF THE SNAKE PEOPLE ○ ISLA DE LOS MUERTOS, LA ○ ISLAND OF THE SNAKE PEOPLE ○ CULT OF THE DEAD ○ MXC ○ LIVING DEATH, THE
SNAKE PIT, THE • 1948 • Litvak Anatole • USA
SNAKE PIT AND THE PENDULUM, THE see **SCHLANGENGRUBE UND DAS PENDEL, DIE** • 1967
SNAKE POISON see **HADI JED** • 1981
SNAKE PRINCE see **SHE WANG-TZU** • 1976
SNAKE PRINCESS see **HEBIHIME DOUCHUH** • 1949
SNAKE PRINCESS, THE see **HEBI HIME-SAMA** • 1940
SNAKE QUEEN, THE see **NYI BLORONG** • 1983
SNAKE RIVER DESPERADOES • 1951 • Sears Fred F. • USA
SNAKE STRIKES BACK, THE • *Han Eagle* • HKG
SNAKE WOMAN, THE • 1961 • Furie Sidney J. • UKN
SNAKES • 1920 • *Van Billy* • SHT • USA
SNAKES AND LADDERS • 1960 • Halas John • ANS • UKN
SNAKES AND LADDERS see **JEU DE L'OIE, LE** • 1981
SNAKES IN EAGLE SHADOW see **SHE-HSING TIAO SHOU** • 1978
SNAKEVILLE AND THE CORSET DEMONSTRATOR • 1914 • *Essanay* • USA
SNAKEVILLE COURTSHIP, A • 1913 • *Joslin Margaret* • USA
SNAKEVILLE EPIDEMIC, A • 1914 • *Essanay* • USA
SNAKEVILLE ROMANCE, A • 1914 • *Clayton Marguerite* • USA
SNAKEVILLE VOLUNTEER, THE • 1914 • *Essanay* • USA
SNAKEVILLE'S BEAUTY PARLOR • 1915 • *Potel Victor* • USA
SNAKEVILLE'S BLIND PIG • 1914 • *Essanay* • USA
SNAKEVILLE'S CHAMPION • 1915 • Clements Roy • USA
SNAKEVILLE'S EUGENIC MARRIAGE • 1915 • *Joslin Margaret* • USA
SNAKEVILLE'S FIRE BRIGADE • 1914 • *Joslin Margaret* • USA
SNAKEVILLE'S HEN MEDIC • 1915 • Clements Roy • USA
SNAKEVILLE'S HOME GUARD • 1914 • *Essanay* • USA
SNAKEVILLE'S MOST POPULAR LADY • 1914 • Clements Roy • USA
SNAKEVILLE'S NEW DOCTOR • 1914 • *Clayton Marguerite* • USA
SNAKEVILLE'S NEW SHERIFF • 1914 • *Essanay* • USA
SNAKEVILLE'S NEW WAITRESS • 1914 • *Essanay* • USA
SNAKEVILLE'S PEACEMAKER • 1914 • Anderson G. M. • USA
SNAKEVILLE'S REFORM WAVE • 1914 • *Essanay* • USA
SNAKEVILLE'S RISING SONS • 1914 • *Essanay* • USA
SNAKEVILLE'S TWINS • 1915 • Clements Roy • USA
SNAKEVILLE'S WEAK WOMAN • 1915 • *Potel Victor* • USA
SNAKY ADULTERY see **JAIN** • 1967
SNAP see **C.O.D.** • 1982
SNAP AND THE BEANSTALK • 1960 • Halas John • ANS • UKN
SNAP GOES EAST • 1960 • Halas John • ANS • UKN
SNAP HAPPY • 1945 • Tytla Bill • ANS • USA
SNAP HAPPY TRAPS • 1946 • Wickersham Bob • ANS • USA
SNAP JUDGMENT • 1917 • Sloman Edward • USA • SLAM BANG JIM
SNAP-SHOT, THE • 1913 • *Pathe* • USA
SNAP SHOTS • 1915 • France Charles H. • *Edison* • USA
SNAPAKA YOHANNAN • 1963 • Subraniam P. • IND
SNAPPHANAR • 1942 • Ohberg Ake • SWD • SCANIAN GUERRILLA
SNAPPY • 1928 • Rollens Jacques • ANS • USA
SNAPPY CABALLERO, THE • 1931 • USA • CABALLEROS
SNAPPY SALESMAN • 1930 • Lantz Walter, Nolan William • ANS • USA
SNAPPY SNAP SHOTS • 1953 • Donnelly Eddie • ANS • USA
SNAPPY SNEEZER • 1929 • Doane Warren • SHT • USA
SNAP'S ROCKET • 1960 • Halas John • ANS • UKN
SNAPSHOT • 1979 • Wincer Simon • ASL • DAY AFTER HALLOWEEN, THE ○ SNAPSHOT: AUSTRALIAN STYLE
SNAPSHOT see **SWEETER SONG, A** • 1976
SNAPSHOT AROUND THE FAMILY TABLE see **STOP CADRU LA MASA** • 1980
SNAPSHOT: AUSTRALIAN STYLE see **SNAPSHOT** • 1979
SNAPSHOT FIEND, THE • 1904 • *Paul R. W.* • USA
SNAPSHOTS • 1915 • *Thanhouser* • USA
SNAPSHOTS see **SWEETER SONG, A** • 1976
SNAPSHOTS AT THE SEASIDE • 1903 • Hepworth Cecil M. • UKN
SNAPSHOTS OF JAVA • 1913 • Melies Gaston • DOC • USA
SNAPSHOTS OF THE CITY • 1961 • Vanderbeek Stan • SHT • USA
SNAPSHOTTING AN AUDIENCE • 1900 • Smith G. A. • UKN
SNARE, THE • 1912 • Wharton Theodore • USA
SNARE, THE • 1918 • Wilson Frank • UKN
SNARE, THE • 1929 • Eveleigh Leslie • UKN
SNARE OF FATE, THE • 1913 • *Thanhouser* • USA
SNARE OF FATE, THE • 1913 • Humphrey William • *Vitagraph* • USA
SNARE OF SOCIETY, THE • 1911 • Salter Harry • USA
SNARE OF THE CITY, THE • 1911 • *Essanay* • USA
SNARES see **PIEGES** • 1939
SNARES OF PARIS • 1919 • Mitchell Howard M. • USA
SNARL, THE • 1917 • West Raymond B. • USA
SNARL OF HATE, THE • 1927 • Smith Noel • USA
SNART 17 • 1984 • Mikkelsen Laila • NRW • SWEET SEVENTEEN
SNATCH • 1980 • Fitchett Christopher • ASL • BLOOD MONEY
SNATCHED • 1973 • Roley Sutton • USA
SNATCHED see **SHOW THEM NO MERCY** • 1935
SNATCHED FROM A BURNING DEATH • 1915 • Gaskill Charles L. • USA
SNATCHED FROM DEATH • 1913 • *Gaumont* • USA
SNATCHED FROM DEATH • 1913 • Calvert Charles? • UKN
SNATCHED FROM THE ALTAR • 1915 • Christie Al • USA
SNATCHERS, THE • 1974 • Monat Donald • SAF
SNAZDY ZIVOT • 1957 • Makovec Milos • CZC
SNEAK, THE • 1913 • *Kalem* • USA
SNEAK, THE • 1919 • Le Saint Edward J. • USA
SNEAK EASILY • 1932 • Meins Gus • SHT • USA
SNEAK, SNOOP AND SWITCH • 1940 • Fleischer Dave • ANS • USA
SNEAK, SNOOP AND SWITCH IN TRIPLE TROUBLE • 1941 • Fleischer Dave • ANS • USA
SNEAK THIEF, THE • 1913 • *Patheplay* • USA
SNEAKERS • 1981 • Duke Daryl • USA
SNEAKERS • 1982 • Scanlan Joseph L. • CND • SPRING FEVER (USA)
SNEAKERS AND SNOOZERS • 1918 • Howe J. A. • SHT • USA
SNEAKING see **NUKIASHI SASHIASHI** • 1934
SNEAKY BOER, THE • 1901 • *Mitchell & Kenyon* • UKN
SNEEZE, THE • 1914 • Plumb Hay • UKN
SNEEZING • 1909 • Yates Frank D. • UKN
SNEEZING BREEZES • 1925 • *Sennett Mack (P)* • SHT • USA
SNEEZING WEASEL • 1938 • Avery Tex • ANS • USA
SNEGUROTCHKA • 1953 • Ivanov-Vano Ivan • ANM • USS • SNOW MAIDEN, THE (USA)
SNEGUROTCHKA • 1969 • Kadotchnikov Pavel • USS • SNOW BEAUTY
SNEHOVA KRALOVNA • 1978 • Schorm Evald • CZC • SNOW QUEEN, THE
SNEHULAK • 1965 • Miler Zdenek • ANS • CZC • SNOWMAN, THE
SNEZENKY A MACHRI • 1982 • Smyczek Karel • CZC • SNOWDROPS AND SHOW-OFFS ○ SNOWDROPS AND ACES
SNEZHNAYA KOROLEVA • 1957 • Atamanov Lev • ANM • USS • SNOW QUEEN, THE
SNEZHNAYA KOROLEVA see **SNYEZHNAYA KOROLYEVA** • 1967
SNEZHNAYA SKAZKA • 1959 • Shengelaya Eldar, Sakharov Alexei • USS • SNOWY FAIRY TALE, A
SNIEGOUROTCHKA • 1914 • Starevitch Ladislas • USS • SNOW MAIDEN, THE
SNIFFKINS DETECTIVE AND THE MISSING CIGARETTE CARDS • 1914 • Collins Edwin J.? • UKN
SNIFFLES AND THE BOOKWORM • 1939 • Jones Charles M. • ANS • USA
SNIFFLES BELLS THE CAT • 1941 • Jones Charles M. • ANS • USA
SNIFFLES TAKES A TRIP • 1940 • Jones Charles M. • ANS • USA
SNIP AND SNAP • 1960 • Halas John • ASS • UKN
SNIP EN RISSIEPIT • 1973 • SAF
SNIPER see **SNAIPER** • 1932
SNIPER, THE • 1952 • Dmytryk Edward • USA
SNIPER, THE • 1980 • Al-Yassiri Fiasal • IRQ
SNIPER'S RIDGE • 1961 • Bushelman John • USA
SNITCH, THE • 1920 • *Franey William* • USA
SNITCH IN TIME, A • 1950 • Bernds Edward • SHT • USA
SNITCHING HOUR, THE • 1922 • Crosland Alan • USA
SNITZ JOINS THE FORCE • 1914 • *Sterling Ford* • USA
'SNO FUN • 1951 • Donnelly Eddie • ANS • USA
SNO-LINE • 1984 • O'Neans Douglas F. • USA • DEATHLINE
SNOB, THE • 1921 • Wood Sam • USA • YOU CAN'T FIGURE WOMEN
SNOB, THE • 1924 • Bell Monta • USA
SNOB BUSTER, THE • 1925 • Rogell Albert S. • USA
SNOBBERY • 1914 • *Nestor* • USA
SNOBS • 1914 • Trimble Larry • UKN
SNOBS • 1915 • Apfel Oscar • USA
SNOBS • 1961 • Mocky Jean-Pierre • FRN
SNOEIEN VAN LOOFHOUT, HET • 1966 • Blansjaar Joh • SHT • NTH
SNOMOBILE • 1973 • Mills Michael, Pindal Kaj • CND • IT'S ONLY A MACHINE
SNOOKEE'S DAY OFF • 1914 • *Sterling* • USA
SNOOKEE'S DISGUISE • 1914 • *Sterling Ford* • USA
SNOOKEE'S FLIRTATION • 1914 • *Sterling Ford* • USA
SNOOKS AS A FIREMAN • 1914 • Kellino W. P. • UKN
SNOOKUMS • 1912-14 • Cohl Emile • *Eclair* • ASS • USA • NEWLYWED SERIES
SNOOKUM'S BIRTHDAY • 1914 • *Royal* • USA
SNOOKUM'S LAST RACKET • 1914 • *Crystal* • USA
SNOOP HOUNDS • 1916 • Beaudine William • USA
SNOOP SISTERS, THE • 1972 • Stern Leonard • TVM • USA • FEMALE INSTINCT
SNOOP SISTERS: FEAR IS A FREE THROW, THE • 1973 • Sagal Boris • TVM • USA
SNOOPER SERVICE • 1945 • Edwards Harry J. • SHT • USA
SNOOPY, COME HOME • 1972 • Melendez Bill • ANM • USA
SNOOPY LOOPY • 1960 • Hanna William, Barbera Joseph • ANS • USA
SNOOZE REEL • 1951 • Kneitel Seymour • ANS • USA
SNOOZIN' BRUIN WOODY • 1971 • Smith Paul J. • ANS • USA
SNORER, THE • 1910 • *Atlas* • USA
SNORING IN HIGH C • 1916 • *Morris Reggie* • SHT • USA
SNORKEL, THE • 1958 • Green Guy • UKN
SNORRI STURLUSON • 1982 • Bertelsson Thrainn • ICL
SNOSTORMEN • 1944 • Ohberg Ake • SWD
SNOUT, THE see **INFORMERS, THE** • 1963
SNOVI, ZIVOT, SMRT FILIPA FILIPOVICA • 1981 • Radivojevic Milos • YGS • DREAMS, LIFE AND DEATH OF FILIP FILIPOVIC
SNOW • 1964 • Jones Geoffrey • SHT • UKN
SNOW • 1981 • Walton Lloyd A. • DOC • CND
SNOW • 1982 • Gibson Robert • ASL • SNOW BUNNIES: NERDS ON VACATION ○ SNOW: THE MOVIE
SNOW • 1982 • Takacs Tibor • CND
SNOW • 1989 • Paz Felipe • SHT • RMN
SNOW-BALL GROVE • 1953 • Levchuk Timofey • USS
SNOW BEAST • 1977 • Wallerstein Herb • TVM • USA
SNOW BEAUTY see **SNEGUROTCHKA** • 1969
SNOW BIRDS • 1932 • White Jules • SHT • USA
SNOW BLINDNESS see **SNOWBLIND** • 1921
SNOW BOUND WITH A WOMAN HATER • 1911 • *Vitagraph* • USA
SNOW BRIDE, THE • 1923 • Kolker Henry • USA
SNOW BUNNIES: NERDS ON VACATION see **SNOW** • 1982
SNOW-BURNER, THE • 1915 • Calvert E. H. • USA
SNOW BUSINESS • 1952 • Freleng Friz • ANS • USA
SNOW CAPERS • 1948 • Cohen Arthur • DCS • USA
SNOW COUNTRY see **YUKIGUNI** • 1957
SNOW COUNTRY (USA) see **YUKIGUNI** • 1965
SNOW CREATURE, THE • 1954 • Wilder W. Lee • USA
SNOW CURE, THE • 1916 • Gillstrom Arvid E. • SHT • USA
SNOW DEMONS see **DIAVOLI DELLO SPAZIO, I** • 1965
SNOW DEVILS (USA) see **DIAVOLI DELLO SPAZIO, I** • 1965
SNOW DOG • 1950 • McDonald Frank • USA
SNOW EXCUSE • 1966 • McKimson Robert • ANS • USA
SNOW-FALL see **HOSZAKADAS** • 1974
SNOW FESTIVAL see **YUKI MATSURI** • 1953
SNOW FIESTA • 1950 • Blais Roger • DCS • CND • FETE DES NEIGES
SNOW FLURRY see **KAZAHANA** • 1959
SNOW FOLLIES • 1939 • Ceballos Larry • SHT • USA
SNOW FOOLIN' • 1949 • Sparber I. • ANS • USA
SNOW GHOST see **KAIDAN YUKIJORO** • 1968
SNOW GIRL, THE • 1915 • Beresford Frank S. • USA
SNOW GIRLS see **FILLES DE NEIGE, LES**
SNOW HAWK, THE • 1925 • Pembroke Scott • SHT • USA
SNOW IN THE DESERT • 1919 • West Walter • UKN
SNOW IN THE SOUTH SEAS (USA) see **MINAMI NO SHIMA NI YUKI GA FURA** • 1961
SNOW IN VENICE • 1971 • Owen Don • DOC • CND
SNOW IS BURNING see **HSUEH TSAI SHAO** • 1987
SNOW JOB • 1969 • Shiffen Arlo • USA
SNOW JOB • 1972 • Englund George • USA • SKI RAIDERS, THE (UKN) ○ GREAT SKI CAPER
SNOW JOB • 1974 • Ferguson Graeme • CND
SNOW MAIDEN, THE • 1911 • *Ambrosio* • ITL
SNOW-MAIDEN, THE • 1969 • Degtyarov Vladimir • ANM • USS
SNOW MAIDEN, THE see **SNIEGOUROTCHKA** • 1914
SNOW MAIDEN, THE (USA) see **SNEGUROTCHKA** • 1953
SNOW MAN, THE • 1908 • *Mccutcheon Walter* • USA
SNOW MAN, THE • 1946 • Rasinski Connie • ANS • USA
SNOW MAN, THE (USA) see **STATUE DE NEIGE, LA** • 1899
SNOW MAN'S LAND • 1939 • Jones Charles M. • ANS • USA
SNOW PLACE LIKE HOME • 1948 • Kneitel Seymour • ANS • USA
SNOW PLACE LIKE HOME • 1966 • Smith Paul J. • ANS • USA
SNOW QUEEN • 1983 • Medak Peter • MTV • USA
SNOW QUEEN, THE • 1958 • *Faber Robert (P)* • ANM • USS
SNOW QUEEN, THE • 1959 • Patton Phil • ANM • USA
SNOW QUEEN, THE • 1976 • Gosling Andrew • UKN
SNOW QUEEN, THE see **SNEZHNAYA KOROLEVA** • 1957
SNOW QUEEN, THE see **SNYEZHNAYA KOROLYEVA** • 1967
SNOW QUEEN, THE see **SNEHOVA KRALOVNA** • 1978
SNOW QUEEN, THE see **LUMIKUNINGATAR** • 1987
SNOW, SAND AND SAVAGES • 1973 • Buckley Anthony • DOC • ASL
SNOW SHOW • 1965-66 • Vanderbeek Stan • USA
SNOW SHOWELER'S SWEETHEART, THE • 1916 • *Yorke Jay C.* • SHT • USA
SNOW SPIDER, THE • Roberts Pennant • UKN
SNOW STORM, THE • 1953 • Iliesu Mirel • DOC • RMN
SNOW STORM AND SUNSHINE • 1916 • *Chamberlin Riley* • SHT • USA
SNOW STUFF • 1916 • Bertram William • USA
SNOW: THE MOVIE see **SNOW** • 1982
SNOW TIME • 1930 • Foster John, Davis Mannie • ANS • USA
SNOW TIME FOR COMEDY • 1941 • Jones Charles M. • ANS • USA
SNOW TIME FOR COMEDY see **NAJVECI SNJEGOVIC** • 1972
SNOW TRAIL see **GINREI NO HATE** • 1947
SNOW TREASURE • 1968 • Jacoby Irving • USA
SNOW USE • 1929 • Lantz Walter, Nolan William • ANS • USA
SNOW WAR, THE • 1980 • Tichenor Harold • DOC • CND
SNOW WAS BLACK, THE (USA) see **NEIGE ETAIT SALE, LA** • 1952
SNOW WHITE • 1903 • *Lubin* • USA
SNOW WHITE • 1913 • *Albert Elsie* • USA
SNOW WHITE • 1916 • *Educational Films* • USA
SNOW WHITE • 1916 • Weston Charles • *Life Photoplay* • USA
SNOW WHITE • 1917 • *Rex* • SHT • USA
SNOW WHITE • 1917 • Dawley J. Searle • *Famous Players* • USA
SNOW WHITE • 1933 • Fleischer Dave • ANS • USA
SNOW WHITE • 1972 • Kolditz Gottfried • GDR
SNOW WHITE • 1987 • Berz Michael • USA • SNOW WHITE AND THE SEVEN DWARFS ○ CANNON MOVIE TALES: SNOW WHITE
SNOW-WHITE see **O SNEHURCE** • 1972
SNOW WHITE AND ROSE RED • 1953 • Reiniger Lotte • ANS • UKN
SNOW WHITE AND ROSE RED (USA) see **SCHNEEWITTCHEN UND ROSENROT** • 1955
SNOW WHITE AND THE SEVEN DWARFS • 1937 • Hand David • ANM • USA
SNOW WHITE AND THE SEVEN DWARFS • 1983 • Medak Peter • MTV • USA
SNOW WHITE AND THE SEVEN DWARFS see **SCHNEEWITTCHEN UND DIE SIEBEN ZWERGE** • 1956
SNOW WHITE AND THE SEVEN DWARFS see **SNOW WHITE** • 1987
SNOW WHITE AND THE SEVEN JUGGLERS see **SCHNEEWITTCHEN UND DIE SIEBEN GAUKLER** • 1962
SNOW WHITE AND THE THREE CLOWNS (UKN) see **SNOW WHITE AND THE THREE STOOGES** • 1961
SNOW WHITE AND THE THREE STOOGES • 1961 • Lang Walter • USA • SNOW WHITE AND THE THREE CLOWNS (UKN)
SNOW WHITE CHRISTMAS, A • 1979 • Wright Kay • ANM • USA
SNOW WHITE (USA) see **SCHNEEWITTCHEN UND DIE SIEBEN ZWERGE** • 1956
SNOW WOMAN • Saikkonen Veli-Matti • FNL

SNOWBALL • 1960 • Jackson Pat • UKN
SNOWBALL EXPRESS • 1972 • Tokar Norman • USA
SNOWBALL PETE • 1914 • *Komic* • USA
SNOWBALLING • 1904 • Haggar William • UKN
SNOWBALLING see **SMOOTH MOVES** • 1984
SNOWBALLING OOM PAUL • 1900 • *Paul R. W.* • UKN
SNOWBIRD, THE • 1916 • Carewe Edwin • USA
SNOWBIRDS • 1981 • Pearson Peter • MTV • CND
SNOWBLIND • 1921 • Barker Reginald • USA • SNOW BLINDNESS
SNOWBLIND • 1968 • Frampton Hollis • USA
SNOWBODY LOVES ME • 1964 • Jones Charles M. • ANS • USA
SNOWBOUND • 1927 • Stone Phil • USA
SNOWBOUND • 1948 • MacDonald David • UKN
SNOWDON AVIARY, THE • 1966 • Gold Jack • SHT • UKN
SNOWDRIFT • 1914 • *Lund O. A. C.* • USA
SNOWDRIFT • 1923 • Dunlap Scott R. • USA
SNOWDROP, A see **HITOHIRA NO YUKI** • 1985
SNOWDROP FESTIVITIES, THE see **SLAVNOSTI SNEZENEK** • 1983
SNOWDROPS • 1920 • Slavinsky Vladimir • CZC
SNOWDROPS • 1964 • Sibianu Gheorghe • ANM • RMN
SNOWDROPS AND ACES see **SNEZENKY A MACHRI** • 1982
SNOWDROPS AND SHOW-OFFS see **SNEZENKY A MACHRI** • 1982
SNOWDROPS BLOOM IN SEPTEMBER see **SCHNEEGLOCKCHEN BLUHN IN SEPTEMBER** • 1974
SNOWED IN • 1926 • Bennet Spencer Gordon • SRL • USA
SNOWED UNDER • 1923 • Stromberg Hunt • USA
SNOWED UNDER • 1936 • Enright Ray • USA
SNOWFIRE • 1958 • McGowan Dorrell, McGowan Stuart E. • USA
SNOWMAN • 1908 • *Bitzer Billy (Ph)* • USA
SNOWMAN • 1940 • Davis Mannie • ANS • USA
SNOWMAN see **JUJIN YUKI-OTOKO** • 1955
SNOWMAN see **LAND OF NO RETURN, THE** • 1975
SNOWMAN, THE • 1901 • *Mitchell & Kenyon* • UKN
SNOWMAN, THE • 1912 • *Solax* • USA
SNOWMAN, THE • 1960 • Buchvarova Radka • ANS • BUL
SNOWMAN, THE • 1966 • Tyrlova Hermina • ANS • CZC
SNOWMAN, THE • 1983 • Jackson Dianne • ANM • UKN
SNOWMAN, THE see **SNEHULAK** • 1965
SNOWMAN FOR AFRICA, A • 1976 • Losansky Rolf • GDR
SNOWMAN'S ROMANCE, A • 1928 • Freund Karl • UKN
SNOWS OF DESTINY (UKN) see **HERR ARNES PENGAR** • 1919
SNOWS OF KILIMANJARO, THE • 1952 • King Henry • USA
SNOWSHOE TRAIL, THE • 1922 • Bennett Chester • USA
SNOWSHOERS, THE see **RAQUETTEURS, LES** • 1958
SNOWTIME see **SHOWTIME** • 1938
SNOWY FAIRY TALE, A see **SNEZHNAYA SKAZKA** • 1959
SNOWY HERON see **SHIRASAGI** • 1941
SNOWY HERON see **SHIRASAGI** • 1959
SNUBBED BY A SNOB • 1940 • Fleischer Dave • ANS • USA
SNUFF see **SLAUGHTER, THE** • 1976
SNUFF BOTTLE see **BAQI ZIDI** • 1988
SNUFFY SKUNK'S PARTY see **SNUFFY'S PARTY** • 1939
SNUFFY SMITH, THE YARD BIRD • 1942 • Cline Eddie • USA • SNUFFY SMITH (UKN) ○ SNUFFY SMITH, YARD BIRD ○ PRIVATE SNUFFY SMITH
SNUFFY SMITH (UKN) see **SNUFFY SMITH, THE YARD BIRD** • 1942
SNUFFY SMITH, YARD BIRD see **SNUFFY SMITH, THE YARD BIRD** • 1942
SNUFFY STUFF, SNUFF • 1914 • Collins Edwin J.? • UKN
SNUFFY'S PARTY • 1939 • Perkins Elmer • ANS • USA • SNUFFY SKUNK'S PARTY
SNUFFY'S SONG • 1962 • Kneitel Seymour • ANS • USA
SNUG IN A JUG • 1933 • Holmes Ben • SHT • USA
SNURREN DIREKT • 1952 • *Ab Imago* • SWD
SNURRIGA FAMILJEN • 1940 • Johansson Ivar • SWD • SPINNING FAMILY
SNY MIMOLETNYE, SNY BEZRABOTNYE SNIATSIA LIS' RAZ • 1913 • Volkov Alexander • USS
SNY NA NEDELI • 1959 • Gajer Vaclav • CZC • DREAMS ON SUNDAY ○ SUNDAY DREAMS
SNYEZHNAYA KOROLYEVA • 1967 • Kazansky Gennadi • USS • SNOW QUEEN, THE ○ SNEZHNAYA KOROLEVA
SO • 1974 • Sipovac Gojko • YGS • SALT
SO ALONE • 1958 • Ford John • SHT • UKN
SO AND SEW • 1936 • Yarbrough Jean • SHT • USA
SO ANGELT MAN KEINEN MANN • 1959 • Deppe Hans • FRG
SO AS NOT TO FORGET see **POUR NE PAS OUBLIER** • 1982
SO BEAUTIFUL IT'S A SIN see **BIBO NI TSUMI ARI** • 1959
SO BIG • 1924 • Brabin Charles J. • USA
SO BIG • 1932 • Wellman William A. • USA
SO BIG • 1953 • Wise Robert • USA
SO BRIGHT THE FLAME (UKN) see **GIRL IN WHITE, THE** • 1952
SO BYE-BYE • 1970 • Olmer Vit • CZC
SO CLOSE TO LIFE see **NARA LIVET** • 1958
SO DARK THE NIGHT • 1946 • Lewis Joseph H. • USA
SO DEAR TO MY HEART • 1948 • Schuster Harold (Live), Luske Hamilton (Anm) • USA
SO DIED A RAT see **COUNTERBLAST** • 1948
SO DOES AN AUTOMOBILE • 1939 • Fleischer Dave • ANS • USA
SO EIN AFFENTHEATER • 1953 • Ode Erik • FRG
SO EIN FLEGEL • 1934 • Stemmle R. A. • FRG
SO EIN FRUCHTCHEN • 1942 • Stoger Alfred • FRG
SO EIN MADEL • 1920 • Gad Urban • FRG
SO EIN MADEL VERGISST MANNICHT • 1932 • Kortner Fritz • FRG, AUS
SO ENDED A GREAT LOVE see **SO ENDETE EINE LIEBE** • 1934
SO ENDETE EINE LIEBE • 1934 • Hartl Karl • FRG • SO ENDED A GREAT LOVE
SO ENDS LOVE see **PUTUS SUDAH KASEH SAYANG** • 1970
SO ENDS OUR NIGHT • 1941 • Cromwell John • USA • FLOTSAM
SO EVIL MY LOVE • 1948 • Allen Lewis • UKN
SO EVIL MY SISTER • 1973 • Le Borg Reginald • USA • PSYCHO SISTERS
SO EVIL SO YOUNG • 1961 • Grayson Godfrey • UKN
SO FALLEN DIE LOSE DES LEBENS • 1918 • Rosenthal Friedrich • AUS
SO FAR FROM HOME see **OMOEBA TOKUE KITAMONDA** • 1981
SO FAR, SO NEAR see **JAK DALEKA STAD, JAK BLISKO** • 1971
SO FINE • 1981 • Bergman Andrew • USA
SO GEFALLST DU MIR • 1941 • Thimig Hans • FRG
SO GOES MY LOVE • 1946 • Ryan Frank • USA • GENIUS IN THE FAMILY, A (UKN)
SO GREAT A MAN see **ABE LINCOLN IN ILLINOIS** • 1939
SO HAPPY TOGETHER • 1967 • Carlos Luciano B. • PHL
SO IS THIS • 1983 • Snow Michael • CND
SO IST DAS LEBEN • 1924 • Rippert Otto • FRG • SO SPIELT DAS LEBEN ○ SUCH IS LIFE
SO IST DAS LEBEN (FRG) see **TAKOVY JE ZIVOT** • 1929
SO-JUN-WAH AND THE TRIBAL LAW • 1912 • *Selig* • USA
SO KUSST NUR EINE WIENERIN • 1927 • Bergen Arthur • FRG
SO LANG' NOCH EIN WALZER VON STRAUSS ERKLINGT • 1931 • Wiene Conrad • FRG
SO LANGE DAS HERZ SCHLAGT • 1958 • Weidenmann Alfred • FRG • AS LONG AS THE HEART BEATS
SO LIEBT UND KUSST MAN IN TIROL • 1961 • Marischka Franz • AUS
SO LIKE A WOMAN • 1911 • *Walturdaw* • UKN
SO LIKE A WOMAN (UKN) see **TEMPTATION** • 1930
SO LIKE HIM • 1919 • Reardon James • UKN
SO LIKE THE FLOWERS see **CHINKASAI** • 1960
SO LITTLE TIME • 1952 • Bennett Compton • UKN
SO LITTLE TIME see **NON HO TEMPO** • 1973
SO LONG AT THE FAIR • 1950 • Darnborough Anthony, Fisher Terence • UKN
SO LONG BLUE BOY • 1973 • Gordon Gerard • USA
SO LONG, COUNT • 1914 • *Lubin* • USA
SO LONG FRIEND see **ADIEU L'AMI** • 1968
SO LONG LETTY • 1920 • Christie Al • USA
SO LONG LETTY • 1929 • Bacon Lloyd • USA
SO LONG, MR. CHUMPS • 1941 • White Jules • SHT • USA
SO LOVELY, SO DEADLY • 1957 • Kohler Will • USA
SO-MANGA • 1981 • SAF
SO MANY DREAMS • 1987 • Carow Heiner • GDR
SO MUCH GOOD IN THE WORST OF US • 1914 • Wilson Frank? • UKN
...SO MUCH NAKED TENDERNESS see **...SO VIEL NACKTE ZARLICHKEIT** • 1968
SO NEAR AND YET SO FAR see **JAK DALEKA STAD, JAK BLISKO** • 1971
SO NEAR, YET SO FAR • 1912 • Griffith D. W. • USA
SO ODER SO IST DAS LEBEN • 1976 • Relin Veit • FRG • SUCH IS LIFE
SO PROUDLY WE HAIL! • 1943 • Sandrich Mark • USA
SO RACHT DIE SONNE • 1915 • Wauer William • FRG
SO RED THE ROSE • 1935 • Vidor King • USA
SO RUNS THE WAT • 1910 • *Reliance* • USA • SO RUNS THE WAY
SO RUNS THE WAY • 1911 • *Gish Lillian* • USA
SO RUNS THE WAY see **SO RUNS THE WAT** • 1910
SO SAAL BAAD • 1967 • *Khan Feroz* • IND
SO SAD ABOUT GLORIA • 1973 • Thomason Harry • USA
SO SHALL YE REAP • 1911 • *Imp* • USA
SO SHALL YE REAP • 1914 • *Frontier* • USA
SO SHALL YE REAP • 1916 • King Burton L. • SHT • USA • AS YE SOW
SO SHINES A GOOD DEED • 1914 • *Reliance* • USA
SO SIND DIE MANNER • 1922 • Jacoby Georg • FRG • NAPOLEONS KLEINER BRUDER ○ KLEINE NAPOLEON, DER
SO SIND DIE MENSCHEN see **ABSCHIED** • 1930
SO. SO. SONACOTRA CEDERA • 1976 • Akika Ali • SHT • FRN
SO SOON TO DIE • 1957 • Brahm John • MTV • USA
SO SORRY, PUSSYCAT • 1961 • Bartsch Art • ANS • USA
SO SPEAKS THE HEART • 1912 • *Leonard Marion* • USA
SO SPIELT DAS LEBEN see **SO IST DAS LEBEN** • 1924
SO SWEET, SO DEAD see **RIVELAZIONI DI UN MANIACO SESSUALE AL CAPO DELLA SQUADRA MOBILE** • 1972
SO SWEET, SO PERVERSE see **COSI DOLCE.. COSI PERVERSA** • 1969
SO THAT MEN ARE FREE • 1962 • Van Dyke Willard • DOC • USA
SO THIS IS AFRICA • 1933 • Cline Eddie • SHT • USA
SO THIS IS ARIZONA • 1922 • Ford Francis • USA
SO THIS IS COLLEGE • 1929 • Wood Sam • USA • COLLEGE DAYS
SO THIS IS FLORIDA • 1926 • *Holmes Burton* • DOC • USA
SO THIS IS GOD'S COUNTRY? (UKN) see **AMERICA, PAESE DI DIO** • 1966
SO THIS IS HAMLET? • 1923 • La Cava Gregory • SHT • USA
SO THIS IS HARRIS • 1932 • Sandrich Mark • SHT • USA
SO THIS IS HOLLYWOOD (UKN) see **IN HOLLYWOOD WITH POTASH AND PERLMUTTER** • 1924
SO THIS IS JOLLYGOOD • 1925 • Brunel Adrian • UKN
SO THIS IS LANCASHIRE • 1933 • Taylor Donald • UKN
SO THIS IS LONDON • 1930 • Blystone John G. • USA
SO THIS IS LONDON • 1933 • Grierson Marion • DOC • UKN
SO THIS IS LONDON • 1939 • Freeland Thornton • USA, UKN
SO THIS IS LOVE • 1928 • Capra Frank • USA
SO THIS IS LOVE • 1953 • Douglas Gordon • USA • GRACE MOORE STORY, THE (UKN)
SO THIS IS MARRIAGE • 1924 • Henley Hobart • USA
SO THIS IS NEW YORK • 1948 • Fleischer Richard • USA
SO THIS IS PARIS • 1916 • Baggot King • SHT • USA
SO THIS IS PARIS • 1926 • Lubitsch Ernst • USA
SO THIS IS PARIS • 1926 • Wallace Richard • SHT • USA
SO THIS IS PARIS • 1954 • Quine Richard • USA
SO THIS IS PARIS GREEN • 1930 • Watson William • USA
SO THIS IS SPRING • 1929 • Aylott Dave, Symmons E. F. • SHT • UKN
SO THIS IS THE AIRFORCE • 1947 • Halas John, Batchelor Joy • ANS • UKN
SO THIS IS WASHINGTON • 1943 • McCarey Ray • USA
SO TIRED • 1929 • Aylott Dave, Symmons E. F. • SHT • UKN
SO TOLL WIE ANNO DAZUMAL • 1962 • Marischka Franz • FRG
...SO VIEL NACKTE ZARLICHKEIT • 1968 • Hendel Gunter • FRG • ...SO MUCH NAKED TENDERNESS
SO WAR DER DEUTSCHE LANDSER • 1955 • Baumeister Albert • FRG
SO WEIT GEHT DIE LIEBE NICHT • 1937 • Seitz Franz • FRG
SO WELL REMEMBERED • 1947 • Dmytryk Edward • UKN
SO WENT THE DAYS • 1977 • Salem Atef • EGY
SO WERDEN SOLDNER GEMACHT • 1968 • Pappe Karlheinz • GDR • THIS IS HOW MEMORIES ARE MADE
SO WHAT WITH BLOOD? see **PARA QUE LA SANGRE?** • 1980
SO, YOU DON'T KNOW KORFF YET? (USA) see **NANU, SIE KENNEN KORFF NOCH NICHT?** • 1938
SO YOU DON'T TRUST YOUR WIFE • 1955 • Bare Richard L. • SHT • USA
SO YOU LOVE YOUR DOG • 1953 • Bare Richard L. • SHT • USA
SO YOU NEVER TELL A LIE • 1952 • Bare Richard L. • SHT • USA
SO YOU THINK THE GRASS IS GREENER • 1956 • Bare Richard L. • SHT • USA
SO YOU THINK YOU CAN'T SLEEP • 1953 • Bare Richard L. • SHT • USA
SO YOU THINK YOU NEED GLASSES • 1942 • Bare Richard L. • SHT • USA
SO YOU THINK YOU'RE A NERVOUS WRECK • 1946 • Bare Richard L. • SHT • USA
SO YOU THINK YOU'RE ALLERGIC • 1945 • Bare Richard L. • SHT • USA
SO YOU THINK YOU'RE NOT GUILTY • 1950 • Bare Richard L. • SHT • USA
SO YOU WANT A RAISE • 1950 • Bare Richard L. • SHT • USA
SO YOU WANT A TELEVISION SET • 1953 • Bare Richard L. • SHT • USA
SO YOU WANT AN APARTMENT • 1948 • Bare Richard L. • SHT • USA
SO YOU WANT TO BE A BABY-SITTER • 1949 • Bare Richard L. • SHT • USA
SO YOU WANT TO BE A BACHELOR • 1951 • Bare Richard L. • SHT • USA
SO YOU WANT TO BE A BANKER • 1954 • Bare Richard L. • SHT • USA
SO YOU WANT TO BE A COWBOY • 1951 • Bare Richard L. • SHT • USA
SO YOU WANT TO BE A DETECTIVE • 1948 • Bare Richard L. • SHT • USA
SO YOU WANT TO BE A GAMBLER • 1948 • Bare Richard L. • SHT • USA
SO YOU WANT TO BE A GLADIATOR • 1955 • Bare Richard L. • SHT • USA
SO YOU WANT TO BE A HANDYMAN • 1951 • Bare Richard L. • SHT • USA
SO YOU WANT TO BE A MUSCLEMAN • 1949 • Bare Richard L. • SHT • USA
SO YOU WANT TO BE A MUSICIAN • 1953 • Bare Richard L. • SHT • USA
SO YOU WANT TO BE A PAPERHANGER • 1951 • Bare Richard L. • SHT • USA
SO YOU WANT TO BE A PLUMBER • 1951 • Bare Richard L. • SHT • USA
SO YOU WANT TO BE A POLICEMAN • 1955 • Bare Richard L. • SHT • USA
SO YOU WANT TO BE A SALESMAN • 1947 • Bare Richard L. • SHT • USA
SO YOU WANT TO BE A V.P. • 1955 • Bare Richard L. • SHT • USA
SO YOU WANT TO BE AN ACTOR • 1949 • Bare Richard L. • SHT • USA
SO YOU WANT TO BE AN HEIR • 1953 • Bare Richard L. • SHT • USA
SO YOU WANT TO BE IN PICTURES • 1947 • Bare Richard L. • SHT • USA
SO YOU WANT TO BE IN POLITICS • 1948 • Bare Richard L. • SHT • USA
SO YOU WANT TO BE ON A JURY • 1955 • Bare Richard L. • SHT • USA
SO YOU WANT TO BE ON THE RADIO • 1948 • Bare Richard L. • SHT • USA
SO YOU WANT TO BE POPULAR • 1949 • Bare Richard L. • SHT • USA
SO YOU WANT TO BE PRETTY • 1956 • Bare Richard L. • SHT • USA
SO YOU WANT TO BE YOUR OWN BOSS • 1954 • Bare Richard L. • SHT • USA
SO YOU WANT TO BUILD A HOUSE • 1948 • Bare Richard L. • SHT • USA
SO YOU WANT TO BUILD A MODEL RAILROAD • 1955 • Bare Richard L. • SHT • USA
SO YOU WANT TO BUY A USED CAR • 1951 • Bare Richard L. • SHT • USA
SO YOU WANT TO ENJOY LIFE • 1952 • Bare Richard L. • SHT • USA
SO YOU WANT TO GET IT WHOLESALE • 1952 • Bare Richard L. • SHT • USA
SO YOU WANT TO GET RICH QUICK • 1949 • Bare Richard L. • SHT • USA
SO YOU WANT TO GIVE UP SMOKING • 1942 • Bare Richard L. • SHT • USA
SO YOU WANT TO GO TO A NIGHT CLUB • 1954 • Bare Richard L. • SHT • USA
SO YOU WANT TO HOLD YOUR HUSBAND • 1950 • Bare Richard L. • SHT • USA
SO YOU WANT TO HOLD YOUR WIFE • 1947 • Bare Richard L. • SHT • USA
SO YOU WANT TO KEEP YOUR HAIR • 1946 • Bare Richard L. • SHT • USA
SO YOU WANT TO KNOW YOUR RELATIVES • 1955 • Bare Richard L. • SHT • USA
SO YOU WANT TO LEARN TO DANCE • 1953 • Bare Richard L. • SHT • USA
SO YOU WANT TO MOVE • 1950 • Bare Richard L. • SHT • USA
SO YOU WANT TO PLAY THE PIANO • 1956 • Bare Richard L. • SHT • USA
SO YOU WANT TO THE PLAY HORSES • 1946 • Bare Richard L. • SHT • USA

SO YOU WANT TO THROW A PARTY • 1950 • Bare Richard L. • SHT • USA
SO YOU WANT TO WEAR THE PANTS • 1952 • Bare Richard L. • SHT • USA
SO YOU WON'T SING, EH? see **SING AND LIKE IT** • 1934
SO YOU WON'T SQUAWK • 1941 • Lord Del • SHT • USA
SO YOU WON'T TALK! • 1935 • Banks Monty • UKN
SO YOU WON'T TALK • 1935 • Beaudine William • USA
SO YOU WON'T TALK • 1940 • Sedgwick Edward • USA
SO YOUNG, SO BAD • 1950 • Vorhaus Bernard • USA
SO YOUNG SO BRIGHT (USA) see **JANKEN MUSUME** • 1955
SO YOUR WIFE WANTS TO WORK • 1956 • Bare Richard L. • SHT • USA
SO YOU'RE GETTING A DIVORCE • 1981 • Wallace Stephen • SHT • ASL
SO YOU'RE GOING ON A VACATION • 1947 • Bare Richard L. • SHT • USA
SO YOU'RE GOING TO A CONVENTION • 1952 • Bare Richard L. • SHT • USA
SO YOU'RE GOING TO BE A FATHER • 1947 • Bare Richard L. • SHT • USA
SO YOU'RE GOING TO HAVE AN OPERATION • 1950 • Bare Richard L. • SHT • USA
SO YOU'RE GOING TO THE DENTIST • 1952 • Bare Richard L. • SHT • USA
SO YOU'RE HAVING IN-LAW TROUBLE • 1949 • Bare Richard L. • SHT • USA
SO YOU'RE HAVING NEIGHBOR TROUBLE • 1954 • Bare Richard L. • SHT • USA
SO YOU'RE TAKING IN A ROOMER • 1954 • Bare Richard L. • SHT • USA
SO ZWITSCHERN DIE JUNGEN • 1964 • Schamoni Peter • SHT • FRG
SOAK THE OLD • 1940 • Lee Sammy • SHT • USA
SOAK THE POOR • 1937 • Bucquet Harold S. • SHT • USA
SOAK THE RICH • 1936 • Hecht Ben, MacArthur Charles • USA
SOAK THE SHEIK • 1922 • Roach Hal • SHT • USA
SOAKING THE CLOTHES • 1915 • Roach Hal • USA
SOAP • 1916 • Smithson Frank • SHT • USA
SOAP AND WATER see **ACQUA E SAPONE** • 1984
SOAP BUBBLES see **SEIFENBLASEN** • 1933
SOAP-BUBBLES see **SEIFENBLASEN** • 1985
SOAP BUBBLES OF TRUTH, THE • 1910 • *Pathe* • SHT • FRN
SOAP BUBBLES (USA) see **BULLES DE SAVON ANIMEES, LES** • 1906
SOAP, COMB, MIRROR see **SOAPPU, SEEPPU, KANNADI** • 1968
SOAP GIRL see **SHABON MUSUME** • 1927
SOAP GIRL, THE • 1918 • Justice Martin • USA
SOAP OPERA • 1964 • Warhol Andy • USA • LESTER PERSKY STORY -A SOAP OPERA, THE ○ LESTER PERSKY STORY, THE
SOAP SUDS STAR, THE • 1915 • *Hastings Carey L.* • USA
SOAP VERSUS BLACKING • 1902 • Booth W. R.? • UKN
SOAPBOX DERBY • 1958 • Conyers Darcy • UKN
SOAPPU, SEEPPU, KANNADI • 1968 • Thirumalai • IND • SOAP, COMB, MIRROR
SOAPSUDS AND SAPHEADS • 1919 • Howe J. A. • SHT • USA
SOAPSUDS AND SIRENS • 1917 • Smith Noel • SHT • USA
SOAPSUDS LADY, THE • 1925 • Cline Eddie • SHT • USA
SOAPY OPERA • 1953 • Rasinski Connie • ANS • USA
SOAPY SOUP • 1907 • Cooper Arthur • UKN
SOB O CEU SA BAHIA • 1956 • Remani Ernesto • BRZ • UNDER THE SKY OF BAHIA
SOB SISTER • 1931 • Santell Alfred • USA • BLONDE REPORTER, THE (UKN) ○ SOB SISTERS
SOB SISTER, THE • 1914 • Turner Otis • USA
SOB SISTERS see **SOB SISTER** • 1931
SOBALVANY • 1956 • Varkonyi Zoltan • HNG • PILLAR OF SALT
SOBO • 1937 • Kumagai Hisatora • JPN • MANY PEOPLE
SOBO see **SOHO** • 1933
SOBOTA • 1944 • Wasserman Vaclav • CZC • SATURDAY
SOBOTA GRAZYNY A. I JERZEGO T. • 1969 • Karabasz Kazimierz • DOC • PLN • SATURDAY IN THE LIFE OF GRAZYNA A. AND JERZY T., A
SOBRE A TERRA E SOBRE O MAR • 1964 • Spiguel Miguel • SHT • PRT
SOBRE EL MUERTO LAS CORONAS • 1959 • Diaz Morales Jose • MXC
SOBRE EL PROBLEMA FRONTERIZO • 1978 • Alvarez Santiago • DOC • CUB
SOBRE HORAS EXTRAS Y TRABAJO VOLUNTARIO • 1973 • Gomez Sara • DOC • CUB
SOBRE LA HERBA VIRGEN • 1977 • Durand Carlos B. • VNZ • ON THE FRESH GRASS
SOBRE LA MISERIA DE LA PEDAGOGIA BAJO CUALQUIERA DE SUS DISFRACES • 1974 • Artero Antonio • SHT • SPN
SOBRE LAS OLAS • 1932 • Zacarias Miguel, Sevilla Raphael J. • MXC
SOBRE LAS OLAS • 1950 • Rodriguez Ismael • MXC
SOBRE UN PRIMER COMBATE • 1971 • Cortazar Octavio • DOC • CUB • CONCERNING A FIRST COMBAT
SOBRE VERDE, EL • 1971 • Gil Rafael • SPN
SOBREDOSIS • 1986 • Ayala Fernando • ARG • OVERDOSE
SOBRENATURAL • 1981 • Martin Eugenio • SPN • SUPERNATURAL
SOBRETODO DE CESPEDES, EL • 1939 • Torres-Rios Leopoldo • ARG
SOBREVIVIENTES ESCOGIDOS • 1973 • *Churubusco Azteca* • MXC
SOBREVIVIENTES, LOS • 1979 • Alea Tomas Gutierrez • CUB • SURVIVORS, THE
SOBRINA DEL SENOR CURA, LA • 1954 • Bustillo Oro Juan • MXC
SOBRINO DE DON BUFFALO BILL, EL • 1944 • Barreiro Ramon • SPN • DON BUFFALO BILL
SOBSTVENNOYE MNYENIYE • 1977 • Karasik Yuli • USS • PERSONAL OPINION
SOCARRON, EL • 1975 • Puig Jaime • SPN
SOCCER • 1931 • Kelley Albert • SHT • USA
SOCCER POKER see **PILKARSKI POKER** • 1988
SOCHAUX, 11 JUIN 1968 • 1968 • FRN
SOCIAL AMBITION • 1918 • Worsley Wallace • USA
SOCIAL ASPIRATIONS • 1913 • Collins Edwin J.? • UKN
SOCIAL BRIARS • 1918 • King Henry • USA
SOCIAL BUCCANEER, THE • 1916 • Conway Jack • USA • SOCIAL BUCCANEERS
SOCIAL BUCCANEER, THE • 1923 • Hill Robert F. • SRL • USA
SOCIAL BUCCANEERS see **SOCIAL BUCCANEER, THE** • 1916
SOCIAL CELEBRITY, A • 1926 • St. Clair Malcolm • USA
SOCIAL CLIMBER, A • 1917 • Thayer Otis B. • SHT • USA
SOCIAL CLUB, A • 1916 • Badger Clarence • USA • SOCIAL CLUB, A
SOCIAL CLUB, A see **SOCIAL CLUB, A** • 1916
SOCIAL CODE, THE • 1923 • Apfel Oscar • USA • TO WHOM IT MAY CONCERN
SOCIAL DECEPTION, A • 1916 • Heffron Thomas N. • SHT • USA
SOCIAL ENEMY NO.1 (UKN) see **NO GREATER SIN** • 1941
SOCIAL ERROR • 1935 • *Commodore* • USA • KIDNAPPED (UKN)
SOCIAL ERROR, A • 1922 • La Cava Gregory • SHT • USA
SOCIAL ERRORS see **ONLY SAPS WORK** • 1930
SOCIAL EXILE, THE see **DECLASSEE** • 1925
SOCIAL GAME see **DRUSTVENA IGRA** • 1973
SOCIAL GANGSTER see **LONESOME LUKE, SOCIAL GANGSTER** • 1915
SOCIAL GHOST, THE • 1914 • *Harris Mildred* • USA
SOCIAL HIGHWAYMAN, THE • 1916 • August Edwin • USA
SOCIAL HIGHWAYMAN, THE • 1926 • Beaudine William • USA • LEAVE IT TO ME
SOCIAL HYPOCRITES • 1918 • Capellani Albert • USA
SOCIAL LAW, THE • 1915 • *Grandin Ethel* • USA
SOCIAL LECTURE, THE • 1898 • Perry Joseph H. • SER • ASL
SOCIAL LEPER, THE • 1917 • Knoles Harley • USA
SOCIAL LION • 1954 • Kinney Jack • ANS • USA
SOCIAL LION, THE • 1915 • Worthington William • USA
SOCIAL LION, THE • 1930 • Sutherland A. Edward • USA • HIGH SOCIETY
SOCIAL OUTCAST, A • 1916 • Wilson Ben • SHT • USA
SOCIAL PIRATE, THE • 1919 • Henderson Dell • USA
SOCIAL PIRATES • 1916 • Horne James W. • USA
SOCIAL PIRATES • 1917 • Reed Walter C. • SHT • USA
SOCIAL PIRATES, THE • 1916 • SER • USA
SOCIAL PRESTIGE • 1928 • Roberts Stephen • SHT • USA
SOCIAL QUICKSANDS • 1918 • Brabin Charles J. • USA
SOCIAL REGISTER • 1934 • Neilan Marshall • USA
SOCIAL SEA LIONS • 1940 • Hines Johnny • SHT • USA
SOCIAL SECRETARY, THE • 1912 • *Hawley Ormi* • USA
SOCIAL SECRETARY, THE • 1913 • *De Lespine Edgena* • USA
SOCIAL SECRETARY, THE • 1916 • Emerson John • USA
SOCIAL-SEX ATTITUDES IN ADOLESCENCE • 1953 • Gorman George • USA
SOCIAL SHOCK ABSORBER, A • 1918 • *Triangle* • USA
SOCIAL SLAVE, A • 1916 • Jaccard Jacques • SHT • USA
SOCIAL TERRORS • 1946 • Roberts Charles E. • SHT • USA
SOCIALIST REALISM see **REALISMO SOCIALISTA** • 1973
SOCIALLY AMBITIOUS • 1915 • *Briscoe Lottie* • USA
SOCIETA DEL MALESSERE see **BARBAGIA** • 1969
SOCIETA OVESTICINO-DINAMO • 1955 • Olmi Ermanno • DOC • ITL
SOCIETE DU SPECTACLE, LA • 1973 • Debord Guy • FRN
SOCIETY • 1955 • *Burman S. D. (M)* • IND
SOCIETY, THE see **SEISHUN NO KAZE** • 1968
SOCIETY AFFAIR • 1982 • McCallum Robert • USA
SOCIETY AND CHAPS • 1912 • Dwan Allan • USA
SOCIETY AND THE MAN • 1911 • Blackton J. Stuart • USA
SOCIETY AT SIMPSON CENTER • 1914 • *Eclair* • USA
SOCIETY BAD MEN • 1920 • Shilling William A. • SHT • USA
SOCIETY BALLOONING • 1906 • *Bitzer Billy (Ph)* • USA
SOCIETY BUG, THE • 1920 • Hayes Ward • SHT • USA
SOCIETY CROOKS see **STRATEGY** • 1915
SOCIETY DAY AT PIPER ROCK • 1913 • *Imp* • USA
SOCIETY DETECTIVE see **DETECTIVE FINN, OR, IN THE HEART OF LONDON** • 1914
SOCIETY DOCTOR see **ONLY EIGHT HOURS** • 1934
SOCIETY DOG SHOW • 1939 • Roberts Bill • ANS • USA
SOCIETY EXILE, A • 1919 • Fitzmaurice George • USA
SOCIETY FEVER • 1935 • Strayer Frank • USA
SOCIETY FOR SALE • 1918 • Borzage Frank • USA
SOCIETY GIRL • 1932 • Lanfield Sidney • USA
SOCIETY GIRL see **MAYFAIR GIRL** • 1933
SOCIETY GOES SPAGHETTI • 1930 • Sandrich Mark • SHT • USA
SOCIETY HOBOES • 1911 • *Yankee* • USA
SOCIETY HYPOCRITES • 1916 • Wilson Ben • SHT • USA
SOCIETY LAWYER • 1939 • Marin Edwin L. • USA • PENTHOUSE
SOCIETY NOTES • 1919 • *Klever Pictures* • SHT • USA
SOCIETY PEOPLE see **YOUTHFUL FOLLY** • 1920
SOCIETY PILOT • 1915 • *Morosco* • USA
SOCIETY PLAYWRIGHT, THE • 1912 • Thornton F. Martin • UKN • POTTED PLAYS NO.1
SOCIETY SCANDAL, A • 1924 • Dwan Allan • USA
SOCIETY SCHEMER, A • 1915 • Mackin John E. • USA
SOCIETY SCRIMMAGE, A • 1917 • *U.s.m.p.* • USA
SOCIETY SECRETS • 1921 • McCarey Leo • USA
SOCIETY SENSATION, A • 1918 • Powell Paul • USA
SOCIETY SHERLOCK, A • 1916 • Garwood William • SHT • USA
SOCIETY SINNER, A see **TYVEN** • 1910
SOCIETY SMUGGLERS • 1939 • May Joe • USA
SOCIETY SNOBS • 1921 • Henley Hobart • USA
SOCIETY STUFF • 1919 • Moore Vin • SHT • USA
SOCIETY TANGO, THE • 1913 • *Selsior Films* • UKN
SOCIETY VISIT, THE • 1915 • *Dangerfield Winnie* • UKN
SOCIETY WOLVES • 1916 • Terriss Tom • USA
SOCIETY WOMAN see **BLONDIE IN SOCIETY** • 1941
SOCIETY WRONGED US see **KINONIA MAS ADIKISE, I** • 1967
SOCIETY'S DRIFTWOOD • 1917 • Chaudet Louis W. • USA
SOCIETY'S GAMES see **JUEGOS DE SOCIEDAD** • 1973
SOCIO, EL • 1945 • Gavaldon Roberto • MXC
SOCIO, IL see **SOCIO INVISIBILE, IL** • 1939
SOCIO DE DIOS, EL • 1986 • Garcia Federico • PRU, CUB
SOCIO INVISIBILE, IL • 1939 • Roberti Roberto Leone • ITL • SOCIO, IL
SOCIOS PARA LA AVENTURA • 1957 • Morayta Miguel • MXC, ARG
SOCK-A-BYE BABY • 1934 • Fleischer Dave • ANS • USA
SOCK-A-BYE BABY • 1942 • White Jules • SHT • USA
SOCK-A-BYE KITTY • 1950 • Kneitel Seymour • ANS • USA
SOCK-A-DOODLE-DO • 1952 • McKimson Robert • ANS • USA
SOCK IT TO ME BABY • 1968 • Campa Lou • USA • HOT BLOODED GALS
SOCK IT TO ME WITH FLESH see **I WANT MORE** • 1970
SOCK ME TO SLEEP • 1935 • Holmes Ben • SHT • USA
SOCKEROO • 1940 • Eason B. Reeves • USA
SOCKERSKRINET • 1938 • Natorp Arthur • SWD • SUGAR BOWL
SOCKO IN MOROCCO • 1954 • Patterson Don • ANS • USA
SOCKS APPEAL • *Columbia* • SHT • USA
SOCRATE • 1971 • Rossellini Roberto • MTV • ITL • SOCRATES
SOCRATE, LE • 1968 • Lapoujade Robert • FRN, FRG • SOCRATES (UKN)
SOCRATES see **SOCRATE** • 1971
SOCRATES (UKN) see **SOCRATE, LE** • 1968
SOD SISTERS • 1969 • Williams Lester* • USA • HEAD FOR THE HILLS
SODA JERKER, THE • 1917 • *Essanay* • SHT • USA
SODA POPPA • 1931 • *Mintz Charles (P)* • ANS • USA
SODA SQUIRT • 1933 • *Iwerks Ub (P)* • ANS • USA
SODA WATER COWBOY • 1927 • Thorpe Richard • USA
SODACHI-ZAKARI • 1967 • Moritani Shiro • JPN • SEVENTEEN
SODER OM LANDSVAGEN • 1936 • Wahlberg Gideon • SWD • SOUTH OF THE MAIN ROAD
SODERKAKAR • 1932 • Hildebrand Weyler • SWD • RAMSHACKLED OF SODER
SODERPOJKAR • 1941 • Stevens Gosta • SWD • BOYS FROM THE SOUTH OF STOCKHOLM
SODHBODH • 1942 • *Sircar B. N. (P)* • IND
SODOM AND GOMORRAH • 1961 • Aldrich Robert, Leone Sergio • USA, ITL, FRN • SODOMA E GOMORRA (ITL) ○ SODOME ET GOMORRHE (FRN)
SODOM AND GOMORRAH -THE LAST SEVEN DAYS • 1975 • *Brancato Sean* • USA
SODOM UND GOMORRA • 1920 • May Joe • FRG
SODOM UND GOMORRA • 1922 • Curtiz Michael • AUS • LEGENDE VON SUNDE UND STRAFE, DIE ○ QUEEN OF SIN AND THE SPECTACLE OF SODOM AND GOMORRAH, THE
SODOMA E GOMORRA (ITL) see **SODOM AND GOMORRAH** • 1961
SODOME ET GOMORRHE (FRN) see **SODOM AND GOMORRAH** • 1961
SODOMISEES, LES • Antony Michel • FRN
SODOMS ENDE • 1913 • *Abel Alfred* • FRG
SODOMS ENDE • 1922 • Basch Felix • FRG
SODRANS REVY • 1951 • Spjuth Arthur • SWD • REVUE AT THE SODRAN THEATRE ○ FARVAL TILL 40-TALET
SODRASBAN • 1964 • Gaal Istvan • HNG • CURRENT (UKN) ○ STREAM, THE
SODY CLERK, THE • 1916 • Beery Wallace • SHT • USA
SOEKIE • 1975 • SAF
SOELDNER, DIE see **DIAMOND MERCENARIES, THE** • 1975
SOEUR ANGELIQUE • 1909 • Carre Michel • FRN
SOEUR ANUARITE, UNE VIE POUR DIEU • 1983 • Masekela Madenda Kiesse • ZRE
SOEURETTE • 1913 • Tourneur Maurice • FRN
SOEURS BRONTE, LES • 1979 • Techine Andre • FRN • BRONTE SISTERS, THE
SOEURS D'ARMES • 1937 • Poirier Leon • FRN
SOEURS DIABOLIQUES, LES • Ricaud Michel • FRN
SOEURS ENNEMIES, LES • 1915 • Dulac Germaine • FRN • ENEMY SISTERS
SOEURS GARNIER, LES see **CONFLIT** • 1938
SOEURS HORTENSIAS, LES • 1935 • Guissart Rene • FRN
SOFERAKI, TO • 1953 • Tzavellas Georges • GRC • TAXI DRIVER
SOFFIO AL CUORE (ITL) see **SOUFFLE AU COEUR, LE** • 1971
SOFI • 1967 • Carlisle Robert • USA
SOFIA • 1948 • Reinhardt John • USA
SOFIA • 1987 • Doria Alejandro • ARG
SOFIA AND SEXUAL EDUCATION see **SOFIA E A EDUCACAO SEXUAL** • 1974
SOFIA CONSPIRACY, THE • 1988 • Vanderkloot William • USA • DEATH GAMES ○ MACE
SOFIA E A EDUCACAO SEXUAL • 1974 • Geada Eduardo • PRT • SOFIA AND SEXUAL EDUCATION
SOFIA PEROVSKAYA see **SOFYA PEROVSKAYA** • 1968
SOFIA STORY see **SOFIISKA ISTORIA** • 1990
SOFIISKA ISTORIA • 1990 • Staneva Nadya • BUL • SOFIA STORY
SOFKA • 1948 • Novakovic Rados • YGS
SOFOR PARCASI • 1967 • Aslan Mehmet • TRK • THAT NO-GOOD CABMAN
SOFT BALL GAME • 1936 • Lantz Walter • ANS • USA
SOFT BEAST see **SHITOYAKANA KEMONO** • 1963
SOFT BEDS, HARD BATTLES • 1973 • Boulting Roy • UKN • UNDERCOVER HERO
SOFT BODY OF DEBORAH, THE see **DOLCE CORPO DI DEBORAH, IL** • 1968
SOFT BOILED • 1923 • Blystone John G. • USA • TEMPERED STEEL ○ YES WE HAVE NO TEMPER
SOFT CATERPILLAR, THE • 1967 • Miler Zdenek • ANS • CZC • VELVET CATERPILLAR, THE
SOFT CUSHIONS • 1927 • Cline Eddie • USA
SOFT FOCUS see **PERFECT TIMING** • 1984
SOFT LIGHTS AND SWEET MUSIC • 1936 • Smith Herbert • UKN
SOFT LIVING • 1928 • Tinling James • USA
SOFT MONEY • 1919 • Roach Hal • SHT • USA
SOFT PLACES • 1978 • Hamilton Wray • USA
SOFT RAIN • 1968 • Jacobs Ken • USA
SOFT RAINS, THE see **GAFFET EL AMTAR** • 1967
SOFT SHOES • 1925 • Ingraham Lloyd • USA

SOFT SKIN, THE (USA) see **PEAU DOUCE, LA** • 1964
SOFT SKIN AND BLACK LACE see **MUNDO PARA MI, UN** • 1959
SOFT SKIN ON BLACK SILK see **MUNDO PARA MI, UN** • 1959
SOFT TENDERFOOT, THE • 1917 • Mix Tom • SHT • USA
SOFT TOUCH OF NIGHT (USA) see **YORU NO HADA** • 1960
SOFT WARM EXPERIENCE, A see **SATIN MUSHROOM, THE** • 1969
SOFTNESS OF CONCRETE, THE • 1961 • Kohanyi Julius • CND
SOFYA PEROVSKAYA • 1968 • Arnstam Leo • USS • SOPHIA PEROVSKAYA ○ SOFIA PEROVSKAYA
SOGA PENDE DEL CIELO, LA • 1979 • Ordosgoitti Napoleon • VNZ • ROPE HANGS FROM THE SKY, THE
SOGARTH AROON • 1912 • *Powers* • USA
SOGEKI • 1968 • Horikawa Hiromichi • JPN • SUN ABOVE, DEATH BELOW
SOGGY BOTTOM USA • 1981 • Flicker Theodore J. • USA
SOGHAT-E-FARANG • 1967 • Madani Hosain • IRN • FOREIGN GIFT
SOGICOT • 1966 • Harzallah Ahmed • DCS • TNS
SOGNI DEL SIGNOR ROSSI, IL • 1978 • Bozzetto Bruno • ITL
SOGNI D'ORO • 1981 • Moretti Nanni • ITL
SOGNI MOSTRUOSAMENTE PROIBITI • 1983 • Parenti Neri • ITL • MONSTROUSLY FORBIDDEN DREAMS
SOGNI MUOIONO ALL'ALBA, I • 1961 • Montanelli Indro, Craveri Mario, Gras Enrico • ITL
SOGNI NEL CASSETTO, I • 1957 • Castellani Renato • ITL • DREAMS IN THE DRAWER
SOGNI PROIBITI DI DON GALEAZZO CURATO DI CAMPAGNA • 1973 • Di Cola Emanuele, Ferrara Gianfranco • ITL
SOGNO A VENEZIA • 1958 • Zucchelli Nino • DOC • ITL
SOGNO D'AMORE • 1943 • Poggioli Ferdinando M. • ITL
SOGNO D'AMORE see **SUONNO D'AMMORE** • 1955
SOGNO DI BUTTERFLY, IL • 1939 • Gallone Carmine • ITL, FRG • PREMIERE DER BUTTERFLY (FRG) ○ DREAM OF BUTTERFLY, THE
SOGNO DI DON CHISCIOTTE, IL • 1915 • Palermi Amleto • ITL
SOGNO DI NATALE • 1910 • *Milano* • ITL • CHRISTMAS DREAM
SOGNO DI TUTTI, IL • 1941 • Biancoli Oreste, Kish Ladislao • ITL
SOGNO DI UN GIORNO, IL • 1916 • Genina Augusto • ITL
SOGNO DI UNA NOTTE DI MEZZA SBORNIA • 1959 • De Filippo Eduardo • ITL
SOGNO DI UNA NOTTE ESTATE • 1984 • Salvatores Gabriele • ITL • MIDSUMMER NIGHT'S DREAM
SOGNO DI ZA LA VIE • 1923 • Ghione Emilio • ITL
SOGNO DI ZORRO, IL • 1952 • Soldati Mario • ITL
SOGNO DI ZORRO, IL • 1976 • Laurenti Mariano • ITL
SOHA, SEHOL, SENKINEK.. • 1989 • Teglasy Ferenc • HNG • NEVER, NOWHERE, TO NO-ONE! (UKN) ○ NEVER, NOWHERE..
SOHN DER GOTTER, DER • 1918 • Wellin Arthur • FRG • JUNGE GOETHE, DER
SOHN DER HAGAR, DER • 1926 • Wendhausen Fritz • FRG • OUT OF THE MIST
SOHN DER MAGD, DER • 1920 • Mack Max • FRG
SOHN DER WEISSEN BERG, DER • 1930 • Bonnard Mario • FRG • GEHEIMNIS VON ZERMATT, DAS ○ SONG OF THE ALPS
SOHN DES GALEERENSTRAFLINGS, DER • 1923 • *Vicor-Film* • FRG
SOHN DES HANNIBAL, DER • 1918 • Larsen Viggo • FRG
SOHN DES HANNIBAL, DER • 1926 • Basch Felix • FRG
SOHN DES MINISTERS, DER • 1915 • *Flink Hugo* • FRG
SOHN DES VERBRECHERS, DER • 1921 • Neff Wolfgang • FRG
SOHN OHNE HEIMAT • 1955 • Deppe Hans • FRG
SOHNE, DIE • 1967 • Vogeler Volker • FRG
SOHNE DER GROSSEN BARIN, DIE • 1966 • Mach Josef • GDR
SOHNE DER HOLLE • 1921 • Bach Rudi • UKN
SOHNE DER NACHT 1 • 1921 • Noa Manfred • FRG • VERBRECHER-GMBH, DIE
SOHNE DER NACHT 2 • 1921 • Noa Manfred • FRG • MACHT DER LIEBE, DIE
SOHNE DES GRAFEN DOSSY, DIE • 1920 • Gartner Adolf • FRG
SOHNE DES GRAFEN STEINFELS, DIE • 1915 • Del Zopp Rudolf • FRG
SOHNE DES HERRN GASPARY, DIE • 1948 • Meyer Rolf • FRG • IM TAL IST SCHON DER FRUHLING..
SOHO • 1933 • Naruse Mikio • JPN • CARELESS ○ SOBO ○ TWO EYES
SOHO • 1944 • Hughes Ken • DCS • UKN
SOHO BLUES see **PERFECT TIMING** • 1984
SOHO CONSPIRACY • 1950 • Williamson Cecil H. • UKN
SOHO INCIDENT • 1956 • Sewell Vernon • UKN • SPIN A DARK WEB (USA) ○ FORTY-FOUR SOHO SQUARE
SOHO MURDERS, THE • 1942 • Haines Ronald • UKN
SOIF D'AMOUR see **FOME DE AMOR** • 1968
SOIF DE L'OR, LA • 1962 • Giraldeau Jacques • DCS • CND
SOIF DES HOMMES, LA • 1949 • de Poligny Serge • FRN
SOIGNE TA DROITE • 1987 • Godard Jean-Luc • SWT, FRN
SOIGNE TON GAUCHE • 1936 • Clement Rene • SHT • FRN
SOIKINA LYUBOV • 1927 • Timoshenko S. • USS • SOIKIN'S LOVE
SOIKIN'S LOVE see **SOIKINA LYUBOV** • 1927
SOIL see **ZEMLYA** • 1930
SOIL, THE see **EARTH** • 1963
SOIL DRIFT see **MULDFLUGTEN** • 1979
SOIL FOR TOMORROW • 1945 • Cherry Evelyn Spice, Cherry Lawrence W. • DOC • CND
SOIL IS THIRSTY, THE see **ZEMLYA ZHAZHDYOT** • 1930
SOIL UNDER YOUR FEET, THE see **TALPALTNYI FOLD** • 1948
SOILED • 1924 • Windermere Fred • USA
SOILERS, THE • 1923 • Roach Hal • SHT • USA
SOILERS, THE • 1932 • Marshall George • SHT • USA
SOINS AUX ASPHYXIES • 1955 • Lanoe Henri • SHT • FRN
SOINS DE L'ENFANCE • Tessier Albert • DCS • CND
SOIR, UN • 1919 • Boudrioz Robert • FRN
SOIR A MARSEILLE, UN • 1937 • de Canonge Maurice • FRN
SOIR A TIBERIADE, UN • 1965 • Bromberger Herve • FRN, ISR
SOIR AU CINEMA, UN • 1962 • Lemaitre Maurice • FRN
SOIR AU FRONT, UN • 1931 • Ryder Alexandre • FRN
SOIR D'ALERTE, UN see **FAUSSE ALERTE** • 1940
SOIR DE BOMBE, UN • 1935 • Cammage Maurice • FRN
SOIR DE LA PLAGE, UN • 1961 • Boisrond Michel • FRN, ITL • QUELLA SERA SULLA SPIAGGIA (ITL) ○ VIOLENT SUMMER (USA)
SOIR DE NOTRE VIE, LE • 1963 • Valentin • SHT • FRN
SOIR DE RAFLE, UN • 1931 • Gallone Carmine • FRN
SOIR DE REVEILLON, UN • 1933 • Anton Karl • FRN
SOIR DES ROIS, LE • 1932 • Daumery John • FRN • SOYEZ LES BIENVENUS
SOIR.. PAR HASARD, UN • 1964 • Govar Yvan • FRN, BLG • AGENT OF DOOM (USA) ○ ONE NIGHT.. BY ACCIDENT
SOIR, UN TRAIN, UN • 1968 • Delvaux Andre • BLG, FRN • ONE NIGHT.. A TRAIN ○ NIGHT.. A TRAIN, A ○ ONE EVENING ON A TRAIN
SOIREE A LA COMEDIE FRANCAISE, UNE • 1934 • Perret Leonce • FRN • COMEDIE FRANCAISE
SOIREE DE GALA • 1935 • Cerf Andre • FRN
SOIREE DU BARON SWENBECK, LA • 1973 • Niogret Hubert • FRN
SOIREE MONDAINE • 1924 • Colombier Piere • FRN
SOIREES DU HAMEAU PROCHE DE DIKANKA, LES • 1962 • Rou Aleksandr • USS
SOIREES D'UNE EPOUSE PERVERTIE, LES • Bernard-Aubert Claude • FRN
SOIRS DE PARIS • 1953 • Laviron Jean • FRN
SOIS BELLE ET TAIS-TOI • 1958 • Allegret Marc • FRN • BE BEAUTIFUL AND SHUT UP (USA) ○ BLONDE FOR DANGER (UKN)
SOIS BELLE ET TAIS-TOI • 1977 • Seyrig Delphine • DOC • FRN
SOIS DA ILHA DE PASCOA, OS (BRZ) see **SOLEILS DE L'ILE DE PAQUES, LES** • 1971
SOIUZKINOZHURNAL NO.77 • 1941 • Vertov Dziga • USS
SOIUZKINOZHURNAL NO.81 • 1941 • Vertov Dziga • USS
SOIXANTE-DIX-SEPT RUE CHALGRIN • 1931 • De Courville Albert • FRN • DU CREPUSCULE A L'AUBE
SOIXANTE-NEUF POSITIONS, LES • 1975 • Beni Alphonse • FRN
SOK OD SLJIVA • 1981 • Baletic Branko • YGS • PLUM JUICE
SOKAKTA KAN VARDI • 1965 • Turkali • TRK
SOKO • 1981 • Mimica Vatroslav • YGS • FALCON, THE
SOKOLOVO • 1975 • USS, CZC
SOKOLS • 1948 • Weiss Jiri • CZC
SOKYU NO MON • 1933 • Yamamoto Kajiro • JPN • GATE TO THE BLUE SKY
SOL • 1965 • Zahariev Edward • DOC • BUL
SOL • 1974 • Brakhage Stan • USA
SOL, EL • 1922 • Barth-Moglia Luis • ARG
SOL DE GLORIA • 1920 • Calles Guillermo • MXC
SOL DE GLORIA see **PESCADORES DE PERLAS** • 1938
SOL DE VERANO • 1963 • Bosch Juan • SPN
SOL E TOUROS • 1949 • Buchs Jose • PRT
SOL EN BOTELLITAS, EL • 1986 • Valladares Edmund • ARG • BOTTLED SUN
SOL EN EL ESPEJO, EL • 1962 • Roman Antonio • SPN
SOL EN LLAMAS • 1961 • Crevenna Alfredo B. • MXC
SOL MADRID see **HEROIN GANG, THE** • 1968
SOL NAD ZLATO • 1982 • Holly Martin • CZC, FRG • SALT IS MORE PRECIOUS THAN GOLD ○ SALT IS WORTH MORE THAN GOLD
SOL NO SE PUEDE TAPAR CON UN DEDO, EL • 1976 • Alvarez Santiago • DOC • CUB
SOL OVER DANMARK • 1935 • Holger-Madsen • DNM • SUN OVER DENMARK
SOL OVER KLARA • 1942 • Lingheim Emil A. • SWD • SUN OVER KLARA (USA) ○ SUNSHINE OVER KLARA
SOL OVER SVERIGE • 1938 • Bornebusch Arne • SWD • SUN OVER SWEDEN
SOL SALE PARA TODOS, EL • 1949 • Urruchua Victor • MXC
SOL SALE TODOS LOS DIAS, EL • 1955 • del Amo Antonio • SPN
SOL SOBRE A LAMA • 1962 • Viany Alex • BRZ
SOL SOBRE O VERDE • 1957 • Spiguel Miguel • SHT • PRT
SOL, SOMMER OG STUDINER • 1923 • Lauritzen Lau • DNM
SOL SVANETII • 1930 • Kalatozov Mikhail • USS • SALT FOR SVANETIA ○ JIM SHVANTE -SVANETIS MARILI ○ DJIM CHUANTE
SOL URBAIN, LE • 1972 • Regnier Michel • DCS • CND
SOL Y SOMBRAS • 1945 • Portas Rafael E. • MXC
SOL ZIEMI CZARNEJ • 1969 • Kutz Kazimierz • PLN • SALT OF THE BLACK COUNTRY ○ SALT OF THE BLACK EARTH ○ TASTE OF THE BLACK EARTH, THE
SOLA • 1931 • Diamant-Berger Henri • FRN • SOLA, TU NE SAIS PAS AIMER
SOLA • 1976 • de la Torre Raul • ARG • ALONE
SOLA, TU NE SAIS PAS AIMER see **SOLA** • 1931
SOLACE OF THE WOODS see **DIAMOND CARLISLE** • 1922
SOLAJA • 1955 • Nanovic Vojislav • YGS
SOLAMENTE NERO • 1978 • Bido Antonio • ITL
SOLAMENTE UNA VEZ • 1953 • Vejar Carlos • MXC
SOLANG' ES HUBSCHE MADCHEN GIBT • 1955 • Rabenalt Arthur M. • FRG
SOLANGE see **HONORABLE CATHERINE, L'** • 1942
SOLANGE DANS NOS CAMPAGNES • 1964 • Carle Gilles • SHT • CND
SOLANGE DU DA BIST • 1953 • Braun Harald • FRG • AS LONG AS YOU'RE NEAR ME (USA)
SOLANGE DU LEBST • 1955 • Reinl Harald • FRG • AS LONG AS YOU LIVE
SOLANGE LEBEN IN MIR IST • 1965 • Reisch Gunter • GDR • AS LONG AS THERE IS LIFE IN ME ○ AS LONG AS I LIVE
SOLANGE NOCH DIE ROSEN BLUH'N • 1956 • Deppe Hans • FRG
SOLANIKA TERRORISTS, THE see **SOLUNSKI ATENTATORI** • 1961
SOLAR AND TIDAL POWER • 1973 • Bonniere Rene • DCS • CND
SOLAR ECLIPSE see **SURJOGRAHAN** • 1976
SOLAR ECLIPSE EXPEDITION AT WALLAL see **ASTRONOMERS AND ABORIGINES** • 1922
SOLAR FILM, THE • 1979 • Bass Saul • SHT • USA
SOLARBABIES • 1986 • Johnson Alan • USA • SOLARWARRIORS
SOLARIS see **SOLYARIS** • 1972
SOLARWARRIORS see **SOLARBABIES** • 1986
SOLCO DI PESCA, IL • 1976 • Liverani Maurizio • ITL
SOLD! • 1913 • Stow Percy • UKN
SOLD • 1915 • Porter Edwin S., Ford Hugh • USA
SOLD see **MODELLHAUS CREVETTE** • 1930
SOLD, A "BEAR" FACT • 1912 • Aylott Dave? • UKN
SOLD AGAIN • 1907 • Mottershaw Frank • UKN
SOLD AND HEALED • 1922 • Dudley Bernard • UKN
SOLD APPETITE, THE see **PRODANNYI APPETIT** • 1928
SOLD AT AUCTION • 1917 • MacDonald Sherwood • USA
SOLD AT AUCTION • 1923 • Parrott Charles • USA
SOLD AT AUCTION • 1931 • Edwards Harry J. • SHT • USA
SOLD FOR CASH see **ON THE STROKE OF THREE** • 1924
SOLD FOR GOLD • 1918 • *Roland Ruth* • SHT • USA
SOLD FOR MARRIAGE • 1916 • Cabanne W. Christy • USA
SOLD INTO EGYPT see **JOSEPH AND HIS BRETHREN** • 1962
SOLD OUT • 1916 • McGill Lawrence?, Hansel Howell? • USA
SOLD TO SATAN • 1916 • Sloman Edward • SHT • USA
SOLD TO THIEVES see **SVEND LANDSTRYGERE, DE** • 1908
SOLDAAT VAN ORANJE • 1977 • Verhoeven Paul* • NTH • SURVIVAL RUN (UKN) ○ SOLDIER OF ORANGE
SOLDADERO, LA • 1966 • Bolanos Jose • MXC
SOLDADOS • 1977 • Ungria Alfonso • SPN • SOLDIERS
SOLDADOS DE PLOMO • 1984 • Sacristan Jose • SPN • TIN SOLDIERS
SOLDADOS DO FOGO • 1958 • dos Santos Nelson Pereira • SHT • BRZ
SOLDADU UNNEHE • 1980 • Pathirajah Dharmasena • IND
SOLDAT BOM • 1948 • Kjellgren Lars-Eric • SWD • PRIVATE BOM
SOLDAT DER MARIE, DER • 1926 • Schonfelder Erich • FRG
SOLDAT DUROC, CA VA ETRE TA FETE • 1974 • Gerard Michel • FRN
SOLDAT ET LES TROIS SOEURS, LE • 1973 • Aubier Pascal • SHT • FRN
SOLDAT INCONNU, LE see **HISTOIRE DU SOLDAT INCONNU** • 1932
SOLDAT IVAN BROVKIN • 1955 • Lukinsky Ivan • USS • PRIVATE IVAN BROVKIN
SOLDAT LAFORET, LE • 1970 • Cavagnac Guy • FRN
SOLDATAMI NYE ROZHDAYUTSYA • 1968 • Stolper Alexander • USS • ONE IS NOT BORN A SOLDIER ○ SOLDIERS AREN'T BORN ○ VENGEANCE ○ NONE ARE BORN SOLDIERS
SOLDATEN-KAMERADEN • 1936 • Huppertz Toni • FRG
SOLDATENSENDER CALAIS • 1960 • May Paul • FRG • HEADQUARTERS STATE SECRET (USA)
SOLDATERKAMMERATER • 1958 • DNM, SWD
SOLDATERKAMMERATER PA BJORNETJENESTE • 1968 • Ottosen Carl • DNM
SOLDATERKAMMERATER PA VAGT • 1960 • Methling Sven • DNM • OPERATION CAMEL (USA)
SOLDATESSA ALLA VISITA MILITAIRE, LA • 1976 • Cicero Nando • ITL
SOLDATESSA ALLE GRANDI MANOVRE, IL • 1978 • Cicero Nando • ITL, FRN • TOUBIB AUX GRANDES MANOEUVRES, LA (FRN)
SOLDATESSE, LE • 1965 • Zurlini Valerio • ITL, FRN, FRG • DES FILLES POUR L'ARMEE (FRN) ○ CAMP FOLLOWERS, THE (USA)
SOLDATI -365 GIORNI ALL'ALBA • 1988 • Risi Marco • ITL • SOLDIERS -365 DAYS UNTIL DAWN
SOLDATI E CAPELLONI • 1967 • Fizzarotti Ettore Maria • ITL • SIAMO TUTTI BEAT ○ SOLDIERS AND BEATNIKS ○ WE ARE ALL SWINGERS
SOLDATI E CAPORALI • 1965 • Amendola Mario • ITL
SOLDATI FARA UNIFORMA • 1960 • Munteanu Francisc • RMN • SOLDIERS WITHOUT UNIFORM
SOLDATI IN CITTA • 1953 • Zurlini Valerio • DCS • ITL
SOLDATO DI VENTURA, IL • 1976 • Festa Campanile Pasquale • ITL, FRN • GRANDE BAGARRE, LA (FRN) ○ SOLDIER OF FORTUNE
SOLDATS SANS UNIFORMES • 1940 • de Canonge Maurice • FRN
SOLDATS SANS UNIFORMES • 1945 • de Meyst E. G. • FRN
SOLDATY • 1956 • Ivanov Alexander • USS • FOUR SOLDIERS FROM STALINGRAD ○ SOLDIERS
SOLDATY SVOBODY • 1977 • USS, BUL, HNG
SOLDI, I • 1965 • Puccini Gianni, Cavedon Giorgio • ITL
SOLDIER, THE • 1966 • Breakston George • USA, YGS • VOJNIK
SOLDIER, THE • 1967 • Power John • DOC • ASL
SOLDIER, THE • 1982 • Glickenhaus James • USA • CODENAME: THE SOLDIER
SOLDIER AND A MAN, A • 1911 • Noy Wilfred • UKN
SOLDIER AND A MAN, A • 1916 • Aylott Dave • UKN
SOLDIER AND THE LADY, THE • 1937 • Nicholls George Jr. • USA • MICHAEL STROGOFF (UKN) ○ ADVENTURES OF MICHAEL STROGOFF
SOLDIER BABY, THE • 1912 • *Reliance* • USA
SOLDIER BLUE • 1970 • Nelson Ralph • USA
SOLDIER BROTHERS OF SUSANNA, THE • 1912 • Melford George • USA
SOLDIER CAME HOME FROM THE FRONT, A see **PRISHOL SOLDAT S FRONTA** • 1972
SOLDIER FRIENDS see **SLUZHILI DVA TOVARISHCHA** • 1968
SOLDIER FROM THE WAR RETURNING see **PRISHOL SOLDAT S FRONTA** • 1972
SOLDIER GIRLS • 1981 • Broomfield Nicholas, Churchill Joan • DOC • USA
SOLDIER IN THE RAIN • 1963 • Nelson Ralph • USA
SOLDIER MAN • 1926 • *Sennett Mack (P)s* • SHT • USA
SOLDIER OF FORTUNE • 1955 • Dmytryk Edward • USA
SOLDIER OF FORTUNE see **SOLDATO DI VENTURA, IL** • 1976
SOLDIER OF LOVE see **FANFAN LA TULIPE** • 1952
SOLDIER OF MISFORTUNE • 1931 • Buzzell Edward • SHT • USA
SOLDIER OF ORANGE see **SOLDAAT VAN ORANJE** • 1977
SOLDIER OF PEACE, A • 1914 • Ince John • USA
SOLDIER OF THE C.S.A., A • 1914 • *Selig* • USA
SOLDIER OF THE LEGION, A • 1917 • Baldwin Ruth Ann • SHT • USA
SOLDIER OF THE NIGHT • 1983 • Wolman Dan • ISR

SOLDIER OF THE TRANSPORT UNIT, THE see **BRATUSHKA** • 1975
SOLDIER OF THE UNITED STATES ARMY, A • 1909 • *Kalem* • USA
SOLDIER OF VICTORY see **ZOLNIERZ ZWYCIESTWA** • 1953
SOLDIER OLD MAN • 1932 • *Mintz Charles (P)* • ANS • USA
SOLDIER ON DUTY see **CAPORALE DI GIORNATA** • 1958
SOLDIER, POLICEMAN AND COOK • 1899 • Cooper Arthur • UKN • AMOROUS COOK, THE
SOLDIER SAILOR • 1945 • Shaw Alexander • UKN
SOLDIER WHO DECLARED PEACE, THE see **TRIBES** • 1970
SOLDIERS see **SOLDATY** • 1956
SOLDIERS see **SOLDADOS** • 1977
SOLDIERS –365 DAYS UNTIL DAWN see **SOLDATI –365 GIORNI ALL'ALBA** • 1988
SOLDIERS, THE see **CARABINIERS, LES** • 1962
SOLDIERS AND BEATNIKS see **SOLDATI E CAPELLONI** • 1967
SOLDIERS AND OTHER COSMIC OBJECTS • 1977 • Brakhage Stan • SHT • USA
SOLDIERS AND WOMEN • 1930 • Sloman Edward • USA
SOLDIERS AREN'T BORN see **SOLDATAMI NYE ROZHDAYUTSYA** • 1968
SOLDIER'S BRIDE (USA) see **JAAKARIN MORSIAN** • 1939
SOLDIER'S COTTAGE, THE • 1946 • Hughes Harry • UKN • COTTAGE PIE
SOLDIER'S COURTSHIP, THE • 1896 • Moul Alfred • UKN
SOLDIER'S DREAM, A • 1917 • *Big U* • SHT • USA
SOLDIER'S DREAM, THE • 1907 • Blackton J. Stuart • USA
SOLDIER'S DUTIES, A see **KRIGSMANS ERINRAN** • 1947
SOLDIER'S DUTY, A • 1912 • Brabin Charles J. • USA
SOLDIER'S FATHER, A see **OTETS SOLDATA** • 1965
SOLDIER'S FRENCH LEAVE, A see **SORTI SANS PERMISSION** • 1898
SOLDIER'S FURLOUGH, A • 1912 • Fielding Romaine • USA
SOLDIER'S GIRL, A • 1915 • *Barker* • UKN
SOLDIER'S HOME • 1976 • Young Robert Malcolm • USA
SOLDIER'S HONOUR, A • 1911 • Martinek H. O. • UKN
SOLDIER'S HONOUR, A • 1914 • Calvert Charles • UKN • BROTHER OFFICERS
SOLDIERS IN SKIRTS (USA) see **TRIPLE ECHO, THE** • 1972
SOLDIERS IN WHITE • 1941 • Eason B. Reeves • SHT • USA
SOLDIER'S JEALOUSY, A • 1907 • Fitzhamon Lewin • UKN
SOLDIER'S JUSTICE see **SEIGI NO TSUWAMONO** • 1927
SOLDIER'S LAST CALL, THE • 1912 • *Republic* • USA
SOLDIER'S LOVE, THE see **VOJNIKOVA LJUBAV** • 1977
SOLDIERS MARCH, THE see **SLI SOLDATI** • 1957
SOLDIERS MARCHED ON, THE see **SLI SOLDATI** • 1957
SOLDIER'S OATH, A • 1915 • Apfel Oscar • USA
SOLDIERS OF CHANCE • 1917 • Scardon Paul • USA
SOLDIERS OF FORTUNE • 1914 • Thomas Augustus • USA
SOLDIERS OF FORTUNE • 1919 • Dwan Allan • USA
SOLDIERS OF FORTUNE (UKN) see **WAR CORRESPONDENT** • 1932
SOLDIERS OF FREEDOM, THE • 1976 • Ozerov Yury, Kurganov S. • USS
SOLDIERS OF INNOCENCE • 1989 • SKR
SOLDIERS OF MISFORTUNE • 1914 • Henderson Dell • USA
SOLDIERS OF PANCHO VILLA see **PANCHO VILLA Y LA VALENTINA** • 1958
SOLDIERS OF THE CROSS • 1900 • Perry Joseph H. • ASL
SOLDIERS OF THE KING • 1933 • Elvey Maurice • UKN • WOMAN IN COMMAND, THE (USA)
SOLDIERS OF THE STORM • 1933 • Lederman D. Ross • USA
SOLDIER'S PAY, A (UKN) see **SOLDIER'S PLAYTHING, A** • 1930
SOLDIER'S PLAYTHING, A • 1930 • Curtiz Michael • USA • SOLDIER'S PAY, A (UKN)
SOLDIER'S PRAYER, A see **NINGEN NO JOKEN III** • 1961
SOLDIER'S RETURN, THE • 1902 • Williamson James • UKN
SOLDIER'S RETURN, THE • 1911 • *Lubin* • USA
SOLDIER'S ROMANCE, A • 1904 • Mottershaw Frank • UKN
SOLDIER'S SACRIFICE, A • 1910 • *Nestor* • USA
SOLDIER'S SONS • 1916 • Melville Wilbert • SHT • USA
SOLDIER'S STORY, A • 1984 • Jewison Norman • USA
SOLDIER'S SWEETHEART, A • 1911 • Aylott Dave? • UKN
SOLDIER'S TALE, A • 1964 • Birkett Michael • UKN
SOLDIER'S TALE, A • 1988 • Parr Larry • NZL
SOLDIER'S TEDIOUS DUTY, A see **CORVEE DE QUARTIER ACCIDENTEE** • 1898
SOLDIERS THREE • 1911 • Baker George D. • USA
SOLDIERS THREE • 1913 • *Bison* • USA
SOLDIERS THREE • 1951 • Garnett Tay • USA
SOLDIERS THREE see **SERGEANTS THREE** • 1962
SOLDIER'S UNLUCKY SALUTATION, A see **SALUT MALENCONTREUX D'UN DESERTEUR** • 1896
SOLDIER'S WEDDING, A • 1907 • Stow Percy • UKN
SOLDIERS WERE MARCHING see **SLI SOLDATI** • 1957
SOLDIER'S WIFE see **I FEEL IT COMING** • 1969
SOLDIERS WITHOUT UNIFORM see **SOLDATI FARA UNIFORMA** • 1960
SOLDIERS WITHOUT UNIFORMS • 1942 • Chauvel Charles • DOC • ASL
SOLE • 1929 • Blasetti Alessandro • ITL
SOLE ANCHE DI NOTTE, IL • 1990 • Taviani Paolo, Taviani Vittorio • ITL, FRN, FRG • SUNSHINE EVEN BY NIGHT
SOLE DI MONTECASSINO, IL • 1945 • Scotese Giuseppe Maria • ITL • SAN BENEDETTO DOMINATORE DEI BARBARI
SOLE E DI TUTTI, IL • 1968 • Paolella Domenico • ITL
SOLE MATES • 1917 • Raymaker Herman C. • USA
SOLE MATES • 1929 • *Mintz Charles (P)* • ANS • USA
SOLE NEGLI OCCHI, IL • 1953 • Pietrangeli Antonio • ITL • SUN IN THE EYES ○ CELESTINA
SOLE NELLA PELLE, IL • 1971 • Stegani Giorgio • ITL • SUN ON THE SKIN (UKN) ○ ONCE AND FOR ALWAYS
SOLE ROSSO (ITL) see **SOLEIL ROUGE** • 1971
SOLE SORGE ANCORA, IL • 1946 • Vergano Aldo • ITL • SUN RISES AGAIN, THE ○ OUTCRY
SOLE SOTTO TERRA, IL • 1971 • Florio Aldo • ITL, SPN • ANDA MUCHACHO, SPARA (SPN) ○ DEAD MEN RIDE (UKN)
SOLE SUPPORT • 1929 • Lamont Charles • SHT • USA
SOLE SURVIVOR • 1969 • Stanley Paul • TVM • USA
SOLE SURVIVOR • 1985 • Eberhardt Thom • USA
SOLE SURVIVOR, THE • 1917 • Grandon Francis J. • SHT • USA
SOLE TORNERA, IL • 1957 • Merighi Ferdinando • ITL
SOLEDAD • 1947 • Zacarias Miguel • MXC
SOLEDAD • 1959 • Gras Enrico, Craveri Mario • DOC • ITL, SPN
SOLEDAD see **REBOZO DE SOLEDAD, EL** • 1952
SOLEDAD see **FRUITS AMERS** • 1967
SOLEIL O • 1969 • Hondo Abib Med • MRT, FRN • OH, SUN
SOLEIL A L'OMBRE, LE see **PRISON EN FOLIE, LA** • 1930
SOLEIL A PAS D'CHANCE, LE • 1975 • Favreau Robert • DOC • CND
SOLEIL A TOUJOURS RAISON, LE • 1941 • Billon Pierre • FRN
SOLEIL DANS L'OEIL, LE • 1961 • Bourdon Jacques • FRN
SOLEIL DE MINUIT, LE • 1943 • Bernard-Roland • FRN
SOLEIL DE PIERRE • 1967 • Baux Jean-Pierre • SHT • FRN
SOLEIL DES AUTRES, LE • 1969 • Faucher Jean • CND
SOLEIL DES HYENES see **SHAMS WA ADH-DHIBA, ASH-** • 1976
SOLEIL DES VOYOUS, LE • 1967 • Delannoy Jean • FRN, ITL • PIU GRANDE COLPO DEL SECOLO, IL (ITL) ○ ACTION MAN (USA) ○ LEATHER AND NYLON
SOLEIL EN FACE, LE • 1979 • Kast Pierre • FRN
SOLEIL ET MITIDJA • 1966 • Riad Mohamed Slimane • SHT • ALG
SOLEIL ET SOMBRE • 1922 • Musidora, Lasseyre Jacques • FRN • SUN AND SHADOW
SOLEIL NOIR • 1918 • Gance Abel • FRN
SOLEIL NOIR • 1966 • de La Patelliere Denys • FRN, ITL • ANGELICA AVVENTURIERA (ITL) ○ DARK SUNLIGHT ○ BLACK SUN
SOLEIL NOIR • 1978 • Mattsson Arne • SWD
SOLEIL PAS COMME AILLEURS, UN • 1972 • Forest Leonard • DOC • CND
SOLEIL PERDU, LE see **CIRCLE OF THE SUN** • 1961
SOLEIL QUI RIT ROUGE, LE • 1973 • Kirchner Bruno-Mario • FRN
SOLEIL ROUGE • 1971 • Young Terence • FRN, ITL, SPN • SOLE ROSSO (ITL) ○ RED SUN (UKN)
SOLEIL SE LEVE EN GRECE, LE • 1958 • Samivel • FRN
SOLEIL SE LEVE EN RETARD, LE • 1976 • Brassard Andre • CND
SOLEILS • 1960 • Vilardebo Carlos • SHT • FRN
SOLEILS DE L'ILE DE PAQUES, LES • 1971 • Kast Pierre • FRN, BRZ, CHL • SOIS DA ILHA DE PASCOA, OS (BRZ) ○ SUNS OF EASTER ISLAND, THE
SOLEMN COMMUNION see **COMMUNION SOLENNELLE, LA** • 1977
SOLEN DER DRAEBTE • 1917 • Davidsen Hjalmar • DNM
SOLEY • 1982 • Roska • ICL
SOLI PER LE STRADE • 1956 • Siano Silvio • ITL
SOLID CONCRETE • 1920 • Semon Larry • SHT • USA
SOLID EXPLANATION, A • 1951 • Bradford Peter • UKN
SOLID GOLD • 1926 • Roberts Stephen • SHT • USA
SOLID GOLD CADILLAC, THE • 1956 • Quine Richard • USA
SOLID IVORY • 1925 • Roach Hal • SHT • USA
SOLID IVORY • 1947 • Lundy Dick • ANS • USA
SOLID JIVE • 1946 • Gould Dave • SHT • USA
SOLID SENDERS • 1945 • Cowan Will • SHT • USA
SOLID SENDERS see **HOW'S ABOUT IT?** • 1943
SOLID SERENADE • 1946 • Hanna William, Barbera Joseph • ANS • USA
SOLID TIN COYOTE, THE • 1966 • Larriva Rudy • ANS • USA
SOLIDARIDAD CUBA Y VIETNAM • 1965 • Alvarez Santiago • DOC • CUB • SOLIDARITY CUBA AND VIETNAM
SOLIDARITE • Colson-Malleville Marie • DOC • FRN
SOLIDARITY • 1973 • Wieland Joyce • CND
SOLIDARITY CUBA AND VIETNAM see **SOLIDARIDAD CUBA Y VIETNAM** • 1965
SOLIDARNOSC • 1981 • Poljinsky Serge • DOC • PLN, FRN
SOLIGA SOLBERG • 1941 • Lingheim Emil A. • SWD • SUNNY MR. SOLBERG
SOLILOQUES DU PAUVRE, LES • 1951 • Drach Michel • SHT • FRN • REVENANT, LE
SOLILOQUY • 1949 • Peries Lester James • SHT • SLN
SOLIMAN BROTHERS • 1967 • Buenaventura Augusto • PHL
SOLIMANO IL CONQUISTATORE • 1961 • Tota Mario, Mimica Vatroslav • ITL, YGS • SOLIMANO IL CONQUISTATORE (YGS) ○ SULEIMAN THE CONQUEROR (USA)
SOLIMANO IL CONQUISTATORE (YGS) see **SOLIMANO IL CONQUISTATORE** • 1961
SOLISTIN ANNA ALT • 1944 • Klinger Werner • FRG • WENN DIE MUSIK NICHT WAR..
SOLITA DE CORDOUE • 1945 • Rozier Willy • FRN
SOLITAIRE • Freeman Mike • USA
SOLITAIRE • 1973 • Chammings Patrick • SHT • FRN
SOLITAIRE, LE • 1913 • Carre Michel • FRN
SOLITAIRE, LE • 1972 • Brunet Alain • FRN, FRG • LONER, THE
SOLITAIRE MAN, THE • 1933 • Conway Jack • USA
SOLITAIRE PASSE A L'ATTAQUE, LE • 1966 • Habib Ralph • FRN, SPN, ITL • SOLITARIO PASA AL ATAQUE, EL (SPN) ○ SOLITARY GOES TO THE ATTACK, THE
SOLITAIRES • 1913 • *Talmadge Norma* • USA
SOLITARIO, EL • 1963 • Martinez Arturo • MXC
SOLITARIO DELLA MONTAGNA, IL • 1931 • De Liguoro Wladimiro • ITL
SOLITARIO PASA AL ATAQUE, EL (SPN) see **SOLITAIRE PASSE A L'ATTAQUE, LE** • 1966
SOLITARY CHILD, THE • 1958 • Thomas Gerald • UKN
SOLITARY CYCLIST, THE • 1921 • Elvey Maurice • UKN
SOLITARY GOES TO THE ATTACK, THE see **SOLITAIRE PASSE A L'ATTAQUE, LE** • 1966
SOLITARY MAN, THE • 1979 • Moxey John Llewellyn • TVM • USA
SOLITARY REFINEMENT • 1965 • Post Howard • ANS • USA
SOLITARY SIN, THE • 1919 • Sullivan Frederick • USA
SOLITI IGNOTI, I • 1958 • Monicelli Mario • ITL • BIG DEAL OF MADONNA STREET, THE (USA) ○ PERSONS UNKNOWN ○ AS USUAL, UNKNOWN ○ BIG DEAL, THE ○ USUAL UNIDENTIFIED THIEVES, THE
SOLITI IGNOTI VENT'ANNI DOPO • 1985 • Todini Amanzio • ITL • BIG DEAL ON MADONNA STREET TWENTY YEARS AFTER
SOLITI RAPINATORI A MILANO, I • 1961 • Petroni Giulio • ITL
SOLITUDE • Sara Sandor • SHT • HNG
SOLITUDE • 1961 • Borowczyk Walerian, Lenica Jan • FRN
SOLITUDE • 1978 • Siegel Lois • CND
SOLITUDE see **LONESOME** • 1928
SOLITUDE DU CHANTEUR DE FOND, LA • 1975 • Marker Chris • DOC • FRN
SOLITUDES • 1973 • Brochu Pierre, Marcoux Pierre • CND
SOLITUDES • 1986 • Macina Michael • CND
SOLITUDINE • 1942 • Pavanelli Livio • ITL • ORA SUPREMA
SOLITUDINE • 1961 • Polselli Renato • ITL
SOLL MAN HEIRATEN? • 1925 • Noa Manfred • FRG • INTERMEZZO EINER EHE IN SIEBEN TAGEN
SOLL UND HABEN • 1924 • Wilhelm Carl • FRG
SOLLAZZEVOLI STORIE DI MOGLI GAUDENTI E MARITI PENITENTI • 1972 • Gastaldi Romano • ITL
SOLNTSE SVETIT VSEM • 1959 • Voinov Konstantin • USS • SUN SHINES FOR ALL, THE (USA) ○ SUN SHINES FOR EVERYBODY, THE
SOLO • 1965 • Cowan Bob • SHT • USA
SOLO • 1965 • Winter Jorn • SHT • USA
SOLO • 1968 • Donat Misha • UKN
SOLO • 1970 • Mocky Jean-Pierre • FRN, BLG • MORAL LOVE (UKN)
SOLO • 1971 • Monfa Ramon • SHT • SPN
SOLO • 1972 • Hoover Mike • USA
SOLO • 1978 • Williams Tony • ASL, NZL
SOLO • 1984 • Dayton Lyman D. • USA
SOLO ANDATA (ITL) see **ALLER SIMPLE, UN** • 1970
SOLO ANTE EL STREAKING • 1975 • Saenz De Heredia Jose Luis • SPN
SOLO CONTRO ROMA • 1962 • Ricci Luciano, Freda Riccardo (U/c) • ITL • VENGEANCE OF THE GLADIATOR (UKN) ○ ALONE AGAINST ROME ○ FALL OF ROME, THE
SOLO CONTRO TUTTI • 1965 • del Amo Antonio • ITL, SPN • HIJO DE JESSE JAMES, EL (SPN)
SOLO DE NOCHE VIENES • 1965 • Vejar Sergio • MXC, GTM
SOLO DIO MI FERMERA • 1957 • Polselli Renato • ITL
SOLO FLIGHT • 1967 • Rowe George • PHL
SOLO FLIGHT • 1975 • Mills Ian • ASL
SOLO FOR ELEPHANT AND ORCHESTRA • 1975 • Lipsky Oldrich • CZC, USS
SOLO FOR SPARROW • 1962 • Flemyng Gordon • UKN
SOLO GRAND AMORE, UN • 1972 • Guerin Claudio • ITL
SOLO LOS DOS • 1968 • Lucia Luis • SPN • BOTH ALONE
SOLO PARA HOMBRES • 1960 • Fernan-Gomez Fernando • SPN
SOLO PARA MARIDOS • 1952 • Soler Fernando • MXC
SOLO PARA TI • 1966 • Cisneros Icaro • MXC
SOLO PER TE • 1937 • Gallone Carmine • ITL, FRG • MUTTERLIED (FRG) ○ ONLY FOR THEE (USA)
SOLO PER TE LUCIA • 1956 • Rossi Franco • ITL
SOLO SAILOR, THE • 1987 • Zschoche Hermann • GDR
SOLO SUNNY • 1979 • Wolf Konrad, Kohlhaase Wolfgang • GDR
SOLO UN ATAUD • 1966 • Alcocer Santos • SPN, FRN • ORGIES DU DOCTEUR ORLOFF, LES (FRN) ○ ORGIES OF DR. ORLOFF, THE ○ ONLY A COFFIN
SOLO UN BACIO • 1983 • Manuli Guido • ANS • ITL
SOLO VERACRUZ ES BELLO • 1948 • Bustillo Oro Juan • MXC
SOLO ZU VIERT see **MEINE FRAU MACHT MUSIK** • 1958
SOLOMON AND SHEBA • 1959 • Vidor King • USA
SOLOMON IN SOCIETY • 1922 • Windom Lawrence C. • USA • HOUSE OF SOLOMON
SOLOMON NORTHRUP'S ODYSSEY • 1984 • Parks Gordon • TVM • USA • HALF-SLAVE, HALF-FREE
SOLOMON'S HEART see **SERDCE SOLOMONA** • 1932
SOLOMON'S RING see **KHATEM SULEIMAN** • 1947
SOLOMON'S SON • 1912 • *Walthall William* • USA
SOLOMON'S TWINS • 1916 • Gilbert Lewis, Frenguelli Alfonse • UKN
SOLOS EN LA MADRUGADA • 1978 • Garci Jose Luis • SPN • ALONE IN THE EARLY HOURS OF THE MORNING ○ ALONE AT DAYBREAK
SOLOTISTAJA DOLINA • 1937 • Shengelaya Nikolai • USS • GOLDEN VALLEY, THE ○ ORANGE VALLEY
SOLOVKI POWER • 1988 • Goldovskia Marina • DOC • USS
SOLSKINSDALEN • 1924 • Gregers Emanuel • DNM
SOLSTANZ • 1975 • Paakspuu Kalli • CND
SOLSTIK • 1953 • Henning-Jensen Bjarne, Henning-Jensen Astrid • DNM
SOLTAN GHALBHA • 1968 • Fardeen Mohamad Ali • IRN • HEART'S KINGDOM
SOLTANTO UN BACIO • 1942 • Simonelli Giorgio C. • ITL
SOLTERA Y CON GEMELOS • 1945 • Salvador Jaime • MXC
SOLTERA Y MADRE EN AL VIDA • 1969 • Aguirre Javier • SPN
SOLTERO • 1985 • de Castro Pio • PHL
SOLTERO, EL • 1977 • Borcosque Carlos Jr. • ARG • BACHELOR, THE
SOLTERO DIFICIL, UN • 1950 • Tamayo Manuel • SPN
SOLTERO Y PADRE EN LA VIDA • 1975 • Aguirre Javier • SPN
SOLTERONES, LOS • 1952 • Delgado Miguel M. • MXC
SOLTEROS DE VERANO • 1961 • Balcazar Alfonso • SPN
SOLUNA • 1967 • Madanes Marcos • ARG
SOLUNSKI ATENTATORI • 1961 • Mitrovic Zika • YGS • SOLANIKA TERRORISTS, THE
SOLUTION BUERRE DE PINOTTES, LA see **PEANUT BUTTER SOLUTION, THE** • 1986
SOLUTION BY PHONE • 1954 • Travers Alfred • UKN
SOLUTION OF THE MYSTERY, THE • 1915 • Eason B. Reeves • USA
SOLUTIONS FRANCAISES • 1939 • Painleve Jean • SHT • FRN
SOLV • 1956 • Roos Jorgen • DOC • DNM
SOLV GIVER ARBEJDE • 1942 • Skot-Hansen Mogens • SHT • DNM
SOLVA SAAL • 1958 • *Burman S. D. (M)* • IND
SOLVAY DOSSIER, THE see **GEHEIMAKTEN SOLVAY** • 1952
SOLVDAASEN MED JUVELERNE • 1910 • *Blom August* • DNM • JEWEL CASE, THE
SOLVEIG ET LE VIOLON TURC • 1974 • Grand-Jouan Jean-Jacques • FRN
SOLVING THE BOND THEFT • 1910 • *Yankee* • USA
SOLVING THE PUZZLE see **CHAMPION DU JEU A LA MODE, LE** • 1910

SOLVMUNN • 1982 • Blom Per • NRW • SILVER MOUTH
SOLYARIS • 1972 • Tarkovsky Andrei • USS • SOLARIS
SOLZHENITSYN'S CHILDREN.. ARE MAKING A LOT OF NOISE IN PARIS • 1978 • Rubbo Michael • CND
SOM ABSTRATO • 1958 • Miller Roberto • BRZ • SOUND ABSTRACT
SOM DU VILL HA MEJ • 1943 • Cederlund Gosta • SWD • AS YOU LIKE ME
SOM EN TJUV OM NATTEN • 1940 • Arvedson Ragnar, Larsson Borje • SWD • LIKE A THIEF IN THE NIGHT
SOM FALLEN FRAN SKYARNA see **PROFESSOR POPPES PRILLIGA PRILLERIER** • 1944
SOM FOLK AR MEST • 1944 • Ekman Hasse • SWD • LIKE MOST PEOPLE
SOM HAVETS NAKNA VIND • 1968 • Hoglund Gunnar • SWD • ONE SWEDISH SUMMER (USA) ○ AS THE NAKED WIND FROM THE SEA ○ NAKED WINDS OF THE SEA, THE ○ NAKED AS THE WIND FROM THE SEA
SOM HON BADDAR FAR HAN LIGGA • 1970 • Hoglund Gunnar • SWD, FRG • NACH STOCKHOLM DER LIEBE WEGEN ○ DO YOU BELIEVE IN SWEDISH SIN
SOM I DROMMAR • 1954 • Gyllenberg Carl • SWD • AS IN DREAMS
SOM MAN BADDAR • 1957 • Larsson Borje • SWD • AS YOU MAKE YOUR BED
SOM NATT OCH DAG • 1969 • Cornell Jonas • SWD • LIKE NIGHT AND DAY
SOMA DAISAKU • 1929 • Inagaki Hiroshi • JPN • GREAT PALISADE, THE
SOMAEND PA SENGEKANTEN • 1976 • Hilbard John • DNM
SOMBRA BLANCA, LA • 1963 • Fernandez Fernando • MXC
SOMBRA DE CHUCHO EL ROTO, LA • 1944 • Galindo Alejandro • MXC
SOMBRA DE CRUZ DIABLO, LA • 1954 • Orona Vicente • MXC
SOMBRA DE LOS HIJOS, LA • 1963 • Baledon Rafael • MXC
SOMBRA DE PANCHO VILLA, LA see **REVOLUCION** • 1932
SOMBRA DE UM SORRISO, A see **TORMENTO** • 1972
SOMBRA DEL CAUDILLO, LA • 1960 • Bracho Julio • MXC
SOMBRA DEL MANO NEGRA, LA • 1963 • Crevenna Alfredo B. • MXC
SOMBRA DEL MURCIELAGO, LA • 1966 • Curiel Federico • MXC • SHADOW OF THE BAT, THE
SOMBRA DEL OTRO, LA • 1957 • Martinez Solares Gilberto • MXC
SOMBRA DEL ZORRO, LA • 1962 • Romero-Marchent Joaquin Luis • SPN
SOMBRA EN DEFENSA DE LA JUVENTUD, LA • 1959 • Salvador Jaime • MXC
SOMBRA EN LA VENTANA, UNA • 1944 • Iquino Ignacio F. • SPN
SOMBRA EN MI DESTINO, UNA • 1944 • Gout Alberto • MXC
SOMBRA, THE SPIDER WOMAN • 1947 • Bennet Spencer Gordon, Brannon Fred C. • USA
SOMBRA VENGADORA, LA • 1954 • Baledon Rafael • MXC
SOMBRA VENGADORA VS. LA MANO NEGRA, LA • 1954 • Baledon Rafael • MXC
SOMBRA VERDE • 1954 • Gavaldon Roberto • MXC
SOMBRAS DE BUENOS AIRES • 1939 • Irigoyen Julio • ARG
SOMBRAS DE CIRCO • 1931 • Millar Adelqui • SPN
SOMBRAS DE GLORIA • 1930 • Stone Andrew L. • USA
SOMBRE DE UN GIRASOL, LA see **CRISIS** • 1968
SOMBRE DIMANCHE • 1948 • Audry Jacqueline • FRN • CHANSON QUI TUE, LA ○ GLOOMY SUNDAY
SOMBRE ILUMINADA, LA • 1948 • Serrano De Osma Carlos • SPN
SOMBRERO • 1952 • Foster Norman • USA
SOMBRERO, EL • 1964 • Balser Robert • ANS • SPN • HAT, THE (USA)
SOMBRERO DE TRES PICOS, EL • 1943 • Bustillo Oro Juan • MXC
SOMBRERO DE TRES PICOS, EL see **TRAVIESA MOLIERNA, LA** • 1935
SOMBRERO KID, THE • 1942 • Sherman George • USA
SOMBRERON, EL • 1950 • GTM
SOMBRES VACANCES see **AGRESSION, L'** • 1974
SOME ACTIVITIES OF THE BERMONDSEY BOROUGH COUNCIL • 1931 • Bush H. W. • UKN
SOME ACTORS • 1915 • Kellino W. P. • UKN
SOME AMERICAN FEMINISTS • 1977 • Guilbeault Luce • CND
SOME ARE SO LUCKY • 1970 • Bonniere Rene • SHT • CND
SOME ARTIST see **CHARITY** • 1919
SOME BABY • 1915 • Roach Hal • USA
SOME BABY • 1917 • *Victor* • SHT • USA
SOME BABY • 1917 • *Ebony* • SHT • USA
SOME BABY • 1918 • Seiter William A. • SHT • USA
SOME BABY • 1922 • Roach Hal • SHT • USA
SOME BLONDES ARE DANGEROUS • 1937 • Carruth Milton • USA • BLONDE DYNAMITE
SOME BOXER • 1916 • Metcalfe Earl • SHT • USA
SOME BOY • 1914 • *Joker* • USA
SOME BOY • 1917 • Turner Otis • USA
SOME BRAVERY • 1916 • *Turpin Ben* • SHT • USA
SOME BRIDE • 1919 • Otto Henry • USA
SOME BULL'S DAUGHTER • 1914 • *Mace Fred* • USA
SOME CALL IT LOVING • 1973 • Harris James B. • USA • DREAM CASTLES ○ DREAM CASTLE
SOME CAME RUNNING • 1958 • Minnelli Vincente • USA
SOME CAVE MAN • 1918 • *Vernon Bobby* • USA
SOME CHAMPS • 1920 • *Cohn Productions* • USA
SOME CHAPERONE • 1915 • Christie Al • USA
SOME CHICKEN • 1916 • Wolbert William • SHT • USA
SOME COLLECTORS • 1914 • Smalley Phillips • USA
SOME COP • 1914 • *De Forrest Charles* • USA
SOME CROOKS • 1914 • *Prescott Vivian* • USA
SOME DANCER • 1917 • Evans Fred, Evans Joe • UKN
SOME DAY • 1935 • Powell Michael • UKN • YOUNG NOWHERES
SOME DECORATORS • 1914 • *Ab* • USA
SOME DETECTIVE! • 1916 • *E & R Jungle Film* • SHT • USA
SOME DETECTIVES • 1916 • Haldane Bert • UKN
SOME DO IT FOR MONEY, SOME DO IT FOR FUN • 1979 • Kramreither Anthony • CND
SOME DOCTOR • 1913 • *Punch* • USA
SOME DOCTOR • 1917 • Jackson Harry • SHT • USA
SOME DOINGS • 1914 • *Crystal* • USA
SOME DOINGS AT LONESOME RANCH • 1913 • *Frontier* • USA
SOME DUEL • 1915 • Baker George D. • USA
SOME DUEL • 1916 • Mix Tom • SHT • USA
SOME ELOPERS • 1913 • *Lubin* • USA
SOME EVENING see **MERRY NIGHT, A** • 1914
SOME FARAWAY LIGHT • 1969 • Lesic Josip • YGS
SOME FISH! • 1914 • Aylott Dave • UKN
SOME FISH • 1916 • *Powers* • SHT • USA
SOME FISH! • 1916 • Buss Harry • UKN
SOME FIXER • 1915 • Christie Al • USA
SOME FOOLS THERE WERE • 1913 • *La Badie Florence* • USA
SOME FUN • 1915 • Evans Fred, Evans Joe • UKN
SOME GAL • 1919 • *Guinan Texas* • SHT • USA
SOME GIRLS • 1988 • Hoffman Michael • UKN • SISTERS
SOME GIRLS DO • 1969 • Thomas Ralph • UKN
SOME GO TO THE MAAZOUN TWICE • 1978 • Aziz Mohamed Abdel • EGY
SOME GOOD IN ALL • 1911 • *Costello Dolores* • USA
SOME GYPSIES ARE HAPPY see **SKUPLJACI PERJA** • 1967
SOME HERO • 1914 • *Prescott Vivian* • USA
SOME HERO • 1916 • *Perez Tweedledum* • SHT • USA
SOME HEROES • 1916 • Clements Roy • SHT • USA
SOME HONEYMOON • 1916 • Christie Al • SHT • USA
SOME JOB • 1918 • Santell Alfred • SHT • USA
SOME JUDGE • 1918 • Richmond J. A. • SHT • USA
SOME KID • 1916 • *Compson Betty* • SHT • USA
SOME KIND OF A NUT • 1969 • Kanin Garson • USA • ONE WITH THE FUZZ, THE
SOME KIND OF HERO • 1972 • Lichtner Marvin • UKN
SOME KIND OF HERO • 1982 • Pressman Michael • USA
SOME KIND OF MIRACLE • 1979 • Freedman Jerrold • TVM • USA
SOME KIND OF NUT see **DOWN AMONG THE Z MEN** • 1952
SOME KIND OF WONDERFUL • 1987 • Deutch Howard • USA
SOME LIAR • 1919 • King Henry • USA
SOME LIARS • 1916 • Miller Rube • SHT • USA
SOME LIKE IT COLD see **A NOI PIACE FREDDO..!** • 1960
SOME LIKE IT COOL • 1961 • Winner Michael • UKN
SOME LIKE IT COOL (USA) see **CASANOVA E COMPAGNI** • 1978
SOME LIKE IT HOT • 1939 • Archainbaud George • USA • RHYTHM ROMANCE
SOME LIKE IT HOT • 1959 • Wilder Billy • USA
SOME LIKE IT HOT see **I'M COLD** • 1954
SOME LIKE IT ROUGH • 1944 • Massingham Richard • UKN
SOME LIKE IT SEXY see **COME BACK PETER** • 1969
SOME LIKE IT VIOLENT • 1968 • Horulu Kemal • USA
SOME LITTLE THINGS OUR TOMMIES LEAVE BEHIND THEM • 1914 • Bocchi Arrigo • UKN
SOME LUCK • 1913 • *Belmont Claude* • USA
SOME MAY LIVE • 1967 • Sewell Vernon • UKN • IN SAIGON: SOME MAY LIVE
SOME MEDICINE MAN • 1916 • Clements Roy • SHT • USA
SOME MONKEY BUSINESS • 1915 • *Mina* • USA
SOME MONKEY BUSINESS see **PIMPLE'S MONKEY BUSINESS** • 1916
SOME MORE OF SAMOA • 1941 • Lord Del • SHT • USA
SOME MOTHER • 1919 • *Strand* • SHT • USA
SOME MOTHER-IN-LAW • 1911 • *Hotely Mae* • USA
SOME MOTHER'S BOY • 1929 • Worne Duke • USA
SOME NATIVES OF CHURCHILL • 1973 • Scott Cynthia • MTV • CND
SOME NERVE • 1913 • Sennett Mack • USA
SOME NERVE see **GENTLEMEN OF NERVE** • 1914
SOME NIGHT • 1916 • Dillon John Francis • USA
SOME NIGHT-MARE • 1914 • *Asher Max* • USA
SOME NIGHTMARE • 1915 • Blystone John G. • SHT • USA
SOME NURSE • 1917 • Curtis Allen • *Strand* • SHT • USA
SOME NURSE • 1917 • Curtis Allen • *Joker* • SHT • USA
SOME OF MY BEST FRIENDS ARE.. • 1971 • Nelson Mervyn • USA • BAR, THE
SOME OF OUR RELATIONS • 1906 • Jeapes Harold • UKN
SOME OF THE PALESTINIANS • 1976 • Hassan Mamoun • UNN, JRD
SOME OF US MAY DIE see **JOURNEY, THE** • 1958
SOME OTHER WOMAN see **NEKA DRUGA ZENA** • 1981
SOME PEOPLE • 1962 • Donner Clive • UKN
SOME PICNIC • 1920 • Washer Frederick H. • UKN
SOME PROFESSOR • 1918 • Jackson Harry • SHT • USA
SOME PULL • 1914 • *Crystal* • USA
SOME PUMPKIN see **KOTSUMA NANKIN** • 1960
SOME PUN'KINS • 1925 • Storm Jerome • USA
SOME RODEO • 1918 • *Christie* • USA
SOME ROGUES AND THE GIRL • 1914 • *Reliance* • USA
SOME ROMANCE • 1915 • *Hamilton Lloyd V.* • USA
SOME RUNNER • 1913 • *Lyons Eddie* • USA
SOME SCOUT • 1927 • Sandrich Mark • SHT • USA
SOME SHIMMIERS • 1920 • Lyons Eddie, Moran Lee • SHT • USA
SOME SHOOTER • 1920 • Gibson Ed Hoot • SHT • USA
SOME SHOW • 1930 • Meins Gus • SHT • USA
SOME SNUFF see **AH! AHH! TISHOO!!!** • 1914
SOME SPECIMENS • 1917 • Chaudet Louis W. • SHT • USA
SOME STATUE • 1917 • Hunter T. Hayes • SHT • USA
SOME STEAMER SCOOPING • 1914 • Costello Maurice • USA
SOME UNIMPORTANT DEAD PEOPLE see **UNOS MUERTOS SIN IMPORTANCIA** • 1977
SOME WAITER! • 1916 • Carney George • UKN
SOME WHITE HOPE? • 1915 • Ince Ralph • USA
SOME WILD OATS • 1920 • Williams C. Jay • USA
SOME WILL, SOME WON'T • 1970 • Wood Duncan • UKN
SOMEBODY CARES • 1967 • Pacheco Lauro • PHL
SOMEBODY IS A TRAITOR see **QUALCUNO HA TRADITO** • 1967
SOMEBODY KILLED HER HUSBAND • 1978 • Johnson Lamont • USA
SOMEBODY LIED • 1917 • Wilson Ben • SHT • USA
SOMEBODY LIED • 1920 • Lyons Eddie, Moran Lee • SHT • USA
SOMEBODY LIED • 1923 • Roberts Stephen (c/d) • SHT • USA
SOMEBODY LOVES ME • 1952 • Brecher Irving S. • USA
SOMEBODY STOLE MY GAL • 1931 • Fleischer Dave • ANS • USA
SOMEBODY UP THERE LIKES ME • 1956 • Wise Robert • USA
SOMEBODY'S BABY • 1915 • *United Film Service* • USA
SOMEBODY'S BABY • 1918 • *Mason Billy* • SHT • USA
SOMEBODY'S DARLING • 1925 • Cooper George A. • UKN
SOMEBODY'S FAULT • 1927 • Taurog Norman • SHT • USA
SOMEBODY'S MOTHER • 1911 • *Lubin* • USA
SOMEBODY'S MOTHER • 1926 • Apfel Oscar • USA
SOMEBODY'S SISTER • 1914 • Martin E. A. • USA
SOMEBODY'S STOLEN OUR RUSSIAN SPY • 1975 • Ward James, Madrid Luis • UKN, SWT
SOMEBODY'S STOLEN THE THIGH OF JUPITER see **ON A VOLE LA CUISSE DE JUPITER** • 1979
SOMEBODY'S WAITING FOR ME • 1931 • Pearson George • SHT • UKN
SOMEBODY'S WIDOW • 1918 • Sidney Scott • USA
SOMEBODY'S WIFIE • 1917 • *Triangle* • USA
SOMEDAY SOON • 1977 • Haldane Don • MTV • CND
SOMEHOW GOOD • 1927 • Raymond Jack • UKN
SOMEONE • 1968 • Rocco Pat • USA
SOMEONE AT THE DOOR • 1936 • Brenon Herbert • UKN
SOMEONE AT THE DOOR • 1950 • Searle Francis • UKN
SOMEONE AT THE DOOR • 1986 • Nikolov Milen • BUL
SOMEONE AT THE TOP OF THE STAIRS • 1974 • Sichel John • TVM • UKN • KISS KISS, KILL KILL (USA)
SOMEONE BEHIND THE DOOR (USA) see **QUALCUNO DIETRO LA PORTA** • 1971
SOMEONE ELSE'S CHILDREN see **CHUZHIE DETI** • 1959
SOMEONE ELSE'S JACKET • 1927 • Ships Boris • USS
SOMEONE FOR THE WELFARE • 1973 • Barraclough Jenny • UKN
SOMEONE I TOUCHED • 1975 • Antonio Lou • TVM • USA
SOMEONE IN THE HOUSE • 1920 • Ince John • USA
SOMEONE IS BLEEDING (UKN) see **SEINS DE GLACE, LES** • 1974
SOMEONE IS WATCHING ME! • 1978 • Carpenter John • TVM • USA
SOMEONE LIKE YOU • 1978 • De Witt Elmo • SAF • IEMAND SOOS JY
SOMEONE MUST PAY • 1919 • Abramson Ivan • USA
SOMEONE, SOMEWHERE (USA) see **QUELQUE PART QUELQU'UN** • 1972
SOMEONE TO LOVE • 1928 • Jones F. Richard • USA
SOMEONE TO LOVE • 1987 • Jaglom Henry • USA
SOMEONE TO REMEMBER • 1943 • Siodmak Robert • USA
SOMEONE TO WATCH OVER ME • 1987 • Scott Ridley • USA
SOMEONE TO WATCH OVER ME see **STRANGE VENGEANCE OF ROSALIE, THE** • 1972
SOMEONE'S BUZZING, OPEN THE DOOR see **ZVONYAT, OTKROYTE DVER** • 1965
SOMEONE'S KILLING THE WORLD'S GREATEST MODELS see **SHE'S DRESSED TO KILL** • 1979
SOMER • 1975 • SAF
SOMEREN JEG FYLTE FEMTEN, DEN • 1976 • Andersen Knut • NRW • SUMMER I BECAME 15, THE
SOMERSAULT see **SARIKAT SAYFEYA** • 1987
SOMERSAULT OF LIFE see **JINSEI TOMBOGAERI** • 1946
SOMERSET MAUGHAM'S QUARTET see **QUARTET** • 1948
SOMETHING ABOUT AMELIA • 1984 • Haines Randa • TVM • USA
SOMETHING ABOUT LOVE • 1988 • Berry Thomas • CND
SOMETHING ABOUT PEACE • 1984 • Bedel Jean-Pierre • MTV • CND • TOUT CA POUR LA PAIX
SOMETHING ALWAYS HAPPENS • 1928 • Tuttle Frank • USA
SOMETHING ALWAYS HAPPENS • 1934 • Powell Michael • UKN
SOMETHING BEAUTIFUL • 1977 • Umboh Wim • INN
SOMETHING BEAUTIFUL see **VALAMI SZEP** • 1971
SOMETHING BIG • 1972 • McLaglen Andrew V. • USA • GUN THAT SHOOK THE WEST, THE
SOMETHING BLONDE see **AURORA** • 1984
SOMETHING CREEPING IN THE DARK see **QUALCOSA STRISCIA NEL BUIO** • 1971
SOMETHING DIFFERENT • 1920 • Neill R. William • USA
SOMETHING DIFFERENT • Kovasznai Gyorgy • ANS • HNG
SOMETHING DIFFERENT see **O NECEM JINEM** • 1963
SOMETHING ELSE see **O NECEM JINEM** • 1963
SOMETHING ELSE -ENTIRELY see **NOE HELT ANNET** • 1985
SOMETHING EVIL • 1970 • Spielberg Steven • TVM • USA
SOMETHING FOR A LONELY MAN • 1968 • Taylor Don • TVM • USA
SOMETHING FOR ALICE see **NECO Z ALENKY** • 1987
SOMETHING FOR EVERYONE • 1970 • Prince Harold • USA • BLACK FLOWERS FOR THE BRIDE ○ COOK, THE ○ ROOK, THE
SOMETHING FOR JOEY • 1977 • Antonio Lou • TVM • USA • QUESTION OF LIFE, A
SOMETHING FOR THE BIRDS • 1952 • Wise Robert • USA
SOMETHING FOR THE BOYS • 1944 • Seiler Lewis • USA
SOMETHING IN BETWEEN see **NESTO ISMEDJU** • 1983
SOMETHING IN COMMON • 1986 • Jordan Glenn • TVM • USA
SOMETHING IN HER EYE • 1915 • *Hardy Oliver* • USA
SOMETHING IN THE AIR see **NECO JE VE VZDUCHU** • 1981
SOMETHING IN THE CITY • 1921 • Gordon Edward R. • UKN
SOMETHING IN THE CITY • 1950 • Rogers Maclean • UKN
SOMETHING IN THE WIND • 1916 • Phillips Bertram • UKN
SOMETHING IN THE WIND • 1947 • Pichel Irving • USA
SOMETHING IS CRAWLING IN THE DARK (USA) see **QUALCOSA STRISCIA NEL BUIO** • 1971
SOMETHING IS DRIFTING ON THE WATER see **HRST VODY** • 1971
SOMETHING IS OUT THERE • 1988 • Colla Richard A. • TVM • USA
SOMETHING IS OUT THERE see **DAY OF THE ANIMALS** • 1977
SOMETHING JUST AS GOOD • 1915 • *World* • USA
SOMETHING LIKE A BAG • 1915 • Wilson Frank? • UKN
SOMETHING LIKE THE TRUTH see **OFFENCE, THE** • 1973
SOMETHING MONEY CAN'T BUY • 1952 • Jackson Pat • UKN
SOMETHING NEW • 1920 • Shipman Nell, Van Tuyle Bert • USA
SOMETHING NICE TO EAT • 1967 • Erulkar Sarah • SHT • UKN
SOMETHING OF VALUE • 1957 • Brooks Richard • USA • AFRICA ABLAZE

SOMETHING OLD -SOMETHING NEW • 1977 • Thoms Albie • DOC • ASL
SOMETHING ROTTEN IN HAVANA • 1913 • *Essanay* • USA
SOMETHING SHORT OF PARADISE • 1979 • Helpern David Jr. • USA
SOMETHING SIMPLE • 1934 • Parrott Charles, Weems Walter • SHT • USA
SOMETHING SO RIGHT • 1982 • Antonio Lou • TVM • USA
SOMETHING SPECIAL see **WILLY MILLY** • 1985
SOMETHING TO ADORE • 1914 • Williams C. Jay • USA
SOMETHING TO CELEBRATE • 1983 • Brittain Don • CND
SOMETHING TO DO • 1919 • Crisp Donald • USA
SOMETHING TO HIDE • 1971 • Reid Alastair • UKN • SHATTERED
SOMETHING TO LIVE FOR • 1952 • Stevens George • USA • MR. AND MRS. ANONYMOUS
SOMETHING TO LIVE FOR see **FORGOTTEN FACES** • 1936
SOMETHING TO SHOUT ABOUT • 1943 • Ratoff Gregory • USA
SOMETHING TO SING ABOUT • 1937 • Schertzinger Victor • USA • BATTLING HOOFER
SOMETHING TO THINK ABOUT • 1920 • De Mille Cecil B. • USA
SOMETHING TO THINK ABOUT • 1962 • Casparius Hans G. • UKN
SOMETHING VENTURED • 1977 • Pearson Peter (c/d) • CND
SOMETHING WAITS IN THE DARK see **ISOLA DEGLI UOMINI PESCE, L'** • 1979
SOMETHING WEIRD • 1968 • Lewis Herschell G. • USA
SOMETHING WENT BUMP • 1970 • Urban Ivan, Stepanek Miroslav, Pojar Bretislav • ANS • CZC
SOMETHING WICKED • 1982 • McDuffie Brian (U/c) • ASL • EARLY FROST
SOMETHING WICKED THIS WAY COMES • 1983 • Clayton Jack • USA
SOMETHING WILD • 1961 • Garfein Jack • USA
SOMETHING WILD • 1986 • Demme Jonathan • USA
SOMETHING WITH CLAWS see **DARK INTRUDER, THE** • 1965
SOMETHING WORTH REMEMBERING see **FULFILLMENT, SOMETHING WORTH REMEMBERING** • 1969
SOMETHING WRONG WITH BESSIE • 1912 • *Kalem* • USA
SOMETHING'S GOTTA GIVE • 1962 • Cukor George • USA
SOMETHING'S HAPPENING see **HIPPIE REVOLT, THE** • 1967
SOMETHING'S ROTTEN • 1979 • Frost Harvey • CND
SOMETHING'S WRONG • 1978 • Raphael Frederic • MTV • UKN
SOMETIME SWEET SUSAN • 1974 • *Reems Harry* • USA
SOMETIMES A GREAT NOTION • 1971 • Newman Paul • USA • NEVER GIVE AN INCH (UKN)
SOMETIMES AUNT MARTHA DOES DREADFUL THINGS • 1971 • Casey Thomas • USA • SOMETIMES AUNT MARTHA DOES TERRIBLE THINGS
SOMETIMES AUNT MARTHA DOES TERRIBLE THINGS see **SOMETIMES AUNT MARTHA DOES DREADFUL THINGS** • 1971
SOMETIMES EVEN THE BRAVE CRY see **KAPOTE KLENE KE I DONATI** • 1967
SOMETIMES GOOD • 1934 • Kellino W. P. • UKN
SOMETIMES IT WORKS • 1914 • Murphy J. A. • USA
SOMETIMES YOU REMEMBER see **TY INOGDA VSPOMINAY** • 1977
SOMEWHERE A VOICE IS CALLING • 1929 • Aylott Dave, Symmons E. F. • SHT • UKN
SOMEWHERE BENEATH THE WIDE SKY see **KONO HIROI SORA NO DOTOKA NI** • 1954
SOMEWHERE BEYOND LOVE see **DELITTO D'AMORE** • 1974
SOMEWHERE DAY, SOMEWHERE NIGHT see **KAHIN DIN KAHIN RAAT** • 1968
SOMEWHERE I HAVE A SON • 1962 • Voitetsky Artur • USS
SOMEWHERE I'LL FIND HIM see **THESE WILDER YEARS** • 1956
SOMEWHERE I'LL FIND YOU • 1942 • Ruggles Wesley • USA • RED LIGHT
SOMEWHERE IN ANY PLACE • 1917 • Semon Larry • SHT • USA
SOMEWHERE IN BERLIN (USA) see **IRGENDWO IN BERLIN** • 1946
SOMEWHERE IN CAMP • 1942 • Blakeley John E. • UKN
SOMEWHERE IN CIVVIES • 1943 • Rogers Maclean • UKN
SOMEWHERE IN DREAMLAND • 1936 • Fleischer Dave • ANS • USA
SOMEWHERE IN EGYPT • 1943 • Davis Mannie • ANS • USA
SOMEWHERE IN ENGLAND • 1940 • Blakeley John E. • UKN
SOMEWHERE IN EUROPE • 1988 • Cruchten Paul • SHT • LXM
SOMEWHERE IN EUROPE see **VALAHOL EUROPABAN** • 1947
SOMEWHERE IN FRANCE • 1915 • Watts Tom • UKN
SOMEWHERE IN FRANCE • 1916 • Giblyn Charles • USA
SOMEWHERE IN FRANCE (USA) see **FOREMAN WENT TO FRANCE, THE** • 1942
SOMEWHERE IN GEORGIA • 1916 • Ridgwell George • USA
SOMEWHERE IN HOLLAND see **ERGENS IN NEDERLAND** • 1940
SOMEWHERE IN MEXICO • 1916 • *Perez Tweedledum* • USA
SOMEWHERE IN MEXICO • 1917 • *Vim* • USA
SOMEWHERE IN PARIS • 1938 • Schwarzwald Milton • USA
SOMEWHERE IN POLITICS • 1949 • Blakeley John E. • UKN
SOMEWHERE IN SAHARA see **SAHARA** • 1943
SOMEWHERE IN SOMEWHERE • 1925 • Roach Hal • SHT • USA
SOMEWHERE IN SONORA • 1927 • Rogell Albert S. • USA
SOMEWHERE IN SONORA • 1933 • Wright Mack V. • USA
SOMEWHERE IN THE CITY see **BACKFIRE** • 1950
SOMEWHERE IN THE MOUNTAINS • 1917 • Fahrney Milton • USA
SOMEWHERE IN THE NIGHT • 1946 • Mankiewicz Joseph L. • USA
SOMEWHERE IN THE PACIFIC • 1942 • Davis Mannie • ANS • USA
SOMEWHERE IN TIME • 1980 • Szwarc Jeannot • USA
SOMEWHERE IN TURKEY • 1918 • Roach Hal • SHT • USA
SOMEWHERE IN WRONG • 1925 • Pembroke Scott • SHT • USA
SOMEWHERE MY LOVE • 1967 • de Guzman Armando • PHL
SOMEWHERE ON LEAVE • 1942 • Blakeley John E. • UKN
SOMEWHERE ON THE BATTLEFIELD • 1916 • Henley Hobart • SHT • USA
SOMEWHERE TO GO see **STED AT VAERE, ET** • 1960
SOMEWHERE TOMORROW • 1983 • Wiemer Robert • USA
SOMEWHERE UNDER THE BROAD SKY see **KONO HIROI SORA NO DOTOKA NI** • 1954
SOMEWHERE UP NORTH • 1953 • Barfod Bent • ANS • DNM
SOMHLOLO • 1985 • SAF • SOMOHOLO
SOMHLOLO 2 • 1985 • SAF
SOMMAR OCH SYNDARE • 1960 • Mattsson Arne • SWD, DNM • SUMMER AND SINNERS
SOMMARAVENTYR, ETT • 1965 • Ersgard Hakan • SWD • ... DA SKA DU FA EN GUNGSTOL AV MIG -EN BLA ○ ANNA, MY DARLING (USA)
SOMMARDANSEN see **HON DANSADE EN SOMMAR** • 1951
SOMMAREN MED MONIKA • 1953 • Bergman Ingmar • SWD • SUMMER WITH MONIKA (UKN) ○ MONIKA (USA)
SOMMARENS TROMPET • 1975 • Axelman Torbjorn • SWD • SUMMER TRUMPET, A
SOMMARFLICKAN • 1956 • Engel Thomas, Bergstrom Hakan • SWD, FRG • SCHWEDENMADEL (FRG) ○ GIRL FOR THE SUMMER
SOMMARLEK • 1951 • Bergman Ingmar • SWD • ILLICIT INTERLUDE (USA) ○ SUMMER INTERLUDE (UKN)
SOMMARNATTENS LEENDE • 1955 • Bergman Ingmar • SWD • SMILES OF A SUMMER'S NIGHT (UKN)
SOMMARNATTER I SKARGARDEN see **KARLEK OCH DYNAMIT** • 1933
SOMMARNOJE SOKES • 1957 • Ekman Hasse • SWD • SUMMER PLACE IS WANTED, A
SOMMARSAGA, EN • 1912 • Sjostrom Victor • SWD • SUMMER TALE, A
SOMMARSAGA, EN • 1941 • Sucksdorff Arne • DOC • SWD • SUMMER'S TALE, A ○ SUMMER TALE, A
SOMMARTAG • 1961 • Troell Jan • DOC • SWD • SUMMER TRAIN
SOMME, DIE • 1930 • Paul Heinz • FRG
SOMME, THE • 1927 • Wetherell M. A. • UKN
SOMMEIL D'ALBERTINE, LE • 1945 • Ledoc Jean • SHT • FRN
SOMMER • 1974 • During Jan Erik • NRW • SUMMER
SOMMER, DEN MAN NIE VERGISST, EIN • 1959 • Jacobs Werner • FRG • TRANEN IN DEINEN AUGEN
SOMMER, SINNE, ERIKA • 1939 • Hansen Rolf • FRG
SOMMERFUGLER • 1972 • Boger Chris • NRW • SUMMER OF SILENCE ○ BUTTERFLY AUTUMN
SOMMERGASTE • 1976 • Stein Peter • FRG • SUMMER GUESTS (UKN)
SOMMERIDYLLE • 1916 • Fleck Jacob, Fleck Luise • AUS
SOMMERKRIG • 1965 • Kjaerulff-Schmidt Palle • DNM • SUMMER WAR
SOMMERLIEBE • 1942 • Engel Erich • FRG
SOMMERLIEBE • 1955 • Barrenstein Franz • GDR
SOMMERLIEBE AM BODENSEE • 1957 • von Oertzen Jaspar • FRG
SOMMERNACHTE • 1944 • Ritter Karl • FRG
SOMMERNACHTSTRAUM, EIN • 1913 • Rye Stellan • FRG • MIDSUMMER NIGHT'S DREAM, A
SOMMERNACHTSTRAUM, EIN • 1925 • Neumann Hans • FRG • MIDSUMMER NIGHT'S DREAM, A (USA) ○ WOOD LOVE (UKN)
SOMMERSPROSSEN • 1968 • Fornbacher Helmut • FRG, SWT, ITL • BEYOND CONTROL (USA) ○ FRECKLES ○ WHAT A WAY TO DIE!
SOMMES-NOUS DEFENDUS? • 1938 • Loubignac Jean • FRN
SOMNABUL • 1929 • Trotz Adolf • FRG • HELLSEHERIN, DIE
SOMNABULIST, THE • 1903 • Collins Alf • UKN • SLEEPWALKER, THE
SOMNABULIST, THE • 1908 • *Essanay* • USA
SOMNABULIST, THE • 1910 • *Nordisk* • DNM
SOMNAMBULES, LES • 1914 • Feuillade Louis • FRN
SOMNAMBULICY • 1957 • Waskowski Mieczyslaw, Nurzynski Antoni • SHT • PLN • SOMNAMBULISTS
SOMNAMBULISMO • 1913 • Caserini Mario • ITL
SOMNAMBULIST, THE • 1911 • *Solax* • USA
SOMNAMBULIST, THE • 1914 • *Chadwick Cyril* • USA
SOMNAMBULISTIC HERO, A • 1909 • *Edison* • USA
SOMNAMBULISTS see **SOMNAMBULICY** • 1957
SOMNAMBULISTS see **SONAMBULOS** • 1978
SOMNIFIA • 1968 • Gonseth Frederic • SWT
SOMOHOLO see **SOMHLOLO** • 1985
SOMOS? • 1982 • Christensen Carlos Hugo • ARG • ARE WE?
SOMOS LOS MEJORES! • 1968 • Padilla Federico • ARG • WE ARE THE BEST
SON • 1914 • *Francis Alec* • USA
SON see **AULAD** • 1968
SON see **BAD BLOOD** • 1989
SON, THE • 1915 • Winter Percy • USA
SON, THE • 1951 • Biggs Julian • CND
SON, THE see **SYN** • 1955
SON, THE see **BONCHI** • 1960
SON, THE see **SYN** • 1970
SON ALTESSE • 1922 • Desfontaines Henri • FRN
SON ALTESSE IMPERIALE • 1933 • Bernard-Derosne Jean, Janson Victor • FRN • TZAREWITCH, LE
SON ALTESSE L'AMOUR • 1931 • Peguy Robert, Schmidt Erich • FRN • SA MAJESTE L'AMOUR
SON ALTESSE ORDONNE see **PRINCESSE, A VOS ORDRES** • 1931
SON ALTESSE VOYAGE see **INCOGNITO** • 1933
SON AUTRE AMOUR • 1933 • Remy Constant, Machard Alfred • FRN • DEDE, SON PERE ET L'AMOUR ○ PAPA
SON AVENTURE • 1919 • Hervil Rene • FRN
SON CARTAS DE AMOR • 1943 • Amadori Luis Cesar • ARG
SON COMES HOME, A • 1936 • Dupont E. A. • USA
SON CONTENTO • 1984 • Ponzi Maurizio • ITL • I'M HAPPY
SON COPAIN see **INCONNUE DE MONTREAL, L'** • 1950
SON CRIME • 1922 • Dieudonne Albert • FRN
SON-DAUGHTER, THE • 1932 • Brown Clarence • USA
SON DERNIER NOEL • 1952 • Daniel-Norman Jacques • FRN
SON DERNIER ROLE • 1945 • Gourguet Jean • FRN
SON ES GROSZ • 1987 • Acs Miklos • HNG • NICE AND BIG
SON ET LUMIERE • 1961 • Beranger • SHT • FRN
SON EXCELLENCE ANTONIN • 1935 • Tavano Charles-Felix • FRN
SON GECE • 1967 • Un Memduh • TRK • LAST NIGHT, THE
SON HATIRA • 1968 • Gorec Ertem • TRK • LAST MEMORIES
SON HEAR MY CRY see **TODOKE HAHA NO SAKEBI** • 1959
SON HEROS • 1918 • Burguet Charles • FRN
SON IMAGE DE LA VILLE • 1977 • Samie Jean-Frederic • DOC • FRN
SON-IN-LAW WHO STAYS ON THE TOP FLOOR, THE see **MAADI VEETU MAAPILLAI** • 1967
SON-IN-LAW'S NIGHTMARE, A • 1912 • *Pathe* • FRN
SON KIZGIN ADAM • 1970 • Davutoglu Zafer • TRK
SON KURBAN • 1967 • Pekmezoglu Oksal • TRK • LAST VICTIM, THE
SON NOM DE VENISES DANS CALCUTTA DESERT • 1976 • Duras Marguerite • FRN
SON O' MINE see **FIGHTING CUB, THE** • 1925
SON O' THE STARS • 1916 • Jaccard Jacques • SHT • USA
SON OF A BADMAN • 1949 • Taylor Ray • USA
SON OF A BITCH • 1979 • Marino Nino • ITL • UOMO AMERICANO, UN
SON OF A BUCCANEER, THE see **FILS DU FLIBUSTIER, LE** • 1922
SON OF A GUN • 1918 • Jones F. Richard • SHT • USA
SON OF A GUN • 1926 • Hurst Paul C. • USA
SON OF A GUN, THE • 1919 • *Anderson Broncho Billy* • USA
SON OF A GUNFIGHTER • 1965 • Landres Paul • USA, SPN • HIJO DEL PISTOLERO, EL (SPN)
SON OF A HUN, THE • 1918 • White Jack • SHT • USA
SON OF A KING see **RAJA VEETU PILLAI** • 1967
SON OF A REBEL CHIEF, THE • 1916 • Mong William V. • SHT • USA
SON OF A SAILOR • 1933 • Bacon Lloyd • USA • SON OF THE GOBS
SON OF A SAMURAI see **SAMURAI NO KO** • 1963
SON OF A STRANGER • 1957 • Morris Ernest • UKN
SON OF ACADEMY LEADER • 1966 • Malanga Gerard • USA
SON OF ALI BABA • 1952 • Neumann Kurt • USA
SON OF ALLAUDIN • 1939 • Vakil Nanubhai • IND
SON OF ALVIN • 1984 • Eastway John • ASL • MELVIN: SON OF ALVIN ○ GIRL-TOY ○ FOREPLAY
SON OF AMR IS DEAD!, THE see **MENSONGE, LE** • 1974
SON OF ATLAS IN THE VALLEY OF LIONS see **URSUS NELLA VALLE DEI LEONI** • 1961
SON OF BELLE STAR • 1953 • McDonald Frank • USA
SON OF BILLY THE KID • 1949 • Taylor Ray • USA
SON OF BIRDMAN • 1969 • *Delta S.f. Group* • SHT • UKN
SON OF BLACK EAGLE, THE see **FIGLIO DI AQUILA NERA, IL** • 1968
SON OF BLOB see **BEWARE! THE BLOB** • 1972
SON OF CAIN, THE • 1916 • Horne James W. • SHT • USA
SON OF CAPTAIN BLOOD, THE(USA) see **HIJO DEL CAPITAN BLOOD, EL** • 1962
SON OF COURAGE • 1930 • Nelson Jack • SHT • USA
SON OF DADA • Preston Richard • ANS • USA
SON OF D'ARTAGNAN (USA) see **FIGLIO DI D'ARTAGNAN, IL** • 1949
SON OF DAVID, A • 1920 • Plumb Hay • UKN
SON OF DAVY CROCKETT, THE • 1942 • Hillyer Lambert • USA • BLUE CLAY (UKN)
SON OF DEAR CAROLINE, THE (USA) see **FILS DE CAROLINE CHERIE, LE** • 1954
SON OF DEMOCRACY, THE • 1918 • SER • USA
SON OF DESTINY (UKN) see **MADAME DE THEBES** • 1915
SON OF DJANGO see **FIGLIO DI DJANGO, IL** • 1967
SON OF DR. JEKYLL, THE • 1951 • Friedman Seymour • USA • SECOND FACE OF DR. JEKYLL, THE
SON OF DRACULA • 1943 • Siodmak Robert • USA • DESTINY
SON OF DRACULA • 1974 • Francis Freddie • UKN • YOUNG DRACULA ○ COUNT DOWNE
SON OF ERIN, A • 1916 • Ivers Julia Crawford • USA
SON OF FATE, THE see **MASTERTJUVEN** • 1915
SON OF FLUBBER • 1963 • Stevenson Robert • USA
SON OF FRANCE, A • 1914 • Pearson George • UKN
SON OF FRANKENSTEIN • 1939 • Lee Rowland V. • USA
SON OF FURY • 1942 • Cromwell John • USA • SON OF FURY -THE STORY OF BENJAMIN BLAKE
SON OF FURY -THE STORY OF BENJAMIN BLAKE see **SON OF FURY** • 1942
SON OF GERONIMO • 1952 • Bennet Spencer Gordon • SRL • USA
SON OF GOD • 1986 • Bae Chang-Ho • SKR
SON OF GOD'S COUNTRY • 1948 • Springsteen R. G. • USA
SON OF GODZILLA • 1963 • *Delta S.f. Group* • SHT • UKN
SON OF GODZILLA see **GOJIRA NO MUSUKO** • 1967
SON OF HASHIMOTO • 1961 • Rasinski Connie • ANS • USA
SON OF HERCULES IN THE LAND OF DARKNESS • *Vadis Dan* • ITL
SON OF HERCULES IN THE LAND OF FIRE, THE (USA) see **URSUS NELLA TERRA DI FUOCO** • 1963
SON OF HERCULES VS. VENUS • 1980 • Baldi Marcello • ITL
SON OF HIS FATHER, A • 1925 • Fleming Victor • USA
SON OF HIS FATHER, THE • 1913 • Smiley Joseph • USA
SON OF HIS FATHER, THE • 1915 • *Holubar Allen* • USA
SON OF HIS FATHER, THE • 1917 • Schertzinger Victor • USA
SON OF HORROR, THE see **PHANTOM OF MORRISVILLE, THE**
SON OF INDIA • 1931 • Feyder Jacques • USA • SON OF THE RAJAH
SON OF INDIA • 1966 • Khan Mehboob • IND
SON OF INGAGI • 1939 • Kahn Richard C., Meyer Herbert • USA
SON OF INGMAR, THE see **INGMARSSONERNA** • 1919
SON OF JAPAN, A • 1913 • Weston Charles • UKN
SON OF KEMAL, THE ENGLISHMAN, THE see **INGILIZ KEMALIN OGLO** • 1968
SON OF KISSING CUP • 1922 • West Walter • UKN
SON OF KONG • 1933 • Schoedsack Ernest B. • USA • JAMBOREE
SON OF LASSIE • 1945 • Simon S. Sylvan • USA
SON OF LIFEBOAT • 1949 • Lewis Jerry • SHT • USA
SON OF MAN, THE see **FIGLIO DELL'UOMO, IL** • 1955
SON OF MARS, A • 1912 • Aylott Dave • UKN
SON OF MINE (UKN) see **POLICE COURT** • 1932

SON OF MONGOLIA see **SYN MONGOLII** • 1936
SON OF MONTE CRISTO, THE • 1940 • Lee Rowland V. • USA
SON OF NEPTUNE, A • 1916 • Mong William V. • SHT • USA
SON OF OKLAHOMA • 1932 • Bradbury Robert North • USA
SON OF OLD GLORY, A • 1911 • *Yankee* • USA
SON OF PALEFACE • 1952 • Tashlin Frank • USA
SON OF ROARING DAN • 1940 • Beebe Ford • USA
SON OF ROBIN HOOD • 1958 • Sherman George • UKN
SON OF RUSTY, THE • 1947 • Landers Lew • USA
SON OF SAMSON (USA) see **MACISTE NELLA VALLE DEI RE** • 1960
SON OF SATAN, A • 1924 • Micheaux Oscar • USA
SON OF SINBAD • 1955 • Tetzlaff Ted • USA • NIGHT IN A HAREM, A
SON OF SLADE see **RETURN OF JACK SLADE, THE** • 1955
SON OF SONTAG, THE • 1925 • Hurst Paul C. • USA
SON OF SPARTACUS, THE see **FIGLIO DI SPARTACUS, IL** • 1962
SON OF SPELLBOUND • 1949 • Lewis Jerry • SHT • USA
SON OF STEEL • 1935 • Lamont Charles • USA
SON OF STIFF TOUR MOVIE • 1981 • Baynes Jeff • DOC
SON OF STRIFE, A • 1917 • *Piedmont Pictures* • USA
SON OF TADJIKISTAN • 1942 • Pronin Vassily • USS
SON OF TARZAN, THE • 1921 • Revier Harry, Flaven Art • SRL • USA
SON OF THE BORDER • 1933 • Nosler Lloyd • USA
SON OF THE DESERT, A • 1928 • McCormick William Merrill • USA
SON OF THE DEVIL see **FILS DU DIABLE, LE** • 1906
SON OF THE DEVIL, THE see **HIJO DEL DIABLO, EL** • 1965
SON OF THE DOG, THE • 1915 • *Reliance* • USA
SON OF THE EXECUTIONER • 1911 • *Great Northern* • DNM
SON OF THE GENERAL • 1990 • Lim Kwon-Taek • SKR
SON OF THE GOBS see **SON OF A SAILOR** • 1933
SON OF THE GODS • 1930 • Lloyd Frank • USA • THUNDER OF THE GODS (UKN)
SON OF THE GOLDEN WEST • 1928 • Forde Eugene J. • USA
SON OF THE GUARDSMAN • 1946 • Abrahams Derwin • SRL • USA
SON OF THE HILLS, A • 1917 • Davenport Harry • USA
SON OF THE IMMORTALS, A • 1916 • Turner Otis • USA
SON OF THE LAND • NKR
SON OF THE LAND, A • 1931 • Ioganson Edward
SON OF THE NAVY • 1940 • Nigh William • USA
SON OF THE NILE, THE see **IBN EL NIL** • 1951
SON OF THE NORTH, A • 1920 • Jaccard Jacques • SHT • USA
SON OF THE NORTHEAST see **LOOK ESARN** • 1982
SON OF THE NORTHEAST II • Kounavudhi Vichit • THL
SON OF THE PLAINS • 1931 • Bradbury Robert North • USA • VULTURES OF THE LAW (UKN)
SON OF THE RAJAH see **SON OF INDIA** • 1931
SON OF THE RED CORSAIR (USA) see **FIGLIO DEL CORSARO ROSSO, IL** • 1960
SON OF THE RED PIRATE see **FIGLIO DEL CORSARO ROSSO, IL** • 1960
SON OF THE REGIMENT • 1946 • Pronin Vassily • USS
SON OF THE RENEGADE • 1953 • Brown Reg?, Canada Roy? • USA
SON OF THE SAHARA • 1967 • Goode Frederic • SRL • UKN
SON OF THE SAHARA, A • 1924 • Carewe Edwin • USA • SULTAN'S SLAVE, THE
SON OF THE SEA see **HAVETS SON** • 1949
SON OF THE SEA, A • 1915 • Batley Ernest G. • UKN
SON OF THE SHEIK, THE • 1926 • Fitzmaurice George • USA
SON OF THE SHUNAMMITE, THE • 1911 • *Gaumont* • FRN
SON OF THE STAR, THE see **HIJO DEL CRACK, EL** • 1953
SON OF THE VAMPIRE see **ANAK PONTIANAK** • 1958
SON OF THE WHITE MARE see **FEHERLOFIA** • 1982
SON OF THE WOLF, THE • 1922 • Dawn Norman • USA
SON OF THOMAS GRAY, THE • 1914 • Ricketts Thomas • USA
SON OF WALLINGFORD, THE • 1921 • Chester George Randolph, Chester George Randolph Mrs. • USA
SON OF ZAMBO • 1938 • Bhavnani Mohan Dayaram • IND
SON OF ZORRO • 1947 • Bennet Spencer Gordon, Brannon Fred C. • SRL • USA
SON ONCLE DE NORMANDIE • 1938 • Dreville Jean • FRN • FUGUE DE JIM BAXTER, LA
SON OR TOR • 1964 • Glut Don • SHT • USA
SON PREMIER ETE see **PREMIER ETE, LE** • 1975
SON PREMIER FILM • 1926 • Kemm Jean • FRN
SO'N RACKERCHEN • 1915 • Karfiol William • FRG
SON RISE: A MIRACLE OF LOVE • 1979 • Jordan Glenn • TVM • USA • SON–RISE: A MIRACLE OF LOVE ○ MIRACLE OF LOVE
SON–RISE: A MIRACLE OF LOVE see **SON RISE: A MIRACLE OF LOVE** • 1979
SON SOZ BENIM • 1967 • Figenli Yavuz • TRK • LAST WORD IS MINE, THE
SON TORNATA PER TE • 1953 • Comencini Luigi • ITL, SWT • HEIDI
SON TORNATE A FIORIRE LE ROSE • 1975 • Sindoni Vittorio • ITL
SON VON ST. MORITZ, DIE • 1923 • Moest Hubert, Weissenberg Friedrich • FRG
SON VURGUN • 1968 • Gorec Ertem • TRK • KURSUNLARIN YAGMURU ○ LAST HOLDUP, THE
SO'N WINDHUND! • 1931 • Wolff Carl Heinz • FRG • KEINEN TAG OHNE DICH
SONAD SKULD • 1915 • Sjostrom Victor • SWD • EXPIATED GUILT
SONADORA, LA • 1917 • Arozamena Edouardo • MXC • DREAMER, THE
SONAMBULIST, THE see **SOVNGAENGERSKEN** • 1914
SONAMBULISTS, THE • 1913 • Dillon Eddie • USA
SONAMBULIST'S CRIME, THE • 1908 • Coleby A. E. • UKN
SONAMBULO, EL • 1973 • *Panorama* • MXC
SONAMBULOS • 1978 • Gutierrez Aragon Manuel • SPN • SLEEPWALKERS ○ SOMNAMBULISTS
SONAR KELLA • 1975 • Ray Satyajit • IND • GOLDEN FORTRESS, THE (UKN)
SONAR NO CUESTA NADA • 1941 • Amadori Luis Cesar • ARG
SONAR, SONAR • 1976 • Favio Leonardo • ARG • TO DREAM, TO DREAM
SONARON CUATRO BALAZOS • 1967 • Navarro Agustin • SPN, ITL • FOUR SHOTS WERE HEARD
SONATA FOR PEN, BRUSH AND RULER • Spinello Barry • SHT • USA
SONATA GALLEGO • 1960 • Castellon Alfredo • SHT • SPN
SONATA NAD OZERO • 1976 • Tsilinski Gunar • USS
SONATA OF SOULS, A • 1911 • *Reliance* • USA
SONATAS • 1959 • Bardem Juan Antonio • MXC, SPN • AVENTURAS DEL MARQUES DE BRADOMIN
SONATE A KREUTZER, LA • 1956 • Rohmer Eric • FRN • KREUTZER SONATA, THE
SONATINE • 1983 • Lanctot Micheline • CND
SONCNI KRIK • 1968 • Hladnik Bostjan • YGS • SUNNY WHIRLPOOL, THE ○ SUNNY CRY ○ SUNCANI KRIK
SONDAG I SEPTEMBER, EN • 1963 • Donner Jorn • SWD • SUNDAY IN SEPTEMBER, A
SONDERBARE LIEBE, EINE • 1984 • Warneke Lothar • GDR
SONDERLING, DER • 1929 • Valentin Karl • FRG
SONDEURS D'ABIME • 1943 • Ichac Marcel • DCS • FRN
SONE, DIE • *Messter Oskar (P)* • FRG
SONERA • 1935-47 • Bose Debaki • IND
SONEZAKI SHINJUH • 1981 • Kurisaki • JPN • DOUBLE SUICIDE AT SONEZAKI
SONEZAKI SINJU • 1977 • Masumura Yasuzo • JPN • LOVERS' SUICIDE IN SONEZAKI
SONG • Taylor Ron • SHT • USA
SONG • 1928 • Eichberg Richard • FRG • SCHMUTZIGES GELD ○ SHOW LIFE
SONG • 1986 • Kuusi Janne • DOC • FNL
SONG 1 • 1964 • Brakhage Stan • SHT • USA
SONG 4 • 1964 • Brakhage Stan • SHT • USA
SONG 5 • 1964 • Brakhage Stan • SHT • USA
SONG 8 • 1964 • Brakhage Stan • SHT • USA
SONG 11 • 1965 • Brakhage Stan • SHT • USA
SONG 12 • 1965 • Brakhage Stan • SHT • USA
SONG 13 • 1965 • Brakhage Stan • SHT • USA
SONG 14 • 1965 • Brakhage Stan • SHT • USA
SONG 16 • 1965 • Brakhage Stan • SHT • USA
SONG 23 see **23RD PSALM BRANCH** • 1967
SONG 26 • 1968 • Brakhage Stan • SHT • USA
SONG 27 (PART II) RIVERS • 1969 • Brakhage Stan • SHT • USA
SONG 28 • 1969 • Brakhage Stan • SHT • USA
SONG 29 • 1969 • Brakhage Stan • SHT • USA
SONG A DAY, A • 1936 • Fleischer Dave • ANS • USA
SONG ABOUT A FLOWER see **SONG ABOUT FLOWERS, THE** • 1959
SONG ABOUT A TIME OF CHERRIES, THE • 1990 • Stage Irene Warner • DNM
SONG ABOUT AN AUROCH, A • Belousov Oleg • ANM • USS
SONG ABOUT FLAX, THE • 1965 • Gedris Marionas Vintzo • SHT • USS
SONG ABOUT FLOWERS, THE • 1959 • Ioseliani Otar • SHT • USS • SONG ABOUT A FLOWER
SONG ABOUT HAPPINESS see **PESNYA O SHCHASTYE** • 1934
SONG ABOUT IRON • 1963 • Kollanyi Agoston • HNG
SONG ABOUT STOCKHOLM see **SANGEN OM STOCKHOLM** • 1947
SONG AND DANCE CONCERT see **CONCERT OF STARS** • 1952
SONG AND DANCE MAN, THE • 1926 • Brenon Herbert • USA
SONG AND DANCE MAN, THE • 1936 • Dwan Allan • USA
SONG AND DANCE OVER THE VISTULA • Ivanov B., Poselsky I. • USS
SONG AND THE SERGEANT, THE • 1918 • Ridgwell George • SHT • USA
SONG AND THE SILENCE, THE • 1969 • Cohen Nathan • USA
SONG AT EVENTIDE • 1934 • Hughes Harry • UKN
SONG BIRD OF THE NORTH, THE • 1913 • Ince Ralph • USA
SONG BIRDS • 1933 • Harlow John • UKN
SONG–COPATION • 1929 • Jeffrey R. E. • UKN
SONG FOR EUROPE, A • 1985 • Goldschmidt John • TVM • UKN, FRG • CRY FOR JUSTICE, A ○ STRENG VERTRAULICH ○ CRIME OF HONOUR
SONG FOR MAN see **PESSEN ZA CHOVEKA** • 1954
SONG FOR MISS JULIE, A • 1945 • Rowland William • USA
SONG FOR PRINCE CHARLIE, A • 1958 • Nieter Hans M. • SHT • UKN
SONG FOR THE DEAD MINERS, A see **KONJUH PLANINOM** • 1966
SONG FOR TOMORROW, A • 1948 • Fisher Terence • UKN
SONG FOR YOU, A see **MY SONG FOR YOU** • 1934
SONG FROM MY HEART, THE (USA) see **WAGA KOI WAGA UTA** • 1969
SONG FROM "THE BELLE OF MAYFAIR" • 1907 • Gilbert Arthur • UKN
SONG FROM THE HEART, A • 1916 • Powell Paul • SHT • USA
SONG HITS ON PARADE • 1936 • Waller Fred • SHT • USA
SONG IN MY HEART, A see **WAGA KOKORONO UTA** • 1977
SONG IN SOHO • 1937 • Hopwood R. A. • UKN
SONG IN THE DARK, THE • 1914 • *Holmes Gerda* • USA
SONG IS BORN, A • 1939 • Roush Leslie • SHT • USA
SONG IS BORN, A • 1948 • Hawks Howard • USA
SONG LANTERN, THE see **UTA ANDON** • 1943
SONG O' MY HEART • 1930 • Borzage Frank • USA
SONG OF A FLOWER BASKET see **HANAKOGO NO UTA** • 1937
SONG OF A FLOWER BASKET see **UTA NO HANAKOGO** • 1946
SONG OF A SAD COUNTRY • 1937 • Weiss Jiri • DOC • CZC
SONG OF ABAYA see **PESNI ABAYA** • 1945
SONG OF AFRICA • 1951 • SAF
SONG OF AIR, A • 1988 • Bennett Merilee • ASL
SONG OF ARIZONA • 1946 • McDonald Frank • USA
SONG OF ASAKUSA see **ASAKUSA NO HADA** • 1950
SONG OF BERNADETTE, THE • 1943 • King Henry • USA
SONG OF BWANA TOSHI, THE see **BUWANA TOSHI NO UTA** • 1965
SONG OF CEYLON • 1934 • Wright Basil • DOC • UKN
SONG OF CHINA • 1936 • Lo Ming-Yau • CHN
SONG OF DEATH see **CHANSON DE LA MORT** • 1973
SONG OF DOLORES (USA) see **COPLA DE LA DOLORES, LA** • 1947
SONG OF ETERNITY • 1975 • Shawqi Khalil • EGY
SONG OF EXPERIENCE • 1985 • Frears Stephen • TVM • UKN
SONG OF FAILURE, THE see **HAIZAN NO UTA WA KANASHI** • 1922
SONG OF FREEDOM • 1936 • Wills J. Elder • UKN
SONG OF FUKAGAWA see **FURYU FUKAGAWA** • 1960
SONG OF GOLD, THE see **ZPEV ZLATA** • 1920
SONG OF GOLDEN GRAIN, THE • 1983 • Gupta Mrinal • IND
SONG OF HAPPINESS see **PESNYA O SHCHASTYE** • 1934
SONG OF HAPPINESS, THE (USA) see **LIED VOM GLUCK, DAS** • 1933
SONG OF HATE, THE • 1915 • Edwards J. Gordon • USA
SONG OF HEROES (UKN) see **KOMSOMOL** • 1932
SONG OF HOME, THE (USA) see **FURUSATO NO UTA** • 1925
SONG OF HOMETOWN, THE see **FURUSATO NO UTA** • 1925
SONG OF IDAHO • 1949 • Nazarro Ray • USA
SONG OF INDIA • 1949 • Rogell Albert S. • USA
SONG OF INDIA see **SADKO** • 1953
SONG OF KENTUCKY, A • 1929 • Seiler Lewis • USA
SONG OF KOLTSOV see **PESN O KOLTSOVE** • 1960
SONG OF LEONARD COHEN, THE • 1981 • Rasky Harry • CND
SONG OF LIFE see **LIED VOM LEBEN, DAS** • 1931
SONG OF LIFE, THE • 1922 • Stahl John M. • USA
SONG OF LIFE, THE see **PISEN ZIVOTA** • 1924
SONG OF LIFE, THE see **JEEVAN SANGEET** • 1968
SONG OF LISBON, THE see **CANCAO DE LISBOA, A** • 1933
SONG OF LOVE • 1947 • Brown Clarence • USA
SONG OF LOVE see **AI NO SANKA** • 1967
SONG OF LOVE see **WAGA INOCHI NO UTA ENKA** • 1968
SONG OF LOVE, THE • 1923 • Franklin Chester M., Marion Frances • USA • DUST OF DESIRE
SONG OF LOVE, THE • 1929 • Kenton Erle C. • USA
SONG OF MAN see **PESSEN ZA CHOVEKA** • 1954
SONG OF MANSHUK see **PESNYA MANSHUK** • 1971
SONG OF MATCHLESS MOONLIGHT, THE see **KANTARO TSUKIYO UTA** • 1952
SONG OF MEXICO see **CANCION DE MEXICO, LA** • 1944
SONG OF MUTSUKO see **MUTCHAN NO UTA** • 1985
SONG OF MY HEART • 1948 • Glazer Benjamin • USA
SONG OF NEVADA • 1944 • Kane Joseph • USA
SONG OF NEW LIFE see **ZEMLYA** • 1930
SONG OF NORWAY • 1955 • Rogers Maclean • UKN
SONG OF NORWAY • 1970 • Stone Andrew L. • USA
SONG OF OLD WYOMING • 1945 • Tansey Robert • USA
SONG OF PARIS • 1952 • Guillermin John • UKN • BACHELOR IN PARIS (USA) ○ CLEMENTINE
SONG OF POTEMKIN, THE see **PODRUGI** • 1936
SONG OF PRAISE see **SANKA** • 1972
SONG OF REMEMBRANCE see **CHANSON DU SOUVENIR, LA** • 1936
SONG OF REVOLT • 1937 • Rowland Roy • SHT • USA
SONG OF RUSSIA • 1943 • Ratoff Gregory • USA • RUSSIA
SONG OF SADNESS, THE see **CANTO DA SAUDADE, O** • 1952
SONG OF SCHEHERAZADE • 1947 • Reisch Walter • USA • FANDANGO
SONG OF SIBERIA see **SKAZANIYE O ZEMLYE SIBIRSKOI** • 1947
SONG OF SILESIA see **KONCERT NA EKRENIE SLASK** • 1956
SONG OF SISTER MARIA, THE (USA) see **SOR INTREPIDA** • 1952
SONG OF SIXPENCE, A • 1917 • Dean Ralph • USA
SONG OF SOHO • 1930 • Lachman Harry • UKN
SONG OF SOLOMON, THE • 1914 • Miller Ashley • USA
SONG OF SONGS, THE • 1913 • *Pilot* • USA
SONG OF SONGS, THE • 1918 • Kaufman Joseph • USA
SONG OF SONGS, THE • 1933 • Mamoulian Rouben • USA
SONG OF STEEL, A see **PESNJ O METALLE** • 1928
SONG OF SUMMER • 1968 • Russell Ken • MTV • UKN
SONG OF SUNNY ITALY, THE • 1914 • Vale Travers • USA
SONG OF SURRENDER • 1949 • Leisen Mitchell • USA • ABIGAIL DEAR HEART ○ NOW AND FOREVER ○ SIN OF ABBY HUNT
SONG OF TEXAS • 1943 • Kane Joseph • USA
SONG OF THE ACCURSED LOVERS, THE see **BALLADE DES AMANTS MAUDITS, LE** • 1967
SONG OF THE ALPS see **SOHN DER WEISSEN BERG, DER** • 1930
SONG OF THE BALALAIKA • 1971 • Diamant-Berger Henri
SONG OF THE BALKAN MOUNTAINS, A • 1934 • Stoychev Peter • BUL
SONG OF THE BIRDS • 1949 • Tytla Bill • ANS • USA
SONG OF THE BIRDS, THE • 1935 • Fleischer Dave • ANS • USA
SONG OF THE BLOOD–RED FLOWER see **LAULU TULIPUNAISESTA KUKASTA** • 1971
SONG OF THE BOATMAN, THE see **SENDO KOUTA** • 1923
SONG OF THE BUCKAROO • 1939 • Herman Al • USA
SONG OF THE CABALLERO • 1930 • Brown Harry J. • USA
SONG OF THE CAMP (USA) see **ROEI NO UTA** • 1938
SONG OF THE CART, THE see **NIGURUMA NO UTA** • 1959
SONG OF THE CITY • 1937 • Taggart Errol • USA
SONG OF THE CLOUDS • 1957 • Armstrong John • UKN
SONG OF THE CORNFIELDS see **ENEK A BUZAMEZOKROL** • 1947
SONG OF THE DAMNED see **ESCAPE FROM DEVIL'S ISLAND** • 1935
SONG OF THE DOVE • 1960 • Ratz Gunter • ANM • GDR
SONG OF THE DRIFTER • 1948 • Hillyer Lambert • USA
SONG OF THE EAGLE • 1933 • Murphy Ralph • USA • BEER BARON, THE
SONG OF THE EXILE • 1989 • Hsu An-Hua • TWN
SONG OF THE FIREMAN see **HORI, MA PANENKO!** • 1967
SONG OF THE FISHERMEN, THE • 1934 • Tsai Chu-Sheng • CHN
SONG OF THE FLAME • 1930 • Crosland Alan • USA
SONG OF THE FLOWER BASKET see **HANAKOGO NO UTA** • 1937
SONG OF THE FOREST (UKN) see **INCANTO DELLA FORESTA, L'** • 1957
SONG OF THE FOREST (USA) see **LESNAYA PESNYA** • 1961
SONG OF THE FORGE • 1937 • Edwards Henry • UKN • VILLAGE BLACKSMITH, THE ○ BLACKSMITH, THE
SONG OF THE GHETTO, THE • 1914 • Humphrey William • USA
SONG OF THE GOODBODY • 1977 • Broughton James • USA

SONG OF THE GREY DOVE see **PIESEN O SIVOM HOLUBOVI** • 1961
SONG OF THE GRINGO • 1936 • McCarthy John P. • USA • OLD CORRAL, THE (UKN)
SONG OF THE HEART, THE • 1915 • Fleming Carroll • USA
SONG OF THE ISLANDS • 1942 • Lang Walter • USA
SONG OF THE LAND • 1953 • Kesler Henry S., Roberts Francis, Harrison Ed N. • DOC • USA
SONG OF THE LANTERN see **UTA ANDON** • 1943
SONG OF THE LARK see **SKRIVANCI PISEN** • 1933
SONG OF THE LOON • 1970 • Herbert Andrew • USA
SONG OF THE MEET see **PISEN O SLETU** • 1949
SONG OF THE MERCHANT KALASHNIKOV see **PESN PRO KOUPTSA KALACHNIKOVA** • 1909
SONG OF THE MOUNTAIN PASS (USA) see **TOGE NO UTA** • 1923
SONG OF THE NARAYAMA see **NARAYAMA BUSHI-KO** • 1958
SONG OF THE NATIVE COUNTRY, THE see **FURUSATO NO UTA** • 1925
SONG OF THE NIGHTINGALE, THE see **VOIX DU ROSSIGNOL, LA** • 1923
SONG OF THE OPEN ROAD • 1944 • Simon S. Sylvan • USA
SONG OF THE PADDLE • 1978 • Mason William • DCS • CND
SONG OF THE PLOUGH • 1933 • Baxter John • UKN • COUNTY FAIR
SONG OF THE PRAIRIE • 1945 • Nazarro Ray • USA • SENTIMENT AND SONG (UKN)
SONG OF THE PRAIRIE see **ARIE PRERIE** • 1949
SONG OF THE RANGE • 1944 • Fox Wallace • USA
SONG OF THE RED LOBSTER, THE see **OJ OJ OJ..** • 1966
SONG OF THE RED RUBY, THE (UKN) see **SANGEN OM DEN RODE RUBIN** • 1970
SONG OF THE RIVERS, THE see **LIED DER STROME, DAS** • 1954
SONG OF THE ROAD • 1937 • Baxter John • UKN
SONG OF THE ROAD, THE see **PATHER PANCHALI** • 1955
SONG OF THE ROAD (USA) see **END OF THE ROAD, THE** • 1936
SONG OF THE SAD IDIOT (USA) see **KANASHIKI HAKUCHI** • 1924
SONG OF THE SADDLE • 1936 • King Louis • USA
SONG OF THE SAILORS, THE see **LIED DER MATROSEN, DAS** • 1958
SONG OF THE SARONG • 1945 • Young Harold • USA
SONG OF THE SCARLET FLOWER see **SANGEN OM DEN ELDRODA BLOMMAN** • 1918
SONG OF THE SCARLET FLOWER see **SANGEN OM DEN ELDRODA BLOMMAN** • 1934
SONG OF THE SCARLET FLOWER, THE see **LAULU TULIPUNAISESTA KUKASTA** • 1938
SONG OF THE SCARLET FLOWER, THE see **SANGEN OM DEN ELDRODA BLOMMAN** • 1956
SONG OF THE SCARLET FLOWER, THE see **LAULU TULIPUNAISESTA KUKASTA** • 1971
SONG OF THE SEA see **CANTO DO MAR, O** • 1954
SONG OF THE SEA SHELL, THE • 1914 • Otto Henry • USA
SONG OF THE SEPHARDI • 1980 • Raphael David • DOC • USA
SONG OF THE SHELL, THE • 1912 • Ince Ralph • USA
SONG OF THE SHIRT • 1980 • Clayton Susan, Curling Jonathan • UKN
SONG OF THE SHIRT, THE • 1908 • Griffith D. W. • USA
SONG OF THE SHIRT, THE • 1924 • ASL
SONG OF THE SHORE, THE • 1914 • *Majestic* • USA
SONG OF THE SIERRAS • 1946 • Drake Oliver • USA
SONG OF THE SIREN (UKN) see **CANTO DE LA SIRENA, EL** • 1946
SONG OF THE SOUL, THE • 1914 • *Swanson Gloria* • USA
SONG OF THE SOUL, THE • 1918 • Terriss Tom • USA
SONG OF THE SOUL, THE • 1920 • Noble John W. • USA
SONG OF THE SOUL (USA) see **CANCION DEL ALMA** • 1937
SONG OF THE SOUP, THE • 1913 • *Kerrigan J. Warren* • USA
SONG OF THE SOUTH • 1946 • Foster Harve, Jackson Wilfred (Anm) • USA
SONG OF THE SUCCUBUS • 1975 • Jordan Glenn • TVM • USA
SONG OF THE TELEGRAPH, THE • 1913 • *Bison* • USA
SONG OF THE THIN MAN • 1947 • Buzzell Edward • USA
SONG OF THE TRAIL • 1936 • Hopton Russell • USA
SONG OF THE UNLOVED, THE see **PISEN NEMILOVA-NEHO** • 1982
SONG OF THE WAGE SLAVE, THE • 1915 • Blache Herbert • USA
SONG OF THE WASTELAND • 1947 • Carr Thomas • USA
SONG OF THE WEST • 1930 • Enright Ray • USA
SONG OF THE WEST see **LET FREEDOM RING** • 1939
SONG OF THE WHALE • 1975 • Stoneman John • MTV • CND
SONG OF THE WHALES see **HAVALERNES SANG** • 1984
SONG OF THE WHITE ORCHID see **BYAKURAN NO UTA** • 1939
SONG OF THE WILDS see **VILDMARKENS SANG** • 1940
SONG OF THE WILDWOOD FLUTE, THE • 1910 • Griffith D. W. • USA
SONG OF THE WOODS • 1916 • Elfelt Clifford S. • SHT • USA
SONG OF TRIUMPHANT LOVE see **PESN TORZHESTVUYUSHCHEI LIUBVI** • 1915
SONG OF TRUCE • 1913 • Campbell Colin • USA
SONG OF VENGEANCE see **FUKUSHU NO UTA GA KIKOERU** • 1968
SONG OF VICTORY • 1942 • Wickersham Bob • ANS • USA
SONG OF VICTORY see **HISSHOKA** • 1945
SONG OF YOUTH • Tsui Wei, Chen Huai-Ai • CHN
SONG OF YOUTH, A see **GENCLIK TURKUSU** • 1967
SONG OF YUEN-CHOW-CHAI see **YUEN-CHAU-CHAI CHIH KO** • 1977
SONG OR TWO, A • 1929 • Jeffrey R. E. • UKN
SONG OVER MOSCOW (USA) see **CHERYOMUSHKI** • 1963
SONG PARADE see **HIT PARADE OF 1951** • 1950
SONG REMAINS THE SAME, THE • 1976 • Clifton Peter, Massot Joe • DOC • UKN
SONG SERVICE • 1930 • Taurog Norman • SHT • USA
SONG SHOPPING • 1933 • Fleischer Dave • ANS • USA
SONG THAT LIVED FOREVER, THE see **SONG TO REMEMBER, A** • 1945
SONG THAT REACHED HIS HEART, THE • 1910 • Dawley J. Searle • USA
SONG THE MAP SINGS • 1937 • Sparling Gordon • CND
SONG TO HER, THE (USA) see **SANGEN TILL HENNE** • 1934
SONG TO REMEMBER, A • 1945 • Vidor Charles • USA • LOVE OF MADAME SAND, THE ○ SONG THAT LIVED FOREVER, THE
SONG WHICH GRANDMOTHER SANG, THE see **OPERABRANDEN** • 1912
SONG WITHOUT END • 1960 • Vidor Charles, Cukor George (U/c) • USA
SONG WRITER, THE see **CHILDREN OF PLEASURE** • 1930
SONG WRITER'S REVUE, THE • 1930 • Lee Sammy • USA
SONG XV see **XV SONG TRAITS** • 1965
SONG XXIII see **23RD PSALM BRANCH** • 1967
SONG YOU GAVE ME, THE • 1933 • Stein Paul L. • UKN
SONGE D'OR DE L'AVARE, LE • 1900 • Melies Georges • FRN • MISER'S DREAM OF GOLD, THE (USA) ○ MISER OR THE GOLD COUNTRY, THE
SONGE D'UN GARCON DE CAFE, LE • 1910 • Cohl Emile • ANS • FRN • REVE DU GARCON DE CAFE, LE ○ HASHER'S DELIRIUM, THE ○ CAFE WAITER'S DREAM
SONGHAYS • 1963 • Sembene Ousmane • SNL • EMPIRE SONRAI, L'
SONGHUA JIAN SHANG • 1947 • Jin Shan • CHN • ALONG THE SUNGARI RIVER
SONGOKU • 1940 • *Tsuburaya Eiji* • JPN
SONGOKU • 1959 • Yamamoto Kajiro • JPN • ADVENTURES OF SUN KUNG
SONGS 2 AND 3 • 1964 • Brakhage Stan • SHT • USA
SONGS 6 AND 7 • 1964 • Brakhage Stan • SHT • USA
SONGS 9 AND 10 • 1965 • Brakhage Stan • SHT • USA
SONGS 17 AND 18 • 1965 • Brakhage Stan • SHT • USA
SONGS 19 AND 20 • 1965 • Brakhage Stan • SHT • USA
SONGS 21 AND 22 • 1965 • Brakhage Stan • SHT • USA
SONGS 24 AND 25 • 1967 • Brakhage Stan • SHT • USA
SONGS AND BULLETS • 1938 • Newfield Sam • USA
SONGS AND DANCES BY THE RIVER MESTA • 1958 • Boyadgieva Lada • DOC • BUL
SONGS AND DANCES OF THE INANIMATE WORLD -THE SUBWAY • 1986 • Hebert Pierre • ANS • CND • CHANTS ET DANSES DU MONDE ANIME -LE METRO
SONGS AND SADDLES • 1938 • Fraser Harry L. • USA
SONGS BY GISELE • 1950 • Blais Roger • DCS • CND
SONGS FOR AFTER A WAR see **CANCIONES PARA DESPUES DE UNA GUERRA** • 1971
SONGS FOR CHILDREN • 1972 • Okamoto Tadashige • ANS • JPN
SONGS FOR CRACOW see **PIOSENKAI DLA KRAKOWA** • 1960
SONGS ILLUSTRATED • 1904 • *Warwick Trading Co* • UKN
SONGS MY MOTHER SANG • 1926 • Croise Hugh • UKN
SONGS OF CHILDHOOD DAYS • 1912 • Porter Edwin S. • USA
SONGS OF ENGLAND • 1925 • Fitzpatrick James A. • SHT • UKN
SONGS OF ERIN • 1951 • Rasinski Connie • ANS • USA
SONGS OF FIRE see **TRAGOUDIA TIS FOTIAS** • 1974
SONGS OF FIRE, THE see **SZARVASSA VALT FIUK** • 1974
SONGS OF HOPE • 1986 • Saretzky Eric • CND, UKN
SONGS OF IRELAND • 1925 • Fitzpatrick James A. • SHT • UKN
SONGS OF MOTORS • 1961 • Grigorov Roumen • DOC • BUL
SONGS OF OUR LIFE see **CANCIONES DE NUESTRA VIDA** • 1975
SONGS OF ROMANCE • 1949 • Cowan Will • SHT • USA
SONGS OF SCOTLAND • 1925 • Fitzpatrick James A. • SHT • UKN
SONGS OF SCOTLAND • 1966 • Henson Laurence, McConnell Edward • UKN
SONGS OF THE BRITISH ISLES • 1925 • Fitzpatrick James A. • SHT • UKN
SONGS OF THE RANGE • 1949 • *Universal* • SHT • USA
SONGS OF THE SEA, THE • 1970 • Munteanu Francisc • RMN, USS
SONGS OF THE SEASON • 1949 • Parker Benjamin R. • SHT • USA
SONGS OF THE VISTULA see **PIESNI NAD WISLA** • 1956
SONGS OF THE WEST COUNTREE • 1926 • Croise Hugh • UKN
SONGS ON THURSDAY AS WELL AS ON SUNDAY see **JEUDI ON CHANTERA COMME DIMANCHE** • 1968
SONGS OVER THE DNIEPER • 1958 • Svetlanov G.
SONGS THAT LIVE • 1951 • Cowan Will • SHT • USA
SONGS WITHOUT WORDS see **CHANSONS SANS PAROLES** • 1958
SONGSTER, THE see **PISNICKAR** • 1932
SONGWRITER • 1984 • Rudolph Alan • USA
SONHAR E FACIL • 1951 • Queiroga Perdigao • PRT
SONHO DE AMOR • 1945 • Porfirio Carlos • PRT
SONHO DE VALSA • 1988 • Soares Ana Carolina Texeira • BRZ • AFTER EIGHT.. FOREVER
SONHO DE VAMPIROS, UM • 1970 • Cavalcanti Ibere • BRZ • VAMPIRE'S DREAM, A
SONHO SEM FIM • 1986 • Escorel Lauro • BRZ • ENDLESS DREAM
SONHOS DE MENINA MOCA • 1988 • Trautman Tereza • BRZ • BEST WISHES
SONIA • 1921 • Clift Denison • UKN
SONIA • 1928 • Sarno Hector V. • USA
SONIA AND THE MADMAN • 1977 • Mustafa Hassam Eddin • EGY
SONIDA PREHISTORICO, EL see **SONIDO DE LA MUERTE, EL** • 1966
SONIDO DE LA MUERTE, EL • 1966 • Nieves Conde Jose Antonio • SPN • SOUND OF HORROR (USA) ○ SONIDA PREHISTORICO, EL ○ PREHISTORIC SOUND, THE ○ PRIGIONIERI DELL'ORRORE
SONJA • 1943 • Faustman Erik • SWD
SONJA • 1978 • Retief Daan • SAF
SONJA -16 AR see **TUMULT** • 1969
SONKA, THE GOLDEN HAND see **SONKA ZOLOTAYA RUCHKA** • 1916
SONKA ZOLOTAYA RUCHKA • 1916 • Yurevsky Y., Kasyanov Vladimir, Chargonin Alexander • SRL • USS • SONKA, THE GOLDEN HAND
SONNAMBULA, LA • 1942 • Ballerini Piero • ITL
SONNAMBULA, LA • 1952 • Barlacchi Cesare • ITL
SONNE, DIE • *Messter Oskar* • FRG
SONNE ASIENS, DIE • 1920 • Heuberger Edmund • FRG • SPRINGFLUT DES HASSES, DIE ○ FLAMMENZEICHEN ○ ASIAN SUN, THE
SONNE BRINGT ES AN DEN TAG, DIE • 1919 • Bauer Leopold • FRG
SONNE GEHT AUF, DIE see **SCHON IST JEDER TAG, DEN DU MIR SCHENSKT, MARIE LOUISE** • 1933
SONNE UND SCHATTEN • 1915 • von Woringen Paul • FRG
SONNE VON ST. MORITZ, DIE • 1954 • Rabenalt Arthur M. • FRG
SONNEBLOM UIT PARYS • 1974 • SAF
SONNEN • 1914 • Blom August • DNM • HER SON
SONNEN FRA VINGARDEN • 1975 • Mossin Ib, Guldbrandsen Peer • DNM
SONNENBRUCKS, DIE • 1951 • Klaren Georg C. • GDR
SONNENKONIG, DIE • 1929 • Steinhoff Hans • FRG
SONNENSCHEIN UN WOLKENBRUCH • 1955 • Nussgruber Rudolf • AUS
SONNENSTRAHL • 1933 • Fejos Paul • AUS • TOGETHER WE TOO (UKN) ○ RAY OF SUNSHINE, A
SONNENSUCHER, DIE • 1958 • Wolf Konrad • GDR • IN SEARCH OF THE SUN
SONNETTE D'ALARME, LA • 1935 • Christian-Jaque • FRN
SONNIGE MARCHEN VOM GLUCK, DAS • 1924 • *Berliner Operetten-Film* • FRG
SONNO SONJUKO • 1939 • Inagaki Hiroshi • JPN • VILLAGE SCHOOL OF EMPEROR SUPPORTERS
SONNTAG DER ANDEREN, DER • 1959 • Hossfeld H. J. • FRG • SUNDAY OF THE OTHERS, THE
SONNTAGMORGEN IN WARSCHAU, EIN see **NIEDZIELNY PORANEC** • 1955
SONNTAGSKIND, DAS • 1956 • Meisel Kurt • FRG
SONNTAGSKINDER • 1941 • von Alten Jurgen • FRG
SONNWENDFEUER • Burghardt Georg • FRG
SONNWENDHOF • 1918 • Leyde Emil • AUS
SONNY • 1922 • King Henry • USA
SONNY • 1985 • SAF
SONNY AND JED (USA) see **BANDA J.S. CRONACA CRIMINALE DEL FAR WEST, LA** • 1972
SONNY BOY • 1916 • Johnson Tefft • USA
SONNY BOY • 1929 • Aylott Dave, Symmons E. F. • SHT • UKN
SONNY BOY • 1929 • Mayo Archie • USA
SONNY BOY • 1988 • Carroll Robert M. • USA
SONNY BOY AND THE DOG SHOW • 1916 • Johnson Tefft • USA
SONNY BOY AT THE BAT • 1916 • Johnson Tefft • USA
SONNY BOY IN SCHOOL DAYS • 1916 • Johnson Tefft • USA
SONNY DUNHAM AND HIS ORCHESTRA • 1944 • Scholl Jack • SHT • USA
SONNY DUNHAM AND HIS ORCHESTRA IN JIVE BUSTERS • 1944 • Collins Lewis D. • SHT • USA
SONNY FORD • 1969 • Ferris Bill, Ferris Josette • USA
SONNY JIM AND THE AMUSEMENT COMPANY LTD. • 1915 • Johnson Tefft • USA
SONNY JIM AND THE FAMILY PARTY • 1915 • Johnson Tefft • USA
SONNY JIM AND THE GREAT AMERICAN GAME • 1915 • Johnson Tefft • USA
SONNY JIM AND THE VALENTINE • 1915 • Johnson Tefft • USA
SONNY JIM AT THE MARDI GRAS • 1915 • Johnson Tefft • USA
SONNY JIM AT THE NORTH POLE • 1914 • Johnson Tefft • USA
SONNY JIM IN SEARCH OF A MOTHER • 1914 • *Connelly Bobby* • USA
SONNY JIM'S FIRST LOVE AFFAIR • 1915 • Johnson Tefft • USA
SONNY ROLLINS LIVE AT LAREN • 1973 • Boelen Frans • NTH
SONNY ROLLINS, MUSICIAN • 1968 • Fontaine Dick • DCS • UKN
SONNY'S LITTLE BIT • 1916 • SAF
SONO FOTOGENICO • 1980 • Risi Dino • ITL • I AM PHOTOGENIC
SONO HITO NO NA WA IENAI • 1951 • Sugie Toshio • JPN • I CANNOT SAY THAT PERSON'S NAME
SONO HITO WA MUKASHI • 1967 • Matsuyama Zenzo • JPN • O LUNA MY PONY!
SONO IO L'ASSASSINO! • 1949 • Montero Roberto Bianchi • ITL
SONO KABE O KUDARE • 1959 • Nakahira Ko • JPN • LET US DESTROY THIS WALL
SONO SARTANA IL VOSTRO BECCHINO • 1969 • Carnimeo Giuliano • ITL • I AM SARTANA: YOUR ANGEL OF DEATH ○ SARTANA, ANGEL OF DEATH
SONO STATO IO! • 1937 • Matarazzo Raffaello • ITL • IT WAS I (USA) ○ I DID IT!
SONO STATO IO • 1973 • Lattuada Alberto • ITL
SONO STATO UN AGENTE C.I.A. • 1978 • Guerrieri Romolo • ITL • COVERT ACTION
SONO UN FENOMENO PARANORMALE • 1985 • Corbucci Sergio • ITL • I AM AN E.S.P.
SONO YO NO BOKEN • 1948 • Yasuda Kimiyoshi • JPN • THAT KIND OF ADVENTURE ○ THAT NIGHT ADVENTURE
SONO YO NO HIMEGOTO • 1957 • Kimura Keigo • JPN • NIGHT HOLDS A SECRET
SONO YO NO TSUMA • 1930 • Ozu Yasujiro • JPN • THAT NIGHT'S WIFE
SONO YO WA WASURENAI • 1962 • Yoshimura Kozaburo • JPN • WE WILL NEVER FORGET THAT NIGHT ○ NIGHT TO REMEMBER, A ○ HIROSHIMA HEARTACHE ○ I WON'T FORGET THAT NIGHT
SONOGONO HACHINOSU NO KODOMOTACHI • 1948 • Shimizu Hiroshi • JPN • CHILDREN OF THE BEEHIVE
SONOKOI MATTA NASHI • 1958 • Nakamura Noboru • JPN
SONONDER • 1971 • Trichardt Carel • SAF
SONORA • 1968 • Balcazar Alfonso • SPN
SONORA • 1968 • Ochoa Jose • SPN
SONORA see **SARTANA NO PERDONE** • 1968

SONORA KID, THE • 1927 • De Lacy Robert • USA
SONORA STAGECOACH • 1944 • Tansey Robert • USA
SONRIA POR FAVOR • 1964 • Balbuena Silvio F., Cano Manuel • SPN
SONRISA DE LA VIRGEN, LA • 1957 • Rodriguez Roberto • MXC • LITTLE ANGEL (USA)
SONRISA DE LOS POBRES, LA • 1963 • Baledon Rafael • MXC
SONS, THE see **SYNI** • 1946
SONS AND DAUGHTERS • 1951 • Sze Tung-San • CHN
SONS AND DAUGHTERS • 1967 • Stoll Jerry • DOC • USA
SONS AND LOVERS • 1960 • Cardiff Jack • UKN
SONS AND MOTHERS (USA) see **SERDTSE MATERI** • 1966
SON'S DEVOTION, A • 1912 • *Lubin* • USA
SON'S DEVOTION, A • 1913 • *Eclair* • USA
SON'S EXAMPLE, A • 1912 • *Melies* • USA
SONS FOR THE RETURN HOME • 1979 • Maunder Paul • NZL
SON'S INGRATITUDE, A • 1912 • *Eclair* • USA
SONS O' GUNS • 1936 • Bacon Lloyd • USA
SONS OF .. see **AWLAD EL EIH** • 1988
SONS OF A SOLDIER • 1913 • *Truesdale Fred* • USA
SONS OF ADVENTURE • 1948 • Canutt Yakima • USA
SONS OF FIERRO see **HIJOS DE FIERRO, LOS** • 1972
SONS OF INGMAR, THE see **INGMARSSONERNA** • 1919
SONS OF KATIE ELDER, THE • 1965 • Hathaway Henry • USA
SONS OF LIBERTY • 1939 • Curtiz Michael • SHT • USA
SONS OF MARTHA • 1907 • Raymond Charles? • UKN
SONS OF MATTHEW • 1949 • Chauvel Charles • ASL • RUGGED O'RIORDANS, THE
SONS OF MEN • 1918 • *Gilbert John* • USA
SONS OF NEW MEXICO • 1950 • English John • USA • BRAT, THE (UKN)
SONS OF SATAN • 1973 • Brooks Lancer • USA
SONS OF SATAN see **BASTARDI, I** • 1968
SONS OF SATAN, THE • 1915 • Tucker George Loane • UKN
SONS OF STEEL • 1988 • Keady Gary L. • ASL
SONS OF THE AIR • 1944 • Knight Castleton • UKN
SONS OF THE DESERT • 1933 • Seiter William A. • USA • FRATERNALLY YOURS (UKN) ○ SONS OF THE LEGION ○ CONVENTION CITY
SONS OF THE GOOD EARTH see **TA-TI NU-ERH** • 1967
SONS OF THE LEGION • 1938 • Hogan James P. • USA
SONS OF THE LEGION see **SONS OF THE DESERT** • 1933
SONS OF THE LO'WAIST GANG • 1967 • Pacheco Lauro • PHL
SONS OF THE MUSKETEERS (UKN) see **AT SWORD'S POINT** • 1951
SONS OF THE NORTHWOODS • 1912 • *Clary Charles* • USA
SONS OF THE PEOPLE see **SYNOWIE LUDU** • 1954
SONS OF THE PIONEERS • 1942 • Kane Joseph • USA
SONS OF THE SADDLE • 1930 • Brown Harry J. • USA
SONS OF THE SEA • 1916 • Wilson Millard K. • SHT • USA
SONS OF THE SEA • 1925 • Woolfe H. Bruce • UKN
SONS OF THE SEA • 1939 • Elvey Maurice • UKN
SONS OF THE SEA • 1942 • Forde Walter • UKN, USA
SONS OF THE SEA see **CHIN-SHUI SHEN** • 1988
SONS OF THE SEA (UKN) see **OLD IRONSIDES** • 1926
SONS OF THE SEA (USA) see **ATLANTIC FERRY** • 1941
SONS OF THE WEST • 1910 • *Nestor* • USA
SONS OF THE WEST • 1922 • *Aywon Film Corp* • USA
SONS OF THUNDER (UKN) see **TITANS, LES** • 1962
SONS OF TOIL, THE • 1915 • *Stanton Richard* • USA
SON'S RETURN, THE • 1909 • Griffith D. W. • USA
SONT MORTS LES BATISSEURS • 1958 • Berne Edouard • FRN
SONTAG DES LEBENS • 1930 • Mittler Leo • FRG
SONTAGSFAHRER • 1963 • Klein Gerhard • GDR • SUNDAY EXCURSION
SONTO • 1981 • SAF
SOOKY • 1931 • Taurog Norman • USA
SOONER OR LATER • 1920 • Ruggles Wesley • USA
SOONER OR LATER • 1978 • Hart Bruce • TVM • USA
SOOO NICHT, MEINE HERREN • 1960 • Burk Michael • AUS
SOOTARANG see **SUTORANG** • 1964
SOOTY SKETCHES • 1909 • Booth W. R. • UKN
SOPHIA see **ZOFIA** • 1977
SOPHIA DE MELLO BREYNER ANDRESEN • 1969 • Monteiro Joao Cesar • SHT • PRT
SOPHIA LOREN: HER OWN STORY • 1980 • Stuart Mel • TVM • USA
SOPHIA PEROVSKAYA see **SOFYA PEROVSKAYA** • 1968
SOPHIA'S IMAGINARY VISITORS • 1914 • Edwin Walter • USA
SOPHIE • Love John • FRN
SOPHIE AND THE FAKER • 1915 • *Joslyn Margaret* • USA
SOPHIE AND THE MAN OF HER CHOICE • 1914 • *Potel Victor* • USA
SOPHIE AND THE SCALE see **SOPHIE ET LES GAMMES** • 1964
SOPHIE CHANGES HER MIND • 1915 • *Joslyn Margaret* • USA
SOPHIE ET LE CRIME • 1955 • Gaspard-Huit Pierre • FRN
SOPHIE ET LES GAMMES • 1964 • Pappe Julien • SHT • FRN • SOPHIE AND THE SCALE
SOPHIE FINDS A HERO • 1914 • *Joslyn Margaret* • USA
SOPHIE GETS STUNG • 1914 • *Joselyn Margaret* • USA
SOPHIE LANG GOES WEST • 1937 • Reisner Charles F. • USA
SOPHIE OF THE FILMS • 1914 • Christie Al • SRL • USA
SOPHIE PICKS A DEAD ONE • 1914 • *Joslyn Margaret* • USA
SOPHIE PULLS A GOOD ONE • 1914 • *Essanay* • USA
SOPHIE SEMENOFF see **MAKING THE GRADE** • 1921
SOPHIE STARTS SOMETHING • 1914 • *Essanay* • USA
SOPHIE THE WITCH see **COPRNICA ZOFKA** • 1989
SOPHIENLUND • 1943 • Ruhmann Heinz • FRG
SOPHIE'S BIRTHDAY PARTY • 1914 • *Potel Victor* • USA
SOPHIE'S CHOICE • 1982 • Pakula Alan J. • USA
SOPHIE'S FATAL WEDDING • 1914 • *Essanay* • USA
SOPHIE'S FIGHTING SPIRIT • 1915 • *Joslin Margaret* • USA
SOPHIE'S HERO • 1913 • *Joslyn Margaret* • USA
SOPHIE'S HOMECOMING • 1915 • *Essanay* • USA
SOPHIE'S LEGACY • 1914 • *Essanay* • USA
SOPHIE'S NEW FOREMAN • 1913 • *Joslin Margaret* • USA
SOPHIE'S PLACE (USA) see **CROOKS AND CORONETS** • 1969
SOPHIE'S SWEETHEART • 1914 • *Joslin Margaret* • USA
SOPHISTICATED GENTS, THE • 1981 • Falk Harry • TVM • USA
SOPHISTICATED VAMPS • Fayman Lynn • SHT • USA
SOPHOMORE, THE • 1929 • McCarey Leo • USA • COMPROMISED (UKN)
SOPHOMORE'S ROMANCE, THE • 1911 • *Essanay* • USA
SOPHY OF KRAVONIA • 1920 • Fontaine Gerard • USA • VIRGIN OF PARIS, THE
SOPLO DE ESPLENDOR • 1973 • Benito Carlos • SPN
SOPOT 57 • 1957 • Hofman Eduard, Skorzewski Edward • DOC • PLN
SOPPY GREEN LOSES A LEGACY • 1912 • Coleby A. E.? • UKN
SOPRALLUOGHI IN PALESTINA • 1964 • Pasolini Pier Paolo • ITL
SOPRAVVISSUTI DELLA CITTA' MORTA, I • 1984 • Margheriti Antonio • ITL • SURVIVORS OF THE DEAD CITY, THE
SOPRAVVISSUTI, I see **ECCE HOMO** • 1969
SOPRAVVISSUTO, IL • 1916 • Genina Augusto • ITL
SOR ALEGRIA • 1952 • Davison Tito • MXC
SOR ANGELICA • 1954 • Romero-Marchent Joaquin Luis • SPN
SOR CITROEN • 1967 • Lazaga Pedro • SPN • SISTER CITROEN
SOR INTREPIDA • 1952 • Gil Rafael • SPN • SONG OF SISTER MARIA, THE (USA)
SOR JUANA INES DE LA CRUZ • 1935 • Peon Ramon • MXC
SOR YE-YE • 1968 • Fernandez Ramon • SPN, MXC • SISTER YE-YE
SORA KAKERU HANAYOME • 1959 • Bansho Yoshiaki • JPN • HIGH-FLYING BRIDE
SORA WA HARETARI • 1925 • Gosho Heinosuke • JPN • NO CLOUDS IN THE SKY ○ SKY SHINES, THE ○ SKY IS CLEAR, THE
SORANO DAIKAIJYU • 1956 • Honda Inoshiro • JPN • RODAN ○ RADON
SORATOBU YUREISEN • 1969 • Ikeda Hiroshi • JPN • FLYING PHANTOM SHIP
SORAYA, QUEEN OF THE DESERT see **SORAYA, REINA DEL DESIERTO** • 1965
SORAYA, REINA DEL DESIERTO • 1965 • SPN • SORAYA, QUEEN OF THE DESERT
SORBET • 1968 • Zwartjes Frans • SHT • NTH
SORBOLE.. CHE ROMAGNOLA! • 1976 • Rizzo Alfredo • ITL
SORCELLERIE CULINAIRE, LA • 1904 • Melies Georges • FRN • COOK IN TROUBLE, THE (USA) ○ CULINARY SORCERY
SORCELLERIE NOCTURNE, LA • 1903 • Velle Gaston • SHT • FRN • NOCTURNAL SORCERY
SORCERER • 1977 • Friedkin William • USA • WAGES OF FEAR, THE (UKN)
SORCERER, THE • 1954 • *Panda* • USA
SORCERER, THE • 1960 • Sens Al • ANS • CND
SORCERER, THE see **SORTILEGES** • 1944
SORCERER, THE see **YOSO** • 1963
SORCERER, THE (UKN) see **TYRANT OF RED GULCH, THE** • 1928
SORCERER FROM OUTER SPACE • 1962-29 • Carpenter John • SHT • USA
SORCERER OF ATHENS, THE • 1931 • Madras • GRC
SORCERER, THE PRINCE AND THE GOOD FAIRY, THE see **SORCIER, LE PRINCE ET LE BON GENIE, LE** • 1900
SORCERERS, THE • 1967 • Reeves Michael • UKN
SORCERER'S APPRENTICE, THE • Calinescu Bob • ANM • RMN
SORCERER'S APPRENTICE, THE • 1933 • SHT • USA
SORCERER'S APPRENTICE, THE • 1955 • Powell Michael • SHT • USA
SORCERER'S APPRENTICE, THE • 1985 • Popescu-Gopo Ion • RMN
SORCERER'S CURSE, THE see **MAGIC SWORD, THE** • 1962
SORCERER'S EYE, THE • 1980 • Jackson G. Philip • MTV • CND
SORCERER'S LOVE see **AMOR BRUJO, EL** • 1967
SORCERER'S REVENGE, THE see **SORCIER, LE** • 1903
SORCERER'S VILLAGE, THE • 1958 • Davis Hassoldt • DOC • VOODOO VILLAGE
SORCERESS • 1982 • Stuart Brian • USA • DEVIL'S ADVOCATE, THE
SORCERESS, THE • 1914 • Smiley Joseph • USA
SORCERESS, THE • 1917 • *Rawlinson Herbert* • SHT • USA
SORCERESS, THE see **HAXAN** • 1955
SORCERESS OF THE STRAND • 1910 • *Eclair* • FRN
SORCEROR'S SCISSORS, THE • 1907 • Booth W. R. • UKN
SORCERY • 1928 • Christensen Benjamin
SORCERY see **MALEFICES** • 1962
SORCIER, LE • 1903 • Melies Georges • FRN • WITCH'S REVENGE, THE (USA) ○ SORCERER'S REVENGE, THE
SORCIER BLANC, LE see **JUNGLE EN FOLIE, LA** • 1952
SORCIER DU CIEL, LE • 1948 • Blistene Marcel • FRN • HEAVEN AND EARTH
SORCIER, LE PRINCE ET LE BON GENIE, LE • 1900 • Melies Georges • FRN • WIZARD, THE PRINCE AND THE GOOD FAIRY, THE (USA) ○ SORCERER, THE PRINCE AND THE GOOD FAIRY, THE
SORCIERE, LA (FRN) see **HAXAN** • 1955
SORCIERES, LES see **DELITTO DEL DIAVOLO, IL** • 1970
SORCIERES DE SALEM, LES • 1957 • Rouleau Raymond • FRN, GDR • HEXEN VON SALEM, DIE (GDR) ○ CRUCIBLE, THE (USA) ○ WITCHES OF SALEM, THE
SORCIERES DU BORD DU LAC, LES (FRN) see **DELITTO DEL DIAVOLO, IL** • 1970
SORCIERES, LES (FRN) see **STREGHE, LE** • 1967
SORDID AFFAIR, A see **UOMO DI PAGLIA, L'** • 1957
SORDID AFFAIR, A see **MALEDETTO IMBROGLIO, UN** • 1959
SORDO, EL • 1958 • Cardona Rene • MXC
SOREKARA • 1985 • Morita Yoshimitsu • JPN • AND THEN
SORELLA • 1920 • Caserini Mario • ITL
SORELLA CONTRO SORELLA • 1920 • Brenon Herbert • ITL • SISTER AGAINST SISTER (USA)
SORELLA DI SATANA, LA (ITL) see **REVENGE OF THE BLOOD BEAST, THE** • 1966
SORELLA DI URSULA, LA • 1978 • Milioni Enzo • ITL
SORELLE, LE • 1969 • Malenotti Roberto • ITL, FRN • SISTERS, THE (UKN)
SORELLE MATERASSI • 1943 • Poggioli Ferdinando M. • ITL • MATERASSI SISTERS, THE
SOREN DASSHUTSU ONNA GUNI TO NISE KYOJIN • 1958 • Magatani Morehei • JPN
SORENSEN AND RASMUSSEN • Viby Margaret, Gregers Emanuel • DNM
SORGA DUNIA DI PINTU NEKA • 1984 • Sulaiman Hengky • INN
SORGLUSTIGA BARBERAREN, DEN • 1927 • Locher Jens • DNM • TRAGICOMIC BARBER
SORIA-MORIA see **DROMDA DALEN, DEN** • 1947
SORLEY MACLEAN'S ISLAND • 1974 • Eadie Douglas • DOC • UKN
SOROCHINSKAYA YAMARKA see **SOROCHINSKY YARMAROK** • 1939
SOROCHINSKI FAIR, THE see **SOROCHINSKY YARMAROK** • 1939
SOROCHINSKY YARMAROK • 1939 • Ekk Nikolai • USS • SOROCHINSKI FAIR, THE ○ SOROCHINSKAYA YAMARKA
SOROK DEVYAT DNEI see **49 DNEY** • 1962
SOROK PERVYI • 1927 • Protazanov Yakov • USS • FORTY-FIRST, THE
SOROK PERVYI • 1956 • Chukhrai Grigori • USS • FORTY-FIRST, THE
SOROK SERDETS • 1931 • Kuleshov Lev • USS • FORTY HEARTS
SORORITY BABIES IN THE SLIMEBALL BOWL-O-RAMA • 1988 • Decoteau David • USA • IMP, THE
SORORITY GIRL • 1957 • Corman Roger • USA • BAD ONE, THE (UKN)
SORORITY HOUSE • 1939 • Farrow John • USA • THAT GIRL FROM COLLEGE (UKN)
SORORITY HOUSE MASSACRE • 1986 • Frank Carol • USA
SORORITY INITIATION • 1914 • *West Billie* • USA
SORORITY SISTER, THE • 1915 • Mitchell Bruce • USA
SORORITY SWEETHEARTS • *Monet Bridgette* • USA
SORPASSO, IL • 1962 • Risi Dino • ITL • EASY LIFE, THE ○ OVERTAKING, THE
SORPRESAS, LAS • 1975 • Fischermann Alberto, Puenzo Luis, Galettini D. C. • ARG • SURPRISES
SORPRESE DEL DIVORZIO, LE • 1939 • Brignone Guido • ITL
SORPRESE DEL VAGONE LETTO, LE • 1941 • Rosmino Gian Paolo • ITL
SORPRESE DELL'AMORE, LE • 1959 • Comencini Luigi • ITL
SORRELL AND SON • 1927 • Brenon Herbert • USA
SORRELL AND SON • 1933 • Raymond Jack • UKN
SORRENTINA see **PUPPETS OF FATE** • 1921
SORRENTO • 1968 • Garces Armando • PHL
SORRISI E CANZONI • 1958 • Capuano Luigi • ITL
SORRISO DEL GRANDE TENTATORE, IL • 1974 • Damiani Damiano • ITL, UKN • TEMPTER, THE (UKN) ○ DEVIL IS A WOMAN, THE (USA)
SORRISO DEL RAGNO, IL • 1971 • Castellani Massimo • ITL
SORRISO DELLA IENA, IL • 1972 • Amadio Silvio • ITL
SORRISO, UNO SCHIAFFO, UN BACIO IN BOCCA, UN • 1975 • Lucherini Enrico, Morra Mario • ITL
SORROW AND THE PITY, THE (USA) see **CHAGRIN ET LA PITIE, LE** • 1970
SORROW AND TREASURE see **GANJ-VA-RANJ** • 1967
SORROW IS ONLY FOR WOMEN see **KANASHIMI WA ONNA DAKENI** • 1958
SORROW OF TWO HEARTS, THE see **DEHADAKA DUKA** • 1968
SORROWFUL EXAMPLE, THE • 1911 • Griffith D. W. • USA
SORROWFUL JONES • 1949 • Lanfield Sidney • USA
SORROWFUL SHORE, THE • 1913 • Griffith D. W. • USA
SORROWFUL SPRING, THE see **DERTLI PINAR** • 1968
SORROWS AND HAPPINESS see **GHAMHA & SHADIHA** • 1968
SORROWS OF A CHAPERONE, THE • 1909 • Fitzhamon Lewin • UKN
SORROWS OF ISRAEL, THE • 1913 • *Imp* • USA
SORROWS OF LOVE, THE • 1916 • Giblyn Charles • USA
SORROWS OF SARAH see **GORE SARRI** • 1913
SORROWS OF SATAN, THE • 1917 • Butler Alexander • UKN
SORROWS OF SATAN, THE • 1926 • Griffith D. W. • USA
SORROWS OF SELINA, THE • 1914 • Aylott Dave • UKN
SORROWS OF THE UNFAITHFUL, THE • 1910 • Griffith D. W. • USA
SORROWS OF THE WAR, THE see **MALHEURS DE LA GUERRE, LA** • 1962
SORROWS OF YOUNG WERTHER, THE see **LEIDEN DES JUNGEN WERTHER, DIE** • 1976
SORRY, CAN'T STOP • 1909 • Aylott Dave • UKN
SORRY I'M LATE see **SCUSATE IL RITARDO** • 1983
SORRY SAFARI • 1962 • Deitch Gene • ANS • USA
SORRY, WRONG NUMBER • 1948 • Litvak Anatole • USA
SORRY YOU'VE BEEN TROUBLED • 1932 • Raymond Jack • UKN • LIFE GOES ON
SORT-OF-GIRL-WHO-CAME-FROM-HEAVEN, THE • 1915 • Ince Ralph • USA
SORTE DROM, DEN see **SCHWARZE TRAUM, DER** • 1911
SORTE HERTUNG, DEN • 1907 • *Holger-Madsen* • DNM
SORTE KANSLER, DEN • 1912 • Blom August • DNM • BLACK CHANCELLOR, THE
SORTE VEJ, DEN • 1987 • Hauge Knud • DOC • DNM • BLACK ROAD, THE
SORTEPER • 1979 • Hartkopp Christian • DOC • DNM • BLACK MAN
SORTI SANS PERMISSION • 1898 • Melies Georges • FRN • SOLDIER'S FRENCH LEAVE, A
SORTIE 234 • 1988 • Langlois Michel • SHT • CND
SORTIE DE SECOURS • 1970 • Kahane Roger • FRN
SORTIE DES ATELIERS VIBERT • 1896 • Melies Georges • FRN • CLOSING HOURS AT VIBERT'S PERFUME FACTORY
SORTIE DES OUVRIERS DE L'USINE LUMIERE see **SORTIE DES USINES, LA** • 1894
SORTIE DES USINES, LA • 1894 • Lumiere Louis • FRN • SORTIE DES OUVRIERS DE L'USINE LUMIERE
SORTIE DU PORT, LA see **BARQUE SORTANT DU PORT** • 1895
SORTIE DU "RUBIS", UNE • 1950 • Cousteau Jacques • FRN • PLONGE DU "RUBIS", UNE
SORTILEGES • 1944 • Christian-Jaque • FRN • BELLMAN, THE (USA) ○ CAVALIER DE RIOUCLARE, LE ○ SORCERER, THE ○ WITCHCRAFT
SORTILEGIO • 1970 • Bonomi Nardo • ITL
SORTING OFFICE • 1935 • Watt Harry (c/d) • DCS • UKN

SORUNGETH SORU • 1967 • Wilson Mike • SLN • THIEF OF THIEVES
SOS CONCORDE see **CONCORDE AFFAIRE '79** • 1979
SOS -EN SEGERSALLSKAPSRESA • 1989 • Aberg Lasse • SWD • S.O.S. SWEDES AT SEA
SOS IN THE MOUNTAINS see **HORSKE VOLANI SOS** • 1929
SO'S YOUR AUNT EMMA! • 1942 • Yarbrough Jean • USA • MEET THE MOB
SO'S YOUR OLD MAN • 1926 • La Cava Gregory • USA
SO'S YOUR UNCLE • 1943 • Yarbrough Jean • USA • LET YOURSELF GO
SOSEIJI GAKKYU • 1956 • Hani Susumu • DOC • JPN • TWIN SISTERS
SOSHI GEKIJO • 1947 • Inagaki Hiroshi • JPN • POLITICAL THEATRE
SOSHIKI BORYOKU • 1967 • Sato Junya • JPN • ORGANISED VIOLENCE
SOSHUN • 1956 • Ozu Yasujiro • JPN • EARLY SPRING
SOSHUN • 1968 • Nakamura Noboru • JPN • SPRING BREEZE
SOSIE, LE • 1915 • Feuillade Louis • FRN
SOSKEN PA GUDS JORD • 1983 • Mikkelsen Laila • NRW • CHILDREN OF THE EARTH
SOSPECHOSA, LA • 1954 • Gout Alberto • MXC
SOSPETTO DI FRANCESCO MASELLI, IL • 1975 • Maselli Francesco • ITL
SOSPIROSA, LA • 1964 • Salce Luciano • ITL
SOSTENUTO • 1987 • Perrenet Armand • SHT • NTH
SOSTER CECILIES OFFER see **HVOR SORGERNE GLEMMES** • 1916
SOSTYAZANIE • 1964 • Mansurov Bulat • USS • CONTROVERSY
SOTA, CABALLO Y REY • 1943 • O'Quigley Roberto • MXC
SOTAERAKKO • 1972 • Mollberg Rauni • MTV • FNL • WAR RECLUSE, THE
SOTANO, EL • 1950 • de Mayora Jaime • SPN
SOTEIO • 1927 • Uchida Tomu • JPN
SOTELO • 1976 • Ruiz Raul • SHT • FRN
SOTLUGG OCH LINLUGG • 1948 • Thermaenius Sven • SWD
SOTO • 1972 • Brandler Alfredo • SHT • VNZ
SOTTACETTI • 1972 • Bozzetto Bruno • ANS • ITL • PICKLES
SOTTO A CHI TOCCA • 1972 • Parolini Gianfranco • ITL
SOTTO DIECI BANDIERE • 1960 • Coletti Duilio, Narizzano Silvio • ITL, UKN, USA • UNDER TEN FLAGS (UKN)
SOTTO GLI OCCHI DELL'ASSASSINO see **TENEBRAE** • 1982
SOTTO IL CIELO STELLATO • 1966 • Castellani Renato • ITL
SOTTO IL RISTORANTE CINESE • 1987 • Bozzetto Bruno • ITL
SOTTO IL SEGNO DELLA SCORPIONE • 1969 • Taviani Paolo, Taviani Vittorio • ITL • UNDER THE SIGN OF SCORPIO
SOTTO IL SOLE DI ROMA • 1948 • Castellani Renato • ITL • UNDER THE SUN OF ROME (USA)
SOTTO IL TALLONE (ITL) see **METAMORPHOSE DES CLOPORTES** • 1965
SOTTO IL VESTITO NIENTE • 1985 • Vanzina Carlo • ITL • NOTHING UNDERNEATH (UKN) ○ NOTHING UNDER THE DRESS
SOTTO LA CROCE DEL SUD • 1938 • Brignone Guido • ITL
SOTTO LA CROCE DEL SUD • 1957 • Zancarella Adriano • ITL
SOTTO.. SOTTO, STRAPAZZATO DA ANOMALA PASSIONE • 1984 • Wertmuller Lina • ITL • BENEATH THE SURFACE, STRICKEN BY ANOMALOUS PASSION ○ SOTTO, SOTTO (USA)
SOTTO, SOTTO (USA) see **SOTTO.. SOTTO, STRAPAZZATO DA ANOMALA PASSIONE** • 1984
SOUBRETTE, THE • 1913 • *White Pearl* • USA
SOUBRETTE, THE • 1917 • Curtis Allen • SHT • USA
SOUBRETTE AND THE SIMP, THE • 1914 • Hotaling Arthur D.? • USA
SOUBRETTE ET LE LUTIN, LA • 1909 • Jasset Victorin • FRN
SOUBRETTE PERVERSE, LA • 1975 • Benazeraf Jose • FRN
SOUBRETTE'S CREDENTIALS, THE • 1899 • *Warwick Trading Co* • UKN
SOUBRETTES DU PLAISIR, LES • Reinhard Pierre B. • FRN
SOUBRETTE'S TROUBLES ON A FIFTH AVENUE STAGE • 1901 • Porter Edwin S. • USA
SOUF, LE • Kerzabi Ahmed • ALG
SOUFFLE AU COEUR, LE • 1971 • Malle Louis • FRN, ITL, FRG • SOFFIO AL CUORE (ITL) ○ MURMUR OF THE HEART (USA) ○ DEAREST LOVE (UKN)
SOUFFLE DE LA LIBERTE, LE see **ANDREA CHENIER** • 1955
SOUFFLE DU DESIR, LE • 1957 • Lepage Henri • FRN
SOUFFRANCES D'UN OEUF MEURTRI, LES • 1967 • Lethem Roland • SHT • BLG
SOUFRIERE, LA • 1976 • Herzog Werner • SHT • FRN
SOUGANDH • 1942 • *Sircar B. N. (P)* • IND
SOUHAITS DE BOUT DE ZAN, LES • 1913 • Feuillade Louis • FRN
SOUHVEZDI PANNY • 1966 • Brynych Zbynek • CZC • SIGN OF THE VIRGIN (USA) ○ CONSTELLATION OF THE VIRGO ○ CONSTELLATION: VIRGO
SOUKROMA VICHRICE • 1967 • Bocan Hynek • CZC • PRIVATE WINDSTORM ○ PRIVATE HURRICANE ○ PERSONAL TEMPEST, A ○ PRIVATE GALE
SOUL see **LAONIANG GOUSAO** • 1987
SOUL ADRIFT, A • 1918 • Blache Alice • USA
SOUL ADRIFT, A see **TARNISHED REPUTATION** • 1920
SOUL AFRICA • 1971 • SAF
SOUL AND BODY • 1921 • Beal Frank • USA
SOUL ASTRAY, A • 1914 • Ricketts Thomas • USA
SOUL AT STAKE, A • 1916 • Garwood William • SHT • USA
SOUL CATCHING BLACK MAGIC, THE see **KOU-HUN CHIANG T'OU** • 1976
SOUL ENSLAVED, A • 1916 • Madison Cleo • USA
SOUL-FIRE • 1925 • Robertson John S. • USA
SOUL FOR SALE, A • 1918 • Holubar Allen • USA
SOUL FOR SALE, A (USA) see **WOMAN WHO DARED, THE** • 1915
SOUL HARVEST, THE see **SOULS IN BONDAGE** • 1923
SOUL HERDER, THE • 1917 • Ford John • SHT • USA
SOUL IN BONDAGE, A • 1913 • Brooke Van Dyke • USA
SOUL IN TRUST, A • 1918 • Hamilton G. P. • USA
SOUL IS GREATER THAN THE WORLD, THE • 1985 • Jarl Stefan • SWD
SOUL LOVER • 1970 • *Stacey Dist.* • USA
SOUL MAN • 1986 • Miner Steve • USA
SOUL MAN, THE • 1916 • Webster Harry Mcrae • SHT • USA
SOUL MARKET, THE • 1916 • Grandon Francis J. • USA
SOUL MASTER, THE • 1917 • Bertsch Marguerite • USA
SOUL MATE, THE • 1914 • Grandon Francis J. • USA
SOUL MATES • 1914 • Hamilton G. P. • USA
SOUL MATES • 1916 • Russell William • USA
SOUL MATES • 1925 • Conway Jack • USA
SOUL MONSTER, THE see **SOUL OF A MONSTER, THE** • 1944
SOUL OF A CHILD, THE • 1916 • Gorman John • USA
SOUL OF A HEEL • 1938 • Lord Del • SHT • USA
SOUL OF A MAGDALENE see **SOUL OF MAGDALEN, THE** • 1917
SOUL OF A MAN, THE • 1921 • Nigh William • USA
SOUL OF A MONSTER, THE • 1944 • Jason Will • USA • SOUL MONSTER, THE ○ DEATH WALKS ALONE
SOUL OF A NATION, THE • 1934 • Williams J. B. • UKN
SOUL OF A PLUMBER, THE • 1917 • *Keystone* • SHT • USA
SOUL OF A ROSE, THE • 1913 • *Hawley Ormi* • USA
SOUL OF A SWORDSMAN see **CHIEN-NU YU-HU** • 1970
SOUL OF A THIEF • 1913 • Dwan Allan • USA
SOUL OF A WOMAN, THE • 1915 • Carewe Edwin • USA
SOUL OF A WOMAN, THE • 1922 • *Novak Jane* • USA
SOUL OF A WOMAN, THE see **DESTINY** • 1915
SOUL OF BROADWAY, THE • 1915 • Brenon Herbert • USA
SOUL OF BRONZE, THE • 1921 • *Houdini Harry* • USA
SOUL OF BUDDHA, THE • 1918 • Edwards J. Gordon • USA
SOUL OF FRANCE, THE • 1929 • Ryder Alexandre • FRN
SOUL OF GUILDA LOIS, THE • 1919 • Wilson Frank • UKN • SOUL'S CRUCIFIXION, A
SOUL OF HONOR, THE • 1914 • Kirkwood James • USA
SOUL OF KURA SAN, THE • 1916 • Le Saint Edward J. • USA
SOUL OF LUIGI, THE • 1914 • Marston Theodore • USA
SOUL OF MAGDALEN, THE • 1917 • King Burton L. • USA • SOUL OF A MAGDALENE
SOUL OF MAN, THE • 1913 • *Levering Joseph* • USA
SOUL OF MEXICO • 1932 • Kirkland David • USA
SOUL OF NIGGER CHARLEY, THE • 1973 • Spangler Larry • USA
SOUL OF PHYRA, THE • 1915 • *Markey Enid* • USA
SOUL OF PIERRE, THE • 1915 • Vale Travers • USA
SOUL OF SATAN, THE • 1917 • Turner Otis • USA
SOUL OF THE ACCORDION, THE (USA) see **ALMA DEL BANDONEON, EL** • 1935
SOUL OF THE BEAST • 1923 • Wray John Griffith • USA • TEN TON LOVE
SOUL OF THE DESERT, THE • 1914 • Miles Mr. • USA
SOUL OF THE SEA see **HAI HUN** • 1957
SOUL OF THE SLUMS • 1931 • Strayer Frank • USA • SAMARITAN, THE (UKN)
SOUL OF THE SOUTH, THE • 1913 • *Ray Charles* • USA
SOUL OF THE VASE, THE • 1915 • Taylor William D. • USA
SOUL OF THE VIOLIN, THE • 1912 • *Solax* • USA
SOUL OF VENICE, THE • 1910 • *Vitagraph* • USA
SOUL OF YOUTH, THE • 1920 • Taylor William D. • USA
SOUL RECLAIMED, A • 1912 • *Essanay* • USA
SOUL SNATCHER, THE • 1965 • Zimmer H. L. • USA
SOUL SOLDIERS • 1970 • Cardos John Bud • USA • RED, WHITE AND BLACK, THE
SOUL TO DEVILS, A see **YAMI NO NAKA NO CHIMIMORYO** • 1971
SOUL TO SOUL • 1913 • *Eclair* • USA
SOUL TO SOUL • 1971 • Sanders Denis • DOC • USA
SOUL TRIUMPHANT • 1917 • Cabanne W. Christy • USA
SOUL WITHOUT WINDOWS, A • 1918 • Vale Travers • USA
SOULIER DE "BEU", LES • 1975 • Plamondon Leo • DCS • CND
SOULIER QUI VOLE, LE • 1980 • Debout Jean-Jacques • FRN
SOULIER TROP PETIT, LE • 1910 • Linder Max • FRN
SOULIERS DE DRANEM, LES • 1908 • Zecca Ferdinand • FRN
SOULIERS DU FACTEUR, LES • 1909 • Jasset Victorin • FRN
SOULIERS EN CROCO, LES see **ALLIGATOR SHOES** • 1981
SOULIOTES • 1970 • Grigoriou Grigoris • GRC • MEN OF SOULS, THE
SOULMATES OF SHANGO see **LORD SHANGO** • 1975
SOULS ADRIFT • 1917 • Knoles Harley • USA
SOULS ADRIFT • 1919 • Perret Leonce • USA
SOULS ADRIFT see **MAD MARRIAGE, THE** • 1925
SOULS AFLAME • 1928 • Wells Raymond • USA
SOULS AT SEA • 1937 • Hathaway Henry • USA
SOUL'S AWAKENING, A • 1922 • Kellino W. P. • UKN
SOULS COURAGEOUS • 1911 • *Reliance* • USA
SOUL'S CRUCIFIXION, A see **SOUL OF GUILDA LOIS, THE** • 1919
SOUL'S CYCLES, THE • 1916 • Davis Ulysses • USA
SOULS DEPARTMENT, THE see **SEFUL SECTORULUI SUFLETE** • 1967
SOULS FOR SABLES • 1925 • McKay James C. • USA
SOULS FOR SABLES (UKN) see **LOVEBOUND** • 1932
SOULS FOR SALE • 1923 • Hughes Rupert • USA
SOULS FOR SALE see **CONFESSIONS OF AN OPIUM EATER** • 1962
SOULS IN BONDAGE • 1916 • Lewis Edgar • USA
SOULS IN BONDAGE • 1923 • Clifford William H. • USA • SOUL HARVEST, THE
SOULS IN CONFLICT • 1955 • Ross Dick, Reeve Leonard • UKN
SOULS IN EXILE (UKN) see **BROKEN HEARTS** • 1926
SOULS IN PAIN • 1930 • Samuelson G. B. • UKN
SOULS IN PAWN • 1915 • Wilson Ben • USA
SOULS IN PAWN • 1917 • King Henry • USA
SOULS IN THE SHADOW • 1912 • *Cornwall Blanche* • USA
SOULS OF CHILDREN, THE see **AMES D'ENFANTS** • 1928
SOULS OF MEN • 1921 • *Jeffries William* • USA
SOULS OF SIN see **MALE AND FEMALE SINCE ADAM AND EVE** • 1961
SOULS OF THE MAD see **AMES DE FOUS** • 1917
SOULS ON THE ROAD see **ROJO NO REIKAN** • 1921
SOULS THAT MEET IN THE NIGHT • 1916 • *Fleitzer Film* • USA
SOUL'S TRAGEDY, A • 1915 • *Clark Bessie* • USA
SOULS TRIUMPHANT • 1917 • O'Brien Jack • USA
SOULS UNITED • 1917 • Grandon Francis J. • SHT • USA
SOUMISE, LA • Whyte Andrew • FRN
SOUMISSIONS PERVERSES • 1977 • Ayranu Lino • FRN
SOUND ABSTRACT see **SOM ABSTRATO** • 1958
SOUND AND FURY IN HAME see **TOHINAA HAMEESSA** • 1977
SOUND AND THE FURY, THE • 1959 • Ritt Martin • USA
SOUND BARRIER, THE • 1952 • Lean David • UKN • BREAKING THE SOUND BARRIER (USA) ○ BREAKING THROUGH THE SOUND BARRIER
SOUND EROTICISM see **EGESZSEGES EROTIKA** • 1985
SOUND OF 7 WHISTLE BOMBS see **NGITNGIT NG PITONG WHISTLE BOMB** • 1968
SOUND OF ANGER, THE • 1968 • Ritchie Michael • TVM • USA
SOUND OF DIFFERENT DRUMMERS, A • 1957 • Frankenheimer John • MTV • USA
SOUND OF FLESH, THE • Stewart John • SHT • USA
SOUND OF FURY, THE (UKN) see **TRY AND GET ME** • 1950
SOUND OF HER VOICE, THE • 1914 • Elvey Maurice • UKN
SOUND OF HORROR (USA) see **SONIDO DE LA MUERTE, EL** • 1966
SOUND OF JAZZ, THE • 1957 • Smight Jack • MTV • USA
SOUND OF LAUGHTER, THE • 1963 • O'Shaughnessey John • USA
SOUND OF LIFE (USA) see **SLEPOY MUZYKANT** • 1961
SOUND OF LOVE, THE • 1979 • Power John • MTV • ASL
SOUND OF MUSIC, THE • 1965 • Wise Robert • USA
SOUND OF SPACE, THE • 1972 • Gagnon Charles • CND
SOUND OF THE CITY • 1973 • Clifton Peter • UKN • ROCK CITY
SOUND OF THE CITY: LONDON 1964-73 • 1981 • Clifton Peter • DOC • UKN
SOUND OF THE MOUNTAIN see **YAMA NO OTO** • 1954
SOUND OF THE TIDE, THE see **KAICHO-ON** • 1981
SOUND OF THE VIOLIN, THE see **KUNSTNERS GENNEMBRUD, EN** • 1915
SOUND OF TRUMPETS, THE see **POSTO, IL** • 1961
SOUND OF WAVES, THE see **SHIOSAI** • 1954
SOUND OFF • 1952 • Quine Richard • USA
SOUND SLEEPER, A • 1909 • Griffith D. W. • USA
SOUNDER • 1972 • Ritt Martin • USA
SOUNDER II see **PART 2 SOUNDER** • 1976
SOUNDLESS CRY see **KONO KOE NAKI SAKEBI** • 1965
SOUNDS FROM THE MOUNTAINS see **YAMA NO OTO** • 1954
SOUNDS KINDA RISKY • 1988 • Spencer James H. • USA
SOUNDS OF STREET CARS see **DODESKA DEN** • 1970
SOUNDS OF SUMMER: THE CONCORD JAZZ FESTIVAL • 1970 • *Kenton Stan* • DOC • USA
SOUNDS OF SYNANON • 1962 • Binder Steve • SHT • USA
SOUNDS OF THE SEVENTIES • 1971 • *Santana* • UKN
SOUNDTRACK • Spinello Barry • SHT • USA
SOUP AND FISH • 1934 • Meins Gus • SHT • USA
SOUP AND FISH BALL, THE • 1918 • Hotaling Arthur D. • SHT • USA
SOUP AND NUTS • 1916 • Curtis Allen • SHT • USA
SOUP FOR NUTS • 1934 • Schwarzwald Milton • SHT • USA
SOUP FOR ONE • 1982 • Kaufer Jonathan • USA
SOUP RUN • 1975 • Magar Guy • SHT • UKN
SOUP SONG, THE • 1931 • *Iwerks Ub (P)* • ANS • USA
SOUP TO MUTTS • 1939 • Kline Lester • ANS • USA
SOUP TO NUTS • 1925 • Watson William • USA
SOUP TO NUTS • 1930 • Stoloff Ben • USA
SOUP TO NUTS see **HERE COMES COOKIE** • 1935
SOUPCON see **IL Y A LONGTEMPS QUE JE T'AIME** • 1979
SOUPCON DE PEUR, UN see **SHAI'UN MINA AL-KHAWF** • 1969
SOUPCONS • 1956 • Billon Pierre • FRN
SOUPE A LA GRIMACE, LA • 1954 • Sacha Jean • FRN
SOUPE AU LAIT • 1959 • Chevalier Pierre • FRN
SOUPE AU POULET • 1963 • Wheeler Rene • FRN
SOUPE AUX CHOUX, LA • 1981 • Girault Jean • FRN
SOUPE AUX POULETS, LA • 1963 • Agostini Philippe • FRN
SOUPE FROIDE, LA • 1974 • Pouret Robert • FRN
SOUPER UM MITTERNACHT, DAS • 1921 • Werckmeister Hans • FRG
SOUPIERE, LA see **REPAS INFERNAL, LE** • 1901
SOUPIRANT, LE • 1962 • Etaix Pierre • FRN • SUITOR, THE
SOUPIRS D'ESPAGNE • 1939 • Perojo Benito • SPN
SOUPIRS PROFONDS • 1975 • Baudricourt Michel • FRN
SOUP'S ON • 1948 • Nichols Charles • ANS • USA
SOUR GRAPES • 1950 • Davis Mannie • ANS • USA
SOUR GRAPES • 1987 • De Bello John • USA • HAPPY HOUR
SOUR GRAPES see **LET'S TRY AGAIN** • 1934
SOUR GRIPES • 1963 • Kneitel Seymour • ANS • USA
SOUR PUSS • 1940 • Clampett Robert • ANS • USA
SOUR SWEET • 1989 • Newell Mike • UKN • SOURSWEET
SOURCE, LA • 1900 • Blache Alice • FRN
SOURCE, THE • 1918 • Crisp Donald?, Melford George? • USA
SOURCE, THE see **VERTIENTE, LA** • 1958
SOURCE, THE see **ZRODLO** • 1963
SOURCE OF HAPPINESS, THE • 1915 • Lloyd Frank • USA
SOURCE OF LOVE, THE see **PRAMEN LASKY** • 1928
SOURCIERS, LES • 1962 • Nacif Abdel-Halim • DCS • ALG
SOURCIERS DES AURES • 1970 • Nacif Abdel-Halim • ALG
SOURD DANS LA VILLE, LE • 1986 • Dansereau Mireille • CND • DEAF TO THE CITY
SOURDE OREILLE, LA • 1980 • Polac Michel • FRN
SOURDOUGH • 1977 • Spinelli Martin J. • USA
SOURDOUGHS, THE see **LOST IN ALASKA** • 1952
SOURIANTE MADAME BEAUDET, LA • 1922 • Dulac Germaine • FRN • SMILING MADAME BEAUDET, THE (USA)
SOURICIERE, LA • 1949 • Calef Henri • FRN
SOURING OF MILK • 1945-52 • Napier-Bell J. B. • DOC • UKN
SOURIRE, LE see **QUATRE SOURIRES, LES** • 1958
SOURIRE AUX LEVRES see **BONJOUR SOURIRE** • 1955
SOURIRE BLEU, LE • 1968 • Lagrange Yvan • FRN • BLUE SMILE, THE
SOURIRE DANS LA TEMPETE, UN • 1950 • Chanas Rene • FRN, FRG
SOURIRE D'OR, LE see **GYLDNE SMIL, DEN** • 1935
SOURIRE VERTICAL, LE • 1973 • Lapoujade Robert • FRN • VERTICAL SMILE, THE
SOURIRES A LA VIE • 1957 • Masson Jean • SHT • FRN
SOURIRES DE LA DESTINEE, LES see **VACANCES PORTUGAISES, LES** • 1963
SOURIS, LA • 1969 • Ifticene Mohamed • ALG
SOURIS BLANCHE, LA • 1911 • Feuillade Louis • FRN
SOURIS BLEUE, LA • 1936 • Ducis Pierre-Jean • FRN

SOURIS BLONDE, LA see BLANC COMME NEIGE • 1931
SOURIS CHEZ LES HOMMES, UNE • 1964 • Poitrenaud Jacques • FRN • DROLE DE CAID, UN
SOURIS, TU M'INQUIETES • 1973 • Danis Aime • CND
SOURSWEET see SOUR SWEET • 1989
SOUS-DOUES, LES • 1980 • Zidi Claude • FRN
SOUS-DOUES EN VACANCE, LES • 1982 • Zidi Claude • FRN
SOUS-DOUES PASSENT LE BAC, LES • 1981 • Zidi Claude • FRN
SOUS LA GRIFFE • 1913-18 • Durand Jean • FRN
SOUS LA GRIFFE • 1921 • Dieudonne Albert • FRN
SOUS LA GRIFFE • 1935 • Christian-Jaque • FRN
SOUS LA JOUG • 1911 • Feuillade Louis • FRN
SOUS LA LUNE DU MAROC • 1933 • Duvivier Julien • FRN • UNDER THE MOON OF MOROCCO (USA)
SOUS LA MASQUE • 1913 • Pouctal Henri • FRN
SOUS LA MENACE • 1917 • Hugon Andre • FRN
SOUS LA PLUIE DE L'AUTOMNE see TAHTA MATAR AL-KHARIF • 1970
SOUS LA PROTECTION • 1935 • Puchalski Eduard • USS
SOUS LA SIGNE DE ROME (FRN) see NEL SEGNO DI ROMA • 1959
SOUS LA SIGNE DU VAUDOUN • 1974 • Abikanlou Pascal • BNN
SOUS LA TERRE • 1931 • Matras Christian • SHT • FRN
SOUS LA TERREUR • 1935 • Cravenne Marcel, Forzano Giovacchino • FRN
SOUS LE CASQUE DE CUIR • 1931 • De Courville Albert • FRN
SOUS LE CIEL DE PARIS see SOUS LE CIEL DE PARIS COULE LE SEINE • 1950
SOUS LE CIEL DE PARIS COULE LE SEINE • 1950 • Duvivier Julien • FRN • UNDER THE PARIS SKY ○ SOUS LE CIEL DE PARIS
SOUS LE CIEL DE PROVENCE (FRN) see ERA DI VENERDI 17 • 1956
SOUS LE CIEL, SUR LA TERRE • 1965 • Vrijman Jan • NTH
SOUS LE MASQUE NOIR • 1958 • Haesaerts Paul • BLG
SOUS LE PEUPLIER see MIN QURB AS-SAFSAF • 1972
SOUS LE SIGNE DE MONTE-CRISTO • 1968 • Hunebelle Andre, Desagnat Jean-Pierre • FRN, ITL • MONTECRISTO '70 (ITL)
SOUS LE SIGNE DU TAUREAU • 1968 • Grangier Gilles • FRN
SOUS LE SOLEIL DE SATAN • 1987 • Pialat Maurice • FRN • UNDER SATAN'S SUN (USA)
SOUS LE VOILE, LA LIBERTE? • 1980 • Deffarge Claude • DOC • FRN
SOUS LES CASQUES DE CUIR • 1930 • Elias Francisco • FRN
SOUS LES DRAPS, LES ETOILES • 1990 • Gariepy Jean-Pierre • CND
SOUS LES PALMES DE MARRAKECH • 1948 • Mineur Jean • SHT • FRN
SOUS LES PHARES • 1917 • Hugon Andre • FRN
SOUS LES PONTS DE PARIS see CLODOCHE • 1938
SOUS LES TOITS DE PARIS • 1930 • Clair Rene • FRN • UNDER THE ROOFS OF PARIS (USA)
SOUS LES YEUX D'OCCIDENT • 1936 • Allegret Marc • FRN • RASUMOFF ○ RASUMOV
SOUS-MARIN BLESSE, LE see MAUDITS, LES • 1946
SOUS-MARIN DE CRISTAL, LE • 1927 • Vandal Marcel • FRN
SOUS-SOL • 1953 • Roy J. C., Malaussena S. • SHT • FRN
SOUS UN AUTRE SOLEIL • 1955 • de Broca Philippe • SHT • FRN
SOUSTO • 1960 • Nemec Jan • CZC • PIECE OF BREAD, A (UKN) ○ LOAF OF BREAD, A ○ BITE TO EAT, A ○ LOAF, THE ○ MORSEL, THE
SOUTAH-DECAN • 1977 • Hatami Ali • IRN
SOUTH, THE see SUR, EL • 1983
SOUTH, THE see SUR • 1987
SOUTH ADVANCING GIRLS see NANSHIN JOSEI • 1939
SOUTH ADVANCING WOMEN see NANSHIN JOSEI • 1939
SOUTH AFRICAN ESSAYS • 1964 • Macartney-Filgate Terence • DOC • USA
SOUTH AFRICANS, THE • 1976 • SAF
SOUTH AMERICAN GEORGE • 1941 • Varnel Marcel • UKN
SOUTH AMERICAN SWAY • 1944 • Negulesco Jean • SHT • USA
SOUTH BEFORE THE WAR, THE • 1910 • *London Cinematograph Co* • UKN
SOUTH BRONX • 1982 • Zichem Frank • DOC • NTH
SOUTH BRONX HEROES • 1985 • Szarka William • USA • REVENGE OF THE INNOCENTS ○ RUNAWAYS
SOUTH CROSS ABOVE US, THE • 1965 • Bolgarin N., Ilyenko V. • USS
SOUTH LIMBURG see SPOORWEGBOUW IN LIMBURG • 1929
SOUTH O' THE NORTH POLE • 1924 • Roach Hal • SHT • USA
SOUTH OF ALGIERS • 1952 • Lee Jack • UKN • GOLDEN MASK, THE (USA) ○ MASK OF PHARAOH
SOUTH OF ARIZONA • 1938 • Nelson Sam • USA
SOUTH OF CALIENTE • 1951 • Witney William • USA
SOUTH OF DEATH VALLEY • 1949 • Nazarro Ray • USA • RIVER OF POISON (UKN)
SOUTH OF DIXIE • 1944 • Yarbrough Jean • USA
SOUTH OF HELL MOUNTAIN • 1974 • Sachs William, Lehman Lewis • USA
SOUTH OF MANIADERO see AL SUR DE MANIADERO • 1970
SOUTH OF MONTEREY • 1946 • Nigh William • USA • ROMANCE OF THE RANCHO
SOUTH OF MY BODY see AO SUL DO MEU CORPO • 1982
SOUTH OF NORTHERN LIGHTS • 1922 • Hart Neal • USA
SOUTH OF PAGO PAGO • 1940 • Green Alfred E. • USA
SOUTH OF PANAMA • 1928 • Hunt Charles J.?, McEveety Bernard F.? • USA
SOUTH OF PANAMA • 1941 • Yarbrough Jean • USA
SOUTH OF RIO • 1949 • Ford Philip • USA
SOUTH OF ST. LOUIS • 1949 • Enright Ray • USA
SOUTH OF SANTA FE • 1919 • *Guinan Texas* • USA
SOUTH OF SANTA FE • 1924 • *Mix Art* • USA
SOUTH OF SANTA FE • 1932 • Glennon Bert • USA
SOUTH OF SANTA FE • 1942 • Kane Joseph • USA
SOUTH OF SANTA FE • 1949 • Cowan Will • SHT • USA
SOUTH OF SONORA • 1930 • *Buffalo Bill, Jr.* • USA
SOUTH OF SONORA • 1937 • Willat Irvin V. • USA
SOUTH OF SUEZ • 1940 • Seiler Lewis • USA
SOUTH OF SUVA • 1922 • Urson Frank • USA
SOUTH OF TAHITI • 1941 • Waggner George • USA • WHITE SAVAGE (UKN)
SOUTH OF TANA RIVER • 1964 • Christensen Bent, Methling Sven • DNM
SOUTH OF TEXAS see SOUTH OF THE BORDER • 1939
SOUTH OF THE BORDER • 1939 • Sherman George • USA • SOUTH OF TEXAS
SOUTH OF THE BOUDOIR • 1940 • Lord Del • SHT • USA
SOUTH OF THE CHISHOLM TRAIL • 1947 • Abrahams Derwin • USA
SOUTH OF THE EQUATOR • 1924 • Craft William James • USA
SOUTH OF THE EQUATOR see WEST OF ZANZIBAR • 1928
SOUTH OF THE MAIN ROAD see SODER OM LANDSVAGEN • 1936
SOUTH OF THE RIO GRANDE • 1932 • Hillyer Lambert • USA
SOUTH OF THE RIO GRANDE • 1945 • Hillyer Lambert • USA
SOUTH OF YOUTH see SEISHUN NO OTO • 1954
SOUTH PACIFIC • 1958 • Logan Joshua • USA
SOUTH PACIFIC 1942 • 1980 • Donovan Paul, MacGillivray Alan • CND • TORPEDOED
SOUTH PACIFIC PLAYGROUND • 1953 • Hall Ken G. • DOC • ASL
SOUTH PACIFIC TRAIL • 1952 • Witney William • USA
SOUTH POLE OR BUST • 1934 • *Terry Paul/ Moser Frank (P)* • ANS • USA
SOUTH POLE PALS • 1966 • Smith Paul J. • ANS • USA
SOUTH RAIDERS see RAIDERS OF THE SOUTH • 1947
SOUTH RIDING • 1938 • Saville Victor • UKN
SOUTH SEA ADVENTURERS • 1932 • USA
SOUTH SEA BUBBLE, A • 1928 • Hunter T. Hayes • UKN
SOUTH SEA ISLAND FILMS • 1908-10 • Barrett Franklyn • SER • NZL
SOUTH SEA LOVE • 1923 • Soloman David • USA • BROADWAY DANCER, THE
SOUTH SEA LOVE • 1927 • Ince Ralph • USA
SOUTH SEA RHYTHMS • 1943 • Yarbrough Jean • SHT • USA
SOUTH SEA ROSE • 1929 • Dwan Allan • USA
SOUTH SEA SINNER • 1949 • Humberstone H. Bruce • USA • EAST OF JAVA (UKN)
SOUTH SEA WOMAN • 1953 • Lubin Arthur • USA • MARINES HAVE A WORD FOR IT, THE
SOUTH SEAS • 1930 • *Pinchot Gifford* • DOC • USA • IN THE SOUTH SEAS WITH MR. AND MRS. PINCHOT ○ TO THE SOUTH SEAS
SOUTH SEAS, THE • 1971 • Heyer John • DOC • ASL
SOUTH SEAS ADVENTURE see CINERAMA -SOUTH SEAS ADVENTURE • 1958
SOUTH SEAS BOUQUET see NANKAI NO HANATABE • 1942
SOUTH SEAS FURY see HELL'S ISLAND • 1955
SOUTH SEASICKNESS • 1935 • Ripley Arthur • SHT • USA
SOUTH TO KARANGA • 1940 • Schuster Harold • USA
SOUTH WEST PACIFIC • 1943 • Hall Ken G. • DOC • ASL
SOUTH WIND see MINAMI KAZE • 1939
SOUTH WIND see MINAMI NO KAZE • 1942
SOUTH WIND, THE see RIH AL-JANUB • 1975
SOUTH WIND AND WAVES see MINAMI NO KAZE TO NAMI • 1961
SOUTH WIND: SEQUEL see ZOKO MINAMI NO KAZE • 1942
SOUTHBOUND DUCKLING • 1955 • Hanna William, Barbera Joseph • ANS • USA
SOUTHBOUND TRAIN see VLAKOM PREMA JUGU • 1981
SOUTHERN BELLES AND CISSY HEATH IN A COON DANCE, THE • 1902 • *Warwick Trading Co* • UKN
SOUTHERN BELLES SPECIALITY DANCE, THE • 1902 • *Warwick Trading Co* • UKN
SOUTHERN BLADE see TIME FOR KILLING, A • 1967
SOUTHERN BLOOD • 1914 • Noy Wilfred • UKN
SOUTHERN BOY OF '61, A • 1912 • *Kalem* • USA
SOUTHERN CINDERELLA, A • 1913 • King Burton L. • USA
SOUTHERN COMFORT • 1940 • Crouch William Forest • SHT • USA
SOUTHERN COMFORT • 1981 • Hill Walter • USA
SOUTHERN COMFORTS • 1971 • *Oft Jacob* • USA
SOUTHERN COURSE, THE see JUZNA PATEKA • 1983
SOUTHERN CROSS see HIGHEST HONOUR: A TRUE STORY, THE • 1984
SOUTHERN CROSS (UKN) see SMITHY • 1946
SOUTHERN CROSSING • 1980 • Guillemot Robert • DOC • ASL
SOUTHERN EXPOSURE • 1934 • *Mintz Charles (P)* • ANS • USA
SOUTHERN EXPOSURE • 1935 • Parrott Charles • SHT • USA
SOUTHERN FRIED HOSPITALITY • 1960 • Hannah Jack • ANS • USA
SOUTHERN FRIED RABBIT • 1953 • Freleng Friz • ANS • USA
SOUTHERN GIRL'S HEROISM, A • 1911 • *Champion* • USA
SOUTHERN HORSE-PITALITY • 1935 • *Terry Paul/ Moser Frank (P)* • ANS • USA
SOUTHERN JUSTICE • 1917 • Reynolds Lynn • USA
SOUTHERN KNIFE NORTHERN SWORD • HKG
SOUTHERN LOVE • 1924 • Wilcox Herbert • UKN • WOMAN'S SECRET, A (USA)
SOUTHERN MAID, A • 1933 • Hughes Harry • UKN
SOUTHERN PRIDE • 1917 • King Henry • USA
SOUTHERN RHODESIA • 1945 • Wright Basil • DOC • UKN
SOUTHERN RHYTHM • 1932 • *Terry Paul/ Moser Frank (P)* • ANS • USA
SOUTHERN ROSES • 1936 • Zelnik Friedrich • UKN
SOUTHERN SCANDAL • 1945 • Crouch William Forest • SHT • USA
SOUTHERN SKIES see WHITE SHADOWS IN THE SOUTH SEAS • 1928
SOUTHERN SOLDIER'S SACRIFICE, A • 1911 • *Tapley Rose* • USA
SOUTHERN STAR, THE • 1969 • Hayers Sidney • UKN, FRN, USA • ETOILE DU SUD, L' (FRN)
SOUTHERN TEHERAN see JONUBE SHAHR • 1959
SOUTHERN TRAIL, THE see JUZNA PATEKA • 1983
SOUTHERN WAR FESTIVAL see DAKSHA YAGNA • 1934
SOUTHERN YANKEE, A • 1948 • Sedgwick Edward • USA • MY HERO! (UKN)
SOUTHERNER, THE • 1944 • Renoir Jean • USA • HOMME DU SUD, L' (FRN) ○ HOLD AUTUMN IN YOUR HAND
SOUTHERNER, THE see PRODIGAL, THE • 1931
SOUTHERNERS, THE • 1914 • Ridgely Richard, Collins John H. • USA
SOUTHIE • 1987 • Bernard Chris • UKN
SOUTHSIDE 1-1000 • 1950 • Ingster Boris • USA • FORGERY (UKN)
SOUTHWARD HO! • 1939 • Kane Joseph • USA
SOUTHWARD HO WITH MAWSON • 1929 • Hurley Frank • DOC • ASL
SOUTHWARD ON THE 'QUEST' • 1923 • Hurley Frank • UKN • SHACKLETON'S EXPEDITION TO THE ANTARCTIC ○ ENDURANCE
SOUTHWEST, THE • 1945 • Rodakiewicz Henwar • SHT • USA • LAND OF ENCHANTMENT: SOUTHWEST U.S.A.
SOUTHWEST PASSAGE • 1954 • Nazarro Ray • USA • CAMELS WEST (UKN)
SOUTHWEST TO SONORA (UKN) see APPALOOSA, THE • 1966
SOUTOS E CASTANHAS • 1939 • Coelho Jose Adolfo • SHT • PRT
SOUVENIR • 1988 • Reeve Geoffrey • UKN • PORK BUTCHER, THE
SOUVENIR see SUMMER WISHES, WINTER DREAMS • 1973
SOUVENIR DE PARIS • 1955 • Theocary • SHT • FRN
SOUVENIR D'ITALIE • 1957 • Pietrangeli Antonio • ITL • IT HAPPENED IN ROME
SOUVENIR FROM CALVARY, A see PAMIATKA Z KALWARII • 1958
SOUVENIR HUNTER, THE • 1912 • *Diamond Films* • UKN
SOUVENIR HUNTERS, THE see SOUVENIRJAGARNA • 1970
SOUVENIR OF CALVARY see PAMIATKA Z KALWARII • 1958
SOUVENIR OF GIBRALTAR • 1975 • Xhonneux Henri • BLG, FRN
SOUVENIR OF PARADISE see VZPOMINKA NA RAJ • 1939-40
SOUVENIR (USA) see AUX YEUX DU SOUVENIRS • 1948
SOUVENIRJAGARNA • 1970 • Gamlin Yngve • SWD • SOUVENIR HUNTERS, THE
SOUVENIRS • 1920 • Kellino W. P. • UKN
SOUVENIRS • 1938 • Pearson George • SHT • UKN
SOUVENIRS D'AMOUR see MA A ADH-DHIKRAYAT • 1960
SOUVENIRS DE CINEMATOGRAPHIE • Guillon Madelaine • SER • FRN
SOUVENIRS DE GUERRE • 1982 • Hebert Pierre • ANS • CND
SOUVENIRS DE MAURIN DES MAURES, LES • 1950 • Hugon Andre • FRN
SOUVENIRS DE PARIS • Gaudard Lucette • FRN • MEMORIES OF PARIS
SOUVENIRS DE PARIS • 1928 • Prevert Pierre, Duhamel M. • FRN • PARIS EXPRESS
SOUVENIRS D'EN FRANCE • 1975 • Techine Andre • FRN • FRENCH PROVINCIAL (USA)
SOUVENIRS DES ANNEES TRAGIQUES • 1976 • Danan Joseph • FRN
SOUVENIRS D'UNE BOUCHE GOURMANDE • 1980 • Antony Michel • FRN
SOUVENIRS FROM SWEDEN • 1961 • Carlsen Henning • DCS • SWD
SOUVENIRS NE SONT PAS A VENDRE, LES • 1948 • Hennion Robert • FRN
SOUVENIRS OF DEATH • 1948 • Cahn Edward L. • SHT • USA
SOUVENIRS PERDUS • 1950 • Christian-Jaque • FRN • LOST PROPERTY
SOUVENIRS, SOUVENIRS • 1984 • Zeitoun Ariel • FRN
SOUWESTO • 1947-69 • Curnoe Greg • CND
SOVEREIGN OF ALL GANGSTERS, THE see GANG NO TEIO • 1967
SOVETSKIE IGRUSHKI • 1924 • Vertov Dziga • ANM • USS • SOVIET PLAYTHINGS ○ SOVIET TOYS
SOVETSKOI ISKUSSTVO • 1944 • Vertov Dziga, Svilova Elizaveta • DOC • USS • SOVIET ART
...SOVIEL NACKTE ZARTLICHKEIT • 1969 • FRG
SOVIET ART see SOVETSKOI ISKUSSTVO • 1944
SOVIET BORDER • 1938 • Ivanov Alexander • USS • ON THE BORDER
SOVIET FRONTIERS ON THE DANUBE • 1941 • Poselsky I. • USS
SOVIET GEORGIA • 1951 • Karmen Roman • DOC • USS
SOVIET MORDOVIA • 1951 • Heifitz Josif • USS
SOVIET PLAYTHINGS see SOVETSKIE IGRUSHKI • 1924
SOVIET RUSSIA TODAY • 1935 • Tisse Eduard • USS
SOVIET TOYS • 1923 • Bushkin A., Ivanov A. • ANS • USS
SOVIET TOYS see SOVETSKIE IGRUSHKI • 1924
SOVIET TURKMENISTAN • 1950 • Karmen Roman • DOC • USS
SOVIET VILLAGE • Chambers Jack • DOC • UKN
SOVIETS GREET NEW TURKEY, THE • 1934 • Arnstam Leo • CMP • USS
SOVIETS ON PARADE • 1933 • Poselsky I. • USS
SOVIETSKAJA NEFT • 1933 • Raizman Yuli • USS
SOVNGAENGERSKEN • 1914 • Holger-Madsen • DNM • SONAMBULIST, THE
SOVRAZNIK • 1965 • Pavlovic Zivojin • YGS • ENEMY, THE ○ NEPRIJATELJ
SOVSEM PROPASHTSHIY • 1974 • Daneliya Georgi • USS
SOVVERSIVI • 1967 • Taviani Paolo, Taviani Vittorio • ITL • AGITATORS ○ SUBVERSIVES, THE
SOWBHAGYAVATHI • 1957 • Jampana • IND
SOWER, THE • 1964 • Kling George • SHT • USA
SOWER REAPS, THE • 1914 • Ricketts Thomas • USA
SOWERS, THE • 1916 • De Mille William C. • USA
SOWERS AND REAPERS • 1917 • Baker George D. • USA
SOWING THE WIND • 1916 • Hepworth Cecil M. • UKN
SOWING THE WIND • 1916 • McGill Lawrence • SHT • USA
SOWING THE WIND • 1921 • Stahl John M. • USA
SOWIZDRZAL SWIETOKRZYSKI • 1977 • Kluba Henryk • PLN • SCAMP FROM SWIETYKRZYZ MOUNTAINS, THE ○ SCAMP, THE
SOY CHARRO DE RANCHO GRANDE • 1947 • Pardave Joaquin • MXC
SOY CHATO, PERO LAS HUELO • 1939 • Zacarias Miguel • MXC • I AM SNUB-NOSED BUT I CAN SMELL (USA)
SOY CHICANO Y JUSTICIERO • 1974 • MXC • I AM CHICANO AND A SEEKER OF JUSTICE
SOY CHICANO Y MEXICANO • 1974 • *Filmicas Agrasanchez* • MXC • I AM CHICANO AND MEXICAN

SOY CUBA see **YA –KUBA** • 1962
SOY EL HIJO DEL GALLERO • 1977 • Hernandez Mario • MXC
SOY MEXICANO DE ACA DE ESTE LADO • 1951 • Contreras Torres Miguel • MXC
SOY MEXICO • 1970 • Reichenbach Francois • SHT • FRN • MEXICO
SOY PURO MEXICANO • 1942 • Fernandez Emilio • MXC • I'M PURE MEXICAN
SOY UN DELINCUENTE • 1976 • de la Cerda Clemente • VNZ • I AM A CRIMINAL
SOY UN DELINCUENTE II see **REINCIDENTE, EL** • 1978
SOY UN GOLFO • 1955 • Morayta Miguel • MXC
SOY UN INFELIZ • 1946 • Hardy Boris H. (c/d) • ARG
SOY UN PROFUGO • 1946 • Delgado Miguel M. • MXC • I'M A FUGITIVE
SOY UN SENORITO • 1934 • Rey Florian • SPN
SOYEZ LES BIENVENUS • 1940 • de Baroncelli Jacques • FRN • NOUVEAUX PAUVRES, LES
SOYEZ LES BIENVENUS! • 1952 • Pierre-Louis • FRN
SOYEZ LES BIENVENUS see **SOIR DES ROIS, LE** • 1932
SOYLENT GREEN • 1973 • Fleischer Richard • USA
SOYLEYIN GENC KIZLARA • 1967 • Tuna Feyzi, Kazankaya Hasan • TRK • TELL IT TO THE GIRLS
SOYOKAZE CHICHI TO TOMONI • 1940 • Yamamoto Satsuo • JPN
SOYONS DONC SPORTIFS • 1909 • Cohl Emile • ANS • FRN • SPORTIVE POET, A
SOYONS GAIS • 1931 • Robison Arthur • FRN • GAI, GAI, DEMARIONS–NOUS
SOYONS SERIEUX see **TOUCHONS DU BOIS** • 1933
SOYUZ VELIKOGO DELA see **S.V.D.** • 1927
SOZDE KIZLAR • 1967 • Saydam Nejat • TRK • THOSE WOULD–BE GIRLS
SPAANSE VLIEG, DIE • 1978 • De Villiers Dirk • SAF • SPANISH FLY, THE
SPAARROUSEL • 1966 • Geesink Joop • SHT • NTH
SPACE • 1965 • Warhol Andy • USA
SPACE 1999: ALIEN ATTACK see **ALIEN ATTACK** • 1977
SPACE 1999: COSMIC PRINCESS see **COSMIC PRINCESS** • 1976
SPACE 1999: DESTINATION MOONBASE ALPHA see **DESTINATION MOONBASE ALPHA** • 1979
SPACE 1999: JOURNEY THROUGH THE BLACK SUN see **JOURNEY THROUGH THE BLACK SUN** • 1975
SPACE AMOEBA see **KESSEN NANKAI NO DAIKAIJU** • 1970
SPACE AND LIGHT • 1973 • Grigor Murray • DOC • UKN
SPACE AND PERSPECTIVE IN PAINTING • 1964 • Takacs Gabor • DOC • HNG
SPACE BETWEEN THE DOOR AND THE FLOOR, THE • 1989 • Chan Pauline • SHT • ASL
SPACE CAMP see **SPACECAMP** • 1986
SPACE CHILDREN, THE • 1958 • Arnold Jack • USA
SPACE CRUISER see **UCHUSENKAN YAMATO** • 1977
SPACE CRUISER: GUARDIAN OF THE GALAXY see **UCHUSENKAN YAMATO** • 1977
SPACE CRUISER YAMATO PART II • 1979 • Masuda Toshio • ANM • JPN
SPACE DEVILS see **DIAVOLI DELLO SPAZIO, I** • 1965
SPACE FIREBIRD see **HINOTORI 2772 AI NO COSMOZONE** • 1980
SPACE FIREBIRD 2772 see **HINOTORI 2772 AI NO COSMOZONE** • 1980
SPACE GREYHOUND see **UCHU KAISOKU–SEN** • 1961
SPACE HUNTER see **SPACEHUNTER: ADVENTURES IN THE FORBIDDEN ZONE** • 1983
SPACE IN THE 70'S • 1971 • *N.a.s.a.* • DCS • USA
SPACE INVASION OF LAPLAND see **RYMDINVASION I LAPPLAND** • 1958
SPACE ISLAND • 1987 • Margheriti Antonio • ITL, FRG • TREASURE ISLAND IN OUTER SPACE
SPACE KID • 1966 • Post Howard • ANS • USA
SPACE KID see **MEATBALLS PART II** • 1984
SPACE LOVE • 1972 • *Distripix Inc* • USA
SPACE MASTER X–7 • 1958 • Bernds Edward • USA • MUTINY IN OUTER SPACE ○ SPACEMASTER X–7
SPACE MEN • 1960 • Margheriti Antonio • ITL • ASSIGNMENT –OUTER SPACE
SPACE MEN APPEAR IN TOKYO see **UCHUJIN TOKYO NI ARAWARU** • 1956
SPACE MISSION OF THE LOST PLANET see **HORROR OF THE BLOOD MONSTERS** • 1970
SPACE MISSION: ZERO HOUR • 1969 • ITL
SPACE MONSTER • 1965 • Katzman Leonard • USA • FIRST WOMAN INTO SPACE ○ FLIGHT BEYOND THE SUN ○ VOYAGE BEYOND THE SUN
SPACE MONSTER DOGORA see **UCHU DAIKAIJU DOGORA** • 1964
SPACE MOUSE • 1959 • Lovy Alex • ANS • USA
SPACE MOVIE • 1983 • Lennick Michael • MTV • CND
SPACE MOVIE, THE • 1980 • Palmer Tony • DOC • UKN
SPACE PATROL see **RAUMPATROUILLE**
SPACE PATROL I • 1955 • Darley Dik • MTV • USA
SPACE PATROL II • 1955 • Darley Dik • MTV • USA
SPACE PIONEERS, A CANADIAN STORY • 1988 • Buttignol Rudy • DOC • CND
SPACE PIRATES • 1957 • *U.s.c.* • SHT • USA
SPACE PLACE • 1969 • Braverman Chuck • USA
SPACE PROBE TAURUS • 1968 • USA
SPACE RAGE • 1985 • Palmisano Conrad E. • USA • BREAKOUT ON PRISON PLANET ○ DOLLAR A DAY, A ○ TRACKERS ○ SPACERAGE ○ TRACKERS: 2180 ○ LAST FRONTIER, THE
SPACE RAIDERS • 1983 • Cohen Howard R. • USA • STAR CHILD
SPACE RIDERS • 1984 • Massot Joe • UKN
SPACE SHIP, THE see **KOSMITCHESKY REIS** • 1935
SPACE SHIP SAPPY • 1957 • White Jules • SHT • USA
SPACE SHIP YAMATO see **UCHUSENKAN YAMATO** • 1977
SPACE SLUTS IN THE SLAMMER • 1988 • Decoteau David • USA
SPACE SOLDIERS see **FLASH GORDON** • 1936
SPACE SOLDIERS CONQUER THE UNIVERSE see **FLASH GORDON CONQUERS THE UNIVERSE** • 1940
SPACE SQUID, THE • 1967 • Culhane Shamus • ANS • USA
SPACE STATION K–9 • 1961 • Lievciuk Timodici • USS
SPACE STATION X–14 see **MUTINY IN OUTER SPACE** • 1965
SPACE THING • 1968 • Elliott B. Ron • USA
SPACE TRAP, THE see **RAUMFALLE, DIE**
SPACE VAMPIRES see **ASTRO–ZOMBIES, THE** • 1968
SPACE VAMPIRES see **LIFEFORCE** • 1985
SPACE WARRIORS 2000 • 1980 • ANM • USA
SPACE–WATCH MURDERS, THE • 1978 • *Steele Barbara* • USA
SPACE WORKS, THE • 1981 • Strick Joseph • USA
SPACEBALLS • 1988 • Brooks Mel • USA
SPACEBORNE • 1978 • Dauber Philip • SHT • USA
SPACEBOY • 1972 • *Marly Florence (P)* • SHT • USA
SPACECAMP • 1986 • Winer Harry • USA • SPACE CAMP
SPACED OUT (USA) see **OUTER TOUCH** • 1979
SPACEFLIGHT IC–1 • 1965 • Knowles Bernard • UKN
SPACEHUNTER: ADVENTURES IN THE FORBIDDEN ZONE • 1983 • Johnson Lamont • USA • ADVENTURES IN THE CREEP ZONE ○ ROAD GANGS ○ SPACE HUNTER
SPACEMAN AND KING ARTHUR, THE (UKN) see **UNIDENTIFIED FLYING ODDBALL** • 1979
SPACEMASTER X–7 see **SPACE MASTER X–7** • 1958
SPACEMEN APPEAR see **UCHU KAIJIN SHUTSUGEN** • 1958
SPACEMEN SATURDAY NIGHT see **INVASION OF THE SAUCER–MEN** • 1957
SPACEPLACE • 1974 • Mygind Annie • UKN
SPACER W BIESZCZADACH • 1958 • Slesicki Wladyslaw • DOC • PLN • WALK IN THE BIESZCZADY MOUNTAINS, A ○ WALK IN THE BIESZCZADY, A
SPACERAGE see **SPACE RAGE** • 1985
SPACERAID '63 see **DAY MARS INVADED EARTH, THE** • 1962
SPACEREK STAROMIEJSKI • 1958 • Munk Andrzej • PLN • WALK IN THE OLD CITY OF WARSAW, A (USA) ○ WALK IN THE OLD TOWN, A
SPACESHIP see **CREATURE WASN'T NICE, THE** • 1981
SPACESHIP OF HUMAN DESTRUCTION see **JINKO EISEN TO JINRUI NO HAMETSU** • 1958
SPACESHIP TO THE UNKNOWN • 1936 • Stephani Frederick • USA • ROCKET SHIP
SPACESHIP TO VENUS see **SCHWEIGENDE STERN, DER** • 1960
SPACESHIP VENUS DOES NOT REPLY see **SCHWEIGENDE STERN, DER** • 1960
SPACEWAYS • English Edward • SHT • USA
SPACEWAYS • 1953 • Fisher Terence • UKN
SPADA BARBARI, LA see **SPADE DEI BARBARI, LE** • 1983
SPADA DEL CID, LA • 1962 • Iglesias Miguel, Baldi Ferdinando • ITL, SPN • HIJAS DEL CID, LA ○ SWORD OF EL CID, THE (USA) ○ ESPADA DEL CID, LA
SPADA DELLA VENDETTA, LA • 1961 • De Marchi Luigi • ITL
SPADA DELL'ISLAM, LA • 1960 • Bomba Enrico • ITL
SPADA E LA CROCE, LA • 1959 • Bragaglia Carlo Ludovico • ITL • SWORD AND THE CROSS, THE (USA) ○ MARIA MADDELENA ○ MARY MAGDALENE
SPADA IMBATTIBILE, LA • 1957 • Fregonese Hugo • ITL
SPADA NELL'OMBRA, UNA • 1961 • Capuano Luigi • ITL
SPADA NORMANNA, LA • 1971 • Mauri Roberto • ITL, SPN, FRN • ESPADA NORMANDA, LA (SPN) ○ NORMAN SWORDSMAN (UKN)
SPADA PER BRANDO, UNA • 1970 • Caltabiano Alfio • ITL
SPADA PER DUE BANDIERE, UNA (ITL) see **LA FAYETTE** • 1963
SPADA PER L'IMPERO, UNA • 1965 • Grieco Sergio • ITL • SWORD OF THE EMPIRE (USA)
SPADACCINO DI SIENA, LO (ITL) see **MERCENAIRE, LE** • 1962
SPADACCINO MISTERIOSO, LO • 1956 • Grieco Sergio • ITL
SPADE COOLEY AND HIS ORCHESTRA • 1949 • Cowan Will • SHT • USA
SPADE COOLEY, KING OF WESTERN SWING • 1945 • Scholl Jack • SHT • USA
SPADE DEI BARBARI, LE • 1983 • Prosperi Franco • ITL • SWORD OF THE BARBARIANS ○ GUNAN, KING OF THE BARBARIANS ○ GUNAN NO.2 ○ INVINCIBLE SWORD, THE ○ SPADA BARBARI, LA
SPADE SENZA BANDIERA • 1961 • Veo Carlo • ITL • SWORD WITHOUT A COUNTRY (USA)
SPADES ARE TRUMPS • 1915 • Beggs Lee • USA
SPADLA S MESICE • 1961 • *Schorm Evald* • CZC
SPAEDBARNET • 1953 • Roos Jorgen • DOC • DNM • NEWBORN, THE
SPAG, THE • 1961 • Mangiamele Giorgio • SHT • ASL
SPAGHETTI • 1916 • *Hardy Babe* • SHT • USA
SPAGHETTI A LA ROMAINE • 1965 • ANS • BLG
SPAGHETTI A MEZZANOTTE • 1981 • Martino Sergio • ITL
SPAGHETTI AND LOTTERY • 1915 • Louis Will • USA
SPAGHETTI HOUSE • 1983 • Paradisi Giulio • ITL
SPAGHETTI IN THE DESERT see **PASTASCIUTTA DEL DESERTO** • 1961
SPAGHETTI TROUBLE • Andersen Yvonne • ANS • USA
SPAHTRUPP HALLGARTEN • 1941 • Fredersdorf Herbert B. • FRG
SPAIN • 1937 • Karmen Roman • DOC • USS
SPAIN see **ISPANIYA** • 1939
SPAIN AGAIN (USA) see **ESPANA OTRA VEZ** • 1968
SPAIN IN FLAMES • 1936 • *Van Dongen Helen (P)* • NTH
SPAIN OUGHT TO KNOW see **ESPANA DEBE SABER** • 1976
SPALICEK • 1947 • Trnka Jiri • ANM • CZC • CZECH YEAR, THE
SPALOVAC MRTVOL • 1968 • Herz Juraj • CZC • CREMATOR, THE (USA) ○ CREMATOR OF CORPSES, THE ○ INCINERATOR OF CADAVERS ○ CARNIVAL OF HERETICS
SPAN OF LIFE, THE • 1914 • Mackey Edward • USA
SPAN OF LIFE, THE • 1916 • *Barrymore Lionel* • USA
SPANGLES • 1926 • O'Connor Frank • USA
SPANGLES • 1928 • Banfield George J. • UKN
SPANGORAMENOS, O • 1967 • Karayannis Kostas • GRC • MISER, THE
SPANIARD, THE • 1925 • Walsh Raoul • USA • SPANISH LOVE (UKN)
SPANIARD'S CURSE, THE • 1958 • Kemplen Ralph • UKN
SPANILA JIZDA • 1963 • Danek Oldrich • CZC • GLORIOUS CAMPAIGN, THE ○ NURNBERG CAMPAIGN, THE
SPANISCHE FLIEGE, DIE • 1931 • Jacoby Georg • FRG
SPANISCHE FLIEGE, DIE • 1955 • Boese Carl • FRG
SPANISCHE GLUTEN • 1924 • Gunsburg Arthur • FRG
SPANISCHE INSELN IM MITTELMEER • 1936 • Nordhaus Gosta • FRG • SPANISH ISLANDS OF THE MEDITERRANEAN, THE
SPANISH ABC • 1938 • Dickinson Thorold, Cole Sidney • DOC • UKN
SPANISH ACRES see **SANTA FE TRAIL, THE** • 1930
SPANISH AFFAIR • 1958 • Siegel Don, Marquina Luis • USA, SPN • AVENTURA PARA DOS (SPN) ○ FLAMENCA
SPANISH–AMERICAN QUICKSTEP, THE • 1913 • *Selsior Films* • UKN
SPANISH–AMERICAN WAR SCENES • 1898 • *Bitzer Billy (Ph)* • USA
SPANISH BLOOD • 1978 • Bugajski Ryszard • MTV • PLN
SPANISH CAPE MYSTERY, THE • 1935 • Collins Lewis D. • USA
SPANISH CAVALIER, THE • 1912 • *Edison* • USA
SPANISH DANCER, THE • 1923 • Brenon Herbert • USA
SPANISH DILEMMA, A • 1912 • Sennett Mack • USA
SPANISH EARTH, THE • 1937 • Ivens Joris • DOC • SPN
SPANISH EYES • 1930 • Samuelson G. B. • UKN
SPANISH FIESTA • 1942 • Negulesco Jean • SHT • USA
SPANISH FLY • 1975 • Kellett Bob • UKN
SPANISH FLY, THE see **SPAANSE VLIEG, DIE** • 1978
SPANISH FURY see **FURIA ESPANOLA** • 1974
SPANISH GARDENER, THE • 1956 • Leacock Philip • UKN
SPANISH GIRL, THE • 1909 • *Essanay* • USA
SPANISH GIRL, THE • 1909 • *Phoenix* • USA
SPANISH GIRLS IN PARIS see **ESPANOLAS EN PARIS** • 1970
SPANISH GYPSY, THE • 1911 • Griffith D. W. • USA
SPANISH INQUISITION, THE see **CREMATION, LA** • 1899
SPANISH ISLANDS OF THE MEDITERRANEAN, THE see **SPANISCHE INSELN IM MITTELMEER** • 1936
SPANISH JADE • 1922 • Robertson John S., Geraughty Tom • UKN
SPANISH JADE, THE • 1915 • Lucas Wilfred • USA
SPANISH LOVE SONG, A • 1911 • Melies Gaston • USA
SPANISH LOVE (UKN) see **SPANIARD, THE** • 1925
SPANISH MADONNA, A • 1915 • Montgomery Frank E. • USA
SPANISH MAIN, THE • 1945 • Borzage Frank • USA
SPANISH OMELET, A • 1914 • *Ab* • USA
SPANISH ONIONS • 1930 • *Terry Paul/ Moser Frank (P)* • ANS • USA
SPANISH PARROT GIRL, THE • 1913 • Parker Lem B. • USA
SPANISH PASSION see **MALVA** • 1924
SPANISH PRELUDE see **PRELUDIO A ESPANA** • 1972
SPANISH REVOLT OF 1836, THE • 1912 • *Kalem* • USA
SPANISH ROMANCE, A • 1908 • *Vitagraph* • USA
SPANISH ROMEO, A • 1925 • Marshall George • SHT • USA
SPANISH SERENADE see **ALBENIZ** • 1947
SPANISH SHOTGUN, THE see **ESCOPETA NACIONAL, LA** • 1978
SPANISH SWORD, THE • 1962 • Morris Ernest • UKN
SPANISH TWIST, A • 1932 • Foster John, Stallings George • ANS • USA
SPANISH VILLAGE • 1957 • Kelly Ron • DOC • CND
SPANISH WOOING, A • 1911 • *Selig* • USA
SPANKING AT SCHOOL see **KLASSENKEILE** • 1968
SPANKING BREEZES • 1926 • Cline Eddie • SHT • USA
SPANKY • 1932 • McGowan Robert • SHT • USA
SPANN AV TID, ET • 1973 • Tuhus Laila • SHT • NRW • PAIL OF TIME, A
SPANSK ELSKOV • 1911 • Gad Urban • DNM
SPANSK ELSOV see **TOD IM SEVILLA, DER** • 1913
SPARA FORTE, PIU FORTE.. NON CAPISCO • 1966 • De Filippo Eduardo • ITL • SHOOT LOUD, LOUDER.. I DON'T UNDERSTAND
SPARA, GRINGO, SPARA • 1968 • Corbucci Bruno • ITL • SHOOT, GRINGO, SHOOT ○ LONGEST HUNT, THE ○ RAINBOW ○ GRINGO
SPARA JOE.. E COSI SIA • 1972 • Miraglia Emilio Paolo • ITL
SPARE A COPPER • 1940 • Carstairs John Paddy • UKN
SPARE BEDROOM • 1971 • Zwartjes Frans • SHT • NTH
SPARE MAN see **ALBERT R.N.** • 1953
SPARE MOMENT, A • 1985 • Creanga Serban • RMN
SPARE PARTS (USA) see **FLEISCH** • 1980
SPARE ROOM, THE • 1932 • Davis Redd • UKN
SPARE THE CHILD • 1955 • Liss Abe • ANS • USA
SPARE THE ROD • 1912 • *Majestic* • USA
SPARE THE ROD • 1954 • Hannah Jack • ANS • USA
SPARE THE ROD • 1954 • Rasinski Connie • ANS • USA
SPARE THE ROD • 1961 • Norman Leslie • UKN
SPARE TIME • 1927 • Sparling Gordon • CND
SPARE TIME • 1939 • Jennings Humphrey • DCS • UKN
SPARE TYRES, THE • 1967 • Lane Michael J. • SHT • UKN
SPARI E BACI A COLAZIONE see **QUICKLY** • 1974
SPARK see **HIBANA** • 1922
SPARK see **HIBANA** • 1956
SPARK, THE • Jones Stuart Wynn • SHT • UKN
SPARK AND THE FLAME, THE • 1915 • Melville Wilbert • USA
SPARK DIVINE, THE • 1919 • Terriss Tom • USA
SPARK ETERNAL, THE • 1914 • *Kb* • USA
SPARK FROM THE EMBERS, THE • 1915 • Ince Thomas H. • USA
SPARK OF MANHOOD, THE • 1914 • Reid Wallace • USA
SPARK PLUG • 1936 • *Mintz Charles (P)* • ANS • USA
SPARKLE • 1976 • O'Steen Sam • USA
SPARKLING CYANIDE • 1983 • Lewis Robert • TVM • USA • AGATHA CHRISTIE'S SPARKLING CYANIDE
SPARKLING WINDS see **FENYES SZELEK** • 1968
SPARKS, THE see **PHIRINGOTI** • 1990
SPARKS OF FATE • 1914 • *Bushman Francis X.* • USA
SPARKS OF FLINT see **TWO–FISTED JEFFERSON** • 1922
SPARKY THE FIREFLY • 1953 • Rasinski Connie • ANS • USA
SPARRING AT N.Y. ATHLETIC CLUB • 1905 • *Bitzer Billy (Ph)* • USA
SPARRING PARTNER • 1924 • Fleischer Dave • ANS • USA
SPARROW, THE see **ASFOUR, EL** • 1973
SPARROW IN A GOURD, THE see **HYOTAN SUZUME** • 1957
SPARROW OF PIGALLE, THE see **PIAF** • 1973
SPARROW OF THE CIRCUS • 1914 • Pollard Harry? • USA
SPARROW SINGS AT NIGHT, THE • 1981 • Wo Lee-Jin • SKR
SPARROWHAWK • 1936 • Field Mary • UKN

SPARROWS • 1926 • Beaudine William • USA • HUMAN SPARROWS (UKN) ○ SCRAPS
SPARROWS CAN'T SING • 1963 • Littlewood Joan • UKN
SPARROWS' MIGRATION, THE • Bablouani Teimouraz • USS
SPARSH • 1978 • Paranjpye Sai • IND • TOUCH
SPARTACO • 1911 • Pasquali Ernesto Maria • ITL
SPARTACO • 1952 • Freda Riccardo • ITL • SPARTACUS THE GLADIATOR (UKN) ○ SINS OF ROME (USA) ○ GLADIATORE DELLA TRACIA, IL ○ SPARTACUS AND THE REBEL GLADIATOR
SPARTACUS • 1960 • Kubrick Stanley • USA
SPARTACUS see **SPARTAK** • 1976
SPARTACUS AND THE REBEL GLADIATOR see **SPARTACO** • 1952
SPARTACUS AND THE TEN GLADIATORS (USA) see **SPARTACUS E I DIECI GLADIATORI** • 1964
SPARTACUS E I DIECI GLADIATORI • 1964 • Iquino Ignacio F. • ITL, SPN, FRN • TRIUNFO DE LOS DIEZ GLADIADORES, EL (SPN) ○ TRIONFO DEI DIECI GLADIATORI ○ SPARTACUS AND THE TEN GLADIATORS (USA) ○ SPARTACUS ET LES DIX GLADIATEURS (FRN)
SPARTACUS ET LES DIX GLADIATEURS (FRN) see **SPARTACUS E I DIECI GLADIATORI** • 1964
SPARTACUS THE GLADIATOR (UKN) see **SPARTACO** • 1952
SPARTAK • 1976 • Derbenev Vadim, Grigorovich Yuri • USS • SPARTACUS
SPARTAKIAD see **SPARTAKIADA** • 1956
SPARTAKIADA • 1929 • Poselsky I. • USS
SPARTAKIADA • 1956 • Fric Martin • DOC • CZC • SPARTAKIAD
SPARTAKIADE, THE • 1960 • Kadar Jan, Klos Elmar • DOC • CZC
SPARTAN FATHER, A • 1913 • *Moore Eugene* • USA
SPARTAN GIRL OF THE WEST, A • 1913 • *Greenwood Winnifred* • USA
SPARTAN GLADIATORS see **RIVOLTA DEI GLADIATORI, LA** • 1958
SPARTAN GLADIATORS, THE see **RIVOLTA DEI SETTE, LA** • 1965
SPARTAN MOTHER, A • 1912 • *Kalem* • USA
SPARTAN SPLEEN, THE • 1916 • *Humphrey Orral* • USA
SPARTREE • 1977 • Borsos Philip • SHT • CND
SPARVIERI DEL RE, GLI • 1959 • Lerner Joseph • ITL
SPARVIERO DEI CARAIBI, LO • 1963 • Regnoli Piero • ITL • CARIBBEAN HAWK (USA) ○ HAWK OF THE CARIBBEAN, THE
SPARVIERO DEL NILO, LO • 1951 • Gentilomo Giacomo • ITL
SPASITYE UTOPAYUSHCHEVO • 1968 • Arsenov Pavel • USS • SAVE THE DROWNING MAN ○ HELP, HE'S DROWNING ○ RESCUE A DROWNING MAN
SPASMO • 1974 • Lenzi Umberto • ITL
SPASMS • 1982 • Fruet William • CND • DEATH BITE
SPASSVOGEL • 1938 • Buch Fritz Peter • FRG
SPATE LIEBE • 1943 • Ucicky Gustav • FRG
SPATE MADCHEN, DAS • 1951 • Hinrich Hans • FRG
SPATE RACHE • 1915 • Del Zopp Rudolf • FRG
SPATNE NAMALOVANA SLEPICE see **GALLINA VOGELBIRDAE** • 1963
SPATS TO SPURS (UKN) see **HENRY GOES ARIZONA** • 1939
SPAVALDI E INNAMORATI • 1959 • Vari Giuseppe • ITL
SPAWN OF THE DESERT • 1923 • Wilson Ben?, King Louis? • USA
SPAWN OF THE NORTH • 1938 • Hathaway Henry • USA
SPAWN OF THE SLITHIS see **SLITHIS** • 1978
SPAZIALE K.1 see **HUMAN DUPLICATORS, THE** • 1965
SPEAK • Latham John • ANS • UKN
SPEAK BODY • 1979 • Armatage Kay • CND
SPEAK EASILY • 1932 • Sedgwick Edward • USA
SPEAK, LITTLE MUTE see **HABLA, MUDITA** • 1973
SPEAK, MUTE GIRL see **HABLA, MUDITA** • 1973
SPEAK NO EVIL • 1914 • *Warfield Irene* • USA
SPEAK OF THE PAST see **AN MILOUSE TO PARELTHON** • 1967
SPEAKEASY • 1929 • Stoloff Ben • USA
SPEAKEASY, THE • 1920 • Jones F. Richard • SHT • USA
SPEAKING DIRECTLY • 1973 • Jost Jon • USA
SPEAKING FROM AMERICA • 1939 • Jennings Humphrey • DCS • UKN
SPEAKING OF ANIMALS • 1941-49 • Lilly Lou, Landers Lew • SHS • USA
SPEAKING OF GLASS see **OVER GLAS GESPROKEN** • 1957
SPEAKING OF MURDER (USA) see **ROUGE EST MIS, LE** • 1957
SPEAKING OF RELATIONS • 1934 • Yates Hal • SHT • USA
SPEAKING OF THE WEATHER • 1937 • Tashlin Frank • ANS • USA
SPEAKING OUR PEACE • 1985 • Klein Bonnie (c/d) • DOC • CND
SPEAKING PARTS • 1988 • Egoyan Atom • CND
SPEAR, THE • 1987 • Santiago Cirio H. • USA
SPEAR DANCE OF 53 STATIONS see **YARIODORI GOJUSANTSUGI** • 1946
SPECIAL • 1967 • Seki Koji • JPN
SPECIAL AGENT • 1935 • Keighley William • USA
SPECIAL AGENT • 1949 • Thomas William C. • USA
SPECIAL AGENT, THE • 1910 • *Vitagraph* • USA
SPECIAL ATHLETES • 1980 • Perris Anthony • MTV • CND
SPECIAL BARDOT see **SHOW BARDOT** • 1968
SPECIAL BOY SOLDIERS OF THE NAVY see **KAIGUN TOKUBETSU SHONEN HEI** • 1972
SPECIAL BULLETIN • 1982 • Zwick Edward • TVM • USA
SPECIAL CIPHER see **CIFRATO SPECIALE** • 1966
SPECIAL CONSTABLE, THE • 1914 • Batley Ernest G. • UKN
SPECIAL COP IN ACTION see **ITALIA A MANO ARMATA** • 1976
SPECIAL CORRECTION see **SPECIJALNO VASPITANJE** • 1978
SPECIAL DAY, A (USA) see **GIORNATA PARTICOLARE, UNA** • 1977
SPECIAL DELIVERY • 1922 • St. John Al • SHT • USA
SPECIAL DELIVERY • 1927 • Arbuckle Roscoe • USA
SPECIAL DELIVERY • 1972 • Lamothe Arthur, Dupuis Francois • DCS • CND
SPECIAL DELIVERY • 1976 • Wendkos Paul • USA
SPECIAL DELIVERY • 1978 • Macauley Eunice, Weldon John • ANS • CND • LIVRAISON SPECIALE
SPECIAL DELIVERY, A • 1916 • *Plump & Runt* • SHT • USA
SPECIAL DELIVERY (USA) see **VOM HIMMEL GEFALLEN** • 1955
SPECIAL DUTY see **DETYRE E POSACINE**
SPECIAL EDITION • 1938 • Davis Redd • UKN
SPECIAL EDUCATION see **SPECIJALNO VASPITANJE** • 1978
SPECIAL EFFECTS • 1984 • Cohen Larry • USA
SPECIAL FORCES • 1967 • Wilthor • PHL
SPECIAL FRIENDSHIP, A • 1987 • Cook Fielder • TVM • USA
SPECIAL GAMES see **GIOCHI PARTICOLARI** • 1970
SPECIAL INSPECTOR • 1939 • Barsha Leon • USA • ACROSS THE BORDER
SPECIAL INVESTIGATOR • 1936 • King Louis • USA
SPECIAL ISSUE see **EDITIE SPECIALA** • 1978
SPECIAL KENNY ROGERS, A • 1975 • Williams Tony • MTV • USA
SPECIAL KIND OF LOVE, A see **SPECIAL OLYMPICS** • 1978
SPECIAL LICENSE, THE • 1909 • Bouwmeester Theo? • UKN
SPECIAL MAGNUM see **BLAZING MAGNUM** • 1977
SPECIAL MARKS –NONE see **BESONDERE KENNZEICHEN: KEINE** • 1956
SPECIAL MESSENGER • 1911 • Olcott Sidney • USA
SPECIAL MISSION TO CARACAS see **MISSION SPECIALE A CARACAS** • 1965
SPECIAL OFFICER, THE • 1913 • Carleton Lloyd B. • USA
SPECIAL OLYMPICS • 1978 • Philips Lee • TVM • USA • SPECIAL KIND OF LOVE, A
SPECIAL PECULIARITIES –NONE see **BESONDERE KENNZEICHEN: KEINE** • 1956
SPECIAL PEOPLE • 1984 • Daniels Marc • TVM • USA • SPECIAL PEOPLE: BASED ON A TRUE STORY
SPECIAL PEOPLE: BASED ON A TRUE STORY see **SPECIAL PEOPLE** • 1984
SPECIAL PRIORITY TRAINS see **OSTRE SLEDOVANE VLAKY** • 1966
SPECIAL QUALITY see **CLASE APARTE** • 1971
SPECIAL REQUEST • 1980 • Tassios Pavlos • GRC
SPECIAL SECTION (USA) see **SECTION SPECIALE** • 1975
SPECIAL SERVICE AGENT • 1964 • Volchek B. • USS
SPECIAL TODAY • 1918 • Drew Sidney, Drew Sidney Mrs. • SHT • USA
SPECIAL TRAIN FOR HITLER see **TRAIN SPECIAL POUR S.S.** • 1976
SPECIAL TRAINS • 1972 • Papic Krsto • SHT • YGS
SPECIAL TREATMENT (UKN) see **POSEBAN TRETMAN** • 1980
SPECIALIST, THE • 1966 • Hill James • SHT • UKN
SPECIALIST, THE • 1975 • Avedis Howard • USA
SPECIALIST, THE see **E SPECIALISTE DEL 44** • 1977
SPECIALISTE, LE (FRN) see **SPECIALISTI, GLI** • 1969
SPECIALISTES, LES • 1984 • Leconte Patrice • FRN
SPECIALISTI, GLI • 1969 • Corbucci Sergio • ITL, FRN, FRG • SPECIALISTE, LE (FRN) ○ DROP THEM OR I'LL SHOOT (UKN)
SPECIALISTS see **STRUCNJACI** • 1969
SPECIALISTS, THE • 1968 • Gregorio A. • PHL
SPECIALISTS, THE • 1968 • Moser Clem
SPECIALISTS, THE • 1971 • Arioli Don • ANS • CND
SPECIALISTS, THE • 1975 • Quine Richard • TVM • USA
SPECIALITY DANCE BY FRED STOREY • 1899 • *Warwick Trading Co* • UKN
SPECIALITY DANCE BY WILLIAM VOKES • 1899 • *Warwick Trading Co* • UKN
SPECIES OF MEXICAN MAN, A • 1915 • Fielding Romaine • USA
SPECIFISCHE GEWICHT, DAS • 1962 • Verhavert Roland • DOC • BLG
SPECIJALIST see **STRUCNJACI** • 1969
SPECIJALNO VASPITANJE • 1978 • Markovic Goran • YGS • SPECIAL EDUCATION ○ SPECIAL CORRECTION
SPECK IN THE WATER see **NUNAL SA TUBIG**
SPECK ON THE WALL, THE • 1914 • Campbell Colin • USA
SPECKLED BAND, THE • 1912 • Treville Georges • UKN
SPECKLED BAND, THE • 1923 • Ridgwell George • UKN
SPECKLED BAND, THE • 1931 • Raymond Jack • UKN
SPECTACLE MAKER, THE • 1934 • Farrow John • SHT • USA
SPECTACLES, THE • Smetana Zdenek • ANS • CZC
SPECTATOR • 1971 • Zwartjes Frans • SHT • NTH
SPECTER, THE • 1908 • *Pathe* • FRN
SPECTER HAUNTS EUROPE, A see **PRIZAK BRODIT PO YEVROPE** • 1923
SPECTER OF EDGAR ALLAN POE • 1972 • Quandour Mohy • USA • SPECTRE OF EDGAR ALLAN POE, THE
SPECTER OF JAGO, THE see **SPETTRO DI JAGO, LO** • 1912
SPECTER OF THE ROSE • 1946 • Hecht Ben • USA • SPECTRE OF THE ROSE (UKN)
SPECTER OF THE VAULT, THE see **SPETTRO DEL SOTTERRANEO, LO** • 1915
SPECTER ON THE BRIDGE see **GOLDEN GATE MURDERS, THE** • 1979
SPECTERS (USA) see **SPETTRI** • 1987
SPECTRE • 1977 • Donner Clive • TVM • USA
SPECTRE see **OUT 1: SPECTRE** • 1970
SPECTRE, LE • 1899 • Melies Georges • FRN • MURDER WILL OUT (USA)
SPECTRE, LE • 1916 • Feuillade Louis • FRN
SPECTRE, THE • 1910 • *Pathe* • FRN
SPECTRE, THE • 1915 • *Santa Barbara* • USA
SPECTRE, THE see **SPETTRO, LO** • 1962
SPECTRE BRIDEGROOM, THE • 1913 • *Francis Alec B.* • USA
SPECTRE DE LA DANSE, LE • 1960 • Delouche Dominique • ANT • FRN
SPECTRE DE M. IMBERGER, LE see **MYSTERE IMBERGER, LE** • 1935
SPECTRE OF DARKNESS see **PRICHOZI Z TEMNOT** • 1921
SPECTRE OF EDGAR ALLAN POE, THE see **SPECTER OF EDGAR ALLAN POE** • 1972
SPECTRE OF THE ROSE, THE • 1989 • Russell Ken • UKN
SPECTRE OF THE ROSE (UKN) see **SPECTER OF THE ROSE** • 1946
SPECTRE VERT, LE • 1930 • Feyder Jacques, Barrymore Lionel • FRN • GREEN GHOST, THE
SPECTRES see **SPETTRI** • 1987
SPECTRES, THE • 1975 • *Conte Richard*
SPECTRUM: I'LL BE GONE • 1971 • Lofven Chris • SHT • ASL
SPECTRUM IN WHITE • 1971 • Siegel Lois • ANS • CND
SPECTRUM–SPECTRUM–SPECTRUM • 1981 • Firus Karen • CND
SPECULATION • 1911 • *Powers* • USA
SPECULATION • 1967 • Riad Mohamed Slimane • SHT • ALG
SPEECH FOR THE DEFENCE see **SLOVO DLYA ZASHCHITY** • 1977
SPEED • 1917 • Walsh James O. • SHT • USA
SPEED • 1919 • *Strand* • SHT • USA
SPEED • 1919 • St. John Al • *Paramount* • SHT • USA
SPEED • 1923 • Seitz George B. • SRL • USA
SPEED • 1925 • Le Saint Edward J. • USA
SPEED • 1931 • Sennett Mack • SHT • USA
SPEED • 1936 • Marin Edwin L. • USA
SPEED • 1972 • Jittlov Mike • SHT • USA
SPEED see **RACING YOUTH** • 1932
SPEED AND SPUNK • 1917 • Semon Larry • SHT • USA
SPEED BEAR, THE • 1913 • *Mace Fred* • USA
SPEED BRENT WINS (UKN) see **BREED OF THE BORDER** • 1933
SPEED CLASSIC, THE • 1928 • Mitchell Bruce • USA
SPEED COP • 1926 • Worne Duke • USA
SPEED CRAZED • 1926 • Worne Duke • USA
SPEED CRAZY • 1959 • Hole William Jr. • USA
SPEED DEMON • 1925 • Bradbury Robert North • USA
SPEED DEMON • 1933 • Lederman D. Ross • USA
SPEED DEMON, THE • 1912 • Sennett Mack • USA
SPEED DEMONS • 1917 • *Pokes & Jabbs* • SHT • USA
SPEED DRIVER • 1982 • Massi Stelvio • ITL, SPN, FRG
SPEED FEVER see **FORMULA UNO FEBBRE DELLA VELOCITA** • 1978
SPEED GIRL, THE • 1921 • Campbell Maurice • USA
SPEED IN THE GAY '90'S • 1932 • Lord Del • SHT • USA
SPEED IS OF THE ESSENCE see **BELIEVE IN ME** • 1971
SPEED KING • 1923 • Jones Grover • USA
SPEED KING, THE • 1915 • *Ostriche Muriel* • USA
SPEED KING, THE see **GREAT CORONA RACE, THE** • 1916
SPEED KINGS • 1915 • *Pokes & Jabbs* • USA
SPEED KINGS, THE • 1913 • Sennett Mack • USA
SPEED LIMIT 65 see **LIMIT, THE** • 1972
SPEED LIMIT, THE • 1913 • *Brennan John E.* • USA
SPEED LIMIT, THE • 1926 • O'Connor Frank • USA
SPEED LOVERS • 1968 • McGaha William • USA
SPEED MAD • 1925 • Marchant Jay • USA
SPEED MAD see **MOTOR MADNESS** • 1937
SPEED MADNESS • 1925 • Mitchell Bruce • USA
SPEED MADNESS • 1931 • Crone George J. • USA
SPEED MANIAC, THE • 1919 • Le Saint Edward J. • USA
SPEED QUEEN, THE • 1913 • Sennett Mack • USA
SPEED REPORTER, THE • 1936 • Ray Bernard B. • USA
SPEED REPORTER, THE (UKN) see **SCAREHEADS** • 1931
SPEED SPOOK, THE • 1924 • Hines Charles • USA
SPEED TEST AT TARANTULA • 1904 • *Bitzer Billy (Ph)* • USA
SPEED THE PLOUGH • 1956 • Privett Bob • ANS • UKN
SPEED THE PLOW • 1939 • Hawes Stanley • UKN
SPEED THE SWEDE • 1923 • Roach Hal • SHT • USA
SPEED TO BURN • 1938 • Brower Otto • USA • RACING BLOOD
SPEED TO SPARE • 1920 • Roach Hal • SHT • USA
SPEED TO SPARE • 1937 • Hillyer Lambert • USA
SPEED TO SPARE • 1948 • Berke William • USA
SPEED VERSUS DEATH • 1910 • Melies Gaston • USA
SPEED WILD • 1925 • Garson Harry • USA
SPEED WINGS • 1934 • Brower Otto • USA
SPEED ZONE see **SPEEDZONE FEVER** • 1989
SPEEDER'S REVENGE, THE • 1914 • *Mack Hughie* • USA
SPEEDING • 1916 • Hartigan P. C. • SHT • USA
SPEEDING HOOFS • 1927 • Chaudet Louis W. • USA
SPEEDING INTO TROUBLE • 1924 • Morrison Lee • UKN
SPEEDING THROUGH • 1926 • Bracken Bertram • USA
SPEEDING VENUS, THE • 1926 • Thornby Robert T. • USA
SPEEDTRAP • 1978 • Bellamy Earl • USA
SPEEDWAY • 1929 • Beaumont Harry • USA
SPEEDWAY • 1968 • Taurog Norman • USA
SPEEDWAY OF DESPAIR, THE • 1914 • Kirkland Hardee • USA
SPEEDY • 1928 • Wilde Ted • USA
SPEEDY GHOST TO TOWN • 1967 • Lovy Alex • ANS • USA
SPEEDY GONZALES • 1955 • *Warner Brothers* • ASS • USA
SPEEDY GONZALES • 1955 • Freleng Friz • ANS • USA
SPEEDY GONZALES, NOIN SEITSEMAN VELJEKSEN POIKA • 1970 • Kokkonen Ere • FNL • SPEEDY GONZALES, SON OF ABOUT SEVEN BROTHERS
SPEEDY GONZALES, SON OF ABOUT SEVEN BROTHERS see **SPEEDY GONZALES, NOIN SEITSEMAN VELJEKSEN POIKA** • 1970
SPEEDY JUSTICE • 1935 • Schwarzwald Milton • SHT • USA
SPEEDY MEADE • 1919 • Lowry Ira M. • USA
SPEEDY SMITH • 1927 • Worne Duke • USA
SPEEDY SPURS • 1926 • Thorpe Richard • USA
SPEEDY THE TELEGRAPH BOY • 1911 • Stow Percy • UKN
SPEEDZONE FEVER • 1989 • Drake Jim • USA • ONE FOR THE MONEY ○ SPEED ZONE
SPEJBL A HURVINEK • 1953 • *Stallich Jan (Ph)* • SHT • CZC
SPEJBL NA STOPE • 1955 • Pojar Bretislav • ANS • CZC • SPEJBL ON THE TRACK ○ SPEJBL ON THE TRAIL
SPEJBL ON THE TRACK see **SPEJBL NA STOPE** • 1955
SPEJBL ON THE TRAIL see **SPEJBL NA STOPE** • 1955
SPEJBLOVO OPOJENI • 1931 • Skupa • CZC • FILM ELATION OF SPEJBL, THE
SPEJLETS SPAADOM • 1914 • Davidsen Hjalmar • DNM
SPELL • 1977 • Cavallone Alberto • ITL • DOLCE MATTATOIO
SPELL, THE • 1913 • *Powers* • USA
SPELL, THE • 1913 • Sturgeon Rollin S. • *Vitagraph* • USA
SPELL, THE • 1977 • Philips Lee • TVM • USA
SPELL, THE • 1987 • Farhang Darioush • IRN
SPELL OF AMY NUGENT, THE (USA) see **SPELLBOUND** • 1941
SPELL OF EVIL • 1973 • Sichel John • TVM • UKN
SPELL OF THE BALL, THE see **LABDA VARASZA, A** • 1962
SPELL OF THE CIRCUS • 1931 • Hill Robert F. • SRL • USA
SPELL OF THE FLOWERS, THE see **CHARME DES FLEURS, LA** • 1910
SPELL OF THE HYPNOTIST see **FRIGHT** • 1956
SPELL OF THE HYPNOTIST, THE • 1912 • *Helios* • USA
SPELL OF THE KNIFE, THE • 1916 • *Landis Margaret* • SHT • USA

SPELL OF THE POPPY, THE • 1915 • Browning Tod • USA
SPELL OF THE PRIMEVAL • 1913 • Le Saint Edward J. • USA
SPELL OF THE RIVER, THE see **REKA CARUJE** • 1945
SPELL OF THE YUKON, THE • 1916 • King Burton L. • USA
SPELLBINDER • 1988 • Greek Janet • USA • WITCHING HOUR
SPELLBINDER, THE • 1928 • Chalmers Thomas • USA
SPELLBINDER, THE • 1939 • Hively Jack • USA
SPELLBINDER, THE (UKN) see **SPIELER, THE** • 1928
SPELLBOUND • 1916 • Horkheimer H. M., Horkheimer E. D. • USA
SPELLBOUND • 1941 • Harlow John • UKN • SPELL OF AMY NUGENT, THE (USA) ◦ PASSING CLOUDS
SPELLBOUND • 1945 • Hitchcock Alfred • USA • HOUSE OF DR. EDWARDES, THE
SPELLBOUND HOUND • 1950 • Hubley John • ANS • USA
SPELLCASTER • 1987 • Zielinski Rafal • USA
SPELNIONE MARZENIA • 1939 • Brazybulski N. • FULFILLED DREAMS (USA)
SPELUNKE • 1928 • Emo E. W. • FRG
SPELUNKE ZUR BLAUEN MEERKATZE, DIE • 1924 • *Wortmann-Film* • FRG
SPENCER'S MOUNTAIN • 1963 • Daves Delmer • USA
SPEND IT ALL • 1970 • Blank Les, Gerson Skip • DOC • USA
SPEND, SPEND, SPEND • 1977 • Goldschmidt John • MTV • UKN
SPENDER, THE • 1913 • Salter Harry • USA
SPENDER, THE • 1915 • Levering Joseph • USA
SPENDER, THE • 1919 • Swickard Charles • USA
SPENDER FAMILY, THE • 1911 • *Essanay* • USA
SPENDER, OR THE FORTUNES OF PETER, THE • 1915 • Mackenzie Donald • USA
SPENDERS, THE • 1921 • Conway Jack • USA • RESPONDENT, THE
SPENDING IT QUICK • 1914 • *Ab* • USA
SPENDING MONEY see **ARGENT DE POCHE, L'** • 1976
SPENDTHRIFT, THE • 1915 • Edwin Walter • USA
SPENDTHRIFT, THE • 1922 • Terry Paul • ANS • USA
SPENDTHRIFT, THE • 1936 • Walsh Raoul • USA
SPENDTHRIFT'S REFORM, THE • 1912 • *Panzer Paul* • USA
SPENT BULLETS see **LAST FLIGHT, THE** • 1931
SPERDUTI NEL BUIO • 1914 • Martoglio Nino • ITL • LOST IN THE DARK
SPERDUTI NEL BUIO • 1947 • Mastrocinque Camillo • ITL
SPERDUTTA DI ALLAH, LA • 1928 • Guazzoni Enrico • ITL
SPERGIURA • 1909 • Maggi Luigi • ITL
SPERIAMO CHE SIA FEMMINA • 1985 • Monicelli Mario • ITL, FRN • LET'S HOPE IT'S A GIRL (USA) ◦ LET'S HOPE IT WILL BE A GIRL
SPERMULA • 1975 • Matton Charles • FRN
SPERRBEZIRK • 1966 • Tremper Will • FRG
SPERREGEBIET: DIAMOND AREA NO.1 • 1972 • SAF
SPESSART INN, THE (USA) see **WIRTSHAUS IM SPESSART, DAS** • 1958
SPESSART ROCKETS see **HERRLICHE ZEITEN IM SPESSART** • 1967
SPETSIALIST PO VISICHKO • 1962 • Vassilev Peter • BUL • MASTER OF ALL TRADES
SPETTERS • 1979 • Verhoeven Paul* • NTH
SPETTRI • 1987 • Avallone Marcello • ITL • SPECTERS (USA) ◦ SPECTRES
SPETTRO DE DR. HICHCOCK, LO see **SPETTRO, LO** • 1962
SPETTRO DEL SOTTERRANEO, LO • 1915 • Del Colle Ubaldo Maria • ITL • SPECTER OF THE VAULT, THE
SPETTRO DI JAGO, LO • 1912 • Lolli Alberto Carlo • ITL • SPECTER OF JAGO, THE
SPETTRO DI MEZZANOTTE, LO • 1915 • *Talia* • ITL • MIDNIGHT SPECTER, THE
SPETTRO, LO • 1962 • Freda Riccardo • ITL • GHOST, THE (USA) ◦ SPETTRO DE DR. HICHCOCK, LO ◦ SPECTRE, THE
SPETTRO VENDICATORE • 1914 • *Roma* • ITL • AVENGING SPECTER, THE
SPHERE, THE • 1971 • Poggi Gianni • ITL
SPHERES • 1969 • McLaren Norman, Jodoin Rene • ANS • CND
SPHERICAL LIGHTNING see **PIORUM KULISTY** • 1975
SPHERICAL SPACE #1 • 1967 • Vanderbeek Stan • SHT • USA
SPHINX • 1918 • Balazs Bela • HNG
SPHINX • 1981 • Schaffner Franklin J. • USA
SPHINX, THE • 1916 • Adolfi John G. • USA
SPHINX, THE • 1933 • Rosen Phil • USA
SPHINX, THE • 1970 • Gavioli Roberto • ANS • ITL
SPHINX, THE see **MORT DU SPHINX, LA** • 1937
SPHINX HAS SPOKEN, THE see **FRIENDS AND LOVERS** • 1931
SPIA CHE VIENE DAL MARE, LA • 1966 • Benvenuti Lamberto • ITL • SPY WHO CAME FROM THE SEA, THE
SPIA SENZA DOMANI, LA see **SELLOUT, THE** • 1975
SPIA SPIONE • 1966 • Corbucci Bruno • ITL
SPIAGGIA, LA • 1954 • Lattuada Alberto • ITL, FRN • BEACH, THE ◦ PENSIONNAIRE, LA
SPIAGGIA DEL DESIDERIO, LA (ITL) see **PLAYA LLAMADO DESEO, UNA** • 1977
SPIAGGIA LIBERA • 1966 • Girolami Marino • ITL
SPIAGGIA LONTANA, UNA • 1970 • Quilici Folco • MTV • ITL
SPICE OF LIFE, THE • 1931 • Elliot Grace • USA
SPICE OF LIFE, THE see **SPORTING YOUTH** • 1924
SPICE OF LIFE, THE (USA) see **CASSE-PIEDS, LES** • 1948
SPICIO AFRICANUS see **SCIPIONE L'AFRICANO** • 1937
SPICK AND SPAN • Szoboszlay Peter • ANS • HNG
SPICY RICE see **DRACHENFUTTER** • 1987
SPICY TIME, A • 1913 • *Imp* • USA
SPIDER • 1985 • SAF
SPIDER see **PAUK** • 1969
SPIDER, THE • 1913 • *Eclair* • USA
SPIDER, THE • 1915 • *Grandin* • USA
SPIDER, THE • 1915 • Windom Lawrence C. • *Essanay* • USA
SPIDER, THE • 1916 • Vignola Robert G. • USA
SPIDER, THE • 1931 • Menzies William Cameron, MacKenna Kenneth • USA
SPIDER, THE • 1939 • Elvey Maurice • UKN
SPIDER, THE • 1945 • Webb Robert D. • USA
SPIDER, THE see **PAUKI** • 1942
SPIDER, THE see **EARTH VS. THE SPIDER, THE** • 1958
SPIDER AND HER WEB, THE • 1914 • Smalley Phillips • USA
SPIDER AND THE FLY, THE • 1916 • Edwards J. Gordon • USA
SPIDER AND THE FLY, THE • 1931 • Jackson Wilfred • ANS • USA
SPIDER AND THE FLY, THE • 1949 • Hamer Robert • UKN
SPIDER AND THE ROSE, THE • 1923 • McDermott John • USA
SPIDER AND THE SCORPION see **GAGAMBA AT SI SCORPIO** • 1969
SPIDER BABY • 1964 • Hill Jack • USA • SPIDER BABY, OR THE MADDEST STORY EVER TOLD ◦ LIVER EATERS, THE ◦ CANNIBAL ORGY, OR THE MADDEST STORY EVER TOLD
SPIDER BABY, OR THE MADDEST STORY EVER TOLD see **SPIDER BABY** • 1964
SPIDER BARLOW CUTS IN • 1915 • Bartlett Charles • USA
SPIDER BARLOW MEETS COMPETITION • 1916 • Bartlett Charles • SHT • USA
SPIDER BARLOW'S SOFT SPOT • 1915 • Bartlett Charles • USA
SPIDER FOOTBALL see **POKFOCI** • 1977
SPIDER GIRL see **IREZUMI** • 1966
SPIDER IN THE BRAIN, A • 1912 • *Itala* • ITL
SPIDER-MAN • 1977 • Swackhamer E. W. • TVM • USA • SPIDERMAN: THE MOVIE
SPIDER-MAN STRIKES BACK • 1978 • Satlof Ron • USA • SPIDERMAN STRIKES BACK
SPIDER -MASTER OF MEN, THE see **SPIDER'S WEB, THE** • 1938
SPIDER RETURNS, THE • 1941 • Horne James W. • SRL • USA
SPIDER TALKS, THE • 1932 • *Terry Paul/ Moser Frank (P)* • ANS • USA
SPIDER TATTOO see **IREZUMI** • 1966
SPIDER WEBS • 1927 • Noy Wilfred • USA
SPIDER WOMAN STRIKES BACK • 1946 • Lubin Arthur • USA
SPIDER WOMAN (UKN) see **SHERLOCK HOLMES AND SPIDER WOMAN** • 1944
SPIDERMAN • 1969 • Glut Don • SHT • USA
SPIDERMAN AND THE DRAGON'S CHALLENGE see **SPIDERMAN: THE DRAGON'S CHALLENGE** • 1979
SPIDERMAN STRIKES BACK see **SPIDER-MAN STRIKES BACK** • 1978
SPIDERMAN: THE DRAGON'S CHALLENGE • 1979 • McDougall Don • USA • SPIDERMAN AND THE DRAGON'S CHALLENGE ◦ CHINESE WEB, THE
SPIDERMAN THE MOVIE • 1989 • Pyun Albert • USA
SPIDERMAN: THE MOVIE see **SPIDER-MAN** • 1977
SPIDERS, THE see **SPINNEN, DIE** • 1919
SPIDERS A GO-GO see **SUPAIDASU NO DAISHINGEKI** • 1968
SPIDERS NO BARITO CHINDOCHU • 1968 • Nishikawa Katsumi • JPN • FUNNY TOUR
SPIDER'S STRATAGEM, THE see **STRATEGIA DEL RAGNO, LA** • 1969
SPIDER'S STRATEGY, THE see **STRATEGIA DEL RAGNO, LA** • 1969
SPIDER'S WEB, THE • 1912 • *Costello Maurice* • USA
SPIDER'S WEB, THE • 1916 • *Washburn Bryant* • SHT • USA
SPIDER'S WEB, THE • 1927 • Micheaux Oscar • USA
SPIDER'S WEB, THE • 1938 • Taylor Ray, Horne James W. • SRL • USA • SPIDER -MASTER OF MEN, THE
SPIDER'S WEB, THE • 1960 • Grayson Godfrey • UKN
SPIDER'S WEB, THE see **TOTER HING IM NETZ, EIN** • 1960
SPIDER'S WEB, THE see **SPINNENETZ, DAS** • 1988
SPIDER'S WEB (UKN) see **FLASHING SPURS** • 1924
SPIE AMANO I FIORI, LE • 1966 • Lenzi Umberto • ITL • SPY LOVES FLOWERS, THE
SPIE CONTRO IL MONDE see **GERN HAB' ICH DIE FRAUEN GEKILLT** • 1966
SPIE FRA LE ELICHE • 1943 • Ferronetti Ignazio • ITL
SPIE UCCIDONO A BEIRUT, LE • 1965 • Martino Luciano, Combret Georges • ITL, FRN • ESPIONS MEURENT A BEYROUTH, LES (FRN) ◦ SECRET AGENT FIREBALL (USA) ◦ SPY KILLERS, THE (UKN) ◦ FIREBALL ◦ KILLERS ARE CHALLENGED ◦ SPY KILLED AT BEIRUT, THE
SPIE UCCIDONO IN SILENZIO, LE (ITL) see **ESPIAS MANTAN EL SILENCIO, LOS** • 1966
SPIE VENGONO DAL SEMIFREDDO, LE • 1966 • Bava Mario • ITL, USA • DR. GOLDFOOT AND THE GIRL BOMBS (USA) ◦ DUE MAFIOSI DELL'F.B.I., I ◦ DR. G. AND THE LOVE BOMBS ◦ TWO MAFIOSI FROM THE F.B.I., THE ◦ SPY CAME FROM THE SEMI-COLD, THE
SPIEGEL DER HELENA, DER see **UNHEIMLICHE WANDLUNG DES ALEX ROSCHER, DIE** • 1943
SPIEGEL DES LEBENS • 1938 • von Bolvary Geza • FRG • LIFE'S MIRROR (USA) ◦ MIRROR, THE
SPIEGEL VAN HOLLAND • 1950 • Haanstra Bert • NTH • MIRROR OF HOLLAND
SPIEGELMENSCH, DER • 1923 • Werfel Franz • FRG • MIRRORMAN, THE
SPIEL • 1944 • Stoger Alfred • FRG
SPIEL AN BORD • 1936 • Selpin Herbert • FRG
SPIEL AUF DER TENNE • 1937 • Jacoby Georg • FRG
SPIEL AUS DEM LEBEN DER ERSTEN VIERHUNDERT, EIN see **FUNFTE STRASSE, DIE** • 1923
SPIEL DER KONIGIN, DAS see **GLAS WASSER, EIN** • 1923
SPIEL DER LIEBE, DAS • 1923 • Schamberg Guido • FRG
SPIEL GLUCKSRITTERN UND SCHONEN FRAUEN, EIN see **JOKEREN** • 1928
SPIEL IM SAND • 1964 • Herzog Werner • SHT • FRG • PLAYING IN THE SAND
SPIEL IM SOMMERWIND • 1938 • von Norman Roger • PLAY IN THE SUMMER BREEZES (USA)
SPIEL IM SPIEL • 1916 • Hanus Emerich • FRG
SPIEL IN FARBEN, EIN see **FARBENSPIEL** • 1934
SPIEL IST AUS, DAS • 1916 • *Abel Alfred* • FRG
SPIEL MIT DEM FEUER • 1931 • Roberts Ralph Arthur • FRG
SPIEL MIT DEM FEUER, DAS • 1918 • von Woringen Paul • FRG
SPIEL MIT DEM FEUER, DAS • 1921 • Wiene Robert, Kroll Georg • FRG
SPIEL MIT DEM SCHICKSAL, DAS • 1924 • Philippi Siegfried • FRG
SPIEL MIT DEM TEUFER, DAS see **INFERNO** • 1920
SPIEL MIT DEM WEIBE, DAS • 1922 • Licho Adolf Edgar • FRG
SPIEL MIT DER LIEBE, DAS • 1928 • Janson Victor • FRG
SPIEL MIT MENSCHEN • 1922 • Lampadius Hanns • FRG
SPIEL MIT STEINEN • 1965 • Svankmajer Jan • ANM • CZC • GAME WITH STONES, A ◦ MOTIFS WITH STONES
SPIEL UM DEN MANN • 1929 • Land Robert • FRG
SPIEL UM JOB, ANTIGONE, DAS GROSSE VORBILD • 1962 • Dieterle William • MTV • FRG
SPIEL VOM TODE, DAS • 1917 • Neuss Alwin • FRG
SPIEL VON KLEINEN SEELEN, EIN see **KIND -EIN HUND, EIN** • 1923
SPIEL VON LIEBE UND TOD, DAS • 1919 • Gad Urban • FRG
SPIELBANKAFFARE • 1957 • Pohl Arthur • GDR, SWT
SPIELER • 1989 • Graf Dominik • FRG • PLAYER ◦ GAMBLER
SPIELER, DER • 1915 • Garas Martin • FRG
SPIELER, DER • 1938 • Lamprecht Gerhard • FRG • ROMAN EINES SPIELERS
SPIELER, DIE • 1919 • Zeyn Willy • FRG
SPIELER, THE • 1928 • Garnett Tay • USA • SPELLBINDER, THE (UKN)
SPIELER AUS LEIDENSCHAFT see **DR. MABUSE, DER SPIELER 1** • 1922
SPIELEREIEN EINER KAISERIN • 1929 • von Strischewski Wladimir • FRG
SPIELERIN, DIE • 1920 • Oswald Richard • FRG
SPIELERIN, DIE • 1927 • Cutts Graham • FRG • CHANCE THE IDOL
SPIELMANN, DER • 1921 • Krause Karl Otto • FRG
SPIELST DU MIT SCHRAGEN VOGELN • 1968 • Ehmck Gustav • FRG • MY SWEDISH MEATBALL (UKN) ◦ SCHRAGE VOGEL ◦ IF YOU PLAY WITH CRAZY BIRDS
SPIELZEUG DER ZARIN, DAS • 1919 • Meinert Rudolf • FRG
SPIELZEUG EINER DIRNE, DAS • 1922 • Illes Eugen, Fiedler-Spies Ernst • FRG
SPIELZEUG SCHONER FRAUEN, DAS • 1927 • Freisler Fritz • FRG
SPIELZEUG VON PARIS, DAS • 1925 • Curtiz Michael • FRG, FRN, AUS • CELIMENE -LA POUPEE DE MONTMARTRE (FRN) ◦ RED HEELS (USA)
SPIES • 1915 • Wilson Frank • UKN
SPIES see **KUROHYO** • 1953
SPIES A-GO-GO • 1963 • Landis James • USA • NASTY RABBIT, THE
SPIES AND SPILLS • 1918 • Semon Larry • SHT • USA
SPIES AT WORK see **SPIONE AM WERK** • 1933
SPIES AT WORK (UKN) see **SABOTAGE** • 1939
SPIES FROM SALONIKA see **MADEMOISELLE DOCTEUR** • 1936
SPIES IN SARONIKO see **KATASKOPI STO SARONIKO** • 1968
SPIES KILL SILENTLY see **ESPIAS MANTAN EL SILENCIO, LOS** • 1966
SPIES, LIES AND NAKED THIGHS • 1989 • Frawley James • USA
SPIES LIKE US • 1985 • Landis John • USA
SPIES' NEST, THE • 1918 • *Universal* • SHT • USA
SPIES OF THE AIR • 1939 • MacDonald David • UKN • OFFICIAL SECRET
SPIES (USA) see **SPIONE** • 1928
SPIES WHO NEVER WERE, THE • 1981 • Rasky Harry • MTV • CND
SPIETATA COLT DEL GRINGO, LA • 1966 • Madrid Jose Luis • ITL
SPIFFKINS EATS FROGS • 1912 • *Lux* • FRN
SPIGOLATRICE DI SAPRI, LA see **ERAN TRECENTO** • 1952
SPIJUN NA STIKLAMA • 1989 • Jelic Milan • YGS • SPY WORE HIGH HEELS, THE
SPIKE OF BENSONHURST see **MAFIA KID** • 1988
SPIKE SHANNON'S LAST FIGHT • 1911 • *Anderson Broncho Billy* • USA
SPIKED HEELS AND BLACK NYLONS • 1967 • Boyd Whit • USA • BLACK NYLONS
SPIKER • 1986 • Tilton Roger • USA
SPIKE'S BIZZY BIKE • 1917 • Hutchinson Craig • SHT • USA
SPIKES GANG, THE • 1974 • Fleischer Richard • USA
SPIKEY'S MAGIC WAND • 1973 • Farlowe Vance • USA
SPIN A DARK WEB (USA) see **SOHO INCIDENT** • 1956
SPIN OF A COIN (UKN) see **GEORGE RAFT STORY, THE** • 1961
SPIN OF DEATH, THE • 1984 • SAF
SPINA DORSALE DEL DIAVOLO, LA • 1970 • Kennedy Burt, Fulgozi Niska • ITL, USA, YGS • DESERTER, THE (USA) ◦ PRELAZ PREKO DJAVOLJE KICME ◦ DJAVOLJA KICMA ◦ DISERTORE, IL ◦ S.O.B.'S, THE
SPINA NEL CUORE, UNA • 1985 • Lattuada Alberto • ITL, FRN • THORN IN THE HEART, A
SPINACH FER BRITAIN • 1943 • Sparber I. • ANS • USA
SPINACH OVERTURE, THE • 1935 • Fleischer Dave • ANS • USA
SPINACH-PACKING POPEYE • 1944 • Sparber I. • ANS • USA
SPINACH ROADSTER, THE • 1936 • Fleischer Dave • ANS • USA
SPINACH VS. HAMBURGERS • 1948 • Kneitel Seymour • ANS • USA
SPINDLE OF LIFE, THE • 1917 • Cochrane George • USA
SPINDRIFT • 1968 • Ryan Michael G. • DCS • NZL
SPINNE, DIE • 1916 • Neuss Alwin • FRG
SPINNE, DIE • 1919 • Wiene Conrad • AUS
SPINNEN, DIE • 1919 • Lang Fritz • FRG • ABENTEUER DES KAY HOOG, DIE ◦ SPIDERS, THE
SPINNEN PART 1, DIE • 1919 • Lang Fritz • FRG • GOLDENE SEE, DER ◦ GOLDEN SEA, THE ◦ GOLDEN LAKE, THE
SPINNEN PART 2, DIE • 1920 • Lang Fritz • FRG • BRILLIANTEN SCHIFF, DAS ◦ DIAMOND SHIP, THE
SPINNENETZ, DAS • 1988 • Wicki Bernhard • FRG • SPIDER'S WEB, THE
SPINNER, A • 1964 • NKR
SPINNER O' DREAMS • 1922 • *Livesey (Mr.)* • USA
SPINNER OF DREAMS • 1918 • Noy Wilfred • UKN
SPINNING A YARN • 1944 • *O'Brien Joseph/ Mead Thomas (P)* • SHT • USA
SPINNING EARTH 1-11 see **CHIKYU WA MAWARU** • 1928
SPINNING FAMILY see **SNURRIGA FAMILJEN** • 1940
SPINNING MICE • 1935 • Gillett Burt, Palmer Tom • ANS • USA
SPINNING WHEEL, THE see **MOUL LE YA, MOUL LE YA** • 1983
SPINNING WHEELS • 1989 • Schmitt Richard • USA
SPINNOLIO • 1977 • Weldon John • ANM • CND

SPINOLAS LETZTES GESICHT • 1915 • *Carmi Maria* • FRG
SPINOUT • 1966 • Taurog Norman • USA • CALIFORNIA HOLIDAY (UKN)
SPINSTER MOTHERS see **LEDIGE MUTTER** • 1928
SPINSTER (UKN) see **TWO LOVES** • 1961
SPINSTERS, THE see **PARA VESTIR SANTOS** • 1955
SPINSTERS AND WIDOWS see **PANNY I WDOWY** • 1990
SPINSTER'S LEGACY, THE • 1911 • *Lubin* • USA
SPION, DER • 1914 • Schmidthassler Walter • FRG
SPION, DER • 1916 • Heiland Heinz Karl • FRG
SPION, DER IN DIE HOLLE GING, DER (FRG) see **CORRIDA POUR UN ESPION** • 1965
SPION FUR DEUTSCHLAND • 1956 • Klinger Werner • FRG
SPIONAGE • 1955 • Antel Franz • AUS
SPIONAGGIO A CASABLANCA (ITL) see **CASABLANCA, NID D'ESPIONS** • 1963
SPIONAGGIO A GIBILTERRA (ITL) see **GIBRALTAR** • 1963
SPIONAGGIO SENZA FRONTIERE (ITL) see **HONORABLE STANISLAS AGENT SECRET, L'** • 1963
SPIONE • 1928 • Lang Fritz • FRG • SPY, THE (UKN) ○ SPIES (USA)
SPIONE, DIE • 1919 • Dupont E. A. • FRG
SPIONE AM WERK • 1933 • Lamprecht Gerhard • FRG • SPIES AT WORK
SPIONE DES KAISERS, DER see **SCHWARZER JAGER JOHANNA** • 1934
SPIONE IM SAVOY-HOTEL • 1932 • Zelnik Friedrich • FRG • GALAVORSTELLUNG DER FRATELLINIS, DIE
SPIONE, LO (ITL) see **DOULOS, LE** • 1962
SPIONE UNTER SICH (FRG) see **GUERRE SECRETE** • 1965
SPIONEN FRA TOKIO • 1910 • Blom August • DNM • RED LIGHT, THE
SPIONIN, DIE • 1921 • Wolff Ludwig • FRG • MATA HARI
SPIRACLE • 1967 • Beavers Robert • SHT • USA
SPIRAL, THE see **SPIRALIA** • 1978
SPIRAL BUREAU, THE • 1976 • Coughlan Ian • MTV • ASL
SPIRAL ROAD, THE • 1962 • Mulligan Robert • USA
SPIRAL STAIRCASE, THE • 1946 • Siodmak Robert • USA
SPIRAL STAIRCASE, THE • 1975 • Collinson Peter • UKN
SPIRALE, LA • 1976 • Mattelart Armand, Meppiel Jacqueline, Mayoux Valerie • DOC • FRN
SPIRALE DI NEBBIA, UNA • 1977 • Visconti Eriprando • ITL
SPIRALIA • 1978 • Zanussi Krzysztof • PLN • SPIRAL, THE
SPIRALS see **KRUSENDULLER** • 1969
SPIRISTISME FIN DE SIECLE see **SPIRITISME ABRACADABRANT** • 1900
SPIRIT • 1989 • Ripley Jonathan • UKN
SPIRIT, THE • 1908 • *Gaumont* • FRN
SPIRIT, THE • 1986 • Bender Joel • USA
SPIRIT, THE • 1987 • Schultz Michael • TVM • USA
SPIRIT, THE see **YU-LING** • 1977
SPIRIT AND THE CLAY, THE • 1914 • Lambart Harry • USA
SPIRIT AND THE FLESH, THE (USA) see **PROMESSI SPOSI, I** • 1941
SPIRIT AWAKENED, THE • 1912 • Griffith D. W. • USA
SPIRIT CHASER, THE see **FROG DREAMING** • 1985
SPIRIT HAND, THE • 1911 • *Thanhouser* • USA
SPIRIT IS WILLING, THE • 1967 • Castle William • USA
SPIRIT OF '17, THE • 1918 • Taylor William D. • USA
SPIRIT OF '23, THE • 1922 • *C.b.c.* • SHT • USA
SPIRIT OF '61, THE • 1916 • *De Carlton Grace* • SHT • USA
SPIRIT OF '76 • 1905 • *Bitzer Billy (Ph)* • USA
SPIRIT OF '76, THE • 1908 • Boggs Frank • USA
SPIRIT OF '76, THE • 1917 • Siegmann George • USA
SPIRIT OF 1976, THE • 1934 • Jason Leigh • SHT • USA
SPIRIT OF ADVENTURE, THE • 1915 • Eason B. Reeves • USA
SPIRIT OF ANNAPOLIS, THE • 1942 • Negulesco Jean • SHT • USA
SPIRIT OF AUDUBON, THE • 1913 • *Swinburne Lawrence* • USA
SPIRIT OF BANG POON VILLAGE • 1981 • Prohmvitake Pakorn • THL
SPIRIT OF CHRISTMAS, THE • 1913 • Humphrey William, Johnson Tefft • USA
SPIRIT OF CULVER, THE • 1939 • Santley Joseph • USA • MAN'S HERITAGE (UKN)
SPIRIT OF ENVY, THE • 1913 • *Thanhouser* • USA
SPIRIT OF GINGER, THE • Wan Ku Chan • ANM • CHN
SPIRIT OF GIVING, THE • 1915 • Pollard Harry? • USA
SPIRIT OF GOD, THE see **SPIRIT OF GOOD, THE** • 1920
SPIRIT OF GOOD, THE • 1920 • Cazeneuve Paul • USA • SPIRIT OF GOD, THE
SPIRIT OF JEALOUSY, THE • 1914 • *Ab* • USA
SPIRIT OF LAFAYETTE, THE • 1919 • Vincent James • USA
SPIRIT OF MERRY CHRISTMAS, THE • 1917 • Drew Sidney, Drew Sidney Mrs. • USA
SPIRIT OF NOTRE DAME • 1931 • Mack Russell • USA • VIGOUR OF YOUTH (UKN)
SPIRIT OF REVENGE, THE • 1916 • *Lily* • SHT • USA
SPIRIT OF ROMANCE, THE • 1917 • Hopper E. Mason • USA
SPIRIT OF ST. LOUIS, THE • 1957 • Wilder Billy • USA
SPIRIT OF STANFORD, THE • 1942 • Barton Charles T. • USA • FIGHTING SPIRIT (UKN)
SPIRIT OF THE BEEHIVE, THE (USA) see **ESPIRITU DE LA COLMENA, EL** • 1973
SPIRIT OF THE BELL, THE • 1915 • Hunt Jay • USA
SPIRIT OF THE BELLS, THE see **GENIE DES CLOCHES, LES** • 1908
SPIRIT OF THE BODY, THE see **RUH EL JASSAD, EL** • 1948
SPIRIT OF THE CHIMES, THE • Melies Georges • FRN
SPIRIT OF THE CONQUEROR OR, THE NAPOLEON OF LABOUR, THE • 1914 • *Phoenix* • USA
SPIRIT OF THE DEAD (USA) see **ASPHYX, THE** • 1972
SPIRIT OF THE FLAG • 1913 • Dwan Allan • USA
SPIRIT OF THE GAME, THE • 1916 • Sullivan Frederick • SHT • USA
SPIRIT OF THE GORGE, THE • 1911 • *Gordon James* • USA
SPIRIT OF THE HEATH, THE • 1921 • Paul Fred, Raymond Jack • UKN
SPIRIT OF THE LAKE, THE • 1909 • *Cines* • ITL
SPIRIT OF THE LIGHT, THE • 1911 • Blackton J. Stuart • USA
SPIRIT OF THE MADONNA • 1914 • *Essanay* • USA
SPIRIT OF THE ORIENT, THE • 1913 • *Costello Maurice* • USA
SPIRIT OF THE PEOPLE (UKN) see **ABE LINCOLN IN ILLINOIS** • 1939
SPIRIT OF THE POND, THE see **MA NO IKE** • 1923
SPIRIT OF THE RANGE, THE • 1912 • *Charleson Mary* • USA
SPIRIT OF THE SWORD, THE • 1910 • *Pathe* • FRN
SPIRIT OF THE TIME see **TIJDGEEST, DE** • 1968
SPIRIT OF THE U.S.A., THE • 1924 • Johnson Emory • USA • SWORDS AND PLOWSHARES ○ OLD HOME, THE
SPIRIT OF THE VIOLIN, THE • 1915 • Le Saint Edward J. • USA
SPIRIT OF THE WEST • 1932 • Brower Otto • USA
SPIRIT OF THE WEST, THE • 1910 • *Yankee* • USA
SPIRIT OF THE WIND • 1979 • Liddle Ralph R. • CND
SPIRIT OF UPLIFT, THE • 1915 • *Thanhouser* • USA
SPIRIT OF VARIETY, THE • 1937 • Wilson Hal • UKN
SPIRIT OF WEST POINT, THE • 1942 • Negulesco Jean • SHT • USA
SPIRIT OF WEST POINT, THE • 1947 • Murphy Ralph • USA
SPIRIT OF WILDERNESS see **KOYA NO TAMASHII** • 1937
SPIRIT OF YOUTH • 1938 • Fraser Harry L. • USA
SPIRIT OF YOUTH, THE • 1929 • Lang Walter • USA
SPIRIT THAT WINS, THE • 1918 • *Ferguson Elsie* • SHT • USA
SPIRIT WORLD OR THE RAJAH'S RUBY, THE • 1927 • *Kenilworth Prod.* • USA
SPIRITISM (USA) see **ESPIRITISMO** • 1961
SPIRITISME ABRACADABRANT • 1900 • Melies Georges • FRN • UP-TO-DATE SPIRITUALISM (USA) ○ SPIRISTISME FIN DE SIECLE
SPIRITISMO • 1920 • *Bertina Francesca* • ITL
SPIRITISMUS • 1920 • Zelnik Friedrich • FRG
SPIRITISTEN • 1914 • Holger-Madsen • DNM • SPIRITUALIST, THE ○ SPIRITS, THE ○ GHOSTS, THE ○ VOICE FROM THE PAST, A
SPIRITO SANTO E LE CINQUE MAGNIFICHE CANAGLIE • 1972 • Mauri Roberto • ITL
SPIRITS • 1920 • Parrott Charles • SHT • USA
SPIRITS • 1929 • Croise Hugh • UKN
SPIRITS, THE • *Tien Ching* • HKG
SPIRITS, THE see **SPIRITISTEN** • 1914
SPIRITS FREE OF DUTY • 1915 • *Horseshoe* • USA
SPIRITS IN THE KITCHEN • 1902 • *Biograph* • USA
SPIRITS OF AN AMBER PAST • 1978 • MacDonald Ramuna • MTV • CND
SPIRITS OF BRUCE LEE • Shang Lung • HKG
SPIRITS OF THE AIR see **SPIRITS OF THE AIR, GREMLINS OF THE CLOUDS** • 1986
SPIRITS OF THE AIR, GREMLINS OF THE CLOUDS • 1986 • Proyas Alexander • ASL • SPIRITS OF THE AIR
SPIRITS OF THE DEAD (USA) see **HISTOIRES EXTRAORDINAIRES** • 1968
SPIRITUAL BOXER, THE • Liu Chia-Liang • HKG
SPIRITUAL CONSTRUCTIONS see **SEELISCHE KONSTRUKTIONEN** • 1927
SPIRITUAL ELOPEMENT, A • 1915 • Ransom Charles • USA
SPIRITUALISM EXPOSED • 1913 • Raymond Charles • UKN • FRAUDULENT SPIRITUALISM EXPOSED ○ SEER OF BOND STREET, THE (USA)
SPIRITUALISM EXPOSED • 1926 • Coleby A. E. • UKN • FAKE SPIRITUALISM EXPOSED
SPIRITUALIST, THE see **SPIRITISTEN** • 1914
SPIRITUALIST, THE see **AMAZING MR. X., THE** • 1948
SPIRITUALIST PHOTOGRAPHER, THE (USA) see **PORTRAIT SPIRITE, LE** • 1903
SPIRITUALISTIC MEETING, A (USA) see **FANTOME D'ALGER, LE** • 1906
SPIRITUALISTIC SEANCE • 1908 • *Pathe* • FRN
SPIRITUALISTIC SEANCE, A • 1911 • *Pathe* • FRN
SPISKROKSVALSEN • 1909 • Magnusson Charles • SWD • WALTZ OF THE POKER
SPISTE HORIZONTER • 1950 • Roos Jorgen (c/d) • DOC • DNM
SPIT-BALL SADIE • 1915 • Roach Hal • USA • SPIT BALL SADIE
SPIT BALL SADIE see **SPIT-BALL SADIE** • 1915
SPITE BRIDE, THE • 1919 • Giblyn Charles • USA
SPITE FLIGHT • 1933 • *Iwerks Ub (P)* • ANS • USA
SPITE HUSBAND, THE • 1916 • Broadwell Robert B. • SHT • USA
SPITE MARRIAGE • 1929 • Sedgwick Edward, Keaton Buster (U/c) • USA
SPITEFUL BRIDAL NIGHT, A see **SHOYA GA NIKUI** • 1968
SPITEFUL UMBRELLA MAKER, THE • 1904 • *Paul R. W.* • UKN
SPITFIRE • 1922 • *Morton Edna* • USA
SPITFIRE • 1934 • Cromwell John • USA • TRIGGER
SPITFIRE, THE • 1914 • *Blackwell Carlyle* • USA
SPITFIRE, THE • 1924 • Cabanne W. Christy • USA
SPITFIRE OF SEVILLE, THE • 1914 • Lloyd Frank • USA
SPITFIRE OF SEVILLE, THE • 1919 • Siegmann George • USA
SPITFIRE: THE FIRST OF THE FEW see **FIRST OF THE FEW, THE** • 1942
SPITFIRE (USA) see **FIRST OF THE FEW, THE** • 1942
SPITTER, THE • Sramek Svatopluk • CZC
SPITTIN' IMAGE • 1983 • Kern Russell S. • USA
SPITTING IMAGE, THE see **ALS TWEE DRUPPELS WATER** • 1963
SPITZEL, DER • 1920 • Neff Wolfgang • FRG
SPITZEN • 1926 • Holger-Madsen • FRG • EID DES FURSTEN ULRICH
SPITZEN DER GESELLSCHAFT, DIE • 1923 • Heidemann Paul • FRG
SPITZEN DER GESELLSCHAFT, DIE • 1990 • Novotny Franz • AUS
SPITZENKLOPPERIN VON VALENCIENNES, DIE • 1923 • Linke Edmund • FRG
SPITZENTUCH DER FURSTIN WOLKOWSKA, DAS • 1917 • Stein Josef? • FRG
SPITZWEG, DER EWIGE HOCHZEITER • 1920 • Frey Karl? • FRG
SPIVS (UKN) see **VITELLONI, I** • 1953
SPLASH! • 1931 • Myers Zion, White Jules • SHT • USA
SPLASH • 1984 • Howard Ron • USA
SPLASH ME NICELY • 1917 • Kellino W. P. • UKN
SPLASH OF LOCAL COLOR, A • 1916 • Henderson Lucius • SHT • USA
SPLASH, TOO • 1988 • Antonacci Greg • TVM • USA
SPLATTER see **FUTURE-KILL** • 1984
SPLATTER -ARCHITECTS OF FEAR • 1986 • Rowe Peter • DOC • USA
SPLATTER UNIVERSITY • 1985 • Haines Richard W. • USA • CAMPUS KILLINGS
SPLAV MEDUZE • 1981 • Godina Karpo • YGS • RAFT OF MEDUSA, THE ○ MEDUSA RAFT, THE ○ RAFT OF THE MEDUSA, THE
SPLEEN see **NACHT DER EINBRUCHER, DIE** • 1921
SPLENDID COWARD, THE • 1918 • Thornton F. Martin • UKN
SPLENDID CRIME, THE • 1926 • De Mille William C. • USA
SPLENDID DAYS, THE see **SEREZHA** • 1960
SPLENDID DISHONOR, A • 1914 • *Bushman Francis X.* • USA
SPLENDID FELLOWS • 1934 • Smith Beaumont • ASL
SPLENDID FOLLY • 1919 • Bocchi Arrigo • UKN
SPLENDID HAZARD, A • 1920 • Rosson Arthur • USA
SPLENDID LIE, THE • 1922 • Horan Charles • USA
SPLENDID ROAD, THE • 1925 • Lloyd Frank • USA
SPLENDID ROMANCE, THE • 1918 • Jose Edward • USA
SPLENDID SACRIFICE, A • 1914 • Le Saint Edward J. • USA
SPLENDID SCAPEGRACE, A • 1913 • Brabin Charles J. • USA
SPLENDID SIN, THE • 1919 • Mitchell Howard M. • USA
SPLENDID SINNER, THE • 1918 • Carewe Edwin • USA
SPLENDID WASTER, THE • 1916 • Shaw Harold • SAF
SPLENDOR • 1935 • Nugent Elliott • USA
SPLENDOR IN THE GRASS • 1961 • Kazan Elia • USA • SPLENDOUR IN THE GRASS (UKN)
SPLENDOR IN THE GRASS • 1981 • Sarafian Richard C. • TVM • USA
SPLENDORI E MISERIE DI MADAME ROYALE • 1970 • Caprioli Vittorio • ITL
SPLENDOUR • 1989 • Scola Ettore • ITL
SPLENDOUR IN THE GRASS (UKN) see **SPLENDOR IN THE GRASS** • 1961
SPLENDOUR OF LOVE see **RAWAAT EL HOB** • 1968
SPLICED AND ICED • 1917 • *Watson Harry Jr.* • SHT • USA
SPLINTERS • 1929 • Raymond Jack • UKN
SPLINTERS IN THE AIR • 1937 • Goulding Alf • UKN
SPLINTERS IN THE NAVY • 1931 • Forde Walter • UKN
SPLIT • 1974 • Lambert Roger • UKN
SPLIT, THE • 1968 • Flemyng Gordon • USA
SPLIT, THE (UKN) see **MANSTER, THE** • 1962
SPLIT CHERRY TREE • 1982 • Konchalovsky Andrei • SHT • USA
SPLIT COMMISSION • 1970 • *Stacey Dist.* • USA
SPLIT DECISIONS • 1988 • Drury David • UKN • KID GLOVES
SPLIT IMAGE see **CAPTURED** • 1981
SPLIT-LEVEL TREEHOUSE • 1963 • *Terrytoon* • ANS • USA
SPLIT LIGHTNING • 1989 • Carver Steve • USA
SPLIT LOVERS • 1969 • *Mitam Productions* • USA
SPLIT NUGGET, THE • 1913 • *Nevius Laura* • USA
SPLIT OF THE SPIRIT • Tan Han-Chang • TWN
SPLIT SECOND • 1953 • Powell Dick • USA
SPLIT SECOND TO AN EPITAPH • 1968 • Horn Leonard • USA
SPLITFACE (UKN) see **DICK TRACY, DETECTIVE** • 1945
SPLITTING HAIRS • 1922 • Kenton Erle C. • SHT • USA
SPLITTING THE BREEZE • 1927 • De Lacy Robert • USA
SPLITTRING • Ozer Muammer • SWD
SPLITTTTTTT • Avidan David • SHT • ISR
SPLITZ • 1984 • Paris Domonic • USA
SPLURGE • 1931 • Elliot Grace • SHT • USA
SPN see **PERSEO L'INVINCIBILE** • 1962
SPN see **COLPO MAESTRO AL SERVIZIO DI SUA MAESTA BRITANNICA** • 1967
SPN see **ROSSO SEGNO DELLA FOLLIA, IL** • 1969
SPN see **NACHT DER VAMPIRE** • 1970
SPN see **VAMPYROS LESBOS -DIE ERBIN DES DRACULA** • 1971
SPN see **TUTTI I COLORI DEL BUIO** • 1972
SPN see **NIGHTMARE CITY** • 1980
SPOD TE UCKE GORI • 1973 • Fanelli Mario • YGS • UNDER THAT UCKA MOUNTAIN
SPOGELSESTOGET • 1976 • Christensen Bent • DNM
SPOGELSET I GRAVKAELDEREN • 1910 • Blom August • DNM • GHOST OF THE VARIETY, THE
SPOGLIAMOCI COSI SENZA PUDOR.. • 1977 • Martino Sergio • ITL • LOVE IN FOUR EASY LESSONS (UKN)
SPOGLIATI, PROTESTA, UCCIDI! • 1973 • De Sisti Vittorio • ITL • QUANDO LA PREDA E L'UOMO
SPOILED CHILD, THE • 1912 • *Johnson Arthur* • USA
SPOILED CHILDREN see **AWLAD EL ZAWAT** • 1931
SPOILED CHILDREN (USA) see **DES ENFANTS GATES** • 1976
SPOILED DARLING • 1968 • *C.i.t. Films* • USA • SPOILED DARLINGS
SPOILED DARLINGS see **SPOILED DARLING** • 1968
SPOILED DARLING'S DOLL, THE • 1913 • *Thanhouser* • USA
SPOILED ROTTEN • 1968 • Dalianidis Ioannis • GRC • PRIZED AS A MATE!
SPOILED WEDDING, A • ANM • CZC
SPOILER, THE • 1972 • Hughes Bill • MTV • ASL
SPOILERS, THE • 1914 • Campbell Colin • USA
SPOILERS, THE • 1923 • Hillyer Lambert • USA
SPOILERS, THE • 1930 • Carewe Edwin • USA
SPOILERS, THE • 1942 • Enright Ray • USA
SPOILERS, THE • 1955 • Hibbs Jesse • USA
SPOILERS, THE • 1976 • Pakdivijit Chalong • THL • S.T.A.B. ○ THONG
SPOILERS OF THE FOREST • 1957 • Kane Joseph • USA
SPOILERS OF THE NORTH • 1947 • Sale Richard • USA
SPOILERS OF THE PLAINS • 1951 • Witney William • USA
SPOILERS OF THE RANGE • 1939 • Coleman C. C. Jr. • USA
SPOILERS OF THE SEA see **FLOR DE MAYO** • 1957
SPOILERS OF THE WEST • 1927 • Van Dyke W. S. • USA
SPOILS • 1934 • Samuelson G. B. • UKN
SPOILS OF THE NIGHT (USA) see **IRO** • 1966
SPOILT CHILD, THE • 1904 • Fitzhamon Lewin • UKN
SPOILT CHILD, THE • 1909 • Fitzhamon Lewin? • UKN
SPOILT CHILD OF FORTUNE, A • 1910 • Fitzhamon Lewin • UKN
SPOJRZENIE NA PLAKAT • 1970 • Papuzinski Andrzej • DOC • PLN • LOOK AT POSTERS, A

SPOJRZENIE NA WRZESIEN • 1971 • Sielenski Maciej • PLN • LOOK AT SEPTEMBER, A
SPOKAR, DET SPOKAR, DET • 1943 • Bolander Hugo • SWD • GHOSTS! GHOSTS!
SPOKBARONEN • 1927 • Edgren Gustaf • SWD • GHOST BARON, THE
SPOKE PA SEMESTER • 1951 • Bernhard Gosta • SWD • GHOST ON HOLIDAY, A
SPOKE TILL SALU • 1939 • Arvedson Ragnar • SWD • GHOST FOR SALE
SPOKET PA BRAGEHUS • 1936 • Ibsen Tancred, Arvedson Ragnar • SWD • GHOST OF BRAGEHUS
SPOKOJI • 1976 • Kieslowski Krzysztof • PLN
SPOKREPORTERN • 1941 • Bauman Schamyl • SWD • GHOST REPORTER, THE
SPOLEM • 1937 • Ford Aleksander • DOC • PLN
SPOLIATEURS, LES • 1972 • Merbah Lamine • ALG
SPOMENEK • 1968 • Antic Miroslav • YGS
SPOMENICIMA NE TREBA VEROVATI • 1958 • Makavejev Dusan • SHT • YGS • DON'T BELIEVE IN MONUMENTS
SPONGE DIVERS see **LOVTSI GUBOK** • 1960
SPONGER, THE • 1953 • Lifanov B. • USS
SPONTANEOUS GENERATION see **GENERATION SPONTANEE** • 1909
SPONTANEOUS MOVEMENT OF PLANTS see **SAMOVOLNE POHYBY ROSTLIN** • 1959
SPONTANEOUS TRANSFORMATION • 1902 • Zecca Ferdinand • FRN
SPOOF! • 1915 • Kellino W. P. • UKN
SPOOF FOR OOF • 1915 • Collins Edwin J.? • UKN
SPOOFING • 1928 • Mack Anthony • SHT • USA
SPOOK AND SPAN • 1958 • Kneitel Seymour • ANS • USA
SPOOK BUSTERS • 1946 • Beaudine William • USA • GHOST BUSTERS
SPOOK-CASTLE IN SALZKAMMERGUT see **SPUKSCHLOSS IM SALZKAMMERGUT** • 1965
SPOOK-CASTLE IN SPESSART, THE see **SPUKSCHLOSS IM SPESSART, DAS** • 1959
SPOOK CHASERS • 1957 • Blair George • USA
SPOOK EASY • 1930 • *Mintz Charles (P)* • ANS • USA
SPOOK HOUSE see **CASA DE LOS ESPANTOS, LA** • 1961
SPOOK LOUDER • 1943 • Lord Del • SHT • USA
SPOOK NO EVIL • 1953 • Kneitel Seymour • ANS • USA
SPOOK RACERS, THE • 1915 • *Hamilton Lloyd V.* • ANS • USA
SPOOK RANCH • 1925 • Laemmle Edward • USA
SPOOK SPEAKS, THE • 1940 • *Keaton Buster* • SHT • USA
SPOOK SPEAKS, THE • 1947 • Yates Hal • SHT • USA
SPOOK SPOOFING • 1927 • McGowan Robert • SHT • USA
SPOOK SPORT • 1941 • Bute Mary Ellen • ANS • USA
SPOOK TO ME • 1945 • White Jules • SHT • USA
SPOOK TOWN • 1944 • Clifton Elmer • USA
SPOOK VAN DONKERGAT, DIE • 1972 • Ginsburg Dianne • SAF • GHOST OF DONKERGAT, THE
SPOOK WARFARE see **YOKAI DAISENSO** • 1968
SPOOK WHO SAT BY THE DOOR, THE • 1973 • Dixon Ivan • USA • CERTAIN HEAT ○ KEEPERS
SPOOKEASY • 1930 • *Columbia* • ANS • USA
SPOOKIES • 1986 • Faulkner Brendan, Doran Thomas, Joseph Eugenie • USA • TWISTED SOULS
SPOOKING ABOUT AFRICA • 1957 • Kneitel Seymour • ANS • USA
SPOOKING OF GHOSTS • 1959 • Kneitel Seymour • ANS • USA
SPOOKING WITH A BROGUE • 1955 • Kneitel Seymour • ANS • USA
SPOOKS • 1912 • *Pathe* • USA
SPOOKS • 1915 • Neilan Marshall • USA • CHRONICLES OF BLOOM CENTER, THE
SPOOKS • 1918 • Phillips R. W. • SHT • USA
SPOOKS • 1922 • White Jack, Kerr Robert • SHT • USA
SPOOKS • 1927 • Wilcox Robert B. • SHT • USA
SPOOKS • 1930 • Lantz Walter • ANS • USA
SPOOKS • 1932 • Iwerks Ub • ANS • USA
SPOOKS • 1936 • Watson William • USA
SPOOKS • 1953 • White Jules • SHT • USA
SPOOKS AND SPASMS • 1917 • Semon Larry • SHT • USA
SPOOKS AT SCHOOL • 1903 • *Biograph* • USA
SPOOKS RUN WILD • 1941 • Rosen Phil • USA
SPOOKTREIN, DE • 1939 • Lamac Carl • NTH • GHOST TRAIN, THE
SPOOKY BUNCH, THE see **CHUANG TAO CHENG** • 1981
SPOOKY HOOKY • 1936 • Douglas Gordon • SHT • USA
SPOOKY MOVIE SHOW, THE see **MASK, THE** • 1961
SPOOKY ROMANCE, A • 1915 • Herman Al • SHT • USA
SPOOKY SWABS • 1957 • Sparber I. • ANS • USA
SPOOKY WOOKY • 1950 • Yates Hal • SHT • USA
SPOOKY-YAKI • 1963 • Kuwahara Bob • ANS • USA
SPOON, THE • 1933 • Marshall George • USA
SPOONERS, THE • 1915 • *Banner* • USA
SPOONEY SAM • 1910 • *Lubin* • USA
SPOONEY SAM • 1912 • *Lubin* • USA
SPOONING • 1906 • Martin J. H.? • UKN
SPOORLOOS • 1988 • Sluizer George • NTH • VANISHING, THE
SPOORWEGBOUW IN LIMBURG • 1929 • Ivens Joris • SHT • NTH • ZUID LIMBURG ○ SOUTH LIMBURG
SPORCA FACCENDA, UNA • 1965 • Mauri Roberto • ITL
SPORCA GUERRA, UNA • 1965 • Tavella Dino • ITL • ABBUFFATORE, L'
SPORCKSCHEN JAGER, DIE • 1926 • Holger-Madsen • FRG
SPORCK'SCHEN JAGER, DIE • 1934 • Randolf Rolf • FRG
SPORE IN DIE MODDER • 1961 • SAF
SPORT DE LA VOILE • 1946 • Sevestre, Motard • SHT • FRN
SPORT DU TONNERRE, UN see **ROARING GAME, THE** • 1952
SPORT ET LES HOMMES, LE • 1961 • Aquin Hubert • DOC • CND
SPORT ETUDE see **ETIUDA SPORTOWA** • 1965
SPORT OF A NATION (UKN) see **ALL-AMERICAN, THE** • 1932
SPORT OF CIRCUMSTANCES • 1915 • Louis Will • USA
SPORT OF FATE, THE • 1913 • Collins Edwin J.? • UKN
SPORT OF KINGS • 1947 • Gordon Robert • USA • HEART ROYAL (UKN)
SPORT OF KINGS, THE • 1919 • *Moore Matt* • USA
SPORT OF KINGS, THE • 1921 • Rooke Arthur • UKN
SPORT OF KINGS, THE • 1931 • Saville Victor, Hunter T. Hayes • UKN
SPORT OF THE GODS, THE • 1921 • Vernot Henry J. • USA
SPORT PAGE see **SPORT PARADE, THE** • 1932
SPORT PARADE, THE • 1932 • Murphy Dudley • USA • SPORT PAGE
SPORT PASSIONNANT: LA CHASSE AUX IMAGES, UN • 1942-43 • Tessier Albert • DCS • CND
SPORT SPOOLS • 1941 • *Bute Mary Ellen* • SHT • USA
SPORT, SPORT, SPORT • 1971 • Klimov Elem • USS
SPORT STICKLERS • 1946 • *Smith Pete* • SHT • USA
SPORT SUPERSTAR • 1978 • Sala Vittorio • DOC • ITL
SPORTICLES • 1958 • Kneitel Seymour • ANS • USA
SPORTING • 1982 • Bozzetto Bruno • ANM • ITL
SPORTING AGE, THE • 1928 • Kenton Erle C. • USA • STRONGER LOVE, THE (UKN)
SPORTING BLOOD • 1909 • *Lubin* • USA
SPORTING BLOOD • 1916 • Bracken Bertram • USA
SPORTING BLOOD • 1931 • Brabin Charles J. • USA • HORSEFLESH
SPORTING BLOOD • 1940 • Simon S. Sylvan • USA • ONE CAME HOME
SPORTING BLOOD, THE see **DANGEROUS COWARD** • 1924
SPORTING CHANCE • 1931 • Herman Al • USA
SPORTING CHANCE see **PERSUADERS: SPORTING CHANCE, THE** • 1972
SPORTING CHANCE, A • 1913 • Collins Edwin J. • UKN
SPORTING CHANCE, A • 1919 • King Henry • *American* • USA • SIGNET OF SHEBA, THE
SPORTING CHANCE, A • 1919 • Melford George • *Paramount* • USA
SPORTING CHANCE, A • 1945 • Blair George • USA
SPORTING CHANCE, THE • 1925 • Apfel Oscar • USA
SPORTING CLUB, THE • 1971 • Peerce Larry • USA
SPORTING DAYS IN THE SOUTH OR THE MAKING OF A CHAMPION • 1909 • *Kalem* • USA
SPORTING DOUBLE, A • 1922 • Rooke Arthur • UKN
SPORTING DUCHESS, THE • 1915 • O'Neil Barry • USA
SPORTING DUCHESS, THE • 1920 • Terwilliger George W. • USA
SPORTING EDITOR, THE • 1912 • *Johnson Arthur* • USA
SPORTING FAME see **NASHI CHEMPIONY** • 1950
SPORTING GOODS • 1928 • St. Clair Malcolm • USA
SPORTING HONOUR • 1951 • Petrov Vladimir • USS
SPORTING HOUSE see **THIS SPORTING HOUSE** • 1969
SPORTING INSTINCT, THE • 1922 • Rooke Arthur • UKN
SPORTING JUSTICE (UKN) see **ROMANCE OF THE WEST** • 1930
SPORTING LIFE • 1918 • Tourneur Maurice • USA
SPORTING LIFE • 1925 • Tourneur Maurice • USA
SPORTING LIFE see **SPORTSKI ZIVOT** • 1977
SPORTING LIFE (UKN) see **NIGHT PARADE** • 1929
SPORTING LOVE • 1936 • Wills J. Elder • UKN
SPORTING LOVER, THE • 1926 • Hale Alan • USA • GOOD LUCK
SPORTING MICE, THE • 1909 • Armstrong Charles • UKN
SPORTING NUTS • 1935 • *Mgm* • SHT • USA
SPORTING OFFER, A • 1911 • Noy Wilfred • UKN
SPORTING TWELVE, THE • 1922 • *Parkinson H. B. (P)* • SER • UKN
SPORTING VENUS, THE • 1925 • Neilan Marshall • USA • HIS SUPREME MOMENT
SPORTING WEST • 1925 • *Williams Big Boy* • USA
SPORTING WIDOW, THE (UKN) see **MADAME RACKETEER** • 1932
SPORTING YOUTH • 1924 • Pollard Harry • USA • THERE HE GOES ○ SPICE OF LIFE, THE
SPORTING YOUTH • 1930 • Taylor Ray, Holmes Ben • USA
SPORTIVE NAVVIES, THE • 1903 • Collins Alf? • UKN
SPORTIVE POET, A see **SOYONS DONC SPORTIFS** • 1909
SPORTIVNAYA SLAVA see **NASHI CHEMPIONY** • 1950
SPORTORAMA • 1963 • *Paramount* • ANT • USA
SPORTS • 1973 • *Halas John (P)* • ANS • UKN
SPORTS AND NATIONS' DANCE, GRAND FINALE AND CURTAIN • 1899 • *Warwick Trading Co* • UKN
SPORTS AND SPLASHES • 1917 • Semon Larry • SHT • USA
SPORTS BILLY see **ADVENTURES OF SPORTS BILLY, THE** • 1982
SPORTS CHAMPIONS • 1941 • Freleng Friz • ANS • USA
SPORTS COACHING see **MODERN SPORTS COACHING** • 1970
SPORTS COMPETITION IN THE FOREST see **ERDEI SPORTVERSENY** • 1951
SPORTS DAM • 1966 • Robertson George C. • CND
SPORTS DAY • 1945 • *Simmons Jean* • SHT • UKN • COLONEL'S CUP, THE
SPORTS ET TRANSPORTS see **ROMANCE OF TRANSPORTATION IN CANADA, THE** • 1952
SPORTS IN MOGGYLAND • 1912 • *Diamond Films* • UKN
SPORTS IN TOYLAND • 1914 • Kinder Stuart? • UKN
SPORTS MEETING see **COUNTRY SPORTS** • 1897
SPORTS ODDITIES • 1949 • *Smith Pete* • SHT • USA
SPORTS ON ICE • 1936 • *Smith Pete* • SHT • USA
SPORTS QUIZ • 1944 • *Smith Pete* • SHT • USA
SPORTS TRIX • 1955 • *Smith Pete* • SHT • USA
SPORTSKI ZIVOT • 1977 • Grgic Zlatko • ANS • YGS • SPORTING LIFE
SPORTSMADEL, DAS • 1915 • Matray Ernst • FRG
SPORTSMAN, THE • 1920 • Semon Larry, Taurog Norman • SHT • USA
SPORTSMAN, THE • 1963 • Bakhtadze Vaktang • ANS • USS
SPORTSMAN, THE • 1976 • SAF
SPORTSMAN'S MEMORIES • 1944 • *Smith Pete* • SHT • USA
SPORTSMAN'S WIFE, A • 1921 • West Walter • UKN
SPORTSMAN'S WORLD • 1969 • Bryant Bill • DOC • USA
SPORTSMEN AND ZIGGY ELMAN'S ORCHESTRA • 1951 • Cowan Will • SHT • USA
SPORTSZERELEM • 1938 • Kardos Leslie • HNG • LOVE OF SPORT (USA)
SPOSA, LA • 1958 • Lozzi Edmondo • ITL
SPOSA BELLA, LA (ITL) see **ANGEL WORE RED, THE** • 1960
SPOSA DEI RE, LA • 1939 • Coletti Duilio • ITL
SPOSA DELLE MORTE, LA • 1916 • Ghione Emilio • ITL
SPOSA ERA BELLISSIMA, LA (ITL) see **MENYASSZONY GYONYORU, A** • 1987
SPOSA IN NERO, LA (ITL) see **MARIEE ETAIT EN NOIR, LA** • 1968
SPOSA NON PUO ATTENDERE, LA • 1950 • Franciolini Gianni • ITL • ALSELMO HA FRETTA ○ BRIDE COULDN'T WAIT, THE
SPOSA NON VESTITA DI BIANCO, LA see **AMANTI SENZA PECCATO** • 1957
SPOSA PER MAO, UNA • 1972 • Principe Albino • ITL
SPOSATA IERI (ITL) see **JEUNES MARIES** • 1953
SPOSERO' SIMON LE BON • 1985 • Cotti Carlo • ITL • I'LL MARRY SIMON LE BON
SPOSI • 1988 • Avati Pupi • ITL • MARRIAGES
SPOSI DELL'ANNO SECONDO, GLI (ITL) see **MARIES DE L'AN II, LES** • 1970
SPOSINA, LA • 1976 • Bergonzelli Sergio • ITL • YOUNG BRIDE, THE ○ UP AND COMING ○ BRIDE, THE
SPOSOB BYCIA • 1965 • Rybkowski Jan • PLN • FRAME OF MIND, A
SPOT see **DOGPOUND SHUFFLE** • 1975
SPOT AS CUPID • 1912 • Kinder Stuart • UKN
SPOT CASH • 1921 • Roach Hal • SHT • USA
SPOT FILMING OF WINDSOR HOTEL FIRE IN NEW YORK • 1899 • Blackton J. Stuart • USA
SPOT IN THE RUG, THE • 1932 • *Sennett Mack (P)* • SHT • USA
SPOT IN THE SHADE, A • 1949 • Lewis Jerry • SHT • USA
SPOT LIGHT • 1925 • Taurog Norman • SHT • USA
SPOT MARKS THE X • 1986 • Rosman Mark • TVM • USA
SPOT OF BOTHER, A • 1938 • MacDonald David • UKN
SPOT OF BOTHER, A • 1952 • *Hall Cameron* • SHT • UKN
SPOT, THE DOG THIEF • 1907 • *Warwick Trading Co* • UKN
SPOT THE MICRODOT • 1970 • Le Grice Malcolm • UKN
SPOTKALI SIE W HAWANIE • 1962 • Hoffman Jerzy, Skorzewski Edward • DCS • PLN • THEY MET IN HAVANA
SPOTKANIA W MROKU • 1960 • Jakubowska Wanda • PLN • ENCOUNTERS IN THE SHADOWS ○ ENCOUNTERS IN THE DARK ○ MEETING AT DUSK ○ BEGEGNUNG IM ZWIELICHT
SPOTKANIA W WARSZAWIE • 1965 • Lomnicki Jan • DOC • PLN • MEETINGS WITH WARSAW ○ MEETINGS IN WARSAW
SPOTKANIE NA ATLANTYKU • 1980 • Kawalerowicz Jerzy • PLN • MEETING ON THE ATLANTIC
SPOTKANIE W "BAJCE" • 1962 • Rybkowski Jan • PLN • CAFE FROM THE PAST
SPOTKANIE W WARSZAWIE • 1955 • Bossak Jerzy (c/d) • DOC • PLN • MEETING IN WARSAW, A
SPOTKANIE W ZOO • 1962 • Laskowski Jan • ANS • PLN • MEETING AT THE ZOO, A
SPOTKANIE Z PRZYRODA • 1971 • Farat Maria Alma • DOC • PLN • ENCOUNTERS WITH NATURE
SPOTKANIE ZE SZPIEGEM • 1964 • Batory Jan • PLN • FAREWELL TO A SPY
SPOTLIGHT • 1938 • Hopwood R. A. • UKN
SPOTLIGHT • 1971 • Tsukioka Sadao • ANS • JPN
SPOTLIGHT, THE • 1927 • Tuttle Frank • USA
SPOTLIGHT NO.1 • 1950 • Sparling Gordon • DCS • CND
SPOTLIGHT NO.2 • 1951 • Sparling Gordon • DCS • CND
SPOTLIGHT NO.3 • 1952 • Sparling Gordon • DCS • CND
SPOTLIGHT NO.4 • 1952 • Sparling Gordon • DCS • CND
SPOTLIGHT NO.5 • 1953 • Sparling Gordon • DCS • CND
SPOTLIGHT NO.6 • 1953 • Sparling Gordon • DCS • CND
SPOTLIGHT ON A MURDERER see **PLEINS FEUX SUR L'ASSASSIN** • 1961
SPOTLIGHT ON GLAMOUR • 1946 • Grey Richard M. • DOC • UKN
SPOTLIGHT ON MURDER see **PLEINS FEUX SUR L'ASSASSIN** • 1961
SPOTLIGHT SADIE • 1919 • Trimble Larry • USA
SPOTLIGHT SCANDALS • 1943 • Beaudine William • USA
SPOTLIGHT SERENADE • 1948 • Parker Benjamin R. • SHT • USA
SPOTS • 1925 • Hiscott Leslie • UKN
SPOTS BEFORE YOUR EYES • 1940 • Hines Johnny • SHT • USA
SPOTTED • 1914 • *Crystal* • USA
SPOTTED • 1918 • *Rhodes Billie* • USA
SPOTTED LILY, THE • 1917 • Salter Harry • USA
SPOTTED NAG, THE • 1919 • Davis James • SHT • USA
SPOTTING • 1934 • Samuelson G. B. • SER • UKN
SPOTTING A COW • 1983 • Driessen Paul • ANM • NTH
SPOZNIENI PRZECHODNIE • 1962 • Holoubek Gustaw, Lapicki Andrzej, Rybkowski Jan, Antczak Jerzy, Wojciech J. • PLN • PASSENGERS WHO ARE LATE ○ THOSE WHO ARE LATE
SPRAGGUE • 1984 • Elikann Larry • TVM • USA
SPRAINED ANKLE, A • 1911 • Fitzhamon Lewin • UKN
SPRAVCA SKANZENU • 1988 • Uher Stefan • CZC • DOWN TO EARTH
SPRAWA DO ZALATWIENIA • 1953 • Rybkowski Jan (c/d) • PLN • UNFINISHED BUSINESS ○ MATTER TO SETTLE, A
SPRAWA GORGONIOWEJ • 1977 • Majewski Janusz • PLN • GORGONIOVA CASE ○ GORGON CASE, THE
SPRAWA NAJWAZNIEJSWA • 1946 • Perski Ludwik • DOC • PLN • MOST IMPORTANT THING, THE
SPRAWA PILOTA MARESZA • 1956 • Buczkowski Leonard • PLN • CASE OF PILOT MARESZ, THE (USA)
SPRAY • 1967 • Huot Robert • SHT • USA
SPREAD EAGLE see **EAGLE AND THE HAWK, THE** • 1950
SPREAD EAGLES • 1968 • *Kirt Films International* • USA
SPREAD IT AROUND • 1970 • *Stacey Dist.* • USA
SPREAD YOUR WINGS: TANYA'S PUPPETS • 1981 • Owen Don • CND
SPREADIN' THE JAM • 1945 • Walters Charles • SHT • USA
SPREADING CLOUD see **WAKARE-GUMO** • 1951
SPREADING DAWN, THE • 1916 • Trimble Larry • USA
SPREADING EVIL, THE • 1919 • Keane James • USA
SPREE • 1897 • *Paul R. W.* • UKN
SPREE • 1967 • Leisen Mitchell, Green Walon • DOC • USA • LAS VEGAS BY NIGHT ○ HERE'S LAS VEGAS
SPREE • 1976 • Spiegel Larry • MXC
SPREE FOR ALL • 1946 • Kneitel Seymour • ANS • USA

SPREE LUNCH • 1957 • Kneitel Seymour • ANS • USA
SPREEWALDMADEL, DAS • 1928 • Steinhoff Hans • FRG
SPRENGBAGGER 1010 • 1929 • Achaz-Duisberg Carl Ludwig • FRG
SPRICH ZU MIR WIE DER REGEN • 1975 • Sirk Douglas • FRG
SPRIG OF SHAMROCK, A • 1913 • *Ross Budd* • USA
SPRIG OF SHAMROCK, A • 1915 • Beaumont Harry • USA
SPRING • 1920 • *De Haven Carter* • USA • TEASING THE SOIL (?)
SPRING • 1953 • Stiopul Savel • RMN
SPRING • 1966 • Donev Donyo • ANS • BUL
SPRING • 1969 • Kruusement Arvo • USS
SPRING see **VESNOY** • 1929
SPRING see **VAREN** • 1951
SPRING see **CH'UN** • 1953
SPRING see **PRINTEMPS, LE** • 1971
SPRING, THE see **IZUMI** • 1956
SPRING, THE see **ZRODLO** • 1963
SPRING, THE see **TCHESHMEH** • 1972
SPRING ADVENTURES OF A GNOME, THE see **WIOSENNE PRZYGODY KRASNALA** • 1959
SPRING AFFAIR • 1960 • Ray Bernard B. • USA
SPRING AND A GIRL see **HARU TO MISUME** • 1932
SPRING AND PORT WINE • 1970 • Hammond Peter • UKN
SPRING AND SAGANAKI • 1958 • Keller Lew • ANS • USA
SPRING AND WINTER • 1951 • Halas John • ANS • UKN
SPRING ANTICS • 1932 • Foster John, Davis Mannie • ANS • USA
SPRING AT SJOSALA see **SJOSALAVAR** • 1949
SPRING AT SKANSEN see **SKANSENVAR** • 1946
SPRING AWAKENING see **HARU NO MEZAME** • 1947
SPRING AWAKENS see **HARU NO MEZAME** • 1947
SPRING BANQUET, A see **HARU KORO NO HANA NO EN** • 1958
SPRING BELL see **HARU NO KANE** • 1985
SPRING BOUQUET, A see **HARU KORO NO HANA NO EN** • 1958
SPRING BREAK • 1983 • Cunningham Sean S. • USA
SPRING BREEZE • 1961 • Helge Ladislav • CZC
SPRING BREEZE see **HARU ICHIBAN** • 1966
SPRING BREEZE see **SOSHUN** • 1968
SPRING CAPRICE see **HARU NO TAWAMURE** • 1949
SPRING CHICKEN, A • 1916 • Henderson Dell • SHT • USA
SPRING CLEANING • 1903 • Williamson James • UKN
SPRING CLEANING • 1907 • *Walturdaw* • UKN
SPRING CLEANING • 1916 • *Myers Harry* • USA
SPRING CLEANING • 1922 • Dudley Bernard • UKN
SPRING CLEANING see **WOMEN WHO PLAY** • 1932
SPRING CLEANING IN THE HOUSE OF SCROGGINS • 1911 • Aylott Dave • UKN
SPRING COMES FROM THE LADIES see **HARU WA GOFUJIN KARA** • 1932
SPRING COMES TO ENGLAND • 1934 • Taylor Donald • DOC • UKN
SPRING COMES TO NIAGARA • 1948 • Sparling Gordon • DCS • CND
SPRING COMES WITH THE LADIES see **HARU WA GOFUJIN KARA** • 1932
SPRING DREAM see **HARU NO KOTEKI** • 1953
SPRING DREAMS see **HARU NO YUME** • 1960
SPRING FAIRY, THE (USA) see **FEE PRINTEMPS, LA** • 1902
SPRING FAIRY, THE (USA) see **FEE PRINTEMPS, LA** • 1906
SPRING FESTIVAL • 1937 • *Mintz Charles (P)* • ANS • USA
SPRING FEVER • 1916 • *Armstrong Billy* • SHT • USA
SPRING FEVER • 1919 • Newmeyer Fred, Roach Hal • SHT • USA
SPRING FEVER • 1923 • Mayo Archie • SHT • USA
SPRING FEVER • 1927 • Sedgwick Edward • USA
SPRING FEVER • 1951 • Davis Mannie • ANS • USA
SPRING FEVER see **RECREATION** • 1914
SPRING FEVER USA • 1988 • Milling William • USA
SPRING FEVER (USA) see **SNEAKERS** • 1982
SPRING FLIRTATION see **HARU NO TAWAMURE** • 1949
SPRING FLOODS see **JARNI VODY** • 1968
SPRING FOR THE THIRSTY, THE • 1965 • Ilyenko Yury • USS • SPRING FOR THIRSTY PEOPLE, A
SPRING FOR THIRSTY PEOPLE, A see **SPRING FOR THE THIRSTY, THE** • 1965
SPRING HANDICAP • 1937 • Hanbury Victor • UKN
SPRING HANDICAP, THE • 1937 • Brenon Herbert • UKN
SPRING IDYLL, A • 1917 • Blackton J. Stuart • SHT • USA
SPRING IN ARMS see **VAR I VAPEN, EN** • 1943
SPRING IN BUDAPEST see **BUDAPEST TAVASZ** • 1955
SPRING IN DALBY PASTURES see **VAR I DALBY HAGE** • 1962
SPRING IN HOLLAND, A see **OCHTEND VAN ZES WEKEN, EEN** • 1966
SPRING IN MOSCOW see **VESNA V MOSKVE** • 1953
SPRING IN PARK LANE • 1948 • Wilcox Herbert • UKN
SPRING IN SOUTHERN ISLANDS see **NANTO NO HARU** • 1925
SPRING IN THE AIR • 1934 • Hanbury Victor, Lee Norman • UKN
SPRING IN THE DESERT, THE • 1913 • *Darkfeather Mona* • USA
SPRING IN THE PARK • 1934 • Lantz Walter, Nolan William • ANS • USA
SPRING IN THE WOODS, THE • 1974 • Laius Leida • USS
SPRING IN WINTERTIME see **TAVASZ A TELBEN** • 1917
SPRING IN ZARECHNAYA STREET see **VESNA NA ZARECHNOI ULITSE** • 1956
SPRING INTO SUMMER see **PLEURE PAS LA BOUCHE PLEINE** • 1974
SPRING IS HERE • 1930 • Dillon John Francis • USA
SPRING IS HERE • 1932 • *Terry Paul/ Moser Frank (P)* • ANS • USA
SPRING LOCK, THE see **SMAEKLAASEN** • 1908
SPRING MADNESS • 1938 • Simon S. Sylvan • USA
SPRING MAGIC see **MARRIAGE MAKER, THE** • 1923
SPRING MEETING • 1941 • Mycroft Walter C. • UKN
SPRING MELODY, A see **PIOSENKA-WIOSENKA** • 1964
SPRING NIGHT • 1935 • *Lichine David* • SHT • USA
SPRING NIGHT, SUMMER NIGHT see **MISS JESSICA IS PREGNANT** • 1970
SPRING OF A NINETEEN YEAR OLD see **JUKU-SAI NO HARU** • 1933
SPRING OF ECSTASY see **KOKOTSU NO IZUMI** • 1967
SPRING OF LIFE see **LIVETS VAR** • 1957
SPRING OF LIFE, THE • 1913 • *Lewis Grace* • USA
SPRING OF LIFE, THE see **IZVOR ZIVOTA** • 1969
SPRING OF SOUTHERN ISLAND see **NANTO NO HARU** • 1925
SPRING OF THE VIRGIN see **DEVICHYA VESNA** • 1960
SPRING OFFENSIVE • 1939 • Jennings Humphrey • DCS • UKN • UNRECORDED VICTORY, AN
SPRING OLYMPICS, OR THE CHOIR CHIEF, THE see **VESENNYAYA OLYMPIADA ILI NACHALNIK KHORA** • 1980
SPRING ON LEPER'S ISLAND see **KOJIMA NO HARU** • 1940
SPRING ON THE FARM • 1934 • Cherry Evelyn Spice • DOC • UKN
SPRING ON THE FARM • 1942 • Keene Ralph • UKN
SPRING ON THE ODER see **VESNA NA ODERYE** • 1968
SPRING ON ZARECHNAYA STREET see **VESNA NA ZARECHNOI ULITSE** • 1956
SPRING ONIONS • 1915 • *Derr George* • USA
SPRING PARADE • 1940 • Koster Henry • USA
SPRING RAIN UMBRELLA see **KYOKAKU HARUSAME-GASA** • 1960
SPRING REUNION • 1957 • Pirosh Robert • USA
SPRING RIVER FLOWS EAST see **YIJIANG CHUNSHUI XIANG DONG LIU** • 1947
SPRING ROUND-UP, THE • 1911 • Melies Gaston • USA
SPRING SHOWER (USA) see **TAVASZI ZAPOR** • 1932
SPRING SNOW see **SHUNSETSU** • 1950
SPRING SONG • 1946 • Tully Montgomery • UKN • SPRINGTIME (USA)
SPRING SONG • 1949 • Sparber I. • ANS • USA
SPRING SONG • 1960 • Halas John • ANS • UKN
SPRING SONG, THE see **PIOSENKA-WIOSENKA** • 1964
SPRING SONGS see **PROLJETNI ZVUCI** • 1960
SPRING SUN, THE see **SHAMS AL-RABIH** • 1968
SPRING SWALLOW (UKN) see **WAN-CH'UN CH'ING-SHIH** • 1989
SPRING SYMPHONY see **FRUHLINGS-SINFONIE** • 1983
SPRING THREE THOUSAND ONE HUNDRED see **JEALOUSY** • 1934
SPRING TIDE see **HARU NO USHIO** • 1950
SPRING TONIC • 1935 • Bruckman Clyde • USA • MAN EATING TIGER
SPRING TUNES see **PROLJETNI ZVUCI** • 1960
SPRING (USA) see **VESNA** • 1947
SPRING VOICES (USA) see **VESENNIE GOLOSA** • 1955
SPRING WATERS see **JARNI VODY** • 1968
SPRING WILL COME SOON, THE • 1962 • Abesadze Otar • USS
SPRING WIND see **FUKEYO HARUKAZE** • 1930
SPRING WIND see **POMLADNI VETER** • 1976
SPRINGBOK • 1976 • Meyer Tommy • SAF
SPRINGEN • 1986 • de Decker Jean-Pierre • BLG • LEAPING
SPRINGENDE HIRSCH ODER DIE DIEBE VON GUNSTERBURG, DER • 1915 • *Witt Vera* • FRG
SPRINGENDE PFERD, DAS see **WENN DIE MASKE FALLT** • 1922
SPRINGER AND THE SS MEN see **PERAK A SS** • 1946
SPRINGER VON PONTRESINA, DER • 1934 • Selpin Herbert • FRG
SPRINGFIELD RIFLE • 1952 • De Toth Andre • USA
SPRINGFLUT DES HASSES, DIE see **SONNE ASIENS, DIE** • 1920
SPRINGHILL • 1971 • Kelly Ron • CND
SPRINGING A SURPRISE • 1912 • *Missimer Howard* • USA
SPRINGPOJKAR AR VI ALLIHOPA • 1941 • Johansson Ivar • SWD • WE ARE ALL ERRAND BOYS
SPRINGS • 1938 • Tharp Grahame • UKN
SPRINGT DIE KETTEN • 1930 • Blum Victor • DOC • FRG • BREAK THE CHAINS
SPRINGTIME • 1915 • Roskam Edwin • USA
SPRINGTIME • 1920 • Robbins Jess • SHT • USA
SPRINGTIME • 1928 • Iwerks Ub • ANS • USA
SPRINGTIME see **VESNOY** • 1929
SPRINGTIME see **VESNA** • 1947
SPRINGTIME see **E PRIMAVERA** • 1949
SPRINGTIME see **DANSHUN** • 1966
SPRINGTIME A LA CARTE • 1918 • Webb Kenneth • SHT • USA
SPRINGTIME FOR CLOBBER • 1958 • Rasinski Connie • ANS • USA
SPRINGTIME FOR HENRY • 1934 • Tuttle Frank • USA
SPRINGTIME FOR PLUTO • 1944 • Nichols Charles • ANS • USA
SPRINGTIME FOR SAMANTHA • 1965 • Linnecar Vera • ANS • UKN
SPRINGTIME FOR THOMAS • 1946 • Hanna William, Barbera Joseph • ANS • USA
SPRINGTIME IN HOLLAND • 1935 • Staub Ralph • USA • TULIP TIME
SPRINGTIME IN ITALY see **E PRIMAVERA** • 1949
SPRINGTIME IN TEXAS • 1945 • Drake Oliver • USA
SPRINGTIME IN THE ROCK AGE • 1940 • Fleischer Dave • ANS • USA
SPRINGTIME IN THE ROCKIES • 1937 • Kane Joseph • USA
SPRINGTIME IN THE ROCKIES • 1942 • Cummings Irving • USA
SPRINGTIME IN THE SIERRAS • 1947 • Witney William • USA
SPRINGTIME IN VIENNA • 1966 • *Hoffberg Productions* • FRG
SPRINGTIME OF LIFE, THE • 1913 • *Ramo* • USA
SPRINGTIME OF LOVE, THE • 1916 • *Lily* • USA
SPRINGTIME OF THE SPIRIT, THE • 1915 • Wilson Ben • USA
SPRINGTIME ON THE VOLGA (USA) see **DEVICHYA VESNA** • 1960
SPRINGTIME RACE see **CORSA DI PRIMAVERA** • 1990
SPRINGTIME SERENADE • 1935 • *Lantz Walter (P)* • ANS • USA
SPRINGTIME TUNE see **MELODI OM VAREN, EN** • 1933
SPRINGTIME (USA) see **SPRING SONG** • 1946
SPRINGWOOD • 1979 • Fraser Chris • DOC • ASL
S'PRISE PARTY 'N' EVER'THING, A • 1919 • Harvey John Joseph • SHT • USA
SPRONG NAAR DE LIEFDE • 1983 • van der Lecq Bas • NTH
SPRUCIN' UP • 1935 • Meins Gus • SHT • USA
SPRUNG IN DEN ABGRUND • 1933 • Piel Harry • FRG • SPUREN IM SCHNEE
SPRUNG IN DIE HOLLE see **MARSCHIER UND KREPIER** • 1962
SPRUNG INS DUNKLE, DER • 1920 • Reicher Ernst • FRG
SPRUNG INS GLUCK, DER • 1927 • Genina Augusto • FRG • SHE'S A GOOD GIRL
SPRUNG INS LEBENS, DER • 1924 • Guter Johannes • FRG • ROMAN EINES ZIRKUSKINDES, DER
SPRUNG INS NICHTS, DER • 1931 • Mittler Leo • FRG
SPRUNG UBER DEN SCHATTEN, DER see **MANN OHNE NAMEN 6, DER** • 1920-21
SPY SPINSTERS, THE • 1912 • *Solax* • USA
SPUD MURPHY'S REDEMPTION • 1913 • Calvert Charles? • UKN
SPUDS • 1927 • Semon Larry • USA
SPUIT ELF • 1965 • Cammermans Paul • NTH
SPUK AUF KATEROW • 1915 • *Rahame-Film* • FRG
SPUK DES LEBENS, DER • 1920 • Bock-Stieber Gernot • FRG
SPUK EINER NACHT, DER see **ZWISCHEN ABEND UND MORGEN** • 1923
SPUK IM OPERNHAUS • Stemmle R. A.? • FRG • GHOST OF THE OPERA
SPUK IM SCHLOSS • 1944 • Zerlett Hans H. • FRG • GHOST IN THE CASTLE
SPUK IN HAUSE DES PROFESSORS, DER • 1914 • May Joe • FRG
SPUKSCHLOSS IM SALZKAMMERGUT • 1965 • Billian Hans, Olsen Rolf • FRG • HAUNTING CASTLE IN SALZKAMMERGUT, THE ○ SPOOK-CASTLE IN SALZKAMMERGUT
SPUKSCHLOSS IM SPESSART, DAS • 1959 • Hoffmann Kurt • FRG • SPOOK-CASTLE IN SPESSART, THE ○ HAUNTED CASTLE, THE
SPUNKY SKUNKY • 1952 • Sparber I. • ANS • USA
SPUNKY THE SNOWMAN • *Fleet* • ANS • USA
SPUR AND SADDLE SERIES • 1919 • SER • USA
SPUR DES ERSTEN, DIE • 1915 • *Messter-Film* • FRG
SPUR DES FALKEN • 1968 • Kolditz Gottfried • GDR, USS • TRAIL OF THE FALCON
SPUR EINES MADCHENS • 1967 • Ehmck Gustav • FRG • TRACE OF A GIRL
SPUR FAHRT NACH BERLIN, DIE • 1952 • Cap Frantisek • FRG • ADVENTURE IN BERLIN
SPUR IM SCHNEE, DIE • 1918 • Dessauer Siegfried • FRG
SPUR IN DER NACHT • 1957 • Reisch Gunter • GDR • TRACKS IN THE NIGHTS
SPUR OF NECESSITY, THE • 1911 • Melies Gaston • USA
SPUR OF THE MOMENT • 1931 • Harwood A. R. • SHT • ASL
SPUREN IM SCHNEE • 1929 • Reiber Willy • FRG • GEFANGENE DER BERNINA, DER
SPUREN IM SCHNEE see **SPRUNG IN DEN ABGRUND** • 1933
SPURS • 1930 • Eason B. Reeves • USA
SPURS AND SADDLES • 1927 • Smith Cliff • USA
SPURS OF SYBIL, THE • 1918 • Vale Travers • USA
SPURS OF TANGO • 1981 • Plaat Henri • SHT • NTH
SPURT OF BLOOD, THE • 1965 • Thoms Albie • SHT • ASL
SPURTING BLOOD • 1988 • Wiederhorn Ken • USA
SPUTNIK see **A PIED, A CHEVAL ET EN SPOUTNIK** • 1958
SPUTNIK SPEAKING • 1959 • Gerasimov Sergei, Volk E., Oganesyan Georgi, Dorman Veniamin • USS • SPUTNIK SPEAKS, THE
SPUTNIK SPEAKS, THE see **SPUTNIK SPEAKING** • 1959
SPY 13 (UKN) see **OPERATOR 13** • 1934
SPY 77 see **ON SECRET SERVICE** • 1933
SPY, THE • 1909 • Fitzhamon Lewin? • UKN
SPY, THE • 1911 • *Selig* • USA
SPY, THE • 1914 • *Searchlight* • UKN
SPY, THE • 1914 • Turner Otis • USA
SPY, THE • 1917 • *Sparkle Comedies* • SHT • USA
SPY, THE • 1917 • Stanton Richard • *Standard* • USA
SPY, THE • 1931 • Viertel Berthold • USA
SPY, THE see **BRIDGE, THE** • 1932
SPY, THE see **SUPAI** • 1965
SPY, THE (UKN) see **SPIONE** • 1928
SPY BREAKER, THE see **CASUS KIRAN** • 1968
SPY BUSTERS see **GUNS IN THE HEATHER** • 1969
SPY CAME FROM THE SEMI-COLD, THE see **SPIE VENGONO DAL SEMIFREDDO, LE** • 1966
SPY CATCHERS, THE • 1914 • Kellino W. P. • UKN
SPY CHASERS • 1955 • Bernds Edward • USA
SPY FEVER • 1911 • Aylott Dave • UKN
SPY FOR A DAY • 1940 • Zampi Mario • UKN • LIVE AND LET LIVE
SPY HAS NOT YET DIED, THE see **KANCHO IMADA SHISEZU** • 1942
SPY HUNT • 1950 • Sherman George • USA • PANTHER'S MOON (UKN) ○ SPY RING
SPY I LOVE, THE (USA) see **COPLAN PREND DES RISQUES** • 1963
SPY IN BLACK, THE • 1939 • Powell Michael • UKN • U-BOAT 29 (USA)
SPY IN ROME • 1968 • Adarsh B. K. • IND
SPY IN THE GREEN HAT, THE • 1966 • Sargent Joseph • MTV • USA
SPY IN THE PANTRY see **TEN DAYS IN PARIS** • 1939
SPY IN THE SKY • 1958 • Wilder W. Lee • *Brodie Steve* • USA
SPY IN WHITE, THE see **SECRET OF STAMBOUL, THE** • 1936
SPY IN YOUR EYE (USA) see **BERLINO, APPUNTAMENTO PER LE SPIE** • 1965
SPY ISN'T DEAD YET, THE see **KANCHO IMADA SHISEZU** • 1942
SPY KILLED AT BEIRUT, THE see **SPIE UCCIDONO A BEIRUT, LE** • 1965
SPY KILLER • 1967 • Wenceslao Jose Pepe • PHL
SPY KILLER, THE • 1969 • Baker Roy Ward • TVM • UKN
SPY KILLERS, THE (UKN) see **SPIE UCCIDONO A BEIRUT, LE** • 1965
SPY LOVES FLOWERS, THE see **SPIE AMANO I FIORI, LE** • 1966
SPY MANIA, THE • 1912 • Aylott Dave? • UKN
SPY OF NAPOLEON • 1936 • Elvey Maurice • UKN
SPY ON THE MASKED CAR see **ANO SHISOSHA O NERAE** • 1967
SPY PIRATE, THE • 1914 • *Keystone* • USA

SPY PIT, THE see **DA BERLINO L'APOCALISSE** • 1967
SPY RING • 1938 • Lewis Joseph H. • USA • INTERNATIONAL SPY
SPY RING see **SPY HUNT** • 1950
SPY SHIP • 1942 • Eason B. Reeves • USA
SPY SMASHER • 1942 • Witney William • SRL • USA
SPY SMASHER • 1964 • Glut Don • SHT • USA
SPY SMASHER RETURNS • 1942 • Witney William • USA
SPY SQUAD see **CAPTURE THAT CAPSULE!** • 1961
SPY STORY • 1976 • Shonteff Lindsay • UKN
SPY STRIKES SILENTLY, THE see **ESPIAS MANTAN EL SILENCIO, LOS** • 1966
SPY SWATTER, THE • 1967 • Larriva Rudy • ANS • USA
SPY TRAIN • 1943 • Young Harold • USA
SPY TRAIN, THE • 1960 • *Halas John (P)* • ANS • UKN
SPY WHO CAME, THE • 1969 • Wertheim Ron • USA
SPY WHO CAME FROM THE SEA, THE see **SPIA CHE VIENE DAL MARE, LA** • 1966
SPY WHO CAME IN FROM THE COLD, THE • 1965 • Ritt Martin • UKN
SPY WHO LOVED ME, THE • 1977 • Gilbert Lewis* • UKN
SPY WHO WENT INTO HELL, THE see **CORRIDA POUR UN ESPION** • 1965
SPY WITH A COLD NOSE, THE • 1966 • Petrie Daniel • UKN
SPY WITH MY FACE, THE • 1965 • Newland John • MTV • USA • DOUBLE AFFAIR, THE
SPY WORE HIGH HEELS, THE see **SPIJUN NA STIKLAMA** • 1989
SPYASHCHAYA KRASAVITSA • 1930 • Vasiliev Sergei, Vasiliev Georgi • USS • WOMAN OF THE SLEEPING FOREST, THE ○ SLEEPING BEAUTY, THE ○ BELLE AU BOIS DORMANT, LA
SPYASHCHAYA KRASAVITSA • 1964 • Dudko Apollinari, Sergeyev Konstantin • USS • SLEEPING BEAUTY, THE (USA)
SPYDA MAN • 1976 • Avalon Phillip • SHT • ASL
SPYING THE SPY • 1918 • Phillips R. W. • SHT • USA
SPYLARKS (USA) see **INTELLIGENCE MEN, THE** • 1965
S*P*Y*S • 1974 • Kershner Irvin • USA • SPYS ○ WET STUFF
SPYS see **S*P*Y*S** • 1974
SPY'S DEFEAT, THE • 1913 • Webster Harry Mcrae • USA
SPY'S FATE, THE • 1914 • *Lubin* • USA
SPY'S MISTAKE PART ONE: ACCORDING TO AN OLD LEGEND PART TWO: BEKAS' RETURN, A see **OSHIBKA REZIDYENTA I: PO STAROY LEGYENDYE II: VOZVRASHCHYENIYE BEKASA** • 1968
SPY'S RUSE, THE • 1915 • *Courtot Marguerite* • USA
SPY'S SISTER, THE • 1915 • Sloman Edward • USA
SPY'S WIFE, THE • 1972 • O'Hara Gerry • SHT • UKN
SQUABBLE FOR A SQUAB, A • 1915 • *Heinie & Louie* • USA
SQUABS AND SQUABBLES • 1918 • Smith Noel • SHT • USA
SQUAD CAR • 1960 • Leftwich Ed • USA
SQUAD TEAM, THE • 1989 • Jonasson Oskar • SHT • ICL
SQUADRA ANTIFURTO • 1976 • Corbucci Bruno • ITL
SQUADRA ANTIGANGSTERS • 1979 • Corbucci Bruno • ITL
SQUADRA ANTIMAFIA • 1978 • Corbucci Bruno • ITL
SQUADRA ANTIRUFFA • 1977 • Corbucci Bruno • ITL
SQUADRA ANTISCIPPO • 1976 • Corbucci Bruno • ITL • COP IN BLUE JEANS, THE (USA)
SQUADRA VOLANTE • 1974 • Massi Stelvio • ITL
SQUADRIGLIA BIANCA • 1942 • Sava Joan • ITL, RMN • ESCADRADRILEI ALBE
SQUADRON 992 • 1940 • Watt Harry • DOC • UKN • FLYING ELEPHANTS
SQUADRON LEADER X • 1942 • Comfort Lance • UKN
SQUADRON NO.5 see **ESKADRILYA N5** • 1939
SQUADRON OF HONOR • 1938 • Coleman C. C. Jr. • USA
SQUADRONE BIANCO • 1936 • Genina Augusto • ITL • WHITE SQUADRON, THE
SQUALL, THE • 1929 • Korda Alexander • USA
SQUAMISH FIVE, THE • 1988 • Donovan Paul • CND
SQUANDERED LIVES (USA) see **DUKE'S SON** • 1920
SQUARCIA see **GRANDE STRADA AZZURRA, LA** • 1957
SQUARE, A see **TER** • 1971
SQUARE, DIE • 1975 • SAF
SQUARE, THE see **TORGET** • 1959
SQUARE AND THE TRIANGLE, THE • Miler Zdenek • ANS • CZC
SQUARE CROOKS • 1928 • Seiler Lewis • USA
SQUARE DANCE • 1944 • Jodoin Rene • ANS • CND • DANCE SQUARED ○ LET'S ALL SING TOGETHER
SQUARE DANCE • 1987 • Petrie Daniel • USA • HOME IS WHERE THE HEART IS
SQUARE DANCE JUBILEE • 1949 • Landres Paul • USA
SQUARE DANCE KATY • 1950 • Yarbrough Jean • USA
SQUARE DEAL, A • 1917 • Knoles Harley • USA
SQUARE DEAL, A • 1918 • Ingraham Lloyd • USA
SQUARE DEAL MAN, THE • 1917 • Hart William S. • USA
SQUARE DEAL SANDERSON • 1919 • Hart William S., Hillyer Lambert • USA
SQUARE DECEIVER, THE • 1917 • Balshofer Fred J. • USA • LOVE ME FOR MYSELF ALONE
SQUARE GAMBLER, THE • 1919 • *Capital* • SHT • USA
SQUARE INCH FIELD • 1968 • Rimmer David • CND
SQUARE JOE • 1921 • *Jeanette Joe* • USA
SQUARE JUNGLE, THE • 1955 • Hopper Jerry • USA
SQUARE MILE MURDER, THE • 1961 • Davis Allan • UKN
SQUARE OF VIOLENCE (USA) see **NASILJE NA TRGU** • 1961
SQUARE PEG, THE • 1958 • Carstairs John Paddy • UKN
SQUARE PEG, THE see **DENIAL, THE** • 1925
SQUARE PEG IN A ROUND HOLE, A see **BOCK I ORTAGARD** • 1958
SQUARE RING, THE • 1953 • Dearden Basil, Relph Michael • UKN
SQUARE ROOT OF ZERO, THE • 1964 • Cannon William • USA • THIS IMMORAL AGE (UKN)
SQUARE SHOOTER • 1935 • Selman David • USA
SQUARE SHOOTER, THE • 1918 • *Hart Neal* • SHT • USA
SQUARE SHOOTER, THE • 1920 • Cazeneuve Paul • USA
SQUARE SHOOTER, THE • 1927 • Wyler William • SHT • USA
SQUARE SHOOTER, THE see **SKIPALONG ROSENBLOOM** • 1951
SQUARE SHOOTING SQUARE • 1955 • Smith Paul J. • ANS • USA
SQUARE SHOULDERS • 1929 • Hopper E. Mason • USA
SQUARE TRIANGLE, THE • 1914 • Bracken Bertram • USA
SQUARED • 1919 • Drew Sidney, Drew Sidney Mrs. • SHT • USA
SQUARED ACCOUNT, A • 1916 • Wolbert William • SHT • USA
SQUARED ACCOUNTS • 1974 • Daniel Leon • BUL
SQUARED CIRCLE, THE (UKN) see **JOE PALOOKA IN THE SQUARED CIRCLE** • 1950
SQUAREHEAD, THE see **MABEL'S MARRIED LIFE** • 1914
SQUAREHEADS OF THE ROUND TABLE • 1948 • Bernds Edward • SHT • USA
SQUARES • 1972 • Murphy Patrick J. • USA • RIDING TALL
SQUARES see **QUADRATE** • 1934
SQUARES, THE • 1971 • Greenberg Bob • ANS • USA
SQUARING IT • 1917 • Marshall George • SHT • USA
SQUARING THE ACCOUNT • 1909 • Aylott Dave? • UKN
SQUARING THE CIRCLE • 1984 • Hodges Mike • UKN
SQUARING THE TRIANGLE • 1914 • *Lubin* • USA
SQUARING THINGS WITH WIFEY • 1913 • *Crystal* • USA
SQUARTATORE DI NEW YORK, LO • 1982 • Fulci Lucio • ITL • NEW YORK RIPPER, THE ○ PSYCHO RIPPER
SQUASHVILLE LADIES' FIRE BRIGADE, THE • 1913 • *Nestor* • USA
SQUASHVILLE ROMANCE, A • 1914 • *Colorado Photo-Play* • USA
SQUASHVILLE SCHOOL, THE • 1914 • Henderson Dell • USA
SQUATTER, THE • 1914 • *Payne Edna* • USA
SQUATTERS, THE • 1914 • Huntley Fred W. • USA
SQUATTER'S CHILD, THE • 1912 • Fahrney Milton • USA
SQUATTER'S DAUGHTER, THE • 1906 • Fitzhamon Lewin • UKN
SQUATTER'S DAUGHTER, THE • 1910 • *Great Western* • USA
SQUATTER'S DAUGHTER, THE • 1910 • Bailey Bert • ASL • LAND OF THE WATTLE
SQUATTER'S DAUGHTER, THE • 1933 • Hall Ken G. • ASL • DOWN UNDER
SQUATTER'S GAL, THE • 1914 • *Anderson Broncho Billy* • USA
SQUATTER'S RIGHTS • 1946 • Hannah Jack • ANS • USA
SQUATTER'S RIGHTS, A • 1912 • *Rex* • USA
SQUATTER'S SON, THE • 1911 • *Pathe Freres* • ASL
SQUATTER'S WIFE'S SECRET, THE • 1918 • ASL
SQUAW AND THE MAN, THE • 1911 • *American* • USA
SQUAW MAN, A • 1912 • *Champion* • USA
SQUAW MAN, THE • 1914 • De Mille Cecil B., Apfel Oscar • USA • WHITE MAN, THE (UKN)
SQUAW MAN, THE • 1918 • De Mille Cecil B. • USA • WHITE MAN, THE
SQUAW MAN, THE • 1931 • De Mille Cecil B. • USA • WHITE MAN, THE (UKN)
SQUAW MAN'S REVENGE, THE • 1912 • *Pathe* • USA
SQUAW MAN'S REWARD, THE • 1913 • *Frontier* • USA
SQUAW MAN'S SON, THE • 1917 • Le Saint Edward J. • USA
SQUAW PATH, THE • 1967 • Culhane Shamus • ANS • USA
SQUAWKIN' HAWK, THE • 1942 • Jones Charles M. • ANS • USA
SQUAWMAN'S AWAKENING, THE • 1913 • *Patheplay* • USA
SQUAWMAN'S SWEETHEART, THE • 1912 • *Pathe* • USA
SQUAW'S DEATH OF GRATITUDE, THE • 1912 • *Pathe* • USA
SQUAW'S DEVOTION, THE • 1911 • *Powers* • USA
SQUAW'S LOVE, THE • 1911 • Griffith D. W. • USA
SQUAW'S LOYALTY, A • 1916 • *Utah* • USA
SQUAW'S RETRIBUTION, A • 1911 • *Bison* • USA
SQUAW'S REVENGE, THE • 1909 • *Bison* • USA
SQUAW'S REVENGE, THE • 1914 • *Darkfeather Mona* • USA
SQUAW'S SACRIFICE, A • 1909 • *Bison* • USA
SQUEAK IN THE DEEP • 1966 • McKimson Robert • ANS • USA
SQUEAKER, THE • 1930 • Wallace Edgar • UKN
SQUEAKER, THE • 1937 • Howard William K. • UKN • MURDER IN DIAMOND ROW (USA)
SQUEAKER, THE (USA) see **ZINKER, DER** • 1965
SQUEAKER'S MATE • 1973 • Baker David • SHT • ASL
SQUEAKS AND SQUAWKS • 1920 • Smith Noel • SHT • USA
SQUEALER, THE • 1930 • Brown Harry J. • USA
SQUEALS ON WHEELS • 1915 • *Mina* • USA
SQUEEDUNK SHERLOCK HOLMES, A • 1909 • *Edison* • USA
SQUEEZE, THE • 1977 • Apted Michael • UKN
SQUEEZE, THE • 1980 • Turner Richard • NZL • NIGHT MOVES
SQUEEZE, THE • 1987 • Young Roger • USA • SKIP-TRACER
SQUEEZE, THE (USA) see **CONTRORAPINA** • 1979
SQUEEZE A FLOWER • 1970 • Daniels Marc • ASL
SQUEEZE PLAY • 1979 • Herz Michael, Weil Samuel • USA
SQUIBS • 1921 • Pearson George • UKN
SQUIBS • 1935 • Edwards Henry • UKN
SQUIBS' HONEYMOON • 1923 • Pearson George • UKN
SQUIBS, M.P. • 1923 • Pearson George • UKN
SQUIBS WINS THE CALCUTTA CUP • 1922 • Pearson George • UKN
SQUILIBRIO MOSSO • 1975 • Esposito Luigi • ITL
SQUILLO • 1967 • Sabatini Mario • ITL
SQUINK CITY FIRE COMPANY • 1912 • *Imp* • USA
SQUIRE AND THE MAID, THE • 1903 • *Warwick Trading Co* • UKN
SQUIRE AND THE NOBLE LORD, THE • 1909 • *Urban-Eclipse* • USA
SQUIRE OF LONG HADLEY, THE • 1925 • Hill Sinclair • UKN • ROMANCE OF RICHES, A
SQUIRE PHIN • 1921 • Wharton Leopold, Townley Robert H. • USA
SQUIRES – BURNS FIGHT • 1908 • *Mcmahon C./ Carroll E. (P)* • ASL
SQUIRE'S DAUGHTER, THE • 1905 • Haggar William • UKN
SQUIRE'S MISTAKE, THE • 1914 • *Stanley Henry* • USA
SQUIRE'S ROMANCE, THE • 1910 • Coleby A. E. • UKN
SQUIRE'S SON, THE • 1914 • West Raymond B. • USA
SQUIRM • 1976 • Lieberman Jeff • USA
SQUIRREL CRAZY • 1951 • Davis Mannie • ANS • USA
SQUIRREL FOOD • 1920 • Parrott James • SHT • USA
SQUIRREL TIME • 1920 • *Howell Alice* • SHT • USA
SQUIRREL WAR • 1947 • Dyer Anson • UKN
SQUIZZY TAYLOR • 1982 • Dobson Kevin • ASL
SR. PRESIDENTE, EL • 1983 • Gomez Manuel Octavio • CUB, NCR, FRN • SENOR PRESIDENTE, EL
SRDCE ZA PISNICKU • 1933 • Hasler • CZC • HEART FOR A SONG, THE
SRDECNY POZDRAV ZE ZEMEKOULE • 1983 • Lipsky Oldrich • CZC • HEARTY GREETING FROM THE EARTH
SREBURNATA LISITSA • 1990 • Roudarov Nikola • BUL • SILVER FOX, THE
SRECA DOLACI U 9 • 1961 • Tanhofer Nikola • YGS • FELICITY ARRIVES AT 9
SRECA NO VRVICI • 1976 • Kavcic Jane • YGS
SRECA U DVOJE • 1969 • Grgic Zlatko, Kolar Boris, Zaninovic Ante • ANS • YGS • HAPPINESS FOR TWO
SRECNA NOVA • 1960 • Strbac Milenko • YGS • HAPPY NEW YEAR
SRECNA NOVA • 1986 • Popov Stole • YGS • HAPPY NEW YEAR 1949
SRECNA PORODICA • 1981 • Mihic Gordan • YGS • HAPPY FAMILY
SRECNO, KEKECI • 1964 • Gale Joze • YGS • MOUNTAIN OF FEAR (UKN)
SREDI DOBRYKH LYUDEY • 1962 • Bryunchugin Yevgeniy, Bukovskiy Anatoliy • USS • MOTHER AND DAUGHTER (USA)
SREDNI VASHTAR • 1981 • Birkin Andrew • SHT • UKN
SREE JAGANNATH • 1950 • Agradoot • IND
SREO SAM CAK I SRECNE CIGANE see **SKUPLJACI PERJA** • 1967
SRETNI UMIRU DVAPUT • 1967 • Sipovac Gojko • YGS • HAPPY ONES DIE TWICE, THE ○ LUCKY DIE TWICE, THE
SRI KRISHNA SATYA BHAMA • 1951 • Paranjpe Raja • IND • PARIJATAK
SRI KRISHNA THULABHARAM • Kameswar Rao D. K. • IND
SRI LANKA • 1975 • Peries Lester James • SLN, UKN • GOD KING, THE (UKN)
SRI LANKA, LOVE AND FAREWELL see **SURI-LANKA, NO AI TO WAKARE** • 1976
SRI MURUGAN • *Ramchandra M. G.* • IND
SRI SIVARATHRI • 1963 • Seetharama Sastry K. R. • IND
SRI VALLI • 1946 • *Saraswati* • IND
SROUBEK'S ADVENTURE see **SROUBKOVO DOBRODRUZSTVI** • 1960
SROUBKOVO DOBRODRUZSTVI • 1960 • Vystrcil Frantisek • ANS • CZC • SROUBEK'S ADVENTURE
SRPNOVA NEDELE • 1960 • Vavra Otakar • CZC • AUGUST SUNDAY ○ SUNDAY IN AUGUST, A
SRUB • 1965 • Jires Jaromil • CZC • LOG CABIN, THE
SS LAGER 5 L'INFERNO DELLE DONNE • 1977 • Garrone Sergio • ITL
SSADIS LAGER KASTRAT KOMMANDATUR see **LAGER SSADIS KASTRAT KOMMANDATUR** • 1976
SSAKI • 1962 • Polanski Roman • PLN • MAMMALS
SSANIN • 1924 • Feher Friedrich, Newolyn Boris • AUS
SSIBOJI • 1987 • Lim Kwon-Taek • SKR • SURROGATE MOTHER ○ SURROGATE WOMAN
SSSHHH! • 1980 • Mann Ron • CND
SSSSNAKE (UKN) see **SSSSSSS** • 1973
SSSSSSS • 1973 • Kowalski Bernard • USA • SSSSNAKE (UKN)
SST -DEATH FLIGHT • 1977 • Rich David Lowell • TVM • USA • SST -DISASTER IN THE SKY ○ DEATH FLIGHT
SST -DISASTER IN THE SKY see **SST -DEATH FLIGHT** • 1977
ST-JEAN-SUR-AILLEURS • 1980 • Forest Leonard • DOC • CND
ST-JEROME • 1968 • Dansereau Fernand • DOC • CND
STA PA • 1976 • Skagen Solve, Knutzen Jan, Nicolayssen Hans Otto, Omdal Skljalg • DOC • NRW
STA SINORA TIS PRODOSIAS • 1968 • Dadiras Dimis • GRC • OUT OF THE BORDERS OF TREASON
STAAL AAN ZEE • 1966 • Moonen Jan • SHT • NTH
STAAL BURGER • 1969 • SAF
STAALKONGENS VILJE see **MORKE PUNKT, DET** • 1913
STAATSANWALT, DER • 1920 • Otto Paul • FRG
STAATSANWALT BRIANDS ABENTEUER 1 • 1920 • Eichberg Richard • FRG • UNGULTIGE EHE, DIE
STAATSANWALT BRIANDS ABENTEUER 2 • 1920 • Eichberg Richard • FRG • DEM WELKENGRAB ENTRONNEN
STAATSANWALT JORDAN • 1919 • Lund Erik • FRG
STAATSANWALT JORDAN • 1926 • Gerhardt Karl • FRG
STAATSANWALT KLAGT AN, DER • 1928 • Trotz Adolf, Sparkuhl Theodor • FRG • HENKER, DER
STAATSANWALTIN CORDA • 1954 • Ritter Karl • FRG
STAB • 1981 • Benton Robert • USA • STILL OF THE NIGHT (UKN)
STAB, THE • 1915 • Butler Fred J. • USA
STAB OF DISGRACE, THE • 1912 • Haldane Bert? • UKN
STABILITY VS. NOBILITY • 1911 • *Selig* • USA
STABLE COMPANIONS • 1922 • Ward Albert • UKN
STABLE DOOR, THE • 1966 • Jackson Pat • UKN
STABLE IN SALVATOR, A see **STAJNIA NA SALWATORZE** • 1967
STABLE ON SALWATOR, THE see **STAJNIA NA SALWATORZE** • 1967
STABLE RIVALS • 1953 • Reeve Leonard • UKN
STABLEMATES • 1938 • Wood Sam • USA
STACEY • 1973 • Sidaris Andy • USA • STACY AND HER GANGBUSTERS
STACHKA • 1925 • Eisenstein Sergei • USS • TOWARDS THE DICTATORSHIP OF THE PROLETARIAT ○ STRIKE (UKN)
STACKARS FERDINAND • 1941 • Jerring Nils • SWD • POOR FERDINAND
STACKARS LILLA SVEN • 1947 • Bolander Hugo • SWD • POOR LITTLE SVEN
STACKARS MILJONARER • 1936 • Ibsen Tancred, Arvedson Ragnar • SWD • POOR MILLIONAIRES
STACKED CARDS • 1926 • Eddy Robert • USA
STACKING • 1987 • Rosen Martin • USA • SEASON OF DREAMS
STACY AND HER GANGBUSTERS see **STACEY** • 1973
STACY'S KNIGHTS • 1983 • Wilson Jim • USA
STAD • 1960 • Troell Jan • SHT • SWD
STADE ZERO see **CIEL SUR LA TETE, LE** • 1964
STADIG OOR DIE KLIPPE • 1969 • SAF
STADIO • 1934 • Campogalliani Carlo • ITL
STADION • 1958 • Jedryka Stanislaw • PLN
STADIUM • 1957 • Szczechura Daniel • ANS • PLN

STADIUM MURDERS, THE see **HOLLYWOOD STADIUM MYSTERY** • 1938
STADT, DIE • 1973 • Klick Roland • FRG • TOWN, THE
STADT ANATOL • 1936 • Tourjansky Victor • FRG • KAMPF UM DAS FLUSSIGE GOLD: OL
STADT DER MILLIONEN, DIE • 1925 • Trotz Adolf • FRG
STADT DER TAUSEND FREUDEN, DIE • 1927 • Gallone Carmine • FRG
STADT DER VERHEISSUNG • 1935 • Ruttmann Walter • FRG
STADT DER VERSUCHUNG, DIE • 1925 • Niebuhr Walter • FRG • CITY OF TEMPTATION, THE
STADT IM NEBEL see **FUNF UNTER VERDACHT** • 1950
STADT IN SICHT • 1923 • Galeen Henrik • FRG
STADT IST VOLLER GEHEIMNISSE, DIE • 1955 • Kortner Fritz • FRG • CITY OF SECRETS (USA) ○ SECRETS OF THE CITY
STADT OHNE JUDEN, DIE • 1924 • Breslauer H. K. • AUS
STADT OHNE JUDEN, DIE • 1987 • Quitta Robert • DOC • AUS • TOWN WITHOUT JEWS, THE
STADT OHNE MITLEID • 1961 • Reinhardt Gottfried • FRG, SWT, USA • VILLE SANS PITIE (SWT) ○ TOWN WITHOUT PITY (USA) ○ SHOCKER
STADT STEHT KOPF, EINE • 1932 • Grundgens Gustaf • FRG
STADT STUTTGART, 100. CANSTATTER VOLKSFEST see **VOLKFEST KANNSTADT** • 1935
STADTSTREICHER • 1966 • Fassbinder R. W. • FRG • CITY TRAMP, THE
STAFETA • 1969 • Kovacs Andras • HNG • RELAY RACE ○ RELAY, THE
STAFF DINNER, THE • 1913 • *Baskcomb A. W.* • UKN
STAFF OF AGE, THE • 1912 • *Moore Joe* • USA
STAFFEN STOLLE STORY, THE see **RATATAA** • 1956
STAFFS • 1927 • Fischinger Oskar • ANS • FRG
STAFFS see **ORGELSTABE** • 1923-27
STAG AND THE WOLF, THE • 1951 • *Sovexportfilm* • ANS • USS
STAG-BEETLES, THE • 1911 • Starevitch Ladislas • ANM • USS
STAG PARTY, THE • 1917 • *Shelley Effie* • USA
STAGE CHILD, THE • 1911 • *Thanhouser* • USA
STAGE COACH DRIVER AND THE GIRL, THE • 1915 • Mix Tom • USA
STAGE COACH LINE (UKN) see **OLD TEXAS TRAIL, THE** • 1944
STAGE CONNECTION see **POZORISNA VEZA** • 1981
STAGE DOOR • 1937 • La Cava Gregory • USA
STAGE DOOR CANTEEN • 1943 • Borzage Frank • USA
STAGE DOOR CARTOON • 1944 • Freleng Friz • ANS • USA
STAGE DOOR FLIRTATION, A • 1914 • *Hotaling Mae* • USA
STAGE DOOR MAGOO see **STAGEDOOR MAGOO** • 1955
STAGE DRIVER, THE • 1909 • *Selig* • USA
STAGE DRIVER'S CHIVALRY, THE • 1913 • *Frontier* • USA
STAGE-DRIVER'S DAUGHTER, THE • 1911 • *Essanay* • USA
STAGE ENTRANCE • 1951 • Seasman Bill • SHT • USA
STAGE ENTRANCE see **SCENINGANG** • 1956
STAGE FOLK see **HAPPY DAYS ARE HERE AGAIN** • 1936
STAGE FRIGHT • 1923 • Roach Hal • SHT • USA
STAGE FRIGHT • 1928 • Roberts Stephen • SHT • USA
STAGE FRIGHT • 1938 • Roberts Charles E. • SHT • USA
STAGE FRIGHT • 1940 • Jones Charles M. • ANS • USA
STAGE FRIGHT • 1950 • Hitchcock Alfred • UKN
STAGE FRIGHT • 1986 • Soavi Michele • USA • AQUARIUS ○ STAGEFRIGHT
STAGE FRIGHT see **SHADOW DANCING** • 1988
STAGE FRIGHTS • 1947 • Hughes Harry • UKN
STAGE HAND, THE • 1920 • Semon Larry, Taurog Norman • SHT • USA • STAGEHAND, THE
STAGE HAND, THE • 1933 • Edwards Harry J. • SHT • USA
STAGE HANDS, THE • 1928 • *De Forest Phonofilm* • SHT • UKN
STAGE HOAX • 1952 • Lantz Walter • ANS • USA
STAGE IS CLEARED FOR MARIKA, THE see **BUHNE FREI FUR MARIKA** • 1958
STAGE KISSES • 1927 • Kelley Albert • USA
STAGE KRAZY • 1933 • *Mintz Charles (P)* • ANS • USA
STAGE MADNESS • 1927 • Schertzinger Victor • USA
STAGE MEMORIES OF AN OLD THEATRICAL TRUNK • 1908 • Porter Edwin S. • USA
STAGE MONEY • 1915 • Marston Theodore • USA • EASY MONEY
STAGE MOTHER • 1933 • Brabin Charles J. • USA
STAGE NOTE, THE • 1910 • Salter Harry • USA
STAGE OF HOPE • 1971 • Siddik Khalid • SHT • KWT
STAGE OF LIFE, THE • 1915 • Montgomery Frank E. • USA
STAGE ROBBERS OF SAN JUAN, THE • 1911 • Dwan Allan • USA
STAGE ROMANCE, A • 1911 • Merwin Bannister • USA
STAGE ROMANCE, A • 1922 • Brenon Herbert • USA
STAGE RUSTLER, THE • 1908 • McCutcheon Wallace • USA
STAGE STRUCK • 1904 • *Warwick Trading Co* • UKN
STAGE STRUCK • 1907 • Porter Edwin S. • USA
STAGE STRUCK • 1911 • *Thanhouser* • USA
STAGE-STRUCK • 1914 • Finley Ned • USA
STAGE STRUCK • 1917 • Morrisey Edward • USA
STAGE STRUCK • 1922 • Roach Hal • SHT • USA
STAGE STRUCK • 1925 • Dwan Allan • USA • SCREEN STRUCK
STAGE STRUCK • 1929 • Terry Paul • ANS • USA
STAGE STRUCK • 1936 • Berkeley Busby • USA
STAGE STRUCK • 1948 • Nigh William • USA
STAGE STRUCK • 1951 • Davis Mannie • ANS • USA
STAGE STRUCK • 1958 • Lumet Sidney • USA
STAGE-STRUCK CARPENTER, A • 1911 • Stow Percy • UKN
STAGE-STRUCK DAUGHTER, THE • 1908 • Brooke Van Dyke • USA
STAGE-STRUCK LIZZIE • 1911 • *Washburn Alice* • USA
STAGE STRUCK MAMIE • 1912 • *Trunnelle Mabel* • USA
STAGE STRUCK SALLY • 1913 • Hotaling Arthur D. • USA
STAGE STUNT • 1929 • Lantz Walter • ANS • USA
STAGE TO BLUE RIVER • 1951 • Collins Lewis D. • USA
STAGE TO CHINO • 1940 • Killy Edward • USA
STAGE TO MESA CITY • 1947 • Taylor Ray • USA
STAGE TO THREE, THE • 1964 • Biggs Julian • CND
STAGE TO THUNDER ROCK • 1964 • Claxton William F. • USA • STAGECOACH TO HELL
STAGE TO TUCSON • 1951 • Murphy Ralph • USA • LOST STAGE VALLEY (UKN)
STAGE VILLAIN, A • 1916 • Curtis Allen • SHT • USA
STAGE WHISPERS (UKN) see **GRIEF STREET** • 1931
STAGECOACH • 1939 • Ford John • USA
STAGECOACH • 1966 • Douglas Gordon • USA
STAGECOACH • 1986 • Post Ted • TVM • USA
STAGECOACH BUCKAROO • 1942 • Taylor Ray • USA
STAGECOACH DAYS • 1938 • Levering Joseph • USA
STAGECOACH DRIVER • 1951 • Collins Lewis D. • USA
STAGECOACH EXPRESS • 1942 • Sherman George • USA
STAGECOACH GUARD, THE • 1915 • Mix Tom • USA
STAGECOACH KID, THE • 1949 • Landers Lew • USA
STAGECOACH OUTLAWS • 1945 • Newfield Sam • USA
STAGECOACH TO DANCERS' ROCK • 1962 • Bellamy Earl • USA
STAGECOACH TO DENVER • 1946 • Springsteen R. G. • USA
STAGECOACH TO FURY • 1956 • Claxton William F. • USA
STAGECOACH TO HELL see **STAGE TO THUNDER ROCK** • 1964
STAGECOACH TO MONTEREY • 1944 • Selander Lesley • USA
STAGECOACH TOM • 1910 • *Columbia* • USA
STAGECOACH WAR • 1940 • Selander Lesley • USA
STAGEDOOR MAGOO • 1955 • Burness Pete • ANS • USA • STAGE DOOR MAGOO
STAGEFRIGHT see **STAGE FRIGHT** • 1986
STAGEHAND, THE see **STAGE HAND, THE** • 1920
STAGIONE ALL'INFERNO, UNA • 1971 • Risi Nelo • ITL
STAGIONE DEI SENSI, LA • 1969 • Franciosa Massimo • ITL
STAGIONI DEL NOSTRO AMORE, LE • 1966 • Vancini Florestano • ITL • SEASONS OF OUR LOVE
STAHLERNE STAHL, DER • 1935 • Wenzler Franz • FRG
STAHLTIER, DAS • 1935 • Zielke Willy • FRG
STAIN, THE • 1912 • *Calvert E. H.* • USA
STAIN, THE • 1914 • Powell Frank • USA
STAIN IN THE BLOOD, THE • 1916 • MacQuarrie Murdock • USA
STAIN OF DISHONOR, THE • 1915 • *Reliance* • USA
STAIN ON THE CONSCIENCE, A see **MRLJA NA SAVJESTI** • 1968
STAIN ON THE SNOW, THE see **NEIGE ETAIT SALE, LA** • 1952
STAINED GLASS AT FAIRFORD, THE • 1955 • Wright Basil • DOC • UKN
STAINED PEARL, THE • 1916 • Huntley Fred W. • SHT • USA
STAINED PENDANT, THE see **SABITA PENDANT** • 1967
STAINLESS BARRIER, THE • 1917 • Heffron Thomas N. • USA
STAIRCASE • 1969 • Donen Stanley • USA
STAIRCASE see **SCHODY** • 1967
STAIRCASE C see **ESCALIER C** • 1984
STAIRCASE TO THE SKY see **LYESTNITSA V NYEBO** • 1967
STAIRS see **SCHODY** • 1967
STAIRS, THE • 1953 • Maddow Ben • DOC • USA
STAIRS OF SAND • 1929 • Brower Otto • USA
STAIRS TO THE SKY see **LYESTNITSA V NYEBO** • 1967
STAIRWAY TO HEAVEN see **STEPHENICE ZA NEBO** • 1984
STAIRWAY TO HEAVEN see **SCHODAMI W GORE..** • 1988
STAIRWAY TO HEAVEN (USA) see **MATTER OF LIFE AND DEATH, A** • 1946
STAIRWAY TO LIGHT • 1945 • Lee Sammy • USA
STAIRWAY TO THE STARS • Safran Fred • SHT • USA
STAJNIA NA SALWATORZE • 1967 • Komorowski Pawel • PLN • STABLE IN SALVATOR, A ○ SALVATOR STABLE, THE ○ STABLE ON SALWATOR, THE
STAKE, THE • 1915 • *Garwood William* • USA
STAKE AND THE FLAME, THE see **RUG SI FLACARA** • 1980
STAKE GREATER THAN LIFE, A see **STAWKA WIEKSZA NIZ ZYCIE** • 1967-69
STAKE OUT, THE see **MEN OF THE NIGHT** • 1934
STAKE OUT, THE see **POLICE STORY** • 1973
STAKE UNCLE SAM TO PLAY YOUR HAND • 1918 • *Frederick Pauline* • SHT • USA
STAKEOUT! • 1962 • Landis James • USA
STAKEOUT • 1987 • Badham John • USA
STAKEOUT ON DOPE STREET • 1958 • Kershner Irvin • USA
STAKING HIS LIFE • 1918 • *W.h. Productions* • USA
STAKKELS KARIN • 1916 • Davidsen Hjalmar • DNM
STAL • 1940 • Lindberg Per • SWD • STEEL
STAL • 1959 • Lomnicki Jan • DOC • PLN • STEEL
STALAG 17 • 1953 • Wilder Billy • USA
STALE FLOWERS see **NIRMALAYAM** • 1973
STALINE • 1984 • Aurel Jean • FRN
STALINGRAD • 1943 • Varlamov Leonid • USS • STORY OF STALINGRAD, THE
STALINGRAD see **STALINGRADSKAYA BITVA** • 1970
STALINGRADSKAYA BITVA • 1950 • Petrov Vladimir • USS • BATTLE OF STALINGRAD, THE
STALINGRADSKAYA BITVA • 1970 • Chukhrai Grigori • USS • BATTLE OF STALINGRAD, THE ○ STALINGRAD
STALIN'S DISCIPLES • 1988 • Levithan Nadav • ISR
STALK THE WILD CHILD • 1976 • Hale William • TVM • USA
STALKED CARDS • 1914 • *Kb* • USA
STALKER • 1979 • Tarkovsky Andrei • USS • WISH MACHINE, THE
STALKING MOON, THE • 1969 • Mulligan Robert • USA • ELITE KILLER, THE
STALLION CANYON • 1949 • Fraser Harry L. • USA
STALLION OF THE SEA • 1979 • Fairfax John C. • DOC • ASL
STALLION ROAD • 1947 • Kern James V., Walsh Raoul (U/c) • USA
STALLONE, LO • 1976 • Longo Tiziano • ITL
STALOWE SERCA • 1948 • Urbanowicz Stanislaw • PLN • STEEL HEARTS ○ HEARTS OF STEEL
STAMBOUL • 1932 • Denham Reginald, Buchowetzki Dimitri • UKN
STAMBOUL QUEST • 1934 • Wood Sam • USA
STAMMBAUM DES DR. PISTORIUS, DER • 1939 • Kulb Karl G. • FRG
STAMMEN LEVER AN • 1938 • Fejos Paul • DCS • SWD • TRIBE LIVES ON, THE
STAMMHEIM see **STAMMHEIM -DER PROZESS** • 1986
STAMMHEIM -DER PROZESS • 1986 • Hauff Reinhard • FRG • STAMMHEIM
STAMP COLLECTING • 1968 • Ratz Gunter • ANM • GDR
STAMP FANTASIA see **KITTE-NO GENSO** • 1959
STAMP OF APPROVAL • 1951 • Garceau Raymond • DCS • CND • AVEC LE SCEAU DU CANADA
STAMP RAMP • 1946 • Hughes Harry • UKN
STAMPEDE • 1929 • Court Treatt C., Court Treatt Stella • UKN
STAMPEDE • 1936 • Beebe Ford • USA
STAMPEDE • 1949 • Selander Lesley • USA
STAMPEDE • 1962 • Poirier Anne-Claire, Fournier Claude • SHT • CND
STAMPEDE • 1978 • Barclay Robert • MTV • CND
STAMPEDE see **CONQUERING HORDE, THE** • 1931
STAMPEDE, THE • 1909 • Boggs Frank • USA
STAMPEDE, THE • 1911 • *Imp* • USA
STAMPEDE, THE • 1911 • Blache Alice • *Solax* • USA
STAMPEDE, THE • 1912 • *Almyr Feature Films* • USA
STAMPEDE, THE • 1916 • *Drouer Robert* • SHT • USA
STAMPEDE, THE • 1921 • Ford Francis • USA
STAMPEDE AT BITTER CREEK see **TEXAS JOHN SLAUGHTER: STAMPEDE AT BITTER CREEK** • 1962
STAMPEDE IN SCARLETT • 1973 • Barclay Robert • SHT • CND
STAMPEDE IN THE NIGHT, THE • 1916 • Jaccard Jacques • SHT • USA
STAMPEDE OF FATE, THE • 1914 • *Gorman Film* • USA
STAMPEDE POT POURRI • 1977 • Barclay Robert • MTV • CND
STAMPEDE THUNDER • 1925 • Gibson Tom • USA
STAMPEDED (UKN) see **BIG LAND, THE** • 1956
STAMPEDIN' TROUBLE • 1925 • Sheldon Forrest • USA
STAMPEN • 1955 • Lagerkvist Hans • SWD • PAWN SHOP
STAMPING GROUND (UKN) see **LOVE AND MUSIC** • 1971
STAN KENTON AND HIS ORCHESTRA • 1962 • Binder Steve • SHT • USA
STAN KENTON AND HIS ORCHESTRA • 1976 • Benson Alan • UKN
STAN KENTON AND HIS ORCHESTRA -ARTISTRY IN RHYTHM • 1945 • Scholl Jack • SHT • USA
STAN POSIADANIA • 1989 • Zanussi Krzysztof • PLN • INVENTORY
STAN THE FLASHER • 1989 • Gainsbourg Serge • FRN
STANARSKO PRAVO LAGUMASA SAFERA • 1974 • Ljubojev Petar • SHT • YGS • DYNAMITE-EXPERT SAFER'S RIGHT-TO-HOUSING
STANCES A SOPHIE, LES • 1970 • Mizrahi Moshe • FRN, CND
STAND ALONE • 1985 • Beattie Alan • USA
STAND AND DELIVER • 1928 • Crisp Donald • USA
STAND AND DELIVER • 1988 • Menendez Ramon • USA • WALKING ON WATER
STAND AND DELIVER (UKN) see **BOWERY BLITZKRIEG** • 1941
STAND AT APACHE RIVER, THE • 1953 • Sholem Lee • USA
STAND BY • 1989 • Veselinovic Ceda • YGS
STAND BY ALL NETWORKS • 1942 • Landers Lew • USA
STAND BY FOR ACTION • 1942 • Leonard Robert Z. • USA • CARGO OF INNOCENTS (UKN) ○ CLEAR FOR ACTION ○ COME HAIL OR HIGH WATER ○ THIS MAN'S NAVY
STAND BY ME • 1986 • Reiner Rob • USA • BODY, THE
STAND BY TO DIE see **FLIGHT FOR FREEDOM** • 1943
STAND BY TO JUMP • 1949 • Blais Roger • DCS • CND
STAND BY YOUR MAN • 1981 • Jameson Jerry • TVM • USA
STAND DER DINGE, DER • 1983 • Wenders Wim • FRG • STATE OF THINGS, THE
STAND EASY, SOLDIER • 1967 • Skanata Krsto • DOC • YGS
STAND EASY (USA) see **DOWN AMONG THE Z MEN** • 1952
STAND-IN • 1937 • Garnett Tay • USA
STAND-IN, THE see **CUOWEI** • 1987
STAND OFF see **TUSZTORTENET** • 1988
STAND PAT • 1922 • Roach Hal • SHT • USA
STAND STRAIGHT see **NAIMRNDHU NIL** • 1968
STAND UP AND BE COUNTED • 1972 • Cooper Jackie • USA
STAND UP AND CHEER • 1934 • MacFadden Hamilton • USA
STAND UP AND FIGHT • 1938 • Van Dyke W. S. • USA
STAND UP AND SING see **EARL CARROLL SKETCHBOOK** • 1946
STAND UP STRAIGHT, DELPHINE see **ISPRAVI SE, DELFINA** • 1978
STAND UP VIRGIN SOLDIERS • 1977 • Cohen Norman • UKN
STANDARD • 1976 • Petruzzellis Stefano • ITL
STANDARD, THE see **STANDARTE, DIE** • 1977
STANDARD BEARER OF THE JEWISH PEOPLE, THE • 1921 • *Fox L.m./ Penser Charles* • SHT • USA
STANDARD TIME • 1967 • Snow Michael • USA
STANDARTE, DIE • 1977 • Runze Ottokar • AUS, FRG, SPN • STANDARD, THE
STANDBY COLLEGIATE see **UMINO WAKADAISHO** • 1965
STANDHAFTE BENJAMIN, DER • 1917 • Wiene Robert • FRG
STANDING BY THE TREASURY see **U POKLADNY STAL** • 1939
STANDING IN THE SHADOWS OF LOVE • 1984 • Crain William • USA
STANDING ROOM ONLY • 1912 • *Thanhouser* • USA
STANDING ROOM ONLY • 1944 • Lanfield Sidney • USA
STANDING TALL • 1978 • Hart Harvey • TVM • USA
STANDRECHTLICH ERSCHOSSEN • 1914 • Gad Urban • FRG
STANDSCHUTZE BRUGGLER • 1936 • Klinger Werner • FRG
STANFIELD • 1968 • Shebib Donald • CND
STANITSA OF DALNAYA, THE • 1940 • Chervyakov Yevgeni • USS
STANLEY • 1972 • Grefe William • USA
STANLEY • 1983 • Storm Esben • ASL
STANLEY see **LIVINGSTONE** • 1925
STANLEY AMONG THE WOO DOO WORSHIPPERS • 1915 • *Watson Roy* • USA
STANLEY AND IRIS • 1989 • Ritt Martin • USA • LETTERS ○ UNION STREET
STANLEY AND LIVINGSTONE • 1939 • King Henry • USA
STANLEY AND THE SLAVE TRADERS • 1915 • *Watson Roy* • USA
STANLEY AT STARVATION CAMP • 1915 • *Watson Roy* • USA
STANLEY IN DARKEST AFRICA • 1915 • *Watson Roy* • USA
STANLEY TAKES A TRIP • 1947 • MacKay Jim, Munro Grant • ANS • CND
STANLEY, THE LION-KILLER • 1914 • Drew Sidney • USA
STANLEY'S CLOSE CALL • 1915 • Montgomery Frank E. • USA
STANLEY'S SEARCH FOR THE HIDDEN CITY • 1915 • *Bonavita Jack* • USA
STANLOW STORY • 1952 • Clarke Douglas • UKN

STANNO TUTTI BENE • 1990 • Tornatore Giuseppe • ITL, FRN • THEY'RE ALL FINE
STANOTTE ALLE 11 see **STASERA ALLE UNDICI** • 1937
STANTON'S LAST FLING • 1913 • Seay Charles M. • USA
STANZA 17-17 PALAZZO DELLE TASSE UFFICIO DELLE IMPOSTE • 1971 • Lupo Michele • ITL
STANZA DEL VESCOVO, LA • 1977 • Risi Dino • ITL • BISHOP'S BEDROOM, THE ○ BISHOP'S ROOM, THE ○ FORBIDDEN ROOM, THE
STANZA DELLE BUONE NOTIZE • 1979 • Petri Elio • ITL • BUONE NOTIZIE, LE
STAR • 1967 • Essid Hamadi • DCS • TNS
STAR! • 1968 • Wise Robert • USA • THOSE WERE THE HAPPY TIMES ○ GERTIE WAS A LADY ○ THOSE WERE THE HAPPY DAYS
STAR see **STAR IS LOST!, A** • 1974
STAR 80 • 1983 • Fosse Bob • USA
STAR, THE • 1913 • *Hennessy Ruth* • USA
STAR, THE • 1953 • Heisler Stuart • USA
STAR, THE • 1953 • Ivanov Alexander • USS
STAR, THE see **LITTLE STAR, THE** • 1965
STAR, THE see **HVEZDA** • 1969
STAR AND CRESCENT, THE • 1913 • *Searchlight Films* • UKN
STAR AND LYRA • 1973 • Alexandrov Grigori • USS
STAR AND THE CROSS, THE see **HAND IN HAND** • 1960
STAR AND THE DEATH OF JOAQUIM MURIETA, THE see **ZVEZDA I SMERT KHOAKINA MURIETY** • 1983
STAR AND THE SAND, THE • 1946 • Gunn Gilbert • DOC • UKN
STAR BOARDER, THE • 1914 • Nicholls George • USA • HASH HOUSE HERO
STAR BOARDER, THE • 1915 • *Royal* • USA
STAR BOARDER, THE • 1917 • Gillstrom Arvid E. • SHT • USA
STAR BOARDER, THE • 1919 • Semon Larry • SHT • USA
STAR BOARDER, THE • 1920 • Davis James • SHT • USA
STAR BOARDERS • 1916 • *Hamilton Lloyd V.* • SHT • USA
STAR CHAMBER, THE • 1983 • Hyams Peter • USA
STAR CHASERS see **SKY'S NO LIMIT, THE** • 1984
STAR CHILD see **SPACE RAIDERS** • 1983
STAR CREATURES, THE see **INVASION OF THE STAR CREATURES** • 1962
STAR CRYSTAL • 1985 • Lindsay Lance • USA
STAR DISAPPEARS, A (USA) see **ETOILE DISPARAIT, UNE** • 1932
STAR DUST • 1917 • Wright Fred E. • SHT • USA
STAR DUST • 1940 • Lang Walter • USA
STAR DUST TRAIL, THE • 1924 • Mortimer Edmund • USA
STAR EXPRESS • 1981 • Zingarelli Italo • ITL
STAR EYES' STRATEGY • 1912 • *Bison* • USA
STAR FALLS FROM HEAVEN, A see **STAR FELL FROM HEAVEN, A** • 1936
STAR FELL FROM HEAVEN, A • 1936 • Merzbach Paul • UKN • STAR FALLS FROM HEAVEN, A
STAR FOR A NIGHT • 1936 • Seiler Lewis • USA
STAR FOR A NIGHT see **BLACK SHEEP** • 1935
STAR FORCE • Kukazama Kiyosumi, Kanaga Minoru • JPN • STAR FORCE: FUGITIVE ALIEN 2
STAR FORCE: FUGITIVE ALIEN 2 see **STAR FORCE**
STAR FROM HEAVEN see **GALLANT BESS** • 1946
STAR GARDEN • 1974 • Brakhage Stan • USA
STAR GAZER, THE • 1914 • *Mcquarrie Murdock* • USA
STAR GLOBE-TROTTER, THE • 1908 • Booth W. R. • UKN
STAR GOES SOUTH, THE see **HVEZDA JEDE NA JIH** • 1957
STAR IMPERSONATIONS • 1930 • Hughes Harry • UKN
STAR IN THE DUST • 1956 • Haas Charles • USA
STAR IN THE NIGHT • 1945 • Siegel Don • SHT • USA
STAR IN THE WEST see **SECOND TIME AROUND, THE** • 1961
STAR INSPECTOR, THE see **ZVYOZDNYI INSPECTOR** • 1980
STAR IS BORED, A • 1956 • Freleng Friz • ANS • USA
STAR IS BORN, A • 1937 • Wellman William A. • USA
STAR IS BORN, A • 1954 • Cukor George • USA
STAR IS BORN, A • 1976 • Pierson Frank R. • USA
STAR IS HATCHED, A • 1938 • Freleng Friz • ANS • USA
STAR IS LOST!, A • 1974 • Howe John • CND • STAR
STAR KNIGHT see **KNIGHT OF THE DRAGON, THE** • 1986
STAR MAIDENS • 1976 • Storch Wolfgang, Gatward James
STAR MAKER, THE • 1939 • Del Ruth Roy • USA
STAR MAKER, THE • 1981 • Antonio Lou • TVM • USA
STAR MAKER, THE see **MARRIAGE CLAUSE, THE** • 1926
STAR MIT FREMDEN FEDERN • 1955 • Mannl Harald • GDR
STAR NAMED WORMWOOD, A see **HVEZDA ZVANA PELYNEK** • 1964
STAR ODYSSEY • 1978 • Brescia Alfonso • ITL
STAR OF ADAM see **OTOKO TO ONNO NO SHINWA** • 1969
STAR OF ASIA • 1937 • Desai Haribhai • IND
STAR OF BETHLEHEM, THE • 1909 • Porter Edwin S. • USA
STAR OF BETHLEHEM, THE • 1912 • Marston Lawrence?, Marston Theodore? • USA
STAR OF BETHLEHEM, THE • 1956 • Reiniger Lotte • ANS • UKN
STAR OF BETHLEHEM, THE • 1960 • Tyrlova Hermina • ANM • CZC
STAR OF BETHLEHEM, THE see **STERN VON BETHLEHEM, DER** • 1922
STAR OF BETHLEHEM, THE see **HVEZDA BETLEMSKA** • 1969
STAR OF CAPTIVE GOOD FORTUNE see **ZVEZDA PLENITELNOVO SCHASTYA** • 1974
STAR OF CHUCKAWALLA, THE • 1916 • Horne James W. • SHT • USA
STAR OF HONG KONG (USA) see **HONKON NO HOSHI** • 1962
STAR OF HOPE, THE see **ZVEZDA NADYEZHDY** • 1980
STAR OF INDIA • 1954 • Lubin Arthur, Anton Edoardo • UKN, ITL, USA • STELLA DELL'INDIA, LA (ITL)
STAR OF INDIA, THE • 1913 • Blache Herbert, Blache Alice • USA
STAR OF INDIA, THE • 1916 • Swickard Charles • SHT • USA
STAR OF KOREA • I Jong-Sun, Om Gil-Son • NKR
STAR OF MARRIED COUPLES see **MEOTO BOSHI** • 1927
STAR OF MIDNIGHT • 1935 • Roberts Stephen • USA
STAR OF MY NIGHT • 1954 • Dickson Paul • UKN
STAR OF MY TOWN, THE • 1972 • Abesadze Otar • USS
STAR OF TEXAS • 1953 • Carr Thomas • USA
STAR OF THE CIRCUS • 1938 • De Courville Albert • UKN • HIDDEN MENACE (USA)
STAR OF THE NORTH • 1914 • *Domino* • USA
STAR OF THE ONE-NIGHT STANDS, THE see **HVEZDA Z POSLEDNI STACE** • 1939
STAR OF THE SEA, THE • 1915 • De Grasse Joseph • USA
STAR OF THE SIDE SHOW, THE • 1912 • *Eline Marie* • USA
STAR OF THE SOUTH, THE • 1911 • *Springbok Film Co* • SAF
STAR OVER NIGHT, A • 1919 • Terwilliger George W. • SHT • USA
STAR PACKER, THE • 1934 • Bradbury Robert North • USA
STAR PARADE see **STARS ON PARADE** • 1936
STAR PILOTS (USA) see **2 + 5 MISSIONE HYDRA** • 1966
STAR PRINCE, THE see **YUSEI OJI** • 1959
STAR QUALITY • 1985 • *York Susannah* • MTV • UKN
STAR REBORN, A • 1912 • *La Badie Florence* • USA
STAR REPORTER • 1982 • Wynne Cordell • MTV • CND
STAR REPORTER, THE • 1911 • *Yankee* • USA
STAR REPORTER, THE • 1912 • *Storey Edith* • USA
STAR REPORTER, THE • 1921 • Worne Duke • USA
STAR REPORTER, THE • 1931 • Powell Michael • UKN
STAR REPORTER IN HOLLYWOOD, THE • 1936 • *Paramount* • SHT • USA
STAR-ROCK see **APPLE, THE** • 1980
STAR ROVER, THE • 1920 • Sloman Edward • USA
STAR SAID NO, THE (UKN) see **CALLAWAY WENT THATAWAY** • 1951
STAR SEX see **CONFESSIONS FROM THE DAVID GALAXY AFFAIR** • 1979
STAR SHALL RISE, A • 1952 • Brahm John • USA
STAR SLAMMER see **PRISON SHIP: THE ADVENTURES OF TARA** • 1987
STAR SLAMMER: THE ESCAPE see **PRISON SHIP: THE ADVENTURES OF TARA** • 1987
STAR SONG • 1984 • Muller John • MTV • CND
STAR SPANGLED BANNER, THE • 1911 • Dawley J. Searle • USA
STAR-SPANGLED BANNER, THE • 1917 • Griffith Edward H. • SHT • USA • STAR SPANGLED BANNER, THE
STAR SPANGLED BANNER, THE see **STAR-SPANGLED BANNER, THE** • 1917
STAR SPANGLED GIRL • 1971 • Paris Jerry • USA • STAR-SPANGLED GIRL
STAR-SPANGLED GIRL see **STAR SPANGLED GIRL** • 1971
STAR SPANGLED RHYTHM • 1942 • Marshall George • USA • STAR-SPANGLED RHYTHM
STAR-SPANGLED RHYTHM see **STAR SPANGLED RHYTHM** • 1942
STAR SPANGLED TO DEATH • 1957 • Jacobs Ken • USA
STAR SQUADRON, THE see **GWIAZDZISTA ESKADRA** • 1930
STAR STUDDED RIDE • 1954 • Menzies William Cameron • SHT • USA
STAR TREK II -THE WRATH OF KHAN • 1982 • Meyer Nicholas • USA
STAR TREK III -THE SEARCH FOR SPOCK • 1984 • Nimoy Leonard • USA
STAR TREK IV -THE VOYAGE HOME • 1987 • Nimoy Leonard • USA
STAR TREK -THE CAGE • 1964 • Butler Robert • MTV • USA • CAGE, THE
STAR TREK: THE MENAGERIE • 1967 • Daniels Marc • MTV • USA • MENAGERIE, THE
STAR TREK -THE MOTION PICTURE • 1979 • Wise Robert • USA • STAR TREK -THE MOVIE
STAR TREK -THE MOVIE see **STAR TREK -THE MOTION PICTURE** • 1979
STAR TREK: THE NEXT GENERATION • 1987 • Allen Corey • TVM • USA
STAR TREK V: THE FINAL FRONTIER • 1989 • Shatner William • USA
STAR UNDER THE COVER OF CLOUD see **MEGHEY DHAAKA TAARA** • 1959
STAR VIRGIN • 1979 • Gator Linus • USA
STAR WARS • 1977 • Lucas George • USA
STAR WITHOUT LIGHT (USA) see **ETOILE SANS LUMIERE** • 1945
STAR WITHOUT SKY see **STERNE OHNE HIMMEL** • 1981
STAR WITNESS, THE • 1917 • McDermott John • SHT • USA
STAR WITNESS, THE • 1931 • Wellman William A. • USA
STAR WORLDS see **BATTLESTAR GALACTICA** • 1978
STARA CINSKA OPERA • 1954 • Kachyna Karel, Jasny Vojtech • CZC • OLD CHINESE OPERA
STARBIRD AND SWEET WILLIAM • 1975 • Hively Jack • USA
STARBIRDS • 1982 • Nagahama Tadao, Part Michael • ANM • JPN
STARBLACK • 1966 • Grimaldi Gianni • ITL
STARBLANKET • 1973 • Brittain Don • CND
STARBOUND • 1984 • SAF
STARBREAKER • 1985 • MacKay Bruce • CND
STARBUCKS, THE • 1912 • Bowman William J. • USA
STARCHASER -THE LEGEND OF ORIN • 1986 • Hahn Steven • ANM • USA
STARCI NA CHMELU • 1964 • Rychman Ladislav • CZC • HOP-PICKERS, THE
STARCRASH (USA) see **SCONTRI STELLARI OLTRE LA TERZA DIMENSIONE** • 1979
STARCROSSED • 1985 • Bloom Jeffrey • TVM • USA
STARDOOM • 1971 • Brocka Lino • PHL
STARDUST • 1921 • Henley Hobart • USA
STARDUST • 1937 • Brown Melville • UKN • MAD ABOUT MONEY (USA) ○ HE LOVED AN ACTRESS
STARDUST • 1974 • Apted Michael • UKN
STARDUST MEMORIES • 1980 • Allen Woody • USA
STARDUST ON THE SAGE • 1942 • Morgan William • USA
STARDUST WHARF see **HOSHIKAGE NO HATOBA** • 1968
STARE POVESTI CESKE • 1952 • Brdecka Jiri, Trnka Jiri • ANM • CZC • OLD LEGENDS OF CZECHOSLOVAKIA ○ OLD CZECH LEGENDS
STARETS VASILI GRYAZNOV • 1924 • Sabinsky • USS • ELDER VASILI GRYAZNOV
STARFIGHTERS, THE • 1964 • Zens Will • USA
STARFISH, THE • 1952 • Cooke Alan, Schlesinger John • DCS • UKN • WITCH OF PENGELLY, THE
STARFLIGHT ONE see **STARFLIGHT: THE PLANE THAT COULDN'T LAND** • 1982
STARFLIGHT: THE PLANE THAT COULDN'T LAND • 1982 • Jameson Jerry • TVM • USA • STARFLIGHT ONE
STARGATE • 1972 • Slater Don • SHT • USA
STARHOPS • 1978 • Peeters Barbara • USA
STARI KHOTTABYCH • 1956 • Kozansky Grigori • USS • FLYING CARPET, THE (USA) ○ OLD KHOTTABYCH
STARINATA MONETA • 1965 • Yanchev Vladimir • BUL • ANCIENT COIN, THE
STARK • 1985 • Holcomb Rod • TVM • USA
STARK FEAR • 1963 • Hockman Ned • USA
STARK LOVE • 1927 • Brown Karl • USA
STARK MAD • 1929 • Bacon Lloyd • USA
STARK: MIRROR IMAGE • 1986 • Nosseck Noel • TVM • USA
STARK NATURE • 1930 • Woods Arthur • UKN
STARKARE AN LAGEN • 1951 • Sjostrand Arnold, Logardt Bengt • SWD • STRONGER THAN THE LAW
STARKASTE, DEN • 1929 • Sjoberg Alf, Lindholm Axel • SWD • STRONGEST ONE, THE ○ STRONGEST, THE
STARKE FERDINAND, DIE • 1976 • Kluge Alexander • FRG • STRONGMAN FERDINAND
STARKE HERZEN • 1937 • Maisch Herbert • FRG
STARKER ALS DIE LIEBE • 1938 • Stockel Joe • FRG
STARKER ALS DIE NACHT • 1954 • Dudow Slatan • GDR • STRONGER THAN THE NIGHT
STARKER ALS PARAGRAPHEN • 1936 • von Alten Jurgen • FRG
STARKERE, DER • 1918 • Wiene Conrad • AUS
STARKERE, DIE • 1953 • Liebeneiner Wolfgang • FRG
STARKERE MACHT, DIE • 1920 • Waldmann Emil • FRG
STARKERE MACHT, DIE see **NACHT DES SCHRECKENS, DIE** • 1929
STARKSTE TRIEB, DER • 1922 • Grundgens Gustaf • FRG
STARLET • 1969 • Kanter Richard • USA
STARLET, THE see **LITTLE STAR, THE** • 1965
STARLIFE • 1983 • Goldsmith Sidney • ANM • CND
STARLIFT • 1951 • Del Ruth Roy • USA
STARLIGHT • 1986 • Wachsberg Orin
STARLIGHT HOTEL • 1987 • Pillsbury Sam • NZL
STARLIGHT OVER TEXAS • 1938 • Herman Al • USA
STARLIGHT PARADE • 1937 • Humphris Eric • UKN
STARLIGHT SERENADE • 1944 • Kavanagh Denis • UKN
STARLIGHT SERENADERS see **ZVJEZDANI KVARTET** • 1969
STARLIGHT SLAUGHTER see **EATEN ALIVE** • 1976
STARLIGHT SLEEP • 1917 • *Essanay* • USA
STARLIGHT THE SQUAW • 1911 • *Bison* • USA
STARLIGHT, THE UNTAMED • 1925 • Webb Harry S. • USA
STARLIGHT'S DEVOTION • 1910 • *American* • USA
STARLIGHT'S MESSAGE • 1916 • *Reid Wallace* • SHT • USA
STARLIGHT'S REVENGE • 1926 • Webb Harry S. • USA
STARLIT GARDEN, THE • 1923 • Newall Guy • UKN
STARMAN • 1984 • Carpenter John • USA
STAROIE I NOVOIE • 1929 • Eisenstein Sergei, Alexandrov Grigori • USS • OLD AND NEW (USA) ○ GENERALNAYA LINIYA ○ GENERAL LINE, THE ○ OLD AND THE NEW, THE ○ STAROYE I NOVOYE
STAROYE I NOVOYE see **STAROIE I NOVOIE** • 1929
STAROZHIL • 1962 • Khamraev Ali • USS • OLD INHABITANT
STARRING IN WESTERN STUFF • 1917 • Mix Tom • SHT • USA
STARRING OF FLORA FINCHURCH, THE • 1915 • Beggs Lee • USA
STARS • 1950 • Randoy Laszlo • HNG
STARS • 1963 • Bottcher Jurgen • DOC • GDR
STARS see **WARA-WARA** • 1930
STARS see **STERNE** • 1959
STARS AND BARS • 1917 • Heerman Victor • SHT • USA
STARS AND BARS • 1988 • O'Connor Pat • UKN
STARS AND BARS see **POLICE CHIEF, THE** • 1916
STARS AND STRIPES • 1940 • McLaren Norman • ANS • USA
STARS AND STRIPES, THE • 1910 • Porter Edwin S. • USA
STARS AND STRIPES FOREVER • 1952 • Koster Henry • USA • MARCHING ALONG (UKN)
STARS AND STRIPES FOREVER, THE • 1913 • *Cunard Grace* • USA
STARS AND VIOLINS • 1944 • Keays Vernon • SHT • USA
STARS AND WATER CARRIERS see **STJERNERNE OG VANDBAERERNE** • 1974
STARS ARE BEAUTIFUL, THE • 1974 • Brakhage Stan • USA
STARS ARE SINGING, THE • 1953 • Taurog Norman • USA
STARS ARE THE EYES OF THE WARRIORS, THE see **ZVEZDE SU OCI RATNIKA** • 1973
STARS BY DAY • 1966 • Talankin Igor • USS • DAY STARS
STARS IN MAY, THE see **MAISKIE ZVEZDY** • 1959
STARS IN MY CROWN • 1913 • *Gem* • USA
STARS IN MY CROWN • 1950 • Tourneur Jacques • USA
STARS IN THE BACK YARD see **PARADISE ALLEY** • 1961
STARS IN THE HAIR, TEARS IN THE EYES see **ZVEZDI V KOSSITE, SULZI V OCHITE** • 1978
STARS IN THE SKY, THE see **SETARE HAYE HAFTASEMOON** • 1968
STARS IN UNIFORM • 1944 • Landers Lew • USA
STARS IN YOUR EYES • 1956 • Elvey Maurice • UKN
STARS LOOK DOWN, THE • 1939 • Reed Carol • UKN
STARS MUST SHINE, THE see **GWIAZDY MUSZA PLONAC** • 1953
STARS OF A SUMMER NIGHT • 1959 • Bryant Gerard • UKN
STARS OF EGER see **EGRI CSILLAGOK** • 1968
STARS OF EGER, THE see **EGRI CSILLAGOK** • 1923
STARS OF GLORY • 1919 • *Perret Leonce* • USA
STARS OF THE RUSSIAN BALLET • 1953 • Rappaport Herbert • USS
STARS ON PARADE • 1936 • Mitchell Oswald, Sanderson Challis • UKN • STAR PARADE
STARS ON PARADE • 1944 • Landers Lew • USA • CALLING ALL STARS
STARS ON THE WINGS • 1955 • Shmaruk I. • USS
STARS OVER ARIZONA • 1937 • Bradbury Robert North • USA
STARS OVER BROADWAY • 1935 • Keighley William • USA
STARS OVER TEXAS • 1946 • Tansey Robert • USA
STARS SHINE, THE (USA) see **ES LEUCHTEN DIE STERNE** • 1938
STARS, THEIR COURSES CHANGE • 1912 • *Rex* • USA
STARS THEIR COURSES CHANGE • 1915 • *Bushman Francis X.* • USA

STARS WHO MADE THE CINEMA • 1952 • Reisz Karel • DCS • UKN
STARSHAYA SESTRA • 1967 • Natanson Georgi • USS • ELDER SISTER, THE
STARSHIP see **LORCA AND THE OUTLAWS** • 1985
STARSHIP INVASIONS • 1977 • Hunt Ed • CND • WAR OF THE ALIENS ○ WINGED SERPENT ○ ALIEN ENCOUNTER ○ PROJECT GENOCIDE
STARSHIP REDWING see **LORCA AND THE OUTLAWS** • 1985
STARSKY AND HUTCH • 1974 • Shear Barry • TVM • USA
STARSTRUCK • 1982 • Armstrong Gillian • ASL
START • 1964 • Vystrcil Frantisek • ANS • CZC
START, THE see **DEPART, LE** • 1968
START, THE see **SKOK** • 1968
START AT THE 18.00 see **DESPEGUE A LAS 18.00** • 1969
START CHEERING • 1938 • Rogell Albert S. • USA • COLLEGE FOLLIES OF 1938
START FROM ZERO see **TUZGOMBOK** • 1975
START OF LIFE • 1983 • Walker John • CND
START SOMETHING • 1919 • Goulding Alf • SHT • USA
START THE MUSIC • 1939 • Yarbrough Jean • SHT • USA
START THE REVOLUTION WITHOUT ME • 1970 • Yorkin Bud • USA • LOUIS, THERE'S A CROWD DOWNSTAIRS! ○ TWO TIMES TWO
START THE SHOW • 1920 • Roach Hal • SHT • USA
STARTING AGAIN AT THREE (UKN) see **RICOMINCIO DA TRE** • 1980
STARTING FROM HATCH • 1953 • Kneitel Seymour • ANS • USA
STARTING FROM THE END see **SHECH THEKE SHURU** • 1968
STARTING LINE • 1948 • Grayson Helen • USA
STARTING OUT see **VSTUPLENIE** • 1962
STARTING OUT see **DEEP END** • 1970
STARTING OVER • 1979 • Pakula Alan J. • USA
STARTING OVER see **PUNCT SI DE LA CAPAT** • 1987
STARTING POINT, THE • 1919 • Collins Edwin J. • UKN
STARTING SOMETHING • 1911 • *Solax* • USA
STARTING SOMETHING • 1913 • *Pathe* • USA
STARTLED LOVER, THE • 1902 • *Biograph* • USA
STARTLING ANNOUNCEMENT, A • 1914 • Stather Frank • UKN
STARTLING CLIMAX, THE • 1917 • Sargent George L. • SHT • USA • DIFFERENT ENDING, A
STARVATION • 1920 • Zimmer George • USA
STARVATION BLUES • 1925 • Roach Hal • SHT • USA
STARVE A FEVER • 1916 • Birch Cecil • UKN
STARVED OUT • 1913 • Miller Ashley • USA
STARVED TO DEATH IN A RESTAURANT • 1916 • *Heinie & Louie* • USA
STARVING FOR LOVE • 1913 • Smalley Phillips • USA
STARY KOWBOJ • 1973 • Giersz Witold • ANS • PLN • OLD COWBOY, THE
STARY PROFESOR • 1962 • Antczak Jerzy • PLN
STARYE STENY • 1974 • Tregubovich Viktor • USS • OLD WALLS, THE
STARYI NAYEZHDNIK • 1940 • Barnet Boris • USS • OLD JOCKEY, THE (UKN)
STARZAN • 1989 • PHL
STARZYKI • 1968 • Jankowski Lucjan • PLN • OLD MINERS, THE ○ OLD MEN, THE
STAS SPOZNIALSKI • 1952 • Nasfeter Janusz • SHT • PLN • STAS THE UNPUNCTUAL
STAS THE UNPUNCTUAL see **STAS SPOZNIALSKI** • 1952
STASERA ALLE UNDICI • 1937 • Biancoli Oreste • ITL • STANOTTE ALLE 11
STASERA MI BUTTO • 1968 • Fizzarotti Ettore Maria • ITL • I'LL TRY TONIGHT
STASERA NIENTE DI NUOVO • 1942 • Mattoli Mario • ITL
STASERA SCIOPERO • 1951 • Bonnard Mario • ITL • STRIKING TONIGHT
STASTNOU CESTU • 1943 • Vavra Otakar • CZC • FAREWELL ○ HAPPY JOURNEY
STASTNOU CESTU • 1974 • Bedrich Vaclav • CZC • HAVE A GOOD TRIP
STASTNY KONEC see **HAPPY END** • 1966
STATE BUONI SE POTETE • 1983 • Magni Luigi • ITL
STATE CARRIAGES AND PRINCE OF WALE'S PROCESSION IN WHITEHALL • 1902 • Hepworth Cecil M. • UKN
STATE CRIMINAL see **GOSUDARSTVENNI PRESTUPNIK** • 1965
STATE DEPARTMENT FILE -649 • 1949 • Newfield Sam • USA • ASSIGNMENT IN CHINA (UKN)
STATE DEPARTMENT STORE see **UNIVERMAG** • 1922
STATE DEPARTMENT STORE see **ALLAMI ARUHAZ** • 1952
STATE FAIR • 1933 • King Henry • USA
STATE FAIR • 1944 • Lang Walter • USA • IT HAPPENED ONE SUMMER
STATE FAIR • 1962 • Ferrer Jose • USA
STATE LINE, THE • 1911 • Salter Harry • USA
STATE OF DIVISION see **DEATH RACE** • 1973
STATE OF EMERGENCY, A • 1986 • Bennett Richard • USA • CHAIN REACTION
STATE OF GRACE • 1990 • Joanou Phil • USA
STATE OF SHOCK see **POWER PLAY** • 1978
STATE OF SIEGE, A • 1979 • Ward Vincent • NZL
STATE OF SIEGE (UKN) see **ETAT DE SIEGE** • 1972
STATE OF SURVIVAL • 1986 • Azzopardi Mario • CND
STATE OF TERROR • 1989 • Kijowski Janusz • PLN
STATE OF THE UNION • 1948 • Capra Frank • USA • WORLD AND HIS WIFE, THE (UKN)
STATE OF THINGS, THE see **STAND DER DINGE, DER** • 1983
STATE OF WONDER • 1984 • Donovan Martin • UKN
STATE PARK • 1987 • Zielinski Rafal • USA
STATE PENITENIARY • 1950 • Landers Lew • USA
STATE POLICE • 1938 • Rawlins John • USA
STATE POLICE (UKN) see **WHIRLWIND RAIDERS** • 1948
STATE REASONS see **RAISON D'ETAT, LA** • 1978
STATE ROOM SECRETS • 1919 • Clements Roy • SHT • USA
STATE SECRET • 1950 • Gilliat Sidney • UKN • GREAT MANHUNT, THE
STATE STREET SADIE • 1928 • Mayo Archie • USA • GIRL FROM STATE STREET, THE (UKN)
STATE TROOPER, THE • 1933 • Lederman D. Ross • USA
STATE VERSUS ELINOR NORTON, THE see **ELINOR NORTON** • 1935
STATE WITNESS, THE • 1916 • McRae Henry • SHT • USA
STATECNE KURATKO • 1960 • Kluge Josef • ANS • CZC • BRAVE CHICKEN, THE
STATECNEM KOVARI, O • 1983 • Sveda Petr • CZC • BRAVE BLACKSMITH, THE
STATELESS see **NO EXIT** • 1962
STATELESS MAN, THE • 1955 • Gherzo Paul • UKN
STATELINE MOTEL (UKN) see **ULTIMA CHANCE, L'** • 1973
STATES • 1967 • Frampton Hollis • USA
STATE'S ATTORNEY • 1932 • Archainbaud George • USA • CARDIGAN'S LAST CASE (UKN)
STATIC • 1986 • Romanek Mark • USA
STATIC IN THE ATTIC • 1939 • Parrott Charles • USA
STATION see **EKI** • 1982
STATION 307 • 1955 • Malle Louis • DCS • FRN
STATION AGENT'S DAUGHTER, THE • 1910 • *Powers* • USA
STATION CONTENT • 1915 • Kelsey Fred A. • USA
STATION CONTENT • 1918 • Hoyt Arthur • USA
STATION FOR TWO, A see **VOKZAL DLIA DVOIKH** • 1983
STATION IN HEAVEN, A see **TENGOKU NO EKI** • 1984
STATION MASTER, THE • 1917 • Gillstrom Arvid E. • SHT • USA
STATION MASTER, THE • 1928 • Moskvin I. M.
STATION MASTER AT LYCKAS, THE see **STINSEN PA LYCKAS** • 1943
STATION MONDAINE • 1951 • Gibaud Marcel • SHT • FRN
STATION SIX SAHARA (UKN) see **ENDSTATION DREIZEHN SAHARA** • 1962
STATION WEST • 1948 • Lanfield Sidney • USA
STATIONMASTER'S WIFE, THE • 1977 • Fassbinder R. W. • MTV • FRG
STATIONS • 1978 • Vukotic Dusan • YGS
STATIONS • 1982 • MacGillivray William D. • MTV • CND
STATIONS • 1984 • McKimmie Jack • SHT • ASL
STATIONS OF THE ELEVATED • 1980 • Kirchheimer Manny • DOC • USA
STATO D'ASSEDIO, LO see **AMORE BREVE, L'** • 1969
STATO INTERESSANTE • 1977 • Nasca Sergio • ITL
STATUA DI CARNE, LA • 1921 • Almirante Mario • ITL
STATUA DI CARNE, LA see **STATUA VIVENTE, LA** • 1943
STATUA DI STALIN, LA • 1962 • Del Fra Lino • ITL
STATUA VIVENTE, LA • 1943 • Mastrocinque Camillo • ITL • STATUA DI CARNE, LA
STATUE • Havettova Jaroslava • ANS • CZC
STATUE, LA • 1905 • Blache Alice • FRN
STATUE, THE • 1913 • *Imp* • USA
STATUE, THE • 1970 • Amateau Rod • UKN
STATUE, THE see **LOVE STATUE, THE** • 1966
STATUE, THE see **SZOBOR** • 1971
STATUE ANIMEE, LA • 1903 • Melies Georges • FRN • DRAWING LESSON, THE (USA) ○ LIVING STATUE, THE ○ LECON DE DESSIN, LA
STATUE DE NEIGE, LA • 1899 • Melies Georges • FRN • SNOW MAN, THE (USA) ○ BONHOMME DE NEIGE, LE
STATUE DEALER, THE • 1905 • *Pathe Freres* • FRN
STATUE DOG, THE • 1910 • *Vitagraph* • USA
STATUE IN THE PARK, THE • 1964 • Georgi Katja, Georgi Klaus • ANS • GDR
STATUE OF MOTHER AND CHILD see **BOSHI ZO** • 1956
STATUE PARADE • 1937 • Keene Ralph, Burnford Paul • UKN
STATUE TO BE PROPPED, A see **POSTAVA K PODPIRANI** • 1963
STATUES ANIMEES, LES • 1906 • Velle Gaston • FRN • ANIMATED STATUES, THE
STATUES ARE LAUGHING, THE see **MUJASEMEHA MEKHANDAD** • 1976
STATUES DE MONSIEUR BASILE, LES • 1978 • Letourneau Diane • CND
STATUES MEURENT AUSSI, LES • 1950 • Resnais Alain, Marker Chris • SHT • FRN
STATUES OF LISBON, THE see **ESTATUAS DE LISBOA** • 1932
STATUS • Sturlis Edward • ANS • PLN
STATUS SEEKERS see **MAPPIRA SHAIN YUKYODEN** • 1968
STAU see **BOTTLENECK** • 1979
STAUB VOR DER SONNE • 1990 • Wagner Petra Katharina • FRG • DUST IN FRONT OF THE SUN
STAVISKY.. • 1973 • Resnais Alain • FRN, ITL • STAVISKY, IL GRANDE TRUFFATORE (ITL) ○ EMPIRE D'ALEXANDRE, L'
STAVISKY, IL GRANDE TRUFFATORE (ITL) see **STAVISKY..** • 1973
STAVITEL CHRAMU • 1919 • Degl Karel, Novotny Antonin • CZC • BUILDER OF THE CATHEDRAL, THE ○ CATHEDRAL BUILDER, THE
STAWKA WIEKSZA NIZ ZYCIE • 1967-69 • Morgenstern Janusz (c/d) • SER • PLN • STAKE GREATER THAN LIFE, A
STAY, THE • 1982 • Beyer Frank • GDR
STAY AS YOU ARE (USA) see **COSI COME SEI** • 1978
STAY-AT-HOMES, THE • 1915 • Cooley Frank • USA
STAY AWAY, JOE • 1968 • Tewkesbury Peter • USA
STAY HOME see **I CAN EXPLAIN** • 1922
STAY HUNGRY • 1976 • Rafelson Bob • USA
STAY NEAR ME DARLING see **MINE KONTA MOU, AGAPIMENE** • 1968
STAY OUT • 1931 • Kelley Albert • SHT • USA
STAY OUT OF THE SOUTH • 1929 • Aylott Dave, Symmons E. F. • SHT • UKN
STAY TUNED FOR MURDER • 1988 • Jones Gary W. • USA
STAYING ALIVE • 1979 • Endelson Robert A. • USA
STAYING ALIVE • 1983 • Stallone Sylvester • USA
STAYING ON • 1980 • Narizzano Silvio, Hussein Waris • TVM • UKN
STAYING THE SAME • 1989 • Grant Lee • USA • BOY'S LIFE
STAZIONE TERMINI • 1953 • De Sica Vittorio • ITL, USA • INDISCRETIONS OF AN AMERICAN WIFE (USA) ○ INDISCRETION (UKN)
STCHASTIE • 1934 • Medvedkin Alexander • USS • HAPPINESS ○ SCHASTE
STEADFAST, THE • 1915 • Smiley Joseph • USA
STEADFAST HEART, THE • 1923 • Hall Sheridan • USA
STEADFAST TIN SOLDIER, THE • 1955 • Caprino Ivo • ANS • DNM
STEADY! see **HOUEN ZO** • 1953
STEADY AS SHE GOES • 1949 • Smith John Kingsford • ASL
STEADY COMPANY • 1915 • De Grasse Joseph • USA
STEADY COMPANY • 1932 • Ludwig Edward • USA • COBBLESTONES
STEADY NOW see **HOUEN ZO** • 1953
STEAGLE, THE • 1971 • Sylbert Paul • USA
STEAK AND ONIONS • 1912 • *Selig* • USA
STEAK TROP CUIT, UN • 1960 • Moullet Luc • SHT • FRN • OVERDONE STEAK
STEAL THE SKY • 1989 • Hancock John • USA
STEAL WOOL • 1957 • Jones Charles M. • ANS • USA
STEALERS, THE • 1920 • Cabanne W. Christy • USA
STEALHEAD • 1976 • Bonniere Rene • SHT • CND
STEALIN' AIN'T HONEST • 1940 • Fleischer Dave • ANS • USA
STEALING A RIDE • 1911 • *Thanhouser* • USA
STEALING A SWEETHEART • 1917 • *Three C* • USA
STEALING HEAVEN • 1988 • Donner Clive • USA
STEALING HOME • 1988 • Kampmann Steven, Aldis Will • USA
STEALING IMAGES • 1990 • Zweig Alan • SHT • CND
STEALING THE COOKED DUCKS • 1909 • Polaski Benjamin • HKG
STEAM BALLET • 1967 • Straiton John S. • SHT • CND
STEAM HEAT • 1963 • Meyer Russ • USA • MR. TEASE AND HIS PLAYTHINGS
STEAM LOCOMOTIVE 1895-1968, THE • 1969 • CMP • UKN
STEAM LOCOMOTIVE C-57 see **KIKANSHA C-57** • 1940
STEAM PIG, THE • 1975 • Ferard Francis • SAF
STEAMBOAT BILL see **STEAMBOAT 'ROUND THE BEND** • 1935
STEAMBOAT BILL, JR. • 1928 • Reisner Charles F., Keaton Buster (U/c) • USA
STEAMBOAT RHYTHM • 1948 • Abrahams Derwin • USA
STEAMBOAT 'ROUND THE BEND • 1935 • Ford John • USA • STEAMBOAT BILL
STEAMBOAT WILLIE • 1928 • Disney Walt, Iwerks Ub • ANS • USA
STEAMBOATS ON RIVER SEINE see **BATEAU-MOUCHE SUR LA SEINE** • 1896
STEAMER ENTERING THE HARBOUR OF JERSEY see **ENTREE D'UN PAQUEBOT PORT DE JERSEY** • 1899
STEAMING • 1984 • Losey Joseph • UKN
STEAMROLLER AND THE VIOLIN, THE see **KATOK I SKRIPKA** • 1961
STECKBRIEF Z 48 see **GEHETZTE MENSCHEN** • 1932
STED AT VAERE, ET • 1960 • Haxthausen Tork • DNM • SOMEWHERE TO GO
STEEL • 1913 • *Eclair* • USA
STEEL • 1936 • Nigh William • USA
STEEL • 1944 • Riley Ronald H. • DCS • UKN
STEEL • 1950 • Huisken Joop • DOC • GDR
STEEL • 1969 • Peries Lester James • SHT • SLN
STEEL • 1970 • Weisbrich Les • ANS • USA
STEEL • 1971 • Zahariev Edward • DOC • BUL
STEEL • 1980 • Carver Steve • USA • LOOK DOWN AND DIE ○ MEN OF STEEL
STEEL see **ACCIAIO** • 1933
STEEL see **STAL** • 1940
STEEL see **STAL** • 1959
STEEL see **LOHA** • 1990
STEEL AGAINST THE SKY • 1942 • Sutherland A. Edward • USA • DANGEROUSLY THEY LIVE
STEEL ARENA • 1973 • Lester Mark L. • USA
STEEL BAYONET, THE • 1957 • Carreras Michael • UKN
STEEL BRIDGE MEN, THE see **MOSTOSTALOWCY** • 1960
STEEL CAGE, THE • 1954 • Doniger Walter • USA
STEEL CAVALRY see **BUGLE SOUNDS, THE** • 1941
STEEL CLAW, THE • 1961 • Montgomery George • USA
STEEL COWBOY, THE • 1978 • Laidman Harvey • TVM • USA
STEEL DAWN • 1987 • Hool Lance • USA
STEEL DOOR, THE see **DEMIR KAPI** • 1967
STEEL FIST, THE • 1952 • Barry Wesley E. • USA
STEEL-FISTED TRIO, THE see **DEMIR YUMRUKLU UCLER** • 1967
STEEL HEARTS • 1917 • McRae Henry • SHT • USA
STEEL HEARTS see **STALOWE SERCA** • 1948
STEEL HELMET, THE • 1951 • Fuller Samuel • USA
STEEL HIGHWAY see **OTHER MEN'S WOMEN** • 1931
STEEL JUNGLE, THE • 1956 • Doniger Walter • USA • I DIED A THOUSAND TIMES
STEEL JUNGLE, THE see **VIOLENT ROAD** • 1958
STEEL KEY, THE • 1953 • Baker Robert S. • UKN
STEEL KING, THE • 1919 • Apfel Oscar • USA
STEEL KINGS see **SHVEDSKI KRALE** • 1968
STEEL KING'S LAST WISH, THE see **MORKE PUNKT, DET** • 1913
STEEL LADY, THE • 1953 • Dupont E. A. • USA • TREASURE OF KALIFA (UKN) ○ SECRET OF THE SAHARA
STEEL MADE IN BULGARIA • 1954 • Kovachev Hristo • DOC • BUL
STEEL MAGNOLIAS • 1989 • Ross Herbert • USA
STEEL MONSTER, THE see **MOST DANGEROUS MAN ALIVE, THE** • 1961
STEEL PLANET see **PLANETA ACERO** • 1972
STEEL PREFERRED • 1926 • Hogan James P. • USA • ENDURING FLAME, THE
STEEL ROLLING MILL, A • 1915 • Sennett Mack • DOC • USA
STEEL TOWN • 1952 • Sherman George • USA
STEEL TOWN see **ZOCELENI** • 1950
STEEL TRAIL, THE • 1923 • Duncan William • SRL • USA
STEEL TRAP, THE • 1952 • Stone Andrew L. • USA
STEEL WORKERS, THE • 1937 • *Lantz Walter (P)* • ANS • USA
STEEL WREATH see **MONGO'S BACK IN TOWN** • 1971
STEEL-WRIST see **CELIK BILEK** • 1967
STEELE JUSTICE • 1987 • Boris Robert • USA
STEELE OF THE ROYAL MOUNTED • 1925 • Smith David • USA
STEELHEART • 1921 • Duncan William • USA
STEELMAN FROM OUTER SPACE, THE see **SUPAH JAIYANTO** • 1956
STEELTOWN • 1943 • Van Dyke Willard • DOC • USA
STEELTOWN • 1967 • Koenig Wolf, Tasker Rex • CND
STEELTOWN STAR • 1976 • Zaritsky John • MTV • CND
STEELYARD BLUES • 1973 • Myerson Alan • USA • FINAL CRASH, THE
STEEP HILLS see **KRUTYE GORKI** • 1956

STEEP PATH, THE see **STRAMNATA PATEKA** • 1961
STEEPLE-CHASE, THE • 1933 • Gillett Burt • ANS • USA
STEEPLE JACKS • 1951 • Rasinski Connie • ANS • USA
STEEPLEJACKS, THE • 1914 • Nash Percy? • UKN
STEERING MY OWN DESTINY see **SAM SOBIE STEREM** • 1971
STEFAN LUCHIAN • 1981 • Margineanu Nicolae • RMN
STEFAN STARZYNSKI, MAYOR OF WARSAW see **DO KRWI OSTATNIEJ** • 1978
STEFANIA (USA) see **STEPHANIA** • 1967
STEFANIE • 1958 • von Baky Josef • FRG
STEFANIE IN RIO • 1960 • Bernhardt Curtis • FRG • STEPHANIE IN RIO (USA)
STEFEK BURCZYMUCHA • 1958 • Nehrebecki Wladyslaw • ANS • PLN • STEFEK THE GRUMBLER
STEFEK THE GRUMBLER see **STEFEK BURCZYMUCHA** • 1958
STEH ICH IN FINSTERER MITTERNACHT • 1927 • Mack Max • FRG
STEIG AUS DEINEM LUFTBALLON • 1985 • Liebenberg J. A. • AUS • GET OUT YOUR BALLOON
STEIN SONG, THE • 1930 • Fleischer Dave • ANS • USA
STEIN UNTER STEINEN • 1916 • Basch Felix • FRG
STEINACH-FILM, POPULARE FASSUNG, DER • 1922 • Kaufmann Nicholas, Thomalla Curt • FRG
STEINACHS FORSCHUNGEN, WISSENSCHAFTLICHE FASSUNG • 1920 • Kaufmann Nicholas, Thomalla Curt • FRG
STEINE GIBT'S -DIE GIBT'S GAR NICHT • 1968 • Schraps Rudolf • GDR • THERE ARE STONES -WHICH DON'T EXIST
STEINE GOTTIN, DIE see **GEHEIMNIS DES HOHEN FALKEN, DAS** • 1950
STEINER -DAS EISERNE KREUZ see **CROSS OF IRON** • 1977
STEINER, DAS EISERNE KRUZ II see **BREAKTHROUGH** • 1978
STEINERNE REITER, DER • 1923 • Wendhausen Fritz • FRG • STONE RIDER, THE
STEINREICHER MANN, EIN • 1932 • Sekely Steve • FRG
STEINZEITBALLADE • 1961 • Kirsten Ralf • GDR
STELA • 1990 • Krelja Petar • YGS • STELLA
STELINHA • 1989 • Faria Miguel • BRZ
STELLA • 1921 • Collins Edwin J. • UKN
STELLA • 1943 • Perojo Benito • ARG
STELLA • 1950 • Binyon Claude • USA
STELLA • 1955 • Cacoyannis Michael • GRC
STELLA • 1983 • Heynemann Laurent • FRN
STELLA • 1989 • Erman John • USA
STELLA see **STELA** • 1990
STELLA DA FALLA • 1972 • Savoldelli Reta Andrea, Sandoz Jacques • SWT
STELLA DALLAS • 1925 • King Henry • USA
STELLA DALLAS • 1937 • Vidor King • USA
STELLA DEL CINEMA, LA • 1931 • Almirante Mario • ITL
STELLA DEL MARE • 1939 • D'Errico Corrado • ITL • VELE DIPINTE
STELLA DELL'INDIA, LA (ITL) see **STAR OF INDIA** • 1954
STELLA I ORLOFI • 1987 • Thorleifsdottir Thorhildur • ICL • ICELANDIC SHOCK STATION, THE
STELLA MARIS • 1918 • Neilan Marshall • USA
STELLA MARIS • 1925 • Brabin Charles J. • USA
STELLA MARIS see **POUR UN SOIR** • 1931
STELLA POLARIS see **GREAT WHITE NORTH, THE** • 1928
STELLA'S CRIME see **ZBRODNIA STELLI** • 1969
STELLVERTRETER, DER • 1918 • *Reicher Ernst* • FRG
STEM VAN HET WATER, DE • 1966 • Haanstra Bert • DOC • NTH • VOICE OF THE WATER, THE
STEMMING I APRIL • 1947 • Henning-Jensen Astrid, Henning-Jensen Bjarne • DNM • IMPRESSIONS OF APRIL
STEN STENSSON COMES BACK see **STEN STENSSON KOMMER TILLBAKA** • 1963
STEN STENSSON COMES TO TOWN see **STEN STENSSON KOMMER TILL STAN** • 1945
STEN STENSSON KOMMER TILL STAN • 1945 • Frisk Ragnar • SWD • STEN STENSSON COMES TO TOWN
STEN STENSSON KOMMER TILLBAKA • 1963 • Larsson Borje • SWD • STEN STENSSON COMES BACK
STEN STENSSON STEEN FRAN ESLOV • 1924 • Ellis Elis • SWD • STEN STENSSON STEEN FROM ESLOV
STEN STENSSON STEEN FRAN ESLOV PA NYA AVENTYR • 1932 • Ellis Elis, Hellstrom Gosta • SWD • STEN STENSSON STEEN FROM ELSOV ON NEW ADVENTURES
STEN STENSSON STEEN FROM ELSOV ON NEW ADVENTURES see **STEN STENSSON STEEN FRAN ESLOV PA NYA AVENTYR** • 1932
STEN STENSSON STEEN FROM ESLOV see **STEN STENSSON STEEN FRAN ESLOV** • 1924
STENALDERMANNEN • 1919 • Brunius Pauline • SHT • SWD
STENANSIKTET • 1973 • Halldoff Jan • SWD • STONE FACE
STENATA • 1957 • Novak Ivo • CZC • PUPPIES
STENKA RAZIN • 1908 • Romashkov Vladimir • USS
STENOGRAPHER, THE • 1914 • Miller Ashley • USA
STENOGRAPHER WANTED • 1912 • *Vitagraph* • USA
STENOGRAPHER WANTED • 1912 • *Kalem* • USA
STENOGRAPHER'S TROUBLES • 1913 • Thompson Frederick A. • USA
STEP • 1978 • Bondarchuk Sergei • USS • STEPPES, THE ○ STYEP ○ STEPPE, THE
STEP ACROSS THE BORDER • 1989 • Humbert Nicolas, Penzel Werner • DOC • SWT
STEP BROTHERS, THE • 1913 • Taylor William D.? • USA
STEP BROTHERS, THE • 1915 • *Santa Barbara* • USA
STEP BY STEP • 1946 • Rosen Phil • USA
STEP BY STEP • 1976 • Shahal Randa • SHT • LBN
STEP BY STEP see **SCHRITT FUR SCHRITT** • 1960
STEP DOWN TO TERROR • 1958 • Keller Harry • USA • SILENT STRANGER, THE (UKN)
STEP DOWN TO TERROR (UKN) see **SILENT STRANGER, THE** • 1924
STEP FORWARD • 1922 • *Sennett Mack (P)* • SHT • USA
STEP LIGHTLY • 1925 • Taurog Norman • SHT • USA
STEP LIVELY • 1917 • Roach Hal • SHT • USA
STEP LIVELY • 1944 • Whelan Tim • USA
STEP LIVELY, JEEVES! • 1937 • Forde Eugene J. • USA
STEP-MOTHER • 1979 • Samanishvili • USS
STEP-MOTHER, THE • 1910 • *Kalem* • USA
STEP-MOTHER, THE see **UVEY ANA** • 1967
STEP-MOTHER SAMANISHVILI • 1927 • Mardzhanishvili Kote • USS
STEP ON IT! • 1922 • Conway Jack • USA
STEP ON IT • 1931 • Fleischer Dave • ANS • USA
STEP ON IT • 1936 • Ray Bernard B. • USA
STEP OUT OF LINE, A • 1970 • McEveety Bernard • TVM • USA
STEP RIGHT UP • 1930 • Meins Gus • SHT • USA
STEPAN KHALTURIN • 1925 • Ivanovsky Alexander • USS
STEPAN RAZIN • 1939 • Preobrazhenskaya Olga • USS
STEPCHILD • 1947 • Flood James • USA
STEPCHILD see **NASANU NAKA** • 1932
STEPCHILDREN (USA) see **CHUZHIE DETI** • 1959
STEPDAUGHTER, THE • 1910 • *Lubin* • USA
STEPDAUGHTER, THE • 1911 • *Yankee* • USA
STEPEN RISKA see **STEPIEN RISKA** • 1969
STEPFATHER see **BEAU-PERE** • 1981
STEPFATHER, THE • 1987 • Ruben Joseph • USA
STEPFATHER II • 1989 • Burr Jeff • USA
STEPFORD CHILDREN, THE • 1987 • Levi Alan J. • TVM • USA
STEPFORD WIVES, THE • 1975 • Forbes Bryan • USA
STEPHANE GRAPPELLY AND HIS QUINTET • 1948 • Shepherd Horace • SHT • UKN
STEPHANE MALLARME • 1960 • Lods Jean • DCS • FRN
STEPHANE, UNA MOGLIE INFEDELE (ITL) see **FEMME INFIDELE, LA** • 1968
STEPHANIA • 1967 • Dalianidis Ioannis • GRC • STEFANIA (USA)
STEPHANIE IN RIO (USA) see **STEFANIE IN RIO** • 1960
STEPHANIE RECTO-VERSO • 1978 • Barny Michel • FRN
STEPHANY • 1972 • Keenan Haydn • SHT • ASL
STEPHEN FOSTER • 1926 • Fitzpatrick James A. • USA
STEPHEN KING'S CAT'S EYE see **CAT'S EYE** • 1985
STEPHEN KING'S GRAVEYARD SHIFT • 1990 • Singleton Ralph S. • USA
STEPHEN KING'S NIGHT SHIFT COLLECTION • 1986 • Darabont Frank, Schiro Jeffrey C., Greco James • USA • NIGHTSHIFT
STEPHEN KING'S SILVER BULLET see **SILVER BULLET** • 1985
STEPHEN STEPS OUT • 1923 • Henabery Joseph • USA
STEPHEN, THE KING see **ISTVAN, A KIRALY** • 1984
STEPHENICE ZA NEBO • 1984 • Pavlovic Miroslav • YGS • STAIRWAY TO HEAVEN
STEPIEN RISKA • 1969 • Averbach Ilya • USS • DEGREE OF RISK ○ RISK, THE ○ STEPEN RISKA
STEPMOTHER • 1985 • SAF
STEPMOTHER, THE • 1910 • *Selig* • USA
STEPMOTHER, THE • 1911 • *Thanhouser* • USA
STEPMOTHER, THE • 1912 • Dwan Allan • USA
STEPMOTHER, THE • 1914 • Salter Harry • USA
STEPMOTHER, THE • 1972 • Avedis Howard • USA
STEPMOTHER, THE see **FEDRA** • 1956
STEPPA, LA • 1962 • Lattuada Alberto • ITL • STEPPE, LA (FRN) ○ STEPPE, THE
STEPPE, THE see **STEPPA, LA** • 1962
STEPPE, THE see **STEP** • 1978
STEPPE, LA (FRN) see **STEPPA, LA** • 1962
STEPPE PEOPLE • 1986 • Vazov Yanoush • BUL
STEPPENWOLF • 1974 • Haines Fred • USA, SWT
STEPPES, THE see **STEP** • 1978
STEPPIN' IN SOCIETY • 1945 • Esway Alexander • USA
STEPPIN' OUT • 1925 • Strayer Frank • USA • IF BUSINESS INTERFERES..?
STEPPIN' OUT • 1979 • Hobbs Lyndall • DCS • UKN
STEPPING ALONG • 1926 • Hines Charles • USA
STEPPING FAST • 1923 • Franz Joseph J. • USA • MODERN MONTE CRISTO, A
STEPPING HIGH • 1928 • Glennon Bert • USA
STEPPING IN SOCIETY see **DOUGHNUTS AND SOCIETY** • 1936
STEPPING INTO SOCIETY (UKN) see **DOUGHNUTS AND SOCIETY** • 1936
STEPPING LIVELY • 1924 • Horne James W. • USA
STEPPING OUT • 1917 • *Belasco Jay* • USA
STEPPING OUT • 1919 • Niblo Fred • USA
STEPPING OUT • 1923 • Roach Hal • SHT • USA
STEPPING OUT • 1929 • Doane Warren, Foster Lewis R. • SHT • USA
STEPPING OUT • 1931 • Reisner Charles F. • USA
STEPPING OUT • 1980 • Noonan Chris • DOC • ASL
STEPPING OUT see **SLINGREVALSEN** • 1981
STEPPING SISTERS • 1932 • Felix Seymour • USA
STEPPING SOME • 1918 • Lyons Eddie, Moran Lee • SHT • USA
STEPPING STONE, THE • 1916 • Barker Reginald • USA
STEPPING STONE TO HAPPINESS • 1901 • *Swan Soap* • UKN
STEPPING STONES • 1931 • Benstead Geoffrey • UKN
STEPPING STONES • 1932 • *Mintz Charles (P)* • ANS • USA
STEPPING TOES • 1938 • Baxter John • UKN
STEPPING WESTWARD • 1915 • *Larkin George* • USA
STEPS • 1972 • Hirschfield Lenny • USA
STEPS, THE see **SCHODY** • 1964
STEPS IN SEX see **SEI NO KAIDAN** • 1968
STEPS IN THE FOG see **KORACI KROZ MAGLE** • 1967
STEPS OF AGE, THE • 1951 • Maddow Ben • DOC • USA
STEPS ON THE BALLET • 1948 • Mathieson Muir • UKN
STEPS TO SOMEWHERE • 1917 • Windom Lawrence C. • SHT • USA
STEPS TO THE MOON see **PASI SPRE LUNA** • 1963
STEPS TOWARDS THE MOON see **PASI SPRE LUNA** • 1963
STEPSISTERS, THE • 1911 • Golden Joseph A. • USA
STEPSON, THE • 1913 • *Nestor* • USA
STEPTOE AND SON • 1972 • Owen Cliff • UKN • STEPTOE AND SON: THE FEATURE
STEPTOE AND SON RIDE AGAIN • 1973 • Sykes Peter • UKN
STEPTOE AND SON: THE FEATURE see **STEPTOE AND SON** • 1972
STEPUTAT & CO • 1938 • Boese Carl • FRG
STERBEN WERD' ICH, UM ZU LEBEN (GUSTAV MAHLER) • 1987 • Lesowsky Wolfgang • AUS • I'LL DIE TO LIVE - GUSTAV MAHLER
STERBENDE ERDE, DIE • 1924 • *Munchener Film-Ind. Heinrich Muller* • FRG
STERBENDE MODELL, DAS • 1918 • Gad Urban • FRG
STERBENDE SALOME, DIE • 1920 • Seitz Franz • FRG
STERBENDE VOLKER 1 • 1922 • Reinert Robert • FRG, ITL • POPULI MORITURI (ITL) ○ HEIMAT IN NOT
STERBENDE VOLKER 2 • 1922 • Reinert Robert • FRG • BRENNENDES MEER
STERBENDEN PERLEN, DIE • 1917 • Meinert Rudolf • FRG
STERBEWALZER • 1914 • *Richter Paul* • AUS
STEREO • 1969 • Cronenberg David • CND
STEREO • 1970 • Carle Gilles • DCS • CND
STEREO FILM • 1953 • Fischinger Oskar • ANM • FRG
STERILE CUCKOO, THE • 1969 • Pakula Alan J. • USA • POOKIE (UKN)
STERIMATOR VESEVO • 1920 • *Gallone Carmine* • ITL
STERLING'S RIVAL ROMEO • 1934 • Horne James W. • SHT • USA
STERMINATORE DEI BARBARI, LO • 1964 • Regnoli Piero • ITL
STERN, DER • Decroix Charles • FRG
STERN DESTINY, A • 1912 • *Pathe* • USA
STERN FALLT VOM HIMMEL, EIN • 1934 • Neufeld Max • AUS
STERN FIEL VOM HIMMEL, EIN • 1961 • von Cziffra Geza • FRG, AUS
STERN PAPA • 1912 • Sennett Mack • USA
STERN VON AFRIKA, DER • 1957 • Weidenmann Alfred • FRG
STERN VON BETHLEHEM, DER • 1922 • Reiniger Lotte • ANS • FRG • STAR OF BETHLEHEM, THE
STERN VON DAMASKUS, DER • 1920 • Curtiz Michael • AUS
STERN VON RIO • 1940 • Anton Karl • FRG
STERN VON RIO • 1955 • Neumann Kurt • FRG
STERN VON SANTA CLARA, DER • 1958 • Jacobs Werner • FRG
STERN VON VALENCIA • 1933 • Zeisler Alfred • FRG
STERN YOUNG MAN, THE see **STROGI YUNOSHA** • 1936
STERNBERG -SHOOTING STAR • 1988 • List Niki • AUS
STERNE • 1959 • Wolf Konrad • GDR, BUL • STARS
STERNE LUGEN NICHT, DIE • 1950 • von Alten Jurgen • FRG
STERNE OHNE HIMMEL • 1981 • Runze Ottokar • FRG • STAR WITHOUT SKY
STERNE UBER COLOMBO • 1953 • Harlan Veit • FRG
STERNSTEIN MANOR, THE see **STERNSTEINHOF** • 1976
STERNSTEINHOF • 1976 • Geissendorfer Hans W. • FRG • STERNSTEIN MANOR, THE
STERREN STRACEN OVERAL • 1953 • Rutten Gerard • NTH
STESSO MARE STESSA SPIAGGIA • 1984 • Pann Angelo • ITL
STET PRIKLYUCHENNI • 1929 • Ptushko Alexander • ANS • USS • 100 ADVENTURES
STEUERLOS • 1924 • Righelli Gennaro • FRG
STEUERMANN HOLK • 1920 • Wolff Ludwig • FRG
STEVE DONOGHUE SERIES • 1926 • West Walter • SER • UKN
STEVE HILL'S AWAKENING • 1914 • Dow Marcus • USA
STEVE MILLER BAND • 1968 • Van Meter Ben • DCS • USA
STEVE O'GRADY'S CHANCE • 1914 • Finley Ned • USA
STEVE, SAMSON AND DELILAH • 1975 • Hawkes Steve • USA
STEVEDORES, THE • 1937 • *Lantz Walter (P)* • ANS • USA
STEVEN'S SWEET SISTERS • 1916 • *Yorke Jay C.* • USA
STEVE'S STEADFAST STEED • 1915 • Mitchell Bruce • USA
STEVIE • 1978 • Enders Robert • UKN
STEVNEMOTE MED GLEMTE AR • 1957 • Mjoen Jon Lennart • NRW • RENDEZVOUS WITH FORGOTTEN YEARS
STEWARD OF SILTALA, THE see **SILTALAN PEHTOORI** • 1933
STEWARDESS, THE • 1968 • Uskov Valeri, Krasnopolsky Vladimir • USS
STEWARDESS SCHOOL • 1986 • Blancato Ken • USA
STEWARDESSEN, DIE • 1972 • Dietrich Erwin C. • FRG • SWINGING STEWARDESSES, THE (UKN) ○ SWINGIN' STEWARDESSES ○ YOUNG SEDUCERS, THE
STEWARDESSES, THE • 1969 • Silliman Alf Jr. • USA • AIRLINE STEWARDESS
STEWED, FRIED AND BOILED • 1929 • Parrott James • SHT • USA
STEWED MISSIONARY • 1904 • Collins Alf? • UKN
STHREE JANMA • 1967 • Prakash Rao K. S. • IND
STI ZOI MAZI SOU PONESA • 1968 • Galatis Dimitris • GRC • LIFE OF GRIEF, A
STICENIK • 1966 • Slijepcevic Vladan • YGS • PROTEGE, THE
STICI PRE SVITANJA BEGSTVO SA ROBIJE • 1979 • Djordjevic Aleksandar • YGS • ESCAPING FROM PRISON
STICK • 1985 • Reynolds Burt • USA
STICK, THE • 1988 • Roodt Darrell • SAF
STICK AND BONE see **PALO Y HUESO** • 1968
STICK 'EM UP DARLINGS (UKN) see **COLPO IN CANNA** • 1975
STICK IT IN YOUR EAR • 1972 • Lewis Herschell G. • USA
STICK THE MONSTER ON THE FIRST PAGE see **SBATTI IL MOSTRO IN PRIMA PAGINA** • 1972
STICK TO YOUR GUNS • 1941 • Selander Lesley • USA
STICK TO YOUR STORY • 1926 • Brown Harry J. • USA
STICK UP, THE • 1978 • Bloom Jeffrey • UKN • MUD
STICKIN' TOGETHER • 1978 • Thorpe Jerry • TVM • USA
STICKPHAST • 1911 • Wilson Frank? • UKN
STICKPIN, THE • 1933 • Hiscott Leslie • UKN
STICKS see **BIT OF KINDLING, A** • 1917
STICKS AND STONES • 1970 • Lopresto Stan • USA
STICKY AFFAIR, A • 1913 • Wilson Frank? • UKN
STICKY AFFAIR, A • 1916 • Stull Walter, Burns Bobby • SHT • USA
STICKY BICYCLE, THE • 1907 • Fitzhamon Lewin • UKN
STICKY FINGERS • 1917 • Davis James • SHT • USA
STICKY FINGERS • 1987 • Adams Catlin • USA
STICKY MY FINGERS -FLEET MY FEET • Hancock John • SHT • USA
STIELKE, HEINZ AGED FIFTEEN • 1987 • Kann Michael • GDR
STIER VON OLIVIERA, DER • 1921 • Buchowetzki Dimitri, Schonfelder Erich • FRG
STIER VON SALANDA, DER • 1918 • Guter Johannes • FRG
STIFF • 1988 • Irvin Sam • USA
STIFFS see **WHIFFS** • 1975
STIFFS see **OUT COLD** • 1988
STIGMA • 1958 • Jackson Stanley R. • DOC • CND
STIGMA • 1972 • Durston David E. • USA
STIGMA • 1981 • Tassios Pavlos • GRC
STIGMA • 1983 • Barbash Uri • ISR
STIGMA, THE • 1912 • *Dowlan William* • USA
STIGMA, THE • 1913 • *Bushman Francis X.* • USA

STIGMA, OR THE BRAND OF SHAME • 1914 • *Kb* • USA
STIGMATE, LE • 1925 • Champreux Maurice, Feuillade Louis • SRL • FRN
STIGMATIZED ONE, THE see **GEZEICHNETEN, DIE** • 1921
STILETTO • 1969 • Kowalski Bernard • USA
STILETTO see **COLD STEEL** • 1987
STILETTO, THE • 1914 • *Foote Courtenay* • USA
STILIGA AUGUSTA • 1946 • Ahrle Elof • SWD • HANDSOME AUGUSTA
STILL • 1970 • Gehr Ernie • SHT • USA
STILL A BROTHER • Greaves William • USA
STILL ALARM, THE • 1903 • Porter Edwin S. • USA
STILL ALARM, THE • 1911 • *Selig* • USA
STILL ALARM, THE • 1918 • Campbell Colin • USA
STILL ALARM, THE • 1926 • Laemmle Edward • USA
STILL CRAZY LIKE A FOX • 1987 • Krasny Paul • TVM • USA
STILL IMAGE • 1976 • Dunford Mike • UKN
STILL IN ONE PIECE ANYWAY • 1975 • MacKay Bruce • MTV • CND
STILL LIFE • 1966 • Baillie Bruce • SHT • USA
STILL LIFE • 1987 • Bruce James • USA
STILL LIFE see **STILLEBEN** • 1969
STILL LIFE see **TABIATE BIDJAN** • 1978
STILL OF THE NIGHT (UKN) see **STAB** • 1981
STILL ON SUNSET MOUNTAIN, THE • 1915 • *Domino* • USA
STILL POINT see **TREVE** • 1983
STILL POINT, THE • 1986 • Boyd-Anderson Barbara • ASL
STILL SMALL VOICE, THE • 1915 • Gaskill Charles L. • USA
STILL SMOKIN' see **CHEECH & CHONG'S STILL SMOKIN'** • 1983
STILL THE BEAVER • 1982 • Stern Steven Hilliard • TVM • USA
STILL VOICE, THE • 1913 • *Drew Sidney* • USA
STILL VOICE, THE • 1916 • Wilson Ben • SHT • USA
STILL WATERS • 1915 • Dawley J. Searle • USA
STILL WATERS RUN DEEP • 1916 • Paul Fred • UKN
STILL WE LIVE see **DOKKOI IKITEIRU** • 1951
STILL WORTHY OF THE NAME • 1908 • Chart Jack • UKN
STILLA FLIRT, EN • 1934 • Molander Gustaf • SWD • QUIET AFFAIR, A
STILLE BETRUGER • 1989 • Lottaz Beat • SWT, FRG • SLEEPY BETRAYERS
STILLE DAGE I CLICHY • 1970 • Thorsen Jens Jorgen • DNM • QUIET DAYS IN CLICHY (USA) ○ NOT SO QUIET DAYS
STILLE LIEFDE, EEN • 1977 • van Nie Rene • NTH • SILENT LOVE, A
STILLE OCEAAN, DE • 1983 • Sinke Digna • NTH
STILLE OZEAN, DER • 1983 • Schwarzenberger Xaver • AUS, FRG • PACIFIC OCEAN, THE
STILLEBEN • 1969 • Lenica Jan • ANS • FRG • STILL LIFE
STILLNESS, THE • 1972 • Golubovic Predrag • SHT • YGS
STILLWATCH • 1987 • Holcomb Rod • TVM • USA
STILTE ROND CHRISTINE M., DE • 1982 • Gorris Marleen • NTH • SILENCE OF CHRISTINE M., THE ○ QUESTION OF SILENCE, A
STILTS, THE see **ZANCOS, LOS** • 1984
STIMME, DIE • 1920 • Gartner Adolf • FRG
STIMME AUS DEM AETHER, DIE • 1939 • Paulsen Harald • FRG
STIMME DER LIEBE, DIE • 1933 • Janson Victor • FRG
STIMME DER SEHNSUCHT, DIE • 1956 • Engel Thomas • FRG
STIMME DES ANDEREN, DIE see **UNTER DEN TAUSAND LATERNEN** • 1952
STIMME DES BLUTES, DIE • 1915 • Schmidthassler Walter • FRG
STIMME DES GEWISSENS, DIE • 1920 • Fleck Jacob, Fleck Luise • AUS
STIMME DES HERZENS • 1942 • Meyer Johannes • FRG
STIMME DES HERZENS, DIE • 1924 • Schwarz Hanns • FRG
STIMME DES HERZENS, DIE • 1937 • Martin Karl Heinz • FRG • SANGER IHRER HOHEIT, DER
STIMME DES TOTEN, DIE • 1916 • Neuss Alwin • FRG
STIMMES DES BLUTES • 1937 • Gallone Carmine • FRG • BLOOD BOND
STIMULANTIA • 1965 • Abramson Hans, Bergman Ingmar, Danielsson Tage, Donner Jorn, Molander Gustaf, Sjoman Vilgot • SWD
STIMULATING MRS. BARTON, THE • 1920 • Drew Sidney Mrs. • SHT • USA
STIN • 1960 • Lehky Vladimir • ANS • CZC • SHADOW, THE
STIN ANAPAFTIKI MERIA • 1981 • Spetsiotis Takis • GRC • ON THE COSY SIDE
STIN VE SVETLE • 1928 • Kokeisl • CZC • SHADOW IN LIGHT
STINE OG DRENGENE • 1969 • Karlsson Finn • DNM • DIARY OF A TEENAGER
STING, THE • 1973 • Hill George Roy • USA
STING II, THE • 1983 • Kagan Jeremy Paul • USA
STING IN THE TAIL, A • 1989 • Schlusser Eugene • ASL
STING OF CONSCIENCE, THE • 1916 • Cochrane George • SHT • USA
STING OF DEATH • 1990 • Oguri Kohei • JPN
STING OF DEATH, THE • 1921 • Paul Fred • UKN
STING OF DEATH, THE • 1966 • Grefe William • USA
STING OF DEATH, THE see **SHA-JEN-CHE SZU** • 1981
STING OF IT, THE • 1915 • Bartlett Charles • USA
STING OF STINGS, THE • 1929 • Parrott James • SHT • USA
STING OF THE LASH, THE • 1921 • King Henry • USA • GREATER LOVE, THE
STING OF THE SCORPION, THE • 1923 • Hatton Richard • USA
STING OF THE WEST, THE see **TEDEUM** • 1972
STING OF VICTORY, THE • 1916 • Haydon J. Charles • USA • LITTLE MUSKETEER, THE
STINGAREE • 1915 • Horne James W. • SRL • USA
STINGAREE • 1916 • *Hornung E. W.* • ASL
STINGAREE • 1934 • Wellman William A. • USA
STINGER STUNG, THE • 1916 • *Humphrey Orral* • USA
STINGER STUNG, THE • 1917 • Curtis Allen • SHT • USA
STINGER STUNG, OR JAKE AND MIKE IN THE OIL FIELDS, THE • 1913 • *Joker* • USA
STINGIEST MAN IN TOWN, THE • 1956 • Petrie Daniel • ANM • USA
STINGRAY • 1978 • Taylor Richard • USA • ABIGAIL WANTED
STINGRAY • 1985 • Colla Richard A. • TVM • USA
STINGRAY: INVADERS FROM THE DEEP • 1964 • Elliott David, Kelly John, Saunders Desmond • ANM • UKN • INVADERS FROM THE DEEP
STINJACKE CIZME see **UND DAMIT TANZEN SIE NOCH IMMER** • 1987
STINKER • 1925 • Shimazu Yasujiro • JPN
STINSEN PA LYCKAS • 1943 • Lingheim Emil A. • SWD • STATION MASTER AT LYCKAS, THE
STINY HORKEHO LETA • 1977 • Vlacil Frantisek • CZC • SHADOWS OF THE HOT SUMMER ○ SHADOWS OF A HOT SUMMER
STIPS • 1951 • Froelich Carl • FRG
STIR • 1980 • Wallace Stephen • ASL
STIR CRAZY • 1980 • Poitier Sidney • USA
STIR PATRA • 1970 • Patrea Purnendu • IND • LETTER FROM THE WIFE
STIRRING DAYS IN OLD VIRGINIA • 1909 • *Selig* • USA
STIRRUP BROTHERS, THE • 1914 • *Johnston J. W.* • USA
STIRRUP CUP SENSATION, THE • 1924 • West Walter • UKN
STITCH IN TIME, A • 1908 • Collins Alf? • UKN
STITCH IN TIME, A • 1919 • Ince Ralph • USA
STITCH IN TIME, A • 1925 • Butler Alexander • UKN
STITCH IN TIME, A • 1963 • Asher Robert • UKN
STITCHES • 1985 • Holcomb Rod (Smithee Alan) • USA
STJAALNE ANSIGT, DET • 1914 • Holger-Madsen • DNM • MISSING ADMIRALTY PLANS, THE ○ ANSIGTET
STJARNSMALL I FRUKOSTKLUBBEN • 1950 • Bernhard Gosta • SWD • KNOCKOUT AT THE "BREAKFAST CLUB" ○ GALOPPERANDE OSTEN, DEN
STJENKA RASIN • 1936 • Volkov Alexander • FRG • WOLGA-WOLGA
STJERNERNE OG VANDBAERERNE • 1974 • Leth Jorgen • DOC • DNM • STARS AND WATER CARRIERS
STO DNEI POSLE DETSTVA • 1975 • Soloviev Sergei • USS • HUNDRED DAYS AFTER CHILDHOOD, A ○ ONE HUNDRED DAYS AFTER CHILDHOOD
STO GOVORIT MOC? • 1924 • Room Abram • USS • WHAT SAY MOC?
STO JE RABNICKI SANJET? • 1959 • Makavejev Dusan • DOC • YGS • WHAT IS A WORKER'S COUNCIL?
STO KATOFLI TIS MIRAS • 1967 • Nomikos George • FRG • ON THE THRESHOLD OF FATE
STO KONI DO STU BRZEGOW • 1978 • Kuzminski Zbigniew • PLN • HUNDRED HORSES TOWARDS A HUNDRED BANKS, A
STO PIECDZIESIAT NA GODZINE • 1971 • Jakubowska Wanda • PLN • AT HUNDRED MILES PER HOUR
STOCK CAR • 1955 • Rilla Wolf • UKN
STOCK CAR see **A TOUT CASSER** • 1953
STOCK-CARS see **A TOUT CASSER** • 1953
STOCK EXCHANGE TRAGEDY, A see **ROMANCE OF WALL STREET, A** • 1911
STOCK IS AS GOOD AS MONEY • 1913 • Martinek H. O.? • UKN
STOCKADE • 1971 • Pomeranz Hans • ASL
STOCKBROKER, THE • 1898 • *Paul R. W.* • UKN
STOCKBROKER, THE see **FOR SIN KARLEKS SKULL** • 1914
STOCKBROKER'S CLERK, THE • 1922 • Ridgwell George • UKN
STOCKHOLM • 1937 • Fitzpatrick James • SHT • USA
STOCKHOLM • 1977 • Zetterling Mai • MTV • CND
STOCKHOLM AT NIGHT • 1989 • Bergenstrahle Marie-Louise De Geer • SWD
STOCKHOLM ET SON ARCHIPEL • 1953 • Sassy Jean-Paul • SHT • FRN
STOCKHOLM STORY see **MANNISKOR I STAD** • 1946
STOCKHOLMSDAMERNAS ALSKLING • 1911 • Hoffman-Uddgren Anna • SWD • DARLING OF THE STOCKHOLM LADIES
STOCKHOLMSFRESTELSER • 1911 • Hoffman-Uddgren Anna • SWD • TEMPTATIONS OF STOCKHOLM
STOCKHOLMSSOMMAR • 1969 • Odulf Tor-Ivan • SWD • SUMMER IN STOCKHOLM
STOCKINGS • 1914 • *Warner'S Features* • USA
STOCKS AND BLONDES • 1928 • Murphy Dudley • USA • BLONDES AND BONDS (UKN)
STOCKS AND BLONDES • 1984 • Greenstands Arthur • USA
STOET VAN REUZEN, EEN • 1966 • Burcksen J., Herblot R. • SHT • NTH
STOFF AUS DEM DIE TRAUME SIND, DER • 1972 • Vohrer Alfred • FRG
STOGGLES' CHRISTMAS DINNER • 1913 • Kellino W. P. • UKN
STOGIES • 1987 • Davidson Martin • USA
STOJ • 1965 • Roos Jorgen • DOC • DNM
STOJAN MUTIKAS • 1954 • Hanzekovic Fedor • YGS
STOKER, THE • 1932 • Franklin Chester M. • USA
STOKER, THE • 1935 • Pearce A. Leslie • UKN • SHOVEL UP A BIT MORE COAL
STOLEN ACTRESS, THE • 1917 • Stonehouse Ruth • SHT • USA
STOLEN AFFECTIONS (USA) see **REVOLTEE, LA** • 1947
STOLEN AIRLINER, THE • 1955 • Sharp Don • UKN
STOLEN AIRSHIP, THE see **UKRADENA VZDUCHOLOD** • 1966
STOLEN AIRSHIP PLANS, THE • 1912 • Kinder Stuart • UKN • REGIMENTAL PET, THE
STOLEN ANTHURIUM, THE • 1915 • *Chamberlain Riley* • USA
STOLEN ASSIGNMENT • 1955 • Fisher Terence • UKN
STOLEN BALLOON, THE see **UKRADENA VZDUCHOLOD** • 1966
STOLEN BICYCLE, THE • 1906 • *Walturdaw* • UKN
STOLEN BIRTHRIGHT, THE • 1914 • Gasnier Louis J. • USA
STOLEN BOOKING, THE • 1916 • Miller Rube • SHT • USA
STOLEN BRIDE, THE • 1906 • Stow Percy • UKN
STOLEN BRIDE, THE • 1913 • O'Sullivan Tony • USA
STOLEN BRIDE, THE • 1927 • Korda Alexander • USA
STOLEN BRIDLE, THE • 1907 • Fitzhamon Lewin • UKN
STOLEN BY GYPSIES • 1905 • Porter Edwin S. • USA
STOLEN BY INDIANS • 1910 • *Champion* • USA
STOLEN CASE, THE • 1915 • Fahrney Milton • USA
STOLEN CHILD, THE • 1923 • *Roubert Matty* • USA
STOLEN CLAIM, THE • 1910 • Porter Edwin S. • USA
STOLEN CLAIM, THE • 1911 • *Vitagraph* • USA
STOLEN CLAIM, THE • 1913 • Melies Gaston • USA
STOLEN CLOTHES, THE • 1909 • Fitzhamon Lewin? • UKN
STOLEN CODE, THE • 1914 • *Reliance* • USA
STOLEN DEATH see **VARASTETTU KUOLEMA** • 1938
STOLEN DESIRE, THE see **NUSUMARETA YOKUJO** • 1958
STOLEN DIRIGIBLE, THE see **UKRADENA VZDUCHOLOD** • 1966
STOLEN DRINK, THE see **QUARRELSOME ANGLERS, THE** • 1898
STOLEN DUCK, THE • 1908 • Mottershaw Frank • UKN
STOLEN FACE • 1952 • Fisher Terence • UKN
STOLEN FACE, THE • 1913 • Eagle Oscar • USA
STOLEN FATHER, THE • 1910 • *Edison* • USA
STOLEN FAVOURITE, THE • 1909 • Stow Percy • UKN
STOLEN FAVOURITE, THE • 1919 • SAF
STOLEN FAVOURITE, THE • 1926 • West Walter • UKN
STOLEN FEAST, THE see **EFTERMIDDAGSGOESTEN** • 1963
STOLEN FORMULA, THE • 1914 • *Melies* • USA
STOLEN FORTUNE, THE • 1910 • *Essanay* • USA
STOLEN FRONTIER, THE see **ULOUPENA HRANICE** • 1947
STOLEN FRUIT • 1906 • Jeapes Harold? • UKN
STOLEN GLORY • 1912 • Sennett Mack • USA
STOLEN GLORY • 1914 • *Powers* • USA
STOLEN GOODS • 1915 • Melford George • USA
STOLEN GOODS • 1924 • McCarey Leo • SHT • USA
STOLEN GREY, THE • 1911 • Melies Gaston • USA
STOLEN GUY, THE • 1905 • Fitzhamon Lewin • UKN
STOLEN HARMONY • 1935 • Werker Alfred L. • USA
STOLEN HEART, THE • 1913 • *Selig* • USA
STOLEN HEART, THE see **GESTOHLENE HERZ, DAS** • 1934
STOLEN HEARTS AND NICKELS • 1915 • *Ritchie Billie* • USA
STOLEN HEAVEN • 1931 • Abbott George • USA
STOLEN HEAVEN • 1938 • Stone Andrew L. • USA
STOLEN HEIR, THE • 1910 • Coleby A. E. • UKN
STOLEN HEIRLOOMS, THE • 1915 • Raymond Charles • UKN
STOLEN HOLIDAY • 1937 • Curtiz Michael • USA
STOLEN HONOR • 1918 • Stanton Richard • USA
STOLEN HONORS • 1916 • *Fuller Mary* • SHT • USA
STOLEN HONOURS • 1914 • Evans Joe • UKN
STOLEN HORSE, THE • 1911 • *Champion* • USA
STOLEN HOURS • 1918 • Vale Travers • USA
STOLEN HOURS, THE • 1963 • Petrie Daniel • UKN • SUMMER FLIGHT
STOLEN IDENTITY • 1953 • Fritsch Gunther V. • USA, AUS
STOLEN IDENTITY, A • 1913 • *Kalem* • USA
STOLEN IDENTITY, A • 1913 • August Edwin • *Powers* • USA
STOLEN IDOL, THE • 1913 • *Leonard Robert* • USA
STOLEN INHERITANCE, THE • 1913 • *Patheplay* • USA
STOLEN INVENTION, THE • 1910 • *Thanhouser* • USA
STOLEN INVENTION, THE • 1912 • *Kalem* • USA
STOLEN INVENTION, THE • 1915 • Montgomery Frank E.? • USA
STOLEN JAIL, THE • 1916 • Ellis Robert • SHT • USA
STOLEN JEWELS, THE • 1908 • Griffith D. W. • USA
STOLEN JEWELS, THE • 1915 • *Gordon Harris* • USA
STOLEN JEWELS, THE • 1916 • *Sunset* • USA
STOLEN JEWELS, THE • 1921 • Gordon Edward R. • UKN
STOLEN JOOLS, THE • 1931 • McGann William • USA • SLIPPERY PEARLS, THE (UKN)
STOLEN KEYHOLE, THE • 1918 • Santell Alfred • SHT • USA
STOLEN KISS • 1920 • Webb Kenneth • USA
STOLEN KISSES • 1929 • Enright Ray • USA
STOLEN KISSES see **BAISERS VOLES, LES** • 1968
STOLEN LETTER, THE • 1912 • *Reliance* • USA
STOLEN LETTERS, THE • 1911 • Fitzhamon Lewin? • UKN
STOLEN LIFE • 1939 • Czinner Paul • UKN
STOLEN LIFE, A • 1946 • Bernhardt Curtis • USA
STOLEN LOAF, THE • 1913 • O'Sullivan Tony • USA
STOLEN LOVE • 1928 • Shores Lynn • USA
STOLEN LOVE see **NUSUMARETA KOI** • 1951
STOLEN LOVE, THE • 1913 • *Imp* • USA
STOLEN MAGIC • 1915 • Sennett Mack • USA
STOLEN MASTER, THE • 1916 • Byrne Jack • SHT • USA
STOLEN MASTERPIECE, THE • 1914 • Martinek H. O. • UKN
STOLEN MASTERPIECE, THE • 1914 • Pollard Harry? • USA
STOLEN MEDICINE • 1967 • Okamoto Tadashige • ANS • JPN
STOLEN MELODY, THE • 1913 • Parker Lem B. • USA
STOLEN MELODY, THE • 1916 • Ayres Sydney • SHT • USA
STOLEN MELODY, THE (UKN) see **RAGTIME** • 1927
STOLEN MOCCASSINS, THE • 1913 • Duncan William • USA
STOLEN MODELS, THE • 1913 • Williams C. Jay • USA
STOLEN MOMENTS • 1920 • Vincent James • USA
STOLEN NECKLACE, THE • 1911 • *Nestor* • USA
STOLEN NECKLACE, THE • 1912 • Rains Fred • UKN
STOLEN NECKLACE, THE • 1933 • Hiscott Leslie • UKN
STOLEN NICKEL, THE • 1912 • Merwin Bannister • USA
STOLEN NOSE, THE see **GESTOHLENE NASE, DIE** • 1955
STOLEN ORDERS • 1918 • Knoles Harley, Kelson George • USA
STOLEN ORE, THE • 1914 • *Reliance* • USA
STOLEN PAPERS, THE • 1912 • Treville Georges • UKN
STOLEN PARADISE • 1941 • Gasnier Louis J. • USA
STOLEN PARADISE, THE • 1917 • Knoles Harley • USA
STOLEN PICTURE • 1912 • Wilson Frank? • UKN
STOLEN PIG, THE • 1904 • Stow Percy • UKN
STOLEN PLANS, THE • 1913 • Brabin Charles J. • USA, UKN
STOLEN PLANS, THE • 1952 • Hill James • UKN
STOLEN PLANS OR THE BOY DETECTIVE • 1908 • Brooke Van Dyke • USA
STOLEN PLAY, THE • 1911 • *Reliance* • USA
STOLEN PLAY, THE • 1917 • Harvey Harry • USA
STOLEN PLEASURE see **TADARE** • 1962
STOLEN PLEASURES • 1927 • Rosen Phil • USA
STOLEN PLUMAGE • 1916 • Ellis Robert • SHT • USA
STOLEN PRINCESS, THE • 1909 • *Tiger* • USA
STOLEN PUPPY, THE • 1904 • Fitzhamon Lewin • UKN
STOLEN PUPS, THE • 1911 • Wilson Frank? • UKN
STOLEN PURSE, THE • 1905 • Stow Percy • UKN
STOLEN PURSE, THE • 1913 • Sennett Mack • USA
STOLEN RADIUM, THE • 1914 • Adolfi John G. • USA
STOLEN RANCH, THE • 1926 • Wyler William • USA
STOLEN REMBRANDT, THE • 1914 • *Holmes Helen* • USA
STOLEN RING, THE • 1912 • *Johnson Arthur* • USA
STOLEN RUBY, THE • 1915 • Vignola Robert G. • USA
STOLEN SACRIFICE, THE • 1916 • Morgan Sidney • UKN
STOLEN SECRETS • 1924 • Cummings Irving • USA
STOLEN SUN, THE • 1945 • ANS • USS

STOLEN SWEETS • 1934 • Thorpe Richard • USA
STOLEN SYMPHONY, THE • 1912 • *Johnson Arthur* • USA
STOLEN TAPESTRIES, THE • 1913 • *Kalem* • USA
STOLEN TIME • 1955 • Deane Charles • UKN • BLONDE BLACKMAILER (USA)
STOLEN TIME (UKN) see **RETURN OF THE DURANGO KID** • 1945
STOLEN TRAIN, THE • 1971 • Yanchev Vladimir • BUL, USS
STOLEN TREATY, THE • 1913 • O'Sullivan Tony • USA
STOLEN TREATY, THE • 1917 • Scardon Paul • USA
STOLEN TRIBUTE TO THE KING, THE • 1913 • *Melies* • USA
STOLEN TRIUMPH, THE • 1916 • Thompson David • USA
STOLEN VIOLIN, THE • 1912 • Collins Edwin J. • UKN
STOLEN VOICE, THE • 1915 • *Warwick Robert* • USA
STOLEN VOICE, THE • 1917 • Crane Frank H.? • SHT • USA
STOLEN WALTZ, A see **STULEN VALS, EN** • 1932
STOLEN WEALTH (UKN) see **BLAZING SIX SHOOTERS** • 1940
STOLEN WILL, THE • 1915 • *Grandin Ethel* • USA
STOLEN WIRELESS, THE • 1909 • Melies Gaston • FRN
STOLEN WOMAN, THE • 1913 • *Cummings Irving* • USA
STOLEN YACHT, THE • 1914 • Powell Paul • USA
STOLZ DER 3 KOMPAGNIE, DER • 1931 • Sauer Fred • FRG
STOLZ DER FIRMA, DER • 1914 • Wilhelm Carl • FRG
STOLZ DER KOMPAGNIE, DER see **PERLE DES REGIMENTS, DIE** • 1925
STOLZ WEHT DIE FLAGGE SCHWARZ-WEISS-ROT • 1916 • Dessauer Siegfried • FRG
STOLZE FRAUEN see **HALLIG HOOGE** • 1923
STOLZE SCHWEIGEN, DAS • 1925 • Eriksen Erich • FRG
STOLZENFELS AM RHEIN • 1927 • Lowenbein Richard • FRG
STOMPIN' FOR MILI • 1955 • Mili Gjon • SHT • USA
STONE • 1974 • Harbutt Sandy • ASL
STONE • 1979 • Allen Corey • TVM • USA
STONE, THE • 1938 • Newman Widgey R. • UKN
STONE AGE • 1931 • Lantz Walter, Nolan William • ANS • USA
STONE AGE, THE • 1917 • Hartman Ferris • USA • HER CAVE MAN
STONE AGE, THE • 1922 • Parrott Charles • SHT • USA
STONE AGE, THE • 1940 • Fleischer Dave • ASS • USA
STONE AGE, THE see **EDAD DE LA PIEDRA, LA** • 1965
STONE AGE ADVENTURE, A • 1915 • Glackens L. M. • ANS • USA
STONE AGE ERROR • 1932 • Foster John, Davis Mannie • ANS • USA
STONE AGE ROMANCE, A • 1929 • *Van Beuren* • ANS • USA
STONE AGE ROMEOS • 1955 • White Jules • SHT • USA
STONE AGE STUNTS • 1930 • Foster John • ANS • USA
STONE AGE TO ATOM AGE • 1961 • Blais Roger • DOC • USA • DE L'AGE DE PIERRE A L'AGE ATOMIQUE
STONE AND LIFE see **KAMEN A ZIVOT** • 1966
STONE AUNTIE, THE see **KAMMENA TETKA** • 1960
STONE BATTLE see **ISHI GASSEN** • 1955
STONE BOY, THE • 1984 • Cain Christopher • USA
STONE COLD DEAD • 1979 • Mendeluk George • CND • SIN SNIPER, THE ○ POINT TWO TWO
STONE CROSS, THE see **KAMENNY KRYEST** • 1968
STONE DANCER • 1968 • Cantrill Arthur, Cantrill Corinne • DOC • ASL
STONE FACE see **STENANSIKTET** • 1973
STONE FLOWER, THE see **KAMENNI TSVETOK** • 1946
STONE FOX • 1987 • Hart Harvey • TVM • USA
STONE GARDEN, THE see **BAGHE SANGUI** • 1975
STONE GUEST, THE see **KAMENNY GOST** • 1967
STONE HAMMER, THE • 1916 • *Supreme* • USA
STONE HEART, THE • 1915 • Collins John H. • USA
STONE IN THE MOUTH see **SASSO IN BOCCA, IL** • 1970
STONE IN THE ROAD, THE • 1914 • Weber Lois, Smalley Phillips • USA
STONE INTO STEEL • 1961 • Dickson Paul • DOC • UKN
STONE KILLER, THE • 1973 • Winner Michael • USA • COMPLETE STATE OF DEATH
STONE OF MAZARIN, THE • 1923 • Ridgwell George • UKN • MAZARIN STONE, THE
STONE OF SILVER CREEK • 1935 • Grinde Nick • USA
STONE ON ROADSIDE, A see **ROBO NO ISHI** • 1938
STONE ON STONE see **BATO SA BATO** • 1967
STONE PILLOW • 1985 • Schaefer George • TVM • USA
STONE RIDER, THE see **STEINERNE REITER, DER** • 1923
STONE SONATA • 1962 • D'Avino Carmen • ANS • USA
STONE THE WOMAN • 1913 • *Mitchell Doris* • USA
STONE, TIME, SONG • 1960 • Lotyanu Emil • SHT • USS
STONE UPON STONE • 1972 • Vabalas Raimondas • USS
STONE WEDDING, THE see **NUNTA DE PIATRA** • 1972
STONE WILL ALSO TURN INTO FRUIT, THE see **KALLUM KANIYAGUM** • 1968
STONE YEARS see **PETRINA CHRONIA** • 1985
STONER • 1974 • Huang Feng • HKG
STONEROLLER'S VILLAGE, THE see **KIVENPYORITTAJAN KULA** • 1979
STONES see **HORROR AT 37000 FEET** • 1972
STONES CRY OUT, THE see **LET THEM LIVE!** • 1937
STONES FOR IBARRA • 1988 • Gold Jack • TVM • USA
STONES OF DEATH • 1988 • Bogle James • ASL • KADAICHA: THE DEATH STONE ○ KADAICHA
STONESTREET: WHO KILLED THE CENTERFOLD MODEL? • 1976 • Mayberry Russ • TVM • USA
STONEWALL JACKSON'S WAY • 1914 • Jones Edgar • USA
STONEY, THE ONE AND ONLY • 1984 • SAF
STONING, A • 1988 • Elikann Larry • USA
STONING, THE • 1915 • Brabin Charles J. • USA
STONY GROUND • 1938 • Alderson John • UKN
STONY ISLAND see **MY MAIN MAN FROM STONY ISLAND** • 1980
STONY LION • 1987 • Jozani Massoud Jafari • IRN
STOOGE, THE • 1953 • Taurog Norman • USA
STOOGE FOR A MOUSE • 1950 • Freleng Friz • ANS • USA
STOOGEMANIA • 1985 • Workman Chuck • USA • PARTY STOOGE
STOOL PIGEON • 1928 • Hoffman Renaud • USA • DECOY, THE (UKN)
STOOL PIGEON, THE • 1913 • *Rex* • USA
STOOL PIGEON, THE • 1915 • Chaney Lon • *Victor* • USA
STOOL PIGEON, THE • 1915 • Powell Paul • *Lubin* • USA
STOOL PIGEON, THE see **TIP-OFF, THE** • 1929
STOOL PIGEON'S REVENGE, A • 1915 • Blystone John G. • USA
STOOLIE, THE • 1972 • Avildsen John G. • USA • ROGER THE STOOLIE
STOOPNOCRACY • 1933 • Fleischer Dave • ANS • USA
STOP • Cadinot Jean-Daniel • FRN
STOP • 1957 • Lavoie Richard, Lavoie Hermenegilde • DCS • CND
STOP! • 1968 • Petersen Mark • UKN
STOP • 1970 • Gunn Bill • USA
STOP • 1971 • Beaudin Jean • CND
STOP! • 1976 • Markovic Darko • SHT • YGS
STOP 88 –THE WARNING LIMIT see **PARADA 88 –O LIMITE DE ALERTA** • 1980
STOP AT NOTHING • 1924 • Seeling Charles R. • USA
STOP CADRU LA MASA • 1980 • Pistiner Ada • RMN • SNAPSHOT AROUND THE FAMILY TABLE ○ FREEZE FRAME AT TABLE
STOP CALLING ME BABY! see **MOI, FLEUR BLEUE** • 1977
STOP, CEASE, HESITATE! • 1919 • Santell Alfred • SHT • USA
STOP CRYING EMPOY, STOP CRYING see **TAHAN NO EMPOY, TAHAN** • 1977
STOP DRIVING US CRAZY • 1960 • Ende Mel M. • SHT • USA
STOP EXCHANGE • 1970 • SAF
STOP FLIRTING • 1925 • Sidney Scott • USA
STOP FOR A MOMENT.. AND FEEL THE PAIN • 1972 • Woods Grahame • CND
STOP IT see **AT DERE TORI** • 1980
STOP KIDDING • 1921 • Roach Hal • SHT • USA
STOP LAUGHING THIS IS SERIOUS • 1967 • Power John • DOC • ASL
STOP, LOOK AND HASTEN! • 1954 • Jones Charles M. • ANS • USA
STOP! LOOK! AND LAUGH! • 1961 • White Jules • CMP • USA
STOP –LOOK –AND LISTEN • 1919 • *Lynne Ethel* • SHT • USA
STOP, LOOK AND LISTEN • 1926 • Semon Larry • USA
STOP, LOOK AND LISTEN • 1949 • Donnelly Eddie • ANS • USA
STOP, LOOK AND LOVE • 1939 • Brower Otto • USA
STOP! LUKE! LISTEN! • 1917 • Roach Hal • SHT • USA
STOP MAKING SENSE • 1984 • Demme Jonathan • USA
STOP ME BEFORE I KILL! (USA) see **FULL TREATMENT, THE** • 1961
STOP-OFF IN NEW MEXICO, A • 1915 • Henderson Dell • USA
STOP PRESS COMEDIES • 1920 • Miller Frank • SER • UKN
STOP PRESS GIRL • 1949 • Barry Michael • UKN
STOP THAT BUS! • 1903 • Stow Percy • UKN • HOW THE OLD MAN CAUGHT THE OMNIBUS (USA)
STOP THAT MAN • 1928 • Ross Nat • USA
STOP THAT NOISE • 1930 • Meins Gus • SHT • USA
STOP THAT NOISE • 1935 • Fleischer Dave • ANS • USA
STOP THAT SHIMMIE • 1920 • Lyons Eddie, Moran Lee • SHT • USA
STOP THAT TANK • 1941 • Iwerks Ub • ANS • USA
STOP THAT WEDDING • 1920 • Lyons Eddie, Moran Lee • SHT • USA
STOP THE FIGHT • 1911 • Evans Fred • UKN
STOP THE OLD FOX see **KAGERO EZU** • 1959
STOP THE WORLD I WANT TO GET OFF • 1966 • Saville Philip • UKN
STOP THE WORLD, I WANT TO GET OFF see **SAMMY STOPS THE WORLD** • 1979
STOP THIEF! • 1901 • Williamson James • UKN
STOP THIEF! • 1913 • Calvert Charles? • UKN
STOP THIEF • 1915 • Fitzmaurice George • USA
STOP THIEF • 1920 • Beaumont Harry • USA
STOP! THINK OF SOMETHING ELSE see **STOPP! TANK PA NAGOT ANNAT** • 1944
STOP TRAIN 349 (USA) see **TRAIN DE BERLIN EST ARRETE** • 1964
STOP YOUR KIDDING • 1917 • *Victor* • SHT • USA
STOP YOUR TICKLING JOCK • 1907 • Gilbert Arthur • UKN
STOP, YOU'RE KILLING ME • 1952 • Del Ruth Roy • USA
STOPFORBUD • 1963 • Leth A. J., Poulsen O. J., Thorsen Jens Jorgen • SHT • DNM
STOPOVER • 1976 • Auzins Igor • MTV • ASL
STOPOVER FOREVER • 1964 • Goode Frederic • UKN
STOPOVER TOKYO • 1957 • Breen Richard L. • USA
STOPP! TANK PA NAGOT ANNAT • 1944 • Ohberg Ake • SWD • STOP! THINK OF SOMETHING ELSE
STOPPED CLOCK, THE • 1913 • O'Sullivan Tony • SHT • USA
STOPPING THE LIMITED • 1914 • *Essanay* • USA
STOPPING THE SHOW • 1932 • Fleischer Dave • ANS • USA
STOPWATCH, THE • 1970 • Esadze Rezo • USS
STOPY • 1960 • Jires Jaromil • CZC • FOOTPRINTS
STOPY NA SITNE • 1968 • Bahna Vladimir • CZC • TRACES ON THE MOUNTAIN SITNO ○ TRACES ON THE SITNO
STORA AVENTYRET, DET • 1953 • Sucksdorff Arne • SWD • GREAT ADVENTURE, THE
STORA FAMNEN • 1940 • Edgren Gustaf • SWD • BIG HUG, A
STORA HOPARE LANE AND HEAVEN see **STORA HOPAREGRAND OCH HIMMELRIKET** • 1949
STORA HOPAREGRAND OCH HIMMELRIKET • 1949 • Folke Gosta • SWD • STORA HOPARE LANE AND HEAVEN
STORA KARLEKEN, DEN • 1938 • Henrikson Anders • SWD • GREAT LOVE, THE
STORA SKRALLEN • 1943 • Jerring Nils • SWD • BIG CRASH
STORCH HAT UNS GETRAUT, DER see **ABENTEUER DER THEA ROLAND, DAS** • 1932
STORCHS TREIKT, DER • 1931 • Emo E. W. • FRG • SIEGFRIED DER MATROSE
STORE, THE see **FLOORWALKER, THE** • 1916
STORE AMATOREN, DEN • 1958 • Ekman Hasse • SWD • GREAT AMATEUR, THE
STORE ATTRAKTION, DEN see **DODSSPRINGET TIL HEST FRA CIRKUSKUPLEN** • 1912
STORE FALD, DET • 1911 • *Holger-Madsen* • DNM • MALSTROMMEN
STORE FLYVER, DEN see **AEDAL DAAD** • 1911
STORE FORVENTNINGER • 1921 • Sandberg Anders W. • DNM • GREAT EXPECTATIONS
STORE HJERTE, DET • 1924 • Blom August • DNM • SIDE LIGHTS OF THE SAWDUST RING ○ LIGHTS FROM CIRCUS LIFE
STORE KEEPER see **COUNTER JUMPER, THE** • 1922
STORE KLAUS OG LILLE KLAUS • 1913 • *Christensen Benjamin* • DNM
STORE MAGT, DEN • 1924 • Blom August • DNM
STORE MIDDAG, DEN • 1914 • Blom August • DNM • GUESTLESS DINNER PARTY, THE
STORIA, LA • 1986 • Comencini Luigi • ITL • HISTORY
STORIA D'AMORE • 1987 • Maselli Francesco • ITL
STORIA D'AMORE, UNA • 1942 • Camerini Mario • ITL
STORIA D'AMORE, UNA • 1969 • Lupo Michele • ITL, FRN • LOVE ME, BABY, LOVE ME (UKN)
STORIA DE FRATELLI E DE CORTELLI • 1973 • Amendola Mario • ITL
STORIA DE UN QUARTIERE • 1950 • Zurlini Valerio • DCS • ITL
STORIA DEI TREDICI • 1917 • Gallone Carmine • ITL
STORIA DEI TREDICI, LA • 1917 • D'Ambra Lucio • ITL
STORIA DEL FORNARETTO DI VENEZIA, LA • 1953 • Solito Giacinto • ITL
STORIA DELLA DAMA DAL VENTAGLIO BIANCO, LA • 1919 • D'Ambra Lucio • ITL
STORIA DI CINQUE CITTA • 1949 • Marcellini Romolo • ITL
STORIA DI CINQUE CITTA (ITL) see **TALE OF FIVE CITIES, A** • 1951
STORIA DI FIFA E DI COLTELLO • 1972 • Amendola Mario • ITL
STORIA DI KARATE, PUGNI E FAGIOLI • 1973 • Ricci Tonino • ITL, SPN
STORIA DI NOTTE, UNA • 1964 • Petrini Luigi • ITL
STORIA DI PIERA • 1983 • Ferreri Marco • ITL • STORY OF PIERA, THE (USA) ○ PIERA'S STORY
STORIA DI PRETE, LADRI E PECCATRICI see **VANGELO SECONDO SAN FREDIANO, IL** • 1978
STORIA DI RAGAZZI E DI RAGAZZE • 1989 • Avati Pupi • ITL • STORY OF BOYS AND GIRLS (UKN)
STORIA DI SAN MICHELE, LA see **AXEL MUNTHE, DER ARZT VON SAN MICHELE** • 1962
STORIA DI UN CRIMINALE (ITL) see **HO!** • 1968
STORIA DI UN ELEFANTE • 1954 • Quilici Folco • SHT • ITL
STORIA DI UN PECCATO • 1918 • Gallone Carmine • ITL
STORIA DI UN PIERROT • 1913 • Negroni Baldassare • ITL • STORY OF A PIERROT, THE
STORIA DI UNA CANAGLIA see **VOYOU, LE** • 1970
STORIA DI UNA CAPINERA • 1943 • Righelli Gennaro • ITL
STORIA DI UNA DONNA, LA • 1920 • Palermi Amleto • ITL • WOMAN'S STORY, A
STORIA DI UNA DONNA (ITL) see **STORY OF A WOMAN** • 1970
STORIA DI UNA MINORENNE • 1956 • Costa Piero • ITL
STORIA DI UNA MONACA DI CLAUSURA • 1973 • Paolella Domenico • ITL • DIARY OF A CLOISTERED NUN (USA)
STORIA LOMBARDA, UNA see **MONACA DI MONZA, LA** • 1969
STORIA MILANESE, UNA • 1962 • Visconti Eriprando • ITL • STORY IN MILAN, A ○ MILANESE STORY, A
STORIA MODERNA –L'APE REGINA, UNA • 1963 • Ferreri Marco • ITL, FRN • LIT CONJUGAL, LE (FRN) ○ CONJUGAL BED, THE (USA) ○ QUEEN BEE ○ APE REGINA, L'
STORIA SENZA PAROLE • 1979 • Proietti Biagio • ITL
STORIE D'AMORE PROIBITE (ITL) see **SECRET DU CHEVALIER D'EON, LE** • 1960
STORIE DELLE INVENZIONI, LA • 1959 • Bozzetto Bruno • ITL • HISTORY OF INVENTIONS, THE ○ STORY OF INVENTIONS, THE
STORIE DI ORDINARIA FOLLIA • 1981 • Ferreri Marco • ITL, FRN • CONTE DE LA FOLIE ORDINAIRE (FRN) ○ TALES OF ORDINARY MADNESS
STORIE DI VITA E MALAVITA • 1975 • Lizzani Carlo • ITL • PROSTITUTION RACKET, THE ○ PROSTITUTE, THE
STORIE SCELLERATE • 1973 • Citti Sergio • ITL, FRN • BAWDY TALES (USA)
STORIE STRAORDINARIE see **HISTOIRES EXTRAORDINAIRES** • 1968
STORIE SULLA SABBIA • 1963 • Fellini Riccardo • ITL
STORIES ABOUT A DOGGY AND A PUSSY see **CAT AND DOG** • 1950-54
STORIES ABOUT LENIN see **RASSKAZY O LENINE** • 1957
STORIES FOR ADULTS see **CUENTOS PARA MAYORES** • 1963
STORIES FROM A FLYING TRUNK • 1980 • Edzard Christine • UKN
STORIES FROM THE CHUQUIAGO see **HISTORIAS DEL CHUQUIAGO** • 1976
STORIES FROM TIERRA SECA see **RELATOS DE TIERRA SECA** • 1979
STORIES OF A BEEHIVE see **ISTORIES MIAS KERITRAS** • 1981
STORIES OF HUMAN INTEREST see **SANMEN KIJI** • 1931
STORIES OF POOR LOVERS see **CRONACHE DI POVERI AMANTI** • 1954
STORIES OF THAT NIGHT see **GESCHICHTEN JENER NACHT** • 1967
STORK • 1971 • Burstall Tim • ASL
STORK AND THE FOX, THE • 1951 • Wasilewski Zenon • ANM • PLN
STORK BITES MAN • 1947 • Endfield Cy • USA
STORK CALIPH, THE see **GOLYAKALIFA, A** • 1917
STORK CLUB, THE • 1945 • Walker Hal • USA
STORK EXCHANGE, THE • 1927 • USA
STORK MARKET, THE • 1931 • *Mintz Charles (P)* • ANS • USA
STORK MARKET, THE • 1949 • Kneitel Seymour • ANS • USA
STORK NAKED • 1955 • Freleng Friz • ANS • USA
STORK PAYS OFF, THE • 1941 • Landers Lew • USA • BACHELORS' BABIES
STORK RAVING MAD • 1958 • Kneitel Seymour • ANS • USA
STORK SOCIETY, THE (USA) see **NACHT MIT HINDERNISSEN, EINE** • 1937
STORK TAKES A HOLIDAY, THE • 1937 • *Mintz Charles (P)* • ANS • USA
STORK TALK • 1962 • Forlong Michael • UKN
STORK'S HOLIDAY • 1943 • Gordon George • ANS • USA
STORK'S MISTAKE, THE • 1942 • Donnelly Eddie • ANS • USA

STORK'S NEST, THE • 1915 • Nigh William • USA • EMMY OF STORK'S NEST
STORM • 1943 • Burnford Paul • USA
STORM • 1959 • Jin Shan • CHN
STORM • 1976 • Levchuk Timofey • USS
STORM • 1986 • Winning David • CND
STORM see **SHTORM** • 1957
STORM see **FENGBAO** • 1959
STORM see **FORTUNA** • 1959
STORM see **FORTUNA** • 1959
STORM see **AANDHI** • 1989
STORM, THE • 1911 • *Imp* • USA
STORM, THE • 1915 • Jaccard Jacques • USA
STORM, THE • 1916 • Reicher Frank • USA
STORM, THE • 1922 • Barker Reginald • USA
STORM, THE • 1925 • Fleischer Dave • ANS • USA
STORM, THE • 1930 • Wyler William • USA
STORM, THE • 1938 • Young Harold • USA
STORM, THE • 1970 • Cardinal Roger • DOC • CND • AL ASSIFA
STORM, THE • 1979 • Yukol Prince Chatri • THL • YELLOW SKY
STORM, THE see **THIELLA, I** • 1929
STORM, THE see **GROZA** • 1934
STORM, THE see **VIHAR** • 1952
STORM, THE see **ARASHI** • 1956
STORM, THE see **MECAVA** • 1978
STORM AT BATALON see **ITEL A BALATON** • 1932
STORM AT DAYBREAK • 1932 • Boleslawski Richard • USA • STRANGE RHAPSODY
STORM AT SEA, A • 1900 • Porter Edwin S. • USA
STORM AT SEA, THE • 1914 • Vignola Robert G. • USA
STORM BIRD, THE • 1914 • *Maison Edna* • USA
STORM BOY • 1976 • Safran Henri • ASL
STORM BREAKER, THE • 1925 • Sloman Edward • USA • TITANS, THE
STORM CAME AND WENT see **ARASHI KITARI SARU** • 1967
STORM CENTER • 1956 • Taradash Daniel • USA
STORM CLOUD see **BAISAKHI MEGH** • 1981
STORM CLOUDS OF VENUS see **PLANETA BURG** • 1962
STORM CLOUDS OVER HAKONE see **HAKONE FUUNROKU** • 1951
STORM CLOUDS OVER MOUNT HAKONE see **HAKONE FUUNROKU** • 1951
STORM DAUGHTER, THE • 1924 • Archainbaud George • USA • STORM'S DAUGHTER, THE
STORM FEAR • 1956 • Wilde Cornel • USA
STORM GIRL • 1922 • Ford Francis • USA
STORM IN A TEACUP • 1937 • Saville Victor, Dalrymple Ian • UKN
STORM IN A TEACUP, A • 1913 • Buckland Warwick? • UKN
STORM IN JAMAICA see **PASSIONATE SUMMER** • 1956
STORM IN TATRA see **BOURE NAD TATRAMI** • 1932
STORM IN THE HOUSE OF WINDS see **THIELLA STO SPITI TON ANEMON** • 1967
STORM OF KANTO, A see **KANTO MO HIROUGOZANSU** • 1967
STORM OF PASSION see **STURME DER LEIDENSCHAFT** • 1931
STORM OF STRANGERS, A • 1972 • Maddow Ben • DCS • USA
STORM OF YOUTH • 1986 • Tan Han-Chang • TWN
STORM ON THE PLANET see **PLANETA BURG** • 1962
STORM ON THE SILVERY PEAKS see **GINREI NO ONJA** • 1961
STORM OVER AFRICA (UKN) see **ROYAL AFRICAN RIFLES** • 1953
STORM OVER ARABIA see **ARABU NO ARASHI** • 1961
STORM OVER ASIA see **POTOMOK CHINGIS-KHAN** • 1928
STORM OVER BENGAL • 1938 • Salkow Sidney • USA
STORM OVER CEYLON see **TEMPESTA SU CEYLON** • 1963
STORM OVER LISBON • 1944 • Sherman George • USA
STORM OVER MONT BLANC see **STURME UBER DEM MONTBLANC** • 1930
STORM OVER PETRA see **TOUFAN BAR FARASE PETRA** • 1968
STORM OVER POLAND see **POWODZ** • 1947
STORM OVER SKAREN • 1938 • Johansson Ivar • SWD • STORM OVER THE SKERRIES
STORM OVER THE ANDES • 1935 • Cabanne W. Christy • USA
STORM OVER THE BELAYA RIVER see **GROZA NAD BYELOY** • 1968
STORM OVER THE NILE • 1955 • Korda Zoltan, Young Terence • UKN
STORM OVER THE PACIFIC, THE see **TAIHEIYO NO ARASHI** • 1960
STORM OVER THE SKERRIES see **STORM OVER SKAREN** • 1938
STORM OVER TIBET • 1952 • Marton Andrew, Benedek Laslo (U/c) • USA • MASK OF THE HIMALAYAS
STORM OVER TJURO • 1954 • Mattsson Arne • SWD
STORM OVER WYOMING • 1950 • Selander Lesley • USA
STORM PLANET see **PLANETA BURG** • 1962
STORM QUEST • 1988 • Sessa Alejandro • USA • STORMQUEST
STORM RIDER, THE • 1957 • Bernds Edward • USA
STORM RIDERS, THE • 1956 • Bare Richard L. • MTV • USA
STORM SIGNAL • 1966 • Drew Robert L. • USA
STORM WARNING • 1946 • Parker Benjamin R. • SHT • USA
STORM WARNING • 1947 • Burnford Paul • USA
STORM WARNING • 1950 • Heisler Stuart • USA
STORM WITHIN, THE (USA) see **PARENTS TERRIBLES, LES** • 1948
STORM WOMAN, THE • 1917 • Baldwin Ruth Ann • SHT • USA
STORMBRINGER see **DAY OF JUDGEMENT, A** • 1981
STORMENS BARN • 1928 • Niska Adolf • SWD • CHILDREN OF THE STORM
STORMFAGELN • 1914 • Stiller Mauritz • SWD • STORMY PETREL
STORMFLOWER • 1921 • Wynne Bert • UKN
STORMIN' HOME • 1985 • Jameson Jerry • TVM • USA
STORMING OF GALLIPOLI, THE see **HERO OF THE DARDANELLES, A** • 1915
STORMING SQUADRON see **NAGURIKOMI KANTAI** • 1961
STORMING THE TRENCHES • 1916 • *Butterworth Frank* • SHT • USA
STORMQUEST see **STORM QUEST** • 1988
STORMRIDER see **GRANDE DUELLO, IL** • 1973
STORM'S DAUGHTER, THE see **STORM DAUGHTER, THE** • 1924
STORMS OF LIFE see **LIVETS STORME** • 1910
STORMS OF LIFE, THE • 1914 • *Balboa* • USA
STORMSWEPT • 1923 • Thornby Robert T. • USA • WRECKAGE
STORMSWEPT • 1954 • Barnett Ivan • UKN
STORMVARSEL • 1968 • Mossin Ib • DNM • GALE-WARNING
STORMY • 1935 • Landers Lew • USA
STORMY CROSSING • 1958 • Pennington-Richards C. M. • UKN • BLACK TIDE (USA)
STORMY ERA (USA) see **SHOWA NO INOCHI** • 1968
STORMY IS MISUNDERSTOOD • 1916 • Birch Cecil • UKN
STORMY KNIGHT, A • 1917 • Clifton Elmer • USA
STORMY MAN see **ARASHI O YOBU OTOKO** • 1957
STORMY MONDAY • 1988 • Figgis Mike • UKN
STORMY PETREL see **STORMFAGELN** • 1914
STORMY PETRELL, THE • 1919 • *Huff Louise* • USA
STORMY SEA, THE see **TA-FENG LANG** • 1976
STORMY SEAS • 1923 • McGowan J. P. • USA
STORMY SEAS • 1932 • *Iwerks Ub (P)* • ANS • USA
STORMY THE THOROUGHBRED see **STORMY, THE THOROUGHBRED WITH AN INFERIORITY COMPLEX** • 1953
STORMY, THE THOROUGHBRED WITH AN INFERIORITY COMPLEX • 1953 • Lansburgh Larry • SHT • USA • STORMY THE THOROUGHBRED
STORMY TRAILS • 1936 • Newfield Sam • USA
STORMY WATERS • 1928 • Lewis Edgar • USA • CAPTAIN OF THE HURRICANE, THE
STORMY WATERS see **OZUSHIO** • 1952
STORMY WATERS (UKN) see **REMORQUES** • 1940
STORMY WEATHER • 1935 • Walls Tom • UKN • GET OUT OF IT ◦ GET OUT
STORMY WEATHER • 1943 • Stone Andrew L. • USA
STORMY WINE • 1976 • Vorlicek Vaclav • CZC
STORSSTROEMBROEN • 1949 • Dreyer Carl T. • SHT • DNM • STORSTROM BRIDGE ◦ BRIDGE OF STORSTROM, THE ◦ STORSTROMS BROEN
STORSTADSFAROR • 1918 • Gothson Manne • SWD • DANGERS OF A BIG CITY
STORSTE I VERDEN, DET • 1919 • Holger-Madsen • DNM • JANES GODE VEN ◦ GREATEST IN THE WORLD, THE ◦ LOVE THAT LIVES, THE
STORSTE KAERLIGHED, DEN • 1914 • Blom August • DNM • MODERS KAERLIGHED, EN ◦ ESCAPED THE LAW, BUT..
STORSTE SPILLET, DET • 1967 • Bohwim Knut • NRW • BIGGEST GAME, THE
STORSTROM BRIDGE see **STORSSTROEMBROEN** • 1949
STORSTROMS BROEN see **STORSSTROEMBROEN** • 1949
STORTEBEKER • 1920 • Wendt Ernst • FRG
STORTJUVEN • 1979 • Hellner Ingegerd • SWD • MASTER-THIEF, THE ◦ BIG THIEF, THE
STORY see **KATHA** • 1982
STORY ABOUT A FACTORY see **PRICA O FABRICI** • 1948
STORY ABOUT AN UNKNOWN ACTOR • 1976 • Zarkhi Alexander • USS
STORY ABOUT BREADMAKING IN THE YEAR 1255 A.D., A • 1948 • Verrall Robert A. • ANM • CND
STORY ABOUT CAT AND DOG • 1954 • Hofman Eduard • CMP • CZC
STORY ABOUT OMAR KHAPTSOKO, A see **TALE ABOUT UMAR KHAPTSOKO, THE** • 1932
STORY ABOUT SANTA CLAUS, A • Anderson Monika • ANM • GDR
STORY ABOUT THE DOTS AND THE LINES, THE • Stecker Alan • SHT • USA
STORY ABOUT THE ROAD see **OPOWIESC O DRODZE** • 1958
STORY BOOKS • 1963 • Boyadgieva Lada • DOC • BUL
STORY FOR ECHIGO, A see **ECHIGO TSUTSUISHI OYASHIRAZU** • 1964
STORY FROM A HOUSING ESTATE see **PANELSTORY** • 1978
STORY FROM ABASHIRI, A see **ABASHIRI BANGAICHI: FUBUKI NO TOSO** • 1967
STORY FROM CHIKAMATSU, A (USA) see **CHIKAMATSU MONOGATARI** • 1954
STORY FROM ECHIGO, A see **ECHIGO TSUTSUISHI OYASHIRAZU** • 1964
STORY FROM LIFE, A • 1916 • Tucker George Loane • SHT • USA
STORY IN MILAN, A see **STORIA MILANESE, UNA** • 1962
STORY IN THE ROCKS see **PALEONTHOLOGIE** • 1959
STORY OF 8 GIRLS, THE • 1965 • Mahon Barry • USA • STORY OF 8 MODELS, THE
STORY OF 8 MODELS, THE see **STORY OF 8 GIRLS, THE** • 1965
STORY OF 100 GHOSTS see **YOKAI HYAKU MONOGATARI** • 1968
STORY OF A BATTLE see **HISTORIA DE UNA BATALLA** • 1962
STORY OF A BELOVED WIFE see **AISAI MONOGATARI** • 1951
STORY OF A CHEAT, THE (USA) see **ROMAN D'UN TRICHEUR, LE** • 1936
STORY OF A COLLIERY DISASTER, THE • 1904 • Hough Harold • UKN
STORY OF A CRIME • 1962 • Hitruck Fedor • ANM • USS
STORY OF A CROSS, THE • 1914 • *B & C* • UKN
STORY OF A DAY, THE see **BIR GUNUN HIKAYYESI** • 1982
STORY OF A DETACHMENT COMMANDO • NKR
STORY OF A DIVE BOMBER, THE see **KHRONIKA PIKIRUYUSHCHEVO BOMBARDIROVSHCHIKA** • 1968
STORY OF A DIVORCE, THE see **PAYMENT ON DEMAND** • 1951
STORY OF A DOUBLE BASS, THE see **ROMAN S BASON** • 1949
STORY OF A DOWNFALL, THE see **JULIA, JULIA -HISTORIEN OM ET FALL** • 1981
STORY OF A DRAGON, THE see **BAJKA O SMOKU** • 1962
STORY OF A FACTORY see **PRICA O FABRICI** • 1948
STORY OF A FIGHTER PLANE, THE see **HISTORIA JEDNOGO MYSLIWCA** • 1958
STORY OF A FOREST GIANT • 1954 • Zguridi Alexander • DOC • USS
STORY OF A GIRL see **BINT MIN EL BANAT** • 1968
STORY OF A GIRL, THE • 1960 • Chiaureli Mikhail • USS
STORY OF A GLOVE, THE see **STORY OF THE GLOVE, THE** • 1915
STORY OF A GOLDEN FISH see **HISTOIRE D'UN POISSON ROUGE** • 1959
STORY OF A HEART, THE • 1975 • Khrabrovitsky Daniil • USS
STORY OF A JUNKIE • 1987 • Kowalski Lech • USA
STORY OF A KISS, THE • 1912 • *Eclair* • USA
STORY OF A LITTLE GIRL WHO WANTED TO BE • 1919 • Starevitch Ladislas • ANM • FRN
STORY OF A LOVE AFFAIR (USA) see **CRONACA DI UN AMORE** • 1950
STORY OF A LOVE STORY, THE (USA) see **QUESTO IMPOSSIBILE OGGETTO** • 1973
STORY OF A MADMAN see **FOLIE DU DOCTEUR TUBE, LA** • 1916
STORY OF A MAN see **HISTORIEN OM EN MAND** • 1944
STORY OF A MAN AND HIS WOMAN, THE see **FREUDUS SEXUALIS** • 1965
STORY OF A MODERN MOTHER, THE • 1907 • Stow Percy • UKN
STORY OF A MOMENT see **CRONICA DE UN INSTANTE** • 1980
STORY OF A MOSQUITO, THE see **HOW A MOSQUITO OPERATES** • 1910
STORY OF A MOTHER see **HISTORIEN OM EN MODER** • 1979
STORY OF A MOUNTAIN, THE see **BIR DAG MASALI** • 1967
STORY OF A NOBODY, THE • 1930 • Gercon Jo, Louis Hershell • USA
STORY OF A NUN see **SHUNDEINI** • 1958
STORY OF A NURSE, THE • NKR
STORY OF A PENNY, THE see **KRAJCAR TORTENETE, EGY** • 1917
STORY OF A PICTURE, THE • 1909 • Fitzhamon Lewin? • UKN
STORY OF A PIECE OF SLATE, THE • 1904 • Hepworth Cecil M. • UKN
STORY OF A PIERROT, THE see **STORIA DI UN PIERROT** • 1913
STORY OF A POOR YOUNG MAN, THE see **NOVELA DE UN JOVEN POBRE, LA** • 1968
STORY OF A POTTER, THE • 1925 • Flaherty Robert • USA • POTTERY MAKER
STORY OF A PRAYER RUG, THE • 1911 • Porter Edwin S. • USA
STORY OF A PUNCH AND JUDY SHOW, THE • 1915 • Buckland Warwick • UKN
STORY OF A REAL MAN see **POVESTE O NASTOYASHCHEM CHELOVEKE** • 1948
STORY OF A RIVER DOWNTOWN, THE see **KAWA NO ARU SHITAMACHI NO HANASHI** • 1955
STORY OF A ROSE see **ROMAN O RUZI** • 1972
STORY OF A ROSE, THE • 1909 • *Kalem* • USA
STORY OF A SECOND, THE • 1959 • Kollanyi Agoston • HNG
STORY OF A SIN, THE (USA) see **DZIEJE GRZECHU** • 1975
STORY OF A SMALL TOWN, THE see **HSIAO CHENG KU-SHIH** • 1979
STORY OF A SOLITARY ROBLES see **HISTORIA DE UN ROBLE SOLO** • 1982
STORY OF A STORY, THE • 1915 • Browning Tod • USA
STORY OF A STRAY DOG, THE • 1907 • *Walturdaw* • UKN
STORY OF A TEENAGER • 1976 • Coscarelli Don, Mitchell Craig • USA • JIM THE WORLD'S GREATEST
STORY OF A THREE DAY PASS, THE (USA) see **PERMISSION, LA** • 1968
STORY OF A TWIG see **TALE OF THE PINE BOUGH** • 1960
STORY OF A VAMPIRE see **YOEN DOKUFU-DEN HANNYA NO OHYAKU** • 1968
STORY OF A VILLAGE see **OKA OORIE KATHA** • 1977
STORY OF A WALLET, THE • 1912 • *Nestor* • USA
STORY OF A WOMAN • 1970 • Bercovici Leonardo • USA, ITL • STORIA DI UNA DONNA (ITL)
STORY OF A WRITER, THE • 1964 • Sanders Terry • DOC • USA
STORY OF A YOUNG COUPLE see **ROMAN EINER JUNGEN EHE** • 1952
STORY OF ADELE H., THE (USA) see **HISTOIRE D'ADELE H., L'** • 1975
STORY OF ALEXANDER GRAHAM BELL, THE • 1939 • Cummings Irving • USA • MODERN MIRACLE, THE (UKN) ◦ ALEXANDER GRAHAM BELL
STORY OF ALFRED NOBEL, THE • 1939 • Newman Joseph M. • SHT • USA • AM I TO BLAME?
STORY OF AMY ROBSTART, THE • 1922 • Ridgwell George • UKN
STORY OF AN ACHIEVEMENT, THE • 1952 • Dickson Paul • DOC • UKN
STORY OF AN ADVENTURER, NAOMI UEMURA see **UEMURA NAOMI MONOGATARI** • 1985
STORY OF AN ARTIST'S STUDIO SECRETS, THE see **ARTIST'S STUDIO SECRETS** • 1964
STORY OF ANN AKHMATOVA, THE see **LICHNOYE DELO ANNY AKHMATOVOY** • 1989
STORY OF ANYBURG U.S.A., THE • 1957 • Geronimi Clyde • ANS • USA
STORY OF ARMY CRUELTY, A see **RIKUGUN ZANGYAKU MONOGATARI** • 1963
STORY OF ASI, WHO LOVED BUT DID NOT MARRY, THE see **ISTORIA ASI KHYACHINOI, KOTORAYA LYUBILA, DANE VYSHLA ZAMUKH** • 1966
STORY OF BARBARA, THE see **HISTORIEN OM BARBARA** • 1967
STORY OF BARNABAS KOS see **PRIPAD BARNABAS KOS** • 1964
STORY OF BIRTH, THE see **BIRTH OF TRIPLETS** • 1964
STORY OF BOB AND SALLY, THE • 1948 • Kenton Erle C. • USA • BOB AND SALLY ◦ SHOULD PARENTS TELL?
STORY OF BOYS AND GIRLS (UKN) see **STORIA DI RAGAZZI E DI RAGAZZE** • 1989
STORY OF CAMILLA, THE see **LOPERJENTEN** • 1983
STORY OF CAPTAIN SCOTT see **NINETY DEGREES SOUTH** • 1933
STORY OF CHIEF JOSEPH, THE • 1975 • *Walter Prods.* • MXC
STORY OF CHRISTMAS, A see **CONTE DE NOEL, UN** • 1902

STORY OF CHRISTMAS, THE • 1973 • Lambart Evelyn • ANS • CND
STORY OF CHRISTMAS NIGHT, THE see **MAJERAYE SHABE JANVEYE** • 1968
STORY OF CINDERELLA, THE see **SLIPPER AND THE ROSE, THE** • 1976
STORY OF CRIME, THE • 1914 • Williams C. Jay • USA
STORY OF CRUELTY OF YOUTH, A see **SEISHUN ZANKOKU MONOGATARI** • 1960
STORY OF CUPID, THE • 1914 • *Newburg Frank* • USA
STORY OF DAVID, A • 1960 • McNaught Bob • UKN • DAVID THE OUTLAW
STORY OF DAVID, THE • 1976 • Segal Alex, Rich David Lowell • TVM • USA
STORY OF DAVID, THE see **KING DAVID** • 1985
STORY OF DAVID GREIG, THE • 1913 • MacNamara Walter • USA
STORY OF DIANA, THE • 1914 • *Selig* • USA
STORY OF DINAH EAST, THE see **DINAH EAST** • 1970
STORY OF DR. CARVER, THE • 1938 • Zinnemann Fred • SHT • USA
STORY OF DR. EHRLICH'S MAGIC BULLET, THE (UKN) see **DR. EHRLICH'S MAGIC BULLET** • 1940
STORY OF DR. JENNER, THE • 1939 • Dunn Henry K. • USA
STORY OF DOCTOR SCHWEITZER, THE see **IL EST MINUIT DR. SCHWEITZER** • 1952
STORY OF DR. WASSELL, THE • 1944 • De Mille Cecil B. • USA
STORY OF ECHIGO, A see **ECHIGO TSUTSUISHI OYASHIRAZU** • 1964
STORY OF EGGS, THE • 1907 • Melies Georges • FRN
STORY OF ESTHER • 1979 • *Principal Victoria* • MTV • USA
STORY OF ESTHER COSTELLO, THE • 1957 • Miller David • UKN • GOLDEN VIRGIN, THE (USA)
STORY OF F, THE • 1970 • Babb Jim • DOC • USA
STORY OF FAST-GROWING WEEDS, THE see **ASUNARI MONOGATARI** • 1955
STORY OF FAUSTA, THE see **ROMANCE DA EMPREGADA** • 1988
STORY OF FIRST LOVE, THE see **HATSUKOI MONOGATARI** • 1957
STORY OF FLOATING WEEDS, A see **UKIGUSA MONOGATARI** • 1934
STORY OF FOLSOM, THE see **INSIDE THE WALLS OF FOLSOM PRISON** • 1951
STORY OF G.I. JOE, THE • 1945 • Wellman William A. • USA • WAR CORRESPONDENT ○ G.I. JOE
STORY OF GEORGE WASHINGTON, THE • 1965 • Mendelsohn Jack • ANS • USA
STORY OF GILBERT AND SULLIVAN, THE • 1953 • Gilliat Sidney • UKN • GREAT GILBERT AND SULLIVAN, THE (USA) ○ GILBERT AND SULLIVAN ○ MR. GILBERT AND MR. SULLIVAN
STORY OF GOOD PEOPLE, THE see **POVEST O DOBRIH LJUDEH** • 1975
STORY OF GOSTA BERLING, THE see **GOSTA BERLINGS SAGA** • 1924
STORY OF HANSEL AND GRETEL, THE • 1951 • Harryhausen Ray • ANS • USA
STORY OF HANSEL AND GRETEL, THE see **POHADKA O JENICKOVI A MARENCE** • 1980
STORY OF HANSEL AND GRETEL, THE (UKN) see **HANSEL UND GRETEL** • 1924
STORY OF HANUMAN AND THE MONKEY-GOD, THE see **VEERANJANEYA** • 1968
STORY OF HYAM TOUCHED, THE • 1913 • Evans Fred? • UKN
STORY OF IMP SANYI, THE • 1967 • Sipo Tamas Szabo • ANS • HNG
STORY OF INVENTIONS, THE see **STORIE DELLE INVENZIONI, LA** • 1959
STORY OF ISRAEL, THE see **THUS SPAKE THEODOR HERZL** • 1967
STORY OF JACOB AND JOSEPH, THE • 1973 • Cacoyannis Michael • TVM • USA
STORY OF JESUS, THE see **JESUS** • 1979
STORY OF JIRO, THE see **JIRO MONOGATARI** • 1988
STORY OF JOANNA, THE • 1975 • Damiano Gerard • USA
STORY OF JOHN M'NEIL, THE • 1911 • Sutherland Halliday • UKN
STORY OF JOSEPH AND HIS BRETHREN, THE see **JOSEPH AND HIS BRETHREN** • 1962
STORY OF JULIANE KOEPCKE, THE see **MIRACOLI ACCADONO ANCORA, I** • 1974
STORY OF KAMILLA, THE see **KAMILLA OG TYVEN** • 1988
STORY OF KIM SKOV, THE see **HISTORIEN OM KIM SKOV** • 1981
STORY OF KING MIDAS, THE • 1953 • Harryhausen Ray • ANS • USA
STORY OF KINUYO see **KINUYO MONOGATARI** • 1930
STORY OF LASSE AND GEIR, THE see **HISTORIEN OM LASSE OG GEIR** • 1975
STORY OF LAVINIA, THE • 1913 • Campbell Colin • USA
STORY OF LENNIE BRUCE -DIRTYMOUTH see **DIRTYMOUTH** • 1970
STORY OF LIFE, THE • 1948 • Bretherton Howard • USA
STORY OF LITTLE ITALY, A • 1914 • Johnston Lorimer • USA
STORY OF LITTLE JOHN BAILEY, THE • 1970 • Driessen Paul • ANS • NTH
STORY OF LITTLE KASIA AND THE BIG WOLF, THE see **O MALEJ KASI I DUZYM WILKU** • 1963
STORY OF LITTLE MOOK, THE see **GESCHICHTE VOM KLEINEN MUCK, DIE** • 1953
STORY OF LITTLE RED RIDING HOOD, THE • 1949 • Harryhausen Ray • ANS • USA
STORY OF LITTLE YOGHURT, THE • 1968 • Driessen Paul • ANS • NTH • LITTLE YOGHOURT
STORY OF LIUPAO VILLAGE • 1957 • Wang Ping • CHN
STORY OF LOST TIME, THE • 1964 • Ptushko Alexander • USS • TALE OF LOST TIME
STORY OF LOUIS PASTEUR, THE • 1936 • Dieterle William • USA • ENEMY OF MAN
STORY OF LOVE see **KASSET GHARAM** • 1946
STORY OF LOVE, THE see **POVESTEA DRAGOSTEI** • 1976
STORY OF LOVE AND ANARCHY see **FILM D'AMORE E D'ANARCHIA: OVVERO STAMATTINA ALLE IO IN VIA DEI FIORI NELLA NOTA CASA DI TOLLERANZA** • 1973
STORY OF LOVE AND HONOUR see **PRIBEH LASKY A CTI** • 1977
STORY OF MAN AND HIS WOMAN, THE see **FREUDUS SEXUALIS** • 1965
STORY OF MANDY, THE see **MANDY** • 1952
STORY OF MANKIND, THE • 1957 • Allen Irwin • USA
STORY OF ME AND HIM, A see **ORE TO AITSU NO MONOGATARI** • 1982
STORY OF MICHAEL FLAHERTY, THE • 1940 • Eldridge John • DOC • UKN
STORY OF MICHALKOWICE, THE • 1955 • Wasilewski Zenon • ANM • PLN
STORY OF MIRAB, THE • 1959 • Khamraev Ali • USS
STORY OF MOLLY X, THE • 1950 • Wilbur Crane • USA • CONVICT MOLLY X
STORY OF MONTANA, A • 1912 • *Anderson Broncho Billy* • USA
STORY OF MONTE CRISTO, THE see **COMTE DE MONTE-CRISTO, LE** • 1961
STORY OF MY LIFE, THE see **MIT LIVS EVENTYR** • 1955
STORY OF MY LOVING WIFE see **AISAI MONOGATARI** • 1951
STORY OF MY STUPIDITY, THE see **BUTASAGOM TORTENETE** • 1966
STORY OF NELL GWYNNE, A • 1922 • Ridgwell George • UKN
STORY OF O, THE see **HISTOIRE D'O** • 1959-61
STORY OF O, THE (USA) see **HISTOIRE D'O, L'** • 1975
STORY OF OIL, THE • 1919 • Saville Victor • DCS • UKN
STORY OF OLD MEXICO, THE • 1910-12 • Melies Gaston • USA
STORY OF OMOLO • 1946 • Wright Basil • DOC • UKN
STORY OF ONE CRIME • 1971 • Hitruck Fedor • ANS • USS
STORY OF PAGE ONE, THE • 1959 • Odets Clifford • USA
STORY OF PIERA, THE (USA) see **STORIA DI PIERA** • 1983
STORY OF PLYMOUTH ROCK, THE • 1917 • *Forum* • SHT • USA
STORY OF POOR HASSAN, THE see **GESCHICHTE VOM ARMEN HASSAN, DIE** • 1958
STORY OF PRETTY BOY FLOYD, THE • 1974 • Ware Clyde • TVM • USA • PRETTY BOY FLOYD
STORY OF PREVIOUS FUTURE see **HISTOIRE DU FUTUR ANTERIEUR** • 1969
STORY OF PRINTING, THE • 1948 • Bradford Peter • UKN
STORY OF PRIVATE POOLEY, THE (UKN) see **SCHWUR DES SOLDATEN POOLEY, DER** • 1962
STORY OF PURE LOVE, A see **JUN-AI MONOGATARI** • 1957
STORY OF Q, THE see **HISTOIRES DE Q** • 1974
STORY OF Q, THE see **HISTOIRE D'Q** • 1975
STORY OF RAPUNZEL, THE • 1951 • Harryhausen Ray • ANS • USA • RAPUNZEL
STORY OF ROBIN HOOD, THE • 1952 • Annakin Ken • USA, UKN • STORY OF ROBIN HOOD AND HIS MERRY MEN, THE (UKN) ○ ROBIN HOOD AND HIS MERRY MEN
STORY OF ROBIN HOOD AND HIS MERRY MEN, THE (UKN) see **STORY OF ROBIN HOOD, THE** • 1952
STORY OF ROSIE'S ROSE, THE • 1911 • Salter Harry • USA
STORY OF RUTH, THE • 1960 • Koster Henry • USA
STORY OF SEABISCUIT, THE • 1949 • Butler David • USA • PRIDE OF KENTUCKY (UKN)
STORY OF SHIRLEY YORKE, THE • 1948 • Rogers Maclean • UKN • SHIRLEY YORKE
STORY OF SHUNKIN see **SHUNKIN MONOGATARI** • 1954
STORY OF SIBERIAN LAND, A see **SKAZANIYE O ZEMLYE SIBIRSKOI** • 1947
STORY OF SIN • 1911 • *Mintus S.* • USS
STORY OF SIN, THE see **DZIEJE GRZECHU** • 1975
STORY OF SOME GOOD PEOPLE, A see **POVEST O DOBRIH LJUDEH** • 1975
STORY OF SPRING, THE see **ALLEGORIA DI PRIMAVERA** • 1949
STORY OF STALINGRAD, THE see **STALINGRAD** • 1943
STORY OF SUE SAN, THE • 1962 • Hu King • HKG
STORY OF SUSAN see **YUAN WANG AI TA JEN!** • 1976
STORY OF SUSAN, THE • 1916 • *World* • USA
STORY OF TABARA, THE see **TABARANAKATHE** • 1986
STORY OF TABARANA, THE see **TABARANAKATHE** • 1986
STORY OF TANK COMMANDER NISHIZUMI, THE see **NISHIZUMI SENSHACHO-DEN** • 1940
STORY OF TEMPLE DRAKE, THE • 1933 • Roberts Stephen • USA
STORY OF THE BASS-CELLO, THE see **ROMAN S BASON** • 1949
STORY OF THE BELL, THE • 1913 • Edwin Walter • USA
STORY OF THE BLOOD-RED ROSE, THE • 1914 • Campbell Colin • USA
STORY OF THE CASPIAN OIL MEN see **POVEST O NEFTYANIKAKH KASPIYA** • 1953
STORY OF THE CASTLE OF OSAKA, THE see **OSAKA-JO MONOGATARI** • 1961
STORY OF THE CHINESE GODS, THE • Tang Chow Lup • ANM • HKG
STORY OF THE CIRCUS, A • 1912 • *Casey Kenneth* • USA
STORY OF THE COMPANY PRESIDENT'S OVERSEAS TRAVELS see **SHACHOU KOUKOU-KO** • 1962
STORY OF THE COUNT OF MONTE CRISTO, THE (USA) see **COMTE DE MONTE-CRISTO, LE** • 1961
STORY OF THE DOG HACHI, A see **HACHIKO MONOGATARI** • 1988
STORY OF THE DRAGON, THE see **HE'S A LEGEND, HE'S A HERO** • 1977
STORY OF THE EYE, THE see **SIMONA** • 1974
STORY OF THE FIVE BROTHERS, THE • Weiler Kurt • ANM • GDR
STORY OF THE FOX, THE (USA) see **ROMAN DE REYNARD, LE** • 1938
STORY OF THE FURIOUS, THE • 1947 • Babochkin Boris • USS
STORY OF THE GHOST BEAR, THE • 1955 • Karpas Jan • ANS • CZC
STORY OF THE GLOVE, THE • 1915 • Drew Sidney • SHT • USA • STORY OF A GLOVE, THE
STORY OF THE GOOD PEOPLE, THE see **POVEST O DOBRIH LJUDEH** • 1975
STORY OF THE HOMELAND • 1955 • Grigorov Roumen • DOC • BUL
STORY OF THE INDIAN LEDGE, THE • 1911 • *Mcdermott Marc* • USA
STORY OF THE KELLY GANG, THE • 1906 • Tait Charles • ASL
STORY OF THE LAST CHRYSANTHEMUMS, THE see **ZANGIKU MONOGATARI** • 1956
STORY OF THE LAST CHRYSANTHEMUMS, THE (USA) see **ZANGIKU MONOGATARI** • 1939
STORY OF THE LATE CHRYSANTHEMUMS, THE see **ZANGIKU MONOGATARI** • 1939
STORY OF THE MAGI, A see **HISTORIA DE LOS REYES, UNA** • 1988
STORY OF THE MATCHES, THE • Hempel Johannes • ANM • GDR
STORY OF THE MEXICAN BORDER, A • 1913 • *Frontier* • USA
STORY OF THE MOTOR-CAR ENGINE, THE • 1958 • Dunning George, Williams Richard • ANS • UKN
STORY OF THE NIGHT see **GESCHICHTE DER NACHT** • 1979
STORY OF THE OLD CEDAR TREE, THE • 1963 • Degtyarov Vladimir • ANS • USS
STORY OF THE OLD GUN, THE • 1914 • *Essanay* • USA
STORY OF THE OLIVE, THE • 1914 • *Ayres Sydney* • USA
STORY OF THE PERVERTED, THE see **FILE X FOR SEX** • 1967
STORY OF THE RAND, A • 1916 • SAF
STORY OF THE RICHEST SPARROW, THE see **POHADKA O NEJBOHATSIM VRABCI** • 1960
STORY OF THE ROSARY, THE • 1920 • Nash Percy • UKN
STORY OF THE SAVAGE MODOC MINE, THE • 1912 • *Broncho* • USA
STORY OF THE SPITFIRE, THE • 1910 • *Champion* • USA
STORY OF THE STREETS, A see **MACHI NO MONOGATARI** • 1924
STORY OF THE SWAN, THE see **HAKUCHO MONOGATARI** • 1956
STORY OF THE TURBULENT YEARS see **POVEST PLAMENNYKH LET** • 1960
STORY OF THE VATICAN, THE • 1941 • Pages Jean • DOC • FRN
STORY OF THE VOYAGES, THE see **SKAZKA STRANSTVILI** • 1983
STORY OF THE WASA, THE • 1982 • Wahlgren Anders • SHT • SWD
STORY OF THE WEST, A • 1911 • *Essanay* • USA
STORY OF THE WHEEL, THE • 1935 • Jennings Humphrey • DCS • UKN
STORY OF THE WILLOW PATTERN • 1917 • *Edison* • SHT • USA
STORY OF THE WILLOW PATTERN, THE • 1914 • France Charles H. • USA
STORY OF THE YANAGAWA CANAL see **YANAGAWA HORIWARI MONOGATARI** • 1988
STORY OF THE YELLOW BOOTEE, THE see **HISTORIA ZOLTEJ CIZEMKI** • 1962
STORY OF THREE GIRLS, THE see **HEKAYET THALASS BANAT** • 1968
STORY OF THREE LOVES, THE • 1953 • Reinhardt Gottfried, Minnelli Vincente • USA
STORY OF TIME, THE • *Leffingwell Robert (P)* • ANS • UKN
STORY OF TOSCA, THE (USA) see **TOSCA** • 1941
STORY OF TWO CHRISTMASES, THE • 1904 • Fitzhamon Lewin • UKN
STORY OF TWO LIVES, THE • 1909 • *Lubin* • USA
STORY OF VENUS, THE • 1914 • MacGregor Norval • USA
STORY OF VERNON AND IRENE CASTLE, THE • 1939 • Potter H. C. • USA • CASTLES, THE
STORY OF VICKIE, THE (USA) see **MADCHENJAHRE EINER KONIGIN** • 1954
STORY OF WILL ROGERS, THE • 1952 • Curtiz Michael • USA
STORY OF WOMEN, A see **AFFAIRE DE FEMMES, UNE** • 1988
STORY OF WOO-VIET, THE see **HU-YUEH-TE KU-SHIH** • 1982
STORY OF WOOL, THE • 1940 • Leacock Philip • DOC • UKN
STORY OF WU-VIET, THE see **HU-YUEH-TE KU-SHIH** • 1982
STORY OF YUGAKU OHARA, THE see **TEMPO SUIKO DEN** • 1976
STORY OF ZONE 2, THE • Lavoie Hermenegilde • DCS • CND
STORY PETREL see **PASAREA FURTUNII** • 1957
STORY THAT COULDN'T BE PRINTED, THE • 1939 • Newman Joseph M. • SHT • USA
STORY THAT THE KEG TOLD ME, THE • 1917 • Crosland Alan • SHT • USA
STORY THE BOOTS TOLD, THE • 1908 • *Vitagraph* • USA
STORY THE CLOCK TOLD, THE • 1915 • Paton Stuart • USA
STORY THE DESERT TOLD, THE • 1913 • *Essanay* • USA
STORY THE GATE TOLD, THE • 1914 • *Lubin* • USA
STORY THE SILK HATS TOLD, THE • 1915 • Lessey George A. • USA
STORY WITHOUT A NAME, THE • 1924 • Willat Irvin V. • USA • WITHOUT WARNING
STORY WITHOUT WORDS, A • 1897 • *Prestwich Mfg. Co.* • UKN
STORYTELLER, THE • 1977 • Markowitz Robert • TVM • USA
STORYTELLING • 1983 • Armatage Kay • CND
STORYTIME • 1968 • Armstrong Gillian • SHT • ASL
STOSSTRUPP 1917 • 1934 • Zoberlein Hans, Schmid-Wildy Ludwig • FRG • SHOCK TROOP
STOSSTRUPP VENUS -5 MADCHEN BLASEN ZUM ANGRIFF • 1974 • Keil George • AUS, FRG • VENUS RAIDERS -5 GIRLS TRUMPET THE ATTACK ○ 2069: A SEX ODYSSEY (USA)
STOT STAR DEN DANSKE SOMAND • 1948 • Ipsen Bodil, Lauritzen Lau Jr. • DNM • PERILOUS EXPEDITION
STOTEN • 1961 • Ekman Hasse • SWD • JOB, THE
STOUBLEN LINDENS, THE see **STUBLENSKITE LIPI** • 1960
STOUT HEART BUT WEAK KNEES • 1914 • Sennett Mack • USA
STOUT HEARTS AND WILLING HANDS • 1931 • Foy Bryan • SHT • USA
STOWAWAY • 1932 • Whitman Phil • USA
STOWAWAY • 1936 • Seiter William A. • USA
STOWAWAY, THE • 1904 • Williamson James • UKN

STOWAWAY, THE • 1909 • *Lubin* • USA
STOWAWAY, THE • 1910 • Fitzhamon Lewin • UKN
STOWAWAY, THE • 1958 • Robinson Lee (c/d) • ASL
STOWAWAY, THE • 1960 • *Halas John (P)* • ANS • UKN
STOWAWAY, THE see **PASSAGER CLANDESTIN, LE** • 1960
STOWAWAY GIRL, THE • 1916 • *Lasky* • USA
STOWAWAY GIRL (USA) see **MANUELA** • 1957
STOWAWAY IN THE SKY see **VOYAGE EN BALLON, LE** • 1960
STOWAWAY TO THE MOON • 1975 • McLaglen Andrew V. • TVM • USA
STOWAWAY WOODY • 1963 • Marcus Sid • ANS • USA
STOWAWAYS • 1949 • Rasinski Connie • ANS • USA
STOWAWAYS see **POTYAUTASOK** • 1989
STOWAWAYS AND STRATEGY • 1917 • Howe J. A. • SHT • USA
STOWAWAYS (USA) see **BLINDE PASSAGIER** • 1937
STOY • 1973 • Nicolayssen Hans Otto • SHT • NRW • NOISE
STRACENA VARTA • 1956 • Makovec Milos • ANM • CZC • LOST SENTRY, THE ○ GUARD, THE ○ ZTRACENA VARTA ○ LOST PATROL, THE
STRACH • 1975 • Krauze Antoni • PLN • FEAR
STRADA, LA • 1954 • Fellini Federico • ITL • ROAD, THE
STRADA BUIA, LA • 1949 • Salkow Sidney, Girolami Marino • ITL • FUGITIVE LADY (USA)
STRADA DEI GIGANTI, LA • 1960 • Malatesta Guido • ITL • VALLEY OF THE DOOMED (USA) ○ ROAD OF THE GIANTS, THE
STRADA FINISCE SUL FIUME, LA • 1950 • Capuano Luigi • ITL • GORGHI NEL FIUME
STRADA LUNGA UN ANNO, LA • 1958 • De Santis Giuseppe • ITL, YGS • CESTA DUGA GODINU DANA (YGS) ○ ROAD A YEAR LONG, THE (USA) ○ YEAR-LONG ROAD
STRADA PER FORT ALAMO, LA • 1965 • Bava Mario • ITL, FRN • ROAD TO FORT ALAMO, THE (USA) ○ ARIZONA BILL
STRADA SENZA USCITA • 1970 • Palmieri Gaetano • ITL • DEAD END (USA)
STRADBROKE INFANTS SCHOOL SOUTH AUSTRALIA • 1973 • Crombie Donald • DOC • ASL
STRADE DI NAPOLI • 1947 • Risi Dino • SHT • ITL
STRADIVARI • 1935 • von Bolvary Geza • FRG
STRADIVARI • 1966 • Papuzinski Andrzej • DOC • PLN
STRADIVARIUS • 1935 • Valentin Albert, von Bolvary Geza • FRN
STRAFBATAILLON 999 • 1960 • Philipp Harald • FRG • PUNISHMENT BATTALION (USA) ○ MARCH TO THE GALLOWS
STRAFF • 1969 • Halldoff Jan • SWD • DREAM OF FREEDOM, A ○ DROM OM FRIHET, EN
STRAFLING AUS STAMBUL, DER • 1929 • Ucicky Gustav • FRG
STRAFLING VON CAYENNE, DER • 1921 • Lasko Leo • FRG
STRAFLINGSKAVALIER, DER • 1927 • Meinhard-Junger Rudolf • FRG
STRAFSACHE VAN GELDERN • 1932 • Wolff Willi • FRG
STRAGE DEI VAMPIRI, LA • 1962 • Mauri Roberto • ITL • SLAUGHTER OF THE VAMPIRES, THE ○ CURSE OF THE GHOULS ○ CURSE OF THE BLOOD-GHOULS (USA)
STRAGGLERS, THE see **SBANDATI, GLI** • 1956
STRAH • 1975 • Klopcic Matjaz • YGS • FEAR
STRAHLEN DES TODES, DIE • 1920 • Bock-Stieber Gernot • FRG
STRAIGHT AND NARROW • 1918 • Parrott Charles • SHT • USA
STRAIGHT AND NARROW PATH, THE • 1915 • *Shirley Arthur* • ASL
STRAIGHT AND NARROW PATH, THE • 1915 • Horne James W. • USA
STRAIGHT BANANA • 1970 • Pickett Lowell • USA
STRAIGHT COURSE, A see **PRYAMAYA LINIYA** • 1968
STRAIGHT CROOK, A • 1918 • *Triangle* • USA
STRAIGHT CROOK, A • 1921 • Roach Hal • SHT • USA
STRAIGHT CROOKS • 1919 • *Lyons Eddie* • SHT • USA
STRAIGHT FROM PARIS • 1921 • Garson Harry • USA
STRAIGHT FROM THE HEART • 1935 • Beal Scott R. • USA
STRAIGHT FROM THE HEART -LOVE SONGS OF THE SOUTH WEST see **DEL MERO CORAZON** • 1979
STRAIGHT FROM THE SHOULDER • 1921 • Durning Bernard J. • USA
STRAIGHT FROM THE SHOULDER • 1936 • Heisler Stuart • USA • JOHNNY GETS HIS GUN
STRAIGHT IS THE WAY • 1921 • Vignola Robert G. • USA
STRAIGHT IS THE WAY • 1934 • Sloane Paul • USA
STRAIGHT JACKET see **DARK SANITY** • 1980
STRAIGHT LINE see **PRYAMAYA LINIYA** • 1968
STRAIGHT ON TILL MORNING • 1972 • Collinson Peter • UKN
STRAIGHT PATH see **NER VAZHI** • 1968
STRAIGHT PATH, A • 1911 • *Reliance* • USA
STRAIGHT, PLACE AND SHOW • 1938 • Butler David • USA • THEY'RE OFF (UKN)
STRAIGHT ROAD, THE • 1914 • Dwan Allan • USA
STRAIGHT SHOOTER • 1939 • Newfield Sam • USA
STRAIGHT SHOOTERS • 1947 • Hannah Jack • ANS • USA
STRAIGHT SHOOTIN' • 1927 • Wyler William • USA • RANGE RIDERS
STRAIGHT SHOOTING • 1917 • Ford John • USA • JOAN OF THE CATTLELANDS
STRAIGHT THROUGH • 1925 • Rosson Arthur • USA • RIDIN' THROUGH
STRAIGHT TIME • 1978 • Grosbard Ulu • USA • NO BEAST SO FIERCE
STRAIGHT TO HEAVEN • 1939 • Leonard Arthur • USA
STRAIGHT TO HELL • 1987 • Cox Alex • UKN
STRAIGHT TO THE HEART see **A CORPS PERDU** • 1988
STRAIGHT TO THE HEART (USA) see **MITTEN INS HERZ** • 1984
STRAIGHT WAY, THE • 1916 • Davis Will S. • USA
STRAIGHTAWAY • 1934 • Brower Otto • USA
STRAIGHTFORWARD BOY, A see **TOKKAN KOZO** • 1930
STRAIGHTJACKET see **SHOCK CORRIDOR** • 1963
STRAINUL • 1964 • Iacob Mihai • RMN • STRANGER, THE
STRAIT see **KAIKYO** • 1983
STRAIT-JACKET • 1964 • Castle William • USA
STRAIT-LACED GIRL, A see **FILLE COUSUE DE FIL BLANC, LA** • 1976
STRAITS OF HUNGER see **KIGA KAIGYO** • 1965
STRAITS OF LOVE AND HATE, THE (USA) see **AIENKYO** • 1937
STRAKOFF THE ADVENTURER see **HVEM ER GENTLEMANTYVEN** • 1915
STRAKONICKY DUDAK • 1955 • Stekly Karel • CZC • BAGPIPER OF STRAKONICE, THE ○ PIPER OF STRAKONICE, THE
STRAMNATA PATEKA • 1961 • Yankov Yanko • USS • STEEP PATH, THE
STRANA COPPIO DI GANGSTERS, UNA • 1979 • *Andress Ursula* • ITL
STRANA LA VITA • 1988 • Bertolucci Giuseppe • ITL • LIFE IS STRANGE
STRANA LEGGE DEL DR. MENGA, LA • 1972 • Merino Fernando • ITL
STRANA ORCHIDES CON CINQUE GOCCE DI SANGUE, UNA see **TUTTI I COLORI DEL BUIO** • 1972
STRANA RODNAYA • 1942 • Shub Esther • DOC • USS • NATIVE COUNTRY, THE
STRANA SOVIETOV • 1937 • Shub Esther • USS • COUNTRY OF THE SOVIETS ○ LAND OF THE SOVIETS
STRANA VOGLIA D'AMARE, UNA see **LOVE BIRDS** • 1969
STRANA VOGLIA DI UNA VEDOVA (ITL) see **DU GRABUGE CHEZ LES VEUVES** • 1963
STRAND OF BLONDE HAIR, A • 1914 • Baker George D. • USA
STRAND, UNDER THE DARK CLOTH • 1990 • Walker John • DOC • CND
STRANDED • 1916 • Burstein Louis • *Vim* • USA
STRANDED • 1916 • Ingraham Lloyd • *Fine Arts* • USA
STRANDED • 1927 • Rosen Phil • USA
STRANDED • 1935 • Borzage Frank • USA
STRANDED • 1986 • Daniel Rod • TVM • USA
STRANDED • 1987 • Fuller Tex • USA • SHOCK WAVE
STRANDED see **VALLEY OF MYSTERY** • 1967
STRANDED see **STRANGER, THE** • 1973
STRANDED ACTOR, THE • 1910-12 • Melies Gaston • USA
STRANDED ACTORS, THE • 1912 • *Lubin* • USA
STRANDED IN ARCADY • 1917 • Crane Frank H. • USA
STRANDED IN PARADISE see **HIS CAPTIVE WOMAN** • 1929
STRANDED IN PARIS • 1926 • Rosson Arthur • USA • YOU NEVER CAN TELL
STRANDED IN PARIS (UKN) see **ARTISTS AND MODELS ABROAD** • 1937
STRANDFEST • Wright Basil • UKN
STRANDGUT • 1924 • Breslauer H. K. • AUS
STRANDGUT • 1925 • *Bjornstadt-Justitz Film-Komp.* • FRG
STRANDGUT DER LEIDENSCHAFT • 1921 • Speyer Jaap • FRG
STRANDGUT ODER DIE RACHE DES MEERES • 1917 • Eichberg Richard • FRG
STRANDHUGG • 1949 • Sucksdorff Arne • DCS • SWD • GOING ASHORE
STRANDING, THE see **STRANDING, SOS ECUADOR** • 1956
STRANDING, SOS ECUADOR • 1956 • van Gasteren Louis A. • NTH • STRANDING, THE
STRANDNIXE, DIE • 1921 • *Flohr Lilly* • FRG
STRANGE ADVENTURE • 1933 • Whitman Phil • USA
STRANGE ADVENTURE, A • 1917 • Neilan Marshall • SHT • USA
STRANGE ADVENTURE, A • 1956 • Witney William • USA • WHITE NIGHTMARE
STRANGE ADVENTURE OF DAVID GRAY, THE (UKN) see **VAMPYR** • 1931
STRANGE ADVENTURE OF NEW YORK DRUMMER • 1899 • Porter Edwin S. • USA
STRANGE ADVENTURES OF A MAGICIAN see **MOSHUSHI DE QIYU** • 1962
STRANGE ADVENTURES OF HERR FRIDOLIN B. see **SELTSAMEN ABENTEUER DES HERRN FRIDOLIN B., DIE** • 1948
STRANGE ADVENTURES OF MR. SMITH, THE • 1937 • Rogers Maclean • UKN
STRANGE AFFAIR • 1944 • Green Alfred E. • USA
STRANGE AFFAIR, THE • 1968 • Greene David • UKN
STRANGE AFFAIR OF UNCLE HARRY, THE • 1945 • Siodmak Robert • USA • ZERO MURDER CASE, THE ○ UNCLE HARRY
STRANGE AFFECTION (USA) see **SCAMP, THE** • 1957
STRANGE AFFINITY see **SHOKKAKU** • 1969
STRANGE ALIBI • 1941 • Lederman D. Ross • USA
STRANGE ALIBI see **STRANGE TRIANGLE** • 1946
STRANGE AND DEADLY OCCURRENCE, THE • 1974 • Moxey John Llewellyn • TVM • USA
STRANGE APPOINTMENT see **STRANO APPUNTAMENTO** • 1951
STRANGE AS IT SEEMS • 1930 • Lantz Walter, Nolan William • ANS • USA
STRANGE AS IT SEEMS • 1931-37 • Hahn Manny Nathan, Fairbanks Jerry • SHS • USA
STRANGE AWAKENING • 1958 • Tully Montgomery • UKN • FEMALE FRIENDS (USA)
STRANGE BARGAIN • 1949 • Price Will • USA
STRANGE BEDFELLOWS • 1964 • Frank Melvin • USA
STRANGE BEDFELLOWS see **FUN ON A WEEKEND** • 1947
STRANGE BEHAVIOR (USA) see **DEAD KIDS** • 1981
STRANGE BIRD see **CUDNA PTICA** • 1969
STRANGE BIRD, A • 1914 • *Belmont Claude* • USA
STRANGE BIRD, THE see **FREMDE VOGEL, DER** • 1911
STRANGE BIRDS • 1930 • *Sennett Mack (P)* • SHT • USA
STRANGE BIRDS see **PTACI KOHACI** • 1965
STRANGE BOARDER, THE • 1920 • Badger Clarence • USA
STRANGE BOARDERS • 1938 • Mason Herbert • UKN
STRANGE BREW • 1983 • Moranis Rick, Thomas Dave • USA
STRANGE CARGO • 1929 • Gregor Arthur, Glazer Benjamin • USA
STRANGE CARGO • 1936 • Huntington Lawrence • UKN
STRANGE CARGO • 1940 • Borzage Frank • USA • NOT TOO NARROW, NOT TOO DEEP
STRANGE CASE, A • 1912 • *Baggot King* • USA
STRANGE CASE, A • 1916 • Mullin Eugene • SHT • USA
STRANGE CASE OF ..!#*%?, THE see **MALTESE BIPPY, THE** • 1969
STRANGE CASE OF BLONDIE, THE • 1954 • Hughes Ken • UKN
STRANGE CASE OF CAPTAIN RAMPER, THE (USA) see **RAMPER, DER TIERMENSCH** • 1927
STRANGE CASE OF CLARA DEANE, THE • 1932 • Gasnier Louis J., Marcin Max • USA • CLARA DEANE
STRANGE CASE OF DISTRICT ATTORNEY M., THE see **FALL DES STAATSANWALTS M..., DER** • 1928
STRANGE CASE OF DR. FAUST, THE see **EXTRANO CASO DEL DR. FAUSTO, EL** • 1969
STRANGE CASE OF DR. JEKYLL AND MISS OSBOURNE, THE see **DOCTEUR JEKYLL ET LES FEMMES** • 1981
STRANGE CASE OF DR. JEKYLL AND MR. HYDE, THE • 1967 • Jarrott Charles • TVM • USA, CND • DR. JEKYLL AND MR. HYDE
STRANGE CASE OF DR. MANNING, THE (USA) see **MORNING CALL** • 1957
STRANGE CASE OF DR. MEADE • 1939 • Collins Lewis D. • USA • NOT FOR GLORY
STRANGE CASE OF DR. RX • 1942 • Nigh William • USA
STRANGE CASE OF MADELEINE, THE see **MADELEINE** • 1950
STRANGE CASE OF MARY PAGE, THE • 1916 • Haydon J. Charles • SRL • USA
STRANGE CASE OF MR. TODMORDEN • 1935 • Tennyson Walter • UKN
STRANGE CASE OF PHILIP KENT, THE • 1916 • Durrant Fred W. • UKN
STRANGE CASE OF PRINCESS KAHN, THE • 1914 • Le Saint Edward J. • USA • HOW LOVE CONQUERED HYPNOTISM
STRANGE CASE OF TALMAS LIND, THE • 1915 • Daly William Robert • USA
STRANGE CASE OF THE MAN AND THE BEAST, THE see **EXTRANO CASO DEL HOMBRE Y LA BESTIA, EL** • 1951
STRANGE CASE OF THE MISSING REMBRANDT, THE see **MISSING REMBRANDT, THE** • 1932
STRANGE CITY see **FREMDE STADT** • 1972
STRANGE COMPANION • 1961 • Davis Mannie • ANS • USA
STRANGE COMPANIONS • 1964 • ANS • HKG
STRANGE COMPULSION • 1964 • Berwick Irvin • USA
STRANGE CONDUCT see **OLIVIA** • 1950
STRANGE CONFESSION • 1945 • Hoffman John • USA • MISSING HEAD, THE
STRANGE CONFESSION see **IMPOSTER, THE** • 1943
STRANGE CONFESSION, A • 1916 • Hunt Jay • SHT • USA
STRANGE CONQUEST • 1946 • Rawlins John • USA
STRANGE CONSPIRACY (UKN) see **PRESIDENT VANISHES, THE** • 1934
STRANGE COUNTESS, THE (USA) see **SELTSAME GRAFIN, DIE** • 1961
STRANGE DEATH OF ADOLF HITLER, THE • 1943 • Hogan James P. • USA
STRANGE DECEPTION see **CRISTO PROIBITO** • 1951
STRANGE DESIRE OF MONSIEUR BARD, THE see **ETRANGE DESIR DE M. BARD, L'** • 1953
STRANGE DESIRES • 1964 • Wilkie B. • SHT • USA
STRANGE DISAPPEARANCE, A • 1915 • Lessey George A. • USA
STRANGE DOOR, THE • 1951 • Pevney Joseph • USA • DOOR, THE
STRANGE DREAM OF PROFESSOR FILUTEK, THE see **DZIWNY SEN PROFESORA FILUTEKA** • 1956
STRANGE DUEL, A • 1971 • Stoyanov Todor • BUL
STRANGE ENCOUNTERS see **PIAOBU QIYA**
STRANGE EVIDENCE • 1914 • *Burbridge Bessie* • USA
STRANGE EVIDENCE • 1933 • Milton Robert • UKN • WIFE IN PAWN
STRANGE EXORCISM OF LYNN HART, THE see **DADDY'S DEADLY DARLING** • 1972
STRANGE EXPERIMENT • 1937 • Parker Albert • UKN
STRANGE FACES • 1938 • Taggart Errol • USA
STRANGE FACES see **IDEGEN ARCOK** • 1974
STRANGE FASCINATION • 1952 • Haas Hugo • USA
STRANGE FATE OF AJEEB KAHANI, THE see **ARVIND DESAI KI AJEEB KAHANI** • 1977
STRANGE FETISHES, THE • 1967 • Blancocello Enrico • USA • STRANGE FETISHES OF THE GO-GO GIRLS, THE
STRANGE FETISHES OF THE GO-GO GIRLS, THE see **STRANGE FETISHES, THE** • 1967
STRANGE GAMBLE • 1948 • Archainbaud George • USA
STRANGE GIRL, THE see **FREMDE MADCHEN, DAS** • 1913
STRANGE GLORY • 1938 • Tourneur Jacques • SHT • USA
STRANGE HANDS ARE HARSH see **XENA HERIA INE PIKRA, TA** • 1968
STRANGE HISTORY OF THE CITIZENS OF SCHILT, THE • Hempel Johannes • ANM • GDR
STRANGE HOLIDAY • 1945 • Oboler Arch • USA • DAY AFTER TOMORROW, THE (UKN)
STRANGE HOLIDAY • 1970 • Brown Mende • ASL
STRANGE HOLIDAY see **DEATH TAKES A HOLIDAY** • 1934
STRANGE HOMECOMING • 1974 • Katzin Lee H. • TVM • USA
STRANGE IDOLS • 1922 • Durning Bernard J. • USA • VOWS THAT MAY BE BROKEN
STRANGE ILLUSION (UKN) see **OUT OF THE NIGHT** • 1945
STRANGE IMPERSONATION • 1945 • Mann Anthony • USA
STRANGE INCIDENT (UKN) see **OXBOW INCIDENT, THE** • 1943
STRANGE INTERLUDE • 1932 • Leonard Robert Z. • USA • STRANGE INTERVAL (UKN)
STRANGE INTERVAL (UKN) see **STRANGE INTERLUDE** • 1932
STRANGE INTRUDER • 1956 • Rapper Irving • USA
STRANGE INTRUSION see **UNHOLY INTRUDERS, THE** • 1956
STRANGE INVADERS • 1983 • Laughlin Michael • USA
STRANGE IRISHMAN • Hickey Kieran • DOC • IRL
STRANGE JOURNEY • 1946 • Tinling James • USA
STRANGE JOURNEY, THE see **EXTRANO VIAJE, EL** • 1964
STRANGE JUSTICE • 1932 • Schertzinger Victor • USA • ALL THE EVIDENCE
STRANGE LADY IN TOWN • 1955 • LeRoy Mervyn • USA
STRANGE LANDS • Gerstein Cassandra M. • SHT • USA
STRANGE LAWS (UKN) see **CHEROKEE STRIP** • 1937
STRANGE LETTERS see **CIUJYE PISMA** • 1976
STRANGE LOVE see **STRANGE LOVE OF MARTHA IVERS** • 1946
STRANGE LOVE, A see **MAERKELIG KAERLIGHED, EN** • 1968

STRANGE LOVE AFFAIR, A • 1986 • de Kuyper Eric, Verstraten Paul • BLG, NTH
STRANGE LOVE AFFAIR, A (UKN) see **BEL MOSTRO, IL** • 1971
STRANGE LOVE OF MARTHA IVERS • 1946 • Milestone Lewis • USA • STRANGE LOVE
STRANGE LOVE OF MOLLY LOUVAIN, THE • 1932 • Curtiz Michael • USA • TINSEL GIRL
STRANGE LOVE STORY, A see **ESTRANHA HISTORIA DE AMOR, UMA** • 1980
STRANGE LOVERS • 1963 • Stambler Robert • USA
STRANGE MARRIAGE see **KULONOS HAZASSAG** • 1951
STRANGE MASQUERADE (USA) see **HERKULESFURDOI EMLEK** • 1977
STRANGE MEETING, A • 1909 • Griffith D. W. • USA
STRANGE MELODY, A • 1914 • *Holloway Carol* • USA
STRANGE MR. GREGORY, THE • 1946 • Rosen Phil • USA
STRANGE MR. VICTOR, THE (UKN) see **ETRANGE M. VICTOR, L'** • 1937
STRANGE MOTHER, THE • 1916 • *Laemmle* • SHT • USA
STRANGE MRS. CRANE, THE • 1948 • Newfield Sam • USA
STRANGE NEW WORLD • 1975 • Butler Robert • TVM • USA
STRANGE NIGHT, THE see **NOTTE PAZZA DEL CONIGLIACCIO, LA** • 1967
STRANGE OBSESSION, THE see **STREGA IN AMORE, LA** • 1966
STRANGE ONE, THE • 1957 • Garfein Jack • USA • END AS A MAN (UKN)
STRANGE ONES, THE (UKN) see **ENFANTS TERRIBLES, LES** • 1949
STRANGE ORCHID WITH FIVE DROPS OF BLOOD, A see **TUTTI I COLORI DEL BUIO** • 1972
STRANGE PATTERNS • 1969 • *Chancellor Films* • USA
STRANGE PEOPLE • 1933 • Thorpe Richard • USA
STRANGE PEOPLE see **STRANNIYE LYUDI** • 1970
STRANGE PLACE TO MEET, A (UKN) see **DROLE D'ENDROIT POUR UNE RENCONTRE** • 1988
STRANGE POSSESSION OF MRS. OLIVER, THE • 1977 • Hessler Gordon • TVM • USA
STRANGE PRINCE, THE see **FREMDE FURST, DER** • 1918
STRANGE RAMPAGE • 1967 • Volpe Ignatius • USA
STRANGE REUNION, A • 1909 • *Phoenix Film* • USA
STRANGE RHAPSODY see **STORM AT DAYBREAK** • 1932
STRANGE RIDER, THE • 1925 • Hayes Ward • USA
STRANGE ROADS (UKN) see **EXPOSED** • 1932
STRANGE ROLE, A see **HERKULESFURDOI EMLEK** • 1977
STRANGE SHADOWS IN AN EMPTY ROOM (USA) see **BLAZING MAGNUM** • 1977
STRANGE SIGNAL, THE • 1914 • *Frontier* • USA
STRANGE STORIES • 1953 • Guillermin John, Chaffey Don • UKN
STRANGE STORY OF BRANDNER KASPER, THE see **SELTSAME GESCHICHTE DES BRANDNER KASPER, DIE** • 1949
STRANGE STORY OF ELSIE MASON, THE • 1912 • *Joyce Alice* • USA
STRANGE TALES • 1969 • Dooley John • UKN
STRANGE TALES see **HISTOIRES EXTRAORDINAIRES** • 1968
STRANGE TEMPTATION see **ALIAS NICK BEAL** • 1948
STRANGE TESTAMENT • 1941 • Lee Sammy • USA • STRANGE WILL OF JULIAN POYDRAS, THE
STRANGE TIME, A see **ABUDASSE KALE** • 1968
STRANGE TO RELATE • 1943 • Newman Widgey R. • UKN
STRANGE TO THE SUDETEN COUNTRY (USA) see **FREMD IM SUDETENLAND** • 1938
STRANGE TOWN see **FREMDE STADT** • 1972
STRANGE TRANSGRESSOR, A • 1917 • Barker Reginald • USA
STRANGE TRIANGLE • 1946 • McCarey Ray • USA • STRANGE ALIBI
STRANGE TRIANGLE see **FURIN** • 1965
STRANGE UNKNOWN, THE • 1915 • Melville Wilbert • USA
STRANGE VENGEANCE OF ROSALIE, THE • 1972 • Starrett Jack • USA • SOMEONE TO WATCH OVER ME
STRANGE VICTORY • 1948 • Hurwitz Leo T. • DOC • USA
STRANGE VOICES • 1987 • Seidelman Arthur Allan • TVM • USA
STRANGE VOYAGE • 1946 • Allen Irving • USA
STRANGE VOYAGE, THE • 1955 • Badzian Teresa • ANM • PLN
STRANGE WAY, THE • 1913 • *Siegmann George* • USA
STRANGE WILL OF JULIAN POYDRAS, THE see **STRANGE TESTAMENT** • 1941
STRANGE WIVES • 1935 • Thorpe Richard • USA
STRANGE WOMAN • 1929 • Pyriev Ivan • USS
STRANGE WOMAN, A see **STRANNAYA ZHENSHCHINA** • 1978
STRANGE WOMAN, THE • 1918 • Le Saint Edward J. • USA
STRANGE WOMAN, THE • 1946 • Ulmer Edgar G. • USA
STRANGE WORLD see **MUNDO EXTRANO** • 1952
STRANGE WORLD, THE see **STRANGE WORLD OF PLANET X, THE** • 1958
STRANGE WORLD OF PLANET X, THE • 1958 • Gunn Gilbert • UKN • COSMIC MONSTER, THE (USA) ○ CREATURES FROM ANOTHER WORLD ○ COSMIC MONSTERS ○ CRAWLING TERROR, THE ○ STRANGE WORLD, THE
STRANGE WORLD OF ZE DO CAIXAO, THE see **ESTRANHO MUNDO DE ZE DO CAIXAO, O** • 1969
STRANGELY POWERFUL EXIT, A see **UNHEIMLICH STARKER ABGANG, EIN** • 1973
STRANGENESS, THE • 1985 • Hillman David Michael • USA
STRANGER, A see **MUUKALAINEN** • 1982
STRANGER, THE • 1910 • Olcott Sidney • USA
STRANGER, THE • 1911 • *Rex* • USA
STRANGER, THE • 1913 • *Baggot King* • USA
STRANGER, THE • 1914 • *White Star* • USA
STRANGER, THE • 1915 • *Grandin* • USA
STRANGER, THE • 1915 • Ayres Sydney • *Powers* • USA
STRANGER, THE • 1917 • Gillstrom Arvid E. • SHT • USA
STRANGER, THE • 1920 • *Universal* • SHT • USA
STRANGER, THE • 1924 • Henabery Joseph • USA
STRANGER, THE • 1946 • Welles Orson • USA
STRANGER, THE • 1973 • Katzin Lee H. • TVM • USA • STRANDED
STRANGER, THE • 1987 • Aristarain Adolfo • ARG, USA
STRANGER, THE see **UKJENT MANN** • 1951
STRANGER, THE see **STRANGER CAME HOME, THE** • 1954
STRANGER, THE see **STRAINUL** • 1964
STRANGER, THE see **DAYUHAN, ANG** • 1968
STRANGER, THE (UKN) see **CHEROKEE KID, THE** • 1927
STRANGER, THE (UKN) see **STRANGER FROM TEXAS, THE** • 1939
STRANGER, THE (UKN) see **INTRUDER, THE** • 1961
STRANGER, THE (USA) see **GHARIB, EL** • 1955
STRANGER, THE (USA) see **STRANIERO, LO** • 1967
STRANGER AMONG HIS OWN PEOPLE see **SVOI SREDI CHUZHIGH, CHUZHOI SREDI SVOIKH** • 1974
STRANGER AND THE FOG, THE see **GHARIBEH VA MEH** • 1974
STRANGER AND THE GUNFIGHTER, THE (USA) see **LA DOVE NON BATTE IL SOLE** • 1975
STRANGER AND THE TAXI-CAB, THE • 1912 • *Secord Willis* • USA
STRANGER AT COYOTE, THE • 1912 • Dwan Allan • USA
STRANGER AT DUMCRIEFF, THE • 1917 • Hurst Paul C. • SHT • USA
STRANGER AT HICKORY NUT GAP, THE • 1914 • *Shay William E.* • USA
STRANGER AT JEFFERSON HIGH, THE • 1981 • Dayton Lyman D. • TVM • USA • RIVALS
STRANGER AT MY DOOR • 1950 • Stafford Brendan J., Leslie Desmond • UKN
STRANGER AT MY DOOR • 1956 • Witney William • USA
STRANGER AT THE DOOR • 1977 • Howe John • CND
STRANGER AT THE MOUNTAIN RANCH, THE • 1913 • *Frontier* • USA
STRANGER CAME HOME, THE • 1954 • Fisher Terence • UKN • UNHOLY FOUR, THE (USA) ○ STRANGER, THE
STRANGER CASE OF MURDER, A see **GASLIGHT** • 1940
STRANGER FROM ARIZONA, THE • 1938 • Clifton Elmer • USA
STRANGER FROM CANTON see **KUAI KO** • 1981
STRANGER FROM CANYON VALLEY, THE • 1921 • Smith Cliff • USA
STRANGER FROM CRUZ DEL SUR STREET see **ESTRANGER – OH! DE LA CALLE CRUZ DEL SUR, EL** • 1985
STRANGER FROM HONG-KONG (USA) see **INCONNU DE HONG-KONG, L'** • 1964
STRANGER FROM PECOS, THE • 1943 • Hillyer Lambert • USA
STRANGER FROM PONCA CITY, THE • 1947 • Abrahams Derwin • USA
STRANGER FROM ST. PETERSBURG • 1978 • Gaidai Leonid • USS
STRANGER FROM SAN MARINO, THE see **SCONOSCIUTO DI SAN MARINO, LO** • 1947
STRANGER FROM SANTA FE • 1945 • Hillyer Lambert • USA
STRANGER FROM SHAOLIN • Lu Chun • HKG
STRANGER FROM SOMEWHERE, A • 1916 • Worthington William • USA
STRANGER FROM TEXAS, THE • 1939 • Nelson Sam • USA • STRANGER, THE (UKN)
STRANGER FROM THE SKY see **FRAMLINGEN FRAN SKYN** • 1956
STRANGER FROM VENUS, A • 1954 • Balaban Burt • UKN • IMMEDIATE DISASTER (USA) ○ VISITOR FROM VENUS, A ○ VENUSIAN, THE
STRANGER IN BETWEEN, THE (USA) see **HUNTED** • 1952
STRANGER IN CAMP, A • 1915 • *Shaw Brinsley* • USA
STRANGER IN CAMP, THE • 1911 • *Lubin* • USA
STRANGER IN HIS OWN HOME, A • 1916 • Moore Matt • SHT • USA
STRANGER IN HOLLYWOOD • 1968 • Slipyj Rodion • USA
STRANGER IN MY ARMS • 1959 • Kautner Helmut • USA • AND RIDE A TIGER
STRANGER IN MY BED • 1986 • Elikann Larry • TVM • USA
STRANGER IN MY HEART, THE see **KALBIMDEKI YABANCI** • 1968
STRANGER IN NEW YORK, A • 1916 • Heffron Thomas N. • SHT • USA
STRANGER IN OUR HOUSE • 1978 • Craven Wes • TVM • USA • SUMMER OF FEAR (UKN)
STRANGER IN SACRAMENTO, A see **STRANIERO A SACRAMENTO, UNO** • 1965
STRANGER IN THE CITY • 1961 • Hartford-Davis Robert • DCS • UKN
STRANGER IN THE FAMILY, A • 1956 • Schweitzer Mikhail • USS
STRANGER IN THE HOUSE • 1967 • Rouve Pierre • UKN • COP-OUT (USA)
STRANGER IN THE HOUSE see **BLACK CHRISTMAS** • 1975
STRANGER IN THE ROCKIES, A • 1913 • *Mecca* • USA
STRANGER IN THE VALLEY, THE • 1915 • Coyle Walter • USA
STRANGER IN THE VILLAGE, A • 1958 • Neretniek A. • USS
STRANGER IN TOWN • 1932 • Kenton Erle C. • USA
STRANGER IN TOWN • 1957 • Pollock George • UKN
STRANGER IN TOWN, A • 1943 • Rowland Roy • USA • MR. JUSTICE GOES HUNTING
STRANGER IN TOWN, A (USA) see **DOLLARO FRA I DENTI, UN** • 1967
STRANGER IS WATCHING, A • 1982 • Cunningham Sean S. • USA
STRANGER KNOCKS, A (USA) see **FREMMED BANKER PA, EN** • 1959
STRANGER LEFT NO CARD, THE • 1953 • Toye Wendy • UKN
STRANGER OF THE HILLS, THE • 1922 • Mitchell Bruce • USA
STRANGER ON A PLANE • 1989 • Mastorakis Nico • USA
STRANGER ON HORSEBACK • 1955 • Tourneur Jacques • USA
STRANGER ON MY BED • 1968 • Bryan Frank • USA
STRANGER ON MY LAND • 1988 • Elikann Larry • TVM • USA
STRANGER ON THE BASS • 1973 • Mylne Christopher • DOC • UKN
STRANGER ON THE PROWL (USA) see **IMBARCO A MEZZANOTTE** • 1952
STRANGER ON THE RUN • 1967 • Siegel Don • TVM • USA
STRANGER ON THE THIRD FLOOR BACK, THE • 1940 • Ingster Boris • USA
STRANGER -PSALM 19, THE • 1927 • Barnett Charles • UKN
STRANGER RETURNS, THE (USA) see **UOMO, UN CAVALLO, UNA PISTOLA, UN** • 1968
STRANGER RIDES AGAIN, THE • 1938 • Davis Mannie • ANS • USA
STRANGER THAN FICTION • 1921 • Barry J. A. • USA
STRANGER THAN FICTION • 1930 • *Foley George* • UKN
STRANGER THAN FICTION • 1934-39 • Ford Charles E. • SHS • USA
STRANGER THAN FICTION • 1940-42 • *O'Brien Joseph/ Mead Thomas (P)* • SHS • USA
STRANGER THAN PARADISE • 1984 • Jarmusch Jim • USA, FRG
STRANGER WAITS, A • 1987 • Lewis Robert • TVM • USA
STRANGER WALKED IN, A (UKN) see **LOVE FROM A STRANGER** • 1947
STRANGER WHO LOOKS LIKE ME, THE • 1974 • Peerce Larry • USA
STRANGER WITH A GUN see **SHEEPMAN, THE** • 1958
STRANGER WITHIN, THE • 1974 • Philips Lee • TVM • USA
STRANGER WITHIN A WOMAN, THE see **ONNA NO NAKA NI IRU TANIN** • 1966
STRANGER WORE A GUN, THE • 1953 • De Toth Andre • USA
STRANGERS • 1974 • Spelvin George • USA
STRANGERS • 1980 • *Mayne Belinda* • USA
STRANGERS • 1989 • Lahiff Craig • ASL
STRANGERS see **I NEVER SANG FOR MY FATHER** • 1970
STRANGERS, THE • 1911 • Porter Edwin S. • USA
STRANGERS, THE • 1962 • Gedris Marionas Vintzo • USS
STRANGERS, THE • 1976 • Darino Eduardo • URG
STRANGERS, THE (USA) see **VIAGGIO IN ITALIA** • 1953
STRANGERS ALL • 1935 • Vidor Charles • USA
STRANGERS AND LOVERS see **DO YOU TAKE THIS STRANGER?** • 1970
STRANGERS AT SUNRISE • 1969 • Rubens Percival • SAF, USA
STRANGER'S BANQUET, THE • 1922 • Neilan Marshall • USA
STRANGERS CAME, THE • 1949 • Travers Alfred • UKN • YOU CAN'T FOOL AN IRISHMAN (USA)
STRANGERS FROM NOWHERE • 1913 • *Solax* • USA
STRANGER'S GUNDOWN, THE (USA) see **DJANGO IL BASTARDO** • 1969
STRANGER'S HAND, THE • 1954 • Soldati Mario • UKN, ITL
STRANGER'S HAND, THE (USA) see **MANO DELLA STRANIERO, LA** • 1954
STRANGERS IN 7A, THE • 1972 • Wendkos Paul • TVM • USA
STRANGERS IN A STRANGE LAND • 1913 • *Powers* • USA • IN A STRANGE LAND
STRANGERS IN A STRANGE LAND: THE ADVENTURES OF A FILM CREW IN THE HEART OF CHINA • 1988 • McKeown Robert • DOC • CND
STRANGERS IN AFRICA • 1971 • *Poran Darr*
STRANGERS IN LOVE • 1932 • Mendes Lothar • USA • BLACK ROBE, THE
STRANGERS IN LOVE • 1983 • Vincent Chuck • USA • IN LOVE
STRANGERS IN OUR MIDST see **ESCAPE IN THE DESERT** • 1945
STRANGERS IN PARADISE • 1983 • Brocka Lino • PHL
STRANGERS IN PARADISE • 1986 • Lommel Ulli • USA
STRANGERS IN THE CITY • 1962 • Carrier Rick • USA
STRANGERS IN THE HOUSE see **INCONNUS DANS LA MAISON, LES** • 1941
STRANGERS IN THE NIGHT • 1944 • Mann Anthony • USA
STRANGERS IN THE NIGHT • 1967 • Pacheco Lauro • PHL
STRANGERS KISS • 1982 • Chapman Matthew • UKN, USA
STRANGERS MAY KISS • 1931 • Fitzmaurice George • USA
STRANGERS' MEETING • 1957 • Day Robert • UKN
STRANGERS OF THE EVENING • 1932 • Humberstone H. Bruce • USA
STRANGERS OF THE NIGHT • 1923 • Niblo Fred • USA • CAPTAIN APPLEJACK ○ AMBROSE APPLEJOHN'S ADVENTURE
STRANGERS ON A HONEYMOON • 1936 • De Courville Albert • UKN • NORTHING TRAMP, THE
STRANGERS ON A TRAIN • 1951 • Hitchcock Alfred • USA
STRANGER'S PLATE, THE • 1911 • *Powers* • USA
STRANGER'S RETURN, THE • 1933 • Vidor King • USA
STRANGERS: THE STORY OF A MOTHER AND DAUGHTER • 1979 • Katselas Milton • TVM • USA
STRANGER'S TRAIL, THE • 1913 • *Frontier* • USA
STRANGERS WHEN WE MEET • 1960 • Quine Richard • USA
STRANGEST CASE, THE (UKN) see **CRIME DOCTOR'S STRANGEST CASE** • 1943
STRANGEST TIE, THE • 1910 • *Kalem* • USA
STRANGHUGG I SOMRAS • 1972 • Ekman Mikael • SWD
STRANGLED EGGS • 1961 • McKimson Robert • ANS • USA
STRANGLED HARMONY • 1915 • *Burns Bobbie* • USA
STRANGLEHOLD • 1931 • Edwards Henry • UKN
STRANGLEHOLD • 1962 • Huntington Lawrence • UKN
STRANGLEHOLD see **GRIP OF THE STRANGLER, THE** • 1958
STRANGLER, THE • 1930 • Smith Percy • UKN
STRANGLER, THE • 1932 • Lee Norman • UKN
STRANGLER, THE • 1964 • Topper Burt • USA
STRANGLER, THE (USA) see **EAST OF PICCADILLY** • 1939
STRANGLER OF BLACKMOOR CASTLE, THE (USA) see **WURGER VON SCHLOSS BLACKMOOR, DER** • 1963
STRANGLER OF THE SWAMP • 1945 • Wisbar Frank • USA
STRANGLER OF THE TOWER • 1966 • Mehringer Hans • FRG
STRANGLER OF VIENNA, THE see **WURGER KOMMT AUF LEISEN SOCKEN, DER** • 1971
STRANGLER V. STRANGLER • 1987 • Savic Bosko
STRANGLER'S CORD, THE • 1915 • *West William H.* • USA
STRANGLER'S GRIP, THE • 1912 • *Stirling Sydney* • ASL
STRANGLER'S MORGUE see **CRIMES OF STEPHEN HAWKE, THE** • 1936
STRANGLERS OF BOMBAY, THE • 1959 • Fisher Terence • UKN
STRANGLERS OF PARIS, THE • 1913 • Gordon James • USA
STRANGLER'S WEB • 1965 • Moxey John Llewellyn • UKN
STRANGLING THREADS • 1923 • Hepworth Cecil M. • UKN
STRANGOLATORE DI VIENNA, LO (ITL) see **WURGER KOMMT AUF LEISEN SOCKEN, DER** • 1971
STRANGULATION see **KOSATSU** • 1978
STRANI CASI DI COLLERICCIO, GLI • 1920 • Lolli Alberto Carlo • ITL
STRANIERA, LA • 1930 • Palermi Amleto, Ravel Gaston • ITL

STRANIERO A PASO BRAVO, UNO • 1968 • Rossi Sergio • ITL

STRANIERO A SACRAMENTO, UNO • 1965 • Bergonzelli Sergio • ITL • STRANGER IN SACRAMENTO, A

STRANIERO FATTI IL SEGNO DELLE CROCE! • 1968 • Fidani Demofilo • ITL

STRANIERO, LO • 1967 • Visconti Luchino • ITL, FRN, ALG • ETRANGER, L' (FRN) ○ STRANGER, THE (USA)

STRANITSY ZHIZN • 1948 • Barnet Boris • USS • PAGES OF LIFE

STRANNAYA ZHENSHCHINA • 1978 • Raizman Yuli • USS • STRANGE WOMAN, A

STRANNIYE LYUDI • 1970 • Shukshin Vassili • USS • STRANGE PEOPLE

STRANO APPUNTAMENTO • 1951 • Hamza D. A. • ITL • STRANGE APPOINTMENT

STRANO RICATTO DI UNA RAGAZZA PER BENE • 1975 • Solvay Paolo • ITL

STRANO VIZIO DELLA SIGNORA WARDH, LO • 1971 • Martino Sergio • ITL, SPN • PERVERSA SENORA WARD, LA (SPN) ○ NEXT! (USA) ○ NEXT VICTIM!, THE

STRAPLESS • 1989 • Hare David • UKN

STRASHNAYA MEST • 1913 • Starevitch Ladislas • USS • TERRIBLE VENGEANCE, THE (USA) ○ TERRIBLE REVENGE, A ○ STRASNAJA MEST' ○ LOVE TAKES HIS VENGEANCE

STRASIDLA Z VIKYRE • 1987 • Cvrcek Radim • CZC • GHOSTS FROM THE ATTIC

STRASILO • 1957 • Mimica Vatroslav • ANS • YGS • SCARECROW

STRASNAJA MEST' see **STRASHNAYA MEST** • 1913

STRASS CAFE • 1980 • Pool Lea • CND

STRASS ET COMPAGNIE • 1916 • Gance Abel • FRN

STRASSE, DIE • 1923 • Grune Karl • FRG • STREET, THE

STRASSE, DIE • 1958 • Kugelstadt Hermann • FRG • STREET, THE

STRASSE DER VERHEISSUNG • 1962 • Moszkowicz Imo • FRG • STREET OF TEMPTATION (UKN)

STRASSE DES BOSEN, DIE see **VIA MALA** • 1944

STRASSE DES VERGESSENS, DIE • 1926 • Paul Heinz • FRG

STRASSE ZUR HEIMAT • 1952 • Mengon Romano • FRG

STRASSEMADCHEN VON BERLIN, DAS • 1922 • Eichberg Richard • FRG

STRASSENBEKANNTSCHAFT • 1948 • Pewas Peter • GDR • STREET ACQUAINTANCE

STRASSENBEKANNTSCHAFTEN AUF ST. PAULI • 1968 • Klinger Werner • FRG • STREET-ACQUAINTANCES OF ST. PAULI

STRASSENMUSIK • 1936 • Deppe Hans • FRG

STRASSENSERENADE • 1953 • Jacoby Georg • FRG

STRASTI PO ANDREYU • 1966 • Tarkovsky Andrei • USS • ANDREI RUBLEV (UKN) ○ PASSION OF ANDREW, THE ○ ANDREI RUBLIOV

STRASZNY DWOR • 1936 • Buczkowski Leonard • PLN • HAUNTED MIRROR, THE

STRATA • 1983 • Steven Geoff • NZL

STRATAGEM see **HARCMODOR** • 1980

STRATAGEM REWARDED • 1908 • *Wrench* • UKN

STRATASPHERE • 1983 • Rasky Harry • CND

STRATEGIA DEL RAGNO, LA • 1969 • Bertolucci Bernardo • ITL • SPIDER'S STRATEGY, THE ○ SPIDER'S STRATAGEM, THE

STRATEGIC AIR COMMAND • 1955 • Mann Anthony • USA

STRATEGIC COMMAND CHIAMA JOE WALKER • 1967 • Parolini Gianfranco • ITL

STRATEGIJA SVRAKE • 1987 • Lavanic Zlatko • YGS • MAGPIE STRATEGY, THE

STRATEGIST, THE • 1915 • MacGregor Norval • USA

STRATEGY • 1911 • *Kerrigan J. Warren* • USA

STRATEGY • 1915 • Weston Harold • UKN • SOCIETY CROOKS

STRATEGY OF ANNE, THE • 1911 • Baker George D. • USA

STRATEGY OF BRONCHO BILLY'S SWEETHEART, THE • 1914 • *Essanay* • USA

STRATEGY OF CONDUCTOR 786, THE • 1914 • *Chamberlin Riley* • USA

STRATEGY OF TERROR • 1969 • Smight Jack • TVM • USA • IN DARKNESS WAITING

STRATFORD ADVENTURE, THE • 1954 • Parker Gudrun, Parker Morten • CND

STRATHMORE • 1915 • Grandon Francis J. • USA

STRATOS FEAR • 1933 • *Iwerks Ub (P)* • ANS • USA

STRATTON STORY, THE • 1949 • Wood Sam • USA

STRAUBERG IST DA • 1978 • Galle Mischa • FRG

STRAUSS DER WALZER KONIG • 1929 • Wiene Conrad • FRG

STRAUSS' GREAT WALTZ (USA) see **WALTZES FROM VIENNA** • 1933

STRAUSS' SALOME see **SALOME** • 1923

STRAV • 1960 • Janevski Slavko • SHT • YGS

STRAVERS • 1987 • Delpeut Peter • NTH

STRAVINSKY • 1965 • Koenig Wolf, Kroitor Roman • DOC • CND

STRAVINSKY PORTRAIT, A • 1968 • Leacock Richard, Liebermann Rolf • USA

STRAW BELLS • 1987 • Ilyenko Yury • USS

STRAW DOGS • 1971 • Peckinpah Sam • USA

STRAW GIRLS see **SLAMARKE DIVOJKE** • 1971

STRAW HAT, THE see **SLAMENY KLOBOUK** • 1972

STRAW MAN, THE • 1915 • Franklin Sidney A., Franklin Chester M. • USA

STRAW MAN, THE • 1953 • Taylor Donald • UKN

STRAW RIDE, A • 1910 • *Atlas* • USA

STRAWANZER • 1983 • Patzak Peter • AUS, FRG • TRAMPS, THE

STRAWBERRIES NEED RAIN • 1970 • Buchanan Larry • USA

STRAWBERRY see **FRUTILLA** • 1980

STRAWBERRY BLONDE, THE • 1941 • Walsh Raoul • USA

STRAWBERRY FIELDS • 1985 • Kuhn Christian • TVM • FRG

STRAWBERRY ROAN • 1945 • Elvey Maurice • UKN

STRAWBERRY ROAN, THE • 1933 • James Alan • USA • FLYING FURY (UKN)

STRAWBERRY ROAN, THE • 1948 • English John • USA • FOOLS AWAKE (UKN)

STRAWBERRY SHORTCAKE AND THE BABY WITHOUT A NAME • 1983 • Selznick Arna • MTV • CND

STRAWBERRY STATEMENT, THE • 1970 • Hagmann Stuart • USA

STRAWBERRY TIME see **KO ZORIJO JAGODE** • 1979

STRAWFIRE see **STROHFEUER** • 1972

STRAWHAIRED FANNY see **FANNY PELOPAJA** • 1984

STRAWMAN see **TAO-TS'AO JEN** • 1988

STRAWS IN THE WIND • 1915 • *Balboa* • USA

STRAWS IN THE WIND • 1924 • Phillips Bertram • UKN

STRAY BULLETS • 1911 • *Essanay* • USA

STRAY CAT see **NORA NEKO** • 1958

STRAY DAYS • 1988 • Ottoni Filippo • USA

STRAY DOG see **NORA INU** • 1949

STRAY SHEEP see **SANSHIRO** • 1955

STRAY SHOT, THE • 1915 • Morgan George • USA

STRAYED FROM THE RANCH • 1910 • *Nestor* • USA

STRAZ NAD BALTYKIEM • 1946 • Bossak Jerzy • DOC • PLN • GUARD ON THE BALTIC

STRAZIAMI MA DI BACI SAZIAMI • 1968 • Risi Dino • ITL, FRN • FAIS MOI TRES MAL, MAIS COUVRE-MOI DE BAISERS (FRN) ○ KILL ME WITH KISSES ○ TEAR ME BUT SATIATE ME WITH YOUR KISSES

STRAZILE AU AMINTIRI • 1962 • Marcus Manole • RMN • STREET REMEMBERS, THE

STREAK CAR COMPANY, THE • Kener Paul W. • USA

STREAK OF LUCK, A • 1925 • Thorpe Richard • USA

STREAK OF YELLOW, A • 1913 • *Joyce Alice* • USA

STREAM, THE see **SODRASBAN** • 1964

STREAM OF LIFE see **GEKIRYU** • 1967

STREAM OF LIFE, THE • 1919 • Plympton Horace G. • USA

STREAM OF YOUTH, THE see **WAKAI KAWA NO NAGARE** • 1959

STREAMERS • 1983 • Altman Robert • USA

STREAMLINE EXPRESS • 1935 • Fields Leonard • USA

STREAMLINED DONKEY, THE • 1941 • *Mintz Charles (P)* • ANS • USA

STREAMLINED GRETNA GREEN • 1937 • Freleng Friz • ANS • USA

STREAMLINED SWING • 1938 • Keaton Buster • SHT • USA

STRECHNI see **VSTRECHNYI** • 1932

STRECKE, DIE • 1927 • Neufeld Max • AUS • GROSSE UN DIE KLEINE WELT, DIE

STREE • 1962 • Shantaram Rajaram • IND • WOMAN

STREET see **MACHI** • 1939

STREET, THE • 1976 • Leaf Caroline • ANS • CND • RUE, LA

STREET, THE see **STRASSE, DIE** • 1923

STREET, THE see **GATAN** • 1949

STREET, THE see **STRASSE, DIE** • 1958

STREET ACQUAINTANCE see **STRASSENBEKANNTSCHAFT** • 1948

STREET-ACQUAINTANCES OF ST. PAULI see **STRASSENBEKANNTSCHAFTEN AUF ST. PAULI** • 1968

STREET ANGEL • 1928 • Borzage Frank • USA

STREET ANGEL, A see **ANGEL DE LA CALLE, UN** • 1966

STREET ARAB see **MONELLO DELLA STRADA, IL** • 1951

STREET ARAB, A • 1909 • Fitzhamon Lewin • UKN

STREET BANDITS • 1951 • Springsteen R. G. • USA

STREET BEAUTIFUL, THE • 1912 • Miller Ashley • USA

STREET CALLED STRAIGHT, THE • 1920 • Worsley Wallace • USA

STREET CAR CHIVALRY • 1903 • Porter Edwin S. • USA

STREET CARS AND CARBUNCLES • 1917 • Smith Dick • SHT • USA

STREET CAT NAMED SYLVESTER, A • 1953 • Freleng Friz • ANS • USA

STREET CORNER • 1948 • Kelley Albert • USA

STREET CORNER • 1953 • Box Muriel • UKN • BOTH SIDES OF THE LAW (USA) ○ GENTLE ARM, THE

STREET CORNER FRAUDS • 1926 • Engholm F. W. • UKN

STREET CORNERS • 1929 • Birdwell Russell J. • USA

STREET DREAMS • 1987 • Paul Stuart • USA

STREET FAKERS • 1915 • *Jamison Bud* • USA

STREET FIGHT see **COONSKIN** • 1975

STREET FLEET see **D.C. CAB** • 1983

STREET GANG • 1982 • Lustig William • USA • VIGILANTE ○ STREET GANGS

STREET GANGS see **STREET GANG** • 1982

STREET GANGS OF HONG KONG • 1974 • *Wang Chung* • HKG

STREET GIRL • 1929 • Ruggles Wesley • USA • BARBER JOHN'S BOY

STREET GIRLS • 1973 • Miller Michael • USA • CRACKERS

STREET HAS MANY DREAMS, THE (UKN) see **MOLTI SOGNI PER LE STRADE** • 1948

STREET HAWK see **STREETHAWK** • 1986

STREET HERO • 1984 • Pattinson Michael • ASL

STREET IN THE SUN see **HI NO ATARU SAKAMICHI** • 1958

STREET IS FULL OF SURPRISES, THE • 1958 • Sidelev Sergei • USS

STREET IS MY BEAT, THE • 1966 • Berwick Irvin • USA

STREET IS NOT A PLAYGROUND, THE • Wiemer Hans Ulrich • ANM • GDR

STREET IS OURS, THE see **A NOUS LA RUE** • 1986

STREET JUGGLER see **MACHI NO TEJINASHI** • 1925

STREET JUSTICE • 1987 • Sarafian Richard C. • USA, CND

STREET KIDS • 1982 • Scott Rob, Tilson Leigh • DOC • ASL

STREET KILLERS (UKN) see **ROMA VIOLENTA** • 1975

STREET KILLING • 1976 • Hart Harvey • TVM • USA

STREET LAW see **REVENGE** • 1979

STREET LEGAL • 1989 • Mackenzie John • USA

STREET LEGION, THE see **LEGION ULICY** • 1932

STREET LISTENS, THE • 1964 • Gazhiu Valeri • SHT • USS

STREET LOVE see **SCARRED** • 1984

STREET MEAT see **STREET MEET** • 1957

STREET MEET • 1957 • Vanderbeek Stan • USA • STREET MEAT

STREET MUSIC • 1972 • Larkin Ryan • SHT • CND • STREET MUSIQUE

STREET MUSIC • 1981 • Bowen Jenny • USA

STREET MUSIQUE see **STREET MUSIC** • 1972

STREET OF ADVENTURE, THE • 1921 • Foss Kenelm • UKN

STREET OF CHANCE • 1930 • Cromwell John • USA

STREET OF CHANCE • 1942 • Hively Jack • USA • BLACK CURTAIN, THE

STREET OF DARKNESS • 1958 • Walker Robert • USA

STREET OF DREAMS • 1988 • Graham William A. • TVM • USA

STREET OF FORGOTTEN MEN, THE • 1925 • Brenon Herbert • USA

STREET OF HOPE, THE see **UMUT SOKAGI** • 1986

STREET OF ILLUSION, THE • 1928 • Kenton Erle C. • USA

STREET OF JAZZ, THE (UKN) see **TIMES SQUARE** • 1929

STREET OF JOY see **AKUSEN TAMANOI -NUKERAREMASU** • 1974

STREET OF LONDON, THE • 1929 • Lee Norman • UKN

STREET OF LOVE see **AI NO MACHI** • 1928

STREET OF MASTERLESS SAMURAI, THE see **RONINGAI** • 1928

STREET OF MEMORIES • 1940 • Traube Shepard • USA

STREET OF MISSING MEN • 1939 • Salkow Sidney • USA

STREET OF MY CHILDHOOD see **BARNDOMMENS GADE** • 1987

STREET OF NO RETURN • 1988 • Fuller Tex • USA

STREET OF SEVEN STARS, THE • 1918 • O'Brien John B. • USA

STREET OF SHADOWS • 1953 • Vernon Richard • UKN • SHADOW MAN (USA)

STREET OF SHADOWS (USA) see **MADEMOISELLE DOCTEUR** • 1937

STREET OF SHAME see **AKASEN CHITAI** • 1956

STREET OF SHANGHAI • 1927 • Gasnier Louis J. • USA

STREET OF SIN, THE • 1928 • Stiller Mauritz, Berger Ludwig (U/c) • USA • KING OF SOHO

STREET OF SIN AND LOVE, THE see **ULICKA HRICHU A LASKY** • 1923

STREET OF SIN (UKN) see **ARZT VON ST. PAULI, DER** • 1968

STREET OF SINNERS • 1957 • Berke William • USA

STREET OF SORROW, THE (USA) see **FREUDLOSE GASSE, DIE** • 1925

STREET OF TEARS, THE • 1924 • Vale Travers • USA

STREET OF TEMPTATION (UKN) see **STRASSE DER VERHEISSUNG** • 1962

STREET OF THE DAMNED see **RUE BARBARE** • 1983

STREET OF THE FLYING DRAGON, THE see **FIVE DAYS TO LIVE** • 1922

STREET OF THE LOST see **RUE BARBARE** • 1983

STREET OF THE PUPPET SHOW see **SHARIAH EL BAHLAWANE** • 1949

STREET OF THE STRANGE ONES, THE see **GARIPLER SOKAGI** • 1967

STREET OF THE YOUNG see **DROGA MLODYCH** • 1935

STREET OF VIOLENCE see **BORYOKU NO MACHI** • 1950

STREET OF WANDERING PIGEONS see **WATARIDORI ITSUKAERU** • 1956

STREET OF WOMEN • 1932 • Mayo Archie • USA

STREET PEOPLE (USA) see **ESECUTORI, GLI** • 1976

STREET PHOTOGRAPHER, THE see **MINUTEROS, LOS** • 1973

STREET PLAYER see **HARRIF, EL** • 1983

STREET PREACHER, THE • 1910 • *Lubin* • USA

STREET REMEMBERS, THE see **STRAZILE AU AMINTIRI** • 1962

STREET REVENGE see **BAMEUI YEOLGI SOGEURO** • 1985

STREET SCENE • 1931 • Vidor King • USA

STREET SCENES see **GAIJO NO SUKECHI** • 1925

STREET SINGER • 1932 • Brice Monte • SHT • USA

STREET SINGER • 1938 • *Sircar B. N. (P)* • IND

STREET SINGER, THE • 1912 • *Joyce Alice* • USA

STREET SINGER, THE • 1937 • de Marguenat Jean • UKN • INTERVAL FOR ROMANCE

STREET SINGERS, THE • 1913 • North Wilfred, Van Wally • USA

STREET SINGER'S SERENADE see **LIMELIGHT** • 1936

STREET SKETCHES (USA) see **GAIJO NO SUKECHI** • 1925

STREET SMART • 1987 • Schatzberg Jerry • USA

STREET SONG • 1935 • Vorhaus Bernard • UKN

STREET-SWEEPERS see **KADUN LAKAISIJAT** • 1989

STREET THIEVES see **ATRACADORES, LOS** • 1961

STREET TO DIE, A • 1985 • Bennett Bill • ASL

STREET TO THE WORLD see **AU BOUT DE MA RUE** • 1958

STREET TRASH • 1986 • Muro Jim • USA

STREET TUMBLERS, THE • 1922 • Wynn George • UKN

STREET UNDER THE SNOW, A • 1978 • Carlsen Henning • DNM

STREET WAIF'S CHRISTMAS, A • 1908 • Porter Edwin S. • USA

STREET WAR see **BLACK GODFATHER, THE** • 1974

STREET WARRIOR see **HIT MAN** • 1972

STREET WARRIOR see **MEAN JOHNNY BURROWS** • 1976

STREET WATCHMAN'S STORY, THE • 1914 • Vernon Charles • UKN

STREET WITH NO NAME, THE • 1948 • Keighley William • USA

STREET WITH THE CUPOLA, THE see **KYUPORA NO ARU MACHI** • 1962

STREET WITHOUT END see **KAJIRINAKI HODO** • 1934

STREET WITHOUT SUN, THE see **TAIYO NO NAI MACHI** • 1954

STREETCAR, THE see **ILUSION VIAJA EN TRANVIA, LA** • 1953

STREETCAR NAMED DESIRE, A • 1951 • Kazan Elia • USA

STREETCAR NAMED REPULSIVE • 1949 • Lewis Jerry • SHT • USA

STREETCAR TO HEAVEN see **DROGA DO NIEBA** • 1958

STREETFIGHTER, THE (UKN) see **HARD TIMES** • 1975

STREETFIGHTER, THE (USA) see **GEKITOTSU SATSUJINKEN** • 1973

STREETFIGHTER COUNTER-ATTACKS, THE see **STREETFIGHTER'S LAST REVENGE, THE** • 1979

STREETFIGHTERS • 1987 • Yuval Peter • USA

STREETFIGHTER'S LAST REVENGE, THE • 1979 • *Chiba Sonny* • JPN • STREETFIGHTER COUNTER-ATTACKS, THE

STREETHAWK • 1986 • Vogel Virgil W. • USA • STREET HAWK

STREET/RACK see **MEAT/RACK** • 1970

STREETS • 1990 • Ruben Katt Shea • USA

STREETS OF EARLY SORROW see **CAMINHOS PARA A ANGUSTIA** • 1963

STREETS OF FIRE • 1983 • Hill Walter • USA

STREETS OF GHOST TOWN • 1950 • Nazarro Ray • USA

STREETS OF GOLD • 1987 • Roth Joe • USA

STREETS OF HOLLYWOOD, THE • 1989 • Davis B. J. • USA

STREETS OF ILLUSION, THE • 1917 • Parke William • USA

STREETS OF ISTANBUL, THE see **ISTANBUL KALDIRIMLARI** • 1968
STREETS OF JUSTICE • 1985 • Crowe Christopher • TVM • USA
STREETS OF L.A., THE • 1979 • Freedman Jerrold • TVM • USA
STREETS OF LAREDO • 1949 • Fenton Leslie • USA
STREETS OF LONDON • 1934 • Thring F. W. • ASL
STREETS OF MAKE BELIEVE, THE • 1915 • Lessey George A. • USA
STREETS OF MISSING WOMEN see **CAFE HOSTESS** • 1940
STREETS OF NEW YORK • 1938 • Nigh William • USA
STREETS OF NEW YORK, THE • 1913 • Vale Travers • USA
STREETS OF NEW YORK, THE • 1922 • King Burton L. • USA
STREETS OF PARIS see **RUE DES PRAIRIES** • 1959
STREETS OF SAIGON, THE see **SAD SONG OF YELLOW SKIN** • 1970
STREETS OF SAN FRANCISCO • 1949 • Blair George • USA
STREETS OF SAN FRANCISCO, THE • 1972 • Grauman Walter • TVM • USA
STREETS OF SIN see **NOT WANTED** • 1949
STREETS OF SORROW (USA) see **HO SOGNATO IL PARADISO** • 1950
STREETS OF YESTERDAY • 1989 • Ne'Eman Yehuda • UKN
STREETWALKER, THE (UKN) see **MARGE, LA** • 1976
STREETWALKIN' • 1985 • Freeman Joan • USA • COOKIE
STREETWISE • 1984 • Bell Martin, Mark Mary Ellen, McCall Cheryl • USA
STREGA, LA • 1907 • *Vitrotti Giovanni (Ph)* • ITL • WITCH, THE
STREGA DE SIVIGLIA, IL • 1911 • *Itala* • ITL • WITCH OF SEVILLE, THE
STREGA IN AMORE, LA • 1966 • Damiani Damiano • ITL • WITCH IN LOVE, THE (UKN) ○ WITCH, THE (USA) ○ STRANGE OBSESSION, THE ○ AURA
STREGHE, LE • 1967 • Pasolini Pier Paolo, Bolognini Mauro, Visconti Luchino, Rossi Franco, De Sica Vittorio • ITL, FRN • SORCIERES, LES (FRN) ○ WITCHES, THE
STREGHE NERE, LE • 1975 • Hoven Adrian • ITL
STREGONI DI CITTA • 1973 • Bettetini Gianfranco • ITL
STREGONI IN TIGHT • 1965 • Marzano Marino • DOC • ITL • AFRICA D'OGGI
STREICH: LOTTE ALS SCHULSCHRECK see **BERLINER RANGE, DIE** • 1920
STREICHHOLZER, KAUFT STREICHHOLZER! • 1916 • Neuss Alwin • FRG
STREICHHOLZKUNSTLER, DER • 1913 • Seeber Guido • ANS • FRG • MATCH MASTER, THE
STREIK • 1974 • Tuhus Oddvar Bull • NRW • STRIKE
STREIK DER DIEBE, DER • 1921 • Abel Alfred • FRG
STREIT UM DEN KNABEN JO • 1937 • Waschneck Erich • FRG • STRIFE OVER THE BOY JO (USA)
STREIT UM DIE RUINEN, DER see **HAPURA, DIE TOTE STADT 2** • 1921
STREJDA • 1959 • Jires Jaromil • SHT • CZC • UNCLE
STREJKEN • 1915 • Sjostrom Victor • SWD • STRIKE, THE
STREKOZA I MURAVEJ • 1912 • *Starevitch Ladislav (P)* • USS
STREKOZA I MURAVEJ • 1935 • Ivanov-Vano Ivan • ANS • USS
STRELLE NEL FOSSO, LE • 1979 • Avati Pupi • ITL
STRELTZI • 1967 • Donev Donyo • BUL • SHARPSHOOTERS ○ MARKSMEN
STREMPELS MIEZE see **MIEZE STREMPELS WERDEGANG** • 1915
STRENG GEHEIM • 1963 • Veiczi Janos • GDR • FOR EYES ONLY
STRENG VERTRAULICH see **SONG FOR EUROPE, A** • 1985
STRENGTH • 1915 • Davis Ulysses • USA
STRENGTH OF A MOUSTACHE, THE see **HIGE NO CHIKARA** • 1931
STRENGTH OF A SAMSON, THE • 1915 • Martin E. A. • USA
STRENGTH OF DONALD MACKENZIE, THE • 1916 • Russell William • USA
STRENGTH OF FAMILY TIES, THE • 1914 • Carleton Lloyd B. • USA
STRENGTH OF GOD, THE see **DEIVA BALAM** • 1959
STRENGTH OF LOVE see **AI WA CHIKARA DA** • 1930
STRENGTH OF MEN, THE • 1913 • *Finley Ned* • USA
STRENGTH OF THE HUMBLE, THE see **FUERZA DE LOS HUMILDES, LA** • 1954
STRENGTH OF THE HUNGARIAN SOIL, THE see **MAGYAR FOLD EREJE, A** • 1917
STRENGTH OF THE PINES • 1922 • Lewis Edgar • USA
STRENGTH OF THE WEAK, THE • 1912 • Porter Edwin S. • USA
STRENGTH OF THE WEAK, THE • 1913 • *Powers* • USA
STRENGTH OF THE WEAK, THE • 1913 • Davenport Charles E. • *Reliance* • USA
STRENGTH OF THE WEAK, THE • 1914 • *Pathe* • USA
STRENGTH OF THE WEAK, THE • 1915 • *Essanay* • USA
STRENGTH OF THE WEAK, THE • 1915 • *Premier* • USA
STRENGTH OF THE WEAK, THE • 1916 • *Buffalo* • SHT • USA
STRENGTH OF THE WEAK, THE • 1916 • Henderson Lucius • *Bluebird* • USA
STRENGTH OF THE WEAK, THE • 1918 • Terriss Tom • USA
STRENGTH O'TEN, THE • 1914 • Ricketts Thomas • USA
STRENGTH THAT FAILED, THE • 1914 • Aylott Dave • UKN
STRENUOUS DREAM, A • 1907 • Blackton J. Stuart • SHT • USA
STRENUOUS LIFE, THE • 1914 • *Madison Cleo* • USA
STRENUOUS LIFE, THE • 1915 • *Brown-Leighton Lyllian* • USA
STRENUOUS RIDE, A • 1914 • *Lubin* • USA
STRENUOUS SCOOP, A • 1914 • *Selig* • USA
STRESEMANN • 1957 • Braun Alfred • FRG
STRESS • 1972 • Prisco Corrado • ITL
STRESS • 1973 • Manuel Pierre, Peche Jean-Jacques • BLG
STRESS • 1984 • Bertucelli Jean-Louis • FRN
STRESS AND EMOTION • 1984 • Spry Robin • CND
STRESS ES TRES, TRES • 1968 • Saura Carlos • SPN • STRESS IS THREE
STRESS IS THREE see **STRESS ES TRES, TRES** • 1968
STRESS OF CIRCUMSTANCE, THE • 1914 • Buckland Warwick? • UKN
STRESS OF THE NEW ADDRESS • 1980 • Wojciechowski Krzysztof • PLN
STRESS OF YOUTH see **TRAPENI** • 1961
STRETCHING OUT • Schulte Larry • ANS • USA
STRIATIONS • 1970 • McLaren Norman • ANS • CND
STRIBRNA OBLAKA • 1938 • Slegl • CZC • SILVER SKIES
STRIBRNY VITR • 1954 • Krska Vaclav • CZC • SILVER WIND, THE ○ SILVERY WIND, THE
STRICH DURCH DIE RECHNUNG • 1932 • Zeisler Alfred • FRG
STRICK DES HENKERS, DER • 1923 • Seitz Franz?, Berger Josef? • FRG
STRICKEN BLIND • 1908 • *Vitagraph* • USA
STRICKEN BLIND • 1909 • *Selig* • USA
STRICKEN HOME, THE • 1910 • Bouwmeester Theo? • UKN
STRICKEN PENINSULA • 1946 • Fletcher Paul • DOC • UKN
STRICKER'S MOUNTAIN • 1986 • Simmonds Alan • CND • STRIKER'S MOUNTAIN
STRICKNADELN, DIE • 1916 • Rippert Otto • FRG
STRICTLY BUSINESS • 1913 • Smalley Phillips • USA
STRICTLY BUSINESS • 1916 • *Stull Walter* • USA
STRICTLY BUSINESS • 1917 • Mills Thomas R. • SHT • USA
STRICTLY BUSINESS • 1932 • Field Mary, Logan Jacqueline • UKN
STRICTLY CONFIDENTIAL • Pogacnik Joze • DCS • YGS
STRICTLY CONFIDENTIAL • 1919 • Badger Clarence • USA
STRICTLY CONFIDENTIAL • 1959 • Saunders Charles • UKN
STRICTLY CONFIDENTIAL (UKN) see **BROADWAY BILL** • 1934
STRICTLY DISHONORABLE • 1931 • Stahl John M. • USA
STRICTLY DISHONORABLE • 1951 • Panama Norman, Frank Melvin • USA
STRICTLY DYNAMITE • 1934 • Nugent Elliott • USA • PHANTOM FAME
STRICTLY DYNAMITE see **FOOTLIGHT SERENADE** • 1942
STRICTLY FOR CASH • 1984 • O'Hara Gerry • UKN
STRICTLY FOR PLEASURE (UKN) see **PERFECT FURLOUGH, THE** • 1958
STRICTLY FOR THE BIRDS • 1963 • Sewell Vernon • UKN
STRICTLY FRESH EGGS • 1903 • *Osterman Kathryn* • USA • CHICKS TO ORDER
STRICTLY FRESH YEGGS • 1934 • Stevens George • SHT • USA
STRICTLY ILLEGAL • 1935 • Ceder Ralph • UKN • HERE COMES A POLICEMAN
STRICTLY IN CONFIDENCE • 1933 • Cook Clyde • UKN • CONFIDENTIAL LADIES
STRICTLY IN THE GROOVE • 1943 • Keays Vernon • USA
STRICTLY MODERN • 1922 • Beaudine William • USA
STRICTLY MODERN • 1930 • Seiter William A. • USA
STRICTLY NEUTRAL • 1915 • Williams C. Jay • USA
STRICTLY PERSONAL • 1933 • Murphy Ralph • USA
STRICTLY PERSONAL • 1988 • Shah Krishna • USA
STRICTLY PRIVATE • 1916 • Myll Louis • SHT • USA
STRICTLY SECRET PREMIERES see **PRISNE TAJNE PREMIERY** • 1967
STRICTLY SECRET PREVIEWS see **PRISNE TAJNE PREMIERY** • 1967
STRICTLY UNCONVENTIONAL • 1930 • Burton David • USA • CIRCLE, THE
STRICTLY UNRELIABLE • 1932 • Marshall George • SHT • USA
STRIDE, SOVIET! see **SHAGAI, SOVIET!** • 1926
STRIDEN GAR VIDARE • 1941 • Molander Gustaf • SWD • FIGHT GOES ON, THE
STRIDULUM • 1979 • Paradisi Giulio • ITL, USA • VISITOR, THE (USA) ○ VISITATORE, IL
STRIFE • 1919 • *Le Guere George* • USA
STRIFE ETERNAL, THE (USA) see **JANE SHORE** • 1915
STRIFE OF THE PARTY, THE • 1931 • Sandrich Mark • SHT • USA
STRIFE OVER THE BOY JO (USA) see **STREIT UM DEN KNABEN JO** • 1937
STRIFE WITH FATHER • 1950 • McKimson Robert • ANS • USA
STRIJD DER GEUZEN, DE • 1912 • Machin Alfred • NTH
STRIJD ZONDER EINDE • 1954 • Haanstra Bert • DOC • NTH, UKN • RIVAL WORLD, THE
STRIKE • 1912 • ASL
STRIKE • 1970 • Carter Peter • CND
STRIKE see **STREIK** • 1974
STRIKE, THE • 1912 • *Solax* • USA
STRIKE, THE • 1913 • *Kalem* • USA
STRIKE, THE • 1914 • *Ostriche Muriel* • USA
STRIKE, THE see **STREJKEN** • 1915
STRIKE, THE see **SIRENA** • 1947
STRIKE, THE see **COMIC STRIP PRESENTS: THE STRIKE** • 1988
STRIKE AT CENTIPEDE MINE, THE • 1915 • *Stanton Richard* • USA
STRIKE AT COALDALE, THE • 1914 • *Walpole Stanley* • USA
STRIKE AT THE GRINGO, THE • 1911 • Melies Gaston • USA
STRIKE AT THE HEART see **COLPIRE AL CUORE** • 1983
STRIKE AT THE LITTLE JONNY MINE, THE • 1911 • *Anderson Broncho Billy* • USA
STRIKE AT THE MINES, THE • 1911 • Porter Edwin S. • USA
STRIKE BACK • 1980 • Schenkel Carl • FRG
STRIKE BREAKER • 1920 • *West Billy* • SHT • USA
STRIKE BREAKER, THE • 1913 • *Nestor* • USA
STRIKE BREAKERS • 1919 • *Lyons Eddie* • SHT • USA
STRIKE COMMANDO • 1986 • Mattei Bruno • ITL
STRIKE FEVER • 1920 • Miller Frank • UKN
STRIKE FORCE • 1975 • Shear Barry • TVM • USA
STRIKE FORCE • 1981 • Lang Richard • TVM • USA
STRIKE IN THE "MAKE YOUNG" BUSINESS, A • 1911 • *Eclair* • FRN
STRIKE IT RICH • 1933 • Hiscott Leslie • UKN
STRIKE IT RICH • 1948 • Selander Lesley • USA
STRIKE IT RICH • 1990 • Scott James • USA
STRIKE LEADER, THE • 1911 • Noy Wilfred • UKN
STRIKE LEADER, THE • 1913 • Apfel Oscar • USA
STRIKE ME DEADLY see **CRAWLING HAND, THE** • 1963
STRIKE ME PINK • 1936 • Taurog Norman • USA
STRIKE OF THE PANTHER, THE • 1987 • Trenchard-Smith Brian • ASL • FISTS OF BLOOD
STRIKE OF THUNDERKICK TIGER • Wong Henry • HKG
STRIKE ON THE RANCH, THE • 1912 • *Pathe* • USA
STRIKE ONE • 1917 • Hutchinson Craig • SHT • USA
STRIKE THE MONSTER ON PAGE ONE see **SBATTI IL MOSTRO IN PRIMA PAGINA** • 1972
STRIKE (UKN) see **STACHKA** • 1925
STRIKE UP THE BAND • 1930 • Fleischer Dave • ANS • USA
STRIKE UP THE BAND • 1940 • Berkeley Busby • USA
STRIKE! (USA) see **RED ENSIGN** • 1934
STRIKEBOUND • 1984 • Lowenstein Richard • ASL
STRIKEBREAKER, THE • 1975 • Heroux Denis • CND
STRIKER • 1976 • Nichol Robert L. • MTV • CND
STRIKER • 1985 • Edmonds Don • USA
STRIKER • 1988 • Castellari Enzo G. • ITL
STRIKER WITH THE NO.9, THE • 1988 • Voulgaris Pantelis • GRC
STRIKERS, THE • 1915 • *Apex* • USA
STRIKERS, THE see **COMPAGNI, I** • 1963
STRIKER'S MOUNTAIN see **STRICKER'S MOUNTAIN** • 1986
STRIKE'S ABC see **ABC DA GREVE** • 1989
STRIKES AND SPARES • 1934 • Feist Felix E. • SHT • USA
STRIKING BACK see **SEARCH AND DESTROY** • 1979
STRIKING BACK see **NEW KIDS, THE** • 1985
STRIKING CHANCE see **HOTSHOT** • 1987
STRIKING MODELS • 1920 • *Christie* • SHT • USA
STRIKING TONIGHT see **STASERA SCIOPERO** • 1951
STRINDBERG • 1979 • Watkins Peter • SWD
STRING BEAN JACK • 1938 • Foster John • ANS • USA
STRING BEANS • 1918 • Schertzinger Victor • USA
STRING OF BEADS, A • 1912 • Melies Gaston • USA
STRING OF PEARLS, A • 1912 • Griffith D. W. • USA
STRING OF PEARLS, A • 1914 • *Holmes Helen* • USA
STRING OF PEARLS, A • 1916 • Page Will • UKN
STRINGENT PREDICTION AT THE EARLY HERMAPHRODITIC STAGE, A • 1961 • Landow George • USA
STRINGIMI FORTE PAPA • 1978 • Tarantini Michele Massimo • ITL
STRINGING THEM ALONG • 1916 • *Judy* • USA
STRINGLOS POV EYINE ARNAKI, O • 1968 • Sakellarios Alekos • GRC • MALE SHREW WHO BECAME A LAMB, THE ○ TAMING OF THE MALE SHREW, THE
STRIP • 1966 • Lamm Steffan, De Fina Don, Davis Peter • UKN
STRIP, THE • 1951 • Kardos Leslie • USA
STRIP, THE • 1973 • Mann Ron • DOC • CND
STRIP CLUBS IN LONDON • 1962 • Sheppard Gordon H. • DOC • CND
STRIP OFF, DOLL see **ZIEH' DICH AUS, PUPPE** • 1968
STRIP POKER • 1912 • *Majestic* • USA
STRIP POKER see **BIG SWITCH, THE** • 1968
STRIP, STRIP, HOORAY! • 1932 • Lee Norman • UKN • LET'S GO NAKED
STRIP-TEASE • 1963 • Poitrenaud Jacques • FRN, ITL • SWEET SKIN (USA)
STRIP-TEASE • 1965 • Lemaire Yvan • BLG
STRIP-TEASE • 1971 • Vajda Bela • HNG
STRIP-TEASE • 1976 • Lorente German • SPN • STRIPTEASE ○ INSANITY
STRIP-TEASE A LA INGLESA • 1975 • Madrid Jose Luis • SPN
STRIP-TEASEUSES, CES FEMMES QUE L'ON CROIT FACILES • 1963 • Roy Jean-Claude • FRN
STRIPED BATHING SUIT, THE • 1912 • *Pates Gwendoline* • USA
STRIPED HORSE IN A RED COLLAR • 1970 • Joseph Stanley • DCS • UKN
STRIPED LOAD, THE • 1961 • Fetin Vladimir • USS • STRIPED VOYAGE, A
STRIPED PARASOL, THE • 1912 • *Majestic* • USA
STRIPED STOCKING GANG, THE • 1915 • Durrant Fred W. • UKN • MRS. CASSELL'S PROFESSION
STRIPED VOYAGE, A see **STRIPED LOAD, THE** • 1961
STRIPES • 1981 • Reitman Ivan • USA
STRIPES AND STARS • 1918 • Hall Walter • SHT • USA
STRIPES AND STARS • 1929 • Lantz Walter • ANS • USA
STRIPES AND STUMBLES • 1918 • Semon Larry • SHT • USA
STRIPPED FOR A MILLION • 1919 • De La Parelle M. • USA
STRIPPED TO KILL • 1987 • Ruben Katt Shea • USA • DECEPTION
STRIPPED TO KILL 2: LIVE GIRLS see **LIVE GIRLS STRIPPED TO KILL II** • 1989
STRIPPER • 1986 • Gary Jerome • DOC • USA
STRIPPER, THE • 1963 • Schaffner Franklin J. • USA • WOMAN OF SUMMER (UKN) ○ CELEBRATION
STRIPPING WIVES see **CASE OF THE STRIPPING WIVES, THE** • 1966
STRIPPO STRAPPO STROPPIO see **CRASH CHE BOTTE!** • 1973
STRIPTEASE • 1957 • Borowczyk Walerian, Lenica Jan • ANS • PLN
STRIPTEASE • 1980 • Armatage Kay • CND
STRIPTEASE see **STRIPTIZ** • 1969
STRIPTEASE see **STRIP-TEASE** • 1976
STRIPTEASE LADY (UKN) see **LADY OF BURLESQUE** • 1943
STRIPTEASE MURDER • 1961 • Morris Ernest • UKN
STRIPTIZ • 1969 • Dragic Nedeljko • ANM • YGS • STRIPTEASE
STRIVING FOR FORTUNE • 1926 • Ross Nat • USA
STROBOSCOPES, LES • 1963 • Borowczyk Walerian • SHT • FRN • MAGASINS DU XIXe SIECLE
STROGI YUNOSHA • 1936 • Room Abram • USS • STERN YOUNG MAN, THE
STROGOFF • 1970 • Visconti Eriprando • ITL, FRN, FRG • MICHELE STROGOFF
STROHFEUER • 1915 • Eichberg Richard • FRG
STROHFEUER • 1972 • Schlondorff Volker • FRG • FREE WOMAN, A (USA) ○ SUMMER LIGHTNING, A ○ STRAWFIRE
STROHWITWER • 1931 • Jacoby Georg • FRG
STROKE OAR, THE • 1912 • *Orlamond William* • USA
STROKE OF A THOUSAND MILLIONS, A see **GOLPE DE MIL MILLONES, UN** • 1966
STROKE OF FATE, THE • 1915 • Smiley Joseph • USA
STROKE OF LUCK, A see **CUCCAGNA, LA** • 1962
STROKE OF MIDNIGHT, THE (USA) see **KORKARLEN** • 1921
STROKE OF NINE, THE • 1970 • *Distripix Inc.* • USA
STROKE OF THE PHOEBUS EIGHT, THE • 1913 • Brabin Charles J. • UKN, USA

STROKE THE CAT'S EARS! see **POHLAD KOCCE USI!** • 1985
STROKER ACE • 1983 • Needham Hal • USA
STROLL, THE • Gutman Walter • USA
STROLL IN THE SUN, A see **VANDRING I SOLEN, EN** • 1978
STROLL ON THE SANDS, A see **LOVERS ON THE SANDS** • 1904
STROLLERS, THE • 1952 • Reinert Emile Edwin
STROLLING HOME WITH ANGELINA • 1906 • Gilbert Arthur • UKN
STROLLING PLAYERS • 1909 • Porter Edwin S. • USA
STROLLING THRU THE PARK • 1949 • Kneitel Seymour • ANS • USA
STROM, DER • 1922 • Basch Felix • FRG
STROM, DER • 1942 • Rittau Gunther • FRG
STROMBOLI • 1951-55 • Tazieff Haroun • SHT • FRN
STROMBOLI see **STROMBOLI, TERRA DI DIO** • 1949
STROMBOLI, TERRA DI DIO • 1949 • Rossellini Roberto • ITL • STROMBOLI
STROMER • 1976 • Refn Anders • DNM • COPPER ○ COP
STROMY A LIDE • 1962 • Schorm Evald • DOC • CZC • TREES AND PEOPLE
STRONG AFFAIR, A • 1914 • *Sterling* • USA
STRONG ARGUMENT, A • 1915 • Nash Percy? • UKN
STRONG ARM NELLIE • 1912 • *Roland Ruth* • USA
STRONG ARM SQUAD, THE • 1916 • Ford Francis • SHT • USA
STRONG BOY • 1929 • Ford John • USA
STRONG EVIDENCE • 1916 • *Vitagraph* • SHT • USA
STRONG FOR LOVE • 1925 • Seiler Lewis • SHT • USA
STRONG IN SPIRIT see **SILNYYE DUKHOM** • 1967
STRONG IS THE FEMALE see **JOSEI WA TSUYOSHI** • 1924
STRONG IS THE SEED • 1949 • Collins Arthur G. • ASL
STRONG MAN, THE • 1926 • Capra Frank • USA
STRONG MAN, THE • 1953-54 • Devlin Bernard • DCS • CND
STRONG MAN, THE • 1973 • Kronik William • TVM • USA
STRONG MAN, THE see **SILNYI CHELOVEK** • 1916
STRONG MAN'S BURDEN, THE • 1913 • O'Sullivan Tony • USA
STRONG MAN'S LOVE, A • 1913 • Noy Wilfred • UKN
STRONG MAN'S WEAKNESS, A see **WILL OF THE PEOPLE, THE** • 1916
STRONG MARK OF IDENTITY, A see **KULONOS ISMERTELOJEL** • 1955
STRONG MEAT see **MARVADA CARNE** • 1986
STRONG MEDICINE • 1981 • Foreman Richard • TVM • USA
STRONG MEDICINE • 1987 • Green Guy • UKN
STRONG MEN, THE see **ANDRES DHEN LIYIZOUN POTE, I** • 1968
STRONG REVENGE, A • 1913 • Sennett Mack • USA
STRONG TO THE FINICH • 1934 • Fleischer Dave • ANS • USA
STRONG TONIC, A • 1909 • *Pathe Freres* • FRN
STRONG WATER • 1975 • Terziev Ivan • BUL
STRONG WAY, THE • 1918 • Kelson George • USA • WAY OF THE STRONG, THE
STRONG WOMAN, WEAK MAN see **TSUYOMUSHI ONNA TO YOWAMUSHI OTOKO** • 1968
STRONGER, THE • 1913 • *Johnston J. W.* • USA
STRONGER, THE • 1976 • Grant Lee • DOC • USA
STRONGER, THE • 1982 • Azzopardi Anthony • MTV • CND
STRONGER CALL, THE • 1913 • *Reliance* • USA
STRONGER HAND, THE • 1914 • *Joy Ernest* • USA
STRONGER LOVE, THE • 1914 • *Imp* • USA
STRONGER LOVE, THE • 1916 • Lloyd Frank, Livingston Jack (U/c) • USA
STRONGER LOVE, THE (UKN) see **SPORTING AGE, THE** • 1928
STRONGER MAN, THE • 1911 • Dwan Allan • USA
STRONGER MAN, THE • 1915 • *Hunt Irene* • USA
STRONGER MIND, THE • 1912 • *Selig* • USA
STRONGER MIND, THE • 1915 • De Grasse Joseph • USA
STRONGER SEX, THE • 1910 • *Lubin* • USA
STRONGER SEX, THE • 1913 • *Baird Leah* • USA
STRONGER SEX, THE • 1930 • Watson William • USA
STRONGER SEX, THE • 1931 • Gundrey V. Gareth • UKN
STRONGER SEX, THE see **SEXO FUERTE, EL** • 1945
STRONGER SEX, THE see **MESU GA OSU O KUIKOROSU: SANBIKI NO KAMAKIRI** • 1967
STRONGER THAN DEATH • 1914 • *Benham Harry* • USA
STRONGER THAN DEATH • 1915 • De Grasse Joseph • USA
STRONGER THAN DEATH • 1920 • Blache Herbert, Bryant Charles • USA • HERMIT DOCTOR OF GAYA, THE
STRONGER THAN DESIRE • 1939 • Fenton Leslie • USA
STRONGER THAN FEAR (UKN) see **EDGE OF DOOM** • 1950
STRONGER THAN LOVE • 1915 • Morgan George • USA
STRONGER THAN STEEL • 1916 • Holubar Allen • SHT • USA
STRONGER THAN THE LAW see **STARKARE AN LAGEN** • 1951
STRONGER THAN THE NIGHT see **STARKER ALS DIE NACHT** • 1954
STRONGER THAN THE SUN • 1980 • Apted Michael • UKN
STRONGER THAN WOMAN'S WILL • 1916 • MacDonald J. Farrell • SHT • USA
STRONGER VOW, THE • 1919 • Barker Reginald • USA
STRONGER WILL, THE • 1916 • *Millais Helena* • UKN
STRONGER WILL, THE • 1928 • McEveety Bernard F. • USA
STRONGEST, THE • 1920 • Walsh Raoul • USA
STRONGEST, THE see **STARKASTE, DEN** • 1929
STRONGEST LINK, THE • 1913 • *Essanay* • USA
STRONGEST MAN IN THE WORLD, THE • 1975 • McEveety Vincent • USA
STRONGEST MAN IN THE WORLD, THE (UKN) see **MACISTE L'UOMO PIU FORTE DEL MONDO** • 1961
STRONGEST ONE, THE see **STARKASTE, DEN** • 1929
STRONGHEART • 1914 • Kirkwood James • USA
STRONGHOLD see **FURIA ROJA** • 1950
STRONGHOLD see **WILDSCHUT** • 1986
STRONGHOLD OF TOUGHS see **GRAJSKI BIKI** • 1967
STRONGMAN FERDINAND see **STARKE FERDINAND, DIE** • 1976
STRONGROOM • 1962 • Sewell Vernon • UKN
STROP • 1962 • Chytilova Vera • SHT • CZC • CEILING
STROPERS VAN DIE LAEVELD • 1962 • SAF
STROSZEK • 1977 • Herzog Werner • FRG
STRUCK BY LIGHTNING • 1919 • *Capital* • SHT • USA
STRUCK BY LIGHTNING • 1989 • Domaradzki Jerzy • ASL
STRUCK GOLD • 1911 • *Nestor* • USA
STRUCK OIL • 1915 • *Mica* • USA
STRUCK OIL • 1919 • Barrett Franklyn • ASL
STRUCNJACI • 1969 • Kolar Boris • ANS • YGS, CND • SPECIALISTS ○ SPECIJALIST
STRUCTURE OF A CRYSTAL see **STRUKTURA KRYSZTALU** • 1970
STRUCTURE OF CRYSTALS, THE see **STRUKTURA KRYSZTALU** • 1970
STRUCTURE OF MATTER, THE • 1951 • Kollanyi Agoston • HNG
STRUCTURE OF UNIONS, THE • 1955 • Koenig Wolf • CND
STRUGGLE • 1967 • Reisenbuchler Sandor • ANS • HNG
STRUGGLE • 1975 • Yannikopoulos Dimitris, Thanasoulas George, Zafiropoulos Ilias, Marangos Thodoros, Ekonomidis Fivos, Papanikolaou Kosta • GRC
STRUGGLE, THE • 1912 • *Vitagraph* • USA
STRUGGLE, THE • 1913 • *Essanay* • USA
STRUGGLE, THE • 1913 • *Broncho* • USA
STRUGGLE, THE • 1913 • Conway Jack, Montgomery Frank E. • *Bison* • USA
STRUGGLE, THE • 1913 • Melford George • *Kalem* • USA
STRUGGLE, THE • 1915 • De Grasse Joseph • USA
STRUGGLE, THE • 1916 • Ince John • USA
STRUGGLE, THE • 1921 • Lederer Otto • USA
STRUGGLE, THE • 1931 • Griffith D. W. • USA
STRUGGLE, THE see **BORZA** • 1935
STRUGGLE AGAINST CANCER, THE see **KAMPEN MOD KRAEFTEN** • 1947
STRUGGLE CONTINUES, THE see **LUTA CONTINUA, LA** • 1971
STRUGGLE EVERLASTING, THE • 1914 • Jones Edgar • USA
STRUGGLE EVERLASTING, THE • 1918 • Kirkwood James • USA
STRUGGLE FOR BREAD • 1950 • Grigorov Roumen • DOC • BUL
STRUGGLE FOR CHINA • 1969 • *Essex Tony (P)* • UKN
STRUGGLE FOR HIS HEART, THE see **KAMPEN OM HANS HJARTA** • 1916
STRUGGLE FOR LIFE see **OUR DAILY BREAD** • 1934
STRUGGLE FOR PEACE • 1950 • Grigorov Roumen • DOC • BUL
STRUGGLE FOR PEDDER • 1974 • Matthews Ross, Dodds Peter • DOC • ASL
STRUGGLE FOR ROME, THE see **KAMPF UM ROM, TEIL 1: KOMM NUR, MEIN LIEBSTES VOGELEIN** • 1969
STRUGGLE FOR THE MATTERHORN see **KAMPF UMS MATTERHORN, DER** • 1928
STRUGGLE FOR THE MATTERHORN see **KAMPF UMS MATTERHORN, DER** • 1934
STRUGGLE IN ITALY see **LOTTE IN ITALIA** • 1969
STRUGGLE IN THE PORT see **SERAA FIL MINAA** • 1955
STRUGGLE IN THE VALLEY see **SERAA FIL WADA** • 1953
STRUGGLE OF HEARTS • 1912 • *Williams Clara* • USA
STRUGGLE OF THE BLIND, THE • 1978 • Papalios Maria • DOC • GRC
STRUGGLE ON THE PIER see **SERAA FIL MINAA** • 1955
STRUGGLE TO SURVIVE see **CH'UNG P'O SZU-WANG HSIEN** • 1981
STRUGGLE UPWARD, THE • 1915 • Castle James W. • USA
STRUGGLE WITH THE ANGELS see **SERAA MAAL MALAIKA** • 1961
STRUGGLING AUTHOR, THE • 1911 • Haldane Bert? • UKN
STRUGGLING HEARTS see **VERGODO SZIVEK** • 1916
STRUKTURA KRYSZTALU • 1970 • Zanussi Krzysztof • PLN • STRUCTURE OF CRYSTALS, THE ○ STRUCTURE OF A CRYSTAL ○ CRYSTAL'S STRUCTURE
STRUL • 1988 • Frick Jonas • SWD • FRAMED
STRUMFLUT • 1914 • Porten Franz • FRG
STRUMPF, DER • 1915 • Sauer Fred • FRG
STRUTTIN' THE MUTTON • 1975 • Tammer Peter • DOC • ASL
STRYCEK Z AMERIKY • 1933 • Vladimirov • CZC • UNCLE FROM AMERICA
STRYKE AND HYDE see **JINXED** • 1982
STRYKER • 1983 • Santiago Cirio H. • USA, PHL
STRZELBA I WEDKA • 1966 • Nehrebecki Wladyslaw • ANS • PLN • RIFLE AND THE FISHING ROD, THE
STRZELNO • 1957 • Jaworski Tadeusz • DOC • PLN
STUBBORN COWBOY, THE • 1967 • Culhane Shamus • ANS • USA
STUBBORN CUPID, A • 1912 • *Nestor* • USA
STUBBORN GUYS BEHIND THE WALLS see **HEI NO NAKA NO KORINAI MENMEN** • 1988
STUBBORN LITTLE GOAT see **KOZIOTOECZEK** • 1953
STUBBORN MOKE, THE • 1908 • Fitzhamon Lewin • UKN
STUBBORN MULE • 1939 • Gillett Burt • ANS • USA
STUBBORNNESS OF GERALDINE, THE • 1915 • Mervale Gaston • USA
STUBBORNNESS OF YOUTH, THE • 1912 • *Lubin* • USA
STUBBS, DER DETEKTIV see **SEINE EXZELLENZ VON MADAGASKAR 2** • 1921
STUBBS' NEW SERVANTS • 1911 • Sennett Mack • USA
STUBBY see **FIMPEN** • 1974
STUBLENSKITE LIPI • 1960 • Dakovski Dako • BUL • STOUBLEN LINDENS, THE
STUCK IN THE STICKS • 1937 • Black Preston • SHT • USA
STUCK ON YOU! • 1983 • Herz Michael, Weil Samuel • USA
STUCK OUT • 1919 • *Supreme Comedies* • USA
STUCK-UP WOLF, THE • 1967 • Culhane Shamus • ANS • USA
STUCK VON HIMMEL, EIN • 1957 • Jugert Rudolf • FRG
STUCKEY'S LAST STAND • 1980 • Goldfarb Lawrence G. • USA
STUD • 1967 • Helge Ladislav • CZC • SHAME
STUD, THE • 1969 • *Gilman Randy* • USA
STUD, THE • 1978 • Masters Quentin • UKN
STUD BROWN • 1975 • Adamson Al • USA • DYNAMITE BROTHERS, THE
STUD. CHEM. HELENE WILLFUER • 1929 • Sauer Fred • FRG
STUD FARM, THE • 1969 • Zacha Jac • USA • STUDY FARM ○ MALE FARM, THE
STUD-FARM, THE see **MENESGAZDA** • 1978
STUDENT see **N'DIANGANE** • 1974
STUDENT AFFAIRS • 1987 • Vincent Chuck • USA • HIGH SCHOOL
STUDENT AND THE HOUSEMAID, THE • 1904 • Williamson James • UKN
STUDENT BODIES • 1981 • Rose Mickey • USA
STUDENT BODY, THE • 1975 • Trikonis Gus • USA
STUDENT CONFIDENTIAL • 1987 • Horian Richard • USA • COUNSELLOR, THE
STUDENT CONNECTION, THE • 1975 • Romero-Marchent Rafael • SPN
STUDENT DAYS see **HSUEH-SHENG-CHICH AI** • 1982
STUDENT EXCHANGE • 1987 • Miller Mollie • TVM • USA
STUDENT FLAT see **SHAKKET EL TALABA** • 1967
STUDENT GEISHA see **KOKOSEI GEISHA** • 1968
STUDENT GING VORBEI, EIN • 1960 • Klinger Werner • FRG
STUDENT LOVE see **BEETHOVEN** • 1927
STUDENT MUMMY, THE see **STUDENTSKA MAMA** • 1935
STUDENT NURSE • 1944 • Searle Francis • DCS • UKN
STUDENT NURSES, THE • 1970 • Rothman Stephanie • USA
STUDENT OF PRAGUE, THE see **STUDENT VON PRAG, DER** • 1913
STUDENT OF PRAGUE, THE see **STUDENT VON PRAG, DER** • 1926
STUDENT OF PRAGUE, THE (UKN) see **STUDENT VON PRAG, DER** • 1935
STUDENT PRINCE see **ALT-HEIDELBERG** • 1923
STUDENT PRINCE, THE • 1954 • Thorpe Richard • USA
STUDENT PRINCE, THE (UKN) see **STUDENT PRINCE IN OLD HEIDELBERG, THE** • 1927
STUDENT PRINCE IN OLD HEIDELBERG, THE • 1927 • Lubitsch Ernst • USA • STUDENT PRINCE, THE (UKN) ○ OLD HEIDELBERG
STUDENT PROSTITUTE see **GAKUSEI SHOFU** • 1968
STUDENT SEIN • Paul Heinz • FRG
STUDENT TEACHERS, THE • 1973 • Kaplan Jonathan • USA
STUDENT, THE SOOT AND THE SMOKE, THE • 1904 • *Paul R. W.* • UKN
STUDENT TOUR • 1934 • Reisner Charles F. • USA
STUDENT UNION see **HARRAD SUMMER** • 1974
STUDENT VACATION • 1979 • Yugala Prince • THL
STUDENT VON PRAG, DER • 1913 • Rye Stellan • FRG • ASYLUM OF HORROR ○ BARGAIN WITH SATAN, A(?) ○ STUDENT OF PRAGUE, THE
STUDENT VON PRAG, DER • 1926 • Galeen Henrik • FRG • MAN WHO CHEATED LIFE, THE (USA) ○ STUDENT OF PRAGUE, THE
STUDENT VON PRAG, DER • 1935 • Robison Arthur • FRG • STUDENT OF PRAGUE, THE (UKN)
STUDENTER I PARIS • 1931 • Mercanton Louis • SWD
STUDENTERKAMMERATERNE • 1916 • Davidsen Hjalmar • DNM
STUDENTERNA PA TROSTEHULT • 1925 • Persson Edvard • SWD • STUDENTS OF TROSTEHULT
STUDENTESSA, LA • 1976 • Piccioni Fabio • ITL
STUDENTIN HELEN WILLFUER • 1956 • Jugert Rudolf • FRG
STUDENTS • 1916 • Hertz Aleksander • PLN
STUDENT'S NIGHT OUT, THE • 1914 • Kellino W. P. • UKN
STUDENTS OF TROSTEHULT see **STUDENTERNA PA TROSTEHULT** • 1925
STUDENT'S PRANK OR A JOKE ON HIS PARENTS • 1908 • *Lubin* • USA
STUDENT'S ROMANCE, THE • 1935 • Kanturek Otto • UKN • I LOST MY HEART IN HEIDELBERG ○ OLD HEIDELBERG
STUDENTSKA MAMA • 1935 • Slavinsky Vladimir • CZC • STUDENT MUMMY, THE
STUDIE 9 see **BRAHM'S HUNGARIAN DANCE** • 1931
STUDIE I • 1952 • Weiss Peter • SHT • SWD • STUDY 1
STUDIE II • 1952 • Weiss Peter • SHT • SWD • HALLUCINATIONER ○ HALLUCINATIONS
STUDIE III • 1953 • Weiss Peter • SHT • SWD • STUDY III
STUDIE IV • 1954 • Weiss Peter • SHT • SWD • FRIGORELSE ○ LIBERATION
STUDIE V • 1955 • Weiss Peter • SHT • SWD • VAXELSPEL ○ GAME OF IMAGINATION
STUDIE WARTEN • 1956 • Grafenstein Heinrich • FRG
STUDIES 1,2,3,4,5,6 • 1946-48 • Whitney John, Whitney James • ANS • USA
STUDIES AND SKETCHES • 1963-65 • Landow George • USA
STUDIES IN ANIMAL MOTION • 1922 • UKN
STUDIES IN EXPRESSION • 1911 • *Gaumont* • UKN
STUDIES IN MOVEMENT (USA) see **ETUDES DE MOUVEMENTS** • 1928
STUDIO CINDERELLA, A • 1917 • *Gail Jane* • SHT • USA
STUDIO ESCAPADE, A • 1915 • Carleton Lloyd B. • USA
STUDIO GIRL, THE • 1918 • Giblyn Charles • USA
STUDIO LEGALE PER UNA RAPINA • 1973 • Boccia Tanio • ITL
STUDIO MURDER MYSTERY, THE • 1929 • Tuttle Frank • USA
STUDIO OF DR. FAUSTUS, THE see **ATEL EINTERIOR** • 1956
STUDIO OF LIFE, THE • 1915 • *Reliance* • USA
STUDIO PESTS • 1929 • Roberts Stephen • SHT • USA
STUDIO ROMANCE, A see **SATSUEIJI ROMANSU-RENAI ANNAI** • 1932
STUDIO ROMANCE (UKN) see **TALENT SCOUT** • 1937
STUDIO SATIRE, A • 1916 • Humphrey Orral • USA
STUDIO STAMPEDE, A • 1917 • Williamson Robin E. • SHT • USA
STUDIO STOOPS • 1950 • Bernds Edward • SHT • USA
STUDIO VISIT, THE • 1946 • *O'Brien Dave* • SHT • USA
STUDS LONIGAN • 1960 • Lerner Irving • USA
STUDUJEME ZA SKOLOU • 1939 • Cikan Miroslav • CZC • WE PLAY TRUANT
STUDY see **RISHU** • 1960
STUDY 1 see **STUDIE I** • 1952
STUDY FARM see **STUD FARM, THE** • 1969
STUDY FOR TWO HANDS, A • Weissova Lenka • CZC
STUDY III see **STUDIE III** • 1953
STUDY IN CHOREOGRAPHY FOR CAMERA, A • 1945 • Deren Maya • SHT • USA • CHOREOGRAPHY FOR CAMERA
STUDY IN FACIAL EXPRESSION, A • 1898 • *Paul R. W.* • UKN
STUDY IN FEET, A • 1903 • *Warwick Trading Co* • UKN
STUDY IN FEET, A • 1914 • Lambart Harry • USA
STUDY IN PAPER • 1965 • Holman L. Bruce • ANM • USA
STUDY IN SCARLET, A • 1914 • *Ford Francis* • USA
STUDY IN SCARLET, A • 1914 • Pearson George • UKN
STUDY IN SCARLET, A • 1933 • Marin Edwin L. • USA

STUDY IN SKARLIT, A • 1915 • Evans Fred, Evans Will • UKN
STUDY IN SOCIOLOGY, A • 1913 • *Majestic* • USA
STUDY IN TERROR, A • 1965 • Hill James • UKN, FRG, USA • SHERLOCK HOLMES GROSSTER FALL (FRG) ○ FOG
STUDY IN TRAMPS, A • 1915 • Beggs Lee • USA
STUDY NO.1 • 1929 • Fischinger Oskar • ANS • FRG
STUDY NO.2 • 1930 • Fischinger Oskar • ANS • FRG
STUDY NO.3 • 1930 • Fischinger Oskar • ANS • FRG
STUDY NO.4 • 1930 • Fischinger Oskar • ANS • FRG
STUDY NO.5 • 1930 • Fischinger Oskar • ANS • FRG
STUDY NO.6 • 1930 • Fischinger Oskar • ANS • FRG
STUDY NO.7 • 1930-31 • Fischinger Oskar • ANS • FRG
STUDY NO.8 • 1931 • Fischinger Oskar • ANS • FRG
STUDY NO.9 • 1931 • Fischinger Oskar • ANS • FRG
STUDY NO.10 • 1932 • Fischinger Oskar • ANS • FRG
STUDY NO.11 • 1932 • Fischinger Oskar • ANS • FRG
STUDY NO.12 • 1932 • Fischinger Oskar • ANS • FRG
STUDY NO.13 • 1933-34 • Fischinger Oskar • ANS • FRG
STUDY NO.14 • 1934 • Fischinger Oskar • ANS • FRG
STUDY OF A DANCE • Woll Yael • USA
STUDY OF A WORKING DAY • 1961 • Kosa Ferenc • HNG • ETUDE ABOUT A WORKING DAY
STUDY OF AN ISLAND see **BESCHREIBUNG EINER INSEL** • 1979
STUDY OF WOMEN, A see **TANULMANY A NOKROL** • 1968
STUDY OPUS 1 -MAN • 1976 • Popescu-Gopo Ion • ANS • RMN
STUFF, THE • 1985 • Cohen Larry • USA
STUFF HEROES ARE MADE OF, THE • 1911 • Powell Frank?, Griffith D. W.? • USA
STUFF OF HEROES see **GREAT MR. NOBODY, THE** • 1941
STUFF THAT AMERICANS ARE MADE OF, THE • 1910 • *Edison* • USA
STUFF THAT DREAMS ARE MADE OF, THE • 1911 • Dawley J. Searle • USA
STUFF THAT DREAMS ARE MADE OF, THE • 1914 • France Charles H. • USA
STUFFED LIONS • 1921 • Reisner Charles F. • SHT • USA
STUFFIE • 1940 • Zinnemann Fred • SHT • USA
STUITER, DE • 1971 • Oonk Jan • SHT • NTH • MARBLE, THE
STUKAS • 1941 • Ritter Karl • FRG
STULEN VALS, EN • 1932 • Marmstedt Lorens • SWD • STOLEN WALTZ, A
STUMBLING • 1916 • Kent Leon D. • SHT • USA
STUMBLING BLOCK, THE • 1911 • *Delaney Leo* • USA
STUMME, DER • 1976 • Meili Gaudenz • MTV • SWT • DUMB, THE
STUMME GAST, DER • 1945 • Braun Harald • FRG
STUMME VON PORTICI, DIE • 1922 • Gunsburg Arthur • FRG
STUMME ZEUGE, DER • 1917 • Piel Harry • FRG
STUMP RUN • 1960 • Dew Edward • USA
STUMP SPEECH • 1900 • *Warwick Trading Co* • UKN
STUMP SPEECH • 1905 • Collins Alf? • UKN
STUNDE DER ENTSCHEIDUNG see **SEMMELWEISS -REITER DER MUTTER** • 1950
STUNDE DER VERGELTUNG, DIE • 1915 • *Morena Erna* • FRG
STUNDE DER VERGELTUNG, DIE • 1918 • Zeyn Willy • FRG
STUNDE DER VERSUCHUNG, DIE • 1936 • Wegener Paul • FRG
STUNDE, DIE DU GLUCKLICH BIST, DIE • 1961 • Jugert Rudolf • FRG
STUNDE GLUCK, EINE • 1930 • Dieterle William • FRG
STUNDE NACH MITTENACHT, DIE • 1920 • Ziener Bruno • FRG
STUNDE NULL • 1977 • Reitz Edgar • FRG • ZERO HOUR
STUNDE WENN DRAKULA KOMMT, DIE (FRG) see **MASCHERA DEL DEMONIO, LA** • 1960
STUNDE X • 1959 • Dorries Bernhard • FRG
STUNDENHOTEL VON ST. PAULI, DAS • 1970 • Olsen Rolf • FRG
STUNG • 1908 • *Essanay* • USA
STUNG! • 1913 • *Patheplay* • USA
STUNG • 1913 • *Eclair* • USA
STUNG! • 1914 • *Kalem* • USA
STUNG • 1915 • *Starlight* • USA
STUNG • 1916 • Van Wally • SHT • USA
STUNG • 1919 • *Henry Gale* • SHT • USA
STUNG • 1922 • USA
STUNG AGAIN • 1920 • *Cohn* • USA
STUNG AGAIN • 1933 • Hackney W. P. • SHT • USA
STUNG BY A WOMAN • 1923 • Phillips Bertram • UKN
STUNG BY GUM • 1916 • Miller Rube • USA
STUNG BY THE BEE • 1914 • *Premier* • USA
STUNNED DETECTIVE VS. KILLING see **SASKIN HAFIYE KILLINGE KARSI** • 1967
STUNT FAMILY, THE • 1978 • Siegel Lois • CND • CASCADEURS, LES
STUNT MAN, THE • 1924 • *Sennett Mack (P)* • SHT • USA
STUNT MAN, THE • 1978 • Rush Richard • USA
STUNT MEN • 1960 • Taras Martin B. • ANS • USA
STUNT PEOPLE • 1990 • Segel Lois • DOC • CND
STUNT PILOT • 1939 • Waggner George • USA
STUNT ROCK • 1978 • Trenchard-Smith Brian • ASL, NTH
STUNT SEVEN • 1979 • Peyser John • TVM • USA • FANTASTIC SEVEN
STUNT SQUAD • Paolella Domenico • ITL
STUNTMAN • 1968 • Baldi Marcello • ITL, FRN • CASCADEUR, LE (FRN)
STUNTMAN, THE see **KASKADER** • 1971
STUNTMEN, THE • 1973 • Trenchard-Smith Brian • DOC • ASL
STUNTS • 1977 • Lester Mark L. • USA • WHO IS KILLING THE STUNTMEN? ○ STUNTS: THE DEADLY GAME ○ DEADLY GAME, THE
STUNTS: THE DEADLY GAME see **STUNTS** • 1977
STUNTS UNLIMITED • 1980 • Needham Hal • TVM • USA
STUPEFIANTS • 1932 • Le Bon Roger, Gerron Kurt • FRN
STUPID BOM see **DUM-BOM** • 1953
STUPID BUT BRAVE • 1924 • St. John Al • SHT • USA
STUPID CUPID, THE • 1944 • Tashlin Frank • ANS • USA
STUPID DEVIL, THE • 1960 • Karpas Jan • ANS • CZC
STUPID FATHERLAND see **PATRIA BOBA, LA** • 1975
STUPID MILLIONAIRE, THE see **SALAK MILYONER** • 1974
STUPID SORCERER, THE see **NINJUTSU MUSHA SHUGYO** • 1956
STUPID YOUNG BROTHER AND WISE OLD BROTHER see **GUTEI KENKEI** • 1931
STUPIDSTITIOUS CAT • 1947 • Kneitel Seymour • ANS • USA
STUPOR DUCK • 1956 • McKimson Robert • ANS • USA
STUPOR SALESMAN • 1948 • Davis Arthur • ANS • USA
STURM AUF DREI HERZEN • 1929 • Neff Wolfgang • FRG
STURM IM WASSERGLAS • 1960 • von Baky Josef • FRG
STURM IM WASSERGLAS see **BLUMENFRAU VON LINDENAU, DIE** • 1931
STURM UBER LA SARRAZ • 1929 • Eisenstein Sergei, Richter Hans, Montagu Ivor • SHT • FRG • KAMPF DES UNABHANGIGEN GEGEN DES KOMMERZIELLEN FILM
STURM UND DRANG see **FRIDERICUS REX (EIN KONIGSSCHICKSAL) 1** • 1922
STURME • 1919 • Lund Erik • FRG
STURME DER LEIDENSCHAFT • 1931 • Siodmak Robert • FRG • STORM OF PASSION ○ TEMPEST, THE
STURME DES LEBENS • 1921 • *Krauss Werner* • FRG
STURME UBER DEM MONTBLANC • 1930 • Fanck Arnold • FRG • AVALANCHE ○ STORM OVER MONT BLANC
STURMFLUT • 1917 • Halm Alfred?, Zeyn Willy? • FRG
STURMFLUT • 1927 • Reiber Willy • FRG
STURMFLUT DER LIEBE • 1929 • Berger Martin • FRG
STURMFLUT DES LEBENS • 1921 • Stein Paul L. • FRG
STURMISCH NIE NACHT • 1930 • Blachnitzky Curt • FRG, AUS
STURMJAHRE • 1947 • Rossak Frank Ward • AUS
STURMSCHWALBE • 1918 • Arnheim Valy • FRG
STURMTRUPPEN • 1976 • Samperi Salvatore • ITL
STURZ, DER • 1979 • Brustellin Alf • FRG • FALL, THE
STURZ DER MENSCHHEIT, DER • 1917 • Heymann Robert • FRG
STURZ IN DIE FLAMMEN, DER • 1920 • Karfiol William • FRG
STURZ INS GLUCK, DER • 1924 • Licho Adolf Edgar • FRG
STURZENDE BERG, DER see **KONIG VON GOLCONDA 2, DER** • 1921
STURZENDE GOTTER • 1922 • Frey Karl • FRG
STURZENDE WASSER • 1923 • *Ernestus-Film* • FRG
STUTTGART: GROSSTADT ZWISCHEN WALD UND REBEN • 1935 • Ruttmann Walter • DOC • FRG
STUTZEN DER GESELLSCHAFT • 1935 • Sirk Douglas • FRG • PILLARS OF SOCIETY (UKN)
STVANI LIDE • 1933 • Feher Friedrich, Svitak • CZC • OUTCASTS
STVORENI SVETA • 1958 • Hofman Eduard • ANM • CZC • CREATION OF THE WORLD, THE (USA)
STVRTY ROZMER • 1983 • Trancik Dusan • CZC • FOURTH DIMENSION, THE
STYEP see **STEP** • 1978
STYLE IS THE MAN HIMSELF, THE • 1970 • Cameron Graham • CND
STYLE OF CHAMPIONS • 1970 • Holmes Cecil • DOC • ASL
STYRIDSATSTYRI • 1957 • Bielik Palo • CZC • FORTY-FOUR
STYRMAN KARLSSONS FLAMMOR • 1925 • Edgren Gustaf • SWD • MR. KARLSSON MATE AND HIS SWEETHEARTS
STYRMAN KARLSSONS FLAMMOR • 1938 • Edgren Gustaf • SWD • MR. KARLSSON MATE AND HIS SWEETHEARTS
SU ADORABLE MAJADERO • 1938 • Gout Alberto • MXC
SU ALTEZA LA NINA • 1962 • Ozores Mariano • SPN
SU DA YANAR • 1987 • Ozzenturk Ali • TRK • WATER ALSO BURNS
SU DESCONSALADO ESPOSA • 1957 • Iglesias Miguel • SPN
SU E GIU • 1965 • Guerrini Mino • ITL
SU ESPOSA DIURNA • 1944 • Cahen Enrique • ARG
SU EXCELENCIA • 1966 • Delgado Miguel M. • MXC
SU EXCELENCIA EL MAYORDOMO • 1942 • Iglesias Miguel • SPN
SU GRAN AVENTURA • 1938 • de Fuentes Fernando • MXC • HIS GREAT ADVENTURE (USA)
SU GRAN ILUSION • 1944 • Magdaleno Mauricio • MXC
SU HERMANA MENOR • 1943 • Cahen Enrique • ARG
SU HERMANO Y EL • 1941 • Marquina Luis • SPN
SU HSIAO-HSIAO • 1967 • Li Ch'En-Feng • HKG • SU SIU SIU
SU NOCHE DE BODAS • 1931 • Mercanton Louis • FRN
SU NOMBRE ES DAPHNE • 1966 • Lorente German • SPN
SU NOMBRE ES MUJER • 1940 • Irigoyen Julio • ARG
SU OSOBNE ZODPOVEDNI • 1946 • Kadar Jan • CZC
SU PRIMER AMOR • 1959 • Ortega Juan J. • MXC • FERIA DE LA CANCION, LA
SU SIU SIU see **SU HSIAO-HSIAO** • 1967
SU ULTIMA AVENTURA • 1946 • Martinez Solares Gilberto • MXC
SU ULTIMA CANCION • 1933 • Auer John H. • MXC
SU ULTIMA NOCHE • 1931 • Franklin Chester M. • USA
SU ULTIMA NOCHE • 1944 • Arevalo Carlos • SPN
SUA ALTEZZA HA DETTO: NO! • 1954 • Basaglia Maria • ITL
SUA ECCELLENZA L'AMBASCIATRICE • 1920 • D'Ambra Lucio • ITL
SUA ECCELLENZA SI FERMO A MANGIARE • 1961 • Mattoli Mario • ITL
SUA EXCELENCIA O MINISTRO • 1975 • Semedo Artur • MTV • PRT
SUA GIORNATA DI GLORIA, LA • 1968 • Bruno Edoardo • ITL • HIS DAY OF GLORY
SUA MAESTA IL SANGUE • 1914 • Roberti Roberto Leone • ITL
SUA STRADA, LA • 1943 • Costa Mario • ITL
SUAVE PATRIA • 1951 • Fernandez Emilio • MXC
SUAVECITO, EL • 1950 • Mendez Fernando • MXC
SUB-A-DUB-DUB see **HELLO DOWN THERE** • 1969
SUBAH KA TARA • 1932 • *Sircar B. N. (P)* • IND
SUBALTERN'S JOKE, THE • 1911 • Fitzhamon Lewin? • UKN
SUBARASHII AKUJO • 1963 • Onchi Hideo • JPN • WONDERFUL BAD WOMAN
SUBARASHIKI DANSEI • 1958 • Inoue Umeji • JPN • THAT WONDERFUL GUY
SUBARASHIKI NICHIYOBI • 1947 • Kurosawa Akira • JPN • ONE WONDERFUL SUNDAY ○ WONDERFUL SUNDAY
SUBARISHIKI MUSUMETACHI • 1959 • Ieki Miyoji • JPN • THOSE WONDERFUL GIRLS
SUBDESARROLLADOS, LOS • 1967 • Merino Fernando • SPN • UNDERDEVELOPED, THE
SUBDUING OF MRS. NAG, THE • 1911 • Baker George D. • USA
SUBE Y BAJA • 1958 • Delgado Miguel M. • MXC
SUBES O BAJAS? • 1970 • Carretero Amaro • ANS • SPN • ARE YOU GOING UP OR DOWN?
SUBHADRA • 1945 • Winayak • IND
SUBIDA AL CIELO • 1951 • Bunuel Luis • MXC • MEXICAN BUS RIDE (USA) ○ ASCENT TO HEAVEN
SUBJECT FOR A SHORT STORY see **SYUZHET DLYA NEBOLSHOVO RASKAZA** • 1968
SUBJECT FOR DISCUSSION • 1943 • Nieter Hans M. • UKN
SUBJECT IS JAZZ, THE • 1958 • King Lynwood • SHS • USA
SUBJECT IS SEX, THE (UKN) see **EPAIS MANTEAU DE SANG, UN** • 1968
SUBJECT LESSON • 1956 • Young Christopher • SHT • USA
SUBJECT WAS ROSES, THE • 1968 • Grosbard Ulu • USA
SUBLIMAL GRAPHICS • Gruenberger John • SHT • USA
SUBLIMATED BIRTH • 1962 • SHT • USA
SUBLIME DECEPTION, A • 1914 • *Melies* • USA
SUBLIME MELODIA • 1955 • Demicheli Tulio • MXC
SUBLIMINAL • 1979 • Pannaccio Elo • ITL
SUBLOKATOR • 1967 • Majewski Janusz • PLN • LODGER, THE ○ TENANT, THE
SUBMARINE • 1910 • *Gaudio Antonio (Ph)* • USA
SUBMARINE • 1928 • Capra Frank • USA
SUBMARINE ALERT • 1943 • McDonald Frank • USA
SUBMARINE BASE • 1943 • Kelley Albert • USA
SUBMARINE COMMAND • 1951 • Farrow John • USA
SUBMARINE CONTROL • 1949 • Privett Bob, Crick Alan • ANS • UKN
SUBMARINE D-1 • 1937 • Bacon Lloyd • USA
SUBMARINE E-57 NEVER SURRENDERS see **SENSUIKAN E-57 KOFUKUSEZU** • 1959
SUBMARINE EYE, THE • 1917 • Kelley J. Winthrop • USA
SUBMARINE GOLD see **WET GOLD** • 1921
SUBMARINE ORZEL • 1959 • Buczkowski Leonard • PLN
SUBMARINE PATROL • 1938 • Ford John • USA
SUBMARINE PILOT, A • 1915 • Avery Charles, Chaplin Sydney • USA • SUBMARINE PIRATE, A
SUBMARINE PIRATE, A see **SUBMARINE PILOT, A** • 1915
SUBMARINE PLANS, THE • 1912 • Southwell Gilbert • UKN
SUBMARINE RAIDER • 1942 • Landers Lew • USA
SUBMARINE SEAHAWK • 1959 • Bennet Spencer Gordon • USA
SUBMARINE SPY, THE • 1914 • *Imp* • USA
SUBMARINE T-9 • 1943 • Ivanov Alexander • USS
SUBMARINE X-1 • 1969 • Graham William A. • UKN
SUBMARINE ZONE see **ESCAPE TO GLORY** • 1940
SUBMARINES AND SIMPS • 1918 • McCray Roy • SHT • USA
SUBMERSION OF JAPAN, THE see **NIHON CHINBOTSU** • 1973
SUBMISSION • 1969 • Savage Allen • USA
SUBMISSION (UKN) see **PETS** • 1973
SUBMISSION (USA) see **SCANDOLO** • 1975
SUBMISSIVE, THE see **UNTERTAN, DER** • 1951
SUBOTOM UVECE • 1957 • Pogacic Vladimir • YGS • SATURDAY EVENING
SUBPOENA SERVER • 1906 • *Bitzer Billy (Ph)* • USA
SUBSTANCE OF JAZZ, THE • 1968 • Baker Baldwin Jr. • SHT • USA
SUBSTANTIAL GHOST, A • 1903 • Collins Alf • UKN
SUBSTITUTE see **SURROGATET (I CIGARRBO'N)** • 1919
SUBSTITUTE, THE • 1911 • *Lubin* • USA
SUBSTITUTE, THE • 1914 • *Kb* • USA
SUBSTITUTE, THE • 1914 • *Thanhouser* • USA
SUBSTITUTE, THE • 1915 • Hotaling Arthur D. • USA
SUBSTITUTE, THE see **SUROGAT** • 1961
SUBSTITUTE, THE see **TOUGHLOVE** • 1985
SUBSTITUTE ENGINEER, THE • 1913 • *Kalem* • USA
SUBSTITUTE FOR PANTS, A • 1914 • *Roland Ruth* • USA
SUBSTITUTE HEIR, THE • 1914 • *Martin E. A.* • USA
SUBSTITUTE HEIRESS, THE • 1912 • *Johnson Arthur* • USA
SUBSTITUTE MINISTER, THE • 1915 • Eason B. Reeves • USA
SUBSTITUTE MODEL, THE • 1912 • Bosworth Hobart • USA
SUBSTITUTE STENOGRAPHER, THE • 1913 • Edwin Walter • USA
SUBSTITUTE WIDOW, THE • 1915 • Paton Stuart • USA
SUBSTITUTE WIFE, THE • 1925 • May Wilfred • USA
SUBSTITUTED JEWEL, THE • 1915 • *Kalem* • USA
SUBSTITUTION • 1970 • Davis Walt • USA
SUBSTITUTION, A • 1912 • *Lubin* • USA
SUBTERANUL • 1967 • Calotescu Virgil • RMN • UNDERNEATH THE SURFACE ○ SUBTERRANEAN, THE
SUBTERFUGE • 1912 • *Selig* • USA
SUBTERFUGE • 1968 • Scott Peter Graham • UKN, USA
SUBTERRANEAN, THE see **SUBTERANUL** • 1967
SUBTERRANEANS • 1988 • Steinmann Danny • USA
SUBTERRRANEANS, THE • 1960 • MacDougall Ranald • USA
SUBUB SURPRISES THE BURGLAR • 1903 • Porter Edwin S. • USA
SUBURB, THE • 1972 • Zafranovic Lordan • SHT • YGS
SUBURBAN, THE • 1915 • Lessey George A. • USA
SUBURBAN ANGELS see **ANJOS DO ARRABALDE** • 1986
SUBURBAN-BUNKUM-MICROBE-GUYOSCOPE, THE • 1903 • Hepworth Cecil M. • UKN
SUBURBAN GIRLS CLUB • 1968 • *Mitam Productions* • USA
SUBURBAN HANDICAP, THE see **KENTUCKY DERBY, THE** • 1922
SUBURBAN HOUSE, THE see **DUM NA PREDMESTI** • 1933
SUBURBAN LEGEND see **KULVAROSI LEGENDA** • 1957
SUBURBAN PAGANS • 1968 • Carse Shannon • USA
SUBURBAN PAL, A • 1914 • *B & C* • UKN
SUBURBAN ROULETTE • 1967 • Lewis Herschell G. • USA
SUBURBAN WIVES • 1971 • Ford Derek • UKN
SUBURBANITE'S INGENIOUS ALARM • 1908 • Porter Edwin S. • USA
SUBURBIA see **WILD SIDE, THE** • 1983
SUBURBIA CONFIDENTIAL • 1966 • Stephen A. C. • USA
SUBURBIO • 1951 • Klimovsky Leon • SPN
SUBVERSION • 1979 • Stanojevic Stanislav • FRN
SUBVERSIVE ACTION see **DIVERSIA** • 1989
SUBVERSIVES, THE see **SOVVERSIVI** • 1967
SUBWAY • 1984 • Besson Luc • FRN
SUBWAY, THE see **MOSKVA STROYIT METRO** • 1934
SUBWAY EXPRESS • 1931 • Newmeyer Fred • USA

SUBWAY IN THE SKY • 1959 • Box Muriel • UKN
SUBWAY OR SPAIN • 1970 • Owen Don • CND
SUBWAY RIDERS • 1981 • Poe Amos • USA
SUBWAY SADIE • 1926 • Santell Alfred • USA
SUBWAY TO PARADISE • 1987 • Hastrup Jannik • ANM • DNM
SUBWAY TO THE STARS • 1987 • Diegues Carlos • BRZ
SUCCES A TOUT PRIX, LE • 1984 • Skolimowski Jerzy • FRN, UKN • SUCCESS IS THE BEST REVENGE (UKN)
SUCCES COMMERCIAL, UN see **Q-BEC MY LOVE OU UN SUCCES COMMERCIAL** • 1969
SUCCES DE LA PRESTIDIGITATION, LE • 1912 • Linder Max • FRN • MAX ESCAMOTEUR
SUCCESS • 1913 • Apfel Oscar • USA
SUCCESS • 1923 • Ince Ralph • USA
SUCCESS • 1963 • Kovacs Andras • HNG
SUCCESS see **PIERWSZY, DRUGI, TRZECI** • 1964
SUCCESS see **AMERICAN SUCCESS COMPANY, THE** • 1979
SUCCESS see **CONFESSIONS OF A MARRIED MAN** • 1982
SUCCESS see **PASTIGENDE KURS** • 1986
SUCCESS see **ERFOLG** • 1990
SUCCESS, THE see **SUKCES** • 1968
SUCCESS, THE (USA) see **SUCCESSO, IL** • 1963
SUCCESS AT ANY PRICE • 1934 • Ruben J. Walter • USA • SUCCESS STORY
SUCCESS IS THE BEST REVENGE (UKN) see **SUCCES A TOUT PRIX, LE** • 1984
SUCCESS OF A CITY WAIF, THE • 1909 • *Empire Films* • UKN
SUCCESS OF SELFISHNESS, THE • 1914 • *Thanhouser Kidlet* • USA
SUCCESS STORY see **SUCCESS AT ANY PRICE** • 1934
SUCCESS: THE CIRCUS see **SIKER: CIRKUSZ** • 1970
SUCCESS WITH DE-FEET • 1913 • *Eclair* • USA
SUCCESSFUL ADVENTURE, A • 1918 • Franklin Harry L. • USA
SUCCESSFUL CALAMITY, A • 1932 • Adolfi John G. • USA
SUCCESSFUL FAILURE, A • 1913 • Mason Billy • USA
SUCCESSFUL FAILURE, A • 1917 • Rosson Arthur • USA
SUCCESSFUL FAILURE, A • 1934 • Lubin Arthur • USA
SUCCESSFUL MAN, A • 1986 • Solas Humberto • CUB
SUCCESSFUL OPERATION, A • 1916 • Fitzmaurice Aubrey • UKN
SUCCESSIVE VICTORIES see **RENSEN RENSHO** • 1930
SUCCESSIVE WIPES • 1976 • Sinden Tony • UKN
SUCCESSO, IL • 1963 • Morassi Mauro, Risi Dino (U/c) • ITL, FRN • SUCCESS, THE (USA)
SUCCUBUS see **SATANIST, THE** • 1968
SUCCUBUS (USA) see **NECRONOMICON -GETRAUMTE SUNDEN** • 1968
SUCE-MOI VAMPIRE • 1976 • Rollin Jean • FRN
SUCEDIO EN ACAPULCO • 1952 • Galindo Alejandro • MXC
SUCEDIO EN BUENOS AIRES • 1954 • Cahen Enrique • ARG
SUCEDIO EN EL FANTASTICO CIRCO TIHANY • 1981 • Carreras Enrique • ARG • IT HAPPENED AT THE FANTASTIC TIHANY CIRCUS
SUCEDIO EN MEXICO • 1957 • Pereda Ramon • MXC
SUCEDIO EN MI ALDEA • 1954 • Santillan Antonio • SPN
SUCEDIO EN SEVILLA • 1954 • Gutierrez Maesso Jose • SPN
SUCESION, LA • 1978 • Gurrola Alfredo • MXC
SUCETTE MAGIQUE, LA • 1975 • Hustaix Lucien • FRN
SUCEUSES, LES • 1979 • Bernard-Aubert Claude • FRN
SUCEUSES INFERNALES • Baudricourt Michel • FRN
SUCH A BIG BOY see **TAKOY BOLSHOY MALCHIK** • 1967
SUCH A BUSINESS • 1914 • *Royal* • USA
SUCH A BUSINESS • 1915 • *Luna* • USA
SUCH A COOK • 1914 • Parrott Charles • USA
SUCH A GORGEOUS KID LIKE ME (USA) see **BELLE FILLE COMME MOI, UNE** • 1972
SUCH A HUGE FISH see **WIELKI POLOW** • 1961
SUCH A HUNTER • 1914 • Baker George D. • USA
SUCH A LITTLE PIRATE • 1918 • Melford George • USA
SUCH A LITTLE QUEEN • 1914 • Porter Edwin S., Ford Hugh • USA
SUCH A LITTLE QUEEN • 1921 • Fawcett George • USA
SUCH A LONG ABSENCE • 1985 • Tsiolis Stavros • GRC
SUCH A MESS • 1914 • Murphy J. A. • USA
SUCH A MISTAKE • 1914 • *Crystal* • USA
SUCH A PICNIC • 1915 • *Superba* • USA
SUCH A PRETTY LITTLE BEACH see **SI JOLIE PETITE PLAGE, UNE** • 1948
SUCH A PRINCESS • 1915 • Matthews H. C. • USA
SUCH A VILLAIN • 1914 • Christie Al • USA
SUCH A WAR • 1915 • *Pyramid* • USA
SUCH AN APPETITE • 1913 • *Lubin* • USA
SUCH GOOD FRIENDS • 1971 • Preminger Otto • USA
SUCH HIGH MOUNTAINS • 1974 • Solntseva Yulia • USS
SUCH IS LIFE • 1913 • *Essanay* • USA
SUCH IS LIFE • 1915 • De Grasse Joseph • USA
SUCH IS LIFE • 1936 • Faye Randall • UKN • MUSIC AND MILLIONS
SUCH IS LIFE • 1963 • Kelly Ron • CND
SUCH IS LIFE see **SO IST DAS LEBEN** • 1924
SUCH IS LIFE see **TAKOVY JE ZIVOT** • 1929
SUCH IS LIFE see **SO ODER SO IST DAS LEBEN** • 1976
SUCH IS LIFE see **ASI ES LA VIDA** • 1977
SUCH IS LIFE: OR, MIND YOUR OWN BUSINESS • 1903 • Collins Alf? • UKN
SUCH IS LIFE (USA) see **ASI ES LA VIDA** • 1940
SUCH IS MY COUNTRY (USA) see **ASI ES MI TIERRA** • 1937
SUCH IS THE KINGDOM • 1911 • *Reliance* • USA
SUCH IS THE LAW • 1930 • Hill Sinclair • UKN
SUCH IS THE WAR • 1914 • BUL
SUCH MEN ARE DANGEROUS • 1930 • Hawks Kenneth • USA • MASK OF LOVE, THE
SUCH MEN ARE DANGEROUS (UKN) see **RACERS, THE** • 1955
SUCH THINGS HAPPEN (UKN) see **LOVE RACKET, THE** • 1929
SUCH THINGS REALLY HAPPEN • 1915 • Hansel Howell? • USA
SUCH WOMEN ARE DANGEROUS • 1934 • Flood James • USA
SUCHE NACH DEM WUNDERBUNTEN VOGELCHEN, DIE • 1964 • Losansky Rolf • GDR
SUCHENDE SEELE, DIE • 1923 • Biebrach Rudolf • FRG
SUCHENDE SEELE, EINE see **MARIONETTEN DES TEUFELS 2** • 1920
SUCHKIND 312 • 1955 • Machaty Gustav • FRG
SUCHY DOK • 1964 • Riesser Jan • PLN • DRY DOCK, A
SUCI SANG PRIMADONA • 1977 • Noer Arifin C. • INN • SUCI THE PRIMADONNA
SUCI THE PRIMADONNA see **SUCI SANG PRIMADONA** • 1977
SUCKER see **LIFE OF JIMMY NOLAN, THE** • 1933
SUCKER, THE (USA) see **CORNIARD, LE** • 1965
SUCKER LIST • 1941 • Rowland Roy • SHT • USA
SUCKER MONEY • 1933 • Reid Dorothy, Shyer Melville • USA • VICTIMS OF THE BEYOND (UKN)
SUCKER.. OR HOW TO BE GLAD WHEN YOU'VE BEEN HAD, THE see **CORNIARD, LE** • 1965
SUCRE, LE • 1968 • Mazif Sid-Ali • SHT • ALG
SUCRE, LE • 1979 • Rouffio Jacques • FRN
SUCRE D'ERABLE ET COOPERATION • 1954 • Proulx Maurice • DCS • CND
SUD • 1963 • Skuibin Vladimir • USS • TRIAL, THE
SUD CHESTI • 1948 • Room Abram • USS • COURT OF HONOR (USA) ○ TRIBUNAL OF HONOUR, THE ○ TRIAL OF HONOUR
SUD ENTRE LES GRIFFES DE L'ENNEMI, LE • 1975 • Nasri Samir • LBN
SUD-EXPRESS • 1963 • Leherissey Jean • DCS • FRN
SUD SUMASSHEDSHICH • 1962 • Roshal Grigori • USS • JUDGMENT OF THE MAD ○ MADMEN'S TRIAL
SUD V SMOLENSKE • 1946 • Shub Esther • DOC • USS • TRIAL IN SMOLENSK, THE
SUDAN • 1945 • Rawlins John • USA • QUEEN OF THE NILE
SUDARIO A LA MEDIA, UN see **CANDIDATO PER UN ASSASSINO** • 1969
SUDARSHAN • 1967 • Mane Dutta • IND
SUDBA • 1978 • Matveyev Yevgeni • USS • DESTINY
SUDBA CHELOVEKA • 1959 • Bondarchuk Sergei • USS • FATE OF A MAN (USA) ○ DESTINY OF A MAN
SUDBINE • 1979 • Golubovic Predrag • YGS • DESTINY
SUDDEN ALARM, A • 1899 • *Warwick Trading Co* • UKN
SUDDEN ATTACK • Sawada • JPN
SUDDEN BILL DORN • 1937 • Taylor Ray • USA
SUDDEN CLOUDS see **KOKHONO MEGH** • 1968
SUDDEN DANGER • 1955 • Cornfield Hubert • USA
SUDDEN DEATH • 1977 • Romero Eddie • PHL
SUDDEN DEATH • 1985 • Shore Sig • USA
SUDDEN DEATH see **FAST ON THE DRAW** • 1950
SUDDEN DEATH see **ONCE YOU KISS A STRANGER** • 1969
SUDDEN DEATH see **2020 TEXAS GLADIATORS** • 1982
SUDDEN FEAR • 1952 • Miller David • USA
SUDDEN FORTUNE OF THE POOR PEOPLE OF KOMBACH, THE see **PLOTZLICHER REICHTUM DER ARMEN LEUTE VAN KOMBACH, DER** • 1970
SUDDEN FRIED CHICKEN • 1946 • Tytla Bill • ANS • USA
SUDDEN FURY • 1975 • Damude Brian • CND
SUDDEN GENTLEMAN, THE • 1917 • Heffron Thomas N. • USA
SUDDEN IMPACT • 1983 • Eastwood Clint • USA
SUDDEN JIM • 1917 • Schertzinger Victor • USA
SUDDEN LONELINESS OF KONRAD STEINER, THE see **PLOTZLICHE EINSAMKEIT DES KONRAD STEINER, DIE** • 1976
SUDDEN LOVE see **KSAFNIKOS EROTAS** • 1984
SUDDEN MONEY • 1939 • Grinde Nick • USA
SUDDEN RAIN see **SHUU** • 1956
SUDDEN RICHES • 1916 • Chautard Emile • USA
SUDDEN TARGET • 1986 • Bare Richard L. • USA
SUDDEN TERROR see **EYEWITNESS** • 1970
SUDDEN WEALTH OF THE POOR PEOPLE OF KOMBACH, THE see **PLOTZLICHER REICHTUM DER ARMEN LEUTE VAN KOMBACH, DER** • 1970
SUDDENLY • 1954 • Allen Lewis • USA
SUDDENLY, A WOMAN! (USA) see **GUDRUN** • 1963
SUDDENLY BAD NAMES see **AKUMYO NIWAKA** • 1965
SUDDENLY IT'S JAZZ • 1963 • Summers Jeremy • SHT • UKN
SUDDENLY IT'S SPRING! • 1944 • Kneitel Seymour • ANS • USA
SUDDENLY, IT'S SPRING • 1947 • Leisen Mitchell • USA
SUDDENLY, LAST SUMMER • 1959 • Mankiewicz Joseph L. • USA, UKN
SUDDENLY, LOVE • 1978 • Margolin Stuart • TVM • USA
SUDDENLY ONE DAY.. (UKN) see **EKDIN ACHANAK** • 1989
SUDDENLY SINGLE • 1971 • Taylor Jud • TVM • USA
SUDDILAGE KATHAWA • 1983 • Bandaranayake Dharmasiri • SLN
SUDEN IM SCHATTEN • 1962 • Spieker Franz-Josef • FRG
SUDLICHE NACHTE • 1953 • Stemmle R. A. • FRG
SUDS • 1920 • Dillon John Francis • USA
SUDS OF LOVE • 1917 • Howe J. A. • SHT • USA
SUDU SUDA • 1968 • Amerasinghe Roland • SLN • SWEETHEART
SUE • 1912 • *Champion* • USA
SUE • 1915 • *Warshauer Dorothy* • USA
SUE MY LAWYER • 1938 • White Jules • SHT • USA
SUE OF THE SOUTH • 1919 • Moore W. Eugene • USA
SUE SIMPKINS' AMBITION • 1912 • Ince Ralph • USA
SUE, SUE, SUE • 1909 • *Warwick Trading Co* • UKN
SUE ULTIME 12 ORE, LE see **E PIU FACILE CHE UN CAMMELLO** • 1950
SUECA ENTRE NOSOTROS, UNA • 1968 • Merino Fernando • ARG • SWEDE AMONG US, A
SUED FOR LIBEL • 1939 • Goodwins Leslie • USA
SUELTATE EL PELO • 1989 • MXC
SUENO DE ANDALUCIA, EL (SPN) see **ANDALOUSIE** • 1950
SUENO DEL CAPORAL, EL • 1922 • Contreras Torres Miguel • MXC • CORPORAL'S DREAM, THE
SUENO DEL MONO LOCO, EL see **MONO LOCO, EL** • 1989
SUENO DEL PONGO, EL • 1970 • Alvarez Santiago • DOC • CUB
SUENO EL CLARIN • 1965 • Gan Jose H. • SPN
SUENOS • 1922 • Barth-Moglia Luis • ARG
SUENOS DE AMOR • 1935 • Bohr Jose • MXC
SUENOS DE GLORIA • 1952 • Gomez Urquiza Zacarias • MXC • DREAMS OF GLORY
SUENOS DE HISTORIA • 1957 • Gan Jose H. • SPN
SUENOS DE MUJER • 1961 • Balcazar Alfonso • SPN
SUENOS DE ORO • 1956 • Zacarias Miguel • MXC, SPN
SUENOS DE TAY-PY • 1951 • Blay Jose Maria, Winterstein Franz • SPN
SUENOS JUVENILES • 1968 • SHT • SPN • JUVENILE DREAMS
SUERTE TE DE DIOS • 1959 • Gazcon Gilberto • MXC
SUEUR NOIRE see **SUEURS NOIRES** • 1975
SUEURS NOIRES • 1975 • Mazif Sid-Ali • ALG • SUEUR NOIRE
SUEZ • 1938 • Dwan Allan • USA
SUFARA', AS- • 1975 • Al-Ktari Naceur • TNS, LBY, FRN • AMBASSADORS, THE ○ AMBASSADEURS, LES ○ ASSOUFARA
SUFFER LITTLE CHILDREN • 1911 • *Kent Charles* • USA
SUFFER LITTLE CHILDREN • 1945 • Newman Sydney • DCS • CND
SUFFER LITTLE CHILDREN • 1976 • Sundstrom Cedric • SAF
SUFFER LITTLE CHILDREN.. FOR SUCH IS THE KINGDOM OF LABOR • 1909 • *Edison* • USA
SUFFER MAMMON see **SUFRE MAMON** • 1987
SUFFER OR DIE • 1979 • Antonioni Michelangelo • ITL
SUFFERIN' BABY, THE • 1915 • Louis Will • USA
SUFFERIN' CATS • 1961 • Smith Paul J. • ANS • USA
SUFFERING AND HAPPINESS OF MOTHERHOOD see **MODERSKAPETS KVAL OCH LYCKA** • 1945
SUFFERING IN CRIME see **AGONIZANDO EN EL CRIMEN** • 1967
SUFFERING IS A WOMAN • 1977 • Yehia Ahmed • EGY
SUFFERING OF SUSAN, THE • 1914 • Morrisey Edward • USA
SUFFERING SHAKESPEARE • 1924 • Roach Hal • SHT • USA
SUFFERING SUFFRAGETTES • 1908 • *Wrench* • UKN
SUFFERINGS OF YOUNG BOHACEK, THE see **UTRPENI MLADEHO BOHACKA** • 1969
SUFFERIN'S CATS • 1943 • Hanna William, Barbera Joseph • ANS • USA
SUFFRAGE AND THE MAN • 1912 • *Eclair* • USA
SUFFRAGETTE, THE • 1913 • *Glynne Agnes* • UKN
SUFFRAGETTE, THE • 1913 • Duncan William? • USA
SUFFRAGETTE, THE see **MODERNA SUFFRAGETTEN, DEN** • 1913
SUFFRAGETTE BATTLE OF NUTTYVILLE, THE • 1914 • Cabanne W. Christy • USA
SUFFRAGETTE IN SPITE OF HIMSELF, A • 1912 • Miller Ashley • USA, UKN
SUFFRAGETTE MINSTRELS, THE • 1913 • Henderson Dell • USA
SUFFRAGETTE SHERIFF, THE • 1912 • *Joyce Alice* • USA
SUFFRAGETTE TAMES THE BANDIT, THE • 1913 • *Frontier* • USA
SUFFRAGETTEN, DEN see **MODERNA SUFFRAGETTEN, DEN** • 1913
SUFFRAGETTEN, DIE • 1913 • Gad Urban • FRG, DNM • SEMMERETSDAMEN
SUFFRAGETTES AND THE HOBBLE SKIRT, THE • 1910 • Bouwmeester Theo? • UKN
SUFFRAGETTE'S DOWNFALL: OR, WHO SAID "RATS", THE • 1911 • Rains Fred • UKN
SUFFRAGETTES IN THE BUD • 1913 • Stow Percy • UKN
SUFFRAGETTE'S REVENGE, THE • 1913 • *Gaumont* • USA
SUFI TALE, A • 1977 • Thomas Gayle • ANM • CND • CONTE DE SUFI, UN
SUFRE MAMON • 1987 • Summers Manuel • SPN • SUFFER MAMMON
SUGAR see **SUKKER** • 1942
SUGAR AND ROSES see **GUL VE SEKER** • 1968
SUGAR AND SPICES • 1930 • Oumansky Alexander • SER • UKN
SUGAR AND SPIES • 1966 • McKimson Robert • ANS • USA
SUGAR BOWL see **SOCKERSKRINET** • 1938
SUGAR CANE ALLEY see **RUE CASES-NEGRES** • 1983
SUGAR CHILE ROBINSON, BILLIE HOLLIDAY, COUNT BASIE AND HIS SEXTET • 1950 • Cowan Will • SHT • USA
SUGAR COLT • 1966 • Giraldi Franco • ITL
SUGAR COOKIES • 1977 • Gershuny Theodore • USA
SUGAR COOKIES • 1988 • Herz Michael • USA
SUGAR COTTAGE see **CUKROVA BOUDA** • 1980
SUGAR DADDIES • 1927 • Guiol Fred • SHT • USA
SUGAR DADDY • 1968 • Crane Larry • USA • GAMES AND VARIATIONS
SUGAR DADDY (USA) see **PAPACITO LINDO** • 1939
SUGAR HILL • 1974 • Maslansky Paul • USA • VOODOO GIRL (UKN) ○ ZOMBIES OF SUGAR HILL, THE
SUGAR, HONEY AND HOT PEPPERS see **ZUCCHERO, IL MIELE E IL PEPPERONCINO, LO** • 1980
SUGAR IS A BUSINESS • 1971 • Wooster Arthur G. • SHT • UKN
SUGAR MANUFACTURE • 1914 • Vidor King • DOC • USA
SUGAR PLUM PAPA • 1930 • Sennett Mack • SHT • USA
SUGAR SHACK see **CUKROVA BOUDA** • 1980
SUGAR STEP, THE • 1928 • *De Forest Phonofilm* • SHT • UKN
SUGARBABY see **ZUCKERBABY** • 1985
SUGARFOOT • 1951 • Marin Edwin L. • USA • SWIRL OF GLORY
SUGARLAND EXPRESS • 1974 • Spielberg Steven • USA
SUGATA SANSHIRO • 1945 • Kurosawa Akira • JPN • SANSHIRO SUGATA ○ LEGEND OF JUDO, THE ○ JUDO SAGA
SUGATA SANSHIRO • 1955 • Tanaka Shigeo • JPN • HE WHO LIVED JUDO
SUGATA SANSHIRO • 1965 • Uchikawa Seiichiro • JPN • JUDO SAGA
SUGATA SANSHIRO PART II see **ZOKU SUGATA SANSHIRO** • 1945
SUGGEST A BETTER WAY • 1970 • Howes Oliver • DOC • ASL
SUGGESTIONATA • 1978 • Rizzo Alfredo • ITL
SUHADA NO WANA • 1967 • Higashimoto Kaoru • JPN • TRAP OF BARE SKIN, THE
SUHNE, DIE • 1917 • Hanus Emerich • FRG
SUHNE DER MARTHA MARX, DIE • 1919 • Halm Alfred • FRG
SUICIDA DA BOCA DO INFERNO, O • 1923 • de Albuquerque Ernesto • PRT
SUICIDAL POET, THE • 1908 • *Lubin* • USA
SUICIDATE MI AMOR! • 1960 • Martinez Solares Gilberto • MXC
SUICIDE • 1965 • Warhol Andy • USA
SUICIDE • 1968 • Kosa Ferenc • SHT • HNG

SUICIDE see **FLICKA OCH HYACINTER** • 1950
SUICIDE -A COMMUNITY'S CONCERN • 1981 • von Puttkamer Peter • DOC • CND
SUICIDE ATTACK • 1951 • Lerner Irving • USA
SUICIDE BATTALION • 1958 • Cahn Edward L. • USA
SUICIDE CLUB, THE • 1909 • Griffith D. W. • USA
SUICIDE CLUB, THE • 1914 • Elvey Maurice • UKN
SUICIDE CLUB, THE • 1973 • Glenn Bill • TVM • USA
SUICIDE CLUB, THE • 1988 • Bruce James • USA
SUICIDE CLUB, THE see **SELBSTMORDERKLUB, DER** • 1920
SUICIDE CLUB, THE (UKN) see **TROUBLE FOR TWO** • 1936
SUICIDE COMMANDO see **COMMANDO SUICIDA** • 1968
SUICIDE COMMANDOS (USA) see **COMMANDO SUICIDA** • 1968
SUICIDE CULT see **ASTROLOGER, THE** • 1977
SUICIDE DE SIR TESTON, LE • 1916 • de Baroncelli Jacques • FRN
SUICIDE DU COLONEL HENRY • 1899 • Melies Georges • FRN
SUICIDE EN PRISON • 1977 • Mankiewicz Francis • CND
SUICIDE FLEET • 1931 • Rogell Albert S. • USA
SUICIDE LEGION see **SUNSET IN VIENNA** • 1937
SUICIDE MISSION • 1956 • Forlong Michael • UKN, NRW • SHELTLANDSGJENGEN (NRW)
SUICIDE MISSION • 1968 • Merino Jose Luis • SPN
SUICIDE MISSION TO SINGAPORE (USA) see **GOLDSNAKE ANONIMA KILLERS** • 1966
SUICIDE MISSION (USA) see **MISION SUICIDA** • 1971
SUICIDE OF A HOLLYWOOD EXTRA see **LIFE AND DEATH OF 9413, A HOLLYWOOD EXTRA, THE** • 1928
SUICIDE PACT, THE • 1913 • Powell Frank • USA
SUICIDE RUN see **TOO LATE THE HERO** • 1970
SUICIDE SEVEN • 1967 • Reyes Efren • PHL
SUICIDE SQUAD • 1936 • Johnston Raymond K. • USA
SUICIDE SQUADRON (USA) see **DANGEROUS MOONLIGHT** • 1941
SUICIDE TROOPS OF THE WATCH TOWER see **BORO NO KESSHITAI** • 1943
SUICIDE'S WIFE, THE • 1979 • Newland John • TVM • USA • NEW LIFE, A
SUICIDO • 1916 • Lolli Alberto Carlo • ITL
SUIKODEN • 1942 • *Tsuburaya Eiji* • JPN
SUING SUSAN • 1912 • Trimble Larry • USA
SUIT ALMOST NEW, THE see **UBRANIE PRAWIE NOWE** • 1963
SUIT AND A SUITOR, A • 1917 • *Bickel George* • USA
SUIT CASE, A • 1909 • *Lubin* • USA
SUIT CASE MYSTERY, THE • 1910 • Seay Charles M. • USA
SUIT OF ARMOR, THE • 1912 • *Bunny John* • USA
SUIT THAT DIDN'T SUIT, THE • 1912 • Stow Percy • UKN
SUITA POLSKA • 1963 • Lomnicki Jan • DOC • PLN • POLISH SUITE
SUITABLE CASE FOR TREATMENT, A see **MORGAN -A SUITABLE CASE FOR TREATMENT** • 1966
SUITCASE, THE see **KOVCEG** • 1968
SUITCASE MYSTERY, THE • 1911 • *Nestor* • USA
SUITCASE WITH DYNAMITE see **KOFFER MIT DYNAMIT** • 1964
SUITE ANGLAISE, LA • 1981 • Cayeux Jean-Paul • FRN
SUITE NO.2 • 1947 • McCormick Hal, Hofflich Albert • SHT • USA
SUITE TEMPIROUETTE • 1954 • *Toonders Martin (P)* • SHT • NTH
SUITED TO A T. • 1931 • Fleischer Dave • ANS • USA
SUITOR, THE • 1920 • Semon Larry, Taurog Norman • SHT • USA
SUITOR, THE see **FIANCEE, THE**
SUITOR, THE see **SOUPIRANT, LE** • 1962
SUITOR FROM THE ROADS, THE see **FRIAREN FRAN LANDSVAGEN** • 1923
SUITOR OF SIAM, THE • 1917 • Smith David • SHT • USA
SUITORS, THE see **KAGIRIARU HI O AINI IKITE** • 1967
SUITORS AND SUITCASES • 1912 • *Lubin* • USA
SUIVEUR OBSTINE OU UN MONSIEUR QUI SUIT LES FEMMES, UN • 1906 • *Deed Andre* • FRN
SUIVEZ CET HOMME! • 1953 • Lampin Georges • FRN
SUIVEZ CETTE AVION • 1990 • Ambard Patrice • FRN
SUIVEZ L'OEUF • 1963 • Robin Pierre • SHT • FRN
SUIVEZ-MOI, JEUNE HOMME! • 1958 • Lefranc Guy • FRN
SUIZO -UN AMOR EN ESPAGNE • Dindo Richard • SWT
SUJAKO MON • 1957 • Mori Issei • JPN • LOVE OF THE PRINCESS ○ SUJAKUMON
SUJAKUMON see **SUJAKO MON** • 1957
SUJATA • 1959 • Roy Bimal • IND
SUJET OU LE SECRETAIRE AUX MILLE ET UN TIROIRS • 1974 • Lledo Joaquin • FRN
SUJSEDI • 1970 • Dragic Nedeljko • ANM • YGS • NEIGHBORS
SUKCES • 1968 • Piwowski Marek • DOC • PLN • SUCCESS, THE
SUKHI SANSAR • 1967 • Sutar Shrikant • IND
SUKI NAREBA KOSO • 1928 • Gosho Heinosuke • JPN • IF YOU LIKE IT ○ BECAUSE I LOVE
SUKKARIYYA, AS- • Al Imam Hassan • EGY
SUKKER • 1942 • Henning-Jensen Bjarne • DNM • SUGAR
SUKOVO TRIO • 1965 • Schorm Evald • MTV • CZC • SUK'S TRIO
SUK'S TRIO see **SUKOVO TRIO** • 1965
SUKURAPPU SHUDAN • 1968 • Tasaka Tomotaka • JPN • SCRAP COLLECTORS LTD.
SUL CAMMINO DEI GIGANTI • 1960 • Zane Angio • ITL
SUL PONTE DEI SOSPIRI • 1953 • Leonviola Antonio • ITL
SULEIMAN THE CONQUEROR (USA) see **SOLIMANO IL CONQUISTATORE** • 1961
SULFATARA • 1955 • De Seta Vittorio • ITL
SULI-BULI • 1983 • Varsanyi Ferenc • HNG • SCHOOLTIME BLUES
SULIMAN TREASURE see **GANJINEH SOLIMAN** • 1967
SULKARY • 1974 • Casals Melchor • CUB
SULLA VIA SI DAMASCO • 1947 • Emmer Luciano, Gras Enrico • ITL
SULL'ALTARE DEL SACRIFICIO • 1912 • Lolli Alberto Carlo • ITL
SULLAM AL-KHALFI, AS- • 1970 • Saiem Atef • EGY • ESCALIER DE SERVICE, L'
SULLE ORME DI GIACOMO LEOPARDI • 1941 • Pasinetti Francesco • ITL
SULLE ROME DI VERDI see **LUOGHI VERDIANI** • 1948
SULLE ROVINE DELL'AMORE • 1913 • Lolli Alberto Carlo • ITL
SULLIVAN CARTOON COMEDIES • 1916 • Sullivan Pat • ASS • USA
SULLIVANS, THE • 1944 • Bacon Lloyd • USA • FIGHTING SULLIVANS, THE
SULLIVAN'S EMPIRE • 1967 • Hart Harvey, Carr Thomas • USA
SULLIVAN'S TRAVELS • 1941 • Sturges Preston • USA
SULOCHANA • 1934 • Chaudhury Ahindra • IND • TEMPLE BELLS
SULT (DNM) see **SVALT** • 1966
SULTAN • 1979 • Tibet Kartal • TRK
SULTAN, THE • 1970 • Deknight Jimmy • USA
SULTAN AND THE EMPEROR, THE • 1987 • Romero Eddie • PHL
SULTAN AND THE ROLLER SKATES, THE • 1914 • Williams C. Jay • USA
SULTAN DESCALZO, EL • 1954 • Martinez Solares Gilberto • MXC
SULTAN OF ZULON, THE • 1915 • Van Wally • USA
SULTAN PEPPER • 1934 • Stallings George • ANS • USA
SULTAN VON JOHORE, DER • 1916 • Piel Harry • FRG
SULTANA • 1989 • Butt Mahmood • PKS
SULTANA, THE • 1916 • *Roland Ruth* • USA
SULTANA ABBASE, THE see **ABBASE SULTAN** • 1968
SULTANA DE L'AMOUR, LA • 1918 • Burguet Charles • FRN
SULTANA OF THE DESERT, A • 1915 • Santschi Thomas • USA
SULTANA SAFYE, LA • 1955 • Martin G. D. • ITL • SULTAN'S WIFE, THE
SULTANE DE L'AMOUR, LA • 1918 • Le Somptier Rene • FRN
SULTANS, LES • 1966 • Delannoy Jean • FRN, ITL • AMANTE ITALIANA, L' (ITL)
SULTAN'S BIRTHDAY • 1944 • Tytla Bill • ANS • USA
SULTAN'S CAT, THE • 1931 • *Terry Paul/ Moser Frank (P)* • ANS • USA
SULTAN'S DAGGER, THE • 1913 • *Melies* • USA
SULTAN'S DAUGHTER, THE • 1943 • Dreifuss Arthur • USA
SULTAN'S SLAVE, THE see **SON OF THE SAHARA, A** • 1924
SULTAN'S WIFE, THE • 1917 • Badger Clarence • SHT • USA
SULTAN'S WIFE, THE see **SULTANA SAFYE, LA** • 1955
SULUDE GODINE • 1989 • Calic Zoran • YGS • NUTSY YEARS
SUMBER ILHAMKU • 1978 • Jaafar Aziz • MLY
SUMIRE MUSUME • 1935 • Yamamoto Kajiro • JPN • VIOLET GIRL
SUMKA DIPKURIERA • 1927 • Dovzhenko Alexander • USS • DIPLOMATIC POUCH, THE ○ TEKA DIPKURYERA
SUMMER • 1930 • Iwerks Ub • ANS • USA
SUMMER • 1955 • Novik William • SHT
SUMMER • 1969 • Proikov Proiko • ANS • BUL
SUMMER see **LETO** • 1949
SUMMER see **SOMMER** • 1974
SUMMER ADVENTURE see **ABENTEUER EINES SOMMERS** • 1974
SUMMER ADVENTURE, A • 1911 • *Selig* • USA
SUMMER AFFAIR see **SUNSHINE ON THE SKIN** • 1979
SUMMER AFFAIR, A see **MOMENT D'EGAREMENT, UN** • 1978
SUMMER AND SINNERS see **SOMMAR OCH SYNDARE** • 1960
SUMMER AND SMOKE • 1961 • Glenville Peter • USA
SUMMER AT 17 • Downey John • USA
SUMMER AT GRANDPA'S, A see **DONGDONG DE JIAQUI** • 1984
SUMMER BACHELORS • 1926 • Dwan Allan • USA
SUMMER BATTLE OF OSAKA, THE see **OSAKA NATSU NO JIN** • 1937
SUMMER BEFORE, THE • 1975 • Brittain Don • CND
SUMMER BEFORE, THE see **ANTES, O VERAO** • 1968
SUMMER BOARDERS • 1917 • Blystone John G. (Spv) • SHT • USA
SUMMER BOARDERS TAKEN IN • 1908 • *Selig* • USA
SUMMER BOARDING • 1917 • De Vonde Chester M. • SHT • USA
SUMMER BY THE BALTIC see **LATO NAD BALTYKIEM** • 1964
SUMMER CAMP • 1979 • Vincent Chuck • USA
SUMMER CAMP see **MEATBALLS** • 1979
SUMMER CAMP NIGHTMARE • 1987 • Dragin Bert L. • USA • BUTTERFLY REVOLUTION, THE
SUMMER CITY • 1977 • Fraser Chris • ASL
SUMMER CLOUD see **BOLONDOS VAKACIO** • 1968
SUMMER CLOUDS see **BOLOND APRILIS** • 1957
SUMMER CLOUDS see **IWASHIGUMO** • 1958
SUMMER DAY, A • Lesiewicz Witold • PLN
SUMMER DAY IN SWEDEN, A • Lindblad Jan • DCS • SWD
SUMMER DAYS • 1920 • *Reelcraft* • USA
SUMMER DAYS see **ZILE DE VARA** • 1968
SUMMER DOG • 1977 • Clayton John • USA
SUMMER FANTASY • 1984 • Nosseck Noel • TVM • USA
SUMMER FEVER • 1987 • Webb William • USA
SUMMER FLIGHT see **STOLEN HOURS, THE** • 1963
SUMMER FLIRTATION, A • 1910 • Golden Joseph A. • USA
SUMMER GIRL • 1983 • Lewis Robert Michael • TVM • USA
SUMMER GIRL, THE • 1911 • Merwin Bannister • USA
SUMMER GIRL, THE • 1916 • August Edwin • USA
SUMMER GIRLS, THE • 1918 • Cline Eddie • SHT • USA
SUMMER GUESTS (UKN) see **SOMMERGASTE** • 1976
SUMMER HEAT • 1980 • McCabe Christy • USA
SUMMER HEAT • 1983 • Starrett Jack • USA • KISS MY GRITS ○ TEXAS LEGEND, A ○ TEXAS BURNS AT NIGHT
SUMMER HEAT • 1987 • Gleason Michie • USA
SUMMER HEAT see **SUMMER SCHOOL TEACHERS** • 1975
SUMMER HOLIDAY • 1948 • Mamoulian Rouben • USA
SUMMER HOLIDAY • 1963 • Yates Peter, Ross Herbert • UKN
SUMMER HOLIDAYS see **AGUAZET SEIF** • 1967
SUMMER I BECAME 15, THE see **SOMEREN JEG FYLTE FEMTEN, DEN** • 1976
SUMMER IDYL, A • 1910 • Griffith D. W. • USA
SUMMER IDYL, A • 1912 • *Majestic* • USA
SUMMER IN HEAT • 1979 • McCabe Christy • USA
SUMMER IN MISSISSIPPI • 1965 • Fox Beryl • DCS • CND
SUMMER IN NARITA see **SANRIZUKA NO NATSU** • 1968
SUMMER IN SAINT TROPEZ, A see **ETE A SAINT-TROPEZ, UN** • 1981
SUMMER IN STOCKHOLM see **STOCKHOLMSSOMMAR** • 1969
SUMMER IN THE CITY (DEDICATED TO THE KINKS) • 1970 • Wenders Wim • FRG
SUMMER IN THE COUNTRY, THE see **PASTORALE** • 1976
SUMMER IN THE FIELDS • 1970 • van der Linden Charles Huguenot • NTH
SUMMER INTERLUDE (UKN) see **SOMMARLEK** • 1951
SUMMER IS FOR KIDS • 1948 • Jackson Stanley R. • DCS • CND
SUMMER IS NEARLY OVER see **ESTATE STA FINENDO, L'** • 1987
SUMMER IS TO BLAME FOR EVERYTHING, THE see **LJETO JE KRIVO ZA SVE** • 1962
SUMMER JOB • 1989 • Madden Paul • USA
SUMMER JOY • 1978 • Czurko Edward • MTV • CND
SUMMER LIGHT (USA) see **LUMIERE D'ETE** • 1942
SUMMER LIGHTNING • 1933 • Rogers Maclean • UKN
SUMMER LIGHTNING • 1988 • Costa-Gavras • USA • SUNDOWN
SUMMER LIGHTNING see **TROUBLESOME WIVES** • 1928
SUMMER LIGHTNING, A see **STROHFEUER** • 1972
SUMMER LIGHTNING (UKN) see **SCUDDHA-HOO, SCUDDA HAY** • 1948
SUMMER LOVE • 1914 • *Lubin* • USA
SUMMER LOVE • 1958 • Haas Charles • USA
SUMMER LOVE • 1968 • Mia Rosa • PHL
SUMMER LOVERS • 1982 • Kleiser Randall • USA
SUMMER MADNESS • 1911 • *Powers* • USA
SUMMER MADNESS (UKN) see **SUMMERTIME** • 1955
SUMMER MAGIC • 1963 • Neilson James • USA
SUMMER MANOEUVRES (UKN) see **GRANDES MANOEUVRES, LES** • 1955
SUMMER MORNINGS • 1974 • Suissa Daniele J. • MTV • CND
SUMMER NIGHT FEVER • 1978 • Gotz Siggi • FRG
SUMMER NIGHT IS SWEET, THE see **LJUVLIG AR SOMMARNATTEN** • 1961
SUMMER NIGHT WITH GREEK PROFILE ALMOND EYES AND THE SCENT OF BASIL see **NOTTE D'ESTATE CON PROFILO GRECO OCCHI A MANDORLA E ODORE DI BASILICO** • 1987
SUMMER NIGHTS ON THE PLANET EARTH see **NAGRA SOMMARKVALLAR PA JORDEN** • 1987
SUMMER OF '42 • 1971 • Mulligan Robert • USA
SUMMER OF '43, THE see **LYETO 43-VO GODA** • 1968
SUMMER OF 58 • 1990 • Rai Mojtaba • IRN
SUMMER OF FEAR (UKN) see **STRANGER IN OUR HOUSE** • 1978
SUMMER OF MEN, THE • 1970 • Gedris Marionas Vintzo • USS • MEN'S SUMMER, THE
SUMMER OF MY GERMAN SOLDIER • 1978 • Tuchner Michael • TVM • USA
SUMMER OF SECRETS • 1976 • Sharman Jim • ASL
SUMMER OF SILENCE see **SOMMERFUGLER** • 1972
SUMMER OF THE 17TH DOLL • 1959 • Norman Leslie • UKN • SEASON OF PASSION (USA)
SUMMER OF THE COLT see **FIERRO OU L'ETE DES SECRETS** • 1988
SUMMER OF THE LION see **LEJONSOMMAR** • 1968
SUMMER ON THE BALTIC see **LATO NAD BALTYKIEM** • 1964
SUMMER ON THE HILL see **NYAR A HEGYEN** • 1967
SUMMER PARADISE (USA) see **PARADISTORG** • 1977
SUMMER PLACE, A • 1959 • Daves Delmer • USA
SUMMER PLACE IS WANTED, A see **SOMMARNOJE SOKES** • 1957
SUMMER RAIN see **AGE OF INNOCENCE** • 1977
SUMMER RAIN see **CHUVAS DE VERAO** • 1977
SUMMER RAIN see **PLUIE D'ETE** • 1986
SUMMER RAIN, A see **ZAPOR** • 1960
SUMMER REBELLION see **KESAKAPINA** • 1969
SUMMER RENTAL • 1985 • Reiner Carl • USA
SUMMER RESIDENTS see **DACHNIKI** • 1967
SUMMER RESIDENTS IN THE COUNTRYSIDE see **DACHNIKI** • 1967
SUMMER RESORT IDYLL, A • 1914 • Seay Charles M. • USA
SUMMER RUN • 1974 • Capetanis Leon • USA
SUMMER SCHOOL • 1987 • Reiner Carl • USA
SUMMER SCHOOL see **LOOSE SCREWS** • 1985
SUMMER SCHOOL TEACHERS • 1975 • Peeters Barbara • USA • SUMMER HEAT
SUMMER SHOWERS see **CHUVAS DE VERAO** • 1977
SUMMER SISTER see **NATSU NO IMOTO** • 1972
SUMMER SKIES • 1911 • *Reliance* • USA
SUMMER SKIN see **PIEL DE VERANO** • 1961
SUMMER SOLDIERS • 1971 • Teshigahara Hiroshi • JPN
SUMMER SOLSTICE • 1981 • Rosenblum Ralph • MTV • USA
SUMMER SOUNDS • 1985 • Lehman Lewis • MTV • CND
SUMMER STOCK • 1950 • Walters Charles • USA • IF YOU FEEL LIKE SINGING (UKN)
SUMMER STORM • 1944 • Sirk Douglas • USA
SUMMER STORM see **NATSU NO ARASHI** • 1956
SUMMER STORY, A • 1988 • Haggard Piers • UKN
SUMMER TALE see **TANASE SCATIU** • 1976
SUMMER TALE, A see **SOMMARSAGA, EN** • 1912
SUMMER TALE, A see **SOMMARSAGA, EN** • 1941
SUMMER TALES see **RACCONTI D'ESTATE** • 1958
SUMMER THE SUN WAS LOST, THE see **NISSHOKU NO NATSU** • 1956
SUMMER TIME • 1910 • *Imp* • USA
SUMMER TIME • 1929 • Foster John • ANS • USA
SUMMER TO REMEMBER, A • 1985 • Lewis Robert • TVM • USA
SUMMER TO REMEMBER, A see **LJETO ZA SECANJE** • 1990
SUMMER TO REMEMBER, A (USA) see **SEREZHA** • 1960
SUMMER TRAGEDY, A • 1910 • Griffith D. W. • USA
SUMMER TRAIL see **MUURAHAISPOLKU** • 1970
SUMMER TRAIN see **SOMMARTAG** • 1961
SUMMER TRUMPET, A see **SOMMARENS TROMPET** • 1975
SUMMER (USA) see **RAYON VERT, LE** • 1986
SUMMER VACATION see **ONE CRAZY SUMMER** • 1986
SUMMER VACATION 1999 (UKN) see **1999-NEN NO NATSU YASUMI** • 1988
SUMMER WAR see **SOMMERKRIG** • 1965
SUMMER WE MOVED TO ELM STREET, THE • 1966 • Watson Patricia • CND
SUMMER WIDOWS • 1911 • *Reliance* • USA

SUMMER WISHES, WINTER DREAMS • 1973 • Cates Gilbert • USA • CARNIVAL ○ DEATH OF A SNOWQUEEN ○ SOUVENIR
SUMMER WITH A COWBOY see **LETO S KOVBOJEM** • 1977
SUMMER WITH ANNA see **VARA CU ANA** • 1988
SUMMER WITH MONIKA (UKN) see **SOMMAREN MED MONIKA** • 1953
SUMMER WITHOUT BOYS, A • 1973 • Szwarc Jeannot • TVM • USA
SUMMER WORLD, A • 1961 • Schaffner Franklin J. • USA
SUMMERFIELD • 1977 • Hannam Ken • ASL
SUMMER'S CHILDREN • 1979 • Kohanyi Julius • CND
SUMMER'S ENDING see **SENSOMMER** • 1988
SUMMER'S LOVE, A see **KARLEKS SOMMAR, EN** • 1979
SUMMER'S NEARLY OVER see **HERE'S TO HARRY'S GRANDFATHER!** • 1970
SUMMER'S TALE, A see **SOMMARSAGA, EN** • 1941
SUMMERSPELL • 1983 • Shanklin Lina • USA
SUMMERTIME • 1931 • *Terry Paul/ Moser Frank (P)* • ANS • USA
SUMMERTIME • 1935 • *Iwerks Ub (P)* • ANS • USA
SUMMERTIME • 1955 • Lean David • USA • SUMMER MADNESS (UKN)
SUMMERTIME FUN see **BEACH BALLS** • 1988
SUMMERTIME KILLER, THE (USA) see **VERANO PARA MATAR, UN** • 1973
SUMMERTIME YANKS see **CHILDREN IN THE CROSSFIRE** • 1984
SUMMERTREE • 1971 • Newley Anthony • USA
SUMMERWIND • 1966 • Dorsky Nathaniel • USA
SUMMIT • 1963 • Vanderbeek Stan • SHT • USA
SUMMIT • 1968 • Bontempi Giorgio • ITL, FRN
SUMMIT OF MOUNT FUJI, THE see **FUJI SANCHO** • 1948
SUMMONING OF EVERYONE, THE • 1956 • Hilliard Richard • USA
SUMMONING SHOT, THE • 1915 • Morgan George • USA
SUMMONING THE SPIRITS (USA) see **EVOCATION SPIRITE** • 1899
SUMMONS, THE see **SCORPION** • 1986
SUMNJIVO LICE • 1954 • Jovanovic Soja, Dinulovic Predrag • YGS • SUSPICIOUS CHARACTER, A
SUMO FESTIVAL see **DOHYOSAI** • 1944
SUMPAH ORANG MINYAK • 1958 • Ramlee P. • MLY, HKG • CURSE OF THE OILY MAN
SUMPAH PONTIANAK • 1958 • *Menado Maria* • MLY • VAMPIRE'S CURSE, THE
SUMPAHAN MAHSURI • 1989 • Sulong Jamil • MLY
SUMPF, DER • 1916 • Mack Max • FRG
SUMPF UND MORAL • 1925 • Walther-Fein Rudolf • FRG
SUMPFBLUME, DIE • 1912 • Larsen Viggo • FRG
SUMPFHANNE, DIE • 1919 • Boese Carl • FRG
SUMPFLILIE, DIE • 1920 • Frey Karl? • FRG
SUMURAI NIPPON • 1931 • Ito Daisuke • JPN
SUMURU • 1967 • Shonteff Lindsay • UKN • 1,000,000 EYES OF SUMURU, THE (USA)
SUMURU • 1968 • Franco Jesus • SPN, FRG, USA • SIEBEN MANNER DER SU-MARU, DIE (FRG) ○ RIO 70 (USA) ○ CIUDAD SIN HOMBRES, LA ○ SEVEN SECRETS OF SU-MARU, THE ○ RIVER 70
SUMURUN • 1908 • Reinhardt Max • FRG
SUMURUN • 1910 • *Salmonova Lyda* • FRG
SUMURUN • 1920 • Lubitsch Ernst • FRG • ONE ARABIAN NIGHT (USA)
SUN • 1971 • Noyce Phil • SHT • ASL
SUN, THE • 1903 • Paul Robert William • UKN • MIDNIGHT SUN AT SCARO, THE
SUN, THE see **NICHIRIN** • 1925
SUN, THE see **NICHIRIN** • 1926
SUN, THE see **NICHIRIN** • 1950
SUN ABOVE, DEATH BELOW see **SOGEKI** • 1968
SUN, AIR AND WATER • 1961 • Mitta Alexander • USS
SUN ALSO RISES, THE • 1957 • King Henry • USA
SUN ALSO RISES, THE • 1984 • Goldstone James • TVM • USA
SUN AND PLANET WHEEL see **CHARKHI-O-FALAK** • 1967
SUN AND RAIN see **TAIYANG YU** • 1987
SUN AND ROSE see **TAIYO TO BARA** • 1956
SUN AND SHADOW see **SOLEIL ET SOMBRE** • 1922
SUN AND SHADOW see **SLANTSETO I SYANKATA** • 1962
SUN AND THE MOON, THE see **VIOLINS CAME WITH THE AMERICANS, THE** • 1986
SUN BARATOM • 1977 • Gemes Jozsef • HNG • FRIEND HEDGEHOG
SUN-BONNET SUE • 1911 • *Yankee* • USA
SUN COMES UP, THE • 1948 • Thorpe Richard • USA • SUN IN THE MORNING
SUN DEMON, THE see **HIDEOUS SUN DEMON, THE** • 1959
SUN DOG TRAILS • 1923 • King Louis • USA
SUN DON'T SHINE ON THE SAME DAWG'S BACK ALL THE TIME, THE • 1969 • Vaitiekunas Vince • CND
SUN DOWN LIMITED, THE • 1924 • Roach Hal • SHT • USA
SUN FLIGHT see **SUNFLIGHT** • 1964
SUN FROM ANOTHER SKY, THE see **SUNCE TUDEG NEGA** • 1968
SUN IN THE EYES see **SOLE NEGLI OCCHI, IL** • 1953
SUN IN THE MORNING see **SUN COMES UP, THE** • 1948
SUN IS FAR AWAY, THE see **DALEKO JE SUNCE** • 1953
SUN IS RISING, THE see **REISE NACH TILSIT, DIE** • 1939
SUN IS UP, THE see **BOY.. A GIRL, A** • 1969
SUN LEGEND OF THE SHOGUNATE'S LAST DAYS see **BAKUMATSU TAIYODEN** • 1958
SUN NEVER SETS, THE • 1939 • Lee Rowland V. • USA
SUN NEVER SETS, THE see **HI WA SHIZUMAZU** • 1954
SUN OF DEATH, THE see **ILIOS TOU THANATOU, O** • 1978
SUN ON A CLOUDY DAY see **SHAMS FI YAUM GHAIM** • 1985
SUN ON THE SKIN (UKN) see **SOLE NELLA PELLE, IL** • 1971
SUN OVER DENMARK see **SOL OVER DANMARK** • 1935
SUN OVER KLARA (USA) see **SOL OVER KLARA** • 1942
SUN OVER SWEDEN see **SOL OVER SVERIGE** • 1938
SUN OVER THE KUROBE GORGE see **KUROBE NO TAIYO** • 1968
SUN RA: A JOYFUL NOISE • 1980 • Mugge Robert • DOC • USA
SUN, RAIN AND FIELD LILY see **SLNKO, DAZD, LALIE POLNE** • 1972
SUN, RAIN AND SMILES • 1962 • Makhnach Leonid • DOC • USS
SUN RISES AGAIN, THE see **SOLE SORGE ANCORA, IL** • 1946
SUN RISES EVERYWHERE see **SURJO SANGRAM** • 1978
SUN RISES ONCE A DAY, THE see **SLONCE WSCHODZI RAZ NA DZIEN** • 1967
SUN SETS AT DAWN, THE • 1950 • Sloane Paul • USA
SUN SETS AT NOON see **MUN TET CHEIN NAY WIN THE** • 1982
SUN SHINES, THE (USA) see **SUT A NAP**
SUN SHINES BRIGHT, THE • 1953 • Ford John • USA
SUN SHINES FOR ALL, THE (USA) see **SOLNTSE SVETIT VSEM** • 1959
SUN SHINES FOR EVERYBODY, THE see **SOLNTSE SVETIT VSEM** • 1959
SUN SHINES FOR YOU TOO, THE see **I DLA WAS SWIECI SLONCE** • 1956
SUN TAI SIL YEN YIN • 1964 • Lo Chen • HKG • BETWEEN TEARS AND SMILES (USA)
SUN, THE PLACE AND THE GIRLS, THE see **NUDES OF THE WORLD** • 1961
SUN-UP • 1919 • Bailey Oliver D. • USA
SUN-UP • 1925 • Goulding Edmund • USA
SUN VALLEY see **SUN VALLEY SERENADE** • 1941
SUN VALLEY CYCLONE • 1946 • Springsteen R. G. • USA
SUN VALLEY SERENADE • 1941 • Humberstone H. Bruce • USA • SUN VALLEY
SUN WILL NEVER SET, THE see **LA TUTFI EL SHEMS** • 1961
SUN WILL RISE see **SURJO SANGRAM** • 1978
SUN WIND see **AURINKOTUULI** • 1980
SUN, WIND AND WOOD see **SUN, WIND, WOOD** • 1978
SUN, WIND, WOOD • 1978 • Henaut Dorothy Todd • DOC • CND • SUN, WIND AND WOOD
SUN WUNGKONG • 1961-65 • Wan Lai-Ming • CHN
SUNA NO KAORI • 1968 • Iwauchi Katsumi • JPN • NIGHT OF THE SEAGULL, THE (USA)
SUNA NO ONNA • 1964 • Teshigahara Hiroshi • JPN • WOMAN IN THE DUNES (USA) ○ WOMAN OF THE DUNES ○ WOMAN IN THE SAND ○ SAND-WOMAN
SUNA NO UTSUWA • 1974 • Nomura Yoshitaro • JPN • CASTLE OF SAND, THE ○ VESSEL OF SAND, A
SUNANO UE NO SHOKUBUTSUGUN • 1964 • Nakahira Ko • JPN • JUNGLE INTERLUDE
SUNBEAM • 1913 • *Powers* • USA
SUNBEAM • 1980 • Vester Paul • UKN
SUNBEAM, THE • 1912 • Griffith D. W. • USA
SUNBEAM, THE • 1916 • Carewe Edwin • USA
SUNBONNET BLUE, A • 1937 • Avery Tex • ANS • USA
SUNBONNET SUE • 1945 • Murphy Ralph • USA • BELLE OF THE BOWERY
SUNBURN • 1970 • Sarafian Richard C. • USA, UKN
SUNBURST • 1975 • Polakoff James • USA
SUNCANI KRIK see **SONCNI KRIK** • 1968
SUNCE TUDEG NEGA • 1968 • Kosovac Milan • YGS • SUN FROM ANOTHER SKY, THE
SUNDANCE AND THE KID see **SUNDANCE CASSIDY AND BUTCH THE KID** • 1975
SUNDANCE CASSIDY AND BUTCH THE KID • 1975 • Pitt Arthur • USA • SUNDANCE AND THE KID
SUNDARI • 1979 • Hossain Amjad • BNG
SUNDAY • 1915 • Lederer George W. • USA
SUNDAY • 1924 • Shimazu Yasujiro • JPN
SUNDAY • 1987 • Grigoriou Anna • SHT • GRC
SUNDAY see **NEDELJA** • 1968
SUNDAY AFTERNOON see **TARDE DEL DOMINGO, LA** • 1957
SUNDAY AFTERNOON see **DOMINGO A TARDE** • 1965
SUNDAY AT 6 O'CLOCK see **DUMINICA LA ORA 6** • 1965
SUNDAY BEACH • 1947 • Jacobs Lewis • USA
SUNDAY, BLOODY SUNDAY • 1971 • Schlesinger John • UKN • BLOODY SUNDAY
SUNDAY BY THE SEA • 1953 • Simmons Anthony • UKN
SUNDAY CALM • 1923 • Roach Hal • SHT • USA
SUNDAY CHILDREN see **NIEDZIELNE DZIECI** • 1977
SUNDAY CHRONICLE, A see **HRONIKO TIS KIRIAKIS** • 1974
SUNDAY CLOTHES • 1931 • *Mintz Charles (P)* • ANS • USA
SUNDAY DAUGHTERS see **VASARNAPI SZULOK** • 1980
SUNDAY DINNER FOR A SOLDIER • 1944 • Bacon Lloyd • USA
SUNDAY DREAMS see **SNY NA NEDELI** • 1959
SUNDAY DRIVE • 1986 • Cullingham Mark • TVM • USA
SUNDAY ENCOUNTER (USA) see **DROLE DE DIMANCHE, UN** • 1958
SUNDAY EXCURSION see **SONTAGSFAHRER** • 1963
SUNDAY FATHER see **TATA DE DUMINICA** • 1974
SUNDAY GAMES see **NEDELNITE MATCHOVE** • 1975
SUNDAY, GO TO MEETIN' TIME • 1936 • Freleng Friz • ANS • USA
SUNDAY IN AUGUST see **DOMENICA D'AGOSTO** • 1950
SUNDAY IN AUGUST, A see **SRPNOVA NEDELE** • 1960
SUNDAY IN HELL, A see **FORARSDAG I HELVEDE, EN** • 1976
SUNDAY IN MELBOURNE • 1959 • Brealey Gil, Olson Paul • ASL
SUNDAY IN NEW YORK • 1963 • Tewkesbury Peter • USA
SUNDAY IN OCTOBER, A see **OKTOBERI VASARNAP** • 1980
SUNDAY IN SEPTEMBER, A see **SONDAG I SEPTEMBER, EN** • 1963
SUNDAY IN THE AFTERNOON see **DOMINGO A TARDE** • 1965
SUNDAY IN THE COUNTRY • 1974 • Trent John • CND, UKN
SUNDAY IN THE COUNTRY (UKN) see **DIMANCHE A LA COMPAGNE, UN** • 1984
SUNDAY IN THE PARK • 1956 • Schlesinger John • DCS • UKN
SUNDAY IN THE PARK • 1970 • Winter Donovan • DOC • UKN
SUNDAY JUNCTION • 1962 • De Laurent Edouard • USA
SUNDAY LARK • 1963 • Semel Sanford • USA
SUNDAY LOVERS • 1980 • Forbes Bryan, Molinaro Edouard, Risi Dino, Wilder Gene • USA, FRN • SEDUCTEURS, LES (FRN)
SUNDAY LOVERS • 1981 • Wilder Donald A. (c/d) • CND
SUNDAY LUNCH see **NEDELJNI RUCAK** • 1983
SUNDAY MATCHES see **NEDELNITE MATCHOVE** • 1975
SUNDAY MORNING (USA) see **NIEDZIELNY PORANEC** • 1955
SUNDAY NIGHT see **VOSKRESNAYA NOCH** • 1977
SUNDAY NIGHT AT THE TROCADERO • 1937 • Sidney George • SHT • USA
SUNDAY OF JUSTICE see **NIEDZIELA SPRAWIEDLIWOSCI** • 1965
SUNDAY OF LIFE, THE (USA) see **DIMANCHE DE LA VIE, LE** • 1967
SUNDAY OF THE OTHERS, THE see **SONNTAG DER ANDEREN, DER** • 1959
SUNDAY ON THE ISLAND OF THE GRAND JATTE see **ZONDAG OP HET EILAND VAN DE GRANDE JATTE, EEN** • 1965
SUNDAY ON THE RIVER • 1960 • Resnick Ken, Hitchens Gordon • USA
SUNDAY PARENTS see **VASARNAPI SZULOK** • 1980
SUNDAY PRANKS see **NIEDZIELNE IGRASZKI** • 1988
SUNDAY PUNCH • 1942 • Miller David • USA
SUNDAY ROMANCE, A see **BAKARUHABAN** • 1957
SUNDAY SCHOOL TREAT, THE • 1906 • *Walturdaw* • UKN
SUNDAY SCHOOL TREAT, THE • 1907 • Stow Percy • UKN
SUNDAY SINNERS • 1941 • Dreifuss Arthur • USA
SUNDAY SUITOR • 1970 • *Mj Productions* • USA
SUNDAY SUN see **ZON OP ZONDAG** • 1964
SUNDAY THEY'LL MAKE ME A SAINT • 1969 • Potts James • UKN
SUNDAY TOO FAR AWAY • 1974 • Hannam Ken • ASL
SUNDAY WOMAN, THE (USA) see **DONNA DELLA DOMENICA, LA** • 1976
SUNDAYING IN FAIRVIEW • 1917 • Windom Lawrence C. • SHT • USA
SUNDAYS AND CYBELE (USA) see **DIMANCHES DE VILLE D'AVRAY, LES** • 1962
SUNDAY'S DINNER • 1907 • Aylott Dave • UKN
SUNDE AM WEIBE • 1926 • Frowein Eberhard • FRG
SUNDE DER HELGA ARNDT, DIE • 1916 • May Joe • FRG
SUNDE DER LISSY KRAFFT, DIE • 1930 • Andersen F. W. • FRG
SUNDE MIT RABATT • 1968 • Lubowski Rudolf • FRG • SIN WITH REBATE
SUNDE UND MORAL • 1929 • Kober Erich • FRG
SUNDEN DER ELTERN • 1919 • Eichberg Richard • FRG
SUNDEN DER VATER, DIE • 1913 • Gad Urban • FRG, DNM • FAEDRENES SYND
SUNDEN VON GESTERN • 1922 • Wullner Robert • FRG
SUNDENBABEL • 1925 • David Constantin J. • FRG
SUNDENBOCK, DER • 1940 • Deppe Hans • FRG
SUNDENBOCK VON SPATZENHAUSEN, DER • 1958 • Fredersdorf Herbert B. • FRG
SUNDENLUST • 1919 • Krafft Uwe Jens? • FRG
SUNDERED TIES • 1912 • Ford Francis • USA
SUNDERIN, DIE • 1919 • Lasko Leo • FRG
SUNDERIN, DIE • 1927 • Bonnard Mario • FRG
SUNDERIN, DIE • 1951 • Forst Willi • FRG • SINNER, THE
SUNDIG UND SUSS • 1929 • Lamac Carl • FRG
SUNDIGE DORF, DAS • 1940 • Stockel Joe • FRG
SUNDIGE DORF, DAS • 1954 • Dorfler Ferdinand • FRG
SUNDIGE GRENZE • 1951 • Stemmle R. A. • FRG
SUNDIGE HAUS, DAS see **VERFUHRTE JUGEND** • 1950
SUNDIGE HOF, DER • 1933 • Osten Franz • FRG • LONA UND IHR KNECHT
SUNDIGE MUTTER • 1921 • Oswald Richard • FRG
SUNDIGE VESTALIN, DIE • 1921 • Seitz Franz • FRG
SUNDIGES BLUT • 1919 • Mack Max • FRG
SUNDOWN • 1924 • Trimble Larry, Hoyt Harry O. • USA
SUNDOWN • 1941 • Hathaway Henry • USA
SUNDOWN • 1989 • Hickox Anthony • USA
SUNDOWN see **SUMMER LIGHTNING** • 1988
SUNDOWN FURY see **JESSE JAMES JR.** • 1942
SUNDOWN IN SANTA FE • 1948 • Springsteen R. G. • USA
SUNDOWN JIM • 1942 • Tinling James • USA
SUNDOWN KID • 1942 • Clifton Elmer • USA
SUNDOWN ON THE PRAIRIE • 1939 • Herman Al • USA
SUNDOWN RIDER, THE • 1932 • Hillyer Lambert • USA
SUNDOWN RIDERS • 1948 • Hillyer Lambert • USA
SUNDOWN SAUNDERS • 1936 • Bradbury Robert North • USA
SUNDOWN SLIM • 1920 • Paul Val • USA
SUNDOWN TRAIL • 1931 • Hill Robert F. • USA
SUNDOWN TRAIL, THE • 1919 • Sturgeon Rollin S. • USA
SUNDOWN TRAIL, THE • 1934 • Tansey Robert • USA
SUNDOWN VALLEY • 1944 • Kline Benjamin • USA
SUNDOWNER, THE • 1911 • *Pathe Freres* • ASL
SUNDOWNERS, THE • 1950 • Templeton George • USA • THUNDER IN THE DUST (UKN)
SUNDOWNERS, THE • 1960 • Zinnemann Fred • UKN, USA
SUNEEMON TORII see **TORII SUNEEMON** • 1942
SUNEHERE DIN • 1949 • *Kapoor Raj* • IND
SUNFLIGHT • 1964 • McDermott Gerald • ANS • USA • SUN FLIGHT
SUNFLOWER • 1965 • White Joshua Wallace • SHT • USA
SUNFLOWER, THE • 1963 • Arsenov Pavel • SHT • USS
SUNFLOWER GIRL see **HIMAWARI MUSUME** • 1953
SUNFLOWER (USA) see **GIRASOLI, I** • 1969
SUNFLOWERS • 1968 • McMillan Ian • UKN
SUNFLOWERS, THE see **GIRASOLI, I** • 1969
SUNGHURSH • 1968 • Rawail H. S. • IND • CONFLICT
SUNJUKA MASTER, THE • 1967 • de Guzman Ruben • PHL
SUNK BY THE CENSUS • 1940 • D'Arcy Harry • SHT • USA
SUNK IN THE SINK • 1949 • White Jules • SHT • USA
SUNKEN, THE (USA) see **GESUNKENEN, DIE** • 1925
SUNKEN ROCKS • 1919 • Hepworth Cecil M. • UKN
SUNKEN SHIPS see **WRAKI** • 1957
SUNKEN SILVER • 1925 • Bennet Spencer Gordon, Seitz George B. • SRL • USA
SUNKEN TREASURE • 1936 • Davis Mannie, Gordon George • ANS • USA
SUNKISSED see **LADY TO LOVE, A** • 1929
SUNKISSED SWEETIES • 1932 • Edwards Harry J. • SHT • USA
SUNKIST STARS AT PALM SPRINGS • 1936 • Rowland Roy • SHT • USA
SUNLESS see **SANS SOLEIL** • 1982
SUNLESS DAYS • 1990 • Shu Kei • DOC • HKG
SUNLESS STREET, THE see **TAIYO NO NAI MACHI** • 1954
SUNLIGHT • 1913 • *Bushman Francis X.* • USA

SUNLIGHT AND SHADOWS • 1916 • Shaw Brinsley • SHT • USA
SUNLIGHT AND SHADOWS see **HANA TO KAIJITSU** • 1967
SUNLIGHT ON COLD WATER (UKN) see **PEU DE SOLEIL DANS L'EAU FROIDE, UN** • 1971
SUNLIGHT SOAP WASHING COMPETITION • 1897 • *Nestles & Lever Brothers* • UKN
SUNLIGHT'S LAST RAID • 1917 • Wolbert William • USA
SUNNY • 1930 • Seiter William A. • USA
SUNNY • 1941 • Wilcox Herbert • USA
SUNNY • 1967 • Mia Rosa • PHL
SUNNY see **ZONNETJE** • 1920
SUNNY CRY see **SONCNI KRIK** • 1968
SUNNY HILL see **SLONECZNE WZGORZE** • 1963
SUNNY ITALY • 1951 • Rasinski Connie • ANS • USA
SUNNY JANE • 1917 • MacDonald Sherwood • USA
SUNNY MR. SOLBERG see **SOLIGA SOLBERG** • 1941
SUNNY OR THE CATTLE THIEF • 1913 • *Gibson Marguerite* • USA
SUNNY SIDE OF THE STREET • 1951 • Quine Richard • USA • ON THE SUNNY SIDE OF THE STREET
SUNNY SIDE UP • 1926 • Crisp Donald • USA • FOOTLIGHTS
SUNNY SIDE UP • 1929 • Butler David • USA
SUNNY SKIES • 1930 • Taurog Norman • USA
SUNNY SMITH • 1913 • *Victor* • USA
SUNNY SOUTH • 1914 • Rolfe Alfred • ASL • WHIRLWIND OF FATE
SUNNY SOUTH • 1931 • Lantz Walter, Nolan William • ANS • USA
SUNNY SOUTH, THE • 1933 • *Terry Paul/ Moser Frank (P)* • ANS • USA
SUNNY SPAIN • 1923 • Roach Hal • SHT • USA
SUNNY SWAMP, THE see **GUNESLI BATAKLIK** • 1978
SUNNY SYDNEY • 1922 • *Segerburg Bert (Ph)* • ASL
SUNNY WHIRLPOOL, THE see **SONCNI KRIK** • 1968
SUNNY YOUTH • 1935 • Koromoitsef Paul
SUNNYSIDE • 1919 • Chaplin Charles • SHT • USA
SUNNYSIDE • 1979 • Galfas Timothy • USA
SUNRISE • 1926 • Longford Raymond (c/d) • ASL
SUNRISE see **ARUNODHAYA** • 1968
SUNRISE see **RICHU** • 1985
SUNRISE –A SONG OF TWO HUMANS see **SUNRISE –A STORY OF TWO HUMANS** • 1927
SUNRISE –A STORY OF TWO HUMANS • 1927 • Murnau F. W. • USA • SUNRISE (UKN) ○ SUNRISE –A SONG OF TWO HUMANS
SUNRISE AT CAMPOBELLO • 1960 • Donehue Vincent J. • USA
SUNRISE TRAIL • 1931 • McCarthy John P. • USA
SUNRISE TRAIL see **BEYOND THE ROCKIES** • 1932
SUNRISE (UKN) see **SUNRISE –A STORY OF TWO HUMANS** • 1927
SUN'S BURIAL, THE see **TAIYO NO HAKABA** • 1960
SUN'S GONNA SHINE, THE • 1967 • Blank Les • SHT • USA
SUN'S HOME, THE see **ASHIYANE KHORSHID** • 1967
SUNS OF EASTER ISLAND, THE see **SOLEILS DE L'ILE DE PAQUES, LES** • 1971
SUNSCORCHED (USA) see **TIERRA DE FUEGO** • 1965
SUNSEED • 1973 • Cohn Frederick • DOC • USA
SUNSET • 1987 • Edwards Blake • USA
SUNSET see **TWO THOROUGHBREDS** • 1939
SUNSET see **AL PONERSE EL SOL** • 1967
SUNSET see **OCASO** • 1967
SUNSET BEACH ON LONG ISLAND • 1967 • Warhol Andy • USA
SUNSET BOULEVARD • 1950 • Wilder Billy • USA
SUNSET CARSON RIDES AGAIN • 1948 • Drake Oliver • USA
SUNSET COVE • 1978 • Adamson Al • USA
SUNSET COVE (UKN) see **MALIBU BEACH** • 1978
SUNSET DERBY, THE • 1927 • Rogell Albert S. • USA
SUNSET GIRLS • *Johnson Terri* • USA • MIDNIGHT PLOWBOY
SUNSET GUN, THE • 1912 • *Mcdermott Marc* • USA
SUNSET HILL see **YUHI NO OKA** • 1964
SUNSET IN EL DORADO • 1945 • McDonald Frank • USA
SUNSET IN NAPLES see **QUANDO TRAMONTA IL SOLE** • 1956
SUNSET IN THE WEST • 1950 • Witney William • USA
SUNSET IN VIENNA • 1937 • Walker Norman • UKN • SUICIDE LEGION
SUNSET IN WYOMING • 1941 • Morgan William • USA
SUNSET JONES • 1921 • Cox George L. • USA
SUNSET LEGION • 1928 • Ingraham Lloyd, Werker Alfred L. • USA
SUNSET LIMOUSINE • 1983 • Hughes Terry • TVM • USA
SUNSET OF POWER • 1936 • Taylor Ray • USA
SUNSET ON THE DESERT • 1942 • Kane Joseph • USA
SUNSET OR HER ONLY ROMANCE • 1912 • *Thornby Robert* • USA
SUNSET PASS • 1929 • Brower Otto • USA
SUNSET PASS • 1933 • Hathaway Henry • USA
SUNSET PASS • 1946 • Berke William • USA
SUNSET PRINCESS, THE • 1918 • *Daw Marjorie* • USA
SUNSET RANGE • 1935 • McCarey Ray • USA
SUNSET SERENADE • 1942 • Kane Joseph • USA
SUNSET SPRAGUE • 1920 • Heffron Thomas N., Cazeneuve Paul • USA
SUNSET STRIP • 1984 • Webb William • USA • L.A. THRILLER
SUNSET STRIP CASE, THE • 1938 • Gasnier Louis J. • USA • HIGH EXPLOSIVE
SUNSET, SUNRISE see **HI WA SHIZUMI, HI WA NOBORU** • 1972
SUNSET TRAIL • 1917 • Melford George • USA
SUNSET TRAIL • 1931 • Eason B. Reeves • USA
SUNSET TRAIL • 1938 • Selander Lesley • USA
SUNSET TRAIL, THE • 1924 • Laemmle Ernst • USA
SUNSEX BOULEVARD • 1982 • Pachard Henri • USA
SUNSHINE • 1912 • Wharton Theodore • USA
SUNSHINE • 1916 • Cline Eddie • SHT • USA
SUNSHINE • 1920 • *Reelcraft* • USA
SUNSHINE • 1973 • Sargent Joseph • TVM • USA
SUNSHINE AFTER STORM • 1908 • Williamson James? • UKN
SUNSHINE AHEAD • 1936 • Orton Wallace • UKN
SUNSHINE ALLEY • 1917 • Noble John W. • USA
SUNSHINE AND CLOUDS OF PARADISE ALLEY, THE • 1915 • Stather Frank • UKN
SUNSHINE AND GOLD • 1917 • King Henry • USA
SUNSHINE AND POWDER SNOW • 1935 • Oliver Bill • DOC • CND
SUNSHINE AND SHADOW • 1911 • *Vitagraph* • USA
SUNSHINE AND SHADOWS • 1914 • Brooke Van Dyke • USA
SUNSHINE AND TEMPEST • 1915 • Haddock William F. • USA
SUNSHINE BOYS, THE • 1975 • Ross Herbert • USA
SUNSHINE CHRISTMAS • 1977 • Jordan Glenn • USA
SUNSHINE CITY • 1973 • Thoms Albie • ASL
SUNSHINE DAD • 1916 • Dillon Eddie • USA
SUNSHINE EVEN BY NIGHT see **SOLE ANCHE DI NOTTE, IL** • 1990
SUNSHINE FOLLOWS RAIN see **DRIVER DAGG FALLER REGN** • 1946
SUNSHINE FOR SOME see **TRI CETRTINE SONCA** • 1959
SUNSHINE HARBOR • 1922 • Hemmer Edward L. • USA
SUNSHINE IN A NET see **SLNKO V SIETI** • 1962
SUNSHINE MAKERS, THE • 1935 • Gillett Burt, Eshbaugh Ted • ANS • USA
SUNSHINE MOLLY • 1915 • Weber Lois, Smalley Phillips • USA
SUNSHINE NAN • 1918 • Giblyn Charles • USA
SUNSHINE OF PARADISE ALLEY • 1926 • Nelson Jack • USA
SUNSHINE ON THE SKIN • 1979 • Casorati George S. • ITL • SUMMER AFFAIR
SUNSHINE OVER KLARA see **SOL OVER KLARA** • 1942
SUNSHINE PART II • 1975 • Haller Daniel, Day Robert • TVM • USA • MY SWEET LADY (UKN)
SUNSHINE PATRIOT, THE • 1968 • Sargent Joseph • USA
SUNSHINE RUN • 1979 • Robinson Chris • USA
SUNSHINE SALLY • 1923 • Harris Lawson • ASL
SUNSHINE SEA, THE • MacGillivray Greg, Freeman Jim • SHT • USA
SUNSHINE SUE • 1910 • Griffith D. W. • USA
SUNSHINE SUE • 1913 • Hotaling Arthur D. • USA
SUNSHINE SUSIE • 1932 • Saville Victor • UKN • OFFICE GIRL, THE (USA)
SUNSHINE THROUGH THE DARK • 1911 • Griffith D. W. • USA
SUNSHINE TRAIL, THE • 1923 • Horne James W. • USA
SUNSPOT see **SURJOGRAHAN** • 1976
SUNSTROKE • 1976 • Piskov Hristo, Aktasheva Irina • BUL
SUNSTROKE • 1984 • Yosha Yaki • ISR
SUNSTROKE see **COLPO DI SOLE** • 1968
SUNSTRUCK • 1972 • Gilbert James • ASL • EDUCATION OF STANLEY EVANS, THE
SUNSWEPT • 1962 • Keatering Michael • UKN
SUNTOK O KARATE • 1968 • Buenaventura Augusto • PHL • PUNCH OR KARATE, A
SUNWIND see **AURINKOTUULI** • 1980
SUO DESTINO, IL • 1939 • Guazzoni Enrico • ITL
SUO MUODO DI FARE, IL see **TENDERLY** • 1968
SUO NOME E DONNA ROSA, IL • 1969 • Fizzarotti Ettore Maria • ITL
SUO NOME ERA POT.. MA.. LO CHIAMAVANO ALLEGRIA • 1971 • Ford D. • ITL
SUO NOME FACEVA TREMARE.. INTERPOL IN ALLARME, IL • 1973 • Lupo Michele • ITL, FRN • HOMME AUX NERFS D'ACIER, L' (FRN) ○ MEAN FRANK AND CRAZY TONY ○ DIO, SEI PROPRIA UN PADRETERNO ○ GANGSTER STORY ○ GUN, THE
SUO NOME GRIDAVA VENDETTA, IL • 1968 • Caiano Mario • ITL
SUO PIU GRANDE AMORE, IL • 1958 • Leonviola Antonio • ITL • HER GREATEST LOVE
SUOMALAISIA ELAINTARINOITA • 1973-75 • Partanen Heikki, Rautoma Riitta • ASS • FNL • FINNISH FABLES
SUOMEN VIIMEINEN SUSI • 1973 • Pakaslahti Jukka • FNL • FINLAND'S LAST WOLF
SUONNO D'AMMORE • 1955 • Corbucci Sergio • ITL • SOGNO D'AMORE
SUOR ANNA ROSA • 1965 • Rolando Giuseppe • ITL
SUOR EMANUELLE • 1978 • Vari Giuseppe • ITL
SUOR LETIZIA • 1956 • Camerini Mario • ITL • AWAKENING, THE ○ LAST TEMPTATION ○ PIU GRANDE AMORE, IL
SUOR MARIA • 1955 • Capuano Luigi • ITL
SUOR OMICIDI • 1979 • Berruti Giulio • ITL • KILLER NUN (UKN)
SUOR TERESA • 1916 • Falena Ugo • ITL
SUOR TERESA see **GRANDE RINUNCIA, LA** • 1951
SUORA GIOVANE, LA • 1965 • Paolinelli Bruno • ITL • NOVICE, THE
SUP SAP BUP DUP • Tang Shu Shuen • HKG
SUPAH JAIYANTO • 1956 • Ishii Teruo • JPN • SUPER GIANT 1 (USA) ○ STEELMAN FROM OUTER SPACE, THE
SUPAH JAIYANTO 2 • 1957 • Ishii Teruo • ANM • JPN • SUPER GIANT 2 ○ RESCUE FROM OUTER SPACE
SUPAI • 1965 • Yamamoto Satsuo • JPN • SPY, THE
SUPAIDASU NO DAISHINGEKI • 1968 • Nakahira Ko • JPN • SPIDERS A GO-GO
SUPE FOR TVA • 1947 • Arvedson Ragnar • SWD • SUPPER FOR TWO
SUPER, EL • 1979 • Ichaso Leon, Jiminez-Leal Orlando • USA, CUB
SUPER CHICK see **SUPERCHICK** • 1973
SUPER CITIZEN see **CH'AO-CHI SHIH-MIN** • 1985
SUPER COOL see **BODY FEVER** • 1972
SUPER COPS, THE • 1974 • Parks Gordon • USA
SUPER CUE MEN • 1949 • Barclay David • SHT • USA
SUPER DIABOLICAL, THE see **AMORE ALL'ITALIANA** • 1966
SUPER DICK (UKN) see **CRY UNCLE** • 1971
SUPER DRAGON see **NEW YORK CHIAMA SUPERDRAGO** • 1966
SUPER DUDE see **HANGUP** • 1974
SUPER–EXPRESS see **KURO NO CHOTOKKYU** • 1964
SUPER FEMALES see **SEXO FUERTE, EL** • 1945
SUPER FIGHT, THE • 1970 • Woroner Murray • USA
SUPER FOOL • 1981 • Liang Puzhi • HKG
SUPER FUZZ • 1981 • Corbucci Sergio • ITL, SPN • SUPERSNOOPER ○ POLIZIOTTO SUPERPIU ○ DANNY THE SUPER SNOOPER
SUPER GIANT see **KOKETSU NO KYOJIN** • 1956-59
SUPER GIANT 1 (USA) see **SUPAH JAIYANTO** • 1956
SUPER GIANT 2 see **SUPAH JAIYANTO 2** • 1957
SUPER GIANT 3 see **KOTETSU NO KYOJIN –KAISEIJIN NO MAJYO** • 1957
SUPER GIANT 4 (USA) see **KOTETSU NO KYOJIN –CHIKYU METZUBO SUNZEN** • 1957
SUPER GIANT 5 (USA) see **JINKO EISEN TO JINRUI NO HAMETSU** • 1958
SUPER GIANT 6 (USA) see **UCHUTEI TO JINKO EISEN NO GEKITOTSU** • 1958
SUPER GIANT 7 (USA) see **UCHU KAIJIN SHUTSUGEN** • 1958
SUPER GIANT 8 (USA) see **AKUMA NO KESHIIN** • 1959
SUPER GIANT 9 (USA) see **DOKUGA OKOKU** • 1959
SUPER GIANT AGAINST THE SATELLITES see **ATTACK FROM SPACE** • 1964
SUPER GIRL • 1988 • PKS
SUPER HE–MAN, THE see **SUPERMACHO, EL** • 1958
SUPER–HEMBRAS, LAS see **SEXO FUERTE, EL** • 1945
SUPER HIGH SCORE • 1990 • Ehmck Gustav • FRG
SUPER–HOOPER–DYNE LIZZIES • 1925 • Lord Del • SHT • USA
SUPER INFRAMAN, THE • 1975 • Hua Shan • HKG • INFRA SUPERMAN, THE
SUPER INVISIBLE MAN see **INAFFERRABILE E INVINCIBILE MR. INVISIBILE, L'** • 1970
SUPER J.J. • 1970 • Bobrowski Edouard • DOC • FRN
SUPER LULU • 1947 • Tytla Bill • ANS • USA
SUPER MOUSE • 1943 • *Terry Paul (P)* • ASS • USA
SUPER MOUSE RIDES AGAIN • 1943 • Davis Mannie • ANS • USA • MIGHTY MOUSE RIDES AGAIN
SUPER–PACIFIC • 1948 • Maudru • SHT • FRN
SUPER PINK • 1966 • Pratt Hawley • ANS • USA
SUPER POWER • 1981 • Lin Chan Wai • HKG • SUPERPOWER
SUPER RABBIT • 1943 • Jones Charles M. • ANS • USA
SUPER–RAPINA A MILANO • 1965 • Celentano Adriano • ITL • ROBBERY ROMAN STYLE (USA)
SUPER SALESMAN • 1947 • Donnelly Eddie • ANS • USA
SUPER SATURDAY • 1972 • *Crowther Leslie* • SHT • UKN
SUPER SCIENTIST, THE see **SUPERSABIO, EL** • 1948
SUPER SEAL • 1976 • Dugan Michael • USA
SUPER SECRET SERVICE, THE • 1953 • Green Charles W. • UKN
SUPER SENSES see **SUPERSENSUAL** • 1967
SUPER SENSUALISTS see **SUPERSENSUAL** • 1967
SUPER–SEX, THE • 1922 • Hillyer Lambert • USA
SUPER SHYLOCK, A see **HENDES MODERS LOFTE** • 1916
SUPER–SISSY, THE see **SUPERFLACO, EL** • 1957
SUPER SLEUTH • 1937 • Stoloff Ben • USA
SUPER SLEUTHS, THE see **SUPERNASEN, DIE** • 1984
SUPER SNOOPER • 1934 • Edwards Harry J. • SHT • USA
SUPER SNOOPER • 1952 • McKimson Robert • ANS • USA
SUPER SPEED • 1925 • Rogell Albert S. • USA
SUPER SPOOK • 1974 • Major Anthony • USA
SUPER SPREAD see **SUPERSPREAD** • 1967
SUPER STUPID • 1934 • Jason Leigh • SHT • USA
SUPER VAN • 1977 • Card Lamar • USA • SUPERVAN
SUPER VISION see **SUPERWIZJA** • 1990
SUPERANDY IL FRATELLO BRUTO DI SUPERMAN • 1979 • Bianchini Paolo • ITL
SUPERARGO AND THE FACELESS GIANTS (USA) see **SUPERARGO EL GIGANTE** • 1967
SUPERARGO CONTRA DIABOLICUS see **SUPERARGO CONTRO DIABOLIKUS** • 1966
SUPERARGO CONTRO DIABOLIKUS • 1966 • Iquino Ignacio F. • ITL, SPN • SUPERARGO VS. DIABOLICUS (USA) ○ SUPERARGO CONTRA DIABOLICUS ○ SUPERARGO EL HOMBRE ENMASCARADO (SPN)
SUPERARGO EL GIGANTE • 1967 • Bianchini Paolo • ITL, SPN • SUPERARGO AND THE FACELESS GIANTS (USA) ○ RE DEI CRIMINALI, IL ○ SUPERDRAGO E I GIGANTI SENZA VOLTO ○ SUPERARGO THE GIANT ○ CRIMINAL KING, THE ○ KING OF CRIMINALS, THE
SUPERARGO EL HOMBRE ENMASCARADO (SPN) see **SUPERARGO CONTRO DIABOLIKUS** • 1966
SUPERARGO THE GIANT see **SUPERARGO EL GIGANTE** • 1967
SUPERARGO VS. DIABOLICUS (USA) see **SUPERARGO CONTRO DIABOLIKUS** • 1966
SUPERBEAST • 1972 • Schenck George • PHL • SUPERBEASTS
SUPERBEASTS see **SUPERBEAST** • 1972
SUPERBITCH see **SI PUO ESSERE PIU BASTARDI DELL'ISPETTORE CLIFF?** • 1973
SUPERBUG, SUPER AGENT • 1976 • Zehetgruber Rudolf • FRG
SUPERBUS • 1969 • Potterton Gerald • CND
SUPERCARRIER • 1987 • Graham William A. • TVM • USA
SUPERCARRIER 2 • 1987 • Graham William A. • TVM • USA
SUPERCARRIER 3: THE LAST BATTLE • 1988 • Allen Corey • TVM • USA
SUPERCHIC see **SUPERCHICK** • 1973
SUPERCHICK • 1973 • Forsyth Ed • USA • SUPERCHIC ○ SUPER CHICK
SUPERCOCK • 1975 • Trikonis Gus • USA
SUPERCOLPO DA SETTE MILIARDI • 1967 • Albertini Bitto • ITL • TEN MILLION DOLLAR GRAB, THE (USA) ○ 1000 CARAT DIAMOND, THE (UKN)
SUPERCROSS see **WINNERS TAKE ALL** • 1987
SUPERDAD • 1974 • McEveety Vincent • USA
SUPERDIABOLICI, I see **AMORE ALL'ITALIANA** • 1966
SUPERDOME • 1978 • Jameson Jerry • TVM • USA
SUPERDRAGO E I GIGANTI SENZA VOLTO see **SUPERARGO EL GIGANTE** • 1967
SUPERDRAGON see **BRUCE LEE STORY, THE** • 1974
SUPERDUPERMAN • 1963 • Glut Don • SHT • USA
SUPERESPECTACULOS DEL MUNDO (SPN) see **SUPERSPETTACOLI NEL MUNDO** • 1962
SUPERFICIE Y FONDO • 1972 • Maldonado C. Enrique • VNZ • SURFACE AND BOTTOM
SUPERFLACO, EL • 1957 • Delgado Miguel M. • MXC • CHIQITO PERO PICOSO ○ SUPER–SISSY, THE
SUPERFLUOUS BABY, A • 1915 • Ransom Charles? • USA
SUPERFLUOUS PEOPLE (USA) see **UBERFLUSSIGE MENSCHEN** • 1926
SUPERFLY • 1972 • Parks Gordon Jr. • USA
SUPERFLY T.N.T. • 1973 • O'Neal Ron • USA
SUPERGANG, THE • *Le Bruce* • HKG

SUPERGIANT see **KOKETSU NO KYOJIN** • 1956-59
SUPERGIRL • 1971 • Thome Rudolf • FRG
SUPERGIRL • 1983 • Szwarc Jeannot • USA
SUPERGRASS, THE • 1985 • Richardson Peter • UKN
SUPERHERO • 1983 • Holland Martin • UKN
SUPERHOMBRE, EL • 1946 • Urueta Chano • MXC • SUPERMAN, THE
SUPERHUMAN • 1979 • Freda Riccardo • ITL
SUPERIMPOSITION • 1968 • Vanderbeek Stan • USA
SUPERIMPOSITION see **SAM NA SAM** • 1977
SUPERINTENDENT SANSHO, THE see **SANSHO DAYU** • 1954
SUPERIOR CLAIM, THE • 1915 • Franz Joseph J. • USA
SUPERIOR FORCE see **VIS MAIOR** • 1974
SUPERIOR LAW, THE • 1913 • *Johnston J. W.* • USA
SUPERIOR SEX, THE • 1928 • *Henry John* • SHT • UKN
SUPERIOR YOUNGSTERS • 1973 • Kong Hung • HKG
SUPERKNIGHT see **AMOROUS ADVENTURES OF DON QUIXOTE & SANCHO PANZA, THE** • 1976
SUPERKNIGHTS see **AMOROUS ADVENTURES OF DON QUIXOTE & SANCHO PANZA, THE** • 1976
SUPERLOCO, EL • 1936 • Segura Juan Jose • MXC
SUPERMACHO, EL • 1958 • Galindo Alejandro • MXC • SUPER HE-MAN, THE
SUPERMAN • 1941 • Fleischer Dave • ANS • USA
SUPERMAN • 1948 • Bennet Spencer Gordon, Carr Thomas • SRL • USA
SUPERMAN • 1960 • Thakur Anant • IND
SUPERMAN • 1962 • Delgado • SHT • CUB
SUPERMAN • 1969 • Rasof Ira, Greenberg Bob • SHT • USA
SUPERMAN • 1978 • Donner Richard • UKN, USA • SUPERMAN: THE MOVIE
SUPERMAN, THE see **SUPERHOMBRE, EL** • 1946
SUPERMAN AND THE JUNGLE DEVIL • 1954 • *Reeves George* • MTV • USA
SUPERMAN AND THE MOLE MEN • 1951 • Sholem Lee • USA • SUPERMAN AND THE STRANGE PEOPLE (UKN) ○ UNKNOWN PEOPLE
SUPERMAN AND THE STRANGE PEOPLE (UKN) see **SUPERMAN AND THE MOLE MEN** • 1951
SUPERMAN FLIES AGAIN • 1954 • Carr Thomas, Blair George • MTV • USA • SUPERMAN'S PERIL
SUPERMAN II • 1980 • Lester Richard, Donner Richard (U/c) • UKN, USA
SUPERMAN III • 1983 • Lester Richard • UKN, USA
SUPERMAN IV: THE QUEST FOR PEACE • 1987 • Furie Sidney J. • USA, UKN • QUEST FOR PEACE, THE
SUPERMAN KI WAPASI • 1960 • *Biswas Anil (M)* • IND
SUPERMAN: THE MOVIE see **SUPERMAN** • 1978
SUPERMAN VS. THE GORILLA GANG • 1965 • Glut Don • SHT • USA
SUPERMAN'S PERIL see **SUPERMAN FLIES AGAIN** • 1954
SUPERMARKET LOVE STORY • 1977 • Brown Alan • UKN
SUPERMARKT • 1974 • Klick Roland • FRG
SUPERMEN see **CHE FANNO I NOSTRI SUPERMEN TRA LE VERGINI DELLA GIUNGLA** • 1970
SUPERNASEN, DIE • 1984 • Prottel Dieter • FRG • SUPER SLEUTHS, THE
SUPERNATURAL • 1933 • Halperin Victor Hugo • USA
SUPERNATURAL see **SOBRENATURAL** • 1981
SUPERNATURAL GANESH see **GANESH MAHIMA** • 1950
SUPERNATURALS, THE • 1986 • Mastroianni Armand • USA • GHOST SOLDIERS
SUPERNUMERARY GIRL, THE see **PREKOBROJNA** • 1962
SUPERPOWER see **SUPER POWER** • 1981
SUPERSABIO, EL • 1948 • Delgado Miguel M. • MXC • SUPER SCIENTIST, THE ○ GENIUS, THE
SUPERSENS see **SUPERSENSUAL** • 1967
SUPERSENSUAL • 1967 • Anders Jan • USA • SUPER SENSUALISTS ○ SUPER SENSES ○ SUPERSENS
SUPERSEVEN CALLING CAIRO see **SUPERSEVEN CHIAMA CAIRO** • 1966
SUPERSEVEN CHIAMA CAIRO • 1966 • Lenzi Umberto • ITL • SUPERSEVEN CALLING CAIRO
SUPERSEXY '64 • 1963 • Loy Mino • DOC • ITL
SUPERSHOW • 1970 • Crome John • UKN
SUPERSNOOPER see **SUPER FUZZ** • 1981
SUPERSONIC MAN • 1979 • Simon Piquer • SPN
SUPERSONIC SAUCER • 1956 • Ferguson S. G. • UKN
SUPERSPEED • 1935 • Hillyer Lambert • USA
SUPERSPETTACOLI NEL MUNDO • 1962 • Montero Roberto Bianchi, Nunes Jose Maria • ITL, SPN • SUPERESPECTACULOS DEL MUNDO (SPN)
SUPERSPREAD • 1967 • Nelson Robert • SHT • USA • SUPER SPREAD
SUPERSTAR see **BINTANG PUJAAN** • 1979
SUPERSTAR see **TA MINGXING** • 1985
SUPERSTARS IN FILM CONCERT • 1971 • Clifton Peter • DOC • USA
SUPERSTITION • 1920 • Laemmle Edward • SHT • USA
SUPERSTITION • 1922 • Dwan Allan • USA
SUPERSTITION • 1982 • Robertson James W. • USA • WITCH, THE
SUPERSTITION see **OUT OF LUCK** • 1923
SUPERSTITION see **VENENOSA, LA** • 1928
SUPERSTITION OF THE BLACK CAT, THE • 1934 • Nazarro Ray • SHT • USA
SUPERSTITION OF THE RABBIT'S FOOT, THE • 1935 • Nazarro Ray • SHT • USA
SUPERSTITION OF THREE ON A MATCH, THE • 1934 • Nazarro Ray • SHT • USA
SUPERSTITION OF WALKING UNDER A LADDER, THE • 1934 • Nazarro Ray • SHT • USA
SUPERSTITIOUS JOE • 1913 • Seay Charles M. • USA
SUPERSTITIOUS MARY • 1913 • *Nestor* • USA
SUPERSTITIOUS SAMMY • 1911 • *Urban Trading Co* • UKN
SUPERSTITIOUS SAMMY • 1915 • *Marshall Boyd* • USA
SUPERSTIZIONE • 1920 • *Novelli Amleto* • ITL
SUPERSTIZIONE • 1949 • Antonioni Michelangelo • DCS • ITL • NON CI CREDO!
SUPERTANKER • 1980 • Ernst Franz • DNM
SUPERTESTIMONE, LA • 1971 • Giraldi Franco • ITL
SUPERTRAIN • 1979 • Curtis Dan • TVM • USA • EXPRESS TO HORROR
SUPERUOMINI, SUPERDONNE, SUPERBOTTE • 1974 • Brescia Alfonso • ITL, HKG, USA
SUPERVAN see **SUPER VAN** • 1977
SUPERVIVIENTES DE LOS ANDES • 1976 • Cardona Rene Jr. • MXC • SURVIVE! (USA) ○ SURVIVAL
SUPERVIXENS, THE • 1975 • Meyer Russ • USA
SUPERWHEELS • 1978 • *Marck Robert* • FRG
SUPERWIZJA • 1990 • Glinski Robert • PLN • SUPER VISION
SUPERZAN AND THE SPACE BOY see **SUPERZAN Y EL NINO DEL ESPACIO** • 1972
SUPERZAN Y EL NINO DEL ESPACIO • 1972 • Lanuza Rafael • MXC • SUPERZAN AND THE SPACE BOY
SUPLEMENT DO "WARSZAWY" • 1954 • Perski Ludwik (c/d) • DOC • PLN • SUPPLEMENT TO WARSAW
SUPLICIO DE CUAUHTEMOC, EL • 1910 • *Union Cinematografica* • MXC • TORTURE OF CUAUHTEMOC, THE
SUPPADAKA NO NENREI • 1959 • Suzuki Seijun • JPN
SUPPADAKA NO SEISHUN • 1958 • Harada Hasuo • JPN
SUPPER AT SIX • 1933 • Shores Lynn • SHT • USA
SUPPER FOR THREE • 1913 • *Crystal* • USA
SUPPER FOR TWO see **SUPE FOR TVA** • 1947
SUPPLEMENT TO WARSAW see **SUPLEMENT DO "WARSZAWY"** • 1954
SUPPLENTE, LA • 1975 • Leoni Guido • ITL
SUPPLICATION see **MOLBA** • 1969
SUPPLICE DE TANTALE, LE • 1901 • Zecca Ferdinand • FRN
SUPPLY see **ABASTECIMIENTO** • 1973
SUPPORT YOUR LOCAL GUNFIGHTER • 1971 • Kennedy Burt • USA • LATIGO
SUPPORT YOUR LOCAL SHERIFF! • 1969 • Kennedy Burt • USA
SUPPOSE I WERE TO MARRY THE CLERGYMAN see **TANK, OM JAG GIFTER MIG MED PRASTEN** • 1941
SUPPOSE THEY GAVE A WAR AND NOBODY CAME? • 1970 • Averback Hy • USA • WAR GAMES ○ OLD SOLDIERS NEVER
SUPPRESSED DUCK • 1965 • McKimson Robert • ANS • USA
SUPPRESSED EVIDENCE • 1912 • *Kalem* • USA
SUPPRESSED EVIDENCE • 1915 • *Anderson Broncho Billy* • USA
SUPPRESSED NEWS • 1914 • Eagle Oscar • USA
SUPPRESSED ORDER, THE • 1916 • Ricketts Thomas • SHT • USA
SUPREMA CONFESSIONE • 1958 • Corbucci Sergio • ITL, FRG • GROSSE SUNDE, DIE (FRG)
SUPREMA LEY • 1936 • Portas Rafael E. • MXC • SUPREME LAW (USA)
SUPREME EPOPEE, LA • 1918 • Desfontaines Henri • FRN
SUPREME IMPULSE, THE • 1915 • Henderson Lucius • USA
SUPREME KID, THE • 1976 • Bryant Peter • CND
SUPREME LAW (USA) see **SUPREMA LEY** • 1936
SUPREME MOMENT, THE • 1913 • *Selig* • USA
SUPREME PASSION, THE • 1921 • Bradley Samuel R. • USA
SUPREME POWER, THE • 1912 • *Powers* • USA
SUPREME SACRIFICE • 1913 • Machin Alfred • NTH
SUPREME SACRIFICE, THE • 1913 • Nicholls George • USA
SUPREME SACRIFICE, THE • 1916 • Belmore Lionel, Knoles Harley • USA
SUPREME SECRET, THE • 1958 • Walker Norman • UKN • GOD SPEAKS TODAY
SUPREME TEMPTATION, THE • 1916 • Davenport Harry • USA
SUPREME TEST, THE • 1912 • *Prout Evebelle* • USA
SUPREME TEST, THE • 1915 • Le Saint Edward J. • USA
SUPREME TEST, THE • 1923 • MacNamara W. P. • USA
SUPREMES JOUISSANCES • 1977 • Mulot Claude • FRN • JOUISSANCES
SUPROVAT • 1977 • Anwar Kabir • BNG • GOOD MORNING
SUPRUGI ORLOVY • 1979 • Donskoi Mark • USS • ORLOV COUPLE, THE ○ ORLOVS, THE
SUR • 1987 • Solanas Fernando • ARG • SOUTH, THE
SUR, EL • 1983 • Erice Victor • SPN, FRN • SOUTH, THE
SUR CES CHEMINS • 1961 • Boigelot Jacques • BLG
SUR FACES • 1977 • Emshwiller Ed • USA
SUR LA BARRICADE • 1907 • Blache Alice • FRN • ENFANT DE LA BARRICADE, L'
SUR LA COTE D'AZUR • 1920 • Puchalski Eduard • PLN
SUR LA COUR see **CRIME DE MONSIEUR LANGE, LE** • 1935
SUR LA ROUTE DE KEY WEST • Cosima Renee • DOC • FRN
SUR LA ROUTE DE SALINA • 1969 • Lautner Georges • FRN, ITL • QUANDO IL SOLE SCOTTA (ITL) ○ ROAD TO SALINA (USA) ○ ROUTE DE SALINA, LA
SUR LA VOIE see **GUI DAO** • 1980
SUR LA VOIE DU BONHEUR • 1931 • Joannon Leo • FRN
SUR LE BANC • 1954 • Vernay Robert • FRN
SUR LE CHEMIN DE LA RECONCILIATION • 1975 • Yonly Rene Bernard • BRK
SUR LE CLAIR RIVAGE • 1921 • Puchalski Eduard • PLN
SUR LE DUNE DE LA SOLITUDE • 1964 • Bassori Timite • IVC • ON THE BANK OF SOLITUDE
SUR LE NIL see **NIL ARZAQ, AN-** • 1972
SUR LE PLANCHER DES VACHES • 1939 • Ducis Pierre-Jean • FRN • PLANCHER DES VACHES, LE
SUR LE PLANETE YGAM • Laloux Rene, Topor Roland • ANS • FRN
SUR LE PONT D'AVIGNON • 1952 • Ladouceur Jean-Paul • ANS • CND
SUR LE PONT D'AVIGNON • 1956 • Franju Georges • DCS • FRN
SUR LE SENTIER DU REQUIEM • 1971 • Dong Jean-Marie • SHT • GBN
SUR LE ZINC • 1958 • Schmid Fred • SWT
SUR LES BORDS DE LA CAMERA • 1932 • Storck Henri • DOC • BLG
SUR LES CHEMINS DE LAMARTINE • 1941 • Tedesco Jean • SHT • FRN
SUR LES ROUTES DE L'ETE • 1936 • Storck Henri • DOC • BLG
SUR LES TOITS • 1897 • Melies Georges • FRN • ON THE ROOFS
SUR L'ORDRE DU BROCHET • 1938 • Rou Aleksandr • USS
SUR QUI DOIT-ON TIRER? see **ALA MAN NAT'LUQ AR-RACAC?** • 1975
SUR UN AIR DE CHARLESTON • 1926 • Renoir Jean • FRN • PARADE SUR UN AIR DE CHARLESTON ○ CHARLESTON (USA) ○ CHARLESTON-PARADE
SUR UN ARBRE PECHE • 1970 • Korber Serge • FRN • UP A TREE
SUR UN MARCHE NORMAND • 1934 • Leherissey Jean • SHT • FRN
SUR UN MILLION, UN see **WAH'ID FI AL-MILIUM** • 1971
SURA CHOWRAYA • 1967 • Mastan M. • SLN • CLEVER BRIGAND, THE
SURABAYA CONSPIRACY, THE • 1975 • Davis Roy • USA
SURAKH • 1973 • Khalifa Omar • TNS • HURLEMENTS ○ SHOUT, A
SURAM CASTLE, THE • 1920 • *Chiaureli Mikhail* • USS
SURAM FORTRESS, THE see **SURAMSKAYA KRYEPOST** • 1923
SURAMSKAYA KRYEPOST • 1923 • Perestiani Ivan • USS • SURAM FORTRESS, THE
SURANGA MHANTYAT MALA • 1967 • Patil Dinkar • IND
SURBOUM see **DECHAINES, LES** • 1950
SURCOS • 1951 • Nieves Conde Jose Antonio • SPN
SURCOS DE NIEBLA • 1978 • Menendez Santiago, Millan Delgado • VNZ • RUTS OF FOG
SURCOS DE SANGRE • 1950 • del Carril Hugo • ARG
SURCOS EN EL MAR • 1956 • Land Kurt • ARG
SURCOUF • 1925 • Luitz-Morat • FRN
SURCOUF, LE TIGRE DES SEPT MERS (FRN) see **SURCOUF, L'EROE DEI SETTE MARI** • 1966
SURCOUF, L'EROE DEI SETTE MARI • 1966 • Bergonzelli Sergio, Rowland Roy • ITL, FRN, SPN • SURCOUF, LE TIGRE DES SEPT MERS (FRN) ○ SEA PIRATE, THE (USA) ○ TIGRE DE LOS SIETE MARES, EL (SPN) ○ TORMENTA SOBRE EL PACIFICO ○ FIGHTING CORSAIR, THE
SURDAS, DEVOTEE TO THE GOD see **BHAKTA SURDAS** • 1938
SURDOUES DE LA 1ere COMPAGNIE, LES • 1980 • Gerard Michel • FRN
SURE CURE • 1927 • Roberts Stephen • SHT • USA
SURE CURE, A • 1911 • *Nestor* • USA
SURE CURE, A • 1913 • *Dickson Charles* • USA
SURE CURE, A • 1914 • *White Pearl* • USA
SURE CURE, THE • 1920 • Seiter William A. • SHT • USA
SURE CURE FOR INDIGESTION see **INDIGESTION: OU, CHIRURGIE FIN DE SIECLE, UNE** • 1902
SURE CURES • 1946 • Barclay David • SHT • USA
SURE DEATH • Sadanaga Masahisa • JPN
SURE FIRE • 1921 • Ford John • USA • BRANSFORD OF RAINBOW RIDGE
SURE FIRE FLINT • 1922 • Henderson Dell • USA
SURE-MIKE • 1925 • Roach Hal • SHT • USA
SURE SHOT, THE • 1916 • *Rancho* • USA
SURE THING, THE • 1985 • Reiner Rob • USA
SURE TIP, THE • 1913 • *Pilot* • USA
SUREKHA HARAN(?) see **VEERGHATOTGACH** • 1949
SURELOCK JONES, DETECTIVE • 1912 • *Thanhouser* • USA
SURELY YOU'LL INSURE • 1915 • Aylott Dave? • UKN
SURESURE • 1960 • Mizuko Harumi • JPN
SURF see **SHIOSAI** • 1954
SURF see **SHIMMERING LIGHT** • 1978
SURF, THE • Johansson Ivar • SWD
SURF AND SEAWEED • 1930 • Steiner Ralph • SHT • USA
SURF AND SOUND • 1954 • Tendlar Dave • ANS • USA
SURF BORED • 1953 • Sparber I. • ANS • USA
SURF BORED CAT • 1967 • Levitow Abe • ANS • USA
SURF GIRL, THE • 1916 • Edwards Harry J. • SHT • USA
SURF HEROES • 1938 • Trego Charles T. • SHT • USA
SURF II • 1984 • Badat Randall • USA • NERDS STRIKE BACK, THE
SURF MAIDENS, THE • 1913 • *Gem* • USA
SURF MOVIES • 1981 • Thoms Albie • DOC • ASL • AUSTRALIAN SURFING PHENOMENON
SURF NAZIS see **SURF NAZIS MUST DIE** • 1987
SURF NAZIS MUST DIE • 1987 • George Peter • USA • SURF NAZIS
SURF PARTY • 1964 • Dexter Maury • USA
SURF SCANDAL • 1917 • Smith Noel • SHT • USA
SURF TERROR see **BEACH GIRLS AND THE MONSTER, THE** • 1965
SURFABOUT 74 • 1974 • Falzon Albert • DOC • ASL
SURFABOUT 75 • 1975 • Elfick David • DOC • ASL
SURFACE AND BOTTOM see **SUPERFICIE Y FONDO** • 1972
SURFACE TENSION • 1968 • Frampton Hollis • SHT • USA
SURFACE TENSION • 1982 • Kennedy Michael • CND
SURFACEMEN see **PALYMUNKASOK** • 1957
SURFACING • 1980 • Jutra Claude • CND
SURFACING ON THE THAMES • 1970 • Rimmer David • SHT • CND
SURFARI • 1967 • Blair Milton • DOC • USA • BLUE SURFARI
SURFBOARD RHYTHM • 1947 • Barclay David, Trego Charles T. • SHT • USA
SURFER, THE • 1987 • Shields Frank • ASL
SURFIN' • 1964 • Shebib Donald • CND
SURFING YEARS, THE • 1966 • Thompson Peter • DOC • ASL
SURFSIDE LOVE see **SURFSIDE SEX** • 1967
SURFSIDE SEX • 1967 • Hennigar William K. • USA • SURFSIDE LOVE
SURFTIDE 77 • 1962 • Frost R. L. • USA • CALL SURFSIDE 77 ○ CALL GIRL 777 ○ SURFTIDE 777
SURFTIDE 777 see **SURFTIDE 77** • 1962
SURGEON, THE • 1912 • Grandon Francis J. • USA
SURGEON OF ABAJO, THE • 1913 • *Frontier* • USA
SURGEON WARREN'S WARD • 1915 • Travers Richard C. • USA
SURGEONS • 1977 • Grubcheva Ivanka • BUL
SURGEON'S CHILD, THE • 1912 • Harris Harry T. • UKN
SURGEON'S EXPERIMENT, THE • 1914 • *Scardon Paul* • USA
SURGEON'S HEROISM, THE • 1912 • Salter Harry • USA
SURGEON'S KNIFE, THE • 1957 • Parry Gordon • UKN
SURGEON'S REVENGE, A • 1916 • *L-Ko* • SHT • USA
SURGEON'S TEMPTATION, THE • 1911 • *Ogle Charles* • USA
SURGERY OF MITRAL STENOSIS • 1961 • Goldberger Kurt • DOC • CZC
SURGING SEAS • 1924 • Chapin James • USA

SURI-LANKA, NO AI TO WAKARE • 1976 • Kinoshita Keisuke • JPN • SRI LANKA, LOVE AND FAREWELL ○ LOVE AND PARTING IN SRI LANKA ○ LOVE AND SEPARATION IN SRI LANKA
SURJO DIGHAL BARI • 1979 • Shaker Masihuddin, Ali Shaikh Neamat • BNG
SURJO SANGRAM • 1978 • Samad Abdus • BNG • SUN RISES EVERYWHERE ○ SUN WILL RISE
SURJOGRAHAN • 1976 • Samad Abdus • BNG • SUNSPOT ○ SOLAR ECLIPSE
SURJOKANNYA • 1977 • Kabir Alamgir • BNG • DAUGHTER OF THE SUN
SURMALE, LE • 1979 • Averty Jean-Christophe • TVM • FRN
SURMENES, LES • 1958 • Doniol-Valcroze Jacques • FRN
SURNAME VIET GIVEN NAME NAM • 1989 • Minh-Ha Trinh • USA
SUROGAT • 1961 • Vukotic Dusan • ANS • YGS • SUBSTITUTE, THE ○ ERSATZ
SUROGATY LYUBVI • 1918 • Tourjansky Victor • USS
SURONIN CHUYA • 1930 • Ito Daisuke • JPN
SURONIN MAKARITORU • 1947 • Ito Daisuke • JPN
SURPRISE • 1923 • Fleischer Dave • ANS • USA
SURPRISE, THE • 1966 • Badzian Teresa • ANM • PLN
SURPRISE BROADCAST • 1941 • Buchanan Andrew • UKN
SURPRISE DU CHEF, LA • 1976 • Thomas Pascal • FRN
SURPRISE FOR FOUR • 1913 • Hotaling Arthur D. • USA
SURPRISE HOUSE, THE • 1916 • *Essanay* • SHT • USA
SURPRISE ITEM • 1934 • *Henry Leonard* • UKN
SURPRISE OF A BOER CAMP, THE • 1901 • *Mitchell & Kenyon* • UKN
SURPRISE OF MY LIFE, THE • 1915 • *Washburn Bryant* • USA
SURPRISE PACKAGE • 1960 • Donen Stanley • UKN
SURPRISE PACKET, A see **AEGTESKAB OG PIGESJOV** • 1914
SURPRISE PACKET, THE • 1913 • Calvert Charles? • UKN
SURPRISE PARTIE • 1974 • Lagrange Yvan • FRN
SURPRISE PARTY • 1937 • Kapps Walter • FRN
SURPRISE-PARTY • 1983 • Vadim Roger • FRN • SURPRISE PARTY
SURPRISE PARTY see **SURPRISE-PARTY** • 1983
SURPRISE PARTY, A • 1914 • MacGregor Norval • USA
SURPRISE PARTY SURPRISED, THE • 1912 • *Lubin* • USA
SURPRISED PARTIES • 1942 • Cahn Edward L. • SHT • USA
SURPRISES see **SORPRESAS, LAS** • 1975
SURPRISES DE LA RADIO, LES • 1940 • Aboulker Marcel • FRN
SURPRISES DE L'AFFICHAGE, LES • 1903-04 • Blache Alice • FRN
SURPRISES DU DIVORCE, LES • 1933 • Kemm Jean • FRN
SURPRISES DU SLEEPING, LES • 1933 • Anton Karl • FRN • COUCHETTE NO.3
SURPRISES D'UNE NUIT DE NOCES, LES • 1951 • Vallee Jean • FRN
SURPRISES OF AN EMPTY HOTEL, THE • 1916 • Marston Theodore • USA
SURPRISIN' EXERCISIN' • 1968 • Anzilotti Cosmo • ANS • USA
SURPRISING A PICKET • 1899 • Ashe Robert • UKN • ATTACK ON A PIQUET
SURPRISING AMSTERDAM • 1966 • Meijer Reinier J. • NTH
SURPRISING ELIZA • 1912 • *Eclair* • USA
SURPRISING ENCOUNTER, A • 1913 • Stow Percy • UKN • MISFITS, THE
SURPRISING ENCOUNTER, A • 1914 • *Melies* • USA
SURPRISING HUNT, THE • 1960 • Dolin Boris • DOC • USS
SURPRISING HUSBAND • 1918 • Baker Graham • SHT • USA
SURPRISING POWDER, A • 1909 • *Cines* • SHT • ITL
SURREAL • 1976 • de Gregorio Eduardo • FRN • SERAGLIO ○ SERAIL
SURRENDER • 1927 • Sloman Edward • USA • PRESIDENT, THE (UKN)
SURRENDER • 1950 • Dwan Allan • USA
SURRENDER • 1987 • Belson Jerry • USA
SURRENDER, THE • 1913 • *Powers* • USA
SURRENDER, THE • 1915 • Entwhistle Harold • USA
SURRENDER, THE • 1931 • Howard William K. • USA
SURRENDER ARMS see **NED MED VAABNENE** • 1914
SURRENDER -HELL! • 1959 • Barnwell John • USA
SURRENDER IN PARADISE • 1976 • Cox Peter • ASL
SURRENDER OF TOURNAVOS, THE see **PRISE DE TOURNAVOS, LA** • 1897
SURREY GARDEN, A • 1896 • Acres Birt • UKN
SURROGATE, THE • 1985 • Carmody Don • CND • BLIND RAGE
SURROGATE, THE see **CHALLENGE, THE** • 1970
SURROGATE MOTHER see **SSIBOJI** • 1987
SURROGATE WOMAN see **SSIBOJI** • 1987
SURROGATET (I CIGARRBO'N) • 1919 • Bruun Einar J. • SWD • SUBSTITUTE
SURROUNDED see **OMRINGAAL** • 1960
SURROUNDED BY WOMEN see **BETWEEN TWO WOMEN** • 1937
SURROUNDED HOUSE, THE see **OMRINGADE HUSET, DET** • 1922
SURROUNDINGS see **OMGIVELSER** • 1973
SURSIS POUR UN ESPION • 1964 • Maley Jean • FRN • HORRIBLE PROFESSION, THE (UKN)
SURSIS POUR UN VIVANT • 1958 • Merenda Victor, Bertolini Ottorino Franco • FRN, ITL • MYSTERE DE LA PENSION EDELWEISS, LE ○ PENSIONE EDELWEISS (ITL)
SURTOUT L'HIVER • 1977 • Gagne Jacques • DOC • CND
SURTUGUN KIZI • 1967 • Egilmez Ertem • TRK • TROLLOP'S DAUGHTER, THE
SURTUR DER SUNNAN • 1965 • Knudsen Osvaldur • DOC • ICL
SURU • 1979 • Okten Zeki • TRK • HERD, THE
SURUBUL LUI MARINICA • 1955 • Popescu-Gopo Ion • SHT • RMN • MARINICA'S BODKIN
SURUGA YUHKYOU-DEN: YABURE TAKKA • 1964 • Tanaka Tokuzo • JPN • GAMBLER'S STORY OF SURUGA: BROKEN IRON FIRE
SURUGA YUKYODEN • 1964 • Tanaka Tokuzo • JPN • ENGAGED IN PLEASURE
SURUJ MIA • 1985 • Arefin Kazal • BNG • MR. SURUJ
SURVEILLEZ VOTRE TENUE • 1949 • Decae Henri • SHT • FRN
SURVEYING • 1970 • Putse V. • USS
SURVEYOR AND THE PONY EXPRESS, THE • 1913 • *Frontier* • USA
SURVEYORS, THE • 1913 • *Excelsior* • USA
SURVIE EN BROUSSE • 1959 • Herman Jean • FRN
SURVIVAL • Noa Manfred • FRG
SURVIVAL • 1976 • Campus Michael • USA
SURVIVAL • 1983 • Noyce Phil • DOC • ASL
SURVIVAL see **PANIC IN YEAR ZERO** • 1962
SURVIVAL see **GUIDE, THE** • 1965
SURVIVAL see **HAMILCHAMA AL HASHALOM** • 1967
SURVIVAL see **SUPERVIVIENTES DE LOS ANDES** • 1976
SURVIVAL 1 • 1985 • SAF
SURVIVAL 2 • 1985 • SAF
SURVIVAL 67 see **HAMILCHAMA AL HASHALOM** • 1967
SURVIVAL 1990 • USA
SURVIVAL ELEMENT see **LAND OF NO RETURN, THE** • 1975
SURVIVAL GAME • 1987 • Freed Herb • USA
SURVIVAL GAME, THE see **SURVIVAL QUEST** • 1987
SURVIVAL IN THE BUSH • 1953-54 • Devlin Bernard • DCS • CND
SURVIVAL IN THE SEA • 1968 • Wormser Richard • DCS • USA
SURVIVAL KIT • 1977 • Altmann Karin • UKN
SURVIVAL OF DANA, THE • 1979 • Starrett Jack • TVM • USA
SURVIVAL OF THE FITTEST, THE • 1911 • *Selig* • USA
SURVIVAL ON CHARTER NO.220 • 1978 • *London Julie* • USA
SURVIVAL QUEST • 1987 • Coscarelli Don • USA • SURVIVAL GAME, THE
SURVIVAL RUN • 1979 • Spiegel Larry • USA
SURVIVAL RUN see **DAMNATION ALLEY** • 1977
SURVIVAL RUN (UKN) see **SOLDAAT VAN ORANJE** • 1977
SURVIVAL ZONE • 1983 • Rubens Percival • SAF
SURVIVALIST, THE see **JACK TILLMAN: THE SURVIVALIST** • 1987
SURVIVANTS DE LA PRE-HISTOIRE • 1955 • Gaisseau Pierre-Dominique • FRN
SURVIVE! (USA) see **SUPERVIVIENTES DE LOS ANDES** • 1976
SURVIVING • 1985 • Hussein Waris • TVM • USA
SURVIVING SHINSENGUMI, THE see **IKINOKOTTA SHINSENGUMI** • 1932
SURVIVOR • 1987 • Shackleton Michael • UKN
SURVIVOR, THE • 1980 • Hemmings David • ASL, UKN
SURVIVOR, THE (USA) see **SCHWUR DES SOLDATEN POOLEY, DER** • 1962
SURVIVORS, THE • 1983 • Ritchie Michael • USA
SURVIVORS, THE see **SARENG BOU** • 1977
SURVIVORS, THE see **SOBREVIVIENTES, LOS** • 1979
SURVIVORS OF THE DEAD CITY, THE see **SOPRAVVISSUTI DELLA CITTA' MORTA, I** • 1984
SURVIVORS OF THE LAST RACE see **REFUGIO DEL MIEDO, EL** • 1973
SURYA KUMARI • 1934 • *Alakananda* • IND
SUS ANOS DORADOS • 1980 • Martinez Lazaro Emilio • SPN • THEIR GOLDEN YEARS
SUS OG DUS PA BY'N • 1968 • Andersen Knut, Mathiesen Mattis, Bohwim Knut • NRW • RIOT AND REVEL ON ORDER
SUSAN • 1974 • Veuve Jacqueline • SWT
SUSAN AND GOD • 1940 • Cukor George • USA • GAY MRS. TREXEL, THE (UKN)
SUSAN AND THE LADS see **ZUZANNA I CHLOPCY** • 1962
SUSAN LENOX see **SUSAN LENOX, HER FALL AND RISE** • 1931
SUSAN LENOX, HER FALL AND RISE • 1931 • Leonard Robert Z. • USA • RISE OF HELGA, THE (UKN) ○ SUSAN LENOX
SUSAN ROCKS THE BOAT • 1916 • Powell Paul • USA • SWEET SEVENTEEN
SUSAN SLADE • 1961 • Daves Delmer • USA
SUSAN SLEPT HERE • 1954 • Tashlin Frank • USA
SUSAN STARR • 1962 • Pennebaker D. A. • USA
SUSANA • 1950 • Bunuel Luis • MXC • DEVIL AND THE FLESH, THE (USA) ○ CARNE Y DEMONIO ○ DEMONIO Y CARNE ○ DEVIL AND FLESH
SUSANA • 1969 • Ozores Mariano • SPN
SUSANA QUIERE PERDER ESO • 1977 • Aured Carlos • SPN
SUSANA TIENE UN SECRETO • 1934 • Perojo Benito • SPN
SUSANA Y YO • 1957 • Cahen Enrique • SPN
SUSANNA.. ED I SUOI DOLCI VIZI ALLA CORTE DEL RE (ITL) see **SUSANNE -DIE WIRTIN VON DER LAHN** • 1967
SUSANNA IN THE BATH (USA) see **SUSANNE IM BADE** • 1937
SUSANNA PASS • 1949 • Witney William • USA
SUSANNA TUTTA PANNA • 1957 • Steno • ITL
SUSANNA (UKN) see **SHEPHERD OF THE OZARKS** • 1942
SUSANNAH OF THE MOUNTIES • 1939 • Seiter William A. • USA
SUSANNE • 1950 • Svendsen Torben Anton • DNM
SUSANNE see **SUZANNE** • 1960
SUSANNE -DIE WIRTIN VON DER LAHN • 1967 • Antel Franz • AUS, ITL, HNG • SUSANNA.. ED I SUOI DOLCI VIZI ALLA CORTE DEL RE (ITL) ○ WIRTIN VON DER LAHN, DIE ○ SWEET SINS OF SEXY SUSAN, THE (UKN) ○ SUSANNE -THE HOSTESS OF THE LAHN ○ ITL ○ DOLCI VIZI DELLA CASTA SUSANNA, I
SUSANNE ET LES BRIGANDS • 1920 • Burguet Charles • FRN
SUSANNE IM BADE • 1937 • von Alten Jurgen • FRG • SUSANNA IN THE BATH (USA)
SUSANNE JAKOBAA KRAFFTIN • 1950 • Galetzki Heinz • FRG
SUSANNE MACHT ORDNUNG • 1930 • Thiele Eugen • FRG
SUSANNE -THE HOSTESS OF THE LAHN see **SUSANNE -DIE WIRTIN VON DER LAHN** • 1967
SUSANNE UND DER ZAUBERRING • 1973 • Stranka Erwin • GDR
SUSAN'S GENTLEMAN • 1917 • Stevens Edwin • USA
SUSAN'S REVENGE • 1910 • Rains Fred • UKN
SUSCEPTIBLE, THE see **CHROUSSOUSIS, O** • 1952
SUSCEPTIBLE DAD • 1911 • *Solax* • USA
SUSE KERKSTRAATEN • 1928 • Rutters H. • FRG
SUSETZ • 1977 • Yosha Yaki • ISR • ROCKINGHORSE
SUSIE OF THE FOLLIES • 1917 • *Quirk Billy* • USA
SUSIE SLIPS ONE OVER • 1917 • *U.s.m.p.* • USA
SUSIE SNOWFLAKE • 1916 • Kirkwood James • USA
SUSIE STEPS OUT • 1946 • Le Borg Reginald • USA • MISS TELEVISION
SUSIE, THE LITTLE BLUE COUPE • 1952 • Geronimi Clyde • ANS • USA
SUSIE THE SLEEPWALKER • 1917 • *U.s.m.p.* • USA
SUSIE THE SLEUTH • 1916 • Baker George D. • SHT • USA
SUSIE TO SUSANNE • 1912 • *Turner Florence* • USA
SUSIE'S NEW SHOES • 1914 • *Pollard Harry* • USA
SUSIE'S SCHEME • 1917 • *U.s.m.p.* • USA
SUSIE'S SUITORS • 1915 • Hotaling Arthur D. • USA
SUSMAN • 1985 • Benegal Shyam • IND • ESSENCE, THE
SUSPECT • 1960 • Boulting Roy, Boulting John • UKN • RISK, THE (USA)
SUSPECT • 1969 • Hodges Mike • MTV • UKN
SUSPECT • 1987 • Yates Peter • USA
SUSPECT, THE • 1913 • *Nestor* • USA
SUSPECT, THE • 1916 • Drew Sidney • USA
SUSPECT, THE • 1944 • Siodmak Robert • USA
SUSPECTED ALIBI see **SUSPENDED ALIBI** • 1957
SUSPECTED ONE, THE see **POD SUMNJOM** • 1956
SUSPECTED: OR, THE MYSTERIOUS LODGER • 1909 • Smith Jack ? • UKN
SUSPECTED PERSON • 1942 • Huntington Lawrence • UKN
SUSPECTED (UKN) see **TRACKED** • 1928
SUSPECTED (UKN) see **TEXAS DYNAMO** • 1950
SUSPECTS, LES • 1956-57 • Devlin Bernard • SHT • CND
SUSPECTS, LES • 1957 • Dreville Jean • FRN
SUSPECTS, LES • 1974 • Wyn Michel • FRN, ITL • PIEUVRE, LA
SUSPENCE • 1919 • Reicher Frank • USA • SUSPENSE
SUSPENDED see **W ZAWIESZENIU** • 1988
SUSPENDED ALIBI • 1957 • Shaughnessy Alfred • UKN • SUSPECTED ALIBI
SUSPENDED CEREMONY, A • 1914 • Pollard Harry • USA
SUSPENDED FORTH • 1969 • Horwitz James • UKN
SUSPENDED ORDEAL, A • 1914 • Lehrman Henry • USA
SUSPENDED SENTENCE • 1913 • Dwan Allan • USA
SUSPENDED SENTENCE • 1914 • *Maison Edna* • USA
SUSPENDED SENTENCE • 1917 • *Compson Betty* • SHT • USA
SUSPENDED VOCATION, THE see **VOCACION SUSPENDIDA, LA** • 1977
SUSPENDIDO EN SINVERGUENZA • 1961 • Ozores Mariano • SPN
SUSPENSE • 1913 • Smalley Phillips, Weber Lois • USA
SUSPENSE • 1930 • Summers Walter • UKN
SUSPENSE • 1946 • Tuttle Frank • USA
SUSPENSE see **SUSPENCE** • 1919
SUSPENSE see **SHOCK TRANSFERT SUSPENCE HYPNOS** • 1977
SUSPENSE A CAIRO POUR AGENT 008 see **A 008 OPERAZIONE STERMINIO** • 1965
SUSPENSE AU DEUXIEME BUREAU • 1959 • de Saint-Maurice Christian • FRN
SUSPENSO EN COMUNISMO • 1955 • Manzanos Eduardo • SPN
SUSPICION • 1910 • *Vitagraph* • USA
SUSPICION • 1918 • Stahl John M. • USA
SUSPICION • 1941 • Hitchcock Alfred • USA • BEFORE THE FACT
SUSPICION • 1971 • Krejcik Jiri • CZC
SUSPICION • 1987 • Grieve Andrew • TVM • UKN
SUSPICION • 1989 • Karim Alaa • EGY
SUSPICION see **VOLPE DALLA CODA DI VELLUTO, LA** • 1971
SUSPICION see **GIWAKU** • 1983
SUSPICION OF MURDER see **GRANGES BRULEES, LES** • 1973
SUSPICIOUS CHARACTER, A see **SUMNJIVO LICE** • 1954
SUSPICIOUS CHARACTERS • 1915 • Ransom Charles • USA
SUSPICIOUS HENRY • 1913 • Thompson Frederick A. • USA
SUSPICIOUS MR. BROWN • 1913 • Haldane Bert? • UKN
SUSPICIOUS WIFE, A • 1914 • *20th Century* • USA
SUSPICIOUS WIVES • 1921 • Stahl John M. • USA
SUSPIRIA • 1977 • Argento Dario • ITL
SUSPIROS DE TRIANA • 1955 • Torrado Ramon • SPN
SUSRET U SNU • 1957 • Kostelac Nikola • ANS • YGS
SUSS GOTT • 1956 • Hoglund Gunnar • SWD • SLEEP WELL
SUSSE LEBEN DES GRAFEN BOBBY, DAS • 1962 • von Cziffra Geza • AUS
SUSSE MADEL, DAS • 1916 • Edel Edmund • FRG
SUSSE MADEL, DAS • 1926 • Noa Manfred • FRG
SUSSE NELLY, DIE • 1915 • Dessauer Siegfried • FRG
SUSSE ZEIT MIT KALIMAGDORA, DIE • 1968 • Lahola Leopold • FRG, CZC • DELECTABLE TIME OF KALIMAGDORA, THE ○ SWEET TIME OF KALIMAGDORA, THE ○ SLADKY CAS KALIMAGDORY
SUSSES GEHEIMNIS, EIN • 1931 • Zelnik Friedrich • FRG
SUSSETEN FRUCHTE, DIE • 1954 • Antel Franz • FRG
SUSSEX FORTNIGHT • 1950 • Hemsley Norman • UKN
SUSSI • 1988 • Justiniano Gonzalo • CHL
SUSSIE • 1945 • Mattsson Arne • SWD
SUSSURRO NEL BUIO, UN • 1976 • Aliprandi Marcello • ITL
SUSTER THERESA see **SISTER TERESA** • 1974
SUSTO QUE PEREZ SE LLEVO • 1940 • Harlan Richard • ARG
SUSUME DOKURITSUKI • 1943 • Kinugasa Teinosuke • JPN • FORWARD FLAG OF INDEPENDENCE
SUSUME JAGUARS TEKIZEN JORIKU • 1968 • Maeda Yoichi • JPN • MAY WAY FOR THE JAGUARS
SUSUZ YAZ • 1963 • Erksan Metin • TRK • DRY SUMMER (USA) ○ I HAD MY BROTHER'S WIFE ○ WATERLESS SUMMER
SUSZA • 1969 • Schabenbeck Stefan, Ryszka Henryk • ANM • PLN • DROUGHT
SUT A NAP • Kalmar Laszlo • HNG • SUN SHINES, THE (USA)
SUTCH-DELAN • 1978 • Hatami Ali • IRN • BROKEN HEARTS
SUTFONGDIK NUIYAN • 1989 • Ou Dingping • HKG • I AM SORRY ○ SITFONGDIK NUIYAN
SUTHERLAND • 1986 • Ianzelo Tony • MTV • CND
SUTIEJKA see **SUTJESKA** • 1974
SUTJESKA • 1974 • Delic Stipe • YGS • FIFTH OFFENSIVE, THE ○ SUTIEJKA
SUTON • 1984 • Paskaljevic Goran • YGS, USA • TWILIGHT TIME ○ TWILIGHT
SUTORANG • 1964 • Dutta Subhash • BNG • CONSEQUENTLY ○ SOOTARANG ○ THEREFORE

SUTTER'S GOLD • 1936 • Cruze James • USA
SUTTOBI KAGO • 1952 • Makino Masahiro • JPN • EXPRESS SEDAN
SUTYI, A SZERENCSEQYEREK • 1938 • Balogh Bela • HNG • SUTYI, THE LUCKY CHILD (USA)
SUTYI, THE LUCKY CHILD (USA) see **SUTYI, A SZERENCSEQYEREK** • 1938
SUUDELMA • 1969 • Talaskivi Jaakko • SHT • FNL • KISS, THE
SUVARNA REKHA • 1963 • Ghatak Ritwik • IND
SUVARNA SUNDARI • 1959 • Raghavaiah V. • IND
SUVINEN SATU • 1925 • Karu Erkki • FNL
SUVISAN COVJEK • 1965 • Majer Branko • YGS
SUVOROV • 1941 • Pudovkin V. I., Doller Mikhail • USS • GENERAL SUVOROV
SUWANEE RIVER • 1925 • Fleischer Dave • ANS • USA
SUWANEE RIVER, THE • 1913 • Kirkland Hardee • USA
SUZANNA • 1922 • Jones F. Richard • USA
SUZANNA'S NEW SUIT • 1914 • Pollard Harry • USA
SUZANNE • 1914 • *Tennant Barbara* • USA
SUZANNE • 1916 • Mercanton Louis, Hervil Rene • FRN
SUZANNE • 1932 • Rouleau Raymond, Joannon Leo • FRN
SUZANNE • 1960 • Colfach Elsa • SWD • SUSANNE
SUZANNE • 1980 • Spry Robin • CND
SUZANNE see **SECOND COMING OF SUZANNE, THE** • 1974
SUZANNE A PARIS • 1956 • Sassy Jean-Paul • SHT • FRN
SUZANNE AU BAIN • 1930 • Storck Henri • DOC • BLG
SUZANNE ET SES BRIGANDS • 1948 • Ciampi Yves • FRN • JOUR ET LA NUIT, LE
SUZANNE & LEONARD • 1984 • Hilbard John • DNM
SUZANNE SIMONIN, LA RELIGIEUSE DE DIDEROT • 1965 • Rivette Jacques • FRN • RELIGIEUSE, LA (UKN) ○ RELIGIEUSE DE DIDEROT, LA ○ NUN, THE (USA)
SUZANNE'S PROFESSION see **CARRIERE DE SUZANNE, LA** • 1963
SUZIE READER -A TRIBUTE • 1985 • Woodland James • MTV • CND
SUZIE SUPERSTAR • 1983 • McCallum Robert • USA
SUZUKAKE NO SANPOMICHI • 1959 • Horikawa Hiromichi • JPN • PATH UNDER THE PLANE-TREES, THE
SUZY • 1936 • Fitzmaurice George • USA
SUZY SAXOPHONE see **SAXOPHON-SUSI** • 1928
SVADBA • 1964 • Kobakhidze Mikhail • SHT • USS • WEDDING, THE
SVADBA • 1973 • Saranovic Radomir • YGS, USS • WEDDING, THE
SVADBA V MALINOVKE • 1967 • Tutyshkin Andrey • USS • WEDDING IN MALINOVKA
SVADLENKA • 1936 • Fric Martin • CZC • SEAMSTRESS, THE
SVAERMERE • 1974 • During Jan Erik • NRW • MOTHWIESE ○ DREAMERS
SVALT • 1966 • Carlsen Henning • SWD, DNM, NRW • SULT (DNM) ○ HUNGER (USA)
SVAMPE • 1990 • Asphaug Martin • NRW
SVARMOR KOMMER • 1932 • Merzbach Paul • SWD • MOTHER-IN-LAW IS COMING
SVARMOR PA VIFT • 1916 • Klercker Georg • SWD • MOTHER-IN-LAW ON THE SPREE
SVARSKOTT PASTORAT, ETT • 1958 • Ohlmarks Ake • SWD
SVART GRYNING • 1988 • Lemos Carlos • SWD • BLACK DAWN
SVART HAV • 1979 • Wingate David • NRW • EMPTY SEA
SVARTA HORISONTER • 1936 • Fejos Paul • DOC • DNM, SWD • BLACK HORIZONS ○ HORIZONS NOIRS
SVARTA MASKERNA, DE • 1912 • Stiller Mauritz • SWD • BLACK MASKS, THE
SVARTA PALMKRONOR • 1968 • Lindgren Lars-Magnus • SWD • BLACK PALM TREES ○ BLACK PALM
SVARTA ROSOR • 1932 • Molander Gustaf • SWD • BLACK ROSES
SVARTA ROSOR • 1945 • Carlsten Rune • SWD • BLACK ROSES
SVARTE FUGLER • 1983 • Glomm Lasse • NRW • BLACK CROWS
SVARTE RUDOLF • 1928 • Edgren Gustaf • SWD • BLACK RUDOLF
SVARTERE ENN NATTEN -EN KJAERLIGHETHISTORIE • 1979 • Wam Svend • NRW • DARKER THAN NIGHT -A LOVE STORY
SVARTSJUKANS FOLJDER • 1916 • Hansen Edmond • SWD • CONSEQUENCES OF JEALOUSY
SVASTICA NEL VENTRE, LA • 1977 • Caiano Mario • ITL
SVATA HRISNICE • 1970 • Cech Vladimir • CZC • HOLY SINNER, THE
SVATBA BEZ PRSTYNKU • 1972 • Cech Vladimir • CZC • WEDDING WITHOUT A RING
SVATBA JAKO REMEN • 1967 • Krejcik Jiri • CZC • UNFORTUNATE BRIDEGROOM ○ HARD AND FAST MARRIAGE, A ○ WEDDING UNDER SUPERVISION
SVATBA V KORALOVEM MORI • 1943 • von Mollendorff • PLN
SVATEJ Z KREJCARKU • 1969 • Tucek Petr • CZC • SAINT FROM THE OUTSKIRTS OF TOWN, THE ○ SAINT FROM THE SUBURBS, THE
SVATY VACLAV • 1929 • Kolar J. S. • CZC • SAINT WENCELAUS
SVE ZELJE SVIJETA • 1966 • Tadej Vladimir • ANS • YGS • ALL THE WISHES OF THE WORLD
SVED AKINEK NYOMA VESZETT, A • 1980 • Bacso Peter • HNG, SWD, FRG • MANNEN SOM GICK UPP I ROK (SWD) ○ MAN WHO WENT UP IN SMOKE, THE
SVEDECTVI • 1961 • Hasa Pavel, Hlavac Roman • CZC • EVIDENCE
SVEDESI, LE • 1961 • Polidoro Gian Luigi • ITL
SVEDOMI • 1949 • Krejcik Jiri • CZC • CONSCIENCE
SVEDSKAYA SPICKA • 1954 • Yuuin Konstantin • USS • SAFETY MATCH, THE
SVEDSKI ARANZMAN • 1989 • Gospic Zoran • YGS • SWEDISH PACKAGE HOLIDAY, THE
SVEGLIATI E UCCIDI (LUTRING) • 1966 • Lizzani Carlo • ITL, FRN • LUTRING.. REVEILLE-TOI ET MEURS (FRN) ○ WAKE UP AND DIE (USA) ○ TOO SOON TO DIE ○ LUTRING
SVEJK NA FRONTE • 1926 • Lamac Carl • CZC • SCHWEIK AT THE FRONT
SVEJK V CIVILU • 1927 • Machaty Gustav • CZC • SCHWEIK IN CIVILIAN LIFE ○ SCHWEIK AS A CIVILIAN
SVEJK V RUSKEM ZAJETI • 1927 • Innemann Svatopluk • CZC • SCHWEIK IN RUSSIAN CAPTIVITY
SVEN KLANG'S COMBO (UKN) see **SVEN KLANGS KVINTETT** • 1976
SVEN KLANGS KVINTETT • 1976 • Olsson Stellan • SWD • SVEN KLANG'S COMBO (UKN) ○ SMALL-TOWN QUINTET, THE
SVEN TUSAN • 1949 • Stevens Gosta • SWD
SVEN TUUVA • 1958 • Laine Edvin • FNL
SVEND LANDSTRYGERE, DE • 1908 • *Holger-Madsen* • DNM • SOLD TO THIEVES
SVENGALI • 1927 • Righelli Gennaro • FRG
SVENGALI • 1931 • Mayo Archie • USA
SVENGALI • 1954 • Langley Noel • UKN
SVENGALI • 1982 • Harvey Anthony • TVM • USA
SVENGALI see **HYPNOTISEUR, DER** • 1914
SVENGALI'S CAT see **MIGHTY MOUSE IN SVENGALI'S CAT** • 1946
SVENGARLIC • 1931 • *Mintz Charles (P)* • ANS • USA
SVENSK STORINDUSTRI, EN • 1953 • Werner Gosta • SHT • SWD
SVENSK TIGER, EN • 1948 • Edgren Gustaf • SWD • SWEDISH TIGER, A
SVENSKA BILDER • 1964 • Danielsson Tage • SWD • SWEDISH PORTRAITS
SVENSKA FLICKOR I PARIS • 1960 • Boman Barbro • SWD • FLAMBOYANT SEX, THE (USA) ○ PARIS PLAYGIRLS ○ FEMMES FLAMBOYANTES, LES ○ FLAMBOYANTS, THE
SVENSKA FLOYD • 1961 • Nyberg Borje • SWD • SWEDISH FLOYD
SVENSKE RYTTAREN • 1949 • Edgren Gustaf • SWD • SWEDISH HORSEMAN, A
SVENSSON ORDNAD ALLT • 1938 • Berthels Theodor • SWD, DNM
SVERCHOK NA PECHI • 1915 • Sushkevich Boris, Uralsky A. • USS • CRICKET ON THE HEARTH
SVERGOGNATA, LA • 1974 • Biagetti Giuliano • ITL
SVERIGE AT SVENSKARNA • 1980 • Olsson Mats Helge • SWD • SWEDEN TO THE SWEDES ○ DRINKING MAN'S WAR, THE
SVET ALFONSO MUCHY • 1980 • Jires Jaromil • DOC • CZC • WORLD OF ALPHONSE MUCHA, THE
SVET BEZ HRANIC • 1931 • Lebl Julius • CZC
SVET DALEKOY ZVEZDY see **SVEV DALEKOI ZVESDY** • 1965
SVET, KDE SE ZEBRA • 1938 • Cikan Miroslav • CZC • WORLD WHERE ONE GOES BEGGING, THE ○ BEGGAR LIFE, THE ○ WORLD OF BEGGARS, THE
SVET NA KAJZARJU • 1952 • Stiglic France • YGS • PEOPLE OF KAJZARJE
SVET NAD ROSSIEI • 1947 • Yutkevich Sergei • USS • LIGHT OVER RUSSIA
SVET OTEVRENY NAHODAM • 1971 • Stekly Karel • CZC • WORLD OPEN TO CHANCES, THE
SVET PATRI NAM • 1937 • Fric Martin • CZC • WORLD BELONGS TO US, THE ○ WORLD IS OURS, THE
SVETACI • 1969 • Podskalsky Zdenek • CZC • MEN ABOUT TOWN
SVETI PESAK • 1968 • Antic Miroslav • YGS • SACRED SAND, THE
SVETLAWA UCCIDERA IL 28 SETTEMBRE see **RAPPORTO FULLER, BASE STOCCOLMA** • 1967
SVETLO PRONIKA TMOU • 1931 • Vavra Otakar • SHT • CZC
SVETLYI GOROD • 1928 • Preobrazhenskaya Olga • USS • BRIGHT TOWN, THE ○ CITE LUMINEUSE, LA
SVETOZAR MARKOVIC • 1981 • Galic Eduard • YGS
SVETYLI PUT • 1940 • Alexandrov Grigori • USS • TANYA (USA) ○ BRIGHT PATH ○ LIGHT WAY, THE
SVEV DALEKOI ZVESDY • 1965 • Pyriev Ivan • USS • LIGHT OF A DISTANT STAR, THE ○ SVET DALEKOY ZVEZDY
SVEZIA, INFERNO E PARADISO • 1968 • Scattini Luigi • DOC • ITL • SWEDEN -HEAVEN AND HELL ○ SWEDEN, HELL AND PARADISE ○ SWEDEN, HEAVEN OR HELL
SVI CRTEZI GRADA • 1959 • Vrbanic Ivo • YGS • ALL DRAWINGS OF THE TOWN ○ ALL THE DRAWINGS OF THE TOWN
SVIDANIE • 1963 • Ishmukhamedov Elyor • USS • RENDEZVOUS
SVINYARKA I PASTUKH • 1941 • Pyriev Ivan • USS • SWINEHERD AND THE SHEPHERD, THE ○ SWINEHERD AND SHEPHERD ○ THEY MET IN MOSCOW
SVIRACHUT (BUL) see **CLOWN AND THE KIDS, THE** • 1968
SVITALO CELOU NOC • 1979 • Matejka Vaclav • CZC • DAWN ALL NIGHT
SVITANI • 1933 • Kubasek Vaclav • CZC • DAWN, THE
SVITATO, LO • 1956 • Lizzani Carlo • ITL
SVOGA TJELA GOSPODAR • 1957 • Hanzekovic Fedor • YGS • MY OWN MASTER
SVOI SREDI CHUZHIGH, CHUZHOI SREDI SVOIKH • 1974 • Mikhalkov Nikita • USS • STRANGER AMONG HIS OWN PEOPLE ○ AT HOME AMONG STRANGERS ○ FRIEND AMONG ENEMIES, ENEMY AMONG FRIENDS
SVRAB • 1969 • Grgic Zlatko, Stalter Pavao • ANS • YGS • SCABIES
SVYATOI CHORT • 1917 • USS • HOLY DEVIL, THE
SWAB THE DUCK • 1956 • Tendlar Dave • ANS • USA
SWAG OF DESTINY • 1913 • *Washburn Bryant* • USA
SWAGGERERS, THE see **NASI FURIANTI** • 1937
SWAGGIE'S STORY, THE • 1923 • Longford Raymond • ASL
SWAGMAN'S STORY • 1912 • Longford Raymond • ASL
SWAIN • 1951 • Markopoulos Gregory J. • SHT • USA • RAIN BLACK MY LOVE
SWAJARA DORAN • 1930 • Painter Baburao • IND
SWALLOW • 1922 • SAF
SWALLOW, THE • 1958 • Lipshits G. • USS
SWALLOW, THE (USA) see **GOLONDRINA, LA** • 1938
SWALLOW STORM, THE see **KIRPLANGIC FIRTINASI** • 1985
SWALLOW THE LEADER • 1949 • McKimson Robert • ANS • USA
SWALLOWS ALWAYS COME BACK see **NAGARDOLA** • 1978
SWALLOWS AND AMAZONS • 1974 • Whatham Claude • UKN
SWAMI • 1976 • Chatterjee Basu • IND
SWAMI SAM • 1914 • Murphy J. A. • USA
SWAMP, THE • 1921 • Campbell Colin • USA
SWAMP, THE see **KAIDAN CHIDORI-GA-FUCHI** • 1956
SWAMP BAIT see **GATOR BAIT** • 1974
SWAMP COUNTRY • 1966 • Patrick Robert • USA
SWAMP DIAMONDS see **SWAMP WOMEN** • 1955
SWAMP FIRE • 1946 • Pine William H. • USA
SWAMP GIRL • 1971 • *Husky Ferlin* • USA
SWAMP OF PASSION • 1982 • Lee Doo-Yong • SKR
SWAMP OF THE BLOOD LEECHES see **ALIEN DEAD, THE** • 1980
SWAMP OF THE LOST MONSTER, THE • 1964 • Baledon Rafael • MXC • SWAMP OF THE LOST SOULS
SWAMP OF THE LOST SOULS see **SWAMP OF THE LOST MONSTER, THE** • 1964
SWAMP THING • 1982 • Craven Wes • USA
SWAMP WATER • 1941 • Renoir Jean • USA • MAN WHO CAME BACK, THE (UKN) ○ ETANG TRAGIQUE, L'(FRN)
SWAMP WOMAN • 1941 • Clifton Elmer • USA
SWAMP WOMEN • 1955 • Corman Roger • USA • SWAMP DIAMONDS ○ CRUEL SWAMP
SWAMY • 1988 • Nag Shankar • IND
SWAN, THE • 1925 • Buchowetzki Dimitri • USA
SWAN, THE • 1956 • Vidor Charles • USA
SWAN, THE see **ONE ROMANTIC NIGHT** • 1930
SWAN GIRL, THE • 1913 • Ince Ralph • USA
SWAN ISLAND see **INSEL DER SCHWANE** • 1983
SWAN LAKE • *Balanchine George* • ITL
SWAN LAKE • Genni Sergio • SWT
SWAN LAKE • Touloubieva Z. • USS
SWAN LAKE • 1949 • Zatouroff Boris • SHT • FRN
SWAN LAKE • 1964 • Draexler-Just • GDR
SWAN LAKE • 1965 • Topaldgikov Stefan • BUL
SWAN LAKE (UKN) see **SCHWANENSEE** • 1967
SWAN LAKE (UKN) see **LEBEDINOYE OZERO** • 1968
SWAN LAKE (USA) see **LEBEDINOYE OZERO** • 1957
SWAN PRINCESS, THE • 1928 • *Sennett Mack (P)* • SHT • USA
SWAN SONG • 1980 • London Jerry • TVM • USA
SWAN SONG see **LABEDZI SPIEW** • 1962
SWAN SONG see **JUE XIANG** • 1985
SWANEE RIVER • 1931 • Cannon Raymond • USA
SWANEE RIVER • 1939 • Lanfield Sidney • USA
SWANKER AND THE WITCH'S CURSE • 1914 • Collins Edwin J.? • UKN
SWANKER MEETS HIS GIRL • 1914 • Collins Edwin J.? • UKN
SWANN IN LOVE (UKN) see **AMOUR DE SWANN, UN** • 1983
SWAP • Gazdag Gyula • HNG
SWAP, THE • Shade John • USA
SWAP, THE • 1986 • Benner Richard • MTV • CND
SWAP, THE see **SWAP AND HOW THEY MAKE IT, THE** • 1966
SWAP, THE see **SAM'S SONG** • 1971
SWAP, THE see **TRAMPA** • 1979
SWAP AND HOW THEY MAKE IT, THE • 1966 • Sarno Joe • USA • SWAP, THE
SWAP MEET • 1979 • Mack Brice • USA
SWAPNA TENCH LOCHNI • 1967 • Chandravadan • IND
SWAPPERS, THE • 1967 • *Mitam Productions* • USA
SWAPPERS, THE see **WIFE SWAPPERS, THE** • 1970
SWARALIPI • 1960 • *Ghatak Ritwik* • IND
SWARM, THE • 1917 • *Cunard Grace* • USA
SWARM, THE • 1966 • Popovic Mica • YGS
SWARM, THE • 1978 • Allen Irwin • USA
SWASH BUCKLED • 1962 • Hanna William, Barbera Joseph • ANS • USA
SWASHBUCKLER • 1976 • Goldstone James • USA • SCARLET BUCCANEER, THE (UKN) ○ SCARLETT BUCKANEER
SWASHBUCKLER, THE (USA) see **MARIES DE L'AN II, LES** • 1970
SWASTIKA • 1973 • Mora Philippe • DOC • UKN
SWASTIKA, THE • 1912 • Melies Gaston • USA
SWAT THAT FLY • 1935 • Fleischer Dave • ANS • USA
SWAT THE CROOK • 1919 • Roach Hal • SHT • USA
SWAT THE FLIRT • 1918 • *Lyons Eddie* • SHT • USA
SWAT THE FLY • 1911 • *Essanay* • USA
SWAT THE KAISER • 1918 • *Fairbanks Douglas* • SHT • USA
SWAT THE SPY • 1918 • Gillstrom Arvid E. • USA
SWAYAM • 1989 • Bhatt Mahesh • IND
SWAYAMVARAM • 1972 • Gopalakrishnan Adoor • IND
SWEAR TO KILL THEM ONE BY ONE see **PILUK IL TIMIDO** • 1968
SWEARING OFF • 1917 • Curtis Allen • SHT • USA
SWEAT see **ASE** • 1929
SWEAT BOX see **SCHWITZKASTEN** • 1978
SWEAT-BOX, THE • 1913 • Henderson Dell • USA
SWEATER, THE • 1915 • Wilson Frank • UKN
SWEATER GIRL • 1942 • Clemens William • USA
SWEATER GIRLS • 1978 • Jones Don • USA
SWEATING SOIL, THE see **TOPRAGIN TERI** • 1982
SWEATMEAT AND WHIP see **ZUCKERBROT UND PEITSCHE** • 1968
SWEDE AMONG US, A see **SUECA ENTRE NOSOTROS, UNA** • 1968
SWEDE-HEARTS • 1917 • Marshall George • SHT • USA
SWEDE LARSON • 1914 • *Leonard Robert* • USA
SWEDEN • 1960 • Van Dyke Willard • DOC • USA
SWEDEN -HEAVEN AND HELL see **SVEZIA, INFERNO E PARADISO** • 1968
SWEDEN, HEAVEN OR HELL see **SVEZIA, INFERNO E PARADISO** • 1968
SWEDEN, HELL AND PARADISE see **SVEZIA, INFERNO E PARADISO** • 1968
SWEDEN TO THE SWEDES see **SVERIGE AT SVENSKARNA** • 1980
SWEDEN TODAY • 1928 • *Johnson Amandus* • DOC • USA
SWEDENHIELMS • 1935 • Molander Gustaf • SWD
SWEDISH AND UNDERAGE see **EVA -DEN UTSTOTTA** • 1969
SWEDISH CONFESSIONS see **JAG VILL LIGGA MED DIN AYSKARE MAMMA** • 1978
SWEDISH DREAM see **LOVE IS A SPLENDID ILLUSION** • 1970
SWEDISH FANNY HILL, THE see **FANNY HILL** • 1968
SWEDISH FLOYD see **SVENSKA FLOYD** • 1961
SWEDISH FLY GIRLS see **CHRISTA** • 1971
SWEDISH HORSEMAN, A see **SVENSKE RYTTAREN** • 1949

SWEDISH LOVE PLAY (UKN) see **CARMILLA** • 1968
SWEDISH LOVE STORY, A see **KARLEKSHISTORIA, EN** • 1969
SWEDISH MISTRESS, THE (USA) see **ALSKARINNAN** • 1962
SWEDISH PACKAGE HOLIDAY, THE see **SVEDSKI ARANZMAN** • 1989
SWEDISH PLAYBIRDS • Lemoine Michel • SWT
SWEDISH PORTRAITS see **SVENSKA BILDER** • 1964
SWEDISH SEX CLINIC • 1981 • Whyte Andrew • SWD • HEAT AND LUST: DIARY OF A SEX THERAPIST ○ HEAT AND LUST ○ RASPOUTINE ○ ECSTASY INC.
SWEDISH SEX GAMES see **INKRAKTARNA** • 1974
SWEDISH SEX KITTEN see **FLOSSIE** • 1974
SWEDISH SUMMER • 1970 • Reddy Dick • DOC • USA
SWEDISH TIGER, A see **SVENSK TIGER, EN** • 1948
SWEDISH WEDDING NIGHT (USA) see **BROLLOPSBESVAR** • 1964
SWEDISH WILDCATS • 1974 • Sarno Joe • SWD
SWEEDIE AND HER DOG • 1915 • *Beery Wallace* • USA
SWEEDIE AND THE DOUBLE EXPOSURE • 1914 • *Beery Wallace* • USA
SWEEDIE AND THE HYPNOTIST • 1914 • *Beery Wallace* • USA
SWEEDIE AND THE LORD • 1914 • *Beery Wallace* • USA
SWEEDIE AND THE SULTAN'S PRESENT • 1915 • *Beery Wallace* • USA
SWEEDIE AT THE FAIR • 1914 • *Beery Wallace* • USA
SWEEDIE COLLECTS FOR CHARITY • 1914 • *Beery Wallace* • USA
SWEEDIE GOES TO COLLEGE • 1915 • Baker Richard Foster?, Hopper E. Mason? • USA
SWEEDIE IN VAUDEVILLE • 1915 • *Beery Wallace* • USA
SWEEDIE LEARNS TO RIDE • 1915 • *Beery Wallace* • USA
SWEEDIE LEARNS TO SWIM • 1914 • *Beery Wallace* • USA
SWEEDIE SPRINGS A SURPRISE • 1914 • *Beery Wallace* • USA
SWEEDIE THE SWATTER • 1914 • *Beery Wallace* • USA
SWEEDIE THE TROUBLE MAKER • 1914 • *Beery Wallace* • USA
SWEEDIE'S CLEAN UP • 1914 • *Beery Wallace* • USA
SWEEDIE'S FINISH • 1915 • *Beery Wallace* • USA
SWEEDIE'S HERO • 1915 • *Beery Wallace* • USA
SWEEDIE'S HOPELESS LOVE • 1915 • *Beery Wallace* • USA
SWEEDIE'S SKATE • 1914 • *Beery Wallace* • USA
SWEEDIE'S SUICIDE • 1915 • *Beery Wallace* • USA
SWEEDY THE JANITOR • 1916 • Beery Wallace • USA
SWEENEY! • 1976 • Wickes David • UKN
SWEENEY 2 • 1978 • Clegg Tom • UKN
SWEENEY AND THE FAIRY • 1913 • France Charles H. • USA
SWEENEY AND THE MILLION • 1913 • France Charles H. • USA
SWEENEY: JACKPOT • 1975 • Clegg Tom • MTV • UKN
SWEENEY TODD • 1926 • Dewhurst George • UKN
SWEENEY TODD • 1928 • West Walter • UKN
SWEENEY TODD • 1984 • *Lansbury Angela* • MTV • USA
SWEENEY TODD, THE DEMON BARBER OF FLEET STREET • 1936 • King George • UKN • DEMON BARBER OF FLEET STREET, THE (USA)
SWEENEY'S CHRISTMAS BIRD • 1914 • Baker George D. • USA
SWEENEY'S DREAM • 1913 • France Charles H. • USA
SWEEP • 1920 • Kellino W. P. • UKN
SWEEP, THE • 1904 • Collins Alf? • UKN
SWEEP, THE • 1922 • Dudley Bernard • UKN
SWEEP! SWEEP! SWEEP! • 1913 • Stow Percy • UKN
SWEEPING AGAINST THE WIND • 1930 • Adamson Victor • USA
SWEEPING FIELDS • 1957 • Stroyeva Vera • USS • PLAINS, MY PLAINS
SWEEPING STATEMENT, A • 1952 • *Hall Cameron* • SHT • UKN
SWEEPINGS • 1933 • Cromwell John • USA
SWEEP'S THREEPENNY BATH, THE • 1909 • *Walturdaw* • UKN
SWEEPSTAKE ANNIE • 1935 • Nigh William • USA • ANNIE DOESN'T LIVE HERE (UKN)
SWEEPSTAKE RACKETEERS (UKN) see **UNDERCOVER AGENT** • 1939
SWEEPSTAKES • 1931 • Rogell Albert S. • USA
SWEEPSTAKES WINNER • 1939 • McGann William • USA
SWEET 16 • 1981 • Sotos Jim • USA • SWEET SIXTEEN
SWEET ADELINE • 1926 • Storm Jerome • USA
SWEET ADELINE • 1927 • Fleischer Dave • ANS • USA
SWEET ADELINE • 1935 • LeRoy Mervyn • USA
SWEET AGONY • 1973 • De Renzy Alex • USA
SWEET ALICE, BEN BOLT • 1912 • *Imp* • USA
SWEET ALOES (UKN) see **GIVE ME YOUR HEART** • 1936
SWEET ALYSSUM • 1915 • Campbell Colin • USA
SWEET AND BELOVED WOMAN, THE see **DOCE MULHER AMADA, A** • 1968
SWEET AND BITTER • 1975 • Velchev Ilya • BUL
SWEET AND BITTER see **EDES ES KESERU** • 1966
SWEET AND HOT • 1958 • White Jules • SHT • USA
SWEET AND LOW • 1914 • Taylor William D. • USA
SWEET AND LOWDOWN • 1944 • Mayo Archie • USA • MOMENT FOR MUSIC
SWEET AND SEXY • 1970 • Sloman Anthony • UKN
SWEET AND SOUR • 1979 • Revach Ze'Ev • ISR
SWEET AND SOUR (USA) see **DRAGEES AU POIVRE** • 1963
SWEET AND THE BITTER, THE • 1962 • Clavell James • CND
SWEET AND TWENTY • 1909 • Griffith D. W. • USA
SWEET AND TWENTY • 1919 • Morgan Sidney • UKN
SWEET AND TWENTY • 1921 • ASL
SWEET BEAT • 1959 • Albert Ronnie • UKN • AMOROUS SEX, THE (USA)
SWEET BIPPY (BLUE) • 1968 • Duffy Kevin • USA
SWEET BIRD OF AQUARIUS • 1970 • Kerwin Harry E. • USA
SWEET BIRD OF YOUTH • 1962 • Brooks Richard • USA
SWEET BODY, THE see **DOLCE CORPO DI DEBORAH, IL** • 1968
SWEET BODY OF DEBORAH, THE (USA) see **DOLCE CORPO DI DEBORAH, IL** • 1968
SWEET BRIDAL NIGHT, A see **AMAI SHOYA** • 1968
SWEET BUNCH see **GLIKIA SIMORIA** • 1983
SWEET BY AND BY • 1921 • Roach Hal • SHT • USA
SWEET CASH see **PLATA DULCE** • 1982
SWEET CHARITY • 1916 • Drew Sidney • SHT • USA
SWEET CHARITY • 1969 • Fosse Bob • USA
SWEET CHEAT • 1949 • Yates Hal • SHT • USA
SWEET COOKIE • 1933 • Marshall George • SHT • USA
SWEET COSTUMES see **BRANDOS COSTUMES** • 1975
SWEET COUNTRY • 1986 • Cacoyannis Michael • GRC
SWEET CREEK COUNTY WAR, THE • 1979 • James J. Frank • USA
SWEET DADDIES • 1926 • Santell Alfred • USA
SWEET DADDY • 1924 • McCarey Leo • SHT • USA
SWEET DAYS OF YOUTH see **GIBBUNURI** • 1986
SWEET DECEPTION • 1913 • Ince Ralph • USA
SWEET DECEPTIONS (USA) see **DOLCI INGANNI, I** • 1960
SWEET DEVIL • 1938 • Guissart Rene • UKN
SWEET DIRTY TONY see **CUBA CROSSING** • 1980
SWEET DREAMS • 1969 • Avildsen John G. • USA
SWEET DREAMS • 1982 • Cowan Tom • ASL
SWEET DREAMS • 1985 • Reisz Karel • USA
SWEET DREAMS, BABY! • 1970 • Simons Peter • BLG
SWEET DREAMS INTERMINGLED WITH NIGHTMARE • 1909 • *Pathe* • FRN
SWEET DRY AND DRY, THE • 1920 • Lyons Eddie, Moran Lee • SHT • USA
SWEET DYNAMITE • 1920 • Morante Milburn • SHT • USA
SWEET ECSTASY (USA) see **DOUCE VIOLENCE** • 1962
SWEET FEED • 1974 • Lofven Chris • SHT • ASL
SWEET GAMES OF LAST SUMMER (UKN) see **SLADKE HRY MINULEHO LETA** • 1969
SWEET GENEVIEVE • 1921 • *Parkinson H. B. (P)* • SHT • UKN
SWEET GENEVIEVE • 1947 • Dreifuss Arthur • USA
SWEET GEORGIA • 1972 • Boles Edward • USA
SWEET HEARTS DANCE • 1988 • Greenwald Robert • USA
SWEET HOME • 1989 • Kurosawa Kiyoshi • JPN
SWEET HOSTAGE • 1975 • Philips Lee • TVM • USA • WELCOME TO XANADU
SWEET HOURS see **DULCES HORAS** • 1981
SWEET HUNTERS • 1969 • Guerra Ruy • BRZ • JAILBIRD ○ TENDRES CHASSEURS
SWEET INNISCARRA • 1934 • Moore Emmett • UKN
SWEET INTERNS, THE see **HANA NO KOIBITOTACHI** • 1968
SWEET IS THE MEAT • 1970 • Soukis Robert • USA
SWEET JAN • 1943 • Keays Vernon • SHT • USA
SWEET JENNY LEE • 1932 • Fleischer Dave • ANS • USA
SWEET JESUS, PREACHER MAN • 1973 • Schellerup Henning • USA
SWEET KILL (UKN) see **AROUSERS, THE** • 1971
SWEET KITTY BELLAIRS • 1916 • Young James • USA
SWEET KITTY BELLAIRS • 1930 • Green Alfred E. • USA
SWEET LADIES, THE see **DOLCI SIGNORE, LE** • 1967
SWEET LAND OF LIBERTY • 1914 • Pollard Harry • USA
SWEET LAVENDER • 1915 • Hepworth Cecil M. • UKN
SWEET LAVENDER • 1920 • Powell Paul • USA
SWEET LIBERTY • 1908 • Collins Alf? • UKN
SWEET LIBERTY • 1986 • Alda Alan • USA
SWEET LIES • 1987 • Delon Nathalie • FRN, USA
SWEET LIES AND TENDER OATHS see **DOUX AVEUX, LES** • 1982
SWEET LIFE, THE see **DOLCE VITA, LA** • 1959
SWEET LIGHT IN A DARK ROOM see **ROMEO, JULIE A TMA** • 1960
SWEET LIGHT IN THE DARK WINDOW see **ROMEO, JULIE A TMA** • 1960
SWEET LITTLE ROCK AND ROLLER • 1987 • Freeman Joan • USA • SATISFACTION
SWEET LORRAINE • 1987 • Gomer Steve • USA
SWEET LOVE • 1972 • Cemano Eduardo • USA
SWEET LOVE, BITTER • 1967 • Danska Herbert • USA • IT WON'T RUB OFF, BABY! ○ BLACK LOVE -WHITE LOVE ○ NIGHT SONG
SWEET LOVE REMEMBERED • 1980 • Elder Bruce • CND
SWEET MAMA • 1930 • Cline Eddie • USA • CONFLICT (UKN)
SWEET MEMORIES • 1911 • Ince Thomas H. • USA
SWEET MEMORIES • 1952 • Barclay David • SHT • USA
SWEET MOVIE • 1974 • Makavejev Dusan • FRN, CND, FRG
SWEET MURDER • 1989 • Rubens Percival • SAF
SWEET MUSIC • 1935 • Green Alfred E. • USA
SWEET NELL OF OLD DRURY • 1911 • Longford Raymond • ASL
SWEET NOVEMBER • 1968 • Miller Robert Ellis • USA
SWEET PATOOTIE • 1920 • Lyons Eddie, Moran Lee • SHT • USA
SWEET PICKLE, A • 1925 • Cline Eddie • SHT • USA
SWEET RACKET see **JUST LIKE A WOMAN** • 1938
SWEET REVENGE • 1909 • Griffith D. W. • USA
SWEET REVENGE • 1913 • *Beery Wallace* • USA
SWEET REVENGE • 1984 • Greene David • TVM • USA
SWEET REVENGE • 1987 • Sobel Mark • USA
SWEET REVENGE • 1987 • Young Terence • USA • RUN FOR YOUR LIFE
SWEET REVENGE see **DANDY, THE ALL-AMERICAN GIRL** • 1977
SWEET REVENGE (USA) see **EDES A BOSSZU** • 1938
SWEET RIDE, THE • 1968 • Hart Harvey • USA
SWEET ROSIE O'GRADY • 1926 • Strayer Frank • USA
SWEET ROSIE O'GRADY • 1943 • Cummings Irving • USA
SWEET SAVAGE • 1979 • Perry Ann • USA • SWEET SAVAGE: BAD GIRL OF THE WEST
SWEET SAVAGE: BAD GIRL OF THE WEST see **SWEET SAVAGE** • 1979
SWEET SAVIOUR • 1971 • Roberts Bob • USA
SWEET SCENT OF DEATH, THE • 1984 • Sasdy Peter • UKN
SWEET SECRET see **AMAI HIMITSU** • 1971
SWEET SERENADE • 1950 • Cowan Will • SHT • USA
SWEET SEVENTEEN see **SUSAN ROCKS THE BOAT** • 1916
SWEET SEVENTEEN see **SNART 17** • 1984
SWEET SEXUAL AWAKENING • *Constant Maria* • GRC • JANE'S SEXUAL AWAKENING
SWEET SICKNESS, A • 1968 • Martin Jon • USA
SWEET SING • 1944 • Berne Josef • SHT • USA
SWEET SINS OF SEXY SUSAN, THE (UKN) see **SUSANNE -DIE WIRTIN VON DER LAHN** • 1967
SWEET SIOUX • 1937 • Freleng Friz • ANS • USA
SWEET SIXTEEN • 1928 • Pembroke Scott • USA
SWEET SIXTEEN see **FREDDIE STEPS OUT** • 1946
SWEET SIXTEEN see **MONIKA: DIE SECHZEHNJAEHRIGEN** • 1975
SWEET SIXTEEN see **SWEET 16** • 1981
SWEET SIXTEEN (UKN) see **FUTURES VEDETTES** • 1955
SWEET SKIN (USA) see **STRIP-TEASE** • 1963
SWEET SMELL OF LOVE see **SWEET SMELL OF SEX, THE** • 1965
SWEET SMELL OF LOVE (USA) see **VERGINE PER UN BASTARDO** • 1966
SWEET SMELL OF PERFUME see **SWEET SMELL OF SEX, THE** • 1965
SWEET SMELL OF SEX, THE • 1965 • Downey Robert • USA • SWEET SMELL OF PERFUME ○ SWEET SMELL OF LOVE
SWEET SMELL OF SUCCESS, THE • 1957 • Mackendrick Alexander • USA
SWEET SOUND OF DEATH • 1965 • Seto Javier • SPN, USA
SWEET SOUNDS • 1976 • Ivory James • USA
SWEET SOUNDS • 1976 • Robbins Richard • USA
SWEET SPIRITS OF THE NIGHTER • *Brendel El* • SHT • USA
SWEET SUBSTITUTE • 1964 • Kent Larry • CND • CARESSED
SWEET SUFFRAGETTES • 1906 • Green Tom? • UKN
SWEET SUGAR • 1972 • Levesque Michel • USA • CHAINGANG GIRLS
SWEET SURRENDER • 1935 • Brice Monte • USA
SWEET SUZY see **BLACKSNAKE!** • 1973
SWEET SWEAT see **AMAI ASE** • 1964
SWEET, SWEET RACHEL • 1971 • Roley Sutton • TVM • USA
SWEET SWEETBACK'S BAADASSSSS SONG • 1971 • Van Peebles Melvin • USA
SWEET TASTE OF JOY • 1970 • Walsh C. • USA
SWEET TIME OF KALIMAGDORA, THE see **SUSSE ZEIT MIT KALIMAGDORA, DIE** • 1968
SWEET TO BE KISSED HARD TO DIE see **NOTTE CHE EVELYN USCI DALLA TOMBA, LA** • 1971
SWEET-TOOTHED BUDULINEK • Zykmund V., Vesela A. • ANM • CZC
SWEET TORONTO • 1972 • Pennebaker D. A. • USA • KEEP ON ROCKIN'
SWEET TORTURE see **AVEUX LES PLUS DOUX, LES** • 1970
SWEET TRAP, THE • 1963 • Wakamatsu Koji • JPN
SWEET TRASH • 1970 • Hayes John • USA
SWEET VENGEANCE • 1970 • Chaudhri Amin • USA
SWEET VIOLENCE see **DOUCE VIOLENCE** • 1962
SWEET VIRGIN see **GOT IT MADE** • 1973
SWEET-VOICED MAN, A see **MARD-E-HANJARE-TALAEI** • 1968
SWEET WILLIAM • 1980 • Whatham Claude • UKN
SWEET WORRIES see **SLADKE STAROSTI** • 1985
SWEETER SONG, A • 1976 • Eastman Allan • CND • SNAPSHOT ○ SNAPSHOTS
SWEETER THE REVENGE • 1915 • Winter Percy • USA
SWEETHEART see **HEUT TANZT MARRIETT** • 1928
SWEETHEART see **SUDU SUDA** • 1968
SWEETHEART, THE see **KOIBITO** • 1951
SWEETHEART DAYS • 1914 • *Imp* • USA
SWEETHEART DAYS • 1921 • St. Clair Malcolm • SHT • USA
SWEETHEART IN MASK see **MASKOVANA MILENKA** • 1940
SWEETHEART OF SIGMA CHI • 1946 • Bernhard Jack • USA
SWEETHEART OF SIGMA CHI, THE • 1933 • Marin Edwin L. • USA • GIRL OF MY DREAMS (UKN)
SWEETHEART OF THE CAMPUS • 1941 • Dmytryk Edward • USA • BROADWAY AHEAD (UKN) ○ BETTY CO-ED
SWEETHEART OF THE DOOMED • 1917 • Barker Reginald • USA
SWEETHEART OF THE FLEET • 1942 • Barton Charles T. • USA
SWEETHEART OF THE GODS (USA) see **LIEBLING DER GOTTER** • 1960
SWEETHEART OF THE NAVY • 1937 • Mansfield Duncan • USA
SWEETHEART SERENADE • 1943 • Negulesco Jean • SHT • USA
SWEETHEARTS • 1938 • Van Dyke W. S. • USA
SWEETHEARTS • 1989 • Talbot Colin • ASL
SWEETHEARTS see **HOPE** • 1919
SWEETHEARTS see **V LYUBLENNYE** • 1970
SWEETHEARTS see **SCHATJES** • 1983
SWEETHEARTS see **PERFECT TIMING** • 1984
SWEETHEARTS AND WIVES • 1930 • Badger Clarence • USA
SWEETHEARTS FOR EVER • 1945 • Richardson Frank • UKN
SWEETHEARTS OF THE U.S.A. • 1944 • Collins Lewis D. • USA • SWEETHEARTS ON PARADE (UKN)
SWEETHEARTS ON PARADE • 1929 • Aylott Dave, Symmons E. F. • SHT • UKN
SWEETHEARTS ON PARADE • 1930 • Neilan Marshall • USA
SWEETHEARTS ON PARADE • 1953 • Dwan Allan • USA
SWEETHEARTS ON PARADE (UKN) see **SWEETHEARTS OF THE U.S.A.** • 1944
SWEETIE • 1923 • Goulding Alf • USA
SWEETIE • 1929 • Tuttle Frank • USA
SWEETIE • 1989 • Campion Jane • NZL, ASL
SWEETKILL see **AROUSERS, THE** • 1971
SWEETNESS OF REVENGE, THE see **PLACER DE LA VENGANZA, EL** • 1987
SWEETNESS OF SIN, THE see **TURM DER VERBOTENEN LIEBE, DER** • 1968
SWEETS • 1970 • USA
SWEETS FOR THE SWEET • 1903 • *Bitzer Billy (Ph)* • USA
SWEETS FROM A STRANGER see **CARAMELLE DA UNO SCONOCIUTO** • 1987
SWEETS OF THE SOUR • 1918 • Baker Graham • SHT • USA
SWEETS TO THE SWEET • 1906 • *Cricks & Sharp* • UKN
SWEETWATER • 1986 • Glomm Lasse • NRW
SWELL GUY • 1946 • Tuttle Frank • USA
SWELL-HEAD, THE • 1927 • Graves Ralph • USA • BIG IDEAS
SWELLED HEAD, A see **HOMME A LA TETE EN CAOUTCHOUC, L'** • 1902
SWELLHEAD • 1935 • Stoloff Ben • USA
SWELLHEAD, THE • 1930 • Flood James • USA • COUNTED OUT (UKN)
SWELLING RIVER, THE see **PERROI VERSHUES** • 1984
SWELLS, THE • 1902 • *Paul R. W.* • UKN
SWELL'S INTERRUPTED NAP, THE • 1903 • *Paul R. W.* • UKN

SWEPT AWAY.. BY AN UNUSUAL DESTINY IN THE BLUE SEA OF AUGUST see **TRAVOLTI DA UN INSOLITO DESTINO NELL'AZZURRO MARE DI AGOSTO** • 1974
SWEPT AWAY.. (USA) see **TRAVOLTI DA UN INSOLITO DESTINO NELL'AZZURRO MARE DI AGOSTO** • 1974
SWIAT BEZ GRANIC • 1931 • Ordynski Ryszard • PLN
SWIAT GROZY • 1968 • Lesiewicz Witold, Petelski Czeslaw, Petelska Ewa • PLN • WORLD OF HORROR
SWIAT ZABITY DESKAMI • 1962 • Stando Robert • PLN • GODFORSAKEN HOLE
SWIATDECTWO URODZENIA • 1961 • Rozewicz Stanislaw • PLN • BIRTH CERTIFICATE, THE
SWIATYNIA MARIACKA • 1961 • Bochenek Zbigniew • PLN • NOTRE DAME OF CRACOW
SWIETO ODRODZENIA: TRASA W-Z OTWARTA! • 1949 • Bossak Jerzy • DOC • PLN • NATIONAL REBIRTH DAY: THE OPENING OF THE W-Z ROUTE
SWIFT LOVER, A (UKN) see **GUN LAW** • 1929
SWIFT SHADOW, THE • 1927 • Storm Jerome • USA
SWIFT VENGEANCE (UKN) see **ROOKIE COP, THE** • 1939
SWIFT WATER • 1952 • Thompson Tony • UKN
SWIFTWIND'S HEROISM • 1912 • *Pathe* • USA
SWIFTY • 1936 • James Alan • USA
SWILIN' RACKET, THE • 1928 • Frissell Varick • DOC • CND • GREAT ARCTIC SEAL HUNT ○ SEAL HUNTING IN THE ARCTIC
SWIM, GIRL, SWIM • 1927 • Badger Clarence • USA
SWIM OR SINK • 1932 • Fleischer Dave • ANS • USA
SWIM PRINCESS, THE • 1928 • Capra Frank • USA
SWIM TEAM see **SWIMTEAM** • 1979
SWIMMER, THE • 1968 • Perry Frank, Pollack Sydney (U/c) • USA
SWIMMER, THE see **PLOVEC** • 1981
SWIMMER TAKE ALL • 1952 • Kneitel Seymour • ANS • USA
SWIMMER'S TALE, THE • 1985 • Stassinos Stratos, Mirmiridis Nassos • ANS • GRC
SWIMMING CLASS • 1904 • *Bitzer Billy (Ph)* • USA
SWIMMING IN WINTER • 1989 • Kasebi Mohammad • IRN
SWIMMING PARTY, THE • 1912 • *Kalem* • USA
SWIMMING POOL, THE • 1975 • Zheljazkova Binka • USS
SWIMMING POOL, THE (USA) see **PISCINE, LA** • 1969
SWIMMING TO CAMBODIA • 1987 • Demme Jonathan • USA
SWIMMY • 1968 • Patel Ishu • ANS • IND
SWIMTEAM • 1979 • Polakoff James • USA • SWIM TEAM
SWINDLE, THE(USA) see **BIDONE, IL** • 1955
SWINDLER, THE • 1915 • Buel Kenean • USA
SWINDLER, THE • 1919 • Elvey Maurice • UKN
SWINDLER, THE see **BEDA WA ELHAGAR, EL** • 1989
SWINDLER MEETS SWINDLER see **TANUKI NO KYUJITSU** • 1967
SWINDLERS, THE • 1914 • *Majestic* • USA
SWINDLERS, THE (UKN) see **BIDONE, IL** • 1955
SWINEHERD, THE • 1957 • Tyrlova Hermina • ANS • CZC
SWINEHERD AND SHEPHERD see **SVINYARKA I PASTUKH** • 1941
SWINEHERD AND THE SHEPHERD, THE see **SVINYARKA I PASTUKH** • 1941
SWING • 1936 • Micheaux Oscar • USA
SWING • 1938 • Hopwood R. A. • UKN
SWING, THE • 1964 • Washburn Richard, Washburn Gladys • SHT • USA
SWING, THE see **SCHAUKEL, DIE** • 1983
SWING ABOARD THE MARY • 1965 • Winter Donovan • DCS • UKN
SWING AND SWAY (UKN) see **SWING IN THE SADDLE** • 1944
SWING AND THE SEESAW, THE • 1906 • *Cricks & Sharp* • UKN
SWING BANDITRY • 1936 • Le Borg Reginald • SHT • USA
SWING CATS JAMBOREE • 1938 • Mack Roy • SHT • USA
SWING CLEANING • 1941 • Fleischer Dave • ANS • USA
SWING, COWBOY, SWING • 1944 • Clifton Elmer • USA • BAD MAN FROM BIG BEND
SWING DING AMIGO • 1966 • McKimson Robert • ANS • USA
SWING FEVER • 1937 • Yarbrough Jean • SHT • USA
SWING FEVER • 1943 • Whelan Tim • USA • RIGHT ABOUT FACE
SWING FROLIC • 1942 • Ceballos Larry • SHT • USA
SWING FROLIC • 1943 • Le Borg Reginald • SHT • USA
SWING HIGH • 1930 • Santley Joseph • USA
SWING HIGH • 1932 • Cummings Jack • SHT • USA
SWING HIGH, SWING LOW • 1937 • Leisen Mitchell • USA
SWING HIGH, SWING SWEET • 1945 • Collins Lewis D. • SHT • USA
SWING HIGH (UKN) see **JIVE JUNCTION** • 1943
SWING HOSTESS • 1944 • Newfield Sam • USA
SWING HOTEL • 1939 • Staub Ralph • SHT • USA
SWING I HJARTER see **MELODI OM VAREN, EN** • 1943
SWING IN THE SADDLE • 1944 • Landers Lew • USA • SWING AND SWAY (UKN)
SWING IT! • 1936 • Goodwins Leslie • SHT • USA
SWING IT, BUDDY (UKN) see **SWING IT PROFESSOR** • 1937
SWING IT, FROKEN! • 1956 • Olin Stig • SWD • SWING IT, MISS!
SWING IT, MAGISTERN • 1940 • Bauman Schamyl • SWD • SWING IT SIR!
SWING IT, MISS! see **SWING IT, FROKEN!** • 1956
SWING IT PROFESSOR • 1937 • Neilan Marshall • USA • SWING IT, BUDDY (UKN)
SWING IT SAILOR • 1938 • Cannon Raymond • USA
SWING IT SIR! see **SWING IT, MAGISTERN** • 1940
SWING IT SOLDIER • 1941 • Young Harold • USA • RADIO REVELS OF 1942 (UKN)
SWING MONKEY SWING • 1937 • *Mintz Charles (P)* • ANS • USA
SWING OUT, SISTER • 1945 • Lilley Edward • USA
SWING OUT THE BLUES see **SWINGOUT THE BLUES** • 1943
SWING PARADE OF 1946 • 1946 • Karlson Phil • USA
SWING SANITARIUM • 1939 • Schwarzwald Milton • SHT • USA
SWING SCHOOL • 1938 • Fleischer Dave • ANS • USA
SWING SERENADE • 1944 • Wilmot Robert • SHT • USA
SWING SHIFT • 1983 • Demme Jonathan • USA • SWINGSHIFT
SWING SHIFT CINDERELLA • 1945 • Avery Tex • ANS • USA
SWING SHIFT MAISIE • 1943 • McLeod Norman Z. • USA • GIRL IN OVERALLS, THE (UKN)
SWING, SISTER, SWING • 1938 • Santley Joseph • USA
SWING SOCIAL • 1940 • Hanna William, Barbera Joseph • ANS • USA
SWING SONG FROM "VERONIQUE" • 1906 • Gilbert Arthur • UKN
SWING SONG FROM "VERONIQUE" • 1907 • *Walturdaw* • UKN
SWING SPAN • 1985 • Pacheco Bruno-Lazaro • MTV • CND
SWING STREET see **MAKE MINE MUSIC** • 1945
SWING STYLES • 1939 • French Lloyd • SHT • USA
SWING SYMPHONY • 1941-46 • *Lantz Walter (P)* • ASS • USA
SWING, TEACHER, SWING (UKN) see **COLLEGE SWING** • 1938
SWING TEASE see **SING AS YOU SWING** • 1937
SWING THAT BAND • 1943 • Dreifuss Arthur • SHT • USA
SWING THAT CHEER • 1938 • Schuster Harold • USA
SWING THE WESTERN WAY • 1947 • Abrahams Derwin • USA • SCHEMER, THE (UKN)
SWING TIME • 1936 • Stevens George • USA
SWING VACATION • 1939 • Yarbrough Jean • SHT • USA
SWING WEDDING • 1937 • Harman Hugh • ANS • USA • MINNIE THE MOOCHER'S WEDDING DAY
SWING WITH BING • 1940 • Pelesie Herbert • SHT • USA
SWING YOU SINNER • 1930 • Fleischer Dave • ANS • USA
SWING, YOU SWINGERS • 1939 • White Jules • SHT • USA
SWING YOUR LADY • 1938 • Enright Ray • USA
SWING YOUR PARTNER • 1943 • Lovy Alex • ANS • USA
SWING YOUR PARTNER • 1943 • McDonald Frank • USA
SWING YOUR PARTNERS • 1918 • Roach Hal • SHT • USA
SWINGER, THE • 1966 • Sidney George • USA
SWINGER'S PARADISE see **WONDERFUL LIFE** • 1964
SWINGIN' AFFAIR, A • 1963 • Lawrence Jay O. • USA
SWINGIN' ALONG • 1962 • Barton Charles T. • USA • DOUBLE TROUBLE ○ SCHNOOK, THE
SWINGIN' AND SINGIN' • 1957 • Cowan Will • SHT • USA
SWINGIN' DOWN THE SCALE • 1946 • Cowan Will • SHT • USA
SWINGIN' IN THE BARN • 1940 • Ceballos Larry • SHT • USA
SWINGIN' IN THE GROOVE • 1960 • Shear Barry • USA
SWINGIN' MAIDEN, THE (USA) see **IRON MAIDEN, THE** • 1962
SWINGIN' ON A RAINBOW • 1945 • Beaudine William • USA
SWINGIN' SET, THE see **GET YOURSELF A COLLEGE GIRL** • 1964
SWINGIN' SINGIN' YEARS, THE • 1960 • Shear Barry • USA
SWINGIN' STEWARDESSES see **STEWARDESSEN, DIE** • 1972
SWINGIN' SUMMER, A • 1965 • Sparr Robert • USA
SWINGIN' SWAPPERS • 1969 • Brand Rex • USA • SWINGING SWAPPERS
SWINGING AT THE CASTLE see **DET SVANGER PA SLOTTET** • 1959
SWINGING BARMAIDS, THE • 1975 • Trikonis Gus • USA • EAGER BEAVERS
SWINGING CHEERLEADERS, THE • 1974 • Hill Jack • USA
SWINGING DOORS, THE • 1915 • MacQuarrie Murdock • USA
SWINGING FINK, THE see **RAT FINK** • 1965
SWINGING JET-AGE • 1968 • Rowe George • PHL
SWINGING LONDON see **PRIMITIVE LONDON** • 1965
SWINGING LONDON EXPOSE see **PRIMITIVE LONDON** • 1965
SWINGING LONDON EXPOSED see **PRIMITIVE LONDON** • 1965
SWINGING PEARL MYSTERY, THE (UKN) see **PLOT THICKENS, THE** • 1936
SWINGING SECRETARY see **OFFICE LOVE-IN, WHITE COLLAR STYLE** • 1968
SWINGING STEWARDESSES, THE (UKN) see **STEWARDESSEN, DIE** • 1972
SWINGING SWAPPERS see **SWINGIN' SWAPPERS** • 1969
SWINGING THE LAMBETH WALK • 1940 • Lye Len • ANS • UKN
SWINGING THE LEAD • 1935 • MacKane David • UKN
SWINGING U.K. • 1964 • Gilpin Frank • UKN • GO GO BIG BEAT (USA)
SWINGING WIVES (UKN) see **NEUE HEISSE REPORT -WAS MANNER NICHT FUR MOGLICH HALTEN, DER** • 1971
SWINGMEN IN EUROPE • 1977 • Mazeas Jean • DOC • FRN
SWINGONOMETRY • 1943 • Shepherd Horace • UKN
SWINGOUT THE BLUES • 1943 • St. Clair Malcolm • USA • SWING OUT THE BLUES
SWING'S THE THING • 1942 • Le Borg Reginald • SHT • USA
SWINGSHIFT see **SWING SHIFT** • 1983
SWINGTAIL • 1969 • Shane Dave • USA
SWINGTIME BLUES • 1942 • Le Borg Reginald • SHT • USA
SWINGTIME HOLIDAY • 1944 • Ceballos Larry • SHT • USA
SWINGTIME IN MEXICO • 1952 • Segura Juan Jose • SHT • USA
SWINGTIME JOHNNY • 1943 • Cline Eddie • USA
SWINKA • 1990 • Magowski Krzysztof • PLN • PIG'S GATE
SWIRL OF GLORY see **SUGARFOOT** • 1951
SWISS ARMY KNIFE WITH RATS AND PIGEONS • 1981 • Breer Robert • USA
SWISS BANK ACCOUNT • 1975 • Anderson Robert** • USA
SWISS CHEESE • 1930 • *Terry Paul/ Moser Frank (P)* • ANS • USA
SWISS CHEEZE FAMILY ROBINSON • 1947 • Davis Mannie • ANS • USA
SWISS CONSPIRACY, THE • 1975 • Arnold Jack • USA, FRG • PER SALDO MORD
SWISS FAMILY ROBINSON • 1940 • Ludwig Edward • USA
SWISS FAMILY ROBINSON • 1961 • Annakin Ken • UKN, USA
SWISS FAMILY ROBINSON • 1975 • Harris Harry • TVM • USA
SWISS GUIDE, THE • 1910 • *Edison* • USA
SWISS HONEYMOON • 1947 • Sikorsky Jan, James Henry C. • UKN
SWISS MADE • 1969 • Yersin Yves, Maeder Fritz, Murer Fredi M. • SWT
SWISS MISS • 1938 • Blystone John G. • USA
SWISS MISS, A • 1951 • Davis Mannie • ANS • USA
SWISS MISS-FIT • 1957 • Lovy Alex • ANS • USA
SWISS MOVEMENT • 1931 • *Mintz Charles (P)* • ANS • USA
SWISS SEA DOG, THE • 1916 • *Falstaff* • USA
SWISS SKI YODELERS • 1940 • Donnelly Eddie • ANS • USA
SWISS TEASE • 1947 • Marcus Sid • ANS • USA
SWISS TOUR see **FOUR DAYS LEAVE** • 1950
SWISS TRICK, A • 1931 • Foster John, Stallings George • ANS • USA
SWISS TRIP • 1934 • Fischinger Oskar • ANS • FRG • RIVERS AND LANDSCAPES
SWISSMAKERS, THE see **SCHWEIZERMACHER, DIE** • 1979
SWIT PAZDZIERNIKA • 1958 • Perski Ludwik • DOC • PLN • DAWN OF OCTOBER, THE
SWITCH • 1975 • Day Robert • TVM • USA
SWITCH • 1979 • Colizzi Giuseppe • ITL
SWITCH, THE • 1963 • Maxwell Peter • UKN
SWITCH, THE • 1974 • Sarno Joe • USA
SWITCH, THE see **PERSUADERS: THE SWITCH, THE** • 1972
SWITCH HITTERS • *Donovan Stacey* • USA
SWITCH IN TIME, A • 1988 • Donovan Paul • USA
SWITCH ON • 1967 • Schepisi Fred • DOC • ASL
SWITCH-TOWER, THE • 1913 • O'Sullivan Tony, Griffith D. W.? • USA
SWITCHBACK RAILWAY, THE • 1898 • Paul Robert William • UKN
SWITCHBLADE SISTERS see **JEZEBELS, THE** • 1975
SWITCHBOARD OPERATOR, THE (UKN) see **LJUBAVNI SLUCAJ ILI TRAGEDIJA SLUZBENICE P.T.T.** • 1967
SWITCHEROO! • 1969 • Donne John • USA
SWITCHES AND SWEETIES • 1919 • Smith Noel • SHT • USA
SWITCHIN' KITTEN • 1961 • Deitch Gene • ANS • USA
SWITCHING CHANNELS • 1988 • Kotcheff Ted • USA
SWITCHMAN'S TOWER, THE • 1911 • *Prior Herbert* • USA
SWITZERLAND • 1955 • Sharpsteen Ben • DOC • USA
SWITZERLAND AND THE ALPS • 1967 • De La Varre Andre Jr. • DOC • USA
SWITZERLAND AND THE SILVER SCREEN see **SCHWEIZER FILM, DER** • 1989
SWOONER CROONER, THE • 1944 • Tashlin Frank • ANS • USA
SWOONERS, THE • 1916 • Drew Sidney • SHT • USA
SWOONING THE SWOONERS • 1945 • Rasinski Connie • ANS • USA
SWORD, THE • 1971 • Pan Lei, Wang Yu • HKG
SWORD, THE see **KEN** • 1964
SWORD, THE see **KARD, A** • 1977
SWORD, THE see **MING CHIEN** • 1980
SWORD, THE (UKN) see **MEITO BIJOMARU** • 1945
SWORD AND DICE see **KARD ES KOCKA** • 1959
SWORD AND LOVE see **KEN WA SHITTEITA** • 1958
SWORD AND THE CROSS, THE see **SCHIAVE DI CARTAGINE, LE** • 1956
SWORD AND THE CROSS, THE (USA) see **SPADA E LA CROCE, LA** • 1959
SWORD AND THE DRAGON, THE(USA) see **ILYA MUROMETS** • 1956
SWORD AND THE FLUTE, THE • 1959 • Ivory James • SHT • USA
SWORD AND THE GEISHA, THE • 1971 • Leigh Malcolm • DCS • UKN
SWORD AND THE KING, THE • 1909 • *Vitagraph* • USA
SWORD AND THE ROSE, THE • 1953 • Annakin Ken • UKN • WHEN KNIGHTHOOD WAS IN FLOWER
SWORD AND THE SORCERER, THE • 1982 • Pyun Albert • USA
SWORD AND THE SUMO RING, A see **IPPON GATANA DOHYOIRI** • 1931
SWORD AND THE SUMO RING, A see **IPPON GATANA DOHYOIRI** • 1934
SWORD AND THE SUMO RING, A see **IPPON GATANA DOHYOIRI** • 1960
SWORD FOR HIRE see **SENGOKU BURAI** • 1952
SWORD GAMBLERS see **TEKKA NO HANAMICHI** • 1968
SWORD IN THE DESERT • 1949 • Sherman George • USA
SWORD IN THE STONE, THE • 1963 • Reitherman Wolfgang • ANM • USA
SWORD OF ALI BABA, THE • 1965 • Vogel Virgil W. • USA
SWORD OF DAMASCUS (USA) see **LADRO DI DAMASCO, IL** • 1963
SWORD OF DAMOCLES, THE • 1914 • *Woodruff Elanor* • USA
SWORD OF DAMOCLES, THE • 1916 • *Pathe* • SHT • USA
SWORD OF DAMOCLES, THE • 1920 • Ridgwell George • UKN
SWORD OF D'ARTAGNAN • 1951 • Boetticher Budd • USA
SWORD OF EL CID, THE (USA) see **SPADA DEL CID, LA** • 1962
SWORD OF ENCHANTMENT, THE see **ZANJIN ZANBA KEN** • 1929
SWORD OF FATE, THE • 1921 • Grant Frances E. • UKN
SWORD OF FLYING DRAGON see **HIRYU NO KEN** • 1937
SWORD OF GIDEON, THE • 1986 • Anderson Michael • UKN, CND • ELEVENTH COMMANDMENT, THE ○ MUNCHEN STRIKE
SWORD OF GRANADA, THE (USA) see **CORAZON Y LA ESPADA, EL** • 1953
SWORD OF HEAVEN • 1985 • Meyers Byron • USA
SWORD OF HONOUR • 1939 • Elvey Maurice • UKN
SWORD OF HONOUR • 1986 • Amenta Pino, Millar Catherine • MTV • ASL
SWORD OF ISLAM • 1962 • Marton Andrew • ITL
SWORD OF JUSTICE • 1978 • Haller Daniel • TVM • USA
SWORD OF JUSTICE, PART II • 1975 • Masumura Yasuzo • JPN
SWORD OF LANCELOT see **LANCELOT AND GUINEVERE** • 1962
SWORD OF MONTE CRISTO, THE • 1951 • Geraughty Maurice • USA
SWORD OF PENITENCE see **ZANGE NO YAIBA** • 1927
SWORD OF SHERWOOD FOREST • 1960 • Fisher Terence • UKN
SWORD OF THE AVENGER • 1948 • Salkow Sidney • USA
SWORD OF THE BARBARIANS see **SPADE DEI BARBARI, LE** • 1983
SWORD OF THE CHILD see **CHIGO NO KEMPO** • 1927
SWORD OF THE CONQUEROR (USA) see **ROSMUNDA E ALBOINO** • 1961
SWORD OF THE EMPIRE (USA) see **SPADA PER L'IMPERO, UNA** • 1965
SWORD OF THE LORD, THE • 1976 • Walker Giles • MTV • CND
SWORD OF THE SPACE ARK • 1977 • JPN
SWORD OF THE VALIANT • 1983 • Weeks Stephen • UKN
SWORD OF VALOR, THE • 1924 • Worne Duke • USA
SWORD OF VENGEANCE • Misumi Kenji • JPN

SWORD OF VENGEANCE III see **KOZURE OHKAMI** • 1973

SWORD OF VENUS • 1952 • Daniels Harold • USA • ISLAND OF MONTE CRISTO (UKN)

SWORD POINTS • 1928 • Sandrich Mark • SHT • USA

SWORD WITHOUT A COUNTRY (USA) see **SPADE SENZA BANDIERA** • 1961

SWORDKILL see **GHOST WARRIOR** • 1985

SWORDS AND HEARTS • 1911 • Griffith D. W. • USA

SWORDS AND PLOWSHARES see **SPIRIT OF THE U.S.A., THE** • 1924

SWORDS AND THE WOMAN (USA) see **I WILL REPAY** • 1923

SWORDS OF BLOOD (UKN) see **CARTOUCHE** • 1962

SWORDS OF DEATH see **SHINKEN SHOBU** • 1969

SWORDS OF MYSTERY see **BYAKKO NITORYU** • 1958

SWORDS OF WAYLAND, THE • 1983 • *Praed Michael* • MTV • UKN

SWORDSMAN see **SIU NGOU GONGWU** • 1990

SWORDSMAN, THE • 1947 • Lewis Joseph H. • USA

SWORDSMAN, THE • 1974 • Shonteff Lindsay • UKN

SWORDSMAN, THE (UKN) see **MIYAMOTO MUSASHI** • 1944

SWORDSMAN AND ENCHANTRESS see **HSIAO SHIH-YI LANG** • 1978

SWORDSMAN MATAEMON ARAKI see **KENGO ARAKI MATAEMON** • 1938

SWORDSMAN OF ALL SWORDSMAN see **I-TAI CHIEN-WANG** • 1969

SWORDSMAN OF SIENA (USA) see **MERCENAIRE, LE** • 1962

SWORDSMAN'S PICTURE BOOK, A see **EHON MUSHASHUGYO** • 1929

SWORN ENEMIES see **SMERTELNI VRAG** • 1971

SWORN ENEMY • 1936 • Marin Edwin L. • USA

SWORN TO SILENCE • 1987 • Levin Peter • USA

S/Y GLADJEN • 1990 • Du Rees Goran • SWD • S/Y JOY

S/Y JOY see **S/Y GLADJEN** • 1990

SYANHAI NO TSUKI • 1941 • *Tsuburaya Eiji* • JPN

SYBIL • 1921 • Denton Jack • UKN

SYBIL • 1976 • Petrie Daniel • TVM • USA

SYBIL see **DUCHESS OF BUFFALO, THE** • 1926

SYBIL JOUNG see **TANZ AUF DEM VULKAN 1, DER** • 1920

SYD AND HIS SWEETHEARTS • 1915 • *Ck* • USA

SYD, THE ATHLETE • 1915 • *Alhambra* • USA

SYD, THE BUM DETECTIVE • 1915 • *Alhambra* • USA

SYD, THE MASHER • 1915 • *De Gray Sydney* • USA

SYDENS BORN • 1911 • Gad Urban • DNM

SYDNEY BY DAY AND NIGHT see **LIVING SYDNEY** • 1914

SYDNEY COMMONWEALTH FESTIVITIES • 1901 • *Baker & Rouse (Ph)* • ASL

SYDNEY ON THE SPREE • 1909 • *Globe Pictures* • ASL • MOTOR BOAT PIRATES ON SYDNEY HARBOUR

SYDNEY SAILING CLUB'S 18-FOOTER CHAMPIONSHIP • 1903 • *Wyndham H. A. (Ph)* • ASL

SYDNEY WHEEL RACE • 1897 • ASL

SYDNEY'S JOUJOUX • 1900 • Blache Alice • SER • FRN

SYDNEY'S SHARP POINTS • 1912 • *Cosmopolitan* • UKN

SYDNEY'S SIRENS OF THE SURF • 1911 • Barrett Franklyn • DOC • ASL

SYD'S BUSY DAY • 1915 • *Alhambra* • USA

SYD'S FINISH • 1915 • *Alhambra* • USA

SYD'S LOVE AFFAIR • 1915 • *Ck* • USA

SYEM NOT V TISHINYE • 1967 • Aksyonov Vitali • DOC • USS • SEVEN NOTES BREAK THE SILENCE ○ SEVEN NOTES IN SILENCE

SYERDTSE DRUGA • 1967 • Grigorieva Renita, Grigoriev Yuri • USS • HEART OF A FRIEND

SYERDTSE.. SYERDTSE • 1977 • Kuliev Ye. • USS • HEART.. THE HEART, THE

SYGNALY • 1959 • Passendorfer Jerzy • PLN • SIGNALS, THE

SYKARIKIN, THE • 1970 • Binetzki Menahem • ISR

SYKLUS • 1977 • During Jan Erik • NRW

SYKSYLLA KAIKKI ON TOISIN • 1978 • Niskanen Mikko • FNL • IN THE AUTUMN ALL WILL BE DIFFERENT ○ IN THE FALL EVERYTHING IS DIFFERENT

SYLPHIDE, LA • 1961 • *Dale Margaret (P)* • MTV • UKN

SYLPHIDES, LES • 1958 • *Fokine Michel* • MTV • UKN

SYLVA • 1945 • Ivanovsky Alexander • USS

SYLVESTER • 1923 • Pick Lupu • FRG • NEW YEAR'S EVE

SYLVESTER • 1985 • Hunter Tim • USA

SYLVESTER see **SILVESTRE** • 1980

SYLVESTER SYNDROME see **VIADUKT** • 1983

SYLVESTERNACHT • 1977 • Sirk Douglas • FRG

SYLVESTERWETTE, DIE • 1919 • *Wessely Molly* • FRG

SYLVI • 1913 • *Puro Teuvo* • FNL

SYLVIA • 1965 • Douglas Gordon • USA

SYLVIA • 1985 • Firth Michael • NZL

SYLVIA • 1986 • Murray Michel • ANS • CND

SYLVIA AND THE GHOST (UKN) see **SYLVIE ET LE FANTOME** • 1946

SYLVIA GRAY • 1914 • Gaskill Charles L. • USA

SYLVIA KRISTEL'S DESIRES • 1987 • Blot Philippe • ARROGANT, THE

SYLVIA OF THE SECRET SERVICE • 1917 • Fitzmaurice George • USA

SYLVIA ON A SPREE • 1918 • Franklin Harry L. • USA

SYLVIA SCARLETT • 1936 • Cukor George • USA

SYLVIA UND IHR CHAUFFEUR see **WALZER UM DEN STEPHANSTURM, EIN** • 1935

SYLVIANE DE MES NUITS • 1956 • Blistene Marcel • FRN

SYLVIA'S GIRLS • 1965 • Dempsey Al • USA

SYLVIA'S LAST PLEDGE • 1918 • *Leslie Gladys* • SHT • USA

SYLVIE • 1973 • Lemke Klaus • FRG

SYLVIE AND THE PHANTOM (USA) see **SYLVIE ET LE FANTOME** • 1946

SYLVIE DESTIN • 1927 • Kirsanoff Dimitri • FRN • DESTINS

SYLVIE ET LE FANTOME • 1946 • Autant-Lara Claude • FRN • SYLVIE AND THE PHANTOM (USA) ○ SYLVIA AND THE GHOST (UKN)

SYLVIE LA PETITE INDIENNE • 1968 • Dansereau Jean • DCS • CND

SYLVIE'S ARK see **HOUSEKEEPING** • 1987

SYMBOL OF DECADENCE see **FRAGMENT OF SEEKING** • 1946

SYMBOL OF SACRIFICE • 1918 • SAF

SYMBOL OF THE UNCONQUERED • 1921 • Micheaux Oscar • USA • WILDERNESS TRAIL, THE

SYMBOLE HYDRO-QUEBEC • 1965 • Rivard Fernand • DCS • CND

SYMETRICS • 1971 • Vanderbeek Stan • ANS • USA • SYMMETRICKS

SYMI, THE ISLAND OF NIREUS • Kladakis F., Korres E. • GRC

SYMMETRICKS see **SYMETRICS** • 1971

SYMMETRY 1 • Stapp Philip • ANS • USA

SYMPATHETIQUE MONSIEUR BONIFACE, LE see **HEROIQUE MONSIEUR BONIFACE, L'** • 1949

SYMPATHY FOR THE DEVIL (UKN) see **ONE PLUS ONE** • 1968

SYMPATHY IN SUMMER • 1971 • Ginnane Anthony I. • ASL

SYMPATHY SAL • 1915 • *Reliance* • USA

SYMPHONIC POEM FABLE OF STANISLAS MONIUSZKO, THE see **POEMAT SYMFONICZNY "BAJKA" STANISLAWA MONIUSZKO** • 1952

SYMPHONIE D'AMOUR see **DISQUE 413, LE** • 1936

SYMPHONIE DER BERGE see **HEILIGEN DREI BRUNNEN, DIE** • 1930

SYMPHONIE DER LIEBE see **EKSTASE** • 1932

SYMPHONIE DES BRIGANDS, LA • 1936 • Feher Friedrich • FRN

SYMPHONIE DES GRAUENS, EINE see **NOSFERATU -EINE SYMPHONIE DES GRAUENS** • 1921

SYMPHONIE DIAGONALE • 1920 • Eggeling Viking • ANS • FRG • DIAGONAL SYMPHONY ○ DIAGONAL SINFONIE

SYMPHONIE EINES LEBENS • 1942 • Bertram Hans • FRG • SYMPHONY OF A LIFE

SYMPHONIE FANTASTIQUE, LA • 1941 • Christian-Jaque • FRN

SYMPHONIE FANTASTIQUE (LA MARCHE AU SUPPLICE HECTOR BERLIOZ), LA • 1987 • Simoneau Guy • SHT • CND

SYMPHONIE IN GOLD • 1956 • Antel Franz • AUS

SYMPHONIE INDUSTRIELLE see **PHILIPS RADIO** • 1931

SYMPHONIE MECANIQUE • 1955 • Mitry Jean • SHT • FRN

SYMPHONIE NR.3 IN ES-DUR, OPUS 55 "EROICA" VON LUDWIG VON BEETHOVEN • 1967 • Colpi Henri • SHT • FRN • BEETHOVEN 3RD SYMPHONY -EROICA (UKN)

SYMPHONIE NR.7 VON LUDWIG VON BEETHOVEN • 1966 • Colpi Henri • SHT • FRN

SYMPHONIE NR.9 VON FRANZ SCHUBERT • 1966 • Colpi Henri • SHT • FRN

SYMPHONIE OF LOVE • Ford Derek • UKN

SYMPHONIE PASSIONNEE see **PRELUDE A LA GLOIRE** • 1949

SYMPHONIE PASTORALE, LA • 1946 • Delannoy Jean • FRN • PASTORAL SYMPHONY

SYMPHONIE PASTORALE, LA see **DENEN KOKYOGAKU** • 1938

SYMPHONIE PAYSANNE • 1944 • Storck Henri • DOC • BLG

SYMPHONIE POUR UN HOMME SEUL • 1956 • Cuny Louis • FRN • SYMPHONY FOR A LONELY MAN

SYMPHONIE POUR UN MASSACRE • 1963 • Deray Jacques • FRN, ITL • SYMPHONY FOR A MASSACRE (USA) ○ SINFONIA PER UN MASSACRO (ITL) ○ CORRUPT, THE (UKN) ○ MYSTIFIERS, THE ○ MYSTIFIES, LES

SYMPHONIE SOUS LE SOLEIL • 1952 • Fehr-Lutz L. • SHT • FRN

SYMPHONIE WIEN • 1951 • Quendlinger Albert • AUS

SYMPHONY • 1969 • Cox Paul • SHT • ASL

SYMPHONY, THE • 1913 • *Rex* • USA

SYMPHONY, THE see **JAZZ MAD** • 1928

SYMPHONY FOR A LONELY MAN see **SYMPHONIE POUR UN HOMME SEUL** • 1956

SYMPHONY FOR A MASSACRE (USA) see **SYMPHONIE POUR UN MASSACRE** • 1963

SYMPHONY HOUR • 1942 • Thomson Riley • ANS • USA

SYMPHONY IN BLACK • 1934 • Waller Fred • SHT • USA

SYMPHONY IN BLACK AND WHITE, A • 1912 • *Eclair* • USA

SYMPHONY IN COAL, A • 1916 • Drew Sidney • SHT • USA

SYMPHONY IN SLANG • 1951 • Avery Tex • ANS • USA

SYMPHONY IN SOULS, A • 1914 • *Rex* • USA

SYMPHONY IN SPINACH • 1948 • Kneitel Seymour • ANS • USA

SYMPHONY IN STEEL • 1932 • Hurley Frank • DOC • ASL

SYMPHONY IN SWING • 1949 • Cowan Will • SHT • USA

SYMPHONY IN TWO FLATS • 1930 • Gundrey V. Gareth • UKN

SYMPHONY OF A CITY see **MANNISKOR I STAD** • 1946

SYMPHONY OF A LIFE see **SYMPHONIE EINES LEBENS** • 1942

SYMPHONY OF EVIL see **CODA** • 1987

SYMPHONY OF LIFE see **SKAZANIYE O ZEMLYE SIBIRSKOI** • 1947

SYMPHONY OF LIFE see **LLAN KI SHAOKAT** • 1954

SYMPHONY OF LIVING • 1935 • Strayer Frank • USA

SYMPHONY OF LOVE see **HARU KORO NO HANA NO EN** • 1958

SYMPHONY OF LOVE AND DEATH see **SIMFONIJA LJUBVI ISMERTI** • 1914

SYMPHONY OF SIX MILLION • 1932 • La Cava Gregory • USA • MELODY OF LIFE (UKN)

SYMPHONY OF SWING • 1939 • *Shaw Artie* • SHT • USA

SYMPHONY OF THE DON BASIN see **ENTUZIAZM** • 1931

SYMPHONY OF THE DONBAS see **ENTUZIAZM** • 1931

SYMPHONY OF THE METROPOLIS see **TOKAI KOKYOGAKU** • 1929

SYMPHONY OF THE STREETS see **GAMLA STAN** • 1931

SYMPHONY OF THE TROPICS see **FAJA LOBBI** • 1960

SYMPHONY ORCHESTRA, THE • 1964 • *Halas John (P)* • ANS • UKN

SYMPOSIUM • 1970 • Kollatos Dimitris • GRC, FRN

SYMPOSIUM ON POPULAR SONGS, A • 1962 • Justice Bill • ANS • USA

SYMPTOMS • 1974 • Larraz Jose R. • UKN, SPN • SINTOMAS (SPN) ○ BLOOD VIRGIN, THE ○ WHEN THE BOUGH BREAKS

SYN • 1955 • Ozerov Yury • USS • SON, THE

SYN • 1970 • Czekala Ryszard • ANM • PLN • SON, THE

SYN MONGOLII • 1936 • Trauberg Ilya • USS • SON OF MONGOLIA

SYNANON • 1965 • Quine Richard • USA • GET OFF MY BACK (UKN)

SYNAPSES • 1972 • Diop Mustapha • NGR

SYNCHROMIE see **SYNCHROMY** • 1971

SYNCHROMY • 1971 • McLaren Norman • ANS • CND • SYNCHROMIE

SYNCHROMY NO.2 • 1936 • Bute Mary Ellen, Nemeth Ted J. • ANS • USA

SYNCHRONIZATION • 1934 • Shillinger Joseph, Jacobs Lewis • ANS • USA

SYNCO-SMOOTH SWING • 1945 • Cowan Will • SHT • USA

SYNCOPATED MELODIES • 1927 • Edwards J. Steven • SHS • UKN

SYNCOPATED MELODY, THE • 1916 • *Unicorn* • USA

SYNCOPATED PICTURE PLAYS • 1923 • Phillips Bertram • SHS • UKN

SYNCOPATED SIOUX • 1940 • Lantz Walter • ANS • USA

SYNCOPATING SUE • 1926 • Wallace Richard • USA • BROADWAY BLUES ○ TIN PAN ALLEY

SYNCOPATION • 1929 • Glennon Bert • USA

SYNCOPATION • 1942 • Dieterle William • USA

SYNCOPE, LA • 1976 • Niermans Edouard • SHT • FRN

SYND • 1928 • Molander Gustaf • SWD • SIN

SYND • 1948 • Sjostrand Arnold • SWD • SIN

SYNDARE I FILMPARADISET • 1956 • Bernhard Gosta • SWD • SINNERS IN THE CINEMA PARADISE

SYNDENS DATTER • 1915 • Blom August • DNM • DEN, DER SEJRER ○ NOBODY'S DAUGHTER

SYNDICATE, THE • 1968 • Goode Frederic • UKN • KENYA - COUNTRY OF TREASURE

SYNDICATE, THE see **JEJAK BERTAPAK** • 1979

SYNDICATE SADISTS see **GIUSTIZIERE SFIDA LA CITTA, IL** • 1975

SYNDICATE VICE • 1980 • Adamson Al • USA • GIRLS' HOTEL

SYNDIG KAERLIGHED • 1915 • Blom August • DNM • EREMITTEN ○ HERMIT, THE

SYNDROME • 1968 • Carver Steve • USA

SYNI • 1946 • Ivanov Alexander • USS • ROAD HOME, THE ○ SONS, THE

SYNIKIA TO ONIRO • 1961 • Alexandrakis Alekos • GRC • QUARTIER LE REVE

SYNNOVE SOLBAKKEN • 1919 • Brunius John W. • SWD • FAIRY OF SOLBAKKEN (USA)

SYNNOVE SOLBAKKEN • 1934 • Ibsen Tancred • SWD

SYNNOVE SOLBAKKEN • 1957 • Hellstrom Gunnar • SWD

SYNONYMIE SYNTAXIQUE ET NUANCES DE LA LOGIQUE • 1972 • Lamothe Arthur • DCS • CND

SYNOWIE LUDU • 1954 • Perski Ludwik • DOC • PLN • SONS OF THE PEOPLE

SYNTHETIC SIN • 1929 • Seiter William A. • USA

SYNTHETIC SOUND EXPERIMENTS • 1932 • Fischinger Oskar • ANS • FRG

SYNTIPUKKI • 1935 • Karu Erkki • FNL • SCAPEGOAT, THE

SYNTYMAPAIVA • 1973 • Janikova-Pakaslathi Eva • SHT • FNL • BIRTHDAY

SYOKSYKIERRE • 1982 • Suominen Tapio • FNL • DOWNWARD SPIRAL ○ GUNPOINT

SYONEN HYORYUKI • 1943 • *Tsuburaya Eiji (Ph)* • JPN

SYPHILIS IN LABOUR see **OSAN TO BAIDOKU** • 1968

SYRIAN IMMIGRANT, THE • 1921 • *Haber Nicholas S.* • USA

SYRINX • 1963 • Chevreuille Pierre • BLG

SYRINX • 1965 • Larkin Ryan • ANS • CND

SYRUP see **SIRUP** • 1989

SYSKONBADD 1782 • 1965 • Sjoman Vilgot • SWD • MY SISTER, MY LOVE (UKN) ○ BED FOR BROTHER AND SISTER

SYSTEEMBOUW • 1966 • Groot Rens • NTH

SYSTEM • 1972 • Majewski Janusz • PLN

SYSTEM, THE • 1953 • Seiler Lewis • USA

SYSTEM, THE • 1963 • Winner Michael • UKN • GIRL-GETTERS, THE (USA)

SYSTEM DES DOKTOR THER UND PROFESSOR FEDER, DAS • 1920 • Oswald Richard • FRG

SYSTEM IS EVERYTHING • 1916 • *Drew Sidney* • USA

SYSTEM OF DR. TARR AND PROFESSOR FEATHER • 1972 • Moctezuma Juan Lopez • MXC • DR. TARR'S TORTURE DUNGEON (USA)

SYSTEME DE LA LANGUE FRANCAISE, LE • 1972 • Lamothe Arthur • SER • CND

SYSTEME DU DOCTEUR GOUDRON ET DU PROFESSEUR PLUME • Chabrol Claude • FRN

SYSTEME DU DOCTEUR GOUDRON ET DU PROFESSEUR PLUME, LE • 1909 • Saidreau Robert • FRN • LUNATICS, THE (USA) ○ DR. GOUDRON'S SYSTEM

SYSTEME DU DOCTEUR GOUDRON ET DU PROFESSEUR PLUME, LE • 1912 • Tourneur Maurice • FRN • LUNATICS, THE (USA)

SYSTEME DU DOCTEUR SOUFLAMORT, LE • 1905 • Melies Georges • FRN • LIFE SAVING UP-TO-DATE (USA)

SYSTEME G, LE • 1983 • Beaudry Michel • MTV • CND

SYSTEME METRIQUE, C'EST PAS SORCIER, LE • 1980 • Beaudry Michel • CND

SYSTRARNA • 1912 • Hoffman-Uddgren Anna • SWD • SISTERS

SYTTEN • 1965 • Meineche Annelise • DNM • ERIC SOYA'S "17" (USA) ○ SEVENTEEN

SYTTEN MINUTTER GRONLAND • 1967 • Roos Jorgen • SHT • DNM

SYUNEN NO HEBI • 1958 • Misumi Kenji • JPN

SYUZHET DLYA NEBOLSHOVO RASKAZA • 1968 • Yutkevich Sergei • USS, FRN • SIUZHET DLYA NEBLOSHOVO RASSKAZA ○ THEME FOR A SHORT STORY ○ SUBJECT FOR A SHORT STORY ○ LIKA, CHEKHOV'S LOVE ○ LIKA, LYUBOV CHEKHOVA ○ PLOT FOR A SHORT STORY, A

SZABAD LELEGZET • 1973 • Meszaros Marta • HNG • GOOD RIDDANCE ○ RIDDANCE ○ FREE BREATHING

SZABADITS MEG A GONOSZTOL • 1978 • Sandor Pal • HNG • DELIVER US FROM EVIL

SZABONE • 1949 • Mariassy Felix • HNG • ANNA SZABO

SZACHOWNICA • 1967 • Duraj Cseslaw • PLN

SZAK, A see **HOGY SZALADNAK FAK** • 1966

SZAKADEK • 1955 • Ranody Laszlo • HNG • ABYSS ○ DISCORD

SZALENCY • 1928 • Buczkowski Leonard • PLN • DEMENTED, THE ○ DAREDEVILS, THE

SZALONY MAJOR • 1972 • Poreba Bohdan • PLN • MAD MAJOR, THE

SZAMARBOR • 1918 • Curtiz Michael • HNG • DONKEY SKIN, THE

SZAMARKOHOGES • 1986 • Gardos Peter • HNG • WHOOPING COUGH
SZAMOK TORTENETE, A • 1962 • Macskassy Gyula, Varnai Gyorgy • ANS • HNG • HISTORY OF NUMBERS, THE ○ 1, 2, 3..
SZANSA • 1970 • Zebrowski Edward • PLN • CHANCE, A
SZANSA • 1980 • Falk Feliks • PLN • CHANCE, THE
SZAR ES A GYOKER FEJLODESE, A • 1961 • Meszaros Marta • DCS • HNG • DEVELOPMENT OF THE STALK AND THE ROOT, THE
SZARADA • 1977 • Komorowski Pawel • PLN • CHARADE
SZARLEJKA • 1955 • Lomnicki Jan • DOC • PLN
SZARNYAS UGYNOK, A • 1988 • Soth Sandor • HNG • PETER IN WONDERLAND
SZARVASSA VALT FIUK • 1974 • Gyongyossy Imre • HNG • SONGS OF FIRE, THE
SZCZESCIARZ ANTONI • 1961 • Haupe Wlodzimierz, Bielinska Halina • PLN • LUCKY TONY
SZCZESCIE ANTKA • 1937 • Bohdziewicz Antoni (c/d) • SHT • PLN • ANTEK'S LUCK
SZEDULES • 1989 • Szasz Janos • HNG • DON'T DISTURB!
SZEGENY DZSONI ES ARNIKA • 1984 • Solyom Andras • HNG • DUCK-AND-DRAKE ADVENTURE, A
SZEGENY GAZDAGOK • 1959 • Ban Frigyes • HNG • FATIA NEGRA
SZEGENYLEGENYEK (NEHEZELETUEK) • 1965 • Jancso Miklos • HNG • HOPELESS ONES, THE (USA) ○ ROUND-UP, THE ○ OUTLAWS ○ POOR OUTLAWS
SZELAM ALEIKUM • 1919 • Linke Edmund • FRG
SZELEBURDI CSALAD • 1982 • Palasthy Gyorgy • HNG • HARUM-SCARUM FAMILY, A
SZEMTOL-SZEMBE • 1970 • Varkonyi Zoltan • HNG • FACE TO FACE
SZEMUVEGESEK • 1969 • Simo Sandor • HNG • THROUGH SPECTACLES ○ BESPECTACLED, THE
SZENT PETER ESERNYOJE • 1917 • Korda Alexander • HNG • ST. PETER'S UMBRELLA
SZENT PETER ESERNYOJE • 1958 • Ban Frigyes • HNG, CZC
SZENTENDRE -TOWN OF PAINTERS see **FESTOK VAROSA - SZENTENDRE, A** • 1964
SZENTJOBI ERDO TITKA, A • 1917 • Curtiz Michael • HNG • SECRET OF ST. JOB FOREST, THE
SZENVEDELY • 1961 • Nepp Jozsef • HNG • PASSION
SZENZACIO • 1922 • Fejos Paul • HNG • QUEEN OF SPADES ○ PIQUE DAME ○ SENSATION
SZENZACIO • 1937 • Sekely Steve, Vajda Ladislao • HNG
SZEP LANYOK, NE SIRJATOK • 1970 • Meszaros Marta • HNG • DON'T CRY, PRETTY GIRLS
SZEP MAGYAR KOMEDIA • 1970 • Banovich Tamas • HNG • LOVELY HUNGARIAN COMEDY
SZEPEK ES BOLONDOK • 1977 • Szasz Peter • HNG • ON THE SIDELINES
SZEPLEANYOK • 1987 • Der Andras, Hartai Laszlo • DOC • HNG • PRETTY GIRLS
SZERELEM • 1970 • Makk Karoly • HNG • LOVE
SZERELEM ELSO VERIG • 1985 • Dobray Gyorgy, Horvath Peter • HNG • LOVE TILL FIRST BLOOD
SZERELEM HAROM EJSZAKAJA, EGY • 1967 • Revesz Gyorgy • HNG • THREE NIGHTS OF A LOVE ○ ONE LOVE IN THREE NIGHTS
SZERELEM MASODIK VERIG • 1988 • Dobray Gyorgy • HNG • LOVE TILL SECOND BLOOD
SZERELEMBOEL NOESUELTEM • 1938 • Sekely Steve • HNG • I MARRIED FOR LOVE ○ I'VE MARRIED FOR LOVE
SZERELMEM ELEKTRA • 1974 • Jancso Miklos • HNG • MY LOVE ELECTRA ○ ELEKTREIA ○ ELECTRA, MY LOVE ○ ELEKTRA
SZERELMES BICIK LISTAK • 1965 • Bacso Peter • HNG • CYCLISTS IN LOVE
SZERELMESFILM • 1970 • Szabo Istvan • HNG • FILM ABOUT LOVE, A ○ LOVE FILM
SZERELMI ALMOK • 1937 • Hille Heinz • FRG
SZERELMI ALMOK -LISZT • 1970 • Keleti Marton • HNG, USS • LOVES OF LISZT, THE
SZERENCSES DANIEL • 1983 • Sandor Pal • HNG • DANIEL TAKES A TRAIN
SZERESSETEK ODOR EMILIAT • 1970 • Sandor Pal • HNG • LOVE EMILIA!
SZERETET • 1963 • Meszaros Marta • SHT • HNG • CARE AND AFFECTION
SZERETOK • 1984 • Kovacs Andras • HNG • AFTERNOON AFFAIR, AN
SZERKEZETTERVEZES • 1960 • Jancso Miklos • SHT • HNG • CONSTRUCTION DESIGN
SZEROKA DROGA • 1949 • Gordon Konstanty • DOC • PLN • WIDE ROAD ○ BROAD HIGHWAY
SZERU TORTENET, EGY • 1975 • Elek Judit • HNG • SIMPLE STORY, A
SZESNASCIE MIEC LAT • 1969 • Piwowski Marek • DOC • PLN • TO BE SIXTEEN YEARS OLD
SZEVASZ, VERA • 1967 • Hersko Janos • HNG • HELLO, VERA
SZIGET A SZARAZFOLDON • 1968 • Elek Judit • HNG • LADY FROM CONSTANTINOPLE, THE (UKN) ○ ISLAND ON THE CONTINENT
SZIKRAZO LANYOK • 1973 • Bacso Peter • HNG • DASHING GIRLS
SZINDBAD • 1971 • Huszarik Zoltan • HNG • SINBAD ○ SINDBAD
SZINES TINTAKROL ALMODOM • 1981 • Ranody Laszlo • HNG • I DREAM ABOUT COLOURS
SZINESNO • 1920 • *Lukas Paul* • HNG
SZINFOLTOK KINABOL • 1957 • Jancso Miklos • SHT • HNG • COLORFUL CHINA ○ COLORS OF CHINA
SZIRMOK, VIRAGOK, KOSORUK • 1985 • Lugossy Laszlo • HNG • PETALS, FLOWERS, WREATHS
SZIUEL SZIVERT • 1939 • Sekely Steve • HNG • HEART FOR HEART
SZIVDOBOGAS • 1961 • Meszaros Marta • SHT • HNG • HEART BEAT
SZIVZUR • 1982 • Boszormenyi Geza • HNG • HEART TREMORS
SZKICE SO PORTRETU REZYSERA • 1970 • Ziarnik Jerzy • DOC • PLN • SKETCHES FOR A DIRECTOR'S PORTRAIT
SZKICE WARSZAWSKIE see **WARSZAWIACY** • 1969
SZKICE WEGLEM • 1957 • Bohdziewicz Antoni • PLN • CHARCOAL SKETCHES
SZKLANA GORA • 1961 • Komorowski Pawel • PLN • GLASS MOUNTAIN, THE
SZKLANA KULA • 1972 • Rozewicz Stanislaw • PLN • CRYSTAL BALL ○ GLASS BALL, THE
SZKOLA • 1958 • Borowczyk Walerian • ANS • PLN • SCHOOL ○ ECOLE, L'
SZKOLA BEZ TABLIC • 1960 • Trzos-Rastawiecki Andrzej • DOC • PLN • SCHOOL WITHOUT BLACKBOARDS
SZKOLA PODSTAWOWA • 1972 • Zygadlo Tomasz • DOC • PLN • PRIMARY SCHOOL
SZOBA KIALTASSAL • 1990 • Xantus Janos • HNG • ROOM WITH CRY
SZOBOR • 1971 • Macskassy Gyula, Varnai Gyorgy • ANS • HNG • STATUE, THE
SZORNYEK EVADJA • 1987 • Jancso Miklos • HNG • SEASON OF MONSTERS
SZOVJET MEZOGAZDASAGI KULDOTTEK TANITASAI • 1951 • Jancso Miklos (c/d) • SHT • HNG • TEACHINGS OF A SOVIET AGRICULTURAL DEPUTATION, THE
SZPITAL • 1962 • Majewski Janusz • PLN • HOSPITAL (UKN)
SZPITAL PRZEMIENIENIA • 1978 • Zebrowski Edward • PLN • HOSPITAL OF TRANSFIGURATION, THE ○ TRANSFIGURATION HOSPITAL
SZSZECIN -MY TOWN • Lesiewicz Witold • DOC • PLN
SZTANDAR • 1965 • Kijowicz Miroslaw • ANS • PLN • BANNER, THE ○ FLAG, THE
SZTANDAR MLODYCH • 1957 • Borowczyk Walerian • SHT • PLN • BANNER OF YOUTH
SZTUKA KOCHANIA • 1989 • Bromski Yacek • PLN • ART OF LOVE, THE
SZTUKA MLODYCH • 1949 • Munk Andrzej • DOC • PLN • ART OF YOUTH, THE ○ ART OF THE YOUNG
SZU-WAN YU-HSI • 1978 • Clouse Robert, Lee Bruce • HNG • BRUCE LEE'S GAME OF DEATH (UKN) ○ GAME OF DEATH
SZURKERUHAS HOLGY, A • 1920 • *Lukas Paul* • HNG
SZURKULET • 1989 • Feher Gyorgy • HNG • TWILIGHT
SZYB L 23 • 1932 • Buczkowski Leonard • PLN • PIT L 23
SZYFRY • 1966 • Has Wojciech J. • PLN • CODE, THE

T

T-34 • 1964 • Kurikhin Nikita, Menaker Leonid • USS
T.A.G., THE ASSASSINATION GAME • 1982 • Castle Nick • USA • TAG ○ KISS ME, KILL ME
T.A.M.I. see **T.A.M.I. SHOW, THE** • 1964
T.A.M.I. SHOW, THE • 1964 • Binder Steve • USA • TEENAGE AWARDS INTERNATIONAL ○ TEENAGE COMMAND PERFORMANCE ○ TEENAGE MUSIC INTERNATIONAL ○ TAMI SHOW, THE ○ T.A.M.I. ○ GATHER NO MOSS
T.A.P.S. see **TAPS** • 1981
T-BIRD GANG • 1958 • Harbinger Richard • USA • PAY-OFF, THE
T-BONE FOR TWO • 1942 • Geronimi Clyde • ANS • USA
T-BONE STEAK DANS LES MANGEUSES D'HOMMES • 1968 • Marchand Gilles, Tremblay Hugues • CND
T CROSS, THE • Beattie Paul • SHT • USA
T. DAN SMITH • 1987 • *Smith T. Dan* • UKN
T FOR TUMBLEWEED • 1962 • *Wexler Haskell (Ph)* • SHT • USA
T.G. BOOGIE WOOGIE • 1945 • Crouch William Forest • SHT • USA
T. HAVILAND HICKS -FRESHMAN • 1917 • Turbett Ben • SHT • USA
T-INQUIETE PAS, CA CE SOIGNE • 1980 • Matalon Eddy • FRN
T-MEN • 1947 • Mann Anthony • USA
T.N.P., LE see **THEATRE NATIONAL POPULAIRE, LE** • 1956
T.N.T. (THE NAKED TRUTH) • 1924 • *Mulhall Jack* • USA • NAKED TRUTH, THE
T.P.A. see **PRESIDENT'S ANALYST, THE** • 1967
T. R. BASKIN • 1971 • Ross Herbert • USA • DATE WITH A LONELY GIRL, A
'T SAL WAARACHTIG WEL GAEN • 1939 • Franken Mannus • INN
T. SVENTON, PRAKTISERANDE PRIVATDETEKTIV • 1972 • Berglund Per • SWD, NRW • TURE SVENTON, PRIVATE DETECTIVE ○ TURE SVENTON -PRIVATDETEKTIV
T.V.A. • 1945 • Vorkapich Slavko • SHT • USA
T.V. FUDDLEHEAD • 1959 • Kneitel Seymour • ANS • USA
T.V. INTERVIEW • 1967 • Vanderbeek Stan • USA
T.V. OF TOMORROW • 1953 • Avery Tex • ANS • USA
T.V. OR NOT T.V. • 1962 • Kneitel Seymour • ANS • USA
'T WAS EEN APRIL • 1935 • Sirk Douglas • NTH
T'A • 1976 • Lung Kang • HKG • NINA
TA' BRILLER PA • 1942 • Weel Arne • DNM
TA CHI • 1962 • Yueh Feng • HKG • LAST WOMAN OF SHANG, THE (USA)
TA CH'IEN SHIH-CHIEH • 1975 • Ting Shan-Hsi • HKG • MY WACKY, WACKY WORLD
TA' DET SOM EN MAND, FRUE see **TAG DET SOM EN MAND, FRUE** • 1974
TA E KOU • 1972 • Roc T'len • HKG • GODFATHER OF HONG KONG ○ NOTORIOUS BANDIT, THE
TA-FENG LANG • 1976 • Chang Hsing-Yen • HKG • STORMY SEA, THE
TA FILIATRA see **LAVETE THESSIS** • 1973
TA HAND OM ULLA • 1942 • Johansson Ivar • SWD • TAKE CARE OF ULLA
TA-HU YING-LIEH • 1982 • Chang P'Ei-Ch'Eng • TWN • MAN OF IMMORTALITY, A
TA HVAD DY VIL HA • 1948 • Palsbo Ole • DNM
TA LUN HUI • 1983 • Hu King, Hsing Li, Pai Ching-Jui • TWN • WHEEL OF LIFE, THE
TA MENG CH'ENG • 1976 • Ta Ko Ch'Eng • HKG • SIMPLE-MINDED FELLOW, THE
TA MINGXING • 1985 • Teng Wenji • CHN • SUPERSTAR
TA NASE PISNICKA CESKA • 1967 • Podskalsky Zdenek • CZC • THAT CZECH SONG OF OURS ○ LOVE WITH A SONG
TA-RA-RA-BOOM-DE-RE • 1922 • *Le Breton Flora* • SHT • UKN
TA-RA-RA-BOOM-DEE-AYE • 1925 • Fleischer Dave • ANS • USA • RA-RA-BOOM-DER-A
TA SHA-HSING YU HSAIO-MEI T'OU • 1978 • Wu Yusen • HKG • FOLLOW THE STAR
TA SHE • 1981 • Mou Tun-Fei • HKG • LOST SOULS
TA-TAI COME AGAIN • 1911 • Armstrong Charles • UKN
TA-TI NU-ERH • 1967 • Hu King • HKG • SONS OF THE GOOD EARTH ○ CHILDREN OF THE GOOD EARTH
TA TRETI • 1968 • Balik Jaroslav • CZC • THIRD ONE, THE
TA-TS'O CHE • 1983 • Yu K'An-P'Ing • TWN • PAPA, CAN YOU HEAR ME SINGING ○ MOONLIGHT
TA TSUI HSIA • 1966 • Hu King • HKG • COME DRINK WITH ME ○ BIG DRUNKEN HERO
TA TU HOU • 1976 • Yang Ch'Uan • HKG • DRUG QUEEN, THE
TAAL NOCH TEKEN • 1966 • Smit Boud • NTH
TAALLA POHJANTAHDEN ALLA • 1968 • Laine Edvin • FNL • HERE, BENEATH THE NORTH STAR
TAALTA TULLAAN, ELAMA! • 1979 • Suominen Tapio • FNL • RIGHT ON, MAN!
TAAN TA YA DAI ATOO YE • 1983 • Nyunt Win • BRM • MISSING YOU ATOO
TABAC A DELHI • 1963-64 • Portugais Louis • DCS • CND
TABAC JAUNE, LE • 1951 • Proulx Maurice • DCS • CND
TABARANAKATHE • 1986 • Kasaravalli Girish • IND • STORY OF TABARANA, THE ○ STORY OF TABARA, THE
TABARE • 1918 • Lezama Luis • MXC
TABARE • 1946 • Lezama Luis • MXC
TABARIN • 1958 • Pottier Richard • FRN, ITL
TABARIN see **ENTRAINEUSE, L'** • 1938
TABARNAC • 1975 • Faraldo Claude • FRN • VIENS CHEZ MOI, TU SERAS PROPHETE
TABASCO KID, THE • 1932 • Horne James W. • SHT • USA
TABASCO ROAD • 1957 • McKimson Robert • ANS • USA
TABATIERE LABRADOR, LA • 1967 • Bonniere Rene • DCS • CND
TABEA, STEHE AUF! • 1922 • Dinesen Robert • FRG
TABI NO OMOSA • 1972 • Saito Koichi • JPN • JOURNEY INTO SOLITUDE
TABI WA AOZORA • 1932 • Inagaki Hiroshi • JPN • TRAVELS UNDER THE BLUE SKY ○ TRAMP UNDER THE BLUE SKY, THE
TABI WA SOYOKKAZE • 1953 • Inagaki Hiroshi • JPN • TRAVELLING WITH A BREEZE
TABIATE BIDJAN • 1978 • Saless Sohrab Shahid • IRN • STILL LIFE
TABIJI • 1953 • Nakamura Noboru • JPN • JOURNEY, THE
TABIJI • 1955 • Inagaki Hiroshi • JPN • LONE JOURNEY, THE
TABIJI • 1967 • Murayama Shinji • JPN • JOURNEY
TABIJI • 1971 • Saito Koichi • JPN
TABIJI • 1987 • Koyama Seijiro • JPN • JOURNEY
TABISUGATA JOSHU NAMARI • 1930 • Ito Daisuke • JPN
TABISUGATA NEZUMIKOZO • 1958 • Inagaki Hiroshi • JPN • RAT KID ON JOURNEY
TABIYAKUSHA • 1940 • Naruse Mikio • JPN • ITINERANT ACTOR, AN ○ TRAVELLING ACTORS
TABLE • 1976 • Gehr Ernie • USA
TABLE AUX CREVES, LA • 1951 • Verneuil Henri • FRN • VILLAGE FEUD, THE
TABLE BAY • 1964 • SAF
TABLE CLOTH GIVEN BY THE NORTH WIND, THE • 1908 • Watanabe Ryuhei • ANS • JPN
TABLE FOR FIVE • 1982 • Lieberman Robert • USA • THESE CHILDREN ARE MINE!
TABLE MAGIQUE, LA • 1908 • de Chomon Segundo • SHT • FRN • MAGIC TABLE, THE
TABLE OF DREAMS see **TABLICZKA MARZENIA** • 1968
TABLE TENNIS • 1936 • Miller David • SHT • USA
TABLE-TOP BALLET • 1949 • Simpson C. F. R. • ANS • UKN
TABLE TOP DOLLY • 1976 • Snow Michael • CND
TABLE TOP RANCH • 1922 • Hurst Paul C. • USA
TABLE TOPPERS • 1950 • Barclay David • SHT • USA
TABLE TOURNANT, LA • 1988 • Grimault Paul • ANM • FRN
TABLE TURNING • 1905 • Fitzhamon Lewin • UKN
TABLEAUX D'UNE EXPOSITION see **PICTURES AT AN EXHIBITION** • 1972
TABLEAUX FUTURISTES ET INCOHERENTS, LES • 1916 • Cohl Emile • ANS • FRN
TABLES OF CONTENTS • 1987 • Tilby Wendy • ANS • CND
TABLES TURNED • 1915 • Horan Charles • USA
TABLES TURNED, THE • 1910 • Martinek H. O. • UKN
TABLES TURNED, THE • 1911 • *Bison* • USA
TABLES TURNED, THE • 1912 • *Baggot King* • USA
TABLES TURNED, THE • 1913 • Kent Charles • USA
TABLES TURNED, THE see **MASQUERADE BANDIT, THE** • 1926
TABLICZKA MARZENIA • 1968 • Chmielewski Zbigniew • PLN • TWO TIMES A DREAM ○ TABLE OF DREAMS
TABOGA • VNZ
TABOO see **TABU** • 1976
TABOO see **TABU** • 1982
TABOO ISLAND see **PLAYA LLAMADO DESEO, UNA** • 1977
TABOOS OF THE WORLD (USA) see **TABU, I** • 1963
TABOR • 1953 • Peclet Georges • FRN
TABOR UHODIT V NEBO • 1976 • Lotyanu Emil • USS • GYPSY CAMP VANISHES INTO THE BLUE, THE
TABU • 1931 • Murnau F. W., Flaherty Robert • USA
TABU • 1976 • Sjoman Vilgot • SWD • TABOO
TABU • 1982 • Bressane Julio • BRZ • TABOO
TABU • 1988 • Baranski Andrzej • PLN
TABU see **MILKA -ELOKUVA TABUISTA** • 1980
TABU (FUGITIVOS DE LAS ISLAS DEL SUR) • 1966 • Seto Javier • SPN, ITL • VERGINE DI SAMOA, LA (ITL) ○ DRUM OF TABU, THE (USA)
TABU, I • 1963 • Marcellini Romolo • DOC • ITL • TABOOS OF THE WORLD (USA)

TABU N.2 • 1965 • Marcellini Romolo • DOC • ITL • MACABRO (USA) ○ MONDO MACABRO ○ IT'S A SICK, SICK WORLD
TABULA RASA-FUNF, DIE TOTEN see **AN EINEM FREITAG UM HALB ZWOLF** • 1961
TABUSSE • 1948 • Gehret Jean • FRN
TAC-WAC • 1981 • Alcoriza Luis • MXC, SPN
TACCHINO, IL • 1923 • Bonnard Mario • ITL
TACCHINO PREPOTENTE, IL • 1939 • Rossellini Roberto • SHT • ITL
TACITURN, THE • Gaitan Jorge • CLM
TACKY SUE'S ROMANCE • 1917 • Stonehouse Ruth • SHT • USA
TACNO U PONOC • 1960 • Feman Mladen • ANS • YGS • LOW MIDNIGHT
TACOS AL CARBON • 1971 • Galindo Alejandro • MXC • BARBECUED TACOS
TACOS ALTOS • 1986 • Renan Sergio • ARG • HIGH HEELS
TACOS JOVEN • 1950 • Diaz Morales Jose • MXC • PODER DE LOS HIJOS, EL
TACOTS, LES • 1974 • Melancon Andre • SHT • CND
TACTICS OF CUPID • 1910 • *Gaumont* • FRN
TACUARA AND CHAMORRO D. see **TACUARA Y CHAMORRO, PICHONES DE HOMBRES** • 1967
TACUARA Y CHAMORRO, PICHONES DE HOMBRES • 1967 • Catrani Catrano • ARG • TACUARA AND CHAMORRO D.
TADAIMA ZEROHIKI • 1957 • Fujiwara Sugio • JPN • MONKEY BUSINESS
TADARE • 1962 • Masumura Yasuzo • JPN • STOLEN PLEASURE ○ CORROSION
TADELLOESER AND WOLFF: RIGHT OR WRONG, MY COUNTRY • 1974 • Fechner Eberhard • FRG
TADEUSZ KULISIEWICZ • 1958 • Brzozowski Jaroslaw • DOC • PLN
TADEUSZ KULISIEWICZ • 1964 • Morgenstern Janusz • DOC • PLN
TADOUSSAC TERRE D'HISTOIRE ET DE BEAUTE • 1947 • Lavoie Hermenegilde • DOC • CND
TADPOLE AND THE WHALE • 1988 • Lord Jean-Claude • CND • GRENOUILLE ET LA BALEINE, LA ○ FROG AND THE WHALE, THE
TAD'S INDOOR SPORTS • 1918 • Nolan William • ASS • USA
TAD'S LITTLE DAFFYDILLS • 1918 • Nolan William, Lantz Walter • ASS • USA
TAD'S SWIMMING HOLE • 1918 • Vidor King • SHT • USA
TADYAK SA LIKOD • 1968 • Wenceslao Jose Pepe • PHL • KICK IN THE BACK
TAENK PA ET TAL • 1969 • Kjaerulff-Schmidt Palle • DNM • THINK OF A NUMBER
TAFFIN • 1988 • Megahy Francis • UKN, IRL • TAFFIN: A DIFFERENT KIND OF HERO
TAFFIN: A DIFFERENT KIND OF HERO see **TAFFIN** • 1988
TAFFY AND THE JUNGLE HUNTER • 1965 • Morse Terry O. • USA
TAFOS TON ERASTON, O • 1968 • Tzimas Nikos • GRC • TOMB OF LOVERS, THE
TAFT FOR A DAY • 1910 • *Motograph* • USA
TAG see **T.A.G., THE ASSASSINATION GAME** • 1982
TAG 56 • 1944 • Henrikson Anders • SWD • TRAIN 56
TAG AUF DEM MARS, EIN • 1920 • Schall Heinz • FRG
TAG DAY • 1909 • *Essanay* • USA
TAG DAY AT SILVER GULCH • 1911 • *Lubin* • USA
TAG DE IDIOTEN • 1982 • Schroeter Werner • FRG
TAG DER AFFEN • 1975 • Meier Uli • MTV • FRG, SWT
TAG DER FREIHEIT: UNSERE WEHRMACHT • 1935 • Riefenstahl Leni • FRG • DAY OF FREEDOM: OUR ARMY
TAG, DER NIE ZU ENDE GEHT, EIN • 1959 • Wirth Franz Peter • FRG
TAG DER ROSEN IM AUGUST.. DA HAT DIE GARDE FORTGEMUSST • 1927 • Mack Max • FRG
TAG DET SOM EN MAND, FRUE • 1974 • Knudsen Mette, Vistrup Li, Rygard Elisabeth • DNM • TAKE IT LIKE A MAN, MA'AM ○ TA' DET SOM EN MAND, FRUE
TAG DR VERGELTUNG, DER • 1915 • Larsen Viggo • FRG
TAG IST SCHONER ALS DER ANDERE, EIN • 1969 • Hoffmann Kurt • FRG
TAG MEJ -ALSKA MEJ see **NANA** • 1970
TAG NACH DER SCHEIDUNG, DER • 1938 • Verhoeven Paul • FRG • DAY AFTER THE DIVORCE, THE (USA)
TAG VOR DER HOCHZEIT, DER • 1952 • Thiele Rolf • FRG
TAGEBUCH • 1975 • Thome Rudolf • FRG • DIARY
TAGEBUCH COLLINS, DAS • 1915 • Eichberg Richard • FRG
TAGEBUCH DER BARONIN W., DAS see **SELIGE EXZELLENZ, DIE** • 1935
TAGEBUCH DER GELIEBTEN, DAS • 1936 • Koster Henry • FRG • MARIE BASCHKIRTZEFF
TAGEBUCH DES APOTHEKERS WARREN, DAS • 1918 • *Leux Lori* • FRG
TAGEBUCH DES DR. HART, DAS • 1916 • Leni Paul • FRG • FELDARZT, DER
TAGEBUCH EINER FRUHREIFEN • 1972 • Casale Nino, Schindler Jurgen • FRG • LOVEPLAY (UKN)
TAGEBUCH EINER KOKOTTE • 1929 • David Constantin J. • FRG
TAGEBUCH EINER TOTEN, DAS see **TAGEBUCH EINER VERLORENEN 1, DAS** • 1918
TAGEBUCH EINER VERLIEBTEN • 1953 • von Baky Josef • FRG • DIARY OF A MARRIED WOMAN
TAGEBUCH EINER VERLORENEN • 1929 • Pabst G. W. • FRG • DIARY OF A LOST GIRL (UKN) ○ DIARY OF A LOST ONE
TAGEBUCH EINER VERLORENEN 1, DAS • 1918 • Oswald Richard • FRG • TAGEBUCH EINER TOTEN, DAS
TAGEBUCH EINER VERLORENEN 2, DAS • 1918 • Oswald Richard • FRG • DIDA IBSENS GESCHICHTE
TAGEBUCH EINES LIEBENDEN • 1977 • Saless Sohrab Shahid • FRG • DIARY OF A LOVER
TAGEBUCH EINES MATROSEN, DAS see **ROBINSON, EIN** • 1940
TAGEMNICA STAREGO ZAMKU • 1956 • Giersz Witold • ANS • PLN • MYSTERY OF THE OLD CASTLE, THE ○ SECRET OF THE OLD CASTLE, THE
TAGES, EINES • 1945 • Kirchhoff Fritz • FRG
TAGET • 1946 • Werner Gosta • SHT • SWD • TRAIN, THE
TAGET GAR KLOCKAN 9 • 1941 • Johansson Ivar • SWD
TAGGART • 1964 • Springsteen R. G. • USA
TAGLIA E TUA E.. L'UOMO L'AMMAZZO IO, LA • 1969 • Mulargia Edoardo • ITL
TAGLIAGOLE, IL (ITL) see **BOUCHER, LE** • 1969
TAGORE see **RABINDRANATH TAGORE** • 1961
TAGSUBER -ABENDS • 1973 • Fritz Roger • FRG • DURING THE DAY -AT NIGHT
TAHAN NA EMPY, TAHAN see **TAHAN NO EMPOY, TAHAN** • 1977
TAHAN NO EMPOY, TAHAN • 1977 • Brocka Lino • PHL • STOP CRYING EMPOY, STOP CRYING ○ TAHAN NA EMPY, TAHAN
TAHIR AND ZHURA see **TAHIR I ZHURA** • 1945
TAHIR I ZHURA • 1945 • Ganiyev Uzbek Nabi • USS • TAHIR AND ZHURA
TAHIRA • 1957 • Wahab Fatin Abdel • EGY
TAHITI HONEY • 1943 • Auer John H. • USA
TAHITI NIGHTS • 1945 • Jason Will • USA
TAHITI OU LA JOIE DE VIVRE • 1956 • Borderie Bernard • FRN
TAHITIAN FISH DRIVE, A • 1913 • Melies Gaston • DOC • USA
TAHRAN MACERASI • 1968 • Inanoglu Turker • TRK • ADVENTURE IN TEHRAN
TAHT AL INQAD • 1983 • Chamoun Jean • LBN • UNDER THE DEBRIS
TAHTA MATAR AL-KHARIF • 1970 • Al-Kechine Ahmed • EGY • SOUS LA PLUIE DE L'AUTOMNE
TAHUNA AL AMM FABRE • 1987 • Rachedi Ahmed • ALG • MILL, THE
TAHYA YA DIDU • 1971 • Zinet Mohamed • ALG • ALGER INSOLITE
TAI-PAN • 1986 • Duke Daryl • USA
T'AI-PEI, WU AI • 1982 • Ho Fan • TWN • TAIPEI MY LOVE
T'AI-SHANG T'AI-HSIA • 1983 • Ch'Ing-Chieh Lin • TWN • SEND IN THE CLOWNS
TAIAN RYOKO • 1968 • Segawa Shoji • JPN • GRAND JOURNEY, THE
TAIFU • 1966 • Mikuni Rentaro • JPN • TYPHOON
TAIFU SODOKI • 1956 • Yamamoto Satsuo • JPN • TYPHOON NO.13
TAIFU TO ZAKURO • 1967 • Sugawa Eizo • JPN • POMEGRANATE TIME
TAIFUN see **POLIZEIAKTE 909** • 1934
TAIFUNHEXE, DIE • 1923 • von Antalffy Alexander • FRG
TAIGA • 1958 • Liebeneiner Wolfgang • FRG
TAIHEIYO HITORI BOCHI see **TAIHEIYO HITORIBOTCHI** • 1963
TAIHEIYO HITORIBOTCHI • 1963 • Ichikawa Kon • JPN • ALONE ON THE PACIFIC (USA) ○ ALONE IN THE PACIFIC ○ MY ENEMY THE SEA ○ ENEMY, THE SEA, THE ○ TAIHEIYO HITORI BOCHI
TAIHEIYO KISEKI NO SAKUSEN KISUKA • 1965 • Maruyama Seiji • JPN • RETREAT FROM KISKA
TAIHEIYO NO ARASHI • 1960 • Matsubayashi Shue • JPN • I BOMBED PEARL HARBOR (USA) ○ STORM OVER THE PACIFIC, THE
TAIHEIYO NO JIGOKU (JPN) see **HELL IN THE PACIFIC** • 1968
TAIHEIYO NO TSUBASA • 1963 • Matsubayashi Shue • JPN • ATTACK SQUADRON
TAIHEIYO NO WASHI • 1953 • Honda Inoshiro • JPN • EAGLE OF THE PACIFIC
TAIHEIYO SENSO TO HIMEYURI BUTAI • 1962 • Komori Kiyoshi • JPN • PACIFIC WAR AND HIMEYURI CORPS
TAII NO MUSUME • 1929 • *Nikkatsu Co.* • JPN
TAIKAPELI • 1984 • Peltomaa Hannu • FNL • MAGIC GAME, THE
TAIKETSU • 1967 • Masuda Toshio • JPN • FRIENDLY ENEMIES
TAIKOKI • 1958 • Osone Tatsuo • JPN
TAIL END • 1938 • Kline Lester • ANS • USA
TAIL-GUNNER JOE • 1977 • Taylor Jud • TVM • USA
TAIL OF A CAT, THE • 1918 • Lyons Eddie, Moran Lee • SHT • USA
TAIL OF A COAT, THE • 1914 • MacGregor Norval • USA
TAIL OF A SHIRT, THE • 1919 • Reese Robert • SHT • USA
TAIL OF THE MONKEY, THE • 1926 • Lantz Walter, Hand David • ANS • USA
TAIL SPIN • 1939 • Del Ruth Roy • USA
TAIL-WIND, THE • 1972 • Boyadgieva Lada • BUL
TAILGATE MAN FROM NEW ORLEANS see **HOMME DE LA NOUVELLE-ORLEANS, L'** • 1958
TAILOR, THE • 1922 • St. John Al • SHT • USA
TAILOR FROM TORZHOK, THE see **ZAKROICHIK IZ TORJKA** • 1925
TAILOR FROM ULM, THE see **SCHNEIDER VON ULM, DER** • 1978
TAILOR MADE MAN, A • 1922 • De Grasse Joseph • USA
TAILOR-MADE MAN, A • 1931 • Wood Sam • USA • IMPOSTOR, THE
TAILOR-MADE ROMANCE, A • 1919 • *Chefee Jack* • SHT • USA
TAILOR MAID • 1920 • *Mason Billy* • SHT • USA
TAILOR OF BOND STREET, THE • 1916 • *Yorke Augustus* • UKN
TAILOR'S BILL, THE • 1915 • Miller Ashley • USA
TAILOR'S MAID, THE (USA) see **PADRI E FIGLI** • 1957
TAILOR'S PLANET, THE • 1983 • Domaradzki Jerzy • PLN
TAILOR'S REVENGE, THE • 1913 • Plumb Hay? • UKN
TAILOR'S STORY, THE see **KREJCOVSKA POVIDKA** • 1954
TAILOR'S TRIMMINGS • 1917 • Miller Rube • SHT • USA
TAILS WIN • 1920 • Watson William • SHT • USA
TAILS YOU LOSE • 1948 • Freedman Laurie • UKN
TAILSPIN TOMMY • 1934 • Landers Lew • SRL • USA
TAILSPIN TOMMY IN THE GREAT AIR MYSTERY • 1935 • Taylor Ray • SRL • USA
TAINA DVUH OKEANOV • 1955 • Pipinashvili Konstantin • USS • ORI OKEANIS SAIDUMLOBEA ○ MYSTERY OF THE OCEANS, THE ○ SECRET OF TWO OCEANS, THE
TAINA KOROLEVY • 1919 • Protazanov Yakov • USS • QUEEN'S SECRET, THE
TAINATA VECHERIA NA SEDMATSITE • 1957 • Dakovski Dako • BUL • SECRET SUPPER OF THE SEDMATSI, THE
TAINSTVENNI OSTROV • 1941 • Pentzlin E., Chelintsev B. M. • USS • MYSTERIOUS ISLAND
TAINT, THE • 1914 • *Hoffman Ruby* • USA
TAINT, THE • 1915 • Olcott Sidney • USA
TAINT, THE • 1916 • *Pathe* • SHT • USA
'TAINT LEGAL • 1940 • D'Arcy Harry • SHT • USA
TAINT OF AN ALIEN, THE • 1914 • *August Edwin* • USA
TAINT OF FEAR, THE • 1916 • Holubar Allen • SHT • USA
TAINT OF MADNESS, THE • 1914 • MacGregor Norval • USA
TAINTED • 1915 • Daly William Robert • USA
TAINTED • 1985 • Matacena Orestes • USA
TAINTED BLOOD • 1915 • *Grandin* • USA
TAINTED FLOWERS see **AKASEN NO HI WA KIEZU** • 1958
TAINTED HORSEPLAY see **KOPYTEM SEM, KOPYTEM TAM** • 1988
TAINTED MONEY • 1914 • King Burton L. • USA
TAINTED MONEY • 1915 • Davis Ulysses • USA
TAINTED MONEY • 1924 • McRae Henry • USA
TAINTED MONEY (UKN) see **SHOW THEM NO MERCY** • 1935
TAINTED (USA) see **VISITEUR, LE** • 1946
TAINYYABI • 1977 • Kabir Alamgir • BNG
TAIPEI MY LOVE see **T'AI-PEI, WU AI** • 1982
TAIPEI STORY • Yang Te-Ch'Ang • TWN
TAIRA CLAN, THE (USA) see **SHIN HEIKE MONOGATARI** • 1955
TAIS-TOI QUAND TU PARLES • 1981 • Clair Philippe • FRN, TNS, ITL
TAISHO • 1940 • Imai Tadashi • JPN
TAISTELUJEN TIE • 1960 • FNL • ROADS OF BATTLE, THE
TAITANFRICHES, LES • Tourane Jean • ANS • FRN
TAIYANG YU • 1987 • Zhang Zeming • CHN • SUN AND RAIN
TAIYO E NO DASSHUTSU • 1963 • Masuda Toshio • JPN • ESCAPE INTO TERROR
TAIYO NO HAKABA • 1960 • Oshima Nagisa • JPN • GRAVE OF THE SUN ○ SUN'S BURIAL, THE
TAIYO NO KARYUDO • 1970 • Onchi Hideo • JPN • HUNTER OF THE SUN
TAIYO NO KISETSU • 1956 • Furukawa Takumi • JPN • SEASON OF THE SUN
TAIYO NO NAI MACHI • 1954 • Yamamoto Satsuo • JPN • STREET WITHOUT SUN, THE ○ SUNLESS STREET, THE
TAIYO NO OJI: HORUSU NO DAIBOKEN • 1968 • Takahata Isao • ANM • JPN • LITTLE NORSE PRINCE VALIANT
TAIYO O NUSUNDA OTOKO • 1979 • Hasegawa Kazuhiko • JPN • MAN WHO STOLE THE SUN, THE
TAIYO TO BARA • 1956 • Kinoshita Keisuke • JPN • ROSE ON HIS ARM, THE ○ SUN AND ROSE
TAIYO WA HIBI NI ARATANATI • 1955 • Nomura Yoshitaro • JPN • NEW EVERY DAY
TAIYOJI • 1929 • Uchida Tomu • JPN • SEA-LOVING SON SAILS AWAY, THE
TAJ MAHAL • 1959 • Ahmed Shri Mushir • IND
TAJEMNICA LEKARZA • 1930 • Ordynski Ryszard • PLN
TAJEMNICA OSKARZONEJ • 1937 • Sikiewicz Bazyli • PLN
TAJEMNY HRAD V KARPATECH • 1981 • Lipsky Oldrich • CZC • MYSTERY CASTLE IN THE CARPATHIANS ○ TAJEMSTVI HRADU V KARPATECH ○ MYSTERIOUS CASTLE IN THE CARPATHIANS, THE
TAJEMSTVI HRADU V KARPATECH see **TAJEMNY HRAD V KARPATECH** • 1981
TAJEMSTVI KRVE • 1953 • Fric Martin • CZC • MYSTERY OF THE BLOOD, THE ○ SECRET OF BLOOD, THE
TAJEMSTVI LEKAROVO • 1930 • Lebl Julius • CZC
TAJEMSTVI VELIKEHO VYPRAVECE • 1972 • Kachyna Karel • CZC • SECRETS OF A GREAT NARRATOR, THE ○ SECRET OF THE BIG NARRATOR
TAJINKO MURA • 1940 • Imai Tadashi • JPN • VILLAGE OF TAJINKO, THE ○ TAJINKO VILLAGE
TAJINKO VILLAGE see **TAJINKO MURA** • 1940
TAJNA NIKOLE TESLE • 1981 • Papic Krsto • YGS • SECRET OF NIKOLA TESLA, THE
TAJO NA NYUEKI • 1967 • Takeda Ario • JPN • AMOROUS LIQUID
TAJROBE • 1975 • Kia-Rostami Abbas • IRN • EXPERIENCE, THE
TAK GOSPODARZA SPOLDZIELCY • 1951 • Bossak Jerzy • DOC • PLN • HOW COOPERATIVES WORK
TAKA TO OKAMI • 1968 • Matsuo Akinori • JPN • EAGLE AND THE WOLF, THE
TAKAMARU AND KIKUMARU see **TAKAMARU KIKUMARU** • 1959
TAKAMARU KIKUMARU • 1959 • Marune Santaro • JPN • TAKAMARU AND KIKUMARU
TAKARA NO YAMA • 1929 • Ozu Yasujiro • JPN • TREASURE MOUNTAIN
TAKARAJIMA ENSEI • 1956 • *Enomoto Kenichi* • JPN • PEACH BOY
TAKAW TUKSO • 1986 • Pascual William • PHL • PRONE TO TEMPTATION
TAKE, THE • 1974 • Hartford-Davis Robert • USA
TAKE A CHANCE • 1918 • Roach Hal • SHT • USA
TAKE A CHANCE • 1933 • Brice Monte, Schwab Laurence • USA
TAKE A CHANCE • 1937 • Hill Sinclair • UKN
TAKE A CUE • 1939 • Feist Felix E. • SHT • USA
TAKE A GIANT STEP • 1959 • Leacock Philip • USA
TAKE A GIANT STEP • 1982 • Jubenvill Ken • MTV • CND
TAKE A GIRL LIKE YOU • 1969 • Miller Jonathan • UKN
TAKE A HARD RIDE (USA) see **PAROLA DI UNA FUORILEGGE.. E LEGGE!, LA** • 1975
TAKE A LETTER, DARLING • 1942 • Leisen Mitchell • USA • GREEN-EYED WOMAN, THE (UKN)
TAKE A LOOK AT ME • 1929 • Aylott Dave, Symmons E. F. • SHT • UKN
TAKE A POWDER • 1953 • Tomlinson Lionel, Vedey Julien • UKN
TAKE A TRIP • 1926 • Fleischer Dave • ANS • USA
TAKE ALL OF ME • 1978 • *Johnson Richard* • ITL
TAKE ALL YOU CAN GET • 1972 • *Dennis Fred* • USA
TAKE BACK YOUR WIFE • 1917 • Beaudine William • SHT • USA
TAKE CARE! FRANCE see **A NOUS DEUX, LA FRANCE!** • 1970
TAKE CARE OF MY LITTLE GIRL • 1951 • Negulesco Jean • USA
TAKE CARE OF ULLA see **TA HAND OM ULLA** • 1942

TAKE CARE OF YOUR NEIGHBOURS • 1979 • *Yousry Mahida* • EGY
TAKE COVER • 1938 • Hiscott Leslie • UKN
TAKE COVER • 1940 • Pearson George • DCS • UKN
TAKE DOCTOR'S ADVICE • 1920 • *Supreme Comedies* • USA
TAKE DOWN • 1978 • Merrill Keith • USA
TAKE HER BY SURPRISE • 1967 • Dorn Rudi • CND • TAKEN BY SURPRISE ○ VIOLENT LOVE
TAKE HER, SHE'S MINE • 1963 • Koster Henry • USA
TAKE IT ALL (USA) see **A TOUT PRENDRE** • 1963
TAKE IT BIG • 1944 • McDonald Frank • USA
TAKE IT BIG see **THEY LEARNED ABOUT WOMEN** • 1929
TAKE IT EASY • 1985 • Hom Jesper • DNM
TAKE IT EASY, IT'S A WALTZ (USA) see **LAISSE ALLER, C'EST UNE VALSE** • 1970
TAKE IT FROM ME • 1926 • Seiter William A. • USA
TAKE IT FROM ME see **TRANSATLANTIC TROUBLE** • 1937
TAKE IT FROM THE TOP • 1966 • Boyko Eugene • CND
TAKE IT LIKE A MAN, MA'AM see **TAG DET SOM EN MAND, FRUE** • 1974
TAKE IT OR LEAVE IT • 1944 • Stoloff Ben • USA
TAKE IT OR LEAVE IT • 1982 • Robinson Dave • UKN
TAKE IT OUT IN TRADE • 1970 • Wood Edward D. Jr. • USA
TAKE IT TO THE LIMIT • 1980 • Starr Peter • DOC • USA
TAKE ME • 1969 • Dwoskin Stephen • USA, UKN
TAKE ME see **TAKE ME NAKED** • 1966
TAKE ME AS I AM (UKN) see **CANAILLES, LES** • 1959
TAKE ME AWAY see **BAWALAH AKU PERGI** • 1981
TAKE ME AWAY, MY LOVE • 1962 • Giannopoulou E. • GRC
TAKE ME BACK TO OKLAHOMA • 1940 • Herman Al • USA
TAKE ME HIGH • 1973 • Askey David • UKN • HOT PROPERTY
TAKE ME HOME • 1928 • Neilan Marshall • USA
TAKE ME, LOVE ME (UKN) see **NANA** • 1970
TAKE ME NAKED • 1966 • Findlay Michael, Findlay Roberta • USA • TAKE ME
TAKE ME OUT TO THE BALL GAME • 1910 • Anderson G. M. • USA
TAKE ME OUT TO THE BALL GAME • 1948 • Berkeley Busby • USA • EVERYBODY'S CHEERING (UKN)
TAKE ME OVER • 1963 • Lynn Robert • UKN
TAKE ME SKIING see **WATASHI WO SKI NI TSURETETTE** • 1988
TAKE ME TO PARIS • 1951 • Raymond Jack • UKN
TAKE ME TO TOWN • 1953 • Sirk Douglas • USA
TAKE ME TO YOUR GEN'RUL • 1962 • Kneitel Seymour • ANS • USA
TAKE ME WHILE I'M WARM see **PLAYGROUND, THE** • 1965
TAKE MY BODY • 1984 • Leblanc Michel • FRN
TAKE MY HAND • 1975 • Fox Beryl • DOC • CND
TAKE MY HEAD • 1970 • Findlay Roberta • USA
TAKE MY LIFE • 1947 • Neame Ronald • UKN
TAKE MY TIP • 1937 • Mason Herbert • UKN
TAKE NEXT CAR • 1922 • Roach Hal • SHT • USA
TAKE NO PRISONERS see **OPERATION: TAKE NO PRISONERS** • 1988
TAKE OFF • 1973 • Nelson Gunvor • SHT • USA
TAKE OFF • 1978 • Weston Armand • USA
TAKE OFF THAT HAT • 1938 • Humphris Eric • UKN
TAKE OFF YOUR CLOTHES AND LIVE • 1963 • Miller Arnold Louis • UKN
TAKE ONE BABY • 1968 • Erulkar Sarah • DCS • UKN
TAKE ONE FALSE STEP • 1949 • Erskine Chester • USA
TAKE SIX • 1963 • Hickox Douglas • UKN
TAKE SOME GIRLS see **WEEKEND WITH THE BABYSITTER** • 1970
TAKE THE 5:10 TO DREAMLAND • 1976 • Conner Bruce • SHT • USA
TAKE THE AIR • 1923 • Roach Hal • SHT • USA
TAKE THE AIR • 1940 • Eason B. Reeves • SHT • USA
TAKE THE HEIR • 1930 • Ingraham Lloyd • USA
TAKE THE HIGH GROUND • 1953 • Brooks Richard • USA
TAKE THE MONEY AND RUN • 1969 • Allen Woody • USA
TAKE THE STAGE (UKN) see **CURTAIN CALL AT CACTUS CREEK** • 1950
TAKE THE STAND • 1934 • Rosen Phil • USA • GREAT RADIO MYSTERY, THE (UKN)
TAKE THIS JOB AND SHOVE IT • 1981 • Trikonis Gus • USA
TAKE THIS MY BODY see **CORPO, IL** • 1974
TAKE TIME TO SMELL THE FLOWERS • 1977 • Caras Chris • USA • COME WITH ME MY LOVE
TAKE TO THE HILLS see **TIRARSE AL MONTE** • 1972
TAKE TWO • 1972 • Dienar Baruch • ISR
TAKE TWO • 1987 • Rowe Peter • CND
TAKE YOUR BEST SHOT • 1982 • Greene David • TVM • USA
TAKE YOUR MEDICINE • 1930 • Cline Eddie • SHT • USA
TAKE YOUR PHOTOGRAPH SIR? • 1901 • *Warwick Trading Co* • UKN
TAKE YOUR PLACE, CITIZEN HUMBLE! • Dukic Radivoje-Lola
TAKE YOUR TIME • 1925 • Bacon Lloyd • SHT • USA
TAKEKURABE • 1955 • Gosho Heinosuke • JPN • GROWING UP ○ COMPARISON OF HEIGHTS ○ DAUGHTERS OF YOSHIWARA
TAKEN BY FORCE • 1987 • Schwain Don • USA
TAKEN BY FORCE see **SLIPPING INTO DARKNESS** • 1988
TAKEN BY STORM • 1914 • Young James • USA
TAKEN BY SURPRISE see **TAKE HER BY SURPRISE** • 1967
TAKEN FOR A RIDE • 1931 • *Mintz Charles (P)* • ANS • USA
TAKEN FOR A RIDE see **BOCKSHORN**
TAKERS, THE • 1971 • *Bush Fred* • USA
TAKERS, THE see **MOMENT OF DANGER** • 1960
TAKETORI MONOGATARI • 1988 • Ichikawa Kon • JPN • LEGEND OF PRINCESS MOON ○ PRINCESS FROM THE MOON
TAKI NO SHIRAITO • 1933 • Mizoguchi Kenji • JPN • WATER MAGICIAN, THE (UKN) ○ WHITE THREADS OF THE WATERFALL ○ WHITE THREADS OF THE CASCADES
TAKI NO SHIRAITO • 1952 • Nobuchi Akira • JPN • WHITE THREADS OF THE CASCADES ○ WATER MAGICIAN, OR THE WHITE THREAD OF THE WATERFALL, THE
TAKIAISPALLO • 1970 • Saikkonen Veli-Matti • FNL • BALL OF BURR
TAKIJI KOBAYASHI • 1974 • Imai Tadashi • JPN • LIFE OF A COMMUNIST WRITER, THE ○ KOBAYASHI TAKIJI
TAKIN' IT OFF • 1984 • Hanson Ed • USA
TAKIN' THE BREAKS • 1946 • Cowan Will • SHT • USA
TAKING A CHANCE • 1912 • Salter Harry • USA
TAKING A CHANCE • 1915 • Fahrney Milton • USA
TAKING A CHANCE • 1916 • Mix Tom • SHT • USA
TAKING A CHANCE • 1928 • McLeod Norman Z. • USA
TAKING A FILM • 1915 • Nash Percy? • UKN
TAKING A LEAP • 1983 • Muller John • DOC • CND
TAKING A REST • 1916 • Drew Sidney • SHT • USA
TAKING CARE • 1988 • Mackey Clarke • CND • PRESCRIPTION FOR MURDER
TAKING CARE OF BABY • 1912 • *Thanhouser* • USA
TAKING CARE OF BABY • 1934 • Cummings Jack • USA
TAKING CARE OF BUSINESS • 1990 • Hiller Arthur • USA
TAKING CHANCES • 1915 • *Deer* • USA
TAKING CHANCES • 1917 • Terwilliger George W. • SHT • USA
TAKING CHANCES • 1922 • Jones Grover • USA
TAKING CHANCES • 1979 • Belec Marilyn A. • CND
TAKING FATHER'S DINNER • 1912 • Wilson Frank? • UKN
TAKING HER MEASURE • 1915 • *Rhodes Billie* • USA
TAKING HIS CHANCE • 1914 • Longford Raymond • SHT • ASL
TAKING HIS MEDICINE • 1911 • Sennett Mack • USA
TAKING HIS PHOTOGRAPH • 1909 • *Edison* • USA
TAKING MOOD, THE • 1969 • Williams Derek • UKN
TAKING OF BEVERLY HILLS, THE • 1990 • Furie Sidney J. • USA
TAKING OF FLIGHT 847, THE • 1988 • Wendkos Paul • TVM • USA • TAKING OF FLIGHT 847: THE ULE DERICKSON STORY, THE
TAKING OF FLIGHT 847: THE ULE DERICKSON STORY, THE see **TAKING OF FLIGHT 847, THE** • 1988
TAKING OF LUKE MCVANE, THE • 1915 • Hart William S., Smith Cliff • USA • FUGITIVE, THE
TAKING OF MUSTANG PETE, THE • 1915 • Mix Tom • USA
TAKING OF PELHAM ONE-TWO-THREE, THE • 1974 • Sargent Joseph • USA
TAKING OF RATTLESNAKE BILL, THE • 1913 • Ince John • USA
TAKING OF SAMELAND, THE • 1984 • Eriksen Skule, Tannvik Kare • DOC • NRW
TAKING OFF • 1971 • Forman Milos • USA • S.P.F.C.
TAKING ORDERS • 1923 • USA
TAKING SIDES (UKN) see **LIGHTNING GUNS** • 1950
TAKING THE BLAME • 1935 • Fleischer Dave • ANS • USA
TAKING THE COUNT • 1916 • *Turpin Ben* • SHT • USA
TAKING THE COUNT • 1918 • *Field Elinor* • USA
TAKING THE COUNT • 1920 • *Collier William* • USA
TAKING THE HONEY OUT OF HONEYMOON • 1916 • Smith David • SHT • USA
TAKING THE TOWN see **QUICK MONEY** • 1937
TAKING THEIR MEDICIN • 1917 • Clements Roy • SHT • USA
TAKING THINGS EASY • 1919 • Edwards Harry J. • SHT • USA
TAKING TIGER MOUNTAIN • 1983 • Smith Kent, Huckabee Tom • UKN
TAKING TIGER MOUNTAIN BY STRATEGY see **ZHI QU WEI HU SHAN** • 1970
TAKING TIME TO FEEL • 1978 • Sommers Frank G. • DOC • CND
TAKING TO THE HILLS see **TIRARSE AL MONTE** • 1972
TAKING UNCLE FOR A RIDE • 1911 • Wilson Frank? • UKN
TAKING WAYS • 1933 • Baxter John • UKN
TAKO • 1987 • Fukushima Michael • ANS • CND • KITE
TAKOVA LASKA • 1959 • Weiss Jiri • CZC • APPASSIONATA ○ THAT KIND OF LOVE
TAKOVY JE ZIVOT • 1929 • Junghans Karl • CZC, FRG • SO IST DAS LEBEN (FRG) ○ THAT'S LIFE ○ SUCH IS LIFE
TAKOY BOLSHOY MALCHIK • 1967 • Fyodorova Marina • USS • SUCH A BIG BOY
TAKT OG TONE I HIMMELSENGEN • 1971 • Methling Sven • DNM • HOW TO CATCH A MAN (UKN)
TAKT, TONE OG TOSSER • 1924 • Lauritzen Lau • DNM
TAKTAZANE SAHRA • 1968 • Safaei Ahmad • IRN • FIRST RIDER OF THE SAHARA
TAKTIK • 1989 • Dahalan Junaidi, Khung Tommy • MLY
TAKTSTOCK RICHARD WAGGNERS, DER • 1918 • Leffler Robert • FRG
TAKU • 1939 • Dawn Norman • USA
TAKUBOKU, THE PASSIONATE POET see **GYONETSU NO SHIJIN TAKUBOKU** • 1936
TAKUKU KANKEI • 1968 • Ogawa Kinya • JPN • MULTIPLE AFFAIRS
TAKYR, THE SLAVE-GIRL see **RABINYA** • 1970
TAL DER SIEBEN MONDE, DAS • 1967 • Kolditz Gottfried • GDR • VALLEY OF THE SEVEN MOONS, THE
TAL DER WITWEN, DAS • 1975 • Vogeler Volker • FRG, SPN • VALLEY OF THE WIDOWS, THE ○ VALLE DE LAS VIUDAS, EL
TAL DES LEBENS, DAS • 1914 • Biebrach Rudolf • FRG
TAL DES LEBENS, DAS see **AMMENKONIG, DER** • 1935
TAL FARLOW • 1980 • Lye Len • SHT • USA
TAL LUIS COSTA, UN • Cortes Luis • SPN
TAL PARA CUAL • 1952 • Gonzalez Rogelio A. • MXC
TALA AND RHYTHM • 1972 • Benegal Shyam • DCS • IND
TALA -INDIAN LOVE SONG • 1907 • Gilbert Arthur • UKN
TALACRE SCHOOL • 1976 • King George* • UKN
TALAKOZAS • Elek Judit • SHT • HNG • ENCOUNTER
TALALKOZAS LUKACS GYORGGYEL • 1972 • Kovacs Andras • MTV • HNG • MEETING GYORGY LUKACS
TALASH • 1969 • *Burman S. D. (M)* • IND
TALATH LESSONS see **THALATHATU LUCUC** • 1966
TALBOT OF CANADA • 1938 • CND
TALCUM POWDER see **BOROTALCO** • 1982
TALE, A • Marucci Salvatore L. • SHT • UKN
TALE, A see **BAJKA** • 1970
TALE A CAMERA TOLD, THE • 1910 • *Defender* • USA
TALE ABOUT A BEETLE, A • 1963 • Nepp Jozsef • ANM • HNG
TALE ABOUT A SOLDIER • 1948 • Brumberg Valentina, Brumberg Zinaida • ANS • USS
TALE ABOUT THE ROAD, A • 1986 • Koulev Henri • ANM • BUL
TALE ABOUT UMAR KHAPTSOKO, THE • 1932 • Raizman Yuli • USS • STORY ABOUT OMAR KHAPTSOKO, A
TALE FOR EVERYONE, A • 1965 • Donev Donyo • ANM • BUL
TALE FROM GENJI, A see **GENJI MONOGATARI** • 1951
TALE FROM THE DECAMERON, A • 1916 • Windom Lawrence C. • SHT • USA
TALE OF 12 POINTS see **MESE A TIZENKET TALALATROL** • 1956
TALE OF A BLACK EYE, THE • 1913 • Sennett Mack • USA
TALE OF A CARPENTER see **DAIKU TAIHEIKI** • 1965
TALE OF A CAT • 1913 • *Solax* • USA
TALE OF A CAT, THE • 1911 • Porter Edwin S. • USA
TALE OF A CAT, THE • 1912 • *Missimer Howard* • USA
TALE OF A CAT, THE • 1914 • *Royal* • USA
TALE OF A CHICKEN, THE • 1914 • *Lubin* • USA
TALE OF A CLOCK, THE • 1913 • *Mason Billy* • USA
TALE OF A COAT, THE • 1905 • Collins Alf? • UKN
TALE OF A COAT, THE • 1914 • Murphy J. A. • USA
TALE OF A COAT, THE • 1916 • Beaudine William • USA
TALE OF A DEAD PRINCESS, THE • 1953 • Ivanov-Vano Ivan • ANM • USS
TALE OF A DOG • 1944 • Endfield Cy • SHT • USA
TALE OF A DOG, A • 1959 • Tendlar Dave • ANS • USA
TALE OF A DOG, THE • 1914 • *Powers* • USA
TALE OF A DOG, THE • 1920 • Buckingham Thomas • SHT • USA
TALE OF A FISH, THE • 1913 • *Grandon Ethel* • USA
TALE OF A GREEDY WOLF • 1919 • ANS • FRG
TALE OF A HAREM, THE • 1908 • *Vitagraph* • USA
TALE OF A HAT, A • 1910 • *Vitagraph* • USA
TALE OF A HAT, THE • 1913 • *Nestor* • USA
TALE OF A HAT, THE • 1914 • *Sterling* • USA
TALE OF A HAT, THE • 1915 • *Kalem* • USA
TALE OF A HAT, THE • 1918 • *Field Elinor* • USA
TALE OF A JOURNEY see **OPOWIESC O DRODZE** • 1958
TALE OF A KITE, THE • 1912 • *Republic* • USA
TALE OF A LINK, THE see **ISTORIA ODNOGO KOLZA** • 1948
TALE OF A LONELY COAST, THE • 1913 • *Leonard Robert* • USA
TALE OF A LONESOME DOG, THE • 1914 • *Victor* • USA
TALE OF A MOUNTAIN see **BIR DAG MASALI** • 1967
TALE OF A MOUSE, THE • 1907 • Martin J. H.? • UKN
TALE OF A RUBBER BOAT, THE • 1912 • *Comet* • USA
TALE OF A SHIRT • 1933 • *Terry Paul/ Moser Frank (P)* • ANS • USA
TALE OF A SHIRT, THE • 1914 • *Mace Fred* • USA
TALE OF A SHIRT, THE • 1915 • Mackenzie Donald • USA
TALE OF A SHIRT, THE • 1916 • Kellino W. P. • UKN
TALE OF A SHIRT, THE • 1922 • Ramster P. J. • ASL
TALE OF A SOLDIER'S RING, THE • 1911 • *Selig* • USA
TALE OF A TAILOR, THE • 1914 • Pollard Harry • USA
TALE OF A TELEGRAM, THE • 1916 • Curtis Glen • SHT • USA
TALE OF A TENDRIL • 1925 • Smith Percy • UKN
TALE OF A THANKSGIVING TURKEY, THE • 1908 • *Essanay* • USA
TALE OF A TOWER • 1971 • Harvey Francis • UKN
TALE OF A TURK, THE • 1916 • Beaudine William • SHT • USA
TALE OF A TYRE • 1915 • *Pollard Snub* • SHT • USA
TALE OF A WOLF • 1958 • Hanna William, Barbera Joseph • ANS • USA
TALE OF AFRICA, A see **AFURIKA MONOGATARI** • 1981
TALE OF AN EGG, THE • 1912 • *Gaumont* • USA
TALE OF ARCHERY AT THE SANJUSANGENDO, A see **SANJU-SANGENDO TOSHIYA MONOGATARI** • 1945
TALE OF CHUN HYANG, THE • NKR
TALE OF CZAR SALTAN, THE see **SKAZKA O TSARE SALTANE** • 1967
TALE OF DEATH VALLEY, A • 1913 • Hamilton G. P.? • USA
TALE OF EBON TINTS, A • 1911 • *Reliance* • USA
TALE OF FIVE CITIES, A • 1951 • Tully Montgomery, Marcellini Romolo, Staudte Wolfgang, Reinert Emile Edwin, von Cziffra Geza • UKN, ITL, FRG • STORIA DI CINQUE CITTA (ITL) ○ TALE OF FIVE WOMEN, A
TALE OF FIVE WOMEN, A see **TALE OF FIVE CITIES, A** • 1951
TALE OF GENJI, A see **GENJI MONOGATARI** • 1951
TALE OF GENJI, THE see **GENJI MONOGATARI** • 1966
TALE OF HIS PANTS, THE • 1915 • Davey Horace • USA
TALE OF HOW TSAR PETER MARRIED OFF HIS MOOR, THE • 1976 • Mitta Alexander • USS
TALE OF JEALOUSY, A • 1905 • *Warwick Trading Co* • UKN
TALE OF JOHN AND MARY, THE see **POHADKA O HONZIKOVI A MARENCE** • 1980
TALE OF LIGHT, THE • 1949 • Werner Gosta • SHT • SWD
TALE OF LOST TIME see **STORY OF LOST TIME, THE** • 1964
TALE OF MAIL, A • 1967 • Canning William, Stear Donald • CND • AU PIED DE LA LETTRE
TALE OF MIDNIGHT, A see **HEKAYET NUS EL LAIL** • 1964
TALE OF OLD TAHITI, A • 1913 • Melies Gaston • USA
TALE OF OLD TUSCAN, A • 1914 • Ridgely Richard • USA
TALE OF RUBY ROSE, THE • 1987 • Scholes Roger • ASL
TALE OF RUSTAM • Kimyagarov Boris • USS
TALE OF SIBERIA, A see **SKAZANIYE O ZEMLYE SIBIRSKOI** • 1947
TALE OF TAILS, A • 1912 • Stow Percy • UKN
TALE OF TAILS, A • 1933 • Shepherd Horace • UKN
TALE OF TALES, THE • 1980 • Norshtein Yuri • ANM • USS
TALE OF TEXAS, A • 1909 • *Centaur* • USA
TALE OF THE ARK, THE • 1909 • Cooper Arthur • ANS • UKN • NOAH'S ARK
TALE OF THE AUSTRALIAN BUSH, A • 1911 • Mervale Gaston • ASL
TALE OF THE BACKWOODS, A • 1910 • *Selig* • USA
TALE OF THE BUNNY PARK, THE • Henson Jim • ANM • UKN • TALE OF THE BUNNY PICNIC, THE ○ BUNNY PICNIC, THE
TALE OF THE BUNNY PICNIC, THE see **TALE OF THE BUNNY PARK, THE**
TALE OF THE C, THE • 1915 • Henderson Lucius • USA
TALE OF THE COCK • 1966 • Derek John, Nelson David • USA • CHILDISH THINGS ○ CONFESSIONS OF TOM HARRIS
TALE OF THE CRUSADES, A • 1908 • *Vitagraph* • USA

TALE OF THE DEAN'S WIFE, THE see **DEAN'S WIFE, THE** • 1970
TALE OF THE DESERT, A • 1914 • *Eclair* • USA
TALE OF THE DOG see **PSI POHADKA** • 1959
TALE OF THE DON, A see **DON STORY, THE** • 1964
TALE OF THE FIDDLE, THE • 1909 • *Urban-Eclipse* • UKN
TALE OF THE FISHERMAN AND THE LITTLE FISH see **SKAZKA O RYBAKE I RYBKE** • 1937
TALE OF THE FJORDS see **DROMDA DALEN, DEN** • 1947
TALE OF THE FOOTHILLS, A • 1911 • *Bison* • USA
TALE OF THE FOOTHILLS, A • 1912 • *Nestor* • USA
TALE OF THE FOX, THE see **ROMAN DE REYNARD, LE** • 1938
TALE OF THE FROG PRINCE • 1982 • Idle Eric • MTV • USA
TALE OF THE HILLS, A • 1915 • Golden Joseph A.? • USA
TALE OF THE HOT DOG, THE • 1910 • *Atlas* • USA
TALE OF THE MAGICIAN, THE • 1964 • *Halas John (P)* • ANS • UKN
TALE OF THE NORTHWEST MOUNTED, A • 1914 • *Broncho* • USA
TALE OF THE PINE BOUGH • 1960 • Dinov Todor • ANM • BUL • STORY OF A TWIG
TALE OF THE PRINCE AND THE THREE DOCTORS, THE • 1966 • Tisachenko O. • ANS • USS
TALE OF THE SAMPO, THE see **SAMMON TARINA** • 1974
TALE OF THE SEA, A • 1910 • *Champion* • USA
TALE OF THE SEA, A • 1910 • *Selig* • USA
TALE OF THE SNOW, A • 1912 • *Champion* • USA
TALE OF THE TOOTH, THE • 1907 • *Walturdaw* • USA
TALE OF THE TUCKER, THE • 1913 • *Kerrigan J. Warren* • USA
TALE OF THE VIENNA WOODS, A • 1934 • Harman Hugh • ANS • USA
TALE OF THE WEST, A • 1909 • *Anderson Broncho Billy* • USA
TALE OF THE WEST, A • 1913 • *Mcdonald Donald* • USA
TALE OF THE WILDERNESS, A • 1912 • Griffith D. W. • USA
TALE OF THE WIND see **HISTOIRE DE VENT, UNE** • 1988
TALE OF THREE WOMEN, A • 1954 • Dickson Paul, Connell Thelma • UKN
TALE OF TIFFANY LUST, THE • 1981 • Metzger Radley H., Kikoine Gerard • USA • BODY LUST
TALE OF TIRE • 1915 • *Essanay* • USA
TALE OF TSAR SALTAN, THE see **SKAZKA O TSARE SALTANE** • 1967
TALE OF TWENTY STORIES, A • 1915 • *L-Ko* • USA
TALE OF TWO CITIES, A • 1911 • Humphrey William • USA
TALE OF TWO CITIES, A • 1917 • Lloyd Frank • USA
TALE OF TWO CITIES, A • 1922 • Rowden W. C. • UKN
TALE OF TWO CITIES, A • 1935 • Conway Jack, Van Dyke W. S. (U/c) • USA
TALE OF TWO CITIES, A • 1958 • Thomas Ralph • UKN
TALE OF TWO CITIES, A • 1980 • Goddard Jim • TVM • USA
TALE OF TWO CITIES, A see **ONLY WAY, THE** • 1925
TALE OF TWO COATS, A • 1910 • *Edison* • USA
TALE OF TWO KITTIES, A • 1944 • Clampett Robert • ANS • USA
TALE OF TWO MICE, A • 1945 • Tashlin Frank • ANS • USA
TALE OF TWO NATIONS, A • 1917 • *August Edwin* • USA
TALE OF TWO TABLES, A • 1913 • Collins Edwin J.? • UKN
TALE OF TWO WORLDS, A • 1921 • Lloyd Frank • USA • WATER LILY, THE
TALE OF TWO WORLDS, A see **MATTER OF LIFE AND DEATH, A** • 1946
TALE OF URSUS, THE see **POEMAT SYMFONICZNY "BAJKA" STANISLAWA MONIUSZKO** • 1952
TALE OF WHEELS see **HJULSAGA, EN**
TALE ON THE TWELVE POINTS see **MESE A TIZENKET TALALATROL** • 1956
TALE-TELLER PHONE, THE • 1928 • Stanley Arthur • UKN
TALE THE TICKER TOLD • 1908 • Porter Edwin S. • USA
TALEB, LE • 1962 • Nacif Abdel-Halim • SHT • ALG
TALENT COMPETITION see **KONKURS** • 1963
TALENT FOR LOVING, A • 1969 • Quine Richard • USA
TALENT SCOUT • 1937 • Clemens William • USA • STUDIO ROMANCE (UKN)
TALENT SHOWCASE • 1951 • Blais Roger • DCS • CND
TALENTED TRAMPS, THE • 1949 • *Gray Billy* • SHT • USA
TALENTED WOMAN, THE see **SAIJO KATAGI** • 1959
TALENTS UNLIMITED • 1968 • Pacheco Lauro • PHL
TALES • 1969 • Gerstein Cassandra M. • DOC • USA
TALES ABOUT CHILDREN • 1963 • Hanibal Jiri • CZC
TALES AFTER THE RAIN see **UGETSU MONOGATARI** • 1953
TALES AND YARNS • Hempel Johannes • ANM • GDR
TALES BY CAPEK see **CAPKOVY POVIDKY** • 1947
TALES FOR MALES • 1970 • ANT • USA
TALES FROM A COUNTRY BY THE SEA see **KAIKOKUKI** • 1928
TALES FROM BEYOND THE GRAVE see **FROM BEYOND THE GRAVE** • 1973
TALES FROM CAPEK see **CAPKOVY POVIDKY** • 1947
TALES FROM MYSTERIOUS BUENOS AIRES see **CUENTOS DE LA MISTERIOSA BUENOS AIRES** • 1981
TALES FROM THE BEYOND see **FROM BEYOND THE GRAVE** • 1973
TALES FROM THE CRYPT • 1972 • Francis Freddie • UKN
TALES FROM THE CRYPT PART II see **VAULT OF HORROR** • 1973
TALES FROM THE DARKSIDE: THE MOVIE • 1990 • Harrison John • USA
TALES FROM THE FIRST REPUBLIC see **POVIDKY Z PRVNI REPUBLIKY** • 1965
TALES FROM THE GIMLI HOSPITAL • 1988 • Maddin Guy • CND
TALES FROM THE LIFE OF A PRAGUE TAXI-DRIVER see **TAXI PROSIM** • 1961
TALES FROM THE NEW WORLD see **ERZAHLUNGEN AUS DER NEUEN WELT** • 1968
TALES FROM THE OLD MONARCHY • 1952 • Hubacek Miroslav • CZC
TALES FROM THE VIENNA WOODS • 1973 • Soul Veronika • ANS • CND
TALES FROM THE VIENNA WOODS see **GESCHICHTEN AUS DEM WIENERWALD** • 1979
TALES FROM THE VIENNA WOODS (USA) see **G'SCHICHTEN AUS DEM WIENERWALD** • 1934
TALES OF 1001 NIGHTS see **POHADKY TISICE A JEDNE NOCI** • 1972
TALES OF A DRAGON see **BAJKA O SMOKU** • 1962
TALES OF A HIGH CLASS HOOKER • 1979 • USA
TALES OF A LONG JOURNEY see **LEGENDA A VONATON** • 1962
TALES OF A SALESMAN • 1965 • Russell Don • USA • TALES OF A TRAVELING SALESMAN
TALES OF A THOUSAND AND ONE NIGHTS, THE (USA) see **CONTES DES MILLE ET UNE NUITS, LES** • 1921
TALES OF A TRAVELING SALESMAN see **TALES OF A SALESMAN** • 1965
TALES OF BEATRIX POTTER • 1971 • Mills Reginald • UKN • PETER RABBIT AND TALES OF BEATRIX POTTER (USA)
TALES OF BUDAPEST see **BUDAPESTI MESEK** • 1976
TALES OF BUDAPEST (USA) see **PESTE MESE** • 1938
TALES OF CAPEK see **CAPKOVY POVIDKY** • 1947
TALES OF CZAR TSALTAN see **SKAZKA O TSARE SALTANE** • 1967
TALES OF DROUGHTY SOIL see **RELATOS DE TIERRA SECA** • 1979
TALES OF ENSIGN STEEL, THE see **FANRIK STALS SAGNER** • 1926
TALES OF EROTIC FANTASY see **CONTES PERVERS** • 1980
TALES OF EROTICA see **GIOCHI PROIBITI DELL'ARETINO PIETRO** • 1972
TALES OF HOFFMAN, THE • 1951 • Powell Michael, Pressburger Emeric • UKN
TALES OF HOFFMANN see **HOFFMANNS ERZAHLUNGEN** • 1911
TALES OF HOFFMANN see **HOFFMANNS ERZAHLUNGEN** • 1924
TALES OF HOFFMANN, THE see **HOFFMANOVY POVIDKY** • 1962
TALES OF HOFFMANN (USA) see **HOFFMANNS ERZAHLUNGEN** • 1916
TALES OF HOFFNUNG • 1964 • *Halas John (P)* • ASS • UKN
TALES OF MANHATTAN • 1942 • Duvivier Julien • USA
TALES OF MYSTERY (UKN) see **HISTOIRES EXTRAORDINAIRES** • 1968
TALES OF ONE NIGHT, THE see **QUARANTE-QUATRE** • 1981
TALES OF ORDINARY MADNESS see **STORIE DI ORDINARIA FOLLIA** • 1981
TALES OF PARIS see **PARISIENNES, LES** • 1962
TALES OF ROBIN HOOD • 1951 • Tinling James • USA
TALES OF SIBERIAN LAND see **SKAZANIYE O ZEMLYE SIBIRSKOI** • 1947
TALES OF TERROR • 1962 • Corman Roger • USA • POE'S TALES OF TERROR
TALES OF THAT NIGHT see **GESCHICHTEN JENER NACHT** • 1967
TALES OF THE BUSH • 1912 • ASL
TALES OF THE FISH PATROL see **JACK LONDON'S TALES OF THE FISH PATROL** • 1923
TALES OF THE GOLD MONKEY • 1982 • Austin Ray • TVM • USA
TALES OF THE NINJA (USA) see **NINJA BUGEICHO** • 1967
TALES OF THE NUNUNDAGA • 1977 • Moxey John Llewellyn • TVM • USA
TALES OF THE PALE AND SILVERY MOON AFTER THE RAIN (UKN) see **UGETSU MONOGATARI** • 1953
TALES OF THE TAIRA CLAN see **SHIN HEIKE MONOGATARI** • 1955
TALES OF THE TYPEWRITER see **MESEK AZ IROGEPROL** • 1916
TALES OF THE UNCANNY see **UNHEIMLICHE GESCHICHTEN** • 1919
TALES OF THE UNCANNY see **UNHEIMLICHE GESCHICHTEN** • 1932
TALES OF THE WEST #1 • 1950 • Cowan Will • ANT • USA
TALES OF THE WEST #2 • 1950 • Cowan Will • ANT • USA
TALES OF THE WEST #3 • 1950 • Cowan Will • ANT • USA
TALES OF THE WEST #4 • 1951 • Cowan Will • ANT • USA
TALES OF TSAR DURANDAI see **SKAZKA O CARE DURANDAE** • 1934
TALES OF TWO SISTERS • 1989 • Riskin Adam • USA
TALES POR CUALES, LOS • 1964 • Martinez Solares Gilberto • MXC
TALES THAT WITNESS MADNESS • 1973 • Francis Freddie • UKN
TALES THE AUTUMN LEAVES TOLD • 1908 • Porter Edwin S. • USA
TALES THE SEARCHLIGHT TOLD • 1908 • Porter Edwin S. • USA
TALFAHRT DES SEVERIN HOYER, DIE • 1922 • Linnekogel Otto • FRG
TALGAI SKULL, THE • 1968 • Haydon Tom • DOC • ASL
TALI MERAH PERKAWINAN • 1983 • Sulaiman Hengky • INN • RED THREAD OF MARRIAGE, THE
TALIHLI AMELE • 1981 • Yilmaz Atif • TRK • LUCKY WORKER, THE
TALIHSIZ MERYEM • 1968 • Duz Aykut • TRK • UNLUCKY MERYEM
TALION, LE • 1921 • Maudru Charles • FRN
TALIRE NAD VELKYM MALIKOVEM • 1977 • Jires Jaromil • CZC • FLYING SAUCERS COMING! ○ FLYING SAUCERS OVER THE TOWN
TALISMAN see **AMULETTEN** • 1911
TALISMAN, DER • 1915 • Seefeld Eddie F. • FRG
TALISMAN, THE • 1911 • *American* • USA
TALISMAN, THE • Molander Gustaf • SWD
TALISMAN, THE • 1966 • Carr John • USA • SAVAGE AMERICAN, THE
TALISMAN, THE • 1986 • Patel Ishu • MTV • CND
TALK, THE see **ROZMOWA** • 1974
TALK ABOUT A LADY • 1946 • Sherman George • USA • DUCHESS OF BROADWAY
TALK ABOUT A STRANGER • 1952 • Bradley David • USA • ENEMY, THE ○ NEXT DOOR NEIGHBOR, THE
TALK ABOUT JACQUELINE • 1942 • Stein Paul L. • UKN
TALK DIRTY TO ME • 1980 • Spinelli Anthony • USA
TALK NAUGHTY TO ME • 1981 • Warfield Chris • USA • CHAMPAGNE FOR BREAKFAST
TALK OF A MILLION • 1951 • Carstairs John Paddy • UKN • YOU CAN'T BEAT THE IRISH (USA)
TALK OF HOLLYWOOD, THE • 1929 • Sandrich Mark • USA
TALK OF THE DEVIL • 1936 • Reed Carol • UKN • MAN WITH YOUR VOICE, A
TALK OF THE DEVIL • 1967 • Searle Francis • UKN
TALK OF THE TOWN • 1918 • Holubar Allen • USA
TALK OF THE TOWN see **SAGS PA STAN, DET** • 1941
TALK OF THE TOWN, THE • 1942 • Stevens George • USA • THREE'S A CROWD
TALK RADIO • 1988 • Stone Oliver • USA
TALKATIVE LADY • 1909 • USA
TALKATIVE TESS • 1913 • *Patheplay* • USA
TALKAUTOBANDEN • 1970 • MacGillivray William D. • CND
TALKED TO DEATH • 1909 • *Lubin* • USA
TALKER, THE • 1912 • *Lubin* • USA
TALKER, THE • 1925 • Green Alfred E. • USA
TALKIES, THE • 1929 • Roberts Stephen • SHT • USA
TALKING ABOUT KIRKALDY.. • 1975 • Clark-Hall Stephen • DOC • UKN
TALKING BEAR, THE see **OURS, L'** • 1960
TALKING CAFTAN, THE • 1969 • Fejer Tamas • HNG
TALKING DOG • 1956 • Lovy Alex • ANS • USA
TALKING FEET • 1937 • Baxter John • UKN
TALKING HANDS • 1936 • Campbell Ivar • UKN • HANDS IN HARMONY
TALKING HEAD, THE • 1904 • *Paul R. W.* • UKN
TALKING HORSE SENSE • 1959 • Kneitel Seymour • ANS • USA
TALKING MAGPIES, THE • 1946 • Davis Mannie • ANS • USA
TALKING PARCEL, THE • 1978 • Cosgrove Brian • ANM • UKN
TALKING THROUGH MY HEART • 1936 • Fleischer Dave • ANS • USA
TALKING TO A STRANGER • 1971 • Till Eric • CND
TALKING TO THE PICTURE • 1913 • *Hemsley Harry May* • UKN
TALKING TURKEY • 1930 • Sandrich Mark • SHT • USA
TALKING WALLS • 1984 • Verona Stephen F. • USA
TALK'S CHEAP see **SNACKA GAR JU..** • 1982
TALKY JONES • 1918 • Matt Allen • SHT • USA
TALL BLOND MAN WITH ONE BLACK SHOE, THE see **MAN WITH ONE RED SHOE, THE** • 1985
TALL BLOND MAN WITH ONE BLACK SHOE, THE (USA) see **GRAND BLOND AVEC UNE CHAUSSURE NOIRE, LE** • 1972
TALL, DARK AND GRUESOME • 1947 • Lord Del • SHT • USA
TALL, DARK AND HANDSOME • 1941 • Humberstone H. Bruce • USA
TALL GUY, THE • 1988 • Smith Mel • UKN • CAMDEN TOWN BOY
TALL HEADLINES, THE • 1952 • Young Terence • UKN • FRIGHTENED BRIDE, THE
TALL IN THE SADDLE • 1944 • Marin Edwin L. • USA
TALL IN THE TRAP • 1962 • Deitch Gene • ANS • USA
TALL LASSE FROM DELSBO see **LANG-LASSE I DELSBO** • 1949
TALL LIE, THE • 1952 • Henreid Paul • USA • FOR MEN ONLY
TALL MAN EXECUTES A JIG, A • 1986 • Winkler Donald • MTV • CND
TALL MAN RIDING • 1955 • Selander Lesley • USA
TALL MEN, THE • 1955 • Walsh Raoul • USA
TALL ORDER • 1948-51 • Harris Roy • DOC • UKN
TALL SHADOWS OF THE WIND see **SAYEHAYE BOLANDE BAD** • 1978
TALL STORY • 1960 • Logan Joshua • USA
TALL STRANGER, THE • 1957 • Carr Thomas • USA
TALL 'T', THE • 1957 • Boetticher Budd • USA
TALL TALE TELLER • 1954 • Rasinski Connie • ANS • USA
TALL TALES • 1941 • Van Dyke Willard, Watts William • SHT • USA
TALL, TAN AND TERRIFIC • 1946 • Pollard Bud • USA
TALL TARGET, THE • 1951 • Mann Anthony • USA
TALL TEXAN, THE • 1953 • Williams Elmo • USA
TALL, THE DARK AND THE HANDSOME, THE • 1968 • San Juan Luis • PHL
TALL, THE SHORT, THE CAT, THE see **LUNGO, IL CORTO, IL GATTO, IL** • 1967
TALL TIMBER • 1926 • Webb Dunstan, Longford Raymond? • ASL
TALL TIMBER • 1928 • Disney Walt • ANS • USA
TALL TIMBER see **PARK AVENUE LOGGER** • 1937
TALL TIMBER see **BIG TIMBER** • 1950
TALL TIMBER TALE • 1951 • Rasinski Connie • ANS • USA
TALL TIMBER TALES • 1925 • Barkas Geoffrey • UKN
TALL TIMBERS • 1937 • Hall Ken G. • ASL
TALL TROUBLE, THE (UKN) see **HELL CANYON OUTLAWS** • 1957
TALL WOMEN, THE (USA) see **SIETE MAGNIFICAS, LAS** • 1966
TALLA • 1967 • Le Grice Malcolm • UKN
TALLER DE LINEA Y 18 • 1971 • Guillen Nicolas • DOC • CUB
TALLONE D'ACHILLE, IL • 1952 • Amendola Mario, Maccari Ruggero • ITL
TALLOS AMARGOS, LOS • 1957 • Ayala Fernando • ARG
TALLY HO! • 1901 • Parker Frank • UKN
TALLY HO! PIMPLE • 1915 • Evans Fred, Evans Joe • UKN
TALLY-HOKUM • 1965 • Post Howard • ANS • USA
TALLYMAN, THE • 1928 • Sandground Maurice • UKN
TALMAGE FARLOW • 1981 • De Stefano Lorenzo • DOC • USA
TALON DE AQUILES, EL • 1976 • Klimovsky Leon • SPN
TALPA • 1955 • Crevenna Alfredo B. • MXC • MANDA, LA
TALPALTNYI FOLD • 1948 • Ban Frigyes • HNG • SOIL UNDER YOUR FEET, THE ○ TREASURED EARTH
TALPRA, GYOZO! • 1983 • Szoreny Rezso • HNG • BE TOUGH, VICTOR
TALPUK ALATT FUTYUL A SZEL • 1976 • Szomjas Gyorgy • HNG • WIND IS WHISTLING UNDER THEIR FEET, THE
TALTO, DALAWA, ISA see **TATLO, DALAWA, ISA** • 1974
TALVISOTA • 1989 • Parikka Pekka • FNL • WINTER WAR, THE
TALYROND, THE • 1965 • Ward Peter • UKN

TAM GDYE DLINNAYA ZIMA • 1968 • Davidson Alexandr • USS • THERE, WHERE THE WINTER IS LONG ○ WHERE THE NIGHTS ARE LONG
TAM NA HORACH • 1920 • Goldin Sidney M. • CZC • IN THE MOUNTAINS
TAM NA KONECNE • 1957 • Kadar Jan, Klos Elmar • CZC • HOUSE AT THE TERMINUS, THE ○ AT THE TERMINAL STATION
TAM O'SHANTER • 1915 • MacQuarrie Murdock • USA
TAM O'SHANTER • 1930 • Jeffrey R. E. • UKN
TAM-TAM • 1975 • Arrieta Adolfo • FRN
TAM-TAM A PARIS • 1963 • Sita-Bella Therese • DCS • CMR
TAM TAM MAYUMBE • 1955 • Napolitano Gian Gaspare, Quilici Folco • ITL, FRN • TOM TOMS OF MAYUMBA (UKN) ○ NATIVE DRUMS (USA)
TAM TAM NELL'OLTRE GIUBA • 1954 • Sandri Carlo • ITL
TAM-TAM, RING OUT! see **ZVUCHI TAM-TAM!** • 1968
TAM ZA LESEM • 1962 • Blumenfeld Pavel • CZC • BEYOND THE FOREST ○ BEYOND THE WOOD
TAMAHINE • 1963 • Leacock Philip • UKN
TAMALE VENDOR, THE • 1931 • Arbuckle Roscoe • USA
TAMANDRA, THE GYPSY • 1913 • Nicholls George • USA
TAMANGO • 1958 • Berry John • FRN, ITL
TAMANO NATURAL see **LIFE SIZE** • 1973
TAMARA • 1968 • Pohland Hansjurgen • FRG
TAMARA ALEXANDROVNA'S HUSBAND AND DAUGHTER see **MUZH I DOCH TAMARI ALEXANDROVNY** • 1989
TAMARA LA COMPLAISANTE • 1937 • Gandera Felix, Delannoy Jean • FRN
TAMARIND SEED, THE • 1974 • Edwards Blake • UKN
TAMAS • 1987 • Nihalani Govind • IND
TAMATAVE LA MARINE • Muntcho Monique • FRN
TAMBIEN DE DOLOR SE CANTA • 1950 • Cardona Rene • MXC
TAMBIEN HAY CIELO SOBRE EL MAR • 1955 • Zabalza Jose Maria • SPN
TAMBOR DEL BRUCH, EL • 1948 • Iquino Ignacio F. • SPN
TAMBORA • 1938 • Fejos Paul • DOC • SWD
TAMBOUR BATTANT • 1933 • Beucler Andre, Robison Arthur • FRN • GRAND AMOUR DE JEUNE DESSAUER, LE ○ AMOURS DE JEUNE DESSAUER, LES ○ MONSIEUR LE MARQUIS
TAMBOUR BATTANT • 1952 • Combret Georges • FRN
TAMBOUR DE PIERRE • 1964 • Rouch Jean • FRN • ELEMENTS POUR UNE ETUDE DE RHYTHME ○ TAMBOUR DES DOGONS, LE
TAMBOUR DES DOGONS, LE see **TAMBOUR DE PIERRE** • 1964
TAMBOUR, LE (FRN) see **BLECHTROMMEL, DIE** • 1979
TAMBOURIN FANTASTIQUE ILLUSION FANTASTIQUE • 1908 • Melies Georges • FRN • KNIGHT OF BLACK ART, THE
TAMBOURINE see **HOT BLOOD** • 1956
TAMBOURINE DANCING QUARTETTE • 1902 • Smith G. A. • UKN
TAMBOURS • 1968 • Marzouk Said • SHT • EGY • DRUMS
TAMBURASI U SPEJBLA A HURVINKA • 1953 • *Stallich Jan (Ph)* • SHT • CZC
TAMBURIN UND KASTAGNETTEN • 1919 • Lasko Leo? • FRG
TAME CAT, A • 1912 • Stow Percy • UKN
TAME CAT, THE • 1921 • Bradley William • USA
TAME MEN AND WILD WOMEN • 1925 • Roach Hal • SHT • USA
TAME SONG FOR A BRAVE PEOPLE, A see **CANCION MANSA PARA UN PUEBLO BRAVO** • 1977
TAMEN ZHENG NIANQING • 1987 • Zhou Xiaowen, Fang Fang Hsiao • CHN • IN THEIR PRIME
TAMER OF WILD HORSES (USA) see **KROTITELJ DIVLJIH KONJA** • 1966
T'AMERO SEMPRE • 1933 • Camerini Mario • ITL • IO T'AMERO SEMPRE
T'AMERO SEMPRE • 1943 • Camerini Mario • ITL
TAMGAK • 1989 • Bretzinger Jurgen • FRG
TAMI SHOW, THE see **T.A.M.I. SHOW, THE** • 1964
TAMIAMI TRAIL • 1929 • Aylott Dave, Symmons E. F. • SHT • UKN
TAMING, THE • 1968 • Arkless Robert • USA
TAMING A COWBOY • 1913 • Hamilton G. P.? • USA
TAMING A GRANDFATHER • 1910 • *Vitagraph* • USA
TAMING A GROUCH • 1915 • *Sloan William* • USA
TAMING A HUSBAND • 1910 • Griffith D. W. • USA
TAMING A SHREW • 1915 • *Hatton Leslie* • UKN
TAMING A TENDERFOOT • 1913 • Duncan William • USA
TAMING A TYRANT • 1911 • *Cooksey Curtis* • USA
TAMING A WOMAN HUNTER • 1910 • *Thanhouser* • USA
TAMING FATHER • 1915 • *Rogers Rena* • USA
TAMING GROUCHY BILL • 1916 • Mix Tom • SHT • USA
TAMING LIZA • 1916 • Evans Joe • UKN
TAMING MRS. SHREW • 1912 • Porter Edwin S. • USA
TAMING OF BETTY, THE • 1913 • Costello Maurice • USA
TAMING OF BIG BEN, THE • 1912 • Kellino W. P. • UKN
TAMING OF DOROTHY, THE (USA) see **HER FAVOURITE HUSBAND** • 1950
TAMING OF FIRE see **UKROSCHENIE OGNIA** • 1972
TAMING OF JANE, THE • 1910 • Salter Harry • USA
TAMING OF KAISER BILL, THE • 1918 • *Murray Mae* • SHT • USA
TAMING OF LUCY, THE • 1917 • Swickard Charles • SHT • USA
TAMING OF MARY, THE • 1912 • *Alberti Viola* • USA
TAMING OF MARY, THE • 1915 • Henderson Lucius • USA
TAMING OF RITA, THE • 1915 • Davis Ulysses • USA
TAMING OF SUNNYBROOK NELL, THE • 1914 • Ayres Sydney • USA
TAMING OF TEXAS PETE, THE • 1913 • Duncan William • USA
TAMING OF THE DRAGON, THE see **POHADKA O DRAKOVI** • 1953
TAMING OF THE FIRE see **UKROSCHENIE OGNIA** • 1972
TAMING OF THE IRON • 1963 • Nasser George • SHT • LBN
TAMING OF THE MALE SHREW, THE see **STRINGLOS POV EYINE ARNAKI, O** • 1968
TAMING OF THE SHREW • 1908 • Griffith D. W. • USA
TAMING OF THE SHREW • 1916 • *Judy* • USA
TAMING OF THE SHREW, THE • 1911 • *Benson Frank* • UKN
TAMING OF THE SHREW, THE • 1915 • Backner Arthur • UKN
TAMING OF THE SHREW, THE • 1920 • Dyer Anson • ANM • UKN
TAMING OF THE SHREW, THE • 1923 • Collins Edwin J. • UKN
TAMING OF THE SHREW, THE • 1929 • Taylor Sam • USA
TAMING OF THE SHREW, THE • 1967 • Zeffirelli Franco • USA, ITL • BISBETICA DOMATA, LA (ITL)
TAMING OF THE SHREW, THE • 1980 • Miller Jonathan • TVM • UKN
TAMING OF THE SHREW, THE see **TROLD KAN TAEMMES** • 1914
TAMING OF THE SHREW, THE see **JAJAUMA NARASHI** • 1966
TAMING OF THE SNOOD, THE • 1940 • *Keaton Buster* • SHT • USA
TAMING OF THE WEST • 1939 • Deming Norman • USA
TAMING OF THE WEST, THE • 1925 • Rosson Arthur • USA
TAMING OF WILD BILL, THE • 1910 • *Lubin* • USA
TAMING OF WILD BILL, THE • 1916 • Bertram William • SHT • USA
TAMING SUTTON'S GIRL • 1957 • Selander Lesley • USA
TAMING TARGET CENTER • 1918 • Campbell William • SHT • USA
TAMING TERRIBLE TED • 1914 • Hotaling Arthur D. • USA
TAMING THE CAT • 1948 • Rasinski Connie • ANS • USA
TAMING THE FIRE see **UKROSCHENIE OGNIA** • 1972
TAMING THE MEKONG • 1965 • Van Dyke Willard • DOC • USA
TAMING THE WEST • 1919 • *National Film Corp. Of America* • SHT • USA
TAMING THE WILD • 1936 • Hill Robert F. • USA • MADCAP (UKN)
TAMING THEIR GRANDCHILDREN • 1913 • *Thanhouser* • USA
TAMING THEIR PARENTS • 1912 • *Lubin* • USA
TAMLIN • 1972 • McDowall Roddy • UKN, USA • DEVIL'S WIDOW, THE (USA) ○ DEVIL'S WOMAN, THE ○ BALLAD OF TAM-LIN, THE
TAMMANY BOARDER, A • 1913 • *Francis Alec B.* • USA
TAMMANY'S TIGER • 1916 • McRae Henry • SHT • USA
T'AMMAZZO, RACCOMANDATI A DIO • 1968 • Civirani Osvaldo • ITL
TAMMY AND THE BACHELOR • 1957 • Pevney Joseph • USA • TAMMY (UKN)
TAMMY AND THE DOCTOR • 1963 • Keller Harry • USA
TAMMY AND THE MILLIONAIRE • 1967 • Miller Sidney, Stone Ezra C., Goodwins Leslie • TVM • USA
TAMMY TELL ME TRUE • 1961 • Keller Harry • USA
TAMMY (UKN) see **TAMMY AND THE BACHELOR** • 1957
TAMO I NATRAG see **ALLER RETOUR** • 1979
TAMPICO • 1944 • Mendes Lothar • USA
TAMPICO • 1971 • *Cinema Jalisco* • MXC
TAMPICO see **GRAN CASINO** • 1946
TAMPON DU CAPISTON, LE • 1930 • Toulout Jean, Francis Joe • FRN
TAMPON DU CAPISTON, LE • 1950 • Labro Maurice • FRN
TAMPOPO • 1985 • Itami Juzo • JPN • DANDELION
TAMS TAMS ET BALAFONS • 1972 • D'Aix Alain • DOC • CND
TAMS-TAMS SE SONT TUS, LES • 1972 • Mora Philippe • GBN
TAN AND TERRIFIC • 1947 • Malkames Don • SHT • USA
TAN BUENO EL GIRO EL COLORADO • 1957 • Salvador Jaime • MXC
TAN-CH'E YU WO • 1983 • T'Ao Te-Ch'En • TWN • BIKE AND I, THE
TAN LINES see **DANGEROUS CURVES** • 1988
TAN-NI-ERH-TE KU-SHIH • 1982 • Liu Wei-Pin • TWN • ORDEALS OF DANIEL, THE
TAN-TAN-DES BOIS • 1952 • Bail Rene • CND
TANA • 1958 • Dhamo Kristaq • ALB
TANA A DVA PISTOLNICI • 1967 • Cvrcek Radim • CZC • TANA AND THE TWO SHARPSHOOTERS ○ BRNO TRAIL, THE
TANA AND THE TWO SHARPSHOOTERS see **TANA A DVA PISTOLNICI** • 1967
TANAAN OLET TAALLA • 1966 • Kurkvaara Maunu • FNL • TODAY YOU'RE HERE
TANAH SABRANG • 1938 • Franken Mannus • NTH, INN • LAND ACROSS SEA, THE
TANAMERA • 1989 • Dobson Kevin, Power John • MTV • ASL
TANAMI • 1928 • MacDonald Alexander • ASL
TANASE SCATIU • 1976 • Pita Dan • RMN • SUMMER TALE
TANCZACY JASTRZAB • 1977 • Krolikiewicz Grzegorz • PLN • DANCING GOSHAWK ○ DANCING HAWK
TANDAS DEL PRINCIPAL, LAS • 1949 • Bustillo Oro Juan • MXC
TANDEM • 1987 • Leconte Patrice • FRN
TANDEM see **VAROSBUJOCSKA** • 1985
TANDES • 1984 • Sulaiman Hengky • INN • KISSES FOR AUNTIE ○ KISAH YANTI
TANDLAEGE PA SENGEKANTEN • 1971 • Hilbard John • DNM • DANISH DENTIST ON THE JOB (UKN) ○ DENTIST ON THE JOB ○ BEDSIDE DENTIST
TANECEK PANNY MARINKY • 1935 • Neufeld Max • CZC
T'ANG-CH'AO HAO-FANG NU • 1984 • Fang Ling-Cheng • HKG
T'ANG-JEN-CHIEH HSAIO-TZU • 1977 • Chang Ch'Eh • HKG • CHINATOWN KID
T'ANG-LANG • 1977 • Liu Chia-Liang • HKG • PRAYING MANTIS ○ SHAOLIN MANTIS
T'ANG-SHAN TA-HSIUNG • 1971 • Lo Wei • HKG • FISTS OF FURY (USA) ○ BIG BOSS, THE
TANGA TIKA • 1953 • Long Dwight
TANGANYIKA • 1954 • De Toth Andre • USA
TANGATA WHENUA • 1974 • Barclay Barry • SER • NZL
TANGE EJDEHA • 1968 • Yasami Siyamak • IRN • DRAGON'S PASS
TANGE SAZEN • 1934 • Ito Daisuke • JPN • SAZEN TANGE
TANGE SAZEN • 1963 • Uchikawa Seiichiro • JPN
TANGE SAZEN HIEN LAI-GIRI • 1966 • Gosha Hideo • JPN • SECRET OF THE URN
TANGENTS • 1983 • Greenwald Barry • CND
TANGERINE • 1979 • McCallum Robert • USA
TANGERINE MAN, THE see **CANDY TANGERINE MAN, THE** • 1975
TANGIER • 1946 • Waggner George • USA
TANGIER ASSIGNMENT • 1955 • Leversuch Ted • UKN
TANGIER INCIDENT • 1953 • Landers Lew • USA
TANGING IKAW • 1968 • de Guzman Armando • PHL • ONLY YOU
TANGLE, THE • 1914 • *Powers* • USA
TANGLE, THE • 1914 • Lambart Harry • *Broadway Star* • USA
TANGLE, THE • 1967 • Latallo Katarzyna, Antosik Wieslaw • ANM • PLN
TANGLE IN HEARTS, A • 1915 • Garrick Richard • USA
TANGLED • 1912 • *Powers* • USA
TANGLED AFFAIR, A • 1913 • Lehrman Henry, Sennett Mack (Spv) • USA
TANGLED ANGLER, THE • 1941 • Tashlin Frank • ANS • USA
TANGLED BY TELEPHONE • 1916 • Ellis Robert • USA
TANGLED CAT, THE • 1914 • *Ostriche Muriel* • USA
TANGLED COURTSHIP, A • 1912 • *Powers* • USA
TANGLED DESTINIES • 1932 • Strayer Frank • USA • WHO KILLED HARVEY FORBES? (UKN)
TANGLED EVIDENCE • 1934 • Cooper George A. • UKN
TANGLED FATES • 1916 • Vale Travers • USA
TANGLED FORTUNES • 1932 • McGowan J. P. • USA
TANGLED HEARTS • 1916 • De Grasse Joseph • *Bluebird* • USA
TANGLED HEARTS • 1916 • Neitz Alvin J. • *Centaur* • USA
TANGLED HEARTS see **WIFE WHOM GOD FORGOT, THE** • 1920
TANGLED HEARTSTRINGS • 1911 • *Yankee* • USA
TANGLED HERDS • 1926 • Bertram William • USA • TANGLED ROMANCE, A (UKN)
TANGLED LINES • 1911 • *Reliance* • USA
TANGLED LIVES • 1910 • *Thanhouser* • USA
TANGLED LIVES • 1911 • Olcott Sidney • *Kalem* • USA
TANGLED LIVES • 1917 • Edwards J. Gordon • USA
TANGLED LIVES • 1918 • Scardon Paul • USA
TANGLED MARRIAGE, A • 1912 • Smalley Phillips • USA
TANGLED MASQUERADE, A • 1910 • *Essanay* • USA
TANGLED PATHS • 1915 • Cabanne W. Christy • USA
TANGLED RELATIONS • 1912 • Salter Harry • USA
TANGLED ROMANCE, A see **COAX ME** • 1919
TANGLED ROMANCE, A (UKN) see **TANGLED HERDS** • 1926
TANGLED SKEIN, A • 1912 • *Republic* • USA
TANGLED SKEINS • 1916 • Hopper E. Mason • SHT • USA
TANGLED TANGOISTS • 1914 • Baker George D. • USA
TANGLED TELEVISION • 1940 • Marcus Sid • ANS • USA
TANGLED THREADS • 1913 • Thornby Robert T. • USA
TANGLED THREADS • 1917 • Forest Alan • SHT • USA
TANGLED THREADS • 1919 • Hickman Howard • USA
TANGLED TIES • 1916 • *Stull Walter* • USA
TANGLED TRAILS • 1921 • Bartlett Charles • USA
TANGLED TRAVELS • 1944 • Geiss Alec • ANS • USA
TANGLED WEB, A • 1912 • *Rex* • USA
TANGLED WEB, THE • 1913 • Apfel Oscar • USA
TANGLED WEB, THE • 1916 • McGill Lawrence?, Hansel Howell? • SHT • USA
TANGLES OF POKES AND JABS, THE • 1915 • *Wizard* • USA
TANGLEWOOD, MUSIC SCHOOL AND MUSIC FESTIVAL see **TANGLEWOOD STORY, THE** • 1950
TANGLEWOOD STORY, THE • 1950 • Maddison • SHT • USA • TANGLEWOOD, MUSIC SCHOOL AND MUSIC FESTIVAL
TANGO • 1913 • Wilson Frank? • UKN
TANGO • 1932 • Hellstrom Gosta • SWD
TANGO • 1933 • Barth-Moglia Luis • ARG
TANGO • 1935 • Rosen Phil • USA
TANGO • 1969 • Mirchev Vassil • BUL
TANGO • 1983 • Rybczynski Zbigniew • ANM • PLN
TANGO 2001 see **TANGO OF PERVERSION** • 1974
TANGO AND POKER • 1916 • *Hippo* • USA
TANGO BAR • 1935 • *Gardel Carlos* • USA
TANGO-BAR • 1935 • Reinhardt John
TANGO BAR • 1988 • Zurinaga Marcos • PRC, ARG
TANGO CAVALIER • 1923 • Seeling Charles R. • USA
TANGO D'ADIEU see **RAPPEL IMMEDIAT** • 1939
TANGO DALLA RUSSIA, UN • 1965 • Ross Berwang • ITL
TANGO DE LA MUERTE, EL • 1917 • Ferreyra Jose • ARG
TANGO DE LA PERVERSION, LE • 1974 • Garnier Pierre-Claude • BLG
TANGO DEL VIUDO, EL • 1967 • Ruiz Raul • CHL • WIDOWER'S TANGO
TANGO DES CHATS • 1930 • ANS • FRN • CAT TANGO
TANGO EN BROADWAY, EL • 1935 • Gasnier Louis J. • SPN
TANGO FLAT, THE • 1914 • *Ab* • USA
TANGO FOR A BEAR see **TANGO PRE MEDVEDA** • 1966
TANGO FUR DICH, EIN • 1930 • von Bolvary Geza • FRG
TANGO IN TUCKERVILLE, THE • 1914 • Seay Charles M. • USA
TANGO INDUSTRI • 1975 • Wam Svend • SHT • NRW
TANGO KONIGIN, DIE • 1913 • Mack Max • FRG
TANGO MAD • 1914 • *Planet* • UKN • CRAZE, THE
TANGO MAD • 1914 • Plumb Hay? • *Hepworth* • UKN
TANGO NOTTURNO • 1937 • Kirchhoff Fritz • FRG
TANGO OF OUR CHILDHOOD, THE • 1986 • Mkrtchan Albert • USS
TANGO OF PERVERSION • 1974 • Carayannis Costa • GRC • TANGO 2001
TANGO PRE MEDVEDA • 1966 • Barabas Stanislav • CZC • TANGO FOR A BEAR
TANGO ROUGE, LE • 1908 • de Rochefort Charles • FRN
TANGO SPREE, A • 1914 • Seay Charles M. • USA
TANGO TANGLE, A • 1913 • *Essanay* • USA
TANGO TANGLE, A • 1914 • *Britannia Films* • UKN
TANGO TANGLES • 1914 • Sennett Mack • USA • CHARLIE'S RECREATION ○ MUSIC HALL
TANGO TRAGEDY, A • 1914 • *Lubin* • USA
TANGO TROUBLES • 1914 • *Royal* • USA
TANGO VS. POKER • 1914 • *Tennant Barbara* • USA
TANGO VUELVE A PARIS, EL • 1947 • *Lamas Fernando* • ARG
TANGO WALTZ, THE • 1913 • *Selsior Films* • UKN
TANGOS L'EXIL DE GARDEL • 1985 • Solanas Fernando • FRN, ARG
TANGRAM, THE • 1914 • Booth W. R. • UKN
TANGSIR • 1974 • Naderi Amir • IRN
TANIA LA BELLA SALVAJE • 1947 • Orol Juan • MXC
TANIAS, LAS • 1971 • Villafuerte Santiago • DOC • CUB
TANIN NO KAO • 1966 • Teshigahara Hiroshi • JPN • FACE OF ANOTHER, THE ○ I HAVE A STRANGER'S FACE

TANITONO • 1945 • Keleti Marton • HNG • SCHOOLMISTRESS, THE
TANITONO, A • 1915 • Curtiz Michael • HNG
TANITVANYOK, A • 1985 • Beremenyi Geza • HNG • DISCIPLES, THE
TANJA, DIE FRAU AN DER KETTE • 1921 • Zelnik Friedrich • FRG
TANJA, DIE NACKTE VON DER TEUFELINSEL • 1967 • Hofherr Julius • FRG • TANJA, THE NUDE OF DEVIL'S ISLAND
TANJA, THE NUDE OF DEVIL'S ISLAND see **TANJA, DIE NACKTE VON DER TEUFELINSEL** • 1967
TANJI SASTOJACK • 1987 • Sijan Slobodan • YGS, USA • SECRET INGREDIENT, THE
TANK • 1984 • Chomsky Marvin • USA
TANK BATTALION • 1958 • Rose Sherman A. • USA • VALLEY OF DEATH, THE (UKN)
TANK BRIGADE, THE see **TANKOVA BRIGADA** • 1955
TANK CARTOONS see **TANKS** • 1916
TANK COMMANDO (UKN) see **TANK COMMANDOS** • 1959
TANK COMMANDOS • 1959 • Topper Burt • USA • TANK COMMANDO (UKN)
TANK FORCE (USA) see **NO TIME TO DIE** • 1958
TANK MALLING • 1989 • Marcus James • UKN
TANK, OM JAG GIFTER MIG MED PRASTEN • 1941 • Johansson Ivar • SWD • SUPPOSE I WERE TO MARRY THE CLERGYMAN
TANK PATROL • 1944 • Eldridge John • DOC • UKN
TANK TOWN TROUPE, THE • 1916 • Edwards Harry J. • USA
TANKBUSTERS • 1975 • Murphy Geoff • SHT • NZL
TANKER • 1969 • Vogeler Volker • FRG
TANKER STORY • 1953 • McNaughton Richard Q. • UKN
TANKMADEL, DAS • 1933 • Behrendt Hans • FRG
TANKOVA BRIGADA • 1955 • Toman Ivo • CZC • TANK BRIGADE, THE
TANKS • 1916 • *Kineto* • SHT • UKN • TANK CARTOONS
TANKS A MILLION • 1941 • Guiol Fred • USA
TANKS ARE COMING, THE • 1941 • Eason B. Reeves • SHT • USA
TANKS ARE COMING, THE • 1951 • Seiler Lewis, Lederman D. Ross • USA
TANKVILLE CONSTABLE, THE • 1912 • *Imp* • USA
TANMESEK A SZEXROL • 1988 • Siklosi Szilveszter • HNG • MORAL STORIES ABOUT SEX
TANNED LEGS • 1929 • Neilan Marshall • USA
TANNENBERG • 1932 • Paul Heinz • FRG
TANNERS, THE • 1962 • Iliesu Mirel • DOC • RMN
TANNHAUSER • 1906 • Porten Franz • FRG
TANNHAUSER • 1913 • *Cruze James* • USA
TANNHAUSER: ACT THREE • 1928 • *British Sound Film Production* • SHT • UKN
TANOSHIKI KANA JINSEI • 1944 • Naruse Mikio • JPN • THIS HAPPY LIFE
TANSSI YLI HAUTOJEN • 1950 • Saakka Toivo • FNL • DANCE OVER THE GRAVES
TANSY • 1921 • Hepworth Cecil M. • UKN
TANT D'AMOUR PERDU • 1958 • Joannon Leo • FRN, ITL • INSAZIABILI, LE (ITL)
TANT GRON, TANT BRUN OCH TANT GREDELIN • 1945 • Lindstrom Rune • SWD • AUNT GREEN, AUNT BROWN AND AUNT LILAC
TANT QUE JE VIVRAI • 1945 • de Baroncelli Jacques • FRN
TANT QUE VOUS SEREZ HEUREUX • 1911 • Feuillade Louis • FRN
TANT QU'IL Y AURA DE L'ANGOISSE • 1966 • Otero Manuel, Leroux Jacques • ANS • FRN
TANT QU'IL Y AURA DES BETES • 1956 • Brassai Jules • FRN • LOVERS AND CROWNS
TANT QU'IL Y AURA DES CAPRICORNES • 1961 • Barral Jean • SHT • FRN
TANT QU'IL Y AURA DES FEMMES • 1955 • Greville Edmond T. • FRN
TANT QU'ON A LA SANTE • 1965 • Etaix Pierre • FRN • AS LONG AS YOU'RE HEALTHY (UKN)
TANT RALIE SE LOSIEHUIS • 1974 • SAF
TANTALIZING FLY, THE • 1919 • Fleischer Dave • ANS • USA
TANTE AURELIE • 1930 • Diamant-Berger Henri • FRN
TANTE CHINOISE ET LES AUTRES • 1959 • Perlov David • FRN
TANTE ESTHER • 1956 • Dewever Jean • FRN
TANTE FRIEDA -NEUE LAUSBUBENGESCHICHTEN • 1965 • Jacobs Werner • FRG
TANTE GUSTI KOMMANDIERT • 1934 • Wolff Carl Heinz • FRG
TANTE JUTTA AUS KALKUTTA • 1953 • Kulb Karl G. • FRG
TANTE SBARRE see **ISTRUTTORIA E CHIUSA, DIMENTICHI, L'** • 1971
TANTE WANDA AUS UGANDA • 1957 • von Cziffra Geza • FRG
TANTE ZITA • 1967 • Enrico Robert • FRN • ZITA
TANTO VA LA GATTA AL LARDO.. • 1978 • Aleandri Marco • ITL
TANTRA, I • 1969 • Payne Gordon • SHT • USA
TANTRUMS see **PEOPLETOYS** • 1974
TANU, A • 1968 • Bacso Peter • HNG • WITNESS, THE
TANUKI NO HANAMICHI • 1964 • Yamamoto Kajiro • JPN
TANUKI NO KYUJITSU • 1967 • Yamamoto Kajiro • JPN • SWINDLER MEETS SWINDLER ○ BADGER'S HOLIDAY
TANUKI NO OSAMA • 1966 • Yamamoto Kajiro • JPN
TANUKI NO TAISHO • 1965 • Yamamoto Kajiro • JPN • THIEF ON THE RUN ○ BADGER GENERAL
TANUKI-SAN'S BIG SUCCESS • 1959 • Reid George M. • ANS • JPN
TANUKI VAGABONDS see **HANAKURABE TANUKI DOCHU** • 1961
TANULMANY A NOKROL • 1968 • Keleti Marton • HNG • STUDY OF WOMEN, A
TANYA (USA) see **SVETYLI PUT** • 1940
TANYA'S ISLAND • 1980 • Sole Alfred • TVM • CND • HORRORS OF SORTS: TANYA'S ISLAND ○ BETE D'AMOUR, LA
TANZ AM SONNABEND -MORD? • 1962 • Thiel Heinz • GDR • SATURDAY EVENING DANCE
TANZ AUF DEM VULKAN • 1938 • Steinhoff Hans • FRG
TANZ AUF DEM VULKAN 1, DER • 1920 • Eichberg Richard • FRG • SYBIL JOUNG ○ DANCE ON THE VOLCANO, THE
TANZ AUF DEM VULKAN 2, DER • 1920 • Eichberg Richard • FRG • TOD DES GROSSFURSTEN, DER
TANZ DER FARBEN • 1938 • *Fischinger Hans (P)* • ANS • FRG • DANCE OF THE COLORS (USA)
TANZ DER LEIDENSCHAFTEN • 1921 • Kayser Charles Willy • FRG
TANZ DES TODES, DER • *Negri Pola* • FRG
TANZ GEHT WEITER, DER • 1930 • Dieterle William • FRG • DANCE GOES ON, THE
TANZ IN DEN ABGRUND, DER • 1920 • Boese Carl • FRG
TANZ IN DER SONNE • 1954 • von Cziffra Geza • FRG
TANZ INS GLUCK • 1951 • Stoger Alfred • AUS
TANZ INS GLUCK, DER • 1930 • Nosseck Max • FRG
TANZ MIT DEM KAISER • 1941 • Jacoby Georg • FRG
TANZ UM LIEBE UND GLUCK, DER • 1921 • Zeyn Willy • FRG
TANZE MIT MIR IN DEN MORGEN • 1962 • Dorre Peter • AUS
TANZENDE DAMON, DER see **FORTUNATO 1** • 1921
TANZENDE HANDE • 1959 • Reinhard Hans • FRG • DANCING HANDS
TANZENDE HERZ, DAS • 1916 • Mack Max • FRG
TANZENDE HERZ, DAS • 1953 • Liebeneiner Wolfgang • FRG • DANCING HEART, THE (USA)
TANZENDE STERNE • 1952 • von Cziffra Geza • FRG
TANZENDE TOD, DER • 1920 • Fleck Jacob, Fleck Luise • AUS
TANZENDE TOD, DER • 1925 • Raffe Rolf • FRG • REX MUNDI
TANZENDE WIEN, DAS • 1927 • Zelnik Friedrich • FRG • AN DER SCHONEN BLAUEN DONAU 2 ○ DANCING VIENNA
TANZENDES GIFT • 1918 • Wolff Ludwig • FRG
TANZER 1, DER • 1919 • Froelich Carl • FRG
TANZER 2, DER • 1919 • Froelich Carl • FRG
TANZER MEINER FRAU, DER • 1925 • Korda Alexander • FRG • DANCING MAD (UKN) ○ DANCE FEVER
TANZERIN, DIE • 1915 • Jacoby Georg • FRG
TANZERIN, DIE • 1987 • Shinoda Masahiro • FRG, JPN
TANZERIN ADINA • 1923 • *Max Mack-Film* • FRG
TANZERIN BARBERINA, DIE • 1920 • Boese Carl • FRG
TANZERIN DES KONIGS, DIE • 1922 • Wolff Willi • FRG
TANZERIN MARION, DIE • 1920 • Feher Friedrich • FRG
TANZERIN NAVARRO, DIE • 1922 • Wolff Ludwig • FRG
TANZERIN TOD • 1920 • Philippi Siegfried • FRG
TANZERIN VON DSCHIAPUR, DIE see **SAFERNDRI, DIE TANZERIN VON DSCHIAPUR** • 1918
TANZERIN VON SANSSOUCI, DIE • 1932 • Zelnik Friedrich • FRG • BARBERINA, DIE TANZERIN VON SANSSOUCI ○ BARBARINA
TANZERINNEN FUR SUD-AMERIKA GESUCHT • 1931 • Speyer Jaap • FRG
TANZERINNEN FUR TANGER • 1977 • Dietrich Erwin C. • SWT, FRN • ISLAND OF THE SAVAGE SEX SLAVES ○ CONFESSIONS OF THE SEX SLAVES ○ NAKED STREET GIRLS
TANZHUSAR, DER • Sauer Fred • FRG
TANZMUSIK • 1935 • Hubler-Kahla J. A. • FRG
TANZSTUDENT, DER • 1928 • Guter Johannes • FRG
TAO • 1923 • Ravel Gaston
TAO-TS'AO JEN • 1988 • Wang T'Ung • TWN • STRAWMAN
TAO WEN • 1989 • Yeh Hung-Wei • TWN • CURSES OF THE KNIFE
TAP • 1913 • *Bison* • USA
TAP • 1989 • Castle Nick • USA
TAP ON THE SHOULDER • 1965 • Loach Kenneth • MTV • UKN
TAP ROOTS • 1948 • Marshall George • USA
TAP! TAP! TAP! • 1915 • Powell Paul • USA
TAPAGE NOCTURNE • 1951 • Sauvajon Marc-Gilbert • FRN
TAPAGE NOCTURNE • 1979 • Breillat Catherine • FRN
TAPAK DEWATA • 1978 • Noyce Phil • DOC • ASL
TAPATIAS NUNCA PIERDEN, LAS • 1964 • Gomez Landero Humberto • MXC
TAPDANCIN' • 1979 • Blackwood Christian • DOC • USA, FRG
TAPECARIA, UMA TRADICAO QUE REVIVE • 1967 • Vasconcelos Antonio-Pedro • SHT • PRT
TAPEHEADS • 1988 • Fishman Bill • USA
TAPERING FINGERS • 1919 • Dillon John Francis • SHT • USA
TAPESTRIES AND LACE • 1967 • Merglova Jan • ANS • CZC
TAPESTRIES OF THE APOCALYPSE see **TAPISSERIES DE L'APOCALYPSE, LES**
TAPESTRY OF PASSION • 1976 • Colberg Alan • USA
TAPETES DE VIANA DO CASTELO • 1967 • Guimaraes Manuel • SHT • PRT
TAPFERE SCHNEIDERLEIN, DAS • 1956 • Spiess Helmut • GDR • BRAVE LITTLE TAILOR, THE
TAPFERE SCHULSCHWANZER, DER • 1967 • Junge Winifried • GDR • BRAVE SCHOOL TRUANT, THE ○ BRAVE TRUANTS, THE
TAPILACAK KADIN • 1967 • Saydam Nejat • TRK • WOMAN TO ADORE, A
TAPINOS KE KATAFRONEMENOS • 1968 • Tegopoulos Apostolos • GRC • HUMBLE AND DESPISED, THE
TAPIS DE MOYSE, LE • 1931 • Greville Edmond T. • SHT • FRN
TAPIS MOQUETTE, LE • 1935 • Leenhardt Roger • DCS • FRN
TAPIS VOLANT, LE • 1960 • Stephane Nicole • FRN • FLYING CARPET, THE
TAPISSERIES DE L'APOCALYPSE, LES • Colson-Malleville Marie • DOC • FRN • TAPESTRIES OF THE APOCALYPSE
TAPPA INTE SUGEN • 1947 • Kjellgren Lars-Eric • SWD • DON'T GIVE UP
TAPPE DELLA GLORIA E DELL'ARDIRE ITALICI, LA • 1924 • Rosa Silvio Laurenti • ITL
TAPPED WIRES • 1913 • Wharton Theodore • USA
TAPPING THE TEMPO • 1938 • Parsons Herbert R. • UKN
TAPPING TOES • 1930 • SHT • USA
TAPPRE SOLDATEN JONSSON, DEN • 1956 • Bergstrom Hakan • SWD
TAPPY TOES • 1968 • Grooms Red • SHT • USA
TAPS • 1981 • Becker Harold • USA • T.A.P.S.
TAPUM, LA STORIA DELLE ARMI • 1958 • Bozzetto Bruno • ANS • ITL • TAPUM, THE HISTORY OF WEAPONS ○ HISTORY OF ARMS
TAPUM, THE HISTORY OF WEAPONS see **TAPUM, LA STORIA DELLE ARMI** • 1958
TAQAT KA TOOFAN • 1988 • Sangeeta • PKS • FORCE
TAQDEER • 1943 • Khan Mehboob • IND • FATE (UKN)
TAQDEER • 1967 • Salam A. • IND • FATE
TAQRIR, AL • 1986 • Laham Doreid • SYR • REPORT, THE
TAR BABIES (UKN) see **FANDO Y LIS** • 1968
TAR-DEALER, THE see **TJAEREHANDLEREN** • 1971
TAR HEEL WARRIOR, THE • 1917 • Hopper E. Mason • USA
TAR SANDS, THE • 1977 • Pearson Peter • MTV • CND
TAR WITH A STAR • 1949 • Tytla Bill • ANS • USA
TARA, DOKHTARE NASHENASS • 1978 • Beyzai Bahram • IRN • TARA, THE UNKNOWN GIRL
TARA POKI • 1971 • Damiani Amasi • ITL
TARA, THE STONECUTTER • 1957 • Wilson John • ANS • USA
TARA, THE UNKNOWN GIRL see **TARA, DOKHTARE NASHENASS** • 1978
TARAHUMARA • 1964 • Alcoriza Luis • MXC • CADA VEZ MAS LEJOS
TARAHUMARA -DRAMA DEL PUEBLO • 1972 • MXC • TARAHUMARA -DRAMA OF THE PEOPLE
TARAHUMARA -DRAMA OF THE PEOPLE see **TARAHUMARA -DRAMA DEL PUEBLO** • 1972
TARAKANOVA • 1930 • Bernard Raymond • FRN
TARAKANOWA • 1938 • Ozep Fedor • FRN • ORLOFF ET TARAKANOWA ○ BETRAYAL
TARALEZHITE SE RAZHDAT BEZ BODLI • 1971 • Petrov Dimitar • BUL • PORCUPINES ARE BORN WITHOUT BRISTLES
TARAMATRI • 1945 • *Ramnik* • IND
TARAN • 1951 • *Biswas Anil (M)* • IND
TARANG • 1978 • Shahani Kumar, Tendulkar Vijay • IND • VIBRATIONS
TARANG • 1984 • Shahani Kumar • IND • WAGES AND PROFIT
TARANTA, LA • 1961 • Mingozzi Gianfranco • DCS • ITL
TARANTEL, DIE • 1920 • Biebrach Rudolf • FRG
TARANTELLA • 1941 • Bute Mary Ellen, Nemeth Ted J. • ANS • USA
TARANTELLA • 1966 • D'Avino Carmen • SHT • USA
TARANTELLA NAPOLETANA • 1953 • Mastrocinque Camillo • ITL
TARANTELLE, LA • 1900 • Blache Alice • FRN
TARANTOLA DAL VENTRE NERO, LA • 1971 • Cavara Paolo • ITL, FRN • BLACK BELLY OF THE TARANTULA, THE (UKN)
TARANTOS, LOS • 1963 • Rovira Beleta Francisco • SPN
TARANTOS Y MONTOYAS see **MONTOYAS Y TARANTOS** • 1988
TARANTULA • 1955 • Arnold Jack • USA
TARANTULA see **TARANTULAS: THE DEADLY CARGO** • 1977
TARANTULA, THE • 1913 • Macpherson Jeanie • USA
TARANTULA, THE • 1916 • Baker George D. • USA
TARANTULAS: THE DEADLY CARGO • 1977 • Hagmann Stuart • TVM • USA • TARANTULA
TARAS BULBA • 1962 • Thompson J. Lee • USA
TARAS BULBA see **REBEL SON, THE** • 1938
TARAS BULBA 1 • 1924 • von Strischewski Wladimir • FRG • TOCHTER DES WOIWODEN, DIE
TARAS BULBA 2 • 1924 • von Strischewski Wladimir • FRG • KOSAKEN-ENDE
TARAS BULBAIL COSACCO • 1963 • Baldi Ferdinando • ITL
TARAS FAMILY, THE see **NEPOKORENNYE** • 1945
TARAS SHEVCHENKO • 1951 • Savchenko Igor • USS
TARASS BOULBA • 1936 • Granowsky Alexis • FRN
TARAWA BEACHHEAD • 1958 • Wendkos Paul • USA
TARDE DE FUTBOL • 1951 • Iquino Ignacio F. • SPN
TARDE DE TOROS • 1955 • Vajda Ladislao • SPN • GRANDE CORRIDA, LA
TARDE DEL DOMINGO, LA • 1957 • Saura Carlos • SHT • SPN • SUNDAY AFTERNOON
TARDE EM ALCACER, UMA • 1933 • do Canto Jorge Brum • SHT • PRT
TARDE OUTRA TARDE, UMA • 1975 • Cobbett William • BRZ • AMOR AOS 40, O
TARDE.. UN LUNES, UNA • 1973 • Castro Alberto Giraldo, Luzardo Julio • CLM • ON A MONDAY AFTERNOON
TARDONA, LA (ITL) see **VIEILLE FILLE, LA** • 1971
TARDONE, LE • 1964 • Girolami Marino • ITL
TARDY CANNON BALL, THE • 1914 • *Crawford Florence* • USA
TARDY RECOGNITION, A • 1913 • Seay Charles M. • USA
TARE, LA • 1911 • Feuillade Louis • FRN
TAREKOMI • 1968 • Segawa Masaharu • JPN • SECRET INFORMATION
TARES • 1918 • Hepworth Cecil M. • UKN
TARES OF THE WHEAT • 1912 • *Imp* • USA
TARGAN, THE FALCON OF THE STEPPES see **BOZKIRLAR SAHINI TARGAN** • 1968
TARGET • 1977 • Wickes David • MTV • UKN
TARGET • 1985 • Penn Arthur • USA
TARGET see **NARROW MARGIN, THE** • 1952
TARGET, THE • 1916 • MacGregor Norval • USA
TARGET, THE • 1952 • Gilmore Stuart • USA
TARGET CAPTAIN KARATE • 1968 • Rowe George • PHL
TARGET EAGLE • 1982 • de la Loma Jose Antonio • SPN, MXC • JUGANDO CON LA MUERTE ○ PLAYING WITH DEATH
TARGET EARTH! • 1954 • Rose Sherman A. • USA
TARGET.. EARTH? • 1980 • Van Rees Joost • USA
TARGET FOR AN ASSASSIN (USA) see **TIGERS DON'T CRY** • 1976
TARGET FOR KILLING (USA) see **GEHEIMNIS DER GELBEN MONCHE, DAS** • 1966
TARGET FOR SCANDAL (UKN) see **WASHINGTON STORY** • 1952
TARGET FOR TODAY • 1944 • Keighley William • DOC • USA
TARGET FOR TONIGHT • 1941 • Watt Harry • DOC • UKN
TARGET: HARRY see **HOW TO MAKE IT** • 1968
TARGET HONG KONG • 1952 • Sears Fred F. • USA
TARGET OF AN ASSASSIN see **TIGERS DON'T CRY** • 1976
TARGET OF DESTINY, THE • 1914 • *Princess* • USA
TARGET OF DREAMS • 1916 • *Mayo Frank* • SHT • USA
TARGET PRACTICE • 1906 • Cooper Arthur • UKN
TARGET PRACTICE • 1915 • *Superba* • USA

TARGET REMOVED see **VERANO PARA MATAR, UN** • 1973
TARGET RISK • 1975 • Scheerer Robert • TVM • USA
TARGET, SEA OF CHINA • 1954 • Adreon Franklin • USA
TARGET SEXY ROSE • 1967 • Feleo Ben • PHL
TARGET: THE A-GO-GO GENERATION • 1967 • Diaz Leody M. • PHL
TARGET UNKNOWN • 1951 • Sherman George • USA • PRISONER OF WAR
TARGET ZERO • 1955 • Jones Harmon • USA
TARGETS • 1968 • Bogdanovich Peter • USA • BEFORE I DIE
TARGETS OF FATE • 1913 • *Reliance* • USA
TARGI GDANSKIE • 1947 • Bossak Jerzy • DOC • PLN • GDANSK TRADE FAIR, THE
TARID EL FARDAWSE • 1965 • Wahab Fatin Abdel • EGY • TARIDU AL-FIRDAWSS ○ RENVOYE DU PARADIS
TARIDU AL-FIRDAWSS see **TARID EL FARDAWSE** • 1965
TARIFF REFORM • 1910 • *Gaumont* • UKN
TARIK AL SHAITAN • 1962 • Atia Kamal • EGY • WAY OF THE DEVIL, THE
TARIK EL MASDUD, EL • 1958 • Abu Saif Salah • EGY • BARRED ROAD, THE ○ T'ARIQ AL-MASDUD, AT-
T'ARIQ AD-DUMU • 1961 • Halim Hilmy • EGY • CHEMIN DES LARMES, LE
T'ARIQ AL-MASDUD, AT- see **TARIK EL MASDUD, EL** • 1958
TARIS CHAMPION DE NATATION see **JEAN TARIS, CHAMPION DE NATATION** • 1931
TARIS OU LA NATATION see **JEAN TARIS, CHAMPION DE NATATION** • 1931
TARIS, ROI DE L'EAU see **JEAN TARIS, CHAMPION DE NATATION** • 1931
TARJETA DE VISITA • 1944 • Obregon Antonio • SPN
TARKA THE OTTER • 1978 • Cobham David • UKN
TARMUL N-ARE SFIRSIT • 1962 • Saucan Mircea • RMN • ENDLESS SHORE, THE
TARNINGEN AR KASTAD • 1960 • Husberg Rolf • SWD • DIE IS CAST, THE
TARNISH • 1924 • Fitzmaurice George • USA
TARNISHED • 1950 • Keller Harry • USA
TARNISHED ANGEL • 1938 • Goodwins Leslie • USA • MIRACLE RACKET
TARNISHED ANGELS, THE • 1957 • Sirk Douglas • USA • PYLON
TARNISHED HEROES • 1961 • Morris Ernest • UKN
TARNISHED LADY • 1931 • Cukor George • USA • NEW YORK LADY
TARNISHED LAND see **ONTLUISTERD LAND** • 1946
TARNISHED REPUTATION • 1920 • Blache Alice • USA • SOUL ADRIFT, A ○ TARNISHED REPUTATIONS
TARNISHED REPUTATIONS see **TARNISHED REPUTATION** • 1920
TARO, BABY DRAGON see **TATSUNOKO TARO** • 1978
TARO, THE DRAGON BOY see **TATSUNOKO TARO** • 1978
TARO, THE SON OF DRAGON • 1968 • Michibayashi Ichiro • ANM • JPN
TARO'S YOUTH see **SEISHUN TARO** • 1967
TAROT • 1973 • Wein Chuck • USA
TAROTS • 1973 • Forque Jose Maria • SPN, FRN
TARPANS see **TARPANY** • 1961
TARPANY • 1961 • Kutz Kazimierz • PLN • WILD HORSES ○ TARPANS
TARPS ELIN • 1957 • Fant Kenne • SWD
TARRED AND FEATHERED • 1920 • *Franey William* • SHT • USA
TARS AND FEATHERS see **SAILOR BE GOOD** • 1933
TARS AND SPARS • 1946 • Green Alfred E. • USA
TARS AND STRIPES • 1935 • Lamont Charles • SHT • USA
TARS ASHORE, THE • 1911 • *Lubin* • USA
TARTAR GIRL, THE see **URSUS E LA RAGAZZA TARTARA** • 1962
TARTAR INVASION (USA) see **URSUS E LA RAGAZZA TARTARA** • 1962
TARTARI, I • 1961 • Thorpe Richard, Baldi Ferdinando • ITL, YGS • TARTARS, THE (USA)
TARTARIN DE TARASCON • 1934 • Bernard Raymond • FRN
TARTARIN DE TARASCON • 1962 • Blanche Francis • FRN
TARTARIN DE TARASCON OU UNE CHASSE A L'OURS • 1908 • Melies Georges • FRN • HUNTING THE TEDDY BEAR
TARTARIN SUR LES ALPES • 1921 • Vorins Henri, Barlatier • FRN
TARTARS, THE (USA) see **TARTARI, I** • 1961
TARTASSATI, I • 1959 • Steno • ITL, FRN • FRIPOUILLARD ET CIE (FRN) ○ OVERTAXED, THE
TARTELETTE, LA • 1967 • Colombat Jacques • ANM • FRN
TARTS, THE • 1965 • Davis Joe • USA
TARTS, THE see **WORST CRIME OF ALL!, THE** • 1966
TARTS AND FLOWERS • 1950 • Tytla Bill • ANS • USA
TARTSUNK KUTYAT • 1975 • Ternovszky Bela • HNG • LET'S KEEP A DOG
TARTU (USA) see **ADVENTURES OF TARTU** • 1943
TARTUFF • 1925 • Murnau F. W. • FRG • TARTUFFE (UKN) ○ TARTUFFE THE HYPOCRITE ○ HERR TARTUFF
TARTUFFE • 1963 • Meyer Jean • FRN
TARTUFFE DE MOLIERE, LE • 1984 • Lasalle Jacques, Depardieu Gerard • FRN
TARTUFFE THE HYPOCRITE see **TARTUFF** • 1925
TARTUFFE (UKN) see **TARTUFF** • 1925
TARZAK CONTRO GLI UOMINI LEOPARDO • 1964 • Veo Carlo • ITL • APE MAN OF THE JUNGLE (USA) ○ TARZAK VS. THE LEOPARD MEN
TARZAK VS. THE LEOPARD MEN see **TARZAK CONTRO GLI UOMINI LEOPARDO** • 1964
TARZAM • 1969 • Burckhardt Rudy • USA
TARZAN '65 see **TARZAN AND THE VALLEY OF GOLD** • 1966
TARZAN '66 see **TARZAN AND THE VALLEY OF GOLD** • 1966
TARZAN AGAINST THE SAHARA see **TARZAN'S DESERT MYSTERY** • 1943
TARZAN AGAINST THE WORLD see **TARZAN'S NEW YORK ADVENTURE** • 1942
TARZAN AND CAPTAIN KISHORE • 1965 • *Azad* • IND
TARZAN AND CIRCUS • 1965 • *Rajdev S. (P)* • IND
TARZAN AND CLEOPATRA • 1964 • *Azad* • IND
TARZAN AND DELILAH • *Darasingh* • IND
TARZAN AND HIS MATE • 1934 • Gibbons Cedric, Conway Jack (U/c) • USA
TARZAN AND JANE REGAINED SORT OF • 1964 • Warhol Andy • USA
TARZAN AND KING KONG • 1963 • *Darasingh* • IND
TARZAN AND MAGICIAN • *Azad* • IND
TARZAN AND THE AMAZONS • 1945 • Neumann Kurt • USA
TARZAN AND THE ARROW OF DEATH see **TARZAN'S MAGIC FOUNTAIN** • 1949
TARZAN AND THE BIG RIVER see **TARZAN AND THE GREAT RIVER** • 1967
TARZAN AND THE GOLDEN LION • 1927 • McGowan J. P. • USA
TARZAN AND THE GORILLA • 1964 • *Azad* • IND
TARZAN AND THE GREAT RIVER • 1967 • Day Robert • USA • TARZAN AND THE BIG RIVER ○ TARZAN IN BRAZIL
TARZAN AND THE GREEN GODDESS (UKN) see **NEW ADVENTURES OF TARZAN, THE** • 1935
TARZAN AND THE HUNTRESS • 1947 • Neumann Kurt • USA
TARZAN AND THE JUNGLE BOY • 1968 • Gordon Robert • USA, SWT
TARZAN AND THE JUNGLE GODDESS (UKN) see **TARZAN'S PERIL** • 1951
TARZAN AND THE JUNGLE QUEEN (UKN) see **TARZAN AND THE SLAVE GIRL** • 1950
TARZAN AND THE LEOPARD WOMAN • 1946 • Neumann Kurt • USA
TARZAN AND THE LOST GODDESS see **NEW ADVENTURES OF TARZAN, THE** • 1935
TARZAN AND THE LOST SAFARI • 1957 • Humberstone H. Bruce, Stoloff Victor • USA, UKN
TARZAN AND THE MERMAIDS • 1948 • Florey Robert • USA
TARZAN AND THE RAINBOW see **TARZAN Y EL ARCO IRIS** • 1972
TARZAN AND THE SHE-DEVIL • 1953 • Neumann Kurt • USA • TARZAN MEETS THE VAMPIRE
TARZAN AND THE SHEIK see **TARZAN'S DESERT MYSTERY** • 1943
TARZAN AND THE SLAVE GIRL • 1950 • Sholem Lee • USA • TARZAN AND THE JUNGLE QUEEN (UKN)
TARZAN AND THE TRAPPERS • 1958 • Humberstone H. Bruce • MTV • USA
TARZAN AND THE VALLEY OF GOLD • 1966 • Day Robert • USA, SWT • TARZAN '65 ○ TARZAN '66
TARZAN COMES TO DELHI • *Darasingh* • IND
TARZAN DO 5° ESQ, O • 1958 • Fraga Augusto • PRT
TARZAN E LA PANTERA NERA • 1973 • Cano Manuel • ITL
TARZAN EN LA GRUTA DEL ORO • 1969 • Cano Manuel • SPN, ITL, PRC • TARZAN IN THE GROTTO OF GOLD ○ TARZAN IN THE GOLDEN CAVE
TARZAN EN LAS MINAS DEL REY SALOMON • 1973 • Merino Jose Luis • SPN
TARZAN ESCAPES! • 1936 • Thorpe Richard, Wellman William A. (U/c) • USA • CAPTURE OF TARZAN, THE ○ TARZAN RETURNS
TARZAN FINDS A MATE • 1965 • Sullivan Michael • SHT • USA
TARZAN FINDS A SON! • 1939 • Thorpe Richard • USA • TARZAN IN EXILE
TARZAN GOES TO INDIA • 1962 • Guillermin John • USA, UKN, SWT
TARZAN IN BRAZIL see **TARZAN AND THE GREAT RIVER** • 1967
TARZAN IN EXILE see **TARZAN FINDS A SON!** • 1939
TARZAN IN GUATEMALA see **NEW ADVENTURES OF TARZAN, THE** • 1935
TARZAN IN ISTANBUL see **TARZAN ISTANBULDA** • 1952
TARZAN IN MANHATTAN • 1989 • Schultz Michael • USA
TARZAN IN THE GOLDEN CAVE see **TARZAN EN LA GRUTA DEL ORO** • 1969
TARZAN IN THE GROTTO OF GOLD see **TARZAN EN LA GRUTA DEL ORO** • 1969
TARZAN IN THE WRONG see **NATURE IN THE WRONG** • 1933
TARZAN ISTANBULDA • 1952 • Atadeniz Orhan • TRK • TARZAN IN ISTANBUL
TARZAN KI BETI • 1937 • Shorey Roop K. • IND
TARZAN, KING OF BRUTE FORCE see **TAUR, IL RE DELLA FORZA BRUTA** • 1963
TARZAN MAMA-MIA • 1989 • Clausen Erik • DNM
TARZAN MEETS THE VAMPIRE see **TARZAN AND THE SHE-DEVIL** • 1953
TARZAN OF THE APES • 1918 • Sidney Scott • USA
TARZAN RETURNS see **TARZAN ESCAPES!** • 1936
TARZAN ROI DE LA FORCE BRUTALE (FRN) see **TAUR, IL RE DELLA FORZA BRUTA** • 1963
TARZAN THE APE MAN • 1932 • Van Dyke W. S. • USA
TARZAN THE APE MAN • 1959 • Newman Joseph M. • USA
TARZAN THE APEMAN • 1981 • Derek John • USA
TARZAN THE FEARLESS • 1933 • Hill Robert F. • USA
TARZAN THE FEARLESS • 1933 • Hill Robert F. • SRL • USA • TARZAN THE INVINCIBLE
TARZAN THE INVINCIBLE see **TARZAN THE FEARLESS** • 1933
TARZAN THE MAGNIFICENT • 1960 • Day Robert • UKN
TARZAN THE MIGHTY • 1928 • Nelson Jack, Taylor Ray • SRL • USA • JUNGLE TALES OF TARZAN
TARZAN THE TIGER • 1929 • McRae Henry • SRL • USA
TARZAN TRIUMPHS • 1943 • Thiele Wilhelm • USA
TARZAN VS. I.B.M. see **ALPHAVILLE, UNE ETRANGE AVENTURE DE LEMMY CAUTION** • 1965
TARZAN Y EL ARCO IRIS • 1972 • Cano Manuel • SPN, ITL, PRC • TARZAN AND THE RAINBOW
TARZAN Y EL MISTERIO DE LA SELVA • 1973 • Iglesias Miguel • SPN • MYSTERY OF THE JUNGLE, THE
TARZAN Y EL TESORO KAWANA • 1974 • Truchado Jose • SPN
TARZANA • 1979 • De Jarnatt Steve • USA
TARZANA SESSO SELVAGGIO • 1969 • Malatesta Guido • ITL • TARZANA, THE WILD GIRL ○ TARZANA'S SAVAGE SEX
TARZANA, THE WILD GIRL see **TARZANA SESSO SELVAGGIO** • 1969
TARZANA'S SAVAGE SEX see **TARZANA SESSO SELVAGGIO** • 1969
TARZANOVA SMRT • 1963 • Balik Jaroslav • CZC • DEATH OF TARZAN, THE (USA) ○ DEATH OF THE APE MAN ○ TARZAN'S DEATH
TARZAN'S AFRICAN JUNGLE see **TARZAN'S HIDDEN JUNGLE** • 1955
TARZAN'S BELOVED • 1964 • *Azad* • IND
TARZAN'S DEADLY SILENCE • 1970 • Friend Robert L., Dobkin Lawrence • MTV • USA • DEADLY SILENCE, THE
TARZAN'S DEATH see **TARZANOVA SMRT** • 1963
TARZAN'S DESERT MYSTERY • 1943 • Thiele Wilhelm • USA • TARZAN AGAINST THE SAHARA ○ TARZAN AND THE SHEIK
TARZAN'S FIGHT FOR LIFE • 1958 • Humberstone H. Bruce • USA
TARZAN'S GREATEST ADVENTURE • 1959 • Guillermin John • USA, UKN
TARZAN'S HIDDEN JUNGLE • 1955 • Schuster Harold • USA • TARZAN'S AFRICAN JUNGLE
TARZAN'S JUNGLE REBELLION • 1970 • Witney William • MTV • USA
TARZAN'S MAGIC FOUNTAIN • 1949 • Sholem Lee • USA • TARZAN AND THE ARROW OF DEATH
TARZAN'S NEW YORK ADVENTURE • 1942 • Thorpe Richard • USA • TARZAN AGAINST THE WORLD
TARZAN'S PERIL • 1951 • Haskin Byron • USA • TARZAN AND THE JUNGLE GODDESS (UKN)
TARZAN'S REVENGE • 1938 • Lederman D. Ross • USA
TARZAN'S SAVAGE FURY • 1952 • Endfield Cy • USA
TARZAN'S SECRET TREASURE • 1941 • Thorpe Richard • USA
TARZAN'S THREE CHALLENGES • 1963 • Day Robert • USA
TARZOON, LA HONTE DE LA JUNGLE • 1974 • Picha, Szulzinger Boris • ANM • BLG, FRN • TARZOON THE SHAME OF THE JUNGLE ○ HONTE DE LA JUNGLE, LA ○ JUNGLE BURGER
TARZOON THE SHAME OF THE JUNGLE see **TARZOON, LA HONTE DE LA JUNGLE** • 1974
TASAJERA • 1976 • Pinto Jorge • DOC • CLM
TASCHENDIEBE • 1920 • Justitz Emil • FRG
TASFIE-KHANEH • 1978 • Kia-Rostami Abbas • IRN • REFINERY, THE
TASHKENT, THE CITY OF BREAD see **TASHKYENT GOROD KHLYEBNY** • 1968
TASHKYENT GOROD KHLYEBNY • 1968 • Abbasov Shukhrat • USS • TASHKENT, THE CITY OF BREAD
TASIO • 1989 • Armendariz Montxo • SPN
TASK FORCE • 1949 • Daves Delmer • USA
TASK TO BE CARRIED OUT see **ZADANIE DO WYKONANIA** • 1965
TASOFARE SAKABA • 1955 • Uchida Tomu • JPN • TWILIGHT BEER HALL
TASSELS IN THE AIR • 1938 • Parrott Charles • SHT • USA
TASSINARO, IL • 1983 • Sordi Alberto • ITL • TAXI DRIVER
TASSINARO A NEW YORK, UN • 1988 • Sordi Alberto • ITL • ITALIAN TAXI DRIVER IN NEW YORK
TASTE FOR FEAR, A • 1987 • Raffani Piccio • ITL • OBSESSION: A TASTE FOR FEAR
TASTE FOR WOMEN, A (USA) see **AIMEZ-VOUS LES FEMMES?** • 1964
TASTE OF ALMONDS, A see **DAKH NA BADEMI, S** • 1967
TASTE OF ASHES, THE • 1959 • Martinson Leslie H. • USA
TASTE OF BLOOD, A • 1967 • Lewis Herschell G. • USA • SECRET OF DR. ALUCARD, THE
TASTE OF BLOOD, THE • 1985 • SAF
TASTE OF BLOOD PART 2 • 1985 • SAF
TASTE OF CATNIP, A • 1966 • McKimson Robert • ANS • USA
TASTE OF EVIL, A • 1971 • Moxey John Llewellyn • TVM • USA
TASTE OF EVIL, A • U Myint Soe • BRM
TASTE OF EXCITEMENT • 1969 • Sharp Don • UKN
TASTE OF FEAR • 1961 • Holt Seth • UKN • SCREAM OF FEAR (USA)
TASTE OF FISH, THE see **SAMMA NO AJI** • 1962
TASTE OF FLESH, A • 1967 • Silverman Louis • USA
TASTE OF GREEN TEA AND RICE, THE see **OCHAZUKE NO AJI** • 1952
TASTE OF HELL, A • 1973 • Yarema Neil, Bradbury Basil • USA
TASTE OF HIS OWN MEDICINE, A • 1913 • Seay Charles M. • USA
TASTE OF HONEY, A • 1961 • Richardson Tony • UKN
TASTE OF HONEY, A SWALLOW OF BRINE, A see **SMELL OF HONEY, A SWALLOW OF BRINE!, A** • 1966
TASTE OF HOT LEAD, A • 1969 • Rotsler William • USA • HOT LEAD
TASTE OF LIFE, A • 1919 • Dillon John Francis • USA
TASTE OF LIFE, A see **BOTTA DI VITA, UNA** • 1988
TASTE OF LOVE, A see **GRANDES PERSONNES, LES** • 1961
TASTE OF MACKEREL, THE see **SAMMA NO AJI** • 1962
TASTE OF MONEY, A • 1960 • Varnel Max • UKN
TASTE OF MONEY, A • 1983 • Mahler Richard • USA
TASTE OF MUSIC • 1976 • Bugajski Ryszard • MTV • PLN
TASTE OF REVENGE, THE see **SAPORE DELLE VENDETTA, IL** • 1968
TASTE OF SEA 2, ONE YEAR LATER, A see **SAPORE DI MARE 2 UN ANNO DOPO** • 1984
TASTE OF SEA, A see **SAPORE DI MARE** • 1983
TASTE OF SIN, A • 1983 • Lommel Ulli • USA • OLIVIA ○ DOUBLE JEOPARDY ○ BEYOND THE BRIDGE ○ FACES OF FEAR
TASTE OF SIN, THE see **SABOR DO PECADO, O** • 1967
TASTE OF SUCCESS, A see **MENESTYKSENMAKU** • 1983
TASTE OF SUMMER, A see **KESAN MAKU** • 1975
TASTE OF THE BLACK EARTH, THE see **SOL ZIEMI CZARNEJ** • 1969
TASTE OF THE SAVAGE • 1974 • Mariscal Alberto • MXC
TASTE OF WATER, THE see **SMAAK VAN WATER, DE** • 1982
TASTE OF WINE, A • 1963 • Davies Bernard • DCS • UKN
TASTE OF WOMAN, TASTE OF MAN see **ONNA TO OTOKO NO AJIKURABE** • 1968
TASTE OF WOMEN see **ANNA NO AJI** • 1967
TASTE OF YOUTH, A • 1970 • *Hale April* • USA
TASTE THE BLOOD OF DRACULA • 1970 • Sasdy Peter • UKN
TASTERS, THE see **ODD TASTES** • 1968
TAT DES ANDERN, DIE • 1951 • Weiss Helmut • FRG
TAT DES ANDREAS HARMER, DIE • 1930 • Deutsch-German Alfred • AUS • DREI MINUTEN VOR ZEHN
TAT VON DAMALS, DIE • 1915 • Kahn William • FRG

TATA DE DUMINICA • 1974 • Constantinescu Mihai • RMN • SUNDAY FATHER
TATA MIA • 1986 • Borau Jose Luis • SPN • MY NANNY ○ NANNY DEAR
TATAK DOUBLE CROSS • 1968 • Gallardo Cesar Chat • PHL • MARK DOUBLE CROSS
TATAK: SACRAMENTADOS • 1968 • Medina Hector • PHL • MARKED: SACRAMENTADOS
TATAKAI HETTAI • 1940 • Kamei Fumio • JPN
TATAL RISIPITOR • Petringenaru Adrian • RMN
TATARJARAS • 1917 • Curtiz Michael • HNG • INVASION
TATCHO • 1905 • *Walturdaw* • UKN
TATER GESUCHT • 1931 • Wolff Carl Heinz • FRG
TATER IST UNTER UNS, DER • 1966 • Fredersdorf Herbert B. • FRG
TATERNICY • 1960 • Sprudin Sergiusz, Utracki Lech • DOC • PLN • TATRA CLIMBERS, THE
TATESHI DAMPEI • 1950 • Makino Masahiro • JPN • FENCING MASTER
TATESHINA NO SHIKI • 1966 • Shindo Kaneto • JPN • FOUR SEASONS OF TATESHINA
TATIANA • 1924 • Litvak Anatole, Petrov Vladimir • USS • HEARTS AND DOLLARS (USA)
TATIE DANIELLE • 1990 • Chatiliez Etienne • FRN
TATJANA • 1923 • Dinesen Robert • FRG
TATJANA • 1977 • Geissendorfer Hans W. • FRG
TATKALA MIMPI BERAKHIR • 1988 • Umboh Wim • INN
TATKO see **OTAC** • 1973
TATLER, THE • 1910 • *Powers* • USA
TATLI-BELA • 1961 • Yilmaz Atif • TRK
TATLO, DALAWA, ISA • 1974 • Brocka Lino • PHL • TALTO, DALAWA, ISA
TATLONG HARI • 1968 • D'Lanor • PHL • THREE KINGS
TATLONG INA • 1988 • O'Hara Mario • PHL • THREE MOTHERS
TATLONG TAONG WALANG DIYOS • 1977 • O'Hara Mario • PHL • THREE YEARS WITHOUT GOD
TATORT BERLIN • 1957 • Kunert Joachim • GDR • IT HAPPENED IN BERLIN
TATOUE, LE • 1968 • de La Patelliere Denys • FRN, ITL • NEMICI PER LA PELLE –IL TATUATO (ITL) ○ MILLION DOLLAR TATTOO
TATOWIERUNG • 1967 • Schaaf Johannes • FRG • DELINQUENT, THE (UKN) ○ TATTOOING ○ TATTOO
TATRA CLIMBERS, THE see **TATERNICY** • 1960
TATRA CUP, THE see **PUCHAR TATR** • 1948
TATRAS ZAUBER • 1933 • Trotz Adolf • FRG
TATSU see **DOBUROKU NO TATSU** • 1962
TATSU THE DRUNKARD see **DOBUROKU NO TATSU** • 1949
TATSUNOKO TARO • 1978 • Urayama Kirio, Kasai Osamu • ANM • JPN • TARO, BABY DRAGON ○ TARO, THE DRAGON BOY
TATTARBLOD see **GUD FADER OCH TATTAREN** • 1954
TATTERED DRESS, THE • 1957 • Arnold Jack • USA
TATTERED DUKE, THE • 1914 • *Roland Ruth* • USA
TATTERED WEB, THE • 1971 • Wendkos Paul • TVM • USA
TATTERLY • 1916 • Lucoque H. Lisle • UKN
TATTERS, A TALE OF THE SLUMS • 1911 • Coleby A. E. • UKN
TATTLE BATTLE, THE • 1913 • Parker Lem B. • USA
TATTLE-TALE ALICE • 1916 • *Howell Alice* • SHT • USA
TATTLE TELEVISION • 1940 • D'Arcy Harry • SHT • USA
TATTLERS, THE • 1920 • Mitchell Howard M. • USA
TATTOO • 1981 • Brooks Bob • USA
TATTOO see **TATOWIERUNG** • 1967
TATTOO see **TATUAJE** • 1976
TATTOO 67 • 1967 • Regnier Michel, Leduc Yves • DCS • CND
TATTOO, THE • 1912 • *Bison* • USA
TATTOO ARI • 1982 • Takahashi Tomoaki • JPN • MAN WITH A TATTOO
TATTOO CONNECTION, THE • 1979 • Lee Tso Nam • HKG
TATTOO MARK, THE • 1914 • Finley Ned • USA
TATTOOED ARM, THE • 1910 • *Lubin* • USA
TATTOOED ARM, THE • 1913 • Reid Wallace • USA
TATTOOED DRAGON • 1981 • HKG
TATTOOED HAND, THE • 1915 • *Ridgely Cleo* • USA
TATTOOED MAN, THE • 1915 • Frank Alexander F. • USA
TATTOOED MAN, THE • De Hirsch Storm • USA
TATTOOED POLICE HORSE, THE • 1964 • Lansburgh Larry • USA
TATTOOED STRANGER, THE • 1950 • Montagne Edward J. • USA
TATTOOED SWORDSWOMAN see **KAIDAN NOBORIRYU** • 1970
TATTOOED TEARS • 1978 • Churchill Joan, Broomfield Nicholas • USA
TATTOOED TEMPTRESS see **IREZUMI MUZAN** • 1968
TATTOOED WILL, THE • 1914 • Batley Ernest G. • UKN
TATTOOING see **TATOWIERUNG** • 1967
TATU BOLA • 1972 • Rocha Glauber • MTV • ITL • ISABEL IS DEATH
TATUAJE • 1976 • Luna Bigas • SPN • PRIMA AVENTURA DE PEPE CARVALHO, LA ○ TATTOO
TAUDIS, LES • 1972 • Regnier Michel • DCS • CND
TAUDIS DOIT ETRE VAINCU, LE • 1912 • O'Galop Marius • ANM • FRN
TAUGENICHTS • 1978 • Sinkel Bernard • FRG • GOOD-FOR-NOTHING, THE
TAUGENICHTS, DER • 1922 • Froelich Carl • FRG
TAUMEL • 1919 • Moest Hubert • FRG
TAUMEL 1924 • 1924 • Schonfelder Erich • FRG
TAUNT, THE • 1915 • Sloman Edward • USA
TAUR, IL RE DELLA FORZA BRUTA • 1963 • Leonviola Antonio • ITL • TARZAN ROI DE LA FORCE BRUTALE (FRN) ○ TARZAN, KING OF BRUTE FORCE ○ THAUR, ROI DE LA FORCE BRUTALE ○ THOR AND THE AMAZON WOMEN ○ TAUR THE MIGHTY ○ TOR, MIGHTY WARRIOR ○ TOR
TAUR THE MIGHTY see **TAUR, IL RE DELLA FORZA BRUTA** • 1963
TAUREAU • 1973 • Perron Clement • CND • BULL, THE
TAUREG THE DESERT WARRIOR see **TUAREG IL GUERRIERO DEL DESERTO** • 1984
TAURO MAQUIAS O LA VOCACION DE RAFAEL ARCOS • 1914 • Elias Francisco • SPN
TAURUS • 1969 • Moeller Gerald • SHT • USA
TAUSE FLERTALL, DET • 1977 • Wam Svend • NRW • SILENT MAJORITY, THE
TAUSEND AUGEN DES DR. MABUSE, DIE • 1960 • Lang Fritz • FRG, FRN, ITL • DIABOLIQUE DOCTEUR MABUSE, LE (FRN) ○ DIABOLICO DR. MABUSE, IL (ITL) ○ 1000 EYES OF DR. MABUSE, THE (USA) ○ EYE OF EVIL ○ SHADOW VS. THE 1000 EYES OF DR. MABUSE, THE
TAUSEND FUR EINE NACHT • 1932 • Mack Max • FRG
TAUSEND LIEDER OHNE TON • 1977 • Holldack Claudia • FRG • THOUSAND SONGS WITHOUT A SOUND, A
TAUSEND MELODIEN • 1956 • Deppe Hans • FRG
TAUSEND ROTE ROSEN BLUHN • 1952 • Braun Alfred • FRG
TAUSEND STERNE LEUCHTEN • 1959 • Philipp Harald • FRG
TAUSEND UND EINE FRAU • 1918 • Raffay Iwa • FRG
TAUTOLOGOS PLUS X • 1975 • Aguirre Javier • SHT • SPN
TAUW • 1970 • Sembene Ousmane • SNL • TAW
TAUWETTER • 1977 • Imhoof Markus • SWT, FRG
TAVASZ A TELBEN • 1917 • Curtiz Michael • HNG • SPRING IN WINTERTIME
TAVASZI SZERELEM • 1921 • von Bolvary Geza • HNG
TAVASZI VIHAR • 1917 • *Lugosi Bela* • HNG
TAVASZI ZAPOR • 1932 • Fejos Paul • HNG • SPRING SHOWER (USA) ○ MARIE –A HUNGARIAN LEGEND ○ MARIE
TAVELURE DU POMMIER ET DU POIRIER, LA • 1955 • Tadie, Lacoste • SHT • FRN
TAVERN, THE • 1975 • Papayiannidis Takis • SHT • GRC
TAVERN BRAWL, THE • 1924 • *Regent Films* • SHT • UKN
TAVERN IN SPESSART, THE see **WIRTSHAUS IM SPESSART, DAS** • 1923
TAVERN-KEEPER'S DAUGHTER, THE • 1908 • Griffith D. W. • USA
TAVERN KEEPER'S SON, THE • 1915 • *Borzage Frank* • USA
TAVERN KNIGHT, THE • 1920 • Elvey Maurice • UKN
TAVERN OF TRAGEDY, THE • 1914 • Crisp Donald • USA
TAVERNA DELLA LIBERTA, LA • 1951 • Cam Maurice • ITL
TAVERNA ROSSA • 1940 • Neufeld Max • ITL • UNO +UNO + UNO ○ 1 + 1 + 1
TAVERNE DU POISSON COURONNE, LA • 1946 • Chanas Rene • FRN • AU POISSON COURONNE
TAVIBOIS • 1952-56 • Tessier Albert • DOC • CND
TAVOLA DEI POVERI, LA • 1932 • Blasetti Alessandro • ITL
TAVOLLET HERCEGE, A • 1989 • Tolmar Tamas • HNG • PRINCE OF ABSENCE, THE
TAVSE PIGER, DE • 1986 • Bro Arne, Wivel Anne • DOC • DNM • SILENT GIRLS, THE
TAW see **TAUW** • 1970
TAWAMURE • 1967 • Yamashita Osamu • JPN • FUN
TAWHIDA • 1976 • Mustafa Hassam Eddin • EGY
TAWNY OWL, THE see **LIFE STORY OF THE TAWNY OWL, THE** • 1936
TAWNY PIPIT • 1944 • Miles Bernard, Saunders Charles • UKN
TAWWE TANNIES • 1984 • Cawood Bromley • SAF • TOUGH ANTS
TAX IS NOT A FOUR-LETTER WORD • 1969 • Mills Michael, Arioli Don • SHT • CND
TAX: THE OUTCOME OF INCOME see **TAX: THE OUTCOME ON INCOME** • 1975
TAX: THE OUTCOME ON INCOME • 1975 • Soul Veronika, Glover Rupert • ANS • CND • TAX: THE OUTCOME OF INCOME
TAXA K 1640 EFTERLYSES • 1956 • Lauritzen Lau Jr. • DNM
TAXANDRIA • 1990 • Servais Raoul • FRG
TAXATION CLIPS • 1974 • Thomas Gayle (c/d) • CND
TAXI • 1919 • Windom Lawrence C. • USA
TAXI! • 1931 • Del Ruth Roy • USA • BLIND SPOT, THE ○ TAXI, PLEASE
TAXI • 1932 • Naumberg Nancy • DOC • USA
TAXI • 1953 • Ratoff Gregory • USA
TAXI • 1963 • Lluch Miguel • SPN
TAXI • 1969 • Stutz Roland • CND
TAXI! • 1970 • Stewardson Joe • SAF
TAXI • 1979 • Hagg Russell • MTV • ASL
TAXI • 1982 • Greenwald Barry • DOC • CND
TAXI see **UOMINI, CHE MASCALZONI.., GLI** • 1932
TAXI see **TAXI, ROULOTTE ET CORRIDA** • 1958
TAXI see **HIT AND RUN** • 1982
TAXI 13 • 1928 • Neilan Marshall • USA
TAXI 13 • 1954 • Larsson Borje • SWD
TAXI 313X7, LE • 1923 • Colombier Piere • FRN
TAXI BARONS • 1933 • Meins Gus • SHT • USA
TAXI BEAUTIES • 1928 • *Sennett Mack (P)* • SHT • USA
TAXI BLUES • 1989 • Longuin Pavel • USS, FRN
TAXI DANCER, THE • 1926 • Millarde Harry • USA
TAXI DE LOS CONFLICTOS, EL • 1970 • Ozores Mariano, Saenz De Heredia Jose Luis • SPN
TAXI DE NUIT • 1935 • Valentin Albert • FRN
TAXI DI NOTTE • 1950 • Gallone Carmine • ITL • SINGING TAXI DRIVER (USA) ○ BAMBINO
TAXI DOLLS • 1929 • *Sennett Mack (P)* • SHT • USA
TAXI DRIVER • 1954 • *Burman S. D. (M)* • IND
TAXI DRIVER • 1975 • Scorsese Martin • USA
TAXI DRIVER see **SOFERAKI, TO** • 1953
TAXI DRIVER see **TASSINARO, IL** • 1983
TAXI FOR TOBRUK (USA) see **TAXI POUR TOBROUK, UN** • 1961
TAXI FOR TWO • 1928 • *Sennett Mack (P)* • SHT • USA
TAXI FOR TWO • 1929 • Esway Alexander, Clift Denison • UKN
TAXI-GATTIN see **WENN MANNER SCHWINDELN** • 1950
TAXI GIRL • 1977 • Tarantini Michele Massimo • ITL
TAXI GIRLS • 1979 • Jaacovi Jaacov • USA
TAXI-KITTY • 1950 • Hoffmann Kurt • FRG
TAXI LOVE SERVIZIO PER SIGNORA • 1977 • Bergonzelli Sergio • ITL
TAXI MAUVE, UN • 1977 • Boisset Yves • FRN, IRL • PURPLE TAXI (USA)
TAXI, MISTER • 1943 • Neumann Kurt • USA
TAXI MYSTERY, THE • 1926 • Windermere Fred • USA
TAXI NACH TOBRUK (FRG) see **TAXI POUR TOBROUK, UN** • 1961
TAXI PARA TOBROUK, UN (SPN) see **TAXI POUR TOBROUK, UN** • 1961
TAXI, PLEASE see **TAXI!** • 1931
TAXI, PLEASE see **TAXI PROSIM** • 1961
TAXI POUR TOBROUK, UN • 1961 • de La Patelliere Denys • FRN, SPN, FRG • TAXI PARA TOBROUK, UN (SPN) ○ TAXI NACH TOBRUK (FRG) ○ TAXI FOR TOBRUK (USA) ○ TAXI TO TOBRUK
TAXI PROSIM • 1961 • Sequens Jiri • CZC • TALES FROM THE LIFE OF A PRAGUE TAXI-DRIVER ○ TAXI, PLEASE
TAXI, ROULOTTE ET CORRIDA • 1958 • Hunebelle Andre • FRN • TAXI
TAXI SCANDAL, A • 1928 • *Sennett Mack (P)* • SHT • USA
TAXI SPOOKS • 1929 • *Sennett Mack (P)* • SHT • USA
TAXI! TAXI! • 1927 • Brown Melville • USA
TAXI TO HEAVEN • 1943 • Rappaport Herbert • USS
TAXI TO PARADISE • 1933 • Brunel Adrian • UKN
TAXI TO THE JOHN see **TAXI ZUM KLO** • 1980
TAXI TO THE LOO see **TAXI ZUM KLO** • 1980
TAXI TO THE TOILET see **TAXI ZUM KLO** • 1980
TAXI TO TOBRUK see **TAXI POUR TOBROUK, UN** • 1961
TAXI TROUBLES • 1931 • Lord Del • SHT • USA
TAXI-TURVY • 1954 • Kneitel Seymour • ANS • USA
TAXI ZUM KLO • 1980 • Ripploh Frank • FRG • TAXI TO THE JOHN ○ TAXI TO THE TOILET ○ TAXI TO THE LOO
TAXICAB MYSTERY, THE • 1911 • *Yankee* • USA
TAXIDERMIST, THE • 1913 • *Nestor* • USA
TAXIDI STA KYTHERA • 1984 • Angelopoulos Theo • GRC • JOURNEY TO CYTHERA ○ VOYAGE TO CYTHERA
TAXIDI STIN PROTEVOUSA • 1981 • Papayiannidis Takis • GRC • VOYAGE TO ATHENS
TAXIMETER CAB, THE • 1909 • Yates Frank D. • UKN
TAXING WOMAN, A see **MARUSA NO ONNA** • 1987
TAXING WOMAN PART II, A see **MARUSA NO ONNA 2** • 1988
TAY HO, THE VILLAGE IN THE FOURTH ZONE • 1973 • Nickel Gitta • DOC • GDR
TAY ROAD BRIDGE, THE • 1956 • Cooper Henry • UKN
TAYINSTVENNAYA STENA • 1968 • Povolotskaya I., Sadkovich M. • USS • RIDDLE OF THE WALL, THE ○ MYSTERIOUS WALL, THE
TAYINSTVENNY MONAKH • 1968 • Koltsaty Arkadi • USS • MYSTERIOUS MONK, THE
TAYLOR MEAD DANCES • 1963 • Morrissey Paul • SHT • USA
TAYLOR MEAD'S ASS • 1966 • Warhol Andy • USA
TAYNA PESHCHYERY KANIYUTA • 1968 • Faisiyev Habibulla • USS • SECRET OF THE KANIYUT CAVE
TAYOPA TREASURE HUNT • 1974 • Cawley Bob • USA • RAIDERS OF THE TREASURE OF TAYOPA ○ TREASURE OF TAYOPA
TAYRONA CASE, THE see **CASO TAYRONA, EL** • 1975
TAYSIDE • 1974 • Marzaroli Oscar • DOC • UKN
TAZA, SON OF COCHISE • 1954 • Sirk Douglas • USA
TAZERKA • Harzallah Ahmed • TNS
TAZNI PTACI • 1961 • Mach Josef • CZC • BIRDS OF PASSAGE
TCAIKOVSKI • 1969 • Talankin Igor • USS, USA • TCHAIKOVSKY ○ CHAIKOVSKI
TCHAIKOVSKY see **TCAIKOVSKI** • 1969
TCHAIKOVSKY MUSIC FESTIVAL • 1963 • DOC • USS
TCHAN KONDELIK A ZET VEJVARA • 1929 • *Vich Vaclav (Ph)* • CZC • KONDELIK –FATHER-IN-LAW, VEJVARA –SON-IN-LAW
TCHAO PANTIN • 1983 • Berri Claude • FRN
TCHEKOV OU LE MIROIR DES VIES PERDUES • 1964 • Goretta Claude • MTV • SWT
TCHERIKE-YE TARA • 1979 • Beyzai Bahram • IRN • BALLAD OF TARA, THE
TCHESHMEH • 1972 • Avanessian Arbi • IRN • SPRING, THE
TCHILAVIEK IZ RESTARANA see **CHELOVEK IZ RESTARANA** • 1927
TCHILI TCHALA THE MAGICIAN see **VARAZSLO, A** • 1970
TCHIN-CHAO, THE CHINESE CONJURER (USA) see **THAUMATURGE CHINOIS, LE** • 1904
TCHOU-TCHOU • 1972 • Hoedeman Co • ANS • CND
TCHOUDESNITSA • 1936 • Medvedkin Alexander • USS • CHUDESNITSA ○ MIRACLE GIRL, THE
TE • 1963 • Szabo Istvan • SHT • HNG • YOU..
TE AMO • 1986 • Calcagno Eduardo • ARG • I LOVE YOU
TE BESARE EN LA BOCA • 1949 • Cortes Fernando • MXC
TE CSAK PIPALJ LADANYI • 1938 • Keleti Marton • HNG • KEEP ON SMOKING, LADANYI
TE LO LEGGO NEGLI OCCHI • 1966 • Mastrocinque Camillo • ITL
TE MARRE PAS, C'EST POUR RIRE! • 1981 • Besnard Jacques • FRN
TE O TSUNAGU KORA • 1947 • Inagaki Hiroshi • JPN • CHILDREN HAND IN HAND
TE O TSUNAGU KORA • 1962 • Hani Susumu • JPN • CHILDREN HAND IN HAND (USA)
TE ODIO Y TE QUIERO • 1956 • Orol Juan • MXC
TE PROMENES-TU SOUVENT SUR UN LAPIN.. • 1974 • Lamothe Arthur • DCS • CND
TE QUIERO • 1978 • Davison Tito • MXC
TE QUIERO CON LOCURA • 1935 • Boland John J. • USA • I'M CRAZY ABOUT YOU
TE QUIERO PARA MI • 1944 • Vajda Ladislao • SPN
TE RETROUVER QUEBEC • 1967 • Lavoie Richard • DCS • CND
TE RONGYOS ELET..! • 1984 • Bacso Peter • HNG • OH, BLOODY LIFE!
TE RUA • 1990 • Barclay Barry • NZL • PIT, THE
TE SIGO ESPERANDO • 1951 • Davison Tito • MXC
TE STO ASPETTANNO • 1956 • Fizzarotti Armando • ITL
TE VE OLIVE • 1931 • de Canonge Maurice • FRN
TE VI EN TV • 1957 • Galindo Alejandro • MXC
TEA AND RICE (USA) see **OCHAZUKE NO AJI** • 1952
TEA AND SYMPATHY • 1956 • Minnelli Vincente • USA
TEA AND TOAST • 1913 • Williams C. Jay?, France Charles H.? • USA
TEA FOR THREE • 1927 • Leonard Robert Z. • USA
TEA FOR TWO • 1950 • Butler David • USA
TEA FOR TWO HUNDRED • 1948 • Hannah Jack • ANS • USA
TEA HOUND, THE • 1919 • Dillon John Francis • SHT • USA
TEA HOUSE MOUSE • 1963 • Kuwahara Bob • ANS • USA
TEA IN THE GARDEN • 1958 • Wieland Joyce • SHT • CND
TEA IN THE HAREM (USA) see **THE AU HAREM D'ARCHIMEDE, LE** • 1984
TEA-LEAF, THE see **RAGMAN'S DAUGHTER, THE** • 1972

TEA LEAVES IN THE WIND • 1938 • Wing Ward • UKN • HATE IN PARADISE
TEA PARTY, THE • 1896 • Paul R. W. • UKN
TEA-POT, THE • 1962 • Haupe Wlodzimierz, Bielinska Halina • ANM • PLN
TEA -WITH A KICK • 1923 • Halperin Victor Hugo (Spv), Kenton Erle C. • USA
TEA WITH THREE OLD LADIES see TEE DER DREI ALTEN DAMEN, DER • 1989
TEACH ME see TEACH ME HOW TO DO IT! • 1967
TEACH ME HOW TO DO IT! • 1967 • Meola Michael • USA • TEACH ME
TEACH ME TO DANCE • 1978 • Wheeler Anne • CND
TEACHARAMMA • 1968 • Puttanna S. R. • IND • LADY TEACHER
TEACHER, THE • 1955 • Uher Stefan • CZC
TEACHER, THE • 1974 • Avedis Howard • USA • SEDUCTRESS, THE
TEACHER, THE • 1986 • Zhirov Yuri • DOC • BUL
TEACHER, THE see UCHITEL • 1939
TEACHER, THE see MAESTRO, IL • 1957
TEACHER, THE see BRIGADISTA, EL • 1978
TEACHER, THE see SANG GURU • 1981
TEACHER AND THE BULLY, THE • 1916 • Gayety • USA
TEACHER AND THE MIRACLE, THE • 1957 • Riethof Carol, Riethof Peter • USA
TEACHER AND THE MIRACLE, THE see MAESTRO, IL • 1957
TEACHER AT ROCKVILLE, THE • 1913 • Grandon Francis J. • USA
TEACHER HOFER see LEHRER HOFER • 1975
TEACHER NANSEN see TIMELAERER NANSEN • 1968
TEACHER OF KRISHNA'S DEVOTEE see KRISHNABHAKTA BODANA • 1944
TEACHER OF ORIENTAL LANGUAGES, THE see UCITEL ORIENTALNICH JAZYKU • 1918
TEACHER, TEACHER • 1926 • Taurog Norman • SHT • USA
TEACHER, TEACHER • 1969 • Cook Fielder • TVM • USA
TEACHER WANTED • 1913 • Lyman Laura • USA
TEACHER WAS A SEXPOT see SEX KITTENS GO TO COLLEGE • 1960
TEACHER WITH THE GOLDEN HAIR, THE see KORITSI ME TA XANTHA MALLIA, TO • 1969
TEACHERS • 1984 • Hiller Arthur • USA
TEACHERS ARE PEOPLE • 1952 • Kinney Jack • ANS • USA
TEACHER'S BEAU • 1935 • Meins Gus • SHT • USA
TEACHER'S FIRST CHILD, THE see FROKENS FORSTA BARN • 1950
TEACHERS IN TRANSFORMATION see LEHRER IM WANDEL • 1963
TEACHER'S MARK CARD, THE see SENSEI NO TSUSHINBO • 1977
TEACHERS ON A SUMMER HOLIDAY see MAGISTRARNA PA SOMMARLOV • 1941
TEACHER'S PEST • 1931 • Fleischer Dave • ANS • USA
TEACHER'S PEST • 1939 • Lord Del • SHT • USA
TEACHER'S PEST • 1950 • Sparber I. • ANS • USA
TEACHER'S PESTS • 1932 • Lantz Walter, Nolan William • ANS • USA
TEACHER'S PET • 1930 • McGowan Robert • SHT • USA
TEACHER'S PET • 1958 • Seaton George • USA
TEACHER'S PET, THE • 1920 • Gibson Hoot • SHT • USA
TEACHING A HUSBAND A LESSON • 1909 • Bouwmeester Theo? • UKN
TEACHING A LIAR A LESSON • 1912 • MacMackin Archer • USA
TEACHING DAD A LESSON • 1913 • Nestor • USA
TEACHING DAD TO LIKE HER • 1911 • Powell Frank?, Griffith D. W.? • USA
TEACHING FATHER A LESSON • 1914 • MacGregor Norval • USA
TEACHING HICKVILLE TO SING • 1913 • Bayne Beverly • USA
TEACHING HIS WIFE A LESSON • 1913 • Seay Charles M. • USA
TEACHING MCFADDEN TO WALTZ • 1911 • Vitagraph • USA
TEACHING OF THE ITTOU STYLE, THE see ITTORYU SHINAN • 1936
TEACHING THE TEACHER • 1921 • Roach Hal • SHT • USA
TEACHINGS OF A SOVIET AGRICULTURAL DEPUTATION, THE see SZOVJET MEZOGAZDASAGI KULDOTTEK TANITASAI • 1951
TEAHOUSE OF THE AUGUST MOON, THE • 1956 • Mann Daniel • USA
TEAM, THE see SIDECAR BOYS • 1974
TEAM APPROACH, THE • 1975 • Dalen Zale R. • CND
TEAM FROM OUR STREET see KOMANDA S NASIEJ ULICY • 1953
TEAM-MATES • 1978 • Jacobson Steven • USA
TEAMSTER, THE • 1911 • Fielding Romaine • USA
TEAMWORK • 1977 • Dunning George • ANM • UKN
TEAR FOR KARAMOJA, A see KARAMOJA • 1962
TEAR GAS SQUAD • 1940 • Morse Terry O. • USA
TEAR ME BUT SATIATE ME WITH YOUR KISSES see STRAZIAMI MA DI BACI SAZIAMI • 1968
TEAR ON THE FACE, A • 1965 • Zaninovic Stejpan • DOC • YGS
TEAR ON THE PAGE, THE • 1915 • Morgan George • USA
TEAR THAT BURNED, THE • 1914 • O'Brien John B. • USA
TEARAWAYS, THE • 1961 • Kelly Ron • UKN
TEARFUL EYES see DHAKRISMENA MATIA • 1967
TEARFUL ROMANCE • 1961 • Klopcic Matjaz • SHT • YGS
TEARIN' INTO TROUBLE • 1927 • Thorpe Richard • USA
TEARIN' LOOSE • 1925 • Thorpe Richard • USA
TEARING AWAY see CAMPANADA, LA • 1979
TEARING DOWN THE SPANISH FLAG • 1898 • Blackton J. Stuart • USA
TEARING OF BRANCHES PROHIBITED see HANAORI • 1968
TEARING THROUGH • 1925 • Rosson Arthur • USA
TEARS see SLEZI • 1914
TEARS see NAMIDA • 1957
TEARS AND LAUGHTER see PLAC A SMICH • 1898
TEARS AND SMILES • 1917 • Bertram William • USA
TEARS AND SORROW see HAPUSLAH AIRMATAMU • 1975
TEARS AND SORROW see LANGIT TIDAK SELALU CERAH • 1979
TEARS AND SUNSHINE • 1915 • Rogers Gene • USA
TEARS ARE FLOWING, THE see SLIOZY KAPALI • 1982
TEARS ARE NOT ENOUGH • 1986 • Zaritsky John • DOC • CND
TEARS DRIED, THE • 1975 • Nagaat • EGY
TEARS DRY IN THE WIND see TRANEN TROCKNET DER WIND • 1967
TEARS FOR A KILLER • 1977 • SAF • AMOR DE ASSASSINO
TEARS FOR SIMON (USA) see LOST • 1956
TEARS IN THE DARK see LUHA SA KARIMLAN • 1968
TEARS IN THE LION'S MANE see NAMIDA O SHISHI NO TATEGAMI NI • 1962
TEARS O' PEGGY • 1912 • Leonard Marion • USA
TEARS OF A MOTHER, THE see BIR ANENIN GOZ YASLARI MUHUR GOZLUM • 1967
TEARS OF AN ONION, THE • 1938 • Fleischer Dave • ANS • USA
TEARS OF BLOOD (USA) see LACRIME DE SANGUE • 1944
TEARS OF GRIEF see DHAKRISMENA MATIA • 1967
TEARS OF HAPPINESS • 1974 • Mouradian Sarky • USA
TEARS OF HIGH SCHOOL LIFE • 1981 • Lim Kwon-Taek • SKR
TEARS OF PEACE see LARMES DE PAIX • 1970
TEARS OF RAGE see DHAKRIA ORGIS • 1967
TEARS OF REMORSE see POLI ARGA YIA DHAKRIA • 1968
TEARS OF SAN FRANCISCO see CHINMEN NU • 1941
TEARS OF THE GEISHA KONATSU see HITORI NERU YO NO KONATSU • 1955
TEARS OF THE OUTCASTS see SADOL KANDULU • 1967
TEARS ON THE LION'S MANE see NAMIDA O SHISHI NO TATEGAMI NI • 1962
TEARS THE WORLD CAN'T SEE see SLZY, KTERE SVET NEVIDI • 1961
TEASE FOR TWO • 1965 • McKimson Robert • ANS • USA
TEASER, THE • 1925 • Seiter William A. • USA
TEASER, THE see IDOL OF THE NORTH, THE • 1921
TEASING GRANDPA • 1901 • Williamson James • UKN
TEASING THE MONKEY • 1899 • Warwick Trading Co • UKN
TEASING THE SOIL • 1920 • Parrott Charles • SHT • USA
TEASING THE SOIL (?) see SPRING • 1920
TEASING THE TORNADO • 1915 • Fielding Romaine • USA
TEATR LALEK • 1954 • Ussorowski Marian • PLN • VISIT TO THE PUPPETS, A
TEATRO see ORIZZONTE DIPINTO, L' • 1941
TEATRO APOLO • 1950 • Gil Rafael • SPN
TEATRO DEL CRIMEN, EL • 1956 • Cortes Fernando • MXC
TEATRO POPULAR • 1975 • de Macedo Antonio • PRT
TEATRO REPELLENTE • 1979 • Solaro Bruno • ITL
TEBESSA, ANNEE ZERO • 1963 • Rachedi Ahmed • SHT • ALG
TEBUKURO O NUGASO ONNA • 1946 • Mori Kazuo • JPN • WOMAN TAKES OFF HER GLOVES, A
TEBUKURO O NUGASU OTOKO • 1946 • Mori Kazuo • JPN • MAN TAKING OFF HIS GLOVES, THE
TEBYE FRONT • 1943 • Vertov Dziga, Svilova Elizaveta • USS • TO THE KAZAKHSTAN FRONT ○ KAZAKHSTAN FRONTU ○ KAZAKHSTAN FRONT, THE ○ ON TO THE FRONT! ○ TO THE FRONT
TECH NEKOLIK DNU.. see A QUELQUES JOURS PRES • 1968
TECHE DE VIDRIO • 1982 • Giral Sergio • CUB • GLASS CEILING
TECHET VOLGA • 1964 • Segel Yakov • USS • VOLGA IS FLOWING, THE
TECHNICAL MOVIE • 1969 • Newman Ira J. • USA
TECHNIK -3 STUNDEN IN JAZZ • 1961 • Hermann Hans H. • SHT • FRG
TECHNIK DER KORPERLICHEN LIEBE • 1968 • Krausser Dietrich • FRG • TECHNIQUE OF PHYSICAL LOVE, THE (UKN)
TECHNIQUE AND RITE see TECNICA E IL RITO, LA • 1971
TECHNIQUE AND THE RITE, THE see TECNICA E IL RITO, LA • 1971
TECHNIQUE DE L'ALIMINIUM • 1949 • Ichac Marcel • DCS • FRN
TECHNIQUE D'UN MEURTRE (FRN) see TECNICA DI UN OMICIDIO • 1966
TECHNIQUE IN A PRIVATE ROOM see KOSHITSU NO TECHNIQUE • 1967
TECHNIQUE OF A FAINT see SHISSHUN NO TECHNIQUE • 1968
TECHNIQUE OF PHYSICAL LOVE, THE (UKN) see TECHNIK DER KORPERLICHEN LIEBE • 1968
TECHNIQUES DU DESSIN • Calderon Philippe • DCS • FRN
TECHNIQUES MINIERES: LE TECHNICIEN EN ARPENTAGE MINIER • 1970 • Lamothe Arthur • DCS • CND
TECHNIQUES OF LOVE • 1974 • Weeran John • FRG
TECHNIQUES OF LOVE, THE • 1970 • First Amendment Inc • USA
TECHNO-CRAZY • 1933 • Lamont Charles • SHT • USA
TECHNOCRACKED • 1933 • Iwerks Ub (P) • ANS • USA
TECHNOLOGICAL THREAT • 1988 • Knoyer Bill • ANM • USA
TECHNORACKET • 1933 • Mintz Charles (P) • ANS • USA
TECHO DE CRISTAL, EL • 1970 • de la Iglesia Eloy • SPN
TECHO DE LA BALLENA, EL see TOIT DE LA BALEINE, LE • 1981
TECI, TECI, KUZA MOJ • 1977 • Kavcic Jane • YGS • HANG ON, DOGGY
TECKMAN MYSTERY, THE • 1954 • Toye Wendy • UKN
TECNICA DI UN AMORE • 1973 • Rondi Brunello • ITL
TECNICA DI UN OMICIDIO • 1966 • Prosperi Franco • ITL, FRN • TECHNIQUE D'UN MEURTRE (FRN) ○ HIRED KILLER, THE (USA) ○ NO TEARS FOR A KILLER
TECNICA DI UNA SPIA (ITL) see OPERAZIONE GOLDSEVEN • 1966
TECNICA E IL RITO, LA • 1971 • Jancso Miklos • MTV • ITL • GIOVANE ATTILA, IL ○ TECHNIQUE AND RITE ○ TECHNIQUE AND THE RITE, THE
TECNICA PARA UN SABOTAGE (SPN) see TECNICA PER UN MASSACRO • 1967
TECNICA PER UN MASSACRO • 1967 • Montero Roberto Bianchi • ITL, SPN • TECNICA PARA UN SABOTAGE (SPN)
TECNICAS DE DUELO • 1988 • Cabrera Sergio • CLM, CUB • MATTER OF HONOUR, A (UKN) ○ DETAILS OF A DUEL
TECNOLOGICOS • 1971 • Fleitas Miguel • DOC • CUB
TECUMSEH • 1972 • Kratzert Hans • GDR
TED • 1967 • Coward Roger • UKN
TED FIO RITO AND HIS ORCHESTRA • 1949 • Cowan Will • SHT • USA
TED HEATH AND HIS MUSIC • 1961 • Henryson Robert • SHT • UKN
TED KENNEDY JR. STORY, THE • 1986 • Mann Delbert • TVM • USA
TED WEEMS AND HIS ORCHESTRA • 1949 • Cowan Will • SHT • USA
TEDDY • 1967 • Kohanyi Julius • SHT • CND
TEDDY • 1969 • Kinnet A. • BLG
TEDDY see PIT, THE • 1981
TEDDY AT THE THROTTLE • 1917 • Badger Clarence • SHT • USA
TEDDY BAR • 1983 • Lyssy Rolf • SWT
TEDDY-BEAR • 1964 • Hitruck Fedor • ANM • USS
TEDDY BEAR see BAMSE • 1969
TEDDY BEAR IN THE MORNING see PORANEK MISIA • 1971
TEDDY BEARS, THE • 1907 • Porter Edwin S. • USA
TEDDY BERGMAN'S BAR-B-Q • 1937 • Schwarzwald Milton • SHT • USA
TEDDY BERGMAN'S INTERNATIONAL BROADCAST • 1936 • Schwarzwald Milton • SHT • USA
TEDDY BOYS see PATOTA, LA • 1961
TEDDY BOYS DELLA CANZONE, I • 1960 • Paolella Domenico • ITL
TEDDY BROWN, XYLOPHONIST • 1929 • Bsfp • SHT • UKN
TEDDY BRUMM • 1958 • Ratz Gunter • ANM • CZC
TEDDY BUCKNER AND HIS DIXIELAND ALL STARS • 1962 • Binder Steve • SHT • USA
TEDDY BY KOURIL • 1919 • Machaty Gustav, Kolar J. S. • CZC • TEDDY'D LIKE A SMOKE ○ TEDDY WANTS TO SMOKE
TEDDY EDWARDS SEXTET • 1962 • Binder Steve • SHT • USA
TEDDY IN JUNGLELAND • 1909 • Blackton J. Stuart • SHT • USA
TEDDY LAUGHS LAST • 1921 • Elmore Milton • UKN
TEDDY RUXPIN: THE ADVENTURES OF TEDDY RUXPIN • 1985 • ANM • USA • ADVENTURES OF TEDDY RUXPIN, THE
TEDDY, THE ACTOR'S SINGING DOG • 1915 • Kineto • UKN
TEDDY, THE ROUGH RIDER • 1940 • Enright Ray • DCS • USA
TEDDY WANTS TO SMOKE see TEDDY BY KOURIL • 1919
TEDDY'D LIKE A SMOKE see TEDDY BY KOURIL • 1919
TEDDYS FRUHLINGSFAHRT • 1915 • Halm Alfred • FRG
TEDDYS GEBURTSTAGSGESCHENK • 1915 • Halm Alfred • FRG
TEDEUM • 1972 • Castellari Enzo G. • ITL, SPN • CON MEN, THE (UKN) ○ STING OF THE WEST, THE
TEE BIRDS, THE • 1959 • Smith Paul J. • ANS • USA
TEE DER DREI ALTEN DAMEN, DER • 1989 • Schmid Daniel • SWT, FRG, FRN • TEA WITH THREE OLD LADIES
TEE FOR TWO • 1925 • Cline Eddie • SHT • USA
TEE FOR TWO • 1945 • Hanna William, Barbera Joseph • ANS • USA
TEEENAGE FRANKENSTEIN (UKN) see I WAS A TEENAGE FRANKENSTEIN • 1957
TEEHAUS ZU DEN ZEHN LOTOSBLUMEN, DAS • 1919 • Richter Ellen • FRG
TEEN ADHAYA • 1968 • Chakravarty Mangal • IND • THREE CHAPTERS
TEEN AGE • 1944 • L'Estrange Dick • USA
TEEN-AGE CRIME WAVE • 1955 • Sears Fred F. • USA
TEEN AGE TRAMP (USA) see THAT KIND OF GIRL • 1963
TEEN-AGERS FROM OUTER SPACE • 1959 • Graeff Tom • USA • GARGON TERROR, THE (UKN) ○ INVASION OF THE GARGON
TEEN BAHURANIYAN • 1968 • Nasan S. S. • IND • THREE DAUGHTERS-IN-LAW
TEEN DEVIYAN • 1965 • Burman S. D. (M) • IND
TEEN KANYA • 1961 • Ray Satyajit • IND • TWO DAUGHTERS ○ THREE DAUGHTERS ○ THREE WOMEN
TEEN MOTHER: A STORY OF COPING • 1983 • Manatis Janine • CND
TEEN VAMP • 1989 • McCullough Jim • USA
TEEN WITCH • 1989 • Walker Dorian • USA
TEEN WOLF • 1985 • Daniel Rod • USA
TEEN WOLF TOO • 1987 • Leitch Christopher • USA
TEENAGE AWARDS INTERNATIONAL see T.A.M.I. SHOW, THE • 1964
TEENAGE BABYLON • 1989 • Wood Graeme • SHT • ASL
TEENAGE BAD GIRL (USA) see MY TEENAGE DAUGHTER • 1956
TEENAGE CAVEMAN • 1958 • Corman Roger • USA • OUT OF THE DARKNESS (UKN) ○ I WAS A TEENAGE CAVEMAN ○ PREHISTORIC WORLD
TEENAGE CHEERLEADER • 1974 • D'Antoni Richard • USA
TEENAGE COMMAND PERFORMANCE see T.A.M.I. SHOW, THE • 1964
TEENAGE CRUISERS • 1979 • Margulies Martin, Denucci Tom • USA
TEENAGE DELINQUENTS (UKN) see NO TIME TO BE YOUNG • 1957
TEENAGE DOLL • 1957 • Corman Roger • USA • YOUNG REBELS, THE
TEENAGE FANTASIES • 1971 • USA
TEENAGE FRANKENSTEIN, THE • 1959 • Glut Don • SHT • USA
TEENAGE FRANKENSTEIN MEETS THE TEENAGE WEREWOLF, THE • 1959 • Glut Don • SHT • USA
TEENAGE GANG DEBS • 1966 • Johnsen S. N. • USA
TEENAGE HITCH-HIKERS • 1975 • Sedley Gerri • USA
TEENAGE INNOCENCE • Warfield Chris • USA • LITTLE MISS INNOCENCE ○ TEENAGE INNOCENTS ○ INNOCENT SEX ○ LITTLE MISS INNOCENT
TEENAGE INNOCENTS see TEENAGE INNOCENCE
TEENAGE JEKYLL AND HYDE • 1963 • Delta S. F. Group • SHT • UKN
TEENAGE LOVERS (UKN) see TOO SOON TO LOVE • 1960
TEENAGE MARRIAGE • 1968 • Lynch Paul • CND
TEENAGE MILLIONAIRE • 1961 • Doheny Lawrence • USA
TEENAGE MONSTER see METEOR MONSTER • 1958
TEENAGE MOTHER • 1968 • Gross Jerry • USA

TEENAGE MUSIC INTERNATIONAL see **T.A.M.I. SHOW, THE** • 1964
TEENAGE MUTANT NINJA TURTLES • 1989 • Barron Steve • USA
TEENAGE NURSES • 1976 • Tribe Oscar • USA
TEENAGE PYSCHO MEETS BLOODY MARY see **INCREDIBLY STRANGE CREATURES WHO STOPPED LIVING AND BECAME CRAZY MIXED-UP ZOMBIES, THE** • 1964
TEENAGE REBEL • 1956 • Goulding Edmund • USA
TEENAGE REBELLION see **MONDO TEENO** • 1967
TEENAGE SEX MAIDS • 1978 • USA
TEENAGE SLUMBER PARTY see **SLUMBER PARTY '57** • 1976
TEENAGE STRANGLER • 1967 • Posner Bill • USA
TEENAGE TEASERS • 1981 • Matalon Eddy • USA
TEENAGE TRAMP see **THAT KIND OF GIRL** • 1963
TEENAGE WASTELAND see **SLEEPAWAY CAMP III** • 1989
TEENAGE WEREWOLF, THE • 1959 • Glut Don • SHT • USA
TEENAGE WOLF PACK (USA) see **HALBSTARKEN, DIE** • 1956
TEENAGE ZOMBIES • 1957 • Warren Jerry • USA
TEENAGER • 1974 • Sindell Gerald Seth • USA
TEENAGER see **SMARKULA** • 1963
TEENAGER, THE see **SESTNACTILETA** • 1918
TEENAGER-MELODIE see **WENN DIE CONNY MIT DEM PETER..** • 1958
TEENAGERS see **ALMURAHIKAT** • 1961
TEENAGERS, LES • 1960 • Din Ahmad Dia Ad- • EGY
TEENAGERS, LES • 1968 • Roustang Pierre • DOC • FRN • TEENAGERS, THE
TEENAGERS, THE see **TEENAGERS, LES** • 1968
TEENAGERS IN SPACE see **OTROKI VO VSELENNOI** • 1975
TEENAGER'S SEX MANUAL see **JUDAI NO SEITEN** • 1953
TEENAGERS' STEPMOTHER • 1975 • USA
TEENIE SWAPPERS, THE • 1969 • *Distripix Inc* • USA
TEENIE TULIP • 1970 • Damiano Gerard • USA • DR. LOVE
TEENY WEENY MEANY • 1966 • Marcus Sid • ANS • USA
TEEPEE FOR TWO • 1963 • Marcus Sid • ANS • USA
TEERTH YATRA • 1958 • Ardash • IND • HOLY PILGRIMAGE
TEESRI KASAM • 1966 • *Kapoor Raj* • IND
TEESRI MANZIL • 1966 • IND
TEETH • 1924 • Blystone John G. • USA
TEETH ARE TO KEEP • 1949 • MacKay Jim, Munro Grant • ANS • CND
TEETH OF THE TIGER, THE • 1919 • Withey Chet • USA
TEGLAFAL MOGOTT • 1980 • Makk Karoly • HNG • BEHIND THE BRICK WALL
TEGNAP • 1959 • Keleti Marton • HNG • YESTERDAY
TEGNAPELOTT • 1981 • Bacso Peter • HNG • DAY BEFORE YESTERDAY, THE
TEHERAN • 1947 • Freshman William, Gentilomo Giacomo • UKN, ITL • PLOT TO KILL ROOSEVELT, THE (USA) ○ APPOINTMENT IN PERSIA ○ CONSPIRACY IN TEHERAN
TEHERAN '43 • 1979 • Alov Alexander, Naumov Vladimir • USS, FRN • NID D'ESPIONS, LE ○ ELIMINATOR, THE
TEHLIKELI ADAM • 1965 • Kazankaya Hasan • TRK
TEHTAAN VARJOSSA • 1969 • Mollberg Rauni • MTV • FNL • IN THE SHADOW OF THE FACTORY
TEHUANTEPEC • 1953 • Contreras Torres Miguel • MXC
TEILHABER, DER • 1918 • Speyer Jaap • FRG
TEILNEHMER ANTWORTET NICHT • 1932 • Sorkin Marc, Katscher Rudolf • FRG
TEIVA • 1963 • Maziere Francis • SHT
TEJANO, EL (SPN) see **TEXICAN, THE** • 1966
TEJEDOR DE MILAGROS, EL • 1961 • del Villar Francisco • MXC • BASKET-MAKER AND THE MIRACLE, THE ○ WEAVER OF MIRACLES, THE ○ MIRACLE WEAVER, THE
TEJO MUYO • 1969 • Tanaka Tokuzo • JPN • HANDCUFFS
TEK KURSUN • 1968 • Tuna Feyzi • TRK • LAST BULLET, THE
TEKA DIPKURYERA see **SUMKA DIPKURIERA** • 1927
TEKETORIA • 1977 • Maar Gyula • HNG • FLARE AND FLICKER
TEKICHU ODAN SANBYAKU RI • 1957 • Mori Issei • JPN • THREE HUNDRED MILES THROUGH ENEMY LINES
TEKKA BUGYO • 1954 • Kinugasa Teinosuke • JPN
TEKKA NO HANAMICHI • 1968 • Matsuo Akinori • JPN • SWORD GAMBLERS
TEKKABA NO KAZE • 1960 • Ushihara Yoichi • JPN • CARDS WILL TELL
TEKKABA YABURI • 1964 • Saito Buichi • JPN • GAMBLER'S BLOOD
TEKKI KUSHU • 1943 • Yoshimura Kozaburo • JPN • ATTACK OF THE ENEMY PLANES, AN ○ ENEMY AIR ATTACK
TEKNO LOVE • 1988 • Toftum Kim • DNM
TEL AVIV - BERLIN • 1987 • Trope Zippi • ISR
TEL AVIV - LOS ANGELES • 1988 • *Topaz Dudu* • ISR
TEL AVIV TAXI • 1956 • Frisch Larry • ISR
TEL EST PRIS QUI CROYAIT PRENDRE • 1901 • Blache Alice • FRN
TEL PERE, TEL FLIC • 1969 • Korber Serge • FRN
TELA DE ARANA • 1963 • Monter Jose Luis • SPN
TELAGA ANGKOR • 1986 • INN
TELARANA, LA • 1954 • Land Kurt • ARG
TELE see **SENGOKU JIEITAI** • 1979
TELEBOX • 1963 • Hickox Douglas • SHS • UKN
TELECOUTURE SANS FIL, LA • 1910 • Cohl Emile • ANS • FRN
TELEFILM • 1928 • Fleischer Dave • ANS • USA
TELEFON • 1962 • Mimica Vatroslav • SHT • YGS • TELEPHONE, THE
TELEFON • 1976 • Grgic Zlatko • ANS • YGS • TELEPHONE, THE
TELEFON • 1977 • Siegel Don • USA
TELEFONDAMEN • 1916 • Lauritzen Lau • DNM
TELEFONI BIANCHI • 1976 • Risi Dino • ITL • CAREER OF A CHAMBERMAID, THE (USA) ○ WHITE TELEPHONES
TELEFONISTA, LA • 1932 • Malasomma Nunzio • ITL
TELEFONKATZCHEN, DAS • 1917 • Karfiol William • FRG
TELEFOOTLERS • 1941 • Carstairs John Paddy • UKN
TELEFTAIO STICHIME • 1989 • Zirinis Costas • GRC • LAST WAGER, THE ○ LAST BET, THE
TELEFTEO PSEMMA, TO • 1957 • Cacoyannis Michael • GRC • MATTER OF DIGNITY, A ○ FINAL LIE, THE
TELEGIAN, THE see **DENSO NINGEN** • 1960
TELEGRAM, THE see **TELEGRAMMA** • 1972
TELEGRAM FROM NEW YORK, A see **NEW YORK EXPRESZ KABEL** • 1921
TELEGRAMA, O • 1954 • Mendes Joao • SHT • PRT
TELEGRAME • 1959 • Naghi Gheorghe, Miheles Aurel • RMN
TELEGRAMMA • 1972 • Bykov Rolan • USS • TELEGRAM, THE
TELEGRAPH OPERATOR, THE • 1913 • *Tennant Barbara* • USA
TELEGRAPH TRAIL, THE • 1933 • Wright Tenny • USA
TELEGRAPHER'S PERIL, THE • 1915 • Terwilliger George W. • USA
TELEGRAPHIC TANGLE, A • 1916 • Drew Sidney • SHT • USA
TELEMACHUS, FRIEND • 1920 • Smith David • SHT • USA
TELEPATHIC WARNING, A • 1908 • Blackton J. Stuart • SHT • USA
TELEPHONE, THE • 1910 • *Delaney Leo* • USA
TELEPHONE, THE • 1957 • Sibianu Gheorghe • ANM • RMN
TELEPHONE, THE • 1988 • Torn Rip • USA
TELEPHONE, THE see **TELEFON** • 1962
TELEPHONE, THE see **TELEFON** • 1976
TELEPHONE AS AN INSTRUMENT OF FEAR, THE • Sturges Howard • SHT • USA
TELEPHONE BELLE, THE • 1917 • *Binns George H.* • USA
TELEPHONE BLUES • 1935 • Schwarzwald Milton • SHT • USA
TELEPHONE BOOK, THE • 1971 • Lyon Nelson • USA
TELEPHONE CALL, THE • 1909 • *Phoenix* • USA
TELEPHONE CALL, THE • 1910 • Fitzhamon Lewin? • UKN
TELEPHONE CALLS, THE • 1985 • Honarmand Mohammad-Reza • IRN
TELEPHONE ENGAGEMENT, A • 1914 • Smalley Phillips • USA
TELEPHONE ENTANGLEMENT, A • 1916 • *Judy* • USA
TELEPHONE GIRL, THE • 1912 • *Storey Edith* • USA
TELEPHONE GIRL, THE • 1924 • St. Clair Malcolm, Pembroke Percy • SRL • USA
TELEPHONE GIRL, THE • 1927 • Brenon Herbert • USA
TELEPHONE GIRL AND THE LADY, THE • 1913 • Griffith D. W. • USA
TELEPHONE OPERATOR • 1938 • Pembroke Scott • USA
TELEPHONE OPERATOR, THE • 1914 • *Lux* • USA
TELEPHONE PUBLIC • 1979 • Perier Jean-Marie • DOC • FRN
TELEPHONE RING IN THE EVENING, A see **DENWA WA YUGATA NI NARU** • 1959
TELEPHONE RINGS IN THE EVENING, THE see **DENWA WA YUGATA NI NARU** • 1959
TELEPHONE ROSE, LE • 1975 • Molinaro Edouard • FRN • PINK TELEPHONE, THE (UKN)
TELEPHONE ROUGE, LE see **ROUBLE A DEUX FACES, LE** • 1969
TELEPHONE SHIP • 1933 • Legg Stuart • DOC • UKN
TELEPHONE SONNE TOUJOURS DEUX FOIS, LE • 1984 • Vergne Jean-Pierre • FRN
TELEPHONE STRATEGY, A • 1914 • *Princess* • USA
TELEPHONE TANGLE, A • 1912 • Coleby A. E. • UKN
TELEPHONE WORKERS • 1933 • Legg Stuart • DOC • UKN
TELEPHONES AND TROUBLES • 1918 • Howe J. A. • SHT • USA
TELEPHONIC DOLLS • Linder Carl • SHT • USA
TELESPHORE, LEGARE, GARDE-PECHE • 1959 • Fournier Claude • DCS • CND
TELETESTS • 1980 • Ruiz Raul • SHT • FRN
TELETHON • 1977 • Rich David Lowell • USA
TELEURGANG VAN DE WATERHOEK, DE see **MIRA** • 1971
TELEVISIE • 1931 • Buchowetzki Dimitri, Salvatori Jack • NTH • SANSATIE DER TOEKOMST, DE
TELEVISION • 1942 • Delacroix Rene • DCS • FRN
TELEVISION see **MAGIE MODERNE** • 1931
TELEVISION CLOSE CIRCUIT • 1989 • Yannopoulos Nikos • MTV • GRC
TELEVISION FAN, THE see **ZAVADA NENI NA VASEMM PRIJIMACI** • 1960
TELEVISION FOLLIES, THE • 1933 • Benstead Geoffrey • UKN
TELEVISION HIGHLIGHTS • 1936 • Schwarzwald Milton • SHT • USA
TELEVISION MANIAC, THE see **ONDOMANE, L'** • 1961
TELEVISION PARTS HOME COMPANION • 1984 • Dear William • USA
TELEVISION SPY • 1939 • Dmytryk Edward • USA • WORLD ON PARADE, THE
TELEVISION TALENT • 1937 • Edmunds Robert • UKN
TELEVISION TURMOIL • 1947 • Yates Hal • SHT • USA
TELEVISIONE • 1931 • de Rochefort Charles • ITL
TELEVISIONUDOS, LOS • 1955 • Delgado Miguel M. • MXC
TELEVIZIUNE • 1931 • D'Esco Phil, Salvatori Jack • RMN
TELHETETLEN MEHECSKE • 1958 • Macskassy Gyula • ANS • HNG • INSATIABLE BEE, THE ○ GREEDY BEE, THE
TELI SIROKKO see **SIROKKO** • 1969
TELJES GOZZEL • 1951 • Mariassy Felix • HNG • FULL STEAM AHEAD
TELJES NAP, EGY • 1988 • Grunwalsky Ferenc • HNG • FULL DAY, A
TELL 'EM NOTHING • 1926 • McCarey Leo • SHT • USA
TELL ENGLAND • 1931 • Asquith Anthony, Barkas Geoffrey • UKN • BATTLE OF GALLIPOLI (USA)
TELL IT LIKE IT IS see **CA IRA, IL FIUME DELLA RIVOLTA** • 1965
TELL IT TO A POLICEMAN • 1925 • Roach Hal • SHT • USA
TELL IT TO A STAR • 1945 • McDonald Frank • USA
TELL IT TO SWEENEY • 1927 • La Cava Gregory • USA
TELL IT TO THE GIRLS see **SOYLEYIN GENC KIZLARA** • 1967
TELL IT TO THE JUDGE • 1928 • Guiol Fred, Yates Hal • SHT • USA
TELL IT TO THE JUDGE • 1949 • Foster Norman • USA
TELL IT TO THE MARINES • 1918 • Gillstrom Arvid E. • USA
TELL IT TO THE MARINES • 1926 • Hill George W. • USA
TELL ME A BADTIME STORY • 1963 • Kneitel Seymour • ANS • USA
TELL ME A RIDDLE • 1980 • Grant Lee • USA
TELL ME ABOUT YOURSELF see **RASSKAZHI MNYE O SEBYE** • 1972
TELL ME IF IT HURTS • 1934 • Massingham Richard • UKN
TELL ME IN THE SUNLIGHT • 1967 • Cochran Steve • USA
TELL ME LIES • 1968 • Brook Peter • UKN
TELL ME MY NAME • 1977 • Mann Delbert • TVM • USA
TELL ME THAT YOU LOVE ME • 1984 • Trope Zippi • CND, ISR
TELL ME THAT YOU LOVE ME, JUNIE MOON • 1970 • Preminger Otto • USA
TELL ME TONIGHT • 1932 • Litvak Anatole • UKN • BE MINE TONIGHT (USA)
TELL ME WHY • 1919 • Barsky • SHT • USS
TELL MORGAN'S GIRL • 1917 • Chaudet Louis W. • SHT • USA
TELL NO TALES • 1939 • Fenton Leslie • USA
TELL-TALE ARM, THE • 1917 • *Reid Wallace* • USA
TELL-TALE BLOTTER, THE • 1909 • *Essanay* • USA
TELL-TALE CINEMATOGRAPH • 1908 • *W.b. & E.* • USA
TELL-TALE FOOTPRINT, THE • 1914 • *Gaumont* • USA
TELL-TALE GLOBE, THE • 1915 • Birch Cecil • UKN
TELL TALE HAT BAND, THE • 1913 • Ford Francis • USA
TELL-TALE HEART, THE • 1927 • Klein Charles • SHT • USA
TELL-TALE HEART, THE • 1928 • Kelin George • SHT • USA
TELL-TALE HEART, THE • 1934 • Hurst Brian Desmond • UKN • BUCKET OF BLOOD (USA)
TELL-TALE HEART, THE • 1941 • Dassin Jules • SHT • USA
TELL-TALE HEART, THE • 1947 • Zarzycki Jerzy • SHT • PLN
TELL-TALE HEART, THE • 1953 • Parmelee Ted • ANS • USA
TELL-TALE HEART, THE • 1953 • Williams J. B. • UKN
TELL-TALE HEART, THE • 1960 • Morris Ernest • UKN • HIDDEN ROOM OF 1000 HORRORS, THE
TELL-TALE HEART, THE • 1966 • *Gottlieb Theodore* • SHT • USA
TELL-TALE HEART, THE • Carver Steve • SHT • USA
TELL-TALE KINEMATOGRAPH, THE • 1908 • Fitzhamon Lewin • UKN
TELL-TALE MESSAGE, THE • 1912 • *Holmes Stuart* • USA
TELL-TALE PARASOL, THE • 1911 • *Powers* • USA
TELL TALE PERFUME, THE • 1910 • *Powers* • USA
TELL-TALE PHOTOGRAPH, THE • 1914 • *Melies* • USA
TELL-TALE REFLECTIONS • 1909 • *Gaumont* • FRN
TELL-TALE SCAR, THE • 1914 • *Foster Morris* • USA
TELL TALE SHIRT, A • 1918 • *Pearce Peggy* • SHT • USA
TELL-TALE STAIN, THE • 1916 • *Puritan* • USA
TELL-TALE STAINS • 1914 • *Nilsson Anna Q.* • USA
TELL-TALE STAR, THE • 1914 • *Lubin* • USA
TELL-TALE TAPS, THE • 1945 • Barralet Paul • UKN
TELL-TALE TELEPHONE, THE • 1906 • Green Tom? • UKN
TELL TALE TRACKS • 1919 • *Lowell John* • SHT • USA
TELL-TALE UMBRELLA, THE • 1912 • Haldane Bert? • UKN
TELL TALE WIRE, THE • 1919 • Eason B. Reeves • SHT • USA
TELL TALES • 1930 • Jeffrey R. E. • UKN
TELL THAT TO THE MARINES • 1918 • Harrison Saul • SHT • USA
TELL THEM NOT TO KILL ME see **DILES QUE NO ME MATEN** • 1986
TELL THEM WILLIE BOY IS HERE • 1969 • Polonsky Abraham • USA • WILLIE BOY
TELL US, OUIJA! • 1920 • SHT • USA
TELL YOUR CHILDREN • 1922 • Crisp Donald • UKN
TELL YOUR CHILDREN see **BURNING QUESTION, THE** • 1940
TELL YOUR WIFE EVERYTHING • 1919 • Christie Al • USA
TELLING THE TALE • 1914 • Aylott Dave • UKN
TELLING THE TALE • 1916 • Birch Cecil • UKN
TELLING THE WORLD • 1928 • Wood Sam • USA • HE LEARNED ABOUT WOMEN
TELLING WHOPPERS • 1926 • Roach Hal • SHT • USA
TELLTALE CLUE, THE • 1917 • Cochrane George • SHT • USA
TELLTALE HAND, THE • 1914 • *Anderson Broncho Billy* • USA
TELLTALE KNIFE, THE • 1911 • *Mix Tom* • USA
TELLTALE KNIFE, THE • 1914 • Mix Tom • USA
TELLTALE LIGHT, THE • 1913 • Sennett Mack • USA
TELLTALE SHELLS, THE • 1912 • Dwan Allan • USA
TELLTALE STEP, THE • 1917 • *Colucci Guido* • USA
TELLTALES see **ZALOBNICI** • 1960
TELO DIANA • 1969 • Richard Jean-Louis • CZC, FRN • CORPS DE DIANE, LE (FRN) ○ BODY OF DIANA, THE
TEMA • 1979 • Panfilov Gleb • USS • THEME
TEMA 13: BATRINETEA • 1984 • Diaconu Cornel • SHT • RMN • OLD AGE
TEMA DI MARCO, IL • 1972 • Antonelli Massimo • ITL • FRAMMENTI D'AMORE ○ MARCO'S THEME ○ MARCO'S THESIS
TEMBELIDES TIS EFORIS KILADAS, I • 1976 • Panayotopoulos Nikos • GRC • LAZY MEN OF THE FERTILE VALLEY, THE ○ IDLERS OF THE FERTILE VALLEY
TEMBI • 1929 • Kearton Cherry • UKN
TEMBO • 1951 • Hill Howard • DOC • USA
TEMERARIO, EL • 1965 • Martinez Arturo • MXC
TEMISCAMING QUEBEC • 1976 • Duckworth Martin • DOC • CND • TEMISCAMINGUE QUEBEC
TEMISCAMINGUE QUEBEC see **TEMISCAMING QUEBEC** • 1976
TEMNIYE SILT -GRIGORII RASPUTIN I YEVO SPODVIZHNIKI • 1917 • Veselonsky S. • USS • DARK POWERS -GRIGORI RASPUTIN AND HIS ASSOCIATES
TEMNO • 1950 • Stekly Karel • CZC • DARKNESS
TEMOIGNAGE DES ENFANTS PALESTINIENS EN TEMPS DE GUERRE see **CHAHADAT AT'FAL FI ZAMAN AL-HARB** • 1972
TEMOIN, LE • 1970 • Walter Anne • FRN, BLG
TEMOIN, LE • 1977 • Mocky Jean-Pierre • FRN, ITL • TESTIMONE, IL (ITL) ○ WITNESS, THE
TEMOIN, THE • 1912 • Feuillade Louis • FRN
TEMOIN DANS LA VILLE, UN • 1959 • Molinaro Edouard • FRN, ITL • APPUNTAMENTO CON IL DELITTO (ITL) ○ WITNESS IN THE CITY
TEMOIN DANS L'OMBRE, LE • 1922 • Herve Jean • FRN
TEMOIN DE MINUIT, LE • 1952 • Kirsanoff Dimitri • FRN
TEMOINS DE JEHOVA • 1962-64 • Fournier Claude • DCS • CND
T'EMPECHES TOUT LE MONDE DE DORMIR! • 1982 • Lauzier Gerard • FRN
TEMPEL DER LIEBE, DER • 1919 • Stein Paul L. • FRG
TEMPELDANSERINDENS ELSKOV • 1914 • Holger-Madsen • DNM • BAYADERE'S REVENGE, THE ○ BAJADERENS HAEVN
TEMPELRAUBER, DER • 1919 • Heiland Heinz Karl • FRG

TEMPER • 1915 • *Walthall Henry B.* • USA
TEMPER AND TEMPERATURE • 1914 • *Lubin* • USA
TEMPER VS. TEMPER • 1914 • Smallwood Ray C. • USA
TEMPERAMENT UNSUITED • 1978 • Cameron Ken • SHT • ASL
TEMPERAMENTAL ALICE • 1913 • *Excelsior* • USA
TEMPERAMENTAL HUSBAND, A • 1912 • Sennett Mack • USA
TEMPERAMENTAL LION • 1940 • Rasinski Connie • ANS • USA
TEMPERAMENTAL WIFE, A • 1919 • Kirkland David • USA
TEMPERAMENTS • 1911 • *Comet* • USA
TEMPERANCE FETE, THE • 1931 • Cutts Graham • UKN
TEMPERANCE LEADER, A • 1910 • *Powers* • USA
TEMPERANCE LECTURE, THE • 1913 • Lepard Ernest • UKN
TEMPERANCE LESSON, A • 1915 • *Aitken Spottiswoode* • USA
TEMPERANCE TOWN, A • 1916 • Heffron Thomas N. • SHT • USA
TEMPERATE ZONE see **MERSEKELT EGOV** • 1970
TEMPERED STEEL • 1918 • Ince Ralph • USA
TEMPERED STEEL see **SOFT BOILED** • 1923
TEMPERED STEEL see **ZOCELENI** • 1950
TEMPERED WITH MERCY • 1910 • Fitzhamon Lewin? • UKN
TEMPEST • 1928 • Taylor Sam • USA
TEMPEST • 1983 • Mazursky Paul • USA
TEMPEST see **BARRAVENTO** • 1961
TEMPEST, THE • 1905 • Urban Charles • UKN
TEMPEST, THE • 1908 • Stow Percy • UKN
TEMPEST, THE • 1911 • *Thanhouser* • USA
TEMPEST, THE • 1912 • *Eclair* • FRN
TEMPEST, THE • 1913 • *Union* • USA
TEMPEST, THE • 1960 • Kalnins Rolands, Krumen V. • USS
TEMPEST, THE • 1969 • *Sherman Roger (P)* • UKN
TEMPEST, THE • 1979 • Gorrie John • TVM • UKN
TEMPEST, THE • 1979 • Jarman Derek • UKN
TEMPEST, THE see **STURME DER LEIDENSCHAFT** • 1931
TEMPEST, THE see **TRIKIMIA** • 1973
TEMPEST, THE (UKN) see **TEMPESTA, LA** • 1958
TEMPEST AND SUNSHINE • 1910 • *Thanhouser* • USA
TEMPEST AND SUNSHINE • 1914 • Crane Frank H. • USA
TEMPEST AND SUNSHINE • 1916 • King Carleton S. • USA
TEMPEST CODY BUCKS THE TRUST • 1919 • Holt George • SHT • USA
TEMPEST CODY FLIRTS WITH DEATH • 1919 • Jaccard Jacques • SHT • USA
TEMPEST CODY GETS HER MAN • 1919 • Holt George • SHT • USA
TEMPEST CODY HITS THE TRAIL • 1919 • Jaccard Jacques • SHT • USA
TEMPEST CODY, KIDNAPPER • 1919 • McRae Henry • SHT • USA
TEMPEST CODY PLAYS DETECTIVE • 1919 • Holt George • SHT • USA
TEMPEST CODY RIDES WILD • 1919 • Jaccard Jacques • SHT • USA • TEMPEST CODY, SHERIFF
TEMPEST CODY, SHERIFF see **TEMPEST CODY RIDES WILD** • 1919
TEMPEST CODY TURNS THE TABLES • 1919 • Holt George • SHT • USA
TEMPEST CODY'S MAN HUNT • 1919 • Jaccard Jacques • SHT • USA
TEMPEST IN A BEDROOM see **TEMPETE DANS UN CHAMBRE A COUCHER, UNE** • 1901
TEMPEST IN MAY see **GEWITTER IM MAI** • 1987
TEMPEST IN THE FLESH (USA) see **RAGE AU CORPS, LA** • 1953
TEMPEST IN TOWN see **REFERENDUM** • 1953
TEMPEST OF LIFE, THE see **TUFANE ZENDEGI**
TEMPEST TOSSED • 1912 • *Melies* • USA
TEMPESTA • 1913 • *Majestic* • USA
TEMPESTA, LA • 1958 • Lattuada Alberto, Antonioni Michelangelo (U/c) • FRN, ITL, YGS • TEMPETE, LA (FRN) ○ TEMPEST, THE (UKN)
TEMPESTA D'ANIME • 1946 • Gentilomo Giacomo • ITL • ANIME IN CATENA
TEMPESTA SU CEYLON • 1963 • Oswald Gerd, Roccardi Giovanni • ITL, FRG, FRN • TODESAUGE VON CEYLON, DAS (FRG) ○ SCARLET EYE, THE (USA) ○ STORM OVER CEYLON
TEMPESTA SUL GOLFO • 1943 • Righelli Gennaro • ITL
TEMPESTAD see **HEROES DE MAR** • 1978
TEMPESTAD EN EL ALMA • 1949 • de Orduna Juan • SPN
TEMPESTADES DA VIDA • 1922 • Lacerda Augusto • PRT
TEMPESTAIRE, LE • 1947 • Epstein Jean • FRN
TEMPESTUOUS LOVE (USA) see **WIE DER STURMWIND** • 1957
TEMPETE • 1939 • Bernard-Deschamps • FRN • TEMPETE SUR PARIS
TEMPETE DANS UN CHAMBRE A COUCHER, UNE • 1901 • Zecca Ferdinand • SHT • FRN • TEMPEST IN A BEDROOM ○ BEWILDERED TRAVELLER, A
TEMPETE, LA (FRN) see **TEMPESTA, LA** • 1958
TEMPETE MERVEILLEUSE, LA • 1949 • de Barros Jose Leitao • BRZ
TEMPETE MERVEILLEUSE, LA see **VENDEVAL MARAVILHOSO** • 1949
TEMPETE SOUS UN CRANE, UNE • 1933 • Bernard Raymond • FRN
TEMPETE SUR LA JETEE DU TREPORT • 1896 • Melies Georges • FRN • PIER AT TREPORT DURING A STORM, THE
TEMPETE SUR L'ASIE • 1938 • Oswald Richard • FRN
TEMPETE SUR LES ALPES • 1945 • Ichac Marcel • DCS • FRN
TEMPETE SUR LES MAUVENTS • 1952 • Dupe Gilbert • FRN, SPN • MAUVENTS, LES
TEMPETE SUR PARIS see **TEMPETE** • 1939
TEMPETES • 1922 • Boudrioz Robert • FRN
TEMPI DURI PER I VAMPIRI • 1959 • Steno • ITL • UNCLE WAS A VAMPIRE (USA) ○ HARD TIMES FOR DRACULA ○ MY UNCLE, THE VAMPIRE ○ HARD TIMES FOR VAMPIRES
TEMPI FELICI see **MAZURKA DI PAPA, LA** • 1938
TEMPI NOSTRI • 1954 • Blasetti Alessandro • ITL, FRN • QUELQUES PAS DANS LA VIE (FRN) ○ ANATOMY OF LOVE, THE (USA) ○ SLICE OF LIFE, A (UKN) ○ OUR TIMES ○ ZIBALDONE N.2
TEMPIO DELL'ELEFANTE BIANCO, IL see **SANDOK, IL MACISTE DELLA GIUNGLA** • 1964
TEMPLE, THE see **AALAYAM** • 1967
TEMPLE BELLS see **SULOCHANA** • 1934
TEMPLE BELLS see **LUANG TA** • 1980
TEMPLE CARPENTER • 1959 • Hani Susumu • DOC • JPN
TEMPLE DE LA MAGIE, LE • 1901 • Melies Georges • FRN • TEMPLE OF THE SUN, THE (USA)
TEMPLE DE L'AMOUR, LE see **MABAD AL-HUBB** • 1961
TEMPLE OF DUSK, THE • 1918 • Young James • USA
TEMPLE OF DUSK, THE see **WITHOUT LIMIT** • 1921
TEMPLE OF MAMMON, THE • 1916 • *Puritan* • SHT • USA
TEMPLE OF MOLOCH, THE • 1914 • West Langdon • USA
TEMPLE OF ROGUES, THE • 1915 • *Apex* • USA
TEMPLE OF SHADOWS, THE see **VESTALE DU GANGE, LA** • 1927
TEMPLE OF TERROR, THE • 1917 • Pearson W. B. • SHT • USA
TEMPLE OF THE DRAGON • 1974 • Chang Ch'Eh • HKG • HEROES TWO
TEMPLE OF THE SUN, THE (USA) see **TEMPLE DE LA MAGIE, LE** • 1901
TEMPLE OF THE SWINGING DOLL • 1960 • Wendkos Paul • TVM • USA
TEMPLE OF THE WHITE ELEPHANTS see **SANDOK, IL MACISTE DELLA GIUNGLA** • 1964
TEMPLE OF THE WILD GEESE see **GAN NO TERA** • 1962
TEMPLE OF VENUS, THE • 1923 • Otto Henry • USA
TEMPLE TOWER • 1930 • Gallaher Donald • USA
TEMPLES DU TEMPS see **TEMPLES OF TIME** • 1972
TEMPLES OF JAPAN • 1913 • Melies Gaston • DOC • USA
TEMPLES OF TIME • 1972 • Canning William • CND • TEMPLES DU TEMPS
TEMPO -AUSTRALIA IN THE SEVENTIES • 1971 • Gow Keith • ASL
TEMPO D'AMARSI • 1957 • Ruffo Elio • ITL
TEMPO D'AMORE (ITL) see **CA N'ARRIVE QU'AUX AUTRES** • 1971
TEMPO DE VIOLENCIA • 1969 • *Carrero Tonia* • BRZ • TIME OF VIOLENCE
TEMPO DEGLI ASSASSINI, IL • 1976 • Andrei Marcello • ITL • SEASON FOR ASSASSINS
TEMPO DEGLI AVVOLTI, IL • 1967 • Cicero Nando • ITL • TIME OF THE VULTURES, THE ○ LAST OF THE BADMEN
TEMPO DELLE BELVE, IL • 1979 • Fontana Bruno • ITL
TEMPO DELL'INIZIO, IL • 1975 • Di Gianni Luigi • ITL
TEMPO DI CHARLESTON CHICAGO 1972 (ITL) see **TIEMPOS DE CHICAGO** • 1968
TEMPO DI CREDERE • 1962 • Racioppi Antonio • ITL
TEMPO DI IMMAGINI • 1970 • Sala Adimaro • ITL
TEMPO DI MASSACRO • 1966 • Fulci Lucio, Vantell Terry • ITL • COLT CANTARONO LA MORTE E FU TEMPO DI MASSACRO, LE ○ BRUTE AND THE BEAST, THE ○ COLT CONCERT ○ TIME OF MASSACRE
TEMPO DI ROMA • 1964 • de La Patelliere Denys • ITL, FRN
TEMPO DI TONNI • 1956 • Sala Vittorio • DOC • ITL
TEMPO DI UCCIDERE • 1990 • Montaldo Giuliano • ITL, FRN • TIME TO KILL
TEMPO DI VILLEGGIATURA • 1956 • Racioppi Antonio • ITL
TEMPO MASSIMO • 1934 • Mattoli Mario • ITL
TEMPO ON TIPTOE • 1938 • Parsons Herbert R. • UKN
TEMPO SI E FERMATO, IL • 1960 • Olmi Ermanno • ITL • TIME STOOD STILL (USA) ○ GRAND BARRAGE, LE ○ TIME HAS STOPPED
TEMPO SUIKO DEN • 1976 • Yamamoto Satsuo • JPN • STORY OF YUGAKU OHARA, THE
TEMPO! TEMPO! • 1929 • Obal Max • FRG
TEMPORADA DE LANGOSTA • 1978 • Gatgens Amando, Mello Victor • DOC • CRC
TEMPORALE ROSY • 1979 • Monicelli Mario • ITL, FRN • ROSY LA BOURRASQUE (FRN) ○ HURRICANE ROSY
TEMPORARILY BROKE (USA) see **PILLANATNYI PEZZAVAR** • 1939
TEMPORARILY YOURS see **YOU'RE TELLING ME** • 1942
TEMPORARY ALIMONY • 1919 • Dillon John Francis • SHT • USA
TEMPORARY DIVORCE • 1986 • Jelic Milan • YGS
TEMPORARY GENTLEMAN, A • 1920 • Durrant Fred W. • UKN
TEMPORARY HUSBAND, A • 1916 • Metcalfe Earl • SHT • USA
TEMPORARY LADY, THE • 1921 • Brunel Adrian • UKN
TEMPORARY MARRIAGE • 1923 • Hillyer Lambert • USA
TEMPORARY PARADISE see **IDEIGLENES PARADICSOM** • 1981
TEMPORARY SHERIFF • 1926 • Hatton Richard • USA
TEMPORARY TRUCE, A • 1912 • Griffith D. W. • USA
TEMPORARY VAGABOND, A • 1920 • Edwards Henry • UKN
TEMPORARY WIDOW, THE • 1930 • Ucicky Gustav • UKN, FRG
TEMPORARY WIVES • 1969 • Shamblin Gene • USA
TEMPORARY WORK see **RAD NA ODREDJENO VREME** • 1981
TEMPS DE FAIRE, LE • 1974 • Dansereau Fernand, Rossignol Yolande • SHT • CND
TEMPS DE LA MANIC, LE • 1989 • Lesaunier Daniel • MTV • CND
TEMPS DE L'AMOUR, LE • 1956 • Lacombe Georges • FRN
TEMPS DE L'AVANT, LE • 1975 • Poirier Anne-Claire • CND • BEFORE THE TIME COMES ○ TIME OF BEFORE, THE
TEMPS DE MOURIR, LE • 1969 • Farwagi Andre • FRN • TWICE UPON A TIME ○ TIME TO DIE, THE
TEMPS DE VIVRE, LE • 1969 • Paul Bernard • FRN
TEMPS DES AMANTS, LE (FRN) see **AMANTI** • 1968
TEMPS DES CERISES, LE • 1937 • Le Chanois Jean-Paul • FRN
TEMPS DES COPAINS, LE • 1962 • Guez Robert • FRN
TEMPS DES DORYPHORES, LE • 1967 • Remy Dominique, de Launay Jacques • CMP • FRN
TEMPS DES ECOLIERS, LE • 1962 • Delvaux Andre • BLG
TEMPS DES EVENEMENTS, LE • 1970 • Moreau Michel • DCS • CND
TEMPS DES LOUPS, LE (FRN) see **TEMPS DES LOUPS -TEMPO DI VIOLENZA, LE** • 1970
TEMPS DES LOUPS -TEMPO DI VIOLENZA, LE • 1970 • Gobbi Sergio • ITL, FRN • TEMPS DES LOUPS, LE (FRN) ○ DILLINGER 70 ○ CARBON COPY ○ HEIST, THE ○ LAST SHOT, THE ○ TIME OF THE WOLVES
TEMPS DES OEUFS DUR, LE • 1957 • Carbonnaux Norbert • FRN
TEMPS DES VACANCES, LE • 1978 • Vital Claude • FRN
TEMPS DU GHETTO, LE • 1961 • Rossif Frederic, Craven Thomas • FRN • WITNESSES, THE (USA)
TEMPS D'UN BALLET, LE • Reichenbach Francois • DOC • FRN
TEMPS D'UN PORTRAIT, LE • 1971 • Goretta Claude • MTV • SWT
TEMPS D'UNE CHASSE, LE • 1972 • Mankiewicz Francis • CND • ONCE UPON A HUNT
TEMPS D'UNE NUIT, LE • 1963 • Bouchet Francis • SHT • FRN
TEMPS D'UNE VENTE, LE • 1974 • Gagne Jacques • SHT • CND
TEMPS MORTS • 1980 • Godard Claude • DOC • FRN
TEMPS MORTS, LES • 1964 • Laloux Rene • ANS • FRN • DEAD TIMES, THE
TEMPS PERDU, LE • 1964 • Brault Michel • SHT • CND • END OF SUMMER, THE
TEMPS REDONNE, LE • 1967 • Fabiani Henri, Levi-Alvares Jean-Louis • DOC • FRN
TEMPTATION • 1911 • *Reliance* • USA
TEMPTATION • 1914 • Calvert Charles • UKN
TEMPTATION • 1916 • De Mille Cecil B. • USA
TEMPTATION • 1923 • Le Saint Edward J. • USA
TEMPTATION • 1930 • Hopper E. Mason • USA • SO LIKE A WOMAN (UKN)
TEMPTATION • 1934 • Neufeld Max • UKN
TEMPTATION • 1936 • Micheaux Oscar • USA
TEMPTATION • 1946 • Pichel Irving • USA • BELLA DONNA
TEMPTATION • 1968 • Benvenuti Lamberto • ITL
TEMPTATION see **ASPHALT** • 1929
TEMPTATION see **YUWAKU** • 1948
TEMPTATION see **POKUSENI** • 1957
TEMPTATION see **YUWAKU** • 1957
TEMPTATION, THE • 1909 • Porter Edwin S. • USA
TEMPTATION AND FORGIVENESS • 1910 • Coleby A. E. • UKN
TEMPTATION AND THE GIRL • 1917 • *Payton Gloria* • SHT • USA
TEMPTATION AND THE MAN • 1916 • Hill Robert F. • USA
TEMPTATION BY NIGHT see **YORU NON HITODE** • 1967
TEMPTATION HARBOUR • 1947 • Comfort Lance • UKN
TEMPTATION HOURS • 1916 • Morgan Sidney • UKN • FRAILTY
TEMPTATION ISLAND (UKN) see **ILE DU BOUT DU MONDE, L'** • 1958
TEMPTATION OF ADAM, THE • 1916 • Green Alfred E. • SHT • USA
TEMPTATION OF BARBIZON, THE see **TENTATION DE BARBIZON, LA** • 1945
TEMPTATION OF CARLTON EARLYE, THE • 1923 • Noy Wilfred • UKN
TEMPTATION OF EDWIN SWAYNE, THE • 1915 • Lloyd Frank • USA
TEMPTATION OF JANE, THE • 1913 • *Gail Jane* • USA
TEMPTATION OF JOHN GRAY, THE • 1909 • *Centaur* • USA
TEMPTATION OF JOSEPH, THE • 1914 • Reed Langford • UKN
TEMPTATION OF MR. PROKOUK, THE see **PAN PROKOUK V POKUSENI** • 1947
TEMPTATION OF MRS. ANTONIE, THE see **POKUSENI PANI ANTONIE** • 1934
TEMPTATION OF PLEASURE see **AKU NO TANOSHISA** • 1954
TEMPTATION OF RODNEY VANE, THE • 1911 • *Joyce Alice* • USA
TEMPTATION OF ST. ANTHONY, THE • 1902 • *Biograph* • USA
TEMPTATION OF ST. ANTHONY, THE • 1905 • Pathe Charles • FRN
TEMPTATION OF ST. ANTHONY, THE see **TENTAZIONE DE S. ANTONIO** • 1911
TEMPTATION OF ST. ANTHONY, THE (USA) see **TENTATION DE SAINT ANTOINE** • 1898
TEMPTATION OF THE FLESH see **NIKUTAI NO YUWAKU** • 1967
TEMPTATION (USA) see **ILE DU BOUT DU MONDE, L'** • 1958
TEMPTATION (USA) see **CHENG-KWAN** • 1968
TEMPTATIONS OF A GREAT CITY see **VED FAENGLETS PORT** • 1910
TEMPTATIONS OF A SHOP GIRL • 1927 • Terriss Tom • USA • HER SISTER
TEMPTATIONS OF SATAN, THE • 1913 • Blache Herbert • USA
TEMPTATIONS OF STOCKHOLM see **STOCKHOLMSFRESTELSER** • 1911
TEMPTATIONS OF TEENAGERS see **JUDAI NO YUWAKU** • 1954
TEMPTATIONS OF THE DEVIL see **ORDOGI KISERTETEK** • 1986
TEMPTATION'S WORKSHOP • 1932 • *Mayfair* • USA • YOUNG BLOOD (UKN)
TEMPTED BUT TRUE • 1912 • *Baggot King* • USA
TEMPTED BY NECESSITY • 1912 • Parker Lem B. • USA
TEMPTER, THE • 1913 • Thornton F. Martin, Callum R. H. • UKN
TEMPTER, THE see **ANTICRISTO, L'** • 1974
TEMPTER, THE (UKN) see **SORRISO DEL GRANDE TENTATORE, IL** • 1974
TEMPTER AND DAN CUPID, THE • 1911 • *Thanhouser* • USA
TEMPTING LUCK see **HUNCH, THE** • 1921
TEMPTING OF MRS CHESTNEY, THE see **GULDETS GIFT** • 1916
TEMPTING THE DEVIL see **ISKUSAVANJE DAVOLA** • 1989
TEMPTRESS, THE • 1911 • *Essanay* • USA
TEMPTRESS, THE • 1911 • *Imp* • USA
TEMPTRESS, THE • 1920 • Hall George Edwardes • UKN
TEMPTRESS, THE • 1926 • Niblo Fred, Stiller Mauritz • USA
TEMPTRESS, THE • 1949 • Mitchell Oswald • UKN
TEMPTRESS, THE • *Croguennec Christine* • FRN

TEMPTRESS, THE see **BYAKUYA NO YOJO** • 1958

TEMPTRESS AND THE MONK, THE (USA) see **BYAKUYA NO YOJO** • 1958

TEMPUS • Ansorge Ernest, Ansorge Giselle • ANS • SWT

TEMPYO NO IRAKA • 1979 • Kumai Kei • JPN • ROOF-TILE OF THE TEMPYO ERA, A ○ SLATES OF THE TENPYO PERIOD ○ TENPYO NO IRAKA

TEN ACRE GOLD BRICK, A • 1913 • Hotaling Arthur D. • USA

TEN AND A HALF WEEKS • 1986 • McCallum Robert • USA • 10½ WEEKS

TEN BILLION DOLLAR VITAGRAPH MYSTERY SERIAL, THE see **FATES AND FLORA FOURFLUSH, THE** • 1914

TEN BLACK WOMEN see **KUROI JUNIN NO ONNA** • 1961

TEN BOB IN WINTER • 1964 • Reckford Lloyd • SHT • UKN

TEN BRIDGES • 1957 • Luke Michael • SHT • UKN

TEN BROTHERS OF SHAOLIN • 1979 • Ting Cheng • HKG

TEN-CARATE HERO, A • 1912 • *Ab* • USA

TEN-CENT ADVENTURE, A • 1915 • Franklin Sidney A., Franklin Chester M. • USA

TEN CENTS A DANCE • 1931 • Barrymore Lionel • USA

TEN CENTS A DANCE • 1945 • Jason Will • USA • DANCING LADIES (UKN)

TEN COMMANDMENTS, THE • 1923 • De Mille Cecil B. • USA

TEN COMMANDMENTS, THE • 1956 • De Mille Cecil B. • USA

TEN COMMANDMENTS, THE • 1988 • Toure Kitia • IVC

TEN DARK WOMEN see **KUROI JUNIN NO ONNA** • 1961

TEN DAYS • 1925 • Worne Duke • USA

TEN DAYS IN DRAGON CITY see **LUNG-CH'ANG SHIH-JIH** • 1969

TEN DAYS IN PARIS • 1939 • Whelan Tim • UKN • MISSING TEN DAYS (USA) ○ SPY IN THE PANTRY

TEN DAY'S LIFE see **TOKAKAN NO JINSEI** • 1941

TEN DAYS THAT SHOOK THE WORLD see **OKTYABR'** • 1928

TEN DAYS THAT SHOOK THE WORLD see **KRASNYE KOLOKOLA** • 1981

TEN DAYS TO DIE see **LETZTE AKT, DER** • 1955

TEN DAYS TO TULARA • 1958 • Sherman George • USA

TEN DAYS WITH THE GUERRILLAS OF FREE MOZAMBIQUE • Cigarini Franco • DOC

TEN DAY'S WONDER (UKN) see **DECADE PRODIGIEUSE, LA** • 1971

TEN DESPERATE MEN see **DIECI GLADIATORI, I** • 1964

TEN DOLLAR RAISE, THE • 1921 • Sloman Edward • USA

TEN DOLLARS OR TEN DAYS • 1920 • *Murray Charles* • SHT • USA

TEN DOLLARS OR TEN DAYS • 1924 • *Sennett Mack (P)* • SHT • USA

TEN FINGERS OF STEEL • 1973 • Kien Lun • HKG • WANG YU -TEN FINGERS OF STEEL

TEN FOR SURVIVAL • 1979 • Halas John • ANS • UKN

TEN FROM YOUR SHOW OF SHOWS • 1973 • Liebman Max • CMP • USA

TEN GIRLS AGO • 1962 • Daniels Harold • CND

TEN GLADIATORS, THE (USA) see **DIECI GLADIATORI, I** • 1964

TEN GOLDEN MEDALS • 1965 • Csoke Jozsef • DOC • HNG

TEN KOLOBRZEG DAYS see **DZIESIEC KOLOBRZESKICH DNI** • 1971

TEN LADIES IN ONE UMBRELLA (USA) see **PARAPLUIE FANTASTIQUE, LE** • 1903

TEN LAKHS see **DUS LAKH** • 1967

TEN LITTLE CYCLISTS, THE • 1953 • Porter Eric • ANS • ASL

TEN LITTLE FARMERS • 1947 • MacKay Jim • ANS • CND

TEN LITTLE INDIANS • 1965 • Pollock George • UKN

TEN LITTLE INDIANS see **AND THEN THERE WERE NONE** • 1974

TEN LITTLE NIGGER BOYS • 1912 • Cooper Arthur • UKN

TEN LITTLE NIGGER BOYS see **DIX PETITS NEGRES**

TEN LITTLE NIGGERS see **AND THEN THERE WERE NONE** • 1974

TEN LITTLE NIGGERS (UKN) see **AND THEN THERE WERE NONE** • 1945

TEN MAN STAR • 1974 • Stoneman John • MTV • UKN

TEN MILLION DOLLAR GRAB, THE (USA) see **SUPERCOLPO DA SETTE MILIARDI** • 1967

TEN MINUTE ALIBI • 1935 • Vorhaus Bernard • UKN

TEN MINUTE EGG, A see **TEN MINUTES EGG, A** • 1924

TEN MINUTES EGG, A • 1924 • McCarey Leo • SHT • USA • TEN MINUTE EGG, A

TEN MINUTES TO KILL • 1933 • Micheaux Oscar • USA

TEN MINUTES TO LIVE • 1932 • Micheaux Oscar • USA

TEN MODERN COMMANDMENTS • 1927 • Arzner Dorothy • USA

TEN MOTHERS see **SEED OF INNOCENCE** • 1980

TEN NIGHTS IN A BAR ROOM • 1903 • *Biograph* • USA

TEN NIGHTS IN A BAR ROOM • 1911 • Boggs Frank • USA

TEN NIGHTS IN A BAR ROOM • 1921 • Apfel Oscar • USA

TEN NIGHTS IN A BAR ROOM • 1931 • O'Connor William A. • USA

TEN NIGHTS IN A BARROOM • 1909 • *Crane Frank* • USA

TEN NIGHTS IN A BARROOM • 1913 • Beggs Lee • USA

TEN NIGHTS IN A BARROOM • 1926 • *Chenault Lawrence* • USA

TEN NIGHTS IN A TEA ROOM • 1919 • Lyons Eddie, Moran Lee • SHT • USA

TEN NIGHTS WITHOUT A BARROOM • 1920 • Cline Eddie • SHT • USA

TEN NO YUGAO • 1948 • Abe Yutaka • JPN • MOONFLOWER OF HEAVEN

TEN NORTH FREDERICK • 1958 • Dunne Philip • USA

TEN O'CLOCK BOAT, THE • 1915 • Mackley Arthur • USA

TEN OF DIAMONDS • 1917 • West Raymond B. • USA

TEN OF DIAMONDS, THE • 1912 • *Rich Vivian* • USA

TEN OF SPADES, THE • 1914 • *Garwood William* • USA

TEN OF SPADES, OR A WESTERN RAFFLE, THE • 1910 • *Bison* • USA

TEN PERCENT WOMAN see **WHAT A WOMAN!** • 1943

TEN PICKNINNIES • 1908 • Porter Edwin S. • USA

TEN PIN TERRORS • 1953 • Rasinski Connie • ANS • USA

TEN SCARS MAKE A MAN • 1924 • Parke William • USA

TEN SECONDS AN HOUR • Bogin Mikhail • SHT • USS

TEN SECONDS TO HELL • 1959 • Aldrich Robert • USA

T'EN SOUVIENS-TU MON AMOUR? see **MARIS DE LEONTINE, LES** • 1947

TEN TALL MEN • 1951 • Goldbeck Willis • USA

TEN THIRTY-TWO IN THE MORNING see **10.32**

TEN THOUSAND AND BROKE • 1931 • Elliot Grace • SHT • USA

TEN THOUSAND BEDROOMS • 1957 • Thorpe Richard • USA

TEN THOUSAND DAYS see **TIZEZER NAP** • 1967

TEN THOUSAND DOLLAR TOE, THE • 1913 • Kirkland Hardee • USA

TEN THOUSAND DOLLARS FOR A MASSACRE see **DIECIMILA DOLLARI PER UN MASSACRO** • 1967

TEN THOUSAND SUNS, THE (UKN) see **TIZEZER NAP** • 1967

TEN TIGERS OF KWANGTUNG • 1981 • HKG

TEN TO CHI O KAKERU OTOKO • 1959 • Masuda Toshio • JPN • SKY IS MINE, THE

TEN TO MIDNIGHT • 1983 • Thompson J. Lee • USA • 10 TO MIDNIGHT

TEN TO SEN • 1958 • Kobayashi Tsuneo • JPN • DEAD END

TEN TON LOVE see **SOUL OF THE BEAST** • 1923

TEN TRZECI • 1958 • Lomnicki Jan • DOC • PLN • THIRD MAN, THE

TEN UNPAID DAYS • 1972 • Vazov Yanoush • BUL

TEN VIOLENT WOMEN • 1982 • Mikels Ted V. • USA

TEN WANTED MEN • 1955 • Humberstone H. Bruce • USA

TEN WHO DARED • 1960 • Beaudine William • USA

TEN WINTERS IN ONE SUMMER • 1969 • Gazhiu Valeri • USS

TEN WOMEN see **ON KADIN** • 1987

TEN WORDS FOR TWENTY-FIVE CENTS • 1911 • *Essanay* • USA

TEN YEAR PLAN, THE • 1945 • Gilbert Lewis* • DCS • UKN

TEN YEARS AFTER see **TIZ EV MULVA** • 1979

TEN YEARS FROM COLOMBO • 1961 • Fraser Donald • DOC • CND

TEN YEARS IN MANITOBA • 1898 • Freer James Simmons • CND

TEN YEARS OF CUBA see **TIZ EVES KUBA** • 1969

TEN YEARS OF EVIL see **AKUDOMA JUNEN** • 1967

TEN YEARS OLD • 1927 • Roach Hal • SHT • USA

TENACIOUS CAT • 1906 • *Pathe* • FRN

TENACIOUS LOVER, THE • 1912 • *Pathe* • USA

TENACIOUS SANTA see **GANBARE SANTA** • 1953

TENACIOUS SOLICITOR, A • 1912 • *Edison* • USA

TENAFLY • 1972 • Colla Richard A. • TVM • USA

TENAGLIE see **TENEBRE** • 1934

TENAMONYA CONFUSION IN THE LAST DAYS OF THE TOKUGAWA REGIME see **BAKUMATSU TENAMONYA OSODO** • 1967

TENAMONYA: GHOST JOURNEY see **TENAMONYA YUREI DOCHU** • 1967

TENAMONYA YUREI DOCHU • 1967 • Matsubayashi Shue • JPN • GHOSTS OF TWO TRAVELERS AT TENAMONYA ○ TENAMONYA: GHOST JOURNEY

TENANT, THE • 1976 • Polanski Roman • USA, FRN • LOCATAIRE, LE (FRN)

TENANT, THE see **SUBLOKATOR** • 1967

TENANTS, THE • 1987 • Mehrjui Dariush • IRN

TENANTS NEXT DOOR, THE see **LOCATAIRES D'A COTE, LES** • 1909

TENANTS OF CASTLES see **KASTELYOK LAKOI** • 1966

TENANTS' RACKET, THE • 1963 • Marcus Sid • ANS • USA

TENCHU see **HITOKIRI** • 1969

TENDA DOS MILAGRES • 1978 • dos Santos Nelson Pereira • BRZ • TENT OF MIRACLES ○ BOUTIQUE DES MIRACLES, LA

TENDA ROSSA, LA (ITL) see **KRASNAYA PALATKA** • 1969

TENDENCIAR • 1967 • Jankovics Marcell • ANS • HNG • TRENDS

TENDER, THE • 1989 • Harmon Robert • USA

TENDER AGE, THE see **LITTLE SISTER, THE** • 1984

TENDER AGE, THE (UKN) see **ADOLPHE OU L'AGE TENDRE** • 1968

TENDER BRANCH, THE • 1972 • Bonniere Rene • SHT • CND

TENDER COMRADE • 1943 • Dmytryk Edward • USA

TENDER CORDS • 1909 • *Urban-Eclipse* • USA

TENDER DRACULA OR CONFESSIONS OF A BLOOD DRINKER (USA) see **TENDRE DRACULA** • 1974

TENDER ENEMY, THE (USA) see **TENDRE ENNEMIE, LA** • 1935

TENDER FEET • 1925 • Mayo Archie • SHT • USA

TENDER FLESH see **WELCOME TO ARROW BEACH** • 1973

TENDER GAME, THE • 1958 • Hubley John, Hubley Faith • ANS • USA

TENDER GRASS see **JENNIE, WIFE/CHILD** • 1965

TENDER-HEARTED CROOK, A • 1913 • O'Sullivan Tony • USA

TENDER HEARTED MIKE • 1912 • *Powers* • USA

TENDER-HEARTED SHERIFF, THE • 1914 • Badger Clarence • USA

TENDER HEARTS • 1909 • Griffith D. W. • USA

TENDER HEARTS see **EDGE OF HELL** • 1956

TENDER HOUR, THE • 1927 • Fitzmaurice George • USA • MARRIAGE OF MARCIA, THE

TENDER HOURS, THE see **TWO WEEKS WITH LOVE** • 1950

TENDER HOURS (UKN) see **DULCES HORAS** • 1981

TENDER IS THE NIGHT • 1962 • King Henry • USA

TENDER IS THE NIGHT • 1985 • Knights Robert • MTV • UKN

TENDER IS THE NIGHT see **TIERNA ES LA NOCHE** • 1990

TENDER LITTLE PUMPKINS see **CALABACITAS TIERNAS** • 1948

TENDER LOVING CARE • 1974 • Edmonds Don • USA • NAUGHTY NURSES

TENDER LUST see **MESU GA OSU KUIKOROSO: KAMAKIRI** • 1967

TENDER MEMORIES • 1918 • *Chapin* • SHT • USA

TENDER MERCIES • 1982 • Beresford Bruce • USA

TENDER MOMENT, THE (USA) see **LECON PARTICULIERE, LA** • 1968

TENDER SCOUNDREL (USA) see **TENDRE VOYOU** • 1966

TENDER SPOTS see **CZULE MIEJSCZ** • 1981

TENDER TALE OF CINDERELLA PENGUIN, THE • 1983 • Perlman Janet • ANS • CND

TENDER TRAP, THE • 1955 • Walters Charles • USA

TENDER WARRIOR • 1970 • Raffill Stewart • USA

TENDER YEARS, THE • 1948 • Schuster Harold • USA

TENDERFEET • 1928 • *Bell Spencer* • USA

TENDERFOOT, THE • 1909 • Boggs Frank • USA

TENDERFOOT, THE • 1910 • *Nestor* • USA

TENDERFOOT, THE • 1917 • Duncan William • USA

TENDERFOOT, THE • 1919 • *Tweede Dan* • SHT • USA

TENDERFOOT, THE • 1932 • Enright Ray • USA

TENDERFOOT, THE • 1966 • Paul Byron • USA

TENDERFOOT BOB'S REGENERATION • 1912 • *Bosworth Hobart* • USA

TENDERFOOT COURAGE • 1927 • Wyler William • SHT • USA

TENDERFOOT DAYS see **KEKEDASHI JIDAI** • 1947

TENDERFOOT FOREMAN, THE • 1912 • *Anderson Broncho Billy* • USA

TENDERFOOT GOES WEST, A • 1937 • O'Neill Maurice • USA

TENDERFOOT HERO, THE • 1913 • *Lubin* • USA

TENDERFOOT MESSENGER, THE • 1910 • *Anderson Broncho Billy* • USA

TENDERFOOT PARSON, THE • 1910 • *Atlas* • USA

TENDERFOOT SHERIFF, THE • 1913 • *Anderson Broncho Billy* • USA

TENDERFOOT'S CLAIM, THE • 1911 • *Kalem* • USA

TENDERFOOT'S GHOST, THE • 1913 • *Frontier* • USA

TENDERFOOT'S LUCK, THE • 1913 • *Roland Ruth* • USA

TENDERFOOT'S MONEY, THE • 1913 • *Walthall Henry B.* • USA

TENDERFOOT'S RETURN, THE • 1913 • *Frontier* • USA

TENDERFOOT'S REVENGE, A • 1912 • *Bison* • USA

TENDERFOOT'S ROUNDUP, THE • 1911 • *American* • USA

TENDERFOOT'S SACRIFICE, THE • 1912 • *Nestor* • USA

TENDERFOOT'S TRIUMPH, THE • 1910 • Powell Frank, Griffith D. W.? • USA

TENDERFOOT'S TRIUMPH, THE • 1915 • Mix Tom • USA

TENDERFOOT'S TROUBLES, THE • 1912 • *Sais Maris* • USA

TENDERHEARTED BOY, THE • 1913 • Griffith D. W. • USA

TENDERHOOKS • 1988 • Callaghan Mary • ASL

TENDERLOIN • 1928 • Curtiz Michael • USA

TENDERLOIN TRAGEDY • 1907 • *Bitzer Billy (Ph)* • USA

TENDERLY • 1968 • Brusati Franco • ITL • GIRL WHO COULDN'T SAY NO, THE (USA) ○ SUO MUODO DI FARE, IL

TENDERNESS see **NIEJNOSTI** • 1968

TENDERNESS see **HELLYYS** • 1972

TENDERNESS see **OMHET** • 1972

TENDERNESS see **BAKSMALLA** • 1973

TENDERNESS AND ANGER see **ZARTLICHKEIT UND ZORN** • 1981

TENDERNESS OF WOLVES, THE see **ZARTLICHKEIT DER WOLFE, DIE** • 1973

TENDERNESS (USA) see **ZARTLICHKEIT** • 1930

TENDRE DRACULA • 1974 • Grunstein Pierre • FRN • TENDER DRACULA OR CONFESSIONS OF A BLOOD DRINKER (USA)

TENDRE ENNEMIE, LA • 1935 • Ophuls Max • FRN • TENDER ENEMY, THE (USA) ○ ENNEMIE, L'

TENDRE ET VIOLENTE ELISABETH • 1960 • Decoin Henri • FRN • PASSIONATE AFFAIR

TENDRE PAPA • Boyer Henri • FRN

TENDRE POULET • 1978 • de Broca Philippe • FRN • DEAR DETECTIVE (USA) ○ DEAR INSPECTOR

TENDRE VOYOU • 1966 • Becker Jean • FRN, ITL • AVVENTURIERO A TAHITI, UN (ITL) ○ TENDER SCOUNDREL (USA)

TENDREMENT VACHE • 1979 • Penard Serge • FRN

TENDRES ADOLESCENTS • Cadinot Jean-Daniel • FRN

TENDRES CHASSEURS see **SWEET HUNTERS** • 1969

TENDRES COUSINES • 1980 • Hamilton David • FRN, FRG • COUSINS IN LOVE

TENDRES DEMOISELLES • Sanders Bob W. • FRN

TENDRES REQUINS • 1967 • Deville Michel • FRN, FRG, ITL • ZARTLICHE HAIE (FRG) ○ AFFECTIONATE SHARKS

TENDRESSE, LA • 1930 • Hugon Andre • FRN

TENDRESSE ORDINAIRE • 1973 • Leduc Jacques • CND • ORDINARY TENDERNESS

TENDRON D'ACHILLE, LE • 1933 • Christian-Jaque • FRN • ACHILLES' HEEL

TENEBRAE • 1982 • Argento Dario • ITL • UNSANE (USA) ○ SOTTO GLI OCCHI DELL'ASSASSINO ○ DARKNESS

TENEBRE • 1934 • Brignone Guido • ITL • CATENA, LA ○ CATENE ○ TENAGLIE

TENEBRES • 1971 • Loubaries Claude • SHT • FRN

TENEMOS 18 ANOS • 1960 • Franco Jesus • SPN • WE ARE 18 YEARS OLD

TENENTE CRAIG MIO MARITO see **TI RITROVERO** • 1949

TENENTE DEI CARABINIERI, IL • 1985 • Ponzi Maurizio • ITL • LIEUTENANT CARIBINIER, THE

TENENTE GIORGIO, IL • 1952 • Matarazzo Raffaello • ITL

TENERIFFE • 1932 • Allegret Yves • FRN

TENG-LUNG CHIEH • 1977 • T'U Chung-Hsun • HKG • LANTERN STREET, THE

TENGAMOS LA GUERRA EN PAZ • 1977 • Martin Eugenio • SPN • LET'S HAVE THE WAR IN PEACE

TENGO DIECISIETE ANOS • 1964 • Forque Jose Maria • SPN

TENGO FE EN TI • 1979 • Alvarez Santiago • DOC • CUB

TENGO QUE ABANDONARTE • 1969 • del Amo Antonio • SPN

TENGOKU NI MUSUBU KOI • 1933 • Gosho Heinosuke • JPN • HEAVEN LINKED WITH LOVE

TENGOKU NO EKI • 1984 • Deme Masanobu • JPN • STATION IN HEAVEN, A

TENGOKU SONOHI-GAERI • 1930 • Uchida Tomu • JPN • RETURN TO HEAVEN

TENGOKU TO JIGOKU • 1963 • Kurosawa Akira • JPN • HIGH AND LOW ○ HEAVEN AND HELL ○ RANSOM, THE

TENI ZABYTYKH PREDKOV see **TINE ZABUTYKH PREDKIV** • 1965

TENICHIBO TO IGANOSUKE • 1926 • Kinugasa Teinosuke • JPN

TENICHIBO TO IGANOSUKE • 1933 • Kinugasa Teinosuke • JPN

TENIS • 1973 • Grgic Zlatko • ANS • YGS • TENNIS

TENIS TAULA 77 • 1975 • Bellmunt Francisco • SHT • SPN

TENKA GOMEN • 1960 • Watanabe Kunio • JPN • COUNTRY IN MY ARMS

TENKA NO FUKU SHOGUN • 1959 • Matsuda Sadatsugu • JPN • SHOGUN TRAVELS INCOGNITO

TENKA NO IGAGOE • 1934 • *Tsuburaya Eiji (Ph)* • JPN

TENKA NO ONI YASHA HIME • 1957 • Mori Masaki • JPN

TENKA O KIRU OTOKO • 1961 • Sasaki Ko • JPN

TENKA O NERU BISHONEN • 1955 • Arai Ryohei • JPN • HANDSOME BOY TRYING TO RULE THE WORLD
TENKA O TORU • 1960 • Ushihara Yoichi • JPN • WHITE-COLLAR DREAMER
TENKA TAIHEI • 1955 • Sugie Toshio • JPN • PEACE OF THE WORLD ○ WORLD IS PEACEFUL, THE
TENKA TAIHEIKI • 1928 • Inagaki Hiroshi • JPN • PEACE OF THE WORLD ○ PEACE ON EARTH
TENKRAT O VANOCICH • 1958 • Kachyna Karel • CZC • THAT CHRISTMAS
TENNESSEE • 1914 • *Mitchell Rhea* • USA
TENNESSEE BUCK see **FURTHER ADVENTURES OF TENNESSEE BUCK** • 1987
TENNESSEE CHAMP • 1953 • Wilcox Fred M. • USA
TENNESSEE JAMBOREE • 1964 • Gannaway Albert C. • USA
TENNESSEE JOHNSON • 1942 • Dieterle William • USA • MAN ON AMERICA'S CONSCIENCE, THE (UKN)
TENNESSEE LOVE STORY, A • 1911 • *Greenwood Winnifred* • USA
TENNESSEE NIGHTS see **TENNESSEE WALTZ** • 1989
TENNESSEE STALLION • 1978 • Hulette Donald • USA
TENNESSEE WALTZ • 1989 • Gessner Nicolas • SWT • TENNESSEE NIGHTS
TENNESSEE WILLIAMS' SOUTH • 1973 • Rasky Harry • CND
TENNESSEE'S PARDNER • 1916 • Melford George • USA
TENNESSEE'S PARTNER • 1955 • Dwan Allan • USA
TENNIS • 1941 • Martin Marcel • SHT • FRN
TENNIS see **TENIS** • 1973
TENNIS CHUMPS • 1949 • Hanna William, Barbera Joseph • ANS • USA
TENNIS CLUB • 1982 • Bozzetto Bruno • ANM • ITL
TENNIS COURT, THE • 1984 • Sasdy Peter?, Frankel Cyril? • TVM • UKN
TENNIS IN RHYTHM • 1949 • *Marble Alice* • SHT • USA
TENNIS RACQUET • 1949 • Kinney Jack • ANS • USA
TENNIS TACTICS • 1937 • Miller David • SHT • USA
TENOR, LE • 1912 • Fescourt Henri • FRN
TENOR, THE • 1915 • Kent Leon D. • USA
TENOR, INC. see **G.m.b.H. TENOR, DER** • 1916
TENORE PER FORZA • 1948 • Freda Riccardo • SHT • ITL
TENPO CHUSHINGURA • 1934 • Inagaki Hiroshi • JPN
TENPO HIKEN ROKU • 1927 • *Tsuburaya Eiji (Ph)* • JPN
TENPYO NO IRAKA see **TEMPYO NO IRAKA** • 1979
TENSAO NO RIO • 1982 • Dahl Gustavo • BRZ • TENSION IN RIO
TENSE ALIGNMENT see **BLACKBIRD DESCENDING** • 1977
TENSE MOMENTS FROM GREAT PLAYS • 1922 • *Parkinson H. B. (P)* • SHS • UKN
TENSE MOMENTS FROM OPERA • 1922 • *Parkinson H. B. (P)* • SHS • UKN
TENSE MOMENTS WITH GREAT AUTHORS • 1922 • *Parkinson H. B. (P)* • SHS • UKN
TENSHI NO KOUKOTSU • 1973 • Wakamatsu Koji • JPN • ANGELIC ORGASM
TENSHI NO YUWAKU • 1968 • Tanaka Yasuyoshi • JPN • ANGEL'S TEMPTATION, AN
TENSION • 1949 • Berry John • USA
TENSION AT TABLE ROCK • 1956 • Warren Charles Marquis • USA
TENSION IN RIO see **TENSAO NO RIO** • 1982
TENSPEED AND BROWN SHOE • 1980 • Swackhamer E. W. • TVM • USA
TENT OF MIRACLES see **TENDA DOS MILAGRES** • 1978
TENT VILLAGE • 1911 • *Lubin* • USA
TENT -WHO OWNS THIS WORLD, THE • 1977 • Du Rees Goran, Olofsson Christina • SWD
TENTACION • 1943 • Soler Fernando • MXC
TENTACION DESNUDA, LA • 1966 • Bo Armando • ARG • WOMAN AND TEMPTATION (USA) ○ NAKED TEMPTATION
TENTACLES see **SHOKKAKU** • 1969
TENTACLES OF THE NORTH • 1926 • Chaudet Louis W. • USA
TENTACLES (USA) see **TENTACOLI** • 1977
TENTACOLI • 1977 • Hellman Oliver • ITL • TENTACLES (USA)
TENTATION, LA • 1929 • de Baroncelli Jacques, Leprince Rene (U/c) • FRN
TENTATION, LA • 1936 • Caron Pierre • FRN
TENTATION DE BARBIZON, LA • 1945 • Stelli Jean • FRN • TEMPTATION OF BARBIZON, THE
TENTATION DE SAINT ANTOINE • 1898 • Melies Georges • SHT • FRN • TEMPTATION OF ST. ANTHONY, THE (USA)
TENTATION D'ISABELLE, LA • 1986 • Doillon Jacques • FRN
TENTATIONS DE MARIANNE, LES • 1972 • Leroi Francis • FRN • I AM SEXY
TENTATIONS (FRN) see **MUNDO PARA MI, UN** • 1959
TENTATIVE D'ASSASSINAT EN CHEMIN DE FER • 1904 • Blache Alice • FRN
TENTATIVE DE FILMS ABSTRAITS • 1930 • Storck Henri • DOC • BLG
TENTATIVO SENTIMENTALE, UN • 1963 • Festa Campanile Pasquale, Franciosa Massimo • ITL, FRN • AMOUR SANS LENDEMAIN (FRN) ○ SENTIMENTAL EXPERIMENT
TENTAZIONE • 1942 • Hinrich Hans, Frosi Aldo • ITL, HNG • FOLLIA DEL GIUDICE PASSMANN, LA
TENTAZIONE DE S. ANTONIO • 1911 • *Ambrosio* • ITL • TEMPTATION OF ST. ANTHONY, THE
TENTAZIONE QUOTIDIANE, LE(ITL) see **DIABLE ET LES DIX COMMANDEMENTS, LE** • 1962
TENTAZIONI PROIBITE • 1964 • Civirani Osvaldo • DOC • ITL
TENTH ANNIVERSARY OF WROCLAW, THE see **W DZIESIECIOLECIE** • 1955
TENTH AVENUE • 1928 • De Mille William C. • USA • HELL'S KITCHEN (UKN)
TENTH AVENUE ANGEL • 1948 • Rowland Roy • USA
TENTH AVENUE KID • 1938 • Vorhaus Bernard • USA
TENTH BROTHER, THE see **DESETI BRAT** • 1983
TENTH CASE, THE • 1917 • Kelson George • USA
TENTH COMMANDMENT, THE • 1914 • Brenon Herbert • USA
TENTH INCARNATION see **DASAVATAR** • 1936
TENTH INCARNATION see **DASH AVTAR** • 1951
TENTH MAN, THE • 1936 • Hurst Brian Desmond • UKN
TENTH MAN, THE • 1988 • Gold Jack • TVM • UKN
TENTH MONTH, THE • 1979 • Tewkesbury Joan • TVM • USA
TENTH OF A SECOND • 1987 • Roodt Darrell • SAF
TENTH STEP, THE see **DESYATY SHAG** • 1967
TENTH STRAW, THE • 1926 • *Paul Peggy* • ASL
TENTH SYMPHONY, THE see **DIXIEME SYMPHONIE, LA** • 1918
TENTH WOMAN, THE • 1924 • Flood James • USA
TENTING TONIGHT ON THE OLD CAMP GROUND • 1943 • Collins Lewis D. • USA
TENTS OF ALLAH, THE • 1923 • Logue Charles A. • USA
TENUE DE SOIREE • 1986 • Blier Bertrand • FRN • EVENING DRESS
TENYA WANYA • 1950 • Shibuya Minoru • JPN • CRAZY UPROAR
TEODORA • 1919 • Carlucci Leopoldo • ITL • THEODORA
TEODORA • 1927 • Maggi Luigi • ITL
TEODORA IMPERATRICE DI BISANZIO • 1909 • Pasquali Ernesto Maria • ITL
TEODORA, L'IMPERATRICE DI BISANZIO • 1954 • Freda Riccardo • ITL, FRN • THEODORE, IMPERATRICE DE BYZANCE (FRN) ○ THEODORA, SLAVE EMPRESS (USA) ○ THEODORA, QUEEN OF BYZANTIUM ○ THEODORE, IMPERATRICE BYZANTINE
TEODORA SANTORO • 1975 • Damiani Amasi • ITL
TEODORO E SOCIO • 1924 • Bonnard Mario • ITL
TEOREMA • 1968 • Pasolini Pier Paolo • ITL • THEOREM (UKN)
TEOREMA DEL SATIRICON, EL • 1973 • Barrero Jose Antonio • SHT • SPN
TEPEPA • 1969 • Petroni Giulio • ITL • VIVA LA REVOLUCION ○ BLOOD AND GUNS
TEPEYAC • 1918 • Gonzalez Carlos • MXC
TEPITO SI! • 1982 • Sluizer George • DOC • NTH
TEPPANYAKI see **T'IEH-PAN-SHAO** • 1984
TEPPICH DES GRAUENS • 1962 • Reinl Harald • FRG, ITL, SPN • TERRORE DI NOTTE, IL (ITL) ○ CARPET OF HORROR, THE (USA)
TEPPICHKNUPFERIN VON BAGDAD, DIE • 1920 • Linke Edmund • FRG
TEPPO DENRAIKI • 1968 • Mori Issei • JPN • SAGA OF TANEGASHIMA
TEQUILA • 1973 • De Micheli I. • ITL
TEQUILA MOCKING BIRD see **ROAD TO ANDALAY** • 1964
TEQUILA SUNRISE • 1988 • Towne Robert • USA
TER • 1971 • Szabo Istvan • DCS • HNG • SQUARE, A
TER WILLE VAN CHRISTENE • 1975 • SAF
TERA NAAM, MERA NAAM • 1987 • Talwar Ramesh • IND • YOUR NAME, MY NAME
TERAPIA AL DESNUDO • 1975 • Lazaga Pedro • SPN
TERBABAS • 1972 • Kadarisman S. • MLY • SINNERS, THE
TERCER BESO, EL • 1942 • Amadori Luis Cesar • ARG
TERCER MUNDO, TERCERA GUERRA MUNDIAL • 1970 • Espinosa Julio Garcia • CUB
TERCERA PALABRA, LA • 1955 • Soler Julian • MXC
TERCERA PUERTA, LA • 1976 • Forque Alvaro • SPN
TERCIO DE QUITES • 1951 • Cortes Fernando • MXC, SPN
TERE GHAR KE SAAMNE • 1963 • *Burman S. D. (M)* • IND
TERE MERE SAPNE • 1971 • *Burman S. D. (M)* • IND
TERELEUR • 1967 • Theberge Andre • SHT • CND
TERESA • 1950 • Zinnemann Fred • USA
TERESA • 1960 • Crevenna Alfredo B. • MXC
TERESA • 1970 • Vergez Gerard • FRN
TERESA • 1988 • Risi Dino • ITL
TERESA BREWER AND THE FIREHOUSE FIVE PLUS TWO • 1951 • Cowan Will • SHT • USA • FIREHOUSE FIVE PLUS TWO, THE
TERESA CONFALONIERI • 1934 • Brignone Guido • ITL
TERESA.. DARLING • 1969 • Stylianou Michel • USA
TERESA DE JESUS • 1961 • de Orduna Juan • SPN
TERESA ETIENNE (ITL) see **THERESE ETIENNE** • 1957
TERESA HENNERT'S ROMANCE see **ROMANS TERESY HENNERT** • 1978
TERESA LA LADRA • 1973 • Di Palma Carlo • ITL • TERESA THE THIEF (UKN)
TERESA RAQUIN • 1915 • Martoglio Nino • ITL
TERESA RAQUIN (ITL) see **THERESE RAQUIN** • 1953
TERESA THE THIEF (UKN) see **TERESA LA LADRA** • 1973
TERESA VENERDI • 1941 • De Sica Vittorio • ITL • DOCTOR BEWARE (USA)
TERI ANKHEN • 1963 • *Burman S. D. (M)* • IND
TERIREM • 1988 • *Lazaridou Olia* • GRC
TERITORYO KO ITO • 1967 • Rizaldy • PHL • THIS IS MY TERRITORY
TERJE VIGEN • 1917 • Sjostrom Victor • SWD • MAN THERE WAS, A
TERM OF TRIAL • 1962 • Glenville Peter • UKN
TERMINA SIEMPRE ASI • 1940 • Susini Enrique T. • IT ALWAYS ENDS THAT WAY (USA)
TERMINAL • 1975 • Breccia Paolo • ITL
TERMINAL CHOICE • 1984 • Larry Sheldon • CND • TRAUMA
TERMINAL ENTRY • 1987 • Kincade John • USA
TERMINAL EXPOSURE • 1987 • Mastorakis Nico • USA • DOUBLE EXPOSURE
TERMINAL FORCE • 1989 • Ray Fred Olen • USA
TERMINAL ISLAND • 1973 • Rothman Stephanie • USA • KNUCKLE-MEN
TERMINAL MAN, THE • 1973 • Hodges Mike • USA
TERMINAL SELF • 1971 • Whitney John Jr. • SHT • USA
TERMINATE WITH EXTREME PREJUDICE see **S.A.S. A SAN SALVADOR** • 1982
TERMINATION • 1966 • Baillie Bruce • SHT • USA
TERMINATOR, THE • 1984 • Cameron James • USA
TERMINI STATION • 1990 • King Allan, Murphy Colleen • CND
TERMINUS • 1960 • Schlesinger John • SHT • UKN
TERMINUS • 1986 • Glenn Pierre-William • FRN, FRG
TERMINUS LOVE see **ENDSTATION LIEBE** • 1957
TERMITES FROM MARS • 1953 • Patterson Don • ANS • USA
TERMITES OF 1938 • 1938 • Lord Del • SHT • USA
TERMS OF ENDEARMENT • 1983 • Brooks James L. • USA
TERNOSECCO • 1987 • Giannini Giancarlo • ITL
TERPSICHORE • 1921 • Del Zopp Rudolf • FRG
TERRA • Munteanu Stefan • ANM • RMN
TERRA ARDENTE • 1960 • Fraga Augusto • SHT • PRT
TERRA BAIXA • 1914 • Elias Francisco • SHT • SPN
TERRA-COTTA WARRIOR, A see **QIN YONG** • 1989
TERRA DA ERMELINDA, A • 1973 • Faria Antonio • SHT • PRT
TERRA DEL MELOFRAMMA • 1947 • Emmer Luciano, Gras Enrico • HNG
TERRA DI FUOCO • 1938 • Ferroni Giorgio, L'Herbier Marcel • ITL
TERRA DI NESSUNO • 1939 • Baffico Mario • ITL • NOBODY'S LAND (USA)
TERRA DI PIRANDELLO • 1951 • Tomei Giuliano • ITL • PIRANDELLO'S COUNTRY
TERRA D'ODIO see **SENTIERO DELL'ODIO, IL** • 1952
TERRA E A VIDA, A • 1960 • Spiguel Miguel • SHT • PRT
TERRA E SEMPRE TERRA • 1951 • Payne Tom • BRZ • LAND IS FOREVER LAND
TERRA EM TRANSE • 1967 • Rocha Glauber • BRZ • EARTH ENTRANCED (USA) ○ EARTH IN REVOLT ○ LAND IN A TRANCE ○ LAND IN ANGUISH
TERRA IN DUE, LA • 1985 • Blank Rosemarie • DOC • NTH
TERRA INCOGNITA • 1959 • Borowczyk Walerian • ANS • FRN
TERRA LADINA • 1949 • Risi Dino • SHT • ITL
TERRA MADRE • 1931 • Blasetti Alessandro • ITL • PASSA LA MORTE
TERRA MAE • 1960 • Fraga Augusto • SHT • PRT
TERRA NOVA • 1963 • Blais Roger • DCS • CND
TERRA PARA ROSE • 1988 • Moraes Tete • BRZ • LAND FOR ROSE
TERRA PORTUGUESA PODE PRODUZIR MAIS, A • 1942 • Coelho Jose Adolfo • PRT
TERRA ROXA • 1986 • Drury David • NRW
TERRA SANTA, TERRA PROMETIDA • 1968 • Ribeiro Antonio Lopes, Spiguel Miguel • SHT • PRT
TERRA SENZA DONNE • 1929 • Gallone Carmine • ITL, FRG • LAND OHNE FRAUEN, DAS (FRG) ○ BRIDE 68
TERRA SENZA TEMPO • 1952 • Prestifilippo Silvestro • ITL
TERRA STRANIERA • 1953 • Corbucci Sergio • ITL
TERRA TREMA, LA • 1950 • Visconti Luchino • ITL • EPISODIO DEL MARE ○ EARTH TREMBLES, THE
TERRACE, THE see **TERRAZZA, LA** • 1979
TERRACE, THE (USA) see **TERRAZA, LA** • 1963
TERRACES • 1977 • Garrett Lila • TVM • USA
TERRAIN VAGUE • 1960 • Carne Marcel • FRN, ITL
TERRAPENE, LA • 1984 • Bouchard Michel • MTV • CND • TERRAPIN, THE
TERRAPIN, THE see **TERRAPENE, LA** • 1984
TERRASSE, LA (FRN) see **TERRAZZA, LA** • 1979
TERRAZA, LA • 1963 • Torre-Nilsson Leopoldo • ARG • TERRACE, THE (USA) ○ ROOF GARDEN, THE
TERRAZZA, LA • 1979 • Scola Ettore • ITL, FRN • TERRASSE, LA (FRN) ○ TERRACE, THE
TERRE, LA • 1921 • Antoine Andre • FRN
TERRE, LA see **ARD, EL** • 1969
TERRE A BOIRE, LA • 1964 • Bernier Jean-Paul • CND
TERRE AU VENTRE, LA • 1978 • Gatlif Tony • FRN
TERRE COMMANDE, LA • 1920 • Bergerat Theo • FRN
TERRE D'AMOUR • 1935 • Cloche Maurice • SHT • FRN
TERRE D'ANGOISSE see **DEUXIEME BUREAU CONTRE KOMMANDANTUR** • 1939
TERRE DE CAIN • 1949 • Petel Pierre • DCS • CND
TERRE DE COURAGE • 1967 • Bendeddouche Ghaouti • DCS • ALG
TERRE DE FEU • 1938 • L'Herbier Marcel • FRN
TERRE DE FLANDRE • 1938 • Storck Henri • DOC • BLG
TERRE DE LA PAIX, LA • 1972 • Shawqi Khalil • SHT • EGY
TERRE DE L'HOMME • 1980 • Lamothe Arthur • SER • CND • INNU-ASI ○ INNU ASI
TERRE DE NOS AIEUX see **ALEXIS TREMBLAY, HABITANT - THE STORY OF A FARMER IN QUEBEC** • 1943
TERRE DE PAIX see **ARD' AS-SALAM** • 1957
TERRE DE REVE see **ARD' AL-AHLAM** • 1957
TERRE DES GLACES • 1949 • Languepin Jean-Jacques • SHT • FRN
TERRE DES TAUREAUX, LA • 1924 • Musidora • FRN • TERRE DES TOROS, LA
TERRE DES TOROS, LA see **TERRE DES TAUREAUX, LA** • 1924
TERRE D'ESPAGNE • 1937 • Renoir Jean • DOC • FRN
TERRE DU DIABLE, LA • 1921 • Luitz-Morat, Vercourt Alfred • FRN
TERRE FLEURIE • 1956 • Mariaud Robert • SHT • FRN
TERRE-NEUVE • 1933 • Rutten Gerard • DOC • NTH
TERRE PROMISE • 1927 • Puchalski Eduard • PLN
TERRE PROMISE, LA • 1925 • Roussell Henry • FRN
TERRE QUI MEURT, LA • 1926 • Choux Jean • FRN
TERRE QUI MEURT, LA • 1936 • Vallee Jean • FRN
TERRE ROUGE • 1988 • Thiltges Jany • SHT • LXM • RED EARTH
TERRE SACREE • 1988 • Pacull Emilio • FRN
TERRE SANGLANTE see **HOMA VAFTIKE KOKKINO, TO** • 1965
TERRE SANS PAIN see **HURDES, LAS** • 1932
TERRES BRULEES • 1934 • Dekeukeleire Charles • CNG
TERRES DE GOLOMPO, LES • 1956 • Vilardebo Carlos • SHT • FRN
TERRES ET FLAMMES • 1951 • Mariaud Robert • SHT • FRN • VALLAURIS
TERREUR • 1924 • Jose Edward, Bourgeois Gerard • FRN • PERILS OF PARIS, THE (USA) ○ TERROR
TERREUR DE DAMES, LA • 1956 • Boyer Jean • FRN • CE COCHON DE MORIN
TERREUR DE LA PAMPA, LA • 1933 • Cammage Maurice • FRN
TERREUR DES BATIGNOLLES, LA • 1931 • Clouzot Henri-Georges • SHT • FRN
TERREUR DES MERS, LA (FRN) see **TERRORE DEI MARI, IL** • 1961
TERREUR EN OKLAHOMA • 1950 • Paviot Paul, Heinrich Andre • SHT • FRN
TERREUR SUR LA SAVANE • 1962 • Allegret Yves • FRN, CNG • KONGA YO
TERREURS DE RIGADIN, LES • 1912 • Monca Georges • FRN • TERRORS OF RIGADIN, THE
TERRIBILE ISPETTORE, IL • 1969 • Amendola Mario • ITL
TERRIBILE TEODORA, IL • 1961 • Montero Roberto Bianchi • ITL
TERRIBILI SETTE, I • 1964 • Matarazzo Raffaello • ITL • CAGASOTTO, I

TERRIBLE ADVENTURE OF CAPTAIN PUSHKIN, THE see **GROZNA PRZYGODA KAPITANA PUSZKINA** • 1964
TERRIBLE ATTEMPT, A • 1909 • *Bison* • USA
TERRIBLE BEAUTY, A • 1960 • Garnett Tay • UKN • NIGHT FIGHTERS, THE (USA)
TERRIBLE BOUT DE PAPIER, LE • 1915 • Cohl Emile • ANS • FRN
TERRIBLE BREAK, A • 1915 • *Mina* • USA
TERRIBLE DE CHICAGO, EL • 1968 • Bosch Juan • SPN • HORROR OF CHICAGO, THE
TERRIBLE DISCOVERY, A • 1911 • Griffith D. W. • USA
TERRIBLE ERUPTION OF MOUNT PELEE AND DESTRUCTION OF ST. PIERRE, MARTINIQUE, THE see **ERUPTION VOLCANIQUE A LA MARTINIQUE** • 1902
TERRIBLE EXPERIENCES OF A FIANCE • 1906 • *Pathe* • SHT • FRN
TERRIBLE FLIRT, A • 1905 • Fitzhamon Lewin • UKN
TERRIBLE GHOST-CAT OF OKAZAKI see **KAIBYO OKAZAKI SODO** • 1954
TERRIBLE GIGANTE DE LAS NIEVES, EL • 1962 • Salvador Jaime • MXC • TERRIBLE SNOW GIANT, THE
TERRIBLE JOE MORAN • 1984 • Sargent Joseph • TVM • USA • ONE BLOW TOO MANY
TERRIBLE KATE • 1917 • *Vim* • USA
TERRIBLE KIDS, THE • 1906 • Porter Edwin S. • USA
TERRIBLE LESSON, A • 1912 • Blache Alice • USA
TERRIBLE LESSON, A • 1913 • *Kalem* • USA
TERRIBLE LESSON, THE • 1914 • O'Sullivan Tony • USA
TERRIBLE NIGHT, A • 1902 • *Biograph* • USA
TERRIBLE NIGHT, A • 1913 • Blache Alice • USA
TERRIBLE NIGHT, A see **NUIT TERRIBLE, UNE** • 1896
TERRIBLE NIGHT, THE see **NOCHE TERRIBLE** • 1967
TERRIBLE NUIT, UNE • 1916 • Burguet Charles • FRN
TERRIBLE ONE, THE • 1915 • Melville Wilbert • USA
TERRIBLE ORDEAL, A see **ILDPROVE, EN** • 1915
TERRIBLE OUTLAW, THE • 1913 • *Eclair* • USA
TERRIBLE PEOPLE, THE • 1928 • Bennet Spencer Gordon • SRL • USA
TERRIBLE PEOPLE, THE (USA) see **BANDE DES SCHRECKENS, DIE** • 1960
TERRIBLE PLANT, A • 1913 • Fitzhamon Lewin? • UKN
TERRIBLE QUICK SWORD OF SIEGFRIED, THE see **SIEGFRIED UND DAS SAGENHAFTE LIEBESLEBEN DER NIBELUNGEN** • 1971
TERRIBLE RAILWAY ACCIDENT, THE see **RAILWAY COLLISION, A** • 1898
TERRIBLE REVENGE, A see **STRASHNAYA MEST** • 1913
TERRIBLE SNOW GIANT, THE see **TERRIBLE GIGANTE DE LAS NIEVES, EL** • 1962
TERRIBLE TED • 1907 • *Bitzer Billy (Ph)* • USA
TERRIBLE TEDDY • 1912 • *Essanay* • USA
TERRIBLE TEDDY THE GRIZZLY KING • 1901 • Porter Edwin S. • USA
TERRIBLE TRAGEDY, A • 1915 • Golden Joseph A.? • USA
TERRIBLE TRAGEDY, A • 1916 • Hevener Jerold T. • SHT • USA
TERRIBLE TROUBADOUR • 1933 • Lantz Walter, Nolan William • ANS • USA
TERRIBLE TRUNK, THE • 1915 • Castle James W. • USA
TERRIBLE TRUTH, THE • 1915 • Reynolds Lynn • USA
TERRIBLE TURK, THE • 1916 • Chaudet Louis W. • SHT • USA
TERRIBLE TURKISH EXECUTIONER, THE (USA) see **BOURREAU TURC, LE** • 1904
TERRIBLE TURKISH EXECUTIONER, OR IT SERVED HIM RIGHT, THE see **BOURREAU TURC, LE** • 1904
TERRIBLE TWINS, THE • 1914 • Neame Elwin • UKN
TERRIBLE TWO, THE • 1914 • Evans Joe • *Phoenix* • UKN
TERRIBLE TWO, THE • 1914 • Plumb Hay? • *Hepworth* • UKN
TERRIBLE TWO -A.B.S., THE • 1915 • Read James • UKN
TERRIBLE TWO ABROAD, THE • 1915 • Read James • UKN
TERRIBLE TWO HAD, THE • 1915 • Read James • UKN
TERRIBLE TWO IN LUCK, THE • 1914 • Read James • UKN
TERRIBLE TWO JOIN THE POLICE FORCE, THE • 1914 • Plumb Hay? • UKN
TERRIBLE TWO, KIDNAPPERS, THE • 1914 • Read James • UKN
TERRIBLE TWO ON THE MASH, THE • 1914 • Evans Joe • UKN
TERRIBLE TWO ON THE STAGE, THE • 1914 • Evans Joe • UKN
TERRIBLE TWO ON THE TWIST, THE • 1914 • Evans Joe • UKN
TERRIBLE TWO ON THE WAIT, THE • 1914 • Read James • UKN
TERRIBLE TWO ON THE WANGLE, THE • 1914 • Read James • UKN
TERRIBLE TWO ON THE WARPATH, THE • 1914 • Evans Joe • UKN
TERRIBLE VENGEANCE, THE (USA) see **STRASHNAYA MEST** • 1913
TERRIBLE WOMAN, A • 1964 • Polak Jindrich • CZC, GDR
TERRIBLES VIVANTES, LES • 1986 • Henaut Dorothy Todd • CND • FIREWORDS
TERRIBLY STUCK UP • 1915 • Roach Hal • USA
TERRIBLY TALENTED • 1948 • Van Dyke Willard, Hammid Alexander • DOC • USA
TERRIER AND THE CHILD, THE see **DOP DOCTOR, THE** • 1915
TERRIER STRICKEN • 1952 • Jones Charles M. • ANS • USA
TERRIFIC THE GIANT • 1952 • Holmes Cecil • ANM • ASL
TERRIFICANTE NOTTE DEL DEMONIO, LA • 1973 • Hunebelle Andre • ITL
TERRIFIED! • 1962 • Landers Lew • USA
TERRIFYING CONFESSIONS OF A CAPTIVE WOMAN see **TERRIFYING CONFESSIONS OF CAPTIVE WOMEN** • 1977
TERRIFYING CONFESSIONS OF CAPTIVE WOMEN • 1977 • Frank Hubert • AUS, FRG, SPN • TERRIFYING CONFESSIONS OF A CAPTIVE WOMAN ○ CAPTIVE WOMEN ○ DIRTY JOBS
TERRITOIRE, LE • 1981 • Ruiz Raul • FRN, PRT • TERRITORY, THE
TERRITOIRE DES AUTRES, LE • 1971 • Vienne Gerard, Bel Francois, Lecompte Jacqueline, Fano Michel • DOC • FRN, BLG
TERRITORIA • 1980 • Surin Alexander • USS • TERRITORY
TERRITORIAL ON THE BRAIN • 1909 • *Anglo-American Films* • UKN
TERRITORY see **TERRITORIA** • 1980
TERRITORY, THE see **TERRITOIRE, LE** • 1981
TERRONAUTS, THE • 1967 • Tully Montgomery • UKN • TERRORNAUTS, THE
TERROR • 1915 • Le Viness Carl M. • USA
TERROR • 1928 • King Louis • USA
TERROR • 1930 • Buehlman Frank J. • USA
TERROR • 1976 • Fredholm Gert • DNM
TERROR • 1979 • Warren Norman J. • UKN • TERROR, THE
TERROR see **TERREUR** • 1924
TERROR see **MOCKERY** • 1927
TERROR see **TERROR MOUNTAIN** • 1928
TERROR see **CASTELLO DELLE DONNE MALEDETTE, IL** • 1973
TERROR see **ANGST** • 1976
TERROR see **SETTIMA DONNA, LA** • 1978
TERROR, THE • 1917 • Wells Raymond • USA
TERROR, THE • 1920 • Jaccard Jacques • USA
TERROR, THE • 1926 • Smith Cliff • USA
TERROR, THE • 1928 • Del Ruth Roy • USA
TERROR, THE • 1938 • Bird Richard • UKN
TERROR, THE • 1963 • Corman Roger, Hellman Monte (U/c) • USA • LADY IN THE SHADOWS ○ NIGHT OF THE TERROR
TERROR, THE see **TERROR** • 1979
TERROR, THE see **TERROR ON TOUR** • 1980
TERROR ABOARD • 1933 • Sloane Paul • USA
TERROR ACTION see **TERRORAKSJONEN** • 1978
TERROR AFTER MIDNIGHT (USA) see **NEUNZIG MINUTEN NACH MITTERNACHT** • 1962
TERROR AMONG US • 1981 • Krasny Paul • TVM • USA
TERROR AND THE TERRIER, THE • 1910 • Coleby A. E. • UKN
TERROR AT ALCATRAZ • 1982 • Hayers Sidney • TVM • USA
TERROR AT BLACK FALLS • 1962 • Sarafian Richard C. • USA
TERROR AT HALFDAY see **MONSTER A GO-GO!** • 1965
TERROR AT LONDON BRIDGE see **BRIDGE ACROSS TIME** • 1985
TERROR AT MIDNIGHT • 1956 • Adreon Franklin • USA • AND SUDDENLY YOU RUN (UKN)
TERROR AT RED WOLF INN see **TERROR HOUSE** • 1972
TERROR BENEATH THE SEA (USA) see **KAITEI DAISENSO** • 1966
TERROR BY NIGHT • 1931 • Freeland Thornton • USA
TERROR BY NIGHT • 1946 • Neill R. William • USA • SHERLOCK HOLMES IN TERROR BY NIGHT
TERROR CASTLE see **VERGINE DI NORIMBERGA, LA** • 1963
TERROR CASTLE see **CASTELLO DELLE DONNE MALEDETTE, IL** • 1973
TERROR CIRCUS • 1973 • Rudolph Alan, Cormier Gerald? • USA • BARN OF THE NAKED DEAD
TERROR-CREATURES FROM THE GRAVE (USA) see **CINQUE TOMBE PER UN MEDIUM** • 1966
TERROR DE LA FRONTERA, EL • 1962 • Gomez Urquiza Zacarias • MXC
TERROR EN EL ESPACIO (SPN) see **TERRORE NELLO SPAZIO** • 1965
TERROR EYES • 1980 • Hughes Ken • USA • NIGHT SCHOOL
TERROR FACES MAGOO • 1959 • Ishii Chris • ANS • USA
TERROR FACTOR see **SCARED TO DEATH** • 1980
TERROR FROM SPACE • 1962-69 • Carpenter John • SHT • USA
TERROR FROM SPACE see **TERRORE NELLO SPAZIO** • 1965
TERROR FROM THE SKY see **TERROR OUT OF THE SKY** • 1978
TERROR FROM THE SUN see **HIDEOUS SUN DEMON, THE** • 1959
TERROR FROM THE YEAR 5000 • 1958 • Gurney Robert Jr. • USA • CAGE OF DOOM (UKN) ○ GIRL FROM 5000 A.D., THE
TERROR FROM UNDER THE HOUSE see **REVENGE** • 1971
TERROR FROM WITHIN • 1974 • Ormerod James • TVM • UKN • WON'T WRITE HOME, MOM -I'M DEAD
TERROR HOUSE • 1972 • Townsend Bud • USA • FOLKS AT RED WOLF INN, THE ○ TERROR AT RED WOLF INN ○ TERROR ON THE MENU
TERROR HOUSE (USA) see **NIGHT HAS EYES, THE** • 1942
TERROR IN 2-A • 1972 • Rose William L. • ITL • GIRL IN ROOM 2A, THE (USA)
TERROR IN A TEXAS TOWN • 1958 • Lewis Joseph H. • USA
TERROR IN THE AISLES • 1984 • Kuehn Andrew J. • CMP • USA
TERROR IN THE CITY • 1966 • Baron Allen • USA • PIE IN THE SKY
TERROR IN THE CRYPT (USA) see **CRIPTA E L'INCUBO, LA** • 1964
TERROR IN THE FOREST see **FOREST, THE** • 1983
TERROR IN THE HAUNTED HOUSE • 1958 • Daniels Harold • USA • MY WORLD DIES SCREAMING
TERROR IN THE JUNGLE • 1968 • Desimone Tom, Jansack Andy, Grattan Alexander • USA
TERROR IN THE JUNGLE see **OPERATION MALAYA** • 1953
TERROR IN THE MIDNIGHT SUN (UKN) see **RYMDINVASION I LAPPLAND** • 1958
TERROR IN THE SKY • 1971 • Kowalski Bernard • TVM • USA
TERROR IN THE SKY see **HOSTAGE FLIGHT** • 1985
TERROR IN THE STREETS see **AKUMA GA YONDEIRU** • 1970
TERROR IN THE SWAMP • 1985 • Catalanotto Joseph • USA • NUTRIA MAN
TERROR IN THE WAX MUSEUM • 1973 • Fenady George • USA
TERROR IN THE WOODS • 1974 • *Testi Fabio*
TERROR IN TOKYO see **ATOUT COEUR A TOKYO POUR OSS 117** • 1966
TERROR IN TOYLAND see **CHRISTMAS EVIL** • 1980
TERROR IS A MAN • 1959 • De Leon Gerardo • USA • CREATURE FROM BLOOD ISLAND ○ BLOOD CREATURE ○ GORY CREATURES, THE
TERROR ISLAND • 1920 • Cruze James • USA • SALVAGE
TERROR MADNESS see **LOCURA DE TERROR** • 1960
TERROR MOUNTAIN • 1928 • King Louis • USA • TOM'S VACATION (UKN) ○ TERROR
TERROR OF ANGER, THE • 1914 • *Thanhouser* • USA
TERROR OF BAR X, THE • 1927 • Pembroke Scott • USA
TERROR OF CONSCIENCE, THE • 1913 • *Vincent James* • USA
TERROR OF DR. CHANEY, THE (UKN) see **MANSION OF THE DOOMED** • 1975
TERROR OF DR. FRANKENSTEIN see **VICTOR FRANKENSTEIN** • 1977
TERROR OF DR. HICHCOCK, THE see **ORRIBILE SEGRETO DEL DR. HICHCOCK, L'** • 1962
TERROR OF DR. MABUSE, THE (USA) see **TESTAMENT DES DR. MABUSE, DAS** • 1962
TERROR OF DRACULA, THE see **NOSFERATU -EINE SYMPHONIE DES GRAUENS** • 1921
TERROR OF FRANKENSTEIN see **VICTOR FRANKENSTEIN** • 1977
TERROR OF GODZILLA, THE see **MEKAGOJIRA NO GYAKUSHU** • 1975
TERROR OF LONDON, THE see **CURSE OF THE WRAYDONS, THE** • 1946
TERROR OF MECHAGODZILLA see **MEKAGOJIRA NO GYAKUSHU** • 1975
TERROR OF PUEBLO, THE • 1924 • *Mix Art* • USA
TERROR OF ROME AGAINST THE SON OF HERCULES (USA) see **MACISTE IL GLADIATORE DI SPARTA** • 1964
TERROR OF SHEBA, THE (USA) see **PERSECUTION** • 1973
TERROR OF THE AIR • 1914 • Wilson Frank • UKN
TERROR OF THE BARBARIANS, THE see **TERRORE DEI BARBARI, IL** • 1959
TERROR OF THE BLACK MASK see **INVINCIBILE CAVALIERE MASCHERATO, L'** • 1964
TERROR OF THE BLOODHUNTERS • 1962 • Warren Jerry • USA
TERROR OF THE DEEP see **DESTINATION INNER SPACE** • 1966
TERROR OF THE FOLD, THE • 1915 • Bowman William J. • USA
TERROR OF THE HATCHET MEN see **TERROR OF THE TONGS, THE** • 1961
TERROR OF THE HOUSE, THE • 1905 • Collins Alf? • UKN
TERROR OF THE ISLANDS see **MAD DOCTOR OF MARKET STREET, THE** • 1942
TERROR OF THE KIRGHIZ see **URSUS IL TERRORE DEI KIGHISI** • 1964
TERROR OF THE MAD DOCTOR, THE see **TESTAMENT DES DR. MABUSE, DAS** • 1962
TERROR OF THE MOUNTAINS, THE • 1915 • *Crawford Florence* • USA
TERROR OF THE NEIGHBOURHOOD, THE • 1905 • Raymond Charles? • UKN
TERROR OF THE NIGHT, A • 1914 • Edwin Walter • USA
TERROR OF THE PLAINS • 1934 • Webb Harry S. • USA
TERROR OF THE PLAINS, A • 1910 • *Yankee* • USA
TERROR OF THE RANGE • 1919 • Paton Stuart • SRL • USA
TERROR OF THE RED MASK (USA) see **TERRORE DELLA MASCHERA ROSSA, IL** • 1960
TERROR OF THE STEPPE (USA) see **PREDONI DELLA STEPPA, I** • 1964
TERROR OF THE TONGS, THE • 1961 • Bushell Anthony • UKN • TERROR OF THE HATCHET MEN
TERROR OF TINY TOWN, THE • 1938 • Newfield Sam • USA
TERROR OF TWIN MOUNTAINS, THE • 1915 • Bertram William • USA
TERROR ON A TRAIN (USA) see **TIME BOMB** • 1952
TERROR ON ALCATRAZ • 1987 • Marcus Philip • USA
TERROR ON BLOOD ISLAND see **BRIDES OF BLOOD** • 1968
TERROR ON HALF MOON STREET (USA) see **MANN MIT DEM GLASAUGE, DER** • 1968
TERROR ON HIGHWAY 91 • 1988 • Jameson Jerry • TVM • USA
TERROR ON TAPE • 1983 • Worms Robert A. Jr. • USA
TERROR ON THE 40TH FLOOR • 1974 • Jameson Jerry • TVM • USA
TERROR ON THE BEACH • 1973 • Wendkos Paul • TVM • USA
TERROR ON THE BRITANNIC see **JUGGERNAUT** • 1974
TERROR ON THE MENU see **TERROR HOUSE** • 1972
TERROR ON THE MIDWAY • 1942 • Fleischer Dave • ANS • USA
TERROR ON TIPTOE • 1936 • Renoir Louis • UKN
TERROR ON TOUR • 1980 • Edmonds Don • USA • TERROR, THE
TERROR OUT OF THE SKY • 1978 • Katzin Lee H. • TVM • USA • TERROR FROM THE SKY
TERROR SHIP (USA) see **DANGEROUS VOYAGE** • 1954
TERROR SQUAD • 1988 • Maris Peter • USA
TERROR SQUAD see **HIJACKING OF THE ACHILLE LAURO, THE** • 1988
TERROR STREET (USA) see **THIRTY-SIX HOURS** • 1954
TERROR STRIKES, THE (UKN) see **WAR OF THE COLOSSAL BEAST** • 1958
TERROR TRAIL • 1933 • Schaefer Armand • USA
TERROR TRAIL • 1946 • Nazarro Ray • USA • HANDS OF MENACE (UKN)
TERROR TRAIL, THE • 1925 • Kull Edward • USA
TERROR TRAIN • 1980 • Spottiswoode Roger • CND
TERROR VISION see **TERRORVISION** • 1986
TERROR WITHIN, THE • 1989 • Notz Thierry • USA
TERRORAKSJONEN • 1978 • Risan Leidulv • NRW • TERROR ACTION
TERRORE see **DANZA MACABRA** • 1964
TERRORE AL KILIMANGIARO see **GRANDE CACCIA, LA** • 1957
TERRORE CON GLI OCCHI STORTI, IL • 1972 • Steno • ITL • CROSS-EYED TERROR, THE
TERRORE DEI BARBARI, IL • 1959 • Campogalliani Carlo • ITL • GOLIATH AND THE BARBARIANS (USA) ○ TERROR OF THE BARBARIANS, THE

TERRORE DEI MANTELLI ROSSI, IL • 1963 • Costa Mario • ITL, FRN, SPN • CAVALIERS DE LA TERREUR, LES (FRN) ○ JINETES DEL TERROR, LOS (SPN) ○ KNIGHTS OF TERROR (USA)

TERRORE DEI MARI, IL • 1961 • Paolella Domenico, Kresel Lee • ITL, FRN • TERREUR DES MERS, LA (FRN) ○ GUNS OF THE BLACK WITCH (USA)

TERRORE DELLA MASCHERA ROSSA, IL • 1960 • Capuano Luigi • ITL • TERROR OF THE RED MASK (USA)

TERRORE DELL'ANDALUSIA, IL see **CARNE DE HORCA** • **1953**

TERRORE DELL'OKLAHOMA, IL • 1960 • Amendola Mario • ITL

TERRORE DI NOTTE, IL (ITL) see **TEPPICH DES GRAUENS** • **1962**

TERRORE NELLO SPAZIO • 1965 • Bava Mario • ITL, SPN, USA • TERROR EN EL ESPACIO (SPN) ○ PLANET OF THE VAMPIRES (USA) ○ PLANET OF TERROR ○ DEMON PLANET, THE ○ OUTLAW PLANET ○ HAUNTED PLANET ○ PLANET OF BLOOD ○ TERROR FROM SPACE

TERRORE SULLA CITTA • 1957 • Majano Anton Giulio • ITL

TERRORISER, THE see **K'UNG-PU FEN-TZU** • **1986**

TERRORIST • 1976 • SAF

TERRORIST, THE see **TERRORISTA, IL** • **1963**

"TERRORIST" HASSAN, THE see **HASSAN TERRO** • **1967**

TERRORIST ON TRIAL: THE UNITED STATES VS. SALIM AJAMI • 1988 • Bleckner Jeff • TVM • USA • HOSTILE WITNESS

TERRORISTA, EL • 1977 • Alcazar Victor • SPN

TERRORISTA, IL • 1963 • De Bosio Gianfranco • ITL, FRN • TERRORISTE, LE (FRN) ○ TERRORIST, THE

TERRORISTE, LE (FRN) see **TERRORISTA, IL** • **1963**

TERRORISTE SUISSE, LE • 1988 • Iseli Christian • DOC • SWT

TERRORISTI A MADRID • 1954 • Torrecilla Rafael, Aleixandre Margarita • ITL, SPN

TERRORISTS, THE see **FATHER'S REVENGE, A** • **1988**

TERRORISTS, THE (USA) see **RANSOM** • **1974**

TERRORNAUTS, THE see **TERRONAUTS, THE** • **1967**

TERRORS • 1930 • Smith Erle O. • UKN

TERROR'S EDGE see **WIND, THE** • **1987**

TERRORS OF A TURKISH BATH • 1916 • *Russell Dan* • SHT • USA

TERRORS OF RIGADIN, THE see **TERREURS DE RIGADIN, LES** • **1912**

TERRORS OF THE JUNGLE • 1913 • *Oakman Wheeler* • USA

TERRORS OF THE JUNGLE, THE • 1915 • *Clifford William* • USA

TERRORS OF WAR, THE • 1917 • Ford Francis • SHT • USA

TERRORS ON HORSEBACK • 1946 • Newfield Sam • USA

TERRORVISION • 1985 • *Reilly Bill* • ANT • USA

TERRORVISION • 1986 • Nicolaou Ted • USA • TERROR VISION

TERRY AND THE PIRATES • 1940 • Horne James W. • SRL • USA

TERRY CARTOON BURLESQUE • 1917 • Terry J. C.? • ASS • USA

TERRY FOX LE COUREUR DE L'ESPOIR see **TERRY FOX STORY, THE** • **1983**

TERRY FOX STORY, THE • 1983 • Thomas Ralph L. • CND • TERRY FOX LE COUREUR DE L'ESPOIR

TERRY OF THE TIMES • 1930 • McRae Henry • SRL • USA

TERRY ON THE FENCE • 1987 • Godwin Frank • UKN

TERRY THE TERROR • 1960 • Kneitel Seymour • ANS • USA

TERRY WHITMORE, FOR EXAMPLE • 1969 • Brodie Bill • DOC • SWD

TERRY'S TEA PARTY • 1916 • Semon Larry • SHT • USA

TERRYTOONS • 1930-54 • *Terry Paul (P)* • ASS • USA

TERU HI KUMORU HI • 1926 • Kinugasa Teinosuke • JPN • SHINING SUN BECOMES CLOUDED, THE

TERUG NAAR HET EILAND • 1950 • van der Linden Charles Huguenot • NTH • BACK TO THE ISLAND

TERUG NAAR OEGSTGEEST • 1987 • van Gogh Theo • NTH • BACK TO OEGSTGEEST

TERUGTOCHT, DE • 1981 • van Eyck Robert • BLG

TERVA • 1976 • Heino Niilo • FNL

TERY YAAD • 1948 • Chand Dawood • PKS

TERZA DIMENZIONE, LA see **COUTEAU DANS LA PLAIE, LE** • **1962**

TERZA IPOTESI SU UN CASO DI PERFETTA STRATEGIA CRIMINALE • 1972 • Vari Giuseppe • ITL

TERZA LICEO • 1954 • Emmer Luciano • ITL • HIGH SCHOOL (USA) ○ JUNIOR YEAR HIGH SCHOOL ○ THIRD LYCEUM

TERZO CANALE • 1970 • Paradisi Giulio • ITL • AVVENTURA A MONTECARLO

TERZO OCCHIO, IL • 1966 • Guerrini Mino • ITL • KILLER WITH THE THIRD EYE, THE ○ THIRD EYE, THE

T'ES FOLLE OU QUOI? • 1982 • Gerard Michel • FRN

T'ES HEUREUSE? MOI, TOUJOURS! • 1982 • Marboeuf Jean • FRN

TESATURA MECCANICA DELLA LINEA A 220,000 VOLT • 1955 • Olmi Ermanno (Spv) • DOC • ITL

TESCHIO D'ORO, IL • 1921 • Campogalliani Carlo • ITL

TESEO CONTRO IL MINOTAURO • 1961 • Amadio Silvio • ITL • WARLORD OF CRETE, THE (UKN) ○ MINOTAUR, THE (USA) ○ MINOTAUR -THE WILD BEAST OF CRETE, THE ○ WILD BEAST OF CRETE, THE ○ THESEUS AGAINST THE MINOTAUR

TESHA • 1928 • Saville Victor • UKN • WOMAN IN THE NIGHT, A (USA)

TESNA KOZA • 1984 • Milosevic Mica • YGS • TIGHT SPOT, A ○ THIN SKIN

TESNA KOZA III • 1989 • Djordjevic Aleksandar • YGS • THIN SKIN III

TESORO DE ATAHUALPA, EL • 1966 • Orona Vicente • MXC, PRU • ATAHUALPA'S TREASURE

TESORO DE CHUCHO EL ROTO, EL • 1959 • Martinez Solares Gilberto • MXC

TESORO DE LA ISLA DE PINOS, EL • 1955 • Orona Vicente • MXC, CUB

TESORO DE LA MUERTE, EL • 1953 • Peon Ramon • MXC • AGUILA NEGRA EN EL TESORO DE LA MUERTE, EL

TESORO DE LAS CUATRO CORONAS, EL • 1983 • Baldi Ferdinando • SPN, ITL • TREASURE OF THE FOUR CROWNS

TESORO DE MAKUBA, EL • 1966 • Elorrieta Jose Maria • SPN, USA • TREASURE OF MAKUBA, THE (USA)

TESORO DE MENTIRAS • 1968 • Gomez Urquiza Zacarias • MXC

TESORO DE MOCTEZUMA, EL • 1966 • Cardona Rene, Cardona Rene Jr. • MXC

TESORO DE PANCHO VILLA, EL • 1935 • Boytler Arcady • MXC

TESORO DE PANCHO VILLA, EL • 1954 • Baledon Rafael • MXC

TESORO DEI BARBARI, IL • 1960 • Ferreri Marco • ITL

TESORO DEL AMAZONES, EL • 1983 • Cardona Rene Jr. • MXC • TREASURE OF THE AMAZON, THE ○ TREASURE OF DOOM

TESORO DEL BENGALA, IL • 1954 • Vernuccio Gianni • ITL

TESORO DEL CAPITAN TORNADO, EL • 1967 • Artero Antonio • SPN

TESORO DEL CASTILLO, EL • 1964 • Fenollar Augusto • SPN

TESORO DEL INDITO, EL • 1960 • Rodriguez Joselito • MXC

TESORO DEL REY SALOMON, EL • 1962 • Curiel Federico • MXC

TESORO DELLA FORESTA PIETRIFICATA, IL • 1965 • Salvi Emimmo • ITL • TREASURE OF THE PETRIFIED FOREST, THE

TESORO DELL'AFRICA, IL (ITL) see **BEAT THE DEVIL** • **1953**

TESORO DI ISACCO, IL • 1918 • Palermi Amleto • ITL

TESORO DI MONTECRISTO, IL (ITL) see **COMTE DE MONTE-CRISTO, LE** • **1953**

TESORO DI ROMMEL, IL • 1965 • Marcellini Romolo • ITL • ROMMEL'S TREASURE (USA)

TESORO EN EL CIELO, UN • 1956 • Iglesias Miguel • SPN

TESORO ESCONDIDO, EL • 1979 • Cardona Rene • MXC

TESORO MIO • 1979 • Paradisi Giulio • ITL • MY DARLING ○ MY DEAREST TREASURE

TESOURO, O • 1958 • Campos Antonio • SHT • PRT

TESOURO PERDIDO see **THESOURO PERDIDO** • **1927**

TESS • 1980 • Polanski Roman • FRN, UKN

TESS OF THE D'URBERVILLES • 1913 • Dawley J. Searle • USA

TESS OF THE D'URBERVILLES • 1924 • Neilan Marshall • USA

TESS OF THE HILLS • 1915 • Vale Travers?, Morgan George? • USA

TESS OF THE HILLS • 1916 • *Supreme* • SHT • USA

TESS OF THE STORM COUNTRY • 1914 • Porter Edwin S. • USA

TESS OF THE STORM COUNTRY • 1922 • Robertson John S. • USA

TESS OF THE STORM COUNTRY • 1932 • Santell Alfred • USA

TESS OF THE STORM COUNTRY • 1961 • Guilfoyle Paul • USA

TESSIE • 1925 • Fitzgerald Dallas M. • USA

TEST see **PAREEKSHA** • **1967**

TEST 88 • 1988 • Hristov Hristo • BUL

TEST 0558 • 1965 • Longpre Bernard • ANS • CND

TEST, THE • 1909 • Griffith D. W. • USA

TEST, THE • 1911 • Dwan Allan • *American* • USA

TEST, THE • 1911 • Salter Harry • *Lubin* • USA

TEST, THE • 1912 • *Selig* • USA

TEST, THE • 1913 • Haldane Bert? • UKN

TEST, THE • 1913 • Lambart Harry • USA

TEST, THE • 1914 • Reid Wallace • *Nestor* • USA

TEST, THE • 1914 • Santschi Thomas • *Selig* • USA

TEST, THE • 1915 • Castle James W. • USA

TEST, THE • 1916 • Blandford Rawdon • NZL

TEST, THE • 1916 • Calvert Charles? • UKN

TEST, THE • 1916 • Fitzmaurice George • USA

TEST, THE • 1923 • Greenwood Edwin • UKN

TEST, THE • 1926 • Elliott William J. • UKN

TEST, THE • 1936 • Ray Bernard B. • USA • TRAPPED (UKN)

TEST, THE • 1961 • Howe John • CND

TEST, THE see **FALSE BRIDE, THE** • **1914**

TEST, THE see **IZPIT** • **1971**

TEST, THE see **TESTET** • **1988**

TEST FLIGHT 263 • 1957 • Villiers David • UKN

TEST FOR LOVE, A • 1937 • Sewell Vernon • DCS • UKN

TEST OF A MAN, THE • 1911 • *Reliance* • USA

TEST OF A MAN, THE • 1915 • McRae Henry • USA

TEST OF AFFECTION, A • 1911 • Stow Percy • UKN

TEST OF CHIVALRY, THE • 1916 • Daly William Robert • SHT • USA

TEST OF COURAGE, THE • 1914 • *Lubin* • USA

TEST OF DONALD NORTON, THE • 1926 • Eason B. Reeves • USA

TEST OF FIDELITY see **ISPYTANIE VERNOSTI** • **1954**

TEST OF FLAME • 1914 • *Domino* • USA

TEST OF FRIENDSHIP, THE • 1908 • Griffith D. W. • USA

TEST OF FRIENDSHIP, THE • 1911 • *Yankee* • USA

TEST OF FRIENDSHIP, THE • 1911 • Merwin Bannister • *Edison* • USA

TEST OF HONOR, THE • 1919 • Robertson John S. • USA

TEST OF LOVE, A (USA) see **ANNIE'S COMING OUT** • **1984**

TEST OF LOVE, THE • 1911 • Porter Edwin S. • USA

TEST OF LOVE, THE • 1914 • *Dd Films* • UKN

TEST OF LOYALTY, THE • 1918 • *Hoffman Michael* • USA

TEST OF PILOT PIRX, THE see **TEST PILOTA PIRXA** • **1978**

TEST OF SINCERITY, THE • 1915 • *Perley Charles* • USA

TEST OF TRUE LOVE, THE • 1914 • *Melies* • USA

TEST OF WOMANHOOD, THE • 1917 • *Holmes Stuart* • USA

TEST PICTURES see **HUIA** • **1975**

TEST PILOT • 1938 • Fleming Victor • USA

TEST PILOT DONALD • 1951 • Hannah Jack • ANS • USA

TEST PILOT PIRX see **TEST PILOTA PIRXA** • **1978**

TEST PILOTA PIRXA • 1978 • Piestrak Marek • PLN • DOZNANIYE PILOTA PIKRSA ○ TEST OF PILOT PIRX, THE ○ TEST PILOT PIRX ○ PIRX TEST-FLIGHT

TEST PILOTS see **OBLATYWACZE** • **1960**

TEST TRIP see **PROBAUT** • **1960**

TEST-TUBE ADULT AND SIMO'S ANGELS, THE see **KOEPUTKIAIKUINEN JA SIMON ENKELIT** • **1979**

TESTA DEL SERPENTE, LA • 1974 • Maesso Jose • ITL, SPN • ORDINE DI UCCIDERE

TESTA DI RAPA • 1966 • Zagni Giancarlo • ITL

TESTA DI SBARCO PER OTTO IMPLACABILI • 1968 • Brescia Alfonso • ITL, FRN • TETE DE PONT POUR HUIT IMPLACABLES (FRN) ○ HELL IN NORMANDY (UKN) ○ BRIDGEHEAD FOR EIGHT RUTHLESS MEN

TESTA IN GIU.. GAMBE IN ARIA • 1973 • Novello Ugo • ITL

TESTA O CROCE • 1969 • Pierotti Piero • ITL

TESTA O CROCE • 1983 • Loy Nanni • ITL

TESTA T'AMMAZZO, CROCE SEI MORTO, MI CHIAMANO ALLELUJA • 1971 • Carnimeo Giuliano • ITL • THEY CALL ME HALLELUJAH

TESTAMENT • 1970 • Gebski Jozef, Halor Antoni • PLN

TESTAMENT • 1974 • Broughton James • USA

TESTAMENT • 1976 • Radivojevic Milos • YGS • WILL, THE

TESTAMENT • 1983 • Littman Lynne • USA

TESTAMENT • 1989 • Akomfrah John • UKN

TESTAMENT, LE see **VERDICT, LE** • **1974**

TESTAMENT DE MOYSE, LE • 1931 • Greville Edmond T. • SHT • FRN

TESTAMENT DE PIERROT, LE • 1904 • Blache Alice • FRN

TESTAMENT DE UN PUEBLO • 1976 • Garcia Munoz M. • SPN • VILLAGE'S TESTAMENT, A

TESTAMENT DES CORNELIUS GULDEN, DAS • 1932 • Emo E. W. • FRG • ERBSCHAFT MIT HINDERNISSEN, EINE

TESTAMENT DES DR. MABUSE, DAS • 1932 • Lang Fritz • FRG • TESTAMENT OF DR. MABUSE, THE (USA) ○ CRIMES OF DR. MABUSE (UKN) ○ LAST WILL OF DR. MABUSE, THE

TESTAMENT DES DR. MABUSE, DAS • 1962 • Klinger Werner • FRG • TERROR OF DR. MABUSE, THE (USA) ○ TERROR OF THE MAD DOCTOR, THE ○ LAST WILL OF DR. MABUSE, THE ○ TESTAMENT OF DR. MABUSE, THE

TESTAMENT DES IVE SIEVERS, DAS • 1922 • Wiene Conrad • FRG

TESTAMENT D'ORPHEE, LE • 1960 • Cocteau Jean • FRN • TESTAMENT OF ORPHEUS OR DON'T ASK ME WHY, THE ○ TESTAMENT OF ORPHEUS (USA) ○ TESTAMENT D'ORPHEE OU NE ME DEMANDEZ PAR POURQUOI, LE

TESTAMENT D'ORPHEE OU NE ME DEMANDEZ PAR POURQUOI, LE see **TESTAMENT D'ORPHEE, LE** • **1960**

TESTAMENT DU DOCTEUR MABUSE, LE • 1933 • Sti Rene, Lang Fritz • FRN

TESTAMENT DU DR. CORDELIER, LE • 1959 • Renoir Jean • FRN • DOCTOR'S HORRIBLE EXPERIMENT, THE (USA) ○ EXPERIMENT IN EVIL (UKN) ○ TESTAMENT OF DR. CORDELIER, THE

TESTAMENT EINES EXZENTRISCHEN, DAS see **AURI SACRA FAMES 2** • **1920**

TESTAMENT OF AN OIL WORKER see **TESTIMONIO DE UN OBRERO PETROLERO** • **1979**

TESTAMENT OF DR. CORDELIER, THE see **TESTAMENT DU DR. CORDELIER, LE** • **1959**

TESTAMENT OF DR. MABUSE, THE see **TESTAMENT DES DR. MABUSE, DAS** • **1962**

TESTAMENT OF DR. MABUSE, THE (USA) see **TESTAMENT DES DR. MABUSE, DAS** • **1932**

TESTAMENT OF FRANKENSTEIN, THE see **TESTAMENTO DEL FRANKENSTEIN, EL** • **1964**

TESTAMENT OF KOPPANY'S AGHA, THE see **KOPPANYI AGA TESTAMENTUMA, A** • **1967**

TESTAMENT OF ORPHEUS OR DON'T ASK ME WHY, THE see **TESTAMENT D'ORPHEE, LE** • **1960**

TESTAMENT OF ORPHEUS (USA) see **TESTAMENT D'ORPHEE, LE** • **1960**

TESTAMENT OF PROFESSOR WILCZUR, THE see **TESTAMENT PROFESORA WILCZURA** • **1939**

TESTAMENT PROFESORA WILCZURA • 1939 • Buczkowski Leonard • PLN • TESTAMENT OF PROFESSOR WILCZUR, THE ○ PROFESSOR WILCZUR'S WILL

TESTAMENTET see **KAERLIGHEDENS TRIUMF** • **1914**

TESTAMENTETS HEMMELIGHED • 1916 • Holger-Madsen • DNM • VOICE OF THE DEAD, THE ○ DODES ROST, DEN ○ NANCY KEITH

TESTAMENTO DE MADIGAN, EL see **MILLIPILLERI** • **1966**

TESTAMENTO DEL FRANKENSTEIN, EL • 1964 • Madrid Jose Luis • SPN • TESTAMENT OF FRANKENSTEIN, THE

TESTAMENTO DEL VIRREY, EL • 1944 • Vajda Ladislao • SPN

TESTAMENTSHEIRAT, DIE • 1918 • Schubert Georg • FRG

TESTAMENTSKLAUSEL, DIE • 1915 • Del Zopp Rudolf • FRG

TESTED BY FIRE • 1914 • *Lockwood Harold* • USA

TESTED BY THE FLAG • 1911 • *Vitagraph* • USA

TESTER TESTED, THE • 1913 • *Eclair* • USA

TESTET • 1988 • Zacharias Ann • SWD • TEST, THE

TESTIGO PARA UN CRIMEN • 1964 • Vieyra Emilio • ARG • VIOLATED LOVE (USA)

TESTIGOS MUERTOS • 1972 • Ordosgoitti Napoleon • VNZ • DEAD WITNESSES

TESTIMONE, IL • 1946 • Germi Pietro • ITL

TESTIMONE, IL (ITL) see **TEMOIN, LE** • **1977**

TESTIMONE DEVE TACERE, IL • 1974 • Rosati Giuseppe • ITL • SILENCE THE WITNESS

TESTIMONIES see **VITTNESBORD OM HENNE** • **1962**

TESTIMONIES OF HER see **VITTNESBORD OM HENNE** • **1962**

TESTIMONIO DE UN OBRERO PETROLERO • 1979 • Guedez Jesus Enrique • VNZ • TESTAMENT OF AN OIL WORKER

TESTIMONY • 1920 • Newall Guy • UKN

TESTIMONY • 1988 • Palmer Tony • UKN

TESTIMONY OF A TABLE IN A RESTAURANT, THE • 1963 • Calotescu Virgil • DOC • RMN

TESTING BILL'S COURAGE • 1914 • *Imp* • USA

TESTING BLOCK, THE • 1920 • Hillyer Lambert • USA

TESTING FIRE, THE • 1914 • *Warfield Irene* • USA

TESTING HIS COURAGE • 1911 • *Walker Lillian* • USA

TESTING OF MILDRED VANE, THE • 1918 • Lucas Wilfred • USA

TESTING OILS FOR TWO-STROKE ENGINES • 1963 • Stewart Derek, Cooper Julian • DCS • UKN

TESTING TIME FOR LOVE, A • 1956 • Medved Jozef • CZC

TETCHED IN THE HEAD • 1935 • *Mintz Charles (P)* • ANS • USA

TETE, LA • 1973 • Bourget • FRN

TETE, LA see **RAS, AR-** • **1976**

TETE A CLAQUES • 1982 • Perrin Francis • FRN

TETE-A-LA-BALEINE • 1958-60 • Bonniere Rene • DCS • CND

TETE-A-TETE • 1977 • Kostenko Andrzej • PLN
TETE AU NEUTRE, LA • 1972 • Gagne Jean • CND
TETE BLONDE • 1949 • Cam Maurice • FRN
TETE CONTRE LES MURS, LA • 1958 • Franju Georges • FRN • KEEPERS, THE (UKN)
TETE COUPEE, LA • 1915 • Feuillade Louis • FRN
TETE DANS LE SAC, LA • 1984 • Lauzier Gerard • FRN
TETE DE NORMANDE ST-ONGE, LA • 1975 • Carle Gilles • CND • NORMANDE
TETE DE PONT POUR HUIT IMPLACABLES (FRN) see **TESTA DI SBARCO PER OTTO IMPLACABILI** • 1968
TETE DE TURC • 1935 • Becker Jacques • FRN • TETE QUI RAPPORTE, UN ○ BOURREAU, LE
TETE DU CLIENT, LA • 1964 • Poitrenaud Jacques • FRN, SPN
TETE D'UN FRERE, LA • Lethem Roland • SHT • BLG
TETE D'UN HOMME, LA • 1932 • Duvivier Julien • FRN
TETE EN FLEURS • 1969 • Longpre Bernard • ANS • CND • MARIE
TETE EN RUINE, LA • 1975 • Gatlif Tony • FRN
TETE FOLLE • 1959 • Vernay Robert • FRN
TETE FROIDE, LA • 1968 • Hella Patrick • BLG
TETE QUI RAPPORTE, UN see **TETE DE TURC** • 1935
TETES BLANCHES see **CATTLE RANCH** • 1961
TETES BRULEES, LES • 1967 • Rozier Willy • FRN, SPN
TETES DE FEMMES, FEMMES DE TETE • 1916 • Feyder Jacques • FRN
TETICKA • 1941 • Fric Martin • CZC • AUNTIE'S FANTASIES
TETKA S FILAKAMI • 1963 • Lyubimov Pavel • USS • AUNT WITH VIOLETS, THE ○ AUNTIE WITH VIOLETS
TETKE PLETKE • 1969 • Grgic Zlatko, Kolar Boris, Zaninovic Ante • ANS • YGS • KNITTING PRETTY
TETNO POLSKIEGO MANCHESTERU • 1929 • Ford Aleksander • PLN • LODZ, THE POLISH MANCHESTER
TETON TORNADO, THE • 1955 • Landers Lew • MTV • USA
TETSU JIRUBA see **JIRUBA TETSU** • 1950
TETSURO NO IKIRU • 1951 • Sekigawa Hideo • JPN • LIFE OF A RAILWAY WORKER
TETSURO NO OKAMI • 1927 • JPN • WOLF OF THE RAILS
TETSUWAN ATOM • 1960 • Tezuka Osamu • ANM • JPN • ASTROBOY
TETSUWAN KISHA • 1926 • Tasaka Tomotaka • JPN • RAILWAY TRAIN
TETSUWAN TOSHO INAO MONOGATARI • 1959 • Honda Inoshiro • JPN
TETTES ISMERETLEN, A • 1957 • Ranody Laszlo • HNG • DANSE MACABRE
TETTO, IL • 1956 • De Sica Vittorio • ITL • ROOF, THE
TEU, TUA • 1981 • de Oliveira Domingos • BRZ • YOURS, HERS ○ HIS, HERS
TEUF-TEUF • 1955 • Jabely Jean • ANM • FRN
TEUFEL, DER • 1918 • Dupont E. A. • FRG
TEUFEL HAT GUT LACHEN, DER • 1960 • Frueh Kurt • SWT • DEVIL MAY WELL LAUGH, THE
TEUFEL IN SEIDE • 1956 • Hansen Rolf • FRG • DEVIL IN SILK (USA)
TEUFEL KAM AUS AKASAWA, DER • 1971 • Franco Jesus • FRG, SPN • DIABLO VENIA DE AKASAWA, EL (SPN) ○ DEVIL WAS COMING FROM AKASAWA, THE
TEUFEL SPIELTE BALALAIKA, DER • 1961 • Lahola Leopold • FRG • UNTIL HELL IS FROZEN
TEUFEL UND CIRCE • 1920 • *Gura Sascha* • FRG
TEUFEL UND DIE MADONNA, DER • 1919 • Boese Carl • FRG • DEVIL AND THE MADONNA, THE
TEUFEL VOM MUHLENBERG, DER • 1955 • Ballmann Herbert • GDR
TEUFELCHEN • 1915 • Matray Ernst • FRG
TEUFELCHEN • 1919 • Muller-Hagen Carl • FRG
TEUFELCHEN • 1921 • Oswald Richard • FRG
TEUFELS-SCHLOSSER, DER • 1919 • Ferdinand Franz • AUS • DEVIL'S LOCKSMITH, THE
TEUFELSANBETER, DIE • 1920 • *Lugosi Bela* • FRG • DEVIL WORSHIPPERS, THE (USA)
TEUFELSKERL, EIN • 1935 • Jacoby Georg • AUS • DEVIL OF A FELLOW, A (USA)
TEUFELSKIRCHE, DIE • 1919 • Mierendorff Hans • FRG
TEUFELSKREIS, DER • 1956 • Balhaus Carl • GDR
TEUFELSMUHLE, DIE • 1920 • Frey Karl? • FRG
TEUFELSREPORTER, DER • 1929 • Laemmle Ernst • FRG
TEUFELSSYMPHONIE • 1922 • Firmans Josef • FRG
TEUFELSWALZER, DER • 1918 • Guter Johannes • FRG
TEURE HEIMAT • 1929 • Wilhelm Carl • FRG • DREI MADCHEN IHR GLUCK
TEUTONEN KOMMEN, DIE • 1962 • Schamoni Peter • SHT • FRG
TEUTONENSCHWERT • 1958 • Thorndike Andrew, Thorndike Annelie • DOC • GDR • OPERATION TEUTONIC SWORD
TEVYA • 1939 • Schwartz Maurice • USA
TEVYE • 1969 • Kohanyi Julius • DCS • CND
TEVYE AND HIS SEVEN DAUGHTERS see **TUVIYAH VE SHEVA BENOTAIV** • 1968
TEVYE UND SEINE SIEBEN TOCHTER (FRG) see **TUVIYAH VE SHEVA BENOTAIV** • 1968
TEX • 1926 • Gibson Tom • USA
TEX • 1982 • Hunter Tim • USA
TEX AND THE LORD OF THE DEEP see **TEX E IL SIGNORE DEGLI ABISSI** • 1985
TEX BENEKE AND HIS ORCHESTRA • 1948 • Cowan Will • SHT • USA
TEX BENEKE AND HIS ORCHESTRA • 1948 • Scholl Jack • SHT • USA
TEX BENEKE AND THE GLENN MILLER ORCHESTRA • 1946 • Cowan Will • SHT • USA
TEX E IL SIGNORE DEGLI ABISSI • 1985 • Tessari Duccio • ITL • TEX AND THE LORD OF THE DEEP
TEX GRANGER • 1948 • Abrahams Derwin • SRL • USA
TEX OF THE TIMBERLANDS • 1920 • Ridgwell George • SHT • USA
TEX RIDES WITH THE BOY SCOUTS • 1938 • Taylor Ray • USA
TEX TAKES A HOLIDAY • 1932 • Neitz Alvin J. • USA • DOLORES THE BEAUTIFUL (UKN)
TEX WILLIAMS AND HIS WESTERN CARAVAN • 1947 • Cowan Will • SHT • USA
TEXAN, THE • 1920 • Reynolds Lynn • USA
TEXAN, THE • 1930 • Cromwell John • USA • BIG RACE, THE (UKN)
TEXAN, THE • 1932 • Smith Cliff • USA
TEXAN MEETS CALAMITY JANE, THE • 1950 • Lamb Ande • USA
TEXAN TWINS, THE • 1912 • *Wilbur Crane* • USA
TEXANO, EL • 1963 • Crevenna Alfredo B. • MXC
TEXANS, THE • 1938 • Hogan James P. • USA
TEXAN'S HONOR, A • 1929 • *Canutt Yakima* • USA
TEXANS NEVER CRY • 1951 • McDonald Frank • USA
TEXAS • 1922 • Bertram William • USA
TEXAS • 1941 • Marshall George • USA
TEXAS ACROSS THE RIVER • 1966 • Gordon Michael • USA
TEXAS ADDIO • 1966 • Baldi Ferdinando • ITL, SPN • AVENGER, THE (UKN) ○ TEXAS ADIOS ○ ADIOS, TEXAS
TEXAS ADIOS see **TEXAS ADDIO** • 1966
TEXAS BAD MAN, THE • 1932 • Laemmle Edward • USA • DEFIANCE (UKN) ○ MARKED MEN
TEXAS BADMAN • 1953 • Collins Lewis D. • USA
TEXAS BEARCAT, THE • 1925 • Eason B. Reeves • USA
TEXAS BILL'S LAST RIDE • 1914 • *Majestic* • USA
TEXAS, BROOKLYN AND HEAVEN • 1948 • Castle William • USA • GIRL FROM TEXAS, THE (UKN)
TEXAS BUDDIES • 1932 • Bradbury Robert North • USA
TEXAS BURNS AT NIGHT see **SUMMER HEAT** • 1983
TEXAS CARNIVAL • 1951 • Walters Charles • USA
TEXAS CHAINSAW MASSACRE 2, THE • 1986 • Hooper Tobe • USA
TEXAS CHAINSAW MASSACRE, THE • 1974 • Hooper Tobe • USA
TEXAS CITY • 1952 • Collins Lewis D. • USA
TEXAS COWBOY, A • 1929 • *Steele Bob* • USA
TEXAS CYCLONE • 1932 • Lederman D. Ross • USA
TEXAS DESPERADOES see **DRIFT FENCE** • 1936
TEXAS DETOUR • 1978 • Avedis Howard • USA
TEXAS DYNAMO • 1950 • Nazarro Ray • USA • SUSPECTED (UKN)
TEXAS FEUD, A • 1913 • *Reliance* • USA
TEXAS FLASH • 1928 • Horner Robert J. • USA
TEXAS GLADIATORS 2020 see **2020 TEXAS GLADIATORS** • 1982
TEXAS GUNFIGHTER • 1932 • Rosen Phil • USA
TEXAS IN 1999 • 1931 • Fleischer Dave • ANS • USA
TEXAS JACK • 1935 • Ray Bernard B. • USA
TEXAS JOHN SLAUGHTER • 1960 • Keller Harry • MTV • USA
TEXAS JOHN SLAUGHTER: STAMPEDE AT BITTER CREEK • 1962 • Keller Harry • MTV • USA • STAMPEDE AT BITTER CREEK
TEXAS JOHN SLAUGHTER: WILD TIMES • 1962 • Keller Harry • MTV • USA
TEXAS JOKE, A • 1910 • Melies Gaston • USA
TEXAS JUSTICE see **LONE RIDER IN TEXAS JUSTICE, THE** • 1941
TEXAS KELLY AT BAY • 1913 • Ford Francis • USA
TEXAS KID see **TEXICAN, THE** • 1966
TEXAS KID, THE • 1920 • Eason B. Reeves • SHT • USA
TEXAS KID, THE • 1943 • Hillyer Lambert • USA
TEXAS KID, OUTLAW (UKN) see **KID FROM TEXAS, THE** • 1950
TEXAS LADY • 1955 • Whelan Tim • USA
TEXAS LAWMEN • 1951 • Collins Lewis D. • USA • LONE STAR LAWMAN
TEXAS LEGEND, A see **SUMMER HEAT** • 1983
TEXAS LIGHTNING • 1981 • Graver Gary • USA
TEXAS MAN, THE see **HORIZONS WEST** • 1952
TEXAS MAN HUNT • 1942 • Newfield Sam • USA
TEXAS MARSHAL • 1941 • Newfield Sam • USA
TEXAS MASQUERADE • 1944 • Archainbaud George • USA
TEXAS PANHANDLE • 1945 • Nazarro Ray • USA
TEXAS PIONEERS • 1932 • Fraser Harry L. • USA • BLOOD BROTHER, THE (UKN)
TEXAS PROJECT, THE see **PLACES IN THE HEART** • 1984
TEXAS RAMBLER, THE • 1935 • Hill Robert F. • USA
TEXAS RANGER, A see **PURE GRIT** • 1923
TEXAS RANGER, THE • 1931 • Lederman D. Ross • USA
TEXAS RANGER, THE see **LAW OF THE RANGE, THE** • 1927
TEXAS RANGERS, THE • 1936 • Vidor King • USA
TEXAS RANGERS, THE • 1951 • Karlson Phil • USA
TEXAS RANGERS RIDE AGAIN • 1941 • Hogan James P. • USA
TEXAS RENEGADES • 1940 • Newfield Sam • USA
TEXAS RIFLES • 1944 • Abrahams Derwin • USA
TEXAS ROAD AGENT see **ROAD AGENT** • 1941
TEXAS ROMANCE -1909, A • 1964 • Benton Robert • SHT • USA
TEXAS ROSE (UKN) see **RETURN OF JACK SLADE, THE** • 1955
TEXAS SERENADE (UKN) see **OLD CORRAL, THE** • 1936
TEXAS SERIAL KILLINGS, THE • 1986 • Dwyer John • USA
TEXAS SPHINX, THE • 1917 • Kelsey Fred A. • SHT • USA
TEXAS STAGECOACH • 1940 • Lewis Joseph H. • USA • TWO ROADS (UKN)
TEXAS STAMPEDE • 1939 • Nelson Sam • USA
TEXAS STEER, A • 1915 • Warren Giles R. • USA
TEXAS STEER, A • 1927 • Wallace Richard • USA
TEXAS STREAK, THE • 1926 • Reynolds Lynn • USA
TEXAS TED'S DEFENCE • 1911 • *Bison* • USA
TEXAS TERROR • 1935 • Bradbury Robert North • USA
TEXAS TERROR, THE • 1926 • *Hoxie Al* • USA
TEXAS TERRORS • 1940 • Sherman George • USA
TEXAS TO BATAAN • 1942 • Tansey Robert • USA • LONG, LONG TRAIL, THE (UKN)
TEXAS TO TOKYO (UKN) see **WE'VE NEVER BEEN LICKED** • 1943
TEXAS TOM • 1950 • Hanna William, Barbera Joseph • ANS • USA
TEXAS TOMMY • 1928 • McGowan J. P. • USA
TEXAS TORNADO • 1932 • Drake Oliver • USA
TEXAS TORNADO, THE • 1928 • Clark Frank Howard • USA
TEXAS TOUGH GUY • 1950 • Yates Hal • SHT • USA
TEXAS TRAIL • 1937 • Selman David • USA
TEXAS TRAIL, THE • 1925 • Dunlap Scott R. • USA
TEXAS TROUBLE SHOOTERS • 1942 • Luby S. Roy • USA
TEXAS WILDCATS • 1939 • Newfield Sam • USA
TEXASVILLE • 1990 • Bogdanovich Peter • USA
TEXICAN, THE • 1966 • Selander Lesley • USA, SPN • TEJANO, EL (SPN) ○ TEXAS KID
TEXT OF LIGHT • 1974 • Brakhage Stan • USA
TEXTILE WORKERS see **ZNAJOME Z LODZI** • 1972
TEXTILES • 1936 • Elder John C. • UKN
TEXTURE OF DECAY • 1947-53 • Vickrey Robert • SHT • USA
TEYZEM • 1985 • Refig Halit • TRK • MY AUNT
TEZAAB • 1988 • *Dikshit Madhuri* • IND
TEZKY ZIVOT DOBRODRUHA • 1941 • Fric Martin • CZC • DIFFICULT LIFE OF AN ADVENTURER, THE ○ ADVENTURE IS A HARD LIFE ○ HARD LIFE OF AN ADVENTURER, THE
TG: PSYCHIC RALLY IN HEAVEN • 1981 • Jarman Derek • UKN
THA KANO PETRA TI KARDHIA MOU • 1968 • Doukas Kostas • GRC • WILD HEART
THA TA KAPSO TA LEFTA MOU • 1968 • Theodoropoulos Angelos • GRC • MONEY TO BURN
THABA • 1976 • SAF
THADDEUS ROSE AND EDDIE • 1978 • Starrett Jack • TVM • USA
THAI MEL AANAI • 1965 • Nathan G. R. • IND
THAIKKU THALAIMAGAN • 1967 • Thirumugam M. A. • IND • FORTUNATE, THE
THAIMI, LA HIJA DEL PESCADOR • 1958 • Orol Juan • MXC, CUB
THAIS • 1914 • Maude Arthur, Crawley Constance • USA
THAIS • 1916 • Bragaglia Anton-Giulio • ITL
THAIS • 1917 • Crane Frank H. • USA
THALA see **OPIUM ET LE BATON, L'** • 1970
THALAMUS LIVES • Lethem Roland • SHT • BLG
THALASS KASSAS • 1968 • el Sahn Ibrahim, Reda Hassan, Nabih Mohamed • EGY • THREE STORIES
THALASSEIES I HANDRES, I • 1967 • Dalianidis Ioannis • GRC • GLASS BEADS FROM THE SEA ○ BLUE BEADS FROM GREECE
THALATH LUSUSS • 1966 • el Sheikh Kamal • EGY • TROIS VOLEURS
THALATH NISA' • 1969 • Abu Saif Salah, Zulficar Mahmoud, Barakat Henry • LBN • TROIS FEMMES
THALATH WUGUH LI AL-HUBB • 1968 • Shukry Mamduh (c/d) • EGY • TROIS VISAGES DE L'AMOUR
THALATHA RIJAL WA IMRA'A • 1960 • Halim Hilmy • EGY • TROIS HOMMES ET UNE FEMME
THALATHA YUHIBUNAHA, ATH- • 1965 • Zulficar Mahmoud • EGY • TOUS LES TROIS L'AIMENT
THALATHATU LUCUC • 1966 • Wahab Fatin Abdel • EGY • TALATH LESSONS ○ TROIS VOLEURS
THALER'S, MEIER'S, SADKOWSKY'S LIFE IN THE EVENING • 1967 • Schoenherr H. H. K. • SWT
THALIRUKAL • 1967 • Money M. S. • IND • "BOKUL" FLOWER, THE
THAMAR, DAS KIND DER BERGE • 1924 • Dinesen Robert • FRG
THAMAR ET AMON • 1961 • Kumel Harry • SHT • BLG
THAMARAI NENJAM • 1968 • Balachandar K. • IND • LOTUS HEART
THAMB LAXMI KUNKU LAVTE • 1967 • Dharamadhikari Datta • IND
THAMES, THE • 1948 • Stringer G. Henry • DOC • UKN
THAMPU • 1978 • Aravindan G. • IND • CIRCUS TENT, THE
THAN LE PECHEUR • 1957 • Schoendoerffer Pierre • SHT • FRN
THANASIS'S CRAZY WORLD see **PALAVOS KOSMOS TOU THANASI, O** • 1979
THANASSIS AND HIS BROTHERS see **THANASSIS KE T' ADHELFIA TOU, O** • 1971
THANASSIS AND THE DICTATOR see **DICTATOR KALI THANASSI** • 1973
THANASSIS IN THE LAND OF SLAPS see **THANASSIS STI HORA TIS SFALIARAS, O** • 1975
THANASSIS KE T' ADHELFIA TOU, O • 1971 • Vengos Thanasis • GRC • THANASSIS AND HIS BROTHERS
THANASSIS STI HORA TIS SFALIARAS, O • 1975 • Katsouridis Dinos, Glykofridis Panos • GRC • EVENTS HIT THANASSIS SMACK ON THE NOSE ○ THANASSIS IN THE LAND OF SLAPS
THANATOPSIS • 1962 • Emshwiller Ed • SHT • USA
THANATOS • 1986 • Gonzalez Christian • MXC
THANATOS TOU ALEXANDROU, O • 1967 • Kollatos Dimitris • GRC • DEATH OF ALEXANDER, THE ○ MORT D'ALEXANDRE, LA
THANGA THAMBI • 1967 • Ramnath-Francis • IND • YOUNGER SISTER AND BROTHER
THANGA VALAYAL • 1968 • Rajendran M. A. V. • IND • GOLDEN BANGLES
THANGAMALAI RAHASYAM • 1957 • Pantulu B. R. • IND • SECRET OF THE GOLDEN HILL
THANK EVANS • 1938 • Neill R. William • UKN
THANK GOD IT'S FRIDAY • 1978 • Klane Robert • USA
THANK GOD, OSMAN BEY see **ALLAH RAZI OLSUN OSMAN BEY** • 1967
THANK HEAVEN FOR SMALL FAVORS (USA) see **DROLE DE PAROISSIEN, UN** • 1963
THANK YOU • 1925 • Ford John • USA
THANK YOU ALL VERY MUCH see **TOUCH OF LOVE, A** • 1969
THANK YOU, AUNT (USA) see **GRAZIE, ZIA** • 1967
THANK YOU, JEEVES • 1936 • Collins Arthur G. • USA • THANK YOU, MR. JEEVES
THANK YOU JESUS FOR THE ETERNAL PRESENT 1 • 1973 • Landow George • USA
THANK YOU JESUS FOR THE ETERNAL PRESENT 2 • 1974 • Landow George • USA
THANK YOU, MADAME (USA) see **IM SONNENSCHEIN** • 1936
THANK YOU MASK MAN • 1968 • Hale Jeffrey • ANS • USA
THANK YOU, MR. JEEVES see **THANK YOU, JEEVES** • 1936
THANK YOU, MR. MOTO • 1937 • Foster Norman • USA
THANK YOU, SIRS see **DEKUJEME, PANOVE** • 1976
THANK YOUR LUCKY STARS • 1943 • Butler David • USA
THANK YOUR STARS (UKN) see **SHOOT THE WORKS** • 1934
THANKING THE AUDIENCE see **VUE DE REMERCIEMENTS AU PUBLIC** • 1900
THANKS A LOT • 1963 • Kaplan Howard S. • USA
THANKS A LOT • 1982 • Muller John • MTV • CND

THANKS A MILLION • 1935 • Del Ruth Roy • USA

THANKS AGAIN • 1931 • Sweet Harry • SHT • USA

THANKS, AUNT see **GRAZIE, ZIA** • 1967

THANKS BE TO LIFE see **GRACIAS A LA VIDA** • 1981

THANKS FOR EVERYTHING • 1938 • Seiter William A. • USA

THANKS FOR LISTENING • 1937 • Neilan Marshall • USA • PARTLY CONFIDENTIAL (UKN)

THANKS FOR THE BOAT RIDE • 1926 • Lamont Charles • SHT • USA

THANKS FOR THE BUGGY RIDE • 1928 • Seiter William A. • USA

THANKS FOR THE FIRE see **GRACIAS POR EL FUEGO** • 1984

THANKS FOR THE LOBSTER • 1914 • Van Wally • USA

THANKS FOR THE MEMORY • 1938 • Archainbaud George • USA

THANKS FOR THE MEMORY • 1938 • Fleischer Dave • ANS • USA

THANKS FOR THE RIDE • 1971 • Woods Grahame • CND

THANKS TO GOD AND THE REVOLUTION see **GRACIAS A DIOS Y LA REVOLUCION** • 1981

THANKSGIVING • 1912 • *Reliance* • USA

THANKSGIVING • 1975 • Wallace Ken • CND

THANKSGIVING PROMISE, THE • 1986 • Bridges Beau • TVM • USA • PROMISE MADE, A

THANKSGIVING SURPRISE, A • 1910 • *Thanhouser* • USA

THANOS AND DESPINA (USA) see **PATRES DU DESORDRE, LES** • 1968

THAR SHE BLOWS • 1969 • Kanter Richard • USA • THAR SHE GOES

THAR SHE GOES see **THAR SHE BLOWS** • 1969

THARK • 1932 • Walls Tom • UKN • THARK, THE HAUNTED HOUSE

THARK, THE HAUNTED HOUSE see **THARK** • 1932

THARTHARA ALA AN-NIL • 1971 • Kamal Hussein • EGY • PALABRES SUR LE NIL

THARUS FIGLIO DI ATTILA • 1962 • Montero Roberto Bianchi • ITL

THASSIOS, O see **THIASOS, O** • 1974

THAT ALL MAY LEARN • 1949 • Jiminez Carlos • MXC

THAT AWFUL BABY • 1905 • Collins Alf? • UKN

THAT AWFUL BROTHER • 1911 • Salter Harry • USA

THAT AWFUL CIGAR • 1902 • Smith G. A. • UKN

THAT AWFUL MAID • 1913 • *Crystal* • USA

THAT AWFUL PIPE • 1909 • Booth W. R. • UKN

THAT AWFUL PIPE • 1913 • Haldane Bert? • UKN

THAT BEDSIDE MANNER see **EMERGENCY WEDDING** • 1950

THAT BLESSED BABY • 1911 • *Nestor* • USA

THAT BOY FROM MISSOURI • 1913 • *Brunette Fritzie* • USA

THAT BOY FROM THE EAST • 1913 • *Eclair* • USA

THAT BOY FROM THE POORHOUSE • 1914 • O'Sullivan Tony • USA • BOY FROM THE POORHOUSE, THE

THAT BRENNAN GIRL • 1946 • Santell Alfred • USA

THAT BRIEF SUMMER see **KORTE SOMMER, DEN** • 1975

THAT BRUTE • 1915 • Murphy J. A. • USA

THAT BRUTE SIMMONS • 1928 • Croise Hugh • UKN • CAMERA COCKTALES

THAT BUSY BEE • 1904 • Collins Alf • UKN

THAT CAT see **AZ PRIJDE KOCOUR** • 1963

THAT CERTAIN AGE • 1938 • Ludwig Edward • USA

THAT CERTAIN FEELING • 1956 • Panama Norman, Frank Melvin • USA

THAT CERTAIN SOMETHING • 1941 • Badger Clarence • ASL

THAT CERTAIN SUMMER • 1972 • Johnson Lamont • TVM • USA

THAT CERTAIN THING • 1928 • Capra Frank • USA

THAT CERTAIN WOMAN • 1937 • Goulding Edmund • USA

THAT CHAMPIONSHIP SEASON • 1982 • Miller Jason • USA • CHAMPIONSHIP SEASON, THE

THAT CHICKEN DINNER • 1912 • *Lubin* • USA

THAT CHINESE LAUNDRY • 1913 • *Imp* • USA

THAT CHINK AT GOLDEN GULCH • 1910 • Griffith D. W. • USA

THAT CHRISTMAS see **TENKRAT O VANOCICH** • 1958

THAT CITY FELLER • 1911 • *Selig* • USA

THAT CODE see **O SIFRE** • 1967

THAT COLD DAY IN THE PARK • 1969 • Altman Robert • USA, CND

THAT COLLEGE LIFE • 1913 • Humphrey William • USA

THAT COUNTRY GAL • 1915 • Douglass James • USA

THAT CRAZY, CRAZY LOVE see **ESE LOCO AMOR LOCO** • 1978

THAT CROWD NEXT DOOR • 1981 • van der Meulen Karst • NTH

THAT CRYING BABY • 1913 • Smalley Phillips • USA

THAT CUCKOOVILLE HORSE RACE • 1914 • *Frontier* • USA

THAT CURSED HOUSE CLOSE TO THE MUSHROOM-BED • *Demick Irina* • ITL

THAT CZECH SONG OF OURS see **TA NASE PISNICKA CESKA** • 1967

THAT DAMNED HOT DAY OF FIRE see **QUEL CALDO MALEDETTO GIORNO DI FUOCO** • 1968

THAT DANGEROUS AGE • 1949 • Ratoff Gregory • UKN • IF THIS BE SIN (USA) ○ CASE OF LADY BROOKES, THE

THAT DARE DEVIL • 1911 • Sennett Mack • USA

THAT DARN CAT • 1965 • Stevenson Robert • USA

THAT DAWGONE DOG • 1917 • Smith Dick • SHT • USA

THAT DAY OF REST • 1948 • Fairbairn Kenneth • UKN

THAT DAY, ON THE BEACH see **HAI-T'AN-SHANG-TE YI T'IEN** • 1983

THAT DEVIL, BATEESE • 1918 • Wolbert William • USA

THAT DEVIL QUEMADO • 1925 • Andrews Del • USA

THAT DIRTY STORY OF THE WEST see **QUELLA SPORCA STORIA DEL WEST** • 1968

THAT DOG • 1913 • *Solar* • USA

THAT DOG GONE DOG • 1917 • *Strand* • USA

THAT DOGGONE BABY • 1916 • *Burns Neal* • USA

THAT DOGGONE DOG • 1910 • *Atlas* • USA

THAT DOGGONE SERENADE • 1915 • *Royal* • USA

THAT DREADFUL DONKEY • 1904 • Mottershaw Frank • UKN

THAT ENGLISHMAN • 1989 • De Villiers Dirk • SAF

THAT ETERNAL PING-PONG • 1902 • Stow Percy • UKN

THAT EXPENSIVE RIDE • 1912 • *Majestic* • USA

THAT FATAL SNEEZE • 1907 • Fitzhamon Lewin? • UKN

THAT FEMALE SCENT (UKN) see **PROFUMO DI DONNA** • 1974

THAT FINE DAY see **TISTEGA LEPEGA DNE** • 1963

THAT FORTSYTE WOMAN • 1949 • Bennett Compton • USA • FORTSYTE SAGA, THE (UKN)

THAT FRENCH LADY • 1924 • Mortimer Edmund • USA

THAT FUNNY FEELING • 1965 • Thorpe Richard • USA

THAT GAL OF BURKE'S • 1916 • Borzage Frank • SHT • USA • THAT GIRL OF BURKE'S

THAT GANG OF MINE • 1940 • Lewis Joseph H. • USA

THAT GIRL ELISA see **FILLE ELISA, LA** • 1956

THAT GIRL FROM BEVERLY HILLS see **TOTE VON BEVERLY HILLS, DIE** • 1964

THAT GIRL FROM COLLEGE (UKN) see **SORORITY HOUSE** • 1939

THAT GIRL FROM PARIS • 1936 • Jason Leigh • USA

THAT GIRL IN WHITE see **AQUELLA JOVEN DE BLANCO** • 1965

THAT GIRL IS A DISCOVERY see **FLICKAN AR ETT FYND** • 1943

THAT GIRL IS A TRAMP • Guy Jack • THAT LADY IS A TRAMP ○ LADY IS A TRAMP, THE ○ THIS GIRL IS A TRAMP

THAT GIRL IS A TRAMP • 1975 • Dietrich Erwin C. • SWT

THAT GIRL MONTANA • 1921 • Thornby Robert T. • USA

THAT GIRL OF BURKE'S see **THAT GAL OF BURKE'S** • 1916

THAT GIRL OF DIXON'S • 1910 • *Edison* • USA

THAT GIRL OKLAHOMA • 1926 • *Mix Ruth* • USA

THAT GOES DOUBLE • *Columbo Russ* • SHT • USA

THAT GOLF GAME • 1948 • *Comet Productions* • SHT • UKN

THAT GOSH-DARN MORTGAGE • 1926 • Cline Eddie • SHT • USA • GOSH-DARN MORTGAGE, THE

THAT GUY AND I see **AITSU TO WATASHI** • 1961

THAT HAGEN GIRL • 1947 • Godfrey Peter • USA

THAT HAMILTON WOMAN • 1941 • Korda Alexander • USA • LADY HAMILTON (UKN)

THAT HAPPY COUPLE see **ESA PAREJA FELIZ** • 1951

THAT HAPPY PAIR (USA) see **ESA PAREJA FELIZ** • 1951

THAT HEAVENLY COOK • 1915 • *Learn Bessie* • USA

THAT I MAY LIVE • 1937 • Dwan Allan • USA

THAT INFERIOR FEELING • 1940 • Wrangell Basil • SHT • USA

THAT INFERNAL MACHINE • 1914 • *Crystal* • USA

THAT IS CALLED DAWN see **CELA S'APPELLE L'AURORE** • 1955

THAT IS THE PORT LIGHT see **ARE GA MINATO NO HIKARI DA** • 1961

THAT JANE FROM MAINE see **IT HAPPENED TO JANE** • 1959

THAT JOYOUS EVE see **MAKKERS STAAKT UW WILD GERAAS** • 1960

THAT JUNE BUG • 1911 • *Solax* • USA

THAT KID FROM THE EAST • 1911 • *Nestor* • USA

THAT KILJUNEN FAMILY see **KILJUSEN HERRASVAKI** • 1982

THAT KIND OF ADVENTURE see **SONO YO NO BOKEN** • 1948

THAT KIND OF GIRL • 1963 • O'Hara Gerry • UKN • TEEN AGE TRAMP (USA) ○ TEENAGE TRAMP

THAT KIND OF GIRL (UKN) see **MODELS INC.** • 1952

THAT KIND OF LOVE see **TAKOVA LASKA** • 1959

THAT KIND OF WOMAN • 1959 • Lumet Sidney • USA

THAT LADY • 1955 • Young Terence • UKN

THAT LADY FROM PEKING • 1970 • Davis Eddie • ASL

THAT LADY IN ERMINE • 1948 • Lubitsch Ernst, Preminger Otto (U/c) • USA

THAT LADY IS A TRAMP see **THAT GIRL IS A TRAMP**

THAT LASS O' LOWRIE'S • 1915 • Leonard Robert Z. • USA

THAT LASS O' LOWRIE'S see **FLAME OF LIFE, THE** • 1923

THAT LASS OF CHANDLER'S • 1929 • Sargent W. J. • UKN

THAT LETTER FROM TEDDY • 1910 • *Defender* • USA

THAT LIFE MAY FLOURISH see **ABY KWILO ZYCIE** • 1962

THAT LITTLE BAND OF GOLD • 1915 • Arbuckle Roscoe • USA

THAT LITTLE BIG FELLOW • 1927 • Fleischer Dave • ANS • USA

THAT LITTLE DIFFERENCE see **QUELLA PICCOLA DIFFERENZA** • 1969

THAT LITTLE GERMAN BAND • 1910 • *Atlas* • USA

THAT LONELY WIDOW • 1916 • Millarde Harry • SHT • USA

THAT LONG NIGHT see **AQUELLA LARGA NOCHE** • 1979

THAT LOVE MIGHT LAST • 1921 • Paul Fred • UKN

THAT LOVING MAN • 1912 • *Eclair* • USA

THAT LUCKY STIFF • 1981 • Vincent Chuck • USA

THAT LUCKY TOUCH • 1975 • Miles Christopher • UKN • HEAVEN HELP US FROM OUR FRIENDS ○ WHO NEEDS FRIENDS

THAT MAD MR. JONES (UKN) see **FULLER BRUSH MAN, THE** • 1948

THAT MAIL ORDER SUIT • 1913 • *Selig* • USA

THAT MAN BOLT • 1973 • Levin Henry, Rich David Lowell • USA, HKG

THAT MAN FROM HONG KONG see **TRIBULATIONS D'UN CHINOIS EN CHINE, LES** • 1965

THAT MAN FROM RIO (USA) see **HOMME DE RIO, L'** • 1963

THAT MAN FROM TANGIER • 1953 • Elwyn Robert • USA

THAT MAN GEORGE (USA) see **HOMME DE MARRAKECH, L'** • 1966

THAT MAN IN ISTANBUL (USA) see **COLPO GROSSO A GALATA BRIDGE** • 1965

THAT MAN JACK • 1925 • Craft William James • USA

THAT MAN MR. IMPOSSIBLE • 1968 • Marquez Artemio • PHL

THAT MAN SAMSON • 1937 • Goodwins Leslie • SHT • USA

THAT MAN'S HERE AGAIN • 1937 • King Louis • USA

THAT MARVELLOUS GRAMOPHONE • 1909 • Fitzhamon Lewin • UKN

THAT MIDNIGHT KISS • 1949 • Taurog Norman • USA

THAT MINSTREL MAN • 1914 • Dillon Eddie • USA

THAT MODEL FROM PARIS • 1926 • Gasnier Louis J., Florey Robert (U/c) • USA • MODEL FROM PARIS

THAT MOTHERS MIGHT LIVE • 1938 • Zinnemann Fred • SHT • USA

THAT MOUSE • 1967 • Rubbo Michael • CND

THAT MUCH-DREADED HELL see **INFIERNO TAN TEMIDO, EL** • 1980

THAT MYSTERIOUS FEZ • 1914 • Plumb Hay? • UKN

THAT NASTY STICKY STUFF • 1908 • Mottershaw Frank • UKN

THAT NAUGHTY GIRL • 1903 • Collins Alf? • UKN

THAT NAUGHTY GIRL (USA) see **CETTE SACREE GAMINE** • 1955

THAT NAVY SPIRIT (UKN) see **HOLD 'EM NAVY** • 1937

THAT NAZTY NUISANCE • 1943 • Tryon Glenn • USA • NAZTY NUISANCE

THAT NIGHT • 1917 • Cline Eddie, Del Ruth Hampton • SHT • USA

THAT NIGHT • 1928 • Heath Arch B. • SHT • USA

THAT NIGHT • 1957 • Newland John • USA

THAT NIGHT ADVENTURE see **SONO YO NO BOKEN** • 1948

THAT NIGHT AT THE BALL see **ES WAR EINE RAUSCHENDE BALLNACHT** • 1939

THAT NIGHT IN LONDON • 1932 • Lee Rowland V. • UKN • OVERNIGHT (USA) ○ BRIGHT LIGHTS OF LONDON

THAT NIGHT IN RIO • 1941 • Cummings Irving • USA • ROAD TO RIO

THAT NIGHT WITH YOU • 1945 • Seiter William A. • USA • ONCE UPON A DREAM

THAT NIGHT'S WIFE see **SONO YO NO TSUMA** • 1930

THAT NO-GOOD CABMAN see **SOFOR PARCASI** • 1967

THAT NOISE • 1961 • Godfrey Bob • SHT • UKN

THAT OBSCURE OBJECT OF DESIRE (USA) see **CET OBSCUR OBJET DU DESIR** • 1977

THAT OL' GHOST TRAIN • 1942 • *Soundies* • SHT • USA

THAT OLD GANG OF MINE • 1925 • Tully May • USA

THAT OLD GANG OF MINE • 1931 • Fleischer Dave • ANS • USA

THAT OTHER GIRL • 1913 • Smalley Phillips • USA

THAT OTHER WOMAN • 1942 • McCarey Ray • USA

THAT OTHERS MAY LIVE see **ULICA GRANICZNA** • 1948

THAT PAIR FROM THESPIA • 1913 • *Carney Augustus* • USA

THAT PARTY IN PERSON • 1929 • Santley Joseph • SHT • USA

THAT PESKY PARROT • 1916 • Ellis Robert • SHT • USA

THAT POOR DAMP COW • 1915 • *Chamberlain Riley* • USA

THAT POOR GIRL see **PAVAPPETTAVAL** • 1967

THAT POPULAR TUNE • 1910 • *Essanay* • USA

THAT PRICKLY FEELING see **FASCINATION** • 1978

THAT QUIET NIGHT • 1920 • France Charles H. • SHT • USA

THAT RAG TIME BAND • 1913 • Sennett Mack • USA

THAT RASCAL • 1932 • Christie Al • USA

THAT REAL MAN • 1975 • Obreshkov O. • BUL

THAT RED-HEADED HUSSY • 1929 • Goulding Alf • USA

THAT RIVIERA TOUCH • 1966 • Owen Cliff • UKN

"THAT ROYLE GIRL" • 1925 • Griffith D. W. • USA • D. W. GRIFFITH'S "THAT ROYLE GIRL"

THAT SAME SUMMER see **RED SKY AT MORNING** • 1970

THAT SECRET SUNDAY • 1986 • Colla Richard A. • TVM • USA

THAT SHAMROCK TOUCH see **LUCK OF THE IRISH, THE** • 1948

THAT SHARP NOTE • 1913 • Dwan Allan • USA

THAT SHARP NOTE • 1916 • *Sheehan John* • SHT • USA

THAT SINKING FEELING • 1980 • Forsyth Bill • UKN

THAT SKATING CARNIVAL • 1910 • Stow Percy • UKN

THAT SOMETHING • 1921 • Wilson Margery?, Underwood Lawrence? • USA

THAT SON OF SHEIK • 1922 • Christie Al • USA

THAT SORT • 1916 • Brabin Charles J. • USA • THAT SORT OF GIRL (UKN)

THAT SORT OF GIRL (UKN) see **THAT SORT** • 1916

THAT SPLENDID NOVEMBER (USA) see **BELLISSIMO NOVEMBRE, UN** • 1968

THAT SPRING LOCK • 1914 • *Komic* • USA

THAT SPRINGTIME FEELING • 1915 • Henderson Dell • USA

THAT SUIT AT TEN • 1913 • Angeles Bert • USA

THAT SUMMER! • 1980 • Cokliss Harley • UKN • TORQUAY SUMMER

THAT SUMMER see **EKINO TO KALOKERI** • 1971

THAT SUMMER OF WHITE ROSES see **DAVOLJI RAJ** • 1989

THAT SWEET WORD "FREEDOM" see **ETO SLADKOE SLOVO-SVOBODA** • 1973

THAT SWINE INSPECTOR STERLING see **QUELLA CAROGNA DELL'ISPETTORE STERLING** • 1968

THAT TENDER AGE see **ADOLESCENTI, LE** • 1964

THAT TENDER TOUCH • 1969 • Vincent Russel • USA

THAT TENNESSEE BEAT • 1966 • Brill Richard • USA

THAT TERRIBLE BARBER'S BOY • 1904 • *Paul R. W.* • UKN

THAT TERRIBLE DOG • 1906 • Mottershaw Frank • UKN

THAT TERRIBLE KID • 1914 • Hotaling Arthur D. • USA

THAT TERRIBLE PEST • 1911 • Aylott Dave? • UKN

THAT TERRIBLE SNEEZE • 1904 • *Paul R. W.* • UKN

THAT TERRIBLE TENDERFOOT • 1917 • *Duncan Bud* • SHT • USA

THAT TEXAS JAMBOREE • 1946 • Nazarro Ray • USA • MEDICINE MAN (UKN)

THAT THEY MAY LIVE • 1942 • Cherry Evelyn Spice, Cherry Lawrence W. • DOC • CND

THAT THEY MAY LIVE (USA) see **J'ACCUSE** • 1937

THAT THING see **ONOVA NESHTO** • 1990

THAT TIME • Rozkopal Zdenek • SHT • PLN

THAT TIRED BUSINESS MAN • 1916 • *Myers Harry* • SHT • USA

THAT TO WILL PASS see **I TO CE PROCI** • 1985

THAT TOUCH OF MINK • 1962 • Mann Delbert • USA

THAT TROUBLESOME COLLAR • 1903 • Paul Robert William • UKN

THAT UNCERTAIN FEELING • 1941 • Lubitsch Ernst • USA

THAT UNCERTAIN FEELING see **ONLY TWO CAN PLAY** • 1962

THAT WAS MY LIFE see **DAS WAR MEIN LEBEN** • 1944

THAT WAS ROCK • 1984 • Binder Steve, Peerce Larry • ANT • USA

THAT WAS THEN.. THIS IS NOW • 1985 • Cain Christopher • USA

THAT WAY TO MADRA see **IK KOM WAT LATER TILL MADRA** • 1965

THAT WAY WITH WOMEN • 1947 • De Cordova Frederick • USA • VERY RICH MAN, A

THAT WHICH I SEE IN MY TELESCOPE see **CE QUE JE VOIS DANS MON TELESCOPE** • 1902

THAT WHICH IS CAESAR'S see **LO DEL CESAR** • 1987

THAT WILD WEST • 1924 • Neitz Alvin J. • USA

THAT WINSOME WINNIE SMILE • 1911 • *Mccoy Gertrude* • USA

THAT WOMAN • 1922 • Hoyt Harry O. • USA
THAT WOMAN see **ARU ONNA** • 1942
THAT WOMAN see **ARU ONNA** • 1954
THAT WOMAN DRIVES ME CRAZY see **KVINNAN GOR MEJ GALEN** • 1949
THAT WOMAN FROM OSAKA see **ARU OSAKA NO ONNA** • 1962
THAT WOMAN LAWYER see **WOMAN LAWYER, A** • 1910
THAT WOMAN OPPOSITE • 1957 • Bennett Compton • UKN • CITY AFTER MIDNIGHT (USA) ○ WOMAN OPPOSITE
THAT WOMAN (USA) see **BERLIN IST EINE SUNDE WELT** • 1966
THAT WONDERFUL GUY see **SUBARASHIKI DANSEI** • 1958
THAT WONDERFUL URGE • 1948 • Sinclair Robert B. • USA
THAT WONDERFUL WIFE • 1916 • *Rhodes Billie* • USA
THAT YOUTH MAY BE ETERNAL see **KONO WAKASA ARU KAGIRI** • 1961
THAT'LL BE THE DAY • 1973 • Whatham Claude • UKN
THAT'S A BAD GIRL see **WHY BE GOOD?** • 1929
THAT'S A DIRTY TRICK • 1970 • *Stacey Dist.* • USA
THAT'S A GOOD GIRL • 1933 • Buchanan Jack • UKN
THAT'S ADEQUATE • 1987 • Hurwitz Harry • USA
THAT'S ADULTERY see **CHO-CHIEN CH'U-SHIH** • 1976
THAT'S ALL AMERICAN • 1917 • Cabanne W. Christy • USA
THAT'S ALL THE LOVE THERE IS • 1989 • Vasilyev Anatoly • USS
THAT'S AN ORDER • 1955 • Irwin John • UKN
THAT'S CARRY ON • 1978 • Thomas Gerald • CMP • UKN
THAT'S DANCING • 1984 • Haley Jack Jr. • CMP • USA
THAT'S DONE IT • 1915 • Birch Cecil • UKN
THAT'S ENTERTAINMENT! • 1974 • Haley Jack Jr. • CMP • USA
THAT'S ENTERTAINMENT PART 2 • 1976 • Kelly Gene • CMP • USA • HOLLYWOOD! HOLLYWOOD!
THAT'S FAIR ENOUGH • 1914 • *Joker* • USA
THAT'S GOOD • 1919 • Franklin Harry L. • USA
THAT'S GRATITUDE • 1934 • Craven Frank • USA
THAT'S HAPPINESS • 1911 • *Thanhouser* • USA
THAT'S HIM • 1918 • Roach Hal • SHT • USA
THAT'S HIS STORY • 1950 • Barclay David • SHT • USA
THAT'S HIS WEAKNESS • 1930 • Argyle John F. • UKN
THAT'S HOW THE COOKIE CRUMBLES see **ZIVI BILI PA VIDJELI** • 1980
THAT'S HOW THEY LOVE IN JALISCO see **ASI SE QUIERE EN JALISCO** • 1942
THAT'S JAZZ • 1973 • Timmins Leslie • SHT • UKN
THAT'S JAZZ see **BYL JAZZ** • 1983
THAT'S LIFE! • 1986 • Edwards Blake • USA
THAT'S LIFE see **TAKOVY JE ZIVOT** • 1929
THAT'S LIFE see **OTO ZIVOT** • 1969
THAT'S MY BABY • 1926 • Beaudine William • USA
THAT'S MY BABY • 1944 • Berke William • USA
THAT'S MY BABY! • 1985 • Yolles Edie, Bradshaw John R. • CND
THAT'S MY BABY! see **TO DOROTHY, A SON** • 1954
THAT'S MY BOY • 1932 • Neill R. William • USA
THAT'S MY BOY • 1951 • Walker Hal • USA
THAT'S MY DADDY • 1928 • Newmeyer Fred • USA
THAT'S MY GAL • 1947 • Blair George • USA
THAT'S MY MAN • 1947 • Borzage Frank • USA • WILL TOMORROW EVER COME? (UKN) ○ GALLANT MAN
THAT'S MY MOMMY • 1955 • Hanna William, Barbera Joseph • ANS • USA
THAT'S MY PUP • 1953 • Hanna William, Barbera Joseph • ANS • USA
THAT'S MY STORY • 1937 • Salkow Sidney • USA
THAT'S MY UNCLE • 1935 • Pearson George • UKN • IRON WOMAN, THE
THAT'S MY WEAKNESS NOW • 1929 • Aylott Dave, Symmons E. F. • SHT • UKN
THAT'S MY WIFE • 1929 • French Lloyd • SHT • USA
THAT'S MY WIFE • 1933 • Hiscott Leslie • UKN
THAT'S NOT RIGHT -WATCH ME! • 1907 • Stow Percy • UKN
THAT'S RIGHT -YOU'RE WRONG • 1939 • Butler David • USA
THAT'S SHOWBIZ • 1973 • Noyce Phil • SHT • ASL
THAT'S THAT • 1923 • Thorpe Richard • SHT • USA
THAT'S THAT • 1928 • Corby Francis • SHT • USA
THAT'S THE PRICE • 1972 • Scott Michael • CND
THAT'S THE SPIRIT • 1924 • Watson William • SHT • USA
THAT'S THE SPIRIT • 1933 • Mack Roy • SHT • USA
THAT'S THE SPIRIT • 1945 • Lamont Charles • USA
THAT'S THE TICKET • 1940 • Davis Redd • UKN
THAT'S THE WAY OF THE WORLD • 1975 • Shore Sig • USA • SHINING STAR
THAT'S THE WAY THE COOKIE CRUMBLES see **ZIVI BILI PA VIDJELI** • 1980
THAT'S TORN IT! • 1914 • Stow Percy • UKN
THAT'S WHAT FRIENDS ARE FOR see **MARSEILLE CONTRACT, THE** • 1974
THAT'S WHAT PUT THE SWEET IN HOME SWEET HOME • 1929 • Aylott Dave, Symmons E. F. • SHT • UKN
THAT'S WHAT WE'RE HERE FOR? • 1976 • Leiterman Richard?, Kaczender Georges? • DOC • CND
THAT'S WHAT YOU THINK • 1951 • Barclay David • SHT • USA
THAT'S WHERE THE ACTION IS • 1965 • De Antonio Emile • MTV • USA
THAT'S WHY see **TIM PADEM** • 1980
THAT'S WHY I LEFT YOU • 1943 • Cahn Edward L. • SHT • USA
THAT'S YOUR FUNERAL • 1972 • Robins John • UKN
THAUMATOPOEA • 1960 • Enrico Robert • FRN
THAUMATURGE CHINOIS, LE • 1904 • Melies Georges • FRN • TCHIN-CHAO, THE CHINESE CONJURER (USA)
THAUR, ROI DE LA FORCE BRUTALE see **TAUR, IL RE DELLA FORZA BRUTA** • 1963
THAW • NKR
THAW (UKN) see **LEDOLOM** • 1931
THAWATH DAVASAK • 1970 • Jayatilaka Amarnath • SHT • SLN
THAWRA AL SHEIKH SALEH AL ALI • 1985 • Suleiman Isam • DOC • SYR • REVOLT OF SHEIK SALEH AL ALI, THE
THAWRAT AL-YAMAN • 1966 • Salem Atef • EGY • REVOLUTION DU YEMEN, LA
THE, LE • 1958 • Shawqi Khalil • SHT • EGY
THE A LA MENTHE, LE • 1984 • Bahloul Bahloul • FRN
THE ANGRY GUN see **PISTOLA PER RINGO, UNA** • 1965
THE ANNA • 1983 • van Zuylen Erik • NTH
THE AU HAREM D'ARCHIMEDE, LE • 1984 • Charef Mehdi • FRN • TEA IN THE HAREM (USA)
THE CHEZ LA CONCIERGE, LE • 1907 • Feuillade Louis • FRN
THE SPIDERS NO DAISODO • 1968 • Morinaga Kenjiro • JPN • HERE COME THE SPIDERS
THE SPIDERS NO GOGO MUKOUMIZUSAKUSEN • 1967 • Saito Buichi • JPN • RECKLESS TACTICS OF THE SPIDERS
THE VISCOUNT, FURTO ALLA BANCA MONDIALE (ITL) see **VICOMTE REGLE SES COMPTES, LE** • 1967
THEA ROLAND (UKN) see **ABENTEUER DER THEA ROLAND, DAS** • 1932
THEATER IN TRANCE • 1981 • Fassbinder R. W. • DOC • FRG
THEATERBESUCH, DER • 1934 • Valentin Karl • FRG
THEATERNACHTE VON BERLIN • 1932 • Wolff Willi • FRG
THEATERPRINZ, DER • 1917 • Hofer Franz • FRG
THEATRE see **SHIBAIDO** • 1944
THEATRE DE M. ET MME. KABAL, LE • 1965 • Borowczyk Walerian • ANM • FRN • CONCERT OF MONSIEUR AND MADAME KABAL, THE ○ CONCERT OF MR. AND MRS. KABAL
THEATRE DES MATIERES, LE • 1977 • Biette Jean-Claude • FRN
THEATRE DU PETIT BOB, LE • 1904 • Velle Gaston • FRN
THEATRE GIRLS • 1979 • Longinotto Kim, Pollack Claire • DOC • UKN
THEATRE NATIONAL POPULAIRE, LE • 1956 • Franju Georges • DCS • FRN • T.N.P., LE
THEATRE OF BLOOD • 1973 • Hickox Douglas • UKN • MUCH ADO ABOUT MURDER
THEATRE OF DEATH • 1967 • Gallu Samuel • UKN • BLOOD FIEND
THEATRE OF LIFE see **JINSEI GEKIJO** • 1936
THEATRE OF LIFE see **JINSEI GEKIJO** • 1952
THEATRE OF LIFE see **JINSEI GEKIJO SEISHUN-HEN** • 1958
THEATRE ROYAL • 1943 • Baxter John • UKN
THEATRE ROYAL see **ROYAL FAMILY OF BROADWAY, THE** • 1930
THEATRE TROUPE KAGERO see **KAGERO-ZA** • 1982
THEATRES EROTIQUES DE PARIS, LES • Hugues Robert • FRN
THEATRICAL CHIMNEY SWEEP, THE see **DUPED OTHELLO, THE** • 1909
THEE AND ME • 1948 • Bishop Terry • DOC • UKN
THEE I LOVE see **FRIENDLY PERSUASION** • 1956
THEFT • 1897 • *Paul R. W.* • UKN
THEFT IN THE DARK, A • 1915 • Brabin Charles J. • USA
THEFT OF THE CROWN JEWELS, THE • 1914 • Buel Kenean • USA
THEFT OF THE MONA LISA, THE (USA) see **RAUB DER MONA LISA, DER** • 1931
THEFT OF THE MUMMIES OF GUANAJUATO, THE see **ROBO DE LAS MOMIAS DE GUANAJUATO, EL** • 1972
THEFT OF THE SECRET CODE, THE • 1913 • *Vitascope* • USA
THEIR ACT • 1916 • Ferguson Edward • SHT • USA
THEIR AFTERNOON OFF • 1911 • *Nestor* • USA
THEIR AGE see **IKALUOKKA** • 1976
THEIR AGREEMENT • 1915 • Drew Sidney • USA
THEIR ANNIVERSARY • 1916 • Wilson Ben • SHT • USA
THEIR ANNIVERSARY FEAST • 1918 • Baker Graham • SHT • USA
THEIR AWFUL PREDICAMENT • 1916 • *Lyons Eddie* • USA
THEIR BABY • 1913 • *Essanay* • USA
THEIR BABY • 1919 • *Depp Harry* • SHT • USA
THEIR BEST FRIEND • 1914 • *Snow Marguerite* • USA
THEIR BEWITCHED ELOPEMENT • 1915 • Curtis Allen • USA
THEIR BIG MOMENT • 1934 • Cruze James • USA • AFTERWARDS (UKN)
THEIR BREAKFAST MEANT LEAD • 1972 • Nagy Ivan • USA • PUSHING UP DAISIES
THEIR BREEZY AFFAIR • 1918 • *Mason Billy* • USA
THEIR BURGLAR • 1911 • *Benham Harry* • USA
THEIR BURGLAR • 1917 • Drew Sidney, Drew Sidney Mrs. • SHT • USA
THEIR CHAPERONE HONEYMOON • 1910 • *Lubin* • USA
THEIR CHARMING MAMA • 1911 • Thompson Frederick A. • USA
THEIR CHEAP VACATION • 1914 • *Beery Wallace* • USA
THEIR CHILD • 1910 • *Thanhouser* • USA
THEIR CHILDREN'S APPROVAL • 1912 • *Francis Alec B.* • USA
THEIR CHRISTMAS TURKEY • 1912 • *Powers* • USA
THEIR COLLEGE CAPERS • 1916 • *Ham Harry* • SHT • USA
THEIR COMBINATION SUIT • 1913 • *Nestor* • USA
THEIR COMPACT • 1917 • Carewe Edwin • USA
THEIR COUNTERFEIT VACATION • 1916 • Walsh James O. • SHT • USA
THEIR COUSIN FROM ENGLAND • 1914 • *Thanhouser* • USA
THEIR DARK SECRET • 1916 • Beaudine William • SHT • USA
THEIR DAY OF REST • 1919 • Seiter William A. • SHT • USA
THEIR DAY OF THANKS • 1910 • *Imp* • USA
THEIR DELAYED HONEYMOON • 1915 • *Ideal* • USA
THEIR DIVORCE • 1916 • Drew Sidney • SHT • USA
THEIR DIVORCE FUND • 1915 • Physioc Wray • USA
THEIR DOMESTIC DECEPTION • 1917 • *St. Clair Malcolm* • USA
THEIR DREAM HOUSE • 1916 • *Myers Harry* • SHT • USA
THEIR EVERYDAY LIFE see **ICH DZIEN POWSZEDNI** • 1963
THEIR FATAL BUMPING • 1914 • Parrott Charles • USA
THEIR FATES SEALED • 1911 • Sennett Mack • USA
THEIR FIRST • 1916 • Drew Sidney • SHT • USA
THEIR FIRST ACQUAINTANCE • 1914 • Crisp Donald?, O'Brien Jack? • USA
THEIR FIRST ANNIVERSARY • 1914 • *Joker* • USA
THEIR FIRST ARREST • 1916 • Beaudine William • SHT • USA
THEIR FIRST BABY • 1911 • *Solax* • USA
THEIR FIRST BABY • 1913 • *Rice Herbert* • USA
THEIR FIRST CIGAR • 1907 • Green Tom? • UKN
THEIR FIRST DIVORCE CASE • 1911 • Sennett Mack • USA
THEIR FIRST EXECUTION • 1913 • Sennett Mack • USA
THEIR FIRST KIDNAPPING CASE • 1912 • Sennett Mack • USA
THEIR FIRST LOVE • 1918 • *Drew Sidney* • USA
THEIR FIRST MISTAKE • 1932 • Marshall George • SHT • USA
THEIR FIRST MISUNDERSTANDING • 1911 • Ince Thomas H., Tucker George Loane • USA
THEIR FIRST QUARREL • 1914 • *Melies* • USA
THEIR FIRST QUARREL • 1915 • Drew Sidney • USA
THEIR FIRST SNOWBALLS • 1907 • *Urban Trading Co* • UKN
THEIR FIRST TINTYPE • 1920 • Jamieson Bud • SHT • USA
THEIR FIRST TRIP TO TOKYO see **TOKYO MONOGATARI** • 1953
THEIR FIRST VACATION • 1922 • St. Clair Malcolm • SHT • USA
THEIR FRIEND, THE BURGLAR • 1915 • Christie Al • USA
THEIR FRONTIER WIVES • 1916 • *Utah* • USA
THEIR GODSON • 1918 • Baker Graham • SHT • USA
THEIR GOLDEN ANNIVERSARY • 1912 • *Brooke Van Dyke* • USA
THEIR GOLDEN WEDDING • 1914 • *Thompson David* • USA
THEIR GOLDEN WEDDING see **GOLDEN WEDDING, THE** • 1915
THEIR GOLDEN YEARS see **SUS ANOS DORADOS** • 1980
THEIR GREAT BIG BEAUTIFUL DOLL • 1913 • *Thanhouser Twins* • USA
THEIR HAPPY HONEYMOON • 1915 • Christie Al • USA
THEIR HAPPY LITTLE HOME • 1915 • France Charles H. • USA
THEIR HERO • 1912 • *Lessey George* • USA
THEIR HERO SON • 1912 • Dwan Allan • USA
THEIR HOBO HERO • 1915 • *Eclair* • USA
THEIR HONEYMOON • 1914 • *Nestor* • USA
THEIR HONEYMOON • 1916 • *Hardy Babe* • SHT • USA
THEIR HOUR • 1915 • *Madison Cleo* • USA
THEIR HOUR • 1928 • Raboch Alfred • USA
THEIR HUSBAND • 1917 • *Triangle* • USA
THEIR HUSBANDS • 1913 • Lehrman Henry • USA
THEIR IDOLS • 1912 • Henderson Dell • USA
THEIR INDIAN FRIEND • 1916 • *Rancho* • USA
THEIR INDIAN UNCLE • 1918 • *Triangle* • USA
THEIR INITIATIONS • 1915 • *Superba* • USA
THEIR INSTALLMENT FURNITURE • 1916 • *Myers Harry* • USA
THEIR INTEREST IN COMMON • 1914 • Sturgeon Rollin S. • USA
THEIR ISLAND OF HAPPINESS • 1915 • *Maison Edna* • USA
THEIR KINGDOM • 1928 • Kalatozov Mikhail • DOC • USS
THEIR LAST BEAN • 1939 • Donnelly Eddie • ANS • USA
THEIR LAST CHANCE • 1911 • *Selig* • USA
THEIR LAST HAUL • 1915 • Blystone John G. • USA
THEIR LAST NIGHT (USA) see **LEUR DERNIERE NUIT** • 1953
THEIR LAST PERFORMANCE • 1916 • *Cooke Ethyle* • SHT • USA
THEIR LEGACY see **KATEI NO JIJYO** • 1962
THEIR LESSON • 1914 • *Selig* • USA
THEIR LITTLE DRUDGE • 1914 • Morrisey Edward • USA
THEIR LITTLE KID • 1918 • *Rhodes Billie* • SHT • USA
THEIR LITTLE ONES • 1914 • *Joker* • USA
THEIR LORDSHIPS DO-RE-ME see **LAXMANA DO-RE-ME** • 1971
THEIR LOVE LESSON • 1917 • *Triangle* • USA
THEIR LUCKY DAY • 1913 • *Nestor* • USA
THEIR MAD MOMENT • 1931 • MacFadden Hamilton, Sprague Chandler • USA
THEIR MASTERPIECE • 1913 • Dwan Allan • USA
THEIR MODEL CAREERS • 1917 • *Stull Walter* • USA
THEIR MOTHER • 1916 • Kent Leon D. • SHT • USA
THEIR MOTHERS-IN-LAW • 1911 • *Lubin* • USA
THEIR MUTUAL CHILD • 1920 • Cox George L. • USA
THEIR MUTUAL FRIEND • 1913 • *Powers* • USA
THEIR MUTUAL FRIEND • 1913 • Thompson Frederick A. • *Vitagraph* • USA
THEIR MUTUAL MISTAKE • 1919 • *Supreme Comedy* • USA
THEIR MUTUAL MOTOR • 1918 • Drew Sidney, Drew Sidney Mrs. • SHT • USA
THEIR NEIGHBOR'S BABY • 1918 • *Ridgeway Fritzi* • USA
THEIR NEW LODGER • 1914 • *Crystal* • USA
THEIR NEW MINISTER • 1911 • *Nestor* • USA
THEIR NIGHT OUT • 1933 • Hughes Harry • UKN • HIS NIGHT OUT
THEIR NOBLE RELATION • 1916 • *Jockey* • USA
THEIR ONE DAY'S WORK • 1912 • *Powers* • USA
THEIR ONE GOOD SUIT • 1913 • Henderson Dell • USA
THEIR ONE LOVE • 1915 • *Fairbanks Madeline* • USA
THEIR ONLY SON • 1911 • *Garcia Al E.* • USA
THEIR ONLY SON • 1914 • Haldane Bert? • UKN
THEIR ONLY SON • 1916 • *Alexander Gus* • SHT • USA
THEIR OWN DESIRE • 1929 • Hopper E. Mason • USA
THEIR OWN WAYS • 1915 • Seay Charles M. • USA
THEIR OWN WORLD see **NANIWA NO KOI NO MONOGATARI** • 1959
THEIR PARENTS • 1913 • Tucker George Loane • USA
THEIR PARENTS' KIDS • 1914 • *Crystal* • USA
THEIR PICNIC • 1914 • *Crystal* • USA
THEIR PROMISE • 1913 • *Essanay* • USA
THEIR PURPLE MOMENT • 1928 • Parrott James • SHT • USA
THEIR QUIET HONEYMOON • 1915 • Christie Al • USA
THEIR QUIET LITTLE HONEYMOON • 1916 • *Drew* • SHT • USA
THEIR SEA VOYAGE • 1910 • *Essanay* • USA
THEIR SEASIDE TANGLE • 1917 • Christie Al • SHT • USA
THEIR SECRET • 1915 • Dowlan William C. • USA
THEIR SECRET AFFAIR (UKN) see **TOP SECRET AFFAIR** • 1956
THEIR SINFUL INFLUENCE • 1915 • Carleton Lloyd B. • USA
THEIR SOCIAL EDUCATION • 1909 • *Edison* • USA
THEIR SOCIAL SMASH • 1916 • Wulze Harry • SHT • USA
THEIR SOCIAL SPLASH • 1915 • Gillstrom Arvid E., Avery Charles • USA
THEIR SOLDIER BOY • 1914 • O'Sullivan Tony • USA
THEIR SPORTING BLOOD • 1918 • Dillon Robert A. • SHT • USA
THEIR STEPMOTHER • 1913 • Martin E. A. • USA
THEIR STRAYING FEET • 1917 • *Triangle* • USA
THEIR TAKING WAYS • 1916 • Beaudine William • SHT • USA
THEIR TWO KIDS • 1913 • *Nestor* • USA
THEIR UNDERCOVER CAPERS • 1918 • *Triangle* • USA

THEIR UPS AND DOWNS • 1914 • *Keystone* • USA
THEIR UPS AND DOWNS • 1914 • *Nestor* • USA
THEIR VACATION • 1914 • *Cunard Grace* • USA
THEIR VACATION • 1916 • *Plump & Runt* • USA
THEIR VILLAGE FRIEND • 1915 • Morgan George • USA
THEIR WATERLOO • 1913 • *Watson Minor* • USA
THEIR WEAK MOMENTS • 1917 • *Triangle* • USA
THEIR WEDDING DAY • 1916 • *Pokes & Jabbs* • USA
THEIR WEDDING GIFTS • 1911 • *Essanay* • USA
THEIR WEEK END • 1916 • Walsh James O. • USA
THEIR WIVES' INDISCRETION • 1913 • *Essanay* • USA
THEIR WIVES' VACATION • 1930 • Roberts Stephen • SHT • USA
THEIR WORDLY GOODS • 1914 • Ayres Sydney • USA
THEIRS IS THE GLORY • 1945 • Hurst Brian Desmond • DOC • UKN
THELEMA ABBEY • 1955 • Anger Kenneth • SHT • UKN
THELMA • 1910 • Marston Theodore • USA
THELMA • 1911 • *Selig* • USA
THELMA • 1912 • *Weeks Alice* • USA
THELMA • 1918 • Coleby A. E., Rooke Arthur • UKN
THELMA • 1922 • Bennett Chester • USA
THELMA JORDON • 1949 • Siodmak Robert • USA • FILE ON THELMA JORDON, THE (UKN)
THELMA: OR, SAVED FROM THE SEA • 1914 • Brett B. Harold • UKN
THELONIUS MONK: STRAIGHT, NO CHASER • 1989 • Zwerin Charlotte • DOC • USA
THEM! • 1954 • Douglas Gordon • USA
THEM see **ILS..** • 1970
THEM EYES • 1919 • Wilson Ben • SHT • USA
THEM NICE AMERICANS • 1958 • Young Tony • UKN
THEM OL' LETTERS • 1914 • *Powers* • USA
THEM THAR HILLS • 1934 • Rogers Charles • SHT • USA
THEM WAS THE GOOD OLD DAYS • 1916 • Williams C. Jay • SHT • USA
THEM WAS THE HAPPY DAYS! • 1916 • Roach Hal • SHT • USA
THEMA AMORE • 1961 • Kluge Alexander • SHT • FRG
THEMA SINIDHISEOS • 1972 • Lykas Petros • GRC • MATTER OF CONSCIENCE, A
THEME see **TEMA** • 1979
THEME AND TRANSITION • 1966 • D'Avino Carmen • SHT • USA
THEME ET VARIATIONS • 1928 • Dulac Germaine • FRN
THEME FOR A SHORT STORY see **SYUZHET DLYA NEBOLSHOVO RASKAZA** • 1968
THEMES D'INSPIRATION • 1938 • Dekeukeleire Charles • BLG
THEMIS • 1920 • *National-Film* • FRG
THEMIS • 1940 • Grant Dwinnel • SHT • USA
THEMROC • 1972 • Faraldo Claude • FRN
THEM'S THE BREAKS • 1982 • Read Melanie • NZL
THEN CAME BRONSON • 1969 • Graham William A. • TVM • USA
THEN CAME THE LEGEND see **LEGENDA** • 1968
THEN CAME THE PAWN • 1930 • Buzzell Edward • SHT • USA
THEN CAME THE WOMAN • 1926 • Hartford David M. • USA
THEN HE DID LAUGH, BUT – • 1912 • Wilson Frank? • UKN
THEN HE JUGGLED • 1913 • Wilson Frank? • UKN
THEN I'LL COME BACK TO YOU • 1916 • Irving George • USA
THEN THE FIRES STARTED see **UZAVRELI GRAD** • 1961
THEN THE ICEMAN CAME • 1915 • *Pathe Exhange* • USA
THEN THERE WERE THREE • 1961 • Nicol Alex • USA, ITL • THREE CAME BACK
THEN YOU'LL REMEMBER ME • 1911 • *Booth Sydney* • USA
THEN YOU'LL REMEMBER ME • 1918 • Waltyre Edward • UKN
THENARDIER, LES • 1933 • Bernard Raymond • FRN
THEO AGAINST THE REST OF THE WORLD see **THEO GEGEN DEN REST DER WELT** • 1980
THEO GEGEN DEN REST DER WELT • 1980 • Bringmann Peter F. • FRG • THEO AGAINST THE REST OF THE WORLD
THEO & THEA • 1989 • Kramer Pieter • NTH
THEO & THEO AND THE SEVEN DWARFS see **THEO & THEO EN DE ONTMASKERING VAN HET TENENKAAS IMPERIUM** • 1990
THEO & THEO EN DE ONTMASKERING VAN HET TENENKAAS IMPERIUM • 1990 • Kramer Pieter • NTH • THEO & THEO AND THE SEVEN DWARFS
THEODOR HIERNEIS ODER: WIE MAN EHEM. HOFKOCH WIRD • 1972 • Syberberg Hans-Jurgen • FRG • LUDWIG'S COOK
THEODOR IM FUSSBALLTOR, DER • 1950 • Emo E. W. • FRG
THEODOR KORNER • 1912 • Porten Franz • FRG
THEODOR KORNER • 1932 • Boese Carl • FRG
THEODOR PISTEK • 1958 • Fric Martin • CZC
THEODORA • 1921 • Ambrosio Arturo • ITL
THEODORA see **TEODORA** • 1919
THEODORA GOES WILD • 1936 • Boleslawski Richard • USA
THEODORA, QUEEN OF BYZANTIUM see **TEODORA, L'IMPERATRICE DI BISANZIO** • 1954
THEODORA, SLAVE EMPRESS (USA) see **TEODORA, L'IMPERATRICE DI BISANZIO** • 1954
THEODORE EST FATIGUE see **SERVICE DE NUIT** • 1931
THEODORE ET CIE • 1933 • Colombier Pierre • FRN
THEODORE, IMPERATRICE BYZANTINE see **TEODORA, L'IMPERATRICE DI BISANZIO** • 1954
THEODORE, IMPERATRICE DE BYZANCE (FRN) see **TEODORA, L'IMPERATRICE DI BISANZIO** • 1954
THEODORE'S TERRIBLE THIRST • 1916 • *Chamberlin Riley* • USA
THEOFILIS • 1988 • *Katalifos Dimitris* • GRC
THEOLOGY AND JAZZ • 1960 • Kiley Tim • SHT • USA
THEOPHRASTUS PARACELSUS • 1916 • Delmont Joseph • FRG • EWIGE LEBEN, DAS
THEOREM OF PYTHAGORAS, THE • 1935 • Salt Brian • UKN
THEOREM (UKN) see **TEOREMA** • 1968
THER THIRUVIZHU • 1968 • Thirumugam M. A. • IND • JOURNEY OF THE CHARIOT
THERE AIN'T NO JUSTICE • 1934 • Horne James W. • SHT • USA
THERE AIN'T NO JUSTICE • 1939 • Tennyson Pen • UKN
THERE AIN'T NO SANTA CLAUS • 1926 • Roach Hal • SHT • USA
THERE AND BACK • 1916 • Semon Larry • SHT • USA
THERE AND BACK • 1917 • *Ovey George* • USA
THERE AND BACK • 1918 • *Sedgwick Edward* • SHT • USA
THERE AND BACK FOR NOTHING? see **FREM OG TILBAKE ER LIKE LANGT?** • 1973
THERE ARE ALSO PEOPLE see **TOZHE LYUDI** • 1960
THERE ARE DEAD THAT ARE SILENT see **HAY MUERTOS QUE NO HACEN RUIDO** • 1946
THERE ARE GIRLS WANTED HERE • 1913 • Stow Percy • UKN
THERE ARE MORE THINGS IN HEAVEN AND EARTH see **DINGE GIBT'S DIE GIBT'S GAR NICHT** • 1966
THERE ARE MOUNTAINS AND RIVERS see **SANGA-ARI** • 1962
THERE ARE NO CROSSES IN THE SEA see **NO HAY CRUCES EN EL MAR** • 1968
THERE ARE NO GODS ON EARTH see **DET FINNS INGA GUDAR PA JORDEN** • 1917
THERE ARE NO STARS IN THE JUNGLE see **EN LA SELVA NO HAY ESTRELLAS** • 1968
THERE ARE NO VILLAINS • 1921 • Veiller Bayard • USA
THERE ARE PEOPLE EVERYWHERE see **VSUDE ZIJI LIDE** • 1960
THERE ARE STONES –WHICH DON'T EXIST see **STEINE GIBT'S –DIE GIBT'S GAR NICHT** • 1968
THERE AT THE BIG RANCH see **ALLA EN EL RANCHO GRANDE** • 1936
THERE AUTO BE A LAW • 1953 • McKimson Robert • ANS • USA
THERE BURNED A FLAME see **DET BRINNER EN ELD** • 1943
THERE CAME A SOLDIER FROM THE FRONT see **PRISHOL SOLDAT S FRONTA** • 1972
THERE CAME THE DAY see **I DOYDE DENYAT** • 1974
THERE FELL A FLOWER • 1911 • *Eclair* • USA
THERE GOES BARDER (USA) see **CA VA BARDER** • 1954
THERE GOES KELLY • 1945 • Karlson Phil • USA
THERE GOES MY GIRL • 1937 • Holmes Ben • USA
THERE GOES MY HEART • 1938 • McLeod Norman Z. • USA
THERE GOES SUSIE • 1934 • Stafford John, Hanbury Victor • UKN • SCANDALS OF PARIS (USA)
THERE GOES THE BRIDE • 1918 • Clements Roy • SHT • USA
THERE GOES THE BRIDE • 1925 • Roach Hal • SHT • USA
THERE GOES THE BRIDE • 1932 • De Courville Albert • UKN
THERE GOES THE BRIDE • 1980 • Marcel Terry • UKN
THERE GOES THE GROOM • 1919 • *Vernon Bobby* • USA
THERE GOES THE GROOM • 1937 • Santley Joseph • USA • DON'T FORGET TO REMEMBER
THERE GROWS A GREEN PINE IN THE WOODS see **U GORI RASTE ZELEN BOR** • 1972
THERE HE GOES • 1925 • *Sennett Mack (P)* • SHT • USA
THERE HE GOES see **SPORTING YOUTH** • 1924
THERE IN THE SUGARMILL • Martinez Gabriel • CLM
THERE IS A DESTINY • 1914 • *Kerrigan J. Warren* • USA
THERE IS A FATHER see **CHICHI ARIKI** • 1942
THERE IS A GREEN HILL FAR AWAY • 1906 • Gilbert Arthur • UKN
THERE IS A NAME FOR EVIL see **NAME FOR EVIL, A** • 1970
THERE IS A SEASON • 1954 • Van Dyke Willard • DOC • USA
THERE IS ALWAYS ANOTHER • 1907 • *Walturdaw* • UKN
THERE IS ANOTHER SUN • 1950 • Gilbert Lewis* • UKN • WALL OF DEATH (USA)
THERE IS NO CROSSING UNDER FIRE see **V OGNYE BRODA NYET** • 1968
THERE IS NO DEATH see **SMART NYAMA** • 1963
THERE IS NO DEATH, BOYS! • 1970 • Mansurov Bulat • USS
THERE IS NO FORGETTING see **IL N'Y PAS D'OUBLI** • 1975
THERE IS NO OTHER WAY see **NIET INEJ CESTY** • 1968
THERE IS NO PLACE LIKE HOME • 1916 • Weber Lois • SHT • USA
THERE IS NO THIRTEEN • 1977 • Sachs William • USA
THERE IS NOTHING FINER THAT BAD WEATHER • 1971 • Andonov Metodi • BUL
THERE IS SKY EVERYWHERE see **VSYUDU YEST NYEBO** • 1968
THERE IS STILL ROOM IN HELL (USA) see **IN DER HOLLE IST NOCH PLATZ** • 1961
THERE IS THE DETAIL see **AHI ESTA EL DETALLE** • 1940
THERE, LITTLE GIRL, DON'T CRY • 1910 • *Selig* • USA
THERE LIVED A BOY • 1959 • Lotyanu Emil • SHT • USS • THERE WAS A BOY
THERE LIVED A THRUSH see **ZIL PEVCIJ DROZD** • 1972
THERE LIVED AN OLD MAN AND AN OLD WOMAN see **ZHILI-BILI STARIK SO STARUKHOI** • 1965
THERE MUST BE A PONY • 1986 • Sargent Joseph • TVM • USA
THERE ONCE LIVED A KING • 1954 • Zeman Borivoj • CZC • ONCE UPON A TIME THERE WAS A KING
THERE ONCE WAS A WOMAN see **REVENGE** • 1971
THERE SERVED TWO COMRADES see **SLUZHILI DVA TOVARISHCHA** • 1968
THERE SHE GOES • 1913 • *Pates Gwendolyn* • USA
THERE THEY GO-GO-GO! • 1956 • Jones Charles M. • ANS • USA
THERE TOO GO I • 1942 • Sparling Gordon • CND
THERE WAS A BOY see **THERE LIVED A BOY** • 1959
THERE WAS A CROOKED MAN • 1960 • Burge Stuart • UKN
THERE WAS A CROOKED MAN.. • 1970 • Mankiewicz Joseph L. • USA
THERE WAS A DOOR • 1957 • Williams Derek • UKN
THERE WAS A FATHER see **CHICHI ARIKI** • 1942
THERE WAS A LAD see **ZHIVET TAKOI PAREN** • 1964
THERE WAS A LITTLE GIRL • 1973 • Graver Gary • USA
THERE WAS A MAN ROAMING • 1966 • Doukov Stoyan • ANM • BUL
THERE WAS A MILLER ON THE RIVER see **JSOUC NA RECE MLYNAR JEDEN** • 1971
THERE WAS A SINGING BLACKBIRD see **ZIL PEVCIJ DROZD** • 1972
THERE WAS A TIME see **ALSO ES WAR SO..** • 1977
THERE WAS A WAR WHEN I WAS A CHILD • Saito Sadaro • JPN
THERE WAS A YOUNG LADY • 1953 • Huntington Lawrence • UKN
THERE WAS A YOUNG MAN • 1937 • Parker Albert • UKN
THERE WAS AN OLD COUPLE (USA) see **ZHILI-BILI STARIK SO STARUKHOI** • 1965
THERE WAS EVENING AND THERE WAS MORNING see **AND THERE WAS AN EVENING AND A MORNING** • 1971
THERE WAS ONCE A FAMILY see **VOLT EGYSZER EGY CSALAD** • 1972
THERE WERE DAYS see **KANAT AYYAM** • 1970
THERE WERE HOBOES THREE • 1913 • Henderson Dell • USA
THERE WERE TEN OF US see **BYLO NAS DESET** • 1963
THERE WERE THREE OF US see **KEEP YOUR POWDER DRY** • 1944
THERE, WHERE THE WINTER IS LONG see **TAM GDYE DLINNAYA ZIMA** • 1968
THERE WILL BE NO LEAVE TODAY see **SEGODNYA OTPUSKA NYE BUDYET** • 1959
THERE WILL BE NO LEAVE TONIGHT see **SEGODNYA OTPUSKA NYE BUDYET** • 1959
THERE YOU ARE! • 1926 • Sedgwick Edward • USA
THEREFORE see **SUTORANG** • 1964
THERE'S A DRAGON A STONE'S THROW AWAY see **ZA HUMNY JE DRAK** • 1982
THERE'S A FIRE, MY DOLLY! see **HORI, MA PANENKO!** • 1967
THERE'S A FUTURE IN IT • 1943 • Fenton Leslie • UKN
THERE'S A GIRL IN MY HEART • 1949 • Dreifuss Arthur • USA
THERE'S A GIRL IN MY SOUP • 1970 • Boulting Roy • UKN
THERE'S A GOOD TIME COMING FOR THE LADIES • 1916 • *Tress Henry* • SHT • UKN
THERE'S A GREEN PINE TREE IN THE FOREST see **U GORI RASTE ZELEN BOR** • 1972
THERE'S A KEY TO EVERY DOOR see **HALL ALLA DORRAR OPPNA** • 1973
THERE'S A LITTLE BIT OF COWBOY IN EVERYONE • 1982 • Wallace Stephen • DOC • ASL
THERE'S A VACANT CHAIR AT HOME SWEET HOME • 1922 • *Parkinson H. B.* • SHT • UKN
THERE'S ALWAY'S A PRICE TAG (USA) see **RETOUR DE MANIVELLE** • 1957
THERE'S ALWAYS A THURSDAY (USA) see **THERE'S ALWAYS THURSDAY** • 1957
THERE'S ALWAYS A WOMAN • 1938 • Hall Alexander • USA
THERE'S ALWAYS ROOM UNDER THE RAINBOW see **UNDER THE RAINBOW** • 1981
THERE'S ALWAYS THURSDAY • 1957 • Saunders Charles • UKN • THERE'S ALWAYS A THURSDAY (USA)
THERE'S ALWAYS TOMORROW • 1934 • Sloman Edward • USA • TOO LATE FOR LOVE
THERE'S ALWAYS TOMORROW • 1956 • Sirk Douglas • USA
THERE'S ALWAYS VANILLA • 1972 • Romero George A. • USA • AFFAIR, THE
THERE'S AN ACE UP MY SLEEVE see **CRIME AND PASSION** • 1975
THERE'S GOOD BOOS TONIGHT • 1948 • Sparber I. • ANS • USA
THERE'S GOOD IN EVERYONE • 1915 • Elvey Maurice • UKN
THERE'S GOOD IN THE WORST OF US • 1913 • Batley Ethyle • UKN
THERE'S GOOD IN THE WORST OF US • 1915 • *Taylor E. Forrest* • USA
THERE'S HAIR • 1915 • Birch Cecil • UKN
THERE'S LIFE IN THE OLD DOG YET • 1908 • Wormald S. • UKN
THERE'S MAGIC IN MUSIC see **HARDBOILED CANARY, THE** • 1941
THERE'S MANY A FOOL • 1917 • Parrott Charles • SHT • USA
THERE'S MANY A SLIP • 1911 • *Reliance* • USA
THERE'S MANY A SLIP • 1912 • *Powers* • USA
THERE'S MANY A SLIP • 1912 • *Essanay* • USA
THERE'S MANY A SLIP • 1915 • Davey Horace • USA
THERE'S MANY A SLIP • 1925 • Butler Alexander • *Reciprocity Films* • SHT • UKN
THERE'S MANY A SLIP • 1925 • Templeman Harcourt • *Royalty Comedies* • UKN
THERE'S MILLIONS IN IT • 1924 • Clift Denison • USA
THERE'S MUSIC IN THE HAIR • 1913 • Trimble Larry • USA
THERE'S MUSIC IN YOUR HAIR • 1941 • *Mintz Charles (P)* • ANS • USA
THERE'S NO BUSINESS LIKE SHOW BUSINESS • 1954 • Lang Walter • USA
THERE'S NO BUSINESS LIKE WAR BUSINESS see **ROSOLINO PATERNO SOLDATO** • 1970
THERE'S NO FOOL LIKE AN OLD FOOL • 1912 • *P & B Films* • UKN
THERE'S NO FORD IN FIRE see **V OGNYE BRODA NYET** • 1968
THERE'S NO OTHER WAY see **NIET INEJ CESTY** • 1968
THERE'S NO PLACE LIKE HELL see **GLORY BOY** • 1973
THERE'S NO PLACE LIKE HOME • 1917 • Weber Lois • USA
THERE'S NO PLACE LIKE HOME see **YI-HSIANG MENG** • 1977
THERE'S NO PLACE LIKE SPACE see **HOLD ON!** • 1966
THERE'S NO TOMORROW (USA) see **SANS LENDEMAIN** • 1939
THERE'S ONE BORN EVERY MINUTE • 1942 • Young Harold • USA • MAN OR MOUSE
THERE'S REASON IN RHUMBA • 1938 • Parsons Herbert R. • UKN
THERE'S SOMETHING ABOUT A SAILOR • 1943 • Green Alfred E. • USA
THERE'S SOMETHING ABOUT A SOLDIER • 1934 • Fleischer Dave • ANS • USA
THERE'S SOMETHING ABOUT A SOLDIER • 1943 • Geiss Alec • ANS • USA
THERE'S SOMETHING FUNNY GOING ON see **VERGINE PER IL PRINCIPE, UNA** • 1965
THERE'S SOMETHING WRONG • 1912 • *Nestor* • USA
THERE'S THAT WOMAN AGAIN • 1939 • Hall Alexander • USA • WHAT A WOMAN (UKN)
THERESE • 1916 • Sjostrom Victor • SWD
THERESE • 1986 • Cavalier Alain • FRN
THERESE see **THERESE DESQUEYROUX** • 1962
THERESE AND ISABELLE • 1969 • Metzger Radley H. • USA, FRG, FRN • THERESE UND ISABELL (FRG)
THERESE DESQUEYROUX • 1962 • Franju Georges • FRN • THERESE
THERESE ETIENNE • 1957 • de La Patelliere Denys • FRN, ITL • TERESA ETIENNE (ITL)

THERESE KRONES see **IHR GROSSTER ERFOLG** • 1934
THERESE MARTIN • 1938 • de Canonge Maurice • FRN
THERESE P.GAGNON BAIE COMEAU • 1981 • Lesaunier Daniel • MTV • CND
THERESE RAQUIN • 1928 • Feyder Jacques • FRN, FRG • DU SOLLST NICHT EHEBRECHEN! (FRG) ○ SHADOWS OF FEAR (USA) ○ THOU SHALT NOT (UKN)
THERESE RAQUIN • 1953 • Carne Marcel • FRN, ITL • TERESA RAQUIN (ITL) ○ ADULTERESS, THE (USA)
THERESE UND ISABELL (FRG) see **THERESE AND ISABELLE** • 1969
THESE ARE HORSES see **ETO LOSHADI** • 1965
THESE ARE THE DAMNED (USA) see **DAMNED, THE** • 1962
THESE CHARMING PEOPLE • 1931 • Mercanton Louis • UKN
THESE CHILDREN ARE MINE! see **TABLE FOR FIVE** • 1982
THESE DANGEROUS YEARS • 1957 • Wilcox Herbert • UKN • DANGEROUS YOUTH (USA)
THESE FEW YEARS • 1986 • Pyke Roger • DOC • CND
THESE FLEETING LOVES see **TRECATOARELE IUBIRI** • 1975
THESE FOOLISH TIMES see **SHIN BAKA JIDAI** • 1946
THESE GHOSTS see **QUESTI FANTASMI** • 1954
THESE GHOSTS see **QUESTI FANTASMI** • 1967
THESE GLAMOUR GIRLS • 1939 • Simon S. Sylvan • USA
THESE OUR CHILDREN see **VINTI, I** • 1952
THESE THINGS HAPPEN see **CHOSES DE LA VIE, LES** • 1970
THESE THIRTY YEARS • 1934 • Pincus David
THESE THOUSAND HILLS • 1959 • Fleischer Richard • USA
THESE THREE • 1936 • Wyler William • USA
THESE WILDER YEARS • 1956 • Rowland Roy • USA • SOMEWHERE I'LL FIND HIM
THESE YOUNG PEOPLE BAD AND TERRIBLE see **WAKAKUTE WARUKUTE SUGOI KOITSURA** • 1962
THESE YOUNGSTERS see **ESEK A FIATALOK** • 1967
THESEUS AGAINST THE MINOTAUR see **TESEO CONTRO IL MINOTAURO** • 1961
THESEUS AND THE MINOTAUR see **MINOTAUR, THE** • 1910
THESOURO PERDIDO • 1927 • Mauro-Humberto • BRZ • TESOURO PERDIDO ○ LOST TREASURE
THESPIAN BANDIT, THE • 1912 • *Conway Jack* • USA
THESSALONIKI 6.5 ON THE RICHTER SCALE • 1979 • Angheli Gay • SHT • GRC
THETA • Roberts Richard • ANS • USA
THETFORD AU MILIEU DE NOTRE VIE • 1978 • Dansereau Fernand, Rossignol Yolande • CND
THETUS • 1979 • Hillman William Byron • USA
THEY ALL COME OUT • 1939 • Tourneur Jacques • USA
THEY ALL DIED LAUGHING (USA) see **JOLLY BAD FELLOW, A** • 1963
THEY ALL DO IT (UKN) see **SADAN ER DE ALLE** • 1968
THEY ALL KISSED THE BRIDE • 1942 • Hall Alexander • USA • HE KISSED THE BRIDE
THEY ALL LAUGHED • 1981 • Bogdanovich Peter • USA
THEY ALL PROFIT • 1965 • Schofield Stanley • UKN
THEY ALL WANT A GIRL • 1914 • Collins Edwin J.? • UKN
THEY ALL WANT SOMETHING see **WHAT A MAN!** • 1930
THEY AND WE • 1929 • Antonovsky B. • ANM • USS
THEY ARE ALL LIKE THAT see **SADAN ER DE ALLE** • 1968
THEY ARE ALSO PEOPLE see **TOZHE LYUDI** • 1960
THEY ARE BURIED ALIVE see **DOTANBA** • 1957
THEY ARE FORSAKEN • 1938 • George W. H. • UKN
THEY ARE GUILY (UKN) see **ARE THESE OUR PARENTS?** • 1944
THEY ARE JOLLY GOOD FELLOWS see **TWO JOLLY GOOD FELLOWS** • 1900
THEY ASKED FOR IT • 1939 • McDonald Frank • USA
THEY BELIEVED HE WAS A SAINT see **UOMO AVVISATO MEZZO AMMAZZATO.. PAROLA DI SPIRITO SANTO** • 1972
THEY BOUGHT A BOAT • 1914 • *Lubin* • USA
THEY BUILT A NATION see **BOU VAN 'N NASIE, DIE** • 1939
THEY CALL HER CLEOPATRA WONG • 1978 • Richardson George • USA • CLEOPATRA WONG
THEY CALL HIM AMEN see **COSI SIA** • 1972
THEY CALL HIM MARCADO (UKN) see **MARCADOS, LOS** • 1975
THEY CALL HIM ROBERT see **YEVO ZOVUT ROBERT** • 1967
THEY CALL IT MURDER • 1971 • Grauman Walter • TVM • USA • D.A. DRAWS A CIRCLE, THE
THEY CALL IT SIN • 1932 • Freeland Thornton • USA • WAY OF LIFE, THE (UKN)
THEY CALL ME BRUCE? • 1983 • Hong Elliot • HKG, USA • FISTFUL OF CHOPSTICKS, A
THEY CALL ME HALLELUJAH see **TESTA T'AMMAZZO, CROCE SEI MORTO, MI CHIAMANO ALLELUJA** • 1971
THEY CALL ME "MISTER" TIBBS • 1970 • Douglas Gordon • USA
THEY CALL ME ROBERT see **YEVO ZOVUT ROBERT** • 1967
THEY CALL ME TRINITY (UKN) see **LO CHIAMAVANO TRINITA** • 1970
THEY CALL THAT AN ACCIDENT see **ILS APPELLENT CA UN ACCIDENT** • 1981
THEY CALL THE WIND KOSAVA see **KOSAVA** • 1975
THEY CALL US MISFITS (USA) see **DOM KALLAR OSS MODS** • 1967
THEY CALL US TRAMPS see **GARIBAN DERLER BIZE** • 1967
THEY CALLED HIM AMEN see **COSI SIA** • 1972
THEY CALLED HIM AMIGO see **SIE NANNTEN IHN AMIGO** • 1958
THEY CALLED HIM BULLDOZER see **LO CHIAMAVANO BULLDOZER** • 1978
THEY CALLED HIM COWARD see **COWARD!** • 1915
THEY CALLED HIM KRAMBAMBULI see **SIE NANNTEN IHN KRAMBAMBULI** • 1972
THEY CALLED IT BABY • 1914 • *Ab* • USA
THEY CALLED IT FIREPROOF • 1963 • Blais Roger • DCS • CND • ON LE PENSAIT A L'EPREUVE DU FEU
THEY CALLED US "LES FILLES DU ROY" see **FILLES DU ROY, LES** • 1974
THEY CAME BY NIGHT • 1940 • Lachman Harry • UKN, USA
THEY CAME FROM ANOTHER WORLD see **INVASION OF THE BODY SNATCHERS** • 1956
THEY CAME FROM BEYOND SPACE • 1967 • Francis Freddie • UKN
THEY CAME FROM WITHIN see **PARASITE MURDERS, THE** • 1975
THEY CAME TO A CITY • 1944 • Dearden Basil • UKN
THEY CAME TO BLOW UP AMERICA • 1943 • Ludwig Edward • USA • SCHOOL FOR SABOTAGE
THEY CAME TO CORDURA • 1959 • Rossen Robert • USA
THEY CAME TO ROB LAS VEGAS (USA) see **LAS VEGAS, 500 MILLONES** • 1968
THEY CAME TOGETHER see **MIDNIGHT COWGIRL** • 1970
THEY CAN'T DIDDLE ME • 1906 • Gilbert Arthur • UKN
THEY CAN'T DIDDLE ME • 1907 • Morland John • UKN
THEY CAN'T HANG ME • 1955 • Guest Val • UKN
THEY CARVE A NEW WAY FORWARD • Keko Endri • DOC • ALB
THEY CAUGHT THE FERRY see **NAEDE FARGEN, DE** • 1948
THEY CHOSE THE SEA • 1960 • Marquis Eric • UKN
THEY CRACKED HER GLASS SLIPPER see **THIRD TIME LUCKY** • 1949
THEY DARE NOT LOVE • 1941 • Whale James • USA
THEY DESPISE FEAR see **ONI PREZIRU STRAH** • 1951
THEY DIDN'T KNOW • 1914 • *Crystal* • USA
THEY DIDN'T KNOW • 1936 • Smith Herbert • UKN
THEY DIED IN THE MIDDLE OF THE RIVER see **MURIERON A LA MITAD DEL RIO** • 1987
THEY DIED WITH THEIR BOOTS ON • 1941 • Walsh Raoul • USA
THEY DIED WITH THEIR GUNS ON see **SILAHLARI ELLERINDE OLDULER** • 1967
THEY DO SUCH THINGS AT BRIGHTON • 1899 • *Evans Will* • UKN
THEY DON'T CLAP LOSERS • 1974 • Power John • MTV • ASL
THEY DON'T WEAR BLACK TIE see **ELES NAO USAM BLACK TIE** • 1981
THEY DON'T WEAR PAJAMAS AT ROSIE'S see **FIRST TIME, THE** • 1968
THEY DRIVE BY NIGHT • 1938 • Woods Arthur • UKN
THEY DRIVE BY NIGHT • 1940 • Walsh Raoul • USA • ROAD TO 'FRISCO, THE (UKN)
THEY FLEW ALONE • 1942 • Wilcox Herbert • UKN • WINGS AND THE WOMAN (USA)
THEY FORGOT THE GAMEKEEPER • 1904 • Williamson James • UKN
THEY FOUGHT FOR THE MOTHERLAND (USA) see **ONI SRAJALIS ZA RODINOU** • 1974
THEY FOUGHT FOR THEIR COUNTRY see **ONI SRAJALIS ZA RODINOU** • 1974
THEY FOUGHT FOR THEIR MOTHERLAND see **ONI SRAJALIS ZA RODINOU** • 1974
THEY FOUND A CAVE • 1962 • Steane Andrew • ASL
THEY GAVE HIM A GUN • 1937 • Van Dyke W. S. • USA
THEY GAVE HIM THE WORKS • 1948 • Swingler Humphrey
THEY GO BOOM • 1929 • Parrott James • SHT • USA
THEY GOT ME COVERED • 1943 • Butler David • USA
THEY HAD TO SEE PARIS • 1929 • Borzage Frank • USA
THEY HAVE A HOMELAND see **U NIKH EST RODINA** • 1951
THEY HAVE A MOTHERLAND see **U NIKH EST RODINA** • 1951
THEY HEADED FOR THE EAST see **ITALIANO, BRAVA GENTE** • 1964
THEY JUST HAD TO GET MARRIED • 1933 • Ludwig Edward • USA • HAPPY DOLLARS
THEY KEEP THE WHEELS TURNING • 1942 • Searle Francis • DCS • UKN
THEY KNEW MR. KNIGHT • 1945 • Walker Norman • UKN
THEY KNEW WHAT THEY WANTED • 1940 • Kanin Garson • USA
THEY KNOW WHAT TO DO see **VEDELI SI RADY** • 1950
THEY LEARNED ABOUT WOMEN • 1929 • Wood Sam, Conway Jack • USA • TAKE IT BIG
THEY LIKE 'EM ROUGH • 1922 • Beaumont Harry • USA
THEY LIVE • 1988 • Carpenter John • USA
THEY LIVE AGAIN • 1938 • Zinnemann Fred • SHT • USA
THEY LIVE BY NIGHT • 1948 • Ray Nicholas • USA • TWISTED ROAD, THE ○ YOUR RED WAGON
THEY LIVE CLOSE BY see **ONI ZHIVUT RYADOM** • 1968
THEY LIVE IN FEAR • 1944 • Berne Josef • USA • AMERICA'S CHILDREN
THEY LOOKED ALIKE • 1915 • Hotaling Arthur D. • USA
THEY LOVE AS THEY PLEASE see **GREENWICH VILLAGE STORY** • 1963
THEY LOVED HIM SO • 1915 • Williams C. Jay • USA
THEY LOVED LIFE see **KANAL** • 1957
THEY MADE HER A SPY • 1939 • Hively Jack • USA
THEY MADE HIM A CRIMINAL see **VITA E BELLA, LA** • 1980
THEY MADE ME A CRIMINAL • 1939 • Berkeley Busby • USA
THEY MADE ME A CRIMINAL see **THEY MADE ME A FUGITIVE** • 1947
THEY MADE ME A FUGITIVE • 1947 • Cavalcanti Alberto • UKN • I BECAME A CRIMINAL (USA) ○ THEY MADE ME A CRIMINAL
THEY MADE ME A KILLER • 1946 • Thomas William C. • USA
THEY MADE ME A KILLER see **BENI KATIL ETTILER** • 1967
THEY MADE THE LAND • 1938 • Field Mary • DOC • UKN
THEY MEET AGAIN • 1941 • Kenton Erle C. • USA
THEY MET AT MIDNIGHT see **PICCADILLY INCIDENT** • 1946
THEY MET IN A TAXI • 1936 • Green Alfred E. • USA
THEY MET IN ARGENTINA • 1941 • Hively Jack, Goodwins Leslie • USA
THEY MET IN BOMBAY • 1941 • Brown Clarence • USA • UNIFORM, THE
THEY MET IN HAVANA see **SPOTKALI SIE W HAWANIE** • 1962
THEY MET IN LONDON • 1942 • Rotha Paul • DOC • UKN
THEY MET IN MOSCOW see **SVINYARKA I PASTUKH** • 1941
THEY MET IN THE DARK • 1943 • Lamac Carl • UKN
THEY MET ON SKI • 1940 • Sokal H. R. • USA
THEY MET ON THE WAY see **PATHEY HOLO DEKHA** • 1968
THEY MIGHT BE GIANTS • 1971 • Harvey Anthony • USA
THEY NEVER CAME BACK • 1932 • Newmeyer Fred • USA
THEY NEVER KNEW • 1914 • Mackley Arthur • USA
THEY NEVER LEARN • 1956 • Kavanagh Denis • UKN
THEY ONLY COME OUT AT NIGHT • 1975 • Duke Daryl • TVM • USA
THEY ONLY KILL THEIR MASTERS • 1972 • Goldstone James • USA
THEY PAID WITH BULLETS (USA) see **TIEMPOS DE CHICAGO** • 1968
THEY PASSED THIS WAY (UKN) see **FOUR FACES WEST** • 1948
THEY PRACTISE ECONOMY • 1916 • *Myers Harry* • SHT • USA
THEY RAID BY NIGHT • 1942 • Bennet Spencer Gordon • USA
THEY RAIDED THE JOINT • 1946 • Crouch William Forest • SHT • USA
THEY RAN FOR MAYOR • 1915 • *Royal* • USA
THEY RAN FOR THEIR LIVES • 1968 • Payne John • USA
THEY RODE WEST • 1954 • Karlson Phil • USA • WHITE FEATHER ○ WOODHAWK, THE
THEY SANG IN SOFIA • 1961 • Stoyanov Yuli • DOC • BUL
THEY SAVED HITLER'S BRAIN see **MADMEN OF MANDORAS, THE** • 1964
THEY SAY -LET THEM SAY • 1914 • Buckland Warwick? • UKN
THEY SERVE ABROAD • 1942 • Boulting Roy • DCS • UKN
THEY SHALL HAVE FAITH see **FOREVER YOURS** • 1944
THEY SHALL HAVE MUSIC • 1939 • Mayo Archie, Heisler Stuart (U/c) • USA • MELODY OF YOUTH (UKN)
THEY SHALL NOT DIE see **SEREGETI DARF NICHT STERBEN** • 1959
THEY SHALL NOT PASS • 1964 • Kuhn Siegfried • USS
THEY SHALL PAY • 1921 • Justice Martin • USA
THEY SHOOT HORSES, DON'T THEY? • 1969 • Pollack Sydney • USA
THEY SHOT THROUGH LIKE A BONDI • 1966 • Buckley Anthony • DOC • ASL
THEY SMILE AGAIN see **UJRA MOSOLYOGNAK** • 1954
THEY SPEAK FOR THEMSELVES • 1942 • Rotha Paul • DOC • UKN
THEY STAKED THEIR LIVES see **MED LIVET SOM INSATS** • 1940
THEY STILL CALL ME BRUCE • 1987 • Yune Johnny, Orr James • USA
THEY STILL CALL ME TRINITY see **CONTINUAVANO A CHIAMARLO, TRINITA** • 1971
THEY STOOGE TO CONGA • 1943 • Lord Del • SHT • USA
THEY TRAVEL BY AIR (FLIGHT OF FANCY) • 1947 • Massingham Richard • UKN • FLIGHT OF FANCY
THEY WANTED PEACE see **GREAT DAWN, THE** • 1938
THEY WANTED TO MARRY • 1937 • Landers Lew • USA
THEY WENT THAT-A-WAY AND THAT-A-WAY • 1978 • Montagne Edward J., McGowan Stuart E. • USA • UNDERCOVER CAPER, THE
THEY WENT TO FIGHT FOR FREEDOM • 1984 • Burton Robert H. • MTV • CND
THEY WENT TO VOSTOK see **ITALIANO, BRAVA GENTE** • 1964
THEY WERE COLLEGE BOYS • 1914 • *Ab* • USA
THEY WERE EXPENDABLE • 1945 • Ford John • USA
THEY WERE FIVE (USA) see **BELLE EQUIPE, LA** • 1936
THEY WERE FOUR • 1917 • Marshall George • SHT • USA
THEY WERE HEROES • 1915 • Christie Al • USA
THEY WERE LEFT JUST BEFORE MARRIAGE see **VESTIDAS Y ALBOROTADAS** • 1968
THEY WERE NOBODY see **NO ERAN NADIE** • 1982
THEY WERE NOT DIVIDED • 1950 • Young Terence • UKN
THEY WERE ON THEIR HONEYMOON • 1913 • France Charles H. • USA
THEY WERE ON THEIR HONEYMOON • 1915 • Lyons Eddie • USA
THEY WERE SISTERS • 1945 • Crabtree Arthur • UKN
THEY WERE SO YOUNG • 1955 • Neumann Kurt • USA, FRG
THEY WERE TEN (USA) see **HEM HAYU ASAR** • 1960
THEY WERE THE FIRST • 1956 • Yegorov Yuri • USS
THEY WHO DARE • 1954 • Milestone Lewis • UKN
THEY WHO DIG PITS • 1914 • *Billington Francelia* • USA
THEY WHO STEP ON THE TIGER'S TAIL see **TORA NO OO FUMA OTOKOTACHI** • 1945
THEY WILL MEET AGAIN see **LEKAA EL TANI, EL** • 1967
THEY WON'T BELIEVE ME • 1947 • Pichel Irving • USA
THEY WON'T FORGET • 1937 • LeRoy Mervyn • USA • DEEP SOUTH
THEY WOULD BANDITS BE • 1914 • Middleton Mr. • USA
THEY WOULD BE ACROBATS • 1909 • Raymond Charles? • UKN
THEY WOULD ELOPE • 1909 • Griffith D. W. • USA
THEY WOULD PLAY CARDS • 1907 • Smith Jack • UKN
THEY WOULDN'T BELIEVE ME • 1925 • Butler Alexander • UKN
THEY WOULDN'T TAKE HIM SERIOUSLY • 1916 • Worthington William • SHT • USA
THEY'RE A WEIRD MOB • 1966 • Powell Michael • UKN, ASL
THEY'RE ALL AFTER FLO • 1915 • Wilson Frank? • UKN
THEY'RE ALL FINE see **STANNO TUTTI BENE** • 1990
THEY'RE ALWAYS CAUGHT • 1938 • Bucquet Harold S. • SHT • USA
THEY'RE COMING TO GET ME • 1926 • *Sale Chic* • SHT • USA
THEY'RE COMING TO GET YOU see **TUTTI I COLORI DEL BUIO** • 1972
THEY'RE CRAZY see **PICCHIATELLI, I** • 1958
THEY'RE OFF • 1917 • Neill R. William • USA
THEY'RE OFF • 1919 • *Parsons Smiling Bill* • USA
THEY'RE OFF • 1922 • Ford Francis • USA
THEY'RE OFF • 1933 • Rawlins John* • UKN
THEY'RE OFF • 1948 • Hannah Jack • ANS • USA
THEY'RE OFF see **KENTUCKY DERBY, THE** • 1922
THEY'RE OFF see **MARRIED FLAPPER, THE** • 1922
THEY'RE OFF (UKN) see **STRAIGHT, PLACE AND SHOW** • 1938
THEY'RE PLAYING WITH FIRE • 1983 • Avedis Howard • USA • PLAYING WITH FIRE
THEY'VE CHANGED FACES see **HANNO CAMBIATO FACCIO** • 1971
THEY'VE KIDNAPPED ANNE BENEDICT see **ABDUCTION OF SAINT ANNE, THE** • 1975
THIASOS, O • 1974 • Angelopoulos Theo • GRC • TRAVELLING PLAYERS, THE ○ TROUPE, THE ○ THASSIOS, O ○ VOYAGE DES COMEDIENS, LE
THICK AND THIN OF IT, THE • 1914 • West Walter • UKN
THICK PUCKER • 1965 • Nelson Robert • SHT • USA
THICK WALLED ROOM, THE see **KABE ATSUKI HEYA** • 1953

THICKER THAN WATER • 1935 • Horne James W. • SHT • USA
THICKER THAN WATER see **RAILROADED** • 1923
THIEF • 1981 • Mann Michael • USA • VIOLENT STREETS
THIEF see **LADRON** • 1971
THIEF, THE • 1910 • *Essanay* • USA
THIEF, THE • 1912 • *Kalem* • USA
THIEF, THE • 1912 • Collins Edwin J.? • UKN
THIEF, THE • 1913 • *Solax* • USA
THIEF, THE • 1915 • Lewis Edgar • USA
THIEF, THE • 1920 • *Reelcraft* • USA
THIEF, THE • 1920 • Giblyn Charles • *Fox* • USA
THIEF, THE • 1922 • Cooper George A. • UKN
THIEF, THE • 1952 • Rouse Russell • USA
THIEF, THE • 1971 • Graham William A. • TVM • USA
THIEF, THE see **BLUDICKA** • 1921
THIEF, THE see **HIRSIZ KIZ** • 1968
THIEF, THE (UKN) see **VOLEUR, LE** • 1967
THIEF AND CULTURE ORDER, A see **KOJIN KOJITSU** • 1961
THIEF AND DOGS see **LISSU WA AL-KILAB, AL-** • 1962
THIEF AND THE BOOK, THE • 1914 • *West Billie* • USA
THIEF AND THE CHIEF, THE • 1915 • *Walpole Stanley* • USA
THIEF AND THE GIRL, THE • 1911 • Griffith D. W. • USA
THIEF AND THE PORTER'S HEAD, THE • 1912 • *Milano* • ITL
THIEF AND THE STRIPPER, THE • 1959 • Kuchar George, Kuchar Mike • SHT • USA
THIEF AND THE WRITER, THE • 1987 • Massoumi Kazem • IRN
THIEF AT THE CASINO, THE • 1908 • Fitzhamon Lewin • UKN
THIEF CATCHER, A • 1914 • Lehrman Henry • USA
THIEF CATCHER, A see **HER FRIEND THE BANDIT** • 1914
THIEF IN A BLACK DRESS see **DOZDE-SIYAHPOUSH** • 1968
THIEF IN PARADISE, A • 1925 • Fitzmaurice George • USA
THIEF IN SILK • 1952 • Planells Salvador • USA, CUB • SAN RIFLE EN LA HABANA ○ LADRON EN SEDA
THIEF IN THE BEDROOM, A see **SANGKAMMARTJUVEN** • 1959
THIEF IN THE DARK, A • 1928 • Ray Albert • USA
THIEF IN THE NIGHT, A • 1913 • *Joyce Alice* • USA
THIEF IN THE NIGHT, A • 1915 • *Lubin (Earl Metcalfe)* • USA
THIEF IN THE NIGHT, A see **BIRD OF PREY, A** • 1916
THIEF IN THE NIGHT, THE • 1915 • *Lubin (Ormi Hawley)* • USA
THIEF IN THE NIGHT, OR SOME GOOD IN ALL, A • 1911 • *Costello Maurice* • USA
THIEF IS SHOGUN'S KIN, THE see **SENRYO-JISHI** • 1958
THIEF MAKER, THE • 1917 • Cochrane George • SHT • USA
THIEF OF BAGDAD see **BAGDAD GAJA DONGA** • 1968
THIEF OF BAGDAD, THE • 1924 • Walsh Raoul • USA
THIEF OF BAGDAD, THE • 1934 • Madhok D. N. • IND
THIEF OF BAGDAD, THE • 1940 • Powell Michael, Berger Ludwig, Whelan Tim, Korda Alexander (U/c), Korda Zoltan (U/c) • UKN
THIEF OF BAGDAD, THE see **BAGDAT HIRSIZI** • 1968
THIEF OF BAGDAD, THE (USA) see **LADRO DI BAGDAD, IL** • 1961
THIEF OF BAGHDAD see **BAGHDAD THIRUDAN** • 1960
THIEF OF BAGHDAD, THE • 1978 • Donner Clive • TVM • UKN, FRN
THIEF OF CORPSES see **LADRON DE CADAVERES** • 1956
THIEF OF DAMASCUS • 1952 • Jason Will • USA
THIEF OF HEARTS • 1984 • Stewart Douglas Day • USA
THIEF OF HEARTS, THE see **HJERTETYVEN** • 1943
THIEF OF PARIS, THE (USA) see **VOLEUR, LE** • 1967
THIEF OF SAN MARENGO, THE see **DIEB VON SAN MARENGO, DER** • 1963
THIEF OF THE DESERT, THE • 1916 • Reynolds Lynn • SHT • USA
THIEF OF THIEVES see **SORUNGETH SORU** • 1967
THIEF OF VENICE, THE (USA) see **LADRO DI VENEZIA, IL** • 1950
THIEF ON HOLIDAY see **MUGAREM FI IJAZA** • 1958
THIEF ON THE RUN see **TANUKI NO TAISHO** • 1965
THIEF OR ANGEL? • 1918 • *Hampton Ruth* • SHT • USA
THIEF WHO CAME TO DINNER, THE • 1973 • Yorkin Bud • USA
THIEF'S WIFE, THE • 1912 • Dwan Allan • USA
THIELLA, I • 1929 • Gaziadis Dimitrios • GRC • STORM, THE
THIELLA STO SPITI TON ANEMON • 1967 • Pallis Byron • GRC • STORM IN THE HOUSE OF WINDS
THIEVES • 1913 • Bowman William J. • USA
THIEVES • 1914 • *Domino* • USA
THIEVES • 1919 • Beal Frank • USA
THIEVES • 1977 • Berry John • USA
THIEVES see **SKELMS** • 1979
THIEVES see **GARATGARAN** • 1981
THIEVES see **CHORON KA BADSHAH** • 1988
THIEVES, THE • 1960 • Kondek Waclaw • ANM • PLN
THIEVES AFTER DARK (USA) see **VOLEURS DE LA NUIT, LES** • 1983
THIEVES AND ROBBERS • 1983 • Corbucci Bruno • ITL
THIEVES AND THE CROSS • 1913 • *Smalley Phillips* • USA
THIEVES' CLOTHES • 1920 • Wright Mack V. • SHT • USA
THIEVES' DECOY, THE • 1910 • Haldane Bert? • UKN
THIEVES FALL OUT • 1941 • Enright Ray • USA • THIRTY DAYS HATH SEPTEMBER
THIEVES' GOLD • 1918 • Ford John • USA
THIEVES' HIGHWAY • 1949 • Dassin Jules • USA • COLLISION ○ HARD BARGAIN ○ THIEVES' MARKET
THIEVE'S HOLIDAY • 1946 • Sirk Douglas • USA • SCANDAL IN PARIS, A (UKN)
THIEVES' HOLIDAY see **HAKUCHU DODO** • 1968
THIEVES LIKE US • 1973 • Altman Robert • USA
THIEVES' MARKET see **THIEVES' HIGHWAY** • 1949
THIEVES OF BANGKOK see **BANGKOK KEY CHOR** • 1986
THIEVING HAND, THE • 1908 • *Vitagraph* • SHT • USA
THIEVING MAGPIE, THE (USA) see **GAZZA LADRA, LA** • 1964
THIEVING PRINCESS, THE see **HIRSIZ PRENSES** • 1967
THIGH LINE LYRE TRIANGULAR • 1961 • Brakhage Stan • SHT • USA
THIGH SPY • 1967 • Hennigar William K. • USA • HIGH SPY
THILAKA AND THILAKAA • 1974 • Jayatilaka Amarnath • SLN
THIMBLE, THIMBLE • 1920 • Griffith Edward H. • SHT • USA
THIN AIR see **BODY STEALERS, THE** • 1969
THIN AND THE OTHERS, THE see **CHDY I INNI** • 1967
THIN BLUE LINE, THE • 1989 • Morris Earl • DOC • USA
THIN DARK LINE, THE • 1910 • *Reliance* • USA
THIN DIME, A • *Pike Bob (P)* • SHT • USA
THIN GOSSIP, THE see **COMMARE SECCA, LA** • 1962
THIN ICE • 1919 • Mills Thomas R. • USA
THIN ICE • 1937 • Lanfield Sidney • USA • LOVELY TO LOOK AT (UKN)
THIN ICE • 1960 • Halas John • ANS • UKN
THIN ICE • 1961 • Johnson Lamont • USA
THIN ICE • 1966 • Vyatich-Berezhnykh Damir • USS
THIN ICE • 1981 • Aaron Paul • TVM • USA
THIN LINE • 1977 • Dale Holly, Cole Janis • DOC • CND
THIN LINE, A see **AL KHEVEL DAK** • 1981
THIN LINE, THE • 1988 • Loucka Andreas A. • USA
THIN LINE, THE see **ONNA NO NAKA NI IRU TANIN** • 1966
THIN MAN, THE • 1934 • Van Dyke W. S. • USA
THIN MAN GOES HOME, THE • 1944 • Thorpe Richard • USA
THIN RED LINE, THE • 1964 • Marton Andrew • USA
THIN SKIN see **TESNA KOZA** • 1984
THIN SKIN III see **TESNA KOZA III** • 1989
THIN TWINS • 1929 • Horne James W. • SHT • USA
THING, THE • Reade Harry • ANS • CUB
THING, THE • 1951 • Nyby Christian, Hawks Howard (U/c) • USA • THING FROM ANOTHER WORLD, THE (UKN)
THING, THE • 1982 • Carpenter John • USA
THING FROM ANOTHER WORLD, THE (UKN) see **THING, THE** • 1951
THING OR TWO IN MOVIES, A • 1915 • Neilan Marshall • USA
THING THAT COULDN'T DIE, THE • 1958 • Cowan Will • USA
THING WE LOVE, THE see **THINGS WE LOVE, THE** • 1918
THING WITH TWO HEADS, THE • 1972 • Frost Lee • USA • MAN WITH TWO HEADS
THINGS ARE LOOKING UP • 1935 • De Courville Albert • UKN • PLEASE TEACHER ○ SCHOOL DAYS
THINGS ARE SELDOM WHAT THEY SEEM • 1912 • *Roland Ruth* • USA
THINGS ARE TOUGH ALL OVER • 1982 • Avildsen Tom • USA • CHEECH AND CHONG: THINGS ARE TOUGH ALL OVER
THINGS AREN'T ALWAYS WHAT THEY SEEM see **APARIENCIAS ENGANAN, LAS** • 1978
THINGS AREN'T RIGHT • 1970 • Spivak Michael • SHT • CND
THINGS CHANGE • 1988 • Mamet David • USA
THINGS EXIST THAT DO NOT EXIST AT ALL see **DINGE GIBT'S DIE GIBT'S GAR NICHT** • 1966
THINGS HAPPEN AT NIGHT • 1948 • Searle Francis • UKN
THINGS I CANNOT CHANGE, THE • 1966 • Ballantyne Tanya • DOC • CND
THINGS IN THE BOTTOM DRAWER, THE • 1915 • Forest Alan • USA
THINGS IN THEIR SEASON • 1974 • Goldstone James • USA
THINGS MEN DO • 1921 • Bradbury Robert North • USA
THINGS OF LIFE, THE (USA) see **CHOSES DE LA VIE, LES** • 1970
THINGS PAST • 1981 • van der Lecq Bas, van Erkel Bram, Logger Roy • NTH
THING'S THE PLAY, THE • 1918 • Ridgwell George • SHT • USA
THINGS TO COME • 1936 • Menzies William Cameron • UKN • SHAPE OF THINGS TO COME, THE ○ WHITHER MANKIND
THINGS TO COME • 1953 • Marx Patricia • ANS • USA
THINGS WE CAN DO WITHOUT • 1953 • Barclay David • SHT • USA
THINGS WE LOVE, THE • 1918 • Tellegen Lou • USA • THING WE LOVE, THE
THINGS WE WANT TO KEEP, THE • 1979 • Howes Oliver • DOC • ASL
THINGS WE WANT TO KNOW • 1915 • Plumb Hay? • UKN
THINGS WILL BE BETTER AGAIN see **ES WIRD SCHON WIEDER BESSER** • 1932
THINGS WIVES TELL • 1926 • Dierker Hugh • USA
THINGYAN MOE • 1986 • Maung Tin Oo • BRM
THINIM STOUT • 1916 • Watt Nate • USA
THINK 20TH • 1967 • Fleischer Richard • USA
THINK DIRTY (USA) see **EVERY HOME SHOULD HAVE ONE** • 1970
THINK FAST, MR. MOTO • 1937 • Foster Norman • USA
THINK FIRST • 1939 • Rowland Roy • SHT • USA
THINK IT OVER • 1917 • Blache Herbert • USA
THINK IT OVER • 1938 • Tourneur Jacques • SHT • USA
THINK MOTHERS • 1915 • Kaufman Joseph • USA
THINK OF A NUMBER see **TAENK PA ET TAL** • 1969
THINK OF THE MONEY • 1915 • Hotaling Arthur D. • USA
THINK OR SINK • 1967 • Culhane Shamus • ANS • USA
THINK THINK • 1969 • Lemon Max • SHT • ASL
THINKIN' BIG see **THINKING BIG** • 1987
THINKING BIG • 1987 • Brownrigg S. F. • USA • THINKIN' BIG
THINNEN STOUT • 1916 • *Humphrey Orral* • USA
THIRA • Sfikas Kostas • SHT • GRC
THIRD, THE see **III-ES, A** • 1919
THIRD, THE see **DRITTE, DER** • 1972
THIRD ACT, THE • 1915 • Vale Travers • USA
THIRD AFTER THE SUN • 1972 • Stoyanov Georgi • BUL • THIRD FROM THE SUN
THIRD ALARM, THE • 1922 • Johnson Emory • USA
THIRD ALARM, THE • 1930 • Johnson Emory • USA
THIRD ALIBI, THE • 1961 • Tully Montgomery • UKN
THIRD ASSASSIN, THE see **DAISAN NO SHIKAKU** • 1959
THIRD BAD NAME, THE see **DAISAN NO AKUMYO** • 1963
THIRD BASE see **SADO** • 1977
THIRD BEGINNING, THE see **HARMADIK NEKIFUTAS** • 1973
THIRD BLOW, THE see **TRETY UDAR** • 1948
THIRD CHARACTER'S TRIPLE DEATH, THE see **TRIPLE MUERTE DEL TERCER PERSONAJE, LA** • 1979
THIRD CIRCLE, THE see **WHERE DO WE GO FROM HERE?** • 1987
THIRD CLASS LOVE see **FAPADOS SZERELEM** • 1959
THIRD CLASS THIEF see **SANTO-KACHO** • 1959
THIRD CLUE, THE • 1934 • Parker Albert • UKN
THIRD COMMANDMENT, THE • 1915 • Moore Tom • USA
THIRD CUP, THE • 1901 • *Warwick Trading Co* • UKN
THIRD DAY, THE • 1965 • Smight Jack • USA
THIRD DEGREE, THE • 1910 • *Actophone* • USA
THIRD DEGREE, THE • 1914 • O'Neil Barry • USA
THIRD DEGREE, THE • 1919 • Terriss Tom • USA
THIRD DEGREE, THE • 1926 • Curtiz Michael • USA
THIRD DEGREE BURN • 1989 • Spottiswoode Roger • USA
THIRD DIMENSIONAL MURDER • 1940 • Sidney George • SHT • USA • THIRD-DIMENSIONAL MURDER
THIRD-DIMENSIONAL MURDER see **THIRD DIMENSIONAL MURDER** • 1940
THIRD DRAGON • 1985 • Hledik Peter • CZC
THIRD EYE, THE • 1920 • Horne James W. • SRL • USA
THIRD EYE, THE • 1929 • Rogers Maclean • UKN
THIRD EYE, THE • 1966 • Anderson Robert • DOC • CND
THIRD EYE, THE see **TERZO OCCHIO, IL** • 1966
THIRD EYE, THE see **UCUNCU GOZ** • 1988
THIRD FACE, THE see **K'UNG-PU-TE CH'ING-JEN** • 1982
THIRD FINGER, LEFT HAND • 1940 • Leonard Robert Z. • USA
THIRD FLOOR LOVE see **AI NO SANGA** • 1950
THIRD FROM THE SUN see **THIRD AFTER THE SUN** • 1972
THIRD GENERATION, THE • 1915 • Shaw Harold • UKN
THIRD GENERATION, THE • 1920 • Kolker Henry • USA
THIRD GENERATION, THE (USA) see **DRITTE GENERATION, DER** • 1979
THIRD GIRL FROM THE LEFT, THE • 1973 • Medak Peter • TVM • USA
THIRD GOD, THE • 1914 • Kinder Stuart • UKN
THIRD GUN, THE • 1929 • Barkas Geoffrey • UKN
THIRD HAND HIGH • 1915 • *Stonehouse Ruth* • USA
THIRD INGREDIENT, THE • 1917 • Mills Thomas R. • SHT • USA
THIRD KEY, THE see **TRECI KLJUC** • 1984
THIRD KEY, THE (USA) see **LONG ARM, THE** • 1956
THIRD KISS, THE • 1919 • Vignola Robert G. • USA
THIRD LINE • 1990 • Ghavidel Amir • IRN
THIRD LOVER, THE (USA) see **OEIL DU MALIN, L'** • 1961
THIRD LYCEUM see **TERZA LICEO** • 1954
THIRD MAN, THE • 1949 • Reed Carol • UKN
THIRD MAN, THE see **TEN TRZECI** • 1958
THIRD MAN ON THE MOUNTAIN • 1959 • Annakin Ken • UKN, USA • BANNER IN THE SKY
THIRD MESHCHANSKAYA see **TRETYA MESHCHANSKAYA** • 1927
THIRD MUSKETEER, THE • 1965 • Bakshi Ralph • ANS • USA
THIRD OF A MAN • 1962 • Lewin Robert • USA
THIRD OF MAY, THE • 1976 • Krolikiewicz Grzegorz • MTV • PLN
THIRD ONE, THE see **TA TRETI** • 1968
THIRD ONE, THE see **DRITTE, DER** • 1972
THIRD ONE, THE see **MOONAMATHORAL** • 1990
THIRD PART OF THE NIGHT, THE see **TRECIA CZESC NOCY** • 1971
THIRD PARTNER, THE • 1915 • Reynolds Lynn • USA
THIRD PARTY, THE • 1914 • *Joker* • USA
THIRD PARTY, THE • 1915 • Marston Theodore • USA
THIRD PARTY RISK • 1955 • Birt Daniel • UKN • DEADLY GAME, THE
THIRD PARTY SPECULATION see **EMILY** • 1979
THIRD PERSON PLURAL • 1978 • Ricketson James • ASL
THIRD PRINCE, THE see **TRETI PRINC** • 1982
THIRD RABBIT, THE • 1937 • Davis Mannie • ANS • USA
THIRD ROAD, THE see **SEVENTH DAWN, THE** • 1964
THIRD ROOM, THE see **III-ES, A** • 1937
THIRD ROUND, THE see **BULLDOG DRUMMOND'S THIRD ROUND** • 1925
THIRD SECRET, THE • 1964 • Crichton Charles • UKN
THIRD SEX, THE (USA) see **ANDERS ALS DU UND ICH** • 1957
THIRD SISTER LIU see **LIU SANJIE** • 1961
THIRD SQUAD, THE see **TRETI ROTA** • 1931
THIRD STRING, THE • 1914 • Tucker George Loane • UKN
THIRD STRING, THE • 1932 • Pearson George • UKN
THIRD THANKSGIVING, THE • 1912 • Dawley J. Searle • USA
THIRD TIME, THE see **TRETIU TAYM** • 1963
THIRD TIME LUCKY • 1931 • Forde Walter • UKN
THIRD TIME LUCKY • 1949 • Parry Gordon • UKN • THEY CRACKED HER GLASS SLIPPER
THIRD TIME UNLUCKY see **CROWN V STEVENS** • 1936
THIRD VICTIM, THE see **GHORBI-YE-SEVOM** • 1967
THIRD VISITOR, THE • 1951 • Elvey Maurice • UKN
THIRD VOICE, THE • 1960 • Cornfield Hubert • USA
THIRD WALKER, THE • 1979 • McLuhan Teri • CND
THIRD WISH, THE see **TRETI PRANI** • 1958
THIRD WITNESS, THE • 1917 • Coleby A. E. • UKN
THIRD WOMAN, THE • 1920 • Swickard Charles • USA
THIRD WOMAN, THE see **DAISAN NON ONNA** • 1959
THIRD WORLD: PRISONER OF THE STREET see **TIERS MONDE: PRISONNIER DE LA RUE** • 1980
THIRORINA, I • 1968 • Avrameas Nikos • GRC • DOOR-WOMAN, THE
THIRST • 1917 • *Swain Mack* • SHT • USA
THIRST • 1920 • *Hallmark* • USA
THIRST • 1960 • Tashkov Yevgyeni • USS
THIRST • 1979 • Hardy Rod • ASL
THIRST see **DESERT NIGHTS** • 1929
THIRST see **SETEA** • 1960
THIRST see **ZEDJ** • 1971
THIRST see **DHAKAM** • 1972
THIRST FOR GOLD, THE • 1912 • *Imp* • USA
THIRST FOR GOLD, THE • 1913 • *Tennant Barbara* • USA
THIRST FOR LOVE see **SED DE AMOR** • 1958
THIRST FOR LOVE, THE see **AI NO KAWAKI** • 1967
THIRST OF BARON BLOOD, THE see **ORRORI DEL CASTELLO DI NORIMBERGA, GLI** • 1972
THIRST (UKN) see **TORST** • 1949
THIRSTY DEAD, THE • 1975 • Becker Terry • USA, PHL
THIRSTY PEOPLE, THE • 1971 • Jamil Mohammed Shoukry • IRQ
THIRSTY TSAR, THE see **ZEDNI CAR** • 1967
THIRSTY YOUTH, THE see **ZIZNIVE MLADI** • 1943
THIRTEEN, THE see **TRINADTSAT** • 1937
THIRTEEN AT DINNER • 1985 • Antonio Lou • TVM • USA • AGATHA CHRISTIE'S THIRTEEN AT DINNER
THIRTEEN AT TABLE • 1913 • *Eclair* • USA
THIRTEEN CANTOS OF HELL • 1957 • King Peter • ANS • UKN
THIRTEEN CLUB, THE • 1905 • *Biograph* • USA
THIRTEEN DAYS see **TRINADESET DNI** • 1964
THIRTEEN DAYS OF LOVE (USA) see **ESCALE** • 1935
THIRTEEN DOWN • 1915 • Totten Lester • USA

THIRTEEN FIGHTING MEN • 1960 • Gerstad Harry • USA

THIRTEEN FRIGHTENED GIRLS • 1963 • Castle William • USA • CANDY WEB, THE ○ 13 FRIGHTENED GIRLS

THIRTEEN GHOSTS • 1960 • Castle William • USA • 13 GHOSTS

THIRTEEN HOURS BY AIR • 1936 • Leisen Mitchell • USA

THIRTEEN MEN AND A GIRL see **LETZTE KOMPANIE, DIE** • 1930

THIRTEEN MEN AND A GUN • 1938 • Zampi Mario • UKN

THIRTEEN MOST BEAUTIFUL BOYS, THE • 1964 • Warhol Andy • USA

THIRTEEN WOMEN • 1932 • Archainbaud George • USA

THIRTEENTH BRIDE OF THE PRINCE, THE • 1986 • Grubcheva Ivanka • BUL

THIRTEENTH CANDLE, THE • 1933 • Daumery John • UKN

THIRTEENTH CHAIR, THE • 1919 • Perret Leonce • USA

THIRTEENTH CHAIR, THE • 1929 • Browning Tod • USA

THIRTEENTH CHAIR, THE • 1937 • Seitz George B. • USA

THIRTEENTH CHAMBER, THE see **TRINACTA KOMNATA** • 1968

THIRTEENTH COMMANDMENT, THE • 1920 • Vignola Robert G. • USA • IMPULSES

THIRTEENTH FLOOR, THE see **13TH FLOOR, THE** • 1988

THIRTEENTH GIRL, THE • 1915 • Marston Theodore • USA

THIRTEENTH GREEN, THE • 1954 • *Howard Ronald* • UKN

THIRTEENTH GUEST, THE • 1932 • Ray Albert • USA • LADY BEWARE

THIRTEENTH HOUR, THE • 1927 • Franklin Chester M. • USA

THIRTEENTH INSTANT, THE • 1940 • Haines Ronald • SHT • UKN

THIRTEENTH JUROR, THE • 1927 • Laemmle Edward • USA

THIRTEENTH LAMB, THE • Oraczewska Zofia • ANS • PLN

THIRTEENTH MAN, THE • 1913 • *Bushman Francis X.* • USA

THIRTEENTH MAN, THE • 1937 • Nigh William • USA • 13TH MAN, THE

THIRTEENTH MAN, THE see **DHEKATOS TRITOS, O** • 1967

THIRTEENTH ROOM, THE see **TRINACTA KOMNATA** • 1968

THIRTIES, THE • 1975 • Mason Bill • DOC • UKN

THIRTIES: GLIMPSE OF AN ARCADE, THE • 1964 • Kelly Ron • DOC • CND

THIRTIETH PIECE OF SILVER, THE • 1920 • Cox George L. • USA

THIRTY • 1915 • *Bushman Francis X.* • USA

THIRTY see **-30-** • 1959

THIRTY A WEEK • 1918 • Beaumont Harry • USA

THIRTY DAY PRINCESS • 1934 • Gering Marion • USA • THIRTY-DAY PRINCESS

THIRTY-DAY PRINCESS see **THIRTY DAY PRINCESS** • 1934

THIRTY DAYS • 1912 • *Comet* • USA

THIRTY DAYS • 1916 • *Hardy Babe* • USA

THIRTY DAYS • 1917 • Christie Al • SHT • USA

THIRTY DAYS • 1922 • Cruze James • USA

THIRTY DAYS see **SILVER LINING, THE** • 1932

THIRTY DAYS AT HARD LABOR • 1912 • *Brower Robert* • USA

THIRTY DAYS HATH SEPTEMBER see **THIEVES FALL OUT** • 1941

THIRTY MINUTES • 1911 • *Reliance* • USA

THIRTY MINUTES OF LOVE see **TRENTA MINUTI D'AMORE** • 1982

THIRTY-NINE STEPS, THE • 1978 • Sharp Don • UKN

THIRTY SECONDS OVER TOKYO • 1944 • LeRoy Mervyn • USA

THIRTY-SIX HOURS • 1954 • Tully Montgomery • UKN • TERROR STREET (USA)

THIRTY-SIX KILLERS • Chyau Juang • HKG

THIRTY THOUSAND see **$30,000** • 1920

THIRTY THOUSAND DOLLARS see **$30,000** • 1920

THIRTY THREE see **TRIDSAT TRI** • 1965

THIRTY-THREE, THE see **TRIDSAT TRI** • 1965

THIRTY-THREE SILVER QUAILS • 1964 • Kachlik Antonin • CZC

THIRTY TIMES YOUR MONEY see **HEJA ROLAND!** • 1966

THIRTY YEARS see **DREISSIG JAHRE** • 1989

THIRTY YEARS BETWEEN • 1921 • *Stewart Vera* • USA

THIRTY YEARS LATER • 1928 • Micheaux Oscar • USA

THIRTY YEARS OF EXPERIMENT • 1951 • Richter Hans • USA

THIRTY YEARS OF FUN • 1963 • Youngson Robert • CMP • USA

THIRUMAL PERUMAI • 1968 • Nagarajan A. P. • IND • FAME OF LORD KRISHNA

THIRUNEELAKANTAR • 1939 • *Thyagaraja M. K.* • IND

THIRUVARUTCHELVAR • 1967 • Nagarajan A. P. • IND • GOD KARTICKEYA

THIS ABOVE ALL • 1942 • Litvak Anatole • USA

THIS ACTING BUSINESS • 1933 • Daumery John • UKN

THIS AND THAT see **QUESTO E QUELLO** • 1984

THIS ANGRY AGE (USA) see **BARRAGE CONTRE LE PACIFIQUE** • 1958

THIS AUCKLAND • 1968 • MacDonald Hugh • DCS • NZL

THIS BADMINTON RACKET • 1936 • Sparling Gordon • DCS • CND

THIS BEAUTIFUL LIFE • 1975 • Rousseva Maria • BUL

THIS BLOOMING BUSINESS OF BILINGUALISM • 1966 • Pearson Peter • DOC • CND

THIS CAN'T HAPPEN HERE (UKN) see **SANT HANDER INTE HAR** • 1950

THIS CHARMING COUPLE • 1949 • Van Dyke Willard • DOC • USA

THIS CHILD IS MINE • 1985 • Greene David • TVM • USA

THIS COULD BE THE NIGHT • 1957 • Wise Robert • USA

THIS COULD BE THE NIGHT see **BIG T.N.T. SHOW, THE** • 1966

THIS CRAZY URGE see **VOGLIA MATTA, LA** • 1962

THIS DAMNED AMERICA! see **VERFLUCHT, DIES AMERIKA!** • 1974

THIS DAY • 1947 • Stark Leonard • USA

THIS DAY AND AGE • 1933 • De Mille Cecil B. • USA

THIS DOESN'T HAPPEN HERE see **SANT HANDER INTE HAR** • 1950

THIS DUSTY WORLD (USA) see **JINKYO** • 1924

THIS EARTH BELONGS TO US see **AFTI I YI INE DIKI MAS** • 1967

THIS EARTH IS MINE • 1959 • King Henry • USA

THIS ENGLAND • 1941 • MacDonald David • UKN • OUR HERITAGE

THIS FILM IS ABOUT RAPE • 1978 • Kreps Bonnie • CND

THIS FILM WILL BE INTERRUPTED AFTER 11 MINUTES BY A COMMERCIAL • 1965 • Landow George • SHT • USA

THIS FREEDOM • 1923 • Clift Denison • UKN

THIS GENERATION: A PRAIRIE ROMANCE • 1934 • Bird Richard • CND

THIS GIRL FOR HIRE • 1983 • Jameson Jerry • TVM • USA

THIS GIRL IS A TRAMP see **THAT GIRL IS A TRAMP**

THIS GREEDY OLD SKIN (USA) see **GAMETSUI YATSU** • 1961

THIS GREEN HELL • 1936 • Faye Randall • UKN

THIS GUN FOR HIRE • 1942 • Tuttle Frank • USA

THIS GUN IS LOADED • 1970 • *Cosmos Films* • USA

THIS HAPPY BREED • 1944 • Lean David • UKN

THIS HAPPY FEELING • 1958 • Edwards Blake • USA • FOR LOVE OR MONEY

THIS HAPPY LIFE see **TANOSHIKI KANA JINSEI** • 1944

THIS HERO STUFF • 1919 • King Henry • USA

THIS HOUSE OF VANITY see **VANITY'S PRICE** • 1924

THIS HOUSE POSSESSED • 1981 • Wiard William • TVM • USA

THIS I LOVE AND THAT I WANT • 1975 • el Imam Hassan • EGY

THIS IMMORAL AGE (UKN) see **SQUARE ROOT OF ZERO, THE** • 1964

THIS INSTANT • 1969 • Lotyanu Emil • USS • THIS MOMENT

THIS IS A FILIPINO see **ITO ANG PILIPINO** • 1967

THIS IS A HIJACK • 1973 • Pollack Barry • USA • AIRPORT S.O.S. HIJACK ○ HIJACK

THIS IS A HOLD-UP • 1982 • Flamholc Leon • SHT • SWD

THIS IS A LIFE? • 1955 • Freleng Friz • ANS • USA

THIS IS A LIVING • 1953 • *Smith Pete* • SHT • USA

THIS IS A PHOTOGRAPH • 1971 • Kish Albert • DOC • CND

THIS IS A RECORDED MESSAGE see **CECI EST UN MESSAGE ENREGISTRE** • 1973

THIS IS AMERICA • 1943 • Fleischer Richard • DSS • USA

THIS IS AMERICA • 1977 • Vanderbes Romano • DOC • USA • CRAZY RIDICULOUS AMERICAN PEOPLE ○ JABBERWALK

THIS IS AN EGG see **TO JEST JAJKO** • 1966

THIS IS AN EMERGENCY • 1979 • Lamb Derek, Macartney-Filgate Terence • CND

THIS IS CALLAN see **CALLAN** • 1974

THIS IS CINERAMA • 1952 • Schoedsack Ernest B. • USA

THIS IS COLOUR • 1942 • Ellitt Jack • DCS • UKN

THIS IS DYNAMITE see **TURNING POINT, THE** • 1952

THIS IS ELVIS • 1981 • Leo Malcolm, Solt Andrew • DOC • USA

THIS IS ENGLAND (USA) see **HEART OF BRITAIN, THE** • 1941

THIS IS FUN! see **ESTO ES ALEGRIA!** • 1967

THIS IS HEAVEN • 1929 • Santell Alfred • USA

THIS IS HOW IT BEGAN.. see **ETO NACHINADOS TAK..** • 1956

THIS IS HOW MAYAKOVSKY BEGAN see **MAYAKOVSKY NACHINALSYA TAK** • 1959

THIS IS HOW MEMORIES ARE MADE see **SO WERDEN SOLDNER GEMACHT** • 1968

THIS IS IT • 1971 • Broughton James • USA

THIS IS IT • 1982 • Snow Michael • CND

THIS IS KARATE see **ITO ANG KARATE** • 1967

THIS IS KATE BENNETT.. • 1982 • Hart Harvey • TVM • USA

THIS IS KOREA • 1951 • Ford John • DOC • USA

THIS IS MY AFFAIR • 1937 • Seiter William A. • USA • HIS AFFAIR (UKN)

THIS IS MY AFFAIR (UKN) see **I CAN GET IT FOR YOU WHOLESALE** • 1951

THIS IS MY ALASKA • 1969 • Shebal Leroy • DOC • USA

THIS IS MY DUCKY DAY • 1961 • Hanna William, Barbera Joseph • ANS • USA

THIS IS MY LIFE see **ITO ANG AKING KASAYSAYAN** • 1967

THIS IS MY LOVE • 1954 • Heisler Stuart • USA

THIS IS MY STREET • 1963 • Hayers Sidney • UKN

THIS IS MY TERRITORY see **TERITORYO KO ITO** • 1967

THIS IS MY WIFE • Trikonis Gus • SHT • USA

THIS IS NEW ZEALAND • 1970 • MacDonald Hugh • DOC • NZL

THIS IS NOT A TEST • 1962 • Gadette Frederic • USA

THIS IS NOT MY ROOM • 1917 • *Vim* • USA

THIS IS NOT THE TIME FOR ROMANCE see **CA N'EST PAS LE TEMPS DES ROMANS** • 1967

THIS IS PHILOSOPHY • 1973 • Nicholson Arch • DOC • ASL

THIS IS POLISH RADIO LODZ SPEAKING see **HALLO, TU POLSKIE RADIO LODZ** • 1945

THIS IS RUSSIA • 1957 • *Wilson Carey/ Feder Sid (P)* • DOC • USA

THIS IS SPINAL TAP • 1985 • Reiner Rob • USA

THIS IS TH' LIFE • 1914 • Otto Henry • *American* • USA

THIS IS THE ARMY • 1943 • Curtiz Michael • USA

THIS IS THE BOWERY • 1941 • Fritsch Gunther V. • USA • ON THE BOWERY

THIS IS THE HOME OF MRS. LEVANT GRAHAME • 1971 • Weill Claudia • SHT • USA

THIS IS THE LAND • 1936 • Agadati B.

THIS IS THE LIFE • 1914 • *Eclectic* • USA

THIS IS THE LIFE • 1914 • *Essanay* • USA

THIS IS THE LIFE • 1914 • Ingraham Lloyd • *Powers* • USA

THIS IS THE LIFE • 1915 • Bertram William • USA

THIS IS THE LIFE • 1917 • Walsh Raoul • USA

THIS IS THE LIFE • 1918 • *Tweede Dan* • SHT • USA

THIS IS THE LIFE • 1933 • De Courville Albert • UKN • SINGING KETTLE, THE

THIS IS THE LIFE • 1935 • Neilan Marshall • USA • MEAL TICKET

THIS IS THE LIFE • 1944 • Feist Felix E. • USA • ANGELA

THIS IS THE LIFE • 1950 • Coronel Sidney A. • UKN

THIS IS THE NIGHT • 1932 • Tuttle Frank • USA • HE MET A FRENCH GIRL

THIS IS THE WEST THAT WAS • 1974 • Cook Fielder • TVM • USA • WEST WAS NEVER LIKE THIS, THE

THIS IS TOMORROW • 1943 • *Nesbitt John* • SHT • USA

THIS IS WAR see **ITO ANG DIGMAAN** • 1968

THIS IS YOUR ARMY • 1954 • Gordon John J. • DOC • USA

THIS ISLAND EARTH • 1955 • Newman Joseph M., Arnold Jack (U/c) • USA • WAR OF THE PLANETS

THIS ISN'T JOHN • 1913 • Hotaling Arthur D. • USA

THIS ISN'T THE LIFE • 1915 • McKim Edwin • USA

THIS JOINT IS JUMPIN' • 1941 • Murray Warren • SHT • USA

THIS JOINT IS JUMPIN' • 1947 • Binney Josh • USA

THIS LADY IS A TRAMP • 1982 • Vincent Chuck • USA

THIS LAND • 1970 • Hammond Arthur • CND

THIS LAND IS FULL OF LIFE see **DIN TILLVAROS LAND** • 1940

THIS LAND IS MINE • 1943 • Renoir Jean • USA

THIS LAND OF OURS see **ESTA TIERRA NUESTRA** • 1959

THIS LIFE I LOVE see **OINARU TABIJO** • 1960

THIS LITTLE GIRL AND THAT LITTLE GIRL • 1907 • Gilbert Arthur • UKN

THIS LITTLE PIGGIE WENT TO MARKET • 1934 • Fleischer Dave • ANS • USA

THIS LOVE FOREVER see **INOCHI KARETEMO** • 1968

THIS LOVE MUST BE KILLED see **TRZEBA ZABIC TE MILOSC** • 1972

THIS LOVE OF MINE see **WO-TE AI** • 1986

THIS LOVE OF OURS • 1945 • Dieterle William • USA • AS IT WAS BEFORE

THIS LOVE THING • 1970 • *Halas John (P)* • ANS • UKN

THIS MAD WORLD • 1930 • De Mille William C. • USA

THIS MADDING CROWD (USA) see **AOBEKA MONOGATARI** • 1964

THIS MAN CAN'T DIE (USA) see **LUNGHI GIORNI DELL'ODIO, I** • 1968

THIS MAN IN PARIS • 1939 • MacDonald David • UKN

THIS MAN IS DANGEROUS • 1941 • Huntington Lawrence • UKN • PATIENT VANISHES, THE

THIS MAN IS DANGEROUS see **CET HOMME EST DANGEREUX** • 1953

THIS MAN IS MINE • 1934 • Cromwell John • USA • TRANSIENT LOVE

THIS MAN IS MINE • 1946 • Varnel Marcel • UKN • CHRISTMAS WEEKEND

THIS MAN IS MINE see **LUSTY MEN, THE** • 1952

THIS MAN IS NEWS • 1938 • MacDonald David • UKN

THIS MAN MUST DIE (USA) see **QUE LA BETE MEURE** • 1969

THIS MAN REUTER (UKN) see **DISPATCH FROM REUTERS, A** • 1940

THIS MAN STANDS ALONE • 1979 • Freedman Jerrold • TVM • USA

THIS MAN -VAUTRIN see **VAUTRIN** • 1943

THIS MAN'S NAVY • 1944 • Wellman William A. • USA

THIS MAN'S NAVY see **STAND BY FOR ACTION** • 1942

THIS MARRIAGE BUSINESS • 1927 • Hiscott Leslie • UKN

THIS MARRIAGE BUSINESS • 1938 • Cabanne W. Christy • USA

THIS MECHANICAL AGE • 1954 • Youngson Robert • SHT • USA

THIS MODERN AGE • 1931 • Grinde Nick, Brown Clarence (U/c) • USA

THIS MODERN AGE NO.1 see **HOMES FOR ALL** • 1947

THIS MODERN AGE NO.2 see **SCOTLAND YARD** • 1947

THIS MODERN AGE NO.3 see **TOMORROW BY AIR** • 1947

THIS MODERN AGE NO.4 see **FABRICS OF THE FUTURE** • 1947

THIS MODERN AGE NO.5 see **THOROUGHBREDS OF THE WORLD** • 1947

THIS MODERN AGE NO.6 see **PALESTINE** • 1947

THIS MODERN AGE NO.7 see **COAL CRISIS** • 1947

THIS MODERN AGE NO.9 see **DEVELOPMENT AREAS** • 1947

THIS MODERN AGE NO.13 see **WILL BRITAIN GO HUNGRY?** • 1947

THIS MODERN AGE NO.15 see **LAND SHORT OF PEOPLE** • 1947

THIS MODERN AGE NO.16 see **BRITISH -ARE THEY ARTISTIC?, THE** • 1947

THIS MODERN AGE NO.20 see **FATE OF AN EMPIRE** • 1948

THIS MOMENT see **THIS INSTANT** • 1969

THIS MUST NOT BE FORGOTTEN see **O TYM NIE WOLNO ZAPOMNIEC** • 1968

THIS NIGHT WILL MAKE YOUR CORPSE INCARNATE see **ESTA NOITE ENCARNAREI NO TEU CADAVER** • 1967

THIS OTHER EDEN • 1959 • Box Muriel • UKN

THIS OXFORD • 1931 • Bowden Frank • UKN

THIS PASSING LIFE see **MUJO** • 1970

THIS PICTURE IS CENSORED see **CENSORED** • 1965

THIS PROPERTY IS CONDEMNED • 1966 • Pollack Sydney • USA

THIS PSYCHIC WORLD • Random Darrell • USA

THIS REBEL AGE see **BEAT GENERATION, THE** • 1959

THIS REBEL BREED • 1960 • Bare Richard L. • USA • THREE SHADES OF LOVE ○ LOLA'S MISTAKE

THIS RECKLESS AGE • 1932 • Tuttle Frank • USA • SECOND CHANCES

THIS RUGGED LAND • 1962 • Hiller Arthur • TVM • USA

THIS SAVAGE LAND • 1968 • McEveety Vincent • TVM • USA • SAVAGE LAND, THE

THIS SCORCHING SEA see **KURUTTA KAJITSU** • 1956

THIS SHOCKING WORLD • 1964 • Proia Gianni • DOC • ITL

THIS SIDE OF HEAVEN • 1932 • Howard William K. • USA • IT HAPPENED ONE DAY

THIS SIDE OF THE LAW • 1950 • Bare Richard L. • USA

THIS SIDE UP • 1906 • Collins Alf? • UKN

THIS SPECIAL FRIENDSHIP (USA) see **AMITIES PARTICULIERES, LES** • 1964

THIS SPORTING AGE • 1932 • Bennison Andrew W., Erickson A. F. • USA

THIS SPORTING HOUSE • 1969 • Sullivan Ron • USA • SPORTING HOUSE

THIS SPORTING LIFE • 1963 • Anderson Lindsay • UKN

THIS STRANGE PASSION see **EL** • 1952

THIS STUFF'LL KILL YA'! • 1971 • Lewis Herschell G. • USA

THIS SUMMER AT 5 see **KESALLA KELLO 5** • 1963

THIS SWEET SICKNESS (UKN) see **DITES-LUI QUE JE L'AIME** • 1977

THIS SWEET WORD -FREEDOM see **ETO SLADKOE SLOVO-SVOBODA** • 1973

THIS, THAT AND THE OTHER • 1971 • Blacetti Giuliano

THIS, THAT AND THE OTHER see **PROMISE OF BED, A** • 1969

THIS THING CALLED LOVE • 1929 • Stein Paul L. • USA

THIS THING CALLED LOVE • 1940 • Hall Alexander • USA • MARRIED BUT SINGLE (UKN)

THIS TIME FOR KEEPS • 1941 • Reisner Charles F. • USA • OVER THE WAVES

THIS TIME FOR KEEPS • 1947 • Thorpe Richard • USA

THIS TIME FOREVER see **YESTERDAY** • 1980

THIS TIME LET'S TALK ABOUT MEN see **QUESTA VOLTA PARLIAMO DI UOMINI** • 1965

THIS TINY WORLD see **KLEINE WERELD, DIE** • 1973

THIS TOWN • 1969 • Evans Hugh • UKN

THIS TRANSIENT LIFE see **MUJO** • 1970

THIS WAS A WOMAN • 1948 • Whelan Tim • UKN

THIS WAS ENGLAND • 1935 • Field Mary • UKN

THIS WAS JAPAN • 1945 • Wright Basil • DOC • UKN

THIS WAS PARIS • 1942 • Harlow John • UKN

THIS WAY OUT • 1915 • Stull Walter, Burns Bobby • USA

THIS WAY OUT • 1918 • *Vernon Bobby* • USA

THIS WAY OUT • 1919 • MacMackin Archer • SHT • USA

THIS WAY OUT • 1920 • *Edwards Neely* • SHT • USA

THIS WAY OUT • 1923 • De Rue Eugene • USA

THIS WAY OUT, PLEASE see **DOCTOR, YOU'VE GOT TO BE KIDDING** • 1967

THIS WAY PLEASE • 1929 • Newfield Sam • SHT • USA

THIS WAY PLEASE • 1937 • Florey Robert • USA

THIS WAY THAT WAY see **ANOTE KONOTE** • 1952

THIS WE CAN DO FOR JUSTICE AND FOR PEACE • 1981 • Harris Kevin • DOC • SAF

THIS WEEK OF GRACE • 1933 • Elvey Maurice • UKN

THIS WIFE FOR HIRE • 1985 • Drake James R. • TVM • USA

THIS WILL DO FOR TODAY • 1977 • Lavut Martin • CND

THIS WILL HAPPEN TOMORROW see **TO, CO ZDARZY SIE JUTRO** • 1972

THIS WINE OF LOVE (USA) see **ELISIR D'AMORE** • 1947

THIS WOMAN • 1924 • Rosen Phil • USA

THIS WOMAN IS DANGEROUS • 1952 • Feist Felix E. • USA

THIS WOMAN IS MINE • 1941 • Lloyd Frank • USA • I, JAMES LEWIS

THIS WOMAN –THIS MAN see **GUILTY OF LOVE** • 1920

THIS WONDERFUL CROOK see **PAS SI MECHANT QUE CA** • 1975

THIS WORLD see **KATAKU** • 1979

THIS YEAR'S BLONDE • 1980 • Erman John • TVM • USA • SECRET LOVE OF MARILYN MONROE, THE

THIS YEAR'S LOVE see **KOTOSHI NO KOI** • 1962

THIS'LL MAKE YOU WHISTLE • 1936 • Wilcox Herbert • UKN

THISTLE, THE • 1934 • Smith Percy • UKN

THISTLEDOWN • 1938 • Woods Arthur • UKN

THISTLES OF BARAGAN, THE see **CIULINII BARAGANULUI** • 1957

THISTLES OF THE BARAGAN, THE see **CIULINII BARAGANULUI** • 1957

THOMAS • 1974 • Dion Jean-Francois • FRN

THOMAS AND.. THE BEWITCHED see **THOMAS E.. GLI INDEMONATI** • 1970

THOMAS CHATTERTON • 1911 • Maggi Luigi • ITL

THOMAS CROWN AFFAIR, THE • 1968 • Jewison Norman • USA • CROWN CAPER, THE

THOMAS E.. GLI INDEMONATI • 1970 • Avati Pupi • ITL • THOMAS AND.. THE BEWITCHED

THOMAS ER FREDLOS • 1967 • Gronlykke Sven • DNM • THOMAS IS AN OUTLAW ○ THOMAS ON THE RUN ○ THOMAS THE RESTLESS ONE

THOMAS GRAALS BASTA BARN • 1918 • Stiller Mauritz • SWD • THOMAS GRAAL'S FIRST CHILD (USA) ○ THOMAS GRAAL'S BEST CHILD(UKN)

THOMAS GRAALS BASTA FILM • 1917 • Stiller Mauritz • SWD • THOMAS GRAAL'S BEST FILM (USA) ○ WANTED A FILM ACTRESS (UKN) ○ WANTED –AN ACTRESS

THOMAS GRAAL'S BEST CHILD(UKN) see **THOMAS GRAALS BASTA BARN** • 1918

THOMAS GRAAL'S BEST FILM (USA) see **THOMAS GRAALS BASTA FILM** • 1917

THOMAS GRAAL'S FIRST CHILD (USA) see **THOMAS GRAALS BASTA BARN** • 1918

THOMAS GRAALS MYNDLING • 1922 • Molander Gustaf • SWD • THOMAS GRAAL'S WARD

THOMAS GRAAL'S WARD see **THOMAS GRAALS MYNDLING** • 1922

THOMAS IS AN OUTLAW see **THOMAS ER FREDLOS** • 1967

THOMAS L'IMPOSTEUR • 1964 • Franju Georges • FRN • THOMAS THE IMPOSTER

THOMAS MUNTZER • 1956 • Hellberg Martin • GDR

THOMAS ON THE RUN see **THOMAS ER FREDLOS** • 1967

THOMAS THE IMPOSTER see **THOMAS L'IMPOSTEUR** • 1964

THOMAS THE RESTLESS ONE see **THOMAS ER FREDLOS** • 1967

THOMASINE AND BUSHROD • 1974 • Parks Gordon Jr. • USA

THOMPSON 1880 • 1966 • Zurli Guido • ITL

THOMPSON'S LAST RUN • 1986 • Freedman Jerrold • TVM • USA • LAST RUN, THE

THOMPSON'S NIGHT OUT • 1908 • *Bitzer Billy (Ph)* • USA

THONG see **SPOILERS, THE** • 1976

THONGPOON KOKPO • 1978 • Chalerm Prince Chatri • THL

THOR • 1985 • SAF

THOR AND THE AMAZON WOMEN see **TAUR, IL RE DELLA FORZA BRUTA** • 1963

THOR IL CONQUISTATORE • 1982 • Ricci Tonino • ITL • THOR THE CONQUEROR

THOR, LORD OF THE JUNGLES • 1913 • Campbell Colin • USA

THOR THE CONQUEROR see **THOR IL CONQUISTATORE** • 1982

THORA VAN DEKEN • 1920 • Brunius John W. • SWD • MOTHER'S FIGHT, A

THORN, THE • 1967 • Georgi Katja • ANS • GDR

THORN, THE • 1980 • Alexander Peter • USA • DIVINE MR. J., THE

THORN AMONG ROSES, A • 1915 • *Mason Dan* • USA

THORN AND THE ROSE, THE • 1916 • Robertson John S. • SHT • USA

THORN AND THE SILK, THE • 1987 • Kimiyaei Massoud • IRN

THORN BIRDS, THE • 1982 • Duke Daryl • TVM • USA

THORN IN THE HEART, A see **SPINA NEL CUORE, UNA** • 1985

THORN INVENTION, A • 1912 • *Rex* • USA

THORN UNDER THE FINGERNAIL, A see **TUSKE A KOROM ALATT** • 1988

THORNS AND ORANGE BLOSSOMS • 1922 • Gasnier Louis J. • USA

THORNS OF PASSION (UKN) see **ROUGHNECK, THE** • 1924

THORNS OF SUCCESS • 1912 • *Trunvelle Mabel* • USA

THORNS OF THE GAY WHITE WAY • 1914 • *Ruby* • USA

THORNTON JEWEL MYSTERY, THE • 1915 • Raymond Charles • UKN

THORNWELL • 1981 • Moses Harry • TVM • USA

THORNY HOBOES see **HORNY HOBO** • 1969

THORNY WAY TO THE STARS, THE see **CHEREZ TERNII K ZVEZDAM** • 1981

THOROBRED • 1922 • Halligan George • USA

THOROUGHBRED • 1936 • Hall Ken G. • ASL

THOROUGHBRED see **RUN FOR THE ROSES** • 1978

THOROUGHBRED, A • 1911 • Dawley J. Searle • USA

THOROUGHBRED, THE • 1916 • Barker Reginald • *Kb* • USA

THOROUGHBRED, THE • 1916 • Bartlett Charles • *American* • USA

THOROUGHBRED, THE • 1925 • Apfel Oscar • USA

THOROUGHBRED, THE • 1928 • Morgan Sidney • UKN

THOROUGHBRED, THE • 1930 • Thorpe Richard • USA • RIDING TO WIN (UKN)

THOROUGHBRED WOMEN GAMBLERS see **SANBIKI NO ONNA TOBAKUSHI** • 1967

THOROUGHBREDS • 1945 • Blair George • USA

THOROUGHBREDS, THE see **RUN FOR THE ROSES** • 1978

THOROUGHBREDS DON'T CRY • 1937 • Green Alfred E. • USA

THOROUGHBREDS OF THE WORLD • 1947 • DOC • UKN • THIS MODERN AGE NO.5

THOROUGHBREDS (UKN) see **SILKS AND SADDLES** • 1929

THOROUGHLY MODERN MILLIE • 1967 • Hill George Roy • USA

THORPE BATES • 1926 • *Deforest Phonofilms* • SHT • UKN

THORS HAMMER • 1983 • Barfod Bent • ANS • DNM • THOR'S HAMMER

THOR'S HAMMER see **THORS HAMMER** • 1983

THORVALD OG LINDA • 1982 • Gronlykke Lene, Gronlykke Sven • DNM • BALLAD OF LINDA, THE

THORVALDSEN • 1949 • Dreyer Carl T., Frank Preben • DCS • DNM

THOSE ATHLETIC GIRLS • 1918 • Cline Eddie • SHT • USA

THOSE AWFUL HATS • 1909 • Griffith D. W. • USA

THOSE BEAUTIFUL DAMES • 1935 • Freleng Friz • ANS • USA

THOSE BITTER SWEETS • 1915 • Jones F. Richard • USA

THOSE BLASTED KIDS see **POKKERS UNGER, DE** • 1947

THOSE BOYS! • 1909 • Griffith D. W. • USA

THOSE BOYS AGAIN • 1906 • Stow Percy • UKN

THOSE CALLOWAYS • 1965 • Tokar Norman • USA • THOSE CRAZY CALLOWAYS

THOSE CHILDREN! • 1915 • Batley Ethyle • UKN

THOSE COLLEGE DAYS • 1914 • Christie Al • USA

THOSE COLLEGE GIRLS • 1915 • Sennett Mack • USA

THOSE COUNTRY KIDS • 1914 • Dillon Eddie, Arbuckle Roscoe • USA

THOSE CRAZY CALLOWAYS see **THOSE CALLOWAYS** • 1965

THOSE CRAZY RASPLYUYEV DAYS see **VESYOLYYE RASPLYUYEVSKIYE DNI** • 1966

THOSE DAMNED SAVAGES see **MAUDITS SAUVAGE, LES** • 1971

THOSE DARING YOUNG MEN IN THEIR JAUNTY JALOPIES (USA) see **MONTE CARLO OR BUST!** • 1969

THOSE DEAR DEPARTED • 1987 • Robinson Ted • ASL

THOSE DIRTY DOGS • 1974 • *Boyd Stephen* • SPN

THOSE DISTANT COUSINS • 1919 • Kellette John William • SHT • USA

THOSE ELEVEN MEN see **ORA EGAROJON** • 1972

THOSE ENDEARING YOUNG CHARMS • 1945 • Allen Lewis • USA

THOSE FANTASTIC FLYING FOOLS (USA) see **JULES VERNE'S ROCKET TO THE MOON** • 1967

THOSE FEMALE HATERS • 1916 • Curtis Allen • SHT • USA

THOSE FLIES • 1908 • Coleby A. E. • UKN • FLIES, THE

THOSE FORGOTTEN BY GOD (USA) see **OLVIDADOS DE DIOS, LOS** • 1939

THOSE FROM THE CASPIAN see **KAPISKIE LIUDI** • 1944

THOSE GENTLEMEN WHO HAVE A CLEAN SHEET see **HERREN MIT DER WEISSEN WESTE, DIE** • 1970

THOSE GERMAN BOWLERS • 1915 • *Sterling* • USA

THOSE GOOD OLD DAYS • 1913 • Sennett Mack • USA

THOSE GOOD OLD DAYS • 1941 • Negulesco Jean • SHT • USA

THOSE GOOD OLD DAYS • 1949 • Barclay David • SHT • USA

THOSE HAPPY DAYS • 1914 • Arbuckle Roscoe, Dillon Eddie • USA

THOSE HARD DAYS see **DIAS DUROS, LOS** • 1970

THOSE HICKSVILLE BOYS • 1912 • Sennett Mack • USA

THOSE HIGH GREY WALLS • 1939 • Vidor Charles • USA • GATES OF ALCATRAZ, THE (UKN) ○ PRISON SURGEON

THOSE JERSEY COWPUNCHERS • 1911 • *Nestor* • USA

THOSE KIDS AND CUPID • 1915 • *Gallagher Ray* • USA

THOSE KIDS FROM TOWN • 1942 • Comfort Lance • UKN

THOSE LIPS, THOSE EYES • 1980 • Pressman Michael • USA

THOSE LITTLE FLOWERS • 1913 • Powell Paul?, Kirkwood James? • USA

THOSE LOVE PANGS • 1914 • Chaplin Charles • USA • RIVAL MASHERS, THE ○ BUSTED HEARTS ○ BUSTED RIVALS

THOSE LOVESICK COWBOYS • 1912 • *Nestor* • USA

THOSE MAGNIFICENT MEN IN THEIR FLYING MACHINES: OR HOW I FLEW FROM LONDON TO PARIS IN 25 HOURS AND.. • 1965 • Annakin Ken, Sharp Don (U/c) • UKN

THOSE NAUGHTY ANGELS • 1974 • Hetherington Neil • SAF

THOSE NUISANCES • 1946 • Hughes Ken • DCS • UKN

THOSE OTHER DAYS • 1941 • Sparling Gordon • CND

THOSE PEOPLE NEXT DOOR • 1953 • Harlow John • UKN

THOSE PERSISTENT OLD MAIDS • 1914 • Christie Al • USA

THOSE PRIMITIVE DAYS • 1916 • *Compson Betty* • SHT • USA

THOSE REDHEADS FROM SEATTLE • 1953 • Foster Lewis R. • USA

THOSE ROOS BOYS AND FRIENDS • 1988 • Boyden Barbara • DOC • CND

THOSE TERRIBLE TELEGRAMS • 1917 • *Sparkle Comedy* • SHT • USA

THOSE TERRIBLE TWINS • 1925 • Ward J. E. • ASL

THOSE THREE FRENCH GIRLS • 1930 • Beaumont Harry • USA

THOSE TROUBLESOME BOYS • 1902 • Williamson James • UKN

THOSE TROUBLESOME TRESSES • 1913 • Baker George D. • USA

THOSE TWO BOYS • 1929 • Roberts Stephen • SHT • USA

THOSE WE LOVE • 1932 • Florey Robert • USA

THOSE WEDDING BELLS • 1917 • Christie Al • SHT • USA

THOSE WERE HAPPY DAYS • 1912 • *Powers* • USA

THOSE WERE THE DAYS • 1934 • Bentley Thomas • UKN • MAGISTRATE, THE

THOSE WERE THE DAYS • 1940 • Reed Theodore • USA • GOOD OLD SCHOOL DAYS (UKN) ○ GOOD OLD SIWASH ○ AT GOOD OLD SIWASH

THOSE WERE THE DAYS • 1946 • Anderson James M. • UKN

THOSE WERE THE DAYS! see **GORJACE D ENEKI** • 1935

THOSE WERE THE DAYS (USA) see **QUE TIEMPOS AQUELLOS** • 1938

THOSE WERE THE HAPPY DAYS • 1914 • *Forde Victoria* • USA

THOSE WERE THE HAPPY DAYS see **STAR!** • 1968

THOSE WERE THE HAPPY TIMES see **STAR!** • 1968

THOSE WERE WONDERFUL DAYS • 1934 • Brown Bernard • ANS • USA

THOSE WHO ARE LATE see **SPOZNIENI PRZECHODNIE** • 1962

THOSE WHO DANCE • 1924 • Hillyer Lambert • USA

THOSE WHO DANCE • 1930 • Beaudine William • USA • HIS WOMAN

THOSE WHO DARE • 1924 • O'Brien John B. • USA

THOSE WHO DWELL IN DARKNESS • 1914 • Raymond Charles? • UKN

THOSE WHO HAVE TO SERVE see **LAS QUE TIENEN QUE SERVIR** • 1967

THOSE WHO JUDGE • 1924 • King Burton L. • USA

THOSE WHO KNOW HOW TO LOVE see **EKINI POU XEROUN N'AGAPOUN** • 1968

THOSE WHO LIVE IN GLASS HOUSES • 1913 • *Leonard Marion* • USA

THOSE WHO LIVE IN GLASSHOUSES • 1925 • Butler Alexander • UKN

THOSE WHO LIVE WHERE THE SOFT WIND BLOWS see **LOS QUE VIVEN DONDE SOPLA EL VIENTO SUAVE** • 1973

THOSE WHO LOVE • 1926 • McDonagh Paulette, Ramster P. J. • ASL

THOSE WHO LOVE • 1929 • Haynes Manning • UKN • MARY WAS LOVE

THOSE WHO MAKE TOMORROW see **ASU O TSUKURU HITOBITO** • 1946

THOSE WHO PAY • 1918 • Wells Raymond • USA

THOSE WHO PLAY THE PIANO see **LOS QUE TOCAN EL PIANO** • 1968

THOSE WHO TOIL • 1916 • Lewis Edgar • USA • TOILERS, THE

THOSE WHO WAIT FOR SPRING see **HARU O MATSU HITOBITO** • 1959

THOSE WITHOUT SIN • 1917 • Neilan Marshall • USA

THOSE WONDERFUL GIRLS see **SUBARISHIKI MUSUMETACHI** • 1959

THOSE WONDERFUL MOVIE CRANKS (UKN) see **BAJECNI MUZI S KLIKOU** • 1979

THOSE WONDERFUL MOVIE MEN WITH A CRANK see **BAJECNI MUZI S KLIKOU** • 1979

THOSE WOULD–BE GIRLS see **SOZDE KIZLAR** • 1967

THOSE YEARS see **AQUELLOS ANOS** • 1972

THOT FAL'N • 1978 • Brakhage Stan • SHT • USA

THOU ART MY JOY (USA) see **DU BIST MEIN GLUCK** • 1936

THOU ART THE MAN • 1916 • Drew Sidney • USA

THOU ART THE MAN • 1920 • Heffron Thomas N. • USA

THOU ART THE MAN see **GUILTY CONSCIENCE, A** • 1921

THOU FOOL • 1926 • Paul Fred • UKN

THOU OLD, THOU FREE (USA) see **DU GAMLA, DU FRIA** • 1938

THOU SHALT HONOR THY WIFE see **DU SKAL AERE DIN HUSTRU** • 1925

THOU SHALT NOT • 1910 • Griffith D. W. • USA

THOU SHALT NOT (?) • 1912 • *Champion* • USA

THOU SHALT NOT • 1914 • Davis Will S. • USA

THOU SHALT NOT • 1919 • Brabin Charles J. • USA

THOU SHALT NOT COMMIT ADULTERY • 1978 • Mann Delbert • TVM • USA

THOU SHALT NOT COVET • 1912 • *Bunny John* • USA

THOU SHALT NOT COVET • 1916 • Campbell Colin • USA

THOU SHALT NOT COVET THY NEIGHBOUR ON THE FIFTH FLOOR see **NO DESEARAS AL VECINO DEL QUINTO** • 1971

THOU SHALT NOT COVET THY NEIGHBOUR'S WIFE see **NO DESEARAS LA MUJER DE TU PROJIMO** • 1968

THOU SHALT NOT FLIRT • 1915 • *L-Ko* • USA

THOU SHALT NOT KILL • 1910 • *Powers* • USA

THOU SHALT NOT KILL • 1913 • Reid Hal • USA

THOU SHALT NOT KILL • 1914 • *Selig* • USA

THOU SHALT NOT KILL • 1915 • *Coghlan Rose* • USA

THOU SHALT NOT KILL • 1940 • Auer John H. • USA

THOU SHALT NOT KILL • 1982 • Rappaport I. C. • TVM • USA

THOU SHALT NOT KILL see **TU NE TUERAS POINT** • 1961

THOU SHALT NOT KILL see **KROTKI FILM O ZABIJANIU** • 1988

THOU SHALT NOT LIE • 1911 • *Reliance* • USA

THOU SHALT NOT LIE • 1915 • Easton Clem • USA

THOU SHALT NOT LOVE • 1922 • *Le Picard Vivian* • USA

THOU SHALT NOT RUBBER • 1913 • *Imp* • USA

THOU SHALT NOT STEAL • 1911 • *Reliance* • USA

THOU SHALT NOT STEAL • 1911 • *Powers* • USA

THOU SHALT NOT STEAL • 1913 • *Rex* • USA

THOU SHALT NOT STEAL • 1914 • Buckland Warwick? • UKN

THOU SHALT NOT STEAL • 1917 • Nigh William • USA

THOU SHALT NOT (UKN) see **THERESE RAQUIN** • 1928

THOU SHALT PAY • 1911 • *Yankee* • USA

THOU VOU FALAKROS PRAKTOR EPIHIRISSIS GIS MADIAM • 1969 • Vengos Thanasis • GRC • BALDHEADED AGENT AND THE LAND OF DESTRUCTION MISSION, THE

THOU, WHICH ART IN HEAVEN • 1988 • Bodjakov Docho • BUL
THOUGH THE SEAS DIVIDE • 1911 • *Vitagraph* • USA
THOUGH YOUR SINS BE AS SCARLET • 1911 • *Vitagraph* • USA
THOUGHT see **MYSL** • 1916
THOUGHT TO KILL • 1953 • Arliss Leslie, Huntington Lawrence, Knowles Bernard • UKN
THOUGHTFULNESS REMEMBERED BY THE UTE • 1910 • *Revier* • USA
THOUGHTLESS BEAUTY, A • 1908 • Fitzhamon Lewin • UKN • FORCED TO CONSENT
THOUGHTLESS WOMEN • 1920 • Goodman Daniel Carson • USA
THOUGHTS IN A LANDSCAPE • 1981 • Sens Al • SHT • CND
THOUGHTS OF TONIGHT • 1915 • French Charles K. • USA
THOUSAND A WEEK, A • 1916 • Beery Wallace • USA
THOUSAND AND ONE HANDS, A see **ALF YAD WA YAD** • 1972
THOUSAND AND ONE NIGHTS, A • 1945 • Green Alfred E. • USA
THOUSAND AND ONE NIGHTS, A • 1968 • Elorrieta Jose Maria • SPN
THOUSAND AND ONE NIGHTS, A • 1969 • Yamamoto Eiichi • ANM • JPN
THOUSAND AND ONE NIGHTS, A see **ALIF LAILA WA LEILA** • 1941
THOUSAND AND ONE NIGHTS, A see **ELIF LAILA WA LAILA** • 1964
THOUSAND AND ONE NIGHTS, A see **POHADKY TISICE A JEDNE NOCI** • 1972
THOUSAND AND ONE NIGHTS, A see **FIORE DELLE MILLE E UNA NOTTE, IL** • 1974
THOUSAND AND ONE NIGHTS IN TOKYO, A see **TOKYO SENICHIYA** • 1938
THOUSAND AND ONE NIGHTS WITH TOHO, A see **TOHO SEN-ICHIYA** • 1947
THOUSAND AND ONE WOMEN, A see **MILLE E UNA DONNA** • 1964
THOUSAND CLARINETS, A see **KDYBY TISIC KLARINETU** • 1964
THOUSAND CLOWNS, A • 1965 • Coe Fred • USA
THOUSAND CRANES see **SENBAZURU** • 1969
THOUSAND CRANES, A see **SENBAZURU** • 1953
THOUSAND CRANES, A see **KHILYADA ZHERAVI** • 1968
THOUSAND CRANES FLYING, A see **SENBAZURU HICHO** • 1959
THOUSAND DAYS, THE • 1942 • Sparling Gordon • DCS • CND
THOUSAND DOLLAR DROP, THE • 1917 • Curtis Allen • SHT • USA
THOUSAND DOLLAR HUSBAND, THE • 1916 • Young James • USA
THOUSAND DOLLAR MARRIAGE see **POP ALWAYS PAYS** • 1940
THOUSAND DOLLARS SHORT, A • 1913 • *Patheplay* • USA
THOUSAND FLOWERS, A • Wickremaratne Dharmasiri • SLN, IND, THL
THOUSAND ISLANDS SUMMER • 1960 • Blais Roger • SHT • CND • QUAND VIENT L'ETE
THOUSAND LITTLE KISSES, A see **ELEF NESHIKOTH KETANOTH** • 1981
THOUSAND-MILE ROAD, A see **DOROGA V TYSYACHU VYERST** • 1968
THOUSAND MILES OF HOLIDAYS, A • 1974 • Pearson Peter • CND
THOUSAND MILLION A YEAR, A • Reeve Leonard • DOC • UKN
THOUSAND MOONS, A • 1976 • Carle Gilles • MTV • CND
THOUSAND PLANE RAID, THE • 1969 • Sagal Boris • USA • 1000 PLANE RAID, THE
THOUSAND PLEASURES, A • 1968 • Findlay Michael • USA
THOUSAND POUND SPOOK, THE see **£1000 SPOOK, THE** • 1907
THOUSAND ROADS -THOUSAND DEATHS see **MIL CAMINOS TIENE LA MUERTE** • 1976
THOUSAND SMILE CHECKUP • 1960 • Taras Martin B. • ANS • USA
THOUSAND SONGS WITHOUT A SOUND, A see **TAUSEND LIEDER OHNE TON** • 1977
THOUSAND SOULS • 1976 • Haanstra Bert • SHT • NTH
THOUSAND THOUGHTS, A see **DAHASAK SITHUVILI** • 1968
THOUSAND TO ONE, A • 1920 • Lee Rowland V. • USA
THOUSAND WINDOWS, A see **TYSYACHA OKON** • 1968
THOUSAND WIVES, A • 1988 • Bat-Adam Michal • ISR
THOUSAND WORDS, A see **MILLE MOTS** • 1973
THOUSAND YEAR MAN, THE • 1956 • Jordan Larry • SHT • USA
THOUSAND-YEAR-OLD BEE, THE see **TISICROCNA VCELA** • 1983
THOUSANDS CHEER • 1943 • Sidney George, Minnelli Vincente (U/c) • USA • AS THOUSANDS CHEER ○ PRIVATE MISS JONES
THRALLS, THE • 1978 • Hastrup Jannik • ANM • DNM
THRALL'S REVOLT, THE • 1978 • Hastrup Jannik • ANM • DNM
THRASHIN' • 1986 • Winters David • USA
THREAD O' SCARLET • 1930 • Godfrey Peter • UKN
THREAD OF DESTINY, THE • 1910 • Griffith D. W. • USA
THREAD OF LIFE, THE • 1912 • Dwan Allan • USA
THREAD OF LIFE, THE • 1916 • Wilson Ben • SHT • USA
THREADING PEARLS • 1916 • *Knickerbocker Star* • SHT • USA
THREADS • 1932 • Samuelson G. B. • USA, UKN
THREADS • 1984 • Jackson Mick • TVM • UKN
THREADS OF DESTINY • 1914 • Smiley Joseph • USA
THREADS OF FATE • 1915 • De Grasse Joseph • USA
THREADS OF FATE • 1916 • *Supreme* • USA
THREADS OF FATE • 1917 • Nowland Eugene • USA
THREADS OF THE RAINBOW • 1968 • Kovachev Hristo • DOC • BUL
THREAT see **ODOSHI** • 1966
THREAT see **UHKKADUS** • 1987
THREAT, THE • 1949 • Feist Felix E. • USA
THREAT, THE • 1960 • Rondeau Charles R. • USA
THREAT, THE • 1988 • Nikolov Milen • BUL
THREAT, THE see **POWER GAME** • 1982
THREAT, THE (UKN) see **SMOKY RIVER SERENADE** • 1947
THREAT IN THE WATER, THE • 1968 • Bigham Richard • UKN
THREATENED CITY, THE see **CIDADE AMEACADA** • 1959
THREATENING SKY, THE (UKN) see **CIEL, LA TERRE, LE** • 1965
THREE • 1969 • Salter James • UKN
THREE • 1969 • Sughrue John J. • USA
THREE see **TRI** • 1965
THREE see **TRE** • 1972
THREE, THE see **TRAJA** • 1969
THREE A.M. • 1976 • McCallum Robert • USA • 3 A.M.
THREE AGES • 1923 • Keaton Buster, Cline Eddie • USA
THREE ALPINISTS, THE • 1909 • *Urban Trading Co* • UKN
THREE AMERICAN BEAUTIES • 1906 • Porter Edwin S. • USA
THREE AMERICANS LP'S see **DREI AMERIKANISCHE LPS** • 1969
THREE AMIGOS! • 1986 • Landis John • USA
THREE AND A DAY • 1939 • Negulesco Jean • SHT • USA
THREE AND ONE • 1974 • Kalik Michael • ISR
THREE AND TWO MORE see **TRES MAS DOS** • 1979
THREE ANGELS AND FIVE LIONS see **TRE ENGLE OF FEM LOVER** • 1983
THREE ANNES, THE see **TRI ANE** • 1959
THREE APPLES, THE • 1979 • Popescu-Gopo Ion • ANM • RMN
THREE APPRENTICES • 1963 • Biggs Julian, Howe John, Burwash Gordon • CND
THREE ARABIAN NUTS • 1951 • Bernds Edward • SHT • USA
THREE AT THE TABLE see **UNKNOWN WIFE, THE** • 1921
THREE AVENGERS, THE (USA) see **INVINCIBILI TRE, GLI** • 1965
THREE BACCHANTS, THE see **TROIS BACCHANTES, LES** • 1900
THREE BACHELORS' TURKEY, THE • 1912 • *Pathe* • USA
THREE BAD MEN • 1926 • Ford John • USA
THREE BAD MEN AND A GIRL • 1915 • Ford Francis • USA
THREE BAD MEN IN A HIDDEN FORTRESS see **KAKUSHI TORIDE NO SAN-AKUNIN** • 1958
THREE BAD SISTERS • 1956 • Kay Gilbert L. • USA
THREE BADGERS see **SANBIKI NO TANUKI** • 1966
THREE BAGS FULL • 1949 • Baxter John • SRL • UKN
THREE BASES EAST • 1925 • Ruggles Wesley • SHT • USA
THREE BEARS • 1925 • Lantz Walter • ANS • USA
THREE BEARS, THE • 1911 • *Prout Eva* • SHT • USA
THREE BEARS, THE • 1934 • *Terry Paul/ Moser Frank (P)* • ANS • USA
THREE BEARS, THE • 1935 • *Iwerks Ub (P)* • ANS • USA
THREE BEARS, THE • 1939 • Davis Mannie • ANS • USA
THREE BITES OF THE APPLE • 1966 • Ganzer Alvin • USA
THREE BLACK BAGS • 1913 • Thompson Frederick A. • USA
THREE BLACK EYES • 1919 • Horan Charles • USA • BLACK EYES
THREE BLACK TRUMPS, THE • 1915 • *Picture Playhouse Film* • USA
THREE BLIND MICE • 1938 • Seiter William A. • USA
THREE BLIND MICE • 1945 • Dunning George • ANS • CND
THREE BLIND MOUSKETEERS • 1936 • Hand David • ANS • USA
THREE BLONDES IN HIS LIFE • 1960 • Chooluck Leon • USA
THREE BOILED-DOWN FABLES • 1914 • *Dunkinson Harry* • USA
THREE BOYS AND A BABY • 1911 • Wilson Frank? • UKN
THREE BRAVE HUNTERS, THE • 1916 • *Big U* • SHT • USA
THREE BRAVE MEN • 1957 • Dunne Philip • USA
THREE BRIDGES FOR THREE SONS see **HAKSUKOI SANNIN MUSUKO** • 1955
THREE BROADWAY GIRLS see **GREEKS HAD A WORD FOR THEM, THE** • 1932
THREE BROTHERS • 1911 • *Vitagraph* • USA
THREE BROTHERS • 1915 • Cabanne W. Christy • USA
THREE BROTHERS see **TRES HERMANOS** • 1943
THREE BROTHERS see **TRE FRATELLI** • 1980
THREE BROTHERS AND THE MIRACULOUS SPRING, THE see **TRI BRATRI A ZAZRACNY PRAMEN** • 1968
THREE BROTHERS AND THE UNDERWORLD see **SAN KYODAI NO KETTO** • 1960
THREE BROTHERS (UKN) see **SIDE STREET** • 1929
THREE BUCKAROOS, THE • 1922 • Balshofer Fred J. • USA
THREE BULLETS FOR A LONG GUN • 1973 • Henkel Peter • SAF
THREE BY JEAN-MARIE STRAUB • 1969 • Straub Jean-Marie • ANT • FRG
THREE CABALLEROS, THE • 1945 • Ferguson Norman, Young Harold • USA
THREE CABLES TO MILAN see **TRE FILI FINO A MILANO** • 1958
THREE CADETS • 1945 • Annakin Ken • DCS • UKN
THREE CALLS, THE • 1911 • *Champion* • USA
THREE CAME BACK see **THEN THERE WERE THREE** • 1961
THREE CAME FROM THE FOREST see **TROE VYSHLI IZ LESA** • 1957
THREE CAME HOME • 1950 • Negulesco Jean • USA
THREE CAME TO KILL • 1960 • Cahn Edward L. • USA
THREE CANADIAN POLITICIANS OF THE THIRTIES • 1961 • Sheppard Gordon H. • DOC • CND
THREE CARD MONTE • 1980 • Rose Les • CND
THREE CASES OF MURDER • 1955 • O'Ferrall George M., Eady David, Toye Wendy • UKN
THREE CHAPTERS see **TEEN ADHAYA** • 1968
THREE CHAPTERS OF LUCK see **DREI KAPITEL GLUCK** • 1961
THREE CHEERS FOR LITTLE MARTHA see **FRAM FOR LILLA MARTA** • 1945
THREE CHEERS FOR LOVE • 1936 • McCarey Ray • USA
THREE CHEERS FOR THE BOYS see **FOLLOW THE BOYS** • 1944
THREE CHEERS FOR THE IRISH • 1940 • Bacon Lloyd • USA
THREE CHERRY PITS, THE • 1910 • *Vitagraph* • USA
THREE CHILDREN • 1913 • *Fisher Kathie* • USA
THREE CHILDREN'S GAMES see **TRES EN RAYA** • 1979
THREE CHIMNEYS see **ENTOTSU NO MIERU BASHO** • 1953
THREE CHIVALROUS MEN see **DAIGASHI** • 1968
THREE CHRISTMASES • 1916 • King Burton L. • SHT • USA
THREE CHRISTMASSES • 1916 • Frenguelli Alfonse • UKN
THREE CHUMPS AHEAD • 1934 • Meins Gus • SHT • USA
THREE CLEAR SUNDAYS • 1965 • Loach Kenneth • MTV • UKN
THREE COCKEYED SAILORS (USA) see **SAILORS THREE** • 1940
THREE COINS IN THE FOUNTAIN • 1954 • Negulesco Jean • USA
THREE COLOMBIAN STORIES • Luzardo Julio, Mejia Alberto • CLM
THREE COLUMNS ON THE CRIME PAGE see **TRE COLONNE IN CRONACA** • 1990
THREE COMRADES • 1938 • Borzage Frank • USA
THREE COMRADES • 1946 • ANS • USS
THREE-CORNERED HAT, THE see **IT HAPPENED IN SPAIN** • 1935
THREE-CORNERED MOON • 1933 • Nugent Elliott • USA
THREE COUNTRY BOYS • 1964 • Biggs Julian, Burwash Gordon, Kenemy John • CND
THREE CRAZY FELLOWS see **DREI TOLLE KERLE** • 1968
THREE CRAZY JERKS • 1988 • Gottlieb Franz J. • USA
THREE CRAZY LEGIONNAIRES (UKN) see **THREE LEGIONNAIRES, THE** • 1937
THREE CROOKED MEN • 1958 • Morris Ernest • UKN
THREE CROSSES see **KRIZOVA TROJKA** • 1948
THREE CROWNS OF THE SAILOR see **TROIS COURONNES DANOIS DES MATELOTS, LES** • 1982
THREE DANISH SAILORS' CROWNS, THE see **TROIS COURONNES DANOIS DES MATELOTS, LES** • 1982
THREE DANJUROS see **DANJURO SANDAI** • 1944
THREE DARING DAUGHTERS • 1947 • Wilcox Fred M. • USA • BIRDS AND THE BEES, THE
THREE DARK HORSES • 1952 • White Jules • SHT • USA
THREE DATES WITH DESTINY see **MALEFICIO** • 1954
THREE DAUGHTERS see **TEEN KANYA** • 1961
THREE DAUGHTERS see **TRI DCERY** • 1967
THREE DAUGHTERS-IN-LAW see **TEEN BAHURANIYAN** • 1968
THREE DAUGHTERS OF THE WEST • 1911 • Dwan Allan • USA
THREE DAWNS TO SYDNEY • 1947 • Eldridge John • DOC • UKN
THREE DAYS see **HOW TO HANDLE WOMEN** • 1928
THREE DAYS AND A CHILD see **SHLOSHA YAMIN VE YELED** • 1966
THREE DAYS AS A VAGABOND see **TRE DAR PA LUFFEN** • 1964
THREE DAYS IN APRIL • 1972 • Perrin Michel • BLG • JAZZ IN BELGIUM
THREE DAYS IN THE GUARDHOUSE see **DREI TAGE MITTELARREST** • 1930
THREE DAYS IN THE GUARDHOUSE see **DREI TAGE MITTELARREST** • 1955
THREE DAYS IN THE LIFE OF VIKTOR CHERNYSHOV see **TRI DNYA VIKTORA CHERNYSHYOVA** • 1968
THREE DAYS OF LOVE (USA) see **DREI TAGE LIEBE** • 1931
THREE DAYS OF THE CONDOR • 1975 • Pollack Sydney • USA
THREE DAYS OF VICTOR CHERNYSHOV see **TRI DNYA VIKTORA CHERNYSHYOVA** • 1968
THREE DAYS OF VICTOR TCHERNYCHEV, THE see **TRI DNYA VIKTORA CHERNYSHYOVA** • 1968
THREE DAY'S RESPITE • 1972 • Sluizer George • BRZ, NTH
THREE DAYS TO LIVE • 1924 • Gibson Tom • USA
THREE DAYS TO LIVE (UKN) see **RED SWORD, THE** • 1929
THREE DAYS WITHOUT GOD see **TRES DIAS SEM DEUS** • 1946
THREE DESPERATE MEN • 1951 • Newfield Sam • USA
THREE DEVILS, THE see **SHAYATIN EL TALATA, EL** • 1964
THREE DIMENSIONAL EXPERIMENTS • 1945 • Grant Dwinnel • SHT • USA
THREE DOLLS FROM HONG KONG (USA) see **ONEICHAN MAKARI TORU** • 1959
THREE DOLLS GO TO HONG KONG see **ONEICHAN MAKARI TORU** • 1959
THREE DOLLS IN COLLEGE see **DAIGAKU NO ONEICHAN** • 1959
THREE DOLLS IN GINZA see **GINZA NO ONE-CHAN** • 1959
THREE DUMB CLUCKS • 1937 • Lord Del • SHT • USA
THREE DUNCES, THE • 1969 • Donev Donyo • ANS • BUL
THREE EGGS IN A GLASS see **TRI VEJCE DO SKLA** • 1937
THREE ENCOUNTERS see **TRI VSTRECHI** • 1948
THREE ETC'S AND THE COLONEL (USA) see **TROIS ETC. DU COLONEL, LES** • 1960
THREE EVILS OF SEX see **SEI NO SAN-AKU** • 1967
THREE FABLES OF LOVE (USA) see **QUATRE VERITES** • 1962
THREE FACES EAST • 1926 • Julian Rupert • USA
THREE FACES EAST • 1930 • Del Ruth Roy • USA
THREE FACES OF EVE, THE • 1957 • Johnson Nunnally • USA
THREE FACES OF FEAR, THE see **TRE VOLTI DELLA PAURA, I** • 1963
THREE FACES OF LOVE see **SEKISHUN** • 1967
THREE FACES OF LOVE (UKN) see **REX HARRISON PRESENTS SHORT STORIES OF LOVE** • 1971
THREE FACES OF SIN (USA) see **PUITS AUX TROIS VERITES, LE** • 1961
THREE FACES OF TERROR, THE see **TRE VOLTI DELLA PAURA, I** • 1963
THREE FACES WEST see **REFUGEE, THE** • 1940
THREE FANTASIES OF PEPE see **TRES FANTASIAS DE PEPE** • 1965
THREE FANTASTIC STORIES see **TRES HISTORIAS FANTASTICAS** • 1965
THREE FANTASTIC SUPERMEN, THE see **FANTASTICI 3 SUPERMEN, I** • 1967
THREE FAT MEN • 1963 • Brumberg Zinaida, Brumberg Valentina • ANM • USS
THREE FAT MEN, THE see **TRI TOLSTYAKA** • 1967
THREE FATHERS FOR ANNA (USA) see **DREI VATER UM ANNA** • 1939
THREE FEET IN A BED • Pottier Richard • FRN
THREE FILMS (BLUE WHITE, BLOOD'S TONE, VEIN) • 1965 • Brakhage Stan • SHT • USA
THREE FILMS: TORONTO • 1970 • Eckert John M. • CND
THREE-FINGERED JACK • 1909 • *Lubin* • USA

THREE-FINGERED KATE -HER SECOND VICTIM, THE ART DEALER • 1909 • Martinek H. O. • UKN
THREE-FINGERED KATE -HER VICTIM THE BANKER • 1910 • Martinek H. O. • UKN
THREE-FINGERED KATE -THE CASE OF THE CHEMICAL FUMES • 1912 • Martinek H. O. • UKN
THREE-FINGERED KATE -THE EPISODE OF THE SACRED ELEPHANTS • 1910 • Martinek H. O. • UKN
THREE-FINGERED KATE -THE PSEUDO-QUARTETTE • 1912 • Martinek H. O. • UKN
THREE-FINGERED KATE -THE WEDDING PRESENTS • 1912 • Martinek H. O. • UKN
THREE FIVES, THE • 1918 • *Boy City Film* • SHT • USA
THREE FLIGHTS UP see **DANCING SWEETIES** • 1930
THREE FOOLISH WEEKS • 1924 • USA • TWO WEEKS AND A HALF
THREE FOOLISH WIVES • 1924 • *Sennett Mack (P)* • SHT • USA
THREE FOR A WEDDING see **DOCTOR, YOU'VE GOT TO BE KIDDING** • 1967
THREE FOR ALL • 1975 • Campbell Martin • UKN
THREE FOR BEDROOM C • 1952 • Bren Milton • USA
THREE FOR BREAKFAST • 1948 • Hannah Jack • ANS • USA
THREE FOR JAMIE DAWN • 1956 • Carr Thomas • USA
THREE FOR THE ROAD • 1975 • Sagal Boris • TVM • USA
THREE FOR THE ROAD • 1987 • Norton B. W. L. • USA
THREE FOR THE SHOW • 1955 • Potter H. C. • USA
THREE FORBIDDEN STORIES see **TRE STORIE PROIBITE** • 1952
THREE FRIENDS • 1912 • Griffith D. W. • USA
THREE FROM ONE STREET see **TROYE S ODNOI ULITSI** • 1936
THREE FROM THE GAS STATION, THE see **DREI VON DER TANKSTELLE, DIE** • 1930
THREE FUGITIVES • 1988 • Veber Francis • USA
THREE FUNNY RASCALS see **TRE SKOJIGA SKOJARE** • 1942
THREE GAMBLERS see **SANNIN NO BAKUTO** • 1967
THREE GAMBLERS, THE • 1913 • *Anderson Broncho Billy* • USA
THREE GAMBLERS, THE see **OTOSHIMAE** • 1967
THREE GARCIAS, THE see **TRES GARCIA, LOS** • 1946
THREE GAY FOOLS see **TRE GLADA TOKAR** • 1942
THREE GEESE, THE • 1914 • *Melies* • USA
THREE GENERATIONS OF DANJURO (USA) see **DANJURO SANDAI** • 1944
THREE GENERATIONS OF THE DANJURO FAMILY see **DANJURO SANDAI** • 1944
THREE GENEROUS MEN see **SE JAVANMARD** • 1968
THREE GHOSTS see **QUESTI FANTASMI** • 1967
THREE GINZA BOYS see **GINZAKKO MONOGATARI** • 1961
THREE GIRLS ABOUT TOWN • 1941 • Jason Leigh • USA
THREE GIRLS AND A GOB see **GIRL, A GUY AND A GOB, A** • 1941
THREE GIRLS AND A MAN • 1912 • Hale Albert W. • USA
THREE GIRLS FROM ROME see **RAGAZZE DI PIAZZA DI SPAGNA, LE** • 1952
THREE GIRLS IN LOVE see **UC SEVDALI KIZ** • 1967
THREE GIRLS LOST • 1931 • Lanfield Sidney • USA
THREE GIRLS ON BROADWAY see **BROADWAY MUSKETEERS** • 1938
THREE GODFATHERS • 1936 • Boleslawski Richard • USA • MIRACLE IN THE SAND
THREE GODFATHERS • 1948 • Ford John • USA
THREE GODFATHERS, THE • 1916 • Le Saint Edward J. • USA
THREE GOLD COINS • 1920 • Smith Cliff • USA
THREE GOLDEN HAIRS OF OLD MAN KNOW-ALL, THE see **TRI ZLATE VLASY DEDA VSEVEDA** • 1963
THREE GOOFY GOBS see **THREE LITTLE SEW AND SEWS** • 1939
THREE GRANDMOTHERS • 1963 • Biggs Julian, Howe John • CND
THREE GREEN EYES • 1919 • Henderson Dell • USA • SCRAP OF PAPER, A
THREE GUN MAN, THE • 1923 • Kenton Erle C. • SHT • USA
THREE GUNS FOR TEXAS • 1968 • Rich David Lowell, Stanley Paul, Bellamy Earl • MTV • USA
THREE GUYS NAMED MIKE • 1950 • Walters Charles • USA
THREE HALFPENNY WORTH OF LEEKS • 1906 • *Walturdaw* • UKN
THREE HAMS ON RYE • 1950 • White Jules • SHT • USA
THREE HARES see **HAROM NYUL, A** • 1972
THREE HATS • 1915 • Vale Travers • USA
THREE HATS FOR LISA • 1965 • Hayers Sidney • UKN
THREE HEARTS • 1910 • *Lubin* • USA
THREE HEARTS FOR JULIA • 1942 • Thorpe Richard • USA
THREE HEROES, THE • 1964 • Topaldgikov Stefan • BUL
THREE HEROINES see **TRI GEROINI** • 1938
THREE HOSTAGES, THE • 1977 • Donner Clive • TVM • UKN
THREE HOURS • 1927 • Flood James • USA • PURPLE AND FINE LINEN
THREE HOURS • Moguy Leonide
THREE HOURS FOR LOVE see **TRI SATA ZA LJUBAV** • 1968
THREE HOURS LATE • 1918 • *Christie* • USA
THREE HOURS TO KILL • 1954 • Werker Alfred L. • USA
THREE HUNDRED AND SIXTY FIVE NIGHTS see **SANBAYAKU ROKUJUGO-YA** • 1948
THREE-HUNDRED MILES FOR STEPHANIE see **300 MILES FOR STEPHANIE** • 1981
THREE HUNDRED MILES THROUGH ENEMY LINES see **TEKICHU ODAN SANBYAKU RI** • 1957
THREE-HUNDRED YEAR WEEKEND, THE see **300 YEAR WEEKEND, THE** • 1977
THREE HUSBANDS • 1950 • Reis Irving • USA • LETTER TO THREE HUSBANDS, A
THREE IMMORAL WOMEN (UKN) see **HEROINES DU MAL, LES** • 1978
THREE IN A CELLAR see **UP IN THE CELLAR** • 1970
THREE IN A CLOSET • 1919 • Lyons Eddie, Moran Lee • SHT • USA
THREE IN A ROW • 1919 • *Strand* • USA
THREE IN EXILE • 1925 • Windermere Fred • USA
THREE IN LOVE see **AFFAIR OF THE FOLLIES, AN** • 1927
THREE IN ONE • 1957 • Holmes Cecil • ASL
THREE IN THE ATTIC • 1968 • Wilson Richard • USA
THREE IN THE CELLAR (UKN) see **UP IN THE CELLAR** • 1970
THREE IN THE RESERVE • Heskiya Zako • BUL
THREE IN THE SADDLE • 1945 • Fraser Harry L. • USA
THREE INSTALLATIONS • 1951 • Anderson Lindsay • SHT • UKN
THREE INTO SEX WON'T GO see **GOURMANDINES, LES** • 1973
THREE INTO TWO WON'T GO • 1969 • Hall Peter • UKN
THREE INVENTIONS, THE • 1910 • Batley Ernest G. • UKN
THREE INVENTORS, THE see **3 INVENTEURS, LES** • 1980
THREE "I's" • 1970 • Ransen Mort • CND
THREE IS A CROWD • 1951 • Rasinski Connie • ANS • USA
THREE IS A CROWD see **RAG. ARTURO DE FANTI BANCARIO-PRECARIO** • 1980
THREE IS A FAMILY • 1944 • Ludwig Edward • USA
THREE JESTING RONIN see **KAIGYAKU SAN ROSHI** • 1930
THREE JOHNS • 1916 • Smith David • SHT • USA
THREE JUMPS AHEAD • 1923 • Ford John • USA • HOSTAGE, THE
THREE KEYS • 1925 • Le Saint Edward J. • USA
THREE KIDS AND A QUEEN • 1935 • Ludwig Edward • USA • BAXTER MILLIONS, THE (UKN)
THREE KINDS OF GIRLS see **JANKEN MUSUME** • 1955
THREE KINDS OF HEAT • 1987 • Stevens Leslie • USA
THREE KINGS see **TATLONG HARI** • 1968
THREE KINGS, THE • 1929 • Steinhoff Hans • UKN
THREE KINGS, THE • 1987 • Damski Mel • TVM • USA
THREE KISSES, THE • 1909 • Porter Edwin S. • USA
THREE KNAVES AND THE HEATHEN CHINESE • 1914 • France Charles H. • USA
THREE LAZY MICE • 1935 • *Lantz Walter (P)* • ANS • USA
THREE LEGIONNAIRES, THE • 1937 • MacFadden Hamilton • USA • THREE CRAZY LEGIONNAIRES (UKN)
THREE: LES POISSONS, JABBERWOCK, OPUS 5 • Williams Lloyd Michael • SHT • USA
THREE LETTERS see **MOONREZHUTHU** • 1968
THREE LETTERS UNDELIVERED see **HAITATSU SARENAI SANTSU NO TEGAMI** • 1979
THREE LIGHTS, THE see **MUDE TOD, DER** • 1921
THREE LITTLE BEERS • 1935 • Lord Del • SHT • USA
THREE LITTLE BOPS, THE • 1957 • Freleng Friz • ANS • USA
THREE LITTLE DUCKS • Yu Tse Kuang • ANS • CHN
THREE LITTLE GIRLS IN BLUE • 1946 • Humberstone H. Bruce • USA
THREE LITTLE MAIDS • 1907 • Morland John • UKN
THREE LITTLE MAIDS FROM SCHOOL • 1906 • Gilbert Arthur • UKN
THREE LITTLE ORPHANS • 1914 • Batley Ethyle • UKN
THREE LITTLE PIGS, THE • 1933 • Gillett Burt • ANS • USA
THREE LITTLE PIGS, THE • 1984 • Storm Howard • MTV • USA
THREE LITTLE PIGSKINS • 1934 • McCarey Ray • SHT • USA
THREE LITTLE PIRATES • 1946 • Bernds Edward • SHT • USA
THREE LITTLE POWDERS • 1914 • *Beery Wallace* • SHT • USA
THREE LITTLE PUPS • 1953 • Avery Tex • ANS • USA
THREE LITTLE SEW AND SEWS • 1939 • Lord Del • USA • THREE GOOFY GOBS
THREE LITTLE SISTERS • 1944 • Santley Joseph • USA
THREE LITTLE SWIGS • 1933 • Gillstrom Arvid E. • SHT • USA
THREE LITTLE TWERPS • 1943 • Edwards Harry J. • SHT • USA
THREE LITTLE VAGABONDS • 1913 • Fitzhamon Lewin • UKN • HOME FOR THE HOLIDAYS
THREE LITTLE WOLVES • 1936 • Hand David • ANS • USA
THREE LITTLE WOODPECKERS • 1965 • Marcus Sid • ANS • USA
THREE LITTLE WORDS • 1950 • Thorpe Richard • USA
THREE LIVE GHOSTS • 1922 • Fitzmaurice George • USA, UKN
THREE LIVE GHOSTS • 1929 • Freeland Thornton • USA
THREE LIVE GHOSTS • 1935 • Humberstone H. Bruce • USA
THREE LIVES • 1953 • Dmytryk Edward • SHT • USA
THREE LIVES • 1972 • Millett Kate, Klechner Susan, Irvine Louva, Mide Robin • USA
THREE LIVES see **TRI ZHIZNI** • 1925
THREE LIVES OF THOMASINA, THE • 1963 • Chaffey Don • USA, UKN
THREE LOAN WOLVES • 1946 • White Jules • SHT • USA
THREE LOVE STORIES • 1968 • Wardy Yaakov • ISR
THREE LOVE STORIES see **TRES HISTORIAS DE AMOR** • 1978
THREE LOVERS, THE • 1911 • Fitzhamon Lewin? • UKN
THREE LOVES see **FRAU, NACH DER MAN SICH SEHNT, DIE** • 1929
THREE LOVES see **MITTSU NO AI** • 1954
THREE LOVES HAS NANCY • 1938 • Thorpe Richard • USA
THREE MAGICIANS, THE see **NINJUTSU MUSHASHUGYO** • 1960
THREE MAIDEN LADIES AND A BULL • Stow Percy • UKN • BEWARE OF THE BULL
THREE MARRIED MEN • 1936 • Buzzell Edward • USA
THREE MAXIMS, THE • 1936 • Wilcox Herbert • UKN • SHOW GOES ON, THE (USA) ○ SHOW MUST GO ON, THE
THREE MEETINGS see **TRI VSTRECHI** • 1915
THREE MEN • 1911 • *Reliance* • USA
THREE MEN • 1980 • Bancroft Shelley • UKN
THREE MEN see **TRI MUZI** • 1959
THREE MEN see **KILME MIESTA** • 1984
THREE MEN AND A BABY • 1987 • Nimoy Leonard • USA
THREE MEN AND A CRADLE (USA) see **TROIS HOMMES ET UN COUFFIN** • 1985
THREE MEN AND A GIRL • 1912 • *Eclair* • USA
THREE MEN AND A GIRL • 1914 • *Crystal* • USA
THREE MEN AND A GIRL • 1919 • Neilan Marshall • USA
THREE MEN AND A GIRL • 1949 • Parry Gordon • UKN • GAY ADVENTURE, THE ○ GOLDEN ARROW
THREE MEN AND A GIRL (UKN) see **KENTUCKY MOONSHINE** • 1938
THREE MEN AND A LITTLE LADY • 1990 • Ardolino Emile • USA
THREE MEN AND A MAID • 1911 • *Vitagraph* • USA
THREE MEN AND A WOMAN • 1914 • Terwilliger George W. • USA
THREE MEN AND LILLIAN (UKN) see **DREI VON DER TANKSTELLE, DIE** • 1930
THREE MEN FROM TEXAS • 1940 • Selander Lesley • USA
THREE MEN FROM THE RESERVE, THE • 1971 • BUL
THREE MEN IN A BOAT • 1920 • Sanderson Challis • UKN
THREE MEN IN A BOAT • 1933 • Cutts Graham • UKN
THREE MEN IN A BOAT • 1956 • Annakin Ken • UKN
THREE MEN IN A CART • 1929 • Phillips Arthur • UKN
THREE MEN IN A TUB • 1938 • Watt Nate • SHT • USA
THREE MEN IN SEARCH OF A TROLL see **TRE MAND FREM FOR EN TROLD** • 1967
THREE MEN IN THE SNOW see **PARADISE FOR THREE** • 1938
THREE MEN IN WHITE • 1944 • Goldbeck Willis • USA
THREE MEN LOOK FOR A WITCH see **TRE MAND FREM FOR EN TROLD** • 1967
THREE MEN MISSING see **ZTRACENCI** • 1957
THREE MEN OF THE NORTH, THE see **KITA NO SANNIN** • 1945
THREE MEN ON A HORSE • 1936 • LeRoy Mervyn • USA
THREE MEN WHO KNEW • 1914 • Crane Frank H. • USA
THREE MESHCHANSKAYA STREET see **TRETYA MESHCHANSKAYA** • 1927
THREE MESQUITEERS, THE • 1936 • Taylor Ray • USA
THREE MILE LIMIT, THE • 1914 • *Britannia Films* • UKN
THREE MILES OUT • 1924 • Willat Irvin V. • USA
THREE MILES UP • 1927 • Mitchell Bruce • USA
THREE MILLION CASE, THE see **PROTSESS O TROYOKH MILLYONAKH** • 1926
THREE MILLION DOLLARS • 1911 • Dwan Allan • USA
THREE MISSING LINKS • 1938 • White Jules • SHT • USA
THREE MISSOURIS, THE • 1902 • *Warwick Trading Co* • UKN
THREE MONUMENTS, THE • Povh Dusan • SHT • YGS
THREE MOTHERS see **TATLONG INA** • 1988
THREE MOUNTAINEERS, THE • 1960 • *Halas John (P)* • ANS • UKN
THREE MOUNTED MEN • 1918 • Ford John • USA
THREE MOVES TO FREEDOM see **SCHACHNOVELLE, DIE** • 1960
THREE MURDERESSES (USA) see **FAIBLES FEMMES** • 1959
THREE MUSKETEERS, THE • 1914 • *Henkel C. V.* • USA
THREE MUSKETEERS, THE • 1921 • Niblo Fred • USA
THREE MUSKETEERS, THE • 1933 • Schaefer Armand, Clark Colbert • SRL • USA
THREE MUSKETEERS, THE • 1935 • Lee Rowland V. • USA
THREE MUSKETEERS, THE • 1939 • Dwan Allan • USA • SINGING MUSKETEER, THE (UKN)
THREE MUSKETEERS, THE • 1948 • Sidney George • USA
THREE MUSKETEERS, THE • 1974 • Lester Richard • UKN • QUEEN'S DIAMONDS, THE
THREE MUSKETEERS, THE see **TROIS MOUSQUETAIRES, LES** • 1913
THREE MUSKETEERS, THE see **TROIS MOUSQUETAIRES, LES** • 1921
THREE MUSKETEERS, THE see **TRI MUSKETERA** • 1938
THREE MUSKETEERS, THE (UKN) see **TRE MOSCHETTIERI, I** • 1909
THREE MUSKETEERS, THE (USA) see **TROIS MOUSQUETAIRES, LES** • 1953
THREE MUSKETEERS, THE (USA) see **TROIS MOUSQUETAIRES, LES** • 1961
THREE MUSKETEERS (PARTS I & II), THE • 1911 • Dawley J. Searle • USA
THREE MUST-GET-THERES, THE • 1922 • Linder Max • USA
THREE NAVAL RASCALS (UKN) see **SHARP SHOOTERS** • 1928
THREE NIGHTS OF A LOVE see **SZERELEM HAROM EJSZAKAJA, EGY** • 1967
THREE NIGHTS OF LOVE (USA) see **TRE NOTTI D'AMORE** • 1964
THREE NON-COMS (USA) see **DREI UNTEROFFIZIERE** • 1939
THREE NUTS FOR CINDERELLA see **TRI ORISKY PRO POPELKU** • 1973
THREE NUTS IN SEARCH OF A BOLT • 1964 • Noonan Tommy • USA
THREE OAKBANK STEEPLES • 1915 • *Krischock H. (Ph)* • ASL
THREE O'CLOCK HIGH • 1987 • Joanou Phil • USA
THREE O'CLOCK IN THE MORNING • 1923 • Thorpe Richard • SHT • USA
THREE O'CLOCK IN THE MORNING • 1923 • Webb Kenneth • USA
THREE OF A KIND • 1911 • *Imp* • USA
THREE OF A KIND • 1911 • *Edison* • USA
THREE OF A KIND • 1912 • *Nestor* • USA
THREE OF A KIND • 1914 • *Royal* • USA
THREE OF A KIND • 1936 • Rosen Phil • USA
THREE OF A KIND • 1943 • Lederman D. Ross • USA
THREE OF A KIND (UKN) see **THREE WISE CROOKS** • 1925
THREE OF HEARTS see **TRES DE COPAS, EL** • 1986
THREE OF MANY • 1917 • Barker Reginald • USA
THREE OF MANY • 1961 • Bottcher Jurgen • DOC • GDR
THREE OF OUR CHILDREN • 1957 • Reed N., Estelle • SHT • UNN
THREE OF THE FILLING STATION, THE see **DREI VON DER TANKSTELLE, DIE** • 1930
THREE OF THEM • 1913 • Wilson Frank? • UKN
THREE OF THEM, THE • 1910 • *Vitagraph* • USA
THREE OF US, THE see **TROYE IZ NAS** • 1989
THREE OF US, THE • 1915 • Noble John W. • USA
THREE OF US, THE see **VI TRE** • 1940
THREE OLD FRIENDS • 1974 • Burstall Tim • SHT • ASL
THREE OLD MAIDS • 1919 • *Austral Photoplays* • ASL
THREE ON A COUCH • 1966 • Lewis Jerry • USA
THREE ON A DATE • 1978 • Bixby Bill • TVM • USA
THREE ON A HONEYMOON • 1934 • Tinling James • USA
THREE ON A LIMB • 1936 • Lamont Charles • SHT • USA
THREE ON A MATCH • 1932 • LeRoy Mervyn • USA
THREE ON A MATCH • 1963 • Fox Beryl, Leiterman Douglas • DOC • CND
THREE ON A MATCH • 1987 • Bellisario Donald P. • TVM • USA
THREE ON A MEATHOOK • 1972 • Girdler William?, Schumann Philip? • USA
THREE ON A ROPE • 1938 • Veer Willard V. • SHT • USA
THREE ON A SPREE • 1961 • Furie Sidney J. • UKN
THREE ON A TICKET • 1947 • Newfield Sam • USA

THREE ON A WEEKEND see **BANK HOLIDAY** • 1938
THREE ON THE TRAIL • 1936 • Bretherton Howard • USA
THREE & ONE-HALF MUSKETEERS • 1961 • Martinez Solares Gilberto • MXC
THREE ORPHAN KITTENS • 1935 • Hand David • ANS • USA
THREE OUTCASTS, THE • 1929 • Smith Cliff • USA
THREE OUTLAWS, THE • 1956 • Newfield Sam • USA
THREE OUTLAWS AND THEIR AFFECTION FOR ONE ANOTHER see **BIYAKKO NO TETSU** • 1968
THREE PAINTERS see **TRES PINTORES**
THREE PAIRS AND A CAT • 1914 • *Patheplay* • USA
THREE PAIRS OF STOCKINGS • 1920 • Curtis Allen • SHT • USA
THREE PALS • 1916 • Berger Rea • USA
THREE PALS • 1926 • McGaugh Wilbur • USA
THREE PASSIONS, THE • 1928 • Ingram Rex • UKN • TROIS PASSIONS, LES
THREE-PENNY OPERA, THE see **MACK THE KNIFE** • 1989
THREE PESTS IN A MESS • 1945 • Lord Del • SHT • USA
THREE PLUS TWO see **TRI Y DVA** • 1963
THREE POEMS see **SHIH SAN SHOU** • 1977
THREE POPLARS IN PLYUSHCHIKHA see **TRI TOPOLYA NA PLYUSHCHIKHYE** • 1968
THREE POPLARS ON PLIUSHCHIKHA STREET see **TRI TOPOLYA NA PLYUSHCHIKHYE** • 1968
THREE PORTRAITS • 1919 • Ivanovsky Alexander • USS
THREE PORTRAITS OF A NON-EXISTENT BIRD see **TROIS PORTRAITS D'UN OISEAU QUI N'EXISTE PAS** • 1963
THREE PRINCESSES see **UGUSUJO NO HANAYOME** • 1959
THREE PRISONERS, THE see **MASSAGUIN EL THALATHA, EL** • 1968
THREE QUEENS, THE • 1913 • *Dayton Frank* • USA
THREE RACKETEERS, THE • 1931 • Elliot Grace • USA
THREE REASONS FOR HASTE • 1909 • *Essanay* • USA
THREE RESURRECTED DRUNKARDS see **KAETTE KITA YOPPARAI** • 1968
THREE RING CIRCUS • 1954 • Pevney Joseph • USA • JERRICO THE WONDER CLOWN ○ THREE-RING CIRCUS ○ BIG TOP, THE
THREE-RING CIRCUS see **THREE RING CIRCUS** • 1954
THREE-RING FLING • 1958 • Lovy Alex • ANS • USA
THREE-RING MARRIAGE • 1928 • Neilan Marshall • USA • DO IT AGAIN
THREE RINGS TWENTY-FIVE see **UC HALJA YIRMIBES** • 1985
THREE ROADS TO TOMORROW • 1958 • Swingler Humphrey • UKN
THREE ROBBERS, THE • Deitch Gene • ANS • USA
THREE ROGUES see **SANBIKI NO AKUTO** • 1968
THREE ROGUES (UKN) see **NOT EXACTLY GENTLEMEN** • 1931
THREE ROMANIAN DANCES • Bostan Elisabeta • SHT • RMN
THREE ROOSTERS, THE see **TRES GALLOS, LOS** • 1989
THREE ROSES • 1915 • *Jones Morgan* • USA
THREE RUSSIAN GIRLS • 1943 • Ozep Fedor, Kesler Henry S. • USA • SHE WHO DARES (UKN)
THREE SACKS OF CUNNING • 1955 • Hodotaeva O., Nosov P. • ANS • USS
THREE SAD TIGERS see **TRES TRISTES TIGRES** • 1968
THREE SAILORMEN AND A GIRL • 1909 • Stow Percy • UKN
THREE SAILORS AND A GIRL • 1953 • Del Ruth Roy • USA
THREE SAPPY PEOPLE • 1939 • White Jules • SHT • USA
THREE SCENES WITH INGMAR BERGMAN see **INGMAR BERGMANIN MA AILMA** • 1976
THREE SCRAPS OF PAPER • 1913 • *Stonehouse Ruth* • USA
THREE SCRATCH CLUE, THE • 1914 • *Bushman Francis X.* • USA
THREE SECONDS TO ZERO HOUR see **BAKUHA SANBYO MAE** • 1967
THREE SECRETS • 1950 • Wise Robert • USA
THREE SEVENS • 1921 • Bennett Chester • USA
THREE SEXATEERS, THE • 1970 • Ruttenberg Robert • USA
THREE SHADES OF LOVE see **THIS REBEL BREED** • 1960
THREE SHELL GAME, THE • 1911 • Dwan Allan • USA
THREE SHORT FILMS • Ring Raymond • ANS • USA
THREE SILENT MEN • 1940 • Bentley Thomas • UKN
THREE SINNERS • 1928 • Lee Rowland V. • USA
THREE SINNERS see **PUITS AUX TROIS VERITES, LE** • 1961
THREE SINNERS (USA) see **MEURTRES** • 1950
THREE SISTERS • 1911 • Griffith D. W. • USA
THREE SISTERS see **TRI SESTRY** • 1964
THREE SISTERS see **PAURA E AMORE** • 1987
THREE SISTERS, THE • 1966 • Strasberg Lee • TVM • USA
THREE SISTERS, THE • 1970 • Olivier Laurence, Sichel John • UKN
THREE SISTERS, THE • 1977 • Bogart Paul • USA
THREE SISTERS OF THE MOOR • 1944 • Larkin John • USA
THREE SISTERS WITH MAIDEN HEARTS see **OTOME-GOKORO SANNIN SHIMAI** • 1935
THREE SLIMS • 1916 • *Summerville Slim* • SHT • USA
THREE SMART BOYS • 1937 • Douglas Gordon • SHT • USA
THREE SMART GIRLS • 1936 • Koster Henry • USA
THREE SMART GIRLS GROW UP • 1939 • Koster Henry • USA
THREE SMART GUYS • 1943 • Cahn Edward L. • SHT • USA
THREE SMART SAPS • 1942 • White Jules • SHT • USA
THREE SOLDIERS • 1932 • Ivanov Alexander • USS
THREE SONGS ABOUT LENIN see **TRI PESNI O LENINYE** • 1934
THREE SONGS OF LENIN see **TRI PESNI O LENINYE** • 1934
THREE SONS • 1939 • Hively Jack • USA
THREE SONS O' GUNS • 1941 • Stoloff Ben?, Niblo Fred? • USA
THREE SONS WENT TO THE AIRFORCE see **TRE SONER GICK TILL FLYGET** • 1945
THREE SORRY TIGERS see **TRES TRISTES TIGRES** • 1968
THREE SOVEREIGNS FOR SARAH • 1985 • Leacock Philip • TVM • USA • THREE SOVEREIGNS FOR SARAH: THE SALEM WITCH HUNT
THREE SOVEREIGNS FOR SARAH: THE SALEM WITCH HUNT see **THREE SOVEREIGNS FOR SARAH** • 1985
THREE SPARE WIVES • 1962 • Morris Ernest • UKN
THREE SPINSTERS, THE see **HAROM SARKANY, A** • 1936
THREE STARS (USA) see **HAROM CSILLAG** • 1960
THREE STARTS see **TRZY STARTY** • 1955
THREE STATE GANG, THE • Peyser John • USA
THREE STEPS FORWARD see **TRZY KROKI NAPRZOD** • 1946
THREE STEPS IN LIFE see **TRZY KROKI PO ZIEMI** • 1965
THREE STEPS IN THE DARK • 1953 • Birt Daniel • UKN
THREE STEPS NORTH (USA) see **TRE PASSI A NORD** • 1951
THREE STEPS ON EARTH see **TRZY KROKI PO ZIEMI** • 1965
THREE STEPS TO THE GALLOWS • 1953 • Gilling John • UKN • WHITE FIRE (USA)
THREE STOOGES, THE • 1934-59 • SHS • USA
THREE STOOGES GO AROUND THE WORLD IN A DAZE, THE • 1963 • Maurer Norman • USA
THREE STOOGES GO WEST, THE (UKN) see **GOLD RAIDERS** • 1951
THREE STOOGES IN ORBIT, THE • 1962 • Bernds Edward • USA • THREE STOOGES MEET THE MARTIANS, THE
THREE STOOGES MEET HERCULES, THE • 1962 • Bernds Edward • USA
THREE STOOGES MEET THE GUNSLINGER (UKN) see **OUTLAWS IS COMING!, THE** • 1965
THREE STOOGES MEET THE MARTIANS, THE see **THREE STOOGES IN ORBIT, THE** • 1962
THREE STOOGES SCRAPBOOK • 1960 • Miller Sidney • USA
THREE STOPS TO MURDER • 1954 • *Conway Tom* • UKN
THREE STORIES see **TRZY OPOWIESCI** • 1953
THREE STORIES see **THALASS KASSAS** • 1968
THREE STRANGE LOVES (USA) see **TORST** • 1949
THREE STRANGE STORIES see **TROIS ESTRANGES HISTOIRES** • 1968
THREE STRANGE STORIES OF EDGAR POE see **HISTOIRES EXTRAORDINAIRES** • 1968
THREE STRANGERS • 1946 • Negulesco Jean • USA
THREE STRIKES AND YOU'RE.. RALPH • 1969 • *American Film Production Co* • USA
THREE STRIKES, YOU'RE OUT • 1917 • *International Film Service* • ANS • USA
THREE STRINGS TO HER BOW • 1911 • *Australian Film Syndicate* • ASL
THREE STRIPES IN THE SUN • 1955 • Murphy Richard • USA • GENTLE SERGEANT, THE (UKN)
THREE STUDENTS, THE • 1923 • Ridgwell George • UKN
THREE STUPID MEN see **CE DIVANE** • 1968
THREE SUBURBAN SPORTSMEN AND A HAT • 1908 • Stow Percy • UKN
THREE SUITORS AND A DOG • 1913 • *Kalem* • USA
THREE SUNDAYS TO LIVE • 1957 • Morris Ernest • UKN
THREE SUPERMEN CLEAN UP, THE see **DREI SUPERMANNER RAUMEN AUF, DIE** • 1967
THREE SUPERMEN IN THE JUNGLE, THE see **CHE FANNO I NOSTRI SUPERMEN TRA LE VERGINI DELLA GIUNGLA** • 1970
THREE SWEDISH GIRLS IN HAMBURG see **DREI SCHWEDINNEN AUF DER REEPERBAHN** • 1980
THREE SWEDISH GIRLS ON THE REEPERBAHN see **DREI SCHWEDINNEN AUF DER REEPERBAHN** • 1980
THREE SWORDS OF ZORRO, THE (USA) see **TRES ESPADAS DEL ZORRO, LAS** • 1963
THREE T COMPANY see **WAN ZHU** • 1988
THREE TALES OF TERROR see **TRILBY** • 1912
THREE TEACHERS • 1962 • Tosheva Nevena • DOC • BUL
THREE TELEGRAMS see **TROIS TELEGRAMMES** • 1950
THREE TEXAS STEERS • 1939 • Sherman George • USA • DANGER RIDES THE RANGE (UKN)
THREE THANKSGIVINGS • 1909 • *Edison* • USA
THREE THE HARD WAY • 1974 • Parks Gordon Jr. • USA
THREE THEMES see **TROIS THEMES** • 1980
THREE THIEVES see **PROTSESS O TROYOKH MILLYONAKH** • 1926
THREE-THOUSAND MILE CHASE, THE see **3,000 MILE CHASE, THE** • 1977
THREE THOUSAND MILES OF DANGER • 1969 • Morrison George • DOC • IRL
THREE TIMES A LADY see **FEMMINE TRE VOLTE** • 1957
THREE TIMES ANA see **TRES VECES ANA** • 1961
THREE TIMES AND OUT • 1915 • *Baggot King* • USA
THREE TIMES AND OUT • 1918 • *Rhodes Billie* • USA
THREE TIMES BUCHAREST see **DE TREI ORI BUCHAREST** • 1967
THREE TIMES SHORT, THREE TIMES LONG • Kim Ho-Sun • SKR
THREE TIMES THREE see **TRZY PO TRZY** • 1965
THREE TO GO • 1970 • Hannant Brian, Howes Oliver, Weir Peter • ASL
THREE TO ONE • 1912 • *Branscombe Lily* • USA
THREE TO ONE • 1913 • *Mack Hughie* • USA
THREE TO ONE AGAINST • 1923 • Cooper George A. • UKN
THREE TONS OF DUST • 1960 • Danek Oldrich • CZC
THREE TOUGH GUYS (USA) see **UOMINI DURI** • 1974
THREE TRAMPS, THE • 1905 • Collins Alf? • UKN
THREE TREASURES, THE see **NIPPON TANJO** • 1959
THREE TROUBLEDOERS • 1946 • Bernds Edward • SHT • USA
THREE TRUTHS IN THE WELL see **PUITS AUX TROIS VERITES, LE** • 1961
THREE UNHOLY VIRGINS • 1965 • *All American Film Producers Inc* • USA
THREE UNLUCKY ONES see **TRES DESGRACIADOS CON SUETE** • 1957
THREE VALISES, THE • 1912 • *Clary Charles* • USA
THREE VETERANS, THE see **TRI VETERANI** • 1983
THREE VIETNAMESE STORIES • 1980 • Noyce Phil • DOC • ASL
THREE VIOLENT PEOPLE • 1956 • Mate Rudolph • USA
THREE WAGERS, THE see **GAY CORINTHIAN, THE** • 1924
THREE WALTZES see **TROIS VALSES** • 1938
THREE WARRIORS • 1977 • Merrill Keith • USA
THREE WAX MEN (USA) see **WACHSFIGURENKABINETT, DAS** • 1924
THREE-WAY MIRROR, THE see **GLACE A TROIS FACES, LA** • 1927
THREE-WAY SPLIT • 1970 • Nizet Charles • USA
THREE WAYS OUT • 1917 • Baker Richard Foster • SHT • USA
THREE WAYS TO LOVE see **CHERRY, HARRY AND RAQUEL** • 1969
THREE WEEK-ENDS • 1928 • Badger Clarence • USA
THREE WEEKS • 1915 • Vekroff Perry N. • USA
THREE WEEKS • 1924 • Crosland Alan • USA • ROMANCE OF A QUEEN, THE (UKN)
THREE WEEKS IN PARIS • 1925 • Del Ruth Roy • USA
THREE WEEKS OF LOVE • 1965 • Brusseau William E. • USA
THREE WEIRD SISTERS, THE • 1948 • Birt Daniel • UKN
THREE WERE THOROUGHBREDS see **RELENTLESS** • 1948
THREE WERE THREE see **TRES ERAN TRES** • 1954
THREE-WHEELED FAIRYTALE • 1970 • Mayers Doe • SHT • USA
THREE WHO LOVED • 1931 • Archainbaud George • USA • HELGA
THREE WHO PAID • 1923 • Campbell Colin • USA
THREE WHO UPSET THE WEST see **VADO, VEDO E SPARA** • 1968
THREE WHO WERE DOOMED (USA) see **HERR ARNES PENGAR** • 1919
THREE WISE CROOKS • 1925 • Weight F. Harmon • USA • THREE OF A KIND (UKN)
THREE WISE FOOLS • 1923 • Vidor King • USA
THREE WISE FOOLS • 1946 • Buzzell Edward • USA
THREE WISE GIRLS • 1932 • Beaudine William • USA
THREE WISE GUYS • 1936 • Seitz George B. • USA
THREE WISE KINGS • 1982 • Corbucci Sergio • ITL
THREE WISE MEN • 1913 • Campbell Colin • USA
THREE WISE MEN, THE • 1916 • Campbell Colin • SHT • USA
THREE WISHES • 1967 • Ratz Gunter • ANM • GDR
THREE WISHES see **TRE DESIDERI, I** • 1937
THREE WISHES see **TRETI PRANI** • 1958
THREE WISHES see **TRE ONSKNINGAR** • 1960
THREE WISHES, THE • 1910 • *Vitagraph* • USA
THREE WISHES, THE • 1915 • *Levering Joseph* • USA
THREE WISHES, THE • 1916 • Henderson Lucius • SHT • USA
THREE WISHES, THE • 1950 • *Films For Children* • SHT • USA
THREE WISHES, THE • 1954 • Reiniger Lotte • ANS • UKN
THREE WISHES FOR JAMIE • 1987 • Young Robert William • TVM • USA
THREE WISHES OF BILLY GRIER, THE • 1984 • Blechman Corey • TVM • USA
THREE WITNESSES • 1935 • Hiscott Leslie • UKN
THREE WITNESSES see **TRAJA** • 1969
THREE WIVES see **LETTER TO THREE WIVES, A** • 1948
THREE WOMEN • 1924 • Lubitsch Ernst • USA
THREE WOMEN • 1934 • Greenwood Edwin • UKN
THREE WOMEN see **SANNIN NO JOSEI** • 1935
THREE WOMEN see **TRZY KOBIETY** • 1956
THREE WOMEN see **TEEN KANYA** • 1961
THREE WOMEN AROUND YOSHINAKA see **YOSHINAKA O MEGURU NO ONNA** • 1956
THREE WOMEN OF FRANCE • 1917 • Baldwin Ruth Ann • SHT • USA
THREE WOMEN (USA) see **PODRUGI** • 1936
THREE WOMEN (USA) see **TROIS FEMMES** • 1951
THREE WORD BRAND • 1921 • Hillyer Lambert • USA • THREE-WORD BRAND, THE
THREE-WORD BRAND, THE see **THREE WORD BRAND** • 1921
THREE WORKSHOP FILMS • 1975 • Maxwell Peter, Weir Peter, Crombie Donald • ASL
THREE WORLDS OF GULLIVER, THE • 1960 • Sher Jack • USA, UKN, SPN
THREE X GORDON • 1918 • Warde Ernest C. • USA
THREE YEARS WITHOUT GOD see **TATLONG TAONG WALANG DIYOS** • 1977
THREE YEARS WITHOUT WOMEN see **TRE ANNI SENZA DONNE** • 1937
THREE YOUNG MEN AND A DREAM GIRL see **KONYAKU SAMBA GARASU** • 1956
THREE YOUNG TEXANS • 1954 • Levin Henry • USA
THREE YUGOSLAVIAN PORTRAITS • 1961 • King Allan • CND
THREEFOLD TRAGEDY, THE • 1922 • Greenwood Edwin • UKN • HENRY THE EIGHTH
THREEPENNY OPERA, THE see **DREIGROSCHENOPER, DIE** • 1930
THREEPENNY OPERA, THE see **OPERA DE QUAT' SOUS, L'** • 1930
THREEPENNY OPERA, THE see **DREIGROSCHENOPER, DIE** • 1962
THREE'S A CROWD • 1927 • Langdon Harry • USA
THREE'S A CROWD • 1933 • Ising Rudolf • ANS • USA
THREE'S A CROWD • 1945 • Selander Lesley • USA
THREE'S A CROWD • 1969 • Falk Harry • USA
THREE'S A CROWD see **TALK OF THE TOWN, THE** • 1942
THREE'S A CROWD see **KNOKKEN VOOR TWEE** • 1982
THREE'S COMPANY • 1953 • Saunders Charles, Fisher Terence • UKN
THREE'S HAPPINESS • 1986 • Grlic Rajko • YGS
THREES, MENAGE A TROIS • 1968 • Anders Jan • USA
THREE'S TROUBLE • 1987 • Thomson Chris • ASL
THREESOME • 1969 • Chase Brandon • USA, DNM • URSULA
THREESOME • 1984 • Antonio Lou • TVM • USA
THRESHING MACHINES WORKED BY POWER see **BATTEUSE A VAPEUR** • 1896
THRESHOLD • 1969 • Jackson Babs • SHT • USA
THRESHOLD • Lovins Jay • SHT • USA
THRESHOLD • 1972 • Le Grice Malcolm • UKN
THRESHOLD • 1981 • Pearce Richard • CND
THRESHOLD see **UMBARTHA** • 1982
THRESHOLD 9 ILLUSIONS see **ILLUSIONS** • 1972
THRESHOLD OF THE VOID, THE see **SEUIL DU VIDE, LE** • 1971
THRIFTY CUBS • 1953 • Davis Mannie • ANS • USA
THRIFTY JANITOR, THE • 1913 • *Edison* • USA
THRIFTY PARSON, THE • 1912 • *Blanchard Eleanor* • USA
THRILL CHASER, THE • 1923 • Sedgwick Edward • USA
THRILL CHASER, THE • 1928 • Horner Robert J. • USA
THRILL DEVIATES, THE see **THRILL KILLER, THE** • 1965
THRILL FOR THELMA, A • 1935 • Cahn Edward L. • SHT • USA
THRILL GIRL, THE see **EXCITEMENT** • 1924
THRILL HUNTER, THE • 1926 • De Rue Eugene?, Strayer Frank? • USA
THRILL HUNTER, THE • 1933 • Seitz George B. • USA
THRILL KILLER, THE • 1965 • *Sack Amusement Enterprises* • USA • THRILL DEVIATES, THE ○ MONDO WEIRDO

THRILL KILLERS, THE • 1965 • Steckler Ray Dennis • USA • MONSTERS ARE LOOSE, THE ○ MANIACS ARE LOOSE, THE
THRILL OF A LIFETIME • 1937 • Archainbaud George • USA
THRILL OF A ROMANCE • 1945 • Thorpe Richard • USA
THRILL OF BRAZIL, THE • 1946 • Simon S. Sylvan • USA
THRILL OF FAIR • 1951 • Kneitel Seymour • ANS • USA
THRILL OF IT ALL, THE • 1963 • Jewison Norman • USA
THRILL OF YOUTH • 1932 • Thorpe Richard • USA
THRILL SEEKERS see **QUAND LES FILLES SE DECHAINENT** • 1973
THRILL SEEKERS, THE • 1927 • Revier Harry • USA
THRILL SEEKERS, THE see **YELLOW TEDDYBEARS, THE** • 1963
THRILLED TO DEATH • 1988 • Vincent Chuck • USA
THRILLER • 1983 • Landis John • USA
THRILLER –EN GRYM FILM • 1974 • Vibenius Bo A. • SWD
THRILLING • 1965 • Scola Ettore, Polidoro Gian Luigi, Lizzani Carlo • ITL
THRILLING ADVENTURES OF COUNT VERACE, THE • 1914 • *Mina* • USA
THRILLING FIGHT ON A SCAFFOLD • 1899 • *Paul R. W.* • USA
THRILLING RACE AGAINST TIME, A • 1910-12 • Melies Gaston • USA
THRILLING RESCUE BY "UNCLE MUN", A • 1912 • *Edison* • USA
THRILLING SHOW, A see **NOVYI ATTRAKTION** • 1957
THRILLING STORIES FROM THE STRAND MAGAZINE • 1924 • *Stoll* • SHS • UKN
THRILLING STORIES FROM THE STRAND MAGAZINE • 1925 • *Stoll* • SHS • UKN
THRILLING STORY, A • 1910 • Aylott Dave • UKN
THRILLING YOUTH • 1926 • Jones Grover • USA
THRILLKILL • 1984 • Kramreither Anthony, D'Andrea Anthony • CND
THROBS AND THRILLS • 1920 • Pratt Gilbert • SHT • USA
THRON FUR CHRISTINE, EINE see **TRONO PARA CRISTY** • 1959
THRONE FOR A LOSS • 1966 • Post Howard • ANS • USA
THRONE FOR A SADDLE, A see **LIGHTNING LARIATS** • 1927
THRONE OF BLOOD see **KUMONOSU–JO** • 1957
THRONE OF CLOUDS see **KUMO NO OZU** • 1929
THRONE OF FIRE, THE see **TRONO DI FUOCO, IL** • 1983
THRONE OF FRANCE, THE see **TRONE DE FRANCE, LE** • 1936
THRONE OF THE WHITE MAN see **HAKUGIN NO OZU** • 1935
THRONGS OF THE EARTH, THE see **CHI NO MURE** • 1970
THRONSTURZER, DER see **RUSSLAND 3** • 1924
THROTTLE PUSHERS • 1933 • White Jules • SHT • USA
THROUGH A GLASS DARKLY (UKN) see **SASOM I EN SPEGEL** • 1961
THROUGH A GLASS WINDOW • 1922 • Campbell Maurice • USA
THROUGH A HIGHER POWER • 1912 • *Rex* • USA
THROUGH A KNOT HOLE • 1915 • *L-Ko* • USA
THROUGH A LENS BRIGHTLY: MARK TURBYFILL • 1966 • Markopoulos Gregory J. • USA
THROUGH AND THROUGH see **NA WYLOT** • 1973
THROUGH ANOTHER MAN'S EYES • 1913 • Kirkland Hardee • USA
THROUGH AUSTIN GLEN • 1906 • *Bitzer Billy (Ph)* • USA
THROUGH AUSTRALIAN WILDS • 1919 • ASL • WITH BIRTLES ON THE TRACK OF SIR ROSS SMITH ○ ACROSS THE TRACK OF ROSS SMITH
THROUGH BABY'S VOICE • 1916 • Cochrane George • SHT • USA
THROUGH BARRIERS OF FIRE • 1913 • August Edwin • USA
THROUGH DANTE'S FLAMES • 1914 • *Howard Lois* • USA
THROUGH DARKENED VALES • 1911 • Griffith D. W. • USA
THROUGH DARKEST AFRICA: IN SEARCH OF WHITE RHINOCEROS • 1927 • Eustace Harry K. • DOC • USA
THROUGH DAYS AND MONTHS see **HI MO TSUKI MO** • 1969
THROUGH DEATH'S VALLEY • 1912 • Northcote Sidney • UKN
THROUGH DIFFERENT EYES see **THRU DIFFERENT EYES** • 1942
THROUGH DUMB LUCK • 1912 • Henderson Dell, Sennett Mack (Spv) • USA
THROUGH EDITH'S LOOKING GLASS • 1915 • *Huling Lorraine* • USA
THROUGH EYES OF LOVE • 1914 • Travers Richard C. • USA
THROUGH FIRE AND WATER • 1914 • *Balboa* • USA
THROUGH FIRE AND WATER • 1917 • Hurst Paul C. • SHT • USA
THROUGH FIRE AND WATER • 1923 • Bentley Thomas • UKN
THROUGH FIRE TO FORTUNE • 1911 • Bouwmeester Theo • UKN
THROUGH FIRE TO FORTUNE OR THE SUNKEN VILLAGE • 1914 • Carleton Lloyd B. • USA
THROUGH FLAMES TO LOVE • 1916 • Webster Harry Mcrae • SHT • USA
THROUGH FLAMING GATES • 1912 • Porter Edwin S. • USA
THROUGH FLAMING PATHS • 1913 • Smiley Joseph • USA
THROUGH HELL TO GLORY (UKN) see **JET ATTACK** • 1958
THROUGH HIS WIFE'S PICTURE • 1911 • Sennett Mack • USA
THROUGH JEALOUS EYES • 1911 • Salter Harry • USA
THROUGH JEALOUSY • 1909 • *Lubin* • USA
THROUGH LIFE'S WINDOW • 1914 • *Costello Maurice* • USA
THROUGH MANY TRIALS • 1913 • *Travers C. T.* • USA
THROUGH MEMORY BLANK • 1912 • *Leonard Marion* • USA
THROUGH NAKED EYES • 1983 • Moxey John Llewellyn • TVM • USA
THROUGH NIGHT TO LIGHT • 1914 • *Balboa* • USA
THROUGH RUSSIA see **PO RUSI** • 1968
THROUGH SHADOW TO SUNSHINE • 1909 • *Lubin* • USA
THROUGH SHADOWED VALES • 1912 • *Baggot King* • USA
THROUGH SOLID WALLS • 1916 • Morton Walter • SHT • USA
THROUGH SPECTACLES see **SZEMUVEGESEK** • 1969
THROUGH STORMY SEAS • 1914 • Brett B. Harold • UKN
THROUGH STORMY WATERS • 1920 • Goddard Frederick • UKN
THROUGH STRIFE • 1913 • Weber Lois, Smalley Phillips • USA
THROUGH THE AGES • 1914 • Aylott Dave • UKN
THROUGH THE BACK DOOR • 1921 • Green Alfred E., Pickford Jack • USA
THROUGH THE BREAKERS • 1909 • Griffith D. W. • USA
THROUGH THE BREAKERS • 1928 • Boyle Joseph C. • USA
THROUGH THE CENTURIES • 1914 • Huntley Fred W. • USA
THROUGH THE CLOUDS • 1910 • *Edison* • USA
THROUGH THE CLOUDS • 1913 • Weston Charles • UKN
THROUGH THE DARK • 1914 • *Reliance* • USA
THROUGH THE DARK • 1924 • Hill George W. • USA
THROUGH THE DARKNESS • 1910 • *Costello Maurice* • USA
THROUGH THE DRIFTS • 1912 • *Lubin* • USA
THROUGH THE EYES OF FRIENDS see **OCZAMI PRZYJACIOL** • 1970
THROUGH THE EYES OF OTHERS • 1985 • Belanger Ray • DOC • CND
THROUGH THE EYES OF THE BLIND • 1914 • Crane Frank H. • USA
THROUGH THE EYES OF THE CAMERA • 1959 • Uher Stefan • CZC
THROUGH THE EYES OF THE WORLD • 1917 • Le Saint Edward J. • USA
THROUGH THE FALSE DOOR see **POR LA PUERTA FALSA** • 1950
THROUGH THE FIRE • 1969 • Jordan David • DOC • NZL
THROUGH THE FIRE • 1988 • Marcum Gary • USA
THROUGH THE FIRES OF TEMPTATION • 1914 • *Warner'S Features* • USA
THROUGH THE FIRING LINE • 1914 • Weston Charles • UKN
THROUGH THE FLAMES • 1912 • *Imp* • USA
THROUGH THE FLAMES • 1912 • *Thanhouser* • USA
THROUGH THE FLAMES • 1912 • Batley Ethyle • UKN
THROUGH THE FLAMES • 1914 • *Kalem* • USA
THROUGH THE FLAMES • 1914 • Turner Otis • *Rex* • USA
THROUGH THE GARDEN • 1971 • Zwartjes Frans • NTH
THROUGH THE KEYHOLE • 1913 • Calvert Charles? • UKN
THROUGH THE KEYHOLE • 1914 • *Brennan John E.* • USA
THROUGH THE KEYHOLE • 1920 • Del Ruth Roy • SHT • USA
THROUGH THE LOOKING GLASS • 1976 • Middleton Jonas • USA
THROUGH THE LOOKING GLASS • 1987 • Slapczynski Richard, Bresciani Andrea • ANM • USA
THROUGH THE LOOKING GLASS see **THRU THE LOOKING GLASS** • 1954
THROUGH THE LOOKING GLASS see **VELVET VAMPIRE, THE** • 1971
THROUGH THE MAGIC PYRAMID • 1981 • Howard Ron • TVM • USA • TIME CRYSTAL, THE
THROUGH THE MIRROR see **KVINDESAND** • 1979
THROUGH THE MURK • 1915 • Swickard Charles • USA
THROUGH THE NEIGHBOR'S WINDOW • 1913 • *American* • USA
THROUGH THE SLUICE GATES • 1913 • *Garwood William* • USA
THROUGH THE SLUMS OF MELBOURNE • 1920 • ASL
THROUGH THE SNOW • 1914 • *Imp* • USA
THROUGH THE STORM • 1914 • *Bushman Francis X.* • USA
THROUGH THE STORM • 1919 • *Capital* • USA
THROUGH THE STORM • 1922 • Plympton Horace G. • USA
THROUGH THE STORM (UKN) see **PRAIRIE SCHOONERS** • 1940
THROUGH THE TELESCOPE • 1913 • *Eclair* • USA
THROUGH THE TOILS • 1919 • Hoyt Harry O. • USA
THROUGH THE VALLEY OF SHADOWS • 1914 • Trimble Larry • UKN
THROUGH THE WALL • 1916 • Sturgeon Rollin S. • USA
THROUGH THE WINDOW • 1911 • *White Pearl* • USA
THROUGH THE WINDOW • 1913 • *Bison* • USA
THROUGH THE WRONG DOOR • 1919 • Badger Clarence • USA • WRONG DOOR, THE
THROUGH THICK AND THIN • 1927 • Eason B. Reeves?, Nelson Jack? • USA
THROUGH TRACKLESS SANDS • 1913 • *Essanay* • USA
THROUGH TRIALS TO VICTORY see **GENNEM KAMP TIL SEJR** • 1911
THROUGH TROUBLED WATERS • 1915 • Davis Ulysses • USA
THROUGH TURBULENT WATERS • 1915 • McRae Duncan • USA
THROUGH TWISTING LANES • 1912 • *Rex* • USA
THROUGHT THE AIR • 1911 • *Baggot King* • USA
THROW A SADDLE ON A STAR • 1946 • Nazarro Ray • USA
THROW AWAY BOOKS, LET'S GO INTO THE STREETS! see **SHO O SUTEYI, MACHI E DEYO** • 1971
THROW AWAY YOUR BOOKS, LET'S GO INTO THE STREETS! see **SHO O SUTEYI, MACHI E DEYO** • 1971
THROW ME TO THE VAMPIRE see **ECHENME AL VAMPIRO** • 1961
THROW MOMMA OFF THE TRAIN • 1987 • DeVito Danny • USA
THROW OF DICE, A • 1913 • Wilson Frank? • UKN
THROW OF DICE, A see **SCHICKSALSWURFEL** • 1929
THROW OF THE DICE see **SCHICKSALSWURFEL** • 1929
THROWBACK see **MAFIA KID** • 1988
THROWBACK, THE • 1920 • Shirley Arthur • ASL
THROWBACK, THE • 1935 • Taylor Ray • USA
THROWING A PARTY • 1940 • Enright Ray • DCS • USA
THROWING LEAD • 1928 • Horner Robert J. • USA
THROWING THE BULL • 1913 • Curtis Allen • USA
THROWING THE BULL • 1946 • Rasinski Connie • ANS • USA
THROWN OFF THE THRONE • 1914 • O'Sullivan Tony • USA
THROWN OUT OF JOINT • 1933 • Goodwins Leslie (c/d) • SHT • USA
THROWN TO THE LIONS • 1916 • Henderson Lucius • USA
THROWN UP STONE, THE see **FELDOBOTT KO** • 1969
THRU DIFFERENT EYES • 1929 • Blystone John G. • USA • PUBLIC OPINION ○ GUILTY
THRU DIFFERENT EYES • 1942 • Loring Thomas Z. • USA • THROUGH DIFFERENT EYES
THRU EYES OF MEN • 1920 • Taylor Charles A. • USA
THRU FIRE AND SMOKE • 1911 • *Santschi Thomas* • USA
THRU THE FLAMES • 1923 • Nelson Jack • USA
THRU THE KEYHOLE • 1920 • Davey Horace • SHT • USA
THRU THE LOOKING GLASS • 1954 • Davis James* • SHT • USA • THROUGH THE LOOKING GLASS
THRU THE MIRROR • 1936 • Hand David • ANS • USA
THRU THIN AND THICKET • 1933 • Sandrich Mark • SHT • USA • THRU THIN AND THICKET: OR, WHO'S ZOO IN AFRICA ○ WHO'S ZOO IN AFRICA
THRU THIN AND THICKET: OR, WHO'S ZOO IN AFRICA see **THRU THIN AND THICKET** • 1933
THUG, DER • 1916 • Neuss Alwin • FRG • IM DIENSTE DER TODESGOTTIN
THUGS WITH DIRTY MUGS • 1939 • Avery Tex • ANS • USA
THUMB FUN • 1952 • McKimson Robert • ANS • USA
THUMB PRINT, THE • 1911 • Brooke Van Dyke • USA
THUMB PRINT, THE • 1913 • *Fischer Margarita* • USA
THUMB PRINT, THE • 1914 • *Melies* • USA
THUMB PRINTS AND DIAMONDS • 1914 • Smiley Joseph • USA
THUMB PRINTS ON THE SAFE, THE • 1915 • Horne James W. • USA
THUMB TRIPPING • 1972 • Masters Quentin • USA
THUMBELINA • 1955 • Reiniger Lotte • ANS • UKN
THUMBELINA • 1964 • Amalrik Leonid • ANM • USS
THUMBELINA • 1970 • Mahon Barry • USA
THUMBELINA • 1983 • Lindsay-Hogg Michael • MTV • USA
THUMBS DOWN • 1927 • Rosen Phil • USA
THUMBS UP! • 1914 • Aylott Dave? • UKN
THUMBS UP • 1943 • Santley Joseph • USA
THUNDER • 1929 • Nigh William • USA
THUNDER see **THUNDER WARRIOR** • 1983
THUNDER 2 see **THUNDER WARRIOR II** • 1985
THUNDER 3 see **THUNDER WARRIOR III** • 1988
THUNDER ACROSS THE PACIFIC (UKN) see **WILD BLUE YONDER, THE** • 1951
THUNDER AFLOAT • 1939 • Seitz George B. • USA
THUNDER ALLEY • 1967 • Rush Richard • USA
THUNDER ALLEY • 1985 • Cardone J. S. • USA
THUNDER AND LIGHTNING • 1977 • Allen Corey • USA
THUNDER AND LIGHTNING see **BLIXT OCH DUNDER** • 1938
THUNDER AT THE BORDER see **WINNETOU UND SEIN FREUND OLD FIREHAND** • 1967
THUNDER BAY • 1953 • Mann Anthony • USA
THUNDER BELOW • 1932 • Wallace Richard • USA
THUNDER BIRDS • 1942 • Wellman William A. • USA
THUNDER COUNTRY • 1974 • *Rooney Mickey* • USA
THUNDER IN CAROLINA • 1960 • Helmick Paul • USA
THUNDER IN DIXIE • 1965 • Naud William T. • USA • THUNDERING WHEELS
THUNDER IN GOD'S COUNTRY • 1951 • Blair George • USA
THUNDER IN HEAVEN • 1966 • Todd Ann • DOC • UKN
THUNDER IN THE AIR • 1935 • Nieter Hans M. • UKN
THUNDER IN THE BLOOD (USA) see **COLERE FROIDE** • 1960
THUNDER IN THE CITY • 1937 • Gering Marion • UKN
THUNDER IN THE DESERT • 1938 • Newfield Sam • USA
THUNDER IN THE DUST (UKN) see **SUNDOWNERS, THE** • 1950
THUNDER IN THE EAST • 1953 • Vidor Charles • USA
THUNDER IN THE EAST (USA) see **BATTLE, THE** • 1934
THUNDER IN THE HILLS see **V HORACH DUNI** • 1946
THUNDER IN THE NIGHT • 1935 • Archainbaud George • USA
THUNDER IN THE PINES • 1948 • Edwards Robert • USA
THUNDER IN THE SUN • 1959 • Rouse Russell • USA
THUNDER IN THE VALLEY • 1947 • King Louis • USA • BOB, SON OF BATTLE (UKN)
THUNDER ISLAND • 1921 • Dawn Norman • USA
THUNDER ISLAND • 1963 • Leewood Jack • USA
THUNDER KID see **ASAMA NO ABARENBO** • 1958
THUNDER LIGHTNING AND SUNSHINE (USA) see **HOCHZEITSTRAUM, EIN** • 1936
THUNDER MOUNTAIN • 1925 • Schertzinger Victor • USA
THUNDER MOUNTAIN • 1935 • Howard David • USA
THUNDER MOUNTAIN • 1947 • Landers Lew • USA
THUNDER MOUNTAIN see **SHEPHERD OF THE HILLS, THE** • 1964
THUNDER OF BATTLE see **CORIOLANO, EROE SENZA PATRIA** • 1965
THUNDER OF DRUMS, A • 1961 • Newman Joseph M. • USA
THUNDER OF SILENCE • 1974 • Todd Ann • DOC • UKN
THUNDER OF THE GODS • 1967 • Todd Ann • DOC • UKN
THUNDER OF THE GODS (UKN) see **SON OF THE GODS** • 1930
THUNDER ON THE HILL • 1951 • Sirk Douglas • USA • BONAVENTURE (UKN)
THUNDER ON THE TRAIL see **THUNDERING TRAIL, THE** • 1951
THUNDER OVER ARIZONA • 1956 • Kane Joseph • USA
THUNDER OVER HAWAII see **NAKED PARADISE** • 1956
THUNDER OVER INYO • 1955 • Landers Lew • MTV • USA
THUNDER OVER PARIS • Mathot Leon • FRN
THUNDER OVER ST. PETERSBURG see **J'AI TUE RASPOUTINE** • 1967
THUNDER OVER SANGOLAND • 1955 • Newfield Sam • USA
THUNDER OVER TANGIER see **MAN FROM TANGIER** • 1957
THUNDER OVER TEXAS • 1934 • Ulmer Edgar G. • USA
THUNDER OVER THE MOUNTAINS see **V HORACH DUNI** • 1946
THUNDER OVER THE PLAINS • 1953 • De Toth Andre • USA
THUNDER OVER THE PRAIRIE • 1941 • Hillyer Lambert • USA
THUNDER PASS • 1954 • McDonald Frank • USA
THUNDER RIDERS • 1928 • Wyler William • USA
THUNDER RIVER FEUD • 1942 • Luby S. Roy • USA
THUNDER ROAD • 1958 • Ripley Arthur • USA
THUNDER ROCK • 1942 • Boulting Roy • UKN
THUNDER RUN • 1986 • Hudson Gary • USA
THUNDER TOWN • 1946 • Fraser Harry L. • USA
THUNDER TRAIL • 1937 • Barton Charles T. • USA • ARIZONA AMES
THUNDER WARRIOR • 1983 • De Angelis Fabrizio • ITL • THUNDER
THUNDER WARRIOR II • 1985 • De Angelis Fabrizio • ITL • THUNDER 2
THUNDER WARRIOR III • 1988 • De Angelis Fabrizio • ITL • THUNDER 3
THUNDER WARRIORS see **AMERICA 3000** • 1985
THUNDERBALL • 1965 • Young Terence • UKN
THUNDERBIRD 6 • 1968 • Lane David • UKN • THUNDERBIRD SIX: THE MOVIE ○ THUNDERBIRD SIX
THUNDERBIRD SIX see **THUNDERBIRD 6** • 1968
THUNDERBIRD SIX: THE MOVIE see **THUNDERBIRD 6** • 1968
THUNDERBIRDS • 1953 • Auer John H. • USA

THUNDERBIRDS see **ISFUGLE** • 1983

THUNDERBIRDS ARE GO • 1966 • Lane David • ANM • UKN • THUNDERBIRDS ARE GO: THE MOVIE

THUNDERBIRDS ARE GO: THE MOVIE see **THUNDERBIRDS ARE GO** • 1966

THUNDERBIRDS: CITY OF FIRE • 1966 • Elliott David • ANM • UKN

THUNDERBIRDS: COUNTDOWN TO DISASTER • 1981 • Elliott David, Lane David, Saunders Desmond • ANM • UKN

THUNDERBIRDS IN OUTER SPACE • 1966 • Lane David, Burgess Brian • ANM • UKN

THUNDERBIRDS: PIT OF PERIL • 1966 • Saunders Desmond • ANM • UKN

THUNDERBIRDS TO THE RESCUE • 1980 • ANM • UKN

THUNDERBOLT • 1910 • *Moulton A. J. (Ph)* • ASL

THUNDERBOLT • 1929 • von Sternberg Josef • USA

THUNDERBOLT • 1935 • Paton Stuart • USA

THUNDERBOLT • 1945 • Sturges John, Wyler William • DOC • USA

THUNDERBOLT, THE • 1912 • *Cruze James* • USA

THUNDERBOLT, THE • 1914 • *Ray Charles* • USA

THUNDERBOLT, THE • 1916 • Bertram William • USA

THUNDERBOLT, THE • 1919 • Campbell Colin • USA

THUNDERBOLT AND LIGHTFOOT • 1974 • Cimino Michael • USA

THUNDERBOLT ANGELS see **NINJA OPERATION 4: THUNDERBOLT ANGELS** • 1988

THUNDERBOLT JACK • 1920 • MacQuarrie Murdock, Ford Francis • SRL • USA

THUNDERBOLT STRIKES, THE • 1926 • *Perrin Jack* • USA

THUNDERBOLTS OF FATE • 1919 • Warren Edward • USA

THUNDERBOLT'S TRACKS • 1927 • McGowan J. P.?, Cohn Bennett? • USA

THUNDERCLAP • 1921 • Stanton Richard • USA

THUNDERCLOUD • 1950 • Marin Edwin L. • USA • COLT '45 (UKN)

THUNDERCLOUD, THE • 1919 • Butler Alexander • UKN

THUNDERCRACK! • 1976 • McDowell Curt • USA

THUNDERGATE • 1923 • De Grasse Joseph • USA

THUNDERGOD • 1928 • Hunt Charles J. • USA

THUNDERGOD, THE see **EMITAI** • 1972

THUNDERGROUND • 1989 • Mitchell David • USA

THUNDERHEAD see **THUNDERHEAD, SON OF FLICKA** • 1945

THUNDERHEAD, SON OF FLICKA • 1945 • King Louis • USA • THUNDERHEAD

THUNDERHOOF • 1948 • Karlson Phil • USA • FURY (UKN)

THUNDERING CARAVANS • 1952 • Keller Harry • USA

THUNDERING DAWN • 1923 • Garson Harry • USA • BOND OF THE RING, THE ○ HAVOC

THUNDERING DAWN see **BAVU** • 1923

THUNDERING FATTY see **DUNDERKLUMPEN** • 1975

THUNDERING FLEAS • 1926 • McGowan Robert • SHT • USA

THUNDERING FRONTIER • 1940 • Lederman D. Ross • USA

THUNDERING GUN SLINGERS • 1944 • Newfield Sam • USA

THUNDERING HERD, THE • 1925 • Howard William K. • USA

THUNDERING HERD, THE • 1933 • Hathaway Henry • USA • BUFFALO STAMPEDE

THUNDERING HOOFS • 1922 • Ford Francis • USA

THUNDERING HOOFS • 1924 • Rogell Albert S. • USA • TIGHT CORNER, A

THUNDERING HOOFS • 1941 • Selander Lesley • USA

THUNDERING JETS • 1958 • Dantine Helmut • USA

THUNDERING LANDLORDS • 1925 • Roach Hal • SHT • USA

THUNDERING MANTIS, THE • 1980 • Yeh Yung-Tsu • HKG • MANTIS FIST FIGHTER

THUNDERING RAILS • 1950 • *Universal* • SHT • USA

THUNDERING ROMANCE • 1924 • Thorpe Richard • USA

THUNDERING SPEED • 1926 • Neitz Alvin J. • USA

THUNDERING TAXIS • 1933 • Lord Del • SHT • USA

THUNDERING TENORS • 1931 • Horne James W. • SHT • USA

THUNDERING THOMPSON • 1929 • Wilson Ben • USA

THUNDERING THROUGH • 1925 • Bain Fred • USA • MODERN KNIGHT, A (UKN)

THUNDERING TOUPEES • 1929 • Roach Hal • SHT • USA

THUNDERING TRAIL, THE • 1951 • Ormond Ron • USA • THUNDER ON THE TRAIL

THUNDERING TRAILS • 1943 • English John • USA

THUNDERING WAVE, THE • 1957 • Frankenheimer John • MTV • USA

THUNDERING WEST, THE • 1939 • Nelson Sam • USA

THUNDERING WHEELS see **THUNDER IN DIXIE** • 1965

THUNDERSTORM • 1956 • Guillermin John • SPN

THUNDERSTORM see **LEIYU** • 1983

THUNDERSTORM, THE see **GROZA** • 1934

THUNDERSTORM OVER THE BELAYA see **GROZA NAD BYELOY** • 1968

THUNDERSTORM SWORD • 1972 • Kwan Chen-Liang • HKG

THURSDAY see **GIOVEDI, IL** • 1962

THURSDAY MORNING MURDERS, THE • 1976 • Nahay Michael • USA

THURSDAY THE 12TH see **PANDEMONIUM** • 1982

THURSDAY'S CHILD • 1943 • Ackland Rodney • UKN

THURSDAY'S CHILD • 1982 • Rich David Lowell • TVM • USA

THURSDAY'S CHILDREN • 1953 • Anderson Lindsay, Brenton Guy • SHT • UKN

THURSDAYS FOR THE POOR see **CZWARTKI UBOGICH** • 1981

THURSDAY'S GAME • 1974 • Moore Robert • TVM • USA • NIGHT CAPER ○ BERK, THE

THURSDAYS, MIRACLE see **JUEVES MILAGRO, LOS** • 1957

THURSDAYS NEVER AGAIN see **V CHETVERG I BOLSHE NIKOGDA** • 1977

THUS ANOTHER DAY see **KYO MO MATA KAKUTE ARINAN** • 1959

THUS BLOWS THE DIVINE WIND see **KAKUTE KAMIKAZE WA FUKU** • 1944

THUS GREW A GREAT LOVE see **ETSI GENNITHIKE MIA MEGALI AGAPI** • 1968

THUS MANY SOULS • 1912 • *Leonard Marion* • USA

THUS SAITH THE LORD • 1913 • *Eclair* • USA

THUS SPAKE THEODOR HERZL • 1967 • Cavalcanti Alberto • DOC • ISR • STORY OF ISRAEL, THE ○ HERZL

THUS THE DIVINE WIND ARRIVES see **KAKUTE KAMIKAZE WA FUKU** • 1944

THUT ALLES IM FINSTERN, EUREN HERRN DAS LICHT ZER ERSPAREN • 1970 • Schmid Daniel • SWT

THWARTED BY NELL PIERCE • 1911 • *Yankee* • USA

THWARTED PLOT, THE • 1913 • *Gebhardt George* • USA

THWARTED VENGEANCE, A • 1911 • *Anderson Broncho Billy* • USA

THX 1138 • 1971 • Lucas George • USA

THX-1138-4EB • 1967 • Lucas George • SHT • USA

THY KINGDOM COME.. THY WILL BE DONE • 1988 • Thomas Anthony • DOC • UKN, USA

THY NAME IS WOMAN • 1924 • Niblo Fred • USA

THY NEIGHBOR'S WIFE • 1953 • Haas Hugo • USA

THY NEIGHBOR'S WIFE • 1986 • Rogers Danielle • USA

THY SOUL SHALL BEAR WITNESS see **KORKARLEN** • 1921

THY WILL BE DONE • 1912 • *Champion* • USA

THY WILL BE DONE • 1913 • *Calvert E. H.* • USA

THYL L'ESPIEGLE see **AVENTURES DE TILL L'ESPIEGLE, LES** • 1956

TI AMERO SEMPRE see **CORTINA DI CRISTALLO** • 1958

TI ASPETTERO ALL'INFERNO • 1960 • Regnoli Piero • ITL • I'LL SEE YOU IN HELL (USA) ○ I'LL WAIT FOR YOU IN HELL

TI ATTENDE UNA CORDA.. RINGO • 1972 • Balcazar Alfonso • SPN

TI COEUR • 1969 • Belanger Fernand • CND

TI CONOSCO, MASCHERINA! • 1944 • De Filippo Eduardo • ITL

TI-CUL TOUGAS • 1976 • Noel Jean-Guy • CND

TI DARO UN POSTO ALL'INFERNO • 1974 • Bianchini Paolo • ITL

TI EKANES STO POLEMO THANASSI • 1970 • Katsouridis Nicos • GRC • WHAT DID YOU DO IN THE WAR, THANASSI?

TI HO SEMPRE AMATO • 1954 • Costa Mario • ITL

TI HO SPOSATO PER ALLEGRIA • 1967 • Salce Luciano • ITL • I MARRIED YOU FOR FUN (USA) ○ I MARRIED YOU FOR GAIETY

TI-HSIA T'UNG-TAO • 1990 • Mak Michael • TWN

TI-JEAN • 1966 • Fournier Claude • DCS • CND

TI-JEAN AU PAYS DU FER • 1958 • Garceau Raymond • DCS • CND

TI-JEAN GOES LUMBERING see **TI-JEAN S'EN VA-T-AUX CHANTIERS** • 1953

TI-JEAN S'EN VA DANS L'OUEST • 1957 • Garceau Raymond • SHT • CND

TI-JEAN S'EN VA-T-AUX CHANTIERS • 1953 • Palardy Jean • SHT • CND • TI-JEAN GOES LUMBERING

TI-KEN A MOSOU see **PLANS MYSTERIEUX, LES** • 1965

TI KI AN GENNITHIKA FTOHOS • 1968 • Petridis Giorgos • GRC • BORN TO SUCCEED

TI-KOYO AND HIS SHARK see **TI-KOYO E IL SUO PESCECANE** • 1962

TI-KOYO E IL SUO PESCECANE • 1962 • Quilici Folco • ITL, FRN, USA • TI-KOYO ET SON REQUIN (FRN) ○ TIKO AND THE SHARK (USA) ○ TI-KOYO AND HIS SHARK

TI-KOYO ET SON REQUIN (FRN) see **TI-KOYO E IL SUO PESCECANE** • 1962

TI-LOUIS MIJOTE UN PLAN • 1973 • Lamothe Arthur • DCS • CND

TI-MINE, BERNIE PIS LA GANG • 1976 • Carriere Marcel • CND

TI-NU HUA • 1976 • Wu Yusen • HKG • PRINCESS CHANG PING

TI PEUPE see **TY-PEUPE** • 1971

TI RITROVERO • 1949 • Gentilomo Giacomo • ITL • TENENTE CRAIG MIO MARITO ○ LIEUTENANT CRAIG -MISSING

TI TA TO see **TROU NORMAND, LE** • 1952

TI-TI JIH-CHI • 1977 • Ch'En Yao-Ch'I • HKG • MISS TATTY'S DIARY

TI YESHYE NYE UMEYESH LYUBIT • 1915 • Boleslawski Richard • USS

TI-YI-LEI-HSING WEI-HSIEN • 1981 • Hsu K'O • HKG • ENCOUNTERS OF THE FIRST KIND

TI-YI-TS'E YUEH-HUI • 1988 • Wang Cheng-Fang • TWN • FIRST DATE

TI-YU • 1975 • Chang Ch'Eh • HKG • HELL

TI-YU T'IEN-T'ANG • 1980 • HKG

TI-YU WU-MEN • 1980 • Hsu K'O • HKG • WE'RE GOING TO EAT YOU

TIA ALEJANDRA, LA • 1978 • Ripstein Arturo • MXC • AUNT CLARA

TIA CANDELA • 1948 • Soler Julian • MXC

TIA DE CARLOS, LA • 1946 • Torres-Rios Leopoldo • ARG

TIA DE CARLOS EN MINIFALDA, LA • 1967 • Fenollar Augusto • SPN • CHARLEY'S AUNT DRESSED IN A MINI-SKIRT

TIA DE LAS MUCHACHAS, LA • 1938 • Bustillo Oro Juan • MXC

TIA TULA, LA • 1964 • Picazo Miguel • SPN • AUNT TULA

TIADA ESOK BAGIMU • 1977 • Shamsuddin Jins • MLY • NO TOMORROW

TIADA WAKTU BICARA • 1974 • Hassan Sandy Suwardi • INN • NO TIME FOR TALK

TIAN PUSA • 1987 • Yen Hao • HKG • BUDDHA'S LOCK

T'IAO HUI • 1977 • Liang Puzhi, Fang Fang Hsiao • HKG • JUMPING ASH

TIAO MEDONHO see **ASSALTO AO TREMO PAGADOR** • 1962

TIAPACA (?) see **TRES ERAN TRES** • 1954

TIARA TAHITI • 1962 • Kotcheff Ted • UKN

TIBBET-KA JADU see **YANGRILLA** • 1938

TIBET • 1976 • Greene Felix • DOC • UKN

TIBET: A BUDDHIST TRILOGY • 1981 • Coleman Graham

TIBETANA see **KASHMIRI RUN** • 1969

TIBURON • 1919 • MXC

TIBURON • 1933 • Peon Ramon • MXC

TIBURONEROS • 1962 • Alcoriza Luis • MXC • SHARK FISHERMEN

TIC, LE • 1908 • Feuillade Louis • FRN

TICHBORNE AFFAIR, THE • 1975 • Schultz Carl • MTV • ASL

TICHTOWN TUMBLERS, THE • 1915 • Batley Ernest G.? • UKN

TICHY TYDEN V DOME • 1969 • Svankmajer Jan • ANS • CZC • SILENT WEEK IN THE HOUSE ○ QUIET WEEK IN A HOUSE, A ○ QUIET WEEK AT HOME, A

TICK.. TICK.. TICK.. • 1969 • Nelson Ralph • USA • TICK.. TICK.. TICK.. A TOWN TURNS INTO A TIME-BOMB

TICK.. TICK.. TICK.. A TOWN TURNS INTO A TIME-BOMB see **TICK.. TICK.. TICK..** • 1969

TICK TOCK MAN, THE • 1919 • Lyons Eddie, Moran Lee • SHT • USA

TICK TOCK TUCKERED • 1944 • Clampett Robert • ANS • USA

TICKET • 1986 • SKR

TICKET FOR THE THEATRE, A • 1911 • Stow Percy • UKN

TICKET FOR TWO, A • 1908 • Fitzhamon Lewin • UKN

TICKET IN TATTS, A • 1911 • Mervale Gaston • ASL

TICKET IN TATTS, A • 1934 • Thring F. W. • ASL

TICKET MANIA • 1906 • *Warwick Trading Co* • UKN

TICKET OF LEAVE • 1922 • Collins Edwin J. • UKN

TICKET OF LEAVE • 1936 • Hankinson Michael • UKN

TICKET OF LEAVE MAN • 1915 • *Superba* • USA

TICKET OF LEAVE MAN, THE • 1912 • Mervale Gaston • ASL

TICKET OF LEAVE MAN, THE • 1913 • *Dragon* • USA

TICKET-OF-LEAVE MAN, THE • 1914 • Gasnier Louis J., Mackenzie Donald • *Wharton* • USA

TICKET-OF-LEAVE MAN, THE • 1914 • Vale Travers • *Ab* • USA

TICKET-OF-LEAVE MAN, THE • 1918 • Haldane Bert • UKN

TICKET OF LEAVE MAN, THE • 1937 • King George • UKN

TICKET TO A CRIME • 1934 • Collins Lewis D. • USA

TICKET TO HAPPINESS, A • 1914 • Farnum Marshall • USA

TICKET TO HEAVEN • 1981 • Thomas Ralph L. • CND

TICKET TO MEXICO • 1955 • Landers Lew • MTV • USA

TICKET TO PARADISE • 1936 • Scotto Aubrey • USA

TICKET TO PARADISE • 1961 • Searle Francis • UKN

TICKET TO PARADISE see **BILJETT TILL PARADISET** • 1962

TICKET TO RED HORSE GULCH, A • 1914 • *Garwood William* • USA

TICKET TO TOMAHAWK, A • 1950 • Sale Richard • USA • SHERIFF'S DAUGHTER, THE

TICKETS, SVP. • 1973 • Perrault Pierre • DCS • CND

TICKLE ME • 1965 • Taurog Norman • USA

TICKLED PINK • 1940 • Ceballos Larry • SHT • USA

TICKLED PINK see **MAGIC SPECTACLES** • 1961

TICKLERS, THE • Tobalina Carlos • USA

TICKLISH AFFAIR, A • 1963 • Sidney George • USA • MOON WALK

TICKLISH BUSINESS • 1929 • Roberts Stephen • SHT • USA

TICKLISH MAN, THE • 1908 • *Lubin* • USA

TICKLISH REUBEN • 1906 • Gilbert Arthur • UKN

TICKLISH TIMOTHY • 1909 • *Gaumont* • SHT • USA

TICKY-TACKY I • 1918 • Lowenbein Richard • FRG • LIEBESATHLET, DER

TICO-TICO NO FUBA • 1952 • Celi Adolfo • BRZ

TID-BITS • 1934 • Doane Warren • SHT • USA

TIDAL VIEWS • 1989 • Ergun Mahinur • TRK

TIDAL WAVE see **PORTRAIT OF JENNIE** • 1948

TIDAL WAVE, THE • 1918 • Stoermer William? • USA

TIDAL WAVE, THE • 1920 • Hill Sinclair • UKN

TIDAL WAVE (UKN) see **S.O.S. TIDAL WAVE** • 1939

TIDAL WAVE (USA) see **NIHON CHINBOTSU** • 1973

TIDE IN THE AFFAIRS OF MEN, A • 1913 • *American* • USA

TIDE OF DEATH • 1912 • Longford Raymond • ASL

TIDE OF DESTINY, THE • 1913 • Parker Lem B. • USA

TIDE OF EMPIRE • 1929 • Dwan Allan • USA

TIDE OF FORTUNE, THE • 1910 • Salter Harry • USA

TIDE OF FORTUNE, THE • 1911 • Bouwmeester Theo • UKN

TIDE OF FORTUNE, THE • 1915 • *Allen Estelle* • USA

TIDE OF THE BATTLE, THE • 1912 • *Cooper Miriam* • USA

TIDE RISING OVER THE BREAKWATER see **MAREE MONTANTE SUR BRISE-LAMES** • 1896

TIDES OF BARNEGAT, THE • 1917 • Neilan Marshall • USA

TIDES OF FATE • 1917 • Cowl George • USA

TIDES OF FUNDY • 1965 • Perry Margaret • DOC • CND

TIDES OF PASSION • 1925 • Blackton J. Stuart • USA

TIDES OF PASSION (USA) see **FLAMES OF PASSION** • 1922

TIDES OF RETRIBUTION, THE • 1915 • MacDonald J. Farrell • USA

TIDES OF SORROW, THE • 1914 • O'Sullivan Tony • USA

TIDES OF TIME, THE • 1915 • Levering Joseph • USA

TIDES THAT MEET • 1915 • *Washburn Bryant* • USA

TIDEWATER TRAMP • 1959 • Keatley Philip • SER • CND

TIDIKAWA AND FRIENDS • 1972 • Doring Jef, Doring Su • ASL

TIDY ENDINGS • 1989 • Millar Gavin • MTV • UKN

TIE ME UP, TIE ME DOWN see **ATAME** • 1989

TIE OF THE BLOOD, THE • 1913 • Parker Lem B. • USA

TIE THAT BINDS, THE • 1910 • *Bison* • USA

TIE THAT BINDS, THE • 1910 • *Essanay* • USA

TIE THAT BINDS, THE • 1911 • *Comet* • USA

TIE THAT BINDS, THE • 1914 • Vroom Frederick • USA

TIE THAT BINDS, THE • 1915 • *Anderson Broncho Billy* • USA

TIE THAT BINDS, THE • 1923 • Levering Joseph • USA

TIED FOR LIFE • 1933 • Gillstrom Arvid E. • SHT • USA

TIED TO ONE'S MEMORIES see **I MINNENAS BAND** • 1916

TIEF IM BOHMERWALD • 1908 • *Messter Oskar (P)* • FRG

TIEFE FURCHEN • 1965 • Kohlert Lutz • GDR

TIEFEN DER GROSSTADT • 1924 • von Strischewski Wladimir • FRG

TIEFLAND • 1922 • Licho Adolf Edgar • FRG

TIEFLAND • 1954 • Riefenstahl Leni • FRG • LOWLAND

T'IEH-CH'I MEN • 1981 • Chang Ch'Eh • HKG • FLAG OF IRON, THE

T'IEH NIU FU HU • 1973 • Tse Tsung Lung • HKG • IRON OX, THE TIGER'S KILLER ○ IRON OX: THE TIGER KILLER

T'IEH-PAN-SHAO • 1984 • Hui Michael • HKG • TEPPANYAKI

TIEH PIEN • 1980 • Hsu K'O • HKG • BUTTERFLY MURDERS

TIEJIA WUDI MALIYA • 1988 • Chung Chi-Man Davi • HKG • I LOVE MARIA

TIEMPO ABIERTO • 1962 • Aguirre Javier • SHT • SPN

TIEMPO DE AMOR • 1964 • Diamante Julio • SPN

TIEMPO DE LOBOS • 1982 • Isaac Alberto • MXC • WOLF SEASON

TIEMPO DE MORIR • 1965 • Ripstein Arturo • MXC • TIME TO DIE

TIEMPO DE MORIR • 1985 • Triana Jorge Ali • CLM, CUB • TIME TO DIE, A

TIEMPO DE PASION • 1963 • Aguirre Javier • SHT • SPN

TIEMPO DE PLAYA • 1961 • Aguirre Javier • SHT • SPN

TIEMPO DE REVANCHA • 1981 • Aristarain Adolfo • ARG • TIME FOR REVENGE

TIEMPO DE SILENCIO • 1986 • Aranda Vicente • SPN • TIME OF SILENCE
TIEMPO DEL DESPRECIO, EL • 1974 • Madanes Claudio • ARG • TIME OF SCORN, A
TIEMPO ES EL VIENTO, EL • 1976 • Alvarez Santiago • DOC • CUB
TIEMPO Y DESTIEMPO • 1975 • *Conacine* • MXC
TIEMPOS DE CASTRO Y GOMEZ APROXIMACION AL GENERAL GABALDON • 1974 • Cordido Ivork • DOC • VNZ • GENERAL GABALDON IN THE TIME OF DICTATORS CASTRO AND GOMEZ
TIEMPOS DE CHICAGO • 1968 • Diamante Julio • SPN, ITL • TEMPO DI CHARLESTON CHICAGO 1972 (ITL) ○ THEY PAID WITH BULLETS (USA)
TIEMPOS DE CONSTITUCION • 1978 • Gordon Rafael • SPN
TIEMPOS DEL JOVEN MARTI, LOS • 1960 • Massip Jose • DOC • CUB
TIEMPOS DOS • 1960 • Aguirre Javier • SHT • SPN
TIEMPOS DUROS PARA DRACULA • 1976 • Darnell Jorge • ARG, SPN • HARD TIMES FOR DRACULA
TIEMPOS ESPANOLES • 1967 • Briz Jose • SHT • SPN
TIEMPOS FELICES • 1949 • Gomez Bascuas Enrique • SPN
TIEMPOS MAYAS • 1912 • MXC
TIEN CHIH PING-PING • 1980 • Chang Kuo-Ming • HKG • COPS AND ROBBERS
TIEN CHYE EE PIE CHU • 1975 • Hui Michael • HKG • LAST MESSAGE, THE
T'IEN-HSIA TI-YI • 1983 • Hu King • TWN • ALL THE KING'S MEN
T'IEN-YA, MING YUEH, TAO • 1977 • Ch'U Yuan • HKG • MAGIC BLADE, THE
TIENDA DE ANTIGUEDADES, LA • 1949 • Elorrieta Jose Maria • SPN
TIENDA DE LA ESQUINA, LA • 1950 • Diaz Morales Jose • MXC
TIENS-TOI BIEN APRES LES OREILLES A PAPA • 1971 • Bissonnette Jean • CND • WHAT THE HELL ARE THEY COMPLAINING ABOUT
TIENS, VOUS ETES A POITIERS • 1916 • Feyder Jacques • FRN
TIERARZT DR. VLIMMEN • 1944 • Barlog Boleslav • FRG
TIERARZT DR. VLIMMEN • 1956 • Rabenalt Arthur M. • FRG
TIERCE A COEUR • 1947 • de Casembroot Jacques • FRN
TIERGARTEN SUDAMERIKA • 1940 • Buhre Werner, Krieg H. • FRG
TIERNA ES LA NOCHE • 1990 • Henriquez Leonardo • VNZ, FRN • TENDER IS THE NIGHT
TIERNA INFANCIA, LA • 1965 • Palomino Felipe • MXC
TIERRA, AMOR Y DOLOR • 1934 • Peon Ramon, Gonzalez Julian S. • MXC
TIERRA BAJA • 1911 • Gallo Mario • ARG
TIERRA BAJA • 1950 • Zacarias Miguel • MXC
TIERRA BRAVA • 1938 • Cardona Rene • MXC
TIERRA BRAVA • 1969 • Klimovsky Leon • SPN
TIERRA BRUTAL (SPN) see **SAVAGE GUNS, THE** • 1962
TIERRA DE FUEGO • 1965 • Stevens Mark, Balcazar Jaime Jesus • SPN, FRG • VERGELTUNG IN CATANO (FRG) ○ SUNSCORCHED (USA) ○ LAND OF FIRE
TIERRA DE GRACIA • 1988 • Lamata Luis Alberto • VNZ • LAND OF GRACE
TIERRA DE HOMBRES • 1956 • Rodriguez Ismael • MXC
TIERRA DE LOS ALVARGONZALEZ, LA • 1969 • Picazo Miguel • SPN • LAND OF THE ALVARGONZALEZ
TIERRA DE PASIONES • 1942 • Benavides Jose Jr. • MXC
TIERRA DE TODOS • 1961 • Isasi Antonio • SPN
TIERRA DE VIOLENCIA • 1965 • de Anda Raul Jr. • MXC
TIERRA DEL FUEGO, A WHOLE NIGHT LONG see **E ANCHTLANG FUURLAND** • 1982
TIERRA DEL FUEGO SE APAGA, LA • 1955 • Fernandez Emilio • ARG
TIERRA DEL MARIACHI, LA • 1938 • de Anda Raul • MXC • COUNTRY OF THE MARIACHI (USA)
TIERRA MADRE see **AMA LUR** • 1966
TIERRA MUERTA • 1949 • Orona Vicente • MXC
TIERRA PROMETIDA • 1970 • Alea Tomas Gutierrez • CUB • PROMISED LAND, THE
TIERRA PROMETIDA, LA • 1974 • Littin Miguel • CHL • PROMISED LAND, THE (USA)
TIERRA QUEMADA • 1968 • Alvarez Alejo • CHL • BURNT LAND
TIERRA SANS PAIN see **HURDES, LAS** • 1932
TIERRA SECA • 1962 • Kantor Oscar I. • ARG • DRY EARTH
TIERRA SEDIENTA • 1945 • Gil Rafael • SPN
TIERRA Y CIELO • 1941 • Ardavin Eusebio F. • SPN
TIERRA Y EL CIELO, LA • 1977 • Gomez Manuel Octavio • CUB • EARTH AND THE SKY, THE
TIERRA Y LIBERTAD • 1978 • Bulbulian Maurice • DOC • CND
TIERRAS BLANCAS, LAS • 1959 • del Carril Hugo • ARG
TIERRAS DE VINO • 1974 • Ardavin Cesar • SHT • SPN
TIERS MONDE: PRISONNIER DE LA RUE • 1980 • Laperrousaz Jerome • DOC • FRN • THIRD WORLD: PRISONER OF THE STREET
TIES see **LEGATO** • 1978
TIES FOR THE OLYMPICS see **KRAWATTEN FUR OLYMPIA** • 1976
TIES OF BLOOD • 1921 • *Clough Inez* • USA
TIES OF BLOOD, THE see **RODNAYA KROV** • 1964
TIETA DE AGRESTE • 1982 • Wertmuller Lina • BRZ
TIFF AND WHAT BECAME OF IT, THE • 1915 • Cooper Toby? • UKN
TIFFANY • *Zarni Anna* • FRG • TIFFANY: TRIANGLE OF LUST
TIFFANY JONES • 1973 • Walker Pete • UKN
TIFFANY MEMORANDUM • 1967 • Grieco Sergio • ITL, FRN
TIFFANY: TRIANGLE OF LUST see **TIFFANY**
TIFUSARI • 1963 • Mimica Vatroslav • SHT • YGS • TYPHOID SUFFERERS ○ TYPHOID ○ TYPHUS
TIGAR • 1979 • Jelic Milan • YGS • TIGER
TIGER see **TIGAR** • 1979
TIGER, DER • 1930 • Meyer Johannes • FRG • TIGER VON BERLIN, DER
TIGER, THE • 1913 • Thompson Frederick A. • USA
TIGER, THE see **TIGRE, IL** • 1967
TIGER, THE see **TIGER MAKES OUT, THE** • 1968
TIGER AKBAR, DER • 1951 • Piel Harry • FRG
TIGER AMONG US, THE see **13 WEST STREET** • 1962
TIGER AND CRANE FISTS see **SHAOLIN HU HO CHEN T'IEN-HSIA** • 1976
TIGER AND TEDDY BEARS • 1978 • Rubbo Michael • CND
TIGER AND THE FLAME, THE see **JHANSI-KI-RANI** • 1953
TIGER AND THE PUSSYCAT, THE (USA) see **TIGRE, IL** • 1967
TIGER ATTACKS, THE • 1959 • *Ventura Lino* • FRN
TIGER BAIT • 1915 • Chaudet Louis W. • USA
TIGER BAND, THE • 1920 • Hamilton G. P. • SRL • USA
TIGER BAY • 1933 • Wills J. Elder • UKN
TIGER BAY • 1959 • Thompson J. Lee • UKN
TIGER BY THE TAIL • 1955 • Gilling John • UKN • CROSS UP (USA)
TIGER BY THE TAIL • 1968 • Springsteen R. G. • USA
TIGER CHILD • 1970 • Brittain Don, Kroitor Roman, Ichikawa Kiichi • CND
TIGER CUB, THE • 1915 • Chaudet Louis W. • USA
TIGER DES ZIRKUS FARINI, DER see **LETZTE SENSATION DES ZIRKUS FARINI, DIE** • 1923
TIGER DOESN'T CRY, THE see **TIGERS DON'T CRY** • 1976
TIGER FANGS • 1943 • Newfield Sam • USA
TIGER FIGHTING • 1977 • Vichien Sa-Nguanthai • HKG
TIGER FLIGHT (USA) see **KYOMO WARE OZORANI ARI** • 1964
TIGER GANG see **KOMMISSAR X: JAGT DIE ROTEN TIGER** • 1971
TIGER GIRL • 1955 • Kosheverova Nadezhda, Ivanovsky Alexander • USS
TIGER GYPSY see **TIGRE GITANO** • 1968
TIGER HUNT IN ASSAM • 1958 • Van Dyke Willard • DOC • USA
TIGER HUNTING IN NORTH INDIA • 1930 • Corbett James • UKN
TIGER IN THE SKY (UKN) see **MCCONNELL STORY, THE** • 1955
TIGER IN THE SMOKE • 1956 • Baker Roy Ward • UKN
TIGER ISLAND • 1930 • Hayle Gerald M. • ASL
TIGER JOE • 1982 • Margheriti Antonio • ITL
TIGER KILLER see **WU SUNG** • 1983
TIGER LEAPS AND KILLS, BUT IT WILL DIE, IT WILL DIE, THE see **TIGRE SALTO Y MATO.. PERO MORIRA.. MORIRA** • 1973
TIGER LIKES FRESH BLOOD (UKN) see **TIGRE AIME LA CHAIR FRAICHE, LE** • 1964
TIGER LIKES FRESH MEAT see **TIGRE AIME LA CHAIR FRAICHE, LE** • 1964
TIGER LILY, THE • 1913 • Brooke Van Dyke?, Ince Ralph? • USA
TIGER LILY, THE • 1919 • Cox George L. • USA
TIGER LOVE • 1924 • Melford George • USA
TIGER MAKES OUT, THE • 1968 • Hiller Arthur • USA • TIGER, THE
TIGER MAN see **LADY AND THE MONSTER, THE** • 1944
TIGER MAN see **TROMBA** • 1949
TIGER MAN see **BAGH BAHADUR** • 1989
TIGER MAN, THE • 1918 • Hart William S. • USA
TIGER MORSE • 1967 • Warhol Andy • USA
TIGER OF BENGAL see **TIGER VON ESCHNAPUR, DER** • 1959
TIGER OF MALAYA see **SANDOKAN** • 1974
TIGER OF MAZANDARAN, THE see **BABR MAZANDARAN** • 1968
TIGER OF SAN PEDRO, THE • 1921 • Elvey Maurice • UKN
TIGER OF THE SEA • 1964 • Ida Tan • JPN • SEA FIGHTERS, THE
TIGER OF THE SEA, THE • 1918 • Shipman Nell • USA
TIGER OF THE SEVEN SEAS (USA) see **TIGRE DEI SETTE MARI, LA** • 1963
TIGER OF YAUTEPEC, THE see **TIGRE DE YAUTEPEC, EL** • 1933
TIGER OVER WALL • 1977 • *Ko Phillip* • HKG
TIGER RAG • Saxon Dave • ANS • USA
TIGER ROSE • 1923 • Franklin Sidney A. • USA
TIGER ROSE • 1929 • Fitzmaurice George • USA
TIGER SHARK • 1932 • Hawks Howard • USA
TIGER SHARK • 1987 • Alston Emmett • USA
TIGER SLAYER, THE • 1915 • Daly William Robert • USA
TIGER STRIKES AGAIN, THE • Hwa I Hung • HKG
TIGER THE 'TEC • 1911 • Fitzhamon Lewin • UKN
TIGER THOMPSON • 1924 • Eason B. Reeves • USA
TIGER TOWN • 1984 • Shapiro Alan • TVM • USA
TIGER TROUBLE • 1945 • Kinney Jack • ANS • USA
TIGER TRUE • 1921 • McGowan J. P. • USA
TIGER VON BERLIN, DER see **TIGER, DER** • 1930
TIGER VON ESCHNAPUR, DER • 1937 • Eichberg Richard • FRG
TIGER VON ESCHNAPUR, DER • 1959 • Lang Fritz • FRG, ITL, FRN • TIGRE DI ESCHNAPUR, LA (ITL) ○ TIGRE DU BENGALE, LE (FRN) ○ TIGRESS OF BENGAL ○ TIGER OF BENGAL
TIGER VON ESCHNAPUR, DER see **INDISCHE GRABMAL II, DAS** • 1921
TIGER WALKS, A • 1964 • Tokar Norman • USA
TIGER WARSAW • 1987 • Chaudhri Amin • USA
TIGER WOMAN, THE • 1917 • Edwards J. Gordon • USA
TIGER WOMAN, THE • 1944 • Bennet Spencer Gordon, Grissell Wallace A. • SRL • USA
TIGER WOMAN, THE • 1945 • Ford Philip • USA
TIGERIN, DIE • 1921 • Wendt Ernst • FRG
TIGER'S CLAW, THE • 1916 • Ellis Robert • SHT • USA
TIGER'S CLAW, THE • 1923 • Henabery Joseph • USA
TIGER'S CLAWS • 1912 • *Pathe* • USA
TIGER'S COAT, THE • 1920 • Clements Roy • USA
TIGER'S CUB • 1920 • Giblyn Charles • USA
TIGERS DON'T CRY • 1976 • Collinson Peter • SAF • TARGET FOR AN ASSASSIN (USA) ○ TARGET OF AN ASSASSIN ○ LONG SHOT, THE ○ AFRICAN RAGE ○ TIGER DOESN'T CRY, THE
TIGERS IN LIPSTICK (USA) see **LETTI SELVAGGI** • 1979
TIGERS IN THE SLUMS see **MGA TIGRE SA LOOBAN** • 1968
TIGERS OF MEMORY see **TIGRES DE LA MEMORIA, LOS** • 1984
TIGERS OF THE HILLS, THE • 1914 • *Kalem* • USA
TIGERS OF THE PLAINS • 1916 • *Big U* • SHT • USA
TIGERS SEKAI WA BOKURA O MATTEIRU • 1968 • Wada Yoshinori • JPN • WORLD IS WAITING FOR US, THE
TIGER'S SHADOW, THE • 1928 • Bennet Spencer Gordon • SRL • USA
TIGER'S SON see **PREP AND PEP** • 1928
TIGER'S TAIL, A • 1964 • Kneitel Seymour • ANS • USA
TIGER'S TALE, A • 1987 • Douglas Peter • USA
TIGER'S TRAIL, THE • 1919 • Ellis Robert, Hurst Paul C. • SRL • USA
TIGER'S TWIN, THE • 1963 • Trusov A. • ANS • USS
TIGERS UNCHAINED • 1916 • Horne James W. • SHT • USA
TIGHT CORNER, A • 1901 • *Mitchell & Kenyon* • UKN
TIGHT CORNER, A • 1932 • Hiscott Leslie • UKN
TIGHT CORNER, A see **THUNDERING HOOFS** • 1924
TIGHT FIT see **AMANTI MIEI** • 1979
TIGHT FIX, A • 1919 • Goulding Alf • SHT • USA
TIGHT LITTLE ISLAND (USA) see **WHISKY GALORE** • 1948
TIGHT REIN, THE • 1916 • Hansel Howell • SHT • USA
TIGHT ROPE TRICKS • 1933 • Foster John, Rufle George • ANS • USA
TIGHT SHOES • 1914 • *Roland Ruth* • USA
TIGHT SHOES • 1923 • Roach Hal • SHT • USA
TIGHT SHOES • 1941 • Rogell Albert S. • USA
TIGHT SKIRTS see **AMOUR A LA CHAINE, L'** • 1965
TIGHT SKIRTS, LOOSE PLEASURES (USA) see **AMOUR A LA CHAINE, L'** • 1965
TIGHT SPOT • 1955 • Karlson Phil • USA
TIGHT SPOT, A see **TESNA KOZA** • 1984
TIGHT SQUEEZE, A • 1914 • Edwin Walter • USA
TIGHT SQUEEZE, A • 1918 • White Jack, Watson William • SHT • USA
TIGHTROPE • 1984 • Tuggle Richard • USA
TIGHTROPE TO TERROR • 1982 • Kellett Bob • UKN
TIGHTWAD, THE • 1914 • Hamilton G. P.? • USA
TIGHTWAD, THE • 1917 • Curtis Allen • SHT • USA
TIGHTWAD ALMOSTS SAVES A DOLLAR • 1912 • *Nestor* • USA
TIGHTWAD BUYS A LAUNDRY • 1914 • *Powers* • USA
TIGHTWAD GETS A BARGAIN • 1912 • *Nestor* • USA
TIGHTWAD PAYS FOR A DOG • 1912 • *Nestor* • USA
TIGHTWAD'S PREDICAMENT • 1913 • Henderson Dell • USA
TIGHTWAD'S PRESENT • 1913 • *Kalem* • USA
TIGIPIO • 1986 • de Castro Pedro Jorge • BRZ
TIGRA, LA • 1954 • Torre-Nilsson Leopoldo • ARG • TIGRESS, THE
TIGRE • 1976 • *Escorpion* • MXC
TIGRE, EL see **ESCUELA DE VALIENTES** • 1961
TIGRE, IL • 1967 • Risi Dino • ITL, USA • TIGER AND THE PUSSYCAT, THE (USA) ○ TIGER, THE
TIGRE, LA • 1911 • Maggi Luigi • ITL
TIGRE AIME LA CHAIR FRAICHE, LE • 1964 • Chabrol Claude • FRN, ITL • TIGRE AMA LA CARNE FRESCA, LA (ITL) ○ TIGER LIKES FRESH BLOOD (UKN) ○ CODE NAME: TIGER (USA) ○ TIGER LIKES FRESH MEAT
TIGRE AMA LA CARNE FRESCA, LA (ITL) see **TIGRE AIME LA CHAIR FRAICHE, LE** • 1964
TIGRE DE CHAMBERI, EL • 1957 • Ramirez Pedro L. • SPN
TIGRE DE GUANAJUATO, EL • 1964 • Baledon Rafael • MXC
TIGRE DE JALISCO, EL • 1946 • Cardona Rene • MXC
TIGRE DE KYBER, EL • 1970 • Merino Jose Luis • SPN, ITL • FURIA DEI KYBER, LA (ITL)
TIGRE DE LOS SIETE MARES, EL (SPN) see **SURCOUF, L'EROE DEI SETTE MARI** • 1966
TIGRE DE SANTA JULIA, EL • 1973 • *Filmicas Agrasanchez* • MXC
TIGRE DE YAUTEPEC, EL • 1933 • de Fuentes Fernando • MXC • TIGER OF YAUTEPEC, THE
TIGRE DEI SETTE MARI, LA • 1963 • Capuano Luigi • ITL, FRN • TIGER OF THE SEVEN SEAS (USA) ○ TIGRE DES MERS, LE (FRN)
TIGRE DES MERS, LE (FRN) see **TIGRE DEI SETTE MARI, LA** • 1963
TIGRE DI ESCHNAPUR, LA (ITL) see **TIGER VON ESCHNAPUR, DER** • 1959
TIGRE DU BENGALE, LE • 1937 • Eichberg Richard • FRN
TIGRE DU BENGALE, LE (FRN) see **TIGER VON ESCHNAPUR, DER** • 1959
TIGRE E ANCORA VIVA, LA see **TIGRE E ANCORA VIVA: SANDOKAN ALLA RISCOSSA, LA** • 1977
TIGRE E ANCORA VIVA: SANDOKAN ALLA RISCOSSA, LA • 1977 • Sollima Sergio • ITL • TIGRE E ANCORA VIVA, LA
TIGRE ENMASCARADO, EL • 1950 • Gomez Urquiza Zacarias • MXC
TIGRE GITANO • 1968 • Junar • PHL • TIGER GYPSY
TIGRE NEGRO, EL • 1961 • Alazraki Benito • MXC
TIGRE PROFUMATA ALLA DINAMITE, LA (ITL) see **TIGRE SE PARFUME A LA DYNAMITE, LE** • 1965
TIGRE REALE • 1916 • Pastrone Giovanni • ITL
TIGRE SALTO Y MATO.. PERO MORIRA.. MORIRA • 1973 • Alvarez Santiago • DOC • CUB • TIGER LEAPS AND KILLS, BUT IT WILL DIE, IT WILL DIE, THE
TIGRE SE PARFUME A LA DYNAMITE, LE • 1965 • Chabrol Claude • FRN, ITL, SPN • TIGRE PROFUMATA ALLA DINAMITE, LA (ITL) ○ ORCHID FOR THE TIGER, AN (UKN)
TIGRE SORT SANS SA MERE, LE see **DA BERLINO L'APOCALISSE** • 1967
TIGRES DE LA MEMORIA, LOS • 1984 • Galettini Carlos • ARG • TIGERS OF MEMORY
TIGRES DE PAPEL • 1978 • Colomo Fernando • SPN • PAPER TIGERS
TIGRES DEL DESIERTO, LOS • 1958 • Delgado Agustin P. • MXC
TIGRES DEL RING, LOS • 1957 • Urueta Chano • MXC
TIGRESA, LA • 1917 • Coss Joaquin • MXC
TIGRESA, LA • 1972 • *Peliculas Rodriguez* • MXC
TIGRESS see **BAGHINI** • 1968
TIGRESS, THE • 1914 • Blache Alice • USA
TIGRESS, THE • 1915 • Johnston Lorimer • USA
TIGRESS, THE • 1927 • Seitz George B. • USA
TIGRESS, THE see **TIGRA, LA** • 1954
TIGRESS OF BENGAL see **TIGER VON ESCHNAPUR, DER** • 1959
TIGRESS OF SIBERIA, THE see **ILSA, LA TIGRESSE DU GOULAG** • 1977
TIGRI DI MOMPRACEN, LE • 1970 • Sequi Mario • ITL
TIGRIS • 1914 • *Itala* • ITL

TIGROS DEL DESIERTO, LOS • Solvay Paolo • SPN • DESERT TIGERS
TIGULLIO MINORE • 1947 • Risi Dino • SHT • ITL
TIH MINH • 1918 • Feuillade Louis • SRL • FRN
TIHERAKIAS, O • 1968 • Thalassinos Errikos • GRC • LUCKY ONE, THE
TIHIYAT BEGLETS • 1971 • Vassilev Peter • BUL • QUIET FUGITIVE, THE
TIJD, DE • 1983 • van der Keuken Johan • NTH • TIME
TIJD OM GELUKKIG TE ZIJN • 1981 • Buyens Frans • BLG • TIME FOR BEING HAPPY
TIJDGEEST, DE • 1968 • van der Keuken Johan • DOC • NTH • SPIRIT OF THE TIME
TIJELO • 1966 • Babaja Ante • SHT • YGS • BODY, THE
TIJERA DE ORO, LA • 1958 • Alazraki Benito • MXC
TIJUANA STORY, THE • 1957 • Kardos Leslie • USA
TIJUANA TOADS • Chiniquy Gerry • ASS • USA
TIKHAYA ODYESSA • 1968 • Isakov Valeri • USS • QUIET ODESSA
TIKHII DON • 1958 • Gerasimov Sergei • USS • QUIET FLOWS THE DON (UKN) ○ AND QUIET FLOWS THE DON
TIKHU DON • 1931 • Preobrazhenskaya Olga • USS • COSSACKS OF THE DON ○ QUIET DON, THE
TIKI-TIKI • 1971 • Potterton Gerald, Stokes Jack, Bykov Rolan • CND
TIKO AND THE SHARK (USA) see **TI-KOYO E IL SUO PESCECANE** • 1962
'TIL DEATH DO US PART see **NOVIA ENSANGRENTADA, LA** • 1972
TIL EN UKJENT see **FLASKEPOST** • 1988
'TIL THE BUTCHER CUTS HIM DOWN • 1971 • Spalding Philip • DOC • USA
'TIL VICTORY (USA) see **JUSQU'A LA VICTOIRE** • 1970
'TIL WE MEET AGAIN • 1940 • Goulding Edmund • USA • WE SHALL ME AGAIN
'TIL WE MEET AGAIN see **TILL WE MEET AGAIN** • 1936
TILASMI HEERA • 1946 • Khan A. M. • IND
TILASMI TALWAR • 1935 • Khan A. M. • IND • NOOR-E-ARAB
TILINTEKO • 1987 • Altonen Veikko • FNL • FINAL ARRANGEMENT, THE
TILISMI TALWAR • 1934 • Desai Nanubhai • IND • SHAIF-E-SULEMANI
TILKI SELIM • 1966 • Hancer Nisan • TRK • CRAFTY SELIM
TILL • 1988 • Tissi Felix • SWT
TILL DEATH • 1978 • Stocker Walter • USA
TILL DEATH DO PART • 1911 • *Reliance* • USA
TILL DEATH DO US PART • 1911 • Fitzhamon Lewin? • UKN
TILL DEATH DO US PART • 1982 • Bond Timothy • CND
TILL DEATH DO US PART see **FOR DODEN OS SKILLER** • 1970
TILL DEATH DO US PART see **NOVIA ENSANGRENTADA, LA** • 1972
TILL DEATH US DO PART • 1913 • *Pilot* • USA
TILL DEATH US DO PART • 1914 • Campbell Colin • USA
TILL DEATH US DO PART • 1968 • Cohen Norman • UKN • ALF 'N' FAMILY (USA)
TILL DIVORCE DO US PART • 1975 • Woods Grahame • CND
TILL DIVORCE DO YOU PART (USA) see **CASTAGNE SONO BUONE, LE** • 1970
TILL EARLY MORNING • 1963 • Laius Leida • USS
TILL EULENSPIEGEL • 1966 • Ophuls Marcel (c/d) • MTV • FRG
TILL EULENSPIEGEL • 1975 • Simon Rainer • GDR
TILL EULENSPIEGEL AND THE BAKER OF BRUNSWICK • Hempel Johannes • ANM • GDR
TILL EULENSPIEGEL AS WATCHMAN • Hempel Johannes • ANM • GDR
TILL EULENSPIEGEL (FRG) see **AVENTURES DE TILL L'ESPIEGLE, LES** • 1956
TILL EULENSPIEGEL UND DER BACKER VON BRAUNSCHWEIG • 1954 • Kempel Johannes • ANS • GDR
TILL GLADJE • 1950 • Bergman Ingmar • SWD • TO JOY
'TILL I COME BACK TO YOU • 1918 • De Mille Cecil B. • USA
TILL MARRIAGE DO US PART (USA) see **MIO DIO, COME SONO CADUTA IN BASSO!** • 1974
TILL MARRIAGE DOES US APART see **ATE QUE O CASAMENTO NOS SEPARE** • 1968
TILL OSTERLAND • 1926 • Molander Gustaf • SWD • TO THE ORIENT
TILL OUR SHIP COMES IN • 1919 • Miller Frank • UKN • MARRIED BLISS
TILL SATERS • 1924 • Ivarsson Harry • NRW
TILL SEX DO US PART (USA) see **TROLL** • 1973
TILL SOON • 1930 • Makarov Georgi • USS
TILL THE BELLS RING • 1933 • Moffatt Graham • UKN
TILL THE CLOUDS ROLL BY • 1946 • Whorf Richard • USA
TILL THE DAY BREAKS • 1913 • *Solax* • USA
TILL THE END AND ONWARD see **DO KONCA IN NAPREJ** • 1990
TILL THE END OF LIFE • 1975 • Fahmy Ashraf • EGY
TILL THE END OF TIME • 1946 • Dmytryk Edward • USA
TILL THE HEART IS THERE see **NENJIRUKKUM VARAI** • 1967
TILL THE SANDS OF THE DESERT GROW COLD • 1914 • *Eclair* • USA
TILL THE STARS DO NOT TWINKLE • 1983 • Ko Young-Nam • SKR
TILL THE SUN DOWN see **YUGURE MADE** • 1981
TILL THE VERY END see **AZ DO OKONCE** • 1985
TILL THERE WAS YOU • 1990 • Seale John • ASL
TILL TOMORROW • 1990 • Trifonov Stanimir • BUL
TILL TOMORROW COMES (USA) see **ASU ARU KAGIRI** • 1962
TILL VICTORY see **JUSQU'A LA VICTOIRE** • 1970
TILL VICTORY ALWAYS see **HASTA LA VICTORIA SIEMPRE** • 1967
TILL WE MEET AGAIN • 1922 • Cabanne W. Christy • USA
TILL WE MEET AGAIN • 1936 • Florey Robert • USA • 'TIL WE MEET AGAIN ○ REUNION
TILL WE MEET AGAIN • 1944 • Borzage Frank • USA
TILL WE MEET AGAIN see **MATA AU HI MADE** • 1932
TILLAS VORMUND • 1915 • *Bois Ilse* • FRG
TILLER GROUP OF DANCERS, THE • 1901 • *Warwick Trading Co* • UKN
TILLER'S SIX DIAMONDS • 1899 • *Warwick Trading Co* • UKN
TILLIE • 1922 • Urson Frank • USA • TILLIE, A MENNONITE MAID
TILLIE, A MENNONITE MAID see **TILLIE** • 1922
TILLIE AND GUS • 1933 • Martin Francis • USA
TILLIE AND THE MORMON MISSIONARY • 1911 • Fitzhamon Lewin • UKN
TILLIE OF THE NINE LIVES • 1917 • *Pitts Zasu* • USA
TILLIE, THE LITTLE SWEDE • 1916 • Madison Cleo, Mong William V. • USA
TILLIE THE TERRIBLE TYPIST • 1915 • *Chamberlain Riley* • USA
TILLIE THE TOILER • 1927 • Henley Hobart • USA
TILLIE THE TOILER • 1941 • Salkow Sidney • USA
TILLIE WAKES UP • 1917 • Davenport Harry • USA
TILLIE'S NIGHTMARE see **TILLIE'S PUNCTURED ROMANCE** • 1914
TILLIE'S PUNCTURED ROMANCE • 1914 • Sennett Mack • USA • CHARLIE'S BIG ROMANCE ○ FOR THE LOVE OF TILLIE ○ MARIE'S MILLIONS ○ TILLIE'S NIGHTMARE
TILLIE'S PUNCTURED ROMANCE • 1928 • Sutherland A. Edward • USA • MARIE'S MILLIONS (UKN)
TILLIE'S TERRIBLE TUMBLES • 1916 • Blystone John G. • SHT • USA
TILLIE'S TOMATO SURPRISE • 1915 • Hansel Howell • USA
TILLSAMMANS MED GUNILLA see **TILLSAMMANS MED GUNILLA MANDAG KVALL OCH TISDAG** • 1965
TILLSAMMANS MED GUNILLA MANDAG KVALL OCH TISDAG • 1965 • Gorling Lars • SWD • WITH GUNILLA MONDAY EVENING AND TUESDAY ○ TILLSAMMANS MED GUNILLA ○ WITH GUNILLA ○ GUILT
TILLY AND THE DOGS • 1912 • Wilson Frank • UKN
TILLY AND THE FIRE ENGINES • 1911 • Fitzhamon Lewin • UKN
TILLY AND THE NUT • 1915 • Wilson Frank • UKN
TILLY AND THE SMUGGLERS • 1911 • Fitzhamon Lewin • UKN
TILLY AT THE ELECTION • 1910 • Fitzhamon Lewin • UKN
TILLY AT THE FOOTBALL MATCH • 1914 • Plumb Hay? • UKN
TILLY AT THE SEASIDE • 1911 • Fitzhamon Lewin? • UKN
TILLY IN A BOARDING HOUSE • 1912 • Plumb Hay? • UKN
TILLY -MATCHMAKER • 1911 • Fitzhamon Lewin • UKN
TILLY OF BLOOMSBURY • 1921 • Wilson Rex • UKN
TILLY OF BLOOMSBURY • 1931 • Raymond Jack • UKN
TILLY OF BLOOMSBURY • 1940 • Hiscott Leslie • UKN
TILLY THE TOMBOY BUYS LINOLEUM • 1910 • Fitzhamon Lewin • UKN
TILLY THE TOMBOY GOES BOATING • 1910 • Fitzhamon Lewin • UKN
TILLY THE TOMBOY PLAYS TRUANT • 1910 • Fitzhamon Lewin • UKN
TILLY THE TOMBOY VISITS THE POOR • 1910 • Fitzhamon Lewin • UKN
TILLY WORKS FOR A LIVING • 1912 • Wilson Frank • UKN
TILLY'S BREAKING UP PARTY • 1913 • Wilson Frank? • UKN
TILLY'S PARTY • 1911 • Fitzhamon Lewin • UKN
TILLY'S UNSYMPATHETIC UNCLE • 1911 • Fitzhamon Lewin • UKN
TILMAN RIEMENSCHNEIDER • 1958 • Spiess Helmut • GDR
TILMIZA WAL OSSTAZ, AL • 1968 • Eddin Ahmed Dia • EGY • PUPIL AND THE PROFESSOR, THE
TILOS A SZERELEM • 1965 • Renyi Tamas • HNG • NO LOVE PLEASE
TILOTTAMA • 1949 • Chatterjee Sanjib • IND
TILT • 1972 • Arioli Don • ANS • CND
TILT! • 1973 • Balducci Richard • FRN
TILT • 1978 • Durand Rudy • USA
TILT TO THE SUN • 1967 • Bowie Ronald • DCS • NZL
TIM • 1912 • *Edison* • USA
TIM • 1979 • Pate Michael • ASL
TIM AND JIM • 1912 • *Lubin* • USA
TIM DRISCOLL'S DONKEY • 1955 • Bishop Terry • UKN
TIM FRAZER JAGT DEN GEHEIMNISVOLLEN MR. K. • 1964 • Hofbauer Ernst • AUS
TIM GROGAN'S FOUNDLING • 1913 • Brooke Van Dyke • USA
TIM MAHONEY, THE SCAB • 1911 • *Vitagraph* • USA
TIM PADEM • 1980 • Kovar Karel • CZC • THAT'S WHY
TIM RALLEY • 1923 • *Filmindustrie Und Lichtspiel* • FRG
TIM SIKEA • 1981 • Payer Roch Christophe • MTV • CND
TIM THE MESSENGER • 1913 • *Phoenix Film Agency* • UKN
TIM, THE TERROR • 1914 • Middleton Mr. • USA
TIM TYLER'S LUCK • 1937 • Beebe Ford, Gittens Wyndham • SRL • USA
TIMANFAYA • 1971 • de la Loma Jose Antonio • SPN • AMOR PROHIBIDO
TIMBER • 1941 • King Jack • ANS • USA
TIMBER • 1942 • Cabanne W. Christy • USA
TIMBER COUNTRY TROUBLE • 1955 • McDonald Frank • MTV • USA
TIMBER INDUSTRY see **TIMMERFABRIEK** • 1930
TIMBER MOVE • 1965 • Prouting Norman • DCS • UKN
TIMBER -OK I CANADA • 1967 • Roos Ole • DCS • DNM
TIMBER QUEEN • 1922 • Jackman Fred • SRL • USA
TIMBER QUEEN • 1943 • McDonald Frank • USA
TIMBER STAMPEDE • 1939 • Howard David • USA
TIMBER TERRORS • 1935 • Tansey Robert • USA • MORTON OF THE MOUNTED (UKN)
TIMBER TOPPERS • 1932 • McCarey Ray • SHT • USA
TIMBER TOWN • 1972 • Howes Oliver • DOC • ASL
TIMBER TRAIL, THE • 1948 • Ford Philip • USA
TIMBER TRAMP • 1973 • Garnett Tay, Keen Chuck D. • USA • BIG PUSH, THE
TIMBER WAR • 1936 • Newfield Sam • USA
TIMBER WOLF • 1925 • Van Dyke W. S. • USA
TIMBER WOLF, THE • 1916 • Cochrane George • SHT • USA
TIMBER WOLF, THE • 1920 • Jaccard Jacques • SHT • USA
TIMBER WOLVES • 1936 • Collins Lewis D. • USA
TIMBERJACK • 1955 • Kane Joseph • USA
TIMBERWORLD, THE • 1920 • *Universal* • USA
TIMBUCTOO • 1933 • Summers Walter, Woods Arthur • UKN
TIMBUCTU (ITL) see **LEGEND OF THE LOST** • 1957
TIMBUKTU • 1959 • Tourneur Jacques • USA
TIME • 1967 • Vukotic Dusan • ANS • YGS
TIME • 1970 • Grottesi Marcello • ITL
TIME • 1973 • Bevc Joze • SHT • YGS
TIME see **MEGALL AZ IDO** • 1981
TIME see **TIJD, DE** • 1983
TIME AFTER TIME • 1979 • Meyer Nicholas • USA
TIME AFTER TIME • 1985 • Hays Bill • UKN
TIME AND A PLACE, A • 1977 • Armstrong Gillian • DOC • ASL
TIME AND HOUR OF AUGUSTO MATRAGA, THE see **HORA E VEZ DE AUGUSTO MATRAGA, A** • 1965
TIME AND MOTION • 1976 • Sinden Tony • UKN
TIME AND TERRAIN • 1948 • Low Colin • ANS • CND
TIME AND THE HOUR • 1915 • Buckland Warwick • UKN
TIME AND THE TOUCH, THE • 1962 • Alazraki Benito • USA
TIME AND TIDE • 1916 • Eason B. Reeves • USA
TIME AND TIDE • 1945 • Rotha Paul • DOC • UKN
TIME AND TIDE see **VREME, VODI** • 1981
TIME AND TIDE (UKN) see **CLOCK, THE** • 1917
TIME AND TIME AGAIN see **ALLE JAHRE WIEDER** • 1967
TIME AVENGES • 1912 • *Reliance* • USA
TIME BANDITS • 1981 • Gilliam Terry • UKN
TIME BOMB • 1952 • Tetzlaff Ted • UKN • TERROR ON A TRAIN (USA)
TIME BOMB • 1971 • Gazhiu Valeri • USS • TIME-BOMB EXPLOSION
TIME BOMB • 1984 • Krasny Paul • TVM • USA
TIME BOMB • 1985-89 • Osman Aziz M. • MTV • MLY
TIME-BOMB EXPLOSION see **TIME BOMB** • 1971
TIME BOMB (USA) see **VENT SE LEVE, LE** • 1959
TIME BURST see **TIME BURST: THE FINAL ALLIANCE** • 1988
TIME BURST: THE FINAL ALLIANCE • 1988 • Yuval Peter • USA • TIME BURST
TIME CAPSULE • 1967 • Lipsett Arthur • CND
TIME CRYSTAL, THE see **THROUGH THE MAGIC PYRAMID** • 1981
TIME FLIES • 1912 • *Carney Augustus* • USA
TIME FLIES • 1913 • Collins Edwin J.? • UKN
TIME FLIES • 1944 • Forde Walter • UKN
TIME FLYER see **BLUE YONDER, THE** • 1985
TIME FOR ACTION (UKN) see **TIP ON A DEAD JOCKEY** • 1957
TIME FOR BEING HAPPY see **TIJD OM GELUKKIG TE ZIJN** • 1981
TIME FOR BURNING, A • 1966 • Jersey William C., Connell Barbara • DOC • USA
TIME FOR DYING, A • 1969 • Boetticher Budd • USA
TIME FOR GIVING, A (UKN) see **GENERATION** • 1969
TIME FOR HEROES, A see **HELL WITH HEROES, THE** • 1968
TIME FOR INDIFFERENCE see **INDIFFERENTI, GLI** • 1964
TIME FOR KILLING, A • 1967 • Karlson Phil, Corman Roger (U/c) • USA • LONG RIDE HOME, THE (UKN) ○ SOUTHERN BLADE
TIME FOR LOVE • 1935 • Fleischer Dave • ANS • USA
TIME FOR LOVE see **DOSLO DOBA DA SE LJUBAV PROBA** • 1981
TIME FOR LOVE, A • 1973 • Schaefer George, Sargent Joseph • TVM • USA
TIME FOR LOVING • 1971 • Miles Christopher • UKN • PARIS WAS MADE FOR LOVERS
TIME FOR MIRACLES, A • 1980 • O'Herlihy Michael • TVM • USA
TIME FOR REVENGE see **TIEMPO DE REVANCHA** • 1981
TIME FOR THE HARVEST • 1963 • Crichton Robin • UKN
TIME FOR THOUGHT • Young Robert • DOC • UKN
TIME FOR TWO see **TWO SMART PEOPLE** • 1946
TIME & FORTUNE VIETNAM NEWSREEL • 1969 • Mekas Jonas • USA
TIME GALLOPS ON • 1952 • Davis Mannie • ANS • USA
TIME GAMES see **PLAYING BEATIE BOW** • 1986
TIME, GENTLEMEN, PLEASE • 1952 • Gilbert Lewis* • UKN • NOTHING TO LOSE
TIME, GENTLEMEN, PLEASE see **POLICEJNI HODINA** • 1960
TIME GUARDIAN, THE • 1987 • Hannant Brian • ASL
TIME HAS STOPPED see **TEMPO SI E FERMATO, IL** • 1960
TIME IN SUMMER • 1968 • Dutkiewicz Ludwik • ASL
TIME IN THE SUN see **QUE VIVA MEXICO!** • 1931
TIME IN THE SUN see **BEZHIN LUG** • 1937
TIME IN THE SUN, A (USA) see **PRINSESSAN** • 1966
TIME IS • 1963 • Levy Don • SHT • UKN
TIME IS JUST A PLACE • 1961 • Glut Don • SHT • USA
TIME IS MERCILESS see **CAS JE NEUPROSNY** • 1978
TIME IS MONEY • 1913 • Brenon Herbert • USA
TIME IS MONEY • 1923 • Sauer Fred • FRG
TIME IS MY ENEMY • 1954 • Chaffey Don • UKN
TIME IS ON OUR SIDE • 1982 • Ashby Hal • DOC • USA
TIME KILLER, THE see **NIGHT STRANGLER, THE** • 1972
TIME LIMIT • 1957 • Malden Karl • USA
TIME LIMIT see **LIMIT, THE** • 1972
TIME LOCK • 1957 • Thomas Gerald • UKN
TIME LOCK NO.776 • 1915 • Reid Hal • USA
TIME-LOCK SAFE, THE • 1910 • *Imp* • USA
TIME LOCKS AND DIAMONDS • 1917 • Edwards Walter • USA
TIME LOST AND TIME REMEMBERED (USA) see **I WAS HAPPY HERE** • 1965
TIME MACHINE, THE • 1960 • Pal George • USA
TIME MACHINE, THE • 1972 • Macartney-Filgate Terence • CND
TIME MACHINE, THE • 1978 • Schellerup Henning • TVM • USA
TIME MONSTERS, THE • 1959 • Glut Don • SHT • USA
TIME OF BEFORE, THE see **TEMPS DE L'AVANT, LE** • 1975
TIME OF CHANGE see **CZAS PRZEMIANY** • 1968
TIME OF CRISIS • 1953 • Keys Richard • SHT • ASL
TIME OF CRISIS see **KRIZNO OBDOBJE** • 1981
TIME OF DESIRE see **VREMIA JELANII** • 1983
TIME OF DESIRE (USA) see **HASTHANDLARENS FLICKOR** • 1954
TIME OF DESTINY, A • 1988 • Nava Gregory • USA
TIME OF GIPSIES, THE see **DOM ZA VESANJE** • 1987
TIME OF HATEM ZAHRAN, THE • 1987 • el Naggar Mohamed • EGY
TIME OF HER LIFE, THE see **PRICE OF A GOOD TIME, THE** • 1918
TIME OF HIS LIFE, THE • 1955 • Hiscott Leslie • UKN
TIME OF HOPE, THE • Cherentsov L. • DOC • USS
TIME OF INDIFFERENCE (USA) see **INDIFFERENTI, GLI** • 1964
TIME OF KALI, THE see **KALIYUGAYA** • 1982

TIME OF LIBERATION HAS COME, THE see **SAAT EL TAHRIR DAKKAT BARRA YA ISTI'MAR** • 1974
TIME OF LOSING FAITH see **FUSHIN NO TOKI** • 1968
TIME OF LOVE • 1990 • Makhmalbaf Mohsen • IRN
TIME OF MASSACRE see **TEMPO DI MASSACRO** • 1966
TIME OF MATURING see **REIFEZEIT** • 1976
TIME OF MIRACLES, THE see **ZAMAN EL AJAB** • 1952
TIME OF MIRACLES, THE see **VREME CUDA** • 1990
TIME OF PARTING see **TIME OF VIOLENCE** • 1987
TIME OF RECKONING, THE see **FUSHIN NO TOKI** • 1968
TIME OF ROSES AND BLOSSOMING FLOWERS see **BARA NO KI NI BARA NO HANA** • 1959
TIME OF ROSES (USA) see **RUUSUJEN AIKA** • 1969
TIME OF SCORN, A see **TIEMPO DEL DESPRECIO, EL** • 1974
TIME OF SILENCE see **TIEMPO DE SILENCIO** • 1986
TIME OF TEARS • 1987 • Mantis Costa • USA • UNCLE
TIME OF THE APES • 1987 • Okunaga Atsuo, Fukazawa Kiyosumi • JPN
TIME OF THE BARBARIANS, THE • 1971 • Reisenbuchler Sandor • ANS • HNG
TIME OF THE CREE • 1976 • Rodgers Bob • MTV • CND
TIME OF THE HEATHEN • 1962 • Kass Peter, Emshwiller Ed • USA
TIME OF THE INNOCENT, THE see **ZEIT DER SCHULDLOSEN, DIE** • 1964
TIME OF THE JACKALS • 1980 • Damiani Damiano • ITL
TIME OF THE ROSES see **RUUSUJEN AIKA** • 1969
TIME OF THE SERVANTS • 1990 • Pavlaskova Irena • CZC
TIME OF THE TAR SANDS • 1974 • Jubenvill Ken • MTV • CND
TIME OF THE VAMPIRE, THE see **VRIJEME VAMPIRA** • 1970
TIME OF THE VULTURES, THE see **TEMPO DEGLI AVVOLTI, IL** • 1967
TIME OF THE WOLF see **ULVETID** • 1981
TIME OF THE WOLF see **VARGENS TID** • 1988
TIME OF THE WOLVES see **TEMPS DES LOUPS -TEMPO DI VIOLENZA, LE** • 1970
TIME OF THE WOLVES see **VARGENS TID** • 1988
TIME OF THEIR LIVES, THE • 1946 • Barton Charles T. • USA • GHOST STEPS OUT, THE
TIME OF THEIR LIVES, THE • 1983 • Cowan Tom • DOC • ASL
TIME OF TRIAL AND HOPE • 1967 • Raizman Yuli • USS
TIME OF TRIUMPH, A • 1986 • Black Noel • TVM • USA
TIME OF UNDUTIFUL CHILDREN see **NIPPON OYAFUKO JIDAI** • 1968
TIME OF VAMPIRES, THE (USA) see **VRIJEME VAMPIRA** • 1970
TIME OF VENGEANCE see **ZEIT DER RACHE** • 1990
TIME OF VIOLENCE • 1987 • Staikov Lyudmil • BUL • TIME OF PARTING
TIME OF VIOLENCE see **TEMPO DE VIOLENCIA** • 1969
TIME OF YOUR LIFE, THE • 1948 • Potter H. C. • USA
TIME OF YOUTH see **MLADI** • 1960
TIME OFF • 1964 • Gass Karl • DOC • GDR
TIME ON MY HANDS • 1932 • Fleischer Dave • ANS • USA
TIME OUT • 1987 • Carlsen Jon Bang • USA, DNM
TIME OUT FOR LESSONS • 1939 • Cahn Edward L. • SHT • USA
TIME OUT FOR LOVE (USA) see **GRANDES PERSONNES, LES** • 1961
TIME OUT FOR MURDER • 1938 • Humberstone H. Bruce • USA • MERIDIAN 7-1212
TIME OUT FOR MURDER see **ONE WILD NIGHT** • 1938
TIME OUT FOR RHYTHM • 1941 • Salkow Sidney • USA
TIME OUT FOR ROMANCE • 1937 • St. Clair Malcolm • USA
TIME OUT FOR SARDINIA • 1970 • Baim Harold • DCS • UKN
TIME OUT FOR TROUBLE • 1938 • Lord Del • SHT • USA
TIME OUT OF MIND • 1947 • Siodmak Robert • USA
TIME OUT OF WAR • 1954 • Sanders Denis • SHT • USA
TIME PAST • 1966 • Cox Paul • SHT • ASL
TIME PAST (USA) see **CZAS PRZESZLY** • 1961
TIME PIECE • 1965 • Henson Jim • SHT • USA • TIMEPIECE
TIME PIECE • 1969 • Kish Albert • DOC • CND • TIMEPIECE
TIME RIDER see **TIMERIDER: THE ADVENTURE OF LYLE SWANN** • 1983
TIME RUNNING OUT (USA) see **TRAQUE, LE** • 1950
TIME SLIP see **SENGOKU JIEITAI** • 1979
TIME STANDS STILL see **MEGALL AZ IDO** • 1981
TIME STOOD STILL • 1956 • De La Varre Andre • SHT • USA
TIME STOOD STILL (USA) see **TEMPO SI E FERMATO, IL** • 1960
TIME TAKES CARE OF EVERYTHING • 1946 • Crouch William Forest • SHT • USA
TIME, THE COMEDIAN • 1925 • Leonard Robert Z. • USA
TIME THE GREAT HEALER • 1914 • Hepworth Cecil M. • UKN
TIME, THE PLACE AND THE GIRL, THE • 1929 • Bretherton Howard • USA
TIME, THE PLACE AND THE GIRL, THE • 1946 • Butler David • USA
TIME TO DIE see **TIEMPO DE MORIR** • 1965
TIME TO DIE, A see **AMELIE OU LE TEMPS D'AIMER** • 1961
TIME TO DIE, A see **SEVEN GRAVES FOR ROGAN** • 1981
TIME TO DIE, A see **TIEMPO DE MORIR** • 1985
TIME TO DIE, THE see **TEMPS DE MOURIR, LE** • 1969
TIME TO HEAL • 1963 • Knight Derrick • UKN
TIME TO KILL • 1942 • Leeds Herbert I. • USA
TIME TO KILL see **TEMPO DI UCCIDERE** • 1990
TIME TO KILL, A • 1955 • Saunders Charles • UKN
TIME TO LIVE see **ZEIT ZU LEBEN** • 1969
TIME TO LIVE, A • 1985 • Wallace Rick • TVM • USA
TIME TO LIVE AND A TIME TO DIE, A (UKN) see **FEU FOLLET, LE** • 1963
TIME TO LIVE AND THE TIME TO DIE, THE see **T'UNG-NIEN WANG-SHIH** • 1985
TIME TO LOVE • 1927 • Tuttle Frank • USA
TIME TO LOVE, A see **VREME LJUBAVI** • 1966
TIME TO LOVE AND A TIME TO DIE, A • 1958 • Sirk Douglas • USA
TIME TO MEND, A see **REMBULAN DAN MATAHARI** • 1980
TIME TO PLAY, A • 1967 • Kane Art • SHT • CND
TIME TO REMEMBER • 1962 • Jarrott Charles • UKN
TIME TO REMEMBER, A • 1988 • Travers Thomas • USA • MIRACLE IN A MANGER
TIME TO RUN • 1973 • Collier James F. • USA
TIME TO SING, A • 1968 • Dreifuss Arthur • USA
TIME TRACKERS • 1989 • Cohen Howard R. • USA
TIME TRAP see **TIME TRAVELERS, THE** • 1964
TIME TRAVELERS • 1970 • Singer Alexander • TVM • USA
TIME TRAVELERS, THE • 1964 • Melchior Ib • USA • TIME TRAP
TIME TRAVELLER see **BU HUO YINGXIONG** • 1985
TIME WALKER • 1982 • Kennedy Tom • USA
TIME WARP • 1981 • Sandler Allan, Emenegger Robert • USA
TIME WARP see **JOURNEY TO THE CENTER OF TIME** • 1967
TIME WARP see **DAY TIME ENDED, THE** • 1978
TIME WARP TERROR see **BLOODY NEW YEAR** • 1987
TIME WARS see **SENGOKU JIEITAI** • 1979
TIME WILL SHOW • 1977 • van Munster Anton • DOC • NTH
TIME WITHIN MEMORY (USA) see **SEIGENKI** • 1973
TIME WITHOUT MEMORY see **SEIGENKI** • 1973
TIME WITHOUT PITY • 1957 • Losey Joseph • UKN
TIME WITHOUT WAR • 1969 • Ivanov-Gapo Branko • YGS
TIMECHECK • 1972 • Hall David • UKN
TIMELAERER NANSEN • 1968 • Stenbaek Kirsten • SHT • DNM • TEACHER NANSEN
TIMELESS TEMIARS • 1956 • Hussain Zain • MLY
TIMELY APPARITION, A • 1909 • *Urban-Eclipse* • FRN
TIMELY BATH, A • 1913 • *Pathe* • USA
TIMELY INTERCEPTION, A • 1913 • Griffith D. W. • USA
TIMELY LESSON, A • 1911 • *Halliday Jack* • USA
TIMELY MEDIATOR see **TOKI NO UJIGAMI** • 1932
TIMELY REPENTANCE, A • 1972 • *Imp* • USA
TIMELY RESCUE, A • 1912 • *Vitagraph* • USA
TIMELY RESCUE, A • 1913 • Johnson Arthur • USA
TIMEPIECE see **TIME PIECE** • 1965
TIMEPIECE see **TIME PIECE** • 1969
TIMERIDER see **TIMERIDER: THE ADVENTURE OF LYLE SWANN** • 1983
TIMERIDER: THE ADVENTURE OF LYLE SWANN • 1983 • Dear William • USA • TIMERIDER ○ TIME RIDER
TIMES ARE DIFFERENT NOW see **INYYE NYNCHYE VREMENA** • 1968
TIMES ARE OUT OF JOINT, THE • 1910 • Cohl Emile • ANS • FRN
TIMES EIGHT • Gardner Frank • SHT • USA
TIMES FOR • 1970 • Dwoskin Stephen • UKN
TIMES GONE BY see **ALTRI TEMPI** • 1952
TIMES HAVE CHANGED • 1923 • Flood James • USA
TIMES OF HARVEY MILK, THE • 1985 • Epstein Robert • DOC • USA
TIMES OF JOY AND SORROW see **YOROKOBI MO KANASHIMI MO IKUTOSHITSUKI** • 1957
TIMES OF KING KRAKUS, THE see **ZAKROLA KRAKUSA** • 1948
TIMES SQUARE • 1929 • Boyle Joseph C. • USA • STREET OF JAZZ, THE (UKN)
TIMES SQUARE • 1980 • Moyle Allan • USA
TIMES SQUARE LADY • 1935 • Seitz George B. • USA
TIMES SQUARE PLAYBOY • 1936 • McGann William • USA • HIS BEST MAN (UKN)
TIMESLIP • 1955 • Hughes Ken • UKN • ATOMIC MAN, THE (USA)
TIMESTALKERS • 1987 • Schultz Michael • TVM • USA
TIMETABLE • 1956 • Stevens Mark • USA
TIMETABLE see **GOZENCHO NO JIKANWARI** • 1972
TIMETABLE BLUES • 1966 • Turner Peter • UKN
TIMETABLE FOR THE DAY AFTER TOMORROW, A see **RASPISANIE NA POSLEZAVTRA** • 1980
TIMI TIS AGAPIS, I • 1984 • Marketaki Tonia • GRC • PRICE OF LOVE, THE
TIMID MAY • 1912 • Sturgeon Rollin S. • USA
TIMID MR. TOOTLES, THE • 1915 • Drew Sidney • USA
TIMID PUP, THE • 1940 • Harrison Ben • ANS • USA
TIMID SCARECROW, THE • 1953 • Donnelly Eddie • ANS • USA
TIMID TABBY • 1957 • Hanna William, Barbera Joseph • ANS • USA
TIMID TERROR, THE • 1926 • Andrews Del • USA
TIMID TOREADOR • 1940 • Clampett Robert, McCabe Norman • ANS • USA
TIMID YOUNG MAN, THE • 1935 • Sennett Mack • SHT • USA
TIMIDO, EL • 1964 • Lazaga Pedro • SPN
TIMING • 1986 • Weinthal Eric • CND
TIMING CUPID • 1914 • Lambart Harry • USA
TIMIOS DROMOS • 1968 • Franyoudakis Mimis • GRC • HONOURABLE WAY, THE
TIMMERFABRIEK • 1930 • *Ivens Joris (Ph)* • DOC • NTH • TIMBER INDUSTRY
TIMON • 1974 • Radic Tomislav • YGS
TIMOR PORTUGUES • 1960 • Spiguel Miguel • SHT • PRT
TIMOTHY DOBBS, THAT'S ME • 1916 • SER • USA
TIMOTHY LEARY'S WEDDING see **YOU'RE NOBODY TILL SOMEBODY LOVES YOU** • 1969
TIMOTHY'S QUEST • 1922 • Olcott Sidney • USA
TIMOTHY'S QUEST • 1936 • Barton Charles T. • USA
TIMOUR ET SON EQUIPE • 1940 • Rasumny Alexander • USS
TIMUR'S OATH see **KLYATVA TIMURA** • 1942
TIN CAN ALLEY • 1924 • Lamont Charles • SHT • USA
TIN CAN CONCERT • 1961 • Hannah Jack • ANS • USA
TIN CAN RATTLE, THE • 1912 • *Lubin* • USA
TIN CAN SHACK, THE • 1915 • *Coxen Ed* • USA
TIN CAN TOURIST, THE • 1937 • Davis Mannie, Gordon George • ANS • USA
TIN DRUM ,THE (UKN) see **BLECHTROMMEL, DIE** • 1979
TIN FLUTE, THE see **BONHEUR D'OCCASION** • 1983
TIN GHOST, THE • 1926 • Roberts Stephen • SHT • USA
TIN GIRL, THE see **RAGAZZA DI LATTA, LA** • 1970
TIN GODS • 1926 • Dwan Allan • USA
TIN GODS • 1932 • Kraemer F. W. • UKN
TIN HAT, THE see **ZELEZNY KLOBOUK** • 1960
TIN HATS • 1926 • Sedgwick Edward • USA
TIN MAN • 1983 • Thomas John G. • USA
TIN MAN, THE • 1935 • Parrott James • SHT • USA
TIN MEN • 1987 • Levinson Barry • USA
TIN PAN ALLEY • 1920 • Beal Frank • USA
TIN PAN ALLEY • 1940 • Lang Walter • USA
TIN PAN ALLEY see **SYNCOPATING SUE** • 1926
TIN PAN ALLEY see **NEW YORK NIGHTS** • 1929
TIN PAN ALLEY CAT • 1960 • Tendlar Dave • ANS • USA
TIN PAN ALLEY CATS • 1943 • Clampett Robert • ANS • USA
TIN PAN ALLEY TEMPOS • 1945 • Cowan Will • SHT • USA
TIN-PLATE CUATRO, THE see **CUATRO DE HOJALATA, EL** • 1979
TIN SOLDIER, A • 1916 • Baker Richard Foster • SHT • USA
TIN SOLDIER AND THE DOLL • 1914 • *Thanhouser Kidlet* • USA
TIN SOLDIERS see **SOLDADOS DE PLOMO** • 1984
TIN STAR, THE • 1957 • Mann Anthony • USA
TIN TAN Y LAS MODELOS • 1959 • Alazraki Benito • MXC
TIN TOY • 1988 • Lassetter John • ANM • USA
TIN-TYPE ROMANCE, A • 1910 • *Vitagraph* • USA
TIN WEDDING PRESENTS • 1910 • *Essanay* • USA
TINAMER • 1988 • Noel Jean-Guy • CND
TINCTURE OF IRON • 1914 • Lyndhurst F. L. • UKN
TINDER BOX, THE • 1907 • Larsen Viggo • SHT • DNM
TINDER BOX, THE (USA) see **FEUERZEUG, DAS** • 1959
TINDERBOX • 1948 • Methling Sven • ANM • DNM
TINDERBOX OR, THE STORY OF A LIGHTER, THE see **DER KOM EN SOLDAT** • 1969
TINE • 1964 • Thomsen Knud Leif • DNM
TINE ZABUTYKH PREDKIV • 1965 • Paradjanov Sergei • USS • SHADOWS OF FORGOTTEN ANCESTORS (USA) ○ SHADOWS OF OUR ANCESTORS ○ SHADOWS OF OUR FORGOTTEN ANCESTORS ○ IN THE SHADOW OF THE PAST ○ TENI ZABYTYKH PREDKOV
TINERETE FARA BATRINETE • 1968 • Bostan Elisabeta • RMN • KINGDOM IN THE CLOUDS (USA) ○ YOUTH WITHOUT OLD AGE ○ YOUTH WITHOUT AGE
TINFOIL see **FAITHLESS** • 1932
TING YI-SHAN • 1964 • Hu King • HKG
TINGBUDAODE SHUOHUA • 1985 • Jiang Dawei • HKG • SILENT LOVE
TINGCHUN MOUNTAIN • 1908 • Lin Ten-Lun • CHN
TINGEL-TANGEL • 1927 • Ucicky Gustav • AUS
TINGEL-TANGEL • 1930 • Speyer Jaap • FRG
TINGELTANGEL • 1922 • Rippert Otto • FRG
TINGELTANGEL see **PRATERHERZEN** • 1953
TINGLER, THE • 1959 • Castle William • USA
TINHORN TROUBADOURS • 1951 • Goodwins Leslie • SHT • USA
"TINI-KLING" -DROMRESA TILL FJARRAN OSTERN • 1951 • *Ehrenborg Lennart/ Ericson Rune (Edt)* • SWD
TINIEBLAS • 1955 • Diaz Morales Jose • MXC
TINIEBLAS QUEDAN ATRAS, LAS • 1947 • Iglesias Miguel • SPN
TINIEST OF STARS, THE • 1913 • *Cruze James* • USA
TINIMBANG KA NGUNI'T KULANG • 1974 • Brocka Lino • PHL • YOU ARE WEIGHED IN THE BALANCE BUT FOUND WANTING ○ HUMAN IMPERFECTIONS ○ YE HAVE BEEN WEIGHED IN THE BALANCE AND FOUND WANTING
TINKER • 1949 • Marshall Herbert • UKN
TINKER OF STUBBINVILLE, THE • 1915 • MacQuarrie Murdock • USA
TINKER, TAILOR, SOLDIER, SAILOR • 1918 • Wilson Rex • UKN
TINKERING WITH TROUBLE • 1915 • Roach Hal • USA
TINKO • 1957 • Ballmann Herbert • GDR
TINKU-EL ENCUENTRO • 1985 • Miranda Juan • BLV • TINKU -THE MEETING
TINKU -THE MEETING see **TINKU-EL ENCUENTRO** • 1985
TINOCO EM BOLANDAS • 1922 • Pinheiro Antonio • PRT
TINSEL • 1918 • Apfel Oscar • USA
TINSEL GIRL see **STRANGE LOVE OF MOLLY LOUVAIN, THE** • 1932
TINSEL TREE • 1941-42 • Anger Kenneth • SHT • USA
TINTANSON CRUSOE • 1964 • Martinez Solares Gilberto • MXC
TINTED VENUS, THE • 1921 • Hepworth Cecil M. • UKN
TINTENFISCHKLUB, DER • 1919 • Boese Carl • FRG
TINTIN AND THE BLUE ORANGES see **TINTIN ET LES ORANGES BLEUES** • 1965
TINTIN AND THE GOLDEN TREASURE see **TINTIN ET LE MYSTERE DE LA TOISON D'OR** • 1961
TINTIN AND THE LAKE OF SHARKS see **TINTIN ET LE LAC AUX REQUINS** • 1972
TINTIN AND THE MYSTERY OF THE GOLDEN FLEECE see **TINTIN ET LE MYSTERE DE LA TOISON D'OR** • 1961
TINTIN AND THE TEMPLE OF THE SUN see **TINTIN ET LE TEMPLE DU SOLEIL** • 1969
TINTIN ET LE CRABE AUX PINCES D'OR • 1946 • Misonne Claude • ANM • BLG
TINTIN ET LE CRABE AUX PINCES D'OR • 1987 • Leblanc Raymond • ANM • BLG, FRN • TINTIN: THE CRAB WITH THE GOLDEN CLAWS ○ CRAB WITH THE GOLDEN CLAWS,THE ○ ADVENTURES OF TINTIN: THE CRAB WITH THE GOLDEN CLAWS
TINTIN ET LE LAC AUX REQUINS • 1972 • Leblanc Raymond, Herge • ANM • FRN, BLG • ADVENTURES OF TINTIN: THE LAKE OF SHARKS, THE ○ TINTIN: THE LAKE OF SHARKS ○ LAKE OF SHARKS, THE ○ TINTIN AND THE LAKE OF SHARKS
TINTIN ET LE MYSTERE DE LA TOISON D'OR • 1961 • Vierne Jean-Jacques • FRN, BLG • TINTIN AND THE MYSTERY OF THE GOLDEN FLEECE ○ TINTIN AND THE GOLDEN TREASURE
TINTIN ET LE TEMPLE DU SOLEIL • 1969 • Monar Lazlo, Herge, Lateste Eddie, Marissen Loe • ANM • FRN, BLG • TINTIN AND THE TEMPLE OF THE SUN
TINTIN ET LES ORANGES BLEUES • 1965 • Condroyer Philippe • FRN, SPN • MISTERIO DE LA NARANJAS AZULES, EL (SPN) ○ TINTIN AND THE BLUE ORANGES ○ MYSTERY OF THE BLUE ORANGES, THE
TINTIN: L'AFFAIRE TOURNESOL • *Belvision* • ANM • FRN
TINTIN: RED RACKHAM'S TREASURE • 1987 • Leblanc Raymond • ANM • BLG, FRN • ADVENTURES OF TINTIN: RED RACKHAM'S TREASURE, THE
TINTIN: THE BLACK ISLAND • 1987 • Leblanc Raymond • ANM • BLG, FRN • ADVENTURES OF TINTIN: THE BLACK ISLAND, THE ○ BLACK ISLAND, THE
TINTIN: THE CALCULUS AFFAIR • Leblanc Raymond • ANM • BLG, FRN • ADVENTURES OF TINTIN: THE CALCULUS CASE, THE ○ CALCULUS AFFAIR, THE ○ ADVENTURES OF TINTIN: THE CALCULUS AFFAIR, THE

TINTIN: THE CRAB WITH THE GOLDEN CLAWS see **TINTIN ET LE CRABE AUX PINCES D'OR** • 1987
TINTIN: THE LAKE OF SHARKS see **TINTIN ET LE LAC AUX REQUINS** • 1972
TINTIN: THE SECRET OF THE UNICORN • 1987 • Leblanc Raymond • ANM • BLG, FRN • ADVENTURES OF TINTIN: THE SECRET OF THE UNICORN
TINTIN: THE SEVEN CRYSTAL BALLS • Leblanc Raymond • ANM • BLG, FRN • ADVENTURES OF TINTIN: THE SEVEN CRYSTAL BALLS, THE ○ SEVEN CRYSTAL BALLS, THE
TINTIN: THE SHOOTING STAR • 1987 • Leblanc Raymond • ANM • BLG, FRN • ADVENTURES OF TINTIN: THE SHOOTING STAR, THE ○ SHOOTING STAR, THE
TINTO CON AMOR • 1967 • Montolio Francisco • SPN
TINTOMARA • 1970 • Abramson Hans • SWD, DNM
TINTORERA • 1977 • Cardona Rene Jr. • MXC • TINTORERA, KILLER SHARK ○ TINTORERA.. BLOODY WATERS ○ TINTORERA: TIGER SHARK
TINTORERA.. BLOODY WATERS see **TINTORERA** • 1977
TINTORERA, KILLER SHARK see **TINTORERA** • 1977
TINTORERA: TIGER SHARK see **TINTORERA** • 1977
TINY HANDS • 1915 • Ayres Sydney • USA
TINY LUND: HARD CHARGER • 1969 • *Bird Lance* • DOC • USA • HARD CHARGER
TINY QUESTION, A see **CHHOTTO JIJNASA** • 1968
TINY SHOES see **CIPELICE NA ASFALTU** • 1956
TINY, SLIM AND FAT • 1917 • *Essanay* • SHT • USA
TINY SPAN see **NIMVAJABI** • 1967
TINY TERRORS OF THE TIMBERLAND • 1946 • Haeseler John A. • SHT • USA
TINY TOT, THE • 1966 • Dembinski Lucjan • ANM • PLN
TINY TOT AND MR. CARLSON, THE • 1969 • Stepantsev Boris • ANM • USS
TINY TROUBLES • 1939 • Sidney George • SHT • USA
TIO DE MI VIDA • 1952 • Soler Julian • MXC
TIO, VERDAD VIENEN DE PARIS? • 1975 • Ozores Mariano • SPN
TIOGA KID, THE • 1948 • Taylor Ray • USA
TIP, THE • 1918 • Roach Hal • SHT • USA
TIP AUF AMALIA • 1940 • Wolff Carl Heinz • FRG
TIP OF THE TONGUE see **DU BOUT DES LEVRES** • 1976
TIP-OFF, THE • 1915 • Hunter T. Hayes • USA
TIP-OFF, THE • 1929 • Jason Leigh • USA • UNDERWORLD LOVE (UKN) ○ STOOL PIGEON, THE
TIP-OFF, THE • 1931 • Rogell Albert S., Murphy Ralph • USA • LOOKING FOR TROUBLE (UKN) ○ EDDIE CUTS IN
TIP-OFF GIRLS • 1938 • King Louis • USA • HIGHWAY RACKETEERS
TIP ON A DEAD JOCKEY • 1957 • Thorpe Richard • USA • TIME FOR ACTION (UKN)
TIP TO HUSBANDS, A • 1911 • *Powers* • USA
TIP TOES see **TIPTOES** • 1927
TIP-TOP • 1928 • Ivanov A. • SHS • USS
TIPASA L'ANCIENNE • 1975 • Allouache Merzak • ALG
TIPI DA SPIAGGIA • 1959 • Mattoli Mario • ITL
TIPO A TODO DAR, UN • 1962 • Cortes Fernando • MXC
TIPO CHE MI PAICE, UN (ITL) see **HOMME QUI ME PLAIT, L'** • 1969
TIPO CON UNA FACCIA STRANA TI CERCA PER UCCIDERTI, UN (ITL) see **AJUSTE DE CUENTAS** • 1973
TIPO DIFICIL DE MATAR, UN • 1965 • Portillo Rafael • MXC, USA
TIPPED OFF • 1920 • Russell Albert • SHT • USA
TIPPED OFF • 1923 • Fox Finis • USA
TIPS • 1916 • Walsh Phil • USA
TIPS • 1923 • USA
TIPS FOR TODAY see **TYPY NA DZIS** • 1959
TIPS ON TRIPS • 1943 • Jason Will • SHT • USA
TIPSY-TOPSY-TURVY • 1897 • Smith G. A. • UKN
TIPTOES • 1927 • Wilcox Herbert • UKN • TIP TOES
TIR A LA CIBLE • 1966 • Sanchez-Ariza Jose • PLN
TIR A VUE • 1984 • Angelo Marc • FRN
TIR GROUPE • 1983 • Missiaen Jean-Claude • FRN
TIRAGE, LE • 1940 • Clement Rene • DCS • FRN • TRIAGE, LE
TIRANA, LA • 1958 • de Orduna Juan • SPN
TIRANDO A GOL • 1965 • Cisneros Icaro • MXC
TIRANDO A MATAR • 1960 • Baledon Rafael • MXC
TIRANNO DEL GARDA, IL • 1956 • Ferronetti Ignazio • ITL
TIRANNO DI PADOVA, IL • 1947 • Neufeld Max • ITL • ANGELO, TYRANT OF PADUA
TIRANNO DI SIRACUSA, IL • 1962 • Bernhardt Curtis, Cardone Alberto • ITL, USA • DAMON AND PYTHIAS (USA) ○ TYRANT OF SYRACUSE, THE ○ DAMONE E PITIAS
TIRANO DE TOLEDO, EL (SPN) see **AMANTS DE TOLEDE, LES** • 1953
TIRARSE AL MONTE • 1972 • Ungria Alfonso • SPN • GO TO THE MOUNTAINS ○ TAKING TO THE HILLS ○ TAKE TO THE HILLS
TIRBARAN • 1974 • Kimiyaei Massoud • IRN • EXECUTION, THE
TIRE DIE • 1960 • Birri Fernando • DOC • ARG • TOSS ME A DIME
TIRE AU FLANC • 1928 • Renoir Jean • FRN • TIRE-AU-FLANC
TIRE AU FLANC • 1933 • Wulschleger Henry • FRN
TIRE AU FLANC • 1949 • Rivers Fernand • FRN
TIRE-AU-FLANC see **TIRE AU FLANC** • 1928
TIRE-AU-FLANC 1962 • 1961 • Truffaut Francois, de Givray Claude • FRN • ARMY GAME, THE (USA) ○ SAD SACK, THE
TIRE PAS SUR MON COLLANT • 1978 • Lemoine Michel • FRN
TIRE TROUBLES • 1923 • Roach Hal • SHT • USA
TIRED ABSENT-MINDED MAN, THE • 1911 • *Vitagraph* • USA
TIRED AND FEATHERED • 1965 • Larriva Rudy • ANS • USA
TIRED BUSINESS MAN, THE • 1927 • Dale Allan • USA
TIRED BUSINESS MEN • 1927 • Roach Hal • SHT • USA
TIRED FEET • 1933 • Gillstrom Arvid E. • SHT • USA
TIRED TAILOR'S DREAM, THE • 1907 • *Dobson F. A. (Ph)* • USA
TIRED TEODOR see **TROTTE TEODOR** • 1931
TIRED TEODOR see **TROTTE TEODOR** • 1945
TIRED WARRIOR, THE see **YORGUN SAVASCI**
TIREE • 1974 • Marzaroli Oscar • DOC • UKN
TIRELIRE, LA • 1984 • Goulet Stella • MTV • CND
TIRELIRE DE BOUT DE ZAN, LA • 1913 • Feuillade Louis • FRN
TIREMAN, SPARE MY TIRES • 1942 • White Jules • SHT • USA
TIREZ S'IL VOUS PLAIT • 1908 • Gasnier Louis J. • FRN
TIREZ SUR LE PIANISTE • 1960 • Truffaut Francois • FRN • SHOOT THE PIANO PLAYER (USA) ○ SHOOT THE PIANIST
TIRIRIT NG MAYA, TIRIRIT NG IBON • 1968 • Carlos Luciano B. • PHL • CHIRRUPPING OF A BIRD, THE
TIRO • 1978 • Bijl Jacob • NTH
TIRO A SEGNO PER UCCIDERE see **GEHEIMNIS DER GELBEN MONCHE, DAS** • 1966
TIRO AL AIRE • 1980 • Sabato Mario • ARG • SHOT IN THE AIR, A
TIRO AL PICCIONE • 1961 • Montaldo Giuliano • ITL
TIRO DE GRACIA • 1969 • Becher Ricardo • ARG
TIRO DE GRACIA, EL • 1957 • Aguilar Rolando • MXC
TIRO POR LA CULATA • Eguiluz Enrique L. • SHT • SPN
TIRO POR LA ESPALDA • 1964 • Roman Antonio • SPN
TIROL IN WAFFEN • 1915 • Biebrach Rudolf • FRG
TIROL LAUGHS AT THAT, THE see **DA LACHT TIROL** • 1967
TIRONS UN COUP, TIRONS EN DEUX • Germont Felix • FRN
'TIS A LONG LANE THAT HAS NO TURNING • 1925 • Butler Alexander • UKN
'TIS AN ILL WIND THAT BLOWS NO GOOD • 1909 • Griffith D. W. • USA
'TIS AN ILL WIND THAT BLOWS NO GOOD • 1912 • *Lubin* • USA
'TIS BETTER TO HAVE LOVED AND LOST • 1911 • *Essanay* • USA
'TIS MOTHER! • 1912 • *Pates Gwendolyn* • USA
'TIS NOW THE VERY WITCHING TIME OF NIGHT • 1909 • *Edison* • USA
'TIS PITY SHE'S A WHORE (USA) see **ADDIO FRATELLO CRUDELE** • 1971
TISCHLEIN DECK DICH, ESELEIN STRECK DICH, KNUPPEL AUS DEM SACK • 1921 • *Kulturabteilung Der Ufa* • FRG
TISH • 1942 • Simon S. Sylvan • USA
TISHINA • 1964 • Basov K. • USS • SILENCE
TISHINA • 1990 • Petkov Dimiter • BUL • SILENCE
TISH'S SPY • 1915 • Calvert E. H. • USA
TISHY • 1923 • Speed Lancelot? • ANS • UKN
TISICROCNA VCELA • 1983 • Jakubisko Juraj • CZC • THOUSAND-YEAR-OLD BEE, THE ○ BEE MILLENIUM, THE
TISSERANDS DU POUVOIR, LES • 1988 • Fournier Claude • CND • MILLS OF POWER, THE
TISTEGA LEPEGA DNE • 1963 • Stiglic France • YGS • THAT FINE DAY
TISZA -AUTUMN SKETCHES see **TISZA -OSZI VAZLATOK** • 1963
TISZA -OSZI VAZLATOK • 1963 • Gaal Istvan • SHT • HNG • TISZA -AUTUMN SKETCHES
TISZAVIRAG • 1938 • von Bolvary Geza • FRG • FLOWER OF THE TISZA (USA)
TISZTA AMERIKA • 1987 • Gothar Peter • HNG, JPN • JUST LIKE AMERICA ○ PURE AMERICA
TISZTELET A KIVETELNEK • 1937 • Rathonyi August
TISZTI KARDBOJT, A • 1915 • Korda Alexander • HNG • OFFICER'S SWORD, THE ○ OFFICER'S SWORDKNOT, THE
TIT-COQ • 1952 • Delacroix Rene, Gelinas Gratien • CND
TIT FOR TAT • 1912 • Thornton F. Martin • UKN
TIT FOR TAT • 1913 • *Essanay* • USA
TIT FOR TAT • 1915 • *Warner'S Features* • USA
TIT FOR TAT • 1916 • *Union Jack* • UKN • VICE VERSA: OR, THE TABLES TURNED
TIT FOR TAT • 1917 • *Henley Hobart* • SHT • USA
TIT FOR TAT • 1920 • *Cohn Productions* • USA
TIT FOR TAT • 1922 • Edwards Henry • UKN
TIT FOR TAT • 1935 • Rogers Charles • SHT • USA
TIT FOR TAT see **NIJE NEGO** • 1979
TIT FOR TAT: OR, A GOOD JOKE ON MY HEAD (USA) see **PRETE POUR UN RENDU: OU, UNE BONNE FARCE AVEC MA TETE, UN** • 1904
TIT WILLOW • 1906 • Gilbert Arthur • UKN
TIT WILLOW • 1907 • Morland John • UKN
TITAN, THE (USA) see **MICHELANGELO** • 1940
TITAN FIND • 1985 • Malone William • USA • CREATURE
TITAN: THE STORY OF MICHELANGELO, THE see **MICHELANGELO** • 1940
TITANENKAMPF • 1916 • Delmont Joseph • FRG
TITANI, I see **TITANS, LES** • 1962
TITANIA, TITANIA AVAGY A DUBLOROK EJSZAKAJA • 1988 • Bacso Peter • HNG • TITANIA, TITANIA OR, THE NIGHT OF THE DOUBLES ○ TITANIA, TITANIA OR NIGHT OF THE REPLICANTS
TITANIA, TITANIA OR NIGHT OF THE REPLICANTS see **TITANIA, TITANIA AVAGY A DUBLOROK EJSZAKAJA** • 1988
TITANIA, TITANIA OR, THE NIGHT OF THE DOUBLES see **TITANIA, TITANIA AVAGY A DUBLOROK EJSZAKAJA** • 1988
TITANIC • *Hameister Willy (Ph)* • FRG
TITANIC • 1943 • Selpin Herbert, Klinger Werner • FRG
TITANIC • 1953 • Negulesco Jean • USA
TITANIC VALS • 1964 • Calinescu Paul • RMN • TITANIC WALTZ
TITANIC WALTZ see **TITANIC VALS** • 1964
TITANS, LES • 1962 • Tessari Duccio • FRN, ITL • ARRIVANO I TITANI (ITL) ○ MY SON, THE HERO (USA) ○ SONS OF THUNDER (UKN) ○ TITANI, I ○ TITANS ARRIVE, THE ○ TITANS, THE
TITANS, THE see **STORM BREAKER, THE** • 1925
TITANS, THE see **TITANS, LES** • 1962
TITANS ARRIVE, THE see **TITANS, LES** • 1962
TITANS OF THE DEEP • 1938 • Barton Charles T. • USA
TITAS EKTI NADIR NAAM • 1973 • Ghatak Ritwik • IND • TITAS IS THE NAME OF A RIVER ○ RIVER CALLED TITAS, A
TITAS IS THE NAME OF A RIVER see **TITAS EKTI NADIR NAAM** • 1973
TITFIELD THUNDERBOLT, THE • 1953 • Crichton Charles • UKN
TITI ROI DES GOSSES • 1926 • Leprince Rene • FRN
TITICUT FOLLIES, THE • 1967 • Wiseman Frederick • DOC • USA
TITILLATION • 1982 • Christian Damon • USA
TITIN DES MARTIGUES • 1937 • Pujol Rene • FRN
TITLE CURE, THE • 1913 • Williams C. Jay • USA
TITLE FOR THE SIN, THE see **PRAVO NA HRICH** • 1932
TITLE SHOT • 1980 • Rose Les • TVM • CND
TITLED TENDERFOOT, THE • 1955 • McDonald Frank • MTV • USA
TITLED TRIO, A • 1915 • *Mina* • USA
TITO IN DEUTSCHLAND • 1965 • Thorndike Andrew, Thorndike Annelie • GDR
TITO SCHIPA • 1929 • Santley Joseph • SHT • USA
TITO SCHIPA CONCERT NO.2 • 1929 • Santley Joseph • SHT • USA
TITO'S GUITAR • 1942 • Wickersham Bob • ANS • USA
TIUTIUN see **TYUTYUN** • 1962
TIVOLI • 1956 • Carlsen Henning • SHT • DNM
TIVOLI • 1974 • Isaac Alberto • MXC
TIVOLI GARDEN GAMES see **TIVOLIGARDEN SPILLER** • 1954
TIVOLIGARDEN SPILLER • 1954 • Henning-Jensen Astrid, Henning-Jensen Bjarne • DNM • TIVOLI GARDEN GAMES
TIYABU BIRU • 1978 • Bathily Moussa • SNL • CIRCUMCISION
TIZ DEKA HALHATATLANSAG • 1967 • Macskassy Gyula, Varnai Gyorgy • ANS • HNG • BIT OF IMMORTALITY, A (USA) ○ 100 GRAMS OF IMMORTALITY
TIZ EV MULVA • 1979 • Lanyi Andras • HNG • TEN YEARS AFTER
TIZ EVES KUBA • 1969 • Gaal Istvan • SHT • HNG • CUBA'S TEN YEARS ○ TEN YEARS OF CUBA
TIZEDES MEG A TOBRIEK, A • 1965 • Keleti Marton • HNG • CORPORAL AND THE OTHERS, THE
TIZEZER NAP • 1967 • Kosa Ferenc • HNG • TEN THOUSAND SUNS, THE (UKN) ○ TEN THOUSAND DAYS
TIZIO, CAIO E SEMPRONIO • 1952 • Marchesi Marcello, Metz Vittorio, Pozzetti Alberto • ITL
TIZNAO • 1982 • Cassuto Dominique • VNZ
TIZOC • 1956 • Rodriguez Ismael • MXC • AMOR INDIO ○ VIRGEN DE TIZOC, LA
TJAEREHANDLEREN • 1971 • Ravn Jens • DNM • TAR-DEALER, THE
TJOCKA SLAKTEN • 1935 • Cederstrand Solve • SWD • NEAR RELATIONS
TJORVEN AND MYSAK see **TJORVEN OCH MYSAK** • 1966
TJORVEN AND SKRALLAN see **TJORVEN OCH SKRALLAN** • 1965
TJORVEN, BATSMAN OCH MOSES • 1964 • Hellbom Olle • SWD • TJORVEN, BOATSWAIN AND MOSES
TJORVEN, BOATSWAIN AND MOSES see **TJORVEN, BATSMAN OCH MOSES** • 1964
TJORVEN OCH MYSAK • 1966 • Hellbom Olle • SWD • TJORVEN AND MYSAK
TJORVEN OCH SKRALLAN • 1965 • Hellbom Olle • SWD • TJORVEN AND SKRALLAN
TJUVARNAS KONUNG see **HON TRODDE DET VAR HAN** • 1943
TKIES KHAF • 1938 • Szaro Henryk • PLN
TKO PJEVA, ZLO NE MISLI • 1971 • Golik Kreso • YGS • HE WHO SINGS MEANS NO EVIL ○ SINGING ONE THINKS NO HARM ○ YOU CAN'T GO WRONG IF YOU SING
TLACUILO • 1988 • Escalona Enrique • ANM • MXC
TLAYUCAN • 1961 • Alcoriza Luis • MXC • PEARL OF THE TLAYUCAN, THE (USA) ○ PEARLS OF ST. LUCIA, THE
TMO 135 • 1965 • Heyer John • DOC • ASL
TNT JACKSON • 1975 • Santiago Cirio H. • USA, PHL • DYNAMITE JACKSON
TO • 1964 • Kjaerulff-Schmidt Palle • DNM • TWO PEOPLE
TO A FINISH • 1921 • Durning Bernard J. • USA
TO A SAFER PLACE • 1988 • Shaffer Beverly • DOC • CND
TO A STRANGER see **FLASKEPOST** • 1988
TO ABBEVILLE COURT-HOUSE • 1913 • *Edison* • USA
TO AIM AT.. see **NERUA** • 1967
TO ALL A GOOD NIGHT • 1983 • Hess David • USA
TO ALL MY FRIENDS ON SHORE • 1971 • Cates Gilbert • TVM • USA
TO AN UNKNOWN see **FLASKEPOST** • 1988
TO AN UNKNOWN GOD see **A UN DIOS DESCONOCIDO** • 1977
TO AND FRO see **ODA-VISSA** • 1962
TO ANOTHER WOMAN • 1916 • Madison Cleo, Mong William V. • SHT • USA
TO BANISH BOREDOM see **SKUKI RADI** • 1968
TO BE see **BYC** • 1967
TO BE 16 see **AVOIR SEIZE ANS** • 1979
TO BE A CROOK (USA) see **FILLE ET DES FUSILS, UNE** • 1965
TO BE A LADY • 1934 • King George • UKN
TO BE A MAN see **CRY OF BATTLE** • 1963
TO BE A MILLIONAIRE see **MANNEN SOM BLEV MILJONAR** • 1980
TO BE A MOTHER, TO BE A WIFE • 1953 • Kamei Fumio • JPN
TO BE A ROSE • 1974 • Levey William A. • USA
TO BE A WOMAN • 1951 • Craigie Jill • DOC • UKN
TO BE A WOMAN • 1968 • Boutel Maurice • USA
TO BE AFRAID AND MAKE OTHERS AFRAID see **ANGST HABEN UND ANGST MACHEN** • 1976
TO BE ALIVE • 1962 • Thompson Francis, Hammid Alexander • SHT • CND
TO BE CALLED FOR • 1914 • Grandon Francis J. • USA
TO BE CONTINUED • 1975 • PLN
TO BE FREE see **IMAGO** • 1970
TO BE OR NOT TO BE • 1916 • Watt Edward • USA
TO BE OR NOT TO BE • 1942 • Lubitsch Ernst • USA
TO BE OR NOT TO BE • 1963 • Rasinski Connie • ANS • USA
TO BE OR NOT TO BE • 1983 • Johnson Alan • USA
TO BE OR NOT TO BE MARRIED • 1917 • Chaudet Louis W. • SHT • USA
TO BE SIXTEEN YEARS OLD see **SZESNASCIE MIEC LAT** • 1969
TO BE SUPERFLUOUS see **BYT LISHNIM** • 1977
TO BE TWENTY see **AVERRE VENT'ANNI** • 1978
TO BE WOMEN see **ESSERE DONNE** • 1964
TO BE YOUNG see **NAAR MAN KUN ER UNG** • 1943

TO BEAT THE BAND • 1935 • Stoloff Ben • USA
TO BED ON A BET • 1965 • *Crystal Productions* • USA
TO BED.. OR NOT TO BED (USA) see **DIAVOLO, IL** • 1963
TO BEEP OR NOT TO BEEP • 1963 • Jones Charles M. • ANS • USA
TO BEGIN AGAIN see **VOLVER A EMPEZAR** • 1983
TO BOO OR NOT TO BOO • 1951 • Sparber I. • ANS • USA
TO BRIGHTON WITH A BIRD see **TO BRIGHTON WITH GLADYS** • 1933
TO BRIGHTON WITH GLADYS • 1933 • King George • UKN • TO BRIGHTON WITH A BIRD
TO BUILD A FIRE • 1970 • Cobham David • UKN
TO BYL CESKY MUZIKANT • 1940 • Slavinsky Vladimir • CZC • HE WAS A CZECH MUSICIAN
TO CATCH A KING • 1984 • Donner Clive • TVM • USA
TO CATCH A SPY (USA) see **ACTION IMMEDIATE** • 1956
TO CATCH A SPY (USA) see **CATCH ME A SPY** • 1971
TO CATCH A THIEF • 1936 • Rogers Maclean • UKN
TO CATCH A THIEF • 1955 • Hitchcock Alfred • USA
TO CATCH A WOODPECKER • 1957 • Lovy Alex • ANS • USA
TO CHASTISE A HUSBAND see **SA TUKTAS EN AKTA MAN** • 1941
TO CHEAT A CHEAT • 1977 • Revach Ze'Ev • ISR
TO CHERISH AND PROTECT • 1915 • Humphrey William • USA
TO CHILDREN see **DZIECIOM** • 1968
TO-CH'ING CHIEN-K'O TUAN-CH'ING TAO • 1979 • Ch'U Yuan • HKG • SENTIMENTAL SWORDSMAN AND THE RUTHLESS BLADE, THE
TO-CH'ING CHIEN-K'O WU-CH'ING CHIEN • 1978 • Ch'U Yuan • HKG • SENTIMENTAL SWORDSMAN, THE ○ LOVER SWORDSMAN, THE
TO CLOTHE THE SAINTS see **PARA VESTIR SANTOS** • 1955
TO, CO ZDARZY SIE JUTRO • 1972 • Solarz Wojciech • PLN • THIS WILL HAPPEN TOMORROW
TO COME AND STAY see **DOCI I OSTATI** • 1965
TO COMMIT A MURDER (USA) see **PEAU D'ESPION** • 1967
TO CROSS THE ORINOCO • Camacho Carlos Antonio • VNZ
TO DIE A LITTLE see **MORIR UN POCO** • 1967
TO DIE A LITTLE see **EIN WENIG STERBEN** • 1981
TO DIE FOR • 1989 • Sarafian Deran • USA
TO DIE FOR NOTHING see **MORIRE GRATIS** • 1968
TO DIE FOR THE COUNTRY • 1989 • PHL
TO DIE FOR YOU see **NANG MAMATAY NG DAHIL SA IYO** • 1968
TO DIE FROM LOVE OF LIFE see **SA MORI RANIT DIN DRAGOSTE DE VIATA** • 1983
TO DIE IN MADRID see **MOURIR A MADRID** • 1962
TO DIE IN PARIS • 1968 • Dubin Charles S., Reisner Allen • TVM • USA
TO DIE LIKE A MAN • 1989 • Wu Ziniu • CHN
TO DIE OF LOVE (USA) see **MOURIR D'AIMER** • 1970
TO DIG A PIT see **CAVAR UN FOSO** • 1966
TO DISTANT SHORES • 1958 • Stoyanov Yuli • DOC • BUL
TO DOROTHY, A SON • 1954 • Box Muriel • UKN • CASH ON DELIVERY (USA) ○ THAT'S MY BABY!
TO DREAM AND TO LIVE • 1974 • Ilyenko Yury • USS
TO DREAM, TO DREAM see **SONAR, SONAR** • 1976
TO DUCK OR NOT TO DUCK • 1943 • Jones Charles M. • ANS • USA
TO EACH HIS OWN • 1946 • Leisen Mitchell • USA
TO EACH HIS OWN see **A CIASCUNO IL SUO** • 1967
TO EACH HIS OWN ROAD see **U KAZHDOVO SVOYA DOROGA** • 1967
TO EAT THE APPLE • 1975 • Roudarov Georgi • BUL
TO EL MUNDO ES GUENO • 1981 • Summers Manuel • SPN • EVERYBODY IS GOOD ○ TO ER MUNDO E GUENO ○ EVERYONE'S GREAT
TO ELVIS, WITH LOVE see **TOUCHED BY LOVE** • 1980
TO ER MUNDO E GUENO see **TO EL MUNDO ES GUENO** • 1981
TO ERR IS HUMAN • 1912 • *Champion* • USA
TO ERR IS HUMAN • 1913 • *American* • USA
TO FIND A MAN • 1972 • Kulik Buzz • USA • SEX AND THE TEENAGER ○ BOY NEXT DOOR, THE
TO FIND MY SON • 1980 • Mann Delbert • TVM • USA
TO FLY • 1976 • *Hammid Alexander* • USA
TO FORGET PALERMO see **DIMENTICARE PALERMO** • 1990
TO FORGET VENICE see **DIMENTICARE VENEZIA** • 1979
TO GO AND COME • 1972 • Bertolucci Giuseppe • MTV • ITL
TO GO ASHORE see **ATT ANGORA EN BRYGGA** • 1965
TO GOOD TO BE TRUE • 1988 • Nyby Christian Ii • TVM • USA
TO GRAB THE RING • 1968 • van der Heyde Nikolai • NTH
TO GROW UP SUDDENLY see **CRECER DE GOLPE** • 1977
TO HARE IS HUMAN • 1956 • Jones Charles M. • ANS • USA
TO HAVE AND HAVE NOT • 1944 • Hawks Howard • USA
TO HAVE AND TO HOLD • 1916 • Melford George • USA
TO HAVE AND TO HOLD • 1922 • Fitzmaurice George • USA
TO HAVE AND TO HOLD • 1951 • Grayson Godfrey • UKN
TO HAVE AND TO HOLD • 1963 • Wise Herbert • UKN
TO HAVE AND TO LOSE • 1915 • Morgan George • USA
TO HEAL A NATION • 1987 • Pressman Michael • TVM • USA
TO HEAR YOUR BANJO PLAY • 1941 • Van Dyke Willard, Lerner Irving • DCS • USA
TO HEIR IS HUMAN • 1944 • Godsoe Harold • SHT • USA
TO HELL AND BACK • 1955 • Hibbs Jesse • USA
TO HELL WITH THE KAISER • 1918 • Irving George • USA
TO HELL WITH THIS PRIEST see **AL DIABLO CON ESTE CURA!** • 1967
TO HEX WITH SEX • 1969 • Nuchtern Simon • USA • HEX WITH SEX, THE
TO HIM THAT HATH • 1918 • Apfel Oscar • USA
TO HIRE: GOOD LOOKING GIRL AND MESSENGER WITH BIKE OF HIS OWN see **SE SOLICITA MUCHACHA DE BUENA PRESENCIA Y MOTORIZADO CON MOTO PROPIA**
TO HONOR AND OBEY • 1917 • Turner Otis • USA
TO HURT AND TO HEAL • 1988 • Sky Laura • DOC • CND
TO INGRID MY LOVE, LISA (USA) see **KOM I MIN SANG** • 1968
TO ITCH HIS OWN • 1958 • Jones Charles M. • ANS • USA
TO JEST JAJKO • 1966 • Brzozowski Andrzej • DOC • PLN • THIS IS AN EGG
TO JOY see **TILL GLADJE** • 1950
TO KILL A BIRD OF PREY see **LOVIND O PASARE DE PRADA** • 1984
TO KILL A CHILD see **ATT DODA ETT BARN** • 1952
TO KILL A CLOWN • 1972 • Bloomfield George • USA
TO KILL A COP • 1978 • Nelson Gary • TVM • USA
TO KILL A JACKAL see **PREGA IL MORTO E AMMAZZA IL VIVO** • 1971
TO KILL A KILLER see **KANTO MUSHOGAERI** • 1967
TO KILL A MOCKINGBIRD • 1962 • Mulligan Robert • USA
TO KILL A PRIEST • 1988 • Holland Agnieszka • FRN, USA
TO KILL A STRANGER • 1985 • Moctezuma Juan Lopez • MXC, USA
TO KILL A WOPPINGBIRD • 1985 • Tichenor Harold • DOC • CND
TO KILL "EL NANI" see **MATAR AL NANI** • 1988
TO KILL OR TO DIE see **MIO NOME E SHANGHAI JOE, IL** • 1973
TO KILL THE SNAKE see **YILANI OLDURSELER** • 1982
TO KILL THIS LOVE see **TRZEBA ZABIC TE MILOSC** • 1972
TO KILL WITH INTRIGUE • 1984 • Lo Wei • HKG
TO L.A... WITH LUST • 1961-62 • Zimmerman Vernon • SHT • USA
TO LATE FOR HAVEN • 1985 • SAF
TO LET • 1919 • Reardon James • UKN
TO LEVENDE OG EN DOD • 1937 • Ibsen Tancred • NRW
TO LIVE see **IKIRU** • 1952
TO LIVE AGAIN see **VOLVER A VIVIR** • 1968
TO LIVE AND DIE IN L.A. • 1985 • Friedkin William • USA
TO LIVE IN PEACE (UKN) see **VIVERE IN PACE** • 1946
TO LIVE ON LOVE see **ZIVJETI OD LJUBAVI** • 1974
TO LIVE ONE'S LIFE see **ZIT SVUJ ZIVOT** • 1963
TO LIVE OUT OF SPITE see **ZIVJETI ZA INAT** • 1973
TO LIVE UNDER THE SUN see **VIVIT AL SOL** • 1967
TO LIVE (USA) see **VIVERE!** • 1937
TO LOVE • 1987 • *Wattanapanit Pim* • THL
TO LOVE see **ATT ALSKA** • 1964
TO LOVE see **KOISURU** • 1975
TO LOVE A MAN see **LYUBIT CHELOVYEKA** • 1972
TO LOVE A MAORI • 1972 • Hayward Rudall C. • NZL
TO LOVE A PERSON see **LYUBIT CHELOVYEKA** • 1972
TO LOVE A VAMPIRE see **LUST FOR A VAMPIRE** • 1970
TO LOVE AGAIN • 1967 • Torres Mar S. • PHL
TO LOVE AGAIN see **AI FUTATABI** • 1972
TO LOVE AND CHERISH • 1913 • Bracken Bertram • USA
TO LOVE AND TO HOLD • 1914 • *Balboa* • USA
TO LOVE SOMEBODY see **MELODY** • 1971
TO MAEND I ODEMARKEN • 1972 • Roos Jorgen • DOC • DNM
TO MAKE THE NATION PROSPER • 1915 • Seay Charles M. • USA
TO MARKET TO MARKET • 1987 • Rouse Virginia • ASL
TO MARY -WITH LOVE • 1936 • Cromwell John • USA
TO MELODY A SOUL RESPONDS • 1915 • Eason B. Reeves • USA
TO MY UNBORN SON • 1943 • Kardos Leslie • SHT • USA
TO NEFERTITI • 1971 • Gross Yoram • ANS • ASL
TO NEW SHORES (UKN) see **ZU NEUEN UFERN** • 1937
TO NEZNATE HADIMRSKU • 1931 • Fric Martin, Lamac Carl • CZC • HADIMRSKU DOESN'T KNOW
TO OBLIGE A LADY • 1931 • Haynes Manning • UKN
TO OBLIGE A VAMPIRE • 1917 • Chaudet Louis W. • SHT • USA
TO ONE'S HEART'S CONTENT see **AV HJARTANS LUST** • 1960
TO OUR CHILDREN'S CHILDREN • 1969 • Halas John • ANS • UKN
TO OUR LOVES see **A NOS AMOURS** • 1983
TO PARIS WITH LOVE • 1955 • Hamer Robert • UKN
TO PARSIFAL • 1963 • Baillie Bruce • SHT • USA
TO PLEASE A LADY • 1950 • Brown Clarence • USA • INDIANAPOLIS
TO PLEASE ONE WOMAN • 1920 • Weber Lois • USA
TO PROUD TO FIGHT • 1916 • *Ovey George* • USA
TO RACE THE WIND • 1980 • Grauman Walter • TVM • USA
TO REDEEM AN OATH • 1915 • Lloyd Frank • USA
TO RENO AND BACK • 1913 • *Baggot King* • USA
TO RENT FURNISHED • 1915 • Eason B. Reeves • USA
TO RUSSIA.. WITH ELTON • 1979 • Clement Dick, La Frenais Ian • DOC • UKN
TO SAIL IS NECESSARY see **ATT SEGLA AR NODVANDIGT** • 1938
TO SATISFY ONE'S CONSCIENCE see **NAVSTRYECHU SOVESTI** • 1967
TO SAVE HER BROTHER • 1912 • *Ogle Charles* • USA
TO SAVE HER DAD • 1913 • Weston Charles • UKN • BESS THE DETECTIVE'S DAUGHTER
TO SAVE HER LIFE • 1915 • Batley Ethyle • UKN
TO SAVE HER SOUL • 1909 • Griffith D. W. • USA
TO SAVE HIM FOR HIS WIFE • 1915 • North Wilfred • USA
TO SAVE HIS LIFE see **DEAD MEN TELL NO TALES** • 1971
TO SAVE THE KING • 1914 • Aylott Dave • UKN • ENEMY WITHIN, THE
TO SEE A COFFIN IN ONE'S DREAM.. see **RAKEV VE SNU VIDETI..** • 1968
TO SEE A COFFIN IN YOUR DREAM see **RAKEV VE SNU VIDETI..** • 1968
TO SEE OR NOT TO SEE see **PSYCHOCRACY, OR TO SEE OR NOT TO SEE** • 1970
TO SERVE THE COMING AGE • 1983 • Spry Robin • DOC • CND
TO SET OUR HOUSE IN ORDER • 1972 • Woods Grahame • CND
TO SET OUR HOUSE IN ORDER • 1984 • Wheeler Anne • CND
TO SET THIS TOWN ON FIRE see **SET THIS TOWN ON FIRE** • 1969
TO SHOOT A MAD DOG • 1976 • Elfick David • DOC • ASL
TO SIR, WITH LOVE • 1966 • Clavell James • UKN, USA
TO SKIN A SPY (UKN) see **AVEC LA PEAU DES AUTRES** • 1966
TO SLEEP SO AS TO DREAM see **YUME MIRUYONI NEMURITAI** • 1985
TO SLEEP WITH ANGER • 1990 • Burnett Charles • USA
TO SMITHEREENS see **BELOW THE BELT** • 1980
TO SO GADI • 1979 • Bevc Joze • YGS • TO SU FAKINI ○ REAL PESTS! ○ PESTS, THE
TO SPEAK OR NOT TO SPEAK • Servais Raoul • ANS • BLG
TO SPIN A COIN see **MONEDA EN EL AIRE, UNA** • 1990
TO SPRING • 1936 • Hanna William • ANS • USA
TO SU FAKINI see **TO SO GADI** • 1979
TO SUSAN WITH LOVE • 1968 • Carlos Luciano B. • PHL
TO TELL THE TRUTH • 1971 • *Kouzkoulos Nicos* • GRC
TO TELL THE TRUTH see **ORACLE, THE** • 1953
TO THE AID OF STONEWALL JACKSON • 1911 • Olcott Sidney • USA
TO THE BITTER END (USA) see **BIS ZUR BITTEREN NEIGE** • 1975
TO THE BLACK LAND see **AU PAYS NOIR** • 1905
TO THE BRAVE BELONG THE FAIR • 1913 • *Nestor* • USA
TO THE CENTER OF THE EARTH see **UNKNOWN WORLD** • 1951
TO THE CITY • 1912 • *Rex* • USA
TO THE COUNT OF BASIE • 1979 • Trowbridge Angus, Jeremy John • UKN, SWD, AUS
TO THE CUSTODY OF THE FATHER • 1908 • Bouwmeester Theo? • UKN
TO THE DEATH • 1915 • Davis Ulysses • USA
TO THE DEATH • 1917 • King Burton L. • USA
TO THE DEVIL A DAUGHTER • 1976 • Sykes Peter • UKN, FRG • BRAUT DES SATANS, DIE (FRG)
TO THE EDGE OF THE WORLD.. see **NA KRAY SVYETA..** • 1976
TO THE END OF THE SILVER-CAPPED MOUNTAINS see **GINREI NO HATE** • 1947
TO THE END OF THE SUN see **HI NO HATE** • 1954
TO THE END OF THE WORLD see **BIS ANS ENDE DER WELT** • 1989
TO THE ENDS OF THE EARTH • 1948 • Stevenson Robert • USA • ASSIGNED TO TREASURY
TO THE FAIR! • 1965 • Hammid Alexander • DOC • USA
TO THE FRONT see **TEBYE FRONT** • 1943
TO THE GLORY OF SOVIET HEROINES see **SLAVA SOVETSKIM GEROINYAM** • 1938
TO THE HANG OUT see **NA MELINE** • 1965
TO THE HIGHEST BIDDER • 1917 • Henderson Lucius • SHT • USA
TO THE HIGHEST BIDDER • 1918 • Terriss Tom • USA
TO THE KAZAKHSTAN FRONT see **TEBYE FRONT** • 1943
TO THE LADIES • 1923 • Cruze James • USA
TO THE LAST DROP OF BLOOD see **ALL'ULTIMO SANGUE** • 1968
TO THE LAST DROP OF BLOOD see **DO KRWI OSTATNIEJ** • 1978
TO THE LAST MAN • 1923 • Fleming Victor • USA
TO THE LAST MAN • 1933 • Hathaway Henry • USA • LAW OF VENGEANCE
TO THE LAST MINUTE see **OS TIN TELEFTEA STIGMI** • 1971
TO THE LIGHTHOUSE • 1983 • Gregg Colin • TVM • UKN
TO THE LORD'S ESTATE see **DO PANSKEHO STAVU** • 1925
TO THE MISS AND HER MALE COMPANY • 1983 • Dobchev Ivan • BUL
TO THE MOON • 1967 • *Cbs* • DCS • USA
TO THE MOON AND BEYOND • 1964 • Trumbull Douglas • DCS • USA
TO THE ORIENT see **TILL OSTERLAND** • 1926
TO THE PUBLIC DANGER • 1948 • Fisher Terence • UKN
TO THE RESCUE • 1917 • *Connelly Bobby* • SHT • USA
TO THE RESCUE • 1932 • Lantz Walter, Nolan William • ANS • USA
TO THE RESCUE • 1952 • Brunius Jacques-Bernard • UKN
TO THE RHYTHM OF MY HEART see **AU RYTHME DE MON COEUR** • 1984
TO THE SHIP see **MEHRI TO PLIO** • 1968
TO THE SHORES OF HELL • 1966 • Zens Will • USA
TO THE SHORES OF TRIPOLI • 1942 • Humberstone H. Bruce • USA
TO THE SKY • 1965 • Mesaros Titus • DOC • RMN
TO THE SOUND OF GUNFIRE see **A SUON DI LUPARA** • 1967
TO THE SOUTH SEAS see **SOUTH SEAS** • 1930
TO THE STARS see **CHEREZ TERNII K ZVEZDAM** • 1981
TO THE TUNE OF BULLETS • 1919 • *Morrison Pete* • SHT • USA
TO THE VICTOR • 1948 • Daves Delmer • USA
TO THE VICTOR see **MAN OF THE PEOPLE** • 1937
TO THE VICTOR see **OWD BOB** • 1938
TO THE VICTOR THE SPOILS • 1912 • *Vampire Films* • UKN
TO THE WALL see **AL PAREDON** • 1970
TO THEIR MUTUAL BENEFIT • 1912 • Coleby A. E.? • UKN
TO TJENESTEPIGER • 1910 • *Blom August* • DNM • RIVAL SERVANTS, THE
TO TRACK A SHADOW • 1967 • Kaczender George • CND
TO TRAP A SPY • 1965 • Medford Don • TVM • USA • VULCAN AFFAIR, THE
TO TURN A TRICK • 1967 • *Simonsen Inga* • USA
TO VICTORY AND BEYOND • 1966 • Mitrovic Zika • YGS
TO WALK ALONE see **NA PRZELAJ** • 1971
TO WHAT RED HELL • 1929 • Greenwood Edwin • UKN
TO WHOM IT MAY CONCERN see **SOCIAL CODE, THE** • 1923
TO WOODY ALLEN, FROM EUROPE WITH LOVE • 1981 • Delvaux Andre • BLG
TO YOUR HEALTH • 1956 • Stapp Philip • ANS • UKN
TOA • 1949 • Guitry Sacha • FRN
TOAD ALLEN'S ELOPEMENT • 1919 • Hale Albert W. • SHT • USA
TOADSTOOLS see **GLJIVA** • 1972
TOAMNA • 1961 • Muresan Mircea • RMN • AUTUMN
TOAST • 1969 • Lomnicki Jan • DOC • PLN
TOAST OF DEATH, THE • 1915 • Sidney Scott • USA
TOAST OF NEW ORLEANS, THE • 1950 • Taurog Norman • USA
TOAST OF NEW YORK, THE • 1937 • Lee Rowland V. • USA
TOAST OF SONG • 1951 • Cowan Will • SHT • USA
TOAST OF THE LEGION (UKN) see **KISS ME AGAIN** • 1931
TOAST TO A YOUNG MISS see **OJOSAN KANPAI** • 1949
TOAST TO MARRIAGE, A see **KANPAI MIAI KEKKON** • 1958
TOAST TO THE YOUNG MISS, A see **OJOSAN KANPAI** • 1949
TOASTER, THE see **TOASTEUR, LE** • 1982
TOASTEUR, LE • 1982 • Bouchard Michel • MTV • CND • TOASTER, THE
TOATLE FAMILIE, DIE • 1981 • Schmidt Ernst Jr. • AUS • TOTAL FAMILY, THE
TOBACCO see **TYUTYUN** • 1962
TOBACCO MANIA • 1909 • *Edison* • SHT • USA

TOBACCO ROAD • 1941 • Ford John • USA
TOBACCO ROODY • 1970 • Buckalew Bethel • USA
TOBBY • 1961 • Pohland Hansjurgen • FRG
TOBENAI CHINMOKU • 1966 • Kuroki Kazuo • JPN • SILENCE HAS NO WINGS (USA)
TOBERMORY • 1931 • Pearson George • SHT • UKN
TOBIAS BREMSER AUF DIENSTREISE • 1972 • Thiel Heinz • GDR
TOBIAS BUNTSCHUH • 1921 • May Joe, Holger-Madsen • FRG
TOBIAS KNAPP, ABENTEUER EINES JUNGGESELLEN • 1950 • Pentzlin Walter • FRG
TOBIAS TURNS THE TABLES • 1913 • Eagle Oscar • USA
TOBIAS WANTS OUT • 1913 • Eagle Oscar • USA
TOBIDASHITA OJOSAN • 1947 • Shibuya Minoru • JPN
TOBIE EST UN ANGE • 1941 • Allegret Yves • FRN
TOBIN'S PALM • 1918 • Webb Kenneth • SHT • USA
TOBIRA O HIRAKU ONNA • 1946 • Kimura Keigo • JPN • WOMAN OPENS THE DOOR, A ○ WOMAN OPENING THE DOOR, THE
TOBISUKE BOKEN RYOKO • 1949 • Nakagawa Nobuo • JPN • TOBISUKE'S ADVENTURES
TOBISUKE'S ADVENTURES see **TOBISUKE BOKEN RYOKO** • 1949
TOBITCHO KANTARO • 1959 • Hisamatsu Seiji • JPN
TOBO CHITAI • 1953 • *Mikuni Rentaro* • JPN • FLIGHT ZONE
TOBO RESSHA • 1966 • Ezaki Jissei • JPN • LAST ESCAPE
TOBO, THE HAPPY CLOWN • 1965 • Rowland William • USA • HAPPY CLOWN, THE
TOBOGGAN • 1934 • Decoin Henri • FRN
TOBOR THE GREAT • 1954 • Sholem Lee • USA
TOBRUK • 1966 • Hiller Arthur • USA • CLIFFS OF MERSA, THE
TOBY • 1978 • Mercero Antonio • SPN
TOBY AND THE TALL CORN • 1954 • Leacock Richard, Van Dyke Willard • DOC • USA
TOBY MCTEAGUE • 1986 • Lord Jean-Claude • CND
TOBY THE PUP • 1930-31 • ASS • USA
TOBY TORTOISE RETURNS • 1936 • Jackson Wilfred • ANS • USA
TOBY TYLER • 1960 • Barton Charles T. • USA • TOBY TYLER, OR TEN WEEKS WITH A CIRCUS
TOBY TYLER, OR TEN WEEKS WITH A CIRCUS see **TOBY TYLER** • 1960
TOBY'S BOW • 1919 • Beaumont Harry • USA
TOCATA Y FUGA DE LOLITA • 1974 • Drove Antonio • SPN • LOLITA'S TOCCATO AND FUGUE
TOCCATA • 1968 • van der Horst Herman • NTH
TOCCATA AND FUGUE • 1940 • Bute Mary Ellen, Nemeth Ted J. • SHT • USA
TOCCATA FOR TOY TRAINS • 1957 • Eames Charles, Eames Ray • SHT • USA
TOCCATA MANHATTA • 1949 • Rogers Roger Bruce • USA
TOCCATE ET FUGUE • 1973 • Audy Michel • SHT • CND
TOCHKA, TOCHKA, ZAPYATAYA.. • 1973 • Mitta Alexander • USS • FULL STOP, FULL STOP, COMMA..
TOCHTER DER ARBEIT, DIE see **FLUCH DER MENSCHHEIT 1, DER** • 1920
TOCHTER DER BERGE, DIE • 1919 • Batz Lorenz • FRG
TOCHTER DER FRAU LARSAC, DIE • 1924 • Neufeld Max • AUS
TOCHTER DER GRAFIN STACHOWSKA, DIE • 1917 • Rippert Otto? • FRG
TOCHTER DER KOMPANIE, DIE • 1951 • von Bolvary Geza, Covaz Tullio • FRG, ITL • FIGLIA DEL REGGIMENTO, LA (ITL)
TOCHTER DER LANDSTRASSE, DIE • 1914 • Gad Urban • FRG
TOCHTER DER WUSTE, DIE see **ORIENT** • 1924
TOCHTER DES BRIGADIER, DIE • 1922 • Porges Friedrich • AUS
TOCHTER DES EICHMEISTERS, DIE • 1916 • Delmont Joseph • FRG
TOCHTER DES HENKERS, DIE • 1919 • Wauer William • FRG
TOCHTER DES HERRN VON DORNBERG, DIE • 1918 • von Woringen Paul? • FRG
TOCHTER DES KUNSTREITERS, DIE • 1927 • Philippi Siegfried • FRG
TOCHTER DES MARQUIS VON CHESTER, DIE • 1923 • Berger Josef • FRG
TOCHTER DES MEHAMED, DIE • 1919 • Halm Alfred • FRG
TOCHTER DES RAJAHS, DIE • 1918 • Zeyn Willy • FRG
TOCHTER DES REGIMENTS, DIE • 1933 • Lamac Carl • FRG • REGIMENTSTOCHTER, DIE
TOCHTER DES SAMURAI, DIE • 1937 • Fanck Arnold • FRG, JPN • LIEBE DER MITSU, DIE
TOCHTER DES SENATORS, DIE see **LIEBE UND LEBEN 2** • 1918
TOCHTER DES WOIWODEN, DIE see **TARAS BULBA 1** • 1924
TOCHTER EINER KURTISANE, DIE see **YVETTE** • 1938
TOCHTER IHRER EXZELLENZ, DIE • 1934 • Schunzel Reinhold • FRG
TOCHTER NAPOLEONS, DIE • 1922 • Zelnik Friedrich • FRG
TOCHUKEN KUMOEMON • 1936 • Naruse Mikio • JPN • ON THE WAY TO SPIDER GATE ○ KUMOEMON TOCHUKEN
TOCQUEVILLE'S AMERICA • 1969 • Bonniere Rene • DOC • CND
TOCSIN, LE • 1920 • Vorins Henri • FRN
TOD AUF ZECHE SILVA, DER • 1916 • Mendel Georg Victor • FRG
TOD AUS DEM OSTEN, DER • 1919 • Hartwig Martin • FRG
TOD AUS DER THEMSE, DIE • 1971 • Philipp Harald • FRG
TOD DER MARIA MALIBRAN, DER • 1971 • Schroeter Werner • FRG • DEATH OF MARIA MALIBRAN, THE
TOD DES ANDERN, DER • 1919 • Oswald Richard • FRG
TOD DES DR. ANTONIO DURCH DIE RENAISSANCE DER GEISTIGE GESELLSCHAFT, DER • 1967 • Lepeniotis Antonis
TOD DES ERASMUS, DER • 1916 • Rippert Otto • FRG
TOD DES FLOHZIRKUSDIREKTORS see **MORT DU DIRECTEUR DE CIRQUE DE PUCES, LA** • 1974
TOD DES FLOHZIRKUSDIREKTORS ODER OTTOCARO WEISS REFORMIERT SEINE FIRMA, DER • 1973 • Koerfer Thomas • SWT • PESTTHEATER
TOD DES GROSSFURSTEN, DER see **TANZ AUF DEM VULKAN 2, DER** • 1920
TOD EINES DOPPELGANGERS, DER • 1967 • Thiele Rolf • FRG, BLG • DEATH OF A DOUBLE, THE ○ ES GEHOREN ZWEI DAZU ○ NOBODY KNOWS
TOD EINES FREMDEN, DER • 1972 • Badiyi Reza • FRG, ISR • DEATH OF A STRANGER (USA) ○ EXECUTION, THE (UKN) ○ ASSASSINATION, THE ○ DEATH MERCHANTS, THE
TOD EINES SCHULERS • 1990 • Patzak Peter • FRG, AUS • DEATH OF A SCHOOLBOY
TOD FAHRT MIT, DER • 1962 • Scully Dennis • FRG, SAF
TOD HAT EIN GESICHT, DER • 1961 • Hasler Joachim • GDR
TOD HOCHZEITSGAST, DER • 1921 • Neufeld Max • AUS
TOD IM ROTEN JAGUAR, DER • 1968 • Reinl Harald • FRG, ITL • MORTE IN JAGUAR ROSSA, LA (ITL) ○ DEATH IN THE RED JAGUAR
TOD IM SEVILLA, DER • 1913 • Gad Urban • FRG, DNM • SPANSK ELSOV
TOD IM SPIEGEL, DER • 1920 • *Vanelli Friedrich Werter* • FRG
TOD IN VENEDIG, DER see **MACHT DES BLUTES 1** • 1921
TOD ODER FREIHEIT • 1977 • Gremm Wolfgang • FRG • DEATH OR FREEDOM
TOD RITT DIENSTAGS, DER (FRG) see **GIORNI DELL'IRA, I** • 1967
TOD UBER SHANGHAI • 1932 • Randolf Rolf • FRG
TOD UND DIE LIEBE, DER • 1919 • Otto Paul • FRG
TOD VERSOHNT, DER • 1920 • *Mundus-Film-Company* • FRG
TOD VON PHALERIA, DER • 1919 • Osten Franz • FRG
TODA BROTHER AND HIS SISTERS, THE see **TODA-KE NO KYODAI** • 1941
TODA BROTHERS, THE see **TODA-KE NO KYODAI** • 1941
TODA BROTHERS AND SISTERS, THE see **TODA-KE NO KYODAI** • 1941
TODA-KE NO KYODAI • 1941 • Ozu Yasujiro • JPN • BROTHERS AND SISTERS OF THE TODA FAMILY, THE ○ TODA BROTHERS AND SISTERS, THE ○ TODA BROTHERS, THE ○ TODA BROTHER AND HIS SISTERS, THE
TODA NUDEZ SERA CASTIGADA • 1973 • Jabor Arnaldo • BRZ • ALL NUDITY SHALL BE PUNISHED (USA) ○ ALL NUDITY WILL BE PUNISHED
TODA UNA VIDA • 1930 • Millar Adelqui • SPN
TODA UNA VIDA • 1944 • Ortega Juan J. • MXC
TODAS AS MULHERES DO MUNDO • 1967 • de Oliveira Domingos • BRZ • ALL THE WORLD'S WOMEN
TODAY • 1917 • Ince Ralph • USA
TODAY • 1917 • Stahl John M. • USA
TODAY • 1930 • Nigh William • USA
TODAY • 1965 • Kandelaki Gela • USS
TODAY see **SEGODNYA** • 1924
TODAY see **SEGODNYA** • 1930
TODAY AND FOR THE REST OF YOUR LIFE • 1970 • Grigoriev Yuri • USS
TODAY AND TOMORROW • 1915 • *Roland Ruth* • USA
TODAY AND TOMORROW • 1937 • Grierson Ruby I. • UKN
TODAY AND TOMORROW see **MA ES HOLNAP** • 1912
TODAY AND TOMORROW: A STORY OF THE MIDDLE EAST • 1945 • Carruthers Robin • UKN
TODAY FOR THE LAST TIME see **DNES NAPOSLED** • 1958
TODAY I HANG • 1942 • Drake Oliver, Merrick George M. • USA
TODAY IN A NEW TOWN • 1963 • Slijepcevic Vladan • YGS
TODAY IS A NEW NUMBER • 1966 • Kosheverova Nadezhda • USS
TODAY IS FOR THE CHAMPIONSHIP • 1980 • Weisburd Dan • DOC • USA
TODAY IS FOREVER see **GRIFFIN AND PHOENIX: A LOVE STORY** • 1976
TODAY ITS ME -TOMORROW YOU see **OGGI A ME, DOMANI A TE** • 1968
TODAY MEXICO, TOMORROW THE WORLD • 1970 • Shillingford Peter • UKN
TODAY OR TOMORROW see **MA VAGY HOLNAP** • 1965
TODAY OR TOMORROW see **VANDAAG OF MORGEN** • 1976
TODAY, TOMORROW AND THE DAY AFTER see **OGGI DOMANI DOPODOMANI** • 1965
TODAY WE LIVE • 1932 • Hawks Howard • USA
TODAY WE LIVE • 1937 • Bond Ralph, Grierson Ruby I. • DOC • UKN
TODAY WE LIVE see **JOUR ET L'HEURE, LE** • 1963
TODAY YOU'RE HERE see **TANAAN OLET TAALLA** • 1966
TODAY'S F.B.I. • 1981 • Vogel Virgil W. • TVM • USA
TODAY'S MLA see **AAJ KA MLA** • 1984
TODAY'S TOMORROW • 1957 • Lewis Henry • UKN
TODBRINGER, DER • 1919 • Larsen Viggo • FRG
TODD KILLINGS, THE • 1971 • Shear Barry • USA • WHAT ARE WE GOING TO DO WITHOUT SKIPPER? ○ DANGEROUS FRIEND, A ○ PIED PIPER OF TUCSON, THE ○ SKIPPER
TODD OF THE TIMES • 1919 • Howe Eliot • USA
TODDLES, SCOUT • 1911 • Fitzhamon Lewin? • UKN
TODDLEUMS • 1913 • *White Pearl* • USA
TODDLIN' ALONG • 1928 • Freund Karl • UKN
TODESARENA, DIE • 1953 • Meisel Kurt • AUS
TODESAUGE VON CEYLON, DAS (FRG) see **TEMPESTA SU CEYLON** • 1963
TODESBOTE, DER • 1920 • Eichgrun Bruno • FRG
TODESCHLEIFE, DIE see **LOOPING THE LOOP** • 1928
TODESCOWBOY, DER • 1919 • Stranz Fred • FRG
TODESFAHRT, DIE • 1919 • Arnheim Valy • FRG
TODESFAHRT DES WEISSEN HAUPTLINGS, DIE • 1920 • Stockel Joe • FRG
TODESFAHRT IM WELTREKORD, DIE • 1929 • Blachnitzky Curt • FRG
TODESFAHRT IN DEN LUFTEN, DIE see **FORTUNATO 2** • 1921
TODESFALLE, DIE see **REITER OHNE KOPF 1, DER** • 1921
TODESFLIEGER, DER • 1921 • Arnheim Valy • FRG
TODESGEHEIMNIS, DAS • 1918 • Moest Hubert • FRG
TODESGOTTIN DES LIEBESCAMPS, DIE • 1981 • Anders Christian • FRG • LOVE CAMP
TODESKARAWANE, DIE • 1920 • Droop Marie Luise, Mouhssinn-Bey E. • FRG • CARAVAN OF DEATH (USA)
TODESKUSS DES DR. FU MAN CHU, DER • 1968 • Franco Jesus • UKN, SPN, FRG • FU MANCHU Y EL BESO DE LA MUERTE (SPN) ○ BLOOD OF FU MANCHU, THE (GBR) ○ KISS & KILL (USA) ○ FU MANCHU AND THE KISS OF DEATH ○ AGAINST ALL ODDS ○ FU MANCHU'S KISS OF DEATH
TODESLEITER, DIE • 1921 • Delmont Joseph • FRG
TODESMASKE, DIE • 1920 • Neff Wolfgang • FRG
TODESRACHER, DER (FRG) see **MUERTO HACE LAS MALETAS, EL** • 1971
TODESRADER VON SOHO, DER • 1972 • Franco Jesus • FRG
TODESREIGEN • Eichberg Richard • FRG
TODESREIGEN, DER • 1922 • Karfiol William • FRG
TODESRITT AM REISENRAD, DER • 1912 • *Planer Franz (Ph)* • FRG
TODESSCHLEIFE, DIE • 1928 • Robison Arthur • FRG • DEATH NOOSE, THE
TODESSCHUSSE AM BROADWAY • 1968 • Reinl Harald • FRG • DEADLY SHOTS IN BROADWAY
TODESSEGLER, DER • 1921 • Stranz Fred • FRG
TODESSEIL DER BLANDIN-TRUPPE, DAS see **DAMON ZIRKUS** • 1923
TODESSMARAGD, DER see **KNABE IN BLAU, DER** • 1919
TODESSPRUNG, DER see **UM KRONE UND PEITSCHE** • 1918
TODESSTERN, DER • 1917 • *Reicher Ernst* • FRG
TODESSTRAHLEN DES DR. MABUSE, DIE • 1964 • Fregonese Hugo • FRG, FRN, ITL • RAYONS MORTELS DU DOCTEUR MABUSE, LES (FRN) ○ SECRETS OF DR. MABUSE (USA) ○ RAGGI MORTALI DEL DR. MABUSE, I (ITL) ○ MIRROR DEATH RAY OF DR. MABUSE, THE ○ FRN ○ DEATH RAYS OF DR. MABUSE, THE
TODESTELEPHON, DAS • 1916 • *Kaiser-Titz Erich* • FRG
TODESURTEIL • 1919 • Berger Martin • FRG
TODESWEG AUF DIE BERNINA, DER • 1930 • Neff Wolfgang • FRG
TODFEIND, FER • 1920 • *Dernburg Ernst* • FRG
TODGEWEIHTEN • 1924 • Illes Eugen • FRG
TODLICHEN TRAUME, DIE see **LIEBESTRAUM** • 1951
TODO ES POSIBLE EN GRANADA • 1954 • Saenz De Heredia Jose Luis • SPN
TODO MODO • 1976 • Petri Elio • ITL
TODO O NADA • 1984 • Vieyra Emilio • ARG • ALL OR NOTHING
TODO POR NADA • 1989 • Lamadrid Alfredo • CHL • ALL FOR NOTHING
TODO UN CABALLERO • 1946 • Delgado Miguel M. • MXC
TODO UN HOMBRE • 1935 • Peon Ramon • MXC
TODO UN HOMBRE • 1943 • Chenal Pierre • ARG
TODO Y NADIE • 1977 • de Pedro Manuel, Campos Fernando Cony, San Miguel Santiago • DOC • VNZ, SPN • ALL AND NOBODY
TODOKE HAHA NO SAKEBI • 1959 • Fukuda Seiichi • JPN • SON HEAR MY CRY
TODOS ERAN CULPABLES • 1962 • Klimovsky Leon • SPN
TODOS LOS COLORES DE LA OSCURIDAD (SPN) see **TUTTI I COLORI DEL BUIO** • 1972
TODOS LOS DIAS SON SABADOS see **DIAS DE CENIZA** • 1978
TODOS LOS DIAS UN DIA • 1977 • Zambrano Roque • DOC • VNZ • EVERY DAY AS ONE DAY
TODOS LOS GRITOS DEL SILENCIO • 1974 • Barco Ramon • SPN
TODOS ME LLAMAN GATO • 1981 • *Tristancho Carlos* • SPN • EVERYBODY CALLS ME GATO
TODOS SOMOS HERMANOS • 1965 • Menendez Oscar • MXC
TODOS SOMOS NECESARIOS • 1956 • Nieves Conde Jose Antonio • SPN, ITL • SIAMO TUTTI NECESSARI (ITL)
TODOS SOMOS RESPONSABLES • 1976 • Busquets Manuel • DOC • CLM
TODOS SON MIS HIJOS • 1951 • Rodriguez Roberto • MXC
TODSPIELER, DER • 1919 • Carstennsen Carlo • FRG
TODY WE KILL.. TOMORROW WE DIE! • 1971 • *Ford Montgomery* • ITL
TOETS • Tholen Tom • NTH
TOETS-TOUCH-TOUCHE • 1968 • Tholen Tom • SHT • NTH
TOFFE JONGENS ONDER DE MOBILISATIE • 1914 • Binger Maurits H. • NTH • FINE FELLOWS DURING THE MOBILISATION
TOFFLAN -EN LYCKLIG KOMEDI • 1967 • Anderberg Torgny • SWD • SLIPPER -A HAPPY COMEDY, THE ○ SLIPPER ○ COWARD
TOG GUN • 1955 • Nazarro Ray • USA
TOGE • 1972 • Saito Koichi • JPN
TOGE NO UTA • 1923 • Mizoguchi Kenji • JPN • SONG OF THE MOUNTAIN PASS (USA)
TOGE O WATARU WAKAI KAZE • 1961 • Suzuki Seijun • JPN
TOGETHER • 1912 • *Halliday Jack* • USA
TOGETHER • 1918 • Lund O. A. C. • USA
TOGETHER • 1956 • Mazzetti Lorenza • UKN
TOGETHER • 1972 • Cunningham Sean S. • DOC • USA • SENSUAL PARADISE (UKN)
TOGETHER • 1976 • Broughton James • USA
TOGETHER see **RAZEM** • 1948
TOGETHER AGAIN • 1944 • Vidor Charles • USA • WOMAN'S PRIVILEGE, A
TOGETHER AGAIN • 1967 • Constantino F. H. • PHL
TOGETHER AND APART • 1987 • Lynd Laurie • SHT • CND
TOGETHER AT LAST • 1987 • Kyronseppa Kari • FNL
TOGETHER BROTHERS • 1974 • Graham William A. • USA
TOGETHER EVEN IF APART see **AYRILSAK DA BERABERIZ** • 1967
TOGETHER FOR DAYS • 1973 • Schultz Michael • USA
TOGETHER IN PARIS see **PARIS WHEN IT SIZZLES** • 1964
TOGETHER IN THE WEATHER • 1945 • Pal George • ANS • USA
TOGETHER (USA) see **AMO NON AMO** • 1979
TOGETHER WE LIVE • 1935 • Mack Willard • USA
TOGETHER WE TOO (UKN) see **SONNENSTRAHL** • 1933
TOGETHERNESS • 1970 • Marks Arthur • USA
TOGETHERNESS • 1975 • Lavut Martin • CND
TOGGER • 1937 • von Alten Jurgen • FRG
TOGLI LE GAMBE DAL PARABREZZA • 1969 • Franciosa Massimo • ITL
TOGYO • 1941 • *Ikebe Ryo* • JPN • FIGHTING FISH

TOGYU NI KAKERU OTOKO • 1960 • Masuda Toshio • JPN • MAN AT THE BULLFIGHT
TOH, E MORTA LA NONNA! • 1969 • Monicelli Mario • ITL • OH, GRANDMOTHER'S DEAD! ○ WELL, GRANDMA'S DEAD
TOHFA • 1988 • Butt Dawood • PKS
TOHFE HEND • 1968 • Jourak Fereydoun • IRN • GIFT FROM INDIA, A
TOHINAA HAMEESSA • 1977 • Hawk Oliver • FNL • SOUND AND FURY IN HAME
TOHNO MONOGATARI • 1983 • Murano Tetsutaro • JPN • LEGEND OF TOHNO
TOHO SEN-ICHIYA • 1947 • Ichikawa Kon • JPN • THOUSAND AND ONE NIGHTS WITH TOHO, A
TOHOKU NO ZUNMUTACHI • 1957 • Ichikawa Kon • JPN • MEN OF TOHOKU, THE ○ MAN OF THE NORTH
TOI C'EST MOI • 1936 • Guissart Rene • FRN
TOI IPPONNO MICHI • 1977 • Hidari Sachiko • JPN • FAR ROAD, THE
TOI KUMO • 1955 • Kinoshita Keisuke • JPN • DISTANT CLOUDS
TOI LE VENIN • 1958 • Hossein Robert • FRN • NIGHT IS NOT FOR SLEEP (UKN) ○ NUDE IN A WHITE CAR (USA) ○ BLONDE IN A WHITE CAR
TOI QUE J'ADORE • 1933 • Valentin Albert, von Bolvary Geza • FRN
TOIHOS, O • 1977 • Pavlidis Stelios • GRC • WALL, THE
TOIL AND TYRANNY • 1915 • *Balboa* • USA
TOILE D'ARAIGNEE MERVEILLEUSE, LA • 1908 • Melies Georges • SHT • FRN • PAINTING OF A MIRACULOUS SPIDER, THE
TOILERS, THE • 1915 • *Hamilton Lloyd V.* • USA
TOILERS, THE • 1919 • Watts Tom • UKN
TOILERS, THE • 1928 • Barker Reginald • USA
TOILERS, THE see **THOSE WHO TOIL** • 1916
TOILERS OF THE SEA • 1914 • *Kerrigan J. Warren* • USA
TOILERS OF THE SEA • 1923 • Neill R. William • USA, ITL
TOILERS OF THE SEA • 1936 • Jepson Selwyn, Fox Ted • UKN
TOILERS OF THE SEA, THE • 1915 • *Sackville Gordon* • USA
TOILET • 1970 • Zwartjes Frans • SHT • NTH
TOILET see **TOILETTE** • 1979
TOILET SECTION CHIEF see **TOIRETTO BUCHOU** • 1961
TOILETTE • 1979 • Pezold Friederike • AUS • TOILET
TOILS OF DECEPTION, THE • 1913 • Eagle Oscar • USA
TOINE • 1932 • Gaveau Rene • FRN
TOIRETTO BUCHOU • 1961 • Kakei Masanori • JPN • TOILET SECTION CHIEF
TOIROS DE MARY FOSTER, OS • 1972 • Campos Henrique • PRT
TOIROS NA FAINA AGRICOLA RIBATEJANA, OS • 1939 • Coelho Jose Adolfo • SHT • PRT
TOIT DE LA BALEINE, LE • 1981 • Ruiz Raul • FRN • TECHO DE LA BALLENA, EL ○ ROOF OF THE WHALE, THE ○ WHALE'S ROOF, THE
TOJIJIRO OF KUTSUKATE see **KUTSUKATE TOKIJIRO** • 1934
TOJIN OKICHI • 1930 • Mizoguchi Kenji • JPN • MISTRESS OF A FOREIGNER (USA)
TOJIN OKICHI • 1931 • Kinugasa Teinosuke • JPN • OKICHI, MISTRESS OF A FOREIGNER ○ OKICHI THE STRANGER
TOJURO NO KOI • 1938 • Yamamoto Kajiro • JPN • LOVES OF A KABUKI ACTOR, THE
TOKA JONE • Hakani Hysen • ALB • OUR SOIL
TOKAI-ICHI NO WAKA-OYABUN • 1961 • Makino Masahiro • JPN
TOKAI KOKYOGAKU • 1929 • Mizoguchi Kenji • JPN • METROPOLITAN SYMPHONY (USA) ○ SYMPHONY OF THE METROPOLIS ○ CITY SYMPHONY
TOKAI NO KAOYAKU • 1960 • Makino Masahiro • JPN • COLLAPSE OF A BOSS
TOKAI O OYOGU ONNA • 1929 • Toyoda Shiro • JPN • COLLAPSE OF A SWIMMING WOMAN, THE
TOKAI SUIKODEN • 1945 • Ito Daisuke, Inagaki Hiroshi • JPN • TOKAI'S SUIKO STORY
TOKAIDO YOTSUYA KAIDAN • 1959 • Nakagawa Nobuo • JPN • GHOST OF YOTSUYA, THE
TOKAI'S SUIKO STORY see **TOKAI SUIKODEN** • 1945
TOKAJI RAPSZODIA • 1938 • Vaszary Janos
TOKAKAN NO JINSEI • 1941 • Shibuya Minoru • JPN • TEN DAY'S LIFE
TOKE • 1973 • *Zapata Carmen* • USA
TOKE see **DANGEROUS TRAFFIC** • 1979
TOKEI • 1987 • Kuramoto So • JPN • ADIEU L'HIVER
TOKEN GESTURE, A • 1970 • Carter Peter • CND
TOKEN GESTURE, A • 1976 • Lanctot Micheline • ANM • CND
TOKI NO UJIGAMI • 1932 • Mizoguchi Kenji • JPN • MAN OF THE MOMENT (USA) ○ MAN OF THE RIGHT MOMENT, THE ○ TIMELY MEDIATOR
TOKIO JOKIO • 1943 • McCabe Norman • ANS • USA
TOKIO SIREN, A • 1920 • Dawn Norman • USA
TOKKAN • 1974 • Okamoto Kihachi • JPN • GO FOR BROKE
TOKKAN KOZO • 1930 • Ozu Yasujiro • JPN • STRAIGHTFORWARD BOY, A
TOKKYU NIPPON • 1961 • Kawashima Yuzo • JPN • ROMANCE EXPRESS (USA)
TOKLAT • 1971 • Davidson Robert W. • USA
TOKOH • 1974 • INN • GREAT LOVER, THE
TOKOLOSHE see **TOKOLOSHE THE EVIL SPIRIT** • 1965
TOKOLOSHE THE EVIL SPIRIT • 1965 • Prowse Peter • SAF • TOKOLOSHE
TOKUGAWA IEYASU • 1965 • Ito Daisuke • JPN
TOKUGAWA IREZUMISHI: SEME JIGOKU • 1970 • Ishii Teruo • JPN • HELL'S TATTOOERS
TOKUGAWA ONNA KEIBATSUSHI • 1968 • Ishii Teruo • JPN • JOYS OF TORTURE, THE
TOKUGAWA ONNA KEIZU • 1968 • Ishii Teruo • JPN • SHOGUN AND THREE THOUSAND WOMEN, THE
TOKYO 196X see **SHOWA GENROKU TOKYO 196X-NEN** • 1968
TOKYO AFTER DARK • 1959 • Herman Norman • USA
TOKYO ANTATCHABURU • 1962 • Murayama Shinji • JPN • TOKYO UNTOUCHABLE
TOKYO BAKUTO • 1967 • Yasuda Kimiyoshi • JPN • GAMBLERS OF TOKYO
TOKYO BATH HAREM see **ONNA UKIYO BURO** • 1968
TOKYO BAY see **TOKYO-WAN** • 1962
TOKYO BOSHOKU • 1957 • Ozu Yasujiro • JPN • TWILIGHT IN TOKYO ○ TOKYO TWILIGHT
TOKYO CENTURY PLAZA see **EKIMAE HYAKUNEN** • 1967
TOKYO CHORUS see **TOKYO NO GASSHO** • 1931
TOKYO CUSTOMS see **TOKYO NO FUZOKU** • 1941
TOKYO DETECTIVE SAGA see **TSUMAARI KOARI TOMOARITE** • 1961
TOKYO EMMANUELLE FUJIN • 1975 • Kato Akira • JPN • EMMANUELLE IN TOKYO
TOKYO FILE 212 • 1951 • McGowan Dorrell, McGowan Stuart E. • USA
TOKYO HONGKONG HONEYMOON see **TOKYO HONGKONG NITSUGETSU RYOKO** • 1958
TOKYO HONGKONG NITSUGETSU RYOKO • 1958 • Nomura Yoshitaro • JPN • TOKYO HONGKONG HONEYMOON
TOKYO INTERNATIONAL TRIAL see **TOKYO SAIBAN** • 1983
TOKYO JOE • 1949 • Heisler Stuart • USA
TOKYO KISHITAI • 1961 • Suzuki Seijun • JPN
TOKYO KNIGHT • 1967 • Kaji Noboru • JPN
TOKYO KOSHINKYOKO • 1929 • Mizoguchi Kenji • JPN • TOKYO MARCH ○ TOKYO SYMPHONY
TOKYO MARCH see **TOKYO KOSHINKYOKO** • 1929
TOKYO MONOGATARI • 1953 • Ozu Yasujiro • JPN • THEIR FIRST TRIP TO TOKYO ○ TOKYO STORY
TOKYO NAGARE MONO • 1966 • Suzuki Kiyonori • JPN
TOKYO NIGHT STORY see **TOKYO YAWA** • 1961
TOKYO NO FUZOKU • 1941 • Shibuya Minoru • JPN • TOKYO CUSTOMS
TOKYO NO GASSHO • 1931 • Ozu Yasujiro • JPN • CHORUS OF TOKYO, THE ○ TOKYO CHORUS
TOKYO NO HITO • 1956 • Nishikawa Katsumi • JPN
TOKYO NO HITOMI • 1958 • Tanaka Shigeo • JPN • EYE PUPILS OF TOKYO
TOKYO NO KOIBITO • 1952 • *Mifune Toshiro* • JPN • TOKYO SWEETHEART
TOKYO NO KYUJITSU • 1958 • Yamamoto Kajiro • JPN • HOLIDAY IN TOKYO, A
TOKYO NO ONNA • 1933 • Ozu Yasujiro • JPN • WOMAN OF TOKYO
TOKYO NO TEKISASU-JIN • 1957 • Oda Motoyoshi • JPN • KNOCKOUT DROPS
TOKYO NO YADO • 1935 • Ozu Yasujiro • JPN • INN IN TOKYO, AN
TOKYO ODORI • 1959 • Ikoma Chisato • JPN • SHOCHIKU FOLLIES
TOKYO OLYMPIAD see **TOKYO ORINPIKKU** • 1965
TOKYO OMNIBUS see **SANBA GARASU SANDAIKAI** • 1959
TOKYO ONIGIRI MUSUME • 1961 • Tanaka Shigeo • JPN
TOKYO ORINPIKKU • 1965 • Ichikawa Kon • JPN • TOKYO OLYMPIAD
TOKYO OSAKA SCOOP see **TOKYO OSAKA TOKUDANE ORAI** • 1936
TOKYO OSAKA TOKUDANE ORAI • 1936 • Toyoda Shiro • JPN • TOKYO OSAKA SCOOP
TOKYO PARIS SEISHUN NO JOKEN • 1970 • Saito Koichi • JPN • RAINBOW OVER PARIS
TOKYO PATROL -SEVEN DETECTIVES see **SHICHININ NON TSUISEKI-SHA** • 1958
TOKYO PATROL -TAXI-DRIVER MURDERS see **MANO DENGONBAN** • 1958
TOKYO POP • 1987 • Kuzui Frannie • USA
TOKYO ROSE • 1945 • Landers Lew • USA
TOKYO SAIBAN • 1983 • Kobayashi Masaki • JPN • FAR EAST MARTIAL COURT, THE ○ TOKYO INTERNATIONAL TRIAL ○ TOKYO TRIAL, THE ○ TOKYO TRIAL OF WAR CRIMINALS
TOKYO SENICHIYA • 1938 • Uchida Tomu • JPN • THOUSAND AND ONE NIGHTS IN TOKYO, A
TOKYO SENSO SENGO HIWA • 1970 • Oshima Nagisa • JPN • MAN WHO LEFT HIS WILL ON FILM, THE (UKN) ○ HE DIED AFTER THE WAR (USA) ○ TOKYO SENSO SENGO HIWA -EIGADE ISHOO NOKOSHITE SHINDA OTOKONO MONOGATARI
TOKYO SENSO SENGO HIWA -EIGADE ISHOO NOKOSHITE SHINDA OTOKONO MONOGATARI see **TOKYO SENSO SENGO HIWA** • 1970
TOKYO SHIGAISEN • 1967 • Nishimura Shogoro • JPN • AFTERMATH OF WAR, THE
TOKYO STORY see **TOKYO MONOGATARI** • 1953
TOKYO SWEETHEART see **TOKYO NO KOIBITO** • 1952
TOKYO SYMPHONY see **TOKYO KOSHINKYOKO** • 1929
TOKYO TRIAL, THE see **TOKYO SAIBAN** • 1983
TOKYO TRIAL OF WAR CRIMINALS see **TOKYO SAIBAN** • 1983
TOKYO TWILIGHT see **TOKYO BOSHOKU** • 1957
TOKYO UNTOUCHABLE see **TOKYO ANTATCHABURU** • 1962
TOKYO-WAN • 1962 • Nomura Yoshitaro • JPN • TOKYO BAY
TOKYO YAWA • 1961 • Toyoda Shiro • JPN • DIPLOMAT'S MANSION, THE ○ TOKYO NIGHT STORY
TOKYO YOITOKO • 1935 • Ozu Yasujiro • JPN • TOKYO'S A NICE PLACE
TOKYO'S A NICE PLACE see **TOKYO YOITOKO** • 1935
TOL'ABLE DAVID • 1921 • King Henry • USA
TOL'ABLE DAVID • 1930 • Blystone John G. • USA
TOL'ABLE ROMEO • 1926 • Roach Hal • SHT • USA
TOLD AT THE TWILIGHT • 1917 • King Henry • USA • TOLD AT TWILIGHT
TOLD AT TWILIGHT see **TOLD AT THE TWILIGHT** • 1917
TOLD BY THE CARDS • 1913 • *Essanay* • USA
TOLD IN COLORADO • 1911 • *Selig* • USA
TOLD IN THE FUTURE • 1913 • *Garwood Billy* • USA
TOLD IN THE GOLDEN WEST • 1910 • *Selig* • USA
TOLD IN THE HILLS • 1919 • Melford George • USA
TOLD IN THE ROCKIES • 1915 • Thayer Otis B. • USA
TOLD IN THE SIERRAS • 1911 • *Selig* • USA
TOLEDO • 1932 • Ledashev A. • USS
TOLERANCE • 1989 • Salfati Pierre-Henri • FRN
TOLERANCE see **TOLERANCIJA** • 1967
TOLERANCE see **GONDVISELES** • 1987
TOLERANCIJA • 1967 • Grgic Zlatko, Ranitovic Branko • ANS • YGS, SWT • TOLERANCE
TOLL, THE • 1914 • Marston Theodore • USA
TOLL BRIDGE TROUBLES • 1942 • Wickersham Bob • ANS • USA
TOLL GATE, THE • 1920 • Hillyer Lambert • USA
TOLL GATE RAIDERS • 1912 • *Nilsson Anna Q.* • USA
TOLL OF FEAR, THE • 1913 • Fielding Romaine • USA
TOLL OF JUSTICE, THE • 1916 • *Miller Walter* • USA
TOLL OF LOVE, THE • 1914 • *Blackstone Lisbeth* • USA
TOLL OF MAMMON, THE • 1914 • Handworth Harry • USA
TOLL OF SIN, THE • 1917 • Eagle Oscar • SHT • USA
TOLL OF THE DESERT • 1935 • Berke William • USA
TOLL OF THE DESERT, THE • 1913 • *Frontier* • USA
TOLL OF THE JUNGLE • 1916 • Santschi Thomas • SHT • USA
TOLL OF THE LAW, THE • 1916 • Powers Francis • SHT • USA
TOLL OF THE MARSHES, THE • 1913 • *Bushman Francis X.* • USA
TOLL OF THE SEA, THE • 1912 • *Macpherson Jeanie* • USA
TOLL OF THE SEA, THE • 1915 • McRae Henry • USA
TOLL OF THE SEA, THE • 1922 • Franklin Chester M. • USA
TOLL OF THE WAR-PATH, THE • 1914 • *Farley Dot* • USA
TOLL OF WAR, THE • 1913 • Ford Francis • USA
TOLL OF YOUTH, THE • 1915 • Lloyd Frank • USA
TOLL TRIEBEN ES DIE ALTEN GERMANEN (FRG) see **QUANDO LE DONNE PERSERO LA CODA** • 1972
TOLLDREISTEN GESCHICHTEN DES HONORE DE BALZAC • 1969 • Zachar Jozef • FRG • BRAZEN WOMEN OF BALZAC, THE (USA) ○ SEX IS A PLEASURE (UKN) ○ KOMM, LIEBE MALD UND MACHE
TOLLE BOMBERG, DER • 1932 • Asagaroff Georg • FRG
TOLLE BOMBERG, DER • 1957 • Thiele Rolf • FRG
TOLLE HEIRAT VON LALO, DIE • 1918 • Pick Lupu • FRG
TOLLE HERZOGIN, DIE • 1926 • Wolff Willi • FRG
TOLLE KISTE, EINE • 1919 • *Wolter Hilde* • FRG
TOLLE KOMTESS, DIE • 1928 • Lowenbein Richard • FRG • CRAZY COUNTESS, THE
TOLLE LOLA, DIE • 1927 • Eichberg Richard • FRG
TOLLE LOLA, DIE • 1953 • Deppe Hans • FRG
TOLLE MISS, DIE see **MISS HOBBS** • 1921
TOLLE NACHT • 1943 • Lingen Theo • FRG
TOLLE NACHT • 1957 • Olden John • FRG
TOLLE NACHT, EINE • 1926 • Oswald Richard • FRG
TOLLE RISCHKA, DIE • 1920 • Lubitsch Ernst • FRG
TOLLE SUSANNE, DIE • 1945 • von Bolvary Geza • FRG
TOLLEN LAUNEN EINES MILLIONARS, DIE see **EULE 1, DIE** • 1927
TOLLER EINFALL, EIN • 1916 • *Bender Henry* • FRG
TOLLER EINFALL, EIN • 1932 • Gerron Kurt • FRG
TOLLER HECHT AUF KRUMMEN TOUREN • 1961 • von Rathony Akos • FRG • PHONY AMERICAN, THE (USA) ○ IT'S A GREAT LIFE
TOLLER TAG, EIN • 1945 • Schuh Oscar F. • FRG
TOLLES FRUCHTCHEN, EIN • 1953 • Antel Franz • AUS
TOLLES HOTEL, EIN • 1956 • Wolff Hans • AUS
TOLLES MADEL, EIN • 1916 • Karfiol William • FRG
TOLLES MADEL, EIN • 1921 • Kalden Hans • FRG
TOLMERS, BEGINNING OR END? • 1974 • Thompson Philip • UKN
TOLONC, A • 1914 • Curtiz Michael • HNG • VAGRANT, THE
TOLPAR • 1978 • Anwar Kabir • BNG • BREAKTHROUGH, THE ○ RUMPUS
TOLSTOI, DER FRIEDENSAPOSTEL see **RUSSLAND 1** • 1924
TOLUBAI -CONNOISSEUR OF RACE-HORSES • Ishenov Sagvnbek • ANM • USS
TOM • 1973 • Clark Greydon • USA
TOM AND CHERIE • 1955 • Hanna William, Barbera Joseph • ANS • USA
TOM AND HIS PALS • 1926 • De Lacy Robert • USA
TOM AND JERRY • 1911 • *Yankee* • USA
TOM AND JERRY • 1931-33 • *Van Beuren* • ASS • USA
TOM AND JERRY -BACHELORS • 1916 • Ireland Frederick J. • SHT • USA
TOM AND JERRY CARTOON KIT, THE • 1962 • Deitch Gene • ANS • USA • TOM-AND-JERRY CARTOON KIT, THE
TOM-AND-JERRY CARTOON KIT, THE see **TOM AND JERRY CARTOON KIT, THE** • 1962
TOM AND JERRY IN THE HOLLYWOOD BOWL • 1950 • Hanna William, Barbera Joseph • ANS • USA
TOM AND JERRY MIX • 1917 • Mix Tom • SHT • USA
TOM BLAKE'S REDEMPTION • 1913 • *Kerrigan J. Warren* • USA
TOM BOY, THE see **WER WIRD DENN WEINEN, WENN MAN AUSEINANDERGEHT** • 1929
TOM BRENEMAN'S BREAKFAST IN HOLLYWOOD see **BREAKFAST IN HOLLYWOOD** • 1946
TOM BRILL STORY, THE • Kagan Norman • SHT • USA
TOM BROWN OF CULVER • 1932 • Wyler William • USA • BROWN OF CULVER
TOM BROWN'S SCHOOLDAYS • 1916 • Wilson Rex • UKN
TOM BROWN'S SCHOOLDAYS • 1940 • Stevenson Robert • UKN • ADVENTURES AT RUGBY (USA)
TOM BROWN'S SCHOOLDAYS • 1951 • Parry Gordon • UKN
TOM BUTLER • 1912 • Jasset Victorin • FRN
TOM CAT see **HOW TO SUCCEED WITH SEX** • 1970
TOM CAT COMBAT • 1958 • Smith Paul J. • ANS • USA
TOM CRINGLE IN JAMAICA • 1913 • Raymond Charles • UKN
TOM, DICK AND HARRY • 1913 • Weston Charles • USA
TOM, DICK AND HARRY • 1917 • *Rhodes Billie* • SHT • USA
TOM, DICK AND HARRY • 1941 • Kanin Garson • USA
TOM, DICK AND HARRY ON THE JOB • 1913 • *Punch* • USA
TOM, DIRK EN HERRIE • 1962 • SAF
TOM DOLLAR • 1967 • Ciorciolini Marcello • ITL, FRN
TOM EDISON -THE BOY WHO LIT UP THE WORLD • 1983 • Schellerup Henning • USA
TOM ET LOLA • 1990 • Arthuys Bertrand • FRN
TOM HORN • 1979 • Wiard William • USA • HORN
TOM HUXLEY'S HEAD • 1910 • *Walturdaw* • UKN
TOM-IC ENERGY • 1965 • Jones Charles M. • ANS • USA
TOM IM NACKEN • 1920 • Sauer Fred • FRG
TOM & JERRY • 1916 • SER • USA
TOM & JERRY NO.6 • 1916 • *Emerald M.p.* • SHT • USA
TOM & JERRY NO.7 • 1916 • *Emerald M.p.* • SHT • USA
TOM & JERRY NO.8 • 1916 • *Emerald M.p.* • SHT • USA
TOM & JERRY NO.9 • 1916 • *Emerald M.p.* • SHT • USA
TOM & JERRY NO.10 • 1916 • *Emerald M.p.* • SHT • USA
TOM JONES • 1917 • Collins Edwin J. • UKN
TOM JONES • 1963 • Richardson Tony • UKN

TOM, LE CHIEN DE L'EXPOSITION COLONIALE • Daix Andre • ANM • FRN
TOM MARTIN –A MAN • 1916 • Nicholls George • SHT • USA
TOM MERRY, LIGHTNING CARTOONIST • 1895 • Acres Birt • UKN
TOM MIX IN ARABIA see **ARABIA** • 1922
TOM MIXUP • 1930 • *A.s.f.i.* • SHT • UKN
TOM MURGER, DER BANKRAUBER • 1920 • Seitz Franz • FRG
TOM OLD BOOT • 1896 • Melies Georges • FRN • TOM OLD BOOT, A GROTESQUE DWARF ○ TOM OLD BOOT, NAIN GROTESQUE
TOM OLD BOOT, A GROTESQUE DWARF see **TOM OLD BOOT** • 1896
TOM OLD BOOT, NAIN GROTESQUE see **TOM OLD BOOT** • 1896
TOM PHILLIPS • 1977 • Rowan David • UKN
TOM SAWYER • 1917 • Taylor William D. • USA
TOM SAWYER • 1930 • Cromwell John • USA
TOM SAWYER • 1973 • Neilson James • TVM • USA
TOM SAWYER • 1973 • Taylor Don • USA
TOM SAWYER, DETECTIVE • 1938 • King Louis • USA
TOM THUMB • Khodatayeva O. • USS
TOM THUMB • 1934 • *Mintz Charles (P)* • ANS • USA
TOM THUMB • 1936 • *Iwerks Ub (P)* • ANS • USA
TOM THUMB • 1958 • Pal George • USA, UKN
TOM THUMB see **PETIT POUCET, LE** • 1905
TOM THUMB see **PULGARCITO** • 1910
TOM THUMB see **PETIT POUCET, LE** • 1912
TOM THUMB see **PETIT POUCET, LE** • 1965
TOM THUMB IN LOVE • 1910 • USA
TOM THUMB IN PERSON • 1943 • *O'Brien Joseph/ Mead Thomas (P)* • SHT • USA
TOM THUMB IN TROUBLE • 1940 • Jones Charles M. • ANS • USA
TOM THUMB (USA) see **PETIT POUCET, LE** • 1900
TOM THUMB (USA) see **PETIT POUCET, LE** • 1909
TOM THUMB (USA) see **PETIT POUCET, LE** • 1912
TOM THUMB (USA) see **PULGARCITO** • 1958
TOM THUMB (USA) see **PETIT POUCET, LE** • 1972
TOM THUMB'S BROTHER • 1941 • Marcus Sid • ANS • USA
TOM THUMP • 1965 • Jones Charles M. • ANS • USA
TOM TIGHT ET DUM DUM • 1903 • Melies Georges • FRN • JACK JAGGS AND DUM DUM (USA) ○ RIVAL MUSIC HALL ARTISTES, THE
TOM TILLING'S BABY • 1912 • *Casey Kenneth* • USA
TOM TIT TOM • *Mock Flora (P)* • SHT • UKN
TOM, TOM, THE PIPER'S SON • 1905 • *Bitzer William (Ph)* • USA
TOM, TOM, THE PIPER'S SON • 1934 • *Terry Paul/ Moser Frank (P)* • ANS • USA
TOM, TOM, THE PIPER'S SON • 1969 • Jacobs Ken • USA
TOM–TOM TOMCAT • 1953 • Freleng Friz • ANS • USA
TOM TOMS OF MAYUMBA (UKN) see **TAM TAM MAYUMBE** • 1955
TOM TURK AND DAFFY • 1944 • Jones Charles M. • ANS • USA
TOM TURKEY AND HIS HARMONICA HUMDINGERS • 1940 • Harman Hugh • ANS • USA
TOM WHISKY OU L'ILLUSIONNISTE TOQUE • 1900 • Melies Georges • FRN • ADDITION AND SUBTRACTION (USA) ○ CRAZY MAGICIAN, THE
TOMA • 1973 • Heffron Richard T. • TVM • USA
TOMAHAWK • 1951 • Sherman George • USA • BATTLE OF POWDER RIVER, THE (UKN)
TOMAHAWK AND THE CROSS, THE (UKN) see **PILLARS OF THE SKY** • 1956
TOMAHAWK TRAIL • 1957 • Selander Lesley • USA • MARK OF THE APACHE (UKN)
TOMAHAWK TRAIL, THE (UKN) see **IROQUOIS TRAIL, THE** • 1950
TOMAS –A CHILD OUT OF REACH see **TOMAS –ET BARN DU IKKE KAN NA** • 1981
TOMAS –ET BARN DU IKKE KAN NA • 1981 • Christensen Mads Egmont, Hertz Lone • DNM • TOMAS –A CHILD OUT OF REACH
TOMASA • 1969 • Kautzner Dieter • FRG
TOMATO KETCHUP KOTEI • 1972 • Terayama Shuji • SHT • JPN • EMPEROR TOMATO–KETCHUP
TOMB, THE • 1986 • Ray Fred Olen • USA
TOMB FOR JOHNNY RINGO, A see **TUMBA PARA JOHNNY RINGO, UNA** • 1967
TOMB FOR THE SHERIFF, A see **TUMBA PARA EL SHERIFF, UNA** • 1967
TOMB OF HORROR see **CINQUE TOMBE PER UN MEDIUM** • 1966
TOMB OF LIGEIA, THE • 1964 • Corman Roger • UKN • LAST TOMB OF LIGEIA ○ TOMB OF THE CAT ○ LIGEIA
TOMB OF LOVERS, THE see **TAFOS TON ERASTON, O** • 1968
TOMB OF THE CAT see **TOMB OF LIGEIA, THE** • 1964
TOMB OF THE CURSED ISLAND, THE see **TUMBA DE LA ISLA MALDITA, LA** • 1972
TOMB OF THE KING, THE see **SEPOLCRO DEI RE, IL** • 1961
TOMB OF THE LIVING DEAD see **MAD DOCTOR OF BLOOD ISLAND** • 1969
TOMB OF THE UNDEAD see **GARDEN OF THE DEAD** • 1972
TOMB OF TORTURE (USA) see **METEMPSYCO** • 1963
TOMBA APERTA.. UNA BARA VUOTA, UNA • 1972 • Bragan A. • ITL
TOMBE DU CIEL • 1946 • Reinert Emile Edwin • FRN
TOMBEAU DE MELIES, LE see **NUIT FANTASTIQUE, LA** • 1941
TOMBEAU HINDOU, LE • 1937 • Eichberg Richard • FRN
TOMBEAU HINDOU, LE (FRN) see **INDISCHE GRABMAL, DAS** • 1959
TOMBEAU SOUS L'ARC DE TRIOMPHE, LE • 1927 • Wiene Robert
TOMBEUR, LE • 1957 • Delacroix Rene • FRN
TOMBOLA • 1962 • Lucia Luis • SPN
TOMBOLO, PARADISE NOIR (FRN) see **TOMBOLO PARADISO NERO** • 1947
TOMBOLO PARADISO NERO • 1947 • Ferroni Giorgio • ITL, FRN • TOMBOLO, PARADISE NOIR (FRN) ○ TOMBOLO (USA)
TOMBOLO (USA) see **TOMBOLO PARADISO NERO** • 1947
TOMBOY • 1912 • *Majestic* • USA
TOMBOY • 1915 • *Saunders Jackie* • USA
TOMBOY • 1940 • McGowan Robert • USA
TOMBOY • 1985 • Freed Herb • USA
TOMBOY, THE • 1909 • Olcott Sidney • USA
TOMBOY, THE • 1911 • *Snow Marguerite* • USA
TOMBOY, THE • 1921 • Harbaugh Carl • USA
TOMBOY, THE • 1924 • Kirkland David • USA
TOMBOY AND THE CHAMP • 1961 • Lyon Francis D. • USA
TOMBOY BESSIE • 1912 • Sennett Mack, Normand Mabel • USA
TOMBOY I MISTERI DEL SESSO • 1977 • Racca Claudio • ITL
TOMBOY OF BAR Z, THE • 1912 • Anderson G. M. • USA
TOMBOY RANCH GIRL, THE • 1912 • *Comet* • USA
TOMBOYS • 1915 • *Kalem* • USA
TOMBOYS, THE • 1905 • *Selig William (P)* • USA
TOMBOY'S RACE, THE • 1913 • *Majestic* • USA
TOMBS OF OUR ANCESTORS see **VARA FADERS GRAVAR** • 1937
TOMBS OF TERROR see **DANZA MACABRA** • 1964
TOMBS OF THE BLIND DEAD (UKN) see **NOCHE DEL TERROR CIEGO, LA** • 1972
TOMBSTONE CANYON • 1932 • James Alan • USA
TOMBSTONE TERROR • 1935 • Bradbury Robert North • USA
TOMBSTONE, THE TOWN TO TOUGH TO DIE • 1942 • McGann William • USA
TOMCAT, THE (USA) see **MINI WEEKEND** • 1967
TOMEI KAIJIN • 1958 • Kobayashi Tsuneo • JPN • INVISIBLE MAN
TOMEI KENSHI • 1970 • Kuroda Yoshiyuki • JPN • INVISIBLE SWORDSMAN
TOMEI NINGEN • 1954 • Oda Motoyoshi • JPN • INVISIBLE MAN
TOMEI NINGEN ARAWARU • 1949 • Adachi Shinsei • JPN • TRANSPARENT MAN, THE
TOMEI–NINGEN TO HAI–OTOKO • 1957 • Murayama Mitsuo • JPN • TRANSPARENT MAN VS. THE FLY MAN, THE ○ MURDERING MITE, THE
TOMEI TENGU • 1958 • Hirozu Mitsuo • JPN
TOMEININGEN EROHAKASE • 1968 • Seki Koji • JPN • INVISIBLE MAN –DR. EROS
TOMFOOLERY • 1970 • Halas John • ANS • UKN
TOMGOU • 1931 • Litvinof • DOC • USS
TOMKINS BUYS A DONKEY • 1908 • Fitzhamon Lewin • UKN
TOMMY • 1931 • Protazanov Yakov • USS • SIBERIAN PATROL ○ SIBIRSKY PATROL
TOMMY • 1937 • Balogh Bela • HNG
TOMMY • 1975 • Russell Ken • UKN
TOMMY • 1981 • SAF
TOMMY 2 • 1983 • SAF
TOMMY AND THE MOUSE IN THE ART SCHOOL • 1902 • Smith G. A. • UKN • LITTLE WILLIE AND THE MOUSE
TOMMY AND THE POLICEMAN'S WHISTLE • 1908 • Collins Alf? • UKN
TOMMY AND THE POWDER • 1910 • *Lux* • FRN
TOMMY AND THE STICKTITE • 1908 • Coleby A. E. • UKN
TOMMY AND THE WHOOPING COUGH • 1912 • Wilson Frank? • UKN
TOMMY ATKINS • 1910 • *Gaumont* • UKN
TOMMY ATKINS • 1915 • Haldane Bert • UKN
TOMMY ATKINS • 1928 • Walker Norman • UKN
TOMMY ATKINS see **COCKNEY SPIRIT IN THE WAR, THE** • 1930
TOMMY ATKINS AND HIS HARRIET ON A BANK HOLIDAY • 1902 • Smith G. A. • UKN
TOMMY ATKINS' DREAM • 1903 • Collins Alf • UKN
TOMMY ATKINS IN THE PARK • 1898 • *Paul R. W.* • UKN
TOMMY DORSEY AND HIS ORCHESTRA • 1951 • Cowan Will • SHT • USA
TOMMY GETS HIS SISTER MARRIED • 1910 • Golden Joseph A. • USA
TOMMY HANDLEY IN MAKING A CHRISTMAS PUDDING • 1933 • *Winads* • SHT • UKN
TOMMY IN DREAMLAND • 1910 • *Essanay* • USA
TOMMY LAD • 1909 • *Walturdaw* • UKN
TOMMY ON A VISIT TO HIS AUNT • 1908 • Cooper Arthur • UKN
TOMMY STEELE STORY, THE • 1957 • Bryant Gerard • UKN • ROCK AROUND THE WORLD (USA)
TOMMY THE TINPOT HERO • 1907 • Collins Alf? • UKN
TOMMY THE TOREADOR • 1959 • Carstairs John Paddy • UKN
TOMMY TRICKER AND THE STAMP TRAVELLER • 1988 • Rubbo Michael • CND • ALBUMINABLE HOMME DES TIMBRES, L' ○ AVENTURIERS DU TIMBRE PERDU
TOMMY TUCKER AND HIS ORCHESTRA • 1947 • Cowan Will • SHT • USA
TOMMY TUCKER'S TOOTH • 1923 • Disney Walt • ANS • USA
TOMMY'S ADVENTURES IN DREAMLAND • 1910 • *Urban* • UKN
TOMMY'S ATONEMENT • 1913 • Kirkland Hardee • USA
TOMMY'S BOX OF TOOLS • 1907 • Hough Harold • UKN
TOMMY'S EXPERIMENTS IN PHOTOGRAPHY • 1905 • Collins Alf? • UKN
TOMMY'S FREEZING SPRAY • 1915 • Birch Cecil • UKN
TOMMY'S GEOGRAPHY LESSON • 1912 • *Edison* • USA
TOMMY'S INITIATION • 1918 • Booth W. R. • UKN
TOMMY'S LAST SHOT • 1901 • *Mitchell & Kenyon* • UKN
TOMMY'S LOCOMOTIVE • 1910 • Stow Percy • UKN
TOMMY'S MONEY SCHEME • 1914 • Wilson Frank? • UKN
TOMMY'S REVENGE • 1901 • *Mitchell & Kenyon* • UKN
TOMMY'S REVENGE • 1904 • *Warwick Trading Co* • UKN
TOMMY'S ROCKING HORSE • 1911 • Melies Gaston • USA
TOMMY'S SISTER • 1912 • Ranous William V. • USA
TOMMY'S STRATAGEM • 1913 • Miller Ashley • USA
TOMMY'S TRAMP • 1914 • Thornby Robert T. • USA
TOMORROW • 1972 • Anthony Joseph • USA
TOMORROW • 1986 • Rosma Juha • FNL
TOMORROW see **DOMANI** • 1974
TOMORROW AND TOMORROW • 1932 • Wallace Richard • USA
TOMORROW AT MIDNIGHT (UKN) see **FOR LOVE OR MONEY** • 1939
TOMORROW AT SEVEN • 1933 • Enright Ray • USA • BLACK ACE, THE
TOMORROW AT TEN • 1962 • Comfort Lance • UKN
TOMORROW BEGINS TODAY: INDUSTRIAL RESEARCH • 1976 • Benegal Shyam • DCS • IND
TOMORROW BY AIR • 1947 • DOC • UKN • THIS MODERN AGE NO.3
TOMORROW FOR A WOMAN see **KVINNAS MORGONDAG, EN** • 1930
TOMORROW I'LL BE FREE see **MANANA SERE LIBRE** • 1988
TOMORROW I'LL WAKE UP AND SCALD MYSELF WITH TEA see **ZITRA VSTANU A OPARIM SE CAJEM** • 1977
TOMORROW IN ALABAMA see **MORGEN IN ALABAMA** • 1984
TOMORROW IS ANOTHER DAY • 1951 • Feist Felix E. • USA
TOMORROW IS ANOTHER DAY see **ASHITA WA ASHITA NO KAZE GA FUKU** • 1958
TOMORROW IS ANOTHER DAY see **MANANA SERS OTRO DIA** • 1967
TOMORROW IS FOREVER • 1946 • Pichel Irving • USA
TOMORROW IS MY FINAL DAY see **YARIN SON GUNDUR** • 1971
TOMORROW IS MY TURN (USA) see **PASSAGE DU RHIN, LE** • 1960
TOMORROW IS SUNDAY see **CROWDED DAY, THE** • 1954
TOMORROW IS THE FINAL DAY see **YARIN SON GUNDUR** • 1971
TOMORROW IS TOO LATE (UKN) see **DOMANI E TROPPO TARDI** • 1950
TOMORROW IT WILL BE FINE see **POGODA NA JUTRO** • 1954
TOMORROW IT'S OVER see **I MORGEN ER DET SLUT** • 1987
TOMORROW MAN, THE see **NINE EIGHTY FOUR –PRISONER OF THE FUTURE** • 1979
TOMORROW MEXICO see **JUTRO MEKSYK** • 1965
TOMORROW MY LOVE see **I MORGEN MIN ELSKEDE** • 1971
TOMORROW NEVER COMES • 1977 • Collinson Peter • UKN, CND
TOMORROW THE WORLD • 1944 • Fenton Leslie • USA
TOMORROW WE DIET • 1951 • Kinney Jack • ANS • USA
TOMORROW WE LIVE • 1936 • Haynes Manning • UKN
TOMORROW WE LIVE • 1942 • King George • UKN • AT DAWN WE DIE (USA)
TOMORROW WE LIVE • 1942 • Ulmer Edgar G. • USA • MAN WITH A CONSCIENCE, THE (UKN)
TOMORROW WE'LL DANCE see **DOMANI SI BALLA** • 1982
TOMORROW WILL BE A SUNDAY see **ASU WA NICHIYOBI** • 1953
TOMORROW WILL BE ANOTHER DAY see **MANANA SERS OTRO DIA** • 1967
TOMORROW WILL BE FRIDAY • 1901 • Williamson James • UKN
TOMORROW WILL BE FRIDAY • 1902 • Moss Hugh • UKN
TOMORROW WILL BE TOO LATE • 1974 • Karpov Alexander, Tyapak M. • USS, CZC
TOMORROW WILL BE TOO LATE see **YARIN COK GEC OLACAK** • 1967
TOMORROW YOU DIE see **CRAWLING HAND, THE** • 1963
TOMORROW'S A KILLER see **PRETTY KILL** • 1986
TOMORROW'S A WONDERFUL DAY • 1949 • Lehmann Siegfried
TOMORROW'S CANBERRA • 1972 • Schepisi Fred • DOC • ASL
TOMORROW'S CHILD • 1982 • Sargent Joseph • TVM • USA • GENESIS
TOMORROW'S CHILDREN • 1934 • Wilbur Crane • USA • UNBORN, THE (UKN)
TOMORROW'S CHILDREN • 1975 • Sky Laura • DOC • CND
TOMORROW'S COSTUME see **ASU ENO SEISO** • 1959
TOMORROW'S DANCERS see **ASHITA NO ODORIKO** • 1939
TOMORROW'S DELO • Pogacnik Joze • DCS • YGS
TOMORROW'S HEADLINES see **BEHIND THE HEADLINES** • 1937
TOMORROW'S ISLAND • 1968 • Crichton Charles • SHT • UKN
TOMORROW'S LOVE • 1925 • Bern Paul • USA
TOMORROW'S MELODY see **MORGONDAGENS MELODI** • 1942
TOMORROW'S MERSEYSIDERS • 1974 • Marquis Eric • UKN
TOMORROW'S PROMISE • 1967 • Owens Edward • USA
TOMORROW'S SATURDAY • 1962 • Grigsby Michael • UKN
TOMORROW'S WARRIOR see **AVRIANOS POLEMISTIS** • 1981
TOMORROW'S WEATHER, THE see **POGODA NA JUTRO** • 1954
TOMORROW'S WORLD • 1981 • Sargent Joseph • USA
TOMORROW'S YOUTH • 1935 • Lamont Charles • USA
TOMOSHIBI • 1954 • Hieki Mioji • JPN
TOMOYUKI YAMASHITA • 1953 • Saeki Kiyoshi • JPN • GENERAL YAMASHITA ○ YAMASHITA TOMOYUKI
TOM'S GANG • 1927 • De Lacy Robert • USA
TOM'S LITTLE STAR • 1920 • Terwilliger George W. • SHT • USA
TOM'S MISFIT • 1909 • *Powhatan* • USA
TOM'S PHOTO FINISH • 1957 • Hanna William, Barbera Joseph • ANS • USA
TOM'S RIDE • 1944 • Catling Darrell • UKN
TOM'S SACRIFICE • 1916 • Mix Tom • SHT • USA
TOM'S STRATEGY • 1916 • Mix Tom • SHT • USA
TOM'S TRAMPING TROUPE • 1917 • Howe J. A. • SHT • USA
TOM'S VACATION (UKN) see **TERROR MOUNTAIN** • 1928
TOMTIT • ANS • USS
TOMURAISHI–TACHI • 1968 • Misumi Kenji • JPN • FUNERAL RACKET, THE ○ UNDERTAKERS
TON KERO TON HELLINON • 1980 • Papastathis Lakis • GRC • WHEN THE GREEKS
TON OMBRE EST LA MIENNE • 1962 • Michel Andre • FRN, ITL • YOUR SHADOW IS MINE (USA)
TON SORT • 1921 • Berger Martin • FRG
TONARI NO TOTORO • 1988 • Mizayaki Hayao • ANM • JPN • TOTORO, THE NEIGHBOURHOOD GHOST
TONARI NO YAECHAN • 1934 • Shimazu Yasujiro • JPN • OUR NEIGHBOUR MISS YAE
TONARI NO YANE NO SHITA • 1931 • Naruse Mikio • JPN • UNDER THE NEIGHBORS' ROOF
TONARI–NO YARO • 1965 • Kuri Yoji • ANS • JPN • MAN NEXT DOOR, THE
TONDEUR DE CHIENS, LE • 1899-00 • Blache Alice • FRN
TONE NO CHISHIBUKI • 1959 • Namiki Kyotaro • JPN • FATAL ARMS

TONE NO KAWAGIRI • 1934 • Inagaki Hiroshi • JPN
TONELLI • 1943 • Tourjansky Victor • FRG
TONG DANG • 1988 • Liu Guochang • HKG • GANGS
TONG MAN, THE • 1919 • Worthington William • USA
TONG WAR see **CHINATOWN NIGHTS** • 1929
TONGDANG WANSUI see **T'UNG-TANG WAN-SUI** • 1989
TONGNIAN WANGSHI see **T'UNG-NIEN WANG-SHIH** • 1985
TONGS • 1989 • Metzger Alan • TVM • USA
TONGS see **TONGS: A NEW YORK CHINATOWN STORY** • 1986
TONGS: A CHINATOWN STORY see **TONGS: A NEW YORK CHINATOWN STORY** • 1986
TONGS: A NEW YORK CHINATOWN STORY • 1986 • Chen Xinjian • HKG • TONGS: A CHINATOWN STORY ○ TONGS
TONGUE AND CHEEK • 1988 • ISR
TONGUE MARK, THE • 1913 • *Mace Fred* • USA
TONGUE OF SCANDAL • 1927 • Clements Roy • USA
TONGUE OF SCANDAL, THE • 1910 • *Vitagraph* • USA
TONGUE TIED • 1970 • *Stacey Dist.* • USA
TONGUES OF FLAME • 1919 • Campbell Colin • USA
TONGUES OF FLAME • 1924 • Henabery Joseph • USA
TONGUES OF MEN, THE • 1916 • Lloyd Frank • USA
TONI • 1928 • Maude Arthur • UKN
TONI • 1935 • Renoir Jean • FRN • AMOURS DE TONI, LES
TONIC, THE • 1928 • Montagu Ivor • UKN
TONIGHT A TOWN DIES see **DZIS W NOCY UMRZE MIASTO** • 1961
TONIGHT AND EVERY NIGHT • 1945 • Saville Victor • USA
TONIGHT AND YOU see **UNDER SUSPICION** • 1931
TONIGHT AT 8.30 (USA) see **MEET ME TONIGHT** • 1952
TONIGHT AT TWELVE • 1929 • Pollard Harry • USA
TONIGHT BELONGS TO US see **MEN IN HER LIFE, THE** • 1941
TONIGHT FOR SURE! • 1962 • Coppola Francis Ford • USA • WIDE OPEN SPACES, THE ○ TONITE FOR SURE
TONIGHT I WILL ENTER YOUR CORPSE see **ESTA NOITE ENCARNAREI SEU CADAVER** • 1966
TONIGHT I WILL PAINT IN FLESH-COLOR see **ESTA NOITE ENCARNAREI SEU CADAVER** • 1966
TONIGHT IN BRITAIN • 1954 • Bryant Gerard • UKN
TONIGHT IS OURS • 1933 • Walker Stuart, Leisen Mitchell (U/c) • USA
TONIGHT LET'S ALL MAKE LOVE IN LONDON • 1968 • Whitehead Peter • DOC • UKN • TONITE LET'S ALL MAKE LOVE IN LONDON
TONIGHT OR NEVER • 1931 • LeRoy Mervyn • USA
TONIGHT OR NEVER see **I NATT ELLER ALDRIG** • 1941
TONIGHT OR NEVER see **CE SOIR OU JAMAIS** • 1960
TONIGHT OR NEVER see **HEUTE NACHT ODER NIE** • 1972
TONIGHT WE DANCE see **DANCING IN MANHATTAN** • 1945
TONIGHT WE RAID CALAIS • 1943 • Brahm John • USA • SECRET MISSION
TONIGHT WE SING • 1953 • Leisen Mitchell • USA
TONIGHT'S THE NIGHT • 1932 • Banks Monty • UKN • BILL TAKES A HOLIDAY
TONIGHT'S THE NIGHT • 1987 • Roth Bobby • TVM • USA
TONIGHT'S THE NIGHT (USA) see **HAPPY EVER AFTER** • 1954
TONIO KROGER • 1964 • Thiele Rolf • FRG, FRN
TONIO, SON OT THE SIERRAS • 1925 • Wilson Ben • USA
TONISCHA • 1929 • Anton Karl • CZC
TONITE FOR SURE see **TONIGHT FOR SURE!** • 1962
TONITE LET'S ALL MAKE LOVE IN LONDON see **TONIGHT LET'S ALL MAKE LOVE IN LONDON** • 1968
TONKA • 1958 • Foster Lewis R. • USA • HORSE CALLED COMANCHE, A
TONKA OF THE GALLOWS see **TONKA SIBENICE** • 1930
TONKA SIBENICE • 1930 • Anton Karl • CZC • TONKA, TART OF THE GALLOWS MOB ○ TONKA OF THE GALLOWS
TONKA, TART OF THE GALLOWS MOB see **TONKA SIBENICE** • 1930
TONNEAU DES DANAIDES, LE • 1900 • Melies Georges • FRN • DAINAID'S BARREL, THE (USA) ○ EIGHT GIRLS IN A BARREL
TONNELIER, LE • 1942 • Rouquier Georges • SHT • FRN
TONNENDE WELLE, DIE • 1921 • Ruttmann Walter • SHT • FRG
TONNERRE, LE • 1921 • Delluc Louis • FRN • EVANGELINE ET LE TONNERRE
TONNERRE DE BREST, SILENCE! • 1984 • Zaninetta Armand, Bastien Didier • BLG
TONNERRE DE DIEU, LE • 1965 • de La Patelliere Denys • FRN, ITL, FRG • MATRIMONIO ALLA FRANCESE (ITL) ○ HERR AUF SCHLOSS BRASSAC (FRG) ○ GOD'S THUNDER (UKN)
TONNERRE DE JUPITER, LE • 1903 • Melies Georges • FRN • JUPITER'S THUNDERBOLTS OR THE HOME OF THE MUSES
TONNERRE SUR L'OCEAN INDIEN (FRN) see **GRANDE COLPO DI SURCOUF, IL** • 1967
TONNERRE SUR SAINT-PETERSBURG see **J'AI TUE RASPOUTINE** • 1967
TONNES DE L'AUDACE, LES • 1960 • Quinet Rene, Sommet Louis • DOC • FRN
TONNY • 1962 • Muller Nils R. • NRW
TONO MONOGATARI • 1983 • Murano Tetsutaro • JPN
TONOSAMA YAJIKITA • 1960 • Sawashima Chu • JPN • SAMURAI VAGABONDS
TONS OF MONEY • 1924 • Crane Frank H. • UKN
TONS OF MONEY • 1931 • Walls Tom • UKN
TONS OF TROUBLE • 1956 • Hiscott Leslie • UKN
TONSORIAL LEOPARD TAMER, THE • 1924 • MacGregor Norval • USA
TONTA DEL BOTE, LA • 1939 • Delgras Gonzalo • SPN
TONTA DEL BOTE, LA • 1971 • de Orduna Juan • SPN
TONTO BASIN OUTLAWS • 1941 • Luby S. Roy • USA
TONTO KID, THE • 1935 • Fraser Harry L. • USA
TONTO QUE HACIA MILAGROS, EL • 1983 • Hernandez Mario • MXC • FOOL WHO MADE MIRACLES, THE
TONTONS FLINGEURS, LES • 1963 • Lautner Georges • FRN, FRG, ITL • MEIN ONKEL, DER GANGSTER (ITL) ○ MONSIEUR GANGSTER (USA) ○ CROOKS IN CLOVER (UKN)
TONY • 1915 • Lessey George A. • USA
TONY AMERICA • 1918 • Heffron Thomas N. • USA
TONY AMERICA see **PUPPETS OF FATE** • 1921
TONY AND MALONEY • 1914 • *Lockwood Harold* • USA
TONY AND MARIE • 1915 • Ince John • USA
TONY AND THE STORK • 1911 • *Baggot King* • USA
TONY AND THE TICK-TOCK DRAGON see **HAHO, OCSI!** • 1971
TONY ARZENTA • 1973 • Tessari Duccio • ITL, FRN • BIG GUNS (FRN) ○ NO WAY OUT (USA)
TONY DOG, DER GEHEIMNISVOLLE TOTE • *Strassburger & Co* • FRG • VIER WOCHEN LEBENDIG BEGRABEN
TONY DRAWS A HORSE • 1950 • Carstairs John Paddy • UKN
TONY KINSEY QUARTET, THE • 1961 • Henryson Robert • SHT • UKN
TONY PASTOR AND HIS ORCHESTRA • 1948 • Cowan Will • SHT • USA
TONY, RANDI AND MARIE • 1973 • Hallis Ron • DOC • CND
TONY ROMAN • 1966 • Fournier Claude • DOC • CND
TONY ROME • 1967 • Douglas Gordon • USA
TONY RUNS WILD • 1926 • Buckingham Thomas • USA
TONY, THE FIDDLER • 1913 • Wharton Theodore • USA
TONY THE GREASER • 1911 • Melies Gaston • USA
TONY, THE GREASER • 1914 • Sturgeon Rollin S. • USA
TONY, THE TENOR • 1915 • *Pilot* • USA
TONY, THE WOP • 1915 • Christie Al • USA
TONY, TOBE PRESKOCILO • 1968 • Plivova-Simkova Vera, Kralova Drahuse • CZC • YOU HAVE A BEE IN YOUR BONNET, TONY ○ TONY YOU ARE NUTS
TONY WOULD BE A COWBOY • 1911 • *Champion* • USA
TONY YOU ARE NUTS see **TONY, TOBE PRESKOCILO** • 1968
TONY'S OATH OF VENGEANCE • 1912 • *Edison* • USA
TONY'S SACRIFICE • 1913 • *Mills Thomas R.* • USA
TOO ARDENT LOVER • 1903 • *Bitzer Billy (Ph)* • USA
TOO BAD, EDDIE • 1916 • Humphrey Orral • SHT • USA
TOO BAD SHE'S BAD (UKN) see **PECCATO CHE SIA UNA CANAGLIA** • 1955
TOO BAZOOKA • 1964 • Kamerling Norman • SHT • USA
TOO BEAUTIFUL FOR YOU (UKN) see **TROP BELLE POUR TOI!** • 1989
TOO BIG • 1987 • Kokkonen Ere • FNL
TOO BUSY TO WORK • 1932 • Blystone John G. • USA
TOO BUSY TO WORK • 1939 • Brower Otto • USA
TOO CLEVER BY HALF • 1916 • Drew Sidney • SHT • USA
TOO CLEVER FOR ONCE see **COCKSURE'S CLEVER RUSE** • 1910
TOO CLEVER TO LIVE see **MAN WHO CRIED WOLF, THE** • 1937
TOO CRAZY see **DOIDA DEMAIS** • 1988
TOO DANGEROUS TO LIVE • 1939 • Norman Leslie, Hankey Anthony • UKN
TOO DANGEROUS TO LOVE (UKN) see **PERFECT STRANGERS** • 1949
TOO DEVOTED WIFE, A • 1907 • Fitzhamon Lewin • UKN
TOO FAR TO GO • 1979 • Cook Fielder • TVM • USA
TOO FAT TO FIGHT • 1918 • Henley Hobart • USA
TOO GOOD TO BE TRUE • 1919 • *Treux Ernest* • SHT • USA
TOO HOP TO HANDLE • 1956 • McKimson Robert • ANS • USA
TOO HOT TO HANDLE • 1930 • Foster Lewis R. • SHT • USA
TOO HOT TO HANDLE • 1938 • Conway Jack • USA
TOO HOT TO HANDLE • 1960 • Young Terence • UKN • PLAYGIRL AFTER DARK
TOO HOT TO HANDLE • 1978 • Schain Don • USA
TOO HUNGRY TO EAT • 1908 • *Urban-Eclipse* • USA
TOO KEEN A SENSE OF HUMOUR • 1911 • Wilson Frank? • UKN
TOO LATE • 1914 • Farnum Marshall • USA
TOO LATE BLUES • 1962 • Cassavetes John • USA
TOO LATE BY A FEW DAYS.. see **A QUELQUES JOURS PRES** • 1968
TOO LATE FOR LOVE see **THERE'S ALWAYS TOMORROW** • 1934
TOO LATE FOR LOVE? see **GODINI ZA LYUBOV** • 1957
TOO LATE FOR TEARS • 1949 • Haskin Byron • USA
TOO LATE THE HERO • 1970 • Aldrich Robert • USA • SUICIDE RUN
TOO LATE TO LOVE (USA) see **POURQUOI VIENS-TU SI TARD?** • 1959
TOO LAZY TO WORK, TOO HONEST TO STEAL • 1902 • *Warwick Trading Co* • UKN
TOO MANY ADMIRERS • 1910 • Coleby A. E. • UKN
TOO MANY AUNTS • 1914 • *Lubin* • USA
TOO MANY BACHELORS • 1915 • *Pearce Peggy* • USA
TOO MANY BILLS • 1919 • *Strand* • USA
TOO MANY BLONDES • 1941 • Freeland Thornton • USA
TOO MANY BRIDES • 1914 • Sennett Mack • USA
TOO MANY BURGLARS • 1911 • Sennett Mack • USA
TOO MANY BURGLARS • 1920 • Lyons Eddie, Moran Lee • SHT • USA
TOO MANY CASEY'S • 1912 • *Shea William* • USA
TOO MANY CHEFS • 1916 • Mix Tom • SHT • USA
TOO MANY CHEFS (UKN) see **WHO IS KILLING THE GREAT CHEFS OF EUROPE?** • 1978
TOO MANY COOKS • 1914 • MacDonald Donald • USA
TOO MANY COOKS • 1921 • Brunel Adrian • UKN
TOO MANY COOKS • 1931 • Seiter William A. • USA
TOO MANY COPS • 1913 • *Kalem* • USA
TOO MANY CROOKS • 1915 • Christie Al • USA
TOO MANY CROOKS • 1919 • Ince Ralph • USA
TOO MANY CROOKS • 1927 • Newmeyer Fred • USA
TOO MANY CROOKS • 1930 • King George • UKN
TOO MANY CROOKS • 1959 • Zampi Mario • UKN
TOO MANY DETECTIVES • 1953 • Burn Oscar, Wall John • UKN
TOO MANY ENGAGEMENTS • 1911 • *Essanay* • USA
TOO MANY GIRLS • 1910 • Porter Edwin S. • USA
TOO MANY GIRLS • 1940 • Abbott George • USA
TOO MANY HIGHBALLS • 1933 • Bruckman Clyde • SHT • USA
TOO MANY HUSBANDS • 1914 • Drew Sidney • USA
TOO MANY HUSBANDS • 1918 • *Triangle* • SHT • USA
TOO MANY HUSBANDS • 1931 • Pearce A. Leslie • SHT • USA
TOO MANY HUSBANDS • 1938 • Campbell Ivar • UKN
TOO MANY HUSBANDS • 1940 • Ruggles Wesley • USA • MY TWO HUSBANDS (UKN)
TOO MANY JOHNNIES • 1914 • *Kalem* • USA
TOO MANY KISSES • 1925 • Sloane Paul • USA
TOO MANY LOVERS (USA) see **CHARMANTS GARCONS** • 1957
TOO MANY MAIDS • 1913 • *Kinemacolor* • USA
TOO MANY MAMAS • 1924 • McCarey Leo • SHT • USA • TOO MANY MAMMAS
TOO MANY MAMMAS see **TOO MANY MAMAS** • 1924
TOO MANY MILLIONS • 1918 • Cruze James • USA
TOO MANY MILLIONS • 1934 • Young Harold • UKN
TOO MANY MOONS see **ZOKU IZUKOE** • 1967
TOO MANY ON THE JOB • 1909 • *Vitagraph* • USA
TOO MANY PARENTS • 1936 • McGowan Robert • USA
TOO MANY PARENTS see **IMAM DVIJE MAME I DVA TATE** • 1968
TOO MANY SMITHS • 1915 • Christie Al • USA
TOO MANY SUSPECTS see **ELLERY QUEEN** • 1975
TOO MANY SWEETHEARTS • 1919 • *Strand* • SHT • USA
TOO MANY TENANTS • 1913 • *Patheplay* • USA
TOO MANY THIEVES • 1968 • Biberman Abner • TVM • USA
TOO MANY TOO SOON • 1961 • Peries Lester James • SHT • SLN
TOO MANY WINNERS • 1947 • Beaudine William • USA
TOO MANY WIVES • 1914 • *Luna* • USA
TOO MANY WIVES • 1919 • *Ham Harry* • SHT • USA
TOO MANY WIVES • 1927 • *Shearer Norma* • USA
TOO MANY WIVES • 1933 • King George • UKN
TOO MANY WIVES • 1937 • Holmes Ben • USA
TOO MANY WIVES • 1951 • Yates Hal • SHT • USA
TOO MANY WOMEN • 1929 • Newfield Sam • SHT • USA
TOO MANY WOMEN • 1932 • Mack Anthony, French Lloyd • SHT • USA
TOO MANY WOMEN • 1942 • Ray Bernard B. • USA
TOO MANY WOMEN (UKN) see **GOD'S GIFT TO WOMEN** • 1931
TOO MUCH • 1987 • Rochat Eric • USA
TOO MUCH ALIKE • 1917 • *Pokes & Jabbs* • SHT • USA
TOO MUCH AUNT • 1911 • *American* • USA
TOO MUCH BEEF • 1936 • Hill Robert F. • USA
TOO MUCH BULL • 1915 • *Handworth Octavia* • USA
TOO MUCH BURGLAR • 1914 • Costello Maurice, Gaillord Robert • USA
TOO MUCH BUSINESS • 1922 • Robbins Jess • USA
TOO MUCH CHAMPAGNE • 1908 • *Vitagraph* • USA
TOO MUCH DOG BISCUIT • 1909 • *Essanay* • USA
TOO MUCH ELEPHANT • 1918 • *Horsley David* • SHT • USA
TOO MUCH ELIXIR OF LIFE • 1915 • *Fralick Allan* • USA
TOO MUCH FOR GALVEZ see **DEMASIADO PARA GALVEZ** • 1981
TOO MUCH FOR LIVING.. TOO LITTLE FOR DYING see **TROPPO PER VIVERE.. POCO PER MORIRE** • 1967
TOO MUCH FOR ONE MAN see **IMMORALE, L'** • 1967
TOO MUCH HARMONY • 1933 • Sutherland A. Edward • USA
TOO MUCH HENRY • 1917 • Drew Sidney, Drew Sidney Mrs. • SHT • USA
TOO MUCH INJUN • 1911 • *Powers* • USA
TOO MUCH JOHNSON • 1920 • Crisp Donald • USA
TOO MUCH JOHNSON • 1938 • Welles Orson • USA
TOO MUCH LIMELIGHT see **HOT WATER** • 1937
TOO MUCH LOBSTER • 1909 • Fitzhamon Lewin? • UKN
TOO MUCH MARRIED • 1914 • *Sisson Vera* • USA
TOO MUCH MARRIED • 1916 • Dillon John Francis • SHT • USA
TOO MUCH MARRIED • 1921 • Dunlap Scott R. • USA
TOO MUCH MONEY • 1926 • Dillon John Francis • USA
TOO MUCH MOTHER-IN-LAW • 1907 • USA
TOO MUCH MOTHER-IN-LAW • 1911 • *Selig* • USA
TOO MUCH MUSTARD see **MAX, PROFESSEUR DE TANGO** • 1912
TOO MUCH OF A GOOD THING • 1902 • Smith G. A. • UKN
TOO MUCH PARCEL POST • 1913 • *Pathe* • USA
TOO MUCH PROTECTION • 1910 • *Lubin* • USA
TOO MUCH REALISM • 1911 • *Kalem* • USA
TOO MUCH SAUSAGE • 1916 • Booth W. R. • UKN
TOO MUCH SPEED • 1921 • Urson Frank • USA
TOO MUCH SUN • 1990 • Downey Robert • USA
TOO MUCH TALK see **OHAYO** • 1959
TOO MUCH TO CARRY see **KDO SVE NEBE NEUNESE** • 1959
TOO MUCH, TOO OFTEN! • 1968 • Silverman Louis • USA • TOO MUCH, TOO SOON
TOO MUCH, TOO SOON • 1958 • Napoleon Art • USA
TOO MUCH, TOO SOON see **TOO MUCH, TOO OFTEN!** • 1968
TOO MUCH TURKEY • 1911 • *Essanay* • USA
TOO MUCH TURKEY • 1914 • *Princess* • USA
TOO MUCH TURKEY • 1915 • Anderson G. M. • USA
TOO MUCH UNCLE see **WIFE WANTED** • 1914
TOO MUCH WIFE • 1922 • Heffron Thomas N. • USA
TOO MUCH WOOING OF HANDSOME DAN • 1912 • *Vitagraph* • USA
TOO MUCH YOUTH • 1925 • Worne Duke • USA
TOO OUTRAGEOUS! • 1988 • Benner Richard • CND
TOO PROUD TO BEG • 1914 • *Reliance* • USA
TOO SCARED TO SCREAM • 1982 • Lo Bianco Tony • USA • DOORMAN
TOO SMALL FOR SUCH A GREAT WAR • 1969 • Gabrea Radu • RMN
TOO SOON TO DIE see **SVEGLIATI E UCCIDI (LUTRING)** • 1966
TOO SOON TO LAUGH, TOO LATE TO CRY • Moberly Luke • USA
TOO SOON TO LOVE • 1960 • Rush Richard • USA • TEENAGE LOVERS (UKN) ○ HIGH SCHOOL HONEYMOON
TOO STRONG see **TROPPO FORTE** • 1985
TOO TIRED • 1919 • Santell Alfred • SHT • USA • TWO TIRED
TOO TOUGH TO KILL • 1935 • Lederman D. Ross • USA
TOO WEAK TO WORK • 1943 • Sparber I. • ANS • USA
TOO WISE WIVES • 1921 • Weber Lois • USA
TOO YOUNG FOR LOVE see **ZU JUNG FUR DIE LIEBE** • 1961
TOO YOUNG FOR LOVE (USA) see **ETA DELL'AMORE, L'** • 1953
TOO YOUNG THE HERO • 1988 • Kulik Buzz • TVM • USA
TOO YOUNG TO KISS • 1951 • Leonard Robert Z. • USA
TOO YOUNG TO KNOW • 1945 • De Cordova Frederick • USA
TOO YOUNG TO LOVE • 1960 • Box Muriel • UKN
TOO YOUNG TO MARRY • 1931 • LeRoy Mervyn • USA • BROKEN DISHES

TOO YOUNG, TOO IMMORAL! • 1962 • Phelan Raymond A. • USA • TWISTED MORALS

TOODLES • 1912 • *Majestic* • USA

TOODLES • 1917 • *Sparkle* • USA

TOODLES, TOM AND TROUBLE • 1915 • *Campbell Colin* • USA

TOOFANI TAKKAR • 1946 • Khan A. M. • IND • TYPHOON TAKKAR

TOOFANI TARZAN • 1937 • Wadia Homi • IND • TYPHOON TARZAN

TOOFANI TARZAN • 1962 • Zamindar A. R. • IND • TYPHOON TARZAN

TOOLBOX MURDERS, THE • 1978 • Donnelly Dennis • USA

TOOLBOX MURDERS II, THE • 1987 • Bare Richard L. • USA

TOOLS OF PROVIDENCE • 1915 • *Hart William S.* • USA

TOOLS OF THE DEVIL • 1984 • Yalden-Tomson Peter • MTV • CND

TOOLSIDAS see **TULSIDAS** • 1934

TOOMORROW • 1970 • Guest Val • UKN

TOONERVILLE FOLKS • 1936 • Gillett Burt, Palmer Tom • ASS • USA

TOONERVILLE PICNIC • 1936 • Gillett Burt • ANS • USA

TOONERVILLE TROLLEY • 1920 • *Mason Dann* • SHT • USA

TOONERVILLE TROLLEY • 1936 • Gillett Burt, Palmer Tom • ANS • USA

TOOT! TOOT! • 1927 • Fleischer Dave • ANS • USA

TOOT, WHISTLE, PLUNK AND BOOM • 1953 • Nichols Charles, Kimball Ward • ANS • USA

TOOTH FOR TOOTH see **ZUB ZA ZUB** • 1912

TOOTH OR CONSEQUENCES • 1947 • Smith Howard • ANS • USA

TOOTH WILL OUT • 1933 • Cadman Frank • UKN

TOOTH WILL OUT, THE • 1951 • Bernds Edward • SHT • USA • YANK AT THE DENTIST, A

TOOTHACHE! • 1913 • *Brennan John* • USA

TOOTHACHES AND HEARTACHES • 1917 • De Vonde Chester M. • SHT • USA

TOOTHLESS BEAVER, THE • 1965 • Rasinski Connie • ANS • USA

TOOTLES BUYS A GUN • 1912 • Aylott Dave? • UKN

TOOTSIE • 1917 • Drew Sidney, Drew Sidney Mrs. • SHT • USA

TOOTSIE • 1982 • Pollack Sydney • USA

TOOTSIES AND TAMALES • 1919 • Smith Noel • SHT • USA

TOP, THE • 1965 • Murakami Jimmy T. • ANS • USA

TOP BANANA • 1954 • Green Alfred E. • USA

TOP CRACK • 1967 • Russo Mario L. F. • ITL

TOP DOG see **WODZIREJ** • 1978

TOP DOG, THE • 1918 • Bocchi Arrigo • UKN

TOP DOGS • 1960 • Halas John • ANS • UKN

TOP END • 1970 • Crombie Donald • SHT • ASL

TOP FLAT • 1935 • Terhune William, Jevne Jack • SHT • USA

TOP FLIGHT • 1964 • Spiro Julian • DCS • UKN

TOP FLOOR GIRL • 1959 • Varnel Max • UKN

TOP GEAR • 1972 • Miller Arnold Louis • DOC • UKN

TOP GUN • 1986 • Scott Anthony • USA

TOP HAND • 1925 • *Bailey Bill* • USA

TOP HAT • 1935 • Sandrich Mark • USA

TOP HAT AND SPUDS NOSE see **KEMENYKALAP ES KRUMPLIORR** • 1978

TOP-HEAVY FROG, THE see **FUKUSUKE** • 1957

TOP-HIT-GIRL • 1969 • Buyens Frans • BLG

TOP JOB (FRG) see **AD OGNI COSTO** • 1967

TOP KIDS • 1987 • Pfleghar Michael • USA

TOP LINE • 1987 • Rossati Nello • ITL

TOP MAN • 1943 • Lamont Charles • USA • MAN OF THE FAMILY (UKN)

TOP MAN see **MY PAL GUS** • 1952

TOP MODEL see **ELEVEN DAYS, ELEVEN NIGHTS: PART 2** • 1988

TOP O' THE MORNING • 1949 • Miller David • USA

TOP O' THE MORNING, THE • 1922 • Laemmle Edward • USA

TOP OF A CONTINENT • 1961 • Crawley Judith • DOC • CND

TOP OF HIS HEAD • 1988 • Mettler Peter • CND

TOP OF NEW YORK, THE • 1913 • *Thanhouser* • USA

TOP OF NEW YORK, THE • 1922 • Taylor William D. • USA

TOP OF THE BILL • 1971 • Miller Arnold Louis • UKN

TOP OF THE BILL (UKN) see **FANNY FOLEY HERSELF** • 1931

TOP OF THE FORM • 1953 • Carstairs John Paddy • UKN

TOP OF THE HEAP • 1972 • St. John Christopher • USA

TOP OF THE TOWN • 1937 • Murphy Ralph • USA

TOP OF THE WORLD • 1955 • Foster Lewis R. • USA

TOP OF THE WORLD, THE • 1925 • Melford George • USA

TOP PRIORITY • 1981 • Patel Ishu • ANS • CND

TOP SECRET • 1950 • Davis Redd • UKN

TOP SECRET • 1952 • Zampi Mario • UKN • MR. POTTS GOES TO MOSCOW (USA)

TOP SECRET • 1978 • Leaf Paul • TVM • USA

TOP SECRET • 1984 • Abrahams Jim, Zucker David, Zucker Jerry • USA

TOP SECRET AFFAIR • 1956 • Potter H. C. • USA • THEIR SECRET AFFAIR (UKN)

TOP SECRET OF TORTURING WOMEN see **GOKUHI ONNA GOMON** • 1968

TOP SENSATION • 1969 • Alessi Ottavio • ITL • SEDUCERS, THE (USA) ○ SENSATION

TOP SERGEANT • 1942 • Cabanne W. Christy • USA

TOP SERGEANT MULLIGAN • 1928 • Hogan James P. • USA

TOP SERGEANT MULLIGAN • 1941 • Yarbrough Jean • USA

TOP SPEED • 1929 • Lamont Charles • SHT • USA

TOP SPEED • 1930 • LeRoy Mervyn • USA

TOP TEN • 1967 • Feleo Ben • PHL

TOPA TOPA • 1938 • Hutchison Charles, Moore Vin • USA • CHILDREN OF THE WILD (UKN)

TOPAZ • 1969 • Hitchcock Alfred • USA

TOPAZ see **SANG GURU** • 1981

TOPAZE • 1932 • Gasnier Louis J. • FRN

TOPAZE • 1933 • D'Arrast Harry D'Abbadie • USA

TOPAZE • 1936 • Pagnol Marcel • FRN

TOPAZE • 1950 • Pagnol Marcel • FRN

TOPCAT • 1960 • Kneitel Seymour • ANS • USA

TOPEKA • 1953 • Carr Thomas • USA

TOPEKA TERROR, THE • 1945 • Bretherton Howard • USA

TOPF, DER • 1963 • Kristl Vlado • SHT • FRG

TOPHAR-MUMIE, DIE • 1920 • Guter Johannes • FRG

TOPI GRIGI, I • 1918 • Ghione Emilio • SRL • ITL

TOPICAL SPANISH • 1971 • Masats Ramon • SPN

TOPICAL TAPS • 1921 • ASL

TOPICAL TRICKS • 1904 • Booth W. R. • UKN

TOPIO STIN OMIHLI • 1988 • Angelopoulos Theo • GRC, ITL, FRN • LANDSCAPE IN THE MIST

TOPKAPI • 1964 • Dassin Jules • USA, FRN • LIGHT OF DAY, THE

TOPLE GODINE • 1966 • Lazic Dragoslav • YGS • FEVERISH YEARS, THE ○ HOT YEARS, THE ○ WARM YEARS, THE

TOPLESS STORY, THE (UKN) see **"OBEN-OHNE" STORY, DIE** • 1965

TOPLITSKY & CO. • 1913 • Nicholls George • USA

TOPO, EL • 1971 • Jodorowsky Alejandro • MXC • MOLE, THE ○ GOPHER, THE

TOPO GIGIO AND THE MISSILE WAR see **TOPPO JIJO NO BOTAN SENSO** • 1967

TOPO GIGIO E I SEI LADRI see **TOPPO JIJO NO BOTAN SENSO** • 1967

TOPO GIGIO: LA GUERRE DEL MISSILE see **TOPPO JIJO NO BOTAN SENSO** • 1967

TOPOS • 1985 • Angelidi Antoinette • GRC • BODY'S LITTLE THEATRE, THE

TOPOS KRANIOU • 1972 • Aristopoulos Konstantinos • GRC • CRANIUM LANDSCAPE ○ PLACE OF A SKULL, A ○ SITE OF A SKULL

TOPPER • 1937 • McLeod Norman Z. • USA

TOPPER • 1979 • Dubin Charles S. • TVM • USA

TOPPER RETURNS • 1941 • Del Ruth Roy • USA

TOPPER TAKES A TRIP • 1939 • McLeod Norman Z. • USA

TOPPER TRIUMPHANT • 1914 • Plumb Hay? • UKN

TOPPO JIJO NO BOTAN SENSO • 1967 • Ichikawa Kon • JPN, ITL • TOPO GIGIO: LA GUERRE DEL MISSILE ○ TOPO GIGIO E I SEI LADRI ○ TOPO GIGIO AND THE MISSILE WAR

TOPRAGIN TERI • 1982 • Baytan Natuk • TRK • SWEATING SOIL, THE

TOPRINI NASZ • 1939 • De Toth Andre • HNG • WEDDING IN JAPAN (USA) ○ WEDDING IN TOPRIN

TOPS IN THE BIG TOP • 1945 • Sparber I. • ANS • USA

TOPS IS THE LIMIT see **ANYTHING GOES** • 1936

TOPS WITH POPS • 1957 • Hanna William, Barbera Joseph • ANS • USA

TOPSY AND EVA • 1927 • Lord Del, Griffith D. W. (U/c) • USA

TOPSY TURKEY • 1948 • Marcus Sid • ANS • USA

TOPSY TURVY • 1984 • Fleming Edward • DNM

TOPSY TURVY see **YASSA MOSSA** • 1953

TOPSY-TURVY DANCE BY THREE QUAKER MAIDENS • 1902 • Smith G. A. • UKN

TOPSY-TURVY JOURNEY (USA) see **GYAKUTEN RYOKO** • 1969

TOPSY-TURVY SWEEDIE • 1914 • *Beery Wallace* • USA

TOPSY TURVY TWINS, THE • 1917 • Stanton Richard • SHT • USA

TOPSY-TURVY VILLA • 1900 • Hepworth Cecil M. • UKN

TOPSY TURVY'S LOVE AFFAIR • 1912 • *Reliance* • USA

TOPSY TV • 1957 • Rasinski Connie • ANS • USA

TOPSY'S DREAM OF TOYLAND • 1911 • Coleby A. E. • UKN

TOQUE DE QUEDA • 1978 • Nunez Inaki • SPN • CURFEW ○ HOUR OF CONFINEMENT

TOR see **TAUR, IL RE DELLA FORZA BRUTA** • 1963

TOR DER FREIHEIT, DAS • 1919 • Schmidthassler Walter • FRG

TOR, KING OF BEASTS • 1962 • Glut Don • SHT • USA

TOR, MIGHTY WARRIOR see **TAUR, IL RE DELLA FORZA BRUTA** • 1963

TOR ZUM FRIEDEN, DAS • 1951 • Liebeneiner Wolfgang • FRG

TOR ZUM PARADIES, DAS see **SELTSAME GESCHICHTE DES BRANDNER KASPER, DIE** • 1949

TORA NO OO FUMA OTOKOTACHI • 1945 • Kurosawa Akira • JPN • MEN WHO TREAD ON THE TIGER'S TAIL, THE ○ WALKERS ON THE TIGER'S TAIL ○ THEY WHO STEP ON THE TIGER'S TAIL

TORA-SAN FINDS A SWEETHEART see **OTOKO WA TSURAIYO, AIAIGASA** • 1975

TORA-SAN GOES TO VIENNA see **OTOKO WA TSURAIYO, TORAJIRO KOKORONO TABIJI** • 1989

TORA-SAN, OUR LOVABLE TRAMP see **OTOKO WA TSURAIYO** • 1969

TORA-SAN PT. 2 (USA) see **ZOKU OTOKOWA TSURAIYO** • 1969

TORA-SAN, THE EXPERT see **OTOKO WA TSURAIYO, HANA MO ARASHI MO TORAJIRO** • 1983

TORA-SAN THE MATCHMAKER • Yamada Yoji • JPN

TORA-SAN'S CHERISHED MOTHER see **ZOKU OTOKOWA TSURAIYO** • 1969

TORA-SAN'S GRAND SCHEME see **SHIN OTOKO WA TSURAIYO** • 1970

TORA-SAN'S SALAD DATE MEMORIAL see **TORAJIRO SARADA KINENBI** • 1988

TORA! TORA! TORA! • 1970 • Fleischer Richard, Masuda Toshio, Fukasaku Kinji • USA, JPN

TORA YA RADITEBLE • 1983 • SAF

TORACHAN NO BOKEN • 1955 • *Toei Doga* • ANS • JPN • ADVENTURES OF LITTLE TIGER

TORAJIRO SARADA KINENBI • 1988 • Yamada Yoji • JPN • TORA-SAN'S SALAD DATE MEMORIAL

TORAK • 1985 • SAF

TORASAN AND A LOVELY MAID see **OTOKO WA TSURAIYO, UWASA NO TORAJIRO** • 1978

TORASAN AND A PAPER BALLOON see **OTOKO WA TSURAIYO, TORAJIRO KAMIFUSEN** • 1982

TORASAN AND HIS FORGET-ME-NOT see **OTOKO WA TSURAIYO, TORAJIRO** • 1973

TORASAN AND THE PAINTER see **OTOKO WA TSURAIYO, TORAJIRO YUYAKE KOYAKE** • 1976

TORASAN, BLUEBIRD OF HAPPINESS see **OTOKO WA TSURAIYO, SHIAWASTE NO AOI TORI** • 1987

TORASAN DREAMS SPRINGTIME see **OTOKO WA TSURAIYO, TORAJIRO HARU NO YUME** • 1979

TORASAN, FROM SHIBAMATA WITH LOVE see **OTOKO WA TSURAIYO, SHIBAMATA YORI AI O KOMETE** • 1985

TORASAN GOES TO HISBISCUS LAND see **OTOKO WA TSURAIYO, HISBISCUS NO HANA** • 1981

TORASAN, HOLD OUT! see **OTOKO WA TSURAIYO, TORAJIRO GAMBARE!** • 1977

TORASAN, HOMEWARD JOURNEY see **ZOKU OTOKOWA TSURAIYO** • 1969

TORASAN LOVES AN ARTIST see **OTOKO WA TSURAIYO, WATASHI NO TORASAN** • 1973

TORASAN MEETS A LADY SCHOLAR see **OTOKO WA TSURAIYO, KATSUSHIKA RISSHI-HEN** • 1975

TORASAN MEETS HIS SCHOOL-MATES see **OTOKO WA TSURAIYO, TORAJIRO JUNJO SHISHU** • 1976

TORASAN, REMIND SHIRETOKE see **OTOKO WA TSURAIYO, SHIRETOKO BOJO** • 1988

TORASAN RIDING HIGH see **OTOKO WA TSURAIYO, TONDERU TORAJIRO** • 1979

TORASAN WHISTLING see **OTOKO WA TSURAIYO, KUCHIBUE O FUKU TORAJIRO** • 1984

TORASAN'S JOURNEY WITH A LADY see **OTOKO WA TSURAIYO, TABI TO ONNA TO TORAJIRO** • 1984

TORASAN'S LOVE IN OSAKA see **OTOKO WA TSURAIYO, NANIWA NO KOI NO TORAJIRO** • 1982

TORASAN'S SONG OF THE SEAGULL see **OTOKO WA TSURAIYO, TORAJIRO KAMOMEUTA** • 1981

TORBELLINO • 1941 • Marquina Luis • SPN

TORBELLINO see **RENCOR DE LA TIERRA, EL** • 1949

TORBIDI MISTERI DELLA SENSUALITA, I • 1977 • Polselli Renato • ITL

TORCH, THE (USA) see **DEL ODIO NACIO EL AMOR** • 1949

TORCH BEARER, THE • 1916 • Russell William, Prescott John • USA

TORCH BEARER, THE see **FROM THE WEST** • 1920

TORCH SINGER • 1933 • Hall Alexander, Somnes George • USA • BROADWAY SINGER (UKN)

TORCH SONG • 1953 • Walters Charles • USA

TORCH SONG, THE see **LAUGHING SINNERS** • 1931

TORCH SONG TRILOGY • 1988 • Bogart Paul • USA

TORCHES see **POCHODNE** • 1960

TORCHES HUMAINES • 1908 • Melies Georges • FRN • JUSTINIAN'S HUMAN TORCHES (USA)

TORCHLIGHT • 1985 • Wright Tom • USA

TORCHLIGHT PROCESSION see **FAKKELGANG** • 1932

TORCHY • 1920 • *Hines Johnny* • USA

TORCHY BLANE IN CHINATOWN • 1939 • Beaudine William • USA

TORCHY BLANE IN PANAMA • 1938 • Clemens William • USA • TROUBLE IN PANAMA (UKN)

TORCHY BLANE -PLAYING WITH DYNAMITE see **TORCHY PLAYS WITH DYNAMITE** • 1939

TORCHY BLANE, THE AMOROUS BLONDE • 1937 • McDonald Frank • USA • ADVENTUROUS BLONDE

TORCHY COMES THROUGH • 1920 • *Hines Johnny* • USA

TORCHY GETS HER MAN • 1938 • Beaudine William • USA

TORCHY IN HIGH • 1920 • *Hines Johnny* • USA

TORCHY PLAYS WITH DYNAMITE • 1939 • Smith Noel • USA • TORCHY BLANE -PLAYING WITH DYNAMITE

TORCHY ROLLS HIS OWN • 1932 • Burr C. C. • USA

TORCHY RUNS FOR MAYOR • 1939 • McCarey Ray • USA

TORCHY TURNS CUPID • 1920 • *Hines Johnny* • USA

TORCHY'S MILLIONS • 1920 • *Hines Johnny* • USA

TORD MAGAD, OREG • 1971 • Simo Sandor • HNG • BE SKILFUL, MAN!

TORDENSKJOLD GAR I LAND • 1943 • Schneevoigt George • DNM

TORDEUSE ORIENTALE, LA • 1955 • Tadie, Lacoste • SHT • FRN

TORE NG DIYABLO • 1969 • Pacheco Lauro • PHL • TOWER OF THE DEVIL

TOREADOR • 1909 • *Warwick Trading Co* • UKN

TOREADOR • 1929 • Aylott Dave, Symmons E. F. • SHT • UKN

TOREADOR, THE • 1919 • Kenton Erle C. • SHT • USA

TOREADORS DON'T CARE see **OLD SPANISH CUSTOMERS** • 1932

TOREDEK AZ ELETROL • 1981 • Gyongyossy Imre, Kabay Barna • HNG • GLIMPSES OF LIFE

TOREDORABLE • 1953 • Kneitel Seymour • ANS • USA

TORERO • 1956 • Velo Carlos • MXC • TORO!

TORERO see **BULLFIGHTER AND THE LADY, THE** • 1951

TORERO, EL see **CHATEAUX EN ESPAGNE** • 1953

TORERO PARA LA HISTORIA, UN • 1972 • Zabalza Jose Maria • SPN

TORERO POR ALEGRIAS • 1955 • Elorrieta Jose Maria • SPN

TORGET • 1959 • Gunwall Per • SWD • SQUARE, THE

TORGUS • 1920 • Kobe Hanns • FRG • TOTENKLAUS

TORI • 1962 • Kivikoski Erkko • SHT • FNL • MARKET PLACE

TORICHTE HERZ, DAS • 1919 • Lund Erik • FRG

TORICHTE JUNGFRAU, DIE • 1935 • Schneider-Edenkoben Richard • FRG

TORII SUNEEMON • 1942 • Uchida Tomu • JPN • SUNEEMON TORII

TORIMONO DOCHU • 1959 • Sawashima Chu • JPN • LORDS AND PIRATES

TORINO ARTISTICA • 1910 • Omegna Roberto • ITL • ARTISTIC AND PANORAMIC VIEWS OF TURIN

TORINO CENTRALE DEL VIZIO • 1979 • Vani Bruno • ITL

TORINO NEI CENT'ANNI • 1961 • Rossellini Roberto • MTV • ITL

TORINO NERA • 1972 • Lizzani Carlo • ITL • BLACK TURIN

TORINO VIOLENTA • 1977 • Ausino Carlo • ITL

TORITATE NO KAGAYAKI • 1982 • Asao Masayuki • JPN • BRILLIANT COLLECTOR, A

TORIWA FUTATABI NAKU • 1954 • *Hidari Sachiko* • JPN

TORMENT • 1924 • Tourneur Maurice • USA

TORMENT • 1949 • Guillermin John • UKN • PAPER GALLOWS

TORMENT • 1986 • Aslanian Samson, Hopkins John • USA

TORMENT see **SCELERATS, LES** • 1960

TORMENT see **FIOCCO NERO PER DEBORAH, UN** • 1974

TORMENT see **TORMENTO** • 1974

TORMENT see **TORMENTA** • 1982

TORMENT, THE • 1916 • *Kerrigan J. Warren* • SHT • USA

TORMENT, THE (USA) see **LLAGA, LA** • 1937

TORMENT (USA) see **HETS** • 1944

TORMENT (USA) see **PEUR ET L'AMOUR, LA** • 1967

TORMENTA • 1923 • Gallone Carmine • ITL • NELLA TORMENTA

TORMENTA • 1955 • Acebal Alfonso, Guillermin John • SPN, USA
TORMENTA • 1982 • Molo Uberto • BRZ • TORMENT
TORMENTA DE ODIOS • 1951 • Amadori Luis Cesar • MXC
TORMENTA EN EL RING • 1962 • Fernandez Fernando • MXC
TORMENTA EN LA CUMBRE • 1943 • Soler Julian • MXC
TORMENTA SOBRE EL PACIFICO see **SURCOUF, L'EROE DEI SETTE MARI** • 1966
TORMENTED • 1960 • Gordon Bert I. • USA
TORMENTED see **OSSESSA, L'** • 1974
TORMENTED FLAME see **JOEN** • 1959
TORMENTED HUSBAND, THE • 1916 • *Myers Harry* • USA
TORMENTED SOULS see **NOUFOUSS HAIRA** • 1968
TORMENTO • 1919 • Mari Febo • ITL
TORMENTO • 1951 • Matarazzo Raffaello • ITL
TORMENTO • 1972 • Sermet Ozen • BRZ • SOMBRA DE UM SORRISO, A ○ SHADOW OF A SMILE
TORMENTO • 1974 • Olea Pedro • SPN • TORMENT ○ ANGUISH
TORMENTO D'AMORE • 1957 • Bercovici Leonardo, Gora Claudio • ITL, SPN
TORMENTO D'ANIME • 1956 • Barlacchi Cesare • ITL
TORMENTO DEL PASSATO • 1954 • Bonnard Mario • ITL
TORMENTO GENTILE • 1916 • Ghione Emilio • ITL
TORMENTOR, THE • 1967 • Moxey John Llewellyn • UKN
TORMENTORS, THE • 1986 • Eagle Boris • USA
TORMENTORS, THE see **OSSESSA, L'** • 1974
TORN ALLEGIANCE • 1984 • Nathanson Alan • SAF
TORN BETWEEN TWO LOVERS • 1979 • Mann Delbert • TVM • USA
TORN BETWEEN TWO VALUES see **SERGEANT RYKER** • 1967
TORN BOOK, THE see **PODARTA KSIAZKA** • 1962
TORN CURTAIN • 1966 • Hitchcock Alfred • USA
TORN DREAM see **SECANGKIR KOPI PAHIT** • 1985
TORN FLAG see **BANDERA ROTA** • 1979
TORN FORMATIONS see **PASSING THROUGH** • 1988
TORN LETTER, THE • 1911 • Haldane Bert? • UKN
TORN LETTER, THE • 1912 • *Davenport Dorothy* • USA
TORN NOTE, THE • 1912 • *Pathe* • USA
TORN NOTE, THE • 1916 • *Lily* • USA
TORN SAILS • 1920 • Bramble A. V. • UKN
TORN SCARF, THE • 1911 • Porter Edwin S. • USA
TORN SHOES see **BROKEN SHOES** • 1934
TORN TO BITS see **MISE A SAC** • 1967
TORN VIRGIN, A see **HIKISAKARETA SHOJO** • 1968
TORNA! • 1954 • Matarazzo Raffaello • ITL
TORNA A NAPOLI • 1949 • Gambino Domenico M. • ITL • SIMME 'E NAPULE, PAISA
TORNA A SORRENTO • 1946 • Bragaglia Carlo Ludovico • ITL
TORNA, CARO IDEAL! • 1939 • Brignone Guido • ITL
TORNA PICCINA MIA! • 1955 • Campogalliani Carlo • ITL
TORNADO • 1943 • Berke William • USA
TORNADO • 1984 • Margheriti Antonio • ITL • TORNADO STRIKE FORCE
TORNADO, THE • 1917 • Ford John • SHT • USA
TORNADO, THE • 1924 • Baggot King • USA
TORNADO IN THE SADDLE, A • 1942 • Berke William • USA • AMBUSHED (UKN)
TORNADO RANGE • 1948 • Taylor Ray • USA
TORNADO STRIKE FORCE see **TORNADO** • 1984
TORNAVARA • 1943 • Dreville Jean • FRN
TORNEO DE LA MUERTE, EL • 1957 • Urueta Chano • MXC
TORNGAT • 1973 • Valcour Pierre • DOC • CND
TORNYAI JANOS see **JANOS TORNYAI** • 1962
TORO! see **TORERO** • 1956
TORO, EL • 1962 • Camino Jaime • SPN • BULL, THE
TORO BRAVO • 1956 • Viladomat Domingo, Cottafavi Vittorio • SPN, ITL • FIESTA BRAVA (ITL)
TORO DA MONTA, UN • 1976 • Mauri Roberto • ITL
TORO NEGRO, EL • 1959 • Alazraki Benito • MXC
TORO, VIDA Y MUERTE, EL • 1962 • Camino Jaime • SHT • SPN
TOROCKOI BRIDE (USA) see **TOROCKOI MENYASSZONY** • 1938
TOROCKOI MENYASSZONY • 1938 • Keleti Marton • HNG • TOROCKOI BRIDE (USA)
TORONTO JAZZ • 1964 • Owen Don • SHT • CND
TORONTO SYMPHONY NO.1 • 1945 • Roffman Julian • CND
TORONTO THE GOOD • 1973 • Chapman Christopher • DOC • CND
TORONTO -THE PEOPLE CITY • 1979 • Azzopardi Anthony • DOC • CND
TOROS, AMOR Y GLORIA • 1943 • de Anda Raul • MXC
TOROS DE COMBAT • Des Vallieres Jean • SHT • FRN
TOROS TRES • 1962 • Aguirre Javier • SHT • SPN
TORPEDO ALLEY • 1953 • Landers Lew • USA
TORPEDO BAY (USA) see **FINCHE DURA LA TEMPESTA** • 1962
TORPEDO BOAT • 1942 • Rawlins John • USA
TORPEDO OF DOOM, THE • 1938 • Witney William, English John • USA
TORPEDO PIRATES • 1918 • Smith Noel • SHT • USA
TORPEDO-PLANES • Aranovitch Semyon • USS
TORPEDO RUN • 1958 • Pevney Joseph • USA
TORPEDO SQUADRON • 1942 • Ford John • DOC • USA
TORPEDO SQUADRON MOVES OUT, THE see **RAIGEKITAI SHUTSUDO** • 1944
TORPEDO-X see **WAKAOYABUN SENRYOHADA** • 1967
TORPEDO ZONE see **GRANDE SPERANZA, LA** • 1954
TORPEDOED see **SOUTH PACIFIC 1942** • 1980
TORPEDOED BY CUPID • 1916 • *Perez Tweedledum* • SHT • USA
TORPEDOED! (USA) see **OUR FIGHTING NAVY** • 1937
TORPIDO YILMAZ • 1965 • Okcugil Cevat • TRK
TORPILLE AERIENNE, LA • 1912 • Mathe Edouard • FRN • AIR TORPEDO, THE
TORQUAY SUMMER see **THAT SUMMER!** • 1980
TORRE DE LOS SIETE JOROBADOS, LA • 1944 • Neville Edgar • SPN • TOWER OF THE SEVEN HUNCHBACKS, THE
TORRE DE LOS SUPLICIOS, LA • 1940 • Sevilla Raphael J. • MXC • TOWER OF TORTURES, THE
TORRE DE MARFIL, LA • 1957 • Blake Alfonso Corona • MXC
TORRE DEI FANTASMI, LA • 1914 • *Tarlarini Mary Cleo* • ITL • TOWER OF THE PHANTOMS, THE
TORRE DEL PIACERE, LA (ITL) see **TOUR DE NESLE, LA** • 1954
TORRE DELL'ESPIAZONE, LA • 1914 • Roberti Roberto Leone • ITL
TORREANI • 1951 • Frohlich Gustav • FRG
TORREJON CITY • 1962 • Klimovsky Leon • SPN
TORRENT, A see **HONRYU** • 1926
TORRENT, LE • 1918 • Mercanton Louis, Hervil Rene • FRN
TORRENT, THE • 1915 • McRae Henry • USA
TORRENT, THE • 1921 • Paton Stuart • USA
TORRENT, THE • 1924 • Bell Monta • USA • IBANEZ' TORRENT
TORRENT, THE • 1924 • Younger A. P., Doner William • USA
TORRENT OF VENGEANCE, THE • 1916 • McRae Henry • SHT • USA
TORRENTE, IL • 1938 • Elter Marco • ITL
TORRENTS • 1946 • de Poligny Serge • FRN
TORREPARTIDA • 1956 • Lazaga Pedro • SPN
TORRES AGUERO • 1958 • Dawidowicz Enrique • ARG
TORRES SNORTEVOLD • 1940 • Ibsen Tancred • NRW • JACOB
TORRID NOON see **GORECHTO PLADNE** • 1965
TORRID TEMPOS • 1940 • Ceballos Larry • SHT • USA
TORRID TOREADOR, THE • 1942 • Donnelly Eddie • ANS • USA
TORRID ZONE • 1940 • Keighley William • USA
TORROS, BRAVOS ET CORRIDAS • 1956 • Sassy Jean-Paul • SHT • FRN
TORSO MURDER MYSTERY, THE (USA) see **TRAITOR SPY** • 1939
TORSO (USA) see **CORPI PRESENTANO TRACCE DI VIOLENZA CARNALE, I** • 1973
TORST • 1949 • Bergman Ingmar • SWD • THREE STRANGE LOVES (USA) ○ THIRST (UKN)
TORTA IN CIELO, UNA • 1970 • Del Fra Lino • ITL • CAKE IN THE SKY (USA)
TORTICOLA CONTRE FRANKENBERG • 1952 • Paviot Paul • FRN
TORTILLA FLAPS • 1958 • Freleng Friz • ANS • USA
TORTILLA FLAT • 1942 • Fleming Victor • USA
TORTILLARDS, LES • 1960 • Bastia Jean • FRN
TORTOISE AND THE HARE, THE • 1921 • Urban Charles • USA
TORTOISE AND THE HARE, THE • 1935 • Jackson Wilfred • ANS • USA
TORTOISE AND THE HARE, THE • 1968 • Hudson Hugh • UKN
TORTOISE AND THE HARE, THE (USA) see **LIEVRE ET LA TORTUE, LE**
TORTOISE BEATS HARE • 1941 • Avery Tex • ANS • USA
TORTOISE WINS AGAIN, THE • 1946 • Rasinski Connie • ANS • USA
TORTOISE WINS BY A HARE • 1943 • Clampett Robert • ANS • USA
TORTOLA DEL AJUSCO, LA • 1960 • Orol Juan • MXC
TORTUE SUR LE DOS, LA • 1977 • Beraud Luc • FRN • LIKE A TURTLE ON ITS BACK ○ TURTLE ON ITS BACK
TORTUGA ARRAU, LA • 1979 • Sole Jorge • DOC • VNZ • ARRAU TORTOISE, THE
TORTUGA VERDE, LA • 1979 • Sole Jorge • DOC • VNZ • GREEN TORTOISE, THE
TORTURA, LA • 1968 • Guzman Patricio • SPN • TORTURE
TORTURA NADZIEI • 1967 • Petelska Ewa, Petelski Czeslaw • MTV • PLN • TORTURE OF HOPE
TORTURE see **TORTURA, LA** • 1968
TORTURE CAGE, THE • 1928 • Paul Fred • UKN
TORTURE CHAMBER OF BARON BLOOD, THE see **ORRORI DEL CASTELLO DI NORIMBERGA, GLI** • 1972
TORTURE CHAMBER OF DR. FU MANCHU, THE see **CASTLE OF FU MANCHU, THE** • 1968
TORTURE CHAMBER OF DR. SADISM, THE see **SCHLANGENGRUBE UND DAS PENDEL, DIE** • 1967
TORTURE DUNGEON • 1970 • Milligan Andy • USA
TORTURE GARDEN • 1967 • Francis Freddie • UKN
TORTURE IM ZEICHEN DES FRIEDENS • 1974 • Bako Klaus, Reick Dieter • GDR
TORTURE ME KISS ME • 1970 • Friedberg David R. • USA
TORTURE MONEY • 1937 • Bucquet Harold S. • SHT • USA
TORTURE OF CUAUHTEMOC, THE see **SUPLICIO DE CUAUHTEMOC, EL** • 1910
TORTURE OF HOPE see **TORTURA NADZIEI** • 1967
TORTURE OF SMILING LIPS • 1974 • el Imam Hassan • EGY
TORTURE PAR L'ESPERANCE, LA • 1928 • Modot Gaston • SHT • FRN
TORTURE SHIP • 1939 • Halperin Victor Hugo • USA
TORTURE ZONE, THE see **FEAR CHAMBER, THE** • 1968
TORTURED FEMALES • 1965 • *Mitam Productions* • USA
TORTURED HEART, A • 1916 • Davis Will S. • USA
TORTURING WOMAN BY TURNS see **ONNA ZEME TARAIMAWASHI** • 1968
TORUKOBORO YOGOTO NO JOHNETSU • 1968 • Ogawa Kinya • JPN • DAILY PASSION AT THE TURKISH BATHS
TORVENYSERTES NELKUL • 1988 • Gulyas Gyula, Gulyas Janos • DOC • HNG • IN KEEPING WITH THE LAW
TOSA NO IPPONZURI • 1981 • Maeda Yoichi • JPN • FISHERMEN'S TOWN IN TOSA
TOSA ONIRA STOUS DROMOUS • 1968 • Konstantinou Panayotis • GRC • DREAMS IN THE STREET
TOSCA • 1917 • De Liguoro Giuseppe • ITL
TOSCA • 1918 • Serena Gustavo • ITL
TOSCA • 1919 • Magnussen Fritz • SWD
TOSCA • 1941 • Koch Carl • ITL • STORY OF TOSCA, THE (USA)
TOSCA • 1956 • Gallone Carmine • ITL
TOSCA see **DAVANTI A LUI TREMAVA TUTTA ROMA** • 1946
TOSCA, LA • 1908 • Calmettes Andre • FRN
TOSCA, LA • 1918 • Jose Edward • USA
TOSCA, LA • 1922 • *Parkinson H. B.* • UKN
TOSCA, LA • 1940 • Koch Carl, Renoir Jean • ITL
TOSCA, LA • 1973 • Magni Luigi • ITL
TOSCANINI: HYMN TO THE NATIONS see **HYMN TO THE NATIONS** • 1946
TOSCANITO Y LOS DETECTIVES • 1950 • Momplet Antonio • ARG
TOSEI TAMATEBAKO • 1925 • Gosho Heinosuke • JPN • CASKET FOR LIVING, A ○ CONTEMPORARY JEWELRY BOX
TOSEININ • 1967 • Saeki Kiyoshi • JPN
TOSEN FRAN STORMYRTORPET • 1917 • Sjostrom Victor • SWD • GIRL FROM STORMY CROFT (USA) ○ WOMAN HE CHOSE, THE (UKN) ○ GIRL FROM THE MARSH CROFT, A ○ GIRL FROM THE STORMY CROFT, A ○ LASS FROM THE STORMY CROFT, THE
TOSEN FRAN STORMYRTORPET • 1947 • Edgren Gustaf • SWD • GIRL FROM THE MARSH CROFT, A
TOSHIGORO • 1958 • Hozumi Toshimasa • JPN
TOSHIGORO • 1968 • Deme Masanobu • JPN • GREEN YEARS, THE ○ PRIME OF LIFE, THE
TOSS ME A DIME see **TIRE DIE** • 1960
TOSS OF A COIN, THE • 1911 • *Pickford Mary* • USA
TOSSEDE PARADIS, DET • 1962 • Axel Gabriel • DNM • CRAZY PARADISE
TOSSING • Kikoine Gerard • FRN
TOSSING EGGS • 1902 • Porter Edwin S. • USA
TOSTAO, A FERO DE OURO • 1970 • Laender Paulo, Leite Ricardo Gomes • BRZ
TOSTI'S GOODBYE • 1929 • Aylott Dave, Symmons E. F. • SHT • UKN
TOT ODER SCHEINTOT • 1919 • Karfiol William • FRG
TOT WATCHERS • 1958 • Hanna William, Barbera Joseph • ANS • USA
TOTAL APPROACH • 1971 • Blais Roger • DCS • CND • APPROCHE GLOBALE
TOTAL FAMILY, THE see **TOATLE FAMILIE, DIE** • 1981
TOTAL RECALL • 1989 • Verhoeven Paul* • USA
TOTAL SERVICE • 1969 • Leduc Jacques (c/d) • CND
TOTAL VEREIST • 1981 • Noever Hans • FRG
TOTAL WAR IN BRITAIN • 1946 • Rotha Paul, Orrom Michael • DOC • UKN
TOTCHKA PARVA • 1956 • Danovski Boian • BUL • FIRST POINT OF THE ORDER, THE
TOTE AUS DER THEMSE, DIE • 1971 • Philipp Harald • FRG • DEAD WOMAN IN THE THAMES, THE
TOTE GAST, DER • 1918 • Kahn William • FRG
TOTE HOTEL, DAS see **GEWISSEN DER WELT 1, DAS** • 1921
TOTE LAND, DAS • 1916 • Zangenberg Einar • FRG
TOTE VON BEVERLY HILLS, DIE • 1964 • Pfleghar Michael • FRG • CORPSE OF BEVERLY HILLS, THE (USA) ○ THAT GIRL FROM BEVERLY HILLS ○ LU (UKN) ○ DEAD WOMAN FROM BEVERLY HILLS
TOTEM • 1963 • Emshwiller Ed, Nikolais Alwin • SHT • USA
TOTEM • 1986 • Bohm Claus • SHT • DNM
TOTEM MARK, THE • 1911 • *Williams Kathlyn* • USA
TOTEM POLE BEGGAR, THE see **EYES OF THE TOTEM** • 1927
TOTEN AUGEN, DIE • 1917 • Matull Kurt? • FRG
TOTEN AUGEN VON LONDON, DIE • 1960 • Vohrer Alfred • FRG • DEAD EYES OF LONDON (USA) ○ DARK EYES OF LONDON, THE
TOTEN BLEIBEN JUNG, DIE • 1968 • Kunert Joachim • GDR • DEAD REMAIN YOUNG, THE ○ DEAD STAY YOUNG, THE
TOTEN ERWACHEN, DIE • 1915 • Gartner Adolf • FRG
TOTEN FISCHE, DIE • 1988 • Synek Michael • AUS • DEAD FISHES, THE
TOTEN RACHEN SICH, DIE • 1918 • Trautmann Ludwig • FRG • TOTEN RACHEN SICH SELBST, DIE ○ DEAD REVENGE THEMSELVES, THE
TOTEN RACHEN SICH SELBST, DIE see **TOTEN RACHEN SICH, DIE** • 1918
TOTENDES SCHWEIGEN • 1920 • Holz Artur • FRG
TOTENGEBET, DAS see **KADDISCH** • 1924
TOTENINSEL • 1920 • Froelich Carl • FRG
TOTENINSEL, DIE • 1955 • Tourjansky Victor • FRG
TOTENKLAUS see **TORGUS** • 1920
TOTENKLAUS, DER • 1921 • Lowenbein Richard • FRG
TOTENKOPF 2, DER • 1921 • *Von Hardt Elga* • FRG
TOTENKOPF, 50,000 MARK-PRAMIENFILM, DER • 1920 • *Weissblaufilm* • FRG
TOTENKOPFREITER • 1917 • Lins-Morstadt Otto • FRG • LEIBHUSAREN UND IHRE GESCHICHTE, DIE
TOTENMAHL AUF SCHLOSS BEGALITZA, DAS • 1923 • Thiele Wilhelm • FRG
TOTENSCHIFF, DAS • 1959 • Tressler Georg • FRG, MXC
TOTENTANZ • 1919 • Rippert Otto • FRG • DANCE OF DEATH
TOTENTANZ, DER • 1912 • Gad Urban • FRG, DNM • DANCE OF THE DEAD, THE (USA) ○ DODEDANSEN
TOTENVOGEL, DER • 1921 • Lasko Leo • FRG
TOTER HING IM NETZ, EIN • 1960 • Bottger Fritz • FRG, YGS • IT'S HOT IN PARADISE (USA) ○ HORRORS OF SPIDER ISLAND ○ HOT IN PARADISE ○ SPIDER'S WEB, THE ○ GIRLS OF SPIDER ISLAND ○ BODY IN THE WEB
TOTER SUCHT SEINEN MORDER, EIN (FRG) see **VENGEANCE** • 1962
TOTER TAUCHER NIMMT KEIN GELD, EIN • 1975 • Reinl Harald • FRG • NO GOLD FOR A DEAD DIVER (UKN)
TOTET NICHT MEHR! • 1919 • Pick Lupu • FRG • MISERICORDIA
TOTETE IN EKSTASE, DIE • 1970 • Franco Jesus • FRG
TOTH FAMILY, THE see **ISTEN HOZTA, ORNAGY UR!** • 1969
T'OTHER DEAR CHARMER • 1918 • Earle William P. S. • USA
TOTO • 1933 • Tourneur Jacques • FRN
TOTO • 1983 • Manttari Anssi • FNL
TOTO see **GAY DECEIVER, THE** • 1926
TOTO A COLORI • 1952 • Steno • ITL • TOTO IN COLOUR
TOTO A PARIGI • 1958 • Mastrocinque Camillo • ITL, FRN • PARISIEN MALGRE LUI (FRN)
TOTO ACROBATE • 1916-24 • Lortac • ANS • FRN
TOTO AL GIRO D'ITALIA • 1948 • Mattoli Mario • ITL
TOTO ALLEGRO FANTASMA see **ALLEGRO FANTASMA, L'** • 1941
TOTO ALL'INFERNO • 1954 • Mastrocinque Camillo • ITL • TOTO IN HELL
TOTO AND THE POACHERS • 1958 • Salt Brian • UKN
TOTO AVIATEUR • 1916-24 • Lortac • ANS • FRN
TOTO CERCA CASA • 1949 • Steno, Monicelli Mario • ITL • TOTO WANTS A HOME
TOTO CERCA MOGLIE • 1950 • Bragaglia Carlo Ludovico • ITL
TOTO CERCA PACE • 1954 • Mattoli Mario • ITL
TOTO CONTRO I QUATTRO • 1963 • Steno • ITL
TOTO CONTRO IL PIRATA NERO • 1964 • Cerchio Fernando • ITL

TOTO CONTRO MACISTE • 1962 • Cerchio Fernando • ITL • TOTO VS. MACISTE
TOTO D'ARABIA • 1965 • de la Loma Jose Antonio • ITL, SPN
TOTO DEVIENT ANARCHISTE • 1910 • Cohl Emile • ANS • FRN
TOTO DI NOTTE N.1 • 1962 • Amendola Mario • ITL
TOTO DIABOLICUS • 1962 • Steno • ITL
TOTO E CAROLINA • 1955 • Monicelli Mario • ITL
TOTO E CLEOPATRA • 1963 • Cerchio Fernando • ITL
TOTO E I RE DI ROMA • 1952 • Steno, Monicelli Mario • ITL
TOTO E LE DONNE • 1952 • Steno, Monicelli Mario • ITL
TOTO E MARCELLINO • 1958 • Musu Antonio • ITL, FRN
TOTO E PEPPINO DIVISI A BERLINO • 1962 • Bianchi Giorgio • ITL
TOTO, EVA E IL PENNELLO PROIBITO • 1959 • Steno • ITL, FRN, SPN
TOTO, FABRIZI E I GIOVANI D'OGGI • 1960 • Mattoli Mario • ITL
TOTO GATE-SAUCE • 1906 • Heuze Andre?, Zecca Ferdinand? • FRN
TOTO IN COLOUR see **TOTO A COLORI** • 1952
TOTO IN HELL see **TOTO ALL'INFERNO** • 1954
TOTO IN THE MOON see **TOTO NELLA LUNA** • 1958
TOTO LASCIA O RADDOPPIA? • 1956 • Mastrocinque Camillo • ITL
TOTO LE MOKO • 1949 • Bragaglia Carlo Ludovico • ITL
TOTO NELLA LUNA • 1958 • Steno • ITL • TOTO IN THE MOON
TOTO OF THE BYWAYS • 1916 • Kohlmar Lee • SHT • USA
TOTO, PEPPINO E I.. FUORILEGGE • 1956 • Mastrocinque Camillo • ITL
TOTO, PEPPINO E.. LA DOLCE VITA • 1961 • Corbucci Sergio • ITL
TOTO, PEPPINO E LA MALAFEMMINA • 1956 • Mastrocinque Camillo • ITL
TOTO, PEPPINO E LE FANATICHE • 1958 • Mattoli Mario • ITL
TOTO SCEICCO • 1950 • Mattoli Mario • ITL • TOTO THE SHEIK ○ TOTO SHEIK
TOTO SEXY • 1963 • Amendola Mario • ITL
TOTO SHEIK see **TOTO SCEICCO** • 1950
TOTO TARZAN • 1950 • Mattoli Mario • ITL
TOTO TERZA UOMO • 1951 • Mattoli Mario • ITL
TOTO THE SHEIK see **TOTO SCEICCO** • 1950
TOTO, UN ANTHOLOGIE • 1978 • Comolli Jean-Louis • CMP • FRN
TOTO, VITTORIO E LA DOTTORESSA • 1957 • Mastrocinque Camillo • ITL, SPN, FRN • MI MUJER ES DOCTOR (SPN) ○ DITES 33 (FRN) ○ LADY DOCTOR, THE (USA)
TOTO VS. MACISTE see **TOTO CONTRO MACISTE** • 1962
TOTO WANTS A HOME see **TOTO CERCA CASA** • 1949
TOTON • 1919 • Borzage Frank • USA
TOTORO, THE NEIGHBOURHOOD GHOST see **TONARI NO TOTORO** • 1988
TOTORUFFA '62 • 1961 • Mastrocinque Camillo • ITL
TOTO'S TROUBLES • 1919 • Roach Hal • SHT • USA
TOTS OF FUN • 1952 • Kneitel Seymour • ANS • USA
TOTSTELLEN • 1975 • Corti Axel • AUS
TOTSUGU HI • 1956 • Yoshimura Kozaburo • JPN • DATE FOR MARRIAGE ○ DAY OF MARRIAGE ○ DAY TO WED, THE
TOTSUSEKI ISEKI • 1966 • Shindo Kaneto • JPN • MONUMENT OF TOTSUSEKI
TOTTE ET SA CHANCE see **DEFENSE D'AIMER** • 1942
TOTTE TOTTE TORIMAKURE • 1968 • Watanabe Yusuke • JPN • DRIFTERS DESUYO
TOTVILLE EYE, THE • 1912 • Merwin Bannister • USA
TOU HORISMOU TO TRENA • 1967 • Filaktos Filippos • GRC • TRAIN OF PARTING, THE
T'OU-PEN NU-HAI • 1983 • Hsu An-Hua • HKG • BOAT PEOPLE
T'OU-T'AI JEN • 1976 • Chang Sen • HKG • REINCARNATION, THE
TOUBAB, LE see **JUNGLE EN FOLIE, LA** • 1952
TOUBIB, LE • 1955 • Govar Yvan • BLG
TOUBIB, LE • 1979 • Granier-Deferre Pierre • FRN • GREATEST ATTACK, THE (UKN) ○ PRELUDE TO APOCALYPSE ○ HARMONIE ○ MEDIC, THE
TOUBIB AUX GRANDES MANOEUVRES, LA (FRN) see **SOLDATESSA ALLE GRANDI MANOVRE, IL** • 1978
TOUCH see **SPARSH** • 1978
TOUCH, THE (USA) see **BERORINGEN** • 1970
TOUCH ALL THE BASES • 1922 • Roach Hal • SHT • USA
TOUCH AND GO • 1955 • Truman Michael • UKN • LIGHT TOUCH, THE (USA)
TOUCH AND GO • 1980 • Maxwell Peter • ASL
TOUCH AND GO • 1986 • Mandel Robert • USA
TOUCH AND GO (USA) see **POUDRE D'ESCAMPETTE, LA** • 1971
TOUCH ME NOT • 1973 • Fifthian Douglas • UKN • HUNTED, THE
TOUCH ME (UKN) see **ICH SPURE DEINE HAUT** • 1968
TOUCH OF A BABE, THE • 1913 • Buckland Warwick? • UKN
TOUCH OF A CHILD, THE • 1913 • *Otto Henry* • USA
TOUCH OF A CHILD, THE • 1914 • *Baggot King* • USA
TOUCH OF A CHILD, THE • 1918 • Hepworth Cecil M. • UKN
TOUCH OF A CHILD'S HAND, THE • 1910 • *Kalem* • USA
TOUCH OF A LITTLE HAND, THE • 1914 • *Chamberlain Riley* • USA
TOUCH OF CLASS, A • 1973 • Frank Melvin • USA
TOUCH OF DEATH • 1962 • Comfort Lance • UKN
TOUCH OF EVIL • 1958 • Welles Orson • USA
TOUCH OF GENIE, A • 1976 • Andersson Karl • USA
TOUCH OF HEALING see **COULISSES DE L'ENTRAIDE** • 1984
TOUCH OF HELL, A see **SERIOUS CHARGE** • 1959
TOUCH OF HER FLESH, THE • 1967 • Findlay Michael • USA • TOUCH OF HER LIFE, THE ○ WAY OUT LOVE
TOUCH OF HER LIFE, THE see **TOUCH OF HER FLESH, THE** • 1967
TOUCH OF HIGH LIFE, A • 1916 • *Mcquire Paddy* • SHT • USA
TOUCH OF HUMAN NATURE, A • 1906 • *Walturdaw* • UKN
TOUCH OF HYDROPHOBIA, A • 1911 • Wilson Frank? • UKN
TOUCH OF LARCENY, A • 1959 • Hamilton Guy • UKN, USA
TOUCH OF LEATHER • 1968 • Ericson Olaf • UKN • DEATH BLOW, THE
TOUCH OF LOVE, A • 1915 • Pollard Harry? • USA
TOUCH OF LOVE, A • 1969 • Hussein Waris • UKN • THANK YOU ALL VERY MUCH ○ MILLSTONE, THE
TOUCH OF MADNESS, A • 1974 • Bonniere Rene • CND
TOUCH OF MELISSA, THE see **CURSE OF MELISSA, THE** • 1971
TOUCH OF NATURE, A • 1911 • Haldane Bert? • UKN
TOUCH OF NATURE, A • 1915 • Nash Percy • UKN
TOUCH OF SATAN, A see **CURSE OF MELISSA, THE** • 1971
TOUCH OF SCANDAL, A • 1984 • Nagy Ivan • TVM • USA
TOUCH OF SHAMROCK, A • 1949 • Shepherd Horace • UKN
TOUCH OF SKIN see **BAIE DU DESIR, LA** • 1964
TOUCH OF THE MOON, A • 1936 • Rogers Maclean • UKN
TOUCH OF THE NIGHT, THE see **DOTKNIECIE NOCY** • 1960
TOUCH OF THE OTHER, A • 1970 • Miller Arnold Louis • UKN
TOUCH OF THE SUN • 1980 • Curran Peter • UKN
TOUCH OF THE SUN, A • 1956 • Parry Gordon • UKN
TOUCH OF THE TIMES, A • 1947-49 • Roemer Michael • USA
TOUCH OF TREASON, A (USA) see **ENNEMIS, LES** • 1961
TOUCH OF ZEN, A see **HSIA NU** • 1968
TOUCH ON THE KEY, THE • 1916 • Le Viness Carl M. • SHT • USA
TOUCH WOOD • 1980 • Armstrong Gillian • DOC • ASL
TOUCH WOOD • 1983 • Keatley Philip • CND
TOUCHABLES, THE • 1961 • Sheridan Jay, Mann Monte, Manning Monroe • USA • NUDE HEAT WAVE
TOUCHABLES, THE • 1968 • Freeman Robert • UKN
TOUCHDOWN • 1931 • McLeod Norman Z. • USA • PLAYING THE GAME (UKN)
TOUCHDOWN see **CHOICES** • 1981
TOUCHDOWN, ARMY! • 1938 • Neumann Kurt • USA • GENERALS OF TOMORROW (UKN)
TOUCHDOWN DEMONS • 1940 • White Volney • ANS • USA
TOUCHDOWN MICKEY • 1932 • Jackson Wilfred • ANS • USA
TOUCHDOWN TO TAKE-OFF • 1953 • Cartwright J. A. D. • UKN
TOUCHE-A-TOUT • 1935 • Dreville Jean • FRN
TOUCHE AND GO • 1957 • Jones Charles M. • ANS • USA
TOUCHE DE BLEUE, UNE • 1988 • Gaignaire Claude Timon • FRN
TOUCHE PAS A MON BINIOU • 1980 • Launois Bernard • FRN
TOUCHE PAS A MON COPAIN • 1976 • Bouthier Bernard • FRN
TOUCHE PAS LA FEMME BLANC see **NON TOCCARE LA DONNA BIANCA** • 1975
TOUCHE, PUSSY CAT • 1954 • Hanna William, Barbera Joseph • ANS • USA
TOUCHED • 1983 • Flynn John • USA
TOUCHED BY LOVE • 1980 • Trikonis Gus • USA • TO ELVIS, WITH LOVE
TOUCHED BY TEMPTATION see **SEXPERTS -TOUCHED BY TEMPTATION** • 1965
TOUCHED ON THE RAW see **KYUSHO ZEME** • 1968
TOUCHEZ PAS A MA CHATTE see **PORNOCHATTES** • 1974
TOUCHEZ PAS AU GRISBI • 1953 • Becker Jacques • FRN, ITL • HONOUR AMONG THIEVES (UKN) ○ GRISBI (USA) ○ DON'T TOUCH THE LOOT ○ PARIS UNDERGROUND ○ HANDS OFF THE LOOT
TOUCHEZ PAS AU ZIZI • 1977 • Rhomm Patrice • FRN
TOUCHEZ PAS AUX BLONDES! • 1960 • Cloche Maurice • FRN
T,O,U,C,H,I,N,G. • 1968 • Sharits Paul J. • SHT • USA
TOUCHING AFFAIR, A • 1910 • *American* • USA
TOUCHING MYSTERY, A • 1910 • *Atlas* • USA
TOUCHING STORY, A • 1934 • Samuelson G. B. • UKN
TOUCHONS DU BOIS • 1933 • Champreux Maurice • FRN • SOYONS SERIEUX
TOUFAN BAR FARASE PETRA • 1968 • Akarame Farough • IRN • STORM OVER PETRA
TOUFAN-E-NOAH • 1967 • Yasami Siyamak • IRN • NOAH'S STORM
TOUGH • 1974 • Jackson Horace • USA
TOUGH see **JAN RAP EN ZIJN MAAT** • 1989
TOUGH, THE see **FATAWA, EL** • 1956
TOUGH ANTS see **TAWWE TANNIES** • 1984
TOUGH AS THEY COME • 1942 • Nigh William • USA
TOUGH ASSIGNMENT • 1949 • Beaudine William • USA
TOUGH EGG, A • 1936 • *Terry Paul/ Moser Frank (P)* • ANS • USA
TOUGH ENOUGH • 1982 • Fleischer Richard • USA
TOUGH GAME, THE see **HARDA LEKEN, DEN** • 1956
TOUGH GIG, A see **DIRTYMOUTH** • 1970
TOUGH GUY • 1936 • Franklin Chester M. • USA
TOUGH GUY • 1970 • JPN
TOUGH GUY see **KENKA TARO** • 1960
TOUGH GUY see **CHUEH-TOU LAO-HU CHUANG** • 1973
TOUGH GUY, THE • 1926 • Kirkland David • USA • HIS BIG PAL
TOUGH GUY FROM 1900, A see **GUAPO DEL 1900, UN** • 1972
TOUGH GUY III see **DAISAN NO AKUMYO** • 1963
TOUGH GUY LEVI • 1912 • *Lubin* • USA
TOUGH GUY OF 1900 see **GUAPO DEL 1900, UN** • 1960
TOUGH GUYS • 1987 • Kanew Jeff • USA
TOUGH GUYS see **CHUEH-TOU LAO-HU CHUANG** • 1973
TOUGH GUYS ARE THERE, THE • 1966 • Lefranc Guy • FRN
TOUGH GUYS DON'T DANCE • 1987 • Mailer Norman • USA
TOUGH KID • 1939 • Bretherton Howard • USA • FIFTH ROUND, THE (UKN)
TOUGH KID'S WATERLOO • 1900 • *Bitzer Billy (Ph)* • USA
TOUGH KNIGHT, A • 1918 • Hotaling Arthur D. • SHT • USA
TOUGH LUCK • 1914 • Griffin Frank C. • USA
TOUGH LUCK • 1915 • *Aubrey James* • USA
TOUGH LUCK • 1917 • *Pokes & Jabbs* • SHT • USA
TOUGH LUCK • 1919 • Roach Hal • SHT • USA
TOUGH LUCK AND TIN LIZZIES • 1917 • Semon Larry • SHT • USA
TOUGH LUCK ON A ROUGH SEA • 1916 • *Russell Dan* • SHT • USA
TOUGH LUCK SMITH • 1914 • Frambers C. A. • USA
TOUGH NINJA: THE SHADOW WARRIOR • Hutton Larry
TOUGH NUTS AND ROUGHS • 1915 • Collins Edwin J.? • UKN
TOUGH ONES, THE see **DELIJE** • 1968
TOUGH TACTICS • 1941-45 • MacDonald David • DOC • UKN
TOUGH TENDERFOOT, THE • 1920 • Murphy Martin • SHT • USA
TOUGH TO HANDLE • 1937 • Luby S. Roy • USA
TOUGH TURF see **TUFF TURF** • 1984
TOUGH TURKEY TROT • 1917 • *Triangle* • USA
TOUGH WINTER, A • 1922 • Roach Hal • SHT • USA
TOUGH WINTER, A • 1930 • McGowan Robert • SHT • USA
TOUGHER THAN LEATHER • 1989 • Rubin Rick • USA
TOUGHER THEY COME, THE • 1950 • Nazarro Ray • USA
TOUGHEST GUN IN TOMBSTONE • 1958 • Bellamy Earl • USA
TOUGHEST MAN ALIVE, THE • 1955 • Salkow Sidney • USA
TOUGHEST MAN IN ARIZONA, THE • 1952 • Springsteen R. G. • USA
TOUGHEST MAN IN THE WORLD, THE • 1984 • Lowry Dick • TVM • USA
TOUGHLOVE • 1985 • Jordan Glenn • TVM • USA • SUBSTITUTE, THE
TOUHA • 1958 • Jasny Vojtech • CZC • DESIRE
TOUHA ZVANA ANADA see **HRST VODY** • 1971
TOUKI-BOUKI • 1973 • Diop Djibril • SNL
TOUL QUEBEC AU MONDE SUA JOBBE • 1975 • Tremblay Robert • CND • QUEBEC SUA JOBBE, LE
TOULA • 1973 • Alassane Moustapha • NGR, FRG
TOULA'S DREAM • 1908 • *Pathe* • FRN
TOULOUSE • 1943 • Clement Rene • DCS • FRN
TOULOUSE-LAUTREC • 1950 • Hessens Robert • FRN
TOUR, LA • 1928 • Clair Rene • FRN
TOUR A LA FOIRE, UN see **CONSEIL DU PIPELET, LE** • 1908
TOUR AU LARGE, LA • 1926 • Gremillon Jean • FRN
TOUR DE BABEL, LA • 1949 • Rony Georges • CMP • FRN
TOUR DE CHANCE • Dimitri Michele • BLG
TOUR DE CHANT • 1932 • Cavalcanti Alberto • FRN
TOUR DE COCHON, UN • 1934 • Tzipine Joseph • FRN
TOUR DE CONTROLE • 1968 • Essid Hamadi • DCS • TNS
TOUR DE FRANCE 1949, LE • 1949 • Beer Jacques • DOC • FRN
TOUR DE FRANCE 1950, LE • 1950 • Beer Jacques • DOC • FRN
TOUR DE FRANCE DE DEUX ENFANTS, LE • 1924 • de Carbonnat Louis • FRN
TOUR DE L'ILE, LE • 1940 • Tessier Albert • DCS • CND
TOUR DE LONDRES: OU, LES DERNIER MOMENTS D'ANNE DE BOLEYN, LA • 1905 • Melies Georges • FRN • TOWER OF LONDON, THE (USA) ○ LAST MOMENTS OF ANNE BOLEYN ○ ANNA DE BOLEYN A LA TOUR DE LONDRES
TOUR DE MANEGE, UN • 1989 • Pradinas Pierre • FRN
TOUR DE NESLE, LA • 1909 • Calmettes Andre • FRN
TOUR DE NESLE, LA • 1937 • Roudes Gaston • FRN
TOUR DE NESLE, LA • 1954 • Gance Abel • FRN, ITL • TORRE DEL PIACERE, LA (ITL) ○ TOWER OF LUST, THE
TOUR DE NESLE, LA • 1969 • Antel Franz • FRN
TOUR DE NESLE, LA see **TURM DER VERBOTENEN LIEBE, DER** • 1968
TOUR DE SASQUATCH • 1984 • Woodland James • CND
TOUR D'ESPAGNE • 1966 • Ardavin Cesar • SHT • SPN
TOUR DU DIABLE, LE • 1990 • Lavoie Richard • DOC • CND
TOUR DU MONDE D'UN POLICIER, LE • 1906 • Velle Gaston • FRN
TOUR DU MONDE EN 80 MINUTES • Cohl Emile • ANM • FRN • AROUND THE WORLD IN 80 MINUTES
TOUR DU MONDE EN BATEAU-STOP, LE • 1954 • Storck Henri • DOC • BLG
TOUR DU MONDE EXPRESS • 1955 • Ichac Marcel • DCS • FRN
TOUR EIFFEL, LA • 1900 • Lumiere Louis • FRN
TOUR MAUDITE, LA • 1901 • Melies Georges • FRN • BEWITCHED DUNGEON (USA) ○ ACCURSED TOWER, THE
TOUR OF DUTY see **NAM: TOUR OF DUTY** • 1987
TOUR OF DUTY 2: UNDER SIEGE • 1987 • Norton B. W. L. • USA
TOUR OF DUTY 3: THE HILL • 1987 • Norton B. W. L. • USA
TOUR OF DUTY 4: THE KILL ZONE • 1988 • Norton B. W. L. • USA
TOUR OF DUTY 5: THE ASSASSIN • 1988 • Sherin Edwin, Posey Stephen L. • USA
TOUR OF DUTY 6: THE BORDER • 1989 • *Knox Terence* • USA
TOUR, PRENDS GARDE!, LA • 1958 • Lampin Georges • FRN, ITL, YGS • AGLI ORDINI DEL RE (ITL) ○ KING ON HORSEBACK (USA)
TOURBIERE, LA • 1965-66 • Garceau Raymond • DCS • CND
TOURBIERS, LES • 1964 • Weyergans Francois • SHT • FRN
TOURBILLON • 1952 • Rode Alfred • FRN
TOURBILLON DE PARIS • 1939 • Diamant-Berger Henri • FRN
TOURBILLON DE PARIS, LE • 1928 • Duvivier Julien • FRN
TOURING WITH TILLIE • 1915 • MacMackin Archer • USA
TOURISM IS A GREAT INVENTION see **TURISMO ES UN GRAN INVENTO, EL** • 1968
TOURISME • 1951 • Bellon Yannick • FRN
TOURISME NAUTIQUE • Tessier Albert • DCS • CND
TOURIST, THE • 1921 • Robbins Jess • USA
TOURIST, THE • 1925 • Arbuckle Roscoe • USA
TOURIST, THE see **TURISTA** • 1962
TOURIST AND THE FLOWER GIRL, THE • 1913 • *Rex* • USA
TOURIST TRAP • 1979 • Schmoeller David • USA
TOURISTES REVENANT D'UNE EXCURSION • 1896-97 • Lumiere Louis • FRN
TOURISTS • 1961 • Topaldgikov Stefan • USS
TOURISTS, THE • 1912 • Sennett Mack • USA
TOURISTS DE LUXE • 1924 • Lamont Charles • SHT • USA
TOURMENT, LE • 1912 • Feuillade Louis • FRN
TOURMENTS • 1953 • Daniel-Norman Jacques • FRN
TOURNAMENT see **TOURNOI, LE** • 1928
TOURNAMENT see **TURNIEJ** • 1959
TOURNAMENT see **SEISHUN** • 1968
TOURNAMENT TEMPO see **GAY BLADES** • 1946
TOURNANT DANGEREUX, LE • 1955 • Bibal Robert • FRN, ITL • CAFFE DEL PORTO, IL (ITL)
TOURNEE see **TURNE** • 1990
TOURNEE DES GRANDS DUCS, LA • 1952 • Pellenc Andre • FRN
TOURNEE TITLES • 1981 • Patel Ishu • ANM • CND • INTERNATIONAL TOURNEE OF ANIMATION

TOURNEUR EN POTERIE • 1897 • Melies Georges • FRN • POTTERYMAKER, A
TOURNOI, LE • 1928 • Renoir Jean • FRN • TOURNOI DANS LA CITE, LE ○ TOURNAMENT
TOURNOI DANS LA CITE, LE see **TOURNOI, LE** • 1928
TOURNOI DE L'ECHARPE D'OR, LE • 1912 • Andreani Henri • FRN
TOUS LES CHEMINS MENENT A ROME • 1948 • Boyer Jean • FRN, ITL • ALL ROADS LEAD TO ROME
TOUS LES DEUX • 1948 • Cuny Louis • FRN
TOUS LES GARCONS S'APPELLENT PATRICK • 1957 • Godard Jean-Luc • SHT • FRN • CHARLOTTE ET VERONIQUE
TOUS LES PARFUMS DE L'ARABIE • 1961 • Kumel Harry • SHT • BLG
TOUS LES TROIS L'AIMENT see **THALATHA YUHIBUNAHA, ATH-** • 1965
TOUS PEUVENT ME TUER • 1957 • Decoin Henri • FRN, ITL • TUTTI POSSONO UCCIDERMI (ITL) ○ ANYONE CAN KILL ME (UKN)
TOUS VEDETTES • 1980 • Lang Michel • FRN
TOUT ARRIVE see **JOUR VIENDRA, UN** • 1933
TOUT CA NE VAUT PAS L'AMOUR • 1931 • Tourneur Jacques • FRN • VIEUX GARCON, UN
TOUT CA POUR LA PAIX see **SOMETHING ABOUT PEACE** • 1984
TOUT CHANTE AUTOUR DE MOI • 1954 • Gout Pierre • FRN
TOUT DEPEND DES FILLES • 1979 • Fabre Pierre • FRN
TOUT ECARTILLE • 1972 • Leduc Andre • CND • ALL SPACED OUT
TOUT FEU TOUT FEMME • 1975 • Richer Gilles • CND
TOUT FEU, TOUT FLAMME • 1982 • Rappeneau Jean-Paul • FRN
TOUT LE MONDE IL EST BEAU, TOUT LE MONDE IL EST GENTIL • 1972 • Yanne Jean • FRN, ITL
TOUT LE MONDE PEUT SE TROMPER • 1982 • Couturier Jean • FRN
TOUT L'OR DU MONDE • 1961 • Clair Rene • FRN, ITL • ALL THE GOLD IN THE WORLD
TOUT L'TEMPS, TOUT L'TEMPS, TOUT L'TEMPS • 1969 • Dansereau Fernand • CND
TOUT PART • 1970 • Fettar Sid-Ali • ALG
TOUT PETIT FAUST, LE • 1910 • Cohl Emile • ANS • FRN • PETIT FAUST, LE ○ VERY SMALL FAUST, THE ○ BEAUTIFUL MARGARET, THE
TOUT PEUT ARRIVER • 1969 • Labro Philippe • FRN • DON'T BE BLUE
TOUT POUR JOUIR • 1978 • Kikoine Gerard • FRN
TOUT POUR L'AMOUR • 1933 • Clouzot Henri-Georges, May Joe • FRN • CHANSON POUR TOI, UNE
TOUT POUR LE TOUT, LE • 1960 • Dally Patrice • FRN, BRZ
TOUT POUR RIEN • 1933 • Pujol Rene • FRN • PETIT CARAMBOUILLEUR, LE
TOUT POUR TOI, MON ENFANT see **MATERNITE** • 1934
TOUT RIEN • Back Frederic • ANM • CND
TOUT S'ARRANGE • 1931 • Diamant-Berger Henri • FRN
TOUT VA BIEN • 1972 • Godard Jean-Luc, Gorin Jean-Pierre • FRN, ITL • CREPA PADRONE TUTTO VA BENE (ITL) ○ ALL IS WELL
TOUT VA BIEN see **NU COMME UN VER** • 1933
TOUT VA TRES BIEN, MADAME LA MARQUISE • 1936 • Wulschleger Henry • FRN
TOUTANKHAMON ET SON ROYAUME • 1952 • de Gastyne Marco • SHT • FRN
TOUTE LA FAMILLE ETAIT LA • 1948 • de Marguenat Jean • FRN • SEDUCTEUR INGENU, LE ○ PORC-EPIC, LE
TOUTE LA FRANCE PAR LE FILM • 1928 • Vorins Henri • SER • FRN
TOUTE LA MEMOIRE DU MONDE • 1956 • Resnais Alain • SHT • FRN • ALL THE MEMORY OF THE WORLD
TOUTE LA VILLE ACCUSE • 1955 • Boissol Claude • FRN • MILLES ET UN MILLIONS, LES
TOUTE MA VIE AU SERVICE DES RICHES • 1978 • Tremblay Robert • CND
TOUTE REVOLUTION EST UN COUP DE DES • 1977 • Straub Jean-Marie, Huillet Daniele • FRN • EVERY REVOLUTION IS A THROW OF THE DICE
TOUTE SA VIE • 1930 • Cavalcanti Alberto • FRN • APPEL DU COEUR, L'
TOUTE UNE NUIT • 1982 • Akerman Chantal • BLG, FRN, NTH • ALL NIGHT LONG
TOUTE UNE VIE • 1974 • Lelouch Claude • FRN, ITL • TUTTA UNA VITA (ITL) ○ AND NOW MY LOVE (USA)
TOUTES FOLLES DE LUI • 1967 • Carbonnaux Norbert • FRN, ITL
TOUTES ISLES • 1958-60 • Bonniere Rene • DCS • CND
TOUTES LES HISTOIRES DE DRAGON ONT UN FOND DE VERITE see **"LIBERATION"** • 1981
TOUT'S REMEMBRANCE, THE • 1910 • *Anderson Broncho Billy* • USA
TOVA SE SLUCHI NA ULITSATA • 1956 • Yankov Yanko • BUL • IT HAPPENED IN THE STREET
TOVARICH • 1937 • Litvak Anatole • USA
TOVARITCH • 1935 • Deval Jacques, Tarride Jean, Fried Germain, Trivas Victor • FRN
TOW see **WITTE VAN SICHEM, DE** • 1980
TOW-GUN PARSON, THE • 1917 • *Dowlan W. C.* • SHT • USA
TOWARD NEW SHORES see **K NOVOMU BEREGU** • 1955
TOWARD THE DECISIVE BATTLE IN THE SKY see **KESSEN NO OZORA E** • 1943
TOWARD THE RAINY SEASON see **TSUYU NO ATOSAKI** • 1956
TOWARD THE UNKNOWN • 1956 • LeRoy Mervyn • USA • BRINK OF HELL (UKN)
TOWARDS BARUYA MANHOOD • 1969 • Dunlop Ian • DOC • ASL
TOWARDS GLORY see **HACIA LA GLORIA** • 1931
TOWARDS NEW TIMES see **MOT NYA TIDER** • 1939
TOWARDS THE ABODE OF GODS (USA) see **DEV GIRI JATRA** • 1932
TOWARDS THE BEGINNING see **U PRAVCU POCETKA** • 1970
TOWARDS THE DICTATORSHIP OF THE PROLETARIAT see **STACHKA** • 1925
TOWARDS THE LIGHT • 1918 • Edwards Henry • UKN
TOWARDS THE LIGHT see **MOD LYSET** • 1919
TOWARDS THE LIGHT see **K SVYETU** • 1968
TOWARDS THE NEW BANK see **K NOVOMU BEREGU** • 1955
TOWARDS THE NORTH see **MARCHA AL NORTE** • 1977
TOWARDS THE SUN see **IDE KU SLONCU** • 1955
TOWARDS THE UNKNOWN see **ILA AYN** • 1957
TOWED IN A HOLE • 1933 • Marshall George • SHT • USA
TOWER, THE • 1953 • Pickering Peter, Ingram John • UKN
TOWER BRIDGE see **PONT DE LA TOUR** • 1896
TOWER HOUSE • 1954 • Brakhage Stan, Cornell Joseph • USA
TOWER IN THE FOREST, THE • 1987 • Johansen Svend • DNM
TOWER OF BABEL, THE • 1987 • Ciric Rasto • ANM • YGS
TOWER OF EVIL • 1972 • O'Connolly Jim • UKN, USA • HORROR OF SNAPE ISLAND (USA) ○ BEYOND THE FOG ○ HORROR ON SNAPE ISLAND
TOWER OF FORBIDDEN LOVE, THE see **TURM DER VERBOTENEN LIEBE, DER** • 1968
TOWER OF IVORY see **OUT OF THE STORM** • 1920
TOWER OF JEWELS, THE • 1920 • Terriss Tom • USA
TOWER OF LIES, THE • 1925 • Sjostrom Victor • USA
TOWER OF LILIES, THE see **HIMEYURI NO TO** • 1953
TOWER OF LONDON • 1962 • Corman Roger • USA
TOWER OF LONDON, THE • 1909 • Williamson James? • UKN
TOWER OF LONDON, THE • 1926 • Elvey Maurice • UKN
TOWER OF LONDON, THE • 1939 • Lee Rowland V. • USA
TOWER OF LONDON, THE (USA) see **TOUR DE LONDRES: OU, LES DERNIER MOMENTS D'ANNE DE BOLEYN, LA** • 1905
TOWER OF LOVE • 1975 • USA
TOWER OF LUST, THE see **TOUR DE NESLE, LA** • 1954
TOWER OF SCREAMING VIRGINS (USA) see **TURM DER VERBOTENEN LIEBE, DER** • 1968
TOWER OF SILENCE • 1975 • Dehlavi Jamil • PKS • TOWERS OF SILENCE
TOWER OF SIN see **TURM DER VERBOTENEN LIEBE, DER** • 1968
TOWER OF STRENGTH • 1919 • Ayrton Randle • UKN • GATES OF DUTY
TOWER OF TERROR see **ASSAULT** • 1971
TOWER OF TERROR, THE • 1941 • Huntington Lawrence • UKN
TOWER OF THE DEVIL see **TORE NG DIYABLO** • 1969
TOWER OF THE PHANTOMS, THE see **TORRE DEI FANTASMI, LA** • 1914
TOWER OF THE SEVEN HUNCHBACKS, THE see **TORRE DE LOS SIETE JOROBADOS, LA** • 1944
TOWER OF TORTURES, THE see **TORRE DE LOS SUPLICIOS, LA** • 1940
TOWERHOUSE see **JUNE**
TOWERING INFERNO, THE • 1974 • Allen Irwin, Guillermin John • USA
TOWERS OF SILENCE see **TOWER OF SILENCE** • 1975
TOWERS OPEN FIRE • 1963 • Balch Anthony • UKN
TOWING • 1978 • *Lyon Sue* • USA
TOWING A BOAT ON THE RIVER see **HALEURS DE BATEAUX, LES** • 1896
TOWN, THE • 1944 • von Sternberg Josef • DOC • USA
TOWN, THE see **GRAD** • 1963
TOWN, THE see **MIASTO** • 1963
TOWN, THE see **STADT, DIE** • 1973
TOWN AND ITS DRAINS, THE see **MACHI TO GESUI** • 1953
TOWN AND VILLAGE • 1968 • Giumale Elhadji Mohamed • SML
TOWN BAND, THE see **SELAMSIZ BANDOSU** • 1987
TOWN BLOODY HALL • 1979 • Pennebaker D. A., Hegedus Chris • USA
TOWN BULLY, THE • 1988 • Black Noel • TVM • USA • INTIMIDATOR, THE
TOWN CALLED BASTARD, A • 1971 • Parrish Robert • UKN, SPN • TOWN CALLED HELL, A
TOWN CALLED BEAUTY, A see **RETURN OF DESPERADO, THE** • 1988
TOWN CALLED HELL, A see **TOWN CALLED BASTARD, A** • 1971
TOWN CALLED TEMPEST, A • 1961 • Kuchar George • SHT • USA
TOWN FOR ASSEMBLY WORKERS, A see **ASSY-TACHI NO MACHI** • 1981
TOWN HALL, TONIGHT • 1911 • *Carney Augustus* • USA
TOWN HAS TURNED TO DUST, A • 1958 • Frankenheimer John • MTV • USA
TOWN IN THE AWKWARD AGE, A see **KAMASZVAROS** • 1962
TOWN IS OUR FUTURE, THE see **KAUPUNGISSA ON TULEVAISUUS** • 1967
TOWN LIKE ALICE, A • 1956 • Lee Jack • UKN • RAPE OF MALAYA, THE
TOWN LIKE ALICE, A • 1981 • Stevens David • MTV • ASL
TOWN MARSHALL, THE • 1911 • *Nestor* • USA
TOWN MEETING OF THE WORLD • 1946 • Wallace Graham • DOC • UKN
TOWN MOUSE AND COUNTRY MOUSE • 1912 • Plumb Hay? • UKN
TOWN MOUSE AND THE COUNTRY MOUSE, THE • 1980 • Lambart Evelyn • ANS • CND
TOWN MUSICIANS, THE • 1954 • Tytla Bill • ANS • USA
TOWN OF ANGER see **IKARI NO MACHI** • 1950
TOWN OF CROOKED WAYS, THE • 1920 • Wynne Bert • UKN
TOWN OF FIRE see **JOEN NO CHIMATA** • 1922
TOWN OF LOVE AND HOPE, A see **AI TO KIBO NO MACHI** • 1959
TOWN OF MY HOPE, THE see **MESTO ME NADEJE** • 1978
TOWN OF NAZARETH, THE • 1914 • *American* • USA
TOWN OF PAINTERS, THE see **FESTOK VAROSA – SZENTENDRE, A** • 1964
TOWN ON TRIAL • 1957 • Guillermin John • UKN
TOWN ON TRIAL, A see **PROCESSO ALLA CITTA** • 1952
TOWN PEOPLE see **MACHI NO HITOBITO** • 1926
TOWN RAT AND THE COUNTRY RAT, THE (USA) see **RAT DE VILLE ET LE RAT DES CHAMPS, LE** • 1926
TOWN SCANDAL, THE • 1923 • Baggot King • USA • CHICKEN THAT CAME HOME TO ROOST, THE ○ CHICKEN, THE
TOWN TAMER • 1965 • Selander Lesley • USA
TOWN THAT CRIED TERROR, THE see **MANIAC** • 1977
TOWN THAT DREADED SUNDOWN, THE • 1977 • Pierce Charles B. • USA
TOWN THAT FORGOT GOD, THE • 1922 • Millarde Harry • USA
TOWN THAT LOST A MIRACLE, THE • 1972 • Barclay Barry • MTV • NZL
TOWN THAT TRIED TO COME BACK, THE • 1916 • Clements Roy • SHT • USA
TOWN WENT WILD, THE • 1944 • Murphy Ralph • USA
TOWN WILL DIE TONIGHT, A see **DZIS W NOCY UMRZE MIASTO** • 1961
TOWN WITHOUT JEWS, THE see **STADT OHNE JUDEN, DIE** • 1987
TOWN WITHOUT PITY (USA) see **STADT OHNE MITLEID** • 1961
TOWNE HALL FOLLIES • 1935 • *Lantz Walter (P)* • ANS • USA
TOWNIES AND HAYSEEDS • 1923 • Smith Beaumont • ASL
TOWNS AND YEARS see **GORODA I GODY** • 1973
TOWNS CHANGE THEIR FACE, THE • 1958 • Makhnach Leonid • DOC • USS
TOWNSEND DIVORCE CASE, THE • 1917 • D'Elba Henri • SHT • USA
TOXI • 1952 • Stemmle R. A. • FRG
TOXIC AVENGER, THE • 1985 • Herz Michael, Weil Samuel • USA • HEALTH CLUB
TOXIC AVENGER II, THE • 1989 • Herz Michael, Weil Samuel • USA
TOXIC LOVE see **AMORE TOSSICO** • 1984
TOXIC ZOMBIES see **BLOODEATERS** • 1980
TOY, THE • 1913 • *Majestic* • USA
TOY, THE • 1982 • Donner Richard • USA
TOY, THE (USA) see **JOUET, LE** • 1976
TOY-BOOTY • Mavrodinova Boika • ANS • BLG
TOY BOX, THE • 1971 • Garcia Ron • USA
TOY FACTORY, THE see **NECROMANCY** • 1972
TOY GRABBERS, THE see **UP YOUR TEDDY BEAR** • 1970
TOY GUN see **REVOLVER DE BRINQUEDO** • 1980
TOY-MAKER OF LEYDEN, THE • 1915 • Barlow Reginald • USA
TOY MUTINY, THE see **VZPOURA HRACEK** • 1947
TOY PHONE, THE • 1912 • *Reliance* • USA
TOY SHOP, THE • 1914 • *Princess* • USA
TOY SHOP, THE • 1928 • *De Forest Phonofilm* • SHT • UKN
TOY SHOPPE • 1934 • Lantz Walter, Nolan William • ANS • USA
TOY SOLDIER, THE • 1916 • Easton Clem • SHT • USA
TOY SOLDIERS • 1983 • Fisher David • USA
TOY TIGER • 1956 • Hopper Jerry • USA
TOY TIME • 1931 • Foster John, Bailey Harry • ANS • USA
TOY TINKERS • 1949 • Hannah Jack • ANS • USA
TOY TOWN ARTILLERY • 1929 • Aylott Dave, Symmons E. F. • SHT • UKN
TOY TOWN HALL • 1936 • Freleng Friz • ANS • USA
TOY TOWN TALES • 1931 • Foster John, Davis Mannie • ANS • USA • TOYLAND ADVENTURE
TOY TROUBLE • 1941 • Jones Charles M. • ANS • USA
TOY WIFE, THE • 1938 • Thorpe Richard • USA • FROU FROU (UKN)
TOYA • 1956 • Heed Eric • NRW
TOYLAND • 1916 • *Wheatley W.w./ Taylor R.f./taylor H.(P)* • ASS • USA
TOYLAND • 1930 • Oumansky Alexander • UKN
TOYLAND • 1932 • *Terry Paul/ Moser Frank (P)* • ANS • USA
TOYLAND ADVENTURE see **TOY TOWN TALES** • 1931
TOYLAND BROADCAST • 1934 • Ising Rudolf • ANS • USA
TOYLAND MYSTERY, A • 1916 • Taylor R. F., Wheatley W. W. • ANS • USA
TOYLAND PREMIERE • 1934 • *Cartune* • ANS • USA
TOYLAND ROBBERY, A • 1916 • *Powers* • SHT • USA
TOYLAND TOPICS • 1928 • ANS • UKN
TOYLAND VILLAIN, THE • 1916 • Taylor Horace • SHT • USA
TOYMAKER, THE • 1912 • *Vitagraph* • USA
TOYMAKER, THE DOLL AND THE DEVIL, THE • 1910 • Porter Edwin S. • USA
TOYMAKER'S DREAM, THE • 1910 • Cooper Arthur • UKN
TOYMAKER'S SECRET, THE • 1910 • *Vitagraph* • USA
TOYO BUKYO-DAN • 1927 • Uchida Tomu • JPN
TOYOTOMI'S RECORD OF PROMOTION see **SHUSSE TAIKOKI** • 1938
TOYS • 1966 • Munro Grant • SHT • CND
TOYS ARE NOT FOR CHILDREN • 1972 • Brasloff Stanley H. • USA • VIRGIN DOLLS
TOYS IN THE ATTIC • 1963 • Hill George Roy • USA
TOYS OF DESTINY • 1912 • *August Edwin* • USA
TOYS OF DESTINY • 1915 • *Rea Isabel* • USA
TOYS OF FATE • 1914 • *Whitman Velma* • USA
TOYS OF FATE • 1918 • Baker George D. • USA
TOYS OF MYSTERY • 1916 • *Unicorn* • USA
TOYS WILL BE TOYS • 1949 • Kneitel Seymour • ANS • USA
TOZHE LYUDI • 1960 • Daneliya Georgi, Talankin Igor • USS • THEY ARE ALSO PEOPLE ○ THERE ARE ALSO PEOPLE
TRA DUE DONNE (ITL) see **RECOURS EN GRACE** • 1960
TRA I GORGHI • 1916 • Gallone Carmine • ITL
TRA MOGLIE E MARITO • 1977 • Comencini Luigi • ITL
TRABALHO DE UM POVO • 1960 • Mendes Joao • SHT • PRT
TRABALHO PRISIONAL • 1954 • Ribeiro Antonio Lopes • SHT • PRT
TRACALEROS, LOS see **NICO EL TRACALERO** • 1977
TRACASSIN OU LES PLAISIRS DE LA VILLE, LE • 1961 • Joffe Alex • FRN
TRACE • 1980 • Elder Bruce • CND
TRACE, LA • 1983 • Favre Bernard • FRN, SWT
TRACE OF A GIRL see **SPUR EINES MADCHENS** • 1967
TRACE OF A TURKEY, THE see **SHICHIMENCHO NO YUKUE** • 1924
TRACE OF DEATH, A see **RASTRO DE MUERTE** • 1980
TRACED BY A KODAK • 1909 • *Kalem* • USA
TRACER, THE see **DESTINAZIONE ROMA** • 1977
TRACES • 1975 • Tremblay Regis • CND
TRACES • 1983 • Holender Jacques • SHT • CND
TRACES see **SAMO LJUDI** • 1957
TRACES see **WECHMA** • 1970
TRACES DU REVE, LES • 1986 • Lafond Jean-Daniel • DOC • CND

TRACES D'UN HOMME, LES • 1981 • Moreau Michel • MTV • CND
TRACES OF A BRUNETTE see **TRAGOVI CRNE DEVOJKE** • 1973
TRACES ON THE MOUNTAIN SITNO see **STOPY NA SITNE** • 1968
TRACES ON THE SITNO see **STOPY NA SITNE** • 1968
TRACHOMA see **TRAKOM** • 1964
TRACING BACK 1907 • 1957 • Calotescu Virgil • DOC • RMN
TRACK 29 • 1988 • Roeg Nicolas • UKN
TRACK AND FIELD QUIZ • 1945 • *Smith Pete* • SHT • USA
TRACK DOWN: HUNT FOR THE GOODBAR KILLER see **TRACKDOWN: FINDING THE GOODBAR KILLER** • 1983
TRACK OF THE CAT • 1954 • Wellman William A. • USA
TRACK OF THE MOON BEAST • 1976 • Ashe Richard • USA
TRACK OF THE VAMPIRE see **BLOOD BATH** • 1966
TRACK OF THUNDER • 1968 • Kane Joseph • USA
TRACK THE MAN DOWN • 1955 • Springsteen R. G. • UKN
TRACK WALKER, THE • 1911 • *Robinson Gertrude* • USA
TRACKDOWN • 1976 • Heffron Richard T. • USA
TRACKDOWN: FINDING THE GOODBAR KILLER • 1983 • Persky Bill • TVM • USA • TRACK DOWN: HUNT FOR THE GOODBAR KILLER
TRACKED • 1911 • *Imp* • USA
TRACKED • 1928 • Storm Jerome • USA • SUSPECTED (UKN)
TRACKED ACROSS THE SEA • 1910 • *Columbia* • USA
TRACKED AND TRAPPED BY BOY SCOUTS • 1909 • *Walturdaw* • UKN
TRACKED BY THE HOUNDS • 1915 • France Charles H. • USA
TRACKED BY THE POLICE • 1927 • Enright Ray • USA
TRACKED BY TIGER • 1911 • Fitzhamon Lewin • UKN
TRACKED BY WIRELESS • 1912 • *Royal Film* • USA
TRACKED DOWN • 1912 • *Bushman Francis X.* • USA
TRACKED IN THE SNOW COUNTRY • 1925 • Raymaker Herman C. • USA
TRACKED THROUGH THE DESERT • 1912 • Fahrney Milton • USA
TRACKED THROUGH THE SNOW • 1915 • *Badgley Helen* • USA
TRACKED TO EARTH • 1922 • Worthington William • USA
TRACKED TO FLORIDA • 1913 • *Punch* • USA
TRACKER, THE • 1988 • Guillermin John • TVM • USA
TRACKERS see **SPACE RAGE** • 1985
TRACKERS: 2180 see **SPACE RAGE** • 1985
TRACKERS, THE • 1971 • Bellamy Earl • TVM • USA • NO TRUMPETS, NO DRUMS
TRACKING A TREACLE TIN • 1910 • Wilson Frank? • UKN
TRACKING OF STINGAREE, THE • 1917 • *Boardman True* • SHT • USA
TRACKING THE BABY • 1913 • Charrington Arthur • UKN
TRACKING THE SLEEPING DEATH • 1938 • Zinnemann Fred • SHT • USA
TRACKING THE ZEPPELIN RAIDERS • 1916 • *Bartlett J.* • UKN
TRACKS • 1922 • Franz Joseph J. • USA
TRACKS • 1976 • Jaglom Henry • USA
TRACKS IN THE NIGHTS see **SPUR IN DER NACHT** • 1957
TRACTOR DRIVERS see **TRAKTORISTI** • 1939
TRACTORIST see **TRAKTORISTI** • 1939
TRACY RIDES • 1935 • Webb Harry S. • USA
TRACY THE OUTLAW • 1928 • Thayer Otis B. • USA
TRAD • 1971 • Trzos-Rastawiecki Andrzej • PLN • LEPROSY
TRADE FAIR • 1952 • Anderson Robert • DOC • CND
TRADE GUN BULLET, THE • 1912 • *Bosworth Hobart* • USA
TRADE MACHINE, THE • 1968 • Potterton Gerald • CND
TRADE MICE • 1938 • *Lantz Walter (P)* • ANS • USA
TRADE SECRET, A • 1913 • *Johnstone Lamar* • USA
TRADE TATTOO • 1937 • Lye Len • DCS • UKN • IN TIME WITH INDUSTRY
TRADE WINDS • 1938 • Garnett Tay • USA
TRADER AIREDALE see **TRADER HOUND** • 1931
TRADER GINSBURG • 1930 • Sandrich Mark • SHT • USA
TRADER HORN • 1930 • Van Dyke W. S. • USA
TRADER HORN • 1973 • Badiyi Reza • USA
TRADER HORNEE • 1970 • Tsanusdi • USA • LEGEND OF THE GOLDEN GODDESS, THE
TRADER HOUND • 1931 • Myers Zion, White Jules • SHT • USA • TRADER AIREDALE
TRADER MICKEY • 1932 • Hand David • ANS • USA
TRADER TOM OF THE CHINA SEAS • 1954 • Adreon Franklin • SRL • USA
TRADGARDSMASTAREN • 1912 • Sjostrom Victor • SWD • GARDENER, THE
TRADIMENTO, IL • 1951 • Freda Riccardo • ITL • PASSATO CHE UCCIDE
TRADIMENTO DI ELENA MARIMON, IL (ITL) see **SECRET D'HELENE MARIMON, LE** • 1953
TRADING HEARTS • 1988 • Leifer Neil • UKN
TRADING HIS MOTHER • 1911 • *Fuller Mary* • USA
TRADING PLACES • 1983 • Landis John • USA
TRADITA • 1954 • Bonnard Mario • ITL • CONCERT OF INTRIGUE (USA) ○ TRADITA LA NOTTE DELLE NOZZE ○ NIGHT OF LOVE
TRADITA LA NOTTE DELLE NOZZE see **TRADITA** • 1954
TRADITION • 1921 • Otto Paul • FRG
TRADITION DE MINUIT, LA • 1939 • Richebe Roger • FRN
TRADITION IN WINE, A • 1968 • McCullough Chris • DOC • ASL
TRADITIONAL DANCE • 1965 • Beresford Bruce • SHT • UKN
TRADITIONAL DANCE AT HYACHINE VILLAGE see **HAYACHINE NO FU** • 1983
TRADITIONAL HUNTER, A see **MATAGI** • 1983
TRADITIONAL TALES see **VEREDAS** • 1978
TRADITIONS ALTAR • 1920 • Worthington William? • USA
TRADITIONS, UP YOURS! see **REND MIG I TRADIONERNE** • 1979
TRADLOST OCH KARLEKSFULLT • 1931 • Lindh Frederick • SWD
TRAELLENE • 1978 • Hastrup Jannik • DNM
TRAELLENES OPROR • 1979 • Hastrup Jannik, Simonsen Kjeld, Steen-Petersen Annemarie • DNM
TRAFEGO E ESTIVA • 1968 • Guimaraes Manuel • SHT • PRT
TRAFFIC • 1915 • Raymond Charles • UKN
TRAFFIC BELMA see **TRAFIK BELMA** • 1967
TRAFFIC COP, THE • 1916 • Mitchell Howard M. • USA
TRAFFIC COP, THE • 1926 • Garson Harry • USA
TRAFFIC IN BABIES • 1914 • Lloyd Frank • USA
TRAFFIC IN CRIME • 1946 • Selander Lesley • USA
TRAFFIC IN HEARTS • 1924 • Dunlap Scott R. • USA
TRAFFIC IN SOLES • 1914 • *Joker* • USA
TRAFFIC IN SOULS • 1913 • Tucker George Loane • USA
TRAFFIC IN SOULS (USA) see **CHEMIN DE RIO, LE** • 1936
TRAFFIC IN WOMEN see **ONNA NO TORIHIKI** • 1967
TRAFFIC JAM see **BOTTLENECK** • 1979
TRAFFIC SIGNS see **SAOBRACAJNI ZNACI** • 1968
TRAFFIC TANGLE • 1930 • Guiol Fred • USA
TRAFFIC TROUBLE • 1967 • Bakshi Ralph • ANS • USA
TRAFFIC TROUBLES • 1931 • Gillett Burt • ANS • USA
TRAFFIC (USA) see **TRAFIC** • 1971
TRAFFICKERS IN SOLES • 1914 • *Feature Photoplay* • USA
TRAFFICONE, IL • 1974 • Corbucci Bruno • ITL
TRAFIC • 1971 • Tati Jacques • FRN, ITL • MONSIEUR HULOT NEL CAOS DEL TRAFFICO (ITL) ○ TRAFFIC (USA)
TRAFIC DE FILLES • 1967 • Maley Jean • FRN • PUNITION, LA
TRAFIC SUR LES DUNES • 1950 • Gourguet Jean • FRN
TRAFICANTES DE LA MUERTE, LOS see **PROFANADORES DE TUMBAS** • 1966
TRAFICS A RIO • 1958 • Davison Tito • MXC
TRAFICS DANS L'OMBRE • 1963 • d'Ormesson Antoine • FRN
TRAFIK BELMA • 1967 • Gultekin Sirri • TRK • TRAFFIC BELMA
TRAFIQUANT, LE • 1911 • Feuillade Louis • FRN
TRAFIQUANTS DE LA MER, LES • 1947 • Rozier Willy • FRN
TRAFRACKEN • 1966 • Lindgren Lars-Magnus • SWD • SADIST, THE (UKN) ○ CROWDED COFFIN, THE ○ COFFIN, THE
TRAGABALAS, EL • 1964 • Baledon Rafael • MXC
TRAGEDIA ALLA CORTE DI SICILIA, UNA • 1914 • Negroni Baldassare • ITL
TRAGEDIA DE AMOR • 1924 • Pinheiro Antonio • PRT
TRAGEDIA DELLA CERNIERA, LA see **CATTIVO SOGGETTO, UN** • 1933
TRAGEDIA DELL'ETNA, LA • 1951 • Paolella Domenico • ITL • ERUPTION OF ETNA, THE
TRAGEDIA DI UN UOMO RIDICOLO • 1981 • Bertolucci Bernardo • ITL • TRAGEDY OF A RIDICULOUS MAN
TRAGEDIA SENZA LACRIME • 1919 • Caserini Mario • ITL
TRAGEDIA SU TRE CARTE • 1922 • D'Ambra Lucio • ITL
TRAGEDIAN, THE • 1908 • *Essanay* • USA
TRAGEDIE DE CARMEN, LA • 1983 • Brook Peter • FRN, UKN, FRG
TRAGEDIE DE LA MINE, LA • 1931 • Beaudoin Robert, Pabst G. W. • FRN
TRAGEDIE DE LOURDES, LA see **CREDO** • 1923
TRAGEDIE IMPERIALE, LA • 1937 • L'Herbier Marcel • FRN • RASPUTIN (USA) ○ DIABLE DE SIBERIE, LE ○ RASPOUTINE ○ FIN DES ROMANOFF, LA
TRAGEDIE RUSSE • 1921 • Puchalski Eduard • PLN
TRAGEDIES OF THE CRYSTAL GLOBE, THE • 1915 • Ridgely Richard • USA
TRAGEDIJA SLUZBENICE P.T.T. see **LJUBAVNI SLUCAJ ILI TRAGEDIJA SLUZBENICE P.T.T.** • 1967
TRAGEDY AT HOLLY COTTAGE • 1916 • Batley Ernest G. • UKN
TRAGEDY AT MIDNIGHT, A • 1942 • Santley Joseph • USA
TRAGEDY IN PANAMA, A • 1915 • Oakman Wheeler • USA
TRAGEDY IN PIMPLE'S LIFE, A • 1913 • Evans Fred, Evans Joe • UKN
TRAGEDY IN SPAIN, A see **RIVALITE D'AMOUR** • 1908
TRAGEDY IN THE ALPS, A • 1913 • Weston Charles • UKN
TRAGEDY IN THE ROCK STYLE • 1988 • Koulish Savva • USS
TRAGEDY IN TOYLAND, A • 1911 • *Kalem* • ANM • USA
TRAGEDY OF A COMIC SONG, THE • 1921 • Elvey Maurice • UKN
TRAGEDY OF A DRESS SUIT, THE • 1912 • Sennett Mack, Dillon Eddie • USA
TRAGEDY OF A RIDICULOUS MAN see **TRAGEDIA DI UN UOMO RIDICOLO** • 1981
TRAGEDY OF AMBITION, THE • 1914 • Campbell Colin • USA
TRAGEDY OF BARNSDALE MANOR, THE • 1924 • Croise Hugh • UKN
TRAGEDY OF BASIL GRIEVE, THE • 1914 • Wilson Frank • UKN • GREAT POISON MYSTERY, THE
TRAGEDY OF BEAR MOUNTAIN, THE • 1915 • *Wolfe Jane* • USA
TRAGEDY OF BIG EAGLE MINE, THE • 1913 • *Wolfe Jane* • USA
TRAGEDY OF JAPAN, A • 1908 • *Vitagraph* • USA
TRAGEDY OF LOVE see **TRAGODIE DER LIEBE** • 1923
TRAGEDY OF SILENCE, THE see **ICH KANN NICHT LANGER SCHWEIGEN** • 1962
TRAGEDY OF THE AEGEAN SEA see **TRAGODIA TOU AEGAEOU** • 1965
TRAGEDY OF THE CORNISH COAST, A • 1912 • Northcote Sidney • UKN
TRAGEDY OF THE DESERT • 1912 • Olcott Sidney • USA
TRAGEDY OF THE HILLS, A • 1915 • Fielding Romaine • USA
TRAGEDY OF THE ICE, A • 1907 • Martin J. H.? • UKN
TRAGEDY OF THE NORTH WOODS, A • 1914 • *Domino* • USA
TRAGEDY OF THE OLDEN TIMES, A • 1911 • Bouwmeester Theo • UKN
TRAGEDY OF THE ORIENT, A • 1914 • Barker Reginald • USA • CURSE OF CASTE, THE
TRAGEDY OF THE RAILS, A • 1915 • Collins John H. • USA
TRAGEDY OF THE SAWMILLS, A • 1906 • Fitzhamon Lewin • UKN
TRAGEDY OF THE STREET see **DIRNENTRAGODIE** • 1927
TRAGEDY OF THE TRUTH, A • 1909 • Gobbett T. J.? • UKN
TRAGEDY OF THE VELDT, A • 1916 • SAF
TRAGEDY OF THE WATERSPRITE, THE see **VODNIKOVA TRAGEDIE** • 1958
TRAGEDY OF WHISPERING CREEK, THE • 1914 • Dwan Allan • USA
TRAGEDY OF YOUTH, THE • 1928 • Archainbaud George • USA
TRAGEDY THAT LIVED, THE • 1914 • Campbell Colin • USA
TRAGEN VINNER • 1916 • Klercker Georg • SWD • PERSEVERANCE DOES IT
TRAGIC CIRCLE, THE • 1915 • Ricketts Thomas • USA
TRAGIC CIRCUS, THE (USA) see **CIRCO TRAGICO, EL** • 1938
TRAGIC DIARY OF ZERO THE FOOL, THE • 1969 • Markson Morley • CND • ZERO THE FOOL
TRAGIC ELOPEMENT: OR, HER TERRIBLE MISTAKE, A • 1903 • *Mitchell & Kenyon* • UKN
TRAGIC EXPERIMENT, A • 1912 • *Fernleigh Jane* • USA
TRAGIC FESTIVAL, THE see **VERBENA TRAGICA** • 1939
TRAGIC FESTIVITY see **VERBENA TRAGICA** • 1939
TRAGIC GHOST STORY OF FUKAGAWA see **KAIDAN FUKAGAWA JOWA** • 1952
TRAGIC HOUR, THE see **BEATRICE CENCI** • 1926
TRAGIC HUNT (USA) see **CACCIA TRAGICA** • 1947
TRAGIC JOKE, A • 1911 • *Eclair* • USA
TRAGIC LOVE • 1909 • Griffith D. W. • USA
TRAGIC MAGIC • 1962 • Smith Paul J. • ANS • USA
TRAGIC MISTAKE, A • 1915 • Batley Ethyle • UKN
TRAGIC MOMENT, A • 1912 • *Republic* • USA
TRAGIC PURSUIT, THE see **CACCIA TRAGICA** • 1947
TRAGIC PURSUIT OF PERFECTION, THE see **LEONARDO DA VINCI: THE TRAGIC PURSUIT OF PERFECTION** • 1953
TRAGIC SHIP, THE see **ELD OMBORD** • 1922
TRAGIC SPELL see **INCANTESIMO TRAGICO** • 1951
TRAGICA NOTTE • 1942 • Soldati Mario • ITL • TRAPPOLA, LA
TRAGICA NOTTE DI ASSISI, LA • 1961 • Pacini Raffaello • ITL • ANGELO DI ASSISI, L'
TRAGICAL TALE OF A BELATED LETTER, THE • 1903 • Stow Percy? • UKN
TRAGICO RITORNO • 1954 • Faraldo Pier Luigi • ITL
TRAGICOMIC BARBER see **SORGLUSTIGA BARBERAREN, DEN** • 1927
TRAGIKOMODIE • 1922 • Wiene Robert • FRG
TRAGIKOMODIE see **PUPPENMACHER VON KIANG-NING, DER** • 1923
TRAGIQUE AMOUR DE MONA LISA, LE • 1910 • Capellani Albert • FRN
TRAGODIA TOU AEGAEOU • 1965 • Maros Basil • DOC • GRC • TRAGEDY OF THE AEGEAN SEA ○ AEGEAN TRAGEDY, THE
TRAGODIE • 1925 • Froelich Carl • FRG
TRAGODIE AUF SCHLOSS ROTTERSHEIM, DIE • 1916 • Fleck Jacob, Fleck Luise • AUS
TRAGODIE DER ENTEHRTEN, DIE • 1924 • Berger Josef • FRG • FRAUEN DER NACHT
TRAGODIE DER GRAFEN ZU SCHONSTADT, DIE see **WER WAR ES?** • 1920
TRAGODIE DER LIEBE • 1923 • May Joe • FRG • LOVE TRAGEDY ○ TRAGEDY OF LOVE
TRAGODIE DER MANJA ORSAN, DIE • 1919 • Eichberg Richard • FRG
TRAGODIE DES KASPAR HAUSER, DIE see **KASPAR HAUSER** • 1915
TRAGODIE EINER ALTERNDEN FRAU, DIE • 1924 • *Stursberg Frau Antonie* • FRG
TRAGODIE EINER EHE • 1926 • Elvey Maurice • FRG
TRAGODIE EINER INTRIGANTIN, DIE see **KITSCH** • 1919
TRAGODIE EINER LEIDENSCHAFT • 1949 • Meisel Kurt • FRG
TRAGODIE EINER LIEBE (FRG) see **VERTIGINE** • 1942
TRAGODIE EINER LIEBESNACHT, DIE • 1924 • Osten Franz • FRG
TRAGODIE EINES GROSSEN, DIE • 1920 • Gunsburg Arthur • FRG • REMBRANDT
TRAGODIE EINES KINDES, DIE see **GEHEIMNISSE VON LONDON, DIE** • 1920
TRAGODIE EINES STAATSANWALTES, DIE • 1924 • Berger Josef • FRG
TRAGODIE EINES VERLORENEN, DIE • 1927 • Steinhoff Hans • FRG
TRAGODIE EINES VERSCHOLLENEN FURSTENSOHNES, DIE see **VERSUNKENE WELT, EINE** • 1922
TRAGODIE EINES VOLKES 1, DIE • 1922 • Schebers Ernst • FRG • SCHMIED VON KOCHEL 1, DER ○ UM THRON UND LAND
TRAGODIE EINES VOLKES 2, DIE • 1922 • Schebers Ernst • FRG • SCHMIED VON KOCHEL 2, DER ○ MORDWEIHNACHT 1705
TRAGODIE IM HAUSE BANG, DIE • 1922 • Mack Max • FRG
TRAGODIE IM HAUSE HABSBURG • 1924 • Korda Alexander • FRG • MAYERLING (USA) ○ DRAMA VON MAYERLING, DAS ○ PRINZ DER LEGENDE, DER
TRAGODIE IM ZIRKUS ROYAL • 1928 • Lind Alfred • FRG
TRAGODIE ZWEIER MENSCHEN, DIE • 1925 • *Helios-Film* • FRG
TRAGOEDIA • 1976 • Brakhage Stan • SHT • USA
TRAGOUDIA TIS FOTIAS • 1974 • Koundouros Nikos • DOC • GRC • SONGS OF FIRE
TRAGOVI CRNE DEVOJKE • 1973 • Randic Zdravko • YGS • TRACES OF A BRUNETTE
TRAGUARDI DI GLORIA • 1957 • Boccia Tanio • DOC • ITL
TRAHISON A STOCKHOLM see **RAPPORTO FULLER, BASE STOCCOLMA** • 1967
TRAICAO INVEROSIMIL • 1971 • Fraga Augusto • PRT
TRAICIONERA • 1950 • Cortazar Ernesto • MXC
TRAIDOR, EL • 1938 • Bohr Jose
TRAIDORES DE SAN ANGEL, LOS • 1967 • Torre-Nilsson Leopoldo • ARG • TRAITORS OF SAN ANGEL, THE
TRAIDORES, LOS • 1973 • Gleyzer Raymundo • ARG • TRAITORS, THE
TRAIGANME LA CABEZA DE ALFREDO GARCIA (MXC) see **BRING ME THE HEAD OF ALFREDO GARCIA** • 1973
TRAIGO MI 45 • 1952 • Orona Vicente • MXC
TRAIL, THE • 1910 • Batley Ernest G. • UKN
TRAIL BEYOND, THE • 1934 • Bradbury Robert North • USA
TRAIL BLAZERS, THE • 1940 • Sherman George • USA
TRAIL BREAKERS, THE • 1914 • McRae Henry • USA
TRAIL DRIVE, THE • 1933 • James Alan • USA
TRAIL DUST • 1924 • Hines Gordon • USA
TRAIL DUST • 1936 • Watt Nate • USA
TRAIL GUIDE • 1952 • Selander Lesley • USA
TRAIL -MEN AGAINST THE RIVER, THE • 1937 • Grey Owl • CND
TRAIL -MEN AGAINST THE SNOW, THE • 1937 • Grey Owl • CND

TRAIL OF '98, THE • 1928 • Brown Clarence • USA
TRAIL OF BOOKS, THE • 1911 • Griffith D. W. • USA
TRAIL OF CARDS, THE • 1913 • Hamilton G. P.? • *American* • USA
TRAIL OF CARDS, THE • 1913 • Martin E. A. • *Selig* • USA
TRAIL OF CHANCE, THE • 1916 • Henderson Lucius • SHT • USA
TRAIL OF COURAGE, THE • 1928 • Fox Wallace • USA
TRAIL OF GOLD, THE • 1912 • *Roland Ruth* • USA
TRAIL OF GRAFT, THE • 1916 • Ellis Robert • USA
TRAIL OF HATE • 1922 • Curran William Hughes • USA
TRAIL OF HATE, THE • 1917 • Ford John • SHT • USA
TRAIL OF KIT CARSON • 1945 • Selander Lesley • USA
TRAIL OF NO RETURN, THE • 1918 • Harvey Harry • SHT • USA
TRAIL OF ROBIN HOOD • 1950 • Witney William • USA
TRAIL OF SAND, THE • 1911 • Haldane Bert • UKN
TRAIL OF SHADOWS, THE • 1917 • Ford John • USA
TRAIL OF TERROR • 1935 • Bradbury Robert North • USA • GANGSTER'S ENEMY NO.1 (UKN)
TRAIL OF TERROR • 1943 • Drake Oliver • USA
TRAIL OF THE ARROW • 1953 • Carr Thomas • USA • ARROW IN THE DUST (UKN)
TRAIL OF THE AXE, THE • 1922 • Warde Ernest C. • USA
TRAIL OF THE CIGARETTE, THE • 1920 • Collins Tom • USA
TRAIL OF THE EUCALYPTUS, THE • 1911 • Dwan Allan • USA
TRAIL OF THE FALCON see **SPUR DES FALKEN** • 1968
TRAIL OF THE FATAL RUBY, THE • 1912 • Haldane Bert? • UKN
TRAIL OF THE HANGING ROCK, THE • 1913 • Lund O. A. C. • USA
TRAIL OF THE HAWK • 1935 • Dmytryk Edward • USA • HAWK, THE
TRAIL OF THE HOLDUP MAN, THE • 1919 • Holt George • SHT • USA
TRAIL OF THE HORSE THIEVES, THE • 1929 • De Lacy Robert • USA • DOUBLE LIVES (UKN)
TRAIL OF THE HOUND, THE • 1920 • Russell Albert • SHT • USA
TRAIL OF THE HUNTER • 1970 • *Jory Victor* • DOC • USA
TRAIL OF THE ITCHING PALM, THE • 1913 • *Allen Joseph* • USA
TRAIL OF THE LAW • 1924 • Apfel Oscar • USA
TRAIL OF THE LONESOME MINE, THE • 1913 • *Nestor* • USA
TRAIL OF THE LONESOME PINE • 1926 • Fleischer Dave • ANS • USA
TRAIL OF THE LONESOME PINE • 1936 • Hathaway Henry • USA
TRAIL OF THE LONESOME PINE, THE • 1914 • Dear Frank L. • USA
TRAIL OF THE LONESOME PINE, THE • 1916 • De Mille Cecil B. • USA
TRAIL OF THE LONESOME PINE, THE • 1923 • Maigne Charles • USA
TRAIL OF THE LOST CHORD, THE • 1913 • Ricketts Thomas • SHT • USA
TRAIL OF THE LOVELORN, THE • 1914 • *Hellar Mildred* • USA
TRAIL OF THE MOUNTIES • 1947 • Bretherton Howard • USA
TRAIL OF THE OCTOPUS, THE • 1920 • Wilson Ben, Worne Duke • SRL • USA
TRAIL OF THE PINK PANTHER, THE • 1982 • Edwards Blake • USA
TRAIL OF THE POMO'S CHARM, THE • 1911 • *Kalem* • USA
TRAIL OF THE ROYAL MOUNTED see **MYSTERY TROOPER, THE** • 1931
TRAIL OF THE RUSTLERS • 1950 • Nazarro Ray • USA • LOST RIVER (UKN)
TRAIL OF THE SERPENT, THE • 1913 • *Imp* • USA
TRAIL OF THE SERPENT, THE • 1915 • Cooley Frank • USA
TRAIL OF THE SHADOW • 1917 • Carewe Edwin • USA
TRAIL OF THE SILVER FOX, THE • 1913 • *Eclair* • USA
TRAIL OF THE SILVER SPURS • 1941 • Luby S. Roy • USA
TRAIL OF THE SNAKE BAND, THE • 1913 • *Essanay* • USA
TRAIL OF THE SWORDFISH, THE • 1931 • *Sennett Mack (P)* • SHT • USA
TRAIL OF THE THIEF, THE • 1916 • Ricketts Thomas • SHT • USA
TRAIL OF THE TIGER • 1927 • McRae Henry • USA
TRAIL OF THE UPPER YUKON, THE • 1915 • Easton Clem • USA
TRAIL OF THE VIGILANTES • 1940 • Dwan Allan • USA
TRAIL OF THE WHITE MAN, THE • 1908 • *Kalem* • USA
TRAIL OF THE WILD WOLF, THE • 1916 • Hill Robert F. • SHT • USA
TRAIL OF THE YUKON • 1949 • Crowley William X.?, Beaudine William? • USA
TRAIL OF TRAPS, THE see **NEMURI KYOSHIRO BURAIHIKAE: MASHO NO HADA** • 1967
TRAIL OF VENGEANCE • 1937 • Newfield Sam • USA
TRAIL OF VENGEANCE, THE • 1924 • Ferguson Al • USA
TRAIL OF VINCE BARRETT, THE • 1933 • Horne James W. • SHT • USA
TRAIL RIDE, THE • 1973 • Hillman William Byron • USA
TRAIL RIDER, THE • 1925 • Van Dyke W. S. • USA
TRAIL RIDERS • 1928 • McGowan J. P. • USA
TRAIL RIDERS • 1942 • Tansey Robert • USA • OVERLAND TRAIL (UKN)
TRAIL STREET • 1947 • Enright Ray • USA
TRAIL THROUGH THE HILLS, THE • 1912 • *Kalem* • USA
TRAIL TO GUNSIGHT • 1944 • Keays Vernon • USA
TRAIL TO LAREDO • 1948 • Nazarro Ray • USA • SIGN OF THE DAGGER (UKN)
TRAIL TO MEXICO • 1946 • Drake Oliver • USA
TRAIL TO RED DOG, THE • 1921 • Franchon Leonard • USA • COLD STEEL
TRAIL TO SAN ANTONE • 1947 • English John • USA
TRAIL TO VENGEANCE • 1945 • Fox Wallace • USA • VENGEANCE (UKN)
TRAIL TO YESTERDAY, THE • 1918 • Carewe Edwin • USA
TRAILBLAZER MAGOO • 1956 • Burness Pete • ANS • USA
TRAILED BY BLOODHOUNDS (USA) see **BLOODHOUNDS TRACKING A CONVICT** • 1903
TRAILED BY THREE • 1920 • Vekroff Perry N. • SRL • USA
TRAILED TO THE HILLS • 1910 • *Essanay* • USA • TRAILED TO THE WEST
TRAILED TO THE PUMA'S LAIR • 1915 • Chaudet Louis W. • USA
TRAILED TO THE WEST see **TRAILED TO THE HILLS** • 1910
TRAILER • 1959 • Breer Robert • USA
TRAILER HORN • 1950 • Hannah Jack • ANS • USA
TRAILER LIFE • 1937 • *Terry Paul (P)* • ANS • USA
TRAILER ROMANCE see **NEXT TIME I MARRY, THE** • 1938
TRAILER THRILLS • 1937 • *Lantz Walter (P)* • ANS • USA
TRAILER TRAGEDY • 1940 • D'Arcy Harry • SHT • USA
TRAILIN' • 1921 • Reynolds Lynn • USA
TRAILIN' BACK • 1928 • McGowan J. P. • USA
TRAILIN' NORTH • 1933 • McCarthy John P. • USA
TRAILIN' TROUBLE • 1930 • Rosson Arthur • USA
TRAILIN' WEST • 1936 • Smith Noel • USA • ON SECRET SERVICE (UKN)
TRAILIN' WEST • 1949 • Templeton George • SHT • USA
TRAILING AFRICAN WILD ANIMALS see **TRAILING BIG GAME IN AFRICA** • 1923
TRAILING ALONG • 1937 • Yarbrough Jean • SHT • USA
TRAILING BIG GAME IN AFRICA • 1923 • Johnson Martin E., Johnson Osa • USA • TRAILING AFRICAN WILD ANIMALS ○ HUNTING AFRICAN ANIMALS
TRAILING DANGER • 1947 • Hillyer Lambert • USA
TRAILING DOUBLE TROUBLE • 1940 • Luby S. Roy • USA
TRAILING TAILOR, THE • 1916 • Beaudine William • SHT • USA
TRAILING THE BLACK HAND • 1910 • *Atlas* • USA
TRAILING THE COUNTERFEITER • 1911 • Sennett Mack • USA
TRAILING THE KILLER • 1932 • Raymaker Herman C. • USA
TRAIL'S END • 1922 • Ford Francis • USA • MAN GETTER, THE
TRAIL'S END • 1949 • Hillyer Lambert • USA
TRAIL'S END, THE • 1916 • Ellis Robert • SHT • USA
TRAIL'S END, THE • 1935 • Herman Al • USA
TRAIL'S END, THE see **ISOBEL** • 1920
TRAIL'S END, THE? see **MAN GETTER, THE** • 1923
TRAILS OF ADVENTURE • 1935 • Wilsey Jay • USA
TRAILS OF DANGER see **TRAILS OF PERIL** • 1930
TRAILS OF DESTINY • 1926 • *Lee-Bradford Corp.* • USA
TRAILS OF PERIL • 1930 • Neitz Alvin J. • USA • TRAILS OF DANGER
TRAILS OF THE GOLDEN WEST • 1931 • De Cordova Leander • USA
TRAILS OF THE WILD • 1935 • Newfield Sam • USA • ARREST AT SUNDOWN (UKN)
TRAILS OF TREACHERY • 1928 • Horner Robert J. • USA
TRAIN 56 see **TAG 56** • 1944
TRAIN 2419 see **RETURN OF CASEY JONES, THE** • 1933
TRAIN, LE • 1964 • Frankenheimer John, Farrel Bernard • FRN, ITL • TRENO, IL (ITL) ○ TRAIN, THE
TRAIN, LE • 1973 • Granier-Deferre Pierre • FRN, ITL • NOI DUE SENZA DOMANI (ITL) ○ LAST TRAIN, THE
TRAIN, THE see **AGITPOEZHD VTSIKA** • 1921
TRAIN, THE see **TAGET** • 1946
TRAIN, THE see **TRAIN, LE** • 1964
TRAIN D'AMOUR, LE • 1935 • Weill Pierre • FRN
TRAIN DANS LA NUIT, UN • 1934 • Hervil Rene • FRN
TRAIN DE 8H.47, LE • 1925 • Pallu Georges • FRN
TRAIN DE 8H.47, LE • 1934 • Wulschleger Henry • FRN
TRAIN DE BERLIN EST ARRETE • 1964 • Hadrich Rolf • FRN, ITL, FRG • TRENO E FERMO A BERLINO, UN (ITL) ○ VERSPATUNG IN MARIENBORN (FRG) ○ STOP TRAIN 349 (USA)
TRAIN DE LA VICTOIRE, LE see **TREN DE LA VICTORIA, EL** • 1964
TRAIN DE LABRADOR, LE • 1967 • Lamothe Arthur • DCS • CND
TRAIN DE PLAISIR • 1935 • Joannon Leo • FRN
TRAIN DE TRANSYLVANIE, LE • 1973 • Robiolles Jacques • FRN
TRAIN D'ENFER • 1965 • Grangier Gilles • FRN, SPN • OPERATION DOUBLE CROSS
TRAIN D'ENFER • 1984 • Hanin Roger • FRN
TRAIN DES SUICIDES, LE • 1931 • Greville Edmond T. • FRN • METROPOLE
TRAIN DESPATCHER, THE • 1911 • *Thanhouser* • USA
TRAIN DRIVER • 1961 • Zhilin Viktor • USS
TRAIN EN MARCHE, LE • 1971 • Marker Chris • FRN • TRAIN ROLLS ON, THE
TRAIN ENTERING A STATION see **RAILWAY TRAFFIC ON THE L.N.W.R.** • 1897
TRAIN FIXATION • 1977 • Dunkley-Smith John • ASL
TRAIN FOR DURANGO, A see **TRENO PER DURANGO, UN** • 1967
TRAIN GOES EAST, THE see **POEZD IDET NA VOSTOK** • 1947
TRAIN GOES TO KIEV, THE see **GODY MOLODYYE** • 1959
TRAIN IN THE SNOW, THE see **VLAK U SNIJEGU** • 1977
TRAIN KILLER, THE see **VIADUKT** • 1983
TRAIN OF DREAMS • 1988 • Smith John N. • DOC • CND
TRAIN OF EVENTS • 1949 • Cole Sidney, Crichton Charles, Dearden Basil • UKN
TRAIN OF FRIENDSHIP TO THE U.S.S.R. see **POCIAGIEM PRZYJAZNI DO Z.S.R.R.** • 1967
TRAIN OF INCIDENTS, A • 1914 • Baker George D. • USA
TRAIN OF PARTING, THE see **TOU HORISMOU TO TRENA** • 1967
TRAIN OF THE CENTRAL COMMITTEE, THE see **AGITPOEZHD VTSIKA** • 1921
TRAIN OF THE CENTRAL EXECUTIVE see **AGITPOEZHD VTSIKA** • 1921
TRAIN OF THE SPECTERS, THE see **TRENO DEGLI SPETTRI, IL** • 1913
TRAIN ON JACOB'S LADDER, MT. WASHINGTON • 1899 • *Bitzer Billy (Ph)* • USA
TRAIN POUR VENISE, LE • 1938 • Berthomieu Andre • FRN
TRAIN RIDE TO HOLLYWOOD • 1975 • Rondeau Charles R. • USA
TRAIN ROBBERS, THE • 1973 • Kennedy Burt • USA, MXC • ROBO DEL TREN, EL (MXC)
TRAIN ROBBERS, THE (UKN) see **ASSALTO AO TREMO PAGADOR** • 1962
TRAIN ROBBERY CONFIDENTIAL (USA) see **ASSALTO AO TREMO PAGADOR** • 1962
TRAIN ROLLS ON, THE see **TRAIN EN MARCHE, LE** • 1971
TRAIN ROUGE, LE • 1973 • Ammann Peter • DOC • SWT • RED TRAIN, THE (USA)
TRAIN SANS YEUX, LE • 1925 • Cavalcanti Alberto • FRN
TRAIN SPECIAL POUR HITLER see **TRAIN SPECIAL POUR S.S.** • 1976
TRAIN SPECIAL POUR S.S. • 1976 • Gartner James • FRN • TRAIN SPECIAL POUR HITLER ○ SPECIAL TRAIN FOR HITLER
TRAIN STOPS HERE, THE see **OSTANOVILSIA POEZD** • 1983
TRAIN THAT DISAPPEARED, THE see **DISAPPEARING TRAINS** • 1966
TRAIN TO ALCATRAZ • 1948 • Ford Philip, Geraughty Gerald • USA
TRAIN TO HEAVEN see **VLAK DO STANICE NEBE** • 1972
TRAIN TO HOLLAND see **IRANY HOLLANDIA** • 1986
TRAIN TO HOLLYWOOD see **POCIAG DO HOLLYWOOD** • 1988
TRAIN TO KRALJEVO, THE see **KRALJEVSKI VOZ** • 1983
TRAIN TO MILAN see **CRIMINALE, IL** • 1963
TRAIN TO THE STARS, A see **TREM PARA AS ESTRELAS, UM** • 1988
TRAIN TO TOMBSTONE • 1950 • Berke William • USA
TRAIN TRIP BY DEGREES • Goldberger Kurt • DOC • CZC
TRAIN TROUBLE • 1940 • Halas John, Batchelor Joy • ANS • UKN
TRAIN WITHOUT A TIMETABLE see **VLAK BEZ VOZNOG REDA** • 1958
TRAIN WRECKERS • 1905 • Porter Edwin S. • USA
TRAIN WRECKERS, THE • 1925 • McGowan J. P. • USA
TRAINBUSTERS • 1943 • Newman Sydney • DCS • CND
TRAINED DOGS • 1902 • Collins Alf? • UKN
TRAINED HOOFS • 1935 • Miller David • SHT • USA
TRAINED NURSE, THE • 1913 • *Crystal* • USA
TRAINED NURSE AT BAR Z, THE • 1911 • Dwan Allan • USA
TRAINED TO KILL • 1988 • Dyal H. Kaye • USA
TRAINED TO KILL see **NO-MERCY MAN, THE** • 1973
TRAINER AND TEMPTRESS • 1925 • West Walter • UKN
TRAINER'S DAUGHTER • 1907 • Porter Edwin S. • USA
TRAINING A HUSBAND • 1912 • *Majestic* • USA
TRAINING A TIGHTWAD • 1913 • *Hotely Mae* • USA
TRAINING CHAMPIONS • 1957 • Mason Richard • DOC • ASL
TRAINING FOR HUSBANDS • 1920 • Cline Eddie • SHT • USA
TRAINING PIGEONS • 1936 • Fleischer Dave • ANS • USA
TRAINS DE PLAISIR • 1930 • Storck Henri • DOC • BLG
TRAINS SANS FUMEE • 1951 • Cantagrel Marc • SHT • FRN
TRAIT D'UNION, LE • 1908 • Melies Georges • FRN • LITTLE PEACEMAKER, THE
TRAITE DE BAVE ET D'ETERNITE • 1951 • Isou Isidore • FRN
TRAITE DES BLANCHES, LA • 1965 • Combret Georges • FRN, ITL • I AM A FUGITIVE FROM A WHITE SLAVE GANG (UKN) ○ TRATTA DELLE BIANCHE, LA (ITL) ○ FRUSTRATIONS (USA) ○ HOT FRUSTRATIONS ○ GIRLS MARKED DANGER
TRAITE DU ROSSIGNOL • 1969 • Flechet Jean • FRN
TRAITEMENT 706, LE • 1910 • Melies Georges • FRN • GUERISON DE L'OBESITE EN 5 MINUTES
TRAITEMENT DE CHOC • 1972 • Jessua Alain • FRN, ITL • UOMO CHE UCCIDEVA A SANGUE FREDDO, L' (ITL) ○ DOCTOR IN THE NUDE (UKN) ○ SHOCK (USA) ○ SHOCK TREATMENT
TRAITEMENT DU HOQUET, LE • 1918 • Bernard Raymond • FRN
TRAITOR see **PREDATEL** • 1926
TRAITOR, THE • 1914 • Weber Lois • USA
TRAITOR, THE • 1915 • Hepworth Cecil M. • UKN • COURT-MARTIALLED
TRAITOR, THE • 1916 • Fahrney Milton • USA
TRAITOR, THE • 1936 • Newfield Sam • USA
TRAITOR, THE see **TRAITORS, THE** • 1957
TRAITOR, THE see **IZDAJNIK** • 1963
TRAITOR, THE see **PRODOTIS, O** • 1967
TRAITOR, THE see **FORRAEDERNE** • 1983
TRAITOR, THE see **DE BRECKER** • 1988
TRAITOR, THE see **FALSCHEN HOND, DE** • 1990
TRAITOR ON THE STAFF, A • 1911 • *Champion* • USA
TRAITOR –PSALM 25, THE • 1927 • Barnett Charles • UKN
TRAITOR SPY • 1939 • Summers Walter • UKN • TORSO MURDER MYSTERY, THE (USA)
TRAITOR TO ART, A • 1916 • Ashley Charles E. • SHT • USA
TRAITOR TO HIS COUNTRY, A • 1914 • *Lubin* • USA
TRAITOR TO HIS COUNTRY, A see **FORRAEDEREN** • 1910
TRAITOR TO HIS KING, A • 1908 • Coleby A. E. • UKN
TRAITOR WITHIN, THE • 1942 • McDonald Frank • USA
TRAITORS see **VERRATER** • 1936
TRAITORS see **NAZO NO YUREISEN** • 1958
TRAITORS, THE • 1957 • McCarthy Michael • UKN • ACCURSED, THE (USA) ○ ACCUSED, THE ○ TRAITOR, THE
TRAITORS, THE • 1962 • Tronson Robert • UKN
TRAITORS, THE see **TRAIDORES, LOS** • 1973
TRAITORS, THE see **FORRAEDERNE** • 1983
TRAITOR'S FATE, THE • 1912 • *Imp* • USA
TRAITOR'S GATE • 1964 • Francis Freddie • UKN, FRG • VERRATEROR, DAS (FRG)
TRAITORS OF SAN ANGEL, THE see **TRAIDORES DE SAN ANGEL, LOS** • 1967
TRAITOR'S REWARD see **JUDASPENGAR** • 1915
TRAITRE, LE • Kosovac Milutin • FRN
TRAITRESS OF PARTON'S COURT, THE • 1912 • Plumb Hay • UKN
TRAJA • 1969 • Bielik Palo • CZC • TRAJA SVEDKOVIA ○ THREE WITNESSES ○ THREE, THE ○ TRIO
TRAJA SVEDKOVIA see **TRAJA** • 1969
TRAJAN'S COLUMN see **COLUMNA** • 1968
TRAJE BLANCO, UN • 1956 • Gil Rafael • SPN
TRAJE DE LUCES, EL • 1946 • Neville Edgar • SPN
TRAJE DE ORO, EL • 1959 • Coll Julio • SPN
TRAKOM • 1964 • Troell Jan • DOC • SWD • TRACHOMA
TRAKTAT O MOKREJ ROBOCIE • 1976 • Piwowski Marek • PLN
TRAKTORISTI • 1939 • Pyriev Ivan • USS • TRACTOR DRIVERS ○ TRACTORIST

TRALLANDE JANTA, EN • 1942 • Larsson Borje • SWD • SINGING LESSON

TRAME, LA see **APRES LE VENT DES SABLES** • 1976

TRAMEL S'EN FICHE see **MYSTERE DE LA TOUR EIFFEL, LE** • 1927

TRAMONTANA, IL • 1966 • Barbano Adriano • ITL

TRAMONTO DEI DORIA, IL • 1921 • Falena Ugo • ITL

TRAMP see **ARCHIMEDE, LE CLOCHARD** • 1959

TRAMP, THE • 1908 • Smith Jack ? • UKN

TRAMP, THE • 1911 • *Thanhouser* • USA

TRAMP, THE • 1914 • Mackenzie Donald • USA

TRAMP, THE • 1915 • Chaplin Charles • *Essanay* • USA • CHARLIE THE HOBO

TRAMP, THE • 1915 • Walsh Raoul • *Reliance* • USA

TRAMP, THE • 1929 • Hayle Gerald M. • SHT • ASL

TRAMP, THE see **SERSERI** • 1967

TRAMP, THE (USA) see **AWARA** • 1953

TRAMP AND THE BABY'S BOTTLE, THE • 1899 • *Riley Brothers* • UKN

TRAMP AND THE BABY'S BOTTLE, THE • 1903 • Haggar William • UKN

TRAMP AND THE BATHER, THE • 1904 • *Warwick Trading Co* • UKN

TRAMP AND THE BEAR, THE • 1912 • *Lubin* • USA

TRAMP AND THE DOG, THE • 1896 • *Selig William N. (P)* • USA

TRAMP AND THE DOG, THE • 1906 • *Selig William N. (P)* • USA

TRAMP AND THE LADY, THE • 1914 • Somers Dalton • UKN

TRAMP AND THE MATTRESS MAKER, THE (USA) see **CADEUSE DE MATELAS, LA** • 1906

TRAMP AND THE NURSING BOTTLE, THE • 1901 • Porter Edwin S. • USA

TRAMP AND THE TENNER, THE • 1914 • *Browne H. A.* • UKN

TRAMP AND THE TURPENTINE BOTTLE: OR, GREEDINESS PUNISHED, THE • 1901 • *Paul R. W.* • UKN

TRAMP AND THE TYPEWRITER, THE • 1905 • Martin J. H.? • UKN

TRAMP AND THE WASHERWOMAN, THE • 1903 • Haggar William • UKN

TRAMP AT THE DOOR • 1987 • Kroeker Allan • CND

TRAMP AT THE SPINSTERS' PICNIC, THE • 1901 • *Paul R. W.* • UKN

TRAMP BICYCLIST, THE • 1910 • *Powers* • USA

TRAMP CHEF, THE • 1916 • Beaudine William • SHT • USA

TRAMP DENTISTS, THE • 1913 • *Joker* • USA

TRAMP ELEPHANT, A • 1912 • *Lubin* • USA

TRAMP IN KILLARNEY, A • 1939 • Byass Nigel • UKN

TRAMP REPORTER, THE • 1913 • *August Edwin* • USA

TRAMP STORY, THE • 1909 • *Essanay* • USA • TRAMP'S STORY, THE

TRAMP STRATEGY • 1911 • *Solax* • USA

TRAMP, TRAMP, TRAMP • 1916 • Christie Al • USA

TRAMP, TRAMP, TRAMP • 1926 • Edwards Harry J., Capra Frank (U/c) • USA

TRAMP TRAMP TRAMP • 1935 • Lamont Charles • SHT • USA

TRAMP, TRAMP, TRAMP • 1942 • Barton Charles T. • USA • CAMP NUTS

TRAMP, TRAMP, TRAMP, THE BOYS ARE MARCHING • 1926 • Fleischer Dave • ANS • USA

TRAMP TROUBLE • 1937 • Goodwins Leslie • SHT • USA

TRAMP UNDER THE BLUE SKY, THE see **TABI WA AOZORA** • 1932

TRAMPA • 1979 • Dyulgerov Georgi • BUL • SWAP, THE

TRAMPA FATAL • 1958 • Fernandez Fernando • MXC

TRAMPA MORTAL • 1962 • Santillan Antonio • SPN

TRAMPA MORTAL, LA • 1961 • Gomez Urquiza Zacarias • MXC

TRAMPA PARA CATALINA • 1961 • Lazaga Pedro • SPN

TRAMPAS • 1978 • de Pedro Manuel • DOC • VNZ • TRAPS

TRAMPING TRAMPS • 1930 • Lantz Walter, Nolan William • ANS • USA

TRAMPLERS, THE (USA) see **UOMINI DAL PASSO PESANTE** • 1966

TRAMPOSOS, LOS • 1959 • Lazaga Pedro • SPN

TRAMPS • 1897 • *Paul R. W.* • UKN

TRAMPS, THE see **MATATABI** • 1973

TRAMPS, THE see **STRAWANZER** • 1983

TRAMPS AND THE ARTIST, THE • 1899 • *Mitchell & Kenyon* • UKN

TRAMPS AND THE PURSE, THE • 1908 • Fitzhamon Lewin • UKN

TRAMPS AND THE WASHERWOMAN, THE • 1904 • Mottershaw Frank • UKN

TRAMPS AND TRAITORS • 1918 • Howe J. A. • SHT • USA

TRAMP'S CYCLING MANIA, THE • 1908 • Booth W. R. • UKN

TRAMP'S DAY OUT, THE • 1911 • *Walturdaw* • UKN

TRAMP'S DREAM • 1901 • Porter Edwin S. • USA

TRAMP'S DREAM, THE • 1906 • Fitzhamon Lewin • UKN

TRAMP'S DREAM, THE • 1913 • *Selsior Films* • UKN

TRAMP'S DREAM OF WEALTH, A • 1907 • Fitzhamon Lewin • UKN

TRAMP'S DUCK HUNT, THE • 1904 • Mottershaw Frank • UKN

TRAMP'S GRATITUDE, THE • 1912 • Dwan Allan • USA

TRAMPS IN CLOVER • 1904 • *Warwick Trading Co* • UKN

TRAMP'S MIRACULOUS ESCAPE • 1901 • Porter Edwin S. • USA

TRAMP'S PARADISE, THE • 1915 • Read James • UKN

TRAMP'S REVENGE, THE • 1904 • Williamson James • UKN

TRAMP'S REVENGE, THE • 1907 • Fitzhamon Lewin • UKN

TRAMP'S REVENGE, THE • 1914 • *Melies* • USA

TRAMP'S STORY, THE see **TRAMP STORY, THE** • 1909

TRAMP'S STRATEGY, A • 1912 • *Graham Charles* • USA

TRAMP'S STRATEGY THAT FAILED • 1901 • Porter Edwin S. • USA

TRAMP'S SURPRISE, THE • 1899 • *Mitchell & Kenyon* • UKN

TRAMP'S SURPRISE, THE • 1902 • Collins Alf? • UKN

TRAMP'S TOILET, THE • 1904 • Collins Alf? • UKN

TRAMP'S UNEXPECTED BATH, THE • 1902 • *Warwick Trading Co* • UKN

TRAMP'S UNEXPECTED SKATE • 1901 • Porter Edwin S. • USA

TRANCE • 1920 • Fleck Luise, Fleck Jacob • AUS • ANITA (USA)

TRANCERS • 1985 • Band Charles • USA • FUTURE COP

TRANCES see **HAL, EL** • 1981

TRANE, DIE • 1970 • Wicki Bernhard • SHT • FRG

TRANEN DIE ICH DIR GEWEINT see **FRUHLINGSRAUSCHEN** • 1929

TRANEN IN DEINEN AUGEN see **SOMMER, DEN MAN NIE VERGISST, EIN** • 1959

TRANEN TROCKNET DER WIND • 1967 • Schier G. H. • FRG • TEARS DRY IN THE WIND

TRANGRESSOR, THE • 1911 • *Nestor* • USA

TRANPORTATION OF FEELINGS • 1969 • Djurkovic Dejan • SHT • YGS

TRANQUILLEMENT PAS VITE: 1re PARTIE QUE S'EST-IL DONC PASSE? • 1972 • Cote Guy-L. • CND

TRANQUILLEMENT PAS VITE: 2e PARTIE COMMUNAUTE DE BASE • 1972 • Cote Guy-L. • CND

TRANQUILLO POSTO DI CAMPAGNA, UN • 1968 • Petri Elio • ITL, FRN • COIN TRANQUILLE A LA CAMPAGNE, UN (FRN) ○ QUIET PLACE IN THE COUNTRY, A (USA)

TRANS-CANADA EXPRESS • 1944 • Newman Sydney • DCS • CND

TRANS-CONTINENTAL RAILWAY • 1914 • ASL

TRANS-EUROP-EXPRESS • 1967 • Robbe-Grillet Alain • FRN, BLG • TRANS-EUROPE EXPRESS

TRANS-EUROPE EXPRESS see **TRANS-EUROP-EXPRESS** • 1967

TRANS SIBERIAN EXPRESS, THE • 1974 • Wilson Rowland B., Hall Russell • UKN

TRANS-SIBERIAN EXPRESS, THE • 1980 • Urazbayev Eldar • USS

TRANSANDINO DEL NORTE, EL • 1948 • Ayala Fernando • DOC • ARG

TRANSATLANTIC • 1931 • Howard William K. • USA

TRANSATLANTIC • Stapp Philip • ANS • USA

TRANSATLANTIC • 1961 • Morris Ernest • UKN

TRANSATLANTIC MERRY-GO-ROUND • 1934 • Stoloff Ben • USA

TRANSATLANTIC TROUBLE • 1937 • Beaudine William • UKN • TAKE IT FROM ME

TRANSATLANTIC TUNNEL (USA) see **TUNNEL, THE** • 1935

TRANSATLANTICO • 1926 • Righelli Gennaro • ITL

TRANSATLANTIQUE • 1983 • Schlumpf Hans-Ulrich • SWT

TRANSATLANTIQUES, LES • 1927 • Colombier Piere • FRN

TRANSCONTINENT EXPRESS (UKN) see **ROCK ISLAND TRAIL** • 1950

TRANSCONTINENTAL BUS see **FUGITIVE LOVERS** • 1933

TRANSCONTINENTAL LIMITED • 1926 • Ross Nat • USA

TRANSES • 1982 • Klopfenstein Clemens • SWT

TRANSES see **HAL, EL** • 1981

TRANSEXUAL, EL • 1977 • Jara Jose • SPN

TRANSEXUAL, EL • 1977 • Klimovsky Leon • SPN

TRANSFER • 1966 • Cronenberg David • CND

TRANSFER OF POWER, THE HISTORY OF THE TOOTHED WHEEL • 1939 • Bell Geoffrey • DOC • UKN

TRANSFER OF SKILL • 1937-45 • Bell Geoffrey • DOC • UKN

TRANSFERT SUSPENCE HYPNOS see **SHOCK TRANSFERT SUSPENCE HYPNOS** • 1977

TRANSFIGURATION • 1964 • Dutkiewicz Ludwik • SHT • ASL

TRANSFIGURATION HOSPITAL see **SZPITAL PRZEMIENIENIA** • 1978

TRANSFIGURATIONS, LES • 1909 • Cohl Emile • ANS • FRN

TRANSFORMACION DE UN AGENTE DE POLICIA • 1973 • Soto Helvio • CHL, FRG • METAMOFOSIS DEL JEFE DE LA POLICIA POLITICA ○ TRANSFORMATION OF A POLICE OFFICER, THE ○ METAMORPHOSIS OF THE CHIEF OF THE POLITICAL POLICE

TRANSFORMATION • 1959 • Emshwiller Ed • SHT • USA • TRANSFORMATIONS

TRANSFORMATION OF A POLICE OFFICER, THE see **TRANSFORMACION DE UN AGENTE DE POLICIA** • 1973

TRANSFORMATION OF MIKE, THE • 1912 • Griffith D. W. • USA

TRANSFORMATION OF PRUDENCE, THE • 1914 • *Gallagher Ray* • USA

TRANSFORMATIONS • 1899-00 • Blache Alice • FRN

TRANSFORMATIONS • 1904 • Blache Alice • FRN

TRANSFORMATIONS • 1914 • Smith F. Percy • UKN

TRANSFORMATIONS • 1988 • Engberg Peter • DCS • DNM

TRANSFORMATIONS • 1988 • Kamen Jay • USA

TRANSFORMATIONS see **TRANSFORMATION** • 1959

TRANSFORMATIONS ELASTIQUE • 1908 • de Chomon Segundo • FRN

TRANSFORMERS, THE see **TRANSFORMERS, THE MOVIE** • 1986

TRANSFORMERS: THE ARRIVAL FROM CYBERTRON • 1985 • Walker John* • ANM • USA

TRANSFORMERS, THE MOVIE • 1986 • Shin Nelson • ANM • USA • TRANSFORMERS, THE

TRANSFORMS • 1970 • Vanderbeek Stan • USA

TRANSFUGE, LE • 1976 • Prigent Yves • FRN

TRANSFUGE, LE • 1984 • Gonseth Frederic • SWT

TRANSFUSION • 1910 • Salter Harry • USA

TRANSGRESSION • 1917 • Scardon Paul • USA

TRANSGRESSION • 1931 • Brenon Herbert • USA • NEXT CORNER, THE

TRANSGRESSION OF MANUEL, THE • 1913 • Dwan Allan • USA

TRANSGRESSIONS OF DEACON JONES, THE • 1912 • *Francis Alec B.* • USA

TRANSGRESSOR, THE • 1913 • *Glaum Louise* • USA

TRANSGRESSOR, THE • 1918 • Levering Joseph • USA

TRANSIENT LADY • 1936 • Buzzell Edward • USA • FALSE WITNESS (UKN)

TRANSIENT LOVE see **THIS MAN IS MINE** • 1934

TRANSIENT LOVES see **TRECATOARELE IUBIRI** • 1975

TRANSIENTS IN ARCADIA • 1918 • Webb Kenneth • SHT • USA

TRANSISTORS • 1961 • Rees Clive • UKN

TRANSISTORS ISAAC ASIMOV • 1973 • Bonniere Rene • DCS • CND

TRANSIT • 1966 • Wicki Bernhard • FRG

TRANSIT • 1980 • Waxman Daniel • ISR

TRANSIT • 1982 • Candilis Takis P. • FRN

TRANSIT • 1982 • Schlumpf Hans-Ulrich • SWT

TRANSIT • 1987 • Roy Richard • SHT • CND

TRANSIT • 1990 • Allio Rene • FRN

TRANSIT A SAIGON • 1962 • Leduc Jean • FRN • INCIDENT IN SAIGON (USA)

TRANSIT CARLSBAD • 1966 • Brynych Zbynek • CZC

TRANSIT GOIN' TO TOWN • 1984 • Jubenvill Ken • MTV • CND

TRANSIT OF VENUS, THE • 1912 • Plumb Hay? • UKN

TRANSIT SUPERVAN • 1969 • Shearer Bob • SHT • UKN

TRANSITION • 1986 • Ianzelo Tony (c/d) • SHT • CND

TRANSITION, LA • 1976 • Akika Ali • SHT • FRN

TRANSITION, THE • 1913 • Sturgeon Rollin S. • USA

TRANSITIONS • 1985 • Low Colin (c/d) • CND

TRANSLATION OF A SAVAGE, THE • 1913 • Edwin Walter • USA

TRANSLATION OF A SAVAGE, THE see **BEHOLD MY WIFE!** • 1920

TRANSMIGRATION OF SOULS see **SEELENWANDERUNG** • 1964

TRANSMISSION D'EXPERIENCE OUVRIERE • 1974 • Vautier Rene • FRN

TRANSMISSIONS HYDRAULIQUES, LES • 1955 • Leenhardt Roger • DCS • FRN

TRANSMUTATION • 1947 • Belson Jordan • ANS • USA

TRANSMUTATIONS IMPERCEPTIBLES • 1904 • Melies Georges • FRN • IMPERCEPTIBLE TRANSMUTATIONS (USA)

TRANSMUTATIONS (USA) see **UNDERWORLD** • 1985

TRANSPARENCY • 1969 • Gehr Ernie • USA

TRANSPARENT CARDS, THE see **CARTES TRANSPARENTES, LES** • 1904

TRANSPARENT DEATH see **MORTE TRANSPARENTE, A** • 1980

TRANSPARENT MAN, THE see **TOMEI NINGEN ARAWARU** • 1949

TRANSPARENT MAN VS. THE FLY MAN, THE see **TOMEI-NINGEN TO HAI-OTOKO** • 1957

TRANSPLANT • 1979 • Graham William A. • TVM • USA

TRANSPLANT (USA) see **TRASPIANTO, IL** • 1970

TRANSPLANTED PRAIRIE FLOWER, A • 1914 • Miller Ashley • USA

TRANSPLANTES, LES • 1975 • Matas Percy • FRN

TRANSPORT, DER • 1961 • Roland Jurgen • FRG • DESTINATION DEATH

TRANSPORT FROM PARADISE see **TRANSPORT Z RAJE** • 1962

TRANSPORT IN THE TOWNS see **TRANSPORTE EN LAS CIUDADES, EL** • 1978

TRANSPORT OF DEATH, THE • 1986 • Pounchev Borislav • BUL

TRANSPORT OF FIRE • 1929 • Ivanov Alexander • USS • FIERY TRANSPORT, THE

TRANSPORT Z RAJE • 1962 • Brynych Zbynek • CZC • TRANSPORT FROM PARADISE

TRANSPORTE EN LAS CIUDADES, EL • 1978 • Lovera Lester • DCS • VNZ • TRANSPORT IN THE TOWNS

TRANSPORTED • 1913 • Lincoln W. J. • ASL

TRANSPORTS, LES • 1973 • Rachedi Ahmed • SHT • ALG

TRANSPORTS URBAINS • 1948 • Gibaud Marcel • SHT • FRN

TRANSVESTITE see **GLEN OR GLENDA?** • 1952

TRANSYLVANIA 6-5000 • 1963 • Jones Charles M. • ANS • USA

TRANSYLVANIA 6-5000 • 1985 • De Luca Rudy • USA

TRAP see **PIEGES** • 1969

TRAP see **TUZAK** • 1977

TRAP, THE • 1913 • August Edwin • *Powers* • USA

TRAP, THE • 1913 • Humphrey William • *Vitagraph* • USA

TRAP, THE • 1914 • *Criterion* • USA

TRAP, THE • 1914 • Ayres Sydney • *American* • USA

TRAP, THE • 1914 • Morty Frank? • *Kb* • USA

TRAP, THE • 1914 • Powell Paul • *Lubin* • USA

TRAP, THE • 1916 • Neitz Alvin J. • SHT • USA

TRAP, THE • 1917 • Ellis Robert • SHT • USA

TRAP, THE • 1918 • Archainbaud George • USA

TRAP, THE • 1919 • Reicher Frank • USA

TRAP, THE • 1922 • Thornby Robert T. • USA • HEART OF A WOLF

TRAP, THE • 1947 • Bretherton Howard • USA • MURDER AT MALIBU BEACH (UKN)

TRAP, THE • 1958 • Panama Norman • USA • BAITED TRAP, THE (UKN)

TRAP, THE • 1966 • Hayers Sidney • UKN, CND • AVENTURE SAUVAGE, L'

TRAP, THE • 1985 • Patroni Griffi Giuseppe • ITL, SPN

TRAP, THE see **PAST** • 1950

TRAP, THE see **ZAMKA** • 1974

TRAP, THE see **FALLEN** • 1975

TRAP CLOSES AT BEIRUT, THE see **TRAPPOLA SCATTA A BEYRUT, LA** • 1966

TRAP DOOR, THE • 1915 • *Ridgely Cleo* • USA

TRAP FOR A KILLER see **RAFLES SUR LA VILLE** • 1957

TRAP FOR CINDERELLA, A (USA) see **PIEGE POUR CENDRILLON** • 1965

TRAP FOR SANTA CLAUS, A • 1909 • Griffith D. W. • USA

TRAP FOR THE ASSASSIN (USA) see **TRAPPOLA PER L'ASSASSINO** • 1966

TRAP HAPPY • 1946 • Hanna William, Barbera Joseph • ANS • USA

TRAP HAPPY PORKY • 1945 • Jones Charles M. • ANS • USA

TRAP OF A LOVE POTION see **BIYAKU NO WANA** • 1967

TRAP OF BARE SKIN, THE see **SUHADA NO WANA** • 1967

TRAP OF LUST see **IROWANA** • 1967

TRAP OF PLEASURE see **KAIRAKU NO WANA** • 1967

TRAP OF THE NIGHT see **YORU NO WANA** • 1967

TRAP ON COUGAR MOUNTAIN • 1972 • Larsen Keith • USA

TRAP THAT FAILED, THE • 1915 • MacQuarrie Murdock • USA

TRAP TO CATCH A BURGLAR, A • 1913 • *Vitagraph* • USA

TRAPALHADAS DE DOM QUIXOTE & SANCHO PANCA, AS • 1980 • Cobbett William • BRZ • MISADVENTURES OF DON QUIXOTE AND SANCHO PANZA, THE

TRAPENI • 1961 • Kachyna Karel • CZC • STRESS OF YOUTH ○ WORRIES ○ PIEBALD ○ LENKA AND PRIM ○ TRIALS OF YOUTH ○ PROUD STALLION, THE

TRAPEZE • 1956 • Reed Carol • USA

TRAPEZE ARTIST, THE • 1934 • *Mintz Charles (P)* • ANS • USA

TRAPEZE DISROBING ACT • 1901 • Porter Edwin S. • USA

TRAPEZE PLEASE • 1960 • Rasinski Connie • ANS • USA

TRAPEZE (UKN) see **SALTO MORTALE** • 1931

TRAPIANTO CONSUNZIONE E MORTE DI FRANCO BROCANI • 1971 • Schifano Mario • ITL

TRAPP-FAMILIE, DIE • 1956 • Liebeneiner Wolfgang • FRG

TRAPP-FAMILIE IN AMERIKA, DIE • 1958 • Liebeneiner Wolfgang • FRG

TRAPP FAMILY, THE • 1961 • Liebeneiner Wolfgang • CMP • FRG

TRAPPE, LA • 1983 • Dinel Pierre • DOC • CND

TRAPPED • 1910 • *Columbia* • USA

TRAPPED • 1914 • *Sais Marin* • USA

TRAPPED • 1915 • *Thorn John* • USA

TRAPPED • 1923 • Fleischer Dave • ANS • USA

TRAPPED • 1925 • *Miller Carl* • USA

TRAPPED • 1931 • Mitchell Bruce • USA

TRAPPED • 1931 • Neumann Kurt • SHT • USA

TRAPPED • 1937 • Barsha Leon • USA

TRAPPED • 1949 • Fleischer Richard • USA

TRAPPED • 1989 • Walton Fred • USA

TRAPPED see **DOBERMAN PATROL** • 1973

TRAPPED see **BAKER COUNTY U.S.A.** • 1981

TRAPPED see **BIRDS OF PREY** • 1984

TRAPPED BENEATH THE SEA • 1974 • Graham William A. • TVM • USA

TRAPPED BY A HELIOGRAPH • 1914 • *American* • USA

TRAPPED BY A SKELETON see **KOSTUR POSTAVLJA ZAMKU** • 1962

TRAPPED BY BLOODHOUNDS, OR THE LYNCHING AT CRIPPLE CREEK • 1905 • *Selig William N. (P)* • USA

TRAPPED BY BOSTON BLACKIE • 1948 • Friedman Seymour • USA

TRAPPED BY FEAR (USA) see **DISTRACTIONS, LES** • 1960

TRAPPED BY FIRE • 1912 • *Bison* • USA

TRAPPED BY G-MEN • 1937 • Collins Lewis D. • USA

TRAPPED BY HIS OWN MARK • 1910 • *Capitol* • USA

TRAPPED BY TELEVISION • 1936 • Lord Del • USA • CAUGHT BY TELEVISION (UKN)

TRAPPED BY THE LONDON SHARKS • 1916 • MacBean L. C. • UKN

TRAPPED BY THE MORMONS • 1922 • Parkinson H. B. • UKN • MORMON PERIL, THE

TRAPPED BY THE TERROR • 1949 • Musk Cecil • UKN

TRAPPED BY WIRELESS • 1912 • *Kalem* • USA

TRAPPED BY WIRELESS see **PANIC ON THE AIR** • 1936

TRAPPED IN A CLOSET • 1914 • *Sterling* • USA

TRAPPED IN A FOREST FIRE • 1913 • Hamilton G. P.? • USA

TRAPPED IN A SUBMARINE (USA) see **MEN LIKE THESE** • 1931

TRAPPED IN LOVE see **NAMI NO TO** • 1960

TRAPPED IN SILENCE • 1986 • Tuchner Michael • TVM • USA

TRAPPED IN TANGIERS see **AGGUATO A TANGERI** • 1958

TRAPPED IN THE AIR • 1922 • McCarty Henry, Meehan James Leo • USA

TRAPPED IN THE CASTLE OF MYSTERY • 1913 • *Warner'S Features* • USA

TRAPPED IN THE SKY • 1939 • Collins Lewis D. • USA • SABOTAGE

TRAPPED IN TIA JUANA • 1932 • *Mayfair* • USA • HER LOVER'S BROTHER (UKN)

TRAPPED (UKN) see **TEST, THE** • 1936

TRAPPER AND THE REDSKIN, THE • 1910 • *Kalem* • USA

TRAPPER BILL, KING OF SCOUTS • 1912 • *Bartlett Charles* • USA

TRAPPER COUNTY WAR, THE • 1988 • Keeter Worth • USA

TRAPPER DAN • 1974 • Windsor Chris • CND

TRAPPER'S DAUGHTER, THE • 1911 • *Vitagraph* • USA

TRAPPER'S DAUGHTER, THE • 1911 • *Reliance* • USA

TRAPPER'S FIVE DOLLAR BILL, THE • 1911 • *O'Connor Edward* • USA

TRAPPER'S MISTAKE, THE • 1913 • *Patheplay* • USA

TRAPPER'S REVENGE, THE • 1915 • Fielding Romaine • USA

TRAPPING OF TWO-BIT TUTTLE, THE • 1917 • Horne James W. • USA

TRAPPING THE BACHELOR • 1916 • Beaudine William • SHT • USA

TRAPPOLA, LA see **TRAGICA NOTTE** • 1942

TRAPPOLA D'AMORE • 1940 • Matarazzo Raffaello • ITL • PRODEZZE DI DICKY, LE ○ DICKY

TRAPPOLA DI FUOCO, LA • 1953 • Petrosemolo Gaetano • ITL

TRAPPOLA PER 4 (ITL) see **LOTOSBLUTEN FUR MISS QUON** • 1966

TRAPPOLA PER 7 SPIE (ITL) see **SIETE ESPIAS EN LA TRAMPA** • 1967

TRAPPOLA PER L'ASSASSINO • 1966 • Freda Riccardo • ITL • TRAP FOR THE ASSASSIN (USA) ○ ROGER LA HONTE

TRAPPOLA PER UN LUPO (ITL) see **DOCTEUR POPAUL** • 1972

TRAPPOLA SCATTA A BEYRUT, LA • 1966 • Kohler Manfred R. • ITL, FRN • TRAP CLOSES AT BEIRUT, THE

TRAPPOLA SI CHIUDE, LA (ITL) see **PIEGE, LE** • 1958

TRAPPOLI PER LUPI see **DOCTEUR POPAUL** • 1972

TRAPS see **TRAMPAS** • 1978

TRAPS AND TANGLES • 1919 • Semon Larry • SHT • USA

TRAQUE, LA • 1975 • Leroy Serge • FRN, ITL

TRAQUE, LE • 1950 • Lewin Boris, Tuttle Frank • FRN, USA • TIME RUNNING OUT (USA) ○ GUNMAN IN THE STREETS (UKN)

TRAQUENARDS • 1969 • Davy Jean-Francois • FRN • EROTIQUE (USA) ○ TRAQUENARDS EROTIQUES

TRAQUENARDS EROTIQUES see **TRAQUENARDS** • 1969

TRARA UM LIEBE • 1931 • Eichberg Richard • FRG

TRAS EL CRISTAL • 1985 • Villaronga Agustin • SPN • BEHIND THE GLASS ○ IN A GLASS CAGE

TRAS LA REJA • 1936 • Dada Jorge M. • MXC

TRAS-OS-MONTES • 1976 • Cordeiro Margarida Martins, Reis Irving • PRT

TRASH • 1970 • Morrissey Paul • USA

TRASH PROGRAM • 1963 • Kneitel Seymour • ANS • USA

TRASHI • 1980 • Lewis Louie • USA

TRASMALLOS • Getino Octavio • SHT • ARG

TRASPIANTO, IL • 1970 • Steno • ITL, SPN • TRASPLANTE A LA ITALIANA (SPN) ○ TRANSPLANT (USA) ○ ITALIAN TRANSPLANT

TRASPLANTE A LA ITALIANA (SPN) see **TRASPIANTO, IL** • 1970

TRASPLANTE DE UN CEREBRO see **CRYSTALBRAIN L'UOMO DAL CERVELLO DI CRISTALLO** • 1970

TRASTEVERE • 1971 • Tozzi Fausto • ITL

TRASTIENDA, LA • 1975 • Grau Jorge • SPN • BACKROOM, THE

TRATTA DELLE BIANCHE, LA • 1952 • Comencini Luigi • ITL • GIRLS MARKED DANGER ○ WHITE SLAVE TRADE ○ SCHIAVE BIANCHE, LA

TRATTA DELLE BIANCHE, LA (ITL) see **TRAITE DES BLANCHES, LA** • 1965

TRATTATO SCOMPARSO, IL • 1933 • Bonnard Mario • ITL

TRAUM DE LIEBENDEN, EIN • 1964 • Jordan Larry • ANS • USA • DREAM OF LOVERS, A

TRAUM DER HERZOGIN, DER • 1920 • *Middendorf Kurt* • FRG

TRAUM DER ZALAVIE, DER see **ZALAMORT** • 1924

TRAUM DES ALLAN GRAY, DER see **VAMPYR** • 1931

TRAUM DES HAUPTMANN LOY, DER • 1961 • Maetzig Kurt • GDR • CAPTAIN LOY'S DREAM

TRAUM DES SANDINO, DER • 1981 • Palla Rudi, Heinrich Margareta • DOC • AUS • DREAM OF GENERAL SANDINO, THE

TRAUM EIN LEBEN, EIN • 1925 • *Haeseki Emil* • FRG

TRAUM' NICHT, ANNETTE • 1949 • Klagemann Eberhard • GDR

TRAUM VOM GLUCK, EIN • 1924 • Stein Paul L. • FRG

TRAUM VOM LIESCHEN MULLER, DER • 1961 • Kautner Helmut • FRG

TRAUM VOM RHEIN, DER • 1933 • Selpin Herbert • FRG

TRAUM VON SCHONBRUNN • 1932 • Meyer Johannes • FRG

TRAUMA • 1962 • Young Robert Malcolm • USA

TRAUMA • 1979 • Martucci Gianni Antonio • ITL

TRAUMA see **EXPOSE** • 1975

TRAUMA see **TERMINAL CHOICE** • 1984

TRAUME VON DER SUDSEE • 1957 • Philipp Harald • FRG

TRAUMENDE MUND, DER • 1932 • Czinner Paul • FRG • DREAMING MOUTH

TRAUMENDE MUND, DER • 1953 • von Baky Josef • FRG • DREAMING LIPS (USA) ○ DREAMING MOUTH

TRAUMEREI • 1944 • Braun Harald • FRG • DREAMING

TRAUMLAND DER SEHNSUCHT • 1960 • Mueller-Sehn Wolfgang • FRG • DREAMLAND OF DESIRE

TRAUMMUSIK • 1940 • von Bolvary Geza • FRG

TRAUMO, EL • 1977 • Klimovsky Leon • SPN

TRAUMREVUE • 1959 • von Borsody Eduard • AUS

TRAUMSCHIFF, DAS • 1956 • Ballmann Herbert • GDR

TRAUMSTADT • 1973 • Schaaf Johannes • FRG • CITY OF DREAMS ○ DREAMTOWN

TRAUMSTRASSE DER WELT • 1958 • Domnick Hans • FRG

TRAUMULUS • 1936 • Froelich Carl • FRG

TRAV, HOPP OCH KARLEK • 1945 • Frisk Ragnar • SWD • TROTTING, HOPE AND CHARITY

TRAVAIL • 1918 • Pouctal Henri • FRN

TRAVAIL, LE see **BAARA** • 1979

TRAVAIL C'EST LA LIBERTE, LE • 1959 • Grospierre Louis • FRN

TRAVAIL MANUEL see **HANDLING** • 1946

TRAVAILLEUR FORESTIER, LE • 1965-66 • Garceau Raymond • DCS • CND

TRAVAILLEURS DE LA MER, LES • 1918 • Antoine Andre • FRN

TRAVAUX DU TUNNEL SOUS L'ESCAUT • 1932 • Storck Henri • DOC • BLG

TRAVEL • 1973 • Kawamoto Kihachiro • ANM • JPN

TRAVEL AND LEISURE • 1971 • Fox Beryl • DOC • CND

TRAVEL GAME, THE • 1958 • Thompson Tony • UKN

TRAVEL LOG • 1978 • Winkler Donald • CND

TRAVEL NOTEBOOK (USA) see **CARNET DE VIAJE** • 1961

TRAVEL OF THE STONE, THE see **SAFARE SANG** • 1977

TRAVEL QUIZ • 1953 • *Smith Pete* • SHT • USA

TRAVEL TO SUN AND SPRING see **FAR TILL SOL OCH VAR** • 1958

TRAVEL TO THE SITE OF THE ACCIDENT see **PUTOVANJE NA MJESTO NESRECE** • 1972

TRAVEL WITH DADDY see **IN VIAGGIO CON PAPA'** • 1983

TRAVELAFFS • 1958 • Sparber I. • DCS • USA

TRAVELAUGHS • 1916 • *Keen-Powers* • ASS • USA

TRAVELIN' FAST • 1924 • *Perrin Jack* • USA

TRAVELIN' ON • 1922 • Hillyer Lambert • USA

TRAVELING BOY • 1950 • Eames Charles, Eames Ray • SHT • USA

TRAVELING EXECUTIONER, THE • 1970 • Smight Jack • USA

TRAVELING HUSBANDS • 1931 • Sloane Paul • USA

TRAVELING SALESLADY • 1935 • Enright Ray • USA

TRAVELING SALESMAN, THE • 1916 • Kaufman Joseph • USA

TRAVELING SALESMAN, THE • 1921 • Henabery Joseph • USA

TRAVELING SALESWOMAN • 1949 • Reisner Charles F. • USA

TRAVELLER, THE • 1990 • Pacheco Bruno-Lazaro • CND

TRAVELLER, THE see **PARDESI** • 1957

TRAVELLER AND THE MASK, THE • 1986 • Pacheco Bruno-Lazaro • MTV • CND

TRAVELLER SECOND CLASS see **PUTNIK DRUGOG RAZREDA** • 1973

TRAVELLERS • 1979 • Comerford Joe • SHT • IRL

TRAVELLERS see **VIAJEROS** • 1990

TRAVELLERS, THE • 1957 • Bare Richard L. • USA

TRAVELLERS FROM THE VESSEL "SPLENDID" see **PUTNICI SA SPLENDIDA** • 1956

TRAVELLER'S JOY • 1949 • Thomas Ralph • UKN

TRAVELLERS OF THE ROAD • 1913 • Hamilton G. P.? • USA

TRAVELLER'S PALM • 1976 • Borenstein Joyce • CND

TRAVELLING ACTORS see **TABIYAKUSHA** • 1940

TRAVELLING COMPANION see **COMPANERO DE VIAJE** • 1977

TRAVELLING COMPANIONS • 1973 • Shukshin Vassili • USS

TRAVELLING LIGHT • 1959 • Keatering Michael • UKN

TRAVELLING LIGHT: THE PHOTOJOURNALISM OF DILIP MEHTA • 1986 • Saltzman Deepa Mehta • DOC • CND, UKN

TRAVELLING MEN • 1987 • Campbell Martin • UKN

TRAVELLING MUSICIANS • 1984 • Kyulumov Igor • BUL

TRAVELLING NORTH • 1986 • Schultz Carl • ASL

TRAVELLING PICTURE SHOW MAN, THE see **PICTURE SHOW MAN, THE** • 1977

TRAVELLING PLAYERS see **GUSHU YIREN** • 1987

TRAVELLING PLAYERS, THE see **UKIGUSA NIKKI** • 1955

TRAVELLING PLAYERS, THE see **THIASOS, O** • 1974

TRAVELLING SHOT • 1985 • Jackson G. Philip • MTV • CND

TRAVELLING SPIRIT see **RYOSO** • 1948

TRAVELLING STILTWALKERS, THE • 1910 • Collins Alf? • UKN

TRAVELLING TUNE, THE • 1960 • Geesink Joop • ANM • NTH

TRAVELLING WITH A BREEZE see **TABI WA SOYOKKAZE** • 1953

TRAVELS OF AKAKI TSERETELI IN RACHA AND LECHKHUMI see **AKAKY TSERETELI'S JOURNEY ALONG THE RACHA AND LECHKHUMA** • 1912

TRAVELS THROUGH LIFE WITH LEACOCK • 1975 • Rasky Harry • CND

TRAVELS UNDER THE BLUE SKY see **TABI WA AOZORA** • 1932

TRAVELS WITH ANITA see **VIAGGIO CON ANITA** • 1979

TRAVELS WITH MY AUNT • 1972 • Cukor George • UKN, USA

TRAVERSATA, LA • 1976 • Risi Nelo • MTV • ITL

TRAVERSATA NERA • 1939 • Gambino Domenico M. • ITL

TRAVERSEE, LA • 1986 • Veuve Jacqueline • SWT

TRAVERSEE DE LA FRANCE, LA • 1961 • Leenhardt Roger (c/d) • DCS • FRN

TRAVERSEE DE LA LOIRE, LA • 1961 • Gourguet Jean • FRN

TRAVERSEE DE L'ATLANTIQUE A LA RAME • 1978 • Laguionie Jean-Francois • ANS • FRN • ROLLING ACROSS THE ATLANTIC

TRAVERSEE DE PARIS, LA • 1956 • Autant-Lara Claude • FRN, ITL • PIG ACROSS PARIS (UKN) ○ FOUR BAGS FULL (USA)

TRAVERSEES • 1983 • Mahmoud Mahmoud Ben • TNS, BLG

TRAVERSES D'HIVER A L'ILE AUX COULDRES, LES • 1958-60 • Bonniere Rene • DCS • CND

TRAVESTI ET CASSURES, NOIR SUR BLANC • 1967 • Beloufa Farouq • ALG

TRAVESTIS DU DIABLE, LES • 1963 • de Bravura • SHT • FRN

TRAVESURAS DE MORUCHA, LAS • 1962 • Iquino Ignacio F. • SPN

TRAVIATA '53 • 1953 • Cottafavi Vittorio • ITL • LOST ONE, THE

TRAVIATA, LA • 1922 • Sanderson Challis • UKN

TRAVIATA, LA • 1927 • Parkinson H. B. • UKN

TRAVIATA, LA • 1953 • Vinti Carlo • ITL

TRAVIATA, LA • 1967 • Lanfranchi Mario • ITL

TRAVIATA, LA • 1982 • Zeffirelli Franco • ITL

TRAVIATA, LA see **SIGNORA DALLE CAMELIE, LA** • 1948

TRAVIESA MOLIERNA, LA • 1935 • D'Arrast Harry D'Abbadie, Soriano Ricardo • SPN • SOMBRERO DE TRES PICOS, EL

TRAVIS LOGAN, D.A. • 1970 • Wendkos Paul • TVM • USA

TRAVIS MCGEE • 1983 • McLaglen Andrew V. • TVM • USA

TRAVOLTI DA UN INSOLITO DESTINO NELL'AZZURRO MARE DI AGOSTO • 1974 • Wertmuller Lina • ITL • OVERCOME BY AN UNUSUAL FATE IN A BLUE AUGUST SEA ○ SWEPT AWAY.. (USA) ○ SWEPT AWAY.. BY AN UNUSUAL DESTINY IN THE BLUE SEA OF AUGUST

TRAVOLTO DAGLI AFFETTI FAMILIARI • 1978 • Severino Mauro • ITL

TRAWLER BOY • 1956 • Lang Gordon • UKN

TRAWLER FISHERMAN • 1970 • Defalco Martin • MTV • CND

TRAWLERS FISHING IN A HURRICANE • 1910-12 • Melies Gaston • USA

TRAXX • 1988 • Gary Jerome • USA

TRAY FULL OF TROUBLE, A • 1920 • Campbell William • SHT • USA

TRAZANJA see **ISKANJA** • 1980

TRE • 1972 • Mace Nicole • NRW • THREE

TRE AMICI, LE MOGLIE E (AFFETTUOSAMENTE) LE ALTRE (ITL) see **VINCENT, FRANCOIS, PAUL.. ET LES AUTRES** • 1974

TRE ANNI SENZA DONNE • 1937 • Brignone Guido • ITL • THREE YEARS WITHOUT WOMEN

TRE AQUILOTTI, I • 1942 • Mattoli Mario • ITL

TRE AVVENTURIERI, I (ITL) see **AVENTURIERS, LES** • 1966

TRE CANAGLIE PER L'INFERNO • 1974 • Pisani Sergio • ITL

TRE CENTURIONI, I • 1965 • Mauri Roberto, Combret Georges • ITL, FRN

TRE CHE SCONVOLSERO IL WEST see **VADO, VEDO E SPARA** • 1968

TRE COLONNE IN CRONACA • 1990 • Vanzina Carlo • ITL • THREE COLUMNS ON THE CRIME PAGE

TRE COLPI DI WINCHESTER PER RINGO • 1966 • Salvi Emimmo • ITL

TRE CORSARI, I • 1952 • Soldati Mario • ITL

TRE CROCI PER NON MORIRE • 1968 • Garrone Sergio • ITL

TRE DAR I BUREN • 1963 • Frisk Ragnar • SWD

TRE DAR PA LUFFEN • 1964 • Frisk Ragnar • SWD • THREE DAYS AS A VAGABOND

TRE DESIDERI, I • 1937 • Gerron Kurt, Ferroni Giorgio • ITL, NTH • DRIE WENSEN, DE (NTH) ○ DRIE WENSCHEN ○ THREE WISHES

TRE DOLLARI DI PIOMBO (ITL) see **TRES DOLARES DE PLOMO** • 1965

TRE E DUE • Gobbi Anna • ITL

TRE ECCETERA DEL COLONELLO, LE (ITL) see **TROIS ETC. DU COLONEL, LES** • 1960

TRE ENGLE OF FEM LOVER • 1983 • Methling Sven • DNM • THREE ANGELS AND FIVE LIONS

TRE FANTASTICI SUPERMEN, I see **FANTASTICI 3 SUPERMEN, I** • 1967

TRE FILI FINO A MILANO • 1958 • Olmi Ermanno • DOC • ITL • THREE CABLES TO MILAN

TRE FRANCHI DI PIETA • 1966 • Batzella Luigi • ITL

TRE FRATELLI • 1980 • Rosi Francesco • ITL • TROIS FRERES (FRN) ○ THREE BROTHERS

TRE FRATELLI IN GAMBA • 1939 • Salvi Alberto • ITL

TRE GENDARMI A NEW YORK (ITL) see **GENDARME A NEW YORK, LE** • 1965

TRE GIORNI IN PARADISO see **CASTELLI IN ARIA** • 1939

TRE GLADA TOKAR • 1942 • Bolander Hugo • SWD • THREE GAY FOOLS

TRE HOMBRES MALOS • 1948 • de Anda Raul • MXC

TRE INNAMORATI, I • 1939 • Malasomma Nunzio • ITL

TRE KAMMERATER, DE • 1912 • Blom August • DNM • 3 COMRADES, THE
TRE LADRI, I • 1954 • De Felice Lionello • ITL, FRN
TRE MAND FREM FOR EN TROLD • 1967 • Thomsen Knud Leif • DNM, SWD • THREE MEN LOOK FOR A WITCH ○ THREE MEN IN SEARCH OF A TROLL
TRE MENO DUE • 1920 • Genina Augusto • ITL
TRE MOSCHETTIERI, I • 1909 • Caserini Mario • ITL • THREE MUSKETEERS, THE (UKN)
TRE NEL MILLE • 1971 • Indovina Franco • ITL
TRE NEMICI, I • 1962 • Simonelli Giorgio C. • ITL
TRE NOTTI D'AMORE • 1964 • Comencini Luigi, Rossi Franco, Castellani Renato • ITL • THREE NIGHTS OF LOVE (USA)
TRE NOTTI VIOLENTE • 1966 • Iquino Ignacio F. • ITL, SPN • TRES NOCHES VIOLENTAS (SPN) ○ WEB OF VIOLENCE (USA)
TRE ONSKNINGAR • 1960 • Gentele Goran • SWD • THREE WISHES
TRE PASSI A NORD • 1951 • Wilder W. Lee • ITL, USA • THREE STEPS NORTH (USA)
TRE PASSI NEL DELIRIO see **HISTOIRES EXTRAORDINAIRES** • 1968
TRE PER UCCIDERE • 1970 • McCohy S. • ITL
TRE PER UNA GRANDE RAPINA • 1973 • Leroy Serge • ITL
TRE PER UNA RAPINA • 1964 • Bongiovanni Gianni • ITL
TRE PISTOLE CONTRO CESARE • 1967 • Peri Enzo • ITL
TRE RAGAZZE CERCANO MARITO • 1944 • Coletti Duilio • ITL • CERCASI MARITO
TRE RAGAZZE VIENNESI • 1942 • Marischka Hubert, Fatigati Giuseppe • ITL, FRG • DREI TOLLE MADELS (FRG)
TRE RAMAZZE IN FUORI GIUOCO • 1974 • Clair Philippe • ITL
TRE SCENER MED INGMAR BERGMAN see **INGMAR BERGMANIN MA AILMA** • 1976
TRE SENTIMENTALI, I • 1920 • Genina Augusto • ITL
TRE SERGENTI DEL BENGALA, I • 1965 • Lenzi Umberto • ITL, SPN • ADVENTURES OF THE BENGAL LANCERS
TRE SIMPATHICE CAROGNE see **RENE LA CANNE** • 1976
TRE SKOJIGA SKOJARE • 1942 • Ahrle Elof, Holmberg Tage • SWD • THREE FUNNY RASCALS
TRE SLAGS KAERLIGHED • 1970 • Ahlberg Mac • DNM • DAUGHTER: I, A WOMAN PART III, THE (USA) ○ I, A WOMAN –3 ○ I AM A WOMAN III
TRE SONER GICK TILL FLYGET • 1945 • Husberg Rolf • SWD • THREE SONS WENT TO THE AIRFORCE
TRE SPIETATI, I • 1964 • Romero-Marchent Joaquin Luis • SPN, ITL
TRE STORIE PROIBITE • 1952 • Genina Augusto • ITL • THREE FORBIDDEN STORIES
TRE STRANIERE A ROMA • 1959 • Gora Claudio • ITL
TRE SUPERMEN A TOKIO (ITL) see **DREI TOLLE KERLE** • 1968
TRE TIGRI CONTRO TRE TIGRI • 1977 • Corbucci Sergio, Steno • ITL
TRE UOMINI IN FRAK • 1933 • Bonnard Mario • ITL • VOCE DEL PADRONE, LA
TRE VOLTI DELLA PAURA, I • 1963 • Bava Mario • ITL, FRN, USA • TROIS VISAGES DE LA PEUR, LES (FRN) ○ BLACK SABBATH (USA) ○ THREE FACES OF FEAR, THE ○ THREE FACES OF TERROR, THE ○ BLACK CHRISTMAS
TRE VOLTI, I • 1965 • Antonioni Michelangelo, Bolognini Mauro, Indovina Franco • ITL
TREACHEROUS POLICEMAN, THE • 1909 • Bouwmeester Theo? • UKN
TREACHEROUS RIVAL, A • 1914 • Kendall Preston, Merwin Bannister • USA
TREACHEROUS SHOT, A • 1912 • *Cooper Marion* • USA
TREACHERY see **PRODOSSIA** • 1964
TREACHERY see **BELANG PERTENDA** • 1971
TREACHERY AND GREED ON THE PLANET OF THE APES • 1974 • *Mcdowall Roddy* • MTV • USA
TREACHERY AT SEA • 1918 • *Universal* • SHT • USA
TREACHERY GAME, THE see **ASSASSINATION RUN, THE** • 1984
TREACHERY OF A SCAR, THE • 1913 • *Kalem* • USA
TREACHERY OF BRONCHO BILLY'S PAL, THE • 1914 • *Anderson Broncho Billy* • USA
TREACHERY OF THE PEQUOTS, THE • 1910 • *Kalem* • USA
TREACHERY OF THE RED MAN • 1916 • *Buffalo* • SHT • USA
TREACHERY ON THE HIGH SEAS (USA) see **NOT WANTED ON VOYAGE** • 1936
TREACHERY RIDES THE RANGE • 1936 • McDonald Frank • USA
TREACHERY RIDES THE TRAIL • 1949 • Moore Charles • SHT • USA
TREAD SOFTLY • 1952 • MacDonald David • UKN
TREAD SOFTLY STRANGER • 1958 • Parry Gordon • UKN
TREAD SOFTLY (UKN) see **SCHUSSE AUS DEM GEIGENKASTEN** • 1965
TREADLE AND BOBBIN • 1954 • Gelentine Wheaton • SHT • USA
TREASON • 1917 • Holubar Allen • USA
TREASON • 1918 • King Burton L. • USA
TREASON • 1933 • Seitz George B. • USA
TREASON OF ANATOLE, THE • 1915 • *Girardot Etienne* • USA
TREASON (UKN) see **REBELLION** • 1936
TREASON (UKN) see **OLD LOUISIANA** • 1937
TREASON (UKN) see **GUILTY OF TREASON** • 1949
TREASURE see **TREASURE OF THE SEA** • 1918
TREASURE, THE • 1915 • *Wise Tom* • USA
TREASURE, THE • 1951 • Leonard Marion • USA
TREASURE, THE • 1961 • Chkheidze Revaz • USS
TREASURE, THE see **SCHATZ, DER** • 1923
TREASURE, THE see **SKARB** • 1949
TREASURE, THE see **NIDHANAYA** • 1971
TREASURE, THE see **GANJ** • 1973
TREASURE, THE see **SHARK'S TREASURE** • 1974
TREASURE AT THE MILL • 1957 • Anderson Max • UKN
TREASURE AT VADUL VECHI, THE see **COMOARA DE CA VADIL VECHI** • 1963
TREASURE BLUES • 1935 • Parrott James • SHT • USA
TREASURE BOX, THE • 1915 • *Ovey George* • USA
TREASURE CANYON • 1924 • *Warner J. B.* • USA
TREASURE GIRL • 1930 • Boleslawski Richard • SHT • USA
TREASURE HUNT • 1952 • Carstairs John Paddy • UKN
TREASURE HUNT • 1985 • SAF
TREASURE HUNT see **WRONG ROAD, THE** • 1937
TREASURE HUNT see **POTRAGA ZA BLAGOM** • 1974
TREASURE HUNT, THE • 1960 • *Halas John (P)* • ANS • UKN
TREASURE HUNTERS, THE • 1910 • *Selig* • USA
TREASURE HUNTERS IN THE HEART OF AFRICA • 1913 • *International Feature Film* • SHT • USA
TREASURE HUNTRESS see **TSUKIHIME KEIZU** • 1958
TREASURE IN MALTA • 1963 • Williams Derek • SRL • UKN
TREASURE ISLAND • Nicholson Nick, Muir Roger
TREASURE ISLAND • 1912 • Dawley J. Searle • USA
TREASURE ISLAND • 1917 • Franklin Chester M., Franklin Sidney A. • USA
TREASURE ISLAND • 1920 • Tourneur Maurice • USA
TREASURE ISLAND • 1934 • Fleming Victor • USA
TREASURE ISLAND • 1941 • Bradley David • USA
TREASURE ISLAND • 1950 • Haskin Byron • UKN
TREASURE ISLAND • 1972 • Hough John • UKN, FRG, SPN • ISLA DEL TESORO, LA
TREASURE ISLAND • 1982 • Heather Dave • UKN • TREASURE ISLAND: THE MUSICAL
TREASURE ISLAND • 1987 • Kikoine Gerard
TREASURE ISLAND see **DOBUTSU TAKARAJIMA** • 1971
TREASURE ISLAND see **OSTROV SOKROVISC** • 1971
TREASURE ISLAND IN OUTER SPACE see **SPACE ISLAND** • 1987
TREASURE ISLAND: THE MUSICAL see **TREASURE ISLAND** • 1982
TREASURE JEST • 1945 • Swift Howard • ANS • USA
TREASURE MOUNTAIN see **TAKARA NO YAMA** • 1929
TREASURE OF ARNE, THE see **HERR ARNES PENGAR** • 1919
TREASURE OF BIRD ISLAND, THE see **POKLAD PTACIHO OSTROVA** • 1952
TREASURE OF BRUCE LEE • 1985 • Velasco Joseph • HKG
TREASURE OF BUDDAH, THE • 1914 • *Gerrard Film* • USA
TREASURE OF CAPTAIN KIDD, THE • 1913 • Ridgely Richard • USA
TREASURE OF CIBOLA, THE • 1916 • Horne James W. • SHT • USA
TREASURE OF DEATH see **FORTY MILLION BUCKS** • 1978
TREASURE OF DESERT ISLE, THE • 1913 • Ince Ralph • USA
TREASURE OF DOOM see **TESORO DEL AMAZONES, EL** • 1983
TREASURE OF FEAR see **SCARED STIFF** • 1945
TREASURE OF HEAVEN, THE • 1916 • Coleby A. E. • UKN
TREASURE OF ICE CAKE ISLAND • 1960 • Halas John • ANS • UKN
TREASURE OF JAMAICA REEF, THE see **EVIL IN THE DEEP** • 1976
TREASURE OF KALIFA (UKN) see **STEEL LADY, THE** • 1953
TREASURE OF LOST CANYON, THE • 1952 • Tetzlaff Ted • USA
TREASURE OF MAKUBA, THE (USA) see **TESORO DE MAKUBA, EL** • 1966
TREASURE OF MATECUMBE • 1976 • McEveety Vincent • USA
TREASURE OF MONTE CRISTO, THE • 1949 • Berke William • USA
TREASURE OF MONTE CRISTO, THE • 1961 • Baker Robert S. • UKN • SECRET OF MONTE CRISTO, THE (USA)
TREASURE OF PANCHO VILLA, THE • 1955 • Sherman George • USA
TREASURE OF RUBY HILLS • 1955 • McDonald Frank • USA
TREASURE OF SAN GENNARO (USA) see **OPERAZIONE SAN GENNARO** • 1966
TREASURE OF SAN LUCAS, THE see **DOWN TWISTED** • 1987
TREASURE OF SAN TERESA, THE • 1959 • Rakoff Alvin • UKN, FRG • HOT MONEY GIRL (USA) ○ RHAPSODIE IN BLEI (FRG) ○ LONG DISTANCE
TREASURE OF SIERRA MADRE, THE see **TREASURE OF THE SIERRA MADRE, THE** • 1948
TREASURE OF SILVER LAKE (USA) see **SCHATZ IM SILBERSEE, DER** • 1962
TREASURE OF TAYOPA see **TAYOPA TREASURE HUNT** • 1974
TREASURE OF THE AMAZON, THE see **TESORO DEL AMAZONES, EL** • 1983
TREASURE OF THE FOREST • 1958 • Blais Roger • DCS • CND • FORET EST UN TRESOR, LA
TREASURE OF THE FOUR CROWNS see **TESORO DE LAS CUATRO CORONAS, EL** • 1983
TREASURE OF THE GOLDEN CONDOR • 1953 • Daves Delmer • USA • CONDOR'S NEST
TREASURE OF THE GROTECEANS, THE see **TRESOR DES GROTOCEANS, LE** • 1980
TREASURE OF THE LOST DESERT • 1982 • Zarindast Tony • USA
TREASURE OF THE MOON GODDESS • 1987 • Garcia Agraz Jose Luis • MXC, USA • RACE TO DANGER
TREASURE OF THE PETRIFIED FOREST, THE see **TESORO DELLA FORESTA PIETRIFICATA, IL** • 1965
TREASURE OF THE PIRATES, THE see **PIRACKI SKARB** • 1960
TREASURE OF THE SEA • 1918 • Reicher Frank • USA • TREASURE
TREASURE OF THE SIERRA MADRE, THE • 1948 • Huston John • USA • TREASURE OF SIERRA MADRE, THE
TREASURE OF THE WHITE GODDESS see **DEVIL HUNTER**
TREASURE OF THE YANKEE ZEPHYR (USA) see **RACE TO THE YANKEE ZEPHYR** • 1981
TREASURE OF WONG LOW, THE • 1934 • Cannon Raymond • USA
TREASURE, OR, THE HOUSE NEXT DOOR, THE • 1909 • *Vitagraph* • USA
TREASURE PLANET • 1983 • Petkov Roumen • ANM • BUL
TREASURE RUNT • 1932 • *Mintz Charles (P)* • ANS • USA
TREASURE SEEKERS • 1915 • *Wolbert William* • USA
TREASURE SEEKERS, THE see **FORTY MILLION BUCKS** • 1978
TREASURE SHIP, THE • 1914 • *Hollister Alice* • USA
TREASURE TRAIN, THE • 1914 • *Baggot King* • USA
TREASURE TROVE • 1911 • *Vitagraph* • USA
TREASURE TROVE • 1912 • *Thanhouser* • USA
TREASURE TROVE • 1914 • Miller Ashley • USA
TREASURE TROVE • 1922 • Miller Frank • UKN
TREASURED EARTH see **TALPALTNYI FOLD** • 1948
TREASURER'S REPORT, THE • 1928 • Chalmers Thomas • SHT • USA
TREASURES FROM TRASH • 1946 • Barclay David • SHT • USA
TREASURES OF KATOOMBA • 1934 • Hurley Frank • DOC • ASL
TREASURES OF SATAN, THE (USA) see **TRESORS DE SATAN, LES** • 1902
TREASURES OF THE PALLAVAS see **PALLAVA SELVANGAL** • 1967
TREASURES OF THE SNOW • 1985 • Pritchard Mike • UKN
TREASURES ON EARTH • 1914 • *Jones Edgar* • USA
TREASURES ON THE WING • 1912 • *Quirk Billy* • USA
TREAT 'EM KIND • 1920 • Goldaine Mark • SHT • USA
TREAT 'EM ROUGH • 1917 • Chaudet Louis W. • SHT • USA
TREAT 'EM ROUGH • 1919 • Reynolds Lynn • USA
TREAT 'EM ROUGH • 1942 • Taylor Ray • USA
TREATING 'EM ROUGH • 1919 • Jackman Fred • SHT • USA
TREATISE ON JAPANESE BAWDY SONGS, A see **NIHON SHUNKAKU** • 1967
TREATMENT, THE see **FULL TREATMENT, THE** • 1961
TREATY TIME AT FORT RAE • 1939 • Finnie Richard S. • DOC • CND
TREBENDE KRAFT • 1921 • Nagy Zoltan • FRG
TRECATOARELE IUBIRI • 1975 • Ursianu Malvina • RMN • THESE FLEETING LOVES ○ TRANSIENT LOVES
TRECE ONZAS DE ORO • 1947 • Delgras Gonzalo • SPN
TRECENTO DELLA SETTIMA, I • 1943 • Baffico Mario • ITL
TRECI KLJUC • 1984 • Tadic Zoran • YGS • THIRD KEY, THE
TRECIA CZESC NOCY • 1971 • Zulawski Andrzej • PLN • THIRD PART OF THE NIGHT, THE ○ TRZECIA CZESC NOCY
TREDICESIMO E SEMPRE GUIDA, IL • 1971 • Vari Giuseppe • ITL
TREDICI UOMINI E UN CANNONE • 1936 • Forzano Giovacchino • ITL, UKN • 13 MEN AND A GUN (UKN)
TREDIE MAGT, DEN • 1912 • Blom August • DNM • SECRET TREATY, THE
TREE, THE • 1969 • Guenette Robert • USA
TREE AND THE BIRD, THE • 1971 • van Maelder Louis • ANS • BLG
TREE AND THE CHAFF, THE • 1913 • Parker Lem B. • USA
TREE CORNERED TWEETY • 1956 • Freleng Friz • ANS • USA
TREE FOR TWO • 1943 • Wickersham Bob • ANS • USA
TREE FOR TWO • 1952 • Freleng Friz • ANS • USA
TREE GROWS IN BROOKLYN, A • 1945 • Kazan Elia • USA
TREE GROWS IN BROOKLYN, A • 1974 • Hardy Joseph • TVM • USA
TREE IMP, THE • 1912 • *Prior Herbert* • USA
TREE IN A TEST TUBE, THE • 1943 • McDonald Charles • SHT • USA
TREE IS A TREE IS A TREE?, A • 1962 • Kneitel Seymour • ANS • USA
TREE MEDIC, THE • 1955 • Lovy Alex • ANS • USA
TREE OF HANDS • 1989 • Foster Giles • UKN
TREE OF HAPPINESS, THE • 1910 • *Pathe* • FRN
TREE OF KNOWLEDGE, THE • 1912 • *Selig* • USA
TREE OF KNOWLEDGE, THE • 1920 • De Mille William C. • USA
TREE OF KNOWLEDGE, THE see **KUNDSKABENS TRAE** • 1981
TREE OF LIBERTY, THE (UKN) see **HOWARDS OF VIRGINIA, THE** • 1940
TREE OF LIFE • 1988 • Aboulkadir • SML
TREE OF LIFE, THE • 1971 • Ferno John • NTH
TREE OF LOVE see **AIGEN KATSURA** • 1937
TREE OF WEALTH, THE • 1944 • Rao A. Bhaskar • IND
TREE OF WOODEN CLOGS, THE see **ALBERO DEGLI ZOCCOLI, L'** • 1978
TREE PEOPLE, THE • 1989 • Markham Monte • USA
TREE SAPS • 1931 • Fleischer Dave • ANS • USA
TREE SURGEON, THE • 1944 • Gordon George • ANS • USA
TREE THINGS • 1968 • *Haugse Bill (P)* • SHT • USA
TREE TRUNK TO HEAD • 1947 • Jacobs Lewis • USA
TREE WE DAMAGED, THE see **DENDRO POU PLIGONAME, TO** • 1987
TREE WITH THE WOODEN CLOGS, THE (UKN) see **ALBERO DEGLI ZOCCOLI, L'** • 1978
TREE WITHOUT ROOTS, A • 1974 • Hristov Hristo • BUL
TREED • 1916 • Miller Rube • SHT • USA
TREEFALL • 1970 • Rimmer David • CND
TREE'S A CROWD • 1958 • Smith Paul J. • ANS • USA
TREES AND JAMAICA DADDY • 1958 • Keller Lew • ANS • USA
TREES AND PEOPLE see **STROMY A LIDE** • 1962
TREES ARE BROWN, THE • 1977 • Dalen Zale R. • CND
TREE'S KNEES, THE • 1930 • Harman Hugh, Ising Rudolf • ANS • USA
TREFF AS see **GEHEIMNIS DER SECHS SPIELKARTEN 3, DAS** • 1921
TREFFEN IN TRAVERS • 1988 • Gwisdek Michael • GDR • RENDEZVOUS IN TRAVERS
TREFFPUNKT AFRIKA! see **ABENTEUERIN VON TUNIS, DIE** • 1931
TREFFPUNKT AIMEE • 1956 • Reinecke Horst • GDR
TREFLE A CINQ FEUILLES, LE • 1971 • Fress Edmond • FRN • HOMME DES CINQ SAISONS, L' ○ MAN FOR FIVE SEASONS, THE
TREFLE D'ARGENT, LE • 1914 • Poirier Leon • FRN
TREGUA, LA • 1974 • Renan Sergio • ARG • TRUCE, THE
TREI MERE • 1979 • Popescu-Gopo Ion • RMN
TREIBENDE FLOSS, DAS • 1917 • *Reicher Ernst* • FRG
TREIBENDE KRAFFT!, DIE • 1921 • Alsen Ola • FRG
TREIBGUT DER GROSSTADT • 1967 • Gabriel Harold • FRG • DRIFTWOOD OF THE CITY
TREIBJAGD AUF EIN LEBEN • 1961 • Lothar Ralph • FRG
TREICHVILLE see **MOI, UN NOIR** • 1957
TREIN ANONIEM • 1968 • Schneider Paul A. M. • SHT • NTH
TREINTA Y NUEVE CARTAS DE AMOR • 1949 • Rovira Beleta Francisco • SPN
TREIZE A TABLE • 1955 • Hunebelle Andre • FRN
TREIZIEME ENQUETE DE GREY, LA • 1937 • Maudru Pierre • FRN
TREIZIEME EPOUSE, LA see **ZAWJA ATH-THALITHA ACHAR, AZ-** • 1961
TREIZIEME JURE, LE see **GRIBOUILLE** • 1937
TREK, THE see **POHOD** • 1968

TREK TO MASHOMBA • 1951 • Sewell Vernon • UKN
TREKSCHUIT, DE • 1932 • Franken Mannus • NTH
TRELAWNEY OF THE WELLS • 1916 • Hepworth Cecil M. • UKN
TRELAWNEY OF THE WELLS see **ACTRESS, THE** • 1928
TRELLOS, PALAVOS KE VENGOS • 1967 • Vengos Thanasis • GRC • MAD, CRAZY AND VENGOS
TRELLOS TAHI TETRAKOSIS, O • 1968 • Karayannis Kostas • GRC • CRAZY MAN WITH FOUR HUNDRED, THE ○ CRAZY MAN WITH BRAINS, A
TREM PARA AS ESTRELAS, UM • 1988 • Diegues Caca • BRZ • TRAIN TO THE STARS, A
TREMARNE CASE, THE • 1924 • Croise Hugh • UKN
TREMBITA • 1968 • Nikolayevski Oleg • USS
TREMBLEMENTS DE CHAIR • Baudricourt Michel • FRN
TREMBLING HOUR, THE • 1919 • Siegmann George • USA
TREMBLING TANG see **FURUERU SHITA** • 1981
TREMOLINA • 1956 • Nunez Ricardo • SPN
TREMOR AS DIE AARDE SKEUR • 1961 • SAF
TREN DE LA VICTORIA, EL • 1964 • Ivens Joris • SHT • CHL • TRAIN DE LA VICTOIRE, LE
TREN DE MATINADA see **PALABRAS DE AMOR** • 1968
TREN FANTASMA, EL • 1926 • Garcia Moreno Gabriel • MXC
TRENCHCOAT • 1983 • Tuchner Michael • USA
TRENCK • 1932 • Neubach Ernst, Paul Heinz • FRG
TRENCK DER PANDUR • 1940 • Selpin Herbert • FRG
TRENDS see **TENDENCIAR** • 1967
TRENDS OF JUNE, THE • 1969 • Zilnik Zelimir • SHT • YGS
TRENDSETTER • 1969 • Linnecar Vera • ANS • USA
TRENER • 1979 • Djordjevic Purisa • YGS • COACH, THE
TRENO, IL (ITL) see **TRAIN, LE** • 1964
TRENO CROCIATO, IL • 1943 • Campogalliani Carlo • ITL • TRENO CROCIATO C.R.15
TRENO CROCIATO C.R.15 see **TRENO CROCIATO, IL** • 1943
TRENO DEGLI SPETTRI, IL • 1913 • Caserini Mario • ITL • TRAIN OF THE SPECTERS, THE
TRENO DEL SABATO, IL • 1964 • Sala Vittorio • ITL • SATURDAY TRAIN, THE
TRENO DELLE 21.15, IL • 1933 • Palermi Amleto • ITL
TRENO E FERMO A BERLINO, UN (ITL) see **TRAIN DE BERLIN EST ARRETE** • 1964
TRENO EXPRESO, EL • 1954 • Klimovsky Leon • SPN
TRENO PER DURANGO, UN • 1967 • Caiano Mario • ITL, SPN • TRAIN FOR DURANGO, A
TRENO PER ISTANBUL, IL • 1979 • Mingozzi Gianfranco • ITL
TRENO POPOLARE • 1933 • Matarazzo Raffaello • ITL
TRENO REALE • 1915 • Campogalliani Carlo • ITL
TRENTA MINUTI D'AMORE • 1982 • Vicario Marco • ITL • THIRTY MINUTES OF LOVE
TRENTA SECONDI D'AMORE • 1936 • Bonnard Mario • ITL
TRENTA WINCHESTER PER EL DIABLO • 1966 • Baldanello Gianfranco • ITL
TRENT'ANNI DI SERVIZIO • 1945 • Baffico Mario • ITL
TRENTE ANS DE LA VIE D'UN SKIEUR • 1972 • Ichac Marcel • DCS • FRN
TRENTE ET QUARANTE • 1945 • Grangier Gilles • FRN
TRENTE MILLE EMPLOYES DE L'ETAT • 1968 • Gagne Jean • DCS • CND
TRENTE SECONDES POUR REVER • 1981 • Leconte Jean-Louis • DOC • CND
TRENT'S FOLLY see **HOUSE OF TRENT, THE** • 1933
TRENT'S LAST CASE • 1920 • Garrick Richard • UKN
TRENT'S LAST CASE • 1929 • Hawks Howard • USA
TRENT'S LAST CASE • 1952 • Wilcox Herbert • UKN
TRENUL DE AUR • 1988 • RMN, PLN • GOLDEN TRAIN, THE
TRENUTKI ODLOCITVE • 1955 • Cap Frantisek • YGS • MOMENT OF DECISION
TRENZA, LA • 1973 • *Churubusco Azteca* • MXC
TREPADORA, LA • 1944 • Martinez Solares Gilberto • MXC
TREPIDAZIONE • 1946 • Frenguelli Tony • ITL
TREPPE, DIE see **VERFUHRTE JUGEND** • 1950
TRES ALEGRES COMADRES, LAS • 1952 • Davison Tito • MXC
TRES ALEGRES COMPADRES, LOS • 1951 • Soler Julian • MXC
TRES AMORES • 1934 • Sackin Moe
TRES AMORES DE LOLA, LOS • 1955 • Cardona Rene • MXC, SPN
TRES ANGELITOS NEGROS • 1958 • Cortes Fernando • MXC
TRES BALAS PERDIDAS • 1960 • Rodriguez Roberto • MXC
TRES BOHEMIOS, LOS • 1956 • Morayta Miguel • MXC
TRES BRIBONES • 1954 • Mendez Fernando • MXC
TRES CALAVERAS, LOS • 1964 • Cortes Fernando • MXC
TRES CANTOS • 1949 • Berlanga Luis Garcia • SPN
TRES CITAS CON EL DESTINO (SPN) see **MALEFICIO** • 1954
TRES COMEDIAS DE AMOR see **CUERNAVACA EN PRIMAVERA** • 1965
TRES COMPADRES, LOS • 1974 • *Filmicas Agrasanchez* • MXC
TRES COQUETONAS, LAS • 1959 • Salvador Jaime • MXC • AMORES DE TRES COLEGIALAS, LOS
TRES DA VIDA AIRADA, OS • 1952 • Queiroga Perdigao • PRT
TRES DE COPAS, EL • 1986 • Cazals Felipe • MXC • THREE OF HEARTS
TRES DE LA CRUZ ROJA • 1962 • Palacios Fernando • SPN
TRES DESGRACIADOS CON SUETE • 1957 • Salvador Jaime • MXC • THREE UNLUCKY ONES
TRES DIAS DE NOVEMBRE • 1976 • Klimovsky Leon • SPN
TRES DIAS SEM DEUS • 1946 • Virginia Barbara • PRT • THREE DAYS WITHOUT GOD
TRES DOLARES DE PLOMO • 1965 • Mercanti Pino • SPN, ITL • TRE DOLLARI DI PIOMBO (ITL)
TRES ELENAS, LAS • 1953 • Gomez Muriel Emilio • MXC
TRES EN RAYA • 1979 • Roma Francisco • SPN • THREE CHILDREN'S GAMES
TRES ERAN TRES • 1954 • Maroto Eduardo G. • SPN • TIAPACA (?) ○ THREE WERE THREE
TRES ESPADAS DEL ZORRO, LAS • 1963 • Blasco Ricardo • SPN, ITL • THREE SWORDS OF ZORRO, THE (USA)
TRES ESPELHOS • 1946 • Vajda Ladislao • PRT
TRES FANTASIAS DE PEPE • 1965 • Puig Jaime • ANS • SPN • THREE FANTASIES OF PEPE
TRES FARSANTES, LOS • 1965 • Fernandez Antonio • MXC
TRES GALLOS, LOS • 1989 • Urquieta Jose Luis • MXC • THREE ROOSTERS, THE
TRES GARCIA, LOS • 1946 • Rodriguez Ismael • MXC • THREE GARCIAS, THE
TRES GORRIONES Y PICO • 1964 • del Amo Antonio • SPN
TRES HERMANOS • 1943 • Benavides Jose Jr. • MXC • THREE BROTHERS
TRES HISTORIAS DE AMOR • 1978 • Busteros Raul • MXC • THREE LOVE STORIES
TRES HISTORIAS FANTASTICAS • 1965 • Madanes Marcos • ARG • THREE FANTASTIC STORIES
TRES HOMBRES BUENOS • 1963 • Romero-Marchent Joaquin Luis • SPN
TRES HOMBRES DEL RIO • 1943 • Soffici Mario • ARG
TRES HOMBRES EN MI VIDA • 1951 • Vejar Carlos • MXC
TRES HOMBRES VAN A MORIR • 1954 • Catalan Feliciano, Chanas Rene • SPN
TRES HUASTECOS, LOS • 1948 • Rodriguez Ismael • MXC
TRES HUCHAS PARA ORIENTE • 1954 • Elorrieta Jose Maria • SPN
TRES INSUFFISANT • 1979 • Berard Herve • FRN
TRES JUSTICEIROS, OS • 1972 • Mendes Nelson Teixeira • BRZ
TRES LECCIONES DE AMOR • 1958 • Cortes Fernando • MXC
TRES MAS DOS • 1979 • Carrer Giancarlo • VNZ • THREE AND TWO MORE
TRES MELODIAS DE AMOR • 1955 • Galindo Alejandro • MXC, SPN
TRES MIL KILOMETROS DE AMOR • 1965 • Delgado Agustin P. • MXC
TRES MOSQUETAROS.. Y MEDIO, LOS • 1956 • Martinez Solares Gilberto • MXC
TRES MOSQUETEROS DE DIOS, LOS • 1966 • Morayta Miguel • MXC
TRES MOSQUETEROS, LOS • 1942 • Delgado Miguel M. • MXC
TRES MUCHACHAS DE JALISCO • 1963 • Gomez Muriel Emilio • MXC
TRES NOCHES EROTICAS DEL MARQUES DE SADE, LAS • 1977 • Molina Jacinto • SPN
TRES NOCHES VIOLENTAS (SPN) see **TRE NOTTI VIOLENTE** • 1966
TRES PALOMAS ALBOROTADAS • 1962 • Gomez Muriel Emilio • MXC
TRES PECADOS, LOS • 1965 • Cortes Fernando • MXC, PRC
TRES PELONAS, LAS • 1957 • Cardona Rene • MXC
TRES PERFECTAS CASADAS, LAS • 1952 • Gavaldon Roberto • MXC
TRES PERROS LOCOS, LOCOS • 1966 • Yague Jesus • SPN
TRES PINTORES • Guzman Rafael • DOC • ITL • THREE PAINTERS
TRES REYES MAGOS, LOS • 1974 • *Conacine* • MXC
TRES RICHES HEURES DE L'AFRIQUE ROMAINE, LES • 1953 • Leherissey Jean • SHT • FRN
TRES ROMEOS Y UNA JULIETA • 1960 • Urueta Chano • MXC
TRES SALVAJES, LOS • 1965 • Martinez Solares Gilberto • MXC
TRES SUECAS PARA TRES RODRIGUEZ • 1975 • Lazaga Pedro • SPN
TRES TRIESTES TIGRES see **TRES TRISTES TIGRES** • 1968
TRES TRISTES TIGRES • 1960 • Gazcon Gilberto • MXC
TRES TRISTES TIGRES • 1968 • Ruiz Raul • CHL • THREE SAD TIGERS ○ TRES TRIESTES TIGRES ○ THREE SORRY TIGERS
TRES VALIENTES CAMARADAS • 1955 • Morayta Miguel • MXC
TRES VECES ANA • 1961 • Kohon David Jose • ARG • THREE TIMES ANA
TRES VILLALOBOS, LOS • 1954 • Mendez Fernando • MXC
TRES VIUDAS DE PAPA, LAS • 1940 • Zacarias Miguel • MXC
TRES VIVALES, LOS • 1957 • Baledon Rafael • MXC
TRESA, SPINE E LACRIME • 1915 • Ghione Emilio • ITL
TRESOR, LE see **BAS DE LAINE OU LE TRESOR, LE** • 1911
TRESOR DE BAUX, LE • 1913 • Jasset Victorin • FRN
TRESOR DE CANTENAC, LE • 1949 • Guitry Sacha • FRN • MIRACLE, UN
TRESOR DE FEMME, UN • 1952 • Stelli Jean • FRN
TRESOR DE L'EGYPTE • 1954 • Samivel • FRN
TRESOR DE NOUVELLE FRANCE, LE • 1980 • Davy Vincent • CND
TRESOR DES GROTOCEANS, LE • 1980 • Hoedeman Co • ANS • CND • TREASURE OF THE GROTECEANS, THE
TRESOR DES HOMMES BLEUS, LE • 1960 • Agabara Edmond, Ferreri Marco • FRN, SPN • SECRETO DE LOS HOMBRES AZULES, EL (SPN) ○ SECRET DES HOMMES BLEUS, LE ○ CARAVANE POUR ZAGORA ○ SECRET OF THE BLUE MEN, THE
TRESOR DES MONTAGNES BLEUES, LE (FRN) see **WINNETOU II** • 1964
TRESOR DES PHARAONS, LE • 1954 • de Gastyne Marco • FRN • MASQUE DE TOUT ANKH AMON, LE
TRESOR DES PIEDS NICKELES, LE • 1949 • Aboulker Marcel • FRN
TRESOR D'OSTENDE, LE • 1955 • Storck Henri • DOC • BLG
TRESOR DU LAC D'ARGENT, LE (FRN) see **SCHATZ IM SILBERSEE, DER** • 1962
TRESORFACH NR.21 • 1917 • Dessauer Siegfried • FRG
TRESORS DE LA VALLEE DES ROIS, LES • 1973-74 • Valcour Pierre • DOC • CND
TRESORS DE SATAN, LES • 1902 • Melies Georges • FRN • TREASURES OF SATAN, THE (USA) ○ DEVIL'S MONEYBAGS, THE
TRESORS DU PORTUGAL • 1955 • Sassy Jean-Paul • SHT • FRN
TRESPASS • 1985 • Zielinska Ida Eva • CND
TRESPASS see **TRESPASSES** • 1986
TRESPASSER, THE • 1929 • Goulding Edmund • USA
TRESPASSER, THE • 1947 • Blair George • USA
TRESPASSER, THE • 1982 • Gregg Colin • TVM • UKN
TRESPASSER, THE (UKN) see **NIGHT EDITOR** • 1946
TRESPASSERS, THE • 1976 • Duigan John • ASL
TRESPASSES • 1986 • Roarke Adam, Bivens Loren • USA • TRESPASS
TRESPASSES see **FINDING KATIE** • 1983
TRESTIGOS, LOS • Elsesser Charles • CHL • WITNESSES, THE
TRETI PRANI • 1958 • Kadar Jan, Klos Elmar • CZC • THREE WISHES ○ THIRD WISH, THE ○ TRI PRANI
TRETI PRINC • 1982 • Moskalyk Antonin • CZC • THIRD PRINCE, THE
TRETI ROTA • 1931 • Innemann Svatopluk • SHT • CZC • THIRD SQUAD, THE
TRETIA MECHT CHANSKAYA see **TRETYA MESHCHANSKAYA** • 1927
TRETIU TAYM • 1963 • Karelov Yevgyeni • USS • LAST GAME, THE (USA) ○ THIRD TIME, THE
TRETTEN AR • 1932 • Schneevoigt George • DNM
TRETY UDAR • 1948 • Savchenko Igor • USS • THIRD BLOW, THE
TRETYA MESHCHANSKAYA • 1927 • Room Abram • USS • THREE MESHCHANSKAYA STREET ○ THIRD MESHCHANSKAYA ○ BED AND SOFA ○ TRETIA MECHT CHANSKAYA
TRETYAKOV GALLERY, THE • 1956 • Kaufman Mikhail • DOC • USS
TREUE HUSAR, DER • 1954 • Schundler Rudolf • FRG
TREUGOLNIK • 1967 • Malyan Ghenrikh • USS • TREYGOLNIK ○ TRIANGLE
TREVE • 1983 • Gervais Suzanne • ANS • CND • STILL POINT
TREVE see **MIGHTY TREVE, THE** • 1937
TREVE, LA • 1969 • Guillemot Claude • FRN • TRUCE, THE (UKN)
TREVICO TORINO • 1973 • Scola Ettore • ITL • TREVICO–TORINO VIAGGIO NEL FIAT–NAM
TREVICO–TORINO VIAGGIO NEL FIAT–NAM see **TREVICO TORINO** • 1973
TREVO DE QUATRO FOLHAS, O • 1936 • de Garcia Eduardo Chianca • PRT
TREVOGA • 1951 • Zhandov Zahari • BUL • ALARM
TREVOZHNAYA MOLODOST • 1955 • Alov Alexander, Naumov Vladimir • USS • TURBULENT YOUTH ○ RESTLESS YOUTH
TREVOZHNOYE UTRO • 1967 • Karsakbaev Abdulla • USS • ANXIOUS MORNING, THE ○ ALARMING MORNING
TREWEY: UNDER THE HAT see **CHAPEAUX A TRANSFORMATIONS** • 1895
TREY O'HEARTS, THE • 1914 • Lucas Wilfred, McRae Henry • SRL • USA
TREYGOLNIK see **TREUGOLNIK** • 1967
TRHANI • 1936 • Wasserman Vaclav • CZC • RAGAMUFFINS, THE ○ RAGGED MEN
TRI • 1965 • Petrovic Aleksandar • YGS • THREE ○ TRIO
TRI ANE • 1959 • Bauer Branko • YGS • THREE ANNES, THE
TRI BRATRI A ZAZRACNY PRAMEN • 1968 • Nemec Jan • CZC • THREE BROTHERS AND THE MIRACULOUS SPRING, THE
TRI CETRTINE SONCA • 1959 • Babic Joze • YGS • SUNSHINE FOR SOME
TRI DCERY • 1967 • Uher Stefan • CZC • THREE DAUGHTERS
TRI DNYA VIKTORA CHERNYSHYOVA • 1968 • Osepyan Mark • USS • THREE DAYS IN THE LIFE OF VIKTOR CHERNYSHOV ○ VICTOR CHERNYSHOV'S THREE DAYS ○ THREE DAYS OF VICTOR CHERNYSHOV ○ THREE DAYS OF VICTOR TCHERNYCHEV, THE
TRI GEROINI • 1938 • Vertov Dziga, Svilova Elizaveta • USS • THREE HEROINES
TRI MUSKETERA • 1938 • Ivanov-Vano Ivan • ANS • USS • THREE MUSKETEERS, THE
TRI MUZI • 1959 • Lehky Vladimir • ANS • CZC • THREE MEN
TRI ORISKY PRO POPELKU • 1973 • Vorlicek Vaclav • CZC • DREI HASELNUSSE FUR ASCHENBRODEL ○ THREE NUTS FOR CINDERELLA
TRI PESNI O LENINYE • 1934 • Vertov Dziga • USS • THREE SONGS ABOUT LENIN ○ THREE SONGS OF LENIN
TRI PRANI see **TRETI PRANI** • 1958
TRI SATA ZA LJUBAV • 1968 • Hadzic Fadil • YGS • THREE HOURS FOR LOVE
TRI SESTRY • 1964 • Samsonov Samson • USS • THREE SISTERS
TRI SISNI see **TRI ZHIZNI** • 1925
TRI TOLSTYAKA • 1967 • Batalov Alexei, Shapiro Iosif • USS • THREE FAT MEN, THE
TRI TOPOLYA NA PLYUSHCHIKHYE • 1968 • Lioznova Tatyana • USS • THREE POPLARS ON PLIUSHCHIKHA STREET ○ THREE POPLARS IN PLYUSHCHIKHA ○ CAFE IN PLIUSHIHA STREET
TRI VEJCE DO SKLA • 1937 • Fric Martin • CZC • THREE EGGS IN A GLASS
TRI VETERANI • 1983 • Lipsky Oldrich • CZC • THREE VETERANS, THE
TRI VSTRECHI • 1915 • Boleslawski Richard • USS • THREE MEETINGS
TRI VSTRECHI • 1948 • Pudovkin V. I., Yutkevich Sergei, Ptushko Alexander • USS • THREE ENCOUNTERS
TRI Y DVA • 1963 • Oganesyan Georgi • USS • THREE PLUS TWO
TRI ZGODBE • 1955 • Kavcic Jane, Pretnar Igor, Kosmac France • YGS
TRI ZHIZNI • 1925 • Perestiani Ivan • USS • THREE LIVES ○ TRI SISNI
TRI ZLATE VLASY DEDA VSEVEDA • 1963 • Fric Martin, Valasek Jan • CZC • THREE GOLDEN HAIRS OF OLD MAN KNOW–ALL, THE
TRIADS –THE INSIDE STORY see **NGO TSOI WAKSEWUI DIK YATTSI** • 1989
TRIAGE, LE see **TIRAGE, LE** • 1940
TRIAL • 1955 • Robson Mark • USA
TRIAL, THE • 1962 • Mansarova Aida (c/d) • USS
TRIAL, THE see **PROZESS, DER** • 1948
TRIAL, THE see **SUD** • 1963
TRIAL, THE see **PROTSESAT** • 1968
TRIAL, THE see **SHAQUE** • 1976
TRIAL, THE (USA) see **PROZESS, DER** • 1962
TRIAL AND ERROR see **FLIGHT FROM DESTINY** • 1941
TRIAL AND ERROR (USA) see **DOCK BRIEF, THE** • 1962
TRIAL AT KAMPILI • 1963 • *Ohki Minoru* • JPN
TRIAL BALLOONS • 1982 • Breer Robert • USA
TRIAL BY COMBAT • 1976 • Connor Kevin • UKN • DIRTY KNIGHT'S WORK (USA) ○ CHOICE OF WEAPONS, A

TRIAL BY FIRE AND WATER see **PROBA OGNIA I WODY** • 1978

TRIAL BY TERROR • 1983 • Brooks Hildy • USA

TRIAL BY TRIGGER • 1944 • McGann William • SHT • USA

TRIAL IN SMOLENSK, THE see **SUD V SMOLENSKE** • 1946

TRIAL MARRIAGE • 1928 • Curran William Hughes • USA • ABOUT TRIAL MARRIAGE

TRIAL MARRIAGE • 1929 • Kenton Erle C. • USA

TRIAL MARRIAGES • 1906 • *Bitzer Billy (Ph)* • USA

TRIAL MARRIAGES • 1907 • *Am & B* • USA

TRIAL OF ABRAHAM'S FAITH, THE • 1909 • *Empire Films* • UKN

TRIAL OF BILLY JACK, THE • 1974 • Laughlin Tom • USA

TRIAL OF BURGOS, THE see **PROCESO DE BURGOS, EL** • 1980

TRIAL OF CHAPLAIN JENSEN, THE • 1975 • Day Robert • TVM • USA

TRIAL OF DONALD DUCK, THE • 1948 • King Jack • ANS • USA

TRIAL OF DONALD WESTHOF, THE see **KAMPF DES DONALD WESTHOF, DER** • 1927

TRIAL OF GIBRALTAR, THE see **PROCESO DE GIBRALTAR** • 1968

TRIAL OF HONOUR see **SUD CHESTI** • 1948

TRIAL OF JESUS see **PROCESO A JESUS** • 1973

TRIAL OF JOAN OF ARC, THE (USA) see **PROCES DE JEANNE D'ARC, LE** • 1961

TRIAL OF LEE HARVEY OSWALD, THE • 1964 • Buchanan Larry • USA

TRIAL OF LEE HARVEY OSWALD, THE • 1977 • Greene David • TVM • USA

TRIAL OF MADAME X, THE • 1948 • England Paul • UKN

TRIAL OF MARTIN CORTES, THE see **JUICIO DE MARTIN CORTES, EL** • 1973

TRIAL OF MARY DUGAN, THE • 1929 • Veiller Bayard • USA

TRIAL OF MARY DUGAN, THE • 1940 • McLeod Norman Z. • USA • CRIME OF MARY ANDREWS, THE

TRIAL OF MIRONOV, THE see **PROZESS MIRONOVA** • 1920

TRIAL OF MR. WOLF, THE • 1941 • Freleng Friz • ANS • USA

TRIAL OF PORTIA MERRIMAN, THE (UKN) see **PORTIA ON TRIAL** • 1937

TRIAL OF SERGEANT RUTLEDGE, THE see **SERGEANT RUTLEDGE** • 1960

TRIAL OF SOULS, A • 1916 • McGill Lawrence?, Hansel Howell? • SHT • USA

TRIAL OF THE CATONSVILLE NINE, THE • 1972 • Davidson Gordon • USA

TRIAL OF THE INCREDIBLE HULK, THE • 1989 • Bixby Bill • TVM • USA

TRIAL OF THE JUDGES, THE see **DIKI TON DIKASTON, I** • 1973

TRIAL OF THE JUNTA, THE see **DIKI TIS CHOUNDAS, I** • 1981

TRIAL OF THE SOCIAL REVOLUTIONARIES, THE see **PROZESS ESEROV** • 1922

TRIAL OF THE THREE MILLIONS, THE see **PROTSESS O TROYOKH MILLYONAKH** • 1926

TRIAL OF THE WITCHES, THE see **PROCESO DE LAS BRUJAS, EL** • 1970

TRIAL OF THREE MILLIONS see **PROTSESS O TROYOKH MILLYONAKH** • 1926

TRIAL OF VIVIENNE WARE, THE • 1932 • Howard William K. • USA

TRIAL ON THE ROAD, THE see **PROVERKA NA DOROGAKH** • 1971

TRIAL PERIOD • 1960 • Gerasimov Vladimir • USS

TRIAL RUN • 1969 • Graham William A. • TVM • USA

TRIAL RUN • 1984 • Read Melanie • NZL

TRIAL TURN, THE • 1928 • *Kenney Horace* • SHT • UKN

TRIAL (USA) see **HUELLA** • 1940

TRIAL WITHOUT JURY • 1950 • Ford Philip • USA

TRIALS AND TRIBULATIONS • 1917 • Green Alfred E. • SHT • USA

TRIALS OF A GYPSY GENTLEMAN, THE see **GENTLEMAN GYPSY, THE** • 1908

TRIALS OF A MERRY WIDOW, THE • 1912 • Calvert Charles? • UKN

TRIALS OF A MILKMAN, THE • 1916 • *Goodman C.* • SHT • UKN • MILKO!

TRIALS OF A MOVIE CARTOONIST • 1916 • *Powers* • SHT • USA

TRIALS OF A SCHOOLMASTER, THE (USA) see **ECOLE INFERNALE, L'** • 1901

TRIALS OF ALEXANDER, THE • 1914 • *Imp* • USA

TRIALS OF ALGER HISS, THE • 1980 • Lowenthal John • USA

TRIALS OF AN IMMIGRANT • 1911 • *Reliance* • USA

TRIALS OF BUD BROWN • 1911 • *Bison* • USA

TRIALS OF CELEBRITY see **GUDERNES YNDLING** • 1919

TRIALS OF FAITH, THE • 1912 • *Robinson Gertrude* • USA

TRIALS OF OSCAR WILDE, THE • 1960 • Hughes Ken • UKN • MAN WITH THE GREEN CARNATION, THE (USA) ○ GREEN CARNATION, THE

TRIALS OF PRIVATE SCHWEIK • 1964 • *Alexander Peter* • FRG • SCHWEIK'S YEARS OF INDISCRETION

TRIALS OF TEXAS THOMPSON, THE • 1919 • Hale Albert W. • SHT • USA

TRIALS OF TRACI, THE • *Lords Traci* • USA

TRIALS OF YOUTH see **TRAPENI** • 1961

TRIANGLE see **TREUGOLNIK** • 1967

TRIANGLE see **TRIANGULO** • 1972

TRIANGLE, LE see **GRAIN DE SABLE, LE** • 1964

TRIANGLE, THE • 1912 • *Edison* • USA

TRIANGLE, THE • 1912 • *Selig* • USA

TRIANGLE CIRCULAIRE, LE see **GRAIN DE SABLE, LE** • 1964

TRIANGLE DE FEU, LE • 1932 • Greville Edmond T., Guter Johannes • FRN

TRIANGLE DE VENUS, LE • 1978 • Frank Hubert • FRN • TRIANGLE OF LUST

TRIANGLE ECORCHE, LE • 1974 • Kalfon Pierre • FRN

TRIANGLE FACTORY FIRE SCANDAL, THE • 1979 • Stuart Mel • TVM • USA

TRIANGLE INVASION see **JAKARTA** • 1988

TRIANGLE MARRIAGE, A • 1914 • *Universal* • USA

TRIANGLE OF LUST see **TRIANGLE DE VENUS, LE** • 1978

TRIANGLE ON SAFARI see **WOMAN AND THE HUNTER, THE** • 1957

TRIANGLE (THE BERMUDA MYSTERY) see **DIABOLICO TRIANGULO DE LA BERMUDAS, EL** • 1977

TRIANGOLO CIRCOLARE, IL (ITL) see **GRAIN DE SABLE, LE** • 1964

TRIANGOLO DEL DELITTO, IL (ITL) see **GROS COUP, LE** • 1963

TRIANGOLO GIALLO, IL • 1917 • Ghione Emilio • SRL • ITL

TRIANGOLO MAGICO, IL see **BRIVIDO** • 1941

TRIANGULITO, EL • 1969 • Forque Jose Maria • SPN

TRIANGULO • 1972 • Moreno Alba Rafael • SPN, PRT, MXC • TRIANGLE

TRIANGULO DE CUATRO • 1975 • Ayala Fernando • ARG • FOUR-SIDED TRIANGLE

TRIBAL LAW, THE • 1912 • Turner Otis • USA

TRIBAL WAR IN THE SOUTH SEAS • 1914 • *Bison* • USA

TRIBE, THE • 1974 • Colla Richard A. • TVM • USA

TRIBE LIVES ON, THE see **STAMMEN LEVER AN** • 1938

TRIBE THAT HIDES FROM MAN, THE • 1970 • Cowell Adrian • DOC • UKN

TRIBES • 1970 • Sargent Joseph • USA • SOLDIER WHO DECLARED PEACE, THE

TRIBE'S PENALTY, THE • 1911 • *Anderson Broncho Billy* • USA

TRIBU • 1934 • Contreras Torres Miguel • MXC

TRIBULATIONS D'UN CHINOIS EN CHINE, LES • 1965 • de Broca Philippe • FRN, ITL • UOMO DI HONG KONG, L' (ITL) ○ UP TO HIS EARS (USA) ○ THAT MAN FROM HONG KONG ○ CHINESE ADVENTURES IN CHINA

TRIBULATIONS D'UN CONCIERGE • 1896 • Melies Georges • FRN • JANITOR IN TROUBLE, A

TRIBULATIONS OF A LOVER • 1909 • *Powhatan* • USA

TRIBULATIONS OF A YOUNG MASTER, THE see **SHAOYEDE MONAN** • 1988

TRIBULLE • 1972 • Floquet Francois • SHS • CND

TRIBUNAL see **GERICHTSTAG** • 1966

TRIBUNAL DE JUSTICIA • 1943 • Galindo Alejandro • MXC • TRIBUNAL OF JUSTICE

TRIBUNAL OF CONSCIENCE, THE • 1914 • *Lubin* • USA

TRIBUNAL OF HONOUR, THE see **SUD CHESTI** • 1948

TRIBUNAL OF JUSTICE see **TRIBUNAL DE JUSTICIA** • 1943

TRIBUNE FILM: BREAK AND BUILD, THE see **TRIBUNE FILM: BREKEN EN BOUWEN, DE** • 1930

TRIBUNE FILM: BREKEN EN BOUWEN, DE • 1930 • Ivens Joris • SHT • NTH • TRIBUNE FILM: BREAK AND BUILD, THE

TRIBUTE • 1981 • Clark Bob • CND • FILS POUR L'ETE, UN

TRIBUTE • 1985 • Leiterman Richard • DOC • CND

TRIBUTE TO A BAD MAN • 1956 • Wise Robert • USA

TRIBUTE TO AMERICA • 1973 • Thoms Albie • DOC • ASL

TRIBUTE TO FANGIO • 1959 • Riley Ronald H. • UKN

TRIBUTE TO LOUIS ARMSTRONG • 1970 • Wein George, Stiber Sidney J. • USA • ANATOMY OF A PERFORMANCE

TRIBUTE TO MARTIN LUTHER KING, A • 1975 • Warren Mark • MTV • USA

TRIBUTE TO MOTHER, A • 1915 • Schrock Raymond L. • USA

TRICET JEONA VE STINU • 1965 • Weiss Jiri • CZC, UKN • 90 DEGREES IN THE SHADE (UKN) ○ 31 STUPNU VE STINU ○ NINETY IN THE SHADE ○ 31° IN THE SHADE

TRICHE, LA • 1984 • Bellon Yannick • FRN

TRICHEURS • 1983 • Schroeder Barbet • FRN, FRG, PRT

TRICHEURS, LES • 1958 • Carne Marcel • FRN, ITL • PECCATORI IN BLUE-JEANS (ITL) ○ CHEATERS, THE (USA) ○ YOUTHFUL SINNERS ○ NOT FOR REAL

TRICHEUSE, LA • 1960 • de Meyst E. G. • FRN

TRICIA'S WEDDING • 1972 • Lester Mark L. • USA

TRICK, DER • 1915 • Sauer Fred • FRG

TRICK AND THE TRADE • 1970 • USA

TRICK BABY • 1973 • Yust Larry • USA • DOUBLE CON, THE

TRICK BICYCLISTS • 1898 • *Haydon & Urry* • UKN

TRICK CYCLIST • 1901 • Porter Edwin S. • USA

TRICK FOR TRICK • 1933 • MacFadden Hamilton • USA

TRICK GOLF • 1934 • Beaudine William • SHT • USA

TRICK OF FATE, A • 1919 • Hickman Howard • USA

TRICK OF FATE, THE • 1915 • Reehm George E. • USA

TRICK OF FORTUNE, A • 1911 • *Reliance* • USA

TRICK OF HEARTS, A • 1928 • Eason B. Reeves • USA • WESTERN SUFFRAGETTES ○ HORSE TRADER, THE

TRICK ON THE BOATMAN, A • 1899 • *Haydon & Urry* • UKN

TRICK OR TREAT • 1952 • Hannah Jack • ANS • USA

TRICK OR TREAT • 1966 • Post Howard • ANS • USA

TRICK OR TREAT • 1976 • Apted Michael • UKN

TRICK OR TREAT • 1982 • Graver Gary • USA

TRICK OR TREAT • 1987 • Smith Charles Martin • USA

TRICK OR TREE • 1961 • Kneitel Seymour • ANS • USA

TRICK OR TWEET • 1959 • Freleng Friz • ANS • USA

TRICK PLAYS • 1931 • Kelley Albert • SHT • USA

TRICK THAT FAILED, THE • 1909 • Griffith D. W. • USA

TRICK-TRACK • 1921 • Albes Emil • FRG

TRICKED • 1915 • Chatterton Thomas • USA

TRICKED BY A PHOTO • 1914 • *Siegmann George* • USA

TRICKED BY A VAMPIRE • 1914 • *Warner's Features* • USA

TRICKED BY HIS PAL • 1914 • *Heron Andrew (P)* • UKN

TRICKED INTO HAPPINESS • 1912 • *Lubin* • USA

TRICKED TRICKSTER, THE • 1911 • *Essanay* • USA

TRICKED (UKN) see **BANDITS OF ELDORADO** • 1949

TRICKERY • 1915 • Lloyd Frank • USA

TRICKING THE GOVERNMENT • 1914 • Olcott Sidney • USA

TRICKING THE TRICKSTER • 1916 • *Unicorn* • USA

TRICKS • 1925 • Mitchell Bruce • USA

TRICKS • 1956 • Balling Erik • DNM

TRICKS see **TRICKS OF THE TRADE** • 1968

TRICKS IN ALL TRADES • 1913 • *Powers* • USA

TRICKS OF AN ERRAND BOY see **ITAZURA KOZO** • 1935

TRICKS OF DECEPTIVE LOVE see **LASKY HRY SALIVE** • 1972

TRICKS OF FATE • 1915 • *Balboa* • USA

TRICKS OF LIFE (USA) see **PAYASADAS DE LA VIDA** • 1934

TRICKS OF THE TRADE • 1913 • *Morley Harry T.* • USA

TRICKS OF THE TRADE • 1968 • Milligan Andy • USA • TRICKS

TRICKS OF THE TRADE • 1989 • Bender Jack • USA

TRICKSTERS, THE • 1916 • Cummings R. E. • USA

TRICKY BUSINESS • 1942 • Donnelly Eddie • ANS • USA

TRICKY CONVICT: OR, THE MAGIC CAP • 1908 • Aylott Dave? • UKN

TRICKY DICKS • 1953 • White Jules • SHT • USA

TRICKY FLUNKIE, THE • 1914 • *Shields Ernest* • USA

TRICKY GIRL see **KARAKURI MUSUME** • 1927

TRICKY NICO see **NICO EL TRACALERO** • 1977

TRICKY ONES, THE see **NICO EL TRACALERO** • 1977

TRICKY PAINTER'S FATE • 1908 • Melies Georges • FRN

TRICKY PRISONER, THE (USA) see **PRISONNIER RECALCITRANT, LE** • 1900

TRICKY STICK, THE • 1914 • Aylott Dave • UKN

TRICKY TROUT • 1961 • Smith Paul J. • ANS • USA

TRICKY TWINS, THE • 1907 • Cooper Arthur? • UKN

TRICOCHE ET CACOLET • 1938 • Colombier Piere • FRN

TRICOFIL C'EST LA CLEF • 1976 • Brault Francois, Lenoir R. • DOC • CND

TRICORNE, LE see **MEUNIERE DEBAUCHEE, LA** • 1935

TRIDENT FORCE • 1988 • Smith Richard* • USA

TRIDEV • 1989 • Rai Rajiv • IND

TRIDSAT TRI • 1965 • Daneliya Georgi • USS • THIRTY THREE ○ THIRTY-THREE, THE

TRIED AND FOUND TRUE • 1910 • Haldane Bert? • UKN

TRIED FOR HIS OWN MURDER • 1915 • Brooke Van Dyke • USA

TRIED IN THE FIRE • 1913 • Buckland Warwick? • UKN

TRIESTE see **TRST** • 1951

TRIESTE, CANTICO D'AMORE • 1954 • Calandri Max • ITL

TRIESTE MIA • 1951 • Costa Mario • ITL

TRIFLE BACKWARD, A • 1933 • Horne James W. • SHT • USA

TRIFLE NOT WITH FIRE • 1912 • *Republic* • USA

TRIFLER, THE • 1912 • *Nestor* • USA

TRIFLER, THE • 1913 • *Rex* • USA

TRIFLERS, THE • 1920 • Cabanne W. Christy • USA

TRIFLERS, THE • 1924 • Gasnier Louis J. • USA

TRIFLES OF IMPORTANCE • 1940 • Wrangell Basil • SHT • USA

TRIFLES THAT WIN WARS • 1943 • Daniels Harold • SHT • USA

TRIFLING WITH HONOR • 1923 • Pollard Harry • USA • YOUR GOOD NAME ○ HIS GOOD NAME

TRIFLING WOMEN • 1922 • Ingram Rex • USA

TRIFOLIATE ORANGE DIARY, THE see **KARATACHI NIKKI** • 1959

TRIGGER see **SPITFIRE** • 1934

TRIGGER FINGER • 1924 • Eason B. Reeves • USA

TRIGGER FINGERS • 1939 • Newfield Sam • USA

TRIGGER FINGERS • 1946 • Hillyer Lambert • USA

TRIGGER HAPPY see **DEADLY COMPANIONS, THE** • 1961

TRIGGER-HAPPY see **YAMI O SAKU IPPATSU** • 1968

TRIGGER JR. • 1950 • Witney William • USA

TRIGGER LAW • 1944 • Keays Vernon • USA

TRIGGER PALS • 1939 • Newfield Sam • USA

TRIGGER SMITH • 1939 • James Alan • USA

TRIGGER TOM • 1935 • Webb Harry S. • USA • DANGEROUS MISSION (UKN)

TRIGGER TRAIL • 1944 • Collins Lewis D. • USA

TRIGGER TREAT • 1960 • Kneitel Seymour • ANS • USA

TRIGGER TRICKS • 1930 • Eason B. Reeves • USA

TRIGGER TRIO, THE • 1937 • Witney William • USA

TRIGGER TWINS, THE (UKN) see **TWIN TRIGGERS** • 1926

TRIGGERMAN • 1948 • Bretherton Howard • USA

TRIGO E O JOIO, O • 1965 • Guimaraes Manuel • PRT

TRIGO LIMPIO • 1967 • Iquino Ignacio F. • SPN • PURE WHEAT

TRIJUMF • 1972 • Sajtinac Borislav • YGS • TRIUMPH

TRIKAL • 1985 • Benegal Shyam • IND

TRIKIMIA • 1973 • Powell Michael • GRC, UKN • TEMPEST, THE

TRILBY • 1908 • Nielsen A. R. • SHT • DNM

TRILBY • 1912 • *Standard* • UKN

TRILBY • 1912 • Fleck Luise, Kolm Anton, Fleck Jacob, Veltee Claudius, Marins Jose Mojica, Candeias Ozvaldo R., Person Luis Sergio • AUS, HNG • THREE TALES OF TERROR ○ TRILOGY OF TERROR

TRILBY • 1913 • *Vitascope* • USA

TRILBY • 1914 • Shaw Harold • UKN

TRILBY • 1915 • Tourneur Maurice • USA

TRILBY • 1922 • *Parkinson H. B. (P)* • UKN

TRILBY • 1923 • Young James • USA

TRILBY BURLESQUE • 1896 • *Paul R. W.* • UKN

TRILBY BY PIMPLE AND CO see **ADVENTURES OF PIMPLE – TRILBY, THE** • 1914

TRILBY'S LOVE DISASTER • 1916 • Mix Tom • SHT • USA

TRILOGIA DI MACISTE, LA • 1919 • Campogalliani Carlo, Moreau Gabriel • ITL

TRILOGIE Z PRAVEKU • 1977 • Schmidt Jan • CZC • TRILOGY FROM THE PRIMEVAL AGES

TRILOGIYA O GORKOM • 1938-40 • Donskoi Mark • USS • GORKY TRILOGY, THE

TRILOGIYA O MAXIME • 1932-38 • Kozintsev Grigori • USS • MAXIM TRILOGY, THE

TRILOGY • 1969 • Perry Frank • TVM • USA • TRUMAN CAPOTE'S TRILOGY

TRILOGY FROM THE PRIMEVAL AGES see **TRILOGIE Z PRAVEKU** • 1977

TRILOGY OF TERROR • 1975 • Curtis Dan • TVM • USA

TRILOGY OF TERROR see **TRILBY** • 1912

TRIM AND A SHAVE, A • 1913 • *Champion* • USA

TRIMMED • 1922 • Pollard Harry • USA

TRIMMED IN FURS • 1933 • Lamont Charles • SHT • USA

TRIMMED IN GOLD • 1926 • *Sennett Mack (P)* • SHT • USA

TRIMMED IN SCARLET • 1923 • Conway Jack • USA

TRIMMED LAMP, THE • 1918 • Ridgwell George • SHT • USA

TRIMMED WITH RED see **HELP YOURSELF** • 1920

TRIMMERS TRIMMED, THE • 1913 • Henderson Dell • USA

TRIMMING A BOOB • 1913 • *Fischer Robert* • USA

TRIMMING OF PARADISE GULCH, THE • 1910 • Boggs Frank • USA

TRINACTA KOMNATA • 1968 • Vavra Otakar • CZC • THIRTEENTH CHAMBER, THE ○ THIRTEENTH ROOM, THE

TRINACTY REVIR • 1945 • Fric Martin, Holman • CZC • GUARD 13 ○ BEAT 13 ○ 13 REVIR

TRINADESET DNI • 1964 • Surchadgiev Stefan • BUL • THIRTEEN DAYS

TRINADTSAT • 1937 • Romm Mikhail • USS • THIRTEEN, THE

TRINCA DEL AIRE, LA • 1951 • Torrado Ramon • SPN
TRINGLEUSES, LES • 1974 • Beni Alphonse • FRN, ITL • MECS.., LES FLICS.., ET LES PUTAINS, LES
TRINIDAD • 1974 • Veitia Hector • CUB
TRINIDAD see TWO YANKS IN TRINIDAD • 1942
TRINIDAD AND TOBAGO • 1964 • Jones Geoffrey • UKN
TRINITA E SARTANA, FIGLI DI.. • 1972 • Siciliano Mario • ITL
TRINITA NOUS VOILA • 1975 • Parolini Gianfranco
TRINITY, THE • 1911 • Baggot King • USA
TRINITY IS MY NAME see LO CHIAMAVANO TRINITA • 1970
TRINITY IS STILL MY NAME (USA) see CONTINUAVANO A CHIAMARLO, TRINITA • 1971
TRINKETS OF TRAGEDY • 1914 • Bushman Francis X. • USA
TRINQUETERO, EL • 1974 • Cineprod. Internacionales • MXC
TRINTA ANOS COM SALAZAR • 1957 • Ribeiro Antonio Lopes • SHT • PRT
TRIO • 1950 • Annakin Ken, French Harold • UKN
TRIO • 1965 • Hofman Eduard • ANS • PLN
TRIO • 1967 • Mingozzi Gianfranco • ITL
TRIO • 1967 • Vas Judit • DOC • HNG
TRIO • 1970 • Celis Louis • BLG
TRIO • 1975 • Grgic Zlatko • ANS • CND
TRIO • 1976 • Brakhage Stan • SHT • USA
TRIO see TRI • 1965
TRIO see TRAJA • 1969
TRIO ANGELOS • 1963 • Barabas Stanislav • CZC
TRIO DE DAMAS • 1960 • Lazaga Pedro • SPN
TRIO DE TRES, UN • 1959 • Orellana Carlos • MXC
TRIO: EVERYBODY'S DOING IT • 1913 • Booth W. R.? • UKN
TRIO FILM • 1968 • Rainer Yvonne • SHT • USA
TRIO INFERNAL • 1974 • Girod Francis • FRN, ITL, FRG • TRIO INFERNALE (ITL) ○ INFERNAL TRIO, THE (USA)
TRIO INFERNALE (ITL) see TRIO INFERNAL • 1974
TRIOMPHE DE LA VIE, LE see ICH LEBE FUR DICH • 1929
TRIOMPHE DE MACISTE, LE (FRN) see TRIONFO DI MACISTE, IL • 1961
TRIOMPHE DE MICHEL STROGOFF, LE • 1961 • Tourjansky Victor • FRN, ITL • TRIUMPH OF MICHAEL STROGOFF, THE (UKN) ○ MICHEL STROGOFF
TRIONFO DEI DIECI GLADIATORI see SPARTACUS E I DIECI GLADIATORI • 1964
TRIONFO DELLA CASTA SUSANNA, IL • 1969 • Antel Franz • ITL
TRIONFO DELL'AMORE, IL • 1938 • Mattoli Mario • ITL • LOVE'S TRIUMPH (USA)
TRIONFO DI ERCOLE, IL • 1964 • De Martino Alberto • ITL, FRN • HERCULES VS. THE GIANT WARRIORS (USA) ○ TRIUMPH OF HERCULES, THE (UKN) ○ HERCULES AND THE TEN AVENGERS
TRIONFO DI MACISTE, IL • 1961 • Boccia Tanio • ITL, FRN • TRIUMPH OF THE SON OF HERCULES (USA) ○ TRIOMPHE DE MACISTE, LE (FRN) ○ TRIUMPH OF MACISTE, THE
TRIONFO DI ROBIN HOOD • 1962 • Lenzi Umberto • ITL • TRIUMPH OF ROBIN HOOD (USA)
TRIP • 1970 • Pati P. • IND
TRIP, A • 1960 • D'Avino Carmen • SHT • USA
TRIP, A • 1963 • Buchvarova Radka • DOC • BUL
TRIP, A • 1969 • Garland Nathan • SHT • USA
TRIP, THE • 1967 • Corman Roger • USA
TRIP, THE • 1967 • Culhane Shamus • ANS • USA
TRIP, THE see WYCIECZKA • 1967
TRIP, THE see VIAGGIO, IL • 1974
TRIP AROUND THE PAN-AMERICAN EXPOSITION, A • 1901 • Porter Edwin S. • USA • TRIP THROUGH THE COLUMBIA EXPOSITION, A
TRIP AROUND THE WORLD see PUK OKO SVIJETA • 1964
TRIP AROUND THE WORLD, A see AROUND THE WORLD WITH NOTHING ON • 1963
TRIP DOWN MEMORY LANE, A • 1965 • Lipsett Arthur • CND
TRIP DOWN THE RIVER, A see REJS • 1970
TRIP FOR TAT • 1960 • Freleng Friz • ANS • USA
TRIP FOR THE GENERAL, A see KLOPKA ZA GENERALA • 1971
TRIP IN A BALLOON see VOYAGE EN BALLON, LE • 1960
TRIP IN SPACE, A see JOURNEY IN THE COSMOS • 1966
TRIP IN THE UNKNOWN see WYCIECZKA W NIEZNANE • 1968
TRIP IN WONDERLAND, A • 1974 • el Saifi Hassan • EGY
TRIP INSIDE A WOMAN'S HEART, A • 1978 • Fahmy Ashraf • EGY
TRIP OF THE "ARCTIC", THE see ADVENTUROUS VOYAGE OF "THE ARCTIC", THE • 1903
TRIP OUT OF TOWN, A see WYCIECZKA Z MIASTA • 1968
TRIP ROUND JENNY • 1975 • Hecht Dina • UKN
TRIP THROUGH SYRIA, A • 1922 • Fares And Debs • USA
TRIP THROUGH THE COLUMBIA EXPOSITION, A see TRIP AROUND THE PAN-AMERICAN EXPOSITION, A • 1901
TRIP THROUGH THE COSMOS, A see WYCIECZKA W KOSMOS • 1961
TRIP THRU A HOLLYWOOD STUDIO, A • 1935 • Staub Ralph • USA
TRIP TO A STAR see VIAGGIO DI UNA STELLA, IL • 1906
TRIP TO AMERICA (USA) see VOYAGE EN AMERIQUE • 1951
TRIP TO BOUNTIFUL, THE • 1986 • Masterson Peter • USA
TRIP TO CHINATOWN, A • 1917 • Richmond J. A. • SHT • USA
TRIP TO CHINATOWN, A • 1926 • Kerr Robert, Marshall George (Spv) • USA
TRIP TO DAVY JONES' LOCKER, A • 1910 • Pathe Freres • FRN
TRIP TO ITALY, A see VIAGGIO IN ITALIA • 1953
TRIP TO JUPITER, A (USA) see VOYAGE A LA PLANETE JUPITER • 1907
TRIP TO KILL (UKN) see CLAY PIGEON • 1971
TRIP TO MARS • Kassner John • ANS • USA
TRIP TO MARS, A • 1910 • Edison • USA
TRIP TO MARS, A • 1920 • Nordisk • DNM
TRIP TO MARS, A • 1920 • W. H. Prods. • ITL
TRIP TO MARS, A • 1924 • Fleischer Dave • ANS • USA
TRIP TO MARS, A see VOYAGE DANS LA LUNE, LE • 1902
TRIP TO MARS, A see HIMMELSKIBET • 1917
TRIP TO MOON, A see TRIP TO THE MOON, A • 1969
TRIP TO PARADISE, A • 1921 • Karger Maxwell • USA
TRIP TO PARIS, A • 1904 • Fitzhamon Lewin • UKN • ENGLISHMAN'S TRIP TO PARIS FROM LONDON, AN (USA)
TRIP TO PARIS, A • 1938 • St. Clair Malcolm • USA
TRIP TO SOUTHEND OR BLACKPOOL, A • 1903 • Williamson James • UKN
TRIP TO TERROR see IS YOUR TRIP REALLY NECESSARY? • 1969
TRIP TO THE COAST • 1973 • Bonniere Rene • SHT • CND
TRIP TO THE DOOR, A • 1971 • Brakhage Stan • USA
TRIP TO THE MOON see REISE AUF DEN MOND • 1959
TRIP TO THE MOON see CHAND PAR CHADAYEE • 1967
TRIP TO THE MOON, A • 1914 • Lubin • USA
TRIP TO THE MOON, A • 1917 • Moss Howard S. • ANM • USA
TRIP TO THE MOON, A • 1933 • University Of Michigan • SHT • USA
TRIP TO THE MOON, A • 1958 • Encyclopedia Britannica • SHT • USA
TRIP TO THE MOON, A • 1963 • Caldura Federico • ITL
TRIP TO THE MOON, A • 1969 • Bartlett Scott • USA • TRIP TO MOON, A
TRIP TO THE MOON, A see VOYAGE DANS LA LUNE, LE • 1902
TRIP TO THE MOON, A (USA) see HOMME DANS LA LUNE, L' • 1898
TRIP TO THE MOON, A (USA) see VIAJE A LA LUNA • 1903
TRIP TO THE POLE, A • 1911 • Pathe Freres • ANS • FRN
TRIP TO THE PYRAMIDS, A • 1904 • Mottershaw Frank • UKN
TRIP TO THE SKY • SHT • FRN
TRIP TO WARSAW, A see WYCIECZKA DO WARSZAWY • 1950
TRIP WITH ANITA, A see VIAGGIO CON ANITA • 1979
TRIPES AU SOLEIL, LES • 1959 • Bernard-Aubert Claude • FRN, ITL • QUESTIONE DI PELLE (ITL) ○ CHECKERBOARD
TRIPLE • 1967 • Cayado Tony • PHL
TRIPLE ACTION • 1925 • Gibson Tom • USA • HURRICANE RANGER, THE
TRIPLE BETRAYAL see NICHI-NICHI O HAISHIN • 1958
TRIPLE BILL • 1970 • Kent Larry • CND
TRIPLE CHECK see TROINAYA PROVERKA • 1970
TRIPLE CLUE, THE • 1920 • Collins Tom • USA
TRIPLE CONJURER AND THE LIVING HEAD, THE (USA) see ILLUSIONNISTE DOUBLE ET LA TETE VIVANTE, L' • 1900
TRIPLE CROSS • 1966 • Young Terence • UKN, FRN • FANTASTIQUE HISTOIRE VRAIE D'EDDIE CHAPMAN, LA (FRN)
TRIPLE CROSS, THE • 1917 • Pokes & Jabbs • SHT • USA
TRIPLE CROSS, THE (UKN) see JOE PALOOKA IN TRIPLE CROSS • 1951
TRIPLE CROSSED • 1959 • White Jules • SHT • USA
TRIPLE DECEPTION (USA) see HOUSE OF SECRETS • 1957
TRIPLE ECHO, THE • 1972 • Apted Michael • UKN • SOLDIERS IN SKIRTS (USA)
TRIPLE ENQUETE • 1946 • Orval Claude • FRN
TRIPLE ENTENTE • 1915 • Feuillade Louis • FRN
TRIPLE ENTENTE • 1917 • Sparkle • USA
TRIPLE-HEADED LADY, THE (USA) see BOUQUET D'ILLUSIONS • 1901
TRIPLE IRONS see NEW ONE-ARMED SWORDSMAN, THE • 1972
TRIPLE JUSTICE • 1940 • Howard David • USA
TRIPLE LADY, THE (USA) see DEDOUBLEMENT CABALISTIQUE • 1898
TRIPLE MORT DU TROISIEME PERSONNAGE, LA (FRN) see TRIPLE MUERTE DEL TERCER PERSONAJE, LA • 1979
TRIPLE MUERTE DEL TERCER PERSONAJE, LA • 1979 • Soto Helvio • SPN, FRN, BLG • TRIPLE MORT DU TROISIEME PERSONNAGE, LA (FRN) ○ THIRD CHARACTER'S TRIPLE DEATH, THE
TRIPLE PASS • 1928 • Barrymore William • USA
TRIPLE PLAY • 1970 • Windom William • TVM • USA
TRIPLE SHOT, THE • 1919 • Kennedy Aubrey M. • USA
TRIPLE THREAT • 1948 • Yarbrough Jean • USA
TRIPLE THREAT see WEST OF PINTO BASIN • 1940
TRIPLE TROUBLE • 1918 • Chaplin Charles, White Leo • SHT • USA
TRIPLE TROUBLE • 1944 • D'Arcy Harry • SHT • USA
TRIPLE TROUBLE • 1948 • Donnelly Eddie • ANS • USA
TRIPLE TROUBLE • 1950 • Yarbrough Jean • USA
TRIPLE TROUBLE (UKN) see KENTUCKY KERNELS • 1934
TRIPLE WINNING, A • 1915 • Morgan George • USA
TRIPLECROSS • 1986 • Greene David • TVM • USA
TRIPLEPATTE • 1922 • Bernard Raymond • FRN
TRIPLES INTRODUCTIONS • 1977 • Mulot Claude • FRN
TRIPLET TROUBLE • 1952 • Hanna William, Barbera Joseph • ANS • USA
TRIPLICE APPUNTAMENTO, IL • 1906 • Velle Gaston • ITL
TRIPODS • 1984 • Theakston Graham, Barry Christopher • MTV • UKN
TRIPOLI • 1950 • Price Will • USA • FIRST MARINES
TRIPOLI BEL SUOL D'AMORE • 1954 • Cerio Ferruccio • ITL • QUATTRO BERSAGLIERI, I
TRIPORTEUR, LE • 1958 • Pinoteau Jack • FRN
TRIPOT CLANDESTIN, LE • 1905 • Melies Georges • SHT • FRN • SCHEMING GAMBLER'S PARADISE, THE (USA)
TRIPOTEUSES, LES • 1975 • Hustaix Lucien • FRN
TRIPTIKH see TRIPTYCH • 1978
TRIPTYCH • 1978 • Khamraev Ali • USS • TRIPTIKH ○ MEVAZAR PORTRAIT
TRIQUE, GAMIN DE PARIS • 1960 • de Gastyne Marco • FRN • FUGITIVES, LES
TRISANDHYA • Marbres Raj • IND
TRISHAGNI • 1988 • Ghosh Nabendu • IND • SANDSTORM, THE
TRISHAW-MAN BA KHET see SIDE-CAR THAMAR BA KHET • 1978
TRISMUS • 1978 • Bugajski Ryszard • MTV • PLN
TRISTAN AND ISOLT • 1981 • Donovan Tom • USA
TRISTAN ET ISEULT • 1972 • Lagrange Yvan • FRN
TRISTAN TZARA, DADAISMENS FADER • 1949 • Roos Jorgen • DOC • DNM
TRISTANA • 1970 • Bunuel Luis • SPN, ITL, FRN
TRISTE CHANSON DE TOUA, LA • 1971 • Abnudi Atiat Al- • SHT • EGY
TRISTE CREPUSCULO • 1917 • de la Bandera Manuel • MXC
TRISTE FIN D'UN VIEUX SAVANT • 1904 • Blache Alice • FRN
TRISTE IMPREGNO • 1914 • Ghione Emilio • ITL
TRISTE NUIT DE NOCES see COUCHER DE LA MARIEE, LE • 1899
TRISTESSE MODELE REDUIT • 1988 • Morin Robert • CND • SADNESS REDUCED TO GO
TRISTI AMORI • 1943 • Gallone Carmine • ITL
TRITON, THE see TRYTON, A • 1917
TRITTICO see SESSO DEL DIAVOLO, IL • 1971
TRITTICO DELL'AMORE, IL • 1920 • Falena Ugo • ITL
TRIUMPH • 1917 • De Grasse Joseph • USA
TRIUMPH • 1924 • De Mille Cecil B. • USA
TRIUMPH see TRIJUMF • 1972
TRIUMPH DER LIEBE • 1947 • Stoger Alfred • AUS
TRIUMPH DES WILLENS • 1934 • Riefenstahl Leni • DOC • FRG • TRIUMPH OF THE WILL
TRIUMPH EINES GENIES, DER see FRIEDRICH SCHILLER • 1940
TRIUMPH OF A GENIUS see FRIEDRICH SCHILLER • 1940
TRIUMPH OF CAESAR, THE • 1971 • Ashton Dudley Shaw • DOC • UKN
TRIUMPH OF DEATH, THE see TRIUNFO DE LA MUERTE, EL • 1969
TRIUMPH OF FAITH, THE • 1912 • Maco Floro • CLM
TRIUMPH OF HERCULES, THE (UKN) see TRIONFO DI ERCOLE, IL • 1964
TRIUMPH OF LESTER SNAPWELL, THE • 1963 • Keaton Buster • SHT • USA
TRIUMPH OF LOVE, THE • 1908 • Urban-Eclipse • USA
TRIUMPH OF LOVE, THE • 1922 • Ramster P. J. • ASL
TRIUMPH OF LOVE (USA) see ICH LEBE FUR DICH • 1929
TRIUMPH OF MACISTE, THE see TRIONFO DI MACISTE, IL • 1961
TRIUMPH OF MICHAEL STROGOFF, THE (UKN) see TRIOMPHE DE MICHEL STROGOFF, LE • 1961
TRIUMPH OF MIND, THE • 1914 • Weber Lois • USA
TRIUMPH OF RIGHT, THE • 1912 • Vitagraph • USA
TRIUMPH OF RIGHT, THE • 1914 • Lubin • USA
TRIUMPH OF RIGHT, THE • 1916 • Lily • USA
TRIUMPH OF ROBIN HOOD (USA) see TRIONFO DI ROBIN HOOD • 1962
TRIUMPH OF SHERLOCK HOLMES, THE • 1935 • Hiscott Leslie • UKN
TRIUMPH OF THE HEART see HJARTATS TRIUMF • 1929
TRIUMPH OF THE RAT, THE • 1926 • Cutts Graham • UKN
TRIUMPH OF THE SCARLET PIMPERNEL, THE • 1928 • Hunter T. Hayes • UKN • SCARLET DAREDEVIL, THE (USA)
TRIUMPH OF THE SON OF HERCULES (USA) see TRIONFO DI MACISTE, IL • 1961
TRIUMPH OF THE SPIRIT • 1989 • Young Robert Malcolm • USA
TRIUMPH OF THE WEAK, THE • 1918 • Terriss Tom • USA
TRIUMPH OF THE WILL see TRIUMPH DES WILLENS • 1934
TRIUMPH OF TRUTH, THE • 1916 • Madison Cleo • SHT • USA
TRIUMPH OF VENUS, THE • 1918 • Hesser Edwin Bower • USA
TRIUMPH OF WINGS, A see TSUBASA NO GAIKA • 1942
TRIUMPH OVER PAIN see GREAT MOMENT, THE • 1944
TRIUMPH TIGER '57 see HEMPAS BAR • 1978
TRIUMPHAL MARCH see MARCIA TRIONFALE • 1976
TRIUMPHAL WINGS see TSUBASA NO GAIKA • 1942
TRIUMPHS OF A MAN CALLED HORSE • 1983 • Hough John • USA, MXC
TRIUMPHS WITHOUT DRUMS • 1941 • Newman Joseph M. • SHT • USA
TRIUNFA LA PANDILLA • 1959 • Porter Julio • MXC
TRIUNFADORES, LOS • 1978 • Duran Javier • MXC
TRIUNFO DA TECNICA • 1970 • de Almeida Manuel Faria • SHT • PRT
TRIUNFO DE LA MUERTE, EL • 1969 • Gutierrez Santos Jose Maria • SHT • SPN • TRIUMPH OF DEATH, THE
TRIUNFO DE LOS DIEZ GLADIADORES, EL (SPN) see SPARTACUS E I DIECI GLADIATORI • 1964
TRIX, DER ROMAN EINER MILLIONENERBIN • 1921 • Zelnik Friedrich? • FRG
TRIXI • 1970 • Dwoskin Stephen • UKN
TRIXIE AND THE PRESS AGENT • 1913 • Kalem • USA
TRIXIE FROM BROADWAY • 1919 • Neill R. William • USA
TRIXIE OF THE FOLLIES • 1917 • Rhodes Billie • SHT • USA
TRO, HAB OG TROLDDOM • 1960 • Balling Erik, Henriksen Finn • DNM • FAITH, HOPE AND WITCHCRAFT
TROBIANA • 1929 • Bindley Victor (P) • ASL
TROCADERO • 1944 • Nigh William • USA
TROCADERO see TROKADERO • 1981
TROCADERO BLEU CITRON • 1978 • Schock Michael • FRN
TROCHE INNY SWIAT • 1959 • Karabasz Kazimierz • DCS • PLN • SLIGHTLY DIFFERENT WORLD, A
TRODLER VON AMSTERDAM, DER • 1925 • Janson Victor • FRG
TROE VYSHLI IZ LESA • 1957 • Voinov Konstantin • USS • THREE CAME FROM THE FOREST
TROFFEI D'AFRICA • 1954 • Quilici Folco • SHT • ITL
TROFFJ • 1980 • Vicek Karolj • YGS • TROPHY
TROG • 1970 • Francis Freddie • UKN
TROIKA • 1930 • von Strischewski Wladimir • FRG
TROIKA • 1940 • von Strischewski Wladimir • FRG
TROIKA • 1969 • Hobbs Fredric, Mueller Gordon • USA
TROIKA ROUGE see TROIKA SUR LA PISTE BLANCHE • 1937
TROIKA SUR LA PISTE BLANCHE • 1937 • Dreville Jean • FRN • TROIKA ROUGE
TROINAYA PROVERKA • 1970 • Brench Alois • USS • TRIPLE CHECK
TROIS AMOURS see PART DE L'OMBRAGE, LA • 1945
TROIS ARGENTINS A MONTMARTRE • 1940 • Hugon Andre • FRN
TROIS ARTILLEURS A L'OPERA • 1938 • Chotin Andre • FRN
TROIS ARTILLEURS AU PENSIONNAT • 1937 • Pujol Rene • FRN
TROIS ARTILLEURS EN VADROUILLE • 1938 • Pujol Rene • FRN

TROIS BACCHANTES, LES • 1900 • Melies Georges • FRN • THREE BACCHANTS, THE
TROIS BALLES DANS LA PEAU • 1933 • Lion Roger • FRN
TROIS CAVALIERS, LES see **FURSAN ATH-THALATHA, AL-** • 1961
TROIS CAVALIERS POUR FORT YUMA • 1968 • Ferroni Giorgio • FRN, ITL, SPN
TROIS CENT DIXSEPTIEME see **317eme SECTION, LA** • 1965
TROIS CENTS A L'HEURE • 1934 • Rozier Willy • FRN
TROIS CENTS SOURDS EN VOIE D'INTEGRATION • 1975 • Moreau Michel • DOC • CND
TROIS CHAMBRES A MANHATTAN • 1965 • Carne Marcel • FRN
TROIS CHANSONS DE LA RESISTANCE • 1944 • Cavalcanti Alberto • SHT • FRN • TROIS CHANTS POUR LA FRANCE
TROIS CHANTS POUR LA FRANCE see **TROIS CHANSONS DE LA RESISTANCE** • 1944
TROIS CONSEILS, LES see **BABUTA** • 1976
TROIS COURONNES DANOIS DES MATELOTS, LES • 1982 • Ruiz Raul • FRN • THREE DANISH SAILORS' CROWNS, THE ○ THREE CROWNS OF THE SAILOR ○ TROIS COURONNES DU MATELOT, LES ○ SAILORS' THREE CROWNS, THE
TROIS COURONNES DU MATELOT, LES see **TROIS COURONNES DANOIS DES MATELOTS, LES** • 1982
TROIS COUSINES, LES • 1946 • Daniel-Norman Jacques • FRN
TROIS DANS UN MOULIN • 1936 • Weill Pierre • FRN
TROIS DE LA CANEBIERE • 1955 • de Canonge Maurice • FRN
TROIS DE LA MARINE • 1934 • Barrois Charles • FRN
TROIS DE LA MARINE • 1957 • de Canonge Maurice • FRN
TROIS DE SAINT-CYR • 1938 • Paulin Jean-Paul • FRN
TROIS DERNIERS HOMMES, LES • 1979 • Perset Antoine • DOC • FRN
TROIS ENFANTS DANS LE DESORDRE • 1966 • Joannon Leo • FRN
TROIS ESTRANGES HISTOIRES • 1968 • Delire Jean • BLG • THREE STRANGE STORIES
TROIS ETC. DU COLONEL, LES • 1960 • Boissol Claude • FRN, ITL • TRE ECCETERA DEL COLONELLO, LE (ITL) ○ THREE ETC'S AND THE COLONEL (USA)
TROIS EXERCICES SUR L'ECRAN D'EPINGLES ALEXEIEFF • 1974 • Drouin Jacques • ANS • CND
TROIS FEMMES • 1951 • Michel Andre • FRN • THREE WOMEN (USA) ○ TROIS FEMMES, TROIS AMES
TROIS FEMMES see **THALATH NISA'** • 1969
TROIS FEMMES, TROIS AMES see **TROIS FEMMES** • 1951
TROIS FILLE EN LIBERTE • Reinhard Pierre B. • FRN
TROIS FILLES DE LA CONCIERGE, LES see **FILLES DE LA CONCIERGE, LES** • 1934
TROIS FILLES EN PORTEFEUILLE • 1916 • de Baroncelli Jacques • FRN
TROIS FILLES FACILES • Korber Serge • FRN
TROIS FILLES VERS LE SOLEIL • 1967 • Beaumont Roger • FRN • EROTIC URGE (UKN)
TROIS FOIS PASSERA • 1973 • Beaudin Jean • SHT • CND
TROIS FONT LA PAIRE, LE • 1957 • Guitry Sacha, Duhour Clement • FRN
TROIS FRERES (FRN) see **TRE FRATELLI** • 1980
TROIS GARCONS, UNE FILLE • 1948 • Labro Maurice • FRN
TROIS HISTOIRES EXTRAORDINAIRES D'EDGAR POE see **HISTOIRES EXTRAORDINAIRES** • 1968
TROIS HOMMES A ABATTRE • 1980 • Deray Jacques • FRN
TROIS HOMMES AU MILLE CARRE • 1966 • Patry Pierre, Kasma Jacques • DCS • CND
TROIS HOMMES EN CORSE • 1950 • Decae Henri • SHT • FRN
TROIS HOMMES EN HABIT • 1933 • Bonnard Mario • FRN
TROIS HOMMES ET UN COUFFIN • 1985 • Serreau Coline • FRN • THREE MEN AND A CRADLE (USA)
TROIS HOMMES ET UNE CORDE • 1933 • Storck Henri • DOC • BLG • TROIS VIES ET UNE CORDE
TROIS HOMMES ET UNE FEMME see **THALATHA RIJAL WA IMRA'A** • 1960
TROIS HOMMES SUR UN CHEVAL • 1969 • Moussy Marcel • FRN, ITL
TROIS JEUNES FILLES NUES • 1928 • Boudrioz Robert • FRN
TROIS JOURS A VIVRE • 1957 • Grangier Gilles • FRN
TROIS JOURS D'AMOUR see **AU-DELA DES GRILLES** • 1948
TROIS JOURS DE BRINGUE A PARIS • 1953 • Couzinet Emile • FRN
TROIS JOURS DE PERM' • 1936 • Monca Georges, Keroul Maurice • FRN
TROIS K • 1918 • de Baroncelli Jacques • FRN
TROIS LECTEURS EN DIFFICULTE • 1968 • Moreau Michel • DOC • CND
TROIS LYS, LES • 1921 • Desfontaines Henri • FRN
TROIS MARINS DANS UN COUVENT • 1949 • Couzinet Emile • FRN
TROIS MARINS EN BORDEE • 1957 • Couzinet Emile • FRN
TROIS MASQUES, LES • 1921 • Krauss Henry • FRN
TROIS MASQUES, LES • 1929 • Hugon Andre • FRN
TROIS-MATS, LE see **TROIS-MATS "MERCATOR"** • 1935
TROIS-MATS "MERCATOR" • 1935 • Ferno John, Storck Henri • SHT • BLG • MERCATOR ○ TROIS-MATS, LE
TROIS MILLIARDS SANS ASCENSEUR • 1972 • Pigaut Roger • FRN, ITL
TROIS MINUTES • 1967 • Lambert Jean-Marie • BLG
TROIS MORTS DANS UN DOLMEN see **DOLMEN TRAGIQUE, LE** • 1947
TROIS MOUSQUETAIRES, LES • 1912 • Calmettes Andre • FRN
TROIS MOUSQUETAIRES, LES • 1913 • Pouctal Henri • FRN • THREE MUSKETEERS, THE
TROIS MOUSQUETAIRES, LES • 1921 • Diamant-Berger Henri • FRN • THREE MUSKETEERS, THE
TROIS MOUSQUETAIRES, LES • 1932 • Diamant-Berger Henri • FRN
TROIS MOUSQUETAIRES, LES • 1953 • Hunebelle Andre • FRN, ITL • FATE LARGO AI MOSCHETTIERI! (ITL) ○ THREE MUSKETEERS, THE (USA)
TROIS MOUSQUETAIRES, LES • 1961 • Borderie Bernard • FRN, ITL • VENGEANCE OF THE THREE MUSKETEERS ○ THREE MUSKETEERS, THE (USA)
TROIS NOUVELLES DE TCHEKHOV • 1967 • Fasquel Maurice • ANT • FRN
TROIS OMBRES, LES • 1914 • Fescourt Henri • FRN
TROIS PASSIONS, LES see **THREE PASSIONS, THE** • 1928
TROIS PETITS TOURS • 1983 • Goulet Stella • MTV • CND
TROIS PISTOLETS CONTRE CESAR • 1967 • Haddad Moussa, Peri C. E. • ALG
TROIS PLACES POUR LE 26 • 1988 • Demy Jacques • FRN
TROIS POINTS C'EST TOUT see **RIEN QUE DES MENSONGES** • 1932
TROIS POMMES A COTE DU SOMMEIL • 1990 • Leduc Jacques • CND
TROIS PORTRAITS D'UN OISEAU QUI N'EXISTE PAS • 1963 • Lapoujade Robert • ANS • FRN • THREE PORTRAITS OF A NON-EXISTENT BIRD
TROIS POUR CENT • 1933 • Dreville Jean • FRN • PETIT MILLIONAIRE, LE
TROIS-RIVIERES • 1949 • Tessier Albert • DCS • CND
TROIS-RIVIERES 71.. • 1971 • Plamondon Leo • DCS • CND
TROIS RIVIERES 1932 • 1932 • Tessier Albert • DCS • CND
TROIS RIVIERES 1934 • 1934 • Tessier Albert • DCS • CND
TROIS-RIVIERES SOUS LA NEIGE, 1937 • 1937 • Tessier Albert • DCS • CND
TROIS.. SIX.. NEUF • 1936 • Rouleau Raymond • FRN
TROIS TAMBOURS, LES • 1939 • de Canonge Maurice • FRN • VIVE LA NATION
TROIS TELEGRAMMES • 1950 • Decoin Henri • FRN • PARIS INCIDENT (USA) ○ THREE TELEGRAMS
TROIS THEMES • 1980 • Alexeieff Alexandre, Parker Claire • FRN • THREE THEMES
TROIS VALSES • 1938 • Berger Ludwig • FRN • THREE WALTZES
TROIS VERITES see **PUITS AUX TROIS VERITES, LE** • 1961
TROIS VIEILLES FILLES EN FOLIE • 1951 • Couzinet Emile • FRN
TROIS VIES ET UNE CORDE see **TROIS HOMMES ET UNE CORDE** • 1933
TROIS VILLES D'ISLAM • 1966 • Essid Hamadi • DOC • TNS
TROIS VISAGES DE LA PEUR, LES (FRN) see **TRE VOLTI DELLA PAURA, I** • 1963
TROIS VISAGES DE L'AMOUR see **THALATH WUGUH LI AL-HUBB** • 1968
TROIS VOLEURS see **THALATH LUSUSS** • 1966
TROIS VOLEURS see **THALATHATU LUCUC** • 1966
TROISIEME CHEMINEE A GAUCHE • 1947 • Mineur Jean • FRN
TROISIEME CRI, LA • 1975 • Niddam Igaal • SWT
TROISIEME DALLE, LA • 1941 • Dulud Michel • FRN
TROISIEME DIMENSION, LA see **COUTEAU DANS LA PLAIE, LE** • 1962
TROISIEME JEUNESSE • 1965 • Dreville Jean • FRN
TROISIEME LARRON, LE • 1916 • Burguet Charles • FRN
TROJAN BROTHERS, THE • 1946 • Rogers Maclean • UKN • MURDER IN THE FOOTLIGHTS
TROJAN HORSE, THE • 1946 • Davis Mannie • ANS • USA
TROJAN HORSE, THE (USA) see **GUERRA DI TROIA, LA** • 1961
TROJAN WAR, THE see **GUERRA DI TROIA, LA** • 1961
TROJAN WOMEN, THE • 1971 • Cacoyannis Michael • USA, GRC
TROJANER see **ZWISCHENFALL IN BENDERATH** • 1956
TROJE I LAS • 1962 • Wohl Stanislaw • PLN
TROKADERO • 1981 • Emmerich Klaus • AUS, FRG • TROCADERO
TROLD KAN TAEMMES • 1914 • Holger-Madsen • DNM • TAMING OF THE SHREW, THE
TROLL • 1973 • Sjoman Vilgot • SWD • TILL SEX DO US PART (USA) ○ SEX TO THE END
TROLL • 1986 • Buechler John • USA
TROLL AND THE PIXY, THE • 1967 • Thomsen Knud Leif • DNM
TROLLALGEN • 1927 • Furst Walter • NRW • MAGIC ELK
TROLLEBOKUNGEN • 1924 • Edgren Gustaf • SWD • KING OF TROLLEBO, THE
TROLLENBERG TERROR, THE • 1958 • Lawrence Quentin • UKN • CRAWLING EYE, THE (USA) ○ CREATURE FROM ANOTHER WORLD
TROLLEY AHOY • 1936 • Gillett Burt • ANS • USA
TROLLEY TROUBLES • 1921 • Roach Hal • SHT • USA
TROLLEY TROUBLES • 1927 • Disney Walt • ANS • USA
TROLLEY TROUBLES • 1931 • Lantz Walter, Nolan William • ANS • USA
TROLLFLOJTEN • 1975 • Bergman Ingmar • MTV • SWD • MAGIC FLUTE, THE (USA)
TROLLOP'S DAUGHTER, THE see **SURTUGUN KIZI** • 1967
TROLLSLANDAN • 1920 • Brunius Pauline • SHT • SWD
TROLOS • 1913 • Blom August • DNM • GOGLERBLOD ○ ARTISTS
TROMA'S WAR! • 1988 • Herz Michael, Weil Samuel • USA
TROMBA • 1949 • Weiss Helmut • FRG • TROMBA, THE TIGER MAN (USA) ○ TIGER MAN
TROMBA, THE TIGER MAN (USA) see **TROMBA** • 1949
TROMBADINHAS, OS • 1979 • Duarte Anselmo • BRZ
TROMBITAS, A • 1979 • Rozsa Janos • HNG • TRUMPETER, THE ○ TRUMPETEER, THE
TROMBONE FROM HEAVEN see **FOLLOW THE BAND** • 1943
TROMBONE TOMMY • 1912 • *Essanay* • USA
TROMBONE TROUBLE • 1944 • King Jack • ANS • USA
TROMBONER'S STRONG NOTE, THE • 1914 • Kellino W. P. • UKN
TROMBONI DI FRA'DIAVOLI, I • 1962 • Simonelli Giorgio C., Lluch Miguel • ITL, SPN • FRA DIAVOLO (SPN)
TROMMELN ASIENS, DIE • 1921 • Krafft Uwe Jens • FRG
TROMMLER, DER • 1969 • Ratz Gunter • ANS • FRG • DRUMMER, THE
TROMPE L'OEIL • 1974 • d'Anna Claude • FRN, BLG
TROMPE-MAIS CONTENT • 1902 • Blache Alice • FRN
TROMPETAS DEL APOCOLIPSIS, LAS • 1969 • Buchs Julio • SPN
TROMPETEN DER LIEBE • 1962 • Schott-Schobinger Hans • FRG, AUS • PFARRER MIT DER JAZZTROMPETE, DER
TROMPETER VON SACKINGEN, DER • 1906-10 • Porten Franz • FRG
TROMPETER VON SACKINGEN, DER • 1918 • Porten Franz • FRG
TROMPETTE ANTI-NEURASTENIQUE, LA • 1915 • Cohl Emile • ANS • FRN
TROMPIE • 1975 • SAF
TRON • 1982 • Lisberger Steven • USA
TRONE DE FRANCE, LE • 1936 • Alexeieff Alexandre • SHT • FRN • THRONE OF FRANCE, THE
TRONO DI FUOCO, IL • 1983 • Prosperi Franco • ITL • THRONE OF FIRE, THE
TRONO DI FUOCO, IL see **PROCESO DE LAS BRUJAS, EL** • 1970
TRONO E LA SEGGIOLA, IL • 1918 • Genina Augusto • ITL
TRONO PARA CRISTY • 1959 • Amadori Luis Cesar • SPN, FRG • THRON FUR CHRISTINE, EINE
TROOP BEVERLY HILLS • 1989 • Kanew Jeff • USA • BE PREPARED
TROOP HAS DISAPPEARED, THE • 1955 • Mimura Akira • JPN
TROOP REVIEW see **DA YUEBING** • 1985
TROOP TRAIN, THE see **LOVE AND THE LAW** • 1919
TROOPER 44 • 1917 • Gahris Roy • USA
TROOPER, THE (UKN) see **FIGHTING TROOPER, THE** • 1934
TROOPER BILLY • 1913 • *Kalem* • USA
TROOPER CAMPBELL • 1914 • Longford Raymond • ASL
TROOPER HOOK • 1957 • Warren Charles Marquis • USA
TROOPER O'BRIEN • 1928 • Gavin John F. • ASL • KEY OF FATE, THE
TROOPER OF TROOP K • 1917 • *Lincoln M.p. Comp.* • SHT • USA
TROOPER O'NEILL • 1922 • Dunlap Scott R., Wallace C. R., Howard William K. • USA
TROOPERS THREE • 1930 • Taurog Norman, Eason B. Reeves • USA
TROOPING OF THE COLOUR • 1961 • Williams R. Maslyn • DOC • ASL
TROOPS GOING TO SOUTH AFRICA • 1900 • Hepworth Cecil M. • UKN
TROOPSHIP (USA) see **FAREWELL AGAIN** • 1937
TROP BELLE POUR TOI! • 1989 • Blier Bertrand • FRN • TOO BEAUTIFUL FOR YOU (UKN)
TROP, C'EST TROP! • 1975 • Kaminka Didier • FRN
TROP CREDULES • 1908 • Durand Jean • FRN
TROP JOLIES POUR ETRE HONNETES • 1972 • Balducci Richard • FRN, ITL, SPN
TROP PETIT MON AMI • 1969 • Matalon Eddy • FRN
TROP TOT, TROP TARD • 1981 • Straub Jean-Marie, Huillet Daniele • FRN
TROP VIEUX! • 1908 • Melies Georges • FRN • OLD FOOTLIGHT FAVOURITE (?)
TROPENBLUT • 1919 • Wellin Arthur • FRG
TROPENGIFT • 1919 • Schomburgk Hans • FRG
TROPENNACHTE • 1930 • Mittler Leo • FRG
TROPERNES DATTER • 1916 • Davidsen Hjalmar • DNM
TROPFEN GIFT, EIN • 1917 • *Kaiser-Titz Erich* • FRG
TROPFEN SCHWARZEN BLUTES, EIN • 1920 • Forsten Hans? • FRG
TROPHEE DU ZOUAVE, LE • 1914 • Ravel Gaston • FRN
TROPHY see **TROFFJ** • 1980
TROPHY ISLAND • 1950 • Williamson Cecil H. • UKN
TROPIC FURY • 1939 • Cabanne W. Christy • USA
TROPIC HOLIDAY • 1938 • Reed Theodore • USA
TROPIC MADNESS • 1928 • Vignola Robert G. • USA • PRICE OF PLEASURE, THE (UKN)
TROPIC OF CANCER • 1970 • Strick Joseph • USA
TROPIC OF ICE • 1987 • Torhonen Lauri • FNL
TROPIC OF SCORPIO • 1968 • Crilly Spence • USA
TROPIC ZONE • 1953 • Foster Lewis R. • USA
TROPICAL BREEZES • 1930 • White H. Brian, Griffiths Sidney G., Goodman A. • UKN
TROPICAL ECSTASY • 1970 • Bo Armando • ARG
TROPICAL EXPRESS see **AFRICAN EXPRESS** • 1975
TROPICAL FISH • 1933 • *Terry Paul/ Moser Frank (P)* • ANS • USA
TROPICAL FLOWER, A • 1983 • Bae Chang-Ho • SKR
TROPICAL HEATWAVE • 1952 • Springsteen R. G. • USA
TROPICAL LAMENT • 1950 • Blais Roger • DCS • CND • CHANSONS CREOLES
TROPICAL LOVE • 1921 • Ince Ralph • USA
TROPICAL NIGHTS • 1928 • Clifton Elmer • USA
TROPICAL ROMEO, A • 1923 • St. John Al • SHT • USA
TROPICAL SNOW • 1988 • Duran Ciro • USA
TROPICAL SOULS see **ALMAS TROPICALES** • 1923
TROPICAL TROUBLE • 1936 • Hughes Harry • UKN
TROPICANA • 1956 • Ortega Juan J. • CUB, MXC
TROPICANA (UKN) see **HEAT'S ON, THE** • 1943
TROPICI • 1969 • Amico Gianni • ITL • TROPICS
TROPICO DI NOTTE • 1961 • Russo Renzo • ITL
TROPICS see **TROPICI** • 1969
TROPISK KAERLIGHED • 1911 • Blom August • DNM • LOVE IN THE TROPICS
TROPPO FORTE • 1985 • Verdone Carlo • ITL • TOO STRONG
TROPPO PER VIVERE.. POCO PER MORIRE • 1967 • Lupo Michele • ITL, FRN • TOO MUCH FOR LIVING.. TOO LITTLE FOR DYING
TROPPO RISCHIO PER UN UOMO SOLO • 1973 • Ercoli Luciano • ITL
TROPPO TARDI T'HO CONOSCIUTA • 1940 • Caracciolo Emanuele • ITL
TROTA CALLES • 1951 • Landeta Matilde • MXC
TROTS • 1952 • Molander Gustaf • SWD • DEFIANCE
TROTTA SCHAAF JOHANNES • 1972 • Schaaf Johannes • FRG
TROTTE TEODOR • 1931 • Edgren Gustaf • SWD • TIRED TEODOR
TROTTE TEODOR • 1945 • Henrikson Anders • SWD • TIRED TEODOR
TROTTER ON THE TROT • 1920 • Aitken Tom • UKN
TROTTER'S GAIT, THE see **PRASHNAI GULSARA** • 1970
TROTTIE TRUE • 1948 • Hurst Brian Desmond • UKN • GAY LADY, THE (USA)
TROTTING, HOPE AND CHARITY see **TRAV, HOPP OCH KARLEK** • 1945
TROTTING THROUGH TURKEY • 1920 • Roach Hal • SHT • USA
TROTTOIR DES ALLONGES, LE see **BOURGEOISE ET LE LOUBARD, LA** • 1977

TROTTOIR ROULANT, LE • 1900 • Melies Georges • FRN
TROTTOIRS DE BANGKOK, LES • 1984 • Rollin Jean • FRN
TROTZ ALLEDEM • 1972 • Reisch Gunter • GDR • IN SPITE OF EVERYTHING ○ DESPITE EVERYTHING
TROTZIGE HERZEN see **ERDE** • 1947
TROU, LE • 1960 • Becker Jacques • FRN, ITL • BUCO, IL (ITL) ○ NIGHT WATCH, THE (USA) ○ HOLE, THE (UKN)
TROU DANS LE MUR, UN • 1931 • Barberis Rene • FRN
TROU DANS LE MUR, UN • 1949 • Couzinet Emile • FRN
TROU DE LA SERRURE, LE • 1903 • Zecca Ferdinand • FRN
TROU NORMAND, LE • 1952 • Boyer Jean • FRN • CRAZY FOR LOVE (USA) ○ TI TA TO
TROUBADOR, THE • 1915 • MacQuarrie Murdock • USA
TROUBADOUR, THE • 1906 • *Pathe* • FRN
TROUBADOUR, THE see **TROVATORE, IL** • 1949
TROUBADOUR, THE see **SA DAGGA** • 1982
TROUBADOUR DE LA JOIE, LE • 1949 • Boucquey Omer • FRN
TROUBADOUR OF THE RANCHO, THE • 1913 • *Powers* • USA
TROUBADOUR'S TRIUMPH, THE • 1912 • Weber Lois • USA
TROUBLE • 1922 • Austin Albert • USA
TROUBLE • 1931 • Foster John, Stallings George • ANS • USA
TROUBLE • 1933 • Rogers Maclean • UKN
TROUBLE • 1988 • Morahan Christopher • UKN
TROUBLE see **ENDISE** • 1975
TROUBLE see **BAS BELASI** • 1977
TROUBLE, THE • 1942 • Donnelly Eddie • ANS • USA
TROUBLE A STOCKING CAUSED, THE • 1913 • *B & C* • UKN
TROUBLE AHEAD see **FALLING IN LOVE** • 1934
TROUBLE ALONG THE WAY • 1953 • Curtiz Michael • USA
TROUBLE AT 16 see **PLATINUM HIGH SCHOOL** • 1960
TROUBLE AT EVERY CORNER see **BAWAT KANTO BASAGULO** • 1968
TROUBLE AT MELODY MESA • 1949 • Connell W. Merle • USA
TROUBLE AT MIDNIGHT • 1938 • Beebe Ford • USA
TROUBLE AT SPRING INN see **YING CH'UN KO CHIH FENG-PO** • 1973
TROUBLE AT TOWNSEND • 1946 • Catling Darrell • UKN
TROUBLE BACK STAIRS (USA) see **KRACH IM HINTERHAUS** • 1935
TROUBLE BELOW STAIRS • 1905 • Martin J. H.? • UKN
TROUBLE BREWING • 1924 • Semon Larry, Davis James • USA
TROUBLE BREWING • 1939 • Kimmins Anthony • UKN
TROUBLE BRUIN • 1961 • Hanna William, Barbera Joseph • ANS • USA
TROUBLE BUBBLES • 1920 • Armstrong William • SHT • USA
TROUBLE BUSTER, THE • 1917 • Reicher Frank • USA
TROUBLE BUSTER, THE • 1925 • Maloney Leo • USA • ROGUES OF THE WEST
TROUBLE BUSTERS • 1933 • Collins Lewis D. • USA
TROUBLE CHASER • 1926 • *Rayart Pictures* • USA
TROUBLE CHASER (UKN) see **LI'L ABNER** • 1940
TROUBLE CHASERS • 1945 • Landers Lew • USA
TROUBLE COMES TO TOWN • 1972 • Petrie Daniel • TVM • USA
TROUBLE DATE • 1960 • Kneitel Seymour • ANS • USA
TROUBLE ENOUGH! • 1916 • Roach Hal • SHT • USA
TROUBLE-FESSES, LE • 1976 • Foulon Raoul • FRN • TROUBLE FESSES, LE
TROUBLE FESSES, LE see **TROUBLE-FESSES, LE** • 1976
TROUBLE-FETE • 1964 • Patry Pierre • CND • TROUBLE FETE
TROUBLE FETE see **TROUBLE-FETE** • 1964
TROUBLE FINDS ANDY CLYDE • 1939 • White Jules • SHT • USA
TROUBLE FOR FATHERS (USA) see **DELISTAVRO KAI GIOS** • 1958
TROUBLE FOR FOUR • 1916 • Robertson John S. • SHT • USA
TROUBLE FOR JUNO • 1957 • Woodhouse Barbara • UKN
TROUBLE FOR THE LEGION see **LEGIONE STRANIERA** • 1953
TROUBLE FOR TWO • 1936 • Ruben J. Walter • USA • SUICIDE CLUB, THE (UKN)
TROUBLE FOR TWO • 1939 • Tennyson Walter • UKN
TROUBLE FOR TWO see **YOUTH ON PAROLE** • 1937
TROUBLE HUNTER, THE • 1920 • Robbins Jess • SHT • USA
TROUBLE IN BAGHDAD • 1963 • Rasinski Connie • ANS • USA
TROUBLE IN BAHIA FOR OSS 117 see **FURIA A BAHIA POUR OSS 117** • 1965
TROUBLE IN HIGH TIMBER COUNTRY • 1980 • Sherman Vincent • TVM • USA
TROUBLE IN MIND • 1986 • Rudolph Alan • USA
TROUBLE IN MOLOPOLIS • 1970 • Mora Philippe • UKN
TROUBLE IN MOROCCO • 1937 • Schoedsack Ernest B. • USA
TROUBLE IN PANAMA (UKN) see **TORCHY BLANE IN PANAMA** • 1938
TROUBLE IN PARADISE • 1932 • Lubitsch Ernst • USA • HONEST FINDER, THE
TROUBLE IN PARADISE • 1988 • Drew Di • TVM • ASL, USA
TROUBLE IN PARADISE • 1989 • de Hert Robbe • BLG
TROUBLE IN SPRING • 1964 • Frid Ya. • USS
TROUBLE IN STORE • 1934 • Cook Clyde • UKN
TROUBLE IN STORE • 1953 • Carstairs John Paddy • UKN
TROUBLE IN SUNDOWN • 1939 • Howard David • USA • KNIGHT IN GHOST TOWN, A
TROUBLE IN TEXAS • 1937 • Bradbury Robert North • USA
TROUBLE IN THE AIR • 1948 • Saunders Charles • UKN
TROUBLE IN THE CITY OF ANGELS see **MAN AGAINST THE MOB** • 1988
TROUBLE IN THE GLEN • 1954 • Wilcox Herbert • UKN
TROUBLE IN THE MORNING see **ASA NO HAMON** • 1952
TROUBLE IN THE SKY (USA) see **CONE OF SILENCE** • 1960
TROUBLE INDEMNITY • 1950 • Burness Pete • ANS • USA
TROUBLE MAKER, THE • 1912 • *Russell William* • USA
TROUBLE MAKER, THE • 1915 • *La Pearl Harry* • USA
TROUBLE MAKERS • 1948 • Le Borg Reginald • USA
TROUBLE MAKERS see **TROUBLEMAKERS** • 1917
TROUBLE MAKERS, THE • 1957 • Frankenheimer John • MTV • USA
TROUBLE MAN • 1972 • Dixon Ivan • USA
TROUBLE ON THE STAGE • 1913 • *Eclair* • USA
TROUBLE ON THE TRAIL • 1954 • McDonald Frank • MTV • USA
TROUBLE OR NOTHING • 1946 • Yates Hal • SHT • USA
TROUBLE PREFERRED • 1948 • Tinling James • USA
TROUBLE SHOOTER, THE • 1924 • Conway Jack • USA
TROUBLE SHOOTER, THE (UKN) see **MAN WITH THE GUN, THE** • 1955
TROUBLE TRAIL • 1924 • Holt George • USA
TROUBLE WAS A DOG • 1958 • Selander Lesley • USA
TROUBLE WITH 2B, THE • 1972 • Smith Peter K. • CMP • UKN
TROUBLE WITH A BATTERY • 1986 • Sarne Mike • UKN
TROUBLE WITH ANGELS, THE • 1966 • Lupino Ida • USA • MOTHER SUPERIOR
TROUBLE WITH DICK, THE • 1986 • Walkow Gary • USA
TROUBLE WITH EVE • 1960 • Searle Francis • UKN • IN TROUBLE WITH EVE (USA)
TROUBLE WITH FRED, THE • 1967 • Robertson George C. • CND
TROUBLE WITH GIRLS, THE • 1969 • Tewkesbury Peter • USA • CHAUTAUQUA
TROUBLE WITH HARRY, THE • 1955 • Hitchcock Alfred • USA
TROUBLE WITH HUSBANDS, THE • 1940 • Roush Leslie • SHT • USA
TROUBLE WITH JOE • 1988 • Andrews David • ANS • CND
TROUBLE WITH JUNIA • 1966 • Woodhouse Barbara • UKN
TROUBLE WITH MONEY, THE see **KOMEDIE OM GELD** • 1936
TROUBLE WITH SPIES, THE • 1987 • Kennedy Burt • USA
TROUBLE WITH WIVES, THE • 1925 • St. Clair Malcolm • USA
TROUBLE WITH WOMEN, THE • 1947 • Lanfield Sidney • USA
TROUBLED see **GELORA** • 1970
TROUBLED ARTISTS • 1909 • *Urban-Eclipse* • USA
TROUBLED CHILDREN • 1964 • Anderson Robert • DSS • CND
TROUBLED HONOUR see **NAMUS BELASI** • 1967
TROUBLED ROAD see **NESPOKOEN PAT** • 1955
TROUBLED TRAIL, THE • 1912 • *Vitagraph* • USA
TROUBLED WATERS • 1913 • *Smalley Phillips* • USA
TROUBLED WATERS • 1916 • Miller Rube • USA
TROUBLED WATERS • 1936 • Parker Albert • UKN
TROUBLED WATERS • 1964 • Goulder Stanley • UKN • MAN WITH TWO FACES (USA)
TROUBLEMAKER • 1988 • Bausch Andy • LXM, FRG
TROUBLEMAKER, THE • 1964 • Flicker Theodore J. • USA
TROUBLEMAKERS • 1917 • Buel Kenean • USA • TROUBLE MAKERS
TROUBLEMAKERS • 1966 • Machover Robert, Fruchter Norman • DOC • USA
TROUBLEMAKERS see **HIGH TENSION** • 1936
TROUBLES see **MAKING A LIVING** • 1914
TROUBLES DE JOHNNY, LES • 1974 • Godbout Jacques • SHT • CND
TROUBLES DE SAINT-PETERSBOURG, LES • 1905 • Nonguet Lucien • FRN
TROUBLES FOR NOTHING • 1916 • Elvey Maurice • UKN
TROUBLES IN THE KINGDOM OF THE SKY see **DA NO TIEN GU** • 1961
TROUBLES OF A BRIDE • 1924 • Buckingham Thomas • USA
TROUBLES OF A BUTLER, THE • 1911 • *Cumpson John R.* • USA
TROUBLES OF A HOUSE AGENT, THE • 1908 • Fitzhamon Lewin • UKN
TROUBLES OF A HYPOCHONDRIAC, THE • 1915 • Birch Cecil • UKN
TROUBLES OF A NEW DRUG CLERK • 1908 • *Selig* • USA
TROUBLES OF A POLICEMAN • 1910 • *Pathe* • USA
TROUBLES OF A SEASIDE PHOTOGRAPHER, THE • 1906 • *Walturdaw* • UKN
TROUBLES OF A STRANDED ACTOR • 1909 • *Lubin* • USA
TROUBLES OF A THEATRE FIREMAN, THE • 1906 • *Walturdaw* • UKN
TROUBLES OF AN AMATEUR DETECTIVE, THE • 1909 • Baker George D. • USA
TROUBLES OF AN HEIRESS, THE • 1914 • Northcote Sidney? • UKN
TROUBLES OF MR.TRISKA, THE • 1949 • Mach Josef • CZC
TROUBLES OF RUFUS, THE • 1915 • *Pathe Exchange* • USA
TROUBLES OF THE TWINS, THE • 1906 • Mottershaw Frank • UKN
TROUBLES OF THE XL OUTFIT • 1912 • Melies Gaston • USA
TROUBLES THROUGH BILLETS (UKN) see **BLONDIE FOR VICTORY** • 1942
TROUBLES WITH HEAT see **KLOPOTY Z CIEPLEM** • 1965
TROUBLESHOOTER, THE • 1988 • Papas Michael
TROUBLESHOOTERS, THE see **WAN ZHU** • 1988
TROUBLESHOOTERS (UKN) see **LAISSE ALLER, C'EST UNE VALSE** • 1970
TROUBLESOME BABY, THE • 1910 • Powell Frank • USA
TROUBLESOME CAT, A • 1914 • *Lubin* • USA
TROUBLESOME COLLAR, THE • 1902 • *Paul R. W.* • UKN
TROUBLESOME DAUGHTERS • 1913 • Thompson Frederick A. • USA
TROUBLESOME DOUBLE, THE • 1971 • Lewis Milo • UKN
TROUBLESOME FIVE, THE see **BELALI BESLER** • 1968
TROUBLESOME FLY, THE • 1902 • *Biograph* • USA
TROUBLESOME MOLE, THE • 1913 • Dillon Eddie • USA
TROUBLESOME PARCEL, A • 1911 • *American* • USA
TROUBLESOME PETE • 1914 • *Sterling* • USA
TROUBLESOME PICTURE, A • 1911 • *Beggs Lee* • USA
TROUBLESOME SATCHEL, A • 1909 • Griffith D. W. • USA
TROUBLESOME SECRETARIES, THE • 1911 • *Vitagraph* • USA
TROUBLESOME STEP-DAUGHTERS, THE • 1912 • Baker George D.?, Trimble Larry? • USA
TROUBLESOME TELEPHONE, THE • 1913 • *Roland Ruth* • USA
TROUBLESOME TRIP, A • 1916 • *U.s.m.p.* • SHT • USA
TROUBLESOME WINK, A • 1914 • Christie Al • USA
TROUBLESOME WIVES • 1928 • Hughes Harry • UKN • SUMMER LIGHTNING
TROUDAG VAN TANT RALIE • 1975 • SAF
TROUDNA LYUBOV • 1974 • Andonov Ivan • BUL • DIFFICULT LOVE, A ○ HARD LOVE, A
TROUGHS OF KAWACHI see **KAWACHI YUKYODEN** • 1967
TROUMBA 67 • 1967 • Grigoriou Grigoris • GRC
TROUPE, THE see **THIASOS, O** • 1974
TROUPE, THE see **HALAHAKA** • 1981
TROUPE DE LA BONNE HUMEUR, LA see **FIRQAT AL-MARAH'** • 1970
TROUPER, THE • 1922 • Harris Harry B. • USA
TROUPER'S HEART, A • 1911 • Dwan Allan • USA
TROUPES ON PARADE • 1938 • Parsons Herbert R. • UKN
TROUPING WITH ELLEN • 1924 • Hunter T. Hayes • USA • PITY THE CHORUS GIRL
TROUS DE BALLES see **ATOMIQUE MONSIEUR PLACIDO, L'** • 1949
TROUSERLESS POLICEMAN, THE • 1914 • *Melies* • USA
TROUSERS • 1920 • Phillips Bertram • UKN
TROUSERS, THE see **HOSE, DIE** • 1927
TROUT, THE see **TRUCHAS, LAS** • 1978
TROUT, THE see **TRUITE, LA** • 1982
TROUT FISHING • 1932 • Reis Irving • SHT • USA
TROUT FISHING, RANGELLY LAKES • 1905 • *Bitzer Billy (Ph)* • USA
TROUVAILLE DE BEBE • 1910 • Feuillade Louis • FRN
TROUVAILLE DE BOUCHU, LE • 1916 • Feyder Jacques • FRN
TROUVAILLES ET BIZARRERIES • 1976 • Garceau Raymond • DCS • CND
TROVATELLA DI MILANO, LA • 1956 • Capitani Giorgio • ITL
TROVATELLA DI POMPEI, LA • 1958 • Gentilomo Giacomo • ITL
TROVATORE, IL • 1910 • Barnett David • UKN
TROVATORE, IL • 1922 • Collins Edwin J. • UKN
TROVATORE, IL • 1927 • Coleby A. E. • UKN
TROVATORE, IL • 1949 • Gallone Carmine • ITL • TROUBADOUR, THE
TROYE IZ NAS • 1989 • Kesayants Dmitry, Melkonyan Gennady, Aivazyan Agasi • USS • THREE OF US
TROYE S ODNOI ULITSI • 1936 • Shpikovsky Nikolai • USS • THREE FROM ONE STREET
TRST • 1951 • Stiglic France • YGS • TRIESTE
TRU-U-UTH, THE see **VERITAAAAAAAA, LA** • 1982
TRUANDS, LES • 1956 • Carlo-Rim • FRN • LOCK UP YOUR SPOONS (UKN) ○ LOCK UP THE SPOONS
TRUANT, THE see **PIONIR I DVOJKA** • 1949
TRUANT HUSBAND, THE • 1920 • Heffron Thomas N. • USA
TRUANT OFFICER DONALD • 1941 • King Jack • ANS • USA
TRUANT, OR HOW WILLIE FIXED HIS FATHER, THE • 1909 • *Vitagraph* • USA
TRUANT SOUL, THE • 1917 • Beaumont Harry • USA
TRUANT STUDENT • 1958 • Smith Paul J. • ANS • USA
TRUANTS • 1907 • *Bitzer Billy (Ph)* • USA
TRUANTS • 1920 • Sandground Maurice • UKN
TRUANTS see **ISKOLAKERULOK** • 1989
TRUANTS, THE • 1922 • Hill Sinclair • UKN
TRUANT'S CAPTURE, THE • 1906 • Stow Percy • UKN
TRUANT'S DOOM, THE • 1912 • *Eline Marie* • USA
TRUBA • 1964 • Zaninovic Ante • ANS • YGS • TRUMPET, THE
TRUBA • 1976 • Grgic Zlatko • ANS • YGS • TRUMPET, THE
TRUBE WASSER • 1960 • Daquin Louis • GDR, FRN • ARRIVISTES, LES (FRN) ○ RABOUILLEUSE, LA ○ MUDDY WATER ○ KREBSFISCHERIN, DIE
TRUC DU BRESILIEN, LE • 1932 • Cavalcanti Alberto • FRN
TRUC DU POTARD, LE see **HALLUCINATIONS PHARMACEUTIQUES OU LE TRUC DU POTARD** • 1908
TRUCE, THE see **TREGUA, LA** • 1974
TRUCE, THE (UKN) see **TREVE, LA** • 1969
TRUCE HURTS, THE • 1948 • Hanna William, Barbera Joseph • ANS • USA
TRUCHAS, LAS • 1978 • Garcia Sanchez Jose Luis • SPN • TROUT, THE
TRUCIDO E LO SBIRRO, IL • 1976 • Lenzi Umberto • ITL
TRUCK • 1975 • Awad Robert • CND
TRUCK, THE see **CAMION, LE** • 1977
TRUCK BUSTERS • 1943 • Eason B. Reeves • USA
TRUCK DRIVER see **LANGTURSCHAUFFOR** • 1981
TRUCK DRIVER, THE • 1963 • Focinic Bosko • SYR
TRUCK STOP see **AMOUR CHEZ LES POIDS LOURDS, L'** • 1978
TRUCK STOP WOMEN • 1974 • Lester Mark L. • USA
TRUCK THAT FLEW, THE • 1943 • Pal George • ANS • USA
TRUCK TURNER • 1974 • Kaplan Jonathan • USA
TRUCKER'S GIRL • 1970 • Davis Bobby • USA
TRUCKER'S TOP HAND • 1924 • Hart Neal • USA
TRUCKIN' MAN • 1975 • Zens Will • USA
TRUCKLOAD OF TROUBLE, A • 1949 • Rasinski Connie • ANS • USA
TRUDE, DIE SECHZEHNJAHRIGE • 1926 • Wiene Conrad • FRG
TRUDE SEKELY • 1975 • Beaudry Michel • CND
TRUDEAU • 1968 • Woods Grahame • CND
TRUDNA MILOSC • 1953 • Rozewicz Stanislaw • PLN • DIFFICULT LOVE
TRUDNO BYT BOGOM • 1988 • Fleischmann Peter • USS, FRG • HARD TO BE A GOD ○ IT'S HARD TO BE GOD
TRUDNOE SCHASTE • 1958 • Stolper Alexander • USS • DIFFICULT HAPPINESS, THE ○ HARD-WON HAPPINESS
TRUE AS A TURTLE • 1957 • Toye Wendy • UKN
TRUE AS STEEL • 1902 • Haggar William • UKN
TRUE AS STEEL • 1924 • Hughes Rupert • USA
TRUE BARBER, THE • D'Bomba Jorg • ANM • GDR
TRUE BELIEVER • 1988 • Ruben Joseph • USA
TRUE BELIEVER, A • 1913 • *Kb* • USA
TRUE BLOOD • 1989 • Kerr Frank • USA • EDGE OF DARKNESS ○ TRUEBLOOD
TRUE BLUE • 1918 • Lloyd Frank • USA
TRUE BOO • 1952 • Sparber I. • ANS • USA
TRUE BRAZIL see **BRASIL VERDADE** • 1968
TRUE BRITAIN, A • 1911 • Bouwmeester Theo • UKN
TRUE CHIVALRY • 1913 • Smalley Phillips • USA
TRUE COLORS • 1990 • Ross Herbert • USA
TRUE CONFESSIONS • 1937 • Ruggles Wesley • USA
TRUE CONFESSIONS • 1981 • Grosbard Ulu • USA
TRUE COUNTRY HEART, A • 1910 • *Bison* • USA
TRUE DIARY OF A VAHINE see **MAEVA** • 1961
TRUE DIARY OF A WAHINE see **MAEVA** • 1961
TRUE END OF THE GREAT WAR, THE see **PRAWDZIWY KONIEC WIELKIEJ WOJNY** • 1957
TRUE FRIENDS see **VERNYE DRUZYA** • 1954
TRUE GAME OF DEATH, THE • 1979 • Che Ten-Tai • HKG

TRUE GANG MURDERS • 1961 • Rosenfeld Sherman • DOC • USA
TRUE GLORY • 1945 • Kanin Garson, Reed Carol • USA
TRUE GRIT • 1969 • Hathaway Henry • USA
TRUE GRIT • 1978 • Heffron Richard T. • TVM • USA
TRUE HEART SUSIE • 1919 • Griffith D. W. • USA
TRUE-HEARTED MINOR, A • 1911 • *Bison* • USA
TRUE HEARTS • 1913 • *Burns Vinnie* • USA
TRUE HEAVEN • 1929 • Tinling James • USA • FALSE COLORS
TRUE INDIAN BRAVE, A • 1910 • *Bison* • USA
TRUE INDIAN'S HEART, A • 1909 • Balshofer Fred J. • USA
TRUE IRISH HEARTS • 1914 • *Chatterton Thomas* • USA
TRUE LIGHT BEAVER FILM: AFTER THE REVOLUTION, THE • Carey Tobe J. • SHT • USA
TRUE LOVE • 1912 • *Reliance* • USA
TRUE LOVE • 1912 • *Pathe* • USA
TRUE LOVE see **KUROI KAFUN** • 1958
TRUE LOVE see **WAHRE LIEBE** • 1989
TRUE LOVE AND A TRAILER • 1913 • *Pridelle Claire* • UKN
TRUE NATURE OF BERNADETTE, THE see **VRAIE NATURE DE BERNADETTE, LA** • 1972
TRUE NOBILITY • 1916 • MacDonald Donald • USA
TRUE NORTH, THE • 1925 • Robertson Jack • USA
TRUE PAL, A • 1910 • *Nestor* • USA
TRUE PATRIOT, A • 1909 • *Lubin* • USA
TRUE SCOUT, A • 1913 • Calvert Charles? • UKN
TRUE SOURCE OF KNOWLEDGE, THE • 1964 • Rubbo Michael • USA
TRUE STORIES • 1986 • Byrne David • USA
TRUE STORIES OF POOR LOVERS see **CRONACHE DI POVERI AMANTI** • 1954
TRUE STORY • 1964 • Gerasimov Vladimir • USS • REAL STORY
TRUE STORY OF A WAHINE see **MAEVA** • 1961
TRUE STORY OF AH Q, THE • 1958 • Yuen Yang-An • HKG
TRUE STORY OF CAMILLE, THE see **DAME AUX CAMELIAS, LA** • 1981
TRUE STORY OF ESKIMO NELL, THE • 1975 • Franklin Richard • ASL • DICK DOWN UNDER
TRUE STORY OF JESSE JAMES, THE • 1956 • Ray Nicholas • USA • JAMES BROTHERS, THE (UKN)
TRUE STORY OF LILLI MARLENE, THE • 1944 • Jennings Humphrey • UKN
TRUE STORY OF LYNN STUART, THE • 1958 • Seiler Lewis • USA • OTHER LIFE OF LYNN STUART, THE
TRUE STORY OF ONEGA, THE • Scabard T. • DOC • USS
TRUE STORY OF THE LYONS MAIL, THE • 1915 • Pearson George • UKN
TRUE TILDA • 1920 • Shaw Harold • UKN
TRUE TILL DEATH • 1907 • *Warwick Trading Co* • UKN
TRUE TILL DEATH • 1912 • Gallagher Ray • USA
TRUE TO HIS DUTY • 1910 • Bouwmeester Theo? • UKN
TRUE TO HIS TRUST • 1910 • *Kalem* • USA
TRUE TO LIFE • 1943 • Marshall George • USA
TRUE TO THE ARMY • 1942 • Rogell Albert S. • USA
TRUE TO THE ARMY see **TRUMPET SERENADE** • 1942
TRUE TO THE NAVY • 1930 • Tuttle Frank • USA
TRUE TO THEIR COLORS • 1917 • Ford Francis? • SHT • USA
TRUE WEALTH see **GEO LE MYSTERIEUX** • 1916
TRUE WEST • 1983 • Sinise Gary • MTV • USA
TRUE WESTERN HEARTS • 1914 • *Ayres Sydney* • USA
TRUE WESTERN HONOR • 1910 • *Bison* • USA
TRUE WESTERNER, A • 1911 • Fahrney Milton • USA
TRUEBLOOD see **TRUE BLOOD** • 1989
TRUER LOVER, THE • 1909 • *Vitagraph* • USA
TRUESTEEL AFFAIR, THE • 1983 • Gunnarsson Sturla • CND
TRUET LYKKE • 1915 • Blom August • DNM • SKUD I MORKET, ET ○ EVIL GENIUS, THE
TRUFFE PIU BELLE DEL MONDO, LE (ITL) see **PLUS BELLES ESCROQUERIES DU MONDE, LES** • 1963
TRUFFLERS, THE • 1917 • Wright Fred E. • USA
TRUHANES • 1984 • Hermoso Miguel • SPN • ROGUES
TRUHANES DE HONOR • 1952 • Maroto Eduardo G. • SPN
TRUITE, LA • 1982 • Losey Joseph • FRN • TROUT, THE
TRULY GOOD LADY, A see **DAME VRAIMENT BIEN, UNE** • 1908
TRULY RURAL • 1917 • *Essanay* • SHT • USA
TRULY RURAL • 1919 • *Strand* • SHT • USA
TRULY RURAL TYPES • 1915 • *Chamberlin Riley* • USA
TRUMAN CAPOTE'S THE GLASS HOUSE see **GLASS HOUSE, THE** • 1972
TRUMAN CAPOTE'S TRILOGY see **TRILOGY** • 1969
TRUMP CARD IS HEARTS, THE see **TRUNFO E COPAS, O** • 1977
TRUMPET, THE see **TRUBA** • 1964
TRUMPET, THE see **TRUBA** • 1976
TRUMPET BLOWS, THE • 1934 • Roberts Stephen • USA • TRUMPET CALLS, THE (UKN)
TRUMPET BOY, A see **TRUMPET SHONEN** • 1955
TRUMPET CALL, THE • 1915 • Nash Percy • UKN
TRUMPET CALL, THE (UKN) see **ROUGH RIDERS** • 1927
TRUMPET CALLS, THE (UKN) see **TRUMPET BLOWS, THE** • 1934
TRUMPET FOR THE COMBO, A • 1965 • Parker Morten • DOC • CND
TRUMPET ISLAND • 1920 • Terriss Tom • USA
TRUMPET OF VICTORY see **IMA WA NAMONAI OTOKO DAGA** • 1958
TRUMPET SERENADE • 1942 • Le Borg Reginald • SHT • USA • TRUE TO THE ARMY
TRUMPET SHONEN • 1955 • Sekigawa Hideo • JPN • TRUMPET BOY, A
TRUMPET TO THE MORN see **TWO FLAGS WEST** • 1950
TRUMPETEER, THE see **TROMBITAS, A** • 1979
TRUMPETER, THE see **TROMBITAS, A** • 1979
TRUMPIN' TROUBLE • 1926 • Thorpe Richard • USA
TRUMPIT • 1955-56 • Jordan Larry • SHT • USA
TRUMPS OVER VIOLENCE (USA) see **OBYKNOVENNYY FASHIZM** • 1965
TRUNFO E COPAS, O • 1977 • Ceitil Rogerio • PRT • TRUMP CARD IS HEARTS, THE
TRUNK, THE • 1961 • Winter Donovan • UKN
TRUNK AN' TROUBLE, A • 1916 • MacMackin Archer • SHT • USA
TRUNK CONVEYOR • 1952 • Anderson Lindsay • SHT • UKN
TRUNK CRIME • 1939 • Boulting Roy • UKN • DESIGN FOR MURDER (USA)
TRUNK MYSTERY, THE • 1914 • Smiley Joseph • USA
TRUNK MYSTERY, THE • 1915 • *Superba* • USA
TRUNK MYSTERY, THE • 1916 • Ellis Robert • SHT • USA
TRUNK MYSTERY, THE • 1927 • Crane Frank H. • USA
TRUNK MYSTERY, THE (UKN) see **ONE NEW YORK NIGHT** • 1935
TRUNK TO CAIRO (USA) see **MIVTZA KAHIR** • 1966
TRUST see **LUOTTAMUS, ELI LENIN JA SUOMI** • 1975
TRUST, LE • 1911 • Feuillade Louis • FRN • BATAILLES DE L'ARGENT, LES
TRUST, THE • 1915 • Chaney Lon • USA
TRUST BEGETS TRUST • 1914 • August Edwin • USA
TRUST DER DIEBE • 1929 • Schonfelder Erich • FRG
TRUST ME • 1989 • Houston Robert • USA
TRUST ME DARLING see **LITA PA MEJ, ALSKLING!** • 1961
TRUST THE NAVY • 1935 • George Henry W. • UKN
TRUST THOSE YOU LOVE • 1910 • Martinek H. O. • UKN
TRUST YOUR WIFE • 1921 • Barry J. A. • USA
TRUST YOUR WIFE (UKN) see **FALL GUY, THE** • 1930
TRUSTED OUTLAW, THE • 1937 • Bradbury Robert North • USA
TRUSTEE OF THE LAW, A • 1912 • *Lubin* • USA
TRUSTING IS GOOD, SHOOTING IS BETTER see **FIDARSI E BENE, SPARARE E MEGLIO** • 1968
TRUSTING WIVES • 1929 • Pearce A. Leslie • USA
TRUSTWORTHY SERVANT, A • 1909 • *Urban Trading Co* • UKN
TRUT! • 1944 • Sucksdorff Arne • DCS • SWD • GULL, THE ○ GULL! ○ CLIFF FACE
TRUTA, A • 1959 • Mendes Joao • SHT • PRT
TRUTH, THE • 1911 • *Nestor* • USA
TRUTH, THE • 1920 • Windom Lawrence C. • USA
TRUTH, THE (USA) see **VERITE, LA** • 1960
TRUTH ABOUT DAN DEERING, THE • 1915 • *Macquarrie Murdock* • USA
TRUTH ABOUT HELEN, THE • 1915 • McGlynn Frank • USA
TRUTH ABOUT HOLLYWOOD, THE see **WHAT PRICE HOLLYWOOD?** • 1932
TRUTH ABOUT HUSBANDS, THE • 1920 • Webb Kenneth • USA
TRUTH ABOUT MEN • 1926 • Clifton Elmer • USA
TRUTH ABOUT MOTHER GOOSE, THE • 1957 • Reitherman Wolfgang, Justice Bill • ANS • USA
TRUTH ABOUT MURDER, THE • 1946 • Landers Lew • USA • LIE DETECTOR, THE (UKN) ○ ALL MEN ARE LIARS ○ MEN ARE SUCH LIARS
TRUTH ABOUT OUR MARRIAGE, THE see **VERITE SUR LE BEBE DONGE, LA** • 1951
TRUTH ABOUT SPRING, THE • 1964 • Thorpe Richard • UKN, USA • PIRATES OF SPRING COVE, THE ○ MISS JUDE
TRUTH ABOUT THE SAVOLTA AFFAIR, THE see **VERDAD SOBRE EL CASO SAVOLTA, LA** • 1980
TRUTH ABOUT WIVES, THE • 1923 • Windom Lawrence C. • USA
TRUTH ABOUT WOMEN, THE • 1924 • King Burton L. • USA
TRUTH ABOUT WOMEN, THE • 1958 • Box Muriel • UKN
TRUTH ABOUT YOUTH, THE • 1930 • Seiter William A. • USA • WHEN WE WERE 21
TRUTH ACHES • 1939 • Roberts Charles E. • SHT • USA
TRUTH AND ILLUSION: AN INTRODUCTION TO METAPHYSICS • 1964 • Vidor King • DCS • USA
TRUTH AND JUSTICE • 1916 • Haldane Bert • UKN
TRUTH CANNOT BE HIDDEN see **HUSZ EVRE EGYMASTOL** • 1962
TRUTH COMES FROM ABOVE, THE see **VERDADE VEM DO ALTO, A** • 1967
TRUTH CRASHED TO EARTH • 1916 • McGill Lawrence?, Hansel Howell? • SHT • USA
TRUTH GAME, THE see **BUT THE FLESH IS WEAK** • 1932
TRUTH IN THE WILDERNESS • 1913 • Johnston Lorimer • USA
TRUTH IS STRANGER THAN FICTION see **ANUBHAVAM PUDUMAI** • 1967
TRUTH JUGGLER, THE • 1922 • Roach Hal • SHT • USA
TRUTH, JUSTICE AND THE AMERICAN WAY • 1963 • *Denaroff Harvey* • SHT • USA
TRUTH OF FICTION, THE • 1915 • Otto Henry • USA
TRUTH SHALL PREVAIL • 1911 • *Yankee* • USA
TRUTH STRANGER THAN FICTION • 1915 • O'Sullivan Tony • USA
TRUTH WAGON, THE • 1914 • Figman Max • USA
TRUTH WILL OUT, THE • 1910 • Stow Percy • UKN
TRUTHFUL LIAR, THE • 1922 • Heffron Thomas N. • USA
TRUTHFUL LIAR, THE • 1924 • Del Ruth Roy • SHT • USA
TRUTHFUL SEX, THE • 1926 • Thomas Richard • USA • WHEN WE ARE MARRIED
TRUTHFUL TELEGRAMS • 1907 • Smith Jack • UKN
TRUTHFUL TULLIVER • 1917 • Hart William S., Smith Cliff • USA
TRUTZE VON TRUTZBERG, DIE • 1921 • Ostermayr Peter • FRG
TRUXA • 1936 • Zerlett Hans H. • FRG
TRUXTON KING • 1923 • Storm Jerome • USA • TRUXTONIA (UKN)
TRUXTONIA (UKN) see **TRUXTON KING** • 1923
TRY AND FIND IT see **HI DIDDLE DIDDLE** • 1943
TRY AND GET IT • 1924 • Tate Cullen • USA
TRY AND GET ME • 1950 • Endfield Cy • USA • SOUND OF FURY, THE (UKN)
TRY-OUT, THE • 1911 • *Edison* • USA
TRY THIS ONE FOR SIZE • 1989 • Hamilton Guy • USA
TRY, TRY AGAIN • 1921 • Roach Hal • SHT • USA
TRYGON FACTOR, THE • 1967 • Frankel Cyril • UKN
TRYING OUT NO.707 • 1913 • *Selig* • USA
TRYING TO FOOL UNCLE • 1912 • Sennett Mack • USA
TRYING TO GET ALONG • 1919 • Jones F. Richard • SHT • USA
TRYING TO GET ARRESTED • 1909 • Griffith D. W. • USA
TRYING TO GET BEDELIA • 1913 • *Reliance* • USA
TRYING TO LIVE see **VERSUCH ZU LEBEN, DER** • 1984
TRYLLEKUNSTNEREN • 1909 • *Nordisk* • SHT • DNM
TRYOUT, THE • 1916 • Stull Walter, Burns Bobby • USA
TRYPTYCH • 1958 • Jordan Larry • SHT • USA
TRYPTYK JAZZOWY • 1960 • Lasota Grzegorz • SHT • PLN • JAZZ TRIPTYCH
TRYST, THE • 1929 • Gilliat Sidney, Burford • SHT • UKN
TRYSTING TREE, THE • 1912 • *White Glen* • USA
TRYTON, A • 1917 • Desy Alfred • AUS • TRITON, THE
TRZEBA ZABIC TE MILOSC • 1972 • Morgenstern Janusz • PLN • THIS LOVE MUST BE KILLED ○ KILL THAT LOVE ○ TO KILL THIS LOVE
TRZECIA CZESC NOCY see **TRECIA CZESC NOCY** • 1971
TRZY KOBIETY • 1956 • Rozewicz Stanislaw • PLN • THREE WOMEN
TRZY KROKI NAPRZOD • 1946 • Perski Ludwik • DOC • PLN • THREE STEPS FORWARD
TRZY KROKI PO ZIEMI • 1965 • Hoffman Jerzy, Skorzewski Edward • PLN • THREE STEPS ON EARTH ○ THREE STEPS IN LIFE
TRZY OPOWIESCI • 1953 • Petelska Ewa, Petelski Czeslaw • PLN • THREE STORIES
TRZY PO TRZY • 1965 • Janik Stefan • ANM • PLN • THREE TIMES THREE ○ FIDDLE-FADDLE
TRZY STARTY • 1955 • Petelska Ewa, Petelski Czeslaw • PLN • THREE STARTS
TSA-CHI WANG-MING TUI • 1979 • Chang Ch'Eh • HKG • DAREDEVILS, THE
TSAHPINIS, O • 1968 • Laskos Orestis • GRC • RASCAL, THE
TSAI-CHIEN, A-LANG • 1970 • Pai Ching-Jui • TWN • GOODBYE, DARLING
TSAI-CHIEN CHUNGKUO • 1974 • T'Ang Shu-Hsuan • HKG • ZAIJIAN ZHONGGUO
TS'AI-LI-FO HSAIO-TZU • 1976 • Chang Ch'Eh • HKG • NEW SHAOLIN BOXERS, THE
TS'AN-TUNG-TE CHAN-CHENG • 1980 • Kong Edwin • DOC • HKG • RISING SUN
TSAO'AN, T'AI-PEI • 1979 • Li Hsing • HKG • GOOD MORNING, TAIPEI
TSAR AND THE GENERAL, THE see **TSAR I GENERAL** • 1966
TSAR I GENERAL • 1966 • Radev Vulo • BUL • TSAR AND THE GENERAL, THE ○ KING AND THE GENERAL, THE ○ CZAR I GENERAL
TSAR I POET • 1927 • Gardin Vladimir • USS • CZAR AND POET
TSAR TO LENIN • 1966 • *Axelbank Herman (P)* • DOC • USA
TSAR WANTS TO SLEEP, THE see **PORUCHIK KIZHE** • 1934
TSARINA'S FAVOURITE, THE see **FAVORIT DER KAISERIN, DER** • 1936
TSARKA MILOST • 1962 • Surchadgiev Stefan • BUL • ROYAL MERCY
TSAR'S BRIDE, THE (USA) see **TSARSKAYA NEVESTA** • 1965
TSAR'S COURIER, THE see **KURIER DES ZAREN, DER** • 1935
TSARSKAYA NEVESTA • 1965 • Gorikker Vladimir • USS • TSAR'S BRIDE, THE (USA)
TSCHERKESSENBLUT • 1919 • Moest Hubert • FRG
TSCHERWONEZ • 1983 • Altorjag Gabor • FRG
TSCHETAN, DER INDIANERJUNGE • 1972 • Bohm Hark • FRG • TSCHETAN, THE RED INDIAN BOY ○ CHETAN, INDIAN BOY
TSCHETAN, THE RED INDIAN BOY see **TSCHETAN, DER INDIANERJUNGE** • 1972
TSCHETSCHENSEN-RACHE • 1920 • Kayser Charles Willy • FRG
TSELEND YA BONOKWANE • 1985 • SAF
TSEMYENT • 1975 • Blank Aleksandr, Linkov Sergey • USS • CEMENT
TSENA CHELOVEKA • 1928 • Donskoi Mark, Averbach Mikhail • USS • PRICE OF MAN, THE ○ VALUE OF MAN ○ MAN'S VALUE ○ LESSON, THE
TSENU SMERTI SPROSI U MYORTVYKH • 1980 • Kiisk Kaliu • USS • ASK THE DEAD THE PRICE OF DEATH
TSIKLOPUT see **ZIKLOPAT** • 1976
TSITELI ESHMAKUNEBI see **KRASNYE DIAVOLIATA** • 1923
TSO-YEH-CHIH TENG • 1983 • Liu Li-Li • TWN • LAST NIGHT'S LIGHT
TSOUF • 1969 • Marangos Thodoros • ANS • GRC
TSUBAKI SANJURO • 1962 • Kurosawa Akira • JPN • SANJURO
TSUBASA • Murano Tetsutaro • JPN • BLUE WINGS, THE
TSUBASA NO GAIKA • 1942 • Yamamoto Satsuo • JPN • TRIUMPHAL WINGS ○ TRIUMPH OF WINGS, A
TSUCHI • 1939 • Uchida Tomu • JPN • EARTH, THE
TSUCHI TO HEITAI • 1939 • Tasaka Tomotaka • JPN • MUD AND SOLDIERS
TSUGARU JONGARA-BUSHI • 1973 • Saito Koichi • JPN • JONGARA
TSUI-CHIA P'AI-TANG • 1982 • Tseng Chih-Wei • HKG • MAD MISSION PART 2: ACES GO PLACES ○ MAD MISSION 2: ACES GO PLACES ○ ACES GO PLACES ○ MAD MISSION 2
TSUI CH'UAN • 1979 • Yuan Ho-P'Ing • HKG • DRUNK MONKEY IN THE TIGER'S EYES
TSUIGAI NAMPANGYAU • 1989 • Chan Kwok-San • HKG • PERFECT MATCH
TSUIOKU NO BARA • 1936 • Tasaka Tomotaka • JPN • MEMORY OF A ROSE
TSUK FUK • 1990 • Yeung Fan • HKG
TSUKI NI TOBU KARI • 1955 • Matsubayashi Shue • JPN • FAREWELL TO INNOCENCE
TSUKI NO DE NO KETTO • 1960 • Ito Daisuke • JPN
TSUKI NO WATARIDORI • 1951 • Kinugasa Teinosuke • JPN • MIGRATORY BIRDS UNDER THE MOON
TSUKI YORINO SHISHA • 1934 • Tasaka Tomotaka • JPN
TSUKIGATA HANPEITA • 1925 • Kinugasa Teinosuke • JPN
TSUKIGATA HANPEITA • 1933 • Ito Daisuke • JPN
TSUKIGATA HANPEITA • 1956 • Kinugasa Teinosuke • JPN
TSUKIHIME KEIZU • 1958 • Watanabe Minoru • JPN • TREASURE HUNTRESS ○ ORIGIN OF PRINCESS MOON, THE
TSUKIMISO • 1959 • Iwaki • JPN
TSUKIWA NOBORINU • 1955 • Tanaka Kinuyo • JPN • MOON HAS RISEN, THE ○ MOON RISES, THE ○ MOONRISE
TSUKIYO NO KASA • 1955 • Hisamatsu Seiji • JPN • UMBRELLA IN MOONLIGHT

TSUKIYORI NO SHISHA • 1954 • Tanaka Shigeo • JPN • MESSENGER FROM THE MOON
TSUMA • 1953 • Naruse Mikio • JPN • WIFE
TSUMA FUTARI • 1967 • Masumura Yasuzo • JPN • TWO WIVES
TSUMA NO HI NO AI NO KATAMINI • 1965 • Tomimoto Sokichi • JPN • WHILE YET A WIFE
TSUMA NO HIMITSU • 1924 • Kinugasa Teinosuke • JPN • SECRET OF A WIFE
TSUMA NO KOKORO • 1956 • Naruse Mikio • JPN • WIFE'S HEART, A
TSUMA TO ONNA KISHA • 1950 • Chiba Yasuki • JPN • WIFE AND WOMAN JOURNALIST
TSUMA TO ONNA NO AIDA • 1976 • Ichikawa Kon, Toyoda Shiro • JPN • BETWEEN WOMEN AND WIVES (USA) ○ BETWEEN WIFE AND LADY (USA)
TSUMA TOSHITE ONNA TOSHITE • 1961 • Naruse Mikio • JPN • LIKE A WIFE, LIKE A WOMAN ○ AS A WIFE, AS A WOMAN ○ OTHER WOMAN, THE
TSUMA WA KOKUHAKU SURU • 1961 • Masumura Yasuzo • JPN • WIFE'S CONFESSION
TSUMA YO BARA NO YONI • 1935 • Naruse Mikio • JPN • WIFE BE LIKE A ROSE ○ FUTARIZUMA ○ QUEST, THE ○ TWO WIVES ○ KIMIKO
TSUMAARI KOARI TOMOARITE • 1961 • Inoue Umeji • JPN • TOKYO DETECTIVE SAGA
TSUMIKI KUZUSHI • 1984 • Saito Mitsumasa • JPN • BROKEN FAMILY
TSUMIKI NO HAKO • 1968 • Masumura Yasuzo • JPN • HOUSE OF WOODEN BLOCKS, THE
TSUMUJI KAZE • 1963 • Nakamura Noboru • JPN • WHIRLWIND
TSURU • 1988 • Ichikawa Kon • JPN • CRANE
TSURUHACHI AND TSURUJIRO see **TSURUHACHI TSURUJIRO** • 1938
TSURUHACHI TSURUJIRO • 1938 • Naruse Mikio • JPN • TSURUHACHI AND TSURUJIRO
TSUYOMUSHI ONNA TO YOWAMUSHI OTOKO • 1968 • Shindo Kaneto • JPN • STRONG WOMAN, WEAK MAN ○ OPERATION NEGLIGEE
TSUYU NO ATOSAKI • 1956 • Nakamura Noboru • JPN • TOWARD THE RAINY SEASON
TSUZURIKATA KYODAI • 1958 • Hisamatsu Seiji • JPN • CHILD WRITERS
TSUZURIKATA KYOSHITSU • 1938 • Yamamoto Kajiro • JPN • COMPOSITION CLASS
TSVET GRANATA see **SAYAT NOVA** • 1969
TSVETI ZAPORDALIGE • 1917 • Gardin Vladimir • USS
TSVETNITE NISCHKI • 1969 • Meitzoff Roman • ANS • BUL • COLORED YARNS
TSVETOK NA KAMNE • 1962 • Paradjanov Sergei • USS • FLOWER ON THE STONE, THE
TSYGAN • 1967 • Matveyev Yevgeni • USS • GIPSY
TU BRULES.. TU BRULES • 1973 • Noel Jean-Guy • CND
TU CHE NE DICI? • 1960 • Amadio Silvio • ITL
TU CHERCHES LA SCIENCE • 1963 • Hamina Mohamed Lakhdar • DCS • ALG
TU DIOS Y MI INFIERNO • 1974 • Romero-Marchent Rafael • SPN
TU ENFANTERAS DANS LA JOIE • 1956-57 • Devlin Bernard • SHT • CND
TU ENFANTERAS SANS DOULEUR • 1956 • Fabiani Henri, Dalmas Louis • SHT • FRN
TU ERES LA LUZ • 1945 • Galindo Alejandro • MXC
TU ES DANSE ET VERTIGE • 1967 • Coutard Raoul • SHT • FRN
TU ES MA VIE see **INTA UMRY** • 1964
TU ES PIERRE • 1959 • Agostini Philippe • DOC • FRN • YOU ARE PETER
TU ESTORS LOCO, BRIONES • 1980 • Maqua Javier • SPN • BRIONES, YOU'RE MAD
TU FOSA SERA LA EXACTA.., AMIGO • 1972 • Bosch Juan • SPN
TU GDZIE ZYJEMY • 1962 • Karabasz Kazimierz (c/d) • DCS • PLN • HERE, WHERE WE LIVE
TU HIJO • 1934 • Bohr Jose • MXC • AMOR DE MADRE
TU HIJO DEBE NACER • 1956 • Galindo Alejandro • MXC
TU IMAGINES ROBINSON • 1968 • Pollet Jean-Daniel • FRN • IMAGINE ROBINSON
TU LUC VAN DOAN • Alemann Claudia • FRG
TU M'APPARTIENDRAS TOUJOURS see **CONDAMNES, LES** • 1947
TU M'APPARTIENS • 1929 • Gleize Maurice • FRN
TU MARIDO NOS ENGANA • 1958 • Iglesias Miguel • SPN
TU M'AS SAUVE LA VIE • 1950 • Guitry Sacha • FRN
TU M'ENVERRAS DES CARTES POSTALES • Titayna • FRN • BE SURE AND SEND ME POSTCARDS
TU MI TURBI • 1982 • Benigni Roberto • ITL • YOU WORRY ME
TU MOISSONNERAS LA TEMPETE • 1968 • Bruckberger Raymond-Leopold • DOC • FRN
TU M'OUBLIERAS • 1931 • Diamant-Berger Henri • FRN
TU MUJER ES LA MIA • 1942 • Portas Rafael E. • MXC
TU NE TUERAS POINT • 1961 • Autant-Lara Claude • FRN, ITL, YGS • NON UCCIDERE (ITL) ○ THOU SHALT NOT KILL ○ NE UBIJ
TU N'EPOUSERAS JAMAIS UN AVOCAT • 1914 • Feuillade Louis • FRN
TU PERDONAS.. YO NO (SPN) see **DIO PERDONA.. IO NO!** • 1967
TU RECUERDO Y YO • 1953 • Delgado Miguel M. • MXC
TU SEI L'UNICA DONNA PER ME see **FIGLIO DELLE STELLE, IL** • 1979
TU SERAS DUCHESSE • 1931 • Guissart Rene • FRN
TU SERAS TERRIBLEMENT GENTILLE • 1968 • Sanders Dirk • FRN • YOU ONLY LOVE ONCE (USA) ○ GENTLE LOVE (UKN)
TU SERAS VEDETTE • 1942 • Mineur Jean • SHT • FRN
TU, SOLO TU • 1949 • Delgado Miguel M. • MXC
TU VIDA ENTRE MIS MANOS • 1954 • Sevilla Raphael J. • MXC
TU Y EL MAR see **MAR Y TU, EL** • 1951
TU Y LA MENTIRA • 1956 • Cardona Rene • MXC
TU Y LAS NUBES • 1955 • Morayta Miguel • MXC, SPN
TU Y YO SOMOS TRES • 1961 • Gil Rafael • SPN
TU.. YO.. NOSOTROS.. • 1970 • *Marco Polo* • MXC
TUA DONNA, LA • 1956 • Paolucci Giovanni • ITL
TUA PER LA VITA • 1955 • Grieco Sergio • ITL
TUA PRESENZA NUDA, LA • 1972 • Montero Roberto Bianchi?, Bianchi Andrea? • ITL
TUAH • 1989 • Jamil Anwardi • MLY
TUAH BADAN • 1970 • Rojik Omar • MLY • BODY'S LUST
TUAN BADUL • 1978 • Sulong Jamil • MLY
TUAN TANAH KEDAWUNG • 1970 • Prijono Ami • INN
TUAREG IL GUERRIERO DEL DESERTO • 1984 • Castellari Enzo G. • ITL, SPN, ISR • TAUREG THE DESERT WARRIOR ○ DESERT WARRIOR
TUB, LE see **APRES LE BAL** • 1897
TUB FILM • 1972 • Beams Mary • USA
TUB NAMED DESIRE, A • 1960 • Kuchar George, Kuchar Mike • USA
TUB RACE • 1903 • Porter Edwin S. • USA
TUBA, THE • 1969 • *Zagreb* • ANS • YGS
TUBA TOOTER, THE • 1932 • Foster John, Stallings George • ANS • USA
TUBBY AND THE CLUTCHING HAND • 1916 • Wilson Frank • SHT • UKN
TUBBY HAYES • 1964 • Scott Robin • SHT • UKN
TUBBY THE TUBA • 1947 • Pal George • ANS • USA
TUBBY THE TUBA • 1977 • Schure Alexander • ANM • USA
TUBBY TURNS THE TABLES • 1916 • Semon Larry • SHT • USA
TUBBY'S BUNGLE-OH! • 1916 • Wilson Frank • SHT • UKN
TUBBY'S DUGOUT • 1916 • Wilson Frank • SHT • UKN
TUBBY'S GOOD WORK • 1916 • Wilson Frank • SHT • UKN
TUBBY'S REST CURE • 1916 • Wilson Frank • SHT • UKN
TUBBY'S RIVER TRIP • 1916 • Wilson Frank • SHT • UKN
TUBBY'S SPANISH GIRLS • 1916 • Wilson Frank • SHT • UKN
TUBBY'S TIP • 1916 • Wilson Frank • SHT • UKN
TUBBY'S TYPEWRITER • 1916 • Wilson Frank • SHT • UKN
TUBBY'S UNCLE • 1916 • Wilson Frank • SHT • UKN
TUBE OF DEATH, THE • 1913 • Butler Alexander • UKN • ANARCHIST'S DOOM, THE
TUBERCULOSE • Tessier Albert • DCS • CND
TUBEROSEN • 1917 • *Berna Elsa* • FRG
TUBOG SA GINTO • 1972 • Brocka Lino • PHL
TUBORG • 1935 • Sandberg Anders W. • DNM
TUCET MYCH TATINKU • 1960 • Hofman Eduard • ANS • CZC • MY TWELVE PAPAS ○ DOZEN DADDIES, A
TUCHTIGEN GEHORT DIE WELT, DEN • 1981 • Patzak Peter • AUS, USA • UPPER-CRUST, THE
TUCK EVERLASTING • 1980 • Keller Frederick King • USA
TUCK ME IN • 1970 • Meola Michael • USA • KEEP ME IN
TUCKER • 1988 • Coppola Francis Ford • USA • TUCKER: THE MAN AND HIS DREAM
TUCKER: THE MAN AND HIS DREAM see **TUCKER** • 1988
TUCSON • 1949 • Claxton William F. • USA
TUCSON JENNIE'S HEART • 1918 • Sargent George L. • SHT • USA
TUCSON RAIDERS • 1944 • Bennet Spencer Gordon • USA
TUDA ZEMLJA • 1957 • Gale Joze • YGS • ON FOREIGN SOIL
TUDO BEM • 1979 • Jabor Arnaldo • BRZ • ALL'S WELL
TUDOR KING • 1979 • Kroeker Allan • CND
TUDOR PRINCESS, A • 1913 • Dawley J. Searle • USA
TUDOR ROSE • 1936 • Stevenson Robert • UKN • NINE DAYS A QUEEN (USA) ○ LADY JANE GREY
TUE LA MORT • 1921 • Navarre Rene • FRN
TUE MANI SUL MIO CORPO, LE • 1970 • Rondi Brunello • ITL
TUE RECHT UND SCHEUE NIEMAND • 1975 • Bruckner Jutta • FRG
TUESDAY AFTERNOON • 1968 • Zimmerman Tom, Swansen Chris • SHT • USA
TUESDAY IN NOVEMBER • 1945 • Berry John • USA
TUESDAY WEDNESDAY • 1985 • Pederson John • CND
TUESDAYS, THURSDAYS, SATURDAYS see **WTORKI, CZWARTKI, SOBOTY** • 1965
TUEUR, LE • 1972 • de La Patelliere Denys • FRN, ITL, FRG • COMMISSARIO LE GUEN E IL CASO GRASSOT, IL (ITL)
TUEUR AIME LES BONBONS, LE (FRN) see **KILLER PER SUA MAESTA, UN** • 1968
TUEURS A GAGES, LES • Squitieri Pasquale • FRN
TUEURS DE SAN FRANCISCO, LES (FRN) see **ONCE A THIEF** • 1965
TUEURS FOUS, LES • 1972 • Szulzinger Boris • FRN, BLG • LONELY KILLERS
TUEURS SANS AME, LES • 1974 • Franju Georges • MTV • FRN
TUFA DE VENETIA • 1977 • Bokor Pierre • RMN • RIEN DE RIEN
TUFANE ZENDEGI • IRN • TEMPEST OF LIFE, THE
TUFF TURF • 1984 • Kiersch Fritz • USA • LOVE FIGHTERS ○ TOUGH TURF
TUFFAH'AT ADAM • 1965 • Wahab Fatin Abdel • EGY • POMME D'ADAM, LA
TUFINO • 1986 • Almodovar Ramon • DCS • PRC
TUGBOAT ANNIE • 1933 • LeRoy Mervyn • USA
TUGBOAT ANNIE SAILS AGAIN • 1940 • Seiler Lewis • USA
TUGBOAT GRANNY • 1956 • Freleng Friz • ANS • USA
TUGBOAT M17 see **SCHLEPPZUG M17** • 1933
TUGBOAT MICKEY • 1940 • Geronimi Clyde • ANS • USA
TUGBOAT PRINCESS • 1936 • Selman David • USA
TUGBOAT ROMEO, A • 1916 • Campbell William, Williams Harry • SHT • USA
TUGGAR AL-MAWT • 1957 • el Sheikh Kamal • EGY • MARCHANDS DE LA MORT, LA
TUGTHUSFANGE NO.97 • 1914 • Blom August • DNM • GAEST FRA EN ANDEN VERDEN, EN ○ OUTCAST'S RETURN, THE
TUISTELUN TIE • 1941 • Orko Risto • FNL
TUISU TAAVI'S SEVEN DAYS • 1971 • Kasper Veljo • USS
TUKARAM • 1915 • Phalke Dada • IND
TUKARAM • 1920 • *Hindustan* • IND
TUKARAM see **SANT TURKARAM** • 1936
TUKKIPOJAN MORSIAN • 1931 • Karu Erkki • FNL • BRIDE OF THE LUMBERJACK, THE ○ LOG-DRIVER'S BRIDE, THE
TUKO SA MADRE KAKAW • 1958 • Abelardo Richard • PHL
TUKOR, EGY • 1971 • Szabo Istvan • DCS • HNG • MIRROR, A
TUKORKEPEK • 1976 • Szoreny Rezso • HNG • REFLECTIONS IN A MIRROR ○ REFLECTIONS
TUKUMA • 1984 • Kjaerulff-Schmidt Palle • DNM
TUL A KALVIN-TEREN • 1955 • Meszaros Marta • DCS • HNG • BEYOND THE SQUARE
TULACKA POHADKA • 1972 • Hofman Eduard • ANS • PLN • VAGRANT'S TALE, THE
TULAK MACOUN • 1939 • Brom Ladislav • CZC • MACOUN THE TRAMP
TULASIDAS, DEVOTEE TO THE GOD see **BHAKTHA TULASIDAS** • 1937
TULAU DEWATA • 1978 • Noyce Phil • DOC • ASL
TULINEN JARVI • 1938 • Orko Risto • FNL
TULIP TIME see **SPRINGTIME IN HOLLAND** • 1935
TULIPA • 1967 • Gomez Manuel Octavio • CUB
TULIPAA • 1980 • Honkasalo Pirjo, Lehto Pekka • FNL • FIREBRAND ○ FLAME-TOP
TULIPANI DI HAARLEM, I • 1970 • Brusati Franco • ITL • LOVE DOES STRANGE THINGS TO PEOPLE ○ TULIPS OF HAARLEM
TULIPANO NERO, IL (ITL) see **TULIPE NOIRE, LA** • 1963
TULIPE NOIRE, LA • 1963 • Christian-Jaque • FRN, ITL, SPN • TULIPANO NERO, IL (ITL) ○ BLACK TULIP, THE
TULIPS • 1980 • Ferris Stan • CND
TULIPS, THE • 1907 • *Pathe* • FRN
TULIPS OF HAARLEM see **TULIPANI DI HAARLEM, I** • 1970
TULIPS SHALL GROW • 1942 • Pal George • ANS • USA
TULIPUNAINEN KYYHKYNEN • 1961 • Kassila Matti • FNL • SCARLET DOVE, THE
TULITIKKUJA LAINAAMASSA • 1978 • Orko Risto, Gaidai Leonid • FNL, USS • OUT TO BORROW MATCHES
TULITIKKUTEHTANN TYTTO • 1989 • Kaurismaki Aki • FNL • GIRL FROM THE MATCH FACTORY
TULL-BOM • 1951 • Kjellgren Lars-Eric • SWD • BOM -THE CUSTOMS OFFICER
TULLIVAPAA AVIOLIITO (FNL) see **VAMMENTES HAZASSAG** • 1981
TULSA • 1949 • Heisler Stuart • USA
TULSA KID, THE • 1940 • Sherman George • USA
TULSI VRINDA • 1970 • IND
TULSIDAS • 1934 • Mukherjee Jyotish • IND • TOOLSIDAS
TUMBA DE LA ISLA MALDITA, LA • 1972 • Salvador Julio • SPN • TOMB OF THE CURSED ISLAND, THE
TUMBA DE LA ISLA MALDITA, LA (SPN) see **CRYPT OF THE LIVING DEAD** • 1973
TUMBA DE VILLA, LA see **CABALLO PRIETO AZABACHE** • 1965
TUMBA DEL PISTOLERO, LA • 1963 • de Ossorio Amando • SPN
TUMBA PARA EL SHERIFF, UNA • 1967 • Caiano Mario • SPN, ITL • BARA PER LO SCERIFFO, UNA (ITL) ○ TOMB FOR THE SHERIFF, A
TUMBA PARA JOHNNY RINGO, UNA • 1967 • Madrid Jose Luis • SPN, FRG • TOMB FOR JOHNNY RINGO, A
TUMBA PARA UN FORAJIDO • 1965 • Madrid Jose Luis • SPN
TUMBLEDOWN RANCH IN ARIZONA • 1941 • Luby S. Roy • USA
TUMBLEDOWN TOWN • 1933 • Foster John, Bailey Harry • ANS • USA
TUMBLEWEED • 1953 • Juran Nathan • USA
TUMBLEWEED GREED • 1969 • Smith Paul J. • ANS • USA
TUMBLEWEED TEMPOS • 1946 • Cowan Will • SHT • USA
TUMBLEWEED TRAIL • 1942 • Newfield Sam • USA
TUMBLEWEED TRAIL • 1946 • Tansey Robert • USA
TUMBLEWEEDS • 1925 • Baggot King • USA
TUMBLEWEEDS • 1939 • Baggot King • USA
TUMBLING RIVER • 1927 • Seiler Lewis • USA • SCOURGE OF THE LITTLE C, THE
TUMBLING TUMBLEWEEDS • 1935 • Kane Joseph • USA
TUMONNOCT ANDROMED • 1967 • Sherstobitov Eudgen • USS • ANDROMEDA NEBULA, THE (USA) ○ ANDROMEDA THE MYSTERIOUS ○ TUMONNOST ANDROMEDY ○ CLOUD OF ANDROMEDA
TUMONNOST ANDROMEDY see **TUMONNOCT ANDROMED** • 1967
TUMUC HUMAC • 1970 • Perier Jean-Marie • FRN
TUMULT • 1969 • Abramson Hans • DNM • RELATIONS (USA) ○ TUMULT -SONJA, AGE 16 ○ SONJA -16 AR
TUMULT see **SMYATENIYE CHUVSTV** • 1978
TUMULT IN DAMASCUS (USA) see **AUFRUHR IN DAMASKUS** • 1939
TUMULT POND • 1962 • Heyer John • DOC • ASL • TUMUT POND
TUMULT -SONJA, AGE 16 see **TUMULT** • 1969
TUMULTES • 1931 • Siodmak Robert • FRN
TUMULTES • 1990 • Van Effenterre Bertrand • FRN
TUMULTO DE PAIXOES • 1958 • Sulistrowski Zygmunt • BRZ, FRG • RUF DER WILDNIS
TUMULTUOUS ELOPEMENT, A • 1909 • Melies Georges • FRN
TUMUT POND see **TUMULT POND** • 1962
TUNA CLIPPER • 1949 • Beaudine William • USA
TUNA FISH KISS • 1968 • Birmelin Bruce • SHT • USA
TUNDE'S FILM • 1973 • Pinhorn Maggie, Ikoli Tunde • UKN
TUNDRA • 1936 • Dawn Norman • USA • MIGHTY TUNDRA, THE (UKN)
TUNDRA, DIE see **KAMPF UM DIE FRAU** • 1932
TUNE IN MY LIFE, A • 1975 • Barakat • EGY
TUNE TIME • 1942 • Le Borg Reginald • SHT • USA
TUNE UP AND SING • 1934 • Fleischer Dave • ANS • USA
TUNE UP THE UKE • 1928 • Freund Karl • UKN
TUNEL • 1979 • Pontecorvo Gillo • SPN • TUNNEL
TUNEL, EL • 1988 • Drove Antonio • SPN • TUNNEL, THE
TUNEL SEIS, EL • 1955 • Urueta Chano • MXC
TUNELUL see **TUNNYEL** • 1967
TUNER OF NOTES, A • 1917 • *Triangle* • USA
TUNES OF GLORY • 1960 • Neame Ronald • UKN
TUNES OF THE TIMES • 1939 • Shepherd Horace • UKN
TUNG • 1966 • Baillie Bruce • SHT • USA
TUNG-FANG YEN SHIH • 1976 • HKG • WEDDING NIGHTS
TUNG FU-JEN • 1969 • T'Ang Shu-Hsuan • HKG • ARCH, THE

T'UNG-NIEN WANG-SHIH • 1985 • Hou Hsiao-Hsien • TWN • TIME TO LIVE AND THE TIME TO DIE, THE ○ TONGNIAN WANGSHI
TUNG NUAN • 1967 • Li Han-Hsiang • HKG • WINTER
T'UNG-PAN T'UNG-HSUEH • 1982 • Ch'Ing-Chieh Lin • TWN
T'UNG-TANG WAN-SUI • 1989 • Yu Weiyen • TWN • TONGDANG WANSUI
TUNGSRAM • 1955 • ANS • HNG
TUNI BOU • 1987 • Nag Hiren • IND
TUNING HIS IVORIES see **LAUGHING GAS** • 1914
TUNING IN • 1929 • *Van Beuren* • ANS • USA
TUNISI TOP SECRET • 1959 • Paolinelli Bruno • ITL
TUNISIAN VICTORY • 1944 • Capra Frank, Boulting Roy • DOC • USA, UKN
TUNISIE, TERRE D'AFRIQUE • 1966 • Essid Hamadi • DOC • TNS
TUNNEL • 1968 • Ghane Nader • IRN
TUNNEL see **TUNEL** • 1979
TUNNEL 28 see **ESCAPE FROM EAST BERLIN** • 1962
TUNNEL, DER • 1915 • Wauer William • FRG
TUNNEL, DER • 1919 • Meinert Rudolf • FRG
TUNNEL, DER • 1933 • Bernhardt Curtis • FRG • TUNNEL, THE
TUNNEL, LE • 1933 • Bernhardt Curtis • FRN
TUNNEL, THE • 1935 • Elvey Maurice • UKN • TRANSATLANTIC TUNNEL (USA)
TUNNEL, THE • 1983 • Pirri Massimo • ITL
TUNNEL, THE see **TUNNEL, DER** • 1933
TUNNEL, THE see **TUNNYEL** • 1967
TUNNEL, THE see **TUNEL, EL** • 1988
TUNNEL BELOW THE STRAIT see **KAIKYO** • 1983
TUNNEL CHILD • 1990 • Riedlsperger Erhard • AUS
TUNNEL OF LOVE, THE • 1958 • Kelly Gene • USA
TUNNEL SOTTO IL MONDO, IL • 1968 • Cozzi Luigi • ITL • TUNNEL UNDER THE WORLD, THE
TUNNEL SOUS LA MANCHE: OU, LE CAUCHEMAR FRANCO-ANGLAIS, LE • 1907 • Melies Georges • FRN • TUNNELING THE CHANNEL (USA) ○ TUNNELLING THE ENGLISH CHANNEL
TUNNEL SYSTEM see **SISTEMA TUNEL** • 1978
TUNNEL TO THE SUN (USA) see **KUROBE NO TAIYO** • 1968
TUNNEL UNDER THE WORLD, THE see **TUNNEL SOTTO IL MONDO, IL** • 1968
TUNNELING THE CHANNEL (USA) see **TUNNEL SOUS LA MANCHE: OU, LE CAUCHEMAR FRANCO-ANGLAIS, LE** • 1907
TUNNELLING THE ENGLISH CHANNEL see **TUNNEL SOUS LA MANCHE: OU, LE CAUCHEMAR FRANCO-ANGLAIS, LE** • 1907
TUNNELS • 1988 • Byers Mark • USA • CRIMINAL ACT
TUNNELS SOUS L'ESCAUT, LES • 1931 • Storck Henri • DOC • BLG
TUNNELVISION • 1976 • Swirnoff Brad, Israel Neal • USA
TUNNEY - GREB BOXING MATCH, THE • 1922 • *J.c. Clark Productions* • DOC • USA
TUNNYEL • 1967 • Munteanu Francisc • RMN, USS • TUNNEL, THE ○ TUNELUL
TUNTEMATON SOTILAS • 1955 • Laine Edvin • FNL • UNKNOWN SOLDIER, THE
TUNTEMATON SOTILAS • 1969 • Kassila Matti, Donner Jorn • FNL • UNKNOWN SOLDIER
TUNTEMATON SOTILAS • 1986 • Mollberg Rauni • FNL • UNKNOWN SOLDIER, THE
TUNTEMATON YSTAVA • 1977 • Thelestam Lars G. • FNL • UNKNOWN FRIEND, THE
TUO DOLCE CORPO DA UCCIDERE, IL • 1970 • Brescia Alfonso • ITL
TUO PIACERE E IL MIO, IL • 1973 • Racca Claudio • ITL
TUO VIZIO E UNA STANZA CHIUSA E SOLO IO NE HO LE CHIAVI, IL • 1972 • Martino Sergio • ITL • EXCITE ME (UKN)
TUP AKKA LAKKO • 1980 • Pasanen Spede • FNL • GIVING UP
TUP-TUP • 1972 • Dragic Nedeljko • ANS • YGS
TUPAC AMARU • 1983 • Garcia Federico • PRU, CUB
TUPAMAROS • 1972 • Lindqvist Jan • DOC • SWD, URG
TUPAPOO • 1938 • Tourneur Jacques • SHT • USA • WHAT DO YOU THINK?
TUPPE, TUPPE, MARESCIA see **E PERMESSO MARESCIALLO?** • 1958
TUPPEN • 1981 • Hallstrom Lasse • SWD • ROOSTER, THE
TUR I NATTEN • 1968 • Roos Ole • DNM • DRIVING IN THE NIGHT
TUR MIT DEN SIEBEN SCHLOSSERN, DIE • 1962 • Vohrer Alfred • FRG • DOOR WITH SEVEN LOCKS, THE (USA)
TURANDOT • 1925 • Noa Manfred • FRG
TURANDOT, PRINCESSE DE CHINE • 1934 • Veber Serge, Lamprecht Gerhard • FRN
TURAS, LAS • 1979 • Henriquez Ana Cristina • DOC • VNZ
TURBAMENTO • 1942 • Brignone Guido • ITL
TURBANTE BLANCO • 1943 • Iquino Ignacio F. • SPN
TURBINA • 1941 • Vavra Otakar • CZC • TURBINE, THE
TURBINA NR.3 • 1927 • Timoshenko S. • USS • TURBINE NO.3
TURBINE • 1941 • Mastrocinque Camillo • ITL • DONNA SENZA NOME, UNA
TURBINE, THE see **TURBINA** • 1941
TURBINE D'ODIO • 1914 • Gallone Carmine • ITL
TURBINE NO.3 see **TURBINA NR.3** • 1927
TURBION • 1938 • Momplet Antonio • ARG
TURBO BLADE see **BIRDS OF PREY** • 1973
TURBULENT LINEN, THE see **LINGE TURBULENT, LE** • 1909
TURBULENT YEARS, THE see **POVEST PLAMENNYKH LET** • 1960
TURBULENT YOUTH see **TREVOZHNAYA MOLODOST** • 1955
TURCHIA see **HAREM SONO DESERTI, GLI** • 1956
TURCO NAPOLETANO, UN • 1953 • Mattoli Mario • ITL
TURE GEHT AUF, EINE • 1933 • Zeisler Alfred • FRG
TURE SVENTON -PRIVATDETEKTIV • 1973 • Berglund Per • NRW, SWD • TURE SVENTON -PRIVATE DETECTIVE
TURE SVENTON -PRIVATDETEKTIV see **T. SVENTON, PRAKTISERANDE PRIVATDETEKTIV** • 1972
TURE SVENTON, PRIVATE DETECTIVE see **T. SVENTON, PRAKTISERANDE PRIVATDETEKTIV** • 1972
TURE SVENTON -PRIVATE DETECTIVE see **TURE SVENTON -PRIVATDETEKTIV** • 1973
TURF CONSPIRACY, A • 1918 • Wilson Frank • UKN
TURF SENSATION, THE (UKN) see **WOMEN FIRST** • 1924
TURFPIRATEN • 1922 • Santen Trude • FRG
TURI E I PALADINI • 1979 • D'Alessandro Angelo • ITL
TURISMO DE CARRETERA • 1968 • Kuhn Rodolfo • ARG • HIGHWAY TOURING
TURISMO DE DON PIO, EL • 1971 • Ardavin Cesar • SHT • SPN
TURISMO ES UN GRAN INVENTO, EL • 1968 • Lazaga Pedro • SPN • TOURISM IS A GREAT INVENTION
TURIST ZEHRA • 1967 • Arikan Kayahan • TRK • ZEHRA THE TOURIST
TURISTA • 1962 • Schorm Evald • SHT • CZC • TOURIST, THE
TURISTAS INTERPLANETARIOS see **ASTRONAUTAS, LOS** • 1960
TURISTAS Y BRIBONES • 1969 • Merino Fernando • SPN
TURK 182! • 1985 • Clark Bob • USA
TURKEY DINNER • 1936 • *Lantz Walter (P)* • ANS • USA
TURKEY HUNT, PINEHURST • 1905 • *Bitzer Billy (Ph)* • USA
TURKEY SHOOT • 1982 • Trenchard-Smith Brian • ASL • ESCAPE 2000 (USA)
TURKEY TIME • 1933 • Walls Tom • UKN
TURKEY TROT: EVERYBODY'S DOING IT • 1912 • *Selsior Films* • UKN
TURKEY TROT TOWN • 1914 • *Anderson Mignon* • USA
TURKEYS see **INDYUKI** • 1958
TURKEYS IN A ROW see **SHICHIMENCHO NO YUKUE** • 1924
TURKEYS: WHEREABOUTS UNKNOWN see **SHICHIMENCHO NO YUKUE** • 1924
TURKISCHEN GURKEN, DIE • 1963 • Olsen Rolf • FRG • TURKISH CUCUMBER, THE (USA) ○ DADDY'S DELECTABLE DOZEN ○ WEDDING PRESENT
TURKISH BATH, THE • 1913 • *Mace Fred* • USA
TURKISH CIGARETTE, A • 1911 • *Walton Fred* • USA
TURKISH CUCUMBER, THE (USA) see **TURKISCHEN GURKEN, DIE** • 1963
TURKISH DELIGHT • 1927 • Sloane Paul • USA
TURKISH DELIGHT (USA) see **TURKS FRUITS** • 1973
TURKISH EXECUTIONER, THE see **BOURREAU TURC, LE** • 1904
TURKISH RING, THE • 1913 • *Belmont Claude* • USA
TURKISH VIDEO • 1985 • Votocek Otakar • SHT • NTH
TURKS AND TROUBLES • 1917 • Semon Larry • SHT • USA
TURKS FRUITS • 1973 • Verhoeven Paul* • NTH • TURKISH DELIGHT (USA) ○ SHELTER OF YOUR ARMS, THE ○ SENSUALIST, THE
TURKSIB • 1929 • Turin Victor • USS
TURKYE: STORIA DI UNA POPOLO OPPRESSO • 1978 • Barberi Franco • ITL
TURLIS ABENTEUER • 1967 • Beck Walter, Merk Ron • GDR • PINOCCHIO (USA)
TURLUPINS, LES • 1979 • Revon Bernard • FRN
TURLUTE DES ANNEES DURES, LA • 1984 • Boutet Richard, Gelinas Pascal • DOC • CND
TURM DER VERBOTENEN LIEBE, DER • 1968 • Antel Franz • FRG, ITL, FRN • TOWER OF SCREAMING VIRGINS (USA) ○ DOLCEZZE DEL PECCATO, LE (ITL) ○ TOWER OF FORBIDDEN LOVE, THE ○ TOWER OF SIN ○ SWEETNESS OF SIN, THE ○ SHE LOST HER YOU KNOW WHAT ○ ITL ○ TOUR DE NESLE, LA
TURM DES SCHWEIGENS, DER • 1925 • Guter Johannes • FRG
TURME DES SCHWEIGENS • 1952 • Bertram Hans • FRG
TURMOIL, THE • 1916 • Jones Edgar • USA
TURMOIL, THE • 1924 • Henley Hobart • USA
TURN AROUND EUGENE see **VOLTATI EUGENIO** • 1980
TURN BACK THE CLOCK • 1933 • Selwyn Edgar • USA
TURN BACK THE HOURS • 1928 • Bretherton Howard • USA • BADGE OF COURAGE, THE
TURN HIM OUT • 1913 • *Leighton Lillian* • USA
TURN IN THE ROAD, THE • 1919 • Vidor King • USA
TURN IT OUT • 1947 • Annakin Ken • DCS • UKN
TURN ME ON! • 1968 • *Lynn Barbara* • USA
TURN OF A CARD, THE • 1918 • Apfel Oscar • USA • TURN OF THE CARD, THE
TURN OF FATE, THE • 1912 • *Gem* • USA
TURN OF THE BADGE see **SANTEE** • 1973
TURN OF THE BALANCE, THE • 1910 • *Costello Maurice* • USA
TURN OF THE CARD, THE see **TURN OF A CARD, THE** • 1918
TURN OF THE CARDS, A • 1914 • Garwood William • USA
TURN OF THE DICE • 1910 • *Imp* • USA
TURN OF THE FURROW • 1944 • Baylis Peter • DOC • USA
TURN OF THE ROAD, THE • 1915 • Johnson Tefft • USA
TURN OF THE ROAD, THE see **KARJOLSTEINEN** • 1978
TURN OF THE SCREW • 1974 • Curtis Dan • TVM • USA, UKN
TURN OF THE SCREW, THE see **OTRA VUELTA DE TUERCA** • 1985
TURN OF THE SOIL • 1946 • Heyer John • DOC • ASL
TURN OF THE TIDE • 1935 • Walker Norman • UKN
TURN OF THE TIDE see **KENTERING** • 1932
TURN OF THE TIDE, THE • 1910 • *Capitol* • USA
TURN OF THE TIDE, THE • 1913 • Leonard Robert Z. • USA
TURN OF THE TIDE, THE • 1914 • Lessey George A. • USA
TURN OF THE WHEEL, THE • 1911 • *Reliance* • USA
TURN OF THE WHEEL, THE • 1915 • *Travers Richard C.* • USA
TURN OF THE WHEEL, THE • 1916 • *Davenport Dorothy* • SHT • USA
TURN OF THE WHEEL, THE • 1918 • Barker Reginald • USA
TURN OFF THE MOON • 1937 • Seiler Lewis • USA
TURN ON TO LOVE • 1969 • Avildsen John G. • USA
TURN ON, TUNE IN, DROP OUT • 1967 • Clark Robin • DOC • USA
TURN OUT THE FIRE BRIGADE • 1900 • Gibbons Walter • UKN
TURN-TALE WOLF, THE • 1952 • McKimson Robert • ANS • USA
TURN THE KEY SOFTLY • 1953 • Lee Jack • UKN
TURN THE OTHER CHEEK (USA) see **PORGI L'ALTRA GUANCIA** • 1974
TURN THE SOIL • 1948 • Robinson Lee (c/d) • DOC • ASL
TURN TO THE RIGHT • 1922 • Ingram Rex • USA
TURNABOUT • 1940 • Roach Hal • USA
TURNABOUT • 1988 • Owen Don • CND
TURNAROUND • 1985 • Solum Ola • NRW, USA • DEADLY ILLUSION
TURNE • 1990 • Salvatores Gabriele • ITL • TOURNEE
TURNED BACK • 1914 • Adolfi John G. • USA
TURNED-ON GIRL • 1970 • Walsh C. • USA
TURNED OUT NICE AGAIN • 1941 • Varnel Marcel • UKN
TURNED TO THE WALL • 1911 • *Edison* • USA
TURNED UP • 1924 • Chapin James • USA
TURNED UP TOES see **LOVE THAT BRUTE** • 1950
TURNER • 1963 • Rowland Anthony M. • UKN
TURNER • 1972 • Rosenblum Ralph • MTV • USA
TURNER AND HOOCH • 1989 • Spottiswoode Roger • USA
TURNERS OF PROSPECT ROAD, THE • 1947 • Wilson Maurice J. • UKN
TURNIEJ • 1959 • Nehrebecki Wladyslaw • ANS • PLN • TOURNAMENT
TURNING see **ZAKRET** • 1977
TURNING IN HELL, A see **JIGOKU NO MAGARIKADO** • 1959
TURNING OF THE ROAD, THE • 1914 • *Ostriche Muriel* • USA
TURNING OF THE WORM • 1910 • *Atlas* • USA
TURNING OVER A NEW LEAF • 1908 • Porter Edwin S. • USA
TURNING POINT see **AUFENTHALT, DIE** • 1983
TURNING POINT, THE • 1911 • *Kirkwood James* • USA
TURNING POINT, THE • 1912 • *Selig* • USA
TURNING POINT, THE • 1912 • *Essanay* • USA
TURNING POINT, THE • 1912 • *Powers* • USA
TURNING POINT, THE • 1913 • *Kalem* • USA
TURNING POINT, THE • 1913 • *Patheplay* • USA
TURNING POINT, THE • 1914 • *Frontier* • USA
TURNING POINT, THE • 1914 • Johnston Lorimer • *American* • USA
TURNING POINT, THE • 1915 • *Associated Film Sales* • USA
TURNING POINT, THE • 1915 • *Reliance* • USA
TURNING POINT, THE • 1915 • Levering Joseph • *Empress* • USA
TURNING POINT, THE • 1920 • Barry J. A. • USA
TURNING POINT, THE • 1952 • Dieterle William • USA • THIS IS DYNAMITE
TURNING POINT, THE • 1977 • Ross Herbert • USA
TURNING POINT, THE see **GIRL LIKE THAT, A** • 1917
TURNING POINT, THE see **VELIKI PERELOM** • 1946
TURNING POINT, THE see **POVOROT** • 1979
TURNING POINT OF JIM MALLOY, THE • 1975 • Gilroy Frank D. • TVM • USA • GIBBSVILLE: THE TURNING POINT OF JIM MALLOY ○ JOHN O'HARA'S GIBBSVILLE
TURNING THE FABLES • 1960 • Kneitel Seymour • ANS • USA
TURNING THE TABLE • 1913 • *Lubin* • USA
TURNING THE TABLES • 1903 • Porter Edwin S. • USA
TURNING THE TABLES • 1906 • Hough Harold • UKN
TURNING THE TABLES • 1909 • *Walturdaw* • UKN
TURNING THE TABLES • 1910 • *Atlas* • USA
TURNING THE TABLES • 1910 • Powell Frank • *Ab* • USA
TURNING THE TABLES • 1911 • *Boulden Edward* • USA
TURNING THE TABLES • 1912 • Collins Edwin J.? • UKN
TURNING THE TABLES • 1919 • Clifton Elmer • USA • WHO'S WHICH
TURNING TO STONE • 1985 • Till Eric • CND • CONCRETE HELL
TURNING WIND, THE see **BARRAVENTO** • 1961
TURNO DI NOTTE (ITL) see **SERVICE DE NUIT** • 1943
TURNOVER • 1970 • Crombie Donald • SHT • ASL
TURNOVER SMITH • 1980 • Kowalski Bernard • TVM • USA
TURNS OF THE WILL • 1911 • *Pathe* • USA
TURNSTILE see **VANDKORSET** • 1944
TURNSTILE, THE • 1911 • *Reliance* • USA
TURQUOISE MINE CONSPIRACY, THE • 1916 • Horne James W. • SHT • USA
TURRI IL BANDITO • 1950 • Trapani Enzo • ITL
TURTLE DIARY • 1985 • Irvin John • UKN
TURTLE DOVES • 1916 • Holmes-Gore Arthur • SHT • USA
TURTLE ON ITS BACK see **TORTUE SUR LE DOS, LA** • 1977
TURTLE SCOOP • 1961 • Kneitel Seymour • ANS • USA
TURTLE SOUP • 1967 • Duga Irene • SHT • USA
TURYN ONSEN NIKKI • 1958 • Matsubayashi Shue • JPN
TUSALAVA • 1929 • Lye Len • ANS • UKN
TUSET STREET • 1968 • Grau Jorge, Marquina Luis • SPN
TUSK • 1979 • Jodorowsky Alejandro • FRN
TUSK TUSK • 1960 • Taras Martin B. • ANS • USA
TUSKE A KOROM ALATT • 1988 • Sara Sandor • HNG • THORN UNDER THE FINGERNAIL, A
TUSKS • 1987 • Moore Tara • USA
TUSSENSPEL BIJ KAARSLICHT • 1959 • van der Linden Charles Huguenot • SHT • NTH • INTERLUDE BY CANDLELIGHT
TUSZTORTENET • 1988 • Gazdag Gyula • HNG • HOSTAGE STORY, A ○ STAND OFF
TUT AND TUTTLE • 1981 • *Barnes Chris* • TVM • USA
TUT OG KJOR • 1976 • Bohwim Knut • NRW
TUT-TUT AND HIS TERRIBLE TOMB • 1923 • Phillips Bertram • UKN
TUTAJOSOK • 1988 • Elek Judit • HNG, FRN • RAFTSMEN ○ MEMORIES OF A RIVER ○ MEMOIRS OF A RIVER
TUTE CABRERO • 1968 • Jusid Juan Jose • ARG
TUTTA COLPA DEL PARADISO • 1985 • Nuti Francesco • ITL • IT'S THE FAULT OF PARADISE
TUTTA LA CITTA CANTA • 1944 • Freda Riccardo • ITL • SEI PER OTTO QUARANTOTTO
TUTTA LA VITA IN UNA NOTTE • 1939 • D'Errico Corrado • ITL
TUTTA LA VITA IN VENTIQUATTR'ORE • 1944 • Bragaglia Carlo Ludovico • ITL
TUTTA UNA VITA (ITL) see **TOUTE UNE VIE** • 1974
TUTTE LE AUTRE REGAZZE LO FANNO see **OLTRAGGIO AL PUDORE** • 1965
TUTTE LE DOMENICHE MATTINA • 1972 • Tuzii Carlo • ITL • EVERY SUNDAY MORNING
TUTTI A CASA • 1960 • Comencini Luigi • ITL, FRN • GRANDE PAGAILLE, LA (FRN) ○ EVERYBODY GO HOME! (USA) ○ BACK HOME
TUTTI A SQUOLA • 1979 • Pingitore Pier Francesco • ITL

TUTTI DEFUNTI.. TRANNE I MORTI • 1977 • Avati Pupi • ITL
TUTTI FIGLI DI MAMMA SANTISSIMA • 1973 • Caltabiano Alfio • ITL
TUTTI FRATELLI NEL WEST.. PER PARTE DI PADRE • 1972 • Grieco Sergio • ITL
TUTTI FRUTTI see **SCATENATO, LO** • 1967
TUTTI GLI UOMINI EL PARLAMENTO • 1979 • Racca Claudio • ITL
TUTTI I COLORI DEL BUIO • 1972 • Martino Sergio • ITL, SPN • TODOS LOS COLORES DE LA OSCURIDAD (SPN) ○ STRANA ORCHIDES CON CINQUE GOCCE DI SANGUE, UNA ○ STRANGE ORCHID WITH FIVE DROPS OF BLOOD, A ○ SPN ○ THEY'RE COMING TO GET YOU
TUTTI INNAMORATI • 1959 • Orlandini Giuseppe • ITL, FRN • EVERYBODY IN LOVE
TUTTI O NESSUNO see **LEGGE DELLA VIOLENZA, LA** • 1969
TUTTI PAZZI MENO IO (ITL) see **ROI DE COEUR, LE** • 1966
TUTTI PER UNO BOTTE PER TUTTI • 1973 • Corbucci Bruno • ITL, SPN, FRG
TUTTI POSSONO ARRICCHIRE TRANNE I POVERI • 1976 • Severino Mauro • ITL
TUTTI POSSONO UCCIDERMI (ITL) see **TOUS PEUVENT ME TUER** • 1957
TUTTLES OF TAHITI, THE • 1942 • Vidor Charles • USA
TUTTO A POSTO E NIENTE IN ORDINE • 1974 • Wertmuller Lina • ITL • EVERYTHING'S READY NOTHING WORKS ○ ALL SCREWED UP ○ EVERYTHING'S IN ORDER BUT NOTHING WORKS
TUTTO E MUSICA • 1963 • Modugno Domenico • ITL
TUTTO IL MONDO RIDE • 1952 • Ferronetti Ignazio • ITL
TUTTO IN COMUNE • 1974 • Alberani Ghigo • ITL
TUTTO PER LA DONNA • 1940 • Soldati Mario • ITL
TUTTO PER TUTTO • 1968 • Lenzi Umberto • ITL, SPN • ALL OUT
TUTTO SUL ROSSO • 1968 • Florio Aldo • ITL
TUTTO SUO PADRE • 1978 • Lucidi Maurizio • ITL
TUTTOBENIGNI • 1985 • Bertolucci Giuseppe • ITL
TUTU • 1969 • Kurkvaara Maunu • FNL
TUTUN ZAMANI • 1959 • Ariburnu • TRK
TUTUNE see **TYUTYUN** • 1962
TUTYU AND TOTYO see **TUTYU ES TOTYO** • 1915
TUTYU ES TOTYO • 1915 • Korda Alexander, Zilahi Gyula • HNG • TUTYU AND TOTYO
TUVIYAH VE SHEVA BENOTAIV • 1968 • Golan Menahem • ISR, FRG • TEVYE UND SEINE SIEBEN TOCHTER (FRG) ○ TEVYE AND HIS SEVEN DAUGHTERS
TUVO LA CULPA ADAN • 1943 • de Orduna Juan • SPN
TUXEDO JUNCTION • 1941 • McDonald Frank • USA • GANG MADE GOOD, THE (UKN)
TUXEDO WARRIOR • 1985 • Sinclair Andrew • USA • AFRICAN RUN, THE
TUYA EN CUERPO Y ALMA • 1944 • Gout Alberto • MXC
TUYA PARA SIEMPRE • 1948 • Martinez Solares Gilberto • MXC
TUZAK • 1977 • Yilmaz Atif • TRK • TRAP
TUZGOMBOK • 1975 • Feher Imre • HNG • START FROM ZERO
TUZKERESZTSEG • 1951 • Ban Frigyes • HNG • BAPTISM BY FIRE
TUZOLTO U.25 see **TUZOLTO UTCA 25** • 1973
TUZOLTO UTCA 25 • 1973 • Szabo Istvan • HNG • 25, FIREMAN'S STREET (USA) ○ TUZOLTO U.25
TVA AR I VARJE KLASS • 1938 • Wallen Sigurd • SWD • TWO YEARS IN EACH FORM
TVA HJARTAN OCH EN KOJA see **KARL FOR SIN HATT** • 1940
TVA HJARTAN OCH EN SKUTA • 1932 • Rodin Gosta • SWD • TWO HEARTS AND A BOAT ○ SKEPPARFROJD
TVA KILLAR OCH EN TJEJ • 1983 • Hallstrom Lasse • SWD • HAPPY WE
TVA KONUNGAR • 1925 • Ellis Elis • SWD • TWO KINGS
TVA KVINNOR • 1947 • Sjostrand Arnold • SWD • TWO WOMEN
TVA KVINNOR • 1974 • Bjorkman Stig, Ahrne Marianne • SWD • TWO WOMEN
TVA LEVANDE OCH EN DOD • 1961 • Asquith Anthony • SWD, UKN • TWO LIVING, ONE DEAD (UKN) ○ TWO LIVING AND ONE DEAD
TVA MAN OM EN ANKA • 1933 • Lindlof John • SWD • TWO MEN AND A WIDOW
TVA MANNISKOR • 1945 • Dreyer Carl T. • SWD • TWO PEOPLE
TVA SKONA JUVELER • 1954 • Husberg Rolf • SWD • TWO RASCALS
TVA SVENSKA EMIGRANTERS AVENTYR I AMERIKA • 1912 • Jaenzon Julius • SWD • ADVENTURES OF TWO SWEDISH EMIGRANTS IN AMERICA, THE
TVA TRAPPOR OVER GARDEN • 1950 • Werner Gosta • SWD • BACKYARD
TVAR • 1973 • Brdecka Jiri • ANM • CZC • FACE, THE
TVAR POD MASKOU • 1970 • Vulchanov Rangel • CZC • FACE UNDER THE MASK ○ MASKED FACE, THE
TVAR V OKNE • 1963 • Solan Peter • CZC • FACE AT THE WINDOW
TVARBALK • 1967 • Donner Jorn • SWD • ROOFTREE ○ CROSS BAR ○ CROSSBEAM
TVENNE BRODER • 1912 • Klercker Georg • SWD
TVERS IGJENNOM LOV • 1979 • Skagen Solve • DOC • NRW • IN SPITE OF THE LAW
TVIGGY • 1969 • Waxman Albert • SHT • CND
TVOI SOVREMENNIK • 1967 • Raizman Yuli • USS • YOUR CONTEMPORARY
TWA CORBIES • 1951 • Halas John • ANS • UKN
TWA HIELAND LADS • 1910 • *Vitagraph* • USA
TWARZ ANIOLA • 1970 • Chmielewski Zbigniew • PLN • ANGEL'S FACE, THE
TWARZA W TWARZ • 1967 • Zanussi Krzysztof • MTV • PLN • FACE TO FACE
'TWAS BUT A DREAM • 1916 • *International Film Service* • SHT • USA
'TWAS EVER THUS • 1911 • *Essanay* • USA
'TWAS EVER THUS • 1915 • Smalley Phillips • USA
'TWAS HENRY'S FAULT • 1919 • *Strand* • SHT • USA
'TWAS ONLY A DREAM see **HUNGER STRIKE, THE** • 1913
'TWAS THE NIGHT BEFORE CHRISTMAS • 1914 • Miller Ashley • USA
TWEE BROEDERS RY SAAM • 1968 • Botha Kappie • SAF • TWO BROTHERS TRAVEL TOGETHER
TWEE VROUWEN • 1978 • Sluizer George, Rood Jurrien • NTH • TWICE A WOMAN ○ SECOND TOUCH
TWEE ZEEUWSCHE MEISJES IN ZANDVOORT • 1914 • Chrispijn Louis H. (c/d) • NTH • TWO GIRLS FROM ZEELAND
TWEEDE SLAAPKAMER, DIE • 1962 • SAF
TWEEDLEDUM BECOMES A HERCULES • 1912 • *Ambrosio* • ITL
TWEEDLEDUM INSURES HIS LIFE • 1913 • *Powers* • USA
TWEEDLEDUM'S BUSY NIGHT • 1916 • *Perez Tweedledum* • SHT • USA
TWEEDLEDUM'S DANCING FITS • 1910 • *Fabre Marcel* • ITL
TWEEDLEDUM'S SCRAMBLED HONEYMOON • 1916 • *Unity Sales* • USA
TWEEDLEDUM'S TORPEDOED BY CUPID • 1916 • *Unity Sales* • USA
'TWEEN TWO LOVES • 1911 • *Pickford Mary* • USA
TWEET AND LOVELY • 1959 • Freleng Friz • ANS • USA
TWEET AND SOUR • 1956 • Freleng Friz • ANS • USA
TWEET DREAMS • 1959 • Freleng Friz • ANS • USA
TWEET MUSIC • 1951 • Sparber I. • ANS • USA
TWEET, TWEET, TWEETY • 1951 • Freleng Friz • ANS • USA
TWEET ZOO • 1957 • Freleng Friz • ANS • USA
TWEETIE PIE • 1947 • Freleng Friz • ANS • USA
TWEETY AND THE BEANSTALK • 1957 • Freleng Friz • ANS • USA
TWEETY'S CIRCUS • 1955 • Freleng Friz • ANS • USA
TWEETY'S S.O.S. • 1951 • Freleng Friz • ANS • USA
TWELFTH HOUR see **V HO DINE DVANASTE** • 1959
TWELFTH HOUR, THE • 1915 • *Imp* • USA
TWELFTH HOUR -NIGHT OF HORROR, THE see **ZWOLFTE STUNDE -EINE NACHTE DES GRAUENS, DIE** • 1930
TWELFTH JUROR, THE • 1909 • *Essanay* • USA
TWELFTH JUROR, THE • 1912 • *Thanhouser* • USA
TWELFTH JUROR, THE • 1913 • Lessey George A. • USA
TWELFTH NIGHT • Hartigan P. C. • USA
TWELFTH NIGHT • 1910 • Kent Charles? • USA
TWELFTH NIGHT • 1953 • Deane Charles • UKN
TWELFTH NIGHT • 1979 • Gorrie John • MTV • UKN
TWELFTH NIGHT • 1986 • Armfield Neil • ASL
TWELFTH NIGHT see **DVENADTSATAYA NOCH** • 1955
TWELFTH NIGHT see **VIZKERESZET** • 1967
TWELVE AND A HALF CENTS • 1969 • Bonniere Rene • CND
TWELVE ANGRY MEN • 1957 • Lumet Sidney • USA
TWELVE CHAIRS, THE • 1970 • Brooks Mel • USA
TWELVE CHAIRS, THE see **DOCE SILLAS, LOS** • 1962
TWELVE CHAIRS, THE see **DVINATSAT STULYEV** • 1971
TWELVE CHAPTERS ABOUT WOMEN see **JOSEI NI KANSURU JUNISHO** • 1954
TWELVE CHAPTERS ON WOMEN see **JOSEI NI KANSURU JUNISHO** • 1954
TWELVE COMPANIONS • 1962 • Karamyan E. • USS
TWELVE CROWDED HOURS • 1939 • Landers Lew • USA
TWELVE DAYS OF CHRISTMAS, THE • *Q3* • ANS • UKN
TWELVE GOLD MEDALLIONS, THE • 1970 • Cheng Kang • HKG
TWELVE GOOD HENS AND TRUE • 1917 • Drew Sidney, Drew Sidney Mrs. • SHT • USA
TWELVE GOOD MEN • 1936 • Ince Ralph • UKN
TWELVE HANDED MEN OF MARS, THE see **MARZIANI HANNO DODICI MANI, I** • 1964
TWELVE HOURS TO KILL • 1960 • Cahn Edward L. • USA
TWELVE HOURS TO LIVE see **E PIU FACILE CHE UN CAMMELLO** • 1950
TWELVE MEN IN A BOX see **JUST OFF BROADWAY** • 1942
TWELVE MILES OUT • 1927 • Conway Jack • USA
TWELVE MONTHS • 1985 • Yabuki Kimio • JPN
TWELVE MONTHS, THE see **O DVANACTI MESICKACH** • 1960
TWELVE MONTHS AFTER • 1898 • *Haydon & Urry* • UKN
TWELVE MONTHS GREEN • 1948 • Clifford William T. • USA
TWELVE O'CLOCK AND ALL AIN'T WELL • 1941 • Donnelly Eddie • ANS • USA
TWELVE O'CLOCK EXPRESS, THE • 1909 • *Urban Trading Co* • UKN
TWELVE O'CLOCK HIGH • 1949 • King Henry • USA
TWELVE PHOTOGRAPHERS see **JUNININ NO SHASHIN-KA** • 1953-57
TWELVE PLUS ONE (USA) see **UNA SU TREDICI** • 1969
TWELVE POUND LOOK, THE • 1920 • Denton Jack • UKN
TWELVE TASKS OF ASTERIX, THE see **DOUZE TRAVAUX D'ASTERIX, LES** • 1976
TWELVE: TEN see **12-10** • 1919
TWELVE TO THE MOON • 1960 • Bradley David • USA • 12 TO THE MOON
TWELVE WILD WOMEN see **MANKILLERS** • 1987
TWELVE WOMEN (USA) see **DOCE MUJERES** • 1939
TWENTIETH CENTURY • 1934 • Hawks Howard • USA
TWENTIETH CENTURY CONJURING see **CLOWNESSE FANTOME, LA** • 1902
TWENTIETH CENTURY FOXES see **FOXES** • 1980
TWENTIETH CENTURY PIRATE, A • 1914 • *Kerrigan J. Warren* • USA
TWENTIETH CENTURY ROGUE see **LOUTYE GHARNE BISTOM** • 1968
TWENTIETH CENTURY SURGEON, A (USA) see **CHIRURGIEN AMERICAIN** • 1897
TWENTIETH CENTURY SURGERY (USA) see **CHIRURGIE DE L'AVENIR, LA** • 1901
TWENTIETH CENTURY TRAMP, THE • 1902 • Porter Edwin S. • USA • HAPPY HOOLIGAN AND HIS AIRSHIP
TWENTY CENTURY FARMER, A • 1913 • *La Badie Florence* • USA
TWENTY CENTURY PIRATE, A • 1918 • *Kerrigan J. Warren* • USA
TWENTY CENTURY SUSIE • 1915 • *Franey William* • USA
TWENTY DAY RESPITE FROM WAR, A see **DVADTSAT DNEI BEZ VOINI** • 1976
TWENTY DAYS WITHOUT WAR see **DVADTSAT DNEI BEZ VOINI** • 1976
TWENTY DOLLAR STAR • 1989 • Leder Paul • USA
TWENTY DOLLARS see **FOOLS AND RICHES** • 1923
TWENTY DOLLARS A WEEK • 1924 • Weight F. Harmon • USA • MAN MAKER, THE (UKN) ○ $20 A WEEK
TWENTY FIRST, THE see **DWUDZIESTA PIERWSZA** • 1964
TWENTY-FIVE YEARS A KING • 1935 • Ginever Aveling • UKN
TWENTY-FOUR EYES see **NIJUSHI NO HITOMI** • 1954
TWENTY-FOUR HOUR MOVIE, THE see ****** (FOUR STARS)** • 1967
TWENTY-FOUR HOURS • 1931 • Gering Marion • USA • HOURS BETWEEN, THE (UKN) ○ 24 HOURS
TWENTY-FOUR HOURS see **NIJUSHI NO HITOMI** • 1954
TWENTY-FOUR HOURS IN CZECHOSLOVAKIA • 1968 • Bairstow David • DOC • CND
TWENTY FOUR HOURS OF A SECRET LIFE see **CHIKAGAI NIJUYO-JIKAN** • 1947
TWENTY-FOUR HOURS OF A WOMAN'S LIFE see **24 HEURES DE LA VIE D'UNE FEMME** • 1968
TWENTY FOUR HOURS OF THE UNDERGROUND STREET see **CHIKAGAI NIJUYO-JIKAN** • 1947
TWENTY-FOUR VARIATIONS • 1940 • Whitney John, Whitney James • ANS • USA
TWENTY GIRLS AND A BAND • 1938 • Goodwins Leslie • SHT • USA
TWENTY GRAND see **RECKLESS LIVING** • 1931
TWENTY HOURS (UKN) see **HUSZ ORA** • 1964
TWENTY LEGS UNDER THE SEA • 1931 • Fleischer Dave • ANS • USA
TWENTY MILLION DOLLAR MYSTERY, THE see **ZUDORA** • 1914
TWENTY MILLION PEOPLE • 1969 • Gelbart Arnie • SHT • CND
TWENTY MILLION SWEETHEARTS • 1934 • Enright Ray • USA • HOT AIR ○ RHYTHM IN THE AIR
TWENTY MINUTES AT THE FAIR • 1916 • *Ritchie Billie* • SHT • USA
TWENTY MINUTES IN MAGIC • 1916 • Humphrey Orral • SHT • USA
TWENTY MINUTES OF LOVE • 1914 • Sennett Mack • USA • COPS AND WATCHERS ○ HE LOVED HER SO
TWENTY-MULE TEAM see **20-MULE TEAM** • 1940
TWENTY-NINE • 1969 • Cummins Brian • SHT • UKN
TWENTY-ONE • 1918 • Worthington William • USA
TWENTY-ONE • 1923 • Robertson John S. • USA
TWENTY ONE DAYS • 1939 • Dean Basil • UKN • TWENTY ONE DAYS TOGETHER (USA)
TWENTY ONE DAYS TOGETHER (USA) see **TWENTY ONE DAYS** • 1939
TWENTY-ONE HOURS AT MUNICH see **21 HOURS AT MUNICH** • 1976
TWENTY-ONE JUMP STREET • 1987 • Manners Kim • TVM • USA • 21 JUMP STREET
TWENTY PLUS TWO • 1961 • Newman Joseph M. • USA • IT STARTED IN TOKYO (UKN) ○ IT HAPPENED IN TOKYO
TWENTY QUESTIONS MURDER MYSTERY, THE • 1950 • Stein Paul L. • UKN • MURDER ON THE AIR
TWENTY-SEVEN DOWN -VARANASI EXPRESS see **SATTAWIS DOWN** • 1973
TWENTY-SIX BAKU COMMISSARS see **DVADTSAT SHESJ KOMISSAROV** • 1936
TWENTY-SIX COMMISSARS, THE • 1929 • Shengelaya Nikolai • USS
TWENTY SIX DAYS IN THE LIFE OF DOSTOEVSKY see **DWATZAT SCHEST DNEJ IS SHISNI DOSTOJEWSKOGO** • 1981
TWENTY THOUSAND LEAGUES UNDER THE SEA • 1905 • USA • AMID THE WONDERS OF THE DEEP
TWENTY THOUSAND LEAGUES UNDER THE SEA • 1973 • Hanna William, Barbera Joseph • ANM • USA • 20,000 LEAGUES UNDER THE SEA
TWENTY THREE PACES TO BAKER STREET • 1956 • Hathaway Henry • USA • 23 PACES TO BAKER STREET
TWENTY-THREE STEPS TO BED see **ARU OSAKA NO ONNA** • 1962
TWENTY-TWO MISHAPS see **DVADZATDVA NESHCHASTIA** • 1930
TWENTY YEARS AFTER • 1914 • Cooper Toby • UKN
TWENTY YEARS IN A STORM see **FUSETSU NIJYUNEN** • 1951
TWENTY YEARS OF CINEMA see **KINO ZA DVADTSAT LET** • 1940
TWENTY YEARS OF SOVIET CINEMA see **KINO ZA DVADTSAT LET** • 1940
TWICE see **DEUX FOIS** • 1971
TWICE A MAN • 1963 • Markopoulos Gregory J. • USA
TWICE A WOMAN see **TWEE VROUWEN** • 1978
TWICE AT ONCE • 1916 • Hutchinson Craig • SHT • USA
TWICE BITTEN see **VAMPIRE HOOKERS** • 1978
TWICE BLESSED • 1945 • Beaumont Harry • USA
TWICE BRANDED • 1936 • Rogers Maclean • UKN
TWICE DEAD • 1988 • Dragin Bert L. • USA
TWICE IN A LIFETIME • 1974 • Daugherty Herschel • TVM • USA
TWICE IN A LIFETIME • 1985 • Yorkin Bud • USA
TWICE IN THE SAME PLACE • 1917 • Davey Horace • USA
TWICE INTO THE LIGHT • 1915 • Berthelet Arthur • USA
TWICE ON A CERTAIN NIGHT see **ARU YO FUTATABI** • 1956
TWICE RESCUED • 1913 • Miller Ashley • USA
TWICE RESCUED • 1915 • Marston Theodore • USA
TWICE ROUND THE DAFFODILS • 1962 • Thomas Gerald • UKN
TWICE-TOLD TALES • 1963 • Salkow Sidney • USA • NATHANIEL HAWTHORNE'S "TWICE-TOLD TALES" ○ CORPSE MAKERS, THE ○ NIGHTS OF TERROR
TWICE TWO • 1920 • Brunel Adrian • UKN
TWICE TWO • 1933 • Parrott James • SHT • USA
TWICE UNDER • 1988 • Crow Dean • USA
TWICE UPON A TIME • 1953 • Pressburger Emeric • UKN
TWICE UPON A TIME • 1979 • Walker Giles • CND
TWICE UPON A TIME • 1983 • Korty John, Swenson Charles • ANM • USA
TWICE UPON A TIME • 1989 • Gutman Nathaniel • FRG
TWICE UPON A TIME see **TEMPS DE MOURIR, LE** • 1969
TWICE UPON A TIME see **SMYKKETYVEN** • 1989
TWICE WON • 1915 • Reehm George E. • USA
TWICKENHAM FERRY • 1913 • *De Lespine Edgena* • USA

TWIDDLE-TWADDLE see **KLIZI-PUZI** • 1968
TWILIGHT • 1912 • *Bushman Francis X.* • USA
TWILIGHT • 1914 • *Warner'S Features* • USA
TWILIGHT • 1919 • Dawley J. Searle • USA
TWILIGHT • 1969 • Sihanouk Norodom
TWILIGHT • 1985 • Bertelsson Thrainn • ICL
TWILIGHT see **WITHOUT HONOR** • 1949
TWILIGHT see **ALKONY** • 1971
TWILIGHT see **DUELLE** • 1976
TWILIGHT see **POKKUVAVIL** • 1981
TWILIGHT see **SUTON** • 1984
TWILIGHT see **SZURKULET** • 1989
TWILIGHT AFFAIR see **DOUBLE YOUR PLEASURE** • 1969
TWILIGHT AND DAWN see **ALKONYOK ES HAJNALOK** • 1961
TWILIGHT BABY, A • 1920 • White Jack • SHT • USA
TWILIGHT BEER HALL see **TASOFARE SAKABA** • 1955
TWILIGHT FOG see **KIRIGAKURE SAIZO** • 1964
TWILIGHT FOR THE GODS • 1958 • Pevney Joseph • USA • DAMNED, THE
TWILIGHT GIRLS, THE (USA) see **COLLEGIENNES, LES** • 1957
TWILIGHT HOUR • 1944 • Stein Paul L. • UKN
TWILIGHT IN THE SIERRAS • 1950 • Witney William • USA
TWILIGHT IN TOKYO • 1990 • Srichuae Thoranong • THL
TWILIGHT IN TOKYO see **TOKYO BOSHOKU** • 1957
TWILIGHT MEETING see **MOTEN I SKYMNINGEN** • 1957
TWILIGHT OF HER LIFE • 1913 • *Lubin* • USA
TWILIGHT OF HONOR • 1963 • Sagal Boris • USA • CHARGE IS MURDER, THE (UKN)
TWILIGHT OF TERROR see **CREPUSCULE D'EPOUVANTE** • 1922
TWILIGHT OF THE DEAD see **PAURA, LA** • 1980
TWILIGHT OF THE GODS see **GODHULI** • 1978
TWILIGHT ON THE PRAIRIE • 1944 • Yarbrough Jean • USA
TWILIGHT ON THE RIO GRANDE • 1947 • McDonald Frank • USA
TWILIGHT ON THE TRAIL • 1937 • Fleischer Dave • ANS • USA
TWILIGHT ON THE TRAIL • 1941 • Bretherton Howard • USA
TWILIGHT PATH (USA) see **DAIKON TO NINJIN** • 1964
TWILIGHT PEOPLE • 1972 • Romero Eddie • USA, PHL • ISLAND OF THE TWILIGHT PEOPLE
TWILIGHT PINK • 1981 • St. Germaine Travis • USA • TWILITE PINK
TWILIGHT STORY, THE see **BOKUTO KIDAN** • 1960
TWILIGHT TIME see **SUTON** • 1984
TWILIGHT TRAVELLERS see **VIAGGIATORI DELLA SERA, I** • 1979
TWILIGHT (USA) see **BELLE AVENTURE, LA** • 1942
TWILIGHT WOMEN (USA) see **WOMEN OF TWILIGHT** • 1952
TWILIGHT ZONE MOVIE, THE see **TWILIGHT ZONE -THE MOVIE** • 1983
TWILIGHT ZONE -THE MOVIE • 1983 • Spielberg Steven, Dante Joe, Miller George, Landis John • USA • TWILIGHT ZONE MOVIE, THE
TWILIGHT'S LAST GLEAMING • 1977 • Aldrich Robert • USA • NUCLEAR COUNTDOWN ○ VIPER THREE
TWILITE GIRLS see **COLLEGIENNES, LES** • 1957
TWILITE PINK see **TWILIGHT PINK** • 1981
TWIN AND SHOSHONE FALLS, THE • 1913 • *Gem* • USA
TWIN BED ROOMS • 1918 • *Bret Tom* • USA
TWIN BEDS • 1920 • Ingraham Lloyd • USA
TWIN BEDS • 1929 • Santell Alfred • USA
TWIN BEDS • 1942 • Whelan Tim • USA
TWIN BRIDES see **WHO'S WHO** • 1915
TWIN BROTHERS • 1909 • Griffith D. W. • USA
TWIN BROTHERS, THE • 1913 • *Phillips Augustus* • USA
TWIN BROTHERS FROM "THE FRENCH MAID" • 1907 • Gilbert Arthur • UKN
TWIN BROTHERS VAN ZANDT, THE • 1914 • Ince John • USA
TWIN CROOKS • 1920 • Buckingham Thomas • SHT • USA
TWIN DETECTIVES • 1976 • Day Robert • TVM • USA
TWIN DRAGON ENCOUNTER • 1988 • Dunlop Paul • USA
TWIN FACES • 1937 • Huntington Lawrence • UKN
TWIN FATES • 1916 • Beaumont Harry • SHT • USA
TWIN FEDORAS, THE • 1917 • Smith David • SHT • USA
TWIN FLAPPERS • 1927 • *Morey Harry* • USA
TWIN FLATS • 1916 • *Hardy Oliver* • USA
TWIN HUSBANDS • 1922 • St. Clair Malcolm • SHT • USA
TWIN HUSBANDS • 1934 • Strayer Frank • USA
TWIN HUSBANDS • 1946 • Yates Hal • SHT • USA
TWIN KIDDIES • 1917 • King Henry • USA
TWIN LIZZIES • 1920 • *Star* • SHT • USA
TWIN PAWNS, THE • 1919 • Perret Leonce • USA • CURSE OF GREED, THE
TWIN PEAKS • 1989 • Lynch David • USA
TWIN ROSES • 1911 • Fitzhamon Lewin • UKN
TWIN SCREWS • 1933 • Parrott James • SHT • USA
TWIN SISTER, THE • 1915 • Hotaling Arthur D. • USA
TWIN SISTERS see **SOSEIJI GAKKYU** • 1956
TWIN SISTERS OF KYOTO see **KOTO** • 1963
TWIN SIX O'BRIEN • 1926 • Horner Robert J. • USA
TWIN SOMBREROS see **GUNFIGHTERS** • 1947
TWIN SOULS • 1916 • *Grey R. Henry* • SHT • USA
TWIN SQUAWS, THE • 1911 • *Powers* • USA
TWIN TOWERS, THE • 1911 • *Edison* • USA
TWIN TRIANGLE, THE • 1916 • Harvey Harry • USA
TWIN TRIGGERS • 1926 • Thorpe Richard • USA • TRIGGER TWINS, THE (UKN)
TWIN TRIPLETS • 1935 • Terhune William • SHT • USA
TWIN TROUBLES • 1917 • Dillon John Francis? • USA
TWIN TRUNK MYSTERY, THE • 1916 • *Armstrong Billy* • USA
TWIN TRUNKS • 1914 • Nash Percy? • UKN
TWINCUPLETS • 1940 • Ripley Arthur • SHT • USA
TWINKLE AND SHINE see **IT HAPPENED TO JANE** • 1959
TWINKLE IN GOD'S EYE, THE • 1955 • Blair George • USA
TWINKLE, TWINKLE, KILLER KANE see **NINTH CONFIGURATION, THE** • 1980
TWINKLE, TWINKLE LITTLE TELSTAR • 1965 • Bartsch Art • ANS • USA
TWINKLE TWINKLE LUCKY STARS • Hong Jinbao • HKG
TWINKLER, THE • 1916 • Sloman Edward • USA
TWINKLETOES • 1926 • Brabin Charles J. • USA
TWINKLETOES GETS THE BIRD • 1941 • Fleischer Dave • ANS • USA
TWINKLETOES IN HAT STUFF • 1941 • Fleischer Dave • ANS • USA
TWINKLETOES -WHERE HE GOES NOBODY KNOWS • 1941 • Fleischer Dave • ANS • USA
TWINKY • 1969 • Donner Richard • UKN • LOLA (USA)
TWINS • 1912 • *Essanay* • USA
TWINS • 1947 • Yudin Konstantin • USS
TWINS • 1988 • Cronenberg David • USA • DEAD RINGERS
TWINS • 1988 • Reitman Ivan • USA • BROTHERS
TWINS, THE • 1911 • Porter Edwin S. • *Rex* • USA
TWINS, THE • 1912 • *Thanhouser* • USA
TWINS, THE • 1913 • *Imp* • USA
TWINS, THE • Tyrlova Hermina • ANS • CZC
TWINS, THE see **DOLLARS AND SENSE** • 1916
TWINS AND THE OTHER GIRL, THE • 1913 • *Thanhouser* • USA
TWINS AND THE STEPMOTHER • 1914 • *Thanhouser* • USA
TWINS AND TROUBLE • 1914 • Seay Charles M. • USA
TWIN'S DOUBLE, THE • 1914 • Ford Francis, Cunard Grace • USA
TWINS OF "DOUBLE X" RANCH, THE • 1913 • *Frontier* • USA
TWINS OF DRACULA see **TWINS OF EVIL** • 1972
TWINS OF EVIL • 1972 • Hough John • UKN • TWINS OF DRACULA ○ GEMINI TWINS, THE ○ VIRGIN VAMPIRES
TWINS OF G. L. RANCH, THE • 1915 • *Fairbanks Madeline* • USA
TWINS OF SUFFERING CREEK • 1920 • Dunlap Scott R. • USA
TWIN'S TEA PARTY, THE • 1896 • Paul Robert William • UKN • CHILDREN AT TABLE
TWIRL • 1981 • Trikonis Gus • TVM • USA
TWIRLIGIG • 1952 • McLaren Norman • ANS • CND, UKN
TWISKER PITCHER, THE • 1937 • Fleischer Dave • ANS • USA
TWIST, THE see **FOLIES BOURGEOISES** • 1976
TWIST AGAIN (USA) see **OPET TWIST, I** • 1964
TWIST ALL NIGHT • 1962 • Hole William Jr. • USA • YOUNG AND THE COOL, THE (UKN) ○ CONTINENTAL TWIST, THE
TWIST AND CRIME • 1963 • Plasencia Arturo • VNZ
TWIST AND SHOUT • 1984 • August Bille • DNM
TWIST AROUND THE CLOCK • 1961 • Rudolph Oscar • USA
TWIST LOCURA DE LA JUVENTUD • 1962 • Delgado Miguel M. • MXC
TWIST, LOLITE E VITELLONI • 1962 • Girolami Marino • ITL
TWIST OF FATE (USA) see **BEAUTIFUL STRANGER, THE** • 1954
TWIST OF SAND, A • 1967 • Chaffey Don • UKN, SAF • GHOST OF WOLFPACK, THE
TWIST PARADE • 1962 • Herman Jean • FRN
TWISTED • 1985 • Holender Adam • USA
TWISTED AFFAIR, A • 1914 • *Columbia* • USA
TWISTED BRAIN see **HORROR HIGH** • 1973
TWISTED GIRLS (UKN) see **ISOLA DELLE SVEDESI, L'** • 1969
TWISTED LIVES see **MENTEURS, LES** • 1961
TWISTED MAN, THE • 1920 • Perret Leonce • USA
TWISTED MORALS see **TOO YOUNG, TOO IMMORAL!** • 1962
TWISTED NERVE • 1968 • Boulting Roy • UKN
TWISTED NIGHTMARE • 1988 • Hunt Paul • USA
TWISTED RAILS • 1935 • Herman Al • USA
TWISTED ROAD, THE see **THEY LIVE BY NIGHT** • 1948
TWISTED SET, THE see **TWISTED SEX, THE** • 1966
TWISTED SEX, THE • 1966 • *Jode Productions* • USA • TWISTED SEX SET, THE ○ TWISTED SET, THE
TWISTED SEX SET, THE see **TWISTED SEX, THE** • 1966
TWISTED SOULS see **SPOOKIES** • 1986
TWISTED TALES • 1925 • Butler Alexander • SHS • UKN
TWISTED TALES • 1926 • Barnett Charles • SHS • UKN
TWISTED TRAIL, THE • 1910 • Griffith D. W. • USA
TWISTED TRAILS • 1916 • Mix Tom • SHT • USA
TWISTED TRIGGERS • 1926 • Thorpe Richard • USA
TWISTER • 1990 • Almereyda Michael • USA
TWITCH, THE • 1974 • Sens Al • ANS • CND
TWITCH OF THE DEATH NERVE see **REAZIONE A CATENA** • 1971
TWITCHING HOUR, THE • 1917 • Curtis Allen • SHT • USA
'TWIXT CUP AND LIP • 1915 • Leigh J. L. V. • UKN
TWIXT LOVE AND AMBITION • 1912 • *Hawley Ormi* • USA
'TWIXT LOVE AND DESIRE • 1917 • Baldwin Ruth Ann • SHT • USA
'TWIXT LOVE AND DUTY • 1908 • *Vitagraph* • USA
TWIXT LOVE AND DUTY: OR, A WOMAN'S HEROISM • 1908 • Coleby A. E. • UKN
TWIXT LOVE AND FIRE • 1913 • Lehrman Henry • USA • BETWIXT LOVE AND FIRE
'TWIXT LOVE AND FIRE • 1914 • Nicholls George • USA
TWIXT LOVE AND FLOUR • 1914 • *Nestor* • USA
TWIXT LOVE AND GOLD • 1910 • *Empire Films* • UKN
TWIXT LOVE AND THE ICEMAN • 1916 • Davey Horace • SHT • USA
TWIXT LOYALTY AND LOVE • 1910 • *Imp* • USA
'TWIXT RED MAN AND WHITE • 1910 • Aylott Dave • UKN
'TWIXT TIME AND TIDE • 1914 • *Cable Films* • UKN
TWO • 1965 • Ray Satyajit • SHT • IND
TWO • 1974 • Trieschmann Charles • USA
TWO see **DVOJE** • 1961
TWO see **KAKSI** • 1972
TWO see **RESAN** • 1977
TWO see **DOS** • 1980
TWO, THE see **DVOYE** • 1965
TWO A.M. • 1919 • *Rodney Earl* • SHT • USA
TWO A.M.: OR, THE HUSBAND'S RETURN • 1896 • *Paul R. W.* • UKN
TWO A PENNY • 1967 • Collier James F. • UKN
TWO ACRES OF LAND see **DO BIGHA ZAMIN** • 1953
TWO AGAINST THE LAW (USA) see **DEUX HOMMES DANS LA VILLE** • 1973
TWO AGAINST THE WORLD • 1932 • Mayo Archie • USA
TWO AGAINST THE WORLD • 1936 • McGann William • USA • CASE OF MRS. PEMBROKE, THE (UKN) ○ ONE FATAL HOUR
TWO-ALARM FIRE, THE • 1934 • Fleischer Dave • ANS • USA
TWO ALONE • 1934 • Nugent Elliott • USA • WILD BIRDS
TWO AND A HALF DADS • 1986 • Bill Tony • USA • 2½ DADS
TWO AND A HALF KILOGRAMMES OF POWER see **DWA I POL KILOGRAMA SILY** • 1966
TWO AND A HALF KILOGRAMMES OF STRENGTH see **DWA I POL KILOGRAMA SILY** • 1966
TWO AND ONE TWO see **DOS MAS UNO DOS** • 1934
TWO AND TWO • 1915 • Williams C. Jay • USA
TWO AND TWO MAKE SIX • 1962 • Francis Freddie • UKN • GIRL SWAPPERS, THE ○ CHANGE OF HEART, A
TWO ANONYMOUS LETTERS see **DUE LETTERE ANONIME** • 1945
TWO APRIL FOOLS • 1954 • White Jules • SHT • USA
TWO ARABIAN NIGHTS • 1927 • Milestone Lewis • USA
TWO ARE GUILTY (USA) see **GLAIVE ET LA BALANCE, LE** • 1962
TWO ARISTOCRATIC PENITENTS • 1913 • Castle James W. • USA
TWO ARTISTS, THE • 1910 • *Wrench Films* • UKN
TWO ARTISTS AND ONE SUIT OF CLOTHES • 1913 • France Charles H. • USA
TWO BACHELOR GIRLS • 1912 • Martinek H. O.? • UKN
TWO BAD BOYS • 1909 • Wilson Frank? • UKN
TWO BAGATELLES • 1952 • McLaren Norman, Munro Grant • ANS • CND
TWO BALLS OF WOOL • 1962 • Tyrlova Hermina • ANM • CZC
TWO BARBERS, THE • 1944 • Donnelly Eddie • ANS • USA
TWO BARK BROTHERS, THE • 1931 • Myers Zion, White Jules • SHT • USA
TWO BATTLES, THE • 1912 • Brooke Van Dyke • USA
TWO BEAUTIFUL CRACKSMEN • 1910 • *Warwick Trading Co* • UKN
TWO BEDS AND NO SLEEP • 1916 • Walsh Phil • USA
TWO BEFORE ZERO • 1962 • Faralla William D. • DOC • USA • RUSSIAN ROULETTE
TWO BIG VAGABONDS (UKN) see **DRIFTER, THE** • 1929
TWO BITS • 1916 • Chatterton Thomas • SHT • USA
TWO-BITS SEATS • 1917 • Windom Lawrence C. • USA
TWO BLACK CROWS • 1929 • Aylott Dave, Symmons E. F. • SHT • UKN
TWO BLACK CROWS IN AFRICA • 1933 • Lamont Charles • SHT • USA
TWO BLACK CROWS IN THE A.E.F. see **ANYBODY'S WAR** • 1930
TWO BLACK SHEEP (UKN) see **TWO SINNERS** • 1935
TWO BLIND MEN, THE (USA) see **DEUX AVEUGLES, LES** • 1900
TWO BLOCKS AWAY see **COHENS AND THE KELLYS, THE** • 1926
TWO BLONDES AND A REDHEAD • 1947 • Dreifuss Arthur • USA
TWO BODYGUARDS, THE see **NIHIKI NO YOJINBO** • 1968
TWO BOLD BAD MEN • 1915 • *Turpin Ben* • USA
TWO BOTTLE BABIES • 1904 • *Bitzer Billy (Ph)* • USA
TWO BOW STRINGS, THE see **DWA SMYCZKI** • 1970
TWO BOYS • 1912 • *Johnson Arthur* • USA
TWO BOYS IN BLUE • 1910 • *Selig* • USA
TWO BRAVE LITTLE HEARTS • 1912 • *Eclair* • USA
TWO BRAVE LITTLE JAPS • 1904 • Williamson James • UKN
TWO BRIDES, THE • 1919 • Jose Edward • USA
TWO BRIGADES see **DWIE BRYGADY** • 1950
TWO BRIGHT BOYS • 1939 • Santley Joseph • USA
TWO BROKEN HEARTS • 1908 • *Vitagraph* • USA
TWO BROTHERS • 1912 • *Pathe* • USA
TWO BROTHERS • 1913 • *Stanley George C.* • USA
TWO BROTHERS • 1934 • Cannon Raymond • USA
TWO BROTHERS see **BRUDER SCHELLENBERG, DIE** • 1926
TWO BROTHERS see **MATIRA MANISHA** • 1967
TWO BROTHERS, THE • 1910 • Griffith D. W. • USA
TWO BROTHERS, THE • 1911 • Stow Percy • UKN
TWO BROTHERS AND A GIRL • 1915 • King Burton L. • USA
TWO BROTHERS AND A SPY • 1912 • Plumb Hay? • UKN
TWO BROTHERS OF THE G.A.R. • 1908 • *Lubin* • USA
TWO BROTHERS RUNNING • 1988 • Robinson Ted • ASL
TWO BROTHERS TRAVEL TOGETHER see **TWEE BROEDERS RY SAAM** • 1968
TWO BROWN BAGS • 1913 • Aylott Dave? • UKN
TWO BROWNS, THE • 1911 • *Champion* • USA
TWO BUDS see **DO KALIYAN** • 1968
TWO, BULDI, TWO see **DVA, BOULDEJ, DVA** • 1930
TWO BY TWO • 1966 • Post Howard • ANS • USA
TWO BY TWO see **DOS POR DOS** • 1968
TWO CAN PLAY • 1926 • Ross Nat • USA • LOVE TEST, THE (UKN)
TWO CAPTAINS see **DVA KAPITANA** • 1956
TWO CARABINEERS, THE see **DUE CARABINIERI, I** • 1984
TWO CASTLES, THE see **DUE CASTELLI, I** • 1963
TWO CAVALIERS, THE • 1977 • Yueh Fung • HKG
TWO-CENT MYSTERY, THE • 1915 • *Badgley Helen* • USA
TWO CENTS WORTH OF HOPE (USA) see **DUE SOLDI DI SPERANZA** • 1951
TWO CENTS WORTH OF HUMAN KINDNESS see **DOLLARS AND SENSE** • 1920
TWO CENTURIES OF BLACK AMERICAN ART • 1976 • *Moss Carlton* • DOC • USA
TWO CHEFS, THE • 1912 • *Rice Herbert* • USA
TWO-CHINNED CHOW • 1923 • Brunel Adrian • UKN
TWO CHIPS AND A MISS • 1952 • Hannah Jack • ANS • USA
TWO CHORUS GIRLS, THE • 1911 • Bouwmeester Theo • UKN
TWO CHRISTMAS HAMPERS • 1911 • Bouwmeester Theo • UKN
TWO CHRISTMAS TIDES • 1909 • *Vitagraph* • USA
TWO CINDERS • 1912 • Trimble Larry • USA
TWO COCKNEYS IN A CANOE see **TWO FOOLS IN A CANOE** • 1898
TWO COLONELS, THE see **DUE COLONNELLI, I** • 1962
TWO COLUMBINES, THE • 1914 • Shaw Harold • UKN
TWO COMRADES-IN-ARMS see **SLUZHILI DVA TOVARISHCHA** • 1968
TWO CONFESSIONS see **KET VALLOMAS** • 1957
TWO CONVICT BROTHERS • 1912 • *Pathe* • USA
TWO CORRIDORS EAST see **BIG LIFT, THE** • 1950
TWO COSMONAUTS AGAINST THEIR WILL see **002 OPERAZIONE LUNA** • 1965
TWO COUSINS • 1908 • *Lubin* • USA

TWO COWARDS, THE • 1913 • Carleton Lloyd B. • USA

TWO CRAZY BUGS see **CRAZY BUGS, THE** • 1908

TWO: CREELY/MCCLURE • 1965 • Brakhage Stan • SHT • USA

TWO CROOKS • 1917 • Heerman Victor • SHT • USA • NOBLE CROOK, A

TWO CROSSES IN DANGER PASS see **DOS CRUCES EN DANGER PASS** • 1967

TWO CROWDED HOURS • 1931 • Powell Michael • UKN

TWO CROWS FROM TACOS • 1956 • Freleng Friz • ANS • USA

TWO CRUSADERS, THE see **DUE CROCIATA, I** • 1968

TWO CUPIDS, THE see **AMOUR NOIR ET AMOUR BLANC** • 1927

TWO-CYLINDER COURTSHIP, A • 1917 • *Rhodes Billie* • USA

TWO DANGEROUS AGENTS see **DUE PERICOLI PUBBLICI, I** • 1965

TWO DAUGHTERS see **TEEN KANYA** • 1961

TWO DAUGHTERS, THE • 1910 • *Imp* • USA

TWO DAUGHTERS OF EVE • 1912 • Griffith D. W. • USA

TWO DAUGHTERS OF HAVANNA • 1911 • *Pathe* • USA

TWO DAYS see **DVA DNYA** • 1927

TWO DAYS -LIKE THE OTHERS see **MINDENNAP ELUNK** • 1963

TWO DAYS OF TURMOIL • 1974 • Surin Alexander • USS

TWO DAYS TO LIVE • 1939 • Tennyson Walter • UKN

TWO DEATHS OF SEAN DOLITTLE • 1975 • Swift Lela • TVM • UKN

TWO DECEIVED OLD MAIDS • 1904 • Collins Alf? • UKN

TWO DECISIONS see **KET ELHATAROZAS** • 1976

TWO DINKY LITTLE DRAMAS OF A NON-SERIOUS KIND • 1914 • Ade George • USA

TWO DOCTORS, THE • 1914 • Lessey George A. • USA

TWO DOLLAR BETTOR • 1951 • Cahn Edward L. • USA • BEGINNER'S LUCK (UKN)

TWO-DOLLAR GLOVES • 1917 • Thayer Otis B. • SHT • USA

TWO DOLLARS, PLEASE! • 1920 • Hall Franklin • USA

TWO DOROTHYS, THE • 1955 • Wasilewski Zenon • ANM • PLN

TWO DOWN, ONE TO GO • 1945 • Capra Frank • DOC • USA

TWO DREAMS OF A NATION: THE FORTIN FAMILY OF QUEBEC AND ALBERTA • 1980 • Richardson Boyce, Dyer John • DOC • CND

TWO-EDGED KNIFE see **FACA DE DOIS GUMES** • 1988

TWO-EDGED SWORD, THE • 1916 • Baker George D. • USA

TWO ELDER CUPIDS • 1914 • Neame Elwin • UKN

TWO ENEMIES see **DO DUSHMAN** • 1968

TWO ENGLISH GIRLS (USA) see **DEUX ANGLAISES ET LE CONTINENT, LES** • 1971

TWO EVIL EYES see **DUE OCCHI DIABOLICI** • 1990

TWO EYES see **SOHO** • 1933

TWO EYES, TWELVE HANDS see **DO ANKHEN BARAH HAATH** • 1958

TWO-FACED QUILLIGAN see **DON JUAN QUILLIGAN** • 1945

TWO-FACED WOLF • 1960 • Hanna William, Barbera Joseph • ANS • USA

TWO-FACED WOMAN • 1941 • Cukor George • USA

TWO FACES see **ANOTHER FACE** • 1935

TWO FACES OF AN ANGEL see **DALAWANG MUKHA NG ANGHEL** • 1968

TWO FACES OF DR. JEKYLL, THE • 1960 • Fisher Terence • UKN • HOUSE OF FRIGHT (USA) ○ JEKYLL'S INFERNO

TWO FACES OF EVIL, THE • 1980 • Gibson Alan • TVM • UKN

TWO FACES OF FEAR, THE (UKN) see **DUE VOLTI DELLA PAURA, I** • 1972

TWO FACES OF GOD see **DWA OBLICZA BOGA** • 1960

TWO FACES OF LOVE see **DALAWANG MUKHA NG PAG-IBIG** • 1967

TWO FACES OF LOVE, THE see **LADY IS A WHORE, THE** • 1972

TWO FAIRY TALES • Pars Heino • ANM • USS

TWO-FAMILY AFFAIR, A • 1914 • *Patheplay* • USA

TWO FATHER CHRISTMASSES, THE • 1913 • Batley Ethyle • UKN

TWO FATHERS, THE • 1910 • Bouwmeester Theo? • UKN

TWO FATHERS, THE • 1911 • Salter Harry • USA

TWO FATHERS, THE • 1912 • *Cooley James* • USA

TWO FATHERS, THE • 1913 • Drouet Robert • USA

TWO FATHERS, THE • 1944 • Asquith Anthony • UKN

TWO FATHERS' JUSTICE • 1985 • Holcomb Rod • TVM • USA

TWO FEATHERS, THE see **DEUX PLUMES, LES** • 1958

TWO FEDORS see **DVA FEDORA** • 1958

TWO FIREMEN, THE see **DUE POMPIERI, I** • 1968

TWO FIST VERSUS SEVEN SAMURAI see **FISTS OF VENGEANCE** • 1974

TWO-FISTED • 1935 • Cruze James • USA • TWO FISTED ○ GETTING SMART

TWO FISTED see **TWO-FISTED** • 1935

TWO-FISTED AGENT (UKN) see **BONANZA TOWN** • 1951

TWO-FISTED BRIDEGROOM, THE see **CIFTE TABANCALI DAMAT** • 1967

TWO FISTED BUCKAROO • 1926 • *Church Fred* • USA

TWO-FISTED GENTLEMAN • 1936 • Wiles Gordon • USA • TWO FISTED GENTLEMAN

TWO FISTED GENTLEMAN see **TWO-FISTED GENTLEMAN** • 1936

TWO-FISTED JEFFERSON • 1922 • Clements Roy • USA • SPARKS OF FLINT ○ FLINTS OF STEEL ○ UNDER ORDERS

TWO-FISTED JONES • 1925 • Sedgwick Edward • USA

TWO FISTED JUSTICE • 1924 • Hatton Richard • USA

TWO-FISTED JUSTICE • 1931 • Durlam G. Arthur • USA

TWO-FISTED JUSTICE • 1942 • Tansey Robert • USA • MIXED JUSTICE (UKN)

TWO-FISTED LAW • 1932 • Lederman D. Ross • USA

TWO FISTED LOVER, THE • 1920 • Laemmle Edward • SHT • USA

TWO-FISTED RANGERS • 1940 • Lewis Joseph H. • USA • FORESTALLED (UKN)

TWO-FISTED SHERIFF • 1937 • Barsha Leon • USA • SHOOTING SHOWDOWN

TWO-FISTED SHERIFF, A • 1925 • Wilson Ben, Hayes Ward • USA

TWO-FISTED STRANGER • 1946 • Nazarro Ray • USA • HIGH STAKES (UKN)

TWO FISTED TENDERFOOT • 1924 • McGowan J. P. • USA

TWO FISTED THOMPSON • 1925 • *Cuneo Lester* • USA

TWO FISTER, THE • 1926 • Wyler William • SHT • USA

TWO-FIVE, THE • 1978 • Kessler Bruce • TVM • USA

TWO + FIVE MISSION HYDRA see **2 + 5 MISSIONE HYDRA** • 1966

TWO FIVES • 1967 • Mozisova Bozena • ANS • CZC

TWO FLAGS WEST • 1950 • Wise Robert • USA • TRUMPET TO THE MORN

TWO FLAMING YOUTHS • 1927 • Waters John • USA • SIDE SHOW, THE (UKN)

TWO FLATS, THE • 1911 • *Washburn Alice* • USA

TWO FLATS AND A SHARP • 1913 • Stow Percy • UKN

TWO FLOWERS see **IRU MALARGAL** • 1967

TWO FOOLS AND THEIR FOLLIES • 1911 • Melies Gaston • USA

TWO FOOLS IN A CANOE • 1898 • Hepworth Cecil M. • UKN • TWO COCKNEYS IN A CANOE

TWO FOOLS THERE WERE • 1916 • *King Cole* • USA

TWO FOR DANGER • 1940 • King George • UKN

TWO FOR THE MONEY • 1942 • French Lloyd • SHT • USA

TWO FOR THE MONEY • 1971 • Kowalski Bernard • TVM • USA

TWO FOR THE MONEY see **ADVENTURE OF THE ACTION HUNTERS, THE** • 1986

TWO FOR THE ROAD • 1967 • Donen Stanley • UKN, USA

TWO FOR THE SEESAW • 1962 • Wise Robert • USA

TWO FOR THE ZOO • 1941 • Fleischer Dave • ANS • USA

TWO FOR TONIGHT • 1935 • Tuttle Frank • USA

TWO FORCES see **KAINUU 39** • 1978

TWO FRAGMENTS OF WORK IN PROGRESS • 1948 • Whitney John, Whitney James • USA

TWO FRESH EGGS • 1930 • Carter Monte • USA

TWO FRIENDS • 1986 • Campion Jane • TVM • ASL

TWO FRIENDS see **DVA DRUGA** • 1955

TWO FRIENDS see **IKI ARKADAS** • 1976

TWO FRIENDS, A MODEL AND A GIRL-FRIEND • 1928 • Popov Alexei • USS

TWO FRIENDS IN THE ARMY see **SLUZHILI DVA TOVARISHCHA** • 1968

TWO FROLICKING YOUTHS, THE • 1909 • *World Film* • USA

TWO FROM TEXAS • 1920 • Feeney Edward • SHT • USA

TWO FROM THE GREAT RIVER see **DWOJE Z WIELKIEJ RZEKI**

TWO FROSTS, THE see **DVA MRAZICI** • 1954

TWO FUGITIVES • 1911 • *Essanay* • USA

TWO FYODORS see **DVA FEDORA** • 1958

TWO GALS AND A GUY • 1951 • Green Alfred E. • USA

TWO GAY BOYS • 1912 • *Powers* • USA

TWO GAY DOGS • 1912 • *Selig* • USA

TWO GENTLEMEN OF THE ROAD • 1910 • *Lubin* • USA

TWO GENTLEMEN SHARING • 1970 • Kotcheff Ted • UKN

TWO GHOSTS AND A GIRL see **DOS FANTASMAS Y UNA MUCHACHA** • 1958

TWO GIRLS • 1911 • *American* • USA

TWO GIRLS • 1914 • MacGregor Norval • USA

TWO GIRLS AND A SAILOR • 1944 • Thorpe Richard • USA • TWO SISTERS AND A SAILOR

TWO GIRLS FOR A MADMAN • 1968 • Brasloff Stanley H. • USA

TWO GIRLS FROM ZEELAND see **TWEE ZEEUWSCHE MEISJES IN ZANDVOORT** • 1914

TWO GIRLS OF THE HILLS • 1913 • *Laughlin Anna* • USA

TWO GIRLS OF THE STREET see **KET LANY AZ UTCAN** • 1939

TWO GIRLS ON BROADWAY • 1940 • Simon S. Sylvan • USA • CHOOSE YOUR PARTNERS (UKN)

TWO GLADIATORS (USA) see **DUE GLADIATORI, I** • 1964

TWO GLASSES, THE • 1913 • *Pilot* • USA

TWO GLUCKS see **LOVE BIRDS** • 1934

TWO GOPHERS FROM TEXAS • 1948 • Davis Arthur • ANS • USA

TWO GRAPES see **DVA ZRNA GROZDJA** • 1955

TWO GREAT GENII, THE • *Chiang Kwang Chou* • HKG

TWO GRENADIERS, THE • 1928 • *British Sound Film Productions* • SHT • UKN

TWO GRILLED FISH (USA) see **FUTATSO-NO YAKIZAKANA** • 1968

TWO GRINNING YOKELS • 1900 • Smith G. A. • UKN

TWO GROOMS FOR A BRIDE (USA) see **RELUCTANT BRIDE, THE** • 1955

TWO GROWNUPS AND A CHILD see **DVOYE I ODNA** • 1989

TWO-GUN BAD MAN, THE • 1915 • *Kriterion* • USA

TWO-GUN BETTY • 1918 • Hickman Howard • USA

TWO GUN CABALLERO • 1931 • Nelson Jack • USA

TWO-GUN CUPID (UKN) see **BAD MAN, THE** • 1941

TWO-GUN GINSBURG • 1929 • Sandrich Mark • SHT • USA

TWO GUN GOOFY • 1952 • Kinney Jack • ANS • USA

TWO GUN GUSSIE • 1918 • Roach Hal • SHT • USA

TWO-GUN HICKS see **PASSING OF TWO-GUN HICKS, THE** • 1914

TWO-GUN JUSTICE • 1938 • James Alan • USA

TWO-GUN LADY • 1956 • Bartlett Richard • USA

TWO GUN LAW • 1937 • Barsha Leon • USA

TWO GUN MAN, THE • 1911 • *Essanay* • USA

TWO-GUN MAN, THE • 1914 • August Edwin • USA

TWO-GUN MAN, THE • 1926 • Kirkland David • USA

TWO GUN MAN, THE • 1931 • Rosen Phil • USA • TWO'S COMPANY (UKN)

TWO-GUN MAN FROM HARLEM • 1938 • Kahn Richard C. • USA

TWO GUN MARSHAL • 1953 • McDonald Frank • MTV • USA

TWO-GUN MICKEY • 1934 • Sharpsteen Ben • ANS • USA

TWO GUN MURPHY • 1928 • *Hoxie Al* • USA

TWO GUN O'BRIEN • 1928 • Horner Robert J. • USA

TWO-GUN OF THE TUMBLEWEEDS • 1927 • Maloney Leo • USA

TWO GUN RUSTY • 1944 • Pal George • ANM • USA

TWO GUN SAP • 1925 • *Farnum Franklyn* • USA

TWO GUN SERMON, THE • 1912 • *Lubin* • USA

TWO GUN SHERIFF • 1941 • Sherman George • USA

TWO GUN TEACHER, THE • 1954 • McDonald Frank • MTV • USA

TWO-GUN TRIXIE • 1919 • *Russell Dan* • SHT • USA

TWO-GUN TROUBADOUR • 1939 • Johnston Raymond K. • USA • LONE TROUBADOUR, THE (UKN)

TWO GUNS AND A BADGE • 1954 • Collins Lewis D. • USA

TWO GUYS FROM MILWAUKEE • 1946 • Butler David • USA • ROYAL FLUSH (UKN)

TWO GUYS FROM TEXAS • 1948 • Butler David • USA • TWO TEXAS KNIGHTS (UKN)

TWO HALF-TIMES IN HELL see **KET FELIDO A POKOLBAN** • 1961

TWO HALVES OF THE HEART, THE see **DVIJE POLOVINE SRCA** • 1983

TWO HEADED GIANT • 1939 • Rasinski Connie • ANS • USA

TWO-HEADED SPY, THE • 1958 • De Toth Andre • UKN

TWO HEADS ON A PILLOW • 1934 • Nigh William • USA

TWO HEART BEATS • 1971 • Imberman Samuel • ISR

TWO HEARTS AND A BOAT see **TVA HJARTAN OCH EN SKUTA** • 1932

TWO HEARTS AND A SHIP • 1915 • Christie Al • USA

TWO HEARTS AND A THIEF • 1913 • *Nestor* • USA

TWO HEARTS AND A THIEF • 1915 • Dillon John Francis • USA

TWO HEARTS IN HARMONY • 1935 • Beaudine William • UKN

TWO HEARTS IN THE RAIN see **MEGURI-AI** • 1968

TWO HEARTS IN WALTZ TIME • 1934 • Gallone Carmine, May Joe • UKN, FRG

TWO HEARTS IN WALTZ TIME see **ZWEI HERZEN IM 3/4-TAKT** • 1930

TWO HEARTS THAT BEAT AS ONE see **TWO SOULS WITH BUT A SINGLE THOUGHT, OR, A MAID AND THREE MEN** • 1913

TWO HEARTS THAT BEAT AS TEN • 1915 • *Beery Wallace* • USA

TWO HENPECKED HUSBANDS see **KAKSI VIHTORIA** • 1939

TWO HENS • Ruutsalo Eino • SHT • FNL

TWO HEROES • 1909 • *Urban-Eclipse* • USA

TWO HEROES, THE • 1911 • *Edison* • USA

TWO HUNDRED GUINEAS REWARD see **ADVENTURES OF DICK TURPIN -200 GUINEAS REWARD, DEAD OR ALIVE, THE** • 1912

TWO HUNDRED MOTELS see **200 MOTELS** • 1971

TWO HUNGRY TRAMPS • 1914 • *Royal* • USA

TWO IMPS, THE • 1905 • Fitzhamon Lewin • UKN

TWO IN A CROWD • 1936 • Green Alfred E. • USA

TWO IN A GREAT CITY see **ZWEI IN EINER GROSSEN STADT** • 1942

TWO IN A MILLION (UKN) see **EAST OF FIFTH AVENUE** • 1933

TWO IN A SLEEPING BAG (USA) see **KLEINES ZELT UND GROSSE LIEBE** • 1956

TWO IN A TAXI • 1941 • Florey Robert • USA • ONE WAY STREET

TWO IN LOVE see **DVOYE** • 1965

TWO IN REVOLT • 1936 • Tryon Glenn • USA

TWO IN THE BUSH see **SAFARI 3000** • 1982

TWO IN THE DARK • 1936 • Stoloff Ben • USA

TWO IN THE SHADOW see **MIDARE-GUMO** • 1967

TWO INTO TWO -ONCE • 1970 • *Stacey Dist.* • USA

TWO JAKES, THE • 1989 • Nicholson Jack • USA

TWO JILLS AND A JACK • 1947 • White Jules • SHT • USA

TWO JOLLY GOOD FELLOWS • 1900 • Smith G. A. • UKN • THEY ARE JOLLY GOOD FELLOWS

TWO JONES • 1915 • *Simon Louis* • USA

TWO KENNEDYS, THE (USA) see **DUE KENNEDY, I** • 1969

TWO KENNEDYS.. A VIEW FROM EUROPE, THE see **DUE KENNEDY, I** • 1969

TWO KENTUCKY BOYS • 1917 • France Floyd • SHT • USA

TWO KINDS OF LOVE • 1920 • Eason B. Reeves • USA

TWO KINDS OF LOVE • 1983 • Bender Jack • TVM • USA

TWO KINDS OF WOMEN • 1922 • Campbell Colin • USA

TWO KINDS OF WOMEN • 1932 • De Mille William C. • USA

TWO KINGS see **TVA KONUNGAR** • 1925

TWO KISSES • 1914 • *Royal* • USA

TWO KNIGHTS see **DWAJ RYCERZE** • 1964

TWO KNIGHTS IN A BARROOM • 1912 • *Edison* • USA

TWO KNIGHTS IN BROOKLYN • 1949 • Neumann Kurt • USA • TWO MUGS FROM BROOKLYN

TWO KUNI LEMEL • 1966 • ISR

TWO LAMPS • 1962 • Wilkosz Tadeusz • ANM • PLN

TWO LANCASHIRE LASSIES IN LONDON • 1916 • Aylott Dave • UKN

TWO-LANE BLACKTOP • 1971 • Hellman Monte • USA

TWO LAPS OF HONOUR • 1961 • Schofield Stanley • UKN

TWO LATINS FROM MANHATTAN • 1941 • Barton Charles T. • USA

TWO LAUGHS • 1917 • *Turpin Ben* • SHT • USA

TWO LAZY CROWS • 1936 • *Mintz Charles (P)* • ANS • USA

TWO LEAP YEAR PROPOSALS • 1904 • Fitzhamon Lewin • UKN

TWO LEFT FEET • 1963 • Baker Roy Ward • UKN

TWO LEFT HANDS see **DWIE LEWE RECE** • 1968

TWO LEGENDS • Aksenchuk Ivan • ANS • USS

TWO LETTER ALIBI • 1962 • Lynn Robert • UKN

TWO LIONS IN THE SUN see **DEUX LIONS AU SOLEIL** • 1980

TWO LIPS AND JULEPS: OR, SOUTHERN LOVE AND NORTHERN EXPOSURE • 1932 • *Tearle Conway* • SHT • USA

TWO LIPS IN HOLLAND • 1926 • Bacon Lloyd?, Marshall George? • SHT • USA

TWO LITTLE ANGELS • 1914 • Fitzhamon Lewin? • UKN

TWO LITTLE BEARS, THE • 1961 • Hood Randall • USA

TWO LITTLE BIRDS see **NIWA NO KOTORI** • 1922

TWO LITTLE BREADWINNERS • 1908 • *Lubin* • USA

TWO LITTLE BRITONS • 1914 • Shaw Harold • UKN

TWO LITTLE DROMIOS • 1914 • *Anderson Mignon* • USA

TWO LITTLE DRUMMER BOYS • 1928 • Samuelson G. B. • UKN

TWO LITTLE FROSTS see **DVA MRAZICI** • 1954

TWO LITTLE GIRLS • 1911 • *Thanhouser* • USA

TWO LITTLE IMPS • 1917 • Buel Kenean • USA

TWO LITTLE INDIANS • 1953 • Hanna William, Barbera Joseph • ANS • USA

TWO LITTLE KITTENS • 1913 • Seay Charles M. • USA

TWO LITTLE LAMBS • 1935 • *Lantz Walter (P)* • ANS • USA

TWO LITTLE MAGIC OXEN see **KET BORS OKROCSKE** • 1955

TWO LITTLE MOTORISTS • 1908 • *Urban-Eclipse* • USA

TWO LITTLE MOTORISTS • 1908 • Booth W. R.? • UKN
TWO LITTLE PALS • 1913 • Buckland Warwick? • UKN
TWO LITTLE PUPS • 1936 • Ising Rudolf • ANS • USA
TWO LITTLE RABBITS see **DOI IEPURASI** • 1952
TWO LITTLE RANGERS • 1912 • Blache Alice • USA
TWO LITTLE SHOES • 1908 • *Lubin* • USA
TWO LITTLE URCHINS, THE see **DEUX GAMINES, LES** • 1920
TWO LITTLE VAGABONDS • 1914 • Lambart Harry • USA
TWO LITTLE VAGABONDS see **DEUX GOSSES, LES** • 1928
TWO LITTLE VAGABONDS: OR, THE PUGILISTIC PARSON • 1903 • Collins Alf? • UKN
TWO LITTLE WAIFS • 1905 • Williamson James • UKN
TWO LITTLE WAIFS • 1914 • *Bison* • USA
TWO LITTLE WAIFS: A MODERN FAIRY TALE • 1910 • Griffith D. W. • USA
TWO LITTLE WOODEN SHOES • 1920 • Morgan Sidney • UKN
TWO LIVES • 1911 • *Selig* • USA
TWO LIVES • 1913 • *Kirkwood James* • USA
TWO LIVES • 1961 • Lukov Leonid • USS
TWO LIVES see **DVOJI ZIVOT** • 1924
TWO LIVES see **ZWEI MENSCHEN** • 1930
TWO LIVES see **DVE ZHIZNI** • 1961
TWO LIVES OF CAROL LETNER, THE • 1981 • Leacock Philip • TVM • USA
TWO LIVING AND ONE DEAD see **TVA LEVANDE OCH EN DOD** • 1961
TWO LIVING, ONE DEAD (UKN) see **TVA LEVANDE OCH EN DOD** • 1961
TWO LOCAL YOKELS • 1945 • White Jules • SHT • USA
TWO LOST WORLDS • 1951 • Dawn Norman • USA
TWO LOVERS • 1928 • Niblo Fred • USA • PASSIONATE ADVENTURE, THE
TWO LOVERS AROUND THE WORLD see **GIRO DEL MONDO DEGLI INNAMORATI DI PEYNET** • 1974
TWO LOVES • 1912 • Melies Gaston • USA
TWO LOVES • 1961 • Walters Charles • USA • SPINSTER (UKN) ○ I'LL SAVE MY LOVE
TWO LUCKY JIMS • 1910 • *American* • USA
TWO LUNATICS • 1913 • Smalley Phillips • USA
TWO MAFIOSI FROM THE F.B.I., THE see **SPIE VENGONO DAL SEMIFREDDO, LE** • 1966
TWO MAFIOSI VS. GOLDGINGER see **DUE MAFIOSI CONTRO GOLDGINGER** • 1965
TWO MAGIC BULLS, THE see **KET BORS OKROCSKE** • 1955
TWO MAIDS • 1910 • *Imp* • USA
TWO-MAN SUBMARINE • 1944 • Landers Lew • USA
TWO MARCHES • 1972 • Povh Dusan • SHT • YGS
TWO MARINES AND A GENERAL see **DUE MARINES E UN GENERALE** • 1966
TWO MEMORIES • 1909 • Griffith D. W. • USA
TWO MEN • 1910 • Salter Harry • USA
TWO MEN • 1912 • *Gem* • USA
TWO MEN • 1912 • *Republic* • USA
TWO MEN • 1934 • Farrow John • USA
TWO MEN AND A GIRL • 1911 • *Powers* • USA
TWO MEN AND A GIRL • 1911 • *Essanay* • USA
TWO MEN AND A GIRL • 1912 • *Selig* • USA
TWO MEN AND A GIRL (UKN) see **HONEYMOON** • 1947
TWO MEN AND A GOAT • 1966 • Horatio Edward Jones • NGR
TWO MEN AND A MAID • 1929 • Archainbaud George • USA
TWO MEN AND A MULE (NO.1) • 1913 • *Reliance* • USA
TWO MEN AND A MULE (NO.2) • 1913 • *Reliance* • USA
TWO MEN AND A MULE (NO.3) • 1913 • *Reliance* • USA
TWO MEN AND A MULE (NO.4) • 1913 • *Reliance* • USA
TWO MEN AND A WARDROBE see **DWAJ LUDZIE Z SZAFA** • 1958
TWO MEN AND A WIDOW see **TVA MAN OM EN ANKA** • 1933
TWO MEN AND A WOMAN • 1913 • Parker Lem B. • USA
TWO MEN AND A WOMAN • 1917 • Humphrey William • USA
TWO MEN AND A WOMAN(?) see **UNCHASTENED WOMAN, THE** • 1918
TWO MEN AND THE LAW • 1912 • *Conway Jack* • USA
TWO MEN IN A BOX • 1938 • Hopwood R. A. • UKN
TWO MEN IN MANHATTAN see **DEUX HOMMES DANS MANHATTAN** • 1959
TWO MEN OF KARAMOJA • 1974 • Jones Eugene S. • DOC • USA • WILD AND THE BRAVE, THE
TWO MEN OF SANDY BAR • 1916 • Carleton Lloyd B. • USA
TWO MEN OF THE DESERT • 1913 • Griffith D. W. • USA
TWO MEN OF TINTED BUTTE • 1919 • Dawn Norman • SHT • USA
TWO MEN WHO WAITED • 1914 • Davies Hal • USA
TWO MERCHANTS, THE • 1913 • Seay Charles M. • USA
TWO MERRY ADVENTURES (USA) see **ZWEI LUSTIGE ABENTEUER** • 1938
TWO MINDS FOR MURDER (UKN) see **QUALCUNO DIETRO LA PORTA** • 1971
TWO-MINUTE WARNING • 1976 • Peerce Larry • USA
TWO MINUTES • 1939 • Taylor Donald • UKN • SILENCE, THE (USA)
TWO MINUTES SILENCE • 1933 • McDonagh Paulette • ASL
TWO MINUTES TO GO • 1921 • Ray Charles • USA
TWO MINUTES TO PLAY • 1937 • Hill Robert F. • USA
TWO MIRACULOUS DAYS • 1972 • Mirsky Lev • USS
TWO MONKS see **DOS MONJES** • 1934
TWO MONKS see **MANDALA** • 1981
TWO-MOON JUNCTION • 1988 • King Zalman • USA
TWO MOONS • 1920 • Le Saint Edward J. • USA
TWO MOONS IN AUGUST see **DHIO FENGARIA TON AVGOUSTO** • 1979
TWO MOTHERS • 1913 • *Patheplay* • USA
TWO MOTHERS • 1916 • Carleton Lloyd B. • SHT • USA
TWO MOTHERS see **ZWEI MUTTER** • 1957
TWO MOTHERS, THE • 1911 • *Essanay* • USA
TWO MOTHERS, THE • 1911 • *Reliance* • USA
TWO MOTHERS, THE (USA) see **DUE MADRI, I** • 1938
TWO MOUSEKETEERS • 1951 • Hanna William, Barbera Joseph • ANS • USA
TWO MRS. CARROLLS, THE • 1947 • Godfrey Peter • USA
TWO MRS. GRENVILLES, THE • 1987 • Erman John • TVM • USA
TWO MRS. WHITES, THE • 1909 • *Vitagraph* • USA
TWO MUGS FROM BROOKLYN see **TWO KNIGHTS IN BROOKLYN** • 1949
TWO MULES FOR SISTER SARA • 1970 • Siegel Don • USA, MXC
TWO MUSKETEERS see **BLAZNOVA KRONIKA** • 1964
TWO MYSTERIOUS MEN see **DWAJ PANOWIE N.** • 1962
TWO NATURES WITH HIM, THE • 1915 • Santschi Thomas • USA
TWO NAUGHTY BOYS • 1909 • Aylott Dave • UKN
TWO NAUGHTY BOYS SPRINKLING THE SPOONS • 1898 • Williamson James • UKN
TWO NAUGHTY BOYS TEASING THE COBBLER • 1898 • Williamson James • UKN
TWO NAUGHTY BOYS UPSETTING THE SPOONS • 1898 • Williamson James • UKN
TWO NECKTIES (USA) see **ZWEI KRAWATTEN** • 1930
TWO NEIGHBOURS see **DOI VECINI** • 1958
TWO NESTS, TWO BIRDS see **DALAWANG PUGAD, DALAWANG IBON** • 1977
TWO NEWS ITEMS • 1916 • Sloman Edward • SHT • USA
TWO NIGHTS WITH CLEOPATRA see **DUE NOTTI CON CLEOPATRA** • 1953
TWO NOTORIOUS MEN STRIKE AGAIN see **AKUMYO NOBORI** • 1965
TWO NYMPHS OF THE WELL, THE • 1953 • Vickman Leon • SHT • USA
TWO O'CLOCK COURAGE • 1945 • Mann Anthony • USA
TWO O'CLOCK IN THE MORNING • 1929 • Marton Andrew • USA • HOUR OF FEAR, THE (UKN)
TWO O'CLOCK TRAIN, THE • 1916 • Dillon Eddie • SHT • USA
TWO OF A KIND • 1912 • *Majestic* • USA
TWO OF A KIND • 1913 • *Nash Edna* • USA
TWO OF A KIND • 1914 • Plumb Hay? • UKN
TWO OF A KIND • 1915 • *Joker* • USA
TWO OF A KIND • 1916 • *Jockey* • USA
TWO OF A KIND • 1916 • Humphrey Orral • *Beauty* • SHT • USA
TWO OF A KIND • 1917 • *Rhodes Billie* • USA
TWO OF A KIND • 1949 • Gilkison Anthony • UKN
TWO OF A KIND • 1951 • Levin Henry • USA • LEFTY FARRELL
TWO OF A KIND • 1982 • Young Roger • TVM • USA
TWO OF A KIND • 1984 • Herzfeld John • USA
TWO OF A KIND see **ROUNDERS, THE** • 1914
TWO OF A SUIT • 1915 • Collins Edwin J.? • UKN
TWO OF A TRADE • 1928 • Malins Geoffrey H. • UKN
TWO OF SCOTCH HOT • 1914 • *A.r. Films* • UKN
TWO OF THE BRAVEST • 1915 • *World* • USA
TWO OF THE FINEST • 1915 • *Weber Joe* • SHT • USA
TWO OF THEM, THE see **OK KETTEN** • 1977
TWO OF US, THE • Li Yu-Ning • TWN
TWO OF US, THE see **VI TVA** • 1939
TWO OF US, THE (USA) see **JACK OF ALL TRADES** • 1936
TWO OF US, THE (USA) see **VIEIL HOMME ET L'ENFANT, LE** • 1967
TWO OFF THE CUFF • 1968 • Godfrey Bob • CMP • UKN
TWO OFFICERS • 1911 • *Fuller Mary* • USA
TWO OLD MEN • 1912 • *Reliance* • USA
TWO OLD MEN WITH WENS • 1959 • *Ninyo & Dentsu* • ANS • JPN
TWO OLD PALS • 1912 • *Selig* • USA
TWO OLD SPORTS • 1900 • Smith G. A. • UKN
TWO OLD SPORTS AT THE MUSIC HALL, THE • 1902 • Smith G. A. • UKN
TWO OLD SPORTS' GAME OF NAP • 1900 • Smith G. A. • UKN • WINNING HAND, THE
TWO OLD SPORTS' POLITICAL DISCUSSION, THE • 1900 • Smith G. A. • UKN
TWO OLD TARS • 1913 • Sennett Mack • USA
TWO ON A BENCH • 1971 • Paris Jerry • TVM • USA
TWO ON A DOORSTEP • 1936 • Huntington Lawrence • UKN
TWO ON A GUILLOTINE • 1965 • Conrad William • USA
TWO ON A TOWER see **PARIS IN SPRING** • 1935
TWO ON THE MOVE see **HIKKOSHI FUFU** • 1928
TWO ON THE TILES • 1951 • Guillermin John • UKN
TWO OR THREE THINGS I KNOW ABOUT HER (UKN) see **DEUX OU TROIS CHOSES QUE JE SAIS D'ELLE** • 1967
TWO ORPHANS, THE • 1906 • Collins Alf? • UKN
TWO ORPHANS, THE • 1911 • Turner Otis • USA
TWO ORPHANS, THE • 1915 • Brenon Herbert • USA
TWO ORPHANS, THE • 1916 • Turner Otis • SHT • USA
TWO ORPHANS, THE see **DEUX ORPHELINES, LES** • 1910
TWO ORPHANS, THE see **ORPHANS OF THE STORM** • 1921
TWO ORPHANS, THE see **DEUX GOSSES, LES** • 1928
TWO ORPHANS, THE see **DEUX ORPHELINES, LES** • 1932
TWO ORPHANS, THE see **DUE ORFANELLE, LE** • 1942
TWO ORPHANS, THE (USA) see **DUE ORFANELLE, LE** • 1966
TWO ORPHANS OF THE G.A.R. • 1909 • *Lubin* • USA
TWO OUTLAWS, THE • 1928 • McRae Henry • USA
TWO OVERCOATS • 1911 • *Vitagraph* • USA
TWO PALS AND A GAL • 1914 • *Joker* • USA
TWO PATHS, THE • 1911 • Griffith D. W. • USA
TWO PEASANTS see **NJIH DVOJICA** • 1955
TWO PENITENTS, THE • 1912 • *Vitagraph* • USA
TWO PENNIES OF HOPE see **DUE SOLDI DI SPERANZA** • 1951
TWO PENNYWORTH OF HOPE see **DUE SOLDI DI SPERANZA** • 1951
TWO PEOPLE • 1973 • Wise Robert • USA
TWO PEOPLE see **TVA MANNISKOR** • 1945
TWO PEOPLE see **TO** • 1964
TWO PERFECT GENTS • 1910 • Wilson Frank? • UKN
TWO PHOTOGRAPHS see **KET FENYKEP** • 1975
TWO PIECES FOR THE PRECARIOUS LIFE • 1961 • Landow George • USA
TWO PISTOLS AND A COWARD see **DUE PISTOLE E UN VIGLIACCO** • 1968
TWO PLUCKY GIRLS • 1911 • *American* • USA
TWO PLUS ONE see **PRATINIDHI** • 1964
TWO POLICEMEN, THE see **DUE VIGILI, I** • 1967
TWO POP-UP FABLES • 1914 • *Essanay* • USA
TWO PORTRAITS see **KET ARCKEP** • 1965
TWO PORTRAITS, THE see **VENGEANCE OF DURAND, OR THE TWO PORTRAITS, THE** • 1913
TWO PORTS AND A MINE see **DOS PUERTOS Y UN CERRO** • 1977
TWO PORTS AND A MOUNTAIN see **DOS PUERTOS Y UN CERRO** • 1977
TWO POUNDER, THE • 1931 • Smith Percy • UKN
TWO POWDERS, THE • 1912 • *Cines* • ITL
TWO PRETTY DANCERS • 1903 • *Paul R. W.* • UKN
TWO PRISONERS see **KET FOGOLY** • 1939
TWO PUBLIC ENEMIES see **DUE PERICOLI PUBBLICI, I** • 1965
TWO PURSES, THE see **TWO SETS OF FURS** • 1913
TWO QUEENS AND A KING • 1981 • Jongerius Otto • NTH
TWO RABBITS see **DOI IEPURASI** • 1952
TWO RANCHMEN, THE • 1913 • *Essanay* • USA
TWO RASCALS see **TVA SKONA JUVELER** • 1954
TWO RED ROSES see **ZWEI ROTE ROSEN** • 1928
TWO REFORMATIONS, THE • 1911 • *Anderson Broncho Billy* • USA
TWO RENEGADES, THE • 1917 • Smith David • SHT • USA
TWO REPAIRS see **DWIE NAPRAWY** • 1964
TWO ROADS, THE • 1911 • *Yankee* • USA
TWO ROADS, THE • 1915 • Shaw Harold • UKN
TWO ROADS (UKN) see **TEXAS STAGECOACH** • 1940
TWO RODE TOGETHER • 1961 • Ford John • USA
TWO ROOMS, THE • 1911 • *Yankee* • USA
TWO ROSES, THE • 1910 • *Thanhouser* • USA
TWO ROSES, THE • 1914 • *Hawley Ormi* • USA
TWO ROSES AND A GOLDEN-ROD • 1969 • Zugsmith Albert • USA
TWO RRRINGOS OF TEXAS see **DUE RRRINGOS NEL TEXAS** • 1967
TWO RUNAWAYS, THE • 1912 • *Kalem* • USA
TWO SACKS OF POTATOES • 1913 • Duncan William • USA
TWO SAURIES see **NIHIKI-NO SAMA** • 1959
TWO SCAMPS, THE see **TWO YOUNG SCAMPS** • 1905
TWO SCENTS' WORTH • 1955 • Jones Charles M. • ANS • USA
TWO SCRAMBLED • 1918 • Roach Hal • SHT • USA
TWO SEATS AT THE OPERA • 1916 • *Garwood William* • SHT • USA
TWO SECONDS • 1932 • LeRoy Mervyn • USA
TWO SENORITAS FROM CHICAGO • 1943 • Woodruff Frank • USA • TWO SENORITAS (UKN)
TWO SENORITAS (UKN) see **TWO SENORITAS FROM CHICAGO** • 1943
TWO SENTENCES, THE • 1915 • Ricketts Thomas • USA
TWO SENTIMENTAL TOMMIES • 1905 • Fitzhamon Lewin • UKN
TWO SETS OF FURS • 1913 • Costello Maurice • USA • TWO PURSES, THE
TWO SHADOWS • 1938 • French Lloyd • SHT • USA
TWO SHALL BE BORN • 1924 • Bennett Whitman • USA
TWO SHOTS IN THE SUN see **DOIS TIROS NO SOL** • 1977
TWO-SIDED COIN see **SEKE DO ROU** • 1968
TWO SIDES, THE • 1911 • Griffith D. W. • USA
TWO SIDES OF A STORY • 1909 • *Essanay* • USA
TWO SIDES OF THE DOLLAR, THE see **DUE FACCE DEL DOLLARO, LE** • 1967
TWO SIDES TO A BOAT • 1913 • *B & C* • UKN
TWO SIDES TO A STORY • 1913 • *August Edwin* • USA
TWO SILENT FRIENDS • 1972 • Fritz-Nemeth Paul • DOC • CND
TWO SINNERS • 1935 • Lubin Arthur • USA • TWO BLACK SHEEP (UKN)
TWO SISTERS • 1929 • Pembroke Scott • USA
TWO SISTERS • 1938 • Blake Ben K. • USA
TWO SISTERS, THE • 1913 • *Thanhouser* • USA
TWO SISTERS AND A SAILOR see **TWO GIRLS AND A SAILOR** • 1944
TWO SISTERS FROM BOSTON • 1946 • Koster Henry • USA
TWO SKITTLE HEADS, THE • 1972 • Bacso Peter • HNG
TWO SLAVES, THE • 1914 • *Reliance* • USA
TWO SLIPS AND A MISS • 1916 • MacMackin Archer • USA
TWO SMALL FISH IN THE SPIDER'S WEB see **KOKOVIOS KE SPAROS STA DIATIA TIS ARAHNIS** • 1967
TWO SMALL TOWN ROMEOS • 1916 • Chaudet Louis W. • SHT • USA
TWO SMART MEN • 1940 • Newman Widgey R. • UKN
TWO SMART PEOPLE • 1946 • Dassin Jules • USA • TIME FOR TWO
TWO SMARTIES • 1914 • *Superba* • USA
TWO SMITHS AND A HALF • 1916 • Greene Clay M. • SHT • USA
TWO SNAILS (USA) see **DVA PUZA** • 1960
TWO SOCIAL CALLS • 1913 • *Holubar Allen* • USA
TWO SOLDIERS see **DVA BOITSA** • 1943
TWO SOLDIERS see **DWAJ ZOLNIERZE** • 1970
TWO SOLDIERS EAST AND WEST see **HELL IN THE PACIFIC** • 1968
TWO SOLITUDES see **DEUX SOLITUDES** • 1978
TWO SONS, THE • 1909 • *Vitagraph* • USA
TWO SONS, THE • 1909 • *Imp* • USA
TWO SONS (UKN) see **BROTHERS** • 1929
TWO-SOULED WOMAN, THE • 1918 • Clifton Elmer • USA
TWO SOULED WOMAN, THE see **UNTAMEABLE, THE** • 1923
TWO SOULS • 1912 • *Thanhouser* • USA
TWO SOULS WITH BUT A SINGLE THOUGHT, OR, A MAID AND THREE MEN • 1913 • Angeles Bert • USA • TWO HEARTS THAT BEAT AS ONE
TWO SPIES • 1913 • *Gaumont* • USA
TWO SPIES, THE • 1912 • *Coombs Guy* • USA
TWO SPOT JOE • 1915 • MacDonald Donald • USA
TWO STAGE SISTERS see **WUTAI JIEMEI** • 1964
TWO STEPCHILDREN • 1914 • Marston Theodore • USA
TWO STONE LANTERNS see **FUTATSU DORO** • 1933
TWO STORIES • 1962 • Amalrik Leonid • ANS • USS
TWO STRANGERS FROM NOWHERE • 1913 • *Solax* • USA
TWO STRAY SOULS • 1915 • Morrissey George • USA
TWO-STROKE ENGINE, THE • 1959 • Orrom Michael • UKN
TWO SUITS • 1910 • *Solax* • USA
TWO SUNDAYS see **DVA VOSKRESENYA** • 1963
TWO SUPERCOPS see **DUE SUPERPIEDI QUASI PIATTI, I** • 1977
TWO TALENTED VAGABONDS • 1908 • Melies Georges • FRN
TWO TARS • 1928 • Parrott James • SHT • USA
TWO TEXAS KNIGHTS (UKN) see **TWO GUYS FROM TEXAS** • 1948

TWO THIEVES • 1913 • *Smalley Phillips* • USA
TWO THIEVES, THE • 1914 • *Mcquarrie Murdock* • USA
TWO THOROUGHBREDS • 1939 • Hively Jack • USA • SUNSET
TWO THOUSAND DOLLARS FOR COYOTE see **DOS MIL DOLARES POR COYOTE** • 1967
TWO THOUSAND MANIACS! • 1964 • Lewis Herschell G. • USA • 2,000 MANIACS
TWO THOUSAND-YEAR ANNIVERSARY OF PECS • 1955 • Kollanyi Agoston • HNG
TWO THOUSAND YEARS' ROAD, THE see **BIN YILLIK YOL** • 1968
TWO TICKETS FOR A DAY SHOW see **DVA BILYETA NA DNEVNOY SEANS** • 1967
TWO TICKETS FOR THE MATINEE see **DVA BILYETA NA DNEVNOY SEANS** • 1967
TWO TICKETS TO BROADWAY • 1951 • Kern James V. • USA
TWO TICKETS TO LONDON • 1943 • Marin Edwin L. • USA
TWO TICKETS TO PARIS! • 1962 • Garrison Greg • USA
TWO TICKETS TO TERROR • 1964 • Adamson Al • USA
TWO TIMES A DREAM see **TABLICZKA MARZENIA** • 1968
TWO TIMES GUIDE see **DUE VOLTE GUIDA** • 1968
TWO TIMES TWO see **START THE REVOLUTION WITHOUT ME** • 1970
TWO TIMES TWO ARE SOMETIMES FIVE see **KETSZER KETTO NEHA 5** • 1954
TWO TIMID ONES, THE see **DEUX TIMIDES, LES** • 1928
TWO TIPSY FELLOWS IN A BOAT • 1898 • *Cinematograph Co* • UKN
TWO TIPSY PALS AND THE TAILOR'S DUMMY • 1899 • *Paul R. W.* • UKN
TWO TIRED see **TOO TIRED** • 1919
TWO TO ONE ON PIMPLE • 1913 • Evans Fred, Evans Joe • UKN
TWO TO TANGO see **MATAR ES MORIR UN POCO** • 1987
TWO TOMBOYS, THE • 1906 • Collins Alf? • UKN
TWO TON BABY SITTER • 1960 • Tendlar Dave • ANS • USA
TWO TONS OF TURQUOISE TO TAOS TONIGHT • 1976 • Downey Robert • USA
TWO TOO MANY • 1913 • McRae Henry • USA
TWO TOO YOUNG • 1936 • Douglas Gordon • SHT • USA
TWO TOPERS • 1905 • *Bitzer Billy (Ph)* • USA
TWO TOUGH KIDS • 1908 • Wormald S. • UKN
TWO TOUGH TENDER FEET • 1918 • Jones F. Richard • SHT • USA
TWO TRAINS A DAY see **NAPONTA KET VONAT** • 1977
TWO TRAMPS • 1907 • *Walturdaw* • UKN
TWO TRAMPS AND THE TAILOR'S DUMMY • 1905 • *Walturdaw* • UKN
TWO TRUMPETS FOR ST. ANDREW • 1968 • Brealey Gil • DOC • ASL
TWO TURKISH EGGS • 1988 • *Piatas Dimitris* • GRC
TWO TWINS • 1923 • Stromberg Hunt • USA
TWO UNDER THE SKY see **DVAMA POD NEBETO** • 1962
TWO UP A TREE • 1913 • *Patheplay* • USA
TWO VALENTINES • 1911 • *Edison* • USA
TWO VANREVELS, THE • 1914 • Ridgely Richard • USA
TWO VICTORIES see **DVE POBEDI** • 1956
TWO VIKINGS, THE see **HAR KOMMER BARSARKARNA** • 1965
TWO VIRTUOUS WOMEN see **ZHEN NU** • 1988
TWO VOICES see **DEUX VOIX** • 1966
TWO WAGONS -BOTH COVERED • 1924 • Wagner Robert • SHT • USA
TWO WAIFS, THE • 1916 • *Supreme* • USA
TWO WAIFS AND A STRAY • 1910 • *Vitagraph* • USA
TWO WARSAWS see **DWIE WARSZAWY** • 1962
TWO WAY STREET • 1931 • King George • UKN
TWO WAY STRETCH • 1960 • Day Robert • UKN • NOTHING BARRED
TWO WAYS • 1956 • Lukov Leonid • USS
TWO WEEKS • 1920 • Franklin Sidney A. • USA
TWO WEEKS AND A HALF see **THREE FOOLISH WEEKS** • 1924
TWO WEEKS IN ANOTHER TOWN • 1962 • Minnelli Vincente • USA
TWO WEEKS IN SEPTEMBER (UKN) see **A COEUR JOIE** • 1967
TWO WEEKS OFF • 1929 • Beaudine William • USA
TWO WEEKS TO LIVE • 1943 • St. Clair Malcolm • USA
TWO WEEKS' VACATION • 1952 • Kinney Jack • ANS • USA
TWO WEEKS WITH LOVE • 1950 • Rowland Roy • USA • TENDER HOURS, THE
TWO WEEKS WITH PAY • 1921 • Campbell Maurice • USA
TWO WERE LONELY, THE see **SAMOTNOSC WE DWOJE** • 1968
TWO WESTERN PATHS • 1913 • *Essanay* • USA
TWO WHITE ARMS • 1932 • Niblo Fred • UKN • WIVES BEWARE (USA)
TWO WHITE ROSES • 1911 • Merwin Bannister • USA
TWO WHO DARED (USA) see **WOMAN ALONE, A** • 1936
TWO WHOLE DAYS see **ZWEI GANZE TAGE** • 1971
TWO WHORES: OR A LOVE STORY WHICH ENDS IN MARRIAGE see **DOS PUTAS, O HISTORIA DE AMOR QUE TERMINA EN BODA** • 1974
TWO WIDOWS • 1913 • Sennett Mack • USA
TWO WINGS see **DOS ALAS** • 1967
TWO WISE MAIDS • 1937 • Rosen Phil • USA
TWO WITHOUT SCARVES • 1958 • Yen Kung • CHN
TWO WIVES see **TSUMA YO BARA NO YONI** • 1935
TWO WIVES see **TSUMA FUTARI** • 1967
TWO WIVES AT ONE WEDDING • 1961 • Tully Montgomery • UKN
TWO WIVES FOR HENRY • 1933 • Brunel Adrian • UKN
TWO WOLVES AND A LAMB • 1911 • *Vitagraph* • USA
TWO WOMEN • 1912 • *Republic* • USA
TWO WOMEN • 1912 • *Powers* • USA
TWO WOMEN • 1915 • Ince Ralph • USA
TWO WOMEN • 1919 • Ince Ralph • USA
TWO WOMEN • 1930 • Roshal Grigori • USS
TWO WOMEN • Moguy Leonide • FRN
TWO WOMEN • 1975 • Ramzi Hassan • EGY
TWO WOMEN see **GHOSTS OF YESTERDAY** • 1918
TWO WOMEN see **TVA KVINNOR** • 1947
TWO WOMEN see **TVA KVINNOR** • 1974
TWO WOMEN see **OK KETTEN** • 1977
TWO WOMEN AND A MAN • 1909 • Griffith D. W. • USA
TWO WOMEN AND ONE HAT • 1915 • MacGregor Norval • USA
TWO WOMEN AND ONE MAN • 1912 • *Smiley Frank* • USA
TWO WOMEN AND TWO MEN • 1912 • Brooke Van Dyke • USA
TWO WOMEN IN GOLD see **DEUX FEMMES EN OR** • 1970
TWO WOMEN OF GOLD see **DEUX FEMMES EN OR** • 1970
TWO WOMEN (USA) see **CIOCIARA, LA** • 1961
TWO WONDROUS TIGERS • 1986 • Cheung Sum • HKG
TWO WORLDS • 1930 • Dupont E. A. • UKN
TWO WORLDS OF ANGELITA, THE see **DOS MUNDOS DE ANGELITA, LOS** • 1982
TWO WORLDS OF JENNIE LOGAN, THE • 1979 • De Felitta Frank • TVM • USA
TWO WORLDS (USA) see **ENDSTATION LIEBE** • 1957
TWO WRONGS MAKE A RIGHT • 1988 • Brown Robert • USA
TWO YANKS IN TRINIDAD • 1942 • Ratoff Gregory • USA • TRINIDAD
TWO YEAR VACATION see **UKRADENA VZDUCHOLOD** • 1966
TWO YEARS BEFORE THE MAST • 1946 • Farrow John • USA
TWO YEAR'S HOLIDAY see **UKRADENA VZDUCHOLOD** • 1966
TWO YEARS IN EACH FORM see **TVA AR I VARJE KLASS** • 1938
TWO YEARS ON THE EDGE OF A PRECIPICE see **DVA GODA NAD PROPASTYU** • 1967
TWO YOUNG SCAMPS • 1905 • *Cricks & Sharp* • UKN • TWO SCAMPS, THE
TWO YOUNG SCAMPS • 1905 • Mottershaw Frank • *Sheffield Photo Co* • UKN
TWONKY, THE • 1953 • Oboler Arch • USA
TWOPENNY MAGIC see **ZWEIGROSCHENZAUBER** • 1929
TWO'S A CROWD • 1950 • Jones Charles M. • ANS • USA
TWO'S COMPANY • Nolan William • ANS • USA
TWO'S COMPANY • 1914 • Ransom Charles • USA
TWO'S COMPANY • 1918 • *Christie* • USA
TWO'S COMPANY • 1936 • Whelan Tim • UKN
TWO'S COMPANY see **SAPS AT SEA** • 1940
TWO'S COMPANY, THREE'S A CROWD • 1908 • *Vitagraph* • USA
TWO'S COMPANY, THREE'S A CROWD • 1913 • Ince Ralph • USA
TWO'S COMPANY, THREE'S NONE • 1904 • *Warwick Trading Co* • UKN
TWO'S COMPANY, THREE'S NONE • 1905 • Haggar William • UKN
TWO'S COMPANY (UKN) see **TWO GUN MAN, THE** • 1931
TY I YA • 1972 • Shepitko Larissa • USS • YOU AND I ○ YOU AND ME
TY INOGDA VSPOMINAY • 1977 • Chukhray Pavel • USS • SOMETIMES YOU REMEMBER
TY-PEUPE • 1971 • Belanger Fernand • CND • TI PEUPE
TYAAG • 1977 • *Burman S. D. (M)* • IND
TYBURN CASE, THE • 1957 • Paltenghi David • UKN
TYCOON • 1947 • Wallace Richard • USA
TYCOON • 1982 • Arcand Denys, Jackson Douglas • MTV • CND • EMPIRE, INC.
TYCOON see **KIZU DARAKE NO SANGA** • 1964
TYDEN V TICHEM DOME • 1947 • Krejcik Jiri • CZC • WEEK IN THE QUIET HOUSE
TYGER TYGER BURNING BRIGHT • 1989 • Sundstrom Neil • SAF
TYING UP THE CORD see **AMMARRANDO EL CORDON** • 1968
TYLER • 1977 • Thomas Ralph L. • MTV • CND
TYNESIDE STORY • 1946 • Gunn Gilbert • DOC • UKN
TYOMIEHEN PAIVAKIRJA • 1967 • Jarva Risto • FNL • NOT BY BREAD ALONE (UKN) ○ WORKER'S DIARY, A ○ DIARY OF A WORKER
TYPE COMME MOI NE DEVRAIT JAMAIS MOURIR, UN • 1976 • Vianey Michel • FRN
TYPES OF INMATES • 1965 • Portugais Louis • DCS • CND • CATEGORIES DE DETENUS
TYPEWRITER TALES see **MESEK AZ IROGEPROL** • 1916
TYPEWRITER'S TALE, A see **MESEK AZ IROGEPROL** • 1916
TYPHOID see **TIFUSARI** • 1963
TYPHOID SUFFERERS see **TIFUSARI** • 1963
TYPHON SUR HAMBOURG • 1968 • Balcazar Alfonso • FRN, ITL, SPN
TYPHON SUR NAGASAKI • 1957 • Ciampi Yves • FRN, JPN • WASURENU BOJO (JPN) ○ TYPHOON OVER NAGASAKI ○ PRINTEMPS A NAGASAKI
TYPHOON • 1940 • King Louis • USA
TYPHOON see **TAIFU** • 1966
TYPHOON, THE • 1914 • Barker Reginald • USA
TYPHOON BILL see **DERELICT** • 1930
TYPHOON LOVE • 1926 • Dawn Norman • USA
TYPHOON NO.13 see **TAIFU SODOKI** • 1956
TYPHOON OVER NAGASAKI see **TYPHON SUR NAGASAKI** • 1957
TYPHOON SHIPMENTS, THE • 1987 • Hellman Monte • USA
TYPHOON TAKKAR see **TOOFANI TAKKAR** • 1946
TYPHOON TARZAN see **TOOFANI TARZAN** • 1937
TYPHOON TARZAN see **TOOFANI TARZAN** • 1962
TYPHOON TREASURE • 1938 • Monkman Noel • ASL
TYPHUS see **TIFUSARI** • 1963
TYPHUS HAS DESTROYED • 1946 • Popovic Mihailo • YGS
TYPICAL BUDGET, A • 1925 • Brunel Adrian • UKN
TYPICAL MEXICAN ASPECTS • 1919 • Wright George D. • USA
TYPIST'S LOVE AFFAIR, A see **FOR HER MOTHER'S SAKE** • 1913
TYPIST'S REVENGE, THE • 1911 • Aylott Dave • UKN
TYPOGRAPHICAL ERROR, A • 1914 • Le Saint Edward J. • USA
TYPY NA BZIS see **TYPY NA DZIS** • 1959
TYPY NA DZIS • 1959 • Hoffman Jerzy, Skorzewski Edward • DCS • PLN • TIPS FOR TODAY ○ TYPY NA BZIS
TYRANN, DER see **COLUMNA** • 1968
TYRANN VON MUCKENDORF, DER • 1915 • *Dreher Konrad* • FRG
TYRANNEI DES TODES • 1920 • Feher Friedrich • FRG
TYRANNENHERRSCHAFT • 1916 • Porten Franz • FRG
TYRANNICAL FIANCE, THE see **TYRANNISKE FASTMANNEN, DEN** • 1912
TYRANNISKE FASTMANNEN, DEN • 1912 • Stiller Mauritz • SWD • TYRANNICAL FIANCE, THE ○ DESPOTIC FIANCE, THE ○ PARSONAGE OF DONVIK, THE
TYRANNY OF THE DARK, THE • 1910 • *Kalem* • USA
TYRANT -FEAR, THE • 1918 • Neill R. William • USA
TYRANT OF CASTILE, THE (USA) see **SFIDA AL RE DI CASTIGLIA** • 1964
TYRANT OF CHIRACAHUA, THE • 1917 • *Sais Marin* • USA
TYRANT OF RED GULCH, THE • 1928 • De Lacy Robert • USA • SORCERER, THE (UKN)
TYRANT OF SYRACUSE, THE see **TIRANNO DI SIRACUSA, IL** • 1962
TYRANT OF THE SEA • 1950 • Landers Lew • USA
TYRANT OF THE VELDT, THE • 1915 • Santschi Thomas • USA
TYRANT'S DREAM, THE • 1909 • *Selig* • USA
TYRANT'S HEART, OR BOCCACCIO IN HUNGARY, THE see **ZSARNOK SZIVE AVAGY BOCCACCIO MAGYARORSZAGON, A** • 1981
TYREE STORY, THE • 1980 • Robertson Michael • DOC • ASL
TYROLESE DOLL, THE • 1911 • *Pathe* • FRN
TYRTEE • 1912 • Feuillade Louis • FRN
TYSTNADEN • 1963 • Bergman Ingmar • SWD • SILENCE, THE (UKN)
TYSTNADENS HUS • 1933 • Malmberg Eric, Carlsten Rune • SWD • HOUSE OF SILENCE (USA)
TYSYACHA OKON • 1968 • Speshnev Alexei • USS • THOUSAND WINDOWS, A
TYTTO KUUNSILLALTA • 1953 • Kassila Matti • FNL • GIRL FROM THE MOON'S BRIDGE, THE
TYUTYUN • 1962 • Korabov Nicolai • BUL • TOBACCO ○ TIUTIUN ○ TUTUNE
TYVEN • 1910 • *Blom August* • DNM • SOCIETY SINNER, A
TYVEPAK • 1920 • Lauritzen Lau • DNM
TZ • 1979 • Breer Robert • USA
TZAK O KAVALLARIS • 1979 • Dadiras Dinos • GRC • JACK THE RIDER
TZANANI FAMILY • 1978 • Davidson Boaz • ISR
TZAREVITCH, LE see **ZARESWITCH, DER** • 1954
TZAREWITCH, LE see **SON ALTESSE IMPERIALE** • 1933
TZIGANE see **GYPSY** • 1937
TZIMIS O TIGRIS • 1966 • Voulgaris Pantelis • SHT • GRC • JIMMY THE TIGER
TZ'U-K'O • 1977 • T'U Chung-Hsun • HKG • ASSASSIN

U

U 9 WEDDIGEN • 1927 • Paul Heinz • FRG • U-BOAT 9 (USA)
U 47 KAPITANLEUTNANT PRIEN • 1958 • Reinl Harald • FRG • U-47 LT. COMMANDER PRIEN (USA)
U-47 LT. COMMANDER PRIEN (USA) see **U 47 KAPITANLEUTNANT PRIEN** • 1958
U 235 • 1954 • Novik William • SHT • FRN
U-238 AND THE WITCH DOCTOR • 1953 • Brannon Fred C. • USA
U-BOAT 9 (USA) see **U 9 WEDDIGEN** • 1927
U-BOAT 29 (USA) see **SPY IN BLACK, THE** • 1939
U-BOAT 39 see **UBAT 39** • 1952
U BOAT 55 see **HAIE UND KLEINE FISCHE** • 1957
U-BOAT PRISONER • 1944 • Landers Lew • USA • DANGEROUS MISTS (UKN)
U-BOOT • 1932 • Paul Heinz • DOC • FRG
U-BOOTE WESTWARTS • 1941 • Rittau Gunther • FRG
U-DELIWE • 1975 • Sabela Simon • SAF • LITTLE ONE, THE
U.F.O'S • Schwartz Lillian, Knowlton Kenneth • ANS • USA
U.F.O. -INVASION U.F.O. see **INVASION UFO** • 1980
U.F.O.'S OVER ALBERTA • 1976 • Windsor Chris • MTV • CND
U.F.O. (UNIDENTIFIED FLYING OBJECTS) • 1956 • Jones Winston • DOC • USA • UNIDENTIFIED FLYING OBJECTS
U GORI RASTE ZELEN BOR • 1972 • Vrdoljak Antun • YGS • THERE'S A GREEN PINE TREE IN THE FOREST ○ PINE TREE ON THE MOUNTAIN ○ PINE-TREE GROWS IN THE MOUNTAIN, A ○ THERE GROWS A GREEN PINE IN THE WOODS
U IME NARODA • 1987 • Nikolic Zivko • YGS • IN THE NAME OF THE PEOPLE
U.K. SWINGS AGAIN • 1964 • Gilpin Frank • UKN • GO GO BIG BEAT (USA)
U KAZHDOVO SVOYA DOROGA • 1967 • Kovalyov Mark • USS • TO EACH HIS OWN ROAD
U KRUTOGO YARA • 1962 • Muratova Kira, Muratov Alexander • USS • SHE-WOLF, THE (USA) ○ ON THE STEEP CLIFF
U.M.C. • 1969 • Sagal Boris • TVM • USA • OPERATION HEARTBEAT (UKN) ○ UNIVERSITY MEDICAL CENTRE
U.N. IN ACTION, THE see **O.N.Z. W AKCJI** • 1949
U.N. IN PERIL • 1960 • Leiterman Douglas • DOC • CND
U NAS V KOCOURKOVE • 1934 • Cikan Miroslav • CZC • WE AT KRAHWINKEL
U NIKH EST RODINA • 1951 • Fainzimmer Alexander, Legoshin Vladimir • USS • THEY HAVE A MOTHERLAND ○ THEY HAVE A HOMELAND
U OLUJI • 1952 • Mimica Vatroslav • YGS • IN THE STORM
U.P. TRAIL, THE • 1920 • Conway Jack • USA
U POKLADNY STAL • 1939 • Lamac Carl • CZC • STANDING BY THE TREASURY
U POZERNOVO STOLBA • 1924 • Bek-Nazarov Amo • USS • AT THE POST OF SHAME ○ IN THE PILLORY ○ PATRICIDE
U PRAVCU POCETKA • 1970 • Djurkovic Dejan • SHT • YGS • TOWARDS THE BEGINNING
U.R.S.S. A COEUR OUVERT, L' • 1961 • Vernay Robert, Karmen Roman • DOC • FRN, USS
U RASKO-RAKU • 1968 • Strbac Milenko • YGS • IN DISAGREEMENT ○ OUT OF STEP
U "ROZY" OD 6-TEJ DO 11-TEJ • 1963 • Halladin Danuta • DOC • PLN • AT "ROZA" FROM 6 TO 11
U.S.A. • Stecker Alan • SHT • USA

U.S. ARMY BAND, THE • 1943 • Negulesco Jean • SHT • USA

U.S. MARSHALS: WACO & RHINEHART • 1987 • Nyby Christian Ii • TVM • USA • WACO AND RHINEHART ○ LINE OF DUTY

U.S. NAVAL MILITIA • 1900 • *Bitzer Billy (Ph)* • USA

U.S. PAVILION FILM (EXPO 86) • 1986 • Chapman Christopher • CND

U.S. REVENUE DETECTIVE, THE • 1910 • *Yankee* • USA

U.S.S. MAINE, HAVANA HARBOR • 1898 • *Bitzer Billy (Ph)* • USA

U.S.S.R. – AMERICA • 1959 • Makhnach Leonid • DOC • USS

U S S R TODAY • 1953 • Bobrov G. • USS

U.S.S. TEAKETTLE see **YOU'RE IN THE NAVY NOW** • 1951

U SAMOVA SINEVO MORYA • 1936 • Barnet Boris, Mardonov S. • USS • BY THE BLUEST OF SEAS ○ RIGHT BY THE BLUE SEA

U SNEDENEHO KRAMU • 1933 • Fric Martin • CZC • EATEN-UP SHOP, THE ○ RUINED SHOPKEEPER, THE ○ RANSACKED SHOP, THE ○ EMPTIED-OUT GROCER'S SHOP, THE

U SV. MATEJE • 1928 • Kokeisl • CZC • BY ST. MATTHIAS

U SVETEHO ANTONICKA • 1933 • Innemann Svatopluk • CZC • BY ST. ANTHONY

U-TURN • 1973 • Kaczender George • FRN • GIRL IN BLUE, THE

UANSTAENDIGE, DE • 1983 • Fleming Edward • DNM • IMPROPER ONES, THE

UB' IMMER TREU UN REDLICHKEIT • 1927 • Schunzel Reinhold • FRG

UBAGURUMA • 1956 • Tasaka Tomotaka • JPN • BABY CARRIAGE

UBANGI • 1931 • Neuman Lewis • USA

UBAR, THE • 1965 • Holmes Cecil • DOC • ASL

UBASIA • 1972 • Steiner Alex • SHT • USA

UBAT 39 • 1952 • Faustman Erik • SWD • U-BOAT 39

UBEL GROSSTES ABER IST DIE SCHULD, DER • 1918 • Moest Hubert • FRG

UBER ALLES –DAS RECHT • 1915 • Schmidthassler Walter • FRG

UBER ALLES DIE LIEBE see **MUNCHNERINNEN** • 1944

UBER ALLES DIE PFLICHT! • 1915 • Turszinsky Walter • FRG

UBER ALLES DIE TREUE • Janson Victor • FRG

UBER ALLES IN DER WELT • 1941 • Ritter Karl • FRG

UBER DEN WOLKEN • 1919 • Piel Harry • FRG

UBER LEBEN • 1978 • Wiener Filmkollektiv • DOC • AUS • ABOUT LIFE

UBER NACHT • 1973 • Thome Karin • FRG • OVER NIGHT

UBERFAHRENE HUT, DER • 1915 • Albes Emil • FRG

UBERFALL • 1927 • Trotz Adolf • FRG

UBERFALL, DER • 1928 • Metzner Erno • FRG • POLIZEIBERICHT UEBERFALL ○ ASSAULT AND BATTERY

UBERFALL AUF DEN EUROPA-EXPRESS, DER • 1920 • Hartt Hanns Heinz • FRG

UBERFALL IM HOTEL see **FALL BENKEN, DER** • 1934

UBERFALL IN FEINDESLAND, EIN • 1915 • Biebrach Rudolf • FRG

UBERFLUSSIGE MENSCHEN • 1926 • Rasumny Alexander • FRG • SUPERFLUOUS PEOPLE (USA)

UBERNACHTUNG IN TIROL • 1973 • Schlondorff Volker • MTV • FRG • OVERNIGHT STAY IN THE TYROL ○ OVERNIGHT IN TIROL

UBERS MEER GEHETZT • 1925 • Stranz Fred • FRG

UBERWINDUNG EINES VERLUSTES • 1964 • Herbst Helmut • ANS • FRG • VICTORY CELEBRATION OF A WAR CASUALTY

UBERWINTERUNG • 1970 • von Mechow Ulf • FRG

UBETAENKSOMME ELSKER, DEN • 1983 • Ploug Claus • DNM • IMPRUDENT LOVER, THE ○ IMPUDENT LOVER, THE

UBI • 1985-89 • Osman Aziz M. • MTV • MLY

UBIISTVO NA UTILITZE DANTE • 1956 • Romm Mikhail • USS • MURDER IN DANTE STREET, THE ○ MURDER ON THE RUE DANTE

UBIJ ME NEZNO • 1981 • Hladnik Bostjan • YGS • KILL ME GENTLY

UBISTVO NA PODMUKAO I SVIREP NACIN I IZ NISKIH POBUBA • 1970 • Mitrovic Zika • YGS • MURDER ○ MURDER COMMITTED IN A SLY AND CRUEL MANNER AND FROM A LOW MOTIVE

UBIT PRI ISPOLNYENII • 1978 • Rozantsev Nikolai • USS • DIED ON DUTY

UBITZI VYKHODYAT NA DOROGU • 1942 • Pudovkin V. I., Tarich Yuri • USS • MURDERERS ARE ON THEIR WAY ○ MURDERERS ARE COMING, THE

UBO THOMSENS HEIMKEHR • 1920 • Larsen Viggo • FRG

UBRANIE PRAWIE NOWE • 1963 • Haupe Wlodzimierz • PLN • HAND-ME-DOWN SUIT, A ○ SUIT ALMOST NEW, THE ○ NEW CLOTHES

UBU • 1978 • Dunbar Geoff • UKN

UBU AND THE GREAT GIDOUILLE see **UBU ET LA GRANDE GIDOUILLE** • 1979

UBU ET LA GRANDE GIDOUILLE • 1979 • Lenica Jan • ANM • FRN • UBU AND THE GREAT GIDOUILLE

UBU ROI • 1977 • Lenica Jan • ANS • FRG • KING UBU

UBUDE ABUPHANGWA • 1982 • SAF

UC HALJA YIRMIBES • 1985 • Olgac Bilge • TRK • THREE RINGS TWENTY-FIVE

UC SEVDALI KIZ • 1967 • Gultekin Sirri • TRK • THREE GIRLS IN LOVE

UCAN ADAM KILLINGE KARSI • 1967 • Atadeniz Yilmaz • TRK • FLYING-MAN VS. KILLING

UCCELLACCI E UCCELLINI • 1966 • Pasolini Pier Paolo • ITL • HAWKS AND SPARROWS (USA) ○ HAWKS AND THE SPARROWS, THE ○ BAD BIRDS AND GOOD BIRDS ○ UGLY BIRDS AND SWEET BIRDS

UCCELLO DALLE PIUME DE CRISTALLO, L' • 1970 • Argento Dario • ITL, FRG • GEHEIMNIS DER SCHWARZEN HANDSCHUHE, DAS (FRG) ○ GALLERY MURDERS, THE (UKN) ○ BIRD WITH THE CRYSTAL PLUMAGE, THE (USA) ○ PHANTOM OF TERROR ○ BIRD WITH THE GLASS FEATHERS, THE

UCCELLO DI FUOCO, L' (ITL) see **ELDFAGELN** • 1952

UCCELLO MIGRATORE, L' • 1972 • Steno • ITL

UCCIDERE IN SILENZIO • 1972 • Rolando Giuseppe • ITL

UCCIDERO UN UOMO (ITL) see **QUE LA BETE MEURE** • 1969

UCCIDETE AGENTE SEGRETO 777–STOP (ITL) see **COPLAN, AGENT SECRET FX18** • 1964

UCCIDETE IL VITELLO GRASSO E ARROSTITELO • 1970 • Samperi Salvatore • ITL

UCCIDETE JOHNNY RINGO • 1966 • Baldanello Gianfranco • ITL

UCCIDETE ROMMEL • 1969 • Brescia Alfonso • ITL

UCCIDEVA A FREDDO • 1967 • Celano Guido • ITL

UCCIDI DJANGO.. UCCIDI PER PRIMO • 1971 • Garrone Sergio • ITL

UCCIDI O MUORI • 1967 • Boccia Tanio • ITL • KILL OR BE KILLED (USA)

UCCISORI, GLI • 1977 • Taglioni Fabrizio • ITL

UCENIE • 1965 • Hanak Dusan • CZC • APPRENTICESHIP

UCHCHAQ AL-HAYAT • 1971 • Halim Hilmy • EGY • AMOUREUX DE LA VIE, LES

UCHITEL • 1939 • Gerasimov Sergei • USS • NEW TEACHER, THE ○ TEACHER, THE

UCHITEL PENIYA • 1972 • Birman Naum • USS • SINGING TEACHER, THE

UCHO • 1970 • Kachyna Karel • CZC • EAR, THE

UCHU DAIKAIJU DOGORA • 1964 • Honda Inoshiro • JPN • DAGORA THE SPACE MONSTER (USA) ○ UCHUDAI DOGORA ○ DOGORA ○ SPACE MONSTER DOGORA ○ DAGORA

UCHU DAIKAIJU GUILALA • 1967 • Nihonmatsu Kazui • JPN • X FROM OUTER SPACE ○ BIG SPACE MONSTER GUILALA ○ GUIRARA ○ GIRARA ○ GUILALA

UCHU DAISENSO • 1959 • Honda Inoshiro • JPN • BATTLE IN OUTER SPACE (USA) ○ WORLD OF SPACE, THE

UCHU KAIJIN SHUTSUGEN • 1958 • Miwa Akira • JPN • SUPER GIANT 7 (USA) ○ SPACEMEN APPEAR

UCHU KAISOKU-SEN • 1961 • Ota Koji • JPN • INVASION OF THE NEPTUNE MEN (USA) ○ SPACE GREYHOUND ○ INVASION FROM A PLANET

UCHU KARA NO KIKAN • 1985 • Nakajima Koichi • JPN • BACK FROM SPACE

UCHU KARA NO MESSEJI see **UCHU KARANO MESSAGE** • 1977

UCHU KARANO MESSAGE • 1977 • Fukasaku Kinji • JPN • MESSAGE FROM SPACE, THE ○ UCHU KARA NO MESSEJI ○ UCHU NI MESSEJI

UCHU NI MESSEJI see **UCHU KARANO MESSAGE** • 1977

UCHU SENKAN YAMATO see **UCHUSENKAN YAMATO** • 1977

UCHUDAI DOGORA see **UCHU DAIKAIJU DOGORA** • 1964

UCHUJIN TOKYO NI ARAWARU • 1956 • Shima Koji • JPN • COSMIC MAN APPEARS IN TOKYO, THE ○ MYSTERIOUS SATELLITE (USA) ○ WARNING FROM SPACE ○ SPACE MEN APPEAR IN TOKYO ○ UNKNOWN SATELLITE OVER OKYO

UCHUSENKAN YAMATO • 1977 • Nishizaki Yoshinobu • ANM • JPN • SPACE CRUISER: GUARDIAN OF THE GALAXY ○ UCHU SENKAN YAMATO ○ SPACE CRUISER ○ SPACE SHIP YAMATO

UCHUTEI TO JINKO EISEN NO GEKITOTSU • 1958 • Ishii Teruo • JPN • DESTRUCTION OF THE SPACE FLEET, THE ○ SUPER GIANT 6 (USA)

UCITEL ORIENTALNICH JAZYKU • 1918 • Kolar J. S., Rautenkranzova Olga • CZC • TEACHER OF ORIENTAL LANGUAGES, THE

UCOPAN BARBADOS PROJECT • 1986 • Zielinska Ida Eva • CND

UCUNCU GOZ • 1988 • Oguz Orhan • TRK • THIRD EYE, THE

UCUNUZU DE MIHLARIM • 1965 • Olgac Bilge • TRK

UCURTRAYI VURMASINLAR • 1988 • Basaran Tunc • TRK • DON'T LET THEM SHOOT THE KITE

UDAHIR PATH • 1943 • Roy Bimal • IND • UDAYER PATHEY

UDARI YESHCHYO UDARI • 1968 • Sadovsky Viktor • USS • SHOOT! SHOOT AGAIN!

UDAYER PATHEY see **UDAHIR PATH** • 1943

UDBRUDTE SLAVE, DEN see **EVENTYR PAA FODREJSEN** • 1911

UDEN EN TRAEVL • 1968 • Meineche Annelise • DNM • WITHOUT A STITCH (USA)

UDEN FAEDRELAND see **FORVISTE, DE** • 1914

UDENRIGSKORRESPONDENTEN • 1983 • Leth Jorgen • DNM • HAITI EXPERIENCE

UDFLYTTERNE • 1972 • Roos Jorgen • DOC • DNM

UDI, AKO HOCES • 1968 • Ostojic Radenko • YGS • COME IN, IF YOU PLEASE

UDIENZA, L' • 1972 • Ferreri Marco • ITL • AUDIENCE, THE

UDOLI VCEL • 1967 • Vlacil Frantisek • CZC • VALLEY OF THE BEES, THE ○ VALLEY OF BEES

UDOLIE VECNYCH KARAVAN • 1968 • Hornak Miroslav • CZC • VALLEY OF ETERNAL CARAVANS, THE

UDVARI LOVEGO • 1918 • *Lukas Paul* • HNG

UDYOGHASTHA • 1967 • Venu • IND • LADY WHO EARNS, THE

UEMURA NAOMI MONOGATARI • 1985 • Sato Junya • JPN • STORY OF AN ADVENTURER, NAOMI UEMURA

UETA JUHYOKU • 1968 • Umesawa Kaoru • JPN • HUNGRY BESTIALITY

UETA KIBA • 1960 • Horiiki Kiyoshi • JPN

UFFICIALE NON SI ARRENDE MAI, NEMMENO DI FRONTE ALL'EVIDENZA: FIRMATA COLONNELLO BUTTIGLIONE, UN see **COLONNELLO BUTTIGLIONE, IL** • 1973

UFO -EXCLUSIVE • 1979 • DOC • USA

UFO INCIDENT, THE • 1975 • Colla Richard A. • TVM • USA

UFO MAN, THE see **UFO-MIES** • 1972

UFO-MIES • 1972 • Pasanen Spede • FNL • UFO MAN, THE

UFO SYNDROME • 1981 • Martin Richard • USA

UFO TARGET EARTH • 1974 • De Gaetano Michael A. • USA

UFORIA • 1980 • Binder John • USA

UFOS ARE REAL • 1979 • Hunt Ed • USA • ALIEN ENCOUNTERS

UFOS: IT HAS BEGUN • 1976 • Rivas Ray • USA

UGETSU MONOGATARI • 1953 • Mizoguchi Kenji • JPN • TALES OF THE PALE AND SILVERY MOON AFTER THE RAIN (UKN) ○ UGETSU (USA) ○ TALES AFTER THE RAIN

UGETSU (USA) see **UGETSU MONOGATARI** • 1953

UGH ME HUNGRY • Gavioli Roberto, Gavioli Gino • ANS • ITL

UGHNIA 'ALA AL-MAMARR • 1972 • Abdel-Khaliq Ali • EGY • CHANSON SUR LE PASSAGE

UGLIES CAN LOVE TOO see **CIRKINLER DE SEVER** • 1982

UGLIES MOVIE, THE • 1920 • ASL

UGLIEST QUEEN ON EARTH, THE • 1909 • *Gaumont* • USA

UGLY AMERICAN, THE • 1963 • Englund George • USA

UGLY AMERICAN, THE see **MEXICANO FEO, EL** • 1983

UGLY BIRDS AND SWEET BIRDS see **UCCELLACCI E UCCELLINI** • 1966

UGLY BOY, THE see **CSUNYA FIJU, A** • 1918

UGLY COCKROACH, THE • 1961 • Sturlis Edward • ANM • PLN

UGLY DACHSHUND, THE • 1966 • Tokar Norman • USA

UGLY DINO, THE • 1940 • Fleischer Dave • ANS • USA

UGLY, DIRTY AND BAD see **BRUTTI, SPORCHI E CATTIVI** • 1976

UGLY, DIRTY AND MEAN see **BRUTTI, SPORCHI E CATTIVI** • 1976

UGLY DUCKLING, THE • 1920 • Butler Alexander • UKN

UGLY DUCKLING, THE • 1931 • Jackson Wilfred • ANS • USA

UGLY DUCKLING, THE • 1939 • Cutting Jack • ANS • USA

UGLY DUCKLING, THE • 1953 • *Encyclopedia Britannica* • SHT • USA

UGLY DUCKLING, THE • 1959 • Comfort Lance • UKN

UGLY KING DOES NOT FORGIVE, THE see **CIRKIN KRAL AFETMEZ** • 1967

UGLY MAN, AN see **BIR CIRKIN ADAM** • 1969

UGLY, MONSTROUS, MIND-ROASTING SUMMER OF O.C. AND STIGGS • 1985 • Altman Robert • USA • O.C. AND STIGGS

UGLY ONES, THE (USA) see **PRECIO DE UN HOMBRE, EL** • 1966

UGLY ONES BY NIGHT see **BRUTTI DI NOTTE** • 1968

UGLY SPINSTER, THE see **OSKLIVA SLECNA** • 1959

UGLY STORY, AN see **SKVENEI ANEKDOT** • 1965

UGLY VILLAGE, THE see **SKAREDA DEDINA** • 1975

UGUBZIARA • 1930 • Rondeli David • USS

UGUISU • 1938 • Toyoda Shiro • JPN • NIGHTINGALE

UGUSUJO NO HANAYOME • 1959 • Matsumura Shoji • JPN • THREE PRINCESSES

UGY EREZTE, SZABADON EL • 1988 • Vitezy Laszlo • DOC • HNG • FLOATING FREE

UHKKADUS • 1987 • Jarl Stefan • DOC • SWD • THREAT

UHLAN see **ULAN** • 1977

UHOHO TANKEN-TAI • 1987 • Negishi Kichitaro • JPN • UNSTABLE FAMILY, AN

UHOL POHLADU • 1985 • Balco Vlado • CZC • POINT OF VIEW

UHUKA see **UHUKA, A KIS BAGOLY** • 1969

UHUKA, A KIS BAGOLY • 1969 • Macskassy Gyula, Varnai Gyorgy • ANS • HNG • NAUGHTY OWL, THE ○ LITTLE OWL, THE ○ UHUKA

UILLEANN PIPES OF FANORE • 1985 • Shaw-Smith David • DCS • IRL

UIRA, UM INDIO EM BUSCA DE DEUS • 1973 • Dahl Gustavo • BRZ

UIRAPURU • 1950 • Zebra Sam • USA

UISQUE.. E UM CIGARRO DEPOIS, UM • 1971 • Tambellini Flavio • BRZ

UITZICHT OP DE HEMEL • 1961 • Dupont Frans • SHT • NTH • PROMISE OF HEAVEN ○ JOY AND LIGHT

UJ FOELDESUR, AZ • 1936 • Gaal Bela • HNG

UJ FOLDESURM, AZ • 1988 • Lanyi Andras • HNG • NEW LANDLORD, THE

UJ GILGAMES • 1963 • Szemes Mihaly • HNG • NEW GILGAMES

UJ ROKON, AZ • 1935 • Gaal Bela • HNG • NEW RELATIVE, THE (USA)

UJALA • 1954 • *Zils Paul (P)* • SHT • IND

UJANG • 1988 • Hafsham Othman • MLY

UJRA MOSOLYOGNAK • 1954 • Meszaros Marta • SHT • HNG • THEY SMILE AGAIN ○ SMILING AGAIN

UJRAELOK • 1921 • Fejos Paul • HNG • RESURRECTED, THE ○ REINCARNATION ○ REVIVED

UKAMAU • 1967 • Sanjines Jorge • BLV

UKANASKNELI JVAROSNEBI • 1934 • Dolidze Siko • USS • LAST CRUSADER, THE

UKANASKNELI MASKARADI see **POSLEDNI MASKARAD** • 1934

UKARE BAIORIN • 1955 • *Toei Doga* • ANS • JPN • MAGIC VIOLIN, THE

UKARE SANDO GASA • 1959 • Tanaka Tokuzo • JPN • PRINCESS SAYS NO, THE

UKELELE SHEIKS • 1926 • Roach Hal • SHT • USA

UKESLUTT • 1976 • Mikkelsen Laila • SHT • NRW

UKHABY ZHIZNI • 1928 • Room Abram • USS • HARD LIFE ○ PITS ○ BUMPS ○ RUTS

UKHOD VELIKOVO STARTZA • 1912 • Protazanov Yakov • USS • DEPARTURE OF A GRAND OLD MAN, THE ○ LIFE OF TOLSTOY, THE

UKHTI • 1970 • Barakat Henry • EGY • MA SOEUR

UKIFUNE • 1957 • Kinugasa Teinosuke • JPN • FLOATING VESSEL

UKIGUMO • 1955 • Naruse Mikio • JPN • FLOATING CLOUDS

UKIGUSA • 1959 • Ozu Yasujiro • JPN • FLOATING WEEDS (USA) ○ DRIFTING WEEDS

UKIGUSA MONOGATARI • 1934 • Ozu Yasujiro • JPN • STORY OF FLOATING WEEDS, A

UKIGUSA NIKKI • 1955 • Yamamoto Satsuo • JPN • DIARY OF UMAGORO'S TRAVELLING THEATRE ○ DUCKWEED STORY ○ TRAVELLING PLAYERS, THE

UKIYO BURO • 1929 • Gosho Heinosuke • JPN • BATH OF THE TRANSITORY WORLD ○ BATH HAREM, THE

UKIYO BURO NO SHIBIJIN • 1958 • Mori Masaki • JPN

UKIYOE see **UKIYOE ZANKOKU MONOGATARI** • 1968

UKIYOE ARTIST see **ONNA UKIYOZOSHI** • 1968

UKIYOE ZANKOKU MONOGATARI • 1968 • Takechi Tetsuji • JPN • UKIYOE

UKJENT MANN • 1951 • Henning-Jensen Astrid, Henning-Jensen Bjarne • NRW • UNKNOWN MAN ○ STRANGER, THE

UKJENTES MARKED, DE • 1968 • Muller Nils R. • NRW • UNKNOWN MARKET, THE

UKLADY A LASKA • 1972 • Schorm Evald • MTV • CZC • INTRIGUE AND LOVE

UKLETI SMO, IRINA • 1974 • Angelovski Kole • YGS • WE ARE BEWITCHED, IRINA

UKOLEBAVKA • 1948 • Tyrlova Hermina • ANS • CZC • LULLABY

UKRADENA VZDUCHOLOD • 1966 • Zeman Karel • CZC • DVA ROKY PRAZDNIN ○ TWO YEAR'S HOLIDAY ○ STOLEN AIRSHIP, THE ○ STOLEN DIRIGIBLE, THE ○ TWO YEAR VACATION ○ STOLEN BALLOON, THE

UKRAINE IN FLAMES see **BITVA ZA NASHA SOVIETSKAYA UKRAINU** • 1943

UKRAINE IN FLAMES see **NEZABYVAYEMOYE** • 1968

UKRAINIAN FESTIVAL • 1965 • Bryunchugin Yevgeniy, Bukovskiy Anatoliy • USS

UKRAINIAN RHAPSODY see **UKRAINSKAYA RAPSODIYA** • 1961

UKRAINSKAYA RAPSODIYA • 1961 • Paradjanov Sergei • USS • UKRAINIAN RHAPSODY

UKRINMAKRINKRIN • 1975 • Rodrigues Carlos Frederico • BRZ

UKRIZOVANA • 1921 • Orlicky Boris • CZC • CRUCIFIED GIRL, THE

UKROSCHENIE OGNIA • 1972 • Khrabrovitsky Daniil • USS • TAMING OF FIRE ○ TAMING OF THE FIRE ○ TAMING THE FIRE

UKUHLUPHEKA • 1982 • SAF

UKULWA • 1982 • SAF

UKUPHINDISELA • 1985 • SAF

UKUSINDISWA • 1981 • SAF

UKUVELEKA • 1985 • SAF

UKUZINGELA • 1985 • SAF

ULAKA • 1984 • SAF

ULAMA, EL • 1985 • Rochin Roberto • DOC • MXC • JUEGO DE PELOTA, EL ○ BALL GAME, THE

ULAMA, EL JUEGO DE LA VIDA Y DE LA MORTE • 1987 • DOC • MXC • ULAMA, GAME OF LIFE AND DEATH

ULAMA, GAME OF LIFE AND DEATH see **ULAMA, EL JUEGO DE LA VIDA Y DE LA MORTE** • 1987

ULAN • 1977 • Okeyev Tolomush • USS • UHLAN

ULAN I DZIEWCZYNA • 1933 • Szaro Henryk • PLN

ULANGA • 1985 • SAF

ULI DER KNECHT • 1954 • Schnyder Franz • SWT

ULI DER PACHTER • 1955 • Schnyder Franz • SWT

ULICA BRZOZOWA • 1947 • Rozewicz Stanislaw, Has Wojciech J. • DCS • PLN • BIRCH STREET

ULICA GRANICZNA • 1948 • Ford Aleksander • PLN • BORDER STREET (UKN) ○ THAT OTHERS MAY LIVE ○ FRONTIER STREET

ULICKA HRICHU A LASKY • 1923 • Binovec Vaclav • CZC • STREET OF SIN AND LOVE, THE

ULICKA V RAJI • 1936 • Fric Martin • CZC • LANE IN PARADISE, A ○ PARADISE ROAD

ULILANG ANGHEL • Agcaoili T. D. • PHL

ULINDIWE • 1984 • SAF

ULISSE • 1954 • Camerini Mario • ITL, USA • ULYSSES (USA)

ULISSE CONTRO ERCOLE • 1961 • Caiano Mario • ITL, FRN • ULYSSES AGAINST THE SON OF HERCULES (USA) ○ ULYSSES AGAINST HERCULES (UKN) ○ HERCULES VS. ULYSSES ○ ULYSSES VS. HERCULES

ULLA MIN ULLA • 1930 • Jaenzon Julius • SWD • ULLA MY ULLA

ULLA MY ULLA see **ULLA MIN ULLA** • 1930

ULLAS WEG • 1916 • von Woringen Paul • FRG

ULLI UND MAREI • 1945 • Hainisch Leopold • FRG • WO DIE ALPENROSEN BLUH'N ○ BERGHOFBAUER, DER

ULOGA MOJE PORODICE U SVETSKOJ REVOLUCIJI • 1971 • Cengic Bato • YGS • ROLE OF MY FAMILY IN WORLD REVOLUTION, THE

ULOUPENA HRANICE • 1947 • Weiss Jiri • CZC • STOLEN FRONTIER, THE

ULRIK FORTAELLER EN HISTORIE • 1972 • Roos Jorgen • DOC • DNM

ULSTER • 1960 • Kelly Ron • DOC • UKN

ULSTER LASS, THE • 1915 • *Gaunthier Gene* • USA

ULTIMA AVENTURA DE CHAFLAN, LA • 1942 • Ojeda Manuel R. • MXC

ULTIMA AVENTURA DEL ZORRO, LA • 1970 • Merino Jose Luis • SPN

ULTIMA AVVENTURA, L' • 1932 • Camerini Mario • ITL • BUON RAGAZZO, UN

ULTIMA AVVENTURA, L' see **ULTIMA FIAMMA** • 1940

ULTIMA CANZONE, L' • 1958 • Mercanti Pino • ITL, SPN

ULTIMA CARICA, L' • 1964 • Savona Leopoldo • ITL

ULTIMA CARROZZELLA, L' • 1943 • Mattoli Mario • ITL • SIETE LIBERO?

ULTIMA CARTA, L' • 1913 • Negroni Baldassare • ITL

ULTIMA CARTA, L' • 1939 • Ballerini Piero • ITL

ULTIMA CENA, L' • 1951 • Giachino Luigi Maria, Reisner Charles F. • ITL

ULTIMA CENA, LA • 1977 • Alea Tomas Gutierrez • CUB • LAST SUPPER, THE

ULTIMA CHANCE, L' • 1973 • Lucidi Maurizio • ITL • STATELINE MOTEL (UKN) ○ LAST CHANCE, THE

ULTIMA CITA, LA • 1936 • Ray Bernard B. • USA

ULTIMA DONNA, L' • 1976 • Ferreri Marco • ITL, FRN • DERNIERE FEMME, LA (FRN) ○ LAST WOMAN, THE (USA)

ULTIMA FALLA, LA (SPN) see **ULTIMA FIAMMA** • 1940

ULTIMA FIAMMA • 1940 • Perojo Benito • ITL, SPN • ULTIMA FALLA, LA (SPN) ○ ULTIMA AVVENTURA, L'

ULTIMA GARA, L' • 1954 • Costa Piero • ITL

ULTIMA GIOVINEZZA (ITL) see **DERNIERE JEUNESSE** • 1939

ULTIMA ILLUSIONE • 1955 • Duse Vittorio • ITL • QUESTA NOSTRA GENTE

ULTIMA IMPRESSA, L' • 1917 • Ghione Emilio • ITL

ULTIMA JUGADA, LA • 1974 • Brell Alfred S. • SPN

ULTIMA LUCHA, LA • 1958 • Soler Julian • MXC

ULTIMA MELODIA, LA • 1938 • Salvador Jaime • MXC • LAST MELODY, THE (USA)

ULTIMA NEMICA, L' • 1938 • Barbaro Umberto • ITL • LAST ENEMY, THE (USA)

ULTIMA NEVE DI PRIMAVERA • 1973 • Del Balzo Raimondo • ITL • LAST SNOWS OF SPRING, THE (UKN)

ULTIMA NOAPTE A COPILARIEI • 1966 • Sistiopul Savel • RMN • LAST NIGHT OF CHILDHOOD, THE

ULTIMA NOCHE, LA • 1948 • Cardona Rene • MXC

ULTIMA NOTTE D'AMORE, L' • 1957 • Ardavin Cesar • ITL, SPN

ULTIMA ORGIA DEL TERZO REICH, L' • 1977 • Canevari Cesare • ITL • GESTAPO'S LAST ORGY

ULTIMA PEGA, A • 1964 • Esteves Constantino • PRT

ULTIMA PREDA DEL VAMPIRO, L' • 1960 • Regnoli Piero • ITL • PLAYGIRLS AND THE VAMPIRE, THE (USA) ○ CURSE OF THE VAMPIRE ○ LAST PREY OF THE VAMPIRE, THE ○ VAMPIRE'S LAST VICTIM, THE

ULTIMA PRIMAVERA, L' • 1919 • Lombardi Dillo • ITL

ULTIMA RAINHA DE PORTUGAL, A • 1951 • de Barros Jose Leitao • SHT • PRT

ULTIMA RECITA DI ANNA PARNELL, L' • 1920 • Serena Gustavo • ITL

ULTIMA SENORA ANDERSON, LA • 1970 • Martin Eugenio • SPN

ULTIMA SENTENZA, L' • 1952 • Bonnard Mario • ITL

ULTIMA THULE • 1968 • Roos Jorgen • DOC • DNM

ULTIMA VIOLENZA, L' • 1957 • Matarazzo Raffaello • ITL

ULTIMA VITTIMA, L' • 1913 • Roberti Roberto Leone • ITL

ULTIMA VOLTA, L' • 1976 • Lado Aldo • ITL • SCIPPATORI, GLI

ULTIMAS BANDERAS, LAS • 1954 • Marquina Luis • SPN

ULTIMAS HORAS, LAS • 1965 • Alcocer Santos • SPN

ULTIMAS IMAGENES DEL NAUFRAGIO • 1989 • Subiela Eliseo • ARG • LAST IMAGES OF THE SHIPWRECK

ULTIMAS POSTALES DE STEPHEN, LAS • 1975 • Ardavin Cesar • SHT • SPN

ULTIMATAS TARDES CON TERESA • 1984 • *Martin Maribel* • SPN • LAST EVENINGS WITH TERESA

ULTIMATE CHASE, THE see **ULTIMATE THRILL, THE** • 1974

ULTIMATE DEGENERATE, THE • 1969 • Findlay Michael, Findlay Roberta • USA

ULTIMATE IMPOSTOR, THE • 1979 • Stanley Paul • TVM • USA

ULTIMATE NINJA, THE • 1986 • Ho Godfrey • HKG

ULTIMATE SACRIFICE, THE • 1911 • Porter Edwin S. • *Rex* • USA

ULTIMATE SOLUTION OF GRACE QUIGLEY, THE see **GRACE QUIGLEY** • 1985

ULTIMATE THRILL, THE • 1974 • Butler Robert • USA • ULTIMATE CHASE, THE

ULTIMATE VOYEUR, THE • 1969 • *Chellee Films* • USA

ULTIMATE WARRIOR, THE • 1975 • Clouse Robert • USA

ULTIMATE WOMAN, THE see **PAROMA** • 1984

ULTIMATUM • 1938 • Wiene Robert, Siodmak Robert (U/c) • FRN

ULTIMATUM • 1973 • Lefebvre Jean-Pierre • FRN

ULTIMATUM ALLA VITA • 1963 • Polselli Renato • ITL

ULTIMAX FORCE • 1986 • Milan Wilfred • USA

ULTIME GRIDA DALLA SAVANA • 1975 • Climati Antonio, Morra Mario • ITL • GRANDE CACCIA, LA ○ SAVAGE MAN, SAVAGE BEAST ○ ZUMBALAH

ULTIME ORE DI UNA VERGINE, LE • 1972 • Piccioli Gianfranco • ITL • DOPPIO A META, UN

ULTIMI, GLI • 1963 • Pandolfi Vito • ITL • LAST, THE

ULTIMI CINQUE MINUTI, GLI • 1955 • Amato Giuseppe • ITL, FRN • CINQ DERNIERES MINUTES, LES (FRN) ○ IT HAPPENS IN ROMA (USA)

ULTIMI DELLA STRADA, GLI • 1940 • Paolella Domenico • ITL

ULTIMI DIECI GIORNI DI HITLER, GLI • 1973 • De Concini Ennio • ITL, UKN • HITLER: THE LAST TEN DAYS (UKN)

ULTIMI FILIBUSTIERI, GLI • 1943 • Elter Marco • ITL

ULTIMI GIORNI, GLI • 1977 • Mingozzi Gianfranco • ITL

ULTIMI GIORNI DI POMPEI, GLI • 1908 • Maggi Luigi • ITL

ULTIMI GIORNI DI POMPEI, GLI • 1913 • Caserini Mario • ITL • LAST DAYS OF POMPEII, THE (USA) ○ PRIEST OF ISIS, THE

ULTIMI GIORNI DI POMPEI, GLI • 1915 • Guazzoni Enrico • ITL

ULTIMI GIORNI DI POMPEI, GLI • 1926 • Gallone Carmine, Palermi Amleto • ITL • LAST DAYS OF POMPEII, THE

ULTIMI GIORNI DI POMPEI, GLI • 1937 • Mattoli Mario • ITL

ULTIMI GIORNI DI POMPEI, GLI • 1950 • Moffa Paolo • ITL

ULTIMI GIORNI DI POMPEI, GLI (ITL) see **DERNIERS JOURS DE POMPEI, LES** • 1948

ULTIMI GIORNI DI POMPEII, GLI (ITL) see **LETZTEN TAGE VON POMPEI, DIE** • 1959

ULTIMI TAUREG, GLI see **CAVALIERI DEL DESERTO, I** • 1942

ULTIMI TRE GIORNI, GLI • 1978 • Mingozzi Gianfranco • MTV • ITL • LAST THREE DAYS, THE

ULTIMI ZAR, GLI • 1926 • Negroni Baldassare • ITL

ULTIMO see **LEBEN KANN SO SCHON SEIN, DAS** • 1938

ULTIMO ADDIO see **DRAMMA NEL PORTO** • 1956

ULTIMO ADDIO, L' • 1942 • Cerio Ferruccio • ITL • ANIME ERRANTI ○ DIAGNOSI

ULTIMO AMANTE, L' • 1956 • Mattoli Mario • ITL

ULTIMO AMOR DE GOYA, EL • 1945 • Salvador Jaime • MXC

ULTIMO AMOR EN TIERRA A DEL FUEGO, EL • 1979 • Bo Armando • ARG • LAST LOVE IN TIERRA DEL FUEGO

ULTIMO AMORE • 1947 • Chiarini Luigi • ITL

ULTIMO BALLO, L' • 1941 • Mastrocinque Camillo • ITL

ULTIMO CABALLO, EL • 1950 • Neville Edgar • SPN

ULTIMO CARTUCHO, EL • 1964 • Gomez Urquiza Zacarias • MXC

ULTIMO CHINALO, EL • 1947 • de Anda Raul • MXC

ULTIMO COMBATTIMENTO, L' • 1941 • Ballerini Piero • ITL

ULTIMO CUPLE, EL • 1957 • de Orduna Juan • SPN

ULTIMO DE LOS VARGAS, EL • 1930 • Howard David • USA

ULTIMO DECAMERONE, L' • 1972 • Alfaro Italo • ITL • DECAMERON N.3 LE PIU BELLE DONNE DEL BOCCACCIO ○ DECAMERON'S JOLLY KITTENS(UKN) ○ DECAMERON N.3

ULTIMO DEI BERGERAC, L' • 1934 • Righelli Gennaro • ITL

ULTIMO DEI FRONTIGNAC, L' • 1911 • Caserini Mario • ITL

ULTIMO DEI VICHINGHI, L' • 1961 • Gentilomo Giacomo • ITL, FRN • DERNIER DES VIKINGS, LE (FRN) ○ LAST OF THE VIKINGS (USA)

ULTIMO DESEO, EL • 1976 • Klimovsky Leon • SPN

ULTIMO DIA DE LA GUERRA, EL • 1969 • Bardem Juan Antonio • SPN, ITL, USA • ULTIMO GIORNO DELLA GUERRA, L' (ITL) ○ LAST DAY OF THE WAR, THE (USA) ○ DEATH ZONE

ULTIMO DIA DE POMPEYO, EL • 1932 • Elias Francisco • SHT • SPN

ULTIMO DIA DEL COMANDANTE GUANIPA, EL • 1971 • Rojas Abigail • VNZ • LAST DAY OF THE COMMANDER GUANIPA, THE

ULTIMO DIA DEL TORERO, EL • 1925 • Trujillo Rafael • MXC

ULTIMO DOMICILIO CONOSCIUTO (ITL) see **DERNIER DOMICILE CONNU** • 1970

ULTIMO DOVERE • 1914 • Ghione Emilio • ITL

ULTIMO E IL PRIMO UOMO, L' • 1969 • Fontoura Antonio Carlos • BRZ

ULTIMO ENCUENTRO • 1967 • Eceiza Antonio • SPN • LAST ENCOUNTER

ULTIMO ENCUENTRO, EL • 1939 • Barth-Moglia Luis • ARG • LAST MEETING, THE (USA)

ULTIMO GIORNO DELLA GUERRA, L' (ITL) see **ULTIMO DIA DE LA GUERRA, EL** • 1969

ULTIMO GIORNO DI SCUOLA PRIMA DELLE VACANZE DI NATALE, L' • 1975 • Baldi Gian Vittorio • ITL

ULTIMO GLADIATORE, L' • 1965 • Lenzi Umberto • ITL • MESSALINA AGAINST THE SON OF HERCULES (USA) ○ EMPRESS MESSALINA MEETS THE SON OF HERCULES

ULTIMO GRUMETE, EL • 1983 • Lopez Jorge • CHL • LAST CABIN BOY, THE

ULTIMO GUAPPO, L' • 1978 • Brescia Alfonso • ITL

ULTIMO GUATEQUE, EL • 1977 • Porto Juan Jose • SPN

ULTIMO HEROE, EL • 1976 • Saenz De Heredia Jose Luis • SPN

ULTIMO HUSAR, EL • 1940 • Marquina Luis • SPN, ITL • AMORE DI USSARO (ITL) ○ ULTIMO USSARO, L'

ULTIMO INCONTRO • 1952 • Franciolini Gianni • ITL

ULTIMO KILLER, L' • 1967 • Vari Giuseppe • ITL, SPN • LAST KILLER, THE

ULTIMO LORD, L' • 1926 • Genina Augusto • ITL

ULTIMO MALON, EL • 1916 • Greca Alcides • ARG

ULTIMO MERCENARIO, EL see **MERCENARIO, EL** • 1968

ULTIMO MERCENARIO, L' (ITL) see **MERCENARIO, EL** • 1968

ULTIMO MEXICANO, EL • 1959 • Bustillo Oro Juan • MXC

ULTIMO MONDO CANNIBALE • 1977 • Deodato Ruggero • ITL • CANNIBAL ○ LAST SURVIVOR, THE

ULTIMO NOME, L' • 1979 • Damiani Damiano • ITL

ULTIMO PARADISO, L' • 1956 • Quilici Folco • DOC • ITL • LAST PARADISE, THE

ULTIMO PERDONO • 1952 • Polselli Renato • ITL

ULTIMO PERRO, EL • 1955 • Demare Lucas • ARG

ULTIMO PROCESO EN PARIS, EL • 1974 • Canalejas Jose A. • SPN

ULTIMO REBELDE, EL • 1956 • Contreras Torres Miguel • MXC • LAST REBEL, THE (USA)

ULTIMO REY DE LOS INCAS, EL • 1967 • Marischka Georg • SPN, ITL, FRG • LAST KING OF THE INCAS, THE

ULTIMO ROUND, EL • 1952 • Galindo Alejandro • MXC

ULTIMO SABADO, EL • 1968 • Balana Pedro • SPN • LAST SATURDAY, THE

ULTIMO SAPORE DELL'ARIA, L' • 1978 • Deodato Ruggero • ITL • LAST FEELINGS (UKN)

ULTIMO SCIUSCIA, L' • 1946 • Gibba • ANS • ITL • LAST STREET BOY, THE (USA)

ULTIMO SCUGNIZZO, L' • 1938 • Righelli Gennaro • ITL

ULTIMO SOGNO • 1921 • Roberti Roberto Leone • ITL

ULTIMO SOLDADO, O • 1980 • da Silva Jorge Alves, Botelho Joao • PRT • LAST SOLDIER, THE

ULTIMO SOLE, L' • 1964 • Bolzoni Adriano • DOC • ITL

ULTIMO TANGO A PARIGI, L' • 1972 • Bertolucci Bernardo • ITL, FRN • DERNIER TANGO A PARIS, LE (FRN) ○ LAST TANGO IN PARIS (UKN)

ULTIMO TANGO A ZAGAROL • 1973 • Cicero Nando • ITL • LAST ITALIAN TANGO, THE (UKN)

ULTIMO TANGO EN MADRID, EL • 1975 • Madrid Jose Luis • SPN • LAST TANGO IN MADRID, THE

ULTIMO TREN DE LA GUERRA, EL • 1977 • Gil Rafael • SPN

ULTIMO TRENO DELLA NOTTE, L' • 1975 • Lado Aldo • ITL

ULTIMO UOMO DELLA TERRA, L' • 1964 • Ragona Ubaldo, Salkow Sidney • ITL, USA • LAST MAN ON EARTH, THE (USA) ○ NIGHT CREATURES, THE ○ VENTO DI MORTE ○ WIND OF DEATH

ULTIMO UOMO DI SARA, L' • 1974 • Onorato Maria Virginia • ITL

ULTIMO USSARO, L' see **ULTIMO HUSAR, EL** • 1940

ULTIMO VARON SOBRE LA TIERRA, EL • 1933 • Tinling James • USA • LAST MAN ON EARTH, THE

ULTIMO VERRANO, EL • 1961 • Bosch Juan • SPN

ULTIMO VIAJE, EL • 1973 • de la Loma Jose Antonio • SPN

ULTIMO ZAR, L' (ITL) see **NUITS DE RASPOUTINE, LES** • 1960

ULTIMOS DE FILIPINAS, LOS • 1945 • Roman Antonio • SPN

ULTIMOS DIAS • 1952 • Roman Antonio • SPN

ULTIMOS DIAS DE LA VICTIMA • 1982 • Aristarain Adolfo • ARG • LAST DAYS OF THE THE VICTIM

ULTIMOS DIAS DE POMPEYO, LOS • 1940 • Portas Rafael E. • MXC

ULTIMOS ROMANTICOS, LOS • 1979 • Borau Jose Luis • VNZ, SPN • LAST ROMANTICS, THE

ULTIMUL CARTUS • 1973 • Nicolaescu Sergiu • RMN • LAST BULLET, THE

ULTISSIME DI NOTTE • 1922 • Ghione Emilio • ITL

ULTRA, JE T'AIME • 1967 • Ledoux Patrick • BLG

ULTRA SEVEN see **URUTORA SEBUN** • 1968

ULTRAJE AL AMOR • 1955 • Portillo Rafael • MXC

ULTRAMAN • 1967 • Hajime, Tsuburaya Eiji • JPN

ULTUS 1: THE TOWNSEND MYSTERY, ULTUS 2: THE AMBASSADOR'S DIAMOND (USA) see **ULTUS, THE MAN FROM THE DEAD** • 1915

ULTUS 3: THE GREY LADY, ULTUS 4:THE TRAITOR'S FATE (USA) see **ULTUS AND THE GREY LADY** • 1916

ULTUS 5: THE SECRET OF THE NIGHT (USA) see **ULTUS AND THE SECRET OF THE NIGHT** • 1916

ULTUS 6: THE THREE BUTTON MYSTERY: ULTUS 7 see **ULTUS AND THE THREE BUTTON MYSTERY** • 1917

ULTUS AND THE GREY LADY • 1916 • Pearson George • UKN • ULTUS 3: THE GREY LADY, ULTUS 4:THE TRAITOR'S FATE (USA)

ULTUS AND THE PHANTOM OF PENGATE • 1918 • Pearson George • UKN

ULTUS AND THE SECRET OF THE NIGHT • 1916 • Pearson George • UKN • ULTUS 5: THE SECRET OF THE NIGHT (USA)

ULTUS AND THE THREE BUTTON MYSTERY • 1917 • Pearson George • UKN • ULTUS 6: THE THREE BUTTON MYSTERY: ULTUS 7

ULTUS, THE MAN FROM THE DEAD • 1915 • Pearson George • UKN • ULTUS 1: THE TOWNSEND MYSTERY, ULTUS 2: THE AMBASSADOR'S DIAMOND (USA)
ULUNYA OF LOHLANGA • 1985 • SAF
ULVETID • 1981 • Ravn Jens • DNM • TIME OF THE WOLF ○ CRY WOLF
ULVOVA MYLLARI • 1983 • Pakkasvirta Jaakko • FNL • HOWLING MILLER, THE ○ OLVOVA MYLLARI
ULYSSA see **VERSPIELTES LEBEN** • 1949
ULYSSE • 1983 • Varda Agnes • FRN
ULYSSES • 1907 • ITL
ULYSSES • 1967 • Strick Joseph • USA, UKN • JAMES JOYCE'S ULYSSES
ULYSSES see **HOMER'S ODYSSEY** • 1909
ULYSSES AGAINST HERCULES (UKN) see **ULISSE CONTRO ERCOLE** • 1961
ULYSSES AGAINST THE SON OF HERCULES (USA) see **ULISSE CONTRO ERCOLE** • 1961
ULYSSES AND THE GIANT POLYPHEMUS (USA) see **ILE DE CALYPSO: OU, ULYSSE ET LE GEANT POLYPHEME, L'** • 1905
ULYSSES (USA) see **ULISSE** • 1954
ULYSSES VS. HERCULES see **ULISSE CONTRO ERCOLE** • 1961
ULZANA (APACHEN, PART 2) • 1974 • Kolditz Gottfried • GDR, RMN
ULZANA'S RAID • 1972 • Aldrich Robert • USA
UM 9 KOMMT HARALD • 1943 • Boese Carl • FRG
UM 500,000 MARK • 1915 • Dessauer Siegfried • FRG
UM AL-ARUSSA • 1963 • Salem Atef • EGY • MERE DE LA MARIEE, LA ○ OM EL AROUSSA ○ BRIDE HAS A MOTHER, THE ○ BRIDE'S MOTHER, THE
UM DAS LACHELN EINER FRAU • 1919 • Wiene Robert • FRG
UM DAS MENSCHENRECHT • 1934 • Zoberlein Hans • FRG
UM DEN BRUCHTEIL EINER SEKUNDE • 1920 • Speyer Jaap • FRG
UM DEN SOHN • 1921 • Larsen Frederik • FRG
UM DER LIEBE WILLEN • 1920 • *Straub Agnes* • FRG
UM DIAMANTEN UND FRAUEN • 1919 • Boese Carl • FRG
UM DIE LIEBE DES DOMPTEURS • 1918 • Heiland Heinz Karl • FRG
UM DIE WELT OHNE GELD • 1927 • Nosseck Max • AUS
UM EIN HAAR.. see **ABENTEUER DER SIBYLLE BRANT, DAS** • 1925
UM EIN KONIGREICH see **KONIG VON GOLCONDA 3, DER** • 1921
UM EIN TOPFCHEN KAVIAR • 1915 • Del Zopp Rudolf • FRG
UM EIN WEIB • 1915 • Schonfeld Carl • FRG
UM EINE MILLION • 1917 • Piel Harry • FRG
UM EINE MILLION • 1924 • Gunsburg Arthur, Delmont Joseph • FRG • PARIS–LONDON–BERLIN
UM EINE NASENLANGE • 1931 • Guter Johannes • FRG
UM EINE NASENLANGE • 1949 • Emo E. W. • FRG
UM EINE STUNDE GLUCK • 1920 • *Andersen Iven* • FRG
UM EINEN GROSCHEN LIEBE see **SCAMPOLO, EIN KIND DER STRASSE** • 1932
UM EINEN STERN • 1915 • Wellin Arthur • FRG
UM EINES WEIBES EHRE • 1923 • Biebrach Rudolf • FRG
UM FREIHEIT UND LIEBE • 1937 • Buch Fritz Peter • FRG
UM FREMDE SCHULD • 1920 • *Berger Friedrich* • FRG
UM HAARSBREITE • 1913 • Biebrach Rudolf • FRG
UM IHRES KINDES GLUCK • 1915 • *Erol Lotte* • FRG
UM KRONE UND PEITSCHE • 1918 • Bluen Georg • FRG • TODESSPRUNG, DER
UM LIEBE UND THRON • 1922 • Osten Franz • FRG
UM NULL UHR SCHNAPPT DIE FALLE ZU • 1966 • Philipp Harald • FRG
UM RECHT UND EHRE • 1925 • Lowenbein Richard • FRG
UM RECHT UND LIEBE • 1923 • Seitz Franz?, Berger Josef? • FRG
UM RHUM UND FRAUENGLUCK see **FRAUENRUHM** • 1920
UM S MARGINAL • 1983 • Caetano Jose De Sa • PRT • ONE MARGINAL S
UM SEINES KINDES GLUCK see **VATER VOSS** • 1925
UM THRON UND LAND see **TRAGODIE EINES VOLKES 1, DIE** • 1922
UM THRON UND LIEBE see **KLEINE HERZOG, DER** • 1924
UM THRON UND LIEBE see **SARAJEVO** • 1955
UM ZWANZIG • 1963 • Radax Ferry • SWT
UMA • 1941 • Yamamoto Kajiro • JPN • HORSE ○ HORSES
UMA CHANDI GOWRI SANKARULA KATHA • 1968 • Reddy K. V. • IND • DIFFERENT INCARNATIONS OF DURGA
UMANITA • 1946 • Salvatori Jack • ITL
UMANO NON UMANO • 1971 • Schifano Mario • ITL
UMANOIDE, L' • 1979 • Lado Aldo • ITL, USA • HUMANOID, THE (USA)
UMARETE WA MITA KEREDO • 1932 • Ozu Yasujiro • JPN • I WAS BORN BUT..
UMARLI RZUCAJA CIEN • 1978 • Dziedzina Julian • PLN • DEAD PERSON'S SHADOW
UMARMT DAS LEBEN see **LEB' WOHL CHRISTINA** • 1945
UMARMUNGEN UND ANDERE SACHEN • 1976 • Richter Jochen • FRG • EMBRACES AND OTHER THINGS
UMBARTHA • 1982 • Patel Jabbar • IND • THRESHOLD
UMBDHALE • 1980 • SAF
UMBER • 1931 • Wright Basil • DOC • UKN
UMBERTO D • 1952 • De Sica Vittorio • ITL
UMBODI • 1984 • SAF
UMBRACLE, EL • Portabella Pedro • SHT • SPN
UMBRELLA • Gokhale G. K. • ANM • IND
UMBRELLA, THE • 1933 • Davis Redd • UKN
UMBRELLA, THE see **ZONTIK** • 1967
UMBRELLA IN MOONLIGHT see **TSUKIYO NO KASA** • 1955
UMBRELLA MAN, THE • 1982 • Noyce Phil • ASL
UMBRELLA MAN, THE see **LONDON BY NIGHT** • 1937
UMBRELLA STORY see **OMBRELLE ET PARAPLUIE** • 1956
UMBRELLA THEY COULD NOT LOSE, THE • 1912 • Wilson Frank? • UKN
UMBRELLA WOMAN, THE • 1986 • Cameron Ken • ASL • GOOD WIFE, THE (UKN)
UMBRELLAS OF CHERBOURG, THE (USA) see **PARAPLUIES DE CHERBOURG, LES** • 1964
UMBRELLAS TO MEND • 1912 • *Bunny John* • USA
UMBRUCH • 1987 • Schlumpf Hans-Ulrich • DOC • SWT
UMDLALI • 1980 • SAF
UMDLALO UMBANGO • 1983 • SAF
UMDLALO UMKHULU • 1982 • SAF
UMETNI RAJ • 1990 • Godina Karpo • YGS • ARTIFICIAL PARADISE
UMFANA • 1984 • SAF
UMFANA II • 1984 • SAF
UMFANA WEKARATE • 1985 • SAF
UMI NO BARA • 1945 • Kinugasa Teinosuke • JPN • ROSE OF THE SEA
UMI NO CHIZU • 1959 • Horiuchi Manao • JPN • MAP OF THE OCEAN
UMI NO G-MEN: TAIHEIYO NO YOJINBO • 1967 • Tanaka Shigeo • JPN • G-MEN OF THE SEA
UMI NO GOZUKU see **MAMPOU HATTENSHI: UMI NO GOZUKU** • 1942
UMI NO HANABI • 1951 • Kinoshita Keisuke • JPN • SEA OF FIREWORKS ○ FIREWORKS OVER THE SEA
UMI NO KOTO • 1966 • Tasaka Tomotaka • JPN • KOTO –THE LAKE OF TEARS ○ LAKE OF TEARS
UMI NO NAI MINATO • 1931 • Murata Minoru • JPN
UMI NO SHOBUSHI • 1961 • Kurahara Koreyoshi • JPN • GAMBLER IN THE SEA
UMI NO WAKADO • 1955 • Hagiwara Ryo • JPN • PEACEFUL SEA
UMI NO YARODOMO • 1957 • Shindo Kaneto • JPN • HARBOUR RATS ○ GUYS OF THE SEA
UMI O WATARU SAIREI • 1941 • Inagaki Hiroshi • JPN • FESTIVAL ACROSS THE SEA
UMI TO DOKUYAKU • 1987 • Kumai Kei • JPN • SEA AND POISON
UMI WA IKITEIRU • 1958 • Hani Susumu • DOC • JPN • LIVING SEA, THE
UMIHEBI DAIMYO • 1960 • Hirozu Mitsuo • JPN
UMINARI KAIDO • 1934 • Yamanaka Sadao • JPN • ROAD TO UMINARI
UMINO WAKADAISHO • 1965 • Furusawa Kengo • JPN • STANDBY COLLEGIATE
UMIR KRVI • 1971 • Velimirovic Zdravko • YGS • BLOOD FEUD
UMJULUKO ME GAZI • 1982 • SAF
UMNYAKAZO • 1981 • SAF
UMONA • 1980 • SAF
UMONI • 1985 • SAF
UMOR PE SFORI • 1954 • Schiopescu Constantza • SHT • RMN • HUMOR OVER STRINGS
UMORISMO NERO • 1965 • Zagni Giancarlo, Forque Jose Maria, Autant-Lara Claude • ITL, SPN, FRN • MUERTE VIAJA DEMASIADO, LA (SPN) ○ HUMORISMO NEGRO ○ BLACK HUMOR ○ HUMOUR NOIR ○ DEATH TRAVELS TOO MUCH
UMPISAHAN MO, AT TATAPUSIN KO • 1967 • Santiago Pablo • PHL • YOU START, AND I'LL FINISH
UMRAO JAAN • 1979 • Ali Muzaffar • IND
UMSIZI • 1985 • SAF
UMUNT AKALAHLWA • 1979 • SAF
UMUT • 1970 • Guney Yilmaz • TRK • HOPE
UMUT DUNYASI • 1974 • Onal Safa • TRK • WORLD OF HOPE, A
UMUT SOKAGI • 1986 • Goren Serif • TRK • STREET OF HOPE, THE
UMUTLU SAFAKLLAR • 1985 • Duru Sureyya • TRK • DAWN OF HOPE, THE
UMUTSUZLAR • 1971 • Guney Yilmaz • TRK • HOPELESS ONES, THE
UMWEG ZUR EHE, DER • 1919 • Wiene Robert?, Wiene Conrad?, Freisler Fritz? • FRG
UMWEGE DES SCHONEN KARL, DIE • 1938 • Froelich Carl • FRG
UMWEGE ZU DIR • 1944 • Thimig Hans • FRG
UMWEGE ZUM GLUCK • 1939 • Buch Fritz Peter • FRG
UMYEI SKAZAT –NYET • 1976 • Narliev Khodzhakuli • USS • KNOW HOW TO SAY NO ○ DARE TO SAY NO
UMZINGELI • 1979 • SAF
UN COUP DE FEU DANS LA NUIT see **COUP DE FEU DANS LA NUIT** • 1942
UN DANS L'AUTRE, ON TIENT LE BON BOUT, L' • Antony Michel • FRN
UN DE LA CANEBIERE • 1938 • Pujol Rene • FRN
UN DE LA COLONIALE see **CANTINIER DE LA COLONIALE, LE** • 1937
UN DE LA LEGION • 1936 • Christian-Jaque • FRN
UN DE LA MONTAGNE • 1933 • de Poligny Serge, Le Henaff Rene • FRN • MAJESTE BLANCHE, LA
UN, DEUX, TROIS.. • 1974 • Shaker • FRN
UN, DEUX, TROIS, QUATRE! • 1960 • Young Terence • FRN • BLACK TIGHTS (USA) ○ COLLANTS NOIRS, LES ○ ONE, TWO, THREE, FOUR
UN, DOS, TRES.., AL ESCONDITE INGLES • 1969 • Zulueta Ivan • SPN • POPLAND
UN, DOS, TRES.., DISPARA OTRA VEZ • 1974 • Demicheli Tulio • SPN
UN DU 22ieme • 1940 • Noxon Gerald • DCS • CND
UN-ERHORTE FRAU, DIE • 1936 • Malasomma Nunzio • FRG • ICH KENNE DICH NICHT MEHR
UN OASPETE LA CINA • 1987 • Constantinescu Mihai • RMN • GUEST AT DINNER, A
UN SURIS IN PLINA VARA • 1963 • Saizescu Geo • RMN • MIDSUMMER DAY'S SMILE, A
UNA DI QUELLE • 1953 • Fabrizi Aldo • ITL
UNA FILM DI • 1964 • Davies Brian • DCS • ASL
UNA OF THE SIERRAS • 1912 • Ince Ralph • USA
UNA SU TREDICI • 1969 • Gessner Nicolas, Lucignani Luciano • ITL, FRN • TWELVE PLUS ONE (USA) ○ 12 + 1 (FRN) ○ LUCKY 13 ○ 13 CHAIRS
UNA SULL'ALTRA • 1969 • Fulci Lucio • ITL, SPN, FRN • HISTORIA PERVERSA, UNA (SPN) ○ ONE ON TOP OF THE OTHER (UKN)
UNA TAL DULCINEA • 1964 • Salvia Rafael J. • SPN
UNACCUSTOMED AS WE ARE • 1929 • Foster Lewis R. • SHT • USA
UNADORNED WEST, THE see **UNDRESSED WEST, THE** • 1964
UNAFRAID, THE • 1915 • De Mille Cecil B. • USA
UNAFRAID, THE • 1917 • King Henry • USA
UNAFRAID, THE see **KISS THE BLOOD OFF MY HANDS** • 1948
UNAKRSNA VATRA (YGS) see **OPERATION CROSS EAGLES** • 1969
UNANSWERED QUESTION, THE • 1987 • van der Keuken Johan • NTH
UNAPPRECIATED GENIUS • 1909 • Porter Edwin S. • USA
UNAPPRECIATED JOKE, THE • 1903 • Porter Edwin S. • USA
UNAPPROACHABLE, THE (UKN) see **UNERREICHBARE, DER** • 1982
UNAS PAGINAS EN NEGRO • 1949 • Fortuny Juan, Seville Armando • SPN
UNA'S USEFUL UNCLE • 1916 • *Emerson* • USA
UNASHAMED • 1932 • Beaumont Harry • USA • WITHOUT SHAME
UNATTAINABLE, THE • 1916 • Carleton Lloyd B. • USA
UNAUTHORISED ROAD see **MACUSHLA** • 1937
UNBALANCED WHEEL, THE see **KICHIGAI BURAKU** • 1957
UNBANDIGES SPANIEN • 1962 • Stein J., Stein K. • GDR
UNBEARABLE BEAR, THE • 1943 • Jones Charles M. • ANS • USA
UNBEARABLE LIGHTNESS OF BEING, THE • 1987 • Kaufman Philip • USA
UNBEARABLE SALESMAN • 1957 • Smith Paul J. • ANS • USA
UNBEATABLE GAME, THE • 1925 • Siple J. Law • USA
UNBEDEUTENDE FRAU, EINE • 1919 • Joseph Erich • FRG
UNBEFLECKTE HAND, DIE see **MANUS IMMACULATA** • 1920
UNBEKANNTE, DIE • 1936 • Wisbar Frank • FRG • UNKNOWN, THE
UNBEKANNTE, DIE see **EULE 2, DIE** • 1927
UNBEKANNTE GAST, DER • 1931 • Emo E. W. • FRG
UNBEKANNTE GEGNER, DER • 1925 • Bock-Stieber Gernot • FRG
UNBEKANNTE MORGEN, DAS • 1923 • Korda Alexander • FRG, AUS • UNKNOWN TOMORROW, THE (UKN)
UNBELIEVABLE GLORY OF THE HUMAN VOICE, THE • 1972 • Williams Tony • MTV • NZL
UNBELIEVABLE STORY, AN • Weiler Kurt • ANM • GDR
UNBELIEVABLE TRUTH, THE • 1989 • Hartley • USA
UNBELIEVER, THE • 1908 • *Tyler Walter* • UKN
UNBELIEVER, THE • 1918 • Crosland Alan • USA
UNBERUHRTE FRAU, DIE • 1925 • David Constantin J. • FRG
UNBESCHRIEBENES BLATT, EIN • 1915 • Delmont Joseph • FRG
UNBESIEGBARON, DIE • 1953 • Pohl Arthur • GDR
UNBEWOHNTE HAUS, DAS • 1920 • Arnheim Valy • FRG
UNBEZAHMBARE ANGELIQUE (FRG) see **INDOMPTABLE ANGELIQUE** • 1967
UNBEZAHMBARE LENI PEICKERT, DIE • 1969 • Kluge Alexander • FRG • INDOMITABLE LENI PEICKERT, THE
UNBLAZED TRAIL • 1923 • Hatton Richard • USA
UNBORN, THE • 1916 • *Bondhill Gertrude* • USA
UNBORN, THE (UKN) see **TOMORROW'S CHILDREN** • 1934
UNBROKEN LINE, THE • 1978 • Beaudry Diane • DOC • CND • NOBLE LIGNEE, LA
UNBROKEN PROMISE, THE • 1919 • Powell Frank • USA
UNBROKEN ROAD, THE • 1915 • *Nash Mary* • USA
UNBURIED PAST, THE • 1913 • *Essanay* • USA
UNCANNY, THE • 1977 • Heroux Denis • CND, UKN • BRRR..
UNCANNY MR. GUMBLE, THE • 1914 • Miller Ashley • USA
UNCAS, EL FIN DE UNA RAZA • 1964 • Cano Mateo • SPN
UNCENSORED • 1942 • Asquith Anthony • UKN • WE SHALL RISE AGAIN
UNCENSORED MOVIES • 1923 • Clements Roy • SHT • USA
UNCENSORED OFFICIAL WAR FILMS • 1921 • ASL
UNCERTAIN GLORY • 1944 • Walsh Raoul • USA
UNCERTAIN LADY • 1934 • Freund Karl • USA
UNCERTAIN SEASON see **NEJISTA SEZONA** • 1987
UNCHAINED • 1955 • Bartlett Hall • USA
UNCHAINED see **MAN WHO BROKE 1,000 CHAINS, THE** • 1987
UNCHAINED, THE see **SCATENATO, LO** • 1967
UNCHAINED GODDESS, THE • 1957 • Hurtz William • DOC • USA
UNCHALLENGEABLE see **ASADHYUDU** • 1968
UNCHANGING SEA, THE • 1910 • Griffith D. W. • USA
UNCHARTED CHANNELS • 1920 • King Henry • USA
UNCHARTED RIVER see **MEIYOUHANGBIAODE HELIU** • 1985
UNCHARTED SEA, THE see **UNCHARTED SEAS** • 1921
UNCHARTED SEAS • 1921 • Ruggles Wesley • USA • UNCHARTED SEA, THE
UNCHARTED WATERS • 1933 • Anstey Edgar • DOC • UKN
UNCHASTENED WOMAN, THE • 1918 • Humphrey William • USA • TWO MEN AND A WOMAN(?)
UNCHASTENED WOMAN, THE • 1925 • Young James • USA
UNCIVIL WARBIRDS • 1946 • White Jules • SHT • USA
UNCIVIL WARRIORS • 1935 • Lord Del • SHT • USA
UNCIVILISED • 1936 • Chauvel Charles • ASL
UNCLAIMED GOODS • 1918 • Sturgeon Rollin S. • USA
UNCLE see **OJISAN** • 1943
UNCLE see **STREJDA** • 1959
UNCLE see **TIME OF TEARS** • 1987
UNCLE, THE • 1964 • Davis Desmond • UKN
UNCLE ABDU'S GHOST see **AFRIT AM ABDU**
UNCLE ABNER'S WILL • 1915 • *Warner'S Features* • USA
UNCLE ANDY HARDY see **LOVE LAUGHS AT ANDY HARDY** • 1946
UNCLE AS CUPID • 1913 • Haldane Bert • UKN
UNCLE BILL • 1912 • *Conway Jack* • USA
UNCLE BILL • 1914 • Ince Ralph • USA
UNCLE BLUE'S NEW BOAT see **FARBROR BLAS NYA BAT** • 1969
UNCLE BOB SHOW, THE • 1989 • Gordon Keith • USA
UNCLE BUCK • 1989 • Hughes John • USA
UNCLE BUYS CLARENCE A BALLOON • 1911 • Wilson Frank? • UKN
UNCLE CRUSTY • 1915 • Seay Charles M. • USA
UNCLE DICK'S DARLING • 1920 • Paul Fred • UKN
UNCLE DONALD'S ANTS • 1952 • Hannah Jack • ANS • USA
UNCLE DUNN DONE • 1912 • *Cosmopolitan* • UKN
UNCLE EXPLAINS • 1949 • Waterhouse John • UKN
UNCLE FRANS see **FARBROR FRANS** • 1926
UNCLE FROM AMERICA see **STRYCEK Z AMERIKY** • 1933
UNCLE FROM AMERICA, THE (USA) see **ZIO D'AMERICA, LO** • 1939

UNCLE FROM SUMATRA, THE see **UNCLE VON SUMATRA, DER** • 1924

UNCLE GEORGE'S TRIP TO LONDON • 1906 • Collins Alf • UKN

UNCLE HARRY see **STRANGE AFFAIR OF UNCLE HARRY, THE** • 1945

UNCLE HECK, BY HECK • 1915 • Steppling John • USA

UNCLE HIRAM'S LIST • 1911 • *West William* • USA

UNCLE JACK see **PIED PIPER MALONE** • 1924

UNCLE JAKE • 1933 • Cline Eddie • SHT • USA

UNCLE JANCO • 1967 • Varda Agnes • SHT • USA • UNCLE YANKO ○ ONCLE JANCO

UNCLE JASPER'S WILL • 1922 • Micheaux Oscar • USA • JASPER LANDRY'S WILL

UNCLE JIM • 1910 • Melies Gaston • USA

UNCLE JOAKIM'S SECRET see **ONKEL JOAKIMS HEMMELIGHED** • 1967

UNCLE JOE • 1910 • Fitzhamon Lewin? • UKN

UNCLE JOE SHANNON • 1978 • Hanwright Joseph C. • USA

UNCLE JOEY • 1941 • Davis Mannie • ANS • USA

UNCLE JOEY COMES TO TOWN • 1941 • Davis Mannie • ANS • USA

UNCLE JOHN • 1915 • *Girardot Etienne* • USA

UNCLE JOHN TO THE RESCUE • 1913 • *Wilbur Crane* • USA

UNCLE JOHN'S ARRIVAL IN STOCKHOLM see **FARBROR JOHANNES ANKOMST TILL STOCKHOLM** • 1912

UNCLE JOHN'S MONEY • 1917 • Cochrane George • SHT • USA

UNCLE JOSH AT THE MOVING PICTURE SHOW • 1902 • Porter Edwin S. • USA

UNCLE JOSH IN A SPOOKY HOTEL • 1900 • Porter Edwin S. • SHT • USA

UNCLE JOSH'S NIGHTMARE • 1900 • Porter Edwin S. • USA

UNCLE MARIN, THE MULTIMILLIONAIRE • 1979 • Nicolaescu Sergiu • RMN

UNCLE MAXIM'S WILL • 1914 • Batley Ethyle? • UKN

UNCLE MOSES • 1932 • Goldin Sidney M., Scotto Aubrey • USA

UNCLE MUN AND THE MINISTER • 1912 • *Flugragh Edna* • USA

UNCLE NICK • 1938 • Cooper Thomas G. • UKN

UNCLE OF THE BRIDE see **LAST OF THE SUMMER WINE: UNCLE OF THE BRIDE** • 1985

UNCLE PETE'S RUSE • 1911 • *Imp* • USA

UNCLE PODGER'S MISHAPS • 1905 • Redfern Jasper • UKN

UNCLE REMUS – BRER RABBIT • 1919 • *Dyer Anson (P)* • ANM • UKN

UNCLE RUBE'S BIRTHDAY (USA) see **FETE AU PERE MATHIEU, LA** • 1904

UNCLE SAM OF FREEDOM RIDGE see **UNCLE SAM OF THE FREEDOM RIDGE** • 1920

UNCLE SAM OF THE FREEDOM RIDGE • 1920 • Beranger George A. • SHT • USA • UNCLE SAM OF FREEDOM RIDGE

UNCLE SAM'S SONGS • 1951 • Cowan Will • SHT • USA

UNCLE SCAM • 1981 • Pileggi Tom, Levanios Michael Jr. • USA

UNCLE SILAS • 1947 • Frank Charles H. • UKN • INHERITANCE, THE (USA)

UNCLE TOM • 1929 • *Sennett Mack (P)* • SHT • USA

UNCLE TOM (UKN) see **ZIO TOM** • 1971

UNCLE TOM WINS • 1909 • Porter Edwin S. • USA

UNCLE TOM WITHOUT THE CABIN • 1919 • Hunt Ray • SHT • USA

UNCLE TOMCAT AND HIS HOUSE OF KITTENS see **UNCLE TOMCAT'S HOUSE OF KITTENS** • 1967

UNCLE TOMCAT'S HOUSE OF KITTENS • 1967 • Purdue Gunther • USA • UNCLE TOMCAT AND HIS HOUSE OF KITTENS

UNCLE TOM'S BUNGALOW • 1937 • Avery Tex • ANS • USA

UNCLE TOM'S CABANA • 1947 • Avery Tex • ANS • USA

UNCLE TOM'S CABIN • 1903 • Porter Edwin S. • USA

UNCLE TOM'S CABIN • 1910 • *Thanhouser* • USA

UNCLE TOM'S CABIN • 1910 • *Pathe* • USA

UNCLE TOM'S CABIN • 1910 • Blackton J. Stuart • *Vitagraph* • USA

UNCLE TOM'S CABIN • 1913 • *Powers* • USA

UNCLE TOM'S CABIN • 1913 • Olcott Sidney • *Kalem* • USA

UNCLE TOM'S CABIN • 1913 • Turner Otis • *Imp* • USA

UNCLE TOM'S CABIN • 1914 • Daly William Robert • *World* • USA

UNCLE TOM'S CABIN • 1918 • Dawley J. Searle • USA

UNCLE TOM'S CABIN • 1922 • *Welsh Bros* • UKN

UNCLE TOM'S CABIN • 1927 • Pollard Harry • USA

UNCLE TOM'S CABIN • 1987 • Lathan Stan • TVM • USA

"UNCLE TOM'S CABIN" TROUPE, AN • 1913 • Henderson Dell • USA

UNCLE TOM'S CABIN (USA) see **ONKEL TOMS HUTTE** • 1965

UNCLE TOM'S CABOOSE • 1920 • Davis James • SHT • USA

UNCLE TOM'S UNCLE • 1926 • Roach Hal • SHT • USA

UNCLE VANYA • 1958 • Goetz John, Tone Franchot • USA

UNCLE VANYA • 1963 • Burge Stuart • UKN

UNCLE VANYA see **DYADYA VANYA** • 1971

UNCLE VON SUMATRA, DER • 1924 • Curtiz Michael • AUS • UNCLE FROM SUMATRA, THE

UNCLE WAS A VAMPIRE (USA) see **TEMPI DURI PER I VAMPIRI** • 1959

UNCLE WILLIE'S BICYCLE SHOP see **ISN'T LIFE WONDERFUL!** • 1953

UNCLE YANKO see **UNCLE JANCO** • 1967

UNCLEAN, THE • 1967 • Noren Andrew • USA

UNCLEAN WORLD, THE • 1903 • Hepworth Cecil M. • UKN

UNCLEAN WORLD: THE SUBURBAN BUNKUM MICROBE-GUYOSCOPE, THE • 1903 • Stow Percy • UKN

UNCLES AND AUNTS • 1989 • Driessen Paul • ANM • NTH

UNCLE'S BIRTHDAY GIFT • 1911 • *Edison* • USA

UNCLE'S DAY WITH THE CHILDREN • 1909 • *Anglo-American Films* • UKN

UNCLE'S DEATH • 1967 • Lugo Alfredo • SHT • VNZ

UNCLE'S DREAM, AN see **DYADYUSHKIN SON** • 1967

UNCLE'S FINISH • 1914 • *Eclectic* • USA

UNCLE'S LAST LETTER • 1915 • *Superba* • USA

UNCLE'S LITTLE ONES • 1916 • *Napoleon & Sally* • SHT • USA

UNCLE'S NAMESAKES • 1913 • *Thanhouser* • USA

UNCLE'S NEW BLAZER • 1915 • *Garwood William* • USA

UNCLE'S PICNIC • 1908 • Williamson James? • UKN

UNCLE'S PICNIC • 1911 • Bouwmeester Theo, Booth W. R.? • UKN

UNCLE'S PRESENT • 1910 • *Empire Films* • UKN

UNCLE'S PRESENT • 1912 • Aylott Dave? • UKN

UNCLE'S PRESENT • 1913 • Aylott Dave • UKN • PRESENT FROM UNCLE, A

UNCLE'S PRESENT RETURNED WITH THANKS • 1907 • *Warwick Trading Co* • UKN

UNCLE'S REJECTED PRESENT • 1908 • Raymond Charles? • UKN

UNCLE'S STRATEGY • 1912 • *Pathe* • USA

UNCLE'S VISIT • 1911 • *Tucker George L.* • USA

UNCLE'S VISIT • 1915 • *Browne H. A.* • UKN

UNCOMMON LOVE, AN • 1983 • Stern Steven Hilliard • TVM • USA

UNCOMMON THIEF, AN see **BEREGIS AVTOMOBILYA!** • 1966

UNCOMMON VALOR • 1982 • Amateau Rod • TVM • USA

UNCOMMON VALOR • 1983 • Kotcheff Ted • USA

UNCOMMONWEALTH see **RZECZ NIEPOSPOLITA** • 1962

UNCONQUERABLE, THE see **NEPOBEDIMYIE** • 1942

UNCONQUERED • 1917 • Reicher Frank • USA

UNCONQUERED • 1947 • De Mille Cecil B. • USA

UNCONQUERED • 1971 • Yang Evan • HKG

UNCONQUERED see **FREEDOM OF THE PRESS** • 1928

UNCONQUERED see **NEPOKORENNYE** • 1945

UNCONQUERED, THE • 1954 • Wood Richard Carver • USA

UNCONQUERED, THE • 1988 • Lowry Dick • TVM • USA

UNCONQUERED, THE see **NEPORAZENI** • 1956

UNCONQUERED BANDIT • 1935 • Webb Harry S. • USA

UNCONQUERED WOMAN • 1922 • Perez Marcel • USA

UNCONSCIOUS • 1980 • Freda Riccardo • ITL

UNCONSCIOUS HUNTER, THE see **HOMENAJE A TARZAN** • 1970

UNCONSECRATED EARTH see **ONGEWIJDE AARDE** • 1967

UNCONTROLLABLE MOTORCYCLE, THE • 1909 • Booth W. R. • UKN

UNCONTROLLED TERRITORY • 1957 • Robinson Lee • DOC • ASL

UNCONVENTIONAL GIRL, THE • 1916 • Hill Robert F. • SHT • USA

UNCONVENTIONAL LINDA see **HOLIDAY** • 1938

UNCONVENTIONAL MAIDA GREENWOOD, THE • 1920 • Drew Sidney Mrs. • SHT • USA

UNCONVENTIONAL YOUTH see **JOVENS PRA FRENTE** • 1968

UNCOVERED WAGON, THE • 1923 • Roach Hal • SHT • USA

UNCOVERED WEEKEND see **FIN DE SEMANA AL DESNUDO** • 1976

UNCULTURED VULTURE • 1947 • Wickersham Bob • ANS • USA

UNCUT DIAMOND, THE • 1916 • *Puritan* • USA

UNCUT DIAMONDS, THE • 1916 • Daly William Robert • *Selig* • SHT • USA

...UND ABENDS IN DIE SCALA • 1958 • Ode Erik • FRG

...UND ALLE DURSTEN NACH LIEBE see **NOCTURNO** • 1935

UND DAMIT TANZEN SIE NOCH IMMER • 1987 • Stoisits Marijana, Rabe Michael • DOC • AUS • STINJACKE CIZME

...UND DANN BYE BYE • 1965 • Gosov Marran • FRG

...UND DAS AM MONTAGMORGEN • 1959 • Comencini Luigi • FRG

...UND DAS IST DIE HAUPTSACHE • 1931 • May Joe • FRG • BALLNICHT, EINE

UND DAS LEBEN GEHT WEITER (FRG) see **A ZIVOT JDE DAL..** • 1935

UND DAS WISSEN IST DER TOD • 1915 • Schmidthassler Walter • FRG

UND DENNOCH KAM DAS GLUCK • 1923 • Lamprecht Gerhard • FRG • SCHWERE TAGE

UND DENNOCH WARD ES MORGEN 1 • 1922 • Linke Edmund • FRG

UND DENNOCH WARD ES MORGEN 2 • 1922 • Linke Edmund • FRG

UND DER AMAZONAS SCHWEIGT • 1963 • Backhaus Helmuth M., Eichhorn Franz • FRG, BRZ • RIVER OF EVIL (USA) ○ BLOOD RIVER

UND DER HIMMEL LACHT DAZU • 1954 • von Ambesser Axel • AUS • BRUDER MARTIN

UND DER REGEN VERWISCHT JEDE SPUR • 1972 • Vohrer Alfred • FRG

...UND DIE GERECHTIGKEIT FAND DEN WEG • 1916 • Neff Wolfgang • FRG

...UND DIE LIEBE LACHT DAZU • 1957 • Stemmle R. A. • FRG • SCHWARZBROT UND KIPFERL

...UND DIE MUSIK SPIELT DAZU • 1943 • Boese Carl • FRG • SAISON IN SALZBURG

UND DU, MEIN SCHATZ, BLEIBT HIER • 1961 • Antel Franz • AUS

UND DU, MEIN SCHATZ, FAHRST MIT • 1936 • Jacoby Georg • FRG

...UND ES KAM, WIE ES KOMMEN MUSSTE! • 1918 • *Treumann Wanda* • FRG

...UND ES LEUCHTET DIE PUSZTA • 1933 • Hille Heinz • FRG, HNG

"...UND ES LOCKT DER RUF AUS SUNDIGER WELT" see **"...UND ES LOCKT EIN RUF AUS SUNDIGER WELT"** • 1925

"...UND ES LOCKT EIN RUF AUS SUNDIGER WELT" • 1925 • Boese Carl • FRG • "...UND ES LOCKT DER RUF AUS SUNDIGER WELT" ○ VERLOREN UND GEWONNEN

...UND EWIG BLEIBT DIE LIEBE • 1954 • Liebeneiner Wolfgang • FRG

...UND EWIG KNALLEN DIE RAUBER • 1962 • Antel Franz • AUS

UND EWIG SINGEN DIE WALDER • 1959 • May Paul • AUS • DUEL WITH DEATH (USA) ○ VENGEANCE IN TIMBER VALLEY ○ BEYOND SING THE WOODS

UND FINDEN DEREINST WIR UNS WIEDER • 1947 • Muller Hans • FRG

UND FUHRE UNS NICHT IN VERSUCHUNG • 1917 • Eichberg Richard • FRG

UND FUHRE UNS NICHT IN VERSUCHUNG • 1957 • Hansen Rolf • FRG

UND FUHRE UNS NICHT IN VERSUCHUNG see **FUHRE UNS NICHT IN VERSUCHUNG** • 1922

UND HATTE DER LIEBE NICHT • 1918 • *Kolberg Ally* • FRG

UND ICH LIEBE DICH DOCH • 1918 • *Trautmann Ludwig* • FRG

UND IMMER RUFT DAS HERZ • 1939 • Freedland Georg • FRG

...UND IMMER RUFT DAS HERZ • 1958 • Freedland Georg, Nosseck Martin • FRG, FNL • MOONWOLF (USA) ○ ZURUCK AUS DEM WELTALL ○ AVARUUSRAKETILLA RAKKAUTEEN

UND JIMMY GING ZUM REGENBOGEN • 1971 • Vohrer Alfred • FRG, AUS • AND JIMMY WENT TO THE RAINBOW'S END

...UND KEINER SCHAMTE SICH • 1960 • Schott-Schobinger Hans • FRG • AND NOBODY WAS ASHAMED

...UND MORGEN FAHRT IHR ZUR HOLLE (FRG) see **DALLE ARDENNE ALL'INFERNO** • 1968

...UND NICHTS ALS DIE WAHRHEIT • 1958 • Wirth Franz Peter • FRG

...UND NOCH FRECH DAZU! • 1959 • von Sydow Rolf • FRG

...UND NOCH NICHT 16 see **SEX UND NOCH NICHT SECHZEHN** • 1968

UND SIE FANDEN SICH WIEDER • 1915 • Del Zopp Rudolf • FRG

UND SIE GENIESSEN DIE LIEBE • 1976 • Wyler Johnny • FRG • JET SEX

...UND SO WAS MUSS UM ACHT INS BETT • 1965 • Jacobs Werner • FRG, AUS

...UND SO WAS NENNT SICH LEBEN • 1960 • von Radvanyi Geza • FRG

UND SOWAS WILL ERWACHSEN SEIN see **WINZERIN VON LANGENLOIS, DIE** • 1957

...UND UBER UNS DER HIMMEL • 1947 • von Baky Josef • FRG • CITY OF TORMENT (USA) ○ ...AND THE SKY ABOVE US

UND WANDERN SOLLST DU RUHELOS.. • 1915 • Oswald Richard • FRG • AND YOU WILL WANDER RESTLESS ○ SCHONE SUNDERIN, DIE ○ BEAUTIFUL SINNER, THE

UND WENN ICH LIEB'.. • 1917 • Rippert Otto • FRG

UND WENN'S NUR EINER WAR' • 1949 • Schleif Wolfgang • GDR

"...UND WER KEIN KREUZ UND LEIDEN HAT.." • 1916 • Matull Kurt • FRG

UND WER KUSST MICH? • 1933 • Emo E. W. • FRG

...UND WER KUSST MICH? • 1956 • Nosseck Max • AUS • HERZ UND EINE SEELE, EIN

UND WIEDER 48! • 1949 • von Wangenheim Gustav • FRG

UNDAMMA BOTTU PEDATA • 1968 • Viswanath K. • IND • WAIT A FEW MOMENTS MORE

UNDEAD, THE • 1956 • Corman Roger • USA

UNDEAD, THE see **FROM BEYOND THE GRAVE** • 1973

UNDEFEATED, THE • 1950 • Dickson Paul • DOC • UKN

UNDEFEATED, THE • 1969 • McLaglen Andrew V. • USA

UNDEFEATED CITY see **MIASTO NIEUJARZMIONE** • 1950

UNDEFEATED WOMAN see **JOKYO ICHIDAI** • 1958

UNDER 18 see **NOCH MINDERJAHRIG** • 1957

UNDER A BARREL • 1916 • Louis Will • SHT • USA

UNDER A CHANGING SKY • 1910 • *Reliance* • USA

UNDER A CLOUD • 1937 • King George • UKN

UNDER A FLAG OF TRUCE • 1912 • Buel Kenean • USA

UNDER A HOT SUN see **UNTER HEISSER ZONE** • 1916

UNDER A SHADOW • 1915 • De Grasse Joseph • USA

UNDER A SKY OF STONE see **UNDER EN STEINHIMMEL** • 1974

UNDER A TEXAS MOON • 1930 • Curtiz Michael • USA

UNDER AGE • 1941 • Dmytryk Edward • USA

UNDER AGE • 1964 • Buchanan Larry • USA

UNDER ANCIENT DESERT SKIES • 1961 • Schneiderov Vladimir • DOC • USS

UNDER ARIZONA SKIES • 1914 • *Larkin Dolly* • USA

UNDER ARIZONA SKIES • 1946 • Hillyer Lambert • USA

UNDER ARREST (UKN) see **BLAZING ACROSS THE PECOS** • 1948

UNDER AZURE SKIES • 1916 • Bertram William • SHT • USA

UNDER BOTH FLAGS • 1910 • Youngdeer James • USA

UNDER BURNING SKIES • 1912 • Griffith D. W. • USA

UNDER CALIFORNIA STARS • 1948 • Witney William • USA

UNDER CAPRICORN • 1949 • Hitchcock Alfred • USA, UKN

UNDER CAPRICORN • 1982 • Hardy Rod • MTV • ASL

UNDER CIRKUSKUPOLEN • 1912 • Klercker Georg • SWD

UNDER COLORADO SKIES • 1947 • Springsteen R. G. • USA

UNDER COVER • 1916 • Vignola Robert G. • USA

UNDER COVER • 1990 • Graf Dominik • FRG

UNDER COVER see **UNDERCOVER** • 1987

UNDER-COVER MAN • 1932 • Flood James • USA

UNDER COVER OF NIGHT • 1936 • Seitz George B. • USA

UNDER COVER OF NIGHT see **JAGTE RAHO** • 1956

UNDER COVER OF NIGHT see **ZIRE POOSTE SHAB** • 1975

UNDER COVER ROGUE see **VOCI BIANCHE, LE** • 1964

UNDER CRIMSON SKIES • 1920 • Ingram Rex • USA • BEACH COMBER, THE

UNDER DESPERATION'S SPUR • 1914 • *Holmes Helen* • USA

UNDER DITT PARASOLL • 1968 • Frisk Ragnar • SWD • UNDER YOUR UMBRELLA

UNDER EARTH see **DEBAJO DEL MUNDO** • 1986

UNDER EASTERN SKIES see **FRAU OHNE NAMEN 1, DIE** • 1927

UNDER EIGHTEEN • 1931 • Mayo Archie • USA

UNDER EN STEINHIMMEL • 1974 • Andersen Knut, Maslennikov Igor • NRW, USS • BENEATH A STONY SKY ○ OCTOBER '44 ○ UNDER A SKY OF STONE

UNDER FALSE COLORS • 1912 • Merwin Bannister • USA

UNDER FALSE COLORS • 1914 • *Thanhouser* • USA

UNDER FALSE COLORS • 1914 • Brooke Van Dyke • *Vitagraph* • USA

UNDER FALSE COLORS • 1917 • Chautard Emile • USA

UNDER FALSE COLOURS see **UNDER FALSK FLAGG** • 1935

UNDER FALSE PRETENCES • 1912 • Dwan Allan • USA

UNDER FALSE PRETENSES • 1918 • Davis James • SHT • USA

UNDER FALSK FLAGG • 1935 • Molander Gustaf • SWD • UNDER FALSE COLOURS

UNDER FIESTA STARS • 1941 • McDonald Frank • USA

UNDER FIRE • 1913 • *Bison* • USA

UNDER FIRE • 1926 • Elfelt Clifford S. • USA

UNDER FIRE • 1957 • Clark James B. • USA

UNDER FIRE • 1983 • Spottiswoode Roger • USA

UNDER FIRE IN MEXICO • 1914 • Nelson J. Arthur • USA

UNDER FOUR FLAGS • 1919 • *World* • USA
UNDER GANGSTER RULE see **BAJO EL IMPERIO DEL HAMPA** • 1968
UNDER HANDICAP • 1917 • Balshofer Fred J. • USA
UNDER HER WING • 1912 • Porter Edwin S. • USA
UNDER HOUSE ARREST see **EN RESIDENCE SURVEILLEE** • 1981
UNDER KAERLIGHEDENS AAG see **SKAEBNES VEJE** • 1913
UNDER KING KRAKUS (USA) see **ZAKROLA KRAKUSA** • 1948
UNDER MEXICALI STARS • 1950 • Blair George • USA
UNDER MEXICAN SKIES • 1912 • *Anderson Broncho Billy* • USA
UNDER MILK WOOD • 1973 • Sinclair Andrew • UKN
UNDER MINDERNES TRAE • 1913 • Holger-Madsen • DNM • GAMLE BAENK, DEN ○ LEFT ALONE
UNDER MONTANA SKIES • 1930 • Thorpe Richard • USA
UNDER MY SKIN • 1950 • Negulesco Jean • USA • BIG FALL, THE ○ MY OLD MAN
UNDER NEVADA SKIES • 1946 • McDonald Frank • USA
UNDER NEW MANAGEMENT • 1915 • Lehrman Henry • USA
UNDER NEW MANAGEMENT • 1946 • Blakeley John E. • UKN • HONEYMOON HOTEL
UNDER NIGHT STREETS • 1958 • Keene Ralph • DOC • UKN
UNDER NORTHERN LIGHTS • 1920 • Jaccard Jacques • USA
UNDER NORTHERN SKIES • 1909 • *Edison* • USA
UNDER NOTICE TO LEAVE see **UPPSAGD** • 1934
UNDER OATH • 1915 • Horne James W. • USA
UNDER OATH • 1922 • Archainbaud George • USA
UNDER ONE ROOF • 1946 • Gilbert Lewis* • DCS • UKN
UNDER ONE ROOF see **POD JEDNOU STRECHOU** • 1938
UNDER ONE ROOF see **POD JEDNYM DACHEM** • 1964
UNDER ORDERS see **TWO-FISTED JEFFERSON** • 1922
UNDER PESTEN see **MENS PESTEN RASER** • 1913
UNDER PRESSURE • 1935 • Walsh Raoul • USA
UNDER PRESSURE see **BAJO PRESION** • 1989
UNDER PROOF • 1936 • Gillett Roland • UKN
UNDER-PUP, THE • 1939 • Wallace Richard • USA
UNDER RODA FANOR • 1931 • Branner Per-Axel • SWD
UNDER ROYAL PATRONAGE • 1914 • Calvert E. H. • USA
UNDER SATAN'S SUN (USA) see **SOUS LE SOLEIL DE SATAN** • 1987
UNDER SAVKLINGENS TAENDER • 1913 • Holger-Madsen • DNM • MECHANICAL SAW, THE ○ USURER'S SON, THE
UNDER SEALED ORDERS (USA) see **MIT VERSIEGELTER ORDER** • 1938
UNDER SECRET ORDERS • 1933 • Newfield Sam • USA
UNDER-SECRETARY'S HONOUR, THE • 1915 • Coleby A. E.? • UKN
UNDER SENTENCE • 1920 • Feeney Edward • SHT • USA
UNDER-SHERIFF, THE • 1914 • Henderson Dell • USA
UNDER SIEGE • Cardona Rene Jr. • MXC
UNDER SIEGE • 1986 • Young Roger • TVM • USA
UNDER SILK GARMENTS see **ITSUWARERU SEISO** • 1951
UNDER SODRA KORSET • 1952 • Nykvist Sven, Bergstrom Olof • SWD • UNDER THE SOUTHERN CROSS
UNDER SOUTHERN SKIES • 1911 • *Powers* • USA
UNDER SOUTHERN SKIES • 1915 • Henderson Lucius • USA
UNDER SOUTHERN STARS • 1937 • Grinde Nick • SHT • USA
UNDER STRANGE FLAGS • 1937 • Willat Irvin V. • USA
UNDER SUNNY SKIES • Ivanov-Barkov Yevgeni • USS
UNDER SUSPICION • 1912 • *Greenwood Winnifred* • USA
UNDER SUSPICION • 1918 • Davis Will S. • USA
UNDER SUSPICION • 1919 • Dowlan William C. • USA
UNDER SUSPICION • 1919 • West Walter • UKN
UNDER SUSPICION • 1931 • Erickson A. F. • USA • TONIGHT AND YOU
UNDER SUSPICION • 1937 • Collins Lewis D. • USA
UNDER SUSPICION see **VOM TATER FEHLT JEDE SPUR** • 1928
UNDER SUSPICION (USA) see **GAME OF LIBERTY, THE** • 1916
UNDER SVALLANDE SEGEL • 1952 • Jute Alex • SWD
UNDER TEN FLAGS (UKN) see **SOTTO DIECI BANDIERE** • 1960
UNDER TEXAS SKIES • 1930 • McGowan J. P. • USA
UNDER TEXAS SKIES • 1940 • Sherman George • USA
UNDER THAT UCKA MOUNTAIN see **SPOD TE UCKE GORI** • 1973
UNDER THE BADGER'S ROCK see **POD JEZEVCI SKALOU** • 1981
UNDER THE BAMBOO TREE • 1905 • *Bitzer Billy (Ph)* • USA
UNDER THE BANNER OF SAMURAI (USA) see **FURIN KAZAN** • 1969
UNDER THE BAZUMKA TREE • 1929 • Aylott Dave, Symmons E. F. • SHT • UKN
UNDER THE BED • 1917 • Chaudet Louis W. • SHT • USA
UNDER THE BED see **CUDZA ZONA I MAZ POD LOZKIEM** • 1962
UNDER THE BED DARLING • 1977 • Grant David • UKN
UNDER THE BIG TOP • 1938 • Brown Karl • USA • CIRCUS COMES TO TOWN, THE (UKN)
UNDER THE BILTMORE CLOCK • 1985 • Miller Neal • TVM • USA
UNDER THE BLACK EAGLE • 1928 • Van Dyke W. S. • USA • DOG OF WAR, THE
UNDER THE BLACK FLAG • 1913 • Turner Otis • USA
UNDER THE BLUE CUPOLA • 1962 • Sibianu Gheorghe • ANM • RMN
UNDER THE BLUE SKY see **NEEL AKASHER NEECHEY** • 1959
UNDER THE BOARDWALK • 1988 • Kiersch Fritz • USA • WIPEOUT
UNDER THE BRIDGE • 1989 • Premaratna H. D. • SLN
UNDER THE BROOKLYN BRIDGE • 1955 • Burckhardt Rudy • SHT • USA
UNDER THE CARIBBEAN see **UNTERNEHMEN XARIFA** • 1954
UNDER THE CHERRY BLOSSOMS see **SAKURA NO MORI NO MANKAI NO SHITA** • 1974
UNDER THE CHERRY MOON • 1986 • Prince • USA
UNDER THE CITY • 1934 • Shaw Alexander • UKN
UNDER THE CITY see **VAROS ALATT, A** • 1953
UNDER THE CLOCK (UKN) see **CLOCK, THE** • 1945
UNDER THE COUNTER SPY • 1954 • Patterson Don • ANS • USA • SECRET AGENT F.O.B.
UNDER THE CRESCENT • 1915 • King Burton L. • SRL • USA
UNDER THE CRIMSON SUNSET see **AKAI YUKI NO TERASARETE** • 1925
UNDER THE DAISIES • 1913 • Brooke Van Dyke • USA
UNDER THE DEBRIS see **TAHT AL INQAD** • 1983
UNDER THE DOCTOR • 1976 • Poulson Gerry • UKN
UNDER THE FALL OF THE CHERRY BLOSSOMS see **SAKURA NO MORI NO MANKAI NO SHITA** • 1974
UNDER THE FIDDLER'S ELM • 1915 • Jones Edgar • USA
UNDER THE FLAG see **SA LILIM NG WATAWAT** • 1967
UNDER THE FLAG OF THE RISING SUN • 1982 • Fukasaku Kinji • JPN
UNDER THE FROZEN FALLS • 1948 • Catling Darrell • UKN
UNDER THE GASLIGHT • 1914 • Marston Lawrence • USA
UNDER THE GERMAN YOKE • 1915 • Noy Wilfred • UKN
UNDER THE GLYCINS see **LEYLAKLAR ALTINDA** • 1968
UNDER THE GREENWOOD TREE • 1918 • Chautard Emile • USA
UNDER THE GREENWOOD TREE • 1929 • Lachman Harry • UKN
UNDER THE GUN • 1950 • Tetzlaff Ted • USA
UNDER THE GUN see **UNDER THE SUN** • 1988
UNDER THE INFLUENCE • 1918 • Drew Sidney, Drew Sidney Mrs. • SHT • USA
UNDER THE INFLUENCE • 1986 • Carter Thomas • TVM • USA
UNDER THE INFLUENCE OF A CERTAIN POWER see **UNTER DEM EINFLUSS EINER KRAFT** • 1987
UNDER THE KURDS • 1915 • Minervin A. • USS
UNDER THE LASH • 1921 • SAF
UNDER THE LASH • 1921 • Wood Sam • USA • SHULAMITE, THE (UKN)
UNDER THE LION'S PAW • 1916 • Hunt Jay • SHT • USA
UNDER THE MAKE-UP • 1913 • Trimble Larry • USA
UNDER THE MASK OF HONESTY • 1914 • *Warner'S Features* • USA
UNDER THE MILITARY FLAG see **GUNKI HATAMEKU SHITANI** • 1972
UNDER THE MISTLETOE • 1903 • Porter Edwin S. • USA
UNDER THE MISTLETOE • 1907 • Aylott Dave • UKN
UNDER THE MISTLETOE BOUGH • 1909 • Stow Percy • UKN
UNDER THE MOON OF MOROCCO (USA) see **SOUS LA LUNE DU MAROC** • 1933
UNDER THE NEIGHBORS' ROOF see **TONARI NO YANE NO SHITA** • 1931
UNDER THE OLD APPLE TREE • 1907 • *Bitzer Billy (Ph)* • USA
UNDER THE OLD APPLE TREE • 1910 • *Vitagraph* • USA
UNDER THE OLIVE TREE see **NON C'E PACE TRA GLI ULIVI** • 1950
UNDER THE PAMPAS MOON • 1935 • Tinling James • USA
UNDER THE PARIS SKY see **SOUS LE CIEL DE PARIS COULE LE SEINE** • 1950
UNDER THE PHRYGIAN STAR see **POD GWIAZDA FRYGIJSKA** • 1954
UNDER THE RAINBOW • 1972 • Goldsmith Sidney • CND
UNDER THE RAINBOW • 1981 • Rash Steve • USA • THERE'S ALWAYS ROOM UNDER THE RAINBOW
UNDER THE RED LIGHT • 1914 • *Literatia* • USA
UNDER THE RED ROBE • 1915 • Noy Wilfred • UKN
UNDER THE RED ROBE • 1923 • Crosland Alan • USA
UNDER THE RED ROBE • 1937 • Sjostrom Victor • UKN, USA
UNDER THE RED SEA see **RED SEA ADVENTURE** • 1952
UNDER THE RIVER • 1959 • Baxter R. K. Neilson • UKN
UNDER THE ROOFS OF PARIS (USA) see **SOUS LES TOITS DE PARIS** • 1930
UNDER THE ROOFS OF THE CITY • 1989 • Hashemi Asghar • IRN
UNDER THE ROUGE • 1925 • Moomaw Lewis H. • USA
UNDER THE SAME SKY • Gogoberidze Lana • USS
UNDER THE SAME SKY see **POD JEDNYM NIEBEM** • 1956
UNDER THE SEAS see **DEUX CENT MILLE LIEUES SOUS LES MERS: OU, LE CAUCHEMAR D'UN PECHEUR** • 1907
UNDER THE SHADOW OF HALEBARDE see **POD SENKOM HALEBARDE** • 1952
UNDER THE SHADOW OF MAGIC • 1955 • Skanata Krsto • DOC • YGS
UNDER THE SHADOW OF THE LAW • 1913 • O'Sullivan Tony • USA
UNDER THE SHEDDING CHESTNUT TREE • 1942 • Wickersham Bob • ANS • USA
UNDER THE SIGN OF CAPRICORN • 1971 • *Sullivan Barry* • USA
UNDER THE SIGN OF SCORPIO see **SOTTO IL SEGNO DELLA SCORPIONE** • 1969
UNDER THE SKIN • 1914 • Vale Travers • USA
UNDER THE SKY OF BAHIA see **SOB O CEU SA BAHIA** • 1956
UNDER THE SOUTHERN CROSS see **UNDER SODRA KORSET** • 1952
UNDER THE SOUTHERN CROSS see **ARMAND AND MICHAELA DENIS UNDER THE SOUTHERN CROSS** • 1954
UNDER THE SOUTHERN CROSS (UKN) see **DEVIL'S PIT, THE** • 1930
UNDER THE SPELL • 1916 • *Smalley Phillips* • SHT • USA
UNDER THE SPREADING BLACKSMITH'S SHOP • 1941 • Lovy Alex • ANS • USA
UNDER THE STAR OF SINGAPORE see **SINGAPORE NO YOWA FUKETE** • 1967
UNDER THE STARS • 1918 • Chapin Benjamin • SHT • USA
UNDER THE STARS AND BARS • 1910 • Melies Gaston • USA
UNDER THE STARS AND STRIPES • 1910 • *Selig* • USA
UNDER THE STARS AND STRIPES • 1919 • *H.w. & L.s. Case Pictures* • USA
UNDER THE SUN • 1988 • Sbardellati Jim • USA • UNDER THE GUN
UNDER THE SUN see **NEL SOLE** • 1967
UNDER THE SUN OF ROME (USA) see **SOTTO IL SOLE DI ROMA** • 1948
UNDER THE TABLE • 1915 • Blystone John G. • USA
UNDER THE TABLE YOU MUST GO • 1969 • Miller Arnold Louis • DOC • UKN
UNDER THE TIDE • 1928 • Paul Fred • UKN
UNDER THE TONTO RIM • 1928 • Raymaker Herman C. • USA
UNDER THE TONTO RIM • 1933 • Hathaway Henry • USA
UNDER THE TONTO RIM • 1947 • Landers Lew • USA
UNDER THE TOP • 1919 • Crisp Donald • USA
UNDER THE TREES see **ONDER DE BOMEN** • 1965
UNDER THE TROPICAL SUN • 1911 • Dawley J. Searle • USA
UNDER THE VOLCANO • 1983 • Huston John • USA
UNDER THE WHIP see **KIRBAC ALTINDA** • 1967
UNDER THE WING OF THE EAGLE • 1963 • Bostan Ion • DOC • RMN
UNDER THE WORLD see **DEBAJO DEL MUNDO** • 1986
UNDER THE YOKE • 1918 • Edwards J. Gordon • USA
UNDER THE YOKE see **POD IGOTO** • 1952
UNDER THE YUM YUM TREE • 1963 • Swift David • USA
UNDER TWO FLAGS • 1912 • Marston Theodore • *Thanhouser* • USA
UNDER TWO FLAGS • 1912 • Nicholls George • *Gem* • USA
UNDER TWO FLAGS • 1915 • Vale Travers • USA
UNDER TWO FLAGS • 1916 • Edwards J. Gordon • USA
UNDER TWO FLAGS • 1922 • Browning Tod • USA
UNDER TWO FLAGS • 1936 • Lloyd Frank • USA
UNDER TWO JAGS • 1923 • Jeske George • SHT • USA
UNDER WESTERN SKIES • 1910 • Barker Reginald • USA
UNDER WESTERN SKIES • 1913 • Christie Al • USA
UNDER WESTERN SKIES • 1921 • Martin George • USA
UNDER WESTERN SKIES • 1926 • Sedgwick Edward • USA
UNDER WESTERN SKIES • 1945 • Yarbrough Jean • USA
UNDER WESTERN SKIES see **WOMAN HUNGRY** • 1931
UNDER WESTERN STARS • 1938 • Kane Joseph • USA
UNDER WHAT STARS see **IKANARU HOSHI NO MOTONI** • 1962
UNDER YOUR HAT • 1940 • Elvey Maurice • UKN
UNDER YOUR SKIN see **KAPY SELAN ALLA** • 1967
UNDER YOUR SPELL • 1936 • Preminger Otto • USA
UNDER YOUR UMBRELLA see **UNDER DITT PARASOLL** • 1968
UNDERACHIEVERS see **NIGHTSCHOOL** • 1987
UNDERBARA LOGNEN, DEN • 1955 • Road Michael • SWD • GENTLE THIEF OF LOVE
UNDERBOSS, THE see **OUR FAMILY BUSINESS** • 1981
UNDERCOVER • 1943 • Nolbandov Sergei • UKN • UNDERCOVER GUERILLAS (USA)
UNDERCOVER • 1983 • Stevens David • ASL
UNDERCOVER • 1987 • Stockwell John • USA • UNDER COVER
UNDERCOVER AGENT • 1939 • Bretherton Howard • USA • SWEEPSTAKE RACKETEERS (UKN)
UNDERCOVER AGENT (USA) see **COUNTERSPY** • 1953
UNDERCOVER CAPER, THE see **THEY WENT THAT-A-WAY AND THAT-A-WAY** • 1978
UNDERCOVER DOCTOR • 1939 • King Louis • USA • FEDERAL OFFENSE
UNDERCOVER GIRL • 1950 • Pevney Joseph • USA
UNDERCOVER GIRL • 1958 • Searle Francis • UKN
UNDERCOVER GIRL see **ASSIGNMENT REDHEAD** • 1956
UNDERCOVER GIRL (UKN) see **UNDERCOVER MAISIE** • 1946
UNDERCOVER GUERILLAS (USA) see **UNDERCOVER** • 1943
UNDERCOVER HERO see **SOFT BEDS, HARD BATTLES** • 1973
UNDERCOVER LOVER see **NO.1 OF THE SECRET SERVICE** • 1978
UNDERCOVER MAISIE • 1946 • Beaumont Harry • USA • UNDERCOVER GIRL (UKN)
UNDERCOVER MAN • 1936 • Ray Albert • USA
UNDERCOVER MAN • 1942 • Selander Lesley • USA
UNDERCOVER MAN, THE • 1949 • Lewis Joseph H. • USA
UNDERCOVER MEN • 1935 • Newfield Sam • USA
UNDERCOVER SCANDALS OF HENRY VIII, THE see **ROYAL FLESH** • 1968
UNDERCOVER WITH THE KKK • 1979 • Shear Barry • TVM • USA • FREEDOM RIDERS, THE
UNDERCOVER WOMAN, THE • 1946 • Carr Thomas • USA
UNDERCURRENT • 1946 • Minnelli Vincente • USA
UNDERCURRENT see **YORU NO KAWA** • 1956
UNDERCURRENT, THE • 1919 • North Wilfred • USA
UNDERCURRENTS • 1973 • Lehman Robin • USA
UNDERCURRENTS • 1984 • Thompson Rob • CND
UNDERDEVELOPED, THE see **SUBDESARROLLADOS, LOS** • 1967
UNDERDOG • 1982 • Cox Paul • DOC • ASL
UNDERDOG see **SECRET LIVES OF THE BRITISH PRIME MINISTERS: MACDONALD, THE** • 1983
UNDERDOG, THE • 1908 • *Kalem* • USA
UNDERDOG, THE • 1932 • Lantz Walter • ANS • USA
UNDERDOG, THE • 1940 • Nigh William • USA
UNDERDOG, THE see **UNTERTAN, DER** • 1951
UNDERGRADS, THE • 1985 • Stern Steven Hilliard • TVM • USA
UNDERGRADUATE, THE • 1970 • Fouracre Ron • UKN
UNDERGRADUATE GIRLS see **LICEALE, LA** • 1975
UNDERGRADUATES, THE • 1906 • Collins Alf? • UKN
UNDERGRADUATE'S VISITOR, THE • 1912 • Raymond Charles? • UKN
UNDERGROUND • 1928 • Asquith Anthony • UKN
UNDERGROUND • 1941 • Sherman Vincent • USA
UNDERGROUND • 1970 • Nadel Arthur H. • UKN, USA • RESISTANCE
UNDERGROUND • 1976 • Wexler Haskell, De Antonio Emile, Lampson Mary • DOC • USA
UNDERGROUND ACES • 1981 • Butler Robert • USA
UNDERGROUND AGENT • 1942 • Gordon Michael • USA
UNDERGROUND CHEATING, THE see **URAGIRI NO ANKOKUGAI** • 1968
UNDERGROUND COMMANDO • 1966 • *Vergara Jose*
UNDERGROUND GUERILLAS (UKN) see **CHETNIKS!** • 1943
UNDERGROUND -IL CLANDESTINO, THE • 1970 • Folkner H. • ITL
UNDERGROUND MAN, THE • 1974 • Wendkos Paul • USA
UNDERGROUND PALACE • 1958 • CND
UNDERGROUND PASSAGE see **IPOGIA DIADROMI** • 1984
UNDERGROUND PASSAGE, THE • 1973 • Kieslowski Krzysztof • MTV • PLN
UNDERGROUND PRINTER • 1934 • Bouchard Thomas • USA
UNDERGROUND RIVER • 1981 • Nichol Robert L. • MTV • CND
UNDERGROUND ROMEO • 1920 • *Romayne Superfilm* • USA
UNDERGROUND RUSTLERS • 1941 • Luby S. Roy • USA
UNDERGROUND TERROR • 1989 • McCalmont James • USA • URBAN NIGHTMARE, AN
UNDERGROUND U.S.A. • 1980 • Mitchell Eric • USA
UNDERGROUND WORLD • 1943 • Kneitel Seymour • ANS • USA
UNDERNEATH THE ARCHES • 1937 • Davis Redd • UKN

UNDERNEATH THE BROADWAY MOON • 1934 • Waller Fred • SHT • USA
UNDERNEATH THE PAINT • 1915 • Gaskill Charles L. • USA
UNDERNEATH THE SURFACE see **SUBTERANUL** • 1967
UNDERSEA ADVENTURE • 1958 • Benson Leon • USA
UNDERSEA DOGS • 1968 • Smith Paul J. • ANS • USA
UNDERSEA GIRL • 1957 • Peyser John • USA
UNDERSEA KINGDOM • 1936 • Eason B. Reeves, Kane Joseph • SRL • USA
UNDERSEA RAIDER see **CLOSE QUARTERS** • 1943
UNDERSTANDING HEART, THE • 1927 • Conway Jack • USA
UNDERSTUDY, THE • 1912 • *Bushman Francis X.* • USA
UNDERSTUDY, THE • 1913 • Johnston Lorimer • USA
UNDERSTUDY, THE • 1917 • Bertram William • USA
UNDERSTUDY, THE • 1922 • Seiter William A. • USA
UNDERSTUDY, THE • 1975 • Velchev Ilya • BUL
UNDERSTUDY, THE see **GRAVEYARD SHIFT II: THE UNDERSTUDY** • 1989
UNDERSTUDY, OR BEHIND THE SCENES, THE • 1915 • Costello Maurice, Gaillord Robert • USA
UNDERTAKER AND HIS PALS, THE • 1966 • Swicegood T. L. P.?, Graham David C.? • USA
UNDERTAKERS see **TOMURAISHI-TACHI** • 1968
UNDERTAKERS, THE • 1969 • Cummins Brian • SHT • UKN
UNDERTAKER'S DAUGHTER, THE • 1915 • *Lubin* • USA
UNDERTAKER'S UNCLE, THE • 1915 • *Potel Victor* • USA
UNDERTOW • 1916 • De Grasse Joseph • USA
UNDERTOW • 1949 • Castle William • USA • BIG FRAME, THE
UNDERTOW • 1956 • Jordan Larry • SHT • USA
UNDERTOW, THE • 1914 • *Maxpherson Jeanie* • USA
UNDERTOW, THE • 1915 • *Essanay* • USA
UNDERTOW, THE • 1915 • *Thanhouser* • USA
UNDERTOW, THE • 1930 • Pollard Harry • USA • GIRL WHO GAVE IN, THE
UNDERWATER! • 1955 • Sturges John • USA
UNDERWATER CITY, THE • 1962 • McDonald Frank • USA
UNDERWATER ODYSSEY, AN see **NEPTUNE FACTOR, THE** • 1973
UNDERWATER ROMANCE see **KINDAN NO SUNA** • 1957
UNDERWATER WARRIOR • 1958 • Marton Andrew • USA
UNDERWATER WARSHIP see **KAITEI GUNKAN** • 1963
UNDERWELLES • 1976 • Aguirre Javier • SHT • SPN
UNDERWORLD • 1927 • von Sternberg Josef • USA • PAYING THE PENALTY (UKN)
UNDERWORLD • 1936 • Micheaux Oscar • USA
UNDERWORLD • 1985 • Pavlou George • UKN • TRANSMUTATIONS (USA)
UNDERWORLD • 1990 • Strick Joseph • USA
UNDERWORLD see **BAS-FONDS, LES** • 1936
UNDERWORLD, THE • 1916 • Julian Rupert • SHT • USA
UNDERWORLD, THE see **ANKO KUGAI** • 1956
UNDERWORLD AFTER DARK see **BIG TOWN AFTER DARK** • 1947
UNDERWORLD BOSS see **MEIDO NO KAOYAKU** • 1957
UNDERWORLD INFORMERS (USA) see **INFORMERS, THE** • 1963
UNDERWORLD LOVE (UKN) see **TIP-OFF, THE** • 1929
UNDERWORLD OF LONDON, THE • 1915 • Weston Charles • UKN
UNDERWORLD SCANDAL see **BIG TOWN SCANDAL** • 1948
UNDERWORLD STORY, THE • 1950 • Endfield Cy • USA • WHIPPED, THE
UNDERWORLD U.S.A. • 1961 • Fuller Samuel • USA
UNDESIRABLE NEIGHBOUR, THE • 1963 • Hales Gordon • UKN
UNDESIRABLE SUITOR, AN • 1914 • *Crystal* • USA
UNDICI GIORNI, UNDICI NOTTI • 1987 • D'Amato Joe • ITL • ELEVEN DAYS ELEVEN NIGHTS
UNDICI MOSCHETTIERI, GLI • 1952 • De Concini Ennio, Saraceni Fausto • ITL
UNDICI UOMINI E UN PALLONE • 1948 • Simonelli Giorgio C. • ITL
UNDIE-WORLD, THE • 1934 • Stevens George • SHT • USA
UNDINE • Gerstein Cassandra M. • SHT • USA
UNDINE • 1912 • Marston Theodore • USA
UNDINE • 1915 • Otto Henry • USA • ANSWER OF THE SEA
UNDINE • 1919 • Neumann Hans • FRG
UNDINE 74 • 1974 • Thiele Rolf • AUS, FRG
UNDISCLOSED see **LETTER OF WARNING, A** • 1932
UNDISPUTED EVIDENCE • 1922 • *Cotton Blossom Film Corp* • USA
UNDIVIDED ATTENTION • 1988 • Gallagher Chris • CND
UNDOING EVIL • 1917 • *Baggot King* • SHT • USA
UNDOING OF SLIM BILL, THE • 1912 • *Nestor* • USA
UNDRESSED • 1928 • Rosen Phil • USA
UNDRESSED KID • 1920 • *Franey William* • SHT • USA
UNDRESSED WEST, THE • 1964 • *Pehlman Carl* • USA • EVERYBODY LIKES MOUNTAIN WOMEN ○ UNADORNED WEST, THE
UNDRESSING see **RIISUMINEN** • 1986
UNDRESSING EXTRAORDINARY: OR, THE TROUBLES OF A TIRED TRAVELLER • 1901 • Booth W. R.? • UKN
UNDSKYLD VIER HER • 1981 • Kristensen Hans • DNM • PARDON US FOR LIVING
UNDULATIONS • Tobalina Carlos • USA
UNDYING FIRE, THE • 1915 • Reehm George E. • USA
UNDYING FLAME, THE • 1917 • Tourneur Maurice • USA
UNDYING MONSTER, THE • 1942 • Brahm John • USA • HAMMOND MYSTERY, THE (UKN)
UNDYING STORY OF CAPTAIN SCOTT, THE see **NINETY DEGREES SOUTH** • 1933
UNDYING STORY OF CAPTAIN SCOTT AND ANIMAL LIFE IN THE ANTARCTIC, THE see **WITH CAPTAIN SCOTT, R.N., TO THE SOUTH POLE** • 1911
UNE CHANTE, L'AUTRE PAS, L' • 1977 • Varda Agnes • FRN • ONE SINGS THE OTHER DOESN'T ○ ONE SINGS THE OTHER DOES NOT
UNE DE LA CAVALERIE • 1938 • Cammage Maurice • FRN
UNE, DEUX, TROIS ETOILES • 1956 • Martin Marcel • SHT • FRN
UNE ET L'AUTRE, L' • 1967 • Allio Rene • FRN • OTHER ONE, THE
UNE NUIT DE NOCES see **NUIT DE NOCES** • 1949
UNE SI GENTILLE PETITE FILLE • 1977 • Matalon Eddy • FRN, CND
UNEARTHLY, THE • 1957 • Peters Brooke L. • USA
UNEARTHLY STRANGER • 1963 • Krish John • UKN • BEYOND THE STARS
UNEASY DREAMS -THE LIFE OF MR. PICKWICK • 1970 • Marre Jeremy • UKN
UNEASY FEET • 1920 • Lascelle Ward • SHT • USA
UNEASY MONEY • 1917 • Beaudine William • SHT • USA
UNEASY MONEY • 1918 • Windom Lawrence C. • USA
UNEASY MONEY (USA) see **ABENTEUER EINES ZEHNMARKSCHEINES, DIE** • 1926
UNEASY PAYMENTS • 1927 • Kirkland David • USA
UNEASY TERMS • 1948 • Sewell Vernon • UKN
UNEASY THREE, THE • 1925 • McCarey Leo • SHT • USA
UNEASY VIRTUE • 1931 • Walker Norman • UKN
UNEHELICHEN, DIE • 1926 • Lamprecht Gerhard • FRG • CHILDREN OF NO IMPORTANCE (USA)
UNEMPLOYED AND UNEMPLOYABLE • 1908 • Fitzhamon Lewin? • UKN
UNEMPLOYED DEVIL, THE • Driessen Paul • ANM • CND
UNEMPLOYED GHOST, THE • 1931 • Scotto Aubrey, Hayes Max E. • SHT • USA
UNEMPLOYMENT: VOICES FROM THE LINE • 1980 • Lasry Pierre • DOC • CND
UNENDING ADVANCE see **KAGIRINAKI ZENSHIN** • 1937
UNENDING LOVE, THE • 1912 • *Rex* • USA
UNENDLICHE FAHRT -ABER REGRENZT • 1965 • Reitz Edgar • SHT • FRG
UNENDLICHE GESCHICHTE, DIE see **NEVERENDING STORY, THE** • 1984
UNENDLICHE WEG, DER • 1943 • Schweikart Hans • FRG • ENDLESS WAY, THE
UNENTSCHULDIGTE STUNDE, DIE • 1937 • Emo E. W. • AUS
UNENTSCHULDIGTE STUNDE, DIE • 1957 • Forst Willi • AUS
UNERKANNTE, DER • 1920 • Neff Wolfgang • FRG
UNERREICHBARE, DER • 1982 • Zanussi Krzysztof • FRG • UNAPPROACHABLE, THE (UKN)
UNEVEN BALANCE, THE • 1914 • *Essanay* • USA
UNEVEN ROAD, THE • 1917 • Windom Lawrence C. • SHT • USA
UNEVENTFUL STORY, AN see **NIECIEKAWA HISTORIA** • 1983
UNEXPECTED, THE • 1914 • *Balboa* • USA
UNEXPECTED, THE • 1916 • Cunard Grace, Ford Francis • SHT • USA
UNEXPECTED, THE • 1981 • Pearson Peter • MTV • CND
UNEXPECTED, THE see **PO ZAKONU** • 1926
UNEXPECTED, THE see **DUNIYA NA MANE** • 1937
UNEXPECTED, THE see **IMPREVISTO, L'** • 1961
UNEXPECTED ANSWER: HOMAGE TO RENE MAGRITTE, THE • 1973 • Borenstein Joyce • CND
UNEXPECTED BATH, THE • 1903 • Hepworth Cecil M. • UKN
UNEXPECTED ENCOUNTER see **HATHAT DEKHA** • 1967
UNEXPECTED FATHER • 1939 • Lamont Charles • USA • SANDY TAKES A BOW (UKN)
UNEXPECTED FATHER see **LITTLE ACCIDENT, THE** • 1930
UNEXPECTED FATHER, THE • 1932 • Freeland Thornton • USA • PAPA LOVES MAMA ○ PUDGE
UNEXPECTED FIREWORKS (USA) see **FEU D'ARTIFICE IMPROVISE, UN** • 1905
UNEXPECTED FORTUNE, AN • 1912 • *Clary Charles* • USA
UNEXPECTED GUEST • 1947 • Archainbaud George • USA
UNEXPECTED GUEST, AN • 1909 • *Lubin* • USA
UNEXPECTED HELP • 1910 • Griffith D. W. • USA
UNEXPECTED HONEYMOON, THE • 1910 • *Imp* • USA
UNEXPECTED HONEYMOON, THE • 1912 • Young James • USA
UNEXPECTED HONEYMOON, THE • 1915 • *Victor* • USA
UNEXPECTED MEETING see **OMBYTE AV TAG** • 1943
UNEXPECTED MEETING, AN • 1913 • *Solax* • USA
UNEXPECTED MRS. POLLIFAX, THE see **MRS. POLLIFAX -SPY** • 1971
UNEXPECTED PEST • 1956 • McKimson Robert • ANS • USA
UNEXPECTED PLACES • 1918 • Hopper E. Mason • USA
UNEXPECTED RECEPTION, THE • 1912 • *Pathe* • USA
UNEXPECTED REVIEW, AN • 1911 • *Vitagraph* • USA
UNEXPECTED REWARD • 1915 • *Liberty* • USA
UNEXPECTED REWARD, AN • 1910 • *Edison* • USA
UNEXPECTED RICHES • 1942 • Glazer Herbert • SHT • USA
UNEXPECTED ROMANCE, AN • 1915 • *Essanay* • USA
UNEXPECTED SANTA CLAUS, AN • 1908 • Porter Edwin S. • USA
UNEXPECTED SCOOP, AN • 1916 • Stanton Richard • SHT • USA
UNEXPECTED SHOT, THE • 1920 • *Jennings Al* • SHT • USA
UNEXPECTED TREASURE • 1918 • *Rains Fred (P)* • SHT • UKN
UNEXPECTED UNCLE • 1941 • Godfrey Peter • USA
UNEXPECTED VISIT: OR, OUR FLAT, THE • 1899 • *Paul R. W.* • UKN
UNEXPECTED VISITOR, THE see **DET KOM EN GAST** • 1947
UNEXPECTED VOYAGER, THE see **VOYAGEUSE INATTENDUE, LA** • 1949
UNEXPECTED WIFE, AN see **YOUTH MUST HAVE LOVE** • 1922
UNEXPLAINED, THE • 1970 • *Encyclopedia Britannica* • DOC • USA
UNFAILING BEAM, THE see **YONG BUXIOSHI DE DIANBO** • 1958
UNFAIR EXCHANGE, AN • 1913 • *Thanhouser Twins* • USA
UNFAIR EXCHANGE IS ROBBERY see **EXCHANGE IS NO ROBBERY** • 1902
UNFAIR GAME, AN • 1910 • *Vitagraph* • USA
UNFAIR LOVE AFFAIR, AN • 1916 • Kerrigan J. M. • IRL
UNFAIR SEX, THE • 1926 • Diamant-Berger Henri • USA
UNFAITHFUL • 1918 • Miller Charles • SHT • USA
UNFAITHFUL • 1931 • Cromwell John • USA
UNFAITHFUL see **UTRO** • 1966
UNFAITHFUL, THE • 1947 • Sherman Vincent • USA
UNFAITHFUL, THE see **INFEDELI, LE** • 1952
UNFAITHFUL LOVE see **AMOR INFIEL, EL** • 1974
UNFAITHFUL MARIJKA, THE see **MARIJKA NEVERNICE** • 1934
UNFAITHFUL NIGHT (UKN) see **NUIT INFIDELE, LA** • 1968
UNFAITHFUL TO HIS TRUST • 1915 • Buel Kenean • USA
UNFAITHFUL WIFE • 1903 • *Bitzer Billy (Ph)* • USA
UNFAITHFUL WIFE see **FEMME INFIDELE, LA** • 1968
UNFAITHFUL WIFE see **FUTEIZUMA** • 1968
UNFAITHFUL WIFE, THE • 1915 • Edwards J. Gordon • USA
UNFAITHFUL WIVES see **FEMME INFIDELE, LA** • 1968
UNFAITHFULLY YOURS • 1948 • Sturges Preston • USA
UNFAITHFULLY YOURS • 1983 • Zieff Howard • USA
UNFAITHFULS, THE (USA) see **INFEDELI, LE** • 1952
UNFILIAL SON, THE • 1909 • Polaski Benjamin • HKG
UNFILLED OATH, THE • 1913 • *Pathe* • USA
UNFINISHED BUSINESS • 1941 • La Cava Gregory • USA
UNFINISHED BUSINESS • 1984 • Owen Don • CND
UNFINISHED BUSINESS • 1986 • Ellis Bob • ASL
UNFINISHED BUSINESS see **SPRAWA DO ZALATWIENIA** • 1953
UNFINISHED CASE, THE • 1916 • *Leonard Robert* • SHT • USA
UNFINISHED CHESS MATCH see **MIKAN NO TAIKYOKU** • 1982
UNFINISHED DANCE, THE • 1947 • Koster Henry • USA
UNFINISHED DESIRE • 1968 • Yu Hyunmok • SKR
UNFINISHED DIARY see **JOURNAL INACHEVE** • 1982
UNFINISHED HOUSE, THE see **CASA NETERMINATA** • 1964
UNFINISHED JOURNEY OF ROBERT F. KENNEDY, THE • 1969 • Stuart Mel • TVM • USA • JOURNEY OF ROBERT F. KENNEDY, THE
UNFINISHED LETTER, THE • 1911 • *Booth Sydney* • USA
UNFINISHED LOVE SONG, THE see **PESN LYUBVI NEDOPETAYA** • 1919
UNFINISHED PIECE FOR MECHANICAL PIANO see **NEOKONTCHENNIA PIESSA DLIA MEKANITCHESKOVO PIANINA** • 1977
UNFINISHED PIECE FOR PLAYER-PIANO see **NEOKONTCHENNIA PIESSA DLIA MEKANITCHESKOVO PIANINA** • 1977
UNFINISHED PORTRAIT, THE • 1915 • Le Saint Edward J. • USA
UNFINISHED SENTENCE, THE see **148 PERC A BEFEJEZETLEN MONDATBOL** • 1974
UNFINISHED SENTENCE IN 148 MINUTES, THE see **148 PERC A BEFEJEZETLEN MONDATBOL** • 1974
UNFINISHED STORY, AN see **NEOKONCHENNAYA POVEST** • 1955
UNFINISHED STORY, AN see **EK ADHURI KAHANI** • 1972
UNFINISHED SYMPHONY (USA) see **LEISE FLEHEN MEINE LIEDER** • 1933
UNFINISHED WAR, THE see **IT BEGAN ON THE VISTULA** • 1966
UNFINISHED WEEKEND see **NEDOKONCENY WEEKEND** • 1971
UNFINISHED WORK FOR MECHANICAL PIANO see **NEOKONTCHENNIA PIESSA DLIA MEKANITCHESKOVO PIANINA** • 1977
UNFIT: OR, THE STRENGTH OF THE WEAK • 1914 • Hepworth Cecil M. • UKN
UNFIT TO PRINT see **SCANDAL STREET** • 1931
UNFIT TO PRINT (UKN) see **OFF THE RECORD** • 1939
UNFOLDMENT, THE • 1922 • Kern George, MacQuarrie Murdock • USA
UNFORESEEABLE NOVELTIES see **IMPREVISIBLES NOUVEAUTES** • 1961
UNFORESEEN, THE • 1917 • O'Brien John B. • USA
UNFORGETTABLE, THE see **NEZABYVAYEMOYE** • 1968
UNFORGETTABLE DIRECTOR OF HOLLYWOOD MOVIES, THE • 1989 • Turgul Yavuz • TRK
UNFORGETTABLE SPRING see **NEPOVTORIMAYA VESNA** • 1957
UNFORGETTABLE STORY see **MARAPURANI KATHA** • 1967
UNFORGETTABLE YEAR OF 1919, THE (USA) see **NEZABYVAYEMI 1919-1 GOD** • 1951
UNFORGETTABLE YEARS, THE • 1957 • Kopalin Ilya • DOC • USS
UNFORGIVEN, THE • 1915 • Johnston Lorimer • USA
UNFORGIVEN, THE • 1960 • Huston John • USA
UNFORGIVEN GUILT, THE see **AFFEDILMEYEN SUC** • 1968
UNFORGOTTEN CRIME see **AFFAIRS OF JIMMY VALENTINE, THE** • 1942
UNFORSEEN COMPLICATION, AN • 1911 • Golden Joseph A. • USA
UNFORSEEN METAMORPHOSIS • 1912-14 • Cohl Emile • ANS • USA • EXPOSITION DE CARICATURES
UNFORTUNATE BATHE, AN • 1908 • Fitzhamon Lewin • UKN
UNFORTUNATE BRIDEGROOM see **SVATBA JAKO REMEN** • 1967
UNFORTUNATE CANVASSER, THE • 1909 • Coleby A. E. • UKN
UNFORTUNATE EGG MERCHANT, THE • 1900 • *Warwick Trading Co* • UKN
UNFORTUNATE INVALID, THE • 1910 • *Walturdaw* • UKN
UNFORTUNATE MISTAKE, AN • 1908 • *Urban-Eclipse* • USA
UNFORTUNATE SEX, THE • 1920 • La Maie Elsier • USA
UNFOUNDED JEALOUSY • 1915 • *Wiggins Lillian* • USA
UNFRIENDLY CALL, AN • 1897 • Acres Birt • UKN
UNFRIENDLY FACES • 1925 • Roach Hal • SHT • USA
UNFRIENDLY FRUIT • 1916 • *Heinie & Louie* • USA
UNFUG DER LIEBE • 1928 • Wiene Robert • FRG
UNG DAM MED TUR • 1941 • Arvedson Ragnar • SWD
UNG FLUKT • 1959 • Kalmar Edith • NRW • WAYWARD GIRL, THE (USA)
UNG KAERLIGHED • 1958 • Rodriguez Andre • DNM • PLEASURES ARE PAID FOR
UNG LEG • 1956 • Allen Johannes • DNM • YOUNG HAVE NO TIME, THE
UNG MAN SOKER SALLSKAP • 1954 • Skoglund Gunnar • SWD • YOUNG MAN SEEKS COMPANY ○ FLICKAN I FONSTRET ○ ESTER OCH ALBERT
UNG OCH KAR see **SKEPPAR MUNTERS BRAVADER** • 1950
UNG SOMMAR • 1954 • Fant Kenne • SWD • YOUNG SUMMER
UNGA GREVEN TAR FLICKAN OCH PRISET • 1924 • Carlsten Rune • SWD • YOUNG COUNT TAKE THE GIRL AND THE PRIZE ○ YOUNG NOBLEMAN, THE (USA)
UNGA HJARTAN • 1934 • Branner Per-Axel • SWD, DNM • YOUNG HEARTS
UNGA HJARTAN see **PRINS GUSTAF** • 1944
UNGALLANT LOVER, THE • 1898 • *Warwick Trading Co* • UKN

UNGARISCHE RHAPSODIE • 1913 • Biebrach Rudolf • FRG • HUNGARIAN RHAPSODY
UNGARISCHE RHAPSODIE • 1928 • Schwarz Hanns • FRG • HUNGARIAN RHAPSODY
UNGARMADEL see **ZIGEUNERBLUT** • 1934
UNGAVA, TERRE LOINTAINE • 1974 • Marchand Pierre, Henrichon Leo • DOC • CND
UNGAVIMBI UMCOLO • 1981 • SAF
UNGDOM AV I DAG • 1935 • Branner Per-Axel • SWD • YOUTH OF TODAY
UNGDOM I BOJOR • 1942 • Henrikson Anders • SWD • YOUTH IN CHAINS
UNGDOM I FARA • 1947 • Holmgren Per Gosta • SWD • YOUTH IN DANGER
UNGDOM OG DAARSKAB (DNM) see **JUGEND UND TOLLHEIT** • 1912
UNGDOM OG LETSIND see **EKSPEDITRICEN** • 1911
UNGDOMMENS RET • 1911 • Blom August • DNM • RIGHT OF YOUTH, THE
UNGE BLOD, DET • 1915 • Holger-Madsen • DNM • BURIED SECRET, THE
UNGEBETENE GAST, DER • 1925 • Mack Max • AUS
UNGEHEUER VON LONDON CITY, DAS • 1964 • Zbonek Edwin • FRG • MONSTER OF LONDON CITY, THE (UKN)
UNGEKLARTER FALL, EIN • 1921 • Ziener Bruno • FRG
UNGEKUSST SOLL MAN NICHT SCHLAFEN GEH'N • 1936 • Emo E. W. • AUS
UNGEN • 1974 • Halle Barthold • NRW • BABY, THE
UNGESCHRIEBENE GESETZ, DAS • 1921 • Boese Carl • FRG
UNGETREUE ECKEHART • 1940 • Marischka Hubert • FRG
UNGETREUE ECKEHART, DER • 1931 • Boese Carl • FRG
UNGKARLSPAPPAN • 1934 • Molander Gustaf • SWD • BACHELOR FATHER
UNGKARLSPARADISET • 1931 • Stenstrom Matts A. • SWD
UNGLASSED WINDOWS CAST A TERRIBLE REFLECTION • 1953 • Brakhage Stan • USA
UNGRATEFUL DAUGHTER-IN-LAW, THE • 1910 • *Yankee* • USA
UNGRATEFUL LAND, THE • 1972 • Scott Cynthia • MTV • CND
UNGREIFBARE, DER • 1916 • Sauer Fred • FRG
UNGT BLOD • 1943 • Johansson Ivar • SWD • YOUNG BLOOD
UNGUARDED GATES see **WHITE SIN, THE** • 1924
UNGUARDED GIRLS • 1929 • Curran William Hughes • USA
UNGUARDED HOUR, THE • 1925 • Hillyer Lambert • USA
UNGUARDED HOUR, THE • 1936 • Wood Sam • USA
UNGUARDED MOMENT, THE • 1956 • Keller Harry • USA
UNGUARDED WOMEN • 1924 • Crosland Alan • USA
UNGULTIGE EHE, DIE see **STAATSANWALT BRIANDS ABENTEUER 1** • 1920
UNHAND ME, VILLAIN • 1916 • *Howell Alice* • SHT • USA
UNHANDY MAN, THE • 1970 • Smith Paul J. • ANS • USA
UNHANGED, THE see **HIRTTAMATTOMAT** • 1972
UNHAPPY CAMPERS • 1988 • Simpson Michael A. • USA • SLEEPAWAY CAMP II: UNHAPPY CAMPERS ○ SLEEPAWAY CAMP 2 ○ NIGHTMARE VACATION 2
UNHAPPY FINISH, AN • 1920 • Davis James • SHT • USA
UNHAPPY HAT, THE see **BOLDOGTALAN KALAP** • 1981
UNHAPPY PAIR, THE • 1913 • *August Edwin* • USA
UNHEIL, DAS • 1972 • Fleischmann Peter • FRG • DISASTER, THE ○ HAVOC
UNHEILBAR • 1917 • Hanus Emerich • FRG
UNHEILBRINGENDE PERLE, DIE • 1913 • May Joe • FRG
UNHEIMLICH STARKER ABGANG, EIN • 1973 • Verhoeven Michael • FRG • STRANGELY POWERFUL EXIT, A
UNHEIMLICHE, DER • 1921 • Wendt Ernst • FRG
UNHEIMLICHE, DER • 1968 • FRG
UNHEIMLICHE, DER see **GROSSE UNBEKANNTE, DER** • 1927
UNHEIMLICHE CHINESE, DER • 1920 • Stranz A. • FRG
UNHEIMLICHE FREMDE, DER see **GEHEIMNISVOLLE WANDERER, DER** • 1915
UNHEIMLICHE GAST, DER • 1922 • Duvivier Julien • FRG • LOGIS DE L'HORREUR, LE ○ SINISTER GUEST, THE
UNHEIMLICHE GESCHICHTEN • 1919 • Oswald Richard • FRG • TALES OF THE UNCANNY
UNHEIMLICHE GESCHICHTEN • 1932 • Oswald Richard • FRG • TALES OF THE UNCANNY
UNHEIMLICHE HAUS 1, DAS • 1916 • Oswald Richard • FRG
UNHEIMLICHE HAUS 2, DAS • 1916 • Oswald Richard • FRG • FREITAG, DER 13
UNHEIMLICHE HAUS 3, DAS see **CHINESISCHE GOTZE, DER** • 1916
UNHEIMLICHE LICHT, DAS • 1920 • Marlo Fred • FRG
UNHEIMLICHE MONCH, DER • 1965 • Reinl Harald • FRG • SINISTER MONK, THE (USA)
UNHEIMLICHE SCHLOSS, DAS • 1920 • Kahn William • FRG
UNHEIMLICHE WANDLUNG DES ALEX ROSCHER, DIE • 1943 • May Paul • FRG • SPIEGEL DER HELENA, DER
UNHEIMLICHE ZIMMER, DAS see **HUND VON BASKERVILLE 3, DER** • 1915
UNHEIMLICHEN 1, DIE • 1923 • *Forum-Film* • FRG
UNHEIMLICHEN 2, DIE • 1923 • *Forum-Film* • FRG
UNHEIMLICHEN HANDE DES DR. ORLAK, DIE see **ORLACS HANDE** • 1925
UNHEIMLICHEN WUNSCHE, DIE • 1939 • Hilpert Heinz • FRG • UNHOLY WISH, THE ○ SINISTER WISH, THE
UNHEIMLICHER MOMENT, EIN • 1970 • Schlondorff Volker • SHT • FRG • FRIGHTENING MOMENT, A
UNHIDDEN TREASURE, THE • 1915 • Johnston Lorimer • USA
UNHINGED • 1983 • Gronquist Don • USA
UNHOLY, THE • 1988 • Vila Camilo • USA
UNHOLY DESIRE see **AKAI SATSUI** • 1964
UNHOLY FOUR, THE (UKN) see **CIAK MULL –L'UOMO DELLA VENDETTA** • 1970
UNHOLY FOUR, THE (USA) see **STRANGER CAME HOME, THE** • 1954
UNHOLY GARDEN, THE • 1931 • Fitzmaurice George • USA
UNHOLY HOUR see **WEREWOLF OF LONDON** • 1935
UNHOLY INTRUDERS, THE • 1956 • Reinl Harald • FRG • STRANGE INTRUSION
UNHOLY LOVE • 1932 • Ray Albert • USA • DECEIT (UKN)
UNHOLY LOVE see **ALRAUNE** • 1927
UNHOLY MATRIMONY • 1966 • John Arthur • USA
UNHOLY NIGHT, THE • 1929 • Barrymore Lionel • USA
UNHOLY PARTNERS • 1941 • LeRoy Mervyn • USA • NEW YORK STORY, THE
UNHOLY QUEST, THE • 1934 • Lotinga R. W. • UKN
UNHOLY ROLLERS • 1972 • Zimmerman Vernon • USA
UNHOLY THREE, THE • 1925 • Browning Tod • USA
UNHOLY THREE, THE • 1930 • Conway Jack • USA
UNHOLY WIFE, THE • 1957 • Farrow John • USA
UNHOLY WISH, THE see **UNHEIMLICHEN WUNSCHE, DIE** • 1939
UNICA LEGGE IN CUI CREDO, L' • 1975 • Giorgi Claudio • ITL
UNICO INDIZIO UNA SCIARPA GIALLA (ITL) see **MAISON SOUS LES ARBRES, LA** • 1971
UNICORN, THE see **ENHORNINGEN** • 1955
UNICORN, THE see **EINHORN, DAS** • 1978
UNICORN FORTRESS, THE • 1969 • *Chao Lei* • HKG
UNICORN IN THE GARDEN, A • 1953 • Hurtz William • ANS • USA
UNICYCLE RACE • 1969 • Swarthe Robert • ANS • USA
UNIDENTIFIED FLYING OBJECTS see **U.F.O. (UNIDENTIFIED FLYING OBJECTS)** • 1956
UNIDENTIFIED FLYING ODDBALL • 1979 • Mayberry Russ • USA • SPACEMAN AND KING ARTHUR, THE (UKN)
UNIDENTIFIED MAN, AN • 1970 • Sens Al • ANS • CND
UNIDOS POR EL EJE • 1941 • Cardona Rene • MXC
UNIFORM, THE • 1966 • Sturlis Edward • ANM • PLN
UNIFORM, THE see **THEY MET IN BOMBAY** • 1941
UNIFORM LOVERS (UKN) see **HOLD 'EM, YALE** • 1935
UNIFORMES ET GRANDES MANOEUVRES • 1950 • Le Henaff Rene • FRN • FERNANDEL JOINS THE ARMY
UNINHABITED PLANET see **BEZLUDNA PLANETA** • 1962
UNINHIBITED, THE (USA) see **PIANOS MECANICOS, LOS** • 1965
UNINTENTIONAL HERO, AN • 1914 • *Lubin* • USA
UNINVITED • 1914 • *Melies* • USA
UNINVITED, THE • 1944 • Allen Lewis • USA
UNINVITED, THE • 1987 • Clark Greydon • USA
UNINVITED, THE (USA) see **INVITATA, L'** • 1969
UNINVITED BLONDE • 1948 • Yates Hal • SHT • USA
UNINVITED GUEST, THE • 1923 • Dewhurst George • UKN
UNINVITED GUEST, THE • 1924 • Ince Ralph • USA • INNOCENT SINNER, THE
UNINVITED GUEST, THE • 1960 • Badzian Teresa • ANM • PLN
UNINVITED GUESTS, THE • 1912 • *Lubin* • USA
UNINVITED LOVE see **NEPROSHENAYA LYUBOV** • 1964
UNINVITED PEST, THE • 1943 • Ising Rudolf • ANS • USA
UNINVITED PESTS, THE • 1946 • Rasinski Connie • ANS • USA
UNION see **SANGAM** • 1964
UNION CITY • 1980 • Reichert Mark • USA
UNION DEPOT • 1932 • Green Alfred E. • USA • GENTLEMAN FOR A DAY (UKN)
UNION MAIDS • 1976 • Reichert Julia, Klein James, Mogulescu Miles • USA
UNION PACIFIC • 1939 • De Mille Cecil B. • USA
UNION PACIFIC RAILROAD SCENES • 1901 • *Bitzer Billy (Ph)* • USA
UNION SACREE • 1915 • Feuillade Louis • FRN
UNION SACREE • 1989 • Arcady Alexandre • FRN
UNION STATION • 1950 • Mate Rudolph • USA
UNION STREET see **STANLEY AND IRIS** • 1989
UNION WAGES • 1932 • Horne James W. • SHT • USA
UNITED AT GETTYSBURG • 1913 • *Imp* • USA
UNITED BUT NOT MIXED (USA) see **JUNTOS, PERO NO REVUELTOS** • 1938
UNITED HARVEST • 1946 • Keene Ralph • DOC • UKN
UNITED IN DANGER • 1914 • Miller Ashley • USA
UNITED STATES ARMY IN SAN FRANCISCO • 1915 • Sennett Mack • DOC • USA
UNITED STATES SMITH • 1928 • Henabery Joseph • USA • FIGHTING MARINE, THE (UKN)
UNITED WE STAND • 1912 • *Nestor* • USA
UNITED WE STAND • 1942 • *Reek Edmund (P)* • DOC • USA
UNITY CANADA • 1984 • Reusch Peter • MTV • CND
UNIVERMAG • 1922 • Vertov Dziga • USS • UNIVERSAL DEPARTMENT STORE ○ STATE DEPARTMENT STORE ○ GUM ○ DEPARTMENT STORE
UNIVERS • 1968 • Otero Manuel • ANM
UNIVERS DES FILLES, L' see **DUNIA AL-BANAT** • 1962
UNIVERS DU SILENCE OU L'ART DE PAUL DELVAUX, L' • 1960 • Haesaerts Luc • DCS • BLG
UNIVERSAL BOY AS THE NEWSBOY'S FRIEND • 1914 • *Roubert Matty* • USA
UNIVERSAL BOY IN CUPID AND THE FISHES • 1914 • *Imp* • USA
UNIVERSAL BOY IN RURAL ADVENTURES, THE • 1914 • *Imp* • USA
UNIVERSAL BOY IN THE GATES OF LIBERTY, THE • 1914 • *Imp* • USA
UNIVERSAL BOY IN THE JUVENILE REFORMER, THE • 1914 • *Imp* • USA
UNIVERSAL BOY IN THE MYSTERY OF THE NEW YORK DOCKS, THE • 1914 • *Imp* • USA
UNIVERSAL BOY (NO.1) • 1914 • *Imp* • USA
UNIVERSAL BOY (NO.2) • 1914 • *Imp* • USA
UNIVERSAL BOY (NO.3) • 1914 • *Imp* • USA
UNIVERSAL BOY SOLVES THE CHINESE MYSTERY • 1914 • *Imp* • USA
UNIVERSAL DEPARTMENT STORE see **UNIVERMAG** • 1922
UNIVERSAL IKE ALMOST A HERO • 1914 • *Universal* • USA
UNIVERSAL IKE AND THE SCHOOL BELLE • 1914 • *Universal* • USA
UNIVERSAL IKE GETS A GOAT • 1914 • Edwards Harry J. • USA
UNIVERSAL IKE GETS A LINE ON HIS WIFE • 1914 • *Universal* • USA
UNIVERSAL IKE HAS HIS UPS AND DOWNS • 1914 • *Carney Augustus* • USA
UNIVERSAL IKE HAS ONE FOOT IN THE GRAVE • 1914 • *Universal* • USA
UNIVERSAL IKE IN SEARCH OF THE EATS • 1914 • *Carney Augustus* • USA
UNIVERSAL IKE IN THE BATTLE OF LITTLE TIN HORN • 1914 • *Carney Augustus* • USA
UNIVERSAL IKE JR. ALMOST GETS MARRIED • 1914 • *Universal* • USA
UNIVERSAL IKE JR. AND HIS MOTHER-IN-LAW • 1914 • *Universal* • USA
UNIVERSAL IKE JR. AND THE VAMPIRE • 1914 • *Universal* • USA
UNIVERSAL IKE JR. AT THE DANCE OF LITTLE L.O. • 1914 • *Universal* • USA
UNIVERSAL IKE JR. BEARLY WON HER • 1914 • *Universal* • USA
UNIVERSAL IKE JR. IN A BATTLE ROYAL • 1914 • *Universal* • USA
UNIVERSAL IKE JR. IN A CASE ON THE DOCTOR • 1914 • *Universal* • USA
UNIVERSAL IKE JR. IN CUPID'S VICTORY • 1914 • *Universal* • USA
UNIVERSAL IKE JR. IN HIS CITY ELOPEMENT • 1914 • *Universal* • USA
UNIVERSAL IKE JR. IN THE DANGERS OF A GREAT CITY • 1914 • *Universal* • USA
UNIVERSAL IKE JR. IS KEPT FROM BEING AN ACTOR • 1914 • *Universal* • USA
UNIVERSAL IKE JR. ON HIS HONEYMOON • 1914 • *Universal* • USA
UNIVERSAL IKE MAKES A MONKEY OF HIMSELF • 1914 • *Carney Augustus* • USA
UNIVERSAL IKE'S LEGACY • 1914 • *Universal* • USA
UNIVERSAL IKE'S WOOING • 1914 • Edwards Harry J. • USA
UNIVERSAL PEACE • 1905 • *Urban Trading Co* • UKN
UNIVERSAL SOLDIER • 1971 • Endfield Cy • UKN
UNIVERSE • 1959 • Low Colin, Kroitor Roman • ANS • CND • NOTRE UNIVERS
UNIVERSE D'UTRILLO, L' • 1954 • Regnier • SHT • FRN
UNIVERSIADE • 1983 • Payer Roch Christophe • MTV • CND
UNIVERSITE DU QUEBEC • 1972 • Labrecque Jean-Claude • DCS • CND
UNIVERSITE INACHEVEE, UNE • 1982 • Cornellier Robert • MTV • CND
UNIVERSITY MEDICAL CENTRE see **U.M.C.** • 1969
UNIVERSITY OF LIFE see **MOI UNIVERSITETI** • 1940
UNIVERSO DI NOTTE • 1962 • Jacovoni Alessandro • DOC • ITL
UNIVERSO PROIBITO • 1963 • Montero Roberto Bianchi • DOC • ITL
UNJUST CURSE see **ADHIKI KATARA** • 1968
UNJUST STEWARD, THE • 1912 • Fitzhamon Lewin • UKN
UNJUST SUSPICION, AN • 1913 • Cabanne W. Christy • USA
UNJUSTLY ACCUSED • 1914 • Hartford David M. • USA
UNJUSTLY ACCUSED see **BALLETTENS DATTER** • 1913
UNKIND LOVE see **LASKA NELASKAVA** • 1969
UNKISSED BRIDE see **MOTHER GOOSE A GO-GO** • 1966
UNKISSED BRIDE, THE see **REBELLIOUS BRIDE, THE** • 1919
UNKISSED MAN, THE • 1929 • McCarey Leo • SHT • USA
UNKNOWN • 1916 • *Chapman Marguerite* • SHT • USA
UNKNOWN 274 • 1917 • Millarde Harry • USA
UNKNOWN, THE • 1913 • *Essanay* • USA
UNKNOWN, THE • 1913 • Fielding Romaine • *Lubin* • USA
UNKNOWN, THE • 1913 • Kirkwood James • *Victor* • USA
UNKNOWN, THE • 1915 • Melford George • USA
UNKNOWN, THE • 1921 • Jones Grover • USA
UNKNOWN, THE • 1927 • Browning Tod • USA
UNKNOWN, THE • 1946 • Levin Henry • USA
UNKNOWN, THE see **UNBEKANNTE, DIE** • 1936
UNKNOWN, THE see **NIEZNANY** • 1965
UNKNOWN, THE see **INCONNUE, L'** • 1966
UNKNOWN, THE see **DESCONHECIDO, O** • 1980
UNKNOWN BATTLE, THE see **HEROES OF TELEMARK, THE** • 1965
UNKNOWN BLONDE • 1934 • Henley Hobart • USA • MAN WHO PAWNED HIS SOUL, THE (UKN)
UNKNOWN BRIDE, THE • 1912 • *Leonard Marion* • USA
UNKNOWN BROTHER, THE • 1915 • *Ayres Sydney* • USA
UNKNOWN CAVALIER, THE • 1926 • Rogell Albert S. • USA
UNKNOWN CHAPLIN • 1983 • Brownlow Kevin, Gill David • DOC • UKN
UNKNOWN CLAIM, THE • 1910 • *Anderson Broncho Billy* • USA
UNKNOWN COUNTRY, THE • 1914 • *Lubin* • USA
UNKNOWN DANGERS • 1926 • Jones Grover • USA
UNKNOWN FRIEND, THE see **TUNTEMATON YSTAVA** • 1977
UNKNOWN FROM SHANDIGOR, THE see **INCONNU DE SHANDIGOR, L'** • 1967
UNKNOWN FUTURE, THE see **MOSTAKBEL EL MAGHOUL, EL** • 1948
UNKNOWN GUEST, THE • 1943 • Neumann Kurt • USA
UNKNOWN HEROES • NKR
UNKNOWN HOUR, THE see **HORA INCOGNITA, LA** • 1964
UNKNOWN ISLAND • 1948 • Bernhard Jack • USA
UNKNOWN LAND • 1972 • Howes Oliver • DOC • ASL
UNKNOWN LANGUAGE, AN • 1911 • *Boulden Edward* • USA
UNKNOWN LOVE • 1918 • Perret Leonce • USA
UNKNOWN LOVER, THE • 1925 • Halperin Victor Hugo • USA
UNKNOWN MAN see **UKJENT MANN** • 1951
UNKNOWN MAN, THE • 1951 • Thorpe Richard • USA • BRADLEY MASEN STORY, THE
UNKNOWN MAN OF SHANDIGOR, THE see **INCONNU DE SHANDIGOR, L'** • 1967
UNKNOWN MARKET, THE see **UKJENTES MARKED, DE** • 1968
UNKNOWN MODEL, THE • 1912 • *Ricketts Josephine* • USA
UNKNOWN OF SHANDIGOR, THE see **INCONNU DE SHANDIGOR, L'** • 1967
UNKNOWN PEOPLE see **SUPERMAN AND THE MOLE MEN** • 1951
UNKNOWN POLICEMAN, THE see **GENDARME DESCONOCIDO, EL** • 1941
UNKNOWN POWERS • 1979 • Como Don • USA
UNKNOWN PURPLE, THE • 1923 • West Roland • USA
UNKNOWN QUANTITY, THE • 1919 • Mills Thomas R. • USA
UNKNOWN RANGER, THE • 1936 • Bennet Spencer Gordon • USA
UNKNOWN REASONS • Mogubgub Fred • SHT • USA
UNKNOWN RIDER, THE • 1929 • Meals A. R. • USA
UNKNOWN SATELLITE OVER OKYO see **UCHUJIN TOKYO NI ARAWARU** • 1956
UNKNOWN SHOW, THE • 1985 • Frost Harvey • MTV • CND

UNKNOWN SOLDIER • 1968 • Shebib Donald • CND
UNKNOWN SOLDIER see **TUNTEMATON SOTILAS** • 1969
UNKNOWN SOLDIER, THE • 1926 • Hoffman Renaud • USA
UNKNOWN SOLDIER, THE see **TUNTEMATON SOTILAS** • 1955
UNKNOWN SOLDIER, THE see **TUNTEMATON SOTILAS** • 1986
UNKNOWN SOLDIER SPEAKS • 1939 • *Rossen Robert* • DOC • USA
UNKNOWN SOLDIER'S PATENT LEATHER SHOES, THE see **LACHENITE OBOUKVI NA NEZNAINYA VOIN** • 1979
UNKNOWN SWORDSMAN, THE • 1970 • *Chin Hsiang Lin* • HKG
UNKNOWN TERROR • 1957 • Warren Charles Marquis • USA
UNKNOWN TOMORROW, THE (UKN) see **UNBEKANNTE MORGEN, DAS** • 1923
UNKNOWN TREASURES • 1926 • Mayo Archie • USA • HOUSE BEHIND THE HEDGE, THE (UKN)
UNKNOWN VALLEY • 1933 • Hillyer Lambert • USA
UNKNOWN VIOLINIST, THE • 1912 • *Kent Charles* • USA
UNKNOWN WIFE, THE • 1921 • Worthington William • USA • THREE AT THE TABLE
UNKNOWN WOMAN • 1935 • Rogell Albert S. • USA
UNKNOWN WOMAN, THE see **OKANDA, DEN** • 1913
UNKNOWN WORLD • 1951 • Morse Terry O. • USA • TO THE CENTER OF THE EARTH
UNKRAUT, DAS • 1962 • Urchs Wolfgang • ANS • FRG • WEED, THE
UNLAWFUL see **KING OF THE UNDERWORLD** • 1939
UNLAWFUL RESTRAINT see **SEQUESTRO DI PERSONA** • 1968
UNLAWFUL TRADE, THE • 1914 • Dwan Allan • USA
UNLAWFUL WEDDING see **ONWETTIGE HUWELIK** • 1970
UNLIKE OTHER GIRLS • 1915 • De Grasse Joseph • USA
UNLOADED '45, THE • 1915 • *Ck* • USA
UNLOADED GUN, THE • 1911 • *Bison* • USA
UNLOADING THE BOAT (HAVRE) see **DECHARGEMENT DE BATEAUX AU HAVRE** • 1896
UNLOVABLE ONE, THE see **PISEN NEMILOVA–NEHO** • 1982
UNLOVED CHILDREN • 1964 • Goldberger Kurt • DOC • CZC
UNLUCKY ANN • 1912 • Fitzhamon Lewin • UKN
UNLUCKY BILL • 1910 • Fitzhamon Lewin? • UKN
UNLUCKY BRIDEGROOM, THE • 1908 • Fitzhamon Lewin • UKN
UNLUCKY DAY, AN • 1905 • Stow Percy • UKN
UNLUCKY DOG • 1943 • Holmes Ben • SHT • USA
UNLUCKY FELLOW NO.13 see **OLYCKSFAGELN NR.13** • 1942
UNLUCKY FELLOW OF THE BLOCK see **KVARTERETS OLYCKSFAGEL** • 1948
UNLUCKY HORSESHOE, THE • 1907 • Hough Harold • UKN
UNLUCKY HORSESHOE, THE • 1909 • *Lubin* • USA
UNLUCKY JIM • 1936 • Marks Harry S. • UKN
UNLUCKY LITTLE ELEPHANT, THE • 1959 • Ratz Gunter • ANM • GDR • CLUMSY LITTLE ELEPHANT, THE
UNLUCKY LOUEY • 1915 • Drew Sidney • USA
UNLUCKY LUKE • 1916 • Borzage Frank • SHT • USA
UNLUCKY MERYEM see **TALIHSIZ MERYEM** • 1968
UNLUCKY NIGHT AT THE BROWNS, AN • 1915 • *Horseshoe* • UKN
UNLUCKY POTLUCK • 1972 • Smith Paul J. • ANS • USA
UNLUCKY PRESENT, AN • 1912 • *Nestor* • USA
UNLUCKY SUITOR, AN • 1915 • *Royal* • USA
UNLUCKY THIEF, THE • 1908 • Fitzhamon Lewin? • UKN
UNLUCKY THIRTEEN • 1914 • Calvert Charles? • UKN
UNLUCKY UMBRELLA, THE see **BIRTHDAY UMBRELLA, A** • 1905
UNMADE BEDS • 1980 • Poe Amos • USA
UNMAILED LETTER, THE • 1910 • *Selig* • USA
UNMAN, WITTERING AND ZIGO • 1971 • Mackenzie John • UKN
UNMARRIED • 1920 • Wilson Rex • UKN
UNMARRIED • 1939 • Neumann Kurt • USA • NIGHT CLUB HOSTESS (UKN) ○ ME AND MY GAL
UNMARRIED see **GLASBERGET** • 1953
UNMARRIED BRIDE see **NIMFIOS ANIMFEFTOS** • 1967
UNMARRIED BRIDE, THE see **LUXURY** • 1921
UNMARRIED GIRL see **KUNWARI** • 1937
UNMARRIED HUSBAND, THE • 1915 • Ince John • USA
UNMARRIED LOOK, THE • 1917 • Drew Sidney, Drew Sidney Mrs. • SHT • USA
UNMARRIED MOTHERS see **OGIFT FADER SOKES** • 1953
UNMARRIED WIVES • 1924 • Hogan James P. • USA
UNMARRIED WOMAN, AN • 1978 • Mazursky Paul • USA
UNMASKED • 1913 • *Patheplay* • USA
UNMASKED • 1917 • Ford Francis, Cunard Grace • SHT • USA
UNMASKED • 1929 • Lewis Edgar • USA
UNMASKED • 1950 • Blair George • USA
UNMASKED BY A KANAKA • 1913 • Melies Gaston • USA
UNMASKING, THE • 1914 • Ayres Sydney • *American* • USA
UNMASKING, THE • 1915 • *Big U* • USA
UNMASKING A RASCAL • 1916 • Horne James W. • SHT • USA
UNMASKING OF MAUD, THE • 1912 • Plumb Hay? • UKN
UNMASKING THE IDOL • 1986 • Keeter Worth • USA
UNMENSCH, DER see **HOMO IMMANIS** • 1919
UNMENTIONABLES, THE • 1915 • Cooper Toby? • UKN
UNMENTIONABLES, THE • 1963 • Freleng Friz • ANS • USA
UNMERITED SHAME • 1912 • *Pathe* • USA
UNMOGLICHE FRAU, DIE • 1936 • Meyer Johannes • FRG • HERRIN VON CAMPINA, DIE
UNMOGLICHE HERR PITT, DER • 1938 • Piel Harry • FRG
UNMOGLICHE LIEBE • 1932 • Waschneck Erich • FRG • VERA HOLGK UND IHRE TOCHTER
UNMOGLICHE MADCHEN, DAS see **FRAULEIN BIMBI** • 1951
UNMORAL • 1928 • Wolff Willi • FRG
UNMORALISCHEN, DIE (FRG) see **GRAIN DE SABLE, LE** • 1964
UNNAMEABLE, THE • 1988 • Quellette Jean-Paul • USA
UNNAMED WOMAN, THE • 1925 • Hoyt Harry O. • USA
UNNATURAL see **ALRAUNE** • 1952
UNNATURAL, THE see **CONTRONATURA** • 1969
UNNATURAL ACT: PART 2, AN • 1986 • Morehead Ned • USA
UNNATURAL CAUSES • 1986 • Johnson Lamont • TVM • USA
UNNATURAL HISTORY • 1925-27 • Lantz Walter, Hand David, Geronimi Clyde • ASS • USA
UNNATURAL HISTORY • 1959 • Levitow Abe • ANS • USA
UNNATURAL LIFE STUDIES • 1924 • Hughes Harry • UKN
UNNECESSARY SEX, THE • 1915 • Harvey John • USA
UNNEPI VACSORA • 1956 • Revesz Gyorgy • HNG • GALA DINNER
UNNEPNAPOK • 1967 • Kardos Ferenc • HNG • RED–LETTER DAYS ○ HOLIDAYS
UNO, L' • 1965 • Bazzoni Camillo • ITL • ONE, THE
UNO A UNO SIN PIEDAD • 1968 • Romero-Marchent Rafael • SPN, ITL • AD UNO AD UNO.. SPIETATAMENTE (ITL)
UNO DEI TRE • 1972 • Serra Gianni • MTV • ITL
UNO DEI TRE (ITL) see **GLAIVE ET LA BALANCE, LE** • 1962
UNO DEL MILLON DE MUERTOS • 1977 • Velasco Andres • SPN
UNO DI PIU ALL'INFERNO • 1968 • Fago Giovanni • ITL • ONE MOVE TO HELL
UNO, DOI, TREI.. • 1975 • Popescu-Gopo Ion • ANM • RMN • 1, 2, 3
UNO DOPO L'ALTRO • 1968 • Iquino Ignacio F. • ITL, SPN • ONE AFTER THE OTHER
UNO ENTRE MUCHOS • 1982 • Zuniga Ariel • MXC • ONE AMONG OTHERS ○ ONE OF MANY
UNO STRANO TIPO • 1963 • Fulci Lucio • ITL
UNO TRA LA FOLLA • 1946 • Cerlesi Ennio • ITL
UNO +UNO + UNO see **TAVERNA ROSSA** • 1940
UNO Y MEDIO CENTRA EL MUNDO • 1971 • *Cinema Marte* • MXC
UNOFFICIAL MANEUVER, THE • 1918 • *Jaxon* • USA
UNOPENED LETTER, THE • 1914 • Kendall Preston • USA
UNORDNUNG UND FRUHES LEID • 1975 • Seitz Franz* • FRG • DISORDER AND EARLY SORROW
UNOS • 1952 • Kadar Jan, Klos Elmar • CZC • KIDNAPPED ○ KIDNAP, THE
UNOS BANKERE FUXE • 1923 • Anton Karl • CZC • ABDUCTION OF BANKER FUXE, THE ○ KIDNAPPING OF BANKER FUX, THE
UNOS MORAVANKY • 1982 • Muchna Milan • CZC • HIJACKING A BRASS BAND
UNOS MUERTOS SIN IMPORTANCIA • 1977 • Brandler Alfredo • VNZ • SOME UNIMPORTANT DEAD PEOPLE
UNOS PASAS DE MUJER • 1941 • Ardavin Eusebio F. • SPN
UNPAID DEBT, AN • 1959 • Shredel Vladimir • USS
UNPAID RANSOM, AN • 1915 • *Phillips Augustus* • USA
UNPAINTED PORTRAIT, THE • 1914 • *Majestic* • USA
UNPAINTED WOMAN, THE • 1919 • Browning Tod • USA
UNPARDONABLE SIN, THE • 1915 • *Ideal* • USA
UNPARDONABLE SIN, THE • 1916 • *Eclair* • SHT • USA
UNPARDONABLE SIN, THE • 1916 • O'Neil Barry • *Shubert* • USA
UNPARDONABLE SIN, THE • 1919 • Neilan Marshall • USA
UNPLANNED ELOPEMENT, AN • 1914 • Calvert E. H. • USA
UNPOPULAR MECHANIC, THE • 1936 • *Lantz Walter (P)* • ANS • USA
UNPOSTED LETTER, THE see **NEOTPRAVLENNOE PISMO** • 1960
UNPRECEDENTED DEFENCE OF THE FORTRESS DEUTSCHKREUTZ, THE see **BEISPIELLOSE VERTEIDIGUNG DER FESTUNG DEUTSCHKREUTZ, DIE** • 1966
UNPROFITABLE BOARDER, THE • 1913 • Williams C. Jay • USA
UNPROMISED LAND see **HURDES, LAS** • 1932
UNPROTECTED • 1916 • Young James • USA
UNPROTECTED FEMALE • 1903 • *Bitzer Billy (Ph)* • USA
UNPUBLISHED STORY • 1942 • French Harold • UKN
UNQUENCHABLE THIRST • 1906 • *Pathe* • FRN
UNQUIET DEATH OF JULIUS AND ETHEL ROSENBERG, THE • 1976 • Goldstein Alvin H. • USA
UNQUIET HOUSE • 1972 • Wright John • CND
UNREAL, THE • Brzezinski Tony • SHT • USA
UNREASONABLE JEALOUSY • 1910 • *Imp* • USA
UNRECOGNIZED MAN OF THE WORLD, THE (USA) see **VERKANNTE LEBEMANN, DER** • 1936
UNRECONCILED see **NICHT VERSOHNT ODER "ES HILFT NUR GEWALT, WO GEWALT HERRSCHT"** • 1965
UNRECORDED VICTORY, AN see **SPRING OFFENSIVE** • 1939
UNREDEEMED PLEDGE, AN • 1914 • *Majestic* • USA
UNRELENTING STRUGGLE • 1945 • Wright Basil • DOC • UKN
UNREMARKABLE BIRTH, AN • 1977-79 • Beaudry Diane • CND
UNREMITTING TENDERNESS • 1977 • Elder Bruce • CND
UNREPEATABLE SPRING see **NEPOVTORIMAYA VESNA** • 1957
UNREST • 1914 • Santschi Thomas • USA
UNREST • 1920 • Cairns Dallas • UKN
UNREST see **NEMIR** • 1983
UNRESTRAINED YOUTH • 1925 • Levering Joseph • USA
UNROMANTIC MAIDEN, AN • 1913 • *Thanhouser* • USA
UNROMANTIC WIFE, AN • 1911 • Wilson Frank? • UKN
UNRUHIGE NACHT • 1958 • Harnack Falk • FRG • RESTLESS NIGHT, THE (USA) ○ ALL NIGHT THROUGH
UNRUHIGE TOCHTER • 1967 • Amon Hansjorg • SWT, FRG • RESTLESS DAUGHTERS
UNRUHIGEN MADCHEN, DIE • 1938 • von Bolvary Geza • AUS • FINALE
UNRULY CHARGE, AN • 1911 • Wilson Frank? • UKN
UNRULY GENERATION, THE see **KURITON SUKUPOLVI** • 1957
UNRULY HARE • 1945 • Tashlin Frank • ANS • USA
UNS ABER IST GEGEBEN, AUF KEINER STATTE ZU RUHEN • 1919 • Eichberg Richard • FRG
UNS DANS LES AUTRES, LES • 1981 • Baudricourt Michel • FRN
UNS ET LES AUTRES, LES • 1981 • Lelouch Claude • FRN • INS AND THE OUTS, THE (USA) ○ BOLERO ○ WITHIN MEMORY
UNS GEFALLT DIE WELT • 1956 • Stemmle R. A. • FRG
UNS, LES AUTRES, LES • 1972 • Ben Salah Mohamed • BLG
UNSANE (USA) see **TENEBRAE** • 1982
UNSATISFIED, THE (UKN) see **INSATISFAITE, L'** • 1971
UNSATISFIED, THE (USA) see **JUVENTUD A LA INTEMPERIE** • 1961
UNSATISFIED LOVE see **LOVE AFTER DEATH** • 1968
UNSCHEDULED TRAIN, THE see **VLAK BEZ VOZNOG REDA** • 1958
UNSCHULD • 1929 • Land Robert • FRG
UNSCHULD IN NOTEN see **MADCHEN AUS DER KONFEKTION, DAS** • 1951
UNSCHULD OHNE KLEID, DIE • 1926 • Halden Karl • FRG
UNSCHULD VOM LANDE, DIE • 1933 • Boese Carl • FRG
UNSCHULD VOM LANDE, DIE • 1957 • Schundler Rudolf • FRG
UNSCRUPULOUS ONES, THE see **CAFAJESTES, OS** • 1962
UNSEEING EYE, THE • 1959 • Muller Geoffrey • UKN
UNSEEING EYES • 1923 • Griffith Edward H. • USA
UNSEEN, THE • 1914 • *Eclair* • FRN
UNSEEN, THE • 1945 • Allen Lewis • USA • HER HEART IN HER THROAT
UNSEEN, THE • 1981 • Foleg Peter • USA
UNSEEN, THE see **HOUSE OF MYSTERY** • 1961
UNSEEN DEFENCE, THE • 1913 • Huntley Fred W. • USA
UNSEEN ENEMIES • 1926 • McGowan J. P. • USA
UNSEEN ENEMIES • 1959 • Clarke Michael • UKN
UNSEEN ENEMY • 1942 • Rawlins John • USA
UNSEEN ENEMY, AN • 1912 • Griffith D. W. • USA
UNSEEN ENEMY, THE (UKN) see **RIDIN' ON** • 1936
UNSEEN FLOWER see **DOOMOORER PHOOL** • 1978
UNSEEN FORCES • 1920 • Franklin Sidney A. • USA
UNSEEN GUARDIANS • 1939 • Wrangell Basil • SHT • USA
UNSEEN HANDS • 1924 • Jaccard Jacques • USA
UNSEEN HEROES (USA) see **BATTLE OF THE V 1** • 1958
UNSEEN INFLUENCE, THE • 1913 • *Kirkwood James* • USA
UNSEEN METAMORPHOSIS • 1913 • *Eclair* • FRN
UNSEEN TERROR, AN • 1913 • *Joyce Alice* • USA
UNSEEN VENGEANCE, THE • 1915 • *American* • USA
UNSEEN WITNESS • 1920 • *Wall David* • USA
UNSEEN WITNESS, THE • 1914 • Wilson Frank? • UKN
UNSELFISH LOVE, AN • 1910 • Dawley J. Searle • USA
UNSENT LETTER, THE see **NEOTPRAVLENNOE PISMO** • 1960
UNSER BOSS IST EIN DAME (FRG) see **OPERAZIONE SAN GENNARO** • 1966
UNSER DOKTOR IST DER BESTE • 1969 • Vock Harald • FRG
UNSER DORF • 1953 • Lindtberg Leopold • SWT, UKN • VILLAGE, THE ○ PESTALOZZIDORF, DAS
UNSER FRAULEIN DOKTOR • 1940 • Engel Erich • FRG
UNSER HAUS IN KAMERUN • 1961 • Vohrer Alfred • FRG
UNSER KLEINE JUNGE • 1941 • Barlog Boleslav • FRG
UNSER MITTWOCH ABEND • 1948 • Krause Georg, Illing Werner • FRG
UNSER TAGLICH BROT • 1926 • David Constantin J. • FRG
UNSER TAGLICH BROT • 1949 • Dudow Slatan • GDR • OUR DAILY BREAD (USA)
UNSER TAGLICHES BROT • 1929 • Jutzi Phil • FRG • HUNGER IN WALDENBURG ○ OUR DAILY BREAD
UNSER WUNDERLAND BEI NACHT • 1959 • Roland Jurgen, Elsner Richard, Hinrich Hans • FRG • MAINLY FOR MEN
UNSERE AFRIKAREISE • 1967 • Kubelka Peter • SHT • AUS
UNSERE ELTERN HABEN DEN AUSWEIS C. • 1983 • Winiger Eduard, Froelicher Mia • DOC • SWT
UNSERE EMDEN • 1926 • Ralph Louis • FRG
UNSERE FAHNE FLATTERT UNS VORAN • 1934 • Steinhoff Hans • FRG
UNSERE KLEINE FRAU • 1938 • Verhoeven Paul • FRG, ITL • MIA MOGLIE SI DIVERTE (ITL)
UNSERE PAUKER GEHEN IN DIE LUFT • 1970 • Vock Harald • FRG
UNSERE TOLLEN NICHTEN • 1963 • Olsen Rolf • AUS
UNSERE TOLLEN TANTEN IN DER SUDSEE • 1964 • Olsen Rolf • AUS
UNSETTLED LAND see **DREAMERS, THE** • 1988
UNSHOD MAIDEN, THE • 1932 • De Mond Albert • SHT • USA
UNSHRINKABLE JERRY MOUSE • 1964 • Jones Charles M. • ANS • USA
UNSICHTBARE, DER • 1963 • Nussbaum Raphael • FRG • INVISIBLE TERROR, THE (USA) ○ INVISIBLE MAN, THE
UNSICHTBARE DIEB, DER • 1920 • Bock-Stieber Gernot • FRG
UNSICHTBARE FRONT, DIE • 1932 • Eichberg Richard • FRG
UNSICHTBARE GAST, DER • 1919 • Feher Friedrich • FRG
UNSICHTBARE GAST, DER • 1921 • Zelnik Friedrich • FRG
UNSICHTBARE GEGNER • 1933 • Katscher Rudolf • FRG, AUS
UNSICHTBARE GEGNER • 1977 • Export Valie • AUS • INVISIBLE ADVERSARY ○ INVISIBLE ADVERSARIES
UNSICHTBARE HANDE • 1917 • Kahn William • FRG
UNSICHTBARE MENSCH, DER • 1916 • Schubert Georg • FRG
UNSICHTBAREN KRALLEN DES DR. MABUSE, DIE • 1962 • Reinl Harald • FRG • INVISIBLE DR. MABUSE, THE (USA) ○ INVISIBLE HORROR, THE ○ INVISIBLE CLAWS OF DR. MABUSE, THE
UNSICHTBARER GEHT DURCH DIE STADT, EIN • 1933 • Piel Harry • FRG • INVISIBLE MAN GOES THROUGH THE CITY, AN ○ MEIN IST DIE WELT ○ DIE WELT IST MEIN! ○ WORLD IS MINE, THE
UNSIGNED AGREEMENT, THE • 1914 • Ford Francis • USA
UNSINKABLE MISS CALABASH see **HSIAO HU–LU** • 1982
UNSINKABLE MOLLY BROWN, THE • 1964 • Walters Charles • USA
UNSKILLED LABOUR • 1913 • Stow Percy • UKN
UNSLEEPING EYE, THE • 1928 • MacDonald Alexander, Sully Wally • ASL, UKN
UNSOPHISTICATED BOOK AGENT • 1910 • *Atlas* • USA
UNSPOKEN GOOD–BYE, THE • 1909 • *Vitagraph* • USA
UNSTABLE FAMILY, AN see **UHOHO TANKEN–TAI** • 1987
UNSTERBLICHE ANTLITZ, DAS • 1947 • von Cziffra Geza • AUS
UNSTERBLICHE GELIEBTE • 1951 • Harlan Veit • FRG
UNSTERBLICHE HERZ, DAS • 1939 • Harlan Veit • FRG
UNSTERBLICHE LUMP, DER • 1930 • Ucicky Gustav • FRG • IMMORTAL VAGABOND, THE (USA)
UNSTERBLICHE LUMP, DER • 1953 • Rabenalt Arthur M. • FRG
UNSTERBLICHE MELODIEN • 1935 • Paul Heinz • FRG • IMMORTAL MELODIES (USA)
UNSTERBLICHER WALZER • 1939 • Emo E. W. • FRG
UNSTERBLICHES LIED, DAS • 1934 • Marr Hans • FRG, CZC
UNSTOPPABLE MAN, THE • 1960 • Bishop Terry • UKN
UNSTRAP ME • 1968 • Kuchar George • USA
UNSUCCESSFUL SUBSTITUTION, AN • 1909 • Porter Edwin S. • USA
UNSUITABLE JOB FOR A WOMAN, AN • 1981 • Petit Christopher • UKN
UNSULLIED SHIELD, AN • 1913 • Brabin Charles J. • USA
UNSUNG HEROES see **WAR DOGS** • 1942
UNSURE RUNTS • 1946 • Swift Howard • ANS • USA
UNSUSPECTED, THE • 1947 • Curtiz Michael • USA

UNSUSPECTED ISLES, THE • 1915 • Haddock William F. • USA
UNTAMEABLE, THE • 1923 • Blache Herbert • USA • WHITE CAT, THE ○ TWO SOULED WOMAN, THE
UNTAMEABLE WHISKERS, THE (USA) see **ROI DU MAQUILLAGE, LE** • 1904
UNTAMED • 1918 • Smith Cliff • USA
UNTAMED • 1929 • Conway Jack • USA • JUNGLE
UNTAMED • 1940 • Archainbaud George • USA
UNTAMED • 1955 • King Henry • USA
UNTAMED see **ARAKURE** • 1957
UNTAMED, THE • 1917 • Henderson Lucius • SHT • USA
UNTAMED, THE • 1920 • Flynn Emmett J. • USA
UNTAMED, THE see **MAN FROM SNOWY RIVER II, THE** • 1987
UNTAMED BREED, THE • 1948 • Lamont Charles • USA
UNTAMED FRONTIER • 1952 • Fregonese Hugo • USA
UNTAMED FURY • 1947 • Scott Ewing • USA
UNTAMED FURY see **MIYAMOTO MUSASHI I** • 1961
UNTAMED HEIRESS • 1954 • Lamont Charles • USA
UNTAMED JUSTICE • 1929 • Webb Harry S. • USA • RUN TO EARTH (UKN)
UNTAMED LADIES • 1918 • *Howell Alice* • SHT • USA
UNTAMED LADY, THE • 1926 • Tuttle Frank • USA
UNTAMED MISTRESS • 1959 • Ormond Ron • USA
UNTAMED SEX see **SECH SCHWEDINNEN IM PENSIONAT** • 1980
UNTAMED WEST see **FAR HORIZONS, THE** • 1955
UNTAMED WOMAN see **ARAKURE** • 1957
UNTAMED WOMEN • 1952 • Connell W. Merle • USA
UNTAMED YOUTH • 1924 • Chautard Emile • USA • BEWARE THE WOMAN ○ BORN OF THE CYCLONE
UNTAMED YOUTH • 1957 • Koch Howard W. • USA
UNTEL PERE ET FILS • 1940 • Duvivier Julien • FRN • HEART OF A NATION (UKN) ○ IMMORTAL FRANCE (USA) ○ COEUR D'UNE NATION, LE ○ RELEVE, LA
UNTER ACHTZEHN see **NOCH MINDERJAHRIG** • 1957
UNTER AUSSCHLUSS DER OEFFENTLICHKEIT • 1927 • Wiene Conrad • FRG
UNTER AUSSCHLUSS DER OEFFENTLICHKEIT • 1937 • Wegener Paul • FRG
UNTER AUSSCHLUSS DER OEFFENTLICHKEIT • 1961 • Philipp Harald • FRG
UNTER BLUTSCHULD • 1923 • *Vonzedlitz Hans* • FRG
UNTER DEM EINFLUSS EINER KRAFT • 1987 • Konig Gerhard • AUS • UNDER THE INFLUENCE OF A CERTAIN POWER
UNTER DEM PFLASTER IST DER STRAND • 1974 • Sanders Helma • FRG
UNTER DEN BRUCKEN • 1945 • Kautner Helmut • FRG
UNTER DEN DACHERN VON ST. PAULI • 1970 • Weidenmann Alfred • FRG
UNTER DEN STERNEN VON CAPRI • 1953 • Linnekogel Otto • FRG
UNTER DEN TAUSAND LATERNEN • 1952 • Engel Erich • FRG • STIMME DES ANDEREN, DIE
UNTER DER DORNENKRONE • 1920 • Randolf Rolf • FRG
UNTER DER LATERNE • 1928 • Lamprecht Gerhard • FRG
UNTER DER MASKE DES JUWELIERS see **GEHEIMNIS DER GLADIATORENWERKE 2, DAS** • 1920
UNTER DER PEITSCHE DES GESCHICKS • 1918 • Henning Hanna • FRG
UNTER DER SCHWARZEN STURMFAHNE • 1933 • von Sonjevski-Jamrowski Rolf • FRG
UNTER EINER DECKE • 1989 • Giger Bernhard • SWT • ACCOMPLICES
UNTER FALSCHER FLAGGE • 1932 • Meyer Johannes • FRG
UNTER FALSCHER MASKE • 1918 • Del Zopp Rudolf • FRG
UNTER GEIERN • 1964 • Vohrer Alfred • FRG, ITL, YGS • LA DOVE SCENDE IL SOLE (ITL) ○ MEDJU JASTREBOVIMA (YGS) ○ FRONTIER HELLCAT (USA) ○ PARMI LES VAUTOURS (FRN) ○ AMONG VULTURES
UNTER GESCHAFTSAUFSICHT see **WEHE, WENN ER LOSGELASSEN** • 1932
UNTER HEISSEM HIMMEL • 1936 • Ucicky Gustav • FRG
UNTER HEISSER SONNE see **UNTER HEISSER ZONE** • 1916
UNTER HEISSER ZONE • 1916 • Piel Harry • FRG • UNDER A HOT SUN ○ UNTER HEISSER SONNE
UNTER JUDEN • 1923 • Christensen Benjamin • DNM • AMONG JEWS
UNTER PALMEN AM BLAUEN MEER • 1957 • Deppe Hans • FRG, ITL • VACANZE A PORTOFINO (ITL)
UNTER RAUBERN UND BESTIEN • 1921 • Wendt Ernst • FRG
UNTERBROCHENE SPUR, DIE • 1982 • Knauer Mathias • SWT • INTERRUPTED TRACKS
UNTERGANG TROJAS, DER see **HELENA 2** • 1924
UNTERM BIRNBAUM • 1974 • Kirsten Ralf • GDR
UNTERM ROCKEN STOSST DAS BOCKCHEN • 1974 • Frank Hubert • FRG
UNTERMANN–OBERMANN • 1969 • Hauff Reinhard • DOC • FRG
UNTERNEHMEN EDELWEISS • 1954 • Paul Heinz • FRG
UNTERNEHMEN GEIGENKASTEN • 1985 • Friedrich Gunther • GDR • OPERATION VIOLIN–CASE
UNTERNEHMEN MICHAEL • 1937 • Ritter Karl • FRG • PRIVATE'S JOB, THE (USA)
UNTERNEHMEN SCHLAFSACK • 1955 • Rabenalt Arthur M. • FRG
UNTERNEHMEN TRANSPORT • 1969 • Meyer Herbert E. • SWT
UNTERNEHMEN XARIFA • 1954 • Hass Hans • SWT • UNDER THE CARIBBEAN
UNTERTAN, DER • 1951 • Staudte Wolfgang • GDR • KAISER'S LACKEY, THE ○ UNDERDOG, THE ○ SUBMISSIVE, THE
UNTERWEGS • 1988 • Baumann Rene, Bischof Marc • SWT • ON THE WAY
UNTIL DEATH • 1913 • Smalley Phillips, Weber Lois • USA
UNTIL DEATH • 1987 • Bava Lamberto • TVM • ITL
UNTIL DEATH DO YOU PART see **BIS DAS DER TOD EUCH SCHEIDET**
UNTIL DEATH US DO PART see **OLUNCEYE KADAR** • 1967
UNTIL HELL IS FROZEN see **TEUFEL SPIELTE BALALAIKA, DER** • 1961
UNTIL I DIE • 1940 • Hecht Ben • USA
UNTIL MAN CAME • 1960 • Junge Winifried • DOC • GDR
UNTIL MARRIAGE SEPARATES US see **ATE QUE O CASAMENTO NOS SEPARE** • 1968
UNTIL MONDAY see **DOZHIVYOM DO PONEDYELNIKA** • 1968
UNTIL SEPTEMBER • 1984 • Marquand Richard • USA
UNTIL THE DAY WE MEET AGAIN see **MATA AU HI MADE** • 1932
UNTIL THE DAY WE MEET AGAIN see **MATA AU HI MADE** • 1950
UNTIL THE END OF THE WORLD see **BIS ANS ENDE DER WELT** • 1989
UNTIL THE SEA • 1913 • Campbell Colin • USA
UNTIL THEY GET ME • 1918 • Borzage Frank • USA
UNTIL THEY SAIL • 1957 • Wise Robert • USA
UNTIL VICTORY DAY see **SHORI NO HI MADE** • 1945
UNTIL WE MEET AGAIN see **MATA AU HI MADE** • 1950
UNTIL WE THREE MEET AGAIN • 1913 • *Buckley May* • USA
UNTIL YOU HAVE MAMMA see **DOKUD MAS MAMINKU** • 1934
UNTILLED FIELDS • 1953 • Bahna Vladimir • CZC
UNTIMELY MAN, THE see **PREZHDEVRYEMENNY CHELOVYEK** • 1973
UNTITLED • Whitney John • SHT • USA
UNTITLED (77) • 1977 • Gehr Ernie • USA
UNTITLED COMEDY • 1898 • Welford Walter D. • UKN
UNTITLED–DANCE • 1937 • Martin Paul • FRG
UNTITLED FILM, AN • 1964 • Gladwell David • UKN
UNTITLED FILM OF GEOFFERY HOLDER'S WEDDING • 1955 • Brakhage Stan, Jordan Larry • USA
UNTO A NEW LAND see **INVANDRARNA** • 1970
UNTO EACH OTHER • 1929 • Coleby A. E. • UKN
UNTO HERSELF ALONE • 1915 • *Roland Ruth* • USA
UNTO THE END • 1919 • Ingraham Harrish • USA
UNTO THE GATES OF HELL see **INTILL HELVETETS PORTAR** • 1948
UNTO THE LEAST OF THESE • 1916 • Baker Richard Foster • SHT • USA
UNTO THE THIRD AND FOURTH GENERATION • 1914 • Le Saint Edward J. • USA
UNTO THE THIRD GENERATION • 1913 • Salter Harry • USA
UNTO THE WEAK • 1914 • *American* • USA
UNTO THOSE WHO SIN • 1916 • Campbell Colin • USA
UNTO US A CHILD IS BORN • 1911 • *Selig* • USA
UNTOUCHABLES, THE • 1987 • De Palma Brian • USA
UNTOUCHABLES, THE see **INTOCCABILI, GLI** • 1969
UNTOUCHABLES: THE SCARFACE MOB see **SCARFACE MOB, THE** • 1962
UNTOUCHED • 1956 • *Montalban Ricardo* • MXC
UNTOUCHED AND PURE • 1970 • Ransen Mort • CND
UNTRAINED SEAL, THE • 1936 • *Mintz Charles (P)* • ANS • USA
UNTYPICAL STORY, AN see **NETEPICHNAYA ISTORIA** • 1978
UNU NO JUNJO • 1956 • Suzuki Seijun • JPN
UNUBERWINDLICHE, DER • 1928 • Obal Max • FRG
UNUS, DER WEG IN DIE WELT • 1921 • Piel Harry • FRG
UNUSUAL BIRTH see **APOORVA PIRAVIGAL** • 1967
UNUSUAL CASE, AN see **CHASTNYI SLUCHAI** • 1934
UNUSUAL COOKING • 1908 • *Pathe* • FRN
UNUSUAL EXHIBITION, THE see **NEOBYKNOVENNAIA VYSTAVKA** • 1968
UNUSUAL FRIENDSHIP OF THE ACTOR JESENIUS, THE see **PODLIVNE PRATELSTVI HERCE JESENIA** • 1985
UNUSUAL MATCH, AN see **NEOVY KNOVENNYI MACH** • 1955
UNUSUAL REQUESTS • 1968 • Anders Jan • USA
UNUSUAL SACRIFICE, AN • 1912 • *Fuller Mary* • USA
UNUSUAL TALES see **HISTOIRES EXTRAORDINAIRES** • 1949
UNUSUAL YEARS see **NEOBYCEJNA LETA** • 1952
UNUTLAN SIR • 1947 • Akat Lutfu • TRK
UNVANQUISHED, THE see **NEPOKORENNYE** • 1945
UNVANQUISHED, THE see **APARAJITO** • 1956
UNVANQUISHED, THE see **NEPORAZENI** • 1956
UNVEILING, THE • 1911 • Griffith D. W. • USA
UNVEILING HAND, THE • 1919 • Crane Frank H. • USA
UNVERBESSERLICHE BARBARA, DIE • 1977 • Warneke Lothar • GDR • INCORRIGIBLE BARBARA
UNVERGANGLICHES LICHT • 1951 • Rabenalt Arthur M. • FRG
UNVERSTANDEN • 1915 • Henning Hanna • FRG
UNVERSTANDENE FRAU, EINE see **NJU** • 1924
UNVOLLKOMMENE EHE, DIE • 1959 • Stemmle R. A. • AUS
UNVOLLKOMMENE LIEBE, DIE • 1940 • Waschneck Erich • FRG
UNWANTED, THE • 1924 • Summers Walter • UKN
UNWANTED BRIDE, THE • 1922 • Greenwood Edwin • UKN
UNWANTED WOMEN see **DONNE SENZA NOME** • 1950
UNWED FATHER • 1974 • Kagan Jeremy Paul • TVM • USA
UNWED MOTHER • 1958 • Doniger Walter • USA
UNWELCOME CHAPERONE, THE • 1909 • Aylott Dave • UKN
UNWELCOME CHILDREN see **KREUZZUG DES WEIBES** • 1926
UNWELCOME GUEST • 1945 • Gordon George • ANS • USA
UNWELCOME GUEST, THE • 1913 • Griffith D. W. • USA
UNWELCOME GUESTS, THE • 1961 • Grooms Red • SHT • USA
UNWELCOME LODGER, AN • 1914 • *B & C* • UKN
UNWELCOME LOVE • 1912 • *Pates Gwendolyn* • USA
UNWELCOME MOTHER, THE • 1916 • Vincent James • USA
UNWELCOME MRS. HATCH, THE • 1914 • Dwan Allan • USA
UNWELCOME SANTA CLAUS, AN • 1911 • Porter Edwin S. • USA
UNWELCOME STRANGER • 1935 • Rosen Phil • USA
UNWELCOME VISITORS (UKN) see **IN EARLY ARIZONA** • 1938
UNWELCOME VISITORS (UKN) see **LONE STAR PIONEERS** • 1939
UNWELCOME WIFE, THE • 1915 • Abramson Ivan • USA
UNWIDERSTEHLICHE, DER • 1937 • von Bolvary Geza • FRG • IRRESISTIBLE MAN, THE (USA)
UNWIDERSTEHLICHE THEODOR, DER • 1917 • *Rieck Arnold* • FRG
UNWILLING AGENT (USA) see **MENSCHEN IM NETZ** • 1959
UNWILLING BIGAMIST, THE • 1912 • *Prior Herbert* • USA
UNWILLING BRIDE, THE • 1912 • Youngdeer James • USA
UNWILLING BRIDE, THE • 1915 • *Royal* • USA
UNWILLING BURGLAR, AN • 1915 • Metcalfe Earl • USA
UNWILLING COWBOY, AN • 1911 • Melies Gaston • USA
UNWILLING HERO, AN • 1921 • Badger Clarence • USA • WHISTLING DICK
UNWILLING INSPECTORS see **REVIZORY PONEVOLE** • 1954
UNWILLING LOVE see **NEPROSHENAYA LYUBOV** • 1964
UNWILLING SAMARITAN, THE see **KOCAR DO VIDNE** • 1966
UNWILLING SEPARATION, AN • 1913 • *Edison* • USA
UNWILLING SINNER, THE see **SJAELETYVEN** • 1915
UNWILLING THIEF, AN • 1915 • West Langdon • USA
UNWINDING IT • 1915 • *Tincher Fay* • USA
UNWORTHY SON, THE • 1912 • *Melies* • USA
UNWRITTEN CHAPTER, AN • 1913 • *Kelly Dorothy* • USA
UNWRITTEN CODE, THE • 1919 • Durning Bernard J. • USA • ALIENS
UNWRITTEN CODE, THE • 1944 • Rotsten Hal • USA
UNWRITTEN LAW, THE • 1916 • *Pike William* • USA
UNWRITTEN LAW, THE • 1925 • Le Saint Edward J. • USA
UNWRITTEN LAW, THE • 1929 • Hill Sinclair • UKN
UNWRITTEN LAW, THE • 1932 • Cabanne W. Christy • USA
UNWRITTEN LAW OF THE WEST • 1913 • Hamilton G. P.? • USA
UNWRITTEN PLAY, THE • 1914 • Marston Theodore • USA
UOMINI, CHE MASCALZONI.., GLI • 1932 • Camerini Mario • ITL • MEN ARE SUCH RASCALS ○ TAXI
UOMINI CHE MASCALZONI!, GLI • 1954 • Pellegrini Glauco • ITL, FRN
UOMINI CONTRO • 1970 • Rosi Francesco • ITL, YGS • ANNO SULL'ALTIPIANO, UN ○ JUST ANOTHER WAR ○ MANY WARS AGO
UOMINI DAL PASSO PESANTE • 1966 • Antonini Alfredo, Sequi Mario • ITL • TRAMPLERS, THE (USA)
UOMINI DEI CIELI see **UOMINI E CIELI** • 1943
UOMINI DURI • 1974 • Tessari Duccio • ITL, USA, FRN • THREE TOUGH GUYS (USA)
UOMINI E BELVE • 1976 • Cottafavi Vittorio • ITL
UOMINI E CIELI • 1943 • De Robertis Francesco • ITL • UOMINI DEI CIELI ○ UOMINI NEI CIELI
UOMINI E LUPI • 1956 • De Santis Giuseppe • ITL, FRN • HOMMES ET LOUPS (FRN) ○ MEN AND WOLVES (USA)
UOMINI E NO • 1979 • Orsini Valentino • ITL
UOMINI E NOBILUOMINI • 1959 • Bianchi Giorgio • ITL
UOMINI E SQUALI • 1976 • Vailati Bruno • ITL
UOMINI IN PIU • 1950 • Antonioni Michelangelo • DCS • ITL
UOMINI MERCE • 1976 • Lizzani Carlo • ITL
UOMINI NEI CIELI see **UOMINI E CIELI** • 1943
UOMINI NELLA NEBBIA • 1955 • Nardi • SHT • ITL
UOMINI NON GUARDANO IL CIELO, GLI • 1952 • Scarpelli Umberto • ITL • SECRET CONCLAVE, THE (USA) ○ PIO X ○ PAPA SARTO
UOMINI NON SONO INGRATI, GLI • 1937 • Brignone Guido • ITL
UOMINI OMBRA • 1954 • De Robertis Francesco • ITL
UOMINI RAPITI • 1965 • Fryd Joseph • ITL • KIDNAPPED MEN
UOMINI SENZA DOMANI • 1947 • Vernuccio Gianni • ITL • NOTTE DI NEBBIA
UOMINI SENZA PACE • 1954 • Saenz De Heredia Jose Luis • ITL, SPN
UOMINI SI NASCE POLIZIOTTI SI MUORE • 1976 • Deodato Ruggero • ITL • LIVE LIKE A COP, DIE LIKE A MAN
UOMINI SONO NEMICI, GLI • 1950 • Giannini Ettore • ITL
UOMINI SUL FONDO • 1941 • De Robertis Francesco • ITL • S.O.S. SUBMARINE
UOMINI VOGLIONO VIVERE, GLI (ITL) see **HOMMES VEULENT VIVRE!, LES** • 1961
UOMO, UN see **GIORNO DEL FURORE, IL** • 1973
UOMO A META, UN • 1966 • De Seta Vittorio • ITL • ALMOST A MAN
UOMO AMERICANO, UN see **SON OF A BITCH** • 1979
UOMO AVVISATO MEZZO AMMAZZATO.. PAROLA DI SPIRITO SANTO • 1972 • Carnimeo Giuliano • ITL, SPN • Y LE LLAMABAN HALCON (SPN) ○ CHIAMAVANO SPIRITO SANTO, LO ○ THEY BELIEVED HE WAS A SAINT
UOMO CHE BRUCIO IL SUO CADAVERE, L' • 1967 • Vernuccio Gianni • ITL
UOMO CHE NON SEPPE TACERE, L' (ITL) see **SILENCIEUX, LE** • 1972
UOMO CHE RIDE, L' • 1966 • Corbucci Sergio • ITL, FRN • MAN WHO LAUGHS, THE (USA) ○ MAN WITH THE GOLDEN MASK, THE
UOMO CHE SFIDO L'ORGANIZZAZIONE, L' • 1975 • Grieco Sergio • ITL
UOMO CHE SORRIDE, L' • 1936 • Mattoli Mario • ITL
UOMO CHE UCCIDEVA A SANGUE FREDDO, L' (ITL) see **TRAITEMENT DE CHOC** • 1972
UOMO CHE VALEVA MILIARDI, L' (ITL) see **HOMME QUI VALAIT DES MILLIARDS, L'** • 1967
UOMO CHE VISSE DUE VOLTE, L' see **CRYSTALBRAIN L'UOMO DAL CERVELLO DI CRISTALLO** • 1970
UOMO CHE VISSE LO SPAZIO, L' • 1966 • Grandi Gastone • ITL
UOMO CHIAMATO APOCALISSE JOE, UN • 1970 • Savona Leopoldo • ITL
UOMO CHIAMATO DAKOTA, UN • 1971 • Sabatini Mario • ITL
UOMO DA BRUCIARE, UN • 1962 • Taviani Paolo, Taviani Vittorio, Orsini Valentino • ITL • MAN FOR BURNING, A ○ MAN TO BURN, A
UOMO DA NULLA, UN • 1977 • Amato Renata • ITL
UOMO DA PAGARE, UN • 1977 • Esposito Luigi • ITL
UOMO DA RISPETTARE, UN • 1972 • Lupo Michele • ITL, FRG • MAN TO RESPECT, A (UKN) ○ MASTER TOUCH, THE (USA) ○ HEARTS AND MINDS
UOMO DAGLI OCCHI DI GHIACCIO, L' • 1971 • De Martino Alberto • ITL
UOMO DAI CALZONI CORTI, L' see **AMORE PIU BELLO, L'** • 1959
UOMO DAI CINQUE PALLONI, L' see **UOMO DAI PALLONCINI, L'** • 1964
UOMO DAI PALLONCINI, L' • 1964 • Ferreri Marco • ITL, FRN • MAN WITH THE BALLOONS, THE (USA) ○ UOMO DAI CINQUE PALLONI, L' ○ BREAK UP
UOMO DAL CERVELLO TRAPIANTATO L' (ITL) see **HOMME AU CERVEAU GREFFE, L'** • 1971
UOMO DAL COLPO PERFETTO, L' • 1967 • Florio Aldo • ITL, SPN • MAN WITH THE PERFECT SHOT, THE
UOMO DAL GUANTO GRIGIO, L' • 1949 • Mastrocinque Camillo • ITL • MAN WITH THE GREY GLOVE, THE (USA)
UOMO DAL LUNGO FUCILE, L' • 1969 • Reinl Harald • ITL

UOMO DAL PENNELLO D'ORO, L' (ITL) see **MANN MIT DEM GOLDENEN PINSEL, DER** • 1971
UOMO DAL PUGNO D'ORO, L' (ITL) see **HOMBRE DEL PUNO DE ORO, EL** • 1966
UOMO DALLA CROCE, L' • 1943 • Rossellini Roberto • ITL
UOMO DALLA MASCHERA DI FERRO, L' (ITL) see **MASQUE DE FER, LE** • 1962
UOMO DALLA PELLE DURA, UN • 1972 • Prosperi Franco • ITL, MNC • RIPPED OFF (USA) ○ BOXER, THE
UOMO DALL'ARTIGLIO, L' • 1931 • Malasomma Nunzio, Steinhoff Hans • ITL, FRG • PRANKE, DIE (FRG)
UOMO DALLE DUE OMBRE, L' (ITL) see **COLD SWEAT** • 1971
UOMO DEL ROMANZO, L' • 1941 • Bonnard Mario • ITL
UOMO DELLA C.I.A., THE see **GOODBYE & AMEN** • 1978
UOMO DELLA LEGIONE, L' • 1940 • Marcellini Romolo • ITL, SPN • HOMBRE DE LA LEGION, EL (SPN) ○ RAGAZZA DI VENEZIA, LA
UOMO DELLA MANCHA, L' (ITL) see **MAN OF LA MANCHA** • 1972
UOMO DELLA MIA VITA, L' (ITL) see **HOMME DE MA VIE, L'** • 1951
UOMO DELLA SABBIA, L' • 1979 • Questi Giulio • ITL
UOMO DELLA STRADA FA GIUSTIZIA, L' • 1975 • Lenzi Umberto • ITL, FRN • FLIC HORS LA LOI, UN (FRN)
UOMO DELLA VALLE MALEDETTA, L' • 1964 • Zeglio Primo • ITL, SPN • HOMBRE DEL VALLE MALDITO, EL (SPN) ○ MAN OF THE ACCURSED VALLEY
UOMO DI CASABLANCA, L' (ITL) see **HOMME DE MARRAKECH, L'** • 1966
UOMO DI CORLEONE, L' • 1977 • Coletti Duilio • ITL
UOMO DI HONG KONG, L' (ITL) see **TRIBULATIONS D'UN CHINOIS EN CHINE, LES** • 1965
UOMO DI PAGLIA, L' • 1957 • Germi Pietro • ITL • SEDUCER, THE ○ MAN OF STRAW ○ SORDID AFFAIR, A ○ SEDUCER –MAN OF STRAW, THE
UOMO DI RIO, L' (ITL) see **HOMME DE RIO, L'** • 1963
UOMO DI SAINT-MICHEL, L' (ITL) see **DOUCEMENT LES BASSES!** • 1971
UOMO DI TOLEDO, L' see **HOMBRE DE TOLEDO, EL** • 1966
UOMO DIFFICILE, L' • 1978 • Cobelli Giancarlo • MTV • ITL
UOMO E IL DIAVOLO, L' (ITL) see **ROUGE ET LE NOIR, LE** • 1954
UOMO E IL SUO MONDO, L' • 1967 • Bozzetto Bruno • ANM • ITL
UOMO E UNA COLT, UN (ITL) see **HOMBRE Y UN COLT, UN** • 1967
UOMO FACILE, UN • 1959 • Heusch Paolo • ITL • EASY MAN, THE
UOMO IN BASSO A DESTRA NELLA FOTO, L' (ITL) see **DEFENSE DE SAVOIR** • 1973
UOMO IN GINOCCHIO, UN • 1979 • Damiani Damiano • ITL
UOMO IN NERO, L' (ITL) see **JUDEX** • 1963
UOMO, LA BESTIA E LA VIRTU, L' • 1953 • Steno • ITL • MAN, BEAST AND VIRTUE
UOMO, LA DONNA E LA BESTIA, L' • 1977 • Cavallone Alberto • ITL
UOMO, L'ORGOGLIO, LA VENDETTA, L' • 1967 • Bazzoni Luigi • ITL, FRG • MAN, PRIDE AND VENGEANCE ○ MIT DJANGO KAM DER TOD (FRG) ○ MAN, PRIDE, REVENGE
UOMO MASCHERATO CONTRO I PIRATA, L' • 1965 • De Angelis Vertunio • ITL
UOMO NELL'OMBRA, L' • 1920 • Maggi Luigi • ITL
UOMO PIANGE SOLO PER AMORE, UN see **DONNE.. BOTTE E BERSAGLIERI** • 1968
UOMO PIU ALLEGRO DI VIENNA, L' • 1925 • Palermi Amleto • ITL
UOMO PIU VELENOSO DEL COBRA, L' • 1971 • Albertini Bitto • ITL, SPN
UOMO PUMA, L' • 1980 • De Martino Alberto • ITL • PUMAMAN, THE ○ PUMA MAN, THE
UOMO RITORNA, UN • 1946 • Neufeld Max • ITL
UOMO SENZA MEMORIA, L' • 1974 • Tessari Duccio • ITL
UOMO SOTTO L'OMBRELLONE, L' • 1981 • Di Carlo Carlo • ITL
UOMO, UN CAVALLO, UNA PISTOLA, UN • 1968 • Vanzi Luigi • ITL, USA, FRG • STRANGER RETURNS, THE (USA) ○ MAN, A HORSE, A PISTOL, A ○ SHOOT FIRST, LAUGH LAST
UOMO UNA CITTA, UN • 1974 • Guerrieri Romolo • ITL
UOMO, UOMO, UOMO • 1977 • Fabbri Lionetto • ITL
UOMO VENUTO DA CHICAGO, L' (ITL) see **CONDE, UN** • 1970
UOMO VENUTO DAL MARE, L' • 1942 • Randone Belisario L., de Ribon Roberto • ITL • GIORNO DI FESTA
UOMO VENUTO DALLA PIOGGIA, L' (ITL) see **PASSAGER DE LA PLUIE, LE** • 1969
UOMO VENUTO PER UCCIDERE, L' (ITL) see **HOMBRE VINO A MATAR, UN** • 1968
UP • 1970 • Lacey Gillian • UKN
UP • 1971 • *Halas John (P)* • ANS • UKN
UP • 1976 • Meyer Russ • USA • RUSS MEYER'S "UP"
UP see **KARMA** • 1988
UP A TREE • 1910 • Powell Frank, Griffith D. W.? • USA
UP A TREE • 1912 • *Majestic* • USA
UP A TREE • 1918 • *Parsons William* • SHT • USA
UP A TREE • 1930 • Arbuckle Roscoe • USA
UP A TREE • 1955 • Hannah Jack • ANS • USA
UP A TREE see **SUR UN ARBRE PECHE** • 1970
UP AGAIN see **UPPAT IGEN** • 1941
UP AGAINST IT • 1912 • *Baggot King* • USA
UP AGAINST IT • 1915 • McKim Edwin • USA
UP AGAINST THE ODDS • 1979 • Doheny Lawrence • TVM • USA • DUKE, THE
UP AGAINST THE SYSTEM • 1969 • Macartney-Filgate Terence • DOC • CND
UP AND AT 'EM • 1922 • Seiter William A. • USA
UP AND AT 'EM • 1924 • Roach Hal • SHT • USA
UP AND COMING see **SPOSINA, LA** • 1976
UP AND DOWN • 1914 • *Mace Fred* • USA
UP AND DOWN • 1917 • Smith David • SHT • USA
UP AND DOWN STAIRS • 1930 • Edwards Harry J. • SHT • USA
UP AND DOWN THE LADDER • 1913 • Trimble Larry • USA
UP AND GOING • 1922 • Reynolds Lynn • USA
UP AND OVER DOWN UNDER • 1966 • Schepisi Fred • DOC • ASL
UP AND RUNNING • 1984 • Beecroft Stuart • MTV • CND
UP, DOWN AND BACK • 1966 • Channell David • UKN
UP FOR MURDER • 1931 • Bell Monta • USA
UP FOR THE CUP • 1931 • Raymond Jack • UKN
UP FOR THE CUP • 1950 • Raymond Jack • UKN
UP FOR THE DERBY • 1933 • Rogers Maclean • UKN
UP FROM THE BEACH • 1965 • Parrish Robert • USA • DAY AFTER, THE
UP FROM THE DEPTHS • 1915 • *Foote Courtenay* • USA
UP FROM THE DEPTHS • 1979 • Griffith Charles B. • USA
UP FRONT • 1951 • Hall Alexander • USA
UP GOES MAISIE • 1945 • Beaumont Harry • USA • UP SHE GOES (UKN)
UP HE GOES • 1967 • Hovmand Annelise • DNM
UP IN A BALLOON • 1913 • Young James • USA
UP IN ALF'S PLACE • 1919 • Jones F. Richard • SHT • USA
UP IN ARMS • 1927 • Taurog Norman • SHT • USA
UP IN ARMS • 1944 • Nugent Elliott • USA
UP IN BETTY'S BEDROOM • 1920 • Morris Reggie • USA
UP IN CENTRAL PARK • 1948 • Seiter William A. • USA
UP IN DAISY'S PENTHOUSE • 1953 • White Jules • SHT • USA
UP IN MABEL'S ROOM • 1926 • Hopper E. Mason • USA
UP IN MABEL'S ROOM • 1944 • Dwan Allan • USA
UP IN MARY'S ATTICK • 1920 • Watson William • USA
UP IN SMOKE • 1958 • Beaudine William • USA
UP IN SMOKE • 1978 • Adler Lou • USA • CHEECH AND CHONG'S UP IN SMOKE
UP IN THE AIR • 1915 • Louis Will • USA
UP IN THE AIR • 1918 • *Rhodes Billie* • USA
UP IN THE AIR • 1940 • Bretherton Howard • USA
UP IN THE AIR • 1969 • Darnley-Smith Jan • UKN
UP IN THE AIR ABOUT MARY • 1922 • *Lorraine Louise* • USA
UP IN THE AIR OVER SADIE • 1914 • *Mace Fred* • USA
UP IN THE CELLAR • 1970 • Flicker Theodore J. • USA • THREE IN THE CELLAR (UKN) ○ 3 IN THE CELLAR ○ THREE IN A CELLAR
UP IN THE CHERRY TREE • 1984 • Evstatieva Marianna • BUL
UP IN THE CLOUDS see **AKASH KUSUM** • 1965
UP IN THE SKY • *D'Amico Victor (P)* • USA
UP IN THE WORLD • 1956 • Carstairs John Paddy • UKN
UP IS DOWN • 1969 • Goldscholl Mildred • ANS • USA
UP JUMPED A SWAGMAN • 1965 • Miles Christopher • UKN
UP JUMPED THE DEVIL • 1940 • Beaudine William • USA
UP JUMPED THE DEVIL • 1941 • *Moreland Mantan* • USA
UP 'N' COMING • 1982 • Daniels Godfrey • USA
UP ON DADDY'S HAT see **OP PA FARS HAT** • 1985
UP ON THE FARM • 1920 • *Claypole Comedies* • USA
UP ON THE FARM • 1924 • Seiler Lewis • SHT • USA
UP OR DOWN • 1917 • Reynolds Lynn • USA
UP PERISCOPE • 1959 • Douglas Gordon • USA
UP POMPEII • 1971 • Kellett Bob • UKN
UP POPPED THE GHOST • 1932 • Stafford Babe • SHT • USA
UP POPS THE DEVIL • 1931 • Sutherland A. Edward • USA
UP POPS THE DUKE • 1931 • Arbuckle Roscoe • USA
UP ROMANCE ROAD • 1918 • King Henry • USA
UP SAN JUAN HILL • 1909 • Boggs Frank • USA
UP SHE GOES • 1918 • *Strand* • USA
UP SHE GOES (UKN) see **UP GOES MAISIE** • 1945
UP THE ACADEMY • 1980 • Downey Robert • USA • MAD MAGAZINE PRESENTS UP THE ACADEMY
UP THE CHASTITY BELT • 1971 • Kellett Bob • UKN
UP THE CONGO • 1929 • O'Brien Alice M. • DOC • USA
UP THE CREEK • 1958 • Guest Val • UKN
UP THE CREEK • 1984 • Butler Robert • USA
UP THE DOWN STAIRCASE • 1967 • Mulligan Robert • USA
UP THE FLUE • 1916 • Miller Rube • SHT • USA
UP THE FLUE • 1917 • *Orth Louise* • SHT • USA • MR. SHOESTRING IN THE HOLE
UP THE FLUE • 1919 • Lyons Eddie, Moran Lee • SHT • USA
UP THE FRONT • 1972 • Kellett Bob • UKN
UP THE JUNCTION • 1965 • Loach Kenneth • MTV • UKN
UP THE JUNCTION • 1967 • Collinson Peter • UKN
UP THE LADDER • 1925 • Sloman Edward • USA
UP THE LADDER WITH TOM BOWLINE • 1909 • *Edison* • USA
UP THE MACGREGORS (USA) see **SETTE DONNE PER I MACGREGOR** • 1967
UP THE MILITARY see **BASIC TRAINING** • 1985
UP THE NAUGHTY STAIRCASE see **INDISCREET STAIRWAY** • 1966
UP THE NAVY • Forsyth Ed • USA
UP THE PENTAGON see **BASIC TRAINING** • 1985
UP THE POLE see **HOW I COOK-ED PEARY'S RECORD** • 1909
UP THE POLL • 1929 • Jeffrey R. E. • UKN
UP THE RIVER • 1896 • *Paul R. W.* • UKN
UP THE RIVER • 1930 • Ford John • USA
UP THE RIVER • 1938 • Werker Alfred L. • USA
UP THE RIVER see **MAN WHO FOUND HIMSELF, THE** • 1925
UP THE RIVER see **CRNE PTICE** • 1967
UP THE ROAD WITH SALLIE see **UP THE ROAD WITH SALLY** • 1918
UP THE ROAD WITH SALLY • 1918 • Taylor William D. • USA • UP THE ROAD WITH SALLIE
UP THE SANDBOX • 1972 • Kershner Irvin • USA
UP THE THAMES TO WESTMINSTER • 1910 • Olcott Sidney • DOC • UKN
UP THE WORLD see **GOODBYE CRUEL WORLD** • 1982
UP THERE ON THOSE MOUNTAINS see **LA-HAUT SUR CES MONTAGNES** • 1946
UP TO A POINT see **HASTA CIERTO PUNTO** • 1984
UP-TO-DATE CLOTHES CLEANING see **CONSEIL DU PIPELET, LE** • 1908
UP-TO-DATE CONJURER, THE • 1900 • *Warwick Trading Co* • UKN
UP-TO-DATE CONJUROR, AN see **ILLUSIONNISTE FIN DE SIECLE, L'** • 1899
UP-TO-DATE COOK, AN • 1914 • *Prescott Vivian* • USA
UP-TO-DATE COURTSHIP, AN • 1914 • France Charles H. • USA
UP-TO-DATE DENTIST, AN see **CHICOT, DENTISTE AMERICAIN** • 1896
UP TO DATE FLYERS see **AVIACIONNAJA NEDELJA NASEKOMYCH** • 1912
UP-TO-DATE LOCHINVAR, AN • 1913 • *Ab* • USA
UP-TO-DATE PICKPOCKETS • 1910 • Rains Fred • UKN
UP-TO-DATE SERVANTS • 1910 • *Essanay* • USA
UP-TO-DATE SPIRITUALISM (USA) see **SPIRITISME ABRACADABRANT** • 1900
UP-TO-DATE STUDIO, AN • 1904 • Stow Percy • UKN
UP-TO-DATE SURGERY (USA) see **INDIGESTION: OU, CHIRURGIE FIN DE SIECLE, UNE** • 1902
UP TO HIS EARS (USA) see **TRIBULATIONS D'UN CHINOIS EN CHINE, LES** • 1965
UP TO HIS NECK • 1954 • Carstairs John Paddy • UKN
UP TO HIS TRICKS • 1904 • Warren John • UKN
UP TO MARS • 1930 • Fleischer Dave • ANS • USA
UP TO THE NECK • 1933 • Raymond Jack • UKN
UP TO THE VISIT • 1989 • Jami Hossein Ghasemi • IRN
UP TRAIN, THE see **SHANG-HSING LIEH-CH'E** • 1982
UP URANUS! • 1971 • Castravelli Claude • CND
UP WITH HAZANA! see **ARRIBA HAZANA!** • 1977
UP WITH HUMOUR see **OP MED HUMORET** • 1943
UP WITH TEPITO! see **QUE VIVA TEPITO!** • 1980
UP WITH THE GREEN LIFT see **OPPAT MED GRONA HISSEN** • 1952
UP WITH THE LARK • 1943 • Brandon Phil • UKN
UP YOUR ALLEY • 1975 • Lieberman Art • USA
UP YOUR ALLEY • 1988 • Logan Bob • USA
UP YOUR ANCHOR see **HAREEMU OHGEN LEMON POPSICLE 6** • 1984
UP YOUR ANCHOR –LEMON POPSICLE VI see **HAREEMU OHGEN LEMON POPSICLE 6** • 1984
UP YOUR LADDER • 1979 • Kaufman Philip • USA
UP YOUR LADDER • 1979 • Ryder Edward, Hayes John • USA • UP YOURS.. A ROCKIN' COMEDY ○ UP YOURS
UP YOUR LEGS FOREVER see **LEGS** • 1970
UP YOUR TEDDY BEAR • 1968 • Mikels Ted V. • USA
UP YOUR TEDDY BEAR • 1970 • Joslyn Don • USA • TOY GRABBERS, THE
UP YOURS see **UP YOUR LADDER** • 1979
UP YOURS.. A ROCKIN' COMEDY see **UP YOUR LADDER** • 1979
UPA UPA DANCE, THE • 1913 • Melies Gaston • DOC • USA
UPAL • 1964 • Kutz Kazimierz • PLN • HEAT, THE
UPHEAVAL see **DORAN** • 1979
UPHEAVAL, THE • 1916 • Horan Charles • USA
UPHILL ALL THE WAY • 1985 • Dobbs Frank Q. • USA
UPHILL CLIMB, THE • 1914 • Campbell Colin • USA
UPHILL PATH, THE • 1918 • Kirkwood James • USA
UPHO SEME see **CRNO SEME** • 1972
UPIOR • 1968 • Lenartowicz Stanislaw • PLN • VAMPIRE
UPIOR W PALACU • 1960 • Hornicka Lidia • ANM • PLN • GHOST CAN'T TAKE IT, THE ○ GHOSTS IN THE CASTLE
UPIR Z FERATU • 1982 • Herz Juraj • CZC • FERAT VAMPIRE
UPKAR • 1967 • Kumar Manoj • IND • GOOD DEED
UPKEEP • 1973 • Hubley John • ANM • USA
UPLAND RIDER, THE • 1928 • Rogell Albert S. • USA
UPLIFT, THE • 1916 • Greene Clay M. • SHT • USA
UPLIFTERS, THE • 1919 • Blache Herbert • USA
UPLIFTING OF MR. BARKER, THE • 1909 • *Edison* • USA
UP'N ATOM • 1947 • Marcus Sid • ANS • USA
UPON THIS ROCK • 1971 • Rasky Harry • DOC • USA
UPONDO NO NKINSELA • 1984 • SAF
UPPAT IGEN • 1941 • Cederlund Gosta • SWD • UP AGAIN
UPPBROTT • 1948 • Sucksdorff Arne • DCS • SWD • OPEN ROAD, THE ○ MOVING ON
UPPDRAG I KOREA • 1951 • Hoglund Gunnar • SWD
UPPDRAGET • 1977 • Arehn Mats • SWD • ASSIGNMENT, THE
UPPEHALLE I MYRLANDET see **FYRA GANGER FYRA** • 1965
UPPER CRUST, THE • 1917 • Sturgeon Rollin S. • USA
UPPER-CRUST, THE see **TUCHTIGEN GEHORT DIE WELT, DEN** • 1981
UPPER HAND, THE • 1914 • Humphrey William • USA
UPPER HAND, THE • 1921 • Paul Fred, Raymond Jack • UKN
UPPER HAND, THE (USA) see **DU RIFIFI A PANAMA** • 1966
UPPER THREE AND LOWER FOUR • 1920 • Santell Alfred • USA
UPPER UNDERWORLD see **RULING VOICE, THE** • 1931
UPPER WORLD • 1934 • Del Ruth Roy • USA
UPPERCUT, THE • 1922 • Roach Hal • SHT • USA
UPPERCUT O'BRIEN • 1929 • Rodney Earle • SHT • USA
UPPERSEVEN L'UOMO DA UCCIDERE • 1966 • De Martino Alberto • ITL, FRG • MANN MIT DEN 1000 MASKEN, DER
UPPSAGD • 1934 • Johansson Ivar • SWD • UNDER NOTICE TO LEAVE
UPRAISING OF ANN, THE • 1913 • Kirkland Hardee • USA
UPRIGHT AND WRONG • 1946 • Dunning George • ANS • CND
UPRIGHT SINNER, THE (USA) see **BRAVE SUNDER, DER** • 1931
UPRISING • 1918 • Rasumny Alexander (c/d) • USS
UPRISING, THE • 1912 • *Ryan Mary E.* • USA
UPRISING, THE • 1917 • *Big U* • SHT • USA
UPRISING, THE see **AUFSTAND, DER** • 1981
UPRISING OF THE UTES, THE • 1910 • *Kalem* • USA
UPROAR IN HEAVEN see **DA NO TIEN GU** • 1961
UPROOTED • 1982 • Frizzell John • CND
UPROOTED, THE see **DISHA** • 1990
UPROOTED FAMILY see **XERRIZOMENI YENIA** • 1967
UPS AND DOWNS • 1911 • *Gardner Helen* • USA
UPS AND DOWNS • 1915 • Stull Walter, Burns Bobby • USA
UPS AND DOWNS DERBY • 1950 • Kneitel Seymour • ANS • USA
UPS AND DOWNS OF A HANDYMAN, THE • 1975 • Sealey John • UKN • CONFESSIONS OF AN ODD-JOB MAN
UPS AND DOWNS OF MURPHY, THE • 1905 • Collins Alf? • UKN
UPS AND DOWNS OF RAFFERTY, THE • 1911 • *Comet* • USA
UPS & DOWNS • 1984 • Almond Paul • CND
UP'S N' DOWN'S • 1930 • Harman Hugh, Ising Rudolf • ANS • USA
UPSIDE DOWN • 1919 • Windom Lawrence C. • USA
UPSIDE DOWN see **HUMAN FLY, THE** • 1896
UPSIDE DOWN see **CLEAN-UP, THE** • 1923

UPSIDE DOWN FEATURE • 1972 • Gidal Peter • UKN
UPSIDE DOWN: OR, THE HUMAN FLIES • 1899 • Booth W. R. • UKN
UPSIDE-DOWN PLANET see **POPLETENA PLANETA** • 1962
UPSTAGE • 1926 • Bell Monta • USA • MASK OF COMEDY, THE
UPSTAIRS • 1919 • Schertzinger Victor • USA
UPSTAIRS.. see **SCHODAMI W GORE..** • 1988
UPSTAIRS AND DOWN • 1919 • Giblyn Charles • USA
UPSTAIRS AND DOWNSTAIRS • 1959 • Thomas Ralph • UKN
UPSTAIRS ROOM, THE • 1970 • Desimone Tom • USA • BEVERLY HILLS CALL BOYS, THE ○ BOYS FROM BEVERLY HILLS, THE
UPSTANDING SITTER, THE • 1947 • McKimson Robert • ANS • USA
UPSTART, THE • 1915 • *Razeto Stella* • USA
UPSTART, THE • 1916 • Carewe Edwin • USA
UPSTART, THE • 1917 • Kerrigan J. M. • IRL
UPSTART, THE see **NADMANTRAPU SIRI** • 1968
UPSTART CROW, THE • 1948 • Williamson Cecil H. • UKN
UPSTATE MURDERS, THE see **SAVAGE WEEKEND** • 1976
UPSTREAM • 1927 • Ford John • USA • FOOTLIGHT GLAMOUR (UKN)
UPSTREAM • 1931 • Elton Arthur • DOC • UKN
UPSTREAM see **GATEWAY OF THE MOON, THE** • 1928
UPSTREAM DOWNSTREAM • 1977 • Auzins Igor • SHT • ASL
UPSWEPT HARE • 1953 • McKimson Robert • ANS • USA
UPTHROWN STONE, THE see **FELDOBOTT KO** • 1969
UPTIGHT • 1968 • Dassin Jules • USA • BETRAYAL
UPTOWN NEW YORK • 1932 • Schertzinger Victor • USA
UPTOWN REVUE • 1937 • Hopwood R. A. • UKN
UPTOWN SATURDAY NIGHT • 1974 • Poitier Sidney • USA
UPTURNED FACE, THE • 1962 • Brennan Richard • SHT • ASL
UPTURNED GLASS, THE • 1947 • Huntington Lawrence • UKN
UPWARD WAY, THE • 1913 • Miller Ashley • USA
UPWORLD • 1989 • Winston Stan • USA
URAGANO AI TROPICI • 1939 • Talamo Gino, Faraldo Pier L. • ITL
URAGANO SUL PO • 1956 • Haechler Horst • ITL, FRG
URAGIRI NO ANKOKUGAI • 1968 • Furuhata Yasuo • JPN • UNDERGROUND CHEATING, THE
URAGIRI NO IROGOTO • 1968 • Nishihara Giichi • JPN • BETRAYAL OF AFFAIRS
URAN KHATOLA • 1955 • Sunny • IND
URANIUM ADVENTURES see **AVVENTURIERI DELL'URANIO, GLI** • 1959
URANIUM BLUES • 1956 • Rasinski Connie • ANS • USA
URANIUM BOOM • 1956 • Castle William • USA
URANIUM CONSPIRACY, THE see **A CHI TOCCA...TOCCA!** • 1978
URANIUM-VERSCHWORUNG, DIE see **A CHI TOCCA...TOCCA!** • 1978
URASHIMA TARO NO KOEI • 1946 • Naruse Mikio • JPN • DESCENDANTS OF TARO URASHIMA, THE
URBA 2000 • 1973-74 • Regnier Michel • SER • CND
URBAN AFFAIR, AN see **ESKIMAE DANCHI** • 1961
URBAN COWBOY • 1979 • Bridges James • USA
URBAN NIGHTMARE, AN see **UNDERGROUND TERROR** • 1989
URBAN PATTERNS • 1970 • Nicholson Arch • DOC • ASL
URBAN WARRIORS • 1989 • Vari Giuseppe • ITL
URBANISME AFRICAIN • 1962 • Rouch Jean • DCS • FRN
URBANISME DE LA CONSTRUCTION EN DUR, L' • 1976 • Dansereau Fernand, Rossignol Yolande • DCS • CND
URBANISME, LE PLAN D'AMENAGEMENT • 1958 • Portugais Louis • DCS • CND
URBANISSIMO • 1967 • Hubley John, Hubley Faith • ANS • CND
URBANOSE • 1972 • Regnier Michel • DSS • CND
URBIEST, DAS • 1924 • *Hirschfeld Richard* • FRG
URCHIN, THE • 1915 • Ince John • USA
URCHINS, THE see **GOLFOS, LOS** • 1959
URCHINS IN NO.57 see **GRABBARNA I 57:AN** • 1935
URFA - ISTANBUL • 1968 • Ergun Nuri • TRK
URGE TO KILL • 1960 • Sewell Vernon • UKN
URGENCES • 1987 • Depardon Raymond • DOC • FRN
URGENT CALL (UKN) see **AGAINST THE LAW** • 1934
URGH! A MUSIC WAR • 1982 • Burbridge Derek • DOC • UKN
URHOVI ZELENGORE see **VRHOVI ZELENGORE** • 1976
URI MURI • 1949 • Ban Frigyes • HNG • GENTRY SKYLARKING
URIEL ACOSTA • 1914 • *Great Players Feature Film Corp* • USA
URIEL ACOSTA • 1920 • Wendt Ernst • FRG
URILANY SZOBAT KERES • 1938 • Balogh Bela • HNG • LADY SEEKS ROOM (USA)
URINAL • 1988 • Greyson John • DOC • CND
URLATORI ALLA SBARRO • 1960 • Fulci Lucio • ITL
URLAUB AUF EHRENWORT • 1937 • Ritter Karl • FRG • FURLOUGH ON WORD OF HONOR (USA)
URLAUB AUF EHRENWORT • 1955 • Liebeneiner Wolfgang • FRG
URLAUB AUF SYLT • 1957 • Thorndike Andrew, Thorndike Annelie • DOC • GDR • HOLIDAY ON SYLT
URLAUB OHNE DICH • 1961 • Licke Hans • GDR
URLAUBSGRUSSE AUS DEM UNTERHOSCHEN • 1974 • Boos Walter • FRG
URLAUBSREPORT -WORUBER REISELEITER NICHT SPRECHEN DURFEN • 1971 • Hofbauer Ernst • FRG
URLO, L' • 1947 • Cerio Ferruccio • ITL
URLO, L' • 1965 • Bazzoni Camillo • SHT • ITL • SCREAM, THE (USA)
URLO, L' • 1968 • Brass Tinto • ITL • HOWL, THE (USA)
URLO CONTRO MELODIA NEL CANTAGIRO '63 • 1964 • Gemmiti Arturo • ITL
URLO DALLE TENEBRE, UN • 1975 • Pannaccio Elo • ITL • WHO ARE YOU SATAN? (USA) ○ NAKED EXORCISM (UKN) ○ EXORCIST 3: CRIES AND SHADOWS, THE ○ ESORCISTA N.2, L'
URLO DEI BOLIDI, L' • 1961 • Guerrasi Leo • ITL
URLO DEI GIGANTI, L' see **HORA CERO: OPERACION ROMMEL** • 1968
URLO DEL VAMPIRO, L' • Fec T. • ITL • CRY OF THE VAMPIRE, THE
URODZAJ • 1959 • Gryczelowska Krystyna • DOC • PLN • HARVEST
URODZENI W 44 • 1965 • Karabasz Kazimierz • DCS • PLN • BORN 1944 ○ BORN IN 44
URODZENI W NIEDZIELE • 1967 • Gradowski Bohdan • DOC • PLN • BORN ON SUNDAY
URODZINY MATYLDY • 1974 • Stawinski Jerzy Stefan • PLN
URODZINY MLODEGO WARSZAWIAKA • 1980 • Petelska Ewa, Petelski Czeslaw • PLN • BIRTHDAY OF THE YOUNG INHABITANTS OF WARSAW
UROK ISTORIJI • 1957 • Arnstam Leo, Piskov Hristo • USS, BLG • LESSON IN HISTORY, A ○ IN THE FACE OF THE WORLD ○ UROKAT NA ISTORIATA
UROK PO ZIGULKA • 1969 • Topouzanov Christo, Panov Asparough • ANS • BUL • VIOLIN LESSON, THE
UROK ZHIZNI • 1955 • Raizman Yuli • USS • LESSON IN LIFE, A ○ LESSON OF LIFE
UROKAT NA ISTORIATA see **UROK ISTORIJI** • 1957
UROS BLESAVI • 1989 • Knezevic Milan • YGS • UROS THE FOOL
UROS THE FOOL see **UROS BLESAVI** • 1969
URS AD-DAM see **ORS AL-DAM** • 1977
URS ZAYN • 1976 • Siddik Khalid • KWT • WEDDING OF ZEIN, THE ○ NOCES DE ZAYN, LES
URSA MAJOR • Silinsky Stewart • SHT • USA
URSULA • Williams Lloyd Michael • SHT • USA
URSULA • 1967 • Zimmer H. L. • USA • SINS OF KITTY
URSULA • 1987 • Pyhala Jaakko • FNL
URSULA see **SLUT, THE** • 1965
URSULA see **THREESOME** • 1969
URSULA see **NUNCA ES TARDE** • 1977
URSULA AND GLENYS • 1987 • Smith Robert, Davies John • UKN
URSULA -FLICKAN FRAN FINNSKOGARNA • 1953 • Johansson Ivar • SWD • URSULA -THE GIRL FROM THE FOREST DEPTHS
URSULA ODER DAS UNWERTE LEBEN • 1967 • Mertens Reni, Marti Walter • SWT
URSULA -THE GIRL FROM THE FOREST DEPTHS see **URSULA -FLICKAN FRAN FINNSKOGARNA** • 1953
URSULA THE HUSSY see **SLUT, THE** • 1965
URSULA THE SLUT see **SLUT, THE** • 1965
URSULE ET GRELU • 1973 • Korber Serge • FRN, ITL
URSUS • 1961 • Campogalliani Carlo • ITL, SPN • MIGHTY URSUS (USA)
URSUS see **POEMAT SYMFONICZNY "BAJKA" STANISLAWA MONIUSZKO** • 1952
URSUS AND THE TARTAR GIRL see **URSUS E LA RAGAZZA TARTARA** • 1962
URSUS E LA RAGAZZA TARTARA • 1962 • Del Grosso Remigio • ITL, FRN • TARTAR INVASION (USA) ○ TARTAR GIRL, THE ○ URSUS AND THE TARTAR GIRL
URSUS GLADIATORE RIBELLE • 1963 • Paolella Domenico • ITL • REBEL GLADIATORS, THE (USA) ○ URSUS, IL GLADIATORE RIBELLE
URSUS, IL GLADIATORE RIBELLE see **URSUS GLADIATORE RIBELLE** • 1963
URSUS IL TERRORE DEI KIGHISI • 1964 • Margheriti Antonio • ITL • HERCULES, PRISONER OF EVIL (USA) ○ TERROR OF THE KIRGHIZ
URSUS IN THE LAND OF FIRE see **URSUS NELLA TERRA DI FUOCO** • 1963
URSUS IN THE VALLEY OF THE LIONS see **URSUS NELLA VALLE DEI LEONI** • 1961
URSUS NELLA TERRA DI FUOCO • 1963 • Simonelli Giorgio C. • ITL • SON OF HERCULES IN THE LAND OF FIRE, THE (USA) ○ URSUS IN THE LAND OF FIRE
URSUS NELLA VALLE DEI LEONI • 1961 • Bragaglia Carlo Ludovico • ITL • URSUS IN THE VALLEY OF THE LIONS ○ VALLEY OF THE LIONS (USA) ○ SON OF ATLAS IN THE VALLEY OF LIONS
URSUSIE see **POEMAT SYMFONICZNY "BAJKA" STANISLAWA MONIUSZKO** • 1952
URTAIN, REY DE LA SELVA.. O ASI • 1969 • Summers Manuel • SPN
URUBU • 1948 • Breakston George, Coplen Yorke • DOC • USA • URUBU THE JUNGLE WARRIOR
URUBU THE JUNGLE WARRIOR see **URUBU** • 1948
URUSAI IMOTOTACHI • 1961 • Masumura Yasuzo • JPN • JUST FOR KICKS
URUTORA SEBUN • 1968 • Tsuburaya Hajime • ANS • JPN • ULTRA SEVEN
URUWASHIKI SAIGETSU • 1955 • Kobayashi Masaki • JPN • BEAUTIFUL YEARS, THE ○ BEAUTIFUL DAYS
URUWASHIKI SHUPPATSU • 1939 • Yamamoto Satsuo • JPN • BEAUTIFUL START
URZAD • 1969 • Majewski Janusz • PLN • OFFICE, THE
US • 1968 • Hammid Alexander (c/d) • USA
US see **BENEFIT OF THE DOUBT** • 1967
US see **OSS** • 1976
US AGAINST THE WORLD • 1975 • Asher William • TVM • USA
US KIDS • 1916 • Warrenton Lule • SHT • USA
US KIDS see **NOUS LES GOSSES** • 1941
US MARINE BAND, THE • 1942 • Negulesco Jean • SHT • USA
US MIECH • 1965 • Kijowicz Miroslaw • ANS • PLN • SMILE, THE
US NAVY BAND, THE • 1943 • Negulesco Jean • SHT • USA
US PAAR • 1974 • *Burman S. D. (M)* • IND
US SERVICE BONDS • 1943 • Negulesco Jean • SHT • USA
US TWO see **A NOUS DEUX** • 1979
USA EN VRAC • 1956 • Lelouch Claude • DCS • FRN
USA TODAY see **MADE IN USA** • 1988
USC BAND AND GLEE CLUB • 1941 • Negulesco Jean • SHT • USA
USE THE BACK DOOR • 1970 • *Kirt Films International* • USA
USE YOUR IMAGINATION • 1933 • Mack Roy • SHT • USA
USED CARS • 1980 • Zemeckis Robert • USA
USEFUL SHEEP • 1912 • Sennett Mack • DOC • USA
USELESS DECEPTION, A • 1913 • *Aldridge Wallace* • UKN
USELESS LIFE OF PITO PEREZ, THE see **VIDA INUTIL DE PITO PEREZ, LA** • 1943
USELESS ONE, THE • 1915 • *Macquarrie Murdock* • USA
USER FRIENDLY • 1989 • Nicholas Gregor • NZL
USERS, THE • 1978 • Hardy Joseph • TVM • USA
USFUR, AL- see **ASFOUR, EL** • 1973
USHA • 1935 • Painter Baburao • IND
USHA HARAN • 1949 • Kumar Shanti • IND
USHA KALYANAM • 1936 • Subramanian K. • IND
USHA SUNDARI • 1930 • *Associated Film Co* • IND
USIA 18 • 1980 • Karya Teguh • INN • AGE OF 18, THE ○ AGE 18
USIGIN ANG MAITIM NA BUDHI • 1967 • Cruz Abraham • PHL • PROSECUTE THE BLACKHEARTED
USIJANJE • 1979 • Draskovic Boro • YGS • RED HOT ○ BURNING
USIKO LWABAFANA • 1984 • SAF
USKI ROTI • Kaul Mani • IND
USKUDARA GIDERKEN see **KATIP** • 1968
USNE KAHA THA • 1960 • *Roy Bhimal (P)* • IND
USO • 1963 • Kinugasa Teinosuke, Yoshimura Kozaburo • JPN • WHEN WOMEN LIE ○ LIES
USODNI TELEFON • 1987 • Kozole Damjan • YGS • FATAL TELEPHONE, THE ○ KOBNI TELEFON
USPORENO KRETANJE • 1980 • Kljakovic Vanca • YGS • SLOW MOTION
UST'A H'ASSAN, AL- see **OSTA HASSEN, EL** • 1952
USTADHA FATMA, AL- • 1952 • Wahab Fatin Abdel • EGY • MAITRE FATMA
USTED PUEDE SER UN ASESINO • 1961 • Forque Jose Maria • SPN
USTED TIENE OJOS DE MUJER FATAL • 1945 • Peon Ramon • MXC
USTED TIENE OJOS DE MUJER FATAL • 1962 • Elorrieta Jose Maria • SPN
USTEDES LOS RICOS • 1948 • Rodriguez Ismael • MXC • YOU THE RICH
USTEDES TIENEN LA PALABRA • 1974 • Gomez Manuel Octavio • CUB • BALL IS IN YOUR COURT, THE ○ NOW IT'S UP TO YOU ○ YOU CAN TALK NOW
USUAL UNIDENTIFIED THIEVES, THE see **SOLITI IGNOTI, I** • 1958
USUAL WAY, THE • 1913 • *Beery Wallace* • USA
USUGESHO • 1985 • Gosha Hideo • JPN • FACE POWDER
USURAIO, L' • 1943 • Hasso Harry • ITL
USURER, THE • 1910 • Griffith D. W. • USA
USURER, THE • 1913 • *Blackwell Carlyle* • USA
USURER'S DUE, THE • 1916 • Powell Paul • SHT • USA
USURER'S GRIP, THE • 1912 • Merwin Bannister • USA
USURER'S SON, THE see **UNDER SAVKLINGENS TAENDER** • 1913
USURIER, L' • 1913 • de Morlhon Camille • FRN
USURPER, THE • 1910 • *Lubin* • USA
USURPER, THE • 1919 • Macrae Duncan • UKN
USURPER, THE • 1919 • Young James • USA
USYNLIGE HAER, DEN • 1945 • Jacobsen Johan • DNM • INVISIBLE ARMADA, THE
UT MINE STROMTID • 1920 • Moest Hubert • FRG
UTA • 1969 • *I.r.m.i. Films* • USA
UTA • 1972 • Jissoji Akio • JPN • POEM
UTA ANDON • 1943 • Naruse Mikio • JPN • SONG OF THE LANTERN ○ SONG LANTERN, THE
UTA ANDON • 1960 • Kinugasa Teinosuke • JPN • LANTERN, THE
UTA NO HANAKOGO • 1946 • Nakamura Noboru • JPN • SONG OF A FLOWER BASKET
UTAE WAKODOTACHI • 1963 • Kinoshita Keisuke • JPN • SING YOUNG PEOPLE
UTAGE • 1967 • Gosho Heinosuke • JPN • REBELLION OF JAPAN ○ FEAST
UTAH • 1945 • English John • USA
UTAH BLAINE • 1957 • Sears Fred F. • USA
UTAH KID, THE • 1930 • Thorpe Richard • USA
UTAH KID, THE • 1944 • Keays Vernon • USA
UTAH TRAIL • 1938 • Herman Al • USA
UTAH WAGON TRAIN • 1951 • Ford Philip • USA
UTAK • 1989 • Feher Gyorgy • HNG • WAY
UTAMARO AND HIS FIVE WOMEN (USA) see **UTAMARO O MEGURU GONIN NO ONNA** • 1946
UTAMARO O MEGURU GONIN NO ONNA • 1946 • Mizoguchi Kenji • JPN • UTAMARO AND HIS FIVE WOMEN (USA) ○ FIVE WOMEN AROUND UTAMARO(UKN)
UTAMARO O MEGURU GONIN NO ONNA • 1959 • Kimura Keigo • JPN • UTAMARO PAINTER OF WOMAN
UTAMARO PAINTER OF WOMAN see **UTAMARO O MEGURU GONIN NO ONNA** • 1959
UTAMARO, THE UKIYOE PAINTER see **UTAMARO, YUMETO SHIRISEBA** • 1976
UTAMARO, YUMETO SHIRISEBA • 1976 • Jissoji Akio • JPN • UTAMARO, THE UKIYOE PAINTER
UTAMATSURI SANDOGASA • 1934 • Ito Daisuke • JPN
UTANC • 1973 • Yilmaz Atif • TRK • SHAME
UTAS ABENTEUERLICHE REISE DURCH ALGERIEN see **ALLAH KERIHM** • 1955
UTAZAS A KOPONYAM KORUL • 1970 • Revesz Gyorgy • HNG • JOURNEY INSIDE MY BRAIN ○ JOURNEY ROUND MY SKULL, A
UTAZAS JAKABBAL • 1972 • Gabor Pal • HNG • MY JOURNEYS WITH JACOB ○ JOURNEY WITH JACOB
UTE • 1981 • Sola Raul • URG
UTE BLASER SOMMARVIND • 1955 • Ohberg Ake • SWD, NRW • UTE BLASER SOMMERVIND (NRW) ○ WHERE THE SUMMER WIND BLOWS
UTE BLASER SOMMERVIND (NRW) see **UTE BLASER SOMMARVIND** • 1955
UTEK • 1967 • Skalsky Stepan • CZC • ESCAPE
UTEK ZE STINU • 1958 • Sequens Jiri • CZC • ESCAPE FROM THE SHADOWS
UTEKAJME, UZ IDE • 1988 • Rapos Dusan • CZC • HURRY, HE'S COMING
UTEKY DOMU • 1980 • Jires Jaromil • CZC • ESCAPES HOME
UTICA CLUB BEER COMMERCIALS • 1960 • Bunin Louis • ANM • USA
UTILE DEVOUEMENT, L' • 1914 • Burguet Charles • FRN
UTILITIES see **GETTING EVEN** • 1981
UTKOZBEN • 1980 • Meszaros Marta • HNG, PLN • ON THE MOVE ○ EN COURS DE ROUTE

UTKOZET BEKEBEN • 1951 • Gertler Viktor • HNG • BATTLE IN PEACE
UTLAGINN • 1982 • Gudmundsson Agust • ICL • OUTLAW, THE
UTOLSO BOHEM, AZ • 1912 • Curtiz Michael • HNG • LAST BOHEMIAN, THE
UTOLSO ELOTTI EMBER, AZ • 1963 • Makk Karoly • HNG • LAST BUT ONE, THE
UTOLSO ELOTTI ITELET, AZ • 1980 • Grunwalsky Ferenc • HNG • LAST JUDGEMENT BUT ONE, THE
UTOLSO HAJNAL, AZ • 1917 • Curtiz Michael • HNG • LAST DAWN, THE
UTOLSO KEZIRAT, AZ • 1986 • Makk Karoly • HNG • LAST MANUSCRIPT, THE
UTOLSO KOR, AZ • 1968 • Gertler Viktor • HNG • LAST CIRCLE, THE
UTOLSO VACSORA • 1961 • Varkonyi Zoltan • HNG • MEMORIES OF A STRANGE NIGHT
UTOLYENIYE ZHAZHDY • 1968 • Mansurov Bulat • USS • QUENCHING OF THE THIRST ○ QUENCHING THIRST ○ QUENCHED THIRST
UTOPIA • 1973 • Kolar Boris • YGS
UTOPIA • 1979 • Azimi Iradj • FRN
UTOPIA • 1983 • Saless Sohrab Shahid • FRG
UTOPIA see **CUERTO REPARTIDO Y EL MUNDO AL REVES** • 1975
UTOPIA OF DEATH • 1940 • *Nesbitt John* • SHT • USA
UTOPIA (USA) see **ATOLL K** • 1952
UTOPIE EN MARCHE, L' • 1980 • Saab Jocelyne • DOC • FRN
UTOSZEZON • 1967 • Fabri Zoltan • HNG • LATE SEASON
UTRENNEYE SHOSSE • 1989 • Fedosov Valery • USS • MORNING HIGHWAY, THE
UTRENNIYE KOLOKOLA • 1968 • Mgeladze Guguli • USS • MORNING BELLS
UTRO • 1966 • Henning-Jensen Astrid • DNM • UNFAITHFUL
UTRO INDIA • 1959 • Karmen Roman • USS • INDIAN MORNING ○ DAWN OF INDIA
UTRO NAD RODINATA • 1951 • Marinovich Anton • BUL • DAWN OVER THE HOMELAND
UTRPENI MLADEHO BOHACKA • 1969 • Filip Frantisek • CZC • SUFFERINGS OF YOUNG BOHACEK, THE ○ HARDSHIPS OF YOUNG BOHACEK, THE
UTRPENIM KE SLAVE • 1919 • Branald Richard F. • CZC • LONG ROAD TO GLORY, THE
UTS CERO • 1971 • Aguirre Javier • SHT • SPN
UTSAV • 1983 • Karnad Girish • IND • FESTIVALS
UTSOTSI • 1978 • SAF
UTSTOTTA, DE • 1931 • Stenstrom Matts A. • SWD • HEMLOSA, DE
UTSUKUSHII HITO • 1954 • Wakasughi Mitsuo • JPN • BEAUTIFUL PERSON
UTSUKUSHIKI AISHU • 1958 • Watanabe Kunio • JPN • PRINCESS OF ANGKOR WAT
UTSUKUSHIKI TAKA • 1937 • Yamamoto Kajiro • JPN • BEAUTIFUL HAWK
UTSUKUSHISA TO KANASHIMI TO • 1965 • Shinoda Masahiro • JPN • WITH BEAUTY AND SORROW
UTTOROK • 1949 • Makk Karoly • HNG
UTU • 1983 • Murphy Geoff • NZL • REVENGE
UTVANDRARNA • 1970 • Troell Jan • SWD • EMIGRANTS, THE (UKN)
UUNO TURHAPURO • 1974 • Kokkonen Ere • FNL • DOPEY NUMBSKULL USELESS-BROOK
UUNO TURHAPURO ARMEIJAN LEIVISSA • 1984 • Kokkonen Ere • FNL • NUMBSKULL EMPTYBROOK IN THE ARMY
UUNO TURHAPURO ESPANJASSA • 1985 • Kokkonen Ere • FNL • NUMBSKULL EMPTYBROOK IN SPAIN
UUNO TURHAPURO II see **PROFESSORI UUNO D. G. TURHAPURO** • 1976
UUNO TURHAPURO MENETTAA MUISTINSA • 1982 • Kokkonen Ere • FNL • NUMBSKULL EMPTYBROOK LOSES HIS MEMORY
UUNO TURHAPURO MUUTTAA MAALLE • 1986 • Kokkonen Ere • FNL • NUMBSKULL EMPTYBROOK MOVES BACK TO THE COUNTRYSIDE
UUNO TURHAPURON AVIOKRIISI • 1981 • Kokkonen Ere • FNL • NUMBSKULL EMPTYBROOK'S MARITAL CRISIS
UUNO TURHAPURON MUISTI PALAILEE PATKITTAIN • 1983 • Kokkonen Ere • FNL • NUMBSKULL EMPTYBROOK'S MEMORY SLOWLY COMES BACK
UVAS DE PORTUGAL -VINDIMAS • 1931 • Coelho Jose Adolfo • SHT • PRT
UVEK SPREMNE ZENE • 1987 • Baletic Branko • YGS • EVER-READY WOMEN
UVEY ANA • 1967 • Erakalin Ulku • TRK • STEP-MOTHER, THE
UVODNI SLOVO PRONESE • 1964 • Pojar Bretislav • ANS • CZC • FEW WORDS OF INTRODUCTION, A ○ ORATOR, THE ○ INTRODUCTORY SPEECH IS BY.., THE
UW MENING GRAAG • 1989 • *Blok Anneke* • NTH • YOUR OPINION PLEASE
UWAGA! • 1958 • Janik Stefan • PLN • ATTENTION! ○ WARNING
UWAGA CHULIGANI! • 1955 • Hoffman Jerzy, Skorzewski Edward • DOC • PLN • LOOK OUT, HOOLIGANS! ○ ATTENTION HOOLIGANS
UWAGA MALARSTWO • 1958 • Waskowski Mieczyslaw • DOC • PLN • ATTENTION PAINTING
UWAKI WA KISHA NI NOTTE • 1931 • Naruse Mikio • JPN • FICKLENESS GETS ON THE TRAIN
UWAKIZUMA • 1967 • Shindo Takae • JPN • FLIRTATIOUS WIFE
UWASA NO MUSUME • 1935 • Naruse Mikio • JPN • GIRL IN THE RUMOUR, THE
UWASA NO ONNA • 1954 • Mizoguchi Kenji • JPN • WOMAN IN THE RUMOR, THE (USA) ○ WOMAN OF RUMOUR, A (UKN) ○ CRUCIFIED WOMAN, A ○ WOMAN OF THE RUMOR, THE
UWAYAKU SHITAYAKU GODOYAKU • 1959 • Honda Inoshiro • JPN • SENIORS, JUNIORS, COLLEAGUES
UXOLO • 1985 • SAF
UYARNTHA MANITHAN • 1968 • Krishnan-Panju • IND • HIGH-MINDED
UYIR MEL AASAI • 1967 • Balu T. N. • IND • WILL TO LIVE
UYIRA MANAMA • 1968 • Gopalakrishnan K. S. • IND • LIFE OR REPUTATION?
UZ JE RANO • 1956 • Hofman Eduard • ANS • PLN • IT'S MORNING
UZ ZASE SKACU PRES KALUZE • 1970 • Kachyna Karel • CZC • I'M JUMPING OVER PUDDLES AGAIN (UKN) ○ JUMPING OVER PUDDLES AGAIN ○ JUMPING THE PUDDLES AGAIN
UZAVRELI GRAD • 1961 • Bulajic Velko • YGS • BOOM TOWN (USA) ○ THEN THE FIRES STARTED ○ WHEN THE FIRES STARTED
UZE • 1976 • Grgic Zlatko • ANS • YGS • ROPE, THE
UZEL NA KAPESNIKU • 1958 • Tyrlova Hermina • ANM • CZC • KNOT IN THE HANDKERCHIEF, THE
UZENET • 1967 • Gyarmathy Livia • DOC • HNG • MESSAGE
UZENZILE AKAKHALELWA • 1981 • SAF
UZICKA REPUBLIKA • 1974 • Mitrovic Zika • YGS • SIXTY-SEVEN DAYS ○ 67 DAYS
UZROK SMRTI NE POMINJATI • 1968 • Zivanovic Jovan • YGS • DO NOT MENTION THE CAUSE OF DEATH ○ DON'T MENTION THE CAUSE OF DEATH
UZUN BIR GECE • 1987 • Duru Sureyya • TRK • LONG NIGHT, A
UZUNGU • 1985 • SAF
UZUSHIO • 1930 • Inagaki Hiroshi • JPN

V

V • 1982 • Johnson Kenneth • TVM • USA
V-1 • 1945 • Lee Jack • DOC • UKN
V 1 see **BATTLE OF THE V 1** • 1958
V-2 OPERATION, THE see **OPERACJA V-2** • 1969
V 26-VO NYE STRELYAT • 1967 • Batyrov Ravil • USS • DON'T SHOOT NO. 26
V BLOUZNENI • 1928 • Kokeisl • CZC • IN A FANTASTIC VISION
V BLUDISKU PAMATI • 1985 • Filan Ludovit • CZC • IN THE LABYRINTH OF MEMORY
V BOJ IDUT ODNI 'STARIKI' • 1973 • Bykov Leonid • USS
V BOLSHOI GORODE • 1927 • Donskoi Mark, Averbach Mikhail • USS • IN THE BIG CITY
V.C. • 1914 • Shaw Harold • UKN • VICTORIA CROSS, THE (USA)
V CENTENARIO DE GIL VICENTE • 1966 • de Almeida Manuel Faria • SHT • PRT
V CHETVERG I BOLSHE NIKOGDA • 1977 • Efros Anatoli • USS • THURSDAYS NEVER AGAIN
V CONGRESSO INTERNACIONAL DA VINHA E DO VINHO, O • 1938 • Coelho Jose Adolfo • SHT • PRT
V.D. • 1961 • Chace Haile • USA • DAMAGED GOODS
V DNI BORBI • 1920 • Perestiani Ivan • USS • IN THE DAYS OF THE STRUGGLE ○ IN THE DAYS OF STRUGGLE
V DOME BOGATOI GOSPOZHI • 1970 • Leimanis Leonidis • USS • AT A RICH LADY'S HOUSE
V DYEN PRAZDNIKA • 1980 • Todorovsky Petr • USS • HOLIDAY
V FOR VICTORY • 1941 • McLaren Norman • ANS • CND
V.G.E. see **VALERIE GISCARD D'ESTAING AU MEXIQUE** • 1979
V GORACH ALA-TAU • 1944 • Vertov Dziga, Svilova Elizaveta • USS • ON THE MOUNTAINS OF ALA-TAU ○ IN THE MOUNTAINS OF ALA-TAU ○ ON MOUNT ALA-TAU
V GORAKH YUGOSLAVII • 1946 • Room Abram • USS • IN THE MOUNTAINS OF YUGOSLAVIA
V GORODE "S" • 1966 • Heifitz Josif • USS • IN THE TOWN OF "S"
V HO DINE DVANASTE • 1959 • Lettrich Andrej • CZC • IN THE NICK OF TIME ○ TWELFTH HOUR
V HORACH DUNI • 1946 • Kubasek Vaclav • CZC • THUNDER OVER THE MOUNTAINS ○ THUNDER IN THE HILLS
V.I.P.'S, THE see **VIPS, THE** • 1963
V KITAI • 1941 • Karmen Roman • USS • IN CHINA
V KUROLNOI STRANE • 1940 • Levandovsky V., Elizarov G. • USS • IN THE LAND OF TOYS
V LASUREVOI STEPI • 1971 • Lonski Valeri, Koltsov Vitali, Bondarev Oleg • USS • SKY-BLUE STEPPE, THE
V LINII OGNIA see **NA LINII OGNYA -OPERATORY KINOKHRONIKI** • 1941
V LYUBLENNYE • 1970 • Ishmukhamedov Elyor • USS • IN LOVE ○ LOVERS, THE ○ VLUBLIONYE ○ SWEETHEARTS ○ VLIUBLYONNIE
V LYUDKYAKH • 1939 • Donskoi Mark • USS • MY APPRENTICESHIP ○ AMONG PEOPLE ○ OUT IN THE WORLD
V NATCHALE SLAVNYKH DEL • 1981 • Gerasimov Sergei • USS
V NAVECHERIETO see **NAKANUNYE** • 1959
V NOC NA VOSKRESENIE • 1969 • *Tsentrnauc-Film* • USS
V OGNE BRODA NET see **V OGNYE BRODA NYET** • 1968
V OGNYE BRODA NYET • 1968 • Panfilov Gleb • USS • NO FORD IN THE FIRE ○ NO FORD THROUGH THE FIRE ○ V OGNE BRODA NET ○ THERE IS NO CROSSING UNDER FIRE ○ THERE'S NO FORD IN FIRE
V OZERA • 1969 • Gerasimov Sergei • USS • AT THE LAKE ○ BY THE LAKE
V PESKAKH SREDNEI AZII • 1943 • Zguridi Alexander • USS • LIFE AND SAND
V PIATOK TRINASTEHO • 1953 • Bielik Palo • CZC • FRIDAY THE THIRTEENTH
V POISKACH RADOSTI • 1939 • Roshal Grigori, Stroyeva Vera • USS • IN SEARCH OF HAPPINESS
V POLNOCH NA KLADBISCHE • 1909 • Khanzhonkov Alexander • USS • AT MIDNIGHT IN THE GRAVEYARD (USA) ○ FATAL WAGER, THE ○ MIDNIGHT IN THE GRAVEYARD
V POLNOTCH NA KLABICHTCHE • 1910 • Goncharov Vasili M. • USS
V.R.C. DERBY • 1897 • ASL
V.R.C. WINTER MEETING • 1898 • ASL
V RAIONYE VYSOTY A • 1941 • Vertov Dziga, Svilova Elizaveta • USS • ELEVATION A ○ HEIGHT A
V SHEST CHASOV VECHERA POSLE VOINY • 1944 • Pyriev Ivan • USS • AT 6 P.M. AFTER THE WAR ○ 6 P.M. 1944
V.T.I.K. TRAIN, THE see **AGITPOEZHD VTSIKA** • 1921
V: THE HOT ONE • 1978 • McCallum Robert • USA
V TIHATA VECHER • 1960 • Shariliev Borislav • BUL • ON A QUIET EVENING
V TOM DOMECKU POD EMAUZY • 1933 • Kanturek • CZC • IN THE LITTLE HOUSE UNDER EMAUZY
V TVOIKH RUKAH ZHIZN • 1959 • Rozantsev Nikolai • USS • YOUR LIFE IS IN THEIR HANDS
V TYENI SMYERTI • 1972 • Piyesis Gunar • USS • IN THE SHADOW OF DEATH
V TYLU U BELYCH • 1925 • Tchaikovsky, Rachimanova • USS
V ZACETKU JE BIL GREH see **AM ANFANG WAR ES SUNDE** • 1954
VA BANQUE • 1920 • Lasko Leo • FRG
VA BANQUE • 1930 • Waschneck Erich • FRG
VA BANQUE see **VABANK** • 1981
VA VOIR MAMAN.. PAPA TRAVAILLE • 1978 • Leterrier Francois • FRN • GO SEE MOTHER.. FATHER IS WORKING ○ YOUR TURN, MY TURN (USA)
VAADESKUDDET • 1915 • Davidsen Hjalmar • DNM
VAAKSA VAARAA • 1965 • Makinen Aito • FNL • CLOSE TO DANGER
VAARWEL • 1973 • Pieters Guido • NTH • ROMANTIC AGONY, THE
VAASNA • 1968 • Prakash Rao T. • IND • DESIRE
VABANK • 1981 • Machulski Juliusz • PLN • VA BANQUE
VACACIONES DEL TERROR • 1989 • MXC
VACACIONES EN ACAPULCO • 1960 • Cortes Fernando • MXC
VACACIONES PARA YVETTE • 1964 • Forque Jose Maria • SPN
VACANCES • 1931 • Boudrioz Robert • FRN
VACANCES • 1938 • Storck Henri • DOC • BLG
VACANCES see **RETOUR AU PARADIS** • 1935
VACANCES A ISCHIA (FRN) see **VACANZE A ISCHIA** • 1957
VACANCES AU LIBAN • 1973 • Nasser George • SHT • LBN
VACANCES AU PARADIS • 1959 • L'Hote Jean • SHT • FRN
VACANCES BLANCHES • 1951 • de Gastyne Marco • SHT • FRN
VACANCES CONJUGALES • 1933 • Greville Edmond T. • SHT • FRN
VACANCES DE L'INSPECTEUR TAHAR, LES • 1975 • Haddad Moussa • ALG
VACANCES DE M. HULOT • 1952 • Tati Jacques • FRN • MR. HULOT'S HOLIDAY (USA) ○ MONSIEUR HULOT'S HOLIDAY
VACANCES DE MAX, LES see **MAX PART EN VACANCES** • 1913
VACANCES DU DIABLE, LES • 1930 • Cavalcanti Alberto • FRN
VACANCES EN ENFER • 1960 • Kerchbron Jean • FRN • CAPTIVE, THE
VACANCES EN ENFER see **IGAZA FI GEHANNAM** • 1949
VACANCES EXPLOSIVES • 1956 • Stengel Christian • FRN
VACANCES FINISSENT DEMAIN, LES • 1953 • Noe Yvan • FRN
VACANCES JOYEUSES, LES see **GARGOUSSE** • 1938
VACANCES ORGANISEES • Sanders Bob W. • FRN
VACANCES PAYEES • 1938 • Cammage Maurice • FRN
VACANCES PORTUGAISES, LES • 1963 • Kast Pierre • FRN • SOURIRES DE LA DESTINEE, LES ○ EGAREMENTS, LES
VACANCES ROYALES • 1980 • Auer Gabriel • FRN
VACANCIERS, LES • 1973 • Gerard Michel • FRN
VACANT LOT, THE • 1990 • MacGillivray William D. • CND
VACANTA CEA MARE • 1988 • Blaier Andrei • RMN • BIG HOLIDAY, THE
VACANZA, LA • 1972 • Brass Tinto • ITL • VACATION
VACANZA BESTIALE, UNA • 1980 • Vanzina Carlo • ITL • BEASTLY VACATION, A
VACANZA DEL DIAVOLO, LA • 1931 • Salvatori Jack • ITL
VACANZE A ISCHIA • 1957 • Camerini Mario • ITL, FRN, FRG • VACANCES A ISCHIA (FRN) ○ HOLIDAY ISLAND (USA)
VACANZE A PORTOFINO (ITL) see **UNTER PALMEN AM BLAUEN MEER** • 1957
VACANZE A VILLA EGEA • 1954 • Alviani Massimo • ITL
VACANZE ALLA BAIA D'ARGENTO • 1961 • Ratti Filippo M. • ITL
VACANZE COL GANGSTER • 1952 • Risi Dino • ITL • VACATION WITH A GANGSTER
VACANZE D'AMORE (ITL) see **VILLAGE MAGIQUE, LE** • 1955
VACANZE DEL SIGNOR ROSSI, LE • 1977 • Bozzetto Bruno • ANM • ITL
VACANZE DI NATALE • 1984 • Vanzina Carlo • ITL • CHRISTMAS HOLIDAYS
VACANZE DI SOR CLEMENTE, LE • 1954 • Mastrocinque Camillo • ITL
VACANZE D'INVERNO • 1959 • Mastrocinque Camillo • ITL • WINTER HOLIDAYS
VACANZE IN AMERICA • 1984 • Vanzina Carlo • ITL • AMERICAN HOLIDAYS
VACANZE IN ARGENTINA • 1961 • Leoni Guido • ITL
VACANZE SULLA COSTA SMERALDA • 1968 • Deodato Ruggero • ITL • HOLIDAYS ON THE COSTA SMERALDA
VACANZE SULLA NEVE • 1966 • Ratti Filippo M. • ITL
VACATION • 1919 • Bertram William • USA
VACATION • 1924 • Fleischer Dave • ANS • USA
VACATION • 1984 • Reusch Peter • MTV • CND
VACATION see **CHHUTI** • 1967
VACATION see **VACANZA, LA** • 1972
VACATION see **NATIONAL LAMPOON'S VACATION** • 1983
VACATION DAYS • 1947 • Dreifuss Arthur • USA
VACATION FROM LOVE • 1938 • Fitzmaurice George • USA
VACATION FROM MARRIAGE (USA) see **PERFECT STRANGERS** • 1945
VACATION IN HAVANNA, A • 1910 • *Edison* • USA
VACATION IN HELL, A • 1979 • Greene David • TVM • USA
VACATION IN RENO • 1946 • Goodwins Leslie • USA
VACATION LOVES • 1930 • Sennett Mack • SHT • USA
VACATION ROMANCE, A • 1916 • *Jockey* • USA
VACATION TIME • 1920 • *De Haven Carter* • SHT • USA
VACATION WITH A GANGSTER see **VACANZE COL GANGSTER** • 1952
VACATION WITH PLAY • 1951 • Sparber I. • ANS • USA

VACATION WITH SYLVESTER see **FERIEN MIT SYLVESTER** • 1990
VACCA E IL PRIGIONIERO, LA (ITL) see **VACHE ET LE PRISONNIER, LA** • 1959
VACCINATING THE VILLAGE • 1914 • *Neilan Marshall* • USA
VACHE ET LE PRISONNIER, LA • 1959 • Verneuil Henri • FRN, ITL, FRG • VACCA E IL PRIGIONIERO, LA (ITL) ○ COW AND I, THE (UKN)
VACIO EN EL ALMA • 1968 • Almeida Sebastian • SPN
VACKER DAG, EN • 1963 • Gentele Goran • SWD
VACKRASTE PA JORDEN, DET • 1947 • Henrikson Anders • SWD • MOST BEAUTIFUL THING ON EARTH, THE
VACUUM CLEANER, THE • 1908 • *Pathe* • FRN
VACUUM CLEANER, THE • 1964 • *Halas John (P)* • ANS • UKN
VACUUM CLEANER, THE • 1982 • Stalter Pavao, Fabiani • ANS • YGS
VACUUM CLEANER NIGHTMARE, THE • 1906 • Booth W. R. • UKN
VACUUM DISTILLATION • 1954 • Verschueren Eduard • UKN, NTH
VACUUM TEST, THE • 1915 • Kent Leon D. • USA
VACUUM ZONE see **SHINKU CHITAI** • 1952
VAD KVINNAN VILL • 1927 • Persson Edvard • SWD • WHAT WOMAN WANTS
VAD SKA VI GORA UN DA • 1958 • Weiss Peter • SHT • SWD • WHAT SHALL WE DO NOW?
VAD VETA VAL MANNEN? • 1933 • Adolphson Edvin • SWD • WHAT DO MEN KNOW?
VADER DES VADERLANDS • 1933 • Teunissen G. J. • NTH
VADERTJE LANGBEEN • 1938 • Zelnik Friedrich • NTH
VADERTJE LANGBEEN • 1955 • SAF
VADO A VIVERE DA SOLO • 1983 • Risi Marco • ITL • I'LL GO AND LIVE BY MYSELF
VADO.. L'AMMAZZO E TORNO • 1967 • Castellari Enzo G. • ITL • FOR A FEW BULLETS MORE (UKN) ○ ANY GUN CAN PLAY (USA) ○ I'LL GO.. I'LL KILL HIM AND COME BACK
VADO, VEDO E SPARA • 1968 • Castellari Enzo G. • ITL, SPN • TRE CHE SCONVOLSERO IL WEST ○ THREE WHO UPSET THE WEST ○ I GO, I SEE AND SHOOT
VADON • 1988 • Andras Ferenc • HNG • WILDERNESS, THE ○ IN THE WILD
VADROZA • 1940 • Balogh Bela • HNG • WILD ROSE (USA)
VADVIZORSZAG • 1952 • Homoki-Nagy Istvan • DOC • HNG • KINGDOM ON THE WATERS, A
VAGABOND • 1967 • Cruz Abraham • PHL
VAGABOND see **VAGABUND** • 1990
VAGABOND, THE • 1911 • Porter Edwin S. • *Rex* • USA
VAGABOND, THE • 1912 • *Republic* • USA
VAGABOND, THE • 1914 • Lloyd Frank • USA
VAGABOND, THE • 1916 • Chaplin Charles • SHT • USA
VAGABOND, THE • 1917 • Hiller Frederick W. • SHT • USA
VAGABOND, THE see **AWARA** • 1953
VAGABOND BIEN-AIME, LE • 1936 • Bernhardt Curtis • FRN • VAGABOND PAR AMOUR
VAGABOND BLACKSMITHS see **SMEDER PA LUFFEN** • 1949
VAGABOND CUB, THE • 1929 • King Louis • USA
VAGABOND CUPID, A • 1913 • *Travers Richard* • USA
VAGABOND KING, THE • 1930 • Berger Ludwig • USA
VAGABOND KING, THE • 1956 • Curtiz Michael • USA
VAGABOND LADY • 1935 • Taylor Sam • USA
VAGABOND LOAFERS • 1949 • Bernds Edward • SHT • USA
VAGABOND LOVE • 1915 • MacDonald Norman?, MacGregor Norval? • USA
VAGABOND LOVE see **AMOR VAGABUNDO** • 1989
VAGABOND LOVER, THE • 1929 • Neilan Marshall • USA
VAGABOND LOVERS see **KIKEN RYOKO** • 1959
VAGABOND LUCK • 1919 • Dunlap Scott R. • USA • LITTLE PRAYER FOR RAIN, A
VAGABOND OF SEX see **SEI NO HORO** • 1967
VAGABOND PAR AMOUR see **VAGABOND BIEN-AIME, LE** • 1936
VAGABOND PRINCE, THE • 1916 • Giblyn Charles • USA
VAGABOND QUEEN, THE • 1929 • von Bolvary Geza • UKN
VAGABOND SOLDIER, THE • 1914 • McRae Henry • USA
VAGABOND TRAIL, THE • 1924 • Wellman William A. • USA
VAGABOND (USA) see **SANS TOIT NI LOI** • 1985
VAGABOND VIOLINIST see **BROKEN MELODY, THE** • 1934
VAGABOND VIOLINIST, THE see **BROKEN MELODY, THE** • 1938
VAGABONDA, LA • 1917 • Falena Ugo • ITL
VAGABONDE see **SANS TOIT NI LOI** • 1985
VAGABONDE, LA • 1931 • Bussi Solange • FRN
VAGABONDI DELLE STELLE, I • 1956 • Stresa Nino • ITL
VAGABONDO, IL • 1942 • Biancoli Oreste, Borghesio Carlo • ITL
VAGABONDS, THE • 1912 • *Selig* • USA
VAGABONDS, THE • 1912 • Olcott Sidney • *Kalem* • USA
VAGABONDS, THE • 1915 • *Foster Morris* • USA
VAGABONDS, THE see **SAALIK, EL** • 1985
VAGABONDS DU REVE, LA • 1949 • Tavano Charles-Felix • FRN • COMEDIENS ERRANTS, LES
VAGABOND'S GALOSHES, THE see **KOLINGENS GALOSCHER** • 1912
VAGABONDS MAGNIFIQUES, LES • 1931 • Dini Gennaro • FRN
VAGABOND'S REVENGE, A • 1915 • Waller Wallett • UKN
VAGABOND'S WALTZ, THE see **KULKURIN VALSSI** • 1941
VAGABUND • 1930 • Weiss Fritz • FRG
VAGABUND • 1990 • Huber Leopold • AUS • VAGABOND
VAGABUND, DER • 1923 • Land Dr.? • FRG
VAGABUNDA • 1950 • Morayta Miguel • MXC
VAGABUNDEN DER LIEBE • 1950 • Hansen Rolf • AUS
VAGABUNDO, EL • 1953 • Gonzalez Rogelio A. • MXC
VAGABUNDO Y LA ESTRELLA, EL • 1960 • Cano Mateo, Merino Jose Luis • SPN
VAGABUNDO Y MILLONARIO • 1958 • Morayta Miguel • MXC
VAGARIES OF FATE, THE • 1914 • *Lubin* • USA
VAGEN GENOM SKA • 1957 • Dahlin Hans • SWD • DERAS OGON SER OSS ○ WAY VIA SKA
VAGEN TILL KLOCKRIKE • 1953 • Skoglund Gunnar • SWD • ROAD TO KLOCKRIKE
VAGEN TILL MANNENS HJARTA • 1914 • Breidahl Axel • SWD • WAY TO THE MAN'S HEART, THE
VAGEN UTFOR • 1916 • Klercker Georg • SWD • WAY DOWNHILL, THE
...VAGHE STELLE DELL'ORSA • 1965 • Visconti Luchino • ITL • SANDRA (USA) ○ OF A THOUSAND DELIGHTS
VAGO SIN OFICIO, UN • 1955 • Gomez Urquiza Zacarias • MXC • PERIQUILLO SARNIENTO, EL
VAGON LI • 1977 • Ilic Dragoslav • YGS • SLEEPING CAR, THE
VAGRANT, THE see **TOLONC, A** • 1914
VAGRANTS, THE see **BARI THEKEY PALIYE** • 1959
VAGRANT'S TALE, THE see **TULACKA POHADKA** • 1972
VAGUES, LES • 1901 • Blache Alice • FRN
VAHAN • 1937 • Kale K. Narayan • IND • BEYOND THE HORIZON (USA)
VAHSI BIR ERKEK SEVDIM • 1968 • Mustafa Niazi • TRK • I'VE LOVED A SAVAGE WOMAN
VAHSI OLUM • 1967 • Akbasli Veli • TRK • SAVAGE DEATH
VAI COL LISCIO • 1976 • Nicotra Gian Carlo • ITL
VAI, GORILLA! • 1975 • Valerii Tonino • ITL
VAI TRABALHAR VAGABUNDO! • 1973 • Carvana Hugo • BRZ • GO TO WORK, VAGABOND!
VAIN DREAMS see **PUSTI SNOVI** • 1968
VAIN JUSTICE • 1915 • Travers Richard C. • USA
VAIN NELJA KERTAA • 1968 • Makinen Aito • FNL • FOUR TIMES ONLY
VAINCRE POUR VIVRE see **HAYAT KHIFA, EL** • 1968
VAINILLA, BRONCE Y MORIR • 1955 • Gonzalez Rogelio A. • MXC
VAINQUEUR, LE • 1932 • Hinrich Hans, Martin Paul • FRN • VEINARD, LE
VAINQUEUR DE LA COURSE PEDESTRE • 1909 • Feuillade Louis • FRN
VAISSEAU SUR LA COLLINE, LE • 1960 • Marcilly Rodolphe • SHT • FRN
VAKASHA • 1983 • SAF
VAKMAN PARAAT • 1956 • van der Linden Charles Huguenot • DOC • NTH • SKILLED HANDS READY
VAKVILAGBAN • 1986 • Gyarmathy Livia • HNG • BLIND ENDEAVOUR
VAL D'ENFER, LE • 1913 • Jasset Victorin • FRN
VAL D'ENFER, LE • 1943 • Tourneur Maurice • FRN
VALACHI PAPERS, THE (UKN) see **COSA NOSTRA** • 1972
VALADAO O CRATERA • 1925 • Mauro-Humberto • BRZ • VALADAO THE DISASTER
VALADAO THE DISASTER see **VALADAO O CRATERA** • 1925
VALAHOL EUROPABAN • 1947 • von Radvanyi Geza • HNG, FRG • IRGENDWO IN EUROPA (FRG) ○ SOMEWHERE IN EUROPE ○ IT HAPPENED IN EUROPE ○ KUKSI
VALAHOL MAGYARORSZAGON • 1988 • Kovacs Andras • HNG • REARGUARD
VALAMI SZEP • 1971 • Bacso Peter • HNG • SOMETHING BEAUTIFUL
VALASZTAS ELOTT • 1953 • Jancso Miklos • SHT • HNG • BEFORE ELECTION
VALBORGSMASSOAFTON • 1935 • Edgren Gustaf • SWD • WALPURGIS NIGHT
VALBRYTNING • 1977 • Josephson Erland • MTV • SWD
VALCHITSATA • 1965 • Vulchanov Rangel • BUL • SHE-WOLF, THE ○ VULCHITSATA
VALD • 1955 • Kjellgren Lars-Eric • SWD • VIOLENCE
VALDEMAR • 1975 • Munoz Tomas • SPN
VALDEZ HORSES, THE see **VALDEZ IL MEZZOSANGUE** • 1974
VALDEZ IL MEZZOSANGUE • 1974 • Sturges John, Coletti Duilio • SPN, ITL, FRN • VALDEZ THE HALFBREED (UKN) ○ CHINO (USA) ○ VALDEZ HORSES, THE ○ WILD HORSES, THE
VALDEZ IS COMING • 1971 • Sherin Edwin • USA
VALDEZ THE HALFBREED (UKN) see **VALDEZ IL MEZZOSANGUE** • 1974
VALE DO CANAA, O • 1971 • Valadao Jece • BRZ
VALECNE TAJNOSTI PRAZSKE • 1926 • Kubasek Vaclav • CZC • PRAGUE WAR SECRECY
VALEHTELIJA • 1980 • Kaurismaki Mika • FNL • LIAR, THE
VALENCIA • 1926 • Buchowetzki Dimitri • USA • LOVE SONG, THE
VALENCIA • 1927 • Speyer Jaap • FRG
VALENTE QUINTERO • 1972 • *Cima* • MXC
VALENTIN • 1973 • Mankiewicz Francis • SHT • CND
VALENTIN DE LA SIERRA • 1968 • Cardona Rene • MXC
VALENTIN DE LAS SIERRAS • 1967 • Baillie Bruce • USA
VALENTIN DOBROTIVY • 1942 • Fric Martin • CZC • VALENTIN THE GOOD
VALENTIN KUZYAEV'S PRIVATE LIFE see **LICHNAYA ZHIZN KUZYAEVA VALENTINA** • 1968
VALENTIN LAZANA • 1979 • Guerrero Francisco • MXC
VALENTIN THE GOOD see **VALENTIN DOBROTIVY** • 1942
VALENTINA • 1980 • Panfilov Gleb • USS • VALENTINA, VALENTINA
VALENTINA • 1983 • Betancor Antonio Jose • SPN
VALENTINA, LA • 1938 • de Lucenay Martin • MXC
VALENTINA, LA • 1965 • Gonzalez Rogelio A. • MXC
VALENTINA -THE VIRGIN WIFE see **MOGLIE VERGINE, LA** • 1976
VALENTINA, VALENTINA see **VALENTINA** • 1980
VALENTINE • 1979 • Philips Lee • TVM • USA
VALENTINE see **SEPARATE WAYS** • 1981
VALENTINE, THE see **OLD MAID'S VALENTINE, THE** • 1900
VALENTINE FOR MARIE, A • 1965 • Hawkins John H., Maas Willard • SHT • USA
VALENTINE GIRL, THE • 1917 • Dawley J. Searle • USA
VALENTINE MAGIC ON LOVE ISLAND • 1980 • Bellamy Earl • TVM • USA • MAGIC ON LOVE ISLAND
VALENTINE WEDDING • 1967 • Borlaza Emmanuel, Torres Mar S., Tapawan Chito B., Mia Rosa, Navarro Marcelino D. • PHL
VALENTINE'S DAY • 1914 • *Eclair* • USA
VALENTINO • 1951 • Allen Lewis • USA
VALENTINO • 1958 • Borghesi Anton Giulio • ITL
VALENTINO • 1977 • Russell Ken • UKN
VALENTINO EN ANGLETERRE • 1923 • Florey Robert • SHT • SWT
VALENTINO MYSTIQUE, THE • 1973 • Killiam Paul • USA
VALENTINO RETURNS • 1987 • Hoffman Peter • USA
VALERI CHKALOV • 1941 • Kalatozov Mikhail • USS • WINGS OF VICTORY (USA) ○ RED FLYER, THE (UKN)
VALERIA DENTRO E FUORI • 1972 • Rondi Brunello • ITL
VALERIA RAGAZZA POCO SERIA • 1958 • Malatesta Guido • ITL
VALERIE • 1957 • Oswald Gerd • USA
VALERIE • 1968 • Heroux Denis • CND
VALERIE A TYDEN DIVU • 1970 • Jires Jaromil • CZC • VALERIE AND HER WEEK OF WONDERS (UKN) ○ VALERIE AND A WEEK OF WONDERS ○ VALERIE AND THE WEEK OF MIRACLES
VALERIE AND A WEEK OF WONDERS see **VALERIE A TYDEN DIVU** • 1970
VALERIE AND HER WEEK OF WONDERS (UKN) see **VALERIE A TYDEN DIVU** • 1970
VALERIE AND THE WEEK OF MIRACLES see **VALERIE A TYDEN DIVU** • 1970
VALERIE GISCARD D'ESTAING AU MEXIQUE • 1979 • Reichenbach Francois • DOC • FRN • V.G.E.
VALERIE TOURNE MAL • Ricaud Michel • FRN
VALET AND THE MAID, THE • 1912 • *Crystal* • USA
VALET DE COEUR, LE see **GRELUCHON DELICAT, LE** • 1934
VALET DE COEUR, UN • 1972 • Gagne Jacques • SHT • CND
VALET GIRLS • 1986 • Zielinski Rafal • USA
VALET MAITRE, LE • 1941 • Mesnier Paul • FRN
VALET WHO STOLE THE TOBACCO, THE • 1906 • Fitzhamon Lewin • UKN
VALET'S VINDICATION, THE • 1910 • *Edison* • USA
VALET'S WIFE, THE • 1908 • Griffith D. W. • USA
VALFANGARE • 1939 • Henrikson Anders • SWD • WHALERS
VALHALLA • 1984 • Varab Jeff • DNM
VALHALLA • 1986 • Madsen Peter • ANM • DNM
VALI • 1967 • Rochlin Sheldon • DOC • USA • VALI -THE WITCH OF POSITANO
VALI SUGRIVA: OR, KANCHANAMALA • 1950 • *Ashok* • IND
VALI -THE WITCH OF POSITANO see **VALI** • 1967
VALIANT, THE • 1929 • Howard William K. • USA
VALIANT, THE • 1962 • Baker Roy Ward, Capitani Giorgio • UKN, ITL • AFFONDAMENTO DELLA VALIANT, L' (ITL)
VALIANT HANS see **BRAVE HANS**
VALIANT HOMBRE, THE • 1949 • Fox Wallace • MTV • USA • ROMANTIC VAQUERO
VALIANT IS THE WORD FOR CARRIE • 1936 • Ruggles Wesley • USA
VALIANT ONES, THE see **CHUNG LIEH T'U** • 1975
VALIANT TAILOR, THE • 1934 • *Iwerks Ub (P)* • ANS • USA
VALIANTS OF VIRGINIA, THE • 1916 • Heffron Thomas N. • USA
VALIBA VIRUNDHU • 1967 • Maran • IND • OPPORTUNITIES FOR THE YOUNG
VALIDITA GIORNI DIECI • 1940 • Mastrocinque Camillo • ITL
VALIENTE • 1964 • Marquina Luis • SPN
VALIENTE BROTHERS • 1967 • Buenaventura Augusto • PHL
VALIENTE, EL DESPIADADO, EL TRAIDOR, EL (SPN) see **CORAGGIOSO, LO SPIETATO, IL TRADITORE, IL** • 1967
VALIENTES DE GUERRERO, LOS • 1973 • *Filmicas Agrasanchez* • MXC
VALIENTES DE JALISCO, LOS see **ENEMIGOS** • 1955
VALIENTES NO MUEREN, LOS • 1961 • Martinez Solares Gilberto • MXC
VALIGIA DEI SOGNI, LA • 1954 • Comencini Luigi • ITL
VALISE, LA • 1973 • Lautner Georges • FRN • GIRL IN THE TRUNK, THE ○ MAN IN THE TRUNK, THE
VALISE DE BARNUM, LA • 1904 • Velle Gaston • FRN • BARNUM'S VALISE
VALISE DIPLOMATIQUE, LA • 1909 • Cohl Emile • ANS • FRN • AMBASSADOR'S DESPATCH, THE ○ BOURSE, LA
VALISE ENCHANTEE, LA • 1903 • Blache Alice • FRN
VALITSA TOU PAPA, I • 1979 • Dadiras Dinos • GRC • PRIEST'S SUITCASE, THE
VALKA • 1960 • Bulajic Velko • YGS
VALKENVANIA • 1990 • Ackroyd Dan • USA
VALKOINEN PEURA • 1952 • Blomberg Erik • FNL • WHITE REINDEER, THE
VALKYRIE, THE • 1915 • Nowland Eugene • USA
VALLAURIS see **TERRES ET FLAMMES** • 1951
VALLE DE LAS ESPADAS, EL • 1963 • Seto Javier • SPN, USA • CASTILIAN, THE (USA) ○ VALLEY OF THE SWORDS
VALLE DE LAS VIUDAS, EL see **TAL DER WITWEN, DAS** • 1975
VALLE DE LOS CAIDOS, EL • 1965 • Marton Andrew • SHT • SPN
VALLE DE LOS HOMBRES DE PIEDRA, EL (SPN) see **PERSEO L'INVINCIBILE** • 1962
VALLE DEI LUNGHI COLTELLI, LA (ITL) see **WINNETOU I** • 1963
VALLE DEL DIAVOLO, LA • 1943 • Mattoli Mario • ITL
VALLE DELLE OMBRE ROSSE, LA (ITL) see **LETZTE MOHIKANER, DER** • 1965
VALLE DELL'ECO TONANTE, LA • 1964 • Boccia Tanio • ITL • HERCULES IN THE DESERT (USA) ○ HERCULES OF THE DESERT ○ VALLEY OF THE THUNDERING ECHO, THE
VALLE DELL'ODIO, LA • 1950 • Zancarella Adriano • ITL
VALLEE, LA • 1972 • Schroeder Barbet • FRN • VALLEY (OBSCURED BY CLOUDS), THE ○ VALLEY, THE
VALLEE DES PHARAONS, LA (FRN) see **SEPOLCRO DEI RE, IL** • 1961
VALLEE DU PARADIS, LA see **CRANEUR, LE** • 1955
VALLEE DU PARADIS, LA see **ODYSSEE DU CAPITAINE STEVE, L'** • 1956
VALLEE FANTOME, LA • 1987 • Tanner Alain • SWT
VALLEE-JARDIN, LA • 1974 • Heroux Denis, Bouchard Justine • SHT • CND
VALLEE JAUNE, LA see **WADI AL-ASFAR, AL-** • 1969
VALLEY, THE see **VOLGY, A** • 1968
VALLEY, THE see **VALLEE, LA** • 1972
VALLEY BETWEEN LOVE AND DEATH, THE see **AI TO SHI NO TANIMA** • 1954
VALLEY FEUD, THE • 1915 • Cooley Frank • USA
VALLEY FOLKS • 1910 • *Nestor* • USA
VALLEY GIRL • 1983 • Coolidge Martha • USA
VALLEY GIRLS • 1983 • Polakoff James • USA • VALS, THE
VALLEY IN A RIVER • 1966 • Kelly Ron • CND
VALLEY IS OURS, THE • 1948 • Heyer John • DOC • ASL

VALLEY (OBSCURED BY CLOUDS), THE see **VALLEE, LA** • 1972
VALLEY OF BEAUTIFUL THINGS, THE • 1917 • Warrenton Lule • SHT • USA
VALLEY OF BEES see **UDOLI VCEL** • 1967
VALLEY OF BLOOD • 1973 • Turner Dean • USA
VALLEY OF BRAVERY, THE • 1926 • Nelson Jack • USA
VALLEY OF DEATH, THE (UKN) see **TANK BATTALION** • 1958
VALLEY OF DECISION, THE • 1916 • Berger Rea • USA
VALLEY OF DECISION, THE • 1945 • Garnett Tay • USA
VALLEY OF DOUBT, THE • 1920 • George Burton • USA
VALLEY OF EAGLES see **VALLEY OF THE EAGLES** • 1951
VALLEY OF ESOPUS • 1906 • *Bitzer Billy (Ph)* • USA
VALLEY OF ETERNAL CARAVANS, THE see **UDOLIE VECNYCH KARAVAN** • 1968
VALLEY OF FEAR • 1947 • Hillyer Lambert • USA
VALLEY OF FEAR, THE • 1916 • Butler Alexander • UKN
VALLEY OF FEAR, THE • 1917 • *Heaney John W.* • USA
VALLEY OF FEAR, THE see **SHERLOCK HOLMES: THE VALLEY OF FEAR** • 1983
VALLEY OF FEAR, THE (UKN) see **SHERLOCK HOLMES UND DAS HALSBAND DES TODES** • 1962
VALLEY OF FIRE • 1951 • English John • USA
VALLEY OF FURY (UKN) see **CHIEF CRAZY HORSE** • 1955
VALLEY OF GOLD, THE (UKN) see **GOLD** • 1932
VALLEY OF GWANGI, THE • 1969 • O'Connolly Jim • USA • VALLEY -WHERE TIME STOOD STILL, THE ○ LOST VALLEY, THE ○ GWANGI
VALLEY OF HATE, THE • 1915 • *Mitchell Rhea* • USA
VALLEY OF HATE, THE • 1924 • Allen Russell • USA
VALLEY OF HEALTH AND QUIET, THE • 1949 • Goldberger Kurt • DOC • CZC
VALLEY OF HELL, THE • 1926 • Smith Cliff • USA
VALLEY OF HUMILIATION, THE • 1915 • Davis Ulysses • USA
VALLEY OF HUNTED MEN • 1942 • English John • USA
VALLEY OF HUNTED MEN, THE • 1928 • Thorpe Richard • USA
VALLEY OF IMMORTALS, THE see **BAJI DESHPANDE** • 1927
VALLEY OF LOST HOPE, THE • 1917 • *Vitagraph* • SHT • USA
VALLEY OF LOST SOULS, THE • 1923 • Fleming Caryl S. • USA
VALLEY OF MYSTERY • 1967 • Leytes Joseph • TVM • USA • STRANDED
VALLEY OF PEACE, THE see **DOLINA MIRU** • 1956
VALLEY OF REGENERATION, THE • 1915 • King Burton L. • USA
VALLEY OF REGRETS, THE • 1911 • *Cashman Harry* • USA
VALLEY OF SILENT MEN, THE • 1915 • Easton H. C. • USA
VALLEY OF SILENT MEN, THE • 1922 • Borzage Frank • USA
VALLEY OF SONG • 1953 • Gunn Gilbert • UKN • MEN ARE CHILDREN TWICE (USA) ○ CHOIR PRACTICE
VALLEY OF TEARS • 1924 • Rasumny Alexander • USS
VALLEY OF TERROR • 1937 • Herman Al • USA
VALLEY OF THE BADMEN (UKN) see **LIGHTNIN' SMITH RETURNS** • 1931
VALLEY OF THE BEES, THE see **UDOLI VCEL** • 1967
VALLEY OF THE COMIC FLOWER, THE • Coke Jack • SHT • USA
VALLEY OF THE DOLLS • 1967 • Robson Mark • USA
VALLEY OF THE DOOMED (USA) see **STRADA DEI GIGANTI, LA** • 1960
VALLEY OF THE DRAGONS • 1961 • Bernds Edward • USA • PREHISTORIC VALLEY (UKN)
VALLEY OF THE EAGLES • 1951 • Young Terence • UKN • VALLEY OF EAGLES
VALLEY OF THE FANGS • 1971 • Cheng Chang Ho • HKG
VALLEY OF THE GHOSTS • 1928 • Samuelson G. B. • UKN
VALLEY OF THE GIANTS • 1919 • Cruze James • USA
VALLEY OF THE GIANTS • 1927 • Brabin Charles J. • USA
VALLEY OF THE GIANTS • 1938 • Keighley William • USA
VALLEY OF THE HEADHUNTERS • 1953 • Berke William • USA
VALLEY OF THE HEADLESS HORSEMAN see **CURSE OF THE HEADLESS HORSEMAN** • 1971
VALLEY OF THE KINGS • 1954 • Pirosh Robert • USA
VALLEY OF THE KINGS • 1964 • Goode Frederic • SRL • USA
VALLEY OF THE LAWLESS • 1936 • Bradbury Robert North • USA
VALLEY OF THE LIONS (USA) see **URSUS NELLA VALLE DEI LEONI** • 1961
VALLEY OF THE MOON, THE • 1914 • Bosworth Hobart • USA
VALLEY OF THE REDWOODS • 1960 • Witney William • USA
VALLEY OF THE SEVEN MOONS, THE see **TAL DER SIEBEN MONDE, DAS** • 1967
VALLEY OF THE STONE MEN see **PERSEO L'INVINCIBILE** • 1962
VALLEY OF THE SUN • 1942 • Marshall George • USA
VALLEY OF THE SWORDS see **VALLE DE LAS ESPADAS, EL** • 1963
VALLEY OF THE TENNESSEE • 1944 • Hammid Alexander • DOC • USA
VALLEY OF THE THUNDERING ECHO, THE see **VALLE DELL'ECO TONANTE, LA** • 1964
VALLEY OF THE WIDOWS, THE see **TAL DER WITWEN, DAS** • 1975
VALLEY OF THE WOLF see **HILL BILLY, THE** • 1924
VALLEY OF THE ZOMBIES • 1946 • Ford Philip • USA
VALLEY OF TOMORROW, THE • 1920 • Flynn Emmett J. • USA
VALLEY OF VANISHING MEN, THE • 1924 • Hart Neal • USA
VALLEY OF VANISHING MEN, THE • 1942 • Bennet Spencer Gordon • SRL • USA
VALLEY OF VENGEANCE • 1944 • Newfield Sam • USA • VENGEANCE (UKN)
VALLEY OF WANTED MEN • 1935 • James Alan • USA • WANTED MEN (UKN)
VALLEY RESOUNDS, THE see **RASUNA VALEA** • 1949
VALLEY TOWN • 1940 • Van Dyke Willard • DOC • USA
VALLEY TRAIN, THE see **RAKEVET HA 'EMEK** • 1989
VALLEY -WHERE TIME STOOD STILL, THE see **VALLEY OF GWANGI, THE** • 1969
VALLFARTEN TILL KEVLAAR • 1921 • Hedqvist Ivan • SWD • PILGRIMAGE TO KEVLAAR (USA)
VALMIKI • 1946 • Pendharkar Bhal G. • IND
VALMIKI • 1963 • Rao C. S. • IND
VALMONT • 1989 • Forman Milos • FRN, USA
VALOR DE UN COBARDE • 1968 • Klimovsky Leon • SPN
VALOR DE VIVIR, EL • 1953 • Davison Tito • MXC
VALOR OF WAR, THE see **HORNET'S NEST** • 1970
VALORIZACAO DE TERRA • 1949 • Coelho Jose Adolfo • SHT • PRT
VALOR'S REWARD • 1915 • *Larkin George* • USA
VALPARAISO, MI AMOR • 1970 • Francia Aldo • CHL • VALPARAISO, MY LOVE
VALPARAISO, MY LOVE see **VALPARAISO, MI AMOR** • 1970
VALPARAISO.. VALPARAISO! • 1971 • Aubier Pascal • FRN
VALS, THE see **VALLEY GIRLS** • 1983
VALS SIN FIN, EL • 1971 • Broido Ruben • MXC
VALSE A TROIS • 1974 • Rivard Fernand • CND
VALSE AU PLAFOND, LA • 1905 • Velle Gaston • FRN
VALSE BLANCHE, LA • 1943 • Stelli Jean • FRN
VALSE BLEUE, LA • 1918 • D'Ambra Lucio • ITL
VALSE BRILLANTE, LA • 1949 • Boyer Jean • FRN
VALSE BRILLANTE DE CHOPIN, LA • 1936 • Ophuls Max • SHT • FRN
VALSE DE BARNABE, LA • 1906 • Velle Gaston • FRN
VALSE DE L'ADIEU, LA • 1929 • Roussell Henry • FRN
VALSE DE L'ADIEU, LA see **CHANSON DE L'ADIEU, LA** • 1934
VALSE DE PARIS, LA • 1949 • Achard Marcel • FRN • PARIS WALTZ, THE (USA)
VALSE DU GORILLE, LA • 1959 • Borderie Bernard • FRN • WALTZ OF THE GORILLA, THE
VALSE ETERNELLE • 1936 • Neufeld Max • FRN
VALSE MIRACULEUSE, LA see **CIBOULETTE** • 1933
VALSE NOOT, DE • Servais Raoul • SHT • BLG • FALSE NOTE, THE
VALSE OF THE PURPLE BUTTERFLIES • 1948 • Petroff Paul • USA
VALSE ROYALE • 1935 • Gremillon Jean • FRN • POUR UN BAISER
VALSE TRISTE • 1977 • Conner Bruce • SHT • USA
VALSE VENIAN DE VIENA Y LOS NINOS DE PARIS, LOS • 1965 • Bustillo Oro Juan • MXC
VALSEUSES, LES • 1974 • Blier Bertrand • FRN • MAKING IT (UKN) ○ GOING PLACES (USA)
VALTER BRANI SARAJEVO • 1972 • Krvavac Hajrudin • YGS • WALTER DEFENDS SARAJEVO
VALTOZO FELHOZET • 1967 • Keleti Marton • HNG • CHANGING CLOUDS
VALTOZO IDOK • 1978 • Kovacs Istvan • HNG • CHANGING TIME
VALUE BEYOND PRICE • 1910 • *Thanhouser* • USA
VALUE FOR MONEY • 1955 • Annakin Ken • UKN
VALUE FOR MONEY • 1971 • Blest David, Tattersall Gale • UKN
VALUE OF MAN see **TSENA CHELOVEKA** • 1928
VALUE OF MOTHER-IN-LAWS, THE • 1913 • *Mason Riley* • USA
VALUE RECEIVED • 1912 • *Melies* • USA
VALUE RECEIVED • 1914 • *Sisson Vera* • USA
VALURILE DUNARI • 1959 • Ionescu Grigore • RMN • RIVER AFLAME
VALURILE DUNARII • 1963 • Ciulei Liviu • RMN • DANUBE WAVES, THE
VALZER DELLA FELICITA, IL see **CANZONE RUBATA, LA** • 1941
VAM CHTO, NASHA VLAST NE NRAVISTYA? • 1989 • Bobrovsky Anatoli • USS • YOU DON'T LIKE THE SYSTEM?
VAMAN AVATAR • 1930 • IND
VAMAN AVATAR • 1934 • Wadia J. B. H. • IND • DANI SAMRAT
VAMHATAR • 1977 • Gaal Istvan • MTV • HNG • CUSTOMS FRONTIER
VAMMENTES HAZASSAG • 1981 • Zsombolyai Janos • HNG, FNL • TULLIVAPAA AVIOLIITO (FNL) ○ DUTY-FREE MARRIAGE
VAMONOS, BARBARA • 1977 • Bartolome Cecilia • SPN • LET'S GO, BARBARA
VAMONOS CON PANCHO VILLA • 1935 • de Fuentes Fernando • MXC • LET'S GO WITH PANCHO VILLA (USA)
VAMONOS PARA LA FERIA • 1960 • Pereda Ramon • MXC
VAMOOSE see **WEST OF CHICAGO** • 1922
VAMOS A CONTAR MENTIRAS • 1962 • Isasi Antonio • SPN
VAMOS A MATAR COMPANEROS! • 1970 • Corbucci Sergio • ITL, SPN, FRG • COMPANEROS! (USA) ○ COMPANEROS ○ LASST UNS TOTEN, COMPANEROS
VAMOS A MATAR SARTANA • 1971 • Pinzauti Mario • ITL
VAMOS A POR LA PAREJITA • 1969 • Paso Alfonso • SPN
VAMOS AL CINE • 1970 • Swarthe Robert • ANS • USA • LET'S GO TO THE MOVIES
VAMP • 1986 • Wenk Richard • USA
VAMP, THE • 1918 • Storm Jerome • USA
VAMP CURE, THE • 1918 • Lyons Eddie, Moran Lee • SHT • USA
VAMP OF THE CAMP, THE • 1917 • Curtis Allen • SHT • USA
VAMP OF VENICE see **VENUS OF VENICE** • 1927
VAMP TILL READY • 1936 • Parrott Charles, Law Harold • SHT • USA
VAMPATA DI VIOLENZA, UNA (ITL) see **GRANDES GUEULES, LES** • 1965
VAMPING • 1984 • Keller Frederick King • USA
VAMPING REUBEN'S MILLIONS • 1917 • Smith Dick • SHT • USA
VAMPING THE VAMP • 1918 • Santell Alfred • SHT • USA
VAMPING VENUS • 1928 • Cline Eddie • USA • IT'S ALL GREEK TO ME
VAMPING VENUS see **PROPERTY MAN, THE** • 1914
VAMPIR-CUADECUC • 1970 • Portabella Pedro • SPN • VAMPYR ○ VAMPIRE
VAMPIR VON SCHLOSS FRANKENSTEIN, DER see **VAMPIRO DE LA AUTOPISTA, EL** • 1970
VAMPIRA • 1974 • Donner Clive • UKN • OLD DRACULA (USA) ○ VAMPIRELLA ○ VAMPIRE ○ OLD DRAC
VAMPIRA INDIANA, LA • 1913 • Roberti Roberto Leone • ITL
VAMPIRAS, LAS • 1968 • Curiel Federico • MXC • VAMPIRE GIRLS, THE ○ VAMPIRES, THE
VAMPIRAS, LAS see **VAMPYROS LESBOS -DIE ERBIN DES DRACULA** • 1971
VAMPIRE • 1920 • Blache Alice • USA
VAMPIRE • 1968 • Tezuka Osamu • ANM • JPN
VAMPIRE • 1979 • Swackhamer E. W. • TVM • USA
VAMPIRE see **VAMPYR** • 1931
VAMPIRE see **UPIOR** • 1968
VAMPIRE see **VAMPIR-CUADECUC** • 1970
VAMPIRE see **VAMPIRA** • 1974
VAMPIRE, LE • 1945 • Painleve Jean • SHT • FRN • VAMPIRE, THE
VAMPIRE, THE • 1910 • *Selig* • USA
VAMPIRE, THE • 1913 • *Searchlight Films* • UKN
VAMPIRE, THE • 1913 • Olcott Sidney, Hunter T. Hayes • USA
VAMPIRE, THE • 1914 • *Eclair* • FRN
VAMPIRE, THE • 1915 • Blache Alice • USA
VAMPIRE, THE see **VAMPIRO, IL**
VAMPIRE, THE see **VAMPYREN** • 1913
VAMPIRE, THE see **VAMPIRE, LE** • 1945
VAMPIRE, THE see **MARK OF THE VAMPIRE** • 1957
VAMPIRE, THE see **PONTIANAK** • 1957
VAMPIRE, THE see **KUNTILANAK** • 1974
VAMPIRE, THE (USA) see **VAMPIRO, EL** • 1957
VAMPIRE A LA MODE • 1928 • *Fox* • USA
VAMPIRE AMBROSE • 1916 • Fishback Fred C. • SHT • USA
VAMPIRE AND SEX, THE see **VAMPIRO Y EL SEXO, EL** • 1968
VAMPIRE AND THE BALLERINA, THE (USA) see **AMANTE DEL VAMPIRO, L'** • 1960
VAMPIRE AT MIDNIGHT • 1988 • McClatchy Gregory • USA
VAMPIRE BAT, THE • 1933 • Strayer Frank • USA
VAMPIRE-BEAST CRAVES BLOOD, THE (USA) see **BLOOD BEAST TERROR, THE** • 1968
VAMPIRE CIRCUS • 1972 • Young Robert • UKN
VAMPIRE CULT, THE see **CULTE DU VAMPIRE, LE** • 1971
VAMPIRE DANCER, THE see **VAMPYRDANSERINDEN** • 1911
VAMPIRE DE DUSSELDORF, LE • 1965 • Hossein Robert • FRN, SPN
VAMPIRE DE LA CINEMATHEQUE, LE • 1971 • Lethem Roland • SHT • BLG
VAMPIRE DOLL, THE (USA) see **CHI O SUU NINGYO** • 1970
VAMPIRE FOR TWO, A see **VAMPIRO PARA DOS, UN** • 1965
VAMPIRE GIRLS, THE see **VAMPIRAS, LAS** • 1968
VAMPIRE HAPPENING, THE see **GEBISSEN WIRD NUR NACHTS -HAPPENING DER VAMPIRE** • 1971
VAMPIRE HOOKERS • 1978 • Santiago Cirio H. • PHL, USA • SENSUOUS VAMPIRES ○ TWICE BITTEN
VAMPIRE IN THE CAVE, THE see **PONTIANAK GUA MUSANG** • 1964
VAMPIRE IN VENICE see **NOSFERATU A VENEZIA** • 1988
VAMPIRE KNIGHTS • 1987 • Peterson Daniel M. • USA
VAMPIRE LOVERS, THE • 1970 • Baker Roy Ward • UKN
VAMPIRE MEN OF THE LOST PLANET see **HORROR OF THE BLOOD MONSTERS** • 1970
VAMPIRE NUE, LA • 1969 • Rollin Jean • FRN • NUDE VAMPIRE, THE (UKN) ○ NAKED VAMPIRE, THE
VAMPIRE OF CASTLE FRANKENSTEIN, THE see **VAMPIRO DE LA AUTOPISTA, EL** • 1970
VAMPIRE OF DR. DRACULA see **MARCA DEL HOMBRE LOBO, LA** • 1968
VAMPIRE OF NOTRE DAME, THE see **VAMPIRI, I** • 1956
VAMPIRE OF THE CIVET-CAT CAVE, THE see **PONTIANAK GUA MUSANG** • 1964
VAMPIRE OF THE DESERT, THE • 1913 • *Gardner Helen* • USA
VAMPIRE OF THE OPERA, THE see **VAMPIRO DELL'OPERA, IL** • 1961
VAMPIRE OF THE TURNPIKE, THE see **VAMPIRO DE LA AUTOPISTA, EL** • 1970
VAMPIRE OR THE STRANGE ADVENTURE OF DAVID GRAY see **VAMPYR** • 1931
VAMPIRE OUT OF WORK, A • 1916 • Drew Sidney • SHT • USA
VAMPIRE OVER LONDON see **MOTHER RILEY MEETS THE VAMPIRE** • 1952
VAMPIRE PEOPLE see **BLOOD DRINKERS, THE** • 1966
VAMPIRE PLAYGIRLS see **PLUS LONGUE NUIT DU DIABLE, LA** • 1971
VAMPIRE RETURNS, THE see **PONTIANAK KEMBALI** • 1963
VAMPIRE THRILLS see **FRISSON DES VAMPIRES, LE** • 1970
VAMPIRE WOMAN see **ZAN-E-KHONASHAM** • 1967
VAMPIRE WOMAN (UKN) see **CRYPT OF THE LIVING DEAD** • 1973
VAMPIRE WOMEN, THE see **VAMPYROS LESBOS -DIE ERBIN DES DRACULA** • 1971
VAMPIRELLA see **VAMPIRA** • 1974
VAMPIRES see **VII** • 1967
VAMPIRES, LES • 1915-16 • Feuillade Louis • SER • FRN • VAMPIRES, THE (USA) ○ ARCH CRIMINALS OF PARIS, THE
VAMPIRES, THE see **VAMPIRI, I** • 1956
VAMPIRES, THE see **MACISTE CONTRO IL VAMPIRO** • 1961
VAMPIRES, THE see **VAMPIRAS, LAS** • 1968
VAMPIRES, THE (USA) see **VAMPIRES, LES** • 1915-16
VAMPIRES AMONG US see **VAMPIRI SU MEDU NAMA** • 1990
VAMPIRE'S COFFIN (USA) see **ATAUD DEL VAMPIRO, EL** • 1957
VAMPIRE'S CURSE, THE see **SUMPAH PONTIANAK** • 1958
VAMPIRES D'ALFAMA • 1963 • Kast Pierre • ANS • FRN
VAMPIRES DE VARSOVIE, LES • 1925 • Bieganski Victor • PLN
VAMPIRE'S DREAM, A see **SONHO DE VAMPIROS, UM** • 1970
VAMPIRE'S GHOST, THE • 1945 • Selander Lesley • USA
VAMPIRES IN HAVANA see **VAMPIROS EN LA HABANA** • 1985
VAMPIRE'S KISS • 1988 • Bierman Robert • USA
VAMPIRE'S LAST VICTIM, THE see **ULTIMA PREDA DEL VAMPIRO, L'** • 1960
VAMPIRE'S LOVER, THE see **AMANTE DEL VAMPIRO, L'** • 1960
VAMPIRE'S NIECE, THE see **MALENKA, LA SOBRINA DEL VAMPIRO** • 1968
VAMPIRES' NIGHT ORGY, THE (USA) see **ORGIA NOCTURNA DE LOS VAMPIROS, LA** • 1972
VAMPIRE'S NOSTALGIA, A • 1968 • Skanata Krsto • DOC • YGS
VAMPIRES OF WARSAW see **WAMPIRY WARSZAWY** • 1914

VAMPIRES OF WARSAW (USA) see **WAMPIRY WARSZAWY** • 1925
VAMPIRE'S TRAIL, THE • 1914 • Vignola Robert G. • USA
VAMPIRESAS 1930 • 1962 • Franco Jesus • SPN
VAMPIRI, I • 1956 • Freda Riccardo • ITL • DEVIL'S COMMANDMENT, THE (USA) ○ VAMPIRE OF NOTRE DAME, THE ○ LUST OF THE VAMPIRE ○ VAMPIRES, THE
VAMPIRI SU MEDU NAMA • 1990 • Calic Zoran • YGS • VAMPIRES AMONG US
VAMPIRISME • 1967 • Duvic David, Chaouat Bernard • SHT • FRN
VAMPIRO, EL • 1957 • Mendez Fernando, Nagle Paul • MXC • VAMPIRE, THE (USA)
VAMPIRO, IL • Pianelli Vittorio Ross • ITL • VAMPIRE, THE
VAMPIRO ACECHA, EL • *Robles German* • MXC • LURKING VAMPIRE, THE
VAMPIRO DE LA AUTOPISTA, EL • 1970 • Madrid Jose Luis • SPN • HORRIBLE SEXY VAMPIRE, THE (USA) ○ VAMPIRE OF THE TURNPIKE, THE ○ VAMPIR VON SCHLOSS FRANKENSTEIN, DER ○ VAMPIRE OF CASTLE FRANKENSTEIN, THE
VAMPIRO DELL'OPERA, IL • 1961 • Polselli Renato • ITL • MOSTRO DELL'OPERA, IL ○ VAMPIRE OF THE OPERA, THE
VAMPIRO NEGRO, EL • 1953 • Barreto Roman Vinoly • ARG • BLACK VAMPIRE, THE
VAMPIRO PARA DOS, UN • 1965 • Lazaga Pedro • SPN • VAMPIRE FOR TWO, A
VAMPIRO SANGRIENTO, EL • 1962 • Morayta Miguel • MXC • BLOODY VAMPIRE, THE (USA) ○ CONDE FRANKENHAUSEN, EL ○ COUNT FRANKENHAUSEN
VAMPIRO Y EL SEXO, EL • 1968 • Cardona Rene • MXC • SANTO EN EL TESORO DE DRACULA ○ SANTO AND DRACULA'S TREASURE ○ VAMPIRE AND SEX, THE
VAMPIROS DE COYOACAN, LOS • 1973 • *Filmicas Agrasanchez* • MXC
VAMPIROS EN LA HABANA • 1985 • Padron Juan • ANM • CUB • VAMPIRES IN HAVANA
VAMPS AND VARIETY • 1919 • Pratt Gilbert • SHT • USA
VAMPYR • 1931 • Dreyer Carl T. • FRN, FRG • VAMPYR OU L'ETRANGE AVENTURE DE DAVID GRAY (FRN) ○ TRAUM DES ALLAN GRAY, DER ○ STRANGE ADVENTURE OF DAVID GRAY, THE (UKN) ○ VAMPIRE ○ CASTLE OF DOOM ○ ADVENTURES OF DAVID GRAY ○ FRG ○ VAMPIRE OR THE STRANGE ADVENTURE OF DAVID GRAY
VAMPYR see **VAMPIR-CUADECUC** • 1970
VAMPYR, DER • 1920 • Stranz A. • FRG
VAMPYR OU L'ETRANGE AVENTURE DE DAVID GRAY (FRN) see **VAMPYR** • 1931
VAMPYR VON ST. LOUIS, DER • 1920 • *Fichtner Erwin* • FRG
VAMPYRDANSERINDEN • 1911 • Blom August • DNM • VAMPIRE DANCER, THE
VAMPYRE see **COUNT YORGA, VAMPIRE** • 1970
VAMPYRE ORGY, THE see **VAMPYRES** • 1974
VAMPYREN • 1913 • Stiller Mauritz • SWD • VAMPIRE, THE
VAMPYRES • 1974 • Larraz Jose R. • UKN • VAMPYRES.. MOST UNNATURAL LADIES ○ VAMPYRES, DAUGHTERS OF DRACULA ○ DAUGHTERS OF DRACULA ○ VAMPYRES, DAUGHTERS OF DARKNESS ○ VAMPYRE ORGY, THE
VAMPYRES, DAUGHTERS OF DARKNESS see **VAMPYRES** • 1974
VAMPYRES, DAUGHTERS OF DRACULA see **VAMPYRES** • 1974
VAMPYRES.. MOST UNNATURAL LADIES see **VAMPYRES** • 1974
VAMPYROS LESBOS -DIE ERBIN DES DRACULA • 1971 • Franco Jesus • FRG, SPN • SIGNO DEL VAMPIRO, EL ○ HERITAGE OF DRACULA, THE ○ HEIRESS OF DRACULA, THE ○ VAMPIRAS, LAS ○ LESBIAN VAMPIRES -THE HEIRESS OF DRACULA ○ VAMPIRE WOMEN, THE ○ SPN ○ SIGN OF THE VAMPIRE, THE
VAN, THE • 1976 • Grossman Sam • USA
VAN BIBBER'S EXPERIMENT • 1911 • Dawley J. Searle • USA
VAN DE VELDE -THE PERFECT MARRIAGE (1) see **VAN DER VELDE -DIE KOLLKOMMENE EHE (1)** • 1968
VAN DER MERWE P.I. • 1985 • SAF
VAN DER VELDE: DAS LEBEN ZU ZWEIT, DIE SEXUALITAT IN DER EHE • 1972 • Gottlieb Franz J. • FRG • EVERY NIGHT OF THE WEEK (UKN)
VAN DER VELDE -DIE KOLLKOMMENE EHE (1) • 1968 • Gottlieb Franz J. • FRG • VAN DE VELDE -THE PERFECT MARRIAGE (1)
VAN ENSOR TOT PERMEKE • 1971 • Deses Greta • BLG
VAN EYCK • 1938 • Cauvin Andre • BLG
VAN GELUK GESPROKEN • 1987 • Verhoeff Pierre • NTH • COUNT YOUR BLESSINGS
VAN GOGH • 1948 • Resnais Alain • SHT • FRN
VAN MORRISON IN IRELAND • 1980 • Radford Michael • DOC • UKN
VAN NOSTRAND TIARA, THE • 1913 • *Ab* • USA
VAN NUYS BLVD. • 1979 • Sachs William • USA
VAN OSTEN JEWELS, THE • 1911 • *Yankee* • USA
VAN PAEMEL FAMILY, THE • 1987 • Cammermans Paul • BLG
VAN THORNTON DIAMONDS, THE • 1915 • Grandon Francis J. • USA
VAN UUR O TOT 24 • 1968 • Korver Pim • SHT • NTH
VAN WARDEN RUBIES, THE • 1913 • *Garwood William* • USA
VANAERDE, DEN • 1914 • Davidsen Hjalmar • DNM
VANASARA • 1968 • Ramachandran L. S., Somaratne S. A. • SLN • JUNGLE BOY
VANCOUVER: A PORTRAIT BY ARTHUR ERICKSON • 1984 • Nicolle Douglas • MTV • CND
VANCOUVER VIGNETTE • 1936 • Sparling Gordon • DCS • CND
VANCOUVER'S CHINATOWN • 1953-54 • Devlin Bernard • DCS • CND
VANDA TERES • 1975 • Vincent Jean-Marie • FRN, SWT
VANDAAG OF MORGEN • 1976 • Kerbosch Roeland • NTH • TODAY OR TOMORROW
VANDALISM • 1977 • Roos Ole • DNM
VANDARHOGG • 1980 • Gunnlaugsson Hrafn • MTV • ICL • WHIPLASH, THE ○ WHIPPING
VANDERBEEKIANA • 1968 • Vanderbeek Stan • USA
VANDERBERG • 1983 • Fruet William, Rowe Peter • SER • CND
VANDERBILT CUP AUTO RACE • 1904 • *Bitzer Billy (Ph)* • USA
VANDERGILT DIAMOND MYSTERY, THE • 1936 • Faye Randall • UKN
VANDERHOFF AFFAIR, THE • 1915 • Vignola Robert G. • USA
VANDET PA LANDET • 1945 • Dreyer Carl T. • DCS • DNM • WATER FROM THE LAND
VANDKORSET • 1944 • Falk Lauritz • SWD • TURNSTILE
VANDRABEN • 1969 • Barfod Bent • ANS • DNM • DROP OF WATER, A (USA)
VANDRING I SOLEN, EN • 1978 • Dahlberg Hans • SWD, GRC • STROLL IN THE SUN, A ○ WALKING IN THE SUN..
VANDRING MED MANEN • 1945 • Ekman Hasse • SWD • WANDERING WITH THE MOON
VANESSA • 1976 • Frank Hubert • FRG
VANESSA, HER LOVE STORY • 1935 • Howard William K. • USA • VANESSA (UKN)
VANESSA (UKN) see **VANESSA, HER LOVE STORY** • 1935
VANG VIR MY 'N DROOM • 1974 • SAF
VANGELO '70 see **AMORE E RABBIA** • 1969
VANGELO SECONDO MATTEO, IL • 1964 • Pasolini Pier Paolo • ITL, FRN • GOSPEL ACCORDING TO ST. MATTHEW, THE (UKN) ○ EVANGILE SELON SAINT-MATHIEU, L' (FRN)
VANGELO SECONDO SAN FREDIANO, IL • 1978 • Brazzi Oscar • ITL • STORIA DI PRETE, LADRI E PECCATRICI
VANGELO SECONDO SIMONE E MATTEO • 1976 • Carnimeo Giuliano • ITL
VANGJUSH MIO • 1966 • Erebara Gesim • ALB
VANILLE FRAISE • 1989 • Oury Gerard • FRN
VANINA see **VANINA ODER DIE GALGENHOCHZEIT** • 1922
VANINA ODER DIE GALGENHOCHZEIT • 1922 • von Gerlach Arthur • FRG • VANINA
VANINA VANINI • 1961 • Rossellini Roberto • ITL, FRN • BETRAYER, THE (USA)
VANISH • 1978 • Kuri Yoji • ANS • JPN
VANISHED • 1971 • Kulik Buzz • TVM • USA
VANISHED DREAM, A • 1911 • *Cines* • ITL
VANISHED HAND, THE • 1928 • Banfield George J., Eveleigh Leslie • UKN
VANISHED LINE RIDER, THE • 1917 • Horne James W. • SHT • USA
VANISHED WORLD see **VERSUNKENE WELT, EINE** • 1922
VANISHING, THE see **SPOORLOOS** • 1988
VANISHING ACT • 1986 • Greene David • USA
VANISHING AFRICA see **KWAHERI** • 1964
VANISHING AMERICAN, THE • 1925 • Seitz George B. • USA • VANISHING RACE, THE
VANISHING AMERICAN, THE • 1955 • Kane Joseph • USA
VANISHING BISHOP, THE • 1917 • *Kalem* • SHT • USA
VANISHING BODY, THE see **BLACK CAT, THE** • 1934
VANISHING BUSKER, THE • 1966 • Brims Ian • DCS • UKN
VANISHING CINDERELLA, THE • 1915 • *Pathe Exchange* • USA
VANISHING CORPORAL, THE (UKN) see **CAPORAL EPINGLE, LE** • 1961
VANISHING CRACKSMAN, THE • 1913 • Lessey George A.?, Wilson Ben? • USA
VANISHING DAGGER, THE • 1920 • Kull Edward, Magowan John F., Polo Eddie • SRL • UKN
VANISHING DUCK • 1958 • Hanna William, Barbera Joseph • ANS • USA
VANISHING FRONTIER • 1924 • Eason B. Reeves • USA
VANISHING FRONTIER see **BROKEN LAND, THE** • 1962
VANISHING FRONTIER, THE • 1932 • Rosen Phil • USA
VANISHING HOOFS • 1926 • McCarthy John P. • USA
VANISHING LADY • 1898 • *Edison* • USA
VANISHING LADY, THE • 1897 • *Paul R. W.* • UKN
VANISHING LADY, THE see **ESCAMOTAGE D'UNE DAME CHEZ ROBERT-HOUDIN** • 1896
VANISHING LEGION, THE • 1931 • Eason B. Reeves • SRL • USA
VANISHING MASK, THE see **HIDDEN DANGERS** • 1920
VANISHING MEN • 1932 • Fraser Harry L. • USA
VANISHING OF OLIVE, THE • 1914 • Ridgely Richard • USA
VANISHING OUTPOST, THE • 1951 • Ormond Ron • USA
VANISHING PIONEER, THE • 1928 • Waters John • USA
VANISHING POINT, THE • 1971 • Sarafian Richard C. • USA
VANISHING PRAIRIE, THE • 1954 • Algar James • DOC • USA
VANISHING PRIVATE, THE • 1942 • King Jack • ANS • USA
VANISHING RACE, THE • 1912 • Dwan Allan • USA • VANISHING TRIBE, THE
VANISHING RACE, THE see **VANISHING AMERICAN, THE** • 1925
VANISHING RIDER, THE • 1928 • Taylor Ray • SRL • USA
VANISHING RIDERS, THE • 1935 • Hill Robert F. • USA
VANISHING SAILS • 1935 • Steuart Ronald • UKN
VANISHING SHADOW, THE • 1934 • Landers Lew • SRL • USA
VANISHING STREET, THE • 1962 • Vas Robert • UKN
VANISHING TRAILS • 1920 • De La Mothe Leon • SRL • USA
VANISHING TRIBE, THE • 1914 • Montgomery Frank E. • USA
VANISHING TRIBE, THE see **VANISHING RACE, THE** • 1912
VANISHING VASES, THE • 1915 • *Sais Marin* • USA
VANISHING VAULT, THE • 1915 • Beggs Lee • USA
VANISHING VIRGINIAN, THE • 1941 • Borzage Frank • USA
VANISHING WEST, THE • 1928 • Thorpe Richard • SRL • USA
VANISHING WESTERNER, THE • 1950 • Ford Philip • USA
VANISHING WILDERNESS • 1974 • Dubs Arthur R., Seilman Heinz • DOC • USA
VANISHING WOMAN, THE • 1917 • Calvert E. H. • SHT • USA
VANITA • 1947 • Pastina Giorgio • ITL
VANITY • 1915 • De Grasse Joseph • USA • SINNER MUST PAY, THE
VANITY • 1917 • O'Brien John B. • USA
VANITY • 1927 • Crisp Donald • USA
VANITY • 1935 • Brunel Adrian • UKN
VANITY AND ITS CURE • 1911 • Salter Harry • USA
VANITY AND SOME SABLES • 1917 • Robertson John S. • USA
VANITY CASE, THE • 1914 • Marston Theodore • USA
VANITY FAIR • 1911 • Kent Charles • USA
VANITY FAIR • 1915 • Brabin Charles J. • USA
VANITY FAIR • 1922 • Rowden W. C. • UKN
VANITY FAIR • 1923 • Ballin Hugo • USA
VANITY FAIR • 1932 • Franklin Chester M. • USA
VANITY OF THE SHOGUN'S MISTRESS, THE see **O-OKU EMAKI** • 1968
VANITY POOL, THE • 1918 • Park Ida May • USA
VANITY STREET • 1932 • Grinde Nick • USA
VANITY THY NAME IS? • 1916 • *Gail Jane* • SHT • USA
VANITY'S PRICE • 1924 • Neill R. William • USA • THIS HOUSE OF VANITY
VANKA • 1942 • Rappaport Herbert • USS
VANKA • 1960 • Bocharov Edvard • USS
VANKA KLIOUTCHIK • 1909 • Goncharov Vasili M. • USS
VANOCE S ALZBETOU • 1968 • Kachyna Karel • CZC • CHRISTMAS WITH ELIZABETH
VANOCNI SEN • 1945 • Zeman Karel • SHT • CZC • CHRISTMAS DREAM, A ○ DREAM OF CHRISTMAS
VANQUISHED, THE • 1953 • Ludwig Edward • USA • GALLANT REBEL
VANQUISHED, THE (USA) see **VINTI, I** • 1952
VANQUISHED FLIRT, THE • 1917 • Miller Rube • SHT • USA
VANQUISHER see **ZWYCIEZCA** • 1977
VANRAJ-KESARI • 1937 • Desai Dhirubhai • IND
VAN'S CAMP • 1973 • Brittain Don, Rose Les • CND
VANSKELIGT VALG, ET see **GULDET OG VORT HJERTE** • 1913
VANTANDE VATTEN • 1964 • Werner Gosta • SHT • SWD • WAITING WATER
VANYUSHIN'S CHILDREN see **DYETI VANYUSHINA** • 1974
VAPAA-DUUNARI VILLE-KALLE • 1984 • Makinen Visa • FNL • FREE-MASON VILLE-KALLE
VAPOR BATH, THE • 1914 • *Komic* • USA
VAPOUR BATH, A • 1912 • Coleby A. E. • UKN
VAQUERO see **RIDE, VAQUERO!** • 1953
VAQUEROS DEL CAUTO • 1965 • Valdes Oscar • DOC • CUB
VAQUERO'S VOW, THE • 1908 • Griffith D. W. • USA
VAQUILLA, LA • 1985 • Berlanga Luis Garcia • SPN • HEIFER, THE ○ LITTLE BULL, THE
VAR HERRE LUGGAR JOHANSSON • 1944 • Wallen Sigurd • SWD • GOD PULLS JOHANSSON'S HAIR
VAR HERRE TAR SEMESTER • 1947 • Winner Peter • SWD, DNM
VAR I DALBY HAGE • 1962 • Troell Jan • SHT • SWD • SPRING IN DALBY PASTURES
VAR I VAPEN, EN • 1943 • Skoglund Gunnar • SWD • SPRING IN ARMS
VAR-MATIN • 1976 • Leenhardt Roger • DCS • FRN
VAR SIN VAG • 1948 • Ekman Hasse • SWD • EACH GOES HIS OWN WAY
VARA CU ANA • 1988 • Lazar Dumitru • RMN • SUMMER WITH ANNA
VARA FADERS GRAVAR • 1937 • Fejos Paul • DCS • SWD, DNM • TOMBS OF OUR ANCESTORS
VARAKOSOK • 1975 • Gyongyossy Imre • HNG • EXPECTANTS ○ EXPECTATIONS
VARAN POKJE • 1936 • Bornebusch Arne • SWD • OUR BOY
VARAN THE UNBELIEVABLE see **DAIKAIJU BARAN** • 1958
VARANDA DOS ROUXINOIS, A • 1939 • de Barros Jose Leitao • PRT
VARASTETTU KUOLEMA • 1938 • Tapiovaara Nyrki • FNL • STOLEN DEATH
VARAT GANG • 1942 • Skoglund Gunnar • SWD • OUR GANG
VARAZSKERINGO • 1918 • Curtiz Michael • HNG • MAGIC WALTZ
VARAZSLO, A • 1970 • Palasthy Gyorgy • HNG • CHILI-CHALA, THE MAGICIAN ○ TCHILI TCHALA THE MAGICIAN
VARDSHUSETS HEMLIGHET • 1917 • Magnussen Fritz • SWD • SECRET OF THE INN
VARELSERNA (SWD) see **CREATURES, LES** • 1966
VAREN • 1951 • Werner Gosta • SHT • SWD • SPRING
VARGA AND HIS BEAUTIES • 1944 • *O'Brien Joseph/ Mead Thomas (P)* • SHT • USA
VARGENS TID • 1988 • Alfredson Hans • SWD, DNM • TIME OF THE WOLVES ○ TIME OF THE WOLF
VARGTIMMEN • 1968 • Bergman Ingmar • SWD • HOUR OF THE WOLF (UKN)
VARHANIK U SV. VITA • 1929 • Fric Martin • CZC • ORGANIST OF ST. VIT, THE ○ ORGANIST AT ST. VITUS, THE
VARI PEPONI, TO • 1976 • Tassios Pavlos • GRC • HEAVY MELON, THE
VARIA KATARA O DIHASMOS • 1968 • Makedon Petros • GRC • HEAVY CURSE OF A SPLIT, THE ○ GOOD AND THE BAD, THE
VARIABLE STUDIES • 1960 • Emshwiller Ed • SHT • USA
VARIACIOK EGY TEMARA • 1961 • Szabo Istvan • SHT • HNG • VARIATIONS UPON A THEME
VARIACIONES • 1963 • Solas Humberto • CUB
VARIATION see **HENSO-KYOKU** • 1975
VARIATION SUR LA GESTE • 1962 • Storck Henri • DOC • BLG
VARIATIONS • Kuchar Mike • USA
VARIATIONS • 1943 • Whitney John, Whitney James • SHT • USA
VARIATIONS see **WARIANTY** • 1970
VARIATIONS GRAPHIQUES SUR TELIDON • 1981 • Moretti Pierre • CND
VARIATIONS NO.5 • 1965 • Vanderbeek Stan • USA
VARIATIONS ON A 7 SECOND LOOP PAINTING • 1970 • Spinello Barry • SHT • USA
VARIATIONS ON A CELLOPHANE WRAPPER • 1970 • Rimmer David • CND
VARIATIONS ON A LOVE THEME see **HA'ISHA BACHEDER HASHENI** • 1967
VARIATIONS ON A MECHANICAL THEME • 1959 • Russell Ken • MTV • UKN
VARIATIONS ON THE SAME THEME • 1978 • Angelidi Antoinette • GRC, FRN • IDEES FIXES (FRN) ○ DIES IRAE
VARIATIONS ON THE THEME OF A DRAGON • 1967 • Dargay Attila • ANS • HNG
VARIATIONS UPON A THEME see **VARIACIOK EGY TEMARA** • 1961
VARIAZONI SINFONICHE • 1949 • Bava Mario • ITL
VARIEDADES DE MEDIANOCHE • 1959 • Cortes Fernando • MXC • ESPECTRO DE TELEVICENTRO, EL

VARIETE • 1925 • Dupont E. A. • FRG • VAUDEVILLE (UKN) ○ VARIETY ○ VARIETES

VARIETE • 1935 • Farkas Nicolas, Gels Jacob • FRG

VARIETES • 1935 • Farkas Nicolas • FRN • VARIETY

VARIETES • 1947-51 • Verneuil Henri • SHT • FRN

VARIETES • 1971 • Bardem Juan Antonio • SPN

VARIETES see **VARIETE** • 1925

VARIETIES ON PARADE • 1951 • Ormond Ron • USA

VARIETY • 1935 • Brunel Adrian • UKN

VARIETY • 1983 • Gordon Bette • USA

VARIETY see **VARIETE** • 1925

VARIETY see **VARIETES** • 1935

VARIETY AND POETRY THEATRE, THE • 1967 • Stoyanov Yuli • DOC • BUL

VARIETY GIRL • 1947 • Marshall George • USA

VARIETY HALF HOUR • 1954 • Baim Harold • SHT • UKN

VARIETY HOUR • 1937 • Davis Redd • UKN

VARIETY IS THE SPICE OF LIFE see **OMBYTE FORNOJER** • 1939

VARIETY JUBILEE • 1943 • Rogers Maclean • UKN

VARIETY LIGHTS (USA) see **LUCI DEL VARIETA** • 1950

VARIETY PARADE • 1936 • Mitchell Oswald • UKN

VARIETY STARS • 1954 • Stroyeva Vera • USS

VARIETY TIME • 1948 • Yates Hal • CMP • USA

VARIETY VIEWS NOS.94-102 • 1941 • *O'Brien Joseph/ Mead Thomas (P)* • SHS • USA • GOING PLACES

VARIETY VIEWS NOS.103-115 • 1942 • *O'Brien Joseph/ Mead Thomas (P)* • SHS • USA • GOING PLACES

VARIETY VIEWS NOS.116-128 • 1943 • *O'Brien Joseph/ Mead Thomas (P)* • SHS • USA

VARIETY VIEWS NOS.129-139 • 1944 • *O'Brien Joseph/ Mead Thomas (P)* • SHS • USA

VARIETY VIEWS NOS.140-148 • 1945 • *O'Brien Joseph/ Mead Thomas (P)* • SHS • USA

VARIETY VIEWS NOS.149-157 • 1946 • *O'Brien Joseph/ Mead Thomas (P)* • SHS • USA

VARIETY VIEWS NOS.158-166 • 1947 • *O'Brien Joseph/ Mead Thomas (P)* • SHS • USA

VARIETY VIEWS NOS.161-173 • 1948 • *O'Brien Joseph/ Mead Thomas (P)* • SHS • USA

VARIETY VIEWS NOS.174-184 • 1949 • *O'Brien Joseph/ Mead Thomas (P)* • SHS • USA

VARIETY VIEWS NOS.185-188 • 1950 • *O'Brien Joseph/ Mead Thomas (P)* • SHS • USA

VARIKKUZHI • 1983 • Nair M. T. Vasudevan • IND • PITFALL, THE

VARIOLA VERA • 1982 • Markovic Goran • YGS

VARIOUS FLOWERS see **HANA NO DAISHOGAI** • 1959

VARIOUS IMAGES • 1964 • Calotescu Virgil • DOC • RMN

VARIOUS POPULAR LIQUORS ILLUSTRATED • 1906 • Martin J. H.? • UKN

VARJU A TORONYORAN • 1939 • Rodriguez A. Endre • CROW ON THE TOWER (USA)

VARLDENS BASTA KARLSSON • 1974 • Hellbom Olle • SWD

VARLDENS MEST ANVANDBARA TRAD • 1937 • Fejos Paul • DCS • SWD, DNM • MOST USEFUL TREE IN THE WORLD, THE

VARMINT, THE • 1917 • Taylor William D. • USA

VARMLANNINGARNA • 1910 • Engdahl Carl • SWD • PEOPLE OF VARMLAND

VARMLANNINGARNA • 1921 • Petschler Eric A. • SWD • PEOPLE OF VARMLAND ○ HARVEST OF HATE

VARMLANNINGARNA • 1932 • Edgren Gustaf • SWD • PEOPLE OF VARMLAND

VARMLANNINGARNA • 1957 • Gentele Goran • SWD • PEOPLE OF VARMLAND

VARNA • 1960 • Vogeler Volker • FRG

VARNATT • 1976 • Solbakken Erik • NRW

VARNEHJERTE, EN • 1916 • Davidsen Hjalmar • DNM

VAROS ALATT, A • 1953 • Hersko Janos • HNG • UNDER THE CITY

VAROS PEREMEN, A • 1957 • Jancso Miklos • SHT • HNG • IN THE OUTSKIRTS OF THE CITY

VAROSBUJOCSKA • 1985 • Sos Maria • HNG • TANDEM

VAROSTERKEP • 1977 • Szabo Istvan • SHT • HNG • CITY MAP

VARSITY • 1928 • Tuttle Frank • USA

VARSITY • 1930 • Legg Stuart • UKN

VARSITY GIRL, THE see **FAIR CO-ED, THE** • 1927

VARSITY RACE, THE • 1914 • Fleming Carroll • USA

VARSITY SHOW • 1937 • Keighley William, Berkeley Busby • USA

VARSITY VANITIES • 1940 • Ceballos Larry • SHT • USA

VARSOI VILAGIFJUSAGI TALAKOZO I-III see **VARSOI VIT I-II-III** • 1955

VARSOI VIT I-II-III • 1955 • Jancso Miklos • SHT • HNG • VARSOI VILAGIFJUSAGI TALAKOZO I-III ○ WARSAW WORLD YOUTH MEETING ○ WORLD YOUTH FESTIVAL IN WARSAW

VARSOVIAN IN KIEV, A see **WARSZAWIAK W KIJOWIE** • 1958

VARSOVIANS, THE see **WARSZAWIACY** • 1969

VARSOVIE QUAND MEME • 1953 • Bellon Yannick • FRN

VARSOVIE-QUEBEC: COMMENT NE PAS DETRUIRE UNE VILLE • 1974 • Regnier Michel • DOC • CND

VART HJARTA HAR SIN SAGA • 1948 • Bugler Bror • SWD • EACH HEART HAS ITS STORY

VARTHOLOMEOS • 1972 • Manousakis Manousos • GRC

VARTICITU KYLA 1944 • 1978 • Linnasalo Timo • FNL • GUARDED VILLAGE 1944, THE

VARUJ! • 1947 • Fric Martin, Bielik Palo • CZC • REITERATE THE WARNING! ○ WARNING

VARVARA see **SELSKAYA UCHITELNITSA** • 1947

VAS-Y, MAMAN! • 1978 • de Buron Nicole • FRN

VASANTHA SENA • 1967 • Ranga B. S. • IND

VASANTHI • 1967 • Wickremasinghe Ananda • SLN

VASARELY • Averty Jean-Christophe • FRN

VASARHELYI SZINEK • 1961 • Meszaros Marta • SHT • HNG • COLOURS OF VASARHELY, THE

VASARNAPI SZULOK • 1980 • Rozsa Janos • HNG • SUNDAY DAUGHTERS ○ SUNDAY PARENTS

VASCO THE VAMPIRE • 1914 • *Roubert Matty* • USA

VASE, LA • 1971 • von Cremer Heinz • SWT

VASE DE NOCES • 1974 • Zeno Thierry • BLG • WEDDING TROUGH

VASECTOMY: A DELICATE MATTER • 1986 • Burge Robert • USA • VASECTOMY: A DELICATE OPERATION

VASECTOMY: A DELICATE OPERATION see **VASECTOMY: A DELICATE MATTER** • 1986

VASEMBER • 1935 • Martonffy Emil • HNG

VASEN • 1962 • Trnka Jiri • ANS • CZC • OBSESSION ○ PASSION

VASENS HEMMELIGHED • 1913 • Blom August • DNM • KINESISKE VASE, DEN ○ CHINESE VASE, THE

VASES OF HYMEN, THE • 1914 • Baker George D. • USA

VASH SYN I BRAT • 1966 • Shukshin Vassili • USS • YOUR SON AND BROTHER

VASHA ZNAKOMAYA • 1927 • Kuleshov Lev • USS • YOUR ACQUAINTANCE ○ JOURNALIST, THE ○ ZHURNALISTA

VASK, VIDENSKAB OG VELVAERE • 1933 • Holger-Madsen • DNM

VASO DE WHISKY, UN • 1958 • Coll Julio • SPN

VASSA • 1982 • Panfilov Gleb • USS

VASSA ZHELEZNOVA • 1953 • Lukov Leonid • USS • MISTRESS, THE

VASSILI BORTNIKOV'S RETURN see **VOZVRASHCHENIE VASSILIYA BORTNIKOVA** • 1953

VASSILY AND VASSILISA see **VASSILY I VASSILISA** • 1983

VASSILY I VASSILISA • 1983 • Poplavskaya Irina • USS • VASSILY AND VASSILISA

VASSILY SOURIKOV • 1959 • Rybakov Anatoly • USS

VASTKUSTENS HJALTAR • 1940 • Lauritzen Lau Jr., O'Fredericks Alice • SWD, DNM • HEROES OF THE WEST COAST

VASVASE SHITAN • 1967 • Zarindast Mohamad • IRN • SATAN'S TEMPTATION

VASVIRAG • 1957 • Hersko Janos • HNG • IRON FLOWER, THE

VASYA -REFORMATOR • 1926 • Dovzhenko Alexander, Lopatinsky F. • USS • VASYA THE REFORMER

VASYA THE REFORMER see **VASYA -REFORMATOR** • 1926

VAT DE • 1985 • Hossain Amjad • BNG • GIVE ME FOOD

VATAN • 1938 • *Biswas Anil (M)* • IND

VATANYOLU -THE JOURNEY HOME • 1989 • Gunay Enis, Konyar Rasim • FRG

VATER, DER • 1943-44 • Engel Erich • FRG

VATER BRAUCHT EINE FRAU • 1952 • Braun Harald • FRG

VATER -DEIN KIND RUFT! • 1908 • FRG

VATER ERBE, DER • 1916 • Trautmann Ludwig • FRG

VATER GEHT AUF REISEN • 1931 • Boese Carl • FRG

VATER MACHT KARRIERE • 1957 • Boese Carl • FRG, AUS

VATER, MUTTER UND NEUN KINDER • 1958 • Engels Erich • FRG

VATER RUCKT EIN see **MIKOSCH RUCKT EIN** • 1928

VATER SEIN DAGEGEN SEHR • 1957 • Meisel Kurt • FRG

VATER UND SOHN • 1918 • Wauer William • FRG

VATER UND SOHN • 1929 • von Bolvary Geza • FRG

VATER UND SOHN see **FRIDERICUS REX (EIN KONIGSSCHICKSAL) 2** • 1922

VATER UND SOHN (FRG) see **MARKURELLS I WADKOPING** • 1930

VATER UNSER BESTES STUCK • 1957 • Luders Gunther • FRG

VATER VOSS • 1925 • Mack Max • FRG • UM SEINES KINDES GLUCK

VATER WERDEN IST NICHT SCHWER.. • 1926 • Schonfelder Erich • FRG

VATERFLUCHT • 1984 • Butler Heinz • SWT

VATERLIEBE • 1915 • Zeyn Willy • FRG

VATERTAG • 1955 • Richter Hans • FRG

VATI MACHT DUMMHEITEN • 1953 • Haussler Johannes • FRG

VATICAN AFFAIR, THE (USA) see **A QUALSIASI PREZZO** • 1968

VATICAN CONSPIRACY, THE see **MORTE IN VATICANO** • 1982

VATICAN STORY see **A QUALSIASI PREZZO** • 1968

VATICANO • 1949 • Manera Guido • DOC • ITL

VATICANO DE PIO XII, EL • 1941 • Bunuel Luis • DCS • SPN • HISTORY OF THE VATICAN, THE

VATROGASCI • 1970 • Mimica Vatroslav • ANS • YGS

VATSALA KALYANAM • 1950 • Panickar T. K. G., Krishnaswami S., Bhatt Nanabhai, Ferenczi Gabor, Dobos Maria, Szoke Andras • IND • COTTON CHICKEN ○ COTTON CHICKEN

VAU-VAU • 1964 • Kolar Boris • YGS • WOW-WOW ○ WOOF! WOOF! ○ BOW WOW

VAUD-O-MAT • 1936 • Schwarzwald Milton • SHT • USA

VAUDEVILLE • 1924 • Fleischer Dave • ANS • USA

VAUDEVILLE DAYS • 1934 • Schwarzwald Milton • SHT • USA

VAUDEVILLE ON PARADE • 1934 • Schwarzwald Milton • SHT • USA

VAUDEVILLE STAR'S VACATION, THE • 1913 • *Patheplay* • USA

VAUDEVILLE (UKN) see **VARIETE** • 1925

VAUDOU AUX CARAIBES • 1981 • de Villiers Gerard • FRN

VAUDOU: ENTRE VIVANTS EN MORTS, LE SANG, LE • 1973 • Magneron Jean-Luc • DOC • FRN • VOODOO: BLOOD BETWEEN LIVING AND DEAD

VAUDRY JEWELS, THE • 1915 • *Maison Edna* • USA

VAULT OF HORROR • 1973 • Baker Roy Ward • UKN, USA • FURTHER TALES FROM THE CRYPT ○ TALES FROM THE CRYPT PART II

VAUTOUR DE LA SIERRA, LE • 1909 • Jasset Victorin • SRL • FRN

VAUTOURS, LES • 1975 • Labrecque Jean-Claude • CND • VULTURES, THE

VAUTRIN • 1915 • Krauss Charles • FRN

VAUTRIN • 1943 • Billon Pierre • FRN • VAUTRIN THE THIEF ○ THIS MAN -VAUTRIN

VAUTRIN THE THIEF see **VAUTRIN** • 1943

VAUXHALL, BEDFORD, ENGLAND • 1965 • Wooster Arthur G. • DCS • UKN

VAVASOUR BALL, THE • 1914 • Brooke Van Dyke • USA

VAXDOCKAN • 1962 • Mattsson Arne • SWD • DOLL, THE ○ WAX DOLL

VAXELSPEL see **STUDIE V** • 1955

VAYA PAR DE GEMELOS! • 1977 • Lazaga Pedro • SPN

VAYA TIPOS • 1954 • Mendez Fernando • MXC

VAYAS CON DIOS, GRINGO • 1966 • Mulargia Edoardo • ITL

VAZHI PIZHACHA SANTHATHI • 1968 • Ramadas O. • IND

VCERA NEDELE BYLA • 1938 • Schorsh Walter • CZC • YESTERDAY IT WAS SUNDAY ○ MALE STESTI

VD • 1972 • Verstappen Wim • NTH

VDAVKY NANYNKY KULICHOVE • 1925 • Krnansky M. J. • CZC • NANYNKA KULICHOVA'S MARRIAGE

VDOVSTVO KAROLINE ZASLER • 1977 • Klopcic Matjaz • YGS • WIDOWHOOD OF KAROLINA ZASLER, THE

VE DVOU SE TO LEPE TAHNE • 1928 • Innemann Svatopluk • CZC • IT'S BETTER TO PULL AT THE SAME END

VEAU, LE • 1908 • Cohl Emile • ANS • FRN

VEAU GRAS, LE • 1939 • de Poligny Serge • FRN

VEC VIDJENO • 1987 • Markovic Goran • YGS

VECCHI E I GIOVANI, I • 1978 • Leto Marco • ITL

VECCHIA GUARDIA • 1933 • Blasetti Alessandro • ITL • OLD GUARD, THE

VECCHIA SIGNORA, LA • 1932 • Palermi Amleto • ITL

VECCHIA SIGNORA, LA see **PEPPINO E LA NOBILE DAMA** • 1959

VECCHIE AMICIZIE • 1956 • Saraceni Fausto • SHT • ITL

VECCHIO CINEMA.. CHE PASSIONE! • 1957 • Crudo Aldo • ITL

VECCHIO NIDO, IL • 1911 • Maggi Luigi • ITL

VECCHIO TESTAMENTO, IL • 1963 • Parolini Gianfranco • ITL • OLD TESTAMENT, THE (USA)

VECERY S JINDRICHEM PLACHTOU • 1954 • Duba Cenek, Zelenda • CZC • EVENINGS WITH JINDRICH PLACHTA

VECES ETAIENT FERMES DE L'INTERIEUR, LES • 1976 • Leconte Patrice • FRN • W.C. SONT FERMES DE L'INTERIEUR, LES ○ ASSASSIN N'EST PAS L'ANTIQUAIRE, L'

VECHERA NA KHUTORE BLIZ DIKANKI • 1961 • Rou Aleksandr • USS • NIGHT BEFORE CHRISTMAS, A (USA)

VECINOS • 1981 • Bermejo Alberto • SPN • NEIGHBOURS

VED FAENGLETS PORT • 1910 • Blom August • DNM • TEMPTATIONS OF A GREAT CITY

VEDA JDE S LIDEM • 1952 • *Kachyna Karel (Ph)* • DOC • CZC • SCIENCE GOES WITH PEOPLE

...VEDA SILAHLARA VEDA.. • 1966 • Conturk Remzi • TRK

VEDELI SI RADY • 1950 • Kachyna Karel, Jasny Vojtech • CZC • THEY KNOW WHAT TO DO

VEDETTES EN PANTOUFLES • 1953 • Guillon Jacques • SHT • FRN

VEDI COME SEI.. LO VEDI COME SEI?!, LO • 1939 • Mattoli Mario • ITL

VEDI NAPOLI E POI MUORI • 1952 • Freda Riccardo • ITL • SEE NAPLES AND DIE (USA) ○ PERFIDO RICATTO

VEDIAMOCI CHIARO • 1984 • Salce Luciano • ITL • LET'S SEE IT CLEARLY

VEDO NUDO • 1969 • Risi Dino • ITL • I SEE EVERYBODY NAKED

VEDOVA, LA • 1939 • Alessandrini Goffredo • ITL

VEDOVA DEL TRULLO, LA • 1979 • Bottari Franco • ITL

VEDOVA ELETTRICA, LA (ITL) see **SEPTIEME CIEL, LE** • 1957

VEDOVA INCONSOLABILE RINGRAZIA QUANTI LA CONSOLARONO • 1973 • Laurenti Mariano • ITL

VEDOVA SCALTRA, LA • 1922 • Gallone Carmine • ITL

VEDOVA TUTTA D'ORO, UNA (ITL) see **VEUVE EN OR, UNE** • 1969

VEDOVA X, LA • 1956 • Milestone Lewis • ITL, FRN • WIDOW, THE (USA) ○ VEUVE, LA

VEDOVE INCONSOLABILI IN CERCA DI.. DISTRAZIONI • 1969 • Gaburro Bruno Alberto • ITL

VEDOVELLA, LA • 1965 • Siano Silvio • ITL, FRN

VEDOVO, IL • 1959 • Risi Dino • ITL • WIDOWER, THE

VEDOVO ALLEGRO, IL • 1950 • Mattoli Mario • ITL

VEENA • 1948 • *Biswas Anil (M)* • IND

VEENA VELI • 1949 • Vyas Vishnu • IND

VEER BABRUVAHAN • 1934 • Desai Jayant • IND

VEER BABRUVAHAN • 1950 • Bhatt Nanabhai • IND

VEER BHIMSEN • 1950 • Desai Jayant • IND

VEERA POOJA • 1967 • Seshagiri Rao A. V. • IND

VEERA PURAN APPU • 1978 • Peries Lester James • SLN • WEERA PURAN APPU ○ REBELLION

VEERANJANEYA • 1968 • Kameswara Rao K. • IND • STORY OF HANUMAN AND THE MONKEY-GOD, THE

VEERGHATOTGACH • 1949 • Bhatt Nanabhai • IND • SUREKHA HARAN(?)

VEERTIG JAREN • 1938 • Greville Edmond T. • DOC • NTH • FORTY YEARS

VEG ZUM NACHBARN • 1963 • Vukotic Dusan • ANS • YGS • WAY TO THE NEIGHBOUR, THE

VEGA$ • 1978 • Lang Richard • TVM • USA

VEGAS STRIP WAR, THE see **VEGAS STRIP WARS, THE** • 1984

VEGAS STRIP WARS, THE • 1984 • Englund George • TVM • USA • VEGAS STRIP WAR, THE

VEGETABLE SOUP • Sztaba Stanley • ANS • USA

VEGETABLE VAUDEVILLE • 1951 • Sparber I. • ANS • USA

VEGETARIAN'S DREAM, A • 1913 • Cohl Emile • ANS • USA

VEGLIONE, LA see **HER BELOVED VILLAIN** • 1920

VEGRE, HETFO • 1971 • Kenyeres Gabor • HNG • IT'S MONDAY, AT LAST

VEGUL • 1974 • Maar Gyula • HNG • AT THE END OF THE ROAD

VEHICLE OF LOVE see **KAATHAL VAHANAM** • 1968

VEIDIFERDIN • 1980 • Indridason Andres • ICL • FISHING TRIP, THE

VEIL, THE • 1958 • Strock Herbert L. • MTV • USA

VEIL, THE • 1974 • Sinclair Arturo • SHT • PRU

VEIL, THE see **HAUNTS** • 1977

VEIL OF BLOOD • 1973 • Sarno Joe • SWT

VEIL OF HAPPINESS, THE see **VOILE DU BONHEUR, LE** • 1923

VEIL OF SLEEP, THE • 1913 • Carleton Lloyd B. • USA

VEILCHEN NR.4 • 1917 • Wiene Robert? • FRG

VEILCHEN VOM POTSDAMER PLATZ, DAS • 1936 • Hubler-Kahla J. A. • FRG • VIOLET OF POTSDAM SQUARE, THE (USA)

VEILCHENFRESSER, DER • 1926 • Zelnik Friedrich • FRG

VEILED ADVENTURE, THE • 1919 • Edwards Walter • USA

VEILED ARISTOCRATS • 1932 • Micheaux Oscar • USA

VEILED LADY, THE • 1913 • Smalley Phillips • USA

VEILED LADY, THE see **FOR SIN FADERS SKYLD** • 1916

VEILED MAN, THE • 1987 • Baghdadi Marun • LBN, FRN • HOMME VOILE, L' (FRN)

VEILED MARRIAGE, THE • 1920 • Buel Kenean • USA

VEILED MYSTERY, THE • 1920 • Grandon Francis J., Cullison Webster, Bowman William J. • SRL • USA
VEILED PRIESTESS, THE • 1915 • *Courtot Marguerite* • USA
VEILED THUNDERBOLT, THE • 1917 • Ellis Robert • SHT • USA
VEILED WOMAN, THE • 1917 • Bantock Leedham • UKN
VEILED WOMAN, THE • 1922 • Ingraham Lloyd • USA
VEILED WOMAN, THE • 1929 • Flynn Emmett J. • USA
VEILLE D'ARMES • 1925 • de Baroncelli Jacques • FRN • IN THE NIGHT WATCH
VEILLE D'ARMES • 1935 • L'Herbier Marcel • FRN • SACRIFICE D'HONNEUR ○ VIGIL, THE
VEILLEE DES VEILLEES, LA • 1976 • Gosselin Bernard • DOC • CND
VEILLEICHT WAR'S NUR EIN TRAUM see **KEIN, EIN HUND, EIN VAGABUND, EIN** • 1934
VEILLEUR DE NUIT, LE see **HARIS, AL-** • 1966
VEILS OF BAGDAD • 1953 • Sherman George • USA
VEIN OF GOLD, A • 1910 • *Essanay* • USA
VEIN OF VIRGINS, A see **SHOJO NO KETSUMIYAKU** • 1967
VEIN STRIPPING • 1952 • Peterson Sidney • USA
VEINARD, LE see **VAINQUEUR, LE** • 1932
VEINARDS, LES • 1962 • Girault Jean, de Broca Philippe, Pinoteau Jack • FRN • PEOPLE IN LUCK
VEINE, LA • 1927 • Barberis Rene • FRN
VEINTE ANOS Y UNA NOCHE • 1941 • de Zavalia Alberto • ARG
VEINTE MIL DOLARES POR UN CADAVER • 1970 • Zabalza Jose Maria • SPN
VEIVISEREN • 1987 • Gaup Nils • NRW • PATHFINDER (UKN) ○ OFELAS
VEJEN TIL BYEN • 1978 • Wanscher Claus, Bonde Jes, Andersen Preben Nygaard • DNM
VEJRHANEN • 1952 • Lauritzen Lau Jr. • DNM
VEL' D'HIV' • 1959 • Rossif Frederic • SHT • FRN
VELA INCANTALA, LA • 1982 • Mingozzi Gianfranco • ITL
VELA PARA EL DIABLO, UNA • 1973 • Martin Eugenio • SPN • CANDLE FOR THE DEVIL, A ○ ONE CANDLE FOR THE DEVIL
VELAZQUEZ Y SU EPOCA • 1962 • Castellon Alfredo • SHT • SPN
VELBLOUD UCHEM JEHLY • 1926 • Lamac Carl • CZC • CAMEL THROUGH THE NEEDLE'S EYE
VELBLOUD UCHEM JEHLY • 1936 • Haas Hugo, Vavra Otakar • CZC • CAMEL THROUGH THE NEEDLE'S EYE
VELD VAN EER, HET • 1983 • Visser Bob • NTH
VELE AMMAINATE • 1931 • Bragaglia Anton-Giulio • ITL
VELE DIPINTE see **STELLA DEL MARE** • 1939
VELEKOIE ZAREVO • 1938 • Chiaureli Mikhail • USS
VELENO DEL PIACERE, IL • 1919 • Righelli Gennaro • ITL
VELGARDHA • 1968 • Motevaselani Mohamad • IRN • WANDERERS, THE
VELHA A FIAR, A • 1964 • Mauro-Humberto • SHT • BRZ
VELHO E A MOCA, O • 1961 • Peyroteo Herlander • SHT • PRT
VELHOS SAO OS TRAPOS • 1980 • Rutler Monique • PRT • OLD RAGS
VELI DI GIOVINEZZA • 1915 • Oxilia Nino • ITL
VELI JOZE • 1980 • Grgic Zlatko • ANS • YGS • BIG JOE
VELIKAYA BITVA NA VOLGE • 1963 • Slavinskaya Mariya • USS • GREAT BATTLE OF THE VOLGA, THE (USA)
VELIKAYA OTECHESTVENNAYA • 1965 • Karmen Roman • USS • GREAT PATRIOTIC WAR, THE
VELIKAYA POBEDA • 1933 • Kaufman Mikhail • USS • GREAT VICTORY, THE
VELIKAYA POBEDA SOVETSKOGO NARODA • 1961 • Kiselyov Fyodor • DOC • USS • GREAT BATTLE OF EUROPE, THE (USA)
VELIKAYA SILA • 1949 • Ermler Friedrich • USS • GREAT FORCE, THE ○ GREAT POWER ○ GREAT STRENGTH
VELIKI GRAZHDANIN • 1938 • Ermler Friedrich • USS • GREAT CITIZEN, A
VELIKI I MALI • 1956 • Pogacic Vladimir • YGS • BIG AND SMALL ○ FUGITIVE IN BELGRADE ○ GREAT AND SMALL
VELIKI MITING • 1951 • Neugebauer Walter, Neugebauer Norbert • ANS • YGS • GREAT MEETING
VELIKI PERELOM • 1946 • Ermler Friedrich • USS • GREAT TURNING POINT, THE ○ TURNING POINT, THE
VELIKI PLAVI PUT see **GRANDE STRADA AZZURRA, LA** • 1957
VELIKI STRAH • 1958 • Vukotic Dusan • ANM • YGS • GREAT FEAR, THE
VELIKII UTESHITEL • 1933 • Kuleshov Lev • USS • GREAT CONSOLER, THE
VELIKII VOIN ALBANII SKANDERBEG • 1953 • Yutkevich Sergei, Stratoberdha Victor • USS, ALB • GREAT ALBANIAN WARRIOR SKANDERBEG, THE ○ GREAT WARRIOR SKANDERBEG, THE ○ SKANDERBEG ○ GREAT WARRIOR, THE
VELIKY PUT • 1927 • Shub Esther • USS • GREAT ROAD, THE
VELJEKSET see **KESYTTOMAT VELJEKSET** • 1970
VELKA NEZNAMA • 1971 • Hobl Pavel • CZC • GREAT UNKNOWN, THE
VELKA PRILEZITOST • 1950 • Wallo K. M. • CZC • GREAT CHANCE, THE
VELKA SAMOTA • 1959 • Helge Ladislav • CZC • GREAT SECLUSION ○ GREAT SOLITUDE
VELKA SYROVA LOUPEZ • 1987 • Pojar Bretislav • ANM • CZC • BIG CHEESE ROBBERY, THE
VELKE DOBRO DU ZSTVI • 1952 • Makovec Milos • CZC
VELKOMMEN TIL LIVET • 1987 • Korst Stine • SHT • DNM • WELCOME TO LIFE
VELKOMMEN TIL VENDSYSSEL • 1954 • Carlsen Henning • SHT • DNM
VELKY PRIPAD • 1946 • Kubasek Vaclav, Mach Josef • CZC • GREAT INCIDENT
VELLUTO NERO • 1976 • Rondi Brunello • ITL • BLACK EMMANUELLE, WHITE EMMANUELLE ○ EMMANUELLE IN EGYPT
VELO DANS L'HERBE, LE • 1973 • Roland Paul • BLG
VELO D'ISIDE, IL • 1913 • Oxilia Nino • ITL
VELODRAME • 1963 • Lapoujade Robert • SHT • FRN
VELVET • 1984 • Lang Richard • TVM • USA
VELVET ALLEY, THE • 1958 • Schaffner Franklin J. • TVM • USA
VELVET AND RAGS • 1911 • *Thanhouser* • USA
VELVET CATERPILLAR, THE see **SOFT CATERPILLAR, THE** • 1967
VELVET FINGERS • 1921 • Seitz George B. • SRL • USA
VELVET HAND, THE • 1918 • Gerrard Douglas • USA
VELVET HANDS see **MANO DI VELLUTO** • 1979
VELVET HOUSE see **CRUCIBLE OF HORROR** • 1971
VELVET HOUSE CORPSE, THE see **CRUCIBLE OF HORROR** • 1971
VELVET PAW, THE • 1916 • Tourneur Maurice • USA
VELVET SMOOTH • 1975 • Fink Michael • USA
VELVET TOUCH, THE • 1948 • Gage John • USA
VELVET TRAP, THE • 1966 • Kennedy Ken • USA
VELVET UNDERGROUND AND NICO, THE • 1966 • Warhol Andy • USA • EXPLODING PLASTIC INEVITABLES, THE ○ PLASTIC INEVITABLES (VELVET UNDERGROUND)
VELVET VAMPIRE, THE • 1971 • Rothman Stephanie • USA • THROUGH THE LOOKING GLASS ○ DEVIL IS A WOMAN, THE ○ CEMETERY GIRLS ○ WAKING HOUR, THE
VELVET WOMAN, THE • 1923 • Bentley Thomas • UKN
VEM DOMER? • 1922 • Sjostrom Victor • SWD • LOVE'S CRUCIBLE (USA) ○ MORTAL CLAY (UKN)
VEM SKOT? • 1917 • Tallroth Konrad • SWD • WHO FIRED?
VEN, HET • 1971 • Zwartjes Frans • SHT • NTH
VEN A CANTAR CONMIGO • 1966 • Zacarias Alfredo • MXC
VENANCIO FLOREZ • 1982 • Castro Juan Carlos Rodriguez • URG
VENCEREMOS • Popovic Dragutin • DOC
VENCEREMOS • 1960 • Fraga Jorge • DOC • CUB
VENDANGES • 1929 • Rouquier Georges • SHT • FRN
VENDANGES, LES • 1922 • Epstein Jean • FRN
VENDEDOR DE ILUSIONES • 1966 • Zabalza Jose Maria • SPN
VENDEDOR DE ILUSIONES, EL • 1971 • Zabalza Jose Maria • SPN
VENDEDOR DE MUNECAS, EL • 1954 • Urueta Chano • MXC
VENDEDORA DE FANTASIAS, LA • 1950 • Tinayre Daniel • ARG • SALESLADY OF DREAMS
VENDEMIAIRE • 1918 • Feuillade Louis • FRN
VENDEMIAIRE see **LISTOPAD** • 1968
VENDETTA • 1901 • Blache Alice • FRN
VENDETTA • 1905 • Zecca Ferdinand • FRN
VENDETTA • 1914 • Mercanton Louis • FRN
VENDETTA • 1919 • Jacoby Georg • FRG • BLUTRACHE
VENDETTA • 1921 • Lubitsch Ernst • FRG
VENDETTA • 1942 • Haines Ronald • UKN
VENDETTA • 1942 • Newman Joseph M. • SHT • USA
VENDETTA • 1950 • Ferrer Mel, Heisler Stuart (U/c), Hughes Howard (U/c), Ophuls Max (U/c), Sturges Preston (U/c) • USA
VENDETTA • 1962 • Mitrovic Zivorad • YGS
VENDETTA • 1966 • Nehrebecki Wladyslaw • ANS • PLN
VENDETTA • 1977 • Manduke Joe • ISR, USA
VENDETTA see **MARIA MORENA** • 1951
VENDETTA see **MURIETA** • 1965
VENDETTA see **KAN DAVASI** • 1967
VENDETTA see **ANGKARA** • 1971
VENDETTA see **ANGELS BEHIND BARS** • 1986
VENDETTA, LA • 1961 • Cherasse Jean-A. • FRN, ITL
VENDETTA, LA (ITL) see **VENGANZA, LA** • 1957
VENDETTA BROTHERS • 1967 • Gallardo Cesar Chat • PHL
VENDETTA DEI BARBARI, LA • 1961 • Vari Giuseppe • ITL • REVENGE OF THE BARBARIANS (USA)
VENDETTA DEI GLADIATORI, LA • 1965 • Capuano Luigi • ITL • REVENGE OF THE GLADIATORS
VENDETTA DEI MORTI VIVENTI, LA see **REBELION DE LAS MUERTAS, LA** • 1972
VENDETTA DEI TUGHS, LA • 1955 • Callegari Gian Paolo, Murphy Ralph • ITL • KILLERS OF THE EAST (USA)
VENDETTA DEL CAVALIERE NERO, LA see **CIECA DI SORRENTO, LA** • 1965
VENDETTA DEL CORSARO, LA • 1951 • Zeglio Primo • ITL • REVENGE OF THE PIRATES (USA) ○ PIRATE'S REVENGE
VENDETTA DELLA MASCHERA DI FERRO (ITL) see **VENGEANCE DU MASQUE DE FER** • 1962
VENDETTA DELLA SIGNORA, LA (ITL) see **BESUCH, DER** • 1964
VENDETTA DI AQUILA NERA, LA • 1952 • Freda Riccardo • ITL • REVENGE OF THE BLACK EAGLE (UKN) ○ REVENGE OF BLACK EAGLE (USA)
VENDETTA DI ERCOLE, LA • 1960 • Cottafavi Vittorio • ITL, FRN • VENGEANCE D'HERCULE, LA (FRN) ○ GOLIATH AND THE DRAGON (USA) ○ VENGEANCE OF HERCULES, THE ○ REVENGE OF HERCULES, THE
VENDETTA DI FUOCO • 1955 • Zona R. • ITL • FIGLI DELL'ETNA, I
VENDETTA DI LADY MORGAN, LA • 1966 • Pupillo Massimo • ITL • REVENGE OF LADY MORGAN, THE ○ LADY MORGAN'S REVENGE
VENDETTA DI MONTECRISTO, LA • 1954 • Vernay Robert • FRN, ITL
VENDETTA DI SPARTACUS, LA • 1964 • Lupo Michele • ITL • REVENGE OF THE GLADIATORS (USA) ○ REVENGE OF SPARTACUS, THE
VENDETTA DI UNA PAZZA, LA • 1952 • Mercanti Pino • ITL
VENDETTA DI URSUS, LA • 1961 • Capuano Luigi • ITL • REVENGE OF URSUS (USA) ○ VENGEANCE OF URSUS ○ MIGHTY WARRIOR, THE
VENDETTA DI ZINGARA • 1952 • Molinari Aldo • ITL • SANGUE DI NOMAD
VENDETTA E IL MIO PERDONO, LA • 1968 • Mauri Roberto • ITL
VENDETTA E UN PIATTO CHE SI SERVE FREDDO, LA • 1971 • Squitieri Pasquale • ITL
VENDETTA EN CAMARGUE • 1949 • Devaivre Jean • FRN • MISS COW-BOY
VENDETTA FOR THE SAINT • 1968 • O'Connolly Jim • MTV • UKN
VENDETTA IN A HOSPITAL • 1915 • *Ritchie Billie* • USA
VENDETTA NEL SOLE • 1949 • Amato Giuseppe • ITL
VENDETTA PER VENDETTA • 1968 • Calloway R. • ITL
VENDETTA.. SARDA • 1952 • Mattoli Mario • ITL
VENDEUR DE BAGUES, LE see **BAIYYA AL-KHAWATIM** • 1965
VENDEUR ITINERANT, LE • 1973 • Lavoie Richard • SHT • CND
VENDEVAL • 1949 • de Orduna Juan • SPN
VENDEVAL MARAVILHOSO • 1949 • de Barros Jose Leitao • PRT, BRZ • TEMPETE MERVEILLEUSE, LA
VENDICATA • 1956 • Vari Giuseppe • ITL
VENDICATORE, IL • 1959 • Dieterle William • ITL, YGS • REVOLT OF THE VOLGA ○ DUBROWSKY ○ AIGLE NOIR, L' ○ REVOLTE SUR LA VOLGA
VENDICATORE DEI MAYAS, IL • 1966 • Malatesta Guido • ITL
VENDICATORE DI KANSAS CITY, IL • 1964 • Navarro Agustin • ITL, SPN
VENDICATORE MASCHERATO, IL • 1964 • Mercanti Pino • ITL, FRN • PIOMBI DI VENEZIA, I ○ GENTLEMEN OF THE NIGHT
VENDICATORI DELL'AVE MARIA, I • 1970 • Albertini Bitto • ITL
VENDITORE DI MORTE, IL • 1971 • Alberto Juan • ITL • PRICE OF DEATH, THE
VENDITORE DI PALLONCINI, IL • 1974 • Gariazzo Mario • ITL • LAST CIRCUS SHOW, THE (USA) ○ BALLOON VENDOR, THE ○ LOST MOMENTS
VENDO CARA LA PELLE • 1968 • Fizzarotti Ettore Maria • ITL • I SELL MY SKIN DEARLY
VENDORS OF DREAMS see **MARCHANDES D'ILLUSIONS** • 1954
VENDREDI 13 HEURES (FRN) see **AN EINEM FREITAG UM HALB ZWOLF** • 1961
VENDREDI -LES CHARS • 1978 • Leduc Jacques • DCS • CND
VENEER see **YOUNG BRIDE** • 1932
VENENO PARA LAS HADAS • 1985 • Enrique Taboada Carlos • MXC • POISON FOR FAIRIES
VENENOSA, LA • 1928 • Lion Roger • FRN • SUPERSTITION
VENENOSA, LA • 1949 • Morayta Miguel • MXC
VENENOSA, LA • 1957 • Morayta Miguel • MXC, ARG
VENERA • 1961 • *Triglav Films* • ANS • YGS • VENUS
VENERABLES TODOS, LOS • 1962 • Antin Manuel • ARG
VENERE • 1933 • Neroni Nicola Fausto • ITL
VENERE BRUNA see **CATTIVO SOGGETTO, UN** • 1933
VENERE CREOLA • 1961 • Ricciardi Lorenzo • ITL
VENERE DEI PIRATI, LA • 1960 • Costa Mario • ITL, FRG • VENUS DER PIRATEN (FRG) ○ QUEEN OF THE PIRATES (USA)
VENERE DEL PIREO, LA • 1974 • Romitelli Giancarlo • ITL
VENERE DELL'ILLE, LA • 1979 • Bava Mario • ITL
VENERE DI CHERONEA, LA • 1957 • Tourjansky Victor, Cerchio Fernando, Rivalta Giorgio • ITL, FRN • APHRODITE DEESSE DE L'AMOUR (FRN) ○ GODDESS OF LOVE, THE
VENERE IMPERIALE (ITL) see **VENUS IMPERIALE** • 1962
VENERE NUDA see **MALIZIE DI VENERE, LE** • 1969
VENERI AL SOLE • 1965 • Girolami Marino • ITL
VENERI IN COLLEGIO • 1965 • Girolami Marino • ITL, SPN
VENERI PROIBITE • 1964 • Loy Mino • DOC • ITL
VENETIAN AFFAIR, THE • 1966 • Thorpe Jerry • USA
VENETIAN ANONYMOUS, THE see **ANONIMO VENEZIANO** • 1970
VENETIAN BIRD • 1952 • Thomas Ralph • UKN • ASSASSIN, THE (USA)
VENETIAN LADY, THE see **VENEXIANA, LA** • 1985
VENETIAN LOOKING-GLASS, THE (USA) see **MIROIR DE VENISE, UNE MESAVENTURE DE SHYLOCK, LE** • 1905
VENETIAN NIGHTS (USA) see **CARNIVAL** • 1931
VENETIAN RED (UKN) see **ROUGE VENETIEN** • 1989
VENETIAN ROMANCE • 1913 • *Chatterton Thomas* • USA
VENETIAN WOMAN, THE (USA) see **VENEXIANA, LA** • 1985
VENETSIANSKIY MAVR • 1961 • Chabukiani Vakhtang • USS • BALLET OF OTHELLO ○ OTHELLO
VENEXIANA, LA • 1985 • Bolognini Mauro • ITL • VENETIAN WOMAN, THE (USA) ○ VENETIAN LADY, THE
VENEZIA, CARNEVALE, UN AMORE • 1981 • Lanfranchi Mario • MTV • ITL
VENEZIA CITTA MINORE • 1958 • Olmi Ermanno • DOC • ITL
VENEZIA IN FESTA • 1947 • Pasinetti Francesco • ITL
VENEZIA, LA LUNA E TU • 1958 • Risi Dino • ITL, FRN • VENISE, LA LUNE ET TOI (FRN) ○ VENICE, THE MOON AND YOU ○ DUE GONDOLIERI, I
VENEZIA MINORE • 1942 • Pasinetti Francesco • ITL
VENEZIA, RIO DELL'ANGELO see **FIAMME SULLA LAGUNA** • 1951
VENEZIA, UNA MOSTRA PER IL CINEMA • 1982 • Blasetti Alessandro • DOC • ITL
VENEZIANISCHE LIEBESPRACHE • 1924 • Feher Friedrich • FRG
VENEZIANISCHE NACHT • 1914 • Reinhardt Max • FRG
VENEZUELA A SU ALTURA • 1972 • Blanco Javier • DOC • VNZ • VENEZUELA AT ITS HEIGHT
VENEZUELA AT ITS HEIGHT see **VENEZUELA A SU ALTURA** • 1972
VENEZUELA LOOKS AHEAD • 1950 • Cole Lionel • UKN
VENEZUELA, PARADIS TERRESTRE • 1936 • de Wavrin Marquis Robert • BLG
VENEZUELA SETENTA ANOS • 1971 • Rebolledo Carlos • VNZ • SEVENTY YEARS VENEZUELA
VENEZUELAN PIANIST see **PIANISTA VENEZOLANA** • 1972
VENGA A FARE IL SOLDATO DA NOI • 1971 • Fizzarotti Ettore Maria • ITL
VENGA A PRENDERE IL CAFFE DA NOI • 1970 • Lattuada Alberto • ITL • COME HAVE COFFEE WITH US (USA)
VENGADOR, EL • 1948 • Aguilar Rolando • MXC
VENGADOR SOLITARIO, EL • 1953 • Peon Ramon • MXC • AGUILA NERA EN LA VENGADOR SOLITARIO, EL
VENGADORAS ENMASCARADAS, LAS • 1962 • Curiel Federico • MXC
VENGADORES, LOS • 1971 • *Churubusco Azteca* • MXC
VENGANZA, LA • 1957 • Bardem Juan Antonio • SPN, ITL • VENDETTA, LA (ITL) ○ HO GIURATO DI UCCIDERTI ○ VENGEANCE
VENGANZA APACHE • 1959 • Mendez Fernando • MXC
VENGANZA DE CLARK HARRISON, LA • 1968 • Madrid Jose Luis • SPN, ITL • CLARK HARRISON'S REVENGE
VENGANZA DE DON MENDO, LA • 1961 • Fernan-Gomez Fernando • SPN

VENGANZA DE HERACLIO BERNAL, LA • 1957 • Gavaldon Roberto • MXC
VENGANZA DE LA MOMIA, LA • 1973 • Aured Carlos • SPN • MUMMY'S REVENGE, THE ○ VENGEANCE OF THE MUMMY
VENGANZA DE LA SOMBRA, LA • 1961 • Gomez Urquiza Zacarias • MXC
VENGANZA DE LAS MUJERES VAMPIRO, LA see **SANTO EN LA VENGANZA DE LAS MUJERES VAMPIRO** • 1968
VENGANZA DE LOS VILLALOBOS, LA • 1954 • Mendez Fernando • MXC
VENGANZA DEL AHORCADO, LA • 1958 • *Clasa-Mohme* • MXC • VENGEANCE OF THE HANGED, THE
VENGANZA DEL CHARRO NEGRO, LA • 1941 • de Anda Raul • MXC
VENGANZA DEL DIABLO, LA • 1954 • Aguilar Rolando • MXC
VENGANZA DEL DOCTOR MABUSE, LA • 1973 • Franco Jesus
VENGANZA DEL LLANERO, LA • 1967 • Ballesteros Pio • SPN
VENGANZA DEL MARINO, LA • 1920 • Buchs Jose • SPN
VENGANZA DEL RESUCITADO, LA • 1961 • Curiel Federico • MXC • VENGEANCE OF THE REVIVED CORPSE, THE
VENGANZA DEL SEXO, LA • 1967 • Vieyra Emilio • ARG • CURIOUS DR. HUMPP, THE (USA) ○ SEX'S VENGEANCE
VENGANZA DEL ZORRO, LA • 1962 • Romero-Marchent Joaquin Luis • SPN • ZORRO, THE AVENGER (USA)
VENGANZA EN EL CIRCO • 1953 • Rodriguez Roberto • MXC
VENGANZA FATAL see **LUCIANO ROMERO** • 1959
VENGANZA O QUE BELLAS SON LAS FLORES, LA • 1979 • Urguelles Thaelman • VNZ • VENGEANCE OR HOW BEAUTIFUL THE FLOWERS ARE
VENGANZA SUPREMA see **MUJERES IN ALMA** • 1934
VENGANZAS DE BETO SANCHEZ, LAS • 1973 • Olivera Hector • ARG • VENGEANCE OF BETO SANCHEZ, THE
VENGEANCE • 1912 • Brenon Herbert • USA
VENGEANCE • 1913 • *Majestic* • USA
VENGEANCE • 1915 • *Travers Richard C.* • USA
VENGEANCE • 1918 • Vale Travers • USA
VENGEANCE • 1930 • Mayo Archie • USA
VENGEANCE • 1936 • Lord Del • CND
VENGEANCE • 1962 • Francis Freddie • UKN, FRG • TOTER SUCHT SEINEN MORDER, EIN (FRG) ○ BRAIN, THE (USA) ○ DEAD MAN SEEKS HIS MURDERER, A
VENGEANCE • 1964 • Hilyard Dene • USA
VENGEANCE see **HAEVNET** • 1911
VENGEANCE see **WHAT PRICE VENGEANCE?** • 1937
VENGEANCE see **ALRAUNE** • 1952
VENGEANCE see **VENGANZA, LA** • 1957
VENGEANCE see **POMSTA** • 1968
VENGEANCE see **SOLDATAMI NYE ROZHDAYUTSYA** • 1968
VENGEANCE see **PERRO, EL** • 1977
VENGEANCE, UN • 1918 • de Baroncelli Jacques • FRN
VENGEANCE AND THE GIRL • 1920 • De La Mothe Leon • USA
VENGEANCE AND THE WOMAN • 1918 • Duncan William, Trimble Larry? • SRL • USA
VENGEANCE BEQUEATHED • 1913 • *Cosmopolitan Film* • USA
VENGEANCE CORSE, LA • 1907 • Feuillade Louis • FRN
VENGEANCE DE DIEU, LA • 1972 • Alberto Juan • SPN
VENGEANCE DE RIRI, LA • 1908 • Cohl Emile • ANS • FRN
VENGEANCE D'EDGAR POE, UNE • 1912 • Capellani Albert • FRN
VENGEANCE DES ESPRITS, LA • 1911 • Cohl Emile • ANS • FRN • VENGEANCE OF THE SPIRITS
VENGEANCE D'HERCULE, LA (FRN) see **VENDETTA DI ERCOLE, LA** • 1960
VENGEANCE DIABOLIQUE • 1918 • *Lynn Emmy* • FRN
VENGEANCE DU BOUDHA, LA see **FONTAINE SACREE OU LA VENGEANCE DE BOUDHA, LA** • 1901
VENGEANCE DU COIFFEUR, LA • 1914 • Machin Alfred • NTH
VENGEANCE DU DOMESTIQUE, LA • 1912 • Linder Max • FRN
VENGEANCE DU FORGERON, LA • 1905-10 • Heuze Andre • FRN
VENGEANCE DU GATE-SAUCE, LA • 1900 • Melies Georges • FRN • COOK'S REVENGE, THE (USA)
VENGEANCE DU MASQUE DE FER • 1962 • De Feo Francesco • FRN, ITL • VENDETTA DELLA MASCHERA DI FERRO (ITL) ○ PRISONER OF THE IRON MASK
VENGEANCE DU SARRASIN, LA see **SCIMITARRA DEL SARACENO, LA** • 1959
VENGEANCE DU SERGENT DE VILLE, LA • 1913 • Feuillade Louis • FRN
VENGEANCE DU SERPENT A PLUMES, LA • 1984 • Oury Gerard • FRN
VENGEANCE DU SURCOUF, LA see **GRANDE COLPO DI SURCOUF, IL** • 1967
VENGEANCE D'UN FEMME, LA • 1989 • Doillon Jacques • FRN
VENGEANCE HATH BEEN HAD • 1911 • *Reliance* • USA
VENGEANCE IN THE SADDLE (UKN) see **BULLETS AND SADDLES** • 1943
VENGEANCE IN TIMBER VALLEY see **UND EWIG SINGEN DIE WALDER** • 1959
VENGEANCE IS MINE • 1904 • Barker Will • UKN
VENGEANCE IS MINE • 1908 • *Tyler Walter* • UKN
VENGEANCE IS MINE • 1912 • *Garwood William* • USA
VENGEANCE IS MINE • 1913 • Campbell Colin • USA
VENGEANCE IS MINE • 1914 • *Lubin* • USA
VENGEANCE IS MINE • 1915 • *Clifton Elmer* • USA
VENGEANCE IS MINE! • 1916 • Broadwell Robert B. • USA
VENGEANCE IS MINE • 1918 • Crane Frank H. • USA
VENGEANCE IS MINE • 1949 • Cullimore Alan J. • UKN
VENGEANCE IS MINE see **NIGHT OF THE STRANGLER** • 1975
VENGEANCE IS MINE see **FUKUSHU SURUWA WARE NI ARI** • 1978
VENGEANCE IS MINE (UKN) see **QUEI DISPERATI CHE PUZZANO DI SUDORE E DI MORTE** • 1970
VENGEANCE LAND • 1986 • Taylor Roderick • USA
VENGEANCE OF A GUNFIGHTER • 1972 • Robinson Richard • USA
VENGEANCE OF A MONSTER, THE see **DAIMAJIN** • 1966
VENGEANCE OF ALLAH, THE • 1915 • Thornton F. Martin • UKN
VENGEANCE OF AQUILLES, THE see **AQUILEO VENGANZA** • 1968
VENGEANCE OF BETO SANCHEZ, THE see **VENGANZAS DE BETO SANCHEZ, LAS** • 1973
VENGEANCE OF DANIEL WHIDDEN, THE • 1912 • Collins Edwin J. • UKN
VENGEANCE OF DR. KUNG, THE see **RACHE DES DR. KUNG, DIE** • 1968
VENGEANCE OF DURAND, THE • 1919 • Terriss Tom • USA
VENGEANCE OF DURAND, OR THE TWO PORTRAITS, THE • 1913 • Blackton J. Stuart • USA • TWO PORTRAITS, THE
VENGEANCE OF EDGAR POE, THE • 1912 • *Lux* • FRN
VENGEANCE OF EGYPT, THE • 1912 • *Gaumont* • FRN
VENGEANCE OF FANTOMAS (USA) see **FANTOMAS REVIENT** • 1965
VENGEANCE OF FATE, THE • 1912 • Giblyn Charles • USA
VENGEANCE OF FU MANCHU, THE • 1967 • Summers Jeremy • UKN, FRG • RACHE DES FU MAN CHU, DIE (FRG)
VENGEANCE OF GALORA, THE • 1913 • O'Sullivan Tony • USA
VENGEANCE OF GOLD, THE • 1914 • *Reliance* • USA
VENGEANCE OF GREGORY WALTERS, THE (UKN) see **FEUD OF THE WEST** • 1936
VENGEANCE OF GUIDO, THE • 1915 • Reynolds Lynn • USA
VENGEANCE OF HATE • 1919 • *Capital* • SHT • USA
VENGEANCE OF HEAVEN, THE • 1913 • Wintrebert M. St. Loup • USA
VENGEANCE OF HERCULES, THE see **VENDETTA DI ERCOLE, LA** • 1960
VENGEANCE OF JACOB VINDAS, THE see **FISKEBYN** • 1920
VENGEANCE OF KALI, THE see **DANCE OF DEATH, THE** • 1938
VENGEANCE OF NAJERRA, THE • 1914 • *Johnstone Lamar* • USA
VENGEANCE OF NANA, THE • 1915 • Weston Charles • UKN
VENGEANCE OF PIERRE, THE • 1923 • *Cuneo Lester* • USA
VENGEANCE OF RANNAH • 1936 • Ray Bernard B. • USA
VENGEANCE OF RANNAH, THE • 1915 • Santschi Thomas • USA
VENGEANCE OF SAMPSON, THE • 1915 • *Powers* • USA
VENGEANCE OF SHE, THE • 1968 • Owen Cliff • UKN
VENGEANCE OF THE AIR, THE • 1914 • Aylott Dave • UKN
VENGEANCE OF THE BARBARIANS see **GET MEAN** • 1976
VENGEANCE OF THE BOZKURTS, THE see **BOZKURTLARIN INTIKAMI** • 1967
VENGEANCE OF THE DEAD • 1910 • *Pathe* • FRN
VENGEANCE OF THE DEAD • 1917 • King Henry • USA
VENGEANCE OF THE DEEP • 1923 • Barringer A. B. • USA
VENGEANCE OF THE FAKIR, THE • 1912 • *Eclair* • USA
VENGEANCE OF THE FORTY-SEVEN RONIN, THE see **CHUSHINGURA** • 1932
VENGEANCE OF THE GIANTS, THE see **DEVLERIN INTIKAMI** • 1967
VENGEANCE OF THE GLADIATOR (UKN) see **SOLO CONTRO ROMA** • 1962
VENGEANCE OF THE HANGED, THE see **VENGANZA DEL AHORCADO, LA** • 1958
VENGEANCE OF THE MUMMY see **VENGANZA DE LA MOMIA, LA** • 1973
VENGEANCE OF THE OPPRESSED • 1916 • Sloman Edward • SHT • USA
VENGEANCE OF THE REVIVED CORPSE, THE see **VENGANZA DEL RESUCITADO, LA** • 1961
VENGEANCE OF THE SKY STONE, THE • 1913 • McRae Henry • USA
VENGEANCE OF THE SPIRITS see **VENGEANCE DES ESPRITS, LA** • 1911
VENGEANCE OF THE THREE MUSKETEERS see **TROIS MOUSQUETAIRES, LES** • 1961
VENGEANCE OF THE VAMPIRE WOMEN, THE see **SANTO EN LA VENGANZA DE LAS MUJERES VAMPIRO** • 1968
VENGEANCE OF THE VAQUERO, THE • 1914 • *Kalem* • USA
VENGEANCE OF THE VIKINGS (UKN) see **ERIK, IL VICHINGO** • 1965
VENGEANCE OF THE WEST • 1942 • Hillyer Lambert • USA • BLACK SHADOW, THE (UKN)
VENGEANCE OF THE WEST see **PAY ME** • 1917
VENGEANCE OF THE WILDS • 1915 • Breitkreutz Big Otto • USA
VENGEANCE OF THE ZOMBIES (USA) see **REBELION DE LAS MUERTAS, LA** • 1972
VENGEANCE OF URSUS see **VENDETTA DI URSUS, LA** • 1961
VENGEANCE OF WINONA, THE • 1914 • *Darkfeather Mona* • USA
VENGEANCE ON DEMAND • 1919 • Chester George Randolph, Chester George Randolph Mrs. • USA
VENGEANCE OR HOW BEAUTIFUL THE FLOWERS ARE see **VENGANZA O QUE BELLAS SON LAS FLORES, LA** • 1979
VENGEANCE THAT FAILED • 1912 • Dwan Allan • USA
VENGEANCE, THE DEMON see **PUMPKINHEAD** • 1988
VENGEANCE: THE STORY OF TONY CIMO • 1986 • Daniels Marc • TVM • USA
VENGEANCE TRAIL, THE • 1921 • Seeling Charles R. • USA
VENGEANCE TRIBUNAL see **DAERAT EL INTIQAM** • 1976
VENGEANCE (UKN) see **VALLEY OF VENGEANCE** • 1944
VENGEANCE (UKN) see **TRAIL TO VENGEANCE** • 1945
VENGEANCE (UKN) see **JOKO INVOCA DIO.. E MUORI** • 1968
VENGEANCE VALLEY • 1950 • Thorpe Richard • USA
VENGEANCE VERSUS MERCY • 1917 • *Oliver Guy* • SHT • USA
VENGERESSE, LA • 1976 • Rivette Jacques • FRN
VENGEUR, LE see **JUGEMENT DE MINUIT, LE** • 1932
VENIAL SIN see **PECCATO VENIALE** • 1974
VENICE • 1930 • *Holmes Burton* • DOC • USA
VENICE ETUDE NO.1 • 1962 • Hugo Ian • SHT • USA
VENICE NITEMARE • 1970 • *Stacey Dist.* • USA
VENICE, THE MOON AND YOU see **VENEZIA, LA LUNA E TU** • 1958
VENICE: THEMES AND VARIATIONS • 1957 • Ivory James • SHT • USA
VENICE VAMP • 1932 • Foster John, Davis Mannie • ANS • USA
VENICE, VENICE • 1990 • Jaglom Henry • USA
VENIDA DEL REY OLMOS, LA • 1974 • Pastor Julian • MXC • COMING OF KING OLMOS, THE
VENIN, LE see **ORAGE** • 1937
VENIN DE LA PEUR, LA (FRN) see **LUCERTOLA CON LA PELLE DI DONNA, UNA** • 1971
VENIR AL MUNDO • 1989 • Torres Miguel • CUB • COMING ALIVE
VENISE ET SES AMANTS see **ROMANTICI A VENEZIA** • 1947
VENISE, LA LUNE ET TOI (FRN) see **VENEZIA, LA LUNA E TU** • 1958
VENIZELOS • 1980 • Voulgaris Pantelis • GRC
VENNER FOR ALTID • 1986 • Henszelman Stefan • SHT • DNM • FRIENDS FOREVER ○ VENNER FOREVER
VENNER FOREVER see **VENNER FOR ALTID** • 1986
VENO D'ORO, LA • 1955 • Bolognini Mauro • ITL
VENOM • 1974 • Sykes Peter • UKN • LEGEND OF SPIDER FOREST (USA)
VENOM • 1981 • Haggard Piers • UKN
VENOM OF THE POPPY, THE • 1911 • *Gordon James* • USA
VENOM (USA) see **GIFT** • 1966
VENONS-EN AU FAIT see **MUFID, AL-** • 1976
VENSKI LES • 1963 • Grigoriev • USS • VIENNA WOODS
VENT, LE • 1972 • Tunis Ron, Jodoin Rene • ANS • CND • WIND, THE
VENT, LE see **FINYE** • 1982
VENT DE GALERNE • 1989 • *Laurier Charlotte* • FRN
VENT DE L'ILLA, EL • 1988 • Gormezano Gerardo • SPN • WIND FROM THE ISLAND
VENT DE NOROIT see **CEUX DU RIVAGE** • 1943
VENT DE SABLE • 1982 • Hamina Mohamed Lakhdar • FRN
VENT DEBOUT • 1923 • Leprince Rene • FRN
VENT DEBOUT • 1952 • Pinoteau Jack • FRN
VENT DEBOUT see **CAP AU LARGE** • 1942
VENT DES AURES, LE see **ASSIFAT AL-AOURAS** • 1967
VENT D'EST, LE • 1969 • Godard Jean-Luc, Gorin Jean-Pierre • FRN, ITL, FRG • VENTO DELL'EST (ITL) ○ WIND VON OSTEN (FRG) ○ WIND FROM THE EAST (USA) ○ EAST WIND
VENT DU SUD see **RIH AL-JANUB** • 1975
VENT QUI CHANTE, LE • 1945 • Palardy Jean • DCS • CND
VENT SE LEVE, LE • 1959 • Ciampi Yves • FRN, ITL • VENTO SI ALZA, IL (ITL) ○ OPERATION TIME BOMB (UKN) ○ TIME BOMB (USA)
VENT SOUFFLE OU IL VEUT, LE see **CONDAMNE A MORT S'EST ECHAPPE, UN** • 1956
VENTA DE VARGAS • 1959 • Cahen Enrique • SPN
VENTA POR PISOS • 1972 • Ozores Mariano • SPN
VENT'ANNI • 1949 • Bianchi Giorgio • ITL
VENTARRON • 1949 • Urueta Chano • MXC
VENTE A ALEMANIA, PEPE • 1970 • Lazaga Pedro • SPN
VENTE A LIGAR AL OESTE • 1971 • Lazaga Pedro • SPN
VENTE DES AMOUREUX, LE • 1971 • Lamorisse Albert • FRN
VENTE D'ESCLAVES AU HAREM • 1897 • Melies Georges • FRN • SLAVE TRADING IN A HAREM
VENTE SOUFFLE OU LE VENT, LE • 1976 • Hanoun Marcel • SHT • FRN
VENTESIMO DUCA, IL • 1943 • De Caro Lucio • ITL
VENTICINQUESIMA ORA, LA (ITL) see **VINGT-CINQUIEME HEURE, LA** • 1966
VENTIQUATTRO ORE.. NON UN MINUTO DI PIU • 1975 • Bottari Franco • ITL
VENTO D'AFRICA • 1949 • Majano Anton Giulio • ITL • KANSIN
VENTO DEL SUD • 1959 • Provenzale Enzo • ITL
VENTO DELL'EST (ITL) see **VENT D'EST, LE** • 1969
VENTO DI MILIONI • 1940 • Falconi Dino • ITL • QUATTRINI A PALATE
VENTO DI MORTE see **ULTIMO UOMO DELLA TERRA, L'** • 1964
VENTO DI PRIMAVERA • 1959 • Rabenalt Arthur M., Del Torre Giulio • ITL, FRG
VENTO MI HA CANTATO UNA CANZONE, IL • 1948 • Mastrocinque Camillo • ITL
VENTO NELLE MANI, IL • 1984 • Risi Claudio • ITL • WIND IN THE HANDS
VENTO NORTE • 1951 • Scliar Salomao • BRZ
VENTO SI ALZA, IL (ITL) see **VENT SE LEVE, LE** • 1959
VENTO VENTO PORTALI VIA CON TE • 1975 • Di Paolo Mario • ITL
VENTOLERA • 1961 • Marquina Luis • SPN
VENTRE DI NAPOLI, IL • 1977 • Ferrara Giuseppe • ITL
VENTRILOQUIST CAT • 1950 • Avery Tex • ANS • USA
VENTRILOQUIST'S TRUNK, THE • 1911 • Thompson Frederick A. • USA
VENTRILOQUO, IL • 1971 • Bene Carmelo • ITL
VENTURERS, THE • 1917 • Mills Thomas R. • SHT • USA
VENTURES OF MARGUERITE, THE • 1915 • Smith Hamilton, Mackin John E., Ellis Robert • SRL • USA
VENUKU • Murphy Geoff • NZL
VENUS • 1929 • Mercanton Louis • FRN
VENUS • 1968 • De Grasse Herbert Jean • USA
VENUS see **VENERA** • 1961
VENUS AGAINST THE SON OF HERCULES (USA) see **MARTE, DIO DELLA GUERRA** • 1962
VENUS AND ADONIS • 1913 • Turner Otis • USA
VENUS AND ADONIS • 1966 • Palazzo Tom • SHT • USA
VENUS AND HER DEVIL see **FRAU VENUS UND IHR TEUFEL** • 1967
VENUS AND THE CAT • 1971 • Bourek Zlatko • ANS • YGS
VENUS AND THE KNUTS • 1915 • Birch Cecil • UKN
VENUS AVEUGLE • 1940 • Gance Abel • FRN
VENUS D'ARLES, LA • 1912 • Denola Georges • FRN
VENUS DE FUEGO, LA • 1948 • Salvador Jaime • MXC
VENUS DE L'OR, LA • 1938 • Mere Charles, Delannoy Jean • FRN
VENUS DER PIRATEN (FRG) see **VENERE DEI PIRATI, LA** • 1960
VENUS DU COLLEGE, LA • 1932 • Duvivier Julien • FRN
VENUS ET ADONIS • 1900 • Blache Alice • SER • FRN
VENUS IM FRACK • 1927 • Land Robert • FRG
VENUS IM PELZ • 1969 • Dallamano Massimo • FRG • VENUS IN FURS
VENUS IMPERIALE • 1962 • Delannoy Jean • FRN, ITL • VENERE IMPERIALE (ITL) ○ IMPERIAL VENUS (USA)
VENUS IN FURS • 1967 • Marzano Joseph • USA

VENUS IN FURS • 1970 • Franco Jesus • UKN, FRG, ITL • VENUS IN PELTZ (FRG) ○ PAROXISMUS (ITL) ○ PUO UNA MORTA RIVIVERE PER AMORE?

VENUS IN FURS see **VENUS IM PELZ** • 1969

VENUS IN PELTZ (FRG) see **VENUS IN FURS** • 1970

VENUS IN THE EAST • 1919 • Crisp Donald • USA

VENUS IN TOWN • 1968 • *Marks Harrison (P)* • UKN

VENUS MAKES TROUBLE • 1937 • Wiles Gordon • USA

VENUS MALDITA, LA • 1966 • Crevenna Alfredo B. • MXC, ARG

VENUS MODEL, THE • 1918 • Badger Clarence • USA

VENUS OF THE SOUTH SEAS • 1924 • Sullivan James R. • USA, NZL

VENUS OF VENICE • 1927 • Neilan Marshall • USA • NAUGHTY CARLOTTA ○ VAMP OF VENICE

VENUS PETER • 1989 • Sellar Ian • UKN

VENUS RAIDERS -5 GIRLS TRUMPET THE ATTACK see **STOSSTRUPP VENUS -5 MADCHEN BLASEN ZUM ANGRIFF** • 1974

VENUS RISING • 1961 • Shapiro Mikhail • USS

VENUS VICTRIX • 1917 • Dulac Germaine • FRN • DANS L'OURAGAN DE LA VIE

VENUS VOM MONMARTRE, DIE • 1925 • Zelnik Friedrich • FRG

VENUS VOR GERICHT • 1941 • Zerlett Hans H. • FRG

VENUSBERG • 1963 • Thiele Rolf • FRG

VENUSIAN, THE see **STRANGER FROM VENUS, A** • 1954

VENUS'S ISLAND see **NISI TIS APHRODITIS, TO** • 1969

VEO Y NO LO CREO, LO • 1975 • *Henaine* • MXC

VER E AMAR • 1930 • de Garcia Eduardo Chianca • PRT

VERA • 1986 • Toledo Sergio • BRZ

VERA see **VERA, UN CUENTRO CRUEL** • 1973

VERA BAXTER see **BAXTER, VERA BAXTER** • 1976

VERA BAXTER OU LES PLAGES DE L'ATLANTIQUE see **BAXTER, VERA BAXTER** • 1976

VERA CRUZ • 1954 • Aldrich Robert • USA

VERA HOLGK UND IHRE TOCHTER see **UNMOGLICHE LIEBE** • 1932

VERA KIROVA • Chichkova Vera • CZC

VERA LUKASOVA • 1939 • Burian E. F. • CZC

VERA PANINA • 1918 • Gad Urban • FRG

VERA ROMEYKE IST NICHT TRAGBAR • 1976 • Willutzki Max • FRG

VERA STORIA DEL GENERALE CUSTER, LA see **NON TOCCARE LA DONNA BIANCA** • 1975

VERA STORIA DELLA SIGNORE DALLE CAMELIE, LA (ITL) see **DAME AUX CAMELIAS, LA** • 1981

VERA STORIA DI FRANK MANNATA, LA (ITL) see **VIVA AMERICA!** • 1969

VERA, THE GYPSY GIRL • 1910 • *American* • USA

VERA THE LAWYER see **ADVOKATKA VERA** • 1937

VERA THE MEDIUM • 1910 • USA

VERA THE MEDIUM • 1916 • Anderson G. M. • USA

VERA, UN CUENTRO CRUEL • 1973 • Molina Josefina • SPN • VERA

VERACHTER DES TODES, DER • 1920 • Piel Harry • FRG

VERANEO EN ESPANA • 1955 • Iglesias Miguel • SPN

VERANO 70 • 1969 • Lazaga Pedro • SPN

VERANO PARA MATAR, UN • 1973 • Isasi Antonio • SPN, ITL, FRN • RICATTO ALLA MALA (ITL) ○ MEURTRES AU SOLEIL (FRN) ○ SUMMERTIME KILLER, THE (USA) ○ TARGET REMOVED

VERANO VIOLENTA • 1966 • Blake Alfonso Corona • MXC

VERAO COINCIDENTE • 1962 • de Macedo Antonio • SHT • PRT

VERA'S HISTORIE • 1984 • Rygard Elisabeth • DOC • DNM

VERA'S TRAINING see **ANGI VERA** • 1979

VERBENA DE LA PALOMA, LA • 1921 • Buchs Jose • SPN

VERBENA DE LA PALOMA, LA • 1936 • Perojo Benito • SPN

VERBENA DE LA PALOMA, LA • 1964 • Saenz De Heredia Jose Luis • SPN

VERBENA TRAGICA • 1939 • Lamont Charles • USA • TRAGIC FESTIVAL, THE ○ TRAGIC FESTIVITY

VERBOGENE GLUTEN • 1925 • Bruun Einar J. • FRG

VERBORGEN LEVEN, HET • 1920 • Binger Maurits H., Doxat-Pratt B. E. • NTH, UKN • HIDDEN LIFE, THE

VERBOTEN! • 1959 • Fuller Samuel • USA

VERBOTENE FRUCHT, DIE • 1921 • Biebrach Rudolf • FRG

VERBOTENE LACHEN, DAS • 1915 • *Projektions-Ag Union* • FRG

VERBOTENE LIEBE • 1920 • Lund Erik • FRG

VERBOTENE LIEBE • 1927 • Feher Friedrich • FRG • LETZTE LIEBE, DIE

VERBOTENE STTADT, DIE see **JAGD NACH DEM TODE 2, DIE** • 1920

VERBOTENE WEG, DER • 1920 • Galeen Henrik • FRG

VERBRANDE BRUG • 1975 • Henderickx Guido • BLG • BURNT BRIDGE ○ BURNED BRIDGE

VERBRANNTE FLUGEL • 1916 • Wellin Arthur • FRG

VERBRECHEN AUF SCHLOSS EHRENFELD, DAS • 1924 • *Film-Handel* • FRG

VERBRECHEN AUS LEIDENSCHAFT see **AUS DEM SCHWARZBUCH EINES POLIZEIKOMMISSARS 2** • 1921

VERBRECHEN IN DER WALLSTREET 13 • 1921 • Neff Wolfgang • FRG

VERBRECHEN NACH SCHULSCHLUSS • 1959 • Vohrer Alfred • FRG • YOUNG GO WILD, THE (USA) ○ AFTER SCHOOL

VERBRECHEN UND LIEBE • 1921 • Neuss Alwin • FRG

VERBRECHEN VON HOUNDSDITCH, DAS • 1921 • Wellin Arthur • FRG

VERBRECHER DER WELTSTADT • 1915 • *Saturn-Film* • FRG

VERBRECHER-GMBH, DIE see **SOHNE DER NACHT 1** • 1921

VERBRECHER IN UNIFORM • 1922 • Firmans Josef • FRG

VERDACHT AUF URSULA • 1939 • Martin Karl Heinz • FRG

VERDAD SOBRE EL CASO SAVOLTA, LA • 1980 • Drove Antonio • SPN, ITL, FRN • TRUTH ABOUT THE SAVOLTA AFFAIR, THE ○ CASO SAVOLTA, EL ○ SAVOLTA AFFAIR, THE

VERDADE VEM DO ALTO, A • 1967 • Nascimento Virgilio T. • BRZ • TRUTH COMES FROM ABOVE, THE

VERDADERA VOCACION DE MAGDALENA, LA • 1971 • Hermosillo Jaime Humberto • MXC • MAGDALENA'S TRUE VOCATION

...VERDAMMT, ICH BIN ERWACHSEN.. • 1975 • Losansky Rolf • GDR

VERDAMMT ZUR SUNDE • 1964 • Weidenmann Alfred • FRG

VERDE CONCELLA • 1968 • Gil Rafael • SPN • GREEN MAIDEN

VERDE EMPIEZA EN LOS PIRINEOS, LO • 1973 • Escriva Vicente • SPN

VERDE ETA, LA • 1957 • Iori Bruno • ITL

VERDE POR FORA, VERMELHO POR DENTRO • 1980 • Costa Ricardo • PRT • GREEN EXTERIOR AND RED INTERIOR

VERDEN ER FULD AF BORN • 1979 • Schmidt Aase • DNM • WORLD FULL OF CHILDREN, A

VERDEN TIL FORSKEL, EN • 1989 • Magnusson Leif • DNM • WORLD OF DIFFERENCE, A ○ ANOTHER WORLD

VERDENS HERKULES • 1908 • *Holger-Madsen* • DNM • HERCULES THE ATHLETE

VERDENS RIGESTE PIGE • 1958 • Lauritzen Lau Jr., O'Fredericks Alice • DNM • RICHEST GIRL IN THE WORLD, THE (USA)

VERDENS UNDERGANG • 1916 • Blom August • DNM • END OF THE WORLD, THE (USA) ○ FLAMMESVAERDET ○ FLAMING SWORD, THE

VERDES ANOS • 1984 • Gerbase Carlos, Brasil Giba Assis • BRZ • GREEN YEARS

VERDES ANOS, OS • 1963 • Rocha Paulo • PRT • GREEN YEARS, THE

VERDES PRADERAS, LAS • 1979 • Garci Jose Luis • SPN • GREEN PASTURES, THE

VERDI • 1913 • De Liguoro Giuseppe • ITL

VERDI BANDIERE DI ALLAH, LE • 1964 • Gentilomo Giacomo, Zurli Guido • ITL • SLAVE GIRLS OF SHEBA (USA)

VERDICT see **VERDICT, LE** • 1974

VERDICT, LE • 1974 • Cayatte Andre • FRN, ITL • ACCUSA E: VIOLENZA CARNALE E OMICIDIO, L' ○ TESTAMENT, LE ○ JURY OF ONE ○ VERDICT

VERDICT, THE • 1914 • Davies Hal • USA

VERDICT, THE • 1915 • *Grandin Ethel* • USA

VERDICT, THE • 1925 • Windermere Fred • USA

VERDICT, THE • 1946 • Siegel Don • USA

VERDICT, THE • 1964 • Eady David • UKN

VERDICT, THE • 1982 • Lumet Sidney • USA

VERDICT FOR TOMORROW • 1961 • Hurwitz Leo T. • DOC • USA

VERDICT OF LAKE BATALON, THE see **ITEL A BALATON** • 1932

VERDICT OF THE DESERT, THE • 1925 • Hart Neal • USA

VERDICT OF THE HEART, THE • 1915 • Noy Wilfred • UKN

VERDICT OF THE SEA • 1932 • Miller Frank, Northcote Sidney • UKN

VERDI'S MUSIC • 1961 • Gorikker Vladimir • USS

VERDUGO, EL • 1920 • *Drehwa-Film-Verleih Und Vertrieb* • FRG

VERDUGO, EL • 1947 • Gomez Bascuas Enrique • SPN

VERDUGO, EL • 1964 • Berlanga Luis Garcia • SPN, ITL • BALLATA DEL BOIA, LA (ITL) ○ NOT ON YOUR LIFE (USA) ○ HANGMAN, THE ○ EXECUTIONER, THE

VERDUGO DE SEVILLA, EL • 1942 • Soler Fernando • MXC

VERDULEROS II, LOS • 1987 • Martinez Solares Gilberto • MXC • GREENGROCERS II, THE

VERDUN, SOUVENIRS D'HISTOIRE • 1931 • Poirier Leon • FRN

VERDUN, VISIONS D'HISTOIRE • 1928 • Poirier Leon • FRN

VEREDA DA SALVACAO • 1965 • Duarte Anselmo • BRZ

VEREDAS • 1978 • Monteiro Joao Cesar • PRT • TRADITIONAL TALES

VEREISTE BRUCKE, DIE • 1973 • Hristov Hristo • USS, GDR

VERENA STADLER • 1940 • Haller Hermann • SWT

VERERBTE TRIEBE • 1929 • Ucicky Gustav • FRG

VERFLIXTE LIEBE, DIE • 1916 • Albes Emil • FRG

VERFLIXTEN JUNGGESELLEN, DIE • 1915 • Bolten-Baeckers Heinrich • FRG

VERFLUCHT, DIES AMERIKA! • 1974 • Vogeler Volker • FRG • THIS DAMNED AMERICA!

VERFLUCHTE, DER • 1921 • Osten Franz • FRG

VERFLUCHTE HUNGER NACH GOLD 1, DER see **AURI SACRA FAMES 1** • 1920

VERFOLGTE UNSCHULD, EINE • 1916 • Albes Emil • FRG

VERFUHRTE, DIE • 1913 • Rye Stellan • FRG • GEHEIMNISSE DER SEELE ○ GEHEIMNISSE DES BLUTES

VERFUHRTE HANDE • 1949 • Kirchhoff Fritz • FRG

VERFUHRTE HEILIGE, DIE • 1919 • Wiene Robert • FRG

VERFUHRTE JUGEND • 1950 • Braun Alfred • FRG • SUNDIGE HAUS, DAS ○ TREPPE, DIE

VERFUHRTEN, DIE • 1919 • Froelich Carl • FRG

VERFUHRUNG AM MEER • 1963 • Zivanovic Jovan • FRG, YGS • SEDUCTION BY THE SEA (USA) ○ OSTRVA ○ ISLANDS

VERFULCHTE HUNGER NACH GOLD 2, DER see **AURI SACRA FAMES 2** • 1920

VERGANGENHEIT RACHT SICH, DIE • 1917 • Gad Urban • FRG

VERGEET MY NIE • 1976 • SAF

VERGELTUNG, DIE • 1923 • Liepski Serge, Burghardt Theodor? • FRG

VERGELTUNG IN CATANO (FRG) see **TIERRA DE FUEGO** • 1965

VERGESSEN • 1959 • Schmaltz Bernhard • FRG

VERGESSENEN JAHRE, DIE • 1962 • Stenzel Otto • AUS

VERGESST MIR MEINE TRAUDEL NICHT • 1957 • Maetzig Kurt • GDR • DON'T FORGET MY TRAUDEL ○ IHR LETZTER FEHLER

VERGETEN MEDEMINNAAR, DE • 1964 • Korporaal John • NTH

VERGIB UNS UNSERE SCHULD see **WEIB AM KREUZE, DAS** • 1929

VERGIFTETE BRUNNEN, DER see **VERGIFTETE STROM, DER** • 1921

VERGIFTETE STROM, DER • 1921 • Gad Urban • FRG • VERGIFTETE BRUNNEN, DER

VERGIFTETES BLUT • 1920 • Sauer Fred • FRG

VERGINE DEL RONCADOR, LA see **YALIS, LA VERGINE DEL RONCADOR** • 1961

VERGINE DI BALI, LA • 1972 • Zurli Guido • ITL, INN • VIRGIN OF BALI, THE

VERGINE DI NORIMBERGA, LA • 1963 • Margheriti Antonio • ITL • CASTLE OF TERROR (UKN) ○ HORROR CASTLE (USA) ○ VIRGIN OF NUREMBURG, THE ○ TERROR CASTLE ○ HORROR CASTLE (WHERE THE BLOOD FLOWS)

VERGINE DI SAMOA, LA (ITL) see **TABU (FUGITIVOS DE LAS ISLAS DEL SUR)** • 1966

VERGINE E DI NOME MARIA see **MALIA** • 1976

VERGINE FOLLE, LA • 1921 • Righelli Gennaro • ITL

VERGINE, IL TORO E IL CAPRICORNO, LA • 1977 • Martino Luciano • ITL

VERGINE IN FAMIGLIA, UNA • 1975 • Delli Azzeri Luca • ITL

VERGINE MODERNA • 1954 • Pagliero Marcello • ITL

VERGINE PER IL PRINCIPE, UNA • 1965 • Festa Campanile Pasquale • ITL, FRN • VIERGE POUR LE PRINCE, UNE (FRN) ○ VIRGIN FOR THE PRINCE, A (UKN) ○ MAIDEN FOR THE PRINCE, A (USA) ○ MAIDEN FOR A PRINCE, A ○ THERE'S SOMETHING FUNNY GOING ON

VERGINE PER UN BASTARDO • 1966 • Ragona Ubaldo, Dein Edward • ITL, FRG • BETT EINER JUNGFRAU, DAS (ITL) ○ SWEET SMELL OF LOVE (USA)

VERGINELLA, LA • 1975 • Sequi Mario • ITL

VERGINI CAVALCANO LA MORTE, LE see **CEREMONIA SANGRIETA** • 1972

VERGINI DI ROMA, LE • 1960 • Cottafavi Vittorio, Bragaglia Carlo Ludovico • ITL, FRN • VIERGES DE ROME, LES (FRN) ○ AMAZONS OF ROME (USA) ○ VIRGINS OF ROME, THE ○ WARRIOR WOMEN

VERGINITA • 1952 • De Mitri Leonardo, Prosperi Giorgio • ITL

VERGINITA • 1975 • Andrei Marcello • ITL

VERGISS DIE LIEBE NICHT • 1953 • Verhoeven Paul • FRG

VERGISS MEIN NICHT • 1935 • Genina Augusto • FRG • FORGET-ME-NOT

VERGISS MEIN NICHT • 1958 • Rabenalt Arthur M. • FRG, ITL • OHNE DICH KANN ICH NICHT LEBEN

VERGISS NICHT DEINE FRAU ZU KUSSEN • 1967 • Kolsto Egil • FRG, DNM • DON'T FORGET TO KISS YOUR WIFE

VERGISS SNEIDER! • 1987 • Spielmann Gotz • AUS • FORGET SNYDER!

VERGISS, WENN DU KANNST • 1956 • Konig Hans H. • FRG, AUS

VERGISS, WENN DU KANNST see **ABENTEUER IM GRANDHOTEL** • 1943

VERGNUGEN, ANSTANDIG ZU SEIN, DAS • 1961 • Dieterle William • MTV • FRG

VERGODO SZIVEK • 1916 • Korda Alexander • HNG • FIGHTING HEARTS ○ BATTLING HEARTS ○ STRUGGLING HEARTS

VERGOGNA, SCHIFOSI! • 1968 • Severino Mauro • ITL • DIRTY ANGELS (UKN) ○ SHAME ON YOU, SWINE

VERGOGNE DEL MONDO, LE • 1968 • Scotese Giuseppe Maria • ITL • PANE AMARO, IL

VERHANGNIS DER SCHONEN SUSI, DAS • 1917 • Alexander Georg • FRG

VERHANGNIS EINER NACHT, DAS • 1917 • Wellin Arthur • FRG

VERHANGNISVOLLE ANDENKEN, DAS • 1918 • Gad Urban • FRG

VERHANGNISVOLLES SPRICHWORT, EIN • 1915 • Del Zopp Rudolf • FRG

VERHEXTE FISCHERDORF, DAS • 1962 • Hartmann Siegfried • GDR

VERHOR UM MITTERNACHT see **PARKSTRASSE 13** • 1939

VERI AZ ORDOG A FELESEGET • 1978 • Andras Ferenc • HNG • IT'S RAIN AND SHINE TOGETHER ○ RAIN AND SHINE

VERIDIQUEMENT VOTRE • 1968 • Leduc Jean • SHT • FRN

VERIGATA • 1964 • Sharlandgiev Ljobomir • BUL • CHAIN, THE

VERIRRTE JUGEND • 1929 • Lowenbein Richard • FRG

VERITA, LA (ITL) see **VERITE, LA** • 1960

VERITA DIFFICILE, LA • 1968 • Pastore Sergio • ITL • DIFFICULT TRUTH, THE

VERITA SECONDO SATANA, LA • 1972 • Polselli Renato • ITL

VERITAAAAAAAA, LA • 1982 • Zavattini Cesare • ITL • TRU-U-UTH, THE

VERITAS VINCIT • 1919 • May Joe • FRG

VERITE • 1977 • Kennedy Michael • CND

VERITE, LA • 1917 • Roussell Henry • FRN

VERITE, LA • 1960 • Clouzot Henri-Georges • FRN, ITL • VERITA, LA (ITL) ○ TRUTH, THE (USA)

VERITE DE FEDKA, LA • 1927 • Preobrazhenskaya Olga • SHT • USS

VERITE SUR LE BEBE DONGE, LA • 1951 • Decoin Henri • FRN • TRUTH ABOUT OUR MARRIAGE, THE

VERITE SUR L'HOMME-SINGE, LA • 1907 • Blache Alice • FRN • BALLET DE SINGE

VERITE SUR L'IMAGINAIRE PASSION D'UN INCONNU • 1974 • Hanoun Marcel • FRN

VERITE TOUTE NUE, LA see **HAQIQA AL-ARIYA, AL-** • 1963

VERITES ACCIDENTELLES, LES see **YEUX ROUGES, LES** • 1982

VERITES ET MENSONGES • 1973 • Reichenbach Francois • DOC • FRN • NOTHING BUT THE TRUTH

VERITES ET MENSONGES (FRN) see **F FOR FAKE** • 1977

VERJUNGTE ADOLAR, DER • 1931 • Jacoby Georg • FRG

VERJUNGTER ADHEMAR (FRG) see **PLAISIRS DE PARIS** • 1932

VERJUNGUNGSKUR, DIE • 1950 • Robbeling Harald • AUS • NACH REGEN FOLGT SONNE

VERKANNT • 1910 • Messter Oskar • FRG

VERKANNT • 1912 • Porten Franz • FRG

VERKANNTE LEBEMANN, DER • 1936 • Boese Carl • FRG • UNRECOGNIZED MAN OF THE WORLD, THE (USA) ○ LEBEMANN

VERKAUFTE BRAUT, DIE • 1915 • Matray Ernst • FRG

VERKAUFTE BRAUT, DIE • 1932 • Ophuls Max • FRG • BARTERED BRIDE, THE

VERKAUFTE GROSSVATER, DER • 1942 • Stockel Joe • FRG

VERKAUFTE GROSSVATER, DER • 1962 • Albin Hans • FRG

VERKAUFTES LEBEN see **MADELEINE UND DER LEGIONAR** • 1958

VERKEERDE NOMMER • 1982 • SAF

VERKENNINGSBORING, DE • 1953 • Haanstra Bert • DCS • NTH, UKN • WILDCAT, THE
VERKLUNGENE MELODIE • 1938 • Tourjansky Victor • FRG • DEAD MELODY (USA)
VERKLUNGENE TRAUME • 1930 • Berger Martin • FRG, RMN • CIULEANDRA (RMN)
VERKLUNGENES WIEN • 1951 • Marischka Ernst • AUS
VERKOMMEN • 1920 • Gunsburg Arthur • FRG • ZU DEN HOHEN DER MENSCHHEIT
VERKRACHTE EXISTENZEN • 1924 • Linke Edmund • FRG
VERLEGENHEITSKIND, DAS • 1938 • Brauer Peter P. • FRG
VERLEUGNETEN JAHRE, DIE see **LANGSAME TOD, DER** • 1920
VERLIEB' DICH NICHT AM BODENSEE • 1935 • Wolff Carl Heinz • FRG
VERLIEB' DICH NICHT IN SIZILIEN see **FRUHLINGSMARCHEN** • 1934
VERLIEBT IN HEIDELBERG • 1964 • Hamel Peter • FRG
VERLIEBT IN OSTERRICH • 1967 • Mueller-Sehn Wolfgang • DOC • AUS • IN LOVE IN AUSTRIA
VERLIEBTE BLASEKOPP, DER • 1932 • Dessauer Siegfried • FRG
VERLIEBTE FIRMA, DIE • 1932 • Ophuls Max • FRG
VERLIEBTE HERZEN • 1939 • Boese Carl • FRG • HEARTS IN LOVE (USA)
VERLIEBTE HOTEL, DAS • 1933 • Lamac Carl • FRG
VERLIEBTE LEUTE • 1954 • Antel Franz • AUS
VERLIEBTER RACKER, EIN • 1915 • Hofer Franz • FRG
VERLIEBTER SOMMER see **HEIDESOMMER** • 1945
VERLIEBTES ABENTEUER • 1938 • Zerlett Hans H. • FRG
VERLOBTE, DIE • 1979 • Rucker Gunther, Reisch Gunter • GDR • FIANCEE, THE
VERLOBTE LEUTE • 1945 • Anton Karl • FRG • DEMENTI, DAS
VERLOBUNG AM WOLFGANGSEE • 1956 • Weiss Helmut • AUS
VERLOCKUNG, DIE • 1988 • Berner Dieter • AUS • SEDUCTION, THE
VERLOEDERING VAN DE SWIEPS, DE • 1967 • Terpstra Erik • NTH • WHIPPING CREAM HERO, THE
VERLOGENE AKT, DER • 1969 • von Sydow Rolf • FRG, ITL • LIZABETH, ADULTERA INNOCENTE (ITL) ○ BORN BLACK (UKN)
VERLOGENE MORAL • 1921 • Kobe Hanns • FRG • BRANDHERD
VERLOREN MAANDAG • 1973 • Monheim Luc • NTH, BLG • GUEULE DE BOIS, LA ○ LUNDI PERDU
VERLOREN PARADIJS, HET • 1978 • Kumel Harry • BLG • PARADIS PERDU, LE ○ LOST PARADISE, THE
VERLOREN UND GEWONNEN see **"...UND ES LOCKT EIN RUF AUS SUNDIGER WELT"** • 1925
VERLORENE, DER • 1951 • Lorre Peter • FRG • LOST ONE, THE (UKN)
VERLORENE BALL, DER • 1959 • Weiler Kurt • GDR
VERLORENE EHRE DER KATHERINA BLUM, DIE • 1975 • Schlondorff Volker • FRG • LOST HONOR OF KATHERINA BLUM, THE (USA)
VERLORENE GESICHT, DAS • 1948 • Hoffmann Kurt • FRG
VERLORENE ICH, DAS • 1923 • Werner-Kahle Hugo • AUS • GEFAHREN DER HYPNOSE ○ DANGERS OF HYPNOSIS, THE ○ LOST SOUL, THE
VERLORENE MELODIE • 1952 • von Borsody Eduard • AUS
VERLORENE PARADIES, DAS • 1917 • Rahn Bruno • FRG
VERLORENE PARADIES, DAS • 1918 • Halm Alfred • FRG
VERLORENE PARADIES, DAS • 1923 • Ruttmann Walter • FRG
VERLORENE SCHATTEN, DER • 1920 • Gliese Rochus • FRG • LOST SHADOW, THE (USA)
VERLORENE SCHUH, DER • 1923 • Berger Ludwig • FRG • CINDERELLA (USA) ○ LOST SHOE, THE
VERLORENE SEELEN • 1921 • Kalden Hans • FRG
VERLORENE SOHN, DER • 1918 • Halm Alfred? • FRG • LUKAS KAPITEL 15
VERLORENE SOHN, DER • 1934 • Trenker Luis • FRG • LOST SON, THE
VERLORENE TAL, DAS • 1934 • Heuberger Edmund • FRG
VERLORENE TOCHTER 1 • 1918 • Kahn William • FRG • LOST DAUGHTERS
VERLORENE TOCHTER 2 • 1919 • Kahn William • FRG • OPFER DER SCHMACH
VERLORENE TOCHTER 3 • 1919 • Kahn William • FRG • MENSCHEN NENNEN ES LIEBE, DIE
VERLORENEN NACHTE • 1926 • Perponcher Friedrich Carl • FRG
VERLORENES LEBEN • 1975 • Runze Ottokar • FRG • LOST LIFE, A
VERLORENES RENNEN • 1948 • Neufeld Max • AUS
VERLORENES SPIEL • 1920 • Seitz Franz • FRG
VERMELHO, AMARELO E VERDE • 1966 • Lopes Fernando • SHT • PRT
VERMILION BOX see **KUNKUMA BHARANI** • 1968
VERMILION DOOR • 1969 • Lo Chen • HKG
VERMILION MARK see **SINDHOOR**
VERMILION PENCIL, THE • 1922 • Dawn Norman • USA
VERMISAT • 1975 • Brenta Mario • ITL
VERMLANDERS • 1910 • Petschler Eric A. • SWD
VERMUMMTE BRAUT, DIE • 1925 • *F.f. Films* • FRG
VERMUMMTEN, DIE • 1920 • Seitz Franz • FRG
VERNAY ET L'AFFAIRE VANDERGHEN • 1960 • Davy Jean-Francois • FRN
VERNE MILLER see **GANGLAND: THE VERNE MILLER STORY** • 1987
VERNI ZUSTANEME • 1945 • Weiss Jiri • DOC • CZC • INTERIM BALANCE
VERNICHTUNG DER MENSCHHEIT, DIE see **HOMUNCULUS 5** • 1917
VERNISSAGE • 1950 • D'Avino Carmen • FRN
VERNON, THE BOUNTIFUL • 1917 • Wright Fred E. • SHT • USA
VERNON'S AUNT • 1930 • Edwards Harry J. • SHT • USA
VERNOST • 1965 • Todorovsky Petr • USS • FAITHFULNESS ○ FIDELITY
VERNOST MATERI see **VYERNOST MATERI** • 1967
VERNYE DRUZYA • 1954 • Kalatozov Mikhail • USS • FAITHFUL FRIENDS ○ CLOSE FRIENDS ○ TRUE FRIENDS ○ LOYAL FRIENDS
VERO E IL FALSO, IL • 1972 • Visconti Eriprando • ITL
VERONA TRIAL, THE see **PROCESSO DI VERONA, IL** • 1962
VERONICA • 1972 • Bostan Elisabeta • RMN
VERONICA • 1977 • Shaffer Beverly • DOC • CND
VERONICA COMES BACK see **VERONICA SE INTOARCE** • 1973
VERONICA KISS • Stevens Mark • USA
VERONICA SE INTOARCE • 1973 • Bostan Elisabeta • RMN • VERONICA COMES BACK
VERONICA TENNANT • 1970 • Bonniere Rene • DCS • CND
VERONICA VOSS see **SEHNSUCHT DER VERONIKA VOSS, DIE** • 1982
VERONICAS SVEDEDUG • 1977 • Rex Jytte • DNM • VERONICA'S VEIL
VERONICA'S VEIL see **VERONICAS SVEDEDUG** • 1977
VERONIKA • 1985 • Vavra Otakar, Macak Jiri • CZC
VERONIKA, DIE MAGD see **WAS DAS HERZ BEFIELT** • 1951
VERONIQUE • 1949 • Vernay Robert • FRN
VERONIQUE • Antoine Jean • SRL • BLG
VERONIQUE ET SON CANCRE • 1958 • Rohmer Eric • SHT • FRN
VERONIQUE NIQUE NIQUE • 1978 • Love John • FRN
VERONIQUE OU L'ETE DE MES 13 ANS • 1974 • Guilmain Claudine • FRN
VERPFUSCHTE HOCHZEITSNACHT, DIE • 1957 • Schleif Wolfgang • FRG
VERRAT AN DEUTSCHLAND • 1955 • Harlan Veit • FRG
VERRAT AUF SCHLOSS TREUENFELS • 1921 • *Kaiser-Titz Erich* • FRG
VERRAT DER GRAFIN LEONIE, DER • 1919 • Justitz Emil • FRG
VERRAT IST KEIN GESELLSCHAFTSSPIEL • 1972 • Staudte Wolfgang • MTV • FRG
VERRAT UND SUHNE • 1923 • *Max Mack-Film* • FRG
VERRATER • 1936 • Ritter Karl • FRG • TRAITORS
VERRATER, DER • 1918 • Boese Carl • FRG
VERRATERIN, DIE • 1911 • Gad Urban • FRG
VERRATEROR, DAS (FRG) see **TRAITOR'S GATE** • 1964
VERROHUNG DES FRANZ BLUM, DIE • 1975 • Hauff Reinhard • FRG • BRUTALISATION OF FRANK BLUM, THE
VERRUCKTE FAMILIE, EINE see **HEUTE BLAU UND MORGEN BLAU** • 1957
VERRUCKTE HOTELZIMMER, DAS • 1918 • Dessauer Siegfried • FRG
VERRUCKTESTE AUTO DER WELT, DAS • 1974 • Zehetgruber Rudolf • FRG • MADDEST CAR IN THE WORLD, THE
VERRUFENEN, DIE • 1925 • Lamprecht Gerhard • FRG • FUNFTE STAND, DER ○ SLUMS OF BERLIN
VERS DE LA GRAPPE, LES • 1955 • Tadie, Lacoste • SHT • FRN
VERS LA COMPETENCE • 1955 • Proulx Maurice • DCS • CND
VERS LA LUMIERE • 1922 • Protazanov Yakov • FRN
VERS L'ABIME • 1934 • Veber Serge, Steinhoff Hans • FRN
VERS L'AVENIR • 1947 • Blais Roger • DCS • CND
VERS LE TRAVAIL • 1916 • Burguet Charles • FRN
VERS L'EXTASE • 1960 • Wheeler Rene • FRN • EXTASE, L'
VERS L'ILE DRAGON see **ILE DES DRAGONS, L'** • 1973
VERS L'IMMORTALITE • 1911 • *Gaumont* • FRN • ELIXIR OF LIFE, THE
VERS L'INCONNU see **NAHWA AL-MAJHUL** • 1960
VERSAILLES • Macovet S. • FRN
VERSAILLES • 1929 • Tayer Elaine • DOC • FRN
VERSAILLES • 1966 • Lamorisse Albert • DOC • FRN
VERSAILLES AFFAIR, THE see **MONSIEUR SUZUKI** • 1959
VERSAILLES NO BARA see **BERUSAIYU NO BARA** • 1978
VERSAILLES (UKN) see **SI VERSAILLES M'ETAIT CONTE** • 1955
VERSATILE LOVERS • 1975 • Chenal Pierre • FRN, ITL
VERSATILE VILLAIN, A • 1915 • Frazee Edwin • USA
VERSCHLEIERTE, DIE • 1920 • Bruck Reinhard • FRG
VERSCHLEIERTE BILD VON GROSZ-KLEINDORF, DER • 1913 • May Joe • FRG
VERSCHLEIERTE DAME, DIE • 1915 • Oswald Richard • FRG
VERSCHLEIERTE MAJA, DIE • 1951 • von Cziffra Geza • FRG
VERSCHLEPPT • 1919 • Boese Carl • FRG
VERSCHLOSSENE TUR, DIE • 1917 • Gad Urban • FRG
VERSCHLUNGENE WEGE • 1919 • *Madeleine Magda* • FRG
VERSCHNEIT • 1920 • Fleck Jacob, Fleck Luise • AUS
VERSCHOLLENE, DER • *Liedtke Harry* • FRG
VERSCHWENDER, DER • 1917 • Fleck Jacob, Fleck Luise • AUS
VERSCHWENDER, DER • 1953 • Hainisch Leopold • AUS
VERSCHWENDER, DER • 1964 • Meisel Kurt • AUS
VERSCHWORUNG ZU GENUA, DIE • 1920 • Leni Paul • FRG • FIESCO
VERSCHWUNDENE FRAU, DIE • 1937 • Emo E. W. • AUS
VERSCHWUNDENE HAUS, DAS • 1922 • Piel Harry • FRG
VERSCHWUNDENE LOS, DAS • 1915 • Piel Harry • FRG
VERSCHWUNDENE MILLION, DIE see **APACHENRACHE 3** • 1920
VERSCHWUNDENE MINIATUR, DIE • 1954 • Schroth Carl-Heinz • FRG
VERSCHWUNDENE TESTAMENT, DAS • 1929 • Randolf Rolf • FRG
VERSCHWUNDENE UNTERSEEBOOT, DAS • 1915 • Schmidthassler Walter? • FRG
VERSE AND WORSE • 1921 • Enright Ray • SHT • USA
VERSIEGELTE LIPPEN • 1917 • Del Zopp Rudolf • FRG
VERSIONE INTEGRALE • 1976 • Russo Nino • ITL
VERSO LA VITA • 1946 • Risi Dino • SHT • ITL
VERSPATUNG IN MARIENBORN (FRG) see **TRAIN DE BERLIN EST ARRETE** • 1964
VERSPIELTES LEBEN • 1949 • Meisel Kurt • FRG • ULYSSA
VERSPREIDING VAN DE VLAAMSE KUNST OVER DE WERELD • 1971 • Degelin Emile • BLG
VERSPRICH MIR NICHTS • 1937 • Liebeneiner Wolfgang • FRG • PROMISE ME NOTHING (USA)
VERSTANDIGUNG • 1965 • *Houwer Rob (P)* • FRG
VERSTECKT (FRG) see **FORBIDDEN** • 1986
VERSUCH ZU LEBEN, DER • 1984 • Feindt Johann • FRG • TRYING TO LIVE
VERSUCHEN SIE MEINE SCHWESTER • 1930 • Lamac Carl • FRG, CZC
VERSUCHUNG • 1955 • Fuchs Friedrich J. • FRG
VERSUCHUNG • 1981 • Zanussi Krzysztof • FRG
VERSUCHUNG IM SOMMERWIND • 1973 • Thiele Rolf • FRG
VERSUNKENE FLOTTE, DIE • 1926 • Noa Manfred • FRG
VERSUNKENE WELT, EINE • 1922 • Korda Alexander • AUS • TRAGODIE EINES VERSCHOLLENEN FURSTENSOHNES, DIE ○ VANISHED WORLD
VERSUNKENE WELTEN • 1922 • Philippi Siegfried • FRG
VERSUS SLEDGEHAMMERS • 1915 • *Edison* • USA
VERSZERZODES • 1983 • Dobray Gyorgy • HNG • BLOOD BROTHERS
VERT GALANT, LE • 1925 • Leprince Rene • FRN
VERTAGTE HOCHZEITSNACHT, DIE • 1924 • Berger Josef • FRG
VERTAGTE HOCHZEITSNACHT, DIE • 1953 • Kulb Karl G. • FRG
VERTAUSCHTE BRAUT, DIE • 1916 • *Krauss Werner* • FRG
VERTAUSCHTE BRAUT, DIE • 1925 • Wilhelm Carl • FRG
VERTAUSCHTE BRAUT, DIE • 1934 • Lamac Carl • FRG
VERTAUSCHTE GESICHTER • 1929 • Randolf Rolf • FRG
VERTAUSCHTE SEELEN • 1917 • Oberlander Hans • FRG
VERTAUSCHTES LEBEN • 1961 • Weiss Helmut • FRG
VERTE MOISSON, LA • 1959 • Villiers Francois • FRN
VERTEIDIGER HAT DAS WORT, DER • 1944 • Klinger Werner • FRG
VERTEIDIGERIN, DIE • 1918 • Halm Alfred • FRG
VERTEIDIGERIN, DIE • 1923 • *Berliner Film-Manufaktur* • FRG
VERTICAL ACCENT, A • 1979 • Crama Nico • SHT • NTH
VERTICAL CLIMB see **VERTIKAL** • 1967
VERTICAL FEATURES REMAKE • 1978 • Greenaway Peter • UKN
VERTICAL LINES see **LINES VERTICAL** • 1960
VERTICAL SMILE, THE see **SOURIRE VERTICAL, LE** • 1973
VERTIENTE, LA • 1958 • Ruiz Jorge • DOC • BLV • SOURCE, THE
VERTIGE see **VERTIGINE** • 1968
VERTIGE, LE • 1926 • L'Herbier Marcel • FRN
VERTIGE, LE • 1935 • Schiller Paul • FRN
VERTIGE, LE • 1972 • Adam Jean-Francois • FRN
VERTIGE D'UN SOIR see **PEUR, LA** • 1936
VERTIGE POUR UN TUEUR • 1970 • Desagnat Jean-Pierre • FRN, ITL • VERTIGINE PER UN ASSASSINO (ITL)
VERTIGES • 1946 • Pottier Richard • FRN • HEURE DU DESTIN, L'
VERTIGES • 1984 • Laurent • FRN
VERTIGINE • 1919 • Negroni Baldassare • ITL
VERTIGINE • 1942 • Brignone Guido • ITL, FRG • TRAGODIE EINER LIEBE (FRG)
VERTIGINE • 1968 • Beaudin Jean • CND • VERTIGE
VERTIGINE BIANCA • 1956 • Ferroni Giorgio • DOC • ITL
VERTIGINE D'AMORE • 1951 • Capuano Luigi • ITL
VERTIGINE PER UN ASSASSINO (ITL) see **VERTIGE POUR UN TUEUR** • 1970
VERTIGO • 1945 • Momplet Antonio • MXC
VERTIGO • 1950 • Ardavin Eusebio F. • SPN
VERTIGO • 1958 • Hitchcock Alfred • USA
VERTIGO see **ZAVRAT** • 1962
VERTIGO DEL CRIMEN, EL • 1970 • Cervera Pascual • SPN
VERTIGO IN MANHATTAN • 1980 • Herralde Gonzalo • SPN, USA • JET LAG (USA)
VERTIKAL • 1967 • Gororukhin Stanislav, Durov Boris • USS • VERTICAL CLIMB
VERTRAUMTE TAGE • 1951 • Reinert Emile Edwin • FRG, FRN • AIGULLE ROUGE, L' (FRN)
VERTREIBUNG AUS DEM PARADIES, DIE • 1977 • Schilling Niklaus • FRG • EXPULSION FROM PARADISE
VERTU DE LUCETTE, LA • 1912 • Feuillade Louis • FRN
VERUCKTE TESTAMENT, DAS see **ALLES WEG'N DEM HUND** • 1935
VERUNTREUTE HIMMEL, DER • 1958 • Marischka Ernst • FRG • EMBEZZLED HEAVEN (USA)
VERURTEILTE DORF, DAS • 1951 • Hellberg Martin • GDR • CONDEMNED VILLAGE, THE
VERUSCHKA • 1971 • Rubartelli Franco • ITL
VERVLAKSTE TWEELING, DIE • 1969 • SAF
VERWANDLUNG, DIE • 1920 • Martin Karl Heinz • FRG
VERWANDTE SIND AUCH MENSCHEN • 1939 • Deppe Hans • FRG
VERWEHTE SPUREN • 1938 • Harlan Veit • FRG • FOOTPRINTS BLOW AWAY, THE
VERWEHTE SPUREN see **AUF GEFAHRLICHEN SPUREN** • 1924
VERWEIGERUNG, DIE see **FALL JAGERSTATTER, DER** • 1972
VERWIRRUNG DER LIEBE • 1959 • Dudow Slatan • GDR • LOVE'S CONFUSION ○ CRAZINESS OF LOVE
VERWORDING VAN HERMAN DURER, DE • 1979 • van der Velde Jean, Seegers Rene, de Winter Leon • NTH • DEMISE OF HERMAN DURER, THE
VERWORFENE, DIE • 1917 • Moest Hubert • FRG
VERWORRENE WEGE • 1918 • Illes Eugen • FRG
VERWUNDBAREN, DIE • 1967 • Tichat Leo • AUS • VULNERABLE ONES, THE ○ ENGEL DER LUST ○ ANGEL OF LUST
VERWUNDSCHENE PRINZESSIN, DIE • 1919 • Lund Erik • FRG
VERWUNSCHENE SCHLOSS, DAS • 1918 • Rippert Otto • FRG
VERY BIG WITHDRAWAL, A • 1979 • Black Noel • USA, CND • MAN, A WOMAN AND A BANK, A
VERY BRADY CHRISTMAS, A • 1988 • Baldwin Peter • TVM • USA
VERY BUSY GENTLEMEN see **PAN NA ROZTRHANI** • 1934
VERY CLOSE ENCOUNTERS OF THE FOURTH KIND see **INCONTRI MOLTO.. RAVVICINATI DEL QUARTO TIPO** • 1978
VERY CLOSE QUARTERS • 1986 • Rif Vladimir • USA
VERY CONFIDENTIAL • 1927 • Tinling James • USA
VERY CRAZY LOVER, A see **AMANTE MUITO LOUCA** • 1980
VERY CURIOUS GIRL, A (USA) see **FIANCEE DU PIRATE, LA** • 1969
VERY EDGE, THE • 1963 • Frankel Cyril • UKN
VERY ENGLISH MURDER, A • 1975 • Samsonov Samson • USS
VERY EYE OF NIGHT, THE • 1956 • Deren Maya • SHT • USA
VERY FRIENDLY NEIGHBORS, THE • 1969 • Zugsmith Albert • USA • FRIENDLY NEIGHBORS
VERY GOOD YOUNG MAN, A • 1919 • Crisp Donald • USA

VERY GRIM FAIRY TALES • 1969 • Gangler Tod, Seder Rufus • SHT • USA
VERY HANDY MAN, A (USA) see **LIOLA** • 1964
VERY HAPPY ALEXANDER (USA) see **ALEXANDRE LE BIENHEUREUX** • 1968
VERY HEAVY METAL see **RIDING HIGH** • 1980
VERY HONORABLE GUY, A • 1934 • Bacon Lloyd • USA • VERY HONOURABLE MAN, A (UKN)
VERY HONOURABLE MAN, A (UKN) see **VERY HONORABLE GUY, A** • 1934
VERY IDEA, THE • 1920 • Windom Lawrence C. • USA
VERY IDEA, THE • 1929 • Rosson Richard • USA
VERY IMPORTANT PERSON • 1961 • Annakin Ken • UKN • COMING OUT PARTY, A (USA)
VERY LAST DAY, THE • 1973 • Ulyanov Mikhail • USS
VERY LATE FOR TEARS see **POLI ARGA YIA DHAKRIA** • 1968
VERY LIKE A WHALE • 1980 • Bridges Alan • TVM • UKN
VERY MERRY CRICKET, A • 1971 • Jones Charles M. • ANS • USA
VERY MISSING PERSON, A • 1972 • Mayberry Russ • TVM • USA
VERY MORAL NIGHT, A see **ERKOLCSOS EJSZAKA, EGY** • 1978
VERY MUCH ALIVE • 1914 • *Mace Fred* • USA
VERY MUCH ENGAGED • 1912 • *Edison* • USA
VERY NAKED CANVAS, THE • 1965 • Jacobsen Jerome • USA
VERY NATURAL THING, A • 1974 • Larkin Christopher • USA
VERY NICE VERY NICE • 1961 • Lipsett Arthur • SHT • CND
VERY POWERFUL VOICE, A • 1911 • Fitzhamon Lewin • UKN
VERY PRIVATE AFFAIR, A (USA) see **VIE PRIVEE, LA** • 1962
VERY PRIVATE MATTER, A see **ASSUNTO MUITO PARTICULAR, UM** • 1984
VERY PRIVATE PARTY, A • 1975 • Fournier Roger • FRN
VERY RICH MAN, A see **THAT WAY WITH WOMEN** • 1947
VERY SILENT TRAVELLER, THE • 1955 • MacDonald David • UKN
VERY SMALL FAUST, THE see **TOUT PETIT FAUST, LE** • 1910
VERY SPECIAL FAVOR, A • 1965 • Gordon Michael • USA • FAVOR, THE
VERY THOUGHT OF YOU, THE • 1944 • Daves Delmer • USA
VERY TRULY YOURS • 1922 • Beaumont Harry • USA
VERY YOUNG LADY, A • 1941 • Schuster Harold • USA
VERY YOUNG PIONEER, A see **SAMII YUNII PIONER** • 1925
VERZAUBERTE TAG, DER • 1944 • Pewas Peter • FRG
VERZAUBERTE WALD, DER • 1928 • Starevitch Ladislas • ANS • FRG • ENCHANTED FOREST, THE (USA)
VERZEIHUNG, SEHEN SIE FUSSBALL • 1983 • GDR • EXCUSE ME, ARE YOU WATCHING FOOTBALL?
VES V POHRANICI • 1948 • Krejcik Jiri • CZC • VILLAGE ON THE FRONTIER, THE
VESELAYA KANAREIKA • 1929 • Kuleshov Lev • USS • HAPPY CANARY, THE ◦ GAY CANARY, THE
VESELE VANOCE ANEB KARLIKOVO ZIMNI DOBRODRUZSTVI • Novak Ilya • ANM • CZC • MERRY CHRISTMAS OR KARLIK'S WINTER ADVENTURE
VESELI DOZIVLJAJ • 1951 • Neugebauer Walter • YGS
VESELICA • 1960 • Babic Joze • YGS • PARTY, THE
VESELY CIRKUS • 1951 • Trnka Jiri • ANS • CZC • HAPPY CIRCUS, THE ◦ MERRY CIRCUS, THE ◦ CIRCUS
VESELYE RASPLIUYEVSKIE DNI see **VESYOLYYE RASPLYUYEVSKIYE DNI** • 1966
VESEL'YE SCENKI IZ ZIZNI ZIVOTNYCH see **GAUDEAMUS** • 1912
VESENNIE GOLOSA • 1955 • Ryazanov Eldar, Gurov S. • USS • SPRING VOICES (USA) ◦ VOICES OF SPRING
VESENNYAYA OLYMPIADA ILI NACHALNIK KHORA • 1980 • Magiton Isaac, Chulyukin Yuri • USS • SPRING OLYMPICS, OR THE CHOIR CHIEF, THE
VESGATHTHO • 1970 • Obeyesekara Vasantha • SLN
VESIKALI YARIM • 1968 • Akat Lutfu • TRK • MY SYNDICATED LOVE ◦ MY WOMAN
VESNA • 1947 • Alexandrov Grigori • USS • SPRING (USA) ◦ SPRINGTIME
VESNA NA ODERYE • 1968 • Saakov Leon • USS • SPRING ON THE ODER
VESNA NA ZARECHNOI ULITSE • 1956 • Khutsiev Marlen, Mironer Felix • USS • SPRING ON ZARECHNAYA STREET ◦ SPRING IN ZARECHNAYA STREET
VESNA V MOSKVE • 1953 • Heifitz Josif, Zarkhi Alexander • USS • SPRING IN MOSCOW
VESNICE NA ROZCESTI • 1945 • Makovec Milos • DOC • CZC
VESNICKO MA STREDISKOVA • 1985 • Menzel Jiri • CZC • MY SWEET LITTLE VILLAGE ◦ MY SWEET VILLAGE
VESNOY • 1929 • Kaufman Mikhail • USS • SPRINGTIME ◦ SPRING
VESPRO SICILIANO • 1950 • Pastina Giorgio • ITL
VESSEL OF SAND, A see **SUNA NO UTSUWA** • 1974
VESSEL OF WRATH • 1938 • Pommer Erich • UKN • BEACHCOMBER, THE (USA)
VESSIOLAIA KANAREIKA • 1929 • *Pudovkin V. I.* • USS • CHEERFUL CANARY, THE
VESTA VICTORIA AS GRACE DARLING • 1902 • *Warwick Trading Co* • UKN
VESTALE DU GANGE, LA • 1927 • Hugon Andre • FRN • TEMPLE OF SHADOWS, THE
VESTER VOV VOV • 1927 • Holger-Madsen • DNM
VESTERHAVSDRENGE • 1950 • Henning-Jensen Astrid, Henning-Jensen Bjarne • DNM • BOYS FROM THE WEST COAST
VESTIDA DE AZUL • 1984 • Gimenez-Rico Antonio • SPN • DRESSED IN BLUE
VESTIDA DE NOVIA • 1966 • Mariscal Ana • SPN • OJOS VERDES ◦ DRESSED AS A BRIDE
VESTIDAS Y ALBOROTADAS • 1968 • Morayta Miguel • MXC • THEY WERE LEFT JUST BEFORE MARRIAGE
VESTIDO DE NOVIA, EL • 1958 • Alazraki Benito • MXC
VESTIGE, A see **OMOKAGE** • 1948
VESTIRE GLI IGNUDI • 1954 • Pagliero Marcello • ITL, FRN • VETIR CEUX QUI SONT NUS
VESTIRE GLI IGNUDI • 1979 • D'Amico Luigi Filippo • ITL
VESUVIUS EXPRESS • 1953 • Lang Otto • SHT • USA
VESYOLY MUSIKANTY • 1937 • Ptushko Alexander • ANS • USS • JOLLY MUSICIANS, THE
VESYOLYE REBYATA • 1934 • Alexandrov Grigori • USS • MOSCOW LAUGHS (USA) ◦ JOLLY FELLOWS, THE ◦ JAZZ COMEDY
VESYOLYYE RASPLYUYEVSKIYE DNI • 1966 • Garin Erast • USS • THOSE CRAZY RASPLYUYEV DAYS ◦ VESELYE RASPLIUYEVSKIE DNI ◦ MERRY RASPLYUYEV DAYS ◦ RASPLYUYEV'S GAY DAYS ◦ GAY RASPLYEV DAYS
VESZPREM –CITY OF BELLS see **HARANGOK VAROSA – VESZPREM** • 1966
VET IN THE DOGHOUSE see **IN THE DOGHOUSE** • 1961
VETAR U MREZI • 1989 • Robar-Dorin Filip • YGS • WIND IN THE NET, THE ◦ WIND IN THE WEB, THE
VETEMENTS CASCADEURS, LES • 1908 • Durand Jean • FRN
VETEMENTS SIGRAND, LES • 1938 • Alexeieff Alexandre • SHT • FRN
VETER • 1959 • Alov Alexander, Naumov Vladimir • USS • WIND, THE
VETER S VOSTOKA • 1941 • Room Abram • USS • WIND FROM THE EAST
VETER V LITSO • 1929 • Heifitz Josif, Zarkhi Alexander • USS • FACING THE WIND ◦ WIND IN THE FACE ◦ HEAD WIND, A
VETERAN, THE • 1913 • *Broncho* • USA
VETERAN, THE • 1926 • Croise Hugh • UKN
VETERAN, THE see **DEATHDREAM** • 1972
VETERAN OF THE G.A.R., A • 1910 • *Lubin* • USA
VETERAN OF WATERLOO, THE • 1933 • Bramble A. V. • UKN
VETERAN POLICE HORSE, THE • 1913 • *Thanhouser* • USA
VETERAN SWORD, THE • 1914 • *Princess* • USA
VETERANS, THE • 1973 • Mason Bill • DOC • UKN
VETERAN'S MASCOT, THE • 1913 • *Solax* • USA
VETERAN'S PENSION, THE • 1911 • Wilson Frank? • UKN
VETERAN'S STORY, A • 1909 • *Empire Films* • UKN
VETERINARY SURGEON'S FOSTER-CHILD, THE see **DYRLAEGENS PLEJEBORN** • 1968
VETIR CEUX QUI SONT NUS see **VESTIRE GLI IGNUDI** • 1954
VETRNE MORE • 1973 • Kuliev Eldar • CZC, USS • WINDY SEA, THE
VETTA • 1957 • Donner Jorn • SHT • FNL • WATER
VETTER AUS DINGSDA, DER • 1934 • Zoch Georg • FRG
VETTER AUS DINGSDA, DER • 1953 • Anton Karl • FRG
VETTER AUS MEXIKO, DER • 1917 • *Rieck Arnold* • FRG
VETTURALE DEL MONCENISIO, IL • 1926 • Negroni Baldassare • ITL
VETTURALE DEL MONCENISIO, IL • 1956 • Brignone Guido • ITL
VETTURALE DEL SAN GOTTARDO, IL • 1942 • Illuminati Ivo, Hinrich Hans • ITL
VEUVE, LA see **VEDOVA X, LA** • 1956
VEUVE CELIBATAIRE, LA see **EPOUX CELEBATAIRES, LES** • 1935
VEUVE COUDERC, LE • 1971 • Granier-Deferre Pierre • FRN, ITL • EVASO, L' (ITL) ◦ WIDOW COUDERC, THE (USA)
VEUVE EN OR, UNE • 1969 • Audiard Michel • FRN, ITL, FRG • VEDOVA TUTTA D'ORO, UNA (ITL)
VEUVE ET L'INNOCENT, LA • 1948 • Cerf Andre • FRN
VEUVE JOYEUSE, LA • 1913 • Chautard Emile • FRN
VEUVE JOYEUSE, LA • 1934 • Lubitsch Ernst • FRN
VEUVE LUBRIQUE, LA • 1975 • Benazeraf Jose • FRN
VEUVES DE QUINZE ANS, LES see **ADOLESCENTI, LE** • 1964
VEUVES EN CHALEUR, LES • 1978 • Bernard-Aubert Claude • FRN
VEUX-TU REPARER MA MAISON • 1973 • Duceppe Pierre • SHT • CND
VEZ ANO SER HIPPY NO HACE DANO, UNA • 1969 • Aguirre Javier • SPN
VEZANI METCHTI • 1956 • Topaldgikov Stefan • BUL • EMBROIDERED DREAMS
VEZEN NO BEZDEZE • 1932 • Vladimirov • CZC • PRISONER OF BEZDEZ, THE
VEZLA DAMA ZAVAZADLA • 1965 • Karpas Jan • ANS • CZC • LADY AND HER LUGGAGE, THE
VI BEHOVER VARANN • 1943 • Faustman Erik • SWD • WE NEED EACH OTHER
VI ER ALLE BROILERE • Greve Bruno • SHT • NRW • WE ARE ALL BROTHERS
VI FIXAR ALLT • 1961 • Frisk Ragnar • SWD
VI FLYGER PA RIO • 1949 • Ohberg Ake • SWD, NRW • VI FLYR PA RIO (NRW) ◦ DESTINATION RIO
VI FLYR PA RIO (NRW) see **VI FLYGER PA RIO** • 1949
VI GAR LANDSVAGEN • 1937 • Wallen Sigurd • SWD • WALKING ALONG THE MAIN ROAD
VI HAENGER I EN TRAD • 1962 • Roos Jorgen • DOC • DNM • WE HANG FROM A THREAD
VI HEMSLAVINNOR • 1942 • Bauman Schamyl • SWD • HEMSLAVINNOR ◦ WE HOUSEMAIDS
VI JUEGOS PANAMERICANOS • 1971 • Fraga Jorge • DOC • CUB
VI MASTHUGGSPOJKAR • 1940 • Jerring Nils • SWD
VI MOTTE STORMEN • 1943 • Janzon Bengt • SWD • WE MET THE STORM
VI OF SMITH'S ALLEY • 1921 • West Walter • UKN
VI PA SALTKRAKAN • 1968 • Hellbom Olle • SWD • WE ON THE ISLAND OF SALTKRAKAN
VI PA SOLGLANTAN • 1939 • Olsson Gunnar • SWD • WE AT SOLGLANTAN (USA) ◦ WE FROM SUNNY GLADE
VI PA VADDO • 1958 • Spjuth Arthur • SWD • WE ON VADDO
VI REDD SEPTET • 1962 • Binder Steve • SHT • USA
VI SOM GAR KOKKENVEIEN (NRW) see **VI SOM GAR KOKSVAGEN** • 1932
VI SOM GAR KOKSVAGEN • 1932 • Molander Gustaf • SWD, NRW • VI SOM GAR KOKKENVEIEN (NRW) ◦ WE GO THROUGH THE KITCHEN
VI SOM GAR SCENVAGEN • 1938 • Wahlberg Gideon • SWD • WE FROM THE THEATRE
VI SPILLOPPER • 1979 • Bohwim Knut • NRW • FLEA IN THE EAR
VI TRE • 1940 • Bauman Schamyl • SWD • THREE OF US, THE
VI TRE DEBUTERA • 1953 • Ekman Hasse • SWD • WE THREE ARE MAKING OUR DEBUT ◦ WE THREE DEBUTANTES
VI TVA • 1930 • Brunius John W. • SWD
VI TVA • 1939 • Bauman Schamyl • SWD • WE TWO (USA) ◦ TWO OF US, THE
VI VAR NAGRA MAN • 1953 • Jute Alex • SWD
VI VIL HA ET BARN • 1949 • O'Fredericks Alice, Lauritzen Lau Jr. • DNM • WE WANT A BABY ◦ WE WANT A CHILD
VIA BORDUAS • 1968 • Belanger Fernand • CND
VIA BUENOS AIRES see **FRANCO DE PORT** • 1937
VIA CABARET • 1913 • Reid Wallace • USA
VIA COL PARA.. VENTO • 1958 • Costa Mario • ITL
VIA CRUCIS • 1918 • Blom August • DNM • GET THEE BEHIND ME
VIA DEGLI SPECCHI • 1983 • Gagliardo Giovanna • ITL • MIRRORS' STREET
VIA DEI BABBUINI, LA • 1974 • Magni Luigi • ITL
VIA DEI CAPELLARI see **LUCIANO (VIA DEI CAPELLARI)** • 1960
VIA DEI CESSATI SPIRITI • 1959 • Baldi Gian Vittorio • ITL
VIA DEL EXITO, LA • 1977 • Punceles Manuel Diaz • VNZ • ROAD TO SUCCESS, THE
VIA DEL PECCATO, LA • 1924 • Palermi Amleto • ITL
VIA DEL PETROLIO, LA • 1965 • Bertolucci Bernardo • MTV • ITL
VIA DEL RHUM, LA (ITL) see **BOULEVARD DU RHUM** • 1971
VIA DEL SUCCESSO CON LE DONNE, LA see **IO PIACCIO** • 1955
VIA DEL SUD, LA • 1953 • Cappellini Enrico • ITL
VIA DELLA DROGA, LA • 1977 • Castellari Enzo G. • ITL
VIA DELLA PROSTITUZIONE, LA • 1978 • D'Amato Joe • ITL • EMMANUELLE AND THE WHITE SLAVE TRADE ◦ EMMANUELLE AND THE WHITE SLAVE TRADERS
VIA DELLE CINQUE LUNE • 1942 • Chiarini Luigi • ITL
VIA DOLOROSA, LA • 1919 • Lolli Alberto Carlo • ITL
VIA EMILIA KM 147 • 1949 • Lizzani Carlo • DOC • ITL
VIA EROTICA 6 • 1967 • Fronz Fritz • AUS
VIA FAST FREIGHT see **FAST FREIGHT, THE** • 1921
VIA LATTEA, LA (ITL) see **VOIE LACTEE, LA** • 1968
VIA LIBRE • 1969 • Giral Sergio • SHT • CUB
VIA LIBRE A LA ZAFRA DEL '64 • 1964 • Alvarez Santiago • DOC • CUB • GREEN LIGHT FOR THE 1964 SUGAR CROP
VIA MACAO • 1965 • Leduc Jean • FRN, PRT
VIA MALA • 1944 • von Baky Josef • FRG • STRASSE DES BOSEN, DIE
VIA MALA • 1961 • May Paul • FRG
VIA MARGUTTA • 1960 • Camerini Mario • ITL, FRN • RUE DES AMOURS FACILES, LA (FRN) ◦ RUN WITH THE DEVIL (USA)
VIA PADOVA 46 • 1954 • Bianchi Giorgio • ITL • SCOCCIATORE, LO
VIA PIU LUNGA, LA • 1917 • Caserini Mario • ITL
VIA POLE NORD • 1954 • Ichac Marcel • DCS • FRN
VIA PONY EXPRESS • 1933 • Collins Lewis D. • USA
VIA RASELLA see **DIECI ITALIANI PER UN TEDESCO** • 1962
VIA THE FIRE ESCAPE • 1914 • Pollard Harry • USA
VIA VENETO • 1965 • Lipartiti Giuseppe • ITL, FRN
VIA WIRELESS • 1915 • Fitzmaurice George • USA
VIACCIA, LA • 1961 • Bolognini Mauro • ITL • LOVE MAKERS, THE ◦ BAD ROAD, THE
VIADUKT • 1983 • Simo Sandor • HNG, FRG, USA • SYLVESTER SYNDROME ◦ TRAIN KILLER, THE ◦ MATUSHKA
VIADUTO DE ALCANTARA • 1971 • de Almeida Manuel Faria • SHT • PRT
VIAGEM AO FIM DO MUNDO • 1968 • Campos Fernando Cony • BRZ • VOYAGE TO THE END OF THE WORLD
VIAGEM DO PRESIDENTE AO NORTE • 1962 • Queiroga Perdigao • SHT • PRT
VIAGEM DO SENHOR PRESIDENTE DA REPUBLICA A MADEIRA • 1955 • Ribeiro Antonio Lopes • SHT • PRT
VIAGEM DO TER • 1969 • Guimaraes Manuel • SHT • PRT
VIAGEM PRESIDENCIAL A ANGOLA • 1954 • Queiroga Perdigao • SHT • PRT
VIAGEM PRESIDENCIAL A INGLATERRA • 1955 • Ribeiro Antonio Lopes • SHT • PRT
VIAGEM PRESIDENCIAL A S. TOME • 1954 • Queiroga Perdigao • SHT • PRT
VIAGENS NA MINHA TERRA • 1980 • Guimaraes Dordio • PRT • JOURNEYS IN MY LAND
VIAGENS PRESIDENCIAIS • 1935 • Contreiras Anibal • SHT • PRT
VIAGER, LE • 1971 • Tchernia Pierre • FRN
VIAGGIATORE DI OGNISSANTI, IL • 1942 • Daquin Louis • ITL, FRN • VOYAGEUR DE LA TOUSSAINT, LE (FRN)
VIAGGIATORI DELLA SERA, I • 1979 • Tognazzi Ugo • ITL • TWILIGHT TRAVELLERS
VIAGGIO, IL • 1921 • Righelli Gennaro • ITL
VIAGGIO, IL • 1974 • De Sica Vittorio • ITL, FRN • JOURNEY, THE (UKN) ◦ VOYAGE, THE (USA) ◦ TRIP, THE
VIAGGIO A MOSCA see **MOSCA DI GIORNO E DI NOTTE** • 1961
VIAGGIO AL CENTRO DELLA LUNA • 1905 • Caserini Mario • SHT • ITL • VOYAGE TO THE CENTER OF THE MOON
VIAGGIO AL SUD • 1949 • Lizzani Carlo • DOC • ITL
VIAGGIO CON ANITA • 1979 • Monicelli Mario • ITL • LOVERS AND LIARS (USA) ◦ TRAVELS WITH ANITA ◦ TRIP WITH ANITA, A
VIAGGIO DE G. MASTORNA, IL • 1967 • Fellini Federico • ITL
VIAGGIO DEL SIGNOR PERRICHON, IL • 1944 • Moffa Paolo • ITL
VIAGGIO DI NOZZE ALL'80% see **OGGI SPOSI** • 1934
VIAGGIO DI NOZZE ALL'ITALIANA • 1965 • Amendola Mario • ITL, SPN • HONEYMOON, ITALIAN STYLE (UKN)
VIAGGIO DI UNA STELLA, IL • 1906 • Velle Gaston • FRN • VOYAGE AROUND A STAR, A (USA) ◦ VOYAGE DANS UNE ETOILE, LE ◦ AROUND A STAR ◦ VOYAGE TO A STAR ◦ TRIP TO A STAR ◦ VOYAGE AUTOUR D'UNE ETOILE
VIAGGIO IN ITALIA • 1953 • Rossellini Roberto • ITL, FRN • AMOUR EST LE PLUS FORT, L' (FRN) ◦ LONELY WOMAN, THE (UKN) ◦ STRANGERS, THE (USA) ◦ VOYAGE TO ITALY ◦ TRIP TO ITALY, A ◦ JOURNEY TO ITALY
VIAGGIO IN ORIENTE • 1953 • Saraceni Fausto • DOC • ITL
VIAGGIO VERSO IL SOLE see **PAZZA DI GIOIA** • 1940
VIAJE, EL • 1970 • Posani Clara • VNZ • VOYAGE, THE
VIAJE, EL • 1976 • *Conacite 1* • MXC

VIAJE A LA LUNA • 1903 • de Chomon Segundo • SPN • TRIP TO THE MOON, A (USA)
VIAJE A LA LUNA • 1957 • Cortes Fernando • MXC
VIAJE A NINGUNA PARTE, EL • 1986 • Fernan-Gomez Fernando • SPN • JOURNEY TO NOWHERE, THE
VIAJE AL CENTRO DE LA TIERRA • 1977 • Simon Piquer • SPN • FABULOUS JOURNEY TO THE CENTRE OF THE EARTH ○ WHERE TIME BEGAN (USA)
VIAJE AL VACIO • 1967 • Seto Javier • SPN
VIAJE DE NOVIOS • 1956 • Klimovsky Leon • SPN
VIAJE DE NOVIOS, UN • 1947 • Delgras Gonzalo • SPN
VIAJE DEL SENOR PRESIDENTE A MANZANILLO, EL • 1908 • Silva Gustavo • MXC
VIAJE FANTASTICO EN GLOBO • 1964 • Ardavin Cesar • SHT • SPN
VIAJE FANTASTICO EN GLOBO • 1974 • *Conacine* • MXC
VIAJE POR ARANJUEZ • 1969 • Ardavin Cesar • SHT • SPN
VIAJE REDONDO • 1919 • Ramos Jose Manuel • MXC
VIAJE SIN DESTINO • 1942 • Gil Rafael • SPN
VIAJE SIN REGRESO, EL • 1946 • Chenal Pierre • ARG
VIAJERA • 1951 • Patino Gomez Alfonso • MXC
VIAJEROS • 1990 • Montero Rafael • MXC • TRAVELLERS
VIAJES DE GULLIVER, LOS • 1976 • Delgado Cruz, de Font Antonio • ANM • SPN
VIAJES ESCOLARES, LOS • 1974 • Chavarri Jaime • SPN
VIALE DELLA CANZONE ,IL • 1965 • Piacentini Tullio • ITL
VIALE DELLE SPERANZA • 1953 • Risi Dino • ITL • HOPE AVENUE
VIANDE, LA • 1958 • Shawqi Khalil • SHT • EGY
VIAPORI –SUOMENLINNA • 1972 • Peippo Antti • FNL
VIAS PARALELAS • 1978 • Sanchez Christian • DOC • CHL • PARALLEL ROUTES
VIASMOS MIAS PATHENOU, O • 1967 • Jackson Stelios • GRC • RAPE OF A VIRGIN, THE
VIATA IN ROZ • 1969 • Pita Dan • SHT • RMN • LIFE IN PINK
VIATA INVINGE • 1951 • Negreanu Dinu • RMN • LIFE TRIUMPHS
VIATA NU IARTA • 1957 • Marcus Manole, Mihu Iulian • RMN • WHEN THE MIST IS LIFTING ○ LIFE DOESN'T SPARE
VIBES • 1988 • Kwapis Ken • USA
VIBES 1-2-3 • 1971 • Foldes Peter • ANM • USA
VIBORA CALIENTE • 1976 • Duran Rojas Fernando • MXC
VIBORAS CAMBIAN DE PIEL, LAS • 1973 • *Churubusco Azteca* • MXC
VIBRACIONES OSCILATORIAS • 1976 • Aguirre Javier • SHT • SPN
VIBRATION • 1984 • Stoyanov Todor • BUL
VIBRATION see **LEJONSOMMAR** • 1968
VIBRATIONS • Hurtado Angel • SHT • USA
VIBRATIONS • 1969 • Sarno Joe • USA • HER "THING".. VIBRATIONS
VIBRATIONS see **TARANG** • 1978
VIBRATIONS SEXUELLES • Rollin Jean • FRN
VIC DYSON PAYS • 1925 • Jaccard Jacques • USA
VICAR, THE see **KYRKOHERDEN** • 1970
VICAR OF BRAY, THE • 1937 • Edwards Henry • UKN
VICAR OF OLOT, THE see **VICARI D'OLOT, EL** • 1980
VICAR OF VEJLBY, THE see **PRAESTEN I VEJLBY** • 1920
VICAR OF WAKEFIELD, THE • 1910 • Marston Theodore • USA
VICAR OF WAKEFIELD, THE • 1912 • Powell Frank • UKN
VICAR OF WAKEFIELD, THE • 1913 • Douglas John • *Planet Films* • UKN
VICAR OF WAKEFIELD, THE • 1913 • Wilson Frank • *Hepworth* • UKN
VICAR OF WAKEFIELD, THE • 1916 • Paul Fred • UKN
VICAR OF WAKEFIELD, THE • 1917 • Warde Ernest C. • USA
VICARI D'OLOT, EL • 1980 • Pons Ventura • SPN • VICAR OF OLOT, THE
VICE AND VIRTUE: OR, THE TEMPTERS OF LONDON • 1915 • Weston Charles • UKN
VICE AND VIRTUE (USA) see **VICE ET LE VERTU, LE** • 1963
VICE DOLLS (USA) see **CLANDESTINES, LES** • 1954
VICE ET LA VERTU, LE • Lethem Roland • SHT • BLG
VICE ET LE VERTU, LE • 1963 • Vadim Roger • FRN, ITL • VIZIO E LA VIRTU, IL (ITL) ○ VICE AND VIRTUE (USA)
VICE GIRLS, LTD. • 1964 • Chaudhri Amin • USA
VICE OF FOOLS, THE • 1920 • Griffith Edward H. • USA
VICE OF SEX see **SEI NO AKUTOKU** • 1968
VICE-PRESIDENT ELECT FAIRBANKS • 1905 • Melies Gaston • USA
VICE RAID • 1959 • Cahn Edward L. • USA
VICE SQUAD • 1931 • Cromwell John • USA
VICE SQUAD • 1953 • Laven Arnold • USA • GIRL IN ROOM 17, THE (UKN)
VICE SQUAD • 1982 • Sherman Gary • USA
VICE VERSA • 1910 • Aylott Dave • UKN
VICE VERSA • 1916 • Elvey Maurice • UKN
VICE VERSA • 1948 • Ustinov Peter • UKN
VICE VERSA! • 1970 • Findlay Michael • USA
VICE VERSA • 1988 • Gilbert Brian • USA
VICE VERSA: OR, THE TABLES TURNED see **TIT FOR TAT** • 1916
VICES AND PLEASURES see **VIZI PRIVATI –PUBBLICHE VIRTU** • 1976
VICES IN THE FAMILY (UKN) see **VIZIO DI FAMIGLIA, IL** • 1975
VICHINGO VENUTO DAL SUD, IL • 1971 • Steno • ITL • VIKING WHO CAME FROM THE SOUTH, THE ○ BLONDE IN THE BLUE MOVIE, THE
VICHY 1969 see **A FLEUR D'EAU** • 1969
VICI BOUDA • 1987 • Chytilova Vera • CZC • WOLF'S HOLE
VICIADOS, OS • 1968 • Chediak Braz • BRZ • HOOKED, THE
VICIEUSE AMANDINE • Sanders Bob W. • FRN
VICIEUSE ET INSATISFAITE • 1977 • Kinaux Henri • FRN
VICINI DI CASA, IL • 1973 • Cozzi Luigi • MTV • ITL
VICINO A TE COL CUORE see **ANIMALI PAZZI** • 1939
VICIO Y LA VIRTUD, EL • 1975 • Lara Polop Francisco • SPN
VICIOUS • 1989 • Zwicky Karl • USA
VICIOUS BLONDE • 1968 • Lindus Allan • USA
VICIOUS BREED, THE • Ragneborn Arne • SWD
VICIOUS CIRCLE see **HUIS-CLOS** • 1954
VICIOUS CIRCLE, THE • 1948 • Wilder W. Lee • USA • WOMAN IN BROWN (UKN)
VICIOUS CIRCLE, THE • 1957 • Thomas Gerald • UKN • CIRCLE, THE (USA)
VICIOUS CIRCLE, THE see **ONDA CIRKELN, DEN** • 1967
VICIOUS CYCLES • 1969 • Brian David, Janson Len, Menville Chuck • SHT • USA
VICIOUS DOCTOR (PART 2) see **ZOKU AKUTOKUI (JOI-HEN)** • 1967
VICIOUS VIKING • 1967 • Smith Paul J. • ANS • USA
VICIOUS YEARS, THE • 1950 • Florey Robert • USA • GANGSTER WE MADE, THE (UKN)
VICISSITUDES OF A TOP HAT, THE • 1911 • Bouwmeester Theo • UKN
VICKI • 1953 • Horner Harry • USA
VICKI • 1970 • SAF
VICKY • 1973 • Bonniere Rene • CND
VICKY VAN • 1919 • Vignola Robert G. • USA • WOMAN NEXT DOOR, THE
VICOLO CIECO see **MORTE NON HA SESSO, LA** • 1968
VICOMTE DE BRAGELONNE, LE • 1954 • Cerchio Fernando • FRN, ITL • VISCONTE DI BRAGELONNE, IL (ITL) ○ LAST MUSKETEER, THE (USA) ○ VISCOUNT OF BRAGELONNE, THE ○ COUNT OF BRAGELONNE, THE
VICOMTE REGLE SES COMPTES, LE • 1967 • Cloche Maurice • FRN, ITL, SPN • THE VISCOUNT, FURTO ALLA BANCA MONDIALE (ITL) ○ ATRACO AL HAMPA (SPN) ○ AVENTURAS DEL VIZCONDE, LAS ○ VISCOUNT, THE (USA) ○ AVENTURES DU VICOMTE, LES
VICTIM • 1961 • Dearden Basil • UKN
VICTIM, THE • 1915 • Siegmann George • USA
VICTIM, THE • 1916 • Davis Will S. • USA
VICTIM, THE • 1917 • Levering Joseph • USA
VICTIM, THE • *Cheung Yick* • HKG
VICTIM, THE • 1972 • Daugherty Herschel • TVM • USA • OUT OF CONTENTION
VICTIM, THE • 1975 • Cronenberg David • CND
VICTIM, THE see **DAMNED DON'T CRY, THE** • 1950
VICTIM, THE see **ALDOZAT, AZ** • 1980
VICTIM: ANATOMY OF A MUGGING, THE see **ACT OF VIOLENCE** • 1979
VICTIM FIVE • 1964 • Lynn Robert • UKN • CODE 7.. VICTIM 5 (USA)
VICTIM OF A CHARACTER, THE see **POTIFARS HUSTRU** • 1911
VICTIM OF A CRISIS • 1909 • *Tiger* • USA
VICTIM OF BRIDGE, A • 1910 • *Edison* • USA
VICTIM OF CIRCUMSTANCE, A • 1912 • *Cooper Miriam* • USA
VICTIM OF CIRCUMSTANCES, A • 1911 • Lehrman Henry, Sennett Mack (Spv) • USA
VICTIM OF CIRCUMSTANCES, A • 1913 • *Thanhouser* • USA
VICTIM OF DECEIT, A • 1913 • *Joyce Alice* • USA
VICTIM OF FIREWATER, A • 1912 • *Pathe* • USA
VICTIM OF HATE, A • 1910 • *Essanay* • USA
VICTIM OF HEREDITY, A • 1913 • *Hollister Alice* • USA
VICTIM OF JEALOUSY, A • 1910 • Griffith D. W. • USA
VICTIM OF MISFORTUNE, A • 1905 • *Paul R. W.* • UKN
VICTIMA, LA see **PIRANAS, LAS** • 1967
VICTIMA DEL ODIO • 1921 • Buchs Jose • SPN
VICTIMAS DEL DIVORCIO • 1952 • Rivero Fernando A. • MXC
VICTIMAS DEL PECADO • 1950 • Fernandez Emilio • MXC
VICTIME DE SA PROBITE • 1908 • Nonguet Lucien • FRN
VICTIMES DE LA FOUDRE, LES • 1906 • Velle Gaston • FRN • VICTIMS OF LIGHTNING, THE
VICTIMES DE LA GUERRE • 1969 • Merbah Lamine • DCS • ALG
VICTIMES DE L'ALCOOL, LES • 1911 • Bourgeois Gerard • FRN
VICTIMES DE L'ALCOOLISME, LES • 1902 • Zecca Ferdinand • FRN • VICTIMS OF ALCOHOLISM, THE
VICTIMES DE L'ALCOOLISME, LES • 1910 • Nonguet Lucien • FRN
VICTIMS • 1979 • Blake Alan • UKN
VICTIMS • 1982 • Freedman Jerrold • TVM • USA
VICTIMS, THE • 1975 • Mustafa Hassam Eddin • EGY
VICTIMS, THE see **DOHAYA, EL** • 1933
VICTIMS FOR VICTIMS see **VICTIMS FOR VICTIMS: THE THERESA SALDANA STORY** • 1984
VICTIMS FOR VICTIMS: THE THERESA SALDANA STORY • 1984 • Arthur Karen • TVM • USA • VICTIMS FOR VICTIMS
VICTIMS OF ALCOHOLISM, THE see **VICTIMES DE L'ALCOOLISME, LES** • 1902
VICTIMS OF BLACKMAIL see **SINS OF HARVEY CLARE, THE** • 1914
VICTIMS OF DIVORCE • 1914 • Russell Martha • USA
VICTIMS OF FATE • 1910 • *Vitagraph* • USA
VICTIMS OF FATE • 1912 • *Pathe* • USA
VICTIMS OF JEALOUSY • 1910 • *Phoenix* • USA
VICTIMS OF LIGHTNING, THE see **VICTIMES DE LA FOUDRE, LES** • 1906
VICTIMS OF PASSION • 1986 • Safran Henri • ASL • LANCASTER MILLER AFFAIR, THE
VICTIMS OF PERSECUTION • 1933 • Pollard Bud • USA
VICTIMS OF SATAN • 1915 • *Regent* • USA
VICTIMS OF SPEED • 1914 • *Komic* • USA
VICTIMS OF TERROR • 1967 • Baim Harold • DCS • UKN
VICTIMS OF THE BEYOND (UKN) see **SUCKER MONEY** • 1933
VICTIMS OF THE MORMONS, THE see **MORMONENS OFFER** • 1911
VICTIMS OF VANITY • 1914 • *Carlyle Francis* • USA
VICTIMS OF VICE see **AMOUR A LA CHAINE, L'** • 1965
VICTIMS OF VIOLENCE • 1981 • Barry Trish • IRL
VICTOIRE DU VAINCU, LA • 1966 • Nasri Samir • LBN
VICTOIRE EN CHANTANT, LA see **NOIRS ET BLANCS EN COULEURS** • 1976
VICTOIRE SUR L'ANNAPURNA • 1953 • Ichac Marcel • DOC • FRN • ANNAPURNA (USA)
VICTOR • 1951 • Heymann Claude • FRN
VICTOR, THE • 1915 • *Beery Wallace* • USA
VICTOR, THE • 1923 • Laemmle Edward • USA
VICTOR, THE see **SIEGER, DIE** • 1918
VICTOR, THE see **SIEGER, DIE** • 1922
VICTOR, THE see **SIEGER, DER** • 1932
VICTOR CHERNYSHOV'S THREE DAYS see **TRI DNYA VIKTORA CHERNYSHYOVA** • 1968
VICTOR FRANKENSTEIN • 1977 • Floyd Calvin • IRL, SWD • TERROR OF DR. FRANKENSTEIN ○ TERROR OF FRANKENSTEIN
VICTOR HERBERT see **GREAT VICTOR HERBERT, THE** • 1939
VICTOR HUGO • 1951 • Leenhardt Roger, Berber Yvonne • DCS • FRN • PERE HUGO, LE
VICTOR I • 1968 • Wenders Wim • SHT • FRG
VICTOR OF THE PLOT, THE • 1917 • Campbell Colin • SHT • USA
VICTOR SJOSTROM –A FILM PORTRAIT • 1982 • Werner Gosta • DOC • SWD
VICTOR VICTORIA • 1982 • Edwards Blake • USA
VICTORIA • 1971 • *Cinemas Trio* • MXC
VICTORIA • 1973 • von Sydow Max • NRW, USA
VICTORIA • 1978 • Widerberg Bo • SWD, FRG
VICTORIA! • 1984 • Ribas Antoni • SPN • VICTORY!
VICTORIA L. see **LEVE SITT LIV** • 1982
VICTORIA, LA • 1974 • Lilienthal Peter • FRG • VICTORY, THE
VICTORIA AND HER HUSSAR see **VIKTORIA UND IHR HUSAR** • 1931
VICTORIA CROSS, THE • 1912 • Reid Hal • USA
VICTORIA CROSS, THE • 1916 • Le Saint Edward J. • USA
VICTORIA CROSS, THE (USA) see **V.C.** • 1914
VICTORIA DE LA V., LA • 1945 • Barth-Moglia Luis • ARG
VICTORIA GIRLS, THE • 1928 • Croise Hugh • UKN • MUSICAL MEDLEY NO.1
VICTORIA GIRLS SKIPPING • 1928 • Croise Hugh • UKN • MUSICAL MEDLEY NO.6
VICTORIA THE GREAT • 1937 • Wilcox Herbert • UKN
VICTORIAN LADY IN HER BOUDOIR • 1896 • Collings Esme • UKN
VICTORINE • 1915 • Powell Paul • USA
VICTORIOUS, THE • 1928 • Chekhova Olga • USS
VICTORS, THE • Bachrach Dora • USA
VICTORS, THE • 1963 • Foreman Carl • UKN, USA
VICTORS, THE • 1968 • Gjika Viktor, Milkani Piro • ALB
VICTORS AND THE VANQUISHED, THE • 1950 • Petrov Vladimir • USS
VICTOR'S AT SEVEN • 1915 • Williams C. Jay • USA
VICTOR'S EGG-O-MAT see **VIKTOROV JAJOMAT** • 1969
VICTORY • 1913 • *Victory Film* • USA
VICTORY • 1919 • Tourneur Maurice • USA
VICTORY • 1928 • Wetherell M. A. • UKN
VICTORY • 1940 • Cromwell John • USA
VICTORY see **POBEDA** • 1938
VICTORY see **MEI HUA** • 1976
VICTORY! see **VICTORIA!** • 1984
VICTORY, THE • 1899 • Ashe Robert • UKN
VICTORY, THE see **VICTORIA, LA** • 1974
VICTORY, THE see **JAIT-RE-JAIT** • 1977
VICTORY, THE see **YESTERDAY** • 1980
VICTORY AND PEACE • 1918 • Brenon Herbert • UKN • INVASION OF BRITAIN, THE (USA)
VICTORY ARMY IN THE MAKING • 1919 • *Miller-Hodkinson* • SHT • USA
VICTORY AT DIEN BIEN PHU, THE • 1988 • DOC • VTN
VICTORY AT ENTEBBE • 1976 • Chomsky Marvin • TVM • USA
VICTORY AT SEA • 1955 • Salomon Henry • DOC • USA
VICTORY CELEBRATION OF A WAR CASUALTY see **UBERWINDUNG EINES VERLUSTES** • 1964
VICTORY IN DARKNESS see **SEGER I MORKER** • 1954
VICTORY IN THE DARK see **SEGER I MORKER** • 1954
VICTORY IN THE SUN see **SHORI NO HI MADE** • 1945
VICTORY IN THE UKRAINE AND THE EXPULSION OF THE GERMANS FROM THE BOUNDARIES OF THE UKR. SOV. LAND see **POBEDA NA PRAVOBEREZHENOI UKRAINE I IZGNANIYE NEMETSIKH ZA PREDELI UKRAINSKIKH SOVIETSKIKH ZEMEL** • 1945
VICTORY IN THE WEST see **SIEG IM WESTEN** • 1941
VICTORY LEADERS, THE • 1919 • Elvey Maurice • UKN
VICTORY LIES IN TRUTH see **SATHYAMAY JAYAM** • 1967
VICTORY MARCH (USA) see **MARCIA TRIONFALE** • 1976
VICTORY OF CONSCIENCE, THE • 1916 • Melford George?, Reicher Frank? • USA
VICTORY OF FAITH see **SIEG DES GLAUBENS** • 1933
VICTORY OF ISRAEL, THE • 1910 • *Vitagraph* • USA
VICTORY OF LIFE see **VITEZSTVI ZIVOTA** • 1954
VICTORY OF SATYAVAMA see **BAMA VIJAYAM** • 1967
VICTORY OF THE FAITH see **SIEG DES GLAUBENS** • 1933
VICTORY OF THE NIGHT see **POBEDITELI NOCHI** • 1927
VICTORY OF VIRTUE, THE • 1915 • Webster Harry Mcrae • USA
VICTORY OF WOMEN, THE (UKN) see **JOSEI NO SHORI** • 1946
VICTORY OR DEFEAT see **SHORI TO HAIBOKU** • 1960
VICTORY OVER DEATH see **NGADHNJIM MBI VDEKJEN**
VICTORY PLAYS • 1932 • Martin Al • SHT • USA
VICTORY QUIZ • 1942 • Jason Will • SHT • USA
VICTORY SONG see **HISSHOKA** • 1945
VICTORY THROUGH AIR POWER • 1943 • Potter H. C., Disney Walt, Hand David, Pearce Perce • USA
VICTORY (USA) see **ESCAPE TO VICTORY** • 1980
VICTORY VEHICLES • 1943 • Kinney Jack • ANS • USA
VICTORY VITTLES • 1942 • Jason Will • SHT • USA
VICTORY WEDDING • 1944 • Matthews Jessie • UKN
VICTUAILLES DE GRETCHEN SE REVOLTENT, LES • 1916 • Cohl Emile • ANS • FRN
VIDA ALEGRE, LA • 1987 • Colomo Fernando • SPN • MERRY LIFE, THE ○ LIFE OF PLEASURE, A
VIDA ALREDEDOR, LA • 1959 • Fernan-Gomez Fernando • SPN
VIDA CAMBIA, LA • 1975 • Torres • MXC
VIDA COLOR DE ROSA, LA • 1951 • Klimovsky Leon • SPN
VIDA CONYUGAL SANA • 1973 • Bodegas Roberto • SPN
VIDA CRIMINAL DE ARCHIBALDO DE LA CRUZ, LA see **ENSAYO DE UN CRIMEN** • 1955
VIDA DE AGUSTIN LARA, LA • 1958 • Galindo Alejandro • MXC
VIDA DE CARLOS GARDEL, A • 1939 • de Zavalia Alberto • ARG
VIDA DE FAMILIA • 1963 • Font Jose Luis • SPN
VIDA DE PEDRO INFANTE, LA • 1963 • Zacarias Miguel • MXC
VIDA DE UM SOLDADO, A • 1930 • Contreiras Anibal • PRT
VIDA DEL PADRE LAMBERT, LA see **SIEMPRE HAY UN MANANA** • 1961
VIDA DIFICIL DE UNA MUJER FACIL • 1977 • Fernandez Unsain Jose Maria • MXC

VIDA DO LINHO • 1943 • Coelho Jose Adolfo • SHT • PRT
VIDA E BELA!?, A • 1982 • Teles Luis Galvao • PRT • IS LIFE BEAUTIFUL?
VIDA E OBRA DE FERREIRA DE CASTRO • 1971 • de Almeida Manuel Faria • SHT • PRT
VIDA EMPIEZA A MEDIANOCHE, LA • 1944 • de Orduna Juan • SPN
VIDA EN BROMA, LA • 1949 • Salvador Jaime • MXC
VIDA EN ROSA, LA • 1989 • Diaz Rolando • CUB • VIE EN ROSE, LA
VIDA EN UN BLOC, LA • 1956 • Lucia Luis • SPN
VIDA EN UN HILO, LA • 1945 • Neville Edgar • SPN
VIDA ENCADENADA, LA • 1948 • Roman Antonio • SPN
VIDA ENTERA, LA • 1987 • Olguin Carlos • ARG • ENTIRE LIFE, THE
VIDA ES MARAVILLOSA, LA • 1955 • Lazaga Pedro • SPN
VIDA ES UN TANGO • 1939 • Romero Manuel • LIFE IS A TANGO (USA)
VIDA INTIMA DE MARCO ANTONIO Y CLEOPATRA, LA • 1946 • Gavaldon Roberto • MXC
VIDA INTIMA DE UN SEDUCTOR CINICO • 1975 • Aguirre Javier • SPN
VIDA INUTIL DE PITO PEREZ, LA • 1943 • Contreras Torres Miguel • MXC • USELESS LIFE OF PITO PEREZ, THE
VIDA NA PENITENCIARIA DE LISBOA, A • 1915 • de Albuquerque Ernesto • PRT
VIDA NO VALE NADA, LA • 1954 • Gonzalez Rogelio A. • MXC
VIDA NUEVA DE PEDRITO DE ANDIA, LA • 1965 • Gil Rafael • SPN
VIDA PARA DOIS, UMA • 1948 • Miranda Armando • PRT
VIDA PARA DOIS, UMA • 1953 • Miranda Armando • BRZ
VIDA PERRA • 1983 • Aguirre Javier • SPN • DOG'S LIFE, A ○ PERRA VIDA
VIDA PERRA DE JUANITA NARBONI, LA • 1978 • Aguirre Javier • SPN
VIDA POR DELANTE, LA • 1958 • Fernan-Gomez Fernando • SPN
VIDA POR OTRA, UNA • 1932 • Auer John H. • MXC
VIDA PRIVADA DE FULANO DE TAL, LA • 1960 • Forn Josep Maria • SPN
VIDA PRIVADA DE UNA SENORITA BIEN see **CALL-GIRL** • 1976
VIDA QUIS ASSIM, A • 1968 • Freund Edward • BRZ • LIFE IS LIKE THAT
VIDA SIGUE IGUAL, LA • 1969 • Martin Eugenio • SPN
VIDA TIENE TRES DIAS, LA • 1954 • Gomez Muriel Emilio • MXC
VIDALITA • 1949 • Saslavsky Luis • ARG
VIDAS • 1983 • Teles Antonio Da Cunha • PRT
VIDAS CONFUSA • 1947 • Mihura Jeronimo • SPN
VIDAS CRUZADAS • 1942 • Marquina Luis • SPN
VIDAS ERRANTES • 1984 • de la Riva Juan Antonio • DOC • MXC • CINE ALAMEDA ○ WANDERING LIVES
VIDAS NUAS • 1967 • Fraga Ody • BRZ • NAKED LIVES
VIDAS ROTAS • 1935 • Ardavin Eusebio F.
VIDAS SECAS • 1963 • dos Santos Nelson Pereira • BRZ • BARREN LIVES ○ DROUGHT ○ SECHERESSE ○ DRY LIVES
VIDAS SEM RUMO • 1956 • Guimaraes Manuel • PRT
VIDE VERDEN, DEN • 1987 • Ernst Franz • DOC • DNM • WIDE WORLD, THE
VIDEO AND JULIA • 1981 • Francken Sandor • NTH
VIDEO DEAD, THE • 1987 • Scott Robert • USA
VIDEO MADNESS • 1983 • Clark Greydon • USA • JOYSTICKS ○ JOY STICKS
VIDEO QUEEN • 1986 • Kool Allen • CND, USA
VIDEO REWIND: THE ROLLING STONES GREAT VIDEO HITS • 1984 • Temple Julien • DOC • UKN
VIDEO-SPACE • 1970 • Vanderbeek Stan • ANS • USA
VIDEO WARS • 1984 • Gianpaolo Mario • ITL
VIDEODROME • 1982 • Cronenberg David • CND, USA
VIDITA NEGRA • 1971 • *Nacionale Cinemas* • MXC
VIDOCQ • 1923 • Kemm Jean • FRN
VIDOCQ • 1938 • Daroy Jacques • FRN
VIDUNDERLIGE HAARELIXIR, DEN • 1909 • *Sonne Petrine* • DNM • MARVELLLOUS CURE, A
VIDYA • 1948 • *Burman S. D. (M)* • IND
VIDYAPATHI • 1937 • Bose Debaki • IND
VIDYAPATI • 1937 • Kapoor Prithviraj • IND
VIE, LA • 1963 • Shawqi Khalil • SHT • EGY
VIE, LA • 1968 • Labrecque Jean-Claude • DOC • CND
VIE, LA see **SAUVE QUI PEUT** • 1980
VIE, UN see **ONNA NO ISSHO** • 1967
VIE, UNE • 1958 • Astruc Alexandre • FRN, ITL • END OF DESIRE (USA) ○ VITA, UNA ○ ONE LIFE
VIE A CHANDIGARH, LA • 1966 • Tanner Alain • DOC • SWT • CITY AT CHANDIGARH, A (UKN) ○ LEBEN IN CHANDIGARH, DAS ○ VILLE A CHANDIGARH, UNE ○ CHANDIGARH
VIE A DEUX, LA • 1958 • Duhour Clement, Guitry Sacha (U/c) • FRN • LIFE TOGETHER
VIE A L'ENVERS, LA • 1964 • Jessua Alain • FRN • LIFE UPSIDE-DOWN (USA) ○ INSIDE OUT ○ LIFE IN HELL
VIE A REBOURS, LA • 1907 • Cohl Emile • ANS • FRN
VIE AMOUREUSE DE L'HOMME INVISIBLE, LA • 1969 • Chevalier Pierre • FRN
VIE CHANTEE, LA • 1950 • Noel-Noel • FRN
VIE COMMENCE DEMAIN, LA • 1950 • Vedres Nicole • DOC • FRN • LIFE BEGINS TOMORROW
VIE COMMENCE EN JANVIER, LA • 1980 • Regnier Michel • DOC • CND
VIE CONJUGALE, LA • 1964 • Cayatte Andre • FRN, ITL • NEL BENE E NEL MALE (ITL) ○ ANATOMY OF A MARRIAGE
VIE CONJUGALE: FRANCOISE, LA • 1964 • Cayatte Andre • FRN, ITL • ANATOMY OF A MARRIAGE: MY DAYS WITH FRANCOISE (USA) ○ PER IL BENE E PER IL MALE(ITL)
VIE CONJUGALE: JEAN-MARC, LA • 1964 • Cayatte Andre • FRN, ITL • ANATOMY OF A MARRIAGE: MY DAYS WITH JEAN-MARC (USA) ○ VITA CONJUGALE, LA (ITL)
VIE CONTINUE, LA • 1948 • Vilardebo Carlos • SHT • FRN
VIE CONTINUE, LA • 1981 • Mizrahi Moshe • FRN • LIFE GOES ON
VIE DANGEREUSE, LA • 1902 • Zecca Ferdinand • FRN
VIE DE BOHEME, LA • 1916 • Capellani Albert • USA • BOHEME, LA
VIE DE BOHEME, LA • 1923 • Righelli Gennaro • ITL, FRG • BOHEME, LA (FRG)
VIE DE BOHEME, LA • 1942 • L'Herbier Marcel • FRN, ITL • BOHEME, LA (ITL)
VIE DE CHATEAU, LA • 1966 • Rappeneau Jean-Paul • FRN • MATTER OF RESISTANCE, A (USA) ○ GRACIOUS LIVING
VIE DE CHIEN, UNE • 1941 • Cammage Maurice • FRN
VIE DE CHIEN, UNE see **MARI REVE, LE** • 1936
VIE DE COUPLE, LA • 1980 • Letourneau Diane • DOC • CND
VIE DE COURTISANE • Benazeraf Jose • FRN
VIE DE FAMILLE, LA • 1984 • Doillon Jacques • FRN
VIE DE GARCON, UNE • 1953 • Boyer Jean • FRN
VIE DE JESUS, LA • Arcady • SHT • FRN
VIE DE JESUS, LA • 1951 • Gibaud Marcel • DOC • FRN
VIE DE JESUS, LA see **PASSION, LA** • 1902
VIE DE PLAISIR, LA • 1943 • Valentin Albert • FRN
VIE DEL CUORE, LE • 1942 • Mastrocinque Camillo • ITL
VIE DEL PECCATO, LE • 1946 • Pastina Giorgio • ITL
VIE DEL PECCATO, LE see **LACRIME DE SANGUE** • 1944
VIE DEL SIGNORE SONO FINITE, LE • 1988 • Troisi Massimo • ITL • WAYS OF THE LORD ARE ENDED, THE
VIE DELL'AMORE, LE see **PERDIZIONE** • 1942
VIE DES ARTISTES, LA • 1938 • Bernard-Roland • FRN
VIE DES AUTRES, LA • 1958 • Dewever Jean • FRN
VIE DES CRIQUETS, LA • 1965 • Lousteau Pierre Roger • SHT • FRN
VIE DES OISEAUX EN MAURITANIE, LA • 1963 • Dragesco Jean • SHT • FRN
VIE DES TRAVAILLEURS ITALIENS EN FRANCE, LA • 1926 • Gremillon Jean • FRN
VIE DEVANT SOI, LA • 1977 • Mizrahi Moshe • FRN • MADAME ROSA (USA)
VIE DRAMATIQUE DE MAURICE UTRILLO, LA • 1949 • Gaspard-Huit Pierre • FRN • VIE TRAGIQUE DE UTRILLO, LA
VIE DROLE, LA • 1913-18 • Feuillade Louis • SER • FRN
VIE DU CHRIST, LA • 1897-98 • Blache Alice • FRN
VIE DU CHRIST, LA • 1906 • Jasset Victorin, Blache Alice, Hatot Georges • FRN • PASSION (USA) ○ LIFE OF CHRIST, THE
VIE DU DETHAM • 1910 • Batisson Rene • VTN
VIE DU MARIN, LA • 1906 • Blache Alice • FRN
VIE DU MOYEN, LE • 1955 • Vilardebo Carlos • SHT • FRN
VIE DU VIDE, LA • 1952 • Baratier Jacques • FRN
VIE D'UN AUTRE, LA see **FILLE DU DIABLE** • 1945
VIE D'UN FLEUVE, LA SEINE, LA • 1933 • Lods Jean • DCS • FRN
VIE D'UN GRAND JOURNAL, LA • 1934 • Epstein Jean (U/c) • FRN
VIE D'UN HOMME, LA • 1938 • Le Chanois Jean-Paul • DOC • FRN
VIE D'UN HONNETE HOMME, LA • 1953 • Guitry Sacha • FRN • VIRTUOUS SCOUNDREL, THE (USA)
VIE D'UN JOUEUR, LA • 1903 • Zecca Ferdinand • FRN
VIE D'UN JOUEUR, LA • 1910 • Nonguet Lucien • FRN
VIE D'UN POETE, LA see **SANG D'UN POETE, LE** • 1930
VIE D'UNE FEMME, LA • 1920 • Gallone Carmine • FRN
VIE EN ROSE, LA • 1947 • Faurez Jean • FRN • LOVES OF COLETTE
VIE EN ROSE, LA see **VIDA EN ROSA, LA** • 1989
VIE EST A NOUS, LA • 1936 • Le Chanois Jean-Paul, Renoir Jean, Becker Jacques, Zwobada Andre, Cartier-Bresson Henri, Unik Pierre, Valiant-Couturier P., Brunius Jacques-Bernard • FRN • PEOPLE OF FRANCE (USA)
VIE EST BELLE, LA • 1956 • Thibault Jean-Marc, Pierre Roger • FRN
VIE EST BELLE, LA • 1958 • Shawqi Khalil • SHT • EGY
VIE EST BELLE, LA • 1988 • Lamy Benoit, Mweze Ngangura • BLG, ZRE, FRN
VIE EST BELLE, LA see **PARIS-CAMARGUE** • 1935
VIE EST COURTE, LA • 1956-57 • Devlin Bernard • SHT • CND
VIE EST DOUCE, LA see **HAYAT HILWA, AL-** • 1966
VIE EST MAGNIFIQUE, LA • 1938 • Cloche Maurice • FRN
VIE EST SI BELLE, LA see **PARIS-CAMARGUE** • 1935
VIE EST UN JEU, LA • 1950 • Leboursier Raymond • FRN
VIE EST UN LONG FLEUVE TRANQUILLE, LA • 1988 • Chatiliez Etienne • FRN
VIE EST UN REVE, LA • 1948 • Severac Jacques • FRN
VIE EST UN ROMAN, LA • 1983 • Resnais Alain • FRN • LIFE IS A BED OF ROSES (USA)
VIE EST UNE FETE, LA see **CA N'ARRIVE QU'AUX AUTRES** • 1971
VIE ET LA PASSION DE JESUS-CHRIST, LA • 1898 • Lumiere Louis • FRN
VIE ET LA PASSION DE JESUS-CHRIST, LA see **PASSION DE NOTRE-SEIGNEUR JESUS-CHRIST, LA** • 1905
VIE ET L'OEUVRE D'ANDRE MALRAUX, LA • 1957 • Keigel Leonard • FRN
VIE ET L'OEUVRE D'EMILE VERHAEREN, LA • 1955 • Haesaerts Paul • BLG
VIE ET MORT EN FLANDRE • 1962 • Degelin Emile • BLG
VIE ET RIEN D'AUTRE, LA • 1988 • Tavernier Bertrand • FRN
VIE FACILE, LA • 1971 • Warin Francis • FRN
VIE HEUREUSE DE LEOPOLD Z., LA • 1965 • Carle Gilles • CND • MERRY WORLD OF LEOPOLD Z., THE
VIE, L'AMOUR, LA MORT, LA • 1968 • Lelouch Claude • FRN, ITL • VITA, L'AMORE, LA MORTE, LA (ITL) ○ LIFE, LOVE, DEATH (UKN)
VIE MIRACULEUSE DE THERESE MARTIN, LA • 1929 • Duvivier Julien • FRN
VIE N'EST PAS UN ROMAN, LA see **JEUNE FILLES DE PARIS** • 1936
VIE NORMAL, LA • 1966 • Charpak Andre • FRN
VIE OU LA MORT, LA • 1912 • Feuillade Louis • FRN
VIE OU MORT see **HAYAT OU MAUT** • 1955
VIE PARISIENNE see **AMOUR CHANTE, L'** • 1930
VIE PARISIENNE, LA • 1935 • Siodmak Robert • FRN
VIE PARISIENNE, LA • 1977 • Christian-Jaque • FRN, ITL, FRG
VIE PASSIONNEE DE CLEMENCEAU, LA • 1953 • Prouteau Gilbert • FRN • PASSIONATE LIFE OF CLEMENCEAU
VIE PERDU, UNE • 1933 • Rouleau Raymond, Esway Alexander (U/c) • FRN • SILENCE DE MORT
VIE PRIVEE • 1941 • Kapps Walter • FRN
VIE PRIVEE, LA • 1962 • Malle Louis • FRN, ITL • VERY PRIVATE AFFAIR, A (USA) ○ VITA PRIVATA (ITL)
VIE QUI ME PLAIT, LA • 1973 • Bartier Pierre, Szulzinger Boris • BLG
VIE QUOTIDIENNE DANS UN VILLAGE SYRIEN, LA see **HAYAT AL-YAWMIYYA FI QARIA SURIYYA, AL-** • 1974
VIE REVEE, LA • 1972 • Dansereau Fernand • CND • DREAM LIFE
VIE SANS JOIE, UNE • 1924 • Dieudonne Albert, Renoir Jean • FRN • CATHERINE ○ BACKBITERS
VIE TELLE QU'ELLE EST • 1911-13 • Feuillade Louis • SER • FRN
VIE, T'EN AS QU'UNE, LA • 1974 • Guedj Denis, Petard Jean-Pierre, Segal Abraham • FRN
VIE TRAGIQUE DE UTRILLO, LA see **VIE DRAMATIQUE DE MAURICE UTRILLO, LA** • 1949
VIEIL AGE, LE • 1962 • Giraldeau Jacques • DCS • CND
VIEIL ANAI, LE • 1979 • Rouch Jean, Dieterlen Germaine • DOC • FRN
VIEIL HOMME ET L'ENFANT, LE • 1967 • Berri Claude • FRN • TWO OF US, THE (USA) ○ CLAUDE
VIEILLE BOITE, UNE • 1975 • Driessen Paul • ANM • CND • OLD BOX, AN
VIEILLE DAME INDIGNE, LA • 1964 • Allio Rene • FRN • SHAMELESS OLD LADY, THE (USA)
VIEILLE FILLE, LA • 1971 • Blanc Jean-Pierre • FRN, ITL • TARDONA, LA (ITL) ○ OLD MAID, THE
VIEILLE RUE ET SCENE PITTORESQUE • 1966 • Meulman Henk • NTH
VIEILLES DAMES DE L'HOSPICE, LES • 1917 • Feyder Jacques • FRN
VIEILLES ESTAMPES • 1904 • Blache Alice • SER • FRN
VIEILLESSE DU PERE MOREUX, LA • 1914 • de Morlhon Camille • FRN
VIEJA MEMORIA, LA • 1977 • Camino Jaime • SPN • OLD MEMORY, THE ○ OLD MEMORIES
VIEJA MEMORIA, LA • 1985 • Camus Mario • SPN • OLD MEMORY, THE
VIEJA MUSICA, LA • 1985 • Camus Mario • SPN • OLD MUSIC, THE
VIEJO AMOR, UN • 1938 • Lezama Luis • MXC • OLD LOVE, AN (USA)
VIEJO BARRIO • 1937 • Navarro Isidoro • ARG
VIEJO BUENOS AIRES, EL • 1942 • Momplet Antonio • ARG
VIEJO DOCTOR, EL • 1940 • Soffici Mario • ARG • OLD DOCTOR, THE
VIEJO NIDO • 1940 • Orona Vicente • MXC
VIEJOS PALACIOS • 1940 • Arevalo Carlos • SHT • SPN
VIEJOS SOMOS ASI, LOS • 1948 • Pardave Joaquin • MXC
VIEL GEKUSST UND NICHT VERGESSEN • 1966 • Pfleghar Michael • FRG • MUCH KISSED BUT NEVER FORGOTTEN
VIEL LARM UM NICHTS • 1964 • Hellberg Martin • GDR • MUCH ADO ABOUT NOTHING
VIEL LARM UM NIXI (FRG) see **NON MI SPOSO PIU** • 1942
VIELE KAMEN VORBEI • 1956 • Pewas Peter • FRG
VIENI AVANTI CRETINO • 1982 • Salce Luciano • ITL • COME ON STUPID
VIENI, VIENI AMORE MIO • 1975 • Caprioli Vittorio • ITL
VIENNA BURGTHEATER see **BURGTHEATER** • 1936
VIENNA, CITY OF SONG see **WIEN, DU STADT DER LIEDER** • 1930
VIENNA IN THE PAST see **WIEN RETOUR** • 1983
VIENNA MAIDENS see **WIENER MADELN** • 1945
VIENNA SCHNITZEL see **WIENER SCHNITZEL** • 1967
VIENNA STRANGLER, THE see **WURGER KOMMT AUF LEISEN SOCKEN, DER** • 1971
VIENNA TALES (USA) see **WIENER G'SCHICHTEN** • 1940
VIENNA WALTZES (USA) see **WIENER WALZER** • 1951
VIENNA WOODS see **VENSKI LES** • 1963
VIENNE 1934 • 1934 • Masson Jean • SHT • FRN
VIENNESE BLOOD see **WIENER BLUT** • 1990
VIENNESE BROOD see **WIENER BRUT** • 1985
VIENNESE MAIDENS (USA) see **WIENER MADELN** • 1945
VIENNESE MELODY, THE see **GREATER GLORY, THE** • 1926
VIENNESE NIGHTS • 1930 • Crosland Alan • USA
VIENNESE POSTAGE STAMP, THE see **VYENSKAYA POCHTOVAYA MARKA** • 1968
VIENNESE WALTZ see **JOHANN STRAUSS, K. UND K. HOFBALLMUSIKDIREKTOR** • 1932
VIENS CHEZ MOI, J'HABITE CHEZ UNE COPINE • 1981 • Leconte Patrice • FRN
VIENS CHEZ MOI, TU SERAS PROPHETE see **TABARNAC** • 1975
VIENS FAIRE L'AMOUR.. CHARLOTTE • Patin Claude • FRN
VIENS, J'AI PAS DE CULOTTE! • 1982 • Pierson Claude • FRN
VIENS JE SUIS CHAUDE • Blanc Michel • FRN
VIENS, MON AMOUR see **LOVE IN A FOUR LETTER WORLD** • 1970
VIENT DE PARAITRE • 1947 • Blais Roger • DCS • CND
VIENT DE PARAITRE • 1949 • Houssin Jacques • FRN
VIENTO DE LIBERTAD • 1975 • Eceiza Antonio • MXC • WIND OF FREEDOM
VIENTO DE SIGLOS • 1945 • Gomez Bascuas Enrique • SPN
VIENTO DEL NORTE • 1954 • Momplet Antonio • SPN
VIENTO DISTANTE • 1965 • Vejar Sergio, Laiter Salomon, Michel Manuel • MXC • NINOS, LOS
VIENTO NEGRO • 1964 • Gonzalez Servando • MXC
VIENTO NORTE • 1939 • Soffici Mario • ARG • NORTH WIND
VIENTO NORTE • 1977 • Soffici Mario • ARG • NORTH WIND
VIENTO SALVAJE • 1972 • *Churubusco Azteca* • MXC
VIER EHEN DES MATTHIAS MERENUS, DIE • 1924 • Funck Werner • FRG
VIER FRAU see **QUATRE D'ENTRE ELLES** • 1968
VIER GEGEN DIE BLANK • 1976 • Petersen Wolfgang • FRG
VIER IM JEEP, DIE • 1951 • Lindtberg Leopold • SWT • FOUR IN A JEEP (USA)
VIER LETZTEN SEKUNDEN DES QUIDAM UHL, DIE • 1924 • Reinert Robert • FRG
VIER MAL LIEBE see **QUARTETT ZU FUNFT** • 1949
VIER MUREN • 1966 • van der Keuken Johan • NTH
VIER MUSKETIERE, DIE • 1935 • Paul Heinz • FRG • FOUR MUSKETEERS, THE (USA)

VIER SCHLUSSEL • 1965 • Roland Jurgen • FRG • FOUR KEYS, THE
VIER TREPPE RECHTS • 1944 • Werther Kurt • FRG
VIER UM DIE FRAU see **KAMPFENDE HERZEN** • 1921
VIER VOM BOB 13, DIE • 1932 • Guter Johannes • FRG
VIER VON DER INFANTERIE see **WESTFRONT 1918** • 1930
VIER WOCHEN LEBENDIG BEGRABEN see **TONY DOG, DER GEHEIMNISVOLLE TOTE**
VIERDE MAN, DE • 1983 • Verhoeven Paul* • NTH • FOURTH MAN, THE (UKN)
VIEREN MARR • 1954 • van der Horst Herman • NTH • LEKKO
VIERGE D'ARGOS, LA • 1911 • Feuillade Louis • FRN
VIERGE DES HALLES, LA see **ROSIERE DES HALLES, LA** • 1935
VIERGE DU RHIN, LA • 1953 • Grangier Gilles • FRN
VIERGE DU ROCHER, LA • 1933 • Pallu Georges • FRN • DRAME DE LOURDES, LE
VIERGE FOLLE, LA • 1928 • Luitz-Morat • FRN
VIERGE FOLLE, LA • 1938 • Diamant-Berger Henri • FRN
VIERGE PARMI LES MORTS VIVANTS, UNE • 1969 • Franco Jesus
VIERGE POUR LE PRINCE, UNE (FRN) see **VERGINE PER IL PRINCIPE, UNA** • 1965
VIERGE POUR SAINT-TROPEZ, UNE • Freedland Georg • FRN
VIERGES, LES • 1962 • Mocky Jean-Pierre • FRN, ITL • VIRGINS, THE (UKN)
VIERGES DE ROME, LES (FRN) see **VERGINI DI ROMA, LE** • 1960
VIERGES ET DEBAUCHEES • Pierson Claude • FRN
VIERGES ET VAMPIRES • 1972 • Rollin Jean • FRN • VIRGINS AND THE VAMPIRES (USA) ○ CRAZED VAMPIRE, THE ○ REQUIEM POUR UN VAMPIRE ○ CAGED VAMPIRES ○ CAGED VIRGINS
VIERGES ROMANES ET GOTHIQUES • 1960 • Haesaerts Luc • DCS • BLG
VIERNES DE LA ETERNIDAD, LOS • 1981 • Olivera Hector • ARG • FRIDAYS OF ETERNITY
VIERTE GEBOT, DAS • 1920 • Oswald Richard • FRG
VIERTE GEBOT, DAS • 1950 • von Borsody Eduard • AUS
VIERTE KOMMT NICHT, DER • 1939 • Kimmich Max W. • FRG
VIERTE VON RECHTS, DIE • 1928 • Wiene Conrad • FRG
VIERTELSTUNDE GROSS-STADTSTATISTIK • 1933 • Fischinger Oskar • ANS • FRG • QUARTER HOUR OF CITY STATISTICS, A
VIERUNDZWANZIG BILDER • 1965 • Houwer Rob • FRG
VIERZEHN MENSCHENLEBEN see **ELETJEL** • 1954
VIETATO AI MINORENNI • 1944 • Massa Mario • ITL
VIETNAM • 1954 • Karmen Roman • DOC • USS
VIETNAM • 1987 • Duigan John, Noonan Chris • MTV • ASL
VIETNAM: AN AMERICAN JOURNEY • 1978 • Richter Robert • DOC • USA
VIETNAM COMMANDOS see **REFUGEE** • 1983
VIETNAM EN GUERRE, LE see **17e PARALLELE: LE VIETNAM EN GUERRE, LE** • 1968
VIETNAM, GUERRA E PACE • 1968 • Antonelli Lamberto • DOC • ITL • VIETNAM, WAR AND PEACE
VIETNAM, GUERRA SENZA FRONTE • 1967 • Perrone Alessandro • DOC • ITL • VIETNAM, WAR WITHOUT A FRONTIER
VIETNAM IN TURMOIL (USA) see **DORAN NO BETONAMU** • 1965
VIETNAM JOURNEY • 1974 • Wexler Haskell, Fonda Jane, Hayden Tom, Burrill Christine, Yahruas Bill • USA • VIETNAM JOURNEY: INTRODUCTION TO THE ENEMY ○ INTRODUCTION TO THE ENEMY
VIETNAM JOURNEY: INTRODUCTION TO THE ENEMY see **VIETNAM JOURNEY** • 1974
VIETNAM SCENE DEL DOPOGUERRA • 1976 • Gregoretti Ugo, Ledda Romano • ITL
VIETNAM, TEXAS • 1990 • Ginty Robert • USA
VIETNAM VERITA • 1970 • Cangini Gabriella • ITL
VIETNAM! VIETNAM! • 1971 • Beck Sherman • USA
VIETNAM, WAR AND PEACE see **VIETNAM, GUERRA E PACE** • 1968
VIETNAM WAR STORY see **WAR STORY 2** • 1989
VIETNAM WAR STORY 2 see **WAR STORY 2** • 1989
VIETNAM, WAR WITHOUT A FRONTIER see **VIETNAM, GUERRA SENZA FRONTE** • 1967
VIEUX AMIS, LES • 1976 • Cote Guy-L. • DOC • CND
VIEUX BIEN, LE • 1956-57 • Devlin Bernard • SHT • CND
VIEUX CHALAND, LE • 1932 • Epstein Jean • FRN
VIEUX DE LA VIEILLE, LES • 1960 • Grangier Gilles • FRN, ITL • OLD GUARD
VIEUX FUSIL, LE • 1975 • Enrico Robert • FRN, FRG • OLD GUN, THE (USA) ○ HIDDEN GUN, THE ○ OLD RIFLE, THE
VIEUX GARCON, UN see **TOUT CA NE VAUT PAS L'AMOUR** • 1931
VIEUX LOUPS BENISSENT LA MORT, LES • 1971 • Kalfon Pierre • FRN
VIEUX MARI, LE see **CULTURE INTENSIVE** • 1904
VIEUX METIERS, JEUNES GENS • 1947 • Palardy Jean • DCS • CND
VIEUX PARIS • 1900 • Melies Georges • FRN
VIEUX PAYS OU RIMBAUD EST MORT, LE • 1977 • Lefebvre Jean-Pierre • CND, FRN • CE VIEUX PAYS OU RIMBAUD EST MORT ○ OLD COUNTRY WHERE RIMBAUD DIED, THE
VIEUX SAVANT, LE • *Studios Misonne* • ANS • BLG • OLD SCIENTIST, THE
VIEW FROM A PARKED CAR • 1970 • Carter Robert • UKN
VIEW FROM POMPEY'S HEAD, THE • 1955 • Dunne Philip • USA • SECRET INTERLUDE (UKN)
VIEW FROM THE 21ST CENTURY, A • 1968 • Fox Beryl • DOC • USA
VIEW FROM THE BRIDGE, A (USA) see **VU DU PONT** • 1962
VIEW FROM THE LOFT • 1975 • Fein Bernard • UKN, FRG
VIEW FROM THE SATELLITE • 1971 • Beresford Bruce • DCS • UKN
VIEW FROM VINEGAR HILL, THE • 1980 • Boyden Barbara • CND
VIEW OF AMERICA, A see **AMERIKAI ANZIKSZ** • 1976
VIEW OF GUANABARA BAY • 1898 • Segreto Alfonso • BRZ
VIEW OF MIDDELHARNIS see **ZWARTE ZAND, HET** • 1954
VIEW OF THE WRECK OF THE MAINE, A see **VISITE DE L'EPAUVE DU MAINE** • 1898
VIEW TO A KILL, A • 1985 • Glen John • UKN
VIEWING SHERMAN INSTITUTE FOR INDIANS AT RIVERSIDE • 1915 • Sennett Mack • DOC • USA
VIEWS OF SAMARANG • 1913 • Melies Gaston • DOC • USA
VIG OZVEGY, A • 1918 • Curtiz Michael • HNG • MERRY WIDOW, THE
VIGGEN 37 • 1974 • Weschelmann Maj • SWD
VIGIE DU CIEL • 1970 • Nasser George • SHT • LBN
VIGIL • 1984 • Ward Vincent • NZL • FIRST BLOOD, LAST RITES
VIGIL, THE • 1914 • Osborne George • USA
VIGIL, THE see **VEILLE D'ARMES** • 1935
VIGIL IN THE NIGHT • 1940 • Stevens George • USA
VIGILANTE see **STREET GANG** • 1982
VIGILANTE 2 see **REVENGE** • 1979
VIGILANTE, THE • 1947 • Fox Wallace • SRL • USA
VIGILANTE EM MISSAO SECRETA, O • 1967 • Fernandes Ary • MTV • BRZ • VIGILANTE ON A SECRET MISSION, THE
VIGILANTE FORCE • 1976 • Armitage George • USA
VIGILANTE HIDEOUT • 1950 • Brannon Fred C. • USA
VIGILANTE ON A SECRET MISSION, THE see **VIGILANTE EM MISSAO SECRETA, O** • 1967
VIGILANTE TERROR • 1953 • Collins Lewis D. • USA
VIGILANTES • 1920 • *Arrow* • USA
VIGILANTES, THE • 1918 • *Bearsstate Film* • USA
VIGILANTES, THE see **FIGHTING BILL FARGO** • 1942
VIGILANTES ARE COMING, THE • 1936 • Wright Mack V., Taylor Ray • SRL • USA
VIGILANTES OF BOOM TOWN • 1947 • Springsteen R. G. • USA
VIGILANTES OF DODGE CITY • 1944 • Grissell Wallace A. • USA
VIGILANTES RETURN, THE • 1947 • Taylor Ray • USA • RETURN OF THE VIGILANTES, THE (UKN)
VIGILANTES RIDE, THE • 1943 • Berke William • USA • HUNTED (UKN)
VIGILE, IL • 1960 • Zampa Luigi • ITL • POLICEMAN, THE ○ COP, THE
VIGILIA DI MEZZA ESTATE • 1959 • Baldi Gian Vittorio • ITL
VIGLIACCHI NON PREGANO, I • 1968 • Siciliano Mario • ITL, SPN • COWARDS DON'T PRAY
VIGNES DU SEIGNEUR, LES • 1932 • Hervil Rene • FRN
VIGNES DU SEIGNEUR, LES • 1958 • Boyer Jean • FRN
VIGNETTE • 1962 • Brown Fred J. • USA
VIGOUR OF YOUTH (UKN) see **SPIRIT OF NOTRE DAME** • 1931
VIGYAZAT, MAZOLVA • 1961 • Korompai Marton • HNG • ATTENTION, WET PAINT
VIHAR • 1952 • Fabri Zoltan • HNG • STORM, THE
VIHREA LESKI • 1968 • Pakkasvirta Jaakko • FNL • GREEN WIDOW
VII • 1967 • Yershov Konstantin, Korpachev Georgi • USS • VAMPIRES ○ VIJ
VIIMEINEN SAVOTTA • 1977 • Laine Edvin • FNL • LAST LUMBER CAMP, THE
VIJ see **VII** • 1967
VIJANDEN, DE • 1968 • Claus Hugo • NTH, BLG • ENEMIES, THE
VIJAYA • 1942 • *Biswas Anil (M)* • IND
VIJETA • 1983 • Nihalani Govind • IND • CONQUEST
VIJF VAN DE VIERDAAGSE, DE • 1974 • van Nie Rene • NTH
VIJFDE ELEMENT, HET • 1966 • Houwer Rob • NTH, FRG • FUNFTE ELEMENT, DAS
VIKEND U TOPOLI • 1981 • Amar Zoran • YGS • WEEKEND IN TOPOLA
VIKEND ZA MILION • 1987 • Trancik Dusan • CZC • WEEKEND FOR A MILLION
VIKI • 1937 • Keleti Marton • HNG
VIKING • 1962 • Barfod Bent • ANS • DNM
VIKING • 1977 • Bonniere Rene • SHT • CND
VIKING, THE • 1928 • Neill R. William • USA
VIKING, THE • 1931 • Frissell Varick, Melford George • USA, CND • NORTHERN KNIGHT ○ WHITE THUNDER
VIKING LONGSHIP • Cartwright J. A. D. • DOC • UKN
VIKING QUEEN, THE • 1914 • Edwin Walter • USA
VIKING QUEEN, THE • 1967 • Chaffey Don • UKN
VIKING VISITORS TO NORTH AMERICA • 1979 • Ianzelo Tony, Kent Anthony • DOC • CND
VIKING WHO CAME FROM THE SOUTH, THE see **VICHINGO VENUTO DAL SUD, IL** • 1971
VIKING WOMEN AND THE SEA SERPENT, THE • 1957 • Corman Roger • USA • VIKING WOMEN VS. THE SEA SERPENT, THE ○ VIKING WOMEN (UKN) ○ SAGA OF THE VIKING WOMEN AND THEIR VOYAGE TO THE WATERS OF THE GREAT SEA SERPENT, THE
VIKING WOMEN (UKN) see **VIKING WOMEN AND THE SEA SERPENT, THE** • 1957
VIKING WOMEN VS. THE SEA SERPENT, THE see **VIKING WOMEN AND THE SEA SERPENT, THE** • 1957
VIKINGO, EL • 1972 • Lazaga Pedro • SPN
VIKINGS, THE • 1958 • Fleischer Richard • USA
VIKING'S BRIDE, THE • 1907 • Fitzhamon Lewin? • UKN
VIKING'S DAUGHTER, THE • 1908 • Blackton J. Stuart • USA
VIKTOR AND VIKTORIA see **VIKTOR UND VIKTORIA** • 1933
VIKTOR KROKHIN'S SECOND TRY see **VTORAYA POPYTKA VIKTORA KROKHINA** • 1977
VIKTOR UND VIKTORIA • 1933 • Schunzel Reinhold • FRG • VIKTOR AND VIKTORIA
VIKTOR UND VIKTORIA • 1957 • Anton Karl • FRG
VIKTORIA • 1935 • Hoffmann Carl • FRG
VIKTORIA UND IHR HUSAR • 1931 • Oswald Richard • FRG • VICTORIA AND HER HUSSAR
VIKTORIA UND IHR HUSAR • 1954 • Schundler Rudolf • FRG
VIKTOROV JAJOMAT • 1969 • Grgic Zlatko, Kolar Boris, Zaninovic Ante • ANS • YGS, FRG • VICTOR'S EGG-O-MAT
VIL DU SE MIN SMUKKE NAVLE? • 1978 • Kragh-Jacobsen Soren • DNM • WANNA SEE MY BEAUTIFUL NAVEL?
VIL SEDUCCION, LA • 1968 • Forque Jose Maria • SPN • VILE SEDUCTION, THE
VILAINE HISTOIRE • 1934 • Christian-Jaque • FRN
VILAINES MANIERES, LES • 1973 • Edelstein Simon • SWT • MAUVAISES MANIERES, LES
VILAMALIA • 1973 • Quinnell Ken • SHT • ASL
VILARINHO DAS FURNAS • 1970 • Campos Antonio • PRT
VILDANDEN • 1963 • Ibsen Tancred • NRW
VILDANDEN • 1974 • Lemkow Tutte • NRW • WILD DUCK, THE
VILDARNA VID DODENS FLOD • 1958 • Anderberg Torgny • SWD • JANGADA -EN BRASILIANSK RAPSODI
VILDE ENGLE, DE • Orsted Claus • SHT • DNM • WILD ANGELS, THE
VILDFAGEL, EN • 1921 • Brunius John W. • SWD • WILD BIRD, A
VILDFAGLAR • 1955 • Sjoberg Alf • SWD • WILD BIRDS
VILDLEDT ELSKOV • 1911 • Blom August • DNM • BANK BOOK, THE
VILDMARKENS SANG • 1940 • Stevens Gosta, Lund Helge • SWD, NRW • SONG OF THE WILDS ○ BASTARD
VILDMARKSRIKE, ETT • 1964 • Lindblad Jan • SWD • KINGDOM IN THE WILDS
VILDMARKSSOMMAR • 1957 • Werner Lars, Haglund Bertil • SWD, UKN • MATTY
VILE SEDUCTION, THE see **VIL SEDUCCION, LA** • 1968
VILJELOS KAERLIGHED • 1915 • Davidsen Hjalmar • DNM
VILL SA GARNA TRO • 1971 • SWD • WANT SO MUCH TO BELIEVE
VILLA! • 1958 • Clark James B. • USA
VILLA ALEGRE • 1956 • Perla Alejandro • SPN
VILLA AUX ENVIRONS DE NEW YORK, UNE • 1982 • Jacquot Benoit • FRN
VILLA BORGHESE • 1953 • Franciolini Gianni • ITL, FRN • AMANTS DE VILLA BORGHESE, LES (FRN) ○ IT HAPPENED IN THE PARK (USA)
VILLA BY THE ZOO, A see **VILLA IM TIERGARTEN, DIE** • 1926
VILLA CARINO • 1967 • Saraceni Julio • ARG • BOSQUE ALOJAMIENTO
VILLA CARINO ESTA QUE ARDE • 1968 • Vieyra Emilio • ARG • VILLA CARINO IS ON FIRE
VILLA CARINO IS ON FIRE see **VILLA CARINO ESTA QUE ARDE** • 1968
VILLA DA VENDERE • 1942 • Cerio Ferruccio • ITL
VILLA DEI MOSTRI, LA • 1950 • Antonioni Michelangelo • DCS • ITL
VILLA DESTIN • 1921 • L'Herbier Marcel • FRN
VILLA DEVALISEE • 1905 • Blache Alice • FRN
VILLA FALCONIERI • 1928 • Oswald Richard • FRG • AT THE VILLA FALCONER
VILLA IM TIERGARTEN, DIE • 1926 • Osten Franz • FRG • VILLA BY THE ZOO, A
VILLA IN THE SUBURBS • 1959 • Chytilova Vera • SHT • CZC
VILLA "LES DUNES" • 1972 • Hartmann-Clausset Madeleine • FRN
VILLA MEPHISTO • 1921 • Seitz Franz • FRG
VILLA MILAGROSA • 1958 • de Guzman Susana • PHL
VILLA MIRANDA • 1972 • Brocka Lino • PHL
VILLA MON REVE • 1961 • Champeaux Albert, Watrin Pierre • FRN • DREAM HOME
VILLA NEGRA see **HATTYUDAL** • 1964
VILLA OF GUADALUPE, THE • 1905 • Barragan Salvador Toscano • MXC
VILLA OF THE MOVIES • 1917 • Cline Eddie • SHT • USA
VILLA PARADISO see **SEGRETO DI VILLA PARADISO, IL** • 1940
VILLA RICA DEL ESPIRITU SANTO • 1945 • Perojo Benito • ARG
VILLA RIDES • 1968 • Kulik Buzz • USA
VILLA SANS-SOUCI, LA • 1955 • Labro Maurice • FRN
VILLA SANTO-SOSPIR, LA • 1952 • Cocteau Jean • FRN
VILLA VENNELY • 1964 • Nyrup Poul • DNM • VILLA VENNELY: HOME OF COPENHAGEN CALL GIRLS (USA) ○ CALL GIRLS OF COPENHAGEN ○ COPENHAGEN CALL GIRLS
VILLA VENNELY: HOME OF COPENHAGEN CALL GIRLS (USA) see **VILLA VENNELY** • 1964
VILLA ZONE • 1975 • Zahariev Edward • BUL
VILLAFRANCA • 1933 • Forzano Giovacchino • ITL
VILLAGE, THE • 1976 • Linnasalo Timo • DOC • FNL
VILLAGE, THE see **UNSER DORF** • 1953
VILLAGE BARBER, THE • 1931 • *Iwerks Ub (P)* • ANS • USA
VILLAGE BLACKSMITH, THE • 1897 • *Paul R. W.* • UKN
VILLAGE BLACKSMITH, THE • 1898 • Cooper Arthur • UKN
VILLAGE BLACKSMITH, THE • 1905 • Stow Percy • UKN
VILLAGE BLACKSMITH, THE • 1908 • Coleby A. E. • UKN
VILLAGE BLACKSMITH, THE • 1913 • *Powers* • USA
VILLAGE BLACKSMITH, THE • 1913 • *Lubin* • USA
VILLAGE BLACKSMITH, THE • 1916 • Mann Hank • SHT • USA
VILLAGE BLACKSMITH, THE • 1917 • Coleby A. E., Rooke Arthur • UKN
VILLAGE BLACKSMITH, THE • 1920 • *International Film Service* • ANS • USA
VILLAGE BLACKSMITH, THE • 1921 • Rowden W. C. • SHT • UKN
VILLAGE BLACKSMITH, THE • 1922 • Ford John • USA
VILLAGE BLACKSMITH, THE • 1933 • *Terry Paul/ Moser Frank (P)* • ANS • USA
VILLAGE BLACKSMITH, THE • 1938 • Davis Mannie • ANS • USA
VILLAGE BLACKSMITH, THE see **SONG OF THE FORGE** • 1937
VILLAGE BRIDE, THE see **MURA NO HANAYOME** • 1927
VILLAGE CHESTNUT, THE • 1918 • Wright Walter, Griffith Raymond • SHT • USA
VILLAGE CHOIR, THE • 1900 • Smith G. A. • UKN
VILLAGE CHOIR, THE • 1913 • *Nestor* • USA
VILLAGE CORRESPONDENT, THE see **SELCOR** • 1975
VILLAGE CUT-UP • 1906 • *Bitzer Billy (Ph)* • USA
VILLAGE CUT-UP, THE see **PUTTING IT OVER** • 1919
VILLAGE DANS PARIS, UN • 1939 • *Clair Rene* • FRN
VILLAGE DANS PARIS: MONTMARTRE • 1940 • Harts • SHT • FRN
VILLAGE DE LA COLERE, LE • 1946 • Andre Raoul • FRN
VILLAGE DE LA FRANCE AUSTRALE • 1954 • Vaudremont • SHT • FRN
VILLAGE DOCTOR, THE • 1988 • Poster Piak • THL
VILLAGE DOCTOR, THE see **SELSKII VRACH** • 1952
VILLAGE DREAMS see **POPE OF GREENWICH VILLAGE, THE** • 1984

VILLAGE DU MILIEU DES BRUMES, LE • 1961 • Chartier • SHT • FRN
VILLAGE EN FOLIE, LE see **HAUT COMME TROIS POMMES** • 1935
VILLAGE ENCHANTE, LE • 1955 • Racicot Marcel, Racicot Real • ANM • CND
VILLAGE FAIR, THE (UKN) see **JOUR DE FETE** • 1949
VILLAGE FESTIVAL, THE see **FIDLOVACKA** • 1931
VILLAGE FEUD, THE see **TABLE AUX CREVES, LA** • 1951
VILLAGE FIRE BRIGADE, THE • 1907 • Williamson James • UKN
VILLAGE FLIRT, THE • 1916 • *Hippo* • USA
VILLAGE GOSSIPS, THE • 1908 • *Selig* • USA
VILLAGE HARVEST see **AROUND THE VILLAGE GREEN** • 1937
VILLAGE HERO, THE • 1911 • Sennett Mack • USA
VILLAGE HOMESTEAD, THE • 1915 • Totten Joseph Byron • USA
VILLAGE IN INDIA, A • 1937-40 • *Cardiff Jack (Ph)* • DCS • UKN
VILLAGE IN THE DUST • 1961 • Chapman Christopher • DOC • CND
VILLAGE IN THE FOG • 1977 • Cheyaroon Permpol • THL
VILLAGE IN THE JUNGLE, THE see **BEDDEGAMA** • 1980
VILLAGE IN THE MIST see **ANGEMAEUL** • 1983
VILLAGE IN THE TAIGA, A see **WIOSKA W TAJDZE** • 1968
VILLAGE IN YOUR PALM, THE see **MESTECKO NA DLANI** • 1942
VILLAGE INTERLUDE, A • 1915 • *Hatton Leslie* • UKN
VILLAGE INVENTOR, THE • 1910 • *Selig* • USA
VILLAGE LOVE STORY, A • 1910 • Haldane Bert? • UKN
VILLAGE MAGIQUE, LE • 1955 • Le Chanois Jean-Paul, Alliata Francesco • FRN, ITL • VACANZE D'AMORE (ITL) ○ MAGIC VILLAGE, THE
VILLAGE MAID see **NAADENA PENNU** • 1967
VILLAGE MILL, THE see **GROMADA** • 1950
VILLAGE MONDIALISTE • 1953 • Haesaerts Paul • BLG
VILLAGE NEAR THE PLEASANT FOUNTAIN, THE see **BYN VID DEN TRIVSAMME BRUNNEN** • 1938
VILLAGE 'NEATH THE SEA, THE • 1914 • *Domino* • USA
VILLAGE OF CATALLI, THE see **CATALLI KOY** • 1968
VILLAGE OF DAUGHTERS • 1962 • Pollock George • UKN
VILLAGE OF EIGHT GRAVESTONES • 1982 • Nomura Yoshitaro • JPN
VILLAGE OF MIST, THE see **ANGEMAEUL** • 1983
VILLAGE OF SIN, THE see **BABI RIAZANSKIE** • 1927
VILLAGE OF TAJINKO, THE see **TAJINKO MURA** • 1940
VILLAGE OF THE DAMNED • 1960 • Rilla Wolf • UKN
VILLAGE OF THE GIANTS • 1965 • Gordon Bert I. • USA
VILLAGE OF THE SHINING SUN see **MURA NI TERU HI** • 1928
VILLAGE OF WIDOWS see **GUAFU CUN** • 1989
VILLAGE OF YASTREBINO • 1965 • Tosheva Nevena • DOC • BUL
VILLAGE ON THE BUG, A see **WIES NAD BUGIEM** • 1965
VILLAGE ON THE FRONTIER, THE see **VES V POHRANICI** • 1948
VILLAGE ON THE RIVER see **DORP AAN DE RIVEIR** • 1958
VILLAGE OUTCAST, THE • 1915 • *Grandin Ethel* • USA
VILLAGE PERDU, LE • 1947 • Stengel Christian • FRN
VILLAGE PERFORMANCE OF HAMLET, A see **PREDSTAVA HAMLETA U MRDUSI DONJOJ** • 1974
VILLAGE PEST, THE • 1913 • *Frontier* • USA
VILLAGE POSTMASTER, THE • 1914 • *Shield Ernest* • USA
VILLAGE REVOLT, THE see **VZBOURENI NA VSI** • 1949
VILLAGE RIVALS, THE • 1912 • *Nestor* • USA
VILLAGE ROGUE, A (USA) see **FALU ROSSZA, A** • 1938
VILLAGE ROMANCE, A • 1911 • Salter Harry • USA
VILLAGE SCANDAL, A • 1911 • Rains Fred • UKN
VILLAGE SCANDAL, A • 1912 • Fitzhamon Lewin? • UKN
VILLAGE SCANDAL, A • 1913 • Haldane Bert? • UKN
VILLAGE SCANDAL, A • 1914 • *Melies* • USA
VILLAGE SCANDAL, A • 1914 • Seay Charles M. • *Edison* • USA
VILLAGE SCANDAL, A • 1915 • Arbuckle Roscoe • USA
VILLAGE SCHOOL • 1940 • Eldridge John • UKN
VILLAGE SCHOOL DAYS • 1914 • *Mace Fred* • USA
VILLAGE SCHOOL MASTER, THE • 1916 • *Supreme* • USA
VILLAGE SCHOOL OF EMPEROR SUPPORTERS see **SONNO SONJUKO** • 1939
VILLAGE SCHOOLTEACHER, THE see **SELSKAYA UCHITELNITSA** • 1947
VILLAGE SHEIK, THE • 1922 • St. John Al • SHT • USA
VILLAGE SHOEMAKERS, THE see **NUMMISUUTARIT** • 1923
VILLAGE SLEUTH, A • 1920 • Storm Jerome • USA
VILLAGE SMITHY, THE • 1915 • Curtis Allen • USA
VILLAGE SMITHY, THE • 1919 • Jones F. Richard • SHT • USA
VILLAGE SMITHY, THE • 1936 • Avery Tex • ANS • USA
VILLAGE SMITHY, THE • 1942 • Lundy Dick • ANS • USA
VILLAGE SMITTY, THE • 1931 • *Iwerks Ub (P)* • ANS • USA
VILLAGE SON see **PESAR-E-DEHATI** • 1967
VILLAGE SPECIALIST, THE • 1932 • *Iwerks Ub (P)* • ANS • USA
VILLAGE SQUIRE, THE • 1935 • Denham Reginald • UKN
VILLAGE TALE • 1935 • Cromwell John • USA
VILLAGE TEACHER see **SELSKAYA UCHITELNITSA** • 1947
VILLAGE TEACHER, A • 1925 • Shimazu Yasujiro • JPN
VILLAGE TRAGEDY, A • 1911 • *Tress Harry (P)* • UKN
VILLAGE VAMPIRE, A • 1916 • Frazee Edwin • SHT • USA
VILLAGE VENUS, A • 1919 • Fishback Fred C. • SHT • USA
VILLAGE VIXEN, THE • 1912 • *Wolf Jane* • USA
VILLAGE WITCH, THE • 1906 • *Pathe* • FRN
VILLAGE'S TESTAMENT, A see **TESTAMENT DE UN PUEBLO** • 1976
VILLAIN • 1971 • Tuchner Michael • UKN
VILLAIN, THE • 1917 • Gillstrom Arvid E. • SHT • USA
VILLAIN, THE • 1979 • Needham Hal • USA • CACTUS JACK (UKN)
VILLAIN FOILED, THE • 1911 • Lehrman Henry, Sennett Mack (Spv) • USA
VILLAIN OF THE PIECE, THE • 1909 • *Warwick Trading Co* • UKN
VILLAIN PURSUES HER see **SINISTER STUFF** • 1934
VILLAIN STILL PURSUED HER, THE • 1913 • Calvert Charles? • UKN
VILLAIN STILL PURSUED HER, THE • 1920 • *Romayne Super-Film* • USA
VILLAIN STILL PURSUED HER, THE • 1937 • *Terry Paul (P)* • ANS • USA
VILLAIN STILL PURSUED HER, THE • 1940 • Cline Eddie • USA
VILLAINOUS PURSUIT, A • 1916 • Walsh James O. • SHT • USA
VILLAINOUS UNCLE, THE • 1914 • *Ab* • USA
VILLAINOUS VEGETABLE VENDOR, THE • 1915 • *Cooper Claude* • USA
VILLAINOUS VILLAIN, A • 1916 • Semon Larry • SHT • USA
VILLAINS AND VIOLINS • 1916 • *Pokes & Jabbs* • USA
VILLAIN'S BROKEN HEART, A • 1920 • Howe J. A. • SHT • USA
VILLAIN'S CURSE, THE • 1932 • *Terry Paul/ Moser Frank (P)* • ANS • USA
VILLAIN'S DOWNFALL, A • 1909 • Fitzhamon Lewin? • UKN
VILLAIN'S WOOING, THE • 1905 • Fitzhamon Lewin • UKN
VILLANELLE DES RUBANS, LA • 1932 • Epstein Jean • FRN
VILLA'S WOMAN GUERRILLA FIGHTER see **GUERRILLERA DE VILLA, LA** • 1967
VILLE, LA • 1970 • Bedard Jean-Thomas • CND • BIG CITY
VILLE, UNE see **MADINA, AL-** • 1971
VILLE A CHANDIGARH, UNE see **VIE A CHANDIGARH, LA** • 1966
VILLE A PRENDRE, LA • 1978 • Brunie Patrick • FRN
VILLE, ALLA TIDERS KILLE see **FAMILJEN BJORCK** • 1940
VILLE ANATOL see **PUITS EN FLAMMES** • 1936
VILLE ANDESON'S ADVENTURES see **VILLE ANDESONS AVENTYR** • 1929
VILLE ANDESONS AVENTYR • 1929 • Wallen Sigurd • SWD • VILLE ANDESON'S ADVENTURES
VILLE-BIDON, LA • 1975 • Baratier Jacques • FRN • VILLE BIDON, LA
VILLE BIDON, LA see **VILLE-BIDON, LA** • 1975
VILLE COMME LES AUTRES, UNE • 1956 • Lelouch Claude • DCS • FRN
VILLE DE VIVRE, UNE • 1967 • Heroux Denis • DOC • CND
VILLE DELLA BRIANZA • 1955-59 • Taviani Paolo, Taviani Vittorio • DCS • ITL
VILLE DES PIRATES, LA • 1983 • Ruiz Raul • FRN, PRT • CIUDAD DE LOS PIRATOS, LA (PRT) ○ PIRATE CITY ○ CITY OF PIRATES
VILLE DES SILENCES, LA • 1979 • Marboeuf Jean • FRN
VILLE DES TROIS-RIVIERES, LA • 1933 • Tessier Albert • DCS • CND
VILLE EST A NOUS • 1975 • Poljinsky Serge • FRN
VILLE ETRANGERE • 1988 • Goldschmidt Didier • FRN
VILLE-MARIE, 7HRS. A.M. • 1954 • Bail Rene • CND
VILLE NOUVELLE, LA • 1980 • Ruiz Raul • SHT • FRN • NEW TOWN, THE
VILLE QUI CHANTE, LA • 1930 • Gallone Carmine • FRN
VILLE SANS PITIE (SWT) see **STADT OHNE MITLEID** • 1961
VILLEGGIATURA, LA • 1973 • Leto Marco • ITL • BLACK HOLIDAY (USA) ○ HOLIDAY, THE
VILLENEUVE PEINTRE-BARBIER • 1964 • Carriere Marcel • DCS • CND
VILLERVALLE I SODERHAVET • 1968 • Anderberg Torgny • SWD • VILLERVALLE IN THE SOUTH SEAS
VILLERVALLE IN THE SOUTH SEAS see **VILLERVALLE I SODERHAVET** • 1968
VILLES-LUMIERES • 1959 • Enrico Robert, de Roubaix Paul • FRN • CITIES OF LIGHTS
VILLIERS DIAMOND, THE • 1938 • Mainwaring Bernerd • UKN
VILNA LEGEND, A • 1949 • Roland George • USA
VIM, VIGOR AND VITALITY • 1936 • Fleischer Dave • ANS • USA
VIMBA ISIPOKO • 1981 • SAF
VIM'S LAST EXERCISE see **COUNT VIM'S LAST EXERCISE** • 1967
VIN CICLISTII • 1968 • Miheles Aurel • RMN • CYCLISTS ARE COMING, THE
VINA VLADIMIRA OLMERA • 1956 • Gajer Vaclav • CZC • GUILT OF VLADIMIR OLMER, THE ○ ON THE THRESHOLD OF LIFE
VINCE IL SISTEMA • 1949 • Risi Dino • SHT • ITL
VINCENT • 1977 • Hock Richard • SHT • NTH
VINCENT • 1983 • Burton Tim • ANS • USA
VINCENT • 1988 • Cox Paul • ASL
VINCENT AND ME • 1990 • Rubbo Michael • CND • VINCENT ET MOI
VINCENT AND THEO • 1990 • Altman Robert • USA, NTH
VINCENT ET MOI see **VINCENT AND ME** • 1990
VINCENT, FRANCOIS, PAUL AND THE OTHERS (USA) see **VINCENT, FRANCOIS, PAUL.. ET LES AUTRES** • 1974
VINCENT, FRANCOIS, PAUL.. ET LES AUTRES • 1974 • Sautet Claude • FRN, ITL • VINCENT, FRANCOIS, PAUL AND THE OTHERS (USA) ○ THE AMICI, LE MOGLIE E (AFFETTUOSAMENTE) LE ALTRE (ITL)
VINCENT MIT L'ANE DANS UN PRE.. • 1975 • Zucca Pierre • FRN
VINCENT PRICE'S DRACULA • 1983 • Muller John • MTV • CND
VINCENT PRICE'S ONCE UPON A MIDNIGHT SCARY see **ONCE UPON A MIDNIGHT SCARY** • 1979
VINCENT THE DUTCHMAN • 1972 • Zetterling Mai • DOC • UKN
VINCENT THE FOWLER • 1979 • Lammers Jean-Olf • SHT • NTH
VINCENT VAN GOGH • 1952 • Hulsker Jan • DOC • NTH
VINCENTA • 1918 • Musidora • FRN
VINDEN FRAN VASTER • 1942 • Sucksdorff Arne • DCS • SWD • WEST WIND ○ WIND FROM THE WEST
VINDEN OCH FLOCHEN • 1951 • Sucksdorff Arne • DCS • SWD • WIND AND THE RIVER, THE
VINDICATED • 1911 • *Thanhouser* • USA
VINDICATION, THE • 1915 • *Centaur* • USA
VINDICATION, THE • 1915 • *Ab* • USA
VINDICATION OF JOHN, THE • 1911 • *Champion* • USA
VINDICATOR see **WHEELS OF FIRE** • 1984
VINDICATOR, THE see **FRANKENSTEIN '88** • 1984
VINDICTA • 1923 • Feuillade Louis • SRL • FRN
VINDICTIVE FIREMAN, THE • 1910 • *Nestor* • USA
VINDINGE WALTZ see **VINDINGEVALS** • 1968
VINDINGEVALS • 1968 • Falck Ake • SWD • WALTZ OF SEX (UKN) ○ VINDINGE WALTZ
VINDUESPLADS • 1964 • Ravn Jens • SHT • DNM
VINE BRIDGE, THE see **LIANBRON** • 1965
VINEGAR TREE, THE see **SHOULD LADIES BEHAVE?** • 1933
VINELLA E DON PEZZOTTA • 1976 • Guerrini Mino • ITL
VINETA • 1923 • Funck Werner • FRG
VINETU II (YGS) see **WINNETOU II** • 1964
VINETU III (YGS) see **WINNETOU III** • 1965
VINETU (YGS) see **WINNETOU I** • 1963
VINEYARD, THE • 1989 • Hong James, Rice Bill, Wong Michael • USA
VINGAR KRING FYREN • 1937 • Hylten-Cavallius Ragnar • SWD • WINGS AROUND THE LIGHTHOUSE
VINGARNA • 1916 • Stiller Mauritz • SWD • WINGS, THE
VINGESKUDT • 1913 • *Christensen Benjamin* • DNM
VINGSLAG I NATTEN • 1953 • Fant Kenne • SWD • WING-BEATS IN THE NIGHT
VINGT ANS APRES • 1922 • Diamant-Berger Henri • FRN
VINGT ANS DE NOTRE VIE • 1962 • Remy Jacques • FRN
VINGT-CINQ ANS DE BONHEUR • 1943 • Jayet Rene • FRN
VINGT-CINQ ANS DE L'OLYMPIA • 1979 • Reichenbach Francois • SER • FRN
VINGT-CINQUIEME HEURE, LA • 1966 • Verneuil Henri • FRN, ITL, YGS • VENTICINQUESIMA ORA, LA (ITL) ○ 25TH HOUR, THE (USA)
VINGT-HUIT JOURS DE CLAIRETTE, LES • 1933 • Hugon Andre • FRN
VINGT MILLE ANS A LA FRANCAISE • 1967 • Forgeot Jacques • DOC • FRN • FRENCH WAY OF LOOKING AT IT, THE (UKN)
VINGT MILLE LIEUES SUR LA TERRE • 1960 • Pagliero Marcello • FRN, USS • 20,000 LEAGUES ACROSS THE LAND (USA) ○ LEON GARROS IS LOOKING FOR HIS FRIENDS
VINGT-QUATRE HEURES D'AMANTS • 1964 • Lelouch Claude • DCS • FRN
VINGT-QUATRE HEURES DE LA VIE D'UN CLOWN • 1946 • Melville Jean-Pierre • SHT • FRN
VINGT-QUATRE HEURES DE PERM' • 1940 • Cloche Maurice • FRN • MARIAGE PAR PROCURATION
VINGT-QUATRE HEURES EN TRENTE MINUTES • 1928 • Lods Jean • SHT • FRN
VINGT-QUATRE HEURES OU PLUS • 1972 • Groulx Gilles • DOC • CND
VINGT-SEPT RUE DE LA PAIX • 1936 • Pottier Richard • FRN
VINGT-SIX FOIS DE SUITE • 1978 • Sauve Alain • MTV • CND
VINHO DE PORTUGAL, UM • 1960 • Mendes Joao • SHT • PRT
VINHO DO PORTO • 1947 • Coelho Jose Adolfo • SHT • PRT
VINHOS BI-SECULARES • 1961 • Guimaraes Manuel • SHT • PRT
VINHOS DE PORTUGAL • 1949 • Marques Carlos • SHT • PRT
VINKEL EN KOLJANDER • 1974 • Sargeant Roy • SAF
VINO BRANI • 1982 • Bocan Hynek • CZC • WINE HARVEST
VINO EL REMOLINO Y NOS ALEVANTO • 1949 • Bustillo Oro Juan • MXC
VINO, WHISKY E ACQUA SALATA • 1963 • Amendola Mario • ITL
VINOLIA SOAP • 1897 • Norton C. Goodwin • UKN • GIRLS PACKING SOAP
VINOPOLIS see **GEHVERSUCHE** • 1982
VINTAGE '28 • 1953 • Angell Robert • UKN
VINTAGE, THE • 1957 • Hayden Jeffrey • USA • HARVEST THUNDER ○ PURPLE HARVEST, THE
VINTAGE MURRUMBIDGEE • 1979 • Hurley Russell • DOC • ASL
VINTAGE OF FATE, THE • 1912 • *Gordon Phyllis* • USA
VINTAGE WINE • 1935 • Edwards Henry • UKN
VINTAGE YEARS, THE • 1975 • Mason Bill • DOC • UKN
VINTE E NOVE IRMAOS • 1965 • Fraga Augusto • PRT
VINTERBORN • 1978 • Henning-Jensen Astrid • DNM • WINTER CHILDREN ○ WINTER-BORN ○ WINTERCHILDREN
VINTI, I • 1952 • Antonioni Michelangelo • ITL • VANQUISHED, THE (USA) ○ NOSTRI FIGLI, I ○ THESE OUR CHILDREN
VINYL • 1965 • Warhol Andy • USA
VIO-GRAFIA • 1975 • Rentzis Thanasis • GRC • BIO-GRAPHY
VIOL, LE • 1967 • Doniol-Valcroze Jacques • FRN, SWD • OVERGREPPET (SWD) ○ QUESTION OF RAPE, A (UKN) ○ VIOL OU UN AMOUR FOU, LE ○ RAPE, THE
VIOL, LE • 1982 • Ricaud Michel • DOC • FRN
VIOL DES VAMPIRES, LES • 1967 • Rollin Jean • FRN • RAPE OF THE VAMPIRES, THE
VIOL DU VAMPIRE ET LA REINE DES VAMPIRES, LE • 1968 • Rollin Jean • FRN
VIOL D'UNE JEUNE FILL DOUCE, LE • 1968 • Carle Gilles • CND • RAPE OF A SWEET YOUNG GIRL, THE
VIOL OU UN AMOUR FOU, LE see **VIOL, LE** • 1967
VIOLA • 1967 • Pereira Dunstan, Davis Richard • SHT • UKN
VIOLACION, LA • 1976 • Lorente German • SPN
VIOLADORES AL AMANECER, LOS • 1978 • Iquino Ignacio F. • SPN
VIOLANTA • 1939 • May Paul • FRG
VIOLANTA • 1942 • May Paul • FRG
VIOLANTA • 1978 • Schmid Daniel • SWT
VIOLANTHA • 1927 • Froelich Carl • FRG
VIOLATED • 1967 • Wakamatsu Koji • JPN
VIOLATED • 1984 • Cannistraro Richard • USA
VIOLATED see **LADIES CLUB, THE** • 1986
VIOLATED ANGELS see **OKASARETA BYAKUI** • 1967
VIOLATED LOVE see **AMOUR VIOLE, L'** • 1977
VIOLATED LOVE (USA) see **TESTIGO PARA UN CRIMEN** • 1964
VIOLATED PARADISE • 1963 • Gering Marion, De Leonardis Robert? • ITL, JPN • DIVING GIRLS' ISLAND, THE ○ DIVING GIRLS OF JAPAN ○ SCINTILLATING SIN ○ SEA NYMPHS
VIOLATION OF CLAUDIA, THE • 1977 • Lustig William • USA
VIOLATION OF JUSTINE, THE see **JUSTINE DE SADE** • 1970
VIOLATION OF SARAH MCDAVID, THE • 1981 • Moxey John Llewellyn • TVM • USA
VIOLATION OF THE BITCH see **VISITA DEL VICIO, LA** • 1978
VIOLATOR, A see **BOKOHAN** • 1968

VIOLATOR, THE (UKN) see **ACT OF VENGEANCE** • 1974
VIOLATORS, THE • 1957 • Newland John • USA
VIOLENCE • 1947 • Bernhard Jack • USA
VIOLENCE see **BORYOKU** • 1952
VIOLENCE see **VALD** • 1955
VIOLENCE, LA • 1963-64 • Portugais Louis • DCS • CND
VIOLENCE AT HIGH NOON see **HAKUCHU NO TORIMA** • 1966
VIOLENCE AT NOON see **HAKUCHU NO TORIMA** • 1966
VIOLENCE ET L'AMOUR, LA • 1968 • Pecas Max • FRN
VIOLENCE ET PASSION see **GRUPPO DI FAMIGLIA IN UN INTERNO** • 1974
VIOLENCE IN THE CINEMA, PART ONE • 1971 • Miller George • SHT • ASL
VIOLENCE IN THE NET see **AMI NO NAKANO BOKO** • 1967
VIOLENCE OF SEX see **SEI NO BOHRYOKU** • 1968
VIOLENCE SUR HOUSTON • 1969 • Reichenbach Francois • SHT • FRN • PRISONS A L'AMERICAINE
VIOLENCE (USA) see **REPLICA DI UN DELITTO** • 1972
VIOLENT AND THE DAMNED, THE (USA) see **MAOS SANGRENTAS** • 1954
VIOLENT BREED, THE see **RAZZA VIOLENTA** • 1984
VIOLENT BREED, THE (UKN) see **KEOMA** • 1976
VIOLENT CITY (UKN) see **CITTA VIOLENTA** • 1970
VIOLENT ECSTASY see **DOUCE VIOLENCE** • 1962
VIOLENT ENEMY, THE • 1969 • Sharp Don • UKN • CAME THE HERO
VIOLENT FANCY, A • 1913 • Stow Percy • UKN
VIOLENT FOUR, THE (USA) see **BANDITI A MILANO** • 1968
VIOLENT HEART, THE • 1958 • Frankenheimer John • MTV • USA
VIOLENT HOUR, THE (UKN) see **DIAL 1119** • 1950
VIOLENT IS THE WORD FOR CURLY • 1938 • Parrott Charles • SHT • USA
VIOLENT JOHN see **IOANNIS O VIEOS** • 1972
VIOLENT JOURNEY, A see **FOOL KILLER, THE** • 1963
VIOLENT JUDOIST, THE see **KODOKAN HAMONJO** • 1968
VIOLENT LAND, THE see **SEARA VERMELHA** • 1963
VIOLENT LIFE, A see **VITA VIOLENTA, UNA** • 1962
VIOLENT LOVE see **TAKE HER BY SURPRISE** • 1967
VIOLENT MEN, THE • 1954 • Mate Rudolph • USA • ROUGH COMPANY (UKN)
VIOLENT MIDNIGHT • 1963 • Hilliard Richard • USA • PSYCHOMANIA
VIOLENT MOMENT • 1959 • Hayers Sidney • UKN
VIOLENT ONES, THE • 1967 • Lamas Fernando • USA
VIOLENT ONES (USA) see **VIOLENTS, LES** • 1957
VIOLENT PATRIOT, THE see **GIOVANNI DELLE BANDE NERE** • 1957
VIOLENT PLAYGROUND • 1958 • Dearden Basil • UKN
VIOLENT PROFESSIONALS, THE (UKN) see **MILANO TREMA: LA POLIZIA VUOLE GIUSTIZIA** • 1973
VIOLENT RAGE • Carras Anthony
VIOLENT ROAD • 1958 • Koch Howard W. • USA • HELL'S HIGHWAY ○ STEEL JUNGLE, THE
VIOLENT SATURDAY • 1955 • Fleischer Richard • USA
VIOLENT SEX AFFAIR see **MYRA'S BED** • 1967
VIOLENT SILENCE, THE see **CHERGUI, EL** • 1978
VIOLENT STRANGERS: WETHERBY see **WETHERBY** • 1985
VIOLENT STREETS see **THIEF** • 1981
VIOLENT SUMMER (USA) see **ESTATE VIOLENTA** • 1959
VIOLENT SUMMER (USA) see **SOIR DE LA PLAGE, UN** • 1961
VIOLENT VIRGIN, THE see **SHOJO GEBA-GEBA** • 1970
VIOLENT YEARS, THE • 1956 • *Headliner Productions* • USA • FEMALE
VIOLENT YEARS, THE • 1956 • Eichhorn Franz • FRG
VIOLENTAS, LAS • 1974 • Miranda Fernando • SPN
VIOLENTATA SULLA SABBIA • 1971 • Cerrato Renzo • ITL
VIOLENTI DI RIO BRAVO, I • 1967 • Siodmak Robert • ITL
VIOLENTI DI ROMA BENE, I • 1976 • Felisatti Massimo, Grieco Sergio • ITL
VIOLENTS, LES • 1957 • Calef Henri • FRN • VIOLENT ONES (USA) ○ COFFIN CAME BY POST, THE
VIOLENZA AL SOLE • 1969 • Vancini Florestano • ITL • ESTATE IN QUATTRO, UN' ○ ISOLA, L' ○ ISLAND, THE ○ PASSION
VIOLENZA CONTRO VIOLENZA • 1973 • Olsen Rolf • ITL
VIOLENZA E L'AMORE, LA see **MITO, IL** • 1963
VIOLENZA PER UN MONACA (ITL) see **ENCRUCIJADA PARA UNA MONJA** • 1967
VIOLENZA: QUINTO POTERE, LA • 1972 • Vancini Florestano • ITL • SICILIAN CHECKMATE
VIOLENZA SEGRETA • 1968 • Moser Giorgio • ITL
VIOLENZA SUL LAGO • 1954 • Cortese Leonardo • ITL
VIOLER ER BLA • 1974 • Refn Peter • DNM • VIOLETS ARE BLUE
VIOLET • 1921 • Holz Artur • FRG
VIOLET see **LJUBICA** • 1979
VIOLET BRIDE, THE • 1913 • *Bostwick Edith* • USA
VIOLET DARE, DETECTIVE • 1913 • *Lamon Isabelle* • USA
VIOLET GIRL see **SUMIRE MUSUME** • 1935
VIOLET OF POTSDAM SQUARE, THE (USA) see **VEILCHEN VOM POTSDAMER PLATZ, DAS** • 1936
VIOLET RAY, THE • 1917 • Ellis Robert • SHT • USA
VIOLET SELLER, THE see **VIOLETERA, LA** • 1959
VIOLET SILK OF FOG, THE • 1980 • Djaya Sjuman • INN
VIOLETERA, LA • 1959 • Amadori Luis Cesar • ITL, SPN • VIOLET SELLER, THE
VIOLETERO, EL • 1960 • Martinez Solares Gilberto • MXC
VIOLETS, THE see **AURA** • 1923
VIOLETS ARE BLUE • 1986 • Fisk Jack • USA
VIOLETS ARE BLUE see **VIOLER ER BLA** • 1974
VIOLETS IN SPRING • 1936 • Neumann Kurt • SHT • USA
VIOLETTE ET FRANCOIS • 1977 • Rouffio Jacques • FRN
VIOLETTE NEI CAPELLI • 1942 • Bragaglia Carlo Ludovico • ITL
VIOLETTE NOZIERE • 1978 • Chabrol Claude • FRN, CND • VIOLETTE (USA)
VIOLETTE (USA) see **VIOLETTE NOZIERE** • 1978
VIOLETTES IMPERIALES • 1924 • Roussell Henry • FRN
VIOLETTES IMPERIALES • 1932 • Roussell Henry • FRN
VIOLETTES IMPERIALES • 1952 • Pottier Richard • FRN
VIOLIN AND ROLLER (USA) see **KATOK I SKRIPKA** • 1961
VIOLIN AND THE DREAM, THE see **HOUSLE A SEN** • 1947
VIOLIN AND THE ROLLER, THE see **KATOK I SKRIPKA** • 1961
VIOLIN CONCERT, THE see **HOUSLOVY KONCERT** • 1962
VIOLIN DE CREMONE, LE • 1968 • Kupissonoff Jacques • SHT • BLG
VIOLIN LESSON, THE see **UROK PO ZIGULKA** • 1969
VIOLIN MAKER, THE • 1915 • Chaney Lon • USA
VIOLIN MAKER OF CREMONA, THE • 1909 • Griffith D. W. • USA
VIOLIN MAKER OF NUREMBERG, THE • 1911 • Blache Alice • USA
VIOLIN OF M'SIEUR, THE • 1914 • Young James • USA
VIOLIN SOLO IN THE ELVES' GARDEN see **RECITAL IN GRADINA CU PITICI** • 1987
VIOLINIST, THE • 1914 • *Holloway Carol* • USA
VIOLINIST, THE • 1959 • Pintoff Ernest • ANS • USA
VIOLINIST OF FLORENCE, THE see **GEIGER VON FLORENZ, DER** • 1926
VIOLINISTE, LE • 1908 • Cohl Emile • ANS • FRN • AGENT ET LE VIOLINISTE, L' ○ VIOLON ET AGENT
VIOLINO DO JOAO, O • 1944 • Alves Jose Bras • PRT
VIOLINS see **VIULUT** • 1973
VIOLINS CAME WITH THE AMERICANS, THE • 1986 • Conway Kevin • USA • SUN AND THE MOON, THE
VIOLIN'S MESSAGE, THE • 1912 • *Johnson Arthur* • USA
VIOLON DE GASTON, LE • 1974 • Melancon Andre • SHT • CND
VIOLON DE GRAND-PERE, LE • 1911 • Carre Michel • FRN
VIOLON ET AGENT see **VIOLINISTE, LE** • 1908
VIOLONS D'INGRES • 1937 • Brunius Jacques-Bernard, Labrousse Georges • SHT • FRN
VIOLONS DU BAL, LES • 1973 • Drach Michel • FRN
VIOLONS PARFOIS, LES • 1977 • Ronet Maurice • MTV • FRN
VIP, MI FRATELLO SUPERUOMO • 1968 • Bozzetto Bruno • ANM • ITL • VIP, MY SUPERMAN BROTHER
VIP, MY SUPERMAN BROTHER see **VIP, MI FRATELLO SUPERUOMO** • 1968
VIPER • 1988 • Maris Peter • USA
VIPER, THE • 1914 • Buel Kenean • USA
VIPER, THE • 1938 • Neill R. William • UKN
VIPER THREE see **TWILIGHT'S LAST GLEAMING** • 1977
VIPERES, LES • 1911 • Feuillade Louis • FRN
VIPERS, THE • Conner Bruce • SHT • USA
VIPS, THE • 1963 • Asquith Anthony • UKN, USA • INTERNATIONAL HOTEL (USA) ○ V.I.P.'S, THE
VIRAGAYA • 1987 • Abeysekera Tissa • SLN • WAY OF THE LOTUS, THE
VIRAGE A 80 • 1974 • Arnaud Michele • DOC • FRN
VIRAGES • 1930 • Jaeger-Schmidt Andre • FRN
VIRAGO OF THE OSTERMAN BROTHERS see **BRODERNA OSTERMANS HUSKORS** • 1925
VIRAGO OF THE OSTERMAN BROTHERS see **BRODERNA OSTERMANS HUSKORS** • 1932
VIRAGVASARNAP • 1969 • Gyongyossy Imre • HNG • PALM SUNDAY
VIRE-VENT • 1948 • Faurez Jean • FRN
VIREE SUPERBE, LA • 1974 • Vergez Gerard • FRN
VIRGEM PROMETIDA, A • 1968 • Cavalcanti Ibere • BRZ • VIRGIN FIANCEE, THE
VIRGEN DE CRISTAL, LA • 1925 • Buchs Jose • SPN
VIRGEN DE GUADALOUPE, LA • 1918 • Gobbett D. W. • MXC • VIRGIN OF GUADALUPE, THE
VIRGEN DE GUADALOUPE, LA • 1976 • *Cinema Calderon* • MXC
VIRGEN DE LA CALLE, LA • 1965 • Orol Juan • MXC, PRC
VIRGEN DE LA CARIDAD, LA • 1930 • Peon Ramon • CUB • VIRGIN OF CHARITY
VIRGEN DE LA SIERRA, LA • 1938 • Calles Guillermo • MXC
VIRGEN DE MEDIANOCHE • 1941 • Galindo Alejandro • MXC
VIRGEN DE TIZOC, LA see **TIZOC** • 1956
VIRGEN DESNUDA, LA • 1949 • Morayta Miguel • MXC
VIRGEN MODERNA, UNA • 1945 • Pardave Joaquin • MXC
VIRGEN MORENA, LA • 1942 • Soria Gabriel • MXC • VIRGIN OF GUADALOUPE, THE
VIRGEN QUE FORJO UNA PATRIA, LA • 1942 • Bracho Julio • MXC • VIRGIN OF GUADALUPE, THE (USA) ○ REINA DE REINAS
VIRGEN ROJA, LA • 1942 • Elias Francisco • MXC
VIRGENES ARDIENTES, LAS • 1977 • Iglesias Miguel • SPN
VIRGILE • 1953 • Carlo-Rim • FRN
VIRGIN see **36 FILLETTE** • 1987
VIRGIN, THE • 1924 • Neitz Alvin J. • USA
VIRGIN, THE • 1982 • Santipracha Somdej • THL
VIRGIN, THE see **KUMARI**
VIRGIN, THE see **PARTHENOS, O** • 1967
VIRGIN AMONG THE LIVING DEAD • 1985 • Franco Jesus • SPN
VIRGIN AND THE GYPSY, THE • 1970 • Miles Christopher • UKN
VIRGIN AND THE SOLDIER, THE see **PETIT MATIN, LE** • 1971
VIRGIN AQUA SEX, THE see **MERMAIDS OF TIBERON, THE** • 1962
VIRGIN.. BUT • 1977 • Saleh Seymon • EGY
VIRGIN CAMPUS see **LEIDENSCHAFTLICHE BLUMCHEN** • 1978
VIRGIN CHERRY see **SHOJO ZAKURA** • 1967
VIRGIN CONFESSIONS see **CHERRY HILL HIGH** • 1976
VIRGIN CRUELTY see **SHOJO ZANKOKU** • 1967
VIRGIN DOLLS see **TOYS ARE NOT FOR CHILDREN** • 1972
VIRGIN FIANCEE, THE see **VIRGEM PROMETIDA, A** • 1968
VIRGIN FOR THE PRINCE, A (UKN) see **VERGINE PER IL PRINCIPE, UNA** • 1965
VIRGIN FROM OYUKI, THE see **MARIA NO OYUKI** • 1935
VIRGIN GODDESS, THE • 1974 • SAF
VIRGIN, GOODBYE see **SHOJO-YO SAYONARA** • 1933
VIRGIN-HUNTER • 1980 • GRC
VIRGIN ISLAND • 1958 • Jackson Pat • UKN • OUR VIRGIN ISLAND
VIRGIN LIPS • 1928 • Clifton Elmer • USA
VIRGIN LOVERS • 1972 • Heroux Denis
VIRGIN NAMED MARY, A (USA) see **PEPPINO E LA VERGINE MARIA** • 1975
VIRGIN OF BALI, THE see **VERGINE DI BALI, LA** • 1972
VIRGIN OF CEDAR, THE see **MADONA DE CEDRO, A** • 1968
VIRGIN OF CHARITY see **VIRGEN DE LA CARIDAD, LA** • 1930
VIRGIN OF GUADALOUPE, THE see **VIRGEN MORENA, LA** • 1942
VIRGIN OF GUADALUPE, THE see **VIRGEN DE GUADALOUPE, LA** • 1918
VIRGIN OF GUADALUPE, THE (USA) see **VIRGEN QUE FORJO UNA PATRIA, LA** • 1942
VIRGIN OF HAMBOUL, THE • 1920 • *Claypole Comedies* • USA
VIRGIN OF NUREMBURG, THE see **VERGINE DI NORIMBERGA, LA** • 1963
VIRGIN OF PARIS, THE see **SOPHY OF KRAVONIA** • 1920
VIRGIN OF SEMINOLE, THE • 1923 • Micheaux Oscar • USA
VIRGIN OF STAMBOUL, THE • 1920 • Browning Tod • USA
VIRGIN OF THE BEACHES see **ANNIE, LA JIERGE DE SAINT TROPEZ** • 1975
VIRGIN OF THE FIRE, THE • 1912 • Davenport Charles E. • USA
VIRGIN OF THE VILLAGE • 1980 • Rorimpandey Frank • INN
VIRGIN PARADISE, A • 1921 • Dawley J. Searle • USA
VIRGIN PRESIDENT, THE • 1968 • Ferguson Graeme • USA
VIRGIN QUEEN, THE • 1923 • Blackton J. Stuart • UKN
VIRGIN QUEEN, THE • 1928 • Neill R. William • SHT • USA
VIRGIN QUEEN, THE • 1955 • Koster Henry • USA
VIRGIN QUEEN OF ST. FRANCIS HIGH, THE • 1987 • Lucente Francesco • USA • PARADISE BUNGALOWS
VIRGIN SOIL UPTURNED • 1961 • Ivanov Alexander • USS
VIRGIN SOIL UPTURNED see **PODNYATAYA TZELINA** • 1940
VIRGIN SOLDIERS, THE • 1969 • Dexter John • UKN
VIRGIN SPRING, THE (UKN) see **JUNGFRUKALLAN** • 1960
VIRGIN VAMPIRES see **TWINS OF EVIL** • 1972
VIRGIN WHO EMBRACES A RAINBOW, A see **NIJI O IDAKU SHOJO** • 1948
VIRGIN WIFE see **MOGLIE VERGINE, LA** • 1976
VIRGIN WIFE, THE • 1926 • *Macfadden True Story Pictures* • USA
VIRGIN WITCH • 1970 • Austin Ray • UKN • LESBIAN TWINS
VIRGIN WITH AN ENCUMBRANCE see **HIMOTSUKI SHOJO** • 1968
VIRGIN WITNESS, THE see **SHOJO GA MITA** • 1966
VIRGIN WIVES (UKN) see **ZUM ZWEITEN FRUHSTUCK** • 1975
VIRGIN YOUTH see **GRAND DADAIS, LE** • 1967
VIRGINAL MIRACLE-MAKER, THE see **PANNA ZAZRACNICA** • 1966
VIRGINIA • 1916 • Madison Cleo • SHT • USA
VIRGINIA • 1941 • Griffith Edward H. • USA
VIRGINIA CITY • 1940 • Curtiz Michael • USA
VIRGINIA COURTSHIP, A • 1921 • O'Connor Frank • USA
VIRGINIA FEUD, A • 1913 • Vignola Robert G. • USA
VIRGINIA HILL STORY, THE • 1974 • Schumacher Joel • TVM • USA
VIRGINIA JUDGE, THE • 1935 • Sedgwick Edward • USA
VIRGINIA ROMANCE, A • 1916 • Belmore Charles • SHT • USA
VIRGINIAN, THE • 1914 • De Mille Cecil B. • USA
VIRGINIAN, THE • 1923 • Forman Tom • USA
VIRGINIAN, THE • 1929 • Fleming Victor • USA
VIRGINIAN, THE • 1946 • Gilmore Stuart • USA
VIRGINIAN OUTCAST • 1924 • Horner Robert J. • USA
VIRGINIA'S HUSBAND • 1928 • Hughes Harry • UKN
VIRGINIA'S HUSBAND • 1934 • Rogers Maclean • UKN
VIRGINIDAD PERDIDA • 1978 • Coll Joaquin • SPN • LOST VIRGINITY
VIRGINIE • 1962 • Boyer Jean • FRN
VIRGINITA see **COME UNA ROSA AL NASO** • 1976
VIRGINITY see **PANENSTVI** • 1937
VIRGINITY see **COME UNA ROSA AL NASO** • 1976
VIRGINITY AND JAIL • 1969 • Lohnisky Vaclav • CZC
VIRGINIUS • 1909 • Blackton J. Stuart • USA
VIRGINIUS • 1912 • Reid Hal • USA
VIRGINQUEST • 1969 • Barclay Robert • MTV • CND
VIRGINS, THE (UKN) see **VIERGES, LES** • 1962
VIRGINS AND THE VAMPIRES (USA) see **VIERGES ET VAMPIRES** • 1972
VIRGIN'S GUILD OF KUTNA HORA see **CECH PANEN KUTNOHORSKYCH** • 1938
VIRGINS OF BALI • 1932 • USA • DJANGER "LOVE RITE OF BALI"
VIRGINS OF KALATRAVA ISLAND • 1967 • Remy Ronald, Roxas Clem M. • PHL
VIRGINS OF ROME, THE see **VERGINI DI ROMA, LE** • 1960
VIRGINS ON THE VERGE see **HILFE, MICH LIEBT EINE JUNGFRAU** • 1969
VIRGIN'S SACRIFICE, A • 1922 • Campbell Webster • USA • WOMAN'S SACRIFICE, A
VIRGINS WANTED see **SHOJO NYUYO** • 1930
VIRGIN'S WEAK POINT, THE see **SHOJO NO JYAKUTEN** • 1968
VIRGO see **ZODIA FECIOAREI** • 1966
VIRGO DE VISANTETA, EL • 1978 • Escriva Vicente • SPN
VIRIDIANA • 1961 • Bunuel Luis • SPN, MXC
VIRILIDAD A LA ESPANOLA • 1975 • Lara Polop Francisco • SPN
VIRILITA • 1974 • Cavara Paolo • ITL
VIRINEA see **VIRINEYA** • 1969
VIRINEYA • 1969 • Fetin Vladimir • USS • VIRINEA
VIRTUD DESNUDA, LA • 1955 • Diaz Morales Jose • MXC
VIRTUE • 1932 • Buzzell Edward • USA
VIRTUE see **K.U.K. BALLETTMADEL, DAS** • 1926
VIRTUE AND MAGIC see **PEPPINO E LA VERGINE MARIA** • 1975
VIRTUE ITS OWN REWARD • 1914 • De Grasse Joseph • USA
VIRTUE OF RAGS, THE • 1912 • Wharton Theodore • USA
VIRTUE RUNS WILD • 1968 • Methling Sven • DNM
VIRTUE TRIUMPHANT • 1916 • Daly William Robert • SHT • USA
VIRTUE'S REVOLT • 1924 • Chapin James • USA
VIRTUOS • Novak Ilya • ANM • CZC • VIRTUOSO
VIRTUOSO see **VIRTUOS**
VIRTUOSO, THE • 1914 • *Fuller Mary* • USA
VIRTUOUS see **BRIDE GOES WILD, THE** • 1948
VIRTUOUS BIGAMIST, THE see **ERA DI VENERDI 17** • 1956
VIRTUOUS DAMES OF PARDUBICE, THE see **POCESTNE PANI PARDUBICKE** • 1944
VIRTUOUS FOOL, A see **BROADWAY GOLD** • 1923
VIRTUOUS HUSBAND, THE • 1931 • Moore Vin • USA • WHAT WIVES DON'T WANT (UKN)
VIRTUOUS HUSBANDS • 1919 • Blystone John G. • SHT • USA

VIRTUOUS ISADORE, THE see **ROSIER DE MADAME HUSSON, LE** • 1931
VIRTUOUS LIARS • 1924 • Bennett Whitman • USA
VIRTUOUS MEN • 1919 • Ince Ralph • USA • BOB STOKES – THE COURAGEOUS
VIRTUOUS MODEL, THE • 1919 • Capellani Albert • USA
VIRTUOUS SCOUNDREL, THE (USA) see **VIE D'UN HONNETE HOMME, LA** • 1953
VIRTUOUS SIN, THE • 1930 • Cukor George, Gasnier Louis J. • USA • CAST IRON (UKN) ○ GENERAL, THE
VIRTUOUS SINNERS • 1919 • Flynn Emmett J. • USA
VIRTUOUS SUSANNAH, THE see **KEUSCHE SUSANNE, DIE** • 1926
VIRTUOUS THIEF, THE • 1919 • Niblo Fred • USA
VIRTUOUS TRAMPS, THE see **DEVIL'S BROTHER, THE** • 1933
VIRTUOUS VAMP, A • 1919 • Kirkland David • USA
VIRTUOUS WIFE, THE see **MEN ARE LIKE THAT** • 1930
VIRTUOUS WIFE, THE (UKN) see **ARIZONA** • 1931
VIRTUOUS WIVES • 1918 • Tucker George Loane • USA
VIRUR, DEVOTEE TO THE GOD see **BHAKTA VIDUR** • 1919
VIRUS (USA) see **FUKKATSU NO HI** • 1979
VIS MAIOR • 1974 • Pavlinic Zlatko • YGS • SUPERIOR FORCE
VISA • 1988 • Reypoor Bahram • IRN
VISA see **LADY WITHOUT PASSPORT, A** • 1950
VISA DE CENSURE • 1967 • Clementi Pierre • FRN
VISA FOR LONDON • 1966 • Grigorov Roumen • DOC • BUL
VISA FOR THE OCEAN • 1975 • Boyadgieva Lada • BUL
VISA POUR L'ENFER • 1958 • Rode Alfred • FRN • PASSEPORT POUR L'ENFER
VISA TO CANTON • 1960 • Carreras Michael • UKN • PASSPORT TO CHINA (USA)
VISA U.S.A. • 1985 • Naranjo Lisandro Duque • CLM, CUB
VISAGE • Breien Anja • SHT • NRW
VISAGE • 1975 • Foldes Peter • ANM • FRN
VISAGE DES P.T.T. • 1964 • Dhomme Sylvain • DCS • FRN
VISAGE PALE • 1986 • Gagnon Claude • CND • PALE FACE
VISAGES, LES • 1967 • Dyja Andre • FRN
VISAGES DE BRONZE • 1957 • Taizant Bernard • SWT • FACES OF BRONZE
VISAGES DE CLEMENCE, LES • 1968 • Brault Francois • DCS • CND
VISAGES DE FEMMES • 1938 • Guissart Rene • FRN
VISAGES DE FEMMES • 1969 • Foldes Peter • ANS • FRN • PORTRAITS OF WOMEN
VISAGES DE FEMMES • 1985 • Ecare Desire • IVC
VISAGES DE FRANCE • 1935 • Kirsanoff Dimitri • DOC • FRN
VISAGES DE LA COOPERATION OUVRIERE • 1958 • Lanoe Henri • SHT • FRN
VISAGES DE LA NUIT see **WUJUH AL-LAYL** • 1968
VISAGES DE PARIS • 1955 • Reichenbach Francois • SHT • FRN
VISAGES D'ENFANTS • 1923 • Rosay Francoise, Feyder Jacques • FRN • FACES OF CHILDREN (USA)
VISAGES -MICHAEL CACOYANNIS • 1976 • Imbert-Vier Huguette • DOC • GRC
VISAGES VIOLES, AMES CLOSES • 1921 • Roussell Henry • FRN
VISCONTE DI BRAGELONNE, IL (ITL) see **VICOMTE DE BRAGELONNE, LE** • 1954
VISCOUNT, THE (USA) see **VICOMTE REGLE SES COMPTES, LE** • 1967
VISCOUNT OF BRAGELONNE, THE see **VICOMTE DE BRAGELONNE, LE** • 1954
VISHNU AVATAR • 1921 • *Madan J. F. (P)* • IND • INCARNATION OF VISHNU
VISHNU PRIVA • 1949 • *Sircar B. N. (P)* • IND
VISHWAMITRA • 1952 • Painter Baburao • IND
VISIBLE MANIFESTATIONS • 1963 • Dunning George • ANS • UKN
VISIBLE WOMAN, THE • 1975 • Fox Beryl • DOC • CND
VISION see **DRISHTI** • 1990
VISION, DIE • 1918 • Schmidthassler Walter • FRG
VISION, THE • 1926 • Maude Arthur • SHT • USA
VISION BEAUTIFUL, THE • 1912 • *Bosworth Hobart* • USA
VISION D'IVROGNE • 1897 • Melies Georges • FRN • DRUNKARD'S DREAM, A (USA)
VISION FOR A NEW WORLD • 1968 • McCullough Chris • SHT • ASL
VISION III • 1958 • Vanderbeek Stan • SHT • USA
VISION IN THE WINDOW, THE • 1914 • Williams C. Jay • USA
VISION OF A CRIME, THE • 1907 • *Lubin* • USA
VISION OF SABBA, THE see **VISIONE DEL SABBA, LA** • 1987
VISION OF THE SHEPHERD, THE • 1915 • Campbell Colin • USA
VISION QUEST • 1985 • Becker Harold • USA • CRAZY FOR YOU
VISION SAHARIENNE • 1939 • Le Tourneur Georgette • DOC • FRN • EMPIRE AU SERVICE DE LA FRANCE, L'
VISIONARI, I • 1968 • Ponzi Maurizio • ITL • VISIONARIES, THE
VISIONARIES, THE see **VISIONARI, I** • 1968
VISIONE DEL SABBA, LA • 1987 • Bellocchio Marco • ITL • VISION OF SABBA, THE ○ VISIONS OF SABBAH, THE
VISIONS.. • 1972 • Katzin Lee H. • TVM • USA • VISIONS OF DEATH
VISIONS • 1977 • Vincent Chuck • USA
VISIONS • 1978 • Arroyd Felix Miguel • USA
VISIONS FROM A JAIL CELL see **MOKUZHONGDE HUANXIANG** • 1988
VISIONS OF A REALITY • 1969 • Erends Ronny • SHT • NTH
VISIONS OF AN OPIUM SMOKER, THE • 1905 • Martin J. H.? • UKN
VISIONS OF CLAIR • 1977 • Erp Thomas • USA
VISIONS OF DEATH see **VISIONS..** • 1972
VISIONS OF EIGHT • 1973 • Forman Milos, Ozerov Yury, Schlesinger John, Zetterling Mai, Ichikawa Kon, Penn Arthur, Lelouch Claude, Pfleghar Michael, Stuart Mel • USA
VISIONS OF EVIL • 1973 • USA
VISIONS OF SABBAH, THE see **VISIONE DEL SABBA, LA** • 1987
VISIONS OF ST. TERESA, THE • Fromberg Gerald • SHT • USA
VISIT • 1963 • Timar Istvan • DOC • HNG
VISIT • 1981 • Lundgren Tapani • SHT • FNL
VISIT see **BESOEKET** • 1966
VISIT, THE • 1956 • Devlin Bernard • SHT • CND
VISIT, THE • 1961 • Gold Jack • UKN
VISIT, THE see **VISITA, LA** • 1963
VISIT, THE see **WIZYTA** • 1975
VISIT, THE (USA) see **BESUCH, DER** • 1964
VISIT AT DUSK, A see **ODWIEDZINY O ZMIERZCHU** • 1966
VISIT AT TWILIGHT see **ODWIEDZINY O ZMIERZCHU** • 1966
VISIT FROM A DEAD MAN • 1974 • Swift Lela • UKN
VISIT FROM SPACE, A (USA) see **POSJET IZ SVEMIRA** • 1964
VISIT FROM THE PRESIDENT see **ODWIEDZINY PREZYDENTA** • 1961
VISIT IN HUNGARY, A • 1965 • Csoke Jozsef • DOC • HNG
VISIT OF SANTA CLAUS, THE see **SANTA CLAUS** • 1898
VISIT OF THE DUKE AND DUCHESS OF YORK, THE • 1901 • Perry Joseph H. • DOC • ASL
VISIT TO A CHIEF'S SON • 1974 • Johnson Lamont • USA
VISIT TO A FOREIGN COUNTRY see **QUEBEC USA** • 1962
VISIT TO A NEW PLANET see **VISIT TO A NUDE PLANET** • 1969
VISIT TO A NUDE PLANET • 1969 • USA • VISIT TO A NEW PLANET
VISIT TO A SMALL PLANET • 1960 • Taurog Norman • USA
VISIT TO A SPIRITUALIST, A • 1906 • Cooper Arthur • UKN
VISIT TO INDIA • Karmen Roman • USS
VISIT TO LIVELY TOWN, A • 1912 • *Lubin* • USA
VISIT TO PICASSO see **VISITE A PICASSO** • 1949
VISIT TO PURDY'S, A • 1983 • Reusch Peter • MTV • CND
VISIT TO SOVIET RUSSIA • 1929 • *Argus Film Co* • DOC • USA
VISIT TO THE KINGS, A see **WIZYTA U KROLOW** • 1965
VISIT TO THE PUPPETS, A see **TEATR LALEK** • 1954
VISIT TO THE SEASIDE, A • 1908 • Smith G. A. • UKN
VISIT TO THE SPIRITUALIST, A • 1899 • Blackton J. Stuart • USA
VISIT TO UNCLE, A • 1909 • *Lubin* • USA
VISIT WITH PABLO CASALS, A • 1957 • Snyder Robert • USA
VISIT WITH PICASSO see **VISITE A PICASSO** • 1949
VISIT WITH TRUMAN CAPOTE, A • 1966 • Maysles Albert, Maysles David • DOC • USA • WITH LOVE FROM TRUMAN
VISIT ZAKOPANE see **VISITEZ ZAKOPANE** • 1963
VISITA, LA • 1963 • Pietrangeli Antonio • ITL • VISIT, THE
VISITA DEL DR. CAMPOS SALLES A BUENOS AIRES • 1900 • Py Eugenio • ARG
VISITA DEL GENERAL MITRE AL MUSEO NACIONAL • 1900 • Py Eugenio • ARG
VISITA DEL VICIO, LA • 1978 • Larraz Jose R. • SPN • VIOLATION OF THE BITCH ○ SEX MANIAC
VISITA PRESIDENCIAL AO BRASIL • 1956 • Ribeiro Antonio Lopes • SHT • PRT
VISITA PRESIDENCIAL AOS ACORES • 1934 • Vieira Manuel Luis • SHT • PRT
VISITA QUE NO TOCO EL TIMBRE, LA • 1954 • Soler Julian • MXC
VISITA QUE NO TOCO EL TIMBRE, LA • 1964 • Camus Mario • SPN
VISITACIONES DE JOSE LUCIANO, LAS • 1982 • Lopez Rigoberto • CUB • JOSE LUCIANO'S VISIT
VISITACIONES DEL DIABLO, LAS • 1968 • Isaac Alberto • MXC • VISITATIONS OF THE DEVIL, THE ○ DEVIL'S VISITATIONS, THE
VISITANTS, THE • 1987 • Sloane Rick • USA
VISITATION, THE • 1947 • Page John, Cooper Henry • UKN
VISITATION, THE • 1974 • Sinclair Arturo • SHT • PRU
VISITATIONS OF THE DEVIL, THE see **VISITACIONES DEL DIABLO, LAS** • 1968
VISITATORE, IL see **STRIDULUM** • 1979
VISITE, LA see **ZIYARA, AZ-** • 1972
VISITE, UNE • 1954 • Truffaut Francois • SHT • FRN
VISITE A CESAR DOMELA • 1947 • Resnais Alain • DCS • FRN
VISITE A FELIX LABISSE • 1947 • Resnais Alain • DCS • FRN
VISITE A HANS HARTNUNG • 1947 • Resnais Alain • DCS • FRN
VISITE A LUCIEN COUTARD • 1947 • Resnais Alain • DCS • FRN
VISITE A MAX ERNST see **JOURNEE NATURELLE** • 1947
VISITE A OSCAR DOMINGUEZ • 1947 • Resnais Alain • DCS • FRN
VISITE A PICASSO • 1949 • Haesaerts Paul • BLG • VISIT WITH PICASSO ○ VISIT TO PICASSO
VISITE AU HARAS • 1951 • Decae Henri • SHT • FRN
VISITE AU PARADIS • 1958 • Novik William • SHT • FRN
VISITE DE L'EPAUVE DU MAINE • 1898 • Melies Georges • FRN • VIEW OF THE WRECK OF THE MAINE, A
VISITE DU GENERAL DE GAULLE AU QUEBEC, LA • 1967 • Labrecque Jean-Claude • DCS • CND
VISITE EN HONGRIE • 1962 • Saleh Tewfik • EGY
VISITE SOUS-MARINE DU MAINE • 1898 • Melies Georges • FRN • DIVERS AT WORK ON THE WRECK OF THE MAINE ○ DIVERS AT WORK ON A WRECK UNDER SEA
VISITEUR, LE • 1946 • Dreville Jean • FRN • TAINTED (USA)
VISITEUR DE L'AUBE, LE see **ZA'IR AL-FAGR** • 1973
VISITEURS DU SOIR, LES • 1942 • Carne Marcel • FRN • DEVIL'S ENVOYS, THE (USA) ○ DEVIL'S OWN ENVOY, THE
VISITEURS SUR LE TROTTOIR ROULANT, LES • 1900 • Melies Georges • FRN
VISITEUSE, LA see **ZA'IRA, AZ-** • 1972
VISITEZ ZAKOPANE • 1963 • Hoffman Jerzy, Skorzewski Edward • DCS • PLN • VISIT ZAKOPANE
VISITING CARD, THE see **KAYNTIKORTTINI** • 1964
VISITING HOURS • 1982 • Lord Jean-Claude • CND • FRIGHT
VISITING NURSE, THE • 1911 • *Selig* • USA
VISITOR see **POSJET IZ SVEMIRA** • 1964
VISITOR, THE (UKN) see **CUGINI CARNALI** • 1974
VISITOR, THE (USA) see **STRIDULUM** • 1979
VISITOR FROM THE GRAVE • 1980 • Sasdy Peter • TVM • UKN
VISITOR FROM VENUS, A see **STRANGER FROM VENUS, A** • 1954
VISITORS • 1985 • SAF
VISITORS, THE • 1972 • Kazan Elia • USA • HOME FREE
VISITORS AND VISITEES • 1915 • Bartlett Charles • USA
VISITORS FROM THE ARCANA GALAXY see **GOSTI IZ GALAKSIJE** • 1981
VISITORS FROM THE GALAXY see **GOSTI IZ GALAKSIJE** • 1981
VISITORS TO NEW YORK see **ZUIHOUDE GUIZU** • 1988
VISKINGAR OCH ROP • 1972 • Bergman Ingmar • SWD • CRIES AND WHISPERS (UKN) ○ WHISPERS AND CRIES (USA)
VISNJA NA TASMAJDANU • 1968 • Jankovic Stole • YGS • CHERRY IN A PARK, A ○ GIRL IN THE PARK
VISOKI NAPON • 1981 • Bulajic Velko • YGS • HIGH VOLTAGE
VISPA TERESA, LA • 1939 • Rossellini Roberto • SHT • ITL
VISPA TERESA, LA • 1944 • Mattoli Mario • ITL
VISPERA, LA • 1982 • Pelayo Alejandro • MXC • DAY BEFORE, THE
VISSZA AZ UTON • 1940 • von Rathony Akos • HNG
VISSZAESOK • 1983 • Kezdi-Kovacs Zsolt • HNG • FORBIDDEN RELATIONS
VISSZASZAMLALAS • 1985 • Erdoss Pal • HNG • COUNTDOWN
VISTA VALLEY P.T.A. • 1980 • Spinelli Anthony • USA
VISTETE CRISTINA • 1958 • Morayta Miguel • MXC
VISTREL see **VYSTREL** • 1967
VISTRIL V GORACH • 1970 • Shamshiev Bolotbek • USS • SHOT IN THE MOUNTAINS KARASH-KARASH, A ○ SHOOTING AT THE KARASH PASS ○ SHOT ON THE KARASH PASS, A ○ GUN-SHOT AT THE MOUNTAIN PASS
VISTULA PEOPLE, THE see **LUDZIE WISLY** • 1937
VISUAL TRAINING • 1969 • Zwartjes Frans • SHT • NTH
VISUAL VARIATIONS ON NOGUCHI • 1945 • Menken Marie • SHT • USA
VISWAMITRA • 1936 • *Srinivas* • IND
VITA, LA see **VITA IN SCATOLA, UNA** • 1967
VITA, UNA see **VIE, UNE** • 1958
VITA A VOLTE E MOLTO DURA, VERO PROVVIDENZA? • 1972 • Petroni Giulio • ITL, FRN, FRG
VITA AGRA, LA • 1964 • Lizzani Carlo • ITL
VITA AVVENTUROSA DI MILADY, LA see **BOIA DI LILLA, IL** • 1953
VITA BRUCIATA, UNA see **LUCIANO** • 1962
VITA BRUCIATA, UNA (ITL) see **JEUNE FILLE ASSASSINEE, LA** • 1974
VITA COL FIGLIO see **INCOMPRESO** • 1966
VITA CONJUGALE, LA (ITL) see **VIE CONJUGALE: JEAN-MARC, LA** • 1964
VITA DA CANI • 1950 • Steno, Monicelli Mario • ITL • IT'S A DOG'S LIFE
VITA DI DONIZETTI, LA see **CAVALIERE DEL SOGNO, IL** • 1946
VITA DI LIGABUE, LA • 1981 • Nocita Salvatore • ITL
VITA DI LUNA-PARK see **ARRIVIAMO NOI!** • 1940
VITA DIFFICILE, UNA • 1961 • Risi Dino • ITL • DIFFICULT LIFE, A ○ HARD LIFE, A
VITA E BELLA, LA • 1943 • Bragaglia Carlo Ludovico • ITL
VITA E BELLA, LA • 1980 • Chukhrai Grigori • ITL, USS • ZHIZN PREKRASNA (USS) ○ LIFE IS WONDERFUL ○ BETRAYED ○ FREEDOM TO LOVE ○ THEY MADE HIM A CRIMINAL
VITA E MORTE • 1916 • Caserini Mario • ITL
VITA FRUN • 1962 • Mattsson Arne • SWD • LADY IN WHITE
VITA FUTURISTA • 1916 • Ginna Arnaldo • ITL
VITA IN GIOCO, LA see **MORIRE A ROMA** • 1973
VITA IN SCATOLA, UNA • 1967 • Bozzetto Bruno • ANS • ITL • LIFE IN A TIN ○ VITA, LA
VITA KATTEN, DEN • 1950 • Ekman Hasse • SWD • WHITE CAT, THE
VITA, L'AMORE, LA MORTE, LA (ITL) see **VIE, L'AMOUR, LA MORT, LA** • 1968
VITA LUNGA UN GIORNO, UNA • 1973 • Baldi Ferdinando • ITL
VITA NOVA, LA • 1975 • Torricella Edoardo • ITL
VITA PER VITA • 1913 • Serena Gustavo • ITL
VITA PRIVATA DI UN PUBBLICO ACCUSATORE • 1975 • Grau Jorge • ITL
VITA PRIVATA (ITL) see **VIE PRIVEE, LA** • 1962
VITA PROVVISORIA, LA • 1962 • Gamna Vincenzo, Broadbent Chris • ITL
VITA RICOMINCIA, LA • 1945 • Mattoli Mario • ITL • LIFE BEGINS ANEW (USA)
VITA RITORNA, LA see **VITA TORNA, LA** • 1943
VITA SEGRETA DI UNA DICIOTTENNE • 1969 • Brazzi Oscar • ITL
VITA SEMPLICE, LA • 1945 • De Robertis Francesco • ITL
VITA SPORTEN, DEN • 1968 • Widerberg Bo (c/d) • DOC • SWD • WHITE GAME, THE ○ WHITE SPORT, THE
VITA TORNA, LA • 1943 • Faraldo Pier Luigi • ITL • RAGAZZA DI VENT'ANNI, UNA ○ VITA RITORNA, LA
VITA VAGGEN, DEN • 1975 • Bjorkman Stig • SWD • DVA KVINNOR: DEN VITA VAGGEN ○ WHITE WALL, THE
VITA VENDUTA, UNA • 1976 • Florio Aldo • ITL
VITA VIOLENTA, UNA • 1962 • Heusch Paolo, Rondi Brunello • ITL • VIOLENT LIFE, A
VITAGRAPH ROMANCE, A • 1912 • Young James • USA
VITAL 2/3RDS, THE • 1973 • Jubenvill Ken • MTV • CND
VITAL QUESTION, THE • 1916 • Drew Sidney • USA
VITAL SIGNS • 1986 • Millar Stuart • TVM • USA
VITAL VITUALS • 1934 • Grinde Nick • SHT • USA
VITAMIN G MAN, THE • 1943 • Sommer Paul, Hubley John • ANS • USA
VITAMIN HAY • 1941 • Fleischer Dave • ANS • USA
VITAMIN THIEF see **ELLOPTAKA VITAMINAT** • 1967
VITAMINS • 1937 • Innes Geoffrey • UKN
VITAMINS A, B, C AND D • 1942 • Parker Gudrun • SER • CND
VITAPHONE VARIETE • 1936 • Mack Roy • SHT • USA
VITE PERDUTE • 1958 • Bianchi Adelchi, Mauri Roberto • ITL • LOST SOULS (USA) ○ LEGGE DEL MITRA, LA ○ LOST LIVES
VITE VENDUTE (ITL) see **SALAIRE DE LA PEUR, LE** • 1953
VITEBSK CASE PART ONE: THE CRIME see **VITEBSKOYE DELO** • 1989
VITEBSKOYE DELO • 1989 • Dashuk Viktor • USS • VITEBSK CASE PART ONE: THE CRIME

VITELLIUS • 1911 • Pouctal Henri • FRN
VITELLONI, I • 1953 • Fellini Federico • ITL • YOUNG AND THE PASSIONATE, THE (USA) ○ SPIVS (UKN) ○ LOAFERS, THE ○ DRIFTERS, THE ○ WASTRELS, THE
VITESSE EST A VOUS, LA • 1961 • Languepin Jean-Jacques • DOC • FRN
VITET E PARA • Dhamo Kristaq • ALB • FIRST YEARS, THE
VITEZSTVI ZIVOTA • 1954 • Rychman Ladislav • CZC • VICTORY OF LIFE
VITR V KAPSE • 1982 • Soukup Jaroslav • CZC • WIND IN MY POCKET, THE
VITRAIL DIABOLIQUE, LE • 1911 • Melies Georges • FRN
VITRINE SOUS LA MER • 1960 • Alepee Georges • SHT • FRN
VITTEL • 1926 • Autant-Lara Claude • DOC • FRN
VITTIMA DELL'AMORE, LA • 1916 • Caserini Mario • ITL
VITTIMA DELL'IDEALE • 1916 • Serena Gustavo • ITL
VITTIMA DESIGNATA, LA • 1971 • Lucidi Maurizio • ITL
VITTNESBORD OM HENNE • 1962 • Donner Jorn • SHT • FNL • TESTIMONIES OF HER ○ TESTIMONIES
VITTORIO DE SICA, IL REGISTA, L'ATTORE, L'UOMO • 1974 • Bragadze Peter • DOC • ITL
VITUS THAVONS GENERALCOUP see **GESTOHLENE PROFESSOR, DER** • 1924
VIU-HAH HAH-TAJA • 1975 • Kokkonen Ere • FNL • WHIZZER, THE
VIUDA ANALUZA, LA • 1976 • Betriu Francisco • SPN
VIUDA CELOSA, LA • 1945 • Cortes Fernando • MXC
VIUDA DE MONTIEL, LA • 1979 • Littin Miguel • MXC, VNZ, CLM • MONTIEL'S WIDOW
VIUDA DESCOCADA • 1980 • Bo Armando • ARG • SHAMELESS WIDOW, A
VIUDA DIFICIL, UNA • 1957 • Ayala Fernando • ARG
VIUDA NEGRA, LA • 1977 • Ripstein Arturo • MXC
VIUDA QUERIA EMOCIONES, LA • 1935 • Elias Francisco • SPN
VIUDA SIN SOSTEN, UNA • 1950 • Cardona Rene • MXC
VIUDAS DE CHA CHA CHA, LAS • 1955 • Delgado Miguel M. • MXC
VIUDAS, LAS • 1966 • Forque Jose Maria, Coll Julio, Lazaga Pedro • SPN
VIUDITA NAVIERA, LA • 1961 • Marquina Luis • SPN
VIUDITA YE-YE, LA • 1968 • Bosch Juan • SPN
VIULUT • 1973 • Pasanen Spede • FNL • VIOLINS
VIVA AMERICA! • 1969 • Seto Javier • SPN, ITL • VERA STORIA DI FRANK MANNATA, LA (ITL) ○ MAFIA MOB (UKN)
VIVA AND LOUIS see **BLUE MOVIE** • 1969
VIVA BANDITO see **QUIEN SABE?** • 1966
VIVA BENITO CANALES! • 1965 • Delgado Miguel M. • MXC
VIVA BUDDY • 1934 • King Jack • ANS • USA
VIVA CHIHUAHUA • 1961 • Martinez Solares Gilberto • MXC
VIVA CISCO KID • 1940 • Foster Norman • USA
VIVA D'ARTAGNAN • 1977 • Crisanti Gabriele, Halas John • ITL
VIVA EL AMOR • 1956 • de la Serna Mauricio • MXC
VIVA EL PERU • 1974 • Zecca Adriano, Zecca Damiano, Condal Elias • ITL
VIVA EL PRESIDENTE see **RECURSO DEL METODO, EL** • 1978
VIVA EL ZORRO • 1974 • *Cine Vision* • MXC
VIVA GRINGO • 1966 • Marischka Georg • ITL
VIVA IL CINEMA! • 1954 • Baldaccini Giorgio, Trapani Enzo • ITL
VIVA IL PRIMO MAGGIO ROSSO • 1969 • Bellocchio Marco (c/d) • ITL
VIVA ITALIA (USA) see **NUOVI MOSTRI, I** • 1977
VIVA JALISCO QUE ES MI TIERRA! • 1959 • Pereda Ramon • MXC
VIVA KNIEVEL! • 1977 • Douglas Gordon • USA
VIVA LA AVENTURA! (SPN) see **DES VACANCES EN OR** • 1969
VIVA LA CAUSA • 1971 • Newman Robert • USA
VIVA LA CLASE MEDIA • 1980 • Garci Jose Luis • SPN • LONG LIVE THE MIDDLE CLASS
VIVA LA JUVENTUD • 1955 • Cortes Fernando • MXC
VIVA LA LIBERTAD • 1965 • Guzman Patricio • SHT • CHL • HAIL TO FREEDOM
VIVA LA MUERTE • Maldoror Sarah • SHT • ANG
VIVA LA MUERTE • 1970 • Arrabal Fernando • FRN, TNS • HURRAH FOR DEATH
VIVA LA MUERTE.. TUA • 1971 • Tessari Duccio • ITL, FRG, SPN • LONG LIVE YOUR DEATH
VIVA LA PARRANDA • 1959 • Cortes Fernando • MXC
VIVA LA REPUBLICA • 1973 • Vega Pastor • CUB
VIVA LA REVOLUCION see **TEPEPA** • 1969
VIVA LA RIVISTA! • 1953 • Trapani Enzo • ITL
VIVA LA SOLDADERA! • 1958 • Contreras Torres Miguel • MXC
VIVA LA TIERRA • 1959 • Garnica Adolfo • MXC
VIVA LA VIE! • 1983 • Lelouch Claude • FRN
VIVA LAS VEGAS • 1963 • Sidney George • USA • LOVE IN LAS VEGAS (UKN)
VIVA LAS VEGAS! (UKN) see **MEET ME IN LAS VEGAS** • 1956
VIVA L'ITALIA • 1961 • Rossellini Roberto • ITL, FRN • GARIBALDI (USA) ○ VIVE L'ITALIA
VIVA LO IMPOSIBLE • 1957 • Gil Rafael • SPN
VIVA MADRID QUE ES MI PUEBLO • 1928 • Delgado Fernando • SPN
VIVA MARIA! • 1966 • Malle Louis • FRN, ITL • BANDIDA
VIVA MAX! • 1969 • Paris Jerry • USA
VIVA MEXICO! • 1934 • Sevilla Raphael J. • MXC
VIVA MI DESGRACIA • 1943 • Rodriguez Roberto • MXC
VIVA PORTUGAL • 1975 • Gerhards Christiane, Oliphant Pierre, Schirmbeck Samuel, Rauch Malte, July Serge • DOC • FRG, FRN
VIVA QUIEN SABE QUERER! • 1959 • Morayta Miguel • MXC, ARG
VIVA RENA • 1967 • Karayannis Kostas • GRC
VIVA REVOLUCION • 1956 • Gavaldon Roberto • MXC • VIVA REVOLUTION (USA)
VIVA REVOLUTION (USA) see **VIVA REVOLUCION** • 1956
VIVA SANTA CRUZ • Roncal Hugo • DCS • BLV
VIVA VILLA! • 1934 • Conway Jack, Hawks Howard (U/c) • USA
VIVA WILLIE • 1934 • *Iwerks Ub (P)* • ANS • USA
VIVA ZALATA • 1976 • Hafez Hassan • EGY
VIVA ZAPATA! • 1952 • Kazan Elia • USA
VIVACIOUS LADY • 1938 • Stevens George • USA
VIVAN LOS NOVIOS! • 1970 • Berlanga Luis Garcia • SPN • LONG LIVE THE BRIDE AND GROOM (USA)
VIVASAAYEE • 1967 • Thirumugam M. A. • IND • FARMER
VIVAT • 1968 • Makarczynski Tadeusz • DOC • PLN
VIVE AMORE see **PANE AMORE E ANDALUSIA** • 1959
VIVE COMO SEA • 1950 • Cardona Rene • MXC
VIVE EAU • 1967 • Roger • SHT • FRN
VIVE HENRI IV, VIVE L'AMOUR • 1961 • Autant-Lara Claude • FRN, ITL
VIVE JOSEPH DELTEIL! • 1971 • Drot Jean-Marie • DOC • FRN
VIVE LA BALEINE • 1972 • Marker Chris, Maret • FRN
VIVE LA CLASSE! • 1932 • Cammage Maurice • FRN
VIVE LA COMPAGNIE • 1933 • Moulins Claude • FRN
VIVE LA FRANCE! • 1918 • Neill R. William • USA
VIVE LA FRANCE! • 1970 • Garceau Raymond • CND
VIVE LA FRANCE! • 1973 • Audiard Michel • DOC • FRN
VIVE LA LEGION see **SERGENT X, LE** • 1931
VIVE LA LIBERTE • 1944 • Musso Jeff • FRN • ON A TUE UN HOMME
VIVE LA LIBERTE • 1972 • Petricic Dusan • ANS • YGS
VIVE LA NATION see **TROIS TAMBOURS, LES** • 1939
VIVE LA SOCIALE! • 1982 • Mordillat Gerard • FRN
VIVE LA VIE • 1937 • Epstein Jean • FRN
VIVE LE SABOTAGE • 1907 • Feuillade Louis • FRN
VIVE LE SKI • 1946 • Blais Roger • DCS • CND
VIVE LE TOUR • 1962 • Malle Louis • DCS • FRN
VIVE LES FEMMES! • 1983 • Confortes Claude • FRN
VIVE LES VACANCES • 1957 • Thibault Jean-Marc • FRN
VIVE L'ITALIA see **VIVA L'ITALIA** • 1961
VIVE MONSIEUR BLAIREAU see **NI VU, NI CONNU..** • 1958
VIVE QUEBEC! • 1988 • Carle Gilles • DOC • CND
VIVEMENT DIMANCHE • 1983 • Truffaut Francois • FRN • LONG SATURDAY NIGHT, THE (USA) ○ CONFIDENTIALLY YOURS ○ FINALLY SUNDAY
VIVENDO, CANTANDO, CHE MALE TI FO? • 1957 • Girolami Marino • ITL
VIVENT LES DOCKERS • 1950 • Menegoz Robert • SHT • FRN
VIVERE! • 1937 • Brignone Guido • ITL • TO LIVE (USA) ○ CANTO D'ADDIO
VIVERE A SBAFO • 1950 • Ferroni Giorgio • ITL
VIVERE ANCORA see **DIECI MINUTI DI VITA** • 1943
VIVERE IN PACE • 1946 • Zampa Luigi • ITL • TO LIVE IN PEACE (UKN)
VIVERE PER VIVERE (ITL) see **VIVRE POUR VIVRE** • 1967
VIVI O PREFERIBILMENTE MORTI • 1969 • Tessari Duccio • ITL, SPN • VIVOS O, PREFERIBLEMENTE MUERTES (SPN)
VIVI RAGAZZA VIVI • 1971 • Artale Lorenzo • ITL
VIVIAMO OGGI see **JOUR ET L'HEURE, LE** • 1963
VIVIAN • 1964 • Conner Bruce • SHT • USA
VIVIANA • 1916 • Eason B. Reeves • SHT • USA
VIVIANA • 1963 • de Almeida Manuel Faria • SHT • PRT
VIVIAN'S BEAUTY TEST • 1914 • *Crystal* • USA
VIVIAN'S BEST FELLOW • 1914 • *Crystal* • USA
VIVIAN'S COOKIES • 1914 • *Crystal* • USA
VIVIAN'S FOUR BEAUS • 1914 • *Crystal* • USA
VIVIAN'S TRANSFORMATION • 1914 • *Crystal* • USA
VIVIDOR, EL • 1955 • Martinez Solares Gilberto • MXC
VIVIDOR, EL • 1978 • Punceles Manuel Diaz • VNZ • SCHEMER, THE
VIVIENDO AL REVES • 1943 • Iquino Ignacio F. • SPN
VIVIETTE • 1918 • Edwards Walter • USA
VIVILLO DESDE CHIQUILLO • 1950 • Gomez Muriel Emilio • MXC
VIVIR A MIL • 1977 • Campos Jose A. • SPN
VIVIR DE SUENOS • 1963 • Baledon Rafael • MXC
VIVIR DEL CUENTO • 1958 • Baledon Rafael • MXC
VIVIR DESVIVIENDOSE see **MOMENTO DELLA VERITA, IL** • 1965
VIVIR EN SEVILLA • 1979 • Garcia Pelayo Gonzalo • SPN • LIFE IN SEVILLA
VIVIR O TODO DAR • 1955 • Martinez Solares Gilberto • MXC
VIVIR UN INSTANTE • 1951 • Demicheli Tulio • ARG
VIVIR UN LARGO INVIERNO • 1964 • de la Loma Jose Antonio • SPN
VIVIRE OTRA VEZ • 1939 • Rodriguez Roberto • MXC • I SHALL LIVE AGAIN (USA)
VIVISECTIONIST, THE • 1915 • Horne James W. • *Kalem* • USA
VIVISECTIONIST, THE • 1915 • Levering Joseph • *Empress* • USA
VIVIT AL SOL • 1967 • Lorente German • SPN • TO LIVE UNDER THE SUN
VIVO O MUERTO • 1959 • Martinez Solares Gilberto • MXC
VIVO PER LA TUA MORTE • 1968 • Bazzoni Camillo • ITL • LONG RIDE FROM HELL, A (USA) ○ I LIVE FOR YOUR DEATH
VIVOS O, PREFERIBILMENTE MUERTES (SPN) see **VIVI O PREFERIBILMENTE MORTI** • 1969
VIVRE • 1928 • Boudrioz Robert • FRN
VIVRE • 1958 • Vilardebo Carlos • SHT • FRN
VIVRE A BONNEUIL • 1974 • Seligmann Guy • DOC • FRN
VIVRE AU PRIMAIRE • 1977 • Lesaunier Daniel • MTV • CND
VIVRE AVEC TOI • 1974 • Dansereau Fernand, Rossignol Yolande • SHT • CND
VIVRE EN CE PAYS • 1965-67 • Sylvestre Claude • SER • CND
VIVRE EN CREOLE • 1982 • D'Aix Alain (c/d) • DOC • CND
VIVRE EN MUSIQUE • 1965 • Regnier Michel • DCS • CND • MASELLA, LES
VIVRE ENSEMBLE • 1973 • Karina Anna • FRN
VIVRE ENSEMBLE: LA REVOLUTION DE LA FAMILLE ELECTRIQUE see **BREATHING TOGETHER: REVOLUTION OF THE ELECTRIC FAMILY** • 1971
VIVRE ENTRE LES MOTS • 1972 • Dansereau Fernand • DOC • CND
VIVRE ICI • 1968 • Goretta Claude • MTV • SWT
VIVRE LA NUIT • 1968 • Camus Marcel • FRN, ITL • RAGAZZA DELLA NOTTE, LA (ITL)
VIVRE LIBRE OU MOURIR • 1980 • Lara Christian • FRN
VIVRE, PAS SURVIVRE • 1974 • Schmidt Jean • DOC • FRN
VIVRE POUR SURVIVRE • 1984 • Pallardy Jean-Marie • FRN, UKN, TRK • WHITE FIRE
VIVRE POUR VIVRE • 1967 • Lelouch Claude • FRN, ITL • VIVERE PER VIVERE (ITL) ○ LIVE FOR LIFE
VIVRE SA VIE • 1962 • Godard Jean-Luc • FRN • MY LIFE TO LIVE (USA) ○ IT'S MY LIFE (UKN)
VIVRE SA VILLE • 1967 • Godbout Jacques • DCS • CND
VIXEN see **JYOTAI** • 1969
VIXEN see **RUSS MEYER'S VIXEN** • 1969
VIXEN, THE • 1910 • *Powers* • USA
VIXEN, THE • 1916 • Edwards J. Gordon • USA • LOVE PIRATE, THE (UKN)
VIXEN, THE see **LUPA, LA** • 1953
VIXEN AND THE HARE, THE see **FOX AND HARE** • 1973
VIXENS, THE • 1969 • Cort Harvey • USA • FRIENDS AND LOVERS ○ WOMEN, THE
VIY • 1967 • Ptushko Alexander • USS
VIZA NO ZLOTO • 1958 • Stiglic France • YGS • FALSE PASSPORT, THE
VIZANTINI RAPSODHIA (IMPERIALE) • 1968 • Skalenakis Giorgos • GRC • BYZANTINE RHAPSODY (IMPERIALE), A
VIZCAYA CUATRO • 1964 • Aguirre Javier • SHT • SPN
VIZCONDE DE MONTECRISTO, EL • 1954 • Martinez Solares Gilberto • MXC
VIZI MORBOSI DI UNA GOVERNANTE, I • 1977 • Ratti Filippo M. • ITL
VIZI PRIVATI -PUBBLICHE VIRTU • 1976 • Jancso Miklos • ITL, YGS • PRIVATE VICES AND PUBLIC VIRTUES (UKN) ○ VICES AND PLEASURES ○ PRIVATE VICES, PUBLIC VIRTUES (USA)
VIZI SEGRETI DELLA DONNA NEL MONDO, I • 1972 • Secelli Silvano • ITL
VIZINHA DO LADO, A • 1945 • Ribeiro Antonio Lopes • PRT
VIZINHOS DO RES DO CHAO, OS • 1947 • Perla Alejandro • PRT
VIZIO DI FAMIGLIA, IL • 1975 • Laurenti Mariano • ITL • VICES IN THE FAMILY (UKN) ○ FAMILY VICES
VIZIO E LA VIRTU, IL (ITL) see **VICE ET LE VERTU, LE** • 1963
VIZIO HA LE CALZE NERE, IL • 1975 • Cimarosa Tano • ITL
VIZITA see **POZOR, VIZITA** • 1981
VIZIVAROSI NYAR • 1965 • Fabri Zoltan • HNG • HARD SUMMER, A
VIZKERESZET • 1967 • Sara Sandor • SHT • HNG • TWELFTH NIGHT
VJETAR I HRAST see **ERA E LISI** • 1981
VJETROVITA PRICA • 1968 • Grgic Zlatko, Kolar Boris, Zaninovic Ante • ANS • YGS • WINDY STORY
V'LA LE BEAU TEMPS • 1943 • Rigal Andre • ANS • FRN
VLAD TEPES • 1979 • Nastase Doru • RMN
VLADIMIR AND ROSA see **VLADIMIR ET ROSA** • 1971
VLADIMIR ET ROSA • 1971 • Godard Jean-Luc, Gorin Jean-Pierre • FRN • VLADIMIR AND ROSA
VLADIMIR ILYITCH LENIN see **LENIN** • 1948
VLAK BEZ VOZNOG REDA • 1958 • Bulajic Velko • YGS • TRAIN WITHOUT A TIMETABLE ○ UNSCHEDULED TRAIN, THE
VLAK DO STANICE NEBE • 1972 • Kachyna Karel • CZC • TRAIN TO HEAVEN
VLAK U SNIJEGU • 1977 • Relja Mate • YGS • TRAIN IN THE SNOW, THE
VLAKARI • 1988 • Lihosit Juraj • CZC • JUNIOR COMMUTERS
VLAKOM PREMA JUGU • 1981 • Krelja Petar • YGS • SOUTHBOUND TRAIN
VLASAKKER, DE • 1982 • Gruyaert Jan • NTH, BLG
VLASCHAARD, DE • 1983 • Gruyaert Jan • BLG • CHAMP DE LIN, LE
VLAST VITA • 1945 • Vavra Otakar, Holman • CZC • WELCOME HOME
VLASTELI BYTA • 1932 • Ptushko Alexander • ANS • USS • HOW RULERS LIVE
VLASTNE SE NIC NESTALO • 1988 • Schorm Evald • CZC • KILLING WITH KINDNESS
VLAZ BEZ JIZDNIHO RADU • 1959 • Bulajic Velko • YGS
VLCI JAMA • 1958 • Weiss Jiri • CZC • WOLF TRAP
VLCIE DIERY • 1948 • Bielik Palo • CZC • FOXHOLES
VLEPE LOUKIANOS • 1969 • Emirzas George • GRC • SEE LUCIAN
VLIEGEN ZONDER VLEUGELS • 1977 • van der Meulen Karst • NTH • FLYING WITHOUT WINGS
VLIEGENDE HOLLANDER, DER • 1957 • Rutten Gerard • NTH
VLINDERVANGER, DIE • 1976 • SAF
VLIUBLYONNIE see **V LYUBLENNYE** • 1970
VLUBIEN PO SOBSTVENNOMU ZHELANIJU • 1983 • Mikailyan Sergei • USS • LOVE BY REQUEST
VLUBLIONYE see **V LYUBLENNYE** • 1970
VLUG VAN DIE SEEMEEU • 1972 • SAF
VLUGTELING, DIE • 1960 • SAF
VM-FIGHTEN PATTERSON-LISTON • 1962 • *Stivell Arne (Edt)* • SWD
VMV 6 • 1936 • Orko Risto • FNL
VNIMANIE CHEREPAKHA • 1969 • Bykov Rolan • USS • ATTENTION TORTOISE!
VO IMYA RODINI • 1943 • Pudovkin V. I., Vasiliev Dimitri • USS • IN THE NAME OF OUR MOTHERLAND ○ IN THE NAME OF THE FATHERLAND
VO IMYA ZHIZNI • 1947 • Heifitz Josif, Zarkhi Alexander • USS • IN THE NAME OF LIFE ○ FOR THE LIVING
VOCACION SUSPENDIDA, LA • 1977 • Ruiz Raul • FRN • VOCATION SUSPENDED, THE ○ VOCATION SUSPENDUE, LA ○ SUSPENDED VOCATION, THE
VOCALIZING • 1936 • Goodwins Leslie • SHT • USA
VOCATION, THE see **KALLELSEN** • 1974
VOCATION D'ANDRE CAREL, LA • 1925 • Choux Jean • SWT
VOCATION IRRESISTIBLE, UNE • 1934 • Delannoy Jean • SHT • FRN
VOCATION SUSPENDED, THE see **VOCACION SUSPENDIDA, LA** • 1977
VOCATION SUSPENDUE, LA see **VOCACION SUSPENDIDA, LA** • 1977
VOCAZIONE, LA see **CRISTIANA MOACA INDEMONIATA** • 1972
VOCE CHE UCCIDE, LA • 1957 • Colombo Aldo • ITL
VOCE DEL CUORE, LA • 1920 • Caserini Mario • ITL
VOCE DEL PADRONE, LA see **TRE UOMINI IN FRAK** • 1933
VOCE DEL SANGUE, LA • 1933 • Ucicky Gustav

VOCE DEL SANGUE, LA • 1954 • Mercanti Pino • ITL
VOCE DEL SILENZIO, LA • 1952 • Pabst G. W. • ITL, FRN • VOICE OF SILENCE, THE (USA) ○ HOUSE OF SILENCE, THE ○ MAISON DU SILENCE, LA
VOCE DELLA LUNA, LA • 1990 • Fellini Federico • ITL, FRN • VOICE OF THE MOON, THE
VOCE 'E NOTTE see **FIGLIA DEL PECCATO, LA** • 1949
VOCE LONTANA, LA • 1933 • Brignone Guido • ITL
VOCE NEL TUO CUORE, UNA • 1950 • D'Aversa Alberto • ITL
VOCE SENZA VOLTO, LA • 1939 • Righelli Gennaro • ITL
VOCE, UNA CHITARRA, UN PO' DI LUNA, UNA • 1956 • Gentilomo Giacomo • ITL
VOCES DE PRIMAVERA • 1946 • Salvador Jaime • MXC
VOCI BIANCHE, LE • 1964 • Festa Campanile Pasquale, Franciosa Massimo • ITL, FRN • SEXE DE ANGES, LE (FRN) ○ WHITE VOICES (USA) ○ COUNTER TENORS, THE ○ UNDER COVER ROGUE ○ CASTRATI, I
VODKA, MR. PALMU see **VODKAA KOMISARIO PALMU** • 1969
VODKAA KOMISARIO PALMU • 1969 • Kassila Matti • FNL • VODKA, MR. PALMU
VODNICKA PODHADKA • 1973 • Hofman Eduard • ANS • PLN • WATER-SPRITE'S TALE, THE
VODNIKOVA TRAGEDIE • 1958 • Kabrt Josef • ANS • CZC • TRAGEDY OF THE WATERSPRITE, THE
VOGEL IM KAFIG, DER • 1917 • Bolten-Baeckers Heinrich • FRG
VOGELHANDLER, DER • 1935 • Emo E. W. • FRG
VOGELHANDLER, DER • 1953 • Rabenalt Arthur M. • FRG
VOGELHANDLER, DER • 1962 • von Cziffra Geza • FRG
VOGELOD CASTLE see **SCHLOSS VOGELOD** • 1921
VOGELOD CASTLE see **SCHLOSS VOGELOD** • 1936
VOGELOD: THE HAUNTED CASTLE see **SCHLOSS VOGELOD** • 1921
VOGEL'S SPECIES see **GALLINA VOGELBIRDAE** • 1963
VOGLIA DA MORIRE, UNA • 1965 • Tessari Duccio • ITL, FRN
VOGLIA DI GUARDERE • 1985 • D'Amato Joe • ITL
VOGLIA MATTA, LA • 1962 • Salce Luciano • ITL • CRAZY DESIRE (USA) ○ THIS CRAZY URGE
VOGLIA MATTA DI DONNA (ITL) see **BAISERS, LES** • 1964
VOGLIAMO I COLONNELLI • 1973 • Monicelli Mario • ITL
VOGLIAMOCI BENE • 1950 • Tamburella Paolo William • ITL • RING AROUND THE CLOCK (USA)
VOGLIO BENE SOLTANTO A TE • 1947 • Fatigati Giuseppe • ITL
VOGLIO TRADIRE MIO MARITO • 1925 • Camerini Mario • ITL
VOGLIO VIVERE CON LETIZIA • 1938 • Mastrocinque Camillo • ITL
VOGLIO VIVERE COSI • 1942 • Mattoli Mario • ITL
VOGLIO VIVERE LA MIA VITA (ITL) see **ARNAUD, LES** • 1967
VOGT DIG FOR DINE VENNER see **HENDES HELT** • 1917
VOGUE–A–LA–MER see **PADDLE TO THE SEA** • 1966
VOGUE MON COEUR • 1935 • Daroy Jacques • FRN
VOGUE VERS L'AMERIQUE, IL • 1975 • Akerman Chantal • BLG
VOGUES • 1937 • Cummings Irving • USA • WALTER WANGER'S VOGUES OF 1938 ○ VOGUES OF 1938 ○ ALL THIS AND GLAMOUR TOO
VOGUES OF 1938 see **VOGUES** • 1937
VOI, PETER, PETER • 1972 • Kassila Matti • FNL • OH, PETER, PETER!
VOICE, THE • 1967 • Soltero Jose • USA • HUMAN VOICE, THE
VOICE, THE see **SES** • 1986
VOICE AT THE TELEPHONE (PART 1), THE • 1914 • *Kb* • USA
VOICE AT THE TELEPHONE (PART 2), THE • 1914 • *Kb* • USA
VOICE FROM BEYOND see **GLOS Z TAMTEGO SWIATA** • 1962
VOICE FROM THE DEAD, A • 1908 • Porter Edwin S. • USA
VOICE FROM THE DEAD, A • 1921 • Paul Fred • UKN
VOICE FROM THE DEEP, A • 1912 • Sennett Mack • USA
VOICE FROM THE FIREPLACE, A • 1910 • *Essanay* • USA
VOICE FROM THE MINARET, THE • 1923 • Lloyd Frank • USA
VOICE FROM THE PAST, A see **SPIRITISTEN** • 1914
VOICE FROM THE SEA, A • 1915 • MacDonald Donald • USA
VOICE FROM THE SKY • 1930 • Wilson Ben • SRL • USA
VOICE FROM THE SKY see **AKASHWANI** • 1934
VOICE FROM THE TAXI, THE • 1915 • *Kalem* • USA
VOICE IN THE DARK • 1989 • Cox Vincent • SAF
VOICE IN THE DARK, A • 1921 • Lloyd Frank • USA • OUT OF THE DARK
VOICE IN THE FOG, THE • 1915 • Reicher Frank • USA
VOICE IN THE MIRROR • 1958 • Keller Harry • USA
VOICE IN THE NIGHT • 1934 • Coleman C. C. Jr. • USA
VOICE IN THE NIGHT, A • 1915 • *Stanley H.* • USA
VOICE IN THE NIGHT, A see **WANTED FOR MURDER** • 1946
VOICE IN THE NIGHT, THE • 1916 • Greene Clay M. • SHT • USA
VOICE IN THE NIGHT, THE (USA) see **FREEDOM RADIO** • 1941
VOICE IN THE WILDERNESS, THE • 1914 • *Bushman Francis X.* • USA
VOICE IN THE WIND • 1944 • Ripley Arthur • USA
VOICE OF ANGELO, THE • 1913 • *Lubin* • USA
VOICE OF BLOOD, THE see **BLODETS ROST** • 1913
VOICE OF BUGLE ANN, THE • 1936 • Thorpe Richard • USA
VOICE OF CONSCIENCE, THE • 1912 • *Thanhouser* • USA
VOICE OF CONSCIENCE, THE • 1912 • Wharton Theodore • *Essanay* • USA
VOICE OF CONSCIENCE, THE • 1915 • France Charles H. • USA
VOICE OF CONSCIENCE, THE • 1917 • Carewe Edwin • USA
VOICE OF CONSCIENCE, THE see **GEBIETERISCHE RUF, DER** • 1944
VOICE OF DESTINY, THE • 1918 • Bertram William • USA
VOICE OF EVA, THE • 1915 • King Burton L. • USA
VOICE OF GIUSEPPE, THE • 1913 • *Essanay* • USA
VOICE OF HIS CONSCIENCE, THE • 1911 • *Solax* • USA
VOICE OF HOLLYWOOD, THE • *Tiffany Pictures* • SHS • USA
VOICE OF IRELAND, THE • 1936 • Haddick Victor • IRL, UKN
VOICE OF KURDISTAN, THE • 1982 • Orion Georges • UKN, ASL
VOICE OF LIBERTY see **OUT OF DARKNESS** • 1941
VOICE OF LOVE, THE • 1916 • Berger Rea • USA
VOICE OF LOVE, THE (USA) see **PRONTO, CHI PARLA?** • 1945
VOICE OF MERRILL, THE • 1952 • Gilling John • UKN • MURDER WILL OUT (USA)
VOICE OF SCANDAL, THE (UKN) see **HERE COMES CARTER** • 1936
VOICE OF SILENCE, THE • 1914 • Ridgely Richard • USA
VOICE OF SILENCE, THE (USA) see **VOCE DEL SILENZIO, LA** • 1952
VOICE OF THE BELLS • 1914 • *Melies* • USA
VOICE OF THE BLOOD see **BLODETS ROST** • 1913
VOICE OF THE CHILD, THE • 1911 • Griffith D. W. • USA
VOICE OF THE CITY • 1929 • Mack Willard • USA
VOICE OF THE DEAD, THE see **TESTAMENTETS HEMMELIGHED** • 1916
VOICE OF THE FUGITIVES • 1977 • Bonniere Rene • SHT • CND
VOICE OF THE GRAVEDIGGER, THE see **VOZ DO COVEIRO, A** • 1943
VOICE OF THE HEART • 1989 • Wharmby Tony • TVM • USA
VOICE OF THE HEART see **HJARTATS ROST** • 1930
VOICE OF THE HURRICANE • 1964 • Fraser George • USA
VOICE OF THE JUNGLE • 1931 • Pollard Bud • USA
VOICE OF THE MILLIONS, THE • 1912 • Taylor Stanner E. V. • USA
VOICE OF THE MOON, THE see **VOCE DELLA LUNA, LA** • 1990
VOICE OF THE NIGHTINGALE, THE (USA) see **VOIX DU ROSSIGNOL, LA** • 1923
VOICE OF THE PEOPLE, THE • 1935-45 • Sainsbury Frank • DOC • UKN
VOICE OF THE STORM, THE • 1929 • Shores Lynn • USA
VOICE OF THE TURKEY • 1950 • Tytla Bill • ANS • USA
VOICE OF THE TURTLE, THE • 1947 • Rapper Irving • USA • ONE FOR THE BOOK
VOICE OF THE VIOLA, THE • 1914 • Reid Wallace • USA
VOICE OF THE VIOLIN, THE • 1909 • Griffith D. W. • USA
VOICE OF THE WATER, THE see **STEM VAN HET WATER, DE** • 1966
VOICE OF THE WATERS • 1918 • SAF
VOICE OF THE WHISTLER • 1946 • Castle William • USA
VOICE OF THE WORLD • 1932 • Elton Arthur • DOC • UKN
VOICE OF THOSE WHO ARE NOT HERE • 1982 • van Zuylen Erik • NTH
VOICE OF WARNING, THE • 1912 • *Greenwood Reine* • USA
VOICE ON THE AIR, A • 1987 • Benchev Detelin • DOC • BUL
VOICE ON THE WIRE, THE • 1917 • Paton Stuart, Wilson Ben • SRL • USA
VOICE OVER • 1982 • Monger Chris • UKN
VOICE SAID GOODNIGHT, A • 1932 • McGann William • UKN
VOICE THAT LED HIM, THE • 1917 • Grandon Francis J. • SHT • USA
VOICE THAT THRILLED THE WORLD, THE • 1943 • Negulesco Jean • SHT • USA
VOICE UPSTAIRS, THE • 1916 • Brenon Herbert • SHT • USA
VOICE WITHIN, THE • 1929 • Archainbaud George • USA
VOICE WITHIN, THE • 1945 • Wilson Maurice J. • UKN
VOICELESS MESSAGE, THE • 1911 • *De Garde Adele* • USA
VOICES • 1920 • De Vonde Chester M. • USA
VOICES • 1968 • Mordaunt Richard • UKN
VOICES • 1973 • Billington Kevin • UKN
VOICES • 1979 • Markowitz Robert • USA
VOICES see **GLOSY** • 1980
VOICES ACROSS THE SEA • 1928 • *Gilbert John* • SHT • USA
VOICES FROM ARCADIA • 1952 • Blais Roger • DCS • CND
VOICES FROM THE PAST • 1915 • Smiley Joseph • USA
VOICES IN THE DARK • 1915 • *Hallam Henry* • USA
VOICES OF EARLY CANADA • 1981 • Rodgers Bob • DOC • CND
VOICES OF MALAYA • 1948 • Elton Ralph • UKN
VOICES OF SARAFINA! • 1989 • Noble Nigel • DOC • USA
VOICES OF SPRING see **VESENNIE GOLOSA** • 1955
VOICES OF THE CITY see **NIGHT ROSE, THE** • 1921
VOICES OF THE TEMPTER, THE • 1916 • Le Saint Edward J. • USA
VOICES UNDER THE SEA • 1951 • Harvey Maurice • DOC • UKN
VOICES WITHIN see **SHATTERED** • 1990
VOICI DES FLEURS • 1963 • de Vaucorbeil Max • SHT • FRN
VOICI LE PAYS D'ISRAEL • 1957 • Leherissey Jean • SHT • FRN
VOICI LE SKI • 1961 • Ertaud Jacques • DOC • FRN
VOICI LE TEMPS DES ASSASSINS • 1956 • Duvivier Julien • FRN • DEADLIER THAT THE MALE (USA) ○ MURDER A LA CARTE
VOIE, LA • 1967 • Riad Mohamed Slimane • ALG • ROAD, THE
VOIE DE LA VICTOIRE, LA • 1972 • Marzouk Said • SHT • EGY • WAY TO VICTORY, THE
VOIE DU PEUPLE, LA • ALG • PEOPLE'S WAY, THE
VOIE DU REVE, LA • 1973 • Sarkissian Harry • IRQ
VOIE LACTEE, LA • 1968 • Bunuel Luis • FRN, ITL, SPN • VIA LATTEA, LA (ITL) ○ MILKY WAY, THE
VOIE SANS DISQUE, LA • 1933 • Poirier Leon • FRN
VOIE TRIOMPHALE, LA • 1936 • Cuny Louis • FRN
VOIENNO–POLEVOI ROMAN • 1983 • Todorovsky Petr • USS • FRONT–LINE ROMANCE, A
VOIJUKU, MIKA LAUANTAI • 1979 • Makinen Visa • FNL • WOW! WHAT A SATURDAY!
VOILA MONTMARTRE • 1934 • Capellani Roger • FRN
VOILA VOUS • 1951 • Dupont Jacques • SHT • FRN
VOILE BLEU, LE • 1942 • Stelli Jean • FRN • BLUE VEIL, THE (USA)
VOILE DES NYMPHES, LE • 1908 • Perret Leonce • FRN
VOILE DU BONHEUR, LE • 1910 • Capellani Albert • FRN
VOILE DU BONHEUR, LE • 1923 • Violet Edouard-Emile • FRN • VEIL OF HAPPINESS, THE
VOILE DU PASSE, LE • 1913 • Jasset Victorin • FRN
VOILES A VAL • 1959 • Perol Guy • SHT • FRN
VOILES BAS ET EN TRAVERS, LES • 1983 • Perrault Pierre • CND
VOILES DANS LE DESERT • 1968 • Kerzabi Ahmed • SHT • ALG
VOINA I MIR • 1915 • Protazanov Yakov, Gardin Vladimir • USS • WAR AND PEACE
VOINA I MIR • 1967 • Bondarchuk Sergei • USS • WAR AND PEACE (USA)
VOINIKUT OT OBOZA see **BRATUSHKA** • 1975
VOIR MIAMI • 1962 • Groulx Gilles • CND
VOIR NAITRE • Diamant-Berger Jerome • DCS • FRN
VOIR PELLAN • 1968 • Portugais Louis • DCS • CND
VOIR VENISE ET CREVER • 1966 • Versini Andre • FRN, FRG, ITL • MORD AM CANALE GRANDE (FRG)
VOISIN TROP GOURMAND, LE • 1915 • Cohl Emile • ANS • FRN
VOISIN, VOISINE • 1911 • Linder Max • FRN
VOISINE DU MELOMANE, LA • 1908 • Bosetti Romeo • FRN
VOISINS see **NEIGHBOURS** • 1952
VOITHIA O VENGOS • 1967 • Vengos Thanasis • GRC • HELP, VENGOS!
VOITURE, LA • 1981 • Koleva Maria • FRN
VOITURE CELLULAIRE, LA • 1906 • Blache Alice • FRN
VOITURE DU POTIER, LA • 1896 • Melies Georges • FRN • POTTER'S CART, THE
VOITURES D'EAU, LES • 1968 • Perrault Pierre • CND • RIVER "SCHOONERS", THE
VOIX D'ACADIE see **SINGING CHAMPIONS** • 1952
VOIX DANS LA NUIT, UNE see **SLIPSTREAM** • 1973
VOIX DE LA CONSCIENCE, LA • 1905-10 • Heuze Andre • FRN
VOIX DE LA PATRIE, LA • 1915 • Perret Leonce • FRN
VOIX DE L'AU–DELA, LA see **VOIX DU REVE, LA** • 1948
VOIX DE L'OCEAN, LA • 1922 • Roudes Gaston • FRN
VOIX DE SON MAITRE, LA • 1977 • Mordillat Gerard, Philibert Nicolas • DOC • FRN
VOIX DES ANCHES, LA • 1957 • Leduc • SHT • FRN
VOIX D'ORLY, LES • 1965 • Lachenay • SHT • FRN
VOIX DU BONHEUR, LA see **RETOUR A BONHEUR** • 1940
VOIX DU CHATIMENT, LA see **VOIX SANS VISAGE, LA** • 1933
VOIX DU LARGE, LA • 1971 • Porcile Francois • FRN
VOIX DU METAL, LA • 1933 • Marca-Rosa Youly • FRN • APPEL DE LA NUIT, L'
VOIX DU PASSE, UNE see **SAWT MINA AL–MAHDI** • 1956
VOIX DU PRINTEMPS, LES see **FRUHLINGSTIMMEN** • 1933
VOIX DU REVE, LA • 1948 • Paulin Jean-Paul • FRN • VOIX DE L'AU–DELA, LA
VOIX DU ROSSIGNOL, LA • 1923 • Starevitch Ladislas • FRN • VOICE OF THE NIGHTINGALE, THE (USA) ○ SONG OF THE NIGHTINGALE, THE
VOIX HUMAINE, LA • 1970 • Delouche Dominique • FRN
VOIX LIBRE • 1944 • Tedesco Jean • SHT • FRN
VOIX QUI MEURT, LA • 1932 • Dini Gennaro • FRN
VOIX SANS VISAGE, LA • 1933 • Mittler Leo • FRN • VOIX DU CHATIMENT, LA
VOJNARKA • 1936 • Borsky Vladimir • CZC
VOJNIK see **SOLDIER, THE** • 1966
VOJNIKOVA LJUBAV • 1977 • Pavlovic Sveta • YGS • SOLDIER'S LOVE, THE
VOKZAL DLIA DVOIKH • 1983 • Ryazanov Eldar • USS • RAILWAY STOP FOR TWO, A ○ STATION FOR TWO, A
VOL, LE • 1925 • Peguy Robert • FRN
VOL A VOILE • 1960 • Benoit Real • DOC • CND
VOL DE REVE • 1983 • Bergeron Philip, Thalman Nadia, Thalman Daniel • ANS • CND
VOL D'ICARE, LE • 1980 • Ceccaldi Daniel • MTV • FRN
VOL D'OISEAU see **A VOL D'OISEAU** • 1962
VOL DU SPHINX, LE • 1984 • Ferrier Laurent • FRN
VOL EN AEROPLANE, UN • 1910 • Machin Alfred • FRN
VOL ETRANGE, UN • 1919 • Desfontaines Henri • FRN
VOLANDO HACIA LA FAMA • 1961 • Franco Jesus • SPN
VOLANIE DEMONOV • 1967 • Lettrich Andrej • CZC • CALL OF THE DEMONS, THE
VOLANTIN • 1961 • Vejar Sergio • MXC
VOLCA NOC • 1955 • Stiglic France • YGS • LIVING NIGHTMARE
VOLCAN, LE see **VOLCANO: AN INQUIRY INTO THE LIFE AND DEATH OF MALCOLM LOWRY** • 1976
VOLCAN INTERDIT, LE • 1966 • Tazieff Haroun, Marker Chris • DOC • FRN
VOLCANIC ERUPTIONS • 1910-12 • Melies Gaston • USA
VOLCANO • 1926 • Howard William K. • USA
VOLCANO • 1942 • Fleischer Dave • ANS • USA
VOLCANO • 1973 • Chapman Christopher • DOC • CND
VOLCANO see **RENDEZ–VOUS DU DIABLE, LES** • 1958
VOLCANO see **KRAKATOA, EAST OF JAVA** • 1969
VOLCANO, THE • 1919 • Irving George • USA
VOLCANO: AN INQUIRY INTO THE LIFE AND DEATH OF MALCOLM LOWRY • 1976 • Brittain Don • DOC • CND • VOLCAN, LE
VOLCANO MONSTER, THE see **GOJIRA NO GYAKUSHYU** • 1955
VOLCANO OF HELLISH DESIRES see **VULKAN DER HOLLISCHEN TRIEBE** • 1968
VOLCANO OF STATION FRONT PLAZA see **KIGEKI EKIMAE KAZAN** • 1968
VOLCANO (USA) see **VULCANO** • 1950
VOLCANS, LES • 1981 • Tazieff Haroun • DOC • FRN
VOLDTEKT see **VOLDTEKT –TILFELLET ANDERS** • 1971
VOLDTEKT –TILFELLET ANDERS • 1971 • Breien Anja • NRW, UKN • RAPE ○ VOLDTEKT
VOLEE PAR LES BOHEMIENS see **RAPT D'ENFANT PAR LES ROMANICHELS** • 1904
VOLETS CLOS, LES • 1972 • Brialy Jean-Claude • FRN • CLOSED SHUTTERS (USA) ○ SHUTTERED WINDOWS
VOLEUR, LE • 1933 • Tourneur Maurice • FRN
VOLEUR, LE • 1967 • Malle Louis • FRN, ITL • THIEF OF PARIS, THE (USA) ○ THIEF, THE (UKN)
VOLEUR DE BAGDAD, LE (FRN) see **LADRO DI BAGDAD, IL** • 1961
VOLEUR DE BICYCLETTES, LE • 1905 • Heuze Andre • FRN
VOLEUR DE CRIMES, LES • 1969 • Trintignant Nadine • FRN, ITL • LADRO DI CRIMINI, IL (ITL) ○ CRIME THIEF, THE
VOLEUR DE FEMMES • 1963 • Rozier Willy • FRN • ROI DES MONTAGNES, LE
VOLEUR DE FEMMES, LE • 1936 • Gance Abel • FRN, ITL • LADRO DI DONNE (ITL)
VOLEUR DE FEUILLES, LE • 1983 • Trabaud Pierre • FRN
VOLEUR DE LA JOCONDE, LE see **ON A VOLE LA JOCONDE** • 1965
VOLEUR DE PARATONNERRES, LE • 1946 • Grimault Paul • ANS • FRN • LIGHTNING–ROD THIEF, THE ○ CHIMNEY THIEF, THE
VOLEUR DE REVES, LE • 1953 • Blais Roger • DCS • CND
VOLEUR DE SCHTROUMPFS, LE • 1960 • Ryssack Eddy • ANS • BLG

VOLEUR DU TIBIDABO, LE • 1965 • Ronet Maurice • FRN, SPN • NOEL AU SOLEIL
VOLEUR ET LES CHIENS, LE see **LISSU WA AL-KILAB, AL-** • 1962
VOLEUR SACRILEGE, LE • 1903 • Blache Alice • FRN
VOLEUR SE PORTE BIEN, LE • 1946 • Loubignac Jean • FRN
VOLEURS DE GLOIRE, LES • 1926 • Marodon Pierre • FRN
VOLEURS DE JOBS, LES • 1979 • Rached Tahani • CND
VOLEURS DE LA NUIT, LES • 1983 • Fuller Samuel • FRN • THIEVES AFTER DARK (USA)
VOLEUSE, LA • 1966 • Chapot Jean • FRN, FRG • SCHORNSTEIN NR.4 (FRG)
VOLEVO I PANTALONI • 1990 • Ponzi Maurizio • ITL • I WANTED THE TROUSERS
VOLGA AND SIBERIA see **VOLGA I SIBERIA** • 1914
VOLGA BOATMAN, THE • 1926 • De Mille Cecil B. • USA
VOLGA EN FEU see **VOLGA EN FLAMMES** • 1933
VOLGA EN FLAMMES • 1933 • Tourjansky Victor • FRN, CZC • VOLHA V PLAMENECH (CZC) ○ VOLGA EN FEU ○ FLAMES ON THE VOLGA
VOLGA I SIBERIA • 1914 • Goncharov Vasili M. • USS • VOLGA AND SIBERIA
VOLGA IS FLOWING, THE see **TECHET VOLGA** • 1964
VOLGA SINGERS, THE • 1930 • *Balcon Michael (P)* • SHT • UKN
VOLGA, VOLGA • 1928 • Tourjansky Victor • USS • WOLGA, WOLGA
VOLGA, VOLGA • 1938 • Alexandrov Grigori • USS
VOLGEND JAAR IN HOLYSLOOT • 1983 • van Morkerken Emile • SHT • NTH • NEXT YEAR IN HOLYSLOOT
VOLGY, A • 1968 • Renyi Tamas • HNG • VALLEY, THE
VOLHA V PLAMENECH (CZC) see **VOLGA EN FLAMMES** • 1933
VOLIO BIH DA SAM GOLUB • 1989 • Stamenkovic Miomir • YGS • I WISH I WAS A DOVE
VOLITE SE, A NE RATUJTE • 1972 • Grgic Zlatko • ANS • YGS • MAKE LOVE, NOT WAR
VOLK IN NOT • 1925 • Neff Wolfgang • FRG
VOLK WILL LEBEN, EIN • 1939 • Stemmle R. A. • FRG • PEOPLE WANTS TO LIVE, A
VOLKFEST KANNSTADT • 1935 • Ruttmann Walter • FRG • STADT STUTTGART, 100. CANSTATTER VOLKSFEST
VOLKSFEIND, EIN • 1937 • Steinhoff Hans • FRG
VOLKSKRANKHEIT KREBS -JEDER ACHTE see **FILM GEGEN DIE VOLKKRANKHEIT KREBS -JEDER ACHTE.., EIN** • 1941
VOLKSWAGENN WAY AHEAD • 1976 • Howard John • DOC • UKN
VOLLDAMPF VORAUS • 1933 • Froelich Carl • FRG
VOLLENDETE SCHICKSAL, DAS • 1919 • Osten Franz • FRG
VOLLES HERZ UND LEERE TASCHEN • 1964 • Mastrocinque Camillo • FRG, ITL • FULL HEARTS AND EMPTY POCKETS (USA)
VOLLEY-BALL • 1966 • Arcand Denys • DOC • CND
VOLLEY FROM THE "AURORA", A • 1966 • Vyshinsky Yu. • USS
VOLLEYBALL • 1968 • Rainer Yvonne • SHT • USA • FOOT FILM
VOLLKOMMENE EHE, DIE • 1967 • Gottlieb Franz J. • FRG
VOLLMACHT ZUM MORD • 1975 • Frankel Cyril • AUS • PERMISSION TO KILL
VOLNAYA PTITSA • 1913 • Bauer Yevgeni • USS • FREED BIRD
VOLNITSA • 1956 • Roshal Grigori • USS • FREE MAN
VOLNYI VETER • 1961 • Trauberg Leonid, Tontichkin A. • USS • FREE WIND
VOLO DEGLI AIRONI, IL • 1920 • Falena Ugo • ITL
VOLOCHAYEVSK DAYS see **VOLOCHAYEVSKIYE DNI** • 1938
VOLOCHAYEVSKIYE DNI • 1938 • Vasiliev Georgi, Vasiliev Sergei • USS • DEFENSE OF VOLOTCHAYEVSK, THE ○ VOLOCHAYEVSK DAYS ○ DAYS OF VOLOCHAYEV, THE ○ FAR EAST ○ INTERVENTION IN THE FAR EAST ○ JOURS DE VOLOTCHAIEV, LES
VOLONTAR, DER • 1919 • Neuss Alwin • FRG
VOLONTARI PER DESTINAZIONE IGNOTA • 1978 • Negrin Alberto • ITL • VOLUNTEERS FOR DESTINATION UNKNOWN
VOLONTARIAT, LE • 1973 • Mazif Sid-Ali • SHT • ALG
VOLONTE • 1915 • Pouctal Henri • FRN
VOLPE DALLA CODA DI VELLUTO, LA • 1971 • Forque Jose Maria • ITL, FRN • SUSPICION
VOLPONE • 1940 • Tourneur Maurice • FRN
VOLSHEBNAYA LAMPA ALADDINA • 1967 • Rytsarev Boris • USS • ALLADIN AND HIS MAGIC LAMP (USA) ○ ALADDIN'S MAGIC LAMP
VOLSHEBNOYE ZERNO • 1942 • Kadochnikov V., Filippov Fyodor • USS • MAGIC SEED, THE
VOLSHEVNOYE ZERKALO • 1958 • Komisarjevsky James, Aksenchuk Ivan, Kristi Leonid • USS • ENCHANTED MIRROR, THE (USA)
VOLT EGYSZER EGY CSALAD • 1972 • Revesz Gyorgy • HNG • THERE WAS ONCE A FAMILY
VOLTA ALLA SETTIMANA, UNA • 1942 • von Rathony Akos • ITL
VOLTA DE JOSE DO TELHADO, A • 1949 • Miranda Armando • PRT
VOLTA REDONDA • 1952 • Waterhouse • BRZ
VOLTAIRE • 1933 • Adolfi John G. • USA
VOLTATI ANDREA • 1979 • Comencini Luigi • ITL
VOLTATI EUGENIO • 1980 • Comencini Luigi • ITL • TURN AROUND EUGENE
VOLTATI.. TI UCCIDO • 1967 • Brescia Alfonso • ITL
VOLTERA, COMUNE MEDIEVALE • 1955 • Taviani Paolo, Taviani Vittorio • DCS • ITL
VOLTI DELL'AMORE, I • 1923 • Gallone Carmine • ITL
VOLTIGE, LA • 1895 • Lumiere Louis • FRN
VOLTINITSA • 1956 • Roshal Grigori • USS • FLAMES ON THE VOLGA ○ SALT OF THE SEA
VOLTRON DEFENDER OF THE UNIVERSE: CASTLE OF LIONS see **VOLTRON DEFENDER OF THE UNIVERSE IN THE CASTLE OF LIONS** • 1984
VOLTRON DEFENDER OF THE UNIVERSE IN THE BATTLE OF ARUS • 1984 • ANM • JPN • VOLTRON DEFENDER OF THE UNIVERSE: PLANET ARUS
VOLTRON DEFENDER OF THE UNIVERSE IN THE CASTLE OF LIONS • 1984 • ANM • JPN • VOLTRON DEFENDER OF THE UNIVERSE: CASTLE OF LIONS
VOLTRON DEFENDER OF THE UNIVERSE IN THE INVASION OF THE ROBOBEASTS • 1984 • ANM • JPN • VOLTRON DEFENDER OF THE UNIVERSE: INVASION OF THE ROBOBEASTS
VOLTRON DEFENDER OF THE UNIVERSE: INVASION OF THE ROBOBEASTS see **VOLTRON DEFENDER OF THE UNIVERSE IN THE INVASION OF THE ROBOBEASTS** • 1984
VOLTRON DEFENDER OF THE UNIVERSE: PLANET ARUS see **VOLTRON DEFENDER OF THE UNIVERSE IN THE BATTLE OF ARUS** • 1984
VOLUNTEER, THE • 1918 • Knoles Harley • USA
VOLUNTEER, THE • 1943 • Powell Michael, Pressburger Emeric • UKN
VOLUNTEER, THE • 1983 • Kennedy Michael • CND, IND
VOLUNTEER BURGLAR, THE • 1914 • *Travers Richard C.* • USA
VOLUNTEER COMMANDOS IN CYPRUS, THE see **FEDAI KOMANDOLAR KIBRISTA** • 1968
VOLUNTEER FIREMAN, THE • 1915 • *Thompson Dave* • USA
VOLUNTEER HEROES see **GONULLU KAHRAMANLAR** • 1968
VOLUNTEER STRIKE BREAKERS, THE • 1913 • *Vitagraph* • USA
VOLUNTEERS • 1985 • Meyer Nicholas • USA
VOLUNTEERS see **DOBROVOLTSY** • 1958
VOLUNTEERS FOR DESTINATION UNKNOWN see **VOLONTARI PER DESTINAZIONE IGNOTA** • 1978
VOLVER • 1982 • Lipszyc David • ARG • COMING BACK
VOLVER A EMPEZAR • 1983 • Garci Jose Luis • SPN • TO BEGIN AGAIN
VOLVER A VIVIR • 1956 • Ardavin Eusebio F. • SPN • COMPADECE AL DELINCUENTE
VOLVER A VIVIR • 1968 • Camus Mario • SPN, ITL • TO LIVE AGAIN
VOLVER.. VOLVER • 1975 • *Aguila* • MXC
VOLVERE A NACER • 1972 • Aguirre Javier • SPN
VOLVORETA • 1976 • Nieves Conde Jose Antonio • SPN
VOM DIEB ZUM BEHERRSCHER see **RUSSLAND 2** • 1924
VOM FREUDENHAUS IN DIE EHE see **MADCHEN OHNE HEIMAT, DAS** • 1926
VOM HIMMEL GEFALLEN • 1955 • Brahm John • FRG, USA • SPECIAL DELIVERY (USA)
VOM LEBEN GETOTET • 1927 • Hofer Franz • FRG
VOM NIEDERRHEIN, DIE • 1933 • Obal Max • FRG • LOWER RHINE FOLKS (USA)
VOM RANDE DES SUMPFES • 1919 • Rahn Bruno • FRG
VOM REGEN IN DIE TRAUFE • 1916 • Albes Emil • FRG
VOM REICHE DER SECHS PUNKTE • 1927 • Rutters H. • FRG
VOM SCHICKSAL ERDROSSELT • 1919 • Neisser Karl • FRG
VOM SCHICKSAL VERWEHT • 1942 • Malasomma Nunzio • FRG
VOM SPIELTEUFEL BEFREIT! • 1915 • Eichberg Richard • FRG
VOM TATER FEHLT JEDE SPUR • 1928 • David Constantin J. • FRG • UNDER SUSPICION
VOM TEUFEL GEJAGT • 1950 • Tourjansky Victor • FRG • CHASED BY THE DEVIL
VOM UHU UND ANDEREN GESICHTERN DER NACHT • 1936 • Schulz Ulrich K. T. • FRG • EAGLE-OWLS AND OWLETS
VOM WERDEN DES MENSCHLICHEN LEBENS see **HELGA** • 1967
VOM ZAREN BIS ZU STALIN • 1961 • Nussbaum Raphael • FRG
VOM ZIRKUS, DIE • 1922 • Kahn William • FRG
VON ALLEN GELIEBT • 1957 • Verhoeven Paul • FRG
VON BUTTIGLIONE STURMTRUPPENFUHRER • 1977 • Guerrini Mino • ITL
VON DER LIEBE BESIEGT • 1956 • Trenker Luis • FRG
VON DER LIEBE LEBEN, DIE • 1919 • Illes Eugen • FRG
VON DER LIEBE REDEN WIR SPATER • 1953 • Anton Karl • FRG
VON DRAKE IN SPAIN • 1962 • Foster Norman, Luske Hamilton • USA
VON HAUT ZU HAUT • 1969 • Scott John • FRG • SKIN TO SKIN (UKN) ○ FROM SKIN TO SKIN
VON METZ INCIDENT, THE • 1988 • Clark Bob • USA • FACE OFF
VON MORGENS BIS MITTERNACHTS • 1920 • Martin Karl Heinz • FRG • FROM MORN TO MIDNIGHT
VON RICHTOFEN AND BROWN • 1971 • Corman Roger • USA • RED BARON, THE (UKN) ○ BATTLE OF THE ACES
VON RYAN'S EXPRESS • 1965 • Robson Mark • USA
VON SIEBEN DIE HASSLICHSTE • 1915 • Del Zopp Rudolf • FRG
VON STUFE ZU STUFE • 1925 • *M. Stambulki & Co* • FRG
VON STUFE ZU STUFE BIS IN DEN TOD • 1919 • Illes Eugen? • FRG
VON WEBER'S LAST WALTZ • 1912 • *O'Moore Barry* • USA
VON ZEIT ZU ZEIT • 1988 • Steiger Clemens • SWT • FROM TIME TO TIME
VONTADE MAIOR, UMA • 1967 • Tudela Carlos • PRT • GREATEST WILL, THE
VOO DA AMIZADE, O • 1962 • Lopes Fernando • SHT • PRT
VOODOO • 1933 • *Wirkus Faustin (P)* • DOC • USA
VOODOO BABY • 1979 • D'Amato Joe • ITL
VOODOO BLACK EXORCIST • 1974 • *Sombrel Aldo*
VOODOO BLOOD BATH see **I EAT YOUR SKIN** • 1964
VOODOO: BLOOD BETWEEN LIVING AND DEAD see **VAUDOU: ENTRE VIVANTS EN MORTS, LE SANG, LE** • 1973
VOODOO BOO-HOO • 1962 • Hannah Jack • ANS • USA
VOODOO DAWN • 1988 • Mangine Joe • USA
VOODOO DEVIL DRUMS • *Toddy* • USA
VOODOO FIRES • 1939 • Henabery Joseph • SHT • USA
VOODOO GIRL (UKN) see **SUGAR HILL** • 1974
VOODOO HEARTBEAT • 1972 • Nizet Charles • USA
VOODOO IN HARLEM • 1938 • Zamora Rudy • ANS • USA
VOODOO ISLAND • 1957 • Le Borg Reginald • USA • SILENT DEATH
VOODOO LAND • 1932 • *Futter Walter (P)* • SHT • USA
VOODOO MAN • 1944 • Beaudine William • USA
VOODOO SPELL, A • 1967 • Bakshi Ralph • ANS • USA
VOODOO TIGER • 1952 • Bennet Spencer Gordon • USA
VOODOO VENGEANCE • 1913 • *World'S Best* • USA
VOODOO VILLAGE see **SORCERER'S VILLAGE, THE** • 1958
VOODOO WOMAN • 1957 • Cahn Edward L. • USA
VOOR RECHT EN VRIJHEID TE KORTRIJK • 1939 • Storck Henri • DOC • NTH
VOOR SONONDER • 1962 • SAF
VOORTREFLIKKE FAMILIE SMIT • 1965 • SAF
VOORTREFLIKKE FAMILIE SMIT • 1975 • SAF
VOORTREKKERS, DE • 1916 • Shaw Harold • SAF • WINNING A CONTINENT
VOORTREKKERS, DIE • 1973 • Millin David • SAF
VOORVLUGTIGE SPIOEN • 1974 • SAF
VOR GOTT UND DEN MENSCHEN • 1955 • Engel Erich • FRG
VOR LIEBE WIRD GEWARNT • 1937 • Lamac Carl • FRG
VOR SONNENUNTERGANG • 1956 • Reinhardt Gottfried • FRG
VOR UNS LIEGT DAS LEBEN • 1948 • Rittau Gunther • FRG • FUNF VOM TITAN, DIE
VORACES, LES (FRN) see **COSI BELLO COSI CORROTTO COSI CONTESO** • 1973
VORAGINE • 1948 • Neville Edgar • ITL
VORAGINE, LA • 1948 • Zacarias Miguel • MXC
VORBESTRAFTEN, DIE • 1927 • Meinert Rudolf • FRG
VORDERHAUS UND HINTERHAUS • 1914 • Gad Urban • FRG, DNM • FORHUS OG BAGHUS (DNM) ○ VORDERTREPPE UND HINTERTREPPE
VORDERHAUS UND HINTERHAUS • 1925 • Oswald Richard • FRG
VORDERTREPPE UND HINTERTREPPE see **VORDERHAUS UND HINTERHAUS** • 1914
VORE VENNERS VINTER • 1923 • Lauritzen Lau • DNM
VORGHITEN DES BALKANBRANDES • 1912 • May Joe • FRG
VORHANG FALLT, DER • 1939 • Jacoby Georg • FRG
VORMITTAGSPUK • 1928 • Richter Hans • SHT • FRG • GHOSTS BEFORE BREAKFAST ○ GHOSTS BEFORE NOON
VOROS FOLD • 1983 • Vitezy Laszlo • HNG • RED EARTH
VOROS GROFNO, A • 1984 • Kovacs Andras • HNG • RED COUNTESS, THE
VOROS MAJUS • 1968 • Jancso Miklos • SHT • HNG • RED MAY
VOROS REKVIEM • 1975 • Grunwalsky Ferenc • HNG • REQUIEM FOR A REVOLUTIONARY ○ RED REQUIEM
VOROS SAMSON, A • 1917 • Curtiz Michael • HNG • RED SAMSON, THE
VOROS TINTA • 1959 • Gertler Viktor • HNG • RED INK
VORREI MORIR • 1918 • *Lukas Paul* • HNG
VORSICHT! HOCHSPANNUNG! LEBENSGEFAHR! • 1920 • Paster Alfred • FRG
VORSICHT, MISTER DODD • 1964 • Grawert Gunter • FRG
VORSTADTGRAFIN • 1926 • Lamac Carl • FRG
VORSTADTVARIETE • 1934 • Hochbaum Werner • AUS • AMSEL VON LICHTENTAL, DIE
VORTEX • 1983 • B. Scott, B. Beth • USA
VORTEX see **DAY TIME ENDED, THE** • 1978
VORTEX, THE • 1913 • Fahrney Milton • USA
VORTEX, THE • 1918 • Hamilton G. P. • USA
VORTEX, THE • 1927 • Brunel Adrian • UKN
VORTEX (USA) see **BLONDY** • 1975
VORTICE • 1954 • Matarazzo Raffaello • ITL
VORUNTERSUCHUNG • 1931 • Siodmak Robert • FRG • PRELIMINARY INVESTIGATION ○ INQUEST
VORWARTS DIE ZEIT • 1968 • Gass Karl • GDR • ONWARDS WITH TIME
VOS GUEULES LES MOUETTES • 1974 • Dhery Robert • FRN
VOSHOZDENIE see **VOSKHOZHDYENIYE** • 1977
VOSKHOZHDYENIYE • 1977 • Shepitko Larissa • USS • ASCENT, THE ○ VOSHOZDENIE
VOSKRESENIE • 1961 • Schweitzer Mikhail • USS • RESURRECTION
VOSKRESNAYA NOCH • 1977 • Turov Viktor • USS • SUNDAY NIGHT
VOSTANIYE RYBAKOV • 1934 • Piscator Erwin • USS • REVOLT OF THE FISHERMEN, THE
VOSTOCHNY KORIDOR • 1968 • Vinogradov Valentin • USS • EASTERN CORRIDOR
VOSTRO SUPER AGENTE FLIT, IL • 1966 • Laurenti Mariano • ITL • FLIT, IMBATTIBILE SUPREMO ○ FLIT, SUPREMELY UNBEATABLE ○ YOUR SUPER AGENT
VOTA A GUNDISALVO • 1977 • Lazaga Pedro • SPN
VOTE 68 • 1968 • Bedel Jean-Pierre • CND
VOTE FOR HUGGETT • 1949 • Annakin Ken • UKN
VOTE FOR MICHALSKI • 1962 • Howe John • CND
VOTE PLUS GUN see **VOTO MAS FUSIL** • 1969
VOTE THAT COUNTS, THE • 1911 • *Thanhouser* • USA
VOTER'S GUIDE, THE • 1906 • Fitzhamon Lewin • UKN
VOTES FOR MEN • 1914 • *Victor* • USA
VOTES FOR WOMEN • 1912 • Reid Hal • USA
VOTES FOR WOMEN -A CARICATURE • 1909 • Armstrong Charles • UKN
VOTO, IL • 1951 • Bonnard Mario • ITL
VOTO DI CASTITA • 1976 • D'Amato Joe • ITL
VOTO DI MARINAIO • 1953 • De Rosa Ernesto • ITL
VOTO MAS FUSIL • 1969 • Soto Helvio • CHL • OATH AND GUN ○ VOTE PLUS GUN
VOTRE DEVOUE BLAKE • 1954 • Laviron Jean • FRN
VOTRE ENFANT M'INTERESSE • 1981 • Carre Jean-Michel • FRN
VOTRE SOURIRE • 1934 • Caron Pierre, Banks Monty • FRN
VOTSARENIYA DOMA ROMANOVIKH • 1913 • Goncharov Vasili M. • USS • ACCESSION OF THE ROMANOV DYNASTY
VOUIVRE, LA • 1989 • Wilson Georges • FRN
VOULEZ-VOUS DANSER AVEC MOI • 1960 • Boisrond Michel • FRN, ITL • SEXY GIRL (ITL) ○ COME DANCE WITH ME (USA)
VOULEZ-VOUS DEVENIR VEDETTE? • 1953 • van Cottom Joe • FRN
VOULEZ-VOUS UN BEBE NOBEL? • 1980 • Pouret Robert • FRN
VOULOIR • 1931 • Jaeger-Schmidt Andre • FRN
VOUS HABITEZ CHEZ VOS PARENTS? • 1983 • Fermaud Michel • FRN
VOUS INTERESSEZ-VOUS A LA CHOSE? • 1973 • Baratier Jacques • FRN, FRG

VOUS N'AUREZ PAS L'ALSACE ET LA LORRAINE • 1977 • Coluche Michel, Monnet Marc • FRN, BLG

VOUS N'AVEZ RIEN A DECLARER? • 1936 • Joannon Leo, Allegret Yves • FRN

VOUS N'AVEZ RIEN A DECLARER? • 1959 • Duhour Clement • FRN

VOUS N'AVEZ RIEN CONTRE LA JEUNESSE • 1958 • Logereau Edouard • SHT • FRN

VOUS NE L'EMPORTEREZ PAS AU PARADIS • 1974 • Dupont-Midy Francois • FRN

VOUS PIGEZ? • 1955 • Chevalier Pierre • FRN, ITL • MAGGIORATO FISICO, IL (ITL) ○ DIAMOND MACHINE, THE (USA) ○ YOU DIG? ○ YOU GET IT?

VOUS SAVEZ-CA M. LE MINISTRE? • 1973 • Favreau Robert • MTV • CND

VOUS SEREZ MA FEMME • 1932 • de Poligny Serge • FRN • POUR AVOIR ADRIENNE ○ ESBROUFFEUR, L'

VOUS SEULE QUE J'AIME • 1939 • Fescourt Henri • FRN • C'EST VOUS SEULE QUE J'AIME

VOUS VERREZ LA SEMAINE PROCHRAINE • 1929 • Cavalcanti Alberto • FRN

VOVKA IN THE KINGDOM OF THE OTHER END OF THE WORLD • 1965 • Stepantsev Boris • ANS • USS

VOW, THE • 1914 • Bracken Bertram • USA

VOW, THE • 1915 • Taylor Stanner E. V. • USA

VOW, THE • 1918 • *Hadley Hopp* • SHT • USA

VOW, THE see **ADAK** • 1980

VOW, THE (USA) see **KLYATVA** • 1946

VOW IN THE DESERT see **NESSA NO CHIKAI** • 1941

VOW OF CHASTITY see **GELUBDE DER KEUSCHHEIT, DAS** • 1919

VOW OF VENGEANCE, THE • 1923 • Moody H. G. • USA

VOW OF YSOBEL, THE • 1912 • *Harte Betty* • USA

VOWS, THE • 1911 • *Reliance* • USA

VOWS THAT MAY BE BROKEN see **STRANGE IDOLS** • 1922

VOX POPULI • 1936 • Edgren Gustaf • SWD

VOY DE GALLO • 1962 • Pereda Ramon • MXC

VOYAGE see **REJS** • 1970

VOYAGE, LE • 1984 • Andrieu Michel • FRN

VOYAGE, THE see **VIAJE, EL** • 1970

VOYAGE, THE (USA) see **VIAGGIO, IL** • 1974

VOYAGE A BIARRITZ • 1962 • Grangier Gilles • FRN, ITL

VOYAGE A KHONOSTROV, LE • 1962 • Ligure Claude • SHT • FRN

VOYAGE A LA PLANETE JUPITER • 1907 • de Chomon Segundo • FRN • TRIP TO JUPITER, A (USA)

VOYAGE A PAIMPOL, LE • 1986 • Berry John • FRN

VOYAGE A TRAVERS L'IMPOSSIBLE, LE • 1904 • Melies Georges • FRN • VOYAGE ACROSS THE IMPOSSIBLE ○ IMPOSSIBLE VOYAGE, AN ○ WHIRLING THE WORLDS

VOYAGE A TROIS • 1949 • Paulin Jean-Paul • FRN

VOYAGE ACROSS THE IMPOSSIBLE see **VOYAGE A TRAVERS L'IMPOSSIBLE, LE** • 1904

VOYAGE AROUND A STAR, A (USA) see **VIAGGIO DI UNA STELLA, IL** • 1906

VOYAGE AROUND MY FATHER, A • 1982 • Rakoff Alvin • TVM • UKN

VOYAGE AU BOUT DE LA FOLIE • Depardon Raymond, Ristelhueber Sophie • DOC • FRN

VOYAGE AU BOUT DU MONDE • 1976 • Cousteau Jacques, Cousteau Philippe • FRN • VOYAGE TO THE EDGE OF THE WORLD (USA) ○ VOYAGE TO THE END OF THE WORLD

VOYAGE AU CENTRE DE LA TERRE • 1909 • de Chomon Segundo • FRN • JOURNEY TO THE CENTRE OF THE EARTH (USA) ○ JOURNEY TO THE MIDDLE OF THE EARTH, A

VOYAGE AU CIEL, LE • Painleve Jean • FRN • VOYAGE TO THE SKY

VOYAGE AU CONGO • 1927 • Allegret Marc (c/d) • DOC • FRN

VOYAGE AU JARDIN DES MORTS • 1978 • Garrel Philippe • FRN

VOYAGE AU PAYS DES LOUFOQUES see **COUPLE IDEAL, LE** • 1945

VOYAGE AU POLE, LE see **A LA CONQUETE DU POLE** • 1912

VOYAGE AUTOMOBILE PARIS – MONTECARLO EN DEUX HEURES, LE see **RAID PARIS – MONTE CARLO EN 2 HEURES, LE** • 1905

VOYAGE AUTOUR D'UNE ETOILE see **VIAGGIO DI UNA STELLA, IL** • 1906

VOYAGE BETWEEN TWO SHORES see **PATESHESTVIE MEZHDU DVA BRYAGA** • 1968

VOYAGE BEYOND THE SUN see **SPACE MONSTER** • 1965

VOYAGE BY NIGHT N see **NACHTMEERFAHRT, DIE** • 1986

VOYAGE CHEZ LES VIVANTS • 1970 • Brandt Henry • DOC • SWT

VOYAGE CHIMERIQUE, LE see **GOIN' DOWN THE ROAD** • 1970

VOYAGE COMPANION, THE see **HAMSAFAR** • 1974

VOYAGE D'ABDULLAH, LE • 1953 • Regnier • SHT • FRN

VOYAGE D'AGREMENT • 1935 • Christian-Jaque • FRN

VOYAGE D'AMELIE, LE • 1974 • Duval Daniel • IND

VOYAGE DANS LA LUNE • 1909 • de Chomon Segundo • FRN • NEW TRIP TO THE MOON (USA) ○ NUEVO A LA LUNA

VOYAGE DANS LA LUNE, LE • 1902 • Melies Georges • FRN • TRIP TO THE MOON, A ○ TRIP TO MARS, A ○ VOYAGE TO THE MOON, THE

VOYAGE DANS LE CIEL • 1937 • Painleve Jean • SHT • FRN

VOYAGE DANS UNE ETOILE, LE see **VIAGGIO DI UNA STELLA, IL** • 1906

VOYAGE DE BADABOU, LE • 1956 • Gruel Henri • SHT • FRN • BABADOU'S VOYAGE

VOYAGE DE BRIGITTE BARDOT AUX U.S.A. • 1966 • Reichenbach Francois • SHT • FRN

VOYAGE DE GULLIVER A LILLIPUT ET CHEZ LES GEANTS, LE • 1902 • Melies Georges • FRN • GULLIVER'S TRAVELS (USA) ○ VOYAGES DE GULLIVER ○ GULLIVER'S TRAVELS AMONG THE LILLIPUTIANS AND THE GIANTS ○ GULLIVER

VOYAGE DE LA FAMILLE BOURRICHON, LE • 1913 • Melies Georges • FRN • VOYAGE OF THE BOURRICHON FAMILY, THE

VOYAGE DE MONSIEUR PERRICHON, LE • 1934 • Tarride Jean • FRN

VOYAGE DE NOCES, LE • 1976 • Trintignant Nadine • FRN, ITL • JALOUSIE 1976 ○ HONEYMOON, THE

VOYAGE DE NOCES, LE see **MAX ET JANE EN VOYAGE DE NOCES** • 1911

VOYAGE DE NOCES EN BALLON • 1908 • Melies Georges • FRN • HONEYMOON IN A BALLOON

VOYAGE DE NOEMIE, LE • Rodde Michel • SWT

VOYAGE DE NUIT • 1981 • Frappier Roger • DOC • CND

VOYAGE DE SIM, LA • 1966 • Alassane Moustapha • ANS • NGR • BON VOYAGE, SIM ○ SIM'S VOYAGE

VOYAGE DES COMEDIENS, LE see **THIASOS, O** • 1974

VOYAGE D'HIVER, LE • 1983 • Handwerker Marian • BLG

VOYAGE DU PERE, LE • 1966 • de La Patelliere Denys • FRN, ITL • DESTINAZIONE MARCIAPIEDE (ITL)

VOYAGE D'UNE VIE, LE see **RIH'LAT AL-UMR** • 1974

VOYAGE EN AFRIQUE • 1910 • Machin Alfred • SER • FRN

VOYAGE EN AMERIQUE • 1951 • Lavorel Henri • FRN • TRIP TO AMERICA (USA) ○ VOYAGE TO AMERICA

VOYAGE EN AMERIQUE AVEC UN CHEVAL EMPRUNTE • 1988 • Chabot Jean • DOC • CND

VOYAGE EN BALLON, LE • 1960 • Lamorisse Albert • FRN • STOWAWAY IN THE SKY ○ TRIP IN A BALLOON ○ BALLOON VOYAGE, THE

VOYAGE EN BOSCAVIE • 1958 • Herman Jean • FRN • JOURNEY IN BOSCAVIA

VOYAGE EN BRETAGNE INTERIEURE • 1978 • Lavoie Richard • DOC • CND

VOYAGE EN CAPITAL • 1977 • Akika Ali, Autissier Anne-Marie • DOC • FRN

VOYAGE EN DOUCE, LE • 1980 • Deville Michel • FRN • SENTIMENTAL JOURNEY (USA) ○ FRENCH LEAVE

VOYAGE EN EGYPTE • 1913 • Machin Alfred • SER • FRN

VOYAGE EN ESPAGNE • 1906 • Blache Alice • SER • FRN

VOYAGE EN GRANDE TARTARIE • 1974 • Tacchella Jean-Charles • FRN • VOYAGE TO GRAND TARTARIE

VOYAGE EN QUESTION, LE • 1962 • Friedman Serge • FRN

VOYAGE IMMAGINAIRE, LE • 1925 • Clair Rene • FRN • IMAGINARY VOYAGE, THE

VOYAGE IMPREVU, LE • 1934 • de Limur Jean • FRN

VOYAGE INTO EVIL see **CRUISE INTO TERROR** • 1978

VOYAGE INTO SPACE • 1965 • *Kaneko Mitsunobu* • JPN • JOHNNY SOKKO AND HIS GIANT ROBOT

VOYAGE OF PETER JOE, THE • 1946 • Hughes Harry • SER • UKN

VOYAGE OF SILENCE (USA) see **SALTO, O** • 1967

VOYAGE OF THE "ARCTIC"; OR, HOW CAPTAIN KETTLE DISCOVERED THE NORTH POLE (USA) see **ADVENTUROUS VOYAGE OF "THE ARCTIC", THE** • 1903

VOYAGE OF THE BOUNTY'S CHILD • 1984 • Edols Michael • ASL

VOYAGE OF THE BOURRICHON FAMILY, THE see **VOYAGE DE LA FAMILLE BOURRICHON, LE** • 1913

VOYAGE OF THE DAMNED • 1976 • Rosenberg Stuart • UKN, SPN

VOYAGE OF THE LEHI IV see **LEHI** • 1963

VOYAGE OF THE ROCK ALIENS • 1984 • Fargo James • USA • WHEN THE RAIN BEGINS TO FALL

VOYAGE OF THE YES, THE • 1972 • Katzin Lee H. • TVM • USA

VOYAGE OPTIQUE • Harber Dick • SHT • USA

VOYAGE POUR L'ENFER DES PASSIONS see **CAIN DE NULLE PART** • 1969

VOYAGE ROYAL see **ROYAL JOURNEY** • 1951

VOYAGE SANS DETOUR • 1973 • Lamothe Arthur • DCS • CND

VOYAGE SANS ESPOIR • 1943 • Christian-Jaque • FRN

VOYAGE-SURPRISE • 1946 • Prevert Pierre • FRN • VOYAGE SURPRISE

VOYAGE SURPRISE see **VOYAGE-SURPRISE** • 1946

VOYAGE SYMPATHETIQUE, UN see **RIHLA LADHIDHA** • 1970

VOYAGE TO A PREHISTORIC PLANET see **VOYAGE TO THE PREHISTORIC PLANET** • 1965

VOYAGE TO A STAR see **VIAGGIO DI UNA STELLA, IL** • 1906

VOYAGE TO AMERICA see **VOYAGE EN AMERIQUE** • 1951

VOYAGE TO ARCTURUS, A • 1971 • Holloway B. J. • USA

VOYAGE TO ATHENS see **TAXIDI STIN PROTEVOUSA** • 1981

VOYAGE TO CYTHERA see **TAXIDI STA KYTHERA** • 1984

VOYAGE TO DANGER (USA) see **ZWISCHEN SHANGHAI UND ST. PAULI** • 1962

VOYAGE TO GRAND TARTARIE see **VOYAGE EN GRANDE TARTARIE** • 1974

VOYAGE TO ITALY see **VIAGGIO IN ITALIA** • 1953

VOYAGE TO MELONIA see **REISEN TIL MELONIA** • 1989

VOYAGE TO NEXT • 1974 • Hubley John • ANM • USA

VOYAGE TO THE BOTTOM OF THE SEA • 1961 • Allen Irwin • USA

VOYAGE TO THE CENTER OF THE MOON see **VIAGGIO AL CENTRO DELLA LUNA** • 1905

VOYAGE TO THE EDGE OF THE WORLD (USA) see **VOYAGE AU BOUT DU MONDE** • 1976

VOYAGE TO THE END OF THE UNIVERSE (USA) see **IKARIE XB-1** • 1963

VOYAGE TO THE END OF THE WORLD see **VIAGEM AO FIM DO MUNDO** • 1968

VOYAGE TO THE END OF THE WORLD see **VOYAGE AU BOUT DU MONDE** • 1976

VOYAGE TO THE MOON, THE see **VOYAGE DANS LA LUNE, LE** • 1902

VOYAGE TO THE OUTER PLANETS • 1973 • Cantwell Colin • SHT • USA

VOYAGE TO THE PLANET OF PREHISTORIC WOMEN see **GILL WOMEN OF VENUS** • 1967

VOYAGE TO THE PREHISTORIC PLANET • 1965 • Harrington Curtis • USA • VOYAGE TO A PREHISTORIC PLANET ○ PREHISTORIC PLANET

VOYAGE TO THE SKY see **VOYAGE AU CIEL, LE**

VOYAGE VERS LA LUMIERE • 1969 • Unia Pierre • SHT • FRN

VOYAGER, THE • 1911 • *Selig* • USA

VOYAGER FROM THE UNKNOWN • 1983 • Parriott James, Colby Rick • USA

VOYAGERS see **ROZWODOW NIE BEDZIE** • 1963

VOYAGES DE GULLIVER see **VOYAGE DE GULLIVER A LILLIPUT ET CHEZ LES GEANTS, LE** • 1902

VOYAGES DE NOCES • 1932 • Fried Germain, Schmidt Erich • FRN • JACQUELINE ET L'AMOUR

VOYAGES DE NOCES EN ESPAGNE • 1912 • Linder Max • FRN

VOYAGES DE TORTILLARD, LES • 1979 • Sander Peter • ANM • CND

VOYAGES EN TURQUIE ET EN ARABIE SEOUDITE • 1963 • Pialat Maurice • DOC • FRN

VOYAGES EXTRAORDINAIRES DE JULES VERNE • 1952 • Aurel Jean • ANS • FRN • EXTRAORDINARY VOYAGES OF JULES VERNE, THE

VOYAGEUR, LE • 1956 • Gruel Henri • ANS • FRN

VOYAGEUR, LE • 1964 • Devlin Bernard • SHT • CND • VOYAGEURS, LES

VOYAGEUR, LE • 1968 • Levie Francoise • BLG

VOYAGEUR, LE see **CHALEURS** • 1970

VOYAGEUR DE LA TOUSSAINT, LE (FRN) see **VIAGGIATORE DI OGNISSANTI, IL** • 1942

VOYAGEUR DU BOUT DU MONDE, LE see **PASSEPORT POUR LE MONDE** • 1958

VOYAGEUR SANS BAGAGES, LE • 1943 • Anouilh Jean • FRN

VOYAGEUR VERS LE NORD, VOYAGEUR VERS LE SUD see **MUSAFIRUN'ILA AL-JANUB, MUSAFIRUN' ILA ASH-SHAMAL** • 1972

VOYAGEURS see **PASAZERKA** • 1963

VOYAGEURS, LES • 1979 • Rodgers Bob • DOC • CND • OIL UNDER ICE

VOYAGEURS, LES see **VOYAGEUR, LE** • 1964

VOYAGEUSE INATTENDUE, LA • 1949 • Stelli Jean • FRN • UNEXPECTED VOYAGER, THE

VOYANTE, LA • 1923 • Mercanton Louis, Abrams Leon • FRN • CLAIRVOYANT, THE

VOYANTS, LES • 1972 • Derouillat Roger • DOC • FRN

VOYDI V MOY DOM • 1968 • Kabulov Anatoli • USS • ENTER MY HOUSE

VOYEUR • 1983 • Eggleston Colin • MTV • ASL

VOYEUR, LE see **GIOCHI PARTICOLARI** • 1970

VOYEUR, THE • 1970 • USA

VOYOU, LE • 1970 • Lelouch Claude • FRN, ITL • SIMON THE SWISS (UKN) ○ CROOK, THE (USA) ○ CRIMINAL, THE ○ STORIA DI UNA CANAGLIA

VOZ DE LA RAZA, LA • 1912 • MXC

VOZ DE MI CIUDAD, LA • 1953 • Demicheli Tulio • ARG

VOZ DO COVEIRO, A • 1943 • Marins Jose Mojica • BRZ • VOICE OF THE GRAVEDIGGER, THE ○ GRAVEDIGGER'S VOICE, THE

VOZ DO OPERARIO, CATEDRAL DO BEM, A • 1930 • Leitao Antonio • SHT • PRT

VOZ DO SANGUE, A • 1965 • Fraga Augusto • PRT

VOZVRASHCHENIE "SVYATOVO LUKI" • 1971 • Bobrovsky Anatoli • USS • RETURN OF "ST. LUCAS", THE ○ RETURN OF ST. LUKE, THE

VOZVRASHCHENIE VASSILIYA BORTNIKOVA • 1953 • Pudovkin V. I. • USS • RETURN OF VASSILI BORTNIKOV, THE ○ VASSILI BORTNIKOV'S RETURN ○ HARVEST, THE

VOZVRASHCHENIYE MAKSIMA • 1937 • Kozintsev Grigori, Trauberg Leonid • USS • RETURN OF MAXIM, THE

VOZVRASHCHYENIYE ULYBKI • 1968 • Mchedlidze Nana, Gordeladze Leyla • USS • SMILE BROUGHT BACK, A ○ RETURN OF A SMILE ○ SMILE RETURNED, THE

VOZVRATA NYET • 1975 • Saltykov Alexei • USS • NO RETURN

VRAI BEAU MARIAGE, UN • 1970 • Carle Gilles • CND

VRAI COUPABLE, LE • 1951 • Thevenard Pierre • FRN

VRAI JEU, LE • 1934 • Leenhardt Roger • DCS • FRN

VRAI VISAGE DE L'AFRIQUE, LE see **CHEZ LES BUVEURS DE SANG** • 1930

VRAI VISAGE DE THERESE DE LISIEUX, LE • 1961 • Agostini Philippe • SHT • FRN

VRAIE HISTOIRE DE GERARD LE CHOMEUR, LA • 1980 • Lledo Joaquin • FRN

VRAIE JEUNE FILLE, UNE • 1975 • Breillat Catherine • FRN

VRAIE NATURE DE BERNADETTE, LA • 1972 • Carle Gilles • CND • TRUE NATURE OF BERNADETTE, THE

VRAIE RICHESSE, LA see **GEO LE MYSTERIEUX** • 1916

VRAIS COUSINS, LES • 1970 • Godbout Jacques • DOC • CND

VRAIS PERDANTS, LES • 1978 • Melancon Andre • DOC • CND

VRAK • 1983 • Toman Ivo • CZC • WRECK, THE

VRANE • 1969 • Kozomora Ljubisa, Mihic Gordan • YGS • CROWS, THE

VRATA • 1972 • Grgic Zlatko • ANS • YGS • DOOR, THE

VRATA OSTAJU OTVORENA • 1959 • Cap Frantisek • YGS • DOOR STAYS OPEN, THE ○ DOOR IS LEFT OPEN, THE

VRATA RAJA • 1967 • Wajda Andrzej • UKN, YGS • BRAMY RAJU (YGS) ○ GATES TO PARADISE ○ GATES OF PARADISE

VRATICU SE • 1957 • Gale Joze • YGS • I WILL RETURN

VRAZDA INZENYRA CERTA • 1968 • Krumbachova Ester • CZC • MURDER OF ENGINEER DEVIL, THE ○ MURDER OF MR. DEVIL, THE ○ KILLING THE DEVIL

VRAZDA PO CESKU • 1967 • Weiss Jiri • CZC • MURDER CZECH STYLE ○ VRAZDA PO NASEM ○ MURDER OUR STYLE

VRAZDA PO NASEM see **VRAZDA PO CESKU** • 1967

VRAZDA V OSTROVNI ULICI • 1933 • Innemann Svatopluk • CZC • MURDER IN ISLAND STREET

VRCHNI, PRCHNI • 1981 • Smoljak Ladislav • CZC • RUN, WAITER, RUN

VREAU SA STIU DE CE AM ARIPI • 1984 • Stan Nicu • RMN • I WANT TO KNOW WHY I HAVE WINGS

VRECKARI • 1967 • Filan Ludovit • CZC • PICKPOCKETS

VREDENS DAG • 1943 • Dreyer Carl T. • DNM • DAY OF WRATH ○ DIES IRAE

VREEMDE VOGEL, EEN • 1967 • Nijgh Lennaert • NTH • OUTSIDER, AN

VREEME WERELD • 1974 • SAF

VREME CUDA • 1990 • Paskaljevic Goran • YGS, UKN • TIME OF MIRACLES, THE

VREME LJUBAVI • 1966 • Petric Vlada, Vucinic Bosko, Rajic Nikola • YGS • TIME TO LOVE, A

VREME, VODI • 1981 • Gapo Branko • YGS • TIME AND TIDE ○ VRIJEME, VODE

VREMIA JELANII • 1983 • Raizman Yuli • USS • TIME OF DESIRE

VRHOVI ZELENGORE • 1976 • Bondarchuk Sergei, Velimirovic Zdravko • YGS • PEAKS OF ZELENGORE, THE (USA) ○ URHOVI ZELENGORE

VRIENDEN, DE • 1971 • van Eyck Robert • BLG • AMIS, LES

VRIJDAG • 1981 • Claus Hugo • BLG • FRIDAY

VRIJEME VAMPIRA • 1970 • Majdak Nikola • ANS • YGS • TIME OF VAMPIRES, THE (USA) ○ TIME OF THE VAMPIRE, THE

VRIJEME, VODE see **VREME, VODI** • 1981

VRITTA • Capell Bill • SHT • USA

VROEGER IS DOOD • 1987 • Schenkkan Ine • NTH • BYGONES

VROEGER KON JE LACHEN • 1982 • Haanstra Bert • NTH • IN THE OLD DAYS YOU COULD LAUGH ○ ONE COULD LAUGH IN FORMER DAYS ○ FORMERLY, YOU HAD A BIG TIME

VROLIKE VRYDAG • 1969 • SAF

VROODER'S HOOCH see **CRAZY WORLD OF JULIUS VROODER, THE** • 1974

VROOM • 1988 • Kidron Beeban • UKN

VROU UIT DIE NAG • 1974 • SAF

VROUW ALS EVA, EEN • 1978 • van Brakel Nouchka • NTH • WOMAN LIKE EVE, A

VROUW TUSSEN HOND EN WOLF, EEN • 1979 • Delvaux Andre • BLG, FRN • FEMME ENTRE CHIEN ET LOUP, UNE (FRN) ○ WOMAN IN A TWILIGHT GARDEN (UKN)

VSADNIK NAD GORODOM • 1967 • Shatrov Igor • USS • RIDER ABOVE THE CITY

VSADNIKI • 1939 • Savchenko Igor • USS • GUERILLA BRIGADE ○ RIDERS

VSADNIKI REVOLUTSII • 1968 • Yarmatov Kamil • USS • HORSEMEN OF THE REVOLUTION

VSE NACHINAETSYA S DOROGI • 1959 • Azarov Vilen, Dostal N. • USS • EVERYTHING BEGINS WITH A JOURNEY ○ EVERYTHING STARTS ON THE ROAD

VSE OSTAETSIA LYUDYAM • 1963 • Natanson Georgi • USS • ALL IS LEFT TO THE PEOPLE

VSE OTLAGAM DA TE ZABRAVYA • 1990 • Gurdev Stefan • BUL • I STILL PUT OFF FORGETTING YOU

VSE PRO LASKA • 1930 • Fric Martin • CZC • ALL FOR LOVE

VSEGO ODNA ZHIZN see **BARE ET LIV –HISTORIEN OM FRIDTJOF NANSEN** • 1968

VSEHOCHLUP • 1979 • Smetana Zdenek • ANS • CZC • ALL-HAIRS

VSEROSSIISKII STAROSTA KALININ • 1920 • Vertov Dziga • USS • KALININ, THE ELDER STATESMAN OF ALL RUSSIA ○ KALININ, STAROST OF RUSSIA ○ VSERUSSKI STARETS KALININ ○ ALL RUSSIAN ELDER KALININ

VSERUSSKI STARETS KALININ see **VSEROSSIISKII STAROSTA KALININ** • 1920

VSICHNI DOBRI RODACI • 1968 • Jasny Vojtech • CZC • EVERYONE A GOOD FELLOW-COUNTRYMAN ○ ALL GOOD FELLOW COUNTRYMEN ○ ALL GOOD CITIZENS ○ OUR COUNTRYMEN ○ ALL THOSE GOOD COUNTRYMEN ○ ALL MY GOOD COUNTRYMEN

VSKRYTIE MOSHCHEI SERGIYA RADONEZHSKOVO • 1920 • Vertov Dziga • USS • DISCOVERY OF SERGEI RADONEZHSKY'S REMAINS ○ EXHUMATION OF THE REMAINS OF SERGEI RADONEZHKOVO, THE

VSTANOU NOVI BOJOVNICI • 1950 • Weiss Jiri • CZC • NEW FIGHTERS SHALL ARISE ○ NEW WARRIORS SHALL ARISE ○ NEW HEROES WILL ARISE

VSTRECHA NA ELBE • 1949 • Alexandrov Grigori • USS • MEETING ON THE ELBE

VSTRECHNYI • 1932 • Ermler Friedrich, Yutkevich Sergei • USS • COUNTERPLAN ○ ONCOMING, THE ○ STRECHNI ○ SHAME ○ POZOR

VSTRETCHA S FRANTZIEI • 1960 • Yutkevich Sergei • DOC • USS • ENCOUNTER WITH FRANCE ○ MEETING WITH FRANCE

VSTRYECHA S PROSHLYM • 1967 • Dolidze Siko • USS • RENDEZVOUS WITH THE PAST

VSTRYECHA V GORAKH • 1967 • Sanishvili Nikolai • USS • ENCOUNTER IN THE MOUNTAINS

VSTUPLENIE • 1962 • Talankin Igor • USS • INTRODUCTION ○ ENTRY, THE ○ STARTING OUT

VSUDE ZIJI LIDE • 1960 • Skalsky Stepan, Hanibal Jiri • CZC • THERE ARE PEOPLE EVERYWHERE

VSYUDU YEST NYEBO • 1968 • Mashchenko Nikolay • USS • THERE IS SKY EVERYWHERE

VT • 1980 • Norman Ron • USA

VTACKOVIA, SIROTY A BLAZNI • 1969 • Jakubisko Juraj • CZC • LITTLE BIRDS, ORPHANS AND FOOLS ○ BIRDS, ORPHANS AND FOOLS

VTIK TRAIN, THE see **AGITPOEZHD VTSIKA** • 1921

VTORAYA POPYTKA VIKTORA KROKHINA • 1977 • Sheshukov Igor • USS • VIKTOR KROKHIN'S SECOND TRY

VTR ST. JACQUES see **VTR ST-JACQUES** • 1969

VTR ST-JACQUES • 1969 • Henaut Dorothy Todd, Klein Bonnie • DOC • CND • VTR ST. JACQUES

VU DU PONT • 1962 • Lumet Sidney • FRN, ITL • SGUARDO DAL PONTE, UNO (ITL) ○ VIEW FROM THE BRIDGE, A (USA)

VUCKO • 1983 • Dragic Nedeljko • ASS • YGS

VUDU SANGRIENTO • 1972 • Cano Manuel • SPN

VUE DE REMERCIEMENTS AU PUBLIC • 1900 • Melies Georges • FRN • THANKING THE AUDIENCE ○ REMERCIEMENTS AU PUBLIC

VUE PANORAMIQUE PRIS DU TRAIN ELECTRIQUE • 1900 • Melies Georges • FRN

VUE PANORAMIQUE PRISE DE LA SEINE • 1900 • Melies Georges • FRN • PANORAMA DE LA SEINE ○ PANORAMA OF RIVER SEINE

VUELO 300 • 1953 • Ayala Fernando • DOC • ARG

VUELO 971 • 1954 • Salvia Rafael J. • SPN

VUELO AL INFIERNO • 1971 • Franco Jesus • SPN

VUELO DE LA MUERTE, EL • 1933 • Calles Guillermo • MXC

VUELO DE LA PALOMA, EL • 1988 • Garcia Sanchez Jose Luis • SPN • FLIGHT OF THE DOVE, THE ○ DOVE'S FLIGHT, THE

VUELTA, LA • 1964 • Madrid Jose Luis • SPN

VUELTA AL NIDO, LA • 1938 • Torres-Rios Leopoldo • ARG

VUELTA AL PARAISO • 1959 • Martinez Solares Gilberto • MXC

VUELTA AL ZANJON • 1974 • de Pedro Manuel • SHT • VNZ • PAINTER JESUS SOTO

VUELTA DEL CHARRO NEGRO, LA • 1941 • de Anda Raul • MXC

VUELTA DEL MEXICO, LA • 1965 • Cardona Rene • MXC

VUELTA DEL TORO, LA • 1924 • Campogalliani Carlo • ARG

VUELVA EL PRIMERO • 1952 • Land Kurt • ARG

VUELVA EL SABADO • 1951 • Cardona Rene • MXC

VUELVE EL DR. SATAN see **DR. SATAN Y LA MAGIA NEGRA, EL** • 1967

VUELVE EL LOBO • 1951 • Orona Vicente • MXC

VUELVE EL NORTENO • 1962 • Munoz Manuel • MXC

VUELVE EL TEXANO • 1965 • Crevenna Alfredo B. • MXC

VUELVE MARTIN CORONA see **ENAMORADO, EL** • 1951

VUELVE, QUERIDA NATI • 1976 • Forque Jose Maria • SPN

VUELVE SAN VALENTIN • 1962 • Palacios Fernando • SPN

VUELVE SEBASTIANA • 1953 • Ruiz Jorge • DOC • BLV • COME BACK SEBASTIANA

VUELVEN LOS ARGUMEDO • 1961 • Munoz Manuel • MXC

VUELVEN LOS CAMPEONES JUSTICIEROS • 1972 • Curiel Federico • MXC • CHAMPIONS OF JUSTICE RETURN, THE

VUELVEN LOS CINCO HALCONES • 1961 • Delgado Miguel M. • MXC

VUELVEN LOS GARCIA • 1946 • Rodriguez Ismael • MXC • GARCIAS RETURN, THE

VUES D'ICI • 1978 • Pinel Vincent, Zarifian Christian • FRN

VUK • 1982 • Darbay Attila • HNG

VUK SA PROKLETIJA • 1968 • Stamenkovic Miomir • YGS • WOLF FROM PROKLETIJE

VUK SAMATNJAK • 1973 • Gluscevic Obrad • YGS • LONE WOLF, THE

VULANE • 1985 • SAF

VULCAN AFFAIR, THE see **TO TRAP A SPY** • 1965

VULCAN ENTERTAINS see **HELL'S FIRE** • 1934

VULCAN, SON OF JUPITER (USA) see **VULCANO FIGLIO DI GIOVE** • 1962

VULCANO • 1950 • Dieterle William • ITL • VOLCANO (USA)

VULCANO FIGLIO DI GIOVE • 1962 • Salvi Emimmo • ITL • VULCAN, SON OF JUPITER (USA)

VULCHITSATA see **VALCHITSATA** • 1965

VULKAN DER HOLLISCHEN TRIEBE • 1968 • Hauser Peter • FRG • VOLCANO OF HELLISH DESIRES

VULKANWERFT IM METALLERSTREIK 1974, DIE • 1975 • Hormann Gunther, Koop Annerose, von Larcher Detlef, Skalla Helga • FRG

VULNERABLE ONES, THE see **VERWUNDBAREN, DIE** • 1967

VULPEJA • 1978 • Diez Miguel Angel • SPN

VULTURE • 1985 • Leder Paul • USA

VULTURE, THE • 1915 • *Anderson Augusta* • USA

VULTURE, THE • 1937 • Ince Ralph • UKN

VULTURE, THE • 1967 • Huntington Lawrence • UKN, USA, CND • MANUTARA

VULTURE, THE see **HA'AYT** • 1981

VULTURE, THE see **DOGKESELYU** • 1983

VULTURE OF SKULL MOUNTAIN, THE • 1917 • Horne James W. • SHT • USA

VULTURES see **GIDDH** • 1984

VULTURES, THE see **VAUTOURS, LES** • 1975

VULTURES AND DOVES • 1912 • *Casey Kenneth* • USA

VULTURES OF LONDON, THE • 1915 • West R. Harley • UKN

VULTURES OF SOCIETY • 1916 • Calvert E. H. • USA

VULTURES OF THE COAST, THE • 1915 • *Apex* • USA

VULTURES OF THE LAW (UKN) see **SON OF THE PLAINS** • 1931

VULTURES OF THE SEA • 1928 • Thorpe Richard • SRL • USA

VULTURE'S PREY, THE • 1922 • SAF

VUMA • 1978 • SAF

VUOLE LUI.. LO VUOLE LEI, LA • 1968 • Amendola Mario • ITL

VUOSI ELAMASTA • 1982 • Niskanen Mikko • FNL • YEAR IN THE LIFE, A

VURGUNCULAR • 1971 • Guney Yilmaz • TRK • WRONGDOERS, THE

VURULDUM BU KIZA • 1968 • Un Memduh • TRK • CRAZY FOR THAT GIRL

VURUN KAHPEYE • 1948 • Akat Lutfu • TRK

VURUN KAHPEYE • 1974 • Refig Halit • TRK • DEATH TO THE WHORE

VVVC JOURNAL • 1929 • Ivens Joris • SHT • NTH

VYBOR TSELI • 1974 • Talankin Igor • USS • CHOICE OF A GOAL, THE ○ CHOICE OF GOAL

VYBORG SIDE, THE see **VYBORGSKAYA STORONA** • 1939

VYBORGSKAYA STORONA • 1939 • Kozintsev Grigori, Trauberg Leonid • USS • NEW HORIZONS ○ VYBORG SIDE, THE

VYENSKAYA POCHTOVAYA MARKA • 1968 • Kasper Veljo • USS • VIENNESE POSTAGE STAMP, THE

VYERNOST MATERI • 1967 • Donskoi Mark • USS • MOTHER'S LOYALTY, A ○ VERNOST MATERI ○ MOTHER'S DEVOTION, A

VYFDE SEISOEN see **FIFTH SEASON** • 1978

VYHRAVAT POTICHU • 1985 • Kralova Drahuse • CZC • WINNING DISCREETLY

VYJIMECNA SITUACE • 1985 • Borek Jaromir • CZC • EXCEPTIONAL SITUATION, AN

VYNALEZ ZKAZY • 1958 • Zeman Karel • CZC • FABULOUS WORLD OF JULES VERNE, THE (USA) ○ INVENTION FOR DESTRUCTION ○ WEAPONS OF DESTRUCTION ○ DIABOLIC INVENTION, THE ○ DEADLY INVENTION, THE ○ INVENTION OF DESTRUCTION

VYSOKA ZED • 1964 • Kachyna Karel • CZC • HIGH WALL, THE

VYSOKOYE ZVANIYE • 1973 • Karelov Yevgyeni • USS • HIGH RANK

VYSOTA • 1957 • Zarkhi Alexander • USS • HEIGHTS, THE ○ GREAT HEIGHT ○ HEIGHT ○ HIGH UP

VYSSI PRINCIP • 1960 • Krejcik Jiri • CZC • HIGHER PRINCIPLE, A

VYSTAVNI PARKAR A LEPIC PLAKATU • 1898 • Krizenecky Jan • CZC • BILL-STICKER AND THE SAUSAGE VENDOR, THE ○ EXHIBITION SAUSAGE VENDOR, THE

VYSTREL • 1967 • Trakhtenberg Naum • USS • SHOT, THE ○ VISTREL ○ PISTOL SHOT, A

VYTVARNA VYCHOVA DETI NA MATERSKYCH SKOLACH • 1958 • Jerabek Jiri • CZC

VZBOURENI NA VSI • 1949 • Mach Josef • CZC • VILLAGE REVOLT, THE

VZDUCHOLOD A LASKA • 1947 • Brdecka Jiri • ANS • CZC • ZEPPELIN AND LOVE, THE ○ LOVE AND THE ZEPPELIN

VZHROSLIE DETI see **VZROSLYI DETI** • 1961

VZLOMSHCHIK • 1987 • Ogorodnikov Valery • USS • BURGLAR

VZORNA VYCHOVA • 1953 • *Stallich Jan (Ph)* • SHT • CZC

VZORNY KINEMATOGRAF JAROSLAVA HASKA • 1955 • Lipsky Oldrich • CZC • HASEK'S EXEMPLARY CINEMATOGRAPH

VZORVANNY AD • 1967 • Lukinsky Ivan • USS • HELL BLOWN UP

VZPOMINKA NA RAJ • 1939-40 • Klos Elmar • CZC • SOUVENIR OF PARADISE

VZPOURA HRACEK • 1947 • Tyrlova Hermina • ANM • CZC • REVOLT OF THE TOYS ○ TOY MUTINY, THE ○ REVOLT OF TOYS, THE ○ REVOLT IN TOYLAND

VZROSLYI DETI • 1961 • Azarov Vilen • USS • GROWN-UP CHILDREN (USA) ○ INFANTILE ADULTS ○ VZHROSLIE DETI

W

W • 1974 • Quine Richard • USA • W: TERROR IS ONE LETTER ○ I WANT HER DEAD

W.A.R. WOMEN AGAINST RAPE • 1987 • Nussbaum Raphael • USA

W.B. BLUE AND THE BEANER • 1988 • Kleven Max • USA

W BIALY DZIEN • 1980 • Zebrowski Edward • PLN • IN BROAD DAYLIGHT

W BIESZCZADACH • 1966 • Raplewski Zbigniew • PLN • IN THE BIESZCZADY HILLS

W BRATNIEJ JUGOSLAWII • 1946 • Bossak Jerzy • DOC • PLN • IN BROTHERLY YUGOSLAVIA

W.C. FIELDS see **NIGHT WITH THE GREAT ONE, A** • 1969

W.C. FIELDS AND ME • 1976 • Hiller Arthur • USA

W.C. FIELDS FILM FESTIVAL see **BEST OF W. C. FIELDS, THE** • 1969

W.C. SONT FERMES DE L'INTERIEUR, LES see **VECES ETAIENT FERMES DE L'INTERIEUR, LES** • 1976

W CHLOPSKIE RECE • 1946 • Buczkowski Leonard • DOC • PLN • INTO THE HANDS OF PEASANTS

W CYRKU • 1954 • Perski Ludwik • DOC • PLN • AT THE CIRCUS

W DJANGO • 1971 • Mulargia Edoardo • ITL

W DZIESIECIOLECIE • 1955 • Perski Ludwik • DOC • PLN • TENTH ANNIVERSARY OF WROCLAW, THE

W DZUNGLI • 1957 • Giersz Witold • ANS • PLN • IN THE JUNGLE

W.E.B. • 1978 • Hart Harvey • TVM • USA

W FABRYCE • 1951 • Nasfeter Janusz • SHT • PLN • IN THE FACTORY

W GROMADZIE DUCHA PUSZCZY • 1957 • Slesicki Wladyslaw (c/d) • DOC • PLN • IN THE COMMUNITY OF THE SPIRIT OF THE WILDERNESS

W.H.I.F.F.S. see **WHIFFS** • 1975

W.I.A. (WOUNDED IN ACTION) • 1966 • Sunasky Irving • USA

W JAKUCJI • 1969 • Bossak Jerzy (c/d) • DOC • PLN • IN YAKUTIA

W KAZDA NIEDZIELE • 1965 • Perski Ludwik • DOC • PLN • EVERY SUNDAY

W KLUBIE • 1963 • Karabasz Kazimierz • DCS • PLN • IN THE CLUB ○ AT THE CLUB

W KLUBIE NA WOLI • 1963 • Gryczelowska Krystyna • DOC • PLN • IN THE WOLA CLUB

W KRAINIE SMUJNEJ BAJKI • 1959 • Jaworski Tadeusz • PLN • IN THE LAND OF THE SAD FAIRY TALE

W KRAINIE TYSIACA I JEDNEJ NOCY • 1969 • Nehrebecki Wladyslaw • ANS • PLN • IN THE LAND OF A THOUSAND AND ONE NIGHTS

W KREGU CISZY • 1960 • Ziarnik Jerzy • DOC • PLN • IN THE CIRCLE OF PEACE ○ IN THE CIRCLE OF SILENCE

W.L.A. GIRL, THE • 1918 • Hepworth Cecil M. • UKN

W LE DONNE • 1970 • Grimaldi Aldo • ITL

W MATNI • 1965 • Janik Stefan • SHT • PLN • IN A TRAP

W PIASKACH PUSTYNI • 1962 • Giersz Witold • ANS • PLN • IN THE SANDS OF THE DESERT

"W" PLAN, THE • 1930 • Saville Victor • UKN

W POGONI ZA ADAMEM • 1969 • Zarzycki Jerzy • PLN • IN PURSUIT OF ADAM ○ POGON ZA ADAMEM ○ CHASING ADAM ○ CHASE AFTER ADAM

W POGONI ZA ZOLTA KOSZULKA • 1954 • Bossak Jerzy • DOC • PLN • IN PURSUIT OF THE YELLOW SHIRT ○ BICYCLE RACE

W PUSTYNI I W PUSZCZY • 1972 • Slesicki Wladyslaw • PLN • IN DESERT AND JUNGLE ○ IN DESERT AND WILDERNESS

W R –MISTERIJE ORGANIZMA • 1971 • Makavejev Dusan • YGS, FRG • W R –MYSTERIES OF THE ORGANISM (USA) ○ MYSTERY OF BODY

W R –MYSTERIES OF THE ORGANISM (USA) see **W R –MISTERIJE ORGANIZMA** • 1971

W.R.N.S. • 1941 • Moffat Ivan • UKN

W RAJU • 1962 • Oraczewska Zofia, Kruk N. • ANS • PLN • IN PARADISE

W.S.P. • 1974 • Anderson J. • SHT • UKN

W SRODKU LATA • 1975 • Falk Feliks • PLN • IN THE MIDDLE OF SUMMER ○ AT THE HEIGHT OF SUMMER

W: TERROR IS ONE LETTER see **W** • 1974

W.W. AND THE DIXIE DANCEKINGS • 1975 • Avildsen John G. • USA

W.W. JACOBS STORIES • 1928 • Malins Geoffrey H. • SHS • UKN

W. WEARY AND T. TIRED • 1905 • Collins Alf? • UKN
W ZAKLETYM KREGU • 1968 • Ziarnik Jerzy • DOC • PLN • IN AN ENCHANTED CIRCLE
W ZAWIESZENIU • 1988 • Krzystek Waldemar • PLN • SUSPENDED
WA ADA AL-HUBB see **WA ADAL'HOB** • 1960
WA ADAL'HOB • 1960 • Wahab Fatin Abdel • EGY • WA ADA AL-HUBB ○ AMOUR EST REVENU, L'
WA GHADAN.. • 1972 • Babay Ibrahim • TNS • ET DEMAIN.. ○ AND TOMORROW?
WA SAQAT'AT FI BAHRIN MIN AL-ASAL • 1976 • Abu Saif Salah • EGY • DANS UN OCEAN DE MIEL
WABASH AVENUE • 1950 • Koster Henry • USA
WABBIT TWOUBLE • 1941 • Clampett Robert • ANS • USA
WABBIT WHO CAME TO SUPPER, THE • 1942 • Freleng Friz • ANS • USA
WAC FROM WALLA WALLA, THE • 1951 • Witney William • USA • ARMY CAPERS (UKN)
WACHSFIGURENKABINETT, DAS • 1924 • Leni Paul • FRG • THREE WAX MEN (USA) ○ WAXWORKS (UKN) ○ WAX MEN, THE
WACHT AM RHEIN • 1915 • Larsen Viggo • FRG
WACHT AM RHEIN • 1926 • Lackner Helene • FRG
WACHT AM RHEIN, DIE see **AUS DES RHEINLANDS SCHICKSALSTAGEN** • 1926
WACHTMEISTER RAHN • 1974 • Lommel Ulli • FRG
WACHTMEISTER STUDER • 1939 • Lindtberg Leopold • SWT
WACKELKONTAKT • 1971 • Maran-Gosoff Tzvetan • FRG
WACKERE SCHUSTERMEISTER, DER • 1936 • Wolff Carl Heinz • FRG
WACKIEST SHIP IN THE ARMY, THE • 1960 • Murphy Richard • USA
WACKIEST WAGON TRAIN IN THE WEST, THE • 1976 • *Tucker Forrest* • USA
WACKIKI WABBIT see **WAIKIKI WABBIT** • 1943
WACKO • 1981 • Clark Greydon • USA
WACKY BLACKOUTS • 1942 • Clampett Robert • ANS • USA
WACKY-BYE BABY • 1948 • Lundy Dick • ANS • USA
WACKY PLAYBOY, THE • 1964 • Edward Steven • USA
WACKY QUACKY • 1947 • Lovy Alex • ANS • USA
WACKY TAXI • 1982 • Grasshoff Alex • USA
WACKY WABBIT, THE • 1942 • Clampett Robert • ANS • USA
WACKY WEED, THE • 1946 • Lundy Dick • ANS • USA
WACKY WIGWAMS • 1942 • Geiss Alec • ANS • USA
WACKY WILDLIFE • 1940 • Avery Tex • ANS • USA
WACKY WORLD OF DR. MORGUS, THE • 1962 • Haig Roul • USA
WACKY WORLD OF MOTHER GOOSE, THE • 1967 • Bass Jules • ANM • USA
WACKY WORM, THE • 1941 • Freleng Friz • ANS • USA
WACO • 1951 • Collins Lewis D. • USA • OUTLAW AND THE LADY, THE (UKN)
WACO • 1966 • Springsteen R. G. • USA
WACO AND RHINEHART see **U.S. MARSHALS: WACO & RHINEHART** • 1987
WACONICHI • 1955 • Proulx Maurice • DCS • CND
WAD AND THE WORM, THE • 1969 • Smith Douglas St. Clair • ANS • USA
WADAAT HUBAK • 1956 • Shahin Youssef • EGY • FAREWELL TO YOUR LOVE ○ WADDATU HUBBAK
WADDATU HUBBAK see **WADAAT HUBAK** • 1956
WADDENZEE -BIRD PARADISE • 1972 • van de Kam Jan • DCS • NTH
WADDLING WILLIE • 1914 • *Pike'S Peak Comp.* • USA
WADE BRENT PAYS • 1914 • Grandon Francis J. • USA
WADERS, THE see **WADLOPERS** • 1959
WADI AL-ASFAR, AL- • 1969 • Shukry Mamduh • EGY • VALLEE JAUNE, LA
WADLOPERS • 1959 • van Morkerken Emile • NTH • WADERS, THE
WAEBULLEO • 1985 • Jang Yeong-Il • SKR
WAFER see **PA D'ANGEL** • 1984
WAFFEN DER JUGEND • 1912 • Wiene Robert?, Muller Friedrich? • FRG
WAFFENKAMMERN DEUTSCHLAND see **DEUTSCHE WAFFENSCHMIEDE, DIE** • 1940
WAGA AI • 1960 • Gosho Heinosuke • JPN • WHEN A WOMAN LOVES ○ MY LOVE
WAGA AI NO KI • 1941 • Toyoda Shiro • JPN • RECORD OF MY LOVE, A
WAGA AI WA YAMA NO KANATA NI • 1948 • Toyoda Shiro • JPN • MY LOVE ON THE OTHER SIDE OF THE MOUNTAIN ○ MY LOVE IS BEYOND THE MOUNTAIN
WAGA ICHIKO JIDAI NO HANZAI • 1951 • Sekigawa Hideo • JPN • MY CRIME WHILE AT THE FIRST HIGHER SCHOOL
WAGA INOCHI NO UTA ENKA • 1968 • Masuda Toshio • JPN • SONG OF LOVE
WAGA KOI NO TABIJI • 1961 • Shinoda Masahiro • JPN • EPITAPH TO MY LOVE
WAGA KOI WA MOENU • 1949 • Mizoguchi Kenji • JPN • MY LOVE HAS BEEN BURNING (UKN) ○ FLAME OF MY LOVE (USA) ○ MY LOVE BURNS
WAGA KOI WAGA UTA • 1969 • Nakamura Noboru • JPN • SONG FROM MY HEART, THE (USA)
WAGA KOISESHI OTOME • 1946 • Kinoshita Keisuke • JPN • GIRL I LOVED, THE ○ GIRL THAT I LOVE, THE
WAGA KOKORONO UTA • 1977 • Yamaguchi Seiichiro • JPN • SONG IN MY HEART, A
WAGA MACHI • 1955 • Kawashima Yuzo • JPN • OUR TOWN
WAGA MICHI • 1974 • Shindo Kaneto • JPN • MY WAY
WAGA SEISHUN NI KUINASHI • 1946 • Kurosawa Akira • JPN • NO REGRETS FOR MY YOUTH ○ NO REGRETS FOR OUR YOUTH ○ NO REGRETS FOR LOST YOUTH
WAGA SEISHUN NO TOKI • 1974 • Morikawa Tokihisa • JPN • DAYS OF MY YOUTH, THE
WAGA SHOGAI NO KAGAYAKERU HI • 1948 • Yoshimura Kozaburo • JPN • DAY OUR LIVES SHINE, THE ○ MY LIFE'S BRIGHT DAY ○ BRIGHT DAY OF MY LIFE, THE
WAGA SHOGAI WA HI NO GOTOKU • 1961 • Sekigawa Hideo • JPN • LIKE FIRE IS MY LIFE ○ MY LIFE IS LIKE FIRE
WAGA TOSO • 1968 • Nakamura Noboru • JPN • MY DESTINY
WAGAHAI WA NEKO DE ARU • 1936 • Yamamoto Kajiro • JPN • I AM A CAT
WAGAHAI WA NEKO DEARU • 1974 • Ichikawa Kon • JPN • I AM A CAT
WAGAYA NI HAHA ARE • 1938 • Shibuya Minoru • JPN • MOTHER STAY AT HOME
WAGAYA WA TANOSHI • 1951 • Nakamura Noboru • JPN
WAGE, THE • 1989 • Javanmard Majid • IRN
WAGER, A • 1913 • *Eclair* • USA
WAGER, THE • 1911 • *Walker Lillian* • USA
WAGER, THE • 1913 • *Reliance* • USA
WAGER, THE • 1913 • Brett B. Harold • UKN
WAGER, THE • 1916 • Baker George D. • USA
WAGER, THE see **KAERLIGHEDS VAEDDEMAALET** • 1914
WAGER, THE see **SIR JAMES MORTIMER'S WAGER** • 1916
WAGER, THE see **OPKLADA** • 1971
WAGER AND THE WAGE EARNERS, THE • 1911 • *Edison* • USA
WAGER BETWEEN TWO MAGICIANS: OR, JEALOUS OF MYSELF, A (USA) see **MATCH DE PRESTIDIGITATION** • 1904
WAGES AND PROFIT see **TARANG** • 1984
WAGES FOR WIVES • 1925 • Borzage Frank • USA
WAGES NO OBJECT • 1917 • Drew Sidney, Drew Sidney Mrs. • SHT • USA
WAGES OF CONSCIENCE • 1927 • Ince John • USA
WAGES OF FEAR, THE (UKN) see **SORCERER** • 1977
WAGES OF FEAR, THE (USA) see **SALAIRE DE LA PEUR, LE** • 1953
WAGES OF SIN • 1903 • *Bitzer Billy (Ph)* • USA
WAGES OF SIN • 1910 • *Nestor* • USA
WAGES OF SIN • 1929 • Micheaux Oscar • USA
WAGES OF SIN, THE • 1908 • *Vitagraph* • USA
WAGES OF SIN, THE • 1914 • *Butler William J.* • USA
WAGES OF SIN, THE • 1918 • Bocchi Arrigo • UKN
WAGES OF SIN, THE • 1922 • *Gabriel Jean* • USA • GOD'S PAY DAY (?)
WAGES OF SINN, THE • 1914 • *Roland Ruth* • USA
WAGES OF TIN, THE • 1924 • Roach Hal • SHT • USA
WAGES OF VIRTUE • 1924 • Dwan Allan • USA
WAGES OF WAR • 1911 • *Vitagraph* • USA
WAGGILY TALE, A • 1958 • Freleng Friz • ANS • USA
WAGHAN LI WAGH • 1976 • Fuad Ahmed • EGY • FACE TO FACE
WAGIB, AL- • 1947 • Barakat Henry • EGY • DEVOIR, LE
WAGNER • 1982 • Palmer Tony • UKN, FRG, AUS
WAGON HEELS • 1945 • Clampett Robert • ANS • USA
WAGON MASTER, THE • 1929 • Brown Harry J. • USA
WAGON OF DEATH, THE • 1914 • *Reliance* • USA
WAGON SHOW, THE • 1928 • Brown Harry J. • USA
WAGON TEAM • 1952 • Archainbaud George • USA
WAGON TRACKS • 1919 • Hillyer Lambert • USA
WAGON TRACKS WEST • 1943 • Bretherton Howard • USA
WAGON TRAIL • 1935 • Fraser Harry L. • USA
WAGON TRAIN • 1940 • Killy Edward • USA
WAGON WHEELS • 1934 • Barton Charles T. • USA • CARAVANS WEST
WAGON WHEELS (UKN) see **KANSAN, THE** • 1943
WAGON WHEELS WEST • 1943 • Eason B. Reeves • SHT • USA
WAGON WHEELS WESTWARD • 1945 • Springsteen R. G. • USA
WAGONMASTER • 1950 • Ford John • USA
WAGONS ROLL AT NIGHT, THE • 1941 • Enright Ray • USA
WAGONS WEST • 1952 • Beebe Ford • USA
WAGONS WESTWARD • 1940 • Landers Lew • USA
WAGS TO RICHES • 1949 • Avery Tex • ANS • USA
WAGTAIL TUNE see **SEKIREI NO KYOKO** • 1951
WAHABTAK HAYATI • 1956 • Wahab Fatin Abdel • EGY • JE T'AI OFFERT MA VIE
WAHAL DUPATHA • 1968 • Abeysekara Shathi • SLN • SLAVE ISLAND
WAHAN KE LOG • 1967 • Ansari N. A. • IND • PEOPLE OF THAT LAND, THE
WAH'ID FI AL-MILIUM • 1971 • Fahmy Ashraf • EGY • SUR UN MILLION, UN
WAHINE see **MAEVA** • 1961
WAHLE DAS LEBEN • 1962 • Leiser Erwin • SWT • CHOOSE LIFE
WAHLVERWANDTSCHAFTEN, DIE • 1975 • Kuhn Siegfried • GDR • ELECTIVE AFFINITIES
WAHN DES PHILIPP MORRIS, DER • 1921 • Biebrach Rudolf • FRG
WAHN IST KURZ, DER • 1918 • Schmidthassler Walter • FRG
WAHNSINN • 1919 • Veidt Conrad • FRG
WAHNSINN, DAS GANZE LEBEN IS WAHNSINN • 1980 • Haffter Peter • FRG • CRAZY, ALL LIFE'S CRAZY
WAHOO BOBCAT, THE • 1971 • Schloss Henry • DOC • USA
WAHRE JAKOB, DER • 1931 • Steinhoff Hans • FRG • MADCHEN VOM VARIETE, DAS
WAHRE JAKOB, DER • 1960 • Schundler Rudolf • FRG
WAHRE LIEBE • 1989 • Kino Kitty • AUS • TRUE LOVE
WAHRE LIEBE, DIE • 1919 • May Joe • FRG
WAHRHEIT UBER ROSEMARIE, DIE • 1959 • Jugert Rudolf • FRG • LOVE NOW, PAY LATER
WAHRSAGERIN VON PARIS, DIE • 1920 • Hartt Heinz S. • FRG
WAH'SH, AL- see **WAHSH, EL** • 1954
WAHSH, EL • 1954 • Abu Saif Salah • EGY • MONSTER, THE ○ WAH'SH, AL-
WAI DIP • 1990 • Mikunsoot Chao • THL • JUNKIE
WAIF, THE • 1911 • *Imp* • USA
WAIF, THE • 1913 • West Raymond B. • USA
WAIF, THE • 1915 • Roubert William L. • USA
WAIF AND THE STATUE, THE • 1907 • Booth W. R.? • UKN
WAIF AND THE WIZARD: OR, THE HOME MADE HAPPY, THE • 1901 • Booth W. R.? • UKN
WAIF HEROINE, THE • 1909 • *Anglo-American Films* • UKN
WAIF OF THE DESERT, A • 1913 • *Nestor* • USA
WAIF OF THE DESERT, A • 1913 • Jones Edgar • *Lubin* • USA
WAIF OF THE PLAINS, A • 1914 • *Warner'S Features* • USA
WAIF OF THE SEA, A • 1912 • *Santschi Thomas* • USA
WAIFS • 1914 • *Ab* • USA
WAIFS • 1918 • Parker Albert • USA
WAIFS, THE • 1915 • Nash Percy? • UKN
WAIFS, THE • 1916 • Sidney Scott • USA
WAIF'S CHRISTMAS, THE • 1908 • *Walturdaw* • UKN
WAIFS OF THE SEA • 1915 • O'Sullivan Tony • USA
WAIF'S WELCOME, A • 1936 • Palmer Tom • ANS • USA
WAIKIKI • 1980 • Satlof Ron • TVM • USA
WAIKIKI MELODY • 1945 • Cowan Will • SHT • USA
WAIKIKI WABBIT • 1943 • Jones Charles M. • ANS • USA • WACKIKI WABBIT
WAIKIKI WEDDING • 1937 • Tuttle Frank • USA
WAIL see **DOKOKU** • 1952
WAISE VOM WEDDING, DIE • 1927 • Neff Wolfgang • FRG
WAISE VON CAPRI, DIE • 1924 • Zelnik Friedrich • FRG • MADEL VON CAPRI, DAS
WAISE VON LOWOOD, DIE • 1919 • Muller-Hagen Carl • FRG
WAISE VON LOWOOD, DIE • 1926 • Bernhardt Curtis • FRG
WAISENHAUSKIND, DAS • 1916 • Schmidthassler Walter • FRG
WAIT • 1968 • Gehr Ernie • USA
WAIT A FEW MOMENTS MORE see **UNDAMMA BOTTU PEDATA** • 1968
WAIT A MINUTE • 1916 • *Stull Walter* • USA
WAIT AND SEE • 1910 • Collins Alf? • UKN
WAIT AND SEE • 1915 • Bertram William • USA
WAIT AND SEE • 1928 • Forde Walter • UKN
WAIT FOR ME • 1920 • Horne James W. • USA
WAIT FOR ME • 1943 • Stolper Alexander, Ivanov B. • USS
WAIT FOR ME, ANNA • 1969 • Vinogradov Valentin • USS
WAIT FOR ME IN HEAVEN see **ESPERAME EN EL CIELO** • 1988
WAIT FOR THE ARRIVAL OF HALLEWYN see **ESPEREN LA LLEGADA DE HALLEWYN** • 1972
WAIT FOR THE DAWN see **ERA NOTTE A ROMA** • 1960
WAIT FOR TOMORROW see **ASHITA HARERUKA** • 1960
WAIT FOR US AT DAWN • 1963 • Lotyanu Emil • USS
WAIT 'TIL THE SUN SHINES NELLIE • 1952 • King Henry • USA
WAIT TILL I CATCH YOU • 1910 • Stow Percy • UKN
WAIT TILL JACK COMES HOME • 1903 • Williamson James • UKN
WAIT TILL THE SUN SHINES, NELLIE • 1932 • Fleischer Dave • ANS • USA
WAIT TILL THE WORK COMES ROUND • 1907 • Gilbert Arthur • UKN
WAIT TILL YOUR MOTHER GETS HOME! • 1982 • Persky Bill • TVM • USA
WAIT UNTIL DARK • 1967 • Young Terence • USA
WAIT UNTIL I GO TO SCHOOL • 1961 • Junge Winifried • DOC • GDR
WAIT UNTIL SPRING, BANDINI (USA) see **BANDINI** • 1988
WAITER • 1985 • Prefontaine Michel • MTV • CND
WAITER, THE see **CAUGHT IN A CABARET** • 1914
WAITER FROM THE RITZ, THE • 1926 • Cruze James • USA
WAITER NO.5 • 1910 • Griffith D. W. • USA
WAITER OF WEIGHT, A • 1912 • *Powers* • USA
WAITER WHO WAITED, THE • 1915 • *La Pearl Harry* • USA
WAITERS, THE • 1969 • Darnley-Smith Jan • UKN
WAITERS' BALL, THE • 1916 • Arbuckle Roscoe, Hartman Ferris • USA
WAITER'S DREAM, THE see **REVE D'UN GARCON DE CAFE** • 1913
WAITERS' PICNIC, THE • 1913 • Sennett Mack • USA
WAITER'S STRATEGY, THE • 1913 • *Lubin* • USA
WAITER'S WASTED LIFE, A • 1918 • White Jack, Watson William • SHT • USA
WAITING • 1925 • Roberts Stephen • SHT • USA
WAITING • 1990 • McKimmie Jack • ASL
WAITING see **OCZEKIWANIE** • 1962
WAITING, THE see **JAGWAL**
WAITING AT THE CHURCH • 1906 • Porter Edwin S. • USA
WAITING AT THE CHURCH • 1911 • *Imp* • USA
WAITING AT THE CHURCH • 1911 • *Thanhouser* • USA
WAITING AT THE CHURCH • 1919 • Lyons Eddie, Moran Lee • SHT • USA
WAITING AT THE CHURCH see **RUNAROUND, THE** • 1931
WAITING FOR.. • 1970 • Basser Ann • USA
WAITING FOR A TRAIN see **ASTEPTIND UN TREN** • 1982
WAITING FOR BABY • 1941 • Roush Leslie • SHT • USA
WAITING FOR CAROLINE • 1967 • Kelly Ron • MTV • CND
WAITING FOR FIDEL • 1974 • Rubbo Michael • CND
WAITING FOR GODOT see **CEKANI NA GODOTA** • 1966
WAITING FOR HIM TONIGHT • 1907 • Morland John • UKN
WAITING FOR HUBBY • 1913 • *Chamberlin Riley* • USA
WAITING FOR LETTERS see **ZHDITE PISEM** • 1960
WAITING FOR LUCAS • 1973 • Barry Ian • SHT • ASL
WAITING FOR MORNING • 1980 • Kroeker Allan • CND
WAITING FOR MORNING see **PLACES IN THE HEART** • 1984
WAITING FOR RAIN see **CEKANI NA DEST** • 1978
WAITING FOR SALAZAR see **DISORGANISED CRIME** • 1989
WAITING FOR SPRING see **HARU O MATSU HITOBITO** • 1959
WAITING FOR THE BRIDE (UKN) see **RUNAROUND, THE** • 1931
WAITING FOR THE LIGHT • 1990 • Monger Chris • USA
WAITING FOR THE MOON • 1987 • Godmilow Jill • USA • ON THE TRAIL OF THE LONESOME PINE
WAITING FOR THE RAIN see **CEKANI NA DEST** • 1978
WAITING FOR TOMORROW see **MENANTI HARI ESOK** • 1976
WAITING GAME, A • 1916 • *Turpin Ben* • SHT • USA
WAITING GIRLS, THE see **CEKANKY** • 1940
WAITING-LIST FOR HELL see **WARTELISTE ZUR HOLLE** • 1967
WAITING ROOM • 1980 • Kawadri Anwar • UKN
WAITING ROOM, THE • 1973 • Sperling Karen • USA
WAITING SOUL, THE • 1917 • King Burton L. • USA
WAITING WATER see **VANTANDE VATTEN** • 1964
WAITING WOMEN (UKN) see **KVINNORS VANTAN** • 1952
WAITRESS! • 1982 • Herz Michael, Weil Samuel • USA
WAITRESS AND THE BOOBS, THE • 1915 • *Kalem* • USA
WAJAH SEORANG LAKI-LAKI • 1971 • Karya Teguh • INN • BALLAD OF A MAN
WAJAN (SON OF A WITCH) • 1934 • Spies Walter • USA, INN • BLACK MAGIC
WAK-WAK, EIN MARCHENZAUBER see **ABENTEUER DES PRINZEN ACHMED, DIE** • 1926
WAKADO NO YUME • 1928 • Ozu Yasujiro • JPN • DREAMS OF YOUTH
WAKAGERI NO IZUMI • 1956 • *Toei Doga* • ANS • JPN • FOUNTAIN OF YOUTH, THE (USA)
WAKAI HIROBA • 1958 • Horiuchi Manao • JPN

WAKAI HITO • 1937 • Toyoda Shiro • JPN • YOUNG PEOPLE
WAKAI HITO • 1952 • Ichikawa Kon • JPN • YOUNG GENERATION ○ YOUNG PEOPLE
WAKAI HITO • 1962 • Nishikawa Katsumi • JPN • FRESH LEAVES
WAKAI HITOTACHI • 1954 • Yoshimura Kozaburo • JPN • PEOPLE OF YOUNG CHARACTER ○ YOUNG PEOPLE
WAKAI KAWA NO NAGARE • 1959 • Tasaka Tomotaka • JPN • STREAM OF YOUTH, THE
WAKAI KOIBITOTACHI • 1959 • Chiba Yasuki • JPN • YOUNG LOVERS
WAKAI SHIGEKI • 1967 • Takeda Ario • JPN • YOUNG STIMULUS
WAKAI SUGATA • 1943 • Toyoda Shiro • JPN • YOUNG FIGURE
WAKAI TOKEIDAI • 1967 • Inoue Akira • JPN • WHIMSY OF CUPID, THE
WAKAKI HI NO CHUJI • 1925 • Kinugasa Teinosuke • JPN
WAKAKI HI NO KANGEKI • 1931 • Gosho Heinosuke • JPN • MEMORIES OF YOUNG DAYS ○ EXCITEMENT OF A YOUNG DAY
WAKAKIHI • 1929 • Ozu Yasujiro • JPN • DAYS OF YOUTH
WAKAKIHI NO AYAMACHI • 1952 • *Hidari Sachiko* • JPN • FAULTS OF YOUTH
WAKAKUTE WARUKUTE SUGOI KOITSURA • 1962 • Nakahira Ko • JPN • THESE YOUNG PEOPLE BAD AND TERRIBLE
WAKAMBA! • 1955 • *Queeny Edgar M. (P)* • DOC • USA
WAKAMONO TACHI • 1967 • Morikawa Tokihisa • JPN • LIVE YOUR OWN WAY (USA) ○ YOUNG ONES, THE ○ WAKAMONOTACHI
WAKAMONO TACHI NO YORU TO HIRU • 1963 • Ieki Miyoji • JPN • INJURED BOY
WAKAMONO YO CHOSEN SEYO • 1968 • Chiba Yasuki • JPN • YOUNG CHALLENGERS
WAKAMONOTACHI see **WAKAMONO TACHI** • 1967
WAKAOKUSAMA ICHIBAN SHOBU • 1952 • Mizuko Harumi • JPN • FIRST STEP OF MARRIED LIFE
WAKAOYABUN KYOJOTABI • 1967 • Mori Issei • JPN • CRIMINAL JOURNEY OF A YOUNG BOSS
WAKAOYABUN O KESE • 1967 • Nakanishi Chuzo • JPN • KILL THE YOUNG BOSS
WAKAOYABUN SENRYOHADA • 1967 • Ikehiro Kazuo • JPN • TORPEDO-X
WAKAOYABUN TANJO • 1967 • Ida Tan • JPN • BIRTH OF A YOUNG HERO
WAKARATE IKIRU TOKI MO • 1961 • Horikawa Hiromichi • JPN • ETERNITY OF LOVE
WAKARE • 1969 • Oba Hideo • JPN • FAREWELL, MY BELOVED (USA)
WAKARE-GUMO • 1951 • Gosho Heinosuke • JPN • DISPERSING CLOUDS ○ DRIFTING CLOUDS ○ DISPERSING CLOUD ○ SPREADING CLOUD
WAKARENU RIYUU • 1988 • Furuhata Yasuo • JPN • REASON FOR NOT DIVORCING
WAKASHACHO DAIFUNSEN • 1967 • Umezu Meijiro • JPN • OUR YOUNG PRESIDENT
WAKASHACHO RAINBOW SAKUSEN • 1967 • Umezu Meijiro • JPN • OPERATION RAINBOW
WAKAZUMA NO NIOI • 1967 • Kataoka Hitoshi • JPN • FRAGRANT YOUNG WIFE
WAKE IN FRIGHT see **OUTBACK** • 1971
WAKE ISLAND • 1942 • Farrow John • USA
WAKE ME WHEN IT'S OVER • 1960 • LeRoy Mervyn • USA
WAKE ME WHEN THE WAR IS OVER • 1969 • Nelson Gene • TVM • USA
WAKE MUKHIN UP see **RAZBUDITYE MUKHINA** • 1968
WAKE OF THE RED WITCH • 1948 • Ludwig Edward • USA
WAKE UP! see **WAKE UP! OR, A DREAM OF TOMORROW** • 1914
WAKE UP AND DIE (USA) see **SVEGLIATI E UCCIDI (LUTRING)** • 1966
WAKE UP AND DREAM • 1934 • Neumann Kurt • USA
WAKE UP AND DREAM • 1946 • Bacon Lloyd • USA • ENCHANTED VOYAGE
WAKE UP AND DREAM (UKN) see **WHAT'S COOKIN'** • 1942
WAKE UP AND FEED • 1936 • Holmes J. B. • UKN
WAKE UP AND LIVE • 1937 • Lanfield Sidney • USA
WAKE UP FAMOUS • 1937 • Gerrard Gene • UKN
WAKE UP LENOCHKA see **RAZBUDITE LENOCHKY** • 1933
WAKE UP! OR, A DREAM OF TOMORROW • 1914 • Cowen Lawrence • UKN • DREAM OF TOMORROW, A ○ WAKE UP!
WAKE UP THE GYPSY IN ME • 1933 • Ising Rudolf • ANS • USA
WAKEFIELD CASE, THE • 1921 • Irving George • USA
WAKEFIELD EXPRESS • 1952 • Anderson Lindsay • SHT • UKN
WAKHEL • *Assis* • EGY
WAKING, THE see **AWAKENING, THE** • 1980
WAKING HOUR, THE see **VELVET VAMPIRE, THE** • 1971
WAKING UP FATHER • 1915 • *Ovey George* • USA
WAKING UP THE TOWN • 1925 • Cruze James • USA • END OF THE WORLD, THE (?)
WAKKAI ONNA NI TE O DASUNA • 1967 • Onishi Takanori • JPN • DON'T TOUCH YOUNG GIRLS
WAKUSEI DAISENSO see **NAKUSEI DAISENSO** • 1977
WALADI, ANA FAKHURUN • 1968 • Nasser George • SHT • LBN
WALANG HARI SA BATAS • 1968 • Cruz Jose Miranda • PHL
WALCO SISTERS, THE • 1914 • *Lubin* • USA
WALCOWNIA • 1956 • Lomnicki Jan • DOC • PLN • ROLLING MILL, THE
WALDBRAND, DER • 1916 • Schmidthassler Walter • FRG
WALDEN: REELS ONE TO FOUR see **DIARIES, NOTES AND SKETCHES** • 1969
WALDO'S LAST STAND • 1940 • Cahn Edward L. • SHT • USA
WALDRAUSCH • 1939 • May Paul • FRG
WALDRAUSCH • 1962 • May Paul • AUS
WALDWINTER • 1936 • Buch Fritz Peter • FRG
WALDWINTER • 1956 • Liebeneiner Wolfgang • FRG
WALES • 1948 • Stringer G. Henry • DOC • UKN
WALES • 1960 • Kelly Ron • DOC • UKN
WALET PIKOWY • 1960 • Chmielewski Tadeusz • PLN • JACK OF SPADES ○ KNAVE OF SPADES
WALIS NI TENTENG • 1965 • Marquez Artemio • PHL
WALK, THE see **ANDADOR, EL** • 1967
WALK A CROOKED MILE • 1948 • Douglas Gordon • USA
WALK A CROOKED PATH • 1970 • Brason John • UKN
WALK A TIGHTROPE • 1963 • Nesbitt Frank • UKN
WALK CHEERFULLY see **HOGARAKA NI AYUME** • 1930
WALK, DON'T RUN • 1966 • Walters Charles • USA
WALK EAST ON BEACON • 1952 • Werker Alfred L. • USA • CRIME OF THE CENTURY (UKN)
WALK IN BEAUTY • 1987 • Eleasari Jacob
WALK IN THE BIESZCZADY, A see **SPACER W BIESZCZADACH** • 1958
WALK IN THE BIESZCZADY MOUNTAINS, A see **SPACER W BIESZCZADACH** • 1958
WALK IN THE CLOUDS, A • 1967 • Kidawa Janusz • DOC • PLN
WALK IN THE FOREST, A • 1975 • Hood Randall • SHT • USA
WALK IN THE OLD CITY OF WARSAW, A (USA) see **SPACEREK STAROMIEJSKI** • 1958
WALK IN THE OLD TOWN, A see **SPACEREK STAROMIEJSKI** • 1958
WALK IN THE SHADOW (USA) see **LIFE FOR RUTH** • 1962
WALK IN THE SPRING RAIN, A • 1970 • Green Guy • USA
WALK IN THE SUN, A • 1946 • Milestone Lewis • USA • SALERNO BEACHHEAD
WALK INTO HELL • 1957 • Robinson Lee • ASL, FRN • ODYSEE DU CAPITAINE STEVE, L' (FRN) ○ WALK INTO PARADISE
WALK INTO PARADISE see **WALK INTO HELL** • 1957
WALK LIKE A DRAGON • 1960 • Clavell James • USA
WALK LIKE A MAN • 1987 • Frank Melvin • USA • BOBO
WALK-OFFS, THE • 1920 • Blache Herbert • USA
WALK ON THE MOON, A • 1988 • Silver Ray • USA
WALK ON THE WILD SIDE • 1962 • Dmytryk Edward • USA
WALK ON WATER, IF YOU CAN see **GA PA VATTNET, OM DU KAN** • 1979
WALK PROUD • 1979 • Collins Robert • USA • GANG
WALK SOFTLY, STRANGER • 1950 • Stevenson Robert • USA • WEEP NO MORE
WALK TALL • 1961 • Dexter Maury • USA
WALK THE DARK STREET • 1956 • Ordung Wyott • USA
WALK THE HOT STREETS (UKN) see **HEISSES PFLASTER KOLN** • 1967
WALK THE PROUD LAND • 1956 • Hibbs Jesse • USA
WALK THE WALK • 1970 • Zacha Jac • USA
WALK THIS WAY • 1916 • Dillon John Francis • USA
WALK THROUGH H, A • 1979 • Greenaway Peter • UKN
WALK UP AND DIE see **BANYON** • 1971
WALK WITH LOVE AND DEATH, A • 1969 • Huston John • USA
WALK WITH THE ANGEL, A • 1990 • Pavlov Ivan • BUL
WALK, -YOU, -WALK! • 1912 • *Roland Ruth* • USA
WALKABOUT • 1971 • Roeg Nicolas • ASL
WALKABOUT EDINBURGH • 1971 • McConnell Edward • DCS • UKN
WALKER • 1988 • Cox Alex • USA
WALKER EVANS -HIS TIME, HIS PRESENCE, HIS SILENCE • 1970 • Pakay Sedat • SHT • USA
WALKERS ON THE TIGER'S TAIL see **TORA NO OO FUMA OTOKOTACHI** • 1945
WALKING • 1968 • Larkin Ryan • ANS • CND • EN MARCHANT
WALKING AFTER MIDNIGHT • 1988 • Kay Jonathon • DOC • CND
WALKING ALONG THE MAIN ROAD see **VI GAR LANDSVAGEN** • 1937
WALKING BACK • 1928 • Julian Rupert • USA
WALKING BACK HOME • 1933 • Stevens George • SHT • USA
WALKING DEAD, THE • 1936 • Curtiz Michael • USA
WALKING DOWN BROADWAY • 1933 • von Stroheim Erich, Walsh Raoul (U/c) • USA
WALKING DOWN BROADWAY • 1938 • Foster Norman • USA
WALKING HILLS, THE • 1949 • Sturges John • USA
WALKING IN THE SUN.. see **VANDRING I SOLEN, EN** • 1978
WALKING MY BABY BACK HOME • 1953 • Bacon Lloyd • USA
WALKING ON AIR • 1936 • Santley Joseph • USA
WALKING ON AIR • 1946 • Ginever Aveling • UKN
WALKING ON.. WALKING see **CAMINANDO PASOS.. CAMINANDO** • 1976
WALKING ON WATER see **STAND AND DELIVER** • 1988
WALKING STICK, THE • 1970 • Till Eric • UKN
WALKING TALL • 1973 • Karlson Phil • USA
WALKING TALL 3: THE FINAL CHAPTER see **FINAL CHAPTER - WALKING TALL** • 1977
WALKING TALL: PART 2 see **PART 2 WALKING TALL** • 1975
WALKING TALL PART 2: VENGEANCE TRAIL see **PART 2 WALKING TALL** • 1975
WALKING TARGET, THE • 1960 • Cahn Edward L. • USA
WALKING THE BABY • 1933 • Scotto Aubrey • USA
WALKING THE EDGE • 1983 • Meisel Norbert • USA
WALKING THE STREETS OF MOSCOW see **YA SHAGAYU PO MOSKVE** • 1964
WALKING THROUGH CHINA see **PROMENADE EN CHINE** • 1934
WALKING THROUGH THE FIRE • 1979 • Day Robert • TVM • USA
WALKING TO HEAVEN see **GYALOG A MENNYORSZAGBA** • 1959
WALKING UPRIGHT see **AUFRECHTE GANG, DER** • 1976
WALKING WALKING see **CAMMINACAMMINA** • 1983
WALKING WOMAN WORK, A see **NEW YORK EYE AND EAR CONTROL** • 1964
WALKOUT, THE • 1923 • Roach Hal • SHT • USA
WALKOVER (USA) see **WALKOWER** • 1965
WALKOWER • 1965 • Skolimowski Jerzy • PLN • WALKOVER (USA)
WALKY TALKY HAWKY • 1946 • McKimson Robert • ANS • USA
WALL, THE • Svankmajer Jan • ANS • CZC
WALL, THE • 1982 • Markowitz Robert • TVM • USA
WALL, THE • 1982 • Parker Alan • UKN • PINK FLOYD -THE WALL
WALL, THE see **OSYNLIGA MUREN, DEN** • 1944
WALL, THE see **MURO, EL** • 1947
WALL, THE see **PARED, LA** • 1962
WALL, THE see **ZID** • 1965
WALL, THE see **MURO, IL** • 1972
WALL, THE see **ZIDUL** • 1974
WALL, THE see **TOIHOS, O** • 1977
WALL, THE see **MUR, LE** • 1983
WALL BETWEEN, THE • 1914 • *Sterling* • USA
WALL BETWEEN, THE • 1915 • Powell Paul • USA
WALL BETWEEN, THE • 1916 • Noble John W. • USA
WALL DRILLER, THE see **FALFURO** • 1985
WALL-EYED NIPPON (USA) see **YABUNIRAMI NIPPON** • 1964
WALL FLOWER, THE • 1922 • Hughes Rupert • USA
WALL FLOWER, THE • 1941 • *Mintz Charles (P)* • ANS • USA
WALL IN JERUSALEM, A (USA) see **MUR A JERUSALEM, UN** • 1968
WALL INVISIBLE, THE • 1918 • Durning Bernard J. • USA
WALL OF DEATH • 1956 • Tully Montgomery • UKN
WALL OF DEATH, THE • Cartwright J. A. D. • DOC • UKN
WALL OF DEATH (USA) see **THERE IS ANOTHER SUN** • 1950
WALL OF FLAME, THE • 1914 • *Mcquarrie Murdock* • USA
WALL OF FLAME, THE • 1916 • *Reid Wallace* • SHT • USA
WALL OF FLESH • 1968 • Sarno Joe • USA
WALL OF FURY • 1962 • Trenker Luis • FRG
WALL OF MONEY, THE • 1913 • Dwan Allan • USA
WALL OF MONEY, THE • 1917 • *Rex* • SHT • USA
WALL OF NOISE • 1963 • Wilson Richard • USA
WALL OF SILENCE, A • 1981 • Ricketson James • DOC • ASL
WALL OF SILENCE, THE see **MURO DEL SILENCIO, EL** • 1972
WALL OF WITCHES, THE see **SCIANA CZAROWNIC** • 1967
WALL OUTSIDE, THE see **COMPANY SHE KEEPS, THE** • 1951
WALL ST. COWBOY • 1939 • Kane Joseph • USA
WALL STREET • 1929 • Neill R. William • USA
WALL STREET • 1987 • Stone Oliver • USA
WALL STREET BLUES • 1924 • *Sennett Mack (P)* • SHT • USA
WALL STREET BLUES • 1946 • Yates Hal • SHT • USA
WALL STREET MYSTERY, THE • 1920 • Collins Tom • USA
WALL STREET TRAGEDY, A • 1916 • Marston Lawrence • USA
WALL STREET WAIL, A • 1913 • *Patheplay* • USA
WALL STREET WALKER • 1970 • *Kirt Films International* • USA
WALL STREET WHIZ, THE • 1925 • Nelson Jack • USA • NEW BUTLER, THE
WALL TIME see **LOST ANGELS** • 1989
WALL TO WALL see **CROSSTALK** • 1982
WALL WALLS see **MUR MURS** • 1980
WALLABY JIM OF THE ISLANDS • 1937 • Lamont Charles • USA
WALLACE JEWELS, THE • 1909 • *Edison* • USA
WALLED IN see **ZAZIDANI** • 1969
WALLENBERG • 1990 • Grede Kjell • SWD • GOOD EVENING, MR. WALLENBERG
WALLENBERG: A HERO'S STORY • 1985 • Johnson Lamont • TVM • USA
WALLENSTEIN 1 • 1925 • Randolf Rolf • FRG
WALLENSTEIN 2 • 1925 • Randolf Rolf • FRG
WALLET, THE • 1952 • Lewis Morton M. • UKN • BLUEPRINT FOR MURDER
WALLFLOWER • 1948 • De Cordova Frederick • USA
WALLFLOWER, THE • 1914 • *Lubin* • USA
WALLFLOWERS • 1928 • Meehan James Leo • USA
WALLINGFORD'S WALLET • 1913 • Lewis Edgar • USA
WALLNERBUB, DER see **JAHR DES HERRN, DAS** • 1950
WALLOP, THE • 1921 • Ford John • USA • HOMEWARD TRAIL, THE
WALLOPING KID • 1926 • Horner Robert J. • USA
WALLOPING TIME, A • 1917 • Stonehouse Ruth • SHT • USA
WALLOPING WALLACE • 1924 • Thorpe Richard • SHT • USA • RANGE RIDERS OF THE GREAT WILD WEST
WALLS • 1985 • Shandel Thomas • CND
WALLS see **FALAK** • 1968
WALLS, THE see **ASWAR, AL-** • 1979
WALLS, THE see **SCIANY** • 1988
WALLS, THE see **MATHILUKAL** • 1990
WALLS AND WALLOPS • 1916 • Semon Larry • SHT • USA
WALLS CAME TUMBLING DOWN, THE • 1946 • Mendes Lothar • USA
WALLS CAME TUMBLING DOWN, THE • 1976 • Rubbo Michael, Lasry Pierre, Weintraub William • CND
WALLS HAVE EYES, THE • 1969 • *Astro-Jemco Film Dist.* • USA
WALLS OF FEAR (USA) see **PLANQUE, LA** • 1961
WALLS OF FIRE • 1973 • Kline Herbert • DOC • USA, MXC
WALLS OF FREEDOM, THE see **FRIHETENS MURAR** • 1978
WALLS OF GLASS see **FLANAGAN** • 1985
WALLS OF GOLD • 1933 • MacKenna Kenneth • USA
WALLS OF HELL, THE • 1964 • De Leon Gerardo, Romero Eddie • USA, PHL • INTRAMUROS (PHL)
WALLS OF JERICHO, THE • 1914 • Hackett James K. • USA
WALLS OF JERICHO, THE • 1948 • Stahl John M. • USA
WALLS OF MALAPAGA, THE (USA) see **AU-DELA DES GRILLES** • 1948
WALLS OF PREJUDICE • 1920 • Calvert Charles • UKN
WALLS OF SING SING, THE • 1908 • *Kalem* • USA
WALLY • 1932 • Brignone Guido • ITL
WALMATHVUVO • 1976 • Obeysekara Vasantha • SLN
WALPURGIS NIGHT • 1932 • Higgin Howard • USA
WALPURGIS NIGHT see **VALBORGSMASSOAFTON** • 1935
WALPURGISNACHT • 1927 • Bauer James • FRG
WALPURGISNACHT • 1954 • Menzel Erich • FRG
WALPURGISZAUBER • 1923 • AUS
WALRUS • 1973 • Leiterman Richard (c/d) • SER • CND
WALRUS GANG, THE • 1917 • Aylott Dave • UKN
WALSH BROTHERS, THE • 1930 • *Balcon Michael (P)* • SHT • UKN
WALSUNGENBLUT • 1964 • Thiele Rolf • FRG • BLOOD OF THE WALSUNGS
WALT DISNEY'S MAGIC CARPET TOUR AROUND THE WORLD • 1971 • Barclay Robert • SHT • CND
WALTER • 1971 • Fedak Waclaw • PLN • GENERAL WALTER
WALTER • 1982 • Frears Stephen • TVM • UKN • LOVING WALTER (USA)

WALTER DEFENDS SARAJEVO see **VALTER BRANI SARAJEVO** • 1972
WALTER E I SUOI CUGINI • 1961 • Girolami Marino • ITL
WALTER FELSENSTEIN • Nickel Gitta • DOC • GDR
WALTER FINDS A FATHER • 1921 • Bamberger Joseph J. • SHT • UKN
WALTER GRAHAM THE HUMAN MARIONETTE • 1905 • *Walturdaw* • UKN
WALTER IV • 1973 • Frydman Gerald • BLG
WALTER MAKES A MOVIE • 1922 • Seymour Tom, Forde Walter • SHT • UKN
WALTER TELLS THE TALE • 1926 • Sloan James B. • SHT • UKN
WALTER THE PRODIGAL • 1926 • Sloan James B. • SHT • UKN
WALTER THE SLEUTH • 1926 • Sloan James B. • SHT • UKN
WALTER WANGER'S VOGUES OF 1938 see **VOGUES** • 1937
WALTER WANTS WORK • 1922 • Seymour Tom, Forde Walter • SHT • UKN
WALTER WILLIAMS • 1926 • *De Forest Phonofilms* • SHT • UKN
WALTER WINS A WAGER • 1922 • Seymour Tom, Forde Walter • SHT • UKN
WALTER'S DAY OUT • 1926 • Sloan James B. • SHT • UKN
WALTER'S PAYING POLICY • 1926 • Sloan James B. • SHT • UKN
WALTER'S TRYING FROLIC • 1922 • Seymour Tom, Forde Walter • SHT • UKN
WALTER'S WINNING WAYS • 1921 • Bowman William J. • SHT • UKN
WALTER'S WORRIES • 1926 • Sloan James B. • SHT • UKN
WALT'S PHOTO • 1914 • *Komic* • USA
WALTZ ACROSS TEXAS • 1982 • Day Ernest • USA
WALTZ AT NOON see **MAHIRU NO ENBUKYOKU** • 1949
WALTZ DREAM see **WALZERTRAUM, EIN** • 1925
WALTZ KING, THE • 1963 • Previn Steven • USA, AUS • JOHAN STRAUSS
WALTZ ME AROUND • 1920 • Roach Hal • SHT • USA
WALTZ ME AROUND AGAIN WILLIE • 1908 • Gilbert Arthur • UKN
WALTZ MELODIES (USA) see **WALZERLANGE** • 1938
WALTZ MUST CHANGE TO A MARCH, THE • 1906 • Gilbert Arthur • UKN
WALTZ MUST TURN TO A MARCH, THE • 1909 • *Warwick Trading Co* • UKN
WALTZ OF SEX (UKN) see **VINDINGEVALS** • 1968
WALTZ OF THE GORILLA, THE see **VALSE DU GORILLE, LA** • 1959
WALTZ OF THE POKER see **SPISKROKSVALSEN** • 1909
WALTZ OF THE TOREADORS • 1962 • Guillermin John • UKN • AMOROUS GENERAL, THE
WALTZ TIME • 1933 • Thiele Wilhelm • UKN
WALTZ TIME • 1945 • Stein Paul L. • UKN
WALTZ TIME IN VIENNA • 1933 • Berger Ludwig
WALTZES FROM VIENNA • 1933 • Hitchcock Alfred • UKN • STRAUSS' GREAT WALTZ (USA)
WALTZING AROUND • 1918 • *Rhodes Billie* • USA
WALTZING AROUND • 1929 • Sweet Harry • SHT • USA
WALTZING MATHILDA • 1944-45 • Ladouceur Jean-Paul • ANS • CND
WALTZING MATILDA • 1933 • Hanna Pat • ASL
WALTZING MATILDA • 1985 • Cusack Michael, Chataway Richard • ANM • ASL
WALTZING POLICEMAN, THE • 1979 • Feltham Kerry B. • SHT • USA
WALTZING REGITZE see **DANSEN MED REGITZE** • 1989
WALZER AN DER NEWA see **PETERSBURGER NACHTE** • 1934
WALZER FUR DICH, EIN • 1934 • Zoch Georg • FRG
WALZER IM SCHLAFCOUPE, EIN • 1930 • Sauer Fred • FRG
WALZER INS GLUCK, EIN see **HERZKONIG** • 1947
WALZER MIT DIR, EIN • 1943 • Marischka Hubert • FRG
WALZER UM DEN STEPHANSTURM, EIN • 1935 • Hubler-Kahla J. A. • AUS • SYLVIA UND IHR CHAUFFEUR
WALZER VON STRAUSS, DER • 1925 • Neufeld Max, Kreisler Otto • FRG, AUS
WALZER VON STRAUSS, EIN • 1932 • Wiene Conrad
WALZERKONIG, DER • 1930 • Noa Manfred • FRG
WALZERKRIEG • 1933 • Berger Ludwig • FRG • WAR OF THE WALTZES ○ COURT WALTZES.., THE
WALZERLANGE • 1938 • Lamac Carl • AUS, FRG • IMMER WENN ICH GLUCKLICH BIN ○ WALTZ MELODIES (USA)
WALZERNACHT, EIN • 1917 • Kaden Danny • FRG
WALZERPARADIES • 1931 • Zelnik Friedrich • FRG
WALZERTRAUM, EIN • 1907 • AUS
WALZERTRAUM, EIN • 1925 • Berger Ludwig • FRG • WALTZ DREAM
WAM! BAM! THANK YOU SPACEMAN • 1975 • Levey William A. • USA
WAMAN AVATAR • 1921 • *National* • IND • BALI RAJA ○ WAMAN, INCARNATION OF GOD
WAMAN, INCARNATION OF GOD see **WAMAN AVATAR** • 1921
WAMBA, A CHILD OF THE JUNGLE • 1913 • Campbell Colin • USA
WAMBA "ENTRE L'EAU ET LE FEU" • 1976 • Kaba Alkaly • DOC • CND, MLI
WAMPIRY WARSZAWY • 1914 • PLN • VAMPIRES OF WARSAW
WAMPIRY WARSZAWY • 1925 • PLN • VAMPIRES OF WARSAW (USA)
WAN • Adachi Masao • JPN • RICE BOWL
WAN-CH'UN CH'ING-SHIH • 1989 • Ch'En Yao-Ch'I • TWN, HKG • SPRING SWALLOW (UKN)
WAN DE JIU SHI XINTIAO • 1989 • Zhang Nuanxin • CHN • IT'S HEARTTHROB THAT WE PLAY
WAN HU CH'IEN CHIA • 1976 • Hu Hsiao-Feng • HKG • FAMILY IN THOUSANDS, A
WAN-JEN-CHAN • 1980 • Kuei Chih-Hung • HKG • KILLER CONSTABLE
WAN PIPEL • 1976 • de la Parra Pim • NTH • ONE PEOPLE
WAN ZHONG • 1988 • Wu Ziniu • CHN • EVENING BELL
WAN ZHU • 1988 • Mi Jiashan • CHN • TROUBLESHOOTERS, THE ○ THREE T COMPANY
WAND, EEN • 1968 • van der Velde Wim • SHT • NTH
WAND-ERFUL WILL • 1916 • Cooper Toby • UKN
WANDA • 1970 • Loden Barbara • USA
WANDA, ELYSE AND PATTI • 1944 • Farrow John • USA
WANDA LA PECCATRICE • 1952 • Coletti Duilio • ITL
WANDA NEVADA • 1979 • Fonda Peter • USA
WANDA (THE SATANIC HYPNOTIST) • 1969 • Corarito Greg • USA
WANDA, THE WICKED WARDEN • 1979 • Franco Jesus
WANDA WHIPS WALL STREET • 1982 • Revene Larry • USA
WANDER LOVE STORY see **WANDERLOVE** • 1970
WANDERER, THE • 1912 • Dwan Allan • USA
WANDERER, THE • 1913 • *Imp* • USA
WANDERER, THE • 1913 • Griffith D. W. • *Ab* • USA
WANDERER, THE • 1926 • Walsh Raoul • USA
WANDERER, THE • 1974 • Hicks Scott (c/d) • ASL
WANDERER, THE • 1988 • Ungar George • ANS • CND
WANDERER, THE (USA) see **GRAND MEAULNES, LE** • 1967
WANDERER AND THE WHOZITT, THE • 1918 • Bruce Robert C. • USA
WANDERER BEYOND THE GRAVE see **ZAGROBNAYA SKITALITSA** • 1915
WANDERER OF THE WASTELAND • 1924 • Willat Irvin V. • USA
WANDERER OF THE WASTELAND • 1934 • Lovering Otho • USA
WANDERER OF THE WASTELAND • 1945 • Killy Edward, Grissell Wallace A. • USA
WANDERER OF THE WEST • 1927 • Williamson Robin E.?, Zivelli Joseph E.? • USA
WANDERER RETURNS, THE • 1914 • Birch Cecil • UKN
WANDERERS see **ZBEHOVIA A PUTNICI** • 1968
WANDERERS see **LANDSTRYKERE** • 1988
WANDERERS see **POUTNICI** • 1988
WANDERERS, THE • 1910 • Olcott Sidney • USA
WANDERERS, THE • 1915 • Wolbert William • USA
WANDERERS, THE • 1979 • Kaufman Philip • USA
WANDERERS, THE see **GENS DU VOYAGE, LES** • 1937
WANDERERS, THE see **VELGARDHA** • 1968
WANDERERS, THE see **MATATABI** • 1973
WANDERER'S NOTEBOOK, A see **HOROKI** • 1962
WANDERERS OF THE DESERT • 1937-40 • *Cardiff Jack (Ph)* • DCS • UKN
WANDERERS OF THE WEST • 1941 • Hill Robert F. • USA
WANDERER'S PLEDGE, THE • 1915 • Morgan George • USA
WANDERER'S RETURN, THE • 1911 • *Powers* • USA
WANDERER'S RETURN: OR, MANY YEARS AFTER, THE • 1909 • Aylott Dave • UKN
WANDERING • 1980 • Hristofis Hristoforos • GRC
WANDERING see **RUTEN** • 1927
WANDERING see **RUTEN** • 1960
WANDERING see **BLOUDENI** • 1965
WANDERING, THE see **RATACIRE** • 1978
WANDERING BIRD (USA) see **AVE SIN RUMBO** • 1937
WANDERING DAUGHTERS • 1923 • Young James • USA
WANDERING DAUGHTERS see **YOUTH ON TRIAL** • 1945
WANDERING FIRES • 1925 • Campbell Maurice • USA • SHOULD A WOMAN TELL? (UKN)
WANDERING FOLK • 1913 • *Bison* • USA
WANDERING FOOTSTEPS • 1925 • Rosen Phil • USA
WANDERING GAMBLER, THE see **HORO ZANMAI** • 1928
WANDERING GIRLS • 1927 • Ince Ralph • USA
WANDERING GYPSY, THE • 1912 • Dwan Allan • USA
WANDERING HORDE, THE • 1916 • Mullin Eugene • SHT • USA
WANDERING HUSBANDS • 1924 • Beaudine William • USA
WANDERING IMAGE, THE see **WANDERNDE BILD, DAS** • 1920
WANDERING JEW, THE • 1923 • Elvey Maurice • UKN
WANDERING JEW, THE • 1933 • Elvey Maurice • UKN
WANDERING JEW, THE • 1933 • Roland George • USA
WANDERING JEW, THE see **EBREO ERRANTE, L'** • 1947
WANDERING JEW, THE (USA) see **JUIF ERRANT, LE** • 1904
WANDERING JEW, THE (USA) see **EBREO ERRANTE, L'** • 1913
WANDERING LIVES see **VIDAS ERRANTES** • 1984
WANDERING MINSTREL, A • 1907 • Morland John • UKN
WANDERING MINSTREL, THE see **RICHESSE ET MISERE; OU, LA CIGALE ET LA FOURMI** • 1899
WANDERING MUSICIAN, THE • 1912 • *Kalem* • USA
WANDERING NEGRO MINSTRELS, THE • 1896 • *Lumiere Cinematographe* • UKN
WANDERING PAPAS • 1925 • Roach Hal • SHT • USA
WANDERING PRINCESS, A see **RUTEN NO OHI** • 1960
WANDERING SOUL, THE see **ASWATHAMA** • 1979
WANDERING SOULS see **ARWA HAIMA** • 1949
WANDERING THE HIGHWAYS see **ORSZAGUTAR** • 1956
WANDERING THROUGH FRENCH CANADA • 1935 • Finnie Richard S. • DOC • CND
WANDERING WILLIES • 1926 • *Sennett Mack (P)* • SHT • USA
WANDERING WITH THE MOON see **VANDRING MED MANEN** • 1945
WANDERINGS OF A SOUL see **SEELENWANDERUNG** • 1964
WANDERINGS OF ULICK JOYCE, THE • 1968 • Lacey Gillian • UKN
WANDERLOVE • 1970 • Fist Fletcher • USA • WANDER LOVE STORY
WANDERLUST (UKN) see **MARY JANE'S PA** • 1935
WANDERN IST HERRN MULLERS LUST • 1973 • Antel Franz • AUS • HIKING IS HERR MULLER'S HOBBY
WANDERNDE AUGE, DAS • 1919 • Del Zopp Rudolf • FRG
WANDERNDE BILD, DAS • 1920 • Lang Fritz • FRG • MADONNA IN SCHNEE ○ WANDERING IMAGE, THE ○ MADONNA IN THE SNOW
WANDERNDE GLUCK, DAS • 1915 • Del Zopp Rudolf • FRG
WANDERNDE KOFFER, DER • 1921 • Hartwig Martin • FRG
WANDERNDE LICHT, DAS • 1916 • Wiene Robert • FRG
WANDERRATTEN • 1918 • Mack Max • FRG
WANDYALANKAS, LES • 1973 • Kaba Alkaly • MLI
WANG-YANG-CHUNG-TE YI-T'IAO CH'UAN • 1980 • Li Hsing • HKG • HE NEVER GIVES UP
WANG YU OF KING BOXER • 1972 • Kien Lun • HKG
WANG YU -TEN FINGERS OF STEEL see **TEN FINGERS OF STEEL** • 1973
WANG YU'S SEVEN MAGNIFICENT FIGHTS see **HAI-YUAN CH'I-HAO** • 1972
WANGENZA • 1977 • SAF
WANGMAGWI • 1967 • Hyukin Kwon • SKR • MONSTER WANGMAGWI
WANING SEX, THE • 1926 • Leonard Robert Z. • USA
WANNA SEE MY BEAUTIFUL NAVEL? see **VIL DU SE MIN SMUKKE NAVLE?** • 1978
WANNEER DIE MASKER VAL • 1955 • SAF
WANNSEE CONFERENCE, THE • 1984 • Schirk Heinz • FRG, AUS
WANPAKU OJI NO OROCHITAIJI • 1963 • Serikawa Yugo • ANM • JPN • LITTLE PRINCE AND THE EIGHT-HEADED DRAGON, THE (USA) ○ PRINCE IN WONDERLAND ○ RAINBOW BRIDGE
WANT A RIDE, LITTLE GIRL? • 1974 • Grefe William • USA • IMPULSE
WANT OF A SUITABLE PLAYHOUSE, THE • 1968 • Vaitiekunas Vince • CND
WANT SO MUCH TO BELIEVE see **VILL SA GARNA TRO** • 1971
WANTA MAKE A DOLLAR • 1917 • Beaudine William • SHT • USA
WANTED • 1937 • King George • UKN
WANTED • 1967 • Ferroni Giorgio • ITL
WANTED? see **WHAT A NIGHT!** • 1931
WANTED see **EFTERLYST** • 1939
WANTED see **FOUR FACES WEST** • 1948
WANTED $5000 see **WANTED FIVE THOUSAND DOLLARS** • 1919
WANTED: A BABY • 1910 • *Powers* • USA
WANTED, A BABY • 1912 • *Lubin* • USA
WANTED -A BABY • 1919 • *Parsons Smiling Bill* • SHT • USA
WANTED -A BAD MAN • 1917 • *Hardy Oliver* • USA
WANTED A BATH CHAIR ATTENDANT • 1910 • Martinek H. O. • UKN
WANTED, A BOY • 1924 • Bentley Thomas • UKN
WANTED -A BROTHER • 1918 • Ensminger Robert • USA
WANTED, A BURGLAR • 1913 • *Edison* • USA
WANTED -A CHAPERONE • 1915 • *Moran Lee* • USA
WANTED: A CHILD • 1909 • Griffith D. W. • USA
WANTED A COWARD • 1927 • Clements Roy • USA
WANTED A FILM ACTRESS (UKN) see **THOMAS GRAALS BASTA FILM** • 1917
WANTED -A GRANDMOTHER • 1912 • *Turner Florence* • USA
WANTED -A HOME • 1916 • Smalley Phillips, Weber Lois • USA
WANTED, A HOME see **DARLING OF NEW YORK, THE** • 1923
WANTED, A HOUSE • 1914 • Beggs Lee • USA
WANTED A HOUSEKEEPER see **NEW HOUSEKEEPER, THE** • 1912
WANTED -A HUSBAND • 1906 • Collins Alf? • UKN
WANTED, A HUSBAND • 1911 • *Urban Trading Co* • UKN
WANTED -A HUSBAND • 1912 • *Rice Herbert* • USA
WANTED A HUSBAND • 1913 • Charrington Arthur • UKN
WANTED -A HUSBAND • 1916 • Davey Horace • SHT • USA
WANTED -A HUSBAND • 1919 • Windom Lawrence C. • USA
WANTED: A MASTER • 1936 • Fritsch Gunther V., Ornitz Arthur • SHT • USA
WANTED -A MOTHER • 1918 • Knoles Harley • USA
WANTED, A MUMMY • 1910 • Coleby A. E. • UKN
WANTED, A NICE YOUNG MAN • 1908 • Aylott Dave? • UKN
WANTED, A NURSE • 1915 • Drew Sidney • USA
WANTED -A PIANO TUNER • 1916 • *Moranti Milburn* • SHT • USA
WANTED, A PLUMBER • 1913 • *Brennan John* • USA
WANTED, A PRACTICE • 1912 • *Powers* • USA
WANTED -A SISTER • 1912 • Young James • USA
WANTED -A STAR • 1920 • Tinsdale A. C. • ASL
WANTED -A STAR • 1921 • *United Theatres & Films Ltd* • ASL
WANTED -A STORY • 1922 • Litson Mason N. • USA
WANTED, A STRONG HAND • 1913 • Brooke Van Dyke • USA
WANTED, A SWEETHEART • 1914 • *Melies* • USA
WANTED A WIDOW • 1916 • *Calthrop Donald* • UKN
WANTED, A WIFE • 1912 • *Reliance* • USA
WANTED -A WIFE • 1912 • Melies Gaston • USA
WANTED A WIFE AND CHILD • 1912 • *Evans Fred* • UKN
WANTED: A WIFE IN A HURRY • 1912 • *Eclair* • USA
WANTED A WIFE (USA) see **ELDER MISS BLOSSOM, THE** • 1918
WANTED -AN ACTRESS see **THOMAS GRAALS BASTA FILM** • 1917
WANTED: AN ARTIST'S MODEL • 1908 • *Lubin* • USA
WANTED, AN HEIR • 1914 • *Roland Ruth* • USA
WANTED AT HEADQUARTERS • 1920 • Paton Stuart • USA
WANTED -BABY see **BACHELOR'S BABY, THE** • 1927
WANTED: BABY-SITTER see **BABYSITTER, LA** • 1975
WANTED BY SCOTLAND YARD (USA) see **DANGEROUS FINGERS** • 1937
WANTED BY THE LAW • 1924 • Bradbury Robert North • USA
WANTED BY THE POLICE • 1913 • *Jefferson William* • USA
WANTED BY THE POLICE • 1938 • Bretherton Howard • USA
WANTED: DEAD OR ALIVE • 1951 • Carr Thomas • USA
WANTED: DEAD OR ALIVE • 1986 • Sherman Gary • USA • WANTED DEAD OR ALIVE
WANTED DEAD OR ALIVE see **WANTED: DEAD OR ALIVE** • 1986
WANTED, FIELD MARSHALS FOR THE GORGONZOLA ARMY • 1911 • Martinek H. O. • UKN
WANTED FIVE THOUSAND DOLLARS • 1919 • Roach Hal • SHT • USA • WANTED $5000
WANTED FOR MURDER • 1919 • Crane Frank H. • USA
WANTED FOR MURDER • 1946 • Huntington Lawrence • UKN • VOICE IN THE NIGHT, A
WANTED: JANE TURNER • 1936 • Reid Cliff?, Killy Edward? • USA
WANTED JOHNNY TEXAS • 1967 • Salvi Emimmo • ITL
WANTED MEN • 1936 • Pember Clifford
WANTED MEN see **WOLVES** • 1930
WANTED MEN (UKN) see **LAW OF THE RIO GRANDE** • 1931
WANTED MEN (UKN) see **VALLEY OF WANTED MEN** • 1935
WANTED: NO MASTER • 1939 • Gross Milt • ANS • USA
WANTED: ONE EGG • 1950 • Barclay David • SHT • USA
WANTED: PERFECT MOTHER • 1970 • Brocka Lino • PHL
WANTED SABATA • 1970 • Mauri Roberto • ITL
WANTED: THE SUNDANCE WOMAN • 1976 • Philips Lee • TVM • USA • MRS. SUNDANCE RIDES AGAIN
WANTED (UKN) see **HIGH VOLTAGE** • 1929
WANTED (UKN) see **POLICE CALL** • 1933

WANTED WOMEN see **JESSI'S GIRLS** • 1975
WANTERS, THE • 1923 • Stahl John M. • USA
WANTING HOUR see **LUSTING HOURS, THE** • 1967
WANTING WEIGHT, THE see **FALSCHE GEWICHT, DAS** • 1971
WANTON, THE (UKN) see **MANEGES** • 1949
WANTON CONTESSA, THE see **SENSO** • 1954
WANTON COUNTESS, THE see **SENSO** • 1954
WANTON JOURNEY • 1961 • *Morishige Hisaya* • JPN
WANTON KISSES see **FREE KISSES** • 1926
WANTON NIECES see **GEILE NICHTEN** • 1978
WANTON OF SPAIN, THE (UKN) see **CELESTINA, LA** • 1968
WANTON OF SPAIN –LA CELESTINA, THE see **CELESTINA, LA** • 1968
WANWAN CHUSHINGURA • 1965 • Shirakawa Daisaku • JPN • DOGGIE MARCH
WAQA'II AL AAM AL MUQBIL • 1986 • Zikra Samir • SYR • EVENTS OF THE COMING YEAR
WAR • 1910 • *Powers* • USA
WAR • 1911 • *Tapley Rose E.* • USA
WAR • 1912 • Reid Hal • USA
WAR • 1913 • *Bison* • USA
WAR • 1915 • Baker George D. • USA
WAR • 1976 • Sharad John S., Griffith David • SHT • UKN
WAR see **RAT** • 1960
WAR, THE • 1958 • Jaworski Tadeusz • DOC • PLN
WAR AFTER THE WAR, THE • 1969 • Shagrir Micha • ISR
WAR AGAINST MRS. HADLEY, THE • 1942 • Bucquet Harold S. • USA
WAR AGAINST WAR • 1960 • Petrovic Aleksandar • YGS
WAR AND A MAN, THE see **NINGEN NO JOKEN I** • 1959
WAR AND LOVE • 1985 • Mizrahi Moshe • USA • CHILDREN'S WAR, THE ○ LOVE AND WAR
WAR AND MATRIMONY • 1917 • *Triangle* • USA
WAR AND MOM'S DREAM, THE • 1916 • Pastrone Giovanni • ANS • ITL
WAR AND ORDER • 1942 • Hasse Charles • DOC • UKN
WAR AND PEACE • 1956 • Vidor King, Soldati Mario • USA, ITL • GUERRA E PACE (ITL)
WAR AND PEACE • 1983 • Schlondorff Volker
WAR AND PEACE see **VOINA I MIR** • 1915
WAR AND PEACE see **SENSO TO HEIWA** • 1947
WAR AND PEACE –1914–1916–1918 see **OORLOG EN VREDE –1914–1916–1918** • 1918
WAR AND PEACE (USA) see **VOINA I MIR** • 1967
WAR AND PEOPLE NO.3 see **SENSO TO NINGEN, KAKETSU-HEN** • 1973
WAR AND PIECES • 1964 • Jones Charles M. • ANS • USA
WAR AND THE WIDOW • 1911 • *Champion* • USA
WAR AND THE WOMAN • 1917 • Warde Ernest C. • USA
WAR AND WOMAN • 1915 • *Pathe Exchange* • USA
WAR ARROW • 1953 • Sherman George • USA
WAR AT HOME • 1915 • *Grandin* • USA
WAR AT HOME, THE • 1915 • *Atlas* • USA
WAR AT HOME, THE • 1979 • Silber Glenn, Brown Barry • DOC • USA
WAR AT HOME, THE see **EDIE** • 1989
WAR AT SEA FROM HAWAII TO MALAYA, THE see **HAWAI-MAREI-OKI KAISEN** • 1942
WAR AT WALLAROO MANSIONS, THE • 1922 • Graeme Kenneth • UKN
WAR BABIES • 1932 • Lamont Charles • SHT • USA
WAR BABY, A • 1915 • O'Neil Barry • USA
WAR BABY, THE • 1914 • Weston Charles • UKN
WAR BETWEEN MEN AND WOMEN, THE • 1972 • Shavelson Melville • USA
WAR BETWEEN THE PLANETS (USA) see **MISSIONE PIANETA ERRANTE** • 1965
WAR BETWEEN THE TATES, THE • 1977 • Philips Lee • TVM • USA
WAR BETWEEN WALI AND SUGRIVA see **SATI TARA** • 1925
WAR BONNET, THE • 1914 • *Darkfeather Mona* • USA
WAR BOY, THE • 1984 • Eastman Allan • CND • POINT OF ESCAPE
WAR BRIDE OF PLUMVILLE, THE • 1916 • Wright Fred E. • SHT • USA
WAR BRIDEGROOM, THE • 1917 • Clements Roy • SHT • USA
WAR BRIDES • 1916 • Brenon Herbert • USA • JOAN OF FLANDERS
WAR BRIDES • 1980 • Lavut Martin • CND
WAR BRIDE'S SECRET, THE • 1916 • Buel Kenean • USA
WAR CAT see **ANGEL OF VENGEANCE** • 1987
WAR CLOUD, THE • 1915 • Weston Harold • UKN
WAR CLOUDS IN THE PACIFIC • 1941 • Legg Stuart • DCS • CND
WAR COMES TO AMERICA • 1945 • Litvak Anatole • DOC • USA • WHY WE FIGHT (PART 7): WAR COMES TO AMERICA
WAR CORRESPONDENCE • 1917 • *Pokes & Jabbs* • SHT • USA
WAR CORRESPONDENT • 1932 • Sloane Paul • USA • SOLDIERS OF FORTUNE (UKN)
WAR CORRESPONDENT see **STORY OF G.I. JOE, THE** • 1945
WAR CORRESPONDENT, THE • 1913 • *Kalem* • USA
WAR CORRESPONDENT, THE • 1913 • Edwards Walter? • *Broncho* • USA
WAR CORRESPONDENT, THE see **KRIGSKORRESPONDENTEN** • 1913
WAR CRY • 1951 • Nazarro Ray • USA
WAR DOGS • 1942 • Luby S. Roy • USA • PRIDE OF THE ARMY ○ UNSUNG HEROES
WAR DOGS • 1943 • Hanna William, Barbera Joseph • ANS • USA
WAR DRUMS • 1957 • Le Borg Reginald • USA
WAR EAGLES see **LONE EAGLE, THE** • 1927
WAR EPISODE see **EPISODE DE GUERRE (GRECO-TURQUE)** • 1897
WAR ES DER IM 3 STOCK? • 1938 • Boese Carl • FRG
WAR EXTRA, THE • 1914 • *Blache* • USA
WAR FEATHERS • 1926 • Roach Hal • SHT • USA
WAR FOR MEN'S MINDS, THE • 1943 • Legg Stuart • SHT • CND • A LA CONQUETE DE L'ESPRIT HUMAIN
WAR GAME, THE • 1962 • Zetterling Mai • UKN
WAR GAME, THE • 1966 • Watkins Peter • MTV • UKN
WAR GAMES see **SUPPOSE THEY GAVE A WAR AND NOBODY CAME?** • 1970
WAR GAMES see **WARGAMES** • 1983
WAR GARDENS • 1918 • *Christie* • USA
WAR GODDESS see **GUERRIERE DAL SENO NUDO, LE** • 1974
WAR GODS OF BABYLON (USA) see **SETTE FOLGORI DI ASSUR, LE** • 1962
WAR-GODS OF THE DEEP (USA) see **CITY UNDER THE SEA, THE** • 1965
WAR HAWKS see **LONE EAGLE, THE** • 1927
WAR HEAD see **ON THE FIDDLE** • 1961
WAR HERO • 1958 • Topper Burt • USA
WAR HERO see **WAR IS HELL** • 1964
WAR HUNT • 1962 • Sanders Denis • USA
WAR HUNT see **WOMAN'S DEVOTION, A** • 1956
WAR IN CHINA • 1915 • *Heather Enid* • UKN
WAR IN SPACE see **NAKUSEI DAISENSO** • 1977
WAR IN THE DARK see **MYSTERIOUS LADY, THE** • 1928
WAR IS A RACKET • 1934 • Koerpel Jacques
WAR IS HELL • 1915 • Batley Ethyle • UKN
WAR IS HELL • 1964 • Topper Burt • USA • WAR MADNESS ○ WAR HERO
WAR IS HELL • 1968 • Nelson Robert, Allen William • USA
WAR IS HELL see **NIEMANDSLAND** • 1931
WAR IS OVER, THE • 1973 • Golubovic Predrag • YGS
WAR IS OVER, THE see **GUERRE EST FINIE, LA** • 1966
WAR IS OVER, MAJOR, THE • 1977 • Bonniere Rene • SHT • CND
WAR ITALIAN STYLE (USA) see **DUE MARINES E UN GENERALE** • 1966
WAR KIDS, THE see **CHICOS DE LA GUERRA, LOS** • 1984
WAR LORD • 1965 • Schaffner Franklin J. • USA
WAR LORD see **WEST OF SHANGHAI** • 1937
WAR LOVER, THE • 1962 • Leacock Philip • UKN, USA
WAR MADNESS see **WAR IS HELL** • 1964
WAR MAMAS • 1931 • Neilan Marshall • SHT • USA
WAR NEWSREEL NO.1 see **BOYEVOYE KINOSBORNIK N.1** • 1941
WAR NEWSREEL NO.3 • 1941 • Yudin Konstantin • USS
WAR NEWSREEL NO.6 • 1941 • Vainshtok Vladimir • USS
WAR NEWSREEL NO.8 • 1941 • Donskoi Mark, Savchenko Igor, Braun Vladimir • USS
WAR NURSE • 1930 • Selwyn Edgar • USA
WAR O' DREAMS, THE • 1915 • Martin E. A. • USA
WAR OF 600 MILLION PEOPLE, THE see **600 MILLION PEOPLE ARE WITH YOU** • 1958
WAR OF CHACO see **GUERRA DEL CHACO, LA** • 1936
WAR OF CHILDREN, A • 1972 • Schaefer George • TVM • USA
WAR OF INSECTS see **KONCHU DAISENSO** • 1968
WAR OF THE ALIENS see **STARSHIP INVASIONS** • 1977
WAR OF THE BUTTONS see **GUERRE DES BOUTONS, LA** • 1961
WAR OF THE CASTLE RANGE, THE • 1913 • *Bison* • USA
WAR OF THE COLOSSAL BEAST • 1958 • Gordon Bert I. • USA • TERROR STRIKES, THE (UKN) ○ REVENGE OF THE COLOSSAL MAN
WAR OF THE GARDENS, THE see **QUERELLES DE JARDINS** • 1982
WAR OF THE GARGANTUAS, THE see **FURANKENSHUTAIN NO KAIJU –SANDA TAI GAILAH** • 1966
WAR OF THE GIANTS see **COMBATE DE GIGANTES** • 1966
WAR OF THE LILLIPUTIENS, THE • 1914 • *Pathe* • USA
WAR OF THE MONSTERS see **GOJIRA TAI GAIGAN** • 1972
WAR OF THE MONSTERS (USA) see **GAMERA TAI BARUGON** • 1966
WAR OF THE PLANETS see **THIS ISLAND EARTH** • 1955
WAR OF THE PLANETS see **COSMOS: WAR OF THE PLANETS** • 1977
WAR OF THE PLANETS see **NAKUSEI DAISENSO** • 1977
WAR OF THE PLANETS (USA) see **DIAFANOIDI PORTANO LA MORTE, I** • 1965
WAR OF THE ROBOTS (USA) see **GUERRA DEI ROBOT, LA** • 1978
WAR OF THE ROSES • 1989 • DeVito Danny • USA
WAR OF THE SATELLITES • 1958 • Corman Roger • USA
WAR OF THE SEXES • 1968 • Shindo Kaneto • JPN
WAR OF THE TONGS, THE • 1917 • *Red Feather* • USA
WAR OF THE TROJANS, THE see **LEGGENDA DI ENEA, LA** • 1962
WAR OF THE WALTZES see **WALZERKRIEG** • 1933
WAR OF THE WILD, THE • 1915 • McRae Henry • USA
WAR OF THE WILDCATS • 1943 • Rogell Albert S. • USA • IN OLD OKLAHOMA
WAR OF THE WIZARDS see **PHOENIX, THE** • 1978
WAR OF THE WORLD, THE • 1914 • *Lewis Pennant Features* • USA
WAR OF THE WORLDS, THE • 1953 • Haskin Byron • USA
WAR OF THE WORLDS –NEXT CENTURY, THE see **WOJNA SWIATOW –NASTEPNE STULECIE** • 1981
WAR OF THE ZOMBIES, THE (USA) see **ROMA CONTRA ROMA** • 1963
WAR OF WARS, THE • 1914 • *Ramo* • USA • FRANCO-GERMAN INVASION, THE
WAR OF WEALTH, THE • 1914 • *Arvidsen Linda* • USA
WAR OF WITS, THE • 1916 • Horne James W. • SHT • USA
WAR ON THE PLAINS • 1912 • Ince Thomas H. • USA • ACROSS THE PLAINS
WAR ON THE RANGE • 1933 • McGowan J. P. • USA
WAR PAINT • 1926 • Van Dyke W. S. • USA • RIDER OF THE PLAINS (UKN)
WAR PAINT • 1953 • Selander Lesley • USA
WAR PARTY • 1965 • Selander Lesley • USA
WAR PARTY • 1989 • Roddam Franc • UKN
WAR PIGEON, THE • 1914 • *All Red Feature* • USA
WAR PRIDES • 1917 • *Finch Flora* • SHT • USA
WAR RECLUSE, THE see **SOTAERAKKO** • 1972
WAR RELIEF • 1917 • Neilan Marshall • SHT • USA
WAR REPORTER'S DIARY • 1982 • Ha Won Choi • SKR
WAR REQUIEM • 1988 • Jarman Derek • UKN
WAR SHEPHERDS • 1988 • Yavor Noam • ISR
WAR SHOCK (UKN) see **WOMAN'S DEVOTION, A** • 1956
WAR STORY 2 • 1989 • Holland Todd, Morris David Burton, Linka Leslie, Toshiyuki Michael, Sholder Jack, King Rick • USA • VIETNAM WAR STORY 2 ○ VIETNAM WAR STORY
WAR STORY, A • 1982 • Wheeler Anne • DOC • CND
WAR TIME ESCAPE, A • 1911 • *Kalem* • USA
WAR-TIME PALS • 1910 • *Powers* • USA
WAR TIME REFORMATION, A see **WARTIME REFORMATION, A** • 1914
WAR TOWN • 1943 • USA
WAR WAGON, THE • 1967 • Kennedy Burt • USA
WAR WAIF, THE • 1917 • Holubar Allen • SHT • USA
WAR WE LEFT BEHIND, THE see **ESPANJANKAVIJAT** • 1980
WAR WITHOUT END • 1936 • Searle Francis • DOC • UKN
WAR YEARS • 1984 • McGuire Patrick • CMP • NZL
WAR ZONE • 1987 • Gutman Nathaniel • USA • WITNESS IN THE WAR ZONE ○ DEADLINE
WARA-WARA • 1930 • Velasco Maidana Jose Maria • BLV • STARS
WARAI-NO NINGEN • 1960 • Kuri Yoji • JPN • PEOPLE
WARAREGA KYOKAN • 1939 • Imai Tadashi • JPN • OUR INSTRUCTOR ○ OUR TEACHER
WARBIRDS • 1988 • Lommel Ulli • USA
WARBONNET see **SAVAGE, THE** • 1952
WARBUS • 1985 • Baldi Ferdinando • USA • WARBUS: RAW COURAGE
WARBUS: RAW COURAGE see **WARBUS** • 1985
WARD NO.9 see **9-ES KORTEREM** • 1955
WARD NO.72 see **72.KOGUS** • 1987
WARD OF THE KING, THE • 1913 • *La Badie Florence* • USA
WARD OF THE MISSION, THE • 1915 • *Ab* • USA
WARD OF THE SENIOR CLASS, THE • 1913 • *Majestic* • USA
WARD OF UNCLE SAM, A • 1910 • *Yankee* • USA
WARDA • 1971 • Francis Yussif • SHT • EGY • FLEUR, UNE
WARDCARE OF PSYCHOTIC PATIENTS • 1941 • Kress Harold F. • DOC • USA
WARDEN'S DAUGHTER, THE • 1941 • Beaudine William • USA
WARDEN'S NIGHTMARE, THE • 1909 • *Pathe* • FRN
WARDI AL-GHARAM • 1951 • Barakat Henry • EGY • FLEURS D'AMOUR
WARDOG • 1986 • Carlstroem Bjorn, Hubenbecher Daniel • USA
WARDOG see **WARDOG: THE KILLING MACHINE** • 1986
WARDOG: THE KILLING MACHINE • 1986 • Wredler Thomas • USA • ASSASSINATION TEAM, THE ○ WARDOGS ○ WARDOG
WARDOGS see **WARDOG: THE KILLING MACHINE** • 1986
WARDROBE, THE • 1960 • Dunning George • ANS • UKN
WARDROBE LADY, THE • 1913 • *Bayne Beverly* • USA
WARDROBE WOMAN, THE • 1915 • Marston Theodore • USA
WARD'S CLAIM, THE • 1914 • Davis Ulysses • USA
WARDS OF SOCIETY, THE • 1914 • *Patheplay* • USA
WARE CASE, THE • 1917 • West Walter • UKN
WARE CASE, THE • 1928 • Haynes Manning • UKN
WARE CASE, THE • 1938 • Stevenson Robert • UKN
WARE FUR KATALONIEN • 1959 • Groschopp Richard • GDR
WARE HITOTSUBU NO MUGI NAREDO • 1964 • Matsuyama Zenzo • JPN • COULD I BUT LIVE
WARE MABOROSHI NO UO O MITARI • 1950 • Ito Daisuke • JPN
WARENHAUSGRAFIN, DIE • 1915 • *Nissen Aud Egede* • FRG
WARENHAUSMADCHEN • 1925 • *Primus-Film* • FRG
WARENHAUSMADCHEN see **KLEINE AUS DER KONFEKTION, DIE** • 1925
WARENHAUSPRINZESSIN, DIE • 1926 • Paul Heinz • FRG
WARERU NO JIDAI • 1959 • Kurahara Koreyoshi • JPN • OUR OWN AGE
WARFARE IN THE SKIES • 1914 • Thompson Frederick A. • USA
WARFARE OF THE FLESH, THE • 1917 • Warren Edward • USA
WARGAMES • 1983 • Badham John • USA • WAR GAMES
WARHEAD see **PRISONER IN THE MIDDLE** • 1975
WARHORSE, THE • 1927 • Hillyer Lambert • USA
WARIANTY • 1970 • Kijowicz Miroslaw • ANS • PLN • VARIATIONS
WARIS • 1954 • *Biswas Anil (M)* • IND
WARKILL • 1968 • Grofe Ferde Jr. • USA, PHL
WARLOCK • 1959 • Dmytryk Edward • USA
WARLOCK • 1989 • Miner Steve • USA
WARLOCK MOON • 1973 • Herbert William • USA
WARLORD, THE • Li Han-Hsiang • HKG
WARLORD OF CRETE, THE (UKN) see **TESEO CONTRO IL MINOTAURO** • 1961
WARLORDS • 1989 • Ray Fred Olen • USA
WARLORDS FROM HELL • 1987 • Henderson Clark • USA
WARLORDS OF ATLANTIS • 1978 • Connor Kevin • UKN • SEVEN CITIES TO ATLANTIS
WARLORDS OF THE 21ST CENTURY see **BATTLETRUCK** • 1983
WARM • 1979 • Yanchev Vladimir • BUL
WARM BED see **WARM, WARM BED, THE** • 1968
WARM BODY, THE see **COLERE FROIDE** • 1960
WARM BODY FOR HELL, A see **CORPO CALDO PER L'INFERNO, UN** • 1968
WARM CORNER, A • 1930 • Saville Victor • UKN
WARM CURRENT, A see **DANRYU** • 1939
WARM CURRENT, A see **DANRYU** • 1957
WARM DECEMBER, A • 1973 • Poitier Sidney • USA, UKN
WARM HEARTS, COLD FEET • 1987 • Frawley James • TVM • USA
WARM IN THE BUD • 1969 • Caringi Rudolph • USA
WARM IT WAS THAT WINTER • Bae Chang-Ho • SKR
WARM MISTY NIGHT, A see **YOGIRI YO KONYA MO ARIGATO** • 1967
WARM NIGHTS AND SECRET PLEASURES see **WARM NIGHTS & HOT PLEASURES** • 1964
WARM NIGHTS & HOT PLEASURES • 1964 • Sarno Joe • USA • WARM NIGHTS AND SECRET PLEASURES
WARM NIGHTS ON A SLOW-MOVING TRAIN • 1987 • Ellis Bob • ASL
WARM RECEPTION, A • 1904 • *Warwick Trading Co* • UKN
WARM RECEPTION, A • 1914 • Cooper Toby • *Clarendon* • UKN
WARM RECEPTION, A • 1914 • Martinek H. O. • *Big Ben Films-Union* • UKN

WARM RECEPTION, A • 1916 • *Hardy Babe* • USA
WARM RECEPTION, A • 1917 • *Morton Alatia* • USA
WARM SUMMER RAIN • 1989 • Gayton Joe • USA
WARM, WARM BED, THE • 1968 • Mahon Barry • USA • WARM BED
WARM WAVES • *Dyleiv Prods.* • SHT • USA
WARM WELCOME, A • 1913 • *Majestic* • USA
WARM WIND see **GARM HAVA** • 1973
WARM YEARS, THE see **TOPLE GODINE** • 1966
WARMAKERS, THE • 1913 • Costello Maurice, Gaillord Robert • USA
WARMI • 1980 • de Eguino Danielle Caillet • BLV
WARMING UP • 1928 • Newmeyer Fred • USA • KNOCKING 'EM OVER
WARMTH • 1969 • Creanga Serban • RMN
WARMTH OF YOUR HANDS, THE • 1972 • Managadze Shota, Managadze Noda • USS
WARN LONDON • 1934 • Hunter T. Hayes • UKN
WARN THAT MAN • 1943 • Huntington Lawrence • UKN
WARNED OFF • 1928 • West Walter • UKN
WARNER BROS MOVIES –A 50-YEAR SALUTE • 1973 • Einhorn Lawrence • USA
WARNER'S WAXWORKS • 1912 • *Thanhouser* • USA
WARNING see **VARUJ!** • 1947
WARNING see **UWAGA!** • 1958
WARNING, THE • 1912 • *Thanhouser* • USA
WARNING, THE • 1914 • *Essanay* • USA
WARNING, THE • 1914 • Crisp Donald • *Majestic* • USA
WARNING, THE • 1914 • Wharton Leopold • *Wharton* • USA
WARNING, THE • 1915 • Cooley Frank • *Mustang* • USA
WARNING, THE • 1915 • Lawrence Edmund • *Triumph Equitable* • USA
WARNING, THE • 1927 • Seitz George B. • USA
WARNING, THE • 1928 • Fogwell Reginald • UKN
WARNING, THE • 1939 • Cavalcanti Alberto • DOC • UKN
WARNING, THE • 1966 • Lofven Chris • SHT • ASL
WARNING, THE • 1982 • Bardem Juan Antonio • BUL, USS, GDR
WARNING, THE • 1985 • Damiani Damiano • ITL
WARNING, THE see **WITHOUT WARNING** • 1980
WARNING CRY, THE • 1914 • *Majestic* • USA
WARNING: EARTHQUAKE • 1970 • Martin Susan • MTV • USA
WARNING FOR SUICIDES, A • Sajko Mako • DCS • YGS
WARNING FROM SPACE see **UCHUJIN TOKYO NI ARAWARU** • 1956
WARNING FROM THE PAST, A • 1914 • Merwin Bannister • USA
WARNING HAND, THE • 1912 • *Bushman Francis X.* • USA
WARNING OF A HOLY WHORE (UKN) see **WARNUNG VOR EINER HEILIGEN NUTTE** • 1970
WARNING SHADOWS see **SCHATTEN** • 1923
WARNING SHOT • 1967 • Kulik Buzz • USA
WARNING SIGN • 1985 • Barwood Hal • USA • BIOHAZARD
WARNING SIGNAL, THE • 1926 • Hunt Charles J. • USA
WARNING! THE S.O.S. CALL OF HUMANITY • 1916 • *Photo Drama* • USA
WARNING TO WANTONS • 1949 • Wilson Donald B. • UKN
WARNUNG VOR EINER HEILIGEN NUTTE • 1970 • Fassbinder R. W. • FRG, ITL • BEWARE OF THE HOLY WHORE (USA) ○ WARNING OF A HOLY WHORE (UKN) ○ BEWARE THE HOLY WHORE
WARPATH • 1951 • Haskin Byron • USA
WARPED ONES, THE see **KYONETSU NO KISETSU** • 1960
WARRA' EL SETAR • 1937 • Salim Kamel • EGY • BEHIND THE CURTAIN
WARRAH • 1982 • Cantrill Arthur, Cantrill Corinne • DOC • ASL
WARRANT, THE • 1911 • *Selig* • USA
WARRANT FOR RED RUBE, THE • 1911 • Melies Gaston • USA
WARRANT–OFFICER PANIN see **MICHMAN PANIN** • 1960
WARRANTY FOR ONE YEAR see **BURGSCHAFT FUER EIN JAHR** • 1980
WARREN CASE, THE • 1934 • Summers Walter • UKN
WARREN DOANE'S BREVITIES • 1933 • Horne James W. • SHT • USA
WARRENDALE • 1967 • King Allan • DOC • CND
WARRENS OF VIRGINIA, THE • 1915 • De Mille Cecil B. • USA
WARRENS OF VIRGINIA, THE • 1924 • Clifton Elmer • USA
WARRING CLANS • Okamoto Kihachi • JPN
WARRING CLANS (USA) see **SENGOKU YARO** • 1963
WARRIOR, THE • 1987 • Cantrell Ray • USA
WARRIOR, THE see **PENDEKAR** • 1976
WARRIOR AND THE DEMON • 1962-69 • Carpenter John • SHT • USA
WARRIOR AND THE NINJA, THE • Jutt H. • HKG
WARRIOR AND THE SLAVE, THE (USA) see **RIVOLTA DEI GLADIATORI, LA** • 1958
WARRIOR AND THE SLAVE GIRL, THE see **RIVOLTA DEI GLADIATORI, LA** • 1958
WARRIOR AND THE SORCERESS, THE see **KAIN DEL PLANETA OSCURO** • 1982
WARRIOR BOLD, A • 1910 • *Edison* • USA
WARRIOR BOLD, A • 1912 • *Brammell Jack* • USA
WARRIOR CHILDREN see **KRIGERNES BORN** • 1979
WARRIOR EMPRESS, THE (USA) see **SAFFO, VENERE DI LESBO** • 1960
WARRIOR GAP • 1925 • Neitz Alvin J. • USA
WARRIOR LOST WORLD see **WARRIOR OF THE LOST WORLD** • 1985
WARRIOR OF DEATH see **PANGLIMA MAUT** • 1975
WARRIOR OF THE LOST WORLD • 1985 • Worth David • USA • WARRIOR LOST WORLD
WARRIOR OF TIGER BAY • 1987 • MLY
WARRIOR QUEEN • 1985 • Vincent Chuck • USA • POMPEII
WARRIOR STRAIN, THE • 1919 • Thornton F. Martin • UKN
WARRIOR WITHIN, THE • 1977 • Rashby Burt • DOC • USA
WARRIOR WOMEN see **VERGINI DI ROMA, LE** • 1960
WARRIORS, THE • 1979 • Hill Walter • USA
WARRIORS, THE see **KELLY'S HEROES** • 1970
WARRIORS, THE (USA) see **DARK AVENGER, THE** • 1955
WARRIORS AND CAPTIVES see **GUERREROS Y CAUTIVAS** • 1988
WARRIOR'S BRIDE, THE • 1917 • *Reid Wallace* • SHT • USA
WARRIOR'S FAITH, A • 1911 • *Bison* • USA
WARRIORS FIVE (USA) see **GUERRA CONTINUA, LA** • 1962
WARRIOR'S HUSBAND, THE • 1933 • Lang Walter • USA
WARRIORS OF DEATH • 1981 • Kyriazi Paul • USA • WEAPONS OF DEATH
WARRIORS OF FAITH see **JAN ROHAC Z DUBE** • 1947
WARRIORS OF THE DEEP • 1936 • Oliver Bill • DOC • CND
WARRIORS OF THE WASTELAND (USA) see **NUOVI BARBARI, I** • 1983
WARRIORS OF THE WIND • 1985 • Komatsubara Kazuo • ANM • JPN
WARRIORS OF YEAR 2072, THE see **GUERRIERI DELL'ANNO 2072, I** • 1984
WARRIOR'S REST see **REPOS DU GUERRIER, LE** • 1962
WARRIOR'S SQUAW, THE • 1911 • *Bison* • USA
WARRIORS THREE • Lau S. H. • HKG • HEROES THREE
WARRIOR'S TREACHERY, A • 1911 • *Bison* • USA
WARS, THE • 1982 • Philips Robin • CND
WAR'S GRIM REALITY • 1914 • Aylott Dave • UKN
WAR'S HAVOC • 1912 • *Nilsson Anna Q.* • USA
WARS OF THE PRIMEVAL TRIBES see **BRUTE FORCE** • 1913
WAR'S WOMEN • 1916 • *Markey Enid* • USA
WARSAW see **WARSZAWA** • 1952
WARSAW see **WARSZAWA 56** • 1956
WARSAW 1945–47 see **WARSZAWA 1945–47** • 1947
WARSAW BRIDGE see **PONT DE VARSOVIE** • 1989
WARSAW CENTRAL STATION see **WARSZAWA GLOWNA** • 1958
WARSAW DEBUT, THE see **WARSZAWSKA PREMIERA** • 1951
WARSAW LAZIENKI, THE see **WARSZAWSKIE LAZIENKI** • 1960
WARSAW MERMAID, THE see **WARSZAWSKA SYRENA** • 1956
WARSAW PEOPLE see **WARSZAWIACY** • 1969
WARSAW PREMIERE, THE see **WARSZAWSKA PREMIERA** • 1951
WARSAW STORY see **WARSZAWSKA OPOWIESC** • 1970
WARSAW SUITE • 1946 • Makarczynski Tadeusz • DOC • PLN
WARSAW WOMEN see **WARSZAWIANKI** • 1962
WARSAW WORLD YOUTH MEETING see **VARSOI VIT I–II–III** • 1955
WARSCHAUER ZITADELLE, DIE • 1930 • Fleck Jacob, Fleck Luise • FRG • CITADEL OF WARSAW, THE
WARSCHAUER ZITADELLE, DIE • 1938 • Buch Fritz Peter • FRG
WARSHIPS BLOW UP IN THE PORT • 1967 • Timonishin Anton • USS
WARSHIPS WITHOUT SMOKE see **GUNGAN SUDENI KEMURI NASHI** • 1950
WARSZAWA • 1952 • Perski Ludwik • DOC • PLN • WARSAW
WARSZAWA 56 • 1956 • Bossak Jerzy (c/d) • DOC • PLN • WARSAW
WARSZAWA 1945–47 • 1947 • Perski Ludwik • DOC • PLN • WARSAW 1945–47
WARSZAWA GLOWNA • 1958 • Lomnicki Jan • DOC • PLN • WARSAW CENTRAL STATION
WARSZAWA W OBRASACH CANALETTA • 1955 • Brzozowski Jaroslaw • PLN • CANALETTO, PAINTER OF WARSAW
WARSZAWIACY • 1969 • Kluba Henryk • PLN • SZKICE WARSZAWSKIE ○ VARSOVIANS, THE ○ WARSAW PEOPLE
WARSZAWIAK W KIJOWIE • 1958 • Perski Ludwik • DOC • PLN • VARSOVIAN IN KIEV, A
WARSZAWIANKI • 1962 • Karabasz Kazimierz • DCS • PLN • WARSAW WOMEN
WARSZAWSKA OPOWIESC • 1970 • Wionczek Roman • PLN • WARSAW STORY
WARSZAWSKA PREMIERA • 1951 • Rybkowski Jan • PLN • WARSAW PREMIERE, THE ○ WARSAW DEBUT, THE
WARSZAWSKA SYRENA • 1956 • Makarczynski Tadeusz • PLN • WARSAW MERMAID, THE
WARSZAWSKI KIEROWCA JERZY WINNICKI • 1973 • Grasveld Fons • DOC • PLN • DAY IN THE LIFE OF A WARSAW BUSDRIVER, A
WARSZAWSKIE LAZIENKI • 1960 • Jaworski Tadeusz • DOC • PLN • LAZIENKI PARK IN WARSAW, THE ○ WARSAW LAZIENKI, THE
WART ON THE WIRE, THE • 1917 • Curtis Allen • SHT • USA
WARTELISTE ZUR HOLLE • 1967 • de Orduna Juan • FRG, ITL, SPN • JERRY LAND CACCIATORE DI SPIE (ITL) ○ WAITING–LIST FOR HELL ○ JERRY LAND, SPY–HUNTER
WARTEZIMMER ZUM JENSEITS • 1964 • Vohrer Alfred • FRG
WARTIME LETTER see **RISALA MIN ZAMAN AL HARB** • 1984
WARTIME MOTHER'S SACRIFICES, A • 1913 • *Broncho* • USA
WARTIME REFORMATION, A • 1914 • Ford Francis • USA • WAR TIME REFORMATION, A
WARTIME ROMANCE, A • 1912 • *Stedman Myrtle* • USA
WARTIME SIREN, THE • 1913 • Melford George • USA
WARTIME SWEETHEART, A • 1909 • *Selig* • USA
WARTIME WOOING, A • 1911 • *Thanhouser* • USA
WARTYWOOING, THE • 1913 • Aylott Dave? • UKN
WARUI YATSU HODO YOKU NEMURU • 1960 • Kurosawa Akira • JPN • WORSE YOU ARE THE BETTER YOU SLEEP, THE ○ BAD SLEEP WELL, THE (USA) ○ ROSE IN THE MUD, A
WARUM HAB ICH BLOSS 2 X JA GESAGT • 1969 • Antel Franz • FRG, ITL • CONFESSIONS OF A BIGAMIST ○ PROFESSIONE BIGAMO
WARUM LAUFT HERR R. AMOK? • 1969 • Fassbinder R. W., Fengler Michael • FRG • WHY DOES HERR R. RUN AMOK?
WARUM LUGST DU, ELISABETH? • 1944 • Kirchhoff Fritz • FRG
WARUM LUGT FRAULEIN KATHE? • 1935 • Jacoby Georg • FRG
WARUM SICH SCHEIDEN LASSEN? • 1926 • Noa Manfred • FRG
WARUM SIND SIE GEGEN UNS? • 1958 • Wicki Bernhard • FRG • WHY ARE THEY AGAINST US?
WARWICK CASTLE • 1926 • Paul Fred • SHT • UKN
WAS BIN ICH OHNE DICH • 1934 • Rabenalt Arthur M. • FRG
WAS DAS HERZ BEFIELT • 1951 • Hainisch Leopold • FRG • VERONIKA, DIE MAGD
WAS DIE NACHT SPRICHT –EINE ERZAHLING • 1987 • Scheugl Hans • AUS • WHAT THE NIGHT TELLS –A TALE
WAS DIE SCHWALBE SANG • 1956 • von Bolvary Geza • FRG
WAS EINE FRAU IM FRUHLING TRAUMT • 1929 • Blachnitzky Curt • FRG
WAS EINE FRAU IM FRUHLING TRAUMT • 1959 • Ode Erik • FRG
WAS EINE FRAU IM FRUHLING TRAUMT see **LEICHTE MUSE** • 1941
WAS ER IM SPIEGEL SAH • 1918 • Wolff Carl Heinz • FRG
WAS FRAUEN TRAUMEN • 1933 • von Bolvary Geza • FRG • WHAT WOMEN DREAM (USA)
WAS GESCHAH IN DIESER NACHT • 1941 • Lingen Theo • FRG
WAS HALTEN SIE VOM TOD DER WILMA MONTESI? • 1977 • von Lutzelburg Helmer • FRG
WAS HE A COWARD? • 1911 • Griffith D. W. • USA
WAS HE A COWARD? • 1913 • Haldane Bert? • UKN
WAS HE A COWARD? • 1915 • *Mcphee Barney* • USA
WAS HE A GENTLEMAN? • 1914 • Finn Arthur • UKN
WAS HE A GERMAN SPY? • 1912 • Plumb Hay • UKN
WAS HE A HERO? • 1914 • *Barnett Chester* • USA
WAS HE A SUFFRAGETTE? • 1912 • *Republic* • USA
WAS HE JUSTIFIED? • 1911 • *Bison* • USA
WAS HE JUSTIFIED? • 1912 • Haldane Bert? • UKN
WAS HIS DECISION RIGHT? • 1914 • Fielding Romaine? • USA
WAS ICH BIN SIND MEINE FILME • 1978 • Weisenborn Christian, Keusch Erwin • DOC • FRG
WAS IST LOS IM ZIRKUS BEELY • 1926 • Piel Harry • FRG
WAS IST LOS MIT NANETTE • 1928 • Holger-Madsen • FRG
WAS IT A DREAM? • 1929 • Aylott Dave, Symmons E. F. • SHT • UKN
WAS IT A DREAM? • 1956 • Negus Olive • UKN
WAS IT A SERPENT'S BITE? • 1909 • Aylott Dave? • UKN
WAS IT BIGAMY? • 1925 • Hutchison Charles • USA
WAS IT HE? • 1914 • Hewitt G. Fletcher • UKN
WAS IT HER DUTY? • 1915 • Castle James W. • USA
WAS IT WORTH WHILE? • 1911 • *Nestor* • USA
WAS JUSTICE SERVED? • 1909 • Griffith D. W. • USA
WAS KINDER DEN ELTERN VERSCHWEIGEN • 1927 • Osten Franz • FRG
WAS KLEINE MADCHEN TRAUMEN see **IN EINER KLEINEN KONDITOREI** • 1930
WAS KOSTET DER SIEG? • 1981 • Bannert Walter • AUS • WHAT PRICE VICTORY?
WAS KOSTET LIEBE? • 1928 • Emo E. W. • FRG
WAS MABEL CURED? • 1912 • *Victor* • USA
WAS MACHT PAPA DENN IN ITALIEN • 1961 • Schwarze Hans D. • FRG
WAS MAN AUS LIEBE TUT • 1915 • Peukert Leo • FRG
WAS MANNER NICHT FUR MOGLICH HALTEN • 1972 • Hofbauer Ernst • FRG
WAS MANNER NICHT WISSEN MUSSEN • 1964 • Puhl Reginald • FRG
WAS PIMPLE (W)RIGHT? • 1915 • Evans Fred, Evans Joe • UKN
WAS SHE A VAMPIRE? • 1915 • Hale Albert W. • USA
WAS SHE GUILTY? • 1922 • Beranger George A. • UKN
WAS SHE JUSTIFIED? • 1911 • *Yankee* • USA
WAS SHE JUSTIFIED? • 1922 • West Walter • UKN • PRUNING KNIFE, THE
WAS SHE RIGHT IN FORGIVING HIM? • 1914 • *Fealy Maude* • USA
WAS SHE TO BLAME? • 1913 • *Rex* • USA
WAS SHE TO BLAME? • 1915 • *Linick & Melchior* • USA
WAS STEINE ERZAHLEN • 1925 • Randolf Rolf • FRG • WENN STEINE REDEN
WAS TREIBT DIE MAUS IM BADENHAUS? • 1976 • Gotz Siggi • FRG
WAS TUN, SYBILLE? • 1938 • Brauer Peter P. • FRG
WAS WARE, WENN..? • 1960 • Klingenberg Gerhard • GDR
WAS WILL BRIGITTE? • 1940 • Martin Paul • FRG
WAS WIRD HIER GESPIELT? • 1940 • Lingen Theo • FRG
WAS WISSEN DENN MANNER • 1933 • Lamprecht Gerhard • FRG
WASCHER–RESL, DIE • 1916 • Portegg R. • FRG
WASCHERMADEL SEINER DURCHLAUCHT, DAS • 1917 • Kaden Danny • FRG
WASEI KENKA TOMODACHI • 1929 • Ozu Yasujiro • JPN • FIGHTING FRIENDS, JAPANESE STYLE
WASH, THE • 1988 • Uno Michael Toshiyuki • USA
WASH DAY TROUBLES • 1895 • Kuhn Edmund • USA
WASHED ASHORE • 1922 • Roach Hal • SHT • USA
WASHEE IRONEE • 1934 • Parrott James • SHT • USA
WASHERWOMAN AND THE SWEEP, THE • 1903 • *Paul R. W.* • UKN
WASHERWOMAN, THE TRAMP AND THE BIKE, THE • 1903 • *Warwick Trading Co* • UKN
WASHERWOMAN'S WAR, THE • 1919 • Lederer Otto • SHT • USA
WASHERWOMEN, THE see **BLANCHISSEUSES, LES** • 1896
WASHI–NO–O TOGE • 1941 • Ito Daisuke • JPN • PASS OF EAGLE'S TAIL
WASHI TO TAKA • 1957 • Inoue Umeji • JPN • EAGLE AND THE HAWK, THE
WASHING A BOER PRISONER IN CAMP • 1900 • *Mitchell & Kenyon* • UKN
WASHING DAY • 1908 • Collins Alf? • UKN
WASHING OUR CLOTHES • 1914 • Sennett Mack • USA
WASHING THE SWEEP • 1898 • Williamson James • UKN
WASHINGTON AFFAIR, THE • 1977 • Stoloff Victor • USA
WASHINGTON AT VALLEY FORGE • 1908 • Olcott Sidney • USA
WASHINGTON AT VALLEY FORGE • 1914 • Ford Francis, Cunard Grace • USA
WASHINGTON, B.C. see **HAIL TO THE CHIEF** • 1973
WASHINGTON COWBOY see **ROVING TUMBLEWEEDS** • 1939
WASHINGTON GIRL see **FOR THE LOVE OF MARY** • 1948
WASHINGTON IN DANGER • 1912 • *Thanhouser* • USA
WASHINGTON MASQUERADE • 1932 • Brabin Charles J. • USA • MAD MASQUERADE (UKN)
WASHINGTON MELODRAMA • 1941 • Simon S. Sylvan • USA
WASHINGTON MERRY–GO–ROUND • 1932 • Cruze James • USA • INVISIBLE POWER (UKN)
WASHINGTON MISTRESS • 1982 • Levin Peter • TVM • USA • BROKEN DREAMS

WASHINGTON STORY • 1952 • Pirosh Robert • USA • TARGET FOR SCANDAL (UKN) ○ MR. CONGRESSMAN
WASHINGTON UNDER THE AMERICAN FLAG • 1909 • Blackton J. Stuart • USA • LIFE OF WASHINGTON, THE
WASHINGTON UNDER THE BRITISH FLAG • 1909 • Blackton J. Stuart (Spv) • USA
WASHINGTON'S WIG WHAM • 1966 • Grooms Red • USA
WASHMA see **WECHMA** • 1970
WASHO UBABA • 1983 • SAF
WASICHU • Domokos Attila • SHT • USA
WASN'T THAT A TIME! • 1981 • Brown Jim • DOC • USA • WEAVERS: WASN'T THAT A TIME!, THE
WASP, THE • 1911 • *Kalem* • USA
WASP, THE • 1914 • Le Saint Edward J. • USA
WASP, THE • 1915 • Eason B. Reeves • USA
WASP, THE • 1918 • Belmore Lionel • USA
WASP WOMAN • 1959 • Corman Roger • USA
WASPS' NEST see **CUIBUL DE VIESPI**
WASSER FUR CANITOGA • 1939 • Selpin Herbert • FRG • WATER FOR CANITOGA
WASSERDOKTOR, DER see **SEBASTIAN KNEIPP -EIN GROSSES LEBEN** • 1958
WASSERTEUFEL VON HIEFLAU, DIE • 1932 • Kober Erich • FRG
WASTE HEAPS see **HALDY** • 1963
WASTE LAND, THE • 1962 • Heyer John • DOC • ASL
WASTE LAND, THE • 1988 • Koulmasis Timon • FRN
WASTE NOT WANT NOT • 1952 • Porter Eric • ANS • ASL
WASTED LIVES • 1915 • Marston Theodore • USA
WASTED LIVES • 1923 • Geldert Clarence • USA
WASTED LIVES • 1925 • Gorman John • USA
WASTED LIVES see **KETTEVALT MENNYEZET** • 1981
WASTED SACRIFICE, A • 1912 • *Thornby Robert* • USA
WASTED YEARS, THE • 1914 • *Carlyle Francis* • USA
WASTED YEARS, THE • 1916 • *Wilbur Crane* • USA
WASTELAND, THE see **PUSTOTA** • 1983
WASTER, THE • 1926 • *Paul Gerson Pictures* • USA
WASTER'S WASTED LIFE, A • 1918 • Hamilton Lloyd • USA
WASTREL, THE (USA) see **RELITTO, IL** • 1961
WASTRELS, THE see **VITELLONI, I** • 1953
WASURENU BOJO (JPN) see **TYPHON SUR NAGASAKI** • 1957
WASURERARETA KORA • 1949 • Inagaki Hiroshi • JPN • FORGOTTEN CHILDREN
WASURERU MONOKA • 1968 • Matsuo Akinori • JPN • I SHALL NOT FORGET
WASYATNAMA • 1945 • *Sircar B. N. (P)* • IND
WAT EEN APPROACH • 1964 • Daalder Renee • SHT • NTH
WAT HUET E GESOT? • 1980 • Scheuer Paul • LXM
WAT JY SAAI • 1979 • Spring Tim • SAF • WHAT YOU SOW
WAT MAAK OOM KALIE DAAR • 1975 • SAF
WAT NU, OUDE MAN? • 1964 • Verhavert Roland • SHT • BLG
WAT ZIEN IK • 1971 • Verhoeven Paul* • NTH • ANY SPECIAL WAY (UKN) ○ BUSINESS IS BUSINESS ○ FUN LIFE OF AN AMSTERDAM STREETWALKER
WATAFLASH see **WHAT A FLASH** • 1971
WATAKUSHI-TACHI NO KEKKON • 1962 • Shinoda Masahiro • JPN • OUR MARRIAGE
WATAKUSHI WA NISAI see **WATASHI WA NISAI** • 1962
WATAN SE DOOR • 1968 • Kamran • IND • FAR FROM THE SOIL
WATANI HABIBI • 1964 • JRD
WATARI AND THE SEVEN MONSTERS • *Yoshinobu Kaneko* • JPN
WATARI IN THE MAGIC WORLD OF NINJAS • *Yoshinobu Kaneko* • JPN
WATARI (NINJA BOY) • 1966 • Funadoko Sadao • JPN
WATARIDORI ITSUKAERU • 1956 • Hisamatsu Seiji • JPN • STREET OF WANDERING PIGEONS
WATASHI NO SUBETE-O • 1954 • Ichikawa Kon • JPN • ALL OF MYSELF
WATASHI TO KANOJO • 1929 • Tasaka Tomotaka • JPN • SHE AND I
WATASHI WA KAI NI NARITAI • 1959 • Hashimoto S. • JPN • I WANT TO BE A SHELLFISH ○ LIPS FORBIDDEN TO TALK
WATASHI WA NISAI • 1962 • Ichikawa Kon • JPN • BEING TWO ISN'T EASY (UKN) ○ I AM TWO YEARS OLD ○ WATAKUSHI WA NISAI
WATASHI WO SKI NI TSURETETTE • 1988 • Baba Yasuo • JPN • TAKE ME SKIING
WATASHIGA SUTETA ONNA • 1969 • Urayama Kirio • JPN • GIRL I ABANDONED, THE
WATASHII WA BELLETT • 1964 • Oshima Nagisa • JPN • IT'S ME HERE, BELLETT ○ I'M HERE BELLETT
WATASHIWA WASURENAI • 1960 • Horiuchi Manao • JPN
WATCH BEVERLY • 1932 • Maude Arthur • UKN
WATCH COMMANDER, THE • 1988 • *Warden Jack* • USA
WATCH DOG see **SAVAGE** • 1972
WATCH DOG, THE • 1923 • Roach Hal • SHT • USA
WATCH DOG, THE • 1945 • Donnelly Eddie • ANS • USA
WATCH DOG IN THE DEEP, THE • 1914 • Brenon Herbert • USA
WATCH FOR THE EYES see **ATTENTION LES YEUX** • 1975
WATCH, GEORGE! • 1927 • Newfield Sam • SHT • USA
WATCH HIM STEP • 1922 • Nelson Jack • USA
WATCH IT SAILOR! • 1961 • Rilla Wolf • UKN
WATCH ME WHEN I KILL • Bido Antonio • ITL
WATCH ON THE LIME • 1949 • Lewis Jerry • SHT • USA
WATCH ON THE RHINE • 1943 • Shumlin Herman, Sherman Vincent • USA
WATCH OUT • 1924 • *Sennett Mack (P)* • SHT • USA
WATCH OUT! • 1953 • Chaffey Don • UKN
WATCH OUT FOR SPIES! see **SE OPP FOR SPIONER!** • 1944
WATCH OUT FOR THE AUTOMOBILE (USA) see **BEREGIS AVTOMOBILYA!** • 1966
WATCH OUT, THE DOCTORS' ROUNDS see **POZOR, VIZITA** • 1981
WATCH OUT, WE'RE MAD see **ALTRIMENTI CI ARRABBIAMO** • 1974
WATCH THE BIRDIE • 1928 • Newfield Sam • SHT • USA
WATCH THE BIRDIE • 1950 • Donohue Jack • USA
WATCH THE BIRDIE • 1953 • Godfrey Bob, Learner Keith, Linnecar Vera, Taylor Dick • ANS • UKN
WATCH THE BIRDIE • 1958 • Lovy Alex • ANS • USA
WATCH THE BIRDIE • 1963 • Russell Ken • MTV • UKN
WATCH THE BIRDIE • 1965 • Alti Giulio • USA
WATCH THE BIRDIE see **ZAOSTRIT PROSIM** • 1956
WATCH THE BIRDIE.. DIE! • 1968 • Doyle Don • USA
WATCH THE BUTTERFLY • 1966 • Tendlar Dave • ANS • USA
WATCH THE SHADOWS DANCE • 1988 • Joffe Mark • ASL
WATCH-TOWER IN THE CARPATHIANS see **ORHAZ A KARPATOKBAN** • 1914
WATCH YOUR BACK, PROFESSOR! see **PAS PA RYGGEN, PROFESSOR!** • 1978
WATCH YOUR CAR see **BEREGIS AVTOMOBILYA!** • 1966
WATCH YOUR HUSBAND • 1920 • Morris Reggie • SHT • USA
WATCH YOUR NEIGHBOR • 1918 • Heerman Victor • SHT • USA
WATCH YOUR STEP • 1918 • *Nestor* • USA
WATCH YOUR STEP • 1920 • Malins Geoffrey H. • UKN
WATCH YOUR STEP • 1922 • Beaudine William • USA • CITY FELLER, THE
WATCH YOUR STEP -MOTHER • 1920 • *Vernon Bobby* • SHT • USA
WATCH YOUR STERN • 1960 • Thomas Gerald • UKN
WATCH YOUR WATCH • 1915 • Collins Edwin J.? • UKN
WATCH YOUR WATCH • 1916 • *Stull Walter* • USA
WATCH YOUR WATCH • 1918 • *Shields Ernie* • SHT • USA
WATCH YOUR WIFE • 1922 • Roach Hal • SHT • USA
WATCH YOUR WIFE • 1926 • Gade Svend • USA
WATCHA WATCHIN' • 1962 • Hanna William, Barbera Joseph • ANS • USA
WATCHDOG, THE • 1939 • Donnelly Eddie • ANS • USA
WATCHED! • 1972 • Parsons John • USA
WATCHER IN THE WOODS, THE • 1980 • Hough John • UKN
WATCHERS • 1988 • Hess Jon • CND
WATCHERS, THE • 1969 • Foster Richard • UKN
WATCHING EYES • 1921 • *Beaumont Edna* • USA
WATCHING EYES • 1921 • Malins Geoffrey H. • SER • UKN
WATCHING FOR THE QUEEN • 1973 • Rimmer David • CND
WATCHMAKER • 1980 • Williams Richard • UKN • BEN TRUMAN 'OPENING TIME'
WATCHMAKER OF ST. PAUL, THE (UKN) see **HORLOGER DE ST. PAUL, L'** • 1973
WATCHMAKER'S INVENTION, THE • 1909 • *Gaumont* • FRN
WATCHMAN, THE see **KAVALKARAN** • 1967
WATCHMAN, THE see **HLIDAC** • 1970
WATCHMAN NO.47 see **HLIDAC C.47** • 1937
WATCHMAN TAKES A WIFE, THE • 1941 • Lord Del • SHT • USA
WATER • 1961 • Stapp Philip • USA
WATER • 1967 • Michaud Henri • SHT • CND
WATER • 1986 • Clement Dick • UKN
WATER see **VETTA** • 1957
WATER see **ZRODLO** • 1963
WATER ALSO BURNS see **SU DA YANAR** • 1987
WATER AS A BLACK BUFFALO see **APA CA UN BIVOL NEGRU** • 1970
WATER BABIES • 1935 • Jackson Wilfred • ANS • USA
WATER BABIES, THE • 1979 • Jeffries Lionel • UKN, PLN
WATER BABIES: OR, THE LITTLE CHIMNEY SWEEP, THE • 1907 • Stow Percy • UKN
WATER BATTLERS • 1948 • Parker Benjamin R. • SHT • USA
WATER BIRDS • 1952 • Sharpsteen Ben • DOC • USA
WATER BUGS • 1941 • Jason Will • SHT • USA
WATER-CARRIER IS DEAD, THE see **SAQQA' MAT, AS-** • 1977
WATER CARRIER OF SAN JUAN, THE • 1915 • *Greenwood Winnifred* • USA
WATER CIRCLE, THE • 1975 • Broughton James • USA
WATER CLUE, THE • 1915 • Julian Rupert • USA
WATER CURE, THE • 1913 • *Thanhauser* • USA
WATER CURE, THE • 1915 • *Joker* • USA
WATER CURE, THE • 1916 • SAF
WATER CURE, THE • 1916 • *Hardy Babe* • USA
WATER CYBORG(S) see **KAITEI DAISENSO** • 1966
WATER CYCLE, THE • 1972 • McDonald Philip • NZL
WATER DOG, THE • 1914 • Lehrman Henry • USA
WATER DUEL • 1900 • *Bitzer Billy (Ph)* • USA
WATER DWELLERS, THE • 1963 • Sparling Gordon • CND
WATER DWELLERS, THE • 1967 • Jeffrey Jim • DOC • ASL
WATER FIGHT, A • 1912 • *Lubin* • USA
WATER FOLK • 1931 • Field Mary, Smith Percy • UKN
WATER FOR CANITOGA see **WASSER FUR CANITOGA** • 1939
WATER FOR DRY LAND: USA -THE SOUTHWEST • 1948 • *De Rochemont Louis (P)* • SHT • USA
WATER FOR FIRE FIGHTING • 1948 • Halas John, Batchelor Joy • ANS • UKN
WATER FOR THE PRAIRIES • 1950 • Cherry Evelyn Spice, Cherry Lawrence W. • DOC • CND
WATER FOUNTAINS • 1986 • Kovachev Oleg • DOC • BUL
WATER FROM THE LAND see **VANDET PA LANDET** • 1945
WATER GIPSIES, THE • 1932 • Elvey Maurice • UKN
WATER HOLE, THE • 1928 • Jones F. Richard • USA
WATER IN OUR LIFE see **SEIKATSU TO MIZU** • 1952
WATER IS SO CLEAR, THE see **GAKI ZOSHI** • 1972
WATER LIGHT • 1957 • Jordan Larry • SHT • USA
WATER LILIES • 1911 • *Vitagraph* • USA
WATER LILY, THE • 1919 • Ridgwell George • USA
WATER LILY, THE see **TALE OF TWO WORLDS, A** • 1921
WATER MAGICIAN, THE (UKN) see **TAKI NO SHIRAITO** • 1933
WATER MAGICIAN, OR THE WHITE THREAD OF THE WATERFALL, THE see **TAKI NO SHIRAITO** • 1952
WATER MARGIN • Chang Ch'Eh • HKG
WATER NYMPH see **MAN OF THE MOMENT** • 1935
WATER NYMPH, THE • 1912 • Sennett Mack • USA
WATER-NYMPH ON THE SIGNET RING see **SELLO A PECSETGYURUN** • 1967
WATER OF LIFE, THE see **ELET VIZE, AZ** • 1970
WATER ON THE BRAIN • 1917 • Curtis Allen • SHT • USA
WATER PLUG, THE • 1920 • *Franey William* • SHT • USA
WATER RAT, THE • 1913 • Eagle Oscar • USA
WATER RAT, THE see **CARMEN VON ST. PAULI, DIE** • 1928
WATER RATS, THE • 1912 • *Payne Edna* • USA
WATER RATS OF LONDON, THE • 1914 • Youngdeer James • UKN
WATER RIGHT WAR, THE • 1912 • *Gerber Neva* • USA
WATER RUSTLERS • 1939 • Diege Samuel • USA
WATER SARK • 1964 • Wieland Joyce • SHT • USA
WATER SPIDER, THE see **ARAIGNEE D'EAU, L'** • 1969
WATER SPORTS • 1935 • McCarey Ray • SHT • USA
WATER SPRITE, THE • 1908 • Blackton J. Stuart • USA
WATER-SPRITE'S TALE, THE see **VODNICKA PODHADKA** • 1973
WATER STARS • 1952 • Gelentine Wheaton • USA
WATER STUFF • 1916 • Bertram William • SHT • USA
WATER TRIX • 1949 • Trego Charles T. • SHT • USA
WATER UNDER THE BRIDGE • 1980 • Auzins Igor • ASL
WATER WAGON, THE • 1912 • *Lubin* • USA
WATER WAGONS • 1925 • *Sennett Mack (P)* • SHT • USA
WATER WALKER • 1984 • Mason William • DOC • CND • WATERWALKER
WATER WAR, THE • 1911 • Dwan Allan • USA
WATER WAR, THE • 1913 • McRae Henry • USA
WATER, WATER, EVERY HARE • 1952 • Jones Charles M. • ANS • USA
WATER, WATER, EVERYWHERE • 1920 • Badger Clarence • USA
WATER WHICH FLOWS UNDER THE BRIDGES, THE see **EAU QUI COULE SOUS LES PONTS, L'** • 1929
WATER WISDOM • 1943 • *Smith Pete* • SHT • USA
WATERBEARER IS DEAD, THE see **SAQQA' MAT, AS-** • 1977
WATERCOLOUR • 1958 • Ioseliani Otar • SHT • USS
WATERCOLOURS see **AKWARELE** • 1978
WATERDEVIL, THE • 1969 • Garceau Raymond • SHT • CND
WATERED STOCK see **BEWARE OF THE LAW** • 1922
WATERFALL, THE • 1974 • Boretsky Yu. • USS
WATERFRONT • 1928 • Seiter William A. • USA
WATERFRONT • 1939 • Morse Terry O. • USA
WATERFRONT • 1944 • Sekely Steve • USA
WATERFRONT • 1950 • Anderson Michael • UKN • WATERFRONT WOMEN (USA)
WATERFRONT AT MIDNIGHT • 1948 • Berke William • USA
WATERFRONT LADY • 1935 • Santley Joseph • USA
WATERFRONT WOLVES • 1924 • Gibson Tom • USA • FAMOUS MORGAN PEARLS, THE
WATERFRONT WOMEN (USA) see **WATERFRONT** • 1950
WATERHOLE #3 • 1967 • Graham William A. • USA
WATERING THE FLOWERS see **ARROSEUR, L'** • 1896
WATERLESS SUMMER see **SUSUZ YAZ** • 1963
WATERLOO • 1928 • Grune Karl • FRG
WATERLOO • 1965 • Kumel Harry • BLG
WATERLOO • 1970 • Bondarchuk Sergei • USS, UKN, ITL • LAST HUNDRED DAYS OF NAPOLEON, THE
WATERLOO BRIDGE • 1931 • Whale James • USA
WATERLOO BRIDGE • 1940 • LeRoy Mervyn • USA
WATERLOO ROAD • 1945 • Gilliat Sidney • UKN • BLUE FOR WATERLOO
WATERMELON, THE see **BATIKHA, EL** • 1972
WATERMELON MAN • 1970 • Van Peebles Melvin • USA • NIGHT THE SUN CAME OUT ON HAPPY HOLLOW LANE, THE ○ NIGHT THE SUN CAME OUT, THE
WATERMELON PATCH, THE • 1905 • Porter Edwin S. • USA
WATERPIPE IN THE KITCHEN GARDEN • 1964 • Vasilchenko V. • USS
WATERPOWER • Damiano Gerard • USA
WATERPROOF WILLIE • 1908 • Booth W. R. • UKN
WATERS ARE RISING, THE • 1966 • Akopyan M. • USS
WATER'S EDGE • 1988 • Krishnamma • UKN
WATERS OF DEATH, THE • 1913 • *Peerless* • USA
WATERS OF LETHE, THE • 1916 • Wolbert William • SHT • USA
WATERS OF LIFE • 1907 • *Gaumont* • FRN
WATERS OF TIME • 1950 • Wright Basil, Launder Bill • DOC • UKN
WATERSHIP DOWN • 1978 • Rosen Martin • ANM • UKN
WATERSMITH • Hindle Will • USA
WATERTIGHT • 1943 • Cavalcanti Alberto • UKN • SHIP SAFETY
WATERWALKER see **WATER WALKER** • 1984
WATERWAYS OF ENGLAND • 1934 • Carr James • DOC • UKN
WATERY ROMANCE, A • 1915 • *Ray Al* • USA
WATERY ROMANCE, A • 1915 • Read James • UKN
WATERY ROMANCE, A • 1920 • Vanderlyn S. • UKN
WATERY WOOING, A • 1916 • Millarde Harry • USA
WATSON'S CLOWN AND DOGS TUG-OF-WAR • 1902 • *Warwick Trading Co* • UKN
WATTLE DAY IN ADELAIDE • 1914 • ASL
WATTOO WATTOO • 1980 • Ballay Hubert • ANS • FRN
WATTS MONSTER, THE see **DR. BLACK, MR. HYDE** • 1976
WATTS UP DOC? see **LIGHT FANTASTIC, THE** • 1972
WATTSTAX • 1973 • Stuart Mel • DOC • USA
WATUSI • 1959 • Neumann Kurt • USA • QUEST FOR KING SOLOMON'S MINES, THE ○ RETURN TO KING SOLOMON'S MINES
WATUSI A GO-GO see **GET YOURSELF A COLLEGE GIRL** • 1964
WAVE, THE • Balasa Sabin • ANS • RMN
WAVE, THE see **REDES** • 1934
WAVE, THE see **FALA** • 1986
WAVE, A WAC AND A MARINE, A • 1944 • Karlson Phil • USA
WAVE OF SPOOKS • 1908 • *Pathe* • FRN
WAVE OF UNREST, A • 1954 • Xie Jin • CHN
WAVELENGTH • 1967 • Snow Michael • USA
WAVELENGTH • 1982 • Gray Mike • USA
WAVELL'S 30,000 • 1942 • Monck John • DOC • UKN
WAVERLEY STEPS • 1947 • Eldridge John • DOC • UKN
WAVES, THE see **NAMI** • 1952
WAVES, THE see **LANG-HUA** • 1976
WAVES, THE see **GOLVEN** • 1982
WAVES AND SPRAY • 1898 • Smith G. A. • UKN
WAVES OF CHANGE • 1970 • MacGillivray Greg, Freeman Jim • DOC • USA
WAVES OF LUST see **ONDATA DI PIACERE, UNA** • 1975
WAWEL CONCERT, THE see **KONCERT WAWEL** • 1960
WAX DOLL see **VAXDOCKAN** • 1962
WAX EXPERIMENTS • 1924-29 • Fischinger Oskar • ANM • FRG
WAX LADY, THE • 1913 • *Thanhauser* • SHT • USA
WAX MEN, THE see **WACHSFIGURENKABINETT, DAS** • 1924
WAX MODEL, THE • 1917 • Hopper E. Mason • USA

WAX MUSEUM see **MYSTERY OF THE WAX MUSEUM, THE** • 1933
WAX WORKS • 1934 • Lantz Walter, Nolan William • ANS • USA
WAXWORK • 1988 • Hickox Anthony • USA
WAXWORKS (UKN) see **WACHSFIGURENKABINETT, DAS** • 1924
WAY see **UTAK** • 1989
WAY AHEAD, THE • 1944 • Reed Carol • UKN • IMMORTAL BATTALION (USA)
WAY BACK, THE • 1914 • Physioc Wray • USA
WAY BACK, THE • 1915 • King Carleton S. • USA
WAY BACK, THE see **CESTA ZPATKY** • 1958
WAY BACK HOME • 1931 • Seiter William A. • USA • OLD GREYHEART (UKN) ○ OLD GREATHEART ○ OTHER PEOPLE'S BUSINESS
WAY BACK WHEN A NIGHTCLUB WAS A STICK • 1940 • Fleischer Dave • ANS • USA
WAY BACK WHEN A RAZZBERRY WAS A FRUIT • 1940 • Fleischer Dave • ANS • USA
WAY BACK WHEN A TRIANGLE HAD ITS POINTS • 1940 • Fleischer Dave • ANS • USA
WAY BACK WHEN WOMEN HAD THEIR WEIGH • 1940 • Fleischer Dave • ANS • USA
WAY DOWN EAST • 1920 • Griffith D. W. • USA
WAY DOWN EAST • 1935 • King Henry • USA
WAY DOWN NORTH • 1920 • Moore Vin • SHT • USA
WAY DOWN SOUTH • 1939 • Vorhaus Bernard • USA
WAY DOWN THE MISSISSIPPI • 1913 • *Selsior Films* • UKN
WAY DOWN YONDER IN THE CORN • 1943 • Wickersham Bob • ANS • USA
WAY DOWNHILL, THE see **VAGEN UTFOR** • 1916
WAY FOR A SAILOR • 1930 • Wood Sam • USA
WAY HE WON THE WIDOW, THE • 1915 • Curtis Allen • USA
WAY HOME, THE • Rekhviashvili Aleksander • USS
WAY HOME, THE • 1914 • Morgan George • USA
WAY IN THE WILDERNESS, A • 1940 • Zinnemann Fred • SHT • USA
WAY IS LONG, THE see **DALEKA JEST DROGA** • 1963
WAY IT GOES, THE see **A TOUT PRENDRE** • 1963
WAY IT IS, THE • 1976 • Parker Gudrun • CND
WAY IT IS, THE • 1981 • Shaffer Beverly • MTV • CND
WAY IT IS, THE • 1986 • Mitchell Eric • USA
WAY MEN LOVE, THE see **BY DIVINE RIGHT** • 1924
WAY OF A GAUCHO • 1952 • Tourneur Jacques • USA
WAY OF A GIRL, THE • 1925 • Vignola Robert G. • USA
WAY OF A MAID, THE • 1911 • *Reliance* • USA
WAY OF A MAID, THE • 1919 • *Strand* • USA
WAY OF A MAID, THE • 1921 • Earle William P. S. • USA
WAY OF A MAN, THE • 1921 • Calvert Charles • UKN
WAY OF A MAN, THE • 1924 • Seitz George B. • SRL • USA
WAY OF A MAN, THE see **MIEHEN TIE** • 1940
WAY OF A MAN WITH A MAID • 1912 • *Costello Maurice* • USA
WAY OF A MAN WITH A MAID, THE • 1918 • Crisp Donald • USA
WAY OF A MOTHER, THE • 1913 • Miller Charles? • USA
WAY OF A MOTHER, THE • 1915 • Conway Jack • USA
WAY OF A RED MAN, THE • 1911 • *Bison* • USA
WAY OF A WOMAN, THE • 1914 • Reid Wallace • USA
WAY OF A WOMAN, THE • 1919 • Leonard Robert Z. • USA
WAY OF A WOMAN, THE see **WONDERFUL WOOING, THE** • 1925
WAY OF A WOMAN'S HEART, THE • 1915 • Beal Frank • USA
WAY OF ALL FISH, THE • 1931 • Sandrich Mark • SHT • USA
WAY OF ALL FLESH, THE • 1927 • Fleming Victor • USA
WAY OF ALL FLESH, THE • 1940 • King Louis • USA
WAY OF ALL FRESHMEN, THE • 1933 • Henabery Joseph • SHT • USA
WAY OF ALL MEN, THE • 1930 • Lloyd Frank • USA • SIN FLOOD (UKN)
WAY OF ALL PANTS, THE • 1927 • Parrott James • SHT • USA
WAY OF ALL PESTS • 1941 • Davis Arthur • ANS • USA
WAY OF AN EAGLE, THE • 1918 • Samuelson G. B. • UKN
WAY OF CARING, A • 1969 • Neal Peter • UKN
WAY OF CHALLENGE see **NINJA OPERATION 2: WAY OF CHALLENGE** • 1987
WAY OF DRAMA, THE see **SHIBAIDO** • 1944
WAY OF HIS FATHER, THE • 1914 • Mainhall Harry • USA
WAY OF LEARNING, A • 1967 • Hooper Tobe • SHT • USA
WAY OF LIFE, A • 1981 • SAF
WAY OF LIFE, THE • 1910 • *Kalem* • USA
WAY OF LIFE, THE • 1913 • Kirkland Hardee • USA
WAY OF LIFE, THE • 1914 • *Lyons Eddie* • USA
WAY OF LIFE, THE (UKN) see **THEY CALL IT SIN** • 1932
WAY OF LIGHT see **YEHUDI MENUHIN -CHEMIN DE LUMIERE** • 1971
WAY OF LOST SOULS, THE see **WOMAN HE SCORNED, THE** • 1929
WAY OF LOVE, THE see **ANBU VAZHI** • 1967
WAY OF MAN, THE • 1909 • Griffith D. W. • USA
WAY OF PATIENCE, THE • 1916 • Windom Lawrence C. • SHT • USA
WAY OF THE BEAST, THE see **KEMONOMICHI** • 1965
WAY OF THE CROSS, THE • 1909 • Blackton J. Stuart (Spv) • USA
WAY OF THE DEVIL, THE see **TARIK AL SHAITAN** • 1962
WAY OF THE DRAGON see **MENG LUNG KUO CHIANG** • 1972
WAY OF THE ENTHUSIASTS see **PUT ENTUZIASTOV** • 1930
WAY OF THE ESKIMO, THE • 1911 • *Selig* • USA
WAY OF THE LAW • 1920 • Craft William James • USA
WAY OF THE LOTUS, THE see **VIRAGAYA** • 1987
WAY OF THE MOUNTAINS, THE • 1912 • *Adair Robert* • USA
WAY OF THE NINJA see **RAGE OF HONOR** • 1986
WAY OF THE REDMAN, THE • 1914 • Mix Tom • USA
WAY OF THE STRONG, THE • 1919 • Carewe Edwin • USA
WAY OF THE STRONG, THE • 1928 • Capra Frank • USA
WAY OF THE STRONG, THE see **STRONG WAY, THE** • 1918
WAY OF THE TRANSGRESSOR, THE • 1911 • *Selig* • USA
WAY OF THE TRANSGRESSOR, THE • 1912 • *American* • USA
WAY OF THE TRANSGRESSOR, THE • 1912 • *Powers* • USA
WAY OF THE TRANSGRESSOR, THE • 1913 • *Solax* • USA
WAY OF THE TRANSGRESSOR, THE • 1915 • Humphrey William • USA
WAY OF THE TRANSGRESSOR, THE • 1923 • Craft William James • USA
WAY OF THE WARRIOR, THE see **BUSHIDO** • 1970
WAY OF THE WEST, THE • 1910 • *Champion* • USA
WAY OF THE WEST, THE • 1911 • Dwan Allan • USA
WAY OF THE WEST, THE • 1934 • Tansey Robert • USA
WAY OF THE WICKED see **CE CORPS TANT DESIRE** • 1958
WAY OF THE WILD • 1935 • Ratcliffe F. W. • UKN
WAY OF THE WIND, THE • 1976 • Tobias Charles • DOC • USA
WAY OF THE WOMAN, THE • 1914 • *Hough Irene* • USA
WAY OF THE WORLD, THE • 1910 • Griffith D. W. • USA
WAY OF THE WORLD, THE • 1911 • *Yankee* • USA
WAY OF THE WORLD, THE • 1914 • *Lewis Pennant Features* • USA
WAY OF THE WORLD, THE • 1916 • Carleton Lloyd B. • USA
WAY OF THE WORLD, THE • 1920 • Coleby A. E. • UKN
WAY OF THE WORLD, THE • 1947 • Komisarjevsky James • UKN
WAY OF YOUTH, THE • 1934 • Walker Norman • UKN
WAY OF YOUTH, THE (USA) see **CHEMIN DES ECOLIERS, LE** • 1959
WAY OUT • 1966 • Yeaworth Irvin S. Jr. • USA
WAY OUT • 1975 • Monheim Luc • NTH
WAY OUT, THE • 1913 • *Costello Maurice* • USA
WAY OUT, THE • 1915 • O'Sullivan Tony • USA
WAY OUT, THE • 1918 • Kelson George • USA
WAY OUT, THE • 1934 • *Sound City* • SHT • UKN
WAY OUT, THE (USA) see **DIAL 999** • 1955
WAY OUT EAST • 1973 • Miller Arnold Louis • DOC • UKN
WAY OUT IN THE COUNTRY • 1967 • Torres Mar S. • PHL
WAY OUT LOVE see **TOUCH OF HER FLESH, THE** • 1967
WAY-OUT SHRINE, THE • 1967 • *Morishige Hisaya* • JPN
WAY OUT STOPLESS see **WAY OUT TOPLESS** • 1967
WAY OUT TOP see **WAY OUT TOPLESS** • 1967
WAY OUT TOPLESS • 1967 • Francis Lewis S. • USA • WAY OUT TOP ○ WAY OUT STOPLESS
WAY OUT WEST • 1930 • Niblo Fred • USA • EASY GOING
WAY OUT WEST • 1937 • Horne James W. • USA
WAY OUTBACK • 1911 • Rolfe Alfred • ASL
WAY PERILOUS, THE • 1913 • *Bushman Francis X.* • USA
WAY ROUND, THE see **OBJIZDKA** • 1968
WAY TO A MAN'S HEART, THE • 1913 • *Thanhouser* • USA
WAY TO BRESSON, THE see **WEG NAAR BRESSON, DE** • 1983
WAY TO HEAVEN, THE • 1914 • Davis Ulysses • USA
WAY TO LIBERTY, THE see **WEG INS FREIE, DER** • 1941
WAY TO LOVE, THE • 1933 • Taurog Norman • USA
WAY TO PARADISE see **PUT U RAJ** • 1971
WAY TO PLEASURE, THE see **PARTIE DE PLAISIR, UNE** • 1974
WAY TO SELL CORSETS • 1904 • *Biograph* • SHT • USA
WAY TO SHADOW GARDEN, THE • 1955 • Brakhage Stan • SHT • USA • WAY TO THE SHADOW GARDEN, THE
WAY TO THE FRONT, THE see **DROGA NA FRONT** • 1975
WAY TO THE GOD, THE see **KAMI E NO MICHI** • 1928
WAY TO THE GOLD, THE • 1957 • Webb Robert D. • USA
WAY TO THE HARBOUR, THE see **PUT K PRICHALU** • 1962
WAY TO THE MAN'S HEART, THE see **VAGEN TILL MANNENS HJARTA** • 1914
WAY TO THE NEIGHBORS, THE • 1982 • Dragic Nedeljko • ANS • YGS • WAY TO YOUR NEIGHBOR
WAY TO THE NEIGHBOUR, THE see **VEG ZUM NACHBARN** • 1963
WAY TO THE SEA, THE • Holmes J. B. • DOC • UKN
WAY TO THE SHADOW GARDEN, THE see **WAY TO SHADOW GARDEN, THE** • 1955
WAY TO THE SKIES, THE see **DROGA DO NIEBA** • 1958
WAY TO THE STARS, THE • 1945 • Asquith Anthony • UKN • JOHNNY IN THE CLOUDS (USA) ○ RENDEZVOUS
WAY TO THE WHARF, THE see **PUT K PRICHALU** • 1962
WAY TO VICTORY, THE see **VOIE DE LA VICTOIRE, LA** • 1972
WAY TO WIN, THE • 1910 • *Imp* • USA
WAY TO YOUR NEIGHBOR see **WAY TO THE NEIGHBORS, THE** • 1982
WAY UP, THE see **WEG NACH OBEN** • 1950
WAY UP IN SOCIETY • 1918 • *Allen Diana* • SHT • USA
WAY UP THAR • 1935 • Sennett Mack • SHT • USA
WAY UP YONDER • 1920 • Sudgeon Leonard S.
WAY UPSTREAM • 1989 • Johnson Terry • UKN
WAY VIA SKA see **VAGEN GENOM SKA** • 1957
WAY, WAY OUT • 1966 • Douglas Gordon • USA
WAY WE LIVE, THE • 1947 • Craigie Jill • DOC • UKN
WAY WE LIVE NOW, THE • 1970 • Brown Barry • USA
WAY WE WERE, THE • 1973 • Pollack Sydney • USA
WAY WEST, THE • 1967 • McLaglen Andrew V. • USA
WAY WOMEN LOVE, THE • 1920 • Perez Marcel • USA
WAYBACKS, THE • 1918 • Sterry Arthur • ASL
WAYFARER see **DENDANG PERANTHU** • 1977
WAYFARER, THE • 1912 • *Selig* • USA
WAYFARERS see **LANDSTRYKERE** • 1988
WAYFARERS, THE • 1916 • *Vosburgh Alfred* • SHT • USA
WAYLAID WOMEN see **SCHWARZE NYLONS -HEISSE NACHTE** • 1958
WAYOUT, WAY IN (USA) see **KOKOSEI BANCHO** • 1970
WAYS AND MEANS • 1968 • Godfrey Bob • ANS • UKN
WAYS AND WALLS see **WEGE UND MAUERN** • 1982
WAYS IN THE NIGHT see **WEGE IN DER NACHT** • 1979
WAYS OF A MAN, THE • 1915 • Giblyn Charles • USA
WAYS OF DESTINY, THE • 1913 • *Pathe* • USA
WAYS OF EATING see **GESTES DU REPAS** • 1958
WAYS OF FATE, THE • 1912 • Dwan Allan • USA
WAYS OF FATE, THE • 1913 • Reid Wallace • USA
WAYS OF LOVE see **AMORE, L'** • 1948
WAYS OF LOVE (USA) see **JOFROI** • 1933
WAYS OF MEN, THE • 1912 • *Powers* • USA
WAYS OF SEEING • 1977 • Cox Paul • SHT • ASL
WAYS OF THE LORD ARE ENDED, THE see **VIE DEL SIGNORE SONO FINITE, LE** • 1988
WAYS OF THE WORLD • 1916 • Le Viness Carl M. • USA
WAYS OF THE WORLD, THE • 1915 • MacBean L. C. • UKN
WAYS TO HEALTH AND BEAUTY see **WEGE ZU KRAFT UND SCHONHEIT** • 1925
WAYSIDE PEBBLE see **ROBO NO ISHI** • 1960
WAYSIDE SHRINE, THE • 1910 • *Vitagraph* • USA
WAYSIDE SINGERS see **KEMBARA SENIMAN JALANAN** • 1985
WAYVILLE SLUMBER PARTY, THE • 1915 • *Bowers Billy* • USA
WAYWARD • 1932 • Sloman Edward • USA
WAYWARD BUS, THE • 1957 • Vicas Victor • USA
WAYWARD CANARY, THE • 1932 • Gillett Burt • ANS • USA
WAYWARD DAUGHTER, A • 1908 • *Essanay* • USA
WAYWARD DAUGHTER, A • 1914 • Brooke Van Dyke • USA
WAYWARD GIRL, THE • 1957 • Selander Lesley • USA
WAYWARD GIRL, THE (USA) see **UNG FLUKT** • 1959
WAYWARD HAT, THE • 1960 • Tendlar Dave • ANS • USA
WAYWARD PUPS • 1937 • Ising Rudolf • ANS • USA
WAYWARD RIVER • 1961 • Garceau Raymond • DCS • CND • CHAUDIERE, LA
WAYWARD SISTER, THE • 1913 • Turner Otis • USA
WAYWARD SISTER, THE • 1916 • *Lubin* • SHT • USA
WAYWARD SON, A • 1915 • Powers Francis • USA
WAYWARD SON, THE • 1913 • *Kalem* • USA
WAYWARD SON, THE • 1914 • *Hutchison Charles* • USA
WAYWARD WIFE, THE see **PROVINCIALE, LA** • 1953
WAYWARD WIVES • 1968 • *Mitam Productions* • USA
WAYWARD YOUTH (UKN) see **RESTLESS YOUTH** • 1928
WAZOU POLYGAME, LE • 1969 • Ganda Oumarou • SHT • NGR
WE A FAMILY • 1968 • Van Hearn J. • USA
WE ACCOMPLISHED see **CUMPLIMOS** • 1962
WE AIM TO PLEASE • 1934 • Fleischer Dave • ANS • USA
WE AIM TO PLEASE • 1977 • Nash Margot • ASL
WE ALL DIE ALONE see **JEDER STIRBT FUR SICH ALLEIN** • 1976
WE ALL GO see **WE ALL GO DOWN** • 1969
WE ALL GO DOWN • 1969 • Damiano Gerard • USA • WE ALL GO
WE ALL LOVED EACH OTHER SO MUCH see **C'ERAVAMO TANTO AMATI** • 1974
WE ALL WALKED INTO THE SHOP • 1906 • Gilbert Arthur • UKN
WE ALL WALKED INTO THE SHOP • 1907 • Morland John • UKN
WE ALL WALKED INTO THE SHOP • 1922 • *Parkinson H. B. (P)* • SHT • UKN
WE ALWAYS LOOKED OUT TO SEA see **ON REGARDAIT TOUJOURS VERS LA MER** • 1982
WE AMERICANS • 1928 • Sloman Edward • USA • HEART OF A NATION, THE (UKN)
WE APES see **NOSOTROS LOS MONOS** • 1972
WE ARE 18 YEARS OLD see **TENEMOS 18 ANOS** • 1960
WE ARE ALL ALONE MY DEAR see **WE'RE ALL ALONE, MY DEAR** • 1977
WE ARE ALL BROTHERS see **VI ER ALLE BROILERE**
WE ARE ALL DEAD DEMONS see **KLABAUTERMANDEN** • 1969
WE ARE ALL DEMONS see **KLABAUTERMANDEN** • 1969
WE ARE ALL ERRAND BOYS see **SPRINGPOJKAR AR VI ALLIHOPA** • 1941
WE ARE ALL FOR PEACE see **MY ZA MIR** • 1951
WE ARE ALL FRIENDS see **SAMI SWOI** • 1967
WE ARE ALL GOOD HERE see **NOS POR CA TODOS BEM** • 1977
WE ARE ALL GUILTY see **AN DE NODO** • 1980
WE ARE ALL MURDERERS (USA) see **NOUS SOMMES TOUS DES ASSASSINS** • 1952
WE ARE ALL NAKED (USA) see **ILS SONT NUS** • 1966
WE ARE ALL SWINGERS see **SOLDATI E CAPELLONI** • 1967
WE ARE ARAB JEWS IN ISRAEL see **NOUS SOMMES DE JUIFS ARABES EN ISMAEL** • 1977
WE ARE BEWITCHED, IRINA see **UKLETI SMO, IRINA** • 1974
WE ARE BUILDERS OF THE COUNTRY see **BUDUJEMY NOWE WSIE** • 1946
WE ARE BUILDING see **WIJ BOUWEN** • 1930
WE ARE BUILDING see **BUDUJEMY** • 1934
WE ARE BUILDING NEW VILLAGES see **BUDUJEMY NOWE WSIE** • 1946
WE ARE BUT LITTLE CHILDREN WEAK • 1913 • Buckland Warwick? • UKN
WE ARE FOR PEACE see **MY ZA MIR** • 1951
WE ARE FRENCH see **BUGLER OF ALGIERS, THE** • 1916
WE ARE FROM KRONSTADT see **MY IZ KRONSTADT** • 1936
WE ARE FROM THE URALS see **MY S URALA** • 1944
WE ARE GETTING DIVORCED see **WIR LASSEN UNS SCHEIDEN** • 1968
WE ARE IN THE NAVY NOW (USA) see **WE JOINED THE NAVY** • 1962
WE ARE MARTIANS • Pavlotskaia Eren • USS • WE MARTIANS
WE ARE NO VIRGINS • 1974 • Sala Henri • FRN • COME AND PLAY
WE ARE NOT ALONE • 1939 • Goulding Edmund • USA
WE ARE NOT ALONE: IS THERE LIFE ON OTHER PLANETS? • 1967 • *Abc* • DOC • USA
WE ARE NOT OF STONE see **NO SOMOS DE PIEDRA** • 1968
WE ARE ON THE ROAD TO GENEVA • 1988 • Song Yeong-Su • SKR • NOW WE ARE GOING TO GENEVA
WE ARE SEVEN • 1936 • Field Mary • UKN
WE ARE SO FOND OF ONIONS • 1908 • *Tyler Walter* • UKN
WE ARE THE BEST see **SOMOS LOS MEJORES!** • 1968
WE ARE THE CHILDREN • 1987 • Young Robert Malcolm • TVM • USA
WE ARE THE CINEMA see **CINE SOMOS NOSOSTROS, EL** • 1979
WE ARE THE GUINEA PIGS • 1980 • Harvey Joan • USA
WE ARE THE LAMBETH BOYS • 1958 • Reisz Karel • UKN
WE ARE THE MARINES • 1942 • de Rochemont Louis • DOC • USA
WE ARE THE RUSSIANS see **MI, RUSSKI NAROD** • 1964
WE ARE TWO see **MI -DVOE MUZHCHIN** • 1963
WE ARE WAITING FOR YOU, LAD! see **ZHDYOM TEBYA, PARENI** • 1973
WE ARE YOUNG • 1967 • Thompson Francis, Hammid Alexander • SHT • CND
WE AT KRAHWINKEL see **U NAS V KOCOURKOVE** • 1934
WE AT SOLGLANTAN (USA) see **VI PA SOLGLANTAN** • 1939
WE BUILD see **BUDUJEMY** • 1934
WE BUILD A SCHOOL • 1961 • D'Bomba Jorg • ANM • GDR

WE CALLED THEM MONTAGUES AND CAPULETS • 1986 • Donev Donyo • ANM • BUL
WE CAN see **SI PODEMOS** • 1973
WE CAN DREAM, CAN'T WE? • 1949 • Barclay David • SHT • USA
WE CAN'T GO HOME AGAIN • 1973 • Ray Nicholas • USA
WE CAN'T HAVE EVERYTHING • 1918 • De Mille Cecil B. • USA
WE CHILDREN FROM BAHNHOF ZOO (USA) see **CHRISTIANE F. WIR KINDER VOM BAHNHOF ZOO** • 1981
WE CLOSE AT TWO ON THURSDAY • 1908 • Gilbert Arthur • UKN
WE COULD DO SOMETHING TOGETHER see **KATI BORI NA KANOUME EMIS I DHIO** • 1972
WE DID IT • 1936 • Fleischer Dave • ANS • USA
WE DIDN'T REALLY MEAN IT • 1978 • Fawbert Fred • SHT • UKN
WE DIE ALONE see **NI LIV** • 1957
WE DINE AT SEVEN • 1931 • Richardson Frank • UKN
WE DIVE AT DAWN • 1943 • Asquith Anthony • UKN
WE DO BELIEVE IN GHOSTS • 1947 • West Walter • UKN
WE DO IT! • 1970 • *Mitam Productions* • USA
WE DO IT BECAUSE • 1942 • Wrangell Basil • SHT • USA
WE DON'T ASK FOR A TRIP TO THE MOON see **NO LES PEDIMOS UN VIAJE A LA LUNA** • 1988
WE DON'T BURY ON SUNDAYS see **ON N'ENTERRE PAS LE DIMANCHE** • 1959
WE DON'T THINK! • 1914 • Plumb Hay? • UKN
WE EAT THE FRUIT OF THE TREES OF PARADISE see **OVOCE STROMU RAJSKYCH JIME** • 1969
WE EXPECT VICTORY THERE see **MY ZHDOM VAS S POBEDOI** • 1941
WE FAW DOWN • 1928 • McCarey Leo • SHT • USA • WE SLIP UP
WE FORGET EVERYTHING see **ON EFFACE TOUT** • 1978
WE FOUND A VALLEY • 1956 • Swingler Humphrey • UKN
WE FRENCH • 1916 • Julian Rupert • USA
WE FROM KRONSTADT see **MY IZ KRONSTADT** • 1936
WE FROM SUNNY GLADE see **VI PA SOLGLANTAN** • 1939
WE FROM THE THEATRE see **VI SOM GAR SCENVAGEN** • 1938
WE GIVE PINK STAMPS • 1965 • Freleng Friz • ANS • USA
WE GO FAST • 1941 • McGann William • USA
WE GO THROUGH THE KITCHEN see **VI SOM GAR KOKSVAGEN** • 1932
WE HAD BETTER CALL IT A DAY see **APAGA Y VAMONOS** • 1981
WE HANG FROM A THREAD see **VI HAENGER I EN TRAD** • 1962
WE HAR MANJE NAMN • 1976 • Zetterling Mai • SWD • WE HAVE MANY NAMES
WE HAVE BEEN THE GUESTS OF CHINA see **KINA VENDEGEI VOLTUNK** • 1957
WE HAVE COME FOR YOUR DAUGHTERS (UKN) see **MEDICINE BALL CARAVAN** • 1971
WE HAVE MANY NAMES see **WE HAR MANJE NAMN** • 1976
WE HAVE NEVER BEEN SO HAPPY see **NUNCA FOMOS TAO FELIZES** • 1984
WE HAVE ONLY ONE LIFE see **MIA ZOI TIN ECHOME** • 1958
WE HAVE OUR MOMENTS • 1937 • Werker Alfred L. • USA
WE HOUSEMAIDS see **VI HEMSLAVINNOR** • 1942
WE HUMANS (UKN) see **YOUNG AMERICA** • 1932
WE INSIST see **NOI INSISTIAMO** • 1965
WE JOINED THE NAVY • 1962 • Toye Wendy • UKN • WE ARE IN THE NAVY NOW (USA)
WE LIVE AGAIN • 1934 • Mamoulian Rouben • USA • RESURRECTION
WE LIVE HERE see **MY ZDES ZHIVEM** • 1957
WE LIVE IN TWO WORLDS • 1937 • Cavalcanti Alberto • DOC • UKN
WE LIVE TODAY see **KYO NI IKIRU** • 1959
WE MARTIANS see **WE ARE MARTIANS**
WE MET AT THE SNACK BAR see **CHIISANA SUNAKKA** • 1968
WE MET THE STORM see **VI MOTTE STORMEN** • 1943
WE MODERNS • 1925 • Dillon John Francis • USA
WE MUST HAVE LOVE see **KARLEK MASTE VI HA** • 1930
WE MUST NOT PART, MY DARLING see **MINE KONTA MOU, AGAPIMENE** • 1968
WE NEED EACH OTHER see **VI BEHOVER VARANN** • 1943
WE NEED VIRGINS see **SHOJO NYUYO** • 1930
WE NEVER SLEEP • 1917 • Roach Hal • SHT • USA
WE OF THE NEVER NEVER • 1982 • Auzins Igor • ASL
WE OF THE URALS see **MY S URALA** • 1944
WE OF THE WEST RIDING • 1946 • Annakin Ken • DOC • UKN • WEST RIDING, THE
WE ON THE ISLAND OF SALTKRAKAN see **VI PA SALTKRAKAN** • 1968
WE ON VADDO see **VI PA VADDO** • 1958
WE ONLY LIVE ONCE see **MIA ZOI TIN ECHOME** • 1958
WE ONLY LIVE WAIS • 1968 • San Juan Luis • PHL • WE ONLY LIVE WISE
WE ONLY LIVE WISE see **WE ONLY LIVE WAIS** • 1968
WE OUTSIDE see **NOSOTROS AGUERA** • 1979
WE PARTED ON THE SHORE • 1907 • Gilbert Arthur • UKN
WE PEOPLE OF SURINAM see **WIJ, SURINAMERS** • 1961
WE PLAY TRUANT see **STUDUJEME ZA SKOLOU** • 1939
WE PROTECT WHAT WE MAKE see **WIR SCHUTZEN, WAS WIR SCHAFFEN** • 1968
WE REFUSE TO DIE • 1942 • Pine William H. • USA
WE SAIL AT MIDNIGHT • 1943 • Ford John • DOC • USA
WE SANG THE ARIZONA see **ZPIVALI JSME ARIZONU** • 1964
WE SEARCH AND STRIKE • 1942 • *Dalrymple Ian (P)* • DOC • UKN
WE SEE THEM THROUGH • 1948 • Kaufman Petus, Alpert Harry • USA
WE SHALL BE CLEVERER NEXT TIME, OLD CHAP see **PRISTE BUDEME CHYTREJSI, STAROUSKU** • 1983
WE SHALL ME AGAIN see **'TIL WE MEET AGAIN** • 1940
WE SHALL REMEMBER THIS DAY see **ZAPOMNIM ETOT DYEN** • 1967
WE SHALL RETURN • 1963 • Goodman Philip S. • USA
WE SHALL RISE AGAIN see **UNCENSORED** • 1942
WE SHALL SEE • 1964 • Lawrence Quentin • UKN
WE SHOULD WORRY • 1918 • Buel Kenean • USA
WE SLIP UP see **WE FAW DOWN** • 1928
WE STILL KILL THE OLD WAY (USA) see **A CIASCUNO IL SUO** • 1967
WE STOLE AWAY • 1964 • Jacobs Ken • USA
WE STUDENTS see **AHNA AL-TALAMD'A** • 1959
WE SWEAR! see **SLUBUJEMY!** • 1952
WE TAKE OFF OUR HATS! • 1930 • Hughes Harry • UKN
WE, THE ANIMALS, SQUEAK • 1941 • Clampett Robert • ANS • USA
WE, THE HEROES see **MITAS ME SANKARIT** • 1980
WE THE LIVING (UKN) see **NOI VIVI** • 1942
WE, THE MOUNTAIN PEOPLE see **KAMING TAGA BUNDOK** • 1968
WE THE POOR see **NOSOTROS LOS POBRES** • 1947
WE, THE RIVER PEOPLE see **KAMING TAGA ILOG** • 1968
WE, THE RUSSIAN PEOPLE see **MI, RUSSKI NAROD** • 1964
WE, THE TOUGH GUYS see **NOI UOMINI DURI** • 1987
WE, THE WOMEN see **SIAMO DONNE** • 1953
WE THINK THE WORLD OF YOU • 1989 • Gregg Colin • UKN
WE THREE ARE MAKING OUR DEBUT see **VI TRE DEBUTERA** • 1953
WE THREE DEBUTANTES see **VI TRE DEBUTERA** • 1953
WE THREE (UKN) see **COMPROMISED** • 1931
WE.. TOGETHER! see **WEDERZIJDS** • 1964
WE TOOK OVER THE CAUSE OF PEACE see **KEZUNKBE VETTUK A BEKE UGYET** • 1951
WE TWO • 1930 • *Morgan A. R.* • SHT • UKN
WE TWO see **WIR-ZWEI** • 1970
WE, TWO MEN see **MI -DVOE MUZHCHIN** • 1963
WE TWO (USA) see **VI TVA** • 1939
WE UNDERSTAND EACH OTHER • Nickel Gitta • DOC • GDR
WE VISIT MOSCOW • 1954 • Wright Kenneth • USA
WE WANT A BABY see **VI VIL HA ET BARN** • 1949
WE WANT A CHILD see **VI VIL HA ET BARN** • 1949
WE WANT OUR MUMMY • 1939 • Lord Del • SHT • USA
WE! WE! MARIE • 1930 • Ray Albert • SHT • USA
WE WENT TO COLLEGE • 1936 • Santley Joseph • USA • OLD SCHOOL TIE, THE (UKN)
WE WERE DANCING • 1941 • Leonard Robert Z. • USA
WE WERE LIKE THIS YESTERDAY, HOW IS IT TODAY? see **GANITO KAMI NOON, PAANO KAYO NGAYON?** • 1977
WE WERE ONE MAN see **NOUS ETIONS UN SEUL HOMME** • 1978
WE WERE SEVEN SISTERS see **ERAVAMO SETTE SORELLE** • 1938
WE WERE SEVEN WIDOWS (USA) see **ERAVAMO SETTE VEDOVE** • 1939
WE WERE SO YOUNG.. see **KAK MOLODY MY BYLI** • 1985
WE WERE STRANGERS • 1949 • Huston John • USA • ROUGH SKETCH
WE WERE TEN see **BYLO NAS DESET** • 1963
WE WERE YOUNG see **A BYAHME MLADI** • 1961
WE WHO ARE ABOUT TO DIE • 1936 • Cabanne W. Christy • USA
WE WHO ARE YOUNG • 1940 • Bucquet Harold S. • USA • I DO
WE WHO ARE YOUNG • 1952 • Simmons Anthony • SHT • UKN
WE WILL ALL MEET IN PARADISE (USA) see **NOUS IRONS TOUS AU PARADIS** • 1977
WE WILL COME BACK see **SEKRETAR RAIKON** • 1942
WE WILL HAVE A HOME see **I BEDZIE MIAL DOM** • 1978
WE WILL NEVER FORGET THAT NIGHT see **SONO YO WA WASURENAI** • 1962
WE WILL NOT GROW OLD TOGETHER see **NOUS NE VIEILLIRONS PAS ENSEMBLE** • 1972
WE WILL REMEMBER see **SENJO NI NAGARERU UTA** • 1965
WE WOMEN • 1925 • Kellino W. P. • UKN
WE WON'T FORGET • 1935-45 • Sainsbury Frank • DOC • UKN
WE WON'T GO TO THE WOODS ANY MORE see **NOUS N'IRONS PLUS UN BOIS** • 1968
WE WON'T GROW OLD TOGETHER see **NOUS NE VIEILLIRONS PAS ENSEMBLE** • 1972
WEAK AND THE WICKED, THE • 1953 • Thompson J. Lee • UKN • YOUNG AND WILLING (USA)
WEAK BUT WILLING • 1926 • Mayo Archie • SHT • USA
WEAK-END PARTY, THE see **EGG, THE** • 1922
WEAK HEARTS AND WILD LIONS • 1919 • Fishback Fred C. • SHT • USA
WEAK-KNEED FROM FEAR OF GHOST-CAT see **KAIBYO KOSHINUKE DAISODO** • 1954
WEAK POINT see **PUNTO DEBIL** • 1974
WEAK SPOT, THE see **FAILLE, LA** • 1975
WEAKER BROTHER, THE • 1912 • Dwan Allan • USA
WEAKER BROTHER, THE • 1914 • Jones Edgar • USA
WEAKER MIND, THE • 1913 • Fielding Romaine • USA
WEAKER SEX, THE • 1914 • *Weber Lois* • USA
WEAKER SEX, THE • 1917 • West Raymond B. • USA
WEAKER SEX, THE • 1948 • Baker Roy Ward • UKN • NO MEDALS FOR MARTHA
WEAKER SEX, THE see **SEXE FAIBLE, LE** • 1934
WEAKER SEX (USA) see **AH JONAN** • 1960
WEAKER STRAIN, THE • 1914 • *Reliance* • USA
WEAKER STRAIN, THE • 1916 • McGill Lawrence?, Hansel Howell? • SHT • USA
WEAKER VESSEL, THE • 1919 • Powell Paul • USA
WEAKER'S STRENGTH, THE • 1914 • *Essanay* • USA
WEAKLING, THE • 1914 • Buel Kenean • USA
WEAKLING, THE • 1916 • *Gilroy Barbara* • SHT • USA
WEAKLY REPORTER, THE • 1944 • Jones Charles M. • ANS • USA
WEAKNESS OF MAN, THE • 1916 • O'Neil Barry • USA • GREATER LOVE, THE
WEAKNESS OF MEN, THE see **LADY IN SILK STOCKINGS, THE** • 1925
WEAKNESS OF STRENGTH, THE • 1916 • Revier Harry • USA
WEALTH • 1921 • Taylor William D. • USA
WEALTH LURE, THE • 1916 • Trinchera Paul • USA
WEALTH OF A NATION • 1938 • Alexander Donald • UKN
WEALTH OF THE POOR, THE • 1915 • *Anderson Broncho Billy* • USA
WEALTHY BROTHER JONATHAN • 1911 • Haldane Bert • UKN • OUR WEALTHY NEPHEW JOHN (USA)
WEAPON, THE • 1913 • Costello Maurice • USA
WEAPON, THE • 1956 • Guest Val • UKN
WEAPONS • 1916 • Dyer Anson • UKN
WEAPONS see **FEGYVER** • 1971
WEAPONS OF DEATH • Caiano Mario
WEAPONS OF DEATH see **WARRIORS OF DEATH** • 1981
WEAPONS OF DESTRUCTION see **VYNALEZ ZKAZY** • 1958
WEAPONS OF LOVE • 1916 • Elfelt Clifford S. • SHT • USA
WEAPONS OF VENGEANCE (USA) see **DIAVOLI DI SPARTIVENTO, I** • 1963
WEAR A VERY BIG HAT • 1965 • Loach Kenneth • MTV • UKN
WEARDALE • 1974 • Dodd Thomas • MTV • UKN
WEARING OF THE GRIN • 1951 • Jones Charles M. • ANS • USA
WEARY DEATH, THE see **MUDE TOD, DER** • 1921
WEARY GOES A-WOOING • 1915 • *Selig* • USA
WEARY HUNTERS AND THE MAGICIAN, THE • 1902 • Porter Edwin S. • USA
WEARY RIVER • 1929 • Lloyd Frank • USA
WEARY STARTS THINGS IN PUMPKINVILLE • 1912 • *Vitagraph* • USA
WEARY WALKER'S WOES • 1915 • *Marshall Boyd* • USA
WEARY WILLIE • 1897 • Smith G. A. • UKN
WEARY WILLIE see **OVERFUL SEAT, AN** • 1898
WEARY WILLIE AND HIS PAL ON THE RAMPAGE • 1902 • UKN
WEARY WILLIE AND THE GARDENER • 1901 • Porter Edwin S. • USA
WEARY WILLIE AND TIRED TIM • 1911 • Martinek H. O. • SER • UKN
WEARY WILLIE AND TIRED TIM -A DEAD SHOT • 1903 • *Warwick Trading Co* • UKN
WEARY WILLIE AND TIRED TIM ON THE MASH • 1908 • *Tyler Walter* • UKN
WEARY WILLIE AND TIRED TIM -THE GUNPOWDER PLOT • 1903 • *Warwick Trading Co* • UKN
WEARY WILLIE AND TIRED TIM TURN BARBERS • 1903 • Haggar William • UKN
WEARY WILLIE IN SEARCH OF HIDDEN TREASURE • 1904 • Browne Tom • UKN
WEARY WILLIE KIDNAPS A CHILD • 1904 • Porter Edwin S. • USA
WEARY WILLIE STEALS A FISH • 1908 • Fitzhamon Lewin • UKN
WEARY WILLIES • 1929 • Lantz Walter, Nolan William • ANS • USA
WEARY WILLIES AND THE POLICEMAN, THE • 1902 • *Warwick Trading Co* • UKN
WEARY WILLIE'S BIRTHDAY • 1916 • Currier Frank • SHT • USA
WEARY WILLIE'S RAGS • 1914 • *Lubin* • USA
WEARY WILLIE'S WILES • 1903 • *Paul R. W.* • UKN
WEARY'S CHRISTMAS DINNER • 1908 • *Vitagraph* • USA
WEARY'S REVENGE • 1912 • *Majestic* • USA
WEASEL STOP • 1956 • McKimson Robert • ANS • USA
WEASEL WHILE YOU WORK • 1958 • McKimson Robert • ANS • USA
WEATHER FORECAST • 1934 • Cherry Evelyn Spice • DOC • UKN
WEATHER MAGIC • 1965 • Anzilotti Cosmo • ANS • USA
WEATHER PICTURE, THE • 1984 • Dodd Thomas • DOC • CND
WEATHER WIZARDS • 1939 • Zinnemann Fred • SHT • USA
WEAVER OF CLAYBANK • 1915 • *Christy Ivan* • USA
WEAVER OF DREAMS • 1918 • Collins John H. • USA
WEAVER OF MIRACLES, THE see **TEJEDOR DE MILAGROS, EL** • 1961
WEAVERS, THE • 1958 • D'Avino Carmen • SHT • USA
WEAVERS, THE see **WEBER, DIE** • 1927
WEAVERS OF FORTUNE • 1922 • Rooke Arthur • UKN • RACING LUCK
WEAVERS OF LIFE • 1917 • Warren Edward • USA
WEAVERS: WASN'T THAT A TIME!, THE see **WASN'T THAT A TIME!** • 1981
WEB see **MISSION MANILA** • 1988
WEB, THE • 1913 • Ince Ralph • USA
WEB, THE • 1917 • Cochrane George • SHT • USA
WEB, THE • 1947 • Gordon Michael • USA • DARK WEB, THE
WEB, THE • 1956 • Watkins Peter • UKN
WEB, THE see **APRES LE VENT DES SABLES** • 1976
WEB OF CHANCE, THE • 1919 • Green Alfred E. • USA
WEB OF CRIME, THE • 1915 • *Saunders Jackie* • USA
WEB OF DANGER, THE • 1947 • Ford Philip • USA
WEB OF DEATH, THE see **WU TU T'IEN LO** • 1977
WEB OF DECEIT, THE • 1920 • Carewe Edwin • USA
WEB OF DESIRE, THE • 1917 • Chautard Emile • USA
WEB OF EVIDENCE (USA) see **BEYOND THIS PLACE** • 1959
WEB OF FATE • 1927 • Fitzgerald Dallas M. • USA
WEB OF FATE, A • 1914 • *Warner'S Features* • USA
WEB OF FATE, THE • 1909 • *Edison* • USA
WEB OF FATE, THE • 1916 • Gilbert Lewis • UKN
WEB OF FEAR (USA) see **CONSTANCE AUX ENFERS** • 1964
WEB OF FEAR (USA) see **YEUX CERNES, LES** • 1964
WEB OF GUILT, THE • 1916 • Horne James W. • SHT • USA
WEB OF HATE, THE • 1915 • Kent Leon D. • USA
WEB OF LIFE, THE • 1917 • *Nord Hilda* • USA
WEB OF PASSION (UKN) see **A DOUBLE TOUR** • 1959
WEB OF SUSPICION • 1959 • Varnel Max • UKN
WEB OF THE LAW, THE • 1923 • Gibson Tom • USA
WEB OF THE SPIDER (USA) see **NELLA STRETTA MORSA DEL RAGNO** • 1971
WEB OF VIOLENCE (USA) see **TRE NOTTI VIOLENTE** • 1966
WEBB PIERCE AND HIS WANDERIN' BOYS • 1955 • Cowan Will • SHT • USA
WEBER, DIE • 1927 • Zelnik Friedrich • FRG • WEAVERS, THE
WEBFOOTED FRIENDS • 1976 • Blotnick Elihu • USA
WEBS • 1972 • Prince Lorraine • ANS • USA
WEBS OF STEEL • 1925 • McGowan J. P. • USA
WEBSTER BOY, THE • 1962 • Chaffey Don • UKN • MIDDLE OF NOWHERE
WECHMA • 1970 • Benani Hamid • MRC • TRACES ○ WASHMA

WECKLEY & SNOOKUMS • 1913 • *Mcmanus George/ Cohl Emile (P)* • ASS • USA
WEDAA YA BONAPARTE, AL- see **ADIEU BONAPARTE** • 1984
WEDDED ANNIVERSARY • 1934 • *Lamont Molly* • SHT • UKN
WEDDED BENEATH THE WAVES • 1910 • *Gaumont* • SHT • FRN
WEDDED BLITZ • 1942 • James Henry • SHT • USA
WEDDING • 1905 • *Bitzer Billy (Ph)* • USA
WEDDING • 1986 • Bakalov Slav • ANS • BUL
WEDDING see **AUORE** • 1962
WEDDING 83 see **PERKAWINAN 83** • 1983
WEDDING, A • 1978 • Altman Robert • USA
WEDDING, THE • 1937 • Garin Erast • USS
WEDDING, THE • 1990 • Afkhami Behruz • IRN
WEDDING, THE see **SVADBA** • 1964
WEDDING, THE see **MAGUL PORUWA** • 1967
WEDDING, THE see **AFRAH** • 1968
WEDDING, THE see **SVADBA** • 1973
WEDDING, THE see **RANJANG PENGANTIN** • 1974
WEDDING, THE see **BODA, LA** • 1986
WEDDING, THE (UKN) see **WESELE** • 1972
WEDDING AT BRANNA see **BROLLOPET I BRANNA** • 1927
WEDDING AT SOLO see **BROLLOPET PA SOLO** • 1946
WEDDING AT ULFASA see **BROLLOPET PA ULFASA** • 1910
WEDDING BELL, THE • 1911 • *Edison* • USA
WEDDING BELLS • 1921 • Withey Chet • USA
WEDDING BELLS • 1933 • *Mintz Charles (P)* • ANS • USA
WEDDING BELLS see **HERE COME THE HUGGETTS** • 1948
WEDDING BELLS AND LUNATICS • 1918 • *Burns Neal* • SHT • USA
WEDDING BELLS AND ROARING LIONS • 1917 • *Sunshine* • SHT • USA
WEDDING BELLS OUT OF TUNE • 1921 • St. Clair Malcolm • SHT • USA
WEDDING BELLS SHALL RING • 1915 • Curtis Allen • USA
WEDDING BELLS (UKN) see **ROYAL WEDDING** • 1950
WEDDING BELTS • 1940 • Fleischer Dave • ANS • USA
WEDDING BILL$ • 1927 • Kenton Erle C. • USA
WEDDING BILLS • 1940 • Mack Roy • SHT • USA
WEDDING BLUES • 1920 • Christie Al • USA
WEDDING BREAKFAST (UKN) see **CATERED AFFAIR, THE** • 1956
WEDDING BY CORRESPONDENCE, A see **MARIAGE PAR CORRESPONDANCE** • 1904
WEDDING DAY • 1963 • Biggs Julian, Howe John, Lemieux Hector • CND
WEDDING DAY see **BAISHEY SHRAVANA** • 1960
WEDDING DAY see **BROLLOPSDAGEN** • 1960
WEDDING DAY, THE see **SHIJIP KANUN NAL** • 1957
WEDDING DAY, THE see **DIA DE LA BODA, EL** • 1968
WEDDING DAY, THE see **PELLI ROJU** • 1968
WEDDING DAY, THE see **JOUR DE NOCES** • 1971
WEDDING DRESS, THE • 1912 • Dwan Allan • USA • HER WEDDING DRESS
WEDDING DURING THE FRENCH REVOLUTION, A see **REVOLUTIONSBRYLLUP** • 1909
WEDDING EVE • 1935 • Barnett Charles • UKN
WEDDING GIFT, THE • 1971 • Bonniere Rene • SHT • CND
WEDDING GOWN, THE • 1913 • Kirkwood James • USA
WEDDING GROUP • 1936 • Bryce Alex, Gullan Campbell • UKN • WRATH OF JEALOUSY (USA)
WEDDING GUEST, THE • 1916 • Jaccard Jacques • SHT • USA
WEDDING II • 1982 • Umboh Wim • INN
WEDDING IN BLOOD (USA) see **NOCES ROUGES, LES** • 1972
WEDDING IN GALILEE see **NOCE EN GALILEE** • 1988
WEDDING IN HELL see **BODA EN EL INFIERNO** • 1941
WEDDING IN JAPAN (USA) see **TOPRINI NASZ** • 1939
WEDDING IN MALINOVKA see **SVADBA V MALINOVKE** • 1967
WEDDING IN THE ECCENTRIC CLUB, THE see **HOCHZEIT IM EXCENTRICCLUB, DIE** • 1917
WEDDING IN TOPRIN see **TOPRINI NASZ** • 1939
WEDDING IN WHITE • 1972 • Fruet William • CND • MARIAGE EN BLANC
WEDDING JOURNEY, THE (USA) see **HOCHZEITRISE, DIE** • 1939
WEDDING KNIGHT, A • 1966 • Post Howard • ANS • USA
WEDDING MARCH see **KEKKON KOSHINKYOKU** • 1951
WEDDING MARCH see **MARCIA NUZIALE** • 1966
WEDDING MARCH, THE • 1912 • *Rex* • USA
WEDDING MARCH, THE • 1928 • von Stroheim Erich • USA
WEDDING NIGHT see **BROLLOPSNATTEN** • 1947
WEDDING NIGHT see **NUIT DE NOCES** • 1949
WEDDING NIGHT see **BROLLOPSNATT, EN** • 1959
WEDDING NIGHT see **NIHTA GAMOU** • 1967
WEDDING NIGHT, THE • 1935 • Vidor King • USA
WEDDING NIGHT AT STJARNEHOV see **BROLLOPSNATT PA STJARNEHOV, EN** • 1934
WEDDING NIGHT ESSAY, A see **ENSAYO DE UNA NOCHE DE BODAS** • 1968
WEDDING NIGHT IN THE DRIZZLE see **HOCHZEITSNACHT IM REGEN** • 1969
WEDDING NIGHT IN THE RAIN see **HOCHZEITSNACHT IM REGEN** • 1969
WEDDING NIGHT (USA) see **I CAN'T.. I CAN'T** • 1969
WEDDING NIGHTS see **TUNG-FANG YEN SHIH** • 1976
WEDDING OF HIMMET AGA, THE • 1916 • TRK
WEDDING OF IAN KNUCK, THE • 1935 • Ivanov Alexander • USS
WEDDING OF LILI MARLENE, THE • 1953 • Crabtree Arthur • UKN
WEDDING OF MR. MARZIPAN see **ZENIDBA GOSPODINA MARCIPANA** • 1963
WEDDING OF MRS. MARZIPAN see **ZENIDBA GOSPODINA MARCIPANA** • 1963
WEDDING OF PRUDENCE, THE • 1914 • *Essanay* • USA
WEDDING OF RASMINE, THE see **RASMINES BRYLLUP** • 1935
WEDDING OF SANDY MCNAB, THE • 1907 • Gilbert Arthur • UKN
WEDDING OF THE BEAR see **LOKIS** • 1926
WEDDING OF THE PAINTED DOLL • *La Roque Rod* • USA
WEDDING OF ZEIN, THE see **URS ZAYN** • 1976
WEDDING ON THE FRINGE, THE • 1989 • Kassissoglou Vassilis • GRC
WEDDING ON THE VOLGA, THE • 1929 • *Schweid Mark* • USA
WEDDING ON WALTONS MOUNTAIN, A • 1982 • Philips Lee • TVM • USA
WEDDING PARTY, THE • 1969 • De Palma Brian, Munroe Cynthia, Leach Wilford • USA
WEDDING PARTY, THE see **BRYLLUPSFESTEN** • 1989
WEDDING PARTY, THE see **LEEDVERMAAK** • 1989
WEDDING PARTY -SWEDISH STYLE • 1973 • Halldoff Jan • SWD
WEDDING PRESENT • 1936 • Wallace Richard • USA
WEDDING PRESENT see **TURKISCHEN GURKEN, DIE** • 1963
WEDDING REHEARSAL • 1932 • Korda Alexander • UKN
WEDDING RIGHT-UP, THE • 1913 • *Johnstone Lamar* • USA
WEDDING RING, THE see **PRSTYNEK** • 1944
WEDDING RING, THE see **ALLIANCE, L'** • 1970
WEDDING RINGS • 1929 • Beaudine William • USA • DARK SWAN, THE
WEDDING SALESMAN, THE see **BONTA NO KEKKON YA** • 1968
WEDDING SECOND TIME AROUND • 1975 • Natanson Georgi • USS
WEDDING SONG, THE • 1925 • Hale Alan • USA
WEDDING -SWEDISH STYLE (UKN) see **BROLLOPSBESVAR** • 1964
WEDDING THAT DIDN'T COME OFF, THE • 1908 • Rosenthal Joe • UKN
WEDDING THAT DIDN'T COME OFF, THE • 1910 • Bouwmeester Theo? • UKN
WEDDING TOOK PLACE.., A see **BYLO WESELE..** • 1968
WEDDING TRIP FROM MONTREAL THROUGH CANADA TO HONG KONG, A • 1910 • *Edison* • USA
WEDDING TROUGH see **VASE DE NOCES** • 1974
WEDDING UNDER SUPERVISION see **SVATBA JAKO REMEN** • 1967
WEDDING WITH STRINGS • 1965 • Kohout Pavel • CZC
WEDDING WITHOUT A RING see **SVATBA BEZ PRSTYNKU** • 1972
WEDDING WORRIES • 1941 • Cahn Edward L. • SHT • USA
WEDDING YELLS • 1927 • Lamont Charles • SHT • USA
WEDDINGS AND BABIES • 1958 • Engel Morris • USA
WEDDINGS ARE WONDERFUL • 1938 • Rogers Maclean • UKN
WEDERZIJDS • 1964 • Rutten Gerard • NTH • WE.. TOGETHER!
WEDGE CLAMP • 1986 • Skagen Peter • DOC • CND
WEDGE-TAILED EAGLE, THE • 1934 • Harvey Frank • SHT • ASL
WEDIJVER, DE • 1966 • Dhondt A. M. • BLG
WEDLOCK • 1918 • Worsley Wallace • USA
WEDLOCK HOUSE: AN INTERCOURSE • 1959 • Brakhage Stan • SHT • USA
WEDLUG ROZKAZU • 1959 • Trzos-Rastawiecki Andrzej • DOC • PLN • ACCORDING TO ORDERS ○ YES, SIR
WEDNESDAY • 1972 • van der Lecq Bas • NTH
WEDNESDAY CHILDREN, THE • 1973 • West Robert D. • USA
WEDNESDAY LUCK see **WEDNESDAY'S LUCK** • 1936
WEDNESDAY MORNING see **CAHILL -U.S. MARSHAL** • 1973
WEDNESDAY'S CHILD • 1934 • Robertson John S. • USA
WEDNESDAY'S CHILD (USA) see **FAMILY LIFE** • 1971
WEDNESDAY'S LUCK • 1936 • Pearson George • UKN • WEDNESDAY LUCK
WEDTIME STORIES • 1943 • Holmes Ben • SHT • USA
WEDTIME STORY, A • 1936 • Goodwins Leslie • SHT • USA
WEE-GEE BROAD • 1967 • *Kirt Films International* • USA
WEE GEORDIE (USA) see **GEORDIE** • 1955
WEE LADY BETTY • 1917 • Miller Charles • USA
WEE MACGREGOR'S SWEETHEART, THE • 1922 • Pearson George • UKN
WEE MEN, THE • 1947 • Tytla Bill • ANS • USA
WEE SANDY • 1962 • Reiniger Lotte • ANS • UKN
WEE WEE, MONSIEUR • 1938 • Lord Del • SHT • USA
WEE WILLIE WILDCAT • 1953 • Lundy Dick • ANS • USA
WEE WILLIE WINKIE • 1937 • Ford John • USA
WEED • 1972 • De Renzy Alex • DOC • USA
WEED, THE see **UNKRAUT, DAS** • 1962
WEED OF CRIME, THE • 1964 • Fukuda Jun • JPN
WEEDS • 1973 • Lim Kwon-Taek • SKR
WEEDS • 1987 • Hancock John • USA • HONOUR AMONG THIEVES
WEEDS see **BURYAN** • 1967
WEEK AT SEA see **SETTIMANA AL MARE, LA** • 1980
WEEK END • 1967 • McNeil David • BLG
WEEK-END • 1968 • Godard Jean-Luc • FRN, ITL • WEEK END: UNA DONNA E UN UOMO DA SABATO A DOMENICO (ITL) ○ WEEKEND
WEEK-END, THE • 1920 • Cox George L. • USA
WEEK-END AT HAPPYHURST, A • 1914 • Seay Charles M. • USA
WEEK-END IM PARADIES • 1932 • Land Robert • FRG
WEEK-END IN HAVANA • 1941 • Lang Walter • USA
WEEK-END MADNESS (UKN) see **AUGUST WEEK-END** • 1936
WEEK-END MARRIAGE • 1932 • Freeland Thornton • USA • WORKING WIVES (UKN)
WEEK END PROIBITO DI UNA FAMIGLIA QUASI PER BENE (ITL) see **CESAR GRANDBLAISE** • 1970
WEEK-END SHOPPING • 1917 • *Ruge Billy* • SHT • USA
WEEK-END SUR DEUX, UN • 1989 • Garcia Nicole • FRN
WEEK-END TOTAL • Calderon Gerald • ANS • FRN
WEEK END: UNA DONNA E UN UOMO DA SABATO A DOMENICO (ITL) see **WEEK-END** • 1968
WEEK-END WITH DEATH see **FIM DE SEMANA COM A MORTE** • 1967
WEEK-ENDS DE CAROLINE, LES • 1980 • Novembre Adrien • FRN
WEEK-ENDS DE NERON, LES (FRN) see **MIO FIGLIO NERONE** • 1956
WEEK-ENDS MALEFIQUES DU COMTE ZAROFF, LES • 1975 • Lemoine Michel • FRN • SEVEN WOMEN FOR SATAN
WEEK ENDS ONLY • 1932 • Crosland Alan • USA
WEEK IN THE QUIET HOUSE see **TYDEN V TICHEM DOME** • 1947
WEEK OF THE ASSASSIN, THE see **SEMANA DEL ASESINO, LA** • 1972
WEEK OF THE MADMEN, THE • 1969 • Cocea Dinu • RMN
WEEKEND • 1964 • Kjaerulff-Schmidt Palle • DNM
WEEKEND • 1972 • SAF
WEEKEND • 1972 • Lavut Martin (c/d) • SER • CND
WEEKEND • 1972 • Manuel Pierre, Peche Jean-Jacques • BLG
WEEKEND • 1990 • Pilz Michael • AUS
WEEKEND see **WOCHENENDE** • 1929
WEEKEND see **WEEK-END** • 1968
WEEKEND A ZUYDCOOTE • 1964 • Verneuil Henri • FRN, ITL • WEEKEND AT DUNKIRK (USA)
WEEKEND AT DUNKIRK (USA) see **WEEKEND A ZUYDCOOTE** • 1964
WEEKEND AT LE MANS see **BOLIDES AU MANS** • 1957
WEEKEND AT THE WALDORF • 1945 • Leonard Robert Z. • USA
WEEKEND BABYSITTER see **WEEKEND WITH THE BABYSITTER** • 1970
WEEKEND FOR A MILLION see **VIKEND ZA MILION** • 1987
WEEKEND FOR THREE • 1941 • Reis Irving • USA
WEEKEND HUSBANDS • 1924 • Griffith Edward H. • USA • PART TIME HUSBANDS
WEEKEND IN PARIS • 1961 • Donner Clive • SHT • UKN
WEEKEND IN TOPOLA see **VIKEND U TOPOLI** • 1981
WEEKEND, ITALIAN STYLE (USS) see **OMBRELLONE, L'** • 1966
WEEKEND LOVER • 1969 • Avery Dwayne • USA • WEEKEND LOVERS
WEEKEND LOVERS see **WEEKEND LOVER** • 1969
WEEKEND MILLIONAIRE (USA) see **ONCE IN A MILLION** • 1936
WEEKEND MURDERS, THE (USA) see **CONCERTO PER PISTOLA SOLISTA** • 1970
WEEKEND NUN, THE • 1972 • Szwarc Jeannot • TVM • USA
WEEKEND OF A CHAMPION • 1971 • Simon Frank • UKN
WEEKEND OF FEAR • 1966 • Danford Joe • USA
WEEKEND OF SHADOWS • 1978 • Jeffrey Tom • ASL
WEEKEND OF TERROR • 1970 • Taylor Jud • TVM • USA
WEEKEND PASS • 1944 • Yarbrough Jean • USA
WEEKEND PASS • 1984 • Bassoff Lawrence • USA
WEEKEND REBELLION • 1970 • *Mahon Barry (P)* • USA
WEEKEND SWINGERS • 1975 • Savage Allen • USA
WEEKEND WAR • 1988 • Stern Steven Hilliard • TVM • USA
WEEKEND WARRIORS • 1986 • Convy Bert • USA • HOLLYWOOD AIRFORCE BASE ○ HOLLYWOOD AIR FORCE
WEEKEND WARRIORS, THE • 1966 • *Collett Gordon* • DOC • USA
WEEKEND WITH A GIRL see **WEEKEND Z DZIEWCZYNA** • 1968
WEEKEND WITH FATHER • 1951 • Sirk Douglas • USA
WEEKEND WITH FIFI • 1969 • *Len Ramon Gar (P)* • USA
WEEKEND WITH KATE • 1989 • Nicholson Arch • ASL
WEEKEND WITH LULU, A • 1961 • Carstairs John Paddy • UKN
WEEKEND WITH THE BABYSITTER • 1970 • Henderson Don • USA • WEEKEND BABYSITTER ○ TAKE SOME GIRLS
WEEKEND WIVES • 1928 • Lachman Harry • UKN • MY WIFE'S HUSBAND
WEEKEND WIVES see **OMBRELLONE, L'** • 1966
WEEKEND Z DZIEWCZYNA • 1968 • Nasfeter Janusz • PLN • WEEKEND WITH A GIRL
WEEKENDS • 1963 • Rutkiewicz Jan • PLN
WEEKLY REELS see **KONO NEDELYA** • 1919
WEEK'S HOLIDAY, A (UKN) see **SEMAINE DE VACANCES, UNE** • 1981
WEEK'S VACATION, A (USA) see **SEMAINE DE VACANCES, UNE** • 1981
WEENIE ROAST, THE • 1931 • *Mintz Charles (P)* • ANS • USA
WEEP, MY EYES see **AGLA GOZLERIM** • 1968
WEEP, MY LIFE see **AGLAYAN BIR OMUR** • 1968
WEEP NO MORE see **WALK SOFTLY, STRANGER** • 1950
WEEP, PEOPLE OF JAPAN -THE LAST PURSUIT PLANE see **NAKE, NIHON KOKUMIN -SAIGO NO SENTOKI** • 1956
WEEPING AFFAIR see **NAKINURETA JOJI** • 1967
WEEPING BLUE SKY see **AOZURA NI NAKU** • 1931
WEEPING FOR A BANDIT see **LLANTO POR UN BANDIDO** • 1964
WEEPING WOMAN, THE see **AGLAYAN KADIN** • 1967
WEERA PURAN APPU see **VEERA PURAN APPU** • 1978
WEERGEVONDEN • 1914 • Chrispijn Louis H. • NTH • FOUND AGAIN
WEERSKANT DIE NAG • 1979 • Marx Franz • SAF
WEG CARL MARIA VON WEBERS, DER see **AUFFORDERUNG ZUM TANZ** • 1935
WEG DER ERLOSUNG, DER • 1918 • Stein Josef • FRG
WEG DER GRETE LESSEN, DER • 1919 • Biebrach Rudolf • FRG
WEG DER TRANEN, DER • 1916 • Neuss Alwin • FRG
WEG, DER ZUR VERDAMMNIS FUHRT 1, DER • 1918 • Rippert Otto • FRG • SCHICKSAL DER AENNE WOLTER, DER
WEG, DER ZUR VERDAMMNIS FUHRT 2, DER • 1919 • Rippert Otto • FRG • HYANEN DER LUST
WEG DES ANTON SCHUBART, DER • 1916 • Gros F. A. • FRG
WEG DES HERZENS, DER • 1937 • Schmidt-Gentner Willy • FRG • PRATER
WEG DES TODES, DER • 1916 • Reinert Robert • FRG
WEG DURCH DIE NACHT, DER • 1929 • Dinesen Robert • FRG
WEG IN DIE VERGANGENHEIT, DER • 1954 • Hartl Karl • AUS
WEG INS FREIE, DER • 1917 • Oswald Richard • FRG
WEG INS FREIE, DER • 1941 • Hansen Rolf • FRG • WAY TO LIBERTY, THE
WEG NAAR BRESSON, DE • 1983 • Rood Jurrien, de Boer Leo • NTH • WAY TO BRESSON, THE
WEG NACH OBEN • 1950 • Thorndike Andrew, Thorndike Annelie • GDR • WAY UP, THE
WEG NACH RIO, DER • 1931 • Noa Manfred • FRG
WEG NACH SHANGHAI, DER see **MOSKAU-SHANGHAI** • 1936
WEG OHNE UMKEHR • 1953 • Vicas Victor • FRG • NO WAY BACK (USA)
WEG ZU GOTT, DER • 1923 • Seitz Franz • FRG • SCHICKSAL DES THOMAS BALT, DAS
WEG ZU ISABEL, DER • 1939 • Engel Erich • FRG
WEG ZUM GUTEN, DER • 1915 • von Horn Andreas • FRG
WEG ZUM LICHT, DER • 1923 • von Bolvary Geza, Rosen Kurt • FRG
WEG ZUM NACHBARN • 1966 • Lenica Jan • ANS • FRG
WEG ZUM NACHBARN 1968 • 1968 • Marks Aleksandar, Jutrisa Vladimir • YGS
WEG ZUR DIR, DER • 1952 • Robbeling Harald • FRG

WEG ZUR SCHANDE, DER see **HAI-TANG** • 1930
WEG ZUR SUHNE, DER • 1915 • Schmidthassler Walter • FRG
WEGE DER LIEBE • 1924 • *Nordfilm* • FRG
WEGE DES LASTERS • 1921 • Hofer Franz • FRG
WEGE DES SCHICKSALS • 1925 • *Reinwald Grete* • FRG
WEGE DES SCHRECKENS see **LABYRINTH DES GRAUENS** • 1921
WEGE, DIE ZUR LIEBE FUHREN • 1918 • *Smolowa Sibyl* • FRG
WEGE IM ZWIELICHT • 1948 • Frohlich Gustav • FRG
WEGE IN DER NACHT • 1979 • Zanussi Krzysztof • MTV • FRG • WAYS IN THE NIGHT ○ NIGHT PATHS ○ PATHS INTO THE NIGHT ○ NACHTDIENST
WEGE UND MAUERN • 1982 • Graf Urs • SWT • WAYS AND WALLS
WEGE ZU KRAFT UND SCHONHEIT • 1925 • Prager Wilhelm • FRG • WAYS TO HEALTH AND BEAUTY
WEGE ZUR GUTEN EHE • 1933 • Trotz Adolf • FRG
WEGEN REICHTEN GESCHLOSSEN • 1968 • Hutter Hans • FRG • CLOSED BECAUSE OF WEALTH
WEGEN VERFUHRUNG MINDERJAHRIGER • 1960 • Leitner Hermann • AUS
WEGWEISER, DER • 1920 • Kottow Hans • AUS
WEH' DEM, DER LIEBT • 1951 • von Slatina Alexander • FRG
WEHE, WENN ER LOSGELASSEN • 1932 • Fric Martin, Lamac Carl • FRG, CZC • UNTER GESCHAFTSAUFSICHT
WEHE, WENN SIE LOSGELASSEN • 1926 • Froelich Carl • FRG
WEHE, WENN SIE LOSGELASSEN • 1958 • von Cziffra Geza • FRG
WEHLOSE OPFER • 1919 • Eichberg Richard • FRG
WEHRHAFTE SCHWEIZ • 1939 • Haller Hermann • SWT
WEHT DIE ANGST, SO WEHT DER WIND • 1983 • Kaufmann Manfred • AUS, FRG • WIND OF FEAR, THE
WEIB • 1920 • *Colanin Victor* • FRG
WEIB AM KREUZE, DAS • 1929 • Brignone Guido • AUS • VERGIB UNS UNSERE SCHULD
WEIB AUF DEM PANTHER, DAS • 1922 • Halm Alfred • FRG
WEIB DES PHARAO, DAS • 1921 • Lubitsch Ernst • FRG • LOVES OF PHARAOH, THE ○ PHARAOH'S WIFE ○ WIFE OF PHARAOH, THE
WEIB, EIN TIER, EIN DIAMANT, EIN • 1923 • Kobe Hanns • FRG • FUNF KAPITEL AUS EINEM ALTEN BUCH
WEIB GEGEN WEIB • 1918 • Gunsburg Arthur • FRG • MORD AN DER NEWA ODER UNTER FALSCHEM PASS
WEIB GIB ACHT! • 1925 • *Fritz Knevels-Film* • FRG
WEIB IM DSCHUNGEL • 1930 • Buchowetzki Dimitri • FRG
WEIB IN FLAMMEN • 1928 • Reichmann Max • FRG
WEIB IN NOT see **DIETER, DER MENSCH UNTER STEINEN** • 1924
WEIBCHEN, DIE • 1970 • Brynych Zbynek • FRG • FEMALES, THE
WEIBERKRIEG, DER • 1928 • Seitz Franz • FRG
WEIBERREGIMENT • 1936 • Ritter Karl • FRG
WEIBERTAUSCH, DER • 1952 • Anton Karl • FRG
WEIBSTEUFEL, DER • 1951 • Liebeneiner Wolfgang • AUS • DEVIL WOMAN
WEIBSTEUFEL, DER • 1966 • Tressler Georg • AUS • DEVIL OF A WOMAN, A
WEIDENMANNSJAHR • 1925 • *Messter-Ostermayr-Film* • FRG
WEIDMANNSHELL see **WILDERER, DER** • 1925
WEIGHED IN THE BALANCE • 1913 • *Moran Lee* • USA
WEIGHED IN THE BALANCE • 1915 • *Thanhouser* • USA
WEIGHED IN THE BALANCE • 1916 • McGill Lawrence?, Hansel Howell? • SHT • USA
WEIGHED IN THE SCALE • 1911 • *Reliance* • USA
WEIGHING THE BABY • 1903 • *Bitzer Billy (Ph)* • USA
WEIGHT FOR ME • 1955 • *Halas John (P)* • ANS • UKN
WEIGHT OF A CROWN • 1914 • Myers Harry • USA
WEIGHT OF A FEATHER, THE • 1912 • *Ridgely Cleo* • USA
WEIGHTS AND MEASURES • 1914 • *Kerrigan J. Warren* • USA
WEIGHTY MATTER FOR A DETECTIVE, A • 1915 • Seay Charles M. • USA
WEIHNACHT • 1963 • Klick Roland • SHT • FRG
WEIL DU ARM BIST, MUSST DU FRUHER STERBEN • 1956 • May Paul • FRG
WEIL DU ES BIST • 1925 • Werckmeister Hans • FRG
WEIL ICH DICH LIEBE • 1918 • *Kolberg Ally* • FRG
WEIN, WEIB, GESANG • 1924 • Achsel Willy • FRG
WEINE NICHT, MUTTER • 1918 • Raffay Iwa? • FRG
WEINIGER'S LAST NIGHT • 1990 • Manker Paulus • AUS
WEIR-FALCON SAGA, THE • 1970 • Brakhage Stan • USA
WEIRD CAT OF NINE LIVES • SKR
WEIRD DEATH TRAP AT UTSUNOMIYA see **KAII UTSUNOMIYA TSURITENJO** • 1956
WEIRD LOVE MAKERS, THE (USA) see **KYONETSU NO KISETSU** • 1960
WEIRD NEMESIS, THE • 1915 • Jaccard Jacques • USA
WEIRD ONE, THE see **WEIRD ONES, THE** • 1962
WEIRD ONES, THE • 1962 • Boyette Pat • USA • WEIRD ONE, THE
WEIRD SCIENCE • 1985 • Hughes John • USA
WEIRD SYMPHONY • 1908 • *Pathe* • FRN
WEIRD TALES see **KWAIDAN** • 1964
WEIRD WEIRDO (UKN) see **GRAND CEREMONIAL, LE** • 1968
WEIRD, WICKED WORLD see **PELO NEL MONDO, IL** • 1964
WEIRD WOMAN • 1944 • Le Borg Reginald • USA
WEIRD WORLD OF L S D, THE • 1967 • Ground Robert • USA
WEISS HAUT AUF SCHWARZEM MARKT • 1969 • FRG
WEISSE ABENTEUER, DAS • 1952 • Rabenalt Arthur M. • FRG
WEISSE DAMON, DER • 1932 • Gerron Kurt • FRG • RAUSCHGIFT ○ WHITE DEMON, THE
WEISSE FRACHT FUR HONGKONG • 1964 • Ashley Helmut, Stegani Giorgio • FRG, ITL, FRN • DA 077 CRIMINALI A HONG KONG (ITL) ○ OPERATION HONG KONG (USA) ○ MYSTERE DE LA JONQUE ROUGE, LE (FRN) ○ SECRET AGENT 077 ○ WHITE CARGO FOR HONG KONG ○ WHITE CARGO
WEISSE FRAU DES MAHARADSCHA, DIE see **LIEBE DES MAHARADSCHA, DIE** • 1936
WEISSE GEISHA, DIE • 1926 • Heiland Heinz Karl, Andersen Valdemar • FRG
WEISSE GOTT, DER • 1931 • Schneevoigt George • FRG, DNM
WEISSE HOLLE MONTBLANC see **FEGEFEUER DER LIEBE** • 1951
WEISSE HOLLE VOM PIZ PALU, DIE • 1929 • Fanck Arnold, Pabst G. W. • FRG • WHITE HELL OF PITZ PALU, THE
WEISSE HOLLE VOM PIZ PALU, DIE • 1935 • Fanck Arnold, Pabst G. W. • FRG
WEISSE MAJESTAT, DIE • 1933 • Kutter Anton • FRG • WHITE MAJESTY
WEISSE PFAU, DER • 1920 • Dupont E. A. • FRG • WHITE PEACOCK, THE
WEISSE RAUSCH, DER • 1931 • Fanck Arnold • FRG • WHITE ECSTASY, THE ○ WHITE FRENZY, THE ○ SKI CHASE, THE ○ WHITE DRUNKENNESS, THE ○ WHITE FLAME, THE
WEISSE REISE • 1980 • Schroeter Werner • FRG, FRN, SWT
WEISSE ROSE, DIE • 1915 • Hofer Franz • FRG
WEISSE ROSE, DIE • 1920 • Obal Max? • FRG
WEISSE ROSE, DIE • 1983 • Verhoeven Michael • FRG • WHITE ROSE, THE
WEISSE ROSEN • 1914 • Gad Urban • FRG
WEISSE SCHATTEN • 1957 • Kautner Helmut • FRG
WEISSE SCHRECKEN, DER • 1917 • Piel Harry • FRG
WEISSE SCHWESTER see **ELISABETH UND IHR NARR** • 1933
WEISSE SKLAVEN • 1936 • Anton Karl • FRG • PANZERKREUZER SEWASTOPOL
WEISSE SKLAVIN 1, DIE • 1921 • Teuber Arthur • FRG • ZWEI EIDE
WEISSE SKLAVIN 2, DIE • 1921 • Teuber Arthur • FRG • SCHWEIGEN DER GROSSTADT, DAS
WEISSE SKLAVIN, DIE • 1927 • Genina Augusto • FRG • WHITE SLAVE, THE
WEISSE SONATE, DIE • 1928 • Seemann Louis • AUS
WEISSE SPINNE, DIE • 1927 • Boese Carl • FRG
WEISSE SPINNE, DIE • 1963 • Reinl Harald • FRG • WHITE SPIDER, THE (USA)
WEISSE TEUFEL, DER • 1930 • Volkov Alexander • FRG • WHITE DEVIL, THE (USA)
WEISSE TOD, DER • 1921 • Gartner Adolf • FRG
WEISSE TOD IN HIMALAYA, DER see **HIMATSCHAL, DER THRON DER GOTTER** • 1931
WEISSE TRAUM, DER • 1943 • von Cziffra Geza • FRG
WEISSE WASCHE • 1942 • Heidemann Paul • FRG
WEISSE WOLKE CAROLIN • Losansky Rolf • GDR • WHITE CLOUD CAROLINE
WEISSE WUSTE, DIE • 1922 • Wendt Ernst • FRG
WEISSEBLAUE LOWE, DER • 1952 • Jacobs Werner, Fischer Olf • FRG
WEISSEN ROSEN VON RAVENSBERG, DIE • 1919 • Chrisander Nils • FRG
WEISSEN ROSEN VON RAVENSBERG, DIE • 1929 • Meinert Rudolf • FRG
WEISSER FLIEDER • 1940 • Rabenalt Arthur M. • FRG
WEISSER HOLUNDER • 1957 • May Paul • FRG
WEISSES BLUT • 1959 • Kolditz Gottfried • GDR • WHITE BLOOD
WEISSES GOLD • 1918 • Mendel Georg Victor • FRG
WEISSES GOLD see **ANGELA** • 1949
WEISST DU NOCH? • 1924 • Krause Karl Otto • FRG
WEIT IST DER WEG • 1960 • Schleif Wolfgang • FRG
WEITE LAND, DAS • 1970 • Beauvais Peter • AUS
WEITE LAND, DAS • 1987 • Bondy Luc • AUS, FRG • DISTANT LAND, THE
WEITE STRASSEN -STILLE LIEBE • *Hoffmann Justa* • GDR • WIDE ROADS -QUIET LOVE
WEITE WEG, DER see **SCHICKSAL IN KETTEN** • 1946
WELCHE BILDER -KLEINE ENGEL -WANDERN DURCH DEIN ANGESICHT? • Hassler Jurg, Hassler Ursula • DOC • SWT
WELCOME BURGLAR, THE • 1909 • Griffith D. W. • USA
WELCOME CHILDREN • 1921 • Mathews Harry C. • USA
WELCOME DANGER • 1929 • Bruckman Clyde • USA
WELCOME DOLLARS see **KALOS ILTHE TO DHOLLARIO** • 1967
WELCOME GRANGER • 1925 • Ruggles Wesley • SHT • USA
WELCOME HOME • 1912 • Plumb Hay? • UKN
WELCOME HOME • 1917 • *Keystone* • SHT • USA
WELCOME HOME • 1917 • Clements Roy • *Nestor* • SHT • USA
WELCOME HOME • 1919 • *Christie* • SHT • USA
WELCOME HOME • 1925 • Cruze James • USA
WELCOME HOME • 1935 • Tinling James • USA
WELCOME HOME • 1989 • Schaffner Franklin J. • USA
WELCOME HOME see **VLAST VITA** • 1945
WELCOME HOME, BOBBY • 1986 • Wise Herbert • TVM • USA
WELCOME HOME, BROTHER CHARLES • 1975 • Fanaka Jamaa • USA
WELCOME HOME JOHNNY • 1974 • Howard James • USA
WELCOME HOME, JOHNNY BRISTOL • 1971 • McCowan George • TVM • USA
WELCOME HOME, ROXY CARMICHAEL • 1990 • Abrahams Jim • USA
WELCOME HOME, SOLDIER BOYS • 1972 • Compton Richard • USA • FIVE DAYS HOME
WELCOME HOME (UKN) see **SNAFU** • 1945
WELCOME IN VIENNA • 1986 • Corti Axel • AUS
WELCOME INTRUDER, A • 1913 • *Mcdowell Claire* • USA
WELCOME KOSTYA! (USA) see **DOBRO POZHALOVAT** • 1964
WELCOME, LITTLE STRANGER • 1919 • Metcalfe Earl • SHT • USA
WELCOME LITTLE STRANGER • 1941 • Rasinski Connie • ANS • USA
WELCOME, MR. BEDDOES see **MAN COULD GET KILLED, A** • 1966
WELCOME, MR. MARSHALL see **BIENVENIDO, MR. MARSHALL** • 1952
WELCOME MR. WASHINGTON • 1944 • Hiscott Leslie • UKN
WELCOME NUDNIK • 1966 • Deitch Gene • ANS • USA
WELCOME OF THE UNWELCOME, THE • 1911 • *Vitagraph* • USA
WELCOME STRANGER • 1924 • Young James • USA
WELCOME STRANGER • 1947 • Nugent Elliott • USA
WELCOME STRANGER (UKN) see **ACROSS THE SIERRAS** • 1941
WELCOME THE QUEEN! • 1954 • Thomas Howard • UKN
WELCOME TO 18 • 1987 • Carr Terry • USA
WELCOME TO ARROW BEACH • 1973 • Harvey Laurence • USA • AND NO-ONE WOULD BELIEVE HER ○ NO ONE WOULD BELIEVE HER ○ TENDER FLESH ○ DERANGED
WELCOME TO BLOOD CITY • 1977 • Sasdy Peter • UKN, CND
WELCOME TO BOHEMIA • 1915 • Van Wally • USA
WELCOME TO BRITAIN • 1943 • Asquith Anthony, Meredith Burgess • DOC • UKN
WELCOME TO BRITAIN • 1976 • Lewin Ben • DOC • UKN
WELCOME TO CANADA • 1990 • Smith John N. • CND
WELCOME TO GERMANY see **PASSAGIER, DER** • 1988
WELCOME TO HARD TIMES • 1967 • Kennedy Burt • USA • KILLER ON A HORSE (UKN)
WELCOME TO L.A. • 1977 • Rudolph Alan • USA
WELCOME TO LIFE see **VELKOMMEN TIL LIVET** • 1987
WELCOME TO MY NIGHTMARE • 1976 • Winters David • DOC • UKN
WELCOME TO OUR CITY • 1922 • Townley Robert H. • USA
WELCOME TO PUBLIC SERVICE • 1985 • Armstrong Mary • DOC • CND
WELCOME TO THE CLUB • 1970 • Shenson Walter • UKN
WELCOME TO THE PARADE • 1987 • Clarfield Stuart • CND
WELCOME TO XANADU see **SWEET HOSTAGE** • 1975
WELDED FRIENDSHIP, A • 1913 • Parker Lem B. • USA
WELFARE • 1975 • Wiseman Frederick • USA
WELFARE OF THE WORKERS • 1940 • Jennings Humphrey, Jackson Pat • DOC • UKN
WELIKATARA • 1971 • Nihalsingha D. B. • SLN
WELKER LORBEER • 1916 • Schmidthassler Walter • FRG
WELL, THE • 1913 • O'Sullivan Tony • USA
WELL, THE • 1951 • Popkin Leo C., Rouse Russell • USA
WELL, THE • 1964 • *Cga Prods.* • ANS • USA
WELL, THE see **KUYU** • 1968
WELL, THE see **POZO, EL** • 1972
WELL, THE see **JING** • 1988
WE'LL BE WAITING FOR YOU, BOY! see **ZHDYOM TEBYA, PAREN!** • 1973
WE'LL BURY YOU • 1962 • Leewood Jack, Thomas Jack W. • DOC • USA
WELL, BY GEORGE! • 1934 • Schwarzwald Milton • SHT • USA
WE'LL CALL HIM ANDREA see **LO CHIAMEREMO ANDREA** • 1972
WELL-DIGGER'S DAUGHTER, THE (USA) see **FILLE DU PUISATIER, LA** • 1940
WELL DONE, HENRY • 1937 • Noy Wilfred • UKN
WELL DONE, SCOUTS! • 1911 • Aylott Dave • UKN
WELL-EARNED DRINK, A • 1909 • *Anglo-American Films* • UKN
WE'LL EAT THE FRUIT OF PARADISE see **OVOCE STROMU RAJSKYCH JIME** • 1969
WELL-FED MAN, THE • 1970 • Mimica Vatroslav • YGS
WELL-FILLED DAY, A see **JOURNEE BIEN REMPLIE, UNE** • 1973
WE'LL FINISH THE JOB • Gurney Philip • DOC • UKN
WE'LL GET BY TILL MONDAY see **DOZHIVYOM DO PONEDYELNIKA** • 1968
WELL, GRANDMA'S DEAD see **TOH, E MORTA LA NONNA!** • 1969
WELL-GROOMED BRIDE, THE • 1946 • Lanfield Sidney • USA
WELL GUARDED TRAINS see **OSTRE SLEDOVANE VLAKY** • 1966
WELL, I'LL BE.. • 1919 • Semon Larry • SHT • USA
WELL I'M - • 1915 • Collins Edwin J. • UKN
WELL MATCHED • 1912 • *Steppling John* • USA
WELL-MEANT DECEPTION, A • 1913 • *Majestic* • USA
WE'LL MEET AGAIN • 1942 • Brandon Phil • UKN
WE'LL MEET ON SUNDAY see **ZOBACZYMY SIE W NIEDZIELE** • 1959
WE'LL NEVER SURRENDER see **NUNCA NOS RENDIREMOS** • 1986
WELL OF LOVE • Hively Jack • USA
WELL OILED • 1947 • Lundy Dick • ANS • USA
WELL PAID STROLL, A see **DOBRE PLACENA PROCHAZKA** • 1965
WELL PLANNED WEST END JEWEL ROBBERY, A • 1919 • Carlton Frank • UKN
WELL SICK MAN, THE • 1913 • Dawley J. Searle • USA
WE'LL SMILE AGAIN • 1942 • Baxter John • UKN
WELL SPENT LIFE, A • 1971 • Blank Les, Gerson Skip • DOC • USA
WELL-SPRING OF MY WORLD see **HERFRA MIN VERDEN GAR** • 1976
WE'LL TAKE HER CHILDREN IN AMONGST OUR OWN • 1915 • Longford Raymond • ASL
WELL-TO-DO GENTLEMAN, A see **LEPSI PAN** • 1971
WELL! WELL! • 1914 • *Asher Max* • USA
WELL.. WELL.. see **OJ OJ OJ..** • 1966
WELL WORN DAFFY • 1965 • McKimson Robert • ANS • USA
WELL, YOUNG MAN? see **HOGY ALLUNK, FIATALEMBER?** • 1963
WELLEN DER LEIDENSCHAFT • 1930 • Gaidarow Wladimir • FRG • KURS AUF DIE EHE
WELLEN SCHWEIGEN, DIE • 1915 • *Porten Henny* • FRG
WELLINGTON • 1957 • Boigelot Jacques • BLG
WELLINGTON see **IRON DUKE, THE** • 1935
WELLINGTON MYSTERY, THE see **WELLINGTONI REJTELY** • 1919
WELLINGTON: THE DUEL SCANDAL see **SECRET LIVES OF THE BRITISH PRIME MINISTERS: THE IRON DUKE, THE** • 1983
WELLINGTONI REJTELY • 1919 • Curtiz Michael • HNG • WELLINGTON MYSTERY, THE
WELLS FARGO • 1937 • Lloyd Frank • USA
WELLS FARGO DAYS • 1944 • Wright Mack V. • SHT • USA
WELLS FARGO GUNMASTER • 1951 • Ford Philip • USA
WELLS OF PARADISE, THE • 1915 • Chatterton Thomas • USA
WELLSPRING OF MY YOUTH see **HERFRA MIN VERDEN GAR** • 1976
WELSH RABBIT, A • 1903 • *Osterman Kathryn* • USA
WELSH SINGER, A • 1915 • Edwards Henry • UKN
WELSHED -A DERBY DAY INCIDENT • 1903 • Collins Alf • UKN

WELSTADTNACHE see **SCHATTEN DER WELTSTADT** • 1925
WELT AM DRAHT • 1973 • Fassbinder R. W. • FRG • WORLD ON A WIRE
WELT DES SCHEINS, DIE • 1920 • Klein-Rohden Rudolf • FRG
WELT DREHT SICH VERKEHRT, DIE • 1947 • Hubler-Kahla J. A. • AUS
WELT IN FLAMMEN 1, DIE • 1923 • Chrisander Nils • FRG • HASS UND LIEBE
WELT IN FLAMMEN 2, DIE • 1923 • Chrisander Nils • FRG
WELT OHNE HUNGER, DIE • 1920 • Wellin Arthur • FRG
WELT OHNE KRIEG (AUS DEN GEHEIMDOKUMENTEN DES PROF. DR. BARNEY) see **KAMPFENDE GEWALTEN ODER WELT OHNE KRIEG** • 1920
WELT OHNE LIEBE, DIE see **DIKTATUR DER LIEBE 2, DIE** • 1921
WELT OHNE LIEBE (DIE FRAU OHNE HERZ), EINE see **DIKTATUR DER LIEBE 2, DIE** • 1921
WELT OHNE MASKE, DIE • 1934 • Piel Harry • FRG • WORLD WITHOUT A MASK, THE
WELT OHNE WAFFEN • 1918 • Wegener Paul • DOC • FRG
WELT OHNE WAFFEN, DIE • 1927 • Bock-Stieber Gernot • FRG • ABRUSTUNG
WELT UND HALBWELT see **GOLDENE ABGRUND, DER** • 1927
WELT WILL BELOGEN SEIN, DIE • 1926 • Felner Peter Paul • FRG • MANN MIT DEM SPLITTER, DER
WELT WILL BETROGEN SEIN, DIE • 1925 • Linke Edmund • FRG
WELTBRAND • 1920 • Gad Urban • FRG • CHRISTIAN WAHNSCHAFFE 1
WELTERUSTEN SCHAT • 1987 • Kos Helga, Vonk Jose • ANS • NTH • GOODNIGHT DARLING
WELTKRIEG 1, DER • 1927 • Lasko Leo • FRG
WELTKRIEG 2, DER • 1927 • Lasko Leo • FRG
WELTMEISTER, DER • 1919 • Lund Erik • FRG
WELTRATSEL MENSCH, DAS see **DARWIN** • 1919
WELTRAUMSCHIFF I STARTET • 1940 • Kutter Anton • FRG
WELTREKORD IM SEITENSPRUNG • 1940 • Zoch Georg • FRG
WELTSPIEGEL, DER • 1918 • Pick Lupu • FRG
WELTSTRASSE SEE –WELTHAFEN HAMBURG see **HAMBURG: WELTSTRASSE SEE** • 1938
WELTTHEATER–SALZBURG ZUR FESTSPIELZEIT • 1950 • Zehenthofer Max • AUS
WEM GEHORT DIE WELT see **KUHLE WAMPE** • 1932
WEM GEHORT MEINE FRAU? • 1929 • Lowenstein Hans Otto • AUS
WEM NIE DURCH LIEBE LEID GESCHAH! • 1922 • Schall Heinz • FRG
WEM NIE VON LIEBE LEID GESCHAH • 1919 • von Woringen Paul • FRG
WEN DIE GOTTER LIEBEN • 1942 • Hartl Karl • FRG • MOZART STORY, THE (USA) ○ MOZART
WEN KUMMERT'S.. • 1960 • Schlondorff Volker • SHT • FRG • WHO CARES..
WEN–T'I HSUEH–SHENG • 1979 • Lin Ch'Ing-Chieh • TWN • PROBLEM STUDENTS
WENCH, THE (USA) see **BAGARRES** • 1948
WEND KUUNI • 1983 • Kabore Gaston • BRK • GOD'S GIFT ○ GIFT OF GOD, THE
WENDEL • 1986 • Schaub Christoph • SWT
WENDELL see **FRATERNITY VACATION** • 1985
WENDY CRACKED A WALNUT • 1989 • Pattinson Michael • ASL
WENGLER AND SONS • 1987 • Simon Rainer • GDR
WENN ABENDS DIE HEIDE TRAUMT • 1952 • Martin Paul • FRG
WENN AM SONNTAGABEND DIE DORFMUSIK SPIELT • 1933 • Klein Charles • FRG
WENN AM SONNTAGABEND DIE DORFMUSIK SPIELT • 1953 • Schundler Rudolf • FRG
WENN BEIDE SCHULDIG WERDEN • 1962 • Leitner Hermann • AUS
WENN COLOMBINE WINKT • 1920 • Illes Eugen • FRG
WENN DAS HERZ DER JUGEND SPRICHT • 1926 • Sauer Fred • FRG
WENN DAS HERZ IN HASS ERGLUHT • 1918 • Matull Kurt • FRG
WENN DAS LEBEN NEIN SAGT • 1919 • Muller-Hagen Carl? • FRG
WENN DAS LEBEN RUFT • 1918 • Leffler Robert • FRG
WENN DAS MEIN GROSSER BRUDER WUSSTE • 1959 • Ode Erik • FRG
WENN DEM ESEL ZU WOHL IST • 1932 • Seitz Franz • FRG • ER UND SEIN TIPPFRAULEIN
WENN DER HAHN KRAHT • 1936 • Froelich Carl • FRG
WENN DER JUNGE WEIN BLUHT • 1926 • Wilhelm Carl • FRG
WENN DER JUNGE WEIN BLUHT • 1943 • Kirchhoff Fritz • FRG
WENN DER VATER MIT DEM SOHNE • 1955 • Quest Hans • FRG
WENN DER WEISSE FLIEDER WIEDER BLUHT • 1929 • Wohlmuth Robert • FRG
WENN DER WEISSE FLIEDER WIEDER BLUHT • 1953 • Deppe Hans • FRG
WENN DIE ABENDGLOCKEN LAUTEN • 1930 • Beck-Gaden Hanns • FRG
WENN DIE ABENDGLOCKEN LAUTEN • 1951 • Braun Alfred • FRG
WENN DIE ALPENROSEN BLUH'N • 1955 • Haussler Richard • FRG
WENN DIE BOMBE PLATZT • 1958 • Emo E. W. • FRG
WENN DIE CONNY MIT DEM PETER.. • 1958 • Umgelter Fritz • FRG • TEENAGER–MELODIE
"WENN DIE FRAU KOCHT –" • 1915 • Rippert Otto • FRG
WENN DIE GARDE MARSCHIERT • 1928 • Steinhoff Hans • FRG
WENN DIE GEIGEN KLINGEN see **IHR JUNGE** • 1931
WENN DIE GLOCKEN HELL ERKLINGEN • 1959 • von Borsody Eduard • AUS
WENN DIE HEIDE BLUHT • 1960 • Deppe Hans • FRG
WENN DIE LIEBE MODE MACHT • 1932 • Wenzler Franz • FRG
WENN DIE LIEBE NICHT WAR'.. • 1920 • Jacobi Joseph Max • FRG
WENN DIE LIEBE NICHT WAR'! • 1925 • Dinesen Robert • FRG
WENN DIE MASKE FALLT • 1912 • Gad Urban • FRG, DNM • NAAR MASKEN FALDER (DNM)
WENN DIE MASKE FALLT • 1922 • Lund Erik • FRG • SPRINGENDE PFERD, DAS
WENN DIE MUSIK NICHT WAR' • 1935 • Gallone Carmine • FRG • LIED DER LIEBE, DAS ○ KRAFT–MAYR, DER ○ LISZT RHAPSODY
WENN DIE MUSIK NICHT WAR.. see **SOLISTIN ANNA ALT** • 1944
WENN DIE MUTTER UND DIE TOCHTER.. • 1928 • Boese Carl • FRG
WENN DIE ROTE HEIDE BLUHT • 1918 • Bach Rudi?, Henning Hanna? • FRG
WENN DIE SCHWALBEN HEIMWARTS ZIEHN • 1927 • Bauer James • FRG • FREMDENLEGIONAR, DER
WENN DIE SOLDATEN.. • 1931 • Fleck Jacob, Fleck Luise • FRG
WENN DIE SONNE WIEDER SCHEINT • 1943 • Barlog Boleslav • FRG • FLACHSACKER, DER
WENN DIE TOTEN ERWACHEN • Mack Max • FRG
WENN DREI DASSELBE TUN.. • 1915 • Schmidthassler Walter • FRG
WENN DU EINE SCHWEIGERMUTTER HAST • 1937 • Stockel Joe • FRG • WHEN YOU HAVE A MOTHER–IN–LAW (USA)
WENN DU EINE TANTE HAST • 1925 • Boese Carl • FRG
WENN DU EINMAL DEIN HERZ VERSCHENKST • 1929 • Guter Johannes • FRG • EQUATOR TRAMP, THE
WENN DU NOCH EINE HEIMAT HAST • 1929 • Philippi Siegfried • FRG
WENN DU NOCH EINE MUTTER HAST.. • 1954 • Stemmle R. A. • FRG • LICHT DER LIEBE, DAS
WENN DU NOCH EINE MUTTER HAST • 1924 • Kertesz Desider • AUS • ZIRKUS BROWN
WENN DU ZU MIR HALST.. • 1962 • Korbschmitt Hans-Erich • GDR • GRUNE MAPPE, DIE ○ IF YOU STAND BY ME
WENN EIN MADCHEN HUBSCH IST • 1919 • Joseph Erich • FRG
WENN EIN MADEL HOCHZEIT MACHT • 1934 • Boese Carl • FRG
WENN EIN WEIB DEN WEG VERLIERT see **CAFE ELECTRIC** • 1927
WENN EINE FRAU LIEBT • 1950 • Liebeneiner Wolfgang • FRG
WENN ES NACHT WIRD AUF DER REEPERBAHN • 1967 • Olsen Rolf • FRG • WHEN NIGHT FALLS ON THE REEPERBAHN
WENN FRAUEN LIEBEN UND HASSEN • 1917 • Speyer Jaap • FRG
WENN FRAUEN SCHWEIGEN • 1937 • Kirchhoff Fritz • FRG • WHEN WOMEN KEEP SILENT
WENN FRAUEN SCHWINDELN • 1957 • Martin Paul • FRG • EUROPAS NEUE MUSIKPARADE
WENN FREI DIE MEERE FUR DEUTSCHE FAHRT..! • 1917 • Schmidthassler Walter • FRG
WENN FREUNDE ZU RIVALEN WERDEN • 1919 • von Woringen Paul? • FRG
WENN ICH CHEF WARE • 1962 • Pohland Hansjurgen • FRG
WENN ICH EINMAL DER HERR GOTT WAR • 1954 • Kutter Anton • FRG, AUS
WENN ICH EINMAL EINE DUMMHEIT MACHE.. see **HOCHZEITSREISE ZU DRITT** • 1932
WENN ICH KONIG WAR! • 1934 • Hubler-Kahla J. A. • FRG • IF I WERE KING (USA)
WENN IN DER EHE DIE LEIBE STIRBT see **KAMPF UM DIE EHE 1, DER** • 1919
WENN LUDWIG INS MANOVER ZIEHT • 1967 • Jacobs Werner • FRG • WHEN LUDWIG GOES ON MANOEUVRES
WENN MADCHEN ZUM MANOVER BLASEN • 1974 • Antel Franz • AUS, FRG • WHEN GIRLS TRUMPET FOR MANOEUVRES
WENN MANNER RICHTEN • 1923 • *Moa-Film* • FRG
WENN MANNER SCHWEIGEN • 1924 • *Imperial-Film* • FRG
WENN MANNER SCHWINDELN • 1950 • Boese Carl • FRG • TAXI–GATTIN
WENN MANNER STREIKEN • 1919 • Edel Edmund • FRG
WENN MANNER VERREISEN • 1939 • Zoch Georg • FRG
WENN MENSCHEN IRREN • 1926 • Ollen Otz • FRG • SCHATTEN DER NACHT
WENN MENSCHEN REIF ZUR LIEBE WERDEN • 1916 • Andra Fern? • FRG
WENN MENSCHEN REIF ZUR LIEBE WERDEN • 1927 • Fleck Jacob, Fleck Luise • FRG • HAUBENLERCHE, DIE
WENN POLDI INS MANOVER ZIEHT • 1956 • Quest Hans • AUS • MANOVERZWILLING
WENN STEINE REDEN see **WAS STEINE ERZAHLEN** • 1925
WENN SUSS DAS MONDLICHT AUF HUGELN SCHLAFT • 1969 • Liebeneiner Wolfgang • FRG
WENN TAUBCHEN FEDERN LASSEN • 1969 • FRG
WENN TOTE SPRECHEN • 1917 • Reinert Robert • FRG
WENN VIER DASSELBE TUN • 1917 • Lubitsch Ernst • FRG
WENN VOLKER STREITEN • 1915 • Lupow Casar • FRG
WENN WIR ALLE ENGEL WAREN • 1936 • Froelich Carl • FRG • IF WE ALL WERE ANGELS (USA)
WENN WIR ALLE ENGEL WAREN • 1956 • Luders Gunther • FRG
WENN ZWEI SICH LIEBEN.. • 1923 • *Vera-Filmwerke* • FRG
WENN ZWEI SICH STREITEN • 1932 • Lindtberg Leopold • SHT • FRG
WENONAH • 1910 • *Powers* • USA
WENONA'S BROKEN PROMISE • 1911 • *Bison* • USA
WENT AWAY BUT DIDN'T RETURN • 1985 • Khan Mohamed • EGY
WENT THE DAY WELL • 1942 • Cavalcanti Alberto • UKN • 48 HOURS (USA)
WEP–TON–NO–MAH, THE INDIAN MAIL CARRIER • 1909 • *Carson* • USA
WER BIN ICH? • 1921 • *Zelenka Maria* • FRG
WER BIST DU? • 1922 • Trotz Adolf • FRG
WER BIST DU? • 1969 • Krausse Werner • ANS • GDR • WHO ARE YOU? (USA)
WER BIST DU DEN ICH LIEBE? • 1949 • von Bolvary Geza • FRG
WER DAS SCHEIDEN HAT ERFUNDEN • 1928 • Neff Wolfgang • FRG
WER DIE HEIMAT LIEBT see **SACHE MIT STYX, DIE** • 1942
WER DIE HEIMAT LIEBT see **HEILIGE ERBE, DAS** • 1957
WER EIN PAAR HOLZLATSCHEN ABGELAUFEN HAT • 1977 • Herrmann Gabriele • GDR
WER EINMAL LUGT ODER VIKTOR UND DIE ERZIEHUNG • 1975 • Kovach June • DOC • SWT
WER FUHR DEN GRAUEN FORD? • 1950 • Pfeiffer Paul • FRG
WER HAT ANGST VORM KLEINEN MANN • 1971 • Prochazka Pavel • FRG • WHO'S AFRAID OF A LITTLE MAN
WER HAT ROBBY GESEHEN? • 1930 • Randolf Rolf • FRG
WER IM GLASHAUS LIEBT.. DER GRABEN • 1970 • Verhoeven Michael • FRG • PEOPLE IN GLASSHOUSES
WER KUSST MADELEINE? • 1939 • Janson Victor • FRG
WER KUSST MICH? • 1917 • *Moja Hella* • FRG
WER KUSST WEN? • 1949 • Friese Wolf Dietrich • AUS • GLUCK MUSST DU HABEN AUS DIESER WELT
WER NICHT IN DER JUGEND KUSST • 1918 • Krause Karl Otto • FRG
WER NIEMALS EINEN RAUSCH GEHABT • 1918 • Bolten-Baeckers Heinrich • FRG
WER NIEMALS EINEN RAUSCH GEHABT.. see **BOCKBIERFEST** • 1930
WER NIMMT DIE LIEBE ERNST? • 1931 • Engel Erich • FRG
WER UNTER EUCH OHNE SUNDE IST.. • 1920 • Sauer Fred • FRG
WER WAGT –GEWINNT! • 1935 • Janssen Walter • FRG • BEZAUBERNDES FRAULEIN
WER WAR ES? • 1920 • Klein-Rohden Rudolf • FRG • TRAGODIE DER GRAFEN ZU SCHONSTADT, DIE ○ SELTSAMES ERLIBNIS, EIN
WER WEISS? • 1917 • Wieder Konrad • FRG
WER WILL UNTER DIE SOLDATEN? • 1960 • Hess Joachim • FRG • WHO WANTS TO BE A SOLDIER?
WER WIRD DENN WEINEN, WENN MAN AUSEINANDERGEHT • 1929 • Eichberg Richard • FRG • TOM BOY, THE
WER WIRFT DEN ERSTEN STEIN! • 1922 • Gunsburg Arthur • FRG
WER WIRFT DEN ERSTEN STEIN? • 1927 • Eriksen Erich • FRG
WER ZULETZT LACHT see **FRITZE BOLLMANN WOLLTE ANGELN** • 1943
WER ZULETZT LACHT, LAHT AM BESTEN • 1971 • Reinl Harald • FRG
WERA MIRZEWA see **FALL DES STAATSANWALTS M..., DER** • 1928
WERDEGANG, EIN see **REIGEN, DER** • 1920
WE'RE ALL ALONE, MY DEAR • 1977 • Cox Paul • SHT • ASL • WE ARE ALL ALONE MY DEAR
WE'RE ALL GAMBLERS • 1927 • Cruze James • USA
WE'RE ALL PRESLEYS see **WSZSCY JEJESTESMY PRESLEYAMI** • 1963
WE'RE BACKING UP • 1909 • *Pathe* • FRN
WE'RE FIGHTING BACK • 1981 • Antonio Lou • TVM • USA
WE'RE GETTING ALONG.. see **KOSZONOM, MEGVAGYUNK..** • 1981
WE'RE GOING TO BE RICH • 1938 • Banks Monty • UKN, USA
WE'RE GOING TO EAT YOU see **TI–YU WU–MEN** • 1980
WERE I THY BRIDE • 1907 • Morland John • UKN
WE'RE IN THE ARMY NOW see **PACK UP YOUR TROUBLES** • 1932
WE'RE IN THE ARMY NOW (UKN) see **PACK UP YOUR TROUBLES** • 1939
WE'RE IN THE HONEY • 1948 • *Paramount* • ANS • USA
WE'RE IN THE LEGION NOW • 1936 • Wilbur Crane • USA
WE'RE IN THE MONEY • 1933 • Ising Rudolf • ANS • USA
WE'RE IN THE MONEY • 1935 • Enright Ray • USA
WE'RE IN THE NAVY NOW • 1926 • Sutherland A. Edward • USA
WE'RE LIVING AT THE CLOISTERS • 1929 • Aylott Dave, Symmons E. F. • SHT • UKN
WE'RE NO ANGELS • 1955 • Curtiz Michael • USA
WE'RE NO ANGELS • 1989 • Jordan Neil • USA
WE'RE NOT DRESSING • 1934 • Taurog Norman • USA
WE'RE NOT MADE OF STONE see **NO SOMOS DE PIEDRA** • 1968
WE'RE NOT MARRIED • 1952 • Goulding Edmund • USA
WE'RE NOT THE JET SET • 1974 • Duvall Robert • USA
WE'RE OFF! see **HOTOVO, JEDEM** • 1947
WE'RE ON OUR WAY TO RIO • 1944 • Sparber I. • ANS • USA
WE'RE ON THE JURY • 1937 • Holmes Ben • USA
WE'RE ONLY HUMAN • 1935 • Flood James • USA
WE'RE RICH AGAIN • 1934 • Seiter William A. • USA
WERE WE REALLY LIKE THIS? see **BYLI JSME TO MY?** • 1990
WERE YOU NOT TO KOKO PLIGHTED • 1907 • Morland John • UKN
WEREWOLF • 1987 • Hemmings David • TVM • USA
WEREWOLF, THE • 1913 • McRae Henry • USA
WEREWOLF, THE • 1956 • Sears Fred F. • USA
WEREWOLF, THE see **LOUP–GAROU, LE** • 1923
WEREWOLF AND THE YETI, THE see **MALDICION DE LA BESTIA, LA** • 1975
WEREWOLF IN A GIRLS' DORMITORY (USA) see **LYCANTHROPUS** • 1962
WEREWOLF OF LONDON • 1935 • Walker Stuart • USA • UNHOLY HOUR
WEREWOLF OF WASHINGTON, THE • 1973 • Ginsberg Milton Moses • USA
WEREWOLF OF WOODSTOCK • 1974 • Moffitt John • USA
WEREWOLF VS. THE VAMPIRE WOMAN, THE (USA) see **NACHT DER VAMPIRE** • 1970
WEREWOLF WOMAN see **LUPA MANNARA, LA** • 1976
WEREWOLF WOMAN see **NAKED WEREWOLF WOMAN** • 1983
WEREWOLF'S SHADOW, THE see **NACHT DER VAMPIRE** • 1970
WEREWOLVES ON WHEELS • 1971 • Levesque Michel • USA
WERFT ZUM GRAUEN HECHT, DIE • 1935 • Wisbar Frank • FRG
WERK SEINES LEBENS, DAS • 1919 • Gartner Adolf? • FRG
WERKELIJKHEID VAN KAREL APPEL, DE • 1962 • Vrijman Jan • SHT • NTH • REALITY OF KAREL APPEL, THE ○ WORLD OF KAREL APPEL, THE

WERKZEUG DES COSIMO, DAS • 1919 • Halm Alfred • FRG
WERNER HERZOG EATS HIS SHOE • 1980 • Blank Les • DOC • USA
WERNER KRAFFT • 1916 • Froelich Carl • FRG
WERT THOU NOT TO KOKO PLIGHTED • 1906 • Gilbert Arthur • UKN
WERTHER • 1910 • Calmettes Andre • FRN
WERTHER • 1911 • Pouctal Henri • FRN
WERTHER • 1922 • Dulac Germaine • FRN
WERTHER • 1926 • Hajsky Milos • CZC
WERTHER • 1985 • *Poncela Eusebio* • SPN
WERTHER see **ROMAN DE WERTHER, LE** • 1938
WERTHER UND LOTTE see **BEGEGNUNG MIT WERTHER** • 1949
WERWOLFE, DER • 1973 • Klett Werner • FRG
WESELE • 1972 • Wajda Andrzej • PLN • WEDDING, THE (UKN)
WESELE KRAKOWSKIE • 1956 • Perski Ludwik (c/d) • DOC • PLN • CRACOW WEDDING
WESOLA II • 1952 • Lesiewicz Witold • SHT • PLN
WESOLE MIASTECZKO • 1958 • Badzian Teresa • PLN • MERRY TOWN, THE ○ LUNA-PARK
WESSADA EL KHALIA, EL • 1957 • Abu Saif Salah • EGY • WISADAT OULKHALIA, EL ○ EMPTY PILLOW, THE ○ WISADA AL-KHALIYA, AL-
WEST 11 • 1963 • Winner Michael • UKN
WEST AND SODA • 1965 • Bozzetto Bruno • ANM • ITL
WEST CASE, THE • 1923 • Coleby A. E. • UKN
WEST END FROLICS • 1937 • Hopwood R. A. • UKN
WEST END JUNGLE • 1961 • Miller Arnold Louis • DOC • UKN
WEST END NIGHTS • 1938 • Haines Ronald • UKN
WEST END PALS • 1916 • Evans Joe • UKN
WEST HEAD • 1973 • Noonan Chris • DOC • ASL
WEST INDIES see **WEST INDIES OU LES NEGRES MARRONS DE LA LIBERTE** • 1979
WEST INDIES OU LES NEGRES MARRONS DE LA LIBERTE • 1979 • Hondo Abib Med • FRN, MRT • NEGRES MARRONS DE LA LIBERTE, LES ○ WEST INDIES
WEST INDIES STORY • 1979 • TNS, MLI, IVC
WEST IS BEST • 1920 • Rosen Phil • SHT • USA
WEST IS EAST see **WEST VS. EAST** • 1922
WEST IS STILL WILD, THE • 1977 • von Mizener Don • USA • MULEFEATHERS
WEST IS WEST • 1920 • Paul Val • USA
WEST IS WEST • 1922 • Marshall George • SHT • USA
WEST IS WEST • 1987 • Rathod David • IND, USA
WEST OF ABILENE • 1940 • Ceder Ralph • USA • SHOWDOWN, THE (UKN)
WEST OF ARIZONA • 1925 • Gibson Tom • USA
WEST OF BROADWAY • 1926 • Thornby Robert T. • USA
WEST OF BROADWAY • 1931 • Beaumont Harry • USA
WEST OF BROADWAY • 1933 • Ray Albert • USA
WEST OF CARSON CITY • 1940 • Taylor Ray • USA
WEST OF CHEYENNE • 1931 • Webb Harry S. • USA
WEST OF CHEYENNE • 1938 • Nelson Sam • USA
WEST OF CHICAGO • 1922 • Dunlap Scott R., Wallace C. R. • USA • VAMOOSE
WEST OF CIMARRON • 1941 • Orlebeck Lester • USA
WEST OF DODGE CITY • 1947 • Nazarro Ray • USA • SEA WALL, THE (UKN)
WEST OF ELDORADO • 1949 • Taylor Ray • USA
WEST OF KERRY • 1938 • Bird Richard • UKN • MEN OF IRELAND (USA) ○ ISLAND MEN
WEST OF LARAMIE • 1949 • Cowan Will • SHT • USA
WEST OF MOJAVE • 1925 • Fraser Harry L. • USA
WEST OF MONTANA (UKN) see **MAIL ORDER BRIDE** • 1963
WEST OF NEVADA • 1936 • Hill Robert F. • USA
WEST OF PARADISE • 1928 • *Cheyenne Bill* • USA
WEST OF PINTO BASIN • 1940 • Luby S. Roy • USA • TRIPLE THREAT
WEST OF RAINBOW'S END • 1938 • James Alan • USA
WEST OF SANTA FE • 1928 • McGowan J. P. • USA
WEST OF SANTA FE • 1939 • Nelson Sam • USA
WEST OF SHANGHAI • 1937 • Farrow John • USA • WAR LORD
WEST OF SINGAPORE • 1933 • Ray Albert • USA
WEST OF SONORA • 1948 • Nazarro Ray • USA
WEST OF SUEZ • 1957 • Crabtree Arthur • UKN • FIGHTING WILDCATS (USA)
WEST OF TEXAS • 1943 • Drake Oliver • USA • SHOOTIN' IRONS
WEST OF THE ALAMO • 1946 • Drake Oliver • USA
WEST OF THE BRAZOS • 1950 • Carr Thomas • USA • RANGELAND EMPIRE
WEST OF THE DIVIDE • 1934 • Bradbury Robert North • USA
WEST OF THE LAW • 1926 • Wilson Ben • USA
WEST OF THE LAW • 1934 • Tansey Robert • SHT • USA
WEST OF THE LAW • 1942 • Bretherton Howard • USA
WEST OF THE PECOS • 1922 • Hart Neal • USA
WEST OF THE PECOS • 1934 • Rosen Phil • USA
WEST OF THE PECOS • 1945 • Killy Edward • USA
WEST OF THE PECOS • 1960 • Freleng Friz • ANS • USA
WEST OF THE RAINBOW'S END • 1926 • Cohn Bennett • USA
WEST OF THE RIO GRANDE • 1921 • Townley Robert H. • USA
WEST OF THE RIO GRANDE • 1944 • Hillyer Lambert • USA
WEST OF THE ROCKIES • 1929 • Carpenter Horace B. • USA
WEST OF THE ROCKIES • 1941 • Connolly Bobby • SHT • USA
WEST OF THE SACRED GEM, THE • 1914 • *Eclectic* • USA
WEST OF THE SANTA FE • 1938 • Nelson Sam • USA
WEST OF THE WATER TOWER • 1924 • Sturgeon Rollin S. • USA
WEST OF TOMBSTONE • 1942 • Bretherton Howard • USA
WEST OF WYOMING • 1950 • Fox Wallace • USA
WEST OF ZANZIBAR • 1928 • Browning Tod • USA • SOUTH OF THE EQUATOR
WEST OF ZANZIBAR • 1954 • Watt Harry • UKN, SAF
WEST ON PARADE • 1934 • Ray Bernard B. • USA
WEST POINT • 1927 • Dwan Allan • SHT • USA • ETERNAL YOUTH
WEST POINT • 1928 • Sedgwick Edward • USA • ETERNAL YOUTH
WEST POINT OF THE AIR • 1935 • Rosson Richard • USA
WEST POINT OF THE SOUTH • 1936 • Rosson Richard • SHT • USA
WEST POINT STORY, THE • 1950 • Del Ruth Roy • USA • FINE AND DANDY (UKN)
WEST POINT WIDOW • 1941 • Siodmak Robert • USA
WEST RIDING, THE see **WE OF THE WEST RIDING** • 1946
WEST SIDE KID, THE • 1943 • Sherman George • USA
WEST SIDE STORY • 1961 • Wise Robert, Robbins Jerome • USA
WEST TEXAS • 1970 • Gadney Alan • USA • WEST TEXAS 1870
WEST TEXAS 1870 see **WEST TEXAS** • 1970
WEST TI VA STRETTO, AMICO.. E ARRIVATO ALLELUJA • 1972 • Carnimeo Giuliano • ITL
WEST TO GLORY • 1947 • Taylor Ray • USA
WEST VIRGINIAN, THE see **REEL VIRGINIAN, THE** • 1924
WEST VS. EAST • 1922 • Perez Marcel • USA • WEST IS EAST
WEST WAS NEVER LIKE THIS, THE see **THIS IS THE WEST THAT WAS** • 1974
WEST WIND • 1915 • *Finley Ned* • USA
WEST WIND see **VINDEN FRAN VASTER** • 1942
WEST WIND: THE STORY OF TOM THOMPSON • 1942 • McInnes Graham • DCS • CND • BOURRASQUE
WEST ZONE see **NYUGATI OVEZET** • 1954
WESTBOUND • 1924 • *Warner J. B.* • USA
WESTBOUND • 1959 • Boetticher Budd • USA
WESTBOUND LIMITED • 1937 • Beebe Ford • USA
WESTBOUND LIMITED, THE • 1923 • Johnson Emory • USA • WESTBOUND NINETY-NINE
WESTBOUND MAIL • 1937 • Blangsted Folmar • USA
WESTBOUND NINETY-NINE see **WESTBOUND LIMITED, THE** • 1923
WESTBOUND STAGE • 1940 • Bennet Spencer Gordon • USA
WESTERBORK see **SCHIJN VAN TWIJFEL, EEN** • 1975
WESTERN • 1965 • Ratz Gunter • ANM • GDR
WESTERN ADVENTURER, A • 1921 • *Fairbanks William* • USA
WESTERN APPROACHES • 1944 • Jackson Pat • UKN • RAIDER, THE (USA)
WESTERN AUSTRALIA -LAND OF OPPORTUNITY • 1920 • *Westralian Films* • ASL
WESTERN BLOOD • 1918 • Reynolds Lynn • USA
WESTERN BLOOD • 1923 • Hunter Robert • USA
WESTERN BORDER, THE • 1915 • Montgomery Frank E. • USA
WESTERN BRIDE, A • 1911 • *Bison* • USA
WESTERN CARAVANS • 1939 • Nelson Sam • USA • SILVER SANDS (UKN)
WESTERN CHILD'S HEROISM, A • 1912 • *Champion* • USA
WESTERN CHIVALRY • 1910 • *Anderson Broncho Billy* • USA
WESTERN CHIVALRY • 1911 • *Lubin* • USA
WESTERN CHIVALRY • 1912 • *Comet* • USA
WESTERN CODE, THE • 1932 • McCarthy John P. • USA
WESTERN COQUETTE, A • 1912 • *Melies* • USA
WESTERN COURAGE • 1927 • Wilson Ben • USA
WESTERN COURAGE • 1935 • Bennet Spencer Gordon • USA
WESTERN COURAGE • 1950 • *Universal* • SHT • USA
WESTERN COURTSHIP • 1908 • Blackton J. Stuart • USA
WESTERN COURTSHIP, A • 1912 • *Lubin* • USA
WESTERN COWGIRL • 1943 • *O'Brien Joseph/ Mead Thomas (P)* • SHT • USA
WESTERN CYCLONE • 1943 • Newfield Sam • USA • FRONTIER FIGHTERS
WESTERN DAZE • 1941 • Pal George • ANS • USA
WESTERN DEMON, A • 1922 • McKenzie Robert • USA
WESTERN DOCTOR'S PERIL, THE • 1911 • Dwan Allan • USA
WESTERN DREAM, A • 1911 • Dwan Allan • USA • WESTERN DREAMER, A
WESTERN DREAMER, A see **WESTERN DREAM, A** • 1911
WESTERN ENGAGEMENT, A • 1925 • Hurst Paul C. • USA
WESTERN EPISODE, A • 1912 • *Bison* • USA
WESTERN FATE • 1924 • Holt George • USA
WESTERN FEUD, A • 1911 • *Nestor* • USA
WESTERN FEUDS • 1924 • Ford Francis • USA
WESTERN FIREBRANDS • 1921 • Seeling Charles R. • USA
WESTERN FRONTIER • 1935 • Herman Al • USA
WESTERN GIRL, A • 1911 • Melies Gaston • USA
WESTERN GIRLS • 1912 • *Essanay* • USA
WESTERN GIRL'S CHOICE, A • 1911 • *Champion* • USA
WESTERN GIRL'S DREAM, A • 1912 • *Mersereau Violet* • USA
WESTERN GIRL'S LOVE, A • 1911 • *Nestor* • USA
WESTERN GIRL'S SACRIFICE, A • 1910 • *Champion* • USA
WESTERN GIRL'S SACRIFICE, A • 1911 • *Essanay* • USA
WESTERN GOLD • 1937 • Bretherton Howard • USA • MYSTERIOUS STRANGER, THE (UKN)
WESTERN GOVERNOR'S HUMANITY, A • 1915 • Fielding Romaine • USA
WESTERN GRIT • 1924 • Cook Ad. • USA
WESTERN HEARTS • 1911 • *Selig* • USA
WESTERN HEARTS • 1912 • *Anderson Broncho Billy* • USA
WESTERN HEARTS • 1913 • *Nestor* • USA
WESTERN HEARTS • 1921 • Smith Cliff • USA
WESTERN HERITAGE • 1948 • Grissell Wallace A. • USA
WESTERN HEROINE, A • 1911 • *Storey Edith* • USA
WESTERN HISTORY • 1971 • Brakhage Stan • USA
WESTERN HONOR see **MAN FROM NOWHERE, THE** • 1930
WESTERN ISLES • 1942 • Bishop Terry • DCS • UKN
WESTERN JAMBOREE • 1938 • Staub Ralph • USA
WESTERN JUSTICE • 1907 • Anderson G. M. • USA
WESTERN JUSTICE • 1910 • *Bison* • USA
WESTERN JUSTICE • 1910 • *Lubin* • USA
WESTERN JUSTICE • 1910 • *Yankee* • USA
WESTERN JUSTICE • 1923 • Caldwell Fred • USA
WESTERN JUSTICE • 1935 • Bradbury Robert North • USA
WESTERN KIMONO, A • 1912 • *Carney Augustus* • USA
WESTERN KNIGHTS • 1930 • Roberts Stephen • SHT • USA
WESTERN LAW THAT FAILED, THE • 1913 • *Essanay* • USA
WESTERN LEGACY, A • 1912 • *Anderson Broncho Billy* • USA
WESTERN LIMITED, THE • 1932 • Cabanne W. Christy • USA • NIGHT EXPRESS, THE (UKN)
WESTERN LOVE • 1913 • Blache Alice • USA
WESTERN LOVE see **LOVE OF THE WEST, THE** • 1911
WESTERN LUCK • 1924 • Beranger George A. • USA
WESTERN MAID, A • 1909 • *Anderson Broncho Billy* • USA
WESTERN MAIL • 1942 • Tansey Robert • USA
WESTERN MASQUERADE, A • 1916 • Mix Tom • SHT • USA
WESTERN MELODY, THE • 1919 • Kennedy Aubrey M. • USA
WESTERN METHODS • 1929 • *Church Fred* • USA
WESTERN MUSKETEER, THE • 1922 • Bertram William • USA
WESTERN NIGHT, A • 1911 • *Edison* • USA
WESTERN ONE-NIGHT STAND, A • 1911 • *Bison* • USA
WESTERN PACIFIC AGENT • 1950 • Newfield Sam • USA
WESTERN PLUCK • 1926 • Vale Travers • USA
WESTERN POSTMISTRESS, A • 1911 • *Pathe* • USA
WESTERN PRINCE CHARMING, A • 1912 • *Hammond Edna* • USA
WESTERN PROMISE • 1925 • *Cuneo Lester* • USA
WESTERN RACKETEERS • 1935 • Horner Robert J. • USA
WESTERN RAYS • 1920 • *Ridgeway Fritzi* • SHT • USA
WESTERN REDEMPTION, A • 1911 • *Essanay* • USA
WESTERN RENEGADES • 1949 • Fox Wallace • USA
WESTERN ROMANCE, A • 1910 • Porter Edwin S. • USA
WESTERN ROMANCE, A • 1913 • Parker Lem B. • USA
WESTERN ROVER, THE • 1927 • Rogell Albert S. • USA
WESTERN RUSE, A • 1911 • *Powers* • USA
WESTERN SISTER'S DEVOTION, A • 1913 • *Anderson Broncho Billy* • USA
WESTERN SKIES • 1933 • Willett Paul B. • USA
WESTERN SPEED • 1922 • Dunlap Scott R., Wallace C. R. • USA
WESTERN STAGE COACH HOLD-UP • 1904 • Porter Edwin S. • USA
WESTERN STORY, THE see **GAL WHO TOOK THE WEST, THE** • 1949
WESTERN SUFFRAGETTES see **TRICK OF HEARTS, A** • 1928
WESTERN TERROR see **BUZZY RIDES THE RANGE** • 1940
WESTERN THOROUGHBRED, A • 1922 • *Mccabe Harry* • USA
WESTERN TRAIL, THE • 1936 • *Terry Paul/ Moser Frank (P)* • ANS • USA
WESTERN TRAILS • 1926 • Carpenter Horace B. • USA
WESTERN TRAILS • 1938 • Waggner George • USA
WESTERN TRAMP, A • 1911 • *Bison* • USA
WESTERN TRIANGLE, A • 1912 • *Republic* • USA
WESTERN UNION • 1941 • Lang Fritz • USA
WESTERN VACATION, A • 1912 • *Nestor* • USA
WESTERN VENGEANCE • 1924 • McGowan J. P. • USA
WESTERN WAIF, A • 1911 • Dwan Allan • USA
WESTERN WALLOP, THE • 1924 • Smith Cliff • USA • ON PAROLE
WESTERN WAY, THE • 1915 • *Anderson Broncho Billy* • USA
WESTERN WELCOME, A • 1910 • Melies Gaston • USA
WESTERN WELCOME, A • 1938 • Goodwins Leslie • SHT • USA
WESTERN WHIRLWIND, THE • 1927 • Rogell Albert S. • USA
WESTERN WHOOPEE • 1930 • Foster John, Bailey Harry • ANS • USA
WESTERN WHOOPEE • 1948 • Cowan Will • SHT • USA
WESTERN WOMAN'S WAY, A • 1910 • *Essanay* • USA
WESTERN WOOING, A • 1919 • Holt George • SHT • USA
WESTERN YESTERDAYS • 1924 • Ford Francis • USA
WESTERN ZONE see **NYUGATI OVEZET** • 1954
WESTERNER, THE • 1935 • Selman David • USA
WESTERNER, THE • 1940 • Wyler William • USA
WESTERNER, THE see **GUN SMOKE** • 1931
WESTERNER AND THE EARL, THE • 1911 • *Thanhouser* • USA
WESTERNERS, THE • 1919 • Sloman Edward • USA
WESTERNER'S WAY, A • 1910 • *Anderson Broncho Billy* • USA
WESTERPLATTE BRONI SIE NADAL • 1967 • Rozewicz Stanislaw • PLN • WESTERPLATTE RESISTS
WESTERPLATTE RESISTS see **WESTERPLATTE BRONI SIE NADAL** • 1967
WESTFRONT 1918 • 1930 • Pabst G. W. • FRG • VIER VON DER INFANTERIE ○ FOUR FROM THE INFANTRY ○ COMRADES OF 1918
WESTLAND CASE, THE • 1937 • Cabanne W. Christy • USA
WESTMINSTER GLEE SINGERS, THE • 1927 • *De Forest Phonofilms* • SHT • UKN • MUSICAL MEDLEY NO.3
WESTMINSTER OF THE WEST, THE • 1934 • Sparling Gordon • DCS • CND
WESTMINSTER PASSION PLAY -BEHOLD THE MAN, THE • 1951 • Rilla Walter • UKN
WESTOSTLICHE HOCHZEIT see **AUFTRAG HOGLERS, DER** • 1950
WESTWARD see **DROGA NA ZACHOD** • 1961
WESTWARD BOUND • 1930 • Webb Harry S. • USA
WESTWARD BOUND • 1944 • Tansey Robert • USA
WESTWARD-BOUND TRAIN, THE see **POEZD IDET NA VOSTOK** • 1947
WESTWARD DESPERADO (USA) see **DOKURITSU GURENTAI NISHI-E** • 1960
WESTWARD HO! • 1919 • Nash Percy • UKN
WESTWARD HO • 1935 • Bradbury Robert North • USA
WESTWARD HO! • 1941 • Dickinson Thorold • DCS • UKN
WESTWARD HO! • 1942 • English John • USA
WESTWARD HO-HUM • 1941 • Beauchamp Clem • SHT • USA
WESTWARD HO THE WAGONS! • 1957 • Beaudine William • USA
WESTWARD PASSAGE • 1932 • Milton Robert • USA
WESTWARD THE WAGON (UKN) see **HITCHED** • 1971
WESTWARD THE WOMEN • 1951 • Wellman William A. • USA
WESTWARD TRAIL, THE • 1948 • Taylor Ray • USA
WESTWARD WHOA • 1924 • Seiler Lewis • SHT • USA
WESTWARD WHOA! • 1936 • King Jack • ANS • USA
WESTWORLD • 1973 • Crichton Michael • USA
WET AND DRY • 1917 • *Watson Harry Jr.* • USA
WET AND WARMER • 1920 • Lehrman Henry • SHT • USA
WET ASPHALT (USA) see **NASSER ASPHALT** • 1958
WET BLANKET POLICY • 1948 • Lundy Dick • ANS • USA
WET DAY, A • 1907 • Stow Percy • UKN
WET DAY AT THE SEASIDE, A • 1900 • *Paul R. W.* • UKN
WET DESTRUCTION OF THE ATLANTIC EMPIRE, THE • 1954 • Kuchar George, Kuchar Mike • USA
WET DREAMS • 1974 • Stuart Falcon • UKN
WET EARTH AND WARM PEOPLE • 1971 • Rubbo Michael • DOC • CND • JALAN JALAN: A JOURNEY TO SUDANESE JAVA
WET GOLD • 1921 • Ince Ralph • USA • SUBMARINE GOLD
WET GOLD • 1984 • Lowry Dick • TVM • USA

WET HARE • 1962 • McKimson Robert • ANS • USA
WET KNIGHT, A • 1932 • Lantz Walter, Nolan William • ANS • USA
WET NIGHT, A • 1926 • Hughes Harry • UKN
WET PAINT • 1911 • *Urban Trading Co* • UKN
WET PAINT • 1926 • Rosson Arthur • USA • FRESH PAINT
WET PAINT • 1946 • King Jack • ANS • USA
WET PARADE, THE • 1932 • Fleming Victor • USA
WET POWDER see **GLUVI BARUT** • 1989
WET RAINBOW • 1974 • Wald Roger, Kane Duddy • USA
WET SHORTS • Desimone Tom • USA
WET STUFF see **S*P*Y*S** • 1974
WET WEATHER • 1922 • Roach Hal • SHT • USA
WETBACK HOUND • 1957 • *Allen Rex* • SHT • USA
WETBACK POWER see **MOJADO POWER** • 1981
WETBACKS • 1956 • McCune Hank • USA
WETBACKS see **ESPALDAS MOJADAS** • 1953
WETHERBY • 1985 • Hare David • UKN • VIOLENT STRANGERS: WETHERBY
WETTE, DIE • 1919 • Wolff Carl Heinz • FRG
WETTE UM EINE SEELE, DIE • 1918 • Boese Carl • FRG
WETTERLEUCHTEN • 1925 • Walther-Fein Rudolf • FRG
WETTERLEUCHTEN AM DACHSTEIN • 1953 • Kutter Anton • AUS • HERRIN VOM SALZERHOF, DIE
WETTERLEUCHTEN UM BARBARA • 1941 • Klinger Werner • FRG
WETTERLEUCHTEN UM MARIA • 1957 • Trenker Luis • FRG
WETTERWART, DER • 1923 • Froelich Carl • FRG
WETTLAUF UMS GLUCK • 1923 • Ziener Bruno • FRG • WOLF OF TIBET, THE
WE'VE COME A LONG WAY • 1944 • Goldberg Jack • USA
WE'VE COME A LONG WAY • 1952 • Halas John, Privett Bob • ANS • UKN
WE'VE COME A LONG WAY TOGETHER • 1974 • Shebib Donald • CND
WE'VE GOT A BONE TO PICK WITH YOU see **PACK, THE** • 1977
WE'VE GOT OUR OWN SONG • 1976 • Jarl Stefan (c/d) • SWD
WE'VE GOT TO GET RID OF THE RATS • 1940 • Carr James • UKN
WE'VE GOT TO HAVE LOVE • 1935 • Brunner Patrick • UKN
WE'VE NEVER BEEN LICKED • 1943 • Rawlins John • USA • TEXAS TO TOKYO (UKN)
WEZEL • 1961 • Karabasz Kazimierz • DCS • PLN • KNOT, THE
WEZWANIE • 1971 • Solarz Wojciech • PLN • CHALLENGE, THE ○ CALL, THE
WHACKEY WORLD OF NUMBERS, THE • 1970 • Clark Steven • ANS • USA
WHACKS MUSEUM • 1933 • *Mintz Charles (P)* • ANS • USA
WHALE FOR THE KILLING, A • 1980 • Heffron Richard T. • TVM • USA
WHALE-HUNT, THE see **WHALE HUNTER, THE** • 1983
WHALE HUNTER, THE • 1983 • Bae Chang-Ho • SKR • WHALE-HUNT, THE
WHALE HUNTING IN JERVIS BAY • 1913 • ASL
WHALE OF A TALE, A • 1975 • Brown Ewing Miles • USA
WHALE WHO WANTED TO SING AT THE MET, THE see **WILLIE THE OPERATIC WHALE** • 1946
WHALERS see **VALFANGARE** • 1939
WHALERS, THE • 1938 • Huemer Dick • ANS • USA
WHALES ARE WAITING, THE • 1975 • Ianzelo Tony • DOC • CND
WHALES OF AUGUST, THE • 1987 • Anderson Lindsay • USA
WHALE'S ROOF, THE see **TOIT DE LA BALEINE, LE** • 1981
WHALING AFLOAT AND ASHORE • 1908 • Paul Robert William • UKN • WHALING ON THE IRISH COAST
WHALING ON THE IRISH COAST see **WHALING AFLOAT AND ASHORE** • 1908
WHAM BAM SLAM • 1955 • White Jules • SHT • USA
WHARF • 1968 • Le Grice Malcolm • UKN
WHARF ANGEL • 1934 • Menzies William Cameron, Somnes George • USA • MAN WHO BROKE HIS HEART, THE
WHARF RAT, THE • 1916 • Withey Chet • USA
WHARF RATS, THE • 1914 • *Hutton Leona* • USA
WHARVES & STRAYS • 1935 • Browne Bernard • UKN
WHAT? • 1971 • Breer Robert • USA
WHAT THE ? • 1915 • Birch Cecil • UKN
WHAT THE..? • 1917 • Beaudine William • SHT • USA
WHAT A BABY DID • 1914 • *Lyons Eddie* • USA
WHAT A BEAUTIFUL DAY see **EN SAN STRALANDE DAG** • 1967
WHAT A BIRTHDAY • 1914 • *Planet Films* • UKN
WHAT A BLONDE • 1945 • Goodwins Leslie • USA • COME SHARE MY LOVE!
WHAT A BOUNDER • 1915 • Kellino W. P. • UKN
WHAT A BOZO! • 1931 • Parrott James • SHT • USA
WHAT A CARRY ON! • 1949 • Blakeley John E. • UKN
WHAT A CARVE UP • 1961 • Jackson Pat • UKN • NO PLACE LIKE HOMICIDE (USA)
WHAT A CHANGE OF CLOTHES DID • 1913 • Costello Maurice • USA
WHAT A CHARMING COUNTRY see **DER ER ET YNDIGT LAND** • 1982
WHAT A CHRISTMAS PARTY see **JULEFROKOSTEN** • 1976
WHAT A CINCH • 1915 • Louis Will • USA
WHAT A CLUE WILL DO • 1917 • Chaudet Louis W. • SHT • USA
WHAT A COUNTRY • 1962 • Mirams Roger • DOC • ASL
WHAT A CRAZY WORLD • 1963 • Carreras Michael • UKN
WHAT A DAY • 1929 • Roberts Stephen • SHT • USA
WHAT A FIND • 1915 • Birch Cecil • UKN
WHAT A FLASH • 1971 • Barjol Jean-Michel • FRN • OH WHAT A FLASH! ○ WATAFLASH
WHAT A GIRL CAN DO • 1924 • *Stuart Edward (P)* • DOC • USA
WHAT A HEAD! • 1931 • Hall Robert • USA
WHAT A HOLIDAY! • 1913 • Calvert Charles? • UKN
WHAT A HUSBAND • 1952 • Taylor Donald • UKN
WHAT A KISS WILL DO • 1914 • Finn Arthur • UKN
WHAT A KNIGHT • 1932 • *Mintz Charles (P)* • ANS • USA
WHAT A LIFE! • 1918 • Reardon James • UKN
WHAT A LIFE • 1932 • *Iwerks Ub (P)* • ANS • USA
WHAT A LIFE • 1939 • Reed Theodore • USA
WHAT A LIFE! • 1948 • Law Michael • UKN
WHAT A LIFE! see **PUTA MISERIA** • 1988
WHAT A LION! • 1938 • Hanna William • ANS • USA
WHAT A LITTLE SNEEZE WILL DO • 1941 • Donnelly Eddie • ANS • USA
WHAT A MAN! • 1930 • Crone George J. • USA • GENTLEMAN CHAUFFEUR, THE (UKN) ○ HIS DARK CHAPTER ○ THEY ALL WANT SOMETHING
WHAT A MAN! • 1937 • Greville Edmond T. • UKN
WHAT A MAN! • 1944 • Beaudine William • USA
WHAT A MAN! (UKN) see **NEVER GIVE A SUCKER AN EVEN BREAK** • 1941
WHAT A MAN, WITHOUT A DOUBT see **QUE HOMBRE TAN SIN EMBARGO** • 1965
WHAT A NIGHT! • 1914 • Weston Charles • UKN
WHAT A NIGHT! • 1924 • Taurog Norman • SHT • USA
WHAT A NIGHT! • 1928 • Sutherland A. Edward • USA • NUMBER PLEASE
WHAT A NIGHT! • 1931 • Banks Monty • UKN • WANTED?
WHAT A NIGHT • 1935 • *Terry Paul/ Moser Frank (P)* • ANS • USA
WHAT A NIGHT! see **MICSODA EJSZAKA** • 1958
WHAT A PERFORMER see **MES NUITS AVEC.. ALICE, PENELOPE, ARNOLD, MAUD ET RICHARD** • 1976
WHAT A PICNIC • 1915 • Birch Cecil • UKN
WHAT A PITY ABOUT DADDY see **DET ER SA SYND FOR FARMAND** • 1968
WHAT A PRETTY GIRL CAN DO • 1910 • Stow Percy • UKN
WHAT A SELL! • 1914 • Plumb Hay? • UKN
WHAT A TERRIBLE ANIMAL see **QUE ANIMAL TAN TERRIBLE**
WHAT A TIME • 1931 • Heath Arch B. • USA
WHAT A WAY TO DIE! see **SOMMERSPROSSEN** • 1968
WHAT A WAY TO GO! • 1964 • Thompson J. Lee • USA
WHAT A WAY TO GO • Rawicz Karl • ASL • BOTTOMS UP
WHAT A WHOPPER • 1921 • Roach Hal • SHT • USA
WHAT A WHOPPER! • 1961 • Gunn Gilbert • UKN
WHAT A WIDOW! • 1930 • Dwan Allan • USA
WHAT A WIFE LEARNED • 1923 • Wray John Griffith • USA • JIM
WHAT A WOMAN! • 1943 • Cummings Irving • USA • BEAUTIFUL CHEAT, THE (UKN) ○ TEN PERCENT WOMAN
WHAT A WOMAN! see **FORTUNA DI ESSERE DONNA, LA** • 1956
WHAT A WOMAN CAN DO • 1911 • *Essanay* • USA
WHAT A WOMAN (UKN) see **THERE'S THAT WOMAN AGAIN** • 1939
WHAT A WOMAN! (UKN) see **BEAUTIFUL CHEAT, THE** • 1945
WHAT A WOMAN WILL DO • 1912 • *Champion* • USA
WHAT A WOMAN WILL DO • 1914 • Weston Charles • UKN
WHAT ABOUT DADDY? • 1942 • Jason Will • SHT • USA
WHAT ABOUT I.F.C.? • 1973 • Nicholson Arch • SHT • ASL
WHAT AM I BID? • 1919 • Leonard Robert Z. • USA
WHAT AM I BID? • 1967 • Nash Gene • USA
WHAT AN EXCUSE • 1927 • Newfield Sam • SHT • USA
WHAT AN EYE • 1924 • Luddy Edward I. • SHT • USA
WHAT ARE BEST FRIENDS FOR? • 1973 • Sandrich Jay • TVM • USA
WHAT ARE FRIENDS FOR? see **MARSEILLE CONTRACT, THE** • 1974
WHAT ARE SCHOOLS FOR? • 1982 • Holland Patricia • UKN
WHAT ARE WE DOING IN THE MIDDLE OF THE REVOLUTION? see **CHE C'ENTRIAMO NOI CON LA RIVOLUZIONE?** • 1972
WHAT ARE WE FIGHTING FOR? • 1943 • Kenton Erle C. • SHT • USA
WHAT ARE WE GOING TO DO WITHOUT SKIPPER? see **TODD KILLINGS, THE** • 1971
WHAT ARE YOU DOING AFTER THE ORGY? see **ROTMANAD** • 1970
WHAT AVAILS THE CROWN • 1912 • *Leonard Marion* • USA
WHAT BECAME OF JACK AND JILL? • 1971 • Bain Bill • UKN • ROMEO AND JULIET -1971
WHAT BECAME OF JANE? • 1914 • Le Saint Edward J. • USA
WHAT BECOMES OF THE CHILDREN? • 1918 • Stahl Walter Richard • USA
WHAT BECOMES OF THE CHILDREN? • 1935 • *Sentinel* • USA • CHILDREN OF DIVORCE (UKN)
WHAT BEFELL THE INVENTOR'S VISITOR (UKN) see **POCHARD ET L'INVENTEUR, LE** • 1902
WHAT CAME TO BAR Q • 1914 • *Essanay* • USA
WHAT CHANGED CHARLEY FARTHING • 1974 • Hayers Sidney • UKN • BANANAS BOAT, THE (USA)
WHAT CHILDREN WILL DO • 1920 • Plympton Horace G. • USA
WHAT COLOR IS THE WIND? • 1984 • Zuniga Frank • USA
WHAT COLOUR HAS LOVE • 1974 • Brynych Zbynek • CZC
WHAT COMES AROUND • 1987 • Reed Jerry • USA
WHAT COULD BE SWEETER! • 1920 • De Haven Carter • USA
WHAT COULD SHE DO? • 1914 • Collins John H. • USA
WHAT COULD THE DOCTOR DO? see **DOCTOR'S DILEMMA, THE** • 1911
WHAT COULD THE POOR GIRL DO? • 1916 • Lyons Eddie • SHT • USA
WHAT COULD THE POOR MAN DO? • 1913 • Stow Percy • UKN
WHAT CUPID DID • 1913 • *Essanay* • USA
WHAT DAD DID • 1912 • *Eclair* • USA
WHAT DARWIN MISSED • 1916 • Griffith Beverly • SHT • USA
WHAT DEMORALIZED THE BARBER SHOP • 1901 • Porter Edwin S. • USA
WHAT DID HE WHISPER? • 1915 • Davis Ulysses • USA
WHAT DID THE LADY FORGET? see **SHUKUJO WA NANI O WASURETAKA** • 1937
WHAT DID WE DO TO HENS see **CO JSME UDELALI SLEPICIM** • 1977
WHAT DID YOU DO AT SCHOOL TODAY? • 1974 • Power John • DOC • ASL
WHAT DID YOU DO IN THE WAR, DADDY? • 1966 • Edwards Blake • USA
WHAT DID YOU DO IN THE WAR, THANASSI? see **TI EKANES STO POLEMO THANASSI** • 1970
WHAT DIDN'T HAPPEN TO MARY • 1914 • *White Pearl* • USA
WHAT DO I TELL THE BOYS AT THE STATION? • 1972 • Nuchtern Simon • USA
WHAT DO MEN KNOW? see **VAD VETA VAL MANNEN?** • 1933
WHAT DO MEN WANT? • 1921 • Weber Lois • USA
WHAT DO THE DIAMONDS SAY? • 1978 • Southcott Pauline • UKN
WHAT DO WE CALL YOU NOW? • 1965 • Chebotaryov Vladimir • USS
WHAT DO WE DO NOW? • 1945 • Hawtrey Charles • UKN
WHAT DO WOMEN WANT? • 1988 • Davidson Boaz?, Golan Menahem? • USA
WHAT DO YOU SAY TO A NAKED LADY? • 1970 • Funt Allen • USA
WHAT DO YOU THINK? • 1937 • Feist Felix E., Tourneur Jacques • SHS • USA
WHAT DO YOU THINK? • 1953-57 • Parker Gudrun • SER • CND
WHAT DO YOU THINK? see **TUPAPOO** • 1938
WHAT DO YOU THINK? see **ANATA WA NANI O KANGAETE IRU KA?** • 1967
WHAT DO YOU WANT JULIE? see **QU'EST-CE QUE TU VEUX JULIE?** • 1976
WHAT DOES A WOMAN NEED MOST • 1918 • *Psycho-Analytic Research* • USA
WHAT DORIS DID • 1916 • Platt George Foster • SHT • USA
WHAT DRINK DID • 1909 • Griffith D. W. • USA
WHAT D'YA KNOW • 1947 • Barclay David • SHT • USA
WHAT D'YE THINK O' THAT! • 1916 • *Napoleon & Sally* • SHT • USA
WHAT D'YER WANT TO TALK ABOUT IT FOR? • 1907 • Morland John • UKN
WHAT EIGHTY MILLION WOMEN WANT • 1913 • *Unique Film* • USA
WHAT EVER HAPPENED TO AUNT ALICE? • 1969 • Katzin Lee H. • USA
WHAT EVER HAPPENED TO BABY JANE? • 1962 • Aldrich Robert • USA
WHAT EVER HAPPENED TO COUSIN CHARLOTTE see **HUSH.. HUSH, SWEET CHARLOTTE** • 1964
WHAT EVER HAPPENED TO GREEN VALLEY? • 1973 • Weir Peter • DCS • ASL
WHAT EVERY GIRL SHOULD KNOW • 1927 • Reisner Charles F. • USA
WHAT EVERY ICEMAN KNOWS • 1927 • Roach Hal • SHT • USA
WHAT EVERY VETERAN SHOULD KNOW • 1945 • *Universal* • SHT • USA
WHAT EVERY WOMAN KNOWS • 1917 • Durrant Fred W. • UKN
WHAT EVERY WOMAN KNOWS • 1921 • De Mille William C. • USA
WHAT EVERY WOMAN KNOWS • 1934 • La Cava Gregory • USA
WHAT EVERY WOMAN LEARNS • 1919 • Niblo Fred • USA
WHAT EVERY WOMAN WANTS • 1919 • Hampton Jesse D. • USA
WHAT EVERY WOMAN WANTS • 1954 • Elvey Maurice • UKN
WHAT EVERY WOMAN WANTS • 1962 • Morris Ernest • UKN
WHAT EXPLODED? see **CO TO BOUCHLO** • 1970
WHAT FARMER JONES SAW AT THE PICTURE SHOW • 1908 • Cooper Arthur • UKN
WHAT FATE ORDAINED • 1912 • *Lubin* • USA
WHAT FATHER SAW • 1913 • Nicholls George • USA
WHAT FOOLS MEN • 1925 • Archainbaud George • USA • JOSEPH GREER AND HIS DAUGHTER
WHAT FOOLS MEN ARE • 1922 • Terwilliger George W. • USA
WHAT FUR • 1933 • Stevens George • SHT • USA
WHAT GEORGE DID • 1913 • *Blanchard Eleanor* • USA
WHAT GIRLS WILL DO • 1913 • *White Glen* • USA
WHAT GOD HATH JOINED TOGETHER • 1913 • *Schaefer Anne* • USA
WHAT GREAT BEAR LEARNED • 1910 • Melies Gaston • USA
WHAT HAPPENED AT 22 • 1916 • Irving George • USA
WHAT HAPPENED AT CAMPO GRANDE? (USA) see **MAGNIFICENT TWO, THE** • 1967
WHAT HAPPENED AT THE WAXWORKS • 1914 • *Motograph* • UKN
WHAT HAPPENED, CAROLINE? see **BETWEEN US GIRLS** • 1942
WHAT HAPPENED IN THE TUNNEL • 1903 • Porter Edwin S. • USA
WHAT HAPPENED ON THE BARBUDA • 1915 • West Langdon • USA
WHAT HAPPENED THEN? • 1934 • Summers Walter • UKN
WHAT HAPPENED TO AUNTY • 1911 • *Essanay* • USA
WHAT HAPPENED TO BROWN • 1909 • Smith Jack ? • UKN
WHAT HAPPENED TO BROWN • 1910 • Aylott Dave • UKN
WHAT HAPPENED TO FATHER • 1915 • Williams C. Jay • USA
WHAT HAPPENED TO FATHER • 1927 • Adolfi John G. • USA
WHAT HAPPENED TO FRECKLES • 1913 • *Pollard Harry* • USA
WHAT HAPPENED TO HARKNESS • 1934 • Rosmer Milton • UKN
WHAT HAPPENED TO HENDERSON see **OFFICER HENDERSON** • 1913
WHAT HAPPENED TO JEAN • 1918 • Walsh Herbert • ASL
WHAT HAPPENED TO JONES • 1915 • Vale Travers • USA
WHAT HAPPENED TO JONES • 1920 • Cruze James • USA
WHAT HAPPENED TO JONES • 1926 • Seiter William A. • USA
WHAT HAPPENED TO KEROUAC? • 1986 • Lerner Richard, MacAdams Lewis • DOC • USA
WHAT HAPPENED TO LIZZIE • 1913 • Stow Percy • UKN
WHAT HAPPENED TO MARY • 1912 • Colеby A. E. • UKN
WHAT HAPPENED TO MARY? • 1913 • Edwin Walter, Dawley J. Searle • SRL • USA
WHAT HAPPENED TO MISS SEPTEMBER • 1974 • Denby Jerry • USA
WHAT HAPPENED TO PEGGY • 1916 • Coyle Walter • SHT • USA
WHAT HAPPENED TO PIMPLE -IN THE HANDS OF THE LONDON CROOK • 1914 • Evans Fred, Evans Joe • UKN
WHAT HAPPENED TO PIMPLE -THE GENTLEMAN BURGLAR • 1914 • Evans Fred, Evans Joe • UKN
WHAT HAPPENED TO PIMPLE -THE SUICIDE • 1913 • Evans Fred, Evans Joe • UKN
WHAT HAPPENED TO POLYNIN • 1971 • Sakharov Alexei • USS

WHAT HAPPENED TO ROSA • 1920 • Schertzinger Victor • USA • ROMANTIC ROSA
WHAT HAPPENED TO SANTIAGO see **LO QUE LE PASO A SANTIAGO** • 1988
WHAT HAPPENED TO SCHULTZ • 1914 • *Joker* • USA
WHAT HAPPENED TO THE DOG'S MEDICINE • 1910 • Martinek H. O. • UKN
WHAT HAPPENED WITH ANDRES LAPETEUS see **SHTO SLUCHILOS S ANDRESOM LAPETEUSOM?** • 1967
WHAT HAPPENS AT NIGHT • 1941 • Rasinski Connie • ANS • USA
WHAT HAVE I DONE TO DESERVE THIS? see **QUE HE HECHO YO MERECER ESTO?** • 1984
WHAT HAVE WE DONE TO THE HENS see **CO JSME UDELALI SLEPICIM** • 1977
WHAT HAVE YOU DONE TO SOLANGE? (USA) see **COSA AVETE FATTO A SOLANGE?** • 1972
WHAT HE DID WITH HIS £5 • 1913 • *B & C* • UKN
WHAT HE FORGOT • 1914 • Hevener Jerold T. • USA
WHAT HER DIARY TOLD • 1913 • *Greenwood Winnifred* • USA
WHAT HO! SHE BUMPS! • 1905 • *Warwick Trading Co* • UKN
WHAT HO! SHE BUMPS • 1937 • Pal George • ANS • NTH
WHAT HO! THE JUNGLE • 1914 • *B & C* • UKN
WHAT I DIDN'T SAY TO THE PRINCE see **CO SJEM PRINCI NEREKLA** • 1975
WHAT I HAVE I HOLD, GENTLEMEN.. • 1980 • Schulhoff Petr • CZC
WHAT I SAID GOES • 1916 • Haydon J. Charles • SHT • USA
WHAT I WANT NEXT • 1949 • Barclay David • SHT • USA
WHAT IF IT BE LOVE see **A ESLI ETO LYUBOV?** • 1961
WHAT IF IT IS LOVE? see **A ESLI ETO LYUBOV?** • 1961
WHAT IF YOU GO? see **PAANO KUNG WALA KA NA?** • 1988
WHAT IN THE WORLD IS WATER • 1968 • Defalco Martin • DOC • CND
WHAT IS A COMPUTER? • 1967 • *Halas John (P)* • ANS • UKN
WHAT IS A JEW TO YOU? • 1986 • Ziegler Aviva • DOC • ASL
WHAT IS A WORKER'S COUNCIL? see **STO JE RABNICKI SANJET?** • 1959
WHAT IS AUTUMN? see **QUE ES EL OTONO?** • 1977
WHAT IS DEMOCRACY? (UKN) see **QUE ES LA DEMOCRACIA?** • 1971
WHAT IS "DUDEK" see **CO TO JEST "DUDEK"** • 1967
WHAT IS HAPPENING TO THE CITY? • 1982 • Vrijman Jan • NTH
WHAT IS HOME WITHOUT THE BOARDER? see **MAISON TRANQUILLE, LA** • 1901
WHAT IS IN A NAME? • 1915 • *Gaumont* • USA
WHAT IS IT MASTER LIKES SO MUCH? • 1905 • Cooper Arthur • UKN
WHAT IS LACKING? • 1947 • Tyrlova Hermina • ANM • CZC
WHAT IS SAUCE FOR THE GOOSE • 1913 • *Melies* • USA
WHAT IS THE FUTURE OF RURAL SETTLEMENTS? see **MAASEUDUN TELEVAISUUS?** • 1970
WHAT IS THE NEWS? see **AMANIE** • 1973
WHAT IS THE USE OF REPINING? • 1913 • Henderson Dell • USA
WHAT IS TO BE, WILL BE • 1910 • *Solax* • USA
WHAT IS YOUR NAME see **KIMI NO NAWA** • 1954
WHAT IT WILL BE • 1910 • *Lux* • FRN
WHAT KATIE DID • 1912 • Seay Charles M. • USA
WHAT KATY DID • 1913 • *Imp* • USA
WHAT KIND OF FOOL AM I? • 1961 • Godfrey Bob • SHT • UKN
WHAT LOLA WANTS see **PAJAMA GAME, THE** • 1957
WHAT LOLA WANTS (UKN) see **DAMN YANKEES** • 1958
WHAT LOVE CAN DO • 1916 • Hunt Jay • USA
WHAT LOVE FORGIVES • 1919 • Vekroff Perry N. • USA
WHAT LOVE WILL DO • 1921 • Howard William K. • USA
WHAT LOVE WILL DO • 1923 • Bradbury Robert North • USA
WHAT MAD PURSUIT? • 1985 • Smith Tony • MTV • UKN
WHAT MADE DAFFY DUCK • 1948 • Davis Arthur • ANS • USA
WHAT MADE HER DO IT? see **NANI GA KANOJO O SO SASETA KA?** • 1930
WHAT MAKES LIZZY DIZZY? • 1942 • White Jules • SHT • USA
WHAT MATTER THE PRICE • 1912 • Collins Edwin J.? • UKN
WHAT MAX SAID see **PALABRAS DE MAX, LAS** • 1977
WHAT MEN LIVE BY • 1939 • Taylor Donald, Sewell Vernon • UKN
WHAT MEN WANT • 1930 • Laemmle Ernst • USA
WHAT MEN WILL DO • 1914 • Weston Charles • UKN
WHAT MIGHT HAVE BEEN • 1912 • *Champion* • USA
WHAT MIGHT HAVE BEEN • 1913 • *Chamberlin Riley* • USA
WHAT MIGHT HAVE BEEN • 1915 • Goldin Sidney M. • *Imp* • USA
WHAT MIGHT HAVE BEEN • 1915 • O'Brien Jack • *Majestic* • USA
WHAT MIGHT HAVE BEEN • 1920 • Ross Jack • UKN
WHAT MIGHT HAVE BEEN see **HER ONLY WAY** • 1918
WHAT MONEY CAN BUY • 1928 • Greenwood Edwin • UKN
WHAT MONEY CAN'T BUY • 1917 • Tellegen Lou • USA
WHAT MONEY WILL DO • 1915 • *Mayo Marvin* • USA
WHAT MOZART SAW ON MULBERRY STREET • 1954 • Burckhardt Rudy, Cornell Joseph • SHT • USA
WHAT NEXT? • 1928 • Forde Walter • UKN
WHAT NEXT? • 1974 • Smith Peter K. • UKN
WHAT NEXT, CORPORAL HARGROVE? • 1945 • Thorpe Richard • USA
WHAT NEXT? (USA) see **CARMILLA** • 1968
WHAT! NO BEER? • 1933 • Sedgwick Edward • USA
WHAT, NO CIGARETTES? • 1945 • Yates Hal • SHT • USA
WHAT NO MAN KNOWS • 1921 • Garson Harry • USA
WHAT, NO MEN? • 1935 • Staub Ralph • SHT • USA
WHAT, NO SPINACH? • 1936 • Fleischer Dave • ANS • USA
WHAT NOW? see **MI LESZ?** • 1966
WHAT OCCURRED ON THE BEACH • 1918 • *Jaxon* • USA
WHAT ON EARTH! • 1966 • Drew Les, Pindal Kaj • ANS • CND
WHAT PAPA GOT • 1913 • Smalley Phillips • USA
WHAT PEARL'S PEARLS DID • 1914 • Smalley Phillips • USA
WHAT POVERTY LEADS TO • 1908 • *Crescent Film* • USA
WHAT PRICE BEAUTY • 1928 • Buckingham Thomas • USA
WHAT PRICE BEAUTY (UKN) see **FALSE FACES** • 1932
WHAT PRICE CRIME? • 1935 • Herman Al • USA
WHAT PRICE CRIME? • 1942 • Haines Ronald • SER • UKN
WHAT PRICE FAME • 1928 • *Ridek Film Co* • USA
WHAT PRICE FAME? (UKN) see **HOLLYWOOD HOODLUM** • 1934
WHAT PRICE FLEADOM • 1948 • Avery Tex • ANS • USA
WHAT PRICE GLORIA? • 1925 • Ruggles Wesley • SHT • USA
WHAT PRICE GLORY • 1926 • Walsh Raoul • USA
WHAT PRICE GLORY • 1952 • Ford John • USA
WHAT PRICE GOOFY? • 1925 • McCarey Leo • SHT • USA
WHAT PRICE HOLLYWOOD? • 1932 • Cukor George • USA • TRUTH ABOUT HOLLYWOOD, THE
WHAT PRICE INNOCENCE? • 1933 • Mack Willard • USA • SHALL THE CHILDREN PAY (UKN)
WHAT PRICE LOVE • 1927 • Revier Harry • USA
WHAT PRICE LOVE see **SHIROIKOYA KOMAKO** • 1960
WHAT PRICE LOVING CUP? • 1923 • West Walter • UKN
WHAT PRICE MELODY? (UKN) see **LORD BYRON OF BROADWAY** • 1930
WHAT PRICE MURDER (USA) see **MANCHE ET LA BELLE, UNE** • 1957
WHAT PRICE PORKY • 1938 • Clampett Robert • ANS • USA
WHAT PRICE SAFETY • 1938 • Bucquet Harold S. • SHT • USA
WHAT PRICE TAXI • 1932 • Lord Del • SHT • USA
WHAT PRICE VENGEANCE? • 1937 • Lord Del • USA • VENGEANCE
WHAT PRICE VICTORY • 1988 • Connor Kevin • TVM • USA
WHAT PRICE VICTORY? see **WAS KOSTET DER SIEG?** • 1981
WHAT SAY MOC? see **STO GOVORIT MOC?** • 1924
WHAT SCHOOLGIRLS DON'T TELL see **SECRETS OF SWEET SIXTEEN: WHAT SCHOOLGIRLS DON'T TELL** • 1974
WHAT SCOTTIE HEARD • 1915 • Birch Cecil • UKN
WHAT SHALL I BE? • 1966 • Buchvarova Radka • BUL • WHAT SHALL I DO?
WHAT SHALL I DO? • 1924 • Adolfi John G. • USA
WHAT SHALL I DO? see **WHAT SHALL I BE?** • 1966
WHAT SHALL IT PROFIT • 1917 • Baker George D. • USA
WHAT SHALL IT PROFIT see **HARD STEEL** • 1942
WHAT SHALL IT PROFIT A MAN • 1913 • Merwin Bannister • USA
WHAT SHALL IT PROFIT A MAN see **MONEY CHANGERS, THE** • 1920
WHAT SHALL WE DO NOW? see **VAD SKA VI GORA UN DA** • 1958
WHAT SHALL WE DO WITH HIM? • 1919 • Revier Harry • USA
WHAT SHALL WE DO WITH OUR OLD? • 1911 • Griffith D. W. • USA
WHAT THE ANGLER CAUGHT • 1909 • Aylott Dave? • UKN
WHAT THE ATOMIC BOMB BROUGHT see **HIROSHIMA NAGASAKI** • 1983
WHAT THE BELL TOLLED • 1912 • *Gem* • USA
WHAT THE BIRDS KNEW see **IKIMONO NO KIROKU** • 1955
WHAT THE BURGLAR GOT • 1914 • *Komic* • USA
WHAT THE BUTLER SAW • 1924 • Dewhurst George • UKN
WHAT THE BUTLER SAW • 1950 • Grayson Godfrey • UKN
WHAT THE CARDS FORETOLD • 1909 • *Edison* • USA
WHAT THE CRYSTAL TOLD • 1914 • *Bennett Belle* • USA
WHAT THE CURATE REALLY DID • 1905 • Fitzhamon Lewin • UKN
WHAT THE DAISY SAID • 1910 • Griffith D. W. • USA
WHAT THE DOCTOR ORDERED • 1912 • Powell Frank, Sennett Mack (Spv) • USA
WHAT THE DOCTOR ORDERED • 1913 • *Kalem* • USA
WHAT THE DRIVER SAW • 1912 • *Buckley May* • USA
WHAT THE EYE DOES NOT SEE see **CO OKO NEVIDI** • 1987
WHAT THE FIRELIGHT SHOWED • 1914 • Wilson Frank? • UKN
WHAT THE GODS DECREE • 1913 • *Krauss Charles* • FRN
WHAT THE GOOD BOOK TAUGHT • 1913 • *Patheplay* • USA
WHAT THE HELL ARE THEY COMPLAINING ABOUT see **TIENS-TOI BIEN APRES LES OREILLES A PAPA** • 1971
WHAT THE HELL, JACK! see **JACK** • 1977
WHAT THE HELL'S GOING ON UP THERE? • 1979 • Lamb Derek • ANS • CND
WHAT THE INDIANS DID • 1911 • *Champion* • USA
WHAT THE MILK DID • 1912 • *Harbaugh Carl* • USA
WHAT THE MOON SAW • 1988 • Amenta Pino • ASL
WHAT THE MOON SAW see **NIEZWYKLA PODROZ** • 1955
WHAT THE NIGHT TELLS –A TALE see **WAS DIE NACHT SPRICHT –EINE ERZAHLING** • 1987
WHAT THE PARROT SAW • 1910 • Stow Percy • UKN
WHAT THE PARROT SAW • 1935 • Newman Widgey R. • UKN
WHAT THE PEEPER SAW (USA) see **NIGHT HAIR CHILD** • 1971
WHAT THE PUPPY SAID • 1936 • Newman Widgey R. • UKN
WHAT THE RIVER FORETOLD • 1915 • Franey William, Franz Joseph J. • USA
WHAT THE SWEDISH BUTLER SAW see **GROOVE ROOM** • 1974
WHAT THE WILD WAVES DID • 1913 • *Nestor* • USA
WHAT THE WIND DID • 1918 • *Rhodes Billie* • USA
WHAT THE WINDOW CLEANER SAW • 1912 • *Cosmopolitan* • UKN
WHAT THREE MEN WANTED • 1924 • Burns Paul • USA
WHAT TIGERS LIKE BEST • 1989 • Nowak Krzysztof • PLN
WHAT TIME IS IT (UKN) see **CHE ORA E** • 1989
WHAT TO DO see **CHTO DELAT'** • 1928
WHAT! (USA) see **FRUSTA E IL CORPO, LA** • 1963
WHAT? (USA) see **CHE?** • 1972
WHAT WAITS BELOW • 1983 • Sharp Don • USA • SECRETS OF THE PHANTOM CAVERNS
WHAT WE ALWAYS KNEW ABOUT THE KOMSOMOL • 1987 • Traikova Ralitsa • DOC • BUL
WHAT WE HAVE ALL BEEN THROUGH see **KAHAN KAHAN SE GUZAR GAVA** • 1981
WHAT WE HAVE HERE IS A PEOPLE PROBLEM • 1976 • Mankiewicz Francis • MTV • CND
WHAT, WHO, HOW • 1957 • Vanderbeek Stan • ANS • USA
WHAT WILL BE, WILL BE • 1911 • *Lubin* • USA
WHAT WILL BECOME OF YOU, ESTHER? see **MI LESZ VELED ESZTERKE?** • 1968
WHAT WILL FATHER SAY • 1918 • *Field Elinor* • USA
WHAT WILL HAPPEN NEXT? • 1918 • *Jaxon* • USA
WHAT WILL MY WIFE SAY see **CO REKNE ZENA** • 1957
WHAT WILL PEOPLE SAY • 1915 • Blache Alice • USA
WHAT WILL THE MOUSE SAY? • 1988 • Pavlov Ivan • BUL
WHAT WILLIAM DID • 1908 • Rosenthal Joe • UKN
WHAT WILLIE DID • 1908 • Mottershaw Frank • UKN
WHAT WIVES DON'T WANT (UKN) see **VIRTUOUS HUSBAND, THE** • 1931
WHAT WIVES WANT • 1923 • Conway Jack • USA
WHAT WOMAN WANTS see **VAD KVINNAN VILL** • 1927
WHAT WOMEN DID FOR ME • 1927 • Roach Hal • SHT • USA
WHAT WOMEN DREAM (USA) see **WAS FRAUEN TRAUMEN** • 1933
WHAT WOMEN GIVE see **MEN MUST FIGHT** • 1932
WHAT WOMEN LOVE • 1920 • Watt Nate • USA
WHAT WOMEN SUFFER • 1909 • *Anglo-American Films* • UKN
WHAT WOMEN SUFFER • 1911 • Rolfe Alfred • ASL
WHAT WOMEN WANT • 1920 • Archainbaud George • USA
WHAT WOMEN WILL DO • 1921 • Jose Edward • USA
WHAT WOULD A GENTLEMAN DO? • 1918 • Noy Wilfred • UKN
WHAT WOULD YOU DO? • 1911 • *Powers* • USA
WHAT WOULD YOU DO? • 1914 • Levering Joseph • USA
WHAT WOULD YOU DO? • 1917 • Windom Lawrence C. • SHT • USA
WHAT WOULD YOU DO? • 1920 • Lawrence Edmund, Clift Denison • USA
WHAT WOULD YOU DO, CHUMS? • 1939 • Baxter John • UKN
WHAT WOULD YOU DO IF – • 1916 • Middleton Edwin • SHS • USA
WHAT WOULD YOU SAY TO SOME SPINACH see **COZ TAKHLE DAT SI SPENAT?** • 1976
WHAT YOU GAVE IS LIFE ITSELF • 1963 • Kollanyi Agoston • HNG
WHAT YOU SOW see **WAT JY SAAI** • 1979
WHATEVER HAPPENED TO THEM ALL? • 1967 • Pearson Peter • CND
WHATEVER HAPPENED TO UNCLE FRED • 1967 • Godfrey Bob • ANS • UKN
WHATEVER IS FUN • *Macmillan Films* • ANS • USA
WHATEVER IT TAKES • 1986 • Demchuk Bob • USA
WHATEVER SHE WANTS • 1921 • Wallace C. R. • USA
WHATEVER THE COST • 1918 • Ensminger Robert • USA
WHATEVER YOU CAN SPARE see **DAJ STO DAS** • 1981
WHAT'LL THE WEATHER BE? • 1915 • Plumb Hay? • UKN
WHAT'LL WE DO WITH UNCLE? • 1917 • Beaudine William • SHT • USA
WHAT'LL YOU HAVE? • 1916 • *Stull Walter* • SHT • USA
WHAT'S A GIRL LIKE YOU DOING IN A PLACE LIKE THIS? see **QUE HACE UNA CHICA COMO TU EN UN SITIO COMO ESTE?** • 1978
WHAT'S A NICE GIRL LIKE YOU..? • 1971 • Paris Jerry • TVM • USA
WHAT'S A NICE GIRL LIKE YOU DOING IN A PLACE LIKE THIS? • 1963 • Scorsese Martin • SHT • USA
WHAT'S A WIFE WORTH? • 1921 • Cabanne W. Christy • USA
WHAT'S BRED.. COMES OUT IN THE FLESH • 1916 • Morgan Sidney • UKN
WHAT'S BREWIN', BRUIN? • 1948 • Jones Charles M. • ANS • USA
WHAT'S BUZZIN' BUZZARD • 1943 • Avery Tex • ANS • USA
WHAT'S BUZZIN', COUSIN • 1943 • Barton Charles T. • USA
WHAT'S COOKIN'? • 1941 • Lantz Walter • ANS • USA • PANTRY PANIC
WHAT'S COOKIN' • 1942 • Cline Eddie • USA • WAKE UP AND DREAM (UKN)
WHAT'S COOKIN', DOC? • 1944 • Clampett Robert • ANS • USA
WHAT'S COOKING? • 1947 • Halas John, Batchelor Joy • ANS • UKN
WHAT'S COOKING? • 1951 • Marshall Herbert • UKN
WHAT'S GOOD FOR THE GANDER see **WHAT'S GOOD FOR THE GOOSE** • 1969
WHAT'S GOOD FOR THE GOOSE • 1969 • Golan Menahem • UKN • WHAT'S GOOD FOR THE GANDER
WHAT'S HAPPENING see **YEAH, YEAH, YEAH, NEW YORK MEETS THE BEATLES** • 1964
WHAT'S HAPPENING –THE BEATLES IN THE U.S.A. see **YEAH, YEAH, YEAH, NEW YORK MEETS THE BEATLES** • 1964
WHAT'S HIS NAME • 1914 • De Mille Cecil B. • USA
WHAT'S IN A NAME? • 1913 • Smiley Joseph • USA
WHAT'S IN A NAME? • 1915 • Birch Cecil • UKN
WHAT'S IN A NAME? • 1915 • Steppling John • USA
WHAT'S IN A NAME? • 1934 • Ince Ralph • UKN
WHAT'S IN A NUMBER • 1948 • Krish John • SHT • UKN
WHAT'S IN IT FOR HARRY? see **HOW TO MAKE IT** • 1968
WHAT'S MY LION? • 1961 • Freleng Friz • ANS • USA
WHAT'S NEW PUSSYCAT? • 1965 • Donner Clive • USA, FRN • QUOI DE NEUF, PUSSYCAT? (FRN)
WHAT'S OPERA, DOC? • 1957 • Jones Charles M. • ANS • USA
WHAT'S OURS? • 1915 • Drew Sidney • USA
WHAT'S PECKIN'? • 1965 • Smith Paul J. • ANS • USA
WHAT'S SAUCE FOR THE GOOSE • 1916 • *Plump & Runt* • SHT • USA
WHAT'S SO BAD ABOUT FEELING GOOD? • 1968 • Seaton George • USA
WHAT'S SWEEPIN'? • 1953 • Patterson Don • ANS • USA
WHAT'S THE JOKE? • 1912 • Aylott Dave? • UKN
WHAT'S THE MATADOR? • 1942 • White Jules • SHT • USA
WHAT'S THE MATTER WITH ANDRES LAPETEUS? see **SHTO SLUCHILOS S ANDRESOM LAPETEUSOM?** • 1967
WHAT'S THE MATTER WITH FATHER? • 1913 • *Bayne Beverly* • USA
WHAT'S THE MATTER WITH FATHER? • 1918 • Blystone John G. • SHT • USA
WHAT'S THE MATTER WITH HELEN? • 1971 • Harrington Curtis • USA • BEST OF FRIENDS
WHAT'S THE USE? • 1912 • *Powers* • USA
WHAT'S THE USE? • 1916 • *Pokes & Jabbs* • SHT • USA
WHAT'S THE USE OF GRUMBLING • 1918 • Edwards Henry • UKN
WHAT'S THE WEATHER LIKE UP THERE? • 1977 • Saltzman Deepa Mehta • DOC • CND
WHAT'S THE WORLD COMING TO? • 1926 • Roach Hal • SHT • USA

WHAT'S UP, DOC? • 1950 • McKimson Robert • ANS • USA
WHAT'S UP, DOC? • 1972 • Bogdanovich Peter • USA
WHAT'S UP FRONT • 1964 • Wehling Bob • USA • FOURTH FOR MARRIAGE, A
WHAT'S UP NO.2 see **WHAT'S UP SUPERDOC?** • 1978
WHAT'S UP NURSE? • 1977 • Ford Derek • UKN
WHAT'S UP SUPERDOC? • 1978 • Ford Derek • UKN • WHAT'S UP NO.2
WHAT'S UP, TIGER LILY? • 1966 • Allen Woody • USA
WHAT'S WORTH WHILE? • 1921 • Weber Lois • USA
WHAT'S WRONG WITH HUNGARIAN FILMS? • 1963 • Fejer Tamas • HNG
WHAT'S WRONG WITH THE PICTURE? • 1971-72 • Landow George • USA
WHAT'S WRONG WITH THE WOMEN? • 1922 • Neill R. William • USA
WHAT'S YOUR DAUGHTER DOING? see **DAUGHTERS OF TODAY** • 1924
WHAT'S YOUR HURRY? • 1909 • Griffith D. W. • USA
WHAT'S YOUR HURRY? • 1920 • Wood Sam • USA
WHAT'S YOUR HURRY? • 1926 • Newfield Sam • SHT • USA
WHAT'S YOUR HUSBAND DOING? • 1919 • Ingraham Lloyd • USA
WHAT'S YOUR I.Q. NO.1 • 1940 • *Smith Pete* • SHT • USA
WHAT'S YOUR I.Q. NO.2 • 1940 • Sidney George • SHT • USA
WHAT'S YOUR NAME see **KIMI NO NAWA** • 1954
WHAT'S YOUR RACKET? • 1934 • Guiol Fred • USA
WHAT'S YOUR REPUTATION WORTH? • 1921 • Campbell Webster • USA
WHAT'S YOURS IS MINE • 1915 • Wilson Frank? • UKN
WHATSOEVER A WOMAN SOWETH • 1914 • *Commerford Thomas* • USA
WHEAT AND TARES • 1915 • *Pennyan Film* • USA
WHEAT AND THE CHAFF, THE • 1916 • Mayo Melvin • SHT • USA
WHEAT AND THE TARES, THE • 1914 • Marston Theodore • USA
WHEAT COUNTRY • 1959 • Blais Roger • DOC • CND • AU PAYS DU BLE
WHEAT KING, THE • 1916 • *Puritan* • USA
WHEAT RIPENS, THE see **ERIK A BUZAKALASZ** • 1939
WHEAT-WHISTLE see **MUGIBUE** • 1955
WHEATLANDS OF EAST ANGLIA • 1935 • Field Mary • UKN • WORKERS TO BE INSURED
WHEEELS #1 • 1958-61 • Vanderbeek Stan • ANS • USA
WHEEELS #2 • 1958-59 • Vanderbeek Stan • ANS • USA
WHEEELS #4 • 1958-65 • Vanderbeek Stan • USA
WHEEL see **CHAKKARAM** • 1968
WHEEL see **CHAKRA** • 1979
WHEEL, THE • Pagot Tony, Pagot Nino • ANM • ITL
WHEEL, THE • 1925 • Schertzinger Victor • USA
WHEEL, THE • 1953 • Brealey Gil • SHT • ASL
WHEEL, THE see **ROUE, LA** • 1922
WHEEL, THE see **MOUL LE YA, MOUL LE YA** • 1983
WHEEL DEALER • 1970 • Gollin Norman • SHT • USA
WHEEL OF ASHES • 1968 • Goldman Peter Emanuel • FRN
WHEEL OF CHANCE • 1928 • Santell Alfred • USA • ROULETTE
WHEEL OF DEATH, THE • 1913 • *Kalem* • USA
WHEEL OF DEATH, THE • 1916 • Coleby A. E. • UKN
WHEEL OF DESTINY, THE • 1912 • *Rex* • USA
WHEEL OF DESTINY, THE • 1927 • Worne Duke • USA
WHEEL OF FATE • 1953 • Searle Francis • UKN • ROAD HOUSE GIRL (USA)
WHEEL OF FATE see **BHAGYA CHAKRAMU** • 1968
WHEEL OF FATE, THE • 1913 • *Reliance* • USA
WHEEL OF FATE, THE see **BHAGYA CHAKRA** • 1935
WHEEL OF FIRE (UKN) see **FUEGO** • 1964
WHEEL OF FORTUNE see **MAN BETRAYED, A** • 1937
WHEEL OF JUSTICE, THE see **WHEEL OF THE LAW, THE** • 1916
WHEEL OF LIFE, THE • 1914 • Reid Wallace • USA
WHEEL OF LIFE, THE • 1929 • Schertzinger Victor • USA
WHEEL OF LIFE, THE see **TA LUN HUI** • 1983
WHEEL OF THE GODS, THE • 1915 • Reehm George E. • USA
WHEEL OF THE LAW, THE • 1916 • Baker George D. • USA • WHEEL OF JUSTICE, THE
WHEELCHAIR, THE see **COCHECITO, EL** • 1960
WHEELED INTO MATRIMONY • 1915 • *Farley Dot* • USA
WHEELER see **PSYCHO FROM TEXAS** • 1982
WHEELER AND MURDOCK • 1972 • Sargent Joseph • TVM • USA
WHEELER DEALERS, THE • 1963 • Hiller Arthur • USA • SEPARATE BEDS (UKN)
WHEELS ACROSS A WILDERNESS • 1967 • Leyland Mike, Leyland Malcolm • ASL
WHEELS AND WOE • 1917 • Dillon John Francis? • USA
WHEELS OF CHANCE, THE • 1922 • Shaw Harold • UKN
WHEELS OF DEATH see **DEATH CAR ON THE FREEWAY** • 1979
WHEELS OF DESTINY • 1934 • James Alan • USA • FLYING FURY
WHEELS OF DESTINY, THE • 1913 • Miller Charles? • USA
WHEELS OF DESTINY, THE • 1914 • Adolfi John G. • USA
WHEELS OF FATE • 1922 • Sanderson Challis • UKN
WHEELS OF FATE see **ROUE, LA** • 1956
WHEELS OF FATE, THE • 1913 • Eagle Oscar • USA
WHEELS OF FIRE • 1984 • Santiago Cirio H. • USA • DESERT WARRIOR ○ VINDICATOR
WHEELS OF JUSTICE • 1909 • *Selig* • USA
WHEELS OF JUSTICE, THE • 1911 • *Williams Kathlyn* • USA
WHEELS OF JUSTICE, THE • 1915 • Marston Theodore • USA
WHEELS OF TERROR • 1987 • Hessler Gordon • USA • MISFIT BRIGADE, THE
WHEELS OF TIME, THE see **IDO KEREKE, AZ** • 1961
WHEELS ON FIRE • 1973 • Young Gary • DOC • ASL
WHEELS ON MEALS • 1984 • Hong Jinbao • HKG
WHEELS WITHIN WHEELS • 1915 • *Mcquarrie Murdock* • USA
WHELP, THE • 1917 • Wilson Millard K. • USA
WHEN A COUNT COUNTED • 1912 • *Anderson Mignon* • USA
WHEN A DOG LOVES • 1927 • McGowan J. P. • USA
WHEN A FELLER NEEDS A FRIEND • 1919 • SER • USA
WHEN A FELLER NEEDS A FRIEND • 1932 • Pollard Harry • USA • WHEN A FELLOW NEEDS A FRIEND (UKN) ○ LIMPY
WHEN A FELLER'S NOSE IS OUT OF JOINT • 1915 • Johnson Tefft • USA
WHEN A FELLOW NEEDS A FRIEND (UKN) see **WHEN A FELLER NEEDS A FRIEND** • 1932
WHEN A GIRL LOVES • 1913 • *Pickford Lottie* • USA
WHEN A GIRL LOVES • 1919 • Weber Lois, Smalley Phillips • USA
WHEN A GIRL LOVES • 1924 • Halperin Victor Hugo • USA
WHEN A GIRL'S BEAUTIFUL • 1947 • McDonald Frank • USA
WHEN A GOD PLAYED THE BADGER GAME see **GIRL WHO COULDN'T GO WRONG, THE** • 1915
WHEN A MAN FEARS • 1911 • *Thanhouser* • USA
WHEN A MAN GROWS OLD see **SENILITA** • 1962
WHEN A MAN IS MARRIED • 1915 • *Alhambra* • USA
WHEN A MAN LOVES • 1911 • Griffith D. W. • USA
WHEN A MAN LOVES • 1920 • Bennett Chester • USA • HIS LADY (UKN)
WHEN A MAN LOVES • 1927 • Crosland Alan • USA • HIS LADY
WHEN A MAN MARRIES • 1913 • *Nestor* • USA
WHEN A MAN RIDES ALONE • 1919 • King Henry • USA
WHEN A MAN RIDES ALONE • 1933 • McGowan J. P. • USA
WHEN A MAN RISKS HIS LIFE see **OTOKO GA INOCHI O KAKERU TOKI** • 1959
WHEN A MAN SEES RED • 1917 • Lloyd Frank • USA
WHEN A MAN SEES RED • 1934 • James Alan • USA
WHEN A MAN WEAKENS • 1916 • *Supreme* • USA
WHEN A MAN'S A MAN • 1924 • Cline Eddie • SHT • USA
WHEN A MAN'S A MAN • 1935 • Cline Eddie • USA • SAGA OF THE WEST
WHEN A MAN'S A PAL • 1920 • *Dalton Emmett* • SHT • USA
WHEN A MAN'S A PRINCE • 1926 • Cline Eddie • SHT • USA
WHEN A MAN'S FICKLE • 1915 • Davey Horace • USA
WHEN A MAN'S MARRIED • 1911 • *Vitagraph* • USA
WHEN A MAN'S MARRIED • 1912 • *Steppling John* • USA
WHEN A MAN'S MARRIED • 1918 • Drew Sidney, Drew Sidney Mrs. • SHT • USA
WHEN A MAN'S SINGLE • 1911 • *American* • USA
WHEN A MAN'S SINGLE • 1916 • Storrie Kelly • UKN
WHEN A STRANGER CALLS • 1979 • Walton Fred • USA
WHEN A WIFE WORRIES • 1916 • Clotworthy Hal • SHT • USA
WHEN A WOMAN ASCENDS THE STAIRS see **ONNA GA KAIDAN O AGARU TOKI** • 1960
WHEN A WOMAN CLIMBS THE STAIRS see **ONNA GA KAIDAN O AGARU TOKI** • 1960
WHEN A WOMAN GUIDES • 1914 • O'Sullivan Tony • USA
WHEN A WOMAN IN LOVE.. (UKN) see **FEMME FIDELE, UNE** • 1976
WHEN A WOMAN IS IN LOVE see **FEMME FIDELE, UNE** • 1976
WHEN A WOMAN LOVES • 1914 • *Eclectic* • USA
WHEN A WOMAN LOVES • 1915 • *Wehlen Emmy* • USA
WHEN A WOMAN LOVES see **ENDAMA TEHOBEL MERAA** • 1933
WHEN A WOMAN LOVES see **WAGA AI** • 1960
WHEN A WOMAN MEDDLES (USA) see **QUAND LA FEMME S'EN MELE** • 1958
WHEN A WOMAN SADDLES A HORSE • 1974 • Narliev Khodzhakuli • USS
WHEN A WOMAN SINS • 1918 • Edwards J. Gordon • USA
WHEN A WOMAN STRIKES • 1919 • Clements Roy • USA
WHEN A WOMAN WAITS • 1915 • *Greenwood Winnifred* • USA
WHEN A WOMAN WASTES • 1913 • *Patheplay* • USA
WHEN A WOMAN WON'T • 1913 • Dwan Allan • USA
WHEN A WOMAN'S 40 • 1914 • Martin E. A. • USA
WHEN ADAM HAD 'EM • 1916 • MacMackin Archer • USA
WHEN ALGY FROZE UP • 1914 • *Chadwick Cyril* • USA
WHEN AMBROSE DARED WALRUS • 1915 • Wright Walter • USA
WHEN AMERICA WAS YOUNG • 1914 • *Broncho* • USA
WHEN AN OLD MAID GETS BUSY • 1912 • *Hedlund Guy* • USA
WHEN ANGELS FALL see **GDY SPADAJA ANIOLY** • 1959
WHEN APPEARANCES DECEIVE • 1915 • *Courtot Marguerite* • USA
WHEN ARIZONA WON • 1919 • *Hamilton Shorty* • USA
WHEN ARTISTS LOVE see **NAR KONSTNARER ALSKA** • 1915
WHEN AUNT MATILDA FELL • 1916 • Christie Al • SHT • USA
WHEN AVARICE RULES • 1915 • *Colwell Goldie* • USA
WHEN BABY FORGOT • 1917 • Moore W. Eugene • USA
WHEN BEARCAT WENT DRY • 1919 • Sellers Oliver L. • USA
WHEN BEAUTY BUTTS IN • 1915 • Clements Roy • USA
WHEN BEAUTY COMES TO KOSKOB • 1915 • *Royal* • USA
WHEN BENGT AND ANDERS SWAPPED WIVES see **NAR BENGT OCH ANDERS BYTTE HUSTRUR** • 1950
WHEN BESS GOT IN WRONG • 1914 • *Meredyth Bess* • USA
WHEN BETTY BETS • 1917 • *Cahill Marie* • SHT • USA
WHEN BIG DAN RIDES • 1919 • *Lowell John* • SHT • USA
WHEN BILLY PROPOSED • 1914 • *Nestor* • USA
WHEN BILLY STRUCK THE STAGE • 1915 • *Santa Barbara* • USA
WHEN BLONDE MEETS BLONDE (UKN) see **ANYBODY'S BLONDE** • 1931
WHEN BOBBY BROKE HIS ARM • 1917 • Seay Charles M. • SHT • USA
WHEN BOBBY FORGOT • 1913 • *Casey Kenneth* • USA
WHEN BOYS ARE FORBIDDEN TO SMOKE • 1908 • Mottershaw Frank • UKN
WHEN BOYS LEAVE HOME (USA) see **DOWNHILL** • 1927
WHEN BROADWAY WAS A TRAIL • 1914 • Lund O. A. C. • USA
WHEN BROTHERS GO TO WAR • 1913 • *King Henry* • USA
WHEN CAESAR RAN A NEWSPAPER • 1929 • Graham Walter • USA
WHEN CALIFORNIA WAS WILD • 1915 • Daly William Robert • USA
WHEN CALIFORNIA WAS WON • 1911 • *Kalem* • USA
WHEN CALIFORNIA WAS YOUNG • 1912 • Sturgeon Rollin S. • USA
WHEN CAMERON PASSED BY • 1915 • McGill Lawrence • USA
WHEN CARNIVAL COMES see **QUANDO O CARNAVAL CHEGAR** • 1972
WHEN CHARLEY WAS A CHILD • 1915 • *Pathe Exchange* • USA
WHEN CHEMISTRY COUNTED • 1913 • *American* • USA
WHEN CHILDHOOD WINS • 1913 • *Patheplay* • USA
WHEN CIDERVILLE WENT DRY • 1915 • *Pathe Exchange* • USA
WHEN CINEMA WAS YOUNG see **KINEMA NO TENCHI** • 1987
WHEN CIVILIZATION FAILED see **IS DIVORCE A FAILURE?** • 1923
WHEN CLUBS WERE CLUBS • 1915 • Aylott Dave • UKN
WHEN CLUBS WERE TRUMPS • 1916 • *Morris Dave* • USA
WHEN COMEDY WAS KING • 1960 • Youngson Robert • CMP • USA
WHEN CONSCIENCE CALLS • 1914 • *Lubin* • USA
WHEN CONSCIENCE SLEEPS • 1915 • Taylor Edward C. • USA
WHEN COUNTRY COUSINS COME TO TOWN • 1913 • *Heron Andrew (P)* • UKN
WHEN COWBOY WAS KING • 1919 • Kennedy Aubrey M. • USA
WHEN CRIPPLES MEET • 1906 • Collins Alf • UKN
WHEN CUPID CAUGHT A THIEF • 1915 • *Nestor* • USA
WHEN CUPID CROSSED THE BAY • 1915 • Christie Al • USA
WHEN CUPID RUNS WILD • 1912 • *Imp* • USA
WHEN CUPID SLEEPS • 1910 • *Atlas* • USA
WHEN CUPID SLIPPED • 1916 • Forde Victoria • SHT • USA
WHEN CUPID WON • 1913 • *Nestor* • USA
WHEN DADDY COMES HOME • 1902 • Stow Percy • UKN
WHEN DADDY WAS WISE • 1912 • *Vitagraph* • USA
WHEN DAMON FELL FOR PYTHIAS • 1917 • Beaudine William • SHT • USA • WHEN DAMON FELL TO PYTHIAS
WHEN DAMON FELL TO PYTHIAS see **WHEN DAMON FELL FOR PYTHIAS** • 1917
WHEN DANGER CALLS • 1927 • Hutchison Charles • USA
WHEN DANGER SMILES • 1922 • Duncan William • USA
WHEN DARKNESS CAME • 1913 • *Thanhouser* • USA
WHEN DARKNESS FALLS see **NAR MORKRET FALLER** • 1960
WHEN DAWN CAME • 1920 • Campbell Colin • USA
WHEN DEATH RODE THE ENGINE • 1914 • *Frazer Robert* • USA
WHEN DEATH UNITED • 1913 • *Rex* • USA
WHEN DESTINY WILLS • 1921 • Baker R. C. • USA
WHEN DINOSAURS RULED THE EARTH • 1970 • Guest Val • UKN
WHEN DO THE DATES RIPEN? see **QUAND MURISSENT LES DATTES?** • 1968
WHEN DO WE EAT? • 1918 • Niblo Fred • USA
WHEN DOCTORS DISAGREE • 1919 • Schertzinger Victor • USA
WHEN DOLLY DIED • 1913 • *Powers* • USA
WHEN DOLLY PASSED AWAY • 1914 • Hotaling Arthur D. • USA
WHEN DREAMS COME TRUE • 1913 • *Thanhouser* • USA
WHEN DREAMS COME TRUE • 1913 • Nicholls George, Sennett Mack (Spv) • *Keystone* • USA
WHEN DREAMS COME TRUE • 1914 • *Pathe* • USA
WHEN DREAMS COME TRUE • 1929 • Worne Duke • USA • LOST AND WON (UKN)
WHEN DREAMS COME TRUE • 1985 • Moxey John Llewellyn • TVM • USA
WHEN DUMBLEIGH SAW THE JOKE • 1915 • Drew Sidney • USA
WHEN DUTY CALLS • 1912 • *Pathe* • USA
WHEN DUTY CALLS • 1913 • *White Pearl* • USA
WHEN EAST COMES WEST • 1911 • Dwan Allan • USA
WHEN EAST COMES WEST • 1922 • Eason B. Reeves • USA
WHEN EAST MEETS WEST • 1914 • *Anderson Mignon* • USA
WHEN EAST MEETS WEST • 1915 • Noy Wilfred • UKN
WHEN EAST MEETS WEST • 1918 • *Betzwood Film* • USA
WHEN EAST MEETS WEST IN BOSTON • 1914 • Edwin Walter • USA
WHEN EDDIE TOOK A BATH • 1915 • Christie Al • USA
WHEN EDDIE WENT TO THE FRONT • 1914 • Christie Al • USA
WHEN EDITH PLAYED JUDGE AND JURY • 1912 • Bosworth Hobart • USA
WHEN EIGHT BELLS TOLL • 1971 • Perier Etienne • UKN
WHEN EMPIRE CALLS • 1914 • *Favourite Films* • UKN
WHEN EMPTY HEARTS ARE FILLED • 1915 • MacMackin Archer • USA
WHEN EVERY DAY WAS THE FOURTH OF JULY • 1978 • Curtis Dan • TVM • USA
WHEN EVERY MAN'S A SOLDIER • 1914 • Stow Percy • UKN
WHEN EXTREMES MEET • 1905 • Collins Alf • UKN
WHEN FALSE TONGUES SPEAK • 1917 • Harbaugh Carl • USA
WHEN FATE DECIDES • 1919 • Millarde Harry • USA
WHEN FATE DECREES • 1913 • *Joyce Alice* • USA
WHEN FATE DISPOSES • 1914 • *Hall Ella* • USA
WHEN FATE FROWNED • 1914 • *Cooper Miriam* • USA
WHEN FATE LEADS TRUMPS • 1914 • Handworth Harry • USA
WHEN FATE REBELLED • 1915 • *Ostriche Muriel* • USA
WHEN FATE WAS KIND • 1914 • *Balboa* • USA
WHEN FATHER BUYS THE BEER • 1910 • Stow Percy • UKN
WHEN FATHER CRAVED A SMOKE • 1913 • *Selig* • USA
WHEN FATHER ELOPED WITH COOK • 1906 • Fitzhamon Lewin • UKN
WHEN FATHER FETCHED THE DOCTOR • 1912 • Aylott Dave? • UKN
WHEN FATHER GOES TO CHURCH • 1913 • *Frontier* • USA
WHEN FATHER GOT A HOLIDAY • 1906 • Stow Percy • UKN
WHEN FATHER HAD HIS WAY • 1912 • *Hawley Ormi* • USA
WHEN FATHER HAD THE GOUT • 1915 • Davey Horace • USA
WHEN FATHER HAS TOOTHACHE see **KUN ISALLA ON HAMMASSARKY** • 1923
WHEN FATHER INTERFERED • 1915 • *Johnson Arthur* • USA
WHEN FATHER LAID THE CARPET ON THE STAIRS • 1905 • Mottershaw Frank • *Sheffield Photo Co* • UKN
WHEN FATHER LAID THE CARPET ON THE STAIRS • 1905 • Stow Percy • *Clarendon* • UKN
WHEN FATHER LEARNT TO BIKE • 1913 • Collins Edwin J.? • UKN
WHEN FATHER MAKES A PUDDING see **BROWN'S PUDDING** • 1904

WHEN FATHER PUT UP THE BEDSTEAD • 1911 • Wilson Frank? • UKN
WHEN FATHER WAS AWAY ON BUSINESS see **OTAC NA SLUZBENOM PUTU** • 1985
WHEN FATHER WAS KIDNAPPED • 1913 • Christie Al • USA
WHEN FATHER WAS THE GOAT • 1915 • Davey Horace • USA
WHEN FATHER WEARS STAYS • 1909 • Stow Percy • UKN
WHEN FIGHTING'S NECESSARY • 1923 • Maloney Leo • USA
WHEN FIRST WE MET • 1911 • *Powers* • USA
WHEN FLIRTING DIDN'T PAY • 1916 • Page Will • UKN
WHEN FRIENDSHIP CEASES • 1913 • Thornby Robert T. • USA
WHEN G.I. JOHNNY COMES HOME • 1945 • Kneitel Seymour • ANS • USA
WHEN G-MEN STEP IN • 1938 • Coleman C. C. Jr. • USA • YOU CAN'T WIN
WHEN GANGLAND STRIKES • 1956 • Springsteen R. G. • USA
WHEN GEORGE HOPS • 1927 • Newfield Sam • SHT • USA
WHEN GHOST MEETS GHOST • 1913 • *Cruze James* • USA
WHEN GIANTS FOUGHT • 1926 • Malins Geoffrey H., Parkinson H. B. • UKN
WHEN GIRLS LEAVE HOME (UKN) see **MISSING GIRLS** • 1936
WHEN GIRLS TRUMPET FOR MANOEUVRES see **WENN MADCHEN ZUM MANOVER BLASEN** • 1974
WHEN GIRLS UNDRESS see **MATRATZEN TANGO** • 1972
WHEN GLASSES ARE NOT GLASSES • 1913 • Brooke Van Dyke • USA
WHEN GOD WILLS • 1914 • Lund O. A. C. • USA
WHEN GOLD IS DROSS • 1912 • Haldane Bert? • UKN
WHEN GRATITUDE IS LOVE • 1915 • Seay Charles M. • USA
WHEN GREEK MEETS GREEK • 1913 • Edwin Walter • USA
WHEN GREEK MEETS GREEK • 1915 • Drew Sidney • USA
WHEN GREEK MEETS GREEK • 1922 • West Walter • UKN
WHEN HANDS ARE IDLE • 1917 • *Castleton Barbara* • SHT • USA
WHEN HARRY MET SALLY • 1989 • Reiner Rob • USA • HARRY, THIS IS SALLY
WHEN HE CAME BACK • 1916 • McDermott John • SHT • USA
WHEN HE DIED • 1911 • *Essanay* • USA
WHEN HE FORGAVE • 1915 • *Warner'S Features* • USA
WHEN HE JUMPED AT CONCLUSIONS • 1913 • *Nestor* • USA
WHEN HE LOST TO WIN • 1913 • *Nestor* • USA
WHEN HE PROPOSED • 1915 • *Lyons Eddie* • USA
WHEN HE SEES • 1913 • Bracken Bertram • USA
WHEN HE WANTS A DOG, HE WANTS A DOG • 1913 • Cohl Emile • ANS • USA
WHEN HE WORE THE BLUE • 1913 • *Nestor* • USA
WHEN HEART WIRES CROSS • 1911 • *Powers* • USA
WHEN HEARTS ARE TRUMPS • 1912 • Christie Al • USA
WHEN HEARTS ARE TRUMPS • 1915 • *Rex* • USA
WHEN HEARTS ARE YOUNG • 1915 • Morrisey Edward • USA
WHEN HEARTS COLLIDE • 1917 • *Triangle Komedy* • USA
WHEN HELEN WAS ELECTED • 1912 • Parker Lem B. • USA
WHEN HELL BROKE LOOSE • 1958 • Crane Kenneth L. • USA
WHEN HELL WAS IN SESSION • 1979 • Krasny Paul • TVM • USA
WHEN HER IDOL FELL • 1915 • Christie Al • USA
WHEN HIRAM WENT TO THE CITY • 1915 • *Asher Max* • USA
WHEN HIS COURAGE FAILED • 1913 • *Nestor* • USA
WHEN HIS DOUGH WAS CAKE • 1915 • Douglass James • USA
WHEN HIS LORDSHIP PROPOSED • 1915 • Christie Al • USA
WHEN HIS SHIP COMES IN • 1914 • Santschi Thomas • USA
WHEN HONOR WAKES • 1915 • O'Neil Barry • USA
WHEN HOOLIGAN AND DOOLIGAN RAN FOR MAYOR • 1915 • Van Wally • USA
WHEN HUBBY ENTERTAINED • 1913 • *Nestor* • USA
WHEN HUBBY FORGOT • 1916 • Beaudine William • SHT • USA
WHEN HUBBY GREW JEALOUS • 1915 • Davey Horace • USA
WHEN HUBBY WASN'T WELL • 1911 • Wilson Frank? • UKN
WHEN HUBBY WENT TO COLLEGE • 1912 • *Powers* • USA
WHEN HUNGRY HAMLET FLED • 1915 • *Huling Lorraine* • USA
WHEN HUSBANDS DECEIVE • 1922 • Worsley Wallace • USA
WHEN HUSBANDS FLIRT • 1925 • Wellman William A. • USA
WHEN HUSBANDS GO TO WAR • 1915 • *Mina* • USA
WHEN I AM DEAD AND WHITE see **KAD BUDEM MRTAV I BEO** • 1968
WHEN I GO.. THAT'S IT! • 1972 • Low Colin • CND
WHEN I GROW UP • 1951 • Kanin Michael • USA
WHEN I GROW UP see **AZ JA BUDU VELKY** • 1963
WHEN I GROW UP see **DA GRANDE** • 1988
WHEN I LEAVE THE WORLD BEHIND • 1916 • *Tress Henry* • SHT • UKN
WHEN I LOST YOU • 1924-26 • Fleischer Dave • ANS • USA
WHEN I SAY I LOVE YOU see **QUANDO DICO CHE TI AMO** • 1967
WHEN I WANT TO CRY, I CAN'T see **CUANDO QUIERO LLORAR NO LLORO** • 1972
WHEN I WANT TO CRY, I DON'T DO IT see **CUANDO QUIERO LLORAR NO LLORO** • 1972
WHEN I WAS A KID, I DIDN'T CARE (USA) see **SI JE SUIS COMME CA, C'EST LA FAUTE DE PAPA** • 1978
WHEN I WAS PRINCE OF ARCADIA see **NAR JAG VAR PRINS UTAV ARKADIEN** • 1909
WHEN I WAS YOUNG • 1969 • Araminas Algirdas • USS
WHEN I YOO HOO • 1936 • Freleng Friz • ANS • USA
WHEN IGNORANCE IS BLISS • 1913 • *Essanay* • USA
WHEN IGNORANCE IS BLISS • 1915 • *Shield Ernie* • USA
WHEN IN LOVE see **ENDAMA NOVHEA** • 1967
WHEN IN ROME • 1952 • Brown Clarence • USA
WHEN IN THE COURSE OF • 1966 • Vanderbeek Stan • ANS • USA
WHEN IS A COUSIN? • 1915 • *Alhambra* • USA
WHEN IT COMES OFF • 1912 • Aylott Dave? • UKN
WHEN IT RAINED IN PARADISE see **KDYZ V RAJI PRSELO** • 1987
WHEN IT RAINS IT POURS • 1916 • Wolbert William • SHT • USA
WHEN IT STRIKES HOME • 1915 • Vekroff Perry N. • USA
WHEN IT STRIKES HOME • 1918 • *Beban George* • SHT • USA
WHEN IT WAS DARK • 1919 • Bocchi Arrigo • UKN
WHEN IT'S ONE OF YOUR OWN • 1914 • *Mcquarrie Murdock* • USA
WHEN IT'S SLEEPY TIME DOWN SOUTH • 1932 • Fleischer Dave • ANS • USA
WHEN JACK COMES HOME • 1909 • Coleby A. E. • UKN
WHEN JACK COMES HOME • 1912 • Stow Percy • UKN
WHEN JACK GOT HIS PAY • 1909 • Coleby A. E. • UKN
WHEN JEALOUSY TUMBLED • 1915 • King Burton L. • USA
WHEN JENKINS WASHED UP • 1906 • Fitzhamon Lewin • UKN
WHEN JERRY CAME TO TOWN • 1916 • *Ovey George* • USA
WHEN JIM RETURNED • 1913 • Reid Wallace • USA
WHEN JOE WENT WEST • 1913 • *Powers* • USA
WHEN JOEY WAS ON TIME • 1912 • *Housman Arthur* • USA
WHEN JOHN BROUGHT HOME HIS WIFE • 1913 • Johnson Arthur • USA
WHEN JOHNNY COMES MARCHING HOME • 1942 • Lamont Charles • USA
WHEN JOHNNY COMES MARCHING HOME see **RIDERS UP** • 1924
WHEN JONES LOST HIS LATCHKEY • 1912 • Wilson Frank? • UKN
WHEN JOSEPH RETURNS.. see **HA MEGJON JOZSEF** • 1975
WHEN JUSTICE ERRS • 1916 • *Fleitzer Film* • USA
WHEN JUSTICE SLEEPS • 1915 • *Balboa* • USA
WHEN JUSTICE WON • 1916 • Calvert E. H. • SHT • USA
WHEN KAPPA KAPPA GAMMA VISITED ONTARIO • 1924 • Sparling Gordon • CND
WHEN KINGS WERE THE LAW • 1912 • Griffith D. W. • USA
WHEN KISSES ARE SWEET • 1915 • *Atlas* • USA
WHEN KNIGHTHOOD WAS IN FLOWER • 1922 • Vignola Robert G. • USA
WHEN KNIGHTHOOD WAS IN FLOWER see **SWORD AND THE ROSE, THE** • 1953
WHEN KNIGHTS WERE BOLD • 1908 • *Bitzer Billy (Ph)* • USA
WHEN KNIGHTS WERE BOLD • 1914 • *Essanay* • USA
WHEN KNIGHTS WERE BOLD • 1915 • *Bray John R. (P)* • ANS • USA
WHEN KNIGHTS WERE BOLD • 1916 • Elvey Maurice • UKN
WHEN KNIGHTS WERE BOLD • 1929 • Whelan Tim • UKN
WHEN KNIGHTS WERE BOLD • 1936 • Raymond Jack • UKN
WHEN KNIGHTS WERE BOLD • 1941 • White Volney • ANS • USA
WHEN KNIGHTS WERE COLD • 1923 • Fouse Frank • USA
WHEN LADIES FLY see **LADIES COURAGEOUS** • 1944
WHEN LADIES MEET • 1933 • Beaumont Harry • USA
WHEN LADIES MEET • 1941 • Leonard Robert Z. • USA
WHEN LAW COMES TO HADES • 1923 • *Beery Noah* • USA
WHEN LEAVES FALL see **LISTOPAD** • 1968
WHEN LEE SURRENDERS • 1912 • Ince Thomas H. • USA
WHEN LENA STRUCK NEW MEXICO • 1913 • *Frontier* • USA
WHEN LIFE FADES • 1913 • *Morrow Elmer L.* • USA
WHEN LIGHT CAME BACK • 1913 • *Francis Alec B.* • USA
WHEN LIGHTS ARE LOW see **WHERE LIGHTS ARE LOW** • 1921
WHEN LILACS BLOSSOM see **NAR SYRENERNA BLOOMAR** • 1952
WHEN LILLIAN WAS LITTLE RED RIDING HOOD • 1913 • Campbell Colin • USA
WHEN LIN CAME HOME • 1916 • Wolbert William • SHT • USA
WHEN LINCOLN PAID • 1913 • Ford Francis • USA
WHEN LINCOLN WAS PRESIDENT • 1913 • *Pilot* • USA
WHEN LIONS ESCAPE • 1914 • *Columbia* • USA
WHEN LIPS ARE SEALED • 1909 • *Lubin* • USA
WHEN LITTLE LINDY SANG • 1916 • Warrenton Lule • SHT • USA
WHEN LIZ LET LOOSE • 1917 • Baldwin Ruth Ann • SHT • USA
WHEN LIZZIE DISAPPEARED • 1916 • Christie Al • SHT • USA
WHEN LIZZIE GOT HER POLISH • 1914 • *Nestor* • USA
WHEN LIZZIE WENT TO SEA • 1915 • *Forde Victoria* • USA
WHEN LONDON BURNED (USA) see **OLD ST. PAULS** • 1914
WHEN LONDON SLEEPS • 1914 • Batley Ernest G. • UKN
WHEN LONDON SLEEPS • 1932 • Hiscott Leslie • UKN
WHEN LONDON SLEEPS (USA) see **MENACE** • 1934
WHEN LOVE AND HONOR CALLED • 1915 • *Anderson Broncho Billy* • USA
WHEN LOVE BREAKS THROUGH • 1980 • Umboh Wim • INN
WHEN LOVE CALLS • Mastrocinque Camillo • ITL
WHEN LOVE CAME TO GAVIN BURKE • 1918 • O'Donovan Fred • IRL
WHEN LOVE COMES • 1922 • Seiter William A. • USA
WHEN LOVE COMES TO THE VILLAGE see **NAR KARLEKEN KOM TILL BYN** • 1950
WHEN LOVE DIES • 1990 • Ove Horace • UKN
WHEN LOVE FORGIVES • 1913 • *Ab* • USA
WHEN LOVE GROWS COLD • 1925 • Hoyt Harry O. • USA
WHEN LOVE GROWS UP • 1913 • *Kinemacolor* • USA
WHEN LOVE HAS GONE see **DVOJE** • 1961
WHEN LOVE IS BLIND • 1919 • Cline Eddie • SHT • USA
WHEN LOVE IS KING • 1916 • Turbett Ben • USA
WHEN LOVE IS LAW • 1916 • *Puritan* • SHT • USA
WHEN LOVE IS LOVE • 1915 • *Bush Pauline* • USA
WHEN LOVE IS LUST see **QUANDO L'AMORE E SENSUALITA** • 1973
WHEN LOVE IS MOCKED • 1915 • Nicholls George • USA
WHEN LOVE IS YOUNG • 1913 • *Essanay* • USA
WHEN LOVE IS YOUNG • 1913 • Smalley Phillips • *Crystal* • USA
WHEN LOVE IS YOUNG • 1922 • *Simpson Russell* • USA
WHEN LOVE IS YOUNG • 1937 • Mohr Hal • USA
WHEN LOVE KILLS see **NAR KARLEKEN DODAR** • 1913
WHEN LOVE LAUGHS • 1915 • *Moore Matt* • USA
WHEN LOVE LAUGHS see **CUANDO EL AMOR RIE** • 1933
WHEN LOVE LEADS • 1912 • *Hawley Ormi* • USA
WHEN LOVE LEADS • 1915 • *Williams Clara* • USA
WHEN LOVE LOSES OUT • 1913 • Smiley Joseph • USA
WHEN LOVE RULES • 1912 • *Rex* • USA
WHEN LOVE TOOK WINGS • 1915 • Arbuckle Roscoe • USA
WHEN LOVE WAS A CRIME (RASSENSCHANDE) see **KIEDY MILOSC BYLA ZBRODNIA (RASSENSCHANDE)** • 1968
WHEN LOVE WAS BLIND • 1911 • *Thanhouser* • USA
WHEN LOVE WAS BLIND • 1917 • Sullivan Frederick • USA
WHEN LOVERS MEET see **LOVER COME BACK** • 1946
WHEN LOVERS PART • 1910 • *Kalem* • USA
WHEN LUCK CHANGES • 1913 • Dwan Allan • USA
WHEN LUDWIG GOES ON MANOEUVRES see **WENN LUDWIG INS MANOVER ZIEHT** • 1967
WHEN LULA DANCED THE HULA • 1917 • *La Salle* • USA
WHEN MACBETH CAME TO SNAKEVILLLE • 1914 • *Joslin Margaret* • USA
WHEN MAGOO FLEW • 1954 • Burness Pete • ANS • USA
WHEN MAMA'S OUT • 1909 • Gobbett T. J. • UKN
WHEN MANDY CAME TO TOWN • 1912 • *Thanhouser* • USA
WHEN MARION WAS LITTLE • 1911 • *Solax* • USA
WHEN MARY GREW UP • 1913 • Young James • USA
WHEN MARY MARRIED • 1913 • *Lubin* • USA
WHEN MARY TOOK THE COUNT • 1917 • *Rhodes Billie* • SHT • USA
WHEN MASONS MEET • 1911 • *Powers* • USA
WHEN MAY WEDS DECEMBER • 1913 • Grandon Francis J. • USA
WHEN MEADOWS BLOOM see **NAR ANGARNA BLOMMAR** • 1946
WHEN MEMORIES ARE STIRRED UP see **JAB YAAD KISIKI AATI HAI** • 1967
WHEN MEMORY CALLS • 1912 • *Selig* • USA
WHEN MEMORY RECALLS • 1914 • *Frontier* • USA
WHEN MEMORY SPEAKS (UKN) see **DESEMBARCOS** • 1989
WHEN MEN ARE BEASTS see **WOMEN IN THE NIGHT** • 1948
WHEN MEN ARE TEMPTED • 1918 • Wolbert William • USA
WHEN MEN BETRAY • 1918 • Abramson Ivan • USA
WHEN MEN BETRAY • 1928 • Micheaux Oscar • USA
WHEN MEN CARRIED CLUBS, WOMEN PLAYED DING DONG! see **QUANDO GLI UOMINI ARMARONO LA CLAVA.. E CON LE DONNE FECERO DIN DON** • 1971
WHEN MEN DESIRE • 1919 • Edwards J. Gordon • USA
WHEN MEN DISCUSS WOMEN see **CUANDO LOS HOMBRES HABLAN DE MUJERES** • 1967
WHEN MEN FORGET • 1913 • Campbell Colin • USA
WHEN MEN HATE • 1913 • Olcott Sidney • USA
WHEN MEN LOVE • 1912 • *Republic* • USA
WHEN MEN WEAR SKIRTS • 1914 • *Roland Ruth* • USA
WHEN MEN WERE MEN • 1925 • *Terry Paul (P)* • ANS • USA
WHEN MEN WOULD KILL • 1914 • Olcott Sidney • USA
WHEN MERCY TEMPERS JUSTICE • 1912 • *Cruze James* • USA
WHEN MICHAEL CALLS • 1971 • Leacock Philip • TVM • USA
WHEN MIGHT WAS RIGHT • 1916 • King Henry • SHT • USA
WHEN MONEY COMES • 1929 • McCarey Leo • SHT • USA
WHEN MOSCOW LAUGHS see **DEVUSHKA S KOROBKOI** • 1927
WHEN MOTHER FELL IN AT CHRISTMAS • 1906 • Stow Percy • UKN
WHEN MOTHER-IN-LAW DICTATES see **NAR SVARMOR REGERAR** • 1914
WHEN MOTHER-IN-LAW REIGNS see **NAR SVARMOR REGERAR** • 1914
WHEN MOTHER IS ILL • 1913 • Stow Percy • UKN
WHEN MOTHER IS OUT • 1983 • Du Khanh • VTN
WHEN MOTHER VISITED NELLIE • 1915 • Hotaling Arthur D. • USA
WHEN MOUNTAIN AND VALLEY MEET • 1913 • Fielding Romaine • USA
WHEN MOUSEHOOD WAS IN FLOWER • 1953 • Rasinski Connie • ANS • USA
WHEN MY BABY SMILES AT ME • 1948 • Lang Walter • USA • BURLESQUE
WHEN MY KNIFE GETS YOU • 1969 • Papic Krsto • SHT • YGS
WHEN MY LADY SMILES • 1915 • *Stonehouse Ruth* • USA
WHEN MY SHIP COMES IN • 1919 • Thornby Robert T. • USA
WHEN MY SHIP COMES IN • 1934 • Fleischer Dave • ANS • USA
WHEN NAPLES SINGS see **NAPOLI CHE CANTA** • 1930
WHEN NATURE CALLS • 1985 • Kaufman Charles • USA • OUTDOORSTERS, THE
WHEN NEW YORK SLEEPS (UKN) see **NOW I'LL TELL** • 1934
WHEN NIGHT FALLS see **AD SOFF HALAYLA** • 1985
WHEN NIGHT FALLS ON THE REEPERBAHN see **WENN ES NACHT WIRD AUF DER REEPERBAHN** • 1967
WHEN NORTH AND SOUTH MEET • 1911 • *Champion* • USA
WHEN ODDS ARE EVEN • 1923 • Flood James • USA
WHEN OLD NEW YORK WAS YOUNG • 1910 • *Vitagraph* • USA
WHEN OPPORTUNITY KNOCKED • 1916 • Millarde Harry • SHT • USA
WHEN OTHER LIPS • 1908 • Raymond Charles? • UKN
WHEN PALS QUARREL • 1911 • *Powers* • USA
WHEN PAPA DIED • 1916 • Dillon John Francis • SHT • USA
WHEN PARIS GREEN SAW RED • 1918 • *Hart Neal* • SHT • USA
WHEN PARIS SLEEPS • 1917 • Bramble A. V. • UKN
WHEN PASSION BLINDS HONESTY see **HULDA RASMUSSEN** • 1911
WHEN PASSIONS RISE • 1915 • Noy Wilfred • UKN
WHEN PATHS DIVERGE • 1913 • Haldane Bert? • UKN
WHEN PEOPLE MEET • 1966 • Werner Gosta • SHT • SWD
WHEN PERSISTENCY AND OBSTINACY MEET • 1912 • *Costello Maurice* • USA
WHEN PIERROT MEETS PIERRETTE • 1913 • *Tennant Barbara* • USA
WHEN PIGEONS FLY see **KAD GOLUBOVI POLETE** • 1968
WHEN PIMPLE WAS YOUNG • 1913 • Evans Fred, Evans Joe • UKN
WHEN PIMPLE WAS YOUNG -HIS FIRST SWEETHEART • 1914 • Evans Fred, Evans Joe • UKN
WHEN PIMPLE WAS YOUNG -YOUNG PIMPLE'S SCHOOLDAYS • 1914 • Evans Fred, Evans Joe • UKN
WHEN PIZARRO, CORTEZ AND ORELLANA WERE FRIENDS see **CUANDO PIZARRO, CORTEZ Y ORELLANA ERAN AMIGOS** • 1979
WHEN QUACKEL DID HYDE • 1920 • Gramlich Charles • USA
WHEN QUEENIE CAME BACK • 1914 • *Beauty* • USA
WHEN ROARING GULCH GOT SUFFRAGE • 1913 • *Frontier* • USA
WHEN ROGUES FALL OUT • 1915 • McGowan J. P. • USA
WHEN ROMANCE CAME TO ANNE • 1914 • Drew William • USA

WHEN ROMANCE RIDES • 1922 • Howe Eliot, Rush Charles O., Hersholt Jean • USA
WHEN ROME RULED • 1914 • *Truex Ernest* • USA
WHEN ROOBARB FOUND SAUCE • 1974 • Godfrey Bob • ANS • UKN
WHEN ROOBARB MADE A SPIKE • 1973 • Godfrey Bob • ANS • UKN
WHEN ROOBARB WAS BEING BORED, THEN NOT BEING BORED • 1974 • Godfrey Bob • ANS • UKN
WHEN ROSEBUDS OPEN see **NAR ROSORNA SLA UT** • 1930
WHEN ROSES BLOOM see **KOGDA TSVETUT ROZY** • 1959
WHEN ROSES WHITHER • 1912 • Young James • USA
WHEN RUBEN CAME TO TOWN • 1911 • *Solax* • USA
WHEN RUBEN COMES TO TOWN • 1908 • Porter Edwin S. • USA
WHEN RUBEN FOOLED THE BANDITS • 1914 • Henderson Dell • USA
WHEN SALT LOSES ITS TASTE see **CUANDO LA SAL PIERDE SU SABOR** • 1975
WHEN SAMUEL SKIDDED • 1915 • Stratton Edmund F. • USA
WHEN SCHULTZ LED THE ORCHESTRA • 1915 • Curtis Allen • USA
WHEN SCOUTING WON • 1930 • Cross J. H. Martin • UKN
WHEN SECONDS COUNT • 1927 • Apfel Oscar • USA
WHEN SEPTEMBER COMES see **KOGDA NASTUPAYET SENTYABR..** • 1977
WHEN SEX WAS A KNIGHTLY AFFAIR (UKN) see **AMOROUS ADVENTURES OF DON QUIXOTE & SANCHO PANZA, THE** • 1976
WHEN SHADOWS FALL • 1915 • Robards Willis • USA
WHEN SHE PLAYED BROADWAY • 1916 • *Hulette Gladys* • SHT • USA
WHEN SHE SAYS NO • 1984 • Aaron Paul • TVM • USA
WHEN SHE WAS ABOUT SIXTEEN • 1912 • *Mcdermott Marc* • USA
WHEN SHE WAS BAD.. • 1979 • Hunt Peter H. • TVM • USA
WHEN SHERMAN MARCHED TO THE SEA • 1913 • *Bison* • USA
WHEN SLIM PICKED A PEACH • 1916 • Clements Roy • SHT • USA
WHEN SLIM WAS HOME CURED • 1916 • Clements Roy • SHT • USA
WHEN SLIPPERY SLIM BOUGHT THE CHEESE • 1915 • *Potel Victor* • USA
WHEN SLIPPERY SLIM MET THE CHAMPION • 1914 • *Potel Victor* • USA
WHEN SLIPPERY SLIM WENT FOR THE EGGS • 1915 • *Essanay* • USA
WHEN SMALTZ LOVES • 1914 • *Sterling Ford* • USA
WHEN SNAKEVILLE STRUCK OIL • 1915 • *Todd Harry* • USA
WHEN SNITZ WAS "MARRIAGED" • 1915 • *Brennan John E.* • USA
WHEN SOCIETY CALLS • 1913 • North Wilfred • USA
WHEN SORROW FADES • 1914 • *Anderson Mignon* • USA
WHEN SORROW WEEPS • 1917 • Windom Lawrence C. • SHT • USA
WHEN SOUL MEETS SOUL • 1912 • MacDonald J. Farrell • SHT • USA
WHEN SOULS ARE TRIED • 1915 • Fielding Romaine • USA
WHEN SPIRITS WALKED • 1913 • *Frontier* • USA
WHEN SPRING COMES see **KETIKA MUSIM SEMI TIBA** • 1987
WHEN SPRING IS HOT see **CIND PRIMAVARA E FIERBINTE** • 1961
WHEN SPRING IS LATE see **KUR PRANVERA VONOHET** • 1980
WHEN SPRING MAKES A MISTAKE see **CUANDO LA PRIMAVERA SE EQUIVOCA** • 1944
WHEN STORKS FLY AWAY • 1964 • Lysenko Vadim • USS
WHEN STRANGERS MARRY • 1933 • Badger Clarence • USA
WHEN STRANGERS MARRY • 1944 • Castle William • USA • BETRAYED
WHEN STRANGERS MEET • 1934 • Cabanne W. Christy • USA
WHEN STRANGERS MEET see **EINER FRISST DEN ANDEREN** • 1964
WHEN STRAWBERRIES RIPEN see **KO ZORIJO JAGODE** • 1979
WHEN STRONG MEN MEET • 1913 • *Champion* • USA
WHEN STUBBS LEAVES THE BOWERY • 1915 • *Santa Barbara* • USA
WHEN SUGAR COOKIES ARE BROKEN see **SATOGASHI GA KOWARERU TOKI** • 1967
WHEN SUMMER COMES • 1922 • Del Ruth Roy • SHT • USA
WHEN SUMMONS COMES • 1932 • Sandrich Mark • SHT • USA
WHEN SVANTE DISAPPEARED see **DA SVANTE FORSVANDT** • 1975
WHEN TAEKWONDO STRIKES • 1974 • Huang Feng • HKG
WHEN THE ALARM BELL RINGS see **NAR LARMLOCKAN LJUDER** • 1913
WHEN THE BATS ARE QUIET • 1987 • Lignini Fabio • ANM • BRZ
WHEN THE BELLS START RINGING see **KAD CUJES ZVONA** • 1969
WHEN THE BIRD FLEW AWAY see **CHEKLA PAIKHRABADA** • 1989
WHEN THE BLIND SEE • 1914 • Powell Paul • USA
WHEN THE BLOOD CALLS • 1913 • *Nestor* • USA
WHEN THE BOUGH BREAKS • 1947 • Huntington Lawrence • UKN
WHEN THE BOUGH BREAKS • 1986 • Hussein Waris • TVM • USA
WHEN THE BOUGH BREAKS see **SYMPTOMS** • 1974
WHEN THE BOYS MEET THE GIRLS • 1965 • Ganzer Alvin • USA • GIRL CRAZY
WHEN THE BRIDES GOT MIXED • 1914 • *Nestor* • USA
WHEN THE CALL CAME • 1915 • *Gaumont* • USA
WHEN THE CALL CAME • 1915 • Goldin Sidney M., De Villiers • *Imp* • USA
WHEN THE CARTRIDGES FAILED • 1914 • Wilson Ben • USA
WHEN THE CAT CAME BACK • 1914 • *Princess* • USA
WHEN THE CAT COMES (USA) see **AZ PRIJDE KOCOUR** • 1963
WHEN THE CAT'S AWAY • 1898 • *Paul R. W.* • UKN
WHEN THE CAT'S AWAY • 1906 • Cooper Arthur • UKN
WHEN THE CAT'S AWAY • 1910 • *Lubin Arthur* • USA
WHEN THE CAT'S AWAY • 1911 • *Pickford Mary* • USA
WHEN THE CAT'S AWAY • 1917 • Chaudet Louis W. • SHT • USA
WHEN THE CAT'S AWAY • 1920 • *Royal Comedy* • USA
WHEN THE CAT'S AWAY • 1928 • Disney Walt, Iwerks Ub • ANS • USA
WHEN THE CAT'S AWAY • 1935 • Ising Rudolf • ANS • USA
WHEN THE CAT'S AWAY • 1935 • Tennyson Walter • UKN
WHEN THE CAT'S AWAY THE MICE PLAY • 1905 • *Walturdaw* • UKN
WHEN THE CHILDREN LEAVE see **CUANDO LOS HIJOS SE VAN** • 1941
WHEN THE CIRCUS CAME TO TOWN • 1913 • Campbell Colin • USA
WHEN THE CIRCUS CAME TO TOWN • 1916 • Smith Sidney • SHT • USA
WHEN THE CIRCUS CAME TO TOWN • 1981 • Sagal Boris • TVM • USA
WHEN THE CLOCK STOPPED • 1913 • *Lubin* • USA
WHEN THE CLOCK STRIKES • 1961 • Cahn Edward L. • USA • CLOCK STRIKES THREE, THE
WHEN THE CLOCK STRUCK NINE • 1921 • *Howarth Lillian* • USA
WHEN THE CLOUDS ROLL BY • 1920 • Fleming Victor, Reed Theodore • USA
WHEN THE COOK FELL ILL • 1914 • Campbell Colin • USA
WHEN THE COOKIE CRUMBLES see **SATOGASHI GA KOWARERU TOKI** • 1967
WHEN THE COUGAR CALLED • 1920 • *Lane Magna* • SHT • USA
WHEN THE CRASH CAME (UKN) see **ALIMONY** • 1924
WHEN THE CROW TURNS WHITE AND THE HERON TURNS BLACK see **PAGPUTI NG UWAK, PAGATIM NG TAGAK** • 1978
WHEN THE DALTONS RODE • 1940 • Marshall George • USA
WHEN THE DEACON SWORE • 1915 • Christie Al • USA
WHEN THE DEAD APPEAR see **MUERTOS SI SALEN, LOS** • 1976
WHEN THE DEAD RETURN • 1911 • Olcott Sidney • USA
WHEN THE DEBT WAS PAID • 1913 • *Majestic* • USA
WHEN THE DESERT CALLS • 1922 • Smallwood Ray C. • USA
WHEN THE DESERT SMILES • 1919 • Hart Neal • USA
WHEN THE DESERT WAS KIND • 1913 • Sturgeon Rollin S. • USA
WHEN THE DEVIL COMMANDS see **DEVIL COMMANDS, THE** • 1941
WHEN THE DEVIL DRIVES • 1907 • Booth W. R. • UKN
WHEN THE DEVIL DRIVES • 1922 • Scardon Paul • USA
WHEN THE DEVIL DRIVES (UKN) see **SAIT-ON JAMAIS** • 1957
WHEN THE DEVIL LAUGHED • 1920 • Jaccard Jacques • SHT • USA
WHEN THE DEVIL WAS WELL • 1937 • Rogers Maclean • UKN
WHEN THE DOCTOR FAILED • 1914 • *Lubin* • USA
WHEN THE DOOR OPENED • 1925 • Barker Reginald • USA
WHEN THE DOOR OPENED see **ESCAPE** • 1940
WHEN THE DOOR WAS CLOSED see **MEDAN PORTEN VAR STANGD** • 1946
WHEN THE EARTH COMES WEST • 1911 • *American* • USA
WHEN THE EARTH TREMBLED • 1913 • *Myers Harry* • USA
WHEN THE FATES SPIN • 1915 • *Essanay* • USA
WHEN THE FIDDLER CAME TO BIG HORN • 1915 • *Sterling Edyth* • USA
WHEN THE FIRE BELL RANG • 1915 • Cooley Frank • USA
WHEN THE FIRE-BELLS RANG • 1912 • Sennett Mack • USA
WHEN THE FIRES STARTED see **UZAVRELI GRAD** • 1961
WHEN THE FLAG FALLS • 1909 • *Lubin* • USA
WHEN THE FLEET SAILED • 1915 • *La Badie Florence* • USA
WHEN THE GANGSTERS CAME TO CHRISTCHURCH • 1933 • Mirams Roger • SHT • NZL
WHEN THE GERMANS CAME • 1915 • Evans Joe • UKN
WHEN THE GERMANS ENTERED LOOS • 1916 • Batley Ernest G. • UKN
WHEN THE GIRLS JOINED THE FORCE • 1914 • Christie Al • USA
WHEN THE GIRLS MEET THE BOYS see **GIRL CRAZY** • 1943
WHEN THE GIRLS TAKE OVER • 1962 • Hayden Russell • USA
WHEN THE GIRLS WERE SHANGHAIED • 1914 • *Nestor* • USA
WHEN THE GODS FALL ASLEEP see **QUANDO OS DEUSES ADORMECEM** • 1972
WHEN THE GODS FORGIVE • 1914 • Davis Ulysses • USA
WHEN THE GODS PLAYED A BADGER GAME • 1915 • De Grasse Joseph • USA
WHEN THE GREEKS see **TON KERO TON HELLINON** • 1980
WHEN THE HAM TURNED • 1914 • Griffin Frank C. • USA
WHEN THE HEART CALLS • 1912 • *Reliance* • USA
WHEN THE HEART CALLS • 1912 • *Selig* • USA
WHEN THE HEART CALLS • 1912 • *Nestor* • USA
WHEN THE HEART CALLS • 1914 • *Imp* • USA
WHEN THE HEART CALLS • 1914 • Wright Fred E. • *Pathe* • USA
WHEN THE HEART CHANGES • 1913 • *Johnson Arthur* • USA
WHEN THE HEART IS WOUNDED see **KAPG PUSO'Y SINUGATAN** • 1967
WHEN THE HEART IS YOUNG • 1917 • Aylott Dave • UKN
WHEN THE HEART RULES • 1912 • *Williams Kathlyn* • USA
WHEN THE HEAVENS FALL see **KUN TAIVAS PUTOAA** • 1972
WHEN THE HOUSE DIVIDED • 1915 • *Royal* • USA
WHEN THE HURRICANES BOUGHT THE LINO • 1914 • Fitzhamon Lewin • UKN
WHEN THE HURRICANES TOOK UP FARMING • 1914 • Fitzhamon Lewin • UKN
WHEN THE HURRICANES VISITED THE DOUGHNUTS • 1913 • Fitzhamon Lewin • UKN
WHEN THE HURRICANES VISITED THE SAWMILLS • 1914 • Fitzhamon Lewin • UKN
WHEN THE HUSBAND TRAVELS (USA) see **OTAN O SYZYGOS TAXEIDEYEI** • 1939
WHEN THE INK RAN OUT • 1914 • Collins Edwin J.? • UKN
WHEN THE KELLYS RODE • 1934 • Southwell Harry • ASL
WHEN THE KELLYS WERE OUT • 1923 • Southwell Harry • ASL
WHEN THE KUNG FU HERO STRIKES • *Pei Betty Ting* • HKG
WHEN THE LAD CAME HOME • 1922 • *Myers Harry* • USA
WHEN THE LAST LEAF FELL • 1913 • *Majestic* • USA
WHEN THE LAW CAME • 1911 • Davis Ulysses • USA
WHEN THE LAW RIDES • 1928 • De Lacy Robert • USA
WHEN THE LEAVES FALL see **LISTOPAD** • 1968
WHEN THE LEGENDS DIE • 1972 • Millar Stuart • USA
WHEN THE LIGHT CAME • 1916 • Chatterton Thomas • SHT • USA
WHEN THE LIGHT CAME IN • 1915 • Kaufman Joseph • USA
WHEN THE LIGHT FADES • 1913 • Dwan Allan • USA
WHEN THE LIGHT SHINES BRIGHTLY IN THE LIGHTHOUSE • 1929 • Aylott Dave, Symmons E. F. • SHT • UKN
WHEN THE LIGHT WANED • 1911 • *Vitagraph* • USA
WHEN THE LIGHTNING STRUCK • 1914 • *Essanay* • USA
WHEN THE LIGHTS GO ON AGAIN • 1944 • Howard William K. • USA
WHEN THE LILY DIED • 1912 • *Powers* • USA
WHEN THE LILY DIED • 1915 • *Early Baby* • USA
WHEN THE LINE GETS THROUGH • 1985 • Ware Clyde • USA
WHEN THE LION COMES see **KAD DODJE LAV** • 1973
WHEN THE LION ROARED • 1915 • *Pathe Exchange* • USA
WHEN THE LITTLE DREAM COMES TRUE • Chung Jin-Woo • SKR
WHEN THE LOSERS WON • 1916 • Christie Al • SHT • USA
WHEN THE MAN IN THE MOON SEEKS A WIFE • 1908 • Stow Percy • UKN
WHEN THE MAN SPEAKS • 1917 • Calvert E. H. • SHT • USA
WHEN THE MEN LEFT TOWN • 1914 • Williams C. Jay • USA
WHEN THE MIDNIGHT CHOO-CHOO COMES TO ALABAM • 1924-26 • Fleischer Dave • ANS • USA
WHEN THE MIND SLEEPS • 1915 • *Tannehill Myrtle* • USA
WHEN THE MINSTRELS CAME TO TOWN • 1916 • Matthews H. C. • SHT • USA
WHEN THE MIST IS LIFTING see **VIATA NU IARTA** • 1957
WHEN THE MISTRESS TOOK HER HOLIDAY • 1907 • Cooper Arthur • UKN
WHEN THE MUMMY CRIED FOR HELP • 1915 • Christie Al • USA
WHEN THE NIGHT CALL CAME • 1914 • Le Saint Edward J. • USA
WHEN THE OCEAN IS BLUE see **HAI-SHUI CHENG LAN** • 1988
WHEN THE PEOPLE AWAKE (UKN) see **CUANDO SE DESPIERTA EL PUEBLO** • 1973
WHEN THE PIE WAS OPENED • 1915 • *Dangerfield Winnie* • UKN
WHEN THE PIE WAS OPENED • 1942 • Lye Len • ANS • UKN
WHEN THE POPPIES BLOOM AGAIN • 1937 • MacDonald David • UKN
WHEN THE POPPIES BLOOM AGAIN see **DOKTER PULDER ZAAIT PAPAVERS** • 1975
WHEN THE PRESS SPEAKS • 1913 • Baker George D. • USA
WHEN THE PRINCE ARRIVED • 1913 • *Rex* • USA
WHEN THE PRISON DOORS OPENED • 1913 • *Lubin* • USA
WHEN THE RAIN BEGINS TO FALL see **VOYAGE OF THE ROCK ALIENS** • 1984
WHEN THE RAIN FALLS see **YAGMUR CISELERKEN** • 1967
WHEN THE RANGE CALLED • 1915 • *Whitman Velma* • USA
WHEN THE RAVEN FLIES see **HRAFNINN FLYGUR** • 1983
WHEN THE RED RED ROBIN COMES BOB BOB BOBBIN' ALONG • 1932 • Fleischer Dave • ANS • USA
WHEN THE RED TURNED GRAY • 1911 • *Reliance* • USA
WHEN THE REDSKINS RODE • 1951 • Landers Lew • USA
WHEN THE RIGHT MAN COMES ALONG • 1913 • Edwin Walter • USA
WHEN THE RIVER WAS THE ONLY ROAD • 1965 • Buckley Anthony • DOC • ASL
WHEN THE ROAD PARTS • 1914 • Taylor William D.? • USA
WHEN THE SCREAMING STOPS see **GARRAS DE LORELEI, LAS** • 1972
WHEN THE SHERIFF GOT HIS MAN • 1911 • *Champion* • USA
WHEN THE SHOW HIT WATERTOWN • 1915 • *Mina* • USA
WHEN THE SKIES FALL see **KUN TAIVAS PUTOAA** • 1972
WHEN THE SLEEPER WAKES • 1904 • Fitzhamon Lewin • UKN
WHEN THE SNOW BLED • 1981 • Arnold Jack • USA
WHEN THE SNOW FALLS THIS WAY see **KIEDY SNIEG PADA TAK** • 1961
WHEN THE SNOWS FELL see **DORODARAKE NO JUNJO** • 1963
WHEN THE SPHINX SPOKE • 1912 • *Powers* • USA
WHEN THE SPIDER TORE LOOSE • 1915 • Lloyd Frank • USA
WHEN THE SPIRIT MOVED • 1915 • Christie Al • USA
WHEN THE STORM IS OVER see **BADAI-PASTI BERLALU** • 1977
WHEN THE STRINGS WEEP see **KDYZ STRUNY LKAJI** • 1930
WHEN THE STUDIO BURNED • 1913 • Marston Theodore • USA
WHEN THE SUGAR CAKE BREAKS see **SATOGASHI GA KOWARERU TOKI** • 1967
WHEN THE SUGAR COOKIE CRUMBLES see **SATOGASHI GA KOWARERU TOKI** • 1967
WHEN THE SUN WENT OUT • 1911 • *Kalem* • USA
WHEN THE TABLES TURNED • 1911 • Melies Gaston • USA
WHEN THE TENTH MONTH COMES see **BAO GIO CHO DEN THANG MUOI** • 1984
WHEN THE TIDE CAME IN • 1915 • *Glaum Louise* • USA
WHEN THE TIDE TURNED • 1915 • *Premier* • USA
WHEN THE TIDE TURNED • 1916 • *Church Frederick* • SHT • USA
WHEN THE TIDE TURNS • 1913 • *Solax* • USA
WHEN THE TIDE TURNS • 1915 • Physioc Wray • USA
WHEN THE TIME COMES • 1987 • Erman John • USA
WHEN THE TOCSIN CALLS see **NAR LARMLOCKAN LJUDER** • 1913
WHEN THE TREES GREW TALL see **KOGDA DEREVYA BYLI BOLSHIMI** • 1962
WHEN THE TREES WERE.. • 1985 • Simm Peeter • USS
WHEN THE TREES WERE TALL (USA) see **KOGDA DEREVYA BYLI BOLSHIMI** • 1962
WHEN THE VIOLIN SIGHS see **KDYZ STRUNY LKAJI** • 1930
WHEN THE WELL WENT DRY • 1913 • *Lubin* • USA
WHEN THE WEST WAS WILD • 1911 • *Nestor* • USA
WHEN THE WEST WAS YOUNG • 1913 • Bowman William J. • USA
WHEN THE WEST WAS YOUNG • 1914 • Campbell Colin • USA
WHEN THE WHALES CAME • 1989 • Rees Clive • UKN

WHEN THE WHEELS OF JUSTICE CLOGGED • 1914 • *Thanhouser* • USA
WHEN THE WIFE'S AWAY • 1905 • Martin J. H.? • UKN
WHEN THE WIFE'S AWAY • 1926 • Strayer Frank • USA
WHEN THE WIND BLOWS • 1920 • Roach Hal • SHT • USA
WHEN THE WIND BLOWS • 1930 • Horne James W. • SHT • USA
WHEN THE WIND BLOWS • 1986 • Murakami Jimmy T. • ANS • UKN
WHEN THE WIND BLOWS see **MAKE WAY FOR TOMORROW** • 1937
WHEN THE WIRES CROSSED • 1915 • *Shumway L. C.* • USA
WHEN THE WOLF HOWLS • 1916 • Madison Cleo, Mong William V. • SHT • USA
WHEN THE WORLD SLEEPS • 1910 • *White Pearl* • USA
WHEN THE WORLD WAS SILENT • 1914 • Brenon Herbert • USA
WHEN THE WORM TURNED • 1913 • *La Badie Florence* • USA
WHEN THEIR DADS FELL OUT • 1915 • Davey Horace • USA
WHEN THEIR WIVES JOINED THE FORCE • 1914 • *Joker* • USA
WHEN THERE ARE FEELINGS see **KUN ON TUNTEET** • 1953
WHEN THERE WASN'T TREASURE • 1974 • Godfrey Bob, Green Peter • ANS • UKN
WHEN THEY GREW JEALOUS • 1914 • *Powers* • USA
WHEN THEY SLEEP • 1957 • Marzano Joseph • SHT • USA
WHEN THEY WERE CO-EDS • 1915 • Christie Al • USA
WHEN THEY WERE KIDS • 1913 • *Pathe* • USA
WHEN THIEF MEETS THIEF (USA) see **JUMP FOR GLORY** • 1937
WHEN THIEVES FALL OUT • 1909 • Bouwmeester Theo? • UKN
WHEN THIEVES FALL OUT • 1914 • Huntley Fred W. • USA
WHEN THIEVES FALL OUT • 1915 • *Jonasson Frank* • USA
WHEN THIEVES FALL OUT • 1917 • Harvey John • SHT • USA
WHEN THINGS GO WRONG • 1916 • Ellis Robert • USA
WHEN THINGS WERE ROTTEN • 1975 • Bonerz Peter, Ruskin Coby, Feldman Marty • MTV • USA
WHEN THREE WAS A CROWD • 1915 • Davey Horace • USA
WHEN TILLY'S UNCLE FLIRTED • 1911 • Fitzhamon Lewin • UKN
WHEN TIME RAN OUT.. • 1980 • Goldstone James • USA • 1985 DAY THE WORLD ENDED, THE
WHEN TOMORROW COMES • 1939 • Stahl John M. • USA • MODERN CINDERELLA, THE
WHEN TOMORROW COMES see **INTERLUDE** • 1967
WHEN TOMORROW DIES • 1966 • Kent Larry • CND
WHEN TONY PAWNED LOUISA • 1913 • *Clayton Ethel* • USA
WHEN TWENTY IS IN LOVE • 1912 • *Rex* • USA
WHEN TWO HEARTS ARE WON • 1911 • Olcott Sidney • USA
WHEN TWO PLAY A GAME • 1916 • Drew Sidney • SHT • USA
WHEN UNCLE SAM WAS YOUNG • 1912 • *Darkfeather Mona* • USA
WHEN UNCLE TOOK CLARENCE FOR A WALK • 1910 • Wilson Frank? • UKN
WHEN UNIVERSAL IKE SETS • 1914 • *Universal* • USA
WHEN URSUS THREW THE BULL • 1914 • *Nestor* • USA
WHEN VICE SHATTERS • 1914 • *Princess* • USA
WHEN VILLAINS WAIT • 1914 • Nicholls George, Henderson Dell • USA
WHEN WAR MEANT PEACE • 1917 • *Triangle* • USA
WHEN WAR THREATENED • 1915 • Powell Paul • *Lubin* • USA
WHEN WAR THREATENED • 1915 • Williams C. Jay • *Joker* • USA
WHEN WE ARE MARRIED • 1943 • Comfort Lance • UKN
WHEN WE ARE MARRIED see **TRUTHFUL SEX, THE** • 1926
WHEN WE ARE OLD • 1983 • Iyoda Seikph • MTV • JPN
WHEN WE CALLED THE PLUMBER IN • 1910 • Stow Percy • UKN
WHEN WE LOOK BACK (UKN) see **FRISCO WATERFRONT** • 1935
WHEN WE WERE 21 see **TRUTH ABOUT YOUTH, THE** • 1930
WHEN WE WERE IN OUR 'TEENS • 1910 • Griffith D. W. • USA
WHEN WE WERE TWENTY-ONE • 1915 • Porter Edwin S., Ford Hugh • USA
WHEN WE WERE TWENTY-ONE • 1921 • King Henry • USA
WHEN WE WERE VERY YOUNG • 1928 • Miller Frank • SER • UKN
WHEN WE WERE YOUNG • 1914 • *Miller'S 101 Ranch* • USA
WHEN WE WERE YOUNG see **KAK MOLODY MY BYLI** • 1985
WHEN WEALTH TORMENTS • 1912 • *Bushman Francis X.* • USA
WHEN WE'RE TOGETHER • 1909 • *Warwick Trading Co* • UKN
WHEN WERE YOU BORN? • 1938 • McGann William • USA
WHEN WIFEY HOLDS THE PURSE STRINGS • 1911 • Sennett Mack, Henderson Dell • USA
WHEN WIFIE SLEEPS • 1915 • Hotaling Arthur D. • USA
WHEN WIFIE'S AWAY • 1941 • D'Arcy Harry • SHT • USA
WHEN WILL YOU GIVE ME MY SHARE? • 1977 • Bugajski Ryszard • MTV • PLN
WHEN WILLIAM'S WHISKERS WORKED • 1915 • *Chamerlain Riley* • USA
WHEN WILLIE COMES MARCHING HOME • 1950 • Ford John • USA • FRONT AND CENTER
WHEN WILLIE WENT WILD • 1915 • Clements Roy • USA
WHEN WIND AND RAIN BEATS ON THE WINDOW see **KOGDA DOZHD I VYETER STUCHAT V OKNO** • 1968
WHEN WINTER WENT • 1925 • Morris Reggie • USA
WHEN WOLVES CRY see **ARBRE DE NOEL, L'** • 1969
WHEN WOMAN HATES • 1909 • *Lubin* • USA
WHEN WOMAN HATES • 1916 • Ward Albert • UKN
WHEN WOMAN WILLS • 1910 • *Reliance* • USA
WHEN WOMEN ARE POLICE • 1913 • *Roland Ruth* • USA
WHEN WOMEN GO ON THE WARPATH • 1913 • Young James, North Wilfred • USA
WHEN WOMEN HAD TAILS (USA) see **QUANDO LE DONNE AVEVANO LA CODA** • 1970
WHEN WOMEN JOINED THE FORCE • 1910 • Martinek H. O. • UKN
WHEN WOMEN KEEP SILENT see **WENN FRAUEN SCHWEIGEN** • 1937
WHEN WOMEN LIE see **USO** • 1963
WHEN WOMEN LOST THEIR TAILS (USA) see **QUANDO LE DONNE PERSERO LA CODA** • 1972
WHEN WOMEN PLAYED DING-DONG see **QUANDO GLI UOMINI ARMARONO LA CLAVA.. E CON LE DONNE FECERO DIN DON** • 1971
WHEN WOMEN RULE • 1908 • Fitzhamon Lewin • UKN
WHEN WOMEN RULE • 1912 • *Stedman Myrtle* • USA
WHEN WOMEN RULE • 1915 • Evans Joe • UKN
WHEN WOMEN RULED THE WORLD • Cooper Arthur
WHEN WOMEN STRIKE • 1911 • *Lubin* • USA
WHEN WOMEN WIN • 1909 • *Lubin* • USA
WHEN WORLDS COLLIDE • 1951 • Mate Rudolph • USA
WHEN YOU AND I WERE YOUNG • 1915 • *Ck* • USA
WHEN YOU AND I WERE YOUNG • 1918 • Blache Alice • USA
WHEN YOU ARE ASLEEP see **KIEDY TY SPISZ** • 1950
WHEN YOU ARE DRY • 1920 • France Charles H. • SHT • USA
WHEN YOU COME HOME • 1947 • Baxter John • UKN
WHEN YOU COMIN' BACK, RED RYDER? • 1979 • Katselas Milton • USA
WHEN YOU HAVE A MOTHER-IN-LAW (USA) see **WENN DU EINE SCHWEIGERMUTTER HAST** • 1937
WHEN YOU HEAR THE BELLS see **KAD CUJES ZVONA** • 1969
WHEN YOU HEAR THE BELLS TOLL see **KAD CUJES ZVONA** • 1969
WHEN YOU HIT -HIT HARD • 1918 • *Ebony* • SHT • USA
WHEN YOUR LOVER LEAVES • 1983 • Bleckner Jeff • TVM • USA
WHEN YOU'RE A LONG WAY FROM HOME • 1916 • *Tress Henry* • SHT • UKN
WHEN YOU'RE IN LOVE • 1937 • Riskin Robert • USA • FOR YOU ALONE (UKN)
WHEN YOU'RE MARRIED see **MABEL'S MARRIED LIFE** • 1914
WHEN YOU'RE SCARED -RUN • 1918 • *Ebony* • SHT • USA
WHEN YOU'RE SMILING • 1950 • Santley Joseph • USA
WHEN YOUTH CONSPIRES (UKN) see **OLD SWIMMIN' HOLE, THE** • 1940
WHEN YOUTH IS AMBITIOUS • 1915 • Kaufman Joseph • USA
WHEN YOUTH MEETS YOUTH • 1912 • *Christy Lillian* • USA
WHEN YOUTH WON OUT • 1915 • *Royal* • USA
WHEN YUBA PLAYS THE RUMBA ON THE TUBA • 1933 • Fleischer Dave • ANS • USA
WHENCE AND WHERE TO see **KUDY KAM** • 1956
WHENCE DOES HE COME • Zecca Ferdinand • FRN
WHENCE DOES HE COME see **QUO VADIS?** • 1901
WHENEVER see **CADA VEZ QUE..** • 1968
WHEN'S YOUR BIRTHDAY? • 1937 • Beaumont Harry • USA
WHERE AFTER THE RAIN? see **KUDA POSLE KISE?** • 1967
WHERE ALL THE CHILDREN WAVE TO THE PASSENGERS • 1961 • Strbac Milenko • YGS
WHERE AM I? • 1923 • Roach Hal • SHT • USA
WHERE AM I? • 1925 • Gillett Burt, Davis Mannie • ANS • USA
WHERE AMBITION LEADS • 1919 • Asher Billy • UKN
WHERE ANGELS GO, TROUBLE FOLLOWS • 1968 • Neilson James • USA
WHERE ARE MY CHILDREN? • 1916 • Weber Lois, Smalley Phillips • USA
WHERE ARE MY TROUSERS? • 1917 • De Haven Carter • SHT • USA
WHERE ARE THE CHILDREN? • 1986 • Malmuth Bruce • USA
WHERE ARE THE DREAMS OF YOUTH see **SEISHUN NO YUME IMA IZUKO** • 1932
WHERE ARE WE HEADING? • 1971 • Nicholson Arch • SHT • ASL
WHERE ARE YOU? see **KE TUMI?** • 1967
WHERE ARE YOU GOING? • 1966 • Vas Judit • DOC • HNG
WHERE ARE YOU GOING? • 1986 • Vulchanov Rangel • BUL
WHERE ARE YOU GOING? see **DOKAD IDZIECIE** • 1961
WHERE ARE YOU GOING ALL NAKED? (UKN) see **DOVE VAI TUTTA NUDA?** • 1969
WHERE ARE YOU GOING TO, MY PRETTY MAID • 1902 • *Warwick Trading Co* • UKN
WHERE ARE YOU, LOUISA? see **GDZIE JESTES LUIZO?** • 1964
WHERE ARE YOU, LUIZO? see **GDZIE JESTES LUIZO?** • 1964
WHERE ARE YOU, MRS. DERY? see **DERYNE, HOL VAN?** • 1975
WHERE ARE YOU, MY ZULFIJA? • 1964 • Khamraev Ali • USS
WHERE ARE YOU NOW, MAXIM? • 1965 • Keosayan Edmond • USS
WHERE ARE YOU TAKING ME? • 1965 • Tammer Peter • DOC • ASL
WHERE ARE YOUR CHILDREN? • 1944 • Nigh William • USA
WHERE ARE YOUR HUSBANDS? • 1920 • *Van Billy* • USA
WHERE BONDS ARE LOOSED • 1919 • Fischer David G. • USA
WHERE BRAINS ARE NEEDED • 1915 • MacQuarrie Murdock • USA
WHERE BREEZES BLOW • 1915 • Dillon Eddie • USA
WHERE BROADWAY MEETS THE MOUNTAINS • 1912 • Dwan Allan • USA
WHERE CAN I GET A WIFE? • 1915 • *Mason Dan* • USA
WHERE CATTLE IS KING • 1933 • Binney Josh • USA
WHERE CHARITY BEGINS • 1913 • Smalley Phillips • USA
WHERE CHIMNEYS ARE SEEN see **ENTOTSU NO MIERU BASHO** • 1953
WHERE COHOES PLAY • 1938 • Oliver Bill • DOC • CND
WHERE DANGER LIVES • 1950 • Farrow John • USA
WHERE DESTINY GUIDES • 1913 • Dwan Allan • USA
WHERE DID OUR LOVE GO? • 1966 • Sonbert Warren • USA
WHERE DID WE MEET? • Roussev Nikola • BUL
WHERE DID YOU GET IT? • 1900 • Smith G. A. • UKN
WHERE DID YOU GET THAT GIRL? • 1941 • Lubin Arthur • USA
WHERE DO WE GO FROM HERE? • 1945 • Ratoff Gregory • USA
WHERE DO WE GO FROM HERE? • 1987 • Vulchanov Rangel • BUL • THIRD CIRCLE, THE
WHERE DO YOU GO? see **DOKAD IDZIECIE** • 1961
WHERE DOES IT HURT? • 1972 • Amateau Rod • USA, UKN
WHERE DOES MORNING COME FROM? see **SAAN DARATING ANG UMAGA** • 1983
WHERE D'YE GET THAT STUFF? • 1916 • *Argosy* • USA
WHERE EAGLES DARE • 1968 • Hutton Brian G., Canutt Yakima • UKN, USA
WHERE EAST IS EAST • 1929 • Browning Tod • USA
WHERE ENMITY DIES • 1915 • *Ab* • USA
WHERE GLORY WAITS • 1917 • Holubar Allen • SHT • USA
WHERE HAPPINESS DWELLS • 1915 • King Burton L. • USA
WHERE HAS POOR MICKEY GONE? • 1964 • Levy Gerry • UKN
WHERE HAVE ALL THE PEOPLE GONE? • 1974 • Moxey John Llewellyn • TVM • USA
WHERE HAZEL MET THE VILLAIN • 1914 • Henderson Dell • USA
WHERE THE HIM OF THE HAIRY HANDS LIVES • 1972 • Joseph Stanley • DCS • UKN
WHERE HISTORY HAS BEEN WRITTEN • 1913 • Pearson George • DCS • UKN
WHERE IS BETA? see **QUEM A BETA?** • 1973
WHERE IS HERE? • 1988 • Gunnarsson Sturio • DOC • CND
WHERE IS MISHA? see **KDE JE MISA?** • 1954
WHERE IS MULCAHEY? • 1910 • *Essanay* • USA
WHERE IS MY CHE-ILD? • 1917 • Smith Noel • SHT • USA
WHERE IS MY DOG? • 1920 • Gibson Harry • SHT • USA
WHERE IS MY FATHER? • 1916 • Adelman Joseph • USA
WHERE IS MY HUSBAND? see **DINTY'S DARING DASH** • 1916
WHERE IS MY MOTHER? • 1917 • Berthelet Arthur • SHT • USA
WHERE IS MY WANDERING BOY THIS EVENING? • 1923 • *Sennett Mack (P)* • SHT • USA
WHERE IS MY WANDERING BOY TONIGHT? • 1909 • Porter Edwin S. • USA
WHERE IS MY WANDERING BOY TONIGHT? • 1922 • Hogan James P., Webb Millard • USA
WHERE IS MY WIFE? • 1916 • *Ritchie Billie* • SHT • USA
WHERE IS THE FRIEND'S HOME? • 1988 • Kia-Rostami Abbas • IRN
WHERE IS THE GENERAL? see **GDZIE JEST GENERAL?** • 1964
WHERE IS THE PLUNGER? • 1970 • Bonniere Rene • SHT • CND
WHERE IS THE THIRD KING? see **GDZIE JEST TRZECI KROL?** • 1967
WHERE IS THIS LADY? • 1932 • Vajda Ladislao, Hanbury Victor • UKN, FRG
WHERE IS THIS WEST? • 1923 • Marshall George • USA
WHERE IS YOUR FRIEND? • 1916 • *Vitagraph* • SHT • USA
WHERE IT'S AT • 1969 • Kanin Garson • USA
WHERE JEALOUSY LEADS • 1912 • *Handworth Octavia* • USA
WHERE LIGHTS ARE LOW • 1921 • Campbell Colin • USA • WHEN LIGHTS ARE LOW
WHERE LOVE DWELLS • 1913 • *Solax* • USA
WHERE LOVE HAS GONE • 1964 • Dmytryk Edward • USA
WHERE LOVE HAS GONE see **DVOJE** • 1961
WHERE LOVE IS • 1917 • *Murdock Ann* • USA
WHERE LOVE IS, THERE GOD IS ALSO • 1912 • Eagle Oscar • USA
WHERE LOVE LEADS • 1916 • Griffin Frank C. • USA
WHERE LOVE SPRINGS see **MACHI NI IZUMI GA ATTA** • 1968
WHERE MEN ARE MEN • 1921 • Duncan William • USA
WHERE MOUNTAINS FLOAT see **HVOR BJERGENE SEJLER** • 1954
WHERE NO VULTURES FLY • 1951 • Watt Harry • UKN, SAF • IVORY HUNTER (USA)
WHERE NOW ARE THE DREAMS OF YOUTH see **SEISHUN NO YUME IMA IZUKO** • 1932
WHERE OH WHERE HAS MY LITTLE DOG GONE? • 1907 • Morland John • UKN
WHERE PATHS DIVERGE • 1914 • *Princess* • USA
WHERE PATHS MEET • 1912 • *Imp* • USA
WHERE PERIL LURKS • 1919 • *Lowell John* • USA
WHERE ROMANCE RIDES • 1925 • Hayes Ward • USA
WHERE SEA AND SHORE BOTH MEET • 1910 • *Reliance* • USA
WHERE SHIPWRECKS ABOUND • 1977 • Stoneman John • MTV • CND
WHERE SHORE AND WATER MEET • 1913 • *Harte Betty* • USA
WHERE SIN LIVES see **ACOSADA** • 1963
WHERE SINNERS MEET • 1934 • Ruben J. Walter • USA • DOVER ROAD, THE (UKN)
WHERE SPRING COMES LATE see **KAZOKU** • 1971
WHERE THE ACTION WAS • 1967 • Keatley Philip (c/d) • SER • CND
WHERE THE BITTERSWEET GROWS, PART 1 • 1980 • Ondaatje Kim • DOC • CND
WHERE THE BOUGH BREAKS • 1970 • Bonniere Rene • CND
WHERE THE BOYS ARE • 1960 • Levin Henry • USA
WHERE THE BOYS ARE '84 • 1984 • Averback Hy • USA
WHERE THE BREAKERS ROAR • 1908 • Griffith D. W. • USA
WHERE THE BUFFALO ROAM • 1938 • Herman Al • USA
WHERE THE BUFFALO ROAM • 1980 • Linson Art • USA
WHERE THE BULLETS FLY • 1966 • Gilling John • UKN • DEATH OF ANGELS
WHERE THE DEVIL CANNOT GO (USA) see **KAM CERT NEMUZE** • 1959
WHERE THE DEVIL SAYS GOODNIGHT see **GDZIE DIABEL MOWI DOBRANOC** • 1956
WHERE THE EAGLE FLIES see **PICKUP ON 101** • 1972
WHERE THE ELEPHANT STOOD see **RUMAH PUAKA** • 1957
WHERE THE FOREST ENDS • 1915 • De Grasse Joseph • USA
WHERE THE FOREST MEETS THE SEA • 1987 • Baker Jeannie • ANS • ASL
WHERE THE GANGES FLOWS see **JIS DESH MEN GANGA BEHIT** • 1961
WHERE THE GREEN ANTS DREAM (UKN) see **WO DIE GRUNEN AMEISEN TRAUMEN** • 1984
WHERE THE HEART IS • 1989 • Boorman John • USA
WHERE THE HEART IS see **SITHA GIYA THANE** • 1967
WHERE THE HEATHER BLOOMS • 1915 • Christie Al • USA
WHERE THE HOP VINE TWINES • 1913 • *Victor* • USA
WHERE THE HOT WIND BLOWS (USA) see **LOI, LA** • 1958
WHERE THE INSPECTOR DOES NOT GO see **KAM NECHODI INSPEKTOR** • 1964
WHERE THE LADIES GO • 1980 • Flicker Theodore J. • TVM • USA
WHERE THE LAW ENDS • 1964 • Skanata Krsto • DOC • YGS
WHERE THE LIGHTHOUSE FLASHES see **DAR FYREN BLINKAR** • 1924
WHERE THE LILIES BLOOM • 1974 • Graham William A. • USA

WHERE THE MONEY WENT • 1912 • *Gardner Helen* • USA
WHERE THE MOUNTAINS MEET • 1913 • *Essanay* • USA
WHERE THE MOUNTAINS MEET • 1914 • *Reliance* • USA
WHERE THE NIGHTS ARE LONG see **TAM GDYE DLINNAYA ZIMA** • 1968
WHERE THE NORTH BEGINS • 1923 • Franklin Chester M. • USA
WHERE THE NORTH BEGINS • 1947 • Bretherton Howard • USA
WHERE THE NORTH HOLDS SWAY • 1927 • Cohn Bennett • USA
WHERE THE OUTBACK ENDS • 1988 • Radwanski Stasch • ASL
WHERE THE PAVEMENT ENDS • 1923 • Ingram Rex • USA
WHERE THE RAINBOW ENDS • 1921 • Lucoque H. Lisle • UKN
WHERE THE RED FERN GROWS • 1974 • Tokar Norman • USA
WHERE THE RIVER BENDS (UKN) see **BEND OF THE RIVER** • 1952
WHERE THE RIVER RUNS BLACK • 1986 • Cain Christopher • USA • LAZARO
WHERE THE ROAD DIVIDED • 1915 • Jones Edgar • USA
WHERE THE ROAD FORKS • 1913 • Ricketts Thomas • USA
WHERE THE ROADS MEET • 1915 • *Empire* • USA
WHERE THE SHAMROCK GROWS • 1911 • Porter Edwin S. • USA
WHERE THE SIDEWALK ENDS • 1950 • Preminger Otto • USA
WHERE THE SPIES ARE • 1966 • Guest Val • UKN, USA • PASSPORT TO OBLIVION ○ ONE SPY TOO MANY
WHERE THE SPIRIT LIVES • 1990 • Pittman Bruce • CND
WHERE THE SUMMER WIND BLOWS see **UTE BLASER SOMMARVIND** • 1955
WHERE THE SUN BEATS (UKN) see **ONDE BATE O SOL** • 1988
WHERE THE SUN SETS • 1910 • *Nestor* • USA
WHERE THE SUN SETS RED • 1918 • *Rancho* • USA
WHERE THE TRAIL DIVIDES • 1914 • Neill James • USA
WHERE THE TRAIL LED • 1915 • *Davenport Dorothy* • USA
WHERE THE TRAILS BEGIN see **WHERE TRAILS BEGIN** • 1927
WHERE THE TRUTH LIES (USA) see **MALEFICES** • 1962
WHERE THE WATER IS CLEAN AND THE GRASS IS GREEN see **GDZIE WODA CZYSTA I TRAWA ZIELONA** • 1977
WHERE THE WEST BEGINS • 1919 • King Henry • USA
WHERE THE WEST BEGINS • 1928 • Horner Robert J. • USA
WHERE THE WEST BEGINS • 1938 • McGowan J. P. • USA
WHERE THE WIND BLOWS • 1910 • *Vitagraph* • USA
WHERE THE WIND DIES see **ADONDE MUERE EL VIENTO** • 1975
WHERE THE WINDS LEAD see **DIT VINDARNA BAR** • 1948
WHERE THE WOLVES HOWL see **WILCZE ECHA** • 1968
WHERE THE WORST BEGINS • 1925 • McDermott John • USA
WHERE THEIR CARAVAN WAS WRESTED • 1915 • *Britannia* • UKN
WHERE THERE IS SOAP THERE IS HOPE • 1912 • *Reliance* • USA
WHERE THERE'S A HEART • 1912 • Dwan Allan • USA
WHERE THERE'S A SWILL THERE'S A SPRAY • 1913 • Calvert Charles? • UKN
WHERE THERE'S A SWILL THERE'S A SWAY • 1913 • Wilson Frank • UKN
WHERE THERE'S A WILL • 1936 • Beaudine William • USA
WHERE THERE'S A WILL • 1955 • Sewell Vernon • UKN
WHERE THERE'S A WILL THERE'S A WAY • 1906 • Williamson James • UKN
WHERE THERE'S A WILL, THERE'S A WAY • 1909 • *Vitagraph* • USA
WHERE THERE'S A WILL THERE'S A WAY • 1911 • *Selig* • USA
WHERE THERE'S A WILL THERE'S A WAY • 1912 • Thornton F. Martin • UKN
WHERE THERE'S A WILL THERE'S A WAY • 1914 • *Grandin Ethel* • USA
WHERE THERE'S A WILL (USA) see **GOOD MORNING, BOYS** • 1937
WHERE THERE'S LIFE • 1947 • Lanfield Sidney • USA
WHERE THERE'S SMOKE • 1961 • Kuwahara Bob • ANS • USA
WHERE THERE'S SMOKE • 1970 • Arioli Don • CND
WHERE THERE'S SMOKE (USA) see **IL N'Y A PAS DE FUMEE SANS FEU** • 1972
WHERE TIME BEGAN (USA) see **VIAJE AL CENTRO DE LA TIERRA** • 1977
WHERE TO? see **ILA AYN** • 1957
WHERE TO, AFTER THE RAIN? see **KUDA POSLE KISE?** • 1967
WHERE TO ESCAPE TO? • 1977 • Emara Hussein • EGY
WHERE TO PUT IT? see **KAM S NIM?** • 1922
WHERE TRAILS BEGIN • 1927 • Smith Noel • USA • WHERE THE TRAILS BEGIN
WHERE TRAILS DIVIDE • 1937 • Bradbury Robert North • USA
WHERE TRAILS END • 1942 • Tansey Robert • USA
WHERE-U-SEER? see **MYSTERY FILM, THE** • 1924
WHERE WAS I? • 1925 • Seiter William A. • USA
WHERE WERE YOU, JACOB? see **JACOB SMITAREN** • 1983
WHERE WERE YOU WHEN THE LIGHTS WENT OUT? • 1968 • Averback Hy • USA
WHERE WILL THEY GO? • 1958 • King Allan • CND
WHERE WILL YOU HIDE? • 1948 • *Audiographic Institute* • ANS • USA
WHERE WINDMILLS RUN see **DAR MOLLARNA GA** • 1956
WHERE WIT WINS • 1913 • *Frontier* • USA
WHERE WIVES WIN • 1916 • *Hastings Carey L.* • SHT • USA
WHERE WORDS FAIL see **DONDE MUEREN LAS PALABRAS** • 1946
WHERE'S BABY? • 1912 • Stow Percy • UKN
WHERE'S CHARLEY? • 1952 • Butler David • UKN
WHERE'S ELMER? • 1934 • Horne James W. • SHT • USA
WHERE'S ELMER? see **ALL-AMERICAN CHUMP** • 1936
WHERE'S GEORGE? • 1935 • Raymond Jack • UKN • HOPE OF HIS SIDE, THE
WHERE'S JACK? • 1969 • Clavell James • UKN
WHERE'S JOHNNY? • 1974 • Eady David • UKN
WHERE'S MISHA? see **KDE JE MISA?** • 1954
WHERE'S MUMMY? • The Wei, Chien Chia Chun • ANS • CHN
WHERE'S MY HUSBAND? • 1915 • *La Pearl Harry* • USA
WHERE'S MY MIND? see **AYNA AQLI?** • 1974
WHERE'S MY NIGHTIE? • 1917 • *Sparkle Comedy* • USA
WHERE'S OLIVER? • 1915 • *La Pearl Harry* • USA
WHERE'S PETE? • 1987 • Purdy Jim • SHT • CND
WHERE'S PICONE? • 1984 • Loy Nanni • ITL
WHERE'S POPPA? • 1970 • Reiner Carl • USA • GOING APE
WHERE'S SALLY? • 1936 • Woods Arthur • UKN
WHERE'S THE BABY • 1913 • *Ab* • USA
WHERE'S THE FIRE? • 1921 • Roach Hal • SHT • USA
WHERE'S THE FIRE? • 1939 • Varnel Marcel • UKN
WHERE'S THE KEY? • 1918 • Reardon James • UKN
WHERE'S WATLING? • 1918 • Thornton F. Martin • UKN
WHERE'S WHOOSIT'S • 1986 • Arsenault Ray • MTV • CND
WHERE'S WILLIE? • 1978 • Florea John • USA • COMPUTER KID, THE ○ COMPUTER WIZARD
WHEREVER LOVE TAKES ME see **SEVENTH DAWN, THE** • 1964
WHEREVER SHE GOES • 1951 • Gordon Michael • ASL • PRELUDE
WHEREVER THERE ARE CHILDREN • 1968 • Perris Anthony • CND
WHEREVER YOU ARE.. see **GDZIESKOLWIRK JEST, JESUS JEST** • 1989
WHEREVER YOU GO see **WO DU HINGEHST** • 1957
WHICH? • 1913 • Lackaye James • USA
WHICH HAM IS SCHNAPPSMEIER'S? • 1914 • MacGregor Norval • USA
WHICH IS WHICH? • 1909 • *Essanay* • USA
WHICH IS WHICH? • 1915 • McKim Edwin • USA
WHICH IS WHICH? • 1926 • Newfield Sam • SHT • USA
WHICH IS WHICH see **HANS RIGTIGE KONE** • 1917
WHICH IS WITCH? • 1915 • Collins Edwin J.? • UKN
WHICH IS WITCH? • 1949 • Freleng Friz • ANS • USA
WHICH IS WITCH? • 1955 • *Halas John (P)* • ANS • UKN
WHICH IS WITCH • 1958 • Kneitel Seymour • ANS • USA
WHICH IS WITCH • 1967 • Bakshi Ralph • ANS • USA
WHICH OF THE TWO • 1912 • Stow Percy • UKN
WHICH SHALL IT BE • 1915 • *Williams Zana* • USA
WHICH SHALL IT BE? • 1924 • Hoffman Renaud • USA • NOT ONE TO SPARE
WHICH SWITCH? • 1924 • Quiribet Gaston • UKN
WHICH WAS LUCKY? • 1918 • *Jaxon* • SHT • USA
WHICH WAS THE HAPPIEST TIME OF YOUR LIFE? • 1909 • *Lubin* • USA
WHICH WAY? • 1916 • Powers Francis • SHT • USA • DAUGHTER OF THE NIGHT, A
WHICH WAY DID HE GO? • 1913 • Baker George D. • USA
WHICH WAY IS UP? • 1977 • Schultz Michael • USA
WHICH WAY TO THE FRONT? • 1970 • Lewis Jerry • USA • JA, JA, MEIN GENERAL! BUT WHICH WAY TO THE FRONT (UKN)
WHICH WAY TO THE RUBBISH DUMP see **APO POU PANE TIS HAVOUZA** • 1979
WHICH WILL YOU HAVE? • 1949 • Taylor Donald • UKN • BARABBAS THE ROBBER (USA)
WHICH WITCH IS WHICH? see **WITCHES' BREW** • 1980
WHICH WOMAN? • 1918 • Browning Tod • USA
WHICH WOULD YOU RATHER BE? • 1915 • *Harris Joseph* • USA
WHICHEVER WAY THE BALL BOUNCES see **KUD PUKLO DA PUKLO** • 1975
WHIFF OF ONIONS, A • 1913 • Coleby A. E.? • UKN
WHIFFLES CUBIST PAINTER see **RIGADIN PEINTRE CUBISTE** • 1912
WHIFFLES' NIGHTMARE • 1912 • Monca Georges • FRN
WHIFFS • 1975 • Post Ted • USA • C.A.S.H. (UKN) ○ W.H.I.F.F.S. ○ STIFFS
WHILE AMERICA SLEEPS • 1939 • Zinnemann Fred • SHT • USA
WHILE AUNTIE BOUNCED • 1914 • *Lubin* • USA
WHILE BABY SLEPT • 1913 • *Chamberlain Riley* • USA
WHILE FATHER TELEPHONED • 1913 • Hunter T. Hayes • USA
WHILE FIRE RAGED • 1914 • *Eclectic* • USA
WHILE I LIVE • 1947 • Harlow John • UKN • DREAM OF OLWEN
WHILE JOHN BOLT SLEPT • 1913 • Merwin Bannister, Collins Hancock • USA
WHILE JUSTICE WAITS • 1922 • Durning Bernard J. • USA • AS A MAN THINKETH
WHILE LONDON SLEEPS • 1926 • Bretherton Howard?, Morosco Walter? • USA
WHILE LONDON SLEEPS see **COCAINE** • 1922
WHILE MCFADDEN LOOKED OUT • 1913 • *Thanhouser* • USA
WHILE MEXICO SLEEPS (USA) see **MIENTRAS MEXICO DUERME** • 1938
WHILE NEW YORK SLEEPS • 1920 • Brabin Charles J. • USA
WHILE NEW YORK SLEEPS • 1938 • Humberstone H. Bruce • USA
WHILE PARENTS SLEEP • 1935 • Brunel Adrian • UKN
WHILE PARIS SLEEPS • 1923 • Tourneur Maurice • USA • GLORY OF LOVE, THE
WHILE PARIS SLEEPS • 1932 • Dwan Allan • USA
WHILE SATAN SLEEPS • 1922 • Henabery Joseph • USA
WHILE SHE POWDERED HER NOSE • 1912 • Trimble Larry • USA
WHILE SHEPHERDS WATCHED • 1913 • Fitzhamon Lewin • UKN
WHILE TENDING MY HOSS • 1920 • *Coburn Wallace* • SHT • USA
WHILE THE AUTO WAITS • 1920 • Totten Joseph Byron • SHT • USA
WHILE THE BAND PLAYED • 1914 • *Ab* • USA
WHILE THE BILLY BOILS • 1921 • Smith Beaumont • ASL
WHILE THE CAT'S AWAY • 1971 • Vincent Chuck • USA
WHILE THE CHILDREN SLEPT • 1913 • *Powers* • USA
WHILE THE CITY SLEEPS • 1928 • Conway Jack • USA
WHILE THE CITY SLEEPS • 1956 • Lang Fritz • USA
WHILE THE CITY SLEEPS see **MEDAN STADEN SOVER** • 1950
WHILE THE COOK SLEPT • 1912 • Coleby A. E.? • UKN
WHILE THE COUNT GOES BATHING • 1913 • Henderson Dell • USA
WHILE THE DEVIL LAUGHS • 1921 • Hill George W. • USA
WHILE THE HOUSEHOLD SLEEPS • 1905 • Martin J. H.? • UKN
WHILE THE PATIENT SLEPT • 1935 • Enright Ray • USA
WHILE THE STARLIGHT TRAVELS • 1913 • *Travers Richard C.* • USA
WHILE THE SUN SHINES • 1947 • Asquith Anthony • UKN
WHILE THE TIDE WAS RISING • 1914 • Wilson Ben • USA
WHILE THERE IS STILL TIME • 1943 • Chauvel Charles • DOC • ASL
WHILE THERE IS STILL TIME • 1957 • Zalakevicius Vitautus • SHT • USS
WHILE THERE'S LIFE • 1913 • *American* • USA
WHILE THERE'S LIFE THERE'S HOPE • 1911 • *Imp* • USA
WHILE THERE'S WAR THERE'S HOPE (USA) see **FINCHE C'E GUERRA C'E SPERANZA** • 1974
WHILE UNDER A HYPNOTIST'S INFLUENCE (UKN) see **MAGNETISEUR, LE** • 1897
WHILE WEDDING BELLS RING OUT • 1912 • *Rex* • USA
WHILE WIFEY IS AWAY • 1914 • Huntley Fred W. • USA
WHILE YET A WIFE see **TSUMA NO HI NO AI NO KATAMINI** • 1965
WHILE YOU SLEEP see **KIEDY TY SPISZ** • 1950
WHILE YOU WAIT • 1916 • Myll Louis • SHT • USA
WHILE YOU'RE ASLEEP see **KIEDY TY SPISZ** • 1950
WHIM, THE see **PRICE OF A GOOD TIME, THE** • 1918
WHIM OF DESTINY, THE • 1913 • *Majestic* • USA
WHIMS OF SOCIETY, THE • 1918 • Vale Travers • USA
WHIMS OF THE GODS • 1922 • Lee Rowland V. • USA
WHIMSICAL ILLUSIONS see **ILLUSIONS FANTAISISTES, LES** • 1909
WHIMSICAL PEOPLE, THE • 1910 • *Pathe* • FRN
WHIMSICAL THREADS OF DESTINY, THE • 1913 • Thompson Frederick A. • USA
WHIMSY OF CUPID, THE see **WAKAI TOKEIDAI** • 1967
WHIP, THE • 1917 • Tourneur Maurice • USA
WHIP, THE • 1928 • Brabin Charles J. • USA
WHIP, THE (USA) see **LATIGO, EL** • 1939
WHIP AND SKIN see **MUCHI TO HADA** • 1967
WHIP AND THE BODY, THE see **FRUSTA E IL CORPO, LA** • 1963
WHIP HAND, THE • 1913 • MacMackin Archer • USA
WHIP HAND, THE • 1951 • Menzies William Cameron • USA • MAN HE FOUND, THE
WHIP LAW • 1950 • Bretherton Howard • USA
WHIP WOMAN, THE • 1928 • Boyle Joseph C. • USA
WHIPLASH • 1948 • Seiler Lewis • USA
WHIPLASH, THE see **VANDARHOGG** • 1980
WHIPPED, THE • 1950 • English John • USA
WHIPPED, THE see **UNDERWORLD STORY, THE** • 1950
WHIPPET RACING • 1931 • Wing Ward • SHT • USA
WHIPPING see **VANDARHOGG** • 1980
WHIPPING BOSS, THE • 1924 • McGowan J. P. • USA
WHIPPING CREAM HERO, THE see **VERLOEDERING VAN DE SWIEPS, DE** • 1967
WHIPS • 1966 • Warhol Andy • USA
WHIP'S WOMEN • 1968 • Denby Jerry • USA
WHIPSAW • 1935 • Wood Sam • USA
WHIRL OF DESTINY, THE • 1913 • *Mundstuk Features* • USA
WHIRL OF LIFE, THE • 1915 • Bailey Oliver D. • USA
WHIRLIGIG • 1958 • Train Michael S., Gittleman Leonard J. • USA
WHIRLIGIG OF LIFE, THE • 1917 • France Floyd • SHT • USA
WHIRLIGIG OF TIME, THE • 1913 • Collins Edwin J. • UKN
WHIRLING DISC, THE • 1915 • Giblyn Charles • USA
WHIRLING THE WORLDS see **VOYAGE A TRAVERS L'IMPOSSIBLE, LE** • 1904
WHIRLPOOL • 1950 • Preminger Otto • USA
WHIRLPOOL • 1959 • Allen Lewis • UKN
WHIRLPOOL • 1970 • Larraz Jose R. • DNM • SHE DIED WITH HER BOOTS ON
WHIRLPOOL see **REMOUS** • 1934
WHIRLPOOL, THE • 1915 • Wright Fred E. • USA
WHIRLPOOL, THE • 1918 • Crosland Alan • USA
WHIRLPOOL, THE • 1933 • Neill R. William • USA
WHIRLPOOL, THE see **LONDON LOVE** • 1926
WHIRLPOOL OF DESTINY, THE • 1916 • Turner Otis • USA
WHIRLPOOL OF FATE (UKN) see **FILLE DE L'EAU, LA** • 1924
WHIRLPOOL OF FLESH see **ONNA NO UZU TO FUCHI TO NAGARE** • 1964
WHIRLPOOL OF LIFE, THE see **FILLE DE L'EAU, LA** • 1924
WHIRLPOOL OF SIN, THE see **GERDABE GONAH** • 1968
WHIRLPOOL OF SPRING see **HARU NO UZIMAKI** • 1954
WHIRLPOOL OF WOMEN (USA) see **ONNA NO UZU TO FUCHI TO NAGARE** • 1964
WHIRLS AND GIRLS • 1929 • Sennett Mack • SHT • USA
WHIRLWIND • 1951 • English John • USA
WHIRLWIND see **TSUMUJI KAZE** • 1963
WHIRLWIND see **DAI TATSUMAKI** • 1964
WHIRLWIND, THE • 1920 • Golden Joseph A. • SRL • USA
WHIRLWIND, THE • 1933 • Lederman D. Ross • USA
WHIRLWIND COURTSHIP ON BRADON'S RANCH, A • 1912 • *Pathe* • USA
WHIRLWIND FINISH, THE • 1918 • McRae Henry • SHT • USA
WHIRLWIND HORSEMAN • 1938 • Hill Robert F. • USA
WHIRLWIND KIDS, THE • 1914 • Fitzhamon Lewin • UKN
WHIRLWIND LOVER, THE (UKN) see **HEROIC LOVER, THE** • 1929
WHIRLWIND OF FATE see **SUNNY SOUTH** • 1914
WHIRLWIND OF LIFE, THE see **GERDBADE ZENDEGI** • 1968
WHIRLWIND OF WHISKERS, THE • 1917 • Santell Alfred? • USA
WHIRLWIND OF YOUTH, THE • 1927 • Lee Rowland V. • USA
WHIRLWIND RAIDERS • 1948 • Keays Vernon • USA • STATE POLICE (UKN)
WHIRLWIND RANGER, THE • 1924 • Hatton Richard • USA
WHIRLWIND RIDER, THE • 1935 • Horner Robert J. • USA
WHIRR OF THE SPINNING WHEEL, THE • 1914 • Wilson Frank • UKN
WHISKERS • 1914 • *Eclectic* • USA
WHISKEY AND SODA (USA) see **ZWEI WHISKY UND EIN SOFA** • 1963
WHISKEY E FANTASMI • 1974 • Margheriti Antonio • ITL
WHISKEY RUNNERS, THE • 1912 • *Stedman Myrtle* • USA
WHISKEY RUNNERS, THE • 1914 • *Domino* • USA
WHISKEY VERSUS BULLETS • 1901 • Smith G. A. • UKN
WHISKEY'S RENEGADES see **SAM WHISKEY** • 1969

WHISKY A MEZZOGIORNO • 1962 • De Fina P. V. Oscar • ITL
WHISKY GALORE • 1948 • Mackendrick Alexander • UKN • TIGHT LITTLE ISLAND (USA) ○ LIQUID TREASURE
WHISKY, WODKA, WIENERIN see **RENDEZ-VOUS IN WIEN** • 1959
WHISKY Y VODKA • 1965 • Palacios Fernando • SPN
WHISPER KILL • 1988 • Nyby Christian Ii • USA • WHISPER KILLS, A
WHISPER KILLS, A see **WHISPER KILL** • 1988
WHISPER MARKET, THE • 1920 • Sargent George L. • USA
WHISPER MY NAME • 1970 • Collier James F. • ISR
WHISPER OF SPRING see **HARU NO SASAYAKI** • 1952
WHISPER TO A SCREAM • 1990 • Bergman Robert • CND
WHISPERED NAME, THE • 1917 • MacDonald Donald • SHT • USA
WHISPERED NAME, THE • 1924 • Baggot King • USA • BLACKMAIL ○ CO-RESPONDENT, THE
WHISPERED WORD, THE • 1913 • *Thornby Robert* • USA
WHISPERED WORD, THE • 1916 • Parke William • SHT • USA
WHISPERERS, THE • 1966 • Forbes Bryan • UKN
WHISPERING • 1922 • *Parkinson H. B. (P)* • SHT • UKN
WHISPERING CANYON • 1926 • Forman Tom • USA
WHISPERING CHORUS, THE • 1917 • De Mille Cecil B. • USA
WHISPERING CITY see **FORTERESSE, LA** • 1947
WHISPERING DEAD BEAUTY see **SASAYAKU SHIBIJIN** • 1963
WHISPERING DEATH • 1975 • Goslar Jurgen • SAF, FRG • FLUSTERNDE TOD, DER (FRG) ○ NIGHT OF THE ASKARI ○ ALBINO ○ DEATH IN THE SUN ○ BLIND SPOT
WHISPERING DEVILS • 1920 • Garson Harry • USA
WHISPERING ENEMIES • 1939 • Collins Lewis D. • USA • WRECKAGE
WHISPERING FOOTSTEPS • 1943 • Bretherton Howard • USA
WHISPERING GABLES • 1927 • Greenwood Edwin • UKN
WHISPERING GHOSTS • 1942 • Werker Alfred L. • USA
WHISPERING IN THE HAYLOFT see **HEUBODENGEFLUSTER** • 1967
WHISPERING JOE (USA) see **SASAYASHI NO JOE** • 1967
WHISPERING PALMS • 1923 • *Cleary Val* • USA
WHISPERING SAGE • 1927 • Dunlap Scott R. • USA
WHISPERING SHADOW, THE • 1933 • Herman Al, Clark Colbert • SRL • USA • WHISPERING SHADOWS
WHISPERING SHADOWS • 1922 • Chautard Emile • USA
WHISPERING SHADOWS see **WHISPERING SHADOW, THE** • 1933
WHISPERING SKULL, THE • 1944 • Clifton Elmer • USA
WHISPERING SMITH • 1916 • McGowan J. P. • USA
WHISPERING SMITH • 1926 • Melford George • USA • OPEN SWITCH, THE
WHISPERING SMITH • 1948 • Fenton Leslie • USA
WHISPERING SMITH HITS LONDON • 1951 • Searle Francis • UKN • WHISPERING SMITH VERSUS SCOTLAND YARD (USA)
WHISPERING SMITH RIDES • 1927 • Taylor Ray • SRL • USA
WHISPERING SMITH SPEAKS • 1935 • Howard David • USA
WHISPERING SMITH VERSUS SCOTLAND YARD (USA) see **WHISPERING SMITH HITS LONDON** • 1951
WHISPERING TONGUES • 1934 • Pearson George • UKN
WHISPERING WHISKERS • 1926 • *Sennett Mack (P)* • SHT • USA
WHISPERING WHOOPEE • 1930 • Horne James W. • SHT • USA
WHISPERING WINDS • 1929 • Flood James • USA
WHISPERING WIRES • 1926 • Ray Albert • USA
WHISPERING WOMEN • 1921 • Keane James • USA
WHISPERS • Sadan Mark • SHT • USA
WHISPERS • 1920 • Earle William P. S. • USA
WHISPERS • 1941 • Wrangell Basil • SHT • USA • DARK RIVER
WHISPERS AND CRIES (USA) see **VISKINGAR OCH ROP** • 1972
WHISPERS IN THE DARK • 1937 • Fleischer Dave • ANS • USA
WHISPERS OF FEAR • 1974 • Davenport Harry Bromley • UKN
WHIST • 1910 • *Essanay* • USA
WHIST! HERE COMES THE PICTURE MAN • 1912 • Plumb Hay? • UKN
WHISTLE, THE • 1921 • Hillyer Lambert • USA
WHISTLE, THE see **DAGE I MIN FARS HUS** • 1968
WHISTLE, THE see **GLASS WHISTLE, THE** • 1970
WHISTLE AT EATON FALLS, THE • 1951 • Siodmak Robert • USA • RICHER THAN THE EARTH (UKN)
WHISTLE BLOWER, THE • 1987 • Langton Simon • UKN
WHISTLE DOWN THE WIND • 1961 • Forbes Bryan • UKN
WHISTLE IN MY HEART, A see **KOTAN NO KUCHIBUE** • 1959
WHISTLE SATELLITE, THE see **SATELITE CHIFLADO, EL** • 1956
WHISTLE STOP • 1946 • Moguy Leonide • USA
WHISTLE STOP see **POLUSTANOK** • 1963
WHISTLER, THE • 1926 • Mander Miles • UKN
WHISTLER, THE • 1944 • Castle William • USA
WHISTLER, THE • 1949 • Lewis Jerry • SHT • USA
WHISTLES AND WINDOWS • 1918 • Semon Larry • SHT • USA
WHISTLES OF MIGRATORY BIRDS see **KUCHIBUE O FUKU WATARIDORI** • 1958
WHISTLIN' DAN • 1932 • Rosen Phil • USA
WHISTLING BET, THE • 1912 • Kellino W. P. • UKN
WHISTLING BOY see **FUEFUKI DORI** • 1954
WHISTLING BULLETS • 1937 • English John • USA
WHISTLING COBBLESTONES see **SIPOLO MACSKAKO** • 1971
WHISTLING COON, THE • 1906 • Gilbert Arthur • UKN
WHISTLING COON, THE • 1907 • *Walturdaw* • UKN
WHISTLING DENTIST, THE • 1975 • Lavut Martin • CND
WHISTLING DICK see **UNWILLING HERO, AN** • 1921
WHISTLING DICK'S CHRISTMAS STOCKING • 1917 • Ridgwell George • SHT • USA
WHISTLING HILLS, THE • 1951 • Abrahams Derwin • USA
WHISTLING HIRAM • 1914 • *Frontier* • USA
WHISTLING IN BROOKLYN • 1943 • Simon S. Sylvan • USA
WHISTLING IN DIXIE • 1942 • Simon S. Sylvan • USA
WHISTLING IN KOTAN see **KOTAN NO KUCHIBUE** • 1959
WHISTLING IN THE DARK • 1932 • Nugent Elliott • USA • SCARED! (UKN)
WHISTLING IN THE DARK • 1941 • Simon S. Sylvan • USA
WHISTLING IN THE NOSE, THE see **FISCHIO AL NASO, IL** • 1967
WHISTLING JIM • 1925 • McGaugh Wilbur • USA
WHISTLING KILLER, THE see **KURENAI NO NAGAREBOSHI** • 1967
WHISTLING WILLIAM • 1913 • Wilson Frank? • UKN
WHITCHURCH DOWN • 1972 • Le Grice Malcolm • UKN • DURATION
WHITE ALLEY, THE • 1916 • *Beaumont Harry* • SHT • USA
WHITE AMAZON see **AMAZONIA INFERNO VERDE** • 1984
WHITE AND BLACK • 1919 • Rasumny Alexander • USS
WHITE AND BLACK see **SHIRO TO KURO** • 1963
WHITE AND BLACK SNOWBALL, THE see **BLACK AND WHITE SNOWBALL, THE** • 1915
WHITE AND UNMARRIED • 1921 • Forman Tom • USA • POINT OF VIEW, THE
WHITE ANGEL, THE • 1936 • Dieterle William • USA
WHITE ANGEL.. BLACK ANGEL see **ANGELI BIANCHI.. ANGELI NERI** • 1969
WHITE APRONS • 1912 • *Eclair* • USA
WHITE ASHES see **LURE OF YOUTH, THE** • 1921
WHITE AVENGER, THE • 1962 • Jutrisa Vladimir, Marks Aleksandar • YGS
WHITE BANNERS • 1938 • Goulding Edmund • USA
WHITE BEAR see **BIALY NIEDZWIEDZ** • 1959
WHITE BEAST see **SHIROI YAJU** • 1950
WHITE BICYCLE, THE see **BEYAZ BISIKLET** • 1986
WHITE BIM THE BLACK EAR see **BELI BIM-CHORNOYE UKHO** • 1977
WHITE BIM WITH A BLACK EAR see **BELI BIM-CHORNOYE UKHO** • 1977
WHITE BIRD • 1971 • Mallory Lawrence • SHT • USA
WHITE BIRD WITH A BLACK MARKING, A see **BYELAYA PTITSA S CHORNOY OTMYETINOY** • 1972
WHITE BIRD WITH A BLACK SPOT, THE see **BYELAYA PTITSA S CHORNOY OTMYETINOY** • 1972
WHITE BIRD WITH THE BLACK MARK, THE see **BYELAYA PTITSA S CHORNOY OTMYETINOY** • 1972
WHITE BLACK SHEEP, THE • 1926 • Olcott Sidney • USA
WHITE BLACKSMITH, THE • 1922 • Roach Hal • SHT • USA
WHITE BLOOD see **WEISSES BLUT** • 1959
WHITE BOAT, THE see **BYELI PAROKHOD** • 1976
WHITE BONDAGE • 1937 • Grinde Nick • USA
WHITE BONNET, THE • 1912 • *Eclair* • USA
WHITE BOYS, THE • 1916 • Wilson Frank • UKN
WHITE BRAVE'S HERITAGE • 1911 • *Kalem* • USA
WHITE BRIDE, THE see **ASMARA KIRANA** • 1970
WHITE BRIDGE see **SHIROI HASHI** • 1956
WHITE BROTHER'S TEST, THE • 1912 • *Powers* • USA
WHITE BUFFALO, THE • 1976 • Thompson J. Lee • USA • HUNT TO KILL
WHITE BUS, THE • 1967 • Anderson Lindsay • UKN
WHITE CALLIGRAPHY • 1967 • Iimura Takahiko • SHT • JPN
WHITE CAPS • 1905 • Porter Edwin S. • USA
WHITE CAPTIVE OF THE SIOUX, THE • 1910 • *Kalem* • USA
WHITE CAPTIVE (UKN) see **WHITE SAVAGE** • 1943
WHITE CARAVAN, THE see **BELYI KARAVAN** • 1964
WHITE CARGO • 1929 • Williams J. B., Barnes Arthur W. • SIL • UKN
WHITE CARGO • 1929 • Williams J. B., Barnes Arthur W. • SND • UKN
WHITE CARGO • 1942 • Thorpe Richard • USA
WHITE CARGO see **WEISSE FRACHT FUR HONGKONG** • 1964
WHITE CARGO FOR HONG KONG see **WEISSE FRACHT FUR HONGKONG** • 1964
WHITE CAT, THE see **UNTAMEABLE, THE** • 1923
WHITE CAT, THE see **VITA KATTEN, DEN** • 1950
WHITE CHIEF, THE • 1908 • *Lubin* • USA
WHITE CHIEF, THE • 1911 • *Powers* • USA
WHITE CHRISTMAS • 1954 • Curtiz Michael • USA
WHITE CIRCLE, THE • 1920 • Tourneur Maurice • USA
WHITE CITY see **PETE TOWNSEND: WHITE CITY, THE MUSIC MOVIE** • 1985
WHITE CITY: PETE TOWNSEND see **PETE TOWNSEND: WHITE CITY, THE MUSIC MOVIE** • 1985
WHITE CLIFF, THE see **SHIROI GAKE** • 1960
WHITE CLIFFS MYSTERY, THE • 1957 • Tully Montgomery • UKN
WHITE CLIFFS OF DOVER, THE • 1944 • Brown Clarence • USA
WHITE CLOUD CAROLINE see **WEISSE WOLKE CAROLIN**
WHITE CLOUD'S SECRET • 1912 • *Nestor* • USA
WHITE COCKATOO, THE • 1935 • Crosland Alan • USA
WHITE-COLLAR DREAMER see **TENKA O TORU** • 1960
WHITE COLT, THE see **RUN WILD, RUN FREE** • 1969
WHITE COMANCHE (USA) see **COMANCHE BLANCO** • 1967
WHITE CORRIDORS • 1951 • Jackson Pat • UKN
WHITE CRADLE INN • 1947 • French Harold • UKN • HIGH FURY (USA)
WHITE CROW, THE • 1988 • Kershner Irvin • USA
WHITE DARKNESS see **BILA TMA** • 1948
WHITE DAWN, THE • 1974 • Kaufman Philip • USA
WHITE DEMON, THE see **WEISSE DAMON, DER** • 1932
WHITE DESERT, THE • 1925 • Barker Reginald • USA
WHITE DEVIL, THE see **HVIDE DJOEVEL, DEN** • 1916
WHITE DEVIL, THE (USA) see **WEISSE TEUFEL, DER** • 1930
WHITE DEVIL-FISH see **SHIROI MAGYO** • 1956
WHITE DISEASE, THE see **BILA NEMOC** • 1937
WHITE DOE'S LOVERS • 1910 • Melies Gaston • USA
WHITE DOG • 1982 • Fuller Samuel • USA
WHITE DOMINO, THE • 1913 • Barker Reginald • USA
WHITE DOVE see **PALOMITA BLANCA** • 1973
WHITE DOVE, THE • 1920 • King Henry • USA
WHITE DOVE, THE see **HOLUBICE** • 1960
WHITE DOVE'S SACRIFICE • 1912 • *Gem* • USA
WHITE DOVE'S SACRIFICE • 1914 • *Sawyer* • USA
WHITE DRAGON • 1986 • Domaradzki Jerzy • PLN
WHITE DRUNKENNESS, THE see **WEISSE RAUSCH, DER** • 1931
WHITE DWARF, THE • 1986 • Humaloja Timo • FNL
WHITE EAGLE • 1922 • Jackman Fred, Van Dyke W. S. • SRL • USA
WHITE EAGLE • 1932 • Hillyer Lambert • USA
WHITE EAGLE • 1941 • Horne James W. • SRL • USA
WHITE EAGLE see **FLYING HORSEMAN, THE** • 1926
WHITE EAGLE, THE see **BYELI OREL** • 1928
WHITE ECSTASY, THE see **WEISSE RAUSCH, DER** • 1931
WHITE ENSIGN • 1934 • Hunt John • UKN
WHITE EXPLOSION • 1970 • Govorukhin S. • USS
WHITE FACE • 1932 • Hunter T. Hayes • UKN
WHITE FAN, THE see **HAKUSEN-MIDARE KURO-KAMI** • 1956
WHITE FANG • 1925 • Trimble Larry • USA
WHITE FANG • 1936 • Butler David • USA
WHITE FANG • 1946 • Zguridi Alexander • DOC • USS
WHITE FANG see **SHIROI KIBA** • 1960
WHITE FANG (UKN) see **ZANNA BIANCA** • 1973
WHITE FANGS see **SHIROI KIBA** • 1960
WHITE FANG'S PERIL • 1911 • *Bison* • USA
WHITE FAWN • 1912 • *Shamrock* • USA
WHITE FAWN'S DEVOTION • 1910 • *Pathe* • USA
WHITE FAWN'S ESCAPE • 1911 • *Bison* • USA
WHITE FEATHER • 1955 • Webb Robert D. • USA
WHITE FEATHER see **THEY RODE WEST** • 1954
WHITE FEATHER, THE • 1913 • Bowman William J. • USA
WHITE FEATHER, THE • 1914 • Elvey Maurice • UKN
WHITE FEATHER VOLUNTEER, A • 1915 • Julian Rupert • USA
WHITE FIELD DURATION • 1972 • Le Grice Malcolm • UKN
WHITE FIRE • 1988 • Ginnane Anthony I. • ASL
WHITE FIRE see **VIVRE POUR SURVIVRE** • 1984
WHITE FIRE (USA) see **THREE STEPS TO THE GALLOWS** • 1953
WHITE FLAG TREACHERY • 1900 • *Mitchell & Kenyon* • UKN
WHITE FLAME • 1928 • *Hamilton Mahlon* • USA
WHITE FLAME, THE see **WEISSE RAUSCH, DER** • 1931
WHITE FLANNELS • 1927 • Bacon Lloyd • USA
WHITE FLESH IS WEAK see **FIONA ON FIRE** • 1978
WHITE FLOOD • 1940 • Meyers Sidney, Maddow Ben • USA
WHITE FLOWER, THE • 1923 • Ivers Julia Crawford • USA
WHITE FLOWERS FOR THE DEAD see **AHASIN POLA WATHA** • 1976
WHITE FORCE • 1987 • Romero Eddie • USA
WHITE FRENZY, THE see **WEISSE RAUSCH, DER** • 1931
WHITE FRONTIER, THE see **SLANDER THE WOMAN** • 1923
WHITE FURY • 1969 • Dubs Arthur R. • DOC • USA
WHITE GAME, THE see **VITA SPORTEN, DEN** • 1968
WHITE GHOST • 1988 • Davis B. J. • USA
WHITE GHOST, THE see **HVIDE DAME, DEN** • 1913
WHITE GODDESS • 1953 • Fox William • MTV • USA • RAMAR OF THE JUNGLE (UKN)
WHITE GODDESS, THE • 1915 • Buel Kenean • USA
WHITE GOLD • 1927 • Howard William K. • USA
WHITE GOLDEN DRAGON • 1936 • SNG
WHITE GORILLA, THE • 1947 • Fraser Harry L. • USA
WHITE GRASS see **BELE TRAVE** • 1977
WHITE GYPSY, THE • 1919 • de Banos Ricardo • SPN
WHITE-HAIRED GIRL, THE • 1950 • Shui Hua, Wang Pu • CHN
WHITE-HAIRED GIRL, THE see **PAI MAO NU** • 1970
WHITE HAND, THE • 1915 • Birch Cecil • UKN
WHITE HAND SOCIETY, THE • 1914 • *Ab* • USA
WHITE HANDS • 1922 • Hillyer Lambert • USA
WHITE HARVEST see **BIALE ZNIWA** • 1978
WHITE HEAT • 1926 • Bentley Thomas • UKN
WHITE HEAT • 1934 • Weber Lois • USA
WHITE HEAT • 1949 • Walsh Raoul • USA
WHITE HEAT see **WHITE HOT** • 1982
WHITE HEATHER see **CIRCLE OF DANGER** • 1951
WHITE HEATHER, THE • 1919 • Tourneur Maurice • USA
WHITE HELL • 1922 • Feikel Bernard • USA
WHITE HELL OF PITZ PALU, THE see **WEISSE HOLLE VOM PIZ PALU, DIE** • 1929
WHITE HELL OF PITZ PALU, THE (USA) see **FOHN** • 1950
WHITE HEN, THE • 1921 • Richardson Frank • UKN
WHITE HERON, THE see **SHIRASAGI** • 1959
WHITE HOOD see **KAITO SHIRO ZUKEN** • 1935
WHITE HOPE, THE • 1912 • *Essanay* • USA
WHITE HOPE, THE • 1915 • Wilson Frank • UKN
WHITE HOPE, THE • 1916 • *Kearns Jack* • ASL
WHITE HOPE, THE • 1917 • *International Film Services* • ANS • USA
WHITE HOPE, THE • 1922 • Wilson Frank • UKN
WHITE HOPE ON CHAMPIONSHIP, THE • 1914 • *Heron Andrew (P)* • UKN
WHITE HORSE, THE see **CABALLO BLANCO, EL** • 1961
WHITE HORSE INN, THE (USA) see **IM WEISSEN ROSSL** • 1960
WHITE HORSEMAN, THE • 1921 • Russell Albert • SRL • USA
WHITE HORSES IN AUGUST see **BIANCHI CAVALLI D'AGOSTO** • 1975
WHITE HORSES OF SUMMER, THE see **BIANCHI CAVALLI D'AGOSTO** • 1975
WHITE HOT • 1982 • Leblanc Michel • FRN • ALPINE ROMANCE ○ WHITE HEAT
WHITE HOT see **CRACK IN THE MIRROR** • 1988
WHITE HOUSE ON THE SHORE, THE see **NAGISA NO SHIROI IE** • 1977
WHITE HUNTER • 1936 • Cummings Irving • USA
WHITE HUNTER • 1965 • Michael George • USA
WHITE HUNTER, BLACK HEART • 1990 • Eastwood Clint • USA
WHITE HUNTRESS (USA) see **GOLDEN IVORY** • 1954
WHITE ILLNESS, THE see **BILA NEMOC** • 1937
WHITE INDIAN, A • 1912 • *Darkfeather Mona* • USA
WHITE KING OF THE ZARAS, THE • 1915 • *Watson Roy* • USA
WHITE LAAGER, THE • 1978 • Davis Peter • DOC • USA
WHITE LACE DRESS, THE see **ROCHIA ALBA DE DANTELA** • 1989
WHITE LADY, THE see **BILA PANI** • 1965
WHITE LAKE • 1990 • Brown Colin • DOC • CND
WHITE LEGION, THE • 1936 • Brown Karl • USA
WHITE LEGS (UKN) see **PATTES BLANCHES** • 1948
WHITE LIE, A • 1909 • *Centaur* • USA
WHITE LIE, A • 1912 • *Nestor* • USA
WHITE LIE, THE • 1912 • *101 Bison* • USA
WHITE LIE, THE • 1918 • Hickman Howard • USA
WHITE LIE, THE • 1925 • Templeman Harcourt • UKN
WHITE LIES • 1913 • *Patheplay* • USA
WHITE LIES • 1914 • *Travers Richard C.* • USA
WHITE LIES • 1920 • Le Saint Edward J. • USA
WHITE LIES • 1935 • Bulgakov Leo • USA
WHITE LIES (UKN) see **BLACK TEARS** • 1927

WHITE LIES (UKN) see **MENTIRAS PIADOSAS** • 1988
WHITE LIGHT OF PUBLICITY, THE • 1915 • Carleton Lloyd B. • USA
WHITE LIGHTNIN' ROAD • 1967 • Ormond Ron • USA
WHITE LIGHTNING • 1953 • Bernds Edward • USA
WHITE LIGHTNING • 1973 • Sargent Joseph • USA
WHITE LILAC • 1935 • Parker Albert • UKN
WHITE LILY LAMENTS, THE (USA) see **SHIRAYURI WA NAGEKU** • 1925
WHITE LINE, THE see **CUORI SENZA FRONTIERE** • 1950
WHITE LINE FEVER • 1975 • Kaplan Jonathan • CND, USA
WHITE LIONS, THE • 1979 • Stuart Mel • USA
WHITE LITE • 1968 • Keen Jeff • UKN
WHITE MADNESS see **WITTE WAN** • 1983
WHITE MAGIC • 1981 • Andonov Ivan • BUL
WHITE MAJESTY see **WEISSE MAJESTAT, DIE** • 1933
WHITE MAMA • 1980 • Cooper Jackie • TVM • USA
WHITE MAN • 1924 • Gasnier Louis J. • USA
WHITE MAN, A • 1909 • *Warwick Trading Co* • UKN
WHITE MAN, THE see **SQUAW MAN, THE** • 1918
WHITE MAN, THE (UKN) see **SQUAW MAN, THE** • 1914
WHITE MAN, THE (UKN) see **SQUAW MAN, THE** • 1931
WHITE MANE (USA) see **CRIN BLANC** • 1953
WHITE MAN'S CHANCE, A • 1909 • Warde Ernest C. • USA
WHITE MAN'S FIREWATER • 1913 • *Nestor* • USA
WHITE MAN'S LAW, THE • 1916 • *Big U* • SHT • USA
WHITE MAN'S LAW, THE • 1918 • Young James • USA
WHITE MAN'S MONEY, THE INDIAN CURSE • 1910 • *Kalem* • USA
WHITE MAN'S THRONE, THE see **HAKUGIN NO OZU** • 1935
WHITE MAN'S WAY, A • 1912 • Thornton F. Martin • UKN
WHITE MARE'S SON, THE see **FEHERLOFIA** • 1982
WHITE MASK, THE • 1915 • Smiley Joseph • USA
WHITE MASKS, THE • 1921 • Holt George • USA
WHITE MEDICINE MAN, THE • 1911 • *Selig* • USA
WHITE MEDICINE MAN, THE • 1911 • Fahrney Milton • *Nestor* • USA
WHITE MEN IN BLACK SKINS • 1967 • Holmes Cecil • DOC • ASL
WHITE MICE • 1926 • Griffith Edward H. • USA
WHITE MISCHIEF • 1988 • Radford Michael • UKN
WHITE MOLL, THE • 1920 • Millarde Harry • USA
WHITE MONKEY, THE • 1925 • Rosen Phil • USA
WHITE MOOR see **DE-AS FI HARAP ALB** • 1965
WHITE MORNING see **SHIROI ASA** • 1964
WHITE MOTH, THE • 1924 • Tourneur Maurice • USA
WHITE MOUSE, THE • 1914 • Campbell Colin • USA
WHITE MOUSE, THE see **BIJELI MIS** • 1961
WHITE NEGRO, THE see **BIALY MURZYN** • 1939
WHITE NIGHT see **FEHER EJSZAKAK** • 1916
WHITE NIGHTMARE see **STRANGE ADVENTURE, A** • 1956
WHITE NIGHTS • 1985 • Hackford Taylor • USA
WHITE NIGHTS see **FEHER EJSZAKAK** • 1916
WHITE NIGHTS see **BELIYE NOCHI** • 1960
WHITE NIGHTS (USA) see **NOTTI BIANCHE, LE** • 1957
WHITE OAK • 1921 • Hillyer Lambert • USA
WHITE ODYSSEY, THE • 1972 • Mirchev Vassil • BUL
WHITE OF THE EYE • 1987 • Cammell Donald • UKN
WHITE ONION, RED ONION see **BAWANG PUTEH, BAWANG MERAH** • 1958
WHITE – ORANGE – GREEN • 1969 • Cantrill Arthur, Cantrill Corinne • ASL
WHITE ORCHID, THE • 1954 • Le Borg Reginald • USA
WHITE ORCHID OF THE HEATING DESERT see **NESSA NO BYAKURAN** • 1951
WHITE OUTLAW, THE • 1925 • Smith Cliff • USA
WHITE OUTLAW, THE • 1929 • Horner Robert J. • USA
WHITE PALACE • 1990 • Mandoki Luis • USA
WHITE PANTHER, THE • 1924 • Neitz Alvin J. • USA
WHITE PANTS WILLIE • 1927 • Hines Charles • USA
WHITE PARADE, THE • 1934 • Cummings Irving • USA
WHITE PARADISE, THE see **BILY RAJ** • 1924
WHITE PEACOCK, THE see **WEISSE PFAU, DER** • 1920
WHITE PEARL, THE • 1915 • Irving Henry George • USA
WHITE PEBBLES • 1927 • Thorpe Richard • USA
WHITE PHANTOM • 1987 • Nelson Dusty • USA • WHITE PHANTOM: ENEMY OF DARKNESS
WHITE PHANTOM: ENEMY OF DARKNESS see **WHITE PHANTOM** • 1987
WHITE PIGEON see **SHIROI HATO** • 1960
WHITE PIGEON see **WILD WHITE PIGEON** • 1986
WHITE PIRATE, THE • 1914 • *Starlight* • USA
WHITE PLEASURE see **SHIROI KAIKAN** • 1968
WHITE PONGO • 1945 • Newfield Sam • USA • ADVENTURE UNLIMITED (UKN) ○ BLOND GORILLA
WHITE PRINCESS OF THE TRIBE, THE • 1910 • *Champion* • USA
WHITE QUEEN TO MOVE see **MOVE OF THE WHITE QUEEN** • 1972
WHITE RAT, THE • 1922 • Cooper George A. • UKN
WHITE RAVEN, THE • 1917 • Baker George D. • USA
WHITE RAVEN, THE see **BELAYA VORONA** • 1941
WHITE, RED AND VERDONE GREEN see **BIANCO, ROSSO E VERDONE** • 1980
WHITE RED MAN, THE • 1911 • Porter Edwin S. • USA
WHITE, RED, YELLOW AND PINK see **BIANCO, ROSSO, GIALLO, ROSA** • 1965
WHITE REINDEER, THE see **VALKOINEN PEURA** • 1952
WHITE RENEGADE, THE • 1931 • Irwin Jack • USA • FOOL'S GOLD (UKN) ○ EMPIRE BUILDERS, THE
WHITE RIDER, THE • 1920 • Craft William James • USA • WHITE RIDERS
WHITE RIDERS see **WHITE RIDER, THE** • 1920
WHITE ROAD, AN ETERNAL PRIEST, SHINRAN see **SHIROI MICHI, SHINRAN** • 1987
WHITE ROCK • 1977 • Maylam Tony • DOC • UKN
WHITE ROCK, THE see **HIS WIFE'S FRIEND** • 1920
WHITE ROCKER, THE • 1948 • Peterson Sidney • USA
WHITE ROOM, THE • 1989 • Rozema Patricia • CND
WHITE ROOM, THE see **CAMERA ALBA** • 1964
WHITE ROOM, THE see **BYALATA STAYA** • 1968
WHITE ROSE see **FEHER ROZSA** • 1920
WHITE ROSE, A • 1913 • *Panzer Paul* • USA
WHITE ROSE, THE • 1915 • *Princess* • USA
WHITE ROSE, THE • 1923 • Griffith D. W. • USA
WHITE ROSE, THE • 1967 • Conner Bruce • SHT • USA
WHITE ROSE, THE see **WEISSE ROSE, DIE** • 1983
WHITE ROSE OF HONG KONG (USA) see **HONKON NO SHIROIBARA** • 1965
WHITE ROSE OF THE WILDS, THE • 1911 • Griffith D. W. • USA
WHITE ROSES • 1910 • Griffith D. W. • USA
WHITE ROSES • 1912 • *Bushman Francis X.* • USA
WHITE ROSES • 1914 • *Hall Ella* • USA
WHITE ROSES • 1989 • Mihlic Zdrvko • UKN
WHITE ROSETTE, THE • 1916 • MacDonald Donald • USA
WHITE SAVAGE • 1943 • Lubin Arthur • USA • WHITE CAPTIVE (UKN)
WHITE SAVAGE see **BIKINI PARADISE** • 1964
WHITE SAVAGE (UKN) see **SOUTH OF TAHITI** • 1941
WHITE SAVIOUR, THE • 1912 • *Bison* • USA
WHITE SCAR, THE • 1915 • Bosworth Hobart, Davis Ulysses • USA
WHITE SEA OF YUSHIMA see **YUSHIMA NO SHIRAUME** • 1955
WHITE SEARCH, THE • 1971 • Barrymore Dick • DOC • USA
WHITE SERPENT, THE see **BYAKU FUJIN NO YUREN** • 1956
WHITE SHADOW, THE • 1924 • Cutts Graham • UKN • WHITE SHADOWS (USA)
WHITE SHADOWS • 1970 • Nielsen Erik Frohn • DNM
WHITE SHADOWS IN THE SOUTH SEAS • 1928 • Van Dyke W. S., Flaherty Robert • USA • SOUTHERN SKIES
WHITE SHADOWS (USA) see **WHITE SHADOW, THE** • 1924
WHITE SHEEP, THE • 1924 • Roach Hal • USA
WHITE SHEIK, THE • 1928 • Knoles Harley • UKN
WHITE SHEIK, THE see **SCEICCO BIANCO, LO** • 1952
WHITE SHIP, THE see **BYELI PAROKHOD** • 1976
WHITE SHOULDERS • 1922 • Forman Tom • USA
WHITE SHOULDERS • 1931 • Brown Melville • USA
WHITE SICKNESS, THE see **BILA NEMOC** • 1937
WHITE SILENCE • 1928 • Klein Charles • USA
WHITE SIN, THE • 1924 • Seiter William A. • USA • UNGUARDED GATES
WHITE SISTER, THE • 1915 • Wright Fred E. • USA
WHITE SISTER, THE • 1923 • King Henry • USA
WHITE SISTER, THE • 1933 • Fleming Victor • USA
WHITE SISTER (USA) see **BIANCO, ROSSO E..** • 1972
WHITE SLAVE see **AMAZONIA INFERNO VERDE** • 1984
WHITE SLAVE, THE • 1913 • *Young Clara Kimball* • USA
WHITE SLAVE, THE see **HVIDE SLAVEHANDEL I, DEN** • 1910
WHITE SLAVE, THE see **WEISSE SKLAVIN, DIE** • 1927
WHITE SLAVE, THE see **BLANKE SLAVIN, DE** • 1969
WHITE SLAVE, THE (USA) see **ESCLAVE BLANCHE, L'** • 1927
WHITE SLAVE CATCHERS, THE • 1914 • *Tincher Fay* • USA
WHITE SLAVE SHIP (USA) see **AMMUTINAMENTO, L'** • 1962
WHITE SLAVE TRADE see **TRATTA DELLE BIANCHE, LA** • 1952
WHITE SLAVERY IN NEW YORK • 1973 • Vickers Milton • USA
WHITE SLAVES see **WHITE SLAVES OF CHINATOWN** • 1964
WHITE SLAVES OF CHINATOWN • 1964 • Mawra Joseph P. • USA • SLAVES OF CHINATOWN ○ WHITE SLAVES
WHITE SLIDE, THE see **BILA SPONA** • 1960
WHITE SLIPPERS • 1924 • Hill Sinclair • UKN • PORT OF LOST SOULS, THE
WHITE SNAKE ENCHANTRESS, THE see **HAKUJA DEN** • 1958
WHITE SNAKE LADY, THE see **CHINESE SHADOW PLAY**
WHITE SNOW OF FUJI see **FUJI NO SHIRAYUKI** • 1935
WHITE SPIDER, THE (USA) see **WEISSE SPINNE, DIE** • 1963
WHITE SPORT, THE see **VITA SPORTEN, DEN** • 1968
WHITE SQUADRON, THE see **SQUADRONE BIANCO** • 1936
WHITE SQUAW, THE • 1908 • *Kalem* • USA
WHITE SQUAW, THE • 1910 • *Yankee* • USA
WHITE SQUAW, THE • 1913 • *Bison* • USA
WHITE SQUAW, THE • 1920 • Joos Therdo? • SHT • USA
WHITE SQUAW, THE • 1956 • Nazarro Ray • USA
WHITE STALLION, THE see **OUTLAW STALLION, THE** • 1954
WHITE STALLION (UKN) see **HARMONY TRAIL** • 1944
WHITE STAR see **LET IT ROCK** • 1988
WHITE STAR, THE • 1915 • Phillips Bertram • UKN
WHITE STEAMER, THE see **BYELI PAROKHOD** • 1976
WHITE STOCKING, THE • 1914 • Kellino W. P. • UKN
WHITE SUN OF THE DESERT, THE see **BELOE SOLNTSE PUOSTINI** • 1971
WHITE SUN OVER THE DESERT see **BELOE SOLNTSE PUOSTINI** • 1971
WHITE TELEPHONES see **TELEFONI BIANCHI** • 1976
WHITE TERROR, THE • 1915 • Paton Stuart • USA
WHITE THREADS OF THE CASCADES see **TAKI NO SHIRAITO** • 1933
WHITE THREADS OF THE CASCADES see **TAKI NO SHIRAITO** • 1952
WHITE THREADS OF THE WATERFALL see **TAKI NO SHIRAITO** • 1933
WHITE THUNDER • 1925 • Wilson Ben • USA
WHITE THUNDER see **VIKING, THE** • 1931
WHITE TIE AND TAILS • 1946 • Barton Charles T. • USA
WHITE TIGER • 1923 • Browning Tod • USA
WHITE TIGER TATTOO (USA) see **IREZUMI ICHIDAI** • 1966
WHITE TO BLACK • 1909 • Wormald S.? • UKN
WHITE TOWER, THE • 1950 • Tetzlaff Ted • USA
WHITE TRAIL, THE • 1915 • *Lariat* • USA
WHITE TRAIL, THE • 1917 • Terwilliger George W. • SHT • USA
WHITE TRAIL, THE see **GJURME TE BARDHA** • 1981
WHITE TRAP, THE • 1959 • Hayers Sidney • UKN
WHITE TRASH ON MOONSHINE MOUNTAIN see **MOONSHINE MOUNTAIN** • 1964
WHITE TREACHERY • 1912 • Dwan Allan • USA
WHITE TRIAL, THE see **PROCESUL ALB** • 1965
WHITE TURKEY, THE • 1916 • Chaudet Louis W. • SHT • USA
WHITE UNICORN, THE • 1947 • Knowles Bernard • UKN • BAD SISTER (USA)
WHITE VAQUERO, THE • 1913 • *Bison* • USA
WHITE VEIL, THE see **WIT SLUIER, DIE** • 1973
WHITE VOICES (USA) see **VOCI BIANCHE, LE** • 1964
WHITE WAGON, THE see **CAMION BLANC, LE** • 1942
WHITE WALL, THE see **VITA VAGGEN, DEN** • 1975
WHITE WARRIOR, THE (USA) see **AGI MURAD, IL DIAVOLO BIANCO** • 1959
WHITE WASHING THE POLICEMAN • 1904 • Haggar William • UKN
WHITE WASHING WILLIAM • 1915 • Miller Rube • USA
WHITE WATER MEN • 1925 • Barkas Geoffrey • UKN
WHITE WATER REBELS • 1982 • Badiyi Reza • TVM • USA
WHITE WATER SUMMER • 1987 • Bleckner Jeff • USA • RITES OF SUMMER
WHITE WHALES • 1987 • Fridriksson Fridrik Thor • ICL
WHITE, WHITE DAY, THE see **BYELY, BYELY DYEN** • 1974
WHITE, WHITE STORKS see **BYELYYE, BYELYYE AISTY** • 1967
WHITE WIDOW, THE see **ROVEDDERKOPPEN** • 1915
WHITE WILDERNESS • 1957 • Algar James • DOC • USA
WHITE WING –A BRAZILIAN DREAM see **ASA BRANCA –UM SONHO BRASILEIRO** • 1982
WHITE WINGS • 1923 • Roach Hal • SHT • USA
WHITE WINGS see **YANKEE CLIPPER, THE** • 1927
WHITE WINGS ON REVIEW • 1903 • Porter Edwin S. • USA
WHITE WINTER HEAT • 1988 • Miller Warren • USA
WHITE WITCH, THE • 1913 • von Herkomer Hubert • UKN
WHITE WITCH DOCTOR • 1953 • Hathaway Henry • USA
WHITE WOLF, THE • 1914 • *Nestor* • USA
WHITE WOMAN • 1933 • Walker Stuart • USA
WHITE YOUTH • 1920 • Dawn Norman • USA
WHITE ZOMBIE • 1932 • Halperin Victor Hugo • USA
WHITECHAPEL • 1920 • Dupont E. A. • FRG • KETTE VON PERLEN UND ABENTEUERN, EINE ○ LONDONER NEBEL
WHITEOAKS OF JALNA, THE • 1972 • Trent John, Woods Grahame • SER • CND
WHITEWASHED WALLS • 1919 • Frame Park • USA
WHITEWASHERS, THE • 1914 • Evans Fred, Evans Joe • UKN
WHITEWASHING THE CEILING • 1914 • Day Will • UKN
WHITEWATER SAM • 1978 • Larsen Keith • USA • RUN OR BURN
WHITHER? see **ILA AYN** • 1957
WHITHER GERMANY? • 1933 • Markham Mansfield • UKN
WHITHER GERMANY? (UKN) see **KUHLE WAMPE** • 1932
WHITHER MANKIND see **THINGS TO COME** • 1936
WHITHER THOU GOEST • 1917 • West Raymond B.? • USA
WHITY • 1970 • Fassbinder R. W. • FRG
WHIZ AND WHISKERS • 1919 • Mann Harry • SHT • USA
WHIZ QUIZ KID • 1964 • Kneitel Seymour • ANS • USA
WHIZZ, WHOOSH, WHAAM! • 1966 • Foldes Peter • ANS • FRN
WHIZZER, THE see **VIU-HAH HAH-TAJA** • 1975
WHO? • 1974 • Gold Jack • UKN • MAN IN THE STEEL MASK, THE ○ MAN WITHOUT A FACE
WHO? see **QUI?** • 1970
WHO AM I? • 1920 • *Conklin Chester* • USA
WHO AM I? • 1921 • Kolker Henry • USA
WHO AM I THIS TIME? • 1981 • Demme Jonathan • TVM • USA
WHO ARE MY PARENTS? • 1922 • Dawley J. Searle • USA • LITTLE CHILD SHALL LEAD THEM, A
WHO ARE THE DEBOLTS? AND WHERE DID THEY GET 19 KIDS? • 1977 • Korty John • DOC • USA
WHO ARE THESE PEOPLE AND WHAT ARE THESE FILMS? • 1973 • Noyce Phil • DOC • ASL
WHO ARE WE? • 1974 • Grgic Zlatko • ANS • CND
WHO ARE WE? see **MAN NAHN U** • 1960
WHO ARE YOU? see **QUI ETES-VOUS, M. SORGE?** • 1960
WHO ARE YOU? see **QUI?** • 1970
WHO ARE YOU MR. SORGE? (USA) see **QUI ETES-VOUS, M. SORGE?** • 1960
WHO ARE YOU POLLY MAGGOO? see **QUI ETES-VOUS, POLLY MAGGOO?** • 1965
WHO ARE YOU SATAN? (USA) see **URLO DALLE TENEBRE, UN** • 1975
WHO ARE YOU? (USA) see **WER BIST DU?** • 1969
WHO BEARS MALICE • 1915 • Jones Edgar • USA
WHO BELIEVES IN THE STORK see **KTO WIERZY W BOCIANY** • 1971
WHO CAN CARRY ON LONGER? • 1962 • Vas Judit • DOC • HNG
WHO CAN KILL A CHILD? see **QUIEN PUEDE MATAR A UN NINO?** • 1975
WHO CARES? • 1919 • Edwards Walter • USA
WHO CARES • 1925 • Kirkland David • USA
WHO CARES • 1969 • Broomfield Nicholas • DOC • UKN
WHO CARES.. see **WEN KUMMERT'S..** • 1960
WHO DARES WINS • 1982 • Sharp Ian • UKN • FINAL OPTION, THE (USA)
WHO DID IT? • 1912 • *Cosmopolitan* • UKN
WHO DISCOVERED THE NORTH POLE? • 1909 • *Lubin* • USA
WHO DOES SHE THINK SHE IS? • 1974 • Jaffe Patricia Lewis, Rodgers Gaby • USA
WHO DONE IT? • 1917 • Beaudine William • SHT • USA
WHO DONE IT? • 1942 • Kenton Erle C. • USA
WHO DONE IT? • 1949 • Bernds Edward • SHT • USA
WHO DONE IT? • 1956 • Dearden Basil • UKN
WHO DUNIT TO WHO? • 1946 • Crouch William Forest • SHT • USA
WHO FEARS THE DEVIL? see **LEGEND OF HILLBILLY JOHN, THE** • 1972
WHO FINDS A FRIEND FINDS A TREASURE see **CHI TROVA UN AMICO TROVA UN TESORO** • 1979
WHO FIRED? see **VEM SKOT?** • 1917
WHO FRAMED ROGER RABBIT • 1988 • Zemeckis Robert • USA
WHO GETS IN? • 1990 • Greenwald Barry • DOC • CND
WHO GETS THE FRIENDS? • 1988 • Garrett Lila • TVM • USA
WHO GETS THE ORDER? • 1911 • Dawley J. Searle • USA
WHO GOES NEXT? • 1938 • Elvey Maurice • UKN
WHO GOES THERE? • 1914 • Miller Ashley • USA
WHO GOES THERE? • 1917 • Earle William P. S. • USA
WHO GOES THERE? • 1952 • Kimmins Anthony • UKN • PASSIONATE SENTRY, THE (USA)
WHO GOES THERE? • Brzezinski Tony • SHT • USA
WHO GOT STUNG? • 1914 • *Selig* • USA
WHO GOT STUNG? • 1915 • *Princess* • USA
WHO GOT STUNG? see **CAUGHT IN THE RAIN** • 1914
WHO GOT THE REWARD? • 1911 • Sennett Mack • USA
WHO HAS SEEN THE WIND • 1977 • King Allan • CND • MAIS QUI A VU LE VENT

WHO HAS THE RIGHT? see **SINO ANG MAY KARAPATAN** • 1968
WHO HIT ME? • 1926 • Roberts Stephen • SHT • USA
WHO-HO-RAY #1 see **WHO HO RAY NO.1** • 1972
WHO-HO-RAY #2 see **WHO HO RAY NO.2** • 1972
WHO HO RAY NO.1 • 1972 • Vanderbeek Stan • USA • WHO-HO-RAY #1
WHO HO RAY NO.2 • 1972 • Vanderbeek Stan • SHT • USA • WHO-HO-RAY #2
WHO I KISSED YESTERDAY see **KOHO JSEM VCERA LIBAL** • 1935
WHO INVENTED THE WHEEL? see **KTO PRIDUMAL KOLESO?** • 1967
WHO IS BETA? see **QUEM A BETA?** • 1973
WHO IS GOING TO OPEN THE DOOR? see **CINE VA DESCHIDE USA?** • 1967
WHO IS GOING TO THE EXHIBITION? • 1964 • Degtyarov Vladimir • ANS • USS
WHO IS GOMEZ? see **GOMESU NO NA WA GOMESU: RYUSA** • 1967
WHO IS GUILTY? see **I KILLED THE COUNT** • 1938
WHO IS GUILTY? see **APRADHI KAUN?** • 1958
WHO IS HAPPIER THAN I? (USA) see **CHI E PIU FELICE DI ME?** • 1938
WHO IS HARRY KELLERMAN AND WHY IS HE SAYING THOSE TERRIBLE THINGS ABOUT ME? • 1971 • Grosbard Ulu • USA
WHO IS HOPE SCHUYLER? • 1942 • Loring Thomas Z. • USA
WHO IS IN THE BOX? • 1913 • Smalley Phillips • USA
WHO IS.. JAMES JONES • 1967 • King Allan • CND
WHO IS JULIA? • 1986 • Grauman Walter • TVM • USA
WHO IS KILLING THE GREAT CHEFS OF EUROPE? • 1978 • Kotcheff Ted • USA, FRG • TOO MANY CHEFS (UKN) ○ SCHLEMMERORGIE, DIE
WHO IS KILLING THE STUNTMEN? see **STUNTS** • 1977
WHO IS NUMBER ONE? • 1918 • Bertram William • SRL • USA
WHO IS RESPONSIBLE see **QRR** • 1971
WHO IS SMOKING THAT ROPE? • 1908 • *Essanay* • USA
WHO IS STRONGEST? • 1952 • Miler Zdenek • ANS • CZC
WHO IS SYLVIA? • 1957 • Haldane Don • SHT • CND
WHO IS THE BLACK DAHLIA? • 1975 • Pevney Joseph • TVM • USA
WHO IS THE BOSS? • 1921 • Brouett Albert • UKN
WHO IS THE BRIDE? see **AROUS KODUME?** • 1960
WHO IS THE GOAT? • 1913 • Smalley Phillips • USA
WHO IS THE GUILTY ONE? see **MUJRIM KAUN?** • 1968
WHO IS THE KING? see **KRAL KIM?** • 1968
WHO IS THE MAN? • 1924 • Summers Walter • UKN
WHO IS THE MURDERER see **KOROSHITANO WA DAREDA** • 1957
WHO IS THE SAVAGE? • 1913 • *Ryan Mary* • USA
WHO IS THINKING SHOULDN'T THINK BAD • 1970 • Golik Kreso • YGS
WHO IS TO BLAME? • 1918 • Borzage Frank • USA
WHO IS WHO? • 1909 • Porter Edwin S. • USA
WHO IS YOUR FRIEND? • 1967 • Vas Judit • DOC • HNG
WHO KILLED AUNT MAGGIE? • 1940 • Lubin Arthur • USA
WHO KILLED BARNO O'NEAL see **NATTENS MYSTERIUM** • 1916
WHO KILLED COCK ROBIN? • 1933 • *Terry Paul/ Moser Frank (P)* • ANS • USA
WHO KILLED COCK ROBIN? • 1935 • Hand David • ANS • USA
WHO KILLED COCK ROBIN? • 1970 • Flynn Harry • USA
WHO KILLED COCK RUBIN? see **MALTESE BIPPY, THE** • 1969
WHO KILLED DOC ROBBIN? • 1948 • Carr Bernard • USA • SINISTER HOUSE (UKN) ○ CURLEY AND HIS GANG ○ CURLEY AND HIS GANG IN THE HAUNTED MANSION
WHO KILLED DOC ROBIN? • 1931 • Kellino W. P. • UKN
WHO KILLED DOC ROBIN? see **DANGEROUS GAME, A** • 1941
WHO KILLED FEN MARKHAM? see **ANGELUS, THE** • 1937
WHO KILLED GAIL PRESTON? • 1938 • Barsha Leon • USA • MURDER IN SPRING TIME
WHO KILLED GEORGE GRAVES? • 1914 • Le Saint Edward J. • USA
WHO KILLED HARVEY FORBES? (UKN) see **TANGLED DESTINIES** • 1932
WHO KILLED JENNY LANGBY? • 1974 • Crombie Donald • DOC • ASL
WHO KILLED JESSIE? see **KDO CHCE ZABIT JESSI?** • 1966
WHO KILLED JOE MERRION? • 1915 • Johnson Tefft • USA
WHO KILLED JOHN DARE? • 1910 • *Yankee* • USA
WHO KILLED JOHN SAVAGE? • 1937 • Elvey Maurice • UKN
WHO KILLED MARY MAGDALENE? see **WHO KILLED MARY WHAT'S'ERNAME?** • 1971
WHO KILLED MARY WHAT'S'ERNAME? • 1971 • Pintoff Ernest • USA • WHO KILLED MARY MAGDALENE? ○ DEATH OF A HOOKER
WHO KILLED OLGA CAREW? • 1913 • *Imp* • USA
WHO KILLED SANTA CLAUS? (USA) see **ASSASSINAT DU PERE NOEL, L'** • 1941
WHO KILLED TEDDY BEAR? • 1965 • Cates Joseph • USA
WHO KILLED THE CAT? • 1966 • Tully Montgomery • UKN
WHO KILLED THE MYSTERIOUS MR. FOSTER see **SAM HILL: WHO KILLED THE MYSTERIOUS MR. FOSTER** • 1971
WHO KILLED THE ROBINS? • 1951 • *Korda Alexander (P)* • SHT • UKN
WHO KILLED VAN LOON? • 1948 • Tomlinson Lionel, Kyle Gordon • UKN
WHO KILLED WALTON? • 1918 • Heffron Thomas N. • USA
WHO KILLED WARING? (UKN) see **BLAZING THE WESTERN TRAIL** • 1945
WHO KILLED WHO? • 1943 • Avery Tex • ANS • USA
WHO KISSED HER? • 1915 • Kellino W. P. • UKN
WHO KNOWS? • 1916 • *King Henry* • SHT • USA
WHO KNOWS? • 1917 • Pratt Jack • USA
WHO KNOWS? • 1918 • *Oro Pictures* • USA
WHO KNOWS A WOMAN'S HEART see **ONNAGOKORO O DAREGA SHIRU** • 1951
WHO LAUGHS LAST • 1920 • Youngdeer James • UKN
WHO LOOKS FOR GOLD see **KDO HLEDA ZLATE DNO** • 1975
WHO LOOKS, PAYS (USA) see **HOMME EST SATISFAIT, L'** • 1906
WHO LOVED HIM BEST? • 1918 • Henderson Dell • USA
WHO LYIN'? • 1928 • Roberts Stephen • SHT • USA
WHO! ME? • 1932 • Stevens George • SHT • USA
WHO ME? • 1942 • Cornelius Henry • SHT • UKN
WHO MISLAID MY WIFE? see **CATTIVI PENSIERI** • 1976
WHO NEEDS FRIENDS see **THAT LUCKY TOUCH** • 1975
WHO NEEDS NUDNIK? • 1966 • Deitch Gene • ANS • USA
WHO OWNS THE ACORNS? • 1966 • Strautman Rasa • ANM • USS
WHO OWNS THE BABY • 1911 • *Lubin* • USA
WHO OWNS TYSSEDAL? see **HVEM EIER TYSSEDAL** • 1976
WHO PAYS? • 1915 • King Henry • SRL • USA • PRICE OF FOLLY
WHO PULLED THE PLUG? see **GOTA KANALEN** • 1982
WHO PULLED THE TRIGGER? • 1916 • McRae Henry • USA
WHO RIDES WITH KANE? see **YOUNG BILLY YOUNG** • 1969
WHO ROBBED THE ROBINS? • 1947 • Dyer Anson • UKN
WHO SAID CHICKEN? • 1917 • Hartigan P. C. • SHT • USA
WHO SAID "MIAO"? • 1962 • Degtyarov Vladimir • ANS • USS
WHO SAID THEY NEVER COME BACK • 1916 • *International Film Service* • SHT • USA
WHO SAVES JESSIE? see **KDO CHCE ZABIT JESSI?** • 1966
WHO SAW HIM DIE? see **OLE DOLE DOFF** • 1968
WHO SAYS I CAN'T RIDE A RAINBOW! • 1971 • Mann Edward • USA
WHO SCENT YOU? • 1960 • Jones Charles M. • ANS • USA
WHO SEEKS A HANDFUL OF GOLD see **KDO HLEDA ZLATE DNO** • 1975
WHO SEEKS REVENGE • 1914 • Smiley Joseph • USA
WHO SEEKS THE GOLD BOTTOM see **KDO HLEDA ZLATE DNO** • 1975
WHO SEES FARTHER • 1984 • Koulev Henri • ANM • BUL
WHO SHALL TAKE MY LIFE? • 1918 • Campbell Colin • USA
WHO SHEDS HIS BLOOD? • 1941 • Crawley Judith • DOC • CND
WHO SHOT BUD WALTON? • 1914 • Adolfi John G. • USA
WHO SLEW AUNTIE ROO? see **WHOEVER SLEW AUNTIE ROO?** • 1971
WHO SO DIGGETH A PIT • 1914 • *Reid Wallace* • USA
WHO SO LOVETH HIS FATHER'S HONOR see **HVO SOM ELSKER SIN FADER** • 1915
WHO STOLE BUNNY'S UMBRELLA • 1912 • Thompson Frederick A. • USA
WHO STOLE PA'S PURSE? • 1915 • Wilson Frank? • UKN
WHO STOLE THE BEER? • 1906 • Stow Percy • UKN
WHO STOLE THE BIKE? • 1902 • *Mitchell & Kenyon* • UKN
WHO STOLE THE BODY (USA) see **BRICOLEURS, LES** • 1962
WHO STOLE THE BRIDEGROOM • 1914 • *Nestor* • USA
WHO STOLE THE DOGGIES? • 1915 • *Hardy Babe* • USA
WHO THREW THE BRICK? • 1920 • Physioc Wray • SHT • USA
WHO VIOLATES THE LAW • 1915 • *Johnson Arthur* • USA
WHO WANTS TO BE A HERO • 1915 • *Selig* • USA
WHO WANTS TO BE A SOLDIER? see **WER WILL UNTER DIE SOLDATEN?** • 1960
WHO WANTS TO KILL JESSIE? see **KDO CHCE ZABIT JESSI?** • 1966
WHO WANTS TO SHOOT CARLOS? see **GEHEIMNISSE IN GOLDENEN NYLONS** • 1966
WHO WANTS TO SLEEP see **LIEBESKARUSSELL, DAS** • 1965
WHO WAS MADDOX? • 1964 • Nethercott Geoffrey • UKN
WHO WAS SHE? see **WOH KAUN THI?** • 1964
WHO WAS THE LADY? • 1960 • Sidney George • USA
WHO WAS THE MAN • 1926 • USA
WHO WAS THE OTHER MAN? • 1917 • Ford Francis • USA
WHO WAS TO BLAME? • 1914 • Kellino W. P. • UKN
WHO WE MUST SHOOT AT see **ALA MAN NAT'LUQ AR-RACAC?** • 1975
WHO WEARS THEM? • 1912 • *Imp* • USA
WHO WERE YOU WITH LAST NIGHT? • 1915 • Birch Cecil • UKN
WHO WILL DECIDE • 1985 • Shaffer Beverly • DOC • CND
WHO WILL I SENTENCE NOW? • 1978 • Richardson Boyce • DOC • CND
WHO WILL LOVE MY CHILDREN? • 1982 • Erman John • TVM • USA
WHO WILL MARRY MARTHA? • 1914 • Evans Joe • UKN
WHO WILL MARRY MARY? • 1913 • Edwin Walter • SRL • USA
WHO WILL MARRY ME? • 1919 • Powell Paul • USA
WHO WILL SAVE OUR CHILDREN? see **WHO'LL SAVE OUR CHILDREN?** • 1978
WHO WILL TEACH YOUR CHILD? • 1948 • Jackson Stanley R. • DOC • CND
WHO WINKED AT THE SOLDIER • 1907 • Jeapes Harold? • UKN
WHO WINS THE WIDOW • 1910 • *Powers* • USA
WHO WORKS IS LOST see **CHI LAVORI E PERDUTO** • 1963
WHO WOULD KILL JESSIE? see **KDO CHCE ZABIT JESSI?** • 1966
WHO WRITES TO SWITZERLAND • 1937 • Cavalcanti Alberto • DOC • UKN
WHOA, BE GONE • 1958 • Jones Charles M. • ANS • USA
WHODUNIT? see **WOH KAUN THI?** • 1964
WHODUNIT? MURDER IN SPACE see **MURDER IN SPACE** • 1985
WHODUNNIT • 1987 • Scherberger Aiken • USA
WHODUNNIT? see **ISLAND OF BLOOD** • 1986
WHOEVER MAY KNOW.. see **KTOKOLWIEK WIE..** • 1966
WHOEVER SLEW AUNTIE ROO? • 1971 • Harrington Curtis • USA, UKN • GINGERBREAD HOUSE ○ WHO SLEW AUNTIE ROO?
WHOEVER WAITS FOR THE SHOES OF A DEAD MAN DIES WITHOUT SHOES see **QUEM ESPERA POR SAPATOS DE DEFUNTO MORRE DESCALCO** • 1970
WHOLE DAM FAMILY AND THE DAM DOG • 1905 • Porter Edwin S. • USA
WHOLE DAMN WAR, THE see **WHOLE DARN WAR, THE** • 1928
WHOLE DARN WAR, THE • 1928 • *Citron Sam* • USA • WHOLE DAMN WAR, THE
WHOLE FAMILY WORKS, THE see **HATARAKU IKKA** • 1939
WHOLE JUNGLE WAS AFTER HIM, THE • 1916 • Bourgeois Paul • SHT • USA
WHOLE LIFE, THE see **GANZE LEBEN, DAS** • 1983
WHOLE NEW WAY OF LIFE, A • 1971 • Benegal Shyam • DCS • IND
WHOLE SHOOTIN' MATCH, THE • 1978 • Pennell Eagle • USA
WHOLE SHOW, THE • 1934 • Schwarzwald Milton • SHT • USA
WHOLE SKY, THE see **SARA AKASH** • 1970
WHOLE TOWN'S TALKING, THE • 1926 • Laemmle Edward • USA
WHOLE TOWN'S TALKING, THE • 1935 • Ford John • USA • PASSPORT TO FAME (UKN)
WHOLE TOWN'S TALKING, THE see **EX-BAD BOY** • 1931
WHOLE TRUTH, THE • 1913 • *Gail Jane* • USA
WHOLE TRUTH, THE • 1958 • Guillermin John • UKN
WHOLE TRUTH, THE • 1964 • Loach Kenneth • MTV • UKN
WHOLE TRUTH, THE see **BLIND JUSTICE** • 1961
WHOLE TRUTH ABOUT COLUMBUS, A • 1970 • Zalakevicius Vitautus • MTV • USS
WHOLE WEEK, A see **OKRAGLY TYDZIEN** • 1977
WHOLE WORLD IS WATCHING, THE • 1969 • Colla Richard A. • TVM • USA
WHOLE WORLD KIN, THE • 1909 • *Edison* • USA
WHOLE WORLD OVER, THE • 1957 • Forest Leonard, Haldane Don • SHT • CND
WHOLESAILING ALONG • 1936 • Boasberg Al • SHT • USA
WHOLESALE PROPOSALS • 1916 • *Gayety* • USA
WHO'LL SAVE OUR CHILDREN? • 1978 • Schaefer George • TVM • USA • WHO WILL SAVE OUR CHILDREN?
WHO'LL SEE FOR THE CHILDREN • 1975 • *Quinn Martin* • MXC
WHO'LL STOP THE RAIN • 1978 • Reisz Karel • USA • DOG SOLDIERS (UKN)
WHOLLY MOSES • 1980 • Weis Gary • USA
WHOLLY SMOKE • 1938 • Tashlin Frank • ANS • USA
WHOM GOD HATH JOINED • 1912 • *Snow Marguerite* • USA
WHOM GOD HATH JOINED • 1914 • *Patheplay* • USA
WHOM GOD HATH JOINED • 1914 • *Eclair* • USA
WHOM GOD HATH JOINED • 1916 • *Puritan* • SHT • USA
WHOM SHALL I MARRY • 1926 • *Lincoln Elmo* • USA
WHOM THE GODS DESTROY • 1916 • Brenon Herbert • USA • WHOM THE GODS WOULD DESTROY
WHOM THE GODS DESTROY • 1916 • Earle William P. S., Blackton J. Stuart • USA
WHOM THE GODS DESTROY • 1934 • Lang Walter • USA
WHOM THE GODS DESTROY see **WHOM THE GODS WOULD DESTROY** • 1919
WHOM THE GODS LOVE • 1936 • Dean Basil • UKN • MOZART (USA)
WHOM THE GODS WISH TO DESTROY see **NIBELUNG, DIE** • 1966
WHOM THE GODS WISH TO DESTROY see **NIBELUNGEN II: KRIEMHILD'S RACHE, DIE** • 1967
WHOM THE GODS WOULD DESTROY • 1915 • Smiley Joseph • USA
WHOM THE GODS WOULD DESTROY • 1919 • Borzage Frank • USA • WHOM THE GODS DESTROY
WHOM THE GODS WOULD DESTROY see **WHOM THE GODS DESTROY** • 1916
WHOOPEE! • 1930 • Freeland Thornton • USA
WHOOPEE BOYS • 1929 • Roberts Stephen • SHT • USA
WHOOPEE BOYS, THE • 1986 • Byrum John • USA
WHOOPEE PARTY, THE • 1932 • Jackson Wilfred • ANS • USA
WHOOPING COUGH see **SZAMARKOHOGES** • 1986
WHOOPING THE BLUES • 1969 • Agins Jack, Paup Rick • SHT • USA
WHOOPS APOCALYPSE • 1982 • Reardon John • MTV • UKN • MUSHROOM BUTTON, THE
WHOOPS APOCALYPSE! • 1987 • Bussman Tom • UKN
WHOOPS! I'M A COWBOY • 1937 • Fleischer Dave • ANS • USA
WHOOPS I'M AN INDIAN • 1936 • Lord Del • SHT • USA
WHORE, A see **BAITA** • 1967
WHORE FOR A WIFE, A see **ZOKU JOROHZUMA** • 1968
WHO'S A DUMMY? • 1941 • D'Arcy Harry • SHT • USA
WHO'S AFRAID? • 1927 • Lamont Charles • SHT • USA
WHO'S AFRAID? see **GHOSTS** • 1913
WHO'S AFRAID OF A LITTLE MAN see **WER HAT ANGST VORM KLEINEN MANN** • 1971
WHO'S AFRAID OF ERNEST HEMINGWAY? see **DEATH IN THE FORENOON**
WHO'S AFRAID OF THE AVANT-GARDE? • 1968 • Leacock Richard • DOC • USA
WHO'S AFRAID OF VIRGINIA WOOLF? • 1966 • Nichols Mike • USA
WHO'S BEEN ROCKING MY DREAMBOAT? • 1941 • Anger Kenneth • SHT • USA
WHO'S BEEN SLEEPING IN MY BED? • 1963 • Mann Daniel • USA
WHO'S BOSS? • 1914 • *Lubin* • USA
WHO'S CHEATING? • 1924 • Levering Joseph • USA
WHO'S COOKIN' WHO? • 1946 • Culhane James • ANS • USA
WHO'S CRAZY • 1965 • Zion Allan, White Thomas • USA
WHO'S CRAZY NOW • 1920 • Davey Horace • SHT • USA
WHO'S CRAZY NOW? see **CRAZY NO KISOUTENGAI**
WHO'S GOT MY HAT? • 1910 • Fitzhamon Lewin • UKN
WHO'S GOT THE ACTION? • 1962 • Mann Daniel • USA
WHO'S GOT THE BLACK BOX? (USA) see **ROUTE DE CORINTHE, LA** • 1967
WHO'S GUILTY? • 1916 • SER • USA
WHO'S GUILTY? • 1945 • Bretherton Howard, Grissell Wallace A. • SRL • USA
WHO'S HARRY CRUMB? • 1989 • Flaherty Paul • USA
WHO'S HER HUSBAND • 1919 • Lyons Eddie, Moran Lee • SHT • USA
WHO'S IN CHARGE • 1983 • King Allan • CND
WHO'S KITTEN WHO? • 1952 • McKimson Robert • ANS • USA
WHO'S LOONEY NOW? • 1914 • *Klaw & Erlanger* • USA
WHO'S LOONEY NOW? • 1916 • *Ab* • SHT • USA
WHO'S LOONEY NOW? • 1917 • Christie Al • SHT • USA
WHO'S LOONEY NOW? • 1936 • Goodwins Leslie • SHT • USA
WHO'S MINDING THE MINT? • 1967 • Morris Howard • USA
WHO'S MINDING THE STORE? • 1963 • Tashlin Frank • USA

WHO'S MURDERING WHOM? see **HVEM MYRDER HVEM** • 1977
WHO'S MY WIFE? • 1926 • Roberts Stephen • SHT • USA
WHO'S SINGING THERE see **KO TO TAMO PEVA?** • 1981
WHO'S SUPERSTITIOUS? • 1943 • Lee Sammy • SHT • USA
WHO'S TAKEN MY PARCEL? • 1906 • *Mitchell & Kenyon* • UKN
WHO'S THAT A-CALLING? • 1905 • Collins Alf? • UKN
WHO'S THAT GIRL? • 1987 • Foley James • USA • SLAMMER
WHO'S THAT KNOCKING AT MY DOOR? • 1967 • Scorsese Martin • USA • I CALL FIRST ○ J.R.
WHO'S THAT SINGING OVER THERE? see **KO TO TAMO PEVA?** • 1981
WHO'S THE BOSS? • 1912 • *Powers* • USA
WHO'S TO BE BLAMED see **SINO ANG DAPAT SISIHIN** • 1967
WHO'S TO BLAME? • 1905 • Cooper Arthur • UKN • WHY THE TYPIST GOT THE SACK
WHO'S TO BLAME? • 1918 • Curtis Allen • SHT • USA
WHO'S TO WIN • 1912 • Thompson Frederick A. • USA
WHO'S WHICH? • 1914 • Birch Cecil • UKN
WHO'S WHICH see **TURNING THE TABLES** • 1919
WHO'S WHO • 1906 • *Selig William N. (P)* • USA
WHO'S WHO • 1909 • *Edison* • USA
WHO'S WHO • 1911 • *Costello Maurice* • USA
WHO'S WHO? • 1912 • *Powers* • USA
WHO'S WHO • 1914 • *Victor* • USA
WHO'S WHO • 1914 • *Melies* • USA
WHO'S WHO • 1914 • Louis Will • *Lubin* • USA
WHO'S WHO • 1915 • *Ovey George* • USA • TWIN BRIDES
WHO'S WHO? • 1921 • Cline Eddie • SHT • USA
WHO'S WHO IN ADELAIDE • 1922 • ASL
WHO'S WHO IN HOG'S HOLLOW • 1914 • *Drew Sidney* • USA
WHO'S WHO IN SOCIETY • 1915 • *Sargeantson Kate* • USA
WHO'S WHO IN SOCIETY • 1915 • Fitzmaurice George • USA
WHO'S WHO IN THE JUNGLE • 1945 • Donnelly Eddie • ANS • USA
WHO'S WHO IN THE ZOO • 1931 • *Sennett Mack (P)* • SHT • USA
WHO'S WHO IN THE ZOO • 1942 • McCabe Norman • ANS • USA
WHO'S WHOOPEE • 1930 • Sullivan Pat, Messmer Otto • ANS • USA
WHO'S YOUR BROTHER? • 1919 • Adolfi John G. • USA
WHO'S YOUR FATHER? • 1918 • Mix Tom • SHT • USA
WHO'S YOUR FATHER? • 1935 • George Henry W. • UKN
WHO'S YOUR FRIEND? • 1916 • Wilson Frank • UKN
WHO'S YOUR FRIEND • 1925 • Sheldon Forrest • USA
WHO'S YOUR LADY FRIEND? • 1937 • Reed Carol • UKN
WHO'S YOUR NEIGHBOR? • 1917 • Drew Sidney • USA
WHO'S YOUR SERVANT? • 1920 • *Wilson Lois* • USA
WHO'S YOUR WIFE? • 1918 • Curtis Allen • SHT • USA
WHO'S ZOO IN AFRICA see **THRU THIN AND THICKET** • 1933
WHO'S ZOO IN HOLLYWOOD • 1941 • Davis Arthur • ANS • USA
WHOSE BABY? • 1913 • *Kinemacolor* • USA
WHOSE BABY? • 1914 • *Crystal* • USA
WHOSE BABY? • 1914 • Collins Edwin J.? • UKN
WHOSE BABY • 1917 • Badger Clarence • *Keystone* • SHT • USA
WHOSE BABY? • 1917 • Beaudine William • *Joker* • SHT • USA
WHOSE BABY ARE YOU? • 1918 • Lyons Eddie, Moran Lee • SHT • USA
WHOSE CHILD AM I? • 1983 • SAF
WHOSE CHOICE • 1976 • London Women'S Film Group • UKN
WHOSE HAND? see **GREAT BRADLEY MYSTERY, THE** • 1917
WHOSE HOOSIERY? • 1917 • *Sparkle* • SHT • USA
WHOSE HUSBAND? • 1915 • Williams C. Jay • USA
WHOSE IS IT? • 1913 • *Lubin* • USA
WHOSE LAW IS IT? see **KINEK A TORVENYE?** • 1979
WHOSE LIFE IS IT ANYWAY? • 1981 • Badham John • USA
WHOSE LITTLE GIRL ARE YOU? see **HVIS LILLE PIGE ER DU?** • 1963
WHOSE LITTLE WIFE ARE YOU? • 1918 • Cline Eddie • SHT • USA
WHOSE TURN IS IT see **NA KOHO TO SLOVO PADNE** • 1980
WHOSE WAS THE HAND • 1912 • ASL
WHOSE WAS THE SHAME? • 1915 • *Bayne Beverly* • USA
WHOSE WIFE? • 1917 • Sturgeon Rollin S. • USA
WHOSE WIFE? • 1918 • *Compson Betty* • SHT • USA
WHOSE WIFE • 1920 • France Charles H. • SHT • USA
WHOSE WIFE IS THIS? • 1913 • *Santschi Tom* • USA
WHOSE ZOO? • 1918 • Hutchinson Craig • SHT • USA
WHOSO DIGGETH A PIT • 1915 • Dewsbury Ralph • UKN
WHOSO FINDETH A WIFE see **WHOSO TAKETH A WIFE** • 1916
WHOSO IS WITHOUT SIN • 1916 • Paul Fred • UKN
WHOSO TAKETH A WIFE • 1916 • Crane Frank H. • USA • WHOSO FINDETH A WIFE
WHOSOEVER SHALL OFFEND • 1919 • Bocchi Arrigo • UKN
WHY? • 1913 • *Eclair* • FRN
WHY? see **PROC?** • 1964
WHY? see **MIERT?** • 1966
WHY? see **DETENUTO IN ATTESA DI GIUDIZIO** • 1971
WHY? see **PROC?** • 1987
WHY AMERICA? see **POURQUOI L'AMERIQUE?** • 1970
WHY AMERICA WILL WIN • 1918 • Stanton Richard • USA
WHY ANNA? see **DIARIO DI UNA SCHIZOFRENICA** • 1968
WHY ANNOUNCE YOUR MARRIAGE? • 1922 • Crosland Alan • USA • DECEIVERS, THE
WHY ARE THEY AGAINST US? see **WARUM SIND SIE GEGEN UNS?** • 1958
WHY AREN'T YOU LAUGHING? see **PROC SE NESMEJES?** • 1922
WHY AUNT JANE NEVER MARRIED • 1913 • *Tennant Barbara* • USA
WHY BABE LEFT HOME • 1913 • *Thanhouser* • USA
WHY BE GOOD? • 1929 • Seiter William A. • USA • THAT'S A BAD GIRL
WHY BEACHES ARE POPULAR • 1919 • *Prevost Marie* • SHT • USA
WHY BEN BOLTED • 1917 • Williamson Robin E. • SHT • USA
WHY BILLINGS WAS LATE • 1915 • MacGregor Norval • USA
WHY BIRDS SIT ON TELEGRAPH POLES see **PROC SEDAJI PTACI NA TELEGRAFNI DRATY** • 1948
WHY BLAME ME? see **HER MOMENT** • 1918
WHY BOTHER TO KNOCK? (USA) see **DON'T BOTHER TO KNOCK** • 1961
WHY BRI? • 1961 • Napier-Bell J. B. • SHT • UKN
WHY BRING THAT UP? • 1929 • Abbott George • USA • BACKSTAGE BLUES
WHY BRONCHO BILLY LEFT BEAR COUNTY • 1913 • *Anderson Broncho Billy* • USA
WHY CHANGE YOUR HUSBAND? (UKN) see **GOLD DUST GERTIE** • 1931
WHY CHANGE YOUR WIFE? • 1920 • De Mille Cecil B. • USA
WHY CHARLSTON DAYS AGAIN? • 1982 • Okamoto Kihachi • JPN
WHY COOKS GO CUCKOO • 1920 • *Ovey George* • USA
WHY DAD WAS HELD UP • 1910 • *Nestor* • USA
WHY, DADDY? • 1944 • Jason Will • SHT • USA
WHY DID BODHI-DHARMA LEAVE FOR THE ORIENT? see **WHY DID BODHY-DHARMA GO EAST?** • 1988
WHY DID BODHY-DHARMA GO EAST? • 1988 • Bae Yong-Kyun • SKR • WHY DID BODHI-DHARMA LEAVE FOR THE ORIENT?
WHY DID I LOVE YOU? see **BAKIT KITA INIBIG?** • 1968
WHY DID YOU PICK ON ME? see **NUOVE AVVENTURE DEL SCERIFFO EXTRA-TERRESTRE, LE** • 1980
WHY DIDN'T THEY ASK EVANS? • 1979 • Davies John, Wharmby Tony • TVM • UKN
WHY DIVORCE? • 1919 • *De Haven Carter* • SHT • USA
WHY DO I DREAM THOSE DREAMS • 1934 • Freleng Friz • ANS • USA
WHY DO WE NEED ALL THE BRASS BANDS? (USA) see **KDYBY TY MUSIKY NEBYLY** • 1963
WHY DO YOU SMILE, MONA LISA? see **PROC SE USMIVAS, MONO LISO?** • 1966
WHY DOES HERR R. RUN AMOK? see **WARUM LAUFT HERR R. AMOK?** • 1969
WHY DOES THE GIRAFFE CRY? • Kadlecek Ludvik • ANS • CZC
WHY DOES THE HYENA LAUGH? • 1929 • Aylott Dave, Symmons E. F. • SHT • UKN
WHY DON'T YOU LEAVE US IN PEACE? see **PERCHE NON CI LASCIATE IN PACE?** • 1971
WHY DON'T YOU SPEAK UP? see **POCHEMU TY MOLCHISH?** • 1967
WHY FATHER GREW A BEARD • 1909 • Booth W. R. • UKN
WHY FATHER LEARNED TO RIDE • 1909 • Fitzhamon Lewin • UKN
WHY FORESAKE ME? • 1983 • SAF
WHY FOXY GRANDPA ESCAPED DUCKING • 1903 • *Bitzer Billy (Ph)* • USA
WHY GEORGE! • 1926 • Lamont Charles • SHT • USA
WHY GERMANY MUST PAY • 1919 • Miller Charles • USA
WHY GET A DIVORCE? • 1918 • *Christie* • USA
WHY GIRLS GO BACK HOME • 1926 • Flood James • USA
WHY GIRLS LEAVE HOME • 1909 • *Edison* • USA
WHY GIRLS LEAVE HOME • 1913 • Williams C. Jay • USA
WHY GIRLS LEAVE HOME • 1921 • Nigh William • USA
WHY GIRLS LEAVE HOME • 1945 • Berke William • USA
WHY GIRLS LOVE SAILORS • 1927 • Guiol Fred • USA
WHY GIRLS SAY NO • 1927 • McCarey Leo • SHT • USA
WHY GO HOME? • 1920 • Parrott Charles, Roach Hal • SHT • USA
WHY GRAND-DADDY WENT TO SEA • 1913 • *Powers* • USA
WHY HE GAVE UP • 1911 • Lehrman Henry, Sennett Mack (Spv) • USA
WHY HE WENT WEST • 1911 • *Champion* • USA
WHY HENRY LEFT HOME • 1918 • Drew Sidney, Drew Sidney Mrs. • SHT • USA
WHY HESITATE? • 1925 • Mayo Archie • SHT • USA
WHY HURRY • 1924 • Christie Al • USA
WHY HUSBANDS FLIRT • 1918 • *Christie* • USA
WHY HUSBANDS GO MAD • 1924 • McCarey Leo • SHT • USA
WHY I AM HERE • 1913 • Ince Ralph • USA
WHY I SING • 1972 • Howe John • CND
WHY I WOULD NOT MARRY • 1918 • Stanton Richard • USA
WHY IS A PLUMBER? • 1929 • McCarey Leo • SHT • USA
WHY IS IT? • 1948 • Barclay David • SHT • USA
WHY IS MONA LISA SMILING? see **PROC SE USMIVAS, MONO LISO?** • 1966
WHY IS THE SKY BLUE? see **BAKIT BUGHAW ANG LANGIT?** • 1981
WHY IS THE STRANGE MR. ZOLOCK INTERESTED IN COMIC STRIPS? see **POURQUOI L'ETRANGE MONSIEUR ZOLOCK S'INTERESSAIT-IL TANT A LA BANDE DESSINEE?** • 1984
WHY IS YOUR HUSBAND UNFAITHFUL? see **POR QUE TE ENGANA TU MARIDO?** • 1968
WHY JENKINS WEARS THE BLUE RIBBON • 1907 • Smith Jack ? • UKN
WHY JIM REFORMED • 1912 • Duncan William • USA
WHY JONES DISCOVERED HIS CLERKS • 1900 • Porter Edwin S. • USA
WHY JONES GOT THE SACK • 1907 • *Walturdaw* • UKN
WHY JONES SIGNED THE PLEDGE • 1906 • Raymond Charles? • UKN
WHY KENTUCKY WENT DRY • 1914 • *Frontier* • USA
WHY LEAVE HOME? • 1929 • Cannon Raymond • USA
WHY LEE! • 1920 • Lyons Eddie, Moran Lee • SHT • USA
WHY LOVE IS BLIND • 1916 • Nicholls George • SHT • USA
WHY MAN CREATES • 1968 • Bass Saul • SHT • USA
WHY MARRIAGE IS A FAILURE • 1904 • *Paul R. W.* • UKN
WHY ME? • 1978 • Lamb Derek, Perlman Janet • ANS • CND
WHY ME? • 1984 • Cook Fielder • TVM • USA
WHY ME? • 1989 • Quintano Gene • USA
WHY MEN FORGET (USA) see **DEMOS** • 1921
WHY MEN GO WRONG • 1922 • *Wondergraph Theatre* • ASL
WHY MEN LEAVE HOME • 1913 • *Imp* • USA
WHY MEN LEAVE HOME • 1914 • *Planet Films* • UKN
WHY MEN LEAVE HOME • 1924 • Stahl John M. • USA
WHY MEN LEAVE HOME see **GOLDEN PIPPIN GIRL, THE** • 1920
WHY MEN RAPE • 1979 • Jackson Douglas • DOC • CND
WHY MEN WORK • 1924 • McCarey Leo • SHT • USA
WHY MR. JONES WAS ARRESTED • 1909 • *Bison* • USA
WHY MR. NATION WANTS A DIVORCE • 1901 • Porter Edwin S. • USA
WHY MRS. JONES GOT A DIVORCE • 1900 • Porter Edwin S. • USA
WHY MRS. KENTWORTH LIED • 1916 • Moore Matt • SHT • USA
WHY MULES LEAVE HOME • 1934 • *Terry Paul/ Moser Frank (P)* • ANS • USA
WHY MUST I DIE? • 1960 • Del Ruth Roy • USA • 13 STEPS TO DEATH (UKN)
WHY NOT see **WHY NOT - A SERENADE OF ESCHATOLOGICAL ECOLOGY** • 1971
WHY NOT? see **POURQUOI PAS?** • 1979
WHY NOT? see **EJA NAIKA** • 1981
WHY NOT - A SERENADE OF ESCHATOLOGICAL ECOLOGY • 1971 • Arakawa • USA • WHY NOT
WHY NOT MARRY? • 1918 • *Bret Tom* • USA
WHY NOT MARRY? • 1922 • Lopez John S. • USA
WHY NOT STAY FOR BREAKFAST? • 1979 • Marcel Terry • UKN
WHY PICK ON ME • 1918 • Roach Hal • SHT • USA
WHY PICK ON ME? • 1937 • Rogers Maclean • UKN
WHY PREACHERS LEAVE HOME • 1914 • *Melies* • USA
WHY RAGS LEFT HOME • 1913 • Pollard Harry • USA
WHY REGINALD REFORMED • 1914 • *Cruze James* • USA
WHY ROCK THE BOAT? • 1974 • Howe John • CND
WHY RUSSIANS ARE REVOLTING • 1970 • Sullivan Neil • USA
WHY SAILORS GO WRONG • 1928 • Lehrman Henry • USA • ROBINSON AND CRUSOE
WHY SAILORS LEAVE HOME • 1930 • Banks Monty • UKN • BARNACLE BILL
WHY SAPS LEAVE HOME (USA) see **INNOCENTS OF CHICAGO, THE** • 1932
WHY SCOTLAND, WHY EAST KILBRIDE • 1970 • McConnell Edward • DOC • UKN
WHY SHOOT THE TEACHER? • 1976 • Narizzano Silvio • CND • PITIE POUR LE PROF!
WHY SHOULD ALBERT PINTO BE ANGRY? see **ALBERT PINTO KO GUSSA KYON AATA HAI** • 1979
WHY SHOULD I LIE? see **WHY WOULD I LIE?** • 1980
WHY SKUNKVILLE WENT DRY • 1914 • *Columbus* • USA
WHY SMITH LEFT HOME • 1919 • Crisp Donald • USA
WHY SPY? see **MAN CALLED DAGGER, A** • 1966
WHY THAT ACTOR WAS LATE see **ACTEUR EN RETARD, L'** • 1908
WHY THE ACTOR WAS LATE see **ACTEUR EN RETARD, L'** • 1908
WHY THE BOARDERS LEFT • 1915 • *Mina* • USA
WHY THE CHECK WAS GOOD • 1911 • *Imp* • USA
WHY THE LODGER LEFT • 1905 • Collins Alf? • UKN
WHY THE MAIL WAS LATE • 1909 • *Lubin* • USA
WHY THE RANGER RESIGNED • 1913 • *Frontier* • USA
WHY THE SHERIFF IS A BACHELOR • 1911 • *Selig* • USA
WHY THE SHERIFF IS A BACHELOR • 1914 • Mix Tom • USA
WHY THE SHERIFF RESIGNED • 1911 • *Yankee* • USA
WHY THE TYPIST GOT THE SACK see **WHO'S TO BLAME?** • 1905
WHY THE WEDDING WAS PUT OFF • 1907 • Williamson James? • UKN
WHY THEY LEFT HOME • 1917 • Beaudine William • SHT • USA
WHY THEY MARRY • 1909 • *Vitagraph* • USA
WHY THOSE STRANGE DROPS OF BLOOD ON THE BODY OF JENNIFER? see **PERCHE QUELLE STRANE GOCCE DI SANGUE SUL CORPO DI JENNIFER?** • 1972
WHY TIGHTWAD TIPS • 1912 • *Brennan John E.* • USA
WHY TOM SIGNED THE PLEDGE • 1912 • *Thanhouser* • USA
WHY TOMMY WAS LATE FOR SCHOOL • 1909 • Booth W. R.? • UKN
WHY TRUST YOUR HUSBAND? • 1921 • Marshall George • USA
WHY, UNCLE! • 1917 • Chaudet Louis W. • SHT • USA
WHY UNESCO? see **PROC UNESCO?** • 1958
WHY UNIVERSAL IKE LEFT HOME • 1914 • *Carney Augustus* • USA
WHY WE FIGHT (PART 1): PRELUDE TO WAR see **PRELUDE TO WAR** • 1942
WHY WE FIGHT (PART 2): NAZIS STRIKE, THE see **NAZIS STRIKE, THE** • 1943
WHY WE FIGHT (PART 3): DIVIDE AND CONQUER see **DIVIDE AND CONQUER** • 1943
WHY WE FIGHT (PART 4): THE BATTLE OF BRITAIN see **BATTLE OF BRITAIN, THE** • 1943
WHY WE FIGHT (PART 5): THE BATTLE OF RUSSIA see **BATTLE OF RUSSIA, THE** • 1943
WHY WE FIGHT (PART 6): THE BATTLE OF CHINA see **BATTLE OF CHINA, THE** • 1944
WHY WE FIGHT (PART 7): WAR COMES TO AMERICA see **WAR COMES TO AMERICA** • 1945
WHY WE HAVE NO LEGS • 1967 • Kluge Josef • ANS • CZC
WHY WE LOST THE WAR see **POR QUE PERDIMOS LA GUERRA?** • 1977
WHY WERE WE EVER BORN? see **IPADUNAY AIYE?** • 1967
WHY WOMEN LOVE • 1925 • Carewe Edwin • USA • SEA WOMAN, THE ○ BARRIERS AFLAME ○ DANGEROUS CURRENTS
WHY WOMEN REMARRY • 1923 • Gorman John • USA
WHY WOMEN SIN • 1920 • King Burton L. • USA
WHY WON'T TOMMY EAT? • 1948 • Crawley Judith • DOC • CND
WHY WORRY? • 1918 • *Lyons Eddie* • SHT • USA
WHY WORRY • Baker Eddie • USA
WHY WORRY? • 1920 • *Moranti Milburn* • SHT • USA
WHY WORRY? • 1923 • Newmeyer Fred, Taylor Sam • USA
WHY WOULD ANYONE WANT TO KILL A NICE GIRL LIKE YOU? • 1969 • Sharp Don • UKN
WHY WOULD I LIE? • 1980 • Peerce Larry • USA • WHY SHOULD I LIE?
WIANO • 1963 • Lomnicki Jan • PLN • DOWRY, THE
WIATR • 1969 • Schabenbeck Stefan • PLN • WIND
WIATR W OCZY see **NOCE I DNIE** • 1974
WICHITA • 1955 • Tourneur Jacques • USA
WICKED • 1931 • Dwan Allan • USA
WICKED see **DURJANA** • 1970

WICKED AS THEY COME • 1956 • Hughes Ken • UKN • PORTRAIT IN SMOKE (USA)
WICKED BOUNDER, A • 1906 • Williamson James • UKN
WICKED CITY, THE • 1916 • Williamson Robin E. • SHT • USA
WICKED CITY, THE (USA) see **HANS LE MARIN** • 1948
WICKED DARLING, THE • 1919 • Browning Tod • USA • ROSE OF THE NIGHT, THE
WICKED DIE SLOW, THE • 1968 • Hennigar William K. • USA
WICKED DREAMS OF PAULA SCHULTZ, THE • 1968 • Marshall George • USA
WICKED DUCHESS, THE (USA) see **DUCHESSE DE LANGEAIS, LA** • 1942
WICKED ELF, THE • *Edison* • USA
WICKED GO TO HELL, THE see **SALAUDS VONT EN ENFER, LES** • 1955
WICKED LADY, THE • 1945 • Arliss Leslie • UKN
WICKED LADY, THE • 1983 • Winner Michael • UKN
WICKED ONES, THE see **HALBSTARKEN, DIE** • 1956
WICKED STEPMOTHER • 1989 • Cohen Larry • USA
WICKED WEST • 1929 • Lantz Walter • ANS • USA
WICKED, WICKED • 1973 • Bare Richard L. • USA
WICKED WIFE (USA) see **GRAND NATIONAL NIGHT** • 1953
WICKED WOLF, THE • 1946 • Davis Mannie • ANS • USA
WICKED WOMAN • 1954 • Rouse Russell • USA
WICKED WOMAN, A • 1934 • Brabin Charles J. • USA
WICKED WORLD see **PELO NEL MONDO, IL** • 1964
WICKEDNESS PREFERRED • 1927 • Henley Hobart • USA • MIXED MARRIAGES
WICKER BASKET, THE see **WIKLINOWY KOSZ** • 1967
WICKER MAN, THE • 1973 • Hardy Robin • UKN
WICKET WACKY • 1951 • Lantz Walter • ANS • USA
WICKHAM MYSTERY, THE • 1931 • Samuelson G. B. • UKN
WICKY-WACKY ROMANCE, A • 1939 • Davis Mannie • ANS • USA
WIDDERBURN HORROR, THE see **HOUSE OF THE BLACK DEATH** • 1965
WIDDICOMBE FAIR see **WIDECOMBE FAIR** • 1928
WIDE ANGLE SAXON • 1975 • Landow George • USA
WIDE-AWAKE DREAMER, THE see **POCHARDIANA OU LE REVEUR EVEILLE** • 1908
WIDE BLUE ROAD, THE (USA) see **GRANDE STRADA AZZURRA, LA** • 1957
WIDE BOY • 1952 • Hughes Ken • UKN
WIDE GREEN VALLEY, THE see **BOLSHAYA ZELYONAYA DOLINA** • 1968
WIDE OPEN • 1927 • Grey John Wesley • USA
WIDE OPEN • 1930 • Mayo Archie • USA
WIDE OPEN • 1974 • Wiklund Gustav • SWD
WIDE-OPEN CITY, THE • 1988 • von Strauss Ulf • DCS • SWD
WIDE-OPEN COPENHAGEN 70 see **PORNOGRAPHY: COPENHAGEN 1970** • 1970
WIDE OPEN FACES • 1926 • Bacon Lloyd • SHT • USA
WIDE OPEN FACES • 1938 • Neumann Kurt • USA
WIDE OPEN SPACES • 1924 • Jeske George • SHT • USA
WIDE OPEN SPACES • 1932 • Rosson Arthur • SHT • USA
WIDE OPEN SPACES • 1947 • King Jack • ANS • USA
WIDE OPEN SPACES • 1950 • Donnelly Eddie • ANS • USA
WIDE OPEN SPACES, THE see **TONIGHT FOR SURE!** • 1962
WIDE OPEN TOWN • 1941 • Selander Lesley • USA
WIDE-OPEN TOWN, A • 1922 • Ince Ralph • USA
WIDE POINT • 1969 • Chamberlain John • USA
WIDE ROAD see **SZEROKA DROGA** • 1949
WIDE ROADS -QUIET LOVE see **WEITE STRASSEN -STILLE LIEBE**
WIDE WORLD, THE see **VIDE VERDEN, DEN** • 1987
WIDE, WRONG WAY, THE • 1917 • Calvert E. H. • SHT • USA
WIDECOMBE FAIR • 1928 • Walker Norman • UKN • WIDDICOMBE FAIR
WIDEO WABBIT • 1956 • McKimson Robert • ANS • USA
WIDERRECHTLICHE AUSUBUNG DER ASTROMONIE • 1967 • Schamoni Peter • FRG
WIDHWA see **KUNWARI** • 1937
WIDOW • 1903 • *Bitzer Billy (Ph)* • USA
WIDOW • 1976 • Thompson J. Lee • TVM • USA
WIDOW see **KUNWARI** • 1937
WIDOW, THE • 1909 • *Essanay* • USA
WIDOW, THE • 1910 • Salter Harry • USA
WIDOW, THE • 1912 • *Comet* • USA
WIDOW, THE • 1914 • Pollard Harry? • USA
WIDOW, THE (USA) see **VEDOVA X, LA** • 1956
WIDOW AND HER CHILD, A • 1910 • *Solax* • USA
WIDOW AND THE GIGOLO, THE see **ROMAN SPRING OF MRS. STONE, THE** • 1962
WIDOW AND THE ONLY MAN • 1904 • *Bitzer Billy (Ph)* • USA
WIDOW AND THE PIG, THE • 1960 • Halas John • ANS • UKN
WIDOW AND THE POLICE OFFICER, THE see **OZVEGY ES A SZAZADOS, AZ** • 1967
WIDOW AND THE TWINS, THE • 1914 • Murphy J. A. • USA
WIDOW AND THE WIDOWER, THE • 1913 • *Rex* • USA
WIDOW BY PROXY • 1919 • Edwards Walter • USA
WIDOW CASEY'S RETURN, THE • 1912 • *Lubin* • USA
WIDOW COUDERC, THE (USA) see **VEUVE COUDERC, LE** • 1971
WIDOW DANGEROUS, THE • 1918 • Watt Allen • SHT • USA
WIDOW FROM CHICAGO, THE • 1930 • Cline Eddie • USA
WIDOW FROM EFFES, THE • Bocek Jaroslav • ANS • CZC
WIDOW FROM MONTE CARLO, THE • 1936 • Collins Arthur G. • USA
WIDOW FROM WINNIPEG, THE • 1913 • *Kalem* • USA
WIDOW IN SCARLET, THE • 1932 • Seitz George B. • USA
WIDOW IS WILLING, THE (USA) see **ESTATE VIOLENTA** • 1959
WIDOW JENKINS' ADMIRERS • 1912 • *Essanay* • USA
WIDOW MAKERS, THE see **SEE HOW THEY RUN** • 1965
WIDOW MALONE • 1916 • Kerrigan J. M. • IRL
WIDOW MALONEY'S FAITH • 1913 • *Domino* • USA
WIDOW MUGGINS' WEDDING • 1914 • *Ab* • USA
WIDOW OF MILL CREEK FLAT, THE • 1910 • *Selig* • USA
WIDOW OF NEVADA, A • 1913 • *Essanay* • USA
WIDOW OF OTAR see **OTAROVA VDOVA** • 1958
WIDOW OF RED ROCK, THE • 1914 • Van Wally • USA
WIDOW OF RICKIE O'NEAL, THE • 1912 • *Selig* • USA
WIDOW TORTURE see **MIBOJIN ZEME** • 1968
WIDOW TWAN-KEE • 1923 • Hill Sinclair • UKN • ONE ARABIAN NIGHT
WIDOW VILLAGE see **GUAFU CUN** • 1989
WIDOW VISITS SPRIGTOWN, THE • 1911 • *Vitagraph* • USA
WIDOW WINKS • 1912 • *Nestor* • USA
WIDOW WINS, THE • 1915 • Middleton Edwin • USA
WIDOWED EMPRESS, THE • 1909 • Polaski Benjamin • HKG
WIDOWER, THE see **VEDOVO, IL** • 1959
WIDOWER, THE see **SAMMA NO AJI** • 1962
WIDOWER, THE see **LOVE AND PAIN (AND THE WHOLE DAMN THING)** • 1972
WIDOWER'S TANGO see **TANGO DEL VIUDO, EL** • 1967
WIDOWERS THREE • 1912 • Melies Gaston • USA
WIDOWER'S WIDOW, THE • 1912 • *Majestic* • USA
WIDOWHOOD OF KAROLINA ZASLER, THE see **VDOVSTVO KAROLINE ZASLER** • 1977
WIDOWS • 1983 • Tonyton Ian • MTV • UKN
WIDOW'S BREEZY SUIT, THE • 1915 • Louis Will • USA
WIDOW'S CAMOUFLAGE, A • 1918 • Curtis Allen • SHT • USA
WIDOW'S CHILDREN, THE • 1914 • *Reliance* • USA
WIDOW'S CHOICE, THE • 1911 • *Lubin* • USA
WIDOW'S CLAIM, THE • 1912 • *Fearnley Jane* • USA
WIDOW'S FOLLY, THE • 1913 • *Nestor* • USA
WIDOW'S HOME, THE see **CASA DELLE VEDOVE, LA** • 1960
WIDOW'S INVESTMENT, THE • 1914 • *Lester Louise* • USA
WIDOW'S ISLAND see **ROMANCE IN FLANDERS, A** • 1937
WIDOW'S KIDS, THE • 1913 • Henderson Dell • USA
WIDOW'S LAST, THE • 1914 • *Nestor* • USA
WIDOW'S LEGACY, THE • 1912 • Coleby A. E. • UKN
WIDOW'S MIGHT, THE • 1912 • Stow Percy • UKN
WIDOW'S MIGHT, THE • 1913 • *Wilder Marshall P.* • USA
WIDOW'S MIGHT, THE • 1914 • *Brennan John E.* • USA
WIDOW'S MIGHT, THE • 1917 • *Otto Jean* • USA
WIDOW'S MIGHT, THE • 1918 • *Capitol* • SHT • USA
WIDOW'S MIGHT, THE • 1918 • De Mille William C. • *Lasky* • USA
WIDOW'S MIGHT, THE • 1935 • Gardner Cyril • UKN
WIDOW'S MITE, THE • 1914 • *Thanhouser* • USA
WIDOW'S NEST • 1977 • *Neal Patricia* • USA
WIDOW'S SECOND MARRIAGE, THE • 1912 • *Bechtel William* • USA
WIDOW'S SECRET, THE • 1915 • Kerrigan J. Warren • USA
WIDOW'S SON, A see **HER ONLY SON** • 1914
WIDOW'S STRATAGEM, THE • 1913 • *Thanhouser* • USA
WIDOW'S SUITORS, THE • 1913 • France Charles H. • USA
WIDOW'S WILES, A • 1912 • *Mace Fred* • USA
WIDOW'S WILES, THE • 1913 • Hotaling Arthur D. • USA
WIDOW'S WOOERS, THE • 1910 • Fitzhamon Lewin? • UKN
WIDTH OF THE PAVEMENT, THE see **LONG DES TROTTOIRS, LE** • 1956
WIDZIADLO • 1984 • Nowicki Marek • PLN • APPEARANCE
WIE BERGLER IN DEN BERGEN SIND EIGENTLICH NICHT SCHULD, DASS WIR DA SIND • 1975 • Murer Fredi M. • DOC • SWT • IT'S NOT REALLY OUR FAULT THAT WE MOUNTAIN DWELLERS ARE WHERE WE ARE
WIE BLEIBE ICH JUNG UND SCHON • 1926 • Neff Wolfgang • FRG • EHEGEHEIMNISSE
WIE DAS MADCHEN AUS DER ACKERSTRASSE DIE HEIMAT FAND 3 • 1923 • Funck Werner? • FRG • MADCHEN AUS DER ACKERSTRASSE 3, DAS
WIE DER BERLINER ARBEITER WOHNT • 1930 • Dudow Slatan • DCS • FRG • HOW THE BERLIN WORKER LIVES
WIE DER HASE LAUFT • 1937 • Boese Carl • FRG
WIE DER STURMWIND • 1957 • Harnack Falk • FRG • NIGHT OF THE STORM, THE (UKN) ◦ TEMPESTUOUS LOVE (USA) ◦ WIE EIN STURMWIND
WIE DIE BLATTER FALLEN • 1912 • Rippert Otto • FRG
WIE DIE ROSE IM MORGENTAU • 1917 • *Moja Hella* • FRG
WIE D'WARRET WURKT • 1933 • Lesch W. • SWT
WIE EIN DIEB IN DER NACHT • 1945 • Thimig Hans • FRG • HERZENSDIEB, DER
WIE EIN STURMWIND see **WIE DER STURMWIND** • 1957
WIE EIN VOGEL AUF DEM DRAHT • 1975 • Fassbinder R. W. • FRG • LIKE A BIRD ON A WIRE
WIE EINST IM MAI • 1926 • Wolff Willi • FRG
WIE EINST IM MAI • 1937 • Schneider-Edenkoben Richard • FRG
...WIE EINST LILI MARLEN • 1956 • Verhoeven Paul • FRG
WIE ER STARB • 1919 • Kahn William? • FRG
WIE FUTTERT MAN EINEN ESEL? • 1975 • Oehme Roland • GDR
WIE HEIRATE ICH MEINEN CHEF • 1927 • Schonfelder Erich • FRG
WIE ICH DETEKTIV WURDE • 1916 • May Joe • FRG
WIE ICH EIN NEGER WURDE • 1970 • Gall Roland • FRG • HOW I BECAME BLACK
WIE ICH ERMORDET WURDE • 1915 • Ralph Louis • FRG
WIE KOMMT EIN SO REIZENDES MADCHEN WIE SIE ZU DIESEM GEWERBE? • 1969 • Tremper Will • FRG, USA • HOW DID A NICE GIRL LIKE YOU GET INTO THIS BUSINESS? (USA)
WIE KONNTEST DU, VERONIKA? • 1940 • Harbich Milo • FRG
WIE MADCHEN HEUTE MANNER LIEBEN see **JET GENERATION** • 1968
WIE MAN MANNER FESSELT • 1934 • Boese Carl • FRG
WIE PLIMPS UND PLUMPS DEN DETEKTIV UBERLISTETEN • 1913 • *Hermann Otto (Anm)* • ANM • FRG
WIE SAG ICH'S MEINEM MANN • 1932 • Schunzel Reinhold • FRG
WIE SAGEN WIR ES UNSERN KINDERN • 1945 • Deppe Hans • FRG
WIE SATAN STARB • 1920 • *Gura Sascha* • FRG
WIE SATAN STARB • 1921 • Rippert Otto • AUS
WIE SCHON, DASS ES DICH GIBT • 1957 • Engel Thomas • AUS
WIE TOTET MAN EINE DAME? see **GEHEIMNIS DER GELBEN MONCHE, DAS** • 1966
WIE WERDE ICH AMANDA LOS? • 1915 • Danuky Nunek • FRG
WIE WERDE ICH FILMSTAR • 1955 • Lingen Theo • FRG
WIE WERDE ICH REICH UND GLUCKLICH? • 1930 • Reichmann Max • FRG
WIECZOR W "SZPAKU" • 1960 • Perski Ludwik • DOC • PLN • EVENING AT "SZPAKS", AN
WIECZOR WIGILIJNY • 1946 • Buczkowski Leonard • DOC • PLN • CHRISTMAS EVE
WIEGENLIED • 1908 • Porten Friedrich • FRG
WIEGENLIED, DAS • 1915 • Mack Max • FRG
WIELICZKA • 1946 • Brzozowski Jaroslaw • DOC • PLN
WIELKA, WIELKA I NAJWIEKSZA • 1962 • Sokolowska Anna • PLN • GREAT WORLD OF LITTLE CHILDREN, THE ◦ BIG WORLD OF LITTLE CHILDREN ◦ GREAT BIG WORLD AND LITTLE CHILDREN ◦ BIG ◦ BIG, THE BIGGER AND THE BIGGEST, THE ◦ LITTLE CAR, THE
WIELKI BIEG • 1988 • Domaradzki Jerzy • PLN • GREAT RACE
WIELKI POLOW • 1961 • Nehrebecki Wladyslaw • ANS • PLN • SUCH A HUGE FISH ◦ GREAT CATCH, THE
WIELKI SZU • 1982 • Checinski Sylwester • PLN • BIG SHAR
WIEN 1910 • 1942 • Emo E. W. • FRG
WIEN – BERLIN • 1926 • Steinhoff Hans • FRG
WIEN, DU STADT DER LIEDER • 1930 • Oswald Richard • FRG • VIENNA, CITY OF SONG
WIEN, DU STADT MEINER TRAUME • 1957 • Forst Willi • AUS
WIEN, DU STADT MEINER TRAUME see **KONIGIN SEINES HERZENS, DIE** • 1928
WIEN RETOUR • 1983 • Aichholzer Josef, Beckermann Ruth • AUS • VIENNA IN THE PAST
WIEN TANZT see **WIENER WALZER** • 1951
WIEN, WIE ES WEINT UND LACHT • 1926 • Walther-Fein Rudolf • FRG
WIEN, WIEN, NUR DU ALLEIN • 1927 • Neff Wolfgang • FRG
WIENER BLUT • 1933 • Wiene Conrad
WIENER BLUT • 1942 • Forst Willi • FRG
WIENER BLUT • 1990 • Berger Helmut • AUS • VIENNESE BLOOD
WIENER BRUT • 1985 • Fadler Hans • AUS • VIENNESE BROOD
WIENER FIAKERLIED see **LIEBE IM DREIVIERTELTAKT** • 1937
WIENER G'SCHICHTEN • 1940 • von Bolvary Geza • FRG • VIENNA TALES (USA)
WIENER HERZEN • 1930 • Sauer Fred • FRG, AUS
WIENER HERZEN see **FAMILIE SCHIMEK** • 1925
WIENER KONGRESS see **KONGRESS AMUSIERT SICH, DER** • 1966
WIENER LIEBSCHAFTEN • 1930 • Land Robert • FRG • GING DA NICHT EBEN DAS GLUCK VORBEI?
WIENER LUFT • 1958 • Hofbauer Ernst • FRG
WIENER LUMPENKAVALIERE see **LUMPENKAVALIERE** • 1932
WIENER MADELN • 1945 • Forst Willi • FRG • VIENNESE MAIDENS (USA) ◦ VIENNA MAIDENS
WIENER MELODIEN • 1947 • Lingen Theo • AUS
WIENER PRATER • 1938 • Schmidt-Gentner Willy • FRG
WIENER SCHNITZEL • 1967 • Lowinger Paul, Ambros Otto, Herbert Hans • AUS • VIENNA SCHNITZEL
WIENER WALZER • 1951 • Reinert Emile Edwin • AUS • VIENNA WALTZES (USA) ◦ WIEN TANZT
WIENFILM 1896–1976 • 1977 • Schmidt Ernst • DOC • AUS
WIERNA RZEKA • 1936 • Buczkowski Leonard • PLN • FAITHFUL RIVER
WIERNA RZEKA • 1988 • Chmielewski Tadeusz • PLN • FAITHFUL RIVER
WIES NAD BUGIEM • 1965 • Halladin Danuta • DOC • PLN • VILLAGE ON THE BUG, A
WIEZA MALOWANA • 1961 • Halladin Danuta • DOC • PLN • PAINTED TOWER, THE
WIFE • 1914 • *Eclair* • USA
WIFE see **TSUMA** • 1953
WIFE see **BHARRYA** • 1968
WIFE see **MOGLIE AMANTE** • 1978
WIFE, THE • 1913 • Cabanne W. Christy • USA
WIFE, THE • 1914 • Kirkwood James • *Klaw & Erlanger* • USA
WIFE, THE • 1914 • Pollard Harry • *Beauty* • USA
WIFE AGAINST WIFE • 1921 • Bennett Whitman • USA
WIFE AND AUTO TROUBLE • 1916 • Henderson Dell • SHT • USA
WIFE AND WOMAN JOURNALIST see **TSUMA TO ONNA KISHA** • 1950
WIFE AT BAY, A • 1916 • Wilson Ben • SHT • USA
WIFE BE LIKE A ROSE see **TSUMA YO BARA NO YONI** • 1935
WIFE BREAKERS, THE • 1919 • Lyons Eddie, Moran Lee • SHT • USA
WIFE BY NIGHT (UKN) see **BELLA DI GIORNO MOGLIE DI NOTTE** • 1971
WIFE BY PROXY, A • 1917 • Collins John H. • USA
WIFE BY PURCHASE, A see **GOD'S LAW AND MAN'S** • 1917
WIFE CAMELIA see **HITOZUMATSUBAKI** • 1967
WIFE DECOY • *Herbert Hugh* • SHT • USA
WIFE, DOCTOR AND NURSE • 1937 • Lang Walter • USA
WIFE FOR A DAY, A • 1912 • Wilson Frank? • UKN
WIFE FOR A NIGHT (USA) see **MOGLIE PER UNA NOTTE** • 1950
WIFE FOR A RANSOM, A • 1916 • Curtis Allen • SHT • USA
WIFE FOR ALFIE, A see **FRAU FUR ALFIE, EINE** • 1989
WIFE FOR AN AUSTRALIAN, A • 1963 • Bareja Stanislaw • PLN
WIFE FOR WIFE • 1915 • Buel Kenean • USA
WIFE FROM THE COUNTRY, A • 1914 • *Reliance* • USA
WIFE HE BOUGHT, THE • 1918 • Salter Harry • USA
WIFE HUNTERS, THE • 1922 • White Bob • USA
WIFE, HUSBAND AND FRIEND • 1939 • Ratoff Gregory • USA
WIFE IN A HURRY, A • 1916 • Kellino W. P. • UKN
WIFE IN DANGER, A (USA) see **MOGLIE IN PERICOLO, UNA** • 1939
WIFE IN LOVE, A see **KOISURU TSUMA** • 1947
WIFE IN NAME ONLY • 1923 • Terwilliger George W. • USA
WIFE IN PAWN see **STRANGE EVIDENCE** • 1933
WIFE IN SUNSHINE • 1916 • Calvert E. H. • SHT • USA
WIFE IN THE ANTIQUE SHOP, A see **JIDAIYA NO NYOBO** • 1983
WIFE INSURANCE • 1937 • Yarbrough Jean • SHT • USA
WIFE KILLER, THE see **ENGLIMA STO KAVOURI** • 1973
WIFE LOST see **NYOBO FUNSHITSU** • 1928
WIFE NUMBER TWO • 1917 • Nigh William • USA
WIFE OF A GENIUS, THE • 1912 • *Essanay* • USA
WIFE OF A THIEF • 1914 • Weston Charles • UKN
WIFE OF AN IMPORTANT MAN, THE see **ZAWGAT RAGOL MOHIM** • 1987

WIFE OF CAIN, THE • 1913 • Gaskill Charles L. • USA
WIFE OF GENERAL LING • 1937 • Vajda Ladislao • UKN • REVENGE OF GENERAL LING, THE (USA)
WIFE OF HASAN-AGA, THE see **HASANAGINICA** • 1967
WIFE OF MARCIUS, THE • 1910 • *Selig* • USA
WIFE OF MONTE CRISTO, THE • 1946 • Ulmer Edgar G. • USA • MONTE CRISTO –MASKED AVENGER
WIFE OF PHARAOH, THE see **WEIB DES PHARAO, DAS** • 1921
WIFE OF SEISAKU, THE see **SEISAKU NO TSUMA** • 1965
WIFE OF SEISHU HANAOKA, THE see **HANAOKA SEISHU NO TSUMA** • 1967
WIFE OF THE CENTAUR • 1924 • Vidor King • USA
WIFE OF THE HILLS, A • 1912 • *Anderson Broncho Billy* • USA
WIFE ON A WAGER, A • 1914 • Reid Wallace • USA
WIFE ON HOLIDAY.. THE MISTRESS IN TOWN, THE see **MOGLIE IN VACANZA, L'AMANTE IN CITTA, LA** • 1980
WIFE ON LOAN, A • 1915 • Birch Cecil • UKN
WIFE ON TRIAL, A • 1917 • Baldwin Ruth Ann • USA
WIFE OR COUNTRY • 1919 • Hopper E. Mason • USA
WIFE OR TWO, A • 1936 • Rogers Maclean • UKN
WIFE O'RILEY, THE • 1931 • Sandrich Mark • SHT • USA
WIFE SAVERS • 1928 • Ceder Ralph • USA
WIFE SWAPPER see **WIFE SWAPPERS, THE** • 1970
WIFE SWAPPERS • 1965 • Bomont Richard W. • USA
WIFE SWAPPERS, THE • 1970 • Ford Derek • UKN • SWAPPERS, THE ○ WIFE SWAPPER
WIFE SWAPPING –FRENCH STYLE (UKN) see **DEBAUCHEE, LA** • 1970
WIFE TAKES A FLYER, THE • 1942 • Wallace Richard • USA • YANK IN DUTCH, A (UKN) ○ HIGHLY IRREGULAR
WIFE TAMERS • 1926 • Roach Hal • SHT • USA
WIFE TAMES WOLF • 1947 • Yates Hal • SHT • USA
WIFE THE WEAKER VESSEL • 1915 • Wilson Frank • UKN
WIFE TO SPARE • 1947 • Bernds Edward • SHT • USA
WIFE TRAP, THE • 1922 • Wullner Robert • FRG
WIFE VERSUS SECRETARY • 1936 • Brown Clarence • USA
WIFE WANTED • 1907 • *Bitzer Billy (Ph)* • USA
WIFE WANTED • 1914 • Ince Ralph • USA • TOO MUCH UNCLE
WIFE WANTED • 1915 • Otto Henry • USA
WIFE WANTED • 1946 • Karlson Phil • USA • SHADOW OF BLACKMAIL (UKN)
WIFE WANTED, A • 1913 • Lehrman Henry, Sennett Mack (Spv) • USA
WIFE WHO DARED, THE • 1915 • *A.a.a.* • UKN
WIFE WHO WASN'T WANTED, THE • 1925 • Flood James • USA
WIFE WHOM GOD FORGOT, THE • 1920 • Humphrey William J. • UKN • TANGLED HEARTS
WIFELESS HUSBAND, THE • 1917 • Calvert E. H. • SHT • USA
WIFEMISTRESS (USA) see **MOGLIE AMANTE** • 1978
WIFE'S AWAKENING, A • 1921 • Gasnier Louis J. • USA
WIFE'S AWAKENING, THE • 1911 • *Imp* • USA
WIFE'S AWAKENING, THE • 1911 • Salter Harry • *Lubin* • USA
WIFE'S BATTLE, A • 1913 • *Reliance* • USA
WIFE'S BUSY DAY • 1914 • *Joker* • USA
WIFE'S CALVARY, A • 1911 • *Bison* • USA
WIFE'S CONFESSION see **TSUMA WA KOKUHAKU SURU** • 1961
WIFE'S DECEIT, A • 1913 • *Weber Lois* • USA
WIFE'S DILEMMA • 1916 • *Hippo* • USA
WIFE'S DISCOVERY, A • 1912 • *Champion* • USA
WIFE'S FOLLY, A • 1917 • Wilson Ben • SHT • USA
WIFE'S FORGIVENESS, A • 1906 • Raymond Charles? • UKN
WIFE'S HEART, A see **TSUMA NO KOKORO** • 1956
WIFE'S INNOCENCE, A • 1916 • *Laemmle* • SHT • USA
WIFE'S LIFE, A • 1950 • Barclay David • SHT • USA
WIFE'S LOVE, A • 1911 • *Powers* • USA
WIFE'S MISTAKE, A • 1912 • *Art Films* • UKN
WIFE'S ORDEAL, A • 1909 • *Edison* • USA
WIFE'S RELATIONS, THE • 1928 • Marshall Maurice • USA • LOST HEIRESS, THE (UKN)
WIFE'S REVENGE: OR, THE GAMBLER'S END, A • 1904 • *Cricks & Sharp* • UKN
WIFE'S ROMANCE, A • 1923 • Heffron Thomas N. • USA • OLD MADRID
WIFE'S SACRIFICE, A • 1916 • Edwards J. Gordon • USA
WIFE'S STRATAGEM, THE • 1914 • Morrisey Edward • USA
WIFE'S SUSPICIONS, A • 1917 • Sargent George L. • SHT • USA
WIFEY MUST FOLLOW HUSBAND • 1913 • *Eclair* • USA
WIFEY'S FLING • 1915 • *Imp* • USA
WIFEY'S INVESTMENT • 1912 • *Pathe* • USA
WIFEY'S MA COMES BACK • 1912 • *Lubin* • USA
WIFEY'S MISTAKE • 1904 • Porter Edwin S. • USA
WIFEY'S STRATEGY • 1908 • Porter Edwin S. • USA
WIFEY'S VISIT HOME • 1914 • *Ab* • USA
WIFFLES AND THE MAGIC WAND • 1912 • *C.g.p.c.* • FRN
WIFIE'S ATHLETIC MAMMA • 1914 • *Lubin* • USA
WIFIE'S FRAME-UP • 1916 • *Gayety* • USA
WIFIE'S MA COMES BACK • 1915 • Hotaling Arthur D. • USA
WIFIE'S MAMMA • 1910 • *Wragland Florence* • USA
WIFIE'S NEW HAT • 1911 • *Lubin* • USA
WIG AND BUTTONS • 1905 • Collins Alf? • UKN
WIG-WAG • 1911 • *Casey Kenneth* • USA
WIGAN EXPRESS, THE • 1934 • *Field Alexander* • SHT • UKN
WIGGLE YOUR EARS • 1929 • McGowan Robert • SHT • USA
WIGGS TAKES THE REST CURE • 1914 • Grandon Francis J. • USA
WIGWAG SYSTEM, THE • 1919 • *Field Elinor* • SHT • USA
WIGWAM, DE see **BRANDENDE STRAAL, DE** • 1911
WIGWAM WHOOPEE • 1948 • Sparber I. • ANS • USA
WIJ BOUWEN • 1930 • Ivens Joris • NTH • WE ARE BUILDING
WIJ, SURINAMERS • 1961 • Creutzberg Peter • NTH • WE PEOPLE OF SURINAM
WIJD EN ZIJD • 1966 • van Gelder Hans • SHT • NTH
WIKLINOWY KOSZ • 1967 • Kijowicz Miroslaw • ANS • PLN • WICKER BASKET, THE
WIL IK WEL DOOD? • 1974 • Grasveld Fons • DOC • NTH • DO I REALLY WANT TO DIE?
WILBUR AND ORVILLE: THE FIRST TO FLY • 1973 • Schellerup Henning • USA
WILBUR AND THE BABY FACTORY • 1970 • Wolfe Tom • USA • BABY FACTORY (UKN) ○ PLEASURE FARM, THE ○ SEX MACHINE
WILBUR CRAWFORDS WUNDERSAMES ABENTEUER see **SEINE FRAU, DIE UNBEKANNTE** • 1923
WILBUR THE LION • 1944 • Pal George • ANM • USA
WILBY CONSPIRACY, THE • 1975 • Nelson Ralph • USA
WILCZE ECHA • 1968 • Scibor-Rylski Aleksander • PLN • ECHOES OF WOLVES ○ WOLF ECHOES ○ WOLVES' ECHOES ○ WHERE THE WOLVES HOWL
WILCZY BILET • 1964 • Bohdziewicz Antoni • PLN • BAD REFERENCE
WILCZYCA • 1983 • Piestrak Marek • PLN • SHE-WOLF, THE
WILD see **FEROZ** • 1983
WILD 90 • 1969 • Mailer Norman • USA
WILD ABOUT HURRY • 1959 • Jones Charles M. • ANS • USA
WILD AFFAIR, THE • 1963 • Krish John • UKN
WILD AFRICA • 1986 • Kool Allen • CND
WILD ALGY OF PICCADILLY • 1918 • Hotaling Arthur D. • SHT • USA
WILD AND BULLY • 1939 • Schwarzwald Milton • SHT • USA
WILD AND THE BRAVE, THE see **TWO MEN OF KARAMOJA** • 1974
WILD AND THE FREE, THE • 1980 • Hill James • TVM • USA
WILD AND THE INNOCENT, THE • 1959 • Sher Jack • USA
WILD AND THE NAKED, THE • 1962 • Roberts Stan • USA
WILD AND THE WANTON, THE see **MARIE DES ISLES** • 1959
WILD AND THE WILLING, THE • 1962 • Thomas Ralph • UKN • YOUNG AND WILLING (USA) ○ YOUNG AND THE WILLING, THE
WILD AND WICKED • 1923 • La Cava Gregory • SHT • USA
WILD AND WILLING see **RAT FINK** • 1965
WILD AND WOLFY • 1945 • Avery Tex • ANS • USA
WILD AND WONDERFUL • 1964 • Anderson Michael • USA • MONSIEUR COGNAC
WILD AND WOODY • 1948 • Lundy Dick • ANS • USA
WILD AND WOOLLY • 1917 • Emerson John • USA
WILD AND WOOLLY • 1931 • Dorian Charles • SHT • USA
WILD AND WOOLLY • 1932 • Lantz Walter, Nolan William • ANS • USA
WILD AND WOOLLY • 1937 • Werker Alfred L. • USA
WILD AND WOOLLY • 1978 • Leacock Philip • TVM • USA
WILD AND WOOLLY WOMEN • 1917 • Clements Roy • SHT • USA
WILD AND WOOLY HARE • 1959 • Freleng Friz • ANS • USA
WILD AND WOOZY WEST, THE • 1942 • Rose Allen • ANS • USA
WILD ANGELS see **DIVLJI ANDELI** • 1970
WILD ANGELS, THE • 1966 • Corman Roger • USA
WILD ANGELS, THE see **VILDE ENGLE, DE**
WILD ARCTIC see **SAVAGE WILD, THE** • 1970
WILD ARNICA • 1917 • *Edison* • SHT • USA
WILD ASS'S SKIN, THE (USA) see **PEAU DE CHAGRIN, LA** • 1909
WILD AT HEART • 1990 • Lynch David • USA
WILD BABIES • 1932 • Mack Anthony, French Lloyd • SHT • USA
WILD BARBARA • 1949 • Cech Vladimir • CZC
WILD BEAR HUNT, THE • Digmelov Alexander • USS
WILD BEAST OF CRETE, THE see **TESEO CONTRO IL MINOTAURO** • 1961
WILD BEASTS see **DRAVCI** • 1948
WILD BEASTS AT LARGE • 1913 • Thompson Frederick A. • USA
WILD BEAUTY • 1927 • McRae Henry • USA
WILD BEAUTY • 1946 • Fox Wallace • USA
WILD BEDS see **LETTI SELVAGGI** • 1979
WILD BILL HICCUP • 1970 • Smith Paul J. • ANS • USA
WILD BILL HICKOK • 1923 • Smith Cliff • UKN
WILD BILL HICKOK RIDES • 1942 • Enright Ray • USA
WILD BILL'S DEFEAT • 1910 • *Defender* • USA
WILD BIRD, A see **VILDFAGEL, EN** • 1921
WILD BIRDS see **TWO ALONE** • 1934
WILD BIRDS see **VILDFAGLAR** • 1955
WILD BLOOD • 1915 • Garwood William • USA
WILD BLOOD • 1929 • McRae Henry • USA
WILD BLUE YONDER, THE • 1951 • Dwan Allan • USA • THUNDER ACROSS THE PACIFIC (UKN) ○ BOMBS OVER JAPAN ○ WINGS ACROSS THE PACIFIC
WILD BORN • 1927 • Gordon Edward R. • USA
WILD BOY • 1934 • De Courville Albert • UKN
WILD BOY see **GARCON SAUVAGE, LE** • 1951
WILD BOY, THE (UKN) see **ENFANT SAUVAGE, L'** • 1970
WILD BOYS OF THE ROAD • 1933 • Wellman William A. • USA • DANGEROUS AGE (UKN) ○ DANGEROUS DAYS
WILD BRIAN KENT • 1936 • Bretherton Howard • USA
WILD BULL OF THE WEST • 1970 • Hopper Jerry • USA
WILD BULL'S LAIR, THE • 1925 • Andrews Del • USA
WILD BUNCH, THE • 1969 • Peckinpah Sam • USA
WILD CAPTAIN, THE • 1973 • Komissarov K. • USS
WILD CARGO • 1934 • Buck Frank • USA
WILD CARGO • 1934 • Denis Armand • DOC • USA
WILD CARGO see **AMMUTINAMENTO, L'** • 1962
WILD CAT, THE • 1915 • Powell Paul • USA
WILD CAT, THE • 1920 • Joos Therdo? • SHT • USA
WILD CAT, THE • 1936 • Pi Rosario • SPN
WILD CAT HETTY see **HELLCAT, THE** • 1928
WILD CAT OF PARIS, THE • 1919 • De Grasse Joseph • USA
WILD CAT –PRIZE FIGHTER (UKN) see **WILDCAT SAUNDERS** • 1936
WILD CAT (UKN) see **WILDCAT TROOPER** • 1936
WILD CAT WELL, THE • 1911 • *Vitagraph* • USA
WILD CATS ON THE BEACH (USA) see **COSTA AZZURRA** • 1959
WILD CHASE, THE • 1965 • Pratt Hawley • ANS • USA
WILD CHERRY TREES see **CHERYOMUSHKI** • 1963
WILD CHILD, THE (USA) see **ENFANT SAUVAGE, L'** • 1970
WILD CHILDREN • 1977 • Fong Yuk-Ping • HKG • YEH HAI CHI
WILD COMPANY • 1930 • McCarey Leo • USA • ROADHOUSE
WILD COUNTRY • 1947 • Taylor Ray • USA
WILD COUNTRY, THE • 1971 • Totten Robert • USA
WILD DAKOTAS • 1956 • Newfield Sam • USA
WILD DAMNED GIRL, THE • Parashakis Paul • GRC
WILD DOG see **JIBARO** • 1985
WILD DOG DINGO see **DINKAYA SOBAKA DINGO** • 1963
WILD DREAM see **HULM AL BARRI, AL** • 1985
WILD DRIFTER see **COCKFIGHTER** • 1974
WILD DUCK, THE • 1983 • Safran Henri • ASL
WILD DUCK, THE see **HAUS DER LUGE, DAS** • 1925
WILD DUCK, THE see **VILDANDEN** • 1974
WILD DUCK, THE see **WILDENTE, DIE** • 1976
WILD ELEPHINKS • 1933 • Fleischer Dave • ANS • USA
WILD EYE, THE (USA) see **OCCHIO SELVAGGIO, L'** • 1967
WILD FEMALES, THE • 1968 • Samoya Carlos • USA • BIRDS OF A FEATHER.. FLOCKING TOGETHER ○ FLOCKING TOGETHER
WILD FIELD • Sen Hong • VTN
WILD FLOWER see **FLOR SILVESTRE** • 1943
WILD FLOWER, THE see **NIYANGALA MAL** • 1974
WILD FLOWER AND THE ROSE, THE • 1910 • *Thanhouser* • USA
WILD FLOWER OF PINO MOUNTAIN, THE • 1913 • *Frontier* • USA
WILD FLOWERS • 1919 • Van Wally • SHT • USA
WILD FLOWERS see **FLEURS SAUVAGES, LES** • 1982
WILD FOR KICKS (USA) see **BEAT GIRL** • 1959
WILD, FREE AND HUNGRY • 1970 • Edwards H. P. • USA
WILD FRONTIER, THE • 1947 • Ford Philip • USA
WILD FRUIT (USA) see **FRUITS SAUVAGES, LES** • 1953
WILD GAME (UKN) see **WILDWECHSEL** • 1972
WILD GEESE • 1927 • Stone Phil • USA
WILD GEESE see **GAN** • 1953
WILD GEESE, THE • 1978 • McLaglen Andrew V. • UKN
WILD GEESE CALLING • 1941 • Brahm John • USA
WILD GEESE CHASE • 1919 • Beaumont Harry • USA
WILD GEESE II • 1985 • Hunt Peter • UKN
WILD GIRL • 1932 • Walsh Raoul • USA • SALOMY JANE (UKN)
WILD GIRL see **WILD, WILD GIRL** • 1965
WILD GIRL, THE • 1914 • *Komic* • USA
WILD GIRL, THE • 1917 • Estabrook Howard • USA
WILD GIRL, THE • 1925 • Bletcher William • USA
WILD GIRL FROM THE HILLS, THE • 1915 • *Marion Frances* • SHT • USA
WILD GIRL OF THE SIERRAS, A • 1916 • Powell Paul • USA
WILD GIRLS OF THE NAKED WEST see **IMMORAL WEST –AND HOW IT WAS LOST, THE** • 1962
WILD GOLD • 1934 • Marshall George • USA
WILD GOOSE, THE • 1921 • Capellani Albert • USA
WILD GOOSE CHASE • 1932 • Foster John, Davis Mannie • ANS • USA
WILD GOOSE CHASE, A • 1908 • Stow Percy • UKN
WILD GOOSE CHASE, A • 1910 • *Champion* • USA
WILD GOOSE CHASE, A • 1915 • De Mille Cecil B. • USA
WILD GOOSE CHASE, THE (USA) see **COURSE A L'ECHALOTTE, LA** • 1975
WILD GOOSE CHASER, THE • 1924 • Bacon Lloyd • SHT • USA
WILD GOOSE ON THE WING, THE see **YEN-ERH TSAI LIN-SHAO** • 1980
WILD GRASS see **BURYAN** • 1967
WILD GUITAR • 1962 • Steckler Ray Dennis • USA
WILD GYPSIES • 1969 • Ray Marc B. • USA
WILD HARE, A • 1940 • Avery Tex • ANS • USA
WILD HARVEST • 1947 • Garnett Tay • USA • BIG HAIRCUT
WILD HARVEST • 1961 • Baerwitz Jerry A. • USA
WILD HEART see **THA KANO PETRA TI KARDHIA MOU** • 1968
WILD HEART, THE (USA) see **GONE TO EARTH** • 1950
WILD HEART OF AFRICA, THE • 1929 • Walker Cub • DOC • USA
WILD HEARTS see **WILDE HARTEN** • 1989
WILD HEATHER • 1921 • Hepworth Cecil M. • UKN
WILD HERITAGE • 1958 • Haas Charles • USA • DEATH RIDES THIS TRAIL
WILD HIGHLANDS • 1961 • Ferguson Ian • UKN
WILD HONEY • 1919 • Grandon Francis J. • USA
WILD HONEY • 1922 • Ruggles Wesley • USA
WILD HONEY • 1942 • Ising Rudolf • ANS • USA
WILD HONEY • 1971 • Edmonds Don • USA
WILD HONEY see **DIKI MYOD** • 1967
WILD HORSE • 1930 • Thorpe Richard, Algier Sidney • USA • SILVER DEVIL (UKN)
WILD HORSE, THE see **KAADU KUDRE** • 1978
WILD HORSE AMBUSH • 1952 • Brannon Fred C. • USA
WILD HORSE CANYON • 1938 • Hill Robert F. • USA
WILD HORSE HANK • 1978 • Till Eric • CND
WILD HORSE MESA • 1925 • Seitz George B. • USA
WILD HORSE MESA • 1933 • Hathaway Henry • USA
WILD HORSE MESA • 1947 • Grissell Wallace A. • USA
WILD HORSE PHANTOM • 1944 • Newfield Sam • USA
WILD HORSE RANGE • 1940 • Johnston Raymond K. • USA
WILD HORSE RODEO • 1937 • Sherman George • USA
WILD HORSE RUSTLERS • 1943 • Newfield Sam • USA
WILD HORSE STAMPEDE • 1943 • James Alan • USA
WILD HORSE STAMPEDE, THE • 1926 • Rogell Albert S. • USA
WILD HORSE VALLEY • 1940 • Webb Ira • USA
WILD HORSES • 1943 • *Smith Pete* • USA
WILD HORSES • 1945 • Anderson Robert • DOC • CND
WILD HORSES • 1983 • Morton Derek • NZL
WILD HORSES • 1985 • Lowry Dick • TVM • USA
WILD HORSES see **TARPANY** • 1961
WILD HORSES, THE see **VALDEZ IL MEZZOSANGUE** • 1974
WILD IN THE COUNTRY • 1961 • Dunne Philip • USA
WILD IN THE SKY • 1972 • Naud William T. • USA • GOD BLESS THE BOMB ○ BLACK JACK
WILD IN THE STREETS • 1968 • Shear Barry • USA
WILD IN THE WINGS see **KOKS I KULISSEN** • 1983
WILD IN THE WOODS • 1970 • *Janus Ii Productions* • USA
WILD INDIAN, THE • 1913 • *Komic* • USA
WILD INJUNS • 1917 • *Pokes & Jabbs* • SHT • USA
WILD INNOCENCE • 1938 • Hall Ken G. • ASL
WILD IRISH ROSE • 1915 • Giblyn Charles • USA
WILD IS MY LOVE • 1963 • Hilliard Richard • USA
WILD IS THE WIND • 1957 • Cukor George • USA
WILD JIM, REFORMER • 1916 • Cooley Frank • SHT • USA
WILD JOE BASS see **ANGRY JOE BASS** • 1976
WILD JUNGLE CAPTIVE (UKN) see **JUNGLE CAPTIVE** • 1944

WILD JUSTICE • 1925 • Franklin Chester M. • USA
WILD KURDISTAN (UKN) see **DURCHS WILDE KURDISTAN** • 1965
WILD LIFE • 1918 • Otto Henry • USA
WILD LIFE • 1959 • Taras Martin B. • ANS • USA
WILD LIFE, THE • 1984 • Linson Art • USA
WILD LIONS AND FEROCIOUS CHEESE • 1920 • Watson William • SHT • USA
WILD LITTLE BUNCH, THE see **14, THE** • 1973
WILD LIVING see **SAINTES NITOUCHES, LES** • 1962
WILD LOVE-MAKERS, THE see **KYONETSU NO KISETSU** • 1960
WILD LOVE (USA) see **INNAMORATI, GLI** • 1955
WILD MAN see **WILDMAN** • 1976
WILD MAN FOR A DAY • 1913 • *Lubin* • USA
WILD MAN FROM BORNEO, THE • 1914 • *Komic* • USA
WILD MAN OF BORNEO, THE • 1902 • Haggar William • UKN
WILD MAN OF BORNEO, THE • 1910 • *Lubin* • USA
WILD MAN OF BORNEO, THE • 1941 • Sinclair Robert B. • USA
WILD MCCULLOCHS, THE see **MCCULLOCHS, THE** • 1975
WILD MEN AND BEASTS OF BORNEO • 1925 • *Hutt Lou (Ph)* • DOC • USA
WILD MEN OF AFRICA • 1920 • Vandenbergh Leonard J. • USA
WILD MEN OF KALAHARI • 1930 • Cadle C. Ernest • DOC • USA
WILD MONEY • 1937 • King Louis • USA
WILD MOUNTAINS see **YE SHAN** • 1985
WILD MUSTANG • 1935 • Fraser Harry L. • USA
WILD NIGHT, A • 1915 • Cooper Toby • UKN
WILD NIGHT, A • 1920 • Santell Alfred • SHT • USA
WILD NORTH, THE • 1951 • Marton Andrew • USA • BIG NORTH, THE
WILD OAT, THE (USA) see **BOULANGER DE VALORGUE, LE** • 1952
WILD OATS • 1915 • Weston Harold • UKN
WILD OATS • 1916 • *Duncan Malcolm* • USA
WILD OATS • 1919 • Williams C. Jay • USA
WILD OATS LANE • 1926 • Neilan Marshall • USA
WILD OLIVE • 1915 • Taylor William D. • USA
WILD ON THE BEACH • 1965 • Dexter Maury • USA
WILD ONE, THE • 1953 • Benedek Laslo • USA • HOT BLOOD
WILD ONE, THE see **HUD** • 1986
WILD ONES OF SAN GIL BRIDGE, THE see **SALVAJES DE PUENTE SAN GIL, LOS** • 1967
WILD ONES ON WHEELS • 1967 • Cusumano Rudolph • USA • DRIVERS TO HELL
WILD ORANGES • 1924 • Vidor King • USA
WILD ORCHID • 1989 • King Zalman • USA
WILD ORCHIDS • 1928 • Franklin Sidney A. • USA
WILD OUTTAKES • 1969 • *Hollywood Cinema Associates* • CMP • USA
WILD OVER YOU • 1953 • Jones Charles M. • ANS • USA
WILD PACK, THE • 1971 • Bartlett Hall • USA • SANDPIT GENERALS, THE
WILD PAIR, THE • 1987 • Bridges Beau • USA
WILD PAPA • 1925 • Roach Hal • SHT • USA
WILD PARTY, THE • 1923 • Blache Herbert • USA • NOTORIETY
WILD PARTY, THE • 1929 • Arzner Dorothy • USA
WILD PARTY, THE • 1956 • Horner Harry • USA
WILD PARTY, THE • 1975 • Ivory James • USA
WILD PASSIONS see **AGRIA PATHI** • 1967
WILD PATH • 1912 • Kent Charles • USA
WILD PONY, THE • 1983 • Sullivan Kevin • CND • WILD STALLION, THE
WILD POSES • 1933 • McGowan Robert • SHT • USA
WILD PRIMROSE • 1918 • Thompson Frederick A. • USA
WILD PUSSYCAT, THE • 1969 • Dadiras Dimis • GRC
WILD RACERS, THE • 1968 • Haller Daniel • USA
WILD REBELS, THE • 1967 • Grefe William • USA
WILD REFUGE • 1974 • Fox Beryl • SER • CND
WILD RENDEZVOUS, THE see **RENDEZ-VOUS SAUVAGE, LE**
WILD REPORTER see **SHIMIZU NO ABAREMBO** • 1959
WILD RIDE • 1960 • Berman Harvey • USA
WILD RIDE, A • 1913 • Campbell Colin • USA
WILD RIDE, A • 1914 • *Sterling* • USA
WILD RIDER, THE • 1919 • Jaccard Jacques • SHT • USA
WILD RIDERS • 1971 • Kanter Richard • USA • IMPURE, THE ○ HEAD
WILD RIDERS LTD. see **WILDER REITER GMBH** • 1967
WILD RIVER • 1960 • Kazan Elia • USA • WOMAN AND THE WILD RIVER, THE
WILD ROOTS OF LOVE (USA) see **PETITS CHATS, LES** • 1959
WILD ROSE (USA) see **VADROZA** • 1940
WILD ROVERS • 1971 • Edwards Blake • USA
WILD SCENE, THE • 1970 • Rowland William • USA
WILD SEARCH see **BUN NGO TSONG TINNGAI** • 1989
WILD SEASON (USA) see **WILDE SEISOEN** • 1967
WILD SEED, THE • 1965 • Hutton Brian G. • USA • REBELLIOUS ONE, THE ○ FARGO ○ DAFFY
WILD SHADOWS see **DIVLJE SENKE** • 1968
WILD SHORE, THE see **NA DIKOM BEREGYE** • 1967
WILD SIDE, THE • 1983 • Spheeris Penelope • USA • SUBURBIA
WILD STALLION • 1952 • Collins Lewis D. • USA
WILD STALLION see **CRIN BLANC** • 1953
WILD STALLION, THE see **WILD PONY, THE** • 1983
WILD STAMPEDE • 1962 • de Anda Raul • MXC
WILD STRAIN, THE • 1918 • Wolbert William • USA
WILD STRAWBERRIES (UKN) see **SMULTRONSTALLET** • 1957
WILD STUD • 1970 • *Jo-Jo Distributors* • USA
WILD STYLE • 1982 • Ahearn Charlie • USA
WILD SUMAC • 1917 • Mong William V. • USA
WILD THING • 1987 • Reid Max • USA
WILD TIMES • 1980 • Compton Richard • TVM • USA
WILD TO GO • 1926 • De Lacy Robert • USA
WILD TORRENT • 1933 • Cheng Bu-Kao • CHN
WILD TRIO see **ABAREMBO SAMBAGARASU** • 1960
WILD WAVES • 1925 • Roberts Stephen • SHT • USA
WILD WAVES • 1928 • Gillett Burt • ANS • USA
WILD WAVES AND WOMEN • 1919 • Griffin Frank C. • SHT • USA
WILD WEED • 1949 • Newfield Sam • USA • DEVIL'S WEED, THE (UKN)
WILD WEST • 1946 • Tansey Robert • USA
WILD WEST, THE • 1925 • Hill Robert F. • SRL • USA
WILD WEST, THE see **SILLY BILLIES** • 1936
WILD WEST DAYS • 1937 • Beebe Ford, Smith Cliff • SRL • USA
WILD WEST DAYS • 1939 • Eason B. Reeves • USA
WILD WEST LOVE • 1914 • Parrott Charles • USA
WILD WEST ROMANCE • 1928 • Hough R. Lee • USA
WILD WEST SHOW, THE • 1928 • Andrews Del • USA • HEY RUBE!
WILD WEST STORY • 1964 • Nyberg Borje • SWD
WILD WEST WHOOPEE • 1931 • Horner Robert J. • USA
WILD WESTERNER, THE • 1919 • Holt George • SHT • USA
WILD WESTERNERS, THE • 1962 • Rudolph Oscar • USA • BROKEN LARIAT, THE
WILD WHEELS • 1969 • Osborne Kent • USA
WILD WHEELS see **RUNNIN' ON EMPTY** • 1982
WILD WHITE PIGEON • 1986 • Soloviev Sergei • USS • WHITE PIGEON
WILD WIFE • 1954 • McKimson Robert • ANS • USA
WILD, WILD GIRL • 1965 • Cartwright Earl • USA • WILD GIRL
WILD, WILD PLANET, THE (USA) see **CRIMINALI DELLA GALASSIA, I** • 1966
WILD WILD PUSSYCAT • 1970 • Cruz Jose Miranda • PHL
WILD, WILD SUSAN • 1925 • Sutherland A. Edward • USA
WILD, WILD WEST • 1920 • *Moranti Milburn* • SHT • USA
WILD WILD WEST REVISITED, THE • 1979 • Kennedy Burt • TVM • USA
WILD, WILD WESTERS, THE • 1911 • Martinek H. O. • UKN
WILD WILD WINTER • 1966 • Weinrib Lennie • USA
WILD, WILD WONG • 1967 • Batista Butch • PHL
WILD WILD WORLD • 1960 • McKimson Robert • ANS • USA
WILD, WILD WORLD • 1965 • Sokoler Bob • ITL
WILD, WILD WORLD OF JAYNE MANSFIELD, THE • 1968 • Knight Arthur • DOC • USA
WILD, WILLING AND SEXY (UKN) see **LIEBE DURCH DIE HINTERTUR** • 1969
WILD WIND see **CHANDAMARUTHA** • 1976
WILD WINGS • 1966 • Anstey Edgar • DOC • UKN
WILD WINGS • 1967 • Carey Patrick • DOC • UKN
WILD WINSHIP'S WIDOW • 1917 • Miller Charles • USA
WILD WOMAN, THE • 1919 • Becker Bruno J. • SHT • USA
WILD WOMEN • 1918 • Ford John • USA
WILD WOMEN • 1970 • Taylor Don • TVM • USA
WILD WOMEN AND TAME LIONS • 1918 • Campbell William • SHT • USA
WILD WOMEN AND WILD WAVES • 1918 • Hall Walter • SHT • USA
WILD WOMEN OF BORNEO • 1932 • Diltz Charles • USA
WILD WOMEN OF CHASTITY GULCH, THE • 1982 • Leacock Philip • TVM • USA
WILD WOMEN OF WONGO • 1958 • Wolcott James L. • USA
WILD WOOLLY WEST, THE • 1914 • *Princess* • USA
WILD WORLD OF BATWOMAN, THE • 1966 • Warren Jerry • USA • SHE WAS A HIPPY VAMPIRE
WILD YEARS, THE • van der Linden Charles Huguenot • NTH
WILD YOUTH • 1918 • Melford George, Blackton J. Stuart (Spv) • USA
WILD YOUTH • 1961 • Schreyer John • USA • NAKED YOUTH
WILD YOUTH • 1985 • Foskos Nick • USA
WILDCAT • 1942 • McDonald Frank • USA
WILDCAT see **GREAT SCOUT AND CATHOUSE THURSDAY, THE** • 1976
WILDCAT, THE • 1917 • MacDonald Sherwood • USA
WILDCAT, THE • 1924 • *Gordon Robert* • USA
WILDCAT, THE • 1926 • Fraser Harry L. • USA
WILDCAT, THE see **VERKENNINGSBORING, DE** • 1953
WILDCAT, THE (USA) see **BERGKATZE, DIE** • 1921
WILDCAT BUS • 1940 • Woodruff Frank • USA
WILDCAT JORDAN • 1922 • Santell Alfred • USA
WILDCAT OF PARIS • 1918 • De Grasse Joseph • USA
WILDCAT OF TUCSON • 1940 • Hillyer Lambert • USA • PROMISE FULFILLED (UKN)
WILDCAT SAUNDERS • 1936 • Fraser Harry L. • USA • WILD CAT -PRIZE FIGHTER (UKN)
WILDCAT TROOPER • 1936 • Clifton Elmer • USA • WILD CAT (UKN)
WILDCAT VALLEY • 1928 • Lamont Charles • SHT • USA
WILDCATS • 1986 • Ritchie Michael • USA • FIRST AND GOAL
WILDCATS OF ST. TRINIANS, THE • 1980 • Launder Frank • UKN
WILDCATTER, THE • 1937 • Collins Lewis D. • USA
WILDE AUGUSTE, DIE • 1956 • Jacoby Georg • FRG
WILDE BLUME, DIE • 1915 • Matray Ernst • FRG
WILDE BOERE, DIE • 1959 • SAF
WILDE FREIGER, DER • 1923 • Randolf Rolf • FRG
WILDE HARTEN • 1989 • Markus Jindra • NTH • WILD HEARTS
WILDE MANN, DER • 1988 • Zschokke Matthias • SWT
WILDE SEISOEN • 1967 • Nofal Emil • SAF • WILD SEASON (USA)
WILDE URSULA, DIE • 1917 • Mendel Georg Victor • FRG
WILDENTE, DIE • 1976 • Geissendorfer Hans W. • AUS, FRG • WILD DUCK, THE
WILDENTE, DIE see **HAUS DER LUGE, DAS** • 1925
WILDER REITER GMBH • 1967 • Spieker Franz-Josef • FRG • WILD RIDERS LTD.
WILDERER, DER • 1918 • Neuss Alwin • FRG
WILDERER, DER • 1925 • Meyer Johannes • FRG • WEIDMANNSHELL
WILDERER VOM SILBERWALD, DER • 1957 • Meyer Otto • FRG
WILDERNESS • 1984 • Chapman Christopher • CND
WILDERNESS see **LOVE'S WILDERNESS** • 1924
WILDERNESS, THE see **VADON** • 1988
WILDERNESS CALLING • 1969 • Hansen Paul O. • DOC • USA
WILDERNESS FAMILY, THE see **ADVENTURES OF THE WILDERNESS FAMILY, THE** • 1976
WILDERNESS FAMILY PART 2 see **FURTHER ADVENTURES OF THE WILDERNESS FAMILY, PART II** • 1978
WILDERNESS MAIL • 1935 • Sheldon Forrest • USA
WILDERNESS MAIL, THE • 1914 • Campbell Colin • USA
WILDERNESS ORPHAN see **ORPHAN OF THE WILDERNESS** • 1936
WILDERNESS TRAIL, THE • 1919 • Le Saint Edward J. • USA
WILDERNESS TRAIL, THE see **SYMBOL OF THE UNCONQUERED** • 1921
WILDERNESS TREASURE • 1962 • Mason William • DOC • CND
WILDERNESS WOMAN, THE • 1926 • Higgin Howard • USA
WILDES BLUT • 1920 • Hanus Emerich • FRG
WILDE'S DOMAIN • 1982 • Tingwell Charles • MTV • ASL
WILDEST!, THE • 1969 • Sully Jim • USA
WILDEST DREAMS • 1988 • Vincent Chuck • USA
WILDFIRE • 1915 • Middleton Edwin • USA
WILDFIRE • 1925 • Hunter T. Hayes • USA
WILDFIRE • 1945 • Tansey Robert • USA • WILDFIRE: THE STORY OF A HORSE (UKN)
WILDFIRE • 1988 • King Zalman • USA
WILDFIRE see **IT'S A DOG'S LIFE** • 1955
WILDFIRE: THE STORY OF A HORSE (UKN) see **WILDFIRE** • 1945
WILDFLOWER • 1914 • Buckland Warwick? • UKN
WILDFLOWER • 1914 • Dwan Allan • USA
WILDFLOWER OF GYIMES (USA) see **GYIMESI VADVIRAG** • 1939
WILDLIFE IN DANGER • 1964 • Holt Seth • DCS • UKN
WILDLIFE RENDEZVOUS, THE • 1959 • Perry Margaret • DOC • CND
WILDMAN • 1976 • Murphy Geoff • NZL • WILD MAN
WILDMAN, THE • 1912 • *Missimer Howard* • USA
WILDNESS OF YOUTH • 1922 • Abramson Ivan • USA
WILDNIS • 1922 • Ziener Bruno • FRG
WILDNIS STIRBT, DIE • 1936 • Fanck Arnold • FRG
WILDROSE • 1984 • Hanson John • USA
WILDSBOUDJIE, DIE • 1946 • SAF
WILDSCHUT • 1986 • Eehart Bobby • BLG, NTH • STRONGHOLD ○ GAMEKEEPER
WILDSCHUTZ, DER • 1953 • Lehner Alfred • AUS
WILDSCHUTZ DES ERZGEBIRGES, KARL STULPNER • 1930 • Siegert Fred • FRG
WILDSCHUTZ JENNERWEIN • 1929 • Beck-Gaden Hanns • FRG
WILDTEMMER, DIE • 1972 • SAF
WILDTOTER, DER see **LEDERSTRUMPF 1** • 1920
WILDVOGEL • 1943 • Meyer Johannes • FRG
WILDWECHSEL • 1972 • Fassbinder R. W. • FRG • WILD GAME (UKN) ○ JAIL BAIT (USA) ○ GAME PASS
WILDWEST IN OBERBAYERN • 1951 • Dorfler Ferdinand • FRG
WILDWOOD FLOWER • 1970 • Dewdney Alexander Keewatin • CND
WILES AND WEDLOCK • 1917 • Kernan Henry • SHT • USA
WILES OF A SIREN, THE • 1914 • *Blackwell Carlyle* • USA
WILES OF CUPID, THE • 1913 • Carleton Lloyd B. • USA
WILFRED PELLETIER, CHEF D'ORCHESTRE DE EDUCATEUR • 1961 • Portugais Louis • DCS • CND
WILFREDO LAM • 1978 • Solas Humberto • CUB
WILFUL AMBROSE • 1915 • Wright Walter • USA
WILFUL COLLEEN'S WAY, A • 1913 • *Edison* • USA
WILFUL MAID, A • 1911 • Fitzhamon Lewin • UKN
WILFUL PEGGY • 1910 • Griffith D. W. • USA
WILFUL PEGGY • 1915 • *Grandin Ethel* • USA
WILFUL WALLOPS FOR WEALTH • 1915 • *Heinie & Louie* • USA
WILFUL WILLIE • 1910 • *Walturdaw* • UKN
WILFUL WILLIE • 1942 • Rasinski Connie • ANS • USA
WILFUL YOUTH • 1927 • Fitzgerald Dallas M. • USA
WILHELM BUSCH ALBUM • 1978 • *Halas John (P)* • ASS • UKN
WILHELM PIECK, THE LIFE OF OUR PRESIDENT see **LEBEN UNSERER PRASIDENTEN, DAS** • 1950
WILHELM TELL • 1923 • Walther-Fein Rudolf, Dworsky Rudolf • FRG
WILHELM TELL • 1934 • Paul Heinz • FRG • LEGEND OF WILLIAM TELL, THE (USA)
WILHELM TELL • 1956 • Stoger Alfred • AUS
WILHELM TELL -BERGEN IN FLAMMEN • 1960 • Dickoff Michel • SWT • GUILLAUME TELL ○ FLAMMENDE BERG
WILHELM VON KOBELL • 1966 • Syberberg Hans-Jurgen • SHT • FRG
WILL • 1968 • Vanderbeek Stan • USA
WILL, THE • 1912 • *Eclair* • USA
WILL, THE • 1921 • Bramble A. V. • UKN
WILL, THE see **AZIMA, EL** • 1939
WILL, THE see **TESTAMENT** • 1976
WILL A WOMAN TELL? • 1916 • *Myers Harry C.* • USA
WILL AND A WAY, A • 1912 • *Anderson Mignon* • USA
WILL AND A WAY, A • 1922 • Haynes Manning • UKN
WILL ANY GENTLEMAN? • 1953 • Anderson Michael • UKN
WILL-BE WEDS, THE • 1913 • *Bayne Beverly* • USA
WILL BLOOD TELL? • 1914 • *Lubin* • USA
WILL BRITAIN GO HUNGRY? • 1947 • DOC • UKN • THIS MODERN AGE NO.13
WILL DO MOUSEWORK • 1956 • Kneitel Seymour • ANS • USA
WILL EVANS HARNESSING A HORSE • 1913 • Wilson Frank? • UKN
WILL EVANS: ON THE DOORSTEP: NOVELETTE: THE JOCKEY • 1907 • Gilbert Arthur • UKN
WILL EVANS THE LIVING CATHERINE WHEEL see **MUSICAL ECCENTRIC, THE** • 1899
WILL, G. GORDON LIDDY • 1982 • Lieberman Robert • TVM • USA
WILL HE DO IT? • 1913 • Collins Edwin J.? • UKN
WILL IT EVER COME TO THIS? • 1911 • *Lubin* • USA
WILL JAMES' SAND • 1949 • King Louis • USA • SAND (UKN)
WILL-O'-THE-WISP • 1913 • Ford Francis • USA
WILL-O'-THE-WISP • 1922 • Cervenkova Thea • CZC
WILL O' THE WISP see **LIEBE DER BRUDER ROTT, DIE** • 1929
WILL O' THE WISP see **ONIBI TORO** • 1958
WILL O' THE WISP see **FEU FOLLET, LE** • 1963
WILL O' THE WISP, THE • 1914 • *Saunders Jackie* • USA

WILL O' THE WISP COMEDIES NOS.1-8 • 1920 • Mannering Cecil • SHS • UKN
WILL O' THE WISP COMEDIES NOS.9-16 • 1920 • Kellino W. P. • SHS • UKN
WILL OF A WESTERN MAID, THE • 1911 • *Champion* • USA
WILL OF DESTINY, THE • 1912 • *Melies* • USA
WILL OF HER OWN, A • 1915 • Elvey Maurice • UKN
WILL OF HIS GRACE, THE see **HANS NADS TESTAMENTE** • 1919
WILL OF JAMES WALDRON, THE • 1912 • Dwan Allan • USA
WILL OF PROVIDENCE, THE • 1911 • *Beggs Lee* • USA
WILL OF THE PEOPLE, THE • 1913 • Merwin Bannister • USA
WILL OF THE PEOPLE, THE • 1916 • Coleby A. E. • UKN • STRONG MAN'S WEAKNESS, A
WILL O'THE WISP see **FLACARI PE COMORI** • 1988
WILL OUR FRIEND SUCCEED IN FINDING THEIR FRIEND.. see **RIUSCIRANNO I NOSTRI EROI A RITROVARE L'AMICO MISTERIOSAMENTE SCOMPARSO IN AFRICA?** • 1968
WILL OUR HEROES BE ABLE TO FIND THEIR FRIEND WHO HAS MYSTERIOUSLY DISAPPEARED IN AFRICA? see **RIUSCIRANNO I NOSTRI EROI A RITROVARE L'AMICO MISTERIOSAMENTE SCOMPARSO IN AFRICA?** • 1968
WILL PENNY • 1968 • Gries Tom • USA
WILL POWER • 1913 • Smalley Phillips • USA
WILL POWER • 1936 • Ripley Arthur • SHT • USA
WILL SUCCESS SPOIL ROCK HUNTER? • 1957 • Tashlin Frank • USA • OH! FOR A MAN! (UKN)
WILL THE EXPRESS OVERTAKE THEM? • 1903 • Rosenthal Joe • UKN
WILL THE GREAT BARRIER REEF CURE CLAUDE CLOUGH? • 1967 • Milson John • SHT • ASL
WILL THE PRESIDENT BETRAY US? see **NOS TRAICIONARA EL PRESIDENTE?** • 1988
WILL THE REAL NORMAN MAILER PLEASE STAND UP • 1968 • Fontaine Dick • CND
WILL THERE REALLY BE A MORNING? • 1982 • Cook Fielder • TVM • USA
WILL THEY NEVER COME? • 1915 • Rolfe Alfred • ASL
WILL TO DIE see **BLOOD LEGACY** • 1971
WILL TO LIVE see **UYIR MEL AASAI** • 1967
WILL TO LIVE, THE see **OWARINAKI INOCHI O** • 1967
WILL TO WIN • 1982 • SAF
WILL TOMORROW EVER COME? (UKN) see **THAT'S MY MAN** • 1947
WILL WILLIE WIN? • 1913 • Hotaling Arthur D. • USA
WILL YOU MARRY ME? • 1911 • *Majestic* • USA
WILL YOU MARRY ME? • 1917 • *Major Film* • USA
WILL YOU MARRY ME? see **BENIMLE EVLENIRMISIN?** • 1968
WILL YOUR HEART BEAT FASTER? see **KAKABAKABA KA BA?** • 1981
WILLA • 1979 • Darling Joan, Guzman Claudio • TVM • USA
WILLAMETTE, MORMOT AND PRIEST • 1974 • Greenwald Barry • CND
WILLARD • 1971 • Mann Daniel • USA
WILLI-BUSCH REPORT, DER • 1980 • Schilling Niklaus • FRG
WILLI TOBLER AND THE FALL OF THE 6TH FLEET see **WILLI TOBLER UND DER UNTERGANG DER SECHSTEN FLOTTE** • 1971
WILLI TOBLER AND THE SINKING OF THE SIXTH FLEET see **WILLI TOBLER UND DER UNTERGANG DER SECHSTEN FLOTTE** • 1971
WILLI TOBLER UND DER UNTERGANG DER SECHSTEN FLOTTE • 1971 • Kluge Alexander • FRG • WILLY TOBLER UND DER UNTERGANG DER 6 FLOTTE ◦ WILLI TOBLER AND THE FALL OF THE 6TH FLEET ◦ WILLI TOBLER AND THE SINKING OF THE SIXTH FLEET
WILLI WIRD DAS KIND SCHON SCHAUKELN • 1972 • Jacobs Werner • FRG
WILLIAM AND DOROTHY • 1978 • Russell Ken • MTV • UKN
WILLIAM AT THE CIRCUS see **WILLIAM COMES TO TOWN** • 1948
WILLIAM "BIG BILL" BROONZY • 1958 • Bruynoghe Yannick • SHT • BLG
WILLIAM COMES TO TOWN • 1948 • Guest Val • UKN • WILLIAM AT THE CIRCUS
WILLIAM DRAKE, THIEF • 1912 • Calvert Charles? • UKN
WILLIAM FARNUM IN A LIBERTY LOAN APPEAL • 1918 • Lloyd Frank • SHT • USA
WILLIAM FAVERSHAM IN A LIBERTY LOAN APPEAL • 1918 • *Paramount* • SHT • USA
WILLIAM FOX MOVIETONE FOLLIES OF 1929 see **FOX MOVIETONE FOLLIES OF 1929** • 1929
WILLIAM HENRY JONES' COURTSHIP • 1914 • Drew Sidney • USA
WILLIAM LYON MACKENZIE: A FRIEND TO HIS COUNTRY • 1961 • Biggs Julian • CND
WILLIAM MCKINLEY AT CANTON, OHIO • 1896 • *Bitzer Billy (Ph)* • USA
WILLIAM TELL • 1901 • *Paul R. W.* • UKN
WILLIAM TELL • 1901 • *Warwick Trading Co* • UKN
WILLIAM TELL • 1925 • Harder Emil
WILLIAM TELL • 1934 • Lantz Walter, Nolan William • ANS • USA
WILLIAM TELL AND THE CLOWN see **GUILLAUME TELL ET LE CLOWN** • 1898
WILLIAM VOSS • 1915 • Meinert Rudolf • FRG
WILLIAM WEBB ELLIS, ARE YOU MAD? • 1971 • Taylor Richard • DOC • UKN
WILLIAMSBURG: THE STORY OF A PATRIOT • 1957 • Seaton George • DOC • USA
WILLIE • 1910 • *Selig* • USA
WILLIE • 1910 • *Imp* • USA
WILLIE • 1914 • Campbell Colin • USA
WILLIE • 1980 • Ebrahimian Ghasem • USA
WILLIE AND JOE BACK AT THE FRONT see **BACK AT THE FRONT** • 1952
WILLIE AND JOE IN TOKYO (UKN) see **BACK AT THE FRONT** • 1952
WILLIE AND PHIL • 1980 • Mazursky Paul • USA
WILLIE AND THE CHINESE CAT see **ALSO ES WAR SO..** • 1977
WILLIE AND THE MOUSE • 1941 • Sidney George • SHT • USA
WILLIE AND THE YANK see **MOSBY'S MARAUDERS** • 1967
WILLIE AND TIM GET A SURPRISE • 1906 • Collins Alf? • UKN
WILLIE AND TIM IN THE MOTOR CAR • 1905 • Stow Percy • UKN
WILLIE BECOMES AN ARTIST • 1912 • Sennett Mack • USA
WILLIE BOY see **TELL THEM WILLIE BOY IS HERE** • 1969
WILLIE DYNAMITE • 1973 • Moses Gilbert • USA
WILLIE -EINE ZAUBERPOSSE see **ALSO ES WAR SO..** • 1977
WILLIE GOES TO SEA • 1915 • Campbell Colin • USA
WILLIE GOODCHILD VISITS HIS AUNTIE • 1907 • Booth W. R.? • UKN
WILLIE MINDS THE DOG • 1913 • Avery Charles, Sennett Mack (Spv) • USA
WILLIE RUNS THE PARK • 1915 • *Rolin* • USA
WILLIE STAYED SINGLE • 1915 • Davis Ulysses • USA
WILLIE SWAPPED PLACES WITH THE BOSS • 1909 • *Waldurdaw* • UKN
WILLIE THE HUNTER • 1912 • *Lubin* • USA
WILLIE THE KID • 1952 • Cannon Robert • ANS • USA
WILLIE THE OPERATIC WHALE • 1946 • Geronimi Clyde, Luske Hamilton • ANS • USA • WHALE WHO WANTED TO SING AT THE MET, THE
WILLIE THE SLEUTH • 1916 • *Jockey* • USA
WILLIE, THE WILD MAN • 1913 • *Thanhouser* • USA
WILLIE WALRUS AND THE AWFUL CONFESSION • 1914 • *Wolbert William* • USA
WILLIE WALRUS PAYS ALIMONY • 1917 • *Wolbert William* • USA
WILLIE WHIPPLE'S DREAM • 1915 • *Kalem* • USA
WILLIE WHOPPER • 1933-34 • Iwerks Ub • ASS • USA
WILLIE WISE AND HIS MOTOR BOAT • 1911 • *Wadsworth William* • USA
WILLIE'S BIRTHDAY PRESENT • 1911 • *Walturdaw* • UKN
WILLIE'S CAMERA • 1903 • *Bitzer Billy (Ph)* • USA
WILLIE'S CONSCIENCE • 1911 • *Hopkins Jack* • USA
WILLIE'S DISGUISE • 1914 • Smalley Phillips • USA
WILLIE'S DOG • 1912 • *Trunnelle Mabel* • USA
WILLIE'S DREAM • 1907 • Mottershaw Frank • UKN
WILLIE'S DREAM OF MICK SQUINTER • 1913 • Aylott Dave? • UKN
WILLIE'S GREAT SCHEME • 1913 • Smalley Phillips • USA
WILLIE'S HAIRCUT • 1914 • MacGregor Norval • USA
WILLIE'S MAGIC WAND • 1907 • Booth W. R. • UKN
WILLIE'S SISTER • 1912 • *Morrison James* • USA
WILLIE'S WINNING WAYS • 1911 • *Yankee* • USA
WILLING WENDY TO WILLIE • 1916 • *Keyes Frances* • SHT • USA
WILLOUGHBY'S MAGIC HAT • 1943 • Wickersham Bob • ANS • USA
WILLOW • 1988 • Howard Ron • USA
WILLOW SPRINGS • 1972 • Schroeter Werner • FRG
WILLOW TREE • 1945 • Hudson Claud • DOC • UKN
WILLOW TREE, THE • 1911 • *Vitagraph* • USA
WILLOW TREE, THE • 1920 • Otto Henry • USA
WILLOW TREE IN THE GINZA, A see **GINZA NO YANAGI** • 1932
WILLOWS OF GINZA see **GINZA NO YANAGI** • 1932
WILLS • 1985 • Walker John • CND
WILLS AND BURKE • 1986 • Weis Bob • ASL
WILLST DU EWIG JUNGFRAU BLEIBEN? • 1968 • Frank Hubert • FRG • DO YOU WANT TO REMAIN A VIRGIN FOREVER? (UKN)
WILLUMSEN see **HISTORIEN OM ET SLOT J.F. WILLUMSEN** • 1951
WILLY • 1963 • Buckhantz Allan A. • MTV • FRG, USA
WILLY AND MYRIAM see **WILLY Y LA MYRIAM, EL** • 1983
WILLY, DER PRIVATDETEKTIV • 1960 • Schundler Rudolf • FRG
WILLY KING OF THE SORCERERS see **WILLY ROI DES SORCIERS** • 1912
WILLY MCBEAN AND HIS MAGIC MACHINE • 1965 • Rankin Arthur Jr. • ANM • USA, JPN
WILLY MILLY • 1985 • Schneider Paul • USA • SOMETHING SPECIAL ◦ I WAS A TEENAGE BOY
WILLY REILLY AND HIS COLLEEN • 1918 • O'Donovan Fred • IRL
WILLY ROI DES SORCIERS • 1912 • FRN • WILLY KING OF THE SORCERERS
WILLY & SCRATCH • 1972 • Emery Robert J. • USA
WILLY SIGNORI AND I COMING FROM AFAR see **WILLY SIGNORI E VENGO DA LONTANO** • 1990
WILLY SIGNORI E VENGO DA LONTANO • 1990 • Nuti Francesco • ITL • WILLY SIGNORI AND I COMING FROM AFAR
WILLY, THE SPARROW • 1989 • Gemes Jozsef • HNG
WILLY TOBLER UND DER UNTERGANG DER 6 FLOTTE see **WILLI TOBLER UND DER UNTERGANG DER SECHSTEN FLOTTE** • 1971
WILLY WALRUS AND THE BABY • 1914 • *Wolbert William* • USA
WILLY WALRUS, DETECTIVE • 1914 • *Wolbert William* • USA
WILLY WILLY • 1970 • Ropert Gregory • SHT • ASL
WILLY WONKA AND THE CHOCOLATE FACTORY • 1971 • Stuart Mel • USA
WILLY WOULD A-WOOING GO • 1913 • Calvert Charles? • UKN
WILLY Y LA MYRIAM, EL • 1983 • Benavente David • DCS • CHL • WILLY AND MYRIAM
WILMA • 1977 • Greenspan Bud • TVM • USA
WILSON • 1944 • King Henry • USA
WILSON OR THE KAISER? see **GREAT VICTORY, WILSON OR THE KAISER?, THE** • 1918
WILSON'S WIFE'S COUNTENANCE • 1910 • *Vitagraph* • USA
WILT • 1989 • Tuchner Michael • UKN
WILTON'S ZOO (USA) see **BOEF JE** • 1938
WILY CHAPERON, THE • 1915 • Pollard Harry • USA
WILY FIDDLER, THE • 1907 • Cooper Arthur • UKN
WILY WEASEL • 1937 • *Lantz Walter (P)* • ANS • USA
WILY WILLIAM'S WASHING • 1913 • Aylott Dave? • UKN
WIMMEN IS A MYSKERY • 1940 • Fleischer Dave • ANS • USA
WIMMIN HADN'T OUGHTA DRIVE • 1940 • Fleischer Dave • ANS • USA
WIMPS • 1987 • Vincent Chuck • USA
WIMSHURST ELECTRIC MACHINE, THE • 1977 • van Zuylen Erik • NTH
WIN, LOSE OR DRAW • 1925 • Maloney Leo • USA
WIN OR LOSE see **LOVE IN BLOOM** • 1935
WIN, PLACE AND SHOW • 1955 • Haldane Don • CND
WIN, PLACE AND SHOWBOAT • 1950 • Sparber I. • ANS • USA
WIN, PLACE OR STEAL • 1975 • Bailey Richard • USA
WIN THAT GIRL • 1928 • Butler David • USA
WIN THEM ALL • Kao Pao Shu • HKG
WIN TO LIVE see **HAYAT KHIFA, EL** • 1968
WINCENTY PSTROWSKI STORY • 1975 • Bugajski Ryszard • MTV • PLN
WINCHESTER '73 • 1950 • Mann Anthony • USA
WINCHESTER '73 • 1967 • Daugherty Herschel • TVM • USA
WINCHESTER CHE NON PERDONA, IL see **BUCKAROO** • 1967
WINCHESTER WOMAN, THE • 1919 • Ruggles Wesley • USA
WIND see **WIATR** • 1969
WIND, THE • 1928 • Sjostrom Victor • USA
WIND, THE • 1987 • Mastorakis Nico • USA, GRC • EDGE OF TERROR, THE ◦ TERROR'S EDGE
WIND, THE see **VETER** • 1959
WIND, THE see **VENT, LE** • 1972
WIND, THE see **FINYE** • 1982
WIND ACROSS THE EVERGLADES • 1958 • Ray Nicholas • USA
WIND AND THE LION, THE • 1975 • Milius John • USA
WIND AND THE OAK, THE see **ERA E LISI** • 1981
WIND AND THE RIVER, THE see **VINDEN OCH FLOCHEN** • 1951
WIND CANNOT READ, THE • 1958 • Thomas Ralph • UKN
WIND, CURVES AND TRAP DOOR • 1948 • Parker Benjamin R. • SHT • USA
WIND FROM AURES see **ASSIFAT AL-AOURAS** • 1967
WIND FROM THE EAST see **VETER S VOSTOKA** • 1941
WIND FROM THE EAST (USA) see **VENT D'EST, LE** • 1969
WIND FROM THE ISLAND see **VENT DE L'ILLA, EL** • 1988
WIND FROM THE SOUTH see **RIH AL-JANUB** • 1975
WIND FROM THE WEST see **VINDEN FRAN VASTER** • 1942
WIND IN MY POCKET, THE see **VITR V KAPSE** • 1982
WIND IN THE FACE see **VETER V LITSO** • 1929
WIND IN THE HANDS see **VENTO NELLE MANI, IL** • 1984
WIND IN THE NET, THE see **VETAR U MREZI** • 1989
WIND IN THE SAILS • 1934 • Franken Mannus, Le Clerq W. L. • NTH
WIND IN THE WEB, THE see **VETAR U MREZI** • 1989
WIND IN THE WILLOWS • 1949 • Algar James, Kinney Jack • ANM • USA
WIND IN THE WILLOWS, THE • 1970 • *Universal Education & Visual Arts* • SHT • USA
WIND IN THE WILLOWS, THE • Salway John • ANM
WIND IN THE WILLOWS, THE • 1983 • Cosgrove Brian, Hall Mark • ANM • UKN
WIND IN THE WILLOWS, THE • 1983 • Rankin Arthur Jr., Bass Jules • ANM • USA
WIND IN THE WILLOWS, THE • 1988 • ANM
WIND IS MY LOVER, THE see **SINGOALLA** • 1949
WIND IS WHISTLING UNDER THEIR FEET, THE see **TALPUK ALATT FUTYUL A SZEL** • 1976
WIND OF CHANGE, THE • 1961 • Sewell Vernon • UKN
WIND OF DEATH see **ULTIMO UOMO DELLA TERRA, L'** • 1964
WIND OF FEAR, THE see **WEHT DIE ANGST, SO WEHT DER WIND** • 1983
WIND OF FREEDOM see **VIENTO DE LIBERTAD** • 1975
WIND OF HATE (USA) see **ANEMOS TOU MISSOUS, O** • 1958
WIND OF HONOUR see **KAZE NO KO** • 1949
WIND OF THE GHOST, THE • Sung Chen Zu • HKG
WIND OF THIS WORLD see **SHABA NO KAZE** • 1928
WIND ON THE HEATH, THE • 1963 • Bijou Leon, Jessop Peter • UKN
WIND ONCE MORE see **KAZE FUTATABI** • 1952
WIND RIDER • 1985 • SAF
WIND ROSE, THE see **WINDROSE, DIE** • 1956
WIND VON OSTEN (FRG) see **VENT D'EST, LE** • 1969
WIND WOMAN AND WANDERER see **KAZE TO ONNA TO TABIGARASU** • 1958
WINDBAG THE SAILOR • 1936 • Beaudine William • UKN
WINDBLOWN HARE, THE • 1949 • McKimson Robert • ANS • USA
WINDBREAKER, THE see **PETOMANE, IL** • 1984
WINDBREAKS FOR THE PRAIRIES • 1942 • Cherry Evelyn Spice, Cherry Lawrence W. • DOC • CND
WINDFALL • 1935 • King George • UKN
WINDFALL • 1955 • Cass Henry • UKN
WINDFALL, THE • 1914 • *Lubin* • USA
WINDFALL IN ATHENS (USA) see **KYRIAKATIKO XYPNIMA** • 1953
WINDFLOWERS: THE STORY OF A DRAFT DODGER • 1968 • Mekas Adolfas • USA
WINDING ROAD, THE • 1920 • Haldane Bert, Wilson Frank • UKN
WINDING STAIR, THE • 1925 • Wray John Griffith • USA
WINDING TRAIL, THE • 1918 • Collins John H. • USA
WINDING TRAIL, THE • 1921 • Martin George • USA
WINDJAMMER • 1929 • Villiers Michael • UKN
WINDJAMMER • 1937 • Scott Ewing • USA
WINDJAMMER • 1958 • de Rochemont Louis, Colleran Bill • DOC • USA
WINDJAMMER, THE • 1926 • Brown Harry J. • USA
WINDJAMMER, THE • 1930 • Orton John • UKN
WINDMILL, THE • 1937 • Woods Arthur • UKN
WINDMILL IN BARBADOS • 1934 • Wright Basil • DOC • UKN
WINDMILL REVELS • 1937 • Hopwood R. A. • UKN
WINDMILLS • 1967 • Marek Dusan • ANS • ASL
WINDMILLS see **MOLINOS DE VIENTO** • 1940
WINDMILLS, THE see **BALLADEN OM CARL-HENNING** • 1969
WINDMILLS OF THE GODS • 1988 • Philips Lee • TVM • USA
WINDOM'S WAY • 1957 • Neame Ronald • UKN
WINDOW • 1964 • Jacobs Ken • USA
WINDOW • 1976 • Brakhage Stan • SHT • USA
WINDOW, THE • 1949 • Tetzlaff Ted • USA
WINDOW, THE • 1976 • Nikolic Zivko • SHT • YGS
WINDOW, THE see **MADO** • 1965
WINDOW CLEANER, THE • 1968 • Leigh Malcolm • SHT • UKN
WINDOW CLEANERS • 1940 • King Jack • ANS • USA
WINDOW DRESSER'S DREAM, THE • 1917 • *U.s.m.p.* • USA

WINDOW DUMMY, THE • 1925 • Bacon Lloyd • SHT • USA
WINDOW IN LONDON, A • 1939 • Mason Herbert • UKN • LADY IN DISTRESS (USA)
WINDOW IN PICCADILLY, A • 1928 • Morgan Sidney • UKN
WINDOW LOOKING OUT ON THE SEA, THE see **OKNO Z WIDOKIEM NA MORZE** • 1978
WINDOW OF DREAMS, THE • 1916 • Mitchell Howard M. • SHT • USA
WINDOW ON THE SEA, THE see **OKNO Z WIDOKIEM NA MORZE** • 1978
WINDOW ON WASHINGTON PARK, THE • 1913 • Trimble Larry • USA
WINDOW OPPOSITE, THE • 1919 • Lawrence Edmund • USA
WINDOW PAINS • 1967 • Smith Paul J. • ANS • USA
WINDOW SHOPPING • 1938 • Marcus Sid • ANS • USA
WINDOW SUITE OF CHILDREN'S SONGS • 1969 • Brakhage Stan • USA
WINDOW TO LET, A • 1910 • Stow Percy • UKN
WINDOW TO THE SKY, A (UKN) see **OTHER SIDE OF THE MOUNTAIN, THE** • 1975
WINDOW WATER BABY MOVING • 1959 • Brakhage Stan • SHT • USA
WINDOWMOBILE • 1977 • Broughton James • USA
WINDOWS • 1979 • Dunkley-Smith John • ASL
WINDOWS • 1980 • Willis Gordon • USA
WINDOWS OF TIME, THE see **IDO ABLAKAI, AZ** • 1969
WINDPRINTS • 1989 • Wicht David • SAF
WINDRIDER • 1986 • Monton Vincent • ASL • MAKING WAVES
WINDROSE, DIE • 1956 • Ivens Joris (Spv), Cavalcanti Alberto, Bellon Yannick, Gerasimov Sergei, Wu Kuo-Yin, Pontecorvo Gillo, Viany Alex • GDR • WIND ROSE, THE ○ LEBEN DER FRAUEN, DAS
WINDS OF AUTUMN, THE • 1976 • Pierce Charles B. • USA
WINDS OF CHANCE • 1925 • Lloyd Frank • USA
WINDS OF CHANGE see **METAMORPHOSES** • 1978
WINDS OF FATE, THE • 1911 • *Ogle Charles* • USA
WINDS OF FOGO, THE • 1970 • Low Colin • DOC • CND
WINDS OF JARRAH, THE • 1983 • Egerton Mark • ASL
WINDS OF KITTY HAWK, THE • 1978 • Swackhamer E. W. • TVM • USA
WINDS OF THE PAMPAS • 1927 • Varney-Serrao Arthur • USA
WINDS OF THE PUSZTA see **PUSZTAI SZEL** • 1938
WINDS OF THE WASTELAND • 1936 • Wright Mack V. • USA
WINDSONG • 1958 • Tourtelot Madeline • SHT • USA
WINDSOR CASTLE • 1926 • Elvey Maurice • UKN
WINDSPLITTER, THE • 1971 • Fiegelson Julius • USA
WINDSTARKE 9 • 1924 • Schunzel Reinhold • FRG • GESCHICHTE EINER REICHEN ERBIN, DIE
WINDSTILL • 1968 • Winzentsen Franz • ANS • FRG
WINDSTROSS, EIN • 1942 • Felsenstein Walter • FRG
WINDWALKER • 1980 • Merrill Keith • USA
WINDWARD ANCHOR, THE • 1916 • Reynolds Lynn • SHT • USA
WINDY • 1935 • Bucquet Harold S. • SHT • USA
WINDY CITY • 1984 • Bernstein Armyan • USA • ALL THE SAD YOUNG MEN
WINDY DAY • 1968 • Hubley John, Hubley Faith • ANS • USA
WINDY DAY, A • 1912 • *Hevener Jerold T.* • USA
WINDY DREAM, A • 1912 • *Pathe* • FRN
WINDY MOUNTAIN • 1955 • Sequens Jiri • CZC
WINDY SEA, THE see **VETRNE MORE** • 1973
WINDY STORY see **VJETROVITA PRICA** • 1968
WINE • 1924 • Gasnier Louis J. • USA
WINE CELLAR BURGLARS see **PIQUEURS DE FUTS, LES** • 1901
WINE GIRL, THE • 1918 • Paton Stuart • USA
WINE HARVEST see **VINO BRANI** • 1982
WINE INDUSTRY, THE • 1915 • ASL
WINE OF COURAGE • 1910 • *Walturdaw* • UKN
WINE OF LIFE, THE • 1924 • Rooke Arthur • UKN
WINE OF MADNESS, THE • 1913 • *Lubin* • USA
WINE OF YOUTH • 1924 • Vidor King • USA
WINE OPENER • 1905 • *Bitzer Billy (Ph)* • USA
WINE, WOMEN AND A LANCE see **SAKE TO ONNA TO YARI** • 1960
WINE WOMEN AND HORSES • 1937 • King Louis • USA
WINE, WOMEN AND REFORMATION • 1913 • *Ammex* • USA
WINE, WOMEN AND SONG • 1915 • *Anderson Broncho Billy* • USA
WINE, WOMEN AND SONG • 1934 • Brenon Herbert • USA
WINE, WOMEN AND WOMEN • 1969 • *Canyon Dist. Co.* • USA
WINE, WOMEN BUT NO SONG • 1931 • Buzzell Edward • SHT • USA
WING AND A PRAYER • 1944 • Hathaway Henry • USA
WING-BEATS IN THE NIGHT see **VINGSLAG I NATTEN** • 1953
WING TO WING • 1951 • Frankel Cyril • DCS • UKN
WING TOY • 1921 • Mitchell Howard M. • USA
WINGED DEVILS (UKN) see **ABOVE THE CLOUDS** • 1933
WINGED DEVILS (UKN) see **FORZA "G"** • 1972
WINGED DIALOG • 1967 • Beavers Robert • SHT • USA
WINGED DIAMONDS • 1917 • Ellis Robert • SHT • USA
WINGED HORSE, THE • 1932 • Lantz Walter, Nolan William • ANS • USA
WINGED HORSEMAN, THE • 1929 • Rosson Arthur, Eason B. Reeves • USA
WINGED IDOL, THE • 1915 • Edwards Walter? • USA
WINGED MESSENGER, THE • 1915 • *Stanton Richard* • USA
WINGED MYSTERY, THE • 1917 • De Grasse Joseph • USA
WINGED SCOURGE, THE • 1943 • *Disney Walt (P)* • ANS • USA
WINGED SERPENT see **STARSHIP INVASIONS** • 1977
WINGED VICTORY • 1944 • Cukor George • USA
WINGED VICTORY see **SHINING VICTORY** • 1941
WINGS • 1927 • Wellman William A. • SIL • USA
WINGS • 1929 • Wellman William A. • SND • USA
WINGS see **KRYLYA** • 1966
WINGS see **SKRZYDLA** • 1966
WINGS, THE see **VINGARNA** • 1916
WINGS ACROSS THE PACIFIC see **WILD BLUE YONDER, THE** • 1951
WINGS AND CLAWS see **ALAS Y GARRAS** • 1967
WINGS AND THE WOMAN (USA) see **THEY FLEW ALONE** • 1942
WINGS AND WHEELS • 1916 • Wright Walter • SHT • USA
WINGS AROUND THE LIGHTHOUSE see **VINGAR KRING FYREN** • 1937
WINGS FOR THE EAGLE • 1942 • Bacon Lloyd • USA • SHADOW OF THEIR WINGS
WINGS IN THE DARK • 1935 • Flood James • USA
WINGS IN THE WILDERNESS • 1975 • Ryan Robert, Gibson Dan • CND
WINGS OF A MOTH, THE • 1913 • Trimble Larry • USA
WINGS OF A SERF see **KRYLYA KHOLOPAL** • 1926
WINGS OF ADVENTURE • 1930 • Thorpe Richard • USA
WINGS OF CHANCE • 1959 • Dew Edward • CND
WINGS OF COURAGE • 1946 • *Mead Thomas (P)* • SHT • USA
WINGS OF DANGER • 1952 • Fisher Terence • UKN • DEAD ON COURSE (USA)
WINGS OF DEATH • 1961 • Davis Allan • UKN
WINGS OF DESIRE (UKN) see **HIMMEL UBER BERLIN, DER** • 1987
WINGS OF DESTINY • 1940 • Kathner Rupert • ASL
WINGS OF DOOM see **FLIGHT TO FAME** • 1938
WINGS OF EAGLES • 1986 • Pyke Roger • CND
WINGS OF EAGLES, THE • 1956 • Ford John • USA
WINGS OF FAME • 1989 • Votocek Otakar • NTH
WINGS OF FIRE • 1967 • Rich David Lowell • TVM • USA • CLOUDBURST, THE
WINGS OF LOVE see **MAID OF THE WEST** • 1921
WINGS OF LOVE, THE • 1910 • *Vitagraph* • USA
WINGS OF MYSTERY • 1963 • Gunn Gilbert • UKN
WINGS OF PRIDE • 1920 • O'Brien John B. • USA
WINGS OF SONG see **KRYLYA PESNI** • 1966
WINGS OF SONG see **KRYLYA PYESNI** • 1967
WINGS OF SONG (UKN) see **LADIES IN LOVE** • 1930
WINGS OF STEEL • 1941 • Eason B. Reeves • SHT • USA
WINGS OF THE APACHE • 1989 • Green David • UKN
WINGS OF THE HAWK • 1953 • Boetticher Budd • USA
WINGS OF THE MORNING • 1937 • Schuster Harold • UKN, USA
WINGS OF THE MORNING, THE • 1919 • Edwards J. Gordon • USA
WINGS OF THE NAVY • 1939 • Bacon Lloyd • USA
WINGS OF THE SERF see **KRYLIA KHOLOPA** • 1926
WINGS OF THE STORM • 1926 • Blystone John G. • USA
WINGS OF THE WEST see **RODEO MIXUP, A** • 1924
WINGS OF VICTORY (USA) see **VALERI CHKALOV** • 1941
WINGS OF YOUTH • 1925 • Flynn Emmett J. • USA
WINGS OVER AFRICA • 1932 • Johnson Martin E. • USA
WINGS OVER AFRICA • 1936 • Vajda Ladislao • UKN
WINGS OVER EMPIRE • 1939 • Legg Stuart • UKN
WINGS OVER EVEREST • 1933 • Montagu Ivor, Barkas Geoffrey • UKN • WINGS OVER THE EVEREST
WINGS OVER HONOLULU • 1937 • Potter H. C. • USA
WINGS OVER THE ATLANTIC • 1937 • Sparling Gordon • CND
WINGS OVER THE CHACO (USA) see **ALAS SOBRE EL CHACO** • 1939
WINGS OVER THE EVEREST see **WINGS OVER EVEREST** • 1933
WINGS OVER THE PACIFIC • 1943 • Rosen Phil • USA
WINGS OVER WYOMING see **HOLLYWOOD COWBOY** • 1937
WINGS, THE FILM • 1979 • Priestley Jack • UKN
WINGS TO SOUTH AFRICA • 1954 • Coffey Frank • DOC • ASL
WINGY MALONE AND THE CLIMAX JAZZ BAND • 1976 • Showler Joe • SHT • CND
WINIFRED THE SHOP GIRL • 1916 • Baker George D. • USA • SHOP GIRL, THE
WINIFRED WAGNER UND DIE GESCHICHTEN DES HAUSES WAHNFRIED 1914-75 • 1976 • Syberberg Hans-Jurgen • DOC • FRG • CONFESSIONS OF WINIFRED WAGNER
WINK OF AN EYE • 1958 • Jones Winston • USA
WINKING IDOL, THE • 1926 • Ford Francis • SRL • USA
WINKING PARSON, THE • 1912 • *Wadsworth William* • USA
WINKING ZULU, THE • 1914 • Hale Albert W. • USA
WINKLE'S GREAT DISCOVERY • 1913 • *Cosmopolitan* • UKN
WIN(K)SOME WIDOW, THE • 1914 • Young James • USA
WINKY ACCUSED OF AN 'ORRIBLE CRIME • 1914 • Birch Cecil • UKN
WINKY AND THE ANTS • 1914 • Birch Cecil • UKN
WINKY AND THE CANNIBAL CHIEF • 1914 • Birch Cecil • UKN
WINKY AND THE GORGONZOLA CHEESE • 1914 • Birch Cecil • UKN
WINKY AND THE LEOPARD • 1914 • Birch Cecil • UKN
WINKY AS A SUFFRAGETTE • 1914 • Birch Cecil • UKN
WINKY AT THE FRONT • 1914 • Birch Cecil • UKN
WINKY BECOMES A FAMILY MAN • 1914 • Birch Cecil • UKN
WINKY, BIGAMIST • 1914 • Birch Cecil • UKN
WINKY CAUSES A SMALLPOX PANIC • 1914 • Birch Cecil • UKN
WINKY DIDDLES THE HAWKER • 1914 • Birch Cecil • UKN
WINKY DONS THE PETTICOATS • 1914 • Birch Cecil • UKN
WINKY GETS PUFFED UP • 1914 • Birch Cecil • UKN
WINKY GETS SPOTTED • 1914 • Birch Cecil • UKN
WINKY GOES CAMPING • 1914 • Birch Cecil • UKN
WINKY GOES SPY CATCHING • 1914 • Birch Cecil • UKN
WINKY IS THE LONG AND SHORT OF IT • 1915 • Birch Cecil • UKN
WINKY LEARNS A LESSON IN HONESTY • 1914 • Birch Cecil • UKN
WINKY, PARK POLICEMAN • 1914 • Birch Cecil • UKN
WINKY, PHOTOGRAPHER • 1915 • Birch Cecil? • UKN
WINKY TAKES TO FARMING • 1914 • Birch Cecil • UKN
WINKY THE TALLYMAN • 1914 • Birch Cecil • UKN
WINKY TRIES CHICKEN RAISING • 1914 • Birch Cecil • UKN
WINKY WAGGLES THE WICKED WIDOW • 1914 • Birch Cecil • UKN
WINKY WILLY AND THE CHERRIES • 1914 • *Melies* • USA
WINKY WINS • 1914 • Birch Cecil • UKN
WINKY'S BLUE DIAMOND • 1915 • Birch Cecil • UKN
WINKY'S CARVING KNIFE • 1914 • Birch Cecil • UKN
WINKY'S CAT • 1914 • Birch Cecil • UKN
WINKY'S FIREWORKS • 1914 • Birch Cecil • UKN
WINKY'S GUILTY CONSCIENCE • 1914 • Birch Cecil • UKN
WINKY'S INSURANCE POLICY • 1914 • Birch Cecil • UKN
WINKY'S INVISIBLE INK • 1914 • Birch Cecil • UKN
WINKY'S JEALOUSY • 1914 • Birch Cecil • UKN
WINKY'S LIFEBOAT • 1914 • Birch Cecil • UKN
WINKY'S MOTHER-IN-LAW • 1914 • Birch Cecil • UKN
WINKY'S NEXT-DOOR NEIGHBOUR • 1914 • Birch Cecil • UKN
WINKY'S RUSE • 1914 • Birch Cecil • UKN
WINKY'S STRATAGEM • 1914 • Birch Cecil • UKN
WINKY'S WEEKEND • 1914 • Birch Cecil • UKN
WINNER, THE • 1913 • *Brunette Fritzie* • USA
WINNER, THE • 1914 • *Essanay* • USA
WINNER, THE • 1914 • Bracken Bertram • *Balboa* • USA
WINNER, THE • 1915 • Calvert Charles • UKN
WINNER, THE • 1926 • Brown Harry J. • USA
WINNER, THE • 1947 • Frolov Andrei • USS
WINNER, THE see **INVINGATORUL** • 1981
WINNER, THE (USA) see **COEUR GROS COMME CAI, UN** • 1962
WINNER AND THE SPOILS, THE • 1912 • Apfel Oscar • USA
WINNER BY A HARE • 1953 • Sparber I. • ANS • USA
WINNER LOSES, THE • 1913 • *Majestic* • USA
WINNER NEVER QUITS, A • 1986 • Damski Mel • TVM • USA
WINNER TAKE ALL • 1918 • Clifton Elmer • USA
WINNER TAKE ALL • 1923 • Roach Hal • SHT • USA
WINNER TAKE ALL • 1924 • Van Dyke W. S. • USA
WINNER TAKE ALL • 1932 • Del Ruth Roy • USA
WINNER TAKE ALL • 1939 • Brower Otto • USA
WINNER TAKE ALL • 1975 • Bogart Paul • TVM • USA
WINNER TAKE ALL • 1984 • SAF
WINNER TAKE ALL (UKN) see **JOE PALOOKA IN WINNER TAKE ALL** • 1948
WINNER TAKES ALL see **BOULEVARD DU RHUM** • 1971
WINNER WINS, THE • 1914 • Bowman William J. • USA
WINNERS, THE • 1972 • Nofal Emil, Sargeant Roy • SAF • MY WAY
WINNERS AND LOSERS • 1989 • *Grantham Leslie* • MTV • UKN
WINNERS AND SINNERS see **CH'I-MOU-MIAO CHI WU FU-HSING** • 1984
WINNER'S CIRCLE, THE • 1948 • Feist Felix E. • USA
WINNER'S CIRCLE, THE see **PREMIERES ARMES** • 1949
WINNERS II • 1976 • Rautenbach Jans • UKN, SAF
WINNERS / LOOSERS • 1986 • Shandel Thomas • MTV • CND
WINNERS OF THE WEST • 1940 • Beebe Ford, Taylor Ray • SRL • USA
WINNERS OF THE WILDERNESS • 1926 • Van Dyke W. S. • USA
WINNERS TAKE ALL • 1987 • Kiersch Fritz • USA • SUPERCROSS
WINNERS TAKE ALL see **ZOO GANG, THE** • 1985
WINNETOU AND HIS FRIEND OLD FIREHAND see **WINNETOU UND SEIN FREUND OLD FIREHAND** • 1967
WINNETOU AND THE HALF-BREED APACHE see **WINNETOU UND DAS HALBBLUT APANATSCHI** • 1967
WINNETOU I • 1963 • Reinl Harald • FRG, ITL, YGS • VALLE DEI LUNGHI COLTELLI, LA (ITL) ○ VINETU (YGS) ○ REVOLTE DES INDIENS APACHES, LA (FRN) ○ APACHE GOLD (USA) ○ WINNETOU THE WARRIOR
WINNETOU II • 1964 • Reinl Harald • FRG, FRN, ITL • TRESOR DES MONTAGNES BLEUES, LE (FRN) ○ GIORNI DI FUOCO (ITL) ○ VINETU II (YGS) ○ LAST OF THE RENEGADES (USA)
WINNETOU III • 1965 • Reinl Harald • FRG, YGS • VINETU III (YGS) ○ DESPERADO TRAIL, THE (UKN)
WINNETOU THE WARRIOR see **WINNETOU I** • 1963
WINNETOU UND DAS HALBBLUT APANATSCHI • 1967 • Philipp Harald • FRG, YGS • WINNETOU AND THE HALF-BREED APACHE
WINNETOU UND SEIN FREUND OLD FIREHAND • 1967 • Vohrer Alfred • FRG, YGS • WINNETOU AND HIS FRIEND OLD FIREHAND ○ THUNDER AT THE BORDER
WINNETOU UND SHATTERHAND IM TAL DER TOTEN • 1968 • Reinl Harald • FRG, ITL, YGS • WINNETOU UND SHATTERHAND IN DEATH VALLEY
WINNETOU UND SHATTERHAND IN DEATH VALLEY see **WINNETOU UND SHATTERHAND IM TAL DER TOTEN** • 1968
WINNIE • 1981 • Spry Robin • CND
WINNIE COLLINS • 1926 • *De Forest Phonofilms* • SHT • UKN
WINNIE THE POOH AND THE BLUSTERY DAY • 1968 • Reitherman Wolfgang • ANS • USA
WINNIE THE POOH AND THE HONEY TREE • 1965 • Reitherman Wolfgang • ANS • USA
WINNIE THE POOH AND TIGGER TOO • 1974 • Lounsbery John • ANS • USA
WINNIE'S DANCE • 1912 • *Mccoy Gertrude* • USA
WINNIE'S WILD WEDDING • 1918 • *Field Elinor* • USA
WINNING • 1969 • Goldstone James • USA
WINNING A BRIDE • 1919 • Wells Robert • SHT • USA
WINNING A CONTINENT • 1924 • Shaw Harold • USA
WINNING A CONTINENT see **VOORTREKKERS, DE** • 1916
WINNING A HEIRESS • 1917 • Quirk William • SHT • USA
WINNING A HOME • 1920 • *Gibson Hoot* • SHT • USA
WINNING A HUSBAND • 1910 • *Powers* • USA
WINNING A PRINCESS • 1909 • *Urban-Eclipse* • USA
WINNING A PRIZE • 1914 • *Albert Elsie* • USA
WINNING A WIDOW • 1909 • *Selig* • USA
WINNING A WIDOW • 1910 • Collins Alf • UKN
WINNING A WIDOW • 1912 • Olcott Sidney • USA
WINNING A WOMAN • 1925 • *Perrin Jack* • USA
WINNING A WOMAN see **$50,000 REWARD** • 1924
WINNING BACK • 1915 • Barker Reginald • USA
WINNING BACK HIS LOVE • 1910 • Griffith D. W. • USA
WINNING BOAT, THE • 1909 • Olcott Sidney • USA
WINNING COAT, THE • 1909 • Griffith D. W. • USA
WINNING DISCREETLY see **VYHRAVAT POTICHU** • 1985
WINNING FREEDOM see **OSVAJANJE SLOBODE** • 1980
WINNING GIRL, THE • 1919 • Vignola Robert G. • USA
WINNING GOAL, THE • 1920 • Samuelson G. B. • UKN
WINNING GRANDMA • 1918 • Bertram William • USA
WINNING HAND, THE • 1913 • *Burns Robert* • USA
WINNING HAND, THE • 1914 • *Carlyle Francis* • USA
WINNING HAND, THE • 1915 • *Reliance* • USA
WINNING HAND, THE see **TWO OLD SPORTS' GAME OF NAP** • 1900
WINNING HIM BACK • 1919 • *Strand* • SHT • USA
WINNING HIS FIRST CASE • 1914 • *Photo Drama Motion Picture Co* • USA

WINNING HIS SPURS see **PREMIERES ARMES** • 1949
WINNING HIS STRIPES • 1913 • Wilson Frank? • UKN
WINNING HIS STRIPES see **HIGH AND HANDSOME** • 1925
WINNING HIS WIFE • 1913 • *Lubin* • USA
WINNING HIS WIFE • 1919 • Terwilliger George W. • SHT • USA
WINNING IS LOSING • 1912 • *Costello Maurice* • USA
WINNING IS THE ONLY THING • 1974 • Shebib Donald • CND
WINNING LOSER, THE • 1913 • *Majestic* • USA
WINNING LOSER, THE • 1915 • *Swayne Marion* • USA
WINNING MISS, A • 1912 • *Baggot King* • USA
WINNING MISTAKE, A • 1914 • *Lubin* • USA
WINNING NUMBER, THE • 1916 • Greene Clay M. • SHT • USA
WINNING OAR, THE • 1927 • McEveety Bernard F. • USA
WINNING OF BARBARA WORTH, THE • 1926 • King Henry • USA
WINNING OF BEATRICE, THE • 1918 • Franklin Harry L. • USA
WINNING OF DENISE, THE • 1914 • Edwards Walter • USA
WINNING OF FATHER, THE • 1910 • *Essanay* • USA
WINNING OF FREEDOM see **OSVAJANJE SLOBODE** • 1980
WINNING OF HELEN, THE • 1912 • *Majestic* • USA
WINNING OF JESS, THE • 1915 • *Gay Charles* • USA
WINNING OF LA MESA, THE • 1912 • Dwan Allan • USA
WINNING OF MISS CONSTRUE, THE • 1916 • Leonard Robert Z., Kirkland David • SHT • USA
WINNING OF MISS LANGDON, THE • 1910 • Porter Edwin S. • USA
WINNING OF SALLY TEMPLE, THE • 1917 • Melford George • USA
WINNING OF THE MOCKING BIRD • 1918 • Watt Allen • SHT • USA
WINNING OF THE WEST • 1922 • *Aywon Film Corp.* • USA
WINNING OF THE WEST, THE • 1953 • Archainbaud George • USA
WINNING OF WHITE DOVE, THE • 1912 • *Pathe* • USA
WINNING OF WONEGA, HE • 1911 • *Bison* • USA
WINNING PAIR, A • 1925 • Lamont Charles • USA
WINNING PAIR, THE • 1917 • Chaudet Louis W. • SHT • USA
WINNING PAPA'S CONSENT • 1911 • *Reliance* • USA
WINNING POSITION, THE see **NOBODY'S PERFECT** • 1968
WINNING PUNCH, THE • 1910 • Salter Harry • *Imp* • USA
WINNING PUNCH, THE • 1912 • Salter Harry • *Victor* • USA
WINNING PUNCH, THE • 1913 • Dillon Eddie • USA
WINNING PUNCH, THE • 1916 • Cline Eddie • SHT • USA
WINNING RUSE, A • 1913 • *Imp* • USA
WINNING STREAK • 1984 • Wilson Jim • USA
WINNING STROKE, THE • 1913 • *Frontier* • USA
WINNING STROKE, THE • 1919 • Dillon Eddie • USA
WINNING TEAM, THE • 1952 • Seiler Lewis • USA
WINNING THE FUTURITY • 1926 • Dunlap Scott R. • USA
WINNING THE GLOVES • 1898 • Williamson James • UKN
WINNING THE LATONIA DERBY • 1912 • *Baggot King* • USA
WINNING THE MAN OVER • 1915 • *Ab* • USA
WINNING THE V.C. • 1900 • *Mitchell & Kenyon* • UKN
WINNING THE WEST • 1946 • Donnelly Eddie • ANS • USA
WINNING THE WEST see **LIGHT OF WESTERN STARS, THE** • 1930
WINNING THE WIDOW • 1915 • Coyle Walter • USA
WINNING THE WIDOW • 1916 • Beaudine William • SHT • USA
WINNING THROUGH (UKN) see **CLASSMATES** • 1924
WINNING TICKET, THE • 1934 • Reisner Charles F. • USA
WINNING TICKET, THE • 1938 • *Captain And The Kids* • ANS • USA
WINNING TRICK, THE • 1914 • North Wilfred • USA
WINNING WALLOP, THE • 1926 • Hutchison Charles • USA
WINNING WASH, THE • 1915 • *Hamilton Lloyd V.* • USA
WINNING WAY, THE • 1910 • Melies Gaston • USA
WINNING WAY, THE (UKN) see **ALL AMERICAN, THE** • 1953
WINNING WHISKERS, THE • 1914 • *Hamilton Lloyd V.* • USA
WINNING WINSOME WINNIE • 1915 • Ince John • USA
WINNING WITH WITS • 1922 • Mitchell Howard M. • USA
WINNINGS OF FRANKIE WALLS, THE • 1980 • Lavut Martin • MTV • CND
WINNINGS OF SILAS PEGG, THE • 1912 • *Rex* • USA
WINONA • 1910 • *Lanning Frank* • USA
WINONA • 1912 • *Champion* • USA
WINS OUT • 1932 • Lantz Walter, Nolan William • ANS • USA
WINSLOW BOY, THE • 1948 • Asquith Anthony • UKN
WINSOME BUT WISE • 1912 • *Solax* • USA
WINSOME WIDOW, THE • 1912 • Raymond Charles? • UKN
WINSOME WINNIE • 1914 • *Beauty* • USA
WINSOME WINNIE'S WAY • 1913 • *Edison* • USA
WINSOR MCCAY • 1911 • *Mccay Winsor* • USA
WINSOR MCCAY AND HIS JERSEY SKEETERS • 1916 • McCay Winsor • SHT • USA
WINSTANLEY • 1975 • Brownlow Kevin • UKN
WINSTON CHURCHILL • 1986 • Jarrott Charles • MTV • CND
WINSTON LEE AND HIS ORCHESTRA NOS.1-8 • 1954 • Shepherd Horace • SHS • UKN
WINSTONE AFFAIR, THE see **MAN IN THE MIDDLE** • 1963
WINTER • 1930 • Gillett Burt • ANS • USA
WINTER see **TUNG NUAN** • 1967
WINTER see **HIGH HOPES** • 1988
WINTER 14 JULIE, DIE • 1977 • SAF
WINTER A GO-GO • 1965 • Benedict Richard • USA
WINTER-BORN see **VINTERBORN** • 1978
WINTER CAMELLIA see **KANTSUBAKI** • 1921
WINTER CARNIVAL • 1939 • Reisner Charles F. • USA
WINTER CARNIVAL • 1949 • Blais Roger • DCS • CND • CARNAVAL D'HIVER
WINTER CHILDREN see **VINTERBORN** • 1978
WINTER CITY see **WINTERSTADT** • 1982
WINTER COMES EARLY • 1977 • McCowan George • CND
WINTER COMES TO KOREA • 1953-54 • Devlin Bernard • DCS • CND
WINTER CONSTRUCTION: IT CAN BE DONE • 1958 • Brittain Don • DOC • CND
WINTER DIARY (UKN) see **DIARIO DE INVIERNO** • 1988
WINTER DRAWS ON • 1948 • *Paramount* • ANS • USA
WINTER DREAMS • 1957 • Frankenheimer John • MTV • USA
WINTER DUSK see **ZIMOVY ZMIERZCH** • 1957
WINTER FLIGHT • 1984 • Battersby Roy • UKN
WINTER FOOTAGE, THE • 1964 • Jacobs Ken • USA
WINTER GARDEN • 1951 • Halas John • ANS • UKN
WINTER GUESTS • 1968 • Bostan Ion • DOC • RMN
WINTER HEAT • 1977 • Goddard Claude • USA
WINTER HOLIDAYS see **VACANZE D'INVERNO** • 1959
WINTER IN AN ARCTIC VILLAGE • 1931 • Finnie Richard S. • DOC • CND
WINTER IN CANADA • 1953 • Cote Guy-L. • DCS • CND • HIVER AU CANADA, L'
WINTER IN LISBON, A • 1990 • Zorrilla Jose Antonio • PRT
WINTER IN MALLORCA see **JURTZENKA** • 1969
WINTER IN NARITA see **SANRIZUKA NO FUYU** • 1970
WINTER IN THE DELTA • 1957 • Iliesu Mirel • DOC • RMN
WINTER INN see **FUYU NO YADO** • 1938
WINTER KEPT US WARM • 1965 • Secter David • CND
WINTER KILL • 1974 • Taylor Jud • TVM • USA • WINTERKILL
WINTER KILL • 1977 • Kent Larry • CND
WINTER KILLS • 1979 • Richert William • USA
WINTER LIGHT (UKN) see **NATTVARDSGASTERNA** • 1963
WINTER MEETING • 1948 • Windust Bretaigne • USA
WINTER OF BLACK SNOW see **RUSKAN JALKEEN** • 1979
WINTER OF OUR DISCONTENT, THE • 1983 • Hussein Waris • TVM • USA
WINTER OF OUR DREAMS, THE • 1981 • Duigan John • ASL
WINTER ON THE FARM • 1933 • Cherry Evelyn Spice • UKN
WINTER PEOPLE, THE • 1988 • Kotcheff Ted • USA
WINTER QUARTERS • Keene Ralph • DOC • UKN
WINTER QUARTERS see **CUARTELES DE INVIERNO** • 1984
WINTER RATES see **OUT OF SEASON** • 1975
WINTER SIROCCO see **SIROKKO** • 1969
WINTER SOLDIER • 1972 • Hamrlin Ken • DOC • USA
WINTER SONGS • 1969 • Gerson Barry • SHT • USA
WINTER SPORTS • 1906 • UKN
WINTER SPORTS AND PASTIMES OF CORONADO BEACH • 1912 • Dwan Allan • DOC • USA • CORONADO NEW YEAR'S DAY
WINTER STORAGE • 1949 • Hannah Jack • ANS • USA
WINTER STORMS (USA) see **WINTER STURME** • 1938
WINTER STRAW RIDE • 1906 • Porter Edwin S. • USA
WINTER STURME • 1938 • Waschneck Erich • FRG • WINTER STORMS (USA)
WINTER SUN see **GET BACK** • 1972
WINTER TAN, A • 1988 • Burroughs Jackie, Frizzell John, Weissman Aerlyn, Clark Louise, Walker John • CND
WINTER TIME • 1943 • Brahm John • USA
WINTER WAR, THE see **TALVISOTA** • 1989
WINTER WAYFARER • 1986 • SKR
WINTER WEEKEND • 1952 • Devlin Bernard • DCS • CND • MESURE POUR RIEN, UNE
WINTER WIND (USA) see **SIROKKO** • 1969
WINTER WOMAN • 1983 • Kim Ho-Sun • SKR
WINTER WONDERLAND • 1947 • Vorhaus Bernard • USA
WINTERCHILDREN see **VINTERBORN** • 1978
WINTERHAWK • 1975 • Pierce Charles B. • USA
WINTERING IN JAKOBSFIELD see **ZIMOVANJE U JAKOBSFELDU** • 1976
WINTERKILL see **WINTER KILL** • 1974
WINTERMARCHEN • 1971 • von Mechow Ulf • FRG • DAVID AND THE ICE AGE
WINTERMELODIE • 1946 • Wieser Eduard • AUS, FRN • AMOURS DE BLANCHE NEIGE, LES (FRN)
WINTERNACHTSTRAUM • 1935 • von Bolvary Geza • FRG
WINTER'S DISCONTENT • 1971 • Woods Grahame • CND
WINTER'S NIGHT IN GAGRA, A • 1986 • Chakhnazarov Karen • USS
WINTERS PAST • 1985 • Jackson G. Philip • MTV • CND
WINTERS SPORTS • 1971 • Leiterman Richard • DOC • CND
WINTER'S TALE, A • 1945 • Ivanov-Vano Ivan • ANS • USS
WINTER'S TALE, A • 1953 • Deane Charles • UKN
WINTER'S TALE, THE • 1910 • Marston Theodore • USA
WINTER'S TALE, THE • 1968 • Dunlop Frank • UKN
WINTERSET • 1936 • Santell Alfred • USA
WINTERSOLDIER • 1972 • USA
WINTERSTADT • 1982 • Giger Bernhard • SWT • WINTERTOWN ○ WINTER CITY
WINTERSTURME • 1924 • Rippert Otto • FRG
WINTERTOWN see **WINTERSTADT** • 1982
WINTHRUP DIAMONDS, THE • 1915 • *Jones Edgar* • USA
WINTON WAKES UP see **BRINGIN' HOME THE BACON** • 1924
WINZERIN VON LANGENLOIS, DIE • 1957 • Konig Hans H. • AUS • UND SOWAS WILL ERWACHSEN SEIN
WIOSENNE PRZYGODY KRASNALA • 1959 • Giersz Witold • ANS • PLN • SPRING ADVENTURES OF A GNOME, THE ○ DWARF'S SPRING ADVENTURES, A ○ GNOMES IN SPRING
WIOSKA W TAJDZE • 1968 • Bossak Jerzy (c/d) • DOC • PLN • VILLAGE IN THE TAIGA, A
WIPE AWAY YOUR TEARS see **HAPUSLAH AIRMATAMU** • 1975
WIPE YER FEET • 1915 • MacGregor Norval • USA
WIPEOUT! see **BOSS, IL** • 1973
WIPEOUT see **UNDER THE BOARDWALK** • 1988
WIPES • Williams Lloyd Michael • SHT • USA
WIPING SOMETHING OFF THE SLATE • 1900 • Hepworth Cecil M. • UKN
WIR ARMEN, KLEINEN MADCHEN • 1926 • Krause Karl Otto • FRG
WIR BEIDEN LIEBTEN KATHERINA • 1945 • Rabenalt Arthur M. • FRG
WIR BITTEN ZUM TANZ • 1941 • Marischka Hubert • FRG
WIR BUMMELN UM DIE WELT • 1949 • Weidenmann Alfred • FRG
WIR FAHREN GEGEN DEN WIND see **FLORENTINE** • 1937
WIR GINGEN EINEN SCHWEREN PFAD • 1918 • Beck Ludwig • FRG
WIR HABEN'S GESCHAFFT • 1916 • Hofer Franz • FRG
WIR HALTEN FEST UND TREU ZUSAMMEN • 1929 • Nossen Herbert • FRG
WIR HAU'N DIE PAUKER IN DIE PFANNE • 1969 • Reinl Harald • FRG
WIR KELLERKINDER • 1960 • Wiedermann Jochen • FRG
WIR KONNEN SOVIEL • 1976 • Tuchtenhagen Gisela, Wildenhahn Klaus • FRG
WIR LASSEN UNS SCHEIDEN • 1968 • Reschke Ingrid • GDR • WE ARE GETTING DIVORCED
WIR MACHEN MUSIK • 1942 • Kautner Helmut • FRG
WIR MAHLEN MI WIND • 1979 • von Swieykowski Heiko • FRG
WIR SCHALTEN UM AUF HOLLYWOOD • 1931 • Reicher Frank, Reisner Charles F. • FRG, USA • HOLLYWOOD REVUE OF 1929
WIR SCHUTZEN, WAS WIR SCHAFFEN • 1968 • Weschke Gunter • GDR • WE PROTECT WHAT WE MAKE
WIR SEH'N UND WIEDER • 1945 • Mayring Philipp L. • FRG
WIR SIND VOM K UND K INFANTERIE-REGIMENT • 1926 • Oswald Richard • FRG
WIR SIND VOM K UND K INFANTERIE-REGIMENT • Hochbaum Werner • FRG
WIR TANZEN AUF DEM REGENBOGEN • 1952 • Rabenalt Arthur M. • FRG, ITL
WIR TANZEN UM DIE WELT • 1939 • Anton Karl • FRG
WIR VON GOTTES GNADEN.. HOHEIT VATER UND SOHN • 1918 • Reicher Ernst • FRG • HOHEIT VATER UND SON
WIR WERDEN DAS KIND SCHON SCHAUKELN • 1952 • Emo E. W. • AUS • SCHAM DICH, BRIGITTE
WIR WOLLEN NIEMALS AUSEINANDERGEHN • 1960 • Reinl Harald • FRG
WIR WUNDERKINDER • 1958 • Hoffmann Kurt • FRG • AREN'T WE WONDERFUL?
WIR-ZWEI • 1970 • Schamoni Ulrich • FRG • WIR ZWEI ○ WE TWO
WIR ZWEI see **WIR-ZWEI** • 1970
WIRBEL DES VERDERBENS see **DAMON DER WELT 2** • 1919
WIRD GEHEIRATET, DER • 1920 • *Treumann Wanda* • FRG
WIRE CHIEF'S REWARD, THE • 1914 • *Kalem* • USA
WIRE DOG see **PERRO DE ALAMBRE** • 1979
WIRE PULLERS, THE • 1916 • Worthington William • SHT • USA
WIRED • 1989 • Peerce Larry • USA
WIRED TO KILL • 1986 • Schaeffer Franky • USA • BOOBY TRAP
WIRELESS • 1915 • Lorraine Harry • UKN
WIRELESS MIRACLE, A • 1912 • *Reliance* • USA
WIRELESS RESCUE, A • 1915 • Marston Theodore • USA
WIRELESS ROMANCE, A • 1910 • *Edison* • USA
WIRELESS VOICE, THE • 1914 • Lewis Edgar • USA
WIRETAPPERS • 1956 • Ross Dick • USA
WIRTIN VOM WORTHERSEE, DIE • 1952 • von Borsody Eduard • FRG, AUS • WIRTIN VON MARIA WORTH, DIE
WIRTIN VON DER LAHN, DIE see **SUSANNE -DIE WIRTIN VON DER LAHN** • 1967
WIRTIN VON MARIA WORTH, DIE see **WIRTIN VOM WORTHERSEE, DIE** • 1952
WIRTIN ZUM WEISSEN ROSS'L, DIE • 1943 • Anton Karl • FRG
WIRTIN ZUR GOLDENEN KRONE, DIE • 1955 • Lingen Theo • AUS
WIRTSHAUS IM SPESSART, DAS • 1923 • Wenter Adolf • FRG • KALTE HERZ, DAS ○ COLD HEART, THE ○ TAVERN IN SPESSART, THE
WIRTSHAUS IM SPESSART, DAS • 1958 • Hoffmann Kurt • FRG • SPESSART INN, THE (USA) ○ INN AT SPESSART, THE
WIRTSHAUS VON DARTMOOR, DAS • 1964 • Zehetgruber Rudolf • FRG • INN ON DARTMOOR, THE (USA)
WISADA AL-KHALIYA, AL- see **WESSADA EL KHALIA, EL** • 1957
WISADAT OULKHALIA, EL see **WESSADA EL KHALIA, EL** • 1957
WISCONSIN UNDER FIRE • 1924 • *Pictorial Sales Bureau* • DOC • USA
WISDOM • 1986 • Estevez Emilio • USA
WISDOM OF BROTHER AMBROSE, THE • 1911 • Fitzhamon Lewin • UKN
WISDOM OF THE WHITE MAN, THE • 1916 • *Hiawatha* • USA
WISE ARISTOTLE GETS STILL WISER see **JAK SE MOUDRY ARISTOTELES STAL JESTE MOUDREJSIM** • 1970
WISE BABY see **FUGITIVES** • 1929
WISE BLOOD • 1979 • Huston John • USA
WISE CRACKER, THE • 1923 • Kenton Erle C. • SHT • USA
WISE DETECTIVES, THE • 1914 • Ritchey C. W. • USA
WISE DRUGGIST, THE • 1910 • *Imp* • USA
WISE DUMMY, A • 1916 • Fahrney Milton • USA
WISE DUMMY, A • 1917 • Hutchinson Craig • SHT • USA
WISE FLIES • 1930 • Fleischer Dave • ANS • USA
WISE FOOL, A • 1921 • Melford George • USA • MONEY MASTER, THE
WISE GIRL • 1937 • Jason Leigh • USA • WOMEN HAVE A WAY
WISE GIRLS • 1929 • Hopper E. Mason • USA • KEMPY
WISE GUY, THE • 1926 • Lloyd Frank • USA • INTO THE NIGHT (UKN) ○ INTO THE LIGHT
WISE GUYS • 1937 • Langdon Harry • UKN
WISE GUYS • 1986 • De Palma Brian • USA
WISE GUYS, THE • 1914 • *Shields Ernest* • USA
WISE GUYS, THE (USA) see **GRANDES GUEULES, LES** • 1965
WISE GUYS PREFER BRUNETTES • 1926 • Roach Hal • SHT • USA
WISE HUSBANDS • 1921 • Reicher Frank • USA
WISE JUDGE, A • 1913 • *Eclair* • USA
WISE KID, THE • 1922 • Browning Tod • USA • KIND DEEDS
WISE LITTLE HEN, THE • 1934 • Jackson Wilfred • ANS • USA
WISE MAN AND THE FOOL, THE • 1916 • Reynolds Lynn • SHT • USA
WISE OLD ELEPHANT, A • 1913 • Campbell Colin • USA
WISE OWL • 1940 • Iwerks Ub • ANS • USA
WISE PURCHASE, A • 1918 • *Griffith Corinne* • SHT • USA
WISE QUACKERS • 1949 • Freleng Friz • ANS • USA
WISE QUACKING DUCK, THE • 1943 • Clampett Robert • ANS • USA
WISE QUACKS • 1939 • Clampett Robert • ANS • USA
WISE QUACKS • 1953 • Davis Mannie • ANS • USA
WISE RUBE, A • 1914 • *Brennan John E.* • USA
WISE SON, A • 1923 • Rosen Phil • USA
WISE TREES, MAGICAL TREES see **SABIOS ARBOLES, MAGIOCS ARBOLES** • 1988
WISE VILLAGE, THE • 1972 • Donev Donyo • ANS • BUL

WISE VIRGIN, THE • 1924 • Ingraham Lloyd • USA
WISE WAITER, A • 1916 • Metcalfe Earl • SHT • USA
WISE WIFE, THE • 1927 • Hopper E. Mason • USA
WISE WIMMIN • 1929 • Roberts Stephen • SHT • USA
WISE WITCH OF FAIRYLAND, THE • 1912 • *Solax* • USA
WISE WIVES • 1919 • Lyons Eddie, Moran Lee • SHT • USA
WISEGUY • 1987 • Holcomb Rod • USA
WISER AGE, THE (USA) see **ONNA NO ZA** • 1962
WISER SEX, THE • 1932 • Viertel Berthold • USA
WISEST FOOL, THE • 1919 • *Jester* • SHT • USA
WISH see **ABHILASHA** • 1968
WISH, THE • 1970 • Duckworth Martin • DOC • CND
WISH FULFILLED, A • 1974 • Druzhinina S. • USS
WISH-FULFILMENT see **ICHHAPURAN** • 1969
WISH MACHINE, THE see **STALKER** • 1979
WISH WHATEVER YOU WANT • 1962 • Nepp Jozsef • ANM • HNG
WISH YOU WERE HERE • 1987 • Leland David • UKN
WISHBONE, THE • 1908 • *Vitagraph* • USA
WISHBONE, THE • 1917 • *U.s.m.p.* • USA
WISHBONE, THE • 1933 • Maude Arthur • UKN
WISHBONE CUTTER • 1978 • Smith Earl E. • USA • SHADOW OF CHIKARA, THE
WISHED ON MABEL • 1915 • Normand Mabel • USA
WISHES • 1934 • Kellino W. P. • UKN
WISHING CHARM, THE • 1909 • *Centaur* • USA
WISHING LAMP, THE • 1916 • Matthews H. C. • SHT • USA
WISHING MACHINE, THE see **CERFVOLANT DU BOUT DU MONDE, LE** • 1957
WISHING MACHINE, THE (USA) see **AUTOMAT NA PRANI** • 1967
WISHING RING, THE • 1914 • Tourneur Maurice • USA
WISHING RING, THE • 1916 • Ellis Robert • USA
WISHING RING MAN, THE • 1919 • Smith David • USA
WISHING SEAT, THE • 1913 • Dwan Allan • USA
WISHING STONE, THE • 1915 • Otto Henry • USA
WISHING TREE, THE see **DREVO ZHELANYA** • 1976
WISHING WELL (USA) see **HAPPINESS OF THREE WOMEN, THE** • 1954
WISKOTTENS, DIE • 1926 • Bergen Arthur • FRG
WISP O' THE WOODS • 1919 • Willoughby Lewis • UKN
WISSELWACHTER, DE • 1987 • Stelling Jos • NTH • POINTSMAN, THE
WISTARIA • 1911 • *Maurice Mary* • USA
WISTERIA see **LILA AKAC** • 1934
WISTFUL WIDOW, THE (UKN) see **WISTFUL WIDOW OF WAGON GAP, THE** • 1947
WISTFUL WIDOW OF WAGON GAP, THE • 1947 • Barton Charles T. • USA • WISTFUL WIDOW, THE (UKN)
WIT AND WORLD OF G. BERNARD SHAW, THE • 1972 • Rasky Harry • CND
WIT SLUIER, DIE • 1973 • De Villiers Dirk • SAF • WHITE VEIL, THE
WIT WINS • 1920 • King Burton L. • USA
WITAJ OJCZYZNO! • 1958 • Ziarnik Jerzy • DOC • PLN • HAIL MOTHERLAND!
WITBLITZ AND PEACH BRANDY • 1978 • SAF
WITCH see **HAXAN** • 1955
WITCH, THE • 1908 • Brooke Van Dyke • USA
WITCH, THE • 1909 • *Le Lion* • FRN
WITCH, THE • 1913 • *Francis Alec B.* • USA
WITCH, THE • 1916 • Powell Frank • USA
WITCH, THE • 1976 • Cimber Matt • USA • WITCH WHO CAME FROM THE SEA, THE
WITCH, THE • 1982 • Roberson James W. • USA
WITCH, THE see **STREGA, LA** • 1907
WITCH, THE see **HEXE, DIE** • 1921
WITCH, THE see **BRUJA, LA** • 1954
WITCH, THE see **HEXE, DIE** • 1954
WITCH, THE see **ONI** • 1972
WITCH, THE see **SUPERSTITION** • 1982
WITCH, THE (USA) see **FEE CARABOSSE: OU, LE POIGNARD FATAL, LA** • 1906
WITCH, THE (USA) see **NOITA PALAA ELAMAAN** • 1952
WITCH, THE (USA) see **STREGA IN AMORE, LA** • 1966
WITCH AND THE BICYCLE, THE see **HEKSEN OG CYKLISTEN** • 1909
WITCH AND THE BICYCLIST, THE (USA) see **HEKSEN OG CYKLISTEN** • 1909
WITCH AND THE CYCLIST, THE see **HEKSEN OG CYKLISTEN** • 1909
WITCH AND WARLOCK see **WITCHCRAFT** • 1964
WITCH BENEATH THE SEA, THE see **MARIZINIA** • 1962
WITCH BITCH see **DEATH SPAR** • 1988
WITCH CRAFTY • 1955 • Smith Paul J. • ANS • USA
WITCH DOCTOR • 1985 • SAF
WITCH DOCTOR see **MEN OF TWO WORLDS** • 1946
WITCH DOCTOR, THE see **ZNACHOR** • 1981
WITCH DOCTOR AND THE VIRGIN, THE see **KWAHERI** • 1964
WITCH FLIGHT • 1977 • Emes Ian • UKN
WITCH GIRL, THE • 1914 • Edwin Walter • USA
WITCH HAS SUCKED THEM UP, THE see **SE LOS CHUPO LA BRUJA** • 1957
WITCH HOUSE, THE see **MALDICION DE LA LLORONA, LA** • 1961
WITCH HUNT • 1987 • Chobocky Barbara • DOC • ASL
WITCH HUNT see **HAJKA** • 1978
WITCH HUNT, THE see **FORFOLGELSEN** • 1981
WITCH IN LOVE, THE (UKN) see **STREGA IN AMORE, LA** • 1966
WITCH KILLER OF BLACKMOOR see **PROCESO DE LAS BRUJAS, EL** • 1970
WITCH LOVE see **AMOR BRUJO, EL** • 1967
WITCH OF ABRUZZI, THE • 1911 • *Le Lion* • FRN
WITCH OF CARABOSSE, THE • 1910 • *Urban-Eclipse* • UKN
WITCH OF PENGELLY, THE see **STARFISH, THE** • 1952
WITCH OF SALEM, THE • 1913 • West Raymond B. • USA
WITCH OF SALEM TOWN, A • 1915 • Henderson Lucius • USA
WITCH OF SEVILLE, THE see **STREGA DE SIVIGLIA, IL** • 1911
WITCH OF THE DARK HOUSE, THE • 1916 • Horne James W. • SHT • USA
WITCH OF THE EVERGLADES, THE • 1911 • Turner Otis • USA
WITCH OF THE GLEN, THE • 1910 • *Warwick* • UKN
WITCH OF THE MOUNTAINS, THE • 1916 • *Nichols Margaret* • SHT • USA
WITCH OF THE RANGE, THE • 1911 • Dwan Allan • USA
WITCH OF THE RUINS, THE • 1910 • *Pathe* • FRN
WITCH OF THE WELSH MOUNTAINS, THE • 1912 • Northcote Sidney • UKN
WITCH OF TIMBUKTU see **DEVIL DOLL, THE** • 1936
WITCH OF WOOKEY AND THE DRUNKEN SAILOR • 1949 • UKN
WITCH RETURNS TO LIFE, THE see **NOITA PALAA ELAMAAN** • 1952
WITCH WHO CAME FROM THE SEA, THE see **WITCH, THE** • 1976
WITCH WITHOUT A BROOM, A (USA) see **BRUJA SIN ESCOBA, UNA** • 1966
WITCH WOMAN, THE • 1918 • Vale Travers • USA
WITCH WOMAN, THE (USA) see **PRASTANKAN** • 1920
WITCHBOARD • 1986 • Tenney Kevin S. • USA
WITCHCRAFT • 1916 • Reicher Frank • USA
WITCHCRAFT • 1964 • Sharp Don • UKN • WITCH AND WARLOCK
WITCHCRAFT • 1965 • Bnisso George, La Freniere Kathy, Robinson Alice • SHT • USA
WITCHCRAFT • 1965 • Vittalachari B. • IND
WITCHCRAFT • 1988 • Spera Robert • USA
WITCHCRAFT see **SORTILEGES** • 1944
WITCHCRAFT see **MALEFICIO** • 1954
WITCHCRAFT see **NAKED GODDESS, THE** • 1959
WITCHCRAFT see **GHOSTHOUSE 2** • 1988
WITCHCRAFT 2 • 1989 • Woods Mark • USA • WITCHCRAFT PART 2: THE TEMPTRESS
WITCHCRAFT '70 (USA) see **ANGELI BIANCHI.. ANGELI NERI** • 1969
WITCHCRAFT PART 2: THE TEMPTRESS see **WITCHCRAFT 2** • 1989
WITCHCRAFT THROUGH THE AGES (UKN) see **HAXAN** • 1921
WITCHERY see **GHOSTHOUSE 2** • 1988
WITCHES see **HEKSENE FRA DEN FORSTENEDE SKOG** • 1977
WITCHES, THE • 1966 • Frankel Cyril • UKN • DEVIL'S OWN, THE (USA)
WITCHES, THE • 1989 • Roeg Nicolas • UKN, USA
WITCHES, THE see **STREGHE, LE** • 1967
WITCHES, THE see **DELITTO DEL DIAVOLO, IL** • 1970
WITCHES AND THE GRINNYGOG, THE • 1983 • *Loftin Zoe* • MTV • UKN
WITCHES ATTACK, THE see **SANTO ATACA LAS BRUJAS** • 1964
WITCHES' BALLAD, THE • 1910 • *Ambrosio* • ITL
WITCHES' BREW • 1980 • Shorr Richard, Strock Herbert L. • USA • WHICH WITCH IS WHICH?
WITCHES' BRIDGE, THE see **PONTE DELLE STREGHE, IL** • 1909
WITCHES' BROOM, THE • 1957 • *Famous Cartoons* • ANS • USA
WITCHES' CAVERN, THE • 1909 • *Selig* • USA
WITCHES CURSE, THE see **MACISTE ALL'INFERNO** • 1962
WITCHES FROM THE STONED FOREST see **HEKSENE FRA DEN FORSTENEDE SKOG** • 1977
WITCHES' MOUNTAIN see **MONTE DE LAS BRUJAS, EL** • 1970
WITCHES MOUNTAIN, THE • *Shepard Patty* • USA
WITCHES' NIGHT see **HAXNATTEN** • 1937
WITCHES OF EASTWICK, THE • 1987 • Miller George • USA
WITCHES OF SALEM, THE see **SORCIERES DE SALEM, LES** • 1957
WITCHES' SABBATH see **BOSZORKANYSZOMBAT** • 1984
WITCHES' SPELL, THE • 1910 • *Urban* • USA
WITCHES: VIOLATED AND TORTURED TO DEATH (USA) see **HEXEN: GESCHANDET UND ZU TODE GEQUALT** • 1972
WITCHES' WALL, THE see **SCIANA CZAROWNIC** • 1967
WITCHFINDER GENERAL • 1968 • Reeves Michael • UKN • EDGAR ALLAN POE'S CONQUEROR WORM ○ CONQUEROR WORM (USA)
WITCHFIRE • 1985 • Privitera Vincent J. • USA
WITCHHAMMER see **KLADIVO NA CARODEJNICE** • 1969
WITCHING, THE see **NECROMANCY** • 1972
WITCHING EYES, THE • 1929 • *Stern Ernest (P)* • USA
WITCHING HOUR see **SPELLBINDER** • 1988
WITCHING HOUR, THE • 1916 • Irving George • USA
WITCHING HOUR, THE • 1921 • Taylor William D. • USA
WITCHING HOUR, THE • 1934 • Hathaway Henry • USA
WITCHING HOUR, THE see **HORA BRUJA, LA** • 1985
WITCHING TIME • 1985 • Leaver Don • TVM • UKN
WITCHITA FILM • 1960 • Branaman Bob • USA
WITCHMAKER, THE • 1969 • Brown William O. • USA
WITCH'S CAT, THE see **MIGHTY MOUSE IN THE WITCH'S CAT** • 1948
WITCH'S CAVE, THE • 1906 • *Pathe* • FRN
WITCH'S CURSE, THE (USA) see **MACISTE ALL'INFERNO** • 1962
WITCH'S DONKEY, THE • 1909 • *Pathe* • FRN
WITCH'S FIDDLE, THE • 1924 • Foster Peter Le Neve • SHT • UKN
WITCH'S LURE, THE • 1921 • *Davide* • USA
WITCH'S MIRROR, THE (USA) see **ESPEJO DE LA BRUJA, EL** • 1960
WITCH'S NECKLACE, THE • 1912 • *Solax* • USA
WITCH'S REVENGE, THE (USA) see **SORCIER, LE** • 1903
WITCH'S RIDERS, THE see **JINETES DE LA BRUJA, LOS** • 1965
WITCH'S SECRET, THE • 1907 • *Pathe* • FRN
WITCH'S SEX, THE see **SESSO DELLA STREGA, IL** • 1972
WITCH'S SONG, THE see **HEXENLIED, DAS** • 1919
WITCH'S SWORD, THE • *Kang Wei* • HKG
WITCH'S TANGLED HARE, A • 1959 • Levitow Abe • ANS • USA
WITH A GIRL AT STAKE • 1915 • Franz Joseph J. • USA
WITH A GRAIN OF SALT • 1913 • *Nestor* • USA
WITH A KODAK • 1912 • Lehrman Henry, Sennett Mack (Spv) • USA
WITH A LIFE AT STAKE • 1916 • Bertram William • SHT • USA
WITH A PIECE OF STRING • 1906 • *Walturdaw* • UKN
WITH A SMILE see **AVEC LE SOURIRE** • 1936
WITH A SONG IN MY HEART • 1952 • Lang Walter • USA
WITH ALL HER HEART • 1920 • Wilson Frank • UKN
WITH ALL MY HEART see **ONNAGOKORO WA HITOSUJI NI** • 1954
WITH AND WITHOUT YOU • 1974 • Nakhapetov Rodion • USS
WITH BABIES AND BANNERS • 1976 • Grey Lorraine • DOC • USA
WITH BATED BREATH see **COL CUORE IN GOLA** • 1967
WITH BEAUTY AND SORROW see **UTSUKUSHISA TO KANASHIMI TO** • 1965
WITH BEST DISHES • 1939 • Schwarzwald Milton • SHT • USA
WITH BIRTLES ON THE TRACK OF SIR ROSS SMITH see **THROUGH AUSTRALIAN WILDS** • 1919
WITH BLOOD AND ROPE • 1989 • Zsigmond Dezso, Erdelyi Janos • DOC • HNG
WITH BOTH LEGS IN THE SKY • 1968 • Junge Winifried • DOC • GDR
WITH BRIDGES BURNED • 1910 • *Edison* • USA
WITH BRIDGES BURNED • 1915 • Miller Ashley • USA
WITH BUFFALO BILL ON THE U.P. TRAIL see **BUFFALO BILL ON THE U.P. TRAIL** • 1926
WITH BYRD AT THE SOUTH POLE • 1930 • *Paramount-Publix Corp.* • DOC • USA
WITH CAPTAIN SCOTT, R.N., TO THE SOUTH POLE • 1911 • Ponting Herbert • UKN • GREAT WHITE SILENCE, THE ○ NINETY DEGREES SOUTH ○ UNDYING STORY OF CAPTAIN SCOTT AND ANIMAL LIFE IN THE ANTARCTIC, THE
WITH CAPTAIN SCOTT TO THE SOUTH POLE see **NINETY DEGREES SOUTH** • 1933
WITH CAR AND CAMERA AROUND THE WORLD • 1929 • *Wanderwell Aloha* • DOC • USA
WITH CHILDREN AT THE SEASIDE see **S DETSA NA MORE** • 1972
WITH CLEAN HANDS see **CU MIINILE CURATE** • 1972
WITH DADDY'S AID • 1915 • *Luna* • USA
WITH DAVY CROCKETT AT THE FALL OF THE ALAMO see **DAVY CROCKETT AT THE FALL OF THE ALAMO** • 1926
WITH DEATH ON YOUR BACK see **CON LA MUERTE EN LA ESPALDA** • 1967
WITH EDGED TOOLS • 1919 • SAF
WITH EUSTACE IN AFRICA • 1922 • *Eustace Harry K.* • USA
WITH EYES SO BLUE AND TENDER • 1913 • *Selig* • USA
WITH FAITH IN GOD see **S VEROM U BOGA** • 1932
WITH FATHER'S HELP • 1915 • Christie Al • USA
WITH FATHER'S HELP • 1922 • Hyland Peggy • UKN
WITH FEAR AND PASSION see **ME FOVO KE PATHOS** • 1972
WITH FIRE AND SWORD see **COL FERRO E COL FUOCO** • 1962
WITH GAGARIN TO THE STARS see **PERVI REJS V ZVEZDAM** • 1961
WITH GENERAL CUSTER AT LITTLE BIG HORN see **GENERAL CUSTER AT THE LITTLE BIG HORN** • 1926
WITH GENERAL PANCHO VILLA IN MEXICO • 1914 • *Rosher Charles (Ph)* • USA
WITH GUNILLA see **TILLSAMMANS MED GUNILLA MANDAG KVALL OCH TISDAG** • 1965
WITH GUNILLA MONDAY EVENING AND TUESDAY see **TILLSAMMANS MED GUNILLA MANDAG KVALL OCH TISDAG** • 1965
WITH HEART IN MOUTH see **COL CUORE IN GOLA** • 1967
WITH HER CARD • 1909 • Griffith D. W. • USA
WITH HER RIVAL'S HELP • 1913 • Smalley Phillips • USA
WITH HOOPS OF STEEL • 1918 • Howe Eliot • USA
WITH HUMAN INSTINCT • 1913 • Martinek H. O.? • UKN
WITH INTENT TO KILL • 1984 • Robe Mike • TVM • USA
WITH INTEREST TO DATE • 1911 • *Edison* • USA
WITH KINGSFORD SMITH TO NEW ZEALAND • 1928 • ASL
WITH KIT CARSON OVER THE GREAT DIVIDE see **KIT CARSON OVER THE GREAT DIVIDE** • 1925
WITH LAURELS AND FIGLEAF see **MIT EICHENLAUB UND FEIGENBLATT** • 1968
WITH LEE IN VIRGINIA • 1913 • Ince Thomas H. • USA
WITH LOVE see **Z LASKY** • 1928
WITH LOVE AND HISSES • 1927 • Guiol Fred • SHT • USA
WITH LOVE AND KISSES • 1936 • Goodwins Leslie • USA
WITH LOVE AND KISSES see **MED KAERLIG HILSEN** • 1971
WITH LOVE AND REGARDS • 1977 • Barakat • EGY
WITH LOVE AND TENDERNESS • 1978 • Vulchanov Rangel • BUL
WITH LOVE FROM TRUMAN see **VISIT WITH TRUMAN CAPOTE, A** • 1966
WITH LOVE IN MIND • 1970 • Cecil-Wright Robin • UKN
WITH LOVE OR WITHOUT LOVE see **IMA LJUBAVI NEMA LJUBAVI** • 1968
WITH LOVE'S EYES • 1913 • Parker Lem B. • USA
WITH MASK AND PISTOL • 1911 • *Urban Trading Co* • UKN
WITH MAWSON IN THE SOUTH • 1912 • ASL
WITH MAWSON TO THE FROZEN SOUTH see **SIEGE OF THE SOUTH** • 1931
WITH MOTORBIKE AND TENT TO TUNISIA • 1961 • Gass Karl • DOC • GDR
WITH MY GUNS see **POR MIS PISTOLAS** • 1968
WITH MY WIFE I CAN'T see **CON MI MUJER NO PUEDO** • 1978
WITH NAKED FISTS • 1923 • *Kennedy Tom* • USA
WITH NEATNESS AND DISPATCH • 1918 • Davis Will S. • USA
WITH NEEDLE AND THREAD • 1966 • Stiopul Savel • RMN
WITH NOBODY • 1975 • Grubcheva Ivanka • BUL
WITH OR WITHOUT • 1916 • Williamson Robin E. • SHT • USA
WITH OUR OWN STRENGTH • 1948 • Heynowski Walter • DOC • GDR
WITH OUR OWN TWO HANDS • 1985 • Raymont Peter • CND
WITH POOPDECK PAPPY • 1940 • Fleischer Dave • ANS • USA
WITH PREJUDICE • 1982 • Storm Esben • MTV • ASL
WITH PREMEDITATION • 1979 • *Amin Mirvaj* • EGY
WITH REGARDS see **NA POKLONY** • 1974
WITH RESPECT • 1954 • Laine Edvin • FNL
WITH SHERIDAN AT MURFREESBORO • 1911 • *Champion* • USA
WITH SITTING BULL AT THE "SPIRIT LAKE MASSACRE" see **SITTING BULL AT THE "SPIRIT LAKE MASSACRE"** • 1927
WITH SIX YOU GET EGGROLL • 1968 • Morris Howard • USA
WITH SLIGHT VARIATIONS • 1914 • Ransom Charles • USA

WITH SPECIAL PRAISE see **MIT VORZUGLICHER HOCHACHTUNG** • 1967
WITH STANLEY IN AFRICA • 1922 • Craft William James, Kull Edward • SRL • USA
WITH STOLEN MONEY • 1915 • Melville Wilbert • USA
WITH STONEWALL JACKSON • 1911 • *Champion* • USA
WITH THE AID OF A ROGUE • 1927 • Payne J. H. • UKN
WITH THE AID OF PHRENOLOGY • 1913 • Dillon Eddie • USA
WITH THE AID OF THE LAW • 1915 • Mix Tom • USA
WITH THE ASSISTANCE OF "SHEP" • 1913 • *Washburn Alice* • USA
WITH THE BEST INTENTIONS see **PARSON PUTS HIS FOOT IN IT, THE** • 1911
WITH THE BURGLAR'S HELP • 1914 • *Lubin* • USA
WITH THE CUBAN WOMEN see **CON LAS MUJERES CUBANAS** • 1974
WITH THE ENEMY'S HELP • 1912 • Griffith D. W. • USA
WITH THE EYES OF LOVE • 1914 • Lessey George A. • USA
WITH THE EYES OF THE BLIND • 1913 • Edwin Walter • USA
WITH THE FLEET IN 'FRISCO • 1908 • *Kalem* • USA
WITH THE HALO ASKEW see **MED GLORIAN PA SNED** • 1957
WITH THE HEADHUNTERS IN PAPUA • 1923 • Hurley Frank • DOC • ASL • WITH THE HEADHUNTERS OF UNKNOWN PAPUA ◦ PARADISE OF PAPUA, THE ◦ IN THE PARADISE OF UNKNOWN PAPUA
WITH THE HEADHUNTERS OF UNKNOWN PAPUA see **WITH THE HEADHUNTERS IN PAPUA** • 1923
WITH THE HELP OF THE LADIES • 1915 • *Welch George* • USA
WITH THE MARINES AT TARAWA • 1944 • Hayward Louis • DOC • USA
WITH THE MOUNTED POLICE • 1912 • *Thanhouser* • USA
WITH THE MUMMIES' HELP • 1917 • *Gibson Margaret* • USA
WITH THE NEXT MAN EVERYTHING WILL BE DIFFERENT see **BEIM NACHSTEN MANN WIRD ALLES ANDERS** • 1989
WITH THE PEOPLE FOR THE COUNTRY see **MED FOLKET FOR FOSTERLANDET** • 1938
WITH THE SPIRITS HELP • 1916 • Chaudet Louis W. • SHT • USA
WITH THE TIDE • 1911 • *Powers* • USA
WITH THE WIND IN HOT SUNLIGHT see **CON EL VIENTO SOLANO** • 1968
WITH THESE HANDS • 1950 • Arnold Jack • DOC • USA
WITH THESE HANDS see **CLINIC XCLUSIVE** • 1971
WITH THINNERS ON TAP • 1961 • Kellett Bob • UKN
WITH THIS RING • 1925 • Windermere Fred • USA
WITH THIS RING • 1978 • Sheldon James • TVM • USA
WITH WILLIAMSON BENEATH THE SEA • 1932 • Williamson J. Ernest • USA
WITH WINGS OUTSPREAD • 1922 • *Terry Fred* • USA
WITH YOU IN MY ARMS see **MED DEJ I MIN ARMAR** • 1940
WITH YOU THE WORLD IS FUN see **S TEBOU ME BAVI SVET** • 1982
WITH YOU THE WORLD THRILLS ME see **S TEBOU ME BAVI SVET** • 1982
WITH YOUR HEART IN YOUR HAND see **CON EL CORAZON EN LA MANO** • 1988
WITHEET • 1966 • Meyering Kees • NTH
WITHERED see **KEMBANG LAYU** • 1970
WITHERED HANDS • 1914 • August Edwin • USA
WITHIN AN ACE • 1909 • Bouwmeester Theo? • UKN
WITHIN AN ACE • 1914 • Marston Theodore • USA
WITHIN AN INCH OF HIS LIFE • 1910 • *Powers* • USA
WITHIN AN INCH OF HIS LIFE • 1914 • *Payne Edna* • USA
WITHIN AND WITHOUT (UKN) see **ESTATE CON SENTIMENTO, UN'** • 1970
WITHIN BOUNDS see **COMPROMIS, HET** • 1968
WITHIN HAIL see **BILOCATION** • 1973
WITHIN MAN'S POWER • 1954 • Webster Nicholas • SHT • USA
WITHIN MEMORY see **UNS ET LES AUTRES, LES** • 1981
WITHIN OUR GATES • 1915 • Harvey Frank • ASL • DEEDS THAT WON GALLIPOLI
WITHIN OUR GATES • 1920 • Micheaux Oscar • USA
WITHIN PRISON WALLS see **RIGHT WAY, THE** • 1921
WITHIN THE CLOISTER see **INTERNO DI UN CONVENTO** • 1977
WITHIN THE CUP • 1918 • West Raymond B. • USA
WITHIN THE ENEMY'S LINES • 1913 • Seay Charles M. • USA
WITHIN THE GATES • 1915 • *Lloyd Charles L.* • USA
WITHIN THE GATES OF PARADISE • 1914 • *Imp* • USA
WITHIN THE HOUR • 1913 • Farnum Marshall • USA
WITHIN THE LAW • 1916 • Luke Monty • ASL
WITHIN THE LAW • 1917 • Earle William P. S. • USA
WITHIN THE LAW • 1923 • Lloyd Frank • USA
WITHIN THE LAW • 1939 • Machaty Gustav • USA
WITHIN THE LAW (UKN) see **PAID** • 1930
WITHIN THE LINES • 1916 • *Mutual* • USA
WITHIN THE NOOSE • 1914 • *Shumway L. C.* • USA
WITHIN THE TEN COUNT • 1913 • *Reliance* • USA
WITHIN THESE WALLS • 1945 • Humberstone H. Bruce • USA
WITHIN THREE HUNDRED PAGES • 1914 • *Essanay* • USA
WITHNAIL AND I • 1987 • Robinson Bruce • UKN
WITHOUT A CLUE see **SHERLOCK AND ME** • 1988
WITHOUT A COUNTRY see **FORVISTE, DE** • 1914
WITHOUT A DOWRY see **BESPRIDANNITSA** • 1936
WITHOUT A HOBBY, IT'S NO LIFE • 1973 • Lavut Martin • DOC • CND
WITHOUT A HOME • 1939 • Martin Alexander
WITHOUT A LIFE OF MY OWN see **XENA HERIA INE PIKRA, TA** • 1968
WITHOUT A PROMISED LAND see **YUEH-CHAN CHIN TS'UN CHE** • 1981
WITHOUT A SOUL see **LOLA** • 1914
WITHOUT A STITCH (USA) see **UDEN EN TRAEVL** • 1968
WITHOUT A TRACE • 1983 • Jaffe Stanley • USA
WITHOUT ANAESTHESIA see **BEZ ZNIECZULENIA** • 1978
WITHOUT ANAESTHETIC see **BEZ ZNIECZULENIA** • 1978
WITHOUT APPARENT MOTIVE (USA) see **SANS MOBILE APPARENT** • 1971
WITHOUT BENEFIT OF CLERGY • 1921 • Young James • USA
WITHOUT CHILDREN (UKN) see **PENTHOUSE PARTY** • 1936
WITHOUT COMPROMISE • 1922 • Flynn Emmett J. • USA
WITHOUT CONSENT • 1932 • Kenton Erle C. • USA
WITHOUT DOWRY see **BESPRIDANNITSA** • 1936
WITHOUT END see **SIN FIN** • 1970
WITHOUT END OR LOOP -DEATH IS NO SOLUTION see **SIN FIN -LA MUERTE NO ES NINGUNA SOLUCION** • 1987
WITHOUT FAMILY, OR.. see **SENZA FAMIGLIA NULLA TENENTI CERCANO AFFETTO** • 1972
WITHOUT FEAR • 1922 • Webb Kenneth • USA
WITHOUT FEAR OF REPROACH see **BEZ STRAKHA UPREKA** • 1963
WITHOUT HER FATHER'S CONSENT • 1910 • Fitzhamon Lewin? • UKN
WITHOUT HONOR • 1918 • Hopper E. Mason • USA
WITHOUT HONOR • 1949 • Pichel Irving • USA • TWILIGHT
WITHOUT HONOR see **MACOMBER AFFAIR, THE** • 1947
WITHOUT HONORS • 1932 • Nigh William • USA
WITHOUT HOPE • 1914 • Mace Fred • USA
WITHOUT LIES see **HAZUGSAG NELKUL** • 1945
WITHOUT LIMIT • 1921 • Baker George D. • USA • TEMPLE OF DUSK, THE
WITHOUT LOVE • 1945 • Bucquet Harold S. • USA
WITHOUT LOVE see **BEZ MILOSCI** • 1980
WITHOUT MERCY • 1925 • Melford George • USA
WITHOUT ORDERS • 1926 • Maloney Leo • USA
WITHOUT ORDERS • 1936 • Landers Lew • USA
WITHOUT PANTS • 1914 • *Crystal* • USA
WITHOUT PITY see **SENZA PIETA** • 1948
WITHOUT REASON AND BY FORCE see **CONTRA LA RAZON Y POR LA FUERZA** • 1973
WITHOUT REGRET • 1935 • Young Harold • USA
WITHOUT RESERVATIONS • 1946 • LeRoy Mervyn • USA
WITHOUT REWARD • 1913 • *Nestor* • USA
WITHOUT RISK (UKN) see **PECOS RIVER** • 1951
WITHOUT SHAME see **UNASHAMED** • 1932
WITHOUT THE OPTION • 1926 • Barnett Charles • UKN
WITHOUT THE PEEL see **SENZA BUCCIA** • 1979
WITHOUT TIME OR REASON • 1962 • Kneitel Seymour • ANS • USA
WITHOUT TITLE see **BES NASLOVA** • 1964
WITHOUT WARNING • 1952 • Laven Arnold • USA
WITHOUT WARNING • 1980 • Clark Greydon • USA • IT CAME WITHOUT WARNING ◦ WARNING, THE
WITHOUT WARNING see **STORY WITHOUT A NAME, THE** • 1924
WITHOUT WARNING see **INVISIBLE MENACE, THE** • 1938
WITHOUT WITNESS see **BEZ SVIDETELEI** • 1983
WITHOUT WITNESSES see **BEZ SVIDETELEI** • 1983
WITHOUT WITNESSES see **HORIS MARTYRES** • 1984
WITHOUT YOU • 1934 • Daumery John • UKN
WITHOUT YOU I'M NOTHING • 1990 • Boskovich John • USA
WITHOUT YOU IT IS NIGHT see **OHNE DICH WIRD ES NACHT** • 1956
WITLESS see **MANK DINNE** • 1968
WITNESS • 1985 • Weir Peter • USA
WITNESS, THE • 1915 • MacDonald Donald • *Paragon* • USA
WITNESS, THE • 1915 • O'Neil Barry • *Lubin* • USA
WITNESS, THE • 1942 • Roush Leslie • SHT • USA
WITNESS, THE • 1959 • Muller Geoffrey • UKN
WITNESS, THE see **ZEUGE, DER** • 1967
WITNESS, THE see **TANU, A** • 1968
WITNESS, THE see **TEMOIN, LE** • 1977
WITNESS "A-3 CENTER" • 1913 • *Essanay* • USA
WITNESS CHAIR, THE • 1936 • Nicholls George Jr. • USA
WITNESS FOR THE DEFENSE, THE • 1919 • Fitzmaurice George • USA
WITNESS FOR THE PROSECUTION • 1957 • Wilder Billy • USA
WITNESS FOR THE PROSECUTION • 1983 • Gibson Alan • TVM • UKN
WITNESS FOR THE STATE, THE • 1917 • Campbell Colin • SHT • USA
WITNESS IN THE CITY see **TEMOIN DANS LA VILLE, UN** • 1959
WITNESS IN THE DARK • 1959 • Rilla Wolf • UKN
WITNESS IN THE WAR ZONE see **WAR ZONE** • 1987
WITNESS OF MANKIND see **NINGEN NO SHOMEI** • 1977
WITNESS OF WILDERNESS see **YASEI NO SHOMEI** • 1978
WITNESS SEAT, THE see **SHONIN NO ISU** • 1965
WITNESS TO MURDER • 1954 • Rowland Roy • USA
WITNESS TO THE WILL, THE • 1914 • Lessey George A. • USA
WITNESS VANISHES, THE • 1939 • Garrett Otis • USA
WITNESSES • 1988 • Burke Martyn • DOC • CND
WITNESSES, THE see **TRESTIGOS, LOS**
WITNESSES, THE (USA) see **TEMPS DU GHETTO, LE** • 1961
WITS AND FITS • 1917 • *U.s.m.p.* • USA
WIT'S END see **G.I. EXECUTIONER** • 1971
WITS VS. WITS • 1920 • Grossman Harry • USA
WITTE VAN SICHEM, DE • 1980 • de Hert Robbe • BLG • FILASSE (FRN) ◦ TOW
WITTE WAN • 1983 • Ditvoorst Adriaan • NTH • WHITE MADNESS
WITTY KITTY • 1960 • Lovy Alex • ANS • USA
WITWENBALL, DER • 1930 • Jacoby Georg • FRG
WITWER MIT 5 TOCHTERN • 1957 • Engels Erich • FRG
WIVE UNDER SUSPICION • 1938 • Whale James • USA
WIVES • 1913 • *Ramo* • USA
WIVES see **HUSTRUER** • 1975
WIVES, THE see **KEY CLUB WIVES** • 1968
WIVES AND LOVERS • 1963 • Rich John • USA • FIRST WIFE
WIVES AND OLD SWEETHEARTS • 1920 • Lyons Eddie, Moran Lee • SHT • USA
WIVES AND OTHER WIVES • 1919 • Ingraham Lloyd • USA
WIVES AND WORRIES • 1918 • *Triangle* • USA
WIVES AT AUCTION • 1926 • Clifton Elmer • USA
WIVES BEWARE (USA) see **TWO WHITE ARMS** • 1932
WIVES NEVER KNOW • 1936 • Nugent Elliott • USA
WIVES OF JAMESTOWN, THE • 1913 • Olcott Sidney • USA
WIVES OF MEN • 1918 • Stahl John M. • USA
WIVES OF MEN, THE • 1915 • MacDonald J. Farrell • USA
WIVES OF THE PROPHET, THE • 1926 • Fitzgerald J. A. • USA
WIVES OF THE RICH • 1916 • Heffron Thomas N. • SHT • USA
WIVES' TALE, A • 1980 • Bissonnette Sophie, Duckworth Martin, Rock Joyce • DOC • CND • HISTOIRE DE FEMMES, UNE
WIVES, TEN YEARS AFTER see **HUSTRUER TI AR ETTER** • 1985
WIVES' UNION, THE • 1920 • France Charles H. • SHT • USA
WIVES WON'T WEAKEN • 1928 • Roberts Stephen • SHT • USA
WIZ, THE • 1978 • Lumet Sidney • USA
WIZARD, THE • 1927 • Rosson Richard • USA
WIZARD, THE see **ZAUBERMANNCHEN, DAS** • 1960
WIZARD, THE see **HEXER, DER** • 1964
WIZARD AND THE BRIGANDS, THE • 1911 • Bouwmeester Theo, Booth W. R.? • UKN
WIZARD OF ANTS, THE • 1941 • Fleischer Dave • ANS • USA
WIZARD OF AUTOS • 1943 • *O'Brien Joseph/ Mead Thomas (P)* • SHT • USA
WIZARD OF BAGHDAD, THE • 1960 • Sherman George • USA
WIZARD OF DEATH see **BEFORE I HANG** • 1940
WIZARD OF GORE, THE • 1970 • Lewis Herschell G. • USA
WIZARD OF LONELINESS, THE • 1988 • Bowen Jenny • USA
WIZARD OF MARS • 1964 • Hewitt David L. • USA • ALIEN MASSACRE, HORRORS OF THE RED PLANET ◦ HORROR OF THE RED PLANET
WIZARD OF OZ • 1910 • Turner Otis • USA
WIZARD OF OZ, THE • 1908 • *Baum L. Frank (P)* • SHS • USA
WIZARD OF OZ, THE • 1925 • Semon Larry • USA
WIZARD OF OZ, THE • 1939 • Fleming Victor, Vidor King (U/c) • USA
WIZARD OF SPEED AND TIME, THE • 1988 • Jittlov Mike • USA
WIZARD OF THE JUNGLE, THE • 1913 • Shaw Harold • USA
WIZARD OF THE SADDLE • 1928 • Clark Frank Howard • USA
WIZARD OF WAUKESHA, THE • 1981 • Orentreich Catherine, Brockman Susan • DOC • USA
WIZARD, THE PRINCE AND THE GOOD FAIRY, THE (USA) see **SORCIER, LE PRINCE ET LE BON GENIE, LE** • 1900
WIZARD WARS see **WIZARDS OF THE LOST KINGDOM** • 1984
WIZARDS • 1977 • Bakshi Ralph • ANM • USA
WIZARD'S APPRENTICE, THE • 1930 • Levee Sidney • SHT • USA
WIZARDS OF THE LOST KINGDOM • 1984 • Olivera Hector • USA, ARG • GUERRA DE LOS MAGOS, LA (ARG) ◦ WIZARD WARS
WIZARDS OF THE LOST KINGDOM II • 1989 • Griffith Charles B. • USA
WIZARD'S PLOT, THE • 1916 • Ellis Robert • SHT • USA
WIZARD'S WALKING STICK, THE • 1909 • Booth W. R. • UKN
WIZARD'S WORLD • 1906 • Paul Robert William • UKN
WIZJA LOKALNA • 1965 • Kidawa Janusz • DOC • PLN • INSPECTION
WIZJA LOKALNA: 1901 • 1980 • Bajon Filip • PLN
WIZYTA • 1975 • Lozinski Marcel • PLN • VISIT, THE
WIZYTA U KROLOW • 1965 • Rybkowski Jan • MTV • PLN • VISIT TO THE KINGS, A
WLODZIMIERZ HAUPE • 1958 • Bielinska Halina • HNG
WNIEBOWSTAPIENIE • 1969 • Rybkowski Jan • PLN • ASCENSION BAY
WO CHE-YANG KUO-LE YI-SHENG • 1985 • Chang Yi • TWN • KUEI-MEI, A WOMAN
WO DER WILDBACH RAUSCHT • 1956 • Richter Walter • FRG
WO DER ZUG NICHT LANGE HALT • 1960 • Hasler Joachim • GDR • NEUER TAG BRICHT AN, EIN
WO DIE ALPENROSEN BLUHN • 1928 • Beck-Gaden Hanns • FRG
WO DIE ALPENROSEN BLUH'N see **ULLI UND MAREI** • 1945
WO DIE ALTEN WALDER RAUSCHEN • 1956 • Stummer Alfons • FRG
WO DIE GRUNEN AMEISEN TRAUMEN • 1984 • Herzog Werner • FRG • WHERE THE GREEN ANTS DREAM (UKN)
WO DIE LERCHE SINGT • 1936 • Lamac Carl • FRG, HNG, SWT
WO DIE LERCHE SINGT • 1956 • Wolff Hans • AUS
WO DU BIST, WIRD MEINE LIEBE SEIN • 1920 • Forsten Hans? • FRG
WO DU HINGEHST • 1957 • Hellberg Martin • GDR • WHEREVER YOU GO
WO EIN WILLE -IST EIN WEG • 1918 • Moest Hubert • FRG
WO ERH HAN-SHENG • 1985 • Chang Yi • TWN • HANG-SHENG, MY SON
WO IST COLETTI? • 1913 • Mack Max • FRG
WO IST HERR BELLING • 1945 • Engel Erich • FRG
WO IST MEIN SCHATZ? • 1916 • Lubitsch Ernst • FRG
WO KO, WO CH'I • 1980 • Sung Ts'Un-Shou • HKG • I SING, I CRY
WO MENSHCEN FRIEDEN FINDEN • 1924 • Konetzky E. • FRG
WO-TE AI • 1986 • Chang Yi • TWN • THIS LOVE OF MINE
WO-TE ERH-TZU SHIH T'IEN-TS'AI • 1990 • Yang Li-Kuo • TWN
WO-TE YEH-YEH • 1981 • K'O Chun-Liang • TWN • MY GRANDPA
WOBBLIES, THE • 1981 • Bird Stewart, Shaffer Deborah • DOC • USA
WOCHENEND IM PARADIES see **LIEBE IM FINANZAMT** • 1952
WOCHENENDBRAUT • 1928 • Jacoby Georg • *Orpid-Film* • FRG
WOCHENENDBRAUT • 1928 • Winar Ernest • *Low & Co* • FRG
WOCHENENDE • 1929 • Ruttmann Walter • FRG • WEEKEND
WOCHENENDZAUBER • 1927 • Walther-Fein Rudolf • FRG
WOCHENTAGS IMMER • 1963 • Burk Michael • FRG
WODA • 1975 • Czekala Ryszard • ANM • PLN
WODZIREJ • 1978 • Falk Feliks • PLN • DANCE LEADER ◦ TOP DOG
WOE OF BATTLE, THE • 1913 • Melford George • USA
WOES OF A MARRIED MAN, THE • 1907 • Cooper Arthur • UKN
WOES OF A STEP-DAUGHTER see **RATAPAN ANAK TIRI** • 1974
WOES OF A WAITRESS, THE • 1914 • Costello Maurice, Gaillord Robert • USA
WOES OF A WEALTHY WIDOW, THE • 1911 • *Bunny John* • USA
WOES OF A WOMAN • 1919 • Lyons Eddie, Moran Lee • SHT • USA
WOES OF GOLF see **POC AR BUILE** • 1974
WOES OF ROLLER SKATERS, THE • 1908 • Melies Georges • FRN
WOGEN DES SCHICKSALS • 1918 • May Joe • FRG

WOH KAUN THI? • 1964 • *Sahda* • IND • WHODUNIT? ○ WHO WAS SHE?
WOHIN DIE ZUGE FAHREN • 1948 • Barlog Boleslav • FRG
WOHLTATERIN DER MENSCHHEIT, DIE see **HERRIN DER WELT 7, DIE** • 1919
WOJNA SWIATOW –NASTEPNE STULECIE • 1981 • Szulkin Piotr • PLN • WAR OF THE WORLDS –NEXT CENTURY, THE
WOKABOUT BILONG TONTEN • 1974 • Howes Oliver • ASL
WOKAI HYAKU MONOGATARI see **YOKAI HYAKU MONOGATARI** • 1968
WOKOL SPRAWY • 1963 • Trzos-Rastawiecki Andrzej • DOC • PLN • AROUND THE MATTER
WOKUJOH NO UZUMAKI • 1968 • Ogawa Kinya • JPN • CONVOLUTION OF LUST, A
WOLA RAFALOWSKA • 1966 • Gryczelowska Krystyna • DOC • PLN
WOLCOTT • 1981 • Bucksey Colin • TVM • UKN
WOLD SHADOW, THE • 1972 • Brakhage Stan • USA
WOLF • 1971 • Sauer Len • SHT • USA
WOLF • 1978 • Mirshekari Ahmad • IRN
WOLF see **OOKAMI** • 1955
WOLF, THE • 1914 • O'Neil Barry • USA
WOLF, THE • 1919 • Young James • USA
WOLF, THE see **FARKAS, A** • 1916
WOLF, THE see **LOBO, EL** • 1971
WOLF AMONG LAMBS, A • 1913 • *Stonehouse Ruth* • USA
WOLF AND HIS MATE, THE • 1918 • Le Saint Edward J. • USA
WOLF AND THE CRANE, THE • Bebderskaya N. • USS
WOLF AND THE LAMB, THE • Todorov Dimiter • ANM • BUL
WOLF AND THE LAMB, THE see **LOUP ET L'AGNEAU, LE** • 1955
WOLF AND THE SEVEN CHILDREN, THE • Nemolayev • ANM • USS
WOLF AND THE WAIF, THE • 1912 • Rains Fred • UKN
WOLF AT THE DOOR • 1932 • *Mintz Charles (P)* • ANS • USA
WOLF AT THE DOOR, THE see **OVIRI** • 1987
WOLF BLOOD • 1925 • Chesebro George, Mitchell George • USA
WOLF CALL • 1939 • Waggner George • USA
WOLF CHASES PIG • 1942 • Tashlin Frank • ANS • USA
WOLF DOG • 1958 • Newfield Sam • USA
WOLF DOG, THE • 1933 • Fraser Harry L., Clark Colbert • SRL • USA
WOLF ECHOES see **WILCZE ECHA** • 1968
WOLF FANGS • 1927 • Seiler Lewis • USA
WOLF FOREST, THE see **BOSQUE DE ANCINES, EL** • 1969
WOLF FROM PROKLETIJE see **VUK SA PROKLETIJA** • 1968
WOLF GIRL, THE • 1915 • *Federal* • USA
WOLF HOUNDED • 1958 • Hanna William, Barbera Joseph • ANS • USA
WOLF HUNT, THE • 1908 • *Abernathy John* • USA
WOLF HUNTERS, THE • 1926 • Paton Stuart • USA
WOLF HUNTERS, THE • 1950 • Boetticher Budd • USA
WOLF IN CHEAP CLOTHING, A • 1936 • *Terry Paul/ Moser Frank (P)* • ANS • USA
WOLF IN CHEAP CLOTHING, THE • 1932 • Buzzell Edward • SHT • USA
WOLF IN SHEEPDOG'S CLOTHING • 1963 • Hanna William, Barbera Joseph • ANS • USA
WOLF IN SHEEP'S CLOTHING, THE • 1910 • *Actophone* • USA
WOLF IN SHEIK'S CLOTHING • 1948 • Sparber I. • ANS • USA
WOLF IN THIEVE'S CLOTHING • 1943 • White Jules • SHT • USA
WOLF LAKE • 1978 • Kennedy Burt • USA • HONOUR GUARD, THE
WOLF LARSEN • 1958 • Jones Harmon • USA
WOLF LARSEN (USA) see **LUPO DEI MARI, IL** • 1975
WOLF LAW • 1922 • Paton Stuart • USA
WOLF LOWRY • 1917 • Hart William S. • USA
WOLF MAN • 1924 • *Sunset Productions* • USA
WOLF–MAN, THE • 1915 • *Lewis Ralph* • USA
WOLF–MAN, THE • 1918 • *Polifilms* • USA
WOLF MAN, THE • 1924 • Mortimer Edmund • *Fox Film Corp.* • USA • BEAST, THE
WOLF MAN, THE • 1941 • Waggner George • USA • DESTINY
WOLF MAN, THE see **HOMEM LOBO, O** • 1971
WOLF OF DEBT, THE • 1915 • Harvey John • USA
WOLF OF LOS ALAMOS • 1917 • Horne James W. • SHT • USA
WOLF OF NEW YORK • 1940 • McGann William • USA
WOLF OF SILA, THE see **LUPO DELLA SILA, IL** • 1949
WOLF OF THE CITY, THE • 1913 • Farnum Marshall • USA
WOLF OF THE MALVENEURS, THE see **LOUP DES MALVENEURS, LE** • 1942
WOLF OF THE RAILS see **TETSURO NO OKAMI** • 1927
WOLF OF THE SEVEN SEAS see **LUPO DEI MARI, IL** • 1975
WOLF OF THE SILA, THE (UKN) see **LUPO DELLA SILA, IL** • 1949
WOLF OF TIBET, THE see **WETTLAUF UMS GLUCK** • 1923
WOLF OF WALL STREET, THE • 1929 • Lee Rowland V. • USA
WOLF PACK • 1922 • Craft William James • USA
WOLF PACK • 1975 • Mason William • DOC • CND
WOLF PACK • 1978 • Manduke Joe • MTV • USA
WOLF RIDERS • 1935 • Webb Harry S. • USA • WOLF RIDES
WOLF RIDES see **WOLF RIDERS** • 1935
WOLF SEASON see **TIEMPO DE LOBOS** • 1982
WOLF SONG • 1929 • Fleming Victor • USA
WOLF TRACKS • 1920 • Wright Mack V. • USA
WOLF TRAP see **VLCI JAMA** • 1958
WOLF UND DIE SIEBEN JUNGEN GEISSLEIN, DER • 1957 • Podehl Peter • FRG • BIG BAD WOLF (USA)
WOLF UNMASKED, THE • 1915 • *Vincent James* • USA
WOLF WITH CHILD see **KOZURE OHKAMI** • 1972
WOLF! WOLF! • 1934 • Lantz Walter, Nolan William • ANS • USA
WOLF! WOLF! • 1944 • Davis Mannie • ANS • USA
WOLF WOMAN, THE • 1916 • Willat Irvin V.?, Edwards Walter? • USA
WOLFE AND MONTCALM • 1959 • Wargon Alan • SHT • CND
WOLFE OR THE CONQUEST OF QUEBEC • 1914 • Olcott Sidney • USA
WOLFEN • 1981 • Wadleigh Michael • USA
WOLFHEART'S REVENGE • 1925 • *Williams Big Boy* • USA
WOLFHOUND • 1916 • *Terry Paul* • ANS • USA
WOLFIN, DIE • 1920 • Brunner Rolf • FRG
WOLFIN VOM TEUFELSMOOR, DIE • 1978 • Pfandler Helmut • AUS • SHE–WOLF OF DEVIL'S MOOR, THE ○ DEVIL'S BED, THE
WOLFISH SUITE • 1988 • Donev Donyo • ANM • BUL
WOLFMAN • 1980 • Keeter Worth • USA • WOLFMAN –A LYCANTHROPE
WOLFMAN –A LYCANTHROPE see **WOLFMAN** • 1980
WOLFMAN OF COUNT DRACULA, THE see **MARCA DEL HOMBRE LOBO, LA** • 1968
WOLFMAN OF GALICIA, THE see **BOSQUE DE ANCINES, EL** • 1969
WOLFPACK • 1988 • Milling William • USA
WOLFPACK (UKN) see **HALBSTARKEN, DIE** • 1956
WOLFPEN PRINCIPLE • 1974 • Darcus Jack • CND • LIBRE COMME DES LOUPS EN CAGE
WOLFRAM • 1950 • Mur Oti • SPN
WOLFS AND THE SHEEP, THE • 1970 • Manfredi Manfredo • ANS • ITL
WOLF'S CLOTHING • 1927 • Del Ruth Roy • USA
WOLF'S CLOTHING • 1936 • Marton Andrew • UKN
WOLF'S DAUGHTER, THE • 1914 • Kent Leon D. • USA
WOLF'S DEN, THE • 1915 • *Davenport Dorothy* • USA
WOLF'S FANGS, THE • 1922 • Apfel Oscar • USA
WOLF'S FANGS, THE • 1930 • Levigard Josef • SHT • USA
WOLF'S HOLE see **VICI BOUDA** • 1987
WOLF'S PARDON, THE • 1947 • Donnelly Eddie • ANS • USA
WOLF'S PREY, THE • 1915 • *Warner'S Features* • USA
WOLF'S PREY, THE • 1915 • *Kalem* • USA
WOLF'S SIDE OF THE STORY • 1938 • Rasinski Connie • ANS • USA
WOLF'S TALE, A • 1944 • Rasinski Connie • ANS • USA
WOLF'S TRACKS • 1923 • *Hoxie Jack* • USA
WOLF'S TRAIL • 1927 • Ford Francis • USA
WOLFSHEAD: THE LEGEND OF ROBIN HOOD • 1969 • Hough John • MTV • UKN
WOLFWOMAN see **LUPA MANNARA, LA** • 1976
WOLGA, WOLGA see **VOLGA, VOLGA** • 1928
WOLGA–WOLGA see **STJENKA RASIN** • 1936
WOLGAMADCHEN, DAS • 1930 • Wohlmuth Robert • FRG, AUS
WOLHAARSTORIES • 1983 • Cawood Bromley • SAF
WOLKENBAU UND FLIMMERSTERN • 1919 • *Lang Fritz* • FRG • CASTLE IN THE SKY AND RHINESTONES
WOLLANDS, DIE • 1973 • Ludcke Marianne, Kratisch Ingo • FRG
WOLNE MIASTO • 1958 • Rozewicz Stanislaw • PLN • FREE CITY
WOLO see **BALETTPRIMADONNAN** • 1916
WOLTER MONGISIDI • 1983 • Rorimpandey Frank • INN
WOLVERINE, THE • 1921 • Bertram William • USA
WOLVES • 1930 • De Courville Albert • UKN • WANTED MEN
WOLVES see **OOKAMI** • 1955
WOLVES, THE • 1972 • Gosha Hideo • JPN
WOLVES, THE see **PERKAWINAN DALAM SEMUSIN** • 1976
WOLVES DON'T EAT MEAT • Khoury Samir • LBN
WOLVES' ECHOES see **WILCZE ECHA** • 1968
WOLVES FROM INSIDE see **LOBOS DE ADENTRO** • 1979
WOLVES' JUNGLE, THE • 1978 • Shahin Mohammed • SYR
WOLVES OF KULTUR • 1919 • Golden Joseph A. • SRL • USA
WOLVES OF SOCIETY • 1915 • Lloyd Frank • USA
WOLVES OF THE AIR • 1927 • Ford Francis • USA
WOLVES OF THE BORDER • 1918 • Smith Cliff • USA
WOLVES OF THE BORDER • 1923 • Neitz Alvin J. • USA
WOLVES OF THE CITY • 1929 • Jason Leigh • USA
WOLVES OF THE CITY see **FURYO BANCHO** • 1968
WOLVES OF THE DEEP (USA) see **LUPI NELL'ABISSO** • 1959
WOLVES OF THE DESERT • 1926 • Wilson Ben • USA
WOLVES OF THE NIGHT • 1919 • Edwards J. Gordon • USA
WOLVES OF THE NORTH • 1921 • Dawn Norman • USA • EVIL HALF, THE
WOLVES OF THE NORTH • 1924 • Duncan William • SRL • USA
WOLVES OF THE RAIL • 1918 • Hart William S. • USA
WOLVES OF THE RANGE • 1918 • Harvey Harry • SHT • USA
WOLVES OF THE RANGE • 1921 • *Livingston Jack* • USA
WOLVES OF THE RANGE • 1943 • Newfield Sam • USA
WOLVES OF THE ROAD • 1925 • Hayes Ward • USA
WOLVES OF THE SEA • 1937 • Clifton Elmer • USA • JUNGLE ISLAND (UKN)
WOLVES OF THE STREET • 1920 • Thayer Otis B. • USA
WOLVES OF THE UNDERWORLD • 1914 • Edwards Walter? • USA
WOLVES OF THE UNDERWORLD (USA) see **PUPPETS OF FATE** • 1933
WOLVES OF WILLOUGHBY CHASE, THE • 1989 • Orme Stuart • UKN
WOLZ see **WOLZ –LEBEN UND VERKLARUNG EINES DEUTSCHEN ANARCHISTEN** • 1974
WOLZ –LEBEN UND VERKLARUNG EINES DEUTSCHEN ANARCHISTEN • 1974 • Reisch Gunter • GDR • WOLZ
WOMAN • 1911 • *Yankee* • USA
WOMAN • 1919 • Tourneur Maurice • USA
WOMAN • 1950 • Pagliero Marcello • FRN
WOMAN see **AURAT** • 1939
WOMAN see **AMORE, L'** • 1948
WOMAN see **ONNA** • 1948
WOMAN see **STREE** • 1962
WOMAN see **AURAT** • 1967
WOMAN see **KONA** • 1982
WOMAN, A • 1912 • Kent Charles • USA
WOMAN, A • 1915 • Chaplin Charles • *Essanay* • USA • CHARLIE AND THE PERFECT LADY ○ PERFECT LADY, A
WOMAN, A • 1990 • Sachdev Arun • IND
WOMAN, A see **MUJER, UNA** • 1976
WOMAN, THE • 1913 • *Broncho* • USA
WOMAN, THE • 1915 • Melford George • *Lasky* • USA
WOMAN, THE see **DIEGUE–BI** • 1970
WOMAN, A MAN, A CITY, A see **MUJER, UN HOMBRE, UNA CIUDAD, UNA** • 1979
WOMAN ABOVE REPROACH, THE • 1920 • *Chase Florence* • USA
WOMAN ACCUSED • 1933 • Sloane Paul • USA
WOMAN AGAINST THE WORLD • 1938 • Selman David • USA
WOMAN AGAINST THE WORLD, A • 1928 • Archainbaud George • USA
WOMAN AGAINST WOMAN • 1914 • Vale Travers • USA
WOMAN AGAINST WOMAN • 1938 • Sinclair Robert B. • USA • ENEMY TERRITORY ○ ONE WOMAN'S ANSWER
WOMAN ALONE • 1956 • Biggs Julian • CND
WOMAN ALONE, A • 1912 • *Majestic* • USA
WOMAN ALONE, A • 1917 • Davenport Harry • USA
WOMAN ALONE, A • 1936 • Frenke Eugene • UKN • TWO WHO DARED (USA)
WOMAN ALONE, A (USA) see **SABOTAGE** • 1936
WOMAN ALONE, THE see **SABOTAGE** • 1936
WOMAN ALTOGETHER see **ONNA NO SUBETE** • 1960
WOMAN ALWAYS PAYS • 1912 • *Imp* • USA
WOMAN ALWAYS PAYS, THE • 1916 • Calvert E. H. • SHT • USA
WOMAN AND A WOMAN, A • 1980 • Bugajski Ryszard (c/d) • PLN
WOMAN AND BEAN SOUP see **ONNA TO MISOSHIRO** • 1968
WOMAN AND HER FOUR MEN, A see **JENCHINA U CHETVERO JEJEU MUJCHINE** • 1983
WOMAN AND HER RESPONSIBILITIES, A see **FRAU MIT VERANTWORTUNG, EINE** • 1978
WOMAN AND LOVER see **SENSUALLY LIBERATED FEMALE, THE** • 1970
WOMAN AND OFFICER 26, THE • 1920 • Lorraine Harry, Haldane Bert • UKN
WOMAN AND PIRATES see **ONNA TO KAIZOKU** • 1959
WOMAN AND PUPPET see **FATINA WAL SOOLUK, AL** • 1976
WOMAN AND TEMPTATION (USA) see **TENTACION DESNUDA, LA** • 1966
WOMAN AND THE BEANCURD SOUP, A see **ONNA TO MISOSHIRO** • 1968
WOMAN AND THE BEAST, THE • 1917 • Warde Ernest C. • USA
WOMAN AND THE BEAST, THE see **MUJER Y LA BESTIA, LA** • 1958
WOMAN AND THE DEVIL, THE see **EMRAA WA SHAITAN** • 1961
WOMAN AND THE HUNTER, THE • 1957 • Breakston George • UKN • TRIANGLE ON SAFARI
WOMAN AND THE LAW • 1918 • Walsh Raoul • USA
WOMAN AND THE LAW, THE • 1913 • *White Pearl* • USA
WOMAN AND THE PIRATES, THE see **ONNA TO KAIZOKU** • 1959
WOMAN AND THE PUPPET, THE • 1920 • Barker Reginald • USA
WOMAN AND THE WILD RIVER, THE see **WILD RIVER** • 1960
WOMAN AND WIFE • 1918 • Jose Edward • USA
WOMAN AND WINE • 1915 • *Elliott William* • USA
WOMAN AT HER WINDOW, A (USA) see **FEMME A SA FENETRE, UNE** • 1976
WOMAN AT PIER THIRTEEN, THE see **I MARRIED A COMMUNIST** • 1949
WOMAN AT THE HELM see **ASSZONY A TELEPEN** • 1962
WOMAN BAIT see **MAIGRET TEND UN PIEGE** • 1957
WOMAN BARBER, THE • 1898 • Smith G. A. • UKN
WOMAN BASKETBALL PLAYER NUMBER FIVE • 1957 • Xie Jin • CHN
WOMAN BEHIND EVERYTHING see **KVINNAN BAKOM ALLT** • 1951
WOMAN BEHIND THE MAN, THE • 1912 • *Cornwall Blanche* • USA
WOMAN BENEATH, THE • 1917 • Vale Travers • USA
WOMAN BETWEEN, THE • 1915 • *A.a.a.* • UKN
WOMAN BETWEEN, THE • 1931 • Mander Miles • UKN • WOMAN DECIDES, THE (USA) ○ CONFLICT
WOMAN BETWEEN, THE • 1931 • Schertzinger Victor • USA • MADAME JULIE (UKN)
WOMAN BETWEEN, THE (UKN) see **WOMAN I LOVE, THE** • 1937
WOMAN BETWEEN FRIENDS, THE • 1918 • Terriss Tom • USA
WOMAN BREED, THE • 1922 • *Frederick Pauline* • USA
WOMAN BY THE LONELY SEA, THE see **ZEKKAI NO RAJO** • 1958
WOMAN CALLED GOLDA, A • 1982 • Gibson Alan • TVM • USA
WOMAN CALLED MOSES, A • 1978 • Wendkos Paul • TVM • USA
WOMAN CALLED SHARAB, A see **ZANI BE–NAME–SHARAB** • 1968
WOMAN CHAMPION, THE see **KANTO ONNA TOBAKUSHI** • 1968
WOMAN CHASES MAN • 1937 • Blystone John G. • USA
WOMAN COMMANDS, A • 1932 • Stein Paul L. • USA
WOMAN CONDEMNED • 1934 • Reid Dorothy • USA
WOMAN CONQUERS, THE • 1922 • Forman Tom • USA
WOMAN DECIDES, THE (USA) see **WOMAN BETWEEN, THE** • 1931
WOMAN DEDICATED TO GOD see **CHARNO KI DASI** • 1959
WOMAN DESTROYED, A (UKN) see **SMASH–UP** • 1947
WOMAN DICE PLAYER, THE see **ONNA TOBAKUSHI TEKKABA YABURI** • 1968
WOMAN DISAPPEARED, A see **FEMME DISPARAIT, UNE** • 1942
WOMAN DISPUTED, THE • 1928 • King Henry, Taylor Sam • USA
WOMAN DISTRESSED, A • 1962 • Kuchar George • SHT • USA
WOMAN DON'T MAKE YOU NAME DIRTY see **ONNA–YO KIMI NO NA O KEGASU NAKARE** • 1930
WOMAN EATER, THE (USA) see **WOMANEATER** • 1958
WOMAN ETERNAL, THE • 1918 • Ince Ralph • USA
WOMAN FOR A DAY • 1915 • *Mina* • USA
WOMAN FOR A SEASON, A • 1969 • Vitandis Gheorghe • RMN
WOMAN FOR ALL MEN, A • 1975 • Marks Arthur • USA
WOMAN FOR ALL REASONS, A see **WOMEN FOR ALL REASONS** • 1969
WOMAN FOR CHARLIE, A see **COCKEYED COWBOYS OF CALICO COUNTY, THE** • 1970
WOMAN FOR HIRE, A see **KIRALIK KADIN** • 1967
WOMAN FOR JOE, THE • 1955 • O'Ferrall George M. • UKN
WOMAN FOR MEN see **MANS KVINNA** • 1945

WOMAN FROM CHINA, THE • 1930 • Dryhurst Edward • UKN
WOMAN FROM HEADQUARTERS • 1950 • Blair George • USA
WOMAN FROM HELL, THE • 1929 • Erickson A. F. • USA
WOMAN FROM LEBANON, THE see **CHATELAINE DU LIBAN, LA** • 1956
WOMAN FROM MELLON'S, THE • 1910 • Griffith D. W. • USA
WOMAN FROM MEVAZAR, THE see **ZHENSHCHINA IZ MEVAZARA** • 1977
WOMAN FROM MONTE CARLO, THE • 1932 • Curtiz Michael • USA
WOMAN FROM MOSCOW, THE • 1928 • Berger Ludwig • USA
WOMAN FROM NOWHERE, THE see **FEMME DE NULLE PART, LA** • 1922
WOMAN FROM ROSE HILL, THE (UKN) see **FEMME DE ROSE HILL, LA** • 1989
WOMAN FROM TANGIER, THE • 1948 • Daniels Harold • USA
WOMAN FROM THE GENROKU ERA, A see **GENROKU ONNA** • 1924
WOMAN FROM THE MOUNTAIN, THE see **DONNA DELLA MONTAGNA, LA** • 1943
WOMAN FROM THE PROPERTY-OWNING MIDDLE CLASS, BORN 1908 see **BESITZ BURGERIN, JAHRGANG 1908** • 1973
WOMAN FROM THE SEA, THE • 1915 • *Saunders Jackie* • USA
WOMAN FROM WARRENS, THE • 1915 • Browning Tod • USA
WOMAN FROM WARSAW, THE • 1956 • Kalatozov Mikhail • USS
WOMAN GAMBLER, THE (USA) see **ONNA TOBAKUSHI** • 1967
WOMAN GAMBLER AND THE NUN, THE see **ONNA TOBAKUSHI AMADERA KAICHO** • 1968
WOMAN GAMBLER COMES, THE see **ONNA TOBAKUSHI NORIKOMU** • 1968
WOMAN GAMBLER -DEATH FOR THE WICKED see **HIBOTANBAKUTO -OINICHI ITADAKIMASU** • 1971
WOMAN GAMBLER, KANTO AFFAIR see **HIBOTAN BAKUTO, ISSHUKU IPPAN** • 1968
WOMAN GAMBLER: ORYU COMES see **HIBOTAN BAKUTO - ORYU SANJO** • 1970
WOMAN GAMBLER'S REVENGE, THE see **ONNA TOBAKUSHI OKUNOIN KAICHO** • 1968
WOMAN GAMBLER'S SUPPLICATION, THE see **ONNA TOBAKUSHI MIDARETSUBO** • 1968
WOMAN GAME, THE • 1920 • Earle William P. S. • USA
WOMAN GIVES, THE • 1920 • Neill R. William • USA
WOMAN GOD CHANGED, THE • 1921 • Vignola Robert G. • USA
WOMAN GOD FORGOT, THE • 1917 • De Mille Cecil B. • USA
WOMAN GOD SENT, THE • 1920 • Trimble Larry • USA
WOMAN HAS NO NAME see **KADININ ADI YOK** • 1987
WOMAN HAS TWO FACES • 1981 • Kim Soo-Yong • SKR
WOMAN HATER • 1948 • Young Terence • UKN
WOMAN HATER, THE • 1909 • *Lubin* • USA
WOMAN HATER, THE • 1910 • *Thanhouser* • USA
WOMAN HATER, THE • 1910 • *Powers* • USA
WOMAN HATER, THE • 1912 • *Kalem* • USA
WOMAN HATER, THE • 1915 • Brabin Charles J. • USA
WOMAN HATER, THE • 1920 • Goldin Sidney M. • UKN
WOMAN HATER, THE • 1925 • Flood James • USA
WOMAN HATER, THE see **KADIN DUSMANI** • 1967
WOMAN HATERS • 1934 • Gottler Archie • SHT • USA
WOMAN HATERS, THE • 1912 • Reid Hal • USA
WOMAN HATERS, THE • 1913 • Lehrman Henry • USA
WOMAN HATER'S BABY, THE • 1915 • *Gaunthier Gene* • USA
WOMAN-HATER'S DEFEAT, THE • 1913 • *Sullivan E. P.* • USA
WOMAN HE CHOSE, THE (UKN) see **TOSEN FRAN STORMYRTORPET** • 1917
WOMAN HE FEARED, THE • 1916 • Millarde Harry • SHT • USA
WOMAN HE LOVED, THE • 1922 • Sloman Edward • USA • HOW A MAN LOVES
WOMAN HE LOVED, THE • 1988 • Jarrott Charles • TVM • USA
WOMAN HE MARRIED, THE • 1915 • *Kromann Ann* • USA
WOMAN HE MARRIED, THE • 1922 • Niblo Fred • USA
WOMAN HE SCORNED, THE • 1929 • Czinner Paul • UKN • WAY OF LOST SOULS, THE
WOMAN HUNGRY • 1931 • Badger Clarence • USA • CHALLENGE, THE (UKN) ○ UNDER WESTERN SKIES
WOMAN HUNT • 1961 • Dexter Maury • USA
WOMAN HUNT see **AU ROYAUME DES CIEUX** • 1949
WOMAN HUNT, THE • 1972 • Romero Eddie • PHL, USA • WOMANHUNT, THE ○ ESCAPE
WOMAN HUNTER, THE • 1972 • Kowalski Bernard • TVM • USA
WOMAN I LOVE, THE • 1929 • Melford George • USA
WOMAN I LOVE, THE • 1937 • Litvak Anatole • USA • WOMAN BETWEEN, THE (UKN) ○ ESCADRILLE
WOMAN I STOLE, THE • 1933 • Cummings Irving • USA
WOMAN IN 47, THE • 1916 • Irving George • USA
WOMAN IN A DRESSING GOWN • 1957 • Thompson J. Lee • UKN
WOMAN IN A LEOPARD-SKIN see **KVINNA I LEOPARD** • 1958
WOMAN IN A TWILIGHT GARDEN (UKN) see **VROUW TUSSEN HOND EN WOLF, EEN** • 1979
WOMAN IN BLACK, THE • 1912 • Cabanne W. Christy • USA
WOMAN IN BLACK, THE • 1914 • *Klaw & Erlanger* • USA
WOMAN IN BLACK, THE • 1914 • *Rex* • USA
WOMAN IN BLACK, THE • 1914 • Costello Maurice, Gaillord Robert • *Vitagraph* • USA
WOMAN IN BLACK, THE • 1916 • Marston Lawrence • USA
WOMAN IN BONDAGE see **IMPASSIVE FOOTMAN, THE** • 1932
WOMAN IN BROWN (UKN) see **VICIOUS CIRCLE, THE** • 1948
WOMAN IN CHAINS, THE • 1923 • Burt William P. • USA • WOMEN IN CHAINS, THE
WOMAN IN CHAINS (USA) see **IMPASSIVE FOOTMAN, THE** • 1932
WOMAN IN CHAINS (USA) see **PRISONNIERE, LA** • 1968
WOMAN IN COMMAND, THE (USA) see **SOLDIERS OF THE KING** • 1933
WOMAN IN DISTRESS • 1937 • Shores Lynn • USA • GRAND OLD WOMAN
WOMAN IN FLAMES, A (USA) see **FLAMBIERTE FRAU, DIE** • 1983
WOMAN IN GREEN, THE • 1945 • Neill R. William • USA • SHERLOCK HOLMES AND THE WOMAN IN GREEN ○ INVITATION TO DEATH
WOMAN IN GREY, THE • 1920 • Vincent James • SRL • USA
WOMAN IN HER THIRTIES (UKN) see **SIDE STREETS** • 1934
WOMAN IN HIDING • 1949 • Gordon Michael • USA • FUGITIVE FROM TERROR
WOMAN IN HIDING see **MANTRAP** • 1953
WOMAN IN HIS HOUSE, THE • 1920 • Stahl John M. • USA
WOMAN IN HIS HOUSE, THE (UKN) see **ANIMAL KINGDOM, THE** • 1932
WOMAN IN LOVE, A • 1970 • Viola Albert T. • USA
WOMAN IN LOVE, A see **IMRA'A ACHIQA** • 1974
WOMAN IN PAWN, A • 1927 • Saville Victor, Greenwood Edwin • UKN
WOMAN IN POLITICS, THE • 1916 • Moore W. Eugene • USA
WOMAN IN QUESTION, THE • 1950 • Asquith Anthony • UKN • FIVE ANGLES ON MURDER (USA)
WOMAN IN RED, THE • 1935 • Florey Robert • USA • NORTH SHORE
WOMAN IN RED, THE • 1984 • Wilder Gene • USA
WOMAN IN ROOM 13 • 1932 • King Henry • USA
WOMAN IN ROOM 13, THE • 1920 • Lloyd Frank • USA
WOMAN IN THE ARTS, A • 1968 • van Nie Rene • SHT • NTH
WOMAN IN THE BOX, THE • 1915 • Davenport Harry • USA
WOMAN IN THE CASE, A • 1911 • Coleby A. E. • UKN
WOMAN IN THE CASE, A • 1916 • Ford Hugh • USA
WOMAN IN THE CASE, A • 1917 • Curtis Allen • SHT • USA
WOMAN IN THE CASE, THE • 1910 • Melies Gaston • USA
WOMAN IN THE CASE, THE • 1916 • *George Willoughby Photoplay* • ASL
WOMAN IN THE CASE, THE (UKN) see **HEADLINE WOMAN, THE** • 1935
WOMAN IN THE CASE (UKN) see **ALLOTMENT WIVES** • 1945
WOMAN IN THE DARK • 1934 • Rosen Phil • USA
WOMAN IN THE DARK • 1952 • Blair George • USA
WOMAN IN THE DUNES (USA) see **SUNA NO ONNA** • 1964
WOMAN IN THE HALL, THE • 1947 • Lee Jack • UKN
WOMAN IN THE HAT see **KOBIETA W KAPELUSZU** • 1984
WOMAN IN THE HOUSE, THE • 1942 • Lee Sammy • USA • FEAR
WOMAN IN THE MOON see **FRAU IM MOND, DIE** • 1929
WOMAN IN THE NET, THE see **AGA DUSEN KADIN** • 1967
WOMAN IN THE NEXT ROOM, THE • 1974 • Yeshurun Isaac • ISR • WOMAN IN THE OTHER ROOM, THE
WOMAN IN THE NIGHT • 1948 • Rowland William • USA
WOMAN IN THE NIGHT, A (USA) see **TESHA** • 1928
WOMAN IN THE OTHER ROOM, THE see **WOMAN IN THE NEXT ROOM, THE** • 1974
WOMAN IN THE PAINTING, THE (USA) see **AMICI PER LA PELLE** • 1955
WOMAN IN THE RUMOR, THE (USA) see **UWASA NO ONNA** • 1954
WOMAN IN THE SAND see **SUNA NO ONNA** • 1964
WOMAN IN THE SUITCASE, THE • 1920 • Niblo Fred • USA
WOMAN IN THE ULTIMATE, A • 1913 • Henderson Dell • USA
WOMAN IN THE WEB, THE • 1918 • Smith David, Hurst Paul C. • SRL • USA
WOMAN IN THE WILDERNESS see **WOMAN OF THE NORTH COUNTRY** • 1952
WOMAN IN THE WINDOW see **RAGAZZA IN VETRINA, LA** • 1960
WOMAN IN THE WINDOW, THE • 1944 • Lang Fritz • USA
WOMAN IN TRANSIT see **FEMME DE L'HOTEL, LA** • 1985
WOMAN IN WHITE see **KVINNA I VITT** • 1949
WOMAN IN WHITE, A (USA) see **JOURNAL D'UNE FEMME EN BLANC, LE** • 1964
WOMAN IN WHITE, THE • 1912 • *Thanhouser* • USA
WOMAN IN WHITE, THE • 1912 • *Gem* • USA
WOMAN IN WHITE, THE • 1917 • Warde Ernest C. • USA
WOMAN IN WHITE, THE • 1929 • Wilcox Herbert • UKN
WOMAN IN WHITE, THE • 1948 • Godfrey Peter • USA
WOMAN INSIDE, THE • 1981 • Van Winkle Joseph • CND
WOMAN IS A FLOWER (UKN) see **FEMININ FLEUR, LA** • 1965
WOMAN IS A WOMAN, A (USA) see **FEMME EST UNE FEMME, UNE** • 1961
WOMAN IS BORN, A see **YARATILAN KADIN** • 1968
WOMAN IS THE JUDGE, A • 1939 • Grinde Nick • USA
WOMAN JUROR, THE • 1926 • Rosmer Milton • UKN
WOMAN KILLED BY LOVE, A • 1978 • *Kamel Madiha (P)* • EGY
WOMAN LAUGHS, A • 1914 • MacGregor Norval • USA
WOMAN LAWYER, A • 1910 • *Powers* • USA • THAT WOMAN LAWYER
WOMAN LIKE EVE, A see **VROUW ALS EVA, EEN** • 1978
WOMAN LIKE SATAN, A (USA) see **FEMME ET LE PANTIN, LA** • 1958
WOMAN LOVED, A • 1913 • *Imp* • USA
WOMAN MEN YEARN FOR, THE • 1928 • *Dietrich Marlene*
WOMAN MICHAEL MARRIED, THE • 1919 • Kolker Henry • USA
WOMAN MISUNDERSTOOD, A • 1921 • Paul Fred, Raymond Jack • UKN
WOMAN MUST BE AFRAID OF MAN, A • 1965 • Tzavellas Georges • GRC
WOMAN NAMED EN, A see **EN TO IU ONNA** • 1971
WOMAN NEEDS LOVING, A (UKN) see **FRAU SUCHT LIEBE, EINE** • 1968
WOMAN NEVER FORGETS, A see **KADIN ASLA UNUTMAZ** • 1968
WOMAN NEXT DOOR, THE • 1915 • *Fenwick Irene* • USA
WOMAN NEXT DOOR, THE see **VICKY VAN** • 1919
WOMAN NEXT DOOR, THE see **LAST CARD, THE** • 1921
WOMAN NEXT DOOR, THE (USA) see **FEMME D'A COTE, LA** • 1981
WOMAN OBSESSED • 1959 • Hathaway Henry • USA
WOMAN OF A MISTY MOONLIGHT see **OBOROYO NO ONNA** • 1936
WOMAN OF A PALE NIGHT see **OBOROYO NO ONNA** • 1936
WOMAN OF AFFAIRS, A • 1928 • Brown Clarence • USA
WOMAN OF ANTWERP see **DEDEE D'ANVERS** • 1947
WOMAN OF ARIZONA, A • 1912 • *Mackley Arthur* • USA
WOMAN OF BRONZE, THE • 1923 • Vidor King • USA
WOMAN OF CLAY, A • 1917 • *Baird Leah* • SHT • USA
WOMAN OF COLOURS, A see **DAME EN COLEURS, LA** • 1984
WOMAN OF DARKNESS see **YNGSJOMORDET** • 1966
WOMAN OF DESIRE see **MEN IN HER LIFE, THE** • 1941
WOMAN OF DESIRE see **MULHER DO DESEJO, A** • 1980
WOMAN OF DESTINY (UKN) see **MARRIAGE BARGAIN, THE** • 1935
WOMAN OF DISTINCTION, A • 1950 • Buzzell Edward • USA
WOMAN OF DOLWYN (USA) see **LAST DAYS OF DOLWYN, THE** • 1949
WOMAN OF EVERYONE, THE see **MULHER DE TODES, A** • 1969
WOMAN OF EVIL, A see **REINE MARGOT, LA** • 1954
WOMAN OF EXPERIENCE, A • 1931 • Brown Harry J. • USA • REGISTERED WOMAN
WOMAN OF FIRE see **MUJER DE FUEGO** • 1988
WOMAN OF FLESH, A • 1927 • *Richardson Charles* • USA
WOMAN OF FRANCE, A • 1918 • *Nazimova Alla* • SHT • USA
WOMAN OF GOOD CHARACTER, A • 1982 • Blyth David • NZL
WOMAN OF HIS DREAMS, THE • 1921 • Shaw Harold • UKN
WOMAN OF ILL REPUTE, A see **MASHO NO ONNA** • 1968
WOMAN OF IMPULSE, A • 1918 • Jose Edward • USA
WOMAN OF IT, THE • 1914 • Campbell Colin • USA
WOMAN OF LIES • 1919 • Hamilton G. P. • USA
WOMAN OF MUSASHINO see **MUSASHINO FUJIN** • 1951
WOMAN OF MY OWN, A see **DESIRE ME** • 1947
WOMAN OF MYSTERY, A • 1958 • Morris Ernest • UKN
WOMAN OF MYSTERY, THE • 1914 • Blache Alice • USA
WOMAN OF MYSTERY, THE • 1916 • Vale Travers • SHT • USA
WOMAN OF NANIWA see **NANIWA ONNA** • 1940
WOMAN OF NERVE, A • 1915 • *Grey Olga* • USA
WOMAN OF NO IMPORTANCE, A • 1912 • *Powers* • USA
WOMAN OF NO IMPORTANCE, A • 1921 • Clift Denison • UKN
WOMAN OF NO IMPORTANCE, A (USA) see **FRAU OHNE BETEUTUNG, EINE** • 1936
WOMAN OF OSAKA, A see **OSAKA NO ONNA** • 1958
WOMAN OF OSAKA, A (USA) see **NANIWA ONNA** • 1940
WOMAN OF OUR TIME, A • 1972 • Tammer Peter • DOC • ASL
WOMAN OF PALE NIGHT see **OBOROYO NO ONNA** • 1936
WOMAN OF PARIS, A • 1923 • Chaplin Charles • USA • PUBLIC OPINION ○ DESTINY
WOMAN OF PLEASURE, A • 1919 • Worsley Wallace • USA
WOMAN OF PLEASURE (USA) see **KANRAKU NO ONNA** • 1924
WOMAN OF REDEMPTION, A • 1918 • Vale Travers • USA
WOMAN OF ROME see **ROMANA, LA** • 1954
WOMAN OF RUMOUR, A (UKN) see **UWASA NO ONNA** • 1954
WOMAN OF SHANGHAI see **SHANHAI NO ONNA** • 1952
WOMAN OF SIN, A • 1913 • *Hunt Irene* • USA
WOMAN OF STRAW • 1964 • Dearden Basil • UKN
WOMAN OF STYLE, A see **SECRET LIVES OF THE BRITISH PRIME MINISTERS: LLOYD GEORGE** • 1983
WOMAN OF SUBSTANCE, A • 1984 • Sharp Don • MTV • UKN, USA
WOMAN OF SUMMER (UKN) see **STRIPPER, THE** • 1963
WOMAN OF THE CIRCUS see **CAROLA LAMBERTI -E!NE VOM ZIRKUS** • 1954
WOMAN OF THE DUNES see **SUNA NO ONNA** • 1964
WOMAN OF THE GANGES see **FEMME DU GANGE, LA** • 1973
WOMAN OF THE GENROKU ERA, A see **GENROKU ONNA** • 1924
WOMAN OF THE GINZA see **GINZA NO ONNA** • 1955
WOMAN OF THE IRON BRACELETS, THE • 1920 • Morgan Sidney • UKN
WOMAN OF THE MIST see **OBOROYO NO ONNA** • 1936
WOMAN OF THE MOON, THE see **DONNA DELLA LUNA, LA** • 1988
WOMAN OF THE MOUNTAINS, THE • 1913 • *Selig* • USA
WOMAN OF THE NORTH COUNTRY • 1952 • Kane Joseph • USA • WOMAN IN THE WILDERNESS
WOMAN OF THE ORIENT see **ORIENTALI, LE** • 1960
WOMAN OF THE OSORE MOUNTAINS, A see **OSOREZAN NO ONNA** • 1965
WOMAN OF THE PEOPLE • 1912 • ASL
WOMAN OF THE PEOPLE, A see **KVINDE AF FOLKET, EN** • 1909
WOMAN OF THE PORT, THE see **MUJER DEL PUERTO, LA** • 1933
WOMAN OF THE RED SEA (UKN) see **AFRICA SOTTO I MARI** • 1953
WOMAN OF THE RIVER (USA) see **DONNA DEL FIUME, LA** • 1955
WOMAN OF THE RUMOR, THE see **UWASA NO ONNA** • 1954
WOMAN OF THE SEA, A • 1926 • von Sternberg Josef, Chaplin Charles • USA • SEA GULL, THE
WOMAN OF THE SEA, THE • 1915 • *Saunders Jackie* • USA
WOMAN OF THE SLEEPING FOREST, THE see **SPYASHCHAYA KRASAVITSA** • 1930
WOMAN OF THE SNOW, THE (UKN) see **YUKI-ONNA** • 1964
WOMAN OF THE TOWN, THE • 1943 • Archainbaud George • USA
WOMAN OF THE WORLD, A • 1915 • *Terriss Tom* • USA
WOMAN OF THE WORLD, A • 1925 • St. Clair Malcolm • USA
WOMAN OF THE WORLD, A (UKN) see **OUTCAST LADY** • 1934
WOMAN OF THE YEAR • 1941 • Stevens George • USA
WOMAN OF THE YEAR • 1976 • Taylor Jud • TVM • USA
WOMAN OF TOKYO see **TOKYO NO ONNA** • 1933
WOMAN OF TOMORROW • 1914 • Chardynin Pyotr • USS
WOMAN OF WONDERS see **DONNA DELLE MERAVIGLIE, LA** • 1985
WOMAN ON BOARD, A see **KVINNA OMBORD, EN** • 1941
WOMAN ON FIRE, A (USA) see **BRUCIA, RAGAZZO, BRUCIA** • 1969
WOMAN ON HER OWN • 1981 • Holland Agnieszka • PLN
WOMAN ON PIER 13, THE (UKN) see **I MARRIED A COMMUNIST** • 1949
WOMAN ON THE BEACH, THE • 1946 • Renoir Jean • USA • FEMME SUR LA PLAGE, LA (FRN) ○ DESIRABLE WOMAN
WOMAN ON THE HILL, THE • 1955 • Bahna Vladimir • CZC
WOMAN ON THE INDEX, THE • 1919 • Henley Hobart • USA
WOMAN ON THE JURY, THE • 1924 • Hoyt Harry O. • USA
WOMAN ON THE ROOF, THE (UKN) see **KVINNORNA PA TAKET** • 1989
WOMAN ON THE RUN • 1950 • Foster Norman • USA

WOMAN ON TRIAL, THE • 1927 • Stiller Mauritz • USA
WOMAN, ONE DAY, A see **FEMME, UN JOUR, UNE** • 1977
WOMAN OPENING THE DOOR, THE see **TOBIRA O HIRAKU ONNA** • 1946
WOMAN OPENS THE DOOR, A see **TOBIRA O HIRAKU ONNA** • 1946
WOMAN OPPOSITE see **THAT WOMAN OPPOSITE** • 1957
WOMAN OR BEAST? see **MUJER O FIERA?** • 1954
WOMAN OR TWO, A see **FEMME OU DEUX, UNE** • 1985
WOMAN PATRIOT see **DANG LENGGANG** • 1971
WOMAN PAYS, THE • 1914 • *Fealy Maude* • USA
WOMAN PAYS, THE • 1915 • Batley Ethyle • UKN
WOMAN PAYS, THE • 1915 • Jones Edgar • USA
WOMAN POSSESSED, A • 1958 • Varnel Max • UKN
WOMAN-PROOF • 1923 • Green Alfred E. • USA • ALL MUST MARRY
WOMAN PROSECUTED FOR TAX EVASION, A see **MARUSA NO ONNA** • 1987
WOMAN PURSUED • 1931 • Boleslawski Richard • USA
WOMAN RACKET, THE • 1929 • Ober Robert, Kelley Albert • USA • LIGHTS AND SHADOWS (UKN)
WOMAN REBELS, A • 1936 • Sandrich Mark • USA • PORTRAIT OF A REBEL
WOMAN RECLAIMED, A • 1915 • Smiley Joseph • USA
WOMAN REDEEMED, A • 1927 • Hill Sinclair • UKN
WOMAN REDEEMED, THE • 1916 • *Empress Marie* • USA
WOMAN SCORNED, A • 1910 • Fitzhamon Lewin? • UKN
WOMAN SCORNED, A • 1911 • Griffith D. W. • USA
WOMAN SCORNED, A • 1913 • *Wilbur Crane* • USA
WOMAN SCORNED, A • 1914 • *Reliance* • USA
WOMAN SCORNED, A • 1914 • *Essanay* • USA
WOMAN SCORNED, A • 1915 • Taylor William D. • USA
WOMAN SEES IT THROUGH, THE see **MOTHER** • 1927
WOMAN STANDING IN THE LIGHT, A see **HIKARI NO TATSU ONNA** • 1920
WOMAN SUFFERS, THE • 1918 • Longford Raymond • ASL
WOMAN SUPREME • 1906 • Jeapes Harold? • *Graphic* • UKN
WOMAN SUPREME • 1906 • Martin J. H.? • *R. W. Paul* • UKN
WOMAN TAKES COMMAND see **KVINNAN TAR BEFELAT** • 1942
WOMAN TAKES OFF HER GLOVES, A see **TEBUKURO O NUGASO ONNA** • 1946
WOMAN TAMER (UKN) see **SHE COULDN'T TAKE IT** • 1935
WOMAN TEMPTED, A • 1926 • Elvey Maurice • UKN
WOMAN TEMPTED ME, THE see **FRELSENDE FILM, DEN** • 1915
WOMAN THAT NIGHT, THE • 1934 • Shimazu Yasujiro • JPN
WOMAN THE GERMANS SHOT • 1918 • Adolfi John G. • USA • CAVELL CASE, THE
WOMAN, THE LION AND THE MAN, THE • 1915 • *Centaur* • USA
WOMAN THERE WAS, A • 1919 • Edwards J. Gordon • USA
WOMAN THEY ALMOST LYNCHED, THE • 1953 • Dwan Allan • USA
WOMAN THOU GAVEST ME, THE • 1919 • Ford Hugh • USA
WOMAN TIMES SEVEN • 1967 • De Sica Vittorio • USA, ITL, FRN • SETTE VOLTE DONNA (ITL) ○ SEPT FOIS FEMME (FRN) ○ WOMAN X 7
WOMAN TO ADORE, A see **TAPILACAK KADIN** • 1967
WOMAN TO BE HANGED, A see **ASILACAK KADIN** • 1985
WOMAN TO WOMAN • 1923 • Cutts Graham • UKN
WOMAN TO WOMAN • 1929 • Saville Victor • UKN
WOMAN TO WOMAN • 1946 • Rogers Maclean • UKN
WOMAN TO WOMAN see **DE MUJER A MUJER** • 1987
WOMAN TRAP • 1929 • Wellman William A. • USA
WOMAN TRAP • 1936 • Young Harold • USA
WOMAN TROUBLE (USA) see **MOLTI SOGNI PER LE STRADE** • 1948
WOMAN UNAFRAID • 1934 • Cowen William J. • USA
WOMAN UNDER COVER, THE • 1919 • Siegmann George • USA
WOMAN UNDER OATH, THE • 1919 • Stahl John M. • USA
WOMAN UNDER THE INFLUENCE, A • 1974 • Cassavetes John • USA
WOMAN UNTAMED, THE • 1920 • Pratt Jack • USA
WOMAN UNVEILED see **ONNA DE ARU KOTO** • 1958
WOMAN UPSTAIRS, THE • 1921 • Paul Fred • UKN
WOMAN USING A SHORT SWORD see **KODACHI O TSUKAU ONNA** • 1944
WOMAN USING A SHORT SWORD see **KODACHI O TSUKAU ONNA** • 1961
WOMAN – VILLA – CAR – MONEY see **FEMME – VILLA – VOITURE – ARGENT** • 1972
WOMAN VS. WOMAN • 1910 • Haldane Bert • UKN
WOMAN, WAKE UP! • 1922 • Harrison Marcus • USA
WOMAN WALKING ALONE ON THE EARTH see **ONNA HITORI DAICHI O YUKU** • 1953
WOMAN WALKS THE EARTH ALONE, A see **ONNA HITORI DAICHI O YUKU** • 1953
WOMAN WANTED • 1935 • Seitz George B. • USA • MANHATTAN MADNESS
WOMAN WENT FORTH, A • 1915 • Kaufman Joseph • USA
WOMAN WHO BECAME MAD, THE see **CILDIRAN KADIN** • 1948
WOMAN WHO BELIEVED, THE • 1922 • Harvey John • USA
WOMAN WHO CAME BACK, THE • 1945 • Colmes Walter • USA
WOMAN WHO CAME FROM THE SEA • 1953 • *Addams Dawn* • ITL
WOMAN WHO CONVICTS MEN, A see **OTOKO O SABAKU ONNA** • 1948
WOMAN WHO CRIED MURDER, THE see **DEATH SCREAM** • 1975
WOMAN WHO DARED, THE • 1911 • *Yankee* • USA
WOMAN WHO DARED, THE • 1915 • Bentley Thomas • UKN • SOUL FOR SALE, A (USA)
WOMAN WHO DARED, THE • 1916 • Middleton George E. • USA
WOMAN WHO DARED, THE (USA) see **CIEL EST A VOUS, LE** • 1943
WOMAN WHO DID, A • 1914 • *K & S Feature Film* • USA
WOMAN WHO DID, THE • 1915 • West Walter • UKN
WOMAN WHO DID, THE see **FRAU MIT DEM SCHLECHTEN RUF, DIE** • 1925
WOMAN WHO DID 'EM, THE • 1916 • *New Agency* • SHT • UKN
WOMAN WHO DID NOT CARE, THE • 1913 • *Darnell Jean* • USA
WOMAN WHO DID NOT CARE, THE • 1916 • Beal Frank • SHT • USA
WOMAN WHO DID NOT CARE, THE • 1927 • Rosen Phil • USA
WOMAN WHO DISAPPEARED, THE see **KVINNAN SOM FORSVANN** • 1949
WOMAN WHO FOLLOWED ME, THE • 1916 • Leonard Robert Z., Kirkland David • SHT • USA
WOMAN WHO FOOLED HERSELF, THE • 1922 • Logue Charles A., Ellis Robert • USA
WOMAN WHO GAMBLES, THE • 1908 • *Lubin* • USA
WOMAN WHO GAVE, THE • 1918 • Buel Kenean • USA
WOMAN WHO IS WAITING see **MACHIBOKE NO ONNA** • 1946
WOMAN WHO KILLED A VULTURE, THE see **GEIER-WALLY, DIE** • 1921
WOMAN WHO KNEW, THE • 1913 • *Cummings Irving* • USA
WOMAN WHO KNOWS WHAT SHE WANTS, A see **ZENA, KTERA VI CO CHCE** • 1934
WOMAN WHO LAUGHS • 1915 • *Lubin* • USA
WOMAN WHO LIED, THE • 1915 • Henderson Lucius • USA
WOMAN WHO MARRIED CLARK GABLE, THE • 1986 • O'Sullivan Thaddeus • SHT • IRL
WOMAN WHO NEEDED KILLING, THE see **DANGEROUS WOMAN, A** • 1929
WOMAN WHO OBEYED, THE • 1923 • Morgan Sidney • UKN • SHALL A WOMAN OBEY
WOMAN WHO PAID, THE • 1915 • Vale Travers?, Reehm George E.? • USA
WOMAN WHO SAW DREAMS, THE • 1988 • Panayotopoulos Nikos • GRC
WOMAN WHO SINGS, THE see **ZHENSHCHINA, KOTORAY POYOT** • 1979
WOMAN WHO SINNED, A • 1924 • Fox Finis • USA
WOMAN WHO TOUCHED THE LEGS, THE see **ASHI NI SAWATTA ONNA** • 1952
WOMAN WHO TOUCHED THE LEGS, THE see **ASHI NI SAWATTA ONNA** • 1960
WOMAN WHO UNDERSTOOD, A • 1920 • Parke William • USA
WOMAN WHO WALKED ALONE, THE • 1922 • Melford George • USA
WOMAN WHO WAS FORGOTTEN, THE • 1930 • Thomas Richard • USA
WOMAN WHO WAS NOTHING, THE • 1917 • Elvey Maurice • UKN
WOMAN WHO WASN'T, THE • 1908 • Collins Alf? • UKN
WOMAN WHO WON, THE see **MAN WHO WAS NEVER KISSED, THE** • 1914
WOMAN WHO WOULD NOT PAY, THE • 1917 • Baldwin Ruth Ann • SHT • USA
WOMAN WHO WOULDN'T DIE, THE (USA) see **CATACOMBS** • 1964
WOMAN WHO WOULDN'T MARRY, A see **KEKKON SHINAI ONNA** • 1987
WOMAN WINS, THE • 1918 • Wilson Frank • UKN
WOMAN WISE • 1928 • Ray Albert • USA
WOMAN WISE • 1937 • Dwan Allan • USA • WOMAN-WISE
WOMAN-WISE see **WOMAN WISE** • 1937
WOMAN WITH A DAGGER see **ZHENSHCHINA S KINZHALOM** • 1916
WOMAN WITH A ROSE, THE • 1915 • *Drew Lillian* • USA
WOMAN WITH FOUR FACES, THE • 1923 • Brenon Herbert • USA
WOMAN WITH LANDSCAPE see **ZENA S KRAJOLIKOM** • 1989
WOMAN WITH NO NAME, THE • 1950 • Vajda Ladislao, O'Ferrall George M. • UKN • HER PANELLED DOOR (USA)
WOMAN WITH RED BOOTS, THE(USA) see **FEMME AUX BOTTES ROUGES, LA** • 1974
WOMAN WITH THE DAGGER, THE see **ZHENSHCHINA S KINZHALOM** • 1916
WOMAN WITH THE FAN, THE • 1921 • Plaissetty Rene • UKN
WOMAN WITH THE KNIFE, THE see **FEMME AU COUTEAU, LA** • 1968
WOMAN WITH THE ORCHID, THE see **FRAU MIT DEN ORCHIDEEN, DIE** • 1919
WOMAN WITH TWO SOULS, THE see **KETLELKU ASSZORY, A** • 1917
WOMAN WITHOUT A FACE see **KVINNA UTAN ANSIKTE** • 1947
WOMAN WITHOUT A FACE (UKN) see **MISTER BUDDWING** • 1965
WOMAN WITHOUT A HEAD, THE see **MUJER SIN CABEZA, LA** • 1943
WOMAN WITHOUT A HEART, A • 1911 • *Powers* • USA
WOMAN WITHOUT A SOUL see **MUJER SIN ALMA, LA** • 1943
WOMAN WITHOUT A SOUL, THE • 1914 • *Majestic* • USA
WOMAN WITHOUT A SOUL, THE • 1915 • Weston Charles • UKN
WOMAN WITHOUT CAMELIAS, THE see **SIGNORA SENZA CAMILIE, LA** • 1953
WOMAN WITHOUT SOUL, A • 1915 • MacDonald J. Farrell • USA
WOMAN! WOMAN! • 1919 • Buel Kenean • USA
WOMAN X 7 see **WOMAN TIMES SEVEN** • 1967
WOMANCOCK • 1965 • Linder Carl • SHT • USA
WOMANEATER • 1958 • Saunders Charles • UKN • WOMAN EATER, THE (USA)
WOMANHANDLED • 1925 • La Cava Gregory • USA
WOMANHOOD • 1917 • Blackton J. Stuart (Spv), Earle William P. S. • USA
WOMANHOOD • 1934 • Hughes Harry • UKN
WOMANHUNT, THE see **WOMAN HUNT, THE** • 1972
WOMANKIND, THE see **LIANGJIA FUNU** • 1985
WOMANLY CURIOSITY • 1914 • *Melies* • USA
WOMANPOWER • 1926 • Beaumont Harry • USA
WOMAN'S ANGLE, THE • 1952 • Arliss Leslie • UKN
WOMAN'S AWAKENING, A • 1917 • Withey Chet • USA
WOMAN'S BETTER NATURE, A • 1910 • *Bison* • USA
WOMAN'S BODY VANISHES see **JOTAI JOHATSU** • 1967
WOMAN'S BURDEN • 1914 • *Weber Lois* • USA
WOMAN'S BUSINESS, A • 1920 • Rolfe B. A. • USA
WOMAN'S CARNAL DESIRE see **ONNA NO SHIKIYOKU** • 1968
WOMAN'S CASE, A see **MIKREH ISHA** • 1969
WOMAN'S CRUSADE • 1931 • Alexandrov Grigori • SWT • WOMAN'S WEAL, WOMAN'S WOE
WOMAN'S CURIOSITY • 1911 • *Lubin* • USA
WOMAN'S DARING, A • 1916 • Sloman Edward • USA
WOMAN'S DEBT, A • 1915 • *Madison Cleo* • USA
WOMAN'S DECISION, A see **BILANS KWARTALNY** • 1975
WOMAN'S DECORATION see **ONNA NO KUNSHO** • 1961
WOMAN'S DESCENT see **ONNA NO SAKA** • 1960
WOMAN'S DEVOTION, A • 1956 • Henreid Paul • USA • WAR SHOCK (UKN) ○ BATTLE SHOCK ○ WAR HUNT
WOMAN'S EXPERIENCE, A • 1918 • Vekroff Perry N. • USA
WOMAN'S EYES, A • 1916 • Carey Harry, Marshall George • SHT • USA
WOMAN'S FACE, A • 1941 • Cukor George • USA
WOMAN'S FACE, A see **KVINNAS ANSIKTE, EN** • 1938
WOMAN'S FACE, A see **ONNA NO KAO** • 1949
WOMAN'S FAITH, A • 1925 • Laemmle Edward • USA • MIRACLE
WOMAN'S FATE see **FRAUENSCHICKSALE** • 1952
WOMAN'S FATE, A see **MIRA MIAS YINEKAS, I** • 1968
WOMAN'S FIGHT, A • 1916 • Blache Herbert • USA
WOMAN'S FOLLY, A • 1910 • Bouwmeester Theo? • *Hepworth* • UKN
WOMAN'S FOLLY, A • 1910 • Noy Wilfred? • *Clarendon* • UKN
WOMAN'S FOLLY, A • 1913 • *Rex* • USA
WOMAN'S FOLLY, A • 1914 • Physioc Wray • USA
WOMAN'S FOOL, A • 1918 • Ford John • USA
WOMAN'S GRATITUDE, A • 1911 • Melies Gaston • USA
WOMAN'S HATE, A • 1913 • Stow Percy • UKN
WOMAN'S HEART see **ONNAGOKORO** • 1959
WOMAN'S HEART, A • 1913 • *Lubin* • USA
WOMAN'S HEART, A • 1926 • Rosen Phil • USA
WOMAN'S HERESY, A see **JASHUMON NO ONNA** • 1924
WOMAN'S HONOR • 1913 • Dwan Allan • USA
WOMAN'S HONOR, A • 1914 • *Victor* • USA
WOMAN'S HONOR, A • 1916 • West Roland • USA
WOMAN'S LAW • 1927 • Fitzgerald Dallas M. • USA
WOMAN'S LAW, THE • 1916 • McGill Lawrence • USA
WOMAN'S LIFE, A see **ONNA NO ISSHO** • 1949
WOMAN'S LIFE, A see **ONNA NO ISSHO** • 1953
WOMAN'S LIFE, A see **ONNA NO ISSHO** • 1955
WOMAN'S LIFE, A see **ONNA NO REKISHI** • 1963
WOMAN'S LOVE, A • 1910 • *Vitagraph* • USA
WOMAN'S LOYALTY, A • 1914 • *Snow Marguerite* • USA
WOMAN'S MAN • 1920 • Gordon Warren • USA
WOMAN'S MAN, A • 1934 • Ludwig Edward • USA
WOMAN'S MANOEUVRING see **ONNA NO TESABAKI** • 1968
WOMAN'S MISSION, A • 1913 • *Melies* • USA
WOMAN'S MISTAKE, A • 1915 • *Kleine George* • USA
WOMAN'S PARADISE (USA) see **FRAUENPARADIES, DAS** • 1939
WOMAN'S PAST, A • 1915 • *Federal* • USA
WOMAN'S PAST, A • 1915 • Powell Frank • *Fox* • USA
WOMAN'S PAST, A • 1915 • Sandberg Anders W. • DNM
WOMAN'S PAST, A see **PARELTHON MIAS YINEKAS, TO** • 1968
WOMAN'S PLACE • 1921 • Fleming Victor • USA
WOMAN'S PLACE, A see **ONNA NO ZA** • 1962
WOMAN'S POWER, A • 1910 • *Powers* • USA
WOMAN'S POWER, A • 1916 • Thornby Robert T. • USA • CODE OF THE MOUNTAINS, THE
WOMAN'S PRIVILEGE, A • 1962 • Bushell Anthony • UKN
WOMAN'S PRIVILEGE, A see **TOGETHER AGAIN** • 1944
WOMAN'S PRIVILEGE IN LEAP YEAR • 1912 • Aylott Dave? • UKN
WOMAN'S RESOLUTION, A see **JOSEI NO KAKUGO** • 1940
WOMAN'S RESURRECTION, A • 1915 • Edwards J. Gordon • USA
WOMAN'S REVENGE, A • 1913 • Smalley Phillips • USA
WOMAN'S REVENGE, A • 1915 • West Langdon • USA
WOMAN'S REVENGE, A see **KADIN INTIKAMI** • 1968
WOMAN'S SACRIFICE, A • 1906 • Green Tom? • UKN
WOMAN'S SACRIFICE, A see **VIRGIN'S SACRIFICE, A** • 1922
WOMAN'S SECRET, A • 1949 • Ray Nicholas • USA
WOMAN'S SECRET, A see **FLAMES OF PASSION** • 1922
WOMAN'S SECRET, A see **FUJINKAI** • 1959
WOMAN'S SECRET, A (USA) see **SOUTHERN LOVE** • 1924
WOMAN'S SHARE, THE • 1915 • Sturgeon Rollin S. • USA
WOMAN'S SIDE, THE • 1922 • Barry J. A. • USA
WOMAN'S SORROWS, A see **NYONIN AISHU** • 1937
WOMAN'S STATUS see **ONNA NO ZA** • 1962
WOMAN'S STORY, A see **STORIA DI UNA DONNA, LA** • 1920
WOMAN'S STORY, A see **ONNA NO REKISHI** • 1963
WOMAN'S STRATAGEM, A • 1913 • *Rex* • USA
WOMAN'S STRATEGY, A • 1910 • *Edison* • USA
WOMAN'S STREET, A • 1989 • Zhang Liang • CHN
WOMAN'S TEMPTATION, A • 1959 • Grayson Godfrey • UKN
WOMAN'S TESTAMENT, A see **JOKYO** • 1960
WOMAN'S TREACHERY, A • 1910 • Bouwmeester Theo? • UKN
WOMAN'S TRIUMPH, A • 1914 • Dawley J. Searle • USA
WOMAN'S URGE, A • 1965 • Hall Ed • USA • NYMPHO
WOMAN'S VANITY • 1910 • *Lubin* • USA
WOMAN'S VANITY, A • 1909 • Bouwmeester Theo? • UKN
WOMAN'S VENGEANCE, A • 1947 • Korda Zoltan • USA • MORTAL COILS
WOMAN'S VENGEANCE, A (UKN) see **MAN FROM SUNDOWN, THE** • 1939
WOMAN'S VICTORY, A see **AFTI POU DHEN LIYISE** • 1967
WOMAN'S VILES, A • 1915 • *Gilmore Paul* • USA • MODEL'S ADVENTURE, THE
WOMAN'S VOICE, A • 1911 • *Essanay* • USA
WOMAN'S WAY, A • 1908 • Griffith D. W. • USA
WOMAN'S WAY, A • 1909 • *Vitagraph* • USA
WOMAN'S WAY, A • 1912 • Melies Gaston • USA
WOMAN'S WAY, A • 1913 • *Essanay* • USA
WOMAN'S WAY, A • 1913 • *Nestor* • USA
WOMAN'S WAY, A • 1913 • *Patheplay* • USA
WOMAN'S WAY, A • 1915 • *Farley Dot* • USA
WOMAN'S WAY, A • 1916 • O'Neil Barry • USA
WOMAN'S WAY, A • 1928 • Mortimer Edmund • USA
WOMAN'S WEAL, WOMAN'S WOE see **WOMAN'S CRUSADE** • 1931

WOMAN'S WEAPONS • 1918 • Vignola Robert G. • USA • WOMEN'S WEAPONS
WOMAN'S WHIM, A • 1912 • *Cosmopolitan* • UKN
WOMAN'S WIT • 1916 • Kerrigan J. M. • IRL
WOMAN'S WIT, A • 1909 • *Essanay* • USA
WOMAN'S WIT, A • 1910 • *Powers* • USA
WOMAN'S WIT, A • 1912 • Buckland Warwick? • UKN
WOMAN'S WIT, A • 1913 • *Kb* • USA
WOMAN'S WOMAN, A • 1922 • Giblyn Charles • USA
WOMAN'S WORLD, A • 1954 • Negulesco Jean • USA
WOMAN'S YOUTH, A see **CHABAB EMRAA** • 1956
WOMB OF POWER • 1979 • *Nihalani Govind (Ph)* • DOC • IND
WOMB TO LET, A see **HARAGASHIONNA** • 1968
WOMBLING FREE • 1978 • Jeffries Lionel • UKN
WOMEN • 1913 • *Calvert E. H.* • USA
WOMEN • 1979 • Meszaros Marta • HNG
WOMEN see **ELLES** • 1966
WOMEN see **FEMMES, LES** • 1969
WOMEN see **NUREN XIN** • 1985
WOMEN, THE • Nickel Gitta • DOC • GDR
WOMEN, THE • 1939 • Cukor George • USA
WOMEN, THE • 1973 • Brakhage Stan • USA
WOMEN, THE see **ZHENSHCHINY** • 1965
WOMEN, THE see **VIXENS, THE** • 1969
WOMEN, THE see **KVINNENE** • 1979
WOMEN AND BLOODY TERROR see **HIS WIFE'S HABIT** • 1970
WOMEN AND DIAMONDS • 1924 • Thornton F. Martin • UKN
WOMEN AND GOLD • 1919 • *Austral Photoplay* • ASL
WOMEN AND GOLD • 1925 • Hogan James P. • USA
WOMEN AND MISO SOUP see **ONNA TO MISOSHIRO** • 1968
WOMEN AND ROSES • 1914 • Reid Wallace • USA
WOMEN AND THE LAW • 1977 • Spring Sylvia • CND
WOMEN AND WAR • 1913 • Dwan Allan • USA
WOMEN AND WAR (USA) see **ARRETEZ LES TAMBOURS** • 1961
WOMEN ARE BAD see **ALL WOMEN ARE BAD** • 1969
WOMEN ARE DANGEROUS (UKN) see **LOVE IS DANGEROUS** • 1933
WOMEN ARE LIKE THAT • 1938 • Logan Stanley • USA • RETURN FROM LIMBO
WOMEN ARE LIKE THAT (USA) see **COMMENT QU'ELLE EST?** • 1960
WOMEN ARE STRONG (USA) see **JOSEI WA TSUYOSHI** • 1924
WOMEN ARE TALKATIVE (USA) see **FEMMES SONT MARRANTES, LES** • 1958
WOMEN ARE THAT WAY • 1932 • *Stuart John* • SHT • UKN
WOMEN ARE TOUGH ANGELS see **FLIGHT ANGELS** • 1940
WOMEN ARE TROUBLE • 1936 • Taggart Errol • USA
WOMEN ARE WARRIORS • 1942 • Beveridge Jane Marsh • DOC • CND • FEMMES DANS LA MELEE, LES
WOMEN ARE WEAK (UKN) see **FAIBLES FEMMES** • 1959
WOMEN AREN'T ANGELS • 1942 • Huntington Lawrence • UKN
WOMEN AROUND LARSSON, THE see **KVINNORNA KRING LARSSON** • 1934
WOMEN AROUND THE SHOGUN, THE see **OOKU MARUHI MONOGATARI** • 1967
WOMEN ARTISTS OF AUSTRALIA • 1980 • Hicks Scott • DOC • ASL
WOMEN AT WAR • 1943 • Negulesco Jean • SHT • USA
WOMEN AT WEST POINT • 1979 • Sherman Vincent • TVM • USA
WOMEN BEHIND BARBED WIRE see **SHIROI HADA TO KIIROI TAICHO** • 1961
WOMEN.. BOTTLES AND SHARPSHOOTERS see **DONNE.. BOTTE E BERSAGLIERI** • 1968
WOMEN CAN'T BE BEATEN see **KIGEKI: ONNAWA DOKYO** • 1970
WOMEN COMMAND, THE see **MUJERES MANDAN, LAS** • 1936
WOMEN DEFEND THE HOME! see **ONNA KOSO IE O MAMORE** • 1939
WOMEN, DO NOT SHAME YOUR NAMES see **ONNA-YO KIMI NO NA O KEGASU NAKARE** • 1930
WOMEN DOCTOR • 1939 • Salkow Sidney • USA
WOMEN DOCTORS see **ARZTRINNEN** • 1983
WOMEN DUELLING (USA) see **DUELLE** • 1976
WOMEN EVERYWHERE • 1930 • Korda Alexander • USA • HELL'S BELLES
WOMEN FAMILY see **JOSEI KAZOKU** • 1963
WOMEN FIGHT FOR PEACE, THE • 1949 • Stiopul Savel • RMN
WOMEN FIRST • 1924 • Eason B. Reeves • USA • TURF SENSATION, THE (UKN)
WOMEN FOR ALL REASONS • 1969 • *Lox Karen* • USA • WOMAN FOR ALL REASONS, A
WOMEN FROM THE BOTTOM OF THE SEA see **KAITEI KARA KITA ONNA** • 1959
WOMEN GO ON FOREVER • 1931 • Lang Walter • USA
WOMEN HAVE A WAY see **WISE GIRL** • 1937
WOMEN IN A WAITING ROOM see **KVINNOR I VANTRUM** • 1946
WOMEN IN BONDAGE • 1943 • Sekely Steve • USA
WOMEN IN CAGES • 1971 • De Leon Gerardo • PHL, USA • BAMBOO DOLLS HOUSE
WOMEN IN CELL BLOCK 7 see **DIARIO SEGRETO DI UN CARCERE FEMMINILE** • 1973
WOMEN IN CHAINS • 1971 • Kowalski Bernard • TVM • USA
WOMEN IN CHAINS, THE see **WOMAN IN CHAINS, THE** • 1923
WOMEN IN HIDING • 1940 • Newman Joseph M. • SHT • USA
WOMEN IN HIS LIFE, THE • 1933 • Seitz George B. • USA • COMEBACK, THE
WOMEN IN LIMBO see **LIMBO** • 1972
WOMEN IN LOVE • 1969 • Russell Ken • UKN
WOMEN IN LOVE see **SINNER'S HOLIDAY** • 1930
WOMEN IN LOVE see **OTAN I YINEKES AGAPOUN** • 1967
WOMEN IN LOVE see **AS ME KRINOUN I YINEKES** • 1968
WOMEN IN NEW YORK see **FRAUEN IN NEW YORK** • 1977
WOMEN IN PARADISE • 1959 • *Jurado Katy* • USA
WOMEN IN PRISON • 1938 • Hillyer Lambert • USA
WOMEN IN PRISON • 1971 • *Barraclough Jenny (P)* • UKN
WOMEN IN PRISON see **KVINNOR I FANGENSKAP** • 1943
WOMEN IN PRISON see **JOSHU TO TOMONI** • 1957
WOMEN IN REVOLT • 1971 • Morrissey Paul, Warhol Andy • USA
WOMEN IN REVOLT see **ANDY WARHOL'S WOMEN** • 1971
WOMEN IN THE NIGHT • 1948 • USA • WHEN MEN ARE BEASTS
WOMEN IN THE SPINNERY see **LORINCI FONOBAN, A** • 1971
WOMEN IN THE WIND • 1939 • Farrow John • USA
WOMEN IN WAR • 1940 • Auer John H. • USA
WOMEN IN WAR see **ARRETEZ LES TAMBOURS** • 1961
WOMEN IN WHITE • 1967 • Wakamatsu Koji • JPN
WOMEN KILLER see **ONNANAKASE** • 1967
WOMEN LEFT ALONE • 1913 • Dwan Allan • USA
WOMEN LOVE DIAMONDS • 1927 • Goulding Edmund • USA
WOMEN LOVE ONCE • 1931 • Goodman Edward • USA
WOMEN MEN FORGET • 1920 • Stahl John M. • USA
WOMEN MEN LIKE • 1928 • *Lake Alice* • USA • ANY WOMAN'S MAN
WOMEN MEN LOVE • 1921 • Bradley Samuel R. • USA
WOMEN MEN MARRY • 1922 • Dillon Eddie • USA
WOMEN MEN MARRY • 1931 • Hutchison Charles • USA
WOMEN MEN MARRY, THE • 1937 • Taggart Errol • USA
WOMEN MUST DRESS • 1935 • Barker Reginald • USA
WOMEN OF ALL NATIONS • 1931 • Walsh Raoul • USA
WOMEN OF DESIRE • 1968 • Sinclair Vincent L. • USA
WOMEN OF DEVIL'S ISLAND see **PRIGIONIERE DELL'ISOLA DEL DIAVOLO, LE** • 1962
WOMEN OF DRACULA, THE see **IMPERIO DE DRACULA, EL** • 1966
WOMEN OF FIRE, THE see **FILLES DU DIABLE, LES** • 1903
WOMEN OF GLAMOR • 1937 • Wiles Gordon • USA • WOMEN OF GLAMOUR
WOMEN OF GLAMOUR see **WOMEN OF GLAMOR** • 1937
WOMEN OF KYOTO see **ONNA NO SAKA** • 1960
WOMEN OF NAZI GERMANY see **HITLER** • 1962
WOMEN OF NISKAVUORI see **NISKAVUOREN NAISET** • 1938
WOMEN OF PARIS see **PARISISKOR** • 1928
WOMEN OF PARIS see **FEMMES DE PARIS** • 1951
WOMEN OF PITCAIRN ISLAND, THE • 1957 • Yarbrough Jean • USA
WOMEN OF RYAZAN see **BABI RIAZANSKIE** • 1927
WOMEN OF SAN QUENTIN • 1984 • Graham William A. • TVM • USA
WOMEN OF SIN (USA) see **MOUCHARDE, LA** • 1958
WOMEN OF THE DESERT • 1913 • Nicholls George • USA
WOMEN OF THE GINZA see **GINZA NO ONNA** • 1955
WOMEN OF THE LAKE see **ONNA NO MISUMI** • 1966
WOMEN OF THE NIGHT (USA) see **YORU NO ONNATACHI** • 1948
WOMEN OF THE PREHISTORIC PLANET • 1966 • Pierce Arthur C. • USA • PREHISTORIC PLANET WOMEN
WOMEN OF THE WEST • 1910 • *Yankee* • USA
WOMEN OF THE WORLD see **WOW** • 1975
WOMEN OF THE WORLD (USA) see **DONNA NEL MONDO, LA** • 1963
WOMEN OF TOKYO see **HANNYO** • 1961
WOMEN OF TRANSPLANT ISLAND see **WONDER WOMEN** • 1973
WOMEN OF TWILIGHT • 1952 • Parry Gordon • UKN • TWILIGHT WOMEN (USA) ○ ANOTHER CHANCE
WOMEN OF TWO WORLDS • 1980 • Ballantyne Tanya • CND
WOMEN OF VALOR • 1986 • Kulik Buzz • TVM • USA
WOMEN OF WILLMAR, THE see **MATTER OF SEX, A** • 1984
WOMEN.. OH, WOMEN! (USA) see **ONNA ONNA ONNA MONOGATARI** • 1963
WOMEN ON THE FIRING LINE see **HIJOSEN NO ONNA** • 1933
WOMEN ON THE VERGE OF A NERVOUS BREAKDOWN (UKN) see **MUJERES AL BORDE DE UN ATAQUE DE NERVIOS** • 1988
WOMEN ON WHEELS see **EASY WHEELS** • 1989
WOMEN -PAST AND PRESENT • 1913 • Parker Lem B. • USA
WOMEN PRISONERS OF DEVIL'S ISLAND, THE see **PRIGIONIERE DELL'ISOLA DEL DIAVOLO, LE** • 1962
WOMEN RACKET (UKN) see **CHEMIN DE RIO, LE** • 1936
WOMEN SHOULD STAY AT HOME see **ONNA KOSO IE O MAMORE** • 1939
WOMEN: SO WE ARE MADE see **NOI DONNE SIAMO FATTE COSI** • 1971
WOMEN TALKING • 1970 • Mackenzie Midge • UKN
WOMEN THEY TALK ABOUT • 1928 • Bacon Lloyd • USA
WOMEN TODAY • 1978 • Alkouli Popi • DOC • GRC
WOMEN WANT.. • 1975 • Kaczender George • CND
WOMEN WHO CRY AT NIGHT see **YORU NAKU ONNA** • 1967
WOMEN WHO DARE • 1928 • King Burton L. • USA
WOMEN WHO GIVE • 1924 • Barker Reginald • USA • WOMEN WHO WAIT
WOMEN WHO GO THROUGH HELL see **SIETE MAGNIFICAS, LAS** • 1966
WOMEN WHO KILL • 1983 • Wallace Stephen • DOC • ASL
WOMEN WHO LEARNED, THE • 1916 • *Imp* • SHT • USA
WOMEN WHO PLAY • 1932 • Rosson Arthur • UKN • SPRING CLEANING
WOMEN WHO WAIT see **FORBIDDEN LOVE** • 1921
WOMEN WHO WAIT see **WOMEN WHO GIVE** • 1924
WOMEN WHO WIN • 1919 • Nash Percy, Durrant Fred W. • UKN
WOMEN WHO WORK (USA) see **MUJERES QUE TRABAJAN** • 1940
WOMEN WILL DO EVERYTHING • 1964 • Szemes Marianne • DOC • HNG
WOMEN WITHOUT HOPE see **MARCHANDES D'ILLUSIONS** • 1954
WOMEN WITHOUT MEN • 1956 • Williams Elmo • UKN • BLONDE BAIT (USA)
WOMEN WITHOUT MEN see **NESSAA BALA RAJAL** • 1952
WOMEN WITHOUT MEN (USA) see **DIRNENTRAGODIE** • 1927
WOMEN WITHOUT NAMES • 1940 • Florey Robert • USA
WOMEN WITHOUT NAMES (USA) see **DONNE SENZA NOME** • 1950
WOMEN WITHOUT UNIFORM see **MILLIONS LIKE US** • 1943
WOMEN WOMEN WOMEN MOIRA • 1970 • Lewis Morton • USA • MOIRA
WOMEN WON'T TELL • 1933 • Thorpe Richard • USA
WOMEN'S CELL see **ZOKU HIROKU ONNA RO** • 1968
WOMEN'S CLUB, THE • 1987 • Weintraub Sandra • USA
WOMEN'S COQUETRY see **ONNA NO BITAI** • 1967
WOMEN'S DESTINY see **FRAUENSCHICKSALE** • 1952
WOMEN'S DREAMS see **KVINNODROM** • 1955
WOMEN'S KINGDOM see **BABYE TSARSTVO** • 1968
WOMEN'S NIGHT see **ONNA BAKARI NO YORU** • 1961
WOMEN'S PRISON • 1955 • Seiler Lewis • USA
WOMEN'S PRISON see **HIROKU ONNA RO** • 1968
WOMEN'S PRISON MASSACRE (USA) see **REVOLTE AU PENITENCIER DE FILLES** • 1983
WOMEN'S REPUBLIC, THE see **REPUBLIKA BABSKA** • 1969
WOMEN'S RIGHTS • 1900 • *Riley Brothers* • UKN
WOMEN'S RIGHTS • 1985 • Woodland James • DOC • CND
WOMEN'S ROOM, THE • 1980 • Jordan Glenn • TVM • USA
WOMEN'S SCROLL see **JOKYO** • 1960
WOMEN'S STREET see **ONNA NO MACHI** • 1940
WOMEN'S SUMMER CAMPS see **ZENSKIE OBOZY LETNIE** • 1938
WOMEN'S TORTURE see **ONNA NO SEME** • 1967
WOMEN'S TOWN see **ONNA NO MACHI** • 1940
WOMEN'S VICTORY (USA) see **JOSEI NO SHORI** • 1946
WOMEN'S WARD • 1989 • Refig Halit • TRK
WOMEN'S WARES • 1927 • Gregor Arthur • USA
WOMEN'S WEAPONS see **WOMAN'S WEAPONS** • 1918
WON AT HIGH TIDE • 1912 • *Lubin* • USA
WON AT THE RODEO • 1913 • *La Badie Florence* • USA
WON BY A CALL • 1912 • *Nestor* • USA
WON BY A CHILD • 1913 • Collins Edwin J.? • UKN
WON BY A FISH • 1912 • Sennett Mack • USA
WON BY A FLUKE • 1915 • Birch Cecil • UKN
WON BY A FOOT • 1917 • *Sutherland Eddie* • USA
WON BY A FOWL • 1916 • *Rhodes Billie* • USA
WON BY A FOWL • 1917 • Beaudine William • SHT • USA
WON BY A HEAD • 1920 • Nash Percy • UKN
WON BY A HOLD-UP • 1910 • *Essanay* • USA
WON BY A MOUSTACHE • 1915 • Mitchell Bruce • USA
WON BY A NECK • 1930 • Arbuckle Roscoe • USA
WON BY A NOSE • 1914 • *Balboa* • USA
WON BY A NOSE • 1915 • *Banner* • USA
WON BY A NOSE • 1920 • Windermere Fred • SHT • USA
WON BY A SKIRT • 1913 • *Nestor* • USA
WON BY A SNAPSHOT • 1912 • Haldane Bert? • UKN
WON BY GRIT • 1917 • Marshall George • SHT • USA
WON BY LOSING • 1916 • Phillips Bertram • UKN
WON BY ONE • 1916 • MacMackin Archer • USA
WON BY STRATEGY • 1904 • Fitzhamon Lewin • UKN
WON BY STRATEGY • 1908 • *Warwick Trading Co* • UKN
WON BY VALOR • 1916 • Hill Robert F. • SHT • USA
WON BY WAITING • 1912 • *Buckley May* • USA
WON BY WARR • 1922 • Collins Edwin J. • UKN
WON BY WIRE • 1914 • *Frontier* • USA
WON BY WIRELESS • 1911 • *Thanhouser* • USA
WON IN A CABINET • 1917 • *Compson Betty* • SHT • USA
WON IN A CLOSET • 1914 • Nicholls George • USA
WON IN THE CLOUDS • 1914 • Turner Otis • USA
WON IN THE CLOUDS • 1928 • Mitchell Bruce • USA
WON IN THE DESERT • 1909 • *Selig* • USA
WON IN THE FIFTH • 1910 • Melies Gaston • USA
WON IN THE FIRST • 1914 • *Joker* • USA
WON IN THE STRETCH • 1917 • King Burton L. • USA
WON ON THE POST • 1912 • Rolfe Alfred • ASL
WON: ONE FLIVVER • 1921 • Reisner Charles F. • SHT • USA
WON THROUGH A MEDIUM • 1911 • Sennett Mack, Henderson Dell • USA
WON THROUGH MERIT • 1915 • Nowland Eugene • USA
WON TON TON, THE DOG WHO SAVED HOLLYWOOD • 1976 • Winner Michael • USA
WON WITH A MAKE-UP • 1916 • Otto Henry • SHT • USA
WON WITH DYNAMITE • 1915 • *Joker* • USA
WONDER BAR • 1934 • Bacon Lloyd • USA
WONDER CHILD see **LITTLE MISS ROUGHNECK** • 1938
WONDER CLOTH, THE • 1915 • Melville Wilbert • USA
WONDER DOG, THE • 1950 • Nichols Charles • ANS • USA
WONDER GLOVES • 1951 • Cannon Robert • ANS • USA
WONDER KID, THE • 1951 • Hartl Karl • UKN, FRG
WONDER MAN • 1945 • Humberstone H. Bruce • USA
WONDER MAN, THE • 1920 • Adolfi John G. • USA
WONDER OF IT ALL, THE • 1974 • Dubs Arthur R. • DOC • USA
WONDER OF LOVE, THE (UKN) see **OSWALT KOLLE: DAS WUNDER DER LIEBE -SEXUALITAT IN DER EHE** • 1968
WONDER OF WOMEN • 1929 • Brown Clarence • USA
WONDER OF WOOL • 1960 • Halas John • ANS • UKN
WONDER PLANE (UKN) see **MERCY PLANE** • 1940
WONDER POT, THE see **HRNECKU VARI!** • 1953
WONDER POWDERS, THE • *Cines* • SHT • ITL
WONDER RING, THE • 1955 • Brakhage Stan, Cornell Joseph • SHT • USA
WONDER WOMAN • 1974 • McEveety Vincent • TVM • USA
WONDER WOMEN • 1973 • O'Neil Robert Vincent • PHL, USA • WOMEN OF TRANSPLANT ISLAND
WONDER WOMEN OF THE WORLD • 1923 • Greenwood Edwin • SHS • UKN
WONDER-WORKING DOCTOR, THE • Schulz Kurt Herbert • ANM • GDR
WONDER WORLD • 1972 • Funakoshi • JPN
WONDERFUL ADVENTURE, A • 1915 • Thompson Frederick A. • USA
WONDERFUL ADVENTURES OF HERR MUNCHHAUSEN, THE see **AVENTURES DE BARON DE CRAC, LES** • 1913
WONDERFUL ADVENTURES OF NILS, THE • 1956 • ANM • USS
WONDERFUL ADVENTURES OF NILS, THE see **NILS HOLGERSSONS UNDERBARA RESA** • 1962
WONDERFUL ADVENTURES OF PIP, SQUEAK AND WILFRED, THE • 1921 • *Astra Films* • ASS • UKN
WONDERFUL BAD WOMAN see **SUBARASHII AKUJO** • 1963
WONDERFUL CHAIR, THE • 1910 • *Brockliss* • UKN
WONDERFUL CHANCE, THE • 1920 • Archainbaud George • USA
WONDERFUL CHARM, THE • 1908 • Melies Georges • FRN
WONDERFUL COAT, THE • 1909 • *Lux* • FRN
WONDERFUL COUNTRY, THE • 1959 • Parrish Robert • USA
WONDERFUL CROOK, THE (USA) see **PAS SI MECHANT QUE CA** • 1975
WONDERFUL DAY see **I'VE GOTTA HORSE** • 1965
WONDERFUL EGGS • 1909 • *Pathe* • FRN

WONDERFUL ELECTRIC BELT, THE see **CEINTURE ELECTRIQUE, LA** • 1907
WONDERFUL ELECTRO-MAGNET, THE • 1909 • *Edison* • USA
WONDERFUL EVENT, THE • 1917 • Windom Lawrence C. • SHT • USA
WONDERFUL EYE, THE • 1911 • Sennett Mack • USA
WONDERFUL FLUID, A • 1908 • *Pathe* • FRN
WONDERFUL GARDEN, THE • 1962 • Snezhko-Blotskaya A. • ANS • USS
WONDERFUL HAIR REMOVER • 1910 • *Gaumont* • UKN
WONDERFUL HAIR RESTORER, A see **LOTION MIRACULEUSE, LA** • 1903
WONDERFUL LAMP, A • 1915 • *Pyramid* • USA
WONDERFUL LAMP, THE see **ALADDIN** • 1923
WONDERFUL LAND OF OZ, THE • 1969 • Mahon Barry • USA
WONDERFUL LIE OF NINA PETROVNA, THE see **WUNDERBARE LUGE DER NINA PETROWNA, DIE** • 1929
WONDERFUL LIFE • 1964 • Furie Sidney J. • UKN • SWINGER'S PARADISE
WONDERFUL LIFE, A • 1922 • Scardon Paul • USA
WONDERFUL LIFE, A • 1951 • Beaudine William • USA
WONDERFUL LIVING FAN, THE (USA) see **MERVEILLEUX EVENTAIL VIVANT, LE** • 1904
WONDERFUL MARRYING MIXTURE • 1910 • *Walturdaw* • UKN
WONDERFUL MOVIE CRANKS see **BAJECNI MUZI S KLIKOU** • 1979
WONDERFUL MOVIE MEN see **BAJECNI MUZI S KLIKOU** • 1979
WONDERFUL NIGHT, A • 1919 • *Parsons Smiling Bill* • SHT • USA
WONDERFUL NIGHTS WITH PETER KINEMA • 1914 • Pearson George • SER • UKN
WONDERFUL NOVEMBER, A see **BELLISSIMO NOVEMBRE, UN** • 1968
WONDERFUL ONE-HORSE SHAY, THE • 1912 • *Lubin* • USA
WONDERFUL ONES, THE see **OMOIDE NO YUBIWA** • 1968
WONDERFUL PILLS • 1909 • *Cines* • ITL
WONDERFUL RAYS, THE • 1913 • *Savoia* • FRN
WONDERFUL REMEDY, A • 1909 • *Pathe* • FRN
WONDERFUL ROSE TREE, THE (USA) see **ROSIER MIRACULEUX, LE** • 1904
WONDERFUL SCARF, THE • 1913 • *Pathe Freres* • FRN
WONDERFUL STATUE, THE • 1913 • Thompson Frederick A. • USA
WONDERFUL STORY, THE • 1922 • Cutts Graham • UKN
WONDERFUL STORY, THE • 1932 • Fogwell Reginald • UKN
WONDERFUL STORY OF SANTA CLAUS • 1948 • Blakeley James • SHT • USA
WONDERFUL SUNDAY see **SUBARASHIKI NICHIYOBI** • 1947
WONDERFUL THING, THE • 1921 • Brenon Herbert • USA
WONDERFUL THINGS • 1958 • Wilcox Herbert • UKN
WONDERFUL THREE see **PAMBIHIRANG TATLO** • 1967
WONDERFUL TIMES • 1951 • Ode Erik • FRG
WONDERFUL TO BE YOUNG! (USA) see **YOUNG ONES, THE** • 1961
WONDERFUL WAGER, THE • 1916 • Plaissetty Rene • SHT • USA
WONDERFUL WIZARD OF OZ, THE • 1987 • *Kidder Margot (Nar)* • ANM • USA
WONDERFUL WOOING, THE • 1925 • Malins Geoffrey H. • UKN • WAY OF A WOMAN, THE
WONDERFUL WORLD OF GIRLS, THE • 1965 • Stootsberry A. P. • USA
WONDERFUL WORLD OF THE BROTHERS GRIMM, THE • 1963 • Levin Henry, Pal George • USA
WONDERFUL YEAR, THE • 1921 • Foss Kenelm • UKN
WONDERFUL YEARS, THE (UKN) see **RESTLESS YEARS, THE** • 1958
WONDERING MAN, THE see **MARD-E-SARGARDAN** • 1967
WONDERLAND • 1931 • Lantz Walter, Nolan William • ANS • USA
WONDERLAND • 1980 • Nichol Robert L. • SHT • CND
WONDERLAND (USA) see **FRUIT MACHINE, THE** • 1988
WONDERLIJK LEVEN VAN WILLEM PAREL, HET • 1955 • Rutten Gerard • NTH
WONDERMAN see **IHMEMIES** • 1979
WONDERS OF ALADDIN, THE (USA) see **MERAVIGLIE DI ALADINO, LE** • 1962
WONDERS OF CREATION see **WUNDER DER SCHOPFUNG** • 1925
WONDERS OF ROME, THE see **MISTERI DI ROMA, I** • 1963
WONDERS OF SURGERY, THE • 1912 • *Majestic* • USA
WONDERS OF THE CONGO • 1931 • Johnson Martin E. • DOC • USA
WONDERS OF THE DEEP see **ROYAUME DES FEES, LE** • 1903
WONDERS OF THE SEA • 1922 • Williamson J. Ernest • DOC • USA
WONDERS OF THE WILD • 1925 • *Burr Nickle Pictures* • DOC • USA
WONDERSHOP • 1975 • Buyens Frans, Staes Guido, van den Eynden Rick • BLG
WONDERWALL • 1968 • Massot Joe • UKN
WONDERWERELD VAN KAMMIE KAMFER, DIE • 1964 • SAF
WONDROUS MELODY, THE • 1914 • *Eclair* • USA
WONDROUS STORY OF BIRTH, THE see **BIRTH OF TRIPLETS** • 1964
WONKEY'S WAGER • 1912 • Wilson Frank? • UKN
WON'T WRITE HOME, MOM -I'M DEAD see **TERROR FROM WITHIN** • 1974
WON'T YOU BUY MY PRETTY FLOWERS? • 1921 • *Parkinson H. B. (P)* • SHT • UKN
WON'T YOU COME HOME? • 1905 • *Warwick Trading Co* • UKN
WON'T YOU THROW ME A KISS • 1907 • Gilbert Arthur • UKN
WON'T YOU WALTZ THE MERRY WIDOW WALTZ WITH ME? • 1909 • *Warwick Trading Co* • UKN
WOO WOO BLUES • 1951 • Quine Richard • SHT • USA
WOO-WOO KID, THE see **IN THE MOOD** • 1987
WOOD AND STONE see **MOKUSEKI** • 1940
WOOD B. WEDD AND THE MICROBES • 1914 • Ransom Charles • USA
WOOD B. WEDD GOES SNIPE HUNTING • 1914 • Ransom Charles • USA
WOOD-BLOCK PRINTING -THE WORLD OF SHIKO MUNAKATA see **HORU -MUNAKATA SHIKO NO SEKAI** • 1975
WOOD-CHOPPER'S CHILD, THE • 1909 • *Edison* • USA
WOOD LOVE (UKN) see **SOMMERNACHTSTRAUM, EIN** • 1925
WOOD NYMPH, THE • 1912 • *Robinson Gertrude* • USA
WOOD NYMPH, THE • 1915 • Calvert E. H. • USA
WOOD NYMPH, THE • 1916 • Powell Paul • USA
WOOD PECKIN' • 1943 • Sparber I. • ANS • USA
WOOD VIOLET, THE • 1912 • Ince Ralph • USA
WOODCHOPPERS • 1929 • Terry Paul • ANS • USA
WOODCROFT CASTLE • 1926 • West Walter • UKN
WOODCUTTER'S DAUGHTER, THE • 1913 • *All-British Films* • UKN
WOODCUTTERS IN THE DEEP SOUTH • 1973 • Rogosin Lionel • USA
WOODCUTTER'S ROMANCE, THE • 1911 • Bouwmeester Theo • UKN
WOODEN ATHLETES, THE • 1912 • Urban Charles • ANM • UKN
WOODEN BOWL, THE • 1912 • *Johnson Arthur* • USA
WOODEN BOWLS, THE see **ECUELLES, LES** • 1983
WOODEN CROSSES see **ROAD TO GLORY, THE** • 1936
WOODEN CROSSES (USA) see **CROIX DE BOIS, LES** • 1931
WOODEN GUN, THE • 1979 • Moshensohn Ilan • ISR
WOODEN HEAD see **MOKUSEKI** • 1940
WOODEN HEADED VETERAN • 1908 • *Pathe* • FRN
WOODEN HORSE, THE • 1950 • Lee Jack • UKN
WOODEN HORSE OF TROY, THE (UKN) see **GUERRA DI TROIA, LA** • 1961
WOODEN HORSEMAN, THE • 1965 • Wasilewski Zenon • ANM • PLN
WOODEN INDIAN, THE • 1909 • *Vitagraph* • USA
WOODEN INDIAN, THE • 1912 • *Edison* • USA
WOODEN INDIAN, THE • 1949 • Rasinski Connie • ANS • USA
WOODEN LEG, THE • 1909 • Griffith D. W. • USA
WOODEN ROSARY, THE see **DREWNIANY ROZANIEC** • 1965
WOODEN SHOES • 1917 • West Raymond B. • USA
WOODEN SHOES • 1933 • *Mintz Charles (P)* • ANS • USA
WOODEN SOLDIER, THE • 1928 • Rollens Jacques • SHT • USA
WOODEN WEDDING see **FIRST HUNDRED YEARS, THE** • 1938
WOODFIRE AT MARTIN'S, THE • 1913 • Martin E. A. • USA
WOODHAWK, THE see **THEY RODE WEST** • 1954
WOODLAND • 1932 • *Terry Frank/ Moser Frank (P)* • ANS • USA
WOODLAND CAFE • 1937 • Jackson Wilfred • ANS • USA
WOODLAND CHRISTMAS IN CALIFORNIA, A • 1912 • *Melies* • USA
WOODLAND CONCERT • 1953 • Ivanov-Vano Ivan • ANS • USS
WOODLAND PARADISE, A • 1913 • Edwin Walter • USA
WOODLAND POND, A • Homoki-Nagy Istvan • DOC • HNG
WOODLAND TRAGEDY, A • 1907 • Jeapes Harold? • UKN
WOODMAN SPARE THAT TREE • 1942 • Wickersham Bob • ANS • USA
WOODMAN SPARE THAT TREE • 1951 • Donnelly Eddie • ANS • USA
WOODMAN'S DAUGHTER, THE • 1913 • Huntley Fred W. • USA
WOODMAN'S DREAM, THE see **NUMBER 16** • 1967
WOODPECKER, THE see **DZIECIOL** • 1970
WOODPECKER AND THE FOX, THE • ANS • USS
WOODPECKER FROM MARS • 1956 • Smith Paul J. • ANS • USA
WOODPECKER HAS NO HEADACHE see **NE BOLIT GOLOVA A DIATLA** • 1975
WOODPECKER IN THE MOON • 1959 • Lovy Alex • ANS • USA
WOODPECKER IN THE ROUGH • 1952 • Lantz Walter • ANS • USA
WOODPECKER NEVER HAS A HEADACHE, THE see **NE BOLIT GOLOVA A DIATLA** • 1975
WOODPECKER OPERATION, THE • 1968 • Okamoto Tadashige • ANS • JPN
WOODPECKER TOLD THE OWL, THE see **OPOWIEDZIAL DZIECIOL SOWIE** • 1952
WOODPECKER WANTED • 1965 • Smith Paul J. • ANS • USA
WOODPIGEON PATROL, THE • 1930 • Smart Ralph, Lucas F. R. • UKN
WOODROW WILSON FILM MEMORIAL, THE • 1924 • *Drugan H. F. (P)* • DOC • USA
WOODS, THE • 1931 • Gerasimov Sergei • USS • FOREST, THE
WOODS ARE FULL OF CUCKOOS, THE • 1937 • Tashlin Frank • ANS • USA
WOODS ARE FULL OF 'EM, THE • 1917 • Hartigan P. C. • SHT • USA
WOODSMAN, THE • 1910 • *Nestor* • USA
WOODSTOCK • 1970 • Wadleigh Michael • DOC • USA
WOODY AND THE BEANSTALK • 1966 • Smith Paul J. • ANS • USA
WOODY HERMAN AND HIS ORCHESTRA • 1948 • Cowan Will • SHT • USA
WOODY HERMAN AND THE SWINGIN' HERD • 1963 • Moore Richard • SHT • USA
WOODY HERMAN'S VARIETIES • 1951 • Cowan Will • SHT • USA
WOODY MEETS DAVY CREWCUT • 1956 • Lovy Alex • ANS • USA
WOODY PLAYS SANTA see **SKI FOR TWO** • 1944
WOODY THE FREELOADER • 1968 • Smith Paul J. • ANS • USA
WOODY, THE GIANT KILLER • 1948 • Lundy Dick • ANS • USA
WOODY WOODPECKER • 1941-72 • *Lantz Walter (P)* • ASS • USA
WOODY WOODPECKER • 1941 • Lantz Walter • ANS • USA • CRACKED NUT, THE
WOODY WOODPECKER IN WOODY DINES OUT • 1945 • Culhane James • ANS • USA
WOODY WOODPECKER, THE SCREWDRIVER • 1941 • Lantz Walter • ANS • USA
WOODY'S CLIP JOINT • 1964 • Marcus Sid • ANS • USA
WOODY'S KOOK-OUT • 1961 • Hannah Jack • ANS • USA
WOODY'S MAGIC TOUCH • 1971 • Smith Paul J. • ANS • USA
WOODY'S NIGHTMARE • 1969 • Smith Paul J. • ANS • USA
WOOED BY A WILD MAN • 1915 • *Kalem* • USA
WOOERS OF MOUNTAIN KATE, THE • 1912 • Dwan Allan • USA • MOUNTAIN KATE
WOOF! • 1989 • Cobham David • UKN
WOOF, WOOF • 1915 • Mackenzie Donald • USA
WOOF! WOOF! see **VAU-VAU** • 1964
WOOING AUNTIE • 1913 • Collins Edwin J.? • UKN
WOOING OF ALICE, THE • 1912 • *Beggs Lee* • USA
WOOING OF AUNT JEMIMA, THE • 1916 • Davey Horace • SHT • USA
WOOING OF BESSIE BUMPKIN, THE • 1914 • *Meredyth Bess* • USA
WOOING OF COFFEE-CAKE KATE, THE • 1918 • Curtis Allen • SHT • USA
WOOING OF LITTLE FAWN, THE • 1912 • *Pathe* • USA
WOOING OF LOUIE, THE • 1915 • *Wright Bertie* • UKN
WOOING OF MILES STANDISH, THE • 1908 • Olcott Sidney • USA
WOOING OF PRINCESS PAT, THE • 1918 • Earle William P. S. • USA
WOOING OF RILEY, THE • 1918 • Bradbury Robert North • SHT • USA
WOOING OF SOPHIE, THE • 1914 • *Essanay* • USA
WOOING OF WATHENA, THE • 1912 • *Emerson Mabel* • USA
WOOING OF WIDOW WILKINS, THE • 1912 • Aylott Dave? • UKN
WOOING OF WINNIFRED • 1911 • *Costello Maurice* • USA
WOOING O'T, THE • 1910 • *Vitagraph* • USA
WOOING THE COOK • 1914 • *Pathe* • USA
WOOLEN UNDER WHERE • 1963 • Jones Charles M. • ANS • USA
WOOLLY TALE, THE • 1964 • Tyrlova Hermina • ANM • CZC
WOP, THE • 1913 • *Shaw Harold* • USA
WORD, THE • 1915 • *Mong William V.* • USA
WORD, THE • 1978 • Lang Richard • TVM • USA
WORD, THE see **ORDET** • 1943
WORD, THE see **ORDET** • 1954
WORD GAMES • 1961 • Keatley Philip • CND
WORD IS EVERYBODY'S, THE see **PALABRA ES DE TODOS, LA** • 1980
WORD IS OUT • 1978 • Adair Peter • DOC • USA
WORD OF A CAT, THE see **KOCICI SIOVO** • 1960
WORD OF HIS PEOPLE, THE • 1914 • *Ray Charles* • USA
WORD OF HONOR • 1981 • Damski Mel • TVM • USA
WORD OF HONOR, THE • 1912 • *Eclair* • USA
WORD OF JOSE, THE • 1913 • *Frontier* • USA
WORDING, DE • 1988 • Duyns Cherry • DOC • NTH
WORDLESS MESSAGE, THE • 1912 • Dwan Allan • USA
WORDLESS MESSAGE, THE • 1913 • Campbell Colin • USA
WORDS AND MUSIC • 1929 • Tinling James • USA
WORDS AND MUSIC • 1948 • Taurog Norman • USA
WORDS AND MUSIC see **WORDS AND MUSIC BY..** • 1919
WORDS AND MUSIC BY.. • 1919 • Dunlap Scott R. • USA • WORDS AND MUSIC
WORDS FOR BATTLE • 1941 • Jennings Humphrey • DCS • UKN
WORDS FOR FREEDOM • 1959 • Holmes Cecil • DOC • ASL
WORDS OF MAX, THE see **PALABRAS DE MAX, LAS** • 1977
WORDSMITH, THE • 1978 • Jutra Claude • CND
WOREK • 1967 • Wilkosz Tadeusz • ANS • CZC • BAGS (USA) ○ SACK, THE
WORK • 1915 • Chaplin Charles • USA • PAPERHANGER, THE ○ PLUMBER, THE
WORK see **BAARA** • 1979
WORK AND PHYSICAL CULTURE • 1958 • Skanata Krsto • DOC • YGS
WORK AND PLAY AT THE DEPOT • 1900 • *Paul R. W.* • UKN
WORK EXPERIENCE • 1989 • Hendrie • SHT • UKN
WORK HABIT, THE • 1913 • O'Sullivan Tony • USA
WORK IN PROGRESS • 1958 • Nasser George • SHT • KWT
WORK IN PROGRESS PARTS I & II • 1970 • Hein Wilhelm, Hein Birgit • FRG
WORK IS A FOUR LETTER WORD • 1967 • Hall Peter • UKN
WORK MADE EASY • 1907 • Blackton J. Stuart • USA
WORK NEWCOMER see **FAD JAL** • 1979
WORK OF ART, THE • 1960 • Kovalyov Mark • USS
WORK OF THE DEVIL, THE see **DAVOLJA POSLA** • 1966
WORK OF THE FIRST AID NURSING YEOMANRY CORPS, THE • 1909 • Butcher Frank E. • UKN
WORK OR FIGHT • 1918 • Hutchinson Craig • SHT • USA
WORK OR PROFESSION? see **MUNKA VAGY HIVATAS?** • 1963
WORK PARTY • 1942 • Lye Len • SHT • UKN
WORKER, THE • 1913 • Davis Will S. • USA
WORKER, THE see **AMEL, EL** • 1943
WORKERS '80 see **ROBOTNICY '80** • 1980
WORKERS AND JOBS • 1935 • Elton Arthur • DOC • UKN
WORKER'S DIARY, A see **TYOMIEHEN PAIVAKIRJA** • 1967
WORKER'S FAMILY, A • NKR
WORKERS LEAVING BRIGHTON RAILWAY STATION • 1897 • Smith G. A. • UKN
WORKERS TO BE INSURED see **WHEATLANDS OF EAST ANGLIA** • 1935
WORKER'S WIFE, A • 1910 • Bouwmeester Theo? • UKN
WORKHORSE see **DOLAPBEYGIRI** • 1982
WORKHOUSE AS THE INMATES EXPECT IT IN 1907, THE • 1906 • *New Bioscope* • UKN
WORKHOUSE GRANNY AGE 93 • 1906 • *Gaumont* • UKN
WORKING AND PLAYING TO HEALTH • 1954 • Van Dyke Willard • DOC • USA
WORKING CHANCE, A • 1976 • Klein Bonnie • DOC • CND • DU COEUR A L'OUVRAGE
WORKING CLASS see **DA GONG HUANGDI** • 1985
WORKING CLASS GOES TO HEAVEN, THE see **CLASSE OPERAIA VA IN PARADISO, LA** • 1971
WORKING CLASS GOES TO PARADISE, THE see **CLASSE OPERAIA VA IN PARADISO, LA** • 1971
WORKING CLASS ON FILM, THE • 1975 • Raymont Peter (c/d) • DOC • CND
WORKING FOR HUBBY • 1912 • *Walker Lillian* • USA
WORKING FOR PEANUTS • 1953 • Hannah Jack • ANS • USA
WORKING GAME, THE • 1967 • Edwards John • UKN
WORKING GIRL • 1988 • Nichols Mike • USA

WORKING GIRLS • 1931 • Arzner Dorothy • USA
WORKING GIRLS • 1986 • Borden Lizzie • USA
WORKING GIRLS, THE • 1974 • Rothman Stephanie • USA
WORKING GIRL'S ROMANCE, A • 1914 • Morrisey Edward • USA
WORKING GIRL'S SUCCESS, THE • 1911 • *Lubin* • USA
WORKING IN AUSTRALIA -HEAVY CONSTRUCTION • 1981 • Pattinson Michael • DOC • ASL
WORKING MAN, THE • 1933 • Adolfi John G. • USA • ADOPTED FATHER, THE
WORKING MOTHERS • 1974-75 • Shannon Kathleen • DSS • CND
WORKING OF A MIRACLE, THE • 1915 • Miller Ashley • USA
WORKING TITLE • 1986 • Scott Ken, Jones Fred • SHT • CND
WORKING TITLE: JOURNEYS FROM BERLIN/1971 • 1971 • Rainer Yvonne • USA, UKN, FRG • JOURNEYS FROM BERLIN ○ JOURNEY FROM BERLIN
WORKING WIVES (UKN) see **WEEK-END MARRIAGE** • 1932
WORKINGMAN'S DREAM, A • 1908 • Blackton J. Stuart • USA
WORKMAN'S HONOUR, A • 1912 • Calvert Charles? • UKN
WORKMAN'S LESSON, THE • 1912 • *Mccoy Gertrude* • USA
WORKMAN'S PARADISE, A • 1902 • Williamson James • UKN
WORKOUT • 1967 • Small Rhonda • ASL
WORKS AND DAYS • 1969 • Frampton Hollis • USA
WORKS LIKE MAGIC • 1911 • *Tress Harry (P)* • UKN
WORKS OF CHARLES DICKENS • 1948 • SHT • USA
WORKS OF THE DEVIL, THE see **PROESTEN I VEJLBY** • 1972
WORKSHOP FOR PEACE • 1954 • Hammid Alexander • SHT • UNN
WORLD • 1970 • Belson Jordan • SHT • USA
WORLD ABOVE, THE • 1913 • *Stonehouse Ruth* • USA
WORLD ACCORDING TO GARP, THE • 1982 • Hill George Roy • USA
WORLD ACCUSES, THE • 1935 • Lamont Charles • USA
WORLD AFFAIRS ARE YOUR AFFAIRS • 1951 • Arnold Jack • DOC • USA
WORLD AFLAME, THE • 1919 • Warde Ernest C. • USA
WORLD AGAINST HIM, THE • 1916 • Crane Frank H. • USA
WORLD AND HIS WIFE, THE • 1915 • *Box Office Attractions* • USA
WORLD AND HIS WIFE, THE • 1920 • Vignola Robert G. • USA
WORLD AND HIS WIFE, THE (UKN) see **STATE OF THE UNION** • 1948
WORLD AND ITS WOMAN, THE • 1919 • Lloyd Frank • USA
WORLD AND THE FLESH • 1932 • Cromwell John • USA
WORLD AND THE WOMAN, THE • 1914 • Vale Travers • USA
WORLD AND THE WOMAN, THE • 1916 • Moore W. Eugene • USA
WORLD APART, A • 1988 • Menges Chris • UKN
WORLD APART, THE • 1917 • Taylor William D. • USA
WORLD AT HER FEET, THE • 1927 • Reed Luther • USA
WORLD AT LARGE, THE • 1913 • *Rex* • USA
WORLD AT THEIR FEET, THE • 1971 • Isaac Alberto • DOC • UKN • WORLD CUP MEXICO 1970
WORLD AT THREE, THE • 1965 • Goode Frederic • DCS • UKN
WORLD AT WAR, THE • 1914 • Youngdeer James • UKN
WORLD BELONGS TO US, THE • Kardos Ferenc • SHT • HNG
WORLD BELONGS TO US, THE see **SVET PATRI NAM** • 1937
WORLD BEYOND, THE • 1978 • *Van Dusen Granville* • TVM • USA
WORLD BEYOND THE MOON • 1953 • *Kemmer Ed* • MTV • USA
WORLD BY NIGHT NO.2 see **MONDO DI NOTTE NUMERO DUE, IL** • 1961
WORLD BY NIGHT (USA) see **MONDO DI NOTTE, IL** • 1960
WORLD CHAMPION • 1953 • Coffey Frank • DOC • ASL
WORLD CHAMPION see **CHEMPION MIRA** • 1954
WORLD CHAMPIONSHIP OF AIR MODELS see **MISTROVSTVI SVETA LETECKYCH MODELARU** • 1957
WORLD CHANGES, THE • 1933 • LeRoy Mervyn • USA
WORLD CONDEMNS THEM, THE see **MONDO LE CONDANNA, IL** • 1953
WORLD CRISIS (USA) see **CRISE MONDIALE** • 1934
WORLD CUP MEXICO 1970 see **WORLD AT THEIR FEET, THE** • 1971
WORLD DANCES, THE • 1954 • Peters Brooke L. • USA
WORLD DOWN HERE, THE see **JINKYO** • 1924
WORLD DOWN THERE, THE see **JINKYO** • 1924
WORLD DRUMS • 1988 • Fichman Niv • DOC • CND
WORLD FESTIVAL OF SONG AND DANCE see **MY ZA MIR** • 1951
WORLD FLIER, THE • 1931 • *Sennett Mack (P)* • SHT • USA
WORLD FOR RANSOM • 1954 • Aldrich Robert • USA
WORLD FOR SALE, THE • 1918 • Blackton J. Stuart • USA
WORLD FULL OF CHILDREN, A see **VERDEN ER FULD AF BORN** • 1979
WORLD GONE MAD, THE • 1933 • Cabanne W. Christy • USA • PUBLIC BE HANGED, THE (UKN)
WORLD GONE WILD • 1988 • Katzin Lee H. • USA
WORLD IN 1981, THE • 1950 • Butler David* • UKN
WORLD IN A BOTTLE, THE see **LAHEV A SVET** • 1963
WORLD IN A MARSH • 1955 • Carrick William, Balfe Maureen • DCS • CND • LIVELY POND, THE ○ ETANG, L'
WORLD IN ACTION, THE • 1942-45 • *Legg Stuart (P)* • SER • CND
WORLD IN FLAMES, THE • 1940 • Richard Albert J. • DOC • USA
WORLD IN HIS ARMS, THE • 1952 • Walsh Raoul • USA
WORLD IN MY CORNER • 1956 • Hibbs Jesse • USA
WORLD IN MY POCKET, THE (USA) see **AN EINEM FREITAG UM HALB ZWOLF** • 1961
WORLD IN OPERA, THE • 1969 • Kotowski Jerzy • ANM • PLN
WORLD IS MINE, THE see **UNSICHTBARER GEHT DURCH DIE STADT, EIN** • 1933
WORLD IS NOT YOURS, BABY PORCUNA, THE see **HINDI SA IYO ANG MUNDO, BABY PORCUNA** • 1978
WORLD IS OURS, THE see **SVET PATRI NAM** • 1937
WORLD IS PEACEFUL, THE see **TENKA TAIHEI** • 1955
WORLD IS RICH, THE • 1948 • Rotha Paul • DOC • UKN
WORLD IS SMALL, THE • 1968 • Tuna Feyzi • TRK
WORLD IS STILL IN ORDER AT SEVEN IN THE MORNING, THE see **MORGENS UM 7 IST DIE WELT NOCH IN ORDUNG** • 1968
WORLD IS WAITING FOR US, THE see **TIGERS SEKAI WA BOKURA O MATTEIRU** • 1968
WORLD IS WATCHING, THE • 1988 • Raymont Peter • DOC • CND
WORLD MELODY see **MELODIE DER WELT** • 1929
WORLD MOVES ON, THE • 1934 • Ford John • USA
WORLD OF 1960 • 1939 • Blake Ben K. • SHT • USA
WORLD OF ABBOTT AND COSTELLO, THE • 1965 • *Rosenberg Max J./ Subotsky Milton (P)* • CMP • USA
WORLD OF AHMED FEZ BENZINE, THE • 1982 • Azzopardi Anthony • MTV • CND
WORLD OF ALPHONSE MUCHA, THE see **SVET ALFONSO MUCHY** • 1980
WORLD OF APU, THE see **APU SANSAR** • 1958
WORLD OF AUTOMATION, THE • 1970 • Rich Denis • SHT • UKN
WORLD OF BEAUTY, A • 1955 • Cowan Will • SHT • USA
WORLD OF BEGGARS, THE see **SVET, KDE SE ZEBRA** • 1938
WORLD OF BUSTER, THE • 1984 • August Bille • MTV • DNM • BUSTER'S WORLD
WORLD OF CHEMISTRY, THE • 1964 • Sluizer George • DCS • NTH
WORLD OF CHILDREN, CHILDREN, A see **ALAM EYAL, EYAL** • 1976
WORLD OF COLUMBUS, THE • 1919 • Griffith D. W. • SHT • USA
WORLD OF DIFFERENCE, A see **VERDEN TIL FORSKEL, EN** • 1989
WORLD OF DONG KINGMAN, THE • 1953 • Howe James Wong • USA
WORLD OF DRACULA • 1979 • Johnson Kenneth • MTV • USA
WORLD OF DRUGS, THE see **MUNDO DE LAS DROGAS, EL** • 1963
WORLD OF FASHION (USA) see **MINI-MIDI** • 1968
WORLD OF FLESH see **HOLLYWOOD'S WORLD OF FLESH** • 1963
WORLD OF FOLLY, A • 1920 • Beal Frank • USA
WORLD OF FREUD, THE see **MONDO FREUDO** • 1966
WORLD OF HANS CHRISTIAN ANDERSEN, THE • 1971 • McCann Chuck, Kilgore Al • ANM • USA, JPN
WORLD OF HANS CHRISTIAN ANDERSEN, THE (USA) see **HANSU KURISHITAN ANDERUSAN NO SEKAI** • 1968
WORLD OF HENRY ORIENT, THE • 1964 • Hill George Roy • USA
WORLD OF HOPE, A see **UMUT DUNYASI** • 1974
WORLD OF HORROR see **SWIAT GROZY** • 1968
WORLD OF INGMAR BERGMAN, THE • 1975 • Donner Jorn • FNL
WORLD OF KAREL APPEL, THE see **WERKELIJKHEID VAN KAREL APPEL, DE** • 1962
WORLD OF KIDS • 1951 • Youngson Robert • SHT • USA
WORLD OF KUNG FU, THE • 1973 • Trenchard-Smith Brian • DOC • ASL
WORLD OF LEGO, THE • 1981 • Fraser Chris • DOC • ASL
WORLD OF LITTLE IG, THE • 1956 • Halas John • ANS • UKN
WORLD OF LITTLE IG, THE • 1962 • Tipper Frank • ANS • UKN
WORLD OF MIRACLES, THE see **MONDO DEI MIRACOLI, IL** • 1959
WORLD OF MOSAIC, THE • 1957 • Cominos N. H. • USA
WORLD OF OBSCENITY see **MONDO OSCENITA** • 1966
WORLD OF PASSION • 1969 • *Topar Productions* • USA
WORLD OF PAUL DELVAUX, THE see **MONDE DE PAUL DELVAUX, LE** • 1946
WORLD OF PLENTY • Graham Sean • DOC • UKN
WORLD OF PLENTY • 1943 • Rotha Paul • DOC • UKN
WORLD OF SIN, A • 1915 • *British Empire* • UKN
WORLD OF SPACE, THE see **UCHU DAISENSO** • 1959
WORLD OF SPORT FISHING, THE • 1972 • *Borgnine Ernest* • USA
WORLD OF STRANGERS, A see **DILEMMA** • 1962
WORLD OF SUZIE WONG, THE • 1960 • Quine Richard • USA, UKN
WORLD OF THE DEAD, THE see **SANTO Y BLUE DEMON EN EL MUNDO DE LOS MUERTOS** • 1969
WORLD OF THE DEPRAVED see **MUNDO DEPRAVADOS** • 1967
WORLD OF THE GERIATRICS, THE • 1985 • Haneda Sumiko • DOC • JPN
WORLD OF THE TALISMAN, THE • ANM • USA
WORLD OF THE VAMPIRES, THE (USA) see **MUNDO DE LOS VAMPIROS, EL** • 1960
WORLD OF THE THREE, THE • 1967 • Kaczender George • CND
WORLD OF TODAY, THE • 1915 • *Ormonde Sylvia* • USA
WORLD OF TOMORROW, THE • 1983 • Bird Lance, Johnson Tom • DOC • USA
WORLD OF TOPO GIGIO, THE • 1965 • Serino Franco
WORLD OF WONDERFUL REALITY, THE • 1924 • Edwards Henry • UKN
WORLD ON A WIRE see **WELT AM DRAHT** • 1973
WORLD ON PARADE, THE see **TELEVISION SPY** • 1939
WORLD ON SHOW, THE • 1958 • Blais Roger • DCS • CND • MONDE A L'ETALAGE, LE
WORLD OPEN TO CHANCES, THE see **SVET OTEVRENY NAHODAM** • 1971
WORLD OWES ME A LIVING, THE • 1945 • Sewell Vernon • UKN
WORLD PREMIERE • 1941 • Tetzlaff Ted • USA
WORLD SAFARI • 1970 • *Olsen Dale (P)* • DOC • USA
WORLD STRUGGLE FOR OIL, THE • 1924 • Butler Hank E. • USA
WORLD TEN TIMES OVER, THE • 1963 • Rilla Wolf • UKN • PUSSYCAT ALLEY (USA)
WORLD, THE DEVIL AND THE FLESH, THE see **MUNDO, DEMONIO Y CARNE** • 1958
WORLD, THE FLESH AND THE DEVIL, THE • 1914 • Thornton F. Martin • UKN
WORLD, THE FLESH AND THE DEVIL, THE • 1932 • Cooper George A. • UKN
WORLD, THE FLESH AND THE DEVIL, THE • 1959 • MacDougall Ranald • USA • END OF THE WORLD
WORLD THINKS TOMORROW, THE • 1968 • Herbert John • UKN
WORLD TO LIVE IN, THE • 1919 • Maigne Charles • USA
WORLD UPSET, THE • 1909 • *Gaumont* • FRN
WORLD UPSTAIRS, THE • 1915 • *Reliance* • USA
WORLD WAR, THE • 1926 • *Zimmer George F. (P)* • DOC • USA
WORLD WAR AND AFTER, THE • 1926 • Nieter Hans M. • UKN
WORLD WAR III BREAKS OUT see **DAI SANJI SEKAI TAISEN-YONJI-ICHI JIKAN NO KYOFU** • 1960
WORLD WAR IN KIDLAND • 1916 • Fitzpatrick James A.* • SHT • USA
WORLD WAR THREE • 1982 • Greene David • TVM • USA
WORLD WAS HIS JURY, THE • 1958 • Sears Fred F. • USA
WORLD WE LIVE IN, THE • 1962 • Watson Patrick • DOC • CND
WORLD WEARY MAN, THE • 1912 • *Baggot King* • USA
WORLD WHERE ONE GOES BEGGING, THE see **SVET, KDE SE ZEBRA** • 1938
WORLD WILL DANCE, THE see **DUNIYA NACHEGI** • 1967
WORLD WILL SHAKE, THE see **MONDE TREMBLERA, LE** • 1939
WORLD WINDOW • 1937-40 • *Cardiff Jack (Ph)* • DCS • UKN
WORLD WITHOUT A MASK, THE see **WELT OHNE MASKE, DIE** • 1934
WORLD WITHOUT BORDERS • 1944 • *O'Brien Joseph/ Mead Thomas (P)* • SHT • USA
WORLD WITHOUT END • 1952 • Rotha Paul, Wright Basil • DOC • UKN
WORLD WITHOUT END • 1956 • Bernds Edward • USA
WORLD WITHOUT SHAME • 1962 • Winter Donovan • UKN • NAKED PEOPLE, THE
WORLD WITHOUT SUN (USA) see **MONDE SANS SOLEIL, LE** • 1964
WORLD WITHOUT WOMEN see **LAST WOMAN ON EARTH, THE** • 1961
WORLD YOUTH FESTIVAL see **IUNOST' MIRA** • 1949
WORLD YOUTH FESTIVAL IN WARSAW see **VARSOI VIT I-II-III** • 1955
WORLDLINGS, THE • 1920 • Harrison Eric • UKN
WORLDLY GOODS • 1924 • Bern Paul • USA
WORLDLY GOODS • 1930 • Rosen Phil • USA
WORLDLY MADONNA, THE • 1922 • Garson Harry • USA
WORLD'S A STAGE, THE • 1953 • Deane Charles • SER • UKN
WORLD'S AFFAIRS, THE • 1933 • *Mintz Charles (P)* • ANS • USA
WORLDS APART • 1921 • Crosland Alan • USA
WORLDS APART • 1980 • Kollek Amos • ISR
WORLD'S APPLAUSE, THE • 1923 • De Mille William C. • USA
WORLD'S BEST BRIDE, THE see **HANAYOME-SAN WA SEKAI ICHI** • 1959
WORLD'S BEST MEN, THE • 1984 • Hu King • HKG
WORLD'S CHAMPION, THE • 1922 • Rosen Phil • USA
WORLD'S DESIRE, THE see **LORD GAVE, THE** • 1915
WORLD'S FAIR see **CARNIVAL** • 1935
WORLD'S FAIR AND WARMER, THE • 1934 • Townley Jack • SHT • USA
WORLD'S GOLD, THE see **ORO DEL MONDO, L'** • 1968
WORLD'S GREAT SNARE, THE • 1916 • Kaufman Joseph • USA
WORLD'S GREATEST ATHLETE, THE • 1973 • Scheerer Robert • USA
WORLD'S GREATEST LOVER, THE • 1977 • Wilder Gene • USA
WORLD'S GREATEST SINNER, THE • 1962 • Carey Timothy • USA
WORLD'S GREATEST SWINDLES see **PLUS BELLES ESCROQUERIES DU MONDE, LES** • 1963
WORLD'S GREATEST THRILLS, THE • 1933 • Butterfield Allyn • SHT • USA
WORLD'S HEAVYWEIGHT CHAMPIONSHIP CONTEST BETWEEN JACK DEMPSEY AND GEORGES CARPENTIER • 1921 • *Fred C. Quimby Inc.* • DOC • USA
WORLD'S IN LOVE, THE (USA) see **GANZE WELT DREHT SICH UM LIEBE, DIE** • 1935
WORLDS IN STRUGGLE see **KINDER DER FINSTERNIS 2** • 1921
WORLD'S MOST BEAUTIFUL GIRLS, THE • 1953 • Hibbs Jesse • SHT • USA
WORLD'S OLDEST LIVING THING, THE • 1914 • Sennett Mack • DOC • USA
WORLD'S PROGRESS FROM STONE AGE TO AIRSHIPS, THE • 1909 • *Gaumont* • FRN
WORLD'S STAGE, THE • 1922 • Campbell Colin • USA
WORLD'S WIZARD, THE • 1906 • Martin J. H.? • UKN
WORLD'S WORST FILM, THE • 1931 • *International Productions* • SHT • UKN
WORLD'S WORST WIZARD, THE • 1915 • Booth W. R. • UKN
WORLD'S YOUNGEST AVIATOR • 1944 • *O'Brien Joseph/ Mead Thomas (P)* • SHT • USA
WORM, THE see **FASHIONABLE FAKERS** • 1923
WORM EATERS, THE • 1975 • Mikels Ted V. • USA
WORM EATERS, THE • 1981 • Robins Herb • USA
WORM TURNS, THE • 1937 • Sharpsteen Ben • ANS • USA
WORM WILL SQUIRM, A • 1912 • *Cosmopolitan* • UKN
WORM WILL TURN, THE • 1909 • *Edison* • USA
WORM'S EYE VIEW • 1951 • Raymond Jack • UKN
WORM'S EYE VIEW, A • 1939 • *Mintz Charles (P)* • ANS • USA
WORMS WILL TURN • 1914 • *Lubin* • USA
WORMWOOD • 1915 • Farnum Marshall • USA
WORMWOOD STAR, THE • 1955 • Harrington Curtis • SHT • USA
WORMWOOD STAR, THE see **GWIAZDA PIOLUN** • 1988
WORRIED GERMAN, THE • 1900 • *Paul R. W.* • UKN
WORRIES see **TRAPENI** • 1961
WORRIES AND WOBBLES • 1917 • Semon Larry • SHT • USA
WORRY, THE • 1927 • Ducey Lillian • USA
WORSE FOR ME.. BETTER FOR YOU see **PEGGIO PER ME.. MEGLIO PER TE** • 1967
WORSE THAN MURDER • 1960 • Leisen Mitchell • MTV • USA
WORSE YOU ARE THE BETTER YOU SLEEP, THE see **WARUI YATSU HODO YOKU NEMURU** • 1960
WORSHIP OF THE FLESH, THE see **ENSETSU MEIJI JAKYODEN** • 1968
WORSHIP THE FIRE see **PAY TRIBUTE TO THE FIRE** • 1972

WORST CRIME OF ALL!, THE • 1966 • Lamb John • USA • WORST CRIME OF ALL, RAPE!, THE ○ MONDO KEYHOLE ○ R—! ○ MONDO KEY ○ TARTS, THE
WORST CRIME OF ALL, RAPE!, THE see **WORST CRIME OF ALL!, THE** • 1966
WORST OF FRIENDS, THE • 1916 • Griffin Frank C. • SHT • USA
WORST SECRET AGENTS see **002 AGENTI SEGRETISSIMI** • 1964
WORST WITCH, THE • 1986 • Young Robert • TVM • UKN
WORST WOMAN IN PARIS?, THE • 1933 • Bell Monta • USA
WORSTELAAR, DE • 1971 • Verhoeven Paul* • SHT • NTH • WRESTLER, THE
WORTH OF A LIFE, THE • 1914 • Sidney Scott • USA
WORTH OF A MAN, THE • 1912 • *Pollard Harry* • USA
WORTH OF A WOMAN, THE • 1915 • Vale Travers • USA
WORTH OF MAN, THE • 1913 • *Ramo* • USA
WORTH WHILE • 1916 • *Washurn Bryant* • SHT • USA
WORTH WINNING • 1989 • Mackenzie Will • USA
WORTHIER MAN, THE • 1915 • Davis Ulysses • USA
WORTHLESS, THE see **ARVOTTOMAT** • 1982
WORTHLESS DUEL, THE see **MIYAMOTO MUSASHI III** • 1963
WORTHY DECEIVER (UKN) see **BIG BLUFF, THE** • 1933
WORUBER MAN NICHT SPRICHT • 1958 • Gluck Wolfgang • FRG • FALSE SHAME (USA)
WORZEL GUMMIDGE DOWN UNDER • 1981 • Hill James • NZL
WOT A NIGHT • 1931 • Foster John, Stallings George • ANS • USA
WOT DOT • 1969 • Batchelor Joy • ANS • UKN
WOT! NO GANGSTERS? • 1946 • White E. W. • UKN
WOTANS TOCHTER • 1915 • Del Zopp Rudolf • FRG
WOTAN'S WAKE • 1962 • De Palma Brian • SHT • USA
WOT'S ALL TH' SHOOTIN' FER • 1940 • White Volney • ANS • USA
WOTTA KNIGHT • 1947 • Sparber I. • ANS • USA
WOTTA NIGHTMARE • 1939 • Fleischer Dave • ANS • USA
WOULD A MANX CAT WAG ITS TAIL IF IT HAD ONE? • 1929 • Aylott Dave, Symmons E. F. • SHT • UKN
WOULD-BE CONJUROR, THE • 1899 • *Riley Brothers* • UKN
WOULD-BE DETECTIVE, THE • 1913 • *Gem* • USA
WOULD-BE DETECTIVES, THE • 1913 • *Sun* • UKN
WOULD-BE GENTLEMAN, THE (USA) see **BOURGEOIS GENTILHOMME, LE** • 1958
WOULD-BE HEIR, THE • 1912 • Dwan Allan • USA
WOULD-BE HERO, A • 1909 • Rosenthal Joe • UKN
WOULD-BE SHRINER, THE • 1912 • Sennett Mack • USA • WOULD-BE SINNER, THE
WOULD-BE SINNER, THE see **WOULD-BE SHRINER, THE** • 1912
WOULD MOMMA ALLOW? see **SALLIIKO AITI**
WOULD YOU BE WILLING? • 1935 • Goulding Alf • SHT • USA
WOULD YOU BELIEVE IT? • 1917 • Windom Lawrence C. • SHT • USA
WOULD YOU BELIEVE IT! • 1929 • Forde Walter • UKN
WOULD YOU BELIEVE IT! • 1938 • Newman Widgey R. • UKN
WOULD YOU BELIEVE IT? see **MAJSTORI, MAJSTORI** • 1982
WOULD YOU BELIEVE ME see **LOVE AND LEARN** • 1947
WOULD YOU FORGIVE? • 1920 • Dunlap Scott R. • USA
WOULD YOU FORGIVE HER? • 1916 • Brooke Van Dyke • SHT • USA
WOULD YOU KILL A CHILD? see **QUIEN PUEDE MATAR A UN NINO?** • 1975
WOULD YOU LIKE TO MARRY ME? see **QUIERE CASARSE CONMIGO?** • 1967
WOULDN'T IT BE NICE • 1981 • Dalen Zale R. • CND
WOUND, THE see **YARA** • 1968
WOUNDED BIRD • 1956 • Pintoff Ernest • ANS • USA
WOUNDED BIRD, THE see **YARALI KUS** • 1967
WOUNDED HEART, A see **KARDIA POU LIYISE TON PONO** • 1968
WOUNDED HEARTS AND WEDDING BELLS • 1918 • Howe J. A. • SHT • USA
WOUNDED IN A FOREST see **RANNY W LESIE** • 1964
WOUNDED IN HONOUR see **MIMI METALLURGICO FERITO NELL'ONORE** • 1972
WOUNDED IN THE FOREST see **RANNY W LESIE** • 1964
WOUNDED LOVE see **AMOUR BLESSE, L'** • 1975
WOUNDED ONE, THE see **PODRANKI** • 1977
WOVON SOLL DER SCHORNSTEIN RAUCHEN see **KEINEN TAG OHNE DICH** • 1933
WOW! • 1969 • Jutra Claude • DOC • CND
WOW • 1975 • Hubley John • ANM • USA • WOMEN OF THE WORLD
WOW! see **MR. PEEK-A-BOO'S PLAYMATES** • 1962
WOW! WHAT A SATURDAY! see **VOIJUKU, MIKA LAUANTAI** • 1979
WOW-WOW see **VAU-VAU** • 1964
WOYZECK • 1967 • Noelte Rudolf • FRG
WOYZECK • 1972 • Cobelli Giancarlo • MTV • ITL
WOYZECK see **WOZZECK** • 1979
WOZEK • 1966 • Petelska Ewa, Petelski Czeslaw • MTV • PLN • CART, THE
WOZZECK • 1947 • Klaren Georg C. • GDR
WOZZECK • 1979 • Herzog Werner • FRG • WOYZECK
WPINK TV: PART 2 • 1986 • Kidder Miles • USA
WRAITH, THE • 1986 • Marvin Mike • USA
WRAITH OF HADDON TOWERS, THE • 1915 • Maude Arthur • USA
WRAITH OF THE TOMB, THE • 1915 • Calvert Charles • UKN • AVENGING HAND, THE
WRAKI • 1957 • Petelska Ewa, Petelski Czeslaw • PLN • SUNKEN SHIPS ○ SHIPWRECKS ○ WRECKS
WRANGLER'S ROOST • 1941 • Luby S. Roy • USA
WRATH • Georgiadis Vassilis • GRC
WRATH • 1917 • Marston Theodore • USA
WRATH OF CACTUS MOORE, THE • 1916 • Mong William V. • SHT • USA
WRATH OF GOD, THE • 1972 • Nelson Ralph • USA
WRATH OF GOD, THE see **IRA DI DIO, L'** • 1968
WRATH OF JEALOUSY (USA) see **WEDDING GROUP** • 1936
WRATH OF LOVE • 1917 • Vincent James • USA
WRATH OF OSAKA, THE • 1913 • Young James • USA
WRATH OF THE GODS see **HEILIGE BERG, DER** • 1926
WRATH OF THE GODS, OR THE DESTRUCTION OF SAKURA JIMA, THE • 1914 • Barker Reginald • USA
WRATH OF THE IMAM, THE see **IMAMIN GAZABI** • 1967
WRATH OF THE SEAS, THE • Noa Manfred • FRG
WRATH OF THE SUN DEMON • 1965 • Glut Don • SHT • USA
WRATHFUL JOURNEY • 1971 • Korabov Nicolai • BUL
WREATH IN TIME, A • 1909 • Griffith D. W. • USA
WREATH OF ORANGE BLOSSOMS, A • 1911 • Powell Frank?, Griffith D. W.? • USA
WRECK, THE • 1913 • Ince Ralph • USA
WRECK, THE • 1913 • Lincoln W. J. • ASL
WRECK, THE • 1917 • Chester George Randolph, Chester George Randolph Mrs. • USA
WRECK, THE • 1919 • Ince Ralph • USA
WRECK, THE • 1927 • Craft William James • USA
WRECK, THE see **VRAK** • 1983
WRECK AND RUIN • 1914 • Noy Wilfred • UKN
WRECK OF THE BATAVIA, THE • 1974 • Beresford Bruce • TVM • ASL
WRECK OF THE DUNBAR • 1912 • Mervale Gaston • ASL • YEOMAN'S WEDDING, THE
WRECK OF THE HESPERUS • 1944 • Davis Mannie • ANS • USA
WRECK OF THE HESPERUS, THE • 1926 • Tilley Frank • UKN
WRECK OF THE HESPERUS, THE • 1927 • Clifton Elmer • USA
WRECK OF THE HESPERUS, THE • 1948 • Hoffman John • USA
WRECK OF THE MARY DEARE, THE • 1959 • Anderson Michael • USA
WRECK OF THE MARY JANE, THE • 1907 • Stow Percy • UKN
WRECK OF THE SINGAPORE, THE (UKN) see **SINGAPORE MUTINY, THE** • 1928
WRECK RAISERS • 1972 • Orton Harold • UKN
WRECKAGE • 1925 • Dunlap Scott R. • USA
WRECKAGE see **STORMSWEPT** • 1923
WRECKAGE see **WHISPERING ENEMIES** • 1939
WRECKAGE see **HYORYU** • 1982
WRECKED LIFE, A • 1913 • *Pathe* • USA
WRECKED TAXI, THE • 1912 • *Benham Harry* • USA
WRECKER, THE • 1928 • von Bolvary Geza • UKN
WRECKER, THE • 1933 • Rogell Albert S. • USA
WRECKER, THE see **SEVEN SINNERS** • 1936
WRECKER OF LIVES, THE • 1914 • Calvert Charles • UKN
WRECKERS, THE • 1912 • *White Glen* • USA
WRECKETY WRECKS • 1933 • Lord Del • SHT • USA
WRECKING AN ARMOURED TRAIN • 1899 • Ashe Robert • UKN
WRECKING BOSS, THE see **CRASH, THE** • 1928
WRECKING CREW • 1942 • McDonald Frank • USA
WRECKING CREW, THE • 1968 • Karlson Phil • USA • HOUSE OF SEVEN JOYS
WRECKS see **WRAKI** • 1957
WRESTED FROM THE SEA see **ZEE ONTRUKT, DER** • 1949
WRESTLER, THE • 1974 • Westman Jim • USA • WRESTLER –THE MAIM EVENT, THE
WRESTLER, THE see **WORSTELAAR, DE** • 1971
WRESTLER, THE see **BEHLIVAN** • 1985
WRESTLER AND THE CLOWN, THE (USA) see **BORETS I KLOUN** • 1957
WRESTLER –THE MAIM EVENT, THE see **WRESTLER, THE** • 1974
WRESTLERS, THE • 1899 • Bhatvadekar Harishchandra S. • IND
WRESTLERS, THE • 1933 • *Sennett Mack (P)* • SHT • USA • WRESTLER'S BRIDE, A
WRESTLERS, THE see **LUTTEURS, LES** • 1982
WRESTLER'S BRIDE, A see **WRESTLERS, THE** • 1933
WRESTLING • 1964 • Menken Marie • SHT • USA
WRESTLING see **LUTTE, LA** • 1961
WRESTLING, N.Y. ATHLETIC CLUB • 1905 • *Bitzer Billy (Ph)* • USA
WRESTLING QUEEN • 1978 • *Vachon Vivian* • USA
WRESTLING-RING FESTIVAL see **DOHYOSAI** • 1944
WRESTLING SEXTETTE, THE see **NOUVELLES LUTTES EXTRAVAGANTES** • 1900
WRESTLING SWORDFISH • 1931 • *Sennett Mack (P)* • SHT • USA
WRESTLING WOMEN VS. THE AZTEC MUMMY, THE (USA) see **LUCHADORAS CONTRA LA MOMIA, LAS** • 1964
WRESTLING WOMEN VS. THE MURDERING DOCTOR, THE see **LUCHADORAS CONTRA EL MEDICO ASESINO, LAS** • 1962
WRESTLING WOMEN VS. THE MURDERING ROBOT, THE see **LUCHADORAS CONTRA EL ROBOT ASESINO, LAS** • 1969
WRESTLING WRECKS • 1953 • Patterson Don • ANS • USA
WRETCHES ARE STILL SINGING, THE • 1980 • Nikolaidis Nikos • GRC
WRIGHT IDEA, THE • 1928 • Hines Charles • USA
WRINGING GOOD JOKE, A • 1900 • Porter Edwin S. • USA
WRIT ON WATER • 1955 • Davis James* • SHT • USA
WRITER, THE see **SCHRIJVER EN DE DOOD, DE** • 1988
WRITING ON THE BLOTTER, THE • 1911 • *Edison* • USA
WRITING ON THE WALL, THE • 1897 • Welford Walter D. • UKN
WRITING ON THE WALL, THE • 1910 • *Thanhouser* • USA
WRITING ON THE WALL, THE • 1915 • *Ridgley Cleo* • USA
WRITING ON THE WALL, THE • 1916 • Johnson Tefft • USA
WRITTEN IN BLOOD see **OPOWIESC W CZERWIENI** • 1974
WRITTEN IN THE SANDS • 1912 • *Vitagraph* • USA
WRITTEN LAW, THE • 1931 • Fogwell Reginald • UKN
WRITTEN OFF see **OTPISANI** • 1975
WRITTEN-OFF RETURN, THE see **POVRATAK OTPISANIH** • 1977
WRITTEN ON THE SAND see **PLAY DIRTY** • 1968
WRITTEN ON THE SKY see **BAR ASMAN NEYESHTE** • 1968
WRITTEN ON THE WIND • 1956 • Sirk Douglas • USA
WRONG ADDRESS, THE • 1915 • *Barclay Don* • USA
WRONG AGAIN • 1920 • *National Film Corp. Of America* • SHT • USA
WRONG AGAIN • 1929 • McCarey Leo • SHT • USA
WRONG ALL ROUND • 1914 • *Komic* • USA
WRONG ALL ROUND • 1914 • *Essanay* • USA
WRONG ALL ROUND • 1917 • *Ebony* • SHT • USA
WRONG AMBITIONS see **AMBIZIONI SBAGLIATE** • 1984
WRONG ARM OF THE LAW, THE • 1962 • Owen Cliff • UKN
WRONG BAG, THE • 1910 • *Atlas* • USA
WRONG BEDS • 1916 • Currier Frank • SHT • USA
WRONG BIRD, THE • 1916 • Davey Horace • SHT • USA
WRONG BIRDS, THE • 1914 • *American* • USA
WRONG BOTTLE, THE • 1911 • *Physioc Wray* • USA
WRONG BOTTLE, THE • 1913 • *Mcdowell Claire* • USA
WRONG BOX, THE • 1910 • *Vitagraph* • USA
WRONG BOX, THE • 1913 • *Solax* • USA
WRONG BOX, THE • 1966 • Forbes Bryan • UKN
WRONG BRIDE, THE • 1912 • *Pathe* • USA
WRONG BURGLAR, THE • 1909 • *Lubin* • USA
WRONG CAB, THE • 1909 • Fitzhamon Lewin • UKN
WRONG CHIMNEY, THE • 1903 • Williamson James • UKN
WRONG CHIMNEY, THE • 1907 • Green Tom? • UKN
WRONG COAT, THE • 1909 • Bouwmeester Theo? • UKN
WRONG DAMN FILM, THE • 1975 • Davidson Carson • USA
WRONG DIRECTION • 1934 • Goulding Alf • SHT • USA
WRONG DOOR, THE • 1916 • De Haven Carter • USA
WRONG DOOR, THE see **THROUGH THE WRONG DOOR** • 1919
WRONG ENVELOPES, THE • 1912 • Fitzhamon Lewin • UKN
WRONG FLAT, THE • 1914 • Lambart Harry • USA
WRONG FLAT, THE • 1918 • *Steiner William (P)* • SHT • USA
WRONG GIRL, THE • 1915 • Van Wally • USA
WRONG GLOVE, THE • 1911 • *Essanay* • USA
WRONG GUYS, THE • 1988 • Bilson Danny, Demeo Paul • USA
WRONG HAND BAG, THE • 1913 • *Lubin* • USA
WRONG HEART, THE • 1916 • Reid Wallace • SHT • USA
WRONG HOUSE, THE • 1915 • Kellino W. P. • UKN
WRONG IS RIGHT • 1982 • Brooks Richard • USA • MAN WITH THE DEADLY LENS, THE (UKN)
WRONG KIND OF GIRL, THE see **BUS STOP** • 1956
WRONG LABEL, THE • 1915 • Easton Clem • USA
WRONG MAN, THE • 1910 • *Essanay* • USA
WRONG MAN, THE • 1917 • Kelsey Fred A. • SHT • USA
WRONG MAN, THE • 1957 • Hitchcock Alfred • USA
WRONG MARY WRIGHT, THE • 1917 • Wilson Millard K. • SHT • USA
WRONG MEDICINE, THE • 1908 • Fitzhamon Lewin? • UKN
WRONG MISS WRIGHT, THE • 1913 • McGill Lawrence • USA
WRONG MISS WRIGHT, THE • 1914 • *Nestor* • USA
WRONG MISS WRIGHT, THE • 1937 • Lamont Charles • SHT • USA
WRONG MR. FOX, THE • 1917 • Jackson Harry • SHT • USA
WRONG MR. PERKINS, THE • 1931 • Varney-Serrao Arthur • UKN
WRONG MR. STOUT, THE see **HIS WIFE'S MISTAKE** • 1916
WRONG MR. WRIGHT, THE • 1916 • Williams C. Jay • SHT • USA
WRONG MR. WRIGHT, THE • 1927 • Sidney Scott • USA
WRONG MOVE see **FALSCHE BEWEGUNG** • 1975
WRONG MOVEMENT (UKN) see **FALSCHE BEWEGUNG** • 1975
WRONG NUMBER • 1959 • Sewell Vernon • UKN
WRONG NUMBER • 1979 • Revach Ze'Ev • ISR
WRONG NUMBER (UKN) see **ARKANSAS SWING, THE** • 1948
WRONG PAIR, THE • 1913 • *Vitagraph* • USA
WRONG PATIENT, THE • 1911 • *Vitagraph* • USA
WRONG PIG, THE • 1910 • *Walturdaw* • UKN
WRONG POISON, THE • 1903 • Williamson James • UKN
WRONG PRESCRIPTION, THE • 1914 • *Reliance* • USA
WRONG ROAD, THE • 1913 • *Fischer Margarita* • USA
WRONG ROAD, THE • 1937 • Cruze James • USA • TREASURE HUNT
WRONG ROAD TO HAPPINESS, THE • 1913 • *Panzer Paul* • USA
WRONG ROMANCE • 1937 • Goodwins Leslie • SHT • USA
WRONG ROOM • 1939 • Brock Lou • SHT • USA
WRONG ROOM, THE • 1916 • *Utah* • USA
WRONG SIDE OF THE ROAD • 1981 • Lander Ned • ASL
WRONG SIDE OF THE TRACKS, THE see **MALA VIDA, LA** • 1973
WRONG SON • 1950 • Fritsch Gunther V. • SHT • USA
WRONG TIMING see **ANTISTRROPHI METRISI** • 1984
WRONG TRAIL, THE • 1910 • *Bison* • USA
WRONG WAIT, THE • 1912 • *Imp* • USA
WRONG WAY BUTCH • 1950 • Barclay David • SHT • USA
WRONG WAY OUT, THE • 1938 • Machaty Gustav • SHT • USA
WRONG WOMAN, THE • 1915 • Ridgely Richard • USA
WRONG WOMAN, THE • 1920 • Abramson Ivan • USA
WRONG WORLD, THE • 1984 • Pringle Ian • ASL
WRONG WRIGHTS, THE • 1917 • *Sparkle* • SHT • USA
WRONGDOERS see **ROSSZEMBEREK** • 1979
WRONGDOERS, THE • 1925 • Dierker Hugh • USA
WRONGDOERS, THE see **VURGUNCULAR** • 1971
WRONGED, THE see **KINONIA MAS ADIKISE, I** • 1967
WRONGED BY MISTAKE • 1918 • *Keystone* • SHT • USA
WRONGFULLY ACCUSED • 1908 • *Essanay* • USA
WRONGLY ACCUSED • 1912 • *Melies* • USA
WRONGLY ACCUSED • 1912 • Davis Ulysses • *Champion* • USA
WRONGLY ACCUSED (UKN) see **BAD MEN OF THE HILLS** • 1942
WRONGS RIGHTED • 1924 • *Gallery Tom* • USA
WRONSKY • 1979 • Pringle Ian • ASL
WRZESIEN 1939 see **WRZESIEN -TAK BYLO** • 1961
WRZESIEN -TAK BYLO • 1961 • Bossak Jerzy (c/d) • DOC • PLN • SEPTEMBER –HOW IT WAS ○ WRZESIEN 1939 ○ SEPTEMBER 1939
WRZOS • 1938 • Starczewski Jerszy • HEATHER (USA)
WSPANIALY MARSZ • 1970 • Giersz Witold • ANS • PLN • GLORIOUS MARCH ○ MAGNIFICENT MARCH, THE
WSPOLNY POKOJ • 1959 • Has Wojciech J. • PLN • ONE ROOM TENANTS (USA) ○ SHARED ROOM
WSROD LUDZI • 1960 • Slesicki Wladyslaw • DOC • PLN • AMONGST PEOPLE ○ AMONG PEOPLE
WSZCY JEJESTESMY PRESLEYAMI • 1963 • Wionczek Roman • DOC • PLN • WE'RE ALL PRESLEYS
WSZYSTKO JEST LICZBA • 1967 • Schabenbeck Stefan • ANS • PLN • EVERYTHING IS A NUMBER ○ REIGN OF NUMBERS ○ NUMBERS

WSZYSTKO NA SPRZEDAZ • 1969 • Wajda Andrzej • PLN • EVERYTHING FOR SALE
WTORKI, CZWARTKI, SOBOTY • 1965 • Gryczelowska Krystyna • DOC • PLN • TUESDAYS, THURSDAYS, SATURDAYS
WU CHIA CHIH PAO • 1976 • Ch'En Yao-Ch'I • HKG • PRICELESS TREASURE
WU-HOU • 1964 • Li Han-Hsiang • HKG • EMPRESS WU (USA)
WU-KO NU-TZU YU YI-KEN SHENG • 1990 • Yeh Hung-Wei • TWN
WU LI CHANG • 1930 • Grinde Nick • USA
WU-LI-TE TI-SHENG • 1983 • Tseng Chuang-Hsiang • TWN • NATURE IS QUIETLY BEAUTIFUL
WU-LIN WAI SHIH • 1978 • Ch'U Yuan • HKG • FOREST OF KNIGHTS
WU SUNG • 1983 • Li Han-Hsiang • HKG • TIGER KILLER
WU-TI T'IEH SHA CHANG • 1973 • Chu Mu • HKG • INVINCIBLE IRON PALM, THE
WU TU T'IEN LO • 1977 • Ch'U Yuan • HKG • WEB OF DEATH, THE
WU T'U WU MIN • 1975 • Li Hsing • HKG • LAND OF THE UNDAUNTED
WUCHERER VON BERLIN, DER see **KRAWATTENMACHER** • 1922
WUJUH AL-LAYL • 1968 • Siddik Khalid • SHT • KWT • VISAGES DE LA NUIT
WULIN ZHI • 1983 • Zhang Huaxun • CHN • PRIDE'S DEADLY FURY
WUN LUNG'S STRATEGY • 1912 • *American* • USA
WUNDER DER LIEBE, DAS see **OSWALT KOLLE: DAS WUNDER DER LIEBE -SEXUELLE PARTNERSCHAFT** • 1968
WUNDER DER MADONNA, DAS • 1916 • Reinert Robert? • FRG
WUNDER DER SCHOPFUNG • 1925 • Kornblum Hanns Walter • FRG • OUR HEAVENLY BODIES (USA) ○ MIRACLES OF CREATION ○ WONDERS OF CREATION
WUNDER DER ZEITEN, DAS see **MENSCHHEIT ANWALT 1, DER** • 1920
WUNDER DES FLIEGENS • 1935 • Paul Heinz • FRG
WUNDER DES MALACHIAS, DAS • 1961 • Wicki Bernhard • FRG • FATHER MALACHY'S MIRACLE (USA) ○ MIRACLE OF MALACHIAS, THE ○ MALACHIAS ○ MIRACLE OF FATHER MALACHIAS, THE
WUNDER DES SCHNEESCHUHS 1, DIE • 1920 • Fanck Arnold, Tauern Dr. • FRG • MARVELS OF SKI
WUNDER DES SCHNEESCHUHS 2, DAS • 1922 • Fanck Arnold • FRG • FUCHSJAGD AUF SKIERN DURCHS ENGADIN, EINE
WUNDER IN NAUMBERG • 1932 • Oertel Curt • FRG
WUNDER VON MAILAND, DAS • 1967 • Strobel Hans Rolf, Tichawsky Heinz • DOC • FRG • MIRACLE OF MILAN, THE
WUNDERBAR KANN EINE SEIN • 1940 • Liebeneiner Wolfgang • FRG
WUNDERBARE LUGE DER NINA PETROWNA, DIE • 1929 • Schwarz Hanns • FRG • WONDERFUL LIE OF NINA PETROVNA, THE
WUNDERFENSTER, DAS • 1952 • Otto Gerda, Otto Hedwig, Krauss Marian • FRG • MIRACLE WINDOW, THE (USA)
WUNDERKIND, DAS • 1916 • Albes Emil • FRG
WUNDERLAMPE, DIE • 1915 • Albes Emil • FRG
WUNDERLICHEN GESCHICHTEN DES THEODOR HUBER, DIE • 1924 • Lowenbein Richard • FRG
WUNDERSAM IST DAS MARCHEN DER LIEBE • 1918 • Connard Leo • FRG
WUNDERSCHONE GALATHEE, DIE • 1950 • Meyer Rolf • FRG
WUNDERUHR, DIE • 1928 • Starevitch Ladislas • FRG, FRN • HORLOGE MAGIQUE, L' (FRN) ○ MAGIC CLOCK, THE (USA)
WUNSCHKONZERT • 1940 • von Borsody Eduard • FRG
WUNSCHKONZERT • 1955 • Ode Erik • FRG
WURGER DER WELT, DER • 1919 • Dupont E. A. • FRG
WURGER KOMMT AUF LEISEN SOCKEN, DER • 1971 • Zurli Guido • FRG, ITL • STRANGOLATORE DI VIENNA, LO (ITL) ○ MAD BUTCHER OF VIENNA, THE ○ VIENNA STRANGLER, THE ○ MEAT IS MEAT ○ MAD BUTCHER, THE ○ STRANGLER OF VIENNA, THE
WURGER VON SCHLOSS BLACKMOOR, DER • 1963 • Reinl Harald • FRG • STRANGLER OF BLACKMOOR CASTLE, THE (USA)
WURRA-WURRA • 1916 • Beaudine William • SHT • USA
WUSA • 1970 • Rosenberg Stuart • USA • HALL OF MIRRORS
WUSTENGRAB, DAS • 1920 • Heiland Heinz Karl • FRG
WUSTENKONIG VON BRANDENBURG, DER • 1973 • Kratzert Hans • GDR
WUSTENRAUSCH • 1923 • von Bolvary Geza • FRG
WUSTENSDIAMANT, DER • 1918 • Meinert Rudolf • FRG
WUTAI JIEMEI • 1964 • Xie Jin • CHN • TWO STAGE SISTERS
WUTHERING HEIGHTS • 1920 • Bramble A. V. • UKN
WUTHERING HEIGHTS • 1939 • Wyler William • USA
WUTHERING HEIGHTS • Erksan Metin • TRK
WUTHERING HEIGHTS • 1970 • Fuest Robert • USA, UKN
WUTHERING HEIGHTS see **POKPOONGEA UHUNDUCK** • 1960
WUTHERING HEIGHTS see **HURLEVENT** • 1986
WUTHERING HEIGHTS see **ARASHI GA OKA** • 1988
WUTHERING HEIGHTS (USA) see **CUMBRES BORRASCOSAS** • 1953
WUXING PEOPLE'S COMMUNE • 1980 • Ianzelo Tony, Richardson Boyce • DOC • CND
WUYA YU MAQUE • 1949 • Zheng Junli • CHN • RAVENS AND SPARROWS ○ CROWS AND SPARROWS
WYCIECZKA • 1967 • Golc Ryszard • DOC • PLN • TRIP, THE
WYCIECZKA DO WARSZAWY • 1950 • Nasfeter Janusz • SHT • PLN • TRIP TO WARSAW, A
WYCIECZKA W KOSMOS • 1961 • Debowski Krzysztof • PLN • PAMIETNIK GWIEZDNE ○ TRIP THROUGH THE COSMOS, A ○ EXCURSION INTO THE COSMOS ○ MEMORIES OF THE STARS
WYCIECZKA W NIEZNANE • 1968 • Ziarnik Jerzy • PLN • EXCURSION TO AUSCHWITZ-BIRKENAU ○ EXCURSION INTO THE UNKNOWN ○ TRIP IN THE UNKNOWN ○ JOURNEY INTO THE UNKNOWN, A ○ ACROSS THE UNKNOWN
WYCIECZKA Z MIASTA • 1968 • Giersz Witold • ANS • PLN • TRIP OUT OF TOWN, A ○ JOURNEY OUT OF THE CITY, THE
WYJSCIE AWARYJNE • 1983 • Zaluski Roman • PLN • EMERGENCY ESCAPE, AN
WYKRES • 1966 • Szczechura Daniel • ANS • PLN • DIAGRAM ○ GRAPH, THE
WYKRZKNIK • Schabenbeck Stefan • ANS • PLN • EXCLAMATION POINT
WYLIE see **EYE OF THE CAT** • 1969
WYN GLADWYN • 1928 • *De Forest Phonofilm* • SHT • UKN
WYNKEN, BLYNKEN AND NOD • 1938 • Heid Graham • ANS • USA
WYNNE AND PENKOVSKY • 1987 • Seed Paul • MTV • UKN
WYNONA'S REVENGE see **WYNONA'S VENGEANCE** • 1913
WYNONA'S VENGEANCE • 1913 • Ford Francis • USA • WYNONA'S REVENGE
WYOMING • 1928 • Van Dyke W. S. • USA • ROCK OF FRIENDSHIP, THE (UKN)
WYOMING • 1940 • Thorpe Richard • USA • BAD MAN OF WYOMING (UKN)
WYOMING • 1947 • Kane Joseph • USA
WYOMING BANDIT, THE • 1949 • Ford Philip • USA
WYOMING HURRICANE • 1944 • Berke William • USA • PROVED GUILTY (UKN)
WYOMING KID, THE • 1947 • Walsh Raoul • USA • CHEYENNE
WYOMING MAIL • 1950 • Le Borg Reginald • USA
WYOMING OUTLAW • 1939 • Sherman George • USA
WYOMING RENEGADES • 1955 • Sears Fred F. • USA
WYOMING ROUNDUP • 1952 • Carr Thomas • USA
WYOMING TORNADO • 1929 • *Acord Art* • USA
WYOMING (UKN) see **SINGLE-HANDED SANDERS** • 1932
WYOMING WHIRLWIND • 1932 • Schaefer Armand • USA
WYOMING WILDCAT • 1941 • Sherman George • USA
WYOMING WILDCAT, THE • 1925 • De Lacy Robert • USA
WYPADEK • 1971 • Czekala Ryszard • PLN • ACCIDENT, THE
WYPRAWA NA CZARNA WYSPE • 1955 • Gryczelowska Krystyna (c/d) • DOC • PLN • EXPEDITION TO THE BLACK ISLAND, AN
WYROK • 1961 • Passendorfer Jerzy • PLN • SENTENCE, THE
WYROK ZYCIA • 1934 • Gardan Juliusz • PLN
WYSCIG POKOJU WARSZAWA - BERLIN - PRAGA see **FRIEDENSFAHRT** • 1952
WYSOKIE LOTY • 1978 • Filipski Ryszard • PLN • HIGH FLIGHT
WYSPA WIELKICH NADZIEI • 1957 • Poreba Bohdan • DOC • PLN • ISLAND OF GREAT HOPES, AN
WYSTRZAL • 1965 • Antczak Jerzy • PLN • PISTOL SHOT, THE ○ SHOT, THE
WYSZEDL W JASNY POGODNY DZIEN • 1973 • Wojciechowski Krzysztof • SHT • PLN • HE LEFT ON A CLEAR FINE DAY ○ HE LEFT ONE FINE DAY ○ HE LEFT ON A BRIGHT CLEAR DAY
WYWIDD Z BALLMAYEREM • 1962 • Wajda Andrzej • PLN • BALLMAYER INTERVIEW, THE

X

X • 1970 • Walsh C. • USA
X • 1985 • Einarson Oddvar • NRW
X see **X -THE MAN WITH THE X-RAY EYES** • 1963
X-3 • 1916 • Hunt Jay • SHT • USA
X 3 OPERAZIONE DINAMITE (ITL) see **FEU AUX POUDRES, LE** • 1956
X-15 • 1961 • Donner Richard • USA
X-15 • 1961 • Leacock Richard • DOC • USA
X-17 TOP SECRET • 1965 • Boccia Tanio • SPN, ITL • AGENTE X-17 OPERAZIONE OCEANO (ITL) ○ XL-7 TOP SECRET
X 25 JAVLJA • 1960 • Cap Frantisek • YGS • X-25 REPORTS
X-25 REPORTS see **X 25 JAVLJA** • 1960
X 312 FLIGHT TO HELL (UKN) see **X 312 -FLUG ZUR HOLLE** • 1971
X 312 -FLUG ZUR HOLLE • 1971 • Franco Jesus • FRG • X 312 FLIGHT TO HELL (UKN)
X BARON, THE see **X-PARONI** • 1964
X-DIAGNOSIS, THE see **DIAGNOZA X** • 1933
X FROM OUTER SPACE see **UCHU DAIKAIJU GUILALA** • 1967
X MARKS THE SPOT • 1931 • Kenton Erle C. • USA
X MARKS THE SPOT • 1942 • Sherman George • USA
X MYSTERIEUX, L' • 1912 • Peguy Robert • FRN
X NOIR, L' • 1915 • Perret Leonce • FRN
X-PARONI • 1964 • Pakkasvirta Jaakko, Jarva Risto, Pasanen Spede • FNL • X BARON, THE ○ BARON X
X.. RACONTE • 1959 • Regnier Michel • SER • CND
X-RAY • 1981 • Davidson Boaz • USA • HOSPITAL MASSACRE ○ MASSACRE HOSPITAL ○ BE MY VALENTINE, OR ELSE..
X-RAY, THE • 1900 • *Warwick* • UKN
X-RAY FIEND, THE see **X-RAYS** • 1897
X-RAY GLASSES, THE see **LUNETTES FEERIQUES, LES** • 1909
X-RAY MIRROR, THE • 1899 • McCutcheon Wallace • USA
X-RAYS • 1897 • Smith G. A. • UKN • X-RAY FIEND, THE
X-RAYS see **RONTGENSTRAHLEN** • 1936
X-RAYS, THE see **RAYONS ROENTGEN, LES** • 1898
X-TERMINATOR, THE • 1986 • Rogel Van • USA
X -THE MAN WITH THE X-RAY EYES • 1963 • Corman Roger • USA • MAN WITH THE X-RAY EYES, THE (UKN) ○ X
X: THE UNHEARD MUSIC • 1986 • Morgan W. T. • USA
X THE UNKNOWN • 1956 • Norman Leslie • UKN
X, Y AND ZEE (USA) see **ZEE AND CO** • 1972
X.Y.Z. • 1960 • Lifchitz Philippe • FRN
X + YY -FORMEL DES BOSEN • 1969 • Piegeler Teja, Jocic P. • FRG • NACKT SIND SEINE OPFER ○ X + YY -FORMULA FOR EVIL
X + YY -FORMULA FOR EVIL see **X + YY -FORMEL DES BOSEN** • 1969
XALA • 1974 • Sembene Ousmane • SNL • CURSE, THE ○ IMPOTENCE
XANADU • 1980 • Greenwald Robert • USA
XANTHIPPE AND SOCRATES • 1962 • ANS • CZC
XAOS • 1984 • Taviani Paolo, Taviani Vittorio • ITL • KAOS
XENA HERIA INE PIKRA, TA • 1968 • Papakostas Giorgos • GRC • WITHOUT A LIFE OF MY OWN ○ STRANGE HANDS ARE HARSH
XENIA • 1989 • Vivancos Patrice • GRC
XEROSCOPY • 1971 • *Halas John (P)* • ANS • UKN
XERRIZOMENI YENIA • 1967 • Tegopoulos Apostolos • GRC • UPROOTED FAMILY
XEW XEW • 1983 • Bah Cheikh Ngaido • SNL
XFILM • 1967 • Schofill John • SHT • USA
XIANGNU XIAOXIAO • 1985 • Zhang Xian • CHN • HUNAN GIRL XIAOXAIO
XIANGNU XIAOXIAO • 1987 • Xie Fei, Lan Wu • CHN • XIAO XIAO -A GIRL FROM HUNAN
XIANGYIN • 1983 • Hu Bingliu • CHN • COUNTRY PEOPLE
XIAO XIAO -A GIRL FROM HUNAN see **XIANGNU XIAOXIAO** • 1987
XIAO'AO JIANGHU • 1988 • Xu Ke • HKG
XIAOHUA • 1979 • CHN • LITTLE FLOWER
XIAOZI BEI • 1980 • Wang Jiayi, Luo Tai • CHN • BUS NUMBER THREE
XICA see **XICA DA SILVA** • 1976
XICA DA SILVA • 1976 • Diegues Carlos • BRZ • XICA
XILO VIKE AP TO PARADISO • 1961 • Sakellarios Alekos • GRC • MAIDEN'S CHEEK
XIPOLITO TAGMA • 1954 • Tallas Gregg R. • GRC • BAREFOOT BATTALION ○ BATTALION DES VA-NU-PIEDS, LE
XIVTH OLYMPIAD -THE GLORY OF SPORT, THE • 1948 • Knight Castleton • UKN • OLYMPIC GAMES OF 1948, THE
XL-7 TOP SECRET see **X-17 TOP SECRET** • 1965
XMAS • 1962 • Nagle Herbert • SHT • USA • CHRISTMAS
XMAS • 1969 • *Fearless Productions* • USA
XMAS GREETING FILM • 1911 • Speer Walter Harold • UKN
XOCHIMILCO see **MARIA CANDELARIA** • 1943
XOXONTLA • 1976 • Mariscal Alberto • MXC
XTRO • 1982 • Davenport Harry Bromley • UKN • JUDAS GOAT
XUEV • 1982 • Brunie Patrick • FRN
XUNAN • 1983 • Keller Margrit, von Gunten Peter • DOC • SWT • LADY, THE
XV SONG TRAITS • 1965 • Brakhage Stan • USA • SONG XV ○ FIFTEEN SONG TRAITS
XVII BOKSERSKIE MISTRZOSTWA POLSKI W LODZI • 1946 • Bossak Jerzy • PLN • 17TH POLISH BOXING CHAMPIONSHIPS IN LODZ
XX JUBILEE see **XX JUBILEUSZOWY** • 1967
XX JUBILEUSZOWY • 1967 • Lomnicki Jan • DOC • PLN • XX JUBILEE
XX VOLTA A PORTUGAL EM BICICLETA • 1957 • Guimaraes Manuel • SHT • PRT
XXII OLYMPIAD: MOSCOW 1980 • 1981 • Ozerov Yury • USS
XXIST MONTE CARLO RALLY 1951 • 1951 • Rankin Douglas, Reid Adrian • UKN
XXX MEDICO • 1940 • Wrangell Basil • SHT • USA • S.O.S. MEDICO
XYLOPHONE SOLO • 1907 • *Walturdaw* • UKN
XYZ MURDERS, THE see **CRIMEWAVE** • 1986

Y

"Y" • Rice Ray • ANS • USA
Y • 1963 • Stern Gern, Maibrakoff Ivan • ANS • USA
Y 17 see **IGREK-17** • 1972
Y A DU COEUR AU PROGRAMME • 1972 • Moreau Michel • DCS • CND
Y A PAS D'MAL A SE FAIRE DU BIEN • 1974 • Mulot Claude • CND
Y A-T-IL UN FRANCAIS DANS LA SALLE? • 1982 • Mocky Jean-Pierre • FRN
Y A-T-IL UN PIRATE SUR L'ANTENNE? • 1983 • Roy Jean-Claude • FRN
Y A TELLEMENT DE PAYS POUR ALLER • 1978 • Bigiaoui Jean, Hagege Claude, Sansoulh Jacques • FRN
Y AHORA QUE, SENOR FISCAL • 1977 • Klimovsky Leon • SPN
Y DIOS LA LLAMO TIERRA • 1960 • Toussaint Carlos • MXC
Y EL CIELO FUE TOMADO POR ASALTO • 1973 • Alvarez Santiago • DOC • CUB
Y EL CUERPO SIGUE AGUANTANDO • 1960 • Klimovsky Leon • SPN
...Y EL DEMONIO CREO A LOS HOMBRES • 1960 • Bo Armando • ARG • HEAT (USA)
...Y EL PROJIMO? • 1974 • del Pozo Angel • SPN
...Y ELIGIO EL INFIERNO • 1958 • Ardavin Cesar • SPN
Y EN A MARRE see **Y'EN A MARRE** • 1959
Y LA MUJER HIZO AL HOMBRE • 1974 • *Conacine* • MXC
Y LE LLAMABAN HALCON (SPN) see **UOMO AVVISATO MEZZO AMMAZZATO.. PAROLA DI SPIRITO SANTO** • 1972
Y MANANA? • 1968 • Degelin Emile • BLG • AND TOMORROW?
Y MANANA SERAN HOMBRES • 1979 • Borcosque Carlos Jr. • ARG • AND TOMORROW THEY'LL BE ADULTS
...Y MANANA SERAN MUJERES! • 1954 • Galindo Alejandro • MXC
...Y MURIO POR NOSOTROS! • 1951 • Rodriguez Joselito • MXC
Y SE LLAMARIA COLOMBIA • 1978 • Norden Francisco • SHT • CLM • IT WILL BE CALLED COLOMBIA
Y-SEVENTEEN see **IGREK-17** • 1972
Y SI ELLA VOLVIERA • 1956 • Orona Vicente • MXC, CUB
Y SI NO ENFADAMOS (SPN) see **ALTRIMENTI CI ARRABBIAMO** • 1974
Y TENEMOS SABOR • 1967 • Gomez Sara • DOC • CUB

YA BABUSHKA, ILIKO I ILLARION • 1963 • Abuladze Tengiz • USS • ME, GRANDMOTHER, ILIKO AND HILLARION ○ ME, BEBIA, ILIKO DA ILARIONI ○ GRANDMOTHER, ILIKO, ILLARION AND ME ○ ILLIKO, ILLARION, GRANDMOTHER AND ME

YA, FRANCIS SKORINA • 1970 • Stepanov Boris • USS • I, FRANCIS SKORINA

YA I MOYA SOVEST • 1915 • Protazanov Yakov • USS • MY CONSCIENCE AND I

YA KAPIL PAPU • 1963 • Frez Ilya • USS • DIMKA (USA)

YA -KUBA • 1962 • Kalatozov Mikhail • USS, CUB • I AM CUBA ○ HERE IS CUBA ○ SOY CUBA

YA LYUBLYU • 1936 • Lukov Leonid • USS • I LOVE

YA NO BASTA CON REZAR • 1971 • Francia Aldo • CHL • ENOUGH PRAYING

Y'A RIEN LA • 1976 • Bulbulian Maurice • DOC • CND

YA RODOM IZ DYETSTVA • 1967 • Turov Viktor • USS • I HAIL FROM CHILDHOOD ○ I'M FROM CHILDHOOD

YA SALAM AL-HUBB • 1962 • Salman Mohammed • LBN • QUE L'AMOUR EST BEAU!

YA SE QUEN ERES • 1970 • *Am Libra* • MXC

YA SEV YA OLDUR • 1967 • Sagiroglu Duygu • TRK • LOVE OR KILL

YA SHAGAYU PO MOSKVE • 1964 • Daneliya Georgi • USS • MEET ME IN MOSCOW (USA) ○ WALKING THE STREETS OF MOSCOW ○ I WALK AROUND MOSCOW ○ I WALK ABOUT MOSCOW

YA SOLDAT, MAMA • 1967 • Zakharias Manos • USS • I AM A SOLDIER, MOTHER

YA SOY UNA MUJER • 1975 • Summers Manuel • SPN • NOW I'M A WOMAN

YA TENEMOS COCHE • 1958 • Salvador Julio • SPN

YA TENGO A MI HIJO • 1946 • Rodriguez Ismael • MXC

YA TIENE COMISARIO EL PUEBLO • 1936 • Martinez Payva Claudio (c/d) • ARG

YA TIENE COMISARIO EL PUEBLO • 1967 • Carreras Enrique • ARG • COMMISSIONER MANAGES THE TOWN HALL, THE

Y'A TOUJOURS MOYEN DE MOYENNER • 1973 • Heroux Denis • FRN

Y'A UN OS DANS LA MOULINETTE • 1974 • Andre Raoul • FRN

YA VAS LYUBIL.. • 1968 • Frez Ilya • USS • I LOVED YOU..

YA VIENE EL CORTEJO • 1939 • Arevalo Carlos • SHT • SPN

YA VSYE POMNYU, RICHARD • 1967 • Kalnins Rolands • USS • I REMEMBER ALL, RICARDS

YA YA MON KOLONEL • Guerrini Mino • FRN

YAABA • 1988 • Ouedraogo Idrissa • BRK, SWT, FRN • GRANDMOTHER

YAAK AND THE ROBOT • Pars Heino • USS

YAB-YUM OP STELTEN (NTH) see **HOT PURSUIT** • 1983

YABAIKITO NARA ZENI NI NARU • 1962 • Nakahira Ko • JPN • DANGER PAYS

YABAN GULU • 1961 • Utku Umit • TRK • DESERT LAUGHS, THE

YABU NO NAKA NO KURONEKO • 1968 • Shindo Kaneto • JPN • BLACK CAT IN THE BUSH ○ KURONEKO ○ BLACK CAT

YABUNIRAMI NIPPON • 1964 • Suzuki Hideo • JPN • WALL-EYED NIPPON (USA)

YABURE-DAIKO • 1949 • Kinoshita Keisuke • JPN • BROKEN DRUM, THE ○ BROKEN WING, THE

YABURE KABURE • 1961 • Kurahara Koreyoshi • JPN • DESPERATION

YABUREZARU MONO • 1964 • Matsuo Akinori • JPN • ETERNAL LIFE

YACATAN • 1960 • Reitz Edgar • FRG

YACHT DE L'AMOUR, LE • Ricaud Michel • FRN

YACHT OF THE SEVEN SINS see **JACHT DER SIEBEN SUNDEN, DIE** • 1928

YACHT RACE, A see **COURSE DE YACHTS, UNE** • 1903

YACHT RACE (RELIANCE-SHAMROCK III), THE see **COURSE DE YACHTS, UNE** • 1903

YACOUT EFFENDI • 1933 • el Rihani Nagib? • EGY

YACUMBU • 1974 • Scheuren Bruno • DOC • VNZ

YADES • 1971 • Merbah Lamine • ALG

YAGMUR CISELERKEN • 1967 • Ergun Nuri • TRK • WHEN THE RAIN FALLS

YAGMUR KACAKLARI • 1987 • Ozkan Yavuz • TRK, FRN • FUGITIVES OF RAIN

YAGODKI LYUBVI • 1926 • Dovzhenko Alexander • USS • JEAN KOLBASINK THE HAIRDRESSER ○ FRUITS OF LOVE, THE ○ MARRIAGE TRAP, THE ○ LOVE'S BERRY ○ YAHIDKA KOKHANNYA

YAGUA • 1941 • Fejos Paul • DOC • PRU

YAGYU BUGEICHO • 1957 • Inagaki Hiroshi • JPN • SECRET SCROLLS (PART I) (USA) ○ YAGYU SECRET SCROLLS ○ YAGYU CONFIDENTIAL

YAGYU BUGEICHO -SORYU HIKEN • 1958 • Inagaki Hiroshi • JPN • SECRET SCROLLS (PART II) ○ NINJUTSU

YAGYU CONFIDENTIAL see **YAGYU BUGEICHO** • 1957

YAGYU ICHIZOKU NO IMBOU • 1977 • Fukasaku Kinji • JPN • INTRIGUE OF THE YAGYU FAMILY, THE

YAGYU SECRET SCROLLS see **YAGYU BUGEICHO** • 1957

YAHALU YEHELI • 1981 • Peries Sumitra • SLN • FRIENDS

YAHIDKA KOKHANNYA see **YAGODKI LYUBVI** • 1926

YAHUDI • 1958 • Roy Bimal • IND

YAHUDI KI LADKI • 1933 • *Sircar B. N. (P)* • IND

YAJIKITA DOCHUKI • 1958 • Chiba Yasuki • JPN • HAPPY PILGRIMAGE

YAJU NO SEISHUN • 1963 • JPN • BRUTE, THE

YAJU NO YONI MIETE • 1962 • Kurahara Koreyoshi • JPN • LIKE A WILD BEAST

YAJU SHISUBESHI • 1959 • Sugawa Eizo • JPN • BEAST SHALL DIE, THE

YAKA-HULA-HICKA-OOOLA • 1924-26 • Fleischer Dave • ANS • USA

YAKETTY YAK • 1974 • Jones David* • ASL

YAKILACAK KITAP • 1968 • Duru Sureyya • TRK • BOOK TO BURN, A

YAKOMAN TO TETSU see **JAKOMAN TO TETSU** • 1949

YAKOV SVERDLOV • 1940 • Yutkevich Sergei • USS

YAKUSA SENSEI • 1960 • Matsuo Akinori • JPN • REFORMER, THE

YAKUSOKU • 1972 • Saito Koichi • JPN

YAKUTA NO UTA • 1960 • Masuda Toshio • JPN

YAKUTIA • 1952 • Grigoriev Roman • DOC • USS

YAKUZA, THE • 1974 • Pollack Sydney • USA • BROTHERHOOD OF THE YAKUZA

YAKUZA BOZU • 1967 • Yasuda Kimiyoshi • JPN • HOODLUM PRIEST, THE (USA)

YAKUZA NO HAKABA • 1976 • Fukasaku Kinji • JPN • GRAVEYARD OF YAKUZA, THE

YAKUZA PAPERS, THE see **JINGI NAKI TATAKAI** • 1972

YAKUZA WAKASHU • 1960 • Hagiwara Ryo • JPN

YAKUZA'S LADIES see **GAKUDA NO ONNATACHI** • 1989

YAL TERCER ANO, RESUCITO • 1980 • Gil Rafael • SPN • AND ON THE THIRD YEAR, HE ROSE AGAIN

YALAN YILLAR • 1968 • Saydam Nejat • TRK • DECEITFUL YEARS

YALANCI YARIM • 1974 • Egilmez Ertem • TRK • MY FALSE BELOVED

YALE LAUNDRY, THE • 1907 • *Am & B* • USA

YALIS, LA VERGINE DEL RONCADOR • 1961 • De Robertis Francesco • ITL • VERGINE DEL RONCADOR, LA

YAM DAABO • 1986 • Ouedraogo Idrissa • BRK • CHOICE, THE

YAMA KURURU • 1921 • Ushihara Kiyohiko • JPN • MOUNTAINS GROW DARK, THE

YAMA NO OTO • 1954 • Naruse Mikio • JPN • SOUNDS FROM THE MOUNTAINS ○ ECHO, THE ○ SOUND OF THE MOUNTAIN

YAMA NO SANKA: MOYURU WAKAMONO-TACHI • 1962 • Shinoda Masahiro • JPN • GLORY ON THE SUMMIT ○ BURNING YOUTH ○ MOYURU WAKAMONOTACHI

YAMA O TOBU HANAGASA • 1949 • Ito Daisuke • JPN

YAMA TO TANI TO KUMO • 1959 • Ushihara Yoichi • JPN • ECHO OF LOVE

YAMABIKO GAKKO • 1952 • Imai Tadashi • JPN • ECHO SCHOOL ○ SCHOOL OF ECHOES

YAMAHA FISH STALL see **YAMAHA YUDANG**

YAMAHA YUDANG • Zhang Liang • CHN • YAMAHA FISH STALL

YAMAMOTO ISOROKU see **RENGO KANTAI SHIREICHOKAN YAMAMOTO ISOROKU** • 1968

YAMANEKO SAKUSEN • 1962 • Taniguchi Senkichi • JPN • OPERATION ENEMY FORT (USA)

YAMASHITA SHONEN MONOGATARI • 1985 • Matsubayashi Shue • JPN • BOYHOOD OF THE JUDO CHAMPION

YAMASHITA TOMOYUKI see **TOMOYUKI YAMASHITA** • 1953

YAMATA • 1919 • Korda Alexander • HNG

YAMBAO • 1956 • Crevenna Alfredo B. • MXC, CUB • YOUNG AND EVIL (USA) ○ CRY OF THE BEWITCHED

YAMI • 1927 • Makino Masahiro • JPN • DARKNESS

YAMI NO KAGEBOSHI • 1938 • Inagaki Hiroshi • JPN • SHADOW OF DARKNESS

YAMI NO NAKA NO CHIMIMORYO • 1971 • Nakahira Ko • JPN • CHIMIMORYO -A SOUL OF DEMONS ○ SOUL TO DEVILS, A

YAMI O SAKU IPPATSU • 1968 • Murano Tetsutaro • JPN • TRIGGER-HAPPY

YAMI O YOKOGIRE • 1959 • Masumura Yasuzo • JPN • ACROSS DARKNESS

YAMILE SOUS LES CEDRES • 1939 • d'Espinay Charles • FRN

YAMKRAW • 1930 • Roth Murray • SHT • USA

YAN DIGA • 1967 • Moati Serge • FRN, NGR

YAN TSOI NAU YEUK • 1989 • Guan Jinpeng • HKG • FULL MOON IN NEW YORK

YANABIE EL SHAMS see **FOUNTAINS OF THE SUN** • 1970

YANAGASE BLUES see **YANAGASE BURUSU** • 1967

YANAGASE BURUSU • 1967 • Murayama Shinji • JPN • YANAGASE BLUES

YANAGAWA HORIWARI MONOGATARI • 1988 • Takahata Isao • DOC • JPN • STORY OF THE YANAGAWA CANAL

YANAPANACUNA • 1970 • Alvarez Santiago • DOC • CUB

YANAS YA HOU! • 1988 • Salem Atef • EGY • PEOPLE.. HELP!

YANCO • 1960 • Gonzalez Servando • MXC

YANG KWEI FEI • 1962 • Li Han-Hsiang • HKG • MAGNIFICENT CONCUBINE, THE (USA)

YANG KWEI FEI (USA) see **YOKIHI** • 1955

YANGAN DOU • 1990 • Ching Siu-Tong • HKG

YANGIN • 1977 • Yilmaz Atif • TRK • FIRE

YANGRILLA • 1938 • Bhavnani Mohan Dayaram • IND • TIBBET-KA JADU

YANGTSE INCIDENT • 1957 • Anderson Michael • UKN • BATTLE HELL (USA) ○ ESCAPE OF THE AMETHYST

YANK AT ETON, A • 1942 • Taurog Norman • USA

YANK AT OXFORD, A • 1937 • Conway Jack • USA, UKN

YANK AT THE DENTIST, A see **TOOTH WILL OUT, THE** • 1951

YANK IN AUSTRALIA, A • 1942 • Goulding Alf • ASL

YANK IN DUTCH, A (UKN) see **WIFE TAKES A FLYER, THE** • 1942

YANK IN ERMINE, A • 1955 • Parry Gordon • UKN

YANK IN INDO-CHINA, A • 1952 • Grissell Wallace A. • USA • HIDDEN SECRET (UKN)

YANK IN KOREA, A • 1951 • Landers Lew • USA • LETTER FROM KOREA (UKN)

YANK IN LIBYA, A • 1942 • Herman Al • USA

YANK IN LONDON, A (USA) see **I LIVE IN GROSVENOR SQUARE** • 1945

YANK IN ROME, A (USA) see **AMERICANO IN VACANZA, UN** • 1946

YANK IN THE R.A.F., A • 1941 • King Henry • USA

YANK IN VIETNAM, A • 1964 • Thompson Marshall • USA • YEAR OF THE TIGER, THE

YANK ON THE BURMA ROAD, A • 1941 • Seitz George B. • USA • CHINA CARAVAN (UKN)

YANKEE • 1966 • Brass Tinto • ITL • AMERICANO, L'

YANKEE, THE see **JANKEN** • 1970

YANKEE AT KING ARTHUR'S COURT, THE (UKN) see **CONNECTICUT YANKEE, A** • 1931

YANKEE BUCCANEER • 1952 • De Cordova Frederick • USA

YANKEE CLIPPER, THE • 1927 • Julian Rupert • USA • WHITE WINGS

YANKEE CONSUL, THE • 1924 • Horne James W. • USA

YANKEE DON • 1931 • Smith Noel • USA • DAREDEVIL DICK (UKN)

YANKEE DOOD IT • 1956 • Freleng Friz • ANS • USA

YANKEE DOODLE • 1911 • *Champion* • USA

YANKEE DOODLE ANDY • 1941 • White Jules • SHT • USA

YANKEE DOODLE BOY • 1929 • Fleischer Dave • ANS • USA

YANKEE DOODLE BUGS • 1954 • Freleng Friz • ANS • USA

YANKEE DOODLE CRICKET • 1974 • Jones Charles M. • ANS • USA

YANKEE DOODLE DAFFY • 1943 • Freleng Friz • ANS • USA

YANKEE DOODLE DANDY • 1942 • Curtiz Michael • USA

YANKEE DOODLE DIXIE • 1913 • *Bosworth Hobart* • USA

YANKEE DOODLE DONKEY • 1944 • Sparber I. • ANS • USA

YANKEE DOODLE DUKE, A • 1926 • Lamont Charles • SHT • USA

YANKEE DOODLE GOES TO TOWN • 1939 • Tourneur Jacques • SHT • USA

YANKEE DOODLE HOME • 1939 • Dreifuss Arthur • SHT • USA

YANKEE DOODLE IN BERLIN • 1919 • Jones F. Richard • SHT • USA • KAISER'S LAST SQUEAL, THE

YANKEE DOODLE, JR. • 1922 • Pratt Jack • USA

YANKEE DOODLE MOUSE, THE • 1943 • Hanna William, Barbera Joseph • ANS • USA

YANKEE DOODLE SWINGSHIFT • 1942 • Lovy Alex • ANS • USA

YANKEE FROM THE WEST, A • 1915 • Siegmann George • USA

YANKEE GIRL, THE • 1915 • Smalley Phillips • USA

YANKEE GO-GETTER, A • 1921 • Worne Duke • USA

YANKEE IN KING ARTHUR'S COURT, A (UKN) see **CONNECTICUT YANKEE IN KING ARTHUR'S COURT, A** • 1948

YANKEE IN MEXICO, A • 1913 • *Patheplay* • USA

YANKEE MADNESS • 1924 • Seeling Charles R. • USA

YANKEE MAN-O-WARSMAN'S FIGHT FOR LOVE • 1908 • Porter Edwin S. • USA

YANKEE PASHA • 1954 • Pevney Joseph • USA

YANKEE PLUCK • 1917 • Archainbaud George • USA

YANKEE PRINCESS, A • 1919 • Smith David • USA

YANKEE SENOR, THE • 1926 • Flynn Emmett J. • USA

YANKEE SPEED • 1924 • Bradbury Robert North • USA

YANKEE WAY, THE • 1917 • Stanton Richard • USA

YANKEEANNA • 1910 • *Imp* • USA

YANKEE'S GIRL REWARD, THE • 1910 • *Yankee* • USA

YANKEL DEM SCHMIDT • 1938 • Ulmer Edgar G. • USA • SINGING BLACKSMITH, THE

YANKI NO! • 1960 • Leacock Richard • DOC • USA • YANQUI NO

YANKO EL GUARDIAN DE LA SELVA • 1962 • Falomir Carlos • MXC • AVENTURAS DEL GUARDIAN, LAS

YANKS • 1920 • Miller Ashley • SHT • USA

YANKS • 1979 • Schlesinger John • UKN, USA

YANKS AHOY • 1943 • Neumann Kurt • USA

YANKS ARE COMING, THE • 1942 • Thurn-Taxis Alexis • USA

YANN, THE TROUBADOUR • 1911 • *Pathe* • USA

YANNIS ZENAKIS • 1974 • Frappier Roger • DCS • CND

YANQUI NO see **YANKI NO!** • 1960

YANTARES DE ESPANA • 1969 • Ardavin Cesar • SHT • SPN

YANTRA • 1959 • Whitney James • ANS • USA

YANZHI KOU • 1988 • Guan Jinpeng • HKG • ROUGE

YAOGUN QINGNIAN • 1988 • Tian Zhuangzhuang • CHN • ROCK KIDS

YAPREK DOKUMU • 1967 • Un Memduh • TRK • FALLING LEAVES, THE

YAPS AND YOKELS • 1919 • Smith Noel • SHT • USA

YAQUI, THE • 1916 • Carleton Lloyd B. • USA

YAQUI CUR, THE • 1913 • Griffith D. W. • USA

YAQUI DRUMS • 1956 • Yarbrough Jean • USA

YAQUI GIRL, THE • 1911 • Youngdeer James • USA

YAQUI JUSTICIERO, EL see **ALMA GRANDE** • 1965

YAQUI'S REVENGE, THE • 1914 • *Gonzales Maria* • USA

YARA • 1968 • Utku Umit • TRK • WOUND, THE

YARALI KARTAL • 1965 • Dursun • TRK

YARALI KUS • 1967 • Aslan Mehmet • TRK • WOUNDED BIRD, THE

YARATILAN KADIN • 1968 • Gulyuz Aram • TRK • WOMAN IS BORN, A

YAREBA YARERUZE ZENIN SHUGO • 1968 • Watanabe Yusuke • JPN • HEROES BY CHANCE

YARI NO GONZA • 1985 • Shinoda Masahiro • JPN • GONZA, THE SPEARMAN

YARIN COK GEC OLACAK • 1967 • Dinler Mehmet • TRK • TOMORROW WILL BE TOO LATE

YARIN SON GUNDUR • 1971 • Guney Yilmaz • TRK • TOMORROW IS MY FINAL DAY ○ TOMORROW IS THE FINAL DAY

YARIODORI GOJUSANTSUGI • 1946 • Mori Kazuo • JPN • SPEAR DANCE OF 53 STATIONS

YARN A-TANGLE • 1914 • *Essanay* • USA

YARN ABOUT YARN, A • 1949 • Rasinski Connie • ANS • USA

YARN OF A BABY'S SHIRT, A • 1911 • *Powers* • USA

YARN OF THE NANCY BELL, THE • 1912 • *Edison* • USA

YARN OF THE NANCY BELLE, THE • 1913 • *Lubin* • USA

YARN OF WOOL, A • 1932 • Foster John, Bailey Harry • ANS • USA

YARO NI KOKKYO WA NAI • 1965 • Nakahira Ko • JPN • BLACK CHALLENGER, THE

YAROSLAVNA, KOROLYEVA FRANTSII • 1979 • Maslennikov Igor • USS • YAROSLAVNA, QUEEN OF FRANCE

YAROSLAVNA, QUEEN OF FRANCE see **YAROSLAVNA, KOROLYEVA FRANTSII** • 1979

YASAMAK HARAM OLDU • 1968 • Karamanbey Cetin • TRK • LIFE HAS BECOME A SIN

YASASHII RAION • 1970 • *Toho* • ANS • JPN

YASEI NO SHOMEI • 1978 • Sato Junya • JPN • WITNESS OF WILDERNESS

YASEMIN • 1988 • Bohm Hark • FRG

YASEMININ TATLI ASKI • 1968 • Yilmaz Atif • TRK • JASMIN'S SWEET LOVE

YASHA-GA-IKE • 1979 • Shinoda Masahiro • JPN • YASHA POND, THE ○ DEMON POND (USA)

YASHA POND, THE see **YASHA-GA-IKE** • 1979

YASHA TOPORKOV • 1960 • Karelov Yevgyeni • USS

YASMINA • 1926 • Hugon Andre • FRN

YASMINA • 1961 • Chanderli Jamal • ALG

YASSA MOSSA • 1953 • Shibuya Minoru • JPN • TOPSY TURVY ○ CONFUSION
YASSIN • 1989 • Ariffin Kamarul • MLY
YATARO-GASA • 1932 • Inagaki Hiroshi • JPN • YATARO'S SEDGE HAT ○ SEDGE HAT, THE
YATARO-GASA • 1960 • Makino Masahiro • JPN • YATARO'S SEDGE HAT
YATARO'S SEDGE HAT see **YATARO-GASA** • 1932
YATARO'S SEDGE HAT see **YATARO-GASA** • 1960
YATHRAYUDE ANTHYAM • 1988 • George K. G. • IND • JOURNEY ENDS
YATIK EMINE • 1975 • Kavur Omer • TRK • EMINE
YATIM MUSTAPHA • 1960 • Rao B. N. • MLY
YATO KAZE NO NAKA O HASHIRU • 1961 • Inagaki Hiroshi • JPN • BANDITS ON THE WIND (USA)
YATRA • 1988 • Ghose Goutam • IND • JOURNEY, THE
YATRIK • 1952 • *Sircar B. N. (P)* • IND
YATSUHAKA-MURA • 1977 • Nomura Yoshitaro • JPN • YATSUHAKA VILLAGE
YATSUHAKA VILLAGE see **YATSUHAKA-MURA** • 1977
YATSUNO KENJU WA JIGOKUDAZE • 1958 • Matsuda Sadatsugu • JPN • HIS HELL-REVOLVER
YAWAHADA SHIGURE • 1967 • Tobita Yoshi • JPN • SHOWER OF TENDER SKIN, A
YAWAR FIESTA • 1975 • Nisiyama Eulogio, Vignati Jorge • DOC • PRU
YAWAR FIESTA • 1980 • Figueroa Luis • PRU
YAWAR MALLKU • 1969 • Sanjines Jorge • BLV • BLOOD OF THE CONDOR (UKN)
YAWARA SEMPU • 1965 • Watanabe Kunio • JPN • BIRTH OF JUDO, THE
YAWARA SEMPU DOTO NO TAIKETSU • 1966 • Nishiyama Masateru • JPN • JUDO SHOWDOWN (USA)
YAWMIYYAT NAIB FI AL-ARYAF • 1968 • Saleh Tewfik • EGY • JOURNAL D'UN SUBSTITUT DE CAMPAGNE EN EGYPTE
YAWMUN BILA GHAD • 1961 • Barakat Henry • EGY • JOUR SANS LENDEMAIN
YAYLA KARTALI • 1968 • Erakalin Ulku • TRK • EAGLE OF THE PLAIN, THE
YAYLA KIZI • 1967 • Evin Semih • TRK • GIRL OF THE PLAIN, THE
YAZERLY, AL • 1972 • Al-Zobidi Kais • SYR
YAZIRLY, AL- • 1974 • Zubaydi Qays Al- • IRQ
YE BANKS AND BRAES • 1919 • Watts Tom • UKN
YE GODS! WHAT A CAST! • 1915 • *Luna* • USA
YE HAPPY PILGRIMS • 1934 • Lantz Walter • ANS • USA
YE HAVE BEEN WEIGHED IN THE BALANCE AND FOUND WANTING see **TINIMBANG KA NGUNI'T KULANG** • 1974
YE MAMA • 1987 • Yao Shougang • CHN • OUTCAST, THE
YE OLD SAW MILL • 1935 • Sennett Mack • USA
YE OLDE MELODIES • 1929 • Fleischer Dave • ANS • USA
YE OLDE MINSTRELS • 1941 • Cahn Edward L. • SHT • USA
YE OLDE SONGS • 1932 • *Terry Paul/ Moser Frank (P)* • ANS • USA
YE OLDE SWAP SHOPPE • 1940 • Iwerks Ub • ANS • USA
YE OLDE TOY SHOP • 1935 • *Terry Paul/ Moser Frank (P)* • ANS • USA
YE OLDE WAXWORKS BY THE TERRIBLE TWO • 1915 • Read James • UKN
YE OLDEN DAYS • 1933 • Gillett Burt • ANS • USA
YE OLDEN GRAFTER • 1915 • Henderson Dell • USA
YE SHAN • 1985 • Yan Xueshu • CHN • IN THE WILD MOUNTAINS ○ WILD MOUNTAINS
Y'E TARD GASTON • 1972 • Favreau Robert • DCS • CND • Y'ETAND, GASTON
YE VENGEFUL VAGABONDS • 1914 • *Razetto Stella* • USA
YE WOOING OF PEGGY • 1917 • Phillips Bertram • UKN
YEAH, YEAH, YEAH, NEW YORK MEETS THE BEATLES • 1964 • Maysles Albert, Maysles David • DOC • USA • WHAT'S HAPPENING -THE BEATLES IN THE U.S.A. ○ WHAT'S HAPPENING
YEAR 1 see **MARRIAGE: YEAR ONE** • 1971
YEAR 1919, THE see **GOD DEVYATNADSATII** • 1938
YEAR 1946, THE see **ROK 1946** • 1946
YEAR 1949, THE see **ROK 1949** • 1949
YEAR 2889 see **IN THE YEAR 2889** • 1966
YEAR 3003, THE • 1962 • *Triglav* • ANS • YGS
YEAR AROUND, THE • 1949 • Cowan Will • SHT • USA
YEAR AS LONG AS LIFE, THE • 1966 • Roshal Grigori • USS
YEAR IN FRANK'S LIFE, A see **ROK FRANKA W.** • 1967
YEAR IN THE LIFE, A see **VUOSI ELAMASTA** • 1982
YEAR-LONG ROAD see **STRADA LUNGA UN ANNO, LA** • 1958
YEAR MY VOICE BROKE, THE • 1987 • Duigan John • ASL
YEAR OF A NIGHT, A • 1932 • Minzenty Gustave • UKN
YEAR OF AWAKENING, THE see **ANO DE LAS LUCES, EL** • 1986
YEAR OF CRISIS see **KRIZNO OBDOBJE** • 1981
YEAR OF FRANEK W., A see **ROK FRANKA W.** • 1967
YEAR OF LIVING DANGEROUSLY, THE • 1983 • Weir Peter • ASL, USA
YEAR OF MONDAYS, A • 1977 • Pounchev Borislav • BUL
YEAR OF QUIET SUN, A see **ROK SPOKOJNEGO SLONCA** • 1985
YEAR OF SCHOOL, A see **ANNO DI SCUOLA, UN** • 1977
YEAR OF SIR IVOR, THE • 1969 • Owens Kit • DOC • UKN
YEAR OF THE CANCER see **JAAR VAN DE KREEFT, HET** • 1975
YEAR OF THE CANNIBALS, THE (USA) see **CANNIBALI, I** • 1970
YEAR OF THE CORTINA, THE • 1964 • Ohlsson Terry, Bond Philip • DCS • UKN • CORTINA CONQUEST
YEAR OF THE CRICKET see **KENNER** • 1968
YEAR OF THE DRAGON • 1985 • Cimino Michael • USA
YEAR OF THE HARE, THE see **JANIKSEN VUOSI** • 1977
YEAR OF THE HORSE, THE • 1966 • Sunasky Irving • USA
YEAR OF THE LOCUST, THE • 1916 • Melford George • USA
YEAR OF THE MOUSE, THE • 1965 • Jones Charles M. • ANS • USA
YEAR OF THE PLAGUE, THE see **ANO DE LA PESTE, EL** • 1978
YEAR OF THE QUIET SUN, THE see **ROK SPOKOJNEGO SLONCA** • 1985
YEAR OF THE SEX DRAGON, THE • Jeremy Ron • USA
YEAR OF THE TIGER, THE see **YANK IN VIETNAM, A** • 1964
YEAR OF THE WOMAN • 1973 • Hochman Sandra • USA
YEAR OF THE YAHOO • 1972 • Lewis Herschell G. • USA
YEAR ONE see **ROK PIERWSWY** • 1960
YEAR ONE (USA) see **ANNO UNO** • 1974
YEAR THE UNIVERSE LOST THE PENNANT, THE • 1961 • Stewart Bhob • SHT • USA • DO-IT-YOURSELF HAPPENING KIT
YEARLING, THE • 1946 • Brown Clarence • USA
YEARNING see **AKOGARE** • 1935
YEARNING see **AKOGARE** • 1955
YEARNING see **MIDARERU** • 1964
YEARNING FOR LOVE see **ATEMLOS VOR LIEBE** • 1970
YEARS ARE SO LONG, THE see **MAKE WAY FOR TOMORROW** • 1937
YEARS BETWEEN, THE • 1946 • Bennett Compton • UKN
YEARS OF CHANGE • 1950 • Van Dyke Willard • DOC • USA
YEARS OF CHANGE see **NEW FRONTIER, THE** • 1950
YEARS OF DREAMS AND REVOLTS see **ANNEES DE REVES, LES** • 1982
YEARS OF FIRE, THE see **POVEST PLAMENNYKH LET** • 1960
YEARS OF HUNGER see **HUNGERJAHRE** • 1980
YEARS OF LIFE, THE see **LETOKRUHY** • 1972
YEARS OF LIGHTNING, DAYS OF DRUMS see **JOHN F. KENNEDY: YEARS OF LIGHTNING, DAYS OF DRUMS** • 1966
YEARS OF OCCUPATION see **HERNAMSARIN** • 1967
YEARS OF THE CUCKOO see **KUCKUCKSJAHRE** • 1967
YEARS OF TRIAL • 1925 • Rasumny Alexander • USS
YEARS OF YOUTH see **GREEN YEARS, THE** • 1942
YEARS TO COME • 1922 • Roach Hal • SHT • USA
YEARS WITHOUT DAYS (UKN) see **CASTLE ON THE HUDSON** • 1940
YEATS COUNTRY • 1965 • Carey Patrick • DOC • IRL
YEDI ADIM SONRA • 1968 • Ucanoglu Yucel • TRK • SEVEN STEPS FROM NOW
YEDI BELALILAR • 1970 • Atasoy Irfan, Guney Yilmaz • TRK • SEVEN NO-GOODS, THE
YEDI DAGIN ASLANI • 1966 • Atadeniz Yilmaz • TRK • MOUNTAIN KING, THE ○ SEVEN WILD LIONS
YEDI KOYUN ZEYNEBI • 1968 • Kan Kemal • TRK • ZEYNEP OF THE SEVEN VILLAGES
YEDINSTVENNAYA • 1976 • Heifitz Josif • USS • ONLY ONE, THE ○ EDINSTVENNAIA ○ ONE AND ONLY, THE
YEELEN • 1987 • Cisse Souleymane • MLI • BRIGHTNESS ○ LIGHT, THE
YEGG AND THE EGGS, THE • 1914 • *Komic* • USA
YEGGMAN, THE • 1912 • *Walthall William* • USA
YEGOR BULYCHOV AND OTHERS • 1953 • Zakhava B. • USS
YEGOR BULYCHOV AND OTHERS see **YEGOR BULYCHOV I DRUGIYE** • 1972
YEGOR BULYCHOV I DRUGIYE • 1972 • Soloviev Sergei • USS • YEGOR BULYCHOV AND OTHERS
YEGUA COLORADA, LA • 1972 • *Cima* • MXC
YEH-CH'IH • 1980 • Yen Hao • HKG • HAPPENING, THE
YEH-CHIH CHI • 1980 • P'An Jung-Min • TWN
YEH GULISTAN HAMARA • 1972 • *Burman S. D. (M)* • IND
YEH HAI CHI see **WILD CHILDREN** • 1977
YEH RAAT PHIR NA AAYEGI • 1966 • Brij • IND
YEH WOH MANZIL TO NAHIN • 1987 • Mishra Sudhir • IND • DESTINATIONS
YEHUDI MENUHIN -CHEMIN DE LUMIERE • 1971 • Reichenbach Francois, Gavoty Bernard, Chevry Bernard • DOC • FRN • YEHUDI MENUHIN -WAY OF LIGHT (UKN) ○ WAY OF LIGHT ○ YEHUDI MENUHIN STORY ○ YEHUDI MENUHIN -ROAD OF LIGHT
YEHUDI MENUHIN -ROAD OF LIGHT see **YEHUDI MENUHIN -CHEMIN DE LUMIERE** • 1971
YEHUDI MENUHIN STORY see **YEHUDI MENUHIN -CHEMIN DE LUMIERE** • 1971
YEHUDI MENUHIN -WAY OF LIGHT (UKN) see **YEHUDI MENUHIN -CHEMIN DE LUMIERE** • 1971
YEI RAI SHAN • 1951 • Ichikawa Kon • JPN • NIGHTSHADE FLOWER ○ IERAISHAN
YEK ETTEFAGHE SADEH • 1973 • Saless Sohrab Shahid • IRN • SIMPLE EVENT, A
YEKATERINA VORONINA see **EKATERINA VORONINA** • 1957
YEKEBEZAN • 1967 • Safaei Reza • IRN • ROBUS
YELLOW AND BLACK see **SENSOMMER** • 1988
YELLOW BACK, THE • 1926 • Andrews Del • USA
YELLOW BALLOON, THE • 1952 • Thompson J. Lee • UKN
YELLOW BAMBOO, THE see **SEMAMBU KUNING** • 1972
YELLOW BIRD • 1912 • Ranous William V. • USA
YELLOW BIRD • 1969 • *Century Cinema Corp.* • USA • CURIOUS YELLOW BIRD
YELLOW BULLET, THE • 1917 • Harvey Harry • USA
YELLOW CAB MAN, THE • 1949 • Donohue Jack • USA
YELLOW CAESAR, THE • 1941 • Cavalcanti Alberto • DOC • UKN • HEEL OF ITALY, THE
YELLOW CAMEO, THE • 1928 • Bennet Spencer Gordon • SRL • USA
YELLOW CANARY • 1943 • Wilcox Herbert • UKN
YELLOW CANARY, THE • 1963 • Kulik Buzz • USA • EVIL COME, EVIL GO
YELLOW CAR, THE see **GULA BILEN, DEN** • 1963
YELLOW CARGO • 1936 • Wilbur Crane • USA
YELLOW CLAW, THE • 1920 • Plaissetty Rene • UKN
YELLOW CONTRABAND • 1928 • Maloney Leo • USA
YELLOW CROW see **KIIROI KARASU** • 1957
YELLOW CRUISE, THE see **CROISIERE JAUNE, LA** • 1933
YELLOW DEVIL, THE see **SCHUT, DER** • 1964
YELLOW DOG • 1973 • Donovan Terence • UKN
YELLOW DOG, THE • 1918 • Campbell Colin • USA
YELLOW DOG CATCHER, THE • 1919 • Blystone John G. • SHT • USA
YELLOW DUST • 1936 • Fox Wallace • USA • MOTHER LODE
YELLOW EARTH see **HUANG TUDI** • 1985
YELLOW EMMANUELLE see **EMANUELLE GIALLA** • 1971
YELLOW FACE • 1921 • Elvey Maurice • UKN
YELLOW FEVER see **FIEBRE AMARILLA** • 1981
YELLOW FIN • 1951 • McDonald Frank • USA
YELLOW FINGERS • 1926 • Flynn Emmett J. • USA
YELLOW FLAME • 1914 • *Broncho* • USA
YELLOW GIRL, THE • 1916 • Keller Edgar • SHT • USA
YELLOW HAIR AND THE FORTRESS OF GOLD • 1984 • Cimber Matt • USA, SPN • YELLOWHAIR AND THE PELOS KID
YELLOW HAIRED KID, THE • 1952 • McDonald Frank • MTV • USA
YELLOW HAND, THE • 1916 • Horne James W. • SHT • USA
YELLOW HANDKERCHIEF OF HAPPINESS, A see **KOFUKU NO KIROI HANKACHI** • 1977
YELLOW HAT, THE • 1966 • Plesch Honoria • UKN
YELLOW HORSE • 1965-66 • Baillie Bruce • SHT • USA
YELLOW HOUND, THE • 1916 • *Supreme* • SHT • USA
YELLOW JACK • 1938 • Seitz George B. • USA
YELLOW JACKET MINE, THE • 1909 • *Selig* • USA
YELLOW JERSEY FOR A WINNER see **GEEL TRUI VIR 'N WENNER** • 1983
YELLOW KILLER, THE see **FROM BANGKOK WITH ORDERS TO KILL** • 1972
YELLOW -LE CUGINE • 1969 • Baldanello Gianfranco • ITL
YELLOW LILY, THE • 1928 • Korda Alexander • USA
YELLOW MASK, THE • 1930 • Lachman Harry • UKN
YELLOW MEN AND GOLD • 1922 • Willat Irvin V. • USA
YELLOW MENACE, THE • 1916 • Steiner William • SRL • USA
YELLOW MERCEDES, THE see **SARI MERSEDES** • 1987
YELLOW MOUNTAIN, THE • 1954 • Hibbs Jesse • USA
YELLOW PAGES see **GOING UNDERCOVER** • 1988
YELLOW PAGES: ROCK AND ROLL • 1980 • Mills Michael • CND
YELLOW PASS, THE see **ZEMLYA V PLENU** • 1928
YELLOW PASSPORT, THE • 1916 • August Edwin • USA
YELLOW PASSPORT, THE (UKN) see **YELLOW TICKET, THE** • 1931
YELLOW PAWN, THE • 1916 • Melford George • USA
YELLOW PERIL • 1908 • *Bitzer Billy (Ph)* • USA
YELLOW PERIL see **CHINESE MAGIC** • 1900
YELLOW PHANTOM • 1935 • Hill Robert F. • USA
YELLOW ROBE, THE see **RAN SALU** • 1967
YELLOW ROLLS-ROYCE, THE • 1964 • Asquith Anthony • UKN
YELLOW ROSE, THE • 1982 • Hart Harvey • TVM • USA
YELLOW ROSE, THE • 1983 • Nastase Doru • RMN
YELLOW ROSE OF TEXAS • 1944 • Kane Joseph • USA
YELLOW SANDS • 1938 • Brenon Herbert • UKN
YELLOW SEAL, THE see **PRAIRIE PIRATE, THE** • 1925
YELLOW SKY • 1949 • Wellman William A. • USA
YELLOW SKY see **STORM, THE** • 1979
YELLOW SLAVE, THE • 1913 • Melies Gaston • USA
YELLOW SLIPPERS, THE (USA) see **HISTORIA ZOLTEJ CIZEMKI** • 1962
YELLOW SQUADRON, THE see **GULA DIVISIONEN** • 1954
YELLOW STAIN, THE • 1922 • Dillon John Francis • USA
YELLOW STAR, THE • 1915 • McGowan J. P. • USA
YELLOW STAR, THE see **GELBE STERN, DER** • 1981
YELLOW STOCKINGS • 1928 • Komisarjevsky Theodor • UKN
YELLOW STREAK, A • 1913 • *Patheplay* • USA
YELLOW STREAK, A • 1915 • Nigh William • *Columbia* • USA
YELLOW STREAK, A • 1927 • Wilson Ben • USA
YELLOW STREAK, THE • 1913 • *Gaden Alexander* • USA
YELLOW STREAK, THE • 1914 • *Garrick Richard* • USA
YELLOW STREAK, THE • 1915 • *Santa Barbara* • USA
YELLOW STREAK, THE • 1915 • King Burton L. • *Selig* • USA
YELLOW STREAK, THE (UKN) see **BOTH BARRELS BLAZING** • 1945
YELLOW SUBMARINE • 1968 • Dunning George • ANM • UKN • BEATLES: YELLOW SUBMARINE
YELLOW SUN see **KIIROI TAIYO** • 1967
YELLOW TAIFUN, THE • 1920 • Jose Edward • USA • YELLOW TYPHOON
YELLOW TEDDYBEARS, THE • 1963 • Hartford-Davis Robert • UKN • GUTTER GIRLS (USA) ○ THRILL SEEKERS, THE
YELLOW TICKET, THE • 1918 • Parke William • USA
YELLOW TICKET, THE • 1931 • Walsh Raoul • USA • YELLOW PASSPORT, THE (UKN)
YELLOW TICKET, THE (USA) see **ZEMLYA V PLENU** • 1928
YELLOW TOMAHAWK, THE • 1954 • Selander Lesley • USA
YELLOW TRAFFIC, THE • 1914 • Blache Alice • USA
YELLOW TYPHOON see **YELLOW TAIFUN, THE** • 1920
YELLOW UMBRELLA, THE • 1917 • Haydon J. Charles • SHT • USA
YELLOW WARD see **GULA KLINIKEN** • 1942
YELLOW WINTON FLYER, THE see **REIVERS, THE** • 1969
YELLOWBACK, THE • 1929 • Storm Jerome • USA • BROUGHT TO JUSTICE (UKN)
YELLOWBEARD • 1983 • Damski Mel • UKN
YELLOWCAKE OPERAZIONE URANO see **A CHI TOCCA... TOCCA!** • 1978
YELLOWHAIR AND THE FORTRESS OF GOLD • 1984 • *Landon Laurene*
YELLOWHAIR AND THE PELOS KID see **YELLOW HAIR AND THE FORTRESS OF GOLD** • 1984
YELLOWNECK • 1955 • Hugh R. John • USA
YELLOWSTONE • 1936 • Lubin Arthur • USA
YELLOWSTONE CUBS • 1963 • *Disney Walt* • USA
YELLOWSTONE HONEYMOON, A • 1915 • *Foster Morris* • USA
YELLOWSTONE KELLY • 1959 • Douglas Gordon • USA
YELP WANTED • 1931 • *Mintz Charles (P)* • ANS • USA
YELYENA NIKOLAYEVNA • 1973 • Yershov Konstantin • USS
Y'EN A MARRE • 1959 • Govar Yvan • FRN, BLG • GARS D'ANVERS, LE ○ Y EN A MARRE
Y'EN A PAS DEUX COMME ANGELIQUE • 1931 • Lion Roger • FRN
Y'EN A PLEIN LES BOTTES • 1976 • Marischka Franz • FRN, FRG
YEN-ERH TSAI LIN-SHAO • 1980 • Liu Li-Li • HKG • WILD GOOSE ON THE WING, THE
YEN REI-SUN • 1921 • Ren Pun-Yen • CHN
YENENDI see **HOMMES QUI FONT LA PLUIE, LES** • 1951
YENS YENSEN OR MISTAKEN FOR A BURGLAR • 1915 • *Vitagraph* • USA
YENTL • 1983 • Streisand Barbara • USA
YEOJAEUI BANRAN • 1985 • Kim Hyeong-Myeong • SKR • FEMALE REBELLION
YEOMAN'S WEDDING, THE see **WRECK OF THE DUNBAR** • 1912
YER DEMIR, GOK BAKIR • 1987 • Livaneli Zulfu • TRK, FRG • IRON EARTH, COPPER SKY

YERAHMIEL THE SHLEMIEL • 1926 • Axelrod Nathan • ISR
YERBERA, LA • 1972 • *Diana* • MXC
YERMA • 1962 • Cavalcanti Alberto
YERMA • 1977 • Ferreri Marco • MTV • ITL
YERMAK TIMOFEIEVITCH • 1908 • Goncharov Vasili M. • USS
YERMANI XANARHONTAI, I • 1947 • Sakellarios Alekos • GRC • GERMANS STRIKE AGAIN, THE ○ ALLEMANDS REVIENNENT, LES
YES • 1964 • Levine Naomi • SHT • USA
YES see **IGEN** • 1964
"YES!" see **KOM I MIN SANG** • 1968
YES see **ANO**
YES.. BUT.. see **NAI MEN ALLA..** • 1972
"YES!" (COUNT THE POSSIBILITIES) see **KOM I MIN SANG** • 1968
YES, DET ER FAR • 1986 • Hilbard John • DNM • YES, IT IS DAD
YES, GIORGIO • 1982 • Schaffner Franklin J. • USA
YES GIRLS, THE • 1972 • Shonteff Lindsay • UKN
YES, HE HAS BEEN WITH ME see **DET AR HOS MIG HAN HAR VARIT** • 1963
YES, I DO • 1967 • Cayado Tony • PHL
YES, IT IS DAD see **YES, DET ER FAR** • 1986
YES, MADAM • 1933 • Hiscott Leslie • UKN
YES, MADAM? • 1938 • Lee Norman • UKN
YES, MR. BROWN • 1932 • Wilcox Herbert, Buchanan Jack • UKN
YES, MONSIEUR HULOT • 1970 • Tati Jacques • FRN
YES, MY DARLING DAUGHTER • 1939 • Keighley William • USA
YES NO MAYBE MAYBENOT • 1967 • Le Grice Malcolm • UKN
YES OR NO? • 1915 • Eason B. Reeves • USA
YES OR NO? • 1920 • Neill R. William • USA
YES OR NO, JEAN-GUY MOREAU • 1979 • Rubbo Michael • CND
YES, SIR see **WEDLUG ROZKAZU** • 1959
YES SIR, MR. BONES • 1951 • Ormond Ron • USA
YES, SIR, THAT'S MY BABY • 1949 • Sherman George • USA
YES SIR, THAT'S MY BABY! see **ONCE UPON A TIME** • 1944
YES SUNDAY, A see **DOMENICA SI', UNA** • 1987
YES, THAT WE CAN see **MEILTAHAN TAMA KAY** • 1974
YES, WE HAVE NO —! • 1923 • Brunel Adrian? • SHT • UKN
YES! WE HAVE NO BANANAS • 1930 • Fleischer Dave • ANS • USA
YES, WE HAVE NO BONANZA • 1939 • Lord Del • SHT • USA
YES WE HAVE NO TEMPER see **SOFT BOILED** • 1923
YES, YES BABETTE • 1926 • Rodney Earle • USA
YES, YES, NANETTE • 1925 • Laurel Stan, Hennecke • SHT • USA
YESENIA • 1971 • *Peliculas Rodriguez* • MXC
YESHCHYO RAZ PRO LYUBOV • 1968 • Natanson Georgi • USS • ONCE AGAIN ABOUT LOVE ○ ONCE MORE ABOUT LOVE ○ ANOTHER LOVE STORY
YESLI DOROG TEBYE TVOY DOM • 1967 • Ordynsky Vassily • USS • IF YOUR HOME IS DEAR TO YOU
YESLI KHOCHESH BYT SCHASTLIVYM • 1974 • Gubenko Nikolai • USS • IF YOU WANT TO BE HAPPY
YESSIR! see **SISSIGNORE** • 1968
YESSONGS • 1973 • Neal Peter • DOC • UKN
YESTERDAY • 1967 • Santiago Pablo • PHL
YESTERDAY • 1980 • Kent Larry • CND • THIS TIME FOREVER ○ SCORING ○ GABRIELLE ○ VICTORY, THE
YESTERDAY • 1984 • Piwowarski Radoslaw • PLN
YESTERDAY • 1986 • Andonov Ivan • BUL
YESTERDAY see **TEGNAP** • 1959
YESTERDAY AND TODAY • 1953 • Greshler Abner J. • DOC • USA
YESTERDAY GIRL see **ABSCHIED VON GESTERN** • 1966
YESTERDAY GOES ON FOR EVER see **BRUTALITAT IN STEIN** • 1960
YESTERDAY IN FACT see **NAPRAWDE WCZORAJ** • 1963
YESTERDAY IS OVER YOUR SHOULDER • 1940 • Dickinson Thorold • UKN
YESTERDAY IT WAS SUNDAY see **VCERA NEDELE BYLA** • 1938
YESTERDAY MACHINE, THE • 1965 • Marker Russ • USA
YESTERDAY THE CHILDREN WERE DANCING • 1968 • Gelinas Gratien • CND
YESTERDAY, TODAY AND TOMORROW see **HIJO AAJA BHOLI**
YESTERDAY TODAY AND TOMORROW see **OCTOBER CINEMA TRUTH** • 1923
YESTERDAY, TODAY AND TOMORROW see **HIER, AUJOURD'HUI ET DEMAIN** • 1970
YESTERDAY, TODAY AND TOMORROW (USA) see **IERI, OGGI, DOMANI** • 1963
YESTERDAY, TODAY, TOMORROW see **HTHES, SIMERA, AVRIO** • 1979
YESTERDAY'S CHILD • 1977 • Allen Corey, Rosenbaum Bob • TVM • USA
YESTERDAY'S ENEMY • 1959 • Guest Val • UKN
YESTERDAY'S GUYS USED NO ARSENIC see **MUCHACHOS DE ANTES NO USABAN ARSENICO, LOS** • 1975
YESTERDAY'S HERO • 1980 • Leifer Neil • UKN, ASL
YESTERDAY'S HERO (UKN) see **HOOSIER SCHOOLBOY, THE** • 1937
YESTERDAY'S HEROES • 1940 • Leeds Herbert I. • USA
YESTERDAY'S TOMORROW see **ZWISCHENGLEIS** • 1978
YESTERDAY'S WIFE • 1923 • Le Saint Edward J. • USA
YET • 1957 • Vanderbeek Stan • SHT • USA
YET SPIES HAVEN'T DIED see **KANCHO IMADA SHISEZU** • 1942
YET WE WERE YOUNG see **A BYAHME MLADI** • 1961
Y'ETAND, GASTON see **Y'E TARD GASTON** • 1972
YETI IL GIGANTE DEL VENTESIMO SECOLO • 1977 • Parolini Gianfranco • ITL • YETI: THE GIANT OF THE 20TH CENTURY ○ YETI (USA)
YETI: THE GIANT OF THE 20TH CENTURY see **YETI IL GIGANTE DEL VENTESIMO SECOLO** • 1977
YETI (USA) see **YETI IL GIGANTE DEL VENTESIMO SECOLO** • 1977
YEUX CERNES, LES • 1964 • Hossein Robert • FRN • WEB OF FEAR (USA)
YEUX DE L'AMOUR, LES • 1960 • de La Patelliere Denys • FRN
YEUX DE MAMAN SONT DES ETOILES, LES • 1971 • Robiolles Jacques • FRN
YEUX D'ELSTIR, LES • 1967 • Magrou Alain • SHT • FRN
YEUX DES OISEAUX, LES • 1982 • Auer Gabriel • FRN, UKN, SWT • EYES OF BIRDS, THE
YEUX DU DRAGON, LES • 1925 • Starevitch Ladislas • FRN • EYES OF THE DRAGON, THE (USA)
YEUX FERMES, LES • 1972 • Santoni Joel • FRN • EYES CLOSED, THE ○ CLOSED EYES, THE
YEUX FERTILES, LES • 1977 • Bellocchio Marco • FRN, ITL
YEUX, LA BOUCHE, LES see **OCCHI, LA BOCCA, GLI** • 1983
YEUX NE PEUVENT PAS EN TOUT TEMPS SE FERMER OU PEUT-ETRE QU'UN JOUR ROME SE PERMETTRA DE CHOISIR A.. • 1970 • Straub Jean-Marie, Huillet Daniele • FRG, ITL • OTHON (UKN) ○ EYES DO NOT WANT TO CLOSE AT ALL TIMES OR PERHAPS ONE DAY ROME WILL PERMIT HERSELF TO CHOOSE IN H...
YEUX NOIRS, LES • 1935 • Tourjansky Victor • FRN • DARK EYES (USA) ○ BLACK EYES
YEUX OUVERTS, LES • 1913 • Feuillade Louis • FRN
YEUX QUI ACCUSENT, LES • 1918 • Burguet Charles • FRN
YEUX QUI FASCINENT, LES • 1916 • Feuillade Louis • FRN
YEUX QUI MEURENT, LES • 1912 • Feuillade Louis • FRN • EYES THAT KILL, THE
YEUX ROUGES, LES • 1982 • Simoneau Yves • CND • VERITES ACCIDENTELLES, LES ○ RED EYES
YEUX SANS VISAGE, LES • 1959 • Franju Georges • FRN, ITL • HORROR CHAMBER OF DR. FAUSTUS, THE (USA) ○ OCCHI SENZA VOLTO (ITL) ○ EYES WITHOUT A FACE (UKN)
YEVGENI ONEGIN • 1911 • Goncharov Vasili M. • USS
YEVGYENI URBANSKI • 1968 • Stashevskaya-Naroditskaya Y. • DOC • USS
YEVO PREVOSHODITIELSTVO • 1927 • Roshal Grigori • USS • YOUR EXCELLENCY ○ HIS EXCELLENCY
YEVO PRIZYV • 1925 • Protazanov Yakov • USS • BROKEN CHAINS ○ HIS CALL
YEVO ZOVUT ROBERT • 1967 • Olshvanger Ilya • USS • THEY CALL HIM ROBERT ○ HIS NAME IS ROBERT ○ CALL ME ROBERT ○ THEY CALL ME ROBERT ○ HE WAS CALLED ROBERT
YEVO ZOVUT SUKHE-BATOR • 1942 • Heifitz Josif, Zarkhi Alexander • USS • HIS NAME IS SUKHE-BATOR
YEZH AR VEZH see **LANGUE DE LA HONTE, LA** • 1979
YHDEKSAN TAPAA LAHESTYA HELSINKIA • 1983 • Donner Jorn • DOC • FNL • NINE WAYS TO APPROACH HELSINKI
YHDEN MIEHEN SOTA • 1973 • Jarva Risto • FNL • ONE MAN'S WAR
YHDEN YON HINTA • 1952 • Laine Edvin • FNL • PRICE OF ONE NIGHT, THE
YI-HSIANG MENG • 1977 • Pai Ching-Jui • HKG • THERE'S NO PLACE LIKE HOME
YI-K'O HUNG TOU • 1980 • Liu Li-Li • HKG • LOVE SEED, A
YI P'ANG JOU • 1976 • Hu Hsiao-Feng • HKG • POUND OF FLESH
YI-YUAN P'IAO-HSIANG • 1983 • Chang P'Ei-Ch'Eng • TWN • PLACE OF REST
YIA MIA TRIPIA DRAHMI • 1968 • Andritsos Kostas • GRC • FOR ONE MOTH-EATEN DRACHMA ○ MONEY FOR JAM
YIA PION HTIPA I KOUDHOUNA • 1968 • Laskos Orestis • GRC • FOR WHOM THE BIG BELL TOLLS
YIA TI KARDIA TIS OREAS ELENIS • 1967 • Tempos Antonis • GRC • FOR THE HEART OF THE BEAUTIFUL HELEN
YIDDISH MAMA, THE see **MY YIDDISHE MAMA** • 1930
YIDDISHER BAND, THE • 1926 • Cullen Robert J. • UKN
YIDDISHER COWBOY, THE • 1909 • *Bison* • USA
YIDDISHER COWBOY, THE • 1911 • Dwan Allan • USA
YIDDLE AND HIS FIDDLE • 1912 • Martinek H. O. • UKN
YIDDLE ON MY FIDDLE • 1912 • Kellino W. P. • UKN
YIDDLE WITH HIS FIDDLE see **YIDL MITN FIDL** • 1937
YIDL MITN FIDL • 1937 • Nowina-Przybylski Jan, Green Joseph • PLN • JUDEL GRA NA SKRZYPKACH ○ YIDDLE WITH HIS FIDDLE
YIELD TO THE NIGHT • 1956 • Thompson J. Lee • UKN • BLONDE SINNER (USA)
YIGE HE BAGE • 1985 • Zhang Junzhao • CHN • ONE AND THE EIGHT, THE
YIGE SIZHE DUI SHENGZHE DE FANGWEN • 1987 • Huang Jianzhong • CHN • QUESTIONS FOR THE LIVING
YIGIT YARALI OLUR • 1966 • Gorec Ertem • TRK
YIJANG CHUNSHUI DONG LIU see **YIJIANG CHUNSHUI XIANG DONG LIU** • 1947
YIJIANG CHUNSHUI XIANG DONG LIU • 1947 • Zheng Junli, Cai Chusheng • CHN • RIVER FLOWS TOWARDS THE EAST, THE ○ SPRING RIVER FLOWS EAST ○ YIJANG CHUNSHUI DONG LIU
YIKILAN GURUR • 1967 • Gultekin Sirri • TRK • BROKEN PRIDE
YIKILAN YUVA • 1967 • Aksoy Orhan • TRK • BROKEN HOME, THE
YILANI OLDURSELER • 1982 • Soray Turkan • TRK • TO KILL THE SNAKE
YILANLARIN OCU • 1985 • Goren Serif • TRK • REVENGE OF THE SERPENTS
YIN AND YANG OF MR. GO, THE • 1970 • Meredith Burgess • USA
YIN-CHIEN HSIANG MA • 1988 • Ho P'Ing • TWN
YIN-YANG • 1968 • Spoecker Peter D. • SHT • USA
YING CH'UN KO CHIH FENG-PO • 1973 • Hu King • HKG • FATE OF LEE KHAN, THE ○ TROUBLE AT SPRING INN
YING LO HIS-YANG P'ING • 1981 • Ch'U Yuan • HKG
YING T'AI CH'I HSUEH • 1976 • Li Han-Hsiang • HKG • LAST TEMPEST, THE
YINGHUNG BUNSIK III -TSIKYEUNGTSI 90 • 1989 • Xu Ke • HKG • BETTER TOMORROW III, A
YINGXIONG BENSE • 1987 • Woo John • HKG, TWN • BETTER TOMORROW
YINYANG JIE • 1988 • Wu Ziniu • CHN • REALM BETWEEN THE LIVING AND THE DEAD, THE ○ BETWEEN LIFE AND DEATH
YIP, YIP, YIPPY • 1939 • Fleischer Dave • ANS • USA
YIQI LIANGFU • 1988 • Chen You • HKG • ONE HUSBAND TOO MANY
YITLEUNG, SINGSING, TAIYEUNG • 1988 • Mak Johnny • HKG • MOON, STARS, SUN
YIWA LIANGQI • 1987 • Chen You • HKG • HAPPY BIGAMIST
YIWAN CHA • 1988 • Wang Wayne • HKG
YKSINTEOIN • 1989 • Lehto Pekka • FNL • SINGLE-HANDED
YKSITYISALUE • 1962 • Kurkvaara Maunu • FNL • PRIVATE PROPERTY
YNGSJOMORDET • 1966 • Mattsson Arne • SWD • WOMAN OF DARKNESS
YO AMO.. TU AMAS.. NOSOTROS • 1974 • *Conacine* • MXC
YO BAILE CON DON PORFIRIO • 1942 • Martinez Solares Gilberto • MXC
YO CREO QUE.. • 1974 • Artero Antonio • SPN
YO DORMI CON UN FANTASMA • 1947 • Salvador Jaime • MXC • I SLEPT WITH A GHOST
YO.. EL AVENTURERO • 1958 • Salvador Jaime • MXC
YO, EL GOBERNADOR • 1965 • Cardona Rene Jr. • MXC, VNZ
YO, EL MUJERIEGO • 1962 • Diaz Morales Jose • MXC
YO, EL VALIENTE • 1964 • Blake Alfonso Corona • MXC
YO FUI EL REY • 1975 • Romero-Marchent Rafael • SPN
YO FUI NOVIO DE POSITA ALVIREZ • 1954 • Gomez Urquiza Zacarias • MXC
YO FUI UNA CALLEJERA • 1951 • Rodriguez Joselito • MXC
YO FUI UNA USURPADORA • 1945 • Morayta Miguel • MXC
YO GIRI NO MAGARIKADO • 1959 • Horiiki Kiyoshi • JPN
YO HABLO A CARACAS • 1978 • Ortiz Alexis, Azpurua Carlos • VNZ • I'M SPEAKING TO CARACAS
YO HE VISTO LA MUERTE • 1967 • Forque Jose Maria • SPN • I HAVE SEEN DEATH
YO, LA PEOR DE TODAS • 1990 • Bemberg Maria Luisa • ARG • I, THE WORST OF ALL
YO LA VI PRIMERO • 1974 • Fernan-Gomez Fernando • SPN • I SAW HER FIRST
YO LOS MATO, TU COBRAS LA RECOMPENSA • 1973 • Montero Roberto Bianchi • SPN
YO MATE • 1955 • Forn Josep Maria • SPN
YO MATE A FACUNDO • 1975 • del Carril Hugo • ARG • I KILLED FACUNDO
YO MATE A JUAN CHARRASQUEADO • 1948 • Urueta Chano • MXC
YO MATE A ROSITA ALVIREZ • 1946 • de Anda Raul • MXC
YO MEREN RANNAULA • 1980 • Kivikoski Erkko • FNL • NIGHT AT THE SEASHORE ○ NIGHT BY THE SEASHORE
YO NO CREO EN LOS HOMBRES • 1954 • Ortega Juan J. • MXC, CUB
YO NO ELEGI MI VIDA • 1949 • Discepolo Enrique Santos, Momplet Antonio • ARG
YO NO ME CASO • 1944 • de Orduna Juan • SPN
YO NO ME CASO COMPADRE • 1959 • Delgado Miguel M. • MXC
YO NO SOY UN ASESINO • 1963 • Zabalza Jose Maria • SPN
YO PECADOR • 1959 • Blake Alfonso Corona • MXC
YO PEDALEO, TU PEDALEAS • 1976 • Castro Alberto Giraldo • DOC • CLM
YO QUIERO QUE ME LLEVEN A HOLLYWOOD • 1931 • Neville Edgar • SPN
YO QUIERO SER HOMBRE • 1949 • Cardona Rene • MXC
YO QUIERO SER MALA • 1949 • Cardona Rene • MXC
YO QUIERO SER TONTA • 1950 • Ugarte Eduardo • MXC
YO SABIA DEMASIADO! • 1959 • Bracho Julio • MXC
YO SOY CHARRO DE LEVITA • 1949 • Martinez Solares Gilberto • MXC
YO SOY CHARRO DONDEQUIERA see **CICLON DE JALISCO, EL** • 1963
YO SOY FULANA DE TAL • 1975 • Lazaga Pedro • SPN
YO SOY GALLO DONDEQUIERA • 1952 • Rodriguez Roberto • MXC
YO SOY MUY MACHO • 1953 • Diaz Morales Jose • MXC
YO SOY TU PADRE • 1927 • Bustillo Oro Juan • MXC
YO SOY TU PADRE • 1947 • Gomez Muriel Emilio • MXC
YO SOY USTED • 1943 • Reiguera Francisco • MXC
YO TAMBIEN SOY DE JALISCO • 1949 • Soler Julian • MXC
YO VAI PAIVA • 1962 • Jarva Risto, Pakkasvirta Jaakko • FNL • NIGHT OR DAY ○ DAY OR NIGHT
YO VENDO UNOS OJOS NEGROS • 1947 • Rodriguez Ismael • MXC, CHL
YO Y EL MARIACHI • 1974 • *Cinema Galindo* • MXC
YO YENGO A MI HIJO • 1946 • Elias Francisco • MXC
YO YO see **YOYO** • 1965
YOAKE ASAAKE • 1953 • Yoshimura Kozaburo • JPN • MORNING DAWN
YOAKE MAE • 1953 • Yoshimura Kozaburo • JPN • BEFORE DAWN (USA) ○ BEFORE THE DAWN
YOAKE NO FUTARI • 1968 • Nomura Yoshitaro • JPN • RAINBOW OVER THE PACIFIC
YOAKE NO KUNI • 1967 • Tokieda Toshie • DOC • JPN • REPORT FROM CHINA ○ YOWAKE NO KUNI ○ DAWNING NATION
YOAKE NO UTA • 1965 • Kurahara Koreyoshi • JPN • AWAKENING, THE
YOAN ASSEN'S WEDDING • 1974 • BUL
YOB, THE see **COMIC STRIP PRESENTS: THE YOB** • 1987
YOBA • 1976 • Imai Tadashi • JPN • OLD WOMAN GHOST, THE
YODELIN' KID FROM PINE RIDGE • 1937 • Kane Joseph • USA • HERO OF PINE RIDGE, THE (UKN)
YODELING YOKELS • 1930 • Harman Hugh, Ising Rudolf • ANS • USA
YOEN DOKUFU-DEN HANNYA NO OHYAKU • 1968 • Ishikawa Yoshihiro • JPN • STORY OF A VAMPIRE
YOG -MONSTER FROM SPACE (USA) see **KESSEN NANKAI NO DAIKAIJU** • 1970
YOGA see **YOGA -EN VEJ TIL LYKKEN** • 1973
YOGA AND THE INDIVIDUAL • 1966 • Murray John B. • DOC • ASL
YOGA -EN VEJ TIL LYKKEN • 1973 • Hasselbalch Hagen • DOC • DNM • YOGA -ROAD TO HAPPINESS ○ YOGA
YOGA -ROAD TO HAPPINESS see **YOGA -EN VEJ TIL LYKKEN** • 1973
YOGEN • 1982 • Hani Susumu • JPN • PROPHECY, THE
YOGHI, DER • 1916 • Gliese Rochus, Wegener Paul • FRG • HAUS DES YOGHI, DAS ○ JOGHI, DER ○ YOGI, THE
YOGI, THE • 1899 • Blackton J. Stuart • USA
YOGI, THE • 1913 • Tucker George Loane • USA

YOGI, THE • FRN
YOGI, THE see **YOGHI, DER** • 1916
YOGI BEAR AND THE MAGICAL FLIGHT OF THE SPRUCE GOOSE • 1984 • Patterson Ray • ANM • USA
YOGIRI NO BOJO • 1966 • Matsuo Akinori • JPN • OUTLINE OF VIOLENCE
YOGIRI NO BURUSU • 1963 • Nomura Takeshi • JPN • FOGGY NIGHT BLUES
YOGIRI NO DAINIKOKUDO • 1958 • Masuda Toshio • JPN
YOGIRI YO KONYA MO ARIGATO • 1967 • Ezaki Mio • JPN • WARM MISTY NIGHT, A
YOGI'S FIRST CHRISTMAS • 1983 • Patterson Ray • ANM • USA
YOGI'S GREAT ESCAPE • Patterson Ray • ANM • USA
YOGORE • 1967 • Yamamoto Shinya • JPN • IMPURITY
YOGOTO NO YUME • 1933 • Naruse Mikio • JPN • EVERYNIGHT DREAMS
YOGURT CULTURE • Chenis Patti-Lee • ANS • USA
YOHO, VALLEE DES MERVEILLES see **YOHO: WONDER VALLEY** • 1952
YOHO: WONDER VALLEY • 1952 • Blais Roger • DCS • CND • YOHO, VALLEE DES MERVEILLES
YOI MUKODONO • 1954 • *Mikuni Rentaro* • JPN • FINE SON-IN-LAW, A
YOIDORE HAKASE • 1966 • Misumi Kenji • JPN • DYNAMITE DOCTOR
YOIDORE TENSHI • 1948 • Kurosawa Akira • JPN • DRUNKEN ANGEL
YOIYAMI SEMAREBA • 1969 • Jissoji Akio • JPN
YOJA NO MADEN • 1956 • Matsuda Sadaji • JPN • PALACE OF SNAKES ○ CONFLICT OF MAGICIANS
YOJASO NO MAWO • 1957 • Magatani Morehei • JPN
YOJIMBO • 1961 • Kurosawa Akira • JPN • BODYGUARD, THE
YOKAI DAISENSO • 1968 • Kuroda Yoshiyuki • JPN • GHOSTS ON PARADE ○ SPOOK WARFARE
YOKAI HYAKU MONOGATARI • 1968 • Yasuda Kimiyoshi • JPN • WOKAI HYAKU MONOGATARI ○ HUNDRED MONSTERS, THE ○ 100 MONSTERS ○ STORY OF 100 GHOSTS
YOKE, THE • 1915 • Vickers James W. • UKN • LOVE'S LEGACY
YOKE OF GOLD, A • 1916 • Carleton Lloyd B. • USA
YOKEL, THE (UKN) see **BOOB, THE** • 1926
YOKEL BOY • 1942 • Santley Joseph • USA • HITTING THE HEADLINES (UKN)
YOKEL BOY MAKES GOOD • 1938 • Lantz Walter • ANS • USA
YOKEL DUCK MAKES GOOD • 1943 • Donnelly Eddie • ANS • USA
YOKEL'S DINNER, THE • 1900 • *Warwick Trading Co* • UKN
YOKE'S ON ME, THE • 1944 • White Jules • SHT • USA
YOKI NA NAKAMA • 1958 • Hirozu Mitsuo • JPN
YOKI NO URAMACHI • 1939 • Yoshimura Kozaburo • JPN • LIVELY ALLEY ○ CHEERFUL ALLEY ○ GAY BACK ALLEY ○ YOKINA URAMACHI
YOKIHI • 1955 • Mizoguchi Kenji • JPN • EMPRESS YANG KWEI FEI, THE (UKN) ○ YANG KWEI FEI (USA) ○ PRINCESS YANG, THE ○ PRINCESS YANG KWEI FEI, THE
YOKINA MIBOJIN • 1964 • Toyoda Shiro • JPN
YOKINA URAMACHI see **YOKI NO URAMACHI** • 1939
YOKIRO • 1984 • Gosha Hideo • JPN • YOKIRO, HOUSE OF PROSTITUTES
YOKIRO, HOUSE OF PROSTITUTES see **YOKIRO** • 1984
YOKO ONO FILM NO.4 • 1967 • Ono Yoko, Cox Anthony • UKN • BOTTOMS ○ NO.4
YOKOGAMI-YABURINO ZENKAMONO • 1968 • Ozawa Shigehiro • JPN • DESPERATE HOODLUM
YOKOHAMA GIRL • 1964 • *Dan Reiko* • JPN
YOKOHAMA YANKEE, A • 1955 • Rasinski Connie • ANS • USA
YOKU • 1958 • Gosho Heinosuke • JPN • HALF A LOAF ○ AVARICE ○ DESIRE
YOKUBO • 1952 • Yoshimura Kozaburo • JPN • DESIRES ○ DESIRE
YOKYO • 1960 • Masumura Yasuzo (c/d) • JPN
YOL • 1982 • Goren Serif, Guney Yilmaz • TRK
YOLA STELLA MARIS • 1916 • Starevitch Ladislas • USS
YOLANDA • 1924 • Vignola Robert G. • USA
YOLANDA • 1942 • Murphy Dudley • MXC
YOLANDA AND THE THIEF • 1945 • Minnelli Vincente • USA
YOLK, THE • 1971 • Lange John C. • ANS • USA
YOLSUZ MEHMET • 1967 • Tengiz Asaf • TRK • MEHMET, THE DECEIVER
YOM EL SADES, EL • 1986 • Shahin Youssef • EGY • SIXTH DAY, THE
YOM MUR, YON HELW • 1987 • Beshara Khairy • EGY • BITTER DAYS, SWEET DAYS
YOMA KIDAN • 1929 • *Tsuburaya Eiji (Ph)* • JPN
YOMIGAERU DAICHI • 1970 • Nakamura Noboru • JPN • REBIRTH OF THE SOIL, THE
YOMMANNIN NO MOKUGEKISHA • 1960 • Horiuchi Manao • JPN • HOT CORNER MURDER
YON SYLISSA • 1977 • Lindstrom Jon • FNL, SWD • HOMEWARD IN DARKNESS ○ HEMAT I NATTEN ○ HOMEWARD IN THE NIGHT ○ HOME AND REFUGE ○ HARRI! HARRI!
YONG BUXIOSHI DE DIANBO • 1958 • Wang Ping • CHN • UNFAILING BEAM, THE ○ CONSTANT BEAM
YONGARY, MONSTER FROM THE DEEP (USA) see **DAI KOESU YONGKARI** • 1967
YONINME NO SHUKUJO • 1948 • Shibuya Minoru • JPN
YONJU HASSAI NO TEIKO • 1956 • Yoshimura Kozaburo • JPN • PROTEST AT FORTY-EIGHT YEARS OLD ○ FORTY-EIGHT YEAR OLD REBEL
YONJUHAICHI-NIN-ME NO DOSHI • 1936 • Ito Daisuke • JPN • FORTY-EIGHTH COMRADE, THE
YONKERS, HANGING OUT • 1973 • Akerman Chantal • USA
YONNA LEFATSENG • 1984 • SAF
YONSAN ILGI • 1988 • Lim Kwon-Taek • SKR • YONSAN'S DIARY
YONSAN'S DIARY see **YONSAN ILGI** • 1988
YOO-HOO • 1932 • Horne James W. • SHT • USA
YOPPARAI TENGOKU • 1962 • Shibuya Minoru • JPN • HEAVEN FOR A DRUNKARD

YOR see **YOR: THE HUNTER FROM THE FUTURE** • 1983
YOR: THE HUNTER FROM THE FUTURE • 1983 • Margheriti Antonio • ITL, TRK • YOR
YORGUN SAVASCI • Refig Halit • TRK • TIRED WARRIOR, THE
YORICKOVA LEBKA • 1919 • Novy Milos • CZC • YORICK'S SKULL
YORICK'S SKULL see **YORICKOVA LEBKA** • 1919
YORK • 1931 • Ucicky Gustav • FRG
YORK MYSTERY, THE • 1924 • Croise Hugh • UKN
YORK STATE FOLKS • 1915 • Jackson Harry • USA
YORKSHIRE DITTY • 1949 • Stringer G. Henry • UKN
YORKSHIRE SCHOOL, A • 1910 • *Edison* • USA
YORKSTOWN, LE SENS D'UNE BATAILLE • 1982 • Ophuls Marcel • MTV • FRN
YOROKOBI MO KANASHIMI MO IKUTOSHITSUKI • 1957 • Kinoshita Keisuke • JPN • TIMES OF JOY AND SORROW ○ LIGHTHOUSE, THE
YORU • 1923 • Mizoguchi Kenji • JPN • NIGHT, THE (USA)
YORU HIRAKU • 1931 • Gosho Heinosuke • JPN • BLOOMING AT NIGHT ○ OPEN AT NIGHT
YORU NAKU ONNA • 1967 • Shindo Takae • JPN • WOMEN WHO CRY AT NIGHT
YORU NO BARA O KESE • 1966 • Masuda Toshio • JPN • KILL THE NIGHT ROSE
YORU NO CHO • 1957 • Yoshimura Kozaburo • JPN • NIGHT BUTTERFLIES ○ BUTTERFLY OF NIGHT
YORU NO EMMACHO • 1961 • Watanabe Kunio • JPN • SMOKE OF NIGHT
YORU NO HADA • 1960 • Kawashima Yuzo • JPN • SOFT TOUCH OF NIGHT (USA)
YORU NO HENRIN • 1964 • Nakamura Noboru • JPN • BEAUTIFUL PEOPLE, THE (UKN) ○ SHAPE OF NIGHT, THE
YORU NO KAWA • 1956 • Yoshimura Kozaburo • JPN • UNDERCURRENT ○ NIGHT RIVER
YORU NO KIBA • 1958 • Inoue Umeji • JPN • FANGS OF THE NIGHT
YORU NO KISEICHU • 1968 • Sawa Kensuke • JPN • PARASITE OF THE NIGHT, A
YORU NO MESU-INU • 1966 • Murayama Shinji • JPN • CHEATING LOVE
YORU NO MESUNEKO • 1928 • Gosho Heinosuke • JPN • CAT OF THE NIGHT
YORU NO NAGARE • 1960 • Naruse Mikio • JPN • LOVELORN GEISHA, THE ○ FLOWING NIGHT ○ EVENING STREAM
YORU NO NAWABARI • 1967 • Murano Tetsutaro • JPN • RULE OVER NIGHT
YORU NO NETTAIGYO • 1965 • Inoue Umeji • JPN • BGS OF GINZA
YORU NO ONNATACHI • 1948 • Mizoguchi Kenji • JPN • WOMEN OF THE NIGHT (USA)
YORU NO SUGAO • 1958 • Yoshimura Kozaburo • JPN • NAKED FACE OF NIGHT, THE ○ LADDER OF SUCCESS, THE
YORU NO TADARE • 1967 • Yamamoto Shinya • JPN • INFLAMMATION OF NIGHT
YORU NO TEHAISHI • 1968 • Murayama Shinji • JPN • NIGHT GUY
YORU NO TOGYO • 1959 • Tanaka Shigeo • JPN • PAPER PIGEON
YORU NO TSUTSUMI see **YORU NO TSUZUMI** • 1958
YORU NO TSUZUMI • 1958 • Imai Tadashi • JPN • ADULTERESS, THE ○ NIGHT DRUM ○ YORU NO TSUTSUMI
YORU NO WANA • 1967 • Tomimoto Sokichi • JPN • TRAP OF THE NIGHT
YORU NO YOROKOBI • 1967 • Mukoi Hiroshi • JPN • NIGHT PLEASURE
YORU NON HAIYAKU • 1959 • Saeki Kozo • JPN • CAST OF NIGHT
YORU NON HITODE • 1967 • Hase Kazuo • JPN • TEMPTATION BY NIGHT
YOSAKOI JOURNEY (USA) see **YOSAKOI RYOKO** • 1969
YOSAKOI RYOKO • 1969 • Segawa Shoji • JPN • YOSAKOI JOURNEY (USA)
YOSEF-VA-ZOLIKHA • 1968 • Reis-Firouz Mehdi • IRN • JOSEPH AND ZOLIKHA
YOSEI GORASU • 1962 • Honda Inoshiro • JPN • YOSEI GORATH ○ GORATH
YOSEI GORATH see **YOSEI GORASU** • 1962
YOSEI NO UTA • 1971 • Hani Susumu • JPN
YOSEMITE, THE • 1914 • Sennett Mack • DOC • USA
YOSEMITE TRAIL, THE • 1922 • Durning Bernard J. • USA
YOSHIDA GOTEN • 1937 • *Yamada Isuzu* • JPN • YOSHIDA PALACE
YOSHIDA PALACE see **YOSHIDA GOTEN** • 1937
YOSHIKO KAWASHIMA • 1989 • He Ping • CHN
YOSHINAKA O MEGURU NO ONNA • 1956 • Kinugasa Teinosuke • JPN • THREE WOMEN AROUND YOSHINAKA
YOSHIWARA • 1937 • Ophuls Max • FRN • KOHANA
YOSHIWARA, DIE LIEBESSTADT DER JAPANER • 1920 • *Durant Allan* • FRG
YOSHIWARA ENJOW • 1987 • Gosha Hideo • JPN • FIRE OVER THE WOMEN'S CASTLE
YOSHIWARA STORY, THE see **HIROKU ONNAGURA** • 1968
YOSO • 1963 • Kinugasa Teinosuke • JPN • BONZE MAGICIAN, THE ○ SORCERER, THE ○ PRIEST AND EMPRESS
YOTSU see **YOTTSU NO KOI NO MONOGATARI** • 1947
YOTSUYA GHOST STORY, THE see **YOTSUYA KAIDAN** • 1949
YOTSUYA GHOST STORY, THE see **YOTSUYA KAIDAN** • 1959
YOTSUYA GHOST STORY, THE see **YOTSUYA KAIDAN** • 1965
YOTSUYA GHOST STORY NEW EDITION see **SHINPAN YOTSUYA KAIDAN** • 1928
YOTSUYA KAIDAN • 1949 • Kinoshita Keisuke • JPN • YOTSUYA GHOST STORY, THE ○ GHOST OF YOTSUYA, THE
YOTSUYA KAIDAN • 1956 • Mori Masaki • JPN • GHOST OF YOTSUYA, THE
YOTSUYA KAIDAN • 1959 • Misumi Kenji • JPN • YOTSUYA GHOST STORY, THE ○ GHOST OF YOTSUYA, THE
YOTSUYA KAIDAN • 1965 • Toyoda Shiro • JPN • YOTSUYA GHOST STORY, THE ○ ILLUSION OF BLOOD ○ GHOST OF YOTSUYA, THE

YOTSUYA KAIDAN -OIWA NO BOREI • 1969 • Mori Issei • JPN • CURSE OF THE NIGHT, THE ○ GHOST OF YOTSUYA, THE
YOTTSU NO KOI NO MONOGATARI • 1947 • Kinugasa Teinosuke, Toyoda Shiro, Yamamoto Kajiro, Naruse Mikio • JPN • FOUR LOVE STORIES ○ FIRST LOVE ○ YOTSU
YOTTSU NO KOI NO MONOGATARI • 1966 • Nishikawa Katsumi • JPN • FOUR LOVES
YOTZ'IM KAVUA • 1979 • Davidson Boaz • ISR • GOING STEADY: LEMON POPSICLE II (USA) ○ GOING STEADY
YOU • 1916 • Shaw Harold • UKN
"YOU" • 1968 • Hunt Paul • USA
YOU.. see **TE** • 1963
YOU, ACROSS THE RIVER OF WRATH see **KIMI YO FUNDO NO KAWA A WATARE** • 1975
YOU ALONE • 1984 • Escamilla Teo • SPN
YOU ALONG O' ME • 1929 • Aylott Dave, Symmons E. F. • SHT • UKN
YOU AND I • 1961 • Makhnach Leonid • DOC • USS
YOU AND I see **BARGAIN, THE** • 1931
YOU AND I see **KIMI TO BOKU** • 1941
YOU AND I see **NEEYUM NAANUM** • 1968
YOU AND I see **TY I YA** • 1972
YOU AND I (USA) see **BERG-EJVIND OCH HANS HUSTRU** • 1918
YOU AND ME • 1938 • Lang Fritz • USA
YOU AND ME • 1975 • Carradine David • USA
YOU AND ME see **TY I YA** • 1972
YOU AND OTHER COMRADES see **DU UND MANCHER KAMARAD..** • 1956
YOU AND YOUR FRIEND see **ANATA TO TOMO NI** • 1955
YOU ARE A CRIMINAL -OBERLANDER! • 1960 • Makhnach Leonid • DOC • USS
YOU ARE A WIDOW, SIR see **PANE, VY JSTE VDOVA** • 1971
YOU ARE ALWAYS IN MY HEART see **HER ZAMAN KALBIMDESIN** • 1967
YOU ARE ALWAYS IN MY HEART see **IN FIECARE ZI MI-E DOR DE TINE** • 1988
YOU ARE ALWAYS LEAVING ME • 1978 • Liappa Frieda • GRC
YOU ARE GUILTY • 1923 • Lewis Edgar • USA
YOU ARE GUILTY TOO see **PARTEA TA DE VINA** • 1963
YOU ARE IN DANGER see **LITTLE GIRL NEXT DOOR, THE** • 1923
YOU ARE LIKE A DAISY see **NOGIKU NO GOTOKI KIMI NARIKI** • 1955
YOU ARE MINE see **SEN BENIMSIN** • 1967
YOU ARE MINE see **IKAW AY AKIN** • 1978
YOU ARE MY ADVENTURE see **DU AR MITT AVENTYR** • 1958
YOU ARE MY DARLING see **JY IS MY LEIFLING** • 1968
YOU ARE MY LOVE see **INTA HABIBI** • 1956
YOU ARE NOT ALONE see **DU ER IKKE ALENE** • 1978
YOU ARE NOT I • 1981 • Driver Sara • USA
YOU ARE ON INDIAN LAND • 1969 • Ransen Mort • CND
YOU ARE PETER see **TU ES PIERRE** • 1959
YOU ARE STUPID, MY BROTHER see **NIISAN NO BAKA** • 1932
YOU ARE THE WORLD FOR ME (USA) see **DU BIST DIE WELT FUR MICH** • 1953
YOU ARE WEIGHED IN THE BALANCE BUT FOUND WANTING see **TINIMBANG KA NGUNI'T KULANG** • 1974
YOU ARE WHAT YOU EAT • 1968 • Feinstein Barry • DOC • USA
YOU BELONG TO ME • 1934 • Werker Alfred L. • USA
YOU BELONG TO ME • 1941 • Ruggles Wesley • USA • GOOD MORNING, DOCTOR (UKN)
YOU BELONG TO ME see **NOW AND FOREVER** • 1934
YOU BELONG TO MY FRIEND see **ARKADASIMIN ASKI** • 1968
YOU BELONG TO MY HEART see **MR. IMPERIUM** • 1951
YOU BETTER WATCH OUT see **CHRISTMAS EVIL** • 1980
YOU BRING THE DUCKS • 1934 • Yates Hal • SHT • USA
YOU CALL ME COLOURED • 1985 • Walker John • CND
YOU CAME ALONG • 1945 • Farrow John • USA
YOU CAME TO MY RESCUE • 1937 • Fleischer Dave • ANS • USA
YOU CAME TOO LATE • 1962 • Kapsakis D. • GRC
YOU CAN • Neiditch Rose • ANS • USA
YOU CAN BE HAD • 1935 • Newfield Sam • SHT • USA
YOU CAN DO IT MEXICAN see **MEXICANO TU PUEDES** • 1985
YOU CAN DRAW • 1938 • van Dongen Helen • NTH
YOU CAN GO A LONG WAY • 1961 • Wilder Donald A. • CND
YOU CAN IF YOU TRY see **ORE NI TSUITE-KOI** • 1965
YOU CAN NEVER TELL see **YOU NEVER CAN TELL** • 1951
YOU CAN SUCCEED TOO (USA) see **KIMIMO SHUSSEGA DEKIRU** • 1964
YOU CAN TALK NOW see **USTEDES TIENEN LA PALABRA** • 1974
YOU CAN'T ALWAYS TELL • 1915 • Garwood William • USA
YOU CAN'T ALWAYS TELL • 1979 • Hicks Scott • SHT • ASL
YOU CAN'T ALWAYS TELL see **RIGHT TO THE HEART** • 1942
YOU CAN'T BEAT IT • 1915 • *Parsons W. B.* • USA
YOU CAN'T BEAT LOVE • 1937 • Cabanne W. Christy • USA
YOU CAN'T BEAT THE IRISH (USA) see **TALK OF A MILLION** • 1951
YOU CAN'T BEAT THE LAW • 1928 • Hunt Charles J. • USA
YOU CAN'T BEAT THE LAW • 1943 • Rosen Phil • USA • PRISON MUTINY
YOU CAN'T BEAT THE LAW see **SMART GUY** • 1944
YOU CAN'T BEAT THEM • 1914 • *Lubin* • USA
YOU CAN'T BELIEVE EVERYTHING • 1918 • Conway Jack • USA
YOU CAN'T BUY EVERYTHING • 1934 • Reisner Charles F. • USA • OLD HANNIBAL
YOU CAN'T BUY LUCK • 1937 • Landers Lew • USA • BORROWED TIME
YOU CAN'T CHEAT AN HONEST MAN • 1939 • Marshall George • USA
YOU CAN'T DO THAT TO ME (UKN) see **MAISIE GOES TO RIO** • 1944
YOU CAN'T DO WITHOUT LOVE (USA) see **ONE EXCITING NIGHT** • 1944
YOU CAN'T ESCAPE • 1956 • Eades Wilfred • UKN
YOU CAN'T ESCAPE FOREVER • 1942 • Graham Jo • USA
YOU CAN'T FIGURE WOMEN see **SNOB, THE** • 1921

YOU CAN'T FOOL AN IRISHMAN (USA) see **STRANGERS CAME, THE** • 1949
YOU CAN'T FOOL YOUR WIFE • 1923 • Melford George • USA
YOU CAN'T FOOL YOUR WIFE • 1940 • McCarey Ray • USA • ROMANTIC MR. HINKLIN, THE
YOU CAN'T FOOL YOUR WIFE see **NUTCRACKER, THE** • 1926
YOU CAN'T GET AWAY WITH IT • 1923 • Lee Rowland V. • USA • ROAD TO NOWHERE, THE
YOU CAN'T GET AWAY WITH IT • 1936 • *Ford Charles E. (P)* • SHT • USA
YOU CAN'T GET AWAY WITH MURDER • 1939 • Seiler Lewis • USA
YOU CAN'T GET MORE BEAUTIFUL see **PIU BELLO DI COSI SI MUORE** • 1982
YOU CAN'T GO HOME AGAIN • 1979 • Nelson Ralph • TVM • USA
YOU CAN'T GO WRONG IF YOU SING see **TKO PJEVA, ZLO NE MISLI** • 1971
YOU CAN'T HAVE EVERYTHING • 1937 • Taurog Norman • USA
YOU CAN'T HAVE EVERYTHING • 1970 • Zweiback Martin • USA • CACTUS IN THE SNOW
YOU CAN'T HURRY LOVE • 1988 • Martini Richard • USA • GREETINGS FROM L.A. ◦ LOVESTRUCK
YOU CAN'T KEEP A GOOD MAN DOWN • 1922 • *Lone Star Motion Picture Co* • USA
YOU CAN'T RATION LOVE • 1944 • Fuller Lester • USA
YOU CAN'T RUN AWAY FROM IT • 1956 • Powell Dick • USA • IT HAPPENED ONE NIGHT
YOU CAN'T RUN AWAY FROM SEX (UKN) see **RUNAWAYS, THE** • 1972
YOU CAN'T SAY NO see **SIE KANN NICHT NEIN SAGEN** • 1914
YOU CAN'T SEE 'ROUND CORNERS • 1969 • Cahill David, De Vigne Jacques • ASL
YOU CAN'T SHOE A HORSEFLY • 1940 • Fleischer Dave • ANS • USA
YOU CAN'T SLEEP HERE (UKN) see **I WAS A MALE WAR BRIDE** • 1949
YOU CAN'T SPELL "SEX" WITHOUT.. X • 1970 • *Kirt Films International* • USA
YOU CAN'T STEAL LOVE see **MURPH THE SURF** • 1975
YOU CAN'T TAKE IT WITH YOU • 1938 • Capra Frank • USA
YOU CAN'T TAKE MONEY (UKN) see **INTERNES CAN'T TAKE MONEY** • 1937
YOU CAN'T WIN • 1948 • Barclay David • SHT • USA
YOU CAN'T WIN see **WHEN G-MEN STEP IN** • 1938
YOU CAN'T WIN 'EM ALL • 1970 • Collinson Peter • UKN • DUBIOUS PATRIOTS, THE
YOU CAN'T WIN THEM ALL see **ONCE YOU KISS A STRANGER** • 1969
YOU COULDN'T BLAME HER • 1919 • *Devore Dorothy* • USA
YOU DIE.. BUT I LIVE see **BANDIDOS** • 1967
YOU DIE EASILY AT GHENTAR see **A GHENTAR SI MUORE FACILE** • 1967
YOU DIG? see **VOUS PIGEZ?** • 1955
YOU DIRTY BOY • 1896 • *Paul R. W.* • UKN
YOU DO, I DO, WE DO • 1972 • Vanderbeek Stan • USA
YOU DON'T BACK DOWN • 1965 • Owen Don • CND
YOU DON'T KNOW WHAT YOU'RE DOING • 1931-32 • Ising Rudolf • ANS • USA
YOU DON'T LIKE THE SYSTEM? see **VAM CHTO, NASHA VLAST NE NRAVISTYA?** • 1989
YOU DON'T NEED PYJAMAS AT ROSIE'S see **FIRST TIME, THE** • 1968
YOU DON'T SMOKE EH? • 1981 • Muller John • DOC • CND
YOU DRIVE ME CRAZY • 1945 • Yates Hal • SHT • USA
YOU FIND IT EVERYWHERE • 1921 • Horan Charles • USA • GIBSON UPRIGHT, THE
YOU FOR ME • 1952 • Weis Don • USA
YOU FREE OLD COUNTRY see **DU GAMLA, DU FRIA** • 1938
YOU GET IT? see **VOUS PIGEZ?** • 1955
YOU GET WHAT YOU PAY FOR see **GET WHAT YOU PAY FOR** • 1970
YOU GO TO MY HEART see **ALL BY MYSELF** • 1943
YOU GOTTA BE A FOOTBALL HERO • 1935 • Fleischer Dave • ANS • USA
YOU GOTTA BE CRAZY • 1987 • Nofal Emil • SAF
YOU GOTTA STAY HAPPY • 1948 • Potter H. C. • USA
YOU, GROWN UP, DON'T KNOW • 1988 • Lee Kyu-Hyong • SKR
YOU HAVE A BEE IN YOUR BONNET, TONY see **TONY, TOBE PRESKOCILO** • 1968
YOU HAVE A MAN IN THE HOUSE see **FI BAYTINA RAJUL** • 1960
YOU HAVE BEEN VERY KIND • 1967 • Bonniere Rene • DOC • CND
YOU HAVE TO RUN FAST • 1961 • Cahn Edward L. • USA • MAN MISSING
YOU KNOW WHAT I MEAN • 1919 • *Parsons William* • SHT • USA
YOU KNOW WHAT SAILORS ARE • 1928 • Elvey Maurice • UKN
YOU KNOW WHAT SAILORS ARE • 1954 • Annakin Ken • UKN
YOU LAUGH LIKE A DUCK • 1980 • Wynne Cordell • MTV • CND
YOU LEAVE ME BREATHLESS • 1938 • Fleischer Dave • ANS • USA
YOU LIE SO DEEP, MY LOVE • 1975 • Rich David Lowell • TVM • USA
YOU LIGHT UP MY LIFE • 1977 • Brooks Joseph • USA
YOU LIVE AND LEARN • 1937 • Woods Arthur • UKN
YOU LUCKY PEOPLE • 1955 • Elvey Maurice • UKN
YOU MADE ME LOVE YOU • 1933 • Banks Monty • UKN
YOU MAY BE NEXT • 1935 • Rogell Albert S. • USA • PANIC ON THE AIR (UKN)
YOU MUST BE CRAZY DARLING! see **AR DU INTE RIKTIGT KLOK?** • 1964
YOU MUST BE JOKING! • 1965 • Winner Michael • UKN
YOU MUST BE JOKING see **IF YOU DON'T STOP IT YOU'LL GO BLIND** • 1975
YOU MUST GET MARRIED • 1936 • Pearce A. Leslie • UKN
YOU NAZTY SPY • 1940 • White Jules • SHT • USA
YOU NEED A DOCTOR • 1915 • *Starlight* • USA
YOU NEVER CAN TELL • 1914 • MacGregor Norval • USA
YOU NEVER CAN TELL • 1915 • *Banner* • USA
YOU NEVER CAN TELL • 1920 • Franklin Chester M. • USA
YOU NEVER CAN TELL • 1951 • Breslow Lou • USA • YOU NEVER KNOW (UKN) ◦ YOU CAN NEVER TELL ◦ ONE NEVER KNOWS
YOU NEVER CAN TELL see **STRANDED IN PARIS** • 1926
YOU NEVER KNOW • 1922 • Ensminger Robert • USA
YOU NEVER KNOW (UKN) see **YOU NEVER CAN TELL** • 1951
YOU NEVER KNOW WOMEN • 1926 • Wellman William A. • USA • LOVE MAGIC
YOU NEVER KNOW YOUR LUCK • 1919 • Powell Frank • USA
YOU NEVER SAW SUCH A GIRL • 1919 • Vignola Robert G. • USA
YOU OLD, YOU FREE see **DU GAMLA, DU FRIA** • 1970
YOU ONLY LIVE ONCE • 1937 • Lang Fritz • USA
YOU ONLY LIVE ONCE see **PERRY RHODAN -SOS AUS DEM WELTALL** • 1967
YOU ONLY LIVE ONCE see **SAMO JEDNOM SE LJUBI** • 1981
YOU ONLY LIVE TWICE • 1967 • Gilbert Lewis* • UKN
YOU ONLY LIVE TWICE see **INSAN IKI KERE YASAR** • 1968
YOU ONLY LOVE ONCE (USA) see **TU SERAS TERRIBLEMENT GENTILLE** • 1968
YOU ORIGINATE FROM THE EARTH see **AF JORD ER DU KOMMET** • 1984
YOU OUGHT TO BE IN PICTURES • 1940 • Freleng Friz • ANS • USA
YOU PAY YOUR MONEY • 1957 • Rogers Maclean • UKN
YOU REMEMBER ELLEN • 1912 • Olcott Sidney • USA
YOU RUINED MY LIFE • 1987 • Ashwell David • TVM • USA
YOU SAID A HATEFUL! • 1934 • Parrott Charles • SHT • USA • YOU SAID A HATFUL!
YOU SAID A HATFUL! see **YOU SAID A HATEFUL!** • 1934
YOU SAID A MOUSEFUL • 1958 • Kneitel Seymour • ANS • USA
YOU SAID A MOUTHFUL • 1932 • Bacon Lloyd • USA
YOU SAID IT SAILOR • 1930 • Van Ronkel Jo • SHT • USA
YOU SAVED MY LIFE • 1910 • *Imp* • USA
YOU SHOULDN'T DIE see **KIMI SHINITAMAU KOTO NAKARE** • 1954
YOU START, AND I'LL FINISH see **UMPISAHAN MO, AT TATAPUSIN KO** • 1967
YOU TALKIN' TO ME? • 1987 • Winkler Charles • USA
YOU TELL 'EM LIONS, I ROAR • 1920 • Watson William • SHT • USA
YOU THE PEOPLE • 1940 • Rowland Roy • SHT • USA
YOU THE RICH see **USTEDES LOS RICOS** • 1948
YOU TOOK THE WORDS RIGHT OUT OF MY HEART • 1938 • Fleischer Dave • ANS • USA
YOU TRY IT • 1911 • *Revier* • USA
YOU TRY SOMEBODY ELSE • 1932 • Fleischer Dave • ANS • USA
YOU WANT SOMETHING • 1916 • Curtis Allen • SHT • USA
YOU WENT AWAY TOO FAR • 1929 • Aylott Dave, Symmons E. F. • SHT • UKN
YOU WERE A PROPHET, MY DEAR see **PROFETA VOLTAL, SZIVEM** • 1968
YOU WERE LIKE A WILD CHRYSANTHEMUM see **NOGIKU NO GOTOKI KIMI NARIKI** • 1955
YOU WERE MEANT FOR ME • 1948 • Bacon Lloyd • USA
YOU WERE NEVER DUCKIER • 1948 • Jones Charles M. • ANS • USA
YOU WERE NEVER LOVELIER • 1942 • Seiter William A. • USA
YOU WERE NEVER UGLIER • 1944 • White Jules • SHT • USA
YOU WHO ARE ABOUT TO ENTER see **I SOM HAR INTRADEN..** • 1945
YOU WILL BE MY HUSBAND (USA) see **MAGA LESZ A FERJEM** • 1938
YOU WILL NOT TASTE PEACE see **NIE ZAZNASZ SPOKOJU** • 1977
YOU WILL REMEMBER • 1940 • Raymond Jack • UKN
YOU WILL SEND ME TO BED, EH? • 1903 • *Bitzer Billy (Ph)* • USA
YOU WORRY ME see **TU MI TURBI** • 1982
YOU WOULDN'T BELIEVE IT • 1920 • Kenton Erle C. • SHT • USA
YOU'D BE SURPRISED • 1926 • Rosson Arthur • USA
YOU'D BE SURPRISED • 1930 • Forde Walter • UKN
YOU'LL DIE see **OLECEKSIN** • 1968
YOU'LL BE MARRIED BY NOON see **MARRIED BEFORE BREAKFAST** • 1937
YOU'LL FIND OUT • 1915 • *Brown W. H.* • USA
YOU'LL FIND OUT • 1940 • Butler David • USA • HERE COME THE BOOGIE MEN
YOU'LL GO FROM THIS SHELL INTO THE COLD OUTSIDE see **PASARAS DE ESE CARACOL AL FRIO DE AFUERA** • 1979
YOU'LL LAUGH see **RIDERA** • 1967
YOU'LL LIKE MY MOTHER • 1972 • Johnson Lamont • USA
YOU'LL NEVER GET RICH • 1941 • Lanfield Sidney • USA
YOU'LL NEVER SEE ME AGAIN • 1973 • Szwarc Jeannot • TVM • USA
YOU'LL REMEMBER ME • 1906 • Gilbert Arthur • UKN
YOUNG AGAIN • 1986 • Stern Steven Hilliard • TVM • USA
YOUNG AMERICA • 1918 • Berthelet Arthur • USA
YOUNG AMERICA • 1919 • Van Loan Philip • SHS • USA
YOUNG AMERICA • 1922 • Berthelet Arthur • USA
YOUNG AMERICA • 1932 • Borzage Frank • USA • WE HUMANS (UKN)
YOUNG AMERICA • 1942 • King Louis • USA
YOUNG AMERICA FLIES • 1940 • Eason B. Reeves • SHT • USA
YOUNG AMERICANS • 1967 • Grasshoff Alex • DOC • USA
YOUNG AMERICANS see **DOWN IN SAN DIEGO** • 1941
YOUNG AND BEAUTIFUL • 1934 • Santley Joseph • USA
YOUNG AND DANGEROUS • 1957 • Claxton William F. • USA
YOUNG AND DUMB • 1922 • St. John Al • SHT • USA
YOUNG AND EAGER (UKN) see **CLAUDELLE INGLISH** • 1961
YOUNG AND EROTIC FANNY HILL, THE see **YOUNG EROTIC FANNY HILL, THE** • 1970
YOUNG AND EVIL (USA) see **YAMBAO** • 1956
YOUNG AND FREE • 1978 • Larsen Keith • USA
YOUNG AND HEALTHY • 1933 • Ising Rudolf • ANS • USA
YOUNG AND HEALTHY • 1943 • Massingham Richard, Strasser Alex • UKN
YOUNG AND HEALTHY AS A ROSE see **MLAD I ZVRAV KAO RUZA** • 1972
YOUNG AND IMMORAL, THE see **SINISTER URGE, THE** • 1961
YOUNG AND IN LOVE see **SKEPPAR MUNTERS BRAVADER** • 1950
YOUNG AND INNOCENT • 1937 • Hitchcock Alfred • UKN • GIRL WAS YOUNG, THE (USA) ◦ SHILLING FOR CANDLES, A
YOUNG AND THE BRAVE, THE • 1963 • Lyon Francis D. • USA • ATTONG
YOUNG AND THE COOL, THE (UKN) see **TWIST ALL NIGHT** • 1962
YOUNG AND THE DAMNED, THE (USA) see **OLVIDADOS, LOS** • 1950
YOUNG AND THE GUILTY, THE • 1958 • Cotes Peter • UKN
YOUNG AND THE OLD KING, THE see **ALTE UND DER JUNGE KONIG, DER** • 1935
YOUNG AND THE PASSIONATE, THE (USA) see **VITELLONI, I** • 1953
YOUNG AND THE WILLING, THE see **WILD AND THE WILLING, THE** • 1962
YOUNG AND WILD • 1958 • Witney William • USA
YOUNG AND WILLING • 1942 • Griffith Edward H. • USA • OUT OF THE FRYING PAN
YOUNG AND WILLING (USA) see **WEAK AND THE WICKED, THE** • 1953
YOUNG AND WILLING (USA) see **WILD AND THE WILLING, THE** • 1962
YOUNG ANIMALS, THE • 1968 • Dexter Maury • USA • BORN WILD
YOUNG APHRODITES (UKN) see **MIKRES APHRODITES** • 1962
YOUNG APOLLO see **MEN OF TOMORROW** • 1932
YOUNG APRIL • 1926 • Crisp Donald • USA
YOUNG AS YOU FEEL • 1931 • Borzage Frank • USA
YOUNG AS YOU FEEL • 1940 • St. Clair Malcolm • USA
YOUNG AT HEART • 1954 • Douglas Gordon • USA
YOUNG BACHELOR'S DREAM, A • 1909 • *Phoenix* • USA
YOUNG BEDMATES see **SCHULMADCHEN-REPORT 10** • 1976
YOUNG BESS • 1953 • Sidney George • USA
YOUNG BILL HICKOK • 1940 • Kane Joseph • USA
YOUNG BILLY YOUNG • 1969 • Kennedy Burt • USA • WHO RIDES WITH KANE?
YOUNG BLOOD • 1932 • Rosen Phil • USA • LOLA (UKN)
YOUNG BLOOD • 1990 • Wannayok Monoo • THL
YOUNG BLOOD see **UNGT BLOD** • 1943
YOUNG BLOOD (UKN) see **TEMPTATION'S WORKSHOP** • 1932
YOUNG BREED see **JEUNES LOUPS, LES** • 1968
YOUNG BRIDE • 1932 • Seiter William A. • USA • LOVE STARVED ◦ VENEER
YOUNG BRIDE, THE see **SPOSINA, LA** • 1976
YOUNG BRITON FOILS THE ENEMY • 1914 • Thornton F. Martin • UKN
YOUNG BRUCE LEE, THE • 1983 • *Lee Bruce* • HKG
YOUNG BUFFALO BILL • 1940 • Kane Joseph • USA
YOUNG CAPTIVES, THE • 1959 • Kershner Irvin • USA
YOUNG CARUSO, THE (USA) see **ENRICO CARUSO** • 1951
YOUNG CASSIDY • 1965 • Cardiff Jack, Ford John (U/c) • UKN, USA
YOUNG CHALLENGERS see **WAKAMONO YO CHOSEN SEYO** • 1968
YOUNG CHARLIE'S HALF DAY • 1915 • *G & Y Films* • UKN
YOUNG CHOPIN see **MLODOSC CHOPINA** • 1952
YOUNG COMPOSER'S ODYSSEY, A • 1986 • Shengelaya Georgi • USS
YOUNG COUNT TAKE THE GIRL AND THE PRIZE see **UNGA GREVEN TAR FLICKAN OCH PRISET** • 1924
YOUNG COUNTRY, THE • 1970 • Huggins Roy • TVM • USA
YOUNG COUPLE, A (USA) see **JEUNE COUPLE, UN** • 1968
YOUNG COUPLES see **YUANGYANF IOU** • 1988
YOUNG CYCLE GIRLS, THE • 1979 • Perry Peter • USA
YOUNG DANIEL BOONE • 1950 • Le Borg Reginald • USA
YOUNG DAYS • 1955 • Kadar Jan, Klos Elmar • CZC
YOUNG DAYS, THE see **MLADE DNY** • 1956
YOUNG DEER'S BRAVERY • 1909 • *Bison* • USA
YOUNG DEER'S GRATITUDE • 1910 • *Bison* • USA
YOUNG DEER'S RETURN • 1910 • *Bison* • USA
YOUNG DESIRE • 1930 • Collins Lewis D. • USA • CARNIVAL GIRL
YOUNG DETECTIVES, THE • 1963 • Gunn Gilbert • SRL • UKN
YOUNG DIANA, THE • 1922 • Capellani Albert, Vignola Robert G. • USA
YOUNG DILLINGER • 1965 • Morse Terry O. • USA
YOUNG DOCTOR, THE • 1911 • *Nestor* • USA
YOUNG DOCTOR IN LOVE • 1982 • Marshall Garry • USA • DOCTORS IN LOVE
YOUNG DR. KILDARE • 1938 • Bucquet Harold S. • USA
YOUNG DOCTORS, THE • 1961 • Karlson Phil • USA
YOUNG DONOVAN'S KID • 1931 • Niblo Fred • USA • DONOVAN'S KID (UKN) ◦ BIG BROTHER
YOUNG DON'T CRY, THE • 1957 • Werker Alfred L. • USA
YOUNG DRACULA see **ANDY WARHOL'S DRACULA** • 1974
YOUNG DRACULA see **SON OF DRACULA** • 1974
YOUNG DYNAMITE • 1937 • Goodwins Leslie • USA
YOUNG EAGLE, THE • Homoki-Nagy Istvan • DOC • HNG
YOUNG EAGLES • 1930 • Wellman William A. • USA
YOUNG EAGLES • 1934 • Bennet Spencer Gordon • SRL • USA
YOUNG EAGLES OF THE KAMIKAZE, THE see **AA YOKAREN** • 1968
YOUNG EINSTEIN • 1986 • Serious Yahoo • ASL
YOUNG EMMANUELLE, A see **NEA** • 1976
YOUNG EROTIC FANNY HILL, THE • 1970 • Sarno Joe • USA • YOUNG AND EROTIC FANNY HILL, THE
YOUNG EVE AND OLD ADAM • 1920 • *Union Photoplays* • UKN
YOUNG FARMERS • 1942 • Eldridge John • DCS • UKN
YOUNG FIGURE see **WAKAI SUGATA** • 1943
YOUNG FRANKENSTEIN • 1974 • Brooks Mel • USA
YOUNG FROG LOOKS FOR HIS FATHER • 1964 • Kochyanov R. • ANS • USS
YOUNG FROLICS see **SINGITHI SURATHAL** • 1968
YOUNG FUGITIVES • 1938 • Rawlins John • USA • AFRAID TO TALK
YOUNG FURY • 1965 • Nyby Christian • USA

YOUNG FURY see **FUUNJI ODA NOBUNAGA** • 1959
YOUNG GENERATION see **WAKAI HITO** • 1952
YOUNG GIANTS • 1983 • Tannen Terrell • USA • MINOR MIRACLE, A
YOUNG GIRL, THE see **DIANKHA-BI** • 1968
YOUNG GIRL AT THE UNIVERSITY see **DAIGAKU NO ONEICHAN** • 1959
YOUNG GIRL DARES TO PASS see **ONEICHAN MAKARI TORU** • 1959
YOUNG GIRLS BEWARE (USA) see **MEFIEZ-VOUS, FILLETTES** • 1957
YOUNG GIRL'S BODY, THE see **CORPO DELLA RAGASSA, IL** • 1979
YOUNG GIRLS OF GOOD FAMILIES see **SAINTES NITOUCHES, LES** • 1962
YOUNG GIRLS OF OKINAWA, THE see **HIMEYURI NO TO** • 1953
YOUNG GIRLS OF ROCHEFORT, THE see **DEMOISELLES DE ROCHEFORT, LES** • 1966
YOUNG GIRLS OF WILKO, THE (UKN) see **PANNY Z WILKO** • 1979
YOUNG GIRL'S TEN RULES, A see **SHAO NU SHIH CHIEH** • 1977
YOUNG GO WILD, THE (USA) see **VERBRECHEN NACH SCHULSCHLUSS** • 1959
YOUNG GOODMAN BROWN • 1972 • Fox Donald • SHT • USA
YOUNG GRADUATES, THE • 1971 • Anderson Robert** • USA
YOUNG GUARD, THE see **MOLODAYA GVARDIYA** • 1948
YOUNG GUNS 2 • 1990 • Murphy Geoff • USA
YOUNG GUNS, THE • 1956 • Band Albert • USA
YOUNG GUNS, THE • 1988 • Cain Christopher • USA
YOUNG GUNS OF TEXAS • 1962 • Dexter Maury • USA
YOUNG GUY GRADUATES (USA) see **FURESSHUMAN WAKADAISHO** • 1969
YOUNG GUY IN RIO see **RIO NO WAKADAISHO** • 1968
YOUNG GUY ON MT. COOK (USA) see **NYUJIRANDO NO WAKADAISHO** • 1969
YOUNG HANNAH, QUEEN OF THE VAMPIRES see **CRYPT OF THE LIVING DEAD** • 1973
YOUNG HARRY HOUDINI • 1987 • Orr James • TVM • USA
YOUNG HAVE NO MORALS, THE see **DRAGUEURS, LES** • 1959
YOUNG HAVE NO TIME, THE see **UNG LEG** • 1956
YOUNG HEARTS • 1952 • Kubasek Vaclav • CZC
YOUNG HEARTS see **UNGA HJARTAN** • 1934
YOUNG HEARTS see **JONGE HARTEN** • 1936
YOUNG HEARTS AND OLD • 1913 • *Patheplay* • USA
YOUNG HELLIONS see **HIGH SCHOOL CONFIDENTIAL** • 1958
YOUNG HERO • 1982 • Lo Chia Po • HKG
YOUNG HOLLYWOOD • 1927 • Thornby Robert T. • USA
YOUNG HOUSEWIFE • Reeve Leonard • DOC • UKN
YOUNG HUSBANDS (USA) see **GIOVANI MARITI** • 1958
YOUNG IDEAS • 1924 • Hill Robert F. • USA • RELATIVITY
YOUNG IDEAS • 1943 • Dassin Jules • USA
YOUNG IN HEART, THE • 1938 • Wallace Richard • USA
YOUNG INVADERS, THE (UKN) see **DARBY'S RANGERS** • 1958
YOUNG IRONSIDES • 1932 • Parrott James • SHT • USA
YOUNG JACOBITES, THE • 1960 • Reeve John • SRL • UKN
YOUNG JESSE JAMES • 1960 • Claxton William F. • USA
YOUNG JOE, THE FORGOTTEN KENNEDY • 1977 • Heffron Richard T. • TVM • USA
YOUNG KILLERS see **HIGH SCHOOL CONFIDENTIAL** • 1958
YOUNG LADIES' DORMITORY, THE • 1905 • Collins Alf? • UKN
YOUNG LADIES OF WILKO, THE see **PANNY Z WILKO** • 1979
YOUNG LADY AND THE CELLIST, THE see **DEMOISELLE ET LE VIOLONCELLISTE, LA** • 1964
YOUNG LADY AS PRESIDENT, A see **OJOSAN SHACHO** • 1954
YOUNG LADY CHATTERLEY • 1977 • Roberts Alan • USA
YOUNG LADY CHATTERLEY II • 1984 • Roberts Alan • USA • PRIVATE PROPERTY
YOUNG LADY FROM THE RIVER BANK, THE see **SLECNA OD VODY** • 1959
YOUNG LADY FROM THE RIVERSIDE, THE see **SLECNA OD VODY** • 1959
YOUNG LADY OF BJORNEBORG, THE see **FROKEN PA BJORNEBORG** • 1922
YOUNG LADY ON HER WAY, A see **OJOSAN TOTO** • 1956
YOUNG LAND, THE • 1959 • Tetzlaff Ted • USA
YOUNG LAWYERS, THE • 1969 • Hart Harvey • TVM • USA
YOUNG LIONS, THE • 1958 • Dmytryk Edward • USA
YOUNG LIONS, THE see **GENC ASLANLAR** • 1967
YOUNG LIPS see **LABBRA ROSSE** • 1960
YOUNG LOCHINVAR • 1911 • *Thanhouser* • USA
YOUNG LOCHINVAR • 1923 • Kellino W. P. • UKN
YOUNG LORD see **BONCHI** • 1960
YOUNG LORD, THE (USA) see **JUNGE LORD, DER** • 1965
YOUNG LORD STANLEY • 1910 • *Thanhouser* • USA
YOUNG LOVE • 1915 • Santschi Thomas • USA
YOUNG LOVE • 1964 • Kobakhidze Mikhail • SHT • USS
YOUNG LOVE see **LIEBELEI** • 1933
YOUNG LOVE see **REKA** • 1933
YOUNG LOVE see **HISTOIRE D'AMOUR, UNE** • 1951
YOUNG LOVE, FIRST LOVE • 1979 • Stern Steven Hilliard • TVM • USA
YOUNG LOVE: LEMON POPSICLE 7 • 1987 • Bennert Walter • ISR
YOUNG LOVER, THE • 1980 • Santipracha Somdej • THL
YOUNG LOVER, THE see **NOZ W WODZIE** • 1961
YOUNG LOVERS see **WAKAI KOIBITOTACHI** • 1959
YOUNG LOVERS, THE • 1949 • Lupino Ida • USA
YOUNG LOVERS, THE • 1954 • Asquith Anthony • UKN • CHANCE MEETING (USA)
YOUNG LOVERS, THE • 1964 • Goldwyn Samuel Jr. • USA • CHANCE MEETING
YOUNG LUST • 1982 • Weis Gary • USA
YOUNG MAGICIAN, THE see **JEUNE MAGICIEN, LE** • 1987
YOUNG MAN AND MOBY DICK, THE see **MLADY MUZ A BILA VELRYBA** • 1978
YOUNG MAN AND THE LION, THE see **JEUNE HOMME ET LE LION, LE** • 1976
YOUNG MAN AND THE WHITE WHALE, THE see **MLADY MUZ A BILA VELRYBA** • 1978
YOUNG MAN NAMED ENGELS, A • 1970 • Georgi Katja, Georgi Klaus, Kurtchevsky Vadim, Hitruck Fedor • ANM • GDR, USS
YOUNG MAN OF MANHATTAN • 1930 • Bell Monta • USA
YOUNG MAN OF MUSIC (UKN) see **YOUNG MAN WITH A HORN** • 1950
YOUNG MAN SEEKS COMPANY see **UNG MAN SOKER SALLSKAP** • 1954
YOUNG MAN WHO FIGGERED, THE • 1915 • Beggs Lee • USA
YOUNG MAN WITH A GUN see **SHASATSU-MA** • 1970
YOUNG MAN WITH A HORN • 1950 • Curtiz Michael • USA • YOUNG MAN OF MUSIC (UKN)
YOUNG MAN WITH IDEAS • 1952 • Leisen Mitchell • USA
YOUNG MANHOOD OF MR. MAGOO, THE see **MAGOO'S YOUNG MANHOOD** • 1958
YOUNG MAN'S BRIDE, THE • 1968 • Gunter George • USA
YOUNG MAN'S FANCY • 1939 • Stevenson Robert • UKN
YOUNG MAN'S FANCY see **YOU'RE A SWEETHEART** • 1937
YOUNG MAN'S FANCY, A • 1920 • St. Clair Malcolm • SHT • USA
YOUNG MASTER, THE see **SHIH-TI CH'U-MA** • 1980
YOUNG MEN, THE see **MUGE** • 1966
YOUNG MILLIONAIRE, THE • 1912 • *Joyce Alice* • USA
YOUNG MISS see **OJOSAN** • 1930
YOUNG MISS see **OJOSAN** • 1937
YOUNG MR. JAZZ • 1919 • Roach Hal • SHT • USA
YOUNG MR. LINCOLN • 1939 • Ford John • USA
YOUNG MR. PITT, THE • 1942 • Reed Carol • UKN
YOUNG MONK, THE see **JUNGE MONCH, DER** • 1978
YOUNG MOTHER HUBBARD • 1917 • Berthelet Arthur • USA
YOUNG MRS. EAMES, THE • 1913 • Grandon Francis J. • USA
YOUNG MRS. ETON • 1912 • *Beaudet Louise* • USA
YOUNG MRS. WINTHROP • 1915 • Ridgely Richard • USA
YOUNG MRS. WINTHROP • 1920 • Edwards Walter • USA
YOUNG NICK AT THE PICNIC • 1915 • Collins Edwin J.? • UKN
YOUNG NOBLEMAN, THE (USA) see **UNGA GREVEN TAR FLICKAN OCH PRISET** • 1924
YOUNG NOWHERES • 1929 • Lloyd Frank • USA
YOUNG NOWHERES see **SOME DAY** • 1935
YOUNG NURSES, THE • 1973 • Kimbro Clinton • USA • SECRETS OF YOUNG NURSES ○ GAMES THAT NURSES PLAY
YOUNG NURSES IN LOVE • 1987 • Vincent Chuck • USA
YOUNG OFFENDERS • 1984 • Nicolle Douglas • DOC • CND
YOUNG OLDFIELD • 1924 • McCarey Leo • SHT • USA
YOUNG ONE, THE • 1960 • Bunuel Luis • MXC • ISLAND OF SHAME (UKN) ○ JOVEN, LA ○ JEUNE FILLE, LA
YOUNG ONES, THE • 1961 • Furie Sidney J. • UKN • WONDERFUL TO BE YOUNG! (USA)
YOUNG ONES, THE see **WAKAMONO TACHI** • 1967
YOUNG ONIONS • 1932 • *Sennett Mack (P)* • SHT • USA
YOUNG PAINTER, THE • 1922 • Blache Herbert • SHT • USA
YOUNG PATRIOT, THE • 1917 • Chaudet Louis W. • SHT • USA
YOUNG PAUL BARONI (UKN) see **KID MONK BARONI** • 1952
YOUNG PEOPLE • 1940 • Dwan Allan • USA
YOUNG PEOPLE see **WAKAI HITO** • 1937
YOUNG PEOPLE see **WAKAI HITO** • 1952
YOUNG PEOPLE see **WAKAI HITOTACHI** • 1954
YOUNG PEOPLE see **MOLODYYE** • 1972
YOUNG PEOPLE FROM BRZOZA see **MLODZI Z BRZOZY** • 1970
YOUNG PEOPLE, REMEMBER see **EMLEKEZZ, IFJUSAGI** • 1955
YOUNG PERSON IN PINK, THE see **GIRL WHO FORGOT, THE** • 1939
YOUNG PHILADELPHIANS, THE • 1958 • Sherman Vincent • USA • CITY JUNGLE, THE (UKN)
YOUNG PHILANTHROPIST, THE • 1914 • *Imp* • USA
YOUNG PHOTOGRAPHER, THE • 1905 • *Cricks & Sharp* • UKN
YOUNG PIMPLE AND HIS LITTLE SISTER • 1914 • Evans Fred, Evans Joe • UKN
YOUNG PIMPLE'S FROLIC • 1914 • Evans Fred, Evans Joe • UKN
YOUNG PIONEER • 1976 • O'Herlihy Michael • TVM • USA
YOUNG PIONEERS' CHRISTMAS • 1976 • O'Herlihy Michael • TVM • USA
YOUNG PUSHKIN • 1937 • Naroditski Arkadi • USS
YOUNG RACERS, THE • 1963 • Corman Roger • USA
YOUNG RAJAH, THE • 1922 • Rosen Phil • USA
YOUNG REBEL, THE see **JOVEN REBELDE, EL** • 1961
YOUNG REBEL, THE (USA) see **AVVENTURE E GLI AMORI DI MIGUEL CERVANTES, LE** • 1967
YOUNG REBELS, THE see **TEENAGE DOLL** • 1957
YOUNG REBELS OF SHINJUKU see **SHINJUKU SODACHI** • 1968
YOUNG REDSKINS, THE • 1909 • Aylott Dave • UKN
YOUNG RIVALS, THE • 1897 • *Paul R. W.* • UKN
YOUNG ROBINSON CRUSOE • 1987 • Irving David • USA
YOUNG ROMANCE • 1915 • Melford George • USA
YOUNG RUNAWAYS, THE • 1968 • Dreifuss Arthur • USA
YOUNG SAMARITAN, THE • 1914 • *Searchlight* • UKN
YOUNG SAMOYED, THE • 1929 • Brumberg Valentina, Brumberg Zinaida • ANS • USS
YOUNG SAMURAI, THE see **SAMURAI NO KO** • 1963
YOUNG SANCHEZ • 1963 • Camus Mario • SPN
YOUNG SAVAGES, THE • 1961 • Frankenheimer John • USA • MATTER OF CONVICTION, A
YOUNG SCAMPS • 1907 • Fitzhamon Lewin • UKN
YOUNG SCARFACE (UKN) see **BRIGHTON ROCK** • 1947
YOUNG SEDUCERS, THE see **STEWARDESSEN, DIE** • 1972
YOUNG SHERLOCK HOLMES • 1985 • Levinson Barry • UKN • YOUNG SHERLOCK HOLMES AND THE PYRAMID OF FEAR
YOUNG SHERLOCK HOLMES AND THE PYRAMID OF FEAR see **YOUNG SHERLOCK HOLMES** • 1985
YOUNG SHERLOCKS • 1922 • McGowan Robert, McNamara Tom • SHT • USA
YOUNG SINNER, THE • 1965 • Laughlin Tom • USA • LIKE FATHER, LIKE SON ○ AMONG THE THORNS ○ CHRISTOPHER WOTAN
YOUNG SINNERS • 1931 • Blystone John G. • USA
YOUNG SINNERS (UKN) see **HIGH SCHOOL BIG SHOT** • 1959
YOUNG SLEUTHS, THE • 1916 • *Butterworth Frank* • SHT • USA
YOUNG SOCIAL WORKER SPEAKS HER MIND, A • 1969 • Macartney-Filgate Terence • DOC • CND
YOUNG SOUL REBELS • 1990 • Julien Isaac • UKN
YOUNG SPRING see **JUNGER FRUHLING** • 1986
YOUNG SQUAW'S BRAVERY, A • 1911 • *Little Anna* • USA
YOUNG STIMULUS see **WAKAI SHIGEKI** • 1967
YOUNG STRANGER, THE • 1957 • Frankenheimer John • USA
YOUNG SUMMER see **UNG SOMMAR** • 1954
YOUNG SWALLOWS SPREAD THEIR WINGS • 1964 • CHN
YOUNG SWINGERS, THE • 1964 • Dexter Maury • USA
YOUNG SWINGERS, THE see **EXOTIC DREAMS OF CASANOVA, THE** • 1971
YOUNG SWORDSMAN see **HIKEN** • 1963
YOUNG, THE EVIL AND THE SAVAGE, THE (USA) see **NUDE.. SI MUORE** • 1968
YOUNG TIGERS, THE see **GIOVANI TIGRI, I** • 1968
YOUNG TOM EDISON • 1940 • Taurog Norman • USA
YOUNG TORLESS (USA) see **JUNGE TORLESS, DER** • 1966
YOUNG TOSCANINI see **GIOVANE TOSCANINI, IL** • 1988
YOUNG VETERAN • 1941 • Cavalcanti Alberto • DCS • UKN
YOUNG VIRGIN, THE see **HAKOIRI MUSUME** • 1935
YOUNG VISITORS, THE • 1984 • Hill James • TVM • UKN
YOUNG WARRIORS, THE • 1967 • Peyser John • USA • BEARDLESS WARRIORS, THE
YOUNG WARRIORS, THE • 1983 • Foldes Lawrence D. • USA
YOUNG WHIRLWIND, THE • 1928 • King Louis • USA
YOUNG WHITE COLLAR: LET'S RUN see **BOCCHAN SHAIN SEISHUN DE TSUPPASHIRE!** • 1967
YOUNG WIDOW • 1946 • Marin Edwin L. • USA
YOUNG WILD WEST CORNERED BY APACHES • 1912 • *Nestor* • USA
YOUNG WILD WEST LEADING A RAID • 1912 • *Field George* • USA
YOUNG WILD WEST ON THE BORDER • 1912 • *Nestor* • USA
YOUNG WILD WEST TRAPPING A TRICKY RUSTLER • 1912 • *Nestor* • USA
YOUNG WILD WEST WASHING OUT GOLD • 1912 • *Nestor* • USA
YOUNG WILD WEST'S PRAIRIE PURSUIT • 1912 • *Nestor* • USA
YOUNG, WILLING AND EAGER (USA) see **RAG DOLL** • 1961
YOUNG WINSTON • 1972 • Attenborough Richard • UKN
YOUNG WIVES' TALES • 1951 • Cass Henry • UKN
YOUNG WOLVES, THE see **JEUNES LOUPS, LES** • 1968
YOUNG WOODLEY • 1929 • Bentley Thomas • SIL • UKN
YOUNG WOODLEY • 1930 • Bentley Thomas • SND • UKN
YOUNG WORLD, A (USA) see **MONDO NUOVO, UN** • 1965
YOUNG YEARS OF OUR COUNTRY see **MOLODOST NASHEI STRANY** • 1946
YOUNGBLOOD • 1978 • Nosseck Noel • USA
YOUNGBLOOD • 1985 • Markle Peter • USA
YOUNGBLOOD HAWKE • 1964 • Daves Delmer • USA
YOUNGER BROTHER see **OTOTO** • 1960
YOUNGER BROTHER, THE • 1911 • *Vitagraph* • USA
YOUNGER BROTHER, THE • 1911 • Merwin Bannister • *Edison* • USA
YOUNGER BROTHERS, THE • 1949 • Marin Edwin L. • USA
YOUNGER GENERATION, THE • 1913 • *Hulette Gladys* • USA
YOUNGER GENERATION, THE • 1929 • Capra Frank • USA
YOUNGER SISTER, THE • 1913 • *Victor* • USA
YOUNGER SISTER, THE • 1913 • Trimble Larry • UKN
YOUNGER SISTER AND BROTHER see **THANGA THAMBI** • 1967
YOUNGEST IN THE FAMILY, THE • 1916 • *Rogers Gene* • SHT • USA
YOUNGEST ONE see **KANCHHI** • 1986
YOUNGEST PROFESSION, THE • 1943 • Buzzell Edward • USA
YOUNGEST SPY, THE see **IVANOVO DETSTVO** • 1962
YOUNITA -FROM GUTTER TO FOOTLIGHTS • 1913 • Haldane Bert? • UKN
YOUNOST PELIA • 1980 • Gerasimov Sergei • USS
YOUR ACQUAINTANCE see **VASHA ZNAKOMAYA** • 1927
YOUR ADDRESS • 1973 • Khrinyuk Yevgyeni • USS
YOUR AUTOMATIC CHOICE • 1958 • Mason Bill • UKN
YOUR BABY AND MINE • 1915 • Mackley Arthur • USA
YOUR BEER see **ANATA NO BIRU** • 1954
YOUR BEST FRIEND • 1922 • Nigh William • USA
YOUR BODY BELONGS TO ME (USA) see **DU GEHORST MIR** • 1959
YOUR BOY AND MINE • 1917 • Clements Roy • SHT • USA
YOUR CHEATIN' HEART • 1964 • Nelson Gene • USA • YOUR CHEATIN' HEART (THE HANK WILLIAMS STORY)
YOUR CHEATIN' HEART (THE HANK WILLIAMS STORY) see **YOUR CHEATIN' HEART** • 1964
YOUR CHILDREN'S SLEEP • Massy Jane • DOC • UKN
YOUR CHILDREN'S TEETH • Massy Jane • DOC • UKN
YOUR CONTEMPORARY see **TVOI SOVREMENNIK** • 1967
YOUR COUNTRY NEEDS YOU • 1914 • Haldane Bert? • UKN
YOUR DAUGHTER -AND MINE • 1920 • *Pauncefort George* • USA
YOUR DAY WILL COME see **LAKA YOM YA ZALEM** • 1951
YOUR DESTINY see **DEIN SCHICKSAL** • 1928
YOUR DOG ATE MY LUNCH MUM! • 1908 • Booth W. R.? • UKN
YOUR EXCELLENCY see **YEVO PREVOSHODITIELSTVO** • 1927
YOUR FRIEND AND MINE • 1923 • Badger Clarence • USA
YOUR GIRL AND MINE • 1914 • Warren Giles R. • USA
YOUR GOOD NAME see **TRIFLING WITH HONOR** • 1923
YOUR HAIR AND SCALP • 1963 • Woodward Ken • UKN
YOUR HALF AND MY HALF • 1915 • *Royal* • USA
YOUR HIGHNESS see **KAKKA** • 1940
YOUR HUSBAND'S PAST • 1926 • Roach Hal • SHT • USA
YOUR KIDS FROM THE STATES see **DINE BORN FRA AMERIKA** • 1969
YOUR LAST ACT • 1941 • Zinnemann Fred • SHT • USA
YOUR LIFE IS IN THEIR HANDS see **V TVOIKH RUKAH ZHIZN** • 1959
YOUR LIPS 3 • 1971 • Le Grice Malcolm • UKN
YOUR LIPS NO.1 • 1970 • Le Grice Malcolm • UKN
YOUR MONEY OR YOUR LIFE see **PENIZE NEBO ZIVOT** • 1932
YOUR MONEY OR YOUR LIFE see **PENGENE ELLER LIVET** • 1982
YOUR MONEY OR YOUR LIFE (UKN) see **BOURSE ET LA VIE, LA** • 1965

YOUR MONEY OR YOUR WIFE • 1960 • Simmons Anthony • UKN
YOUR MONEY OR YOUR WIFE • 1972 • Reisner Allen • TVM • USA
YOUR MOST HUMBLE AND OBEDIENT SERVANT • 1969 • Sykes Jeremy • DOC • NZL
YOUR MOVE • 1973 • Parker Gudrun • CND
YOUR NAME BROWN? • 1914 • Finn Arthur • UKN
YOUR NAME, MY NAME see **TERA NAAM, MERA NAAM** • 1987
YOUR NEIGHBOUR'S SON see **DIN NABOS SON** • 1981
YOUR OBEDIENT SERVANT • 1917 • Griffith Edward H. • USA
YOUR ONLY FRIEND • 1915 • *Ramona* • USA
YOUR ONLY YOUNG TWICE see **HAPPY YEARS, THE** • 1950
YOUR OPINION PLEASE see **UW MENING GRAAG** • 1989
YOUR OWN BACK YARD • 1925 • Roach Hal • SHT • USA
YOUR OWN BLOOD see **RODNAYA KROV** • 1964
YOUR OWN HANDS • 1956 • Voitetsky V. • USS
YOUR OWN LAND see **DIN TILLVAROS LAND** • 1940
YOUR PAST IS SHOWING (USA) see **NAKED TRUTH, THE** • 1957
YOUR PAW, FRIEND! see **DAY LAPU, DRUG!** • 1967
YOUR PLACE OR MINE • 1982 • Day Robert • TVM • USA
YOUR PORTRAIT • van Zuylen Erik • NTH
YOUR RED WAGON see **THEY LIVE BY NIGHT** • 1948
YOUR RELATIVES ARE BEST see **SLAKTEN AR BAST** • 1944
YOUR RELATIVES ARE WORST see **SLAKTEN AR VARST** • 1936
YOUR SHADOW IS MINE (USA) see **TON OMBRE EST LA MIENNE** • 1962
YOUR SINS COUNT see **LICZE NA WASZE GRZECHY** • 1963
YOUR SMILING FACE see **HUAN YEN** • 1979
YOUR SON AND BROTHER see **VASH SYN I BRAT** • 1966
YOUR SUPER AGENT see **VOSTRO SUPER AGENTE FLIT, IL** • 1966
YOUR TECHNOCRACY AND MINE • 1933 • *Benchley Robert* • SHT • USA • YOUR TECHNOLOGY AND MINE
YOUR TECHNOLOGY AND MINE see **YOUR TECHNOCRACY AND MINE** • 1933
YOUR TERM HAS COME, BABY see **ECELIN GELDI YAVRUM** • 1967
YOUR THREE MINUTES ARE UP • 1973 • Schwartz Douglas • USA
YOUR TICKET IS NO LONGER VALID • 1980 • Kaczender George • CND, FRN • FINISHING TOUCH ○ SLOW DESCENT INTO HELL, A ○ AU-DELA DE CETTE LIMITE VOTRE TICKET N'EST PLUS VALABLE
YOUR TIME ON EARTH see **DIN STUND PA JORDEN** • 1972
YOUR TURN, DARLING (USA) see **A TOI DE FAIRE, MIGNONNE** • 1963
YOUR TURN, MY TURN (USA) see **VA VOIR MAMAN.. PAPA TRAVAILLE** • 1978
YOUR UNCLE DUDLEY • 1935 • Tinling James, Forde Eugene J. • USA
YOUR VERY GOOD HEALTH see **CHARLEY IN "YOUR VERY GOOD HEALTH"** • 1946-47
YOUR WIFE AND MINE • 1919 • *Dorrington Eve* • USA
YOUR WIFE AND MINE • 1927 • O'Connor Frank • USA
YOUR WIFE -THE UNKNOWN CREATURE see **OSWALT KOLLE: DEINE FRAU, DAS UNBEKANNTE WESEN** • 1969
YOUR WITNESS • 1950 • Montgomery Robert • UKN • EYE WITNESS (USA)
YOU'RE A BIG BOY NOW • 1966 • Coppola Francis Ford • USA
YOU'RE A LUCKY FELLOW, MR. SMITH • 1943 • Feist Felix E. • USA
YOU'RE A SAP, MR. JAP • 1942 • Gordon Dan • ANS • USA
YOU'RE A SWEETHEART • 1937 • Butler David • USA • BROADWAY JAMBOREE ○ YOUNG MAN'S FANCY
YOU'RE AN EDUCATION • 1938 • Tashlin Frank • ANS • USA
YOU'RE DARN TOOTIN' • 1928 • Kennedy Edgar • SHT • USA • MUSIC BLASTERS, THE
YOU'RE DRIVING ME CRAZY • 1931 • Fleischer Dave • ANS • USA
YOU'RE DRIVING ME CRAZY! • 1978 • Grant David • UKN
YOU'RE FIRED • 1919 • Cruze James • USA
YOU'RE FIRED • 1925 • *Bailey Bill* • USA
YOU'RE FOR ME see **IF I'M LUCKY** • 1946
YOU'RE HUMAN LIKE THE REST OF US • 1967 • Johnson B. S. • UKN
YOU'RE IN THE ARMY NOW • 1941 • Seiler Lewis • USA
YOU'RE IN THE ARMY NOW (USA) see **O.H.M.S.** • 1937
YOU'RE IN THE MOVIES • 1985 • Nofal Emil • SAF
YOU'RE IN THE NAVY NOW • 1951 • Hathaway Henry • USA • U.S.S. TEAKETTLE
YOU'RE LYING see **NI LJUGER** • 1969
YOU'RE MINE, I'M YOURS see **IKAW AY AKIN, AKO AY SA IYO** • 1968
YOU'RE MY DREAM see **PANGARAP KO'Y IKAW, ANG** • 1967
YOU'RE MY EVERYTHING • 1949 • Lang Walter • USA
YOU'RE NEVER TOO YOUNG • 1955 • Taurog Norman • USA
YOU'RE NEXT • 1916 • Van Wally • SHT • USA
YOU'RE NEXT • 1919 • Perez Marcel • USA
YOU'RE NEXT • 1921 • Roach Hal • SHT • USA
YOU'RE NO GOOD • 1966 • Kaczender George • SHT • CND
YOU'RE NOBODY TILL SOMEBODY LOVES YOU • 1969 • Pennebaker D. A. • USA • TIMOTHY LEARY'S WEDDING
YOU'RE NOT ALONE • 1986 • De Simone Franco • DOC • CND
YOU'RE NOT ALONE see **DU ER IKKE ALENE** • 1978
YOU'RE NOT BUILT THAT WAY • 1936 • Fleischer Dave • ANS • USA
YOU'RE NOT SO TOUGH • 1940 • May Joe • USA
YOU'RE NUDE see **MEZTELEN VAGY** • 1972
YOU'RE O.K. CHAP see **OKEY KA CHOY** • 1967
YOU'RE ONLY YOUNG ONCE • 1938 • Seitz George B. • USA
YOU'RE ONLY YOUNG TWICE! • 1952 • Bishop Terry • UKN
YOU'RE OUT OF LUCK • 1941 • Bretherton Howard • USA
YOU'RE PINCHED • 1920 • Roach Hal • SHT • USA
YOU'RE PUTTING ME ON • 1969 • Klugman Don B. • USA
YOU'RE TELLING ME • 1932 • Mack Anthony, French Lloyd • SHT • USA
YOU'RE TELLING ME • 1934 • Kenton Erle C. • USA
YOU'RE TELLING ME • 1941 • Peake Bladon • UKN
YOU'RE TELLING ME • 1941 • Rotha Paul • DOC • UKN
YOU'RE TELLING ME • 1942 • Lamont Charles • USA • TEMPORARILY YOURS
YOU'RE THE DOCTOR • 1938 • Lockwood Roy • UKN
YOU'RE THE ONE • 1941 • Murphy Ralph • USA
YOU'RE THE ONE • 1979 • Bell John • SHT • ASL
YOU'RE TOO CARELESS WITH YOUR KISSES • 1933 • Ising Rudolf • ANS • USA
YOU'RE UNDER ARREST • 1979 • Arioli Don, Koenig Wolf • ANS • CND
YOU'RE WANTED ON THE PHONE, SIR • 1914 • Kellino W. P. • UKN
YOURS FOR THE ASKING • 1936 • Hall Alexander • USA
YOURS, HERS see **TEU, TUA** • 1981
YOURS, MINE AND OURS • 1968 • Shavelson Melville • USA • HIS, HERS AND THEIRS
YOURS TO COMMAND • 1927 • Kirkland David • USA
YOURS TRULY • 1943 • Roush Leslie • SHT • USA
YOUTH • 1915 • Handworth Harry • USA
YOUTH • 1917 • Fielding Romaine • USA
YOUTH • 1935 • Lukov Leonid • USS
YOUTH • 1977 • Xie Jin • CHN
YOUTH see **SEISHUN** • 1925
YOUTH see **SHONEN-KI** • 1951
YOUTH see **MLADI** • 1960
YOUTH see **SEISHUN** • 1968
YOUTH see **JEUNESSE, UNE** • 1983
YOUTH AFLAME • 1945 • Clifton Elmer • USA
YOUTH AND ADVENTURE • 1925 • Horne James W. • USA
YOUTH AND ART • 1914 • Ricketts Thomas • USA
YOUTH AND HIS AMULET, THE (USA) see **GEN TO FUDO MYOO** • 1962
YOUTH AND JAZZ • 1962 • Royem Ulf Balle • NRW
YOUTH AND JEALOUSY • 1913 • Dwan Allan • USA
YOUTH AND TENDERNESS see **JUVENTUDE E TERNURA** • 1968
YOUTH ASTRAY • 1928 • Ostermayr Peter • FRG
YOUTH BELONGS TO US! see **BOCCHAN SHAIN: SEISHUN WA ORE NO MONODA** • 1967
YOUTH CLUB, THE see **KLUBBEN** • 1978
YOUTH CONQUERORS, THE • 1929 • Gelovani Mikhail • USS
YOUTH COVERED WITH MUD see **DORODARAKE NO SEISHUN** • 1954
YOUTH ENDURING CHARM • 1916 • Kirkwood James • USA
YOUTH FOCUS ON THEIR CITY • 1978 • Darino Eduardo • URG
YOUTH FOR SALE • 1924 • Cabanne W. Christy • USA • YOUTH TO SELL
YOUTH GETS A BREAK • 1941 • Losey Joseph • SHT • USA
YOUTH IN CHAINS see **UNGDOM I BOJOR** • 1942
YOUTH IN DANGER see **UNGDOM I FARA** • 1947
YOUTH IN FURY see **KAWAITA MIZUUMI** • 1960
YOUTH IN LOVE see **INNAMORATI, GLI** • 1955
YOUTH IN POLAND see **YOUTH OF POLAND, THE** • 1957
YOUTH IN REVOLT (USA) see **ALTITUDE 3200** • 1938
YOUTH IN SEARCH OF MORALITY • 1966 • Fox Beryl • DOC • CND
YOUTH IS AT WORK • 1946 • Stiglic France • YGS
YOUTH IS TOMORROW • 1939 • Legg Stuart • DCS • CND
YOUTH KILLER, THE see **SEISHUN NO SATSUJIN-SHA** • 1976
YOUTH MARCH (USA) see **GIOVINEZZA GIOVINEZZA** • 1969
YOUTH MARCHES ON • 1938 • Parfitt Eric, Fraser George • UKN
YOUTH MUST HAVE LOVE • 1922 • Franz Joseph J. • USA • UNEXPECTED WIFE, AN
YOUTH OF ATHENS • 1949 • Batapoulos Takis • GRC
YOUTH OF CHOPIN, THE see **MLODOSC CHOPINA** • 1952
YOUTH OF FORTUNE, A • 1916 • Turner Otis • USA
YOUTH OF HEIJI ZENIGATA, THE see **SEISHUN ZENIGATA HEIJI** • 1953
YOUTH OF JAPAN, THE see **NIHON NO SEISHUN** • 1968
YOUTH OF MAXIM, THE see **YUNOST MAKSIMA** • 1935
YOUTH OF OUR COUNTRY, THE see **MOLODOST NASHEI STRANY** • 1946
YOUTH OF OUR FATHERS see **YUNOST NASHIKH OTSOV** • 1958
YOUTH OF POLAND, THE • 1957 • Maysles Albert, Maysles David • DOC • USA • YOUTH IN POLAND
YOUTH OF RUSSIA, THE • 1934 • Lynn Henry
YOUTH OF SHIP • NKR
YOUTH OF "THE LAND OF ANGELS", THE see **ANGYALFOLDI FIATOLOK** • 1955
YOUTH OF THE WORLD, THE see **IUNOST' MIRA** • 1949
YOUTH OF TODAY see **UNGDOM AV I DAG** • 1935
YOUTH OF TODAY (USA) see **JUGEND VON HEUTE** • 1938
YOUTH ON PARADE • 1942 • Rogell Albert S. • USA
YOUTH ON PAROLE • 1937 • Rosen Phil • USA • TROUBLE FOR TWO
YOUTH ON TRIAL • 1945 • Boetticher Budd • USA • WANDERING DAUGHTERS
YOUTH PRESIDENT see **SEISHUN DAITORYO** • 1966
YOUTH REGAINED • 1906 • Cooper Arthur • UKN
YOUTH RUNS WILD • 1944 • Robson Mark • USA • ARE THESE OUR CHILDREN?
YOUTH SPEAKS see **KOMSOMOL** • 1932
YOUTH TAKES A FLING • 1938 • Mayo Archie • USA
YOUTH TAKES A HAND (UKN) see **BEHIND PRISON WALLS** • 1943
YOUTH TO SELL see **YOUTH FOR SALE** • 1924
YOUTH TO YOUTH • 1922 • Chautard Emile • USA
YOUTH TO YOUTH see **PRASTANKAN** • 1920
YOUTH TRAVEL • 1965 • Kelly Ron • CND
YOUTH TRIUMPHANT see **ENEMIES OF CHILDREN** • 1923
YOUTH (USA) see **JUGEND** • 1938
YOUTH WILL BE SERVED • 1940 • Brower Otto • USA
YOUTH WITH A VIOLIN, THE • 1982 • Czurko Edward • SHT • CND
YOUTH WITHOUT AGE see **TINERETE FARA BATRINETE** • 1968
YOUTH WITHOUT DOCUMENTS see **KIROKUNAKI SEISHUN** • 1967
YOUTH WITHOUT OLD AGE see **TINERETE FARA BATRINETE** • 1968
YOUTHFUL AFFAIR, A • 1918 • Drew Sidney, Drew Sidney Mrs. • SHT • USA
YOUTHFUL CHEATERS • 1923 • Tuttle Frank • USA
YOUTHFUL FOLLY • 1920 • Crosland Alan • USA • SOCIETY PEOPLE
YOUTHFUL FOLLY • 1934 • Mander Miles • UKN
YOUTHFUL HACKENSCHMIDTS • 1907 • *Urban Trading Co* • UKN
YOUTHFUL HERO, A • 1909 • Coleby A. E. • UKN
YOUTHFUL KNIGHT, A • 1913 • Edwin Walter, Merwin Bannister • USA
YOUTHFUL SINNERS see **TRICHEURS, LES** • 1958
YOUTHFUL TARO see **SEISHUN TARO** • 1967
YOUTHFUL YEARS see **MLADA LETA** • 1952
YOUTHQUAKE • 1977 • Miller Max B. • DOC • USA
YOUTHS, THE see **JOVENES, LOS** • 1960
YOUTH'S DESIRE • 1920 • *Bennett Joseph* • USA
YOUTH'S ENDEARING CHARM • 1916 • Dowlan William C. • USA
YOUTH'S GAMBLE • 1925 • Rogell Albert S. • USA
YOUTH'S GHOST STORY, THE see **SEISHUN KAIDAN** • 1955
YOUTH'S OATH see **KLIATVA MOLODYCH** • 1944
YOU'VE BEEN A PROPHET, MY DEAR see **PROFETA VOLTAL, SZIVEM** • 1968
YOU'VE COME A LONG WAY, KATIE • 1982 • Sarin Vic • CND
YOU'VE COME BACK, YOU'RE STILL HERE! • 1965 • Jacobs Ken • USA
YOU'VE GOT TO BE SMART • 1967 • Kadison Ellison • USA
YOU'VE GOT TO PAY • 1913 • *Balboa* • USA
YOU'VE GOT TO WALK IT LIKE YOU TALK IT OR YOU'LL LOSE THAT BEAT • 1971 • Locke Peter • USA
YOU'VE REALLY GOT ME see **DEVERAS ME ATRAPASTE** • 1983
YOVITA (USA) see **JOWITA** • 1967
YOWAKE NO KUNI see **YOAKE NO KUNI** • 1967
YOYO • 1965 • Etaix Pierre • FRN • YO YO
YPOTRON -FINAL COUNTDOWN (USA) see **AGENTE LOGAN MISSIONE YPOTRON** • 1966
YPOTRON (SPN) see **AGENTE LOGAN MISSIONE YPOTRON** • 1966
YPRES • 1925 • Summers Walter • UKN
YSANI THE PRIESTESS • 1934 • Sherry Gordon • UKN
YSTAVAT, TOVERIT • 1989 • Mollberg Rauni • FNL • FRIENDS, COMRADES
YU-HUO FEN CH'IN • 1980 • Liu Ch'Eng-Han • HKG • HOUSE OF THE LUTE
YU-LING • 1977 • Li Han-Hsiang • HKG • SPIRIT, THE
YU-MA TS'AI-TZU • 1983 • Wan Jen • TWN • AH FEI
YU MEI-JEN • *Ling-Po Ivy* • TWN • BEAUTIFUL CARP SPIRIT, THE (USA)
YU NI MAO NI • 1980 • Liang Puzhi • HKG • NO BIG DEAL
YUAI KEKKON • 1930 • Toyoda Shiro • JPN • FRIENDSHIP MARRIAGE
YUAN • 1980 • Ch'En Yao-Ch'I • HKG • PIONEERS, THE
YUAN-HSIANG JEN • 1980 • Li Hsing • HKG • MY NATIVE LAND
YUAN NU • 1988 • Tan Han-Chang • TWN • ROUGE OF THE NORTH
YUAN WANG AI TA JEN! • 1976 • Chen Chi Hua • HKG • INJUSTICE! MY LORD! ○ KUAN-JEN! WO YAO.. ○ I WANT MORE ○ CONFESSIONS OF A CONCUBINE ○ STORY OF SUSAN
YUAN-YUEH WAN-TAO • 1978 • Ch'U Yuan • HKG • FULL MOON SCIMITAR
YUANGYANF IOU • 1988 • Zheng Dongtian • CHN • YOUNG COUPLES
YUANLIZHANZHENGDE NIANDAI • 1988 • Hu Mei • CHN • FAR FROM WAR
YUBADARAWA • 1964 • Holmes Cecil • DOC • ASL
YUBASININ KIZI • 1968 • Gulyuz Aram • TRK • CAPTAIN'S DAUGHTER, THE
YUBUE • 1967 • Nishikawa Katsumi • JPN • LOST LOVE
YUCATECO HONORIS CAUSA, UN • 1965 • Martinez Arturo • MXC
YUEH-CHAN CHIN TS'UN CHE • 1981 • Chiang Chih-Ming, T'Ung Lu • HKG • WITHOUT A PROMISED LAND
YUEN-CHAU-CHAI CHIH KO • 1977 • Fong Yuk-Ping • HKG • SONG OF YUEN-CHOW-CHAI
YUEYAER • 1988 • Huo Zhuang, Xu Xiaoxing • CHN • CRESCENT MOON
YUGANDA SEX • 1968 • Yamashita Osamu • JPN • DISTORTED SEX
YUGANTHAYO • 1983 • Peries Lester James • SLN • END OF AN ERA
YUGATO • 1953 • Yamamoto Kajiro • JPN
YUGO, EL • 1946 • Urruchua Victor • MXC
YUGURE MADE • 1981 • Kuroki Kazuo • JPN • TILL THE SUN DOWN
YUHI GA NAITEIRU • 1967 • Morinaga Kenjiro • JPN • EVENING SUN IS CRYING, THE
YUHI NI AKAI NO KAO • 1961 • Shinoda Masahiro • JPN • KILLERS ON PARADE ○ MY FACE RED IN THE SUNSET
YUHI NO OKA • 1964 • Matsuo Akinori • JPN • SUNSET HILL
YUI TO HI • 1977 • Gagnon Claude • JPN
YUJO • 1975 • Miyazaki Akira • JPN • FRIENDSHIP
YUKA FROM MONDAY see **GETSUYOBI NO YUKA** • 1964
YUKAI HODO • 1983 • Ito Toshiya • JPN • KIDNAP NEWS
YUKI FUJIN EZU • 1950 • Mizoguchi Kenji • JPN • PICTURE OF MADAME YUKI, THE (USA) ○ PORTRAIT OF MADAME YUKI (UKN) ○ SKETCH OF MADAME YUKI
YUKI MATSURI • 1953 • Hani Susumu • DOC • JPN • SNOW FESTIVAL
YUKI NO MOSHO • 1967 • Misumi Kenji • JPN • SHROUD OF SNOW, THE
YUKI NO WATARIDORI • 1957 • Murayama Mitsuo • JPN • MIGRATORY BIRDS OF SNOW
YUKI NO YO NO KETTO • 1954 • Kinugasa Teinosuke • JPN • DUEL OF A SNOWY NIGHT, THE
YUKI-ONNA • 1964 • Kobayashi Masaki • JPN • WOMAN OF THE SNOW, THE (UKN)
YUKI YUKITE SHINGUN • Hara Kazuo • DOC • JPN • FORWARD, ARMY OF GOD
YUKIGUNI • 1957 • Toyoda Shiro • JPN • SNOW COUNTRY
YUKIGUNI • 1965 • Oba Hideo • JPN • SNOW COUNTRY (USA) ○ LOVE IN THE SNOW
YUKIKO • 1955 • Imai Tadashi • JPN

YUKINOJO HENGE • 1935 • Kinugasa Teinosuke • JPN • YUKINOJO'S DISGUISE ○ REVENGE OF YUKINOJO, THE ○ YUKINOJO'S REVENGE

YUKINOJO HENGE • 1959 • Makino Masahiro • JPN

YUKINOJO HENGE • 1963 • Ichikawa Kon • JPN • REVENGE OF YUKINOJO, THE ○ ACTOR'S REVENGE, AN

YUKINOJO'S DISGUISE see **YUKINOJO HENGE** • 1935

YUKINOJO'S REVENGE see **YUKINOJO HENGE** • 1935

YUKIONNA see **KAIDAN YUKIJORO** • 1968

YUKIONNA NO ASHIATO • 1959 • Kato Bin • JPN • FOOTMARK OF A SNOW FAIRY

YUKIONNA, WOMAN OF THE SNOW see **KAIDAN YUKIJORO** • 1968

YUKIWARISO • 1951 • Tasaka Tomotaka • JPN • HEPATICA

YUKIYUKITE SHINGUN • 1988 • DOC • JPN • SACRED SOLDIERS MARCHED, THE

YUKO AND THE LIVING CHAIR see **FUTARI NO IDA** • 1976

YUKOKU • 1965 • Mishima Yukio • JPN • RITES OF LOVE AND DEATH ○ PATRIOTISM

YUKON FLIGHT • 1940 • Staub Ralph • USA • RENFREW OF THE ROYAL MOUNTED IN YUKON FLIGHT

YUKON GOLD • 1952 • McDonald Frank • USA

YUKON HAVE IT • 1958 • Lovy Alex • ANS • USA

YUKON JAKE • 1924 • *Sennett Mack (P)* • SHT • USA

YUKON MANHUNT • 1951 • McDonald Frank • USA

YUKON OLD, YUKON NEW • 1961 • Howe John • DOC • CND

YUKON PATROL • 1940 • Witney William, English John • USA

YUKON PATROL, THE see **KING OF THE ROYAL MOUNTED** • 1940

YUKON VENGEANCE • 1954 • Beaudine William • USA

YUKONERS, THE • 1956 • King Allan • CND

YUKOVSKY see **ZHUKOVSKY** • 1951

YUL 871 • 1966 • Godbout Jacques • CND

YULE • 1929 • Aylott Dave • UKN

YULE LAFF • 1962 • Kneitel Seymour • ANS • USA

YULE LOG, THE • 1914 • Denton Jack • UKN

YULETIDE REFORMATION, A • 1910 • Rains Fred • UKN

YULIA VREVSKA see **YULIYA VREVSKAYA** • 1978

YULIYA VREVSKAYA • 1978 • Korabov Nicolai • USS, BUL • JULIA VREVSKAYA ○ YULIA VREVSKA

YULSKII DOZHD see **LYULSKI DOZHD** • 1967

YUM MIN UMRI • 1960 • Salem Atef • EGY • JOUR DANS MA VIE, UN

YUM-YUM GIRLS, THE • 1976 • Rosen Barry • USA

YUMA • 1970 • Post Ted • TVM • USA

YUME DE ARITAI • 1962 • Tomimoto Sokichi • JPN • IF IT WERE A DREAM

YUME MIRU HITOBITO • 1953 • Nakamura Noboru • JPN

YUME MIRUYONI NEMURITAI • 1985 • Hayashi Kaizo • JPN • TO SLEEP SO AS TO DREAM

YUME NO YORU HIRAKU • 1967 • Noguchi Haruyasu • JPN • DREAMS COME TRUE AT NIGHT

YUME TO SHIRISEBA • 1952 • Nakamura Noboru • JPN

YUMEMI-DOJI • 1958 • *Toei* • ANS • JPN • FABLE OF A DREAMER, THE (USA) ○ DREAM BOY

YUMIHARI-ZUKI • 1955 • *Azuma Chiyonosuki* • JPN • CRESCENT MOON, THE

YUMINGAI NO JUDAN • 1963 • Iizuka Masuichi • JPN • OPERATION DIAMOND

YUNAGI • 1957 • Toyoda Shiro • JPN • EVENING CALM

YUNAK MARKO • 1953 • Dinov Todor • ANS • BUL • MIGHTY MARKO, THE ○ BRAVE MARCO ○ JUNAK MARKOS ○ MARKO THE HERO

YUNBOGI NO NIKKI • 1965 • Oshima Nagisa • SHT • JPN • YUNBOGI'S DIARY (UKN) ○ DIARY OF YUNBOGI, THE

YUNBOGI'S DIARY (UKN) see **YUNBOGI NO NIKKI** • 1965

YUNG-CH'UN TA-HSIUNG • 1978 • Wang Hsing Lei • HKG • DRAGON LIVES, THE ○ KING OF KUNG FU ○ HE'S A HERO ○ HE'S A LEGEND ○ HE'S A LEGEND, HE'S A HERO

YUNOST MAKSIMA • 1935 • Kozintsev Grigori, Trauberg Leonid • USS • YOUTH OF MAXIM, THE

YUNOST MIRA see **IUNOST' MIRA** • 1949

YUNOST NASHIKH OTSOV • 1958 • Kalik Moisei, Rytsarev Boris • USS • YOUTH OF OUR FATHERS ○ OUR FATHER'S YOUTH

YUPPIDU • 1975 • Celentano Adriano • ITL

YUPPIE FANTASIA, THE see **SIU NAMYAN CHOWGEI** • 1988

YUPPIES • 1985 • Vanzina Carlo • ITL

YURAKUCHO DE AIMASHO • 1958 • Shima Koji • JPN • CHANCE MEETING

YUREI HANJO-KI • 1961 • Saeki Kozo • JPN • MY FRIEND DEATH

YUREI-JIMA NO OKITE • 1961 • Sasaki Ko • JPN

YUREI OOINI IKARU • 1943 • Shibuya Minoru • JPN • ANGRY GHOST, THE

YUREI RESSHA • 1949 • Nobuchi Akira • JPN • GHOST TRAIN

YUREI TAKUSHI • 1956 • JPN • GHOST IN A CAB

YUREISEN • 1957 • Matsuda Sadatsugu • JPN • GHOST SHIP

YURI NOSENKO, KGB • 1986 • Jackson Mick • TVM • UKN

YUSEI OJI • 1959 • Wakabayashi Eijiro • JPN • PRINCE OF SPACE (USA) ○ INVADERS FROM THE SPACE SHIP ○ INVADERS FROM SPACE ○ STAR PRINCE, THE

YUSHA NOMI (JPN) see **NONE BUT THE BRAVE** • 1965

YUSHIMA NO SHIRAUME • 1955 • Kinugasa Teinosuke • JPN • ROMANCE OF YUSHIMA, THE ○ WHITE SEA OF YUSHIMA

YUSHU HEIYA • 1963 • Toyoda Shiro • JPN • MADAME AKI

YUST FROM SWEDEN • 1916 • Leonard Robert Z. • SHT • USA

YUSUF AND KENAN see **YUSUF ILE KENA** • 1980

YUSUF FROM KUYUCAK see **KUYUCAKLI YUSUF** • 1985

YUSUF ILE KENA • 1980 • Kavur Omer • TRK • YUSUF AND KENAN

YUVANA DON BABA • 1968 • Gulyuz Aram • TRK • COME BACK HOME, DADDY

YUWAKU • 1948 • Yoshimura Kozaburo • JPN • TEMPTATION ○ SEDUCTION

YUWAKU • 1957 • Nakahira Ko • JPN • TEMPTATION

YUYAKE-KUMO • 1956 • Kinoshita Keisuke • JPN • CLOUDS AT TWILIGHT

YUYUN, A PATIENT IN A MENTAL HOSPITAL see **YUYUN PASIEN RUMAH SAKIT JIWA** • 1980

YUYUN PASIEN RUMAH SAKIT JIWA • 1980 • Noer Arifin C. • INN • YUYUN, A PATIENT IN A MENTAL HOSPITAL

YUZBASI KEMAL • 1967 • Atadeniz Yilmaz • TRK • CAPTAIN KEMAL

YVES MONTAND CHANTE • 1956 • Yutkevich Sergei, Slutsky Mikhail • DOC • FRN, USS • YVES MONTAND SINGS ○ POET IV MONTAN

YVES MONTAND SINGS see **YVES MONTAND CHANTE** • 1956

YVETTE • 1917 • Tourjansky Victor • USS

YVETTE • 1927 • Cavalcanti Alberto • FRN

YVETTE • 1938 • Liebeneiner Wolfgang • FRG • TOCHTER EINER KURTISANE, DIE

YVETTE DARNAC • 1929 • *B.s.f.p.* • SHT • UKN

YVETTE, DIE MODEPRINZESSIN • 1922 • Zelnik Friedrich • FRG

YVETTE'S MILLIONS see **MILLIONEN DER YVETTE, DIE** • 1956

YVONGELISATION • 1973 • D'Aix Alain (c/d) • DOC • CND

YVONNE • 1915 • Aylott Dave • UKN

YVONNE FROM 6 TO 9 • 1969 • *Blake Sam* • USA

YVONNE FROM PARIS • 1919 • Flynn Emmett J. • USA

YVONNE LA BELLA DONNA • 1915 • Serena Gustavo • ITL

YVONNE LA NUIT • 1949 • Amato Giuseppe • ITL

YVONNE, THE FOREIGN SPY • 1912 • *Imp* • USA

Z

Z • 1968 • Costa-Gavras • FRN, ALG

Z • 1972 • Grgic Zlatko • ANS • YGS

Z.7. OPERACION REMBRANDT (SPN) see **MARK DONEN AGENTE Z 7** • 1966

Z BLATA DO LOUZE • 1934 • Innemann Svatopluk • CZC • OUT OF THE FRYING PAN INTO THE FIRE

Z CESKYCH MYLYNU • 1929 • Innemann Svatopluk, Seidl • CZC • FROM THE CZECH MILLS

Z CINSKEO ZAPISNIKU • 1954 • Kachyna Karel, Jasny Vojtech • CZC • FROM A CHINESE NOTEBOOK

Z DAY, THE • 1985 • Nicolaescu Sergiu • RMN

Z LASKY • 1928 • Slavinsky Vladimir • CZC • WITH LOVE

Z MEHO ZIVOTA • 1955 • Krska Vaclav • CZC • FROM MY LIFE

Z MEHO ZIVOTA • 1970 • Schorm Evald • MTV • CZC • FROM MY LIFE

Z MEN see **ATTACK FORCE Z** • 1981

Z.P.G. (USA) see **ZERO POPULATION GROWTH** • 1972

Z TAMTEJ STRONY OKIENKA • 1963 • Ziarnik Jerzy • DOC • PLN • AT THE OTHER SIDE OF THE WINDOW

Z-TZU T'E KUNG TUI (TWN) see **ATTACK FORCE Z** • 1981

Z7 OPERATION REMBRANDT (USA) see **MARK DONEN AGENTE Z 7** • 1966

ZA BOREM ZA LASEM • 1961 • Nehrebecki Wladyslaw • ANS • PLN • BEYOND THE FORESTS, BEYOND THE WOODS ○ BEYOND THE WOOD

ZA DVUMYA ZAYTSAMI • 1961 • Ivanov V. • USS • KIEV COMEDY: OR, CHASING TWO HARES ○ KIEV COMEDY, A

ZA HUMNY JE DRAK • 1982 • Pinkava Josef, Cvrcek Radim • CZC • THERE'S A DRAGON A STONE'S THROW AWAY ○ DRAGON DOWN THE LANE

ZA LA FRAK • 1920 • Ghione Emilio • ITL

ZA LA MORT • 1914 • Ghione Emilio • SRL • ITL

ZA LA MORT CONTRA ZA LA MORT • 1921 • Ghione Emilio • ITL

ZA NAMI MOSKVA • 1968 • Begalin Mazhit • USS • MOSCOW IS BEHIND US

ZA RANNICH CERVANKU • 1934 • Rovensky Josef • CZC • ROSY DAWN, THE

ZA RODNOU HROUDU • 1930 • Kminek • CZC • FOR NATIVE SOIL

ZA ROK • 1976 • Lenartowicz Stanislaw • PLN

ZA SADA BEZ DOBROG NASLOVA • 1987 • Karanovic Srdjan • YGS • FILM WITHOUT A NAME

ZA SCIANA • 1971 • Zanussi Krzysztof • MTV • PLN • BEHIND THE WALL (USA) ○ NEXT DOOR

ZA SVOBODU NARODA • 1920 • Binovec Vaclav • CZC • FOR THE FREEDOM OF THE NATION

ZA TRNKOVYM KEREM • 1981 • Gajer Vaclav • CZC • BEHIND THE BLACKTHORN BUSH

ZA VITRINOI UNIVERMAGA • 1955 • Samsonov Samson • USS • BEHIND THE SHOP WINDOWS ○ SHOP WINDOWS

ZA WAMI POJDA INNI • 1949 • Bohdziewicz Antoni • PLN • OTHERS WILL FOLLOW

ZA WASZA I NASZA WOLNOSC • 1968 • Perski Ludwik, Machnacz Leonid • DOC • PLN, USS • FOR YOUR FREEDOM AND OURS

ZA WINY NIEPOPELNIONE • 1939 • Bodo Eugene • FOR CRIMES NOT THEIRS (USA)

ZA ZIVOT RADOSTNY • 1951 • Kachyna Karel, Jasny Vojtech • CZC • FOR A JOYFUL LIFE

ZAA LE PETIT CHAMEAU BLANC • 1960 • Bellon Yannick • FRN

ZAAK M.P., DE • 1960 • Haanstra Bert • NTH • M.P. CASE, THE ○ MANNEKEN PIS CASE, THE

ZAAK VAN LEVEN OF DOOD, EEN • 1983 • Schouten George • NTH

ZAAT • 1972 • Barton Dan • USA • BLOOD WATERS OF DR. Z, THE

ZABAGLIONE • 1966 • Robin Georges • UKN

ZABARDAST • 1988 • PKS

ZABAWA • 1961 • Leszczynski Witold • PLN • GAME, A ○ PLAY

ZABAWA • 1961 • Majewski Janusz • PLN • GAME, THE

ZABAWA W DOROSLYCH • 1966 • Zukowska Jadwiga • JPN • PLAYING AT GROWN-UPS

ZABIC NA KONCU • 1990 • Wojcik Wojciech • PLN • KILL AT THE END

ZABIH • 1974 • Motevaselani Mohamad • IRN

ZABIJ MNIE, GLINO • 1988 • Bromski Yacek • PLN • KILL ME, PIG ○ KILL ME, COP

ZABIJAKA • 1967 • Lenartowicz Stanislaw • MTV • PLN

ZABIJCIE CZARNA OWCE • 1972 • Passendorfer Jerzy • PLN • KILL THE BLACK SHEEP

ZABIJET JE SNADNE • 1972 • Schorm Evald • CZC • KILLING IS EASY

ZABIL JSEM EINSTEINA, PANOVE • 1969 • Lipsky Oldrich • CZC • GENTLEMEN, I HAVE KILLED EINSTEIN ○ I KILLED EINSTEIN, GENTLEMEN ○ I KILLED EINSTEIN

ZABITA NEDELE • 1970 • Vihanova Drahomira • CZC • KILLED SUNDAY ○ LOST SUNDAY, A ○ KILLING A SUNDAY

ZABLITZKY'S WATERLOO • 1915 • *Pierard Jean-Pierre* • USA

ZABORAVLJENI II • 1989 • Bajic Darko • YGS • FORGOTTEN II, THE

ZABOU see **SCHIMANSKI 2** • 1987

ZABRISKIE POINT • 1969 • Antonioni Michelangelo • USA, ITL

ZACA LAKE MYSTERY, THE • 1915 • Otto Henry • USA

ZACARANI DVORAC U DUDINCINA • 1951 • Vukotic Dusan • YGS • ENCHANTED CASTLE IN DUDINCI, THE ○ HAUNTED CASTLE AT DUDINCI, THE

ZACAZONAPAN • 1974 • *Filmadora Chapultepec* • MXC

ZACHARIAH • 1971 • Englund George • USA

ZACHAROVANNAYA DESNA • 1965 • Solntseva Yulia • USS • ENCHANTED DESNA, THE ○ DESNA, THE

ZACIATOK SEZONY • 1987 • Zahon Zoro • CZC • SEASON'S OPENING

ZACMIENIE SLONCA • 1955 • Urbanowicz Stanislaw • PLN • ECLIPSE OF THE SUN

ZACZAROWANY ROWER • 1955 • Sternfeld Silik • PLN • MAGIC BICYCLE, THE

ZACZELO SIE NAD WISLA see **IT BEGAN ON THE VISTULA** • 1966

ZACZELO SIE W HISZPANII • 1950 • Munk Andrzej • DOC • PLN • IT BEGAN IN SPAIN ○ IT STARTED IN SPAIN

ZADAH TELA • 1984 • Pavlovic Zivojin • YGS • BODY SCENT

ZADANIE DO WYKONANIA • 1965 • Trzos-Rastawiecki Andrzej • DOC • PLN • TASK TO BE CARRIED OUT

ZADNUSZKI • 1961 • Konwicki Tadeusz • PLN • HALLOWE'EN ○ ALL HALLOWS EVE ○ ALL SOULS DAY

ZADUSNICE • 1963 • Lazic Dragoslav • YGS

ZAFRA • 1959 • Demare Lucas • ARG

ZAGALATONES • 1971 • Corona Juan • VNZ • AGGRESSIVE TEENAGERS, THE

ZAGANELLA E IL CAVALIERE • 1932 • Serena Gustavo, Mannini Giorgio • ITL

ZAGLADA BERLIN • 1945 • Bossak Jerzy • DOC • PLN • ANNIHILATION OF BERLIN, THE ○ FALL OF BERLIN, THE

ZAGOR E L'ERBA MUSICALE • 1974 • Garolda G. A., De Mas P. L. • ITL

ZAGOVOR OBRECHENNYKH • 1950 • Kalatozov Mikhail • USS • CONSPIRACY OF THE DOOMED

ZAGRANICHNII POKHOD SUDOV BALTIISKOGO FLOTA KREISERE 'AURORA' I UCHEBNOGO SUDNA 'KOMSOMOLTS' • 1925 • Vertov Dziga • USS

ZAGRLJAJ • 1989 • Vrdoljak Antun • YGS • EMBRACE, THE

ZAGROBNAYA SKITALITSA • 1915 • Tourjansky Victor • USS • WANDERER BEYOND THE GRAVE

ZAHADA MODREHO POKOJE • 1933 • Cikan Miroslav • CZC • MYSTERY OF THE BLUE ROOM, THE

ZAHLTAG • 1972 • Noever Hans • FRG • PAY-DAY

ZAHRADA • 1968 • Svankmajer Jan • ANS • CZC • GARDEN, THE

ZAHRADU • 1975 • Pojar Bretislav • ANM • CZC • GARDEN, THE

ZAHRAT AL QANDUL • 1985 • Chamoun Jean • LBN • ASPALATHUS FLOWER

ZAHYO MONOGATARI • 1963 • Ikehiro Kazuo • JPN • RABBLE TACTICS

ZAIDA, DIE TRAGODIE EINES MODELLS • 1923 • Holger-Madsen • FRG

ZAIJIAN ZHONGGUO • 1974 • T'Ang Shu-Hsuan • HKG • CHINA BEHIND

ZAIJIAN ZHONGGUO see **TSAI-CHIEN CHUNGKUO** • 1974

ZAIKO-BAIKO • 1970 • Chavdarov Georgi • ANS • BUL

ZA'IR AL-FAGR • 1973 • Shukry Mamduh • EGY • VISITEUR DE L'AUBE, LE

ZA'IRA, AZ- • 1972 • Barakat Henry • EGY • VISITEUSE, LA

ZAIRA, LA • 1971 • Louhichi Taieb • TNS

ZAJACZEK • 1964 • Laskowski Jan • ANS • PLN • LITTLE RABBIT, THE

ZAKALEC • 1977 • Kijowski Janusz • PLN • SLACK-BAKED BREAD

ZAKAZANE PIOSENKI • 1947 • Buczkowski Leonard • PLN • FORBIDDEN SONGS (USA)

ZAKHAR BERKUT • 1972 • Osyka Leonid • USS

ZAKHMI AURAT • 1989 • Kashmiri Iqbal • PKS

ZAKII • 1983 • Piault Marc-Henri • DOC • FRN

ZAKIAD • 1990 • Kotlarczyk Teresa • PLN • REFORMATORY

ZAKKYO KAZOKU • 1956 • *Tanaka Kinuyo* • JPN • MIXED FAMILY

ZAKLETE REWIRY see **DVOJI SVET V HOTELU PACIFIK** • 1975

ZAKON • 1989 • Naumov Vladimir • USS • LAW, THE

ZAKON VELIKOI LYUBVI • 1945 • Dolin Boris • USS • LAW OF THE GREAT LOVE, THE

ZAKONE BOLSHOI ZEMLI see **ALITET UKHODIT V GORY** • 1949

ZAKRET • 1977 • Brejdygant Stanislaw • PLN • TURNING

ZAKROICHIK IZ TORJKA • 1925 • Protazanov Yakov • USS • TAILOR FROM TORZHOK, THE

ZAKROLA KRAKUSA • 1948 • Wasilewski Zenon • ANS • PLN • UNDER KING KRAKUS (USA) ○ TIMES OF KING KRAKUS, THE

ZALACAN, EL AVENTURERO • 1954 • de Orduna Juan • SPN

ZALAMORT • 1924 • Ghione Emilio • FRG • TRAUM DER ZALAVIE, DER

ZALICZENIE • 1968 • Zanussi Krzysztof • MTV • PLN • CLASS CERTIFICATE ○ EXAMINATION, AN ○ PASS MARK ○ EXAM, THE

ZALIMLER DE SEVER • 1967 • Engin Ilhan • TRK • CRUEL ALSO LOVE, THE

ZALM • 1966 • Schorm Evald • CZC • PSALM, THE

ZALOBNICI • 1960 • Novak Ivo • CZC • TELLTALES

ZALOGA • 1952 • Fethke Jan • PLN • CREW, THE

ZALZALA • 1952 • Zils Paul • IND

ZAMACH • 1958 • Passendorfer Jerzy • PLN • ANSWER TO VIOLENCE

ZAMALLU • 1928 • Perestiani Ivan • USS

ZAMAN • 1983 • Le Bon Patrick • BLG

ZAMAN EL AJAB • 1952 • el Imam Hassan • EGY • TIME OF MIRACLES, THE

ZAMAN YA HUBB • 1971 • Salem Atef • EGY • IL Y A LONGTEMPS, O AMOUR!

ZAMBA • 1949 • Berke William • USA • ZAMBA THE GORILLA (UKN) ○ GIRL AND THE GORILLA, THE

ZAMBA THE GORILLA (UKN) see **ZAMBA** • 1949

ZAMBO • 1937 • Bhavnani Mohan Dayaram • IND • SHER-E-JUNGLE

ZAMBO IL DOMINATORE DELLA FORESTA • 1972 • Albertini Bitto • ITL • ZAMBO KING OF THE JUNGLE (USA)

ZAMBO KING OF THE JUNGLE (USA) see **ZAMBO IL DOMINATORE DELLA FORESTA** • 1972

ZAMBOANGA • 1937 • *Filippine* • USA • FURY IN PARADISE (UKN)

ZAMEK W LESIE • 1971 • Szczechura Daniel • ANS • PLN • CASTLE IN THE FOREST, THE

ZAMILOVANA TCHYNE • 1914 • Pech Antonin • CZC • MOTHER-IN-LAW IN LOVE

ZAMKA • 1974 • Ilic Aleksandar • YGS • TRAP, THE

ZAMPO Y YO • 1965 • Lucia Luis • SPN

ZAN BOKO • 1988 • Kabore Gaston • BRK

ZAN-E-KHONASHAM • 1967 • Oskouei Mostafa • IRN • VAMPIRE WOMAN

ZAN RE DELLA GIUNGLA • 1969 • Cano Manuel • ITL

ZANBOURAK • 1973 • Gaffari Farrokh • IRN • RUNNING CANON, THE

ZANCOS, LOS • 1984 • Saura Carlos • SPN • STILTS, THE

ZANDER THE GREAT • 1925 • Hill George W. • USA

ZANDORI'S SECRET • 1914 • *Sylvaine Renee* • FRN

ZANDUNGA, LA • 1936 • de Fuentes Fernando • MXC

ZANDUNGA PARA TRES • 1953 • Rodriguez Roberto • MXC

ZANDY'S BRIDE • 1974 • Troell Jan • USA • FOR BETTER, FOR WORSE

ZANGE NO YAIBA • 1927 • Ozu Yasujiro • JPN • SWORD OF PENITENCE

ZANGIKU MONOGATARI • 1939 • Mizoguchi Kenji • JPN • STORY OF THE LAST CHRYSANTHEMUMS, THE (USA) ○ STORY OF THE LATE CHRYSANTHEMUMS, THE

ZANGIKU MONOGATARI • 1956 • *Hasegawa Kazuo* • JPN • STORY OF THE LAST CHRYSANTHEMUMS, THE

ZANGIR • 1986 • Malik Pervaiz • PKS • CHAIN, THE

ZANGUEZOUR • 1938 • Bek-Nazarov Amo • USS

ZANHA-VA SHOHARHA • 1967 • Fatemi Nezam • IRN • HUSBANDS AND WIVES

ZANI BE-NAME-SHARAB • 1968 • Shervan Amir • IRN • WOMAN CALLED SHARAB, A

ZANIK DOMU USHERU • 1981 • Svankmajer Jan • ANM • CZC • FALL OF THE HOUSE OF USHER, THE

ZANIK SERCA • 1970 • Gradowski Bohdan • DOC • PLN • ATROPHY OF THE HEART

ZANIKLY SVET RUKAVIC • 1982 • Barta Jiri • ANM • CZC • LOST WORLD OF GLOVES, THE

ZANIM OPADNA LISCIE • 1963 • Slesicki Wladyslaw • DOC • PLN • BEFORE THE LEAVES FALL

ZANJIN ZANBA KEN • 1929 • Ito Daisuke • JPN • MAN-SLASHING HORSE-PIERCING SWORD ○ SWORD OF ENCHANTMENT, THE

ZANKI: SEITAIJIKKEN • 1967 • Komori Haku • JPN • EXPERIMENTS ON THE HUMAN BODY

ZANKYO ABAREHADA • 1967 • Saeki Kiyoshi • JPN • RIOTOUS SKIN OF THE OUTLAW

ZANKYO MUJO • 1968 • Ida Tan • JPN • HEART OF STONE

ZANKYO NO SAKAZUKI • 1967 • Tanaka Tokuzo • JPN • LAST GALLANTRY, THE

ZANNA BIANCA • 1973 • Fulci Lucio • ITL, FRN, SPN • CROC-BLANC (FRN) ○ WHITE FANG (UKN)

ZANNA BIANCA ALLA RISCOSSA • 1975 • Ricci Tonino • ITL

ZANNA BIANCA E IL CACCIATORE SOLITARIO • 1976 • Brescia Alfonso • ITL

ZANNA BIANCA E IL GRANDE KID • 1978 • Bruschini Vito • ITL

ZANNIN • 1967 • Komori Haku • JPN • CRUELTY

ZANNIN MARUHI ONNA ZEME • 1968 • Umesawa Kaoru • JPN • SECRET STORY OF CRUELTY -WOMAN TORTURE

ZANSETSU • 1968 • Nishikawa Katsumi • JPN • ETERNAL LOVE

ZANY ADVENTURES OF ROBIN HOOD, THE • 1984 • Austin Ray • TVM • USA

ZANY CARTOONIST, THE see **MAT GELAP** • 1990

ZANZABUKU • 1956 • Cotlow Lewis • DOC • UKN

ZANZARONI, I • 1967 • La Rosa Ugo • ITL • BIG MOSQUITOES, THE

ZANZE see **FORTUNA DI ZANZE, LA** • 1933

ZANZIBAR • 1940 • Schuster Harold • USA

ZANZIBAR • 1989 • Pascal Christine • FRN

ZAOCHUN ERYUE • 1963 • Xie Tieli • CHN • EARLY SPRING

ZAOSTRIT PROSIM • 1956 • Fric Martin • CZC • WATCH THE BIRDIE ○ CLOSE-UP PLEASE!

ZAP • 1969 • Anger Kenneth • USA • INVOCATION OF MY DEMON BROTHER (UKN)

ZAP-IN see **MISS NYMPHET'S ZAP-IN** • 1970

ZAPADNIA • 1932 • Medvedkin Alexander • USS

ZAPATA • 1971 • *Aguilar Antonio* • MXC

ZAPATAS BANDE • 1914 • Gad Urban • FRG

ZAPATILLAS VERDES, LAS • 1955 • Cardona Rene • MXC

ZAPATO CHINO, EL • 1979 • Sanchez Christian • CHL • CHINESE SHOE, THE

ZAPE • 1980 • Lares Luis • UKN

ZAPFENSTREICH • 1925 • Wiene Conrad • FRG

ZAPFENSTREICH AM RHEIN • 1930 • Speyer Jaap • FRG

ZAPIS ZBRODNI • 1975 • Trzos-Rastawiecki Andrzej • PLN • RECORD OF A CRIME ○ CRIMINAL RECORDS

ZAPISKI PECHORINA • 1967 • Rostotsky Stanislav • USS • HERO OF OUR TIME, A ○ PECHORIN'S NOTES

ZAPISNIK ZMIZELEHO • 1978 • Jires Jaromil • DOC • CZC • DIARY OF ONE WHO DISAPPEARED, THE ○ NOTEBOOK OF THINGS GONE

ZAPOMNIM ETOT DYEN • 1967 • Korsh-Sablin Vladimir • USS • WE SHALL REMEMBER THIS DAY

ZAPOR • 1960 • Kovacs Andras • HNG • SUMMER RAIN, A

ZAPOROSH SA DUNAYEM • 1939 • Ulmer Edgar G. • USA • COSSACKS ACROSS THE DANUBE ○ COSSACKS IN EXILE

ZAPPA • 1983 • August Bille • DNM

ZAPPATORE • 1929 • Serena Gustavo • ITL

ZAPPATORE, LO • 1950 • Furlan Rate • ITL • RINNEGO MIO FIGLIO

ZAPPED! • 1982 • Rosenthal Robert J. • USA

ZAPPED AGAIN • 1989 • Rosenthal Robert J. • USA

ZAPROSZENIE DO WNETRZA • 1978 • Wajda Andrzej • DOC • PLN • INVITATION TO THE INSIDE

ZAR UND ZIMMERMANN • 1970 • Hess Joachim • MTV • FRG

ZARAA, AL- • 1921 • Shakly Shamama • TNS

ZARABANDA BING.. BING • 1967 • Forque Jose Maria • SPN, ITL, FRN

ZARAGOZA • 1968 • Santos Teodorico C. • PHL

ZARAK • 1957 • Young Terence, Canutt Yakima, Gilling John • UKN

ZARCO, EL • 1920 • Ramos Jose Manuel • MXC

ZARCO, EL • 1957 • Delgado Miguel M. • MXC

ZARDA, LA • Ferchiou Sofia • TNS

ZARDOZ • 1974 • Boorman John • UKN

ZARE • 1927 • Bek-Nazarov Amo • USS

ZARESWITCH, DER • 1928 • Fleck Jacob, Fleck Luise • FRG

ZARESWITCH, DER • 1933 • Janson Victor • FRG

ZARESWITCH, DER • 1954 • Rabenalt Arthur M. • FRG • TZAREVITCH, LE

ZAREX • 1958 • Abelardo Richard • PHL

ZARIJOVE NOCI • 1957 • Jasny Vojtech • CZC • SEPTEMBER NIGHTS

ZARKI • 1971 • Kadijevic Djordje • YGS

ZARTE HAUT IN SCHWARZER SEIDE • 1961 • Pecas Max • FRG, FRN • DE QUOI TU TE MELES, DANIELA! (FRN) ○ DANIELLA BY NIGHT (USA)

ZARTLICHE HAIE (FRG) see **TENDRES REQUINS** • 1967

ZARTLICHEN VERWANDTEN, DIE • 1930 • Oswald Richard • FRG

ZARTLICHES GEHEIMNIS • 1956 • Schleif Wolfgang • FRG • FERIEN IN TIROL

ZARTLICHKEIT • 1930 • Lowenbein Richard • FRG • TENDERNESS (USA)

ZARTLICHKEIT DER WOLFE, DIE • 1973 • Lommel Ulli • FRG • TENDERNESS OF WOLVES, THE

ZARTLICHKEIT UND ZORN • 1981 • Flutsch Johannes • DOC • SWT • TENDERNESS AND ANGER

ZASADIL DEDEK REPU • 1945 • Trnka Jiri • ANS • CZC • GRANDPA PLANTED A BEET

ZASEDA • 1969 • Pavlovic Zivojin • YGS • AMBUSH

ZASIHLA ME NOC • 1985 • Herz Juraj • CZC • CAUGHT BY THE NIGHT

ZASTAVA • 1949 • Marjanovic Branko • YGS

ZASTAVE • 1973 • Jovanovic Zoran • YGS • FLAGS

ZATAH • 1985 • Strnad Stanislav • CZC, PLN • POLICE RAID

ZATO ICHI AND A CHEST OF GOLD see **ZATO ICHI SENRYO KUBI** • 1964

ZATO ICHI CHIKEMURI KAIDO • 1967 • Misumi Kenji • JPN • ZATOICHI CHALLENGED (USA)

ZATO ICHI JIGOKUTABI • 1967 • Misumi Kenji • JPN • SHOWDOWN FOR ZATOICHI (USA)

ZATO ICHI KENKA-DAIKO • 1968 • Misumi Kenji • JPN • BLIND SWORDSMAN SAMARITAN, THE

ZATO ICHI KENKATABI • 1968 • Yasuda Kimiyoshi • JPN • ZATOICHI (USA)

ZATO ICHI KYOJOTABI • 1963 • Tanaka Tokuzo • JPN • MASSEUR ICHI THE FUGITIVE

ZATO ICHI MONOGATARI • 1962 • Misumi Kenji • JPN • LIFE AND OPINION OF MASSEUR ICHI, THE ○ BLIND SWORDSMAN

ZATO ICHI NIDAN-GIRI • 1965 • Inoue Akira • JPN

ZATO ICHI NO UTA GA KIKOERU • 1966 • Tanaka Tokuzo • JPN • BLIND SWORDSMAN'S VENGEANCE, THE ○ ZATOICHI'S SONG IS HEARD

ZATO ICHI RO-YABURI • 1967 • Yamamoto Satsuo • JPN • BLIND SWORDSMAN'S RESCUE, THE ○ ZATOICHI ROUYABURI ○ ZATOICHI BREAKING OUT OF PRISON

ZATO ICHI SENRYO KUBI • 1964 • Ikehiro Kazuo • JPN • ZATOICHI: A THOUSAND DOLLAR PRICE ON HIS HEAD ○ ZATO ICHI AND A CHEST OF GOLD

ZATO-ICHI TEKKA-TABI • 1967 • Yasuda Kimiyoshi • JPN • BLIND SWORDSMAN'S CANE SWORD, THE ○ ZATOICHI'S GAMBLING TRAVELS

ZATO ICHI TO YOJINBO • 1970 • Okamoto Kihachi • JPN • ZATOICHI MEETS YOJIMBO (USA)

ZATOICHI: A THOUSAND DOLLAR PRICE ON HIS HEAD see **ZATO ICHI SENRYO KUBI** • 1964

ZATOICHI BREAKING OUT OF PRISON see **ZATO ICHI RO-YABURI** • 1967

ZATOICHI CHALLENGE LETTER see **ZATOICHI HATASHIJO** • 1968

ZATOICHI CHALLENGED (USA) see **ZATO ICHI CHIKEMURI KAIDO** • 1967

ZATOICHI HATASHIJO • 1968 • Yasuda Kimiyoshi • JPN • BLIND SWORDSMAN AND THE FUGITIVES, THE ○ ZATOICHI CHALLENGE LETTER

ZATOICHI MEETS HIS EQUAL • Yasuda Kimiyoshi • JPN, HKG • ZATOICHI MEETS THE ONE-ARMED SWORDSMAN

ZATOICHI MEETS THE ONE-ARMED SWORDSMAN see **ZATOICHI MEETS HIS EQUAL**

ZATOICHI MEETS YOJIMBO (USA) see **ZATO ICHI TO YOJINBO** • 1970

ZATOICHI ROUYABURI see **ZATO ICHI RO-YABURI** • 1967

ZATOICHI (USA) see **ZATO ICHI KENKATABI** • 1968

ZATOICHI: WILD FIRE FESTIVAL see **ZATOUICHI ABARE HIMATSURI** • 1970

ZATOICHI'S GAMBLING TRAVELS see **ZATO-ICHI TEKKA-TABI** • 1967

ZATOICHI'S SONG IS HEARD see **ZATO ICHI NO UTA GA KIKOERU** • 1966

ZATOUICHI ABARE HIMATSURI • 1970 • Misumi Kenji • JPN • ZATOICHI: WILD FIRE FESTIVAL

ZATRUDNENIE • 1967 • Andonov Ivan • BUL • EMBARRASSMENT

ZAUBER DER BOHEME • 1937 • von Bolvary Geza • AUS • CHARM OF LA BOHEME, THE (USA)

ZAUBER DER DOLOMITEN • 1959 • FRG

ZAUBERBERG, DER • 1982 • Geissendorfer Hans W. • FRG • MAGIC MOUNTAIN, THE

ZAUBERFLOTE, DIE • 1976 • Hess Joachim • FRG • MAGIC FLUTE, THE

ZAUBERGEIGE, DIE • 1944 • Maisch Herbert • FRG

ZAUBERMANNCHEN, DAS • 1960 • Engel Christoph • GDR • RUMPELSTILZCHEN ○ WIZARD, THE

ZAUBERPUPPE, DIE • 1929 • FRG

ZAUNGASTE DES LEBENS • 1925 • *Royal-Film-Corp* • FRG

ZAVADA NENI NA VASEMM PRIJIMACI • 1960 • Brdecka Jiri • ANS • CZC • TELEVISION FAN, THE

ZAVALLILAR • 1975 • Guney Yilmaz, Yilmaz Atif • TRK • POOR ONES, THE ○ MISERABLE ONES, THE

ZAVAZA • 1972 • Zaluski Roman • PLN • EPIDEMIC, THE

ZAVET POD: VINOVA • 1923 • Molas Zet • CZC

ZAVINIL TO EINSTEIN see **MUZ Z PRVNIHO STOLETI** • 1961

ZAVODYSE SMERTI • 1981 • Herz Juraj • CZC • RACING AGAINST DEATH

ZAVRACHTANE • 1967 • Boyadgieva Lada • BUL • RETURN

ZAVRAT • 1962 • Kachyna Karel • CZC • VERTIGO

ZAWAG ALLA TARIKA EL HADISSA • 1968 • Karim Salah • EGY • MARRIAGE IN THE MODERN MANNER

ZAWGA AL THANIA, AL • 1967 • Abu Saif Salah • EGY • SECOND WIFE, THE ○ ZAWGA EL SANIA, EL ○ ZOGA EL SANIA, EL ○ ZAWJA ATH-THANIYA, AZ-

ZAWGA EL SANIA, EL see **ZAWGA AL THANIA, AL** • 1967

ZAWGA LI KHAMSA RIGAL • 1970 • Shawkat Saifeddine • EGY • EPOUSE POUR CINQUE HOMMES, UNE

ZAWGAT RAGOL MOHIM • 1987 • Khan Mohamed • EGY • WIFE OF AN IMPORTANT MAN, THE

ZAWGATI MINA AL-HIBBI • 1972 • Salem Atef • EGY • MA FEMME EST UNE HIPPIE

ZAWGATI WA AL-KALB • 1970 • Marzouk Said • EGY • MA FEMME ET LE CHIEN ○ MY WIFE AND THE DOG ○ ZAWGATI WAL KALB

ZAWGATI WAL KALB see **ZAWGATI WA AL-KALB** • 1970

ZAWGATUN MIN BARISS • 1966 • Salem Atef • EGY • EPOUSE DE BARISS, UNE

ZAWJA ATH-THALITHA ACHAR, AZ- • 1961 • Wahab Fatin Abdel • EGY • TREIZIEME EPOUSE, LA

ZAWJA ATH-THANIYA, AZ- see **ZAWGA AL THANIA, AL** • 1967

ZAWODNICY • 1964 • Kosinski Bohdan • DOC • PLN • COMPETITORS, THE

ZAWSZE RODZI SIE CHLEB • 1969 • Gryczelowska Krystyna • DOC • PLN • BREAD IS ALWAYS BORN

ZAYAVLYENIYE O LYUBVI • 1979 • Averbach Ilya • USS • DECLARATION OF LOVE

ZAZA • 1909 • Pasquali Ernesto Maria • ITL

ZAZA • 1915 • Porter Edwin S., Ford Hugh • USA

ZAZA • 1923 • Dwan Allan • USA

ZAZA • 1938 • Cukor George • USA

ZAZA • 1942 • Castellani Renato • ITL

ZAZA • 1955 • Gaveau Rene • FRN

ZAZA THE DANCER • 1913 • Haldane Bert • UKN

ZAZDROSC • 1967 • Zukowska Jadwiga • PLN • JEALOUSY

ZAZDROSC I MEDYCYNA • 1939 • Bohdziewicz Antoni • PLN • JEALOUSY AND MEDICINE

ZAZDROSNY TRZMIEL • 1965 • Nehrebecki Wladyslaw • ANS • PLN • JEALOUS BUMBLE BEE, THE

ZAZIDANI • 1969 • Rakonjac Kokan • YGS • WALLED IN

ZAZIE DANS LE METRO • 1960 • Malle Louis • FRN • ZAZIE (USA) ○ ZAZIE IN THE UNDERGROUND

ZAZIE IN THE UNDERGROUND see **ZAZIE DANS LE METRO** • 1960

ZAZIE (USA) see **ZAZIE DANS LE METRO** • 1960

ZAZRACNY HLAVOLAM • 1967 • Taborsky Vaclav • CZC • MIRACULOUS BRAIN TEASER, THE ○ MIRACULOUS PUZZLE

ZBABELEC • 1961 • Weiss Jiri • CZC • COWARD, THE

ZBEHOVIA A PUTNICI • 1968 • Jakubisko Juraj • CZC, ITL • DESERTER AND THE NOMADS, THE (USA) ○ DISERTORE E I NOMADI, IL (ITL) ○ DESERTERS AND PILGRIMS ○ POUTNICI ○ ZBEHOVIA A TULACI ○ WANDERERS

ZBEHOVIA A TULACI see **ZBEHOVIA A PUTNICI** • 1968

ZBOGOM OSTAJ, BUNKERU NA RECI • 1972 • Djordjevic Purisa • YGS • FAREWELL, RIVERSIDE PILLBOX

ZBOJNICKI • 1955 • Perski Ludwik (c/d) • DOC • PLN • HIGHLAND ROBBERS' FOLK DANCE, THE

ZBOJNIK JURKO • Kubal Viktor • ANM • CZC • JURKO THE OUTLAW

ZBOROV • 1938 • Holman J. Alfred, Slavicek Jiri • CZC

ZBRODNIA STELLI • 1969 • Szczechura Daniel • ANS • PLN • STELLA'S CRIME

ZBRODNIARZ I PANNA • 1963 • Nasfeter Janusz • PLN • CRIMINAL AND THE LADY, THE ○ MURDERER AND THE GIRL, THE

ZBRODNIARZ, KTORY UKRADL ZBRODNIC • 1969 • Majewski Janusz • PLN • CRIMINAL WHO STOLE THE CRIME, THE

ZBYSZEK see **ZBYSZEK CYBULSKI** • 1969

ZBYSZEK CYBULSKI • 1969 • Laskowski Jan • PLN • ZBYSZEK

ZDE JSOU LVI • 1958 • Krska Vaclav • CZC • SCARS OF THE PAST ○ HIC SUNT LEONES ○ HERE ARE LIONS

ZDJECIA PROBNE • 1978 • Holland Agnieszka, Kedzierski Pawel, Domaradzki Jerzy • PLN • FILM TEST, THE ○ SCREEN TESTS

ZDRAVSTVAI MOSKVA • 1945 • Yutkevich Sergei • USS • HALLO MOSCOW! ○ GREETINGS MOSCOW!

ZDRAVSTVUJ, ZIZN! • 1962 • Zarkhi Alexander • USS • HELLO, LIFE!

ZDRAVSTVYI, ETO YA! • 1965 • Dovlatyan Frunze • USS • GREETINGS, IT IS I! ○ HALLO, IT'S ME! ○ HOW DO, IT'S ME!

ZDRAVSTVYITE DETI • 1962 • Donskoi Mark • USS • HOW DO YOU DO, CHILDREN? ○ HELLO CHILDREN

ZE ANALFABETO • 1952 • Marques Carlos • SHS • PRT

ZE DO BURRO • 1972 • Ferreira Eurico • PRT, MZM

ZE SOBOTY NA NEDELI • 1931 • Machaty Gustav • CZC • FROM SATURDAY TO SUNDAY

ZE SVETA LESNICH SAMOT • 1933 • Krnansky M. J. • CZC • FROM THE WORLD OF WOOD COTTAGES ○ FOR FOREST LONELINESS

ZEAMI • 1974 • Harada Susumu • JPN

ZEB VS. PAPRIKA • 1924 • Ceder Ralph • SHT • USA

ZEB, ZACK AND THE ZULUS • 1913 • Hotaling Arthur D. • USA

ZEB, ZEKE AND THE WIDOW • 1910 • *Lubin* • USA

ZEBRA • 1971 • SAF
ZEBRA FORCE • 1977 • Tornatore Joe • USA
ZEBRA IN THE KITCHEN • 1965 • Tors Ivan • USA
ZEBRA KILLER, THE see **PANIC CITY** • 1974
ZEBRAS • *Halgelback John* • ANS • SWD
ZEB'S MUSICAL CAREER • 1913 • Williams C. Jay • USA
ZEC S PET NOGU see **LEPURI ME PESE KEMBE** • 1983
ZECA • 1972 • Sluizer George • DOC • NTH, BRZ
ZECHENKIND, DAS • 1916 • *Wiesse Hanni* • FRG
ZECHMEISTER • 1981 • Summereder Angela • AUS
ZED AND TWO NOUGHTS, A • 1985 • Greenaway Peter • UKN • ZOO: A ZED AND TWO NOUGHTS
ZEDER • 1983 • Avati Pupi • ITL • ZEDER: VOICES FROM DARKNESS ○ REVENGE OF THE DEAD
ZEDER: VOICES FROM DARKNESS see **ZEDER** • 1983
ZEDJ • 1971 • Osmanli Dimitri • YGS • THIRST
ZEDNI CAR • 1967 • Dukanovic Milo • YGS • THIRSTY TSAR, THE
ZEE AND CO • 1972 • Hutton Brian G. • UKN • X, Y AND ZEE (USA)
ZEE ONTRUKT, DER • 1949 • van der Horst Herman • NTH • WRESTED FROM THE SEA
ZEEBRUGGE • 1924 • Woolfe H. Bruce, Bramble A. V. • UKN
ZEEDIJK FILM STUDIE • 1927 • Ivens Joris • NTH • ZEEDYK FILM STUDY ○ FILMSTUDY -ZEEDIJK
ZEEDYK FILM STUDY see **ZEEDIJK FILM STUDIE** • 1927
ZEELAYA MELAD • 1986 • BRM
ZEFT • 1984 • Seddiki Tayeb • MRC
ZEGEN • 1988 • Imamura Shohei • JPN • GO-BETWEEN, A
ZEGNAJ PARO • 1973 • Antoniszczak Ryszard • PLN • GOODBYE STEAM
ZEHIRLI CICEK • 1967 • Dinler Mehmet • TRK • POISONED FLOWER, THE
ZEHIRLI DUDAKLAR • 1967 • Karamanbey Cetin • TRK • POISONED LIPS
ZEHIRLI HAYAT • 1967 • Inanoglu Turker • TRK • POISONED LIFE
ZEHN MILLIARDEN VOLT • 1920 • Gartner Adolf • FRG
ZEHN MINUTEN MOZART • 1930 • Reiniger Lotte • ANS • FRG
ZEHNTAUSEND see **HUTET EURE TOCHTER** • 1962
ZEHRA THE TOURIST see **TURIST ZEHRA** • 1967
ZEICHEN DER DREI, DAS • 1919 • Hartt Hanns Heinz • FRG • PLANE DER KALIFORNISCHEN GOLDMINEN ODER DAS ZEICHEN DER DREI KREUZE, DIE
ZEICHEN DES MALAYEN, DAS • 1920 • Boese Carl • FRG
ZEILEN • 1962 • Hoving Hattum • SHT • NTH • SAILING
ZEIN WEIB'S LIEBENIK • 1931 • Goldin Sidney M. • USA • HIS WIFE'S LOVER
ZEISTERS see **FAT GUY GOES NUTZOID** • 1986
ZEIT DER KIRSCHEN IST VORBEI, DIE (FRG) see **GRAND DADAIS, LE** • 1967
ZEIT DER RACHE • 1990 • Peschke Anton • AUS • TIME OF VENGEANCE
ZEIT DER SCHERZE IST VORBEI ODER DER SPRINTER, DIE • 1983 • Boll Christopher • FRG
ZEIT DER SCHULDLOSEN, DIE • 1964 • Fantl Thomas • FRG • TIME OF THE INNOCENT, THE
ZEIT IST BOSE, DIE • 1982 • Kuert Beat • SWT • EVIL TIMES
ZEIT MIR DIR, DIE • 1948 • Hurdalek Georg • FRG
ZEIT ZU LEBEN • 1969 • Seemann Horst • GDR • TIME TO LIVE
ZEITGENOSSEN • 1983 • Lauscher Ernst Josef • AUS • CONTEMPORARIES
ZEITUNGSRIESE, DER • 1915 • Matull Kurt • FRG
ZEJSCIE DO PIEKLA • 1966 • Kuzminski Zbigniew • PLN • DESCENT TO HELL
ZEKKAI NO RAJO • 1958 • Nomura Kosho • JPN • WOMAN BY THE LONELY SEA, THE
ZELDA • 1974 • Cavallone Alberto • ITL
ZELDA, THE GYPSY • 1911 • *Yankee* • USA
ZELENA KNIZKA • 1948 • Mach Josef • CZC • GREEN BOOK, THE
ZELENA LETA • 1985 • Muchna Milan • CZC • GREEN YEARS
ZELENE OBZORY • 1962 • Novak Ivo • CZC • GREEN HORIZONS
ZELENIE TSEPOCHKI • 1970 • Aronov Grigori • USS • GREEN CHAINS
ZELEZNICARI • 1963 • Schorm Evald • DOC • CZC • RAILWAYMEN
ZELEZNY KLOBOUK • 1960 • Kabrt Josef • ANS • CZC • IRON HELMET, THE (USA) ○ TIN HAT, THE
ZELIG • 1983 • Allen Woody • USA
ZELLE, DIE • 1971 • Bienek Horst • FRG • CELL, THE
ZELLY AND ME • 1988 • Rathbone Tina • USA
ZELYONAYA KARYETA • 1967 • Frid Ya. • USS • GREEN CARRIAGE, THE
ZELYONYI PAUK • 1916 • Volkov Alexander • USS • GREEN SPIDER, THE
ZEM SPIEVA • 1933 • Plicka Karel • CZC • EARTH IS SINGING, THE ○ EARTH SINGS, THE ○ SINGING LAND, THE ○ SINGING EARTH, THE
ZEMALJSKI DANI TEKU • 1980 • Paskaljevic Goran • YGS • DAYS ARE PASSING, THE ○ EARTH DAYS PASS BY
ZEME ZEMI • 1962 • Schorm Evald • CZC • COUNTRY OF COUNTRIES, THE ○ COUNTRY TO COUNTRY ○ LAND, THE
ZEMLYA • 1930 • Dovzhenko Alexander • USS • SONG OF NEW LIFE ○ EARTH ○ SOIL
ZEMLYA I LYUDI • 1955 • Rostotsky Stanislav • USS • LAND AND PEOPLE
ZEMLYA OTTSOV • 1968 • Aimanov Shaken • USS • LAND OF OUR FATHERS
ZEMLYA SANNIKOVA • 1973 • Mkrtchan Albert, Popov Leonid • USS • ISLAND IN THE SNOW ○ SANNIKOV'S LAND
ZEMLYA V PLENU • 1928 • Ozep Fedor • USS • YELLOW TICKET, THE (USA) ○ YELLOW PASS, THE ○ EARTH IN CHAINS
ZEMLYA ZHAZHDYOT • 1930 • Raizman Yuli • USS • EARTH THIRSTS, THE ○ SOIL IS THIRSTY, THE
ZEMMA see **ZENMA** • 1951
ZEMSTA • 1957 • Bohdziewicz Antoni • PLN • REVENGE
ZEMYA • 1957 • Zhandov Zahari • BUL • EARTH ○ LAND
ZEN, LE • 1971 • Desjardins Arnaud • DOC • FRN
ZEN GUTS • Ringo David • SHT • USA
ZENA, KTERA VI CO CHCE • 1934 • Binovec Vaclav • CZC • WOMAN WHO KNOWS WHAT SHE WANTS, A
ZENA S KRAJOLIKOM • 1989 • Matic Ivica • YGS • WOMAN WITH LANDSCAPE
ZENABEL • 1969 • Deodato Ruggero • ITL
ZENDEGUI • 1969 • Karimi Nosrattolah • ANS • IRN • LIFE
ZENGIN MUTFAGI • 1988 • Sabuncu Basar • TRK • KITCHEN OF THE RICH, THE
ZENGIN VE SERSERI see **HAYATA DONUS** • 1967
ZENI NO ODORI see **DOKONJO MONOGATARI -ZENI NO ODORI** • 1964
ZENICA • 1957 • Zivanovic Jovan, Stefanovic Milos • YGS
ZENIDBA GOSPODINA MARCIPANA • 1963 • Mimica Vatroslav • YGS • WEDDING OF MR. MARZIPAN ○ WEDDING OF MRS. MARZIPAN ○ MR. MARZIPAN'S MARRIAGE
ZENIGATA HEIJI • 1967 • Yamanouchi Tetsuya • JPN • COIN-THROWING DETECTIVE, THE
ZENIGATA HEIJI TORIMONO HIKAE • 1958 • Saeki Kiyoshi • JPN
ZENKA MONO • 1968 • Yamashita Kosaku • JPN • MARKED MAN, THE
ZENMA • 1951 • Kinoshita Keisuke • JPN • GOOD FAIRY, THE ○ ZEMMA
ZENOBIA • 1939 • Douglas Gordon • USA • ELEPHANTS NEVER FORGET (UKN) ○ IT'S SPRING AGAIN
ZENOBIA see **MADAME ZENOBIA** • 1973
ZENSCAPES • 1962 • Menken Marie • USA
ZENSCINAVAMPIR • 1915 • Tourjansky Victor • USS
ZENSHIN ZENSHIN MATA ZENSHIN • 1967 • Wada Yoshinori • JPN • GO FORWARD, FORWARD AND STILL FORWARD
ZENSKIE OBOZY LETNIE • 1938 • Bohdziewicz Antoni (c/d) • SHT • PLN • WOMEN'S SUMMER CAMPS
ZENTA TO SANPEI MONOGATARI • 1957 • Yamamoto Kajiro • JPN
ZENTRALE RIO • 1939 • Engels Erich • FRG
ZENU ANI KVETINOU NEUHODIS • 1966 • Podskalsky Zdenek • CZC • NEVER STRIKE A WOMAN EVEN WITH A FLOWER ○ NEVER HIT A WOMAN WITH A FLOWER
ZEPPEKI NO ONI-MUSUME • 1959 • Shimura Toshio • JPN • CLIFF OF THE GHOST GIRL, THE
ZEPPELIN • 1971 • Perier Etienne • UKN
ZEPPELIN • 1981 • Glomm Lasse • NRW
ZEPPELIN AND LOVE, THE see **VZDUCHOLOD A LASKA** • 1947
ZEPPELIN ATTACK ON NEW YORK • 1917 • *Rothacker* • SHT • USA
ZEPPELIN'S LAST RAID, THE • 1918 • Willat Irvin V. • USA
ZEPPELINS OF LONDON • 1916 • Birch Cecil • UKN
ZERBROCHENE KRUG, DER • 1937 • Ucicky Gustav • FRG • BROKEN JUG, THE
ZERKALO • 1974 • Tarkovsky Andrei • USS • MIRROR (UKN)
ZERO • 1928 • Raymond Jack • UKN
ZERO • 1960 • Asquith Anthony • UKN
ZERO • 1968 • Markson Morley • CND
ZERO BOYS, THE • 1985 • Mastorakis Nico • USA
ZERO CITY (UKN) see **GOROD ZERO** • 1989
ZERO DE CONDUITE • 1933 • Vigo Jean • FRN • ZERO FOR CONDUCT (USA)
ZERO DEGREES • 1986 • Woodland James • DOC • CND
ZERO FIGHTER see **ZEROSEN KUROKUMO IKKA** • 1962
ZERO FIGHTER see **DAI KUSEN** • 1966
ZERO FOR CONDUCT (USA) see **ZERO DE CONDUITE** • 1933
ZERO FOR ZEP • 1984 • SAF
ZERO GIRLS • 1965 • Findlay Michael • USA • SIN SYNDICATE, THE ○ JAZZ ME BABY
ZERO HOUR! • 1957 • Bartlett Hall • USA
ZERO HOUR see **ROAD TO GLORY, THE** • 1936
ZERO HOUR see **STUNDE NULL** • 1977
ZERO HOUR, A • 1921 • Roach Hal • SHT • USA
ZERO HOUR, THE • 1918 • Vale Travers • USA
ZERO HOUR, THE • 1923 • *Cuneo Lester* • USA
ZERO HOUR, THE • 1939 • Salkow Sidney • USA
ZERO HOUR: OPERATION ROMMEL see **HORA CERO: OPERACION ROMMEL** • 1968
ZERO IN AMORE see **E ARRIVATO L'ACCORDATORE** • 1952
ZERO IN THE UNIVERSE • 1966 • Moorse Georg • USA
ZERO MURDER CASE, THE see **STRANGE AFFAIR OF UNCLE HARRY, THE** • 1945
ZERO NO HAKKEN • 1963 • Kuri Yoji • ANS • JPN • DISCOVERY OF ZERO, THE
ZERO NO INJU • 1968 • Hayasaka Hiroshi • JPN • OBSCENE ANIMAL OF ZERO
ZERO OPTION • 1988 • Hellings Sarah • USA
ZERO PILOT see **OZORA NO SAMURAI** • 1976
ZERO POPULATION GROWTH • 1972 • Campus Michael • UKN, USA • Z.P.G. (USA) ○ FIRST OF JANUARY, THE ○ EDICT
ZERO THE FOOL see **TRAGIC DIARY OF ZERO THE FOOL, THE** • 1969
ZERO THE HERO • 1954 • Kneitel Seymour • ANS • USA
ZERO, THE HOUND • 1941 • Fleischer Dave • ANS • USA
ZERO TO SIXTY • 1978 • Weis Don • USA
ZEROSEN KUROKUMO IKKA • 1962 • Masuda Toshio • JPN • ZERO FIGHTER
ZERSCHOSSENE TRAUME • 1976 • Patzak Peter • AUS, FRN, FRG • APPAT, L' (FRN) ○ BAIT, THE
ZERSTREUTE DICHTER, DER • 1915 • Del Zopp Rudolf • FRG
ZERT • 1968 • Jires Jaromil • CZC • JOKE, THE
ZERTIGO DIAMOND CAPER, THE • 1980 • Asselin Paul • USA
ZERWANY MOST • 1962 • Passendorfer Jerzy • PLN • BROKEN BRIDGE, THE
ZES JAREN • 1946 • Josephson H. M., van der Linden Charles Huguenot • NTH • SIX YEARS
ZESTOKE GODINE • 1980 • Ristic Zika, Baitrov Ravil • USS, YGS • FORCEFUL YEARS, THE ○ BITTER YEARS, THE
ZESTOS MENAS AUGOUSTOS, HO • 1966 • Kapsaskis Sokrates • GRC • HOT MONTH OF AUGUST, THE (USA)
ZETA ONE • 1969 • Cort Michael • UKN
ZETTAI TASU • 1965 • Nakamura Noboru • JPN • ABSOLUTE MAJORITY
ZETTAI ZETSUMEI see **KOKUSAI HIMITSU KEISATSU: ZETTAI ZETSUMEI** • 1967
ZETTELDAMMERUNG • 1979 • Kaiser Alfred • DOC • AUS • PAMPHLET TWILIGHT
ZEUGE, DER • 1967 • Heynowski Walter, Scheumann Gerhard • GDR • WITNESS, THE
ZEUGEN GESUCHT • 1930 • Heuberger Edmund • FRG
ZEUGENDE TOD, DER • 1920 • Sarnow Heinz • FRG
ZEUGIN AUS DER HOLLE, DIE • 1966 • Mitrovic Zika • FRG, YGS
ZEUZERE DE ZEGOUZIE • 1970 • Noel Jean-Guy • SHT • CND
ZEX see **ESCAPEMENT** • 1957
ZEX, THE ELECTRONIC FIEND see **ESCAPEMENT** • 1957
ZEYNEP OF THE SEVEN VILLAGES see **YEDI KOYUN ZEYNEBI** • 1968
ZEYNO • 1970 • Yilmaz Atif • TRK
ZEZET • 1961 • Issa Sayyed • EGY
ZEZOWATE SZCZESCIE • 1960 • Munk Andrzej • PLN • DE LA VEINE A REVENDRE ○ SCHIELENDE GLUCK, DAS ○ BAD LUCK
ZGODBA KI JE NI • 1967 • Klopcic Matjaz • YGS • NON-EXISTENT STORY, A ○ ON THE RUN
ZGODNIE Z ROZKAZEM • 1970 • Karabasz Kazimierz • DCS • PLN • ACCORDING TO ORDERS
ZHAN SHEN TAN • 1972 • Wang Yu • HKG • BEACH OF THE WAR GODS ○ BEACH OF WAR GODS
ZHAVORONKI PRILETAYUT PYERVYMI • 1968 • Rudzitis Maris • USS • SKYLARKS ARE THE FIRST TO RETURN ○ SKYLARKS FLY HOME FIRST
ZHDITE PISEM • 1960 • Karasik Yuli • USS • WAITING FOR LETTERS
ZHDYOM TEBYA, PARENI • 1973 • Batyrov Ravil • USS • WE'LL BE WAITING FOR YOU, BOY! ○ WE ARE WAITING FOR YOU, LAD!
ZHELEZNYI POTOK see **ZHELYEZNY POTOK** • 1967
ZHELYEZNY POTOK • 1967 • Dzigan Yefim • USS • IRON FLOOD, THE ○ ZHELEZNYI POTOK
ZHEN NU • 1988 • Huang Jianzhong • CHN • TWO VIRTUOUS WOMEN
ZHENIKH S TOGO SVETA • 1958 • Gaidai Leonid • USS • BRIDEGROOM FROM THE OTHER WORLD ○ FIANCEE FROM THE OTHER WORLD
ZHENITBA BALZAMINOVA • 1965 • Voinov Konstantin • USS • MARRIAGE OF BALZAMINOV, THE (USA) ○ BALZAMINOV'S MARRIAGE
ZHENSHCHINA IZ MEVAZARA • 1977 • Khamraev Ali • USS • WOMAN FROM MEVAZAR, THE
ZHENSHCHINA, KOTORAY POYOT • 1979 • Orlov Alexandr • USS • WOMAN WHO SINGS, THE
ZHENSHCHINA S KINZHALOM • 1916 • Protazanov Yakov • USS • WOMAN WITH A DAGGER ○ WOMAN WITH THE DAGGER, THE
ZHENSHCHINNI see **ZHENSHCHINY** • 1965
ZHENSHCHINY • 1965 • Lyubimov Pavel • USS • RUSSIAN WOMEN, THE ○ WOMEN, THE ○ ZHENSHCHINNI
ZHENYA, ZHENECHKA AND THE KATYUSHA see **ZHENYA, ZHENECHKA I KATYUSHA** • 1967
ZHENYA, ZHENECHKA I KATYUSHA • 1967 • Motyl Vladimir • USS • ZHENYA, ZHENECHKA AND THE KATYUSHA
ZHEREBYONOK • 1960 • Fetin Vladimir • USS • COLT, THE
ZHESTOKOST • 1959 • Skuibin Vladimir • USS • CRUELTY
ZHI QU WEI HU SHAN • 1970 • CHN • TAKING TIGER MOUNTAIN BY STRATEGY
ZHIL PEVCHI DROZD see **ZIL PEVCIJ DROZD** • 1972
ZHILI-BILI STARIK SO STARUKHOI • 1965 • Chukhrai Grigori • USS • THERE LIVED AN OLD MAN AND AN OLD WOMAN ○ THERE WAS AN OLD COUPLE (USA) ○ COUPLE, THE
ZHILI-BYLI SEM'SIMEONOV • 1989 • Franks Hercs, Eisner Vladimir • USS • ONCE UPON A TIME THERE LIVED SEVEN SIMEONS
ZHITEL NYEOBITAYEMOVO OSTROVA see **ZITEL NEOBITAJEMOVO OSTROVA** • 1915
ZHIVET TAKOI PAREN • 1964 • Shukshin Vassili • USS • BOY LIKE THAT, A ○ THERE WAS A LAD
ZHIVOI TRUP • 1929 • Ozep Fedor • USS, FRG • LEBENDE LEICHHAM, DER (FRG) ○ LIVING CORPSE, THE
ZHIVOI TRUP • 1953 • Vengerov Vladimir • USS • LIVING CORPSE, THE
ZHIVOI TRUP • 1969 • Vengerov Vladimir • USS • LIVING CORPSE, THE
ZHIVYE GEROI • 1959 • Zalakevicius Vitautus, Zhebrunas Arunas, Gedris Marionas Vintzo, Bratkauskas Balis • USS • LIVING HEROES
ZHIVYE I MERTVYE • 1964 • Stolper Alexander • USS • LIVING AND THE DEAD, THE
ZHIZN • 1927 • Donskoi Mark • USS • LIFE
ZHIZN I SMYERT FERDINANDA LYUSA • 1977 • Bobrovsky Anatoli • USS • LIFE AND DEATH OF FERDINAND LYUS, THE
ZHIZN KHOROSHAYA SHTUKA, BRAT! • 1967 • Askerov Ramiz, Vojazos Antonis • USS • LIFE'S A FINE THING, BROTHER!
ZHIZN PREKRASNA (USS) see **VITA E BELLA, LA** • 1980
ZHIZN V SMERTI • 1914 • Bauer Yevgeni • USS • LIFE IN DEATH
ZHIZN V TSITADEL • 1947 • Rappaport Herbert • USS • LIFE IN THE CITADEL ○ LIFE IN A CITADEL
ZHIZN ZA ZHIZN • 1916 • Bauer Yevgeni • USS • LIFE FOR A LIFE, A
ZHONGHUA NUER • 1949 • Ling Zhifeng, Zhai Jiang • CHN • DAUGHTERS OF CHINA
ZHUFU • 1957 • Sang Hu • CHN • NEW YEAR SACRIFICE
ZHUKOVSKY • 1951 • Pudovkin V. I., Vasiliev Dimitri • USS • YUKOVSKY
ZHUMORESKI • 1925 • Vertov Dziga • USS • HUMORESQUE ○ IUMORESKI
ZHURAVUSHKA • 1969 • Moskalenko N. • USS
ZHURNALIST • 1967 • Gerasimov Sergei • USS • JOURNALIST
ZHURNALISTA see **VASHA ZNAKOMAYA** • 1927
ZHUZHUNA'S DOWRY • 1930 • Palavandishvili S. • USS
ZIA D'AMERICA VA A SCIARE, LA • 1958 • Montero Roberto Bianchi • ITL
ZIA DI CARLO, LA • 1943 • Guarini Alfredo • ITL
ZIA PICCHIATELLA, LA see **ZIA SMEMORATA, LA** • 1941
ZIA SMEMORATA, LA • 1941 • Vajda Ladislao • ITL • PASSAGIO A LIVELLO ○ ZIA PICCHIATELLA, LA
ZIBALDONE N.1 see **ALTRI TEMPI** • 1952
ZIBALDONE N.2 see **TEMPI NOSTRI** • 1954

ZIBAYE KHATARNAK • 1967 • Eshghi Salar • IRN • DANGEROUSLY BEAUTIFUL

ZID • 1965 • Zaninovic Ante • ANS • YGS • WALL, THE

ZIDDI • 1964 • *Burman S. D. (M)* • IND

ZIDORE OU LES METAMORPHOSES • 1921 • Feuillade Louis • FRN

ZIDUL • 1974 • Vaeni Constantin • RMN • WALL, THE

ZIEGFELD FOLLIES • 1945 • Minnelli Vincente, Sidney George, Ayres Lemuel, Del Ruth Roy • USA

ZIEGFELD FOLLIES PROLOGUE, THE • 1948 • Bunin Louis • ANM • USA

ZIEGFELD GIRL • 1941 • Leonard Robert Z. • USA

ZIEGFELD, THE MAN AND HIS WOMEN • 1978 • Kulik Buzz • TVM • USA

ZIEH' DICH AUS, PUPPE • 1968 • von Rathony Akos • FRG • STRIP OFF, DOLL

ZIEL IN DEN WOLKEN • 1938 • Liebeneiner Wolfgang • FRG • GOAL IN THE CLOUDS (USA)

ZIELARZE Z KAMIENNEJ DOLINY • 1952 • Has Wojciech J. • PLN • FLOWERS OF THE VALLEY

ZIEMIA CZEKA • 1954 • Lomnicki Jan • DOC • PLN • EARTH WAITS, THE

ZIEMIA I WEGIEL • 1961 • Jankowski Lucjan • PLN • EARTH AND COAL

ZIEMIA KOSZALINSKA • 1961 • Wionczek Roman • DOC • PLN • KOSZALIN REGION, THE

ZIEMIA OBIECANA • 1974 • Wajda Andrzej • PLN • LAND OF PROMISE (UKN) ○ PROMISED LAND (USA)

ZIEMIA OPOLSKA • 1959 • Hoffman Jerzy, Skorzewski Edward • DCS • PLN • OPOLE REGION, THE

ZIEMIA WIELKOPOLSKA • 1961 • Ziarnik Jerzy • DOC • PLN • GREAT POLAND REGION, THE

ZIG ET PUCE SAUVENT NENETTE • 1952 • Noe Yvan, Rollin Georges • SHT • FRN

ZIG ZAG see **ZIGZAG** • 1950

ZIG-ZAG OF FORTUNE see **ZIG-ZAG UDACHI NEZABUVAEMOE** • 1969

ZIG-ZAG OF SUCCESS, THE see **ZIG-ZAG UDACHI NEZABUVAEMOE** • 1969

ZIG-ZAG STORY • 1983 • Schulmann Patrick • FRN

ZIG-ZAG UDACHI NEZABUVAEMOE • 1969 • Ryazanov Eldar • USS • ZIG-ZAG OF SUCCESS, THE ○ ZIG-ZAG OF FORTUNE

ZIG-ZIG • 1974 • Szabo Laszlo • FRN, ITL • ZIG ZIG NON SI POSSONO STRAPPARE LE STELLE (ITL)

ZIG ZIG NON SI POSSONO STRAPPARE LE STELLE (ITL) see **ZIG-ZIG** • 1974

ZIGANO see **ZIGANO, DER BRIGANT VOM MONTE DIAVOLO** • 1925

ZIGANO, DER BRIGANT VOM MONTE DIAVOLO • 1925 • Piel Harry • FRG • ZIGANO

ZIGARETTEN GRAFIN, DIE • 1922 • Neff Wolfgang • FRG

ZIGEUNER DER NACHT • 1932 • Schwarz Hanns • FRG

ZIGEUNERBARON • 1935 • Hartl Karl • FRG

ZIGEUNERBARON, DER • 1927 • Zelnik Friedrich • FRG

ZIGEUNERBARON, DER • 1954 • Rabenalt Arthur M. • FRG • GYPSY BARON

ZIGEUNERBARON, DER • 1962 • Wilhelm Kurt • FRG, FRN

ZIGEUNERBLUT • 1911 • Gad Urban • FRG • GYPSY BLOOD

ZIGEUNERBLUT • 1920 • Krause Karl Otto • FRG

ZIGEUNERBLUT • 1934 • Klein Charles • FRG • UNGARMADEL

ZIGEUNERLIEBCHEN • 1928 • D'Algy Antonio • FRG

ZIGEUNERLIEBE • 1922 • Walsh Thomas E. • AUS

ZIGEUNERPRIMAS, DER • 1929 • Wilhelm Carl • FRG

ZIGEUNERWEISEN • 1918 • Meinert Rudolf • FRG

ZIGEUNERWEISEN • 1940 • von Bolvary Geza • FRG • GYPSY WAYS (USA)

ZIGEUNERWEISEN • 1980 • Suzuki Seijun • JPN

ZIGGY STARDUST AND THE SPIDERS FROM MARS • 1983 • Pennebaker D. A. • DOC • UKN

ZIGGY'S GIFT • 1982 • Williams Richard • ANS • USA

ZIGOMAR • 1911 • Jasset Victorin • SRL • FRN

ZIGOMAR CONTRE NICK CARTER • 1912 • Jasset Victorin • FRN

ZIGOMAR EELSKIN (UKN) see **ZIGOMAR, PEAU D'ANGUILLE** • 1912

ZIGOMAR, PEAU D'ANGUILLE • 1912 • Jasset Victorin (c/d) • SRL • FRN • ZIGOMAR EELSKIN (UKN)

ZIGOTO • 1911 • Durand Jean • SER • FRN

ZIGZAG • 1950 • Stauffacher Frank • SHT • USA • ZIG ZAG

ZIGZAG • 1970 • Colla Richard A. • USA • FALSE WITNESS (UKN)

ZIGZAG • 1974 • Buyens Frans • BLG

ZIGZAGS • 1983 • Melancon Andre • CND

ZIJEME V PRAZE • 1934 • Vavra Otakar • SHT • CZC

ZIKKARON • 1971 • Coderre Laurent • ANS • CND

ZIKLOPAT • 1976 • Hristov Hristo • BUL • CYCLOPS, THE ○ TSIKLOPUT

ZIL PEVCIJ DROZD • 1972 • Ioseliani Otar • USS • THERE WAS A SINGING BLACKBIRD ○ ONCE THERE WAS A THRUSH ○ SINGING THRUSH, THE ○ THERE LIVED A THRUSH ○ ZHIL PEVCHI DROZD ○ ONCE A BLACKBIRD SANG

ZILCHI • 1989 • Riddiford Richard • NZL

ZILE DE VARA • 1968 • Nita Ion • RMN • SUMMER DAYS

ZILE FIERBINTI • 1976 • Nicolaescu Sergiu • RMN • HOT DAYS

ZILIARA, I • 1968 • Karayannis Kostas • GRC • JEALOUS WIFE, THE

ZILLAH, A GYPSY ROMANCE see **PORTRAIT, THE** • 1911

ZILLAH, A STORY OF GYPSY LIFE • 1909 • *Anglo-American Films* • UKN

ZILLI NAZIFE • 1967 • Un Memduh • TRK

ZIMBA GIBI DELIKANLI • 1964 • Conturk Remzi • TRK

ZIMBO • 1958 • Wadia Homi • IND

ZIMMER 13 • 1964 • Reinl Harald • FRG • ROOM 13 (USA)

ZIMMER 36 • 1988 • Fischer Markus • SWT

ZIMMERMADCHEN.. DREIMAL KLINGELN • 1933 • Heuberger Edmund • FRG

ZIMOVANJE U JAKOBSFELDU • 1976 • Bauer Branko • YGS • WINTERING IN JAKOBSFIELD

ZIMOVY ZMIERZCH • 1957 • Lenartowicz Stanislaw • PLN • WINTER DUSK

ZINA • 1986 • McMullen Ken • UKN

ZINC LAMINE ET ARCHITECTURE • 1958 • Berr • SHT • FRN

ZINC OINTMENT • 1971 • Dolan Marianne • SHT • CND

ZINDA LASH • 1932 • *Sircar B. N. (P)* • IND

ZINDAGI • 1940 • *Sircar B. N. (P)* • IND

ZINDAGI AUR MAUT • 1965 • Ansari N. A. • IND

ZINDAGI ZINDAGI • 1972 • *Burman S. D. (M)* • IND

ZINDIGI • 1939 • Barua Pramathesh Chandra • IND

ZINGARA • 1969 • Laurenti Mariano • ITL

ZINGARO • 1935 • *Gulab* • IND

ZINGARO, LO see **GITAN, LE** • 1975

ZINGO, SON OF THE SEA • 1914 • *Ambrosio* • ITL

ZINKER, DER • 1931 • Lamac Carl, Fric Martin • FRG

ZINKER, DER • 1965 • Vohrer Alfred • FRG • SQUEAKER, THE (USA)

ZINKERS DOOR DE WESTERSCHELDE • 1966 • van Nie Rene • NTH

ZINZABELLE A PARIS • 1949 • Starevitch Ladislas, Bo Soniko • ANM • FRN

ZIO ADOLFO IN ARTE FUHRER • 1978 • Castellano, Pipolo • ITL

ZIO D'AMERICA, LO • 1939 • Benedetti A. • UNCLE FROM AMERICA, THE (USA)

ZIO INDEGNO, LO • 1990 • Brusati Franco • ITL • DISREPUTABLE UNCLE, THE

ZIO TOM • 1971 • Jacopetti Gualtiero, Prosperi Franco* • ITL • FAREWELL UNCLE TOM (USA) ○ UNCLE TOM (UKN) ○ ADDIO ZIO TOM

ZIP AND HIS GANG • 1915 • *L-Ko* • USA

ZIP AND ZEST • 1919 • Pratt Gilbert • SHT • USA

ZIP 'N' SNORT • 1960 • Jones Charles M. • ANS • USA

ZIP THE DODGER • 1914 • Arbuckle Roscoe? • USA

ZIPPING ALONG • 1953 • Jones Charles M. • ANS • USA

ZIPSTONES • 1975 • Bongers Bob • ANS • NTH

ZIR-E-GONBAD-E-KABOUD • 1967 • Reis-Firouz Mehdi • IRN • BENEATH THE SKY

ZIRAFA V OKNE • 1968 • Cvrcek Radim • CZC • GIRAFFE IN THE WINDOW, A

ZIRE POOSTE SHAB • 1975 • Goleh Freydoon • IRN • UNDER COVER OF NIGHT

ZIRKUS BROWN see **WENN DU NOCH EINE MUTTER HAST** • 1924

ZIRKUS DES LEBENS • 1921 • Guter Johannes • FRG

ZIRKUS KOMMT, DER • 1966 • Houwer Rob • FRG

ZIRKUS LEBEN • Paul Heinz • FRG

ZIRKUS RENZ • 1926 • Neff Wolfgang • FRG

ZIRKUS RENZ • 1943 • Rabenalt Arthur M. • FRG • RENZ CIRCUS, THE

ZIRKUS-ROMANZE, EINE see **MAGYARENFURSTIN, DIE** • 1923

ZIRKUS SARAN see **KNOX UND DIE LUSTIGEN VAGABUNDEN** • 1935

ZIRKUS SCHNABELMAN • 1920 • Valentin Karl • FRG

ZIRKUSBLUT • 1916 • Oswald Richard • FRG

ZIRKUSDIVA, DIE • 1924 • Kahn William? • FRG

ZIRKUSGRAFIN • *Andra Fern* • FRG

ZIRKUSKONIG, DER • 1924 • Linder Max, Violet Edouard-Emile • AUS, FRN • ROI DU CIRQUE, LE (FRN) ○ CIRCUSMANIA (UKN) ○ KING OF THE CIRCUS ○ CLOWN AUS LIEBE

ZIRKUSMADEL, DAS see **SCHWERE JUNGE, DER** • 1921

ZIRKUSMADEL, EIN • 1916 • Wilhelm Carl? • FRG

ZIRKUSPRINZESSIN, DIE • 1925 • Gartner Adolf • FRG

ZIRKUSPRINZESSIN, DIE • 1928 • Janson Victor • FRG

ZIS BOOM BAH • 1941 • Nigh William • USA • JAZZ MAD

ZISE VIA TIN AGAPI MAS • 1968 • Tempos Antonis • GRC • DO NOT FORSAKE MY LOVE ○ ASK FOR MY LOVE

ZISKA LA DANSEUSE ESPIONNE • 1922 • Andreani Henri • FRN

ZIT' • 1935 • Room Abram • USS

ZIT SVUJ ZIVOT • 1963 • Schorm Evald • DOC • CZC • TO LIVE ONE'S LIFE ○ LIVING ONE'S LIFE

ZITA see **TANTE ZITA** • 1967

ZITEL NEOBITAJEMOVO OSTROVA • 1915 • Starevitch Ladislas • USS • HABITANT OF THE DESERT ISLE, THE (USA) ○ INHABITANT OF A DESERT ISLE ○ ZHITEL NYEOBITAYEMOVO OSTROVA

ZITELLONI, GLI • 1958 • Bianchi Giorgio • ITL, SPN

ZITONTAS TI TIHI STA XENA • 1967 • Douros Thimios • GRC • SEARCH FOR A BETTER LIFE, THE

ZITRA TO ROZTOCIME, DRAHOUSKU • 1977 • Schulhoff Petr • CZC • LET'S MAKE WHOOPEE TOMORROW, DARLING..! ○ LET'S STEP ON IT TOMORROW, DARLING

ZITRA VSTANU A OPARIM SE CAJEM • 1977 • Polak Jindrich • CZC • TOMORROW I'LL WAKE UP AND SCALD MYSELF WITH TEA

ZITS • 1986 • Shermann Arthur • USA

ZIVA ISTINA • 1973 • Radic Tomislav • YGS • REAL TRUTH, THE

ZIVI BILI PA VIDJELI • 1980 • Gamulin Bruno, Puhlovski Milivoj • YGS • THAT'S THE WAY THE COOKIE CRUMBLES ○ THAT'S HOW THE COOKIE CRUMBLES

ZIVJECE OVAJ NAROD • 1947 • Popovic Nikola • YGS

ZIVJETI OD LJUBAVI • 1974 • Golik Kreso • YGS • TO LIVE ON LOVE

ZIVJETI ZA INAT • 1973 • Ilyenko Yury • USS, YGS • TO LIVE OUT OF SPITE

ZIVOT I DELA BESMRTNOG VOZDA KARADJORDJE • 1911 • Stojadinovic I. • YGS

ZIVOT JE LEP • 1985 • Draskovic Boro • YGS • LIFE IS BEAUTIFUL

ZIVOT JE MASOVNA POJAVA • 1971 • Idrizovic Mirza • YGS • LIFE IS A MASS PHENOMENON

ZIVOT JE NAS • 1948 • Gavrin Gustav • YGS

ZIVOT JE PES • 1933 • Fric Martin • CZC • DOG'S LIFE, A

ZIVOT SEL KOLEM • 1913 • Mejkal Rudolf • CZC • LIFE PASSED BY

ZIVOT VOJENSKY, ZIVOT VESELY • 1934 • Svitak • CZC • MILITARY LIFE, PLEASANT LIFE

ZIVOTEM VEDLA JE LASKA • 1928 • Rovensky Josef • CZC • LOVE LEAD THEM THROUGH LIFE

ZIYARA, AZ- • 1972 • Zubaydi Qays Al- • IRQ • VISITE, LA

ZIZA IZ IDRIJE • 1947 • Rajic Nikola, Petrovic Miodrag • YGS

ZIZANIE, LA • 1978 • Zidi Claude • FRN

ZIZEN • 1949 • Kubasek Vaclav • CZC

ZIZIS EN FOLIE, LES • 1977 • Roy Jean-Claude • FRN

ZIZKOVSKA ROMANCE • 1958 • Brynych Zbynek • CZC • LOCAL ROMANCE, A

ZIZNIVE MLADI • 1943 • Krnansky M. J. • CZC • THIRSTY YOUTH, THE

ZJOEK • 1987 • van Zuylen Erik • NTH

ZKAZENA KREV • 1913 • Wiesmer Alois • CZC • ROTTEN BLOOD

ZKROCENI ZLEHO MUZE • 1987 • Polednakova Marie • CZC, FNL • POWERPLAY

ZLATA KATERINA • 1934 • Slavinsky Vladimir • CZC • GOLDEN KATHERINE

ZLATA RENETA • 1965 • Vavra Otakar • CZC • GOLDEN RENNET, THE ○ GOLDEN QUEENING, THE

ZLATA ZENA • 1920 • Slavinsky Vladimir • CZC • GOLDEN WOMAN, THE

ZLATE CASY • 1978 • Uher Stefan • CZC • GOLDEN DAYS, THE

ZLATE KAPRADI • 1963 • Weiss Jiri • CZC • GOLDEN BRACKEN ○ GOLDEN FERN, THE

ZLATE PTACE • 1932 • Kminek • CZC • LITTLE GOLD BIRD, THE

ZLATE SRDECKO • 1916 • Fencl Antonin • CZC • GOLDEN HEART, THE ○ HEART OF GOLD

ZLATNA PRACKA • 1968 • Dukic Radivoje-Lola • YGS • GOLDEN SLING, THE

ZLATNIAT ZAB • 1962 • Marinovich Anton • BUL • GOLDEN TOOTH, THE

ZLATOROG • 1918 • Randolf Rolf • FRG

ZLATOVLASKA • 1954 • Tyrlova Hermina, Dudesek Jan • ANS • CZC • GOLDEN CURLS ○ GOLDILOCKS

ZLATY KLICEK • 1922 • Kvapil Jaroslav • CZC • LITTLE GOLD KEY, THE

ZLATYE GORI • 1931 • Yutkevich Sergei • USS • GOLDEN MOUNTAINS ○ GOLDEN HILLS

ZLE PARE • 1956 • Stojanovic Velimir • YGS

ZLOCIN V DIVCI SKOLE • 1965 • Menzel Jiri, Rychmann Ladislav, Novak Ivo • CZC • CRIME AT THE GIRLS' SCHOOL ○ CRIME IN THE GIRLS' SCHOOL ○ CRIME AT A GIRLS' SCHOOL

ZLOCIN V MODRE HVEZDE • 1973 • Kachlik Antonin • CZC • CRIME OF THE BLUE STAR

ZLOCIN V SANTANU • 1968 • Menzel Jiri • CZC • CRIME IN THE CAFE CHANTAN ○ CRIME IN THE NIGHT CLUB ○ CRIME AT THE NIGHT CLUB ○ CRIME IN A NIGHT CLUB

ZLOTE KOLO • 1971 • Wohl Stanislaw • MTV • PLN • GOLD RING

ZLOTO • 1961 • Has Wojciech J. • PLN • GOLDEN DREAMS ○ GOLD

ZLY CHLOPIEC • 1950 • Wajda Andrzej • PLN • EVIL BOY, THE ○ BAD BOY, THE

ZMIANA WARTY • 1958 • Bielinska Halina, Haupe Wlodzimierz • ANS • PLN • CHANGING OF THE GUARD

ZMITANA see **HRST VODY** • 1971

ZMLUVA S DIABLOM • 1967 • Zachar Jozef • CZC • DEAL WITH THE DEVIL

ZMORY • 1979 • Marczewski Wojciech • PLN • NIGHTMARES

ZMRZLY DREVAR • 1962 • Brdecka Jiri • ANM • CZC • FROZEN LOGGER, THE

ZNACHOR • 1938 • Waszynski Michael • PLN • MIRACLE MAN, THE (USA)

ZNACHOR • 1981 • Hoffman Jerzy • PLN • WITCH DOCTOR, THE

ZNAJOME Z LODZI • 1972 • Gryczelowska Krystyna • DOC • PLN • TEXTILE WORKERS

ZNAK BEDY • 1986 • Ptashuk Mikhail • USS • SIGN OF DISASTER ○ ILL OMEN

ZNAKI NA DRODZE • 1971 • Piotrowski Andrzej J. • PLN • SIGNS ON THE ROAD

ZNAMENI RAKA • 1967 • Herz Juraj • CZC • SIGN OF THE CRAB, THE ○ SIGN OF CANCER, THE ○ MARK OF CANCER, THE

ZNATIZELJA • 1966 • Dovnikovic Borivoj • ANS • YGS • CURIOSITY

ZNOI • 1963 • Shepitko Larissa • USS • HEAT WAVE, THE ○ HEAT

ZO • 1957 • Yamamoto Kajiro • JPN • ELEPHANT, AN

ZO O KUTTA RENCHU • 1947 • Yoshimura Kozaburo • JPN • FELLOWS WHO ATE THE ELEPHANT, THE

ZOARD MESTER • 1917 • Curtiz Michael • HNG • MASTER ZOARD

ZOBACZYMY SIE W NIEDZIELE • 1959 • Lenartowicz Stanislaw • PLN • WE'LL MEET ON SUNDAY

ZOCELENI • 1950 • Fric Martin • CZC • TEMPERED STEEL ○ STEEL TOWN

ZODIA FECIOAREI • 1966 • Marcus Manole • RMN • VIRGO

ZODIAC COUPLES, THE • 1970 • Stein Bob, Roberts Alan • USA

ZODIAC KILLER, THE • 1971 • Hanson Tom • USA

ZOE • 1953 • Brabant Charles • FRN

ZOEKEN NAAR EILEEN • 1987 • van den Berg Rudolf • NTH • SEARCHING FOR EILEEN

ZOFENSTREICHE • 1915 • Moest Hubert • FRG

ZOFF • 1971 • Pieper Eberhard • FRG

ZOFIA • 1915 • Moest Hubert • FRG

ZOFIA • 1977 • Czekala Ryszard • PLN • SOPHIA

ZOGA EL SANIA, EL see **ZAWGA AL THANIA, AL** • 1967

ZOI ENOS ANTHROPOU, I • 1968 • Ziagos Spiros • GRC • LIFE OF A MAN, THE

ZOKO MINAMI NO KAZE • 1942 • Yoshimura Kozaburo • JPN • SOUTH WIND: SEQUEL

ZOKU AKUTOKUI (JOI-HEN) • 1967 • Fukuda Seiichi • JPN • VICIOUS DOCTOR (PART 2)

ZOKU BANKA JIGOKU • 1929 • Inagaki Hiroshi • JPN • ELEGY OF HELL II-III

ZOKU BOTCHAN SHAIN • 1954 • Yamamoto Kajiro • JPN • MR. VALIANT RIDES AGAIN

ZOKU HEITAI YAKUZA • 1965 • Tanaka Tokuzo • JPN • PRIVATE AND THE C.O., THE

ZOKU HIROKU ONNA RO • 1968 • Yasuda Kimiyoshi • JPN • WOMEN'S CELL

ZOKU IZUKOE • 1967 • Moritani Shiro • JPN • TOO MANY MOONS

ZOKU JIROCHI FUJI • 1960 • Mori Issei • JPN • JIROCHI THE CHIVALROUS
ZOKU JOROHZUMA • 1968 • Hashimoto Tadanori • JPN • WHORE FOR A WIFE, A
ZOKU JUDAI NO SEITEN • 1953 • Saeki Kozo • JPN • DANGEROUS AGE
ZOKU KINDAN NO SUNA • 1958 • Horiuchi Manao • JPN
ZOKU: MIDAREGAMI HADAIROJIGAKE • 1967 • Fukuda Seiichi • JPN • SKIN TRICK
ZOKU NAMONAKU MAZUSHIKU UTSUKUSHIKU: CHICHI TO KO • 1967 • Matsuyama Zenzo • JPN • OUR SILENT LOVE ○ CHICHI TO KO
ZOKU NIHON BOKO ANKOKUSHI BOGYAKUMA • 1967 • Wakamatsu Koji • JPN • RAPIST, THE
ZOKU NIKU • 1968 • Mukoi Hiroshi • JPN • FLESH, THE
ZOKU NIKUTAI JOYU NIKKI • 1968 • Sasaki Moto • JPN • DIARY OF A SEXY ACTRESS
ZOKU NINGEN KAKUMEI • 1975 • Masuda Toshio • JPN • HUMAN REVOLUTION, PART II ○ HUMAN REVOLUTION: SEQUEL
ZOKU OOKU MARUHI MONOGATARI see **OOKU MARUHI MONOGATARI** • 1967
ZOKU OTOKOWA TSURAIYO • 1969 • Yamada Yoji • JPN • TORA-SAN PT. 2 (USA) ○ TORA-SAN'S CHERISHED MOTHER ○ AM I TRYING PART II ○ TORASAN, HOMEWARD JOURNEY
ZOKU OTOSHIMAE • 1968 • Ishii Teruo • JPN • FINAL DECISION, THE
ZOKU ROKYOKU KOMORIUTA • 1967 • Takamori Ryuichi • JPN • DADDY'S LULLABY
ZOKU SEX DOCTOR NO KIROKU • 1968 • Yuge Taro • JPN • MASKED DOCTOR, THE
ZOKU SHACHO GYOJOKI • 1966 • Matsubayashi Shue • JPN • FIVE GENTS ON THE SPOT
ZOKU SHACHO HANJOKI • 1968 • Matsubayashi Shue • JPN • FIVE GENTS AND A CHINESE MERCHANT
ZOKU SHACHO SANDAIKI • 1958 • Matsubayashi Shue • JPN
ZOKU SHACHO SENICHIYA see **SHACHO SEN-ICHIYA** • 1967
ZOKU SOSHIKI BORYOKU • 1967 • Sato Junya • JPN • ORGANISED VIOLENCE (TWO)
ZOKU SUGATA SANSHIRO • 1945 • Kurosawa Akira • JPN • SUGATA SANSHIRO PART II ○ JUDO SAGA II
ZOKU TOSEININ • 1967 • Saeki Kiyoshi • JPN • GAMBLERS' WORLD (TWO), THE
ZOKU YAKUZA BOZU • 1968 • Ikehiro Kazuo • JPN • PRIEST AND THE GOLD MINT
ZOLDAR • 1965 • Gaal Istvan • HNG • GREEN YEARS, THE ○ GREEN FLOOD
ZOLLENSTEIN • 1917 • Jones Edgar • USA
ZOLNIERZ ZWYCIESTWA • 1953 • Jakubowska Wanda • PLN • PUPPET OF WARSAW, THE ○ SOLDIER OF VICTORY
ZOLOTAIA ANTILOPA • 1954 • Atamanov Lev • USS • GOLDEN ANTELOPE, THE
ZOLOTAYA GOLOVA MSTITELYA • 1989 • Khmadamov Alisher • USS • GOLDEN HEAD OF THE AVENGER, THE
ZOLOTOI ESHELON • 1961 • Gurin Ilya • USS • GOLDEN TRAIN, THE
ZOLOTOI KLYUCHIK • 1939 • Ptushko Alexander • ANM • USS • LITTLE GOLDEN KEY, THE ○ GOLDEN KEY
ZOLOTOY TELYONOK • 1968 • Schweitzer Mikhail • USS • GOLDEN CALF, THE
ZOLOTYE VOROTA • 1969 • Solntseva Yulia • USS • GOLDEN GATES, THE
ZOLTAN see **DRACULA'S DOG** • 1978
ZOLTAN.. HOUND OF DRACULA see **DRACULA'S DOG** • 1978
ZOLTAN, HOUND OF HELL see **DRACULA'S DOG** • 1978
ZOMBI 2 • 1979 • Fulci Lucio • ITL • ZOMBIE FLESH EATERS ○ ISLAND OF THE LIVING DEAD ○ ZOMBIE
ZOMBIE see **ZOMBI 2** • 1979
ZOMBIE 3 see **NOTTI DEL TERRORE, LE** • 1980
ZOMBIE, THE see **PLAGUE OF THE ZOMBIES, THE** • 1965
ZOMBIE AFTERMATH see **AFTERMATH** • 1979
ZOMBIE BRIGADE • 1988 • Pattison Barrie • ASL
ZOMBIE CHILD see **CHILD, THE** • 1977
ZOMBIE CREEPING FLESH see **INFERNO DEI MORTI-VIVENTI** • 1981
ZOMBIE FLESH EATERS see **ZOMBI 2** • 1979
ZOMBIE HIGH • 1987 • Link Ron, Toberoff Marc? • USA
ZOMBIE HOLOCAUST see **REGINA DEI CANNIBALI, LA** • 1979
ZOMBIE HORROR see **NOTTI DEL TERRORE, LE** • 1980
ZOMBIE ISLAND MASSACRE • 1984 • Carter John N. • USA
ZOMBIE LAKE see **LAC DES MORTS-VIVANTS, LE** • 1980
ZOMBIE NIGHTMARE • 1987 • Bravman Jack • USA
ZOMBIES • 1978 • Romero George A. • USA • ZOMBIES – DAWN OF THE DEAD (UKN) ○ DAWN OF THE DEAD
ZOMBIES see **I EAT YOUR SKIN** • 1964
ZOMBIES, THE see **PLAGUE OF THE ZOMBIES, THE** • 1965
ZOMBIES –DAWN OF THE DEAD (UKN) see **ZOMBIES** • 1978
ZOMBIES' LAKE see **LAC DES MORTS-VIVANTS, LE** • 1980
ZOMBIES OF MORA-TAU • 1957 • Cahn Edward L. • USA • DEAD THAT WALK, THE (UKN)
ZOMBIES OF SUGAR HILL, THE see **SUGAR HILL** • 1974
ZOMBIES OF THE STRATOSPHERE • 1952 • Brannon Fred C. • SRL • USA
ZOMBIES ON BROADWAY • 1945 • Douglas Gordon • USA • LOONIES ON BROADWAY (UKN)
ZOMBIETHON • 1986 • Dixon Ken • CMP • USA
ZON • 1920 • Boudrioz Robert • FRN
ZON, DE • 1970 • Bex Ludo • BLG
ZON OP ZONDAG • 1964 • van der Hoeven Jan • DOC • NTH • SUNDAY SUN
ZONA PERICOLOSA • 1951 • Maselli Francesco • DOC • ITL
ZONA ROJA • 1975 • Fernandez Emilio • MXC • RED ZONE
ZONDAG OP HET EILAND VAN DE GRANDE JATTE, EEN • 1965 • Weisz Frans • SHT • NTH • SUNDAY ON THE ISLAND OF THE GRAND JATTE
ZONE 2-V • 1988 • Gagov Chavdar • BUL
ZONE 413 • Mideke Michael, Potash Morton • SHT • USA
ZONE, LA • 1928 • Lacombe Georges • FRN
ZONE DE LA MORT, LA • 1917 • Gance Abel • FRN • ZONE OF DEATH, THE (USA)
ZONE DE TURBULENCE • 1984 • D'Aix Alain • MTV • CND
ZONE DESIGNEE, LE ROLE DES GOUVERNEMENTS • 1968 • Dansereau Fernand • DCS • CND
ZONE FRONTIERE • 1949 • Gourguet Jean • FRN
ZONE GRISE • 1979 • Murer Fredi M. • SWT
ZONE INTERDITE see **FAIZA, AL-** • 1975
ZONE MOVEMENT • 1956 • Brakhage Stan • SHT • USA
ZONE OF DEATH, THE • 1928 • Paul Fred • UKN
ZONE OF DEATH, THE (USA) see **ZONE DE LA MORT, LA** • 1917
ZONE ROUGE • 1986 • Enrico Robert • FRN
ZONE TROOPERS • 1986 • Bilson Danny • USA
ZONGA EL ANGEL DIABOLICO • 1957 • Orol Juan • MXC
ZONGAR • 1918 • MacFadden Barnar • USA
ZONGORA A LEVEGOBEN • 1976 • Bacso Peter • HNG • PIANO IN MID-AIR, A
ZONK • 1950 • SAF
ZONNETJE • 1920 • Binger Maurits H., Doxat-Pratt B. E. • NTH, UKN • SUNNY ○ JOY
ZONTAR: THE THING FROM VENUS • 1966 • Buchanan Larry • USA
ZONTIK • 1967 • Kobakhidze Mikhail • SHT • USS • UMBRELLA, THE
ZOO • 1962 • Haanstra Bert • NTH
ZOO • 1965 • Cantrill Arthur, Cantrill Corinne • ASL
ZOO • 1988 • Comencini Cristina • ITL
ZOO see **INVITE DE LA ONZIEME HEURE, L'** • 1945
ZOO see **CHIDIAKHANA** • 1967
ZOO: A ZED AND TWO NOUGHTS see **ZED AND TWO NOUGHTS, A** • 1985
ZOO BABY • 1957 • Eady David • UKN
ZOO, BY NIGHT, A see **ZOO LA NUIT, UN** • 1987
ZOO DIARY see **DOBUTSUEN NIKKI** • 1957
ZOO GANG, THE • 1985 • Watson John, Densham Pen • USA • WINNERS TAKE ALL
ZOO IN BUDAPEST • 1933 • Lee Rowland V. • USA
ZOO IN STANLEY PARK, THE • 1953-54 • Devlin Bernard • DCS • CND
ZOO IS COMPANY • 1961 • Hanna William, Barbera Joseph • ANS • USA
ZOO LA NUIT, UN • 1987 • Lauzon Jean-Claude • CND • ZOO, BY NIGHT, A ○ NIGHT ZOO
ZOO ON REPAIR • 1987 • Lerner Remont • ANM
ZOO ROBBERY, THE • 1973 • McCarthy Matt, Black John • UKN
ZOO SEM GRADES • 1971 • Spiguel Miguel • SHT • PRT
ZOO SHIP • 1985 • Shorr Richard • USA
ZOO STORY see **DOBUTSUEN NIKKI** • 1957
ZOO-ZERO • 1978 • Fleischer Alain • FRN • ZOO ZERO
ZOO ZERO see **ZOO-ZERO** • 1978
ZOOALS IK BEN • 1920 • Binger Maurits H., Doxat-Pratt B. E. • NTH • AS GOD MADE HER
ZOOM AND BORED • 1957 • Jones Charles M. • ANS • USA
ZOOM AT THE TOP • 1962 • Jones Charles M. • ANS • USA
ZOOM-ZOOM APOLLO • 1969 • Marquez Artemio • PHL
ZOONI • 1989 • Ali Muzaffar • IND
ZOOPSIE • 1973 • Giraldeau Jacques • ANS • CND
ZOOS OF THE WORLD • 1968 • Rasky Harry • MTV • USA
ZOOT CAT, THE • 1944 • Hanna William, Barbera Joseph • ANS • USA
ZOOT SUIT • 1981 • Valdez Luis • USA
ZOPF UND SCHWERT • 1926 • Janson Victor • FRG
ZOPF UND TURBAN • 1920 • Linke Edmund • FRG
ZORA see **SILENT NIGHT, BLOODY NIGHT** • 1972
ZORAS IL RIBELLE • 1959 • Saenz De Heredia Jose Luis • ITL, SPN
ZORBA THE GREEK • 1964 • Cacoyannis Michael • USA, GRC • ZORMBA (GRC)
ZORI PARISCHA • 1937 • Roshal Grigori • USS • DAWN IN PARIS ○ PARIS COMMUNE
ZORIKAN LO STERMINATORE • 1964 • Mauri Roberto • ITL • ZORIKAN THE BARBARIAN (USA)
ZORIKAN THE BARBARIAN (USA) see **ZORIKAN LO STERMINATORE** • 1964
ZORINA • 1948 • Ortega Juan J. • MXC
ZORMBA (GRC) see **ZORBA THE GREEK** • 1964
ZORNIGEN JUNGEN MANNER, DIE • 1960 • Rilla Wolf • FRG • ANGRY YOUNG MEN, THE
ZORNS LEMMA • 1970 • Frampton Hollis • USA
ZORRITA EN BIKINI, LA • 1975 • Iquino Ignacio F. • SPN
ZORRITA MARTINEZ • 1975 • Escriva Vicente • SPN
ZORRO • 1961 • Romero-Marchent Joaquin Luis • SPN
ZORRO • 1975 • Tessari Duccio • ITL, FRN
ZORRO ALLA CORTE DI SPAGNA • 1962 • Capuano Luigi • ITL • MASKED CONQUEROR, THE (USA) ○ ZORRO AT THE SPANISH COURT
ZORRO ALLA CORTE D'INGHELTERRA • 1969 • Montemurro Francesco • ITL
ZORRO AND THE THREE MUSKETEERS see **ZORRO E I TRE MOSCHETTIERI** • 1963
ZORRO AT THE SPANISH COURT see **ZORRO ALLA CORTE DI SPAGNA** • 1962
ZORRO CABALGA OTRA VEZ, EL • 1965 • SPN, ITL • BEHIND THE MASK OF ZORRO (USA)
ZORRO CABALLERO DE LA JUSTICIA, EL • 1971 • Merino Jose Luis • SPN, ITL • ZORRO IL CAVALIERE DELLA VENDETTA (ITL)
ZORRO CONTRO MACISTE • 1964 • Lenzi Umberto • ITL • SAMSON AND THE SLAVE QUEEN (USA) ○ ZORRO VS. MACISTE
ZORRO DE JALISCO, EL • 1940 • Benavides Jose Jr. • MXC
ZORRO DE MONTERREY, EL • 1970 • Merino Jose Luis • SPN
ZORRO E I TRE MOSCHETTIERI • 1963 • Capuano Luigi • ITL • ZORRO AND THE THREE MUSKETEERS
ZORRO ESCARLATA, EL • 1958 • Baledon Rafael • MXC
ZORRO ESCARLATA EN LA VENGANZA DEL AHORCADO, EL • 1958 • Baledon Rafael • MXC
ZORRO IL CAVALIERE DELLA VENDETTA (ITL) see **ZORRO CABALLERO DE LA JUSTICIA, EL** • 1971
ZORRO IL DOMINATORE • 1969 • Merino Jose Luis • ITL, SPN
ZORRO IL RIBELLE • 1966 • Pierotti Piero • ITL
ZORRO JUSTICIERO, EL • 1971 • Romero-Marchent Rafael • SPN
ZORRO MARCHESE DI NAVARRA • 1969 • Montemurro Francesco • ITL
ZORRO PIERDE EL PELO, EL • 1950 • Lugones Mario C. • ARG
ZORRO RIDES AGAIN • 1937 • Witney William, English John • SRL • USA
ZORRO THE AVENGER • 1960 • Barton Charles T. • MTV • USA
ZORRO, THE AVENGER (USA) see **VENGANZA DEL ZORRO, LA** • 1962
ZORRO THE GAY BLADE • 1981 • Medak Peter • USA
ZORRO VENGADOR, EL • 1961 • Gomez Urquiza Zacarias • MXC
ZORRO VS. MACISTE see **ZORRO CONTRO MACISTE** • 1964
ZORRO'S BLACK WHIP • 1944 • Bennet Spencer Gordon, Grissell Wallace A. • SRL • USA
ZORRO'S FIGHTING LEGION • 1939 • Witney William, English John • SRL • USA
ZOSSIA see **SIX CHEVAUX BLEUS** • 1967
ZOSYA • 1967 • Bogin Mikhail • USS, PLN • ZOZYA
ZOTZ! • 1962 • Castle William • USA
ZOUHEI MONOGATARI • 1963 • Ikehiro Kazuo • JPN • LOW-RANK SOLDIERS
ZOUL WIJHAIN • 1949 • Sameh Walieddine, Diaeddin Ahmed • EGY • MAN WITH TWO FACES, THE
ZOUT VOOR DE WIELEN • 1966 • Breyer Charles • NTH
ZOUZOU • 1934 • Allegret Marc • FRN
ZOYA • 1944 • Arnstam Leo • USS
ZOZOS, LES • 1973 • Thomas Pascal • FRN
ZOZYA see **ZOSYA** • 1967
ZPEV ZLATA • 1920 • Kolar J. S. • CZC • SONG OF GOLD, THE
ZPIVALI JSME ARIZONU • 1964 • Sklenar Vaclav • CZC • WE SANG THE ARIZONA
ZPOMALENY ZIVOT • 1962 • Goldberger Kurt • CZC • LIFE IN SLOW MOTION
ZRAK • 1978 • Grgic Zlatko • ANS • YGS • ENDLESS DEVILRY, AN
ZRALE VINO • 1981 • Vorlicek Vaclav • CZC • MATURE WINE
ZRCADLENI • 1965 • Schorm Evald • CZC • REFLECTIONS ○ REFLECTION
ZRODLO • 1963 • Jaworski Tadeusz • DOC • PLN • SOURCE, THE ○ SPRING, THE ○ WATER
ZRYW NA SPLYW • 1956 • Nehrebecki Wladyslaw • ANS • PLN • DASH TO THE CANOE RALLY
ZSARNOK SZIVE see **ZSARNOK SZIVE AVAGY BOCCACCIO MAGYARORSZAGON, A** • 1981
ZSARNOK SZIVE AVAGY BOCCACCIO MAGYARORSZAGON, A • 1981 • Jancso Miklos • HNG, ITL • TYRANT'S HEART, OR BOCCACCIO IN HUNGARY, THE ○ CUORE DEL TIRRANO, IL (ITL) ○ ZSARNOK SZIVE ○ HEART OF A TYRANT
ZSIGMOND MORICZ 1879–1942 see **MORICZ ZSIGMOND 1879–1942** • 1956
ZTRACENA STOPA • 1956 • Kachyna Karel • CZC • LOST TRAIL, THE ○ LOST TRACK, THE
ZTRACENA TVAR • 1965 • Hobl Pavel • CZC • LOST FACE, THE ○ BORROWED FACE, THE
ZTRACENA VARTA see **STRACENA VARTA** • 1956
ZTRACENCI • 1957 • Makovec Milos • CZC • THREE MEN MISSING
ZU BEFEHL, FRAU FELDWEBEL • 1956 • Jacoby Georg • FRG
ZU BEFEHL, HERR UNTEROFFIZIER • 1931 • Schonfelder Erich • FRG • PECHVOGEL, DER
ZU BOSER SCHLACHT SCHLEICH' ICH HEUT NACHT SO BANG • 1970 • Kluge Alexander • FRG • IN SUCH TREPIDATION I SHALL CREEP OFF TONIGHT TO THE EVIL BATTLE
ZU DEN HOHEN DER MENSCHHEIT see **VERKOMMEN** • 1920
ZU HILFE! • 1920 • Gunsburg Arthur • FRG
ZU JEDEM KOMMT EINMAL DIE LIEBE see **ALTE LIED, DAS** • 1930
ZU JEDER STUNDE • 1960 • Thiel Heinz • GDR
ZU JUNG FUR DIE LIEBE • 1961 • Balque Erica • FRG • TOO YOUNG FOR LOVE
ZU NEUEN UFERN • 1937 • Sirk Douglas • FRG • LIFE BEGINS ANEW (USA) ○ TO NEW SHORES (UKN) ○ PARAMATTA ○ BAGNE DE FEMMES
ZU SPAT • 1911 • Froelich Carl • FRG
ZU STRASSBURG AUD DER SCHANZ • 1934 • Osten Franz • FRG • AT THE STRASSBURG (USA)
ZU WARRIORS FROM THE MAGIC MOUNTAIN see **SHU SHAN** • 1983
ZUB ZA ZUB • 1912 • Pech Antonin • CZC • TOOTH FOR TOOTH
ZUCCHERO, IL MIELE E IL PEPPERONCINO, LO • 1980 • Martino Sergio • ITL • SUGAR, HONEY AND HOT PEPPERS
ZUCHTHAUS-KAVALIERE • 1925 • *Georg Anders-Film* • FRG
ZUCKER FUR DEN MORDER (FRG) see **KILLER PER SUA MAESTA, UN** • 1968
ZUCKER UND ZIMT • 1915 • Lubitsch Ernst, Matray Ernst • FRG
ZUCKERBABY • 1985 • Adlon Percy • FRG • SUGARBABY
ZUCKERBROT UND PEITSCHE • 1968 • Gosov Marran • FRG • MIT ZUCKERBROT UND PEITSCHE ○ SWEATMEAT AND WHIP ○ LUCK OF THE GAME, THE
ZUCKERKANDL • 1968 • Hubley John, Hubley Faith • ANS • USA
ZUDORA • 1914 • Sullivan Frederick, Hansel Howell • SRL • USA • ZUDORA IN THE TWENTY MILLION DOLLAR MYSTERY ○ TWENTY MILLION DOLLAR MYSTERY, THE
ZUDORA IN THE TWENTY MILLION DOLLAR MYSTERY see **ZUDORA** • 1914
ZUFLUCHT • 1928 • Froelich Carl • FRG • REFUGE
ZUG FAHRT AB, EIN • 1942 • Meyer Johannes • FRG
ZUG NASSOUI • 1983 • Yeshurun Isaac • ISR • MARRIED COUPLE
ZUGELLOSES BLUT • 1917 • *Negri Pola* • FRG
ZUGURT AGA • 1985 • Colgecen Nesli • TRK • AGHA
ZUGVOGEL • 1947 • Meyer Rolf • FRG
ZUHANAS KOZBEN • 1987 • Tolmar Tamas • HNG • FALL, THE
ZUHURUN BARRIYYA • 1972 • Francis Yussif • EGY • FLEURS SAUVAGES
ZUI AI • 1987 • Zhang Aijia • HKG • PASSION
ZUID LIMBURG see **SPOORWEGBOUW IN LIMBURG** • 1929
ZUIDERZEE • 1933 • Ivens Joris • NTH • ZUYDERZEE

ZUIDERZEE DIKE • 1931 • *Van Dongen Helen (Ed)* • NTH

ZUIHOU YIGE DONGRI • 1987 • Wu Ziniu • CHN • LAST DAY OF WINTER, THE

ZUIHOUDE FENGKUANG • 1987 • Zhou Xiaowen • CHN • DESPERATION

ZUIHOUDE GUIZU • 1988 • Xie Jin • CHN, HKG • VISITORS TO NEW YORK ○ LAST ARISTOCRATS, THE

ZUKUNFT AUS ZWEITER HAND see **SCHICKSAL AUS ZWEITER HAND** • 1949

ZUKUNFTIGEN GLUCKSELIGKEITEN, DIE • 1989 • van der Kooij Fred • SWT, FRG • FUTURE FELICITIES

ZULA HULA • 1937 • Fleischer Dave • ANS • USA

ZULU • 1963 • Endfield Cy • UKN, SAF

ZULU DAWN • 1979 • Hickox Douglas • UKN, SAF

ZULU KING, THE • 1913 • Hotaling Arthur D. • USA

ZULU-LAND • 1911 • *Selig* • USA

ZULU LOVE • 1928 • Freund Karl • UKN

ZULU TOWN • 1917 • SAF

ZULU'S DEVOTION, A • 1916 • SAF

ZULU'S HEART, THE • 1908 • Griffith D. W. • USA

ZUM BEISPIEL: EHEBRUCH see **OSWALT KOLLE: ZUM BEISPIEL: EHEBRUCH** • 1969

ZUM GOLDENEN ANKER • 1931 • Korda Alexander • FRG

ZUM PARADIES DER DAMEN • 1922 • Pick Lupu • FRG

ZUM TEE BEI DE. BORSIG • 1963 • Hess Joachim • MTV • FRG

ZUM TEUFEL MIT PER PENNE, DIE see **LUMMEL VON DER ERSTEN BANK II: ZUM TEUFEL MIT PER PENNE, DIE** • 1968

ZUM TODE GEHETZT • 1912 • Gad Urban • FRG, DNM • DODENS GAADE (DNM)

ZUM ZUM ZUM -LA CANZONA CHE MI PASSA PER LA TESTA • 1968 • Corbucci Bruno • ITL • ZUM, ZUM, ZUM -THE SONG THAT GOES THROUGH MY HEART

ZUM ZUM ZUM N.2 • 1969 • Corbucci Bruno • ITL • ZUM ZUM ZUM N.2 (SARA CAPITATO ANCHE A VOI)

ZUM ZUM ZUM N.2 (SARA CAPITATO ANCHE A VOI) see **ZUM ZUM ZUM N.2** • 1969

ZUM, ZUM, ZUM -THE SONG THAT GOES THROUGH MY HEART see **ZUM ZUM ZUM -LA CANZONA CHE MI PASSA PER LA TESTA** • 1968

ZUM ZWEITEN FRUHSTUCK • 1975 • Frank Hubert • FRG • VIRGIN WIVES (UKN)

ZUMA BEACH • 1978 • Katzin Lee H. • TVM • USA

ZUMBALAH see **ULTIME GRIDA DALLA SAVANA** • 1975

ZUND SCHNURE • 1974 • Hauff Reinhard • FRG

ZUNDHOLZER • 1960 • Krauss Uwe, Gehric Peter • FRG • MATCHES

ZUQAQ AL-MIDAQQ • Al Imam Hassan • EGY • PASSAGE DES MIRACLES

ZUQAQ AS-SAYYID AL-BULT'Y • 1967 • Saleh Tewfik • EGY

ZUR BESSERUNG DER PERSON • 1982 • Butler Heinz • SWT • FOR THE IMPROVEMENT OF THE INDIVIDUAL

ZUR CHRONIK VON GRIESHUUS "UM DAS ERBE VON GRIESHUUS" • 1925 • von Gerlach Arthur • FRG • CHRONICLES OF THE GREY HOUSE, THE (UKN) ○ CHRONIK VON GRIESHUUS, DIE ○ CHRONICLES OF THE GRAY HOUSE, THE (USA) ○ AT THE GREY HOUSE ○ CHRONIK VON GRIESHUUS

ZUR SACHE SCHATZCHEN • 1968 • Spils May • FRG • JUNKER HINRICHS VERBOTENE LIEBE ○ COME TO THE POINT, TREASURE

ZUR STRECKE GEBRACHT • 1917 • Piel Harry • FRG

ZURCHER SECHSELAUTEN-UMZAG • 1901 • Hipleh-Walt Georges • SWT

ZURCHER VERLOBUNG, DIE • 1957 • Kautner Helmut • FRG • AFFAIRS OF JULIE, THE (USA)

ZURDO, EL • 1964 • Martinez Arturo • MXC

ZURICH - BERN - BASEL • 1989 • Imbach Thomas • SWT

ZURUCK AUS DEM WELTALL see **...UND IMMER RUFT DAS HERZ** • 1958

ZUSTER BROWN • 1921 • Doxat-Pratt B. E., Binger Maurits H. • NTH, UKN • NURSE BROWN

ZUT L'HIPPOPATAME • 1929 • Daix Andre • ASS • FRN

ZUTA • 1974 • Tadej Vladimir • YGS • GINGER

ZUVIEL AN BORD, EINER • 1935 • Lamprecht Gerhard • FRG

ZUYDER ZEE • 1907 • Morland John • UKN

ZUYDER ZEE • 1908 • Gilbert Arthur • UKN

ZUYDERZEE see **ZUIDERZEE** • 1933

ZUZANA LEARNS TO WRITE • Lehky Vladimir • ANS • CZC

ZUZANNA I CHLOPCY • 1962 • Mozdzenski Stanislaw • PLN • SUSAN AND THE LADS

ZUZU, THE BAND LEADER • 1913 • Sennett Mack • USA

ZVANYI UZHIN • 1962 • Ermler Friedrich • SHT • USS

ZVENI, NASHA YUNOST! • 1959 • Boykov V. • USS • CONCERT OF YOUTH

ZVENIGORA • 1928 • Dovzhenko Alexander • USS • ZVENYHORA

ZVENYHORA see **ZVENIGORA** • 1928

ZVEROLOVY • 1959 • Nifontov Gleb • USS • HUNTING IN SIBERIA (USA)

ZVEZDA I SMERT KHOAKINA MURIETY • 1983 • Grammatikov Vladimir • USS • STAR AND THE DEATH OF JOAQUIM MURIETA, THE

ZVEZDA NADYEZHDY • 1980 • Keosayan Edmond • USS • STAR OF HOPE, THE

ZVEZDA PLENITELNOVO SCHASTYA • 1974 • Motyl Vladimir • USS • STAR OF CAPTIVE GOOD FORTUNE

ZVEZDE SU OCI RATNIKA • 1973 • Jankovic Branimir Tori • YGS • STARS ARE THE EYES OF THE WARRIORS, THE

ZVEZDI V KOSSITE, SULZI V OCHITE • 1978 • Nichev Ivan • BUL • STARS IN THE HAIR, TEARS IN THE EYES

ZVIRATA VE MESTE • 1988 • Kristek Vaclav • CZC • ANIMALS IN THE CITY

ZVIRATKA A PETROVSTI • 1946 • Trnka Jiri • ANS • CZC • ANIMALS AND THE BRIGANDS, THE ○ ANIMALS AND BRIGANDS

ZVJEZDANI KVARTET • 1969 • *Zagreb* • ANS • YGS • STARLIGHT SERENADERS

ZVONY PRE BOSYCH • 1965 • Barabas Stanislav • CZC • KNELL FOR THE BAREFOOTED

ZVONYAT, OTKROYTE DVER • 1965 • Mitta Alexander • USS • SOMEONE'S BUZZING, OPEN THE DOOR ○ GIRL AND THE BUGLER, THE (USA) ○ OPEN THE DOOR WHEN THE BELL RINGS

ZVUCHI TAM-TAM! • 1968 • Beisembayev Sharip • USS • TAM-TAM, RING OUT!

ZVYOZDNYI INSPECTOR • 1980 • Kovalyov Mark • USS • STAR INSPECTOR, THE

ZVYOZDNYYE BRATYA • 1962 • Bogolepov Dimitriy • USS • RENDEZVOUS IN SPACE

ZVYOZDY I SOLDATY (USS) see **CSILLAGOSOK, KATONAK** • 1967

ZWAAR MOEDIGE VERHALEN VOOR BIJ DE CENTRALE VERWARMING • 1975 • van Brakel Nouchka, Damen Ermie, van der Lecq Bas, Pieters Guido • NTH • MELANCHOLY FIRESIDE TALES ○ MELANCHOLY TALES

ZWANGSLIEBE IM FREISTAAT • 1919 • Schubert Georg • FRG

ZWANZIG MADCHEN UND DIE PAUKER • 1970 • Jacobs Werner • FRG

ZWARE JONGENS • 1983 • de Hert Robbe • BLG • ROUGH DIAMONDS

ZWARIOWANA NOC • 1967 • Kuzminski Zbigniew • PLN • CRAZY NIGHT ○ MAD NIGHT, A

ZWARTE HAND, HET see **ZWARTE ZAND, HET** • 1954

ZWARTE ZAND, HET • 1954 • van der Linden Charles Huguenot • DOC • NTH • VIEW OF MIDDELHARNIS ○ ZWARTE HAND, HET

ZWARTE ZON, DER • 1970 • Le Bon Patrick • BLG

ZWARTZIEK • 1974 • Bijl Jacob • MTV • NTH • JEALOUSY

ZWEI • 1965 • Klick Roland • FRG

ZWEI ALS FRISEURE, DIE • 1930 • *Augusta-Film* • FRG

ZWEI BAYERN IM HAREM • 1957 • Stockel Joe • FRG

ZWEI BAYERN IM URWALD • 1957 • Bender Ludwig • FRG

ZWEI BAYERN IN ST. PAULI • 1956 • Konig Hans H. • FRG

ZWEI BLAUE AUGEN • 1955 • Ucicky Gustav • FRG

ZWEI BRUDER • 1929 • Dubson Michael • FRG • RIVALEN DER LIEBE

ZWEI EIDE see **WEISSE SKLAVIN 1, DIE** • 1921

ZWEI FRAUEN • 1911 • Stark Kurt • FRG

ZWEI FRAUEN • 1938 • Zerlett Hans H. • FRG

ZWEI GANZE TAGE • 1971 • Ophuls Marcel • MTV • FRG • TWO WHOLE DAYS

ZWEI GIRLS VOM ROTEN STERN • 1966 • Drechsel Sammy • FRG, AUS, FRN • AFFAIR OF STATE, AN (USA)

ZWEI GLUCKLICHE HERZEN see **BISSCHEN LIEBE FUR DICH, EIN** • 1932

ZWEI GLUCKLICHE MENSCHEN • 1943 • Emo E. W. • FRG

ZWEI GLUCKLICHE PAARE • 1915 • Mack Max • FRG

ZWEI GLUCKLICHE TAGE • 1916 • Albes Emil • FRG

ZWEI GLUCKLICHE TAGE • 1932 • Walther-Fein Rudolf • FRG

ZWEI GUTE KAMERADEN • 1933 • Obal Max • FRG

ZWEI HERZEN IM 3/4-TAKT • 1930 • von Bolvary Geza • FRG • TWO HEARTS IN WALTZ TIME

ZWEI HERZEN IM MAI • 1958 • von Bolvary Geza • FRG

ZWEI HERZEN UND EIN SCHLAG • 1931 • Thiele Wilhelm • FRG

ZWEI HERZEN UND EIN THRON • 1955 • Schott-Schobinger Hans • AUS • HOFJAGD IN ISCHL

ZWEI HERZEN VOLLER SELIGKEIT • 1957 • Holmann J. A. • FRG

ZWEI HIMMELBLAUE AUGEN • 1931 • Meyer Johannes • FRG

ZWEI IM SONNENSCHEIN • 1933 • Jacoby Georg • FRG

ZWEI IN EINEM ANZUG • 1950 • Stockel Joe • FRG

ZWEI IN EINEM AUTO • 1931 • May Joe • FRG • REISE INS GLUCK, DIE

ZWEI IN EINEM AUTO • 1951 • Marischka Ernst • AUS • DU BIST DIE SCHONSTE FUR MICH! ○ ZWEI IN EINEM BLAUEN AUTO

ZWEI IN EINEM BLAUEN AUTO see **ZWEI IN EINEM AUTO** • 1951

ZWEI IN EINER GROSSEN STADT • 1942 • von Collande Volker • FRG • TWO IN A GREAT CITY

ZWEI KINDER • 1924 • Hilber Richard Clement • FRG

ZWEI KRAWATTEN • 1930 • Basch Felix, Weichart Richard • FRG • TWO NECKTIES (USA)

ZWEI KUNSTLER • 1915 • Del Zopp Rudolf • FRG

ZWEI LUSTIGE ABENTEUER • 1938 • Hartl Karl • FRG • TWO MERRY ADVENTURES (USA)

ZWEI MATROSEN AUF DER ALM • 1957 • Hamel Peter • FRG

ZWEI MENSCHEN • 1923 • Schwarz Hanns • FRG

ZWEI MENSCHEN • 1930 • Waschneck Erich • FRG • TWO LIVES

ZWEI MENSCHEN • 1952 • May Paul • FRG

ZWEI MUTTER • 1957 • Beyer Frank • GDR • TWO MOTHERS

ZWEI ROTE ROSEN • 1928 • Land Robert • FRG • TWO RED ROSES

ZWEI SCHWARZE LATERNEN • 1921 • Abter Adolf • FRG

ZWEI SUPERTYPEN RAUME AUF see **PADRONI DELLA CITTA, I** • 1977

ZWEI UND DIE DAME, DIE • 1925 • Neuss Alwin • FRG

ZWEI UNTER MILLIONEN • 1961 • Vicas Victor • FRG

ZWEI UNTERM HIMMELSZELT • 1927 • Guter Johannes • FRG

ZWEI VOM SUDEXPRESS, DIE • 1932 • Wohlmuth Robert • FRG

ZWEI WELTEN • 1919 • Wiene Conrad • AUS

ZWEI WELTEN • 1922 • Lowenbein Richard • FRG

ZWEI WELTEN • 1929 • Hochbaum Werner • FRG

ZWEI WELTEN • 1930 • Dupont E. A. • FRG

ZWEI WELTEN • 1940 • Grundgens Gustaf • FRG

ZWEI WELTEN see **LIEBE UND LEBEN 3** • 1918

ZWEI WHISKY UND EIN SOFA • 1963 • Grawert Gunter • FRG • WHISKEY AND SODA (USA) ○ OPERATION MOONLIGHT

ZWEIERLEI BLUT • 1912 • *Fleck Jacob* • AUS

ZWEIERLEI MASS • 1963 • Verhoeven Paul • FRG

ZWEIERLEI MORAL • 1930 • Lamprecht Gerhard • FRG

ZWEIGROSCHENZAUBER • 1929 • Richter Hans • FRG • TWOPENNY MAGIC

ZWEIKAMPF • 1966 • Brandner Uwe • FRG

ZWEIMAL HOCHZEIT • 1930 • Emo E. W. • FRG

ZWEIMAL LUX • 1930 • Heuberger Edmund • FRG

ZWEIMAL VERLIEBT see **LIEBE FREUNDIN** • 1949

ZWEIMAL ZWEI IM HIMMELBETT • 1937 • Deppe Hans • FRG

ZWEITE ERWACHEN DER CHRISTA KLAGES, DER • 1978 • von Trotta Margarethe • FRG • SECOND AWAKENING OF CHRISTA KLAGES, THE

ZWEITE FRAU, DIE • 1917 • Oswald Richard • FRG

ZWEITE FRUHLING, DER • 1975 • Lommel Ulli • FRG • SECOND SPRING, A

ZWEITE GLEIS, DAS • 1962 • Kunert Joachim • GDR • SECOND TRACK, THE

ZWEITE ICH, DAS • 1917 • Hofer Franz • FRG

ZWEITE LEBEN, DAS • 1916 • *Kortner Fritz* • AUS

ZWEITE LEBEN, DAS • 1921 • Halm Alfred • FRG

ZWEITE LEBEN, DAS • 1954 • Vicas Victor • FRG, FRN • DOUBLE DESTIN (FRN) ○ DOUBLE LIFE, A (USA) ○ DOUBLE DESTINY

ZWEITE LEBEN DES FRIEDRICH WILHELM GEORG PLATOW, DAS • 1974 • Kuhn Siegfried • GDR

ZWEITE MUTTER, DIE • 1925 • Bolten-Baeckers Heinrich • FRG

ZWEITE SCHUSS, DER • 1923 • Krol Maurice • FRG

ZWEITE SCHUSS, DER • 1943 • Fric Martin • FRG • SECOND SHOT, THE

ZWERG NASE • 1921 • Tuszinsky Ladislaus • AUS • DWARF NOSE

ZWERVERS, DE • 1971 • Staes Guido • BLG

ZWIELICHT • 1940 • van der Noss Rudolf • FRG

ZWIERZETA ARENY • 1966 • Lomnicki Jan • DOC • PLN • ANIMALS OF THE ARENA, THE

ZWILLINGE VOM ZILLERTAL, DIE • 1957 • Reinl Harald • FRG

ZWILLINGSSCHWESTERN, DIE • 1916 • Otto Paul? • FRG

ZWISCHEN ABEND UND MORGEN • 1923 • Robison Arthur • FRG • SPUK EINER NACHT, DER ○ BETWEEN EVENING AND MORNING

ZWISCHEN DEN ELTERN • 1938 • Hinrich Hans • FRG

ZWISCHEN FLAMMEN UND BESTIEN • 1923 • Stranz Fred • FRG

ZWISCHEN FLAMMEN UND FLUTEN • 1921 • Wolff Carl Heinz • FRG

ZWISCHEN GESTERN UND MORGEN • 1947 • Braun Harald • FRG

ZWISCHEN GLUCK UND KRONE • 1959 • Schundler Rudolf • FRG

ZWISCHEN HALFTE 11 UND 11 • 1917 • Dessauer Siegfried • FRG

ZWISCHEN HAMBURG UND HAITI • 1940 • Waschneck Erich • FRG

ZWISCHEN HIMMEL UND ERDE • 1942 • Braun Harald • FRG

ZWISCHEN HIMMEL UND ERDE see **BRUDER** • 1923

ZWISCHEN HIMMEL UND HOLLE • 1934 • Seitz Franz • FRG • LIEBE LASST SICH NICHT ERZWINGEN

ZWISCHEN LIEBE UN PFLICHT see **SCHOPFER, DER** • 1928

ZWISCHEN LIEBE UND MACHT • 1922 • Stranz Fred • FRG

ZWISCHEN LIPP' UND KELCHESRAND • 1919 • Bach Rudi • FRG

ZWISCHEN NACHT UND MORGEN • 1919 • Philippi Siegfried • FRG

ZWISCHEN NACHT UND MORGEN • 1931 • Lamprecht Gerhard • FRG • DIRNENTRAGODIE

ZWISCHEN NACHT UND MORGEN • 1944 • Braun Alfred • FRG • AUGEN DER LIEBE

ZWISCHEN NACHT UND SUNDE • 1922 • Hofer Franz • FRG

ZWISCHEN SHANGHAI UND ST. PAULI • 1962 • Schleif Wolfgang • FRG, ITL • VOYAGE TO DANGER (USA)

ZWISCHEN SPREE UND PANKE see **GROSSTADTKINDER** • 1929

ZWISCHEN STROM UND STEPPE • 1938 • von Bolvary Geza • FRG • PUSZTALIEBE

ZWISCHEN TOD UND LEBEN • 1918 • Wellin Arthur • FRG

ZWISCHEN UNS DIE BERGE • 1956 • Schnyder Franz • SWT • LIED DER HEIMAT, DAS

ZWISCHEN VIERZEHN UND SIEBZEHN • 1929 • Emo E. W. • FRG

ZWISCHEN ZEIT UND EWIGKEIT • 1956 • Rabenalt Arthur M., Nieves Conde Jose Antonio • FRG, SPN • ENTRE HOY Y LA ETERNIDAD (SPN) ○ BETWEEN TIME AND ETERNITY (USA)

ZWISCHEN ZWEI FRAUEN • 1925 • *Maakfilm* • FRG

ZWISCHEN ZWEI HERZEN • 1934 • Selpin Herbert • FRG • BETWEEN TWO HEARTS (USA)

ZWISCHEN ZWEI KRIEGEN • 1977 • Farocki Harun • FRG • BETWEEN TWO WARS

ZWISCHEN ZWEI WELTEN • 1919 • Gartner Adolf • FRG

ZWISCHENFALL IN BENDERATH • 1956 • Veiczi Janos • GDR • INCIDENT IN BENDERATH ○ RACIAL INCIDENT ○ TROJANER

ZWISCHENGLEIS • 1978 • Staudte Wolfgang • MTV • FRG • YESTERDAY'S TOMORROW ○ MEMORIES

ZWISCHENLANDUNG IN PARIS (FRG) see **ESCALE A ORLY** • 1955

ZWOLF HERZEN FUR CHARLY • 1949 • Andelfinger Fritz • FRG

ZWOLFJAHRIGE KRIEGSHELD, DER • 1915 • Schmidthassler Walter • FRG

ZWOLFTE STUNDE, DIE • 1930 • Ronger Waldemar • FRG • NACHT DES GRAUENS, EINE

ZWOLFTE STUNDE -EINE NACHTE DES GRAUENS, DIE • 1930 • Murnau F. W. • SND • FRG • TWELFTH HOUR -NIGHT OF HORROR, THE ○ NACHT DES GRAUENS, EINE

ZWYCIEZCA • 1977 • Zulawski Andrzej • PLN • VANQUISHER

ZYANKALI • 1948 • Neufeld Max, Robbeling Harald • AUS

ZYCIE J PILSUDSKIEGO • 1935 • Ordynski Ryszard • PLN

ZYCIE JEST PIEKNE • 1959 • Makarczynski Tadeusz • PLN • LIFE IS BEAUTIFUL ○ LIFE IS MARVELOUS

ZYCIE LUDZKIE W TWOIM REKU • 1951 • Nasfeter Janusz • SHT • PLN • HUMAN LIFE IN YOUR HANDS

ZYCIE RAL JESZCZE • 1964 • Morgenstern Janusz • PLN • LIFE ONCE AGAIN ○ LIFE ONCE MORE

ZYCIE RODZINNE • 1971 • Zanussi Krzysztof • PLN • FAMILY LIFE

ZYCIE WENETRZNE • 1988 • Koterski Marek • PLN • INNER LIFE

ZYCIE ZA ZYCIE • 1990 • Zanussi Krzysztof • PLN • LIFE FOR LIFE

ZYCIE ZACZYNA SIE WCZESNIE • 1961 • Ziarnik Jerzy • DOC • PLN • LIFE BEGINS EARLY

ZYCIORYS • 1974 • Kieslowski Krzysztof • PLN • LIFE-STORY

ZYGFRYD • 1986 • Domalik Andrzej • PLN • SIEGFRIED
ZYGMUNT KOLOSOWSKI • 1947 • Nawroski Zygmunt
ZYRAFA • 1966 • Nehrebecki Wladyslaw • ANS • PLN • GIRAFFE, THE
ZYWOT MATEUSZA • 1968 • Leszczynski Witold • PLN • LIFE OF MATTHEW, THE ○ DAYS OF MATTHEW, THE